Webster's Third New International Dictionary

OF THE ENGLISH LANGUAGE

UNABRIDGED

NOAH WEBSTER

OCTOBER 16, 1758 — MAY 28, 1843

THE significance of Noah Webster's *Dictionary* and his *Spelling Book* can be appreciated only when they are viewed against the background spanned by his life. He was born on an eighty-acre Connecticut farm the year before Wolfe's victory on the Plains of Abraham, and lived to see American pioneers penetrate overland into California and Oregon. He was a small boy when the Stamp Act aroused the colonists, and a student at Yale when college classes were dispersed into the interior towns by the menace of British landing parties. He marched with his father against Burgoyne. In 1785, moved by the incompetence of the Confederation of thirteen sovereign states, he wrote a widely circulated argument for national union. In 1787 he issued an influential pamphlet advocating the adoption of the Federal Constitution. From 1793 to 1798 he owned, managed, and edited a daily and a weekly newspaper in New York City, supporting the Federalist policies of Washington and Adams. Living under the first ten presidents, he witnessed the acquisition of Louisiana Territory and Florida, the admission of thirteen additional states, and the approaching annexation of Texas.

Out of the patriotism and nationalism inspired by this sweep of events came the conviction that lusty young America needed its own school books, its own uniform language, and its own intellectual life. Into the attainment of these ends Webster flung himself with insatiable curiosity and indomitable energy. His *Blue-Backed Speller* (which taught not only spelling but pronunciation, common sense, morals, and good citizenship) was partly provoked by his efforts to use Dilworth's English spelling book while he was teaching school in Connecticut, New York, and Philadelphia. His dictionaries (*Compendious*, 1806; *American*, 1828) were suggested partly by his resentment against the ignorance concerning American institutions shown in contemporary British dictionaries. All his life he was a defender and interpreter of the American political "experiment", with all its cultural implications.

His dictionaries and his *Spelling Book* grew out of an intimate and vital familiarity with American life. He knew the farm, the law, the city, the school, and politics. He knew the country as a whole—he had traveled (1785–1786) by horse, by carriage, and by sailing vessel from Massachusetts to South Carolina, persuading state legislatures to pass laws for the protection of copyright. He was a spelling reformer, an orchardist, a gardener, and an experimental scientist. He was admitted to practice before the United States Supreme Court. He became and remained a devoted Calvinistic churchman. He wrote scores of articles, books, and pamphlets on literary, economic, political, philological, practical, and scientific subjects —on banks, epidemics, insurance, the French Revolution, the decomposition of white-lead paint, the Jay Treaty, and the rights of neutral nations in time of war. He edited Governor Winthrop's Journal. He wrote and published a revised and emended version of the Bible.

He assumed all the local duties and responsibilities of a citizen. He was clerk and committeeman of his Hartford school district. He was a member for a time of the General Assembly of Connecticut and for a time of the General Court of Massachusetts. He was councilman and alderman in New Haven and judge of the County Court. In Amherst he was town moderator. He was a director of the Hampshire Bible Society, a vice-president of the Hampshire and Hampden Agricultural Society, and a founder of the Connecticut Academy of Arts and Sciences. He was active in the establishment of both Amherst Academy and Amherst College, and was president of the Board of Trustees of the Academy. In New Haven he campaigned for the introduction of an adequate water supply, and took active part in a movement to plant elms along the streets.

In 1807 he wrote: "I hope to be able to finish my Complete Dictionary. . . . It will require the incessant labor of from three to five years." In 1812 he moved to Amherst, Massachusetts, where for ten years he labored from point to point about the large circular table that held the dictionaries and grammars of twenty languages. In 1824 he sailed to spend a year in the libraries of Paris, London, and Cambridge in order to consult books not available in America. In 1828, at the age of seventy, he at length published *An American Dictionary of the English Language* in a two-volume edition of 2500 copies.

The *American Dictionary* stands practically beyond praise or comparison. The excellence of the definitions has received ample acknowledgment. But some other features of Webster's work have never been adequately recognized: First, the inclusion of thousands of modern technical and scientific terms, making it more than a purely literary dictionary. Second, the discovery of the correct principle for arranging the definitions, with the etymologically primary meaning first. And third, the etymologies, which are mines of pertinent and valuable information, as appears when they are compared, not only with the results of an added century of research, but especially with the scanty or fragmentary treatment of Johnson, Junius, and Skinner, and the speculations of Horne Tooke.

Webster brought out a revised edition of the *Dictionary* in 1841, just before his death. The *Spelling Book* had meanwhile undergone many revisions and improvements. These two books, written to illuminate and explain to the American people both their language and their culture, were his contribution to American civilization.

The publishers and the editors of this latest edition of *Webster's Dictionary* have worked under the constant responsibility of maintaining Noah Webster's standards of integrity and clarity in meeting the needs of the whole modern English-speaking world.

Webster's Third New International Dictionary

OF THE ENGLISH LANGUAGE
UNABRIDGED

A Merriam-Webster
REG. U.S. PAT. OFF.

Utilizing all the experience and resources of more than one hundred years of Merriam-Webster® dictionaries

EDITOR IN CHIEF
PHILIP BABCOCK GOVE, Ph.D.
AND
THE MERRIAM-WEBSTER
EDITORIAL STAFF

MERRIAM-WEBSTER INC., *Publishers*
SPRINGFIELD, MASSACHUSETTS, U.S.A.

A GENUINE MERRIAM-WEBSTER

The name *Webster* alone is no guarantee of excellence. It is used by a number of publishers and may serve mainly to mislead an unwary buyer.

Merriam-Webster™ is the name you should look for when you consider the purchase of dictionaries or other fine reference books. It carries the reputation of a company that has been publishing since 1831 and is your assurance of quality and authority.

Library of Congress Cataloging in Publication Data
Main entry under title:

Webster's third new international dictionary of the English language, unabridged: a Merriam-Webster/editor in chief, Philip Babcock Gove and the Merriam-Webster editorial staff.
p. cm.
ISBN 0-87779-201-1 (blue sturdite).—ISBN 0-87779-202-X (carrying case).—ISBN 0-87779-206-2 (imperial buckram).
1. English language—Dictionaries. I. Gove, Philip Babcock, 1902–1972. II. Merriam-Webster, Inc.
PE1625.W36
423-dc20

MADE IN THE UNITED STATES OF AMERICA

52535455QKY050403

CONTENTS

Tables

(at or near *italicized* word)

Full-Page Illustrations

PREFACE

Webster's Third New International Dictionary is a completely new work, redesigned, restyled, and reset. Every line of it is new. This latest unabridged Merriam-Webster is the eighth in a series which has its beginning in Noah Webster's *American Dictionary of the English Language*, 1828. On Webster's death in 1843 the unsold copies and publishing rights of his dictionary were acquired by George and Charles Merriam, who in 1847 brought out a revision edited by Noah Webster's son-in-law, Professor Chauncey A. Goodrich of Yale College. The 1847 edition became the first Merriam-Webster unabridged dictionary*. G. & C. Merriam Company now offers Webster's Third New International Dictionary to the English-speaking world as a prime linguistic aid to interpreting the culture and civilization of today, as the first edition served the America of 1828.

As the number of students in school and college jumps to ever-increasing heights, the quantity of printed matter necessary to their education increases too. Not only are more words used more often with these increases; words must be used more economically and more efficiently both in school and out. More and more do people undertaking a new job, practicing a new hobby, or developing a new interest turn to how-to pamphlets, manuals, and books for both elementary instruction and advanced guidance. Where formerly they had time to learn by doing, they now need to begin by reading and understanding what has been recorded. A quick grasp of the meanings of words becomes necessary if one is to be successful. A dictionary opens the way to both formal learning and to the daily self-instruction that modern living requires. It is the key also to the daily newspaper and to a vast number of other periodicals that demand our attention. This edition has been prepared with a constant regard for the needs of the high school and college student, the technician, and the periodical reader, as well as of the scholar and professional. It undertakes to provide for the changes in public interest in all classes of words as manifested by what people want to read, discuss, and study. The dictionary more than ever is the indispensable instrument of understanding and progress.

G. & C. Merriam Company have produced this Third New International at a cost of over $3,500,000. The budgetary and technical planning underlying its production has been directed and coordinated since 1953 by the Company's president, Mr. Gordon J. Gallan. His activity, understanding, and cooperation have contributed indispensably to its editorial completion and have made possible the maintenance of a Merriam-Webster permanent office staff constituted according to need. This staff is in effect a faculty which specializes in different branches of knowledge much as a small college faculty does. Listed among the resident editors are a mathematician, a physicist, a chemist, a botanist, a biologist, a philosopher, a political scientist, a comparative religionist, a classicist, a historian, and a librarian as well as philologists, linguists, etymologists, and phoneticians whose specialty is the English language itself. Their academic affiliations and their degrees can be seen one by one in the "Merriam-Webster Editorial Staff" that follows this preface. Besides the office staff over two hundred other scholars and specialists have served as outside consultants in supplementary reviewing, revising, and submitting new definitions in subjects in which they are authorities. The range and experience of this special knowledge appear in the listing of their names alphabetically after the editorial staff.

In conformity with the principle that a definition, to be adequate, must be written only after an analysis of usage, the definitions in this edition are based chiefly on examples of usage collected since publication of the preceding edition. Members of the editorial staff began in 1936 a systematic reading of books, magazines, newspapers, pamphlets, catalogs, and learned journals. By the time of going to press the collection contained just under 4,500,000 such new examples of recorded usage, to be added to more than 1,665,000 citations already in the files for previous editions. Further, the citations in the indispensable many-volume *Oxford English Dictionary*, the new citations in Sir William Craigie's four-volume *Dictionary of American English* and Mitford M. Mathews' two-volume *Dictionary of Americanisms*, neither of which was available to the editors of the preceding edition, and the uncounted citations in dozens of concordances to the Bible and to works of English and American writers and in numerous books of quotations push the citation background for the definitions in this dictionary to over ten million. This figure does not include freely consulted text matter in the office library of reference books. Nor does it include thousands of textbooks in the private and academic libraries of the editors and consultants, nor books consulted in the Springfield City Library whose librarians have generously given the editorial staff ready and frequent access to its large and valuable word-hoard.

While dictionaries of special subjects, glossaries, indexes, and checklists are collected and examined to verify the existence of special words, no word has been entered in this dictionary merely on the authority of another dictionary, special or general, and no definition in this dictionary has been derived from any other dictionary (except, of course, Merriam-Webster predecessors). Learned and industrial organizations have created numerous committees of nomenclature to collect, define, and standardize the terminology in their fields. Some of the staff editors serve as advisory members of such committees. Nevertheless prescriptive and canonical definitions have not been taken over nor have recommendations been followed unless confirmed by independent investigation of usage borne out by genuine citations.

The primary objective of precise, sharp defining has been met through development of a new dictionary style based upon completely analytical one-phrase definitions throughout the book. Since the headword in a definition is intended to be modified only by structural elements restrictive in some degree and essential to each other, the use of commas either to separate or to group has been severely limited, chiefly to units in apposition or in series. The new defining pattern does not provide for a predication which conveys further expository comment. Instead of encyclopedic treatment at one place of a group of related terms, each term is defined at its own place in the alphabet. Every phrase in lowercase roman type following a heavy black colon and running to the next heavy colon or to a divisional number or letter is a complete definition of one sense of the word to which it is attached. Defining by synonym is carefully avoided by putting all unqualified or undifferentiated terms in small capital letters. Such a term in small capitals should not be considered a definition but a cross-reference to a definition of equivalent meaning that can be substituted for the small capitals.

A large number of verbal illustrations mostly from the mid-twentieth century has been woven into the defining pattern with a view to contributing considerably to the user's interest and understanding by showing a word used in context. The illustration is often a brief combination of words that has actually been used in writing and when this is so the illustration is attributed to its author or source. More than 14,000 different authors are quoted for their use of words or for the structural pattern of their words but not for their opinions or sentiments.

A number of other features are (1) the recognition and separate entry (with part-of-speech label) of verb-plus-adverb compounds (as *run down*) that function like one-word verbs in every way except for having a separable suffix, (2) the recognition (by using the label *n* for noun) that substantive open compounds (as *clothes moth*) belong in the same class as nouns written solid or hyphened, (3) the recognition (by using the label *often attrib*) of nouns that often function as adjectives but otherwise do not behave like the class of adjectives, (4) the indication (by inserting suffix-symbols, as -s or -es, -ed/-ing/-s or -es, -er/-est) of the inflectional forms of nouns, verbs, adjectives, and adverbs at which the forms are not written out in full, (5) the recognition (by beginning entries with a lowercase letter and by inserting either the label *cap, usu cap, often cap*, or *sometimes cap*) that words vary considerably in capitalization according to circumstances and environment, (6) the recognition (by not using at all the status label *colloquial*) that it is impossible to know whether a word out of context is colloquial or not, and (7) the incorporation of abbreviations alphabetically in the main vocabulary.

In continuation of Merriam-Webster policy the editors of this new edition have held steadfastly to the three cardinal virtues of dictionary making: accuracy, clearness, and comprehensiveness. Whenever these qualities are at odds with each other, accuracy is put first and foremost, for without accuracy there could be no appeal to Webster's Third New International as an authority. Accuracy in addition to requiring freedom from error and conformity to truth requires a dictionary to state meanings in which words are in fact used, not to give editorial opinion on what their meanings should be.

In the editorial striving for clearness the editors have tried to make the definitions as readable as possible. Even so, the terminology of many subjects contains words that can be adequately and clearly explained only to those who have passed through preliminary stages of initiation, just as a knowledge of algebra is prerequisite for trigonometry. A dictionary demands of its user much understanding and no one person can understand all of it. Therefore there is no limit to the possibilities for clarification. Somewhat paradoxically a user of the dictionary benefits in proportion to his effort and knowledge, and his contribution is an essential part of the process of understanding even though it may involve only a willingness to look up a few additional words.

Comprehensiveness requires maximum coverage with a minimum of compromise. The basic aim is nothing less than coverage of the current vocabulary of standard written and spoken English. At the same time the scientific and technical vocabulary has been considerably expanded to keep pace with progress especially in physical science (as in electronics, nuclear physics, statistics, and soil science), in technology (as in rocketry, communications, automation, and synthetics), in medicine, and in the experimental phases of natural science. Therefore space has been found not only for new terms but also for new uses of old terms, for English like other living languages is in a metabolic process of constant change. The changes affect not only word stock but meaning, syntax, morphology, and pronunciation.

The demands for space have made necessary a fresh judgment on the claims of many parts of the old vocabulary. This dictionary is the result of a highly selective process in which discarding material of insubstantial or evanescent quality has gone hand in hand with adding terms that have obtained a place in the language. It confines itself strictly to generic words and their functions, forms, sounds, and meanings as distinguished from proper names that are not generic. Selection is guided by usefulness, and usefulness is determined by the degree to which terms most likely to be looked for are included. Many obsolete and comparatively useless or obscure words have been omitted. These include in general words that had become obsolete before 1755 unless found in well-known major works of a few major writers.

In definitions of words of many meanings the earliest ascertainable meaning is given first. Meanings of later derivation are arranged in the order shown to be most probable by dated evidence and semantic development. This arrangement applies alike to all meanings whether standard, technical, scientific, historical, or obsolete. No definitions are grouped alphabetically by subject labels. In fact this edition uses very few subject labels. It depends upon the definition for incorporating necessary subject orientation.

The pronunciation editor is Mr. Edward Artin. This edition shows as far as possible the pronunciations prevailing in general cultivated conversational usage, both informal and formal, throughout the English-speaking world. It does not attempt to dictate what that usage should be. It shows a

*The successors in the Merriam-Webster series are *American Dictionary of the English Language*, popularly known as the *Unabridged*, 1864, edited by Dr. Noah Porter, president of Yale College; *Webster's International Dictionary*, 1890, Noah Porter, editor in chief; *Webster's New International Dictionary*, 1909, Dr. William Torrey Harris, U. S. Commissioner of Education, editor in chief, and F. Sturges Allen, general editor; *Webster's New International Dictionary, Second Edition*, 1934, Dr. William Allan Neilson, president of Smith College, editor in chief, and Dr. Thomas A. Knott, general editor.

wide variety of acceptable pronunciations based on a large file of transcriptions made by attentive listening to actual educated speech in all fields and in all parts of the country—the speech of those expecting to be completely understood by their hearers. The facility with which such speech can be checked today by television, radio, and recordings has made it possible to show more representative and more realistic pronunciations than in the past.

To this end the Merriam-Webster pronunciation key has been revised. Many of the symbols of preceding editions have been retained, some with slight alteration, a few substitutions have been made, and some symbols that have outlived their usefulness have been dropped altogether. It is still fundamentally a diacritical key that makes use of many of the conventions of English spelling and is based on the principles that every distinct significant sound should have a distinct symbol to represent it and that no sound should be represented in more than one way. The elimination of symbols for all nonsignificant differences in sound makes it possible for transcriptions to convey to speakers in different parts of the English-speaking world sounds proper to their own speech. The new pronunciation alphabet is designed to represent clearly the standard speech of educated Americans.

It should be clearly understood that in striving to show realistic pronunciations definite limitations are fixed by the very nature of a dictionary. Each word must be isolated and considered apart from its place in connected spoken discourse. It is impracticable to show in a dictionary many kinds of variations—rising or falling pitch, syllabic emphasis or lack of emphasis, contraction or prolongation of sounds—to which the pronunciation of a word is susceptible under the influence of other words temporarily associated with it. Some of these variations are discussed under several headings in "Guide to Pronunciation", which contains also several paragraphs on the subject of correctness in pronunciation.

The etymologist for this edition is Dr. Charles R. Sleeth. In the etymologies the aim has been to retrace step by step the line of transmission by which the words have come down to modern English from the language in which they are first recorded. The present work adheres in this respect to the sound general principles governing the presentation of word histories in previous editions and indeed applies them with a consistency that has not previously been attained. With particular care it traces back to Middle English every word which is recorded in Middle English; also it carefully distinguishes the age of borrowings from French by giving the source language as Old French if the word came into English before 1300, as Middle French if it came into English between 1300 and 1600, and as French only if it came into English in the seventeenth century or later.

The etymologies fall into four general groups based on the origins of English words. Native words (as *hound*) that have been in the language as long as it has existed are traced back first through Middle English to Old English and then to Germanic languages other than English and to Indo-European languages other than Germanic. Old and well-established borrowings (as *chief*, *add*, and *dialect*) that have been in English since medieval or Renaissance times and come from languages, usually French, Latin, or often indirectly Greek, which belong, like English, to the Indo-European language family are traced back through their immediate source to their ultimate source in as much detail as native words. Many more recent borrowings (as *éclair*, *anile*, *hubris*, *sforzando*, *lariat*, *dachshund*, *smorgasbord*, *galore*, *muzhik*, and *karma*) are incorporated into the network of Indo-European etymology more thoroughly than in earlier dictionaries by going beyond the immediate source to either a list of cognates or a cross-reference to another entry. Borrowings (as *bushido*, *tepee*, *sheikh*, *sampan*, and *taboo*) from non-Indo-European languages are traced to the immediate source and analyzed into their parts if in the source language they are compounds or derivatives.

In the modern technical vocabulary of the sciences it is difficult if not impossible to adhere strictly to the principle of tracing step by step the line of transmission of a word, because such vocabulary has expanded rapidly in numerous fields and has been transmitted freely across language boundaries. Very few works of reference give full or systematic information about the language of origin of technical terms in any one field, and consequently it is impossible for the etymological staff of a general dictionary to garner and present such information about the technical terms of all fields. The present work attempts a new solution of this problem by introducing the label ISV (for International Scientific Vocabulary), for use in the etymology of such words when their language of origin is not positively ascertainable but they are known to be current in at least one language other than English. Examples of the use of ISV and further details about it are given in "Explanatory Notes", 7.6. Some ISV words (like *haploid*) have been created by taking a word with a rather general and simple meaning from one of the languages of antiquity, usually Latin or Greek, and conferring upon it a very specific and complicated meaning for the purposes of modern scientific discourse. More typically, however, ISV words are compounds or derivatives, made up of constituents that can be found entered in their own alphabetical position with their own ulterior etymology, again generally involving Latin or Greek. In either case an ISV etymology as given in the present work incorporates the word into the system of Indo-European etymology as well as if the immediate source language were known and stated. At the same time, use of ISV avoids the often untenable implication that the word in question was coined in English, and recognizes that the word as such is a product of the modern world and gets only its raw materials, so to speak, from antiquity.

The scheme of biological classification used has been concerted in consultation between Dr. Mairé Weir Kay, staff biologist, and specialists in the several divisions of taxonomy. It is planned to coordinate in the broadest way with current professional usage and specifically avoids undue reliance on any single school or system. The total taxonomic coverage is far more extensive than this characterization might imply and is designed to include and link with the preferred scheme both historically important though now disused terminology and the more important terms pertinent to divergent schools of professional thought (as in the question of whether the leguminous plants constitute one or several families).

Words that are believed to be trademarks have been investigated in the files of the United States Patent Office. No investigation has been made of common law trademark rights in any word since such investigation is impracticable. Those that have current registrations are shown with an initial capital and are also identified as trademarks. The inclusion of any word in this dictionary is not, however, an expression of the publishers' opinion on whether or not it is subject to proprietary rights. Indeed, no definition in this dictionary is to be regarded as affecting the validity of any trademark.

This dictionary has a vocabulary of over 450,000 words. It would have been easy to make the vocabulary larger although the book, in the format of the preceding edition, could hardly hold any more pages or be any thicker. By itself, the number of entries is, however, not of first importance. The number of words available is always far in excess of and for a one-volume dictionary many times the number that can possibly be included. To make all the changes mentioned only to come out with the same number of pages and the same number of vocabulary entries as in the preceding edition would allow little or no opportunity for new words and new senses. The compactness and legibility of Times Roman, a typeface new to Merriam-Webster dictionaries, have made possible more words to a line and more lines to a column than in the preceding edition, and a larger size page makes a better proportioned book.

The preparation of this edition has absorbed 757 editor-years. This figure does not include the time of typists, photocopiers, and clerical assistants or the time of over 200 consultants. The book appears, like its predecessor, after more than ten years of active full-time preparation. It is hardly necessary to observe that no one editor could harmonize all the diverse and disparate matter by reading and criticizing every line or even determine and keep firm control over editorial policy, nor could an editorial board of fixed membership. Instead the editor in chief has used his editors one by one and has delegated multiple responsibilities to them individually as occasion required. In this way members of the Merriam-Webster staff have been grouped and regrouped to form hundreds of task forces performing simultaneously thousands of missions. The editor can say with gratitude and relief that the accomplishment is not a one-man dictionary. "What individual", asks Noah Webster in his preface, "is competent to trace to their source, and define in all their various applications, popular, scientific, and technical, sixty or seventy thousand words!"

WEBSTER'S THIRD NEW INTERNATIONAL DICTIONARY is a collaborative effort. Without the cooperation of the scholarly, scientific, and technical world, the specialized guidance of our outside consultants, and the ingenuity of the compositors and printers, G. & C. Merriam Company and its permanent editorial staff could not have brought the work to its successful culmination. Those most deeply involved with overall responsibility deserve special mention here. Three associate editors, Mr. Artin, Dr. Kay, and Dr. Sleeth, have already been named in this preface. Among others who have shared large responsibilities are these associate editors: Miss Anne M. Driscoll, Dr. Philip H. Goepp, Mr. Hubert P. Kelsey, Dr. Howard G. Rhoads, and Dr. H. Bosley Woolf; two assistant editors, Miss Ervina E. Foss and Mrs. Laverne W. King; and the departmental secretary, Mrs. Christine M. Mullen.

It is now fairly clear that before the twentieth century is over every community of the world will have learned how to communicate with all the rest of humanity. In this process of intercommunication the English language has already become the most important language on earth. This new Merriam-Webster unabridged is the record of this language as it is written and spoken. It is offered with confidence that it will supply in full measure that information on the general language which is required for accurate, clear, and comprehensive understanding of the vocabulary of today's society.

Springfield, Mass. PHILIP B. GOVE
June 1, 1961

MERRIAM-WEBSTER EDITORIAL STAFF

EDITOR IN CHIEF

PHILIP B. GOVE (1946–1972)
A.B., Dartmouth College; A.M., Harvard University; Ph.D., Columbia University; Litt.D., Dartmouth College
Formerly teacher at Rice Institute and at New York University
(managing editor 1950–1952; general editor 1952–1960)

ASSOCIATE EDITORS

EDWARD ARTIN (*1934–1974)
Harvard University

JOHN P. BETHEL (*1934–1958)
B.A., McGill University; A.M., Ph.D., Harvard University
Formerly teacher at Buffalo (N.Y.) State Teachers College
(general editor 1935–1952; senior associate editor 1952–1958)

DANIEL COOK (1952–1957)
B.S.(Ed.), M.A., University of Wisconsin; Ph.D., University of California
Formerly teacher at Duke University and at University of California

ANNE M. DRISCOLL (1937–1961)
A.B., Smith College

PHILIP H. GOEPP (1952–1967)
Ph.D., Johns Hopkins University
Formerly teacher at City College (N.Y.) and at University of Rochester

LUCIUS H. HOLT (*1934–1946)
B.A., M.A., Ph.D., Yale University **
Formerly teacher at United States Military Academy
(managing editor 1934–1946)

MAIRÉ WEIR KAY (1946–1978)
B.A., University of Kansas; M.A., Ph.D., University of Washington
Formerly teacher at Wells College

HUBERT P. KELSEY (1935–1972)
B.A., M.A., University of Michigan

DONALD W. LEE (1946–1948; 1953–1957)
B.A., Pennsylvania State College; M.A., Duke University; Ph.D., Columbia University
Formerly teacher at United States Naval Academy and at University of Pittsburgh

EDWARD F. OAKES (*1934–1957)
B.A., M.A., Williams College; A.M., Harvard University
Formerly teacher at Union College and at University of Michigan

HOWARD G. RHOADS (1952–1965)
A.B., University of Pennsylvania; A.M., Harvard University; Ph.D., University of Pennsylvania
Formerly teacher at Beaver College, at College of Wooster, at Harvard University, at Lehigh University, at Lingnan University (China), and at Temple University

CHARLES R. SLEETH (1951–1962)
A.B., A.M., West Virginia University; B.A., Oxford University; M.A., Ph.D., Princeton University
Formerly teacher at Greensboro College, at University of Oklahoma, and at Princeton University

H. BOSLEY WOOLF (1955–1975)
A.B., Emory & Henry College; Ph.D., Johns Hopkins University; Litt. D., Emory & Henry College
Formerly teacher at Louisiana State University
(managing editor from 1960)

ASSISTANT EDITORS

FREEMAN B. ANDERSON (1952–1953)
A.B., Bucknell University; Ph.D., Stanford University

WARREN B. AUSTIN (1958–1963)
B.A., City College (N.Y.); Ph.D., Columbia University
Formerly teacher at City College (N.Y.)

MILDRED F. BAXTER (1954–1960)
A.B., Vassar College; M.A., Ph.D., University of Michigan

WARREN B. BEZANSON (1954–1956)
B.A., Guilford College; B.Ed., Central Connecticut State College; M.A., University of North Carolina; Ph.D., University of Maryland
Formerly teacher at Washington College and at University of Maryland

LUCILLE C. BROUILLET (1940–1956)
B.S., University of Massachusetts

ROBERT B. COSTELLO (1960–1962)
B.A., Wesleyan University

F. STUART CRAWFORD (1959–1973)
B.A., Amherst College; M.A., Oxford University; Ph.D., Harvard University
Formerly teacher at Amherst College, Miami University (Ohio) and at Boston University

PHILIP W. CUMMINGS (1958–1962)
B.A., Bowdoin College; M.A., Ph.D., University of Pittsburgh

VIRGINIA L. DONIGIAN (1950–1961)
B.S., Boston University

AUDREY R. DUCKERT (1953–1956)
B.S.(Ed.), M.A., University of Wisconsin; Ph.D., Radcliffe College

ROSE F. EGAN (*1934–1945)
B.A., Syracuse University; M.A., Columbia University
Formerly teacher at Smith College

This table contains only those who have been in full-time residence for at least one year.

FRANK FLETCHER (1953–1959)
A.B., M.A., Brown University; Ph.D., University of Michigan
Formerly teacher at University of Michigan and Cornell University

ERVINA E. FOSS (*1934–1968)
A.B., Mount Holyoke College

MARIAN M. FOX (1958–1962)
B.A., University of Massachusetts
Formerly teacher at Dalton (Mass.) High School

EDWARD A. H. FUCHS (1943–1952)
Ph.B., Ph.D., University of Chicago
Formerly teacher at Indiana University and Centre College of Kentucky

JEROME J. FUSSELL (1951–1955)
B.J., University of Missouri; M.A., Ph.D., University of Chicago

J. EDWARD GATES (1956–1962)
B.A., Maryville College; B.D., Yale University; S.T.M., Harvard University; Ph.D., Hartford Seminary Foundation
Formerly teacher at Gerard Institute (Sidon, Lebanon)

E. WARD GILMAN (1958–1997)
B.A., Bowdoin College; A.M., Boston University

MYRON J. GLADSTONE (1952–1956)
S.B., M.A., Harvard University

SAMUEL J. GOLUB (1947–1949)
B.S., M.S., University of Massachusetts; Ph.D., Harvard University
Formerly teacher at University of Massachusetts

LUCILE GREBENC (1952–1960)
University of California

---

* also on the editorial staff of WEBSTER'S NEW INTERNATIONAL, Second Edition, 1934
** also on the editorial staff of WEBSTER'S NEW INTERNATIONAL, 1909

WILLIAM H. HAWLEY (1959–1961)
A.B., Dartmouth College; M.A., Middlebury College; LL.B., Western New England College
Formerly teacher at Mt. Hermon School, at St. Paul's School, at Williston Academy, and at the Peddie School

CHRISTOPHER T. HOOLIHAN (1955–1959)
B.A., St. Meinrad Seminary; M.A., Catholic University of America
Formerly teacher at St. Meinrad Seminary

BETTIE (SHULL) HUGHES (1956–1957)
B.S. in Ed., A.M., University of Missouri
Formerly teacher at Westboro (Mo.) Consolidated High School, at Lathrop (Mo.) High School, and at University of Missouri

BENJAMIN KEEN (1956–1959)
B.A., Muhlenberg College; M.A., Lehigh University; Ph.D., Yale University
Formerly teacher at Yale University, at Amherst College, and at University of West Virginia

GRACE A. KELLOGG (1941–1984)
B.A., American International College

FRANCIS M. KELLY, JR. (1959–1961)
B.A., University of Rochester; M.A., Ph.D., Columbia University
Formerly teacher at Hunter College and at University of Michigan

LAVERNE W. KING (1949–1973)

HENRY KRATZ (1955–1960)
A.B., State University College of Education at Albany, New York; A.M., Ph.D., Ohio State University
Formerly teacher at Ohio State University, at University of Michigan, and at University of Massachusetts

MALCOLM R. LEETE (1935–1937)
B.A., Harvard University

ELSIE MAG (*1934–1968)
A.B., Smith College
Formerly teacher at Ludlow (Mass.) High School

MILDRED A. MERCIER (1956–1962)
B.S. in Ed., Ohio University; M.A., Western Reserve University; B.S. in L.S., Columbia University
Formerly teacher at South High School (Lima, Ohio) and at Celina (Ohio) High School

RALF F. MUNSTER (1951–1955)
A.B., M.A., Ph.D., Duke University
Formerly teacher at Duke University and at University of Georgia

HAROLD E. NIERGARTH (1959–1965)
B.A., University of Michigan

JOSEPH A. PALERMO (1940–1943)
A.B., Temple University; A.M., Ph.D., Princeton University
Formerly teacher at Temple University

FRANK G. PICKEL (1957–1959)
A.B., Oberlin College; Ph.D., University of Chicago
Formerly teacher at Washington University (St. Louis), at University of Washington, and at University of Vermont

ROBERT J. QUINLAN (1958–1962)
A.B., M.A., Ph.D., Yale University

RAYMOND RHINE (1953–1958)
A.B., A.M., Syracuse University
Formerly teacher at Felt Mills (N.Y.) High School, at Black River (N.Y.) High School, at Babylon (N.Y.) High School, at Syracuse University, and at Springfield College

M. ELUNED ROBERTS (1952–1962)
A.B., M.A., University of Vermont
Formerly teacher at Westbrook Junior College

THOMAS H. B. ROBERTSON (1958–1962)
A.B., Bluffton College
Formerly teacher at Wilbraham (Mass.) Academy

HUBERT H. ROE (*1934–1967)

MIRIAM H. ROOT (1946–1962)
A.B., Keuka College; B.S., Columbia University

DONALD B. SANDS (1953–1957)
B.A., Lehigh University; A.M., Ph.D., Harvard University
Formerly teacher at University of Arkansas, at University of Maine, at Bowdoin College, and at Harvard University

JANET D. SCOTT (1955–1960)
A.B., Vassar College; S.M., University of Chicago

DONALD J. SHARF (1957–1961)
B.A., M.A., Wayne State University; Ph.D., University of Michigan

LESTER C. SHERMAN (1950–1959)
B.A., Wayne State University; M.A., University of Michigan
Formerly teacher at Drake University

SIDNEY A. SIMMONS (1950–1956)
B.S.A., Ontario College of Agriculture; M.A., University of Toronto
Formerly teacher at Ontario College of Agriculture

HARRIET SMITH (1957–1961)
A.B., Mt. Holyoke College; M.S., Columbia University; M.A., University of Massachusetts

ADELE K. SULLIVAN (1951–1968)
B.A., Connecticut College

SOL STEINMETZ (1958–1961)
B.A., Yeshiva University
Formerly teacher at Yavne Academy (Brooklyn, N.Y.)

GEORGE M. SWANSON (1955–1958)
A.B., Drake University

SIDNEY THOMAS (1958–1961)
B.A., City College (N.Y.); M.A., Ph.D., Columbia University
Formerly teacher at City College (N.Y.), at Brooklyn College, and at Queens College

EVERETT E. THOMPSON (*1934–1949)
B.A., M.A., Amherst **
College; Litt. D., Syracuse University

JARVIS TODD (1947–1951)
A.B., Wabash College; M.A., University of Kentucky
Formerly teacher at University of Dayton

LEROY D. WELD (1951–1955)
B.S., M.S., Ph.D., State University of Iowa
Formerly teacher at Coe College

BAXTER D. WILSON (1952–1955)
A.B., The Citadel; M.A., Ph.D., University of Virginia

RAYMOND R. WILSON (1950–1976)
B.A., Northwestern State College (Oklahoma); M.A., West Texas State College

RENATE (WOLFF) WOLF (1952–1956)
B.A., Goucher College; M.Ed., Smith College; M.A., Ph.D., Bryn Mawr College
Formerly teacher at Wilkes College and at Wellesley College

EDITORIAL ASSISTANTS

DOROTHY L. ARTIN (*1934–1942; 1957)
B.S., University of Massachusetts

JOHN D. BARLOW (1954–1956)
B.A., Bates College

HOWARD K. BATTLES (1951–1955)
B.A., M.A., University of Minnesota

RUTH Y. BERRY (1958–1962)
S.B., Simmons College; M.A., American International College

GRACE E. BROPHY (1960–1963)
A.B., Grove City College

DOLORES D. CIERI (1951–1954)
Beaver College

MIRIAM E. COHEN (1957–1959)
New England Conservatory of Music

ROBERT W. CONBOY (1952–1970)
A.B., University of Miami; A.M., Vanderbilt University
Formerly teacher at Pfeiffer Junior College and at Riverside Military Academy

HILDA H. CONKLING (1959–1960)

THERESE (HAFEY) CORRIDAN (1946–1952)
B.A., College of Our Lady of the Elms

DOROTHY K. CRONE (1954–1955)
A.B., Smith College

MARIANNE E. DUFRESNE (1957–1959)
A.B., University of Vermont
Formerly teacher at Delevan (N.Y.) High School

ERWIN L. EISOLD (1940–1943)
B.A., Centre College of Kentucky

JOHN T. FLAHIVE (1951–1954)
B.S., Arnold College of Hygiene and Physical Education; M.A., Columbia University

HAROLD J. FLAVIN (1956–1957)
B.A., Tusculum College; M.F.S., University of Maryland; M.S. in L.S., Drexel Institute

LUCILLE B. GILCREAST (1958–1959)
B.S., Boston University

RITA L. GOYETTE (1946–1952)

HARVEY R. GRAVELINE (1959–1960)
A.B., Boston University

RUTH F. GREEN (1951–1954)
B.S.E., Massachusetts State Teachers College (Westfield); M.Ed., Springfield College

ALICE A. GUIMOND (1953–1954; 1955–1957)
B.A., American International College; M.A., University of Illinois; Ph.D., University of Wisconsin

MABEL B. HANCHETT (1942–1952)

SHIRLEY H. HENDERSON (1954–1955)
B.S., State Teachers College at Edinboro (Penn.)

JAMES M. HENRY, JR. (1958–1960)

BARBARA A. HOLLAND (1953–1955)
A.B., M.A., University of Pennsylvania

VERNON L. INGRAHAM (1951–1953)
B.A., University of New Hampshire; M.A., Amherst College; Ph.D., University of Pennsylvania

RUTH S. JOHNSON (1959–1961)
A.B., Oberlin College
Formerly teacher at Connellsville (Penn.) High School and at Northampton (Mass.) High School

CHARNA (LYTELL) KATZMAN (1952–1954)
B.A., American International College

IRENE (BARONIAN) KING (1950–1956)
B.A., American International College

DORIS R. KNIGHT (1958–1959; 1960–1961)
B.A., M.A., University of Massachusetts

MARY ELLEN KNIGHT (1957–1964)
B.A., University of New Hampshire; A.M., Boston University

ARTHUR G. LAMIRANDE (1959–1961)
B.A., American International College

EMILE O. LARUE (1956–1957)
B.A., Université Laval
Formerly teacher at Loyola College (Montreal), at Assumption College, and at Clark University

EDITH M. LOWE (1959–1966)
B.A., Milwaukee-Downer College
Formerly teacher at Wausau (Wis.) High School and at Bay Path Junior College

EULELAH G. LYON (1957–1963)
A.B. in Th., Gordon College

CHARLES P. MCCORMICK, JR. (1958–1961)
B.S., M.Ed., Springfield College

JUDITH (LEITCH) MARQUESS (1958–1959)
B.A., Queens College

PATRICIA F. MARTIN (1957–1971)
Wayne State University

JEAN (YOUNGDALE) MAYER (1953–1954)
B.S., University of Minnesota; M.Ed., University of Massachusetts

JOHN O. MAYHUGH (1941–1942)
B.A., M.A., University of Texas

BETTY MELTZER (1959–1967)
B.A., Goddard College

M. PORTIA MICKEY (1951–1954)
A.B., Oberlin College
Formerly teacher at North China Union Women's College and at Doshisha University (Japan)

LORNA (HOLBROOK) MUI (1953–1955)
B.S., M.A., Columbia University

EMILY (NOSS) MUTTER (1951–1952)
A.B., Mt. Holyoke College

GERTRUDE F. NEW (1957–1964)
Massachusetts State Teachers College (Westfield)

ANNE (BAKER) O'BRIEN (1951–1956)

RAYMOND L. PANIGHETTI (1959–1960)
B.A., American International College

JOHN E. PETRONE (1957–1961)
B.A.(J.), University of Wisconsin

MARIE T. PLOUFFE (1959–1960)
B.A., American International College

CHARLEEN A. PRENTICE (1952–1953)
B.A., American International College; M.Ed., Springfield College

WALTER A. REPPUCCI (1958–1959)
B.S.F.S., Georgetown University; M. Ed., Massachusetts State College at Westfield; J.D., Western New England College

BARBARA A. RICHMOND (1952–1956)
A.B., Smith College

ALICE (DUNN) ROBERTS (1952–1953)
A.B., Smith College

HAZEL B. ROSSI (1957–1959)
University of Massachusetts

WALTER E. SEARS (1951–1955)
A.B., Harvard University

DORIS N. SHERWOOD (1954–1966)

WALTER J. SKOCZOLEK (1951–1955)
B.S. in Ed., Massachusetts State Teachers College (Hyannis); A.M., Boston University
Formerly teacher at Springfield (Mass.) Technical High School and at Boston (Mass.) High School of Commerce

JANE F. SMITH (1958–1962)
B.A., Cornell University

GEORGIANA (WARD) STRICKLAND (1955–1957)
B.A., Middlebury College

THOMAS J. SULLIVAN (1954–1956)
A.B., Holy Cross College
Formerly teacher at Holy Cross College

KATHLEEN W. THOMPSON (1957–1958)
A.A., A.B., George Washington University

LUCY (RICH) THOMPSON (1940–1942)
A.B., Vassar College

ELSIE A. TOURVILLE (1951–1952)

CHARLES WESTCOTT (*1934–1946)

IDA N. WOLFSON (1954–1956)

DOROTHY M. ZIEMANN (1951–1955)
B.A., American International College; A.M., Ed.M., Boston University

ETHEL S. ZIMMERMAN (1958–1959)
B.S., University of Massachusetts

SECRETARIAL AND CLERICAL ASSISTANTS

MAUDE L. BARNES (1960–1978)
Massachusetts State Teachers College (Framingham)

LILLIAN (BOUDREAU) CARPENTER (1953–1957)

ANNA M. CURTO (1953–1961)

BEATRICE (BREAULT) DAUNAIS (1951–1956)

MARY C. DILLON (1959–1968)
Massachusetts State Teachers College (Westfield)

ESTHER (HARRINGTON) GAUTHIER (1958–1962; 1969–1973)

MARY A. GRIFFIN (1953–1961)

ELEANOR (BRAULT) HARVEY (1952–1957)

EDITH (MOORE) HEATHCOTE (1938–1941)

ALICE HOYT (*1934–1940)

HELEN (MCGUIRE) JUTT (1943–1957)

SHEILA M. KELLY (1955–1961)

FLORIDA L. KING (1956–1961)

SADIE LAGODITZ (1946–1952)

CHRISTINE (MAYHER) MULLEN (*1934–1964)

MAE C. NIELSEN (1956–1965)

ARABELLE POLLOCK (1952–1957)

ROSAMOND (LYLE) PORTER (1948–1951)
B.A., Wells College

NELL (SABALASKA) SHERWOOD (1947–1952)

ROSE D. STICKEL (1959–1962)

EVELYN G. SUMMERS (1959–1978)

FRANCES V. SUNDQUIST (1952–1956)

ROBERTA M. TEEHAN (1935–1944)

ROSE (DEWEY) THERRIEN (1954–1959)

BERTHA P. TIMBIE (1946–1962)
Sargent School of Physical Education

SARA N. TRACY (1954–1963)

MARIE P. TRUE (1953–1957)

MARGARET (COLE) VANCINI (1947–1951)

HELEN F. VYE (1952–1956)

NELLIE T. WILLCUTT (1958–1964)

PEARL (GREEN) WYMA (*1934–1946)

OUTSIDE CONSULTANTS

THIS LIST of outside consultants contains 202 names. It is a partial list of specialists not on our own Merriam-Webster staff, for it includes only those who were asked to handle a considerable body of related terms as distinguished from other hundreds of outsiders whose opinions were sought by letter, telephone, or visit. To all these others we are grateful, but it would be impracticable to name every one. Those who are named have worked on terms in the subject mentioned opposite their name. This does not necessarily mean that they actually phrased the definitions in that subject. Because of the requirements of styling and of integrating definitions with each other and with overall policies not always easily explained to outsiders, responsibility for any definition cannot in fairness be placed on an outside consultant. The staff editors are solely responsible for the printed form of all definitions in this dictionary.

ABBOTT, KENNETH M. **Etymology: Greek and Latin**
A.B., Harvard University; Ph.D., University of Illinois
Professor of Classical Languages, Ohio State University
Coauthor: *Index Apuleianus; Index Verborum Ciceronis Epistularum*

ALLEN, MARTHA F. **Camp Fire Girls**
A.B., Mississippi State College for Women; A.M., Columbia University
National Director, Camp Fire Girls Inc.

ANDERSON, FRANK W., JR. **Air Force**
B.A., Birmingham-Southern College; M.A., Ph.D., University of North Carolina
Managing Editor: *Air University Quarterly Review*
Editor: *Great Flying Stories*

ANDERSON, RUTH TRIPP **Salvation Army**
Member of Salvation Army Editorial Staff

ARAND, LOUIS A. **Roman Catholicism**
A.B., A.M., S.T.B., St. Mary's Seminary and University; S.T.L., Catholic University of America; S.T.D., Anglico University (Rome)
President, Divinity College, Catholic University of America
Author: *St. Augustine: Faith, Hope and Charity*
Coauthor: *Doctrine and Devotion*
Editor: *The Spiritual Life*

ARENSBERG, CONRAD M. **Peoples and Tribes of Europe**
A.B., Ph.D., Harvard University
Professor of Anthropology, Columbia University
Author: *Irish Countryman; Family and Community in Ireland*
Coauthor: *Measuring Human Relations; Trade and Markets in the Early Empires*
Editor: *Human Organization*

BANNER, PAUL H. **Economics**
B.A., University of Michigan; M.P.A., Ph.D., Harvard University
Chairman, Research Committee, Western and Southwestern Trunkline Railroads
Lecturer in Economics, Washington University

BARROWS, ROBERT S. **Physics of Photography**
B.A., Kalamazoo College
Research Physicist, Eastman Kodak Company
Author: chapters or sections in *Theory of the Photographic Process* (Mees, rev.ed.) and *Fundamentals of Photographic Theory* (James and Higgins); several papers on photographic sensitometry

BASOLO, FRED **Chemical Elements Table, Periodic Table**
B.Ed., Southern Illinois Normal University; M.S., Ph.D., University of Illinois
Professor of Chemistry, Northwestern University
Author: numerous scientific publications
Coauthor: *Mechanisms of Inorganic Reactions*

BAUER, EDWARD E. **Concrete and Masonry**
B.S., C.E., M.S., University of Illinois
Professor of Civil Engineering, University of Illinois
Author: *Plain Concrete; Highway Materials*
Contributor: *Engineering News Record*

BECKMAN, THEODORE N. **Marketing**
B.S., A.M., Ph.D., Ohio State University
Professor of Marketing, Ohio State University
Author: *Credits and Collections in Theory and Practice*
Coauthor: *Principles of Marketing; Wholesaling; Cases in Credits and Collections*

BENDER, ERNEST **India and Pakistan**
A.B., Temple University; Ph.D., University of Pennsylvania
Research Associate Professor of Modern Indo-Aryan Languages and Literatures, University of Pennsylvania
Editor and translator: *The Nalarāyadavadanticarita*

BITTINGER, CHARLES *Color:* **Spectrum**
Student, Massachusetts Institute of Technology; student, École des Beaux Arts; Academician, National Academy of Design; Captain, U.S.N.R. (Ret.)
Contributor: *U.S. Naval Institute Proceedings; National Geographic Magazine*

BLACK, KNOX C. **Communications**
A.B., A.M., Ph.D., Harvard University
Scientific Advisor to SACEUR, Supreme Headquarters Allied Powers Europe and to SHAPE in Paris, France

BLACK, MAX **Logic**
B.A., University of Cambridge; Ph.D., D. Lit., University of London
Professor of Philosophy, Cornell University
Author: *Language and Philosophy; The Nature of Mathematics; Critical Thinking; Problems of Analysis*
Editor: *Philosophical Analysis; The Social Theories of Talcott Parsons*
Coeditor: *Journal of Symbolic Logic; Philosophical Review*

BLAKELEY, HAROLD W. **Military Science**
Graduate: Field Artillery School; Command and General Staff School; Army War College
Major General, U.S. Army (Ret.)
Author: *The Employment of Land Mines; The 32d Infantry Division in World War II*
Contributor: *N. Y. Times, N. Y. Herald Tribune, Reporter*, and misc. military journals

BOGEN, JULES I. **Finance and Banking**
B.S., A.M., Ph.D., Columbia University
Professor of Finance, Graduate School of Business Administration, New York University
Author: *Corporation Finance*
Coauthor: *Investment Banking; Money and Banking*
Editor: *Financial Handbook*

BOUDREAU, RICHARD P. **Etymology: Romance**
B.A., Seton Hall University; M.A., Ph.D., Princeton University
Assistant Professor of French, La Salle College

BOWIE, HAROLD E. **Mathematics**
B.A., M.A., University of Maine
Professor of Mathematics, American International College
Contributor: misc. mathematics publications

BOYD, WILLIAM C. **Immunology and Serology**
A.B., A.M., Harvard University; Ph.D., Boston University
Professor of Immunochemistry, Boston University School of Medicine
Author: *Genetics and the Race of Man; Races and People;* textbooks and articles in technical journals

BREWER, ALLEN F. *Color Plate:* **Horses**
B.F.A., Yale University
Free-lance artist; president of EQUI-LITH
Contributor: *Encyclopaedia Britannica;* veterinary manuals; national turf and harness horse publications

BROWN, JAMES M., III **Glass**
B.A., (hon.) M.A., Amherst College; M.A., Harvard University
Director, Corning Glass Center

BROWN, KARL **Library Science**
A.B., University of Kansas; B.S., New York State Library School
Free-lance editor and bibliographer; Library Consultant, St. Martin's Press (N.Y.C.)
Author: *Guide to Reference Collections of the New York Public Library*
Editor: *New York Public Library; Library Journal*

BROWN, ROY H. **Art**
A.B., Queens College; A.M., Columbia University
Instructor, Garland Junior College; Art Director, Houghton Mifflin Company

BRUMMITT, WYATT B. **Amateur Photography**
B.Litt., Columbia University
Manager, Historical Projects, Eastman Kodak Company
Coauthor: *This Is Photography*
Editor: *Pictures*

BUSSOW, CARL **Pavement Construction**
B.S., Cooper Union; B.S., Polytechnic Institute of Brooklyn
Consulting Chemist and Paving Engineer
Contributor: misc. articles

CALAMIA, ERIC **Pipes and Tobacco**
Managing Director, Retail Tobacco Dealers of America Inc.

CARPENTER, FRANK M. **Entomology**
A.B., M.S., D.Sc., Harvard University
Professor of Entomology, Alexander Agassiz Professor of Zoology, and Curator of Fossil Insects, Museum of Comparative Zoology, Harvard University
Author: misc. articles on insect evolution and taxonomy

CASKEY, JAMES E., JR. **Meteorology**
B.S., Furman University; M.A., Duke University; Certificate of Professional Competence in Meteorology, University of Chicago
Meteorologist Editor: U.S. Weather Bureau
Editor: *Monthly Weather Review*

CHAMBERLAIN, NEIL W. **Labor**
A.B., M.A., Western Reserve University; Ph.D., Ohio State University
Professor of Economics, Yale University
Author: *The Union Challenge to Management Control; Collective Bargaining; Social Responsibility and Strikes; The Impact of Strikes; A General Theory of Economic Process; Labor*

CHILD, EDWIN B. *Portrait of Noah Webster*
A.B., (hon.) M.A., Amherst College
Artist

CHRISTENSEN, CLYDE M. **Mycology**
B.S., M.S., Ph.D., University of Minnesota
Professor of Plant Pathology, University of Minnesota
Author: *Common Edible Mushrooms; Molds and Man; Keys to the Common Fleshy Fungi;* numerous research papers in plant pathology, mycology

CLENCH, WILLIAM J. **Mollusks**
B.S., (hon.) D.Sc., Michigan State University; M.S., Harvard University; M.S., Ph.D., University of Michigan
Curator of Mollusks, Harvard Museum of Comparative Zoology
Special Editor in Zoology, *Webster's New International Dictionary, Second Edition*
Editor and contributor: *Johnsonia;* occasional papers on mollusks

COBURN, C. GILBERT **Coffee**
B.J., University of Missouri
Director of Public Relations, Pan-American Coffee Bureau

COLE, FAY-COOPER **Archaeology**
B.S., Sc.D., Northwestern University; Ph.D., Columbia University; LL.D., University of Chicago; LL.D., Beloit College
Professor Emeritus of Anthropology, University of Chicago
Author: *Peoples of Malaysia; The Bukidnon*
Coauthor: *Kincaid, A Prehistoric Illinois Metropolis*
Contributor: articles for encyclopedias

CONKLIN, HAROLD C. **Etymology and Definitions: Austronesian**
A.B., University of California (Berkeley); Ph.D., Yale University
Associate Professor of Anthropology, Columbia University
Author: *Hanunóo-English Vocabulary; Hanunóo Agriculture*

CORNEY, GEORGE M. **Radiography**
B.A., Cornell University
Research Associate, Eastman Kodak Company
Contributor: *Handbook of Nondestructive Testing; Radiation Hygiene Handbook*

CREED, ROBERT P. **Etymology: Derivative and Germanic**
B.A., Swarthmore College; M.A., Ph.D., Harvard University
Assistant Professor of English, Brown Univ.
Author: articles and reviews on Old English

DALL, WILLIAM B. **Textile Machinery and Processes**
B.A., Amherst College
Managing Editor, *Textile World*

DARKIS, FREDERICK R. **Tobacco**
B.S., M.S., Ph.D., University of Maryland
Vice-president and Director of Research, Liggett and Myers Tobacco Company
Author: misc. articles on tobacco

DAY, CYRUS L. **Knots**
B.S., Harvard University; A.M., Columbia University; Ph.D., Harvard University
Professor of English, University of Delaware
Author: *The Art of Knotting and Splicing*
Editor: *Songs of Dryden; Songs of D'Urfey*
Cocompiler: *English Song-Books*

DECAMP, DAVID **Etymology: Scientific**
B.A., Hillsdale College; M.A., University of New Mexico; Ph.D., University of California
Assistant Professor of English, University of Texas
Author: *Jamaican Creole*
Contributor: *Orbis*

DEIGNAN, HERBERT G. **Ornithology**
A.B., Princeton
Curator, Birds, U.S. National Museum, Smithsonian Institution
Author: *The Birds of Northern Thailand; Type Specimens of Birds in the United States National Museum; Check-list of the Birds of Thailand*

DILGER, WILLIAM C. *Color Plates:* **State Birds, Water Birds**
B.S., M.S., Ph.D., Cornell University
Director of Research and Assistant Professor of Ornithology, Cornell University
Contributor: *Wilson Bulletin; Auk; Evolution; Zeitschrift für Tierpsychologie*

DIXON, ALBERT, JR. **Accounting**
C.P.A., Massachusetts, Connecticut; B.C.S., Northeastern University; LL.D., Western New England College
Partner, Ernst & Ernst
Trustee, Western New England College

DODGE, AUSTIN A. **Pharmacy**
Ph.C., Valparaiso University; B.S., Ph.D., University of Wisconsin
Professor of Pharmacognosy, School of Pharmacy, University of Mississippi
Assistant Editor: *Remington's Practice of Pharmacy*

DRAVES, CARL Z. **Dye Table**
B.S., M.S., Ph.D., University of Washington
Instructor in Chemistry, Brooklyn College
Author: "Textile Chemical Specialties," *1933 Technical Manual and Year Book of American Association of Textile Chemists and Colorists*
Contributor: *Journal of Optical Society of America; American Dyestuff Reporter; Melliand Textilberichte; Encyclopedia of Chemical Technology*

DUNNIGAN, MARY CATHERINE **Brewing**
B.A., Mary Washington College; M.L.S., Columbia University
Librarian, U.S. Brewers Foundation, Inc.
Author: *Beer and Ale in Old New York*

EATON, GEORGE T. **Chemistry of Photography**
B.A., Brandon College; B.S., Acadia University; M.A., McMaster University
Head of Processing Research Department; Assistant Head of Applied Photography Division, Research Laboratories, Eastman Kodak Company
Author: *Photochemistry; in Black-and-White and Color Photography*
Contributor: *Americana Annual*

ELBERT, SAMUEL H. **Etymology and Definitions: Polynesian**
A.B., Grinnell College; Ph.D., Indiana University
Professor of Pacific Languages and Linguistics, University of Hawaii
Coauthor: *Hawaiian-English Dictionary*

EMENEAU, MURRAY B. **Etymology: Indic and Dravidian**
B.A., Dalhousie University; B.A., M.A., Oxford University; Ph.D., Yale University
Professor of Sanskrit and General Linguistics, University of California (Berkeley)
Author: *Kota Texts; Kolami, a Dravidian Language; Sanskrit Sandhi and Exercises; Studies in Vietnamese (Annamese) Grammar*
Coauthor: *A Dravidian Etymological Dictionary*
Contributor: educational publications

FAIRBAIRN, HAROLD W. **Petrology and Geochronology**
B.Sc., Queen's University; A.M., Ph.D., Harvard University
Professor of Geology, Massachusetts Institute of Technology
Author: *Structural Petrology of Deformed Rocks*

FEDERER, CHARLES A., JR. **Astronomy**
B.S., City College of New York
Editor and Publisher: *Sky and Telescope*

FERGUSON, CHARLES A. **Language Tables: Afro-Asiatic (Arabic)**
A.B., A.M., Ph.D., University of Pennsylvania
Director, Center for Applied Linguistics (Washington, D.C.)
Coauthor: *Lessons in Contemporary Arabic*
Editor: *Contributions to Arabic Linguistics*
Coeditor: *Linguistic Diversity in South Asia*

FERGUSON, WALTER W. *Color Plates:* **Gems, Insects, Monkeys**
Artist; formerly a staff artist for the American Museum of Natural History

FLOROVSKY, GEORGES **Eastern Orthodoxy**
Diploma, Graduate Studies, University of Odessa; D.D., St. Andrews University; S.T.D., Boston University; Th.D., University of Salonika
Professor of Eastern Church History, Harvard Divinity School
Author: *Eastern Fathers of the Fourth Century; Byzantine Fathers of the Fifth through the Eighth Centuries; Ways of Russian Theology*
Contributor: *Cahiers théologiques de l'actualité protestante; A History of the Ecumenical Movement*

FORD, ROBERT S. **Taxation**
A.B., Texas Christian University; A.M., University of California; Ph.D., Columbia University
Associate Dean, Rackham Graduate School and Professor of Economics, University of Michigan
Author: *Michigan Highway Finance*
Contributor: technical and professional journals

FOSTER, FRED W. **Cartography**
A.B., M.S., Ph.D., University of Michigan
Professor of Geography, University of Illinois
Editor: *Atlas of Illinois Resources; Commercial Atlas*
Contributor: numerous articles on interpretation of aerial photographs

FRIED, HENRY B. **Horology**
Graduate of the University of the State of New York Industrial Teachers' Training College
Technical Director: American Watchmakers' Institute; Watch Material Distributors' Association of America
Horological Consultant: *Jewelers' Circular-Keystone*
Author: *Watch Repairers' Manual; Bench Practices for Watch Repairers; The Watch Escapement; The Universal Watch Parts Catalogue*

FULFORD, MARGARET **Mosses and Liverworts**
B.A., B.E., A.M., University of Cincinnati; Ph.D., Yale University
Professor of Botany, Fellow of the Graduate School, University of Cincinnati
Author: *Bazzania in Central and South America; Young Stages in the Leafy Hepaticae; Distribution Patterns of the Genera of Leafy Hepaticae of South America*

GARRATT, GEORGE A. **Forestry**
B.S., Michigan State College; M.F., Ph.D., Yale University; (hon.) Sc.D., University of the South
Dean, School of Forestry, and Pinchot Professor of Forestry, Yale University
Author: *The Mechanical Properties of Wood*
Coauthor: *Wood Preservation*

GILLETTE, GEORGE A. **Photographic Trade Names**
E.E., Rensselaer Polytechnic Institute; LL.B., Fordham University Law School
Assistant Director of Patent Department, Eastman Kodak Company

GLEASON, HENRY A. **Plant Taxonomy (Flowering Plants)**
B.S., A.M., University of Illinois; Ph.D., Columbia University
Head Curator Emeritus, New York Botanical Garden
Author: *A Revision of the North American Vernonieae; The Vegetation of the Inland Sand Deposits of Illinois; Some Applications of the Quadrat Method; The Vegetational History of the Middle West; The Individualistic Concept of the Plant Association; Botan-*

ical Results of the Tyler-Duida Expedition; Plants of the Vicinity of New York
Coauthor: *The New Britton and Brown Illustrated Flora of the Northeastern United States and Adjacent Canada; Plant Ecology of Porto Rico*
Contributor: numerous articles on botanical research

GLEASON, HENRY A., JR. **Language Names**
B.S., Cornell; Ph.D., Hartford Seminary Foundation
Professor of Linguistics, Hartford Seminary Foundation
Author: *An Introduction to Descriptive Linguistics*

GODLOVE, ISAAC H. **Color**
B.S., A.M., Washington University; Ph.D., University of Illinois
Chemist and Physicist, DuPont Company and General Aniline and Film Corporation
Special Editor in Color, *Webster's New International Dictionary, Second Edition*
Author: articles on color physics and psychology
Coauthor: *The Science of Colors; The Smithsonian Tables of Physical Constants*

GOLLON, FRANK R. **Photographic Trade Names**
B.S., C.E., City College of New York; LL.B. George Washington University
Patent Attorney, Eastman Kodak Company

GORDON, LEWIS H. **Etymology: Italian and French**
A.B., A.M., Princeton University; Ph.D., Cornell University
Professor of Italian and French, Brown Univ.
Author: *Supplementary Concordance to Minor Italian Works of Dante*

GRIMWOOD, W. K. **Sound Motion Pictures**
B.S., Massachusetts Institute of Technology
Research Associate, Eastman Kodak Company
Contributor: articles on sound recording and television

GRISWOLD, ERWIN N. **Law**
A.B., A.M., Oberlin College; LL.B., S.J.D., Harvard University; L.H.D., Tufts College and Case Institute of Technology; LL.D., thirteen universities and colleges
Dean and Langdell Professor of Law, Harvard Law School
Author: *Spendthrift Trusts; Cases on Federal Taxation; The Fifth Amendment Today*
Coauthor: *Cases on Conflict of Laws*
General Editor: American Casebook Series
Contributor: legal periodicals; *Geographical Review*

GROSSENHEIDER, RICHARD P. *Color Plates:* **Butterflies and Moths, Cats, Shells**
Free-lance artist

GUMPERTZ, WERNER H. **Building and Building Materials**
S.B., S.M., Bldg. E., Massachusetts Institute of Technology
Consulting Engineer and President, Simpson Gumpertz and Heger Inc.
Contributor: *Technology Review, Journal of Engineering Education, Civil Engineering*

GUNN, HAROLD D. **Africa: Peoples and Tribes**
B.A., Southern Methodist University; M.A., University of London
Assistant Professor of Anthropology and African History, Lincoln University (Pa.)
Author: *Peoples of the Plateau Area of Northern Nigeria; Pagan Peoples of the Central Area of Northern Nigeria; Handbook of the African Collections of the Commercial Museum of Philadelphia*
Coauthor: *Peoples of the Middle Niger Region, Northern Nigeria*

HAMILTON, RICHARD W. *Star Charts*
B.S., Polytechnic Institute of Brooklyn
Chart Curator of the American Association of Variable Star Observers

HARRIS, ZELLIG S. **Language Tables: Afro-Asiatic**
A.B., A.M., Ph.D., University of Pennsylvania
Professor of Linguistic Analysis, University of Pennsylvania
Author: *Development of Canaanite Dialects; Methods in Structural Linguistics;* several monographs
Contributor: articles to technical journals

HARRISON, G. DONALD **Pipe Organs**
President of Aeolian-Skinner Company

HECKMAN, RICHARD C. **Physics**
B.S., Antioch College; M.A., Ph.D., Duke University
Research Physicist, C. F. Kettering Foundation
Associate Professor of Physics, Antioch College

HEDGES, J. EDWARD **Insurance**
A.B., Baker University; M.B.A., University of Kansas; Ph.D., Johns Hopkins University; LL.D., Baker University
Professor of Insurance, Indiana University
Author: *Practical Fire and Casualty Insurance; Commercial Banking and the Stock Market before 1863*
Coauthor: *Compensation of Life Insurance Agents; Public Law 15 and the Insurance Agent*
Contributor: *Economic Problems of War;* educational and business publications

HENRY, ROBERT S. **Railroads**
A.B., LL.B., Vanderbilt University; Litt.D., University of Chattanooga
Vice-president, Association of American Railroads
Author: *Trains; This Fascinating Railroad Business; The Story of the Confederacy; "First with the Most" Forrest; The Story of the Mexican War; The Story of Reconstruction*
Editor: *As They Saw Forrest*

HIBBS, FENELLA W. **Girl Guiding**
Public Relations Secretary, Girl Guides Association, London

HIMMELSBACH, G. R. **Brewing**
B.A., M.A., Indiana University
Head, Department of Information, U.S. Brewers' Foundation Inc.

HINE, WADSWORTH C. *Line drawings for cuts*
Student, Cleveland Institute of Art
Commercial artist

HOENIGSWALD, HENRY M. **Etymology: Greek and Latin**
D.Litt., University of Florence (Italy)
Professor of Linguistics, Univ. of Pennsylvania
Author: *Spoken Hindustani; Language Change and Linguistic Reconstruction*

HOOTMAN, JAMES A. **Aeronautics**
B.S., Randolph-Macon College; M.S., Mississippi State College; Ph.D., University of Virginia
Executive Secretary, Inventions and Contributions Board, National Aeronautics and Space Administration
Contributor: *American Journal of Science, Physics Review,* National Advisory Committee for Aeronautics reports

HUGHES, CHARLES H. **Nautical**
Student, Massachusetts Institute of Technology
Naval Architect and Engineer
Author: *Motor Boats; Handbook of Ship Calculations and Construction*
Contributor: *New International Year Book*

HURD, CHARLES D. **Chemistry**
B.S., Syracuse University; Ph.D., Princeton University; (hon.) Sc.D., Syracuse Univ.
Clare Hamilton Hall Research Professor of Chemistry, Northwestern University
Author: *The Pyrolysis of Carbon Compounds; Open-Chain Nitrogen Compounds*
Contributor: articles in various fields of chemistry

HURD, FRED W. **Traffic Regulations**
B.S., University of Missouri; Certificate in Highway Traffic, Yale University
Director, Bureau of Highway Traffic, Yale University
Coauthor: *Traffic Engineering*

HYMES, DELL H. **Etymology: American Indian**
B.A., Reed College; M.A., Ph.D., Indiana University
Associate Professor of Anthropology and Linguistics, Univ. of California (Berkeley)
Contributor: *Anthropological Linguistics, Current Anthropology*

IVES, CHARLES E. **Motion Picture Technology**
Research Associate, Eastman Kodak Company
Coauthor: papers on motion picture film, instrument design, and photographic development

JACKSON, Robert J. **Rugs**
B.Ch.E., Northeastern University; M.S., Massachusetts Institute of Technology
Director of Engineering and Research, Bigelow-Sanford Carpet Company Inc.

JAMES, THOMAS H. **Photo Theory and Development Theory**
A.B., M.A., Ph.D., University of Colorado
Senior Research Associate, Eastman Kodak Company
Author: *Fundamentals of Photographic Theory*
Editor: *Photographic Science and Engineering*
Contributor: *Encyclopedia of Chemical Technology;* numerous research papers

JONES, WILLIAM R. **Etymology: Greek and Latin**
A.B., A.M., Ph.D., Univ. of Illinois
Associate Professor of Classical Languages, Ohio State University

JOOS, MARTIN **Cryptography**
A.M., Ph.D., University of Wisconsin
Professor of German and Linguistics, University of Wisconsin
Author: *Acoustic Phonetics; Middle High German Courtly Reader; Readings in Linguistics*
Contributor: articles in linguistic journals

JUDD, DEANE B. **Color**
A.B., M.A., Ohio State University; Ph.D., Cornell University
Physicist, Colorimetry, National Bureau of Standards; President, Munsell Color Foundation
Author: *Color in Business, Science, and Industry*
Editor: *Journal of the Optical Society of America*
Contributor: chapters in science books and articles

KELLENBERGER, HUNTER **Etymology: Romance**
A.B., Kenyon College; A.M., Ph.D., Princeton University
Professor of French, Brown University
Author: *The Influence of Accentuation on French Word Order*
Contributor: *The Case for Basic Education*

KIMPTON, KENNETH **Hardware**
B.S., University of Rochester
Associate Professor, Electrical Department, Rochester Institute of Technology

KINGSLAKE, RUDOLF **Optics of Photography**
B.Sc., M.Sc., D.Sc., Imperial College of Science and Technology (London)
Director of Optical Design, Eastman Kodak Company
Author: *Lenses in Photography*
Contributor: scientific papers, articles, and chapters in books

KNOWLTON, ARCHER E. **Engineering**
B.S., M.S., Trinity College (Conn.); E.E., Yale University
Associate Professor of Electrical Engineering, Yale University
Electrical Engineer, Connecticut Public Utilities Commission
Author: *Electrical Power Metering*
Senior Associate Editor: *Electrical World*

KORAB, HARRY E. **Soft Drinks**
B.S., University of Maryland
Technical Service Director, American Bottlers of Carbonated Beverages
Author: *Technical Problems of Bottled Carbonated Beverage Manufacture; Outline of Water Treating Methods*
Contributor: *American Society of Refrigeration Engineers Data Book*

KOSSOFF, A. DAVID **Etymology: Romance**
A.B., Amherst College; A.M., Ph.D., Brown University
Associate Professor of Spanish, Brown University
Author: *The Poetic Vocabulary of Fernando de Herrera*
Contributor: articles on Herrera

KRONEN, LEIF C. **Leather**
A.B., Nebraska Wesleyan University; LL.B., University of Nebraska
Secretary of Tanners' Council of America Inc.

KURATH, GERTRUDE PROKOSCH **Dance Ethnology**
B.A., M.A., Bryn Mawr College
Dance Editor: *Ethno-musicology*
Director: Dance Research Center
Author: books on Indian musicology and dance, folkways records
Dance Editor: *Topical Encyclopedia*
Contributor: articles on music and dance ethnology in journals, encyclopedias and the *Dictionary of Folklore*

LADRIÈRE, JAMES C. **Prosody**
Ph.B., University of Detroit; A.M., Ph.D., University of Michigan
Professor of English, Catholic University of America; Visiting Professor of Comparative Literature, University of Louvain and Harvard University
Author: *Directions in Contemporary Criticism and Literary Scholarship*
Coauthor: *English Institute Essays; Sound and Poetry*
Contributor: various articles on prosody

LAFAR, ARTHUR B. **Cocktails**
Formerly, President, Angostura-Wuppermann Corporation

LAMBDIN, THOMAS O. **Etymology: Semitic and Hamitic**
A.B., Franklin and Marshall College; Ph.D., Johns Hopkins University
Assistant Professor of Hebrew, Harvard Univ.
Contributor: articles on the Semitic and Egyptian languages

LAWSON, RICHARD H. **Etymology: Scientific**
B.A., M.A., University of Oregon; Ph.D., University of California
Assistant Professor of German, San Diego State College
Contributor: articles on Old High German and Modern German literature

LEBEL, C. J. **Audio Devices**
S.B., S.M., Massachusetts Institute of Technology
Vice-president, Audio Devices Inc.; President and Chief Engineer, Audio Instrument Company Inc.
Contributor: articles in engineering and scientific journals

LEROUX, ANDRE **Liquors and Cordials**
B.A., Lehigh University
President, Leroux and Company Inc.

LESLAU, WOLF **Language Tables: Afro-Asiatic (Ethiopic, Cushitic)**
Lic. ès Lettres, Dr. ès Lettres, Sorbonne
Professor of Hebrew and Semitic Linguistics, University of California (Los Angeles)
Author: *Short Grammar of Tigre; A Dictionary of Moca*

LEWIS, HENRY **Etymology: Celtic**
M.A., D. Litt., University College (Cardiff); (hon.) D.Litt.Celt., National University of Ireland
Professor Emeritus of University of Wales; formerly, Professor of Welsh Languages and Literature, University College of Swansea
Author: *Llawlyfr Cernyweg Canol; Llawlyfr*

Llydaweg Canol; Datblygial yr Iaith Gymraeg; Brut Dingestow
Coauthor: *A Concise Comparative Celtic Grammar*
Editor: *Peniarth 53; Welsh New Testament; Welsh Old Testament; Welsh Apocrypha;* etc.
Coeditor: *Welsh Congregational Hymnbook;* etc.
Contributor: *Encyclopaedia Britannica;* Welsh journals

LOVELAND, ROGER P. **Photomicrography**
B.A., Grinnell College; M.Sc., Ohio State University
Head, Photomicrography Department, Eastman Kodak Company
Author: *Photomicrography*
Contributor: misc. papers

LOWE, RONALD L. **Matches**
A.B., DePauw University
Sales Promotion Manager, Diamond Match Division, Diamond National Corporation

LUNN, HERBERT W. **Boy Scouts**
Assistant to the Director, Editorial Service, National Council of Boy Scouts of America

LUTZ, HAROLD J. **Forestry**
B.S., Michigan State College; M.F., Ph.D., Yale University
Morris K. Jesup Professor of Silviculture, Yale University
Coauthor: *Forest Soils*

LYMAN, HENRY **Marine Sport Fisheries**
A.B., Harvard University
Publisher: *Salt Water Sportsman*
Author: *Bluefishing*
Coauthor: *Striped Bass Fishing; Weakfishing*

LYMAN, TAYLOR **Metals**
A.B., Stanford University; S.M., Harvard University; Ph.D., Notre Dame University
Editor: *Metals Handbook*

MCGHEE, ADDISON F., JR. **Distilling**
B.S., Alabama Polytechnic Institute
Director of Public Relations, Kentucky Rural Electric Corporation; formerly, Community Relations Manager, Brown-Forman Distilling Corporation
Author: *He's in the Armored Force; History of Fort Knox*
Contributor: misc. articles in magazines, newspapers

MCLANATHAN, RICHARD B. K. **Minor Arts**
A.B., Ph.D., Harvard University
Director, Munson-Williams-Proctor Institute; formerly, Curator, Museum of Fine Arts, Department of Decorative Arts of Europe and America (Boston)

MCMILLAN, DONALD M. **Salvation Army**
Graduate, Salvation Army Officers' Training College
National Commander, Salvation Army in U.S.

MARTIN, GEORGE WILLARD **Mycology**
Litt.B., M.S., Rutgers University; Ph.D., University of Chicago
Emeritus Professor of Botany, State University of Iowa
Author: *Outline of the Fungi*
Coauthor: *The Myxomycetes*
Contributor: articles in botanical journals; *Dictionary of the Fungi*

MARTIN, JOHN H. **Agriculture**
B.S., Oregon State College; M.S., University of Maryland; Ph.D., University of Minnesota
Agriculturist, Research Service, U.S. Department of Agriculture
Author: *Principles of Field Crop Production*
Contributor: *Encyclopaedia Britannica, Cyclopedia American*

MATHER, KIRTLEY F. **Geology**
B.S., Sc.D., Denison University; Ph.D., University of Chicago; Sc.D., Colby College; Litt.D., Union College; L.H.D., Bates College; LL.D., Beloit College
Professor Emeritus of Geology, Harvard University
Author: *Old Mother Earth;* numerous other books
Coauthor: *Source Book of Geology*
Contributor: U.S. Geological Survey papers and bulletins; papers in technical periodicals; popular articles

MATTHEWS, GLENN E. **Photography and Motion Pictures**
B.Sc., M.Sc., University of Minnesota
Technical Editor, Research Laboratories, Eastman Kodak Company
Special Editor in Photography, *Webster's New International Dictionary, Second Edition*
Coauthor: *Photographic Chemicals and Solutions*
Contributor: *New International Encyclopedia, National Encyclopedia Yearbook, Americana Encyclopedia Yearbook, American Annual of Photography, Yearbook of Science, Photography Yearbook, Photographic Progress*

MEES, CHARLES E. K. **Photography**
B.Sc., D.Sc., University of London; (hon.) D.Sc., University of Rochester, Alfred University
Vice-president in charge of Research, Eastman Kodak Company
Special Editor in Photography, *Webster's New International Dictionary, Second Edition*
Author or coauthor of several books

MEGARGEE, EDWIN Color Plate: **Dogs**
Student, Georgetown University, Drexel Institute, Art Students League
Painter, Author, and Illustrator: *Dogs; Horses; The Dogs' Dictionary; Gun Dogs at Work*

MERRILL, LINDSEY **Music**
Mus.M., Yale University
Professor of Music, Bucknell University
Editor: *Trio Sonatas by J. S. Bach*

MERTON, ROBERT K. **Sociology**
A.B., LL.D., Temple University; M.A., Ph.D., Harvard University
Professor of Sociology, Columbia University
Author: *Social Theory and Social Structure; Science, Technology, and Society in 17th Century England; Mass Persuasion*
Coauthor: *The Focussed Interview*
Coeditor: *Continuities in Social Research; Reader in Bureaucracy; The Student-Physician; Sociology Today*

MEYER, WALTER H. **Forestry**
B.A., M.F., Ph.D., Yale University
Harriman Professor of Forest Management, Yale University
Coauthor: *Forest Mensuration; Forest Valuation*

MILLER, PAUL R. **Plant Pathology**
B.S., Indiana University; M.S., Purdue University; Ph.D., George Washington University
Plant Pathologist, Crops Research Division, U.S. Department of Agriculture
Author: numerous scientific papers

MINSHALL, ROBERT **Etymology: Romance and Celtic**
A.B., M.A., Ph.D., Princeton University
Assistant Professor of German, University of Scranton
Author: *Indo-European */y in Armenian; Indo-European */y in Albanian*

MITCHELL, GEORGE F. **Tea**
B.S., Clemson Agricultural College
Tea consultant; formerly, Plant Manager, Maxwell House Tea Division, General Foods Corporation
Author: monographs and articles on tea

MONACHINO, JOSEPH **Taxonomy**
B.S., St. John's University (N.Y.)
Associate Custodian of the Herbarium, New York Botanical Gardens
Author: taxonomic studies on *Manilkara, Ryania,* and various genera of Apocynaceae

MOREHEAD, ALBERT H. **Card Games, Gambling Games**
Bridge Editor, New York Times
Author: *The New Complete Hoyle; Official Rules of Card Games;* numerous other books

MORGAN, ANN H. **Zoology**
A.B., Ph.D., Cornell University
Professor of Zoology, Mount Holyoke College
Author: *Field Book of Ponds and Streams; Animals in Winter; Kinships of Animal and Man*

MORGRET, CHARLES O. **Railroads**
B.A., George Washington University; M.A., American University
Manager, Public and Special Services, Association of American Railroads
Author: *Careers in the American Railroad Industry*

MORRIS, ROBERT A. **Color and Colorimetry**
B.S., University of Michigan
Technical Associate, Eastman Kodak Company
Contributor: *Progress in Photography; Television Engineering Handbook*

MORTON, CONRAD V. **Ferns**
A.B., University of California
Curator, Division of Ferns, United States National Museum

MOYES, VICTOR J. **Applied Photography and Equipment**
S.B., S.M., Massachusetts Institute of Technology
Curator, Patent Department Museum, Eastman Kodak Company

MUEHLER, LOWELL E. **Chemistry of Photography**
B.S., Rose Polytechnic Institute
Research Associate: Photographic Chemistry, Research Laboratories, Eastman Kodak Company
Coauthor: papers on the chemistry and technology of photographic processing and after-treatments

MUNROE, W. O. **Industrial Management**
A.B., St. Mary's College (Kansas)
Formerly, Works Manager, The Baldwin Locomotive Works (1929–38)
Author: shop manuals and procedure instructions for various industries

MYERS, GEORGE S. **Ichthyology**
A.B., A.M., Ph.D., Stanford University
Professor of Biology and Curator of Zoology Collections, Stanford University
Editor: *Stanford Ichthyological Bulletin*
Associate Editor: *The Aquarium*
Managing Editor: *Aquarium Journal*

NELSON, CLARENCE N. **Physics of Photography**
B.A., St. Olaf College; M.S., Ohio State University
Research Physicist, Eastman Kodak Company
Contributor: articles on sensitivity of photographic materials, aerial photography, color photography

NEWHALL, BEAUMONT **History of Photography**
A.B., A.M., Harvard University
Director, George Eastman House
Author: *The History of Photography; The Daguerreotype in America*
Coauthor: *Masters of Photography*

NICKERSON, DOROTHY **Colorimetry**
Color Technologist, Chief of Standardization Section, Cotton Division, United States Department of Agriculture
Contributor: articles on color measurements and specifications, color, and illumination problems in color grading and standardization

NOEL, JOHN V., JR. **Navigation and Seamanship**
B.S., United States Naval Academy; M.A., Stanford University
Captain, United States Navy
Author: *Naval Terms Dictionary; Division Officer's Guide; Watch Officer's Guide*
Coauthor: *Shiphandling*
Editor: *Knight's Modern Seamanship*

ODELL, LOREN B. **Paints and Varnish**
B.S., North Dakota Agricultural College
President, James Bute Company

ODUM, EUGENE P. **Ecology**
A.B., A.M., University of North Carolina; Ph.D., University of Illinois
Alumni Foundation Distinguished Professor of Zoology, University of Georgia
Author: *Fundamentals of Ecology*
Contributor: articles in scientific journals

OWEN, GWILYM E. **Physics**
Ph.B., Lafayette College; Ph.D., University of Pennsylvania
Professor of Physics, Antioch College
Special Editor in Physics, *Webster's New International Dictionary, Second Edition*
Contributor: articles on the growing of quartz crystals, the conductivity of electrolytes at temperatures near the critical temperature of water, the responsibility of scientists, history of science, and the teaching of physics

PARKER, HAYWOOD, JR. **Applied Photography and Equipment**
A.B., M.S., University of North Carolina
Supervisor of Technical Publications, Eastman Kodak Company

PATTERSON, AUSTIN M. **Chemistry**
A.B., Princeton University; Ph.D., Johns Hopkins University; (hon.) D.Sc., Antioch College
Vice-president and Professor of Chemistry, Antioch College
Special Editor in Chemistry, *Webster's New International Dictionary* and *Webster's New International Dictionary, Second Edition*
Author: *French-English Dictionary for Chemists; German-English Dictionary for Chemists*
Coauthor: *Ring Index: A List of Ring Systems Used in Organic Chemistry; Guide to the Literature of Chemistry*
Editor: *Chemical Abstracts*
Contributor: numerous articles on chemistry

PEEL, ROBERT **Christian Science**
A.B., A.M., Harvard University
Formerly, editorial writer for *Christian Science Monitor*
Author: *Christian Science: Its Encounter with American Culture*

PENZL, HERBERT **Etymology: Iranian**
Ph.D., Vienna University
Professor of German, University of Michigan
Author: *A Grammar of Pashto*
Contributor: articles in general, Germanic, and Oriental linguistics

PERROT, PAUL N. **Glass**
Director, The Corning Museum of Glass, Corning Glass Center
Author: *Three Great Centuries of Venetian Glass*
Contributor: *Antiques*

PERRY, JAMES W. **Non-numerical Computer Applications**
B.S., M.S., North Carolina State College; S.M., Massachusetts Institute of Technology
Professor, College of Engineering, University of Arizona
Author: *Chemical Russian, Self-Taught; Scientific Russian*
Coauthor: *Surface Active Agents; Machine Literature Searching; Centralized Information Services*
Coeditor: *Punched Cards; Information Systems in Documentation; Tools for Machine Literature Searching*

PHILLIPS, CRAIG Color Plates: **Fishes, Tropical Fishes**
A.B., University of Miami
Assistant Director, National Aquarium, United States Fish and Wildlife Service
Coauthor: *Sea Pests*

PIOTRASCHKE, CHARLES F. **Hardware**
A.A.S., Rochester Institute of Technology; B.S., University of Rochester
Assistant Professor of Electrical Engineering, Rochester Institute of Technology

PLUMMER, GAYTHER L. **Plant Ecology**
B.S., Butler University; M.S., Kansas State College; Ph.D., Purdue University
Assistant Professor, Department of Botany, University of Georgia
Contributor: articles on plant species

POSTER, FRANCES W. **Girl Scouts**
A.B., University of Maryland; M.A., Columbia University
Director of Publications, Girl Scouts of the United States of America

PRESCOTT, G. W. **Phycology**
B.A., University of Oregon; M.A., Ph.D., University of Iowa
Professor of Botany and Plant Pathology, Michigan State University
Author: *Algae of the Western Great Lakes Area; How to Know the Fresh-water Algae*
Coauthor: *Fundamentals of Plant Science*

QUIMBY, HAROLD R. **Shoes**
Formerly, Executive Secretary, National Shoe Manufacturers' Association

RASCHIG, F. ELMER **Freemasonry**
A.B., Indiana University
Grand Secretary General Supreme Council 33 Scottish Rite of Northern Masonic Jurisdiction U.S.A.

RASHKIS, HAROLD A. **Psychiatry, Neurology**
A.B., University of Miami; A.M., Ph.D., Columbia University; M.D., University of Pennsylvania
Senior Research Psychiatrist, Eastern Pennsylvania Psychiatric Institute
Author: articles on psychology and psychiatry

RASKIN, EUGENE **Architecture**
A.B., B.Arch., Columbia University
Associate Professor of Architecture, School of Architecture, Columbia University
Author: *Architecturally Speaking*

REMINGTON, CHARLES L. **Entomology**
B.S., Principia College; A.M., Ph.D., Harvard University
Associate Professor of Zoology, Yale University
Associate Curator of Entomology, Peabody Museum
Author: several articles on entomology

RUDGE, WILLIAM E. **Printing**
President, Rudge Associates Inc.
Editor and Publisher: *Print*

SCHNERR, WALTER J. **Etymology: Romance**
A.B., A.M., Ph.D., University of Pennsylvania
Associate Professor of Romance Languages, Brown University

SCHOLES, SAMUEL R. **Ceramics**
A.B., Ripon College; Ph.D., Yale University; (hon.) Sc.D., Alfred University
Formerly, Dean of New York State College of Ceramics
Emeritus Professor, Alfred University
Author: *Modern Glass Practice; Opportunities in Ceramics*
Editor: *Glass Industry Handbook*

SCHOPF, JAMES M. **Paleobotany**
B.A., University of Wyoming; M.S., Ph.D., University of Illinois
Supervising Geologist, Fuels Branch, Coal Laboratory, United States Geological Survey, Ohio State University
Author: technical articles on conifer embryology, paleobotany, and coal geology

SEEMANN, HERMAN E. **Radiography**
A.B., Oberlin College; Ph.D., Cornell University
Physicist, Eastman Kodak Company
Author: papers on physical problems of medical and industrial radiography

SEYMOUR, MERRILL W. **Color and Colorimetry**
B.S., University of Minnesota; M.A., Ph.D., Princeton University
Research Associate, Eastman Kodak Company

SHAND, ERROL B. **Glass**
B.S., McGill University
Technical Consultant, formerly Staff Research Engineer, Corning Glass Works
Author: *Glass Engineering Handbook*

SHIPMAN, FRANK M. **Distilling**
B.S., Georgetown College; M.S., University of Louisville; Ph.D., Iowa State College
Technical Director and Vice-president, Brown-Forman Distillers Corporation

SMITH, DAVID M. **Forestry**
B.S., University of Rhode Island; M.F., Ph.D., Yale University
Associate Professor, School of Forestry, Yale University
Coauthor: *Practice of Silviculture*

SMITH, GILBERT M. **Phycology**
B.S., (hon.) Sc.D., Beloit College; Ph.D., University of Wisconsin
Formerly, Professor of Botany, Stanford University
Author: *A Textbook of General Botany; Fresh Water Algae of the United States; Marine Algae of the Monterey Peninsula; Cryptogamic Botany*

SNELL, HAMPTON K. **Transportation**
A.B., A.M., University of Wisconsin; Ph.D., Yale University
Professor of Marketing and Transportation, College of Business Administration, University of Texas
Author: *Coordination of Rail, River, and Road Transportation in Egypt; Air Transportation;* numerous monographs, papers, reports of studies

SOUTHWICK, CHARLES A., JR. **Packaging**
B.S., Massachusetts Institute of Technology
Technical Editor: *Modern Packaging; Modern Packaging Encyclopedia*
Contributor: *Colloid Chemistry; Storage of Cereal Grains and Their Products;* numerous articles in packaging field

SPRAGUE, ATHERTON H. **Mathematics**
B.A., Amherst College; M.A., Ph.D., Princeton University
Professor of Mathematics, Amherst College
Author: *Plane and Spherical Trigonometry; Trigonometry and Analytical Geometry; Calculus*

STALLINGS, JAMES H. **Soils**
B.S., Agricultural and Mechanical College of Texas; M.S., Ph.D., Iowa State College
Principal Soil Conservationist, Agricultural Research Service, U.S. Department of Agriculture
Author: *Soil Conservation; Soil: Use and Improvement*
Contributor: numerous technical articles and reviews

SUTERMEISTER, EDWIN **Paper and Paper Manufacturing**
B.S., Massachusetts Institute of Technology
Chief Chemist, S. D. Warren Company
Author: *Chemistry of Pulp and Paper Making; The Story of Papermaking*
Contributor: numerous articles to technical journals

TARKINGTON, RAIFE G. **Photogrammetry, Military Photography**
B.S., Virginia Polytechnic Institute
Associate Head, Applied Photography Division, Kodak Research Laboratories
Contributor: *Photogrammetric Engineering; Signal*

TAYLOR, NORMAN **General Botany**
Student, Cornell University; (hon.) D.Sc., Washington College
Curator, Brooklyn Botanic Garden
Special Editor in Botany, *Webster's New International Dictionary, Second Edition*
Author: *Taylor's Encyclopedia of Gardening; Taylor's Garden Guide; Flight from Reality; Cinchona in Java; Guide to Garden Flowers; Guide to the Wild Flowers*

TAYLOR, ROBERT E. **Etymology: French**
A.B., Reed College; A.M., Ph.D., Columbia University
Associate Professor of French, New York University
Seminar Associate, Columbia University
Associate Editor, Renaissance Society of America
Author: studies on Sade, French 17th & 18th centuries; bibliographies of French literature and general Renaissance literature

TAYLOR, ROY W. **Wine**
B.S., University of Illinois
Public Relations Director, Wine Institute

THAYER, CLARK L. **Horticulture**
B.S., University of Massachusetts
Head of Department of Floriculture, University of Massachusetts
Author: *Spring Flowering Bulbs*

THOMPSON, J. ERIC S. **Maya Calendar**
Student, Cambridge University; LL.D., University of Yucatan
Member of Department of Archaeology, Carnegie Institution of Washington
Author: *The Rise and Fall of Maya Civilization*
Contributor: numerous articles on Maya and Mexican archaeology and ethnology

THOMSON, C. L. **Horticulture**
B.S.A., University of Toronto; M.S., University of Minnesota
Professor of Vegetable Crops, University of Massachusetts

THORSEN, MARGARET A. **Sports**
B.A., Carleton College; M.S., Wellesley College; Ph.D., New York University
Associate Professor of Physical Education, Springfield College

TRIBOLET, HAROLD W. **Bookbinding**
Manager, Department of Extra Binding, R. R. Donnelley and Sons Company
Contributor: magazine articles, reviews of technical books

TUIT, FRANK E., II **Law**
A.B., Amherst College; student, Harvard Law School
Lawyer, Register of Probate Court for County of Hampshire, Massachusetts

TURNER, LORENZO D. **Etymology: African**
A.B., A.M., Harvard University; Ph.D., University of Chicago
Professor of English, Roosevelt University
Author: *Anti-Slavery Sentiment in American Literature Prior to 1865; Africanisms in the Gullah Dialect*
Coauthor: *Readings from Negro Authors*

TWADDELL, W. FREEMAN **Grammar, Linguistics**
A.B., Duke University; A.M., Ph.D., Harvard University
Professor of Linguistics and German, Brown University
Author: numerous monographs, textbooks (German language, *Faust*), teacher training materials in Egypt and Japan
Contributor: articles and reviews on linguistics and philology

TYSON, VICTOR E., JR. **Navigation**
B.S., University of New Hampshire; B.S., U.S. Merchant Marine Academy
Captain, United States Marine Service
Assistant Superintendent, United States Merchant Marine Academy

VAN DEUSEN, W. P. **Graphic Reproduction Photography**
A.B., Princeton
Technical Staff Assistant to Research Director's Office, Eastman Kodak Company

VOEGELIN, CHARLES F. **Etymology: American Indian**
A.B., Stanford University; Ph.D., University of California
Professor of Anthropology, Indiana University
Author: monographs and papers on aboriginal languages of native Americans and anthropological theory
Editor: *International Journal of American Linguistics;* Indiana University publications in anthropology and linguistics

WANGAARD, FREDERICK F. **Forestry**
B.S., University of Minnesota; M.S., Ph.D., New York State College of Forestry; (hon.) M.A., Yale University
Professor of Forest Products, Yale University
Author: *Mechanical Properties of Wood*

WATERS, EVERETT O. **Tools**
A.B., Ph.B., M.E., Yale University
Emeritus Strathcona Professor of Mechanical Engineering, Yale University
Special Editor in Tools, *Webster's New International Dictionary, Second Edition*
Coauthor: *Principles of Machine Design*

WERNER, H. O. **Naval Science**
A.B., M.A., Brown University; M.A., Ph.D., Harvard University
Professor, United States Naval Institute
Coauthor: *The United States and World Sea Power; Men in Arms; Sea Power*

WEXLER, HARRY **Meteorology**
S.B., Harvard University; Sc.D., Massachusetts Institute of Technology
Director of Meteorological Research, United States Weather Bureau
Author: scientific articles

WIENS, HEROLD J. **Peoples of Asia**
A.B., University of California; A.M., Ph.D., University of Michigan
Associate Professor of Geography, Yale University
Author: *China's March toward the Tropics*
Coauthor: *Pattern of Asia*

WILLEY, NORMAN L. **Etymology: Scientific and Technical**
A.B., Syracuse University; A.M., Harvard University; LL.B., People's College; Ph.D., University of Michigan
Professor Emeritus of Germanic languages, University of Michigan
Contributor: articles in technical journals

WINCHELL, HORACE **Mineralogy, Crystallography, Gemmology**
B.A., M.A., University of Wisconsin; M.A., Ph.D., Harvard University
Associate Professor of Mineralogy, Yale University
Contributor: articles on physical and systematic mineralogy and optical crystallography

WINER, HERBERT I. **Forestry**
B.A., M.F., Ph.D., Yale University
Assistant Professor of Lumbering, Yale University

WOOLSTON, HELENE **Etymology: Maori**
M.A., University of Hawaii
Lecturer, Auckland University

EXPLANATORY CHART

THE CENTER COLUMN on this page contains entries taken from the dictionary. One or more parts of each entry has an oval line linked to a box in the margin. The term in the box is our name for the circled convention. The number in the box refers to a section in the "Explanatory Notes" following.

abbr **3.3, 19.1**
angle bracket **13.1**
author quoted **13.2.1, 13.2.2**
binomial **14.1, 14.2**
boldface type **1.1, 22.1**
capitalization label **5.2**
centered period **1.6**
cognate cross-reference **1.7.3, 16.3.1**
comb form **3.3, 21.1**
definition
directional cross-reference **16.1, 16.1.2**
ditto marks **2.8.1**
double hyphens **2.7.2**
equal variant **1.7.1**
etymology **7.**
functional label **3.1**
homographs **1.4**
hyphened compound **1.1, 2.7.2**
inflectional cross-reference **4.6, 4.12, 16.4**
inflectional form **4.1**
lightface type **1.1**
lowercase **5.1**
main entry **1.1, 22.1**
often attrib **6.**
open compound **1.1, 2.7.2**
pl but sing in constr **4.3**
prefix **3.3, 21.1**

pa *abbr* **1** paper **2** piaster

⁴pa·ce \ˈpāsē\ *prep* [L, abl. of *pac-, pax* peace — more at PEACE] **:** with all due respect or courtesy to ⟨~ the feminists, I believe my own sex is largely responsible for this . . . impertinent curiosity —Katharine F. Gerould⟩

pacific herring *n, usu cap P* **:** a herring (*Clupea pallasii*) of the northern Pacific ocean

¹pac·tion \ˈpakshən\ *n* -s [MF, fr. L *paction-, pactio,* fr. *pactus* (past part. of *pacisci* to agree, contract) + *-ion-, -io* -ion] **1** *chiefly Scot* **:** AGREEMENT, COMPACT, BARGAIN ⟨made ~ tween them twa⟩ — **pac·tion·al** \-shənᵊl, -shnəl\ *adj*

pants \ˈpants, ˈpaan-, ˈpain-\ *n pl but sometimes sing in constr, often attrib* [short for *pantaloons,* pl. of *pantaloon*] **1** *also* **pant a** (1) **:** PANTALOON 2 (2) **:** TROUSERS, SLACKS **b** *chiefly Brit* **:** men's short underpants **c :** PANTIE **2 pant** *n sing* **:** half or one leg of a pair of pants — **with one's pants down :** in an embarrassing position (as of being unprepared for an emergency) ⟨caught *with its pants down* by the surprise attack⟩

panty *var of* PANTIE

pa·per·ful \ˈpāpə(r),fu̇l\ *n, pl* **paperfuls** *also* **papersful** \-(r),fu̇lz, -(r)z,fu̇l\ **:** as much as will fill a paper ⟨a ~ of pins⟩

papyro- *comb form* [Gk, fr. *papyros* papyrus] **1 :** papyrus

pas·to·ral·ize \ˈpast(ə)rə,līz\ *vt* -ED/-ING/-S *see -ize in Explan Notes* **1 :** to render pastoral or rural; *specif* **:** to convert to a pastoral economy or social organization

pas·tor·ate \ˈpast(ə)rət, ˈpaas-, ˈpais-, ˈpás-, *usu* -əd·+V\ *n* -s [ML *pastoratus,* fr. LL *pastor* pastor (fr. L, shepherd) + L *-atus* -ate] **1** **a :** the office, state, jurisdiction, or tenure of office of a pastor **b :** a body of pastors **2 :** PARSONAGE

ˈpat·a·go·ni·an \ˌpadə;gōnyən, -atə;-, -nēən\ *adj, usu cap* [*Patagonia,* region in southern So. America belonging partly to Argentina and partly to Chile + E *-an*] **1 :** of, relating to, or characteristic of Patagonia **2 a :** of, relating to, or characteristic of the people of Patagonia **b** *obs* **:** GIGANTIC

²patagonian \ʺ\ *n* -s **1** *cap* **:** a native or inhabitant of Patagonia; *esp* **:** one of the aboriginal Indian stock — compare TEHUELCHE

pat·e·fac·tion \ˌpadəˈfakshən\ *n* -s [L *patefaction-, patefactio,* fr. *patefactus* (past part. of *patefacere*) + *-ion-, -io* -ion] *archaic* **:** DISCLOSURE, MANIFESTATION, REVELATION

patent-coated \ˈ==;==\ *adj, of paperboard* **:** vat-lined on one or both sides with an uncoated white liner

patent hammer *or* **patent ax** *n* **:** BUSHHAMMER

pat·er·is·sa \ˌpadəˈrisə\ *n* -s [NGk *pateritsa,* fr. MGk *pateriza,* perh. dim. of Gk *pater-, patēr* father — more at FATHER] *Eastern Church* **:** a crosier surmounted by a small cross from whose base issue two serpents

pa·tine \pəˈtēn\ *n* -s [F, fr. ML & NL *patina* — more at PATINA] **1 :** PATEN **2 :** PATINA ⟨time has bestowed a ~ of oxidation on these vessels —Dorothy Adlow⟩

²patine \ʺ\ *vt* -ED/-ING/-S **:** PATINATE

¹pa·to·la \pəˈtōlə\ *n* -s [Gujarati *patolū,* fr. Skt *patola*] **1 :** a silk cloth of India **2 :** a wedding sari woven in Gujarat, India, in chiné technique

²patola \ʺ\ *n* -s [Tag] *Philippines* **:** a dishcloth gourd (*Luffa acutangula*) that is eaten green or cooked

patty-cake \ˈ==,=\ *n* [by alter.] **:** PAT-A-CAKE

paul·in·ize \-lə,nīz\ *vb* -ED/-ING/-S *often cap* [*pauline* + *-ize*] *vi* **:** to follow the teachings of the apostle Paul ~ *vt* **:** to indoctrinate with Paulinism

pawky \ˈpȯkī\ *adj* [obs. E (northern dial.) *pawk* trick + E *-y*] **1** *chiefly Brit* **:** artfully shrewd **:** CANNY ⟨that favorite of fiction, the ~ rich old lady who incessantly scores off her parasitical descendants —*Punch*⟩ **2** *chiefly Scot* **a :** LIVELY, UNINHIBITED **b :** BOLD, FORWARD ⟨a rude and ~ child⟩

paws *pl of* PAW, *pres 3d sing of* PAW

paymaster general *n, pl* **paymasters general 1 :** a military officer in command of the pay department of an army or navy

Pb *symbol* [L *plumbum*] lead

peanut tube *n* **:** a small vacuum tube

peanut worm *n* **:** SIPUNCULID

pen·ni·less \ˈpenᵊləs, -nəl-\ *adj* [ME *peniles,* fr. *peni* penny + *-les* -less] **:** destitute of money **:** extremely poor ⟨in one day the rich man . . . saw himself ~, landless, a bankrupt among creditors —J.G.Lockhart⟩ **syn** see POOR

phy·sique \fəˈzēk\ *n* -s [F, fr. *physique,* adj., physical, bodily, fr. L *physicus* natural, fr. Gk *physikos* — more at PHYSIC] **1 :** bodily makeup or type **:** the structure, constitution, appearance, or strength of the human body ⟨a muscular ~⟩

syn BUILD, CONSTITUTION, HABIT: PHYSIQUE designates the total bodily or physical construction or qualities of an individual ⟨tall of stature, slender in *physique* —H.W.H.Knott⟩ ⟨his five-foot-nine-inch *physique* —*Current Biog.*⟩ BUILD, usu. interchangeable with PHYSIQUE, often stresses the geometrically determinable qualities of the physique ⟨a man of rather square *build*⟩ ⟨leisure and heredity gave me a husky *build*⟩ CONSTITUTION is the overall makeup of an individual comprising both mental and physical qualities ⟨extremely high-spirited, my greatest advantage was that my *constitution* did not allow me to be depressed —Osbert Sitwell⟩ ⟨a frail *constitution* necessitated his living in the South —H.E.Starr⟩ ⟨wealthy by inheritance but saving by *constitution* —Ellen Glasgow⟩ HABIT, usu. occurring with a qualifier, is generally confined to characteristic mental or moral quality, makeup, or disposition ⟨the country is where he has gone to indulge a contemplative *habit* —L.J.Halle⟩

²poster \ʺ\ *n* -s *often attrib* [²*post* + *-er*] **1 :** a bill or placard intended to be posted in a public place; *specif* **:** one that is decorative or pictorial **2 :** POSTER STAMP

post flag *n* [²*post*] **:** the national flag measuring 19 feet fly by 10 feet hoist ordinarily used at a military post (as of the U.S. Army)

¹posthaste \(ˈ)ˈ=;=\ *n* [⁴*post* (courier) + *haste*] **:** speed in traveling (as of a post or courier) **:** great haste — used chiefly in the phrase *in posthaste*

practical politics *n pl but sing or pl in constr* **1 :** matter for concrete action as distinguished from theoretical discussion

prac·tic·ing *or* **prac·tis·ing** \ˈpraktəsiŋ, -sēŋ\ *adj* **:** actively engaged in an indicated career or way of life ⟨a ~ physician⟩ ⟨~ Catholics⟩

¹pro- *prefix* [ME, fr. OF, fr. L, fr. Gk, fr. *pro* — more at FOR] **1 a :** earlier than **:** prior to **:** before ⟨*pro*anthropus⟩ ⟨*pro*baptismal⟩ ⟨*Pro*mammalia⟩ **b :** rudimentary **:** PROT- ⟨*pro*embryo⟩ **2 :** situated before **:** located in front of **:** anterior to

pro-and-con \ˈ=;=;=\ *vb* **pro-and-conned; pro-and-conned; pro-and-conning; pro-and-cons :** DEBATE

primary stress **2.2**
pronunciation **2.**
regional label **8.3.4**
run-on entry (derivatives) **17.1.1**
run-on entry (phrasal) **17.2**
secondary stress **2.2**
secondary variant **1.7.2**
see -ize in Explan Notes **23.1**
sense letter **12.2**
sense number **12.1**
small capitals **16.0, 16.2**
status label **8., 8.1.2**
subject guide phrase **10.1**
subject label **9.1**
suffixal cross-reference **4.4, 4.10, 16.5**
superscript **1.4, 1.5**
swung dash (boldface) **3.2**
swung dash (lightface) **13.1**
symbol **3.3, 20.1**
symbolic colon **11.1**
synonymous cross-reference **16.2**
synonymy cross-reference **18.2**
synonymy paragraph **18.1**
uppercase
usage note **15.1**
verbal illustration **13.1**
verb principal parts **4.7**

EXPLANATORY NOTES

A careful reading of these explanatory notes will make it easier for the user of this dictionary to comprehend the information contained at each entry. Here are brief explanations of the different typefaces, different labels, significant punctuation, symbols, and other conventions by which a dictionary can achieve compactness. The chief divisions are:

1. THE MAIN ENTRY

1.1 A heavy black letter or a combination of heavy black letters (**boldface type**) set flush with the left-hand margin of each column of type is a main entry or entry word. The combination consists usually of letters set solid (*about*) or of letters separated by one or more spaces (*art song*) or of letters joined by a hyphen (*air-dry*). What follows each such boldface entry in lightface type on the same line and on indented lines below explains and justifies its inclusion in the dictionary. The boldface entry together with this added matter is also called an entry.

1.2 The main entries follow one another in this dictionary from *a* to *zyzzogeton* in alphabetical order letter by letter. For example, *above the line* follows *abovestairs* (not *above all*) as if it were printed *abovetheline* with no spaces in the middle. Entry words containing an arabic numeral (*3-D*, *1080* "ten-eighty") are alphabetized as if the numeral were spelled out. Entry words derived from proper names beginning with abbreviated forms of *Mac-* (*McCoy*) are alphabetized as if spelled *mac-*. Entries often beginning with *St.* or *Ste.* in common usage have the abbreviation spelled out *saint* (*Saint Martin's summer*).

1.3 A thumb index with tabs lettered from *A* through *Z* is cut into the fore edge of this dictionary to aid in locating the pages beginning with each letter. As a further aid to finding a wanted entry, a pair of guide words is printed at the top of nearly every page. These are the first and last words of a sequence of boldface words on one page of the dictionary. Entries alphabetically between the word in the upper left corner (as *addressee* on page 25) and the word in the upper right corner (as *adhere*) are defined on the same page.

1.4 When one entry has exactly the same written form as another that follows it, the two are distinguished by superior numbers preceding each word:

> [1]**arc**
> [2]**arc**

Sometimes such homographs are related, like the two *arcs*, which are different parts of speech derived from the same root. At other times, there is no relationship beyond the accident of spelling:

> [1]**are** ⟨the boys *are* here⟩
> [2]**are** ⟨one *are* equals 100 square meters⟩

Whether homographs are related or not, their order is usually historical: the one first used in English, insofar as the dates can be established, is entered first.

1.5 Such superscripts are used only when all the letters, spaces, and hyphens of two or more entries are identical (except for foreign accent marks). A variation in form calls for a new series of superscripts. In general, words precede word elements made up of the same letters, and lowercase type precedes uppercase type.

1.6 The centered periods within entry words indicate division points at which a hyphen may be put at the end of a written line, thus for *ar·chae·ol·o·gy:*

	ar-
chaeology	archae-
ology	archaeol-
ogy	archaeolo-
gy	

Such periods are not shown after a single initial letter (*aplomb*, not *a·plomb*) or before a single terminal letter (*ar·ea*, not *ar·e·a*) because printers seldom cut off one letter only. Many printers try to avoid cutting off two letters only, especially at the end. They might divide *ar·cha·ic* into *ar-/chaic* but not into *archa-/ic*. Other words (*April*, *apron*) that are not often divided in printing do not show a centered period. For a full discussion of word division, see the following article headed "Divisions in Boldface Entry Words".

1.6.1 A double hyphen ⸗ at the end of a line (as between *pro* and *British* at [1]*hyphen* 1b) stands for a hyphen that belongs normally at that point in a hyphened word (as *pro-British*) and should be retained when the word is written out as a unit on one line.

1.7.1 When a main entry is followed by the word *or* and another spelling or form, the two spellings or forms are equal variants. Their order is usually alphabetical, and the first is no more to be preferred than the second, or third, or fourth, if three or four are joined by *or*. Both or all are standard and any one may be used according to personal inclination or personal style preferences:

> **an·gel·ic** . . . *or* **an·gel·i·cal**
> **ar·dor** *or* **ar·dour**
> **arc of recess** *or* **arc of recession**
> **angel cake** *or* **angel food** *or* **angel food cake**

If the alphabetical order of variants joined by *or* is reversed, they remain equal variants. The one printed first may be slightly more common but not enough to justify calling them unequal:

> **cad·dis** *or* **cad·dice**

1.7.2 When another spelling or form is joined to the first entry by the word *also* instead of *or*, the spelling or form after *also* is a secondary variant and occurs less frequently than the first form:

> **car·bo·ther·mic** . . . *also* **car·bo·ther·mal**

The secondary variant belongs to standard usage and may for personal or regional reasons be preferred by some. If there are two secondary variants, the second is joined to the first by *or*. Once the italic *also* is used to signal a secondary variant, all following variants are joined by *or:*

> **aso·ka** . . . *also* **as·ak** *or* **as·ok**

No evaluation below secondary is implied. Absence of a variant does not mean that there is no variant; for example, some variants have been arbitrarily omitted.

1.7.3 Standard variants are reentered at their own places alphabetically whenever their spelling places them alphabetically more than five inches away from the main entry. The form of entry is

> **loth** *var of* LOATH
> **rime** *var of* RHYME

in which *var of* stands for "variant of". These two entries result from the main entries *loath or loth* and *rhyme or rime.*

2. THE PRONUNCIATION

2.1 The matter between reversed virgules \ \ is the pronunciation in symbols shown in the chart headed "Pronunciation Symbols" and discussed in greater detail in the "Guide to Pronunciation". A centered period · shows syllable divisions only when a given sequence of sounds can be syllabified in more than one way without employing deliberate pause, as discussed in detail in the section on "Divisions in Boldface Entry Words". All other sequences have only one reasonably possible syllabication (as in the sounds of *admit*) or have no determinable syllabication (as in the sounds of *easter*). In either case they are pronounceable in a normal manner when the sound sequence is pronounced. These centered periods in the respelling for pronunciation often do not correspond with centered periods in the boldface entry. Thus in our analysis the first syllable of the pronunciation of *metric* ends with \e\ and the second syllable begins with \t\, but printers usually divide the word between the *t* and the *r*.

2.2 A high-set mark ˈ indicates primary accent or stress; a low-set mark ˌ indicates a secondary accent. The two are often set one over the other ¦ to indicate stress variation. Two occurrences of ¦ within a pronunciation indicate that in some contexts the first syllable so marked has secondary stress and the second so marked has primary stress, in other contexts vice versa:

> **ben·e·fi·cial** \¦benə¦fishəl\

The occurrence of (ˈ) on the first syllable and of ¦ on the second syllable indicates that in some contexts the first syllable has a degree of stress we would leave unmarked and that the second syllable has primary stress but that in other contexts the first syllable has primary stress and the second has secondary stress:

> **fic·ti·tious** \(ˈ)fik¦tishəs\

The order primary-secondary is especially common when another word, especially one with stress on the first syllable, follows without pause, as when the first word is attributive. Stress marks show the stress of the first vowel that follows; they are not necessarily indicators of syllable division and often do not correspond with the centered periods in the boldface entry.

2.3 The presence of variant pronunciations simply indicates that not all educated speakers pronounce the word the same way. Some variant pronunciations (as \ˈbərd\ and \ˈbə̄d\ for *bird*) are the kind that one speaker uses but another does not for the reason that their dialects are different and that the speech habits of one are different from those of the other. One of these pronunciations is predictable from a knowledge of a speaker's pronunciation of other words. Other variants (as for *disparate*) are not predictable from a speaker's pronunciation of other words. Some speakers stress *disparate* on the second syllable; others stress it on the first. Words with predictable variant pronunciations usually show them when the word is of frequent occurrence in highly literate language but only one pronunciation when it is not. Words with unpredictable variant pronunciations show any that has currency, whatever the frequency of the word.

2.4 When a word shows more than one unpredictable variant, variants not preceded by *also* or *sometimes* or by a label (as *substand*) do not differ greatly in frequency in educated speech. The order in which they appear has no significance. Variants preceded by *also* are appreciably less frequent. Variants preceded by *sometimes* are infrequent. Before predictable variants no *also* or *sometimes* occurs, whatever the frequency of a variant, except that *also* precedes a variant that is less common in one class of words than in another. Thus \er\, which is variant to \ar\ with fewer speakers in *harry* than in *hairy*, is preceded by *also* at the first but not at the second.

2.5.1 Parentheses mean that whatever is indicated by the symbol or symbols between them is present in the pronunciation of some speakers and absent from the pronunciation of other speakers, or that it is present in some utterances and absent from other utterances of the same speaker, or that its presence or absence is uncertain:

> **nu·mer·ous** \ˈn(y)üm(ə)rəs\
> **floc·cu·lence** \ˈfläkyələn(t)s\

Such pronunciations could alternatively have been shown, at greater cost of space, as \ˈnümərəs, ˈnyü-, -mrəs\

2.5.2 The symbols (r, with no closing parenthesis, at the end of the transcription of a word, as *seminar*, means that speakers who do not usually pronounce the \r\ when a consonant or a pause follows may pronounce it when a vowel follows without pause.

2.6.1 When a defined word that is at its own alphabetical place has less than a full pronunciation, the missing part is to be supplied from a pronunciation in a preceding entry, from a preceding pronunciation for a variant spelling in the same entry, or from a preceding pronunciation within the same pair of reversed virgules:

> **floc·cu·lence** \ˈfläkyələn(t)s\ *also* **floc·cu·len·cy** \-nsē\
> [1]**floc·cu·lent** \-nt\

The hyphen at *flocculency* and at *flocculent* indicates that the first part of the pronunciation is missing. The missing part is to be supplied from the pronunciation at *flocculence.*

2.6.2 The lightface vertical bar is used to facilitate the placement of a variant pronunciation. It occurs chiefly at a point immediately preceding or immediately following a variation.

> **flight·i·ly** \ˈflīd·|ᵊlē, -īt|, |ᵊli, |ə̇l-\
> **flight·i·ness** \|ēnə̇s, |in-\

At *flightily* in the four-character unit -īt| (hyphen + bar i + t + vertical bar) the īt is a variation of īd· and the hyphen stands for the ˈfl that precedes īd· and the vertical bar stands for the ᵊlē that follows īd·; in the unit |ᵊli the ᵊli is a variation of ᵊlē and the vertical bar stands for both ˈflīd· and ˈflīt; in the unit |ə̇l- the vertical bar stands for both ˈflīd· and ˈflīt and the hyphen stands for the variants ē and i of the final syllable. This system makes it possible to show economically several variant pronunciations for *flightily:*

> \ˈflīd·ᵊlē, ˈflītᵊlē, ˈflīd·ᵊli, ˈflītᵊli, ˈflīd·ə̇lē, ˈflītə̇lē, ˈflīd·əli, ˈflītəli\

At *flightiness* the vertical bar in the unit |ēnə̇s stands for both ˈflīd· and ˈflīt from the pronunciation at *flightily;* the vertical bar in the unit |in- stands for ˈflīd· and ˈflīt and the hyphen stands for ə̇s from the preceding ēnə̇s.

2.7.1 A slanted double hyphen in transcriptions represents all the sounds of a syllable:

> **per·pet·u·ate** \pə(r)ˈpechəˌwāt . . . \
> **per·pet·u·a·tion** \⸗ˌ⸗⸗ˈwāshən\
> **per·pet·u·a·tor** \⸗ˈ⸗⸗ˌwād·ə(r) . . . \

The first three syllables of each of these consecutive entries have the same sounds. The double hyphens at *perpetuation* and *perpetuator* show this sameness. The stress, however, differs. The stress on the second syllable is primary in *perpetuate* and *perpetuator* but secondary in the middle word.

2.7.2 Open compounds of two or more English words usually have no pronunciation (as at *barn dance*). Such members of solid or hyphened compounds as are whole English words often show only the stress indicated by double hyphens and stress marks:

heartache \'⸗ˌ⸗\
waterworthy \'⸗⸗ˌ⸗⸗\
fort·let \'⸗lə̇t\
cata·baptist \¦kad·ə¦⸗⸗\

The sounds of the syllables represented by such double hyphens can be found at the main entry of the elements (as at *heart* and *ache*, at *fort*, and at *baptist*). Thus in the consecutive entries

den·e·ga·tion \ˌdenə̇'gāshən\
denehole \'⸗ˌ⸗\

the value of the syllables of the second should be sought at *dene* and at *hole*, not in the representation of the first two syllables in the pronunciation at *denegation*.

2.8.1 A ditto mark " in a pronunciation stands for the sounds of the nearest preceding pronounced entry. The orthographic division for this preceding entry also applies unless another is shown. For an entry having the same sequence of letters as a preceding entry but not followed by reversed virgules, no commitment about pronunciation is made:

[1]**carp** \'kärp, 'kȧp\
[2]**carp** \"\
carp *abbr*

[1]**in·dict** \ə̇n'dīt, *usu* -īd·+V\ *vt*
[2]**indict** *vt* . . . *obs*

keelboat \'⸗ˌ⸗\
keel·boat·man \"mən\

[1]**keel·er** \'kēlə(r)\
[2]**keeler** \"\
[3]**keeler** \"\
kee·ler polygraph \"-\

[2]*carp* has the same pronunciation as [1]*carp*, but no pronunciation is to be understood for *carp* the abbreviation. No pronunciation is to be understood for the obsolete [2]*indict*. (In general, words obsolete in their entire range of meaning have an indicated pronunciation only if they occur in Shakespeare.) The stress on the first two syllables of *keelboatman* is the same as for *keelboat;* the sounds for *keel* and *boat* should be sought at the entry for each. [2]*keeler* and [3]*keeler* have the same pronunciation and division as [1]*keeler; keeler* in *keeler polygraph* has the same pronunciation as [1]*keeler* but its division differs.

2.8.2 If the entry at which the value of a ditto mark is to be sought contains variants not identical in pronunciation, the value of the ditto mark is the pronunciation of the variant of the same spelling in a preceding entry:

[1]**ap·o·dal** \'apədᵊl\ *also* **ap·o·dan** \-dən, -dᵊn\ *or* **ap·o·dous** \-dəs\
[2]**apodal** \"\ *also* **apodan** \"\

2.9 When a word is composed of a combining form or prefix and a whole English word, often the transcription consists of a pronunciation for the first element followed by a plus sign. The plus sign means that the sounds and the orthographic division for the second element should be sought at the entry for that word. If other compounds with the same first element follow, their pronunciation may be shown by the formula \"+\:

geo·positive \¦jē(ˌ)ō+\
geo·potential \"+\

In many contexts a primary stress shown for the second element at its entry may alter to secondary in the compound.

2.10 The symbol *R* preceding variants indicates the pronunciation of speakers who consistently pronounce most postvocalic *r*'s; –*R* indicates the pronunciation of speakers who consistently have no \r\ sound for any *r* for which educated usage sanctions pronunciation without the sound. At

gov·er·nor *R* 'gəv(ə)nər *also* -vərnər, –*R* -v(ə)nə(r\

the purpose of the labeling is to indicate that speakers who ordinarily have \r\ for postvocalic *r* (as for the last *r* in *governor*) often do not have \r\ for the first *r* in the word (see DISSIMILATION in "Guide to Pronunciation"). Some speakers sometimes drop, sometimes retain \r\ in the same environment (as in *card, art*), many consistently drop \r\ in some environments (as in *card, art*) but consistently pronounce it in others (as in *bird, hurt*). Our –*R* transcriptions, however, do not record this usage.

2.11 The low-set minus sign ˍ cancels a stress at the same point in a pronunciation shown elsewhere, as in a preceding variant or in a pronunciation for a preceding word in another entry:

cam·era·man \'⸗(⸗)⸗ˌman, -ˍmən . . . \
[1]**mer·cu·ri·al** \¦mər¦kyu̇rēəl, ˍmə(r)'k- . . . \
ac·tiv·ism \'aktə̇ˌvizəm . . . \
[1]**ac·tiv·ist** \-ˍvə̇st\

2.12 The symbol ÷ precedes variants which occur in educated speech but to the acceptability of which many take strong exception, as to the second variant at *cu·po·la* \'kyüpələ, ÷ -pəˌlō\ because of the rarity or unprecedentedness of \ō\ for *a*, or to the second variant at *gon·do·la* \'gändələ, ÷ gän'dōlə\ because the stress in the language of origin is on the first syllable. Sometimes the variant to which exception is taken is the commonest of all and is given first, as at *sacrilegious*. If not repeated, ÷ applies only to the variant that it immediately precedes.

3. FUNCTIONAL LABELS

3.1 An italic label that indicates part of speech or some other functional classification follows the pronunciation or, if no pronunciation is given, the main entry. The eight traditional parts of speech are thus indicated:

ac·tive . . . *adj*	(adjective)
across . . . *adv*	(adverb)
al·though . . . *conj*	(conjunction)
alas . . . *interj*	(interjection)
act . . . *n*	(noun)
across . . . *prep*	(preposition)
he . . . *pron*	(pronoun)
act . . . *vb*	(verb)

3.2 If a verb is both transitive and intransitive, the labels *vt* and *vi* introduce the subdivisions:

act . . . *vb* . . . *vt* . . . **~** *vi*

The character **~** is a boldface swung dash used to stand for the main entry (as *act*) and mark the subdivisions of the verb.
If there is no subdivision, *vt* or *vi* takes the place of *vb:*

ac·ti·fy . . . *vt*

Definition of a verb as transitive does not preclude intransitive usage, although it may be uncommon. On occasion most transitive verbs get used intransitively.

3.3 Other italicized labels sometimes occurring in the same position as the part-of-speech label are:

atty *abbr*	(abbreviation, see 19)
anth- . . . *comb form*	(combining form, see 21)
ante- . . . *prefix*	
Ac *symbol*	(symbol, see 20)
may . . . *verbal auxiliary*	
whoa . . . *v imper*	(imperative verb)
me·thinks . . . *vb impersonal*	(impersonal verb)

Occasionally, two or more functional labels are combined, as in *n or adj;* see also 19.3.

4. INFLECTIONAL FORMS

4.1 A plural for nearly all standard nouns is explicitly or implicitly shown in this dictionary. If a plural is irregular in any way, the form is given in full in boldface following the label *n, pl:*

man . . . *n, pl* **men**
mouse . . . *n, pl* **mice**
da·tum . . . *n, pl* **da·ta**
mother-in-law . . . *n, pl* **mothers-in-law**

4.2 If there are two or more plurals, all are written out in full and joined by *or* or *also* to indicate whether the forms are equal or secondary variants (see also 1.7.1 and 1.7.2):

fish . . . *n, pl* **fish** *or* **fishes**
court-martial . . . *n, pl* **courts-martial** *also* **court-martials**
fun·gus . . . *n, pl* **fun·gi** . . . *also* **funguses**
beef . . . *n, pl* **beefs** . . . *or* **beeves** . . . *also* **beef**
crux . . . *n, pl* **cruxes** . . . *also* **cru·ces**

4.3 Nouns that are plural in form and regularly used in plural construction are labeled *n pl* (without a comma):

en·vi·rons . . . *n pl*
feazings *n pl*
da·na·i·dae . . . *n pl*

If the plural form is not always construed as a plural, the label continues with an applicable qualification:

ge·net·ics . . . *n pl but sing in constr*
pol·i·tics . . . *n pl but sing or pl in constr*
math·e·mat·ics . . . *n pl but usu sing in constr*

in which *sing in constr* stands for "singular in construction" and means that the entry word takes a singular verb.

4.4 A noun that has only a regular English plural formed by adding the suffix *-s* or the suffix *-es* or by changing a final *-y* to *-i-* and adding the suffix *-es* is indicated by an -S or -ES following the label *n:*

bird . . . *n* -S
love . . . *n* -S
wish . . . *n* -ES
sky . . . *n* -ES
ba·by . . . *n* -ES

All standard English nouns can have regular English plurals. Such endings are given analogically in this dictionary to nouns that may be little used in the plural. All that their presence means in cases of doubtful frequency is that these plurals are available for use if needed; it does not bar the use of a non-English plural if known.

4.5 Plurals are usually omitted at compounds containing a terminal element that corresponds to a whole English word whose plural is regular and is shown at its own place. At

blackbird . . . *n*
arrow grass *n*
cake-eater . . . *n*
bio·ecology . . . *n*

the plurals are omitted because they can be found at *bird, grass, eater,* and *ecology.* At words (as *bioecology*) that may be unfamiliar, an etymology consisting of the elements of a compound word shows the element at which an omitted plural can be looked up. Plurals are often not indicated at nonstandard terms. At compounds with doubtful irregular plurals, the plural forms are written out in full. For a full discussion on the way English plurals are formed see the following article headed "Plurals".

4.6 A plural form that falls alphabetically more than five inches from the main entry is entered at its own alphabetical place:

bows *pl of* BOW
boxes *pl of* BOX
mice . . . *pl of* MOUSE
geni·i *pl of* GENIUS

Such an entry does not specify whether it is the only plural; it simply tells where to look for relevant information. At *genius* the variant plurals *geniuses* and *genii* are shown. The plural *geniuses* is not a main entry because it falls within five inches alphabetically of the main entry of *genius.*

4.7 The principal parts of all standard verbs are explicitly or implicitly given in this dictionary. These principal parts, besides the main entry, are four: the past, the past participle, the present participle, and the present 3d singular. They are printed in that order in boldface whenever any one of them has an irregular or unexpected combination of letters:

see . . . *vb* **saw** . . . **seen** . . . **seeing** . . . **sees**
make . . . *vb* **made** . . . **made** . . . **making** . . . **makes**
hit . . . *vb* **hit** . . . **hit** . . . **hitting** . . . **hits**
trap . . . *vb* **trapped** . . . **trapped** . . . **trapping** . . . **traps**
cha·grin . . . *vt* **chagrined** . . . **chagrined** . . . **chagrining** . . . **chagrins**
dye . . . *vb* **dyed** . . . **dyed** . . . **dyeing** . . . **dyes**
tie . . . *vb* **tied** . . . **tied** . . . **tying** . . . **ties**
volley . . . *vb* **volleyed** . . . **volleyed** . . . **volleying** . . . **volleys**
emcee . . . *vb* **emceed** . . . **emceed** . . . **emceeing** . . . **emcees**

4.8 Whenever any of the four parts has a variant all parts are written out in full:

sky . . . *vb* **skied** *or* **skyed** . . . **skied** *or* **skyed** . . . **skying** . . . **skies**
burn . . . *vb* **burned** . . . *or* **burnt** . . . **burned** *or* **burnt** . . . **burning** . . . **burns**
ring . . . *vb* **rang** . . . *also* **rung** . . . **rung** . . . **ringing** . . . **rings**
show . . . *vb* **showed** . . . **shown** . . . *or* **showed** . . . **showing** . . . **shows**
dwell . . . *vb* **dwelt** . . . *also* **dwelled** . . . **dwelt** *also* **dwelled** . . . **dwelling** . . . **dwells**
drink . . . *vb* **drank** . . . *or dial* **drunk** . . . **drunk** . . . *or archaic* **drunk·en** . . . **drinking** . . . **drinks**

4.9 If the four spaces usually occupied by inflectional forms cannot (for lack of evidence) all be filled, the surviving forms that can be given are identified by an italic label:

aby or **abye** . . . *vb, past or past part* **abought**

4.10 Verbs are considered regular when they have in their past a terminal *-ed* which is added with no other change except dropping a final *-e* or changing a final *-y* to *-i-*. The principal parts for these verbs are indicated by adding -ED/-ING/-S or -ED/-ING/-ES to represent the past and past participle endings (*-ed*), the present participle ending (*-ing*), and the present 3d singular ending (*-s* or *-es*):

bark . . . *vb* -ED/-ING/-S
wish . . . *vb* -ED/-ING/-ES
stone . . . *vb* -ED/-ING/-S
ba·by . . . *vt* -ED/-ING/-ES

4.11 Principal parts are usually omitted at compounds containing a terminal element or related homograph whose principal parts are regular and are shown at its own place. At

freewheel . . . *vi*
overdrive . . . *vt*
un·wrap . . . *vt*

the principal parts are not given because they can be found at *wheel, drive,* and *wrap.* An etymology consisting of the elements of a compound verb shows the element at which omitted principal parts can be looked up. Principal parts are often not given at nonstandard terms or at verbs of relatively low frequency.

4.12 A principal verb part that falls alphabetically more than five inches away from the main entry is entered at its own alphabetical place if there is no entry that is a homograph:

burned *past of* BURN
shoving *pres part of* SHOVE
denies *pres 3d sing of* DENY

4.13 All adjectives and adverbs that have comparatives and superlatives with the suffixes *-er* and *-est* have these forms explicitly or implicitly shown in this dictionary. They are written out in full in boldface when they are irregular or when they double a final consonant:

red . . . *adj* **redder** . . . **reddest**
cheer·ful . . . *adj, sometimes* **cheerfuller** . . . *sometimes* **cheerfullest**
well . . . *adv* **bet·ter** . . . **best**

4.14 When they are formed by simple addition of *-er* and *-est* with no change except dropping of final *-e* or changing of final *-y* to *-i-*, these forms are indicated by -ER/-EST following the part-of-speech label:

green . . . *adj* -ER/-EST
lucky . . . *adj* -ER/-EST
re·mote . . . *adj, often* -ER/-EST
soon . . . *adv* -ER/-EST
ear·ly . . . *adv* -ER/-EST

4.15 Comparatives and superlatives are usually omitted at compounds containing a constituent element whose inflection is shown at its own place. At

kind·heart·ed . . . *adj*
un·lucky . . . *adj*

kinderhearted and *unluckiest* are omitted because -ER and -EST are shown at *kind* and at *lucky*. Similarly the comparatives and superlatives of adverbs are often omitted when an adjective homograph shows them, as at *flat* and *hot*.

4.16 Comparatives and superlatives that fall alphabetically more than five inches away from the main entry are entered at their own alphabetical places:

hotter *comparative of* HOT
hottest *superlative of* HOT

4.17 Showing *-er* and *-est* forms does not imply anything more about the use of *more* and *most* with a simple adjective or adverb than that the comparative and superlative degrees can often be expressed in either way (*luckier* or *more lucky*, *smoothest* or *most smooth*).

4.18 A few pronouns have identified case forms:

her . . . *pron, objective case of* SHE

5. CAPITALIZATION

5.1 Except for trademarks and some abbreviations and symbols the main entries in this dictionary are set lowercase. The extent to which usage calls for an initial uppercase letter is indicated in one of five ways. Four of these consist of an italic label:

cap = almost always capitalized initially
usu cap = more often capitalized than not; capitalized approximately two to one
often cap = as likely to be capitalized as not; acceptable one way or the other
sometimes cap = more often not capitalized than capitalized; not usually capitalized

The fifth is absence of one of these labels, which indicates that the word is almost never capitalized except under irrelevant circumstances (as beginning a sentence:

french . . . *n, cap*
christian . . . *adj, usu cap*
french . . . *adj, usu cap*
french·ify . . . *vb* . . . *often cap*
die·sel . . . *adj, sometimes cap*

5.2 When an entry has more than one letter in question, the label specifies the capitalization required by usage:

french anemone . . . *usu cap F*
black-eyed su·san . . . *usu cap S*
brown betty . . . *usu cap 2d B*
french canadian . . . *usu cap F&C*
neo-thomist . . . *often cap N & usu cap T*

6. ATTRIBUTIVE NOUNS

6.1 The label *often attrib* in italics added to the label *n* at a main entry indicates that the noun is often used as an adjective equivalent in attributive position before a substantive (as in *air passage*, *cabbage soup*):

air . . . *n* -S *often attrib*
cab·bage . . . *n* -S *often attrib*
din·ner . . . *n* -S *often attrib*
fox . . . *n, pl* **foxes** *or* **fox** *often attrib*
pep·per . . . *n* -S *often attrib*
shoul·der . . . *n* -S *often attrib*
va·ca·tion . . . *n* -S *often attrib*

6.2 While any noun is likely to get used attributively sometimes, the label *often attrib* is confined to those having such widespread general frequent attributive use that they could be entered and defined as adjectives or adjectival elements. The label is not used when there is an entered adjective homograph (as *milk, adj* and *dog, adj*). Also, it is not used at open compounds that may be often used attributively when hyphened (as *X ray* in *X-ray microscope*).

7. THE ETYMOLOGY

7.1 The matter in boldface square brackets preceding the definition is the etymology. Meanings given in roman type within these brackets are not definitions of the main entry, but meanings of the Middle English, Old English, or non-English words within the brackets. Such etymological meanings may or may not be the same as one or more of the meanings of the main entry. For the meanings of abbreviations in an etymology, see the pages headed "Abbreviations Used in This Dictionary".

7.2 It is the purpose of the etymology to trace a main vocabulary entry as far back as possible in English, as to Old English; to tell from what language and what form it came into English; and to trace the pre-English source as far back as possible. These etyma (or a part of them) are printed in italic type.

7.3 The etymology usually gives the Middle English and Old English forms of native words in the manner illustrated by the following examples:

earth . . . *n* . . . [ME *erthe*, fr. OE *eorthe* . . .]
day . . . *n* . . . [ME, fr. OE *dæg* . . .]

7.3.1 When a word is traced back to Middle English but not to Old English, it is found in Middle English but not in the texts that have survived from the Old English period, even though it cannot be shown to have been borrowed from any other language, and even though it may have cognates in the other Germanic languages:

girl . . . *n* . . . [ME *girle, gerle, gurle* young person of either sex]
poke . . . *vb* . . . [ME *poken;* akin to MD *poken* to poke, stick . . .]

7.3.2 When a word is traced back directly to Old English with no intervening mention of Middle English, it has not survived continuously from Old English times to the present, but died out after the Old English period and has been revived in modern times for its historical or antiquarian interest:

ge·mot *or* **ge·mote** . . . *n* . . . [OE *gemōt* . . .]

7.4 For words borrowed into English from other languages, the etymology gives the language from which the word is borrowed and the form or a transliteration of the word in that language if the form differs from that in English:

etch . . . *vb* . . . [D *etsen* . . .]
flam·boy·ant . . . *adj* [F . . .]
judge . . . *vb* . . . [ME *juggen*, fr. OF *jugier* . . .]
ab·bot . . . *n* . . . [ME *abbod, abbed*, fr. OE *abbod, abbad*, fr. LL *abbat-, abbas* . . .]

7.5.1 Sometimes no etymology is given for words (including open compounds) created in Modern English by the combination of existing constituents. This generally indicates that the identity of the constituents is expected to be evident to the user without guidance. Examples:

blackfish . . . *n* **1 :** any of several dark-colored fishes
black·ly *adv* **:** in a black manner

7.5.2 At other times the etymology states one or both of the constituents of such words, especially when it is felt that their identity is not necessarily self-evident:

ac·ti·va·ble . . . *adj* [*activate* + *-able*]
man·ga·nite . . . *n* . . . [*mangan-* + *-ite*]
black·guard . . . *n* [[1]*black* + *guard*]
indian bison *n* . . . [[2]*indian* 1]

No hard-and-fast line, however, can be drawn between these two methods of treatment.

7.6 A considerable part of the technical vocabulary of the sciences and other specialized studies consists of words or word elements that are current in two or more languages with only such slight modifications as are necessary to adapt them to the structure of the individual language in each case. Many words and word elements of this kind have become sufficiently a part of the general vocabulary of English to require entry in a general dictionary of our language. On account of the vast extent of the relevant published material in many languages and in many scientific and other specialized fields, it is impracticable to ascertain the language of origin of every such term, yet it would not be accurate to formulate a statement about the origin of any such term in a way that could be interpreted as implying that it was coined in English. Accordingly, whenever a term that is entered in this dictionary belongs recognizably to this class of internationally current terms, and no positive evidence is at hand to show that it was coined in English, the etymology recognizes its international status and the possibility that it originated elsewhere than in English by use of the label ISV (for International Scientific Vocabulary). In some instances a statement as to probable language of origin is added after a semicolon. Examples:

end·oral . . . *adj* [ISV *end-* + *oral*]
en·do·scope . . . *n* [ISV *end-* + *-scope;* prob. orig. formed in F]
hap·loid . . . *adj* [ISV, fr. Gk *haploeidēs* single . . .] **1 :** having the gametic number of chromosomes or half the number characteristic of the somatic cells
-ene . . . *n suffix* . . . [ISV, fr. Gk *-ēnē* (fem. patronymic suffix)] **:** unsaturated carbon compound

7.6.1 Occasionally the label ISV is used, not to indicate that the entire entry form belongs to the International Scientific Vocabulary, but to identify as internationally current (though non-Latin) one of the constituents of a compound word formed in New Latin:

cho·les·ter·ol·emia *also* **cho·les·ter·ol·ae·mia** . . . *n* . . . [NL, fr. ISV *cholesterol* + NL *-emia, -aemia*]

7.7.1 An etymology beginning with the name of a language (including ME or OE) and not giving the foreign (or Middle English or Old English) form indicates that the foreign (or Middle English or Old English) form is the same as that in present-day English:

for . . . *prep* [ME, fr. OE . . .]
fos·sa . . . *n* . . . [L, cavity, ditch, trench . . .]

7.7.2 An etymology beginning with the name of a language (including ME or OE) and not giving the foreign (or Middle English or Old English) meaning indicates that the foreign (or Middle English or Old English) meaning is the same as that expressed in the first or only definition in the entry:

bea·con . . . *n* . . . [ME *beken*, fr. OE *bēacen* sign . . .] **1 :** a signal fire
de·note . . . *vt* . . . [MF *denoter*, fr. L *denotare* . . .] **1 :** to serve as indication of

7.8.1 Small superscript figures preceding forms mentioned in an etymology identify them in each case as a particular member of a set of numbered homographic entries in this dictionary. Such figures are normally used with unlabeled (Modern English) forms; but sometimes, for convenience, they are used with forms labeled OE, ME, NL, or ISV, provided these are completely identical in spelling with the corresponding Modern English form. Examples:

chucker . . . *n* . . . [[6]*chuck* + *-er*]
in·definable . . . *adj* [[1]*in-* + *definable*]
in·dec·or·ous . . . *adj* [L *indecorus*, fr. *in-* [1]in- + *decorus* decorous]
bi·fluoride . . . *n* . . . [ISV [1]*bi-* + *fluoride*]
sad·ness *n* . . . [ME *sadnesse* seriousness, firmness, fr. [1]*sad* + *-nesse* -ness]

7.8.2 Small superscript figures following words or syllables in an etymology refer in each case to the tone of the word or syllable which they follow, and accordingly are used only with forms cited from tone languages:

sam·pan *also* **san·pan** . . . *n* . . . [Chin(Pek) *san*[1] *pan*[3], fr. *san*[1] three + *pan*[3] board, plank]
voo·doo *also* **vou·dou** . . . *n* . . . [. . . Ewe *vo*[1]*du*[3] tutelary deity, demon]

7.9 When the source of a word appearing as a main entry is unknown, the formula "origin unknown" is usually used. Only rarely and in exceptional circumstances does absence of an etymology mean that it has not been possible to furnish any informative etymology; this is the case, however, with some ethnic names. More usually it means that no etymology is felt to be necessary; this is the case, for instance, with a very large proportion of the entries identified as variants or taxonomic synonyms and with Modern English coinages of the kind mentioned in paragraph 7.5.1. In one situation, absence of an etymology has a distinct and positive significance, namely in the second and later items in a set of homographic entries; here it indicates derivation by functional shift, in Modern English, from the last preceding homograph that has an etymology.

7.10.1 For native words the etymology gives cognates where possible from other Germanic or Indo-European languages, especially Old High German, Old Norse, Gothic, Latin, Greek, and Sanskrit. Similarly, for a very large proportion of the words borrowed into English from other Indo-European languages, not only Latin and Greek but also Sanskrit, the Germanic languages, the Romance languages, the Slavic languages, and the rest, the etymology gives a like indication of the Indo-European cognates. Examples:

bench . . . *n* . . . [ME, fr. OE *benc;* akin to OHG *bank* bench, ON *bekkr*]
bear . . . *vb* . . . [ME *beren*, fr. OE *beran;* akin to OHG *beran* to carry, ON *bera*, Goth *bairan*, L *ferre*, Gk *pherein*, Skt *bharati* he carries]
dic·tion . . . *n* . . . [LL & L; LL *diction-, dictio* word, fr. L, delivery in public speaking, fr. *dictus* (past part. of *dicere* to say) + *-ion-, -io* -ion; akin to OE *tēon* to accuse, OHG *zīhan* to accuse, ON *tjā* to show, Goth *gateihan* to tell, L *dicare* to dedicate, Gk *deiknynai* to show, *dikē* right, judgment, Skt *diśati* he shows]
meld . . . *vb* . . . [G *melden* to announce, report, fr. OHG *meldōn;* akin to OE *meldian* to announce, reveal, inform on, *meld* proclamation . . . OHG *melda* betrayal, OSlav *moliti* to ask for, request, pray . . .]

7.10.2 Considerations of space of course make it inadvisable to give a full display of cognates at every possible entry; what is more usually done is to direct the user by a "more at" cross-reference to another entry where such a full display of cognates is given:

edict . . . *n* . . . [L *edictum*, fr. neut. of *edictus*, past part. of *edicere* to declare, decree, fr. *e-* + *dicere* to say — more at DICTION]

7.11 Besides the use of "akin to" to denote ordinary cognate relationship, as in several examples in the preceding paragraph, there is in some etymologies a somewhat special use of "akin to" as part of a longer formula "of — origin; akin to —". This longer formula indicates that a word was borrowed from some language belonging to a group of languages, the name of the group being inserted in the blank just before *origin;* that for some reason it is not possible to say with confidence that the word in question is a borrowing of a particular attested word in a particular language of the source group; and that the word or words cited in the blank after "akin to" are a cognate or cognates of the word in question as attested within the source group. Examples:

guard . . . *vb* . . . [MF *garder*, fr. OF *garder, guarder* to ward, guard, of Gmc origin; akin to OHG *wartēn* to watch, take care — more at WARD]
cant . . . *n* . . . [ME, prob. fr. MD or ONF; MD, edge, fr. ONF, fr. L *cantus, canthus* iron ring round a carriage wheel, perh. of Celt origin; akin to W *cant* rim, Bret *cant* circle; akin to Gk *kanthos* corner of the eye, Russ *kut* corner]

This last example shows the two uses of "akin to" in explicit contrast with each other. The words cited immediately after "of Celt origin; akin to" are Celtic cognates of the presumed Celtic source word from which the Latin word was borrowed; the words cited after the second "akin to" are further cognates from other Indo-European languages.

8. STATUS LABELS

8.0 A status label in italics sometimes appears before a definition. It provides a degree of usage orientation by identifying the character of the context in which a word ordinarily occurs. Status labels are of three kinds: temporal, stylistic, and regional.

8.1.1 The temporal label *obs* for "obsolete" means that no evidence of standard use since 1755 has been found or is likely to be found:

abastardize *vt* . . . *obs*
abhorrency *n* . . . *obs*
absume *vt* . . . *obs*

obs is a comment on the word being defined, not on the thing defined by the word. When obsoleteness of the thing is in question, it is implied in the definition (as by *onetime*, *formerly*, or historical reference):

longbow . . . *n* . . . **:** the great bow of medieval England
man·tel·et . . . *n* . . . **:** a movable shelter formerly used by besiegers as a protection when attacking

8.1.2 The temporal label *archaic* means standard after 1755 but surviving in the present only sporadically or in special contexts:

be·like . . . *adv* . . . *archaic*
oak·en . . . *adj* . . . *archaic*
spir·i·tu·ous . . . *adj* . . . *archaic*

archaic is a comment on the word being defined, not on the thing the word represents.

8.2.1 The stylistic label *slang* is affixed to terms especially appropriate in contexts of extreme informality, having usually a currency not limited to a particular region or area of interest, and composed typically of clipped or shortened forms or extravagant, forced, or facetious figures of speech:

clary . . . *n* . . . *slang*
cornball . . . *n* . . . *slang*
happy dust *n* . . . *slang*
lu·lu . . . *n* . . . *slang*

There is no completely satisfactory objective test for slang, especially in application to a word out of context. No word is invariably slang, and many standard words can be given slang connotations or used so inappropriately as to become slang.

8.2.2 The stylistic label *substand* for "substandard" indicates status conforming to a pattern of linguistic usage that exists throughout the American language community but differs in choice of word or form from that of the prestige group in that community:

drown . . . *vb* . . . *substand* **drownd·ed**
his·self . . . *also* **his·sel** . . . *pron* . . . *substand*

This label is not regional.

8.2.3 The stylistic label *nonstand* for "nonstandard" is used for a very small number of words that can hardly stand without some status label but are too widely current in reputable context to be labeled *substand:*

ir·regardless . . . *adj* . . . *nonstand*

8.3.1 The regional label *dial* for "dialect" when unqualified indicates a regional pattern too complex for summary labeling usually because it includes several regional varieties of American English or of American and British English:

husky . . . *n* . . . *dial*

8.3.2 The combined label *dial Brit* and the combined label *dial Eng* indicate substandard currency in a provincial dialect of the British Commonwealth or England:

clart . . . *dial Brit*
slape . . . *adj* . . . *dial Eng*

8.3.3 A standard word requiring a specified regional restriction in the U.S. will have one of the seven labels *North, NewEng, Midland, South, West, Southwest,* and *Northwest.* These correspond loosely to the areas in Hans Kurath's *Word Geography of the Eastern United States* (1949). Examples:

dreadful . . . *adv, chiefly North*
jolt-wagon . . . *n, Midland*
can·ni·kin . . . *n* . . . *NewEng*
mountain pheasant *n, South*
cay·use . . . *n* . . . *West*
jor·na·da . . . *n* . . . *Southwest*
muck·a·muck . . . *vb* . . . *Northwest*

No collective label (as *U.S.*) is used to indicate currency in all regions of the U.S.

8.3.4 A regional label that names a country indicates standard currency in the named part of the whole English language area. Examples:

derry . . . *n* . . . *Austral*
cau·been . . . *n* . . . *Irish*
abeigh . . . *adv* . . . *Scot*
cabbage tree *n* . . . *NewZeal*
ca·nuck . . . *n* . . . *chiefly Canad*
pet·rol . . . *n* . . . *Brit*

9. SUBJECT LABELS

9.1 A prefixed subject label in italics names an activity or branch of knowledge in relation to which a word usually has a special meaning not identical with any other meaning it may have apart from the labeled subject. An abbreviated subject label can be found in the list of "Abbreviations Used in This Dictionary". Examples:

con·junct . . . *adj* . . . **5** *music*
break . . . *vt* . . . **4** . . . **c** *cricket*
con·choi·dal . . . *adj* . . . **2** *mineralogy*
con·sec·u·tive . . . *adj* . . . **3** . . . **b** *Semitic grammar*

10. SUBJECT GUIDE PHRASES

10.1 More common than the subject label in this dictionary is the subject guide phrase. This is a brief italicized phrase that points to something with which the word is associated:

con·chyl·i·at·ed . . . *adj* . . . *of a dye*
con·cor·dant . . . *adj* . . . **3** *of twins*
fire . . . *vi* . . . **1** . . . **d** (1) *of flax*
break *vi* . . . **6** . . . **d** (1) *of a fish or whale*

11. THE SYMBOLIC COLON

11.1 This dictionary uses a boldface character recognizably distinct from the usual roman colon as a linking symbol between the main entry and a definition. It stands for an unexpressed simple predicate that may be read "is being here defined as (or by)". It indicates that the supporting orientation immediately after the main entry is over and thus facilitates a visual jumping from word to definition:

black·ly *adv* **:** in a black manner
blackfish \ˈ=,=\ *n* **1 :** any of several dark-colored fishes
bis·cay·ner \ˈbi(ˌ)skānər\ *also* **bis·cay·neer** \ˌ==ˈni(ə)r\ *n* -s *usu cap* [obs. *Biskaine, Biscayne* Biscayan (fr. *Biscay*, province of Spain) + *-er* or *-eer*] **:** a seaman or ship from Biscay

11.2 Words that have two or more definitions have two or more symbolic colons. The signal for another definition is another symbolic colon:

daunt·less . . . **:** marked by courageous resolution **:** incapable of being daunted, intimidated, or subdued
avail·a·ble . . . **3 :** such as may be availed of **:** capable of use for the accomplishment of a purpose **:** immediately utilizable

11.3 If there is no symbolic colon, there is no definition. For what sometimes takes the place of a definition see 15.2, 16.3, 19.1, 20.1.

12. SENSE DIVISION

12.1 Boldface arabic numerals separate the senses of a word that has more than a single sense:

x . . . **1 :** . . . **2 :** . . . **3 :**
sev·en·teenth . . . *adj* . . **1 :** being number 17 in a countable series . . . **2 :** being one of 17 equal parts into which something is divisible

12.2 Boldface lowercase letters separate coordinate subsenses of a numbered sense or sometimes of an unnumbered sense:

x . . . **1 :** . . . **2 a :** . . . **b :** . . . **c :** . . . **3 :**
howl . . . *n* . . . **1 :** a loud protracted mournful rising and falling cry . . . **2 a :** a prolonged cry of distress . . . **b :** a yell or outcry of disappointment, rage, or protest

x . . . **1 :** . . . **2 :** . . . **:** as **a :** . . . **b :** . . . **c :**
bridge·man . . . *n* . . . **1 :** one who works on a bridge: as **a :** one who tends the landing bridge where a ferryboat docks . . . **b :** one who operates the machinery for opening and closing drawbridges . . . **c :** a member of a construction crew that builds bridges . . . **2 :** one who works on the loading platform of an icehouse

x . . . **:** . . . **:** as **a :** . . . **b :** . . . **c :**
huge . . . *adj* . . . **:** very large or extensive: as **a :** of great size or area . . . **b :** of sizable scale or degree . . . **c :** of limitless scope or character

x . . . **1 :** . . . **2 :** . . . **:** **a :** . . . **b :** . . . **c :**
gag . . . *vb* . . . *vt* **1 :** to apply a gag to: **a :** to stop the mouth of . . . **b :** to pry or hold open . . . **c :** to silence by the force of authority . . . **2 :** to cause to heave

12.2.1 The lightface colon (as in the preceding formulas) indicates that the definition immediately preceding it binds together or subsumes the coordinate subsenses that follow it:

main stem *n* **:** a main trunk or channel: as **a :** the main course of a river or stream . . . **b :** the main line of a railroad **c :** the main street of a city or town

12.2.2 The word *as* may or may not follow this lightface colon. Its presence indicates that the subsenses following are typical or significant examples which are not exhaustive. Its absence indicates that the subsenses following are exhaustive with respect to evidence for dictionary inclusion.

12.3 Lightface numbers in parentheses indicate a further division of subsenses:

x . . . **1 a :** . . . **b** (1) **:** . . . (2) **:** . . . **c :** . . . **2 :**
lead . . . *vi* . . . **2 a :** to be first or foremost in some respects . . . **b** (1) **:** to begin or open a passage or course of action . . . (2) **:** to play the first card of a trick, round, or game (3) **:** to direct the first of a series of blows at an opponent in boxing

12.4 The system of separating by numbers and letters reflects something of the semantic relationship between various senses of a word. It is only a lexical convenience. It does not evaluate senses or establish an enduring hierarchy of importance among them. The best sense is the one that most aptly fits the context of an actual genuine utterance.

12.5 The order of senses is historical: the one known to have been first used in English is entered first. This ordering does not imply that each sense has developed from the immediately preceding sense. Sense 1 may give rise to sense 2 and sense 2 to sense 3. As often as not, however, each of several senses derived in independent lines from sense 1 has served as the source of a number of other meanings. Sometimes an arbitrary arrangement or rearrangement is the only reasonable and expedient solution to the problems of ordering senses.

12.6.1 An italic functional label or other information given between a main entry and the etymology of a multisense word applies to all senses and subsenses unless a limiting label (as *pl*) or symbol (as -s) is inserted immediately after a divisional number or letter and before the symbolic colon or unless in any way clearly inapplicable. Examples of limiting labels:

can·tha·ris . . . *n* . . . **1** *pl* **can·thar·i·des** . . . **2 canthar·ides** *pl but sing or pl in constr* . . . **3** *cap*
frit·il·lar·ia . . . *n* . . . **1** *cap* **:** a genus of bulbous herbs . . . **2** -s **:** any plant, bulb, or flower of the genus *Fritillaria*
alexandrian . . . *adj* . . . **1 a** *usu cap* **:** of or relating to Alexander the Great **b** *often cap* **:** characterized by the ideas prevalent after Alexander the Great
front . . . *adj* . . . **2** *comparative sometimes* **fronter :** articulated at or toward the front of the oral passage

12.6.2 The etymology also applies to all senses and subsenses unless another etymology in boldface brackets is given after a sense number or letter:

can·on . . . *n* . . . [ME *canoun* . . .] . . . **6** [LGk *kanōn*, fr. Gk] **:** a contrapuntal musical composition

12.6.3 An italic status label, subject label, or guide phrase does not apply to all the senses of a multisense word. When divisional numbers are present, such a label is inserted after the number:

daisy cutter *n* **1** *slang* **:** . . . **2** *slang* **:** . . . **3** *slang* **:**
de·ject . . . *vt* . . . **2 a** (1) *obs* **:** to lower esp. in rank or condition **:** ABASE, HUMBLE (2) *archaic* **:** to reduce esp. in force, degree, or quality **:** WEAKEN, LESSEN **b :** to make gloomy
de·fine . . . *vb* . . . **6 a** *math* **:** . . . **b :**
fish . . . *vb* . . . *vi* . . . **4** *of a Salvationist* **:** to speak with individuals

It then applies to lettered and parenthetically numbered subsenses that follow. It does not apply to succeeding boldface-numbered senses:

glance . . . *vt* . . . **2** *obs* **a :** to allude to **b :** to barely touch **:** GRAZE **3 :**

Senses 2a and 2b are both obsolete but not sense 3. If it falls between a boldface letter and the symbolic colon or between a lightface number in parentheses and the symbolic colon, it applies only to the immediately following sense.

13. VERBAL ILLUSTRATIONS

13.1 The matter enclosed in a pair of angle brackets illustrates an appropriate use of the word in context. The word being illustrated is replaced by a swung dash which stands for the same form of the word as the main entry or by a swung dash plus an italicized suffix which can be added without any change of letters to the form of the main entry. Otherwise the word is written in full and italicized:

av·id . . . *adj* . . . **2** . . . ⟨an ~ reader⟩ ⟨an ~ gardener⟩
firm . . . *adj* . . . **1** . . . **b** (1) . . . ⟨walked with a ~ tread⟩ ⟨a ~ handshake⟩
fix . . . *vb* . . . *vt* . . . **4** . . . **c** . . . (2) . . . ⟨the jury had been ~*ed*⟩
fritter . . . *vb* . . . **1** . . . ⟨foolishly ~*ing* away time and energy⟩
shake . . . *vb* . . . **3 a :** . . . ⟨were *shaking* in their shoes⟩

13.2.1 A person's name or an italicized title included in the angle brackets acknowledges the authorship or source of a quoted verbal illustration:

just . . . *adv* . . . **4 a** . . . ⟨I'm ~ your interpreter —Ernest Hemingway⟩
lim·it . . . *n* . . . **1a** . . . ⟨at the exact northern ~ of this valley —*Amer. Guide Series: Minn.*⟩
shake . . . *vb* . . . **3 a** . . . ⟨his voice *shook* and became shrill —Kenneth Roberts⟩

13.2.2 Suspension periods indicate an omission in quoted matter. Sometimes spelling, punctuation, or capitalization has been normalized without notation usually because the brief quotation is so far removed from its original context that such matters are no longer significant and may be actually misleading.

14. THE TAXONOMIC ENTRY

14.1 A main entry that defines the name of a kind of plant or animal (as rose) or a technical category of plants or animals (as Rosaceae) is a taxonomic entry. Such entries employ in part a formal codified New Latin terminology developed and used by biologists in accord with international codes of botanical and of zoological nomenclature to identify and to indicate the relations of plants and animals. In this terminology each kind of organism has one and only one correct name that for a species (binomial or species name) consists of a singular capitalized genus name combined with an uncapitalized specific epithet or trivial name which is an appositive or genitive noun or an adjective agreeing in case, number, and gender with the genus name (as in *Rosa setigera*). For a variety or subspecies (trinomial or variety name or subspecies name) the name adds a similar varietal or subspecific epithet (as in *Rosa setigera tomentosa*). Such binomials and trinomials are in this dictionary routinely italicized and enclosed in parentheses and ordinarily immediately follow the primary orienting noun:

ca·ran·dá . . . *n* . . . **1 :** a tropical palm (*Copernicia australis*)
bar·row's goldeneye . . . *n* . . . **:** a No. American goldeneye (*Bucephala islandica*)
red-shafted flicker *n* **:** a flicker (*Colaptes caper collaris*)

By their use an absolute technical identification is made.

14.2 A binomial or trinomial so used is a technical device and does not have separate entry. The name of a genus used in such a combination normally does have an entry unless directly or indirectly oriented (as by specific mention of a higher category or through another vernacular or a technical adjective) to a higher taxonomic category (as a family, order, or class):

northern anthracnose *n* . . . caused by a fungus (*Kabatulla caulivora*) of the family Tuberculariaceae
man·go . . . *n* . . . **4:** any of a genus (*Anthracothrax*) of hummingbirds
rainbow runner *n* **:** a . . . carangid food and sport fish (*Elegatis bipinnulatus*) but
indian laurel . . . *n* . . . **1 :** an Asiatic tree (*Persea indica*)

14.3 Occasionally two binomials appear in one parenthesis in a taxonomic entry:

redstart . . . *n* . . . **2** . . . birds of the genus *Phoenicurus* (as the black redstart, *P. ochruros* syn. *P. titys* of Europe)
blacknose dace . . . *n* **:** a common No. American dace (*Rhinichthys atronasus* or *Atratulus atronasus*)

The first form indicates that the binomial following *syn* (for "synonym") is technically invalid but so widely known or generally used as to justify mention. The second is used when there is professional lack of agreement about the correct name.

14.4 A genus name used more than once in an unnumbered entry or in a numbered sense of an entry is routinely abbreviated in uses after the first:

go·ran . . . *n* . . . **:** either of two Indian mangroves (*Ceriops roxburghiana* and *C. candolleana*)
nas·tur·tium . . . *n* . . . **2** -s **:** any plant of the genus *Tropaeolum* (as *T. majus* and *T. minus*)
ich·thy·oph·thir·i·us . . . *n* . . . *cap* **:** a genus of oval holotrichous ciliates comprising a single species (*I. multifiliis*)

14.5 Names of taxonomic categories higher than the genus are capitalized plural nouns often used with singular verbs, are not italicized or abbreviated in normal use, and in this dictionary are routinely oriented in rank when used in defining:

turtle . . . *n* . . . **1 :** a reptile of the order Testudinata
scar·a·bae·oid . . . **1 :** a beetle of Scarabaeidae or a closely related family
achari·ace·ae . . . a family of herbs and subshrubs (order Parietales)

Such names when used in other entries will be found entered at their own alphabetical place.

14.6 A taxonomic entry of the form **x** *syn of* Y means that *x* is in all respects (as grammatical number, capitalization, meaning, and taxonomic rank) equivalent to *y* but that it is for some reason (as a flaw of spelling or form, a faulty application, or a lack of priority) technically inferior to and less valid than *y*.

14.7 An italic guide phrase (as *in some classifications*) used to introduce the text of a taxonomic entry is a warning device and implies that the taxon defined though not strictly a synonym in the taxonomic sense is not as generally acceptable as one lacking such a qualifier.

15. USAGE NOTES

15.1 A usage note is introduced by a lightface dash. Two or more successive usage notes are separated by a semicolon. A usage note provides information about the use of the word being defined and so always modifies the word that is the main entry. It may be in the form of a comment on idiom, syntax, semantic relationship, status, or various other matters:

fresh·en . . . *vt* . . . **4 :** . . . — usu. used with *up*
collar . . . *vb* . . . *vi* **:** . . . — used of a steel bar in a rolling mill
al·le·gro . . . *adv (or adj)* . . . **:** . . . — used as a direction in music
free·ma·son . . . *n* . . . **2 :** . . . — called also *Mason*
co·he·sion . . . *n* . . . **3 :** . . . — distinguished from *adhesion*

15.2 A usage note may stand in place of a definition and without the symbolic colon. Some function words have little or no semantic content, and most interjections express feelings but otherwise are untranslatable into substitutable meaning. Many other words (as some oaths and imprecations, calls to animals, specialized signals, song refrains, and honorific titles), though genuinely a part of the English language, have a usage note instead of a definition:

gee . . . *interj* . . . — often used as an introductory expletive for emphasis and sometimes to express surprise or enthusiasm
at . . . *prep* . . . **1** — used as a function word to indicate presence in, on, or near
ahoy . . . *interj* . . . — used in hailing ⟨ship ~⟩
hey . . . *interj* . . . — used to call attention or to incite, to express interrogation, surprise, or exultation, or with indefinite meaning in the burden of a song

16. CROSS-REFERENCES

16.0 Various word relationships requiring that matter at one place in a dictionary show special awareness of matter at another place are taken care of by a system of cross-references. A sequence of lightface small capitals used anywhere in a definition is identical letter-by-letter with a boldface main entry (or with one of its inflectional forms) at its own alphabetical place. This sequence is a cross-reference; its boldface equivalent elsewhere is what is cross-referenced to and is not itself a cross-reference.

16.1 A cross-reference following a lightface dash and beginning with either *see* or *compare* is a directional cross-reference. It explicitly directs one to look somewhere else for further information. It never stands for a definition but (with a few exceptions) is always appended to one. Such a cross-reference is separated from another cross-reference or from a usage note by a semicolon.

16.1.1 A cross-reference using the verb *see* means that the boldface entry word to which it is appended is mentioned in the same meaning and function at the entry cross-referenced to. The information at this entry which is cross-referenced to adds to the meaning of the boldface word to which the cross-reference is attached or supplements it in some significant way (as by adding to one definition of *house* the cross-reference "see BUNGALOW, COTTAGE, MANSION; APARTMENT BUILDING, BOARDINGHOUSE, DWELLING HOUSE, LODGING HOUSE, ROOMING HOUSE, TENEMENT HOUSE"):

horn . . . *n* . . . **1 a** (1) **:** one of the paired bony processes that arise from the upper part of the head of many ungulate mammals . . . — see ANTLER
ant·ler . . . *n* . . . **:** a horn of an animal of the deer family

16.1.2 A cross-reference using the verb *compare* means that the boldface entry word to which it is appended is not mentioned (except perhaps incidentally) at the entry cross-referenced to. The additional information at this entry which is cross-referenced to is related in some pertinent way (as by similarity, contrast, or complement):

apoc·o·pe . . . *n* . . . **:** the loss of one or more sounds or letters at the end of a word . . . — compare APHAERESIS, SYNCOPE
syn·co·pe . . . *n* . . . **2 a :** the loss of one or more sounds or letters in the interior of a word

16.2 A cross-reference following a symbolic colon is a synonymous cross-reference. It may stand alone as the only definitional matter for a boldface entry or for a sense or subsense of an entry. It may be one of a group of definitions joined in series by symbolic colons. In either case the cross-reference means that the definitions at the entry cross-referenced to are substitutable as definitions for the boldface entry or the sense or subsense at which the cross-reference appears:

con·cep·ti·ble . . . *adj* . . . **:** CONCEIVABLE
con·cen·tra·tion . . . *n* . . . **4 :** DENSITY 1
concentric cable *n* **:** COAXIAL CABLE
con·cen·tric . . . *adj* . . . **1** . . . **b :** having a common axis (as of two or more cones or moraines) **:** formed about the same axis **:** COAXIAL
in·vent . . . *vt* . . . **2 :** to think up or imagine **:** concoct mentally **:** FABRICATE

16.2.1 Two or more synonymous cross-references are sometimes introduced by a symbolic colon and joined to each other by a comma. This indicates that there are two or more sets of definitions at other entries which are substitutable in various contexts:

con·cept . . . *n* . . . **:** THOUGHT, IDEA, NOTION
con·cede . . . *vb* . . . **2 :** ADMIT, ACKNOWLEDGE

16.2.2 A synonymous cross-reference sometimes accounts for a usage note introduced by *called also* at the entry cross-referenced to:

ra·ad . . . *n* . . . **:** ELECTRIC CATFISH
electric catfish *n* . . . — called also *raad*
fairy bell *n* **1** . . . **:** FOXGLOVE 1
foxglove . . . *n* . . . **1** . . . — called also *fairy bell, fingerflower, fingerroot*

16.3.1 A cross-reference following an italic *var of* is a cognate cross-reference. It is explained and illustrated in 1.7.3 as applied to standard variants.

16.3.2 A limiting label before the *var of* in a cognate cross-reference indicates in what way an entry word is nonstandard:

air *Scot var of* EYRE
alarum clock *chiefly Brit var of* ALARM CLOCK
ast . . . *dial var of* ASK
colour . . . *chiefly Brit var of* COLOR
defuse *obs var of* DIFFUSE

16.3.3 A cross-reference following an italic *syn of* is also a cognate cross-reference. See 14.6.

16.4 A cross-reference following an italic label identifying an entry as an inflectional form of a singular noun, of an adjective or adverb, or of an infinitive verb is an inflectional cross-reference. These are illustrated in 4.6, 4.12, and 4.16.

16.5 A cross-reference following a functional label is a suffixal cross-reference. These are illustrated at 4.4, 4.10, and 4.14. Each of these suffixes is an entry at its own alphabetical place where the way in which it is suffixed is explained.

16.6 A cross-reference may or may not be identified by a superscript number before it or by a lightface sense number or letter after it. A synonymous cross-reference to a homograph is not identified by part of speech: nouns refer to nouns, adjectives to adjectives. Cross-references to verbs sometimes distinguish between *vt* and *vi*.

17. RUN-ON ENTRIES

17.1.1 A main entry may be continued after a lightface dash by a boldface derivative of itself. This is a run-on entry. Its boldface is always in alphabetical order with respect to the word it is run on to. It has a functional label but no definition:

en·vi·able . . . *adj* . . . — **en·vi·able·ness** . . . *n* -ES
epi·phenomenal . . . *adj* . . . — **epi·phenomenally** . . . *adv*
equi·distant . . . *adj* . . . — **equidistantly** *adv*

17.1.2 An additional run-on entry sometimes follows:

er·ro·neous . . . *adj* . . . — **er·ro·neous·ly** *adv* — **er·ro·neous·ness** *n* -ES

17.2 A main entry may be continued after a lightface dash by a boldface phrase containing the main entry word or an inflected form of it. This also is a run-on entry. It often is not in alphabetical order. It may or may not have a functional label but it has a definition:

ac·count . . . *n* . . . — **in account with** *prep* . . . — **on account of** *prep*
bad . . . *adj* . . . — **in a bad way** . . . — **too bad**
deep . . . *adj* . . . — **in deep water**
run . . . *vb* . . . — **run across** . . . — **run a temperature** . . . — **run foul of** . . . — **run riot** . . . — **run to seed** . . . — **run wild**

set . . . *vb* . . . — **set about** . . . — **set aside** . . . — **set forth** . . . — **set one's cap for** . . . — **set one's hand to**

17.3 A run-on entry is an independent entry with respect to function and status. Labels at the main entry do not apply unless they are repeated.

18. SYNONYMIES

18.1 This dictionary contains over a thousand paragraphs in which synonymous words are briefly discriminated and given verbal illustrations. Each paragraph follows the entry of one of the words of a group under consideration and is signaled by the boldface abbreviation **syn** indented. The paragraph is a synonymy. The first one appears at the word *abjure* and considers *abjure, renounce, forswear, recant,* and *retract.*

18.2 Words considered in a synonymy refer at their own alphabetical places to its location by running on the boldface letters **syn** and the word:

re·nounce . . . **syn** see ABJURE
for·swear . . . **syn** see ABJURE

19. ABBREVIATIONS

19.1 An entry having the label *abbr* is an abbreviation and what follows it is an expansion rather than a definition. No symbolic colon is used:

bbl *abbr* barrel
abp *abbr, often cap* archbishop

19.2 An abbreviation formed from the initial letters of two or more words appears in unspaced capital letters.

BCD *abbr* bad conduct discharge
GA *abbr* **1** general agent **2** general assembly

19.3 Some abbreviations function also as substantives and have a combined label:

TD *abbr or n* -s . . . touchdown

20. SYMBOLS

20.1 An entry having the label *symbol* has an expansion or interpretation rather than a definition. No symbolic colon is used:

Ga *symbol* gallium
y *symbol* **1** unknown quantity **2** an ordinate **3** *cap* admittance **4** *cap* yttrium

21. COMBINING FORMS

21.1 A main entry that begins or ends with a hyphen is a word element that forms part of an English compound. The identifying label, besides the hyphen, is *comb form* for "combining form", or if the element is used only as an affix, the label is *prefix* or *suffix*. A suffix or terminal combining form that always determines syntactic function is further identified by addition of a part-of-speech label (as *adj suffix* or *n comb form*):

nas- *or* **naso-** *also* **nasi-** *comb form*
pre- *prefix*
-able *also* **-ible** . . . *adj suffix*
-age . . . *n suffix* -s
cephal- *or* **cephalo-** *comb form* . . . **1 :** head ⟨*cephaitis*⟩ ⟨*cephalometer*⟩ **2 :** cephalic and ⟨*cephalofacial*⟩

21.2 This dictionary enters combining forms for two reasons: chiefly to make easier the writing of etymologies of words in which they occur over and over again; and to recognize meaningful elements that are constantly being used to form new words not yet authenticated for dictionary inclusion. A compound consisting of a known word and a known combining form is not censurable merely by being absent from the dictionary.

22. THE VOCABULARY ENTRY

22.1 The following definition appears at its own alphabetical place in the dictionary:

vocabulary entry *n* **:** a word (as the noun *book*), hyphened or open compound (as the verb *book-match* or the noun *book review*), word element (as the affix *pro-*), abbreviation (as *agt*), verbalized symbol (as *Na*), or term (as *man in the street*) entered alphabetically in a dictionary for the purpose of definition or identification or expressly included as an inflectional form (as the noun *books* or the verbs *booked* and *saw*) or as a derived form (as the noun *godlessness* or the adverb *globally*) or related phrase (as *one for the book*) run on at its base word and usu. set in a type (as boldface or small capitals) readily distinguishable from that of the running text which defines, explains, or identifies the entry

As defined, this term applies to all the entries as they are printed alphabetically from *a* to *zyzzogeton*, with or without hyphens, all their boldface variants, all the run-on entries, and all inflectional forms whether written out in boldface or indicated by small-capital suffixes.

23. -ER, -OR, -IZE

23.1 -ER, -OR, or -IZE. A "*see -er in Explan Notes*" as at *center*, a "*see -or in Explan Notes*" as at *honor*, or a "*see -ize in Explan Notes*" as at *synchronize* refers to variant spellings discussed in sections 2.7, 2.12, and 2.10 in the article headed "Spelling".

24. FACTOTUMS

24.1 The letter-forms illustrated at the beginning of each letter of the alphabet are a capital surrounded by lowercase roman (upper left), lowercase italic (upper right), and small and large script or black letter (across the bottom).

DIVISIONS IN BOLDFACE ENTRY WORDS

1. The centered periods in boldface main entries indicate places at which a hyphen may be put as the last character in a line of print or writing when the rest of the word must be put at the beginning of the following line. We have made an effort to insert the periods only at places where hyphens would actually be used by publishing houses whose publications show a conscientious regard for end-of-the-line divisions. Such publishers probably never divide *oleo* between the *e* and the *o* (if there is room for a hyphen, there is room for the *o*). They avoid dividing between the *o* and the *l* except in extremely narrow measure (as when an illustration narrows a column). They avoid divisions like *prea·damic* and *cardi·ovascular*, in which a letter from one element of a compound containing an English word is placed with the other element. We show no division marks at all in the word *oleo*, none between the *a* and *d* of *adamic* or *preadamic*, and none between the *i* and *o* of *cardiovascular*. Divisions avoided by publishers are sometimes printed in dictionaries probably as a concession to those who believe that syllabic division is a guide to pronunciation. However, it is the pronunciation of a word that governs its orthographic division rather than the other way around. This summary of the division practices followed in this dictionary includes a few alternatives that may recommend themselves for use and discusses objections to some of the division practices that have long been followed by dictionaries and in turn by publishers.

2.1 A compound formed of two elements each of which is an independent English word may be divided between the two elements: *nose·bleed*, *up·end*. No divisions have been shown for these compounds in this dictionary under a belief that no writer or printer need consult a dictionary for such information.

2.2 Compounds formed of an English word and an element (prefix, suffix, or combining form) that is not an independent English word are difficult to reduce to rule. In general, the more freely attachable those elements are to English words, the more apt compounds containing them are to be divided between the two constituents if the consonant or consonant group at the point of junction is one that could be either word-final or word-initial in English with the phonetic value it has in the compound. Thus, compounds with syllable-increasing inflectional suffixes are divided before the suffix: *stat·ed*, *stat·ing*, *fil·ing*, *fill·ing*, *whit·er*, *whit·est*. Such divisions are too well known to be shown in this dictionary. Divisions are made before such suffixes as the noun-forming suffix *-er* and the adjective-forming suffix *-ish*: *stat·er*, *whit·ish*. Most words in *-or* with a consonant preceding are usually divided before the preceding consonant when the break must be made between the vowels of the last and next-to-the-last syllables (as in *mortga·gor*) although a variant spelling in *-er* is usually divided after the consonant (as in *mortgag·er*). A more realistic procedure would be to show alternative divisions for words which, like *tribal*, *affective*, *defendant*, and *zincoid*, exhibit variation, just as we show variant spellings and variant pronunciations. But even the minimal number of divisions that it has long been traditional to show constitutes a disfigurement of the entry word, which in reading matter has syllable indications only at the end of a line.

3. The unsatisfactoriness of the practice of allowing pronunciation to determine place of division when no morpheme boundary is involved is best illustrated by words of the type of *apparatus* and *cyclic*, which have pronunciation variants that call for inconsistent divisions. Thus, \ˈsīklik\ calls for *cy·clic*, but \ˈsiklik\ calls for *cyc·lic*. To print the word as *cy·c·lic* is something so precedentless that it would arouse strong resistance among dictionary users. An alternative that is less disturbing, that has good precedent in other parts of the English-speaking world, and that promises to require a minimum of dictionary thumbing for the typesetters and proofreaders who are the ones most concerned with orthographic divisions, is the divorcing of such division from pronunciation as much as possible. All dictionaries and all careful dividers use such divisions as *offi·cial*, *posi·tion*, and *divi·sion*, in which a short vowel stands at the end of a line or syllable.

4. If divisions such as these are accepted with equanimity, it seems unlikely that a short vowel would be strongly resisted at the end of a syllable when the consonant between it and the following vowel is one other than *c*, *t*, or *s* with the phonetic values they have in the words cited. Books published recently in Great Britain contain such line-final short vowels which not only do not disturb the reader but are not even noticed by him in the course of reading at normal tempo. (British publishers seem not to attach much importance to consistency of division, and most British dictionaries do not show divisions in entry words.) Any publisher who would like to reduce the expense of division checking by typesetter and proofreader and of resetting could start with the following practice: When no morpheme boundary is involved, put a single consonant (except *x*, which is really two consonants: compare *toxin*, *tocsin*) with the vowel that follows it. Examples:

ap·pa·ra·tus	*Co·lo·ra·do*
cy·clic	*pa·na·te·la*
ci·ty	*di·gi·ta·lis*
mi·li·ta·ry	*Abi·ti·bi*

In *Abi·ti·bi*, there is no division between the *A* and the following *b* because leaving a single letter at the end of a line is usually avoided, now probably from custom but originally probably from the obvious fact that the reader can seldom, if ever, know how to read a single letter without knowing what letters follow it.

5. We have eliminated many of the division marks called for by traditional dictionary practice —such division marks as *o·le·o*, *sepi·a*, *min·icamera*, and *mon·osyllable*. With less success at consistency, we have avoided showing a division at points where variant pronunciations would imply two divisions, as at the entry *sapient* whose *a* is both \ā\ and \a\. If a dictionary user pronounces \a\ in *sapient*, then he may find the division *sa·pient* disturbing and may wish for a system under which he can choose the division *sap·ient*. Because of the need for a maximum of division points, we have usually not omitted division marks out of regard for variant pronunciations if it would deprive the divider of a division point at the end of two consecutive syllables. A variant preceded by the qualifier *sometimes*, the sign ÷, or some such label as *dial* has also usually not been regarded as justifying omission of a divider. Although unavoidable inconsistencies may be noticed in our divisions, no reader is apt to notice any at the righthand margin of a printed page set in strictest accord with our divisions. The showing of alternative divisions (as for *sapient*) or a discussion of division in an entry is impracticable. Division, from whatever necessity, presents a problem that has no positive solution.

6. Other classes of words in which we are unable to avoid the appearance of inconsistency are hyphened compounds (as *self-centered*) and compounds composed of an English word and an initial combining form (as *rhinencephalon*). Because the hyphen used at the end of a line is identical with the hyphen that occurs between the *f* and *c* of a word like *self-centered*, many find objectionable the breaking of such a word at the end of a line at any point other than the hyphen. The reason no doubt is that *self-centered* looks as much like (*self-cen*)(*tered*) as it does like (*self*)-(*centered*), and may give the reader a slight pause. An end-of-the-line division that coincides with the orthographic hyphen is to be preferred, even at the expense of some contrivance, if the measure is wide enough to permit it. In *Mason-Dixon line*, for example, where the word preceding and the word following the orthographic hyphen are both quite short, every effort should be made to avoid dividing between *a* and *s* and between *x* and *o*; and in *master-at-arms*, which has two orthographic hyphens to start with, to avoid dividing between the *s* and *t* of *master*. But if a line will contain all except the last syllable of a word like *self-determination*, few will object to setting off *-tion*. If there are on either side of the orthographic hyphen two word components both of which occur freely in English, the boundary between these components is the next-best place for the typographic hyphen. In *self-centeredness*, for example, breaking the word between the *d* and *n* is much better than breaking it between the *n* and *t*. In fact, the word is really (*self-centered*)(*ness*) rather than (*self*)(*centeredness*). Divisions such as that between the *n* and *t*, however, occur in publications whose typography and proofreading are overall of a very high order. Probably no such publication would divide immediately before a single letter preceding or immediately after a single letter following an orthographic hyphen—for example, before the first *i* or after the second *i* of *semi-ionic*. Such divisions would also be avoided if the word were solid instead of hyphened.

7. Dictionaries have usually put a division mark before the final consonant of the combining form in such compounds as *rhinencephalon*, *otacoustic*, in which the vowel before that final consonant is long and in which the second element is an independent English word that begins with a vowel and that retains its pronunciation unchanged in the compound. Dividing *rhinencephalon* between the *i* and the immediately following *n* conceals the make-up of the word, difficult at best for any except the specialist, and fails to provide the resourceful reader with a clue for intelligent guessing that would be provided by a division between the first *n* and the *e*. Since a clue to meaning is more valuable to the average reader than a clue to pronunciation, we have departed from precedent in the division of words of this class. A division such as *hydr·argillite*, however, would confuse by suggesting a mispronunciation for the combining form. So we have not divided such words as these at the morpheme boundary.

8. The following brief summarization replaces the considerably longer list of rules contained in preceding editions of this work, a list so detailed as to be difficult to remember and follow.

8.1 A single lowercase letter at the end of a word is never separated from the rest of the word. (In *India* the *i* and *a* are never separated. In *grade-A milk* the *A* is possibly sometimes set at the beginning of a line in narrow measure.)

8.2 Dividing after a single letter at the beginning of a word in which an orthographic hyphen is not the second character is usually avoided except in narrow measure. (In *again* and *Abel* the first letter is found separated from the rest of the word in the publications of typographically careful publishers chiefly in such narrow columns as those of pocket New Testaments. Such publications would probably show greater toleration toward setting the "*H-*" of *H-shaped* and the "*2-*" of *2-celled* at the end of a line.)

8.3 Solid compounds that consist of whole English words and that require dividing between the last syllable of one component and the first syllable of the next are divided at the boundary between the components. (*Newspaper* is divided between the *s* and the first *p*, *breakup* between the *k* and the *u*. In a compound like *newspaper*, the between-component division between *s* and *p* is somewhat to be preferred to the within-component division between *a* and the following *p* if the measure is wide enough so that the first alternative is possible.)

8.4 When a word composed of a whole English word, with pronunciation unaltered from its lexical pronunciation, and a prefix freely attachable to English words (as *anti-*, *non-*, *post-*, *pre-*, *pro-*, *semi-*) or a syllable-increasing suffix freely attachable to English words (as the present participle suffix *-ing* of *holding*, the comparative and superlative suffixes *-er* and *-est* of *moister* and *moistest*, the adjective suffix *-ish* of *girlish*, the adjective and adverb suffixes *-ly* of *lowly* and *coyly*, the agent-noun suffix *-er* of *toiler*) requires division between vowels belonging to different components, the division is made at the boundary between the components.

8.5 A non-syllable-increasing suffix, as the *-ed* of *turned*, is not separated from the rest of the word by most U. S. publishers but divisions such as *turn-ed* are numerous in some books printed in Great Britain. A word is accounted unaltered when the sounds remain the same even though the stress in the compound may, at least in certain contexts, differ, as in *Hollywoodian*.

8.6 A word is accounted whole even though a final silent *e* is dropped. Thus, *whaling* belongs with the words mentioned in paragraph 8.4 and is divided between the *l* and *i*. The British appear to adhere as strictly to the division of these words between components as do careful American publishers. However, in American publications that take less care with division, one also sees such divisions as *toi·ler*, *fligh·ty*, in which something of the base is taken over with the suffix. Although the between-components division here seems logical, it is not easy to answer effectively an objection that *toi·ler* is not different from *rela·tion*. (The latter has a phonetic reason that the former does not. But the phonetics of *toiler* would not be a bar to the division *toi·ler:* compare *toi·let*.) Several dictionaries now or formerly put the *g* or *q* of words ending in *-gue* or *-que* with the suffix when a word-initial syllable-increasing suffix follows, showing such divisions as *pla·guing*, *pi·quing*, *pla·guy*, *cli·quish*.

8.7 *-y* as in *frisky* and *flighty* is a freely attachable suffix but would not be separated from the rest of the word any more than the single letter *a* of *India* would. Divisions such as *fris·ky*, *fligh·ty*, however, may be found in publications not much concerned about the matter. Publishers who follow the dictionaries for the division of words like *mangey* find such words treated sometimes as *mang*(*e*)+*-ey* and sometimes as *mange*+*-y*, and divide or refrain from dividing accordingly. There is probably a feeling that *mang·ey* suggests a first syllable rhyming with *fang*, but divisions like *rang·ing* appear not to elicit this feeling to the same extent.

8.8 The comparative adjectives *longer, stronger,* and *younger* are usually divided after the *g* although division before the *g* would be in better agreement with the standard pronunciation, which has a sound \g\ not found in the positive forms and not ascribable to the suffix. *England* and by extension *English* are often divided after the *g* to keep the *land* intact but we have adopted the division before the *g*.

8.9 *-en* is not as freely attachable as other suffixes mentioned. (As a past-participle and noun-plural ending it seldom or never occurs outside the small handful of words in which it has long been established) but it is of Old English origin and deserves comment. When *-en* is coupled with an English word to form a verb or an adjective (as in *broaden, oaken*), each component retains its own consonants, except in words like *hasten, moisten,* in which the \t\ of the base disappears and for which division between the *s* and *t* is usual. In past participles the *en* usually stands by itself when the pronunciation of what precedes is the same as that of the infinitive or past-tense form (as *tak•en, shak•en, fall•en, shrunk•en*) or takes a preceding consonant when the pronunciation of what precedes is different from that of the infinitive (as *cho•sen, fro•zen*).

8.10 In compounds of affix and whole English word, division immediately before a single vowel at the end of a prefix or immediately after a single vowel at the beginning of a suffix is better avoided (as between the *m* and *i* of *semicircle* or between the *d* and *i* of *Hollywoodian*). The alternative requires little or no more effort.

8.11 Except when morpheme-final, as in *missing,* divide between two consecutive identical intervocalic consonants: *ab•bot, al•lot, mis•sion, expres•sion, swim•ming, ad•der* ("snake"), *add•er* ("one that adds"). (Spanish-derived *ll,* when not anglicized \l\, is often divided before the first *l,* as in *Trujillo*.)

8.12 Some suffixes of frequent occurrence in words borrowed from other languages have been naturalized to the extent that they are freely added to whole English words to form words in which the boundary between the components is an optimum dividing place: *Russian•ize, social•ize, Shakespear•ean, Roosevelt•ian* (but *Jeffersonian,* in which the first component differs from its uncompounded phonetic form in more than mere stress, is much less often treated as so divisible).

8.13 In general, it is best not to regard English proper names as English word plus suffix in dividing. The safest course is to employ such divisions as *Ba•ker, Mil•ler, Wel•ler,* even though many such words are in origin suffix-containing compounds. Such names are ordinarily not taken literally today. The pitfalls of looking for suffixes in proper names is shown by a word like *Wheeling,* which is often divided *Wheel•ing.* But the name of the West Virginia city is probably of Indian origin and the identity of the first part with English *wheel* and of the second part with the English present-participle suffix pure accident.

9. Perhaps the most inconsistently divided class of words in English consists of words whose first part is a whole English word (except that the spelling may exhibit loss of a final silent *e* and the pronunciation may exhibit shift of stress) and whose second part is a suffix of frequent occurrence in words borrowed directly from a foreign language and of more or less definite meaning, or is a short sequence of letters of infrequent occurrence and of vague or no meaning except to a language specialist. Examples of this class of words are *pompous, labyrinthine, legendary, missionary, lemonade, servant, service, licensee, patentee, lobar, lubricator, mastoiditis, millionaire, meditative.* (Words of the type *momentous, laborious* do not belong because, although the spelling of the first part is that of an English word, the sounds are not.) Some words at least of this class so often show two divisions between the vowels of the abutting syllables of the components (the division being made either at the boundary between components or before the last letter of the first component) that the dictionary practice of showing no more than one division between two consecutive syllable cores is misleading. The members of this group that are most often subject to variation are those in which the first component ends in two consonants or in a long vowel (as *pompous, lobar, legendary*). The members that are least subject to variation are those in which the first component ends in a single consonant with a completely unstressed vowel preceding (as *legionary, lemonade*). In the second group, the single consonant is usually kept with the first component. *-ator* is usually divided between *a* and *t* (but *-ater,* with the same meaning, is usually divided between *t* and *e*).

10. Between two consecutive syllables not composed of two meaningful elements, the following basic rules are usually followed by American publishers. The latter often prescribe that a specific dictionary should be taken as a guide in such matters as division and spelling.

10.1 A single consonant or a digraph goes with the preceding vowel if the vowel is stressed and short, with the following vowel if the preceding vowel is long or has weaker stress than the vowel next following: *civ•ic, vap•id, Loch•invar, Ach•eson, feath•er; sa•vor, Si•nai, Gra•ham, Ra•chel, ei•ther, se•cede, ma•chine.*

NOTE: \ā\, \ȧ\, \au̇\, \ē\, \ī\, \ō\, \ȯ\, \ȯi\, \ü\ are long vowels, \a\, \aa\, \e\, \i\, \u̇\, \ˌə\ are short. An *a* pronounced \ä\ is in most cases treated as a long vowel (as in *fa•ther, sona•ta*) whereas an *o* pronounced \ä\ is treated as a short vowel (as in *both•er*). \ȯ\ is long when it does not immediately precede \r\ (as in *Ta•ney, Chautau•qua*). Before \r\, it is long when the spelling is other than *o* (as in *lau•rel, Law•rence*) or when an alternative pronunciation is \ō\ (as in *Dorian*); it is short when an alternative pronunciation is \ä\ (as in *Dor•ic, mor•al*). \i\ and \u̇\ are long before \r\ when their spelling is *e* and *u,* respectively (as in *se•rial, fu•rious; ser•ial, fur•ious* would suggest \ˈserēəl\, \ˈfər•ēəs\).

10.2 *x* (which ordinarily is pronounced as two consonants \ks\ or \gz\) goes with the preceding vowel (as in *ex•act*). Those who believe that a division that fits any of two or more variant pronunciations is acceptable may wish to divide *Artaxerxes* between *a* and the *x* immediately following, \z\ being one variant for the first *x* there.

10.3 A *c* not pronounced \k\ or \s\, an *s* not pronounced \s\ or \z\, a *t* not pronounced \t\ or \d•\, and a *g* not pronounced \g\ go with a following *i* or *e* even when the preceding vowel is short (*pre•cious, offi•cial, vi•sion, posi•tion, pi•geon, reli•gion, prodi•gious*). The same dividers have not usually, however, employed a parallel placement of the letter *s* when it is preceded by a short vowel and pronounced \zh\ but followed by the letter *u* (*cas•ual, vis•ual, meas•ure, pleas•ure, treas•ure;* in these last three, there is a variant with the long vowel \ā\ preceding), nor for *t* when its pronunciation is \ch\ and its environment is the same (*fat•uous, rit•ual*); nor for *d* when its pronunciation is \j\ (voiced cognate of \ch\) and its environment is the same (as in *grad•ual, decid•uous*). The explanation probably is that the divisions for these words were based on pronunciations that are not now and probably have never been usual or even common in this country. Thus, Jones's *English Pronouncing Dictionary,* based on southern British speech, shows, in its first pronunciation for *visual, ritual,* and *gradual,* characters whose equivalents in our alphabet are \zy\, \ty\, and \dy\ respectively, instead of the \zh\, \ch\, and \j\ respectively that are almost universal in U. S. speech. In the dictionary we have changed over to the divisions *ca•sual, vi•sual, mea•sure, plea•sure, trea•sure* but have retained such divisions as *rit•ual* and *grad•ual* for the reason that even in the pronunciations that have resulted from assimilation, \t\ and \d\ respectively are the sounds that immediately follow the short vowel (\ch\=\t+sh\, \j\=\d+zh\).

10.4 A single *r* immediately preceded by the letter *e* pronounced \-ə\ and immediately followed by another vowel is usually put with the preceding *e* (as in *feder•ation, ciner•ary, toler•able*), although when any other vowel letter precedes under the same circumstances the *r* is usually put with the vowel letter that follows (as in *ado•ration, admi•rable, decla•ration, satu•rable*). Probably responsible is an apprehension that a division like *cine•rary* would suggest a pronunciation like \ˈsīn,rerē\, although such divisions as *dele•terious* and *ade•quate,* employed by the same dividers, are open to the same objection.

10.5 Practice has varied in the division of words in which a single consonant (usually *l* or *n*) is preceded by a long vowel and followed by an *i* pronounced \y\ (as in *Australian, communion*). In the past, the divisions *Austral•ian* and *commun•ion* have probably been the usual ones in dictionaries but *Austra•lian* and *commu•nion* appear to us to be better, especially since in some words of this class the *i* is alternatively pronounced \ē\ rather than \y\.

11. The practices followed for the division of two or more medial consonants (*consonants* is to be understood to include consonantal digraphs, as the *ch* of *puncheon* and the *ch* and *th* of *ichthyology*) are given in the following summary. These rules are for consonant clusters within which or at either end of which there is no boundary between the elements of a compound one or both of which is an English word.

11.1 When two identical consonants occur medially, a division is made between the consonants (as in *col•lie, mil•lion, camel•lia*). When two identical consonants are followed by another consonant but the entire consonant sequence is pronounced as a single sound, the division is also between the identical consonants (as in *Bud•dha, Mat•thew, bac•chanalian, sap•phire*). (These sequences are trigraphs.) When two identical consonants are followed by another consonant that is separately pronounced, the division is after the second identical consonant (as in *Press•ley, Meiss•ner, Hauss•mann, Hoff•mann, Ripp•mann, Will•kie*), except that before *le* pronounced \əl\ or \ᵊl\ the division is between the identical consonants (as in *bab•ble, mid•dle, baf•fle, tus•sle, muz•zle*). When the identical consonants are preceded by another consonant, the division is between the identical consonants *Nils•son, Jans•sen.*

11.2 When two consonants that are not identical are preceded by a short stressed vowel, the division is usually between the consonants (as in *bar•ley, ad•junct, whis•per, pub•lic, met•ric, arith•metic, expul•sion, conten•tion*). *ck* and *dg* are usually divided after the second member (as in *knick•er•bock•er, gadg•et*) but such treatment of *dg* (except in two-morpheme words like *edg•ing*) appears to us to be inconsistent with d-j in *adjunct,* and we have divided *gad•get.* When the first consonant is followed by *-le* pronounced \əl\ or \ᵊl\, the division is before the first consonant (as in *tre•ble, tri•ple, dou•ble*).

11.3 When two consonants that are not identical are preceded by a long stressed vowel or by a vowel that has less stress than the one immediately following, the division is before the first consonant if it is a stop (*p, t, c* or *k, b, d, g*) followed by *l* or *r* (except that *tl* and *dl,* which do not occur word-initially in English except in a few borrowed words, have the division before the first consonant only when this consonant is followed by *-le* or by an inflected form of *-le,* as in *ti•tle, enti•tling, noo•dle, At•lantic, ad•lumine*): *du•plicate, ca•pricious, ni•tric, trea•cle, mi•crometer, Bi•ble, cele•brate, hy•drant, hiero•glyphic, photo•graph.* The sequences *tl* and *dl* in *ti•tle* and *noo•dle* and *zl* in *muz•zle* are unusual in that they stand at the beginning of a syllable although they do not stand at the beginning of any except borrowed English words. The sequence *le* itself is unusual in that the phonetic items consisting of syllabic consonant and of vowel plus consonant are usually spelled with vowel letter first and consonant letter second. The sequence *ck* is usually treated as a digraph and kept together, with division after the *ck* (as in *knick•erbock•er*). *ck* is not, however, a digraph in the sense that the *ch* of *Wichita* is; it is much in the nature of a variant of *kk* (compare *chucker,* variant of *chukker*), and divisions like *grac•kle,* sometimes seen, can hardly be open to any serious objection. Dividing *lac•key* would parallel *lac•quer.* When two unidentical consonants other than those listed above occur, the division is usually between the consonants: *clois•ter, aus•picious, an•gel, Daim•ler.*

11.4 When three or more consonants occur between vowels, regardless of the nature of the preceding vowel, at least one consonant goes with it; if the placing of only one consonant with the preceding vowel would leave with the vowel that follows a consonant sequence that does not begin a genuine English word with the phonetic value it has intervocalically, two consonants are placed with the preceding vowel: *claus•trophobia, Neus•trian, mis•creant, im•bricated, ex•tricate, sump•ter, ad•script.* In a word like *sumpter* the \mpt\ is a difficult phonetic cluster and the \p\ is often lost by way of simplification, so that *pt* in *sumpter* often has the same pronunciation as the *pt* of *ptomaine,* but such accidental loss of a medial consonant does not constitute a reason for such divisions as *sum•pter.*

11.5 In words borrowed from foreign languages consonant sequences retaining a pronunciation close to that of the foreign language are sometimes divided as in that language (as they commonly are in our dictionary), and sometimes divided as they would be in English words: *vignette, tortilla, zabaglione.*

SPELLING

0. The following sections describe the spelling of English derivatives and variants. They do not aim to account for it. Examples are typical, not exhaustive.

The words *vowel* and *consonant* here refer to letters, not to sounds. The letters *a, e, i, o* are vowels; *u, w, y* are sometimes vowels, sometimes consonants; the other letters are consonants.

u is a consonant when it immediately follows *q* (*quit, liquid, quoin, pique*); when it is pronounced \w\ or is silent immediately following *g* (*anguish, guide*); when it is pronounced \w\ immediately following *s* (*suave*). Otherwise it is a vowel (*accuse, blue, snafu, suet, gulf, ague*).

w is a vowel when it immediately follows a vowel letter in the same syllable (*awe, law, ewe, dew, grow, cow*), and has no \w\ corresponding to it in the pronunciation as represented in this dictionary. It is a consonant in other positions (*way, swan, award*), where it has a \w\ corresponding to it in the pronunciation (but *answer* has no \w\ in the pronunciation).

y is a consonant when it is followed in the same syllable by any vowel except silent *e* (*yap, yet, youth, ye*). Otherwise it is a vowel (*dye, eye, boy, alley, gray, by, deny, gyp, synonym, many*).

1. DERIVATIVES

1.0.1 English derivatives are chiefly derivatives in which one element is an English word and the other is another English word or an affix that is readily attachable to a variety of English words. A number of suffixes from foreign languages (esp. from Greek and Latin) occur with great frequency in English words, often preceded by letters that spell an English word to whose meaning the suffix merely makes an addition. But such suffix-bearing formations have in the main been produced not by adding a suffix to an English word but by adding a suffix to the foreign source of the English word — unions either made in the foreign language and borrowed into English or made in English on the analogy of other unions in the foreign language. Accordingly, often the spelling of such suffixal formations is not the sum of the spelling of the English derivative of the foreign root plus the spelling of the anglicized form of the suffix, and such formations cannot be explained without a consideration of non-English spellings, which is beyond the province of these rules (except that a certain amount of such detail has been presented in the treatment of *-able/-ible*). Examples of spellings that these rules do not attempt to explain are: *crystallize* (has the meaning of *crystal* plus the meaning that *-ize* frequently gives, but the two *l*'s are on the analogy of Greek *krystallos*); *excellent* (from Latin *excellens, -entis;* compare English *excel* with one *l*); *libidinous* (traces orthographically to Latin *libidinosus* rather than English *libido*); *tranquillize* (the two *l*'s trace to Latin *tranquillus;* the more frequent one-*l* variant is based directly on English *tranquil*); *metallic* (from Greek *metallikos* and *metallon* rather than English *metal*); *pontifical* (from the Latin word *pontific-* rather than English *pontiff*).

1.0.2 In derivatives of the preceding type alteration of stress and vowel values is of frequent occurrence, whereas in most of the derivatives next discussed the addition merely adds sounds to the base without disturbing the latter's stress and sounds. Rules for adding a suffix to an English word are of such involvement and extent that the consultant who desires help on some one specific detail only is advised to locate that detail by the boldface subdivision.

1.1 Words ending in -x are unchanged before any suffix:

coax → coaxed, coaxing
fix → fixable, fixed, fixer, fixing
jinx → jinxed, jinxing
Manx → Manxman
Marx → Marxist
six → sixty

1.2 Words ending in -c remain unchanged

1.2.1 before *a, o, u* or a consonant:

frolic → frolicsome
sac → saclike
talc → talcose, talcous
zinc → zincate, zincoid, zincous

1.2.2 before suffixal *e, i,* and *y* add *k* if the pronunciation of the *c* remains hard but add nothing if the pronunciation of the *c* becomes soft:

bivouac → bivouacked, bivouacking
critic → criticism, criticize
frolic → frolicked, frolicking
mimic → mimicked, mimicking
music → musician
physic → physicist
picnic → picnicked, picnicking
toxic → toxicity

1.3 Words ending in consonant plus -c usually remain unchanged before any suffix, but forms with an inserted *k* occur occasionally:

arc → arced/sometimes *arcked, arcing*/sometimes *arcking*
disc → disced, discing
zinc → zinced/zincked, zinciferous, zincing/zincking, zincite, zincky/zincy/but also *zinky*
talc → talcky

1.4 Some base words in this class have variants in which *-k* replaces *-c*. Such variants remain unchanged before any suffix.

1.4.1 Words ending in a single consonant except x or c immediately preceded by two or more vowels in the same syllable remain unchanged before any suffix:

air → aired, airing, airy
appeal → appealed, appealing
boil → boiled, boiling
brief → briefed, briefer, briefly
cloud → clouded, cloudless
cool → cooled, cooler, coolest, cooling, coolly
curtail → curtailed, curtailing, curtailment
head → headed, headless, heady
prowl → prowled, prowler, prowling
recoil → recoiled, recoiling
suit → suitable, suitor
tail → tailed, tailless
zeal → zealot, zealous
zoom → zooming

EXCEPTION:
wooly/but *woolly* is more frequent

1.4.2 Words ending in a single consonant immediately preceded by a single vowel bearing primary stress double the consonant before a suffixal vowel but not before a suffixal consonant:

abet → abetted, abetting, abettor
bag → baggage
begin → beginner
clan → clannish
drop → droplet, dropped
fit → fitness, fitting
glad → gladden, gladly
gyp → gypped, gypping
hot → hotly, hotter
lug → luggage
spot → spotless, spotted
trek → trekker, trekking

EXCEPTIONS:
chagrin → chagrined, chagrining
combat → combated, combating
(pronunciations having widespread currency in British speech, but little or none in U.S. are \shə'grēn\ or 'shagrin\ and \'kämbət\; see 1.4.3; the forms *combatted, combatting* are often found in U.S. writing; but *chagrinned, chagrinning,* though justifiable on the basis of logic and pronunciation, are less common variants).
control → controled, controling
(less frequent than the two *l* forms, but preferred by some to preserve the long vowel sound; for the same reason, derivatives of *extol* and *patrol* sometimes have single *l* spellings)
defer → deference
prefer → preferable, preference
refer → reference
transfer → transference
(when the stress is altered, the derivative has a single *r*, but some derivatives of *-er* verbs have an alternative single *r* spelling even when the stress remains the same: *transfer → transferable/transferrable*)
gas → gaseous, gasify but *gassed, gassing*

1.4.3 Words ending in a single consonant immediately preceded by a single vowel bearing secondary stress vary greatly in their derivatives:

some always double the consonant:

handicap → handicapped, handicapping
humbug → humbugged, humbugging
zigzag → zigzagged, zigzagging

some have single consonant only:

catalog → cataloged, cataloging
(but *catalogue → catalogued, cataloguing,* which present no problem)
chaperon → chaperoned, chaperoning
(the single *n* is probably due to the long vowel sound, as well as to the occasional appearance of the alternative form *chaperone*)
parallel → paralleled, paralleling
(the single *l* serves to avoid the awkward appearance of two pairs of *l*'s)
pyramid → pyramided, pyramiding

some have both forms:

bayonet → bayoneted/bayonetted, bayoneting/bayonetting
benefit → benefited/benefitted, benefiting/benefitting
carburet → carbureted/carburetted, carbureting/carburetting, carburetor/carburettor
combat → combated/combatted, combating/combatting
kidnap → kidnapped/kidnaped, kidnapping/kidnaping
nonplus → nonplussed/nonplused, nonplussing/nonplusing
program → programmed/programed, programming/programing
(the variant spellings may not have the same pronunciation; rather, the two-consonant spelling represents a pronunciation (or in *kidnap* a former pronunciation) with definite secondary stress on the last syllable of the base word, whereas the one-consonant spelling represents a pronunciation with no stress on the last syllable of the base word; in *carburetor* it may reflect the pronunciation \ˌrāt\ instead of \ˌret\

1.4.4 Words ending in a single consonant immediately preceded by one or more vowels without stress remain unchanged before any suffix:

bargain → bargained, bargaining
callous → calloused, callously
carom → caromed, caroming
credit → credited, crediting, creditor
gallop → galloped, galloping
gladden → gladdened, gladdening
solid → solider, solidest, solidify, solidly
waver → wavered, wavering

EXCEPTIONS:
(1) a large group of words doubles a final consonant immediately preceded by a single unstressed vowel before a suffixal vowel; in British use this is the regular practice; in U.S. use it is usually an accepted alternative to the one-consonant spelling. To this class belong words with unstressed final syllable ending in *-l* (except *parallel,* sometimes pronounced \-ləl\, esp. in Britain; compare 1.4.3) as well as some words ending in *-s* or *-t*. Derivatives of compounds of these words follow the same rules as derivatives of the simplex words. The following list includes the most important of these words:

apparel	*drivel*	*marshal*	*shovel*
barrel	*duel*	*marvel*	*shrivel*
bevel	*enamel*	*medal*	*signal*
bias	*equal*	*metal*	*snivel*
bowel	*focus*	*model*	*spiral*
cancel	*fuel*	*panel*	*stencil*
carol	*funnel*	*parcel*	*symbol*
cavil	*gambol*	*pedal*	*tassel*
channel	*gravel*	*pencil*	*tinsel*
chisel	*grovel*	*peril*	*total*
counsel	*gruel*	*pistol*	*towel*
cudgel	*jewel*	*pummel*	*trammel*
devil	*kennel*	*quarrel*	*travel*
dial	*label*	*ravel*	*trowel*
dishevel	*laurel*	*revel*	*tunnel*
dowel	*libel*	*rival*	*victual*

(2) two *l*'s are more common in adjectives like *gravelly, tinselly* than in derivatives with other suffixes; the double consonant prevents these words from being read as two-syllabled adverbs (*gravelly, adj; gravely, adv*)
(3) for derivatives of *worship* the one-*p* and two-*p* forms are about equally common:
worship → worshiped/worshipped, worshiping/worshipping, worshiper/worshipper

1.5 Words ending in a single consonant that is silent remain unchanged before any suffix:

chamois → chamoised, chamoising
crochet → crocheted, crocheting
hurrah → hurrahed, hurrahing
picot → picoted, picoting
pooh-pooh → pooh-poohed, pooh-poohing

EXCEPTION:
ricochet → ricocheted/ricochetted, richocheting/ricochetting
(this is not a true exception, for whereas the single-consonant spelling reflects a pronunciation in which the *t* is silent (\ˈrikəˈshā\), the double-consonant form reflects the pronunciation \ˈrikəˈshet\— compare 1.4.3.

1.6 Words ending in two or more consonants the last of which is not c remain unchanged before any suffix:

art→ *artistic, artless*
attach→ *attached, attachment*
buzz→ *buzzed, buzzer, buzzing*
condemn→ *condemnatory, condemned, condemning*
length→ *lengthen, lengthy*
odd→ *oddity, oddly*
sighed→ *sighing*
stiff→ *stiffen, stiffer, stiffly, stiffness*
thrall→ *thralldom*
trick→ *tricked, tricking, trickster*
thirst→ *thirsty*
wrong→ *wronged, wrongly*

EXCEPTIONS:
(1) words ending in *-ll* often drop one *l* before a suffixal consonant and in forming compounds (in Britain the one *l* spelling is by far the more common for such words; in the U.S. it is a widespread variant):

dull→ *dulness* *skill*→ *skilful*
fill→ *fulfil, fulfilment* *will*→ *wilful*
roll→ *enrol* *thrall*→ *enthral, thraldom*

(2) the second *l* of final *-ll* frequently disappears before suffixal *l;* it always disappears before *-ly* (*droll*→ *drolly; dull*→ *dully; full*→ *fully*); before *-less* it may disappear, but hyphened forms, retaining all three *l*'s are more frequent (*hull-less, will-less*); with *-like*, the hyphened form, retaining all three *l*'s is usual (*bell-like, bull-like, scroll-like*)

1.7 Words ending in silent -e drop the vowel before a suffixal vowel but remain unchanged before a suffixal consonant:

bone→ *boned, boning*, but *boneless*
complete→ *completed, completing*, but *completeness*
curve→ *curvature, curved, curving*, but *curvesome*
imagine→ *imaginable, imagining*, but *imagines*
clique→ *cliquish*, but *cliques*
bugle→ *bugling, bugler*
gentle→ *gentler, gentlest*, but *gentleness*

Although both are often called silent, the *e* at the end of words of the type *bone* and *giraffe* differs from the *e* at the end of words of the type *bugle* and *tickle* in this respect: the vowel letter that immediately precedes the final consonant or consonant group of *bone* and *giraffe* stands for a vowel sound that is the nucleus of the final or only syllable of the word whereas the vowel letter in the same position in *bugle* and *tickle* does not. The *-e* in *bugle* may be regarded as a vowel letter that is pronounced but that is out of position in the orthography of the word. Although such an *e* is usually dropped from the spelling before a suffixal vowel, the extra syllable that it represents in the form of the word before suffixation may remain present in the pronunciation, *bugling* for example being either \'byügliŋ\ or \'byügəliŋ\ and *ticklish* being either \'tiklish\ or \'tikəlish\. Words ending in a single pronounced *-e* (other than those bearing an accent, covered in 1.9) are rare; the few existing examples drop the *-e* before a suffix beginning with an *e*, but remain unchanged before all other suffixes:

Dante→ *Dantesque*
dele (vb)→ *deles, deled, deleing*

EXCEPTIONS:
(1) proper names ending in single *-e* preceded by one or more consonants usually keep the *e* before the suffix *-an;* in the derivatives so formed the *e* is sounded, whether or not it is silent in the base:

Coleridge→ *Coleridgean* usually preferred to */Coleridgian*
Europe→ *European* *Chile*→ *Chilean*
Nietzsche→ *Nietzschean*
Shakespeare→ *Shakespearean* usually preferred to */Shakespearian*

(2) *mile*→ *mileage* much more frequent than */milage*
nurse→ *nursling* the common form rather than */nurseling*

(3) before the suffix *-ly* words ending in consonantal *-le* usually drop the *-le:*
gentle→ *gently* *simple*→ *simply*
subtle→ *subtly*/but also *subtlely*
supple→ *supply*/but more frequently *supplely* probably to avoid confusion with the verb *supply*

(4) some words ending in *-re* retain the *-e* before a suffixal vowel:

acre→ *acreage* *nacre*→ *nacreous*

(5) words ending in *-ce* or *-ge* usually retain the *-e* before any suffixal letter except *e, i*, or *y*, thus preserving the softness of the *c* or *g:*

age→ *ageless* (but *aging/ageing*)
change→ *changeable, changeless* (but *changing*)
courage→ *courageous, encouragement* (but *encouraged, encouraging*)
grace→ *graceful* (but *disgraced, disgracing*)
peace→ *peaceable*
replace→ *replaceable* (but *replacing*)
range→ *rangy*/but also *rangey*

A *d* preceding *g* may in a few cases act as a preserver of the soft sound and permit the dropping of the *-e:*

abridge→ *abridgment*/but *abridgement* especially in Britain
acknowledge→ *acknowledgment*/but *acknowledgement* especially in Britain
judge→ *judgment*/but *judgement* especially in Britain
lodge→ *lodgment*/but *lodgement* especially in Britain

(6) although final *-e* regularly drops before the suffix *-able*, some adjectives in *-able* have alternatives retaining the *-e:*

like→ *likable/likeable*
live→ *livable/liveable*
love→ *lovable/loveable*
move→ *movable/moveable*
size→ *sizable/sizeable*

British usage is more inclined than U.S. usage to retain the form with *e;* recent or nonce formations, especially from polysyllabic base words, usually appear without the *e;* but formations based on verbs ending in *-le* or *-re* usually retain the *e:*

automobile→ *automobilable*
isolate→ *isolatable*

but:

handle→ *handleable* *whistle*→ *whistleable*
settle→ *settleable* *wrinkle*→ *wrinkleable*

(7) usage fluctuates considerably with regard to dropping or retaining final *-e* before derivatives formed with the suffix *-y;* many have both the *-ey* and the *-y* alternative:

cage→ *cagey/cagy* *phone*→ *phony/phoney*
home→ *homey/homy* *poke*→ *pokey/poky*
horse→ *horsey/horsy* *stage*→ *stagy/stagey*
mouse→ *mousy/mousey*
stone→ *stony/stoney*

and some words have only one form in common usage:

rose→ *rosy* *slave*→ *slavey*
shade→ *shady*

(8) the silent *-e* remains in some present participles to distinguish them from the corresponding forms of other verbs:

dye→ *dyeing* (in contrast to *dying*)
singe→ *singeing* (in contrast to *singing*)
springe→ *springeing* (in contrast to *springing*)
swinge→ *swingeing* (in contrast to *swinging*)

1.8 Words ending in -e preceded by a vowel drop the final *-e* before suffixal *-a-* and *-e-*:

argue→ *arguable, argued*
awe→ *awed* *toe*→ *toed*
blue→ *blued, bluer, bluest*
free→ *freed, freer, freest*
issue→ *issuance, issued*
lie→ *liar* *vie*→ *vied*

EXCEPTIONS:
(1) words ending in *-ee* usually retain both *e*'s before *a* and always before suffixal *-i-*:

agree→ *agreeable, agreeing*
flee→ *fleeing*
foresee→ *foreseeable*
free→ *freeing*

-ie in an accented syllable becomes *-y* before suffixal *-i-*:

die→ *dying* *lie*→ *lying*
tie→ *tying* *vie*→ *vying*

-ie in an unaccented syllable remains unchanged before suffixal *-i-*:

stymie→ *stymieing* *sortie*→ *sortieing*

-oe remains unchanged before suffixal *-i-*:

canoe→ *canoeing* *shoe*→ *shoeing*
hoe→ *hoeing* *toe*→ *toeing*

-ue usually drops *-e* before suffixal *-i-*:

accrue→ *accruing* *pursue*→ *pursuing*
argue→ *arguing* *true*→ *truing, truism*
ensue→ *ensuing*

-ye alternatively keeps or drops *-e* before suffixal *-i-*:

eye→ *eyeing/eying* (compare *dyeing*)

retain *-e* when forming adjectives with the suffix *-y*:

glue→ *gluey* *tissue*→ *tissuey*

usually remain unchanged before a suffixal consonant:

agree→ *agreement* *accrue*→ *accruement*
free→ *freedom* *blue*→ *blueness*
woe→ *woeful*/but also *woful*

but:

argue→ *argument* *true*→ *truly*
awe→ *awful* (but *awesome*) *due*→ *duly*

1.9 Verbs derived from the French and ending in -é usually form their past and past participle in *-éd*, less often in *-éed;* they form their present participle in *-éing:*

appliqué→ *appliquéd, appliquéing*
visé→ *viséd*/also *viséed*

1.10 Words ending in -y preceded by a consonant usually change the *-y* to *i* before any suffixal letter except *i* and the possessive sign *'s:*

beauty→ *beautiful, beautify*
body→ *bodily, embodiment*
cliquy→ *cliquier, cliquiest*
contrary→ *contrariwise*
copy→ *copyist* *icy*→ *iciest, icily*
defy→ *defiant, defying*
deny→ *denial, denying*
fancy→ *fanciful, fancying*
happy→ *happiness*
likely→ *likelihood* *mercy*→ *merciless*
merry→ *merrier, merriest, merriment*
thirty→ *thirtyish* *weary*→ *wearisome*

but:

everybody→ *everybody's*
Mary→ *Mary's*

Verbs of this classification form the third person singular by changing the *-y* to *i* and adding *-es*, in analogy with the past and past participle in which *-y* regularly changes to *i* before *-ed*.

EXCEPTIONS:
(1) one-syllable words usually retain *-y* before *-ly* and *-ness:*

dry→ *dryly, dryness* *sly*→ *slyly, slyness*
shy→ *shyly, shyness*
wry→ *wryly, wryness*

(2) comparatives and superlatives of one-syllable adjectives alternatively retain *-y* or replace it with *i:*

shy→ *shier/shyer, shiest/shyest*
dry→ *drier, driest*/more common than *dryer, dryest*

(3) *fly*→ *flier/flyer*

(4) *-y* remains unchanged
before *-like* and *-ship:*
lady→ *ladylike*
secretary→ *secretaryship*
in derivatives of *baby* and *lady:*
baby→ *babyhood* *lady*→ *ladykin*
in *busyness* (busy state) to distinguish it from *business* (enterprise)
in some rarely used forms:
hobby→ *hobbyless* *Tory*→ *Torydom*

(5) *-y* may be lost completely before suffixal *-i-*, especially when separated by one or more syllables from the primary stress of the base word:

accompany→ *accompanist/accompanyist*
military→ *militarism, militarist, militarize*
soliloquy→ *soliloquize*
voluntary→ *voluntarism*

1.11 Words ending in -y preceded by a vowel usually remain unchanged before any suffix:

alloy→ *alloys* *attorney*→ *attorneys*
convey→ *conveyance, conveyor*
enjoy→ *enjoying, enjoyment*
gray→ *graying, grayish, grayness*
play→ *played, playing, player, playful, playlet*

EXCEPTIONS:
(1) *day*→ *daily* *say*→ *saith*
lay→ *laid* *slay*→ *slain*
pay→ *paid*

(2) *gay*→ *gaiety/gayety, gaily/gayly*
stay→ *stayed*

(3) comparatives and superlatives of adjectives ending in *-ey* replace these two letters with *i:*

gluey→ *gluier, gluiest, gluily*
phoney→ *phonier, phoniest, phonily*

A number of adjectives ending in *-ey* preceded by a consonant have alternative forms without *e* (*phoney/phony*). For these alternatives the spellings *-ier, -iest* are covered in 1.10.

(4) adjectives ending in *-wy* change the *-y* to *i* before any suffix:

dewy→ *dewier, dewiest, dewily, dewiness*
showy→ *showier, showiest, showily, showiness*

1.12 Words ending in a vowel except e or y, when adding a suffix beginning with a consonant, remain unchanged:

China→ *Chinaman* *photo*→ *photostat*
coo→ *coos* *radio*→ *radiogram*
law→ *lawful* *taxi*→ *taximan*

1.13.1 Verbs ending in a vowel except e or y, when adding a suffix beginning with a vowel, remain unchanged before their inflectional suffixes:

alibi→ *alibied, alibiing*
boo→ *booed* *coo*→ *cooed, cooing*
radio→ *radioed, radioing*
shanghai→ *shanghaied, shanghaiing*
show→ *showed, showing*
ski→ *skied, skiing, skier*
snafu→ *snafus, snafued*
taboo→ *tabooed, tabooing*
tattoo→ *tattooed, tattooing*
taxi→ *taxis, taxiing*/but also *taxying*

EXCEPTIONS:
verbs ending in single *-o* usually insert *e* before adding *-s* for the third person singular:

echo→ *echoes* *lasso*→ *lassoes*

For the plural of nouns ending in a single *-o* (*potato*), see "Plurals".

1.13.2 Nouns ending in a vowel when adding one of the suffixes -esque, -ism, -ist usually remain unchanged especially if the base word is short and the final vowel is essential to its recognition:

Dada→ Dadaism	*Tao→ Taoism*
Dali→ Daliesque	*Tito→ Titoism*
solo→ soloist	*Zola→ Zolaesque*

EXCEPTIONS:
cello→ cellist
chiaroscuro→ chiaroscurist
Leonardo→ Leonardesque
Michelangelo→ Michelangelesque
Nazi→ Nazism/but also *Naziism*
propaganda→ propagandist
quattrocento→ quattrocentist

1.13.3 Geographical and personal names ending in -a regularly drop the *-a* before the suffix *-an/-ian:*

Africa→ African	*America→ American*
Alberta→ Albertan	*Canada→ Canadian*
North Carolina→ North Carolinian	
Seneca→ Senecan	*Victoria→ Victorian*
Venezuela→ Venezuelan	

1.13.4 Some geographical names ending in -o drop the *-o* before *-an/-ian:*
Borneo→ Bornean
Mexico→ Mexican
Morocco→ Moroccan
Ontario→ Ontarian
San Diego→ San Diegan
San Francisco→ San Franciscan

1.13.5 Scientific terms of Greek or Latin origin ending in -a regularly drop the *-a* before a suffix beginning with a vowel:
pleura→ pleural
urea→ urease, ureic
urethra→ urethral

1.13.6 Words ending in -o insert *e* before suffixal *-y:*
goo→ gooey *mosquito→ mosquitoey*

1.13.7 Geographical and personal names ending in -o or a combination of vowels pronounced \ō often insert *n* or *v* before *-an/-ian:*
Buffalo→ Buffalonian
Cicero→ Ciceronian
Draco→ Draconian
Harrow→ Harrovian
Marlow→ Marlovian
(compare *Peru→ Peruvian*)
Thoreau→ Thoreauvian
Toronto→ Torontonian

but some geographical names ending in *-o* remain unchanged before *-an:*
Chicago→ Chicagoan
Colorado→ Coloradoan

1.14 When adding a prefix that forms a new word, a base word usually remains unchanged:
act→ enact
call→ recall
change→ exchange
danger→ endanger
deck→ bedeck
fill→ fulfill
prove→ disprove
roll→ enroll
veil→ unveil

EXCEPTIONS:
words ending in *-ll* often drop one *l* when adding a prefix; this practice, common in Britain, is widespread also in the U.S., but the unchanged (*-ll*) forms prevail in this country:
fill→ fulfil, fulfilment
roll→ enrol
thrall→ enthral

By analogy even some infinitives which are not derivatives of English base words sometimes drop one *l*. For these words, too, the one *-l* spelling prevails in Britain, whereas in the U.S. it exists side by side with the *-ll* form:
distil/distill
instal/install
instil/instill

1.15 Two or more words joining to form a compound usually retain the full spelling of both component words:

billfold	*self-conscious*
father-in-law	*sidestep*
freedom-loving	*well-bred*
love-lies-bleeding	*wholehearted*
makeup	*widespread*
man-of-war	*workhouse*
narrow-minded	

For the spelling of such compounds (separate, closed, or hyphened) see the section on "The Writing of Compounds".

EXCEPTIONS:
many compounds which are long-established in the language and in which the full literal force of one or both elements has been weakened or lost have dropped a letter from one, sometimes both, of the original elements:
almighty, almost, alone, already, also, although, altogether, always
withal, therewithal, wherewithal
welcome, welfare
Candlemas, Christmas, Lammas, Michaelmas
artful, hateful, rueful, woeful/woful
chilblain
fulfill
namesake
neckerchief
numskull/but also *numbskull*
pastime
until
wherever

Many words which are not readily recognizable as compounds resulted from the joining of two words in the Old or Middle English periods (*lord*, from OE *hlāfweard*, bread keeper; *threshold*, from ME *threshwold*, (a piece of) wood to tread (on); *woman* from OE *wīfmann*, a wife man).

2. VARIANTS

2.0 Many English words may be spelled in more than one way. The variant used may be a matter of individual choice, or it may be regional. One form may be usual in one region (as the U.S.), and a variant may be usual in another region (as Britain). Some of the more conspicuous U.S./British variations are:

U.S.	BRITISH	EXAMPLE	SEE
-ction	*-xion*	*connection/connexion*	**2.5**
-dg-	*-dge*	*judgment/judgement*	**1.7**
e	*ae, oe*	*eolian/aeolian* *ecology/oecology*	**2.2**
-er	*-re*	*theater/theatre*	**2.7**
-ize	*-ise*	*organize/organise*	**2.10**
-l-	*-ll-*	*leveling/levelling*	**1.4.4**
-ll-	*-l-*	*enrollment/enrolment*	**1.6**
-or	*-our*	*humor/humour*	**2.12**
-s-	*-c-*	*defense/defence*	**2.14**

The variations treated in the following sections are not regional unless the contrary is stated.

2.1 -able/-ible. English has a large group of adjectives in *-able*, another in *-ible;* the force of the suffix in both groups is the same. Many of these adjectives are from Latin adjectives in *-abilis* and *-ibilis; -abilis* occurs after first-conjugation stems, *-ibilis* after stems of the other conjugations. With *-abilis* the stem used is the present, with *-ibilis* it is sometimes the present, sometimes the participial. Examples: (first conjugation) *laudabilis;* (second, third, fourth conjugations respectively, present stem) *horribilis, credibilis, audibilis;* (second, third, fourth conjugations respectively, participial stem) *risibilis, defensibilis, sensibilis.* These and many other such Latin adjectives have been borrowed by English, with change of *-ilis* to *-le*. In addition, many others have been analogically formed in English, or in French and borrowed by English. Since Latin provides precedent for either the present or the participial stem with *-ibilis*, two quite or substantially synonymous *-ible* words with different stems have in some cases been introduced into English (*corrodible/corrosible, submergible/submersible*). Further, *-able* has become a productive suffix in English and has been attached to a multitude of English verbs. Many of these that are Latin-derived are (*a*) from second-, third-, and fourth-conjugation stems, or (*b*) from first-conjugation participial stems, with none of which *-abilis* occurs. Hence, English has a few variants of the type *preventible/preventable* (class *a*) and a probably larger number of the type *educable/educatable* (class *b*).

2.2 e/ae, e/oe. The digraphs *ae/æ* and *oe/œ* of Latin and of Greek transliterated into Latin are sometimes retained in English derivatives and borrowings, sometimes reduced to *e*. Sometimes one form strongly prevails throughout English, and variants are infrequent: *economy, enigma, estuary, ether, Caesar, Aegean, aer-* words (as *aerial, aeronautics*). When variants are frequent, the one-letter variant is nearly always in greater favor in U.S. use than in British:
anemia/anaemia
anesthetic/anaesthetic
diarrhea/diarrhoea
edema/oedema
esophagus/oesophagus
estrogen/oestrogen
etiology/aetiology
fetus/foetus
hemoglobin/haemoglobin
maneuver/manoeuvre (fr. French)

2.3.1 chemistry suffixes for compounds, classes of compounds, and radicals: -an/-ane, -id/-ide, -in/-ine, -ol/-ole, -on/-one, -oyl/-yl, -yne/-ine. Words in *-ane* usually designate saturated carbon compounds (as paraffin hydrocarbons and many cyclic hydrocarbons) and in the U.S. also completely hydrogenated parent heterocyclic compounds (as *dioxane*); words in *-an* designate other chemical compounds (as *furan, pyran*) including in Britain completely hydrogenated parent heterocyclic compounds (as *dioxan*). *-ide* has superseded *-id* except in a few terms (notably *lipid* as preferred by most biochemists). In organic chemical names *-ine* designates bases; *-in* designates compounds that are neutral or not distinctly basic or acidic (as glycerides, proteins, porphyrins, and some six-membered heterocyclic compounds). In systematic names *-ol* designates alcohols and phenols, whereas *-ole* designates other compounds (as most five-membered heterocyclic compounds and some others). Words in *-one* designate ketones, quinones, lactones, or other compounds containing a carbonyl group and also sulfones and sultones; in *-on*, other compounds (as *nervon*). *-oyl* is now preferred to *-yl* by the International Union of Pure and Applied Chemistry for most organic acid radicals (as *carbamoyl, phthaloyl*). With one or two exceptions *-yne* has superseded *-ine* in systematic names for carbon compounds containing triple bonds (as hydrocarbons of the acetylene series).

2.3.2 -ene/-en. The spelling *thiophene* is used in the U.S., whereas *thiophen* is used in Britain. (In both countries *-ene* is used especially for carbon compounds containing double bonds, as olefin hydrocarbons and aromatic hydrocarbons.)

2.3.3 -e. In systematic chemical names a final *e* (as in the name of a hydrocarbon) is dropped before a suffix beginning with a vowel (as *butane, butanol*, but *butanediol*).

2.4 -ant/-ent. English contains a large group of words ending in *-ant* and another in *-ent*, both pronounced \ənt\. Most of the *-ant* words stem from Latin present participles of the first conjugation (*radiant*, from Latin *radians, -antis*), the *-ent* words from Latin present participles of the other conjugations (*regent*, from Latin *regens, -entis*); but not always (*tenant*, ultimately from a Latin verb of the second conjugation, owes its *a* to Old French). The two endings do not differ in force, and, though usually all English words that derive from the present participle of the same Latin verb have *a* only or *e* only, in each of the following families of such derivatives there is variation:

a almost always	*e* almost always	*a* usually	*e* usually	*a* and *e* with about equal frequency
	repell...ncy		*repell...nt* *impell...nt*	
		propell...nt *expell...nt*		
pend...nt noun	*pend...ncy* *depend...nt* adj. *independ...nt*, *-...nce, -...ncy*			*pend...nt* adj. *depend...nt* noun
ascend...nt, -...nce *descend...nt*				*ascend...ncy*
	transcend...nt, -...nce, -...ncy			
tend...nce "care" *intend...nt, -...nce, -...ncy* *attend...nt, -...nce*	*tend...ncy*			
	superintend...nt, -...nce, -...ncy			

2.5 -ction/-xion. Most nouns ending in \kshən\ are spelled *-ction* only; a few are alternatively *-ction/-xion;* a few are *-xion* only. Those that are *-ction* only are ultimately from a Latin verb whose participial stem ends in *-ct: direction*, from *directio* from *direct(us)*. Those that are alternatively *-ction/-xion* are ultimately from a Latin verb whose participial stem ends in *-x* and whose present stem ends in *-ct;* the participial stem is the source of the *-xion* variant, the present stem is the source, usually via an English verb, of the *-ction* variant: thus *inflexion* is from *inflexio* from *inflex(us)*; *inflection* is *inflexion* with *x* assimilated to the *ct* of English *inflect*, from *inflect(ere)*, an assimilation catalyzed by the analogy of nouns like *direction*. Nouns that are *-xion* only are ultimately from Latin verbs of which the present stem does not end in *-ct* and which accordingly have not procreated English verbs in *-ct: crucifixion, transfixion,* and *fluxion.*

-CTION/-XION		
	U.S.	BRITISH
defle...ion	*ct* prevails *x* rare	*x* probably prevails
genufle...ion	*ct* prevails	*x* prevails
infle...ion	*ct* prevails *x* rare	*x* prevails
refle...ion	*ct* prevails *x* rare	*ct* prevails
conne...ion	*ct* prevails *x* rare	*x* prevails
comple...ion	*x* prevails *ct* rare*	*x* prevails *ct* rare

*in spite of the fact that there is a fairly common U.S. form *complected*

2.6.1 em-/im-, en-/in-. The Latin preposition or adverb *in,* in such English derivatives as *inoculate, intrude, invent,* occurs as a prefix in many Latin verbs and verb derivatives. Sometimes the *in-* is unchanged (*inoculare, intrudere, invenire*). At other times the phonetic influence of an initial consonant of the base that follows the *in-* changes the *n* to a consonant having the same articulation as the base-initial consonant. The change is to *m* before *m, b,* and *p* (*immigrare, imbibere, implorare*), to *l* before *l* (*illuminare*), to *r* before *r* (*irradiare*).

2.6.2 French — Old and Modern — has borrowed many of these compounds and retained the Latin spelling of the prefix (*inoculer, inventer, immigrer, imbiber, implorer, illuminer, irradier*). However, Latin *in* became *en* in French, and when similar compounds were constructed in French on French words as a base the vowel used in the prefix was *e.* The assimilation of the *n* to *m* before *m, b,* and *p* continued (*emmener, embaumer, employer*); the assimilation of the *n* to *l* and *r* before *l* and *r* respectively did not (*enlargier, enrager*).

2.6.3 English, like French, has borrowed many of the Latin compound verbs and retained the Latin spelling of the prefix (*inoculate, invent, immigrate, imbibe, implore, illuminate, irradiate*). English has borrowed also from French many forms in *em-* and *en-* (*embalm, employ, enlarge*). English has taken over also the prefixes *im-, in-, em-, en-* and attached them to English nouns and adjectives to make verbs, or to verbs to make other verbs (*imbed, encage, enkindle*). As in French formations, *-m* is usually used before *m, b, p* (*immarble/emmarble, imbed/embed, impanel/empanel*) but in the compound having *mesh* as base both *m* and *n* are found prefixally.

2.6.4 Of the borrowings from French *em-* and *en-* forms, and of the formations within English, some have now *e* now *i* as the prefixal vowel (*enclose/inclose, embed/imbed, embitter/imbitter*); others, some of which formerly showed the same variation, are found with *e* only or with *i* only (*embalm, encamp, impeach*). *i* is more frequent before *m* than before *n.*

2.6.5 In most of the intra-English formations the prefix adds little or nothing semantically to the base. Before an adjective or noun it serves chiefly as a sign that the adjective or noun has been made a verb. This verb-forming prefix is closest to being completely functionless when it is added to a verb: thus *kindle* and *enkindle* are not easily discriminable. If the prefix makes a substantial semantic contribution, usually the prefixal vowel is *i* and the prefixal consonant is *n* whatever letter follows (*inborn, inbound, inbuilt, inbred*/but *imbred* occasionally).

2.7 -er/-re. Some English words, mostly derived from French words in *-re,* which in turn are mostly derived from Greek or Latin, alternatively end in *-er/-re.* But the *-er,* of different origin, that is a productive suffix freely attachable to English bases (*writer, header, four-poster, New Yorker*) does not have the variant *-re.* Most of the variants are usually *-er* in U.S., *-re* in Britain:

caliber/calibre   *sepulcher/sepulchre*
center/centre   *somber/sombre*
fiber/fibre   *specter/spectre*
luster/lustre

EXCEPTIONS:

(1) in both U.S. and British use *-re* is usually the form after *c,* the immediately following *r* ensuring the hardness of the *c* (*acre, chancre, involucre, lucre, massacre, mediocre, nacre, wiseacre*). But after *g* (which, like *c,* may be hard or soft) the same is not true (U.S. *meager*/Britain *meagre;* but both countries prefer *eager, ogre*).

(2) U.S. and British usage both prefer *cadre* \ˈkadrē\, *macabre, timbre* "tone quality". The latter (often \ˈtambə(r)\) is not to be confused with *timber* "wood" (\ˈtimbə(r)\), a different word, which has only *-er* in both countries.

(3) although *meter/metre,* the metric-system unit of measurement (which is ultimately from Greek *metron*), and its compounds (*centimet-, decimet-, millimet-*) are *-re* in Britain, *meter* (which is *mete+ -er*) is universal in both countries for any device for measuring (electric *meter*), as is also *-meter* as the second element of many names for specific measuring devices (*altimeter, barometer, galvanometer, gasometer, ohmmeter, speedometer, thermometer, voltmeter, volumeter*). Some of these compounds are simply a joining or telescoping of an English first element and *meter* "measuring device", but most are not. In a few the quality of the *e* that follows the *m* is the same as in the simplex word; in most this *e* is of a different quality and without stress. In metric-system names the sound values in *-meter/-metre* are the same as in the simplex.

(4) although *meter/metre* "rhythm" is *metre* in Britain, for names of individual measures (*trimeter, tetrameter, pentameter, hexameter*) *-meter* is the spelling there as well as in the U.S. In these, too, the *e* following the *m* is without stress.

(5) both *theater/theatre* have wide currency in the U.S., only the second in Britain. In New York City, the theatrical center of the U.S., the spelling is usually *theatre.*

(6) *neuter* and *sober* are in both countries *-er* only.

2.8.1 -er/-or. These are the most common endings in English for agent nouns. This *-or* does not have a variant *-our* except in *saviour.* A few agent nouns have *a* rather than *e* or *o* before the *r* (*beggar, liar, pedlar* sometimes). Such nouns of this class as are based on a Latin perfect stem, whether the nouns are formed in English from an English verb so based or are taken from the Latin or, with somewhat altered spelling, from French (*author*) usually have *-or:*

actor   *fabricator*   *negotiator*
arbitrator   *incisor*   *objector*
collector   *inspector*   *operator*
conductor   *lubricator*   *supervisor*
confessor   *mediator*   *translator*
detector   *motor*   *victor*

2.8.2 Other agent nouns usually have *-er,* such as nouns based on Latin present stems and nouns based on verbs of Germanic origin:

convoker   *modifier*   *slicer*
designer   *organizer*   *stitcher*
digger   *producer*   *subscriber*
distiller   *rider*   *usurper*
drawer   *robber*   *voyager*
invader   *redeemer* (compare *Redemptorist*)
commuter (compare *commutator*)

2.8.3 Occasionally, however, an English agent noun, although its base is from a Latin perfect stem, has *-er* for suffix, as a less frequent variant of *-or.* In such pairs the *-or* form is on the analogy of Latin, the *-er* form is the English suffix added to an English verb that is from the same Latin perfect stem as the *-or* noun (*executor*/ archaic *executer*). Conversely, sometimes an agent noun, though its base is from a Latin present stem, has *-or* alone or as a variant of *-er.* Sometimes false analogy may be responsible: some Latin present stems have the same final consonant or consonant cluster as some Latin perfect stems (compare the present participle *reflect*[*ere*] and the past participle *elect*[*us*]); the coiner of *reflector* may have used as his model a quite regular formation of the type *elector.* So also *adaptor* and *advisor* are unexpected (compare *adapt*[*are*], *advis*[*are*]), *captor* and *supervisor* are regular (compare *capt*[*us*], *supervis*[*us*]).

2.8.4 Old French is the source of numerous *-or* agent nouns. Many are law terms or have a legal sense, and of these many have correlatives in *-ee* (*bailor, bailee*). Most of the terms below have variants in *-er,* and *-er* is the usual spelling in nonlegal use of such terms as have both legal and nonlegal senses:

abettor   *consignor*   *promisor*
alienor   *donor*   *releasor*
bailor   *mortgagor*   *surrenderor*
bargainor   *obligor*   *transferor*
barrator   *pawnor*   *vendor*
confirmor   *pledgor/pledgeor*   *visitor*
bettor (avoidance of homography with *better* "more good" may have been a factor)

2.9. -ph-/-f-. \ˈsəlfə(r)\ as a chemical term and chemical terms based on it are usually spelled *sulf-* by U.S. scientists, *sulph-* by British scientists. Nonscientists in both countries usually spell *sulph-.*

2.10. -ize/-ise. Ancient Greek has a verb suffix *-izein,* which descended into postclassical Latin as *-izare* and into French as *-iser.* English has borrowed verbs (all of more than one syllable) containing this suffix from all three languages (*ostracize, pulverize, moralize*). In addition, English has isolated the suffix and used it quite freely, attaching it to bases both Greek (*criticize, mechanize*) and non-Greek (to Latin bases, *anglicize;* to English nouns, *victimize, memorize, dockize;* to English adjectives, *normalize, victorianize;* to proper names, *londonize, fletcherize*). In U.S. use the suffix is nearly always spelled *-ize,* even in words from French, in which the spelling is *-iser.* In Britain, however, many not only retain *s* in borrowings from French but use *s* instead of *z* in borrowings from Greek and Latin and in English formations. Many others in Britain, however, including several influential publications, use *-ize* in all words in which \īz\ is descended from Greek *-izein.*

EXCEPTIONS:

(1) although \īz\ in *exorci-e* and *chasti-e* derives (in the second somewhat circuitously) from Greek *-izein,* there is a strong preference for *s* over *z* in these words.

(2) the ending \īz\ in some English verbs (and a few nouns) not only is from etyma spelled with *s* rather than *z* but has no etymological relationship to the ending discussed in the preceding paragraph. For *appri-e* "inform" *s* strongly prevails in both the U.S. and Britain; for *appri-e* "evaluate", a rarer word, *z* seems to prevail in the U.S. and to be as common as *s* in Britain. For *adverti-e s* strongly prevails in both countries. In Britain *z* seems to prevail in *amorti-e, assi-e, recogni-e,* strongly prevails in *aggrandi-e, capsi-e, cogni-e, gormandi-e;* in the U.S. *z* alone occurs or strongly prevails in all seven words. The verb *merchandi-e* occasionally has *z,* the noun seldom. The following are usually found with *s:*

advise   *devise*   *improvise*
comprise   *disguise*   *revise*
compromise   *enterprise*   *supervise*
demise   *excise*   *surmise*
despise   *franchise*   *surprise*

(3) in the small group of words *analy-e, dialy-e, electroly-e, paraly-e,* in which *-ly-e* derives from the Greek noun *lysis, s* seems to be somewhat more common than *z* in Britain but *z* is much more common than *s* in the U.S.

2.11 -ol/-oul. In the words *mold/mould, molder/moulder, molt/moult,* and *smolder/smoulder,* the *u* is likely to be more often dropped than kept in the U.S., is almost always kept in Britain. *Molten* (from *melt*) has no variant with *u.*

2.12 -or/-our. English contains a group of *r*-final nouns that are descended from Latin nouns having nominative *-or,* that are not agent nouns (compare 2.8.1), and that are usually spelled *-or* in the U.S. but *-our* in Britain:

ardor/ardour   *labor/labour*
color/colour   *rigor/rigour*
fervor/fervour   *tumor/tumour*
honor/honour

The first such borrowings into English were from early Old French, and the termination in both lending and borrowing language was *-or* or *-ur.* In French as spoken in Britain after the Norman Conquest the ending became *-our.* English borrowings from this Anglo-French retained the *-our,* and earlier borrowings from continental French became *-our* by assimilation. After the Renaissance made Latin more widely known, words of this category were usually borrowed, in their Latin spelling, with *-or* as the ending. Many words once spelled *-our* in English are in Britain now written *-or,* but others are not. In the U.S. the *-our* spelling is seldom used in these words.

EXCEPTIONS:

(1) although the *-our* ending formerly occurred also in agent nouns, *saviour* is the only important survival.

(2) *glamour* and *saviour* are the only two *-our* forms that have wide currency in the U.S.

(3) not all *-or/-our* words derive ultimately from Latin *-or* words (*arbor* "latticework", *armor, behavior, harbor, neighbor*).

In Britain, *u* is usually retained before suffixes that had their origin within English (*favourer, flavourful, humourless, neighbourhood, neighbourly, vapourish*); before Latin suffixes that are not freely addable to English words *u* usually disappears (*coloration, honorary, honorific, odoriferous, odorous*); before Greek and Latin suffixes that have been naturalized (*-able, -ism, -ist, -ite, -ize*) the spelling varies.

2.13 -ped/-pede (from Latin *pes, pedis,* foot). *-pede* is more common than *-ped* after *milli-* and possibly the only form after *veloci-* and *centi-.* After other elements *-ped* is usual and is probably the only form that is now used after *bi-* and *quadru-.*

2.14 -c-/-s-.

defence/defense   *pretence/pretense*
offence/offense   *vice/vise* "tool"

In all four words *c* is the preference in Britain, *s* in the U.S.; *defensive, offensive,* and *pretension,* however, are the usual word forms in both countries.

licence/license
practice/practise

U.S. usually spells *license* both noun and verb with *s;* Britain almost invariably spells the noun with *c,* usually spells the verb with *s.* U.S. uses *c* more often than *s* in the noun *practice,* uses one letter about as often as the other in the verb *practise;* Britain strongly prefers *c* in the noun (*s* seems nonexistent), *s* in the verb. Although noun and verb were once undifferentiated, on both sides of the Atlantic *prophecy* is more common for the noun, *prophesy* for the verb.

PLURALS

1. The plurals of English nouns are regularly formed in writing by the suffixation of the letter *-s* (*hat→hats*) or the letters *-es* (*cross→crosses*) and in speaking by the addition of the sound \s\ (\hat→hats\), the sound \z\ (\bȯi→bȯiz\), or the sound \əz\ (\krȯs→krȯsəz\). Although there are many exceptions to be noted, this regularity is so dominant that in theory all English nouns may be said to be capable of an analogical plural in the letters *-s* or *-es,* and in practice little hesitation in so forming a new or unknown plural should be felt. Native speakers of English have no difficulty in using the sounds of pluralization in accordance with regular patterns. This treatment of plurals will be limited to written words, typically selected, not exhaustive.

2. -s. Most nouns simply add *-s:*

bag→bags *button→buttons*
book→books *violet→violets*

3. silent -e. Nouns ending in *-e* that is silent regularly add *-s:*

collapse→collapses *race→races*
college→colleges *ride→rides*
hedge→hedges *size→sizes*

4. -es. Nouns ending in *-s, -z, -x, -ch,* or *-sh* regularly add *-es:*

buzz→buzzes *gas→gases*
dash→dashes *torch→torches*
fox→foxes

5. consonant + -y. Nouns ending in *-y* preceded by a consonant regularly change *-y* to *-i-* and add *-es:*

army→armies *pity→pities*
baby→babies *sally→sallies*
courtesy→courtesies *sky→skies*
lady→ladies

except proper names:

Germany→Germanys *Kinny→Kinnys*
Kathy→Kathys *Mary→Marys*
Kentucky→Kentuckys

6. -quy. Nouns ending in *-quy* regularly change *-y* to *-i-* and add *-es:*

colloquy→colloquies *soliloquy→soliloquies*

7. vowel + -y. Nouns ending in *-y* preceded by a vowel (except those ending in *-quy*) regularly add *-s:*

attorney→attorneys *chimney→chimneys*
bay→bays *guy→guys*
boy→boys *key→keys*

8. vowel + -o. Nouns ending in *-o* preceded by a vowel regularly add *-s:*

cameo→cameos *studio→studios*
duo→duos *trio→trios*
embryo→embryos *zoo→zoos*
Romeo→Romeos

9. consonant + -o. Most nouns ending in *-o* preceded by a consonant add *-s:*

alto→altos *jocko→jockos*
bozo→bozos *piano→pianos*
burro→burros *poncho→ponchos*
chromo→chromos *silo→silos*
ego→egos *two→twos*
hippo→hippos

but other nouns ending in *-o* preceded by a consonant add *-es:*

bubo→buboes *hero→heroes*
bucko→buckoes *jo→joes*
echo→echoes *potato→potatoes*
embargo→embargoes

The consonant or cluster preceding the *-o* does not determine whether the plural will add *-s* or *-es.* A few nouns add either:

banjo→{banjos, banjoes} *innuendo→{innuendos, innuendoes}*
bravo→{bravos, bravoes} *motto→{mottos, mottoes}*
buffalo→{buffalos, buffaloes} *mulatto→{mulattos, mulattoes}*
calico→{calicos, calicoes} *proviso→{provisos, provisoes}*
cargo→{cargos, cargoes} *tobacco→{tobaccos, tobaccoes}*
domino→{dominos, dominoes} *tornado→{tornados, tornadoes}*
halo→{halos, haloes} *zero→{zeros, zeroes}*

10. -oo. Nouns ending in *-oo* regularly add *-s:*

coo→coos *kangaroo→kangaroos*
cuckoo→cuckoos *tattoo→tattoos*

11. -i. Most nouns ending in *-i* add *-s:*

macaroni→macaronis *ski→skis*
rabbi→rabbis

but a few add either *-s* or *-es:*

alkali→{alkalis, alkalies} *taxi→{taxis, taxies}*

12. -f. A few nouns ending in *-f* change the *-f* to *-v-* and add *-es:*

leaf→leaves *thief→thieves*
self→selves *wolf→wolves*

but some of these also add *-s* without consonant change:

beef→{beeves, beefs} *loaf→{loaves, loafs}*
calf→{calves, calfs} *wharf→{wharves, wharfs}*

13. -fe. A few nouns ending in *-fe* change *-f-* to *-v-* and add *-s:*

knife→knives *life→lives*

14. uniliteral words. Single letters, numbers, figures, and signs add either apostrophe and *-s* or just *-s:*

A→{A's, As} *1920→{1920's, 1920s}*
A→{A's, As} *△→{△'s, △s}*
a→{a's, as} *#→{#'s, #s}*
4→{4's, 4s}

15.1 nouns formed from abbreviations. Abbreviations formed by literation and used as nouns add either apostrophe and *-s* or more often just *-s:*

GI→{GI's, GIs} *IQ→{IQ's, IQs}*
G. I.→{G. I.'s, G. I.s} *Ph.D.→{Ph.D.'s, Ph.D.s}*

15.2 Abbreviations formed by truncation or contraction usually add *-s* without apostrophe:

apt→apts *cap→caps*
bbl→bbls *ms→mss*
bx→bxs *mt→mts*

but some become plural without any change:

1 *hr*→4 *hr* 1 *oz*→4 *oz*
1 *in*→4 *in* 1 *qt*→4 *qt*
1 *mo*→4 *mo* 1 *yd*→4 *yd*

15.3 Some single-letter abbreviations double an initial consonant:

c.→cc. (chapters) *v.→vv.* (verses, violins)
p.→pp. (pages) *M.→MM.* (Messieurs)

16. -en. One noun usually adds *-en:*

ox→oxen

and another changes the stem and adds *-en:*

child→children

and one sometimes changes the stem and adds *-en:*

brother→brethren

17. umlaut. Six nouns change the medial vowel:

foot→feet *man→men*
goose→geese *mouse→mice*
louse→lice *tooth→teeth*

Compounds in which one of these is the final element likewise change:

dormouse→dormice *eyetooth→eyeteeth*
Dutchman→Dutchmen *forefoot→forefeet*
Englishman→Englishmen *woman→women*

18. foreign endings. Many nouns of foreign origin retain the foreign plural; most of them have also a regular English *-s* or *-es* plural, which is often preferred, although sometimes a foreign plural signals a difference in meaning (compare *stadia* and *stadiums*).

18.1 Latin. Most of these common anglicized foreign words come from Latin:

alga→algae *formula→formulae*
alumna→alumnae *larva→larvae*
antenna→antennae *minutia→minutiae*

alumnus→alumni *focus→foci*
bacillus→bacilli *fungus→fungi*
cactus→cacti *radius→radii*

apex→apices *executrix→executrices*
appendix→appendices *index→indices*
codex→codices *matrix→matrices*

addendum→addenda *erratum→errata*
aquarium→aquaria *medium→media*
datum→data *ovum→ova*
emporium→emporia *residuum→residua*

corpus→corpora *genus→genera*
femur→femora *opus→opera*

crux→cruces *lex→leges*
dux→duces *pons→pontes*
gens→gentes *rex* "king"*→reges*

gravamen→gravamina *nomen→nomina*

apparatus→apparatus *nexus→nexus*
meatus→meatus *series→series*
custos→custodes *imago→imagines*

18.2 Greek. The second largest group of anglicized foreign words comes from Greek:

analysis→analyses *nemesis→nemeses*
basis→bases *parenthesis→parentheses*
crisis→crises *thesis→theses*
ellipsis→ellipses
genesis→geneses

automaton→automata *ganglion→ganglia*
criterion→criteria *phenomenon→phenomena*
ephemeron→ephemera

carcinoma→carcinomata *lemma→lemmata*
miasma→miasmata
dogma→dogmata *schema→schemata*

aphis→aphides *iris→irides*
ephemeris→ephemerides *proboscis→proboscides*

necropolis→necropoleis

cyclops→cyclopes *phalanx→phalanges*
larynx→larynges *sphinx→sphinges*

logos→logoi

18.3 Italian. A comparatively small number of Italian plurals have become anglicized:

bambino→ bambini *palazzo→ palazzi*
bandit→ banditti *seraglio→ seragli*
cicerone→ ciceroni *solo→ soli*
dilettante→ dilettanti *tempo→ tempi*
libretto→ libretti
monsignor→ monsignori

18.4 French. A small number of French plurals have been anglicized:

adieu→ adieux *bureau→ bureaux*
beau→ beaux *plateau→ plateaux*
madame→ mesdames *monsieur→messieurs*

18.5 miscellaneous.

cherub→ cherubim (Hebrew)
fellah→ fellahin (Arabic)
halakah→ halakoth (Hebrew)
Kohen→ Kohanim (Hebrew)
señor→ señores (Spanish)
seraph→ seraphim (Hebrew)

19.1 compounds. Two-word compounds consisting of initial noun plus adjective hyphened or open customarily pluralize the noun:

cousin-german→ cousins-german
heir apparent→ heirs apparent
knight-errant→ knights-errant
vicar-general→ vicars-general

but not invariably; sometimes the adjective is construed as a noun and a regular suffix is alternatively added to it:

attorney general→{attorneys general, attorney generals}
battle royal→{battles royal, battle royals}
beau ideal→{beaus ideal, beau ideals}
court-martial→{courts-martial, court-martials}
notary public→{notaries public, notary publics}
poet laureate→{poets laureate, poet laureates}
sergeant major→{sergeants major, sergeant majors}

In similar-appearing compounds in which the second word is a noun a regular suffix is added at the end:

brigadier general → brigadier generals
judge advocate → judge advocates
lieutenant colonel→ lieutenant colonels

A few similar compounds have double plurals:

gentleman-usher→ gentlemen-ushers
lord justice → lords justices
thing-in-itself → things-in-themselves

19.2 Three-word compounds consisting of initial noun plus prepositional phrase hyphened or open customarily pluralize the initial noun:

aide-de-camp → aides-de-camp
attorney-at-law → attorneys-at-law
brother-in-law → brothers-in-law
chargé d'affaires → chargés d'affaires
coat of mail → coats of mail
man-of-war → men-of-war

20. animals. Many names of fishes, birds, and mammals have both a plural with a suffix and a zero plural that is identical with the singular. Some have one or the other. Some present a choice according to meaning or according to a special interest of the user

20.1 The following such names form a plural with a suffix (except occasionally when modified by an adjective like *wild, native, sea, mountain*):

bird	→ *birds*	*monkey*	→ *monkeys*
cow	→ *cows*	*owl*	→ *owls*
crow	→ *crows*	*parrot*	→ *parrots*
cuckoo	→ *cuckoos*	*penguin*	→ *penguins*
dog	→ *dogs*	*pig*	→ *pigs*
eagle	→ *eagles*	*rat*	→ *rats*
goat	→ *goats*	*robin*	→ *robins*
hawk	→ *hawks*	*shark*	→ *sharks*
hen	→ *hens*	*sparrow*	→ *sparrows*
lark	→ *larks*	*starling*	→ *starlings*
loon	→ *loons*	*swallow*	→ *swallows*
mole	→ *moles*	*vulture*	→ *vultures*

20.2 The following have both plurals of which the zero plural is likely to be preferred by those who hunt or fish:

albatross → {*albatross*, *albatrosses*}
antelope → {*antelope*, *antelopes*}
bear → {*bear*, *bears*}
beaver → {*beaver*, *beavers*}
buck → {*buck*, *bucks*}
buffalo → {*buffalo*, *buffalos*}
doe → {*doe*, *does*}
duck → {*duck*, *ducks*}
eel → {*eel*, *eels*}
flounder → {*flounder*, *flounders*}
fox → {*fox*, *foxes*}
hare → {*hare*, *hares*}
herring → {*herring*, *herrings*}
lobster → {*lobster*, *lobsters*}
mink → {*mink*, *minks*}
minnow → {*minnow*, *minnows*}
partridge → {*partridge*, *partridges*}
quail → {*quail*, *quails*}
rabbit → {*rabbit*, *rabbits*}
raccoon → {*raccoon*, *raccoons*}
sardine → {*sardine*, *sardines*}
seal → {*seal*, *seals*}
shrimp → {*shrimp*, *shrimps*}
skunk → {*skunk*, *skunks*}
smelt → {*smelt*, *smelts*}
squid → {*squid*, *squids*}
squirrel → {*squirrel*, *squirrels*}
stag → {*stag*, *stags*}
stork → {*stork*, *storks*}
swan → {*swan*, *swans*}
tiger → {*tiger*, *tigers*}
tortoise → {*tortoise*, *tortoises*}
tuna → {*tuna*, *tunas*}
turtle → {*turtle*, *turtles*}

20.3 The following have both plurals of which the zero plural is the commoner but the plural with a suffix is used to signify diversity in kind or species (*trouts* of the Rocky mountains; *fishes* of the Atlantic):

bass → {*bass*, *basses*}
bream → {*bream*, *breams*}
carp → {*carp*, *carps*}
cod → {*cod*, *cods*}
elk → {*elk*, *elks*}
fish → {*fish*, *fishes*}
haddock → {*haddock*, *haddocks*}
halibut → {*halibut*, *halibuts*}
mackerel → {*mackerel*, *mackerels*}
perch → {*perch*, *perches*}
pike → {*pike*, *pikes*}
pollack → {*pollack*, *pollacks*}
pout → {*pout*, *pouts*}
roe → {*roe*, *roes*}
springbok → {*springbok*, *springboks*}
trout → {*trout*, *trouts*}
waterbuck → {*waterbuck*, *waterbucks*}

20.4 The following customarily prefer the zero plural:

bison → *bison*
cattle → *cattle*
chamois → *chamois*
dace → *dace*
deer → *deer*
grouse → *grouse*
moose → *moose*
muskellunge → *muskellunge*
pickerel → *pickerel*
shad → *shad*
sheep → *sheep*
swine → *swine*

21. numbers. A small number of general terms for numbers or quantities have both a plural form with suffix and a zero plural used in some constructions:

brace	→ {*brace*, *braces*}	*million*	→ {*million*, *millions*}
dozen	→ {*dozen*, *dozens*}	*score*	→ {*score*, *scores*}
hundred	→ {*hundred*, *hundreds*}	*thousand*	→ {*thousand*, *thousands*}

22. peoples. Many names of tribal origin have a zero plural and also an anglicized plural with suffix:

Abnaki	→ {*Abnaki*, *Abnakis*}	*Congo*	→ {*Congo*, *Congos*}
Bantu	→ {*Bantu*, *Bantus*}	*Eskimo*	→ {*Eskimo*, *Eskimos*}
Carib	→ {*Carib*, *Caribs*}	*Mohawk*	→ {*Mohawk*, *Mohawks*}

23. -ese. Most names derived from a place name and ending in *-ese* have only a zero plural:

Burmese → *Burmese*
Cantonese → *Cantonese*
Ceylonese → *Ceylonese*
Chinese → *Chinese*
Genovese → *Genovese*
Japanese → *Japanese*
Maltese → *Maltese*
Portuguese → *Portuguese*
Sudanese → *Sudanese*
Tyrolese → *Tyrolese*
Viennese → *Viennese*

CAPITALIZATION

1. The essential distinction in the use of capitals and lowercase letters beginning words lies in the particularizing or individualizing significance of capitals as against the generic or generalizing significance of lowercase. A capital is used with proper nouns, that is, nouns that distinguish some individual person, place, or thing from others of the same class, and with proper adjectives, that is, adjectives that take their descriptive meaning from what is characteristic of the person, place, or thing named by the noun. Most proper nouns and proper adjectives used not in the primary signification but in a derived, secondary, or special sense (as *cashmere*, the fabric; *quixotism*, *herculean*) are written usually without capitalization.

2. A capital letter in normal practice in continuous textual matter:

2.1 begins the first word of a sentence or an expression standing for a sentence ⟨You urge in vain.⟩ ⟨Recant my views?⟩ ⟨Never!⟩

2.2 usually begins a direct formal quotation ⟨God said, Let there be light —Gen 1:3⟩

2.3 usually begins a direct question within a sentence even though not quoted ⟨The eighteenth century asked of any action, Is it decorous?⟩

2.4 often and traditionally begins a line of verse:

Our fears in Banquo
Stick deep; and in his royalty of nature
Reigns that which would be fear'd —Shak.

2.5 usually begins proper nouns, words used as proper nouns, and their derivatives used in the primary sense ⟨George→Georgian⟩ ⟨Spain→Spanish⟩ ⟨Americanism⟩ ⟨New-Yorky⟩ ⟨Roman customs⟩ but verbs are less often capitalized than adjectives or nouns ⟨anglicize⟩

2.6 represents the first person pronoun ⟨he and I disagree⟩

2.7 usually begins the names of peoples, races, tribes, and languages ⟨Phoenician⟩ ⟨Japanese⟩ ⟨Iroquois⟩ ⟨Indo-European⟩ ⟨Latin⟩

2.8 begins titles of honor, academic and religious titles, and professional and business titles used before proper nouns and epithets used in place of proper nouns ⟨Queen Elizabeth I⟩ ⟨His Eminence the Cardinal Archbishop of New York⟩ ⟨Iron Chancellor⟩ ⟨Citizen King⟩ ⟨Old Hickory⟩ ⟨the Hoosier Poet⟩ ⟨All-America team⟩ ⟨Associate Professor John Doe⟩ ⟨Chief Engineer John Doe⟩ ⟨Treasurer John Doe⟩ but not usually when used after ⟨Henry VIII, king of England⟩ ⟨King George V, emperor of India⟩

2.9 begins official and government titles and titles of nobility (as *president, governor, senator, speaker of the House, secretary for defense, postmaster general, prime minister*) when preceding a proper name or used in direct address; as ⟨U.S. Minister John Doe⟩ ⟨Secretary John Doe⟩ ⟨His Honor the Mayor⟩ ⟨Mr. President⟩

⟨Your Honor⟩ but ⟨John Adams, president of the U.S.⟩

2.10 begins official names of national or international governmental bodies or documents and sometimes short forms of these used specifically or with a capitalized name but not usually any short forms or modified forms of them in general reference ⟨The Constitution of the United States⟩ ⟨the Eightieth Congress⟩ ⟨the Federal Reserve system⟩ ⟨Federal Reserve banks⟩ ⟨the Federal Communications Commission⟩ ⟨Charter of the United Nations (*or* the Charter)⟩ ⟨the Security Council (*or* the Council)⟩ ⟨the International Bank⟩ but ⟨according to the constitution⟩ ⟨administration policies⟩ ⟨federal agency⟩

2.11 usually begins nouns and often also adjectives that refer to the Deity and pronouns and pronominal adjectives referring to the Deity when not closely preceding or following their antecedent naming Deity ⟨God⟩ ⟨the Supreme Being⟩ ⟨the Almighty⟩ ⟨Allah⟩ ⟨Great Manito⟩ ⟨Providence⟩ ⟨Lord⟩ ⟨the Trinity⟩ ⟨Holy Ghost⟩ ⟨trust Him who doeth all things well; take time to think about God and his beneficence⟩ ⟨The Almighty has his own purposes —Abraham Lincoln⟩ ⟨so lonely 'twas, that God himself scarce seemed there to be —S.T.Coleridge⟩ ⟨Lamb of God, who takest away the sins of the world, only in thy grace shall my soul be healed —Katherine Anne Porter⟩

2.11.1 Some writers and a few hymnals capitalize a pronoun or pronominal adjective referring to Deity, even when close to the antecedent naming Deity and thus not requiring a capital for clarity of reference ⟨a personal God, creator and governor of all, Who will bring His children into fellowship with Himself⟩ ⟨Jesus and His disciples⟩ ⟨"My Jesu, as Thou wilt"⟩ ⟨teach me, my God and King, in all things Thee to see —George Herbert⟩ ⟨God's in His heaven — all's right with the world —Robert Browning⟩ ⟨all Thy works, O Lord, shall bless Thee —*Oxford Amer. Hymnal*⟩

2.12 usually begins names for the Bible or parts, versions, or editions of it and names of other sacred books and often derivative adjectives when the adjective refers explicitly to the Bible or Scriptures (otherwise not capitalized) ⟨Bible⟩ ⟨Vedas⟩ ⟨the Scriptures⟩ ⟨Old Testament⟩ ⟨Pentateuch⟩ ⟨Apocrypha⟩ ⟨Gospel of Mark⟩ ⟨Apocalypse⟩

2.13 begins names of creeds and confessions, religious denominations, monastic orders, and *Church* when used to designate a specific body or edifice ⟨Apostles' Creed⟩ ⟨the Thirty-nine Articles of the Church of England⟩ ⟨Hunt Memorial Church⟩

2.14 usually begins holidays and holy days generally, the months of the year, and the days of the week ⟨Fourth of July⟩ ⟨Good Friday⟩ ⟨Holy Week⟩ ⟨Labor Day⟩ ⟨January⟩ ⟨next Tuesday⟩

2.15 begins names of congresses, councils, and expositions, of organizations and institutions, of governmental departments, and of political parties (but not the word *party*) ⟨the Yalta Conference⟩ ⟨the Security Council of the United Nations⟩ ⟨Louisiana Purchase Exposition⟩ ⟨the Progressive party⟩ ⟨the Smithsonian Institution⟩ ⟨Bureau of Engraving and Printing⟩ ⟨Congress of Industrial Organizations⟩

2.16 begins names of specific courts of law ⟨Circuit Court of the United States for the 2d Circuit (*but* the circuit court)⟩ ⟨the Michigan Court of Appeals (*but* the state court of appeals)⟩

2.17 begins names of treaties, laws, acts, important events, historical epochs, literary periods, wars ⟨Versailles Treaty⟩ ⟨the Crusades⟩ ⟨Middle Ages⟩ ⟨the Enlightenment⟩ ⟨the Civil War⟩ ⟨War of 1812⟩

2.18 usually begins names of geological eras, periods, epochs, strata, and names of prehistoric divisions ⟨Carboniferous⟩ ⟨Upper Jurassic⟩ ⟨Age of Reptiles⟩ ⟨Neolithic age⟩

2.19 begins names of genera but not of species in binomial scientific names in zoology and botany ⟨a marine worm (*Nereis diversicolor*)⟩ ⟨*Spiraea latifolia*⟩

2.20 begins New Latin names of classes, families, and all other groups above genera in zoology and botany but not derivative adjectives or nouns ⟨Gastropoda *but* gastropod⟩ ⟨Ranunculaceae *but* ranunculaceous⟩

2.21 usually begins a breed name ⟨Belgian hare⟩ ⟨Airedale terrier⟩ ⟨Guernsey bull⟩

2.22 begins names of planets, constellations, asteroids, stars, and groups of stars but not sun, earth, and moon unless listed with other astronomical names ⟨Mercury⟩ ⟨the planet Venus⟩ ⟨Pleiades⟩ ⟨Big Dipper⟩

2.23 usually begins generic geographical terms that form an integral part of a specific proper name (as *bay, borough, colony, continent, county, district, hemisphere, island, lake, mountain, pass,* and likewise *avenue, boulevard, bridge, park, road, square, street*) ⟨Hudson Bay⟩ ⟨Grand Canyon⟩ ⟨Niagara Falls⟩ ⟨Long Island⟩ ⟨Crater Lake⟩ ⟨Blue Ridge⟩ ⟨Park Drive⟩ but ⟨the Atlantic coast of Labrador⟩ ⟨Pacific islands⟩ ⟨Swiss mountains⟩ ⟨the Ohio river valley⟩ ⟨Indian ocean⟩ ⟨Florida keys⟩ ⟨Sahara desert⟩ ⟨born in Chekiang province⟩ ⟨on the Ohio river⟩ ⟨Oak avenue⟩ ⟨the Leeward and Windward islands⟩ ⟨at the confluence of the Missouri and Platte rivers⟩

2.24 usually begins generic political terms that form an integral part of a specific proper name, denoting a political division (as *colony, department, dominion, empire, kingdom, republic, state, territory*) ⟨the Holy Roman Empire⟩ ⟨the Province of Quebec⟩ ⟨the State of Ohio⟩ ⟨the Third Republic⟩

2.25 usually begins names of definite geographical divisions ⟨the Orient⟩ ⟨the Old World⟩ ⟨the Middle East⟩ ⟨the Middle West⟩

2.26 usually begins points of the compass used to designate geographical portions of a country or divisions of the world and also nouns or adjectives derived therefrom ⟨the South⟩ ⟨the Northwest⟩ ⟨a Northerner⟩ but not when used to denote direction only ⟨due east⟩ ⟨go west⟩

2.27 usually begins abstract ideas or inanimate objects personified and names of seasons only when personified or sometimes when referred to specifically or with special connotations ⟨do the bidding of Nature⟩ ⟨the Winter at Valley Forge⟩ ⟨the Plague Year of 1665⟩ ⟨where Spring her verdant mantle cast⟩

2.28 usually begins all words in titles of books, periodicals, essays, poems except unemphatic prepositions, conjunctions and articles ⟨Shakespeare's *Taming of the Shrew*⟩ ⟨the *Journal of the American Medical Association*⟩ ⟨"Phosphorus: Bearer of Light and Life," *Scientific American* 178:101 *ff.*⟩ and except in cataloging and often in bibliographies when only the first word and proper names are capitalized.

2.29 usually begins the article *the* when part of a proper name or title or when incorporated as part of the legal name but usually not in referring to newspapers and magazines in running text ⟨The Honorable John Doe⟩ but ⟨the *Chicago Daily News*⟩ ⟨the *Saturday Evening Post*⟩

2.30 usually begins particles in American names but in foreign names only when not preceded by a forename, a professional title, or title of nobility or of courtesy ⟨Reginald De Koven⟩ ⟨Della Crusca⟩ ⟨Von Moltke (Count von Moltke)⟩

2.31 usually begins German common nouns that have not been anglicized, when used in English text ⟨Frau⟩ ⟨Junker⟩ ⟨Luftwaffe⟩ but anglicized German nouns may be written with a small initial letter ⟨blitzkrieg⟩ ⟨gestalt⟩ ⟨leitmotiv⟩ ⟨pumpernickel⟩ ⟨rathskeller⟩ ⟨sauerkraut⟩ ⟨turnverein⟩

2.32 usually represents academic degrees ⟨A. B.⟩ ⟨LL.D.⟩ ⟨Ph.D.⟩

2.33 begins names of registered trademarks.

ITALICIZATION

1. Foreign words and phrases that are not fully naturalized are usually italicized in English context. This is done in manuscript or typescript by single underlining. The choice of roman or italic text properly belongs to the user on the basis of subject matter and expected readers. A dictionary cannot prescribe or even record in a matter so subjective. These examples simply show words and phrases that are often italicized in English context ⟨*ancien régime*⟩ ⟨*anschluss*⟩ ⟨*cognoscente*⟩ ⟨*de trop*⟩ ⟨*dolce far niente*⟩ ⟨*jeu d'esprit*⟩ ⟨*mañana*⟩ ⟨*noblesse oblige*⟩ ⟨*rapprochement*⟩ ⟨*zeitgeist*⟩

2. Titles of books (not parts of books), plays, works of art, magazines, newspapers are usually italicized but not the Bible or its books ⟨Stevenson's *Treasure Island*⟩ ⟨Verdi's *Il Trovatore*⟩ ⟨Michelangelo's *David*⟩ ⟨the *Christian Science Monitor*⟩ ⟨*Saturday Evening Post*⟩

3. Names of ships and aircraft are usually italicized ⟨Lindbergh's *Spirit of St. Louis*⟩ ⟨the carrier *Lexington*⟩

4. Names of long-range missiles and man-made satellites are often italicized.

5. A word spoken of as a word, a phrase as a phrase, a letter as a letter (except that a letter indicating shape is printed in type most nearly depicting the shape; thus, V-shaped; I beam) are usually italicized.

6. New Latin scientific names of genera, species, subspecies, and varieties (but not groups of higher rank, as phyla, classes, orders) in botanical and zoological names are italicized ⟨a thick-shelled quahog (*Mercenaria mercenaria*)⟩

THE WRITING OF COMPOUNDS

1. DEFINITION

1.1 A *compound*, as the term is used here, is a word or word group of two or more elements at least one of which is an independent word of the same language. The elements in an English compound are variously written solid, open, or hyphened when they are all English words that can be written independently. When one of the elements in an English compound is not an independent English word, the elements are usually solid (*watery, anticlerical, predate*) or hyphened (*de-emphasize*).

1.2 To show in a dictionary all of the stylings that are found for English compounds would necessitate excluding other information much more likely to be sought by the dictionary user. This dictionary therefore limits itself almost without exception to a single styling for a compound. When a compound occurs frequently and one styling predominates, this styling is used. When a compound is rare or when the examples indicate that two or three stylings are approximately equal in frequency, the choice is based on the analogy of parallel compounds or is made arbitrarily.

2. COMPOUNDS CONTAINING AN ELEMENT THAT IS NOT AN INDEPENDENT WORD

2.1 The dependent element in most compounds formed within English is a prefix or a suffix. It is added to several or many English words and exerts the same modification of sense on all of them.

2.1.1 Prefixes in borrowed compounds. In prefix-containing foreign-language compounds borrowed into English, if the prefix ends and the base word begins with the same vowel letter, a hyphen is often used between the two vowels, or a diaeresis is sometimes placed over the second vowel (*co-operate/coöperate*) but usually the form is solid (*cooperate*). If two vowels that are not identical come together at the point of juncture, usually neither hyphen nor diaeresis is used (*coalesce, coerce*). If the junctural letters are two consonants, or a vowel and a consonant, or a consonant and vowel, neither hyphen nor diaeresis is used (*collect, diagram, anarchy*).

2.1.2 Prefixes in compounds formed within English. In prefix-containing compounds formed in English a prefix and a base word are seldom open-styled. Some combinations are usually close-styled (*in-* and *un-*, as in *inexpressible, untenable*), some are usually hyphened (*ex-* in *ex-president*), some are frequently styled either way (*anti-, co-, extra-, non-, pre-, semi-*). With prefixes of this last class the hyphened styling is usual when the prefix ends with a vowel letter and the base word begins with the same letter (*anti- + intellectualism, infra- + angelic, semi- + independent*); the hyphened styling is less frequent when the junctural letters are two vowels that are not identical (*de- + adjectival, fore- + oath*); but solid styling is usual when the junctural letters are two consonants, or a vowel and a consonant (*non- + metallic, non- + alcoholic, extra- + legal*).

2.1.3 When the base word begins with a capital, a hyphen is usual (*un- + American*).

2.1.4 Some elements commonly regarded as prefixes function as adjectives when they stand open before a noun (*a pseudo liberal; quasi independence*). But a styling like *a semi annual sale* is seldom seen outside newspaper advertisements.

2.1.5 When a prefix governs two or more words, it is almost invariably followed by a hyphen, and the styling of the group of words to which the hyphen applies varies: sometimes the members of the group are left spaced, sometimes they are hyphened (*an ex-vice president/an ex-vice-president, pre-World War prices/pre-World-War prices, the ex-Republican majority leader/the ex-Republican-majority-leader*). Although spaced styling in such cases is often ambiguous, mere substitution of hyphens for spaces is not always a solution.

2.1.6 Sometimes the same succession of letters forms two words that contain the same prefix but that are different in sense, pronunciation, and styling, one word being solid and the other hyphened. In such cases the solid compound was formed in and borrowed from another language, the hyphened compound was formed in English; the second element may or may not be ultimately the same word etymologically in both cases (*recover* "to get back", *re-cover* "to cover again"; *recreation* "play", *re-creation* "a creating again").

2.2 Suffix-containing compounds. Suffixes are close-styled (*shoeless, meanness, freer*), except that a succession of three identical consonants is hyphened (*hull-less*) if one is not dropped (*hulless*).

2.2.1 Some independent English words (*like, worthy*) which are sometimes regarded as suffixes when they are joined to the word they govern may be joined by a hyphen: *Christlike/Christ-like, praiseworthy/praise-worthy*.

2.2.2 When a suffix is added to two or more words that are written separate before suffixation, the styling of these words varies (*baby farming/baby-farming, bitter-ender/bitter ender, otherworldly/other-worldly*). The composition of some of these compounds, especially those that end in *-er*, may be ambiguous. Thus *lime-juicer* "a British ship" is *lime juice + -er;* whereas *lime juicer* "a device for squeezing or juicing limes" is *lime + juicer*. Both words might appear in any of three stylings — hyphened, open, or solid.

2.3.1 Other real or apparent compounds of this category. In other compounds in which one element is also an independent English word and the other is not or seems not to be, some are usually solid (*raspberry, bonfire, bookmobile, cheeseburger*), others are usually spaced (*bez antler, tonka bean, shea tree*).

2.3.2 In some words that appear to be similar compounds the apparent independent English word is an assimilation to an English word (*crayfish, gillyflower, safflower, gridiron, andiron*). The solid styling is usual for such apparent compounds.

3. NOUN COMPOUNDS WHOSE COMPONENTS ARE WHOLE ENGLISH WORDS

3.1 Noun + noun, as in *fruit + cake, cherry + pie, ox + bow, shoulder + blade, car + load, calamity + howler, emancipation + proclamation.*

3.1.1 In most noun-plus-noun compounds the first noun is uninflected and singular. Some of these compounds are freely styled in all three ways (*prize fighter / prizefighter / prize-fighter*). Some are rarely seen, at least in American English, other than solid (*newspaper, typewriter, pineapple*). Some are usually open (*gunnery officer, secretary bird*). Since there is a long precedent for the purely uniting function of the hyphen, it is not out of place in almost any noun-plus-noun compound where both elements are lowercase (*ox-bow, power-transmission, security-regulations*), but it seems to be used less often today than it formerly was. The compounds in which it is most likely to be used are those that would be written solid except that they contain at the point of juncture letters in a sequence unusual within an English word so that apprehension of this point may be retarded. Thus the hyphen is often not so much a uniter of words as it is a separator of letters.

3.1.2 Typically, two-noun noun compounds that are often or usually solid are fairly short, are of frequent occurrence, are concrete rather than abstract, and have primary stress on the first element and secondary stress on the second element (*notebook, paperweight, grasshopper, battlewagon, newspaperman, holidaymaker*). Five-syllable solid compounds, such as the last, are comparatively rare. Compounds that sometimes have even stress usually solidify only if short and very common (*corn + meal, air + mail, life + blood, arm + chair, eye + tooth, pot + luck, bed + rock, jaw + bone, barb + wire, car + load, bow + knot, death + bed, bell + wether*).

3.1.3 Falling accentuation (primary stress on first element and secondary stress on second element) is almost a prerequisite to solidification. Observation of how compounds in the spoken language are stressed provides information of possibly more value than an examination of how compounds in the written language are styled. A large proportion of the compounds that are written solid may with equal acceptability be open or hyphened (*matchbox/match box/match-box*); but in the spoken language falling stress may be acceptable whereas even stress may not be, except when one is making a contrast between one compound and another with the same first element (*matchbox, matchstick*); in such contrasts supersession of the "normal" stress is regular. But the accentuation of compounds, like the accentuation of noncompound phrases, is a matter of usage, which does not fall into neat patterns. In some cases the meaning of a compound is a reliable guide to its accentuation, in other cases not. The native speaker knows that if *wood + box* means "a box made of wood" the stress is \ˈ=ˈ=\ and that if it means "a box in which wood is placed" the stress is \ˈ=ˌ=\. On the other hand he may be unable to be sure of the stress of another compound even after reading a definition of it. Some speakers stress a compound one way, and other speakers another way. To make rules that would cover the stress of all compounds seems impossible. Certain conditions seem to make for one kind of stress or the other; these conditions leave the stress on many compounds unexplained.

3.1.4 In what follows

A = *1st half of a two-part compound*
B = *2d half of a two-part compound*
C = *3d part of a three-part compound*

The relative specificity of B seems to account for many variations in stress between compounds whose elements stand in the same logical relationship to each other: the more specific, the less general and inclusive B is, the more likely the compound is to have even stress; thus *ˈtown + ˈhall* but (in the same sense) *ˈtown + ˌhouse: hall* is a more specific term than *house*, whose wide applicability is shown by the combinations or phrases *doll + house, chicken + house, discount + house, mail + order + house*, the *houses* of Congress or Parliament, the *house* of Rothschild. Other examples: *ˈfinger + ˈnail* (sometimes) but *ˈfinger + ˌtip, ˈalligator + ˈpear* but *ˈalligator + ˌweed, ˈtimothy + ˌgrass* but *ˈtimothy + ˈhay, ˈchurch + ˌservice* but *ˈchurch + ˈliturgy, ˈcorner + ˈstore* but *ˈcorner + ˌstone, ˈkey + ˈsignature* but *ˈkey + ˌnote, ˈdesk ˈdrawer* but *ˈdesk ˌleg*.

3.1.5 Compounds that name something which requires the synchronous association or combination of what is named by A and what is named by B are usually even-stressed: *ˈleather + ˈshoe* but *ˈshoe + ˌleather* (*shoe + leather* can exist even though it may never be made into a shoe, or has ceased to exist in the form of a shoe), *ˈbottle + ˈbeer* but *ˈbeer + ˌbottle, ˈpaper + ˈbook* but *ˈbook + ˌpaper, ˈbeef + ˈsoup* and *ˈbeef + ˈstew* but *ˈbeef + ˌbroth* (the last is merely a product of beef flesh, which is not present in the broth as it is in the soup and stew). Among the most numerous members of this category are compounds in which A names a thing of a sort that is the sole or an essential ingredient of B: *ˈcherry + ˈpie* (cherries or something of the sort — berries, apples, apricots, peaches — are a necessary part of a pie), *ˈgold + ˈcup, ˈglass + ˈpendant, ˈkid + ˈgloves, ˈrye + ˈbread*. When A is a thing of a sort that is secondary or incidental to B, falling stress is more likely: *ˈfruit + ˌcake, ˈraisin + ˌbread* (cake and bread can be quite plain, without anything of the order of raisins or other fruit). Compounds of the first category mentioned in this paragraph may have falling stress if B is lacking in specificity: *ˈglass + ˌware, ˈpaper + ˌgoods*.

3.1.6 When A and B stand in an appositive relationship to each other, the stress is usually even: *ˈbaby + ˈboy, ˈwoman + ˈdriver. Boy + friend*, however, has falling stress. It differs from the first two compounds in not being literal when it does not mean any friend who is a boy.

3.1.7 Metonymic compounds (compounds that name an entire thing by naming some feature of the thing, the first element sometimes being metaphorical) invariably have falling stress. They rarely have open styling. If they are not long and if there is no troublesome series of letters at the juncture, they are commonly solid: *sheath + bill, frog + mouth, paper + back, egg + head, leather + neck, butter + fingers;* otherwise they are usually hyphened: *violet + ear*.

3.1.8 There is a numerous class of words in which the second element is a verb plus *-er* or *-ing* and in the definition of which the first element is the object of the verb or the object of a preposition following the verb: *orange + sucker, potato + digger, baby + sitter*. These nearly always have falling accent, and appear quite freely in all three possible stylings. The hyphen is more often used in this class than it is in most other classes.

3.1.9 The relationship of the three elements in the preceding class of compounds can be represented thus: (A) (B, suffix). There is another class of compounds in which two elements are followed by a suffix (one of which may be *-er*, as in the preceding class) but in which the relationship of the three elements is different. Such compounds are *broad jumper* and *Bay Stater* in which the relationship is (A,B) (suffix), not (A) (B, suffix). Another such compound is *gold + medal + -ist*. Such compounds follow the accentuation of the two-part compound to which the suffix is added: *ˈbroad + ˌjump (er), ˈBay + ˌState (r), ˈgold + ˈmedal (ist)*. Such compounds exhibit all three stylings. In noun compounds of the class (A,B) (suffix), both of the first two elements need not be nouns: *bitter + end + -er, America + first + -er*.

3.2 Noun+(')s+noun, as in *fool(')s+cap, cock(')s + comb, woman(')s + club, women(')s + club*, or **noun+s(')+noun,** as in *boys(')+club, ladies(')+room.*

3.2.1 When these have a literal meaning, they are often written open, and with an apostrophe before the *s* if the first element is in the singular (*red as a cock's comb, a man's house is his castle*) or in the plural but not ending in *-s* (*children's clothes*). A few literal compounds of this class, however, are solid and without apostrophe, especially by assimilation to a form that is usual or frequent for an extended sense; thus *cockscomb* occurs for both the comb of a cock and a garden plant; *menswear* and *womenswear* occur usually. If the elements are written solid the apostrophe is not used, whether the first element is singular or plural (*foolscap*/never *fool'scap, menswear*/probably never *men'swear*). If the first element is singular and the elements are spaced, the apostrophe is not omitted: *a fool's cap, a man's thoughts, a woman's thoughts.*

3.2.2 When the compound is literal in meaning and open, and the first element is a plural ending in *-s* or is the possessive of a collective singular, the apostrophe is often omitted in titles in which the first element means "for the use of" or "operated by": *farmers(') cooperative, a students(') dictionary, People(')s Industrial Bank, Ladies(') Aid Society*. When the first element is the possessive of a plural that does not end in *-s*, omission of the apostrophe seems to be less frequent: *women's club/womens club.*

3.2.3 The first element may in some cases be either singular or plural: *woman's club/women's club/womens club.*

3.2.4 Compounds in which the first element has a possessive *s* are very common in an extended or figurative sense, especially in plant names. Use of the apostrophe seems to be usual for such compounds and the hyphen is sometimes used. There is often variation between a singular and a plural first element: *baby's breath/babies' breath, lady's slipper/ladies' slipper, lady's-eardrop/ladies'-eardrop.* The solid form without apostrophe also occurs: *cockscomb, foolscap, swansdown.*

3.3 Adjective + noun, as in *blue + bird, black + tern, red + head, blue + blood.*

3.3.1 When an adjective and an immediately following noun are used with full literalness of meaning and nonattributively, the two are written with a space between and are spoken with level stress: *I saw a* ˈ*blue* ˈ*bird* (a bird that was blue; variety unknown), *a doll with a* ˈ*red* ˈ*head*. But when there is some abridgment of full literalness, the adjective and the noun may be written solid or hyphened and be spoken with falling stress: *I saw one jay and two* ˈ*blue*ˌ*birds* (two ˈ*blue* ˈ*birds* of the variety known to scientists as *Sialis sialis;* the jay is also a ˈ*blue* ˈ*bird*); *redheads are proverbially hot-tempered.* Here again, however, as in the case of noun + noun compounds, specificity is important: the more specific the second element of the compound, the more likely the compound is to be written spaced and pronounced with even stress. Thus a typical dictionary definition of *blue + bird* begins "any of several birds more or less blue above", and a typical definition of *black + tern* begins "any of several small terns with black plumage"; but the first is usually ˈ*blue*ˌ*bird*, the second is usually ˈ*black* ˈ*tern.*

3.3.2 Metonyms with an adjective as the first element, like those with a noun as the first element, have falling stress and are usually solid or hyphened: ˈ*red +* ˌ*head*, ˈ*hot +* ˌ*spur*, ˈ*free +* ˌ*stone*, ˈ*blue +* ˌ*stocking*, ˈ*yellow +* ˌ*jacket.*

3.3.3 Adjective + noun pairs in which the application of the adjective to the noun is not a literal one commonly have falling stress and may be hyphened or solid; but the solid styling is less frequent than for specifying compounds like *black + bird: sick + call, cold + chisel, easy + chair.* Some of these can also be analyzed as noun + noun compounds (a call for the sick).

3.3.4 A few literal even-stressed adjective + noun compounds are styled in any of the three possible ways: *good + will, long + suffering, loving + kindness.*

3.4 Verb + noun, as in (a) *kill + joy, pick + pocket, cure + all, turn + coat, skin + flint, sling + shot, tattle + tale,* and (b) as in *bake + shop, turn + table, drip + coffee, try + square.*

3.4.1 In the (a) class the second element is the direct object of the verb. Words of this class have falling stress and are not open-styled. They are usually solid if short and if there are no troublesome letter combinations, like *e + a* in *cure + all,* which makes a hyphen usual.

3.4.2 In the compounds in class (b) the second element is not the direct object of the first element. It is impossible to be sure whether the first element of many compounds of this class is to be regarded as a verb or a noun. No practical difficulty arises from this because the styling and stress of these compounds parallels that of noun + noun compounds: all three stylings occur, and the stress is falling in some cases, level in others.

3.5 Particle + noun, as in *down + pour, down + draft, down + card, out + come, out + house, on + rush, on + going, on + position.*

3.5.1 A particle, as used here, is one of a small class of words that have sometimes adverbial, sometimes adjectival, sometimes prepositional force. When a verbal idea is present in the noun that is the second element, as it commonly is when the second element is identical in spelling with a corresponding verb, or when the second element ends in *-ing*, such compounds are rarely open, and the solid styling is more frequent than the hyphened: *down + pour, on + going.* When the second element is a concrete noun without any verbal idea and the first element has adjective force, all three stylings may occur: *down + card, down + pipe, off + horse, out + garrison, through + street, up + train.*

3.6 Noun + adjective, as in *battle + royal, court + martial, cousin + german, letters + patent, postmaster + general, sum + total.* These occur both hyphened and spaced.

3.7 Verb or verb derivative + adverb, as in *write + up, lean + to, pin + up, cut + up, shoo + in, follow + through, grown + up, get + together, shut + in, damping + off, goings + on, passer + by, hanger + on.*

3.7.1 Both the solid and the hyphened stylings are common for such of these nouns as do not have a first element ending in the suffix *-ing* or *-er*. The hyphen prevails when both junctural letters are vowels, as in *write + up, shoo + in.* For compounds whose first element ends in the suffix *-ing*, both the hyphened and the open styling are common. For compounds whose first element ends in the suffix *-er*, the hyphened or solid styling is usual, the open styling occasional.

4. VERB COMPOUNDS WHOSE COMPONENTS ARE WHOLE ENGLISH WORDS

4.1 A verb and an adverb that accompanies and follows it usually have a space between them: *to throw out a ball, to throw a ball out, to talk loudly.* An adverb preceding a verb usually has a space following: *he loudly demanded reform, I well remember the day, he soon returned;* but the words considered as particles (in 3.5.) are usually not followed by a space but are close-styled, less often hyphened: *to uproot*/less often *up-root an evil.*

4.2 When a solid or hyphened noun compound is used as a verb by functional change, the styling of the noun compound is generally retained. Thus one who uses the solid or hyphened styling for the nouns *snow + shoe, sand + bag, court + martial* will probably use the same styling in *to snow + shoe across a field, to sand + bag a dike, to court + martial a soldier.*

4.3 For compound verbs that do not belong to any of the categories enumerated in the preceding paragraphs all three stylings are found. The hyphened styling is the most frequent; the open styling seems to be less common in formal than in informal English. Examples: *to double + space a manuscript, to heat + treat a metal, to cold + roll steel, to rotten + egg a speaker.*

4.4 A verb compound that has a verb as its second element and that has the suffix *-ing* at the end of the verb may be hyphened when an object follows but either hyphened or spaced when no object follows. Thus the same writer may write *heat-treating these metals is not recommended* but *for these metals, heat treating is not recommended.* In the latter, *heat + treatment,* whose usual styling is probably open, could be substituted.

5. ADVERB COMPOUNDS

5.1 Compound adverbs of the type illustrated by *to run hot + foot to the window, to go bare + foot, recommended sight + unseen, to win hands + down, to dive in head + first* are infrequently found, and at least two stylings can be found for all of these and for some, three. Combinations of adjective + noun are likely to be solid (*hotfoot*), but if the first element is a plural noun or the second a past participle, the form is likely to be open (*arms akimbo, feet first, sight unseen*).

5.2 Compound adverbs like *light + hearted + -ly* usually follow the styling of the corresponding compound adjective. See 6.5.

5.3 Some compounds with adverbial force consist of a preposition followed by a noun, with loss of the commonly preceding article: *down + town, up + stream, below + stairs, between + decks, over + board.* Although each of the three stylings occurs, the solid is probably usual for most.

6. ADJECTIVE COMPOUNDS

6.1 Noun or adjective + adjective or participle, as in *snow + white, home + grown, red + hot, rusty + red, bitter + sweet, acrid + smelling, smoke + filled.* These are usually hyphened, occasionally solid (when the compound is short and common), or less frequently open (more often in predicative than in attributive position).

6.2 Adverb + adjective or participle, as in *well + known, better + known, widely + acclaimed, very + ignorant, twice + told.* The solid styling sometimes occurs for these compounds when the first element is a word freely usable as an adverb (*straight + forward, plain + spoken*). Most adverb + adjective compounds are either hyphened or open. In attributive position an adverb + adjective compound is most likely to be open if the first element is an adverb ending in *-ly* (*an extremely + important matter*); is most likely to be hyphened if the first element is an adverb that is identical in spelling with an adjective: *a slow + moving van.* Here a hyphen between *slow* and *moving* tells the reader that the writer has in mind a van of no particular variety that is moving slowly; a space between *slow* and *moving* would leave the expression open to the interpretation that the van is a variety known as a moving van and that it is slow; if the latter were the writer's intent, he might very well make it clear by inserting a hyphen between *moving* and *van*, even though he might use the open styling in *the moving + van has arrived.* In predicative position, open styling is more frequent than in attributive position; it is the most frequent styling by far when the first element has only adverbial use (*his hair is now + gray, he was once + wealthy*); it is less frequent when the first element is a form that is used as both adverb and adjective (*the van was large and slow + moving, he is plain + spoken*).

6.3 Particle + participle, as in *out + spoken, up + swept, in + curving, out + bound.* These are solid or, less often, hyphened, whether attributive or predicative.

6.4 Noun or adjective + noun, as in *home + town boy, seed + case integument, stove + pipe hat, grandfather + clock collector, short + term loan, small + store owner.* Pairs that are consistently solid or hyphened in nonattributive position are usually so in attributive position: *the seedcase/seed-case is tough, the seedcase/seed-case integument, twenty blackbirds, a blackbird hater.* Sometimes a writer who uses the spaced styling nonattributively uses the solid styling attributively: *cut with a jig saw; a jigsaw puzzle.* Ordinarily, however, noun pairs that are open-styled nonattributively are either hyphened or open attributively; the open styling is more common in informal than formal English. Noun + noun + noun groups are probably less often ambiguous than adjective + noun + noun groups and accordingly are probably less often written with a space between A and B. Thus *feed + store owner* presents little or no ambiguity, whereas *small + store owner* written with a space between *small* and *store* is apprehensible, if the context affords no help, either as "owner of a small store" or "store owner who is small". If the first is the meaning intended, many would insert a hyphen between *small* and *store;* if the second many would insert a hyphen between *store* and *owner.*

6.5 Adjective or noun + noun + -ed, as in *red + head + -ed, club + foot + -ed, hot + temper + -ed, cloud + cap + -ped.* In these the middle element and the suffix are always solid. The first and middle elements are seldom spaced, whether in predicative or attributive position; are usually hyphened; are solid in a few short compounds of frequent occurrence.

6.6 Adjective or participle + particle, as in *to be hard + up, to be done + in, to be fed + up, warmed + over cabbage, a turned + down collar.* These are usually spaced in predicative position, hyphened in attributive position. When a prefix is added, the prefix and the middle element are usually written solid; the middle element and the particle are either spaced or hyphened in predicative position, hyphened in attributive position: *an un + heard + of accomplishment, such appliances were un + dreamed + of in those days.*

6.7 Preposition-initial adjective compounds, as in *down + stream, up + hill, over + seas, out + of + date, on + the + house, down + in + the + mouth.* Two-part compounds with no article between are usually solid, less often hyphened or open, in attributive position; in predicative position both solid and open stylings are common: *an up + hill pull, over + seas possessions, the race will be down + stream.* Compounds having three or more parts are open or hyphened in predicative position, usually hyphened in attributive position: *book is out + of + date, an out + of + date book, looked down + in + the + mouth.*

6.8 When something in the typography makes the interrelationship of a multiple-word adjective obvious, the hyphen is usually omitted:

A Jim Crow law	(capital letters)
an *a priori* argument	(italics)
his "big shot" talk	(quotation marks)

In an expression like *April + fool joke, Indian + club enthusiast,* where the typography of one member of the attributive (*April*) does not parallel that of the other (*fool*), the hyphen is frequently or usually present (*April-fool joke*).

6.9 Compound adjectives not covered by any of the categories enumerated above are usually hyphened: *a pop + up toaster, a middle + of + the + road course, his never + the + twain + shall + meet policy.* The solid styling is found occasionally for some shorter compounds, as *pop + up.* The open styling is more common in informal than formal English: *a middle of the road course.*

MERRIAM-WEBSTER PRONUNCIATION SYMBOLS

For greater detail and for some symbols not shown below see "Guide to Pronunciation"

ə .....banana, collect

ˈə, ˌə humdrum

ə̄ .....as in one pronunciation used by *r*-droppers for bird (alternative \əi\)

ə̇ .....two-value symbol equivalent to the unstressed variants \ə\, \i\, as in habit, duchess (\ˈhabə̇t\ = \ˈhabət, -bit\)

ᵊ .....immediately preceding \l\, \n\, \m\, \ŋ\, as in battle, mitten, and in one pronunciation of cap and bells \-ᵊm-\, lock and key \-ᵊŋ-\; immediately following \l\, \m\, \r\, as in one pronunciation of French table, prisme, titre

əi ....as in one pronunciation used by *r*-droppers for bird (alternative \ə̄\)

ər ....operation; stressed, as in bird as pronounced by speakers who do not drop *r;* stressed and with centered period after the \r\, as in one pronunciation of burry (alternative \ə̄r\) and in one pronunciation of hurry (alternative \ə·r\); stressed and with centered period between \ə\ and \r\, as in one pronunciation of hurry (alternative \ər·\)

a .....mat, map

ā .....day, fade, date, aorta

ä .....bother, cot; most American speakers have the same vowel in father, cart

ȧ .....father as pronounced by speakers who do not rhyme it with bother; farther and cart as pronounced by *r*-droppers

aa ...bad, bag, fan as often pronounced in an area having New York City and Washington, D. C., on its perimeter; in an emphatic syllable, as before a pause, often \aaə\

ai ....as in some pronunciations of bag, bang, pass

au̇ ...now, loud, some pronunciations of talcum

b .....baby, rib

ch ....chin, nature \ˈnāchə(r)\ (actually, this sound is \t\ + \sh\)

d .....elder, undone

d· ....as in the usual American pronunciation of latter, ladder

e .....bet, bed

ˈē, ˌē beat, nosebleed, evenly, sleepy

ē .....as in one pronunciation of evenly, sleepy, envious, igneous (alternative \i\)

ee ....(in transcriptions of foreign words only) indicates a vowel with the quality of *e* in *bet* but long, not the sound of *ee* in *sleep: en arrière* \äⁿnȧryeer\

eu̇ ...as in one pronunciation of elk, helm

f .....fifty, cuff

g .....go, big

h .....hat, ahead

hw ...whale as pronounced by those who do not have the same pronunciation for both *whale* and *wail*

i ......tip, one pronunciation of banish (alternative unstressed \ē\), one pronunciation of habit (alternative \ə\; see ə̇)

ī .....site, side, buy (actually, this sound is \ä\ + \i\, or \ȧ\ + \i\)

iu̇ ....as in one pronunciation of milk, film

j .....job, gem, edge, procedure \prəˈsējə(r)\ (actually, this sound is \d\ + \zh\)

k .....kin, cook, ache

k̲ .....as in one pronunciation of loch (alternative \k\), as in German ich-laut

l ......lily, pool

m ....murmur, dim, nymph

n .....no, own

ⁿ .....indicates that a preceding vowel is pronounced with the nasal passages open, as in French *un bon vin blanc* \œⁿbōⁿvaⁿbläⁿ\

ŋ .....sing \ˈsiŋ\, singer \ˈsiŋə(r)\, finger \ˈfiŋgə(r)\, ink \ˈiŋk\

ō .....bone, snow, beau; one pronunciation of glory

ȯ .....saw, all, saurian; one pronunciation of horrid

œ ....French bœuf, German Hölle

œ̄ ....French feu, German Höhle

ȯi ....coin, destroy, strawy, sawing

ōō ...(in transcriptions of foreign words only) indicates a vowel with the quality of *o* in *bone* but longer, not the sound of *oo* in *food: comte* \kōōⁿt\

p .....pepper, lip

r .....rarity, one pronunciation of tar

s .....source, less

sh ....with nothing between, as in shy, mission, machine, special (actually, this is a single sound, not two); with a stress mark between, two sounds as in death's-head \ˈdeths,hed\

t .....tie, attack; one pronunciation of latter (alternative \d·\)

th ....with nothing between, as in thin, ether (actually, this is a single sound, not two); with a stress mark between, two sounds as in knighthood \ˈnīt,hu̇d\

t̲h̲ ....then, either (actually, this is a single sound, not two)

ü .....rule, fool, youth, union \ˈyünyən\, few \ˈfyü\

u̇ .....pull, wood, curable \ˈkyu̇rəbəl\

ue ....German füllen, hübsch

ue̅ ....French rue, German fühlen

v .....vivid, give

w ....we, away

y .....yard, cue \ˈkyü\, union \ˈyünyən\

ʸ .....(in transcriptions of foreign words only) indicates that during the articulation of the sound represented by the preceding character the tip of the tongue has substantially the position it has for the articulation of the first sound of *yard,* as in French *digne* \dēnʸ\

yü ....youth, union, cue, few

yu̇ ....curable

z .....zone, raise

zh ...with nothing between, as in vision, azure \ˈazhə(r)\ (actually, this is a single sound, not two); with a stress mark between, two sounds as in rosehill \ˈrōz,hil\

For greater detail on most of the following see the beginning of "Guide to Pronunciation" and that part of "Explanatory Notes" dealing with pronunciation (section numbers for the latter are included below)

**** ....slant line used in pairs to mark the beginning and end of a transcription: \ˈpen\

ˈ .....mark preceding a syllable with primary (strongest) stress: \ˈpenmən,ship\

ˌ .....mark preceding a syllable with secondary (next-strongest) stress: \ˈpenmən,ship\

ˈˌ .....combined marks preceding a syllable whose stress varies between primary and secondary: *backbone* \ˈ=ˈˌ=\ (§2.2)

- .....inferior minus sign canceling a stress in the same position in a preceding pronunciation or emphasizing that a following syllable is without stress: *optimism* \ˈäptə,mizəm\, *optimist* \-ˌmə̇st\ (§2.11)

· .....mark of syllable division inserted in a sequence of sounds that can have more than one syllable division: *nitrate* \ˈnī·,trāt\ (§2.1)

= .....symbol for the sounds of a syllable: *backbone* \ˈ=ˈˌ=\ (§§2.7.1, 2.7.2)

(), (..indicate that what is symbolized between or after is present in some utterances but not in others: *factory* \ˈfakt(ə)rē\, *bar* \ˈbär, ˈbȧ(r\ (§§2.5.1, 2.5.2)

" .....ditto mark, indicating that a preceding pronunciation is to be repeated: ¹*poise* \ˈpȯiz\ *v,* ²*poise* \"\ *n* (§§2.8.1, 2.8.2)

+ ....in an incomplete pronunciation signifies that the missing part is to be sought elsewhere in the vocabulary: *geopositive* \ˌjē(,)ō+\ (pronunciation of *-positive* is to be sought at POSITIVE) (§2.9)

+V..means "when a vowel sound follows without pause, as in a suffix or another word"

| .....facilitates the placement of a variant pronunciation: *flightily* \ˈflīd·|ᵊlē, -īt|, |ᵊli, |əl-\ (§2.6)

R ....labels certain pronunciations used by speakers who do not drop *r* (§2.10)

−*R* ...labels certain pronunciations used by speakers who drop *r* (§2.10)

÷ ...indicates that many regard as unacceptable the one pronunciation immediately following: *cupola* \ˈkyüpələ, ÷-pə,lō\, *sacrilegious* \÷ˈˌsakrəˈˌlijəs, -lēj-\ (§2.12)

. . . ...indicates an omission to be supplied from a preceding entry or an entry elsewhere: *dilettantish* \ˈˌ==ˈˌt. . .ntish\ (four variants for the *a* are to be supplied from ¹DILETTANTE)

GUIDE TO PRONUNCIATION

By Edward Artin, Pronunciation Editor

This is a presentation of facts adequate, it is hoped, to explain the way we use our symbols in pronunciation indications in the vocabulary and to enable the consultant to infer certain pronunciations not actually shown from pronunciations that we do show. This is not a treatise on phonetics; many elementary facts of phonetics are not discussed at all (for example, the nature of most articulations). Those who desire such information should consult any of a number of good textbooks on phonetics.

The matter in this "Guide" is arranged under headings that so far as possible are in alphabetical order. Criteria for the alphabetization of some of the items have not been established by usage.

Headings that are not, that do not contain, or that are not formed by addition to, the 26 letters of the English alphabet appear ahead of everything else. Between the beginning of the first of such items and the end of the last no scheme of ordering is attempted.

The character \ə\ and modifications of it appear next.

The character \ŋ\ appears between the *n*, \n\ items and the *o*, \ō\, \ȯ\ items.

Ligatured characters are alphabetized as if they were separate letters (e.g., \œ\ is alphabetized as if it were \oe\).

A character entered as an orthographic letter appears ahead of the same character entered as a symbol of our pronunciation alphabet.

The same symbol may appear in two or more of the following forms: plain or unmodified; with diacritic above or below; reduced in size and set high as a superior character. For a symbol having two or more of these forms the alphabetization is as follows:

(1) single plain symbol, as \a\, \th\
(2) single symbol with horizontal bar above or below, as \ā\, \t͟h\
(3) single symbol with two dots, as \ä\
(4) single symbol with one dot, as \ȧ\
(5) single symbol set as a small superior, thus: \ᵊ\, \ᵊ̄\, \ᵊ̇\, \ᵊ\
(6) multiple-character symbols come at the end of the last single symbol based on the first character of the multiple symbol. Thus \aa\ comes at the end of the series \a\, \ā\, \ä\, \ȧ\, not between \a\ and \ā\. Such multiple symbols are alphabetized without regard to diacritics or to the size of any component character, except that when such disregard results in duplication the order is as stated in (1)–(5) above. Thus \ai\ precedes \äi\ and \o͞o\ precedes \ȯȯ\

**\ ** see the section on phonemicity.

( ) two parentheses mean that whatever is indicated by the symbol or symbols between them is present in the pronunciation of some speakers and absent from the pronunciation of other speakers, or that it is present in some utterances and absent from other utterances of the same speaker, or that its presence or absence is something difficult to be sure of.

nu·mer·ous \ˈn(y)üm(ə)rəs\
floc·cu·lence \ˈfläkyələn(t)s\
chick·a·dee \ˈchikə(ˌ)dē, . . .\

Such pronunciations could alternatively have been shown, at greater cost of space, as \ˈnümərəs, ˈnyü-, -mrəs\, etc.

Parentheses are often placed around one of the members of a digraph symbol when there are two pronunciation variants one of which is symbolized by the digraph and the other of which is symbolized by one member of the digraph.

var·i·ous \. . ., ˈva(a)r-, . . .\ [\ˈva(a)r-\ = \ˈvar-, ˈvaar-, *or vice versa*\]
su·mac \ˈs(h)üˌmak, . . .\ [\ˈs(h)ü-\ = \ˈshü-, ˈsü-, *or vice versa*\]
fair \ˈfa(a)(ə)r, . . .\ [\ˈfa(a)(ə)r\ = \ˈfaər, ˈfar, ˈfaaər, ˈfaar, *or any other order*\]

There will possibly be those who will object to such symbolization on the ground that, for example, \sh\ is a single sound, not two, that \sh\ really has no \h\ in it, and that it is bad to suggest that \sh\ can be converted to \s\ by omitting a final \h\ sound. Our view is that \s(h)\ is no more objectionable than \sh\, and that dictionary users who demand \sh\ should be prepared to accept \s(h)\.

In an abbreviated variant pronunciation following a punctuation mark one of two parentheses in a preceding pronunciation may be repeated simply to provide a locator for the substitution of the second variant in a preceding pronunciation.

cre·do \ˈkrē(ˌ)dō, ˈkrā(-\ [the \ā\ replaces \ē\ between \ˈkr\ and the first parenthesis]

An r that stands at the end of a transcription will often be found parenthesized, and the parenthesizing takes either of two forms: a left-handed parenthesis stands before the r and no right-handed parenthesis follows, as in \ˈmär, ˈmȧ(r\ at ¹*mar;* a parenthesis stands on either side as in \ˈbät͟hə(r)\ at ¹*bother*. The single parenthesis will be found only in a pronunciation in which there are at least two variants separated by a comma, and never in the first variant. A preceding variant ending in r without parenthesis shows the pronunciation of those who have as many \r\ sounds in their speech as there are letters *r* and letter sequences *rr* in the spelling (but see the section on dissimilation). A variant with a single parenthesis preceding the r shows the pronunciation of those who often do not have or who never have immediately before a consonant or a pause the sound, made usually by a lifting and curling backward of the tip of the tongue, that is transcribed \r\. For details of the environments in which \(r\ is pronounced and those in which it is not, see the section on \r\.

A transcription with a parenthesis on each side of a final r, as \ˈbät͟hə(r)\ at *bother*, is an abbreviated way of writing the transcription \ˈbät͟hər, ˈbät͟hə(r\, with explanation as for \ˈmär, ˈmȧ(r\ in the preceding paragraph. The abbreviated transcription can be used for *bother* but not for *mar* for the reason that the vowel symbol immediately preceding the r is the same for both kinds of speech in *bother* but not in *mar*. Since by definition above the single parenthesis means that r occurs in some environments but usually not in others, we could not use \ˈbät͟hə(r\ alone as our transcription, which would not hold for those who have r in all environments. Our explanation of double parenthesis, however, in the first sentence of this section makes the two-parenthesis transcription applicable to both *r*-keepers and *r*-droppers.

= see 2.7.1, 2.7.2 in "Explanatory Notes".

+ see 2.9 of "Explanatory Notes", and stress marks and ". . ." in this "Guide".

When a stress marking (ˈ) or ¦ appears on a syllable in the item that precedes the plus sign, the marking ¦ is to be understood as superseding a primary stress in the pronunciation that is to be supplied for the last part of the compound.

The plus sign is not necessarily an indicator of the etymological make-up of the word in whose pronunciation it is used. The etymology in square brackets, immediately following the pronunciation, is the proper source of such information. Thus the etymology of *su·per·naturalism* is plainly shown as [¹*supernatural* + *-ism*] but as a time-saving and space-saving device the pronunciation is shown as \ˌsüpə(r)+\ (that is, "+ the pronunciation at *naturalism*").

When the spelling that the plus sign directs the consultant to refer to in order to complete the pronunciation has two or more entries belonging to different parts of speech not identical in pronunciation, the pronunciation to be supplied is that of the spelling whose part of speech is the same as that of the compound. Thus for ¹*concorporate*, an adjective, add the pronunciation given for the adjective *corporate*, and for ²*concorporate*, a verb, add the pronunciation given for the verb *corporate*. If the compound has inflected forms for which the pronunciation is desired, this information should be sought at the entry for the word that is the last part of the compound.

When the second syllable of a word has primary stress, anything less than primary stress is not marked on the first syllable (except when the vowel of the first syllable is \ə\), although first syllables often have a degree of stress that we mark as secondary stress on any syllable except the first. Thus no stress mark appears before the \mī-\ at *microscopist* and *microscopy*, although , would appear before the \-mī\ of *biomicroscopy* if we were transcribing that compound in full. We usually forgo such nicety of stress indication when we use the plus formula, however, and the pronunciation of *biomicroscopy* is shown as \"+\ (read ¦bīō for the ditto).

The reason for the use of \"+\ instead of \"\ alone as the pronunciation of a word for which the value of the ditto is to be picked up from a preceding entry is illustrated by the following sequence of entries:

neo·arsphenamine \¦nē(ˌ)ō+\
neo-assyrian \"+\
¹*neo-babylonian* \"+\
²*neo-babylonian* \"\

Use of \"\ alone at *neo-assyrian* and ¹*neo-babylonian* could mean that these two words have the same pronunciation as *neoarsphenamine*. Use of \"\ alone at ²*neo-babylonian* means that that word does have the same pronunciation as the entry preceding, ¹*neo-babylonian*.

When an initial combining form has variants and appears in a number of compounds, we often list the variants in the entry for the combining form alone, devise a formula that we equate to the variants, and pronounce compounds in which the combining form so pronounced appears by means of the formula and a plus sign.

elec·tro- *in pronunciations below*, ≠¦≠≠ = ə¦lek(ˌ)trō *or* ē¦- *or* -ˌtrə\ . . .
¹*electrodeposit* \≠¦≠≠ *at* ELECTRO- +\

The principal stress in the combining-form entry is altered if the stress in the compound differs.

In entries pronounced with the plus formula, usually no division marks are shown in the second part. This part may be divided at the places indicated at the entry where the pronunciation is to be sought. Divisions between the beginning of the compound and the beginning of the second element are usually shown, except that in compounds like ¹*electrodeposit* both the pronunciation and the divisions for the first part are to be sought at the entry for the initial combining form. In such compounds a division may also be made between the two components; in fact, this division is preferable to any other.

Many printers avoid dividing after a single initial letter, and no division is shown between the components of a compound when the first is a single letter, as in *asexual.*

| the vertical bar, ascender-high and descender-deep so that it will be as distinct as possible from \l\, is frequently used in transcriptions in which one or more variants are shown as an orientation mark to make it easier for the consultant to locate the part of the pronunciation in which the variation occurs. Our usual method of fixing the point of variation is to repeat, to both the left and the right of the variation or to one side only, one or more characters that are common to the variants and that fulfill other functions in the transcription (sound symbol, stress mark, parenthesis). But when contiguous variations occur, or when a character that would ordinarily be used occurs more than once in a transcription, a character whose sole function is that of a locator is desirable. The vertical locator is inserted in the first variant and is repeated in the same position in one or more variants that follow:

flight·i·ly \ˈflīd·|ᵊlē, -īt|, |ᵊli, |əl-\. See 2.6 in "Explanatory Notes".

Two vertical bars have been used with some frequency to facilitate the presentation of three contiguous variations, as in

gen·er·a·tive \ˈjenəˌrā|d·|iv, ˈjen(ə)rə|, |t|, |ēv *also* |əv\

In the variants presented after the first mark of punctuation variants of the first of the three contiguous parts end with a vertical bar, variants of the second have a vertical bar on each side, and variants of the third begin with a vertical bar.

" see 2.8.1, 2.8.2 in "Explanatory Notes".

. see "Divisions in Respelled Pronunciations".

We hear a difference between the usual American pronunciation of the two items *fly twitch* and *flight witch* and the two items *sent reagents* and *sentry agents*, for the members of each of which pairs most transcribers would show identical sequences of sound symbols. On the other hand, we do not hear a difference between the two items *wool fox* and *wolf ox*, nor between the two items *wool freight* and *wolf rate*, for the members of each of which pairs most transcribers would also show identical sequences of sound symbols. (The qualification is to be understood that our observations are based upon the pronunciation of all items without pause, punctuative or hesitative. That some are nonsense items is of no moment.) We conclude therefore that an alteration of the boundary between meaningful elements in a sequence, or that the introduction of such a boundary into a sequence that lacks it, can cause a phonetic difference in some sequences but not in others. It makes sense to treat this phonetic difference as a difference of syllable division rather than as a difference between certain sounds in the pairs of sequences, which actually it is: such an interpretation will be more readily understood by those who do not know phonetics, and a single symbol for syllable division will do work that alternatively requires several additional sound symbols. Our symbol for a syllable division is a centered period, • ; we would use it in one position in a full transcription of items like *fly twitch* and *sentry agents* (\-ī•tw-\, \-n•tr-\) and in another position in items like *flight witch* and *sent reagents* (\-īt•w-\, \-nt•r-\); we would not use it at all in a full transcription of any of the items *wool fox, wolf ox, wool freight, wolf rate.* (Actually, we usually omit it in items of the first group when they are compounds of two English words and the pronunciation is limited to stress indication.) Our stress marks are not simultaneously indicators of syllable division, as they are in some systems of transcription, and their placement when no • accompanies them is arbitrary (see "Divisions in Respelled Pronunciations"). Thus our transcription at *astronomer* is \ə'stränəmə(r)\ but it is impossible to know from a comparison of normally pronounced English items containing the sequence \st\ whether the syllable division is before the \s\, between the \s\ and \t\, or after the \t\. In short, our policy in this book is to indicate a syllable division (use the mark •) only in sequences.

Examples of our use of •:

be•tween \bə̇'twēn . . .\ [\tw\ different from that of *rabbit warren.*]

sight \. . . *usu* -īd•+V\ [The voiced sound that most Americans have between the first two vowels of *sight over* is different from the voiced sound that some speakers (e.g., some British speakers) have between the first two vowels of *side over* or *Cy Dover.*]

bur•ry \'bər•|ē . . .\ . . . **:** abounding in or containing burs . . . [Many have \'bər•ē\ for this but \'hə•rē\ for *hurry.*]

alma-ata \¦almə•ə¦tä\ [The centered period is necessary here because in our system a doubled symbol with nothing between indicates a long monosyllabic vowel.]

For \r(•)\ at the end of a transcription, as at *knur*, see the section on \r(•)\.

ˍ the low-set minus sign usually cancels a stress at the same point in a pronunciation shown elsewhere, as in a preceding variant within the same reversed virgules or in a pronunciation for a preceding word in the same or another entry.

cam•era•man \'=(=)=,man, -ˍmən\

¹*mer•cu•ri•al* \¦mər¦kyu̇rēəl, ˍmə(r)'k-, . . .\

ac•tiv•ism \'aktə̇,vizəm\

¹*ac•tiv•ist* \-ˍvə̇st\

Occasionally ˍ merely emphasizes that the syllable that follows is without stress, as when it stands at the beginning of the first pronunciation shown for a monosyllable.

from \ˍf(r)əm, . . . \

¹*-y also -ey* \ˍē, i\

If the compound word *binaural* had been transcribed in full in the vocabulary, the stress indication would have been ¦ and would have been placed immediately ahead of the symbol \n\, as explained in "Divisions in Respelled Pronunciations". In some areas of the vocabulary we used a formula of the type \(')bī¦n+ˍ-\ for such compounds (see the plus sign), in which the purpose of the mark ˍ is to cancel the stress appearing before the first vowel at the entry *aural* in favor of the placement of stress indication for the same syllable before the \n\ in the compound, and so to guard against the interpretation that our intention as to stress is \(')bī¦n'ȯrəl\. However, since we do not employ stress marks to double as syllable dividers, formulas of the type \(')bī¦n+ˍ-\ may carry nicety of stress-mark placement to excess. The shift of stress indication for *au* from ' at *aural* to ¦ at *binaural* is implied by (') or ¦ in the first member of the compound, as it of necessity must be when the plus formula is used for a compound whose second member has no stress on the first syllable. Hence in most of the vocabulary we use a formula of the type found at *exostracize*, \eks+\ (instead of \ek's+ˍ-\).

÷ see 2.12 in "Explanatory Notes".

. . . the three-dot ellipsis is often used between sound symbols preceding and following for a pronounced part that will be found in a corresponding position in a preceding pronunciation either within the same or in a preceding entry.

humpty-dumpty \¦həm(p)tē¦dəm(p)tē, -ti . . . ti\

It may be so used for one or more of the following reasons: what it stands for may be of such length that to repeat it would consume space and distract the reader's attention from the part of the word to which we wish to draw it; it may emphasize that the pronounced parts preceding and following are concomitant variants; a duplication of sound symbols in the part of the pronunciation the ellipsis stands for may make the provision of orienting symbols from this part difficult. For additional examples see *dilettantist* and *catalogue raisonné* in the vocabulary.

Occasionally . . . is used at the end of a pronunciation consisting of stress indication only for a multiplicity of variants that it would be clumsy to indicate otherwise.

high-temperature \'=¦= . . .\ [see *temperature*]

In a formula such as that found in the pronunciation of the three-part entry

sul•fo•benzoic acid \¦səl(,)fō+. . . -\

the three dots stand for the second of the three parts. The dots together with the hyphen that follows tell the consultant that to find the pronunciation of the entire entry he must look at two other entries, *benzoic* or *benzoic acid*, and *acid*.

\ə when a stress mark (' or ,) stands at the beginning of the syllable in which it occurs, this symbol, called *schwa*, is pronounced as in *bud* or *nut* or the last syllable of *aqueduct;* when the syllable in which it stands is without stress mark, it is pronounced as in the first syllable of *alone* or *occur* or as in the second syllable of *colony* or as in the last syllable of *abbot* or *famous* or *sabbath* or *circus*.

Formerly nearly all phonetic alphabets used for the vowel of *bud* a symbol different from that for the vowel of the second syllable of *abbot*, and some alphabets still do. Some who are familiar only with these alphabets find the use of \ə\ in stressed syllables objectionable when they encounter it for the first time. But use of \ə\ as a symbol for both unstressed and stressed vowel is rapidly increasing, and abandonment of a separate symbol for the vowel of *bud* parallels abandonment of former symbols for half-long a, e, and o in whose stead ā, ē, and ō without stress mark are entirely adequate.

\ə̄ used by *r*-droppers for the *-ir* of *stir* and the *-irre-* of *stirred*, and used by many *r*-droppers for the *-ur-* of *sturdy* and the *-ir-* of *bird*. It is a single sound and not a diphthong.

An *r*-dropper, symbolized by *–R* in transcriptions in this dictionary, in no case makes immediately before a pause or a consonant the *r*-sound that is characterized by the raising and bending backward of the tongue tip. Complete *r*-droppers are comparatively rare, and in the U.S. possibly nonexistent. A not uncommon phenomenon is a speaker who pronounces *bird* and the first syllable of *further* the way an *r*-keeper does but who drops the *r* of the second syllable of *further* and of words like *farm* and *form*.

In words like *bird* and *sturdy* (words not having *r* as the last letter in the orthography and not derived from such words) but not in words like *stir, stirred, stirs,* many *r*-droppers in the New York City area and in the southeastern U.S. have instead of the vowel \ə̄\ the diphthong \əi\ (see the section on \əi\). A variant vowel used by some speakers for words like *bird* and *stir* but not shown in this dictionary is \əə\ — that is, \'ə\, the vowel of *bud*, lengthened. With such speakers *bud* and *bird* have the same vowel, but it is appreciably longer in *bird*. With *r*-droppers in the U.S. the pronunciation of words like *furry* and *stirring* (two-element words whose second element is a vowel suffix or a vowel-initial suffix) is either \'fə̄rē\, \'stə̄riŋ\ or more often \'fər•ē\, \'stər•iŋ\, the latter being also the pronunciation of *r*-keepers. See the section on \ər(•)\.

\ə̄\ is often used by *r*-droppers as an anglicization of any of the vowels \œ\, \œ̄\, \œœ\, \œ̄œ\ in words borrowed from a foreign language. Example: \-sə̄z\ for the second syllable of *berceuse* which in French is \-sœ̄œz\. This \ə̄\ anglicization is even used to some extent by *r*-keepers although it is not a sound that they use in fully English words. See \œ\.

\ə̇ used in unstressed syllables only; the dot is not a diacritic indicating that \ə̇\ stands for something different from \ə\. Rather \ə̇\ is a compound or two-part symbol, the two components being \ə\ and the dot of the symbol \i\. \ə̇\ is used when \ə\ occurs in some dialects and \i\ in others, or when the same speaker may have \ə\ in ordinary speech but \i\ in formal speech, or in an initial position where either \ə\ or \i\ may occur depending on what precedes. Less space is required to transcribe, for instance, *rapid* as \'rapə̇d\ than to transcribe it as \'rapəd, -pid\. In positions in which we show \ə̇\, most dictionaries have long shown only \i\ — or even \e\ alternatively or alone when the orthography has *e*, as in the second syllable of *ticket*. \i\ is the pronunciation of some Americans and of most speakers of Received Standard, but most Americans make exact rhymes of *quotaed* and *quoted*, of *ballad* and *valid*, of *abbot* and *rabbit* and *rabbet*. The first member of each of these groups is shown with only \ə\ or its equivalent as the unstressed vowel.

Our system includes the three symbols \ə\, \i\, and \ə̇\ and uses \ə̇\ to mean either \ə\ or \i\. A system (or a modification of it) used by many linguists includes the three symbols \ə\, \i\, and "barred *i*", produced by overprinting the \i\ with a hyphen), and uses barred *i* in most of the places where we use \ə̇\. As used by most, it appears to be intended as a symbol for a sound distinct from \ə\ and \i\ — articulated with the tongue higher than for \ə\ and farther back than for \i\. Although it is quite true that the unstressed sound we symbolize \ə\ varies in its articulation more than any other vowel, the variation seems purely a matter of phonetic environment. If speakers do not consistently articulate within the same environment three distinct vowels symbolized by \ə\ and \i\ and barred *i*, then we need no equivalent for an unstressed barred *i*.

Barred *i* has also been used to symbolize a stressed vowel heard from some Southern speakers in the first syllable of *sister*, produced by drawing the tongue back in the direction of \u̇\. We have not used a symbol for this vowel in the vocabulary because the geographical and lexical incidence of the vowel does not seem to be well enough known. Some students of American speech insist that a symbol for such a stressed vowel is necessary for adequate transcription of the full range of variants heard for the adverb *just* from speakers in all parts of the U.S., on the ground that this adverb frequently has a vowel that is not the vowel of the adjective *just*, not the vowel of the noun *gist*, and not the vowel of the noun or verb *jest*. We agree but we are not convinced that (outside those areas of the South where the first vowel of *sister* is not \i\) pronunciations of the adverb *just* when the vowel is not stressed \ə\, \i\, or \e\ have any more stress to them than does the pronunciation of the *gest* of *largest*. The full range of variants for the adverb *just* is reasonably well covered for the English-speaking world as a whole when it is indicated that the vowel is \ə\, \i\, or (less frequent than the other two in standard speech) \e\, all either stressed or unstressed.

In transcriptions of uncommon words, as a space-saving device, \ə̇\ only is used where \ē\ is heard as a variant of \ə\ and \i\ as in the antepenultimate syllable of words in *-ical* or in the second syllable of *Libyco-Berber*. Such practice is not inconsistent with the widely followed practice of transcribing as \i\ the last vowel of words like *happy*, a vowel for which the symbol \ē\ better represents the usual U.S. pronunciation. The \ē\ variant is usually included in transcriptions of common words.

If we were attempting to cover British as well as American pronunciation, we would use \ə̇\ much more freely than we do in vocabulary pronunciations. In British usage an unstressed vowel whose orthographic counterpart is *i* or *e* is usually \i\, but American usage more often has \ə\ than \i\ in unstressed syllables. Even with American speakers who most often have \i\, its range is much more restricted.

\ᵊ (preceding \l\, \n\, \m\, \ŋ\; for ᵊ following \l\, \m\, \r\, see \lᵊ\, \mᵊ\, \rᵊ\) printed as a superior character means that a consonant following it is a syllabic consonant, that is, a consonant that immediately follows another consonant without any vowel between. Nearly all phoneticians are agreed that \n\ and \l\ are often syllabic in English although some use no symbol that indicates syllabicity. Some transcribers of pronunciations in dictionaries who use a special symbol for syllabicity with \n\ and \l\ find no occasion to attach the symbol to \m\ or \ŋ\, but this does not necessarily mean that they deny the existence of syllabic \m\ and \ŋ\. There is variation in the interpretation and transcription of the sound of the *er* in the three-syllabled pronunciation of *coppery* and in *r*-keepers' pronunciation of *copper*, some phoneticians regarding these sounds as a syllabic \r\.

Apparently there are many, especially among writers of textbooks on phonics and teachers in the elementary schools, who are of the opinion that there can be no syllable without a vowel. Every dictionary in line of succession from, and including, Noah Webster's original dictionary of 1828 shows vowelless syllables. For instance, the unabridged Webster dictionaries that preceded this pronounce the word *kitten* as follows:

1828	kit'n
1847	kit'tn
1864	kĭt'tn
1890	kĭt't'n
1909	kĭt''n
1934	kĭt''n

As a realistic representation of what takes place in articulation when a syllabic consonant is pronounced, the representation employed by Noah Webster in 1828 is difficult to improve: the consonant alone is used without the addition of any symbol for syllabicity. Something additional must be used when the syllabic consonant is not final in a sequence and is followed by a vowel; thus \kitnish\ does not adequately represent a three-syllabled pronunciation of *kittenish*, but its inadequacy can be rectified by inserting a hyphen after the syllabic consonant, thus: \kitn-ish\). Our latest school dictionaries transcribe *kitten* as \'kit-n\, and with the abolition of unnecessary marks of syllable division in this book our transcription could have been \'kitn\. However, this book departs from this method of transcribing syllabic consonants for two reasons:

(1) In some environments some monosyllabic particles (for example, *and*) often have no vowel sound but have a syllabic consonant as their first or only sound. Although in the transcription of words of more than one syllable a special symbol for syllabicity is not essential, without one the indication of a syllabic consonant in a monosyllable is a matter of some difficulty, and in this book the user has a right to expect a minute listing of all the variants commonly heard for such monosyllabic particles as *and*. (2) In our school dictionaries, a syllabic consonant followed in the same word by a vowel is indicated as syllabic by the printing of a hyphen (in these books a mark of syllable division) after the consonant, as in \'fas-n-,āt\ for *fascinate* and \,fas-n-'ā-shən\ for *fascination*. We have found that these transcriptions have been often understood to show *fascinate* as having two syllables only or *fascination* three syllables only, so we attempt to forestall misinterpretations such

as these by using a small superior schwa before the syllabic consonant.

Some transcribers symbolize a syllabic consonant by a full-size \ə\ followed by the symbol for the consonant, for example, the sound that follows the second consonant of *wooden* being transcribed \ən\. Either or both of two lines of reasoning seem to motivate this procedure:

(1) There are speakers who have a vowel between the \d\ and \n\ of words like *wooden*. Even those who rarely or never have the vowel-plus-\n\ pronunciation would not apprehend that pronunciation as anything but the word *wooden*. There are few if any speakers who consistently have \d\ plus syllabic \n\ in one kind of context and have \d\ plus \ə\ plus \n\ in another context, and therefore the two pronunciations are seldom in contrast. Why then go to the trouble of having an additional method of symbolization for a syllabic consonant?

(2) The pronunciation without any vowel in the second syllable of *wooden* is the usual one, but a speaker's ingrained pronunciation habits can be depended upon to make him pronounce a syllabic consonant in the right places even though the transcription shows \ə\ before the consonant.

Against these arguments several counter arguments can be posed:

In the pronunciation heard, with few exceptions, for a word like *wooden* from speakers who are communicating with friends and are not trying to impress, there is no vowel in the syllable that contains the \n\. Some speakers do insert the vowel \ə\ before the consonant especially when they have a large audience containing hearers who may expect a more formal kind of pronunciation than the speaker ordinarily uses. That there are others in any such audience, however, who do not expect the speaker to alter his normal style of speech to this extent must be the experience of many or most who have done a great deal of radio or television listening in the company of others. When a television news broadcaster pronounces *threaten* with a vowel in the second syllable, a listener, although ignorant of phonetics, must be instantly aware that the pronunciation differs from what years of hearing English spoken have shown to be the usual pronunciation of *threaten*. Most speakers of English who pronounce a vowel in the second syllable of *wooden* or *threaten* probably do so because the spelling contains a vowel letter before the *n*. These speakers make a literal-minded interpretation of the presence of the written vowel, and do not see that they have introduced a vowel sound unnaturally. They can point to transcriptions that represent the same succession of symbols — \tən\ — the initial sounds of *tonight* and the final sounds of *threaten*. The utterances *lye denotes* and *Leyden oats* differ in that the first would ordinarily be pronounced with a vowel between the \d\ and the \n\ (with American speakers this vowel would often or usually be \ə\) whereas the second would ordinarily not have a vowel between the \d\ and the \n\. Some linguists would assert that there would be a difference of juncture between these two items whether there is or is not a vowel \ə\ in the second syllable of the second item — that in spite of identity of sounds and stresses and intonation there is something in the way these otherwise identical items are uttered that makes it clear to a hearer that the word boundaries are not the same. However, as readers know who are familiar with our vocabulary pronunciations or who have read the section on *juncture* in this "Guide", it is our view that often it is impossible to identify word boundaries phonetically. The difference between *lye denotes* consistently pronounced with \ən\ after the \d\ and *Leyden oats* consistently pronounced with a syllabic \n\ after the \d\ is the only one consistently made. Such a consistently made difference is phonemic.

Transcribers who use the symbol \ə\ in the second syllable of words like *wooden* will apparently be in difficulty if they decide to record certain widespread pronunciations that all of them seem to have thus far avoided — the pronunciation of *seven*, for instance, in which the second consonant is \b\ rather than \v\ and the last consonant is \m\ rather than \n\. The consultant who interprets a transcription like \ˈthretən\ literally and pronounces the word with a vowel in the last syllable will be saying something that may be heard from numerous other speakers but the consultant who interprets a transcription like \ˈsebəm\ in the same way would be using a pronunciation almost without precedent.

There can be no better way of indicating no vowel between two consonants than to print them with nothing between them — e.g., to transcribe \ˈsebm\ (one pronunciation of *seven*) and \ˈkäntn-ənt\ (one pronunciation of *continent*), or to follow the long-established IPA practice of using a modifier underneath the symbol for the syllabic consonant, at least whenever the syllabic consonant is followed by an unstressed vowel in the same word. Some dictionary users, however, prefer some sort of symbol between the two consonants, and the raised symbol \ᵊ\ should provide an acceptable compromise between the extreme of no modifier at all and the extreme of a full-sized \ə\, which tends to encourage overpronunciation.

Transcribers of dictionary pronunciations who employ a special way of indicating that a consonant is syllabic treat \n\ and \l\ as syllabic in a high percentage of cases. Some dictionaries show no syllabic \m\ or \ŋ\ in any of their pronunciations, although the very best speakers from time to time use a syllabic \m\ and less often a syllabic \ŋ\. (On these, see the entries \ᵊm\ and \ᵊŋ\.) The phonetic entity that corresponds to the *er* of the spelling *differ* or to the *or* of the spelling *honor* in the speech of *r*-keepers, and often in the speech of *r*-droppers when a word beginning with a vowel sound follows without pause, is variously interpreted. Some phoneticians regard this entity as the vowel \ə\ pronounced with a raising or turning back (retroflexion) of the tip of the tongue and use for it the symbol \ə\ with a symbol for retroflexion attached. Other phoneticians regard the sound as a syllabic \r\ and use a transcription that parallels that for syllabic \n\ or \l\. Still others transcribe \ər\. Of this number some regard the item as two sounds, others are willing to grant its singleness but find the two-symbol transcription more practicable since it more closely parallels the orthographic spelling, does not require the additional specially made symbol that use of a single symbol might, and makes it possible to show both the *r*-keepers' and the *r*-droppers' pronunciation by merely parenthesizing or italicizing the r. Whereas the latest school dictionaries in the Merriam-Webster series transcribe the *er* of *wither* as a syllabic r — \ˈwit͟h-r\ — this dictionary transcribes the same word \ˈwit͟hə(r)\. In the school dictionaries only the pronunciation of *r*-keepers is shown and it seemed advisable to attempt to indicate syllable boundaries in pronunciations (*attempt* because the exact location of many syllable boundaries in speech is highly uncertain). If these had been the only considerations affecting the transcription of words like *wither*, any of the three mentioned methods of transcribing the final part of the word would have served equally well. But there was the further consideration that derivatives formed by the addition of a vowel or vowel-initial suffix to many such words have pronunciation variants one of which has one syllable less than the other, *withering* and *withery*, for example, being either three-syllabled or two-syllabled. Such variation occurs often, especially in the present participle of verbs. By treating the sound of the *er* in the three-syllabled pronunciation of *withery* as a syllabic consonant \r\ we can show the variation thus: \ˈwit͟h-r(-)ē\, which means \ˈwit͟h-r-ē, ˈwit͟h-rē\ or \ˈwit͟h-rē, ˈwit͟h-r-ē\, the parentheses indicating the alternative presence or absence of the phonetic item symbolized between them. For the present participle *withering*, following after *wither* transcribed \ˈwit͟h-r\ at the beginning of the main entry, the indication of this variation can even be reduced to \-r(-)ing\. If the transcription of *wither* had been given as \ˈwit͟h-ər\, a parentheses formula for the two variants of *withering* would have entailed either \ˈwit͟h-(-ə)r(-)ing\ or \ˈwit͟h-(ə-)ring\, the first clumsy with its two pairs of parentheses one of which encloses two characters instead of one, the second having two characters parenthesized instead of one and having one division changed from what it is in the form without a suffix. The alternative to a parentheses formula would have been one of the two fairly long ones \ˈwit͟h-ər-ing, ˈwit͟h-ring\ or \-ər-ing, ˈwit͟h-ring\. Omission of the first syllable from the second variant in the last formula would have been ambiguous and even if done would have yielded a formula that is still longer than the \-r(-)ing\ formula. Primarily because the \-r(-)ing\ formula for the present-participle variation is the shortest one we were able to contrive for use in a transcription system in which syllable boundaries are indicated, \r\ is treated as being capable of being a syllabic consonant in the school dictionaries, in one of which the formula is extensively used.

The present book shows for well-known entries the pronunciation of both *r*-keepers and *r*-droppers and does not attempt to show boundaries for all syllables. Because of these two practices in this book we transcribe *wither* as \ˈwit͟h-ə(r)\ and *withering* as \ˈwit͟h(ə)riŋ\. This last is to be regarded as merely one of several possible ways of representing exactly the same two variant pronunciations that are represented by \ˈwit͟h-r(-)ing\ in our other dictionaries. We could achieve somewhat closer parallelism between the two systems by representing in this book the *r*-keepers' pronunciation of *wither* as \ˈwit͟hᵊr\ and the two variants of *withering* as \ˈwit͟h(ᵊ)riŋ\ (paralleling \ˈbət(ᵊ)niŋ\ for *buttoning*), but a transcription \ˈwit͟hᵊ(r)\ is impossible since \ˈwit͟hᵊ\ is impossible.

In this dictionary we use the same symbols for the *r*-keepers' pronunciation of the stressed *ur* in the first syllable of *murmur* and the unstressed *ur* in the second syllable of that word, \ˈmərmər\. In the school dictionaries we do not, transcribing \ˈmərm-r\, for two reasons:

(1) Primarily, there might be strong opposition to showing a syllabic consonant in a stressed syllable, since the average dictionary user has never encountered a system that so employs a syllabic consonant.

(2) Although the sound of the stressed *ur* in *murmur* is a single sound, the sound of the *ir* in *firm* and the *ur* of *fur* is often a double sound when these monosyllables are in prepausal position, particularly if they are emphasized, and transcribing the *ir* of *firm*, the *ur* of *fur*, and the first *ur* of *murmur* as two sounds has phonetic justification. The vowel of *ray* is apt to be diphthongal and the vowel of the first syllable of *raking* is apt to be monophthongal in most American speech, but sound phonetic practice calls for regarding these variations as nonsignificant and using the same symbol or symbols in both situations.

We transcribe the *ir* of *firm* and *firmer* as if it were pronounced as two successive sounds. We are not certain that this is the only phonetic item answering to a vowel letter and an *r* in the spelling that is sometimes pronounced as a single sound. We often pronounce the *ar* of *army* so, and if we use a single symbol for the *ir* in *firm(er)* we ought also to use a single symbol for the *ar* of *army*. But to add symbols to a pronunciation alphabet unnecessarily seems unwise and useless. It is simpler and adequate to use a vowel symbol followed by \r\, with the understanding that the \r\ may represent either a second, independent sound or merely a modification of the preceding sound. Of the four consonants — \l\, \n\, \m\, \ng\ — that we treat as capable of being syllabic, the first three are shown as syllabic in the school dictionaries in many environments in which they are treated as \ə\ plus consonant in this book. The chief reason for this is the same as for treating the *er* of *wither* as a syllabic \r\: if we show the pronunciation of *hyphen* as \ˈhī-n\ and of *rival* as \ˈrīv-l\, we can show the two variant pronunciations of the present participles by simply parenthesizing a single character in the brief formulas \-n(-)ing\ and \-l(-)ing\. When syllable divisions in transcriptions are dispensed with, as in this book, it is possible to treat the *al* of *rival* as vowel plus \l\, the double pronunciation of the present participle being shown by the simple parenthesizing of a single character \ˈrīv(ə)liŋ\.

If the reader will pronounce each of the following items with the consonant between the two vertical bars as a syllabic consonant and then as \ə\ plus consonant, there should be no doubt that the two pronunciations of each word are markedly different:

(1) \ˈkit|n|\ (*kitten*)
(2) \ˈred|n|\ (*redden*)
(3) \ˈkēp|m|\ (*keep 'em*)
(4) \ˈgrab|m|\ (*grab 'em*)
(5) \ˌkəp|m|ˈsȯsə(r)\ (*cup and saucer*)
(6) \ˈseb|m|\ (*seven*)
(7) \ˌläk|ŋ|ˈkē\ (*lock and key*)
(8) \ˌeg|ŋ|ˈkəp\ (*egg and cup*)

For items (1) and (2) a pronunciation \ən\ instead of \ᵊn\ is heard with some frequency especially in formal speech, but even in such speech it does not sound quite natural to many listeners. For items (3) and (4) both \ᵊm\ and \əm\ sound natural. For items (5) and (6) the \əm\ pronunciation sounds utterly unnatural, as does the \əŋ\ pronunciation for items (7) and (8). For the phonetic entity between vertical bars in items (5)–(8) \ən\ is a perfectly natural alternative (in item (6), when \v\ precedes) and if any experimenters believe that \əm\ and \əŋ\ sound normal in these items they are probably pronouncing or hearing \ən\ instead. In all eight items the first vertical bar is immediately preceded by a stop consonant that is homorganic with (i.e., that has the same basic articulation as) the consonant between the two. This book treats the nasal consonants \n\, \m\, and \ŋ\ as capable of being syllabic after such a homorganic consonant. If the preceding homorganic consonant is in turn preceded by a consonant, in many cases the first of the three consonants inhibits the syllabicity of the third. Thus *London* is nearly always \ˈləndən\, although *fountain* is as often \ˈfau̇ntᵊn\ as \ˈfau̇ntən\.

The same criteria used for the possible syllabicity of the nasal consonants after homorganic stops point to the advisability of treating \l\ as capable of syllabicity after the homorganic stops \t\ and \d\ and also after the homorganic nasal \n\ (which is classifiable as a nasal stop), as in *metal*, *meddle*, and *final*. As with \n\, pronunciation of these words with \əl\ instead of \ᵊl\ is sometimes heard in formal speech. With most American speakers such pairs as *metal : medal* are quite identical in pronunciation, the consonant preceding the \l\ being a variety of \d\ (see the section on \d·\).

We have found it difficult to decide about the transcription of the group of words in which the consonant sound preceding \n\, \l\, or \m\ is a homorganic consonant other than a stop.*

---

*\ŋ\ is not involved here because it is the only velar consonant other than stops. Consonant successions like \ln\, \rn\, \rl\ in words like *sullen*, *barren*, *barrel* are not considered, for this reason: these successions can be pronounced monosyllabically, as in one pronunciation of *kiln*, in *barn*, and in one pronunciation of *Carl* (see section on *rl*), and the usual practice among phoneticians for these two-consonant successions capable of monosyllabic pronunciation (as successions like \tn\ and \bm\ are not) is to transcribe a vowel between them when they are pronounced as in *sullen*, *barren*, and *barrel*, just as \v\ and \d\ are \-vd\ in the monosyllable *lived* but \-və̇d\ in the disyllable *livid*.

The following words illustrate this classification:

(1) \ˈbās|n|\ (*basin*)
(2) \ˈrēz|n|\ (*reason*)
(3) \ˈōsh|n|\ (*ocean*)
(4) \ˈvizh|n|\ (*vision*)
(5) \ˈskəch|n|\ (*scutcheon*)
(6) \ˈpij|n|\ (*pigeon*)
(7) \ˈnāth|n|\ (*Nathan*)
(8) \ˈhēth̲|n|\ (*heathen*)

---

(9) \ˈgris|l|\ (*gristle*)
(10) \ˈēz|l|\ (*easel*)
(11) \ˈsōsh|l|\ (*social*)
(12) \ˈyüzh|l|\ (*usual*)
(13) \ˈsach|l|\ (*satchel*)
(14) \ˈaj|l|\ (*agile*)
(15) \ˈeth|l|\ (*ethyl*)
(16) \bə̇ˈkwēth̲|l|\ (*bequeathal*)

---

(17) \ˈstəf|m|\ (*stuff 'em*)
(18) \ˌdef|m|ˈāsh|n|\ (*defamation*)
(19) \ˈlēv|m|\ (*leave 'em*)
(20) \ˈsev|m|\ (*seven*)

The two chief kinds of data used in determining what our transcription of each of these types of word should be were (1) our records, accumulated over an extended period of listening, of our impression as to whether a consonant was syllabic or was preceded by a vowel \ə\ and (2) the impression arrived at after much pronouncing by ourselves such items (often containing made-up words or nonsensical names) as *May Sinnott: mace a knot: Maysa Nott: Mason Ott*, which could differ from one another only in the presence or absence of a vowel before the consonant being explored (items containing a pause were out of order). After repeated alternate attempts to pronounce \ən\ and then \ᵊn\ in the consonant successions in items (3)–(6), the successions all sound alike whether in our made-up test items there is a word boundary before the first member of the consonantal succession, after the second member, or between the two. Such an outcome determines an arbitrary choice of either \ən\ or \ᵊn\ for these words, and the equivalent of \ᵊn\ is used in the school dictionaries; in this book the syllable core of these words is represented, except for a few interjections, in all cases where the consonants \n\, \l\, \m\, and \ŋ\ are not involved, by a vowel symbol. Such representation also avoids transcribing the last part of *fission* as \-ᵊn\ and the first part of *another* as \əˈn-\, with their suggestion that *fission others* and *fish another's* do not sound alike.

Words of the type illustrated in (1) and (2) are transcribed with ᵊn because pairs like *Mason Ott* and *May Sinnott* seem distinct and because our records contain notations of pronunciations of words like *reason* with overpronunciations having \ən\ at the end. The difference between \zᵊn\ and \zən\, however, is by no means as easy to hear as the difference between \dᵊn\ and \dən\, and when an unstressed vowel precedes the \s\ or \z\ a clear distinction between \sən\ and \sᵊn\ seems impossible, *Jefferson Ott* and *Jeffersa Nott* and *Jeffer Sinnott* all sounding the same to us. Hence we transcribe \ˈgärsᵊn\ (*Garson*) but \ˈjefərsən\ (*Jefferson*).

Items (7) and (8) are more difficult, but a distinction can be heard between \thən\ and \thᵊn\ and between \th̲ən\ and \th̲ᵊn\; \ən\ is regular when a vowel follows the \n\ without pause, being heard in *unearth a nape, unearth an ape, Bertha Nape*, and *earthen ape;* and either \ən\ or \ᵊn\ is apt to occur when a consonant or a pause follows the \n\, \ən\ and \ᵊn\ in such position being in free variation. We have therefore shown \ən\ after \th\ and \th̲\, to the exclusion of \ᵊn\.

To make \əl\ and \ᵊl\ in items (9)–(16) sound distinct and like normal English is also difficult, and we accordingly transcribe \əl\ after the consonants listed there. A number of transcribers show a syllabic \l\ in words like *gristle* and *dazzle*, but this may be primarily because of the analogy of the orthography, in which there is no vowel letter immediately before the *l*.

After \v\ in items (19) and (20) \ᵊm\ and \əm\ are possible and are quite distinct: \ˈsevəm\ for *seven* would sound strange to probably all educated persons whose native language is English whereas \ˈsevᵊm\ sounds quite natural to nearly all and is a part-time pronunciation of many, most of whom are entirely unaware that they are hearing or pronouncing an \m\ at the end of the word, are unwilling to believe that any educated speaker so pronounces, and actually denounce the pronunciation as worthy only of the most illiterate.

The syllabic \m\ of \vᵊm\ has an articulation different from that of most \m\'s in English, being formed not with the lips but with the lower lip and the upper front teeth, by assimilation to the \v\. The same kind of \m\ is heard in *nymph* and *symphony*. Its lip-teeth articulation is an almost inevitable result of its environment and in most transcription requires no special symbol. \vᵊm\, however, has a very strong tendency to become \bᵊm\ which is somewhat easier to utter and has the usual two-lip variety of \m\.

Certain common speech items having *v* and *m* in the orthography may have any of the three variants \vəm\, \vᵊm\, \bᵊm\, as *government, leave 'em* (these three pronunciations for *government* are not limited to *r*-droppers). Possibly even an uncommon item like *Novum Organum* would be heard with all three. It seems likely that an item like *Neva Martin*, in which what precedes the letter *M* is a word that in isolation is pronounced with a final vowel, would usually have only the variant \vəm\, although it might be generalizing too much to rule out \vᵊm\ and \bᵊm\ altogether. For all *v . . . m* items a pronunciation \bəm\ does not sound natural.

A number of *v . . . n* items have any of the three variants \vən\, \vᵊm\, \bᵊm\, as *seven, eleven, davenport*. For these, either \vəm\ or \bəm\ does not sound natural. *b . . . m* items like *rob 'em* are either \bᵊm\ or \bəm\. For these, \vᵊm\ or \vəm\ would not sound natural.

Items of the type illustrated in (17) and (18) — *stuff 'em, defamation* — do not offer as many complications as do those just discussed. The \f\ does not tend to become \p\, as \v\ does to become \b\, and the \m\ does not tend, to an extent at least that would appear to require notice in transcriptions in this dictionary, to appear in words in which the corresponding orthograpic item is *n*, as *hyphen*. The variants \fəm\ and \fᵊm\ both occur freely for items like *stuff 'em* and *sophomore* (the last also has a two-syllable variant) but \fᵊm\ would probably be a pretty rare variant in an item like *Josepha Moore*.

In words exemplified in the following list, there is a syllable core between an \l\, \n\, or \m\ and the next preceding consonant, which is not homorganic (successions in which a nasal is preceded by a nasal are discussed later; no words in which unstressed \əŋ\ is a possibility are shown because such a succession probably does not occur in normal English, and \ᵊŋ\ occurs only as an occasional variant):

(1) *triple*	(9) *ribbon*	(17) *ligament*
(2) *babble*	(10) *weaken*	(18) *blossom*
(3) *fickle*	(11) *wagon*	(19) *chasm*
(4) *struggle*	(12) *stiffen*	(20) *Gotham*
(5) *baffle*	(13) *seven*	(21) *rhythm*
(6) *bevel*		(22) *Beecham*
(7) *camel*	(14) *bottom*	(23) *Bridgham*
	(15) *madam*	(24) *Gresham*
(8) *happen*	(16) *oakum*	

Although words of the type *triple* and *babble*, and of the type *chasm* and *rhythm*, have been shown as having syllabic \l\ or syllabic \m\ in many books containing transcriptions, an \əl\, \ən\, or \əm\ in these words distinct from an \ᵊl\, \ᵊn\, or \ᵊm\ is undetectable, and we accordingly transcribe all these words with \əl\, \ən\, \əm\. Some of these words having an *n* in the spelling have pronunciation variants in which, by assimilation to the preceding consonant, the \n\ becomes \m\ (homorganic with preceding \v\, \p\, or \b\) or \ŋ\ (homorganic with preceding \k\ or \g\). In such variants the \m\ or \ŋ\ is syllabic and is transcribed \ᵊm\ or \ᵊŋ\. Such variants are shown for common words (as *happen* and *seven*), but for other words they are to be understood as occasional pronunciations largely limited to extremely rapid speech or to predisposing environments. (Thus, \-gᵊŋ\ would be less frequent for *dragon* immediately before a pause than for *dragon* in *dragon claw*, an environment in which the nasal is not merely preceded but also followed by a consonant having the same place of articulation as \ŋ\).

It seems likely that some who transcribe words like *triple, fickle, chasm*, and *prism* with a syllabic consonant \l\ or \m\ do so in continuance of a tradition that originated in a day when transcribers stood more in awe of spelling than the more enlightened do today. Transcriptions of *rifle* and *supple* that do not parallel those of *rival, opal*, and *oval*, and transcriptions of *chasm* and *prism* that do not parallel those of *blossom* and *gruesome* are suspect. There are of course passages of poetry in which the pronunciation of an *-sm* word as \-zəm\ would roughen the meter — a phrase like "a chasm of granite rock" in a line requiring iambics. But what is required in such a passage is not the use of \ᵊm\ instead of \əm\ but the use of a pronunciation in which the \z\ and the \m\ stand to each other in the same relationship as in the word *jazzman*. Such a pronunciation is easy enough to make clear by the use of spaces in the transcription: \ə kaz məv granə̇t räk\. Any attempt at the entry *chasm* to transcribe such a pronunciation of the *sm* would probably elude even most of the phonetically sophisticated, unless an explanation were given. Some might say that such a pronunciation is merely an example of poetic license and as deserving of ready dismissal as the pronunciation \th̲\ required for the definite article in "and dashed th' ambitious hopes" or the pronunciation required for *loathed* in "the loathèd hut they left behind". Such elision of a vowel between certain consonants and a following word-final \m\ that precedes an unstressed vowel occurs in prose utterance as well (the more rapid the utterance, the more likely its occurrence) and it also occurs before word-final \l\, \n\, and even \ŋ\, despite the fact that its occurrence before \ŋ\ would require that \ŋ\ be regarded as preceding a vowel in the same syllable, something that \ŋ\ is supposed never to do in normal English. Thus such pronunciations as the following are heard frequently:

\ə mit nə(v) wu̇l\ (*a mitten of wool*)
\tə sēz nə rōst\ (*to season a roast*)
\ə kak lə(v) gēs\ (*a cackle of geese*)
\th̲ə pē plə(v) rōm\ (*the people of Rome*)
\th̲ə {sev nə(v) / sev mə(v) / seb mə(v)} kləbz\ (*the seven of clubs*)
\th̲ē ənthüzēaz mə vȯl\ (*the enthusiasm of all*)
\th̲ə rith̲ mə velēəts līn\ (*the rhythm of Eliot's line*)
\ə̇t wōn(t) hap {nəgen / məgen}\ (*it won't happen again*)
\ə wag ŋə dā\ (*a wagon a day*)
\bak ŋəp th̲ə kär\ (*backing up the car*)

Except for an occasional entry word (as ²*couple*) that has prevocalic occurrence in a frequently pronounced phrase, such variants are not shown. Such information is more likely to be sought in a discussion of phonetics than at individual entries in a dictionary, and constant repetition of a formula adequate to make this difficult-to-transcribe variation clear is felt to be unjustified.

The preceding remarks have touched on the pronunciation of a word like *chasm* in prevocalic position. Also to be found in poetry are such passages as "the chasm 'twixt rock and rock" (Browning), with *chasm* preconsonantal and in a position where optimally smooth meter requires a monosyllable. Uttering *chasm* here in a way that would be normal in any prose passage produces a very jarring rhythm.

Transcriptions of *chasm* that have appeared in some of our earlier dictionaries are (kăzm) and (kăz'm). (kăz'm) parallels the transcription of words like *dazzle* and *button* in having an apostrophe (symbol indicating a following consonant as syllabic) before the final consonant but differs from them in having no stress mark before the apostrophe (in our earlier dictionaries a stress mark following any syllable except the last indicated not merely stress but also a syllable boundary). The transcribers of both (kăzm) and (kăz'm) may have been influenced by an awareness of the monosyllabicity desirable for *chasm* in some poetic passages and may have intended these transcriptions to represent either a disyllabic or a monosyllabic pronunciation. The orthography may have caused them not to realize that the variations occurring for *chasm* are paralleled in words like *couple* and *mitten* (which have a vowel letter either after or immediately before the last consonant whereas *chasm* has such a letter in neither position). The briefest possible transcription for such variation is \ˈkaz(ə)m\, \ˈkəp(ə)l\, \ˈmit(ᵊ)n\, although the intent of such a transcription would probably be lost on most dictionary users.

Many or most *r*-droppers have syllabic consonants not only in words of the type *cotton* and *curtain* (in which the orthography has a vowel letter or vowel letters between the two consonants involved) but also in words of the type *modern* \-dᵊn\, *pattern* \-tᵊn\, *lantern* \-ntᵊn\, *international* \ˌintᵊn-\, *utterly* \ˈəd·ᵊlē\, and *government* \ˈgəvᵊmənt, ˈgəbᵊmənt\ (in which there is a vowel letter and an *r* between the two consonant letters in the orthography). The two pronunciations just shown for *government* occur frequently in the speech of *r*-keepers as well. Although it has been claimed or implied in transcriptional practice that there are *r*-droppers who consistently keep the members of such a pair as *Patton: pattern* distinct in their pronunciation, making the first \ˈpatᵊn\ and the second \ˈpad·ən\ or \ˈpatən\, there can be no doubt that pronunciations such as \ˈpatᵊn\ for *pattern* are common in *r*-dropping speech in both the U.S. and Great Britain.

Between some successions of two sounds, the minimum transition in English is a non-syllable-forming one: for example, the transition from \ī\ to \n\ in *brine*, from \r\ to \n\ in *r*-keepers' *barn*, from \g\ to \d\ in *drugged*, from \l\ to \n\ in one pronunciation of *kiln*, all monosyllabic words. Between other successions of two sounds (the successions discussed in some detail in the preceding paragraphs), the minimum transition is a syllable-forming one: for example, the transition from \d\ to \n\ in *hidden*, from second \p\ to \l\ in *people*, from \z\ to \m\ in *chasm*, from \k\ to \r\ in *acre**. When both a minimum and a more-than-minimum transition can be heard, a vowel is present in the more-than-minimum transition and a vowel symbol should be shown in the transcription. Thus *Bryan* is \ˈbrīən\ not \ˈbrīᵊn\ (compare monosyllabic \ˈbrīn\ *brine*), *baron* is \ˈbarən\ not \ˈbarᵊn\ (compare monosyllabic \ˈbärn\ *barn*), *rugged* is \ˈrəgəd\ or \ˈrəgid\ not \ˈrəgᵊd\ (compare monosyllabic \ˈdrəgd\ *drugged*). Successions incapable of less than disyllabic transition offer the complications that some are clearly capable of both a minimum disyllabic transition and a more-than-minimum disyllabic transition (\d\ and \n\ for instance, as in *hidden*) whereas others are not. Some phoneticians, feeling it unnecessary to take cognizance of such

*In some other languages, as French, \l\, \m\, and \r\ are in such position pronounced in such a way as to make possible a monosyllabic transition between them and a preceding consonant of the type illustrated. The qualification should also be added that we are speaking of successions of sounds in which the second is in prepausal position: since the desideratum in these considerations is to see what happens to a succession when an attempt is made to attach it to a single vowel, to introduce a word like *jitney*, in which the members of the succession are susceptible to distribution between a preceding and a following vowel, is to introduce a different criterion.

transitional variation, transcribe alike all transitions that are disyllabic, either treating the second consonant of all such successions as having a vowel before it or as being syllabic. Transcribers who record both types of transition do not always agree to which classification a given succession belongs. Those who wish to distinguish them should use \ᵊ\ between consonant symbols for the minimum transition and \ə\ for the more-than-minimum — for example, \ˈhidᵊn\ for the minimum, \ˈhidən\ for the more-than-minimum, in *hidden*.

For words like *linen, allyl, minimum,* and *goaded,* in which the two sounds of the succession are identical consonants, the transcription is with a vowel (\ə\ or in many cases either \ə\ or \i\) rather than \ᵊ\, the transition being more-than-minimum. The minimum transition for such a consonant pair is that heard in a word like *meanness,* where the transition from \n\ to \n\ consists of a mere holding or prolongation of the articulation of the \n\ that is also regardable as a doubling of the consonant and is usually transcribed by writing the symbol twice. Citing *meanness* (a word with a vowel both preceding and following the consonant pair) violates the criteria announced earlier as a basis for this particular part of our discussion, but it is only in such words that this type of transition ordinarily occurs in English. In some languages, however, it occurs within the bounds of a single syllable as a regular phenomenon, and is occasionally used in English for effect. Thus Carl Sandburg pronounces *Lincoln* \ˈliŋŋkən\ in reading from his works.

Although there are those who use transcriptions of the type \ˈkämᵊn\ *common* and \ˈvenᵊm\ *venom* (just as there are those who use transcriptions of the type \ˈbrīᵊn\ *Bryan* and \ˈmelᵊn\ *melon*), such transcriptions are out of line with the criteria we have used in that they employ the symbol of syllabicity for a more-than-minimum transition. The minimum transition for two different nasals is one in which the mouth closure for the second is simultaneous with a part or all of the closure for the first. Presumably only the articulation that is nearest the breath stream is acoustically identifiable, the outer one being blocked off by the inner one from forming any part of the resonance chamber. Such transitions do not occur in normal English nor in any of the languages with whose phonetics we have any firsthand acquaintance but they are quite easy to make. Mischa Elman once pronounced his surname over the radio as \ˈelm\ plus a nasal \n\ whose articulation began during the closure for \m\ and was held until the pause that follows the surname, as was also apparently the closure for the \m\. Whether this pronunciation should be considered disyllabic or monosyllabic is something easily argued.

**\ ᵊ ** (following \l\, \m\, \r\; for ᵊ preceding \l\, \n\, \m\, \ŋ\, see the sections \ᵊl\, \ᵊn\, \ᵊm\, \ᵊŋ\) in some foreign languages, of which French is the best known, two consonants the second of which is \l\, \m\, or \r\ can occur at the end of a word without any vowel between them. However, whereas in English the second member of the pair is voiced and the pair is disyllabic, in French the second member of the pair is voiceless (even when the first member is voiced) and the pair is monosyllabic. We indicate such a pronunciation of a pair of consonants by placing the symbol ᵊ after rather than before the second member. Examples from French of words for which such a pronunciation is one variant:

couple \küplᵊ\ *titre* \tētrᵊ\
table \täblᵊ\ *mordre* \mȯrdrᵊ\
prisme \prēsmᵊ, -ēzmᵊ\

In French such words may have any of four pronunciation variants, representable in our system as follows:

table \täbl(ᵊ), -b(lə)\

The four variants shown are

1. \täblᵊ\
2. \täbl\
3. \täblə\
4. \täb\

In French prose, 1 occurs before a pause, as does 4 chiefly in rapid or informal speech; 2 occurs before a word that begins with a vowel sound and that follows without pause; 3 and 4 occur before a word that begins with a consonant sound and that follows without pause, 4 occurring esp. in rapid or informal speech and in set phrases such as *maître d'hôtel.* The meaning of a transcription like 2 will be misunderstood by many, who will interpret it as disyllabic. In the following examples, spaces are used to indicate where the syllable boundaries are usually regarded as being in French, in order to facilitate an understanding of our transcriptions. Examples:

1. *amour-propre* \à mür prȯprᵊ— *three syllables*\
2. *la table est belle* \lȧ tà ble bel—*four syllables*\
3. *table de bois* \tà blə də bwä —*three syllables*\
4. *amour-propre* \à mür prȯp— *three syllables*\ ; *table de bois* \tàb də bwä — *three syllables*\

**\ əi ** as in a pronunciation of *bird* that is widely used in greater New York City and in a strip of the deep South extending from North Carolina to Louisiana. This pronunciation is commonly represented by the letters *oi,* as in the spelling *boid* for *bird,* but the \ȯi\ suggested by this spelling is rarely or never the pronunciation actually used. In the South this pronunciation appears to be less regarded by educated speakers as one to be avoided than in the New York City area.

\əi\ does not occur as a variant of \ər\ and \ə̄\ in words having no sound after the \ər\ or \ə̄\, nor in formations based on such words — that is, \əi\ does not occur, in educated speech at least, in words like *spur, spurred, spurring, furry.* Nor does \əi\ occur in educated speech as a variant of \ər\ in words in which \ər\ is followed by a vowel, as *hurry, flourish.*

**\ ᵊl ** the usual sound of the *le* of *battle* and *muddle,* of the *al* of *vital,* of the *el* of *model* and *funnel,* of the *ile* of *futile.* The \ᵊ\ is a diacritic and \ᵊl\ is a single sound, not two, an \l\ sound that serves as the nearest thing to a vowel in its syllable. Especially on formal occasions and with speakers not fully sure of themselves the two sounds \əl\ do sometimes occur instead of \ᵊl\. The \əl\ variant is usually not shown. When a word ending in \t\, \d\, or \n\ precedes without pause, words shown as beginning \əl-\ (as *allow, alone*) may have \ᵊl-\ instead, as in *not alone.*

**\ ᵊm ** often heard for the words *'em* and *and* when \p\, \b\, or \v\ precedes, as in *stop 'em, grab 'em, save 'em, up and down, rub and buff, stove and poker.* A preceding \v\ may be assimilated to \b\, as in the third and sixth examples above; if the \v\ remains \v\, the \ᵊm\ articulation is lip-teeth rather than lip-lip. \vᵊm\ and \bᵊm\ are also often heard for the *ven* of words like *seven* and *eleven* and for the *vernm* of *government.* The \ᵊ\ is a diacritic and \ᵊm\ is a single sound, not two, an \m\ sound that serves as the nearest thing to a vowel in its syllable. The two sounds \əm\ are not heard as a variant for \ᵊm\ when the orthographic correlate is *n* (*government* is not an exception because the orthographic correlate there is *m* not *n,* the first \n\ being lost possibly through the dissimilatory influence of the second \n\). When a word ending in \p\, \b\, or \m\ precedes without pause, words shown in the vocabulary as beginning \əm-\ sometimes have \ᵊm-\ instead, as in *save ammonia.*

**\ ᵊn ** as the usual *an* of *Satan* and *en* of *wooden.* The \ᵊ\ is a diacritic and \ᵊn\ is a single sound, not two, an \n\ sound that serves as the nearest thing to a vowel in its syllable. Especially on formal occasions and with speakers not fully sure of themselves the two sounds \ən\ do sometimes occur instead of \ᵊn\. The \ən\ variant is usually not shown. When a word ending in \d\ or \t\ precedes without pause, words shown as beginning \ən-\, \ȧn-\, or \in\ (as *announce, engage*) may have \ᵊn\ instead, as in *made announcements, can't engage.*

**\ ᵊŋ ** sometimes heard as a variant for vowel plus \n\ or \ŋ\ when \k\ or \g\ precedes and somewhat more often when \k\ or \g\ also follows, as in *chicken coop, breaking ground, dog and gun.* The \ᵊ\ is a diacritic and \ᵊŋ\ is a single sound, not two, an \ŋ\ sound that serves as the nearest thing to a vowel in its syllable. When a word ending in \k\ or \g\ precedes without pause, words shown as beginning \ȧnk-\ or \ȧng-\ sometimes have \ᵊŋk\ or \ᵊŋg\ instead, as in *break engagements, big encouragement.*

**\ ər ** (see also the section on \ər·, ə·r\) when in a syllable bearing either of the stresses ˈ ˌ, and when word-final or followed by a consonant sound, \ər\ is the sound used by *r*-keepers for the *ir* of *stir,* the *ear* of *search,* or the *ir* of *circularity.* When the \ə\ of \ər\ is not preceded by a stress mark, \ər\ is the sound used by *r*-keepers for the *er* of *walker* and by both *r*-keepers and *r*-droppers for the *ar* of *arise,* the *er* of *veneration,* and the *er* of *bakery* when that word is pronounced in three syllables and not two.

Many transcribers regard what we transcribe as \ər\ as a single sound (stressed or unstressed) and use a single symbol instead of \r\ preceded by a vowel symbol. Such transcribers regard the articulation as a single one in which the body of the tongue is in the position for some such vowel as \ə\ or \ə̄\ at the same time that the tip is in substantially the position for the sound following the \n\ in *unroll.* Even if the pronunciation that we symbolize \ər\ is one sound, there appears to be no great objection to transcribing it as if the components of the articulation were successive rather than simultaneous, and such a transcription is now the usual practice of many linguists in this country. Such a practice makes it possible to show both the *r*-keepers' and the *r*-droppers' pronunciation of a word like *winner* by merely parenthesizing the \r\, thus: \ˈwinə(r)\.* Furthermore, it is by no means sure that, if \ər\ is a single sound, it is the only such sound in English: *arc* may be just as much a two-sound word as *irk.*

**\ ər·, ə·r ** used in words in which \ə\ is stressed and a vowel immediately follows the \r\. The first of the two transcriptions is also used at the end of words, since any word is capable of being followed by a vowel-initial word.

\ər·\ with a vowel sound following is the same sound as that written without the centered dot when a consonant sound follows — that is, it is the sound used by *r*-keepers for the *ir* of *bird* or the *irre* of *stirred.* It is also the sound used by *r*-keepers for the *irr* of *stirring* (most U.S. *r*-droppers have the same sound in this word, a smaller number have \ə̄r\) and by *r*-keepers for the *ir* of *Sir Albert* (some U.S. *r*-droppers have the same sound, some say \sə̄ˈalbət\, and fewer say \sə̄ˈralbət\, the usual pronunciation in southern British speech, as is \ə̄r\ for *stirring*). \ər·\ is also the pronunciation used by most *r*-keepers for the *urr* of *hurry* and the *our* of *courage,* words that differ from the linguistic items *stirring* and *Sir Albert* in not being composed of two meaningful English units.

Most U.S. *r*-droppers, speakers of southern British, and *r*-keepers in some areas of the U.S. pronounce the *urr* of *hurry* and the *our* of *courage* in a way that we transcribe \ə·r\. In \ər·\ whatever we represent by the \ə\and the \r\ is in the same syllable: the syllable division occurs after the \r\. But in the pronunciation that we represent \ə·r\ the \ə\and the \r\ seem very definitely to be distributed between successive syllables. Therefore, we have made the distinction between the two by a difference in the placement of the centered period, a syllable-boundary indicator. One of the most expected places for the occurrence of the \ə·r\ pronunciation is in the circus barker's spiel "Hurry! Hurry! Hurry!" where, it seems likely, \ə·r\ is used even by speakers who ordinarily have \ər·\ in such words. This sound may be produced by saying the first two sounds of *hum* without sounding the \m\ and then adding the first two sounds of *react.*

In transcriptions of uncommon words rhyming with *stir,* like *claqueur* \klaˈkər(·)\, the parenthesized period means that the period is to be omitted when a consonant or a pause follows (as in \klaˈkərz\ *claqueurs*) but is to be retained, without the parentheses, when a vowel sound follows without pause (as in \əklaˈkər·ənthəˈbalkənē\ *a claqueur in the balcony*). \-ˈkə·rən-\ for this last phrase would be a pronunciation that does not ordinarily occur in educated standard speech.

In words as common as *hurry* both the \ər·\ and the \ə·r\ variant are shown, in the expectation that it will be chiefly in the more frequent words that phonetic detail will be sought in this book. But for a word having as little currency among nonspecialists as *gurry* the transcription is shown simply as \ˈgərē\, since either of two likely interpretations placed on the \ər\ will be acceptable.

In words like *stirring, burry,* formed by adding an active vowel or vowel-initial suffix to words of the type *stir,* the \ə·r\ variant is not usually heard, although it appears to be an occasional, and the usual British, variant of the noun *furrier* and a rare variant of *furry* (and therefore of the comparative adjective *furrier*) in British speech. In words of the type *occurrence,* which are from, or which parallel words existing in, a foreign language, notably Latin, and which if formed in English were formed by using a suffix now relatively inactive in English, an \ə·r\ variant is quite regular with speakers who have \ə·r\ in *hurry.*

**\ əu̇ ** as in one pronunciation of *bulb* — see section on \l\.

**\ əw ** this succession of symbols followed by a vowel symbol (as in \ˈstrenyəwəs\ for *strenuous,* \ˌsichəˈwāshən\ for *situation*) occurs instead of the \u̇\ or \ō\ followed by a vowel that is employed by a number of transcribers. The starting point in the reasoning that led to a decision to use \əw\ was a very strong conviction that the members, or that the shorter member and a part of the longer member, of such pairs as the following are exact rhymes (some of the words and names below are made up and some of the combinations are nonsensical):

silhouette
Scylla wet
Genoese
Jenna Weeze
Manuella
Manya Weller
Halloween
Valhalla wean
willowy Ona
Willa Weona
habituate
bitch a wait
Venezuela
Venn is a weal (or *wale*)

Granting the homophony of the members of those pairs, without any attempt to explore the phonetics of the matter, we transcribe \əw\ for the following two reasons: (1) Transcribers have been unanimous, or nearly so, in using \ə\ and \w\ in transcriptions of items of the sort we have shown in each pair as the second member, but the same transcriber ordinarily uses \u̇\ when the spelling has *u* and \ō\ when the spelling has *o.* If homophony is granted, then it must be that transcribers are using two symbols (\u̇\ and \ō\) for what is really the same sound or succession of sounds. Such variation violates one of the most fundamental tenets of transcription. (2) If we decide to transcribe *silhouette* and

*Parenthesizing of \r\ after a vowel in a stressed syllable will in most cases not yield the *r*-droppers' pronunciation.

Scylla wet both \silu̇et\ or \silōet\ rather than \siləwet\, then providing variant transcriptions at both words of the type *Scylla* and words of the type *wet* that will take care of their pronunciation in isolation and their pronunciation in succession, with the *w*-initial word second, is a task so formidable as to be prohibitive. If we transcribe both *silhouette* and *Scylla wet* with \əw\, however, then the transcription for *Scylla* and for *wet* in isolation is also the transcription for them in succession in that order. Thus only at words of the type *follow* and *value* must variants be provided for isolation and succession differences where a variant in \-əw\ is provided to take care of the usual or a common pronunciation in items like *following, follow up, valuer, value alteration.*

\a as in *hat, gap, has-been, have-not;* some speakers have \a\ also in one, two, or all of the three words *hash, hang, ask*. Other speakers have in *hash* and *ask* a vowel that we symbolize \aa\ or \aaə\; they have the latter vowel also in *halve* and in the emphatic pronunciation of the verb *can,* words which may be distinct from the emphatic form of *have* and from the noun *can* ("container"), the latter two having \a\. Other speakers have in *hash, hang, ask* a vowel that we symbolize \ai\; they also have the latter vowel in *halve* and, if the word is in their vocabulary, probably also in *salvy*, words which if so pronounced are distinct in the vocabulary of most from the emphatic form of *have* and from *savvy*, the latter two usually having \a\. Still other speakers have in *ask* a vowel that we symbolize \ȧ\; they also usually have the latter vowel in one or more of the words *halve, heart, salvy*, words which then are distinct from the emphatic form of *have*, from *hat*, and from *savvy*, the latter three having \a\. See the sections on \aa(ə)\, \ai\, and \ȧ\.

The sound in the vowel of *hat* may vary according to the dialect, but our symbol for all varieties is \a\. To speakers who have \aa(ə)\ in their vocabulary the vowel used in *hat* in other dialects may sound to them like or much like their \aa(ə)\. The \a\ of speakers whose vocabulary includes both \a\ and \aa(ə)\ may sound to speakers of other dialects like or much like \ȧ\. The vowel of *hat* in Scottish dialect is a sound that has a quality like that often heard for the *ear* of *heart* in eastern New England or southern British speech or for the *o* of *hot* in most U.S. speech (that is, that has an \ȧ\ or \ä\ quality) but that is always very short. For the Scottish vowel, a symbol different from that for the standard vowel of *hat* is often employed in dictionaries. However, since the standard-English vowel of *hat* does not occur in the type of Scottish transcribed in this dictionary and it and the Scottish vowel of *hat* are not in contrast, there is no necessity for using a different symbol to transcribe the Scottish sound. The speaker of Scottish will use the sound natural to him in *hat* when he sees \a\ in a transcription, just as the American and the southern Englishman each interprets \ō\ for the vowel of *toe* in his own way, although their vowels are usually markedly different.

\ā as the vowel of *day, fade, date, aorta*, when emphatic usually more diphthongal in British speech than in most American speech. When it is a diphthong, the second element is \i\ and the first element is either the vowel of *debt* or the vowel used in *day* when that vowel is a monophthong.

\ä as used in *cot* and *cod* by those who pronounce these words differently from *caught* and *cawed*. The quality of the vowel of *cot* and *cod* varies, in length and in quality. In southern British speech, it is consistently short but in the U.S. may be quite long, especially before a voiced consonant. The vowel of most southern Englishmen and of many eastern New Englanders is pronounced with the tongue higher and further back and with the lips more rounded than the vowel of the average American, to whom the others' vowel may sound more like that of his *caught* or *cawed*. Our symbol \ä\ is to be interpreted as covering all varieties of vowel used in the English-speaking world for the vowel of *cot* and *cod* by speakers who pronounce these words differently from *caught* and *cawed*. Although this vowel is more often spelled with *o* in English than with any other letter, we use \ä\ rather than \o\ or an *o*-based character in our transcription for this reason: We must be able to show that in the speech of most or many Americans the first two italicized items in each of the groups of three below are identical in sound and that the third item in each group consists of the same sounds in the same order but with the additional sound \r\ present immediately after the vowel under discussion:

Fothergill	*bock* beer
father	*Bach*
farther	*bark*
bomb	*mock*
balm	*mach*
barm	*mark*

The first two orthographies in each group show that either \a\ or \o\ with or without a diacritic would be a symbol with precedent in English orthography for the words without *r* in the spelling or \r\ in the pronunciation. For this last class of words, however, \a\ is a better symbol than \o\ because \o\ before an \r\ suggests the vowel of *cord* rather than of *card*.

When one transcribes, as sound transcriptional practice requires, on the principle of one symbol to a sound, it is impossible to have all transcriptions of a language as orthographically lawless as English look right. A vowel with an articulatory position as far forward as that of *fair* and *fare* is usually represented orthographically by *a* or a letter group containing *a* and has traditionally been represented in transcriptions by \a\ with a diacritic over it. On the other hand, a vowel with an articulatory position as far back as that of *all* and *saw* is often represented orthographically by *a* or a letter group containing *a* and is represented in some pronunciation systems by \a\ with a diacritic over it. The use of \a\ with a diacritic over it to represent a vowel with an in-between articulatory position should therefore occasion no surprise. In a phonetic alphabet widely used by American linguists today, the vowel of *cot* is \a\. In the alphabet of the International Phonetic Association, which is used by many transcribers of American speech, the symbol used for the vowel in this word is one that resembles a script or italic *a* or Greek alpha.

For any who may require in their transcribing a symbol for the unrounded vowel that occurs in *cot* and a symbol for the rounded vowel that occurs in the same word and is distinct from the vowel of *caught*, we suggest \ä\ for the unrounded vowel and \o\ for the rounded. It was common practice in dictionaries, and is still the practice in some dictionaries, to use symbols for four distinct vowels in the range from front \ȧ\ to back \ȯ\ — symbols equivalent to \ȧ\, \ä\, \o\, and \ȯ\ respectively. Although there may be dialects of English in which a distinction is consistently made between four classes of words on the basis of four vowels representable by \ȧ\, \ä\, \o\, and \ȯ\, we have no reason to believe that there are speakers enough who make such a distinction to justify its notice in our dictionary. Perhaps a knowledge that the usual or a frequent British vowel and the usual American vowel in *cot* are different accounts for some American transcribers' employing four symbols rather than three. The desideratum in the formulation of a phonetic alphabet, however, is not the provision of a one-character symbol for every minute shade of sound but the provision of the barest minimum necessary to represent the distinctions consistently made in the speech of any one speaker. For distinctions any finer than this, the phonetician may use modifiers. When the explanation is made that \ä\ is the vowel of *cot*, whatever the quality of that vowel may be; that any whose vowel (in *cart*, for example, in the speech of *r*-droppers) is consistently between that of *cot* and the further-forward and higher vowel of *cat* have a vowel that we symbolize \ȧ\; that any whose vowel (in *caught* or *quart*, for example) is consistently between that of *cot* and the further-back and higher vowel of *coat* have a vowel that we symbolize \ȯ\, we have provided symbols enough to transcribe all the vowel distinctions that most speakers make in this range.

Of the best-known dialects of English, none appears to have more than three vowels in this range, and some appear to have only two. Any who may have concluded from the presence in southern British of a rounded vowel in *cot* which is distinct from the unrounded vowel of *cart* and from the even more rounded vowel of *caught* that there are four vowels between \a\ and \ō\ should observe that Daniel Jones and Henry Wyld transcribe only three. The number of such words that are phonetically distinct in southern British probably does not differ materially from the number that are distinct in the speech of U.S. *r*-keepers who do not level pairs like *cot* and *caught*. Such U.S. speakers make no distinction between such words as *Spaak* and *Spock* but southern British speakers make no distinction between such words as *Spaak* and *spark*. It seems likely that the mistaking of one word for another in this group is greater than average. If so, an explanation is to be sought not merely in the fact that some speakers have two vowels instead of the three of other speakers but also in the fact that with speakers who have the same number of vowels the distribution of the vowels is subject to much variation, as was just illustrated in the words *Spaak*, *Spock*, and *spark*. Ordinary words known in all dialects cause little difficulty, for the same reason that such identically pronounced words as *meet* and *meat* seldom cause difficulty: the context in nearly every case leaves the hearer in no doubt as to what word the speaker is using. But unknown or little-known words — surnames and the names of small geographical entities, for example — can sometimes cause perplexity.

In our transcriptions we have attempted to use only the minimum number of symbols required to show the distinctions that occur in any one major dialect of English. Since the discussion that follows involves the comparative phonetics of a group of words showing a high degree of variation and overlapping in some of the major dialects of English, we will use symbolizations that do not occur in the dictionary. Those that do we will enclose in lightface square brackets rather than in our usual reverse slant lines. [ȧ] represents a vowel that has a tongue position somewhat lower and further back than \a\; it is the vowel usually heard in *part* and usually or often heard in *pass* in eastern New England speech. [ä] is the vowel that the majority of Americans use in *pot*. [o] is the vowel that is used in southern British speech in *pot*. It differs from the usual American vowel in the same word in being pronounced with the lips rounded and often or usually in having a tongue position slightly higher and further back. [ȯ] is the vowel used in the first syllable of *order* and in *sawed* by speakers with whom *sawed* and *sod* are distinct. Doubling a vowel symbol indicates a lengthening of the sound it represents; [oo] indicates a vowel of the same quality as [o] but longer; [oo] does not represent the vowel of *hoot* or *hook*.

Such pairs as *order : ardor, born : barn*, in which a consonant sound immediately follows whatever pronunciation is given the *or* or *ar*, are no more than sporadically leveled in any well-known dialect. There appears to be some leveling in the Southern Mountain dialect and perhaps in Utah. In a section of southern Illinois the first part of the word *Borneo* is pronounced exactly like *barn*. Speakers of the dialects of the Atlantic and Gulf coasts and of Texas, from New York City to El Paso, in which [o] occurs with some frequency in the first syllable of *ardor* and in *barn*, with or without an \r\ following the vowel, are apt to be misunderstood as pronouncing *order* and *born* instead by the speakers of dialects in which *ardor* and *barn* have [ä] or [ȧ]; but the percentage of misunderstandings appears to be no higher when both speaker and listener have the same distinction than in the case of other vowel pairs equally close in articulation.

With the majority of American speakers, such pairs as *Mahler : Moller, father : Fother*gill, *Brahms : Brom's, khaki : cocky* (when the *a* of *khaki* is not \a\), and *Bach's : box* (when the *ch* of *Bach's* is not \k̲\) are exact rhymes. When they are, the vowel of both is usually [ä], but in Southern Mountain speech may be [o]. These two vowels are represented by \ä\ in our dictionary transcriptions.

In some dialects of English (especially those in which *r*-dropping occurs, as eastern New England, southern Coastal, southern British, and New York City), the vowels of such pairs are usually or often not homophonous. The stressed vowel of *Mahler* may be [ȧ] (as in eastern New England and southern British), a vowel articulated further forward in the mouth than the stressed vowel of *Moller*, lacking the rounding that usually or often accompanies the vowel of *Moller*, and in southern British at least usually longer than that vowel. The vowel of *Mahler* may be [ää] or [äə] (as in southern Coastal and New York City), a vowel having the same quality at the beginning as the vowel of *Moller* but appreciably longer because of prolongation or because of the presence of a slight [ə] off-glide at the end. The vowel of *Mahler* may be [oo] (as also in southern Coastal and New York City), a vowel with the quality of [o], the rounded vowel heard in southern British *not*, but longer. All of these three vowels or vowel characteristics that make the stressed vowel of *Mahler* distinct from the stressed vowel of *Moller* are symbolized in the dictionary pronunciations by \ȧ\. If only southern Coastal and New York City speech were being transcribed, the vowel of *Mahler*, when it differs from that of *Moller*, could very well be transcribed as \ää\. This could be made to provide for the [oo] variant as well by an explanation that lengthened \ä\ is often accompanied by rounding. That *Mahler* and *Moller* are sometimes homophonous and sometimes not could be shown by the transcriptions \ˈmä(ä)lə(r)\ and \ˈmälə(r)\ respectively. Speakers of dialects in which the stressed vowel of *Mahler* is [oo] may easily be misunderstood by hearers not familiar with the dialect as saying *mauler* instead of *Mahler*. Whether within such dialects the stressed vowels of *Mahler, mauler*, and *Morley* are ever completely leveled is doubtful. With southern speakers who have [oo] in *Mahler*, the stressed vowel of *mauler* (but not, it appears, that of *Morley*) is often a diphthong [ȯu̇], acoustically quite distinct from [oo].

In *r*-keeping speech pairs like *Spaak : spark* are distinct because one member contains an \r\ and the other does not. In *r*-dropping speech such pairs usually are homophones, but sometimes in such speech *Spaak* goes with *Spock* rather than with *spark*, as it does in most *r*-keeping speech. Our symbol for the vowel of *Spaak* when it is homophonous with that of *Spock* is \ä\; for the vowel of *Spaak* when it is not homophonous with that of *Spock*, \ȧ\.

In *r*-keeping speech pairs like *spark : Spock, Farley : folly, harmony : hominy* are distinct because one member contains an \r\ and the other does not. In some such dialects (as Middle Atlantic and the *r*-keeping speech of Texas), the vowel of *spark* is apt to be rounded ([ˈspȯrk]) whereas the vowel of *Spock* is apt to be unrounded ([ˈspäk]), but we can transcribe \ˈspärk\ and \ˈspäk\ and explain that \ä\ followed by \r\ may be rounded. Such an explanation holds both for words like *spark*, in which a consonant follows the \r\, and for words like *moral* and *horrid*, in which a vowel follows the \r\.

In some *r*-dropping dialects (as eastern New England and southern British) a pretty consistent qualitative distinction is made between the vowels of *spark* and *Spock*, and often in addition a quantitative or durational distinction as well. If the quantitative difference is lacking, the qualitative one sets the words apart. (Incidentally, the eastern New England vowel of *spark* is usually markedly different in quality from the southern British vowel in the same word, \ȧ\ standing in the former for a vowel much closer to that of *cat* and \ȧ\ being in the latter a vowel much the same in quality, and often in quantity also, as the vowel that most Americans have in *cot*.) Although some American phoneticians have observed that the southern British vowel in *cot* does not always have the rounding that the writings and transcriptions of British phoneticians seem to claim for it, the extent of the leveling of *spark* and *Spock* is beyond much question not as great as in the dialects next discussed.

With *r*-dropping speakers (as in the coastal Southern states and in New York City) who never have more than a quantitative difference between the vowels of *spark* and *Spock*, this difference of duration frequently breaks down, with the resultant homophony of such pairs. Some who have written on this type of leveling attribute it to a lengthening of the [ä] of the *r*-less member of the pair, chiefly before voiced consonants, the tendency to lengthening being greater before these than before voiceless consonants. But the leveling may be due also to a shortening of the vowel of *spark*. The tendency of a vowel to be short in duration increases with its distance from the last syllable of a word, and such words at least as *harmony* and *hominy*, in which the [ä] is in the third syllable from the end, both sometimes have a fairly short [ä] and are homophonous. Such leveling is not indicated in our transcription. A variant \ä\ is to be understood as occurring with varying frequency for all words transcribed with the variants \är\ and \ȧ\ (in uncommon words, with \är\ only) before a consonant. Our omission of the third variant does not mean that we regard the variant as substandard but rather reflects the uncertainty that exists as to the extent of the variation.

In some areas (as western Pennsylvania, eastern New England, and parts of the Far West) the members of such pairs as *cod : cawed, rot : wrought* may have the same vowel, or may undergo a range of variation from [ä] through [o] to [ȯ]. In *r*-dropping dialects, as that of eastern New England, such leveling may extend not merely to *cod* and *cawed* but to *cord* as well. *Card* and *cord* probably are not leveled to any great extent, although, as pointed out earlier, the vowel of *card* has some degree of rounding in some dialects. For a transcription of the speech of *r*-keepers who level *cod : cawed*, but not *card : cawed*, two symbols (as \ä\ and \ȯ\) are necessary in the range between \a\ and \ō\ to take care of the *card : cawed* distinction. For a transcription of the speech of *r*-droppers who level *cod : cawed : cord*, two symbols (as \ȧ\ and \ä\ or \ȧ\ and \o\ or \ȧ\ and \ȯ\) are necessary in the range between \a\ and \ō\ to take care of the distinction between *card* and *cod : cawed : cord*. For any speakers who may level *card : cord* as well as *cod : cawed*, only one symbol (\ȧ\ or \ä\ or \o\ or \ȯ\) is necessary in the range between \a\ and \ō\.

The leveling of words like *cod* and of words like *cawed* and *cord* is not transcribed after the entry words. We have refrained from transcribing it in order to simplify the transcriptions. Users of the pronunciations are to understand that the symbol \ȯ\ and the symbol \ä\, when the latter corresponds to the letter *o* in the spelling (as in *cod*), or corresponds to the letter *a* in the spelling and is preceded by the sound \w\ or \y\ and is not followed by the sound \r\ plus a consonant (as in *watch, yacht, warrant* but not in *yarn*), are merely, as far as certain dialects are concerned, two symbols for the same sound.

A further complication is the fact that the first vowel of *utter* in southern British speech is usually more like the usual American [ä] in *otter* than the usual American first vowel in *utter*, so that in an ambiguous context an Englishman's *utter* is apt to be heard by an American as *otter*.

**\ ȧ ** as any of several phonetically different vowel sounds that in the speech of *r*-droppers make *card* distinct from *cad* on the one hand and from *cod* on the other, or from *cod* on the one hand and from *cawed* on the other.

In the speech typical of eastern New England and southern England, the vowel transcribed \ȧ\ at *card* is articulatorily between the \a\ of *cad* and the \ä\ of *cod*. The New England vowel is closer to the vowel of *cad* than is the British vowel. In both eastern New England and southern British speech \ȧ\ is usual or frequent in a small group of words that have come to be known as the *ask* words. In all but a few words of this group, the vowel, orthographically *a* or *au*, is followed by one of the voiceless fricatives \f\, \s\, \th\, or by \m\ or \n\ plus a consonant. They are more often pronounced by American speakers with \a\ or (with a few exceptions, at least for \ai\) \aa(ə)\ or \ai\.

In one kind of *r*-dropping speech heard in the southeastern U.S. and in New York City, the vowel transcribed \ȧ\ at *card* is the same in quality as the vowel transcribed \ä\ at *cod* but usually of greater duration (see the statement about exceptions at the section on \ä\). Some transcribers treat the greater duration as a prolongation of the \ä\ sound, others as a diphthongization of the \ä\ sound to \äə\. In the South, with the exception of a small area of coastal Virginia, \ȧ\ occurs in the *ask* words only in conscious imitation of the speech of areas in which its use is natural. Its occurrence in New York City is also chiefly imitative, but *aunt* and *rather* have \ȧ\ (or \ä\) with some frequency. Because any word for which only an \a\ pronunciation is shown in this book may with many New York City speakers have a vowel of a quality like that of eastern New England \ȧ\, this latter vowel is perhaps to be regarded as merely a nonsignificant variant of \a\ in their speech.

In another kind of *r*-dropping speech heard in the southeastern U.S. and in New York City, the vowel transcribed \ȧ\ at *card* is articulatorily between that of *cod* and that of *cawed*. Speakers with whom the \ȧ\ is of such quality do not have \ȧ\ in the *ask* words. Any New York City speakers who may use in the *ask* words a vowel of the quality that is transcribed \ȧ\ for other dialects are to be regarded as using a nonsignificant variety of \a\. See the preceding paragraph.

Some transcribers use the symbol \ȧ\ for the vowel of most Scottish speakers in words which in most dialects are pronounced with \a\, \aa(ə)\, or \ai\, as *cat, man, bag*. This Scottish vowel is of much the same quality as eastern New England \ȧ\ but usually markedly shorter. We use for it the symbol \a\. See the section on \a\.

See also the section on \ä\.

**\ aa \, \ aaə ** chiefly in what is known as the Middle Atlantic region, an area that has New York City and Washington, D.C. on its perimeter. This vowel occurs in one or more of the following groups of words:

(1) words like *bare, fair,* and *Sayre*.

(2) words like *Cary, hairy, vary*, in which typically the sound \r\ represented by a single *r* in the spelling is followed by a vowel sound and is preceded by a vowel sound whose orthographic representation is *a* or a vowel sequence containing *a*. With speakers who have \aa(ə)\ in these words the members of the following groups are usually or often distinct: *Cary, carry, Kerry; hairy, Harry; vary, very*.

(3) words like *sail, sailor, Haley*, which in other dialects usually contain the sequence \āl\ or (when not immediately followed by a vowel sound) \āəl\. With speakers who have \aa(ə)l\ in these words, *barely* and *Bailey* may be exact rhymes. \aa(ə)\ in this group of words is reported to be less frequent among cultivated speakers.

(4) most words that have in other dialects the vowel \a\ or \ai\ in the last syllable immediately followed by one of the following consonants:

\b\, \d\, \g\, \j\
\f\, \v\, \th\, \th̲\, \s\, \z\, \sh\
\m\, \n\

When a suffix is added to such words, the vowel usually remains the same, except that the \ə\ final element is usually lost. Before some of the above consonants or some consonant groups of which one of the above is the first member, \aa\ also occurs in syllables that are not final without the help of a suffix addition. The consonants just shown are classified into three groups as an aid to the memory. The first group consists of voiced stops (\j\ is actually a double sound, \d\ + \zh\, the first constituent of which is a voiced stop), the second group consists of voiced and unvoiced fricatives (\zh\ is not listed because there is no fully English word that ends in \aa(ə)zh\), and the third group consists of two of the three nasal consonants. With speakers who have \aa(ə)\ in these words, the vowel of *cab* is readily perceived as markedly different from the vowel of *cap* (although those who do not have \aa(ə)\ may have trouble hearing the distinction); *can* ("container" or "to put in a container") may be distinct from the emphatic form of *can* ("to be able"), and *halve* may be distinct from the emphatic form of *have*, in that the first member of each pair has \aa(ə)\ whereas the second has \a\; *fad* and *fared* when they are identical in stress may be exact rhymes.

In accord with our system of doubling a symbol to indicate duration, \aa\ is longer than \a\. In one variant it is of substantially the same quality as \a\, in a second and possibly commoner variant it is formed with a higher tongue position than \a\ (approaching the tongue position for \e\), and in a third and comparatively infrequent variant it is \ȧ\ (see section on \ȧ\). Sometimes \aa\ is followed by a distinct \ə\ off-glide, indicated by three transcriptions \aa\, \aa(ə)\, \aaə\. When the \ə\ is present, it is the overall length of the diphthong that distinguishes or helps to distinguish the vowel from \a\, but to indicate that what we transcribe \aa\ is longer when the \aa\ is a monophthong than when it is the first part of a diphthong would unnecessarily complicate the transcription.*

**\ ää ** as the sound \ä\ when it is appreciably long in duration and is distinct from the shorter \ä\ for the reason that both may occur in the same environment. Thus, the German words *Stadt* and *Staat*, in the dialect of German usually regarded as standard, consist of the sounds \sh\, \t\, a vowel of \ä\ quality, and \t\, but the \ä\ in *Stadt* is not as long as the \ä\ in *Staat*. In our system the German pronunciations are transcribed \ˈshtät\ and \ˈshtäät\ respectively. When such foreign words are pronounced in an English context by one whose native language is English, the durational difference is often lost.

Although the [ä] : [ää] difference in duration serves to distinguish otherwise identical words, as *cod* and *card*, in the *r*-dropping dialects of the southeastern U.S. and New York City, we do not employ [ää] in our symbolization of this difference. In *r*-dropping English speech as a whole there are several values of the vowel spelled *ar* in *card* that make that word distinct from *cod*, and all of these values, including [ää], are subsumed under the symbol \ȧ\.

**\ a(a)(ə) ** \e(ə)\ is to be understood as a variant when it does not appear in a vocabulary transcription, as at *cudbear*.

**\ aaⁿ ** as the sound of the *ein* in the French pronunciation of French *enceinte* — that is, a lengthened \aⁿ\. See section on \ⁿ\.

**\ ääⁿ ** as the sound of the *ande* in the French pronunciation of French *bande* — that is, a lengthened \äⁿ\. See section on \ⁿ\.

**\ a(a)rV ** \erV\ and \ārV\ are to be understood as variants when they do not appear in a vocabulary transcription, as at *myaria*.

accentuation see the section on stress marks.

**\ ai ** articulated as a tense monophthong with the tongue higher than for \a\ or as a diphthong having approximately the beginning and ending limits indicated by the \ai\ transcription. Although using the two-symbol transcription is more convenient than devising another diacritic, the sound is in its less emphatic utterances at least a monophthong.

It occurs before some but not all of the consonants listed in classification (4) in the section on \aa\ and \aaə\; it does not occur in words that belong to the other three classifications there; and it occurs before one consonant not listed in any of the four classifications there — the nasal \ŋ\. The occurrence of \ai\ in the dialect of a native of southern Illinois compares as follows with the occurrence of \aa(ə)\ : \ai\ is almost invariable before \g\ even in syllables far removed from the last but does not occur before \b\ and \j\ and occurs before \d\ only in a few words (*bad, glad, mad*), chiefly when they are emphatic. \ai\ occurs before \f\, \v\, \th\, \th̲\, and \s\ chiefly in final and near-final syllables (as in *half, bath, baths*, the variant \ˈshaivz\ of *shafts*, and *pass*) and before \sh\ even in syllables distant from the last (as in *passionate*); it does not occur before \z\ (in *jazz* for instance) nor in emphatic *have* or *has to*. \ai\ does not occur before \m\ or \n\ when one of these is the only consonant that follows (as in *ram, ran*, except that *man* may have \ai\ when it is emphatic, as in the interjectional phrase "Man oh man!") but it does occur before certain consonant sequences of which \m\ or \n\ is the first member (as in *sample, answer*). Before \ŋ\, \ai\ may occur in any syllable whereas \aa(ə)\ appears not to occur before \ŋ\ at all. In some parts of the southern U.S., particularly in uncultivated speech, the incidence of \ai\ seems to be wider than in the speech just described.

Precisely what the phonetic relationship is between \aa(ə)\ and \ai\ is uncertain. If both are diphthongs in their maximum-stress occurrences, then the difference in the ending positions of the diphthongs (\ə\ in one case, \i\ in the other) constitutes a distinction. If both vowels are in some of their occurrences monophthongs, then the difference is not so palpable. Both are fairly long vowels, and length therefore is an unlikely basis of difference. With some speakers \aa\ is of the same quality and tongue height as \a\ but longer, whereas with speakers who have \ai\, that vowel is always higher than the speaker's \a\ during all or a part of its articulation — *all* if \ai\ is a monophthong, *a part* if \ai\ is a diphthong. When one adds to this the fact that the \a\ (as in *cap*) of many Middle Atlantic speakers is an appreciably different vowel from the \a\ (as in *cap*) of speakers in most of the rest of the country, it is obvious that \aa\ must often be a quite different vowel from monophthongal \ai\. The \a\ in *cap* of many Middle Atlantic speakers is obviously a vowel with considerable \ȧ\ coloration in it. Speakers in other parts of the country use in *cap* a vowel that is much the same in quality (if not in length) as the monophthongal variety of \aa\ vowel in *cast*. Before certain consonants and with some speakers, the Middle Atlantic vowel that we transcribe \aa\ may be the same as the vowel that we transcribe \ai\. Since the words in which \aa(ə)\ is used instead of \a\ and \ai\ is used instead of \a\ are far from being always the same, it would cause difficulty to try to make only one of these two symbols do the work of both in a given transcription.

There are even fewer pairs of words that are distinguished solely by the difference between \a\ and \ai\ than there are pairs that are distinguished solely by the difference between \a\ and \aa(ə)\. In the speech of some *halve* is usually distinct from emphatic *have* and *salvy* from *savvy* in that the first member of each pair

---

*This account is based to a large extent on that of Allan F. Hubbell in his *Pronunciation of English in New York City* (1950) but he is in no way responsible for our interpretation of his data.

has \ai\ and the second \a\. The same is probably true of the pair *bad : bade* in the speech of many.

**\ äi\, \ ȧi ** in the dictionary we have shown no pronunciation for the present participle of the few verbs which have as a final sound \ä\ or \ȧ\ (as *sol-fa*), with the implication that the transcription if shown would be \-äiŋ\, \-ȧiŋ\, \-äēŋ\, \-ȧēŋ\. Since, as stated in the section on \ī\, the first component of the diphthong represented \ī\ is usually \ä\ or \ȧ\ and the second component is or may be \i\, the question arises as to whether the vowel sequence immediately preceding the \ŋ\ of such present participles may not be identical with the sequence in *fine*. For the reasons stated in the section on \ȯi\, random-listening evidence on this matter is difficult to come by. When the last syllable of a verb ending in \ä\ or \ȧ\ is under primary stress (as in *hurrahing*), the \ä\ or \ȧ\ usually seems longer than the \ä\ or \ȧ\ of *fine;* when the \ä\ or \ȧ\ syllable has less than primary stress (as in some utterances of *sol-faing*) the two sequences are more apt to be leveled.

**\ āl ** words transcribed with this succession of symbols, as *sail, alien,* often have \aa(ə)l\ instead in Middle Atlantic speech. The \aa(ə)l\ variant is not shown in transcriptions in the vocabulary.

**\ aⁿ ** see section on \ⁿ\.

**\ äⁿ ** see section on \ⁿ\.

anglicization see section on foreign words.

**\ ār ** occurs in the deep South and in Scotland in words like *barbarian* and *various,* and in Scotland in words like *fair*. In the dictionary \ār\ is not shown for any except Scottish words of the latter type, and is shown only for common words of the former type.

**\ au̇ ** as the sound of *ow* in *now, ou* in *loud,* and *ou* in *out,* and used by many instead of \al\ in some words when certain labial or velar consonants follow, as in *scalp, Ralph, album, valve, talcum.* When \au̇\ is not an alternative to \al\, the first part of the diphthong may have a range from unrounded \ä\ to \e\, the \e\ occurring especially in dialect. The in-between varieties with \a\ or \ȧ\ are commoner, and it is difficult to be sure whether one is hearing \a\ or \ȧ\ unless there is prolongation of this part of the diphthong, as in the speech of some areas. \ȧ\ or an equivalent is the symbol usually employed for the first part of the sound, but fully as good a case can be made for \a\. There may be prejudice against the use of \a\ because of the exaggerated length of this sound in the diphthong often heard in styles of Southern speech regarded by many as substandard. Such length is not a necessary concomitant of the sound in this diphthong.

In a coastal area of the southern U.S. extending from Virginia to So. Carolina and in some areas of eastern Canada, still another variety of this diphthong occurs — one in which the first element is \ə\ or \ə̄\ or \ō\. Those who have this variety in their speech have the other also, the first occurring before voiceless consonants (as in *out*) and the second before voiced consonants and finally (as in *loud, now*). Although the two varieties strike even the most untrained ear as widely different, it is not necessary to have two different symbols since their occurrence is determined by the phonetic context.

When \au̇\ is alternative to \al\, the range of \a\ is no wider than that of \a\ when it is followed by a sound other than \u̇\. Although using \au̇\ in the transcription of one class of words in which there is and of another class in which there is not a wide range of variation is not an ideal procedure, neither are the other two possibilities: (1) using \au̇\ as the alternative to \al\ but \ȧu̇\ or some other variant for words of the type *out* and *loud;* this would not as readily convey the information that the diphthong in the two classes may be identical; (2) giving the full range of at least five variants for words like *out* and *loud* but only \au̇\ when the variant is \al\. This would have made transcribing too space- and time-consuming.

Although we do not show the possibility in vocabulary pronunciations, with some speakers who have \a\ as the first element of their diphthong in *loud,* the sequence of sounds that we transcribe \al\ in some words and \au̇l\ in others, depending on the spelling, is probably actually \au̇l\ in both classes. Such pairs as *Al : owl, Cal : cowl, Hal : howel, Halley : Howley, Alice Ide : owl aside* are sometimes identical (the second member of the \l\-final pairs is subject to the intrusion of a parasitic \ə\ sound after the \u̇\, the first is not). The variety of \l\ used by most Americans outside the South in words such as those cited is known as the dark variety, in which the back of the tongue is in a position for \u̇\ or a neighboring vowel. Since the back of the tongue must reach this position before the tip makes the contact for the articulation of an \l\, the intrusion of an \u̇\ or of a closely related vowel sound seems highly probable.

The use of \au̇\ instead of \al\ before \y\, as in *medallion, Italian,* belongs chiefly to substandard speech. See section on \l\.

**\ b ** as in *baby, knob.*

**\ b̲ ** as in the Spanish pronunciation of *hablar*. Whereas for \b\ the lips are in contact and form a closure along their entire extent, for \b̲\ the lips are close together without closure.

brackets, square [ ] lightface square brackets are used in this guide instead of slant enclosures to enclose transcriptions that are phonetic rather than phonemic.

British dialect see section on foreign words.

centered period see separate section on "Divisions in Respelled Pronunciations".

**\ ch ** based on English orthography, for the sound \t\ followed by the sound \sh\ in the same syllable, as in *chin, pitcher, fixture, Christian.* The sounds that come between the two vowels in the words *cha-cha* (dance) and *hotshot* can in both cases be regarded as \t\ followed by \sh\ but as being in the same syllable in the first (\ˈchä,chä\) and distributed between the two syllables in the second (\ˈhät,shät\). If our transcription for what precedes the first vowel in *cha-cha* had been \tsh\, the transcription for *cha-cha* and *hotshot* would have been \ˈtshä-,tshä\ and \ˈhät-,shät\ respectively.

For words of the type *mention, essential,* and *provincial,* transcriptions of the type \-nshən\ and \-nshəl\ have enjoyed a long tradition in dictionaries. At least in American speech and in common words of this type \t\ almost always intrudes between the \n\ and \sh\, and we transcribe \-nchən\ and \-nchəl\.

comparatives of adjectives see sections on INFLECTED FORMS, DIVISION OF and on INFLECTED FORMS, PRONUNCIATION OF.

correctness in pronunciation

The term *correct pronunciation* is often used. Yet it is probable that many who use the term would find it difficult to give a precise and clear definition of the sense in which they use it. As every kind of correctness implies a standard of measurement, so in pronunciation it is intimately bound up with the question of standard pronunciation. It has been stated that there are certain extensive regional types of cultivated English speech that have spread far beyond the area of their local origin, as the southern British or American speech is which *r* is not dropped. It might be reasonably maintained that it would be incorrect for an educated native of London or Oxford to say \ˈask\ or to pronounce the *r* in *farm,* just as it would be incorrect for the midwestern American to say \ˈȧsk\ or \ˈfȧm\; for in both cases it is contrary to the standard which prevails in each region. From the nature of the case, when the essential facts are considered, correctness of pronunciation must be a flexible term. It is perhaps as accurate a definition as can be made to say that a pronunciation is correct when it is in actual use by a sufficient number of cultivated speakers. This is obviously elastic, depending both on knowledge — never accurately ascertainable — of the number of users, and on judgment as to the cultivation of the speakers. Mere majorities, without consideration of historical linguistic background and regional distribution, are not decisive. For example, the fact that more speakers in the English-speaking world habitually use *R* American than any other single type cannot vitiate the standing of the southern British pronunciation for the educated Englishman.

It has been frequently maintained, and more often assumed, that some single type should be looked upon as solely standard. But this is not the prevailing view of those who are familiar with the essential facts (the detailed differences of pronunciation in the different types, their historical development and relations, the various conditions — chiefly uncontrollable — which in the past have brought certain types into prominence) and who, therefore, possess that breadth of view and freedom from local prejudice that result from acquaintance with those phonetic features, often strikingly different, that have attained to approved usage in the standard types of English and other languages. The following statements are worthy of consideration:

Daniel Jones, M.A., emeritus head of the department of Phonetics, University College, London:

"I have no intention of becoming either a reformer of pronunciation or a judge who decides what pronunciations are 'good' and what are 'bad'. My aim is to observe and record accurately, and I do not believe in the feasibility of imposing one particular form of pronunciation on the English-speaking world. I take the view that people should be allowed to speak as they like. And if the public wants a standardized pronunciation, I have no doubt that some appropriate standard will evolve itself. If there are any who think otherwise, it must be left to them to undertake the invidious task of deciding what is to be approved and what is to be condemned" — from *English Pronouncing Dictionary,* N.Y., 1956, p. xvi.

"I do not consider it possible at the present time to regard any special type as 'Standard' or as intrinsically 'better' than other types." . . . "The term 'Received Pronunciation' . . . is often used to designate this type of pronunciation. This term is adopted here for want of a better. I wish it, however, to be understood that other types of pronunciation exist which may be considered equally 'good' " — from *An Outline of English Phonetics,* 8th ed., N.Y., 1956, p. 12.

A. Lloyd James, M.A., late University reader in Phonetics, School of Oriental Studies, London; linguistic adviser to the British Broadcasting Corporation; and secretary of the B.B.C. Advisory Committee on Spoken English:

"The listener who writes to ask the 'correct way' of pronouncing a word quite evidently assumes that there *is* a 'correct way'. In all these queries and criticisms there is implied the idea of a standard pronunciation. We have a standard yard, a standard pound weight, a standard sovereign, and a standard pint. The yard does not vary from Aberdeen to Plymouth, and the pint pot contains as much in Mayfair as in Bethnal Green. Unfortunately speech is not capable of rigid measurement, and there is no standard of pronunciation. Pronunciation varies from district to district, from class to class, from character to character, in proportion to the local, social, or moral difference that separates them. . . . It is quite evident that we are not entitled to conclude that there is *one* standard pronunciation, *one* and *only one* right way of speaking English. There are varieties that are acceptable throughout the country, and others that are not" — from *Broadcast English,* I., 2d ed., London, 1931, pp. 11 f.

Samuel Moore, Ph.D., late professor of English in the University of Michigan, and editor of the *Middle English Dictionary:*

"When we consider all the varieties of English spoken by those who are admitted to speak 'good English' in the different British colonies and in different parts of the United States, we must recognize that there is still no Standard Spoken English in any strict sense of the term. In every part of the English-speaking world some type of spoken English, that which is used by the educated and superior class within the community, is considered 'good English', as contrasted with the 'Vulgar English' and local dialects spoken by other classes of the community. If we use the term Standard Spoken English at all we must recognize that it is merely a convenient way of speaking of the various kinds of 'good English' that are current in various parts of the English-speaking world" — from *Historical Outlines of English Phonology and Morphology,* 1929, p. 114.

George Philip Krapp, Ph.D., late professor of English in Columbia University:

"A sufficient definition of the term standard will perhaps be found in the statement that speech is standard when it passes current in actual use among persons who must be accounted as among the conservers and representatives of the approved social traditions of a community" — from *The English Language in America,* N.Y., 1925, II, 7.

Edward S. Sheldon, late professor of Romance Languages in Harvard University, and editor of etymologies for Webster's *International,* 1909, and *New International Dictionaries,* Second Edition, 1934:

"The so-called standard language is not a fixed and infallible standard, but is itself constantly changing with the course of time, and is different in the different places where it is spoken" — from "What is a Dialect?" *Dialect Notes,* I, 287.

Otto Jespersen, late professor of English in the University of Copenhagen:

"Our chief concern will be with the normal speech of the educated class, what may be called Standard English" — from *Essentials of English Grammar,* N.Y. [1933], p. 16.

The question, what degree of uniformity exists in the various cultivated types of English speech, depends on what differences one chooses to emphasize, and what to ignore. At present all cultivated types, when well spoken, are easily intelligible to any speaker of English, and there is a very large percentage of practical identity in the speech sounds used. For example, it has been found that, in a thousand words from *The Legend of Sleepy Hollow* as they would be pronounced by a native of Rochester, N.Y., and a native of London, respectively, there are 125 words that would differ in the use of \r\, 36 in the sound of *o* as in *not,* 11 in the sound of *a* as in *ask,* and 4 in the use of the secondary accent. These four differences may be looked upon as the differences of pronunciation in the two types most noticeable to the average person, and one of these, the short *o,* might often pass unnoticed. In most other respects the same phonetic symbols would be used to represent the two types.

Since the establishment of orthoepy as a feature of English dictionaries, the standard assumed has been considerably changed, and has of necessity been made broader. While usage is still and must always be the standard, it is no longer the usage of a particular locality, since the pronunciation of no one locality can now claim admitted precedence. Nor can the pronunciation of any one person, or group of persons, be taken as a standard for all, for such pronunciation is in some cases more advanced, in others more archaic, than the average. Orthoepists of former generations are authorities for the present generation only in so far as their work agrees with good present usage.

The standard of English pronunciation, then, so far as a standard may be said to exist, is the usage that now prevails among the educated and cultured people to whom the language is vernacular; but, as shown above, since somewhat different pronunciations are used by the cultivated in different regions too large to be ignored, we must admit the fact that uniformity of pronunciation is not to be found throughout the English⸗speaking world, though there is a very large percentage of practical uniformity.

The function of a pronouncing dictionary is to record as far as possible the pronunciations prevailing in the best present usage rather than to attempt to dictate what that usage should be. In so far as a dictionary may be known and acknowledged as a faithful recorder and interpreter of such usage, so far and no farther may it be appealed to as an authority.

In the case of diverse usages of extensive prevalence, the dictionary must recognize each of them.

There is a constantly increasing body of technical terms which, being more often written than spoken, are often called "book words". For many of these no accepted usage can properly be said to exist, and their pronunciations must be determined on the analogies of words more often spoken, or according to the accepted rules of pronunciation for the languages from which they are derived.

\d as in *dried, deduce*. See section on \d·\ immediately following.

\d· when one starts from pause and utters the word *die*, the consonant is produced by breaking a closure produced by the tongue against the front of the palate, to the accompaniment of vibration of the vocal cords. When one starts from pause and utters the word *tie*, the consonant is produced by breaking the same closure but without vibration of the vocal cords. The basic difference between the two sounds is that one is voiced and the other is voiceless, and when hearing conditions are not unfavorable, the two can usually be easily enough distinguished without the help of context. In the pronunciation of the *dd* of *ladder* and of the *tt* of *latter* used by some speakers (British, most consistently), the same readily heard distinction is made. Most U.S. speakers, however, do not use closure (stop) consonants in the words *ladder* and *latter* but a voiced flap consonant and the two words cannot be distinguished out of context. This flap consonant is either very similar to or identical with the sound often heard from British speakers for the *r* of *very*, the spelling *veddy* often being used by Americans to mimic this pronunciation.

The voiced flap consonant appears to be normal for *d(d)* in American speech when a vowel immediately precedes and a vowel or \ᵊl\ immediately follows, regardless of the stress of the two syllables (*ladder, tidal, parody, made-up, grade A, adorn*). It also appears to be normal for *t(t)* in American speech in the same environment when the second vowel is unstressed (*latter, title, parity*) and when the second word is stressed and *t(t)* ends a word or a word within a word (*at Omaha, pick it up, great A, butt end, separatism*). In words in which *t(t)* is not word-final, a vowel with primary stress precedes, and a vowel with secondary stress follows, both the flap and the voiceless stop (\t\) are quite common (*veto, Hittite, Mithridates*). Exceptionally, the flap is fairly frequent for the first *t* of *potato* (and is, of course, usual for the second *t*).

Some speakers seem to level *d(d)* and *t(t)* before \ᵊn\, in pairs like *ridden : written*. Such leveling is not as familiar to us and has not been shown in our transcriptions. The leveling sound before \ᵊn\ is probably a voiced stop rather than a flap.

Most transcribers use a special symbol for the flapped sound. We have employed another approach, however. As previously pointed out, when one starts from pause and pronounces *die* or *tie*, the beginning sound is a stop, voiced for *die*, voiceless for *tie*. The voiced flap sound does not occur finally before a pause but a typical occurrence of it is for word-final, and hence syllable⸗final, *t(t)* before a vowel. The flap that occurs for *d(d)* and *t(t)* in American English is always a single sound that follows a vowel and precedes a vowel or syllabic consonant (the \r\ that occurs in *r*-keeping speech in a word like *forty* is more vowel than consonant — see the section on \r\). Vowels and syllabic consonants are syllable nuclei, and there is accordingly a syllable boundary between what precedes and what follows the voiced flap sound. It has seemed altogether practicable to treat the alveolar voiced stop \d\ as a syllable-initial \d\ (transcription \·d\) and to treat the alveolar voiced flap as a syllable-final \d\ (transcription \d·\). Since both the flap and the voiced alveolar stops are heard for intervocalic *d(d)*, the syllable divisor · is not used in the transcription of such words. Since a voiced stop is not used for *t(t)* before a vowel or \ᵊl\, the flap pronunciation of such words is always indicated by placing the · after the \d\. For all *t(t)* words that are commonly pronounced with the voiced flap in American English, a pronunciation with the voiceless alveolar stop is usual in some dialects (as British) and occurs with more or less frequency, especially for emphasis, as an alternative pronunciation. Examples of our transcription of *d(d)* and *t(t)* before a vowel or \ᵊl\:

ladder \ˈladə(r)\ (=\ˈlad·ə(r)\ *or* \ˈla·də(r)\)

latter \ˈlad·ə(r), -atə(r)\ (\ˈla·də(r)\ is not a normal pronunciation)

editor \ˈedəd·ə(r), -ətə(r)\

competitor \kəmˈped·əd·ə(r), -etətə(r)\ (this formula is to be understood as also covering a permutation like \-ed·ətə(r)\)

adapt \əˈdapt\ (=\ə·ˈdapt\ *or* \əd·ˈapt\)

attack \əˈtak\

For uncommon *t(t)* words, usually only the \d·\ variant is shown in the vocabulary. \t\ is always to be understood as an acceptable variant of \d·\.

Some observers who grant the leveling of the consonant in pairs like *ladder : latter* insist that the pairs are nevertheless distinct in that the vowel preceding the consonant is longer for the *d(d)* than for the *t(t)* word. We have not been sufficiently convinced of such a distinction to show it.

When *t* is initial in a word with an unstressed vowel or first vowel and follows without pause a word ending with a voiced consonant, or when in the same word *t* precedes an unstressed vowel and is preceded by a voiced consonant which in turn is preceded by an unstressed vowel, the *t* is probably often a stop \d\ (not \d·\), as in *a dog to watch, hang together, seventy*.

dissimilation see the vocabulary definition. \r\ dissimilation by *R* speakers (see section on *R*) is the most frequent kind in English. When the \r\ affected is preconsonantal, or word-final and therefore potentially prepausal, it is necessary to use the labels *R* and *–R* in order to make it clear that the omission occurs in *R* speech. A mere transcription \sə(r)ˈprīz\ at *surprise*, for example, would justifiably be interpreted as meaning that \sərˈprīz\ is the *R* and \səˈprīz\ the *–R* pronunciation, whereas actually \səˈprīz\ is frequent *R* as well.

Dissimilation of \l\ is probably next most frequent after \r\ in English, probably accounting, for example, for the frequent pronouncing of only the second *l* of *ophthalmologist* and *Guadalcanal* and of only the first *l* of *Wilhelmina*. (The last two words are not included in the vocabulary.)

ditto mark see 2.8.1, 2.8.2 in "Explanatory Notes".

division see "Divisions in Respelled Pronunciations" following \zü\. There is also an earlier section entitled "Divisions in Boldface Entry Words", not strictly in the field of pronunciation although to a great extent determined by pronunciation.

double hyphen (⸗) see 2.7.1, 2.7.2 in "Explanatory Notes".

doubling the doubling or repeating of a symbol indicates a sound of greater duration than is indicated by the symbol standing single. In the variants \ˈmanlē\ and \ˈmaanlē\ for *manly*, \aa\ is a vowel of greater duration than \a\; in \ˈshtäät\, German pronunciation of German *Staat*, and \ˈshtät\, German pronunciation of German *Stadt*, \ää\ is a vowel of greater duration than \ä\; in \ˈhīnəs\ *highness* and \ˈfīnnəs\ *fineness*, \nn\ is a consonant of greater duration than \n\. In the case of vowels, there may be a slight difference of quality in addition to the difference in duration but it is not necessary to transcribe this too: it can be regarded as a by-product of the lengthening.

Because of the practices of English orthography and of other pronunciation alphabets, a word of warning is necessary about certain of these doubled symbols that will be found in transcriptions of foreign words and phrases. \ee\ is a vowel having a quality like that of the *e* in *red* but of greater duration, not a vowel having the quality of the *ee* in *reed;* \ō ō\ and \ȯȯ\ are long vowels having a quality like that of the *o* in *coerce* and the *o* in *sort* respectively, not vowels having the quality of the *oo* in *boot* or *foot*.

\e as in *bet, bed*, and the first syllable of *merry;* in some American speech, the vowel of the first syllable of *marry* and the vowel or the core vowel of words like *bear* and *bare*.

Some speakers who have \a\ or \aa\ in most words of the type *bear, bare*, have \e\ in a small number of words of this type (among them *care, chair, scare, scarce*, emphatic *where*) in which the preceding sound is articulated with the tongue high in the mouth. Apparently by assimilative influence, the \a(a)\ is replaced by the higher \e\.

Some speakers have \a\ or \aa\ in emphatic *there* but \e\ in emphatic *their* and in *theirs*.

In words of the type *barbarian, various*, the same speakers have \e\ in some and \a(a)\ in others. Some appear to interchange \e\ and \a(a)\ in the same word. In the deep South and in Scottish, \ā\ occurs in these words. For uncommon words, we have usually transcribed \a(a)\. \e\ and \ā\ are always to be understood as variants of this \a(a)\.

\ē as in *beat, bead*, and the first syllable of *beady*, and the unstressed vowel used by most American speakers, and apparently also by most Canadian and Australian speakers, in the second syllable of *lady, cities*, and as a prevocalic in *piano, serious, meander*. In some parts of the southern U.S., \i\ appears to prevail in these unstressed syllables, and British phoneticians transcribe \i\ although reporting that the British vowel is sometimes \e\ (vowel of *bet*) or something approaching it. \i\ is favored by some who, while admitting that \ē\ better represents the quality of the usual American vowel, have misgivings that \ē\ in transcriptions may foster a tendency to overpronounce (i.e., to pronounce an \ē\ with full secondary stress).

To hold down the number of variants in transcriptions, only \ē\ has been shown for the *i* of *piano* and *serious* and the first *e* of *meander*. It may be, as some transcribers appear to believe, that \ē\ is used in such words by speakers who have \i\ in *lady*, but \i\ is surely frequent enough to justify the blanket recognition here of \i\ as an always-to-be-understood variant of unstressed \ē\.

\ee used only in the transcription of words from foreign languages; of long duration and with a quality like that of the *e* in English *red*, not like that of *ee* in English *reed*.

\ēr occurs in the deep South and in Scotland in words like *serial, serious, weary*, and in Scotland in words like *hear, mere, veer*.

It is not shown for any except Scottish words of the latter type, and is shown only for common words of the former type.

\eu̇ as a frequent variant of \el\ when certain consonant sounds follow, as in *elk, elm, help, twelve*. The use of \eu̇\ instead of \el\ before \y\, as in *hellion, rebellious*, belongs chiefly to substandard speech. See section on \l\.

\f as in *five, traffic, puff*.

foreign words for foreign words borrowed unchanged into English and italicized by some writers to signify that they are regarded as falling short of complete naturalization, we nevertheless often show in the vocabulary a pronunciation somewhat anglicized. Even an approximation to some foreign sounds is difficult or impossible for the average speaker of English who does not have a speaking knowledge of the foreign language, and even when a sound close to the foreign sound exists in English it may be passed over in favor of one that is usual in the same environment in English words. Thus the Italian name *Garibaldi* is usually pronounced by English speakers with the first vowel as in *garrison* and the third as in *bald*, although the vowel of *garb* is closer to the one vowel that occurs in both syllables in Italian. The speaker who is sufficiently conversant with the phonetics of a foreign language to be capable and desirous of using the full foreign pronunciation is unlikely to use an English dictionary as a source, and we have accordingly often not given the foreign pronunciation even as a variant. In general we give foreign pronunciations when known usage has shown them or similar pronunciations to be within the capabilities of educated English speakers inexpert in the foreign language, or when no anglicization is known to us to be established and the foreign pattern is such that there is insufficient analogy to make an anglicized pattern safely predictable.

For the same reasons we also show a standard⸗English pronunciation pattern for words or parts of words belonging to British dialect, including Scottish. Thus the vowel of *clat* is shown as \a\, the vowel of *fat* in standard English, and the vowel of *darg* is shown as \ä\, one of the vowels of *bargain* in standard English, although the two words have the same vowel in much British dialect. It seems pointless to give only \a\ for words like *fat* that belong to standard English as well as to British dialect and to give some other vowel for a word like *clat* that belongs exclusively to British dialect and that rhymes with *fat* in that dialect. A dictionary key that tells the speaker of standard English who is completely ignorant of British dialect that *clat* has the vowel of *fat* provides that consultant with a pronunciation that in his ignorance of dialect he would be well advised to use; a speaker of the British dialect Scottish who finds \a\ for *clat* in a dictionary and finds *fat* cited as a key word for \a\ is not misled; a speaker of standard English who knows something about Scottish knows that his vowel in *fat* is not Scottish dialect's vowel in *fat*, and also knows what vowel does occur there instead of his vowel.

French words fully French pronunciations are shown without any stress marks, in accord with the usual practice of transcribers of French.

\g as in *get, got, tiger, big*.

\g̅ as for *g* in Spanish *luego;* a non-English voiced fricative sound, made with the tongue in approximately the position for \g\ in English *go* but without closure.

glottal stop a phonetic effect (symbol \ʔ\) produced by a complete closure in the throat (more specifically, a closure of the vocal cords) that makes it impossible for breath to issue from the lungs. It is the same phenomenon that bottles up the breath before a cough or before the clearing of the throat. In speech it may occur between silence and a sound, between two sounds, or between a sound and silence. In some languages (as standard English, with the exception of a few interjections such as \ʔmʔm\ or \ ʔəʔə\ for *no*), the glottal stop occurs only as an accidental, in some cases almost inevitable, sound, and adds no significance to the context in which it occurs: if it were omitted the meaning of the context would not be altered. Thus, this sound often occurs between \ə\ and a following vowel sound (as in *ultra-atomic, ultraism*) or before the vowel in a vowel-initial word that is under emphasis (as "Eggs!" or, with an intonation of annoyance or disbelief, "Eggs?"). In speech usually regarded as nonstandard and not recorded in this book, the glottal stop in certain contexts replaces \d·\ or \t\ of standard speech, as in \ˈwȯʔə(r)\ for *water.* Omission of the stop in such cases might cause misunderstanding if the context were ambiguous enough, since \ˈwȯə(r)\ is a pronunciation of *war.* In the type of German speech usually regarded as standard, a glottal stop occurs with great frequency before or at the beginning of words stressed on the first syllable and having no consonant letter preceding the first-syllable vowel; it is usually retained when the word follows another member in a compound. Such a glottal stop is symbolized by some transcribers but not by others. Whether it is phonemic or not, it is symbolized in this book in fully German transcriptions of words in which it occurs because its absence hinders ready comprehension by a German listener. We believe that a certain number of departures from strict phonemicity are advisable in the sporadic fully foreign pronunciations.

-gu-, -qu-; division of words containing for the end-of-the-line division of words like *leaguing* and *cataloguer* and *piquing*, in which *gu* is pronounced \g\, *qu* is pronounced \k\, and a following *e* is dropped before a syllable-increasing English suffix is added, see section on inflected forms, division of.

When the pronounced vowel that follows the *u* is not an English suffix or a part of one, the most satisfactory division between the two syllables is immediately preceding the *g* or *q*, as in *belea·guer, li·quor, che·quered.*

\gy in at least three coastal areas of the South — Virginia, South Carolina, eastern Texas — a \y\ sound often intrudes between \g\ and certain or all of the members of the vowel series from \ē\ to \ä\. Thus, *garden* is often \ˈgyädᵊn\ in Charleston. These variants are not shown in this book.

\h as in *hat, ahead;* in the anglicized pronunciation of Spanish-derived words, \h\ is the usual pronunciation before a stressed vowel of a sound that in some dialects at least of Spanish is \k̲\ — for example, for the *x* of *Don Quixote.*

\hw used for the *wh* of *whet* by speakers whose *whet* and *wet* are not pronounced the same. Some phoneticians regard \hw\ not as two sounds but as one, a voiceless \w\. With most American speakers *whet* and *wet* differ in pronunciation but with most southern British speakers they do not.

\i as in *bit, bid, here, hear.*

\ī as in *try, light, guide, aisle.* \ī\ is a diphthong, not a single sound, with heaviest stress on the first element. Its beginning position ranges from the position for the \ȧ\ heard in *ask* in eastern New England to the position for the unrounded \ä\ heard from most U.S. speakers for the vowel of *hot, heart;* its ending position ranges from that for monophthongal \ā\ to that for \i\. In eastern Virginia and in an area of Canada having Toronto as its metropolis, the position of the first element before voiceless consonants is approximately that of the \ˈə\ of *nut.* In the southern U.S., the second part of the \ȧi\ or \äi\ variety of the diphthong may disappear, and finally and before voiced consonants, less often before voiceless consonants, the pronunciation may be simply \ȧ\ or unrounded \ä\, as in \ˈwȧvz\ or \ˈwävz\ for *wives.*

See section on \äi\.

incomplete pronunciations many of the pronunciations shown in this dictionary are for a part of the entry only and the user is to seek the missing part somewhere else in the dictionary. Two of the most frequently used indicators that a sound symbol or a sequence of sound symbols is not a complete pronunciation for the whole of a boldface entry are the ordinary single hyphen and the vertical bar (for the latter see the paragraph on | and 2.6 of "Explanatory Notes"). A hyphen at the left-hand side of a roman-type item within reversed virgules means that something is missing at the beginning (\-līn\); a hyphen at the right-hand side means that something is missing at the end (\ˈkōd-\); a hyphen to both left and right means that something is missing at both beginning and end (\-tȯr-\). If the missing part is the pronunciation of a word or of words pronounced at its or their own alphabetical place in the vocabulary, the missing part should be sought there.

law of ti·ti·us \-ˈtētsēəs\ [missing part at *law* and *of*]
gresh·am's law \ˈgreshəmz-\ [missing part at *law*]

Otherwise the missing part is to be supplied from the corresponding part of a variant pronunciation that appears before a preceding punctuation mark within the same reversed virgules, or from a pronunciation for another spelling that precedes in the same or another entry.

1*sa·line* \ˈsā͵lēn, -līn\ [substitute \ˈsā\ for the hyphen]
cod·i·fy \ˈkädə͵fī, ˈkōd-\ [substitute \ə͵fī\ for the hyphen]
sen·a·to·ri·al \¦senə¦tōrēəl, -tȯr-\ [substitute \¦senə¦\ for the first hyphen and \ēəl\ for the second]
anal·y·sis \əˈnaləsə̇s\ *n, pl* *analy·ses* \-ə͵sēz\ [substitute \əˈnal\ for the hyphen]

1*or·gan·ic* \(ˈ)ȯ(r)¦ganik, -nēk\ . . .
2*organic* \"\ . . .
or·gan·i·cal \-nə̇kəl, -nēk-\ . . .
or·gan·i·cal·ly \-k(ə)lē, -li\ [for the first hyphen at *organical* substitute \(ˈ)ȯ(r)¦ga\ from 1*organic;* for the first hyphen at *organically* substitute \(ˈ)ȯ(r)¦ganə, -nē\ from 1*organic* and *organical*]

We usually repeat something from the preceding pronunciation to indicate where in this pronunciation that which is different in the following pronunciation is to serve as a replacement. Often both something to the left and something to the right of the variant part is repeated. Thus in \ˈsā͵lēn, -līn\ the repeated \l\ and \n\ show that \ī\ may replace the \ē\ between those two characters. A locator repeated may be something other than a sound symbol, as a stress mark or a parenthesis.

per·sist \pə(r)ˈsist *also* -ˈzi-\
cre·do \ˈkrē(͵)dō, ˈkrā(-\

When we use a consonantal locator on one side of a vowel variant and no locator on the other side, it is to be understood that the vowel adjacent to the locator in a following pronunciation replaces the vowel adjacent to the locator in a preceding pronunciation and is not inserted after that vowel. Thus in \ˈkōdə͵sēz, -äd-\ for *codices* at *codex,* \-äd-\ is to be read \ˈkäd-\ not \ˈkōäd-\.

Variants of the vowel of a monosyllable or of a sound whose symbolization differs from that of the variant in that one has a diacritic and the other does not or has a different diacritic are sometimes shown without a locator on either side.

bask \ˈbask, -aa(ə)-,-ai-,-ȧ-\
broomy \ˈbrümē, -u̇-\
hu·chen \ˈhükən, -k̲-\

Printing the last three variants for *bask* without spaces between is merely a space-saving device that we often employ when two or more variants of each other are printed in succession.

If no hyphen or vertical bar appears at the beginning of a pronunciation, the pronunciation for the first part of the word is complete and nothing is to be supplied ahead of what is shown; if no hyphen or vertical bar appears at the end of a pronunciation, the pronunciation for the last part of the word is complete and nothing is to be supplied at the end of what is shown.

1*good-bye or good-by* \gu̇dˈbī, gədˈbī, gəˈbī, ˈbī\ [the last variant, \ˈbī\, is a pronunciation for the entire word and not for only the part *bye* or *by.*]
2*pretty* \. . ., *before 'near' often* ˈpru̇t *or* ˈprit\ [\ē\ or \i\ is not to be supplied at the end of the last two variants. The pronunciations intended are \ˈpru̇tni(ə)r\, etc.]

A user who is familiar with the pronunciation practices of the preceding edition of this work should observe that the giving of variants differs in the two in that in this book no attempt is made to always have a variant begin at a syllable beginning and end at a syllable ending.

inflected forms, division of when no division is shown for an inflected form, a form with zero inflection or a form inflected by the addition of an ending that does not add a syllable may be divided at any point where a division is shown in the inflectional base:

2*mul·let*→ pl *mul·let* or *mul·lets*
in·ter·vene→ *in·ter·vened*→ *in·ter·venes*

If the ending adds a syllable and the spelling of the base does not change, a division may be made between the two components, as well as at any point at which a division is shown in the base:

church→ *church·es*
con·strain→ *con·strained*→ *con·strain·ing*→ *con·strains*
ap·proach→ *ap·proached*→ *ap·proach·ing*→ *ap·proach·es*
re·tort→ *re·tort·ed*→ *re·tort·ing*→ *re·torts*
2*stout*→ *stout·er*→ *stout·est*

In a syllable-increased form in which the final consonant of the inflectional base is doubled, a division is made between the doubled consonants:

re·but→ *re·but·ted*→ *re·but·ting*→ *re·buts*

When both of two identical consonants immediately preceding a syllable-increasing ending belong to the inflectional base, a division is made after the second consonant:

bluff·ing

For variants like *conn/con* a syllable-increased form can be divided in either of two ways:

conn also *con, conn·ing* or *con·ning*

In a syllable-increased form in which a final *e* of the base is dropped before the ending, a division is made between the letter that preceded the *e* and the ending:

rate→ *rat·ed*→ *rat·ing*
glue→ *glu·ing*
plague→ *plagu·ing*
pique→ *piqu·ing*
gro·tesque→ *gro·tesqu·er*→ *gro·tesqu·est*

In syllable-increased forms like those in the last three lines, in which *gu* or *qu,* with *u* silent, appears immediately before the ending, some prefer to divide immediately before the *g* or *q* if it is not immediately preceded by a short vowel or, in the case of *g,* by *n* (*haran·guing* would suggest the substandard pronunciation \həˈraŋgiŋ\):

pi·quing
pla·guing
grotes·quer

For plurals identical in form with the singular, or formed by adding *-s* or *-es,* usually neither pronunciation nor division is shown. For other plurals pronunciation and division are shown, except that (1) divisions common to both plural and singular are usually omitted and (2) the pronunciation and division of the last part of a compound whose last part is an independent English word must usually be sought at the entry for the independent word. The last or the only centered period in a plural is the last point at which a division should be made in it:

ep·i·the·li·um→ pl *epithe·lia*

The plural may be divided like the singular except that no division should be made after that between the *e* and *l.*

The centered period between two consecutive vowels in the plural supersedes a differently placed period between the same two vowels in the singular. In *ge·nus,* pl *gen·era* a division is not to be understood between the *e* and *n* of the plural as well as between the *n* and *e.* It is true, as explained in the section on "Divisions in Boldface Entry Words", that divisions such as *ge·nera* do occur, especially in British publications, but our policy is to show only one division between two consecutive vowels. A plural of the type not needing division and pronunciation does have pronunciation when it is the first variant plural (as at 2*virtuoso* where *virtuosos* is first and *virtuo·si* second). When a plural of this type is the second variant plural, pronunciation and division are omitted (as at *tibia* where *tibi·ae* is first and *tibias* second).

inflected forms, pronunciation of

The pronunciation of any inflected forms not pronounced is the pronunciation shown at the entry for the inflectional base plus the pronunciation or one of the pronunciations shown for the inflectional ending. These ending entries are, for nouns, 1-S, 1-ES; for verbs, 1-ED, 1-ING, 3-S, 2-ES, 2-EST, 1-ETH; for adjectives, 1-ER, 1-EST. The definitions at some of these contain information that will facilitate the ascertainment of the pronunciation for the entire word.

-ing in vocabulary words formed by attaching this ending to a verb, usually no pronunciation is shown, whether the inflected form is a main entry or is a run-on entry, if the pronunciation of that part of the word preceding the *-ing* is the same as the pronunciation of the base verb. When such is not the case, usually the only pronunciation shown for the *-ing* is \-iŋ\ or, for common words entered with hanging indention, \-iŋ, -ēŋ\. It is to be understood, however, that in some dialects or under some circumstances the *-ing* may be otherwise pronounced. See the entry 1-ING in the vocabulary for a detailed list of variants.

\iŋ when stressed, as in *sing, forefinger,* \āŋ\ and perhaps less often \eŋ\ are variants especially in the southern U.S. These variants are not shown. When unstressed, as in *running,* \ēŋ\ is a frequent variant and is shown for words that are common.

\ir\, \iər\, \iə in words of the type of *inferior, hear, pierce,* variants occur that are not shown in the vocabulary or that are not shown for uncommon words.

Words of the type of *inferior* are shown in the vocabulary as containing the sequence \ir\ followed by a vowel. In the deep South they may contain \ēr\ instead of \ir\, and the \ēr\ variant is to be understood for uncommon words for which it is not shown. In southern British speech all words of this type usually have \ə\ between the \i\ and \r\, and some may be pronounced with \yə̄\ instead of \iə\.

Words of the type of *hear* are shown in the vocabulary as having \ir\ or \iər\ in *R* speech and before a vowel in *–R* speech, and as having \iə\ in *–R* speech elsewhere. Words of the type of *pierce* are shown as having \iə\, with no \r\ following, in *–R* speech. In some words of both types \yə̄\ may occur instead of \iə\ in southern

British speech. The same variant occurs in a very few words in which the part of the orthography that answers to \iə\, \yə\ in the pronunciation contains no *r*, as in the *thea* fragment of *theater*.*

\iu̇ as in one pronunciation of the *il* in *film, milk*. See section on \l\.

\j as in *j*ug, ba*dg*e, a*g*ile. Some linguists treat the sound of the italicized letters in the words cited as the sound \d\ followed by the sound \zh\ in the same syllable, others transcribe it with a single symbol.

\k as in *k*i*ck*, pa*ch*yderm, ba*cch*ic.

\k̲ as for *ch* in German *siech* and *Bach;* a non-English voiceless fricative sound, made with the tongue in a range of positions from approximately that of the \k\ in English *keep* to that of the \k\ in English *cool* but without closure.

With particular reference to German, it was formerly the usual transcriptional practice to have two symbols for this range of sounds, one symbol for the front varieties and another for the back varieties. It is now common practice, however, to regard a single symbol as adequate to the phonemic transcription of the entire range of sounds, and the symbol \k̲\ is so used in the transcription of the comparatively small number of words for which a full German pronunciation, or something approaching it, is given. Whether or not a single symbol is adequate for transcribing German for Germans, a single symbol suffices in this book, in which any word or phrase borrowed unchanged in spelling from a foreign language is treated as an item occurring in English context. Whatever variety of \k̲\ may come naturally in a particular word to an educated speaker of English addressing another speaker of English is unlikely to seem out of place in English context. In German the use of one symbol instead of two presents the problem that certain pairs of words (very small in number, apparently) which when spoken in isolation are distinguishable are transcriptionally identical (*Pfauchen, pfauchen*, both \ˈpfäu̇k̲ən\ but with a front \k̲\ in the first and a back \k̲\ in the second). If, as it appears may be the case for all except the intervocalic occurrences of \k̲\, a simple set of rules can be drawn up that will fix its front or back position on the basis of phonetic environment alone, an expediential device for transcribing its quality intervocalically is to treat the front variety as syllable-initial, the back variety as syllable-final, and to employ such transcriptions as \ˈpfäu̇·k̲ən\ *Pfauchen*, \ˈpfäu̇k̲·ən\ *pfauchen*, \äk̲·ˈälis\ *Achelis*.

\ky in at least three coastal areas of the South — Virginia, South Carolina, eastern Texas — a \y\ sound often intrudes between \k\ and certain or all of the members of the vowel series from \ē\ to \ä\. Thus, *card* is often \ˈkyȧd\ in Charleston. These variants are not shown.

\l as in *leaf, loot, police, allude, feel, fool*. Articulations of \l\ vary widely, from the clear *l* in some pronunciations of *leaf* to the dark *l* of *fool*. In both sounds the tip of the tongue is in contact with the teethridge. For the clear *l* the top of the tongue is convex; for the dark *l* the top of the tongue is concave and at the back is in the articulatory position for \ü\ or a neighboring vowel. The clearest *l* in American speech is not as clear as in some foreign languages, and some phoneticians treat all occurrences of \l\ in the speech of most Americans as dark. The almost invariable practice of all transcribers, whatever their views, is to use only one symbol for all varieties in English. In the U.S. the clearest \l\'s occur in the speech of some Southern speakers, whose pronunciation of the intervocalic \l\ in words like *salad, Alice, willing* contrasts sharply with that of Northern speakers. The difference between the two can be shown by the transcriptions \ˈsa·lid\, \ˈa·lis\, \ˈwi·liŋ\ for the Southern speakers and \ˈsal·əd\, \ˈal·əs\, \ˈwil·ēŋ\ for the Northern. It is possible that \ˈsau̇l·əd\ and \ˈau̇l·əs\ (in which \a\ is the vowel of *apt*) would be proper transcriptions for the dark *l* articulations of the first two words and that *Alice* and *owl us* would be rhymes with some speakers. Such transcriptions have not been shown in this book.

When the vowel articulation preceding an \l\ is one that pulls the back of the tongue forward of the dark *l* articulatory position, a very clear \ə\ may result while the tongue is in transition between the two positions. Words like *ale, eel*, and *oil*, in which the last vowel represented by the spelling is front, often have as much of an \ə\ as *betrayal, perigeal*, or *loyal*, especially when a pause or a consonant follows. Before a pause or a consonant, pairs like *reel : ideal, trail : betrayal, vile : vial, oil : royal* may be exact rhymes. The pronunciation with epenthetic \ə\ is shown as a variant for such words. The back vowel \u̇\ in a word like *owl* is so far fronted when the first half of the diphthong has the quality of the \a\ in *pat* that a clear \ə\ frequently intrudes, and the variant with \ə\ is shown in this book. Between other back vowels and \l\ the \ə\ has not been shown although the \ə\ sometimes appears after \ü\ when that vowel is fronted by the articulation of a preceding tongue-front consonant, as in *schedule, mule*.

\u̇\ often occurs, in some dialects at least, instead of \l\ before the lip consonants \p\, \b\, \m\, \f\, \v\, and before the back-of-the-tongue consonant \k\, especially when these consonants are word-final — that is, only the back half of the articulation of a dark *l* occurs, the contact between tongue tip and teethridge being absent: *help, bulb, elm, self, twelve, elk*. With some Southern speakers, *help, self*, and *twelve* have nothing whatever corresponding to an *l*.

Less often than in the class of words just mentioned, \u̇\ occurs instead of \l\ when \y\ immediately follows, as in *million, hellion*. The \u̇\ variant is not shown before \y\ in this book.

\l^{ə} as in one pronunciation of French *peuple*. Like \$^{ə}$l\, \l^{ə}\ is a single sound differing from \$^{ə}$l\ in being voiceless rather than voiced and in not adding an extra syllable, the \pœpl^{ə}\ pronunciation of *peuple* being a single syllable. The \$^{ə}$\ after the \l\ is always parenthesized to indicate the usual pronunciation when a vowel-initial word follows without pause. Thus *peuple anglais* is \pœ plä^{n} glā\, three syllables, with \pl\ as in French *plaisir*. Compare section on \$^{ə}$\.

\lch as in *belch, gulch;* sometimes \lsh\ in U.S. speech and more often so in British speech.

-lds usually no pronunciation is shown for noun and verb inflected forms produced by adding *-s* to a base in *-ld*, as *fields, welds*. The pronunciation \l(d)z\ is to be understood.

\lü as in *lute, lewd, clue, ablution, absolute, revolution;* that is, words in which the orthographic representation is not *loo* and which are mostly from Latin and Greek. In words like the first three, the variant \lyü\ (=\lyü\ or \liü\) appears to be frequent in southern British speech but is rare in U.S. speech and is not shown. In words like the last two, in which the \l\ is intervocalic and the sequence \lyü\ can easily be syllabicated \l·yü\ instead of \·lyü\, the variant with \y\ is less rare in the U.S. and is shown after an *also*.

\l^{y} as *gli* in Italian *figlio* and *ll* in the Castilian Spanish pronunciation of *olla;* the sound can be approximated by trying to pronounce \l\ while the tip of the tongue is held behind the lower front teeth.

\m as in *maim, hammer, nymph;* the usual articulation of \m\ is with the lips in contact to form a closure but when an \f\ or \v\ sound immediately precedes or follows the closure is made by the lower lip against the upper front teeth, as in *nymph, triumph, triumvir, Hoffman(n)* and the pronunciation \ˈsev^{ə}m\ for *seven*.

\m^{ə} as in one pronunciation of French *prisme;* \m^{ə}\ is a single sound differing from \$^{ə}$m\ in being voiceless rather than voiced and in not adding an extra syllable, the \prēsm^{ə}\ or \-ēzm^{ə}\ pronunciation of *prisme* being a single syllable. The \$^{ə}$\ after the \m\ is always parenthesized to indicate the usual pronunciation when a vowel-initial word follows without pause. Thus *prisme oblique* is \prē smȯ blēk\ or \prēz mȯ blēk\, three syllables, with \m\ as in French *smille* or *mille*. Compare section on \$^{ə}$\.

\n as in *known, manly, enrage, tenth*.

**\$^{n}$** indicates that the preceding vowel is pronounced through the nose, that is, with the velum lowered and the nostrils open at the back. Vowels are not infrequently so uttered in American English but the nasality is an accident and a nasal vowel does not function as something different from the same vowel without the nasality. In some languages, however, as French and Portuguese, the difference between a vowel without nasality and the same vowel with nasality may make two different words of two sequences of sounds otherwise identical. French has four nasal vowels and they are often exemplified by the four-word phase *un bon vin blanc* ("a good white wine"), which in our symbols would be transcribed \œ^{n}bō^{n}va^{n}blä^{n}\.

In a transcription like \kōō^{n}t\ at *comte*, in which \ōō\ indicates a sound the same in quality as \ō\ but of greater duration (not a vowel with the quality of *oo* in English *boot*), the diacritic \$^{n}$\ applies to both preceding characters.

-nds usually no pronunciation is shown for noun and verb inflected forms produced by adding *-s* to a base in *-nd*, as *friends, sends*. The pronunciation \n(d)z\ is to be understood.

ng see section on \ŋ\.

\n^{y} as *gn* in French *agneau* and Italian *bagno* and *ñ* in Spanish *cañón*. The sound can be approximated by trying to pronounce \n\ while the tip of the tongue is held behind the lower front teeth.

\ŋ as in *hang* \ˈhaŋ\, *hanger* \ˈhaŋə(r)\, *anger* \ˈaŋgə(r)\, *singer* \ˈsiŋə(r)\, *finger* \ˈfiŋgə(r)\, *linger* \ˈliŋgə(r)\. The sound of the *ng* in *hang* and of the *n* in *anger* is a single sound not the sound \n\ followed by the sound \g\, although the transcription \ng\ for this single sound is used in some of the smaller members of this series to avoid the use of characters that are not letters of the ordinary English alphabet.

\ō as in *bone, snow, coerce;* \ō\ has a strong tendency to become diphthongal, with \u̇\ as a second element, when it is in a position of emphasis, as when it is word-final, under primary stress, and before a pause. In southern British speech and in some American speech, especially in the Philadelphia area, the diphthongization is more frequent and the first element is often \ə\ or \ə̄\. The symbol \ō\ is to be understood to cover all these variants.

In a group of some fifty words, chiefly monosyllables, and their derivatives, transcribed with \ō\, some New England speakers, chiefly rural, have a vowel that has been described, and that apparently is articulated, in more than one way but that sounds to most ears unaccustomed to it like the vowel of *cut*. At least some New England speakers make homophones of *cut* and *coat*. The users of this vowel constitute only a small fraction of the English-speaking world and appear to be on the decrease, and so this variant is not shown.

In a small area that includes the cities of Charleston and Savannah, words transcribed with \ō\ followed by a consonant often have \ōə\ instead, as in \ˈkōət\ for *coat*. This variant is not shown.

\ȯ as in *corn, saw, all, cause*. In the southern U.S., there is often a diphthongal variant (not used in this book) for at least all of the key words cited except *corn*. In this variant the first element is much the same as the monophthong that occurs with other speakers in these words and the second element is \u̇\ or even \ü\.

\œ as in French *bœuf*, German *Hölle;* \œ\ can be approximated by pronouncing \e\ with moderately rounded lips.

\œ̄ as in French *feu*, German *Höhle;* \œ̄\ can be approximated by pronouncing \ā\ with strongly rounded lips.

\œ^{n} see section on \$^{n}$\.

\ȯi as in *coin, boy*. In the southern U.S. and chiefly before a consonant in the same word, the second element is sometimes lost or replaced by \ə\. Random listening for misapprehension of two-morpheme items as one-morpheme and vice versa is not as productive of evidence for these pairs as it is for certain other pairs whose identity is disputed — e.g., for *latter : ladder* and *a name : an aim*. Even for these common items, highly ambiguous contexts are infrequent, and there are no or few words in *-oing* in English and but few in *-awy*. With most Americans speaking at normal tempo occurrences of \ȯ\ followed by \i\ without pause are phonetically identical, regardless of whether the two components belong to the same morpheme or to two. Whether, however, such sequences are to be regarded as one syllable or two is a more difficult matter. But *strawy* and the last part of *destroy* are identical, and *coin* and *boy* are more disyllabic than monosyllabic. In the speech of New York City the first half of the diphthong \ȯi\ is overlong.

In transcriptions of the full German pronunciation of German words, \ȯi\ is used for the vowel sequence of words like *neu*, whose second member in German is usually a lip-rounded vowel more properly transcribed \ȯœ\ or \ȯœ̄\.

\ō^{n} see section on \$^{n}$\.

\ōō used only in the transcription of words from foreign languages; of long duration and with a quality like that of the *o* in English *coerce*, not like that of *oo* in English *boot*.

\ȯȯ used only in the transcription of words from foreign languages; of long duration and with a quality like that of the *o* in English *sort*, not like that of *oo* in English *foot* or *boot*.

\ōō^{n} as \ōō\ nasalized, as in French *comte*. See sections on \ōō\ and on \$^{n}$\.

\ōr as in *board, boarder, glory;* many speakers have this sequence in their speech only when the \ō\ and the \r\ belong to separate morphemes, as in *pro rata* and the \ə\-less pronunciation of *grower*. With these speakers, in other items \ȯ\ occurs instead of \ō\. For words common in the literary language, both the \ō\ and \ȯ\ variants are shown. For other words, usually only the \ō\ variant is shown and the \ȯ\ variant is to be understood. Thus, only \-ōr-\ is shown at *auctorial* and \-ȯr-\ is to be understood, as can be ascertained

*Daniel Jones, *Outline of English Phonetics*, New York (1956), §442*a*.

by examining the transcription at the entry for a common word (like *editorial*) for which \-ōrēəl\ is the first variant shown; only \-fō(ə)r\ is shown at *gonophore* and \-fȯ(ə)r\ is to be understood, as well as \-fōə\ and \-fȯ(ə)\ for *r*-droppers, as can be seen by examining the transcription for a common word like *semaphore*.

In words like *glory* and *glorious*, in which a vowel follows the \ōr\, the pronunciation of many speakers in the deep South, whose vowel is \ōə\, is appreciably different from the pronunciation of others in the South and from that of speakers in other parts of the country who have \ōr\ rather than \ȯr\, in that with the first group the \r\ is more consonantal than with the second group, whose \r\ is in the nature of the second half of a diphthong. The first variant may be transcribed \ˈglō·ri\, the second and probably more common variant \ˈglōr·ē, -ōr·i\.

\ȯr as in *moral, horrible*, in which a vowel follows the \r\. Both \ȯr\ and \är\ occur in these words in U. S. speech. \är\ strongly predominates in the South, and is frequent along the Atlantic coast in the North. \är\ strongly predominates in British speech, where the \ä\ is usually somewhat lip-rounded and different from the \ä\ of most U. S. speech. \ȯr\ probably prevails in the U. S. and is shown first for nearly all words for which both variants are shown. For words of this group not common in literary English, usually only the \ȯr\ variant is shown but the \är\ variant is to be understood. For a few such words in which the \r\ is or may be followed by \ō\, as *borrow* and *sorrow*, many have \är\ who have \ȯr\ in other words of the group. The pronunciation for words like *borrow* is shown as \är *also* ȯr\. Dissimilation has been suggested as an explanation of the difference. \är\ is not to be understood for \ȯr\ in words in which the vowel that follows the \r\ is that of a suffix freely addable to English words. \är\ is quite normal for *abhorrence* and *abhorrent*, but if it occurs for *abhorring* or *abhorrer* it probably does so from the analogy of a word like *abhorrence*. The analogy of *horror*, for example, for which \är\ is a normal variant, may sometimes produce \är\ in *abhorrer*.

\p as in *pay, lip, upper*.

phonemicity our endeavor has been to make the transcriptions of fully English items phonemic. Because of the inevitability, however, that they will not in every respect agree with every evaluator's ideas of phonemicity, and because we have deliberately not striven for phonemicity in our transcription of certain nonanglicized pronunciations, we enclose our transcriptions in virgules having a slant the opposite of the virgules conventionally employed for phonemic transcription. In the comparatively small number of nonanglicized pronunciations of words from foreign languages that occur in this dictionary of the English language, we have transcribed a variant that is purely allophonic in the foreign language (for example, the [ŋ] variant of \n\ in Spanish and Italian) if the variation is phonemic in English.

plurals see sections on INFLECTED FORMS, DIVISION OF and on INFLECTED FORMS, PRONUNCIATION OF.

present participles many present participles have two pronunciations, one that is the pronunciation of the base verb or of one form of it plus the pronunciation shown in the vocabulary for *-ing*, a second with one syllable less.

> [1]*flick·er* \ˈflikə(r)\ . . . *flickering* \-k(ə)riŋ\ [i.e., the present participle is \ˈflikəriŋ\ or \ˈflikriŋ\]
>
> *fat·ten* \ˈfatᵊn\ . . . *fattening* \-t(ᵊ)niŋ\ [i.e., the present participle is \ˈfatᵊniŋ\ or \ˈfatniŋ\]

When such a variation occurs, at all but wholly dialect or very rare verbs the present participle is subentered and pronounced. Usually only \-iŋ\ is shown at the end but it is to be understood that other variants of \-iŋ\ may occur; see [1]-ING in the vocabulary. When more than one identically spelled verb is entered the present-participle pronunciation may be shown only for the common one or ones or for the first.

principal parts of verbs see sections on INFLECTED FORMS, DIVISION OF and on INFLECTED FORMS, PRONUNCIATION OF.

punctuation marks variants are usually separated by a comma in the vocabulary but sometimes by a semicolon. See the paragraph on variants.

-qu-: division of words containing see sections on *-gu-* and on inflected forms, division of.

R used in vocabulary pronunciations and in this "Guide" as a label for the speech of those who always have the sound \r\ before a consonant or pause when *r* or *rr* in the spelling provides justification, except for occasional loss by dissimilation as in the first syllable of *surprise*. The term "*r*-keeper" has been used in a few places for a speaker of this type of speech, to supply the need for an antonym of "*r*-dropper".

–R used in vocabulary pronunciations and in this "Guide" as a label for the speech of those who have no \r\ sound before a consonant or pause. Our use of this label ignores speakers who in this position sometimes have \r\ and sometimes do not in the same class of words, or who usually have \r\ only in a limited number of classes from which educated usage sanctions its omission. Thus some speakers usually have \r\ before consonant or pause only in syllables of the type of *spurn* or *spur*. Speakers whose omission of \r\ is maximal and those whose omission is only partial are both known as "*r*-droppers" but in this "Guide" the term is restricted to the former.

\r as in *rid, arouse, merry* as pronounced by all speakers of standard English, and as in one pronunciation of *carbarn, lizard, murder*.

Words such as the last three are not uniformly pronounced. Most Americans have for these *r*'s a sound which, though it may usually differ appreciably from the prevocalic second sound in *crow*, is distinct from any other sound in the language and can be symbolized by \r\. The \r\ and the vowel sound that answers to a letter preceding the *r* in the orthography may be articulated simultaneously, as in *purr* and perhaps also in *par*, and some transcribers prefer a single symbol for the double articulation. Favoring the use of \r\ preceded by a vowel symbol, however, is the fact that the articulations, usually or often simultaneous, may alternatively be successive, particularly under emphasis, and that the two-symbol transcription parallels the transcription for items like *dear*, whose corresponding articulations are only or usually successive. Other speakers (as in the southeastern United States, eastern New England, New York City, and southern England) with varying degrees of regularity do not make in words like *carbarn, lizard, murder* the articulation that we transcribe \r\. The sum total of what they do instead is commonly called *r*-dropping, a term that is misleading to the extent that it may suggest that syllables in which some have \r\ and some do not are identical except that with the latter one member of a linear series has been removed, with consequent durational shortening. Trying to gauge the comparative duration of what *R* and *–R* speakers respectively say for what is between the \k\ and \d\ of *card* runs into complications. A vowel of the quality of that in *card*, if it occurs and is of substantially the same quality in the speech of both in items in which the spelling does not have *r*, may not be of the same duration in the two dialects. Further, it may be difficult or impossible to dissociate the vowel and the \r\ in *R* speech: the \r\ may be simultaneous with the whole or the last part of the vowel, or may be initiated after the vowel begins and continue after the vowel ends. In most classes of words with postvocalic *r* in the orthography things happen in the pronunciation that make these words as distinct from maximally similar words spelled without *r* as in *R* speech. The relationships in *–R* speech between the vowels used for items containing postvocalic *r* in the spelling and the vowels used for items not containing such an *r* are:

(1) The pronunciation of a spelling item containing the letter *r* may be identical with the pronunciation of an item not containing *r*:

tort and *taut* may be identical, with [ȯ] or [ȯȯ] (long [ȯ]) or [ȯə] for both *or* and *au*. *Card* and *cod* are often identical (as in the speech of New York City), with [ää] for both *ar* and *o*, [ää] occurring for the latter because of the tendency of certain final consonants, as voiced stops, to lengthen a preceding vowel. The consonants that when word-final tend to lengthen a preceding vowel and to produce such leveling are \b\, \d\, \g\, \j\, \m\, \n\, \sh\. Although published statements on *–R* speech take little note of the possible leveling of *ar* and *o* as in *cart* and *cot* for the opposite reason that the vowel for the *r*-containing item has the shortness normal for the *o* of an item like *cot*, in certain contexts at least that are most favorable to vowel shortness (distance in syllables from the end of a word as in *parsimony*, stress weaker than primary as in *arcade*) such leveling may occur. To hold down the amount of detail in our vocabulary transcriptions, we have not indicated there the levelings here discussed.

Pairs like *manners : mannas* \-nəz\, *scapulars : scapulas* \-ləz\, *rushers : Russia's* \-shəz\, *goer : Goa* \-ōə\, *Ballard : ballad* \-ləd\ are identical.

The following pairs may be identical, some chiefly in eastern New England and southern British speech, both members containing [ää] or [ȧ] ([ȧ] here, in square brackets, transcribes a vowel that is between \ä\ and \a\ in quality; within reversed virgules in vocabulary transcriptions, \ȧ\ stands for both [ää] and [ȧ]; see the section on \ȧ\): *farther : father, spars : spas, aren't : aunt, arms : alms, carve : calve, farced : fast, parsed : past*.

(2) The pronunciations of both items with and items without *r* in the spelling may contain the same sounds in the same sequence but be distinct because the vowel is longer in the items with *r*.

Pairs like *cart* and *cot* so differ with a high degree of consistency in the South and in New York City, pairs like *card* and *cod* with much less consistency. See (1) preceding.

Pairs like *bird* and *bud* may so differ, and the difference may be shown by the transcriptions [ˈbəəd] and [ˈbəd] respectively. The words more often differ in that *bird* has [ə̄] instead of [əə], [ə̄] indicating a vowel differing in quality from that of *bud*. Within reversed virgules in transcriptions, \ə̄\ stands for both [ə̄] and [əə].

(3) Items with and items without orthographic *r* may differ in that in the pronunciation of the former the vowel common to both has \ə\ following: *beard* \ˈbiəd\ : *bid* \ˈbid\, *erred* \ˈeəd\ : *Ed* \ˈed\, *court* \ˈkōət\ : *coat* \ˈkōt\, *poorly* \ˈpu̇əlē\ : *pulley* \ˈpu̇lē\, *sired* \ˈsīəd\ : *side* \ˈsīd\, *scour* \ˈskau̇ə\ : *scow* \ˈskau̇\, *coir* \ˈkȯiə\ : *coy* \ˈkȯi\. Some speakers may frequently have \ȯə\ in words like *tort* but usually only \ȯ\ in words like *taut*. Because of a tendency for English vowels to shorten in proportion to their distance in syllables from the end of a word, it was decided at the beginning of transcription to show \ȯə\ as well as \ȯ\ for *r* words of this class only in the ultima and penultima — e.g., in *norm* and *normal* but not in *normalize* or *normality*. The precedent, however, of words that show \ȯə\ only or alternatively in at least all stressed syllables and of other words that show only \ȯ\ in all syllables has made for some inconsistency in the transcriptions.

The \ȯə\ of some transcribers and the \ȯȯ\ of others (see 2) may sometimes be merely a difference of interpretation of the same phonetic entity. We do not show a transcription \ȯə\ for words of the type *taut, law*. For *–R* dialects in which *tort* and *taut* are both \ˈtȯət\ the variant \ȯ\ should be regarded as having the value \ȯə\. Some transcribers might regard the entity transcribed \ää\ in (1) as in pairs like *card : cod, cart : cot*, as \äə\ instead.

The Middle Atlantic vowel symbolized \aa\ is often followed by \ə\ in monosyllables or in the last syllable of words without *r* in the spelling, with leveling of pairs like *paired : pad*, as indicated by the variants \ˈpaaə\ at *pair* and \ˈpaa(ə)d\ at *pad*.

In drawled speech, especially common in the South but not here transcribed, the vowel \ə\ frequently occurs between certain vowels and a following consonant, as in \ˈbiəd\ for *bid*. Whether pairs like *beard : bid* are leveled in the South and if so to what extent is a question that needs further investigation.

(4) An item containing *r* may differ in *–R* pronunciation from all items not containing *r* in that a vowel is used for the *r* item that lacks \r\ quality and that is different from any other the speaker uses. Thus the vowel \ə̄\ is limited to words like *bird, German*, except as it may occur as a replacement for \œ\, \œ̄\, \œœ\, \œ̄œ\ in words originating in a foreign language, as *Goebbels, Goethe*. The diphthong \əi\ is used for the *ir* of *bird* by many speakers in the New York City area and in the deep South.

(5) The speech of some is partly *–R* and partly *R*. Speakers whose speech habits were formed near a boundary between *–R* and *R* areas sometimes have and sometimes lack \r\ in words of the same class (*card, cart, hearth*) or even in the same word. Many speakers have in words of the class *bird, dirt, mirth* the same pronunciation as *R* speakers — \ər\ — but a basically *–R* pronunciation in other classes of words.

What happens before a vowel in *–R* speech to a word in which \r\ is the last symbol shown in transcriptions for *R* speech needs some discussion.

When before an initial vowel in a following word there is a pause whose correlate in the written language is a punctuation mark, there usually is no \r\ at the end of a preceding word when there would be no \r\ if a consonant followed: *Why should I care? Others don't.*

When there is no pause between two such words, *–R* speech may have an \r\ or may not: *a door opened*. When there is no \r\ a glottal stop may occur between the two words. Such a glottal stop is not transcribed in this dictionary.

When the vowel that follows is a suffix or the first sound of a suffix, \r\ regularly occurs in all standard *–R* speech: *starry, starring*.

A word like *dear* is not pronounced with an \r\ at the end in *–R* speech when a consonant or pause follows ("*dear friend*", "*Dear? Eighty dollars!*"), but is often pronounced with an \r\ when a vowel word follows without pause (*dear experience*). A word like *idea* also is not pronounced with an \r\ when a consonant or pause follows, but like *dear* frequently does have an \r\ before a closely following vowel with many speakers who pronounce an \r\ in *dear* in the same situation, in spite of the fact that *idea* has no *r* in the orthography. Such an \r\, called "intrusive *r*", is frequent in the northeastern United States and southern England but is rare or nonexistent in the southern United States. It usually follows \ə\, \ȯ\, \ȧ\, or \ä\ and may occur before a vowel in a following word or, perhaps less often and with greater deprecation from some listeners, before a suffixed vowel: *idea of importance, law and order, Omaha and Lincoln, drawing, withdrawal, sol-faing*. Our transcriptions have taken notice of intrusive *r* probably only at *idea*, where the variant with \r\ was mentioned both because it seemed a distortion to omit it from a complement of variants so sizable and because *idea* has come to be regarded as something of a shibboleth for the occurrence of intrusive *r*. Two kinds of parenthesizing of an \r\ at the end of a transcription will be found: "(r)", with a parenthesis on each side, and "(r", with no closing parenthesis:

dod·der \'dädə(r)\
ˡ*bar* \'bär, 'bȧ(r\

In transcriptions with two parentheses the form with r is the *R* pronunciation and in some environments the *–R* pronunciation also, the form without r is the *–R* pronunciation in other environments. In that fraction of a transcription that follows a comma or semicolon and that ends with r preceded but not followed by a parenthesis, the form with as well as the form without r is limited to *–R* speech (as \'bȧr\ as well as \'bȧ\); the form preceding the comma or semicolon (as \'bär\) is the *R* pronunciation and with *–R* speakers whose \ȧ\ is to be construed as [ää] is alternative to [ää] before a vowel.

In words that rhyme with *spur* and are common enough to call for maximum variant coverage, the *R* and *–R* pronunciations are labeled.

In a pronunciation like that at

fear \'fi(ə)r, -iə\

\'fi(ə)r\ is the *R* pronunciation in all environments and the *–R* pronunciation in some, \'fiə\ is the *–R* pronunciation in other environments.

To provide a degree of clarification of the pronunciations of such words impossible in most of our transcriptions, to enable the consultant to be sure of our intent as to the pronunciation of inflected forms not transcribed, and to enable the consultant to supply the *–R* pronunciation of uncommon words for which that pronunciation is not shown, we transcribe in detail below the infinitive, past, and present participle of one verb of each of the classes into which verbs are divisible on the basis of the pronunciation of the last syllable.

fear *R*, *–R+suffixal vowel, some –R+following-word vowel* 'fir, 'fiər; *–R+consonant or pause, some –R+following-word vowel* 'fiə\ *feared* *R* 'fi(ə)rd, *–R* 'fiəd\ *fearing* *R & –R* 'fi(ə)riŋ\ (the greater the stress or emphasis the greater the likelihood of \-iər(-)\ rather than \-ir(-)\)

bare *R*, *–R+suffixal vowel, some –R+following-word vowel* 'bar, 'ber, 'baar, 'baər, 'beər, 'baaər; *–R+consonant or pause, some –R+following-word vowel* 'baə, 'beə, 'baaə\ *bared* *R* 'ba(ə)rd, 'be(ə)rd, 'baa(ə)rd, *–R* 'baəd, 'beəd, 'baaəd\ *bearing* *R & –R* 'ba(ə)riŋ, 'be(ə)riŋ, 'baa(ə)riŋ\

bar *R* 'bär; *–R+consonant or pause, some –R+following-word vowel* 'bȧ; *some –R+suffixal vowel, some –R+following-word vowel* 'bȧr; *some –R+suffixal or following-word vowel* 'bär (*with some speakers whose* 'bȧ = 'bää\) *barred* *R* 'bärd, *–R* 'bȧd\ *barring* *R* 'bȧriŋ, *–R* 'bȧriŋ *or* 'bäriŋ\

spur *R+consonant* 'spər, *+vowel* 'spər·; *–R+consonant or pause* 'spə̄, *+suffixal vowel* 'spər· *also* 'spə̄r, *+following-word vowel* 'spər· *or* 'spə̄ *also* 'spə̄r\ *spurred* *R* 'spərd, *–R* 'spə̄d\ *spurring* *R* 'spər·iŋ, *–R* 'spər·iŋ *also* 'spə̄riŋ\ (the centered period means that only one of the two variants that occur for the *urr* of a word like *hurry* occurs in *spurring;* see the section on \ˌər\; the variants \ər·\, \ə̄r\ differ in that although both have substantially the same two articulations the articulations are simultaneous or overlapping for \ər·\ but consecutive for \ə̄r\, the latter being of greater duration than the former)

dodder *R*, *–R+suffixal vowel, some –R+following-word vowel* 'dädər; *–R+consonant or pause, some –R+following-word vowel* 'dädə\ *doddered* *R* 'dädərd, *–R* 'dädəd\ *doddering* *R & –R* 'däd(ə)riŋ\ (in most words of this class, with unstressed final syllable, a variation occurs for the present participle that it is more convenient to record at the subentry for that form)

war, warred, warring *as for variants with* ȯ *at* STORE *below*\

store *R*, *–R+suffixal vowel, some –R+following-word vowel* 'stōr, 'stōər, 'stȯr, 'stȯər; *–R+consonant or pause, some –R+following-word vowel* 'stōə, 'stȯ, 'stȯə\ *stored* *R* 'stō(ə)rd, 'stȯ(ə)rd, *–R* 'stȯ(ə)d\ *storing* *R & –R* 'stō(ə)riŋ, 'stȯ(ə)riŋ\

tour *R*, *–R+suffixal vowel, some –R+following-word vowel* 'tu̇r, 'tu̇ər; *–R+consonant or pause, some –R+following-word vowel* 'tu̇ə\ *toured* *R* 'tu̇(ə)rd, *–R* 'tu̇əd\ *touring* *R & –R* 'tu̇(ə)riŋ\

tire *R*, *–R+suffixal vowel, some –R+following-word vowel* 'tīr, 'tīər; *–R+consonant or pause, some –R+following-word vowel* 'tīə\ *tired* *R* 'tī(ə)rd, *–R* 'tīəd\ *tiring* *R & –R* 'tī(ə)riŋ\

tower *R*, *–R+suffixal vowel, some –R+following-word vowel* 'tau̇r, 'tau̇ər; *–R + consonant or pause, some –R+following-word vowel* 'tau̇ə\ *towered* *R* 'tau̇(ə)rd, *–R* 'tau̇əd\ *towering* *R & –R* 'tau̇(ə)riŋ\

**\ r(·) ** see \ə·r, ər·\ and \r\. Words that rhyme with *stir* and that are not common often have \r(·)\ as the final items in their transcriptions, as *knur* \'nər(·)\. The parenthesized centered period means that before a following vowel such words do not have one of the two pronunciations that are common in standard speech for the *urr* of *hurry*. For the full range of pronunciations that are heard for a word like *knur* see \r\ in this "Guide" or the pronunciation of rhyming words in the vocabulary.

**\ rᵊ ** as in one pronunciation of French *lustre*. \rᵊ\ is a single voiceless sound that does not add an extra syllable, the \lu̅estrᵊ\ pronunciation of *lustre* being a single syllable. The \ᵊ\ after the \r\ is always parenthesized to indicate the usual pronunciation when a vowel-initial word follows without pause. Thus *lustre antique* is \lu̅e strän tēk\, three syllables, with \str\ as in French *strate*. See section on \ᵊ\.

***r*-dropper** see section headed *–R*.

***r*-keeper** see section headed *R*.

**\ rr ** in some languages, as Spanish, the difference between a trilled *r* (made with two or more taps of the tongue) and a single-tap *r* is phonemic, distinguishing words otherwise identical. In transcriptions of the Spanish pronunciation of words borrowed from the Spanish \rr\ has been used for the trilled *r*. For languages which have a trilled *r* only or in which the difference between two varieties is of no significance, \r\ alone is adequate.

**\ rü ** as in *rude, peruse, verruca;* that is, words in which the orthographic representation is not *roo* and that are mostly from Latin and Greek. The variant \ryü\ or \riü\ occurs in such words to a very limited extent in U.S. speech and so is not shown for any of the words listed above. Occasionally when \'rü\ and \ˌr(y)ə\ are gradational variants (as in *garrulity, garrulous*), the \ryü\ variant may be less limited in its extent and then is shown.

**\ s ** as in *so, less, lesser*.

On the showing of \z\ and \s\ variants for the *s* of words like *abstain, teamster, instigate* (in which a voiced consonant precedes and a voiceless sound follows), see the section on \z\.

sandhi see the vocabulary definition. Only to a very limited extent is account taken in vocabulary pronunciations of the variations that occur at the beginning of words because of the nature of the last sound of a preceding word, or of the variations that occur at the end of words because of the nature of the first sound of a following word. In common words whose last sound is \t\ when the word is pronounced in isolation, we record that before vowels \d·\ usually occurs instead, as at *complete*. At *and* and *you* we record variations that these words undergo as a result of environment. At *'em* we record that a preceding word ordinarily \v\-final may before \ᵊm\ have \b\ instead of \v\. We do not, however, record at words whose final sound is shown as \s\ or \z\ that instead the sound is usually \sh\ or \zh\ respectively when a word following without pause begins with \sh\, \y\, or \zh\, as in *horseshoe, the pace you've set, the size you want, this gendarme*. We do not record at words whose first sound is shown as \b\, \d\, or \g\ that when a word ending in \s\ precedes without pause these three stops may not differ in pronunciation from the stops respectively transcribed \p\, \t\, and \k\ in *spy, stay, sky*, with frequent homophony of such pairs as *this buy : the spy, this day : the stay, this guy : the sky* (compare our transcriptions at *disband, disdain*, and *disguise*). We do not record at words shown as having a given consonant at the end of an unstressed final syllable and at words shown as having the same consonant as their first sound that when such a consonant-final word precedes such a consonant-initial word without pause often only one consonant is articulated, with homophony of such pairs as *Asian nights : Asia nights.* We do not record at words shown as beginning with unstressed \əl-\ or \il-\, \əm-\ or \im-\, \ən-\ or \in-\ that when certain consonants precede without pause some of the words of the first group may begin \ᵊl-\ instead (as in *not allowed*), some of the words of the second group may begin \ᵊm-\ instead (as in *the help employed*), and some of the words of the third group may begin \ᵊn-\, \ᵊm-\, or \ᵊŋ\ instead (as in *good encyclopedia, stop entirely*, and *dog encountered* respectively). These sandhi variants that we omit from vocabulary entries are more satisfactorily covered by being cataloged in a discussion of phonetics. Most of them happen automatically and usually without any awareness of the speaker that he is not using the pronunciations that dictionary vocabularies usually limit themselves to.

**\ sch ** as in *mischief, exhaustion*. Many transcribe only \sch\ in such words but a sequence whose first member is \sh\ rather than \s\, or at least whose first member seems to be closer to \sh\ than to \s\, is frequent when the vowel that precedes is front and is as high as \e\, as in *mischief, question*, the tongue position for a vowel of this height being closer to the tongue position for \sh\ than for \s\. After other vowels, whose tongue position is less conducive to \sh\, that consonant is less frequent and is not shown as a variant in the vocabulary, as at *bastion, combustion, exhaustion*.

Scottish see section on foreign words.

semicolon a semicolon rather than a comma sometimes separates variant pronunciations. A semicolon does not mean that what follows it is less acceptable or less frequent than what precedes it. It is in general used as a safeguard against regarding a variant or a label as applicable to an item or a part of an item following the semicolon. Examples:

adversary *R* 'advə(r),serē, *–R* -vəˌs-; -ri\ (if a comma had been used instead of the semicolon, the meaning would be that the variant -ri is limited to *–R* speech)

cayuga \kē'ügə, 'kyü-; kā'(y)ü-,kī'(y)ü-, *attrib* (')=¦==\ [the *attrib* (')=¦== does not apply to anything before the semicolon]

aficionada \əˌfisēə'nädə, əˌfēsēə'-,əˌfishə'-, aˌf-, -ȧdə; -ˌfēthēə'nät͟hə, -nȧ-\ (such variants as \i\, \s\, and \sh\ are unlikely when the last consonant in the word is t͟h)

luxembourg or *luxemburg* \'ləksəm,bu̇rg, -bu̇əg *also* 'lük- *or* -ˌbərg *or* -ˌbə̄g *or* -ˌbəig; 'ləksəm,bərg, -bə̄g, -ˌbəig *also* -bu̇rg *or* -bu̇əg\ (the label *also* does not apply to 'ləksəm,bərg, which is probably as frequent as the 'lu̇k- variant; and construing the *also* to apply to the last four final-syllable variants would produce a contradiction with the first part of the pronunciation. Use of the semicolon facilitates the presentation of the relationship between the vowel quality of the first and final syllables)

**\ sh ** as in *shy, dish, sure, mission*. \sh\ is a single sound, not two, and has in it no \s\ sound or \h\ sound.

**\ shch ** see section on \sch\.

-sia, -sian as in *magnesia, euthanasia, Andalusian*. For many words ending in *-sia* or *-sian* as many as ten variants occur: \-zhə(n), -zhēə(n), -shə(n), -shēə(n), *chiefly Brit* -ziə(n), -zyə(n), -zhyə(n), -siə(n), -syə(n), -shyə(n)\. We do not show this range of variants at any entry in the vocabulary. For common words for which we have records we limit the transcriptions to the variants that appear to be most frequent in American speech, and for uncommon words we often show \-zh(ē)ə\ as the two variants that an averaging of the records of commoner words suggests as most likely.

stress marks see 2.2 in "Explanatory Notes"; on the placement of stress marks, see "Divisions in Respelled Pronunciations"; the mark ˌ is treated in a separate part of the "Guide". The brief discussion of stress in "Explanatory Notes", while true as far as it goes, omits some details. Actually, words like *beneficial* (vocabulary stress marking \¦==¦==\), *fictitious* (vocabulary stress marking \(')=¦==\), and *campaign* (vocabulary stress marking \(')=¦=\) undergo an even wider variation of stress than "Explanatory Notes" shows. Thus *beneficial* may also be \'=='==\ (as in *Beneficial though it is . . .*) or \ˌ==ˌ==\ (as in *beneficial diet*), *fictitious* may also be \'='==\ or \ˌ=ˌ==\ (as in *fictitious story*), and *campaign* may be \='=\ (as in *a hard campaign*), \'=ˌ=\, \'='=\, or \ˌ=ˌ=\ (as in *campaign promises*).

A high percentage of adjectives traditionally transcribed with a primary stress as the last of two or more stresses (as *beneficial, scrophulariaceous*), and many adjectives traditionally transcribed with a primary stress on the second syllable but no stress on the first (as *fictitious, magnanimous, dissociative*) are marked in the vocabulary with the indicators of variation of stress. (Two successive primary stresses were mentioned as a possible stress variant for *beneficial;* three successive primaries seem unlikely but three successive secondaries may easily occur, as in the fourth word of *one of the scrophulariaceous herbs*.) A high percentage of words belonging to other parts of speech and traditionally transcribed with two or more stresses the last of which is a primary on the last syllable (as *campaign, acquiesce, catamaran*) are transcribed with the markings for stress variation because of the frequency with which primary stress recedes in them or is reduced to secondary when another word follows without pause (*acquiesce readily, catamaran sailing*). It is possibly a safe generalization to say that there is no word having two or more stresses the last of which is primary when the word is pronounced in isolation that does not in some contexts undergo recession or reduction of the last stress, whatever the part of speech and whichever the syllable that bears the last stress. Thus in the item *Smith's explanation, Johnson's explanation, Wilson's explanation — they're all questionable*, probably neither of the two stressed syllables in any of the three words *explanation* would be uttered with primary stress. But such a stress pattern would occur in fewer contexts for a noun that in isolation lacks primary on the ultima than for a noun that possesses it, and our stress marking for *explanation* is \ˌ=='==\.

For two-member compounds the second member of which is an independent English word the vocabulary usually shows only the pronunciation of the first member followed by a plus sign. If ¦ or (') occurs in the transcription of the first member, it is to be understood that the compound as a whole is subject to stress variation. When in compounds whose pronunciation is shown by the plus-sign formula the second member normally has secondary stress only, the plus sign is followed by ˌ-.

mac·ro·fauna \ˌmakrō+\
mac·ro·prism \ˈmakrō+ˌ-\

Many words for which variable stress is indicated are both adjective and noun. If for such a word that has no stress on the last syllable the adjective entry is first, we usually show the pronunciation of the noun following simply as \ˈ\. If the noun entry is first, we usually show for it a pronunciation in which the only primary stress is the last and show variation of stress for the adjective following by means of stress marks and double hyphens. Thus our pronunciation for ¹*organic, adj* is \(ˈ)ȯ(r)¦ganik, -nēk\ and for ²*organic, n* is \ˈ\. If ¹*organic* had been the noun instead our pronunciation would have been \ȯ(r)ˈganik, -nēk\ and the pronunciation for ²*organic, adj* would have been \(ˈ)=¦==\. Showing no stress variation for the noun in such cases is an oversimplification: even a noun without stress on the last syllable does sometimes undergo stress recession but much less often than does the adjective.

The nouns that usually have last-syllable primary stress when pronounced immediately before a pause are shown with the marks for recession of stress. If, in words with last-syllable stress, this stress is often secondary rather than primary before a pause their stress may be indicated by two variants separated by a comma.

¹*av·oir·du·pois* \ˌavə(r)dəˈpȯiz, ˈ===ˌ=\

**\ sü ** as in *sue, suit, assume;* that is, words in which the orthographic representation is not *soo* and that are mostly from Latin and Greek. The variant \syü\ or \siü\ appears to be frequent in southern British speech but is rare in U.S. speech and so is not shown.

superlatives of adjectives see sections on INFLECTED FORMS, DIVISION OF and on INFLECTED FORMS, PRONUNCIATION OF.

syllables see separate section on "Divisions in Boldface Entry Words" and "Divisions in Respelled Pronunciations".

symbol names the terms *bar, one-dot,* and *two-dot* can be used with the name of a character in this way: \ā\ is "bar a", \t͟h\ is "bar t-h", \ȯ\ is "one-dot o", \ü\ is "two-dot u". Symbols with no modifier are *plain:* \a\ is "plain a", \i\ is "plain i" because the dot is not a modifier.

**\ t ** as in *tights, attend, Atlantic.* See section on \d·\.

With chiefly substandard speakers in the New York City area the precise phonetic form of the consonant answering to *t* or *tt* between a preceding stressed vowel and a following \ᵊl\ is the glottal stop, as in *title, battle* (symbol, not shown in the transcription of such words in the vocabulary, [ˀ]). In Scotland the glottal stop is used in the same environment, and before an unstressed vowel as in *water, bitter,* by a higher percentage of cultured speakers than in New York City.

In words like *winter, plenty, gentlemen,* in which what corresponds to the *nt* of the spelling is preceded by a stressed vowel and followed by an unstressed vowel or \ᵊl\, the \t\ is either feebly articulated or absent in much American speech, pairs like *winter : winner* being difficult or impossible to distinguish without the help of context. Certainly the usual American pronunciation is in strong contrast to the usual southern British pronunciation, in which there is a strongly articulated, aspirated, distinctly heard \t\ that probably is to be regarded as the first sound of the syllable to which the unstressed vowel or \ᵊl\ belongs, any \t\ that may occur in the American pronunciation probably being best regarded as belonging to the syllable that contains the \n\. One way of transcribing the difference between the two pronunciations would be \ˈwin(t)·ə(r), ˈwin·tə(r\. Orthoepic commentary usually decries the absence or weakness of the \t\ in such words but the pronunciation is too widespread in all levels of American speech to be ignored. The \t\-less pronunciation is noticed in the vocabulary only in an occasional word for which multiple variants are shown or from which the absence is regarded as apt to be especially conspicuous, as at *gentleman,* the emphasis on the plural of this word in the formula "Ladies and Gentlemen" at the beginning of an address making the absence quite noticeable. A two-variant pronunciation such as that shown above for *winter* is to be understood in the vocabulary for all words of this class, with the label "÷" preceding the \-n(t)· -\ variant to signify the deprecation of orthoepists.

With chiefly substandard speakers in the New York City area a pronunciation somewhat like the British often occurs, except that the tongue position is further forward, the tip frequently being against the lower front teeth.

**\ th ** as in *thin, ether.* \th\ is a single sound, not two, and has in it no \t\ sound or \h\ sound. The basic difference between \th\ and \t͟h\ is that the first is pronounced without and the second with vibration of the vocal cords.

**\ t͟h ** as in *then, either.* \t͟h\ is a single sound, not two, and has in it no \t\ sound or \h\ sound. The basic difference between \th\ and \t͟h\ is that the first is pronounced without and the second with vibration of the vocal cords.

-ths plurals of singulars ending in *-th* pronounced \th\ with vowel preceding and without pronunciation in the vocabulary are to be understood to be \ths\, as *myths.* Plurals with the variants \t͟hz\ and \ths\ (not always in this order) are pronounced in the vocabulary. The \t͟h\ of \t͟hz\ is often weakly articulated; in fact, it may be that in some pronunciations regarded as containing \t͟h\ what is so regarded is an extension of the length of the preceding vowel rather than a consonantal articulation.

**\ ū ** this symbol, used in most diacritical alphabets for the sounds following the \f\ of *few* and often for the sounds between the \f\ and \r\ of *fury,* is replaced in this dictionary by \yü\ and \yu̇\, which are not only phonetically more realistic but also transcriptionally more economical in permitting the showing of two variants by parenthesization, as in \ˈn(y)ü\ for *new.*

**\ u̇ ** as in *pull, wood, injurious.* See section on \u̇r\.

\u̇\ is usually shown as the second part or ending position of the diphthong of *loud* but in most articulations a point this high is not reached, the ending position being closer to \ō\. Other diphthongs with this ending position occur as variants in certain classes of words in which other speakers pronounce a vowel followed by \l\. See section on \l\.

**\ ue ** as in German *füllen, hübsch;* \ue\ can be approximated by pronouncing \i\ with moderately rounded lips.

**\ u̅e̅ ** as in French *rue,* German *fühlen;* \u̅e̅\ can be approximated by pronouncing \ē\ with strongly rounded lips.

**\ ü ** as in *rule, moon, few* \ˈfyü\, *union* \ˈyünyən\. Compare the section on \yü\.

\ ü \ plus unstressed vowel in vocabulary pronunciations, \u̇\ if not shown is to be understood as a variant of \ü\ in such position, as in *fluid, gluey, skua.*

**\ u̇r \, \ u̇ər \, \ u̇ə ** in words of the type of *injurious, furious, tour, pure,* variants occur that are not shown in the vocabulary or that are not shown for uncommon words.

Words of the type of *injurious* are shown in the vocabulary as containing the sequence \u̇r\ followed by a vowel. In the deep South they may contain \ür\ instead of \u̇r\, and the \ür\ variant is to be understood for uncommon words for which it is not shown. In southern British speech all words of this type usually have \ə\ between the \u̇\ and \r\ and may have \ōər\ as a variant; the most common words may also have \ȯr\ or \ȯər\ as a variant, and for one such word at least (*injurious*) \ər\ is also shown.

Words of the type of *pure* are shown in the vocabulary as having \u̇r\ or \u̇ər\ in *R* speech and before a vowel in *–R* speech, and as having \u̇ə\ in *–R* speech elsewhere. In southern British speech the \ə\ appears to be usually present between \u̇\ and \r\; in all such words a variant \ōə(r\ is heard, and the most common words may also have \ȯə(r\ or \ȯ(r\.

V used in the formula "*usu* -ād·+V" as at *wait;* chosen for the formula as being an abbreviation for "vowel" but "+V" is to be interpreted as meaning "*+ vowel or ᵊl following without pause*".

**\ v ** as in *vote, level, give.* Under the assimilative influence of a following \ᵊm\, the lip-teeth sound \v\ may have as a variant the two-lip sound \b\, as in *give 'em, government.* See section on \ᵊm\.

variants see 2.3, 2.4 in "Explanatory Notes". If the consultant knows or has reason to believe that an uncommon word has less than a full complement of the predictable variants that we usually give for common words, he can supply the omitted variants by examining the variants for better-known words that rhyme or the variants for a rhyming part of such words. He will need to observe certain precautions mentioned in this "Guide". The \əi\ variant shown at a word of the type of *bird,* for example, does not hold for a word of the type of *preferred.* See \əi\.

**\ w ** as in *we, sweep, away.* See sections on \əw\, \hw\.

**\ wʸ ** as *hu* in French *huile* or *u* in French *nuit;* \wʸ\ can be approximated by rounding the lips as for \w\ while the tongue makes the articulation for \y\.

x for words of the type of *exact, exult,* in which the sounds that correspond to the *x* of the spelling are preceded by an unstressed and followed by a stressed vowel, the vocabulary usually shows only the value \gz\ for the *x.* For such words some speakers have \ks\ instead.

**\ y ** as in *yard, yours, European* \ˌyu̇rə¦pēən\, *cue* \ˈkyü\, *union* \ˈyünyən\. See section on \yü\.

**\ ʸ ** not a symbol for a sound but a diacritic signifying a modification of the sound of the preceding symbol, the modification consisting of articulating the sound while the tongue is in approximately the position for the sound \y\, with the tip back of the lower front teeth. See the sections on \lʸ\, \nʸ\, \wʸ\.

Frequently at the end of the articulation of \nʸ\ or \lʸ\ an independent \y\ sound is heard, without anything else accompanying, [nʸy], [lʸy], but it is usually considered unnecessary to transcribe this off-glide.

The sound \wʸ\ could with equal logic have been symbolized by a full-size y followed by a superior w to denote lip rounding, but \wʸ\ is preferred because \w\ is the usual anglicization, as in \swād\ for *suede,* from a French word pronounced \swʸed\.

**\ yə ** as in *ammunition.* Some transcribers prefer \yu̇\ to \yə\ as the transcription in an unstressed medial syllable of *u* or *eu.* In normal-tempo speech it is difficult to hear the difference between unstressed \yə\ and \yu̇\. A distinct \yu̇\ is probably more common in British speech than in American and is heard in the latter in emphatic or deliberate utterance. In initial syllables, as in *unite* and *uranium,* \yü\, \yu̇\, and \yə\ are all three heard although the vocabulary does not show all three. When such words are pronounced starting from pause, the \yə\ variant is more apt to occur before \r\ than before other consonants, and the vocabulary transcriptions for the initial vowel are not identical for all words.

**\ yü \, \ yu̇ ** these two transcriptions replace the ū of previous editions of this dictionary, \yu̇\ occurring before \r\ as in *European* and \yü\ elsewhere as in *unity.* These two transcriptions not only better display the nature of the sounds but also make it possible to show two pronunciations for a word like *new* simply by parenthesizing, \ˈn(y)ü\, the (y) signifying that *new* may either be pronounced like the *noo-* of *noose* or have between \n\ and \ü\ a sound that does not occur in *noose.* See sections on \lü\, \sü\.

When certain consonants precede in the same syllable the first component may be [i] instead of [y]. In the variety with [y] the second component has greater stress than the first but in the variety with [i] the first component has stress equal to or greater than that of the second. It is not necessary to show in the vocabulary the variant [iü] or [iu̇], which is merely the variety of \yü\ or \yu̇\ that occurs under certain conditions.

See section on \yə\.

**\ z ** as in *zone, freezer, raise.*

Most transcribers treat as \s\ the sound of the *s* in words like *abstain, teamster, instigate, redskin, brownstone,* in which a voiced consonant precedes and a voiceless sound follows. But it is doubtful that there is any difference between most utterances of the *-mst-* of *teamster* and the *-m's t-* of *the team's terrific,* of the *-dsk-* of *redskin* and the *-d's k-* of *Red's kin,* of the *-nst-* of *brownstone* and the *-n's t-* of *Brown's tone,* in the second member of which pairs transcribers just as regularly treat the sound of the *s* as \z\. What happens in both *brownstone* and *Brown's tone* when they are identical is probably the same thing that phoneticians agree happens to the last sound of *Brown's* or *brows* when those words have only pause following, as at the end of a sentence: the last sound starts out voiced, by carryover from the voiced sound preceding, but becomes voiceless.

This devoicing might be shown in minute transcription intended primarily for scholars by the symbol \z\ with a small circle underneath, such a circle being widely used by phoneticians for devoicing, or even by a transcription \brau̇nz-stōn\, but for an item like *Brown's* which has at the end the same sequence of voice and voicelessness a plain \z\ alone is usually employed. For items like *abstain, teamster, instigate* we show two variants for the *s,* \z\ and \s\, the latter probably being frequent or usual in emphatic utterance. We provide only stress indications at the vocabulary entries of compounds like *redskin* and *brownstone,* although only \s\ is shown at SKIN and STONE. If transcriptions with sound symbols were shown for such compounds our transcription at REDSKIN would be \ˈredzˌkin, -dˌsk-\. Compare the section on sandhi.

When the preceding voiced consonant is a nasal, when the next vowel is without stress, and when the *s* is definitely \s\ and not \z\, the voiceless stop homorganic with the nasal often occurs parasitically before the \s\: *teamster* \ˈtēmpstə(r)\, *monster* \ˈmäntstə(r)\, *gangster* \ˈgaŋkstə(r)\.

**\ zh ** as in *vision.* \zh\ is a single sound, not two, and has in it no \z\ sound or \h\ sound.

**\ zü ** as in *presume, resume;* that is, words in which the orthographic representation is not *zoo* and which are mostly from Latin and Greek. The variant \zyü\ or \ziü\ appears to be frequent in southern British speech but is rare in U.S. speech and so is not shown.

DIVISIONS IN RESPELLED PRONUNCIATIONS

1. American general dictionaries have for a long time attempted to mark the boundaries of all the syllables in a respelled pronunciation. Many linguists and phoneticians, however, have no certainty as to precisely where these divisions are and sometimes no certainty even as to how many syllables a word has. The three words *gore, goer, Goa* are pronounced alike by many U. S. speakers, and yet it is general practice to treat the first as a monosyllable only and the other two as disyllables only. It has also been general practice to treat a single consonant as being in the following syllable when preceded by a long stressed vowel or an unstressed vowel and as being in the same syllable with a preceding short stressed vowel, although consonantal quality has more to do with syllable boundaries than does vocalic quality.

2. Because of the extremes of opinion with regard to syllable boundaries, whatever course a dictionary adopts will meet with some opposition. Some students maintain that in some languages there is no such thing as a phonetically recognizable boundary between words when they follow one another without pause. Other students of language and probably most laymen believe that if practically any succession of two words is pronounced in isolation, the boundary is determinable from the pronunciation alone, even though a sequence like *a never-ready* may be misapprehended as *an ever-ready* (and vice versa) when the context is ambiguous. The word *adder* originally had an initial *n* whereas *nickname* originally lacked an initial *n*, the respective loss and gain resulting from mistaking the constituents when such words as *a* or *an, my* or *mine* preceded.

3. In most American speech the sound used for the letter *t* varies according to its position in a word. This variance is a basis of our treatment of syllables in the respellings. Thus most Americans would not speak *ten trips/tent rips* or *Kay Tolliver/Kate Oliver* identically. Our treatment does not attempt to cover in full southern British speech in which a *t* is often pronounced the same whether it appears to the left or to the right of a word boundary.

4. In American speech the following consonant sounds when preceded by a stressed vowel usually sound one way when a word boundary is immediately to the left of the corresponding orthographic *t* and another way when the boundary is to the immediate right of the *t:*

\t,d·\ *wry tangle/right angle*
\nt\ *men told/meant old*
\tr\ *stay trite/state right*
\ltr\ *bell trick/belt Rick*
\ntr\ *ten trips/tent rips*
\tw\ *no twill/note Will*
\ltw\ *Hall twin/halt Wynn*
\ntw\ *Doane twin/don't win*
\ty\ *why Tunis/white Eunice* (*when Tunis is* \'tyü-\ and not \'tü-\)
\lty\ *spell Tunis/spelt Eunice*
\nty\ *scan Tunis/scant Eunice*
\tsh(=t·sh)\ *Leete shin*
\ch(=·tsh)\ *Lee chin/Leech Inn*

5. When any consonant except \r\ occurs immediately before any of the preceding sequences except the last, the sequence resulting, if it is not one of those listed above, sounds the same regardless of word boundary. The following sequences sound the same: *black tie/blacked eye, cur stray/curse tray/curst ray, lop twigs/lopped wigs, miff Tunis/miffed Eunice.*

6. When the \l\ or \n\ in the preceding list is syllabic or is preceded by an unstressed vowel, the difference usually heard when a stressed vowel precedes is reduced or may disappear. A complication for the \nt\-plus-vowel sequence is the possibility that a difference heard may be due to complete loss of the \t\ when a word boundary follows rather than to a difference in the syllable placement of the \t\, as in the second item in *flew and told/fluent old.*

7. When any of the sequences in the preceding list susceptible of two syllabifications occurs within a word at a point where there is no boundary between meaningful elements that a speaker may be trying to maintain, the syllabification is usually that which occurs when a *t* is to the right of a word boundary: \t\ instead of \d·\ for the *tt* of *attack*, \n·t\ instead of \nt·\ for the *nt* of *entire*, \·tr\ instead of \t·r\ for the *tr* of *metric*, \·tyü\ instead of \t·yü\ for the *tu* of *mature* (when \y\ is not absent from the word). Exceptions are \d·\, sometimes heard instead of \t\ for the first *t* of *potato;* \t·w\ instead of \·tw\ for the *tw* of *Antwerp* (though \·tw\ possibly occurs sometimes in British speech); \nt·r\, sometimes heard instead of \n·tr\, chiefly in substandard speech for the *ntr* of words like *country* and *contribution.*

8. If in our transcriptions our symbol for the *ch* of *chin* and *each* were \tsh\, in order to make it clear that this \tsh\ differs from the \t·sh\ of *Leete shin* and to be consistent with our use of two differently placed dots in all the other divisionally different items, it would be necessary to use a dot in another position when the sequence is intervocalic (as in *Lee chin/Leech Inn*) and to make a commitment as to the syllable division of these two morpheme-different homophonous pairs, something that we do not do for other such pairs. In that case consistency could have been achieved by removing all pre-\t\ dots.

9. Presumably the sounds represented by the *d* preceding and the *g* following the space in *bad gendarme* (when the speaker's pronunciation of the *g* is \zh\) stand to the sound represented by the *dge* of *badge of honor* as the corresponding parts of *Leete shin/Leech Inn/Lee chin* do, the first being \d·zh\ and the second \j=·dzh\. But words beginning with \zh\ are so rare in English that random listening will yield little or nothing in the way of evidence.

10. In this dictionary the roles of the stress mark and the syllable divider are kept distinct; the stress mark does not simultaneously serve as a syllable divider as in some pronunciation systems. Our stress marks are ' and ˌ our syllable divider is ·. For a consonant or for a sequence of consonants preceding a stressed vowel that is not the first vowel in a word, our procedure is as follows: If the consonant or sequence is one that always sounds the same wherever the corresponding word division may be, no divider is used, and the stress mark is placed before the first consonant sound or sequence of consonant sounds that can begin English words that are not mere borrowings: *astrology* \ə'sträləjē\, *mellite* \'meˌlīt\, *guest rope* \'geˌstrōp\, *Rhode Island* \(')rōˈdīlənd\, *McCoy* \mə'kȯi\, *hypnosis* \hip'nōsə̇s\, *agnostic* \ag'nästik\. If, for a given sequence, a difference of word boundary in the orthography is paralleled by a difference in the pronunciation, we indicate for each occurrence of the sequence which of the two pronunciations it has by inserting the syllable divider and placing the stress mark immediately after the divider: *antagonize* \an·'tagəˌnīz\, *contrive* \kən·'trīv\, *between* \bə̇·'twēn\, *solitude* \'sälə·ˌtyüd\, *patrician* \pə·'trishən\. When the vowel that follows the consonants is without stress, only the divider is used: *metric* \'me·trik\, *matriarch* \'mā·trēˌärk\, *country* \'kən·trē\, *contribution* \ˌkän·trə'byüshən\. In derivatives formed by adding the suffix *-ry* to an English word ending in *t* immediately preceded by a vowel, *l*, or *n*, the division is sometimes before, sometimes after, the \t\, and no divider is used: *puppetry* \'pəpə̇trē\.

10.1 The sequence \ntr\ in a word like *country* is sometimes, chiefly in substandard speech, \'kənt·rē\ rather than \'kən·trē\. The \nt·r\ variant is not shown for these.

10.2 For \nt\ followed by an unstressed vowel, both \nt·\ and \n·t\ occur, and no divider has been used in the transcription: *winter* \'wintə(r)\, *bunting* \'bəntiŋ\. The \n·t\ division for these is much less frequent in American than in British speech. In American speech what many hear as \nt·\ is probably often simply \n\, pairs like *winter/winner* probably often being homophonous. \nt\ is often subject to variation in American speech when a vowel with secondary stress follows. There has been some inconsistency in the transcribing of these, and both of the following formulas, which are the same in intent, will be found: *pimento* \pə̇'ment·(ˌ)ō,-en·(ˌ)tō\, *adventism* \'adˌvenˌtizəm\.

10.3 \d\ is one of two single consonants with which the divider is used. When the orthographic correspondent of \d\ is *t(t)*, the \d\ is always followed by the divider: *lattice* \'lad·ə̇s\, *at all* \əd·'ȯl\. When the orthographic correspondent of \d\ is *d(d)*, no divider is used and the \d\ is to be interpreted as transcribing the variation \d·, ·d\: *modest* \'mädə̇st\, *adopt* \ə'däpt\ (for words like the latter it is to be understood that for the \d·\ variant the stress is on the other side of the \d\). See the section on \d·\.

10.4 \r\ is the other single consonant with which the divider is used. The preceding vowel is always a stressed \ə\. For *hurry* the transcription \'hər·ē\ indicates a pronunciation in which the quality of the \ə\ is strongly affected by the \r\ and the two sounds may be regarded as in the same syllable, as they are in stressed *her* (in fact, the \ə\ and the \r\ may be simultaneously articulated and a single sound). The transcription \'hə·rē\ indicates a pronunciation in which the quality of the \'ə\ is much the same as the quality it has when it precedes any other consonant than \r\. \ə·r\ is probably familiar to some of the many Americans in whose speech it does not normally occur as the pronunciation usually used by circus-sideshow barkers (or by actors enacting the part) for the middle of *Hurry!* (See the section on \ər\.) In transcriptions of words not widely known in the literary language, no divider is used with the \r\, and this is to be interpreted as transcribing the same \ər·, ə·r\ variation: *dhurrie* \'dərē\.

10.5 When stressed \ər\ is followed by a consonant or a pause, the variety that occurs in American speech is the variety heard in stressed *her*. In the transcription of words like *piqueur* \-'kər(·)\, the parentheses mean that the divider is to be dispensed with when a consonant follows, as in transcribing the plural \-'kərz\, but retained when a vowel follows without pause, as in "the piqueur assisted" \-'kər·ə'sistə̇d\.

10.6 An \r\ within a word preceded by stressed \ō\ and followed by a stressed vowel is placed before, rather than after, the stress mark, as at *dorad* \'dōrˌad\, because in the prevailing pronunciation in the U. S. the division seems definitely to be \ōr·\. The centered period is not used, however, because the \ō·r\ variant is frequent in the deep South. See the section on \ōr\.

10.7 With some British speakers the sequence \tl\, as in *Atlantic*, very definitely sounds as it does at the beginning of a borrowed word like *Tlascala*, but because such a pronunciation of the \tl\ is not often heard in this country, we have transcribed \ət'lantic\. British practice could be shown by either of the two formulas mentioned above, \ət·'lantik, ə·'tl-\ or \ə'tlantik\.

10.8 Two successive identical vowels that are not in the same syllable are separated by a divider: *Alma-Ata* \ˌalmə·əˈtä\. Two successive identical vowel symbols not so separated indicate a same-syllable vowel that is or that may be regarded as of the same quality as the vowel indicated by only one of the symbols but longer: *champion* \'chaampēən\, *feuille* \fœœy\. See the section on \aa\.

10.9 In some cases the divider is put to a quite different use, serving merely to make up for deficiencies caused by the use of a digraph for a single sound. Thus, \sh\ is used to represent a single sound in *shoe* but two sounds in *gas house* and *less heroic*. \th\, likewise, is used to transcribe a single sound in *think* but two sounds in *knothole* and *not heroic*. In a transcription of sequences like *gas house* and *knothole*, in which the vowel following the \h\ is stressed, the presence of a stress mark between the two letters is sufficient. When the vowel following the \h\ is unstressed, the centered period needs to be used, as in one of the pronunciations for *imposthume* \ə̇m'päs·thəm\.

10.10 It is impracticable to attempt to show, in the transcription of single words, where a stress mark and where and when the divider would occur in connected discourse. Except for final stressed \ər\, this has not been attempted. When only part of an entry has been transcribed because the other part is pronounced at its own alphabetical place, it has usually not been practicable to position the stress mark as it would have been positioned if the entry had been transcribed in full. Thus, the transcription *Bartram oak* is \'bär·trəm-\. If a pronunciation had been shown for the second word, the full respelling would have been \'bär·trə'mōk\, with stress mark before rather than after the \m\. When an entire pronunciation or a part of a pronunciation consists of double hyphens only, full-transcription placement of stress marks is often impossible and the divider has also usually been omitted: *boathook* \'=ˌ=\, *sightworthy* \'=ˌ==\.

PUNCTUATION

The chief marks of punctuation and reference, with their names

The chief uses of the most important punctuation marks are explained in the numbered sections below.

, comma
; semicolon
: colon
. period *or* full stop
— dash *or* em dash
– dash *or* en dash
~ swung dash
? question mark *or* interrogation point
¿? question marks, Spanish
! exclamation point
( ) parentheses *or* curves
[ ] brackets, square
⟨⟩ brackets, angle
’ *or* ' apostrophe
- hyphen
= *or* ≠ double hyphen
´ (é) acute accent
` (è) grave accent
ˆ (ô) *or* ⌢ *or* ~ circumflex
~ (ñ) tilde
¯ (ō) macron

˘ (ŭ) breve
¨ (oö) diaeresis
¸ (ç) cedilla
∧ caret
“ ” *or* " " quotation marks
« » quotation marks, French
» « *or* „ “ quotation marks, German
‘ ’ *or* ' ' quotation marks, single
“ *or* ” *or* " ditto marks
/ virgule *or* slant
\ reversed virgule
{ *or* } *or* ⏞ brace
. . . *or* * * * *or* —— ellipsis
. . . suspension points
* asterisk
† dagger
‡ double dagger
§ section *or* numbered clause
‖ parallels
¶ *or* ⁋ paragraph
☞ index *or* fist
⁂ *or* ⁂ asterism

0.1 Speech consists not merely of sounds but of organized sound sequences that follow various structural patterns and are uttered with significant modifications of pitch and stress and significant pauses. Besides representing the basic sounds of speech, the English writing system accordingly utilizes signs called punctuation marks to separate groups of words and to convey some indication of the varying pitch and volume and especially the pauses in the flow of speech sounds.

0.2 A pause in speech is accompanied by a significant adjustment in the pitch of the voice, which may rise, fall, or remain the same. There may also be an increase or decrease in stress with or without actual cessation of sound. Three principal types of pauses are readily perceptible in English speech:

(1) The fading pause, a falling into silence with a full stop, is marked by a lowering of pitch and decrease of stress until the production of sound ceases. This pause signifies the termination of an utterance and in writing is usually indicated by the period or the semicolon. (2) The rising pause is characterized by an upturn in pitch often combined with a lengthening of word sounds just before the break. This pause is used to set off word groups within utterances, especially whenever there is anticipation of supplementary or explanatory matter to follow, and is usually indicated in writing by a comma or, at the end of a question, by a question mark. (3) The sustained pause occurs whenever there is a break without any change in the pitch of the voice or when the same pitch is continued across a break. This pause is often indicated in writing by a comma, particularly when a rising pause would also be appropriate. The sustained pause is indicated also by such marks as a dash or ellipsis where a person stops speaking without altering the pitch of his voice, as when he is interrupted.

0.3 Much written expression consists of discourse never actually spoken but formulated in the writer's mind and immediately expressed in writing. Somewhat more formal in its structural patterns than actual speech, such written expression is nevertheless a reflection of the spoken language, is itself capable of being spoken, and is therefore punctuated as the written expression of actual speech.

0.4 As will be indicated, punctuation marks are often used in an arbitrary or mechanical manner not directly related to language structure or to patterns of speech sounds. To a considerable extent, however, punctuation may be explained in terms of the structural divisions of speech — sentences, clauses, phrases, and other word groups — and some of the more obvious elements of pitch, stress, and pause that indicate their separation or their relationship.

1. THE PERIOD

1.1 Like a fading pause and full stop in speech, a period usually terminates a sentence that is neither interrogative nor exclamatory ⟨The mountain is 5,000 feet high. If the climbers have a good day, they will reach the top in a few hours. At the summit they will eat the lunch which has been prepared, and then they will start down early enough to reach the bottom before dark.⟩

1.1.1 Utterances terminated by a fading pause do not always have a complete subject-predicate structure. In the context of consecutive speech, however, the meaning of such utterances is entirely clear, and in writing they are usually terminated with a period ⟨"Tell me when you came in." "Just now."⟩ ⟨"Please close the door." "Certainly."⟩

1.1.2 Structurally incomplete or fragmentary elements terminating in a period occur frequently in modern narrative writing and are usually terminated with a period ⟨The sound of artillery through the night. The enemy again. Banging away to keep everyone nervous and awake.⟩

1.2 A period often follows an abbreviation ⟨Reedville, Mass., pop. 879⟩ ⟨cap. or l. c.⟩ ⟨7 a. m.⟩ ⟨30 mins.⟩ ⟨lg. pkg.⟩ ⟨no. 72⟩ ⟨5s. 6d.⟩ ⟨bks. marked o. p.⟩ ⟨dept. bulls.⟩ ⟨50 pp.⟩ ⟨U. S. S. *Wyoming*⟩ ⟨Dr. John H. Doe, 7 Pine St., New York, N. Y.⟩ ⟨Dec. 7, 1941⟩ ⟨Lt. Col. John Doe⟩

1.2.1 Periods do not usually follow abbreviations of compound names of international organizations and government agencies, official abbreviations designating equipment, and a large number of similar compound abbreviations usually written without spaces ⟨NATO⟩ ⟨UN⟩ ⟨UNESCO⟩ ⟨TVA⟩ ⟨VT fuze⟩ ⟨pfc⟩ ⟨EST⟩

1.2.2 Periods usually follow common contractions made by omitting medial letters ⟨secy.⟩ ⟨advt.⟩ ⟨mfg.⟩ ⟨recd.⟩

1.2.3 Some publishers, chiefly British, often do not put a period after *Mr*, *Mrs*, and *Dr* ⟨Dr and Mrs John H. Doe⟩

1.2.4 A period does not follow symbols of chemical elements ⟨*Al*⟩ ⟨*Cu*⟩ ⟨*U 235*⟩

1.2.5 Such terms as 1st, 2d, 3d, 4th, 8vo, and 12mo are not abbreviations and do not require a period.

1.2.6 Isolated letters of the alphabet used as designations do not require a period ⟨T square⟩ ⟨A 1⟩ ⟨I beam⟩

1.2.7 After titles of books and articles, after headings, and in display printing, printers usually omit a period at the ends of lines, as well as other punctuation except an essential question mark or an exclamation point.

1.3 A period is necessary before a decimal and between dollars and cents in figures ⟨16.63 ft.⟩ ⟨.32 cal.⟩ ⟨$12.17⟩

1.4 A period may or may not follow a Roman numeral. In particular contexts usage is often quite uniform; thus a period is used after a roman numeral designating a chapter of a book in the Bible ⟨2 Sam. xix. 12⟩ but no period is used after a roman numeral following a personal name ⟨Elizabeth II of England⟩

1.5 Dictionaries use centered periods to indicate division between syllables of words where division is not otherwise indicated by accent marks or hyphens.

2. THE QUESTION MARK

2.1 A question mark usually indicates in writing the incompleteness or anticipation conveyed in speech by any of various intonation patterns and frequently though not exclusively by a rising pause. The word order may be that of a question or a statement ⟨When did he leave?⟩ ⟨You say he never came back?⟩ ⟨An Oxford degree — or was it foreign travel? — lured him to England.⟩

2.1.1 A question mark does not follow an indirect question, which has the intonation pattern and fading pause of a positive statement ⟨They are asking him where he plans to go.⟩

2.1.2 A request expressed in interrogative form for the sake of courtesy usually ends in a period corresponding to the fading pause of a positive statement ⟨Will you kindly fill out this questionnaire and return it to the personnel office.⟩

2.1.3 When used as the terminal mark of a direct quotation, the question mark, as well as the exclamation point, usually takes the place of a comma or period which would otherwise be used at that point in the sentence ⟨After he had affixed the title "What is Progress?" he folded the manuscript of his speech.⟩

2.2 A question mark, usually enclosed in parentheses, often follows arbitrarily after a word, phrase, or date to indicate uncertainty of its accuracy or to mark a gap in available information ⟨Omar Khayyám, Persian poet (?–1123?)⟩

3. THE EXCLAMATION POINT

3.1 An exclamation point follows an expression or statement that is an exclamation and corresponds to a heavy, relatively high-pitched terminal stress in speech ⟨Oh no! Not that!⟩ ⟨I wish he would!⟩ ⟨Do you think we will stand for this any longer!⟩ ⟨Hurry! We need help!⟩

4. THE COMMA

4.0 Of all the marks of punctuation the comma offers the most difficulty in use and the widest range for individual choice. Though often marking rhetorical or elocutionary pauses, the comma is used primarily to separate or to set off in a group. It sometimes distinguishes nonrestrictive modifiers from restrictive modifiers. Since the genus-terms of definitions in this dictionary are intended to be modified only by differentiae that are restrictive in some degree, the use of commas either to separate or to group is severely limited chiefly to units in apposition or in series.

4.1 *Commas That Set Off.* A word, phrase, or clause is often inserted in a sentence to supply explanatory or supplementary information. In speech the rising pause or sometimes the sustained pause sets off such material when it is of relatively minor importance and is not essential to the main idea. In writing commas usually indicate the subordinate status of such matter. These commas always make a pair unless the element set off begins or ends a sentence.

4.1.1 Commas usually set off words, phrases, and other sentence elements that are parenthetical or independent. Items of this sort are contrasting expressions, prefatory exclamations, the name of a person directly addressed, and expressions like *he said* in direct quotations ⟨Work, not words, is what is needed.⟩ ⟨The outcome, though hardly to our liking, is better than expected.⟩ ⟨The animals, nervous and restless, pace interminably in their cages.⟩ ⟨He is often late, to be sure, but we can rely on him in a crisis.⟩ ⟨"Listen, John," he said, "drive carefully."⟩ ⟨Oh bosh, pay no attention to him (the comma that goes with the comma after *bosh* gives way to the capital *O*).⟩

4.1.2 Commas usually set off appositional or modifying words, phrases, or clauses that do not limit or restrict the main idea of a sentence. Such constructions are termed nonrestrictive ⟨George, his own brother, is turning against him.⟩ ⟨John, whom we saw yesterday, is away today.⟩ ⟨His father, dressed in a new gray suit, came early for the ceremony.⟩
The second of the pair of commas in the next three gives way to the period that closes the sentence ⟨There stood John, smiling quietly to himself.⟩ ⟨We leave at 3 o'clock, when the bell rings.⟩ ⟨The formation is of great interest to geologists, although most of us would hardly notice it.⟩

4.1.2.1 When inserted or appended words, phrases, or clauses are restrictive or essential to the main idea of a statement, they are spoken without the pauses or other significant intonation that would indicate matter of minor importance. In writing, commas are likewise unnecessary ⟨His friend George is turning against him.⟩ ⟨The man whom we saw yesterday is not here today.⟩ ⟨The man dressed in the new gray suit is his father.⟩ ⟨John is the boy standing in the rear and smiling to himself.⟩ ⟨We leave when the bell rings.⟩ ⟨He will come if his safe-conduct is guaranteed.⟩

4.1.2.2 Sometimes the presence or absence of commas corresponding to spoken pauses constitutes the sole means of determining whether a phrase or clause is essential or nonessential, restrictive or nonrestrictive ⟨Our friends, who live out of town, do not like the new parking laws/ Our friends who live out of town do not like the new parking laws.⟩ ⟨The men, draining the swamp, searched all day for the boy/The men draining the swamp searched all day for the boy.⟩ ⟨We do not visit him, because he always serves liquor/We do not visit him because he always serves liquor.⟩

4.1.3 Commas set off transitional words and expressions (as *on the contrary, on the other hand, consequently, furthermore, moreover, nevertheless, therefore*) whenever they are or would be spoken with the adjacent rising or sustained pauses that indicate subordinate matter ⟨The question, however, remains unsettled.⟩ ⟨Nevertheless, we shall go.⟩ ⟨On the contrary, under the rules a vote is in order.⟩

4.1.3.1 Such expressions may occur in context so as to be spoken without significant pauses and may likewise require no punctuation ⟨We shall therefore proceed with the operation.⟩ ⟨The weaklings will consequently be forced to drop out.⟩ ⟨A clear-cut decision is on the other hand too much to expect.⟩

4.2.1 *Commas That Separate.* Various expressions are often used in sentences to introduce or qualify something that follows. To separate these elements in speech a rising or sustained pause denotes the end of the introductory information and the beginning of the main part of the statement. In writing, a comma accordingly often separates an introductory word or phrase from the rest of the sentence, particularly when the introductory material is long or when ambiguity might otherwise occur ⟨Unfortunately, we shall have to decline the invitation.⟩ ⟨In the first place, you will get very little information from him.⟩ ⟨To gain popularity, he betrayed his convictions.⟩ ⟨Immediately upon reaching the surface, he swam to shore.⟩ ⟨Seeing the dog approaching, he ran off down the street.⟩

4.2.2 Whenever in spoken English there is an enumeration of items, a rising or sustained pause separates and distinguishes each member of the series. In writing, a comma likewise usually separates words, phrases, or clauses that occur in a series ⟨The estate is to be divided among Robert, John, and William.⟩ ⟨Trees, trees, trees were all we could see.⟩ ⟨He opened the can, removed the contents, and replaced the lid.⟩ ⟨The one who befriended us, watched over us, and gave us help is now no more.⟩ ⟨The prisoner will not talk, he refuses to eat, and he pounds the bars continually.⟩

4.2.2.1 Before *and* or *or* introducing the final term in a closed series, writers usually put a comma ⟨*a, b,* and *c*⟩ ⟨a coat, a hat, and a pair of gloves⟩ ⟨scientific, technical, and learned periodicals⟩ but sometimes omit it in a short series ⟨a coat, a hat and a pair of gloves⟩ ⟨*a, b* and *c*⟩

4.2.2.2 Modifying words in an open series preceding a noun are often separated and distinguished in speech by pauses and in writing by commas ⟨a rural, agricultural, idyllic life⟩ ⟨journalistic, literary, popular publications⟩. Sometimes, however, the pause and hence the comma may be unnecessary when the second modifier relates more closely to the noun than the first, or when the first modifier applies to the second modifier and the noun as a unit ⟨a quiet rural atmosphere⟩ ⟨a vivid red tie⟩ ⟨a brilliant military strategist⟩

4.2.3 Statements or clauses joined by a coordinating conjunction are separated in speech by a sustained or rising pause. In writing, a comma usually effects this separation ⟨He seemed inattentive, but not a word escaped him.⟩ ⟨His face showed his disappointment, for he knew he had failed.⟩ ⟨He did not like intruders of the sort that now confronted him, nor did he see any way of avoiding them.⟩ ⟨She knew very little about him, and he volunteered nothing.⟩

4.2.3.1 When the statements or clauses joined by a coordinating conjunction are brief and unambiguous, and usually when the subject is the same, the comma may be omitted ⟨He will suffer but he will recover.⟩

4.2.3.2 A comma alone without the conjunction sometimes separates brief and closely related statements or clauses. In such instances a sustained or slightly falling pause may occur in speech rather than the fading pause and full stop designated by the period ⟨The boy went to the store, then he went home.⟩ ⟨Don't bother, it doesn't make any difference.⟩ ⟨He would always remember, the experience was now a part of him.⟩ This comma may or may not be permissive in the treatment of the comma fault in various handbooks of composition.

4.2.3.3 When a conjunction joins two predicative constructions that have the same subject, the clarifying pause in speech may be slight or imperceptible. In writing, a comma is likewise not considered necessary except to avoid ambiguity ⟨The car teetered for a moment on the edge of the road and then plunged down the embankment.⟩ ⟨Sailing an iceboat is thrilling sport but requires great skill.⟩

4.2.4 Corresponding to the rising or sustained pause necessary in speech to distinguish items in addresses and dates, a comma usually separates such matter in writing ⟨Born January 1, 1900, in Delhi, India, the university's outstanding student received his college degree in June, 1922.⟩ ⟨Apply for the booklet at the Superintendent of Documents, Washington 25, D. C.⟩

4.2.4.1 Usage is about evenly divided, however, when the day is not given ⟨in June 1922⟩ or ⟨in June, 1922⟩

4.2.4.2 Sometimes writers omit the comma after the year ⟨born January 1, 1900 in India⟩

4.2.5 When such expressions as *namely, that is, i. e., e. g., viz.* introduce an illustration or example, a comma that corresponds in function to a rising or sustained pause in speech usually separates it from what follows ⟨There are two ways to do the job: namely, a right way and a wrong way.⟩ ⟨He forbade future forays; that is, there were to be no more raids on the neighbors' gardens.⟩

4.2.6 A comma usually indicates the place of an omitted word or word group to achieve a separation like that effected in speech by a sustained or rising pause ⟨The tractor is used for hauling; the bulldozer, for excavating.⟩

4.2.7 Like a sustained or rising pause in speech, a comma usually separates a direct quotation from the rest of a sentence or context ⟨"Make way for liberty," he cried.⟩ ⟨He asked abruptly, "Which way do you vote?"⟩ ⟨As some say, "Virtue is its own reward."⟩

4.3 *Commas Used Arbitrarily.* The comma often functions in an arbitrary manner as a mechanical device.

4.3.1 In numbers the comma usually separates thousands, millions, and other groups of three digits except in dates, page numbers, and street numbers, and in numbers of four digits ⟨an altitude of 7525 feet⟩ ⟨3600 rpm⟩

4.3.2 A comma usually sets off inverted names in bibliographies and reference lists ⟨Doe, John, Jr.⟩

4.3.3 A comma usually separates a proper name and an academic or honorary title, also two or more such titles in succession ⟨John Doe, M.A., Ph.D., President⟩

4.3.4 A comma is the customary mark after the salutation in personal letters and after the complimentary close in all letters ⟨Dear Jack,⟩ ⟨Sincerely yours,⟩ ⟨Yours very truly,⟩

4.4.1 One may avoid excessive or uncertain use of the comma by eliminating commas, excepting those used arbitrarily, where there are no significant pauses. In terms of structure, a comma does not usually separate closely related grammatical sequences ⟨The advice his father gave him/ remained long in his mind.⟩ ⟨The result of the long and detailed planning was/ that the forces were well prepared for the battle.⟩ ⟨The flea-bitten, shaggy/ dog padded desolately down the alley.⟩ ⟨The long, happy, and successful trip/ was one he will never forget.⟩ ⟨His new car is a fast/ and powerful machine.⟩

4.4.2 It is equally important to insert a comma to prevent misreading or ambiguity. The need for a rising or sustained pause in speech usually indicates that a comma is necessary in writing ⟨Inside, the fire was burning brightly.⟩ ⟨Ever since, the little man comes at dark to clean the kitchen.⟩ ⟨Whoever lost it, lost an invaluable treasure.⟩ ⟨To Ruth, John appeared as a mighty warrior on a white horse.⟩ ⟨In 1925, 25 percent of the graduates of the school went on to college.⟩ ⟨The railroad had no resources, but the trains were somehow kept running.⟩ ⟨As the car struck, the utility pole fell with a crash.⟩

5. THE SEMICOLON

5.1 In general the semicolon functions as a weak period or as a strong comma. As a weak period the semicolon corresponds to a fading pause and full stop in speech similar to but perhaps not quite as final as that represented by a period. As a strong comma the semicolon corresponds to a rising or sustained pause in speech possibly longer or slightly more definitive than that represented by a comma.

5.1.1 As a weak period a semicolon usually separates independent statements or clauses joined together in one sentence without a conjunction. Such statements or clauses are usually closely related ⟨Make no terms; resist until the last breath.⟩ ⟨A fool babbles continuously; a wise man holds his tongue.⟩

5.1.2 As a weak period a semicolon usually separates two statements or clauses when the second begins with a sentence connector or conjunctive adverb, as *accordingly, also, consequently, furthermore, hence, however, indeed, moreover, nevertheless, otherwise, so, still, then, therefore, thus, yet* ⟨You have recommended this man; therefore I will give him a trial.⟩ ⟨His conduct has always been exemplary; nevertheless he will not be permitted to go.⟩

5.1.3 As a strong comma a semicolon usually separates phrases or clauses that are themselves broken up by punctuation ⟨The country's resources consist of large ore deposits; lumber, waterpower, and fertile soils; a favorable climate; and a strong, rugged people.⟩ ⟨When the presently available natural resources are greatly depleted, man will have to develop new sources of food and power; and then will come the real test of his energies his imagination, and his ingenuity.⟩

5.1.4 A semicolon sometimes separates arbitrarily in lists of names with addresses, titles, or figures where a comma alone would not clearly separate items or references ⟨Genesis 3:1–19; 4:1–16⟩

6. THE COLON

6.1 The colon, corresponding to a fading or sustained pause in speech, is a rhetorical mark of supplementation. It links clauses, phrases, or less often single words; it indicates that what follows it coordinates with some element of what precedes or sometimes with all of what precedes back to the beginning of a sentence. Specific types of supplementation are mentioned in parentheses after the examples ⟨The same forced yes-or-no choice appears on referenda on public questions: the voter cannot express approval of some parts and disapproval of others unless amended. (elaboration)⟩ ⟨It vigorously opposes clandestine marriages: that is, marriages which were made outside the auspices of the Church. (definition)⟩ ⟨His ambition must be stirred: his greed must be played upon. (balance)⟩ ⟨The following items of equipment are necessary: sleeping bag, ground cloth, cooking utensils, and a small axe. (enumeration)⟩ ⟨Representatives of ten countries presented papers at the formal meetings, including: Brazil, England, France, Holland, India, Italy, Japan, the United States, the U. S. S. R., and West Germany —Allen Kent. (enumeration)⟩ ⟨The author never exploits any whimsical or romantic elements in this subject: he maintains throughout the decent, workmanlike attitude he has set himself. (restatement)⟩ ⟨Local currencies, like local laws, were not suppressed: they were encouraged to improve. (antithesis)⟩ ⟨His death raised the possibility that his political heirs might seek the final solution for insolvent, disorganized governments: war. (summation)⟩ ⟨The question is this: will the removal of restrictions lead to freedom or license? (apposition)⟩
Usually what precedes a colon is general and what follows is specific but sometimes the relation is reversed ⟨Physics and biology, evolution and anthropology, conservation and religion: he discusses them all.⟩
Sometimes paired colons correlate ⟨He has ambition: it must be stirred. He has a belief in fair play: it must be honored.⟩
Frequently the colon is reinforced by anticipatory phrasing (as *thus, namely, for example, as follows*).

6.2 A colon functions as a mechanical device in set formulas involving separation of parts, as when relating the antecedent of a ratio to its consequent ⟨12 : 19⟩ or one ratio to another ⟨12 : 19 : : x : 57⟩ or when relating subdivisional units in a descending series to specify or particularize one member, especially in time-telling by hour, minute, and second ⟨2:31:30⟩, in bibliographical reference by volume and page ⟨*National Geographic* 33:89⟩ or by chapter and verse ⟨Luke 2:12⟩ or by place and publisher ⟨Springfield : G. & C. Merriam Co.⟩, or in accounting by pounds, shillings, and pence ⟨46 : 6 : 11⟩

6.3 A colon symbolizes a conventional separation or emphatic pause after a formal salutation in a letter ⟨Dear Sir:⟩ or an address ⟨Mr. Chairman, Ladies and Gentlemen:⟩ or between a book title and a subtitle not otherwise differentiated ⟨*Victory : A History of the Recent Struggle*⟩

6.4 A colon introduces a quotation especially when quotation marks are omitted and when the quoted matter is indented ⟨We quote from the text: "Greater love hath no man".⟩:

He reads these words from Ruth:
Whither thou goest, I will go.

Mother: Where did you go?
Child: I won't tell.

A colon joins terms that are being contrasted or compared and is sometimes centered or spaced ⟨Seventeenth century rhymes include *prayer: afar* and *brass : was : ass.*⟩ ⟨The stature of the two sexes shows very nearly the same female : male proportions.⟩

7. THE DASH

7.0 In its function in writing and in the speech intonation to which it corresponds, the dash is similar to the comma and the colon, and a pair of dashes is similar to parentheses.

7.1 A dash usually marks an abrupt change or suspension in the thought or structure of a sentence ⟨If you will listen I will explain — but perhaps another time will be better.⟩ ⟨The mountain we climbed is higher than — oh, never mind how high it is.⟩ ⟨He was — how shall I put it — a controversial figure to say the least.⟩ ⟨"Yes, but I — er — I'll have to —" and he stopped hopelessly.⟩

7.2 A dash often makes parenthetic, appositional, or explanatory matter stand out clearly or emphatically ⟨Three of the country's most important products — oil, steel, and wheat — are produced in greater quantities than ever before.⟩ ⟨Two of our group — Eddie and John — came walking down the street.⟩ ⟨He is willing to discuss all problems — those he has solved and those for which there is no immediate solution.⟩

7.3 A dash often occurs before a summarizing statement or clause ⟨Oil, steel, and wheat — these are the sinews of industrialization.⟩

7.4 A dash sometimes sets off appositional or parenthetic matter that is introduced by such expressions as *namely, for example, that is* ⟨Sports develop two valuable traits — namely, self-control and the ability to make quick decisions.⟩

7.5 A dash often mechanically precedes the name of an author or source at the end of a quoted passage ⟨There is a tide in the affairs of men which, taken at the flood, leads on to fortune —William Shakespeare⟩ ⟨"In the beginning God created the heavens and the earth" —Genesis 1:1⟩

7.6 A long dash often functions as a notational device to indicate the omission of a word or of letters in a word ⟨yelling —— loudly⟩ ⟨Mr. M—— of New York⟩ ⟨go to the d——l⟩

7.7 A short dash — slightly larger than a hyphen — often serves as an arbitrary equivalent of *to and including* between numbers or dates and in compounding capitalized two-word names with the hyphen ⟨pages 40–98⟩ ⟨the decade 1951–60⟩ ⟨the New York–Lisbon plane⟩

8. PARENTHESES

8.1 Parentheses often set off parenthetic matter when the interruption is more marked than that usually indicated by commas ⟨Three old destroyers (all now out of commission) will be scrapped.⟩ ⟨He is hoping (as we all are) that this time he will succeed.⟩

8.2 Parentheses often set off supplementary or explanatory matter that is not a part of the main statement or not a structural element of the sentence ⟨The more distant mountain (I think you have climbed it before) is our goal.⟩ ⟨The diagram (Fig. 3) illustrates the action of the pump.⟩ ⟨The Springfield (Illinois) stop is the first on the tour.⟩

8.3 Parentheses often mechanically enclose sequential numbers or letters in a series (but do not take the place of required punctuation) ⟨We must clearly set forth (1) our long-term goals, (2) our immediate objectives, and (3) the means at our disposal.⟩

8.4 Parentheses usually arbitrarily enclose an arabic number confirming a number expressed in words ⟨Delivery will be made in thirty (30) days.⟩ ⟨Payment due is twenty dollars ($20.00).⟩

9. BRACKETS

9.1 Brackets usually set off mechanically a word or phrase that is extraneous or incidental to the context, such as editorial interpolations ⟨He wrote, "I am just as cheerful as when you was [sic] here".⟩ ⟨A fly is said to be a two-winged dipterous [does that make four wings?] insect.⟩ ⟨The officer in charge [General Doe] had to countersign the order.⟩

9.2 Brackets often function as parentheses within parentheses ⟨Bowman Act (22 Stat., ch. 4, § [or sec.] 4, p. 50).⟩

10. ELLIPSIS *or* SUSPENSION POINTS

10.1 Consisting usually of three spaced periods or asterisks and corresponding in effect to a sustained pause in speech, an ellipsis often indicates an interrupted or unfinished sentence. Wherever an ellipsis is terminal, a period follows ⟨"I shall . . . that is . . . if we can only . . . ." He faltered and stopped speaking.⟩ ⟨"Cut the line and cast. . . ." His voice was lost in the crash of the next wave.⟩

10.2 An ellipsis often occurs as a notational device to indicate an omission in quoted matter, as a word or a group of consecutive words unessential or undesirable for quotation ⟨"Oh say can you see . . . what so proudly we hailed . . .?"⟩

10.3 An ellipsis on a line by itself in poetry indicates the omission of one or more lines of verse. Sometimes it consists of periods spaced and extended in number to the full measure of the line:

Thus driven
By the bright shadow of that lovely dream,
. . . .
He fled

—P. B. Shelley

11. THE CENTERED PERIOD

11.1 A centered period in a dictionary entry indicates syllabic or end-of-line division ⟨dy•nam•ic⟩. (For discussion and examples see "Divisions in Respelled Pronunciations" and "Divisions in Boldface Entry Words".)

12. THE HYPHEN (For discussion and examples of hyphens see "The Writing of Compounds".)

12.1.1 A hyphen is a mark of separation or division at the end of a line which terminates with a syllable of a word that is to be carried over to the next line ⟨mill- [end of line] stone⟩ ⟨pas-sion⟩

12.1.2 A hyphen divides letters or syllables to give the effect of stuttering, sobbing, or halting ⟨S-s-sammy⟩ ⟨ah-ah-ah⟩ ⟨y-y-es⟩

12.1.3 A hyphen suspends the second part of a hyphened compound used in combination with another hyphened compound ⟨a six- or eight= cylindered engine⟩ ⟨in ten- and twenty-dollar bills⟩

12.1.4 Hyphens indicate a word spelled out letter by letter ⟨p-r-o-b-a-t-i-o-n⟩

12.2 A hyphen before a word element indicates that it is a suffix or a terminal combining form ⟨-ous⟩ ⟨-ship⟩

12.3 A hyphen after a word element indicates that it is a prefix or initial combining form ⟨anti-⟩ ⟨fore-⟩

12.4 Hyphens before and after a word element indicate that it is a medial word element ⟨-o-⟩

13. QUOTATION MARKS

13.1 Quotation marks often enclose a direct quotation from a speaker or from a text or other written matter ⟨"When I am dead," said one of the keenest of modern minds, one of the greatest of modern poets, "lay a sword on my coffin, for I was a soldier in the war for the liberation of humanity."⟩
Quotation marks are not used to enclose oft= quoted familiar phrases (as *to err is human*). Quotation marks are not used to enclose indirect quotations ⟨*direct* — The man said, "I am going home."⟩ ⟨*indirect* — The man said that he was going home.⟩

13.2 In long quotations, excepting extracts from plays, left-hand quotation marks are placed at the beginning of every paragraph included in the quotation in addition to those placed at the beginning and at the end of the selection.

13.3 Quotation marks are usually not used when the quoted matter is set in smaller type or in paragraphs indented on both sides.

13.4 Single quotation marks enclose a quotation within a quotation; or if single quotation marks are used primarily, double quotation marks enclose a quotation within a quotation ⟨The witness said, "I distinctly heard him say, 'Don't be late'; then I heard the door close".⟩

13.5 Quotation marks usually enclose titles of short poems, paintings, lectures, articles, and parts or chapters of books. (Titles of whole books, periodicals, and newspapers are usually italicized in context.)

13.5.1 In American usage printers usually place a period or comma inside closing quotation marks whether it belongs logically to the quoted matter or to the whole sentence or context ⟨The package is labeled "Handle with Care."⟩ ⟨The golden rule, "Do unto others as you would have them do unto you," is easier to remember than to practice.⟩ But when a logical or exact distinction is desired in specialized work in which clarity is more important than usual (as in this dictionary), a period or comma can be placed outside quotation marks when it belongs not to the quoted matter but to a large unit containing the quoted matter ⟨The package is labeled "Handle with Care".⟩ ⟨This act may be cited as the "Army-Navy Medical Services Corps Act of 1947".⟩ ⟨The Prime Minister, after reporting the negotiations, declared resolutely, "Our only course is to resist aggression".⟩ ⟨Replying with the one word "Bunk", he subsided.⟩

13.5.2 Only one other mark accompanies closing quotation marks, whether the quotation and the whole sentence or context call for the same mark or for different marks ⟨Did he keep asking you, "What is your number?"⟩ ⟨We shouted in unison, "Where do you think you're going?"⟩ ⟨Just as he screamed, "I will not!" he slammed the door.⟩ ⟨Is this the gratitude I receive, to have you bellow, "Get out of here and don't come back!"⟩

13.5.3 A colon or semicolon is usually placed outside of quotation marks ⟨"Fame is proof that people are gullible"; with this quotation he retired in silence.⟩

13.5.4 A colon or semicolon is sometimes placed inside the quotation marks when it belongs inseparably to the quotation ⟨"Sirs:" is a salutation used in letters to a newspaper.⟩; however, a terminal colon or semicolon of quoted matter incorporated in a sentence usually gives place to appropriate end punctuation.

13.5.5 A question mark or exclamation point is usually placed inside or outside the quotation marks according to whether it belongs to the quoted matter or to the whole sentence or clause that includes the quotation ⟨Can you forget his angry exit after he shouted "Include me out"?⟩ ⟨"And what do you think of this new novel?" his friend asked.⟩

13.6 Quotation marks, often single quotation marks, sometimes enclose technical terms unfamiliar to the reader; words used in an unusual sense; and coined words, trade or shop jargon, or slang for which the writer implies a slight apology ⟨An "em" is a unit of measure used in printing.⟩ ⟨The plates of copper are hung by "corrosion hooks" in the acid.⟩ ⟨This venture is a "wildcat" invented to prey upon the unwary.⟩ ⟨We've had enough of your "unshrinkable" shirts.⟩ ⟨He is "goofy" according to their lingo.⟩

14. THE APOSTROPHE

14.0 An apostrophe and *s* are usually added to a noun to indicate ownership or a relation analogous to ownership. This possessive form is a survival of the *es* ending in Old and Middle English, from which the vowel sound has disappeared in Modern English except in nouns ending with the sound \s\, \z\, \sh\, \zh\, \ch\, or \j\. In early Modern English the *s* of the possessive was often dropped from the possessive of nouns already ending in an *s* or *z* sound, both in speaking and in writing, leaving only the apostrophe in writing, as is evident in various idioms and in poetry. Since the middle of the 19th century, however, the form with the apostrophe and *s* has been generally adopted for the possessives in which the extra syllable is not awkward to pronounce in context.

14.1 An apostrophe and *s* form the possessive case of singular or plural nouns that do not end in an *s* or *z* sound ⟨boy's⟩ ⟨carpenter's⟩ ⟨dog's⟩ ⟨president's⟩ ⟨at his wit's end⟩ ⟨garage's responsibility⟩ ⟨Senator Doe's constituency⟩ ⟨the church's policy⟩ ⟨men's⟩ ⟨Descartes's philosophy⟩ ⟨Delacroix's painting⟩

14.2 An apostrophe either with or without *s* forms the possessive case of singular nouns ending in an *s* or *z* sound.

14.2.1 Singular nouns ending in an *s* or *z* sound that consist of one syllable or have a primary or secondary accent on the last syllable usually add an apostrophe and *s* to form the possessive case ⟨the class's recitation⟩ ⟨the press's description⟩ ⟨the fox's tail⟩ ⟨King James's reign⟩ ⟨Laplace's theories⟩ ⟨the marquise's jewels⟩

14.2.2 Singular nouns ending in an *s* or *z* sound that consist of more than one syllable and have no primary or secondary accent on the last syllable often add the apostrophe and *s* to form the possessive case unless the additional syllable with the *s* or *z* sound would be unpleasant or difficult to pronounce in context. Sometimes such a syllable is necessary to avoid ambiguity in pronunciation. Usage is divided in this matter (1) ⟨an audience's/

audience' reaction⟩ ⟨the waitress's/ waitress' duties⟩ ⟨the phoenix's/ phoenix' nest⟩ ⟨for appearance's/ appearance') sake⟩ (2) ⟨Dr. Adams'/ Adams's services⟩ ⟨the octopus'/ octopus's snaky appearance⟩ ⟨Dickens'/ Dickens's novels⟩

14.2.3 With some exceptions various classical and biblical names are treated as in 14.2.1 and 14.2.2 ⟨Zeus's son⟩ ⟨Mars's help⟩ ⟨Venus's/ Venus'⟩ ⟨Judas's/ Judas'⟩ but ⟨Brutus'/ Brutus's⟩ ⟨Odysseus'/ Odysseus's⟩, and ⟨Jesus'⟩ ⟨Moses'⟩ ⟨Pythagoras's/ Pythagoras'⟩ ⟨Herodotus's/ Herodotus'⟩⟨Oedipus's/Oedipus'⟩, but ⟨Aristophanes'/ Aristophanes's⟩ ⟨Socrates'/ Socrates's⟩ ⟨Thucydides'/ Thucydides's⟩

14.3 An apostrophe without *s* usually forms the possessive case of plural nouns ending in an *s* or *z* sound ⟨consumers' protest⟩ ⟨foxes' holes⟩ ⟨the Joneses' invitation⟩ ⟨the two chateaux' occupants⟩ but ⟨geese's⟩ ⟨lice's⟩ ⟨mice's⟩

14.4 An apostrophe and *s* usually form the possessive case of various indefinite pronouns ⟨anybody's⟩ ⟨anyone's⟩ ⟨everybody's⟩ ⟨everyone's⟩ ⟨somebody's⟩ ⟨someone's⟩ but no apostrophe is used in the possessive pronouns *his, hers, its, ours, yours, theirs.*

FORMS OF ADDRESS

An exhaustive list of all alternative forms of address permissible in polite correspondence would extend far beyond the scope of this dictionary; especially in informal correspondence there is a great variety of possible salutations. In the table below we have usually put the most formal address and salutation first. Differences of local usage, however, inevitably introduce many exceptions. In the United States "My dear Mrs. Smith" is more formal than "Dear Mrs. Smith"; in Great Britain the reverse is true. In business correspondence the addressee's address is placed before the salutation; in most official and some social correspondence, it is placed at the foot of the letter, below and to the left of the signature. Social invitations to a married man are customarily addressed to the man and his wife; as, Senator and Mrs. ——; The President and Mrs. ——; Lord and Lady ——; Their Excellencies, the German Ambassador and Madam ——; etc.

It will be noted that some of the addresses given below begin with the word "To," whereas most do not. There is no hard-and-fast rule. We have tried to suggest merely the more customary usage. Insertion or omission of the word "To" is optional. It will also be noted that the same word may be spelled differently according to the residence of the persons addressed. For example, in the United States the spellings *honor* and *honorable* are preferred; but in Great Britain, *honour* and *honourable.* In the address abbreviations are commonly used but they should never be used in the salutation or beginning of a letter.

*Such salutations as My Lord, Your Lordship, etc., are not ordinarily used in the United States of America, but should be used by an American writing to dignitaries of foreign countries entitled to such a title or mark of respect.

†When the person addressed holds several titles, as one from birth, another by marriage, and another by profession, the highest title should be preferred.

‡Clerical, naval, and military prefixes are written before other titles; initials indicative of distinction are written after the title and name; an officer should be addressed by his official title when the communication refers to official business.

A

abbot
address: The Right Reverend —— ——, O.S.B. (or other initials of the order), Abbot of ——; *or* The Right Rev. Abbot ——
begin: Right Reverend and dear Father

administrator same as governor

air force officers like army officers

alderman (in Canada and U.S.)
address: Honorable —— ——
begin: Dear Sir

ambassador†
address: His Excellency, The American Ambassador; *or* The Honorable —— ——, American Ambassador; *or* His Excellency, —— ——, Ambassador of Brazil at ——; *or* His Excellency, Her Majesty's Ambassador for the United Kingdom (the personal name or hereditary or professional title may be added after the words *His Excellency; His Excellency* is usually abbreviated to *H.E.*)
begin: Sir (*or* with the personal title, as Your Grace, etc.); *or* Excellency

ambassador and his wife
address: His Excellency, The —— Ambassador and Mrs. —— ——; *or* The Honorable —— ——, —— Ambassador and Madam —— ——
begin: Your Excellencies

apostolic delegate see papal nuncio

archbishop (Anglican)
address: The Most Reverend His Grace the Lord Archbishop of ——
begin: My Lord Archbishop; *or* Your Grace
In formal documents the archbishops of Canterbury and York are addressed as The Most Reverend Father in God ——, by Divine Providence Lord Archbishop of ——

archbishop (Roman Catholic)
address: The Most Reverend —— ——, D.D., Archbishop of ——
begin: Your Excellency

archdeacon
address: The Venerable The Archdeacon of ——; *or* The Venerable —— ——, Archdeacon of ——
begin: Venerable Sir

army officers
In the United States in letters from civilians:
address: The Commander in Chief, Army of the United States; *or* Lieutenant General ——, Commanding Officer, Army of the United States; Colonel (highest rank and full title) —— ——, U.S.A.; Lieutenant —— ——, U.S.A. (in case of retired officers U.S.A. is omitted)
begin: Sir; *or* (informal) My dear General —— (not My dear Lieutenant General ——); *or* Dear Commander —— (not Dear Paymaster Commander ——); and for all officers below the rank of captain, My dear (*Rank*) ——
In the British army and navy when an officer has a hereditary title or rank, his military or naval rank will ordinarily be prefixed to this; as, Admiral the Right Honourable the Earl of ——; General the Right Honourable Lord ——; but lieutenants in the army and sublieutenants in the navy are not addressed by their military or naval rank; thus, —— ——, Esq., 10th Hussars (not Lieutenant —— ——)
begin: Sir; *or* Dear General ——; *or* Dear Lord —— (but not Dear General Lord ——)

assemblyman
address: The Honorable —— ——, Member of Assembly; *or* Assemblyman ——
begin: Sir; *or* Dear Sir; *or* My dear Mr. ——

assistant secretary (assistant to a cabinet officer)
address: Honorable —— ——, Assistant Secretary of ——; *or* The Assistant Secretary of the —— Department
begin: Sir; *or* Dear Sir; *or* My dear Mr. ——; *or* Dear Mr. —— (never Mr. Secretary)

associate justice
address: The Honorable —— ——, United States Supreme Court; *or* Mr. Justice ——, The Supreme Court
begin: My dear Mr. Justice; *or* Dear Justice ——

attorney general see cabinet officers

auditor of the treasury
address: The Honorable —— ——, Auditor of the Treasury; *or* The Auditor of the Treasury
begin: Sir; *or* Dear Sir

B

baron
address: The Right Honourable Lord ——; *or* The Lord ——
begin: My Lord

baroness
address: The Right Honourable the Baroness ——; *or* The Right Honourable Lady ——; *or* The Lady ——
begin: Madam

baronet
address: Sir John ——, Bt. *or* Bart.
begin: Sir

baronet's wife see lady

baron's daughter
address: (if unmarried) The Honourable Helen ——; *or* (if married to a commoner or to the son of a baron or viscount or the younger son of an earl) The Honourable Mrs. ——; *or* (if her husband has a married brother) The Honourable Mrs. John ——; *or* (if married to a knight or baronet) The Honourable Lady ——. If she is married to a man of higher title, use feminine of husband's title
begin: Madam (or use higher title if one exists)

baron's son
address: The Honourable —— ——
begin: Sir
(in Scotland the eldest son is sometimes addressed as Master of ——)

baron's son's wife† like baron's married daughter

baron's wife = baroness

Benedictine see priest

bishop (Anglican)
address: The Right Reverend the Lord Bishop of ——; *or* The Lord Bishop of ——; *or* (very formal) The Right Reverend Father in God, ——, by Divine Permission Lord Bishop of ——
In formal documents the Bishop of Durham is addressed as The Most Reverend Father in God ——, by Divine Providence Lord Bishop of Durham
begin: My Lord Bishop; *or* My Lord

bishop (Methodist)
address: The Reverend —— ——, D.D.
begin: Reverend Sir; *or* Dear Sir; *or* Dear Bishop ——; *or* My dear Bishop

bishop (Protestant Episcopal)
address: To the Right Reverend —— ——, Bishop of ——
begin: Right Reverend and Dear Sir; *or* (informal) Dear Bishop ——; *or* My dear Bishop

bishop (Roman Catholic)
In England
address: The Lord Bishop of ——; *or* The Right Reverend —— ——, Bishop of ——
begin: My Lord Bishop; *or* My Lord
In the U.S.
address: The Most Reverend —— ——, Bishop of ——
begin: Your Excellency
In Italy
address: To His Excellency, the Most Illustrious and Most Reverend Monsignor ——, Bishop of ——
begin: Most Illustrious and Most Reverend Lord; *or* Excellency

brother of a religious order
address: Brother ——, (followed by the initials of the order)
begin: Dear Brother ——

C

cabinet officers (United States)
address: The Honorable the Secretary of State (or Defense, Agriculture, etc.); The Honorable the Secretary of the Treasury; The Honorable the Postmaster General; *or* The Honorable —— ——, Secretary of State, etc.; *or* The Secretary of State; The Attorney General, etc.
begin: Sir; *or* Dear Sir; *or* My dear Mr. Secretary; *or* My dear Mr. Attorney General

canon
address: The Very Reverend Canon —— ——; *or* The Very Reverend ——, Canon of ——
begin: Very Reverend Canon; *or* Dear Canon ——
canon regular see priest regular
cardinal
address: His Eminence John Cardinal H——
begin: Your Eminence*
cardinal (if also an archbishop)
address: His Eminence —— Cardinal ——, Archbishop of ——
Carthusian see priest
chargé d'affaires
address: The Chargé d'Affaires of ——; *or* ——, Esq., Chargé d'Affaires; *or* Mr. —— ——, Chargé d'Affaires
begin: Dear Sir; *or* Sir; *or* My dear Mr. —— (use military, naval, or hereditary title, if there is one)†
chief justice of the Supreme Court of Canada
address: The Honourable —— ——, Chief Justice of Canada
begin: Sir
chief justice of the United States
address: The Chief Justice of the United States; *or* The Chief Justice, The Supreme Court, Washington, D.C.; *or*, if to the chief justice and his wife, The Chief Justice and Mrs. ——
begin: Sir; *or* My dear Mr. Chief Justice
children see baron's daughter, baron's son, duke's eldest son; children of a peeress in her own right married to a commoner receive the same courtesy titles as though their father were a peer of the mother's rank
Cistercian see priest
clergyman
address: The Reverend —— —— (Rev. and Mrs. —— ——); *or* (if a doctor of divinity) The Rev. Dr. —— ——; *or* The Reverend —— ——, D.D.
begin: Dear Sir; *or* Reverend Sir; *or* My dear Mr. (or Dr.) ——; *or* Dear Mr. (or Dr.) ——; see also archbishop, bishop, priest (most authorities disapprove the use of *Rev.* with the last name alone)
clerk (Anglican Church)
address: The Reverend —— ——; *or* (if the son of a duke or marquess) The Reverend Lord —— ——; *or* (if the son of an earl, viscount, or baron) The Rev. The Hon. —— ——†
begin: Reverend Sir; *or* Sir
clerk (below the order of priesthood in Roman Catholic Church)
address: The Reverend —— ——
begin: Reverend Sir; *or* Dear Mr. ——
clerk of the Senate *or* House
address: The Honorable —— ——, Clerk of ——
begin: Sir; *or* Dear Sir
commissioner of a bureau (as U.S. Commissioner of Education)
address: The Honorable —— ——, Commissioner of the Bureau of Education
begin: Sir; *or* Dear Sir
common forms
man
address: Mr. —— ——
begin: Dear Sir; My dear Sir; My dear Mr. ——; *or* Dear Mr. ——
pl. address: Messrs. —— —— and —— ——
begin: Gentlemen
married woman
address: Mrs. John Doe
begin: Dear Madam; My dear Madam; My dear Mrs. Doe; *or* Dear Mrs. Doe
pl. address: Mmes. —— —— and —— ——
begin: Mesdames; *or* Ladies
unmarried woman
address: Miss Doe (eldest daughter); *or* Miss Jane Doe (younger daughter)
begin: Dear Madam; My dear Miss Doe; etc.
pl. address: The Misses Doe
begin: Ladies; *or* Mesdames
comptroller of Treasury
address: The Honorable —— ——, Comptroller of the Treasury
begin: Sir; *or* Dear Sir
congressman
address: Honorable —— ——, House of Representatives, Washington, D.C.; *or* Honorable John Doe, Representative in Congress, Springfield, Mass.
(some authorities disapprove the use of the prefix Hon. without first name or initials)
begin: Sir; *or* Dear Sir; *or* My dear Mr. ——
consul
address: To the American Consul at ——; *or* —— ——, Esq., American Consul at ——; *or* Mr. —— ——, United States Consul at ——; *or* To —— ——, Esq., Her Majesty's Consul for the United Kingdom
begin: Dear Sir
countess
address: To the Right Honourable The Countess of ——; *or* The Countess ——
begin: Madam

D

dame
address: Dame —— —— (followed with initials of the order, or if the lady has a higher title, with these initials after that title)†
begin: Madam
deacon (Anglican and Protestant Episcopal)
address: The Reverend Deacon ——
begin: Reverend Sir
(for deacons of other churches there is no special form of address)
dean (cathedral)
address: The Very Reverend the Dean of ——
begin: Very Reverend Sir; *or* Sir
dean (Roman Catholic)
address: The Very Reverend —— ——, V.F.
begin: Very Reverend Father
dean of a college *or* graduate school
address: Dean —— ——
begin: Dear Sir (*or* Madam); *or* Dear Dean ——
diplomat see ambassador, chargé d'affaires, minister (diplomatic); for diplomats of lower rank, having no other title, use common forms
divorced woman
(ordinarily *Mrs.* with her maiden name as a prename instead of her ex-husband's prename is preferred; some divorced women prefer to resume the *Miss;* the form of address preferred by the woman herself, if that is known, should be used unless there has been a court decision; divorced peeresses lose officially any title gained by marriage; courtesy use of former title is optional)
doctor of divinity
address: —— ——, D.D.; *or* Dr. —— ——; *or* Rev. Dr. ——
begin: Dear Sir; *or* My dear Dr. ——; *or* Dear Dr. ——; *or* Reverend and Dear Sir; *or* Reverend Doctor
doctor of philosophy, laws, medicine, etc.
address: A—— B——, Ph.D. [LL.D.] [M.D.]; *or* Dr. A—— B——; (Dr. and Mrs. A—— B——; etc.)
begin: Dear Sir; *or* My dear Dr. B——; *or* Dear Dr. B——
(if a higher title is applicable, it should be preferred; see professor, president of a college)†
domestic prelate of the pope
address: The Right Reverend Monsignor —— ——, Domestic Prelate (or D.P.)
begin: Right Reverend Monsignor; *or* Dear Monsignor ——
dowager see widow
duchess
address: Her Grace the Duchess of ——; *or* The Most Noble the Duchess of ——
begin: Madam; *or* Your Grace
duchess of the blood royal
address: Her Royal Highness The Duchess of ——
begin: Madam; *or* May it please your Royal Highness
duke
address: His Grace the Duke of ——; *or* The Most Noble the Duke of ——
begin: My Lord Duke; *or* Your Grace
duke of the blood royal
address: His Royal Highness The Duke of ——
begin: Sir; *or* May it please your Royal Highness
duke's daughter†
address: The Lady Mary ——; *or* The Right Honourable Lady ——
begin: Madam; *or* My Lady
(if her husband holds a title of nobility, either by right or courtesy, the wife is ordinarily addressed according to her husband's title)
duke's eldest son
address: The Most Honourable the Marquess ——; *or* The Marquess of ——
begin: My Lord Marquess; *or* My Lord
duke's eldest son's daughter same as baron's daughter
duke's eldest son's eldest son use grandfather's third title
duke's eldest son's wife
address: The Most Honourable the Marchioness of ——
begin: My Lady Marchioness
duke's wife = duchess
duke's younger son
address: The Right Honourable Lord —— ——
begin: My Lord
duke's younger son's wife
address: Lady —— ——
begin: Madam; *or* My Lady; *or* Your Ladyship

E

earl
address: The Right Honourable The Earl of ——; *or* The Earl of ——
begin: My Lord
earl's daughter like duke's daughter
earl's eldest son
address: The Right Honourable the Viscount ——; *or* The Right Honourable Lord ——
begin: My Lord Viscount ——
earl's wife = countess
earl's younger son same as baron's son
earl's younger son's wife†
address: Honourable Mrs. ——
begin: Madam
envoy same as minister (diplomatic)
esquire
address: —— ——, Esq.
begin: Sir; *or* Dear Sir; *or* Dear Mr. ——
(*Esq.* is never used if the person is addressed by any other title, even *Mr.*)

F

French common forms
(these forms are acceptable for nearly all diplomats other than English-speaking)
man
address: M. —— ——
begin: Monsieur
pl. address: Messrs. ——
begin: Messieurs
married woman
address: Mme. —— ——
begin: Madame
pl. address: Mmes. —— —— et —— ——
begin: Mesdames
unmarried woman
address: Mlle. —— ——
begin: Madame (formal); *or* Mademoiselle (informal)
pl. address: Mlles. —— —— et —— ——
begin: Mesdames

G

German common forms
man
address: Herrn —— ——
begin: Sehr geehrter Herr
pl. address: Herren —— ——
begin: Geehrte Herren
married woman
address: Frau —— ——
begin: Sehr geehrte Frau ——
unmarried young woman
address: Fräulein —— ——
begin: Mein liebes Fräulein (cordial)
governor
address (in Massachusetts and in New Hampshire and by courtesy in some other states) His Excellency, The Governor of ——; *or* His Excellency —— ——; *or* (in other states of the U.S.) The Honorable the Governor of ——; *or* The Honorable —— ——, Governor of ——
begin: Sir; *or* Dear Sir
governor-general of an independent commonwealth
address: His Excellency —— —— (personal title and name), Governor-General of ——
begin: Sir (or according to rank)
governor-general of Canada†
address: His Excellency The Right Honourable —— ——, (plus personal rank or title, if any)
begin: My Lord; *or* Sir (according to rank)
governor-general's wife (British dominions)†
address: Her Excellency —— ——
begin: Madam

H

honorary chamberlain to the pope same as papal chamberlain

I

internuncio see papal nuncio
Italian common forms
man
address: Gentilissimo Signore ——
begin: Gentilissimo Signore
pl. address: Spettabile Ditta ——
begin: Spettabile Ditta
married woman
address: Distinta Signora ——
begin: Distinta Signora
unmarried woman
address: Esimia Signorina —— ——
begin: Esimia Signorina

J

judge (in Canada)
address: The Honourable Mr. Justice —— (if of a superior court or of the circuit court of Montreal); *or* His Honour Judge —— (if of a lower court)
begin: Sir
judge (in England and the British dominions [except as noted elsewhere in this table])
address: Honourable Mr. Justice ——; *or* (when a knight) Honourable Sir ——
begin: Sir
judge (in U.S.)
address: The Honorable —— ——, United States District Judge (or Chief Judge of the Court of Appeals, etc.)
begin: Dear Sir; *or* My dear Judge ——
see also chief justice, associate justice
judge of City of London court *or* of a county court in England *or* of a court in British colonies
address: His Honour Judge ——
begin: Sir; *or* Dear Sir
junior added to a son's name to distinguish him from his father with the same name, —— ——, Jr.; *or* —— ——, Jr., Ph.D.; *or* jr.
justice see associate justice, chief justice, judge

K

king
address: The King's Most Excellent Majesty; *or* His Most Gracious Majesty, King ——
begin: Sir; *or* May it please your Majesty
king's counsel
address: To —— ——, Esq., K.C.
begin: Sir; *or* Dear Sir
knight
address: Sir —— —— (initials of his order, if any, as K.C.B.)
begin: Sir
knight's wife see lady

L

lady
address: Lady ——; *or* (if the daughter of a baron or viscount) Hon. Lady ——; *or* (if the daughter

of an earl, marquess, or duke) Lady Florence ——
begin: Madam; My Lady; Your Ladyship
lady mayoress see lord mayor's wife
lawyer
address: —— ——, Esq.; *or* Mr. —— ——, Attorney-at-Law
begin: Dear Sir; My dear Mr. ——; etc.
(Mr. —— ——, Esq. is incorrect)
lieutenant governor
address: The Honorable —— ——, Lieutenant Governor of ——; (British) His Honour The Lieutenant Governor of ——†
begin: Sir; *or* Dear Sir
lord advocate†
address: To the Right Honourable the Lord Advocate; *or* The Right Honourable —— ——
begin: Sir
lord chancellor†
address: The Right Honourable the Lord High Chancellor; *or* The Right Honourable —— (hereditary title), Lord High Chancellor
begin: My Lord (or according to rank)
lord chief justice of England†
address: To the Lord Chief Justice of England; *or* To the Rt. Hon. Baron ——, Lord Chief Justice of England
begin: Sir
lord mayor (of London, York, Belfast, Melbourne, Sydney, Brisbane, Hobart, Adelaide, and Perth)
address: The Right Honourable Lord Mayor of ——; *or* The Right Honourable ——, Lord Mayor of ——
(all other lord mayors are addressed as The Right Worshipful)
begin: My Lord
lord mayor's wife
address: Mrs. —— ——
begin: Madam
lord of appeal in ordinary same as baron
lord of appeal in ordinary's children same as baron's children
lord of appeal in ordinary's wife same as baroness
lord of council and session
address: Honourable Lord ——
begin: My Lord
lord of council and session's wife
address: Lady ——
begin: Madam
lord provost
address: The Honourable the Lord Provost; *or* The Honourable ——, Lord Provost of ——; *or* (in Edinburgh and Glasgow) The Right Honourable the Lord Provost, etc.
begin: Sir

M

maid of honor
address: The Honourable Miss ——
begin: Madam
marchioness
address: The Most Honourable the Marchioness of ——
begin: Madam
marquess
address: The Most Honourable the Marquess of ——; *or* The Marquess of ——
begin: My Lord Marquess
marquess's children like duke's children
married woman see common forms
master of the rolls
address: To the Right Honourable the Master of the Rolls
begin: Sir
mayor (in Canadian cities and towns, and English boroughs)
address: His Worship, The Mayor of ——
begin: Sir
mayor (in English cities)
address: The Right Worshipful the Mayor of ——
begin: Sir (see also lord mayor)
mayor (in the U.S.)
address: The Honorable —— ——, Mayor of ——; *or* The Mayor of the City of ——
begin: Sir; *or* Dear Sir; *or* Dear Mr. Mayor; *or* My dear Mr. Mayor
member of parliament (*or* **of a provincial legislative council** *or* **of a provincial legislature,** etc.) the ordinary form of address followed by M.P. (*or* M.L.C., *or* M.P.P., *or* M.L.A., etc.)
military officers see army officers
minister (diplomatic)
address: The Honorable —— ——, Minister of Costa Rica; *or* Her Majesty's Minister for the United Kingdom
begin: Sir (or with personal title, as My Lord, Your Grace, etc.); *or* My dear Mr. Minister
minister of a provincial cabinet of Canada
address: The Honourable —— ——, Minister of ——
begin: Sir
minister of religion see clergyman, priest, rabbi
moderator (of the General Assembly of the Church of Scotland)
address: The Right Reverend —— ——
begin: Right Reverend Sir
monk see priest regular, clerk
monsignor see domestic prelate, papal chamberlain, protonotary apostolic, vicar general
mother superior of a sisterhood
address: The Reverend Mother Superior, Convent of ——; *or* Reverend Mother ——, O.S.D. (*or* other initials of the order); *or* Mother ——, Superior, Convent of ——
begin: Reverend Mother; *or* Dear Madam; *or* Dear Reverend Mother (informal); *or* My dear Reverend Mother ——

N

naval officers
address: The Admiral of the Navy of the United States; *or* Admiral ——, Commanding United States Navy; Captain —— ——, U.S.N.
begin: Sir; *or* (informal) My dear Admiral ——; Dear Commander ——; but for officers below the rank of commander, Dear Mr. ——
nun see sister of a religious order
nuncio see papal nuncio

P

papal ablegate
address: The Right Reverend Monsignor ——, Ablegate of His Holiness the Pope
begin: Right Reverend Monsignor
papal chamberlain
address: The Very Reverend Monsignor —— ——
begin: Very Reverend and dear Monsignor
papal chaplain same as papal chamberlain
papal nuncio *or* **internuncio** *or* **apostolic delegate**
address: His Excellency, The Papal Nuncio (*or* Internuncio *or* Apostolic Delegate) to ——
begin: Your Excellency
parliament, member of see member of parliament
patriarch (Eastern Church)
address: His Beatitude the Patriarch of ——; *or* His Beatitude the Lord ——, Patriarch of ——
begin: Most Reverend Lord; *or* Your Beatitude
patriarch (Roman Catholic Church)
address: His Excellency, the Patriarch (Archbishop) of ——
begin: Your Excellency
peer see duke, marquess, earl, baron
pope
address: To His Holiness Pope ——
begin: Most Holy Father; Your Holiness
postmaster general see cabinet officers
preacher general
address: The Venerable and Very Reverend Father —— ——, O.P., P.G.
begin: Very Reverend Father
premier of a province of Canada
address: The Honourable ——, Premier of the Province of ——
begin: Sir
president of a Canadian legislative council
address: The Honourable ——, The President of the Legislative Council
begin: Sir
president of a college *or* **university**
address: —— ——, LL.D. (*or* if he is not an LL.D., the initials of his highest degree), President of —— University (*or* President, —— University); *or* President —— ——
If he is a clergyman, Reverend —— ——, LL.D., President of —— University
begin: Dear Sir; *or* Dear President ——
president of a theological seminary
address: The Rev. President —— ——
begin: Dear Sir; *or* Dear President ——
president of state senate
address: The Honorable —— ——, President of the Senate of ——
begin: Sir
president of the Senate of the United States
address: The Honorable, The President of the Senate of the United States; *or* The Honorable —— ——, President of the Senate
begin: Sir
president of the United States
address: The President, The White House (*His Excellency* should not be used)
begin: Mr. President; *or* The President; *or* My Dear Mr. President
priest (Roman Catholic Church)
regular (except as noted below)
address: Reverend —— ——, O.S.M. (*or* other initials of his order)
begin: Dear Father —— (religious name)
Benedictine, Cistercian, *or* **canon regular**
address: The Reverend Dom —— ——, C.R.L. (*or* other initials of his order)
begin: Reverend Father; *or* Dear Father ——
Carthusian
address: The Venerable Father Dom —— ——, O.Cart.
begin: Venerable Father; *or* Dear Father ——
secular
address: Reverend —— ——, (followed by the initials of his degree)
begin: Reverend and dear Father
prime minister of Canada
address: The Right Honourable —— ——, P.C., Prime Minister of Canada
begin: Sir
prime minister of the United Kingdom
address: The Right Honourable —— ——, P.C., M.P., Prime Minister
begin: Sir
prince of the blood royal
address: His Royal Highness Prince —— (given name)
begin: Sir
see also duke of the blood royal
prince of Wales
address: His Royal Highness The Prince of Wales
begin: Sir; *or* May it please your Royal Highness
princess of the blood royal
address: Her Royal Highness the Princess —— (given name)
begin: Madam
see also duchess of the blood royal
princess of Wales
address: Her Royal Highness The Princess of Wales
begin: Madam
prior, claustral
address: The Very Reverend Dom —— ——, O.C. (*or* other initials of his order); *or* The Very Reverend Father Prior, —— Abbey
begin: Very Reverend Father; *or* Dear Father Prior
prior, conventual
address: The Very Reverend the Prior of ——; *or* The Very Reverend Father (*or* Dom) —— ——, O.P. (*or* other initials of his order), Prior of ——; *or* The Very Reverend Father Guardian, O.F.M.; *or* The Very Rev. —— ——, Prior (*or* Guardian) of ——
begin: Very Reverend Father; *or* Dear Father Prior; *or* Very Reverend and Dear Father
prioress
address: The Very Reverend the Prioress of ——; *or* The Very Reverend Mother (*or* Dame) —— ——, (followed by the initials of her order), Prioress of ——
begin: Very Reverend Mother; *or* Dear Mother Prioress
privy chamberlain to the pope same as papal chamberlain
privy councillor (British imperial)†
address: To the Right Honourable —— ——, P.C.
begin: Sir
If other titles are used, they should come after *The Right Honourable;* as, The Right Honourable Sir John ——
privy councillor (of Canada)
address: The Honourable —— ——
begin: Sir
professor in a college *or* **university**
address: Professor —— ——; *or* —— ——, Ph.D. (*or* LL.D., M.D., etc., using only the initials of his highest degree, if the degrees are in the same field), Professor of ——
begin: Dear Sir; *or* My dear Professor ——; *or* Dear Professor ——; *or* My dear Professor; etc.
professor in a theological seminary
address: The Reverend Professor —— ——; *or* The Rev. —— ——, D.D.; *or* Professor —— ——
begin: Dear Sir; *or* Dear Professor ——
protonotary apostolic
address: The Right Reverend Monsignor —— ——, Protonotary Apostolic (or P.A.)
begin: Right Reverend Monsignor; *or* Dear Monsignor ——
provincial of a religious order
address: The Very Reverend Father Provincial, O.F.M. (*or* other initials of his order); *or* The Very Reverend Father —— ——, Provincial, S.J.
begin: Very Reverend and dear Father
provost see lord provost
provost (Roman Catholic Church)
address: The Very Reverend Provost ——
begin: Very Reverend Provost; *or* Dear Provost
puisne judge of the Supreme Court of Canada
address: The Honourable Mr. Justice ——
begin: Sir

Q

queen
address: The Queen's Most Excellent Majesty; *or* Her Gracious Majesty, The Queen
begin: Madam; *or* May it please your Majesty
queen mother
address: Her Gracious Majesty Queen ——
begin: Madam; *or* May it please your Majesty

R

rabbi
address: Rabbi —— ——; *or* Rev. —— ——
begin: Reverend Sir; *or* Dear Sir; *or* My dear Rabbi ——; *or* Dear Rabbi ——
(if he holds a doctor's degree, Dr. may be substituted for Rabbi)
recorder
address: His Honour Recorder ——
begin: Sir
rector of a religious house *or* **of a seminary**
address: The Very Reverend —— ——, O.S.B. (*or* other initials of the order), Rector, Brothers of St. Francis (*or* Brother)
begin: Very Reverend and dear Father
representative see congressman

S

Scottish land court chairman same as lord of council and session
secretary of agriculture, state, defense, etc. see cabinet officer
secretary of state (England)
address: His Majesty's Principal Secretary of State for the —— Department (this may be preceded by hereditary title)
begin: according to rank (Your Grace, My Lord, etc.)
senator (Canadian)
address: The Honourable —— ——
begin: Dear Sir; Dear Senator ——; etc.
senator (U.S.)
address: The Honorable —— ——, The United

States Senate, Washington, D.C.
begin: Dear Sir; *or* My dear Senator
senior added to a father's name to distinguish him from a son of the same name; as, —— ——, Sr.; *or* —— ——, Sr., Ph.D.; *or* sr.
señor see Spanish common forms
serjeant-at-law
address: Serjeant ——; *or* Mr. Serjeant ——
begin: Sir; *or* Dear Sir
sister of a religious order
address: Sister ——, (followed by the initials of the order)
begin: Dear Sister; *or* My dear Sister; *or* Dear Sister ——; *or* My dear Sister ——
solicitor general (Canada)
address: The Honourable ——
begin: Sir
solicitor general (U.S.)
address: The Solicitor General
begin: Sir; *or* Dear Sir; *or* Dear Mr. ——
Spanish common forms
man
address: Señor —— ——
begin: Muy señor mío
pl. address: Señores —— ——
begin: Muy señores nuestros
married woman
address: Señora de ——; or Señora Doña —— de ——
begin: Muy estimada señora
unmarried woman
address: Señorita ——; *or* Señorita Doña ——
begin: Muy distinguida señorita
speaker of a provincial legislature of Canada
address: The Honourable ——, The Speaker of (name of legislature)
begin: Dear Mr. Speaker
speaker of the House of Commons (Canada)
address: The Honourable ——, The Speaker of the House of Commons
begin: Dear Mr. Speaker
speaker of the House of Representatives of the United States
address: The Honorable —— ——, Speaker of the House of Representatives
begin: Sir; *or* Mr. Speaker; *or* My dear Mr. Speaker
speaker of the Senate (Canada)
address: The Honourable —— ——, Speaker of the Senate
begin: Dear Mr. Speaker
state senator like senator (U.S.)
superior general of a religious community of priests
address: The Most Reverend Father —— (followed by the initials of the order), Superior General of the —— Fathers
begin: Most Reverend Father General
superior general of a religious order (female)
address: The Reverend Mother ——, (followed by the initials of her order), Superior General of ——
begin: Reverend Mother
Supreme Court see chief justice, associate justice

U

undersecretary of state (U.S.)
address: The Undersecretary of State; *or* The Honorable ——, Undersecretary of State
begin: Sir; *or* Dear Sir; *or* Dear Mr. ——
unmarried woman see common forms

V

vicar-general
address: The Right Reverend Monsignor —— ——, V.G.; *or* The Right Reverend the Vicar-General
begin: Right Reverend and dear Monsignor
vice-chancellor (law) same as judge (in England)
vice-consul similar to consul
vice-president
address: The Vice-President; *or* The Honorable, The Vice-President of the United States; *or* The Honorable —— ——, Vice-President of the United States
begin: Mr. Vice-President; *or* Sir; *or* My dear Mr. Vice-President
viceroy
address: His Excellency, The Lord Lieutenant of Ireland (The Viceroy of India)
begin: Excellency
viscount
address: The Right Honourable the Viscount ——; *or* The Viscount ——
begin: My Lord
viscountess
address: The Right Honourable the Viscountess ——; *or* The Viscountess ——
Begin: Madam
viscount's children same as baron's children

W

widow
(ordinarily addressed by her former title: as, Mrs. John Doe, not Mrs. Jane Doe, unless the latter form is preferred by the person herself; but if her married son, stepson, or grandson now holds a title of nobility formerly held by her late husband, the word dowager may be added before (or after) her title to distinguish her from the younger lady of the same title; as, Her Grace the Dowager Duchess of ——; The Dowager Lady ——; when such relationship does not exist, she may be distinguished by using her given name; as, The Right Honourable Jane, Countess of ——; the latter form is now generally preferred by ladies entitled to the distinction *Dowager;* officially a widow who remarries is not recognized as having any claim to bear the title of her deceased husband, but courtesy usually accords her this title)

ABBREVIATIONS USED IN THIS DICTIONARY

AA .... Associate in Arts
AAS ...... Associate in Applied Science
ab .... about
AB .... Bachelor of Arts
abbr ...... abbreviation
Abd ...... Abdias
AB in Th .. Bachelor of Arts in Theology
abl .... ablative
AC .... alternating current
acad ...... academy
acc or
accus ..... accusative
act .... active
A.D. ...... anno Domini
adj .... adjective
adv .... adverb
advt .... advertisement
Aeol ...... Aeolic
AF .... Anglo-French
Afr .... Africa, African
Afrik ...... Afrikaans
Agg .... Aggeus
agric ...... agriculture
A.H. ...... anno Hegirae
Ala .... Alabama
Alb .... Albanian
alter ...... alteration
a.m. ...... ante meridiem
AM .... amplitude modulation, Master of Arts
Am or
Amer ..... America, American
AmerF .... American French
AmerInd ... American Indian
AmerSp or
AmSp .... American Spanish
anat ...... anatomy
anthrop .... anthropological, anthropology
aor .... aorist
Apoc ...... Apocalypse
appar ..... apparently
Apr .... April
Ar .... Arabic
Aram ...... Aramaic
archeol .... archeology
archit ..... architecture
arith ...... arithmetic
Ariz .... Arizona
Ark .... Arkansas
Arm .... Armenian
art .... article
assoc or
assn ...... association
ASSR ..... Autonomous Soviet Socialist Republic
Assyr ..... Assyrian
Assyr-Bab .. Assyro-Babylonian
astrol ..... astrology
astron .... astronomy
ASV ...... American Standard Version
at.no. ..... atomic number
attrib ..... attributive, attributively
at.wt. ..... atomic weight
aug .... augmentative
Aug .... August
Austral .... Australia
Av .... Avestan
AV .... Authorized Version
b .... born
BA .... Bachelor of Arts
Bab .... Babylonian
bacteriol ... bacteriology
BA(J) ..... Bachelor of Arts in Journalism
Bar .... Baruch
BArch ..... Bachelor of Architecture
bart .... baronet
BBC .... British Broadcasting Corporation
B.C. ...... before Christ, British Columbia
BChE ..... Bachelor of Chemical Engineering
BCS ...... Bachelor of Commercial Science
BD .... Bachelor of Divinity
Bé .... Baumé
BE .... Bachelor of Education, Bachelor of Engineering
BEd .... Bachelor of Education
bef .... before
Bel .... Bel and the Dragon
Belg ...... Belgian, Belgium
Beng ...... Bengali
BFA .... Bachelor of Fine Arts
biochem .... biochemistry
biog .... biographical, biography
biol .... biologic, biological, biology
BJ .... Bachelor of Journalism
bk .... book
BldgE ..... Building Engineer
BLitt or
BLit .... Bachelor of Letters, Bachelor of Literature
bot .... botany
Braz ...... Brazilian
Bret .... Breton
brig .... brigadier
Brit .... Britain, British
bros .... brothers
BS .... Bachelor of Science
BSA ...... Bachelor of Science in Agriculture
BSc .... Bachelor of Science
BSEd or
BSE ...... Bachelor of Science in Education
BSFS ..... Bachelor of Science in Foreign Service
BS in CE .. Bachelor of Science in Chemical Engineering, Bachelor of Science in Civil Engineering
BS in ChE . Bachelor of Science in Chemical Engineering
BS in Ed .. Bachelor of Science in Education
BS in LS .. Bachelor of Science in Library Science, Bachelor of Science in Library Service
bt .... baronet
Btu .... British thermal unit, British thermal units
Bulg ...... Bulgarian
bull .... bulletin
C .... centigrade
cal .... calendar, caliber
Calif ...... California
Canad ..... Canada, Canadian
CanF ..... Canadian French
Cant ...... Cantonese
cap .... capital, capitalized
capt .... captain
Cast ...... Castilian
cat .... catalog
Catal ...... Catalan
caus .... causative
cc .... cubic centimeter, cubic centimeters
CE .... Chemical Engineer, Civil Engineer
Celt .... Celtic

cen central
cent century
cgs centimeter-gram-second
Chald Chaldean
chem chemical, chemistry
Chin Chinese
Chron Chronicles
cm centimeter, centimeters
co company, county
col colonel
Col Colossians
coll college
colloq colloquial
Colo Colorado
com common
comb combination, combining
compar or *comp* comparative
conj conjunction
Conn Connecticut
cons consonant
constr construction
contr contraction
Copt Coptic
Cor Corinthians
Corn Cornish
corp corporation
cos cosine
CPA Certified Public Accountant
CRL Canons Regular of the Lateran
crystallog crystallography
cu cubic
cwt hundredweight
cycl cyclopedia
Czech Czechoslovak, Czechoslovakia, Czechoslovakian
d denarius, denarii, penny, pence
D Dutch
Dan Daniel, Danish
dat dative
D.C. District of Columbia
DC direct current
DD Doctor of Divinity
Dec December
def definite
Del Delaware
dept department
Deut Deuteronomy
dial dialect
dict dictionary
dim diminished, diminutive
DLitt or *DLit* Doctor of Letters, Doctor of Literature
dom dominant
Dor Doric
doz dozen
DP domestic prelate
dr debit, doctor
DSc Doctor of Science
Du Dutch
DV Douay Version
E east, eastern, English
eccl ecclesiastic, ecclesiastical
Eccles Ecclesiastes
Ecclus Ecclesiasticus
ecol ecological, ecology
econ economics
ed edition
EdM Master of Education
educ education, educational
EE Electrical Engineer
EFris East Frisian
e.g. exempli gratia
EGmc East Germanic
Egypt Egyptian
embryol embryology
emu electromagnetic unit, electromagnetic units
encyc encyclopedia
Eng England, English
engin engineering
Eph Ephesians
Esd Esdras
Esk Eskimo
esp especially
esq esquire
EST eastern standard time
Esth Esther
esu electrostatic unit, electrostatic units
etc et cetera
Eth Ethiopic
ethnol ethnology
eve evening
Exod Exodus
explan explanatory
Ezech Ezechiel
Ezek Ezekiel
f following
F Fahrenheit, French
FBI Federal Bureau of Investigation
Feb February
fem feminine
ff following
fig figurative, figuratively, figure
Finn Finnish
fl flourished
Fla Florida
Flem Flemish
FM frequency modulation
fo or *f* folio
f.o.b. free on board
fps foot-pound-second
fr from
Fr French
freq frequent, frequentative, frequently
Fri Friday
Fris Frisian
ft feet, foot
fund fundamental
fut future
g acceleration of gravity
G German
Ga Georgia
gal gallon, gallons
Gal Galatians
gaz gazette
gen general, genitive
Gen Genesis
geog geographic, geographical
geol geologic, geological, geology
geom geometry
Ger German
GI government issue
Gk Greek
gm gram, grams
Gmc Germanic
Goth Gothic
govt government
Gt Brit Great Britain
h hour, hours
Hab Habacuc, Habakkuk
Hag Haggai
handbk handbook
HE his excellency
Heb Hebrew, Hebrews
HG High German
hist historical, history
Hitt Hittite
HMS Her Majesty's Ship, His Majesty's Ship
hon honorable, honorary
hort horticulture
Hos Hosea
hp horsepower
ht height
Hung Hungarian
Icel Icelandic
i.e. that is
IE Indo-European
Ill Illinois
IMF International Monetary Fund
imit imitative
imp or *imper* imperative
imperf imperfect
in inch, inches
inc incorporated
incho inchoative
Ind Indiana
indic indicative
infin infinitive
infl influenced
inst institute, institution, institutional
instr instrumental
interj interjection
internat or *internatl* international
interrog interrogative
intrans intransitive
inv inversion
Ion Ionic
IPA International Phonetic Alphabet
Ir Irish
Ire Ireland
IrGael Irish Gaelic
irreg irregular
Isa Isaiah, Isaias
ISV International Scientific Vocabulary
It or *Ital* Italian
ital italic, italicized
Jan January
Jap Japanese
Jas James
Jav Javanese
Jer Jeremiah, Jeremias
jg junior grade
Jn John
JND just noticeable difference
Jos Josue
Josh Joshua
jour journal
JPS Jewish Publication Society
jr junior
Jth Judith
Judg Judges
K Kelvin (scale)
Kans Kansas
KC king's counsel
KCB Knight Commander of the Bath
kg kilogram, kilograms
kgps kilogram per second, kilograms per second
km kilometer, kilometers
KP kitchen police
kt knight
Ky Kentucky
L Latin
La Louisiana
LaF Louisiana French
Lam Lamentations
lang language, languages
lat latitude
lb pound, pounds
l.c. lowercase
Lev Leviticus
lg large
LG Low German
LGk Late Greek
LH lower half
LHD Doctor of Humanities
LHeb late Hebrew
lieut lieutenant
lit literal, literally, literary
Lith Lithuanian
LittB or *LitB* Bachelor of Letters, Bachelor of Literature
LittD or *LitD* Doctor of Letters, Doctor of Literature
Lk Luke
LL Late Latin
LLB Bachelor of Laws
LLD Doctor of Laws
loc locative
long longitude
LP long-playing
lt. lieutenant
ltd limited
LXX Septuagint
m meridies (L., noon), meter, meters, minute, minutes
M monsieur
MA Master of Arts
Macc Maccabees
Maced Macedonian
Mach Machabees
mag magazine
maj major
Mal Malachi, Malachias
manuf manufacture, manufacturing
Mar March
masc masculine
Mass Massachusetts
math mathematics
MBA Master of Business Administration
MBret Middle Breton
Md Maryland
MD Doctor of Medicine, Middle Dutch
Me Maine
ME Middle English
mech mechanical
med medical, medicine
MEd Master of Education
met metropolitan
meteorol meteorology
Mex Mexican, Mexico
MexSp Mexican Spanish
MF Master of Forestry, Middle French
mfg manufacturing
MFlem Middle Flemish
MFS Master of Foreign Study
mg milligram, milligrams
MGk Middle Greek
MHeb Middle Hebrew
MHG Middle High German
Mic Micah
Mich Micheas, Michigan
mil military
min minor, minute, minutes
Minn Minnesota
MIr Middle Irish
misc miscellaneous
Miss Mississippi
Mk Mark
mks meter-kilogram-second
ml milliliter, milliliters
ML Medieval Latin
MLA member of the legislative assembly
MLC member of the legislative council
MLG Middle Low German
Mlle mademoiselle
MLS Master of Library Science
mm millimeter, millimeters
Mme madame
Mo Missouri
mod modern
modif modification
Mon Monday
Mont Montana
MP member of parliament, military police
MPA Master of Public Administration
MPer Middle Persian
mph miles per hour
MPP member of provincial parliament
MS manuscript, Master of Science
MSc Master of Science
MS in LS Master of Science in Library Science
MSS manuscripts
MSw Middle Swedish
mt mount, mountain
Mt Matthew
MusM Master of Music
MW Middle Welsh
mythol mythology
n noun
N north, northern
Nah Nahum
nat or *natl* national
NATO North Atlantic Treaty Organization
naut nautical
N.C. North Carolina
NCAA National Collegiate Athletic Association
NCE New Catholic Edition
N. Dak. North Dakota
NE northeast
Nebr Nebraska
Neh Nehemiah
neut neuter
Nev Nevada
NewEng New England
NewZeal New Zealand
NGk New Greek
NGmc North Germanic
N.H. New Hampshire
NHeb New Hebrew
N.J. New Jersey
NL New Latin
N. Mex. New Mexico
no north, number
nom nominative
nonattrib nonattributively
nonstand nonstandard
Norw Norwegian
Nov November
n pl noun plural
N.S. Nova Scotia
NT New Testament
Num Numbers
numis numismatic, numismatical, numismatics
NW northwest
NWT Northwest Territories
N.Y. New York
NYC New York City
N.Z. New Zealand
O Ohio, old
Obad Obadiah
OBret Old Breton
obs obsolete
OBulg Old Bulgarian
OC Cistercian Order
O Cart Carthusian Order
OCatal Old Catalan
occas occasionally
OCorn Old Cornish
Oct October
OD Old Dutch
ODan Old Danish
OE Old English
OF Old French
OFM Order of Friars Minor
OFris Old Frisian
OFrk Old Frankish
OHG Old High German
OIcel Old Icelandic
OIr Old Irish
OIt Old Italian
Okla Oklahoma
OL Old Latin
old-fash old-fashioned
OLF Old Low Franconian
ON Old Norse
ONF Old North French
ONorw Old Norwegian
Ont Ontario
o.p. out of print
OP Order of Preachers
OPer Old Persian
OPg Old Portuguese
OPol Old Polish
OProv Old Provençal
OPruss Old Prussian
Oreg Oregon
orig originally
ORuss Old Russian
OS Old Saxon
OSB Order of St. Benedict
Osc Oscan
OScan Old Scandinavian
OSD Order of St. Dominic
OSlav Old Slavic
OSM Order of the Servants of Mary
OSp Old Spanish
OSw Old Swedish
OT Old Testament
OTurk Old Turkish
OW Old Welsh
oz ounce, ounces
p page
Pa Pennsylvania
PA protonotary apostolic
PaG Pennsylvania German
paleontol paleontology
Par Paralipomenon

part .... participle
pass .... passive
pathol .... pathology
PC .... privy councilor
Pek .... Pekingese
Per or *Pers* .... Persian
perf .... perfect
perh .... perhaps
pers .... person
Pet .... Peter
pfc .... private first class
Pg or *Port* .... Portuguese
PG .... preacher general
pharm .... pharmacy
PhB .... Bachelor of Philosophy
PhC .... Pharmaceutical Chemist
PhD .... Doctor of Philosophy
Phil .... Philippians
Philem .... Philemon
philos .... philosophy
PhilSp .... Philippine Spanish
photog .... photography
phr .... phrase
physiol .... physiology
pkg .... package
pl .... plural
p.m. .... post meridiem
Pol .... Polish
polit .... political
pop .... population
poss .... possessive
pp .... pages
prep .... preposition
pres .... present, president
Pr Man .... Prayer of Manasseh
prob .... probably
pron .... pronoun, pronunciation
prond .... pronounced
pronunc .... pronunciation
protect .... protection
prov .... province
Prov .... Provençal, Proverbs
prox .... proximo
Ps .... Psalms
psychol .... psychology
PTA .... Parent-Teacher Association
pub .... public
publ .... publication
rap .... rapid
RD .... rural dean
recd .... received
redupl .... reduplication
ref .... reference
refl .... reflexive
rel .... relative
relig .... religion
rep .... republic
repr .... representatives
resp .... respectively
ret .... retired
rev .... reverend, review
Rev .... Revelation
rev. ed. .... revised edition
R.I. .... Rhode Island
Rom .... Roman, Romance, Romanian, Romans
ROTC .... Reserve Officers' Training Corps
rpm .... revolutions per minute
RR .... railroad
RSV .... Revised Standard Version
rt hon .... right honorable
Rum .... Rumanian
Russ .... Russian
s .... shilling, shillings
S .... south, southern
S.A. .... South Australia
Sam .... Samuel
Sat .... Saturday
SB .... Bachelor of Science
Sc .... Scots
S.C. .... South Carolina
Scand .... Scandinavian
ScD .... Doctor of Science
ScGael .... Scottish Gaelic
sci .... science
Scot .... Scotland, Scottish
S. Dak. .... South Dakota
SE .... southeast
sec .... second, seconds, section
secy .... secretary
Sem .... Semitic
Sept .... September
Serb .... Serbian
Shak .... Shakespeare
sin .... sine
sing .... singular
SJ .... Society of Jesus
SJD .... Doctor of Juridical Science
Skt .... Sanskrit
Slav .... Slavic
SM .... Master of Science
so .... south
SoAfr .... South Africa
soc .... social, society
sociol .... sociology
Sol .... Solomon
Soph .... Sophonias
South .... Southern
Sp or *Span* .... Spanish
specif .... specific, specifically
sp. gr. .... specific gravity
sq .... square
sr .... senior
SSR .... Soviet Socialist Republic
st .... saint, street
stand .... standard
stat .... statute
STB .... Bachelor of Sacred Theology, Bachelor of Theology
STD .... Doctor of Sacred Theology
ste .... saint
STL .... Licentiate of Sacred Theology
STM .... Master of Sacred Theology, Master of Theology
subj .... subjunctive
substand .... substandard
Sun .... Sunday
superl .... superlative
supp .... supplement
Sus .... Susanna
Sw or *Swed* .... Swedish
SW .... southwest
syll .... syllable
syn .... synonym, synonymy
Syr .... Syriac
Tag .... Tagalog
tech .... technical, technological, technology
technol .... technology
tel .... telegraph, telephone
Tenn .... Tennessee
Tex .... Texas
ThD .... Doctor of Theology
theol .... theological
Thess .... Thessalonians
Thurs .... Thursday
Tim .... Timothy
Tit .... Titus
Tob .... Tobias, Tobit
Toch .... Tocharian
Toch A .... Tocharian A
Toch B .... Tocharian B
trans or *transl* .... translated, translation
Tues .... Tuesday
Turk .... Turkish
TV .... television
TVA .... Tennessee Valley Authority
UH .... upper half
Ukr .... Ukrainian
Umbr .... Umbrian
UN .... United Nations
UNESCO .... United Nations' Educational, Scientific and Cultural Organization
univ .... university
US .... United States
USA .... United States of America
USN .... United States Navy
USNR .... United States Naval Reserve
USS .... United States Ship
USSR .... Union of Soviet Socialist Republics
usu .... usual, usually
v .... velocity, verb, versus, vowel
Va .... Virginia
var .... variant
vb .... verb
VF .... vicar forane
VG .... vicar-general
vi .... verb intransitive
v imper .... verb imperative
viz .... videlicet
VL .... Vulgar Latin
voc .... vocative
vocab .... vocabulary
vol .... volume
vt .... verb transitive
Vt .... Vermont
VT .... variable time
W .... Welsh, west, western
Wall .... Walloon
Wash .... Washington
Wed .... Wednesday
WFris .... West Frisian
WGmc .... West Germanic
Wis or *Wisc* .... Wisconsin
Wisd .... Wisdom
Wisd Sol .... Wisdom of Solomon
W. Va. .... West Virginia
Wyo .... Wyoming
YMCA .... Young Men's Christian Association
yr .... year
yrbk .... yearbook
YWCA .... Young Women's Christian Association
Zach .... Zacharias
Zech .... Zechariah
Zeph .... Zephaniah
zool .... zoological, zoology

SPECIAL SYMBOLS

[ ].... boldface square brackets contain etymology
:...... boldface symbolic colon signals a definition or sense
~..... boldface or lightface swung dash stands for the preceding boldface entry word
⟨ ⟩.... lightface angle brackets contain a verbal illustration
=...... lightface double hyphen at end-of-line is a hyphen that should be retained
☞...... fistnote (see definition)
+..... plus sign in etymology joins words or word elements
†...... dagger precedes a death date

ADDENDA SECTION

WEBSTER'S THIRD NEW INTERNATIONAL DICTIONARY

a* *abbr* **1** *cap* adenine **2** atto- *herein*

A and R *abbr* artists and repertory

ab \ˈab\ *n* -S [short for *abdominal*] : an abdominal muscle — usu. used in pl. ⟨highly developed ~s⟩

a band *n, usu cap A* [*a*nisotropic *band*] : one of the cross striations in striated muscle that contains myosin filaments and appears dark under the light microscope and light in polarized light

ABD \ˌā(ˌ)bēˈdē\ *n* -S [*all but dissertation*] : a doctoral candidate who has completed the required course work and examinations but not the dissertation

ab·dom·i·no·plas·ty \abˈdämənōˌplastē\ *n* -ES [*abdomin-* + *-plasty*] : cosmetic surgery of the abdomen that typically involves removal of excess skin and fat and tightening of the abdominal muscles — called also *tummy tuck*

ab·duc·tee \ˌabˌdəkˈtē\ *n* -S : one who has been abducted ⟨UFO ~s⟩

abe·lian \əˈbēlyən, -lēən\ *adj, often cap* [Niels *Abel* †1829 Norw. mathematician + E *-ian*] : COMMUTATIVE 2 ⟨~ ring⟩ ⟨the real numbers under addition comprise an ~ group⟩

ab initio \ˌabiˈnishēō\ *adj* [L, from the beginning] : starting from or based on first principles ⟨predicted by *ab initio* calculations⟩

abio·gen·ic \ˌāˌbīōˈjenik\ *adj* [*²a-* + *biogenic*] : not produced by the action of living organisms — **abio·gen·i·cal·ly** \-nək(ə)lē\ *adv*

ab·la·tor \aˈblād·ə(r)\ *n* -S [*ablate* + *¹-or*] : a material that provides thermal protection (as to the outside of a spacecraft on reentry) by ablating

abled \ˈābəld\ *adj* [back-formation fr. *disabled*] : capable of unimpaired function ⟨~ teachers⟩ ⟨the senior citizens, those less ~ in some way —Richard Hair⟩ — compare DIFFERENTLY ABLED *herein*

able·ism \ˈābəlizəm\ *n* -S [*¹able* + *-ism*] : discrimination or prejudice against individuals with disabilities — **able·ist** \-ləst\ *adj*

ABM \ˌā(ˌ)bēˈem\ *n* -S : ANTIBALLISTIC MISSILE *herein*

aboard* *adv (or adj)* **1** : in or into a group, association, or organization ⟨her second promotion since coming ~⟩ **2** *baseball* : on base

aboriginal* *n, often cap* : ABORIGINE *herein* — **aboriginal*** *adj, often cap*

aborigine* *n, often cap* : a member of any of the indigenous peoples of Australia

abort* *n* : the premature termination of an action, procedure, or mission relating to a rocket or spacecraft ⟨a launch ~⟩

abort·er \ˈ⸗ə(r)\ *n* -S [*¹abort* + *²-er*] : a female that aborts ⟨a chronic ~⟩

¹ABS \ˌā(ˌ)bēˈes\ *n* -ES [*a*crylonitrile-*b*utadiene-*s*tyrene] : a tough rigid plastic used esp. for automobile parts and building materials

²ABS *abbr* antilock brake system; antilock braking system

ab·scis·ic acid \(ˌ)abˌsizik-\ *n* [*abscisic* fr. *abscision* + *-ic*] : a growth-inhibiting plant hormone $C_{15}H_{20}O_4$ widespread in nature and made synthetically that typically promotes leaf abscission and dormancy and has an inhibitory effect on cell elongation — called also *abscisin II, dormin*

ab·scis·in *also* **ab·scis·sin** \abˈsisᵊn\ *n* -S [*abscis*ion, *abscission* + *-in*] : any of several plant hormones that tend to promote leaf abscission and inhibit various growth processes; *esp* : ABSCISIC ACID *herein*

ab·seil \ˈäpˌzīl, -īəl\ *vi* -ED/-ING/-S [*abseil*, n.] *chiefly Brit* : ²RAPPEL — **ab·seil·er** \-ə(r)\ *n* -S

absolute convergence *n* : convergence of a mathematical series when the absolute values of the terms are taken

ab·so·lut·ive \ˌabsəˈlüd·iv *also* -lyü-\ *adj* [*¹absolute* + *¹-ive*] : of, relating to, or being an inflectional morpheme that typically marks the subject of an intransitive verb or the direct object of a transitive verb in an ergative language

ab·sorp·ti·om·e·try \abˌsȯrpshēˈämətrē\ *n* -ES [*absorption* + *-metry*] : the use of an absorptiometer to determine the amount of radiation absorbed (as by living tissue)

absurd* *adj* **1** : having no rational or orderly relationship to man's life : MEANINGLESS; *also* : lacking order or values ⟨adults have condemned them to live in what must seem like an ~ universe —Joseph Featherstone⟩ **2** : dealing with the absurd or with absurdism

absurd *n* -S [*absurd*, adj. (herein)] : the state or condition in which man exists in an irrational and meaningless universe and in which man's life has no meaning outside his own existence

ab·surd·ism \əbˈsərdˌizəm, ab-, -ˈz-\ *n* -S [*absurd* (herein) + *-ism*] : a philosophy based on the belief that man exists in an irrational and meaningless universe and that his search for order brings him into conflict with his universe

¹ab·surd·ist \-dəst\ *n* -S [*absurd* (herein) + *¹-ist*] : a proponent or adherent of absurdism; *esp* : a writer who deals with absurdist themes

²absurdist \"\ *adj* : of, relating to, or dealing with absurdism

abyssal plain *n* : any of the great flat sediment-covered areas of ocean floor

-ac \ˌak, *in a few words* ik *or* ək\ *n suffix* -S [Gk *-akos* of relating to, var. of *-ikos* ¹-ic after noun stems ending in *i*] : one affected with ⟨hemophili*ac*⟩ ⟨nostalgi*ac*⟩

AC* *abbr* **1** air conditioning **2** area code *herein*

aca·de·mese \əˌkadəˈmēz, ˌakəd-, -ēs\ *n* -S [*academic* + *²-ese*] : a style of writing held to be characteristic of academic people

academic* *n academics pl* : academic subjects

acanth·amoeba \əˌkanthəˈmēbə\ *n* [NL, fr. *acanth-* + *amoeba*] **1** *cap* : a genus of free-living amoebas (family Acanthamoebidae of the order Amoebida) found esp. in soil and freshwater either in the form of feeding and asexually replicating trophozoites or dormant double-walled cysts and including several (as *A. culbertsoni* and *A. castellanii*) which are pathogenic in humans causing infections of the eye, skin, respiratory tract, and brain **2** : any amoeba of the genus *Acanthamoeba*

aca·pul·co gold \ˌäkəˈpül(ˌ)kō-, ˌak-, -ül-\ *n, usu cap A & often cap G* [*Acapulco*, Mexico] : marijuana grown in Mexico that is held to be very potent

acathisia *var of* AKATHISIA *herein*

acceptable* *adj* : capable of being endured : TOLERABLE ⟨maximum ~ damage from nuclear attack⟩ ⟨an ~ level of risk⟩

access *vt* -ED/-ING/-ES [*access*, n.] : to get at : gain access to ⟨index registers can be ~*ed* by the programmer —*Datamation*⟩

access time *n* **1** : the lag between the time stored information (as in a computer) is requested and the time it is delivered **2** : television airtime during prime viewing hours that is reserved for exclusive use by local broadcasters

¹ac·com·mo·da·tion·ist \əˌkäməˈdāsh(ə)nəst\ *n* -S [*accommodation* + *¹-ist*] : a black who adapts to the ideals or attitudes of whites ⟨making Uncle Toms, compromisers, and ~*s* . . . thoroughly ashamed —Ossie Davis⟩

²accommodationist *adj* : favoring or practicing accommodation or compromise

accretion disk *n* : a disk of usu. gaseous matter surrounding a massive celestial object (as a black hole) in which the matter gradually spirals in toward and accretes onto the object as a result of gravitational attraction

accrual *adj* [*accrual*, n.] : relating to or being a method of accounting that recognizes income when earned and expenses when incurred regardless of when cash is received or disbursed

AC/DC \ˈā(ˌ)sēˈdē(ˌ)sē\ *adj* [so called fr. the likening of a bisexual person to an electrical appliance which can operate on either alternating or direct current] : BISEXUAL 1b

ace* *vt* **1** : to defeat, displace, or dispose of : gain a decisive advantage over — usu. used with *out* **2** : to earn the grade of A on (an examination)

ace inhibitor *n, usu cap A&C&E* [*a*ngiotensin *c*onverting *e*nzyme (herein)] : any of a group of antihypertensive drugs (as captopril) that relax arteries and promote renal excretion of salt and water by inhibiting the activity of angiotensin converting enzyme

aces *adj* [fr. pl. of *¹ace*] : TOPS

ac·e·tab·u·lo·plas·ty \ˌasəˈtabyə(ˌ)lōˌplastē, -i\ *n* -ES [*acetabulum* + *-o-* + *-plasty*] : plastic surgery on the acetabulum intended to restore its normal state (as by repairing or enlarging its cavity)

ac·et·amin·o·phen \əˌsēd·əˈminəfən, ˌasəd-\ *n* -S [*acet-* + *amin-* + *phenol*] : a crystalline compound $C_8H_9NO_2$ that is a hydroxy derivative of acetanilide and is used in chemical synthesis and in medicine instead of aspirin to relieve pain and fever

ac·e·to·hex·amide \ˌasəd·ōˈheksəməd, əˌsē-, -ˌheksˈaməd, -ˌmīd\ *n* -S [*acetyl* + *cyclohexyl* + *amide*, chemical family to which ureas belong] : a sulfonylurea drug $C_{15}H_{20}N_2O_4S$ used in the oral treatment of some of the milder forms of diabetes in adults to lower the level of glucose in the blood

ace·tyl coA \əˈsēd·ᵊlˌkōˈā; ˌasəd·ᵊl-, -əˌtēl-\ *n, usu cap C* [*acetyl coenzyme A*] : ACETYL COENZYME A

acetylcysteine \əˈsēd·ᵊl-, ˌasəd·ᵊl-, -əˌtēl-\ *n* [*acetyl* + *cysteine*] : a mucolytic agent $C_5H_9NO_3S$ used esp. to reduce the viscosity of abnormally viscid respiratory tract secretions

achieved *adj* [fr. past part. of *achieve*] : brought to or marked by a high degree of development or refinement : FINISHED ⟨fully ~ poems⟩

achi·ral \āˈkī(ə)rəl, a-\ *adj* [*²a-* + *chiral* (herein)] : of, relating to, or being a molecule that is superimposable on its mirror image : not chiral ⟨~ substrates⟩

acid* *n* : LSD

acidhead \ˈ⸗ˌ⸗\ *n* [*acid* (herein) + *head* (as in *hophead*)] : a person who frequently uses LSD

acid house *n* : house music that usu. features a driving tempo and heavily distorted synthesized sound effects : HOUSE *herein*

acid jazz *n* : popular dance music containing elements of jazz

acid precipitation *n* : precipitation (as rain or snow) having increased acidity caused by environmental factors (as sulfur dioxide and nitrogen oxides from the combustion of fossil fuels)

acid rain *n* : acid precipitation esp. in the form of rain

acid rock *n* : rock music with lyrics and sound relating to or suggestive of drug-induced experiences

acid snow *n* : acid precipitation in the form of snow

acid·uria \ˌasəˈd(y)u̇rēə, ˌaas-, -ür-\ *n* -S [NL, fr. *acidum* acid + *-uria*] : the condition of having acid in the urine esp. in abnormal amounts — see AMINOACIDURIA *herein*

acid–washed *or* **acid–wash** \ˈ⸗ˌ⸗\ *adj* : of, relating to, or being a fabric or a garment that has been treated with a bleach solution to produce a faded appearance

ACL \ˌāˌsēˈel\ *n* -S : ANTERIOR CRUCIATE LIGAMENT *herein*

ACLS *abbr* advanced cardiac life support

acorn woodpecker *n* : CALIFORNIA WOODPECKER

acoustic* *adj* **1** *also* **acoustical*** : of, relating to, or being a musical instrument whose sound is not electronically modified **2 a** : being a musical group or performer that uses acoustic instruments **b** : being or involving a musical performance on acoustic instruments

acoustic *n* -S [*acoustic*, adj. (herein)] : an acoustic musical instrument (as a guitar)

acoustic microscope *n* : a microscope in which ultrasound is used to scan a sample and then is converted to an electrical signal from which an image is reconstructed on a video screen — **acoustic microscopy** *n*

acoustic neuroma *n* : a nonmalignant usu. slow-growing tumor involving the Schwann cells of a vestibular nerve that may cause deafness, tinnitus, disturbance of the sense of balance, and serious complications if not treated

acous·to–optic \əˈküstō+\ *also* **acous·to–optical** \"+\ *adj* [*¹acoustic* + *-o-* + *optic, optical*] : of or relating to the use of ultrasound to modulate or change the direction of light in solids

acquaintance rape *n* : DATE RAPE *herein*

acquire* *vt* : to locate and hold (a desired object) in a detector ⟨~ a target by radar⟩

acquired immune deficiency syndrome *n* : AIDS *herein*

acquired immunodeficiency syndrome *n* : AIDS *herein*

acquired taste *n* : someone or something that is not easily or immediately liked or appreciated

ac·ri·tarch \ˈakrəˌtärk\ *n* -S [Gk *akritos* confused, uncertain (fr. *a-* ²a- + *kritos*, verbal of *krinein* to separate, decide) + *archē* beginning — more at CERTAIN, ARCHI-] : any of a group of fossil one-celled marine planktonic organisms of uncertain and possibly various taxonomic affinities that are held to represent the earliest known eukaryotes

ac·ro·lect \ˈakrəˌlekt, -rō-\ *n* -S [*acr-* + *-lect* (as in *dialect*)] : the language variety of a speech community closest to the standard or prestige form of a language — compare BASILECT *herein* — **ac·ro·lect·al** \ˌ⸗⸗ˈlektᵊl\ *adj*

acro·mio·clavicular \əˌkrōmē(ˌ)ō, aˌ-+\ *adj* [*acromio-* + *clavicular*] : relating to or being the joint connecting the acromion and the clavicle ⟨~ arthritis⟩

across* *prep* **1** : so as to find or meet ⟨stumbled ~ my old yearbook in the hall closet⟩ **2 a** : THROUGHOUT ⟨obvious interest ~ the nation —Robert Goralski⟩ **b** : so as to include or take into consideration all classes or categories ⟨~ differences, they insist, there can be no rational dialogue —Huston Smith⟩

acrylic* *n* **1** : a paint in which the vehicle is an acrylic resin **2** : a painting done in an acrylic resin

act* *n* **1** : a performance or presentation identified with a particular individual or group **2** : the sum of a person's actions or effects that serve to create an impression or set an example ⟨a hard ~ to follow⟩

actinomycin D *n* : DACTINOMYCIN *herein*

ac·ti·no·spec·ta·cin \akˌtinōˈspektəsən, ˌ⸗⸗-, ˌ⸗tən-\ *n* -S [*actinomycete* + NL *spectabilis* (specific epithet of *Streptomyces spectabilis*, species of actinomycete) + E *-mycin*] : SPECTINOMYCIN *herein*

action* *n* **1** : financial gain or an opportunity for financial gain ⟨a piece of the ~⟩ **2** : sexual activity **3** : the most vigorous, productive, or exciting activity in a particular field, area, or group ⟨go where the ~ is⟩

ac·tion·er \ˈaksh(ə)nər\ *n* -S : a film dominated by a high degree of exciting action

action figure *n* : a small-scale figure usu. of a superhero used esp. as a toy

action painting *n, sometimes cap A&P* : nonrepresentational painting marked esp. by thickly textured surfaces and by the use of improvised techniques (as dribbling, splattering, or smearing) to create apparently accidental pictorial effects — **action painter** *n*

action potential *n* : a momentary reversal in the electric potential across a plasma membrane (as of a nerve cell or muscle fiber) that occurs when a cell has been activated by a stimulus

activation analysis *n* : NEUTRON ACTIVATION ANALYSIS *herein*

active* *adj* **1** : requiring the expenditure of energy ⟨~ calcium ion uptake⟩ **2** : of or relating to the collection, storage, and redistribution of the sun's heat esp. with the aid of pumps and blowers ⟨an ~ solar energy system⟩ **3** : functioning by the emission of radiant energy or sound ⟨an ~ sensor⟩ ⟨~ sonar⟩ **4** : characterized by emission of large amounts of electromagnetic energy ⟨an ~ galactic nucleus⟩

active site *n* : a region esp. of a biologically active protein (as an enzyme) where catalytic activity takes place and whose shape permits the binding only of a specific reactant molecule

active transport *n* : the movement of a chemical substance by the expenditure of energy against a gradient in concentration or electric potential across a plasma membrane and opposite to the direction of normal diffusion

active·wear \ˈ⸗⸗ˌ⸗\ *n* -S : SPORTSWEAR

acu·pressure \ˈakyü+ˌ\ *n* [*acu-* (as in *acupuncture*) + *pressure*] : the application of pressure (as with the thumbs or fingertips) to the same discrete points on the body stimulated in acupuncture that is used for its therapeutic effects (as the relief of tension or pain) — see SHIATSU *herein* — **acu·pres·sur·ist** \ˈ⸗⸗ˌpreshərəst\ *n* -S

acute lymphoblastic leukemia *also* **acute lymphocytic leukemia** *n* : leukemia that is marked by an abnormal increase in the number of lymphoblasts, that is characterized by rapid onset and progression of symptoms which include fever, anemia, pallor, fatigue, appetite loss, bleeding, thrombocytopenia, granulocytopenia, bone and joint pain, and enlargement of the lymph nodes, liver, and spleen, and that occurs chiefly during childhood — abbr. *ALL*

acute myelogenous leukemia *also* **acute myeloid leukemia** *n* : leukemia that is marked by an abnormal increase in the number of myeloblasts esp. in bone marrow and blood, that is characterized by symptoms similar to those of acute lymphoblastic leukemia, and that may occur either in childhood or adulthood — abbr. *AML*

ACV *abbr* **1** actual cash value **2** air-cushion vehicle

acy·clo·vir \ˌāˈsīklōˌvir\ *n* [*²a-* + *cyclo-* + *virus*; fr. its containing less cyclic structure than its naturally occurring analogue guanosine] : a cyclic nucleoside $C_8H_{11}N_5O_3$ used esp. to treat the symptoms of the genital form of herpes simplex

AD* *abbr* Alzheimer's disease

Ada \ˈādə\ *trademark* — used for a structured computer programming language

ADA *abbr* adenosine deaminase *herein*

ad·ap·ta·tion·ist \ˌaˌdapˈtāshənəst *also* ˌadəpˈt- *or* əˌdapˈt-\ *adj* [*adaptation* + *²-ist*] : explaining or seeking to explain the evolution of the traits of an organism in terms of their adaptive function or survival value — **adaptationist** *n*

adaptive optics *n pl but often sing in constr* : a telescopic system that improves image resolution by compensating (as by adjustment of a flexible mirror) for distortions caused by atmospheric turbulence

add* *n* : an instance of addition ⟨the computer does an ~ in 7 microseconds⟩

ADD *abbr* attention deficit disorder *herein*

add–in \ˈadˌin\ *adj* : being or able to be added to and enclosed within an existing system (as a computer) ⟨an *add-in* graphics board⟩ — **add–in** *n* -S

additive identity *n* : an identity element (as 0 in the group of whole numbers under the operation of addition) that in a given mathematical system leaves unchanged any element to which it is added

additive inverse *n* : a number of opposite sign with respect to a given number so that addition of the two numbers gives zero ⟨the *additive inverse* of 4 is –4⟩

¹add–on \ˈ⸗ˌ⸗\ *adj* **1** : being or able to be added on ⟨*add-on* accessories⟩ **2** : of or relating to add-ons **3** : that can be added to ⟨an *add-on* certificate of deposit⟩

²add–on \ˈ⸗ˌ⸗\ *n* -S : something added on: as **a** : a sum or amount added on **b** : something (as an accessory or an added feature) that enhances the thing it is added to

ad·dress·able \əˈdresəbəl\ *adj* [*¹address* + *-able*] **1** : able to be addressed : directly accessible **2** : of or relating to a subscription television system that uses decoders addressable by the system operator — **ad·dress·abil·i·ty** \ˌ⸗ˌ⸗⸗ˈbiləd·ē, -ətē, -i\ *n* -S

ad·e·no·acanthoma \ˌadᵊn(ˌ)ō+\ *n, pl* **adenoacanthomas** *or* **adenoacanthomata** [*aden-* + *acanthoma*] : an adenocarcinoma with epithelial cells differentiated and proliferated into squamous cells

ad·e·no·ma·toid \ˌadᵊnˈōməˌtȯid\ *adj* [NL *adenomat-*, *adenoma* + E *¹-oid*] : relating to or resembling an adenoma ⟨~ tumors of the fallopian tube⟩

adenosine deaminase *n* : an enzyme which catalyzes the conversion of adenosine to inosine and whose deficiency causes a form of severe combined immunodeficiency disease as a result of the accumulation of toxic metabolites which inhibit DNA synthesis — abbr. *ADA*

adenosine mo·no·phos·phate \-ˌmä(ˌ)nōˈfäsˌfāt, -ˌmōn-\ *n* [*mon-* + *phosphate*] : AMP *herein*

ad·e·no·sis \ˌadᵊnˈōsəs\ *n, pl* **adeno·ses** \-ōˌsēz\ [NL, fr. *aden-* + *-osis*] : a disease of glandular tissue; *esp* : one involving abnormal proliferation or occurrence of glandular tissue

ade·no·syl·methionine \əˈdenəsəl-, ˌadᵊnˈōs-, -ˌsil+\ *n* [*adenosine* + *-yl* + *methionine*] : the active sulfonium form of methionine $C_{15}H_{22}N_6O_5S$ that acts as a methyl group donor in various biochemical transmethylation reactions (as the formation of epinephrine or creatine), that is formed when methionine reacts with ATP, and that is an intermediate in the formation of homocysteine; *S*-adenosylmethionine

ad·e·no·virus \ˈadᵊnō+\ *n* [*adenoid* + *-o-* + *virus*] : any of a family (Adenoviridae) of icosahedral DNA viruses orig. identified in human adenoid tissue, causing respiratory diseases (as catarrh), and including some capable of inducing malignant tumors in experimental animals — **ad·e·no·viral** \"+\ *adj*

ad·e·nyl·ate cy·clase \əˈdenᵊlət-, -lˌāt-; ˌadᵊnˈilət-\ *n* [*adenylate* fr. *adenyl* + *¹-ate*] : an enzyme that catalyzes the formation of cyclic AMP from ATP

adenyl cy·clase *n* : ADENYLATE CYCLASE *herein*

ADHD *abbr* attention deficit/hyperactivity disorder *herein*

ad–hoc·ra·cy \(ˌ)adˈhäkrəsē, -ōk-, -si\ *n* -ES [*ad hoc* + *-cracy*] : a temporary organization or committee set up to accomplish a specific task; *also* : a system of government utilizing such organizations

adipocyte* *n* : a fat-containing cell of adipose tissue

adip·sia \āˈdipsēə, əˈ-\ *n* -S [NL, fr. Gk *a-* ²a- + *dipsa* thirst + NL *¹-ia*] : loss of thirst; *also* : abnormal and esp. prolonged abstinence from the intake of fluids

adjustable rate mortgage *n* : a mortgage having an interest rate which is usu. initially lower than that of a fixed rate mortgage but is adjusted periodically according to the cost of funds to the lender — abbr. *ARM*

ad·ju·vant* \ˈajəvənt, -jüvänt, aˈjüvənt\ *n* : a substance enhancing the immune response to an antigen

admass \ˈ⸗ˌ⸗\ *n, often attrib* [*ad*vertising + *mass*] *chiefly Brit* : a system of marketing that attempts to influence consumers by mass-media advertising; *also* : a society thus influenced

ADDENDA

ado·bo \əˈdōbō, *Sp* äˈt͟hōbō\ *n* -s [Sp, marinade, fr. *adobar* to prepare, marinate, fr. OF *adober* to arm (a knight), prepare, fr. *a-* (fr. L *ad-*) + *-dober*, of Gmc origin; akin to OE *dubbian* to dub — more at DUB] : a Philippine dish of fish or meat usu. marinated in a sauce containing vinegar and garlic, browned in fat, and simmered in the marinade

adoptive immunotherapy *n* : treatment esp. for cancer in which lymphocytes are removed from a patient, cultured with an interleukin to induce their transformation into lymphokine-activated killer cells, and returned to the patient's body along with the interleukin

ad·re·nal·ized \əˈdrenəlˌīzd, -ˈdrē-\ *adj* [*adrenal*ine + *-ize* + [1]*-ed*] : filled with a sudden rush of energy : EXCITED

ad·re·no·cor·ti·co·steroid \əˌdrēnō,kȯrd·əkō+\ *n* [*adrenocortical* + *-o-* + *steroid*] : a steroid (as cortisone or hydrocortisone) obtained from, resembling, or having physiological effects like those of the adrenal cortex

ad·re·no·cor·ti·co·tro·pin \-ˈtrōpən, -äp-\ *also* **ad·re·no·cor·ti·co·tro·phin** \-ˈtrōfən, -äf-\ *n* [*adrenocorticotropic* or *adrenocorticotrophic* + *-in*] : ADRENOCORTICOTROPIC HORMONE

ad·re·no·leu·ko·dys·tro·phy \ *n* [*adren-* + *leukodystrophy* (herein)] : a demyelinating disease of the central nervous system that is inherited as an X-linked recessive trait affecting males in childhood and that is characterized by progressive blindness, deafness, tonic spasms, and mental deterioration — abbr. *ALD*

ad·re·no·medullary \əˌdrēnō, -ren-+\ *adj* [*adren-* + *medullary*] : relating to or derived from the medulla of the adrenal glands ⟨~ extracts⟩

Adri·a·my·cin \ˌādrēəˈmīsᵊn\ *trademark* — used for a preparation of the hydrochloride of doxorubicin

adult* *adj* : dealing in or with explicitly sexual material : PORNOGRAPHIC ⟨~ bookstore⟩ ⟨~ movie⟩

adult–onset diabetes *n* : TYPE 2 DIABETES *herein*

adult respiratory distress syndrome *n* : respiratory failure in adults or in children that results from diffuse injury to the endothelium of the lung (as in sepsis, chest trauma, massive blood transfusion, aspiration of the gastric contents, or diffuse pneumonia) and is characterized by pulmonary edema with an abnormally high amount of protein in the edematous fluid and by respiratory distress and hypoxemia

advance directive *n* : a legal document (as a living will) signed by a living competent person in order to provide guidance for medical and health-care decisions (as the termination of life support and organ donation) in the event that the person becomes incompetent to make such decisions

advanced level *n, usu cap A* : A LEVEL 1 *herein*

advance man* *n* : an aide (as of a political candidate) who makes a security check or handles publicity in advance of personal appearances by his employer

ad·vect \(ˈ)adˈvekt\ *vt* -ED/-ING/-S [back-formation fr. *advection*] : to transport esp. horizontally by the movement of tides, currents, or air masses ⟨~ heat⟩ ⟨~ plankton⟩

ad·ver·bi·al \(ˈ)adˈvərbēəl, adˈv-, -əb-\ *n* -s : a word, phrase, or clause that functions as an adverb

ad·ver·sar·i·al *R* ˌadvə(r)ˈserēəl, *–R* -vəˈs-\ *adj* [*adversary* + [1]*-al*] : of, relating to, or having the characteristics of an adversary or adversary procedures : ADVERSARY

advertorial* *n* : an advertisement that imitates editorial format

advocacy journalism *n* : journalism that advocates a cause or expresses a viewpoint — **advocacy journalist** *n*

aeon* *n* : a unit of geologic time equal to one billion years

ae·quo·rin \ēˈkwȯrən, -ōr-\ *n* -s [NL *Aequorea* + E *-in*] : a bioluminescent protein of jellyfish (genus *Aequorea*) that emits light in response to the addition of calcium or strontium and is used to demonstrate the presence and distribution of calcium in cells

aerial* *n* : an acrobatic maneuver performed (as by skiers and gymnasts) in the air; *also* : a downhill ski event in which skiers execute aerials

aero·al·ler·gen \ *n* [*aer-* + *allergen*] : an allergen carried in the air

aerobic* *adj* : involving, utilizing, or resulting from aerobics ⟨~ exercises⟩ ⟨~ fitness⟩

aer·o·bi·cize \ˌa(ə)ˈrōbəˌsīz, ˌe(ə)-, ˌā(ə)-\ *vb* -ED/-ING/-S [*aerobic* (herein) + *-ize*] *vt* : to bring (the body) to a good physical condition through aerobics ~ *vi* : to engage in aerobics — **aer·o·bi·ciz·er** \-ə(r)\ *n* -s

aer·o·bics \ˌa(ə)ˈrōbiks, ˌe(ə)-, ˌā(ə)-\ *n pl but sing or pl in constr* [fr. *aerobic*, after such pairs as *calisthenic* : *calisthenics*] : a system of physical conditioning designed to improve respiratory and circulatory function by exercises (as running, walking, or swimming) that increase oxygen consumption

aer·on·o·my \a(ə)ˈränəmē, e(ə)ˈ-, ˌā(ə)ˈ-\ *n* -ES [*aer-* + *-nomy*] : a science that deals with the physics and chemistry of the upper atmosphere of planets — **aer·on·o·mer** \-mə(r)\ *n* -s — **aer·o·nom·ic** \ˌa(ə)rəˈnämik, ˌe(ə)r-, ˌāər-\ *also* **aer·o·nom·i·cal** \-mə̇kəl\ *adj* — **aer·on·o·mist** \a(ə)ˈränəmə̇st, e(ə)ˈ-, ˌā(ə)ˈ-\ *n* -s

aero·plankton \ˌa(ə)rə, ˌe(ə)rə, ˌāərə, -rō+\ *n* [*aer-* + *plankton*] : small airborne organisms (as small insects or fungus spores)

[1]**aero·space** \ˈa(ə)rə, ˈe(ə)r-, ˈāər-, -rō+\ *n* [*aer-* + *space*] **1** : space comprising the earth's atmosphere and the space beyond **2** : a branch of physical science that deals with aerospace **3** : the aerospace industry

[2]**aerospace** \"\ *adj* : of or relating to aerospace, to vehicles used in aerospace or the manufacture of such vehicles, or to travel in aerospace ⟨~ research⟩ ⟨~ medicine⟩

AFDC *abbr* aid to families with dependent children

affective disorder *n* : MOOD DISORDER *herein*

affective fallacy *n* : the error in literary criticism of judging a work on the basis of its effect on the reader

af·fect·less \ˈafekt+\ *adj* [[1]*affect* + *-less*] : showing or expressing no emotion; *also* : UNFEELING ⟨a ruthless ~ sociopath⟩ — **af·fect·less·ly** \"+\ *adv* — **af·fect·less·ness** \"+\ *n* -ES

affinity card *n* : a credit card that is issued in affiliation with a particular organization (as a charity or a hotel chain) and whose use earns a benefit for the organization or consumer

affinity chromatography *n* : chromatography in which a macromolecule (as a protein) is isolated and purified by passing it in solution through a column that has been treated with a substance having a ligand for which the macromolecule has an affinity that causes it to be retained on the column

affinity group *n* : a group of people having a common interest or goal or acting together for a specific purpose (as for a chartered tour)

affirmative action *n* : an active effort to improve employment or educational opportunities for members of minority groups and women; *also* : a similar effort to promote the rights or progress of other disadvantaged persons

af·ford·able \əˈfō(ə)rdəbəl, -ó(ə)rd-, -ōəd-, -óəd-\ *adj* [*afford* + *-able*] : that can be afforded ⟨~ housing⟩ ⟨~ prices⟩ — **af·ford·abil·i·ty** \ˈbiləd·ē, -ətē, -i\ *n* -ES

af·ghan·i·stan·ism \afˈganəˌstaˌnizəm, -taaˌn-, -ˌstəˌ-\ *n* -s *usu cap* [*Afghanistan* + *-ism*; fr. the remoteness of Afghanistan from America] : the practice (as by a journalist) of concentrating on problems in distant parts of the world while ignoring controversial local issues

af·la·tox·in \ˌaflәˈtäksən\ *n* [NL *Aspergillus flavus*, species of mold + E *toxin*] : any of several carcinogenic mycotoxins that are produced esp. in stored agricultural crops (as peanuts) by molds (as *Aspergillus flavus*)

AFP *abbr* alpha-fetoprotein *herein*

a–frame* *n, cap A* [fr. the resemblance of the shape of the facade to a capital A] : a building (as a house) that typically has triangular front and rear walls and a roof reaching to or nearly to the ground

af·ri·cana \ˌafrəˈkänə, -ˈkanə, -ˈkaa(ə)nə\ *n pl, usu cap* [*Africa* + *-ana*] : materials (as books, documents, or artifacts) relating to African history and culture

african–american \ *n, cap both As* : AFRO-AMERICAN — **african–american** *adj, usu cap both As*

africanized bee *also* **africanized honeybee** *n, usu cap A* : a honeybee that originated in Brazil as an accidental hybrid between an aggressive African subspecies (*Apis mellifera scutellata*) and previously established European honeybees and has spread to Mexico and the southernmost U.S. where it breeds with local bees producing populations retaining most of the African bee's traits — called also *killer bee*

african swine fever *n, usu cap A* : an acute highly contagious usu. fatal virus disease of swine that is caused by a spherical virus containing one linear double-stranded molecule of DNA, that resembles but is more severe than hog cholera, that is indigenous to Africa where wild swine (as the warthog and bushpig) act as natural reservoirs of the disease, and that has spread to and caused epidemics in the western hemisphere

af·ro \ˈa(ˌ)frō\ *n* -s *usu cap* [*Afro-*] : a hairstyle with an evenly rounded shape — **af·roed** \ˈa(ˌ)frōd\ *adj, usu cap*

af·ro·cen·tric \ˌ-trik\ *adj, usu cap* [*afr-* + *-centric*] **1** : centered on or deriving from Africa or Africans ⟨~ research⟩ ⟨~ clothing⟩ **2** : emphasizing or promoting emphasis on African culture and the contributions of Africans to the development of western civilization ⟨an ~ curriculum⟩ — **af·ro·cen·tric·i·ty** \ˈtrisəd·ē, -i\ *n* -ES *usu cap* — **af·ro·cen·trism** \ˌaˌfrōˈsenˌtrizəm\ *n* -s *usu cap* — **af·ro·cen·trist** \-trist\ *n or adj, usu cap*

afterburner* *n* : a device for burning or catalytically destroying unburned or partially burned carbon compounds in exhaust (as from an automobile)

aftershock* *n* : an aftereffect of a distressing or traumatic event

after–tax \ *adj* [[2]*after* + *tax*] : remaining after payment of taxes and esp. of income tax ⟨*after-tax* income⟩

agar·ose \ˈägəˌrōs, -ōz\ *n* -s [*agar* + [2]*-ose*] : a polysaccharide obtained from agar that is used esp. as a supporting medium in gel electrophoresis

age·ism *also* **agism** \ˈā(ˌ)jizəm\ *n* -s [[1]*age* + *-ism* (as in *racism*)] : prejudice or discrimination against a particular age-group and esp. against the elderly — **age·ist** *also* **agist** \-əst\ *adj*

agent orange *n, usu cap A&O* : an herbicide widely used as a defoliant in the Vietnam War that is composed of 2,4-D and 2,4,5-T and contains dioxin as a contaminant

age spots *n pl* : benign flat spots evenly colored with darker pigment that occur on sun-exposed skin (as of the hands) esp. of persons 50 years old or older

ag·gior·na·men·to \əˌjȯrnəˈmen(ˌ)tō\ *n* -s [It, fr. *aggiornare* to bring up to date, fr. *a-* to (fr. L *ad-*) + *giorno* day, fr. LL *diurnum* — more at JOURNEY] : a bringing up to date ⟨the enthusiasts of ~ and the defenders of older, stricter ways —*Time*⟩

aggregate* *n* : MONETARY AGGREGATE *herein*

aggressive* *adj* : more severe, intensive, or comprehensive than usual esp. in dosage or extent ⟨~ chemotherapy⟩

ag·grieve·ment \əˈgrēvmənt *also* aˈ-\ *n* -s [*aggrieve* + [1]*-ment*] : the quality or state of being aggrieved

ag·gro *also* **ag·ro** \ˈag(ˌ)rō\ *n* -s [by shortening & alter. fr *aggravation*] **1** *Brit* : EXASPERATION, IRRITATION ⟨in any case it is not worth the ~ it causes —*The Sun (London)*⟩ **2** *Brit* : a rivalry or grievance esp. public in nature marked by mistrust, rancor, and often violence ⟨the railwaymen could cause trouble again in May . . . even if their ~ about inter-union differentials is resolved —*Economist*⟩ **3** *Brit* : violence against persons and property that is usu. deliberate but not specific in its aims ⟨shots fired and tyres let down as the ~ flares —Gilbert Johnson⟩

agin·ner \əˈginə(r)\ *n* -s [[2]*agin* + [2]*-er*] *slang* : one who opposes change

ag·no·lot·ti \ˌänyəˈlȯt(t)ē\ *n, pl* **agnolotti** [It, pl. of *agnolotto*, *agnellotto*, alter. of (assumed) *anegliotto*, alter. of *anellotto*, dim. of *anello* ring, fr. L *anellus*, dim. of *anus* ring — more at ANUS] : a usu. crescent-shaped dumpling filled with vegetables, seafood, or meat

agnostic* *n* : a person unwilling to commit to an opinion about something ⟨most researchers remain ~s, awaiting some observation or theoretical development —Charles Meegan⟩

agnostic* *adj* : NONCOMMITTAL 1 ⟨stubbornly ~ about the free market —Sarah Wright⟩

[1]**a–go–go** \äˈgō(ˌ)gō, əˈg-\ *n* -s [*Whisky à Gogo*, café and discotheque in Paris, France, fr. F *whisky* whiskey + *à gogo* galore, fr. MF] : a nightclub for dancing to live or recorded popular music : DISCOTHEQUE

[2]**a–go–go** \"\ *adj* **1** : of, relating to, or being an a-go-go or the music or dances performed there ⟨*a-go-go* dancers⟩ **2** : being in a whirl of motion ⟨arms *a-go-go*⟩ **3** : being in the latest style ⟨psychiatry *a-go-go*—Charles Schulz⟩

agonist* *n* : a chemical substance (as a drug) capable of combining with a specific receptor on a cell and initiating the same reaction or activity typically produced by the binding of an endogenous substance — compare ANTAGONIST 2b *in the Dict*

agonistic* *adj* : of, relating to, or being aggressive or defensive social interaction (as fighting, fleeing, or submitting) between individuals usu. of the same species ⟨~ behavior⟩

agony aunt *n, chiefly Brit* : a person who writes an advice column

ago·ra \ˌägəˈrä\ *n, pl* **ago·rot** \-ˈrōt\ [NHeb *ăgōrāh*, fr. Heb, a small coin] **1** : a monetary unit of Israel representing $^1/_{100}$ of a shekel — see MONEY table *in the Dict* **2** : a coin representing one agora

ag·o·ra·phobe \ˈagərəˌfōb\ *n* -s [back-formation fr. *agoraphobia*] : AGORAPHOBIC *herein*

ag·o·ra·pho·bic \-ik\ *n* -s : a person affected with agoraphobia

agran·u·lo·cy·to·sis \əˌgranyəlōˌsīˈtōsə̇s\ *n, pl* **agranulocyto·ses** \-ōˌsēz\ [NL, fr. [2]*a-* + *granulocytosis*] : an acute condition marked by a severe decrease in the number of granulocytes and characterized by fever, prostration, chills, and ulceration esp. of mucous membranes (as of the throat or rectum)

agrav·ic \(ˈ)āˈgravik\ *adj* [[2]*a-* + *gravity* + [1]*-ic*] : of or relating to a theoretical condition of no gravitation

ag·ri·power \ˈagrə+\ *n* [*agriculture* + *power*] : the economic and political power of an agriculturally productive nation

ag·ro·chemical \ˌa(ˌ)grō+\ *or* **ag·ri·chemical** \ˌagrə+\ *n* [*agrochemical* fr. *agro-* + *chemical*; *agrichemical* fr. *agriculture* + *chemical*] : an agricultural chemical (as an herbicide or an insecticide) — **agrochemical** *or* **agrichemical** *adj*

ag·ro·ecosystem \ˌa(ˌ)grō+\ *n* [*agro-* + *ecosystem*] : the organisms and environment of an agricultural area considered as an ecosystem

ag·ro·forestry \"+\ *n* [*agro-* + *forestry*] : land management involving the growing of trees in association with food crops or pastures — **ag·ro·forester** \"+\ *n*

ag·ro–industrial \"+\ *also* **ag·ri–industrial** \ˌagrə+\ *adj* [*agro-industrial* fr. *agro-* + *industrial*; *agri-industrial* fr. *agriculture* + *industrial*] **1** : of or relating to production for both industrial and agricultural purposes ⟨a nuclear-powered *agro-industrial* complex for producing electric power and desalted seawater⟩ **2** : of or relating to an industry (as the production of farm tools or fertilizer) directly related to agriculture — **ag·ro–industry** \"+\ *also* **ag·ri–industry** \ˌagrə+\ *n*

ag·ro·nome \ˈagrəˌnōm\ *n* -s [Russ or F; Russ *agronom*, fr. F *agronome*, fr. *agronomie*, after such pairs as F *astronomie* astronomy : *astronome* astronomer] : AGRONOMIST

ag·ro·pastoral \ˌa(ˌ)grō+\ *adj* [*agro-* + [2]*pastoral*] : of or relating to a practice of agriculture that includes both the growing of crops and the raising of livestock — **ag·ro·pastoralism** \"+\ *n*

AHA \ˌāˌāchˈā\ *n* -s : ALPHA HYDROXY ACID *herein*

ahi \ˈähē\ *or* **ahi tuna** *n* -s [Hawaiian *ʻahi* yellowfin tuna] : either of two tunas of the genus *Thunnus* that occur in the Atlantic, Pacific, and Indian oceans: **a** : the yellowfin tuna (T. albacares) that was formerly split into two species of the genus *Neothunnus* **b** : a fish (T. obesus) similar to the yellowfin tuna

-aholic *or* **-oholic** \-əˈhȯlik, -ˈhäl-\ *n comb form* -s [*alcoholic*] **1** : one who feels compulsively the need to (do something) ⟨shop*aholic*⟩ ⟨win*aholic*⟩ **2** : one who likes (something) to excess ⟨golf*aholic*⟩

AI* *abbr* artificial intelligence *herein*

AID *abbr* artificial insemination by donor

AIDS \ˈādz\ *n* : a disease of the human immune system that is characterized cytologically esp. by reduction in the numbers of CD4-bearing helper T cells to 20 percent or less of normal thereby rendering the subject highly vulnerable to life-threatening conditions (as Pneumocystis carinii pneumonia) and to some that become life-threatening (as Kaposi's sarcoma) and that is caused by infection with HIV commonly transmitted in infected blood esp. during illicit intravenous drug use and in bodily secretions (as semen) during sexual intercourse — called also *acquired immune deficiency syndrome, acquired immunodeficiency syndrome*

AIDS–related complex \ *n* : a group of symptoms (as fever, weight loss, and lymphadenopathy) that is associated with the presence of antibodies to HIV and is followed by the development of AIDS in a certain proportion of cases — abbr. *ARC*

AIDS virus *n* : HIV *herein*

ai·ki·do \ˌīkēˈdō, īˈkē(ˌ)dō\ *n* -s [Jap *aikidō*, fr. *ai-* together, mutual + *ki* breath, spirit + *dō* way, art] : a Japanese art of self-defense employing locks and holds and utilizing the principle of nonresistance to cause an opponent's own momentum to work against him

ai·o·li \(ˈ)īˈōlē, (ˈ)āˈ-, -li, F áyȯlē\ *n* -s [Prov, fr. *ai* garlic (fr. L *allium*) + *oli* oil, fr. L *oleum* — more at ALLIUM, OIL] : a mayonnaise flavored with garlic and sometimes other ingredients (as red pepper)

air* *n* **1** : a football offense utilizing primarily the forward pass ⟨trailing by 20 points, the team took to the ~⟩ **2** : an air-conditioning system ⟨equipped with ~⟩

air bag *n* : an automobile safety device consisting of a bag designed to inflate automatically esp. in front of an occupant in case of collision to protect that person from pitching into solid parts (as the windshield or dashboard)

air ball *n* : a shot in basketball that misses the rim and backboard

airbus \ *n* : a short-range or medium-range subsonic jet passenger airplane

air cavalry *n* : an army unit that is transported by aircraft and carries out the traditional cavalry missions of reconnaissance and security

air–cushion vehicle *n* : a vehicle that is supported above the surface of land or water by a cushion of air produced by downwardly directed fans

air dam *n* : a device attached to the underside of the front of an automobile to improve stability and aerodynamic performance by reducing airflow under the car and to aid engine cooling by increasing the flow of air to the engine compartment

air date *n* : the scheduled date of a broadcast

air·er \ˈe(ə)rə(r), ˈa(-\ *n* -s *Brit* : a frame on which clothes are aired or dried

airfall \ *n* : the deposition of material (as ash) ejected from a volcano

airfare \ *n* : fare for travel by airplane

air guitar *n* : an imaginary guitar that one pretends to play; *also* : the action of playing air guitar

airhead \ *n* : a mindless or stupid person — **airheaded** \ *adj*

air–kiss \ *vt* : to make a kissing gesture at without touching ⟨*air-kissed* the guests⟩ — **air kiss** *n*

airmobile \ *adj* [*air* + *mobile*, adj.] : of, relating to, or being a military unit whose members are transported to combat areas usu. by helicopter

air piracy *n* : the hijacking of an airplane — **air pirate** *n*

airplay \ *n* : the playing of a recording on the air by a radio station

airshed \ *n* -s [*air* + *-shed* (as in *watershed*)] : the air supply of a given region; *also* : the geographical area covered by such an air supply

air show *n* : an exhibition of aircraft and aviation skills

air taxi *n* : a small commercial airplane used as needed for short flights between localities not served by scheduled airlines

airtime \ *n* : the time or any part thereof that a radio or television station is on the air

aka *abbr* also known as

aka·thi·sia *also* **aca·thi·sia** \ˌakaˈthizh(ē)ə, ˌa-, -ēzh-\ *n* -s [NL, fr. Czech *akathisie*, fr. [2]*a-* + Gk *kathisis* sitting (fr. *kathizein* to sit down) + Czech *-ie* [1]-ia — more at KATHISMA] : a condition characterized by uncontrollable motor restlessness

ak–47 \ˌāˌkāˌ\ *n* -s *usu cap A&K* [Russ *a*utomat *K*alashnikova 1947 Kalashnikov automatic rifle of 1947] : a Soviet-designed 7.62 mm (.30 cal.) gas-operated magazine-fed rifle for automatic or semiautomatic fire

à la carte *also* **a la carte*** *adj* : of, being, or offering a list of options from which to select

à la grecque \ˌäləˈgrek, ˌal-\ *adj, often cap G* [F, lit., in the Greek manner] *of food* : served in a sauce of olive oil, lemon juice, and seasonings

albatross* *n* [fr. the albatross killed by the ancient mariner and subsequently hung about his neck in the poem *The Rime of the Ancient Mariner* (1798) by S.T. Coleridge †1834 Eng. poet] **1** : something that causes persistent deep concern or anxiety ⟨an ~ of guilt that he has volunteered to carry —Jack Holland⟩ **2** : something that makes accomplishment particularly difficult : ENCUMBRANCE ⟨this regulatory ~ inhibits any marketing scheme that might lure commuters —Charles Luna⟩

album quilt *n* : a quilt made of squares containing appliquéd designs or pictures

al·bu·te·rol \alˈbyüd·əˌrōl, -ˈbyütə-\ *n* -s [prob. fr. [2]*al*pha + *butyl* + *tert-* + *diol*] : a drug $C_{13}H_{21}NO_3$ used to treat asthma as an aerosol or as the sulfate in tablet form

al·cid \ˈalsə̇d\ *n* -s [NL *Alcidae*] : any of the family Alcidae of diving birds

ALD *abbr* adrenoleukodystrophy *herein*

al den·te \(ˌ)älˈden·(ˌ)tā, -ál-, -al-\ *adj* [It, lit., to the tooth] *of food* : cooked just enough to retain a somewhat firm texture ⟨fresh pasta cooked *al dente*—*Vogue*⟩ ⟨hosannahs for precisely *al dente* carrots —Gael Greene⟩

al·di·carb \ˈaldəkärb\ *n* -s [prob. fr. *alde*hyde + *-i-* + *carba*mate] : a persistent highly toxic agricultural carbamate pesticide $C_7H_{14}N_2O_2S$ used against insects, mites, and nematodes

al·do·ste·ron·ism \alˈdästəˌrōˌnizəm, ˌaldōstəˈr-\ *n* -s [*aldosterone* + *-ism*] : a condition that is characterized by excessive excretion of aldosterone and typically by loss of body potassium, muscular weakness, and elevated blood pressure

ale·a·tor·ic \ˌālēəˈtȯrik\ *adj* [L *aleator* dice player, gambler (fr. *alea* dice game) + E *-ic*] : characterized by chance or random elements ⟨~ music⟩

aleatory* *adj* : ALEATORIC *herein*

a level *n, usu cap A* **1** : the second of three standardized British examinations in a secondary school subject used as a qualification for university entrance; *also* : successful completion of an A-level examination in a particular subject — called also *advanced level*; compare O LEVEL *herein*, S LEVEL *herein* **2 a** : the level of education required to pass an A-level examination **b** : a course leading to an A-level examination

alexander technique *n, usu cap A&T* [after Frederick Matthias *Alexander* †1955 Eng. (Tasmanian-born) actor and teacher] : a technique for positioning and moving the body so as to release muscular tension

alf·vén wave \ˌäl(f)ˈvān-, -ven-\ *n, usu cap A* [after Hannes *Alfvén* †1995 Swed. astrophysicist] : a transverse electromagnetic wave that propagates along the lines of force in a magnetized plasma

ALG *abbr* antilymphocyte globulin *herein*; antilymphocytic globulin *herein*

algebra* *n* : LINEAR ALGEBRA 2 *herein*

al·gol \ˈalˌgäl, -ˌgȯl\ *n* -s *usu cap A or all cap* [*algo*rithmic *l*anguage] : an algebraic and logical language for programming a computer

algorithm* *n* : a procedure for solving a mathematical problem (as finding the greatest common divisor) in a finite number of steps that frequently involves repetition of an operation; *broadly* : a step-by-step procedure for solving a problem or accomplishing an end esp. by a computer — **algorithmic*** *adj* — **al·go·rith·mi·cal·ly** \-mək(ə)lē, -mēk-, -li\ *adv*

al·gor mor·tis \ˌalgō(ə)rˈmȯrtəs\ *n* [NL, fr. L, lit., coldness of death] : the gradual cooling of the body following death

al·ice–in–won·der·land \ˈ===ˈ==ˌ=\ *adj, usu cap A&W* [fr. *Alice's Adventures in Wonderland* (1865) by Lewis Carroll †1898 Eng. storywriter] : suitable to a world of fantasy or illusion

alien* *n* : EXTRATERRESTRIAL *herein*

ali·es·ter·ase \ˌalēˈestəˌrās, -āz\ *n* [*ali*phatic + *esterase*] : an esterase that promotes the hydrolysis of ester links esp. in aliphatic esters of low molecular weight

ali·go·té \ˌalēgōˈtā\ *n* -s *usu cap* [F *aligoté, alligotet*, a secondary grape variety of Burgundy, perh. fr. F dial. (Burgundy), alter. (influenced by F dial. *haricoter* to cultivate poor ground, work for meager returns) of MF *haligoté*, pp. of *haligoter, harigoter* to cut in pieces — more at HARICOT] **1** : a white wine made from the Aligoté grape and sometimes mixed with cassis to make an aperitif **2** : a white grape native to Burgundy

a–line \ˈ=ˌ=\ *adj, cap A* [fr. the resemblance of such a garment's outline to that of a capital A] : having a flared bottom and a close-fitting top — used of a garment ⟨an *A-line* skirt⟩

alin·gual \(ˈ)āˈliŋgwəl *sometimes* -gyəw-\ *adj* [²*a-* + *-lingual* (as in *bilingual*)] : not fluent in any language

a–list \ˈ=ˌ=\ *n, usu cap A, often attrib* [fr. the convention of using A to designate the first or best] : a list or group of individuals of the highest level of society, excellence, or eminence

alit·er·a·cy \ˌāˈlidərəsē, -ˈlitərə-, -ˈli-trə-, -si\ *n* [²*a-* + *literacy*] : the quality or state of being able to read but uninterested in doing so — **alit·er·ate** \ˌāˈlid-ərət, ˈlitərət, ˈli-trət\ *adj or n*

ali·yah* *or* **ali·ya** \ˌaləˈ(y)ä, äˈlē(ˌ)-, əˈlē(y)ə\ *n* -s : immigration of Jews into Israel

alkaline battery *n* : a long-lived dry cell that has an alkaline electrolyte which decreases corrosion of the cell — called also *alkaline cell*

alkylating agent *n* : a substance that causes replacement of hydrogen by an alkyl group esp. in a biologically important molecule; *specif* : one with mutagenic activity that inhibits cell division and growth and is used to treat some cancers

al·kyl·phe·nol \ˌ==ˈ==\ *n* [*alkyl* + *phenol*] : a derivative of phenol having one or more alkyl groups attached to the carbon ring

al·le·lo·chem·i·cal \əˌ=ˌ==ˈ===\ *n* [*allelo-* + ²*chemical*] : a toxic chemical produced by a plant in order to defend itself against herbivores or competing plants

al·le·lo·path·ic \əˌlēləˈpathik, -ˌlel-\ *adj* [*allelopathy* + *-ic*] : of, relating to, or exhibiting allelopathy

alley* *n* : either of two areas in a baseball outfield lying between the normal positions of the center fielder and the left or right fielder ⟨lined a double up the ~ in left center field⟩

al·ley–oop \ˌalēˈüp, ˌaliˈyüp\ *n* [alter. (influenced by ¹*alley*) of earlier *allez-oop*, cry of a circus acrobat about to leap, prob. fr. F *allez*, 2d pers. pl. imper. of *aller* to go + E *oop*, alter. of *up*] : a basketball play in which a leaping player catches a pass above the basket and immediately dunks the ball; *also* : the usu. looping pass thrown in such a play

all–night·er \(ˌ)ȯˈnīd·ə(r)\ *n* -s : something (as a party or a study session) that lasts throughout the night

al·lo·antibody \ˌalō+\ *n* [*all-* + *antibody*] : ISOANTIBODY

al·lo·antigen \ˈ"+\ *n* [*all-* + *antigen*] : ISOANTIGEN — **al·lo·an·tigenic** \ˈ"+\ *adj*

al·lo·ge·ne·ic \ˌaləjəˈnēik, -lō-\ *also* **al·lo·gen·ic** \-ˈjenik\ *adj* [*allogeneic* fr. *all-* + *-geneic* (as in *syngeneic* — herein); *allogenic* fr. *all-* + *-genic*] : involving, derived from, or being individuals of the same species that are sufficiently unlike genetically to interact antigenically ⟨~ skin grafts⟩ ⟨~ donors⟩ — compare SYNGENEIC *herein*, XENOGENEIC *herein*

al·lo·graft \ˈalō=, ˈalə=\ *n* [*all-* + *graft*; fr. its being a graft from another individual] : a homograft between allogeneic individuals — **allograft** *vt*

al·lo·immune \ˌalō+\ *adj* [*all-* + *immune*] : of, relating to, or characterized by isoimmunization ⟨~ reactivity⟩

al·lo·pu·ri·nol \ˌalōˈpyu̇rəˌnȯl, -ˌnōl\ *n* -s [*all-* + *purine* + *-ol*] : a drug $C_5H_4N_4O$ used to promote excretion of uric acid esp. in the treatment of gout

al·lo·saur \ˈaləˌsȯr\ *n* -s [NL *Allosaurus*] : any of a family (Allosauridae) of large theropod dinosaurs usu. having three digits on each arm and hand and living from the late Jurassic to the late Cretaceous; *esp* : ALLOSAURUS *herein*

allosaurus* *n* -ES : any of the genus *Allosaurus* of theropod dinosaurs

al·lo·ste·ric \ˌaləˈsterik, -ti(ə)r-\ *adj* [*all-* + *steric*] : of, relating to, undergoing, or being alteration of chemical activity by combination with another substance at a point other than the active site ⟨~ enzymes⟩ — **al·lo·ste·ri·cal·ly** \-rək(ə)lē\ *adv* — **al·los·te·ry** \əˈlästərē, ˌaləˈsterē\ *n* -ES

al·lo·transplant \ˌal(ˌ)ō+\ *vt* [*all-* + *transplant*] : to transplant between genetically different individuals — **allotransplant** *n* — **al·lo·transplantation** \ˈ"+\ *n*

allotype* *n* : an alloantigen that is part of a plasma protein (as an immunoglobulin) — compare IDIOTYPE *herein*, ISOTYPE *herein* — **al·lo·typic** \ˌalə+\ *adj* — **al·lo·typically** \ˈ"+\ *adv* — **al·lo·typy** \ˈ=ˌ=ˌtīpē\ *n* -ES

all–out* *adj* : FULL-BLOWN 2 ⟨an *all-out* ban⟩

al·lo·zyme \ˈ=ˌ=ˌzīm\ *n* -s [*all-* + *-zyme*] : any of the variants of an enzyme that are determined by alleles at a single genetic locus — **al·lo·zy·mic** \ˌ==ˈzīmik\ *adj*

all–terrain vehicle \ˈ=ˌ=ˌ=-\ *n* : a small motor vehicle with three or four wheels that is designed for use on various types of terrain

all–wheel \ˈ=ˈ=\ *adj* : acting esp. independently on or by means of all four wheels of an automotive vehicle ⟨*all-wheel* drive⟩

aloe* *n* : ALOE VERA 2 *herein*

aloe vera \ˈaˌlōˈverə, ˈvirə\ *n* [NL, species name, fr. *Aloe* + L *vera*, fem. of *verus* true — more at VERY] **1** : a plant of the genus *Aloe* (*A. barbadensis* syn. *A. vera*) whose leaves furnish an emollient extract used esp. in cosmetics and skin creams **2** : an extract of the aloe vera plant; *also* : a preparation composed predominantly of such an extract

alongside* *prep* : in addition to ⟨a special category ~ the awards it annually presents —*Horizon*⟩

à l'orange \ä̇lȯrä^nzh\ *adj* [F] : prepared or served with oranges

alpha* *n* **1** : ALPHA WAVE **2** : an alpha individual (as in a wolf pack)

alpha* *adj* : socially dominant esp. in a group of animals ⟨challenging the ~ wolf in their pack —Suzanne Core⟩

al·pha \ˈalfə, ˈau̇fə\ *adj* [by shortening] : ALPHABETIC ⟨an ~ sort⟩

alpha–adrenergic \ˈ=ˌ=ˌ=ˈ==\ *adj* : of, relating to, or being an alpha-receptor ⟨*alpha-adrenergic* blocking action⟩

alphabet soup* *n* : a hodgepodge esp. of initials (as of the names of organizations)

alpha decay *n* : the radioactive decay of an atomic nucleus by emission of an alpha particle

alpha–fe·to·protein \ˌ==ˌfēd-ō+\ *n* [²*alpha* + *feto-* + *protein*] : a fetal blood protein present abnormally in adults with some forms of cancer (as of the liver) and normally in the amniotic fluid of pregnant women but with very low levels tending to be associated with Down's syndrome in the fetus and very high levels with neural tube defects (as spina bifida) in which the tube remains open — abbr. *AFP*

alpha–helix *n* : the coiled structural arrangement of many proteins consisting of a single chain of amino acids that is stabilized by hydrogen bonds — compare BETA-SHEET *herein*, DOUBLE HELIX *herein* — **alpha–helical** \ˌ=ˈ===\ *adj*

alpha hydroxy acid *n* : any of various carboxylic acids with a hydroxyl group attached at the alpha position; *specif* : one (as glycolic acid, malic acid, or lactic acid) that occurs in natural products (as fruits, sugar cane, or yogurt) and is used in cosmetics for its exfoliating effect on the surface layer of skin — called also *AHA*

alpha interferon *n* : an interferon produced by various white blood cells that inhibits viral replication, suppresses cell proliferation, and regulates immune response and that is used in a form obtained from recombinant DNA to treat various diseases (as hairy cell leukemia and AIDS-related Kaposi's sarcoma) — called also *interferon alpha*; compare BETA INTERFERON *herein*, GAMMA INTERFERON *herein*

alpha–ketoglutaric acid \ˈ==ˈ===ˌ==-\ *n* : the alpha keto isomer of ketoglutaric acid formed in various metabolic processes (as the Krebs cycle)

al·pha·met·ic \ˌalfəˈmed·ik\ *n* -s [*alpha*betic + arith*metic*] : a mathematical puzzle consisting of a numerical computation with letters substituted for numbers which are to be restored through mathematical reasoning

alpha–1–antitrypsin \ˈ==ˈwən¦=(ˌ)=+\ *n* [²*alpha* + ¹*anti-* + *trypsin*] : a trypsin-inhibiting serum protein which inhibits the digestive action of elastase on the tissues of the lungs and whose deficiency is associated with the development of emphysema

alpha–receptor \ˈ===ˌ=\ *n* : any of a group of receptors that are postulated to exist on cell surfaces of some effector organs and tissues innervated by the sympathetic nervous system to explain the specificity of certain adrenergic agents in activating or blocking only some sympathetic activities (as vasoconstriction, relaxation of intestinal muscle, and contraction of most smooth muscle) — compare BETA-RECEPTOR *herein*

alpine* *adj, usu cap* : of, relating to, or being competitive ski events consisting of slalom and downhill racing — compare NORDIC *herein*

al·pra·zo·lam \alˈprāzōlam\ *n* [*alprazol-* (perh. fr. rearrangement of letters in *triazole* and *benzodiazepine* — herein) + *-am* (as in *diazepam* — herein)] : a benzodiazepine tranquilizer $C_{17}H_{13}ClN_4$ used esp. in the treatment of mild to moderate anxiety

al·pros·ta·dil \alˈprästədil\ *n* [prob. fr. ²*al*pha + *prosta*glan*di*n (herein) + *-il*, alter. of *-yl*] : a vasodilating prostaglandin $C_{20}H_{34}O_5$ used esp. to treat erectile dysfunction

ALS* *abbr* amyotrophic lateral sclerosis *herein*

alternating series *n* : a mathematical series in which consecutive terms are alternatively positive and negative

alternative* *adj* **1** : existing or functioning outside the established cultural, social, or economic system ⟨~ newspaper⟩ ⟨whose kids went to the same ~ nursery school —Cyra McFadden⟩; *also* : different from the usual or conventional ⟨~ fuels⟩ **2** : of, relating to, or being rock music that is regarded as an alternative to established rock, is typically influenced by hard rock and punk and sometimes by hip-hop and pop, and is commonly associated with younger audiences and their culture ⟨~ music⟩ ⟨the ~ market⟩

alternative* *n* : alternative rock music

alternative medicine *n* : any of various systems of healing or treating disease (as chiropractic, homeopathy, or faith healing) not included in the traditional medical curricula taught in the U.S. and Britain

alternative school *n* : an elementary or secondary school with a nontraditional curriculum

altruism* *n* : behavior by an animal that is not beneficial to or may be harmful to itself but that benefits the survival of its species — **altruist*** *n* — **altruistic*** *adj* — **altruistically*** *adv*

al·ve·o·lo·plas·ty \alˈvēə(ˌ)lōˌplastē\ *or* **al·veo·plas·ty** \ˈalvē(ˌ)ō-\ *n* -ES [*alveoloplasty* fr. *alveol-* + *-plasty*; *alveoplasty* fr. L *alveus* cavity + E *-o-* + *-plasty*] : surgical shaping of the dental alveoli and alveolar processes esp. after extraction of several teeth or in preparation for dentures

am·a·ni·tin \ˌaməˈnēt³n\ *n* -s [ISV *amanit-* (fr. NL *Amanita*, genus name of *Amanita phalloides*, species name of the death cup) + *-in*; orig. formed in G] : a highly poisonous cyclic peptide produced by the death cup that selectively inhibits RNA polymerase in mammalian cells

aman·ta·dine \əˈmantəˌdēn\ *n* -s [*amantad-* (fr. anagram of *adamantane*) + *amine*] : a drug used esp. as the hydrochloride $C_{10}H_{17}N \cdot HCl$ to prevent infection (as by an influenza virus) by interfering with virus penetration into host cells and in the treatment of Parkinson's disease

am·a·ret·to \ˌaməˈred·ō, -etō\ *n* [It, dim. of *amaro* bitter, fr. L *amarus*] **1 amaret·ti** \-dē, -tē\ *pl* : macaroons made with bitter almonds **2** -s, *usu cap* : an almond-flavored liqueur

ama·ro·ne \ämäˈrōnā\ *n* -s *usu cap* [It, fr. It dial. (Veneto), lit., tart, very dry, aug. of *amaro* tart, bitter, fr. L *amarus* bitter] : a robust dry red Italian wine with a high alcohol content

am·bi·plasma \ˈambə, ˈaam-, -bē+\ *n* [*ambi-* + *plasma*] : a hypothetical plasma that is held to consist of matter and antimatter

am·bi·polar \ˈ"+\ *adj* [*ambi-* + *polar*] : relating to or consisting of both electrons and positive ions moving in opposite directions ⟨~ diffusion⟩

am·er·asian \ˌamər+\ *n, cap* [*Amer-* + *Asian*] : a person of mixed American and Asian descent; *esp* : one fathered by an American and esp. an American serviceman in Asia — **amerasian** \ˈ"\ *adj, usu cap*

american depositary receipt *n, usu cap A&D&R* : a negotiable receipt that represents ownership of a foreign stock held in trust (as by the foreign branch of a U.S. bank) for an American citizen and that can be traded in dollars like shares of domestic companies

american dream *n, usu cap A & often cap D* : an American social ideal that stresses egalitarianism and esp. material prosperity; *also* : the prosperity or life that is the realization of this ideal ⟨wanted his piece of the *American Dream*⟩

american eel *n, usu cap A* : a yellow to greenish-brown eel of the genus *Anguilla* (*A. rostrata*) that is lighter below, has 103 to 111 vertebrae, is found in fresh and coastal waters along the Atlantic coasts of No. America, and is held to spawn in or near the Sargasso Sea

american kestrel *n, usu cap A* : SPARROW HAWK 2

amer·i·can·o·pho·bia \əˌmerəkənəˈfōbēə, -ˌkan-\ *n, usu cap* [*American* + *-o-* + *-phobia* (as in *claustrophobia*)] : hatred of the U.S. or American culture — **amer·i·cano·phobe** \=ˈ===ˌfōb, =ˈkanəˌfōb\ *n* -s *usu cap*

american oyster *n, usu cap A* : the common commercial oyster (*Crassostrea virginica*) that occurs along the eastern coast of No. America from Prince Edward Island to the Gulf of Mexico

american pit bull terrier *n, usu cap A* : a dog of a breed that was developed to combine the traits of terriers and bulldogs and esp. those useful in fighting and that has extremely powerful jaws and great strength and tenacity — called also *pit bull terrier*

american sad·dle·bred \ˈ=ˌ=ˌ=\ *n, usu cap A* : AMERICAN SADDLE HORSE

american shorthair *n, usu cap A* : a domestic cat of a breed that has a short thick coat of variable color and pattern and is descended from cats brought to America by European settlers; *broadly* : SHORTHAIR

american sign language *n, usu cap A&S&L* : a sign language for the deaf in which meaning is conveyed by a system of articulated hand gestures and their placement relative to the upper body

american staffordshire terrier *n, usu cap A&S* : a strong stocky dog of a breed having an ancestry similar to that of the American pit bull terrier

amer·i·ka \əˈmerəkə\ *n* -s *usu cap* [G *Amerika*; fr. the likening of the U.S. to Nazi Germany] : the fascist or racist aspect of American society — **amer·i·kan** \-kən\ *adj, usu cap*

ame·slan \ˈaməˌslan\ *n* -s *usu cap* : AMERICAN SIGN LANGUAGE *herein*

ames test \ˈāmz-\ *n, usu cap A* [after Bruce Nathan *Ames* b1928 Am. biochemist] : a test for identifying potential carcinogens by studying the frequency with which they cause histidine-producing genetic mutants in bacterial colonies of the genus *Salmonella* (*S. typhimurium*) initially lacking the ability to synthesize histidine

am·e·thop·ter·in \ˌaməˈthäpt(ə)rən\ *n* -s [*amin-* + *meth-* + *pteroyl* + *-in*] : METHOTREXATE *herein*

ami·cus \əˈmēkəs\ *n, pl* **ami·ci** \-ē(ˌ)kē\ : AMICUS CURIAE

amil·o·ride \əˈmilōrīd, -ō-\ *n* -s [*ami*dino- + *chlor-* + *amide*] : a diuretic $C_6H_8ClN_7O$ that promotes sodium excretion and potassium retention

ami·no·ac·id·uria \ˌ=¦=ˌasə̇dyu̇rēə, -u̇r-\ *n* -s [NL, fr. E *amino acid* + NL *-uria*] : a condition in which one or more amino acids are excreted in excessive amounts

ami·no·gly·co·side \=¦==+\ *n* -s [*amin-* + *glycoside*] : any of a group of antibiotics (as streptomycin and neomycin) that inhibit bacterial protein synthesis and are active esp. against gram-negative bacteria

ami·no·transferase \=¦==+\ *n* [*amin-* + *transferase*] : TRANSAMINASE

ami·no·triazole \=¦==+\ *n* [*amin-* + *triazole*] : AMITROLE *herein*

am·i·trip·ty·line \ˌaməˈtriptəˌlēn\ *n* -s [*amin-* + *tript-* (alter. of *trypt-* — as in *tryptophan*) + *-yl* + ²*-ine*] : a tricyclic antidepressant drug $C_{20}H_{23}N$ administered in the form of its hydrochloride salt and used to treat migraine headaches and neuropathic pain as well as depression

am·i·trole \ˈaməˌtrōl\ *n* -s [*amin-* + *triazole*] : a systemic herbicide $C_2H_4N_4$ used in areas other than food croplands

amnesia* *n* : the selective overlooking or ignoring of events or acts that are not favorable or useful to one's purpose or position

am·nio \ˈamnēō\ *n* -s [by shortening] : AMNIOCENTESIS *herein*

am·nio·cen·te·sis \ˌamnēōsen-ˈtēsə̇s\ *n, pl* **amniocente·ses** \-ˈtēˌsēz\ [NL, fr. *amnio-* + *centesis*] : the surgical insertion of a hollow needle through the abdominal wall and into the uterus of a pregnant female to obtain amniotic fluid esp. to examine the fetal chromosomes for an abnormality and for the determination of sex — called also *amnio*

am·ni·og·ra·phy \ˌamnēˈägrəfē\ *n* -ES [*amnio-* + radio*graphy*] : radiographic visualization of the outlines of the uterine cavity, placenta, and fetus after injection of a radiopaque substance into the amnion

am·ni·os·co·py \ˌ=ˈäskəpē\ *n* -ES [*amnio-* + *-scopy*] : visual examination of the amniotic cavity and its contents by means of an endoscope — **am·nio·scope** \ˈamnēəˌskōp\ *n*

amniotic sac *n* : AMNION 1

amor* *n, usu cap* [fr. *Amor*, an asteroid of this class] : any of a class of asteroids esp. having orbits that extend from just beyond the orbit of Earth to beyond the orbit of Mars — compare APOLLO *herein*

amox·i·cil·lin \ä(ˌ)mäksəˈsilən\ *n* -s [*am*in- + ²*oxy-* + *penicillin*] : a semisynthetic penicillin $C_{16}H_{19}N_3O_5S$ derived from ampicillin

amox·y·cil·lin \ˈ", -ksē-\ *Brit var of* AMOXICILLIN *herein*

amp \ˈamp, ˈaa(ə)-\ *n* -s [by shortening] : AMPLIFIER

AMP \ˌāˌemˈpē\ *n* -s [*a*denosine *mono*phosphate] : a mononucleotide of adenine $C_{10}H_{12}N_5O_3H_2PO_4$ that was orig. isolated from mammalian muscle and is reversibly convertible to ADP and ATP in metabolic reactions — called also *adenosine monophosphate*; see CYCLIC AMP *herein*

am·phi·path·ic \ˌamfəˈpathik\ *adj* [*amphi-* + *-pathic*] : AMPHIPHILIC *herein*

am·phi·phil·ic \ˌ==ˈfilik\ *adj* [*amphi-* + *-philic*] : of, relating to, consisting of, or being one or more molecules (as of a glycolipid or sphingolipid) in a biological membrane having a polar water-soluble terminal group attached to a water-insoluble hydrocarbon chain

am·pho·ter·i·cin \ˌamfəˈterəsən\ *n* -s [*amphoteric* + *-in*] : either of two antibiotic drugs obtained from a soil actinomycete of the genus *Streptomyces* (*S. nodosus*); *esp* : AMPHOTERICIN B *herein*

amphotericin B *n* : the amphotericin that is used against deep-seated and systemic fungal infections

am·pi·cil·lin \ˌampəˈsilən\ *n* -s [*amin-* + *penicillin*] : a penicillin $C_{16}H_{19}N_3O_4S$ that is effective against gram-negative and gram-positive bacteria and is used in anhydrous forms, as the trihydrate, or as the sodium salt to treat various infections of the urinary, respiratory, and intestinal tracts

amplification* *n* : a usu. massive replication of genetic material and esp. of a gene or DNA sequence (as in a polymerase chain reaction) — **amplify*** *vt*

amyg·da·lot·o·my \əˌmigdəˈlätəmē, -läd-\ *n* -ES [*amygdala* + *-o-* + *-tomy*] : destruction of part of the amygdala of the brain (as for the control of epilepsy) esp. by surgical incision

am·y·lo·bar·bi·tone \ˌaməlō+\ *n* [*amyl-* + *barbitone*] *Brit* : AMOBARBITAL

amyotrophic lateral sclerosis *n* : a rare fatal progressive degenerative disease that affects pyramidal motor neurons, usu. begins in middle age, and is characterized esp. by increasing and spreading muscular weakness — abbr. *ALS*; called also *Lou Gehrig's disease*

anabolic steroid *n* : any of a group of usu. synthetic hormones that increase constructive metabolism and are sometimes abused by athletes in training to increase temporarily the size of their muscles

an·a·dama bread \ˌanəˈdamə-, -dám-\ *n* [origin unknown] : a leavened bread made with flour, cornmeal, and molasses

anaerobic* *adj* : of, relating to, or being activity in which the body incurs an oxygen debt ⟨~ exercise⟩ ⟨an ~ workout⟩ ⟨~ sports⟩ — **anaerobically*** *adv*

anagenesis* *n* : evolutionary change within a single lineage in which one group replaces another without branching into distinct forms — compare CLADOGENESIS *herein* — **anagenetic*** *adj* — **ana·ge·net·i·cal·ly** \ˌanəjəˈned·ək(ə)lē\ *adv*

an·a·heim \ˈanəˌhīm\ *n* -s *usu cap* [fr. *Anaheim*, Calif.] : a long tapered green usu. mild chili pepper

analemma* *n* : a plot or graph of the position of the sun in the sky that is measured at one locale at a certain time of day (as noon) throughout the year and that has the shape of a figure 8

an·a·log *also* **an·a·logue** \ˈan³lˌȯg, -äg\ *adj* **1** : of, relating to, or being an analogue **2** **a** : of, relating to, or being the representation of data by continuously variable physical quantities **b** : of or relating to an analog computer **c** : being a timepiece having both hour and minute hands

analogue* *also* **analog*** *n* **1** : a chemical compound that is structurally similar to another but differs slightly in composition (as in the replacement of one atom by an atom of a different element or in the presence of a particular functional group) **2** : a food product made by combining a less expensive food (as soybeans or whitefish) with additives to give the appearance and taste of a more expensive food (as beef or crab meat)

anal–retentive \ˌ===ˈ==\ *adj* : exhibiting or typifying personality traits (as frugality and obstinacy) held to be psychological consequences of toilet training — **anal retentive** *n* — **anal retentiveness** *n*

analysis of variance : any of several statistical techniques for analyzing the variation in a number of samples of equal or unequal size by partitioning the total sum of the squares of the deviations of each of the elements in all samples from the mean of all elements into components corresponding to the factors contributing to the variation — abbr. *ANOVA*

an·a·lyte \ˈanəˌlīt\ *n* -s [fr. *analysis*, after such pairs as E *electrolysis* : *electrolyte*] : a chemical compound that is the subject of a chemical analysis

analytic* *adj* **1** *of a function of a real variable* : capable of being expanded in a Taylor's series in powers of $x - h$ in some neighborhood of the point h **2** *of a function of a complex variable* : differentiable at every point in some neighborhood of a given point or points

anamnestic* *adj* : of or relating to a second rapid increased production of antibodies in response to an immunogenic substance after serum antibodies from a first response can no longer be detected in the blood

ana·plas·tic \ˌanəˈplastik\ *adj* [*ana-* + *-plastic*] : characterized by,

composed of, or being cells which have reverted to a relatively undifferentiated state ⟨~ carcinomas⟩
anatolian shepherd *n, usu cap A* : any of a breed of large rugged working dogs of Turkish origin that are used esp. to guard flocks of sheep or goats — called also *Anatolian, Anatolian shepherd dog*
an·a·tom·i·co- \ˌanəˈtäməˌ(ˌ)kō\ *or* **anat·o·mo-** \əˈnad·ə(ˌ)mō\ *comb form* [*anatomic*] : anatomical and : anatomical ⟨*anatomicopathological*⟩ ⟨*anatomoclinical*⟩
an·autogenous \ˌan+\ *adj* [*an-* + *autogenous* (herein)] : requiring a meal esp. of blood to produce eggs ⟨~ mosquitoes⟩
an·cho \ˈänchō\ *n* -S [AmerSp (*chile*) *ancho*, lit., wide chili] : a poblano chili pepper esp. when mature and dried to a reddish black
anchor* *n* **1** : an anchorman or anchorwoman **2** : a large store that attracts customers and other businesses to a shopping center or mall
anchor* *vt* : to act or serve as anchor for ⟨~ the evening news⟩
an·chor·man \ˈ==ˌman, -mən\ *n, pl* **anchormen 1** : a broadcaster (as on a newscast) who introduces reports by other broadcasters and usu. reads the news **2** : MODERATOR 3d
anchorpeople \ˈ==ˌ==\ *n pl* : ANCHORPERSONS *herein*
anchorperson \ˈ==ˌ==\ *n* : an anchorman or anchorwoman
anchorwoman \ˈ==ˌ==\ *n, pl* **anchorwomen** : a woman who anchors a broadcast
AND \ˈand\ *n* -S : a logical operator equivalent to the sentential connective *and* ⟨~ gate in a computer⟩
andalusian* *n, usu cap* : any of a breed of horses of Spanish origin that have a high-stepping gait
andouille \(ˌ)änˈdüwē, an-, -ˈdwē\ *or* **andouille sausage** *n* -S [F, fr. (assumed) VL *inductilia*, neut. pl. of (assumed) *inductilis* made by insertion, fr. L *inductus* (past part. of *inducere* to insert, bring in) + *-ilis* -ile — more at INDUCE] : a highly spiced smoked pork sausage
an·dra·go·gy \ˈandrəˌgäjē, -ˌgōjē, -ˌgägē\ *n* -ES [*andr-* + *-agogy* (as in *pedagogy*)] : the art or science of teaching adults — **an·dra·gog·i·cal** \ˌ==ˈgäjəkəl\ *adj*
an·dro·cen·trism \ˌandrōˈsentrizəm\ *n* -S [*androcentric* + *-ism*] : emphasis or insistence on the centrality of males and maleness in the human experience
an·dro·gen·ize \anˈdräjəˌnīz\ *vt* -ED/-ING/-S [*androgen* + *-ize*] : to treat or influence with male sex hormone esp. in excessive amounts ⟨neonatally *androgenized* female rats⟩
androgynous* *adj* **1 a** : neither specifically feminine or masculine ⟨the ~ pronoun *them*⟩ ⟨the themes cross the sexual divide to the darkest place of our ~ soul —Anne Roiphe⟩ **b** : suitable to or for either sex ⟨an ~ school of clothing design —Angelo d'Arcangelo⟩ ⟨the best fiction is ~: designed by a writer . . . for a reader of either sex —Doris Grumbach⟩ **2** : having traditional male and female roles obscured or reversed ⟨the possibility of a new ~ way of life —Gerda Lerner⟩ — **an·drog·y·nous·ly** \-lē, -li\ *adv* — **an·drog·y·nous·ness** \-nəs\ *n*
an·dro·stene·di·one \ˌandrəˈstēnˈdīˌōn, -ˈstēndēˌ-\ *n* -S [*androsterone* + *-ene* + *-dione*] : a steroid sex hormone $C_{19}H_{26}O_2$ that is secreted by the testis, ovary, and adrenal cortex and is a precursor of testosterone and estrogen
anecdotal* *adj* : based on or consisting of reports or observations of usu. unscientific observers ⟨~ evidence⟩
anemic* *adj* **1** : lacking interest or savor: as **a** : INSIPID 1 ⟨~ wines⟩ **b** : INSIPID 2 ⟨an ~ reputation⟩ **2** : lacking in substance or quantity ⟨~ returns on an investment⟩ ⟨~ attendance⟩
angel* *n* : a radar echo caused by something not visually discernible
angel dust *n* : PHENCYCLIDINE *herein*
angel–hair pasta *also* **angel hair** *n* [trans. of It *capelli d'angelo*] : pasta made in very thin strings
an·gel·man syndrome \ˈānjəlmən\ *also* **angelman's syndrome** \-mənz\ *n, usu cap A* [after Harry *Angelman* †1996 Eng. pediatrician] : a genetic disorder characterized by severe mental retardation, seizures, ataxic gait, jerky movements, lack of speech, microcephaly, and frequent smiling and laughter
angel skin coral *n* : a pale pink coral of the genus *Corallium* (esp. *C. secundum*) used in making jewelry
an·gi·o·graph·ic \ˈ==ˈ==\ *adj* : of, relating to, utilizing, or used in angiography ⟨~ assessment⟩ ⟨~ procedures⟩ — **an·gi·o·graph·i·cal·ly** \ˈ===(ə)\ *adv*
an·gi·op·a·thy \ˌanjēˈäpəthē, anˈjäp-\ *n* -ES [*angi-* + *-pathy*] : a disease of the blood or lymph vessels
an·gi·o·plas·ty \ˈ===ˌ=\ *n* -ES [*angi-* + *-plasty*] : surgical repair of a blood vessel; *esp* : BALLOON ANGIOPLASTY *herein*
an·gio·sarcoma \ˌanj(ē)ō, -jēə+\ *n* [*angi-* + *sarcoma*] : a rare malignant vascular tumor (as of the liver or breast)
an·gio·ten·sin \ˌ===ˈten(t)sən\ *n* -S [blend of *angiotonin* and *hypertensin*] **1** : either of two forms of a kinin of which one has marked physiological activity and the other is its physiologically inactive precursor; *esp* : ANGIOTENSIN II **2** : a synthetic amide derivative of angiotensin II used to treat some forms of hypotension
an·gio·ten·sin·ase \-səˌnās, -āz\ *n* -S [*angiotensin* (herein) + *-ase*] : any of several enzymes in the blood that hydrolyze angiotensin
angiotensin converting enzyme *n* : a proteolytic enzyme that converts the physiologically inactive form of angiotensin into angiotensin II — see ACE INHIBITOR *herein*
angiotensin converting enzyme inhibitor *n* : ACE INHIBITOR *herein*
angiotensin II \-ˈtü\ *n* : a protein with vasoconstrictive activity that increases blood pressure, stimulates the release of aldosterone, is composed of a chain of eight amino acid residues, and is the physiologically active form of angiotensin
an·glo·cen·tric \ˌaŋglōˈsentrik\ *adj, usu cap* [*anglo-* + *-centric*] : centered on or giving priority to England or things English ⟨an ~ view of history⟩
[1]**an·glo·phone** \ˈaŋgləˌfōn\ *or* **an·glo·phon·ic** \ˈ==ˈfänik\ *adj, often cap* [*anglophone* fr. F, fr. *anglo-* Anglo- + *-phone* (as in *francophone*); *anglophonic* fr. *anglophone* + *-ic*] : of, having, or belonging to an English-speaking population esp. in a country where two or more languages are spoken
[2]**anglophone** \"\ *n* -S *usu cap* : an English-speaking person esp. in a country where two or more languages are spoken
angry young man *n* [*Angry Young Man*, autobiography (1951) of Leslie A. Paul †1985 Eng. journalist] **1** : one of a group of mid-20th century British writers whose works express the bitterness of the lower classes toward the established sociopolitical system and toward the mediocrity and hypocrisy of the middle and upper classes **2** : an outspoken critic of or protester against a social or economic condition or injustice
angular perspective *n* : TWO-POINT PERSPECTIVE
animal* *n* : an individual with a particular interest or aptitude ⟨a political ~⟩
animal control *n* : an office or department responsible for enforcing ordinances relating to the control, impoundment, and disposition of animals
animal model *n* : an animal sufficiently like humans in its anatomy, physiology, or response to a pathogen to be used in medical research in order to obtain results that can be extrapolated to human medicine; *also* : a pathological or physiological condition that occurs in such an animal and is similar to a human condition
animal rights *n pl* : rights (as that to fair and humane treatment) regarded as belonging fundamentally to all animals
an·i·ma·tron·ic \ˌanəməˈtränik\ *adj* [short for *audio-animatronic* (herein)] : of, relating to, or being a puppet or similar figure that is animated by means of electromechanical devices — **an·i·ma·tron·i·cal·ly** \-(ə)lē\ *adv*
an·i·ma·tron·ics \ˌanəməˈträniks\ *n pl but sing or pl in constr* : technology dealing with animatronic animation
an·ky·lo·sau·rus \ˈaŋkəlōˈsȯ(ə)rəs\ *n* [NL, fr. *ankyl-* + *-saurus*] **1** *cap* : a No. American genus of large ankylosaurs (family Ankylosauridae) of the late Cretaceous that were herbivorous dinosaurs walking on all four legs and having the body, head, and tail covered with bony plates studded with spikes and a tail ending in a bony club **2** -ES : a dinosaur of the genus *Ankylosaurus*
ankylosing spondylitis *n* : RHEUMATOID SPONDYLITIS
anneal* *vb* ~ *vt* : to heat and then cool (nucleic acid) in order to separate strands and induce combination at lower temperatures esp. with complementary strands of a different species ~ *vi* : to be capable of combining with complementary nucleic acid by a process of heating and cooling ⟨some bacterial nucleic acid ~s well with eukaryotic DNA⟩
annihilate* *vb* ~ *vt* : to cause (as a particle and its antiparticle) to vanish or cease to exist by coming together and changing into other forms of energy (as photons) ⟨matter and antimatter ~ each other⟩ ~ *vi* : to undergo annihilation ⟨an elementary particle and its antiparticle ~ when they meet⟩
annual percentage rate *n* : a measure of the annual percentage cost of consumer credit (as in installment buying or a charge account) that is required by law to appear on statements of credit accounts and is variously computed but always takes into consideration the amount financed, the amount of the finance charges, and the schedule of repayment — abbr. *APR*
anod·al \ˈaˌnōdᵊl, ˌaˈ-\ *adj* [*anode* + [1]*-al*] : of, relating to, attracted to, or originating at an anode : ANODIC 3a ⟨an ~ current⟩ — used esp. in the life sciences — **anod·al·ly** \-ē\ *adv*
ano·genital \ˈānō+\ *adj* [[2]*ano-* + *genital*] : of, relating to, or involving the genital organs and the anus ⟨an asymptomatic ~ infection⟩
anointing of the sick : EXTREME UNCTION
anorectic* *also* **anoretic*** *adj* : ANOREXIC 1b *herein*
anorectic* *also* **anoretic*** *n* : ANOREXIC *herein*
[1]**an·o·rex·ic** \ˌanəˈreksik, -nō-\ *adj* [*anorexia* + [1]*-ic*] **1 a** : ANORECTIC **b** : relating to, characteristic of, or affected with or as if with anorexia nervosa ⟨~ patients⟩ : excessively skinny ⟨~ models⟩ **2** : characterized by privation or deficiency ⟨operations slimmed to ~ proportions —Brian Dumaine *et al*⟩
[2]**anorexic** *n* -S : a person affected with or as if with anorexia nervosa
ANOVA *abbr* analysis of variance *herein*
an·ovu·lant \aˈnävyələnt, -ōv-\ *n* -S [*an-* + *ovulation* + *-ant*] : an anovulatory drug — **anovulant** *adj*
an·ovulation \(ˈ)an+\ *n* [*an-* + *ovulation*] : failure or absence of ovulation
anovulatory* *adj* : suppressing ovulation ⟨~ drugs⟩
anoxic* *adj* : greatly deficient in oxygen ⟨~ water⟩
an·ox·y·gen·ic \ˈ=ˈ==ˈ=\ *adj* [*an-* + *oxygenic*] : being or carrying out photosynthesis in which oxygen is not produced as a by-product ⟨~ purple bacteria⟩
answer* *n* : one that imitates, matches, or corresponds to another ⟨picture books—the book business's ~ to the movies —Edward Hoagland⟩
answering machine *n* : a machine that receives telephone calls by playing a recorded message and usu. by recording messages from callers
answering service *n* : a commercial service that answers telephone calls for its clients
ante* *n* : STAKE 4a, b — often used in the phrase *up the ante* ⟨he knows he can up the *ante* by asking to live with Dad —Myriam W. Misrach⟩
an·te·grade \ˈ==+\ *adj* [*ante-* + *grade*] : ANTEROGRADE *herein*
antenna* *n* : a special sensitivity, alertness, or receptiveness — usu. used in pl. ⟨helped in her career by sensitive political *antennae*⟩
anterior cruciate ligament *n* : a cruciate ligament of each knee that is attached in front to the more medial aspect of the tibia, that passes upward, backward, and laterally through the middle of the knee to attach to the femur, that functions to prevent hyperextension of the knee and to keep the femur from sliding backward in relation to the tibia, and that is subject to sports injury esp. by tearing — called also *ACL*
anterograde* *adj* : occurring or performed in the normal or forward direction of conduction or flow: as **a** : occurring along nerve processes away from the cell body ⟨~ axonal transport⟩ **b** : occurring in the normal direction or path of blood circulation ⟨restoration of ~ flow in an occluded coronary artery⟩
anthem* *n* **1** : a popular song typical of or identified with a particular group, movement, or subculture ⟨a punk rock ~⟩; *broadly* : a piece of music : SONG ⟨new love ~s and steaming gospel numbers —Nat Hentoff⟩ **2** : something (as a slogan or belief) resembling an anthem in being associated with or typical of a group, movement, or period ⟨complex and imaginative art, the ~ of discontent —Earl Shorvis⟩ ⟨his novel . . . became the ~ of the decadent fin-de-siècle 1890s —Paul Gray⟩ — **an·them·ic** \anˈthemik\ *adj*
an·thra·cy·cline \ˌan(t)thrəˈsīˌklēn, -ˌklən\ *n* -S [*anthr-* + *-cycline* (as in *tetracycline*)] : any of a class of antineoplastic drugs (as doxorubicin) derived from an actinomycete of the genus *Streptomyces* (esp. *S. peucetius*)
anthropic principle *n* : either of two principles in cosmology: **a** : conditions that are observed in the universe must allow the observer to exist — called also *weak anthropic principle* **b** : the universe must have properties that make inevitable the existence of intelligent life — called also *strong anthropic principle*
an·thro·po·nym \anˈthräpəˌnim, ˈan(t)thrəpə-\ *n* [*anthrop-* + *-onym*] : a person's name; *esp* : SURNAME 2a — **an·thro·po·nym·ic** \=ˌ==ˈnimik, ˌ===-\ *adj*
an·thro·po·sere \anˈthräpə, ˈan(t)thrəpə+ˌ\ *n* [*anthrop-* + [5]*sere*] : NOOSPHERE *herein*
an·thro·po·sphere \"+ˌ\ *n* [*anthrop-* + *sphere*] : NOOSPHERE *herein*
an·ti·abortion \ˈanˌtī, ˈantē, ˈantə+\ *adj* [[1]*anti-* + *abortion*] : opposed to abortion and esp. to the legalization of abortion ⟨~ activists⟩ — **antiabortionist** \"+\ *n*
an·ti·aging \"+\ *adj* [[1]*anti-* + *aging*, gerund of [2]*age*] : used or tending to prevent or lessen the effects of aging ⟨~ skin creams⟩
anti–AIDS \"+\ *adj* [[1]*anti-* + *AIDS* (herein)] : used to treat or delay the development of AIDS ⟨the *anti-AIDS* drug AZT⟩
an·ti·allergic \ˈanˌtī, ˈantē, ˈantə+\ *also* **an·ti·allergenic** \"+\ *adj* [[1]*anti-* + *allergic* or *allergenic*] : tending to relieve or control allergic symptoms — **antiallergic** *also* **antiallergenic** *n* -S
anti–american \"+\ *adj, usu cap 2d A* : opposed or hostile to the people or the government policies of the U.S. — **anti–americanism** \"+\ *n, usu cap 2d A*
an·ti·androgen \"+\ *n* [[1]*anti-* + *androgen*] : a substance that tends to inhibit the production, activity, or effects of a male sex hormone — **an·ti·androgenic** \"+\ *adj*
an·ti·anginal \"+\ *adj* [[1]*anti-* + *anginal*] : used or tending to prevent or relieve angina pectoris ⟨~ drugs⟩
an·ti·anxiety \"+\ *adj* [[1]*anti-* + *anxiety*] : tending to prevent or relieve anxiety ⟨~ drugs⟩
an·ti·arrhythmic \"+\ *adj* [[1]*anti-* + *arrhythmia* + [1]*-ic*] : counteracting or preventing cardiac arrhythmia ⟨an ~ agent⟩ — **antiarrhythmic** *n* -S
an·ti–art \ˈanˌtī, ˈantē, ˈantəˌ+\ *n* [[1]*anti-* + *art*] : art based on premises antithetical to traditional or popular art forms; *specif* : DADA
an·ti·arthritic \ˈ=(ˌ)=+\ *or* **an·ti·arthritis** \ˈ=(ˌ)=+\ *adj* [[1]*anti-* + *arthritic* or *arthritis*] : tending to relieve or prevent arthritic symptoms — **antiarthritic** *n*
an·ti·atom \ˈ=(ˌ)=+ˌ\ *n* [[1]*anti-* + *atom*] : an atom comprised of antiparticles
an·ti·authoritarian \ˈanˌtī, ˈantē, ˈantə+\ *adj* [[1]*anti-* + *authoritarian*] : opposed or hostile to authoritarians or authoritarianism — **an·ti·authoritarianism** \"+\ *n*
an·ti·auxin \"+\ *n* [[1]*anti-* + *auxin*] : a plant substance that opposes or suppresses the natural effect of an auxin
an·ti·ballistic missile \"+. . .-\ *n* [[1]*anti-* + *ballistic missile*] : a missile for intercepting and destroying a ballistic missile
an·ti·baryon \"+\ *n* [[1]*anti-* + *baryon* (herein)] : an antiparticle of a baryon (as an antiproton or antineutron)
an·ti·black \"+\ *adj* [[1]*anti-* + *black*] : opposed or hostile to people belonging to a black race — **an·ti·black·ism** \-ˌizəm\ *n* -S
an·ti·bond·ing \"+\ *adj* [[1]*anti-* + *bonding*, gerund of [4]*bond*] : relating to, being, or occupying a molecular orbital which tends to inhibit bonding between atoms ⟨~ orbitals⟩ ⟨an ~ electron⟩; *broadly* : tending to inhibit bonding between atoms
an·ti·business \"+\ *adj* [[1]*anti-* + *business*] : antagonistic toward business and esp. big business
an·ti·busing \"+\ *adj* [[1]*anti-* + *busing* (herein)] : opposed to the busing of schoolchildren ⟨~ parents⟩ ⟨~ campaign⟩
an·ti·cancer \"+\ *adj* [[1]*anti-* + *cancer*] : used or effective against cancer ⟨~ drugs⟩ ⟨~ treatments⟩
an·ti·carcinogenic \"+\ *adj* [[1]*anti-* + *carcinogenic*] : tending to inhibit or prevent the activity of a carcinogen or the development of carcinoma ⟨foods with ~ properties⟩ — **an·ti·carcinogen** \"+\ *n*
an·ti·caries \"+\ *adj* [[1]*anti-* + *caries*] : tending to inhibit the formation of caries ⟨~ effects⟩ ⟨an ~ toothpaste additive⟩
an·ti·choice \"+\ *adj* [[1]*anti-* + [1]*choice*] : ANTIABORTION *herein* — **an·ti·choic·er** *n* -S
an·ti·coagulation \"+\ *n* [[1]*anti-* + *coagulation*] : the process of hindering the clotting of blood esp. by treatment with an anticoagulant — **an·ti·coagulate** \"+\ *vt* — **an·ti·coagulatory** \"+\ *adj*
an·ti·codon \"+\ *n* [[1]*anti-* + *codon* (herein)] : a triplet of nucleotide bases in transfer RNA that identifies the amino acid carried and binds to a complementary codon in messenger RNA during protein synthesis at a ribosome
an·ti·convulsant \"+\ *also* **an·ti·convulsive** \"+\ *adj* [[1]*anti-* + *convulsant* or *convulsive*] : used or tending to control or prevent convulsions (as in epilepsy) — **anticonvulsant** *also* **anticonvulsive** *n* -S
an·ti·crop \"+\ *adj* [[1]*anti-* + [1]*crop*] : destructive to or directed against crops ⟨~ chemical weapons⟩
[1]**an·ti·depressant** \ˈanˌtī, ˈantē, ˈantə+\ *also* **an·ti·depressive** \"+\ *adj* [[1]*anti-* + *depressant* or *depressive*] : used or tending to relieve or prevent psychic depression
[2]**antidepressant** *n* : an antidepressant drug — called also *energizer, psychic energizer*; see TRICYCLIC ANTIDEPRESSANT *herein*
an·ti·desiccant \"+\ *n* [[1]*anti-* + [2]*desiccant*] : ANTITRANSPIRANT *herein*
an·ti·deuteron \"+\ *n* [[1]*anti-* + *deuteron*] : the antimatter counterpart of a deuteron
an·ti·diabetic \"+\ *adj* [[1]*anti-* + *diabetic*] : tending to relieve diabetes ⟨~ drugs⟩ — **antidiabetic** *n* -S
an·ti·diarrheal \"+\ *adj* [[1]*anti-* + *diarrheal*] : tending to prevent or relieve diarrhea — **antidiarrheal** *n* -S
an·ti·diuresis \"+\ *n* [[1]*anti-* + *diuresis*] : reduction in or suppression of the excretion of urine
antidiuretic hormone *n* : VASOPRESSIN
an·ti·drug \"+\ *adj* [[1]*anti-* + [1]*drug*] : acting against or opposing illicit drugs or their use ⟨~ activist⟩ ⟨~ program⟩
an·ti·dumping \"+\ *adj* [[1]*anti-* + *dumping*] : designed to discourage the importation and sale of foreign goods at prices substantially lower than domestic prices ⟨~ tariffs⟩
an·ti·electron \"+\ *n* [[1]*anti-* + *electron*] : POSITRON
an·ti·emetic \"+\ *adj* [[1]*anti-* + *emetic*] : used or tending to prevent or check vomiting ⟨~ drugs⟩ — **antiemetic** *n*
an·ti·epileptic \"+\ *adj* [[1]*anti-* + *epileptic*] : tending to suppress or prevent epilepsy ⟨~ treatment⟩ — **antiepileptic** *n*
an·ti·establishment \"+\ *adj* [[1]*anti-* + *establishment* (herein)] : opposed or hostile to the social, economic, and political principles of a ruling class (as of a nation)
an·ti·establishmentarian \"+\ *adj* [*antiestablishment* (herein) + *-arian*] : ANTIESTABLISHMENT *herein* — **antiestablishmentarian** *n* -S — **an·ti·establishmentarianism** \"+\ *n* -S
an·ti·estrogen \"+\ *n* [[1]*anti-* + *estrogen*] : a substance that inhibits the physiological action of an estrogen — **an·ti·estrogenic** \"+\ *adj*
an·ti·feminist \"+\ *adj* [[1]*anti-* + *feminist*] : opposed to feminism — **an·ti·feminism** \"+\ *n* — **antifeminist** *n*
an·ti·fertility \"+\ *adj* [[1]*anti-* + *fertility*] : having the capacity or tending to reduce or destroy fertility : CONTRACEPTIVE ⟨~ agents⟩ ⟨~ action⟩
an·ti·flu·o·ri·da·tion·ist \ˈ=(ˌ)=ˌflu̇rəˈdāsh(ə)nəst, -ˌōr-, -ˌȯr-\ *n* -S [[1]*anti-* + *fluoridation* + *-ist*] : a person who is vigorously opposed to the fluoridation of public water supplies
an·ti·foul·ant \ˈ=(ˌ)=ˈfau̇lənt\ *n* -S [[1]*anti-* + [4]*foul* + [1]*-ant*] : a substance (as paint for use on the bottom of a boat) designed to prevent, reduce, or eliminate fouling
antifreeze* *n* : any of various substances (as proteins or alcohols) that are found in some living organisms (as certain fish, amphibians, and insects) and serve to lower the freezing point of body fluids esp. by limiting ice crystal growth
an·ti·fungal \ˈanˌtī, ˈantē, ˈantə+\ *adj* [[1]*anti-* + *fungal*] : destroying fungi or inhibiting their growth : FUNGICIDAL, FUNGISTATIC ⟨~ drugs⟩ ⟨~ activity⟩ ⟨~ chemotherapy⟩ — **antifungal** *n*
an·ti·fur \"+\ *adj* [[1]*anti-* + [3]*fur*] : opposed to the killing of fur-bearing animals for their pelts
an·ti·gay \"+\ *adj* [[1]*anti-* + [1]*gay*] : opposed or hostile to homosexuals
antigenic determinant *n* : EPITOPE *herein*
antigen–presenting cell \ˈ===ˈ==\ *n* : any of various cells (as a macrophage or a B cell) that take up and process an antigen into a form that when displayed at the cell surface in combination with a molecule of the major histocompatibility complex is recognized by and serves to activate a specific helper T cell
an·ti·glare \ˈanˌtī, ˈantē, ˈantə+\ *adj* [[1]*anti-* + [2]*glare*] : reducing or preventing glare
an·ti·globulin \"+\ *n* [[1]*anti-* + *globulin*] : an antibody that combines with and precipitates globulin
[1]**an·ti·gravity** \"+\ *adj* [[1]*anti-* + *gravity*] : reducing, canceling, or protecting against the effect of gravity
[2]**antigravity** \"+\ *n* : a hypothetical effect resulting from cancellation or reduction of a gravitational field
an·ti·helium \"+\ *n* [[1]*anti-* + *helium*] : the antimatter counterpart of helium
an·ti·hemophilic factor *also* **antihemophilic globulin** \"+. . .-\ *n* [[1]*anti-* + *hemophilic*] : FACTOR VIII *herein*
an·ti·hero \"+\ *n* [[1]*anti-* + *hero*] : a protagonist who is notably lacking in heroic qualities — **an·ti·heroic** \"+\ *adj*
an·ti·heroine \"+\ *n* [[1]*anti-* + *heroine*] : a female antihero
an·ti·human \"+\ *adj* [[1]*anti-* + *human*] : acting or being against humans; *also* : reacting strongly with human antigens ⟨~ antibodies⟩
an·ti·hydrogen \"+\ *n* [[1]*anti-* + *hydrogen*] : the antimatter counterpart of hydrogen
an·ti·hypertensive \"+\ *adj* [[1]*anti-* + *hypertension* + *-ive*] : used or effective against high blood pressure — **antihypertensive** *n*
an·ti–idiotype \"+\ *n* [[1]*anti-* + *idiotype* (herein)] : an antibody that binds to the antigen combining site of another antibody either suppressing or enhancing the immune response — **an·ti–idiotypic** \"+\ *adj*
an·ti–immunoglobulin \"+\ *adj* [[1]*anti-* + *immunoglobulin*] : acting against specific antibodies ⟨*anti-immunoglobulin* sera⟩ — **anti–immunoglobulin** *n*
an·ti–infective \"+\ *adj* [[1]*anti-* + *infective*] : used against or tending to counteract or prevent infection ⟨*anti-infective* agents⟩ — **anti–infective** *n* -S
an·ti–inflammatory \ˈanˌtī, ˈantē, ˈantə+\ *adj* [[1]*anti-* + *inflammatory*] : counteracting inflammation — **anti–inflammatory** *n* -ES
an·ti–intellectual \"+\ *adj* [[1]*anti-* + *intellectual*] : opposing or hostile to intellectuals or to an intellectual view or approach ⟨an *anti-intellectual* know-nothingism: forget politics, forget art, forget history —Samuel Hynes⟩ — **anti–intellectual** *n*
an·ti·lepton \"+\ *n* [[1]*anti-* + [3]*lepton*] : an antiparticle (as a positron or an antineutrino) of a lepton

an·ti·leukemic \"+\ *also* **an·ti·leukemia** \"+\ *adj* [[1]*anti-* + *leukemic* or *leukemia*] : counteracting the effects of leukemia

an·ti·life \"+\ *adj* [[1]*anti-* + *life*] **1** : antagonistic or antithetical to life or to normal human values ⟨authoritarian, ~ political regimes —Richard Hoff⟩ **2** : PROABORTION *herein* — often used disparagingly

an·ti·litter \"+\ *adj* [[1]*anti-* + *litter*] : intended to prevent or discourage the littering of public areas ⟨~ laws⟩

an·ti·lock \"+\ *adj* [[1]*anti-* + [3]*lock*] : being a braking system for a motor vehicle designed to keep the wheels from locking by electronically controlled pulsed application of the brake for each wheel

an·ti·lymphocyte globulin \"+. . .\ *n* [[1]*anti-* + *lymphocyte*] : serum globulin containing antibodies against lymphocytes that is used similarly to antilymphocyte serum

an·ti·lymphocyte serum \"+. . .\ *n* : a serum containing antibodies against lymphocytes that is used for suppressing graft rejection caused by lymphocyte-controlled immune responses in organ or tissue transplant recipients

an·ti·lymphocytic globulin \"+. . .\ *n* [[1]*anti-* + *lymphocytic*] : ANTILYMPHOCYTE GLOBULIN *herein*

an·ti·lymphocytic serum \"+. . .\ *n* : ANTILYMPHOCYTE SERUM *herein*

an·ti·manic \"+\ *adj* [[1]*anti-* + [1]*manic*] : counteracting or preventing mania and esp. mania associated with bipolar disorder

an·ti·missile \"+\ *adj* [[1]*anti-* + *missile*] : designed as a defense against missiles ⟨an ~ system⟩

antimissile missile *n* : a missile for intercepting another missile in flight; *esp* : ANTIBALLISTIC MISSILE *herein*

an·ti·mitotic \ˌan‚tī, ¦antē, ¦antə+\ *adj* [[1]*anti-* + *mitotic*] : inhibiting or disrupting mitosis ⟨~ drugs⟩ ⟨~ activity⟩ — **antimitotic** *n* -S

an·ti·mutagenic \"+\ *adj* [[1]*anti-* + *mutagenic*] : reducing the rate of mutation ⟨~ substances⟩

an·ti·mycotic \"+\ *adj or n* [[1]*anti-* + *mycotic*] : ANTIFUNGAL *herein*

an·ti·neoplastic \"+\ *adj* [[1]*anti-* + *neoplastic*] : inhibiting or preventing the growth and spread of neoplasms or malignant cells ⟨treated with ~ drugs⟩ — **antineoplastic** *n* -S

an·ti·noise \"+\ *adj* [[1]*anti-* + *noise*] : designed or acting to reduce noise level ⟨an ~ ordinance⟩

an·ti·novel \"+\ *n* [part trans. of F *antiroman*] : a work of fiction that lacks most or all of the traditional features (as coherent structure or character development) of the novel — **an·ti·novel·ist** \"+\ *n*

an·ti·nuclear \"+\ *adj* **1** [[1]*anti-* + *nucleus* + *-ar*] : being antibodies or autoantibodies that react with components and esp. DNA of cell nuclei and that tend to occur frequently in connective tissue diseases (as systemic lupus erythematosus, rheumatoid arthritis, and Sjögren's syndrome) **2** [[1]*anti-* + *nuclear*] : opposing the use or production of nuclear power plants or nuclear weapons

an·ti·nuke \¦=(ˌ)=¦n(y)ük\ *adj* [by shortening & alter.] : ANTINUCLEAR 2 *herein*

an·ti·obscenity \"+\ *adj* [[1]*anti-* + *obscenity*] : designed to prevent or restrict the dissemination of obscene materials

an·ti·oncogene \"+\ *n* [[1]*anti-* + *oncogene* (herein)] : TUMOR SUPPRESSOR GENE *herein*

an·ti·ozon·ant \¦=(ˌ)=¦ōˌzōnənt\ *n* -S [[1]*anti-* + *ozone* + [1]*-ant*] : a substance that opposes ozonization or protects against it

an·ti·parasitic \"+\ *adj* [[1]*anti-* + *parasitic*] : acting against parasites ⟨~ drugs⟩

an·ti·parkinsonian \"+\ *also* **an·ti·parkinson** \¦=(ˌ)=ˈpärkənsən\ *adj* [[1]*anti-* + *parkinsonian* or *parkinson's* (*disease*)] : tending to relieve parkinsonism ⟨~ drugs⟩

an·ti·particle \ˈan‚tī, ˈantē, ˈantə+\ *n* [[1]*anti-* + *particle*] : an elementary particle that is identical to another elementary particle in mass but opposite to it in electric and magnetic properties (as sign of charge) and that when brought together with its counterpart produces mutual annihilation; *specif* : an elementary particle not found in ordinary matter

an·ti·political \ˌan‚tī, ¦antē, ¦antə+\ *adj* [[1]*anti-* + *political*] : opposing or reacting against traditional political policies and principles

an·ti·politician \"+\ *n* [[1]*anti-* + *politician*] : a politician who appears to be antipolitical

an·ti–politics \"+\ *n pl but sing or pl in constr* [[1]*anti-* + *politics*] : reaction against or rejection of the practices or attitudes associated with traditional politics

an·ti·pollution \"+\ *adj* [[1]*anti-* + *pollution*] : intended to prevent, reduce, or eliminate pollution — **an·ti·pol·lu·tion·ist** \-shənəst\ *n* -S

an·ti·poverty \"+\ *adj* [[1]*anti-* + *poverty*] : of or relating to action designed to relieve poverty ⟨~ programs⟩

an·ti·psychotic \"+\ *n* [[1]*anti-* + *psychotic*] : any of the powerful tranquilizers (as the phenothiazines or butyrophenones) used esp. to treat psychosis and believed to act by blocking dopamine nervous receptors — called also *neuroleptic* — **antipsychotic** *adj*

an·ti·quark \"+\ *n* [[1]*anti-* + *quark* (herein)] : the antiparticle of a quark

antique* *vb* ~ *vi* : to shop around for antiques

an·ti·racism \"+\ *n* [[1]*anti-* + *racism*] : adherence to the view that racism is a social evil — **an·ti·racist** \"+\ *n or adj*

an·ti·radical \"+\ *adj* [[1]*anti-* + *radical*] : opposed to radicals or radicalism

an·ti·reflective \"+\ *adj* [[1]*anti-* + *reflective*] : being or coated with an antireflection film ⟨~ lenses⟩

an·ti·rejection \"+\ *adj* [[1]*anti-* + *rejection*] : used or tending to prevent organ or tissue transplant rejection ⟨~ drugs⟩

anti–roll bar \"+\ *n* [[1]*anti-* + [1]*roll*] : SWAY BAR

an·ti·satellite \"+\ *adj* [[1]*anti-* + [1]*satellite*] : of, relating to, or being a system designed for the destruction or incapacitation of satellites

an·ti·science \"+\ *n* [[1]*anti-* + *science*] : a system or attitude or cult that rejects scientific methods or the value of science to humans; *also* : one that denies the value of basic scientific research — **antiscience** *adj* — **an·ti·scientific** \"+\ *adj*

an·ti·seizure \"+\ *adj* [[1]*anti-* + *seizure*] : preventing or counteracting seizures ⟨~ medications⟩

an·ti·sense \"+\ *adj* [[1]*anti-* + *-sense* (as in *nonsense* — herein)] : having a sequence complementary to a segment of genetic material; *specif* : of, being, relating to, or possessing a sequence of DNA or RNA that is complementary to and pairs with a specific messenger RNA blocking it from being translated into protein and serving to inhibit gene function ⟨~ RNA⟩ ⟨~ drug therapy⟩ ⟨~ research⟩ — compare MISSENSE *herein*, NONSENSE *herein*

an·ti·sex \"+\ *or* **an·ti·sexual** \"+\ *adj* [[1]*anti-* + *sex* or *sexual*] : antagonistic toward sex; *esp* : tending or intended to reduce or eliminate the sex drive or sexual activity

an·ti·sexist \"+\ *adj* [[1]*anti-* + *sexist* (herein)] : opposed to sexism — **an·ti·sexism** \"+\ *n* — **antisexist** *n*

an·ti·skid \"+\ *adj* [[1]*anti-* + *skid*] : designed to prevent skidding ⟨~ brakes⟩

an·ti·smog \"+\ *adj* [[1]*anti-* + *smog*] : designed to reduce pollutants that contribute to the formation of smog

an·ti·smok·ing \"+\ *adj* [[1]*anti-* + *smoking*, gerund of [2]*smoke*] : opposed to tobacco smoking ⟨~ groups⟩ ⟨~ ads⟩

an·ti·static \ˌan‚tī, ¦antē, ¦antə+\ *also* **an·ti·stat** \ˌan‚tī¦stat, ¦antē-, ¦antə-\ *adj* [*antistatic* fr. [1]*anti-* + *static*, n.; *antistat* short for *antistatic*] : reducing, removing, or preventing the buildup of static electricity — **antistatic** *n*

an·ti·streptococcal *or* **an·ti·streptococcic** \ˌan‚tī, ¦antē, ¦antə+\ *adj* [[1]*anti-* + *streptococcal* or *streptococcic*] : tending to destroy or inhibit the growth and reproduction of streptococci ⟨~ antibodies⟩

antisymmetric* *adj* **1** : relating to or being a relation (as "is a subset of") that implies equality of any two quantities for which it holds in both directions ⟨the relation *R* is ~ if *aRb* and *bRa* implies *a* = *b*⟩ **2** : being a wave function of a particle (as an electron or a nucleus in a molecule) that changes sign when the particle is interchanged with another similar particle which occupies a different energy state

an·ti·thrombotic \"+\ *adj* [[1]*anti-* + *thrombotic*] : used against or tending to prevent thrombosis ⟨~ agents⟩ ⟨~ therapy⟩

an·ti·tran·spi·rant \"+\ *n* -S [[1]*anti-* + *transpiration* + [1]*-ant*] : a substance (as pine oil) that is usu. sprayed on plant surfaces (as of the leaves and stems) to reduce transpiration and inhibit water loss — called also *antidesiccant*

an·ti·tuberculous \"+\ *or* **an·ti·tuberculosis** \"+\ *also* **an·ti·tubercular** \"+\ *adj* [[1]*anti-* + *tuberculous* or *tuberculosis* or *tubercular*] : used or effective against tuberculosis ⟨~ drugs⟩

an·ti·tumor \"+\ *also* **an·ti·tumoral** \"+\ *adj* [[1]*anti-* + *tumor* or *tumoral*] : preventing or inhibiting the formation or growth of tumors : ANTICANCER *herein* ⟨~ agents⟩ ⟨~ activity⟩

antitussive* *n* -S : an antitussive agent

an·ti·ulcer \"+\ *adj* [[1]*anti-* + *ulcer*] : tending to prevent or heal ulcers ⟨~ drug research⟩

an·ti–utopia \"+\ *n* [[1]*anti-* + *utopia*] : DYSTOPIA *herein* — **an·ti–utopian** \"+\ *adj or n*

antiviral* *adj* : ANTIVIRUS *herein*

an·ti·viral \"+\ *n* [*antiviral*, adj.] : an antiviral agent

an·ti·virus \"+\ *adj* [[1]*anti-* + *virus* (herein)] : relating to or being software designed to detect and usu. delete computer viruses

an·ti·war \"+\ *adj* [[1]*anti-* + *war*] : opposed to war ⟨~ demonstrations⟩

an·ti·white \"+\ *adj* [[1]*anti-* + *white*] : opposed or hostile to people belonging to a light-skinned and esp. the Caucasian race — **an·ti·whit·ism** \¦=(ˌ)=¦(h)wīdˌizəm\ *n* -S

an·ti·world \ˈan‚tī, ˈantē, ˈantə+‚\ *n* [[1]*anti-* + *world*] : the hypothetical antimatter counterpart of a world

anx·io·lyt·ic \ˌaŋzēōˈlid·ik, ˌaŋ(k)sē-, -itik, -ēk\ *n* -S [*anxiety* + *-o-* + *-lytic*] : a drug that relieves anxiety — **anxiolytic** *adj*

ao dai \¦aŭ¦dī, ¦a-\ *n, pl* **ao dais** [Vietnamese *áo dài*, fr. *áo* jacket, tunic (of Chinese origin; akin to Chin (Pek) *ao*[3] jacket) + *dài* long] : the traditional dress of Vietnamese women that consists of a long tunic with slits on either side and wide trousers

A–OK \¦ā(ˌ)ō¦kā\ *adj* [[1]*a* + *OK*] : very definitely OK

aor·to·coronary \(ˌ)āˌȯrd·ō+, -rtō-\ *adj* [*aort-* + *coronary*] : of, relating to, or joining the aorta and the coronary arteries

aor·to·iliac \"+\ *adj* [*aort-* + *iliac*] : of, relating to, or joining the abdominal aorta and the iliac arteries ⟨an ~ bypass graft⟩

apartheid* *n* : SEPARATION, SEGREGATION ⟨cultural ~⟩

APC \ˌāˌpēˈsē\ *n* -S [*a*rmored *p*ersonnel *c*arrier] : an armored vehicle used to transport military personnel

ape \ˈāp\ *adj* [[1]*ape*] : being beyond restraint : CRAZY, WILD — usu. used in the phrase *go ape* ⟨went ~ over another girl —*Boston Sunday Globe Mag.*⟩

aperture card *n* : a punched card for data processing in which one or more frames of a microfilmed document are mounted

aperture synthesis *n* : a technique in radio astronomy in which two or more radio telescopes are varied in position and spacing to simulate a large telescope having a collecting area with a diameter approximately equal to the largest spacing between the smaller telescopes

APEX \ˈāˌpeks\ *n* -ES [*a*dvance *p*urchase *ex*cursion] : a class of reduced airfares requiring payment a specified number of days in advance and a round trip of specified duration

ap·gar score \ˈapˌgär, -ˌgȧ(r\ *n, usu cap A* [after Virginia *Apgar* †1974 Am. anesthesiologist] : an index used to evaluate the condition of a newborn infant based on a rating of 0, 1, or 2 for each of the five characteristics of color, heart rate, response to stimulation of the sole of the foot, muscle tone, and respiration with 10 being a perfect score

apha·si·ol·o·gy \əˈfāz(h)ēˈäləjē, -ji\ *n* -ES [*aphasia* + *-ology*] : the study of aphasia including its linguistic, psychological, and neurological aspects — **apha·si·ol·o·gist** \-jəst\ *n* -S

aphe·re·sis* \ˌafəˈrēsəs\ *n* : withdrawal of blood from a donor's body, removal of one or more blood components (as plasma, blood platelets, or white blood cells), and transfusion of the remaining blood back into the donor — called also *pheresis*

apo \ˈapō\ *n* -S [by shortening] : APOLIPOPROTEIN *herein* — usu. used with a letter or letter and number

apo·apsis \¦apō+\ *n, pl* **apo·ap·ses** *or* **apo·apsides** \"+\ [NL, fr. *apo-* + *apsis*] : the apsis that is farthest from the center of attraction : the high point in an orbit — compare PERIAPSIS *herein*

apo·lipoprotein \¦apə, ¦apō+\ *n* [*apo-* + *lipoprotein*] : a protein that combines with a lipid to form a lipoprotein — often used with a letter or letter and number

apollo* *n, usu cap, often attrib* [fr. *Apollo*, an asteroid of this class] : any of a class of asteroids having orbits that extend from inside to beyond Earth's orbit — compare AMOR *herein*

apo·lune \ˈapəˌlün\ *n* -S [*apo-* (as in *apogee*) + *-lune* (fr. L *luna* moon — more at LUNAR)] : the point in the path of a body orbiting the moon that is farthest from the center of the moon

apo·protein \¦apə, ¦apō+\ *n* [*apo-* + *protein*] : a protein that combines with a prosthetic group to form a conjugated protein

ap·o·pto·sis \ˌapəˈtōsəs, ˌapäp-, ˌapō-, ˌapäp-\ *n* [NL, fr. Gk *apoptōsis* a falling off, fr. *apopiptein* to fall off, fr. *apo-* + *piptein* to fall — more at FEATHER] : a genetically directed process of cell self-destruction that is marked by the fragmentation of nuclear DNA, is activated either by the presence of a stimulus or by the removal of a stimulus or suppressing agent, is a normal physiological process eliminating DNA-damaged, superfluous, or unwanted cells, and when halted (as by genetic mutation) may result in uncontrolled cell growth and tumor formation — called also *programmed cell death* — **ap·o·ptot·ic** \-ˈtäd·ik\ *adj*

app \ˈap\ *n* -S [by shortening] : APPLICATION *herein*

appalachian* *n, cap* : a white native or resident of the Appalachian mountain area

appellation* *n* [F] : a geographical name (as of a viticultural region, village, or vineyard) under which a winegrower is authorized to identify and market wine; *also* : the area designated by such a name

apple–pie* *adj* [fr. the tradition that apple pie is a quintessentially American dish] : of, relating to, or characterized by traditionally American values ⟨concerned with the recovery of a lot of *apple-pie* virtues after an era of turmoil and flux —E.B.Fiske⟩

ap·plet \ˈaplət\ *n* -S [*app*lication + *-et*] : a short computer application esp. for performing a simple specific task

application* *n* : a program (as a word processor or a spreadsheet) that performs one of the important tasks for which a computer is used

approach–approach conflict \=¦==¦=-\ *n* : psychological conflict that results when a choice must be made between two desirable alternatives — compare APPROACH-AVOIDANCE CONFLICT *herein*, AVOIDANCE-AVOIDANCE CONFLICT *herein*

approach–avoidance conflict \=¦==¦==-\ *also* **approach–avoidance** *n* : psychological conflict that results when a goal is both desirable and undesirable — compare APPROACH-APPROACH CONFLICT *herein*, AVOIDANCE-AVOIDANCE CONFLICT *herein*

appropriate technology *n* : technology that is suitable to the social and economic conditions of the geographic area in which it is to be applied, is environmentally sound, and promotes self-sufficiency on the part of those using it

APR *abbr* annual percentage rate *herein*

après–ski \¦äˌprā¦skē, ¦a-\ *n, often attrib* [F, fr. *après* (*le*) *ski* after skiing] : social activity (as at a ski lodge) after a day's skiing

aqua·cul·tur·ist *also* **aqui·cul·tur·ist** \¦akwə¦kəlch(ə)rəst, ¦äk-\ *n* : a person who specializes in aquaculture

Aqua–Lung \ˈakwəˌləŋ,ˈäkwəˌləŋ\ *trademark* — used for an underwater breathing apparatus

aqua·naut \ˈakwəˌnȯt, ˈäk-, -ˌnät\ *n* -S [*aqua-* + *-naut* (as in *astronaut*)] : a scuba diver who lives beneath the surface of water for an extended period and carries on activities both inside and outside an underwater shelter

aquaplane* *vi, chiefly Brit* : HYDROPLANE *herein*

aquarian* *n, usu cap* : AQUARIUS *herein*

aquar·i·an \əˈkwa(a)rēən, -wer-, -wär-\ *adj, usu cap* [*aquarian*, n. (herein)] : relating to or characteristic of an Aquarius ⟨that little bit of *Aquarian* perversity —*Annabel*⟩

aquarius* *n, usu cap* : one born under the astrological sign Aquarius

arabesque* *n* : an elaborate or intricate pattern ⟨~*s* of alliteration —C.E.Montague⟩ ⟨richly pierced by an ~ of wormholes —John Chase⟩

arabian oryx *n, usu cap A* : an endangered oryx (*Oryx leucoryx*) orig. occurring from Syria to the southern Arabian Peninsula and now surviving in captivity and in herds reintroduced into the wild

ara·chid·o·nate \ˌarəˈkidᵊnˌāt\ *n* -S [*arachidonic* acid + [1]*-ate*] : a salt or ester of arachidonic acid

arach·no·phobe \əˈraknəˌfōb\ *n* -S [*arachn-* + *-phobe*] : an individual affected with arachnophobia

arach·no·pho·bia \əˌraknəˈfōbēə\ *n* -S [NL, fr. *arachn-* + *phobia*] : pathological fear or loathing of spiders — **arach·no·pho·bic** \-ˈfōbik\ *adj or n*

ar·a·mid \ˈarəməd\ *n* -S [*aromatic polyamide*] : any of a group of lightweight but very strong heat-resistant synthetic aromatic polyamide materials that are fashioned into fibers and used esp. in textiles; *also* : a fiber manufactured from an aramid

arb \ˈärb, ˈȧb\ *n* -S [by shortening] : ARBITRAGER

arbitrage* *n* : the purchase of the stock of a takeover target esp. with a view to selling it profitably to the raider

ar·bo·rio rice *also* **arborio** \ärˈbȯrēō-\ *n* -S *often cap A* [fr. *Arborio*, village in Piedmont region of Italy] : a short-grain rice that has a creamy texture when cooked and is typically used in risotto

ar·bo·vi·rol·o·gy \ˌärbəˌvīˈräləjē\ *n* [*arbovirus* + *-ology* (as in *virology*)] : a branch of virology that deals with the arboviruses — **ar·bo·vi·rol·o·gist** \-jəst\ *n* -S

ar·bo·vi·rus \¦ärbə¦vīrəs\ *n* [*ar*thropod-*bo*rne *virus*] : any of various RNA viruses (as an arenavirus or flavivirus) transmitted principally by arthropods and including the causative agents of encephalitis, yellow fever, and dengue — **ar·bo·vi·ral** \-¦vīrəl\ *adj*

arc* *n* : TRAJECTORY, SPAN

ARC *abbr* AIDS-related complex *herein*

arcade* *n* : an amusement center having coin-operated games

ar·chaea \ärˈkēə\ *n pl* [NL, fr. Gk *archaia*, neut. pl. of *archaios* ancient — more at ARCHAE-] **1** *cap* : a domain of primitive microorganisms comprising the archaebacteria when considered as equal in taxonomic rank to the other prokaryotes and to the eukaryotes **2** : microorganisms belonging to the domain Archaea — **ar·chae·an** \-ˈkēəl\ *adj* — **ar·chae·an** *adj or n*

ar·chae·bac·te·ri·um \ˌärkē+\ *also* **ar·chaeo·bac·te·ri·um** \¦=== *or* =¦== *at* ARCHAE-+\ *n* [NL, fr. *archae-* + *bacterium*] : any of a class (Archaeobacteria), a separate kingdom (Archaeobacteria) or a domain (Archaea) of primitive microorganisms including methane-producing forms, some red halophilic forms, and others of harsh hot acidic environments — **ar·chae·bac·te·ri·al** \"+\ *adj*

ar·chaeo·astronomy *also* **ar·che·o·astronomy** \¦==(ˌ)= *or* =¦== *at* ARCHAE-+\ *n* [*archae-* + *astronomy*] : the study of the astronomy of ancient cultures — **ar·chaeo·astronomer** *also* **ar·che·o·as·tronomer** \"+\ *n*

archipelago* *n* : something resembling an archipelago; *esp* : a group or scattering of similar things ⟨an ~ of small parks within the city⟩

architecture* *n* : the manner in which the components of a computer or computer system are organized and integrated

ar·cho·saur \ˈärkəˌsȯ(ə)r\ *n* -S [NL *Archosauria*] : a member of the reptilian subclass Archosauria

arc minute *n* : MINUTE 2

ar·col·o·gy \ärˈkäləjē\ *n* -ES [*arc*hitectural *ecology*] : a city intended to be contained in a single structure

arc second *n* : [4]SECOND 1

arcuate nucleus *n* : any of several cellular masses in the thalamus, hypothalamus, or medulla oblongata

area code *n* [so called fr. its designation of major subdivisions of the territory of the United States] : a 3-digit code used in dialing long-distance telephone calls

area rug *n* : a rug covering only part of a floor

arena stage *n* : a theater stage surrounded or nearly surrounded by the audience; *specif* : the stage of an arena theater

are·na·vi·rus \ə¦rēnə¦vīrəs, ¦erənə-, ¦ärənə-\ *n* [NL, alter. of *arenovirus*, fr. L *arena* sand + NL *-o-* + *virus*; so called fr. the fine granules seen in cross sections of the virion] : any of a family (Arenaviridae) of single-stranded RNA viruses that have a grainy appearance due to the presence of ribosomes in the virion, that include the causative agents of lymphocytic choriomeningitis and Lassa fever, and that are usu. transmitted to humans by infected wild rodents through contamination of food and personal items or by inhalation of the airborne virus

ar·eo·cen·tric \¦a(a)rēō¦sen·trik, -ēə¦-\ *adj* [*areo-* + *-centric*] : having or relating to the planet Mars as a center

ar15 \ˈāˈär(ˈ)fifˈtēn\ *or* **ar15 rifle** *n* -S *usu cap A&R* [fr. *Ar*malite, the manufacturer] : a .223 caliber gas-operated semiautomatic rifle that is essentially a civilian version of the M16

argon laser *n* : a laser that emits light esp. in the blue and green regions of the visible spectrum, operates by means of a high-voltage current through ionized argon gas, and is used esp. in laser surgery

arguable* *adj* : that can be plausibly or convincingly argued ⟨an explanation is offered that if not self-evident is at least ~ —G.W.Johnson⟩ — **arguably*** *adv*

Ar·gy·rol \ˈärjəˌrȯl, -ˌrōl\ *trademark* — used for a silver-protein compound whose aqueous solution is used as a local antiseptic esp. for mucous membranes

arhythmic \¦ā+\ *also* **arhythmical** \"+\ *adj* [[2]*a-* + *rhythmic* or *rhythmical*] : ARRHYTHMIC ⟨struck by the ~ quality of their reading —Charles Drake⟩

ar·i·an \ˈa(a)rēən, ˈer-, ˈär-\ *n* -S *usu cap* [*Aries* + E *-an*] : ARIES *herein*

aries* *n, usu cap* : one born under the astrological sign Aries

ARM *abbr* adjustable rate mortgage *herein*

arm and a leg *n* : an exorbitant price ⟨have fun without shelling out an *arm and a leg*—Genevieve Stuttaford⟩

armpit* *n* : the least desirable place : PIT *herein* ⟨77th Street Station . . . was the ~ of detective duty —Joseph Wambaugh⟩

arm–twist·ing \ˈ=ˌ==\ *n* : the use of direct personal pressure in order to achieve a desired end ⟨for all the *arm-twisting*, the . . . vote on the measure was unexpectedly tight —*Newsweek*⟩ — **arm–twist** *vb* — **arm–twis·ter** *n*

arm wrestling *n* : INDIAN WRESTLING 2b — **arm–wres·tle** *vb* — **arm–wres·tler** *n*

ar·nold·ian \ärˈnōldēən\ *adj, usu cap* [Matthew *Arnold* †1888 Eng. poet & critic + E *-ian*] : of or relating to Matthew Arnold or his works

aro·ma·tase \əˈrōməˌtās\ *n* -S [*aromatic* + *-ase*] : an enzyme or complex of enzymes that promotes the conversion of an androgen (as testosterone) into estrogens (as estradiol)

aromatherapy \=¦=¦===\ *n* [F *aromathérapie*, fr. L & Gk *arōma* + F *thérapie*] : massage of the body and esp. the face with a preparation of fragrant essential oils extracted from herbs, flowers, and fruits; *broadly* : the use of aroma to enhance a feeling of well-being — **aromatherapist** *n*

around the world *n* : the action of orally stimulating many parts of the body for sexual gratification

array* *vt* : to arrange or display in or as if in an array ⟨the . . . data are ~*ed* in descending order —Ed Burnett⟩

array* *n* **1** : an arrangement of computer memory elements in a single plane **2** : a group of elements forming a complete unit ⟨an ~ of solar cells⟩ **3** : a data structure in which similar elements of data are arranged in a table

array processor *n* : a computer peripheral designed to perform fast numerical calculations on large amounts of data

arrest* *vb* ~ *vi* : to undergo cardiac arrest ⟨the patient ~*ed*⟩

ar·res·tant \ə'restənt\ *n* -S [[1]*arrest* + [1]*-ant*] : a substance that stimulates an insect to stop locomotion

art de·co \ˌär(t)dā'kō; (ˈ)är(t)'dā(ˌ)kō, -de-; -ā(t)-\ *n, often cap A&D* [F *Art Déco*, fr. *Exposition Internationale des Arts Décoratifs et Industriels Modernes*, an exposition of modern decorative and industrial arts held in Paris, France, in 1925] : a popular architectural and decorative style of the 1920s and 1930s characterized esp. by bold outlines and colors, by streamlined and geometric forms, and by the use of man-made materials

ar·thro·gry·po·sis \ˌär,thrōgrə'pōsəs, ˌä,th-\ *n* [NL, fr. *arthr-* + *gryposis*] **1** : congenital fixation of a joint in an extended or flexed position **2** : any of a heterogeneous group of congenital conditions characterized by reduced mobility of multiple joints due to contractures causing fixation of the joints in extension or flexion

ar·throl·o·gy \är'thräləjē\ *n* -ES [*arthr-* + *-logy*] : a science concerned with the study of joints

ar·thro·scope \'ärthrəˌskōp\ *n* [ISV *arthr-* + *-scope*] : a fiber-optic instrument surgically inserted through an incision near a joint (as the knee) and used to visually examine the joint interior

ar·thros·co·py \-'thräskəpē\ *n* -ES [*arthroscope* (herein) + [2]*-y*] : examination of a joint with an arthroscope; *also* : surgery on a joint using an arthroscope — **ar·thro·scop·ic** \ˌ==ˈskäpik\ *adj*

arthrosis* *n* : a degenerative disease of a joint

ar·throt·o·my \är'thräd·əmē\ *n* -ES [ISV *arthr-* + *-tomy*] : incision into a joint

ar·tic \ä'tik\ *n* -S [short for *articulated lorry*] *Brit* : SEMITRAILER 2

artifact* *n* : something characteristic of or resulting from a particular human institution, period, trend, or individual ⟨the vast Hollywood system . . . that produced so many ~*s* that are still resonant for us —Elizabeth Kendall⟩ ⟨self-consciousness . . . turns out to be an ~ of our education system —*Times Lit. Supp.*⟩

artificial intelligence *n* **1** : the capability of a machine to imitate intelligent human behavior (as reasoning, learning, or the understanding of speech) **2** : a branch of computer science dealing with the simulation of intelligent behavior in computers

art·mo·bile \'ärtmōˌbēl, ˈät-\ *n* -S [*art* + *-mobile*] : a trailer that houses an art collection designed for exhibition on road tours

art mo·derne \ˌär(t)mȯ'de(ə)rn\ *n, often cap A&M* [F, lit., *modern art*] : ART DECO *herein*

art–rock \'=,=\ *n* : rock music that incorporates elements of traditional or classical music — **art–rocker** \'=,==\ *n*

artsy \'ärtsē, -i\ *adj* -ER/-EST [[2]*art* + *-sy* (as in *folksy*)] : ARTY

aru·gu·la \ə'rüg(y)ələ\ *n* [prob. from It dial.; akin to It dial. (Lombardy) *arigola* garden rocket, It *ruca* — more at ROCKET] : GARDEN ROCKET 1

ary·te·noi·dec·to·my \ˌarəˌtēˌnȯi'dektəmē, əˌrit[ə]nˌȯi-\ *n* -ES [[2]*arytenoid* + *-ectomy*] : excision of an arytenoid cartilage

ASAP *abbr* as soon as possible

ascending colon *n* : the part of the large intestine that extends from the cecum to the bend on the right side below the liver — compare DESCENDING COLON *herein*, TRANSVERSE COLON *in the Dict*

ASCII \'as(ˌ)kē\ *n* [*A*merican *S*tandard *C*ode for *I*nformation *I*nterchange] : a code for representing alphanumeric information

asexual* *adj* : devoid of sexuality ⟨an ~ relationship⟩

as far as *prep* : with reference to : as for — not often in formal use; used in speech and speechlike prose ⟨*as far as* being mentioned in the Ten Commandments, I think it is —Billy Graham⟩

asian–american \ˈ===ˈ===\ *n, cap both As* : an American of Asian descent — **asian–american** *adj, usu cap both As*

asian elephant *n, usu cap A* : ASIATIC ELEPHANT

asian tiger mosquito *n, usu cap A* : a black-and-white striped Asian mosquito of the genus *Aedes* (*A. albopictus*) that transmits the causative viruses of several diseases (as dengue and Japanese B encephalitis) in Asia and that has been introduced into the U.S.

ASL *abbr* American Sign Language *herein*

as·par·tame \'aspə(r)ˌtām, ə'spär,tām\ *n* -S [*aspart*ic acid + *pheny*lalanine + *me*thyl *e*ster] : a crystalline compound $C_{14}H_{18}N_2O_5$ that is a diamide synthesized from phenylalanine and aspartic acid and that is used as a low-calorie sweetener

as·par·to·kinase \əˌspärd·ō+\ *n* [*aspart*ic acid + *-o-* + *kinase*] : an enzyme that catalyzes the phosphorylation of aspartic acid by ATP

as·per·ger's syndrome \'äspərgərz-\ *n, usu cap A* [after Hans *Asperger* †1980 Austrian pediatrician] : a developmental disorder characterized by impaired social and occupational skills, by normal language and cognitive development, and by restricted, repetitive, and stereotyped patterns of behavior, interests, and activities often with above average performance in a narrow field against a general background of deficient functioning — called also *Asperger's disorder, Asperger syndrome*

asphalt jungle *n* : a big city or a specified part of a big city ⟨the *asphalt jungle* around Times Square —E.R.Bentley⟩

-ass \ˌas, ˌaa(ə)s, ˈais *also* ˈäs\ *adv* [[4]*ass*] — used as a postpositive intensive esp. with words of derogatory implication ⟨fancy-*ass*⟩; often considered vulgar

assaultive* *adj* : having an intense or abrasive effect on the senses or emotions

assault rifle *n* [trans. of G *sturmgewehr*] : any of various automatic or semiautomatic rifles with large capacity magazines designed for military use

assault weapon *n* : any of various automatic or semiautomatic firearms; *esp* : ASSAULT RIFLE *herein*

as·sem·blage* \ə'semblij; ˌaˌsä(ⁿ)m'bläzh\ *n* **1** : an artistic composition made from scraps, junk, and odds and ends (as of paper, cloth, wood, stone, or metal) **2** : the art of making assemblages — **as·sem·blag·ist** \-jəst, -zhə-\ *n* -S

assembler* *n* **1** : a computer program that automatically converts instructions written in assembly language into machine language **2** : ASSEMBLY LANGUAGE

assembly* *n* **1** : the translation of assembly language to machine language by an assembler **2** : ASSEMBLY LANGUAGE *herein*

assembly language *n* : a programming language that consists of instructions which are mnemonic codes for corresponding machine language instructions and that is usu. unique to a particular processor or family of processors

assertiveness training *n* : a method of training individuals to act in a bold self-confident manner

assess* *vt* : to charge (a player or team) with a foul or penalty

asset* *n* : something useful in an effort to foil or defeat an enemy: as **a** : a piece of military equipment **b** : SPY

asshole \'=,=\ *n* [[4]*ass* + *hole*] **1** : ANUS — usu. considered vulgar **2** : a stupid or incompetent person : BLOCKHEAD — usu. considered vulgar **3** : the least attractive or desirable part or area — usu. considered vulgar

assist* *n* : a mechanical or electromechanical device that provides assistance

assisted living *n, often attrib* : a system of housing and limited care that is designed for senior citizens who need some assistance with daily activities but do not require care in a nursing home and that usu. includes private quarters, meals, personal assistance, housekeeping aid, monitoring of medications, and nurses' visits ⟨an *assisted living* facility⟩

assisted suicide *n* : suicide by a patient facilitated by means (as a drug prescription) or by information (as an indication of a lethal dosage) that is provided by a physician aware of the patient's intent — called also *physician-assisted suicide*

ass–kissing \'=,==\ *n* : obsequious flattery or attentiveness — usu. considered vulgar — **ass–kisser** \'=,==\ *n*

associative neuron *or* **association neuron** *n* : an internuncial neuron

AST* *abbr* Alaska standard time

asteroid belt *n* : a region of interplanetary space between the orbits of Mars and Jupiter in which most asteroids are found

as·ti spu·man·te \ˌästē(ˌ)spü'män(ˌ)tā, ˌas-, -sti-, -spə'-, -tē\ *n, usu cap A & often cap S* [It, lit., sparkling Asti] : a sweet sparkling white wine made in and around the village of Asti in Piedmont

astral projection *n* : the occult phenomenon of out-of-body travel

as·tro·biology \ˌas(ˌ)trō+\ *n* [*astr-* + *biology*] : EXOBIOLOGY *herein* — **as·tro·biological** \"+\ *adj* — **as·tro·biologist** \"+\ *n*

as·tro·bleme \'astrəˌblēm\ *n* -S [*astr-* + Gk *blēma* throw, missile, wound from a missile, fr. *ballein* to throw — more at DEVIL] : a scar on the earth's crust made by the impact of a meteorite

as·tro·chemistry \ˌastrō+\ *n* [*astr-* + *chemistry*] : the chemistry of celestial bodies and interstellar space — **as·tro·chemist** \"+\ *n*

as·tro·dynamics \ˌas(ˌ)trō+\ *n pl but sing or pl in constr* [*astr-* + *dynamics*] : celestial mechanics applied to space vehicles — **as·tro·dynamic** \"+\ *adj* — **as·tro·dy·nam·i·cist** \ˌas(ˌ)trōdī'naməsəst *sometimes* -də-\ *n* -S

as·tro·geology \ˌas(ˌ)trō+\ *n* [*astr-* + *geology*] : a branch of geology that deals with celestial bodies — **as·tro·geologic** \ˌastrō+\ *adj* — **as·tro·geologist** \ˌas(ˌ)trō+\ *n or adj*

As·tro·turf \'astrəˌtərf, -ˌtrō-\ *trademark* — used for an artificial grass that resembles carpeting

asynchronous transfer mode *n, often cap A&T&M* : a digital network communications system that allows high-speed broadband transmissions

atavism* *n* : recurrence of or reversion to a past style, manner, outlook, approach, or activity ⟨architectural ~⟩

ATC *abbr* air traffic control

atemporal \(ˈ)ā+ˈ\ *adj* [[2]*a-* + *temporal*] : independent of or unaffected by time : TIMELESS

aten·o·lol \ə'tenəlȯl, -ōlōl, -lȯl, -läl, -tēn-\ *n* -S [perh. fr. *a*ntihyper*ten*sive (herein) + *-olol* (as in *propranolol* — herein)] : a beta-blocker $C_{14}H_{22}N_2O_3$ used in the treatment of hypertension

atheoretical \ˌā+\ *adj* [[2]*a-* + *theoretical*] : not based on or concerned with theory

ath·ero·genesis \ˌathərō+\ *n* [*athero-* + *genesis*] : the formation of atheroma

ath·ero·gen·ic \ˌathərō'jenik\ *adj* [*athero-* + *-genic*] : relating to or causing atherogenesis ⟨an ~ diet⟩ — **ath·ero·ge·nic·i·ty** \-jə'nisəd·ē, -ətē\ *n* -ES

-a·thon \əˌthän\ *n comb form* -S [*marathon*] **1** : event or activity lasting a long time often for the purpose of raising funds ⟨jog*athon*⟩ **2** : an excess of something ⟨practical joke-*athon*⟩

athymic \(ˈ)ā+ˈ\ *adj* [[2]*a-* + [2]*thymic*] : lacking a thymus ⟨congenitally ~ mice⟩

at·lan·ti·cism \ət'lantəˌsizəm\ *n* -S *usu cap* [*Atlantic* + *-ism*] : a policy of military, political, and economic cooperation between European and North American powers — **at·lan·ti·cist** \-ntəsəst\ *n or adj, usu cap*

ATM \ˌā(ˌ)tē'em\ *abbr or n* -S : automated teller machine *herein*

at·mo·sphe·ri·um \ˌatmə'sfirēəm\ *n* -S [blend of *atmosphere* and *planetarium*] **1** : an optical device for projecting images of meteorological phenomena (as clouds) on the inside of a dome **2** : a room housing an atmospherium

atoxic \(ˈ)ā+ˈ\ *adj* [[2]*a-* + *toxic*] : not toxic ⟨~ antibiotics⟩

ATPase \ˌā,tē'pēˌās, -ˌāz\ *n* -S [*ATP* + *-ase*] : ADENOSINE TRIPHOSPHATASE

at·ra·zine \'a·trəˌzēn\ *n* -S [ISV, perh. fr. *amin-* + *triazine*] : a photosynthesis-inhibiting persistent herbicide $C_8H_{14}ClN_5$ used esp. to kill annual weeds and quack grass

atrial fibrillation *n* : AURICULAR FIBRILLATION

atrial natriuretic peptide *or* **atrial natriuretic factor** *n* : a peptide hormone secreted by myocytes of the cardiac atria that in pharmacological doses promotes salt and water excretion and lowers blood pressure

at·ro·pin·iza·tion \ˌa·trəpənə'zāshan, -ˌpēn-, -ˌī'z-\ *n* -S [*atropine* + *-ization*] : the physiological condition of being under the influence of atropine

attackman \ə'=(ˌ)=\ *n, pl* **attackmen** : a player (as in lacrosse) assigned to an offensive zone or position

attention deficit disorder *n* : a syndrome of disordered learning and disruptive behavior that is not caused by any serious underlying physical or mental disorder and that has several subtypes characterized primarily by symptoms of inattentiveness or primarily by symptoms of hyperactivity and impulsive behavior (as in speaking out of turn) or by the significant expression of all three — abbr. *ADD;* called also *minimal brain dysfunction*

attention deficit/hyperactivity disorder *n* : ATTENTION DEFICIT DISORDER *herein* — abbr. *ADHD*

attitude* *n* : a negative, hostile, or aggressive frame of mind

at·to- \ˌad·(ˌ)ō, ˌatə\ *comb form* [ISV, fr. Dan or Norw *atten* eighteen (fr. ON *āttjān*) + *-o-* — more at EIGHTEEN] : one quintillionth (10^{-18}) part of ⟨*atto*gram⟩

at·trit \ə'trit, a·'-\ *or* **at·trite** \-'trīt\ *vt* -ED/-ING/-S [back-formation fr. *attrition*] : to weaken or reduce by attrition

attrition* *n* : a usu. gradual loss of personnel from causes normal or peculiar to a given situation (as death, retirement, and resignation in a labor force or failure and dropout among students) often without filling the vacancies

ATV \ˌā,tē'vē\ *n* -S : ALL-TERRAIN VEHICLE *herein*

au bleu \(ˌ)ō'blœ̄, -'blā, -'blü\ *adj (or adv)* [F, lit., to the blue; fr. the fact that the skin of fish cooked in this manner turns blue] : cooked by boiling in acidulated water immediately after being killed and cleaned but without being washed or scaled — used esp. of trout

au·di·al \'ȯdēəl\ *adj* [*audio* + [1]*-al*] : of, relating to, or affecting the sense of hearing : AURAL — **au·di·al·ly** \-əlē, -li\ *adv*

au·di·bi·lize \'ȯdəbəˌlīz\ *vi* -ED/-ING/-S [*audible*, n. (herein) + *-ize*] : AUDIBLE *herein*

[1]**audible** *n* -S [*audible*, adj.] : a substitute offensive play or defensive formation called at the line of scrimmage in football

[2]**audible** *vi* -ED/-ING/-S : to call an audible ⟨*audibled* to a long pass play that fell incomplete —David Boyce⟩

audio–an·i·ma·tron·ic \ˌȯdē(ˌ)ōˌanəmə'tränək\ *adj* [fr. *Audio-Animatronics*, a trademark] : being or consisting of a lifelike electromechanical figure of a person or animal that has synchronized movement and sound

au·dio·cassette \"+\ *n* [*audio-* + *cassette* (herein)] : an audio recording mounted in a cassette

au·dio–lingual \"+\ *adj* [*audio-* + *lingual*] : involving the use of listening and speaking drills in language learning

au·dio·tape \'ȯdēōˌtāp\ *n* [*audio-* + *tape*] : a tape recording of sound

au·dio·visuals \ˌȯdēō+\ *n pl* [*audiovisual*] : instructional materials (as filmstrips accompanied by recordings) that make use of both hearing and sight

audit trail *n* : a record of a sequence of events (as actions performed by a computer) from which a history of those events may be reconstructed

auger electron spectroscopy *n, usu cap A* : an instrumental method for determining the chemical composition of a material's surface by means of analysis of the energies of Auger electrons emitted from the surface — called also *Auger spectroscopy*

augmented matrix *n* : a matrix whose elements are the coefficients of a set of simultaneous linear equations with the constant terms of the equations entered in an added column

au gra·tin \ō'grät[ə]n, ȯ'-, -rat-\ *n, pl* **au gratins** : a container in which au gratin dishes may be cooked and served

auntie* *n* : a usu. middle-aged male homosexual who seeks the companionship of younger men

aunt sally* *n, usu cap A&S, Brit* : an object of criticism or contention; *esp* : a person, condition, or argument set up to invite criticism or be easily refuted

au pair *n, pl* **au pairs** [*au pair*, adj.] : a usu. young foreign person who cares for children and does domestic work for a family in return for room and board and the opportunity to experience another culture

aus·form \'ȯsˌfȯ(ə)rm, -ō(ə)m\ *vt* -ED/-ING/-S [*aus*tenitic + de*form*; fr. the deformation's taking place while the steel is still in the austenitic form] : to subject (steel) to deformation and then to quenching and tempering in order to increase the strength, ductility, and resistance to fatigue failure

aus·tral \ȯ'sträl\ *n, pl* **aus·tral·es** \-'sträləs\ *also* **aus·trals** [Sp, fr. *austral*, adj., southern, fr. L *australis* — more at AUSTRAL] : the basic monetary unit of Argentina 1985–91

australia antigen *also* **australian antigen** *n, usu cap 1st A* : HEPATITIS B SURFACE ANTIGEN *herein*

aus·tra·li·ana \ȯˌstrālē'anə, äˌ-, əˌ-, -'anə\ *n pl, usu cap* [*Australia* + E *-ana*] : collected material (as books) relating to Australia

australian shepherd *n, usu cap A* : any of a breed of agile intelligent short-tailed working dogs developed in the U.S. for herding livestock

au·teur \ō'tər, -tœər\ *n* -S [F, originator, author, fr. OF *autor* — more at AUTHOR] **1** : a film director whose practice accords with the auteur theory **2** : an artist whose style and practice are distinctive

au·teur·ism \-ˌizəm\ *n* -S [*auteur* (herein) + *-ism*] : AUTEUR THEORY *herein* — **au·teur·ist** \-əst\ *n or adj*

auteur theory *n* : a view of film making in which the director is considered the primary creative force in a motion picture

authentic* *adj* : true to one's own personality, spirit, or character ⟨an ~ and unselfconscious middle-class primitive —Philip Roth⟩

autism* *n* : a developmental disorder that appears by age three and is characterized by impairment of the ability to form normal social relationships, by impairment of the ability to communicate with others, and by stereotyped behavior patterns — **autistic*** *adj*

au·tis·tic \ȯ'tisˌtik, -ˌtək, ˌä-\ *n* -S [*autistic*, adj.] : a person affected with autism

au·to·ci·dal \ˈ==ˈsīd[ə]l\ *adj* [*aut-* + *-cide* + [1]*-al*] : controlling or eradicating populations of noxious insects (as the screwworm) by reducing their capacity to produce viable or fertile offspring (as by the introduction of sterile males) ⟨~ procedures⟩ ⟨~ effects⟩

au·to·cide \'==ˌsīd\ *n* -S [[2]*auto-* + *-cide*] : suicide by crashing one's automobile

au·to·clav·able \ˈ==ˈklāvəbəl\ *adj* [[2]*autoclave* + *-able*] : able to withstand the action of an autoclave

au·to·correlation \ˈ==+\ *n* [*aut-* + *correlation*] : the correlation between the two members of pairs of values of a function of a mathematical or statistical variable taken at usually constant intervals that indicates the degree of periodicity of the function

au·to·crine \'ȯd·ōkrin\ *adj* [*aut-* + *-crine* (as in *endocrine*)] : of, relating to, promoted by, or being a substance secreted by a cell and acting on surface receptors of the same cell ⟨~ stimulation of T-cell growth⟩ ⟨~ growth of some breast cancers —M.E.Lippman⟩ — compare PARACRINE *herein*

au·to·cross \'==+ˌ\ *n* -ES [[2]*auto* + *motocross*] : an automobile gymkhana

au·to·di·al \'==ˌ=(=)\ *n, often attrib* [*aut-* + [1]*dial*] : a system or feature of a system by which a device (as a telephone or computer) automatically dials a preprogrammed telephone number — **autodial** *vt* — **au·to·di·al·er** \'==ˌ=(=)=\ *n* -S

au·to·ex·po·sure \ˈ===ˈ=\ *n, often attrib* [*aut-* + *exposure*] : a system by which a camera automatically adjusts exposure (as by changing the aperture or shutter speed) according to ambient lighting conditions

au·to·focus \'==+ˌ\ *n* [*aut-* + *focus*] : a system by which a camera automatically focuses on an object in its field of view

autogenic* *adj* : of or relating to any of several relaxation techniques that actively involve the patient (as by self-hypnosis, meditation, or biofeedback) in attempts to control physiological variables (as body temperature or blood pressure) ⟨~ training⟩

autogenous* *also* **autogenic*** *adj* : not requiring a meal of blood to produce eggs ⟨~ mosquitoes⟩ — **autogeny*** *n*

au·to·ges·tion \ˈ==ˈjes(h)chən\ *n* -S [F *autogestion*, fr. *auto-* aut- + *gestion* administration, fr. L *gestion-, gestio* performance — more at GESTION] *chiefly Brit* : control and management of an enterprise (as a factory) by representatives of the workers

au·to·immune \ˈ==+\ *adj* [back-formation fr. *autoimmunization*] : of, relating to, or caused by antibodies or T cells that attack molecules, cells, or tissues of the organism producing them ⟨~ diseases⟩ — **au·to·immunity** \"+\ *n* — **au·to·immunize** \"+\ *vt*

au·to·ionization \ˈ==+\ *n* [*aut-* + *ionization*] : a process by which an excited atom becomes ionized and goes to a lower energy state by emitting one of two or more excited electrons that together possess energy exceeding the atom's ionization energy; *esp* : such a process yielding an electron having an energy equivalent to that of a photon of optical wavelength — compare AUGER EFFECT *in the Dict* — **au·to·ionize** \"+\ *vb*

au·to·ma·nia \ˈ==ˈmānyə, -əˈmā-, -nēə\ *n* [[2]*auto-* + *mania*] : undue dependence on or concern with having an automobile esp. for recreation

au·to·manipulation \ˈ==+\ *n* [*aut-* + *manipulation*] : physical stimulation of the genital organs by oneself — **au·to·manipulative** \"+\ *adj*

automated teller machine *also* **automatic teller machine** *or* **automated teller** *or* **automatic teller** *n* : a computerized electronic machine that performs basic banking functions (as handling check deposits or issuing cash withdrawals)

automatic* *n* : AUDIBLE *herein*

automatic pilot* *n* : a state or condition in which activity or behavior is regulated automatically in a predetermined or instinctive manner ⟨burnt-out cases operating on *automatic pilot* —Winifred Gallagher⟩

au·toph·a·gy \ȯ'täfəjē\ *n* -ES [*aut-* + *-phagy*] : digestion of cellular constituents by enzymes of the same cell — **au·toph·a·gic** \-jik\ *adj*

autopilot* *n* : AUTOMATIC PILOT *herein*

au·to·regulation \ˈȯd·(ˌ)ō, ˈȯ(ˌ)tō, -ə+\ *n* [*aut-* + *regulation*] : the maintenance of relative constancy of a physiological process by an organ or tissue under varying conditions; *esp* : the maintenance of a constant supply of blood to an organ in spite of varying arterial pressure ⟨the influence of vasoactive agents on ~ of renal flow —P.C.Johnson *et al*⟩ — **au·to·regulate** \ˈ==+\ *vb* — **au·to·regulative** \ˈ==+\ *adj* — **au·to·regulatory** \ˈ==+\ *adj*

auto–reverse \'==ˌ=\ *n* [*aut-* + [3]*reverse*] : a feature of an audiocassette player by which the direction of play of the tape is automatically reversed at the end of one side in order to play the other side

au·to·route \'ȯd·əˌrüt, -d·ō-, 'äd-; *F* ōtōrüt, ō-\ *n* [F, fr. *auto* automobile (fr. *automobile*) + *route* road, fr. OF — more at ROUTE] : a high-speed multilane motor road

au·to·stra·da \ˌaùd·ō'strädə, ˌȯd-\ *n, pl* **autostradas** *or* **autostrade** \-äd(ˌ)ā\ [It, fr. *auto*mobile automobile (fr. F) + *strada* street, fr. LL *strata* paved road — more at STREET] : a high-speed multilane motor road first developed in Italy

au·to·transfusion \ˈȯd·ō+, ˈȯtō-, -ə+\ *n* [*aut-* + *transfusion*] : return of blood lost by or taken from a patient to his or her own circulatory system

autoworker \'==ˌ=\ *n* [[2]*auto* + *worker*] : a person employed in the automobile manufacturing industry

auxo·troph \'ȯksəˌtrōf, -äf\ *n* -S [*auxo-* + *-troph* (as in *autotroph*)] : an auxotrophic strain or individual

auxo·tro·phic \ˌȯksə'trōfik, -äf-\ *adj* [*auxo-* + *-trophic*] : requiring a specific growth substance beyond the minimum required for normal metabolism and reproduction of the parental or wild-type strain ⟨~ mutants of bacteria⟩ — **aux·ot·ro·phy** \ȯk'sätrəfē\ *n* -ES

avalanche diode *n* : a silicon semiconductor device in which the voltage drop remains constant and independent of current beyond a certain applied voltage and which is used in surge protectors

avale·ment \àvål(ə)mäⁿ\ *n* -S [F, lit., swallowing, fr. *avaler* to lower, swallow, fr. MF — more at AVALE] : the technique of allowing the knees to flex and thus absorb bumps when skiing and turning at high speed so that the skis will remain in constant contact with the snow

avant \¦ä¦vänt, ¦a-\ *adj* [F *avant-* fore-, front, fr. *avant* before, fr. L *abante* forward — more at AVAUNT] : culturally or stylistically advanced ⟨~ jazz⟩

avascular necrosis *n* : necrosis of bone tissue due to impaired or disrupted blood supply (as that caused by traumatic injury or disease) and marked by severe pain in the affected region and by weakened bone that may flatten and collapse

avatar* *n* : an electronic image that represents and is manipulated by a computer user in a virtual space (as in a computer game or an on-line shopping site) and that interacts with other objects in the space

aversion* *n* : a tendency to extinguish a behavior or to avoid a thing or situation and esp. a usu. pleasurable one because it is or has been associated with a noxious stimulus ⟨conditioning of food ~*s* by drug injection⟩

aversion therapy *n* : therapy intended to suppress an undesirable habit or behavior (as smoking or overeating) by associating the habit or behavior with a noxious or punishing stimulus (as electric shock)

aversive* *adj* : tending to avoid or causing avoidance of a noxious or punishing stimulus ⟨behavior modification by ~ stimulation⟩ ⟨~ conditioning⟩ — **aver·sive·ly** \-lē\ *adv* — **aver·sive·ness** *n*

av·go·lem·o·no \ˌävgōˈlemə(ˌ)nō\ *n* -s [NGk *augolemono*, fr. *augo* egg (fr. Gk *ōion*) + *-lemono*, fr. *lemoni* lemon — more at EGG, LEMON] : a soup or sauce made of chicken stock, egg yolks, and lemon juice

aviator glasses *n pl* [fr. their resemblance to the aviator sunglasses formerly issued to U.S. military pilots] : eyeglasses having a lightweight metal frame and relatively large usu. tinted lenses

avogadro's number *var of* AVOGADRO NUMBER

avoidance* *n* : an anticipatory response undertaken to avoid a noxious stimulus ⟨conditioned ~ in mice⟩

avoidance–avoidance conflict \¦=¦==¦==-\ *n* : psychological conflict that results when a choice must be made between two undesirable alternatives — compare APPROACH-APPROACH CONFLICT *herein*, APPROACH-AVOIDANCE CONFLICT *herein*

avoid·ant \əˈvȯidᵊnt\ *adj* [*avoid* + [2]*-ant*] : characterized by turning away or by withdrawal or defensive behavior ⟨the ~ detached schizophrenic patient —Norman Cameron⟩

AWACS \ˈāˌwaks\ *n, pl* **AWACS** [*a*irborne *w*arning *a*nd *c*ontrol *s*ystem] : a long-range military surveillance system for use in an airplane

aw–shucks \¦ȯ¦shəks\ *adj* : being or marked by an unsophisticated, self-conscious, or self-effacing manner

ax* *or* **axe*** *n* : any of several musical instruments (as a guitar or a saxophone)

ax·ion \ˈaksē(ˌ)än\ *n* -s [*axial* + [2]*-on*] : a hypothetical subatomic particle of low mass and energy that in certain versions of quantum chromodynamics is postulated to exist because there are no violations of charge conjugation and parity in strong nuclear interactions

aya·tol·lah \ˌīəˈtōlə, -tälə, -təlä, ˈ==ˌ==; ˌīə·təˈlä\ *n* -s [Per, lit., sign of God, fr. Ar *āya* sign, miracle + *allāh* God] **1** : a religious leader among Shiite Muslims — used as a title of respect esp. for one who is not an imam **2** : a powerful self-righteous leader or administrator

aza·thi·o·prine \ˌazəˈthīəˌprēn, -ˌprən\ *n* -s [*aza-* + *thi-* + *purine*] : a purine antimetabolite $C_9H_7N_7O_2S$ that is used esp. as an immunosuppressant

azeri \əˈzerē, ˈäzərē\ *n* -s *usu cap* [Turk *Azeri* or Azerbaijani *azäri* fr. Pers *āzarī*, fr. Ar *ādharī*, fr. *Ādhar-*, short for *Ādharbayjān* Azerbaijan] : AZERBAIJANI

az·i·do·thy·mi·dine \əˌzīdōˈthīmədən, -dēn\ *n* -s [*azido-* + *thymidine*] : AZT *herein*

azin·phos·meth·yl \ˌāzᵊn(ˌ)fäsˈmethəl, ˌaz-\ *n* [*azine* + *phos*phorus + *methyl*] : an organophosphorus pesticide $C_{10}H_{12}N_3O_3PS_2$ used against insects and mites

AZT \ˌā(ˌ)zēˈtē\ *n* -s [*az*ido*t*hymidine (herein)] : an antiviral drug $C_{10}H_{13}N_5O_4$ that inhibits replication of some retroviruses (as HIV) and is used to treat AIDS — called also *azidothymidine, ZDV, zidovudine*

azu·le·jo \ˌäsüˈlā(ˌ)hō, -zü-, -thü-\ *n* -s [Pg or Sp] : a glazed ceramic tile orig. of Portugal and Spain that is usu. decorated in rich colors and esp. blue

azy·gog·ra·phy \¦ā(ˌ)zī¦gägrəfē, əˌzīˈgäg-\ *n* -ES [ISV *azygo-* + *-graphy*] : roentgenographic visualization of the azygous system of veins after injection of a radiopaque medium

ba·ba gha·noush \ˌbäbəgəˈnüsh\ *or* **ba·ba gha·nouj** \-gəˈnüzh\ *n* [Ar dial. *bābaghanūj*] : an appetizer or spread made chiefly of eggplant, tahini, garlic, olive oil, and lemon

bab·ka \ˈbäbkə, ˈbab-\ *n* -s [Pol, dim. of *baba* baba] : a glazed sweet bread made with dried fruit (as raisins)

baby boom *n, often attrib* : a marked rise in birthrate (as in the U.S. immediately following the end of World War II)

baby boomer *n* : a person born during a baby boom

baby bust *n* [fr. *baby boom* (herein), after *boom* : *bust*] : a marked decline in birthrate (as in the U.S. in the 1960s and 1970s)

baby buster *n* : a person born during a baby bust

baby–doll \ˈ==ˌ=\ *n, often attrib* : a short dress or pajamas that are loose-fitting and often adorned with lace or ribbon

baby–sit* *vi* : to stay with and care for any offspring ⟨the male *baby-sits*, uncovering the eggs if the mound gets too hot —*Nat'l Geographic World*⟩ ~ *vt* : to stay with and look after the welfare of : MIND, TEND ⟨*baby-sit* the house plants⟩

bach·e·lor·ette \ˌbach(ə)ləˈret\ *n* -s [*bachelor* + *-ette*] : a young unmarried woman

back* *vt* : to provide a musical accompaniment for — often used with *up* ⟨a song is categorized as "country" if it is ~*ed* up with a steel guitar —Robert Windeler⟩ — **back into** : to get into inadvertently

back–and–forth* *n* : DISCUSSION, GIVE-AND-TAKE; *also* : EXCHANGE 1

backbeat \ˈ=ˌ=\ *n* [*back*ground + *beat*] : a steady pronounced rhythm stressing the second and fourth beats in a four-beat measure

back burner *n* [fr. the custom of allowing food to simmer on the back burner] : the condition of being out of active consideration or development ⟨directed the board to put on a *back burner* follow-up studies —Dan Berger⟩ ⟨*back burner* projects⟩

back channel *n* : a secret, unofficial, or irregular means of communication — **back–channel** \¦=¦=\ *adj*

back–comb \ˈ=ˌ=\ *vt* : [3]RUFF 3; *broadly* : to comb (hair) in a direction opposite to the one in which it lies naturally

backcourt* *n* : the basketball players who play the backcourt

back forty *n* [[3]*back* + *forty* (*acres*)] : a remote and uncultivated or undeveloped piece of land of indefinite size (as on a farm)

background* *n* : a level of computer processing at which the processor uses time not required for a primary task to work on a less important task — compare FOREGROUND *herein*

back·ground·er \ˈbakˌgraündə(r)\ *n* : an informal statement in which a spokesperson (as for a government or a corporation) provides background information on a particular matter

background radiation *n* : the microwave radiation pervading the universe that exhibits a corresponding blackbody temperature of 2.7K and that is the principal evidence supporting the big bang theory — called also *cosmic background radiation, cosmic microwave background, microwave background*

backhander* *n* **1** *Brit* : BRIBE **2** : a shot made in ice hockey with a back-handed stroke

back judge *n* : a football official whose duties include keeping the official time and identifying eligible pass receivers

backlash* *n* : a strong adverse reaction (as to a recent political or social development) ⟨big success also means big ~ —Jeffrey Schmalz⟩

backmarker \¦=¦==\ *n* [[1]*back* + *marker*] : ALSO-RAN

back of beyond : an extremely remote place; *esp* : the outback of Australia

back–office \¦=¦==\ *adj* [*back office*] : of or relating to the inner workings of a business or institution : INTERNAL 1a ⟨*back-office* operations⟩

back·pack·er \ˈ=ˌ=ə(r)\ *n* -s : one who backpacks

back·plane \ˈ=ˌ=\ *n* [[1]*back* + [4]*plane*] : a support surface in a computer with the electrical connections necessary to join the internal components of the computer

back–room \ˈ=ˌ=\ *adj* [*back room*] : made or operating in an inconspicuous way : BEHIND-THE-SCENES ⟨*back-room* deals⟩ ⟨*back=room* operations⟩

back–street \¦=(ˌ)=\ *adj* [*back street*] : SURREPTITIOUS ⟨*back-street* abortions⟩

back up* *vt* : to make a backup of (a computer file or data) to protect against accidental loss; *also* : to make backups of all the files on (a hard disk)

backup* *n* **1** : one that serves as a substitute or alternative ⟨the second spacecraft would be a ~ in case of failure⟩ **2** : ACCOMPANIMENT 1 ⟨the tunes included banjo and guitar ~⟩ **3** : a copy of computer data (as a file, a program, or all the files of a hard disk); *also* : the act or an instance of making a backup

backup \¦=¦=\ *adj* **1** : serving as a backup ⟨a ~ guidance system⟩ **2** : serving as an accompaniment ⟨he records as a soloist with ~ musicians —Ellen Sander⟩

backward compatible *adj* : compatible with older equipment or previous versions of software — **backward compatibility** *n*

backwrap \ˈ=ˌ=\ *n* [[1]*back* + [3]*wrap*] : a wraparound garment (as a skirt) designed so that the ends of the garment are at the back

bac·lo·fen \ˈbakləˌfen, ˌ==ˈ=\ *n* -s [origin unknown] : a gamma=aminobutyric acid analogue $C_{10}H_{12}ClNO_2$ used as a relaxant of skeletal muscle esp. in treating spasticity (as in multiple sclerosis)

bacteria* *n, pl* **bacteria** *or* **bacterias** : BACTERIUM 2 — not usu. used technically ⟨caused by a ~ borne by certain tiny ticks —*Wall Street Jour.*⟩ ⟨etching circuit parts the width of a single ~ —David Thurber⟩ ⟨several area reservoirs harbored high levels of fecal ~*s*—*Denver Post*⟩

bacterial vag·i·no·sis \-ˌvajəˈnōsəs\ *n, pl* **bacterial vagino·ses** \-ōˌsēz\ [*vaginosis* fr. NL, fr. *vagina* + *-osis*] : vaginitis that is marked by a grayish vaginal discharge usu. of foul odor and that is associated with the presence of a bacterium (esp. *Gardnerella vaginalis* syn. *Haemophilus vaginalis*)

bac·te·rio·cin \bakˈtirēəsən\ *n* -s [ISV *bacteri-* + *-cin* (as in *colicin*); orig. formed as F *bactériocine*] : an antibacterial agent (as colicin) produced by bacteria

bac·te·rio·rhodopsin \=¦===+\ *n* [*bacteri-* + *rhodopsin*] : a purple=pigmented protein that is found in the outer membrane of a bacterium of the genus *Halobacterium* (*H. halobium*) and converts light energy into chemical energy in the synthesis of ATP

bac·u·lo·vi·rus \¦bakyülō¦vīrəs\ *n* [NL, fr. L *baculum* staff, stick + NL *-o-* + *virus* — more at BACTERIUM] : any of a family (Baculoviridae) of DNA viruses that consist of one or more enveloped nucleocapsids, that infect arthropods and esp. insects, and that have been used as biological control agents for insect pests and experimentally in recombinant DNA technology as vectors for the expression of eukaryotic genes

bad* *adj* **badder**; **baddest** *slang* **1** : GOOD, GREAT ⟨one of the *baddest* songwriters to be found anywhere —*Black Collegian*⟩ **2** : TOUGH 8

[1]**badass** \¦=¦=\ *adj* [[2]*bad* + *-ass* (herein)] : ready and willing to cause or get into trouble : MEAN, TOUGH ⟨down on the ground in a great big ring lived a ~ lion who knew he was king —*The Signifying Monkey*⟩ ⟨pretending to be a ~ gunslinger —L.L.King⟩ — often considered vulgar; sometimes used as a term of approval

[2]**badass** *n* : a person who is badass — often considered vulgar

bad–mouth \ˈ=ˌmaůth, -th\ *vt* [E dial. *bad mouth*, n., curse, spell, trans. of a West African phrase like Vai *dàn*ʸ*àmà* curse, lit., bad mouth] : to criticize severely : make disparaging remarks about — **bad–mouth·er** \-ə(r)\ *n*

bad news *n pl but sing in constr* : a troublesome situation or person ⟨he's *bad news*; stay away from him⟩

bafflegab \ˈ==ˌ=\ *n* [[2]*baffle* + [3]*gab*] : GOBBLEDYGOOK

bag* *n* **1** : frame or state of mind ⟨when a person acts stupidly, he is "in his stupid ~" —Junius Griffin⟩ **2** : something suited to one's taste : something one likes or does well : SPECIALTY ⟨hasn't been my ~ so far, but I'm a very dedicated actor —Dick Van Dyke⟩ **3 a** : an individual's typical way of life ⟨can't expect people who are in another ~ to accept my ~ —Jerry Rubin⟩ **b** : a characteristic manner of expression ⟨more than any other singer in the soul ~ —Albert Goldman⟩ **4** : something that frustrates or impedes : HANG-UP **5** : a small packet of a narcotic drug (as heroin or marijuana) **6 bags** *pl, Brit* : a large amount or number : LOT ⟨fancied a job with ~*s* of variety —*Punch*⟩

bag* *vt* **1** : to achieve or complete successfully : WIN ⟨*bagged* a 30-foot putt⟩; *also* : to climb (a mountain peak) successfully **2** : to give up, forgo, or abandon esp. for something more desirable or attainable ⟨~ college for a good job —Shannon Dortch⟩

bag·gies \ˈbagēz\ *n pl* : baggy pants or shorts

Bag·gies \ˈbagēz\ *trademark* — used for transparent plastic bags that are used chiefly for food storage

bag lady *n* : a homeless woman who roams the streets of a large city carrying her possessions in a shopping bag

baguette* *n* : a long thin loaf of French bread; *also* : a long thin roll

bagwash \ˈ=ˌ=\ *n* [[1]*bag* + [2]*wash*] *Brit* : LAUNDRY 1b; *esp* : WET WASH

ba·ha·sa in·do·ne·sia \bəˌhäsəˌindəˈnēzhə, -ēshə, -ēzēə, -ēsēə\ *n, cap B&I* [Indonesian *bahasa Indonesia* fr. *bahasa* language (fr. Malay, fr. Skt *bhāṣā*, fr. *bhāṣate* he speaks; akin to Gk *phanai* to say) + *Indonesia* Indonesian, Indonesia — more at BAN] : INDONESIAN 3b

bailout* *n* : a rescue (as of a corporation) from financial distress ⟨massive Government ~*s* of big business —*Time*⟩

bail out *vi* [[6]*bail* + *out*] **1** : to back away from a pitch in baseball **2** : to jump off a surfboard or skis in order to avoid an accident **3** : to get out : LEAVE, DEPART ⟨some guests *bailed out* early —Laura Stevenson⟩

bait and switch *n* : a sales tactic in which a customer is attracted by the advertisement of a low-priced item but is then encouraged to buy a higher-priced one; *broadly* : a technique for falsely leading a person to expect a certain outcome or experience

ba·jan \ˈbājən\ *n* -s *cap* [by shortening & alter. fr. *Barbadian*] : a native or inhabitant of Barbados — **ba·jan** \"\ *adj, usu cap*

ba·ker–nunn camera \ˌbākə(r)ˈnən-\ *n, usu cap B&N* [after James G. Baker *b*1914 Am. optical designer and Joseph Nunn Am. engineer] : a large camera for tracking earth satellites

bake sale *n* : a fund-raising event at which homemade foods (as cakes and cookies) are offered for sale

balancing act *n* : an attempt to cope with several often conflicting factors or situations at the same time ⟨social life . . . becomes a *balancing act* between the realms of politics, economics and religion —Mark Lilla⟩

balinese* *n, usu cap* : a domestic cat of a breed that originated as a spontaneous mutation of the Siamese and is identical to it in type and in coat color and eye color but has a long silky coat and plumelike tail

ball* *n* **balls** *pl* : NERVE 3b, c — often considered vulgar ⟨don't have enough ~*s* to try out their new material in front of a real audience —*East Village Other*⟩

ball* *vb* [[1]*ball* (testis)] *vt* : to have sexual intercourse with — usu. considered vulgar ~ *vi* : to have sexual intercourse — usu. considered vulgar

ball–and–stick model *n* : a graphic or physical representation of a molecule in which the atoms are balls joined usu. by pegs representing bonds — compare SPACE-FILLING MODEL *herein*

ball control *n* : an offensive strategy (as in football or basketball) in which a team tries to maintain possession of the ball for extended periods of time

ball game* *n* **1** : a set of circumstances to be dealt with : SITUATION ⟨once that blaze surged across the river, it would be a whole new *ball game*—Jeffrey J. Smith⟩ **2** : CONTEST, COMPETITION ⟨pit crews . . . inform their driver if he is in the *ball game*—Sylvia Wilkinson⟩

ball girl *n* **1** : a female tennis court attendant who retrieves balls for the players **2** : a female attendant who retrieves foul balls during a baseball game

ballistic* *adj* **1** : being or characterized by a repeated bouncing movement ⟨~ stretching⟩ **2** : extremely and usu. suddenly excited, upset, or angry : WILD ⟨went ~⟩

ball of wax : a vaguely specified set of related objects or circumstances ⟨will you go to the file safe, please, get the whole *ball of wax*, and lay it out here —*New Yorker*⟩ ⟨knows who's having troubles, who's sleeping with who, the whole *ball of wax*—Grover Lewis⟩

balloon angioplasty *n* : dilatation of an artery stenosed by atherosclerotic plaque by the passage of a balloon catheter through the vessel to the area of disease where inflation of the catheter compresses the plaque against the vessel wall

balloon catheter *also* **balloon–tipped catheter** *n* : a catheter that has two lumens and an inflatable tip which can be expanded by the passage of gas, water, or a radiopaque medium through one of the lumens and that is used esp. to measure blood pressure in a blood vessel or to expand a partly closed or obstructed bodily passage or tube (as a coronary artery)

bal·lot·tine \ˈbalōˌtēn, ˌ==ˈ=, -lō-, -lə-\ *n* -s [F, dim. of *ballotte* rolled, stuffed meat, dim. of *balle* bundle, fr. OF *bale* — more at BALE] : boned meat, poultry, or fish that is stuffed with seasoned meats or vegetables, rolled and tied into a bundle shape, and usu. braised

ballpark** *n* : a range (as of prices, views, or capabilities) within which comparison, compromise, or competition is possible ⟨the views of the two sides are being brought closer . . . . We are in the same general ~ —H.A.Kissinger⟩ ⟨price of $3500 puts it in the same ~ —*Datamation*⟩ — **in the ballpark** : approximately correct

ballpark \¦=¦=\ *adj* : approximately correct ⟨a 20 percent increase would be a good ~ figure —H.L.MacOdrum⟩

balls out *adv* [*balls*, pl. of [1]*ball* (testis)] : at the maximum attainable speed or capacity : all out ⟨running *balls out* to be as far up front as possible —Patricia N. Warren⟩ ⟨detachments in Gonaïves . . . are operating *balls out* while here in Limbé everybody is daydreaming —Bob Shacochis⟩ — often considered vulgar

balls–out \ˈbȯlz¦aůt\ *adj* [*balls out* (herein)] **1** : characterized by maximum intensity : ALL-OUT, FULL-OUT ⟨a *balls-out* effort⟩ — often considered vulgar **2** : characterized by bold aggressiveness ⟨a *balls-out* rock climber⟩ — often considered vulgar

balls–up \ˈbȯlzˌəp\ *n* -s [*balls*, pl. of [1]*ball* (testis)] *Brit* : FOUL-UP — sometimes considered vulgar

ballsy \ˈbȯlzē, -zi\ *adj* -ER/-EST [*balls* (pl. of [1]*ball*) + [1]*-y*] : aggressively tough : GUTSY ⟨a ~ little guy, and . . . the most perfect writer of my generation —Norman Mailer⟩

bal·lute \bəˈlüt, ˈbaˌlüt\ *n* -s [*balloon* + *parachute*] : a small inflatable parachute for stabilization and deceleration of a jumper or object usu. before a conventional parachute opens

bal mu·sette \ˌbälmüˈzet\ *n* [F *bal-musette* dance accompanied by accordion music, fr. *bal* gathering for social dancing + (*accordéon*) *musette* accordion tuned to resemble the sound of a musette — more at BALL, MUSETTE] : a French dance hall with an accordion band

balsamic vinegar *n* [trans. of It *aceto balsamico*, lit., curative vinegar] : an aged Italian vinegar made from the must of white grapes

balsam woolly adelgid *also* **balsam woolly aphid** *n* : a woolly adelgid (*Adelges piceae*) native to Europe that has been introduced accidentally into the U.S. where it is a serious and usu. lethal pest of fir trees (as the balsam fir and Fraser fir) — see WOOLLY ADELGID *herein*

baltimore chop *n, usu cap B* [so called fr. its perfection by the Baltimore baseball team of the 1890s] : a batted ball in baseball that usu. bounces too high for an infielder to make a putout at first base

ba·nach algebra \ˈbäˌnäk-, -ˌnək-\ *n, usu cap B* [after Stefan *Banach* †1945 Pol. mathematician] : a linear algebra over the field of real or complex numbers that is also a Banach space for which the norm of the product of x and y is less than or equal to the product of the norm of x and the norm of y for all x and y belonging to it

ban·ach space *n, usu cap B* : a normed vector space for which the field of multipliers comprises the real or complex numbers and in which every Cauchy sequence converges to a point in the space

ba·nal·ize \bəˈnälˌīz, -ˈnál-; bəˈnal-, ba-, bā-; ˈbānᵊl-\ *vt* -ED/-ING/-S [[1]*banal* + *-ize*] : to make banal ⟨*banalized* the art . . . by mass=producing a few popular designs —Bernard Leach⟩

ba·nan·as \bəˈnanəz\ *adj* [fr. pl. of *banana*] : CRAZY ⟨spelling the English language drives everyone ~ —G.H.Poteet⟩

banana seat *n* : an elongated bicycle saddle that often has an upward-curved back

bananas fos·ter \-ˈfōstə(r), -ˈfäs-\ *n pl but sing in constr, often cap B & usu cap F* [after Richard *Foster*, friend of New Orleans restaurateur Owen E. Brennan, at whose restaurant the dish was first made] : a dessert of bananas in a caramel sauce flamed (as with rum) and served with ice cream

band–aid \¦=¦=\ *adj, usu cap B&A* [fr. *Band-Aid*, a trademark] : offering, making use of, or serving as a temporary or expedient remedy or solution ⟨for decades, the city [sewage] system has been subject to *Band-Aid* remedies —*Atlanta Jour. & Constitution*⟩

B and B *abbr or n* bed-and-breakfast *herein*

band collar *n* : a stand-up close-fitting buttoned collar

B and D *abbr or n, sometimes not cap* [*b*ondage *and d*iscipline] : sadomasochistic practices

B and E *abbr* breaking and entering

band·gap \ˈ=ˌ=\ *n* [[1]*band* + *gap*] : the difference in energy between the valence band and the conduction band of a solid material (as an insulator or semiconductor) that consists of the range of energy values forbidden to electrons in the material

bandwidth* *n* : the capacity for data transfer of an electronic communications system ⟨graphics consume more ~ than text does⟩; *esp* : the maximum data transfer rate of such a system ⟨a ~ of 56 kilobits per second⟩

bang* *n* — **bang for the buck** *also* **bang for one's buck** : value received from outlay or effort ⟨investment is yielding less *bang for the buck*—*Fortune*⟩

bang–bang \¦=¦=\ *adj* **1 a** : having a sudden forceful or attention=grabbing effect : PUNCHY ⟨*bang-bang* headlines⟩ **b** : executed or happening so quickly as to make judgement (as by an umpire or referee) difficult ⟨a *bang-bang* play at first base⟩ **2** : characterized by violent or fast-paced action ⟨a *bang-bang* movie⟩

bang·er \ˈbaŋə(r), -aiŋ-\ *n* -s [[1]*bang* + [2]*-er*] **1** [perh. fr. the noise sausages often make while frying] *Brit* : SAUSAGE **2** *Brit* : FIRECRACKER **3** *Brit* : a noisy dilapidated automobile

[1]**ban·gla·deshi** \ˌbaŋgləˈdeshē, bäŋ-, -lä-, -ˈdāsh-\ *n, pl* **bangladeshis** *also* **bangladeshi** *cap* [Bengali *bā̃lādeśī*, fr. *Bā̃lādeś* Bangladesh, Bengal, fr. *bā̃lā* Bengal + *deś* country, fr. Skt *deśa* point, place, region, fr. *diśati* he shows; akin to Gk *deiknynai* to show — more at TOKEN] : a native or resident of Bangladesh

[2]**bangladeshi** *adj, usu cap* : of, relating to, or characteristic of Bangladesh or its people

ban·jax \ˈbanˌjaks\ *vt* -ED/-ING/-ES [origin unknown] *chiefly Irish* : DAMAGE, RUIN; *also* : SMASH

bankable* *adj* : sure to bring in a profit ⟨only one ~ female star

whose name can guarantee financing of a movie —Judy Klemesrud〉 — **bank·abil·i·ty** \ˌ==ˈbiləd·ē\ *n*
bank card \ˈ=ˌ=\ *n* [[4]*bank* + [3]*card*] : a credit card, debit card, or ATM card issued by a bank
bankers' hours *n pl* : short working hours
banquet lamp *n* : a tall elaborate kerosene table lamp
ban·tu·stan \ˈban(ˌ)tüˌstan, ˈbantəˌs-, ˈbän(ˌ)tüˌstän, ˌ=(ˌ)=ˈ=\ *n* -s *usu cap* [*Bantu* + *-stan* (as in *Hindustan*)] : any of several all-black enclaves in the Republic of So. Africa during the period of apartheid that had a limited degree of self-government — called also *homeland*
bar·ba·res·co \bärbäˈreskō\ *n* -s *usu cap* [It, fr. *Barbaresco*, village in the Piedmont region, Italy] : a robust red wine from the Piedmont region of Italy
bar·be·ra \bärˈberä, -bir-\ *n* -s *usu cap* [It, variety of dark grape, wine made from this grape, fr. It dial. (Piedmont), perh. alter. of (assumed) *albera*, modif. of L *albuelis* variety of vine] : a usu. full-bodied red wine from the Piedmont region of Italy; *also* : a similar wine made elsewhere (as California) from the grapes of the same variety
bar·bie \ˈbä(r)bē\ *n* -s [[1]*barbecue* + *-ie*] *chiefly Austral* : BARBECUE 1, 2
barcelona chair *n, usu cap B* [fr. *Barcelona*, Spain, site of the 1929 International Exposition for which the chair was designed] : an armless chair with leather-covered cushions on a stainless steel frame
bar code *n* : a code consisting of a group of printed and variously patterned bars and spaces and sometimes numerals that is designed to be scanned and read into computer memory and that contains information (as identification) about the object it labels — see UNIVERSAL PRODUCT CODE *herein* — **bar–coded** \ˈ=ˌ==\ *adj* — **bar coding** *n*
bar·do·li·no \ˌbärd[ə]lˈē(ˌ)nō, -dəˈlē-\ *n* -s *usu cap* [It, fr. *Bardolino*, village on Lake Garda, Italy] : a light red Italian wine
barefoot doctor *n* [trans. of Chin (Pek) *ch'ih[4]-chiao[3]-yi[1]-shêng[1]*] : an auxiliary medical worker trained to provide basic health care in rural areas of the People's Republic of China
barf \ˈbärf, ˈbȧf\ *vi* -ED/-ING/-s [origin unknown] : VOMIT — **barf** *n* -s
bargaining chip *n* : something that can be used to gain concessions in a negotiation
bar·gel·lo \bärˈjelō\ *n* -s [fr. the *Bargello*, museum in Florence, Italy; fr. the use of this stitch in the upholstery of 17th cent. chairs at the Bargello] : a needlework stitch that produces a zigzag pattern
bar girl *n* **1** : BARMAID **2** : a prostitute who frequents bars **3** : B-GIRL
bar·iat·rics \ˌbarēˈaˌtriks\ *n pl but sing in constr* [*bar-* + *-iatrics*] : a branch of medicine that deals with the treatment of obesity — **bar·iat·ric** \-ik\ *adj* — **bar·ia·tri·cian** \-ēəˈtrishən\ *n* -s
bar·low lens \ˈbärˌlō\ *n, usu cap B* [after Peter *Barlow* †1862 Eng. mathematician and optician] : a diverging lens used to increase the magnifying power of a telescope
bar mitzvah *vt* **bar mitzvahed; bar mitzvahed; bar mitzvahing; bar mitzvahs** *often cap B&M* : to administer the ceremony of bar mitzvah to
barn burner *n* : one that arouses much interest or excitement 〈the game promises to be a real *barn burner*〉
barn sale *n* : GARAGE SALE *herein*
bar·o·clin·ic \ˌbarəˈklinik\ *adj* [ISV *bar-* + *-clinic*] : relating to a state of a fluid (as the atmosphere) in which surfaces of constant pressure intersect those of constant density
ba·ro·lo \bäˈrō(ˌ)lō, bə-\ *n* -s *usu cap* [It, fr. *Barolo*, village in the Piedmont region, Italy] : a dry red Italian wine
barometer* *n* : STANDARD, TEST 〈a ∼ to measure high school talent —Jeff Fellenzer〉
baro·re·cep·tor \ˌbarōrəˈseptə(r), -ōrē-\ *also* **bar·o·cep·tor** \ˈbarōˌs-\ *n* -s [*bar-* + *receptor*] : a receptor in the walls of large arteries (as the carotid sinus and arch of the aorta) that is sensitive to changes in blood pressure — called also *pressoreceptor*
bar·quette \ˌbärˈket\ *n* -s [F, lit., small boat, dim. of *barque* boat, bark — more at BARK] : a small boat-shaped pastry shell
barracuda* *n* : one that uses aggressive, selfish, and sometimes unethical methods to obtain goals esp. in business
barr body \ˈbär-, ˈbȧ(r-\ *n, usu cap 1st B* [after Murray Llewellyn *Barr* †1995 Canad. anatomist] : a densely staining inactivated condensed X chromosome that is present in each somatic cell of most female mammals and is used as a test of genetic femaleness (as in a fetus or an athlete) — called also *sex chromatin*
barrel* *n* : a supply or collection of similar things 〈people graduating from college who are at the lowest part of the ∼ —Albert Shanker〉
bar·tók·ian \ˌbärˈtäkyən, -tók-, -kēən\ *adj, usu cap* [Béla *Bartók* †1945 Hung. composer + E *-an*] : of, relating to, or suggestive of Béla Bartók or his musical compositions
barware \ˈ=ˌ=\ *n* [[1]*bar* + [4]*ware*] : glassware or utensils used in preparing and serving alcoholic beverages
bary·on \ˈbarēˌän\ *n* -s [*bary-* + [2]*-on*] : any of a group of elementary particles (as a nucleon or a lambda particle) that are subject to the strong force and are held to be a combination of three quarks — **bary·on·ic** \ˌbarēˈänik\ *adj*
baryon number *n* : a number equal to the number of baryons minus that of antibaryons in a system of elementary particles
base* *n* **1** : a number that is multiplied by a rate or of which a percentage or fraction is calculated 〈to find the interest on $90 at 10% multiply the ∼ 90 by .10〉 **2** : the economic factors on which in Marxist theory all legal, social, and political relations are formed **3** : a price level at which a security previously actively declining in price resists further price decline **4** : any of the five purine or pyrimidine bases of DNA and RNA that include cytosine, guanine, adenine, thymine, and uracil **5** : a point to be considered 〈is covering . . . detailed material and is trying to touch every ∼ —R.L.Tobin〉 **6** : FREEBASE *herein*
base angle* *n* : either of the angles of a triangle that have one side in common with the base
[1]**base·band** \ˈ=ˌ=\ *n* [[3]*base* + [1]*band*] : the band of frequencies that carries information in electronic communications and usu. modulates a carrier signal
[2]**baseband** *adj* : of or relating to a communications system in which information is transmitted using a single unmodulated band of frequencies — compare BROADBAND *herein*
base exchange *n* : a post exchange on a naval or an air force base
baseline** \ˈ=ˌ=\ *n, often attrib* **1** : a usu. initial set of critical observations or data used for comparison or a control **2** : a starting point 〈a kind of ∼ from which all discussions . . . must proceed —Nicholas Lemann〉
[1]**base pair** *n* : one of the pairs of nucleotide bases on complementary strands of nucleic acid that consist of a purine on one strand joined to a pyrimidine on the other strand by hydrogen bonds holding together the two strands much like the rungs of a ladder and that include adenine linked to thymine in DNA or to uracil in RNA and guanine linked to cytosine in both DNA and RNA
[2]**base pair** *vi* : to participate in formation of a base pair 〈adenine *base pairs* with thymine〉
base unit *n* : one of a set of simple units in a system of measurement that is based on a natural phenomenon or established standard and from which other units may be derived 〈the *base units* of SI are the meter, kilogram, second, ampere, kelvin, mole, and candela〉
bash* *n* **1** : a festive social gathering : PARTY **2** *chiefly Brit* : TRY, ATTEMPT 〈I want to have a ∼ at different kinds of books —Colleen McCollough〉
bash* *vt* : to assail verbally and esp. publicly 〈∼*ing* members of her own party〉
BA·SIC \ˈbāsik, -zik\ *n* -s [*B*eginner's *A*ll-purpose *S*ymbolic *I*nstruction *C*ode] : a simplified high-level language for programming and interacting with a computer
basi·lect \ˈbazəˌlekt, ˈbāzə-, -sə-\ *n* -s [*basi-* + *-lect* (as in *dialect*)] : the least prestigious language variety of a community — compare ACROLECT *herein* — **basi·lec·tal** \ˌ==ˈlekt[ə]l\ *adj*
basis* *n* : a set of linearly independent vectors in a vector space such that any vector in the vector space can be expressed as a linear combination of them with appropriately chosen coefficients
basket* *n* **1** : a category or collection of items 〈direct their money into a ∼ of funds used for loans —*N.Y. Times*〉 **2** : MARKET BASKET 2 **3** : an aggregate of values (as of selected currencies or commodities) the average of which serves as a monetary standard **4** *slang* : male genitalia **5** : a ring around the lower end of a ski pole that keeps the pole from sinking too deep in snow **6** : a selection of financial instruments (as equities, futures, or options) the underlying values of which reflect the fluctuations of their markets
basket case* *n* : one that is totally worn out, incapacitated, or inoperable 〈dad's a *basket case* by the time he gets out to Yellowstone from the East —Harold Graham〉 〈reveal the Northeast to be an economic *basket case*—Michael Kramer〉 〈many models end up emotional *basket cases*—Gwen Kinkead〉
bas·ma·ti rice *also* **bas·ma·ti** \ˌbäzˈmäd·ē, -tē *also* ˌbaz-\ *n* -s [Hindi *bāsmatī*, lit., something fragrant, fr. *bās* odor, stench (fr. Skt *vāsa* perfume) + *-matī* possessing, fr. Skt, fem. of *-mant-*, *-mān*, by-form of *-vān*; akin to Gk *-ent-*, *-eis* possessing, Hitt *-want-*] : a cultivated aromatic long grain rice originating in southern Asia
ba·so·tho \bəˈsütü, -ˈsüd-‑\ *n, pl* **basotho** *or* **basothos** *usu cap* [Sotho, pl. of *Mosotho* Southern or Northern Sotho person, fr. *mo-*, class prefix + *-sotho*, perh. alter. of *motho* human being] : BASUTO 1
bass–ack·ward \ˌbasˈakwə(r)d, -aa(ə)s-, -ais- *sometimes in NE* -ȧs-\ *or* **bass–ackwards** \-dz\ *adv (or adj)* [anagram of *ass-backward*] : in a backward or inept way
batch* *n, often attrib* : a group of jobs (as programs) which are submitted for processing on a computer and whose results are obtained at a later time 〈∼ processing〉 — compare TIME-SHARING *herein*
batch file *n* : a computer file containing a series of commands to be executed automatically and sequentially by the operating system
bat–eared fox \ˈ=ˌ=\ *n* : LONG-EARED FOX
bath* *n* : a financial setback : LOSS 〈heard that you took a ∼ on the South African securities —J.K.Galbraith〉
ba·tracho·toxin \bəˌtrakə, ˌbaˌtrakō+\ *n* [ISV *batrach-* + *toxin*] : a toxic steroid alkaloid $C_{31}H_{42}N_2O_6$ extracted from the skin of several So. American frogs (genus *Phyllobates*)
battered child syndrome *n* : the complex of grave physical injuries (as fractures, hematomas, and contusions) that results from gross abuse (as by a parent) of a young child
battered woman syndrome *also* **battered woman's syndrome** *or* **battered wife syndrome** *or* **battered women's syndrome** *n* : the highly variable symptom complex of physical and psychological injuries exhibited by a woman repeatedly abused esp. physically by her mate
baud* *n, pl* **baud** *also* **bauds** : a variable unit of data transmission speed (as one bit per second)
baud·e·lair·ean *also* **baud·e·lair·ian** \bōdˈlerēən, ˌbōd[ə]lˈer-, ˌ=a(a)r-\ *adj, usu cap* [Charles Pierre *Baudelaire* †1867 Fr. poet + E *-an*] : of, relating to, or characteristic of Baudelaire or his writings
[1]**bayes·ian** \ˈbāzēən, -āzhən\ *adj, usu cap* [Thomas *Bayes* †1761 Eng. mathematician + E *-an*] : being, relating to, or involving statistical methods (as of decision making or inference) that assign probabilities or distributions to events, statements, and parameters based on prior knowledge or best guesses before statistical experiments are performed and data collected and that use applications of Bayes' theorem to revise the probabilities or distributions after experimentation and data collection
[2]**bayesian** *n* -s *usu cap* : a statistician who advocates or uses Bayesian methods
bayes' theorem \ˈbāz-\ *also* **bayes's theorem** \-əz\ *n, usu cap B* [Thomas *Bayes*] : a theorem about conditional probabilities: the probability that an event A occurs given that another event B has already occurred is equal to the probability that the event B occurs given that A has already occurred multiplied by the probability of occurrence of event A and divided by the probability of occurrence of event B
ba·zil·lion \bəˈzilyən\ *n* -s [alter. of *zillion*] : a large indeterminate number — **bazillion** *adj*
ba·zoom \bəˈzüm\ *n* -s [prob. alter. of *bosom*] : a woman's breast
BBA \ˌbē(ˌ)bēˈā\ *abbr or n* -s : a bachelor of business administration
b–ball \ˈbēˌbȯl\ *n, sometimes cap 1st B* [by shortening] : BASKETBALL
b–boy \ˈbēˌbȯi\ *n, usu cap 1st B* [prob. fr. *break* (herein) or *b*reak beat (sequence of breaks created by manually backing up the needle on two record turntables) + *boy*] : a male who engages in the pursuits of hip-hop culture or adopts its styles
BBS \ˌbē(ˌ)bēˈes\ *abbr or n, pl* **BBSs** *or* **BBSes** [*b*ulletin *b*oard *s*ystem] : an electronic bulletin board system
BCD \ˌbē(ˌ)sēˈdē\ *n* -s [*b*inary *c*oded *d*ecimal] : a code for representing alphanumeric information (as on magnetic tape); *also* : a code for representing decimal digits in a computer
b cell *n, usu cap B* [*B* prob. fr. *b*ursa-derived (produced by the bursa of Fabricius)] : any of the lymphocytes that have antigen-binding antibody molecules on the surface and that comprise the antibody-secreting plasma cells when mature — called also *B lymphocyte*; compare T CELL *herein*
beach bag *n* : a capacious bag for articles used at the beach
beach bunny *n* : a girl or woman who frequents the beach
beachwear \ˈ=ˌ=\ *n* : clothing for wear at the beach
beamwidth \ˈ=ˌ=\ *n* : the angular diameter of the region adjoining an antenna through which the reception of the signal is best
bean* *n* **1 beans** *pl* : EXUBERANCE — used in the phrase *full of beans* **2 beans** *pl* : NONSENSE — used in the phrase *full of beans*
beanbag* *n* : any of various pellet-filled bags used for furniture (as a chair) or for household articles (as the base of an ashtray)
bean counter *n* [[1]*bean* (dollar) + [2]*counter*] : one involved in corporate financial decisions and esp. one reluctant to spend money 〈no union . . ., a minimum of red tape, and no *bean counters* breathing down his neck restricting investment —Faye Rice〉
bean threads *n pl* : translucent noodles made from mung beans — called also *cellophane noodles*
bearded collie *n* : any of a breed of large working dogs that originated in Scotland and have a long rough coat and drooping ears
bear–hug \ˈ=ˌ=\ *vt* : to embrace in a bear hug
beat* *vb* ∼ *vt* : to score against (a goalkeeper)
beat box *n* : an electronic device that simulates the sound of drums — called also *drum machine*
beat off* *vb* ∼ *vi* : MASTURBATE — used of a male; usu. considered vulgar
beat up* *vb* — **beat up on** : to attack physically or verbally 〈borderline sociopaths . . . *beat up on* even bigger meanies —Steven Flax〉 〈wouldn't gain much by *beating up on* our universities —S.D.Bryen〉
beau·coup \ˈbü(ˌ)kü, ˈbō-, -(ˌ)küp; ˌ=ˈ=\ *adj* [F, n., much, a great deal, fr. *beau* fine, beautiful + *coup* blow, stroke — more at BEAU, COPE] *slang* : great in quantity or amount : MANY, MUCH 〈wants to spend ∼ bucks —Heidi Henneman〉
beaujolais nouveau *n, usu cap B & sometimes cap N* [F, lit., new beaujolais — more at BEAUJOLAIS, NOUVEAU] : a beaujolais wine that is released shortly after a grape harvest and is sold for immediate consumption
beaut *adj* [*beaut*, n.] *Austral & NewZeal* : EXCELLENT 3
beautiful people *n pl, often cap B&P* : wealthy or famous people whose life-style is usu. expensive and well-publicized 〈to this festival came the stars, the magnates, the *beautiful people*, and the crowds —Roland Gelatt〉
beauty* *n* : a quantum characteristic that accounts for the existence and lifetime of the upsilon particle; *also* : a particle having this characteristic
beauty contest* *n* : a presidential primary election in which the popular vote does not determine the number of convention delegates a candidate receives
beauty part *n* : the most desirable or beneficial aspect of something
beaver* *n* [[1]*beaver*] : the pudenda of a woman — usu. considered vulgar
bea·ver \ˈbēvə(r)\ *vi* **beavered; beavered; beavering** \-v(ə)riŋ\; **beavers** [fr. the proverbial energy of the animal] *chiefly Brit* : to work diligently — usu. used with *away* 〈my subconscious, ∼*ing* away independently, suddenly came up with that dazzlingly brilliant punch line —*Yorkshire Post*〉
beck·er muscular dystrophy \ˈbekər-\ *or* **becker's muscular dystrophy** \-ərz-\ *n, usu cap B* [after Peter Emil *Becker* *b*1908 Ger. geneticist] : a less severe form of Duchenne muscular dystrophy with later onset and slower progression of the disease that is inherited as an X-linked recessive trait and is characterized by dystrophin of deficient or abnormal molecular weight
beck·ett·ian \beˈketēən\ *adj, usu cap* [Samuel *Beckett* †1989 Irish author + E *-an*] : of, relating to, or suggestive of the works or characters of Samuel Beckett
becque·rel \ˌbekəˌrel, bekˈrel\ *n* -s [after Antoine H. *Becquerel* †1908 Fr. physicist] : a unit of radioactivity equal to one disintegration per second
bed–and–breakfast *n* : an establishment (as an inn or guesthouse) offering lodging and breakfast
bed·da·ble \ˈbedəbəl\ *adj* [[2]*bed* + *-able*] : suitable for taking to bed 〈tolerated brains in women who were too old to be ∼ —Peter Quennell〉
[1]**bed·dy–bye** \ˌbedēˌbī\ *n* [baby talk, fr. *bed*] : [3]BYE-BYE
[2]**beddy–bye** \"\ *adv* : [4]BYE-BYE
bed·form \ˈ=ˌ=\ *n* : features developed by fluid flow over a deformable bed (as sand or seabed)
bed–hop \ˈ=ˌ=\ *vi* : to engage in sex promiscuously
bed–sit \ˈ=ˌ=\ *n* [by shortening] *Brit* : BED-SITTING-ROOM
[1]**bed·so·nia** \bedˈsōnēə\ [NL, fr. Samuel P. *Bedson* †1969 Brit. bacteriologist + NL *-ia*] *syn of* CHLAMYDIA
[2]**bedsonia** \"\ *n, pl* **bedsoni·ae** \-nēˌī\ : CHLAMYDIA 1 *herein*
bedworthy \ˈ=ˌ==\ *adj* [[1]*bed* + *worthy*] *chiefly Brit* : BEDDABLE *herein*
beef·alo \ˈbēfəˌlō\ *n* [blend of [1]*beef* and *buffalo*] **1** *usu cap* : a breed of beef cattle developed in the U.S. that is genetically ⅝ domestic bovine and ⅜ No. American buffalo (*Bison bison*) **2** *pl* **beefalos** *or* **beefaloes** *often cap*: an animal of the Beefalo breed
beefsteak tomato *n* : a very large globe-shaped red tomato with dense flesh
beef wellington *n, usu cap W* [prob. fr. the name *Wellington*] : a fillet of beef covered with pâté de foie gras and enclosed in pastry
beehive* *n* : a woman's hairdo in a conical shape
beeper* *n* : a device that beeps; *specif* : a small radio receiver that beeps when signaled to alert the person carrying it and usu. displays a short message (as a telephone number) — called also *pager*
bee–stung \ˈ=ˌ=\ *adj* : having a red puffy appearance as if from being stung by a bee 〈*bee-stung* lips〉
beeswax* *n* : BUSINESS — used chiefly by children in the phrases *mind your own beeswax, none of your beeswax*
before* *conj* **1** : so that . . . do not 〈get out of there ∼ you get dirty〉 **2** : until the time that 〈miles to go ∼ I sleep —Robert Frost〉 **3 a** : or else . . . not 〈must be convicted ∼ he can be removed from office〉 **b** : or else 〈get out of here ∼ I call a cop〉
beggar's chicken *n* : a traditional Chinese dish of marinated and stuffed chicken wrapped in lotus leaves and roasted in a shell of clay
behavioral scientist *n* : a specialist in behavioral science
behavior modification *also* **behavior therapy** *or* **behavioral therapy** *or* **behaviorial modification** *n* : psychotherapy that is concerned with the treatment (as by desensitization or aversion therapy) of observable behaviors rather than underlying psychological processes and that applies principles of learning to substitute desirable responses and behavior patterns for undesirable ones (as phobias or obsessions) — **behavior therapist** *or* **behaviorial therapist** *n*
beige* *adj* : lacking distinction : VANILLA *herein*
beignet* *n* : a light square doughnut usu. sprinkled with powdered sugar
[1]**be·la·rus·an** \ˌb(y)eläˈrüsən, ˌb(y)ä-, -lə-\ *or* **be·la·rus·ian** \"ˈrüsēən\ *or* **be·la·rus·sian** \"ˈrəshən\ *n* -s *cap* [*Belarusan*, *Belarusian* fr. *Belarus*, country in Eastern Europe (formerly the Belorussian S.S.R.) + E *-an*; *Belarussian* alter. (influenced by *Belarus*) of *Belorussian*] : a native or inhabitant of Belarus
[2]**belarusan** *or* **belarusian** *or* **belarussian** *adj, usu cap* : of or relating to Belarus or the Belarusans
belgian malinois *n, usu cap B&M* : MALINOIS
belgian tervuren \-(ˌ)tərˈvyürən, -ter-\ *n, usu cap B&T* [fr. *Tervuren*, commune in Brabant, Belgium] : any of a breed of working dogs closely related to the Belgian sheepdog but having abundant long straight fawn-colored hair with black tips
belgian waffle *n, usu cap B* : a waffle having large depressions that is usu. topped with fruit and whipped cream
bell curve *n* : a bell-shaped curve; *specif* : NORMAL CURVE
belle epoque *or* **belle époque** \ˌbelāˈpȯk\ *n, often cap B&E* [F *belle époque* beautiful age] : a period that represents the height of artistic or cultural development (as for a society); *specif* : the period in France around the turn of the century
bells \ˈbelz\ *n pl* [by shortening] : BELL-BOTTOMS
bells and whistles *n pl* : items or features that are useful or decorative but not essential : FRILLS
bell–shaped \ˈ=ˌ=\ *adj* : relating to, being, or approximating a normal curve or a normal distribution
bell's theorem *n, usu cap B* [after John Stewart *Bell* †1990 Irish physicist] : a theorem in quantum physics: two particles that have interacted will continue to influence each other instantaneously following separation
bellwether* *n* : an indicator of trends
bellyboard \ˈ=ˌ=\ *n* [[1]*belly* + *board*] : a small buoyant board usu. less than three feet long that is used in surf riding
belly dancer *n* : one who performs a belly dance — **belly dance** *vi*
belly–up \ˌ==ˈ=\ *adj* : done for; *esp* : BANKRUPT 〈twelve thousand businesses have gone *belly-up* this year —L.A.Iacocca〉
belt* *vi* : to sing loudly — **bel·ter** *n* -s
belted–bias tire \ˌ==ˈ==-\ *n* : BIAS-BELTED TIRE *herein*
belt up *vi, Brit* : to shut up
be·me·gride \ˈbeməˌgrīd, -ēm-\ *n* -s [*beta* + *ethyl* + *methyl* + *glutaric acid* + *imide*] : an analeptic drug $C_8H_{13}NO_2$ used esp. to counteract the effect of barbiturates
bench mark* *n, usu* **benchmark** \ˈ=ˌ=\ : a standardized problem by which computer systems or programs are compared
benchmark \ˈ=ˌ=\ *vt* : to test (as a computer system) by a benchmark problem in order to measure performance
bench·mark·ing \ˈ=ˌ=-iŋ\ *n* -s : study of a competitor's product or business practices in order to improve the performance of one's own company
bench press* *n* : a lift in weight lifting in which from a supine position on a bench a lifter presses the weight from chest level straight up to full extension of the arms; *also* : a competitive event involving this lift — **bench–press** \ˈ=ˌ=\ *vt*
bench seat *n* : a seat in an automotive vehicle that extends the full width of the passenger section
benedict's solution *n, usu cap B* [after Stanley Rossiter *Benedict* †1936 Am. chemist] : a blue solution containing sodium carbon-

ate, sodium citrate, and cupric sulfate which yields a red, yellow, or orange precipitate upon warming with a reducing sugar (as glucose or maltose)

ben·e·fi·cials \-z\ *n pl* [fr. *beneficial*, adj.] : organisms (as ladybugs, lacewings, predatory mites, and bacteria) that feed on or parasitize pests of crops, gardens, and turf

benign neglect *n* : an attitude or policy of ignoring an often undesirable situation that one is perceived to be responsible for dealing with

benign prostatic hyperplasia *also* **benign prostatic hypertrophy** *n* : adenomatous hyperplasia of the periurethral part of the prostate gland that occurs esp. in some men over 50 years old and that tends to obstruct urination by constricting the urethra

be·nin \bəˈnin, -ˈnēn; ˈbenən\ *adj, usu cap* [fr. *Benin*, republic in West Africa and former kingdom in Nigeria] : of or relating to Benin : of the kind or style prevalent in Benin

ben·ning·ton \ˈbeniŋtən\ *or* **bennington ware** *also* **bennington pottery** *n* -s *usu cap B* : ceramic ware including earthenware, stoneware, and Parian ware produced at Bennington, Vt.; *esp* : earthenware with brown or mottled glaze

ben·o·myl \ˈbenə͵mil, -nō͵-\ *n* -s [*benz-* + *-o-* + *-myl* (by shortening & alter. fr. *methyl*)] : a derivative $C_{14}H_{18}N_4O_3$ of carbamate and benzimidazole used esp. as a systemic fungicide on agricultural crops and ornamental plants

bent* *adj, slang* **1** : different from what is normal or usual: as **a** *chiefly Brit* : DISHONEST, CORRUPT ⟨a basically straight guy making it in an unrepentantly ~ world —*Times Lit. Supp.*⟩ **b** : ECCENTRIC, CRAZY ⟨she was so ~ that she's probably a woman who ought to be locked up somewhere —Robert Redford⟩ **c** : HOMOSEXUAL **2** : extremely upset or angry — often used in the phrase *bent out of shape*

bent note *n* : a variable microtonal lowering of the third, seventh, and occas. fifth degrees of the major scale

ben·to box \ˈbentō-\ *n* [Jap *bentō* box lunch] : a multicompartment box used for containing the different courses of a usu. Japanese lunch

ben·zo·di·az·e·pine \¦benzō͵dīˈazə͵pēn, -͵pən\ *n* -s [*benz-* + *di-* + *az-* + *-epine* (fr. *hepta-* + ²*-ine*)] : any of a group of aromatic lipophilic amines (as diazepam and chlordiazepoxide) used esp. as tranquilizers

ben·zo·mor·phan \͵benzōˈmȯr͵fan\ *n* -s [*benz-* + *-morph* + ³*-an*] : any of a group of synthetic compounds including some potent analgesics (as phenazocine or pentazocine)

ben·zyne \ˈben͵zīn\ *n* -s [*benzene* + *-yne*] : an unsaturated cyclic hydrocarbon C_6H_4 derived from and structurally similar to benzene but having one of the double bonds of benzene replaced by a triple bond

be·rim·bau \bāˈrēⁿ(m)͵bau̇\ *n* [Brazilian Pg, fr. Pg, Jew's harp] : a musical instrument of Brazil that consists of a gourd resonator and a single string which is struck with a stick

berm *vt* [*berm*, n.] **1** : to provide with a berm (as of earth) **2** : to form into a berm ⟨he ~*ed* the earth up to the bottom of the big windows —Philip Langdon⟩

bermuda bag *n, usu cap 1st B* : a round or oval handbag with a wooden handle and removable cloth covers

bermuda petrel *n, usu cap B* : CAHOW

bermuda triangle *n, usu cap B&T* [fr. *Bermuda Triangle*, roughly triangular area of the Atlantic Ocean with Bermuda as one of its apexes into which boats and aircraft have allegedly disappeared without trace] : a place, state, or set of circumstances in which something (as a plan) is usu. regrettably thwarted or nullified ⟨talented young women with dreams . . . disappeared into the *Bermuda Triangle* of their husbands' ambitions —Susan Littwin⟩

ber·noul·li's equation \bərˈnülē-, ¦ber͵nü¦lē-\ *also* **ber·noul·li equation** *n, usu cap B* **1** [after Jacques *Bernoulli* †1705 Swiss mathematician] : a nonlinear differential equation of the first order that has the general form

$$\frac{dy}{dx} + f(x)y = g(x)y^n$$

and that can be put in linear form by dividing through by y^n and making the change of variable $Y = y^{-n+1}$ **2** [after Daniel *Bernoulli* †1782 Swiss mathematician and scientist] : an equation used in fluid mechanics that relates pressure, velocity, density, and gravitational acceleration — compare BERNOULLI EFFECT *in the Dict*, BERNOULLI'S THEOREM 2 *in the Dict*

bernoulli's principle \"-\ *n, usu cap B* [after Daniel *Bernoulli*] : BERNOULLI EFFECT

ber·noul·li trial \"-\ *n, usu cap B* [after Jacques *Bernoulli*] : one of the repetitions of a statistical experiment having two mutually exclusive outcomes with constant probability of occurrence

be·som pocket \ˈbēzəm-, ˈbiz-, ˈbis-\ *n* [origin unknown] : a pocket with welting or edging around the opening

best boy *n* : the chief assistant to the gaffer in motion-picture or television productions

best–case \ˈ=͵=\ *adj* : based on, being, or relating to a projection of future events that assumes only the best possible circumstances ⟨a *best-case* scenario⟩

best–efforts \¦=¦==\ *adj, of security underwriting* : not involving a firm commitment on the part of an underwriter to take up any unsold shares or bonds of an issue being underwritten

beta* *n* **1** : a measure of the risk potential of a stock or investment portfolio expressed as a ratio of the stock's or portfolio's volatility to the volatility of the market as a whole **2** *often attrib* : a nearly complete prototype of a product (as software) not yet ready for commercial release ⟨~ version⟩

beta–adrenergic \¦==͵==¦==\ *adj* : of, relating to, or being a beta-receptor ⟨*beta-adrenergic* blocking action⟩

beta–adrenergic receptor *n* : BETA-RECEPTOR *herein*

beta–am·y·loid \¦==ˈ==͵=\ *also* **beta–amyloid protein** *n* : an amyloid that is derived from a larger precursor protein and is a component of the neurofibrillary tangles and plaques characteristic of Alzheimer's disease

beta–blocker \ˈ==ˈ==\ *n* : any of a group of drugs (as propranolol) that combine with and block the activity of a beta-receptor so as to decrease the heart rate and force of contractions and to lower high blood pressure and that are used esp. to treat hypertension, angina pectoris, and ventricular and supraventricular arrhythmias — **beta–blocking** \ˈ==ˈ==\ *adj*

beta decay *n* : a radioactive nuclear transformation governed by the weak force in which a nucleon (as a neutron) changes into a nucleon (as a proton) of the other type with the simultaneous emission of a beta particle and a neutrino or antineutrino without change in the mass number

beta–en·dor·phin \¦==en¦dȯrfən\ *n* : an endorphin of the pituitary gland with much greater analgesic potency than morphine that occurs free and as the terminal sequence of 31 amino acids in the polypeptide chain of beta-lipotropin

beta globin *n* : the chain of hemoglobin that is designated beta and that when deficient or defective causes various anemias (as beta-thalassemia or sickle-cell anemia)

beta–glu·can \¦=ˈ=͵=, -͵=\ *n* : any of several polysaccharides consisting of glucose units and including one found in endosperm cell walls of cereal grains (as barley and oats)

beta interferon *n* : an interferon that is produced esp. by fibroblasts, possesses antiviral activity, and is used in a form obtained from recombinant DNA esp. in the treatment of multiple sclerosis marked by recurrent attacks alternating with periods of remission — compare ALPHA INTERFERON *herein*, GAMMA INTERFERON *herein*

beta–lac·tam \ˈ==ˈ=͵=, -=ˈ=\ *n* : any of a large class of natural and semisynthetic antibiotics (as the penicillins and cephalosporins) with a lactam ring

beta–lac·ta·mase \ˈ==ˈlakta͵mās, -tə-; -͵lakˈta͵mās\ *n* -s [²*beta* + *lactam* + *-ase*] : PENICILLINASE

beta–lipotropin \¦==͵==¦==\ *n* : a lipotropin of the adenohypophysis of the pituitary gland that contains beta-endorphin as the terminal sequence of 31 amino acids in its polypeptide chain

be·ta·meth·a·sone \¦==¦methə͵zōn, -͵sōn\ *n* -s [²*beta* + *-methasone* (as in *dexamethasone* — herein)] : a potent glucocorticoid $C_{22}H_{29}FO_5$ that is isomeric with dexamethasone and has anti-inflammatory activity

beta–oxidation \¦==͵==¦==\ *n* : stepwise catabolism of fatty acids in which two-carbon fragments are successively removed from the carboxyl end of the chain

beta particle* *n* : a high-speed electron or positron

beta–receptor \¦==¦==\ *n* : any of a group of receptors that are postulated to exist on cell surfaces of some effector organs and of tissues innervated by the sympathetic nervous system in order to explain the specificity of certain adrenergic agents in activating or blocking only some sympathetic activities (as vasodilation, increase in muscular contraction and beat of the heart, and relaxation of smooth muscle in the bronchi and intestine) — compare ALPHA-RECEPTOR *herein*

beta–sheet \¦==¦=\ *or* **beta–pleat·ed sheet** \¦==¦==\ *n* : the structural arrangement of many proteins in which two or more short regions of the polypeptide chain align adjacently and are stabilized by hydrogen bonds into sheets with a pleated or accordionlike appearance — compare ALPHA-HELIX *herein*

beta test* *n* : a field test of the beta version of a product (as software) esp. by testers from outside the company developing it that is conducted prior to commercial release — **beta test** *vt* — **beta tester** *n*

beta–thalassemia \ˈ==͵=ˈ===\ *n* : thalassemia in which the hemoglobin chain designated beta is affected and which comprises Cooley's anemia in the homozygous condition and a thalassemia minor in the heterozygous condition

be·tha·ne·chol \bəˈthānə͵kȯl, -ōl\ *n* -s [*beth-* (blend of ²*beta* and *methyl*) + *-ane* + *choline*] : a parasympathomimetic agent administered in the form of its chloride $C_7H_{17}ClN_2O_2$ and used esp. to treat gastric and urinary retention

beurre blanc \ˈbərˈbläⁿ\ *n* [F, lit., white butter] : a sauce made from a base of wine, vinegar, or lemon juice cooked down and flavored with herbs and often stock and blended with softened butter

beurre ma·nié \ˈbərmänˈyā\ *n* [F, lit., handled butter] : flour and butter kneaded together and used as a thickener in sauces

BFA *abbr* bachelor of fine arts

BGH *abbr* bovine growth hormone

b–girl \ˈbē¦gərl\ *n* [*b-* (as in *b-boy* — herein) + *girl*] : a usu. young woman who adopts the pursuits or styles of hip-hop culture

Bh *symbol* bohrium *herein*

BHA \¦bē¦āchˈā\ *n* -s [*b*utylated *h*ydroxy*a*nisole] : a phenolic antioxidant $C_{11}H_{16}O_2$ used esp. to preserve fats and oils in food, cosmetics, and pharmaceuticals

bhan·gra \ˈbäŋgrä, -rə\ *n* -s [Panjabi *bhaṁgṛā*, a kind of folk dance] : popular music originating chiefly in England and marked by features of traditional Punjabi music and of disco

BHT \¦bē¦āchˈtē\ *n* -s [*b*utylated *h*ydroxy*t*oluene] : a phenolic antioxidant $C_{15}H_{24}O$ used esp. to preserve fats and oils in food, cosmetics, and pharmaceuticals

bi \ˈbī\ *adj* [by shortening] : BISEXUAL 1b — **bi** *n* -s

bi–* *or* **bio–*** *comb form* : biographical ⟨*biopic*⟩ : biographical and ⟨*biocritical*⟩

bi·a·fran \bēˈafrən, bī-, -äf-, -āf-\ *n* -s *cap* [*Biafra*, name assumed by seceding region of Nigeria (1967–1970) + E *-an*] : a native or inhabitant of the onetime secessionist Republic of Biafra — **biafran** *adj, usu cap*

bi·aly \bēˈalē\ *n, pl* **bialys** [Yiddish, short for *bialystoker*, fr. *bialystoker* of Bialystok, fr. *Białystok*, city in northeast Poland] : a flat roll that has a depressed center and is usu. covered with onion flakes

bias–belted tire \¦==¦==-\ *n* : a pneumatic tire with a belt (as of steel or fiber glass) around the tire under the tread and on top of the ply cords set diagonally to the center line of the tread

biased* *adj* **1** : tending to yield or select one outcome more frequently or less frequently than others in a statistical experiment ⟨a ~ coin⟩ ⟨a ~ sample⟩ **2** : having an expected value different from the quantity or parameter estimated ⟨a ~ estimate⟩ **3** : not having minimum probability of rejecting the null hypothesis when it is true ⟨a ~ statistical test⟩

bias–ply tire \¦==¦=-\ *n* : a pneumatic tire having crossed layers of ply cord set diagonally to the center line of the tread

bi·ath·lete \bīˈath͵lēt\ *n* -s [blend of *athlete* and *biathlon* (herein)] : an athlete who competes in a biathlon

bi·ath·lon \bīˈathlən, -͵län\ *n* -s [ISV ¹*bi-* + *-athlon* (as in *pentathlon*)] : a composite athletic contest consisting of cross-country skiing and rifle sharpshooting

bibb lettuce \ˈbib-\ *also* **bibb** *n, usu cap B* [after Major John *Bibb*, 19th cent. Am. grower] : a butterhead lettuce of a variety that has a small head and dark green color

bible–thump·er \ˈ==͵==\ *n, usu cap B* : an overzealous advocate of Christian fundamentalism — **bible–thump·ing** \ˈ==¦==\ *adj, usu cap B*

bib·lio·ther·a·py \͵biblēōˈtherəpē\ *n* [*biblio-* + *therapy*] : the use of reading materials for help in solving personal problems or for psychiatric therapy

bi·carpellate \(ˈ)bīˈkärpə͵lāt, -͵lət\ *adj* [¹*bi-* + *carpellate*] : having two carpels

bi·chon fri·se \¦bē¦shōⁿfrēˈzā\ *n, pl* **bichons frises** *or* **bichon frises** \-ōⁿfrēˈzā(z)\ [modif. of F *bichon à poil frisé* curly-furred lapdog] : any of a breed of small sturdy dogs of Mediterranean origin having a thick wavy white coat

bi·coastal \¦bī+\ *adj* [¹*bi-* + *coastal*] : of or relating to or living or working on both the East and West coasts of the U.S. ⟨pioneers in ~ living, continuing to write for the theater in New York, our home, and going out West periodically to do a movie —Betty Comden & Adolph Green⟩

bi·component \"+\ *adj* [¹*bi-* +²*component*] : being a fiber made of two polymers having slightly different physical properties so that the fiber has a permanent crimp and fabrics made from it have inherent bulk and stretchability

bi·cu·cul·line \(ˈ)bī¦k(y)ükyə͵lēn, -͵lən\ *n* -s [¹*bi-* + *cucull-* (fr. *cucullaria*, specific epithet of *Dicentra cucullaria*, Dutchman's-breeches, in which the substance occurs) + *-ine*] : a convulsant alkaloid $C_{20}H_{17}NO_6$ obtained esp. from plants of the family Fumariaceae and having the capacity to antagonize the action of gamma-aminobutyric acid in the central nervous system

bi·cultural \¦bī+\ *adj* [¹*bi-* + *cultural*] : of, relating to, or including two distinct cultures ⟨~ education⟩ — **bi·cul·tur·al·ism** \¦bī¦kəlch(ə)rə͵lizəm\ *n* -s

bicycle kick *n* : a kick in soccer that is executed by somersaulting backwards and moving the legs in a pedaling motion in order to strike the ball in midair

bicycle shorts *n* : tight-fitting shorts made usu. of spandex and worn orig. by bicyclists

bi·dialectal \"+\ *adj* [¹*bi-* + *dialectal*] : fluent in the use of two dialects of the same language — **bidialectal** *n* -s

bi·dialectalism \"+\ *n* -s : facility in using two dialects of the same language; *also* : the teaching of Standard English to pupils who normally use a nonstandard dialect

bi·di·a·lec·tal·ist \¦bī͵dīə¦lektələst\ *n* : a person who favors the promotion and development of bidialectalism by schools esp. for speakers whose primary dialects are not standard

bi·don·ville \͵bē͵dōⁿˈvē(ə)l\ *n* -s [F, fr. *bidon* metal can, canteen (fr. MF) + *ville* city, fr. OF, village — more at VILLAGE] : a settlement of jerry-built dwellings on the outskirts of a city (as in France or Africa)

bi·functional \¦bī+\ *adj* [¹*bi-* + *functional*] : having two functions ⟨~ neurons⟩; *esp* : DIFUNCTIONAL *herein* ⟨~ reagents⟩

big* *n* : MAJOR LEAGUE 1a — usu. used in pl. ⟨a chance to play in the ~*s*⟩

big bang *n* **1** *sometimes cap both Bs* : the cosmic explosion that marked the beginning of the universe according to the big bang theory — compare BIG CRUNCH *herein* **2** *often cap both Bs* : a development having a quick or strong impact ⟨the *big bang* of Cubism that changed the course of modern art —Grace H. Glueck⟩

big bang theory *n, sometimes cap both Bs* : a theory in astronomy: the universe originated billions of years ago in an explosion from a single point of nearly infinite energy density — compare STEADY STATE THEORY *herein*

big beat *n, often cap both Bs* : music (as rock and roll) characterized by a heavy persistent beat

big buck *n* : a large sum of money — usu. used in pl. ⟨looking to make *big bucks* as free agents —E.M.Swift⟩; often hyphenated in sing. when used attrib. ⟨a *big-buck* proposition⟩

big C \ˈ=͵=\ *n, usu cap B* : CANCER 2

big crunch *n, often cap B&C* : a hypothetical cosmological event in which all matter in the universe collapses to a singularity and which is posited to be a possible fate of the universe if the density of matter in it is sufficiently high — compare BIG BANG *herein*

big daddy *n, often cap B&D* : one preeminent esp. by reason of power, size, or seniority : one representing paternalistic authority

big deal *n* : something of special importance — sometimes used ironically as an interjection

bigfoot \ˈ=͵=\ *n, pl* **bigfeet** *or* **bigfoots** *often cap* [fr. the size of the footprints ascribed to it] **1** : SASQUATCH *herein* **2** : BIG SHOT

big hair *n* : hair that is styled and teased to occupy an unusually large amount of space above and around the head

big one* *n* : a thousand dollars ⟨the house . . . would go for two hundred *big ones* now —John Updike⟩

big science *n, often cap B&S* : large-scale scientific research consisting of projects funded usu. by a national government or group of governments

big–time \ˈ=͵=\ *adv* [*big time*] : in a major or large-scale way ⟨the new show bombed *big-time*⟩; *also* : to a large degree ⟨you owe me *big-time*⟩

bi·jec·tion \bīˈjekshən\ *n* -s [¹*bi-* + *-jection* (as in *injection*)] : a mathematical function that is a one-to-one and onto mapping — compare INJECTION *herein*, SURJECTION *herein* — **bi·jec·tive** \-ktiv, -ēv\ *adj*

bijou* *n* : something delicate, elegant, or highly prized

bike* *n* **1** : MOTORCYCLE **2** : MOTORBICYCLE 2 **3** : a light 2-wheeled cart used at horse shows and in harness races : SULKY **4** : STATIONARY BICYCLE *herein*

biker* *n* : MOTORCYCLIST; *esp* : one who belongs to an organized gang

bikeway \ˈ=͵=\ *n* : a thoroughfare for bicycles

bik·ie \ˈbīkē\ *n* -s [*bike* + *-ie*] : BIKER *herein*

bikini* *n* **1** : a man's brief swimsuit **2** : a man's or woman's low-cut briefs

bi·ki·nied \bəˈkēnēd\ *adj* [*bikini* + ¹*-ed*] : wearing a bikini

bi·layer \ˈbī+\ *n* [¹*bi-* + *layer*] : a film or membrane with two molecular layers ⟨a ~ of phospholipid molecules⟩ — **bilayer** *adj*

¹bi–level \ˈ=¦==\ *adj* [¹*bi-* + *level*] **1** : having two levels of freight or passenger space **2** : having two floors with a ground-level entry situated between the floors

²bi–level \"+\ *n* : a bi-level house

bilingual *adj* : of or relating to bilingual education

bilingual education *n* : education in an English-language school system in which minority students with little fluency in English are taught in their native tongue

bill·able \ˈbiləbəl\ *adj* [⁵*bill* + *-able*] : that can be billed ⟨a lawyer's ~ hours⟩ ⟨time ~ to a specific project⟩

billboard *vt* -ED/-ING/-S : to promote by a conspicuous display on or as if on a billboard

bil·li–bi *also* **bil·ly–bi** \¦bilē¦bē, -li¦-\ *n* -s [F, fr. *Billy B.*, nickname of William B. Leeds, Jr. †1972 Am. industrialist; fr. his partiality for it] : a soup made of mussel stock, white wine, and cream and served hot or cold

bi·lo·qui·al·ism \(ˈ)bī¦lōkwēə͵lizəm\ *n* -s [¹*bi-* + *-loquial* (as in *colloquial*) + *-ism*] : BIDIALECTALISM *herein* — **bi·lo·qui·al·ist** \-kwēələst\ *n or adj*

bim·bette \¦bim¦bet\ *n* -s [*bimbo* + *-ette*] : an attractive but empty-headed woman

bi·na·rism \ˈbīnə͵rizəm\ *n* -s [F *binarisme*, fr. *binaire* binary (fr. LL *binarius*) + *-isme* -ism — more at BINARY] : a mode of thought predicated on stable oppositions (as good and evil or male and female) that is seen in post-structuralist analysis as an inadequate approach to areas of difference; *also* : a specific dichotomy subscribed to or reinforced in such thought ⟨the ~*s* of West and East, of heterosexuality and homosexuality —J.A.Boone⟩

binary* *adj* **1** : involving a choice or condition of two alternatives only (as on-off or yes-no) **2** : involving binary notation **3** : utilizing two harmless ingredients that upon combining form a lethal substance (as a gas) ⟨~ weapon⟩

binary notation *n* : expression of a number with a base of 2 using only the digits 0 and 1 with each digital place representing a power of 2 instead of a power of 10 as in decimal notation

binary pulsar *n* : a binary system in which one star is a pulsar; *also* : the pulsar of such a system

binge \ˈbinj\ *vi* **binged; binged; bingeing** *or* **binging; binges** [*binge*, n.] : to go on a binge; *esp* : to go on an eating binge : eat compulsively or greedily esp. as a symptom of bulimia ⟨the urge to ~ on chocolate cookies —Sylvia Sachs⟩ ⟨a self-destructive pattern of smoking, starving, and ~*ing*—Carol Tavris⟩ — **binger** *n*

bio·accumulation \¦bīō+\ *n* [²*bi-* + *accumulation*] : the accumulation of a substance (as a pesticide) in a living organism — **bioaccumulate** *vb* — **bio·accumulative** *adj*

bio·active \"+\ *adj* [²*bi-* + *active*] : having an effect on a living organism ⟨~ materials⟩ ⟨~ molecules with potential for use as drugs⟩ — **bio·activity** \"+\ *n*

bio·astronautics \"+\ *n pl but sing or pl in constr* [²*bi-* + *astronautics*] : the medical and biological aspects of astronautics — **bioastronautical** \"+\ *adj*

bio·au·tog·ra·phy \͵bīōȯˈtägrəfē\ *n* -ES [²*bi-* + *autograph* + ²*-y*] : the identification or comparison of organic compounds separated by chromatography by means of their effect on living organisms and esp. microorganisms — **bio·au·to·graph** \-ˈȯd·ə͵graf\ *n* — **bio·au·to·graph·ic** \¦bīō͵ȯd·ə¦grafik\ *adj*

bio·availability \¦bīō+\ *n* [²*bi-* + *availability*] : the degree and rate at which a substance (as a drug) is absorbed into a living system or is made available at the site of physiological activity — **bioavailable** \"+\ *adj*

bio·chip \"+\ *n* [²*bi-* + ¹*chip* (integrated circuit)] : a hypothetical computer logic circuit or storage device in which the physical or chemical properties of large biological molecules (as proteins) are used to process information

bio·cid·al \¦bīō¦sīdᵊl\ *adj* [²*bi-* + *-cidal*] : destructive to life

bio·clean \¦bīō+\ *adj* [²*bi-* + *clean*] : free or almost free of harmful or potentially harmful organisms (as bacteria) ⟨a ~ room⟩

bio·compatibility \"+\ *n* [²*bi-* + *compatibility*] : the condition of being compatible with living tissue or a living system by not being toxic, injurious, or physiologically reactive and not causing immunological rejection — **bio·compatible** \"+\ *adj*

bio·control \"+\ *n* [²*bi-* + *control*] : BIOLOGICAL CONTROL

bio·conversion \"+\ *n* [²*bi-* + *conversion*] : conversion of organic materials (as wastes) into an energy source (as methane) by processes (as fermentation) involving living organisms

bio·critical \"+\ *adj* [²*bi-* (biographical) + *critical*] : of, relating to, or being a study of the life and work of someone (as a writer or moviemaker)

bio·degradable \¦bīō+\ *adj* [²*bi-* + *degradable* (herein)] : capable of being broken down esp. into innocuous products by the action of living things (as microorganisms) ⟨a ~ pesticide⟩ ⟨~ packaging⟩ — **bio·de·grad·abil·i·ty** \¦==͵==¦biləd·ē\ *n* —

biodegradable *n* — **bio·degradation** \¦bīō+\ *n* — **bio·degrade** \"+\ *vb*

bio·deterioration \"+\ *n* [²*bi-* + *deterioration*] : the breakdown of materials by microbial action

bio·diversity \"+\ *n* [²*bi-* + *diversity*] : biological diversity in an environment (as the whole world or a tropical rain forest) as indicated by numbers of different species of plants and animals

bio·electronics \¦bīō+\ *n pl but sing in constr* [²*bi-* + *electronics*] **1** : a branch of the life sciences that deals with electronic control of physiological function esp. as applied in medicine to compensate for defects of the nervous system **2** : a branch of science that deals with the role of electron transfer in biological processes — **bio·electronic** \"+\ *adj*

bioenergetics* *n pl but sing in constr* : a system of therapy that combines breathing and body exercises, psychological therapy, and the free expression of impulses and emotions and that is held to increase well-being by releasing blocked physical and psychic energy — **bioenergetic*** *adj*

bioengineering* *n* : the biological or medical application of engineering principles (as the theory of control systems in models of the nervous system) or engineering equipment (as in the construction of artificial organs) — called also *biomedical engineering* — **bio·engineer** \¦bīō+\ *n or vt*

bio·environmental \¦bīō+\ *adj* [²*bi-* + *environmental*] : of, relating to, affecting, or utilizing living things, their environment, and the interactions between them ⟨~ effects of pollution⟩ ⟨~ pest control⟩

bio·equivalence \"+\ *n* [²*bi-* + *equivalence*] : the property wherein two drugs with identical active ingredients (as a brand name drug and its generic equivalent) or two different dosage forms (as tablet and oral suspension) of the same drug possess similar bioavailability and produce the same effect at the site of physiological activity — **bio·equivalent** \"+\ *adj*

bio·ethics \"+\ *n pl but usu sing in constr* [²*bi-* + *ethics*] : a discipline dealing with the ethical implications of biological research and applications esp. in medicine — **bio·ethic** \"+\ *n* — **bio·ethical** \"+\ *adj* — **bio·ethicist** \"+\ *n* -s

bio·feedback \"+\ *n* [²*bi-* + *feedback*] : the technique of making unconscious or involuntary bodily processes (as heartbeat or brainwaves) perceptible to the senses (as by use of an oscilloscope) in order to manipulate them by conscious mental control

bio·film \"+\ *n* [²*bi-* + ¹*film*] : a thin usu. resistant layer of microorganisms (as bacteria) that form on and coat various surfaces (as of water pipes and catheters)

bio·fouling \"+\ *n* [²*bi-* + *fouling*] : the gradual accumulation of waterborne organisms (as bacteria or protozoa) on the surfaces of engineering structures in water that contributes to corrosion of the structures and to a decrease in efficiency of moving parts

bio·fuel \"+\ *n* [²*bi-* + ¹*fuel*] : a fuel (as wood or ethanol) composed of or produced from biological raw materials — compare FOSSIL FUEL *herein*

bio·gas \"+\ *n* [²*bi-* + *gas*] : a mixture of methane and carbon dioxide produced by the bacterial decomposition of animal and vegetable wastes and used as a fuel

biogenesis* *n* : the synthesis of chemical compounds or structures in the living organism — **biogenetic*** *adj* — **biogenetically*** *adv*

bio·geo·coe·nose *or* **bio·geo·coe·nose** \ˌbīō¦jēōsə¦nōz, -nōs\ *n* -s [Russ *biogeotsenoz*, fr. NL *bi-* ²*bi-* + *ge-* + *-coenosis* (as in *biocoenosis*)] : BIOGEOCOENOSIS *herein*

bio·geo·coe·no·sis *or* **bio·geo·ce·no·sis** \-¦jēōsə¦nōsə̇s\ *n, pl* **biogeocoeno·ses** *or* **biogeoceno·ses** \-ō,sēz\ [NL, fr. ²*bi-* + *ge-* + *-coenosis* (as in *biocoenosis*)] : ECOSYSTEM — **bio·geo·coe·notic** \-nädˌik\ *adj*

bio·hazard \¦bīō+\ *n* [²*bi-* + *hazard*] : a biological agent or condition (as an infectious organism or insecure laboratory procedures) that constitutes a hazard to humans or the environment; *also* : a hazard posed by such an agent or condition — **bio·hazardous** \"+\ *adj*

bio·informatics \"+\ *n pl but sing in constr* [²*bi-* + *informatics* (herein)] : the collection, classification, storage, and analysis of biochemical and biological information using computers esp. as applied in molecular genetics and genomics — **bio·in·for·mat·ic** \-ik\ *adj*

bio·inorganic \"+\ *adj* [²*bi-* + *inorganic*] : of, relating to, or concerned with the application of inorganic chemistry and its techniques to the study of biological processes and substances in which inorganic substances are important constituents or play important roles

bio·instrumentation \"+\ *n* [²*bi-* + *instrumentation*] : the development and use of instruments for recording and transmitting physiological data (as from astronauts in flight); *also* : the instruments themselves

biological* *also* **biologic*** *adj* : connected by direct genetic relationship rather than by adoption or marriage ⟨his ~ father⟩

biological clock *n* : an inherent timing mechanism in a living system that is inferred to exist in order to explain various cyclical behaviors and physiological processes

bio·marker \"+\ *n* [²*bi-* + *marker*] : a distinctive biological or biologically derived indicator (as a biochemical metabolite in the body or an organic compound in rock) of a process, event, or condition (as aging, disease, or oil formation)

biomass* *n* : plant materials and animal waste used as a source of fuel

bio·material \¦bīō+\ *n* [²*bi-* + *material*] : a natural or synthetic material (as a metal or polymer) that is suitable for introduction into living tissue esp. as part of a medical device (as an artificial heart valve or joint)

bio·medical \"+\ *adj* [²*bi-* + *medical*] **1** : of or relating to biomedicine ⟨~ studies⟩ **2** : of, relating to, or involving biological, medical, and physical science — **bio·medically** \"+\ *adv*

biomedical engineering *n* : BIOENGINEERING *herein* — **biomedical engineer** *n*

bio·medicine \¦bīō+\ *n* [²*bi-* + *medicine*] : medicine based on the application of the principles of the natural sciences and esp. biology and biochemistry; *also* : a branch of medical science concerned esp. with the capacity of human beings to survive and function in abnormally stressful environments and with the protective modification of such environments

bio·membrane \"+\ *n* [²*bi-* + *membrane*] : a membrane either on the surface or in the interior of a cell that is composed of protein and lipid esp. in sheets only a few molecules thick and that limits the diffusion and transport of materials

bio·mimetic \"+\ *adj* [ISV ²*bi-* + *mimetic*] : relating to, based on, or produced by the application of biomimetics ⟨a ~ catalyst⟩ ⟨synthetic ~ systems⟩ ⟨a ~ approach⟩

bio·mimetics \"+s\ *n pl but sing in constr* [*biomimetic* (herein) + *-ics*] : the study of the formation, structure, or function of biologically produced substances and materials (as enzymes or silk) and biological mechanisms and processes (as protein synthesis or photosynthesis) esp. for the purpose of synthesizing similar products by artificial mechanisms which mimic natural ones

bio·mineralization \"+\ *n* [²*bi-* + *mineralization*] : the formation or accumulation of minerals by organisms esp. into biological tissues or structures (as bones, teeth, and shells)

bio·molecule* *n* : an organic molecule and esp. a macromolecule (as a protein or nucleic acid) in a living organism — **bio·molecular** \"+\ *adj*

bi·on·ic \(ˈ)bī¦änik\ *adj* [²*bi-* + *-onic* (as in *electronic*)] **1** : of or relating to bionics **2 a (1)** : having natural biological capability or performance enhanced by or as if by electronic or electromechanical devices ⟨our future may lie not with the ~ man but with natural man —Susan Schiefelbein⟩ **(2)** : comprising or made up of artificial body parts that enhance or substitute for a natural biological capability ⟨a ~ heart⟩ **b** : better than ordinary : SUPER ⟨the developer of this ~ tuber . . . admits that it's not the perfect potato —*Saturday Rev.*⟩

bi·on·ics \bīˈäniks\ *n pl but sing in constr* [²*bi-* + *-onics* (as in *electronics*)] : a branch of science concerned with the application of data about the functioning of biological systems to the solution of engineering problems

bio·organic \¦bīō+\ *adj* [²*bi-* + *organic*] : of, relating to, or concerned with the organic chemistry of biologically significant substances

bio·pesticide \"+\ *n* [²*bi-* + *pesticide*] : a pesticide consisting of naturally occurring or genetically engineered microorganisms (as bacteria)

bio·pharmaceutics \"+\ *n pl but sing in constr* [²*bi-* + *pharmaceutics*] : the study of the relationships between the physical and chemical properties, the dosage, and the form of administration of a drug and its activity in the living body — **bio·pharmaceutical** \"+\ *adj or n*

bio·pic \ˈbīōˌpik\ *n* -s [²*bi-* (biographical) + *picture*] : a movie about the life of a usu. famous person

bio·politics \¦bīō+\ *n pl but sing or pl in constr* [²*bi-* + *politics*] : politics concerned with influencing environmental public policy and decision making — **bio·political** \"+\ *adj*

bio·polymer \"+\ *n* [²*bi-* + *polymer*] : a polymer (as a protein or a polysaccharide) formed in a biological system

biopsy *vt* -ED/-ING/-ES [*biopsy*, n.] : to perform a biopsy on ⟨confirmed liver tumors were *biopsied*—*Amer. Family Physician*⟩ ⟨used for *~ing* breast tissue suspected of being malignant —E.M.Kennedy⟩

bio·reactor \"+\ *n* [²*bi-* + *reactor*] : a device or apparatus in which living organisms and esp. bacteria synthesize useful substances (as interferon) or break down harmful ones (as in sewage)

bio·region \"+\ *n* [²*bi-* + *region*] : a region whose limits are naturally defined by topographic and biological features (as mountain ranges and ecosystems) — **bio·regional** \"+\ *adj*

bio·regionalism \"+\ *n* [blend of *bioregion* (herein) and *regionalism*] : an environmentalist movement to make political boundaries coincide with bioregions — **bio·regionalist** \"+\ *n or adj*

bio·remediation \"+\ *n* [²*bi-* + *remediation*] : the treatment of pollutants or waste (as in an oil spill, contaminated groundwater, or an industrial process) by the use of microorganisms (as bacteria) that break down the undesirable substances — **bio·remediate** \"+\ *vt*

bio·research \"+\ *n* [²*bi-* + *research*] : research in biological science

bio·rhythm \"+\ *n* [²*bi-* + *rhythm*] : an innately determined rhythmic biological process or function (as sleep behavior); *also* : an innate rhythmic determiner of such a process or function — **bio·rhythmic** \"+\ *adj* — **bio·rhythmically** \"+\ *adv* — **bio·rhythmicity** \"+\ *n*

BIOS *abbr* Basic Input/Output System

bio·safety \"+\ *n, often attrib* [²*bi-* + *safety*] : safety with respect to the effects of biological research on humans and the environment

bio·satellite \"+\ *n* [²*bi-* + *satellite*] : an artificial satellite for carrying a living human being, animal, or plant

bio·science \¦bīō+\ *n* [²*bi-* + *science*] : BIOLOGY 1a; *also* : LIFE SCIENCE *herein* — **bio·scientific** \"+\ *adj* — **bio·scientist** \"+\ *n*

bio·sensor \"+\ *n* [²*bi-* + *sensor*] : a device that is sensitive to a physical or chemical stimulus (as heat or a particular ion) and transmits information about a life process (as of an astronaut)

bio·solid \"+\ *n* [²*bi-* + ³*solid*] : solid organic matter recovered from a sewage treatment process and used esp. as fertilizer — usu. used in pl.

bio·speleology \"+\ *n* [²*bi-* + *speleology*] : the biological study of cave-dwelling organisms — **bio·speleologist** \"+\ *n*

bio·synthesize \"+\ *vt* [²*bi-* + *synthesize*] : to produce by biosynthesis

bio·tech \ˈbīōˌtek\ *n* -s [by shortening] : BIOTECHNOLOGY 1

bio·technical \¦bīō+\ *adj* [²*bi-* + *technical*] : BIOTECHNOLOGICAL

bio·technologist \¦bīō+\ *n* [*biotechnology* + ¹*-ist*] : a specialist in biotechnology

bio·telemetry \"+\ *n* [²*bi-* + *telemetry*] : the remote detection and measurement of a human or animal function, activity, or condition (as heart rate or body temperature) — **bio·telemetric** \"+\ *adj*

bio·transformation \"+\ *n* [²*bi-* + *transformation*] : the transformation of chemical compounds within a living system

bio·tur·ba·tion \ˌbīōtər¦bāshən\ *n* -s [ISV ²*bi-* + *-turbation* (as in E *congeliturbation*); orig. formed in G] : the restructuring of sedimentary deposits (as in a lake bottom or oceanic benthos) by moving organisms (as worms and burrowing clams) — **bio·tur·ba·ted** \-d.ə̇d\ *adj*

bipolar* *adj* **1** : characterized by the alternation of manic and depressive states ⟨a ~ disorder⟩ **2** : relating to, being, or using a transistor in which both electrons and holes are utilized as charge carriers

bi·quinary \(ˈ)bī+\ *adj* [¹*bi-* + *quinary*] : of, based on, being, or relating to a mixed-base system of numbers in which each decimal digit *n* is represented as a pair of digits *xy* where $n = 5x + y$ and *x* is written in base 2 as 0 or 1 and *y* is written in base 5 as 0, 1, 2, 3, or 4 ⟨decimal 9 is represented by ~ 14⟩

birch·er \ˈbərchər\ *n* -s *usu cap* [John Birch Society, conservative political organization + E *-er*] : a member or adherent of the John Birch Society — **birch·ite** \-ˌchīt, *usu* -īd.+V\ *n or adj, usu cap*

bird* *n* **1** : something (as an aircraft, rocket, or satellite) resembling a bird esp. in flying or being aloft **2** : an obscene gesture of contempt made by pointing the middle finger upward while keeping the other fingers down — usu. used with *the*; called also *finger* **3** [by shortening fr. *bird lime*, rhyming slang for *time*] *Brit* : a term in prison

birman* *n, usu cap* : a long-haired domestic cat of a breed originating in Burma and resembling the Siamese in eye color and coat pattern but much stockier in build and with paws symmetrically marked with white

birr \ˈbi(ə)r\ *n, pl* **birr** *also* **birrs** [Amharic *bərr*, lit., silver] **1** : the basic monetary unit of Ethiopia — see MONEY table *in the Dict* **2** : a note representing one birr

birth *adj* [*birth*, n.] : BIOLOGICAL *herein* ⟨spent years searching for her ~ parents⟩

birth control pill *n* : any of various preparations that usu. contain a combination of a progestin (as norethindrone) and an estrogen (as ethinyl estradiol) but sometimes only a progestin, are taken orally esp. on a daily basis, and act as contraceptives typically preventing ovulation by suppressing secretion of gonadotropins (as luteinizing hormone) — called also *contraceptive pill, oral contraceptive*

birth defect *n* : a physical or biochemical defect (as cleft palate or phenylketonuria) that is present at birth and may be inherited or environmentally induced

birthing center *n* : a facility usu. staffed by nurse-midwives that provides a less institutionalized setting than a hospital for women who wish to deliver by natural childbirth

birthing room *n* : a comfortably furnished hospital room where both labor and delivery take place and in which the baby usu. remains during the hospital stay

birth·right *adj* [*birthright*, n.] : being a member of a group by birth ⟨a ~ Quaker⟩

biryani *also* **biriani** \bi(ə)rˈyänē, ˌbirēˈänē, -i\ *n* -s [Hindi *biryānī*, fr. *biryān* roasted, fr. Per; prob. akin to MPer *barshtan* to roast, Skt *bhṛjjati* he roasts — more at FRY] : an Indian dish of meat, fish, or vegetables cooked with rice flavored esp. with saffron or turmeric

bis·cot·to \bə̇ˈskäd.ō, -ä(ˌ)tō\ *n, pl* **biscot·ti** \-äd.ē, -ä(ˌ)tē, -i\ [It, biscuit, cookie, fr. (*pane*) *biscotto*, lit., bread baked twice, fr. *pane* bread + *biscotto* twice-baked, fr. *bis-* twice (fr. L *bis*) + *cotto*, past part. of *cuocere* to bake, cook, fr. (assumed) VL *cocere*, alter. of L *coquere* — more at BIS, COOK] : a crisp cookie or biscuit of Italian origin flavored usu. with anise and filberts or almonds

bi·stable \(ˈ)bī+\ *adj* [¹*bi-* + *stable*] : having two stable states ⟨a ~ electrical element⟩ — **bi·stability** \¦bī+\ *n*

bi·static \"+\ *adj* [¹*bi-* + *static*] : involving the use of a transmitter and receiver at separate locations ⟨~ radar⟩

bi–swing \"+\ *adj* [¹*bi-* + *swing*; perh. because of the freedom allowed by this garment] *of a coat or jacket* : made with a pleat or gusset at the back of the arms to permit more freedom of movement

bit* *n* [³*bit*] **1** : a characteristic situation, appearance, behavior, or action ⟨book burning, unless it's an embassy library, is strictly a Fascist ~ —Gene Williams⟩ ⟨I never have dates or call up a girl and meet her and take her out, that whole ~ —Arthur Garfunkle⟩ **2** : an action or mode of behavior likened to a theater role or sketch ⟨starts in with one of her crazy lunatic *~s*—Judith Rossner⟩ **3** : subject under consideration : MATTER ⟨as for the ~ about marriage being a woman's be-all and end-all —Letty C. Pogrebin⟩ — often used as a general indirect reference to something specified or implied ⟨the blouson top . . . matches exactly. The blouson ~ is piped in suede —Lois Long⟩

bit* *n* [⁷*bit*] : the physical representation (as in a computer tape or memory) of a bit by an electrical pulse, a magnetized spot, or a hole whose presence or absence indicates data

bitch·in' *also* **bitch·in** *or* **bitch·en** \ˈbichən\ *adj* [prob. short for *sonofabitching*, fr. *son of a bitch* + ¹*-ing* (perh. as euphemism for *fucking*)] **1** *slang* : remarkably bad : DETESTABLE ⟨of all the ~ luck⟩ **2** *slang* : remarkably good or cool ⟨a ~ car⟩

bite* *vb* — **bite the bullet** : to face up to an unpleasant situation by taking action ⟨we are now seeing responsible industries beginning to *bite the bullet* and clean up waste sites —Harold Gershowitz⟩

bite* *n* **1** : SOUND BITE *herein* ⟨a 10-second news ~⟩ ⟨answers questions in quick *~s* —Monica Collins⟩ **2** : a brief catchy presentation that is usu. one of a series ⟨information *~s*⟩ ⟨video *~s*⟩

bite plate *n* : a removable usu. plastic dental appliance used in orthodontics and prosthodontics to assist in therapy or diagnosis: as **a** : a U-shaped device worn in the upper or lower jaw and used esp. to reposition the jaw or prevent bruxism by covering the occlusal surfaces of the teeth so that they cannot be brought into contact **b** : RETAINER *herein*

bite–size \ˈ=ˌ=\ *also* **bite–sized** \ˈ=¦=\ *adj* **1** : of a size that can be eaten in one bite ⟨*bite-size* pieces of chicken⟩ **2** : being or made small or brief esp. so as to be easily manageable ⟨*bite-size* tasks⟩ ⟨*bite-size* essays⟩

bit–map \ˈ=ˌ=\ *n* **1** : an array of binary data representing a bit-mapped image or display; *also* : a file containing such data **2** : a bit-mapped image or display

bit–mapped \ˈ=¦=\ *adj* : of, relating to, or being a digital image or display for which an array of binary data specifies the value of each pixel ⟨*bit-mapped* graphics⟩

bi·unique \(ˈ)bī+\ *adj* [¹*bi-* + *unique*] : being a correspondence between two sets that is one-to-one in both directions ⟨the ~ correspondence between the points on a straight line and the real numbers⟩ ⟨a phonemic transcription should be ~⟩ — **bi·uniqueness** \"+\ *n*

bi·zar·ro \bə̇ˈzärō\ *adj* [alter. (prob. influenced by *Bizarro*, grotesque duplicate of Superman in the *Superman* comic-book series who inhabits a "bizarro world") of *bizarre*] : characterized by a bizarre, fantastic, or unconventional approach : OUTLANDISH ⟨the director's ~ vision⟩ ⟨a ~ comedy⟩ — **bizarro** *n* -s

bi·zen ware \bēˈzen-\ *n, usu cap B* [part trans. of Jap *bizen-yaki*, fr. *Bizen*, former province in Japan, where it was made + Jap *yaki* pottery] : a Japanese ceramic ware produced since the 14th century that is typically a dark bronzy stoneware often with smears of natural ash glaze

black* *adj* **1** : of or relating to the Afro-American people or their culture ⟨~ literature⟩ ⟨~ college⟩ ⟨~ pride⟩ ⟨~ studies⟩ **2** : typical or representative of the most readily perceived characteristics of black culture ⟨trying to sound ~⟩ ⟨played *~er* jazz⟩ **3 a** : of or relating to covert intelligence operations **b** : employed in covert intelligence operations **4** : characterized by black humor ⟨that ~, bitterly funny book, full of pain —Edmund Morris⟩

black* *vt, chiefly Brit* : to declare (as a business or industry) subject to boycott by trade-union members

black and tan* *n, chiefly Brit* : a drink consisting of a dark beer (as stout or porter) and ale or beer of a paler color

black–and–white \ˈ==ˈ=\ *n* : SQUAD CAR

black angus *n, usu cap B&A* : ABERDEEN ANGUS

black bean* *n* : a black soybean commonly used usu. fermented in Oriental cuisine

¹black belt *n* **1** : an area characterized by rich black soil **2** *often cap both Bs* : an area densely populated by blacks

²black belt \ˈ=ˈ=\ *n* [so called fr. the color of the belt of the uniform worn by the holder of the rating] **1** : a rating of expert in various arts of self-defense (as judo and karate) **2** : one who holds a black belt

blackboard jungle *n* : an urban school whose students are generally belligerent and disorderly

black box *n* **1** : a usu. complicated electronic device that functions and is packaged as a unit and whose internal mechanism is usu. hidden from or mysterious to the user; *broadly* : anything that has mysterious or unknown internal functions or mechanisms ⟨the secrecy of Soviet society makes it a *black box* to Western observers —James Fallows⟩ ⟨the cancer cell is no longer an impenetrable *black box* —R.A.Weinberg⟩ **2** : a crash-worthy device in aircraft for recording cockpit conversations and flight data; *also* : a similar device in another type of vehicle (as an automobile or ship) esp. for recording vehicle performance data

black comedy *n* [trans. of F *comédie noire*] : comedy that employs black humor; *also* : a situation or a series of events that resembles black comedy ⟨his odyssey from illness to diagnosis was a *black comedy* —Glenn Garelik⟩

black dwarf *n, pl* **black dwarfs** : a very cool star that emits no detectable light and that is the cooled remnant of a white dwarf; *also* : BROWN DWARF

black·ened \ˈblakənd\ *adj* [fr. past part. of *blacken*] : coated with a mixture of cayenne pepper and other spices and cooked in a frying pan over extremely high heat ⟨~ redfish⟩

black english *n, usu cap B & cap E* : a nonstandard variety of English spoken by some Afro-Americans — called also *Black English vernacular*

black forest cake *n, usu cap B&F* [*Black Forest*, region in Germany] : a rich usu. chocolate layer cake with cherries

black hat *n* **1** : VILLAIN 5 **2** : a mark or symbol of villainy ⟨corporate executives tired of wearing the *black hat* for their environmentalist opponents⟩

black hole *n* **1** : a hypothetical celestial object that has a gravitational field so strong that light cannot escape it and that is believed to be created in the collapse of a very massive star **2** : one that resembles a black hole: as **a** : one into which something disappears ⟨do not foresee the international debt situation dragging the banking system into a financial *black hole* —*Business Week*⟩ **b** : something unseen or undetected ⟨the *black hole* of error revealed —Mavis Gallant⟩ **c** : an empty space : VOID ⟨paused, as if he had suddenly come upon a *black hole* in the space of his ambition —Anatole Broyard⟩

black humor *n* [trans. of F *humour noir*] : humor marked by the use of usu. morbid, ironic, grotesquely comic episodes — **black–humored** \¦=¦==\ *adj* — **black humorist** *n*

black ice* *n* **1** : a thin film of ice on paved surfaces (as roads) that is difficult to see **2** : nearly transparent ice on a body of water

blacklight trap \ˈ=ˌ=ˌ=\ *n* : an insect trap using a form of black light for attraction

black lung *n* : a disease of the lungs caused by habitual inhalation of coal dust (as by miners) — called also *black lung disease*

black money *n* : income (as from a black market or from gambling) that is not reported to the government for tax purposes
black muslim *n, usu cap B&M* : a member of a chiefly black group that professes Islamic religious belief
black nationalist *n, often cap B&N* : one of a group of militant blacks who advocate separatism from the whites and the formation of self-governing black communities — **black nationalism** *n, often cap B&N*
blackness* *n* **1** : the aggregate of qualities characteristic of the black races **2** : NEGRITUDE *herein*
black panther *n, usu cap B&P* : a member of an organization of militant American blacks
black power *n, often cap B&P* : the power of American blacks esp. as applied to the achieving of their political and economic rights
black smoker *n* : a vent in a geologically active region of the sea floor from which issues superheated water laden with minerals (as sulfide precipitates)
blacks·ploi·ta·tion *var of* BLAXPLOITATION *herein*
black studies *n pl* : studies (as in history and literature) relating to the culture of American blacks
blacktown \ˈ=ˌ=\ *n* : the predominantly black section of a city
blade* *vi* : to skate on in-line skates — **blad·er** \-ər\ *n* -S
blahs \ˈbläz, -ȧz\ *n pl* [²*blah* + ¹*-s*] **1** : a feeling of boredom, lethargy, or general dissatisfaction — usu. used with *the* **2** : a state marked by a lack of excitement, originality, activity, or effectiveness — usu. used with *the* ⟨peppers banish the recipe ~ —Babs S. Harrison⟩
blanc de blancs *or* **blanc de blanc** \ˌblänⁿdəˈblänⁿ\ *n, pl* **blanc de blancs** [F, lit., white from whites] : a still or sparkling white wine made from white grapes only
blanc de noirs *or* **blanc de noir** \ˌblänⁿdəˈnwär\ *n, often cap B&N* [F, lit., white from blacks] : a still or sparkling white wine that is made from red or black grapes
blasé* *also* **blase** *adj* : UNCONCERNED
blast* *n* **1** : an enjoyably exciting experience, occasion, or event ⟨have a ~⟩; *esp* : PARTY ⟨a beer ~⟩ **2** : HOME RUN
blast* *vi* : to proceed rapidly ⟨~ around . . . at moderately high speeds on windy little roads —P.J. O'Rourke⟩ ~ *vt* : to play loudly ⟨the stereo *~ed* old show tunes⟩
blast cell \ˈblast-\ *or* **blast** *n* -S [*-blast*] : an immature cell; *esp* : a usu. large blood-cell precursor (as a myeloblast) that is in the earliest stage of development in which it is recognizably committed to development along a particular cell lineage
blast crisis \ˈ"+\ *also* **blast·ic crisis** \-ik-\ *n* [*blastic* fr. *blast* (herein) + ¹*-ic*] : the terminal stage of chronic myelogenous leukemia that is characterized by a marked increase in the proportion of blast cells, by fever and pain in the bones, and by increased severity of anemia, thrombocytopenia, and splenomegaly
blastogenesis* *n* : the transformation of lymphocytes into larger cells capable of undergoing mitosis
blas·to·my·cin \ˌblastōˈmīsᵊn\ *n* -S [*blastomyc-* (fr. NL *Blastomyces dermatitidis*, fungus species) + *-in* — more at BLASTOMYCES] : a preparation of growth products of the causative agent (*Blastomyces dermatitidis*) of No. American blastomycosis that is used esp. to test for this disease
blax·ploi·ta·tion *also* **blacks·ploi·ta·tion** \ˌblakˌsplȯiˈtāshən\ *n* -S [blend of *blax* (alter. of *blacks*) and *exploitation*] : the exploitation of blacks by producers of black-oriented films
bleb* *n* : something resembling a bleb; *esp* : a vesicular outpocketing of a plasma or nuclear membrane — **bleb·bing** *n* -S
bleed* *n* : the escape of blood from vessels : HEMORRHAGE ⟨a massive gastrointestinal ~⟩
¹bleep \ˈblēp\ *n* -S [imit.] **1** : a short high-pitched sound (as from electronic equipment) **2** — used in place of an obscene or vulgar expletive
²bleep \"\ *vt* -ED/-ING/-S : BLIP *herein*
³bleep \"\ *interj* — used in place of an expletive
bleeper \-ə(r)\ *n* -S [¹*bleep* (herein) + ²*-er*] *chiefly Brit* : a device that emits bleep signals
blended family *n* : a family that includes children from a previous marriage of one or both spouses
bleo·my·cin \ˌblēəˈmīsᵊn\ *n* -S [alter. of *phleomycin* antibiotic derived from the same source, from *phleo-* (of unknown origin) + *-mycin*] : a mixture of glycoprotein antibiotics derived from a streptomyces (*Streptomyces verticillus*) and used in the form of its sulfate as an antineoplastic agent
bleph·a·ro·plas·ty \ˈblefərōˌplastē\ *n* -ES [*blephar-* + *-plasty*] : plastic surgery on an eyelid esp. to remove fatty or excess tissue
BLEVE *abbr, sometimes not cap* boiling liquid expanding vapor explosion
blind side* *n* : the side away from which one is looking
blindside *vt* **1** : to hit from the blind side **2** : to strike suddenly and unexpectedly : surprise unpleasantly ⟨insure that we don't get *blindsided* by some unfortunate sudden development —*New Yorker*⟩
blind trust *n* : an arrangement by which a person in a sensitive position protects himself from possible conflict of interest charges by placing his financial affairs in the hands of a fiduciary and giving up all right to know about or intervene in their handling
blip* *n* **1** : an interruption of sound occurring as a result of blipping **2** : a transient sharp move up or down (as in a quantity commonly shown on a graph) ⟨the systems account for a ~ in sales⟩ **3** : something relatively small or inconsequential within a larger context ⟨made a ~ on the pop music scene in the 1960's —Rob Hoerburger⟩ ⟨a tiny ~ of civilization in the midst of the vast . . . wilderness —Dean Kuipers⟩
blip* *vt* : to remove (recorded matter) from a magnetic tape so that there is an interruption in the reproduced sound or picture ⟨swearwords *blipped* by a censor⟩
bliss out *vi* **blissed out; blissed out; bliss·ing out; bliss·es out** : to experience bliss or ecstasy — **blissed out** \ˈblist-\ *adj*
blister pack *n* : a package holding and displaying merchandise in a clear plastic case sealed to a sheet of cardboard
blitz* *n* : a rush on a passer in football by the linebackers or defensive backs
blitz* *vb* ~ *vt* **1** : to rush (a passer) in football from a position as a linebacker or defensive back **2** : to have (as a linebacker) blitz ~ *vi of a linebacker or defensive back* : to make a rush on the passer in football — **blitz·er** *n* -S
bl la·cer·tae object \-ləˈsərtē-, -d·ē-\ *also* **bl lac object** \-ˈlak-\ *n, usu cap B & both Ls* [*BL Lacertae*, original designation for the first such object to be discovered, fr. *BL*, designation for the 89th variable star in a constellation + NL *Lacertae*, gen. of *Lacerta*, a constellation] : a celestial object that is similar to a quasar in the intensity of its radiation and is recognizable by its radio emissions
block* *vt* : to work out (as the principal positions and movements) for the performers (as of a play); *also* : to work out the players' positions and movements for (as a scene or a play) — often used with *out*
block·bust·ing \ˈ=ˌbəstiŋ\ *n* -S [¹*block* (space in a city) + *-busting*, gerund of ²*bust*] : profiteering by first inducing white property owners to sell hastily and often at a loss by appeals to fears of depressed values because of threatened minority encroachment and then reselling at inflated prices — **block·bust·er** \-ə(r)\ *n*
block club *n* : an organized group of residents in an urban neighborhood
block grant* *n* : an unrestricted federal grant
blocking* *n* : the planning and working out of the principal positions and movements of stage performers (as for a play) ⟨camera shots, musical cues, ~, makeup, costumes and the rest were run through —Robert Jacobson⟩
blood* *n* : a black American male — used esp. among blacks
blood–brain barrier \ˈ=ˈ=-\ *n* : a naturally occurring barrier created by the modification of brain capillaries (as by reduction in fenestration and formation of tight cell-to-cell contacts) that prevents many substances from leaving the blood and crossing the capillary walls into the brain tissues
blood doping *n* : a technique for temporarily improving athletic performance in which oxygen-carrying red blood cells previously withdrawn from an athlete are injected back just before an event — called also *blood packing*
blood thinner *n* : a drug used to prevent the formation of blood clots by hindering coagulation of the blood
bloody–minded \ˈ==ˈ==\ *adj* **1** : willing to accept violence or bloodshed **2** *often Brit* : stubbornly contrary or obstructive : CANTANKEROUS — **bloody–mindedness** *n* -ES *chiefly Brit*
bloom* *n* : an abundant or excessive growth of plankton
bloop* *vt* : to hit (a fly ball) usu. just beyond the infield in baseball ⟨*~ed* a single to center field⟩
bloop \ˈblüp\ *n* -S *often attrib* [*bloop*, v. (herein)] : BLOOPER 3b
blot* *n* : a sheet of cellulose nitrate or nylon that contains spots of immobilized macromolecules (as of DNA, RNA, or protein) or their fragments and is used to identify specific components of the spots by applying a molecular probe (as a complementary nucleic acid or a radiolabeled antibody) — see NORTHERN BLOT *herein*, SOUTHERN BLOT *herein*, WESTERN BLOT *herein*
blouse* *vb* ~ *vt* : to cause to blouse ⟨trousers are *bloused* over the boots⟩ ⟨big, loose shapes (which the fainthearted may ~ over a belt) —Anne-Marie Shiro⟩
blou·son \ˈblau̇ˌzän, -ˌsän, -ˌsᵊn; ˈblüˌzän\ *n* -S [F, dim. of *blouse* blouse] : a garment (as a dress or blouse) having a close waistband with a blousing of material over it
blow* *vt* **1** : FELLATE *herein* — usu. considered vulgar **2** : SMOKE ⟨a few had started *~ing* grass in their early teens —Daniel Greene⟩ **3** : to defeat decisively ⟨has simply *blown* competitors from the field —Roger Sale⟩ **4** : to move quickly ⟨~ past him in the final yards⟩ — **blow one's cool** : to lose one's composure — **blow one's cover** : to reveal one's real identity : give one's cover away — **blow one's mind 1** : to overwhelm with wonder or bafflement **2** : to undergo or cause to undergo a psychedelic experience — **blow out of the water** : to show to be incorrect or inferior ⟨wanted to *blow* the old truths *out of the water*⟩
blow* *n* [perh. fr. ⁵*blow*] *slang* : COCAINE
blow away* *vt* **1** : to kill by gunfire : shoot dead **2** : to impress very strongly and usu. favorably ⟨a single idea, well conceived and well executed, can still *blow* us all *away* —*advt*⟩ **3** : to defeat or outperform by a wide margin
blow–dried \ˈ=ˌ=\ *adj* : having blow-dried hair; *also* : being well-groomed but superficial and without substance ⟨a set fairly oozing with *blow-dried* men and bleached bombshell women —Elaine Warren⟩
blow–dry \(ˈ)=ˌ=\ *vb* [back-formation fr. *blow-dryer*] *vt* : to dry and usu. style (hair) with a blow-dryer ~ *vi* : to dry hair with a blow-dryer — **blow–dry** \ˈ=ˌ=\ *n*
blow–dryer \ˈ=ˌ==\ *n* -S [¹*blow* + ²*drier*] : a handheld hair dryer
blower* *n, Brit* : TELEPHONE
blowjob \ˈ=ˌ=\ *n* [*blow*, v. (herein) + ¹*job*] : the act of stimulating the penis orally usu. to orgasm — usu. considered vulgar
blow off* *vt* **1** : to refuse to take notice of, honor, or deal with : IGNORE ⟨decided to *blow off* two billion viewers —Harry Homburg⟩ **2** : to fail to attend or show up for ⟨*blew off* an official dinner⟩
blowout* *n* : an easy one-sided victory
blow out* *vt* **1** : to defeat easily **2** : to damage severely ⟨she *blew out* her right knee in the marathon⟩
BLS \ˌbē(ˌ)elˈes\ *abbr or n* -S **1** : a bachelor of liberal studies **2** : a bachelor of library science
BLT \ˌbē(ˌ)elˈtē\ *n* -S : a bacon, lettuce, and tomato sandwich
blue box *n* : an electronic device attached to a telephone that emits signals enabling the user to make illegal free long-distance calls
blue corn *n* : Indian corn that has bluish kernels used to make flour and that is grown esp. in the southwestern U.S.
blue–eyed* *adj* **1** : performed by whites ⟨listening to *blue-eyed* soul⟩ **2** : being white ⟨a *blue-eyed* soul singer⟩
blue flu *n* [fr. the color of a police uniform] : SICK-OUT *herein*; *specif* : a sick-out staged by policemen
bluegrass* *n* [fr. the *Blue Grass Boys*, performing group, fr. *Bluegrass State*, nickname of Kentucky] : country music played on unamplified stringed instruments (as banjo, fiddle, guitar, and mandolin) and characterized by free improvisation and close usu. high-pitched harmony — **blue·grass·er** \ˈ=ˌ=ə(r)\ *n* -S
blue heaven *n, slang* : amobarbital or its sodium derivative in a blue tablet or capsule
blue point *adj, of a domestic cat* : having a bluish cream body coat with dark gray points
blueshift *n* : the displacement of the spectrum of an approaching celestial body toward shorter wavelengths as a consequence of the Doppler effect — compare RED SHIFT *in the Dict* — **blue-shift·ed** \ˈ=ˌ==\ *adj*
bluesman \ˈ=(ˌ)=\ *n, pl* **bluesmen** : a musician who plays or sings the blues
blues–rock \ˈ=ˈ=\ *n* : music combining blues and rock 'n' roll
bluesy \ˈblüzē, -i\ *adj* -ER/-EST [²*blues* + ¹*-y*] : resembling, characteristic of, or suited to the blues
blunt* *n* : a cigar in which part or all of the tobacco has been replaced by marijuana
blunt trauma *n* : an injury caused by a blunt object or surface ⟨the patient died of *blunt trauma* to the head⟩
blusher* *n* : a cosmetic applied to the face to give a usu. pink color or to accent the cheekbones
blush wine *n* : any of various pinkish table wines
b lymphocyte *n, usu cap B* [bone-marrow-derived *lymphocyte*] : B CELL *herein*
BM* *abbr or n* : a bachelor of music
BME \ˌbē(ˌ)emˈē\ *abbr or n* -S **1** : a bachelor of mechanical engineering **2** : a bachelor of mining engineering **3** : a bachelor of music education
BMX *abbr* bicycle motocross
BO* *abbr* best offer
board* *n* **1** : BLACKBOARD **2 a boards** *pl* : the low wooden wall enclosing a hockey rink **b** (1) : BACKBOARD — usu. used in pl. (2) : a rebound in basketball **c** : SURFBOARD **3** : a sheet of insulating material carrying circuit elements and terminals so that it can be inserted in an electronic apparatus (as a computer) **4** : MIXING BOARD *herein* **5** : BULLETIN BOARD *herein* — **on board*** : in or into a working relationship
boardsailing \ˈ=ˌ=\ *n* [¹*board* + *sailing*, fr. gerund of ²*sail*] : WINDSURFING *herein* — **boardsailor** \ˈ=ˌ==\ *n*
boat* *n* : BOAT FORM
boa·tel \(ˈ)bōˈtel\ *n* -S [blend of *boat* and *hotel*] : a waterside hotel equipped with docks to accommodate persons traveling by boat
boat people *n pl* : refugees fleeing by boat
boat–rock·er \ˈ=ˌ==\ *n* : one that rocks the boat : one who challenges the status quo ⟨as an unreconstructed *boat rocker*, I always question conventional wisdom —Harvey Steiman⟩ — **boat–rock·ing** \ˈ=ˌ==\ *adj or n*
boat shoe *n* [so called fr. the original use of such shoes on the decks of small boats] : a canvas or leather low-cut shoe with a sole designed to prevent slipping
bob·bing \ˈbäbiŋ\ *n* -S [⁹*bob*] : BOBSLEDDING
bocage* *n* : a supporting and ornamental background (as of shrubbery and flowers) for a ceramic figure
bock·wurst \ˈbäkˌ=\ *n* -S [G, fr. *bock* bock beer + *wurst* sausage; fr. the traditional consumption of the sausage with bock beer around the time of the Feast of Corpus Christi — more at BOCK BEER, BRATWURST] : a seasoned sausage made chiefly of veal
bod* *n* [by shortening] : BODY
bodh·ran \ˈbō(ˌ)rän, -rən\ *n* -S [IrGael *bodhrán*, fr. MIr, fr. *bodar* rough-sounding, lit., deaf, fr. OIr — more at BOTHER] : a shallow handheld Irish drum
bodice ripper *n* : a historical or Gothic romance typically featuring scenes in which the heroine is subjected to violence
body bag *n* : a zippered bag (as of rubber) in which a human corpse is placed (as for transportation)
body builder *n* : one who engages in body building
body building *n* : the developing of the body through physical exercises and diet; *specif* : the developing of the physique for competitive exhibition
body checker *n* : one that body checks
body clock *n* : the internal mechanisms that schedule periodic bodily functions and activities — usu. not used technically
body count *n* **1** : a count of dead bodies (as of killed enemy soldiers) **2** : the number of persons involved in a particular activity
body language *n* : the bodily movements, gestures, and mannerisms by which a person or animal communicates with others
body mechanics *n pl but sing or pl in constr* : systematic exercises designed esp. to develop coordination, endurance, and poise
body shirt *n* **1** : a woman's close-fitting top made with a sewn-in or snapped crotch **2** : a close-fitting shirt or blouse
body stocking *n* : a usu. sheer close-fitting one-piece garment for the torso that often has sleeves and legs
bodysuit \ˈ==ˌ=\ *n* : a close-fitting one-piece garment for the torso
bodysurf \ˈ=ˌ=\ *vi* : to ride on a wave without a surfboard by planing on the chest and stomach — **bodysurfer** \ˈ==ˌ==\ *n*
bodywork* *n* : therapeutic touching or manipulation of the body by using specialized techniques
body wrap *n* : a full-body treatment for the skin usu. offered at a spa or salon
boff \ˈbäf, ˈbȯf\ *vt* -ED/-ING/-S [prob. fr. slang *boff* hit, strike, alter. of ²*buff*] : to have sexual intercourse with — often considered vulgar
bof·fo \ˈbäf(ˌ)ō\ *adj* [*boffo*, n., short for *boffola*] : extraordinarily successful : SENSATIONAL
bog \ˈbäg\ *n* -S [short for obs. *boghouse* privy, fr. *bog* to defecate (of unknown origin) + ¹*house*] *Brit* : TOILET, LOO
bo·gart \ˈbōˌgärt\ *vt* -ED/-ING/-S [prob. after Humphrey *Bogart* †1957 Am. film actor] : BULLY, INTIMIDATE ⟨activists *~ed* their way into the . . . offices —Sarah Ferguson⟩
¹bo·ho \ˈbōhō\ *adj* [²*Bohemian* + ¹*-o*] : BOHEMIAN 3
²boho *n* -S : BOHEMIAN 2
bohr effect \ˈbō(ə)r-, ˈbȯ(ə)r-\ *n, usu cap B* [after Christian *Bohr* †1911 Dan. physiologist] : the decrease in oxygen affinity of a respiratory pigment (as hemoglobin or hemocyanin) in response to decreased blood pH resulting from increased carbon dioxide concentration
bohr·i·um \ˈbōrēəm, ˈbȯr-\ *n* -S [NL, fr. Niels *Bohr* †1962 Dan. physicist + NL *-ium*] : a short-lived radioactive element of atomic number 107 that is produced artificially — symbol *Bh*
boiloff** \ˈ=ˌ=\ *n* -S : the vaporization of a liquid (as liquid oxygen)
bok choy \ˈbäkˈchȯi, -ˈjȯi\ *n* [Chin (Cant) *baahk-choi*, lit., white vegetable] : a Chinese cabbage (*Brassica chinensis*) that forms an open head with long white stalks and green leaves
bok·mål \ˈbu̇kˌmȯl, ˈbōk-\ *n* -S *usu cap* [Norw, fr. *bok* book (fr. ON *bōk*) + *mål* language, fr. ON *māl* — more at BOOK, MAIL] : RIKSMÅL
bol·li·to mis·to \bȯˈlēd·ōˈmē(ˌ)stō, -ētōˈ-\ *n, pl* **bol·li·ti mis·ti** \-ēd·ēˈmēstē, -ētēˈ-\ [It, lit., mixed boiled dish] : a dish of mixed meats (as lamb, veal, beef, and sausage) boiled with vegetables
bo·lo tie \ˈbō(ˌ)lō-\ *or* **bola tie** *n* [prob. fr. ¹*bola*] : a cord fastened around the neck with an ornamental clasp and worn as a necktie
bolus* *n* : a dose of a substance (as a drug) given intravenously; *specif* : a large dose given for the purpose of rapidly achieving the needed therapeutic concentration in the bloodstream
bomb* *n* **1** : ATOM BOMB; *also* : nuclear weapons in general — usu. used with *the* ⟨when the ~ has taken the place of God . . . as the ultimate disposer of the earth —H.C.Schonberg⟩ **2** : an unsuccessful performance or production : FLOP ⟨a terrible ~ of a movie —Paul Newman⟩; *broadly* : FAILURE **3** *chiefly Brit* : an old car **4** *Brit* : a lot of money : FORTUNE ⟨demonstrating how to avoid the flu and save a ~ on the central heating —Richard Gordon⟩ **5** *Brit* : a great success : HIT — often used in the phrases *go a bomb* or *go like a bomb* **6** : a long pass in football
bomb* *vb* ~ *vi* **1** : FAIL; *esp* : to fail to win audience approval **2** *slang* : to move rapidly ⟨realized that there was more to [ski] racing than *~ing* down her native hill —Adam Shaw⟩
bom·bay \bämˈbā\ *n* -S *usu cap* [fr. *Bombay*, India] : a domestic cat of a breed originating as a cross between the American Shorthair and the Burmese that is characterized by a shiny black short-haired coat and gold or copper eyes
bombed \ˈbämd\ *adj* [fr. past part. of ²*bomb*] : intoxicated by alcohol or drugs : HIGH, DRUNK
bomber* *n* : BOMBER JACKET *herein*
bomber jacket *n* : a usu. leather jacket made to resemble a military-issue flight jacket
bomb·let \ˈbämlət\ *n* -S [¹*bomb* + *-let*] : a small bomb
bona fides* \ˈbōnəˈfīˌdēz, -ˌfīdz\ *n* **1** : evidence of one's good faith or genuineness — usu. pl. in constr. ⟨when the war ended . . . [his] *bona fides* were unambiguously established —E.J.Epstein⟩ **2** : evidence of one's qualifications or achievements — usu. pl. in constr.
bonce* *n, Brit* : HEAD, PATE
bondage* *n* : sadomasochistic sexual practices involving the physical restraint of one partner
bonded* *adj* : composed of two or more layers of the same or different fabrics held together by an adhesive ⟨~ jersey⟩
bonding* *n* **1** : the formation of a close relationship (as between a mother and child or between a person and an animal) esp. through frequent or constant association **2** : a dental technique in which a material (as plastic or porcelain) is attached to a tooth surface to correct minor defects (as chipped or discolored teeth)
bonding *adj* [fr. pres. part. of ⁴*bond*] : relating to, being, or occupying a molecular orbital which tends to promote bond formation between atoms ⟨a ~ electron⟩
bone–chil·ling \ˈ=ˌchiliŋ\ *adj* : intensely cold ⟨*bone-chilling* weather⟩; *also* : penetrating, disturbing, or intense in emotional or physical effect ⟨*bone-chilling* drama⟩ ⟨a *bone-chilling* wind⟩
bonehead \ˈ=ˌ=\ *adj* [*bonehead*, n.] : being a college course intended for students lacking fundamental skills : REMEDIAL ⟨teaches ~ English⟩
bong \ˈbȯŋ, ˈbäŋ\ *n* -S [Thai *bɔ̄ŋ* hollow piece of wood or bamboo] : a simple water pipe for smoking marijuana that consists of a bottle or vertical tube partially filled with a liquid (as water or liqueur) and a smaller offset tube ending in a bowl
bo·ni·a·to \ˌbōnēˈätō, -d·ō\ *n* -S [AmerSp, perh. fr. Taino] : a sweet potato having white dry flesh with little sweetness that is usu. grown in subtropical regions (as Cuba and southern Florida)
bonk \ˈbäŋk, ˈbȯŋk\ *vt* [imit.] : HIT ⟨baseball players getting *~ed* on the head by routine fly balls —Gary Cartwright⟩
bon·kers \ˈbäŋkə(r)z, ˈbȯŋ-\ *adj* [prob. fr. *bonk* (herein) + *-ers* (as in *crackers*)] : CRAZY, MAD ⟨if I don't work, I go ~ —Zoe Caldwell⟩
bo·no·bo \bəˈnōbō; ˈbänəbō, -nō-\ *n* -S [perh. fr. Mongo or Ngando (Bantu languages of the Democratic Republic of the Congo)] : a rare anthropoid ape (*Pan paniscus*) of the family Pongidae that has a more slender build and longer limbs than the related common chimpanzee (*P. troglodytes*) and that inhabits a small geographic region in equatorial Africa south of the Congo river — called also *pygmy chimpanzee*
boo \ˈbü\ *n* -S [origin unknown] : MARIJUANA
boob* *n, Brit* : MISTAKE, BLOOPER
boob \ˈbüb\ *n* -S [short for ²*booby*] : BREAST — sometimes considered vulgar
boobird \ˈ=ˌ=\ *n* -S : a home fan at a sporting event who boos one or more members of the home team
boob tube *n* [¹*boob* + *tube* (television); fr. the notion that television programming is foolish or is viewed by foolish people] : TELEVISION; *esp* : a television set
boo·gie *also* **boo·gy** \ˈbügē, ˈbügē\ *vi* **boogied; boogieing** *or* **boogying; boogies** [short for *boogie-woogie*] : to dance to rock music

book* *vt, Brit, of a referee* : to note the name or number of (as a soccer player) for a serious infraction of the rules ~ *vi slang* : LEAVE, GO

bookmark* *n* : a menu entry or icon on a computer that is most often created by the user and that serves as a shortcut for returning to a previously viewed location (as in a document or on the Internet) ⟨create a ~ for that Web site⟩

bookmark *vt* : to create a computer bookmark for ⟨~*ed* the home page⟩

bookshelf *adj* [*bookshelf*, n.] : designed to occupy a small amount of space : COMPACT ⟨~ speakers⟩

boom* *n* [²*boom*] : a temporary floating barrier used to contain an oil spill

boom* *n* [⁴*boom*] : an upsurge in activity, interest, or popularity ⟨a folk music ~⟩

boom *adv* [⁴*boom*] : without delay or hesitation : SUDDENLY ⟨then ~, he was fired⟩ — often used interjectionally to indicate suddenness

boom box *n* [⁴*boom* + ²*box*; fr. its use at high volume in public places] : a large portable radio and often tape player with two attached speakers — called also *box, ghetto blaster*

boomer* *n* **1** [by shortening] : BABY BOOMER *herein* **2** : a submarine armed with nuclear missiles

boonies \ˈbünēz, -iz\ *n pl* [*boon*docks + *-ie* + ¹*-s*] *slang* : BACKCOUNTRY, BOONDOCKS

booster cables *n pl* : JUMPER CABLES *herein*

boot \ˈbüt\ *vb* **boot·ed; boot·ing** [short for *bootstrap* (herein)] *vt* **1** : to load (a program) into a computer from a disk **2** : to start or ready for use esp. by booting a program — often used with *up* ⟨~ up a computer⟩ ~ *vi* **1** : to become loaded into a computer's memory from a disk ⟨the program ~*s* automatically⟩ **2** : to become ready for use esp. by booting a program ⟨the computer ~*s* quickly⟩ — often used with *up* — **boot·a·ble** *adj*

boot camp* *n* **1** : a place or undertaking that resembles boot camp esp. by requiring one to endure rigorous training or initiation ⟨a *boot camp* for prospective truck drivers⟩ **2** : a facility or program in which young offenders are forced to participate in a rigidly structured routine that includes physical drills and firm discipline

bootstrap* *n* : a computer routine consisting of a few initial instructions by means of which the rest of the instructions are brought into the computer

bootstrap* *adj* **1** : being or relating to a process that is self-generated or self-sustaining **2** : being or relating to a device that is self-acting **3** : of or relating to a hypothesis of particle physics which assumes that all strongly interacting particles are composite systems made up of other strongly interacting particles

bootstrap \ˈ=,=\ *vt* **1** : BOOT *herein* **2** : to promote or develop by initiative and effort with little or no assistance ⟨the junior-grade professional woman may face stiff opposition when she tries to ~ her way up —Lisa C. Wohl⟩ — **bootstrapper** \ˈ=,==\ *n*

boo·ty *also* **boo·tie** \ˈbüd·ē, -tē; -i\ *n, pl* **booties** [alter. of an English-based creole word; akin to Sea Islands Creole (Gullah) *bʌti* buttocks, Jamaican Creole, Krio *bati*; all fr. (assumed) Early Mod E *bottie* buttocks, fr. ¹*bott*om + *-ie*] : BUTTOCKS

booze–up \ˈ=,=\ *n* -s [fr. *booze up*, v.] *chiefly Brit* : a drinking spree

bop* *n* : JIVE 1

bop *vi* **bopped; bopped; bopping; bops** [prob. fr. *bop*, n. (herein)] **1** : to go quickly or unceremoniously : POP **2** : to dance or shuffle along to or as if to bop music

borderline* *adj* : characterized by psychological instability in several areas (as interpersonal relations, behavior, mood, and identity) often with impaired social and vocational functioning but with brief or no psychotic episodes ⟨a ~ personality disorder⟩

borderline \ˈ==,=\ *adv* : not actually but very close to being : ALMOST ⟨is ~ senile⟩

bor·de·tel·la \ˌbȯrdāˈtelə\ *n, cap* [NL, fr. Jules *Bordet* †1961 Belg. bacteriologist + NL *-ella*] : a genus of bacteria comprising very short gram-negative strictly aerobic coccuslike bacilli and including the causative agent (*B. pertussis*) of whooping cough

born–again \ˌ==ˌ=\ *adj* [fr. the statement "Except a man be *born again*, he cannot see the Kingdom of God"—John 3:3 (AV)] **1** : of, relating to, or being a Christian who has made a renewed or confirmed commitment of faith esp. after an intense religious experience **2** : having returned to or having newly adopted an activity, a conviction, or a persona esp. with a proselytizing zeal ⟨a *born-again* conservative⟩ **3** : newly restored, transformed, or revitalized : given a new life ⟨proud of their *born-again* Victorian house⟩ — **born–again** *n* -s

bor·ges·ian \bȯrˈhāzhēən\ *n, usu cap* [Jorge Luis *Borges* †1986 Argentine writer + E ²*-an*] : of, relating to, or suggestive of Jorge Luis Borges or his writings

borough* *n* : a civil division of the state of Alaska corresponding to a county in other states

bor·sa·li·no \ˌbȯrsəˈlē(ˌ)nō\ *or* **borsalino hat** *n* -s *usu cap B* [It, fr. *Borsalino*, the manufacturer] : a wide-brimmed soft felt hat for men

borscht belt *also* **borsch belt** *n, often cap both Bs* : BORSCH CIRCUIT

bos·sa no·va \ˌbäsəˈnōvə, ˌbȯs-\ *n* [Pg, lit., new trend] **1** : a Brazilian dance characterized by the sprightly step pattern of the samba and a subtle bounce **2** : music resembling the samba with jazz interpolations

bo·ta \ˈbōd·ə, -ōtə\ *n* -s [Sp, fr. LL *buttis* cask, flask — more at BUTT] : a leather pouch for carrying wine

bo·tan·i·ca \bəˈtanikə, bō-, -nēkə\ *n* -s [AmerSp *botánica*, fr. Sp, fem. of *botánico* botanical] : a shop that specializes in articles (as herbs, charms, and statues) employed esp. by devotees of santeria

bot·ti·cel·lian \ˌbäd·əˈchelēən, -ätə-, -lyən\ *adj, usu cap* [Alessandro *Botticelli* †1510 Ital. painter + E *-an*] : of, relating to, or having the characteristics of the painter Botticelli or his work

bottle* *n* [prob. back-formation fr. Brit. slang *no bottle* useless, worthless] *slang Brit* : METTLE, COURAGE

bottle–feed \ˈ==,=\ *vt* : to feed (as an infant) with a bottle

bottleneck* *or* **bottleneck guitar** *n* : a style of guitar playing in which an object (as a metal bar or the neck of a bottle) is pressed against the strings for a glissando effect

bottling* *n* : a bottled beverage; *esp* : WINE

bottom* *n* : the bass or baritone instruments of a band

bottom* *vi* **1** *of a security market* : to decline to a point where demand begins to exceed supply and a rise in prices is imminent — usu. used with *out* **2** : to reach a point where a decline is halted or reversed — usu. used with *out*

bottom* *adj* : having a quantum characteristic that accounts for the existence and lifetime of upsilon particles and that has a value of zero for most known particles ⟨~ quark⟩

bot·tomed \ˈbäd·əmd, -ätə-\ *adj* : having a bottom esp. of a specified kind — usu. used in combination ⟨a broad-*bottomed* boat⟩

bottom–feeder *n* **1** : a fish that feeds at the bottom **2** : one that is of the lowest status or rank **3** : an opportunist who seeks quick profit usu. at the expense of others or from their misfortune

bottomless* *adj* **1** : NUDE **2** : featuring nude entertainers ⟨a ~ bar⟩

bottom line *n* **1 a** : the line at the bottom of a financial report that shows the net profit or loss **b** : financial considerations (as cost or profit or loss) **c** : the final result : OUTCOME, UPSHOT **d** : final statement : SUMMARY, CONCLUSION **2 a** : the essential or salient point : CRUX **b** : the primary or most important consideration

bottom–line \ˌ==ˌ=\ *adj* **1** : concerned only with cost or profits ⟨*bottom-line* publishing, with little real concern for editorial values —*Newsweek*⟩ **2** : PRAGMATIC, REALISTIC ⟨a realist, dealing in facts, in *bottom-line* emotions —Allene Talmey⟩

bottom–up *adj* [fr. the phrase *from the bottom up*] : progressing upward from the lowest levels (as of a stratified organization or system)

bottom woman *n, slang* : a pimp's favorite or most dependable prostitute

bou·bou \ˈbüˌbü\ *n* -s [F, fr. Malinke *bubu*] : a long flowing garment worn in parts of Africa

bouillabaisse* *n* : POTPOURRI ⟨a ~ of essays⟩

boul·der·ing \ˈbōld(ə)riŋ\ *n* -s [¹*boulder* + ³*-ing*] : practice in the techniques of rock climbing

boulevard* *adj* : produced primarily to entertain ⟨~ farce⟩

bounce* *vt* **1** : to write (a check) on an account having insufficient funds **2** : to present (as an idea) to another person in order to elicit helpful suggestions or to gain approval — usu. used with *off*

bouncer* *n* **1** : ⁴BUMPER 1f **2** : a batted baseball that bounces

bounded *adj* : having a mathematical bound or bounds ⟨a set ~ above by 25 and ~ below by –10⟩

bouque·tière \ˌbu̇k(ə)ˈtye(ə)r, -tēˈe(-\ *adj* [F, (*à la*) *bouquetière*, lit., in the manner of a flower seller; F *bouquetière* woman who sells flowers, fem. of *bouquetier* flower seller, fr. *bouquet* bouquet + *-ier* -eer] : garnished with vegetables ⟨rack of lamb ~⟩

bour·gie \ˈbu̇rzhē, ˈbüzhē\ *adj* [fr. *bourgie*, n., fr. ¹*bourge*ois + *-ie*] : BOURGEOIS 2 — **bourgie** *n* -s

bour·gui·gnonne \ˌbu̇rgēnˈyȯn\ *also* **bour·gui·gnon** \-ˈyōⁿ\ *adj, often cap* [F, (*à la*) *bourguignonne*; F *bourguignonne*, fem. of *bourguignon* of Burgundy, fr. *Bourgogne* Burgundy, region in France] : prepared or served in the manner of Burgundy (as with a sauce made with red Burgundy wine) ⟨beef ~⟩

bour·ride \bu̇ˈrēd, bə-\ *n* -s [F, fr. Prov *bourrido*, alter. of *boulido* something boiled, fr. *bouli*, to boil, fr. L *bullire* — more at BOIL] : a fish stew similar to bouillabaisse that is usu. thickened with egg yolks and strongly flavored with garlic

boutique* *n* : a small company that offers highly specialized products or services — often used attributively ⟨~ wineries⟩ ⟨an independent investment ~⟩

bou·zou·ki *also* **bou·sou·ki** \bu̇ˈzükē, bəˈ-\ *n, pl* **bouzoukis** *also* **bouzoukia** \-kēə\ [NGk *mpouzouki*] : a long-necked stringed musical instrument of Greek origin

bovine spon·gi·form encephalopathy \-ˈspənjiˌfȯrm-\ *n* [*spongiform* spongelike fr. *spongi-* + *-form*] : a progressive fatal disease of the central nervous system of adult domestic cattle that resembles scrapie of sheep and goats and is prob. caused by a prion transmitted by infected tissue in food — abbr. *BSE*; called also *mad cow disease*

bow shock \ˈbau̇-\ *n* [so called fr. a similarity to the wave pattern produced at the bow of a ship] : the shock wave formed by the collision of the supersonic charged particles of a stellar wind with another medium (as the magnetosphere of a planet)

bow thruster *n* : an auxiliary propulsion device at the bow of a ship to aid in maneuvering

box* *n* **1** : the female genitalia — usu. considered vulgar **2 a** : TELEVISION; *esp* : a television set **b** : a usu. self-contained piece of electronic equipment **c** : BOOM BOX *herein* **3** : a house or office building resembling a box esp. in shape

boxer* *n* [¹*boxer*] **boxers** *pl* : BOXER SHORTS

boy·chick \ˈbȯiˌchik\ *n* -s [Amer. Yiddish *boytshik*, lit., little boy, fr. E *boy* + Yiddish *-tshik*, dim. suffix, of Slav origin; akin to Pol *-czyk*, Ukrainian *-chyk*, dim. suffix] : a young man : BOY

boy toy \ˈ=,=\ *n* : a usu. young man considered as an object of sexual desire

bozo* *n* : a foolish or incompetent person

bp* *abbr* base pair

BP \ˌbēˈpē\ *abbr or n* -s **1** : beautiful people *herein* **2** : batting practice

bpi *abbr* bits per inch; bytes per inch

bps *abbr* bits per second

brace* *n* **brac·es** *pl* : a nonremovable orthodontic appliance usu. of metallic wire that is used esp. to exert pressure to straighten misaligned teeth

brachio·ce·phal·ic artery \¦brakē(ˌ)ōsə¦falik-\ *n* [*brachi-* + *-cephalic*] : INNOMINATE ARTERY

brachiocephalic trunk \". . .-\ *n* [*brachi-* + *-cephalic*] : INNOMINATE ARTERY

brachiocephalic vein \". . .-\ *n* [*brachi-* + *-cephalic*] : INNOMINATE VEIN

brachy·the·ra·py \ˌbrakēˈ===\ *n* [ISV *brachy-* + *therapy*] : radiotherapy in which the source of radiation is placed (as by implantation) in or close to the area being treated

bra·ci·o·la \ˌbräch(ē)ˈōlə\ *or* **bra·ci·o·le** \-lā\ *n* -s [*braciola* fr. It, fr. *brace* live coal (fr. OIt *bragia*) + *-ola* -ole, fr. L; *braciole* fr. It, pl. of *braciola* — more at BRAZE] : a thin slice of meat (as steak) usu. wrapped around a savory filling and often cooked in wine

bracket creep *n* : movement into a higher tax bracket as a result of income rises intended to offset the effects of inflation

bra·dy·ki·nin \¦brādə¦kīnən\ *n* [*brady-* + *kinin* (herein)] : a kinin that is formed locally in injured tissue, acts in vasodilation of small arterioles, is held to play a part in inflammatory processes, and is composed of a chain of nine amino acids

bragging rights *n pl* : entitlement to boast about one's status, superiority, or achievement

brain* *n* : something that performs the functions of a brain; *esp* : an automatic device (as a computer) used for control, guidance, or computation ⟨the ~ of a missile⟩

brain–dead \ˈ=,=\ *adj* **1** : characterized by brain death **2** : lacking intelligence or vitality ⟨ideas both smart and *brain-dead* —Stanley Bing⟩

brain death *n* : final cessation of activity in the central nervous system esp. as indicated by a flat electroencephalogram for a predetermined length of time

brain drain *n* : the departure of educated or professional people from one country, economic sector, or field for another usu. for better pay or living conditions

brain–drain \ˈ=¦=\ *vt* : to entice to move to another country or job for a higher salary or better working conditions

brain hormone *n* **1** : a hormone that is secreted by neurosecretory cells of the insect brain and that stimulates the prothoracic glands to secrete ecdysone **2** : any of various hormones (as serotonin and melatonin) produced in or acting on the vertebrate brain or central nervous system — not usu. used technically

brain·i·ac \ˈbrānēˌak\ *n* -s [prob. fr. *Brainiac*, superintelligent villain in the *Superman* comic-book series] : a person characterized by unusual brainpower

bra·less \ˈbräləs, -rȧl-, *sometimes* -rȯl-\ *adj, of a woman* : wearing no bra — **bralessness** *n* -ES

branch* *n* : a part of a computer program executed as a result of a program decision

branch* *vi* : to follow one of two or more branches (as in a computer program)

bran·dade \bräⁿdȧd\ *n* -s [F, fr. Prov *brandado*, lit., act of stirring, fr. *branda* to stir, agitate, fr. OProv *brandar*, fr. *bran* sword, of Gmc origin — more at BRANDISH] : a seasoned puree of fish and esp. of salt cod

Bran·gus \ˈbraŋgəs, -aiŋ-\ *trademark* — used for polled solid black beef cattle of a breed developed from a Brahman-Angus cross

brassware \ˈ=,=\ *n* : articles made of brass

brave new world *n, sometimes cap B&N&W* [fr. the dystopian novel *Brave New World* (1932) by Aldous Huxley †1963 Eng. novelist] : a future world, situation, or development; *also* : a recent development or recently changed situation

brax·ton–hicks contractions \ˈbrakstənˈhiks-\ *n pl, usu cap B&H* [after John *Braxton Hicks* †1897 Eng. gynecologist] : relatively painless nonrhythmic contractions of the uterus that occur during pregnancy with increasing frequency over time but are not associated with labor

breadboard \ˈ=,=\ *vt* [*breadboard*, n.] : to make an experimental arrangement of (an electronic circuit) on a breadboard

break* *n* **1** : a usu. solo instrumental passage in jazz, folk, country, or popular music **2** : BREAKDOWN 2a

breakaway* *n* : a sudden acceleration by one or more bicyclists pulling away from the pack in a race

break–bulk \ˈ=¦=\ *adj* : of or relating to materials shipped in conventional individual packages and not containerized

break dancing *n* [*break* (herein); fr. the performance of acrobatic dances during a cued series of instrumental breaks in pop songs] : dancing in which individual dancers perform a series of often acrobatic moves — **break–dance** \ˈ=,=\ *vb* — **break–danc·er** \ˈ=,==\ *n*

break·even \ˈ=¦==\ *n* -s [*break even*] **1** : BREAK-EVEN POINT **2** : the condition in a nuclear fusion reactor of equality of the energy expended in causing the reactions to occur and the energy produced by the reactions

break out* *vi* : to make a break from a restraining condition or situation ⟨*broke out* of a slump⟩ ~ *vt* : to separate from a mass of data ⟨*break out* newsstand sales⟩

breakout* *n* : a breakdown of statistical data

breakout *adj* [*breakout*, n.] : being or relating to a sudden or smashing success esp. in comparison to previous efforts ⟨a ~ book⟩

breakthrough* *n* : a person's first notable success

breathable* *adj* : allowing air to pass through ⟨a ~ synthetic fabric⟩ — **breath·a·bil·i·ty** \ˌbrēthəˈbiləd·ē, -ətē, -i\ *n* -ES

Breath·a·ly·zer \ˈbrethəˌlīzə(r)\ *trademark* — used for a device that determines the alcohol content of a breath sample

breathe* *vi, of wine* : to develop flavor and bouquet by exposure to air

brecht·ian \ˈbrektēən, -k-\ *adj, usu cap* [Bertolt *Brecht* †1956 Ger. dramatist + E *-an*] : of, relating to, or suggestive of Bertolt Brecht or his writings

bre·tyl·i·um \brəˈtilēəm, bre-\ *n* [*brom-* + *ethyl* + ammon*ium*] : an antiarrhythmic drug administered in the form of its tosylate $C_{18}H_{24}BrNO_3S$ in the treatment of ventricular fibrillation and tachycardia and formerly used as an antihypertensive

brew·pub \ˈ=,=\ *n* : a restaurant that sells beverages brewed on the premises

brew·ski \ˈbrüskē\ *n, pl* **brew·skies** *or* **brew·skis** [²*brew* + *-ski* (suffix in Slavic surnames)] *slang* : BEER 4

bri·co·lage \ˌbrēkōˈläzh, ˌbri-\ *n* -s [F, fr. *bricoler* to do odd jobs, make or fix in a haphazard fashion, fr. MF, to rebound, move in a zigzag course, fr. *bricole* catapult — more at BRICOLE] : construction (as of a sculpture or a structure of ideas) achieved by using whatever comes to hand; *also* : something constructed in this way

bri·co·leur \ˌbrēkōˈlə(r), -ˈlœr, ˌbri-\ *n* -s [F, fr. *bricoler*] : one who engages in bricolage

bride's basket \ˈ=,==\ *n* [so called fr. such bowls' frequently being given as wedding presents in the late 19th century] : an ornate usu. colored glass bowl fitted with a handle and mounted on a silver-plated base

bridesmaid* *n* : one that finishes just behind the winner

bridge loan *n* : a short-term loan used to finance an enterprise, investment, or government prior to obtaining other funds

brig·a·doon \¦brigə¦dün\ *n* -s *usu cap* [fr. *Brigadoon*, imaginary village in Scotland in the musical *Brigadoon* (1947) by Alan Jay Lerner †1986 Am. playwright and Frederick Loewe †1988 Am. (Austrian-born) composer] : a place that is idyllic, unaffected by time, or remote from reality

bright* *n* : a bright color — usu. used in pl.

bringdown \ˈ=,=\ *n* [*bring down*, v.] : COMEDOWN, LETDOWN

brit \ˈbrit\ *n* -s *cap* [by shortening] : BRITON 2

british shorthair *n, usu cap B* : any of a breed of domestic cats resembling the American Shorthair but stockier in build with a closer-lying coat

brittle* *adj* : affected with or being a form of type 1 diabetes characterized by large and unpredictable fluctuations in blood glucose level

bro \ˈbrō\ *n* -s [by shortening & alter.] **1** : BROTHER **2** : SOUL BROTHER *herein*

broad·band \ˈ=¦=\ *adj* **1** : operating at, responsive to, or comprising a wide band of frequencies — compare NARROWBAND *herein* **2** : of, relating to, or being a communications network in which a frequency range is divided into multiple independent channels for simultaneous transmission of signals (as voice, data, or video) usu. by cable — compare BASEBAND *herein*

broad·scale \¦=¦=\ *adj* : broad in extent, range, or effect

broadsheet* *n, chiefly Brit* : a newspaper with pages of a size larger than those of a tabloid

broadside* *vb* ~ *vt* : to hit broadside ⟨the car was *broadsided* by a truck⟩

broken* *adj* : disunited by divorce, separation, or the desertion of one parent ⟨~ homes⟩ ⟨a ~ family⟩

broker* *n* : POWER BROKER *herein*

broker* *vt* : to arrange, settle, or control as a broker ⟨~ a convention⟩ ⟨accustomed to diversity and disagreement, to ~*ing* policy between the various factions —*Wall Street Jour.*⟩

bro·kered \ˈbrōkə(r)d\ *adj* [fr. past part. of *broker* (herein)] : arranged or controlled by brokers and esp. power brokers ⟨a ~ political convention⟩

bro·mo·crip·tine \ˌbrōmōˈkripˌtēn\ *n* -s [by shortening & alter. fr. *bromoergocryptine*, fr. ISV *brom-* + *ergocryptine*, an ergot derivative, fr. ²*ergo-* + Gk *kryptos* hidden + ISV ²*-ine*] : a polypeptide alkaloid $C_{32}H_{40}BrN_5O_5$ that is a derivative of ergot and mimics the activity of dopamine in selectively inhibiting the secretion of prolactin by the pituitary gland

bro·mo·de·oxy·uridine \¦brōmō(ˌ)dē¦äksē+\ *n* [*brom-* + *deoxy-* + *uridine*] : a mutagenic analogue $C_9H_{11}O_5NBr$ of thymidine that induces chromosomal breakage esp. in heterochromatic regions and has been used to selectively destroy actively dividing cells; 5-bromodeoxyuridine — abbr. *BUdR*

bro·mo·ura·cil \ˌbrōmōˈyu̇rəˌsil, -məˈ-, -ˌsəl\ *n* [*brom-* + *uracil*] : a mutagenic uracil derivative $C_4H_3N_2O_2Br$ that is an analogue of thymine and pairs readily with adenine and sometimes with guanine during bacterial or phage DNA synthesis

bron·cho·constriction \¦bräŋ(ˌ)kō, -än(-+\ *n* [*bronch-* + *constriction*] : constriction of the bronchial air passages — **bron·cho·constrictive** \"+\ *adj*

bron·cho·constrictor \"+\ *adj* [*bronch-* + *constrictor*] : causing or involving bronchoconstriction ⟨~ effects⟩ ⟨~ responses⟩ — **bronchoconstrictor** *n*

bron·cho·pulmonary \"+\ *adj* [*bronch-* + *pulmonary*] : of, relating to, or affecting the bronchi and the lungs ⟨arterial branches that supply the ~ segments of the lungs⟩

bronzer* *n* : a cosmetic that makes the skin look tanned

broomball \ˈ=,=\ *n* : a game like hockey that is played on ice by players wearing shoes instead of skates and using special brooms to propel a ball

brown bag·ging \ˈbrau̇nˈbagiŋ\ *n* **1** : the practice of carrying a bottle of liquor into a restaurant or club where setups are available but where the sale of liquor by the drink is illegal **2** : the practice of carrying one's lunch (as to work) usu. in a brown paper bag — **brown–bag** \ˈ=,=\ *vb or adj* — **brown bag·ger** \-gə(r)\ *n*

brown dwarf *n* : a celestial object that is much smaller than a normal star and has insufficient mass for nuclear fusion to begin but that is hot enough to radiate energy esp. at infrared wavelengths

brown fat *n* : a mammalian heat-producing tissue occurring esp. in human fetuses and newborn infants and in hibernating animals — called also *brown adipose tissue*

brown·field \ˈ=,=\ *n, often attrib* : a tract of land that has been developed for industrial purposes, polluted, and abandoned ⟨a ~ site⟩ ⟨clean up the city's ~*s*⟩ — compare GREENFIELD *herein*

brownie point *n, sometimes cap B* : a credit regarded as earned esp. by currying favor (as with a superior)

brown lung disease *or* **brown lung** *n* : BYSSINOSIS

brown recluse spider *also* **brown recluse** *n* [*recluse* prob. fr. NL *reclusa*, specific epithet, fr. LL, fem. of *reclusus* shut up; fr. its living chiefly in dark corners — more at RECLUSE] : a venomous spider of the genus *Loxosceles* (*L. reclusa*) introduced esp. into the southern and central U.S. that has a violin-shaped mark on the cephalothorax and produces a dangerous cytotoxin which can cause necrotic lesions

brownware \ˈ=,=\ *n* **1** : a brown-glazed earthenware formerly widely used for utility pottery **2** : typically primitive pottery that fires to a brown or reddish color

brown water *n* : an inland or coastal waterway esp. when murky or colored brown by silt, tannins, or pollutants — compare BLUE WATER *in the Dict*

brown–water \ˈ=¦=\ *adj* : of, relating to, operating in, or characteristic of brown waters ⟨a *brown-water* navy⟩

brows·able \ˈ==ə\ *adj* : suitable for browsing through ⟨a ~ anthology⟩ ⟨~ merchandise⟩

browse* *vt* : to access (a network) by means of a browser — **browsing** *n*

browser* *n* **1** : an open case for holding phonograph records that is designed for ease in browsing **2** : a computer program used for accessing sites or information on a network (as the World Wide Web)

bru·schet·ta \brüˈshed·ə, -ˈsked·ə\ *n* -S [It *bruschetta, bruschetto,* fr. It dial. (Tuscany), fr. *bruscare* to toast, burn, prob. fr. (assumed) VL *brusicare,* freq. of *brusare,* by-form of *brusiare* to burn] : thick slices of bread grilled, rubbed with garlic, drizzled with olive oil, often topped with tomatoes and herbs, and usu. served as an appetizer

brush back *vt* : to throw a brushback to ⟨hard to set up a hitter if you can't *brush* him *back*—Red Schoendienst⟩

brushback \ˈ=¦=\ *n* [⁴*brush* + *back*] : a pitch thrown near the batter's head in baseball in an attempt to make him move back from home plate

bru·tal·ism \ˈbrüd·ᵊl,izəm, -üt°l-\ *n* -S [*brutal* + *-ism*] : a style in art and esp. architecture using exaggeration and distortion to create its effect (as of massiveness or power) — **bru·tal·ist** \-ᵊləst\ *adj or n*

BS* *abbr, often not cap* bullshit — sometimes considered vulgar

b–school \ˈbē¦=\ *n, usu cap B* [*business*] : a school of business within a university

BSE *abbr* bovine spongiform encephalopathy *herein*

BSEE \ˌbē,es,ēˈē\ *abbr or n* -S **1** : a bachelor of science in electrical engineering **2** : a bachelor of science in elementary education

b side *n, usu cap B* : FLIP SIDE *herein; also* : a song on the flip side of a record

BST *abbr* bovine somatotropin

bt \bēˈtē\ *n* -S *usu cap B* [NL *Bacillus thuringiensis,* species name, lit., Thuringian bacillus; fr. its discovery in larvae of Mediterranean flour moths from a mill in Thuringia] : a variable bacterium of the genus *Bacillus* (*B. thuringiensis*) that produces various crystal proteins during sporulation some of which are toxic to various insect larvae esp. of the orders Lepidoptera, Diptera, and Coleoptera; *also* : a preparation of this bacterium often modified by genetic engineering for use as a biopesticide having activity against specific insects

bub·ba \ˈbəbə\ *n* -S *often cap* [fr. *Bubba,* a stereotypical nickname of white Southerners] : REDNECK — often used disparagingly

bubble* *n* **1** : something (as a plastic or an inflatable structure) that is more or less semicylindrical or dome-shaped **2** : BALLOON 2d **3** : MAGNETIC BUBBLE *herein* — **on the bubble** : subject to being bumped from an automobile race by reason of having the lowest qualifying speed; *broadly* : being at risk of exclusion or replacement ⟨teams *on the bubble* at tournament time⟩

bubble car *n* : a small often three-wheeled British automobile with a transparent bubble-shaped roof; *broadly* : any automobile with a similar top

bubblegum** *n* : bubblegum rock music

bubblegum \ˈ==,=\ *adj* [fr. the fact that bubble gum is chewed chiefly by children] : appealing to, characteristic of, or being preteens or adolescents ⟨~ songs⟩ ⟨the ~ set⟩

bubblehead \ˈ==,=\ *n* : a foolish or stupid person — **bubble–headed** \ˈ==,==\ *adj*

bubble memory *n* : a computer memory that uses magnetic bubbles to store information

bub·kes *also* **bup·kes** \ˈbəpkəs, ˈbüp-\ *n pl but sing in constr* [Yiddish *bubkes* (prob. short for *kozebubkes,* lit., goat droppings), pl. of *bubke, bobke,* dim. of *bub, bob* bean, of Slav origin; akin to Pol *bób* bean, Ukrainian *bob-, bib;* akin to L *faba* bean — more at BEAN] : the least amount : BEANS ⟨won't win ~ this year —Ivan Maisel⟩; *also* : NOTHING ⟨received ~ at nomination time —Lewis Beale⟩

buc·co·lingual \ˌbəkō+\ *adj* [*bucco-* + *lingual*] **1** : relating to or affecting the cheek and the tongue **2** : of or relating to the buccal and lingual aspects of a tooth ⟨the ~ width of a molar⟩ — **buc·co·lingually** \"+\ *adv*

buck* *n* : a sum of money esp. to be gained ⟨greed and the desire to make a quick ~ —*London Times*⟩ ⟨pursuing the tourist ~ —Albin West⟩ ⟨it entreats in the name of art; it hopes to make a ~, too —John Corry⟩ ⟨agents who look only for the biggest ~ —Sol Stein⟩; *also* : MONEY ⟨tactics . . . the Pentagon has used in its pursuit of the public ~ —Robert Claiborne⟩ — usu. used in pl. ⟨for the big ~*s* you've got to give people meaningful material —Russell Baker⟩ ⟨the public image of art as ~*s*—Barbara Rose⟩

buckle up *vi* : to fasten one's seat belt

buck·min·sterful·le·rene \ˌbək,minstər,fu̇ləˈrēn\ *n* [R. *Buckminster Fuller* †1983 Am. engineer + E *-ene;* fr. the resemblance of its molecules to the geodesic domes designed by Fuller] : a spherical fullerene C_{60} that is an extremely stable form of pure carbon, consists of interconnected pentagons and hexagons suggestive of the geometry of a geodesic dome, and is believed to be a major constituent of soot

buck rog·ers \ˌbək¦räjə(r)z\ *adj, usu cap B&R* [*Buck Rogers,* science-fiction comic strip created by Philip Nowlan †1940 Am. writer and Richard Calkins †1962 Am. artist] : marked by futuristic high-tech qualities : suggestive of science fiction

bucky·ball \ˈbəkē,bȯl\ *n* [*bucky-* (fr. *buck*minsterfullerene — herein — + ⁴*-y*) + ¹*ball*] : a molecule of buckminsterfullerene

bucky·tube \ˈ",t(y)üb\ *n* [*bucky-* (as in *buckyball* — herein) + ¹*tube*] : a microscopic hollow cylinder composed of pure carbon with a molecular arrangement similar to that of fullerenes

buddy *adj* [*buddy,* n.] : featuring a friendship or partnership between the two main usu. male characters ⟨a ~ movie⟩

bu·do \ˈbüd(,)ō\ *n* -S [Jap *budō* martial arts] : the Japanese martial arts (as karate, aikido, and kendo)

BUdR *abbr* bromodeoxyuridine

buff* *or* **buffed** \ˈbəft\ *adj* [⁵*buff; buffed* fr. past part. of ⁶*buff*] : having a physique enhanced by body building exercises

buffalo wing *n* [fr. *Buffalo,* N.Y.] : a deep-fried chicken wing coated with a spicy sauce and usu. served with a blue cheese dressing

buffer* *vt* **1** : to supply with a buffer ⟨~*ed* computer terminals⟩ **2** : to collect (as data) in a buffer

bugger all *n* [fr. the phrase *bugger all* (damn it all)] *slang Brit* : NOTHING ⟨we knew *bugger all* about growing oranges —Peter Kerr⟩

bug off \ˈbəgˈȯf, *also* -äf\ *vi* [short for ²*bugger*] : to go away : LEAVE — usu. used as a command

bug out* *vi* **1** : to depart esp. in a hurry **2** : to evade a responsibility ⟨an excuse to *bug out* of exams⟩

building society *n, Brit* : SAVINGS AND LOAN ASSOCIATION

bul·bo·spon·gi·o·sus muscle \ˌbəl(,)bō,spənjēˈōsəs-, -,spän-\ *n* [NL, fr. *bulb-* + L *spongiosus* spongy] : BULBOCAVERNOSUS

bulimia* *n* : a serious eating disorder that occurs chiefly in females, is characterized by episodes of compulsive overeating typically followed by self-induced vomiting or laxative or diuretic abuse, and is often accompanied by guilt, depression, and self-criticism

¹bu·lim·ic \b(y)üˈlimik\ *adj* [*bulimia* + *-ic*] : of, relating to, or affected with bulimia ⟨~ patients⟩

²bulimic *n* -S : a person affected with bulimia

bulk up *vi* : to gain weight esp. by becoming more muscular ~ *vt* : to cause to bulk up

bull dyke *n* : an aggressively masculine lesbian — often used disparagingly

bulletin board* *n* : a program on a computer system that allows users to read and write public notices and is accessed usu. by modem

bullet train *n* : a high-speed passenger train

bull·shot \ˈbu̇l,shät\ *n* [*bull-* (shortening & alter. of *bouillon*) + ¹*shot*] : a drink made of vodka and bouillon

bully pulpit *n* [²*bully* + ¹*pulpit;* fr. the observation by Theodore Roosevelt †1919, 26th U.S. president, that "the White House is a *bully pulpit*"] : a prominent public position (as a political office) that provides an opportunity for expounding one's views; *also* : such an opportunity

bum *vt* **bummed; bummed; bumming; bums** [prob. back-formation fr. *bummer* (herein)] : DISAPPOINT, DEPRESS — usu. used with *out* ⟨this is starting to *bum* me out⟩

bum·mer \ˈbəmə(r)\ *n* -S [⁸*bum* + ²*-er*] **1** : something bad or unpleasant; *esp* : an unpleasant experience (as a bad reaction to a hallucinogenic drug) **2 a** : something of low quality : STINKER **b** : something that is a disappointment

bumper* *n* [⁴*bumper*] : a brief interval on radio or television filled with music, video shots, or voice-overs that marks a break usu. between a program and a commercial

bumper car *n* : a small electric car made to be driven around in an enclosure and to be bumped into others (as at an amusement park)

bumper sticker *n* : a strip of adhesive paper or plastic bearing a printed message (as a candidate's name or a slogan) and designed to be stuck on a vehicle's bumper

bun* *n* : BUTTOCKS — usu. used in pl.

BUN \ˌbē,yüˈen\ *n* -S [*blood urea nitrogen*] : the concentration of nitrogen in the form of urea in the blood

bundle* *n* **1** : a person embodying a specified quality or characteristic ⟨a ~ of energy⟩ **2** : a package offering related goods or services at a single price ⟨software ~*s* that include a self-teaching guide⟩

bundle* *vt* : to include (a product or service) with a related product for sale at a single price ⟨software is *bundled* with computer hardware⟩

Bundt \ˈbənt\ *trademark* — used for a cake pan having a tube in the center and scalloped sides

bun·ga·ro·toxin \ˌbəŋgərōˈtäksən\ *n* [*bungar-* (fr. NL *Bungarus,* genus name of the krait) + *-o-* + *toxin* — more at BUNGARUS] : a potent polypeptide neurotoxin that is obtained from krait venom and yields three electrophoretic fractions of which the one designated *α* is used esp. to label acetylcholine receptors at neuromuscular junctions because it binds irreversibly to them and blocks their activity — often used with one of the Greek prefixes *α-, β-,* or *γ-* to indicate the electrophoretic fractions

bungee cord *n* : an elasticized cord used esp. as a fastening or shock-absorbing device

bungee jumping *n* : the activity or sport of jumping from a height while attached to an elasticized cord — **bungee–jump** *n* — **bungee–jump** *vi* — **bungee jumper** *n*

bunker mentality *n* : a state of mind esp. among members of a group that is characterized by chauvinistic defensiveness and self-righteous intolerance of criticism

bunny* *n* [fr. *Bunny,* a service mark used for a waitress whose minimal attire includes a tail and ears resembling those of a rabbit] : a pretty girl esp. considered as an object of sexual desire

bun·ra·ku \bünˈrä(,)kü, ˈbün(,)r-\ *n* -S *usu cap* [Jap, fr. *Bunraku,* 19th cent. puppet troupe and theater in Osaka, fr. *bun* literature + *raku* ease, pleasure] : Japanese puppet theater featuring large costumed wooden puppets, onstage puppeteers, and a chanter who speaks all the lines

bupkes *var of* BUBKES *herein*

bup·pie \ˈbəpē\ *n* -S *sometimes cap* [¹*b*lack + *yuppie* (herein)] : a college-educated Afro-American adult who is employed in a well-paying profession and lives or works in or near a large city

bu·pro·pi·on \byüˈprōpēän, -ən\ *n* -S [ISV *butyl* + *-propion,* alter. of *propiophenone* (herein)] : a drug $C_{13}H_{18}ClNO$ used in the form of its hydrochloride as an antidepressant and as an aid to stop smoking usu. without the side effects of depressed libido and weight gain

buq·sha \ˈbu̇kshə *also* ˈbək-\ *n, pl* **buqsha** *or* **buqshas** [Ar] **1** : a monetary unit of Yemen equal to ¹⁄₄₀ rial — see MONEY table *in the Dict* **2** : a note or coin representing one buqsha

burb \ˈbərb\ *n* -S [by shortening] : SUBURB

bu·reau·cra·tese \ˌbyu̇rə¦krad·ˈēz, ˈbyü-, -rō-, -aˈtēz; byü¦räkrə¦tēz, byü-; *also* -ˈēs\ *n* : a style of language held to be characteristic of bureaucrats and marked by the prevalence of abstractions, jargon, euphemisms, and circumlocutions

bur·kitt's lymphoma \¦bərkəts-, ¦bə̄k-\ *also* **burkitt lymphoma** \-kət-\ *n, usu cap B* [after Denis Parsons *Burkitt* †1993 Brit. surgeon] : a malignant lymphoma that affects primarily the upper and lower jaws, orbit, retroperitoneal tissues situated near the pancreas, kidneys, ovaries, testes, thyroid, adrenal glands, heart, and pleura, that occurs esp. in children of central Africa, and that is associated with Epstein-Barr virus

burkitt's tumor *also* **burkitt tumor** \ˈ=¦=-\ *n, usu cap B* : BURKITT'S LYMPHOMA *herein*

burn* *vt* **1** : to use up : CONSUME ⟨~ calories⟩ **2** : to beat or score on (an opposing team or player) ⟨~*ed* the defense with a touchdown pass⟩ **3** : to subject to misfortune or mistreatment — often used in passive ⟨~*ed* in love⟩ ⟨banks ~*ed* by the financial collapse⟩

burn* *n* **1** : the firing of a rocket engine in flight **2** *slang* : an instance of dishonest dealing : SWINDLE, GYP

burn bag *n* : a bag for holding classified papers that are to be destroyed by burning

burn–in \ˈ=,=\ *n* -S [*burn in*] : the continuous operation of a device (as a computer) as a test for defects or failure prior to putting it to use

burnout* *n* **1** : the process or an instance of burning out **2 a** : the cessation of operation of a jet or rocket engine as the result of exhaustion of or shutting off of fuel **b** : the point in the trajectory of a rocket engine at which burnout occurs **3 a** : exhaustion of physical or emotional strength usu. as a result of prolonged stress or frustration **b** : a person suffering from burnout **4** : a person showing the effects of drug abuse

burrito* *n* : a flour tortilla rolled or folded around a filling (as of meat, beans, or cheese) and usu. baked

bur·sec·to·my \ˌbərˈsektəmē, ˌbə(r)ˈ-\ *n* -ES [¹*bursa* + *-ectomy*] : excision of a bursa (as the bursa of Fabricius of a chicken) — **bur·sec·to·mize** \(ˌ)=ˈ==,mīz\ *vt* -ED/-ING/-S

burst* *vt* : to separate (as a perforated continuous paper form) into sheets

burster* *n* **1** : the celestial source of an outburst of radiation (as X rays) **2** : a machine that separates at perforations business forms produced and printed on one long sheet

bury* *vt* **1** : to succeed emphatically or impressively in making (a shot in a game) ⟨~ a jumper⟩ **2** : to defeat overwhelmingly

bus* *n* **1** : a spacecraft or missile that carries one or more detachable devices (as probes or warheads) **2** : a set of parallel conductors in a computer or computer system that forms a main data transmission path

bush \ˈbu̇sh\ *adj* [¹*bush* (minor league)] : falling below acceptable standards : UNPROFESSIONAL ⟨the travesty was not that the speedway went the show-business route, but that the execution was so ~ —J.S.Radosta⟩

bush hat *n* [¹*bush* (backcountry)] : a broad-brimmed hat worn orig. as part of an Australian military uniform

bush·hog \ˈ=¦hȯg, -äg\ *vb* [fr. *Bush Hog,* proprietary name for a rotary cutter towed by a tractor] *vi, chiefly South & Midland* : to clear land of trees and brush ~ *vt, chiefly South & Midland* : to clear of trees and brush

businessman's risk *n* : an investment (as a stock) with a moderately high risk factor that is bought with an eye to growth potential and capital gains or sometimes tax advantages rather than for income

businesspeople \ˈ==¦=\ *n pl* : persons active in business

businessperson \ˈ==,==\ *n* : a person active in business

bus·ing *also* **bus·sing** \ˈbəsiŋ\ *n* -S [fr. gerund of ²*bus*] : the act of transporting by bus; *specif* : the transporting of children to a school outside their residential area as a means of establishing racial balance in the school

bust* *vt* **1** *slang* : ARREST **2** *slang* : RAID — **bust one's chops** : to give one a hard time

bust* *n* **1** *slang* : a police raid **2** *slang* : ARREST 2b(1)

bust* *or* **busted*** *adj* : having failed or come to nothingness ⟨a new friendship gone ~⟩

bus·tier \ˌbüstēˈā, ˌbəs-, -ˈtyā; ÷ˈbəstē(ə)r\ *n* -S [F, fr. *buste* bust + *-ier* ²-er — more at BUST] : a tight-fitting often strapless top worn as a brassiere or outer garment

bustout \ˈ=,=\ *n* -S [*bust out*] *slang* : a confidence scheme in which an established business is taken over, a large stock of merchandise is purchased on credit and quickly sold, and the business is then abandoned or bankruptcy is declared

bust–up* *n, chiefly Brit* : an outbreak of dissension or hostility : ALTERCATION; *also* : a rough argument or fight : SCUFFLE

bu·sul·fan \byüˈsəlfən\ *n* -S [*butane* + *sulf*onate + ³*-an*] : an antineoplastic agent $C_6H_{14}O_6S_2$ used in the treatment of chronic myelogenous leukemia

busway* *n* : an expressway or a lane of one that is reserved for the exclusive use of commuter buses

Bu·ta·zol·i·din \ˌbyüd·əˈzäləˌdēn, -ˌdən\ *trademark* — used for a preparation of phenylbutazone

butch* *n* [*butch,* adj. (herein)] : one who is butch

¹butch \ˈbu̇ch\ *adj* [prob. fr. *Butch,* a nickname for boys and esp. tough boys] **1** : significantly masculine in appearance or manner **2** : playing the male role in a homosexual relationship

²butch \"\ *n* -ES [by shortening] : BUTCHER 5

butcher block *n* : a heavy board made by bonding together thick strips of hardwood

butcher–block \ˈ=¦=\ *adj* : having a top made of or resembling butcher block ⟨a *butcher-block* table⟩

bute \ˈbyüt\ *n* -S [by shortening] : PHENYLBUTAZONE

butterfly effect *n* : a property of chaotic mathematical or physical systems (as the atmosphere) by which an extremely small change in initial conditions (as the flapping of a butterfly's wings) can lead to large–scale unpredictable variation in the future state of the system (as the severity of a tornado)

but·ter·fly·er \ˈbəd·ər,flī(ə)r, ˈbəd·ə,flīə, -ətə-\ *n* -S : a swimmer who specializes in the butterfly

butterhead \ˈ==,=\ *n* : BUTTER LETTUCE *herein*

butter lettuce *n* : a butterhead lettuce: as **a** : BOSTON LETTUCE **b** : BIBB LETTUCE

button* *n* **1** : a mescal button chewed for its hallucinogenic effect **2** : a button that has the real or symbolic capability of initiating a nuclear attack **3** : a hidden sensitivity that can be manipulated by another person to produce a desired response ⟨really knows how to push her ~*s*⟩ **4** : a usu. box-shaped icon on a computer screen that initiates a specific software function when clicked on with a mouse

button–down* *or* **but·toned–down** \ˈbət³n¦daůn\ *adj* [fr. the fact that button-down shirts are felt to be conservative] : conservatively traditional or conventional; *esp* : adhering to conventional norms in dress and behavior ⟨*button-down* businessmen⟩

button–down \ˈ==,=\ *n* -S : a shirt with a button-down collar

buttoned–up \ˈ==ˈ=\ *adj* : coldly reserved or standoffish

button man *n* [perh. fr. *buttons* (bellboy)] : a low-ranking member of an underworld organization who is given disagreeable and often dangerous assignments

button mushroom *n* : a commonly cultivated white to brown mushroom of the genus *Agaricus* (*A. bisporus* syn. *A. brunnescens*); *esp* : one that is white with a rather bland flavor and that is marketed while small and immature with the pileus not yet expanded — compare CREMINI *herein,* PORTOBELLO *herein*

butt out *vi* [*butt (in)* + ¹*out*] : to cease interference or involvement ⟨told him to *butt out* of my personal affairs⟩

bu·tut \ˈbü,tüt\ *n, pl* **butut** *or* **bututs** [Wolof *butuut,* lit., something small, fr. *tuuti* to be small] **1** : a monetary unit of Gambia equal to ¹⁄₁₀₀ dalasi — see MONEY table *in the Dict* **2** : a coin representing one butut

butylated hy·droxy·anisole \-hī¦dräksē+\ *n* [ISV *hydroxy-* + *anisole*] : BHA *herein*

butylated hy·droxy·toluene \"+\ *n* [ISV *hydroxy-* + *toluene*] : BHT *herein*

butyl nitrite *n* : a colorless pungent liquid $C_4H_9NO_2$ that is an ester of normal butyl alcohol and nitrous acid and is inhaled by drug abusers for its stimulating effects which are similar to those of amyl nitrite

bu·ty·ro·phe·none \ˌbyüd·ə(ˌ)rōfəˈnōn, -ˈfē,nōn\ *n* [*butyr-* + *phen-* + *-one*] : any of a class of antipsychotic drugs (as haloperidol) used esp. in the treatment of schizophrenia

buy* *vb* — **buy the farm** : to get killed : DIE

buyback \ˈ=,=\ *n* -S [fr. the phrase *buy back*] **1** : the act or an instance of purchasing something or a part of something previously sold **2** : the repurchase by a corporation of shares of its own common stock on the open market (as in an effort to avert a take-over by another corporation)

buy–in \ˈbī,in\ *n* -S [*buy in*] : the act or process of buying in esp. to cover a short on a stock or commodity exchange

buy into* *vt* : BUY 8

buyout \ˈ=,=\ *n* -S [*buy out*] **1** : an act or instance of buying out ⟨a ~ of residual rights⟩ ⟨a leveraged ~ of a corporation⟩ **2** : a financial incentive offered to an employee in exchange for an early retirement or voluntary resignation

buzz* *n* : FAD, CRAZE

buzz cut *n* [prob. fr. ²*buzz* (rasping sound) + ²*cut;* fr. the sound of the electric clippers used to cut the hair close] : CREW CUT — **buzz–cut** \ˈ=,=\ *adj*

buzz off *vi* : to leave forthwith : go away — usu. used as a command

buzz session *n* : a small informal group discussion

buzzword \ˈ=,=\ *n* [²*buzz* + *word*] **1** : an important-sounding and often technical word or phrase associated with a special group or activity and used chiefly to impress others **2** : a word enjoying a popular vogue

b vitamin *n, usu cap B* : any vitamin of the vitamin B complex

BX \(ˈ)bēˈeks\ *abbr or n, pl* **BXs** \-eksəz\ : base exchange *herein*

BY *abbr, usu not cap* billion years

bycatch \ˈ=,=\ *n* : the portion of a commercial fishing catch that consists of marine animals caught unintentionally ⟨the shrimp trawler's ~ included sea turtles and finfish⟩

BYOB *abbr* bring your own beer; bring your own booze; bring your own bottle

bypass* *n* : a surgically established shunt; *also* : a surgical procedure for the establishment of a shunt ⟨a triple coronary ~⟩

byte \ˈbīt\ *n* -S [alter. of ²*bite* (morsel)] : a unit of computer information or data-storage capacity that consists of a group of eight bits and that is used esp. to represent an alphanumeric character

byzantine* *adj, usu cap* **1** : of, relating to, or characterized by a devious and usu. surreptitious manner of operation ⟨the government, with its own *Byzantine* sources of intelligence —Wesley Pruden⟩ **2** : intricately involved : LABYRINTHINE ⟨searching in the *Byzantine* complexity of the record —B.L.Collier⟩

BZ \(ˈ)bē¦zē\ *n* [*BZ,* army code name, perh. fr. *benzilate* ester of benzilic acid, fr. *benzilic* acid + ¹*-ate*] : a benzilic acid ester war gas $C_{21}H_{23}NO_3$ that when breathed produces incapacitating physical and mental effects

c* *n, cap* : a structured programming language designed to produce compact and efficient object code after compilation and to allow access to hardware functions of a computer

c* *abbr, cap* cytosine
c* *symbol* **1** *cap* charge conjugation *herein* **2** *usu ital* speed of light
cabana set *n* : a two-piece beachwear ensemble for men consisting of loosely fitting shorts and a short-sleeved jacket
cabernet sau·vi·gnon \ˌ≈≈ˈsōvēˈnyōⁿ\ *n* [F, fr. *cabernet*, a grape variety of the Médoc region + *sauvignon*, a grape variety of SW France, alter. of MF *sarvinien*] : a dry red wine made from a single cultivated variety of black grape
cable* *n* : CABLE TELEVISION *herein*
ca·ble·cast \ˈ≈≈ˌ≈\ *vt* **cablecast** *also* **cablecasted; cablecast** *also* **cablecasted; cablecasting; cablecasts** [*cable* (*television*) (herein) + *-cast* (as in *broadcast*)] : to telecast by cable television — **cablecast** *n* — **ca·ble·cast·er** \-ə(r)\ *n*
cable television *or* **cable TV** *n* : a system of television reception in which signals from distant stations are picked up by a master antenna and sent by cable to the individual receivers of paying subscribers
cablevision \ˈ≈≈ˌ≈≈\ *n* : CABLE TELEVISION *herein*
ca·cha·ça *or* **ca·cha·ca** \kəˈshäsə\ *n* -S [Pg] : a clear Brazilian rum
cache* *or* **cache memory** *n* : a computer memory with a very short access time used for storage of frequently used instructions or data
cack–hand·ed \ˈkakˌhandəd\ *adj* [E dial. *cack*, *keck* awkward, of unknown origin] **1** *Brit* : LEFT-HANDED **2** *Brit* : CLUMSY, AWKWARD
CAD *abbr* computer-aided design; coronary artery disease
cadenza* *n* : an exceptionally brilliant part of an artistic and esp. a literary work
caer·phil·ly \ke(ə)rˈfilē, kär-, kī(ə)r-, kə(r)-\ *n* -ES *usu cap* [fr. *Caerphilly*, urban district in Wales] : a mild white friable cheese of Welsh origin
cae·sar salad \ˌsēzə(r)-\ *n, usu cap C* [after *Caesar* Cardini †1956 Am. (Ital.-born) restaurateur, at whose restaurant in Tijuana, Mexico, the recipe was originated] : a tossed salad made typically with romaine, garlic, anchovies, and croutons and dressed with olive oil, coddled egg, lemon juice, and grated cheese
ca·fé filtre \ˌkaˌfāˈfiltə(r), *F* käfāfēltrᵊ\ *n* [F *café-filtre*, fr. *café* coffee + *filtre* filter] : coffee made by passing hot water through ground coffee and a filter
caff \ˈkaf\ *n* -S [by shortening & alter.] *Brit* : CAFÉ
caf·fein·a·ted \ˈkafəˌnād·əd\ *adj* [back-formation fr. *decaffeinated*] **1** : stimulated by or as if by caffeine ⟨~ workers⟩ **2** : containing caffeine
caf·fè latte \ˈkäfā-, ˈka-\ *n* [It *caffè latte, caffelatte, caffellatte*, short for *caffè e latte* coffee and milk] : espresso mixed with hot or steamed milk
cage* *n* **1** : a sheer one-piece dress that has no waistline, is often gathered at the neck, and is worn over a close-fitting underdress or slip **2** : an arrangement of atoms or molecules so bonded as to enclose a space in which another atom or ion (as of a metal) can reside
CAGS *abbr* certificate of advanced graduate study
CAI *abbr* computer-aided instruction; computer-assisted instruction
ca·jun \ˈkā(ˌ)jən\ *adj, usu cap* [*Cajun*, n.] **1** : of, relating to, or characteristic of the Cajuns ⟨*Cajun* French⟩ ⟨*Cajun* music⟩ **2** : being, relating to, or prepared in a style of cooking originating among the Cajuns and characterized by the use of hot seasonings (as cayenne pepper) ⟨*Cajun* shrimp⟩
cal·a·mari \kaləˈmärē, kä-; ˈkaləˌmerē, -ri\ *n* -S [It, pl. of *calamaro*, fr. It dial., fr. ML *calamarium* inkpot, pen-case, fr. L *calamus* reed pen; fr. the inky substance ejected by the squid and the shape of its shell — more at CALAMUS] : squid used as food
ca·la·ma·ta *var of* KALAMATA
cal·ci·phy·lax·is \ˌkalsəfəˈlaksəs\ *n, pl* **calciphylax·es** \-akˌsēz\ [NL, fr. *calc-* + *-phylaxis* (as in *prophylaxis*)] : an adaptive response that follows systemic sensitization by a calcifying factor (as a D-vitamin) and a challenge (as with a metallic salt) and involves local inflammation and sclerosis with calcium deposition — **cal·ci·phy·lac·tic** \ˌ≈≈ˈlaktik\ *adj* — **cal·ci·phy·lac·ti·cal·ly** \-tək(ə)lē, -li\ *adv*
cal·ci·to·nin \ˌkalsəˈtōnən\ *n* -S [*calc-* + *-tonin* (as in *serotonin*)] : a polypeptide hormone esp. from the thyroid gland that tends to lower the level of calcium in the blood plasma — called also *thyrocalcitonin*
cal·ci·tri·ol \ˌkalsəˈtrīˌōl, -ˌōl\ *n* -S [*calc-* + *-triol*] : a physiologically active metabolic derivative $C_{27}H_{44}O_3$ of cholecalciferol that is synthesized in the liver and kidney and stimulates the intestinal absorption of calcium — called also *dihydroxycholecalciferol*
calcium channel blocker *or* **calcium blocker** *n* : any of a class of drugs (as verapamil) that prevent or slow the influx of calcium ions into smooth muscle cells esp. of the heart and that are used esp. to treat some forms of angina pectoris and some cardiac arrhythmias
calcium propionate *n* : a mold-inhibiting calcium salt $(CH_3CH_2COO)_2Ca$ used chiefly as a food preservative (as in bread)
calculus* *n* : a system or arrangement of intricate or interrelated parts ⟨the ~ of forces in world affairs —Martin Mayer⟩
cal·do ver·de \ˌkaldōˈve(ə)rdə, ˌkäldüˈverdē\ *n* [Pg, green broth] : a soup that is a puree of potatoes and greens served with smoked sausages
ca·len·drics \kəˈlendriks, ˌka-\ *n pl but sing or pl in constr* [*calendrical* + *-ics*] : the reckoning and recording of time over long periods : the creation and maintenance of a calendar
calibrate* *vt* **1** : to adjust precisely for a particular function ⟨each airport's systems are *calibrated* at least every five months —J.N.Wilford⟩ **2** : to measure precisely; *esp* : to measure against a standard
ca·li·ci·vi·rus \kəˈlisəˌvīrəs, -ˈlēsē-, -ˈlēchē-\ *n* [NL, fr. L *calic-, calix* cup + *-i-* + NL *virus* — more at CHALICE] : any of a family (Caliciviridae) of single-stranded RNA viruses that have 32 cup-shaped depressions arranged symmetrically on the surface and that include the causative viruses of a form of hepatitis and vesicular exanthema
cal·i·for·ni·ana \kaləˌfōrnēˈänə, -ˌfō(ə)n-, -ˈanə, -ˈaa(ə)nə\ *n pl, usu cap* [*California* + E *-ana*] : materials concerning or characteristic of California, its history, or its culture
caliper* *n* : an assembly designed to press a frictional material (as a brake pad) against the sides of a rotating wheel or disk in some brake systems
call* *vt* **1** : to indicate and keep track of balls and strikes in (a baseball game) **2** : to manage (as a team's strategy during a game) by giving the signals or orders ⟨the coach ~*s* every play from the sidelines⟩ **3** : to temporarily transfer control of computer processing to (as a subroutine or procedure) — **call on*** : to solicit a response (as an answer or comment) from ⟨the teacher always *called on* her first⟩
call* *n* **1** : a temporary transfer of control of computer processing to a particular set of instructions (as a subroutine or procedure) **2** : DECISION ⟨not an easy ~ for parents to make⟩
¹cal·la·loo *also* **cal·a·loo** *or* **calalu*** *or* **cal·la·lou** \ˌkaləˌlü\ *n* -S [*calalu*] : a soup or stew made with greens (as calalu or spinach), okra, and crabmeat or pork
²callaloo *var of* CALALU
call–and–response \ˈ≈≈≈\ *n* : a statement quickly followed by an answering statement; *also* : a musical phrase in which the first and often solo part is answered by a second and often ensemble part
callback** *n* : a recall by a manufacturer of a recently sold product (as an automobile) for correction of a defect
call boy** *n* : a male homosexual prostitute
caller ID *also* **caller identification** *n* : a telephone service that allows a subscriber to identify the telephone number of a caller before answering the call
call forwarding *n* : a telephone service that allows a subscriber to have incoming calls automatically forwarded to a different number
cal·li·graph \ˈkaləˌgraf\ *vt* -ED/-ING/-S [back-formation fr. *calligraphy*] : to produce or reproduce in a calligraphic style
call in* *vb* — **call in sick** : to report by telephone that one will be absent because of illness
call–in \ˈ≈(ˌ)≈\ *adj* [*call in*] : allowing listeners or viewers to engage in on-the-air telephone conversations with the host or a guest ⟨a *call-in* program⟩
calling card* *n* : a sign or evidence that someone or something is or has been present; *broadly* : an identifying mark
call up* *vt* : to retrieve from the memory of a computer esp. for display and user interaction
call waiting *n* : a telephone service that signals (as by a click) to the subscriber when an incoming call is received during a call in progress
cal·mod·u·lin \kalˈmäjəlin, -dyůlin\ *n* -S [*cal*cium + *modul*ator + *-in*] : a calcium-binding protein that mediates cellular metabolic processes (as muscle-fiber contraction) by regulating the activity of specific calcium-dependent enzymes
caló* *n* -S : any of several Spanish argots; *esp* : an argot used by Chicano youths in cities of the U.S. Southwest
cal·vin cycle \ˈkalvən-\ *also* **calvin–ben·son cycle** \-ˈben(t)sən-\ *n, usu cap 1st C&B* [after Melvin *Calvin* †1997 and Andrew *Benson* b1917 Am. biochemists] : the cycle of enzyme-catalyzed reactions of photosynthesis not requiring the presence of light that occurs in the chloroplasts of plants and in many bacteria and that involves the fixation of carbon dioxide and the formation of a six-carbon sugar — compare LIGHT REACTION *herein*
cal·zo·ne \kalˈzōn, -(ˌ)nä, -(ˌ)nē; kälˈzōnä\ *n, pl* **calzone** *or* **calzones** *or* **cal·zo·ni** \-(ˌ)nē\ [It (sing. of *calzoni* trousers), aug. of *calza* stocking, fr. ML *calcea*, fr. L *calceus* shoe, fr. *calc-, calx* heel; fr. the resemblance of its shape to that of a pants leg — more at CALK] : a baked or fried turnover of pizza dough stuffed with various fillings usu. including cheese
CAM *abbr* computer-aided manufacturing
cam·cord·er \ˈkamˌkȯ(r)də(r)\ *n* -S [*camera* + *recorder*] : a small portable combined video camera and VCR
cam·e·lot \ˈkaməˌlät\ *n* -S *usu cap* [fr. the musical *Camelot* by Alan J. Lerner †1986 Am. playwright and Frederick Loewe †1988 Am. (Austrian-born) composer which portrayed an ideal world in the Arthurian setting] : a time, place, or atmosphere of idyllic happiness
cameo* *n* : a brief dramatic role performed by a well-known actor or actress and often limited to a single scene; *broadly* : a brief appearance ⟨hit four home runs in a late September ~ in the majors⟩
cameraperson \ˈ≈(≈)≈ˌ≈≈\ *n* : a man or woman who operates a camera
camerawoman \ˈ≈(≈)≈ˌ≈≈\ *n, pl* **camerawomen** : a woman who operates a camera
camerawork \ˈ≈(≈)≈ˌ≈\ *n* [*camera* + ¹*work*] : the photography produced by a motion-picture or television camera
¹camo \ˈkamō\ *adj* [by shortening & alter.] : CAMOUFLAGE *herein*
²camo \"\ *n* -S : a combination of colors and patterns typical of camouflage; *also* : a camouflage garment or outfit
camouflage *adj* [*camouflage*, n.] : made in colors or patterns typical of camouflage ⟨a ~ jacket⟩
¹camp \ˈkamp, -aa(ə)-, -ai-\ *n* -S [origin unknown] **1** : exaggerated effeminate mannerisms (as of speech or gesture) exhibited esp. by homosexuals; *also* : a homosexual displaying such mannerisms **2** : something that is so outrageously artificial, affected, inappropriate, or out-of-date as to be considered amusing **3** : something self-consciously exaggerated or theatrical — **camp·i·ly** \-pəlē, -li\ *adv* — **camp·i·ness** *n* -ES — **campy** *adj* -ER/-EST
²camp \"\ *adj* : of, relating to, being, or displaying camp ⟨~ send-ups of the songs of the fifties and sixties —John Elsom⟩
³camp \"\ *vi* -ED/-ING/-S : to engage in camp : exhibit the qualities of camp ⟨he . . . was ~*ing*, hands on hips, with a quick eye to notice every man who passed by —R.M.McAlmon⟩
camper* *n* : a portable dwelling (as a collapsible structure folded into a small trailer or a specially equipped automotive vehicle) for use during casual travel and camping
camphor glass *n* : glass with a cloudy white appearance resembling gum camphor
camp shirt *n* : a woman's shirt having a notched collar and usu. patch pockets
camp·to·the·cin \ˌkamptəˈthēsən\ *n* -S [NL *Camptotheca*, genus name (fr. *campto-* + *-theca*) + E *-in*] : an alkaloid $C_{20}H_{16}N_2O_4$ from the wood of a Chinese tree (*Camptotheca acuminata*) of the family Nyssaceae that has shown some antileukemic and antitumor activity in animal studies; *also* : a semisynthetic or synthetic derivative of this
cam·pylo·bac·ter \ˌkampəlōˌbaktər, kamˈpilə-\ *n* [NL, genus name, fr. *campylo-* (fr. Gk *kampylos* bent, curved) + *-bacter*] **1** *cap* : a genus of slender spirally curved rod bacteria of the family Spirillaceae that are gram-negative, microaerophilic, and motile with a characteristic motion resembling a corkscrew, that do not form spores, and that include forms formerly included in the genus *Spirillum* or *Vibrio* of which some are pathogenic for domestic animals or man **2** -S : a bacterium of the genus *Campylobacter*
can* *n, slang* : an ounce of marijuana
canada day *n, usu cap C&D* : DOMINION DAY 1
ca·na·di·ana \kəˌnādēˈanə\ *n pl, usu cap* [*Canadian* + *-ana*] : materials (as historical documents and artifacts) concerning or characteristic of Canada, its civilization, or its culture; *also* : a collection of such materials
canalization* *n* : the developmental buffering and homeostatic processes by which a particular kind of organism forms a relatively constant phenotype although individuals may have a variety of genotypes and environmental conditions may vary
canard* *n* : a small airfoil in front of the wing of an aircraft that increases the aircraft's stability
cancer* *n, usu cap* : one born under the astrological sign Cancer
can·cer·ian \kanˈserēan, -ˈsi(ə)r-\ *n* -S *usu cap* [*Cancer* + *-ian*] : CANCER *herein*
can–do \ˈ≈ˈ≈\ *adj* [fr. the phrase *can do*] : characterized by an eager willingness to accept and meet challenges ⟨a gung ho *can-do* attitude⟩ ⟨the *can-do* character of a self-created nation —Barbara W. Tuchman⟩
C and W *abbr* country and western *herein*
candy–ass \ˈ≈≈ˌ≈\ *n* : SISSY 2b — sometimes considered vulgar — **candy–assed** *adj*
candy floss *n* **1** *chiefly Brit* : COTTON CANDY **2** *usu* **candyfloss** *chiefly Brit* : something attractive but insubstantial
candy strip·er \-ˌstrīpə(r)\ *n* [*candy stripe* + ²*-er*; fr. the red and white stripes of her uniform] : a teenage volunteer nurse's aide
can·na·bi·noid \ˈkanəbəˌnȯid, kəˈnabə-\ *n* -S [ISV, fr. NL *cannabis* + ISV *-n-* (as in E *cannabinol* or L *cannabinus* hempen) + ¹*-oid*] : any of various chemical constituents (as THC or cannabinol) of cannabis or marijuana
can·nel·li·ni bean *also* **cannellini** \ˌkanəˈlēnē-\ *n, pl* **cannellini** *also* **cannellinis** [It *cannellini*, pl. of *cannellino* kind of hard candy, variety of white bean resembling the candy, prob. fr. *cannella* cinnamon (used to flavor the candy) — more at CANNELURE] : a white kidney bean
cannibalize* *vt* **1** : to use or draw on material of (as earlier work or another person) ⟨chose to ~ existing technology rather than build a new model from the ground up —Thomas O'Donnell & Jill Andresky⟩ **2** : to make use of (a part taken from one thing) in building, repairing, or creating something else **3** : to take (sales) away from an existing product by selling or being sold as a similar but new product usu. from the same manufacturer; *also* : to affect (as an existing product) adversely by cannibalizing sales
can·no·li \kəˈnōlē, ka-\ *n pl but sing or pl in constr* [It, pl. of *cannolo* small cylinder, tube, dim. of *canna* tube, fr. L *canna* reed — more at CANE] : a tube of pastry fried in deep fat and filled with a sweetened mixture of ricotta cheese, cream, and flavoring
cannon net *n* : a net that is left on the ground until birds or mammals are in position and then is spread over them by the simultaneous firing of several projectiles
can of worms : PANDORA'S BOX
can·o·la \kaˈnōlə, kə-\ *n* -S [fr. *Canola*, a trademark] **1** : a variety of rape plant having seeds that are low in erucic acid and are the source of canola oil **2** : CANOLA OIL *herein*
canola oil *n* -S : an edible vegetable oil that is obtained from the seeds of canola and is high in monounsaturated fatty acids
canonical form *n* : the simplest form of a matrix; *specif* : the form of a square matrix that has zero elements everywhere except along the principal diagonal
can·tha·xan·thin \ˌkan(t)thəˈzanˌthin\ *n* [ISV *cantha-* (fr. NL *Cantharellus cinnabarinus*, species of mushroom from which it was isolated) + *xanthin* — more at CANTHARELLUS] : a naturally occurring carotenoid $C_{40}H_{52}O_2$ used esp. as a color additive for food
can't–miss \ˈ≈ˌ≈\ *adj* [fr. the phrase *can't miss*] : certain to have a favorable result, performance, or reception : SUREFIRE ⟨a *can't-miss* pitching prospect⟩ ⟨a *can't-miss* plot⟩
canton china *n, usu cap 1st C* : porcelain Canton ware esp. when blue and white
canton enamel *n, usu cap C* [fr. *Canton*, China] : Chinese enamelware of Limoges type
cantonese* *n, usu cap* : a style of Chinese cooking that emphasizes freshness of ingredients, subtle but distinct tastes and textures, and relatively mild sauces
cap* *n* [¹*cap*] **1** *Brit* : DUTCH CAP *herein* **2** : an upper limit : CEILING ⟨a salary ~⟩ **3** : the symbol ∩ indicating the intersection of two sets — compare CUP *herein* **4** : a cluster of molecules or chemical groups bound to one end or a region of a cell, virus, or molecule ⟨the cell surface receptors were redistributed into ~*s*⟩
cap* *vt* **1** : to form a chemical cap on ⟨the *capped* end of a messenger RNA⟩ **2** : to prevent from growing or spreading : set an upper limit on ⟨legislation . . . that would ~ credit card rates —Peter Pae & Georgette Jasen⟩ ~ *vi* : to form or produce a chemical cap ⟨erythrocytes and fibroblasts usually do not ~⟩
capacitate* *vt* : to cause (sperm) to undergo capacitation
capacitation* *n* : the change undergone by sperm in the female reproductive tract that enables them to penetrate and fertilize an egg
cap·el·li·ni \ˌkapəˈlēnē\ *n* -S [It, pl. of *capellino* dim. of *capello* hair, fr. L *capillus*] : pasta made in long thin strings smaller in diameter than vermicelli and spaghetti
capillary electrophoresis *n* : electrophoresis performed in a capillary tube
capital gains distribution *n* : the part of the payout of an investment company to its shareholders that consists of realized profits from the sale of securities and technically is not income
capital–intensive \ˌ≈(≈)≈(ˈ)≈ˌ≈≈\ *adj* : having a high capital cost per unit of output; *esp* : requiring greater expenditure in the form of capital than of labor
capital structure *n* : the makeup of the capitalization of a business in terms of the amounts and kinds of equity and debt securities : the equity and debt securities of a business together with its surplus and reserves
cap·i·tate \ˈkapəˌtāt\ *n* -S [by shortening] : CAPITATUM
Cap·lets \ˈkapləts\ *trademark* — used for capsule-shaped medicinal tablets
ca·po \ˈkä(ˌ)pō, ˈka-, ˈkȧ-\ *n* -S [It, head, chief, fr. L *caput* — more at HEAD] **1** : the head of a branch of a crime syndicate **2** : ⁵BOSS 2 ⟨~ of the network's news division⟩
ca·po·ei·ra \ˌkäp(ə)ˈwārə\ *n* -S [Brazilian Pg, kind of martial art, ruffian skilled in this art, fugitive slave living in the forest, fr. *capão* island of forest in a clear-cut area (fr. Tupi *kaápaũ*, fr. *kaá* forest + *paũ* round) + *-eira*, fem. of *-eiro* ²-er] : a Brazilian dance of African origin that incorporates martial arts movements such as kicks and chops
ca·po·na·ta \ˌkäpəˈnäd·ə, -ätə\ *n* -S [It dial. (Sicily) *capunata*, sailor's dish of biscuit steeped in oil and vinegar, chopped vegetable assortment served similarly, fr. Catal *caponada* dry bread soaked in oil and vinegar, perh. fr. *capó* capon (fr. L *capon-, capo*) + *-ada* -ade — more at CAPON] : a relish of chopped eggplant and assorted vegetables
capper* *n* : something that concludes or surpasses that which preceded it : FINALE, CLIMAX, CLINCHER
cap·puc·ci·no *or* **cap·uc·ci·no** \ˌkapəˈchēnō, ˌkäpů-\ *n* -S [It, lit., Capuchin; fr. the likeness of its color to that of a Capuchin's habit — more at CAPUCHIN] : espresso coffee topped with frothed hot milk or cream and often flavored with cinnamon; *also* : a cup of cappuccino
cap·reo·my·cin \ˌkaprēōˈmīsᵊn\ *n* -S [NL *capreolus* (specific epithet of *Streptomyces capreolus*) + E *-mycin*] : an antibiotic obtained from a bacterium of the genus *Streptomyces* (*S. capreolus*) that is used to treat tuberculosis
capricorn* *n, usu cap* : one born under the astrological sign Capricorn
cap·ri·cor·ni·an \ˌkaprəˈkȯrnēən, -rēˌk-, -ó(ə)n-\ *n* -S *usu cap* [*capricorn* + E *-ian*] : CAPRICORN *herein*
capri pants *n pl, often cap C* [fr. *Capri*, island in the Bay of Naples, Italy] : close-fitting pants that have tapered legs with a slit on the outside of the leg bottom, extend almost to the ankle, and are used for informal wear esp. by women
cap·sid \ˈkapsəd\ *n* -S [ISV *caps-* (fr. L *capsa* case) + ⁴*-id*; orig. formed as F *capside* — more at CASE] : the protein shell of a virus particle that surrounds its nucleic acid — **cap·sid·al** \-dᵊl\ *adj*
cap·so·mer \ˈkapsəmər\ *or* **cap·so·mere** \-ˌmi(ə)r\ *n* -S [*capsid* (herein) + *-o-* + *-mer, -mere*] : one of the subunits making up a viral capsid
cap·su·li·tis \ˌkaps(y)əˈlīd·əs, -ītəs\ *n* -ES [NL, fr. E ¹*capsule* + NL *-itis*] : inflammation of a capsule (as that of the crystalline lens)
cap·su·lot·o·my \ˌkaps(y)əˈläd·əmē, -ätə-, -mi\ *n* -ES [¹*capsule* + *-o-* + *-tomy*] : incision of a capsule esp. of the crystalline lens (as in a cataract operation)
cap·tan \ˈkapˌtan\ *n* -S [perh. short for *mercaptan*] : a fungicide $C_9H_8Cl_3NO_2S$ that is used on agricultural crops and as a bacteriostat in soaps
cap·to·pril \ˈkaptəˌpril\ *n* -S [*mercapt-* + *proline* + *-il*] : an antihypertensive drug $C_9H_{15}NO_3S$ that is an ACE inhibitor
capture* *n* : the act of recording in a permanent file ⟨data ~⟩
capture* *vt* : to record in a permanent file (as in a computer)
car·a·van·eer \ˌkarə(ˌ)vaˈni(ə)r, -ˌvaˈ-, -niə(r\ *n* -S [*caravan* + *-eer*] : CARAVANNER *herein*
car·a·van·ner *or* **car·a·van·er** \ˈkarəˌvanə(r), -vaan- *also* ˈker- *esp Brit* ˌ≈≈ˈ≈\ *n* -S [*caravan* + ²*-er*] **1** : one that travels in a caravan **2** *Brit* : one who goes camping with a trailer
carb \ˈkärb\ *or* **car·bo** \ˈkärˌbō\ *n* -S [by shortening] : CARBOHYDRATE; *also* : a high-carbohydrate food — usu. used in pl. ⟨munching out on *carbos* —Cyra McFadden⟩
car·ba·maz·e·pine \ˌkärbəˈmazəˌpēn\ *n* -S [*carbamoyl* + *-azepine* (as in *benzodiazepine* — herein)] : a tricyclic anticonvulsant and analgesic $C_{15}H_{12}N_2O$ used in the treatment of trigeminal neuralgia and epilepsy
car·ba·ryl \ˈkärbəˌril, -ˌrəl\ *n* -S [*carbamate* + *aryl*] : a nonpersistent carbamate insecticide $C_{12}H_{11}O_2N$ effective against numerous crop, forage, and forest pests — see SEVIN
car bed *n* : a portable bed for an infant that is designed for use in an automobile
carbene* *n* : any of a class of usu. highly reactive chemical compounds containing an uncharged divalent carbon atom that are formed esp. as intermediates in chemical reactions
car·ben·i·cil·lin \ˌkär(ˌ)benəˈsilən\ *n* -S [*carb-* + *benzyl* + *penicillin*] : a broad-spectrum semisynthetic penicillin $C_{17}H_{18}N_2O_6S$ that is effective against gram-negative bacteria (as pseudomonas) and that acts esp. by inhibiting cell-wall synthesis
car·bo·cat·ion \ˌkärbōˈkadˌīən, -ˌīˌän, -ˈkaˌtī-\ *n* [ISV *carb-* + *cation*; orig. formed in F] : CARBONIUM

car·bo·fur·an \ˌkärbōˈfyüˌran\ *n* [*carb-* + *furan*] : a highly toxic broad-spectrum carbamate pesticide $C_{12}H_{15}NO_3$ used on crops
car·bo·line \ˈkärbəˌlēn\ *n* -s [*carb-* + *indole* + *pyridine*] : any of various isomers that have the formula $C_{11}H_8N_2$ and are structurally related to indole and pyridine
carbo–load \ˈ⁼⁼ˌ⁼\ *vi* [*carbohydrate* + [1]*load*] : to consume a large amount of carbohydrates through food intake usu. in order to improve performance in an upcoming athletic event (as a marathon)
car bomb *n* : an explosive device concealed in an automobile for use as a weapon of terrorism
car·bo·na·ra \ˌkärbəˈnärə\ *n* -s [It dial. (*alla*) *carbonara*, lit., in the manner of the charcoal burner, fem. of *carbonaro* charcoal burner or seller — more at CARBONARI] : a dish of hot pasta into which other ingredients (as raw eggs, bacon or ham, and grated cheese) have been mixed — often used as a postpositive modifier ⟨spaghetti ~⟩
carbon dating *n* : the determination of the age of old material (as of an archaeological find) by means of the content of carbon 14 — called also *carbon 14 dating, radiocarbon dating* — **carbon–date** \ˈ⁼⁼ˌ⁼\ *vt*
carbon fiber *n* : a very strong lightweight synthetic fiber made esp. by carbonizing acrylic fiber at high temperatures
carbonless* *adj* : being or composed of paper that makes multiple copies without intervening layers of carbon paper ⟨~ forms⟩
car·bon·nade \ˌkärbəˈnäd\ *n* -s [F, lit., grilled meat, fr. It *carbonata*, fr. *carbone* charcoal, coal (fr. L *carbon-, carbo*) + *-ata* -ade] : a beef stew cooked in beer
carbon spot* *n* : a small black spot on a coin
carbon star *n* : a reddish star of low surface temperature containing a high proportion of carbon and other heavier elements
carbon 12 *n* : an isotope of carbon of mass number 12 that is the most abundant carbon isotope
car·bo·rane \ˈkärbəˌrān\ *n* -s [blend of *carbon* and *borane*] : any of a class of thermally stable compounds $B_nC_2H_{n+2}$ that are used in the synthesis of polymers and lubricants
car·bu·ret·ed \ˈkärbəˌrād·əd, -byə-, *esp by chemists* -ˌred·əd\ *adj* [*carburetor* + [1]*-ed*] : equipped with a carburetor ⟨a ~ engine⟩
car·byne \ˈkärˌbīn\ *n* -s [*carb-* + *-yne*] : any of several crystalline forms of carbon in which it is linked in chains containing alternating single and triple bonds
car·ci·no·embryonic antigen \ˈkärsᵊn(ˌ)ō+. . .-\ *n* [*carcin-* + *embryonic*] : a glycoprotein present in fetal gut tissues during the first two trimesters of pregnancy and in peripheral blood of patients with some forms of cancer (as of the digestive system or breast) — abbr. *CEA*
car coat *n* : a three-quarter-length overcoat
card* *n* **1** : CREDIT CARD **2** : a flat stiff piece of material (as plastic) bearing electronic circuit components for insertion into a larger electronic device (as a computer) **3** : an issue esp. with emotional appeal that is brought into play to achieve a desired end (as a campaign victory) ⟨played the race ~⟩
card* *vt* : to ask for identification (as in a bar)
card–car·ry·ing \ˈ⁼ˌ⁼⁼⁼\ *adj* [so called fr. the assumption that such a member carries a membership card] **1** : being a full-fledged member esp. of a Communist party **2 a** : being strongly identified with a group (as of people with a common interest) ⟨*card-carrying* members of the ecology movement —Richard Neuhaus⟩ **b** : characterized as having a clear specific identity ⟨*card-carrying* skeptics —Junius Ellis⟩
card·enol·ide \kärˈdēnᵊlˌīd\ *n* -s [*card*iac + but*enolide* ring, a constituent of cardenolide] : any of numerous organic compounds with a characteristic ring structure many of which are found in plants (as some milkweeds), have an effect on the vertebrate heart like that of digitalis, and cause vomiting
car·di·nal·i·ty \ˌkärdᵊnˈaləd·ē\ *n* -ES [*cardinal (number)* + *-ity*] : the number of elements in a given mathematical set
cardinal number* *n* : the property that a mathematical set has in common with all sets that can be put into one-to-one correspondence with it
cardinal's hat *n* : GALERO *herein*
car·dio \ˈkärdē(ˌ)ō\ *adj* [by shortening] : CARDIOVASCULAR *herein*
car·dio·accelerator *also* **car·dio·acceleratory** \ˈkärdē(ˌ)ō+\ *adj* [*cardi-* + *accelerator* or *acceleratory*] : speeding up the action of the heart — **car·dio·acceleration** \"+\ *n*
car·dio·active \"+\ *adj* [*cardi-* + *active*] : having an influence on the heart ⟨~ drugs⟩ — **car·dio·activity** \"+\ *n*
car·dio·circulatory \"+\ *adj* [*cardi-* + *circulatory*] : of or relating to the heart and circulatory system ⟨temporary ~ assist⟩
car·dio·dynamics \"+\ *n pl but sing or pl in constr* [*cardi-* + *dynamics*] : the dynamics of the heart's action in pumping blood — **car·dio·dynamic** \"+\ *adj*
car·dio·gen·ic \ˈ⁼⁼(ˌ)ō¦jenik *also* -jēn-\ *adj* [*cardi-* + *-genic*] : originating in the heart : caused by a cardiac condition ⟨~ shock⟩
car·dio·meg·a·ly \ˌkärdēōˈmegəlē\ *n* -ES [*cardi-* + *-megaly*] : enlargement of the heart
car·dio·myopathy \ˈkärdē(ˌ)ō+\ *n* [*cardi-* + *myopathy*] : a structural or functional disease of heart muscle that is marked esp. by hypertrophy of cardiac muscle, by enlargement of the heart, by rigidity and loss of flexibility of the heart walls, or by narrowing of the ventricles but is not due to a congenital developmental defect, to coronary atherosclerosis, to valve dysfunction, or to hypertension
car·dio·pulmonary \"+\ *adj* [*cardi-* + *pulmonary*] : of or relating to the heart and lungs ⟨the ~ system⟩ ⟨a ~ bypass that diverts blood from the entrance to the right atrium through an oxygenator directly to the aorta⟩
cardiopulmonary resuscitation *n* : a procedure designed to restore normal breathing after cardiac arrest that includes the clearance of air passages to the lungs, the mouth-to-mouth method of artificial respiration, and heart massage by the exertion of pressure on the chest — abbr. *CPR*
car·dio·sclerosis \ˈkärdē(ˌ)ō+\ *n, pl* **cardioscleroses** [NL, fr. *cardi-* + *sclerosis*] : induration of the heart caused by formation of fibrous tissue in the cardiac muscle
car·dio·thoracic \"+\ *adj* [*cardi-* + *thoracic*] : relating to, involving, or specializing in the heart and chest ⟨a ~ surgeon⟩ ⟨~ surgery⟩
car·dio·toxic \"+\ *adj* [*cardi-* + *toxic*] : having a toxic effect on the heart — **car·dio·toxicity** \"+\ *n*
cardiovascular* *adj* : used, designed, or performed to cause a temporary increase in heart rate (as to improve heart function and reduce the risk of heart disease) ⟨a ~ workout⟩ ⟨treadmills, stationary bicycles, and other ~ equipment⟩
car·dio·ver·sion \ˈ⁼⁼(ˌ)ō¦vərzhən *also* |shən\ *n* -s [*cardi-* + *version* (turning of an organ or fetus)] : application of an electric shock in order to restore normal heartbeat
care* *vb* — **care less** : not to care — used positively and negatively with the same meaning ⟨I could *care less* what happens⟩ ⟨I couldn't *care less* what happens⟩
caregiver \ˈ⁼ˌ⁼⁼\ *n* : a person who provides direct care (as for children or the chronically ill) — **caregiving** \ˈ⁼ˌ⁼⁼\ *n*
care package \ˈke(ə)r-, ˈkeə-, ˈka(a)(ə)r-, ˈka(a)ə-\ *n* [fr. *CARE package*, a charity food parcel sent to needy Europeans after World War II by CARE (Cooperative for American Remittances to Europe)] : a package of useful or pleasurable items that is sent or given to another (as a college student)
cargo pocket *n* : a large pocket usu. with a flap and a pleat
car·io·static \ˌka(a)rēō+\ *adj* [*cario-* + *static*] : tending to inhibit the formation of dental caries ⟨the ~ action of fluorides⟩
ca·ri·so·pro·dol \kəˌrīsəˈprōˌdȯl, -īzə-, -dōl\ *n* -s [*carbamate* + *isopropyl* + *-diol*] : a drug $C_{12}H_{24}N_2O_4$ related to meprobamate that is used to relax muscle and relieve pain
car·jack·ing \ˈkärˌjakiŋ, ˈkȧ(r)-\ *n* -s [[1]*car* + hi*jack* + [3]*-ing*] : the theft of an automobile from its driver by force or intimidation — **car·jack** \-ˌjak\ *vt* -ED/-ING/-S — **car·jack·er** \-ə(r)\ *n* -s
car·ne asa·da \ˌkärnäəˈsädə, -äˈsäthə\ *n* [Sp, grilled meat] : marinated and grilled strips of steak often topped with spicy condiments or sauce and sometimes served in a burrito or taco
car·ni·tas \ˌkärˈnēd·əz, -ˈnētäs\ *n pl* [MexSp, pl. of *carnita*, dim. of Sp *carne* meat, fr. L *carn-, caro* flesh — more at CARNAL] : small chunks or strips of meat and esp. pork that are fried or roasted until crisp
carnival glass *n, often cap C* [so called fr. its frequent use for prizes at carnival booths] : pressed glass with an iridescent finish mass-produced in a variety of colors (as frosty white or deep purple) in the U.S. in the early 20th century
car·no·saur \ˈkärnəˌsȯ(ə)r, -ȯ(ə)\ *n* -s [NL *Carnosauria*] : any of the group Carnosauria (as an allosaur or a tyrannosaur) of theropod dinosaurs
carousel* *n* : a revolving case or tray used for storage or display
carp \ˈkärp, ˈkȧp\ *n* -s [[1]*carp*] : COMPLAINT
car·pac·cio \kärˈpäch(ē)ō\ *n* -s [It *filetto Carpaccio* fillet Carpaccio, after Vittore *Carpaccio* †1525 Venetian painter known for his use of reds and whites] : thinly sliced raw meat or fish served with a sauce — often used as a postpositive modifier ⟨beef ~⟩
carpal tunnel *n* : a passage between the flexor retinaculum of the hand and the carpal bones that is sometimes a site of compression of the median nerve
carpal tunnel syndrome *n* : a condition caused by compression of the median nerve in the carpal tunnel and characterized esp. by weakness, pain, and disturbances of sensation in the hand and fingers
carpetbag steak *n* : a thick piece of steak in which a pocket is cut and stuffed (as with oysters)
carpool \ˈ⁼ˌ⁼\ *vb* [*car pool*, n.] *vt* : to take turns driving ⟨~ children to school⟩ ~ *vi* : to participate in a car pool ⟨~*ed* with coworkers⟩ — **carpool·er** \ˈ⁼ˌpülə(r)\ *n*
carrier* *n* : an entity (as a hole or an electron) capable of carrying an electric charge
carrier bag *n, Brit* : SHOPPING BAG *herein*
carrot–and–stick \ˈ⁼⁼⁼ˌ⁼\ *adj* : characterized by the alternating use of reward and punishment
carry* *vb* — **carry the can** *chiefly Brit* : to bear alone and in full an often hazardous responsibility
carry* *n* : a quantity that is transferred in addition from one number place to the adjacent one of higher place value
carry–cot \ˈ⁼⁼ˌ⁼\ *n, Brit* : a portable bed for an infant
carryon \ˈ⁼⁼ˌ⁼\ *n* -s [[1]*carry* + [2]*on*] : a piece of luggage suitable for being carried aboard an airplane by a passenger — **carry–on** \ˈ⁼⁼ˌ⁼\ *adj*
[1]**carryout** \ˈ⁼⁼ˌ⁼\ *adj* [[1]*carry* + [1]*out*] : TAKEOUT *herein*
[2]**carryout** \ˈ⁼⁼ˌ⁼\ *n* -s **1** : prepared food packaged to be consumed away from its place of sale **2** : an establishment that sells carryout
car seat *n* : a portable seat for an infant or small child that attaches to an automobile seat and holds the child safely
cartesian plane *n, usu cap C* : a plane whose points are labeled with Cartesian coordinates
cartesian product *n, usu cap C* : a set that is constructed from two given sets and comprises all pairs of elements such that one element of the pair is from the first set and the other element is from the second set
cartoon* *n* : a simplistic, unrealistic, or one-dimensional portrayal or version (as of a person) : CARICATURE
car·toon·ish \kärˈtünish\ *adj* : resembling a cartoon — **car·toon·ish·ly** \-lē\ *adv*
car·toony \kärˈtünē\ *adj* : CARTOONISH *herein*
car·top·per \ˈkärˌtäpər; ˈkȧ-, -pə(r\ *n* -s [*cartop* + [2]*-er*] : a small boat that may be transported on top of a car
cartridge* *n* **1** : a removable case containing a magnetic tape or one or more disks and used as a computer storage medium **2** : a case for holding integrated circuits containing a computer program ⟨a video-game ~⟩
case* *n* **1** : one of a set of relational semantic categories in the deep structure of a sentence that help determine the meaning of the sentence **2** : oneself considered as an object of harassment ⟨get off my ~⟩ ⟨they'd been on his ~ ever since his school grades had started to drop —*New Yorker*⟩
casebook* *n* : a compilation of primary and secondary documents relating to a central topic together with scholarly comment, exercises, and study aids that is often designed to serve as a source book for short papers (as in a course in composition) or as a point of departure for a research paper
case grammar *n* : a grammar that describes the deep structure of sentences in terms of the relation of a verb to a set of semantic cases
case officer *n* : an intelligence officer who recruits agents and manages their activities
ca·sette \kəˈset, ka-\ *n* -s [by alter.] **1** : CASSETTE 3 **2** : CASSETTE *herein*
cash bar *n* : a bar (as at a wedding reception) at which drinks are sold — compare OPEN BAR *herein*
cash cow *n* : something (as an established product or corporate division) that yields a dependable profit without additional capital investment
cash desk *n, Brit* : a counter at which a cashier works
cash flow *n* **1** : a measure of an organization's liquidity that usu. consists of net income after taxes plus noncash charges (as depreciation) against income **2** : a flow of cash ⟨maintaining an international *cash flow* —C.H.Stern⟩ ⟨the faster the speed of *cash flow*, the better the fiscal health of the publishing company —*Book Production Industry*⟩; *esp* : one that provides solvency ⟨colleges obtained bank loans in July to maintain a *cash flow* until tuition money came in —L.B.Mayhew⟩
cash·less \ˈkashləs\ *adj* : not having or involving cash; *specif* : relying largely or entirely on monetary transactions that use electronic means rather than cash
cash out *vi* : to convert (noncash assets) to cash ⟨*cash out* stocks⟩ ~ *vi* : to convert noncash assets to cash — **cash–out** \ˈ⁼ˌ⁼\ *n* -s
ca·si·no \kəˈsē(ˌ)nō\ *adj* [*casino*, n.] : baked or broiled on the half shell usu. with a topping of green pepper and bacon — often used postpositively ⟨clams ~⟩ ⟨oysters ~⟩
cas·sa·ta \kəˈsäd·ə, ka-, -ätə\ *n* -s [It, fr. It dial. (Sicily), perh. alter. of OIt *casiata* egg and cheese pastry, fr. *cascio* cheese, fr. L *caseus* — more at CHEESE] : a cake filled with ricotta cheese, candied fruit, and chocolate
cas·se·grain \ˈkasəˌgrān, *F* kásgrañ\ *also* **cassegrainian** *adj, usu cap C* : of, relating to, or being the system of optics used in a Cassegrainian telescope ⟨~ focus⟩
cassette* *n* : a usu. flat case or container that holds a substance, device, or material which is difficult, troublesome, or awkward to handle and that can easily be inserted into or removed from a machine; *esp* : a usu. plastic cartridge containing magnetic tape with the tape on one reel passing to the other without having to be threaded
casting couch *n* : a couch in an entertainment executive's office on which aspiring actresses are reputed to perform sexual acts in exchange for desired roles; *broadly* : the practice of abusing one's power to obtain sexual partners
cas·tro·ism \ˈkas(ˌ)trōˌizəm *sometimes* -äs-\ *n* -s *usu cap* [Fidel *Castro* b1927 Cuban political leader + E *-ism*] : the political, economic, and social principles and policies of Fidel Castro — **cas·tro·ist** \-ōˌist, -ō,əst\ *n or adj, usu cap* — **cas·tro·ite** \-ōˌīt\ *n or adj, usu cap*
CAT *abbr* **1** clear-air turbulence *herein* **2** computed axial tomography *herein*; computerized axial tomography *herein*
catalytic converter *n* : an automobile exhaust-system component containing a catalyst which causes conversion of harmful gases (as carbon monoxide and unconsumed hydrocarbons) into mostly harmless products (as water and carbon dioxide)
ca·taph·o·ra \kəˈtaf(ə)rə\ *n* -s [*cata-* + ana*phora*] : the use of a grammatical substitute (as a pronoun) that has the same reference as a following word or phrase
cat·a·phor·ic \ˈkad·əˈfȯrik\ *adj* : of or relating to cataphora; *esp* : being a word or phrase (as a pronoun) that takes its reference from a following word or phrase (as *her* in "before her Jane saw nothing but desert") — compare ANAPHORIC *in the Dict*
catastrophe* *n* : a violent usu. destructive natural event (as a supernova)
catastrophe theory *n* : mathematical theory and conjecture concerned with the use of topology to explain events (as an earthquake or a stock market crash) characterized by major abrupt changes
catch* *vt* : to meet with ⟨I might ~ them in the evenings at a local motel —Bryan Di Salvatore⟩ — often used as an informal farewell at parting ⟨~ you later⟩ ~ *vi* : to kick over ⟨the engine finally *caught*⟩
catchment area* *n* : the geographical area served by an institution ⟨describe the *catchment areas* and social backgrounds of the various schools she examined —*Times Lit. Supp.*⟩
catch–22 \ˈ⁼ˌ⁼ˈ⁼\ *n, pl* **catch–22's** *or* **catch–22s** *often cap C* [fr. *Catch-22*, the paradoxical rule found in the novel *Catch-22* (1961) by Joseph Heller †1999 Am. author, fr. [2]*catch* (difficulty) + *22*] **1** : a problematic situation for which the only solution is denied by a circumstance inherent in the problem or by a rule ⟨the show-business *catch-22*—no work unless you have an agent, no agent unless you've worked —Mary Murphy⟩; *also* : the circumstance or rule that denies a solution ⟨this *Catch-22* principle of the tax code: . . . any transaction which has no substantive object other than to reduce one's taxes—does not qualify to reduce one's taxes —Andrew Tobias⟩ **2 a** : an illogical, unreasonable, or senseless situation ⟨continuing the *Catch-22* logic, he explained that the agents busted in with guns drawn "to reduce the potential for violence" —Michael Drosnin⟩ **b** : a measure or policy whose effect is the opposite of what was intended ⟨a medical *catch-22*: some experts now believe that the examination . . . may actually cause more cases of breast cancer than it helps to cure —*Newsweek*⟩ **c** : a situation presenting two equally undesirable alternatives : DILEMMA ⟨"*catch-22*" If I don't jog, it's bad. If I jog in polluted city air, it's bad —Jim Berry⟩ **3** : CATCH 7 ⟨the puritanical *Catch-22* that runs through our society—pleasure, it warns, must be paid for —Janet S. King⟩
catch–up *adj* [*catch-up*, n.] : intended to catch up to a theoretical norm or a competitor's accomplishments
catch up* *vi* : to reach a state of parity or a state of being able to cope ⟨some kindergartners without preschool education have difficulty *catching up*⟩ — often used with *with* ⟨will take years of spending to *catch up* with the immense needs⟩
catechism* *n* : something resembling a catechism esp. in being a rote response or formulaic statement
cat·e·chol·amine \ˌkad·əˈkōləˌmēn, -äl-\ *n* [*catechol* + *amine*] : any of various substances (as epinephrine, norepinephrine, and dopamine) that contain a benzene ring with two adjacent hydroxyl groups and a side chain of ethylamine and that function as hormones or neurotransmitters or both
cat·e·chol·amin·er·gic \ˌ⁼⁼¦⁼⁼(ˌ)mē¦nərjik, -ˌmə¦-\ *adj* [*catecholamine* + *-ergic* (herein)] : involving, liberating, or mediated by catecholamine ⟨~ neurons in the brain⟩ ⟨~ transmission in the nervous system⟩
category* *n* : a mathematical class of objects (as groups or topological spaces) together with a set of structure-preserving mappings (as homomorphisms or continuous functions) between the members of the class such that the operation of applying one mapping after another to produce a single combined mapping is associative and the set of mappings includes an identity element — **categorical*** *adj*
cat·e·na·tive \ˈkad·əˌnād·iv, ˈkatᵊnˌād·iv, -atə-, -ātiv\ *or* **catenative verb** *also* **catenative auxiliary** *n* -s [[1]*catenate* + [2]*-ive*] : a verb often followed by a function word (as *to* or *on*) that occupies a position other than final in a succession of two or more verbs together forming the main part of the predicate of a sentence (as *ought* in "I ought to go home now" and *try* and *keep* in "they tried to keep on working")
cathedral* *adj, of women's formal apparel* : having a length that reaches the floor and trails behind ⟨~ veil⟩
ca·tho·dal \ˈkathˌōdᵊl, kathˈ-\ *adj* : of, relating to, or attracted to a cathode : CATHODIC 1a ⟨~ potentials⟩ ⟨~ hemoglobins⟩ — used esp. in the life sciences — **ca·tho·dal·ly** \ˈ⁼ˈ⁼ᵊlē\ *adv*
cat scan \ˈkat-, ˌsēˌāˈtē-\ *n, usu cap C&A&T* [computed axial tomography] : a sectional view of the body made by computed tomography — called also *CT scan* — **cat scanning** *n, usu cap C&A&T*
cat scanner *n, usu cap C&A&T* : a medical instrument consisting of integrated X-ray and computing equipment and used for computed tomography — called also *CT scanner*
cat suit *n* [prob. fr. the use of such garments as cat costumes, as in the 1953 science-fiction film *Cat-Women of the Moon*] : a close-fitting one-piece garment that covers the torso and legs and sometimes the arms
cattle call *n* : a mass audition
CATV *abbr* community antenna television *herein*
cau·chy sequence \ˈkōshē-, kōˈshē-\ *n, usu cap C* [after Augustin-Louis *Cauchy* †1857 Fr. mathematician] : a sequence of elements in a metric space such that for any positive number no matter how small there exists a term in the sequence for which the distance between any two consecutive or nonconsecutive terms beyond this term is less than an arbitrarily small positive number ⟨the sequence 1, ½, ⅓, ¼, . . ., $^1/_n$, . . . is a *Cauchy sequence*⟩
caucus* *n* : a group of people united to promote an agreed-upon cause ⟨emergence of radical ~*es* in most professional and academic organizations —L.J.Magid⟩
cau·ri \ˈkaürē\ *n, pl* **cauris** [F, cowrie shell, fr. Hindi *kaurī* — more at COWRIE] : a monetary unit of Guinea equal to $^1/_{100}$ syli — see MONEY table *in the Dict*
CAV \ˌsē(ˌ)āˈvē\ *n* -s [constant angular velocity] : a videodisc recording format in which the disc spins at a constant rate and the same number of frames is recorded on each track
cavalier king charles spaniel *n, usu cap both Cs&K* [[1]*cavalier* + *King Charles spaniel*] : a dog of a breed of toy spaniels that was developed in Great Britain from English toy spaniels and comprises active friendly dogs having a tapered muzzle and long silky coat — compare KING CHARLES SPANIEL *in the Dict*
CB \ˌsēˈbē\ *n* -s : CITIZENS BAND *herein*; *also* : the radio transmitting and receiving set used for citizens-band communications
CBC *abbr* complete blood count
CBD* *abbr* central business district
cber \(ˌ)sēˈbēə(r)\ *n* -s *usu cap C&B* [*CB* (herein) + [2]-er] : one that operates a CB radio
CBW *abbr* chemical and biological warfare
CCD \ˌsē(ˌ)sēˈdē\ *n* -s : CHARGE-COUPLED DEVICE *herein*
CCTV *abbr* closed-circuit television
CD \ˌsēˈdē\ *n* -s : COMPACT DISC *herein*
CD8 \ˌsē(ˌ)dēˈāt\ *n* -s *often attrib* [cluster of differentiation antigen + *8*] : a glycoprotein found on the surface esp. of killer T cells that usu. functions to facilitate recognition by killer T cell receptors of antigens complexed with molecules of a class that are found on the surface of most nucleated cells and are the product of genes of the major histocompatibility complex
CD4 \-ˈfōr, -ˈfȯr\ *n* -s *often attrib* [cluster of differentiation antigen + *4*] : a large glycoprotein that is found on the surface esp. of helper T cells, that is the receptor for HIV, and that usu. functions to facilitate recognition by helper T cell receptors of antigens complexed with molecules of a class that are found on the surface of antigen-presenting cells (as B cells and macrophages) and are the product of genes of the major histocompatibility complex
CD–I \ˌsēˌdēˈī\ *n* [compact disc interactive] : a compact disc that contains audio, video, and text information — compare CD-ROM *herein*
cDNA \ˈsēˌdē(ˌ)eˈnā\ *n* -s [complementary] : a DNA that is

complementary to a given RNA which serves as a template for synthesis of the DNA in the presence of a reverse transcriptase
CDP *abbr* certificate in data processing
CD–ROM \ˌsēˌdēˈräm\ *n* -s [compact *d*isc *r*ead-*o*nly *m*emory] : a compact disc containing data that can be read by a computer — compare CD-1 *herein*
CEA *abbr* carcinoembryonic antigen *herein*
ce·co·pexy \ˈsēkəˌpeksē, -kō-\ *n* -ES [*cec-* + *-pexy*] : a surgical operation to fix the cecum to the abdominal wall
ce·di \ˈsādē\ *n* -s [Twi *sedi* cowrie shell] **1** : the basic monetary unit of Ghana — see MONEY table *in the Dict* **2** : a note representing one cedi
cef·tri·ax·one \ˌseftrīˈaksōn\ *n* -s [*cef-* (alter. of *cepha*losporin — herein) + *-triaxone*, of unknown origin] : a semisynthetic cephalosporin antibiotic $C_{18}H_{18}N_8O_7S_3$ that is administered parenterally in the form of its sodium salt
ce·leb·ri·ty·hood \səˈlebrədēˌhu̇d, -ətē-, -ti-\ *n* : the state of being a celebrity
cell* *n* **1** : a basic subdivision of a computer memory that is addressable and can hold one basic operating unit (as a word) **2** : FUEL CELL *herein* **3** : a manufacturing unit that produces a group of related products **4** : any of the small sections of a geographic area of a cellular telephone system
cellar master *n* : a person who supervises the making of wine in a winery
cell cycle *n* : the complete series of events from one cell division to the next — see G 1 PHASE *herein*, G 2 PHASE *herein*, M PHASE *herein*, S PHASE *herein*
cell line *n* : a cell culture selected for uniformity from a cell population derived from a usu. homogeneous tissue source (as an organ) ⟨a newly established *cell line* derived from human endometrial carcinoma —*Biol. Abstracts*⟩
cell–mediated *adj* : relating to or being the part of immunity or the immune response that is mediated primarily by T cells and esp. cytotoxic T cells rather than by antibodies secreted by B cells ⟨~ immunity⟩ ⟨~ reactions⟩ — compare HUMORAL *herein*
cellophane noodles *n pl* [so called fr. their translucency] : BEAN THREADS *herein*
cell phone *n* : a cellular telephone
cellular* *adj* : of, relating to, or being a radiotelephone system in which a geographical area (as a city) is divided into small sections each served by a transmitter of limited range so that any available radio channel can be used in different parts of the area simultaneously
cellular *n* -s : a cellular telephone
cellular automaton *n* **1** : a hypothetical computing machine that can reproduce itself **2** : an element in a computer simulation composed of semiautonomous interacting elements; *specif* : any of such elements that are visualized on a computer screen as square or hexagonal cells comprising an array, grid, or lattice, that are controlled by similar but separate software routines or hardware devices, that can exist in a number of states, that are influenced by the states of their neighbors, and that are used to simulate diverse complex systems (as neuronal activity in a brain or traffic flow patterns)
cel·lu·lite \ˈselyəˌlīt, -ˌlēt\ *n* -s [F, lit., accumulation of subcutaneous fat, cellulitis, fr. *cellule* cell (fr. L *cellula*, fr. *cella* cell + *-ula* -ule) + *-ite* -itis — more at CELL] : lumpy fat found in the thighs, hips, and buttocks of some women
cent* *n* : a common monetary unit of most countries of the European Union equivalent to $^1/_{100}$ euro — see *birr, dollar, euro, gulden, leone, lilangeni, rand, rupee, shilling, Somali shilling, yuan* at MONEY table *in the Dict*
centavo* *n* : a monetary unit of Brazil equivalent to $^1/_{100}$ real — see MONEY table *in the Dict*
center* *n* : the center of the circle inscribed in a regular polygon
centered* *adj* : emotionally stable and secure — **cen·tered·ness** \-nəs\ *n* -ES
centerfold \ˈ≈ˌ≈\ *n* **1** : a foldout that is the center spread of a magazine **2** : a picture (as of a nude) on a centerfold; *also* : a model featured in such a picture
center–of–mass system* *n* : a frame of reference in which the center of mass is at rest
centerpiece* *n* : one that is of central importance or interest in a larger whole ⟨some women make a husband or lover the ~ of their lives —Carol Tavris⟩ ⟨the farm's ~, a two-acre barn —Anita M. Mobley⟩
center stage *n* **1** : CENTER 3e **2** : a central or highly prominent position — **center stage** *adj (or adv)*
centime* *n* : a monetary unit of Equatorial Guinea equivalent to $^1/_{100}$ ekuele — see MONEY table *in the Dict*
cen·ti·mil·lion·aire \ˌsentəˈmilyəˌna(a)(ə)r\ *n* [*centi-* + *millionaire*] : one whose wealth is estimated at one hundred million (as of dollars or pounds) or more
cen·ti·mor·gan \ˈsentəˌmȯrgən, -ˌmȯ(ə)g-\ *n* [*centi-* + *morgan* (herein)] : a genetic unit equivalent to $^1/_{100}$ of a morgan
central angle *n* : an angle formed by two radii of a circle
central casting *n, sometimes cap both Cs* : the department of a movie studio responsible for casting actors esp. viewed as a source of people who are stereotypical of their role in appearance, behavior, or nature ⟨a politician right out of *central casting*⟩
central dogma *n* : a generalization in genetics and molecular biology subject to several exceptions that genetic information is coded in self-replicating DNA and undergoes unidirectional transfer to messenger RNAs in transcription which act as templates for protein synthesis in translation
central limit theorem *n* : any of several fundamental theorems of probability and statistics giving the conditions under which the distribution of a sum of independent random variables can be found approximately by using the normal distribution; *esp* : a special case of the central limit theorem which is much applied in sampling: the distribution of the mean of a sample from a population with finite variance approaches the normal distribution as the number in the sample becomes large
central processing unit *n* : CPU *herein*
central tendon *n* : a 3-lobed aponeurosis located near the central portion of the diaphragm caudal to the pericardium and composed of intersecting planes of collagenous fibers
cen·tri·lobular \ˌsen·trə+\ *adj* [*centri-* + *lobular*] : relating to or affecting the center of a lobule ⟨~ necrosis in the liver⟩; *also* : affecting the central parts of the secondary pulmonary lobules of the lung ⟨~ emphysema⟩
cen·trism \ˈsenˌtrizəm\ *n* -s [*centr-* + *-ism*] : a political philosophy of avoiding extremes of right or left — **centrist** \-trist\ *adj*
CEO \ˌsēˌēˈō\ *n* -s *sometimes not cap* : the chief executive officer of a business concern or corporation
ceph·a·lex·in \ˌsefəˈleksən\ *n* -s [*cephal*osporin (herein) + *-ex-* (of unknown origin) + *-in*] : a semisynthetic cephalosporin $C_{16}H_{17}N_3O_4S$ with a spectrum of antibiotic activity similar to the penicillins
ceph·a·lopelvic disproportion \ˌsefə(ˌ)lō+. . .-\ *n* [*cephal-* + *pelvic*] : a condition in which a maternal pelvis is small in relation to the size of the fetal head
ceph·a·lor·i·dine \ˌsefəˈlȯrəˌdēn, -ˈlär-\ *n* -s [prob. fr. *cephalosporin* (herein) + *-idine*] : a semisynthetic broad-spectrum antibiotic $C_{19}H_{17}N_3O_4S_2$ derived from cephalosporin
ceph·a·lo·spo·rin \ˌsefələˈspōrən, -ˈspȯr-\ *n* -s [ISV *cephalospor-* (fr. NL *Cephalosporium*, genus name) + *-in*; perh. orig. formed in It] : any of several beta-lactam antibiotics produced by an imperfect fungus (genus *Acremonium* syn. *Cephalosporium*) or made semisynthetically
ceph·a·lo·thin \ˈsefələ(ˌ)thin\ *n* -s [*cephalo*sporin (herein) + *thi-* + *-in*] : a semisynthetic broad-spectrum antibiotic $C_{16}H_{15}N_2NaO_6S_2$ that is an analogue of a cephalosporin and is effective against penicillin-resistant staphylococci
cer·amide \ˈse(ə)rəˌmīd, ˈsi(ə)r-, -ˌməd; səˈramˌīd, -məd\ *n* [*cerebroside* + *amide*] : any of a group of amido sphingolipids formed by linking a fatty acid to sphingosine and found widely in small amounts in plant and animal tissue
cereal leaf beetle *n* : a small reddish brown black-headed Old World chrysomelid beetle (*Oulema melanopus*) that feeds on cereal grasses and is a serious pest of U.S. grain crops
ce·re·bral–pal·sied \ˈ≈≈ˈpȯlzēd, ˈ≈≈≈-\ *adj* : affected with cerebral palsy
cerebrovascular accident *n* : STROKE 5b
ce·ren·kov *also* **che·ren·kov** \chərˈ(y)eŋkəf\ *adj, usu cap C* **1** : of, relating to, or being Cerenkov radiation or the process that produces such radiation **2** : being a device that makes use of Cerenkov radiation ⟨*Cerenkov* counter⟩
ce·ru·lo·plas·min \səˌrülōˈplazmən, ˌser(y)əl-\ *n* -s [ISV *cerulo-* (fr. L *caeruleus* dark blue) + *plasma* + *-in*; prob. orig. formed in Sw] : a blue copper-binding serum oxidase that is deficient in Wilson's disease and that may catalyze the conversion of ferrous iron in tissues to ferric iron
cervical cap *n* : a usu. rubber or plastic contraceptive device in the form of a thimble-shaped molded cap smaller than a diaphragm that fits snugly over the uterine cervix and blocks sperm from entering the uterus — called also *Dutch cap*
cer·vico·thoracic \ˌsərvə(ˌ)kō+\ *adj* [*cervic-* + *thoracic*] : of or relating to the neck and thorax ⟨~ sympathectomy⟩
cer·vico·vaginal \"+\ *adj* [*cervic-* + *vaginal*] : of or relating to the uterine cervix and the vagina ⟨~ flora⟩ ⟨~ carcinoma⟩
cesium clock *n* : an atomic clock regulated by the natural vibration frequency of cesium atoms
cesium 137 *n* : a radioactive isotope of cesium that has the mass number 137 and a half-life of about 12 months and that is a by-product of nuclear fission
ce·tol·o·gist \sēˈtäləjəst\ *n* -s : a zoologist who is a specialist in cetology
ce·tri·mide \ˈsē·trəˌmīd, ˈse·t-\ *n* [*cetyl* + *tri-* + *methyl* + *-ide*] : a mixture of bromides of ammonium used esp. as a detergent and antiseptic
CEU *abbr* continuing education unit
CF *abbr* cystic fibrosis
CFA *abbr* certified financial analyst
CFC \ˌsē(ˌ)efˈsē\ *abbr or n* -s chlorofluorocarbon *herein*
CFP *abbr* certified financial planner
CFS *abbr* chronic fatigue syndrome *herein*
chain printer *n* : a line printer in which the printing element is type carried on a continuous chain
chain rule *n* : a mathematical rule concerning the differentiation of a function of a function (as *f*[*u*(*x*)]) by which under suitable conditions of continuity and differentiability one function is differentiated with respect to the second considered as an independent variable and then the second function is differentiated with respect to its independent variable ⟨if $v=u^2$ and $u=3x^2+2$ the derivative of *v* by the *chain rule* is $2u(6x)$ or $12x(3x^2+2)$⟩
chainwheel \ˈ≈ˌ≈\ *n* : SPROCKET WHEEL
chair* *n* : CHAIR FORM
chairperson \ˈ≈ˌ≈≈\ *n* [[1]*chair*man + *person*] **1** : the presiding officer of a meeting or an organization or a committee **2** : the administrative officer of a department of instruction (as in a college)
chairside \ˈ≈ˌ≈\ *adj* [[1]*chair* + *-side* (as in *bedside*)] : relating to, performed in the vicinity of, or assisting in the work done on a patient in a dentist's chair ⟨a dental ~ assistant⟩ ⟨a good ~ manner⟩
chakra* *n* : any of several points of physical or spiritual energy in the human body according to yoga philosophy
chal·lenged \ˈchalənjd\ *adj* : having a disability or deficiency : HANDICAPPED 1 *herein* ⟨skiing programs for physically ~ athletes —Craig Hansell⟩ ⟨mentally ~ clients who are diagnosed with schizophrenia —Michelle Runge⟩
cha·lu·pa \chäˈlüpä, chəˈlüpə\ *n* -s [MexSp, fr. Sp, boat, skiff, fr. F *chaloupe* — more at CHALOUPE] : a fried corn tortilla sometimes shaped like a boat and usu. filled with a savory mixture (as of meat, vegetables, or cheese) — compare TOSTADA *in the Dict*
chamberlain* *n* : an often honorary papal attendant; *specif* : a priest having a rank of honor below domestic prelate
cham·pers \ˈshampə(r)z\ *n pl but sing in constr* [*champ*agne + *-ers* (as in *starkers* — herein)] *Brit* : CHAMPAGNE
chan·dler wobble \ˈchan(d)lər-\ *also* **chan·dler's wobble** \-lərz-\ *n, usu cap C* [after Seth Carlo *Chandler* †1913 Am. astronomer] : an elliptical oscillation of the earth's axis of rotation with a period of 14 months whose cause has not been determined
chan·dra·se·khar limit \ˌchəndrəˈshā(ˌ)kär-\ *n, usu cap C* [after Subrahmanyan *Chandrasekhar* †1995 Am. (Indian-born) physicist] : the maximum mass at which a star near the end of its life cycle can become a white dwarf and above which the star will collapse to form a neutron star or black hole : a stellar mass equal to about 1.4 solar masses
change* *n* **1** : a negligible additional amount ⟨only six minutes and ~ left in the game⟩ **2** : CHANGE OF PACE 2
changeover* *n* : a pause in a tennis match during which the players change ends of the court
changing room *n, Brit* : CHANGEROOM; *esp* : LOCKER ROOM
channel* *n* **1** : a path along which information passes or an area (as of magnetic tape) on which it is stored **2** : a transition passage in jazz : BRIDGE **3** : GUTTER 2f **4** : one who conveys thoughts or energy from a source believed to be outside one's body or conscious mind; *specif* : one who speaks for a nonphysical being (as while in a trance) — compare MEDIUM 7 *in the Dict* **5** : a passage created in a selectively permeable membrane by a conformational change in membrane proteins ⟨an inflow of sodium ions through the cell's sodium ~s⟩ — see CALCIUM CHANNEL BLOCKER *herein*
channel* *vt* : to serve as a channel or intermediary for ⟨gets $15 . . . for ~*ing* the archangel Gabriel —Otto Friedrich⟩ — **channeler*** *n*
channel surfing *n* : the activity or practice of surfing through television programs usu. by use of a remote control to find something of interest — **channel–surf** *vi* — **channel surf** *n* — **channel surfer** *n*
chaos* *n* : the inherent unpredictability in the behavior of a complex natural system (as the atmosphere, boiling water, or the beating heart) — **chaotic*** *adj* — **chaotically*** *adv*
chaos theory *n* : a branch of mathematical and physical theory that deals with the nature and consequences of chaos and chaotic systems — **chaos theorist** *n*
chao·tro·pic \ˌkāōˈtrōpik, -ˈträp-\ *adj* [*chaos* + *-tropic*] : disrupting the structure of water, macromolecules, or a living system so as to promote activities inhibited by such structure
chapter 11 *or* **chapter 11 bankruptcy** *n, usu cap C* [fr. Chapter 11 of the U.S. Bankruptcy Code] : bankruptcy as provided under Chapter 11 of the Bankruptcy Code which governs corporate reorganization ⟨declared *Chapter 11*, after defaulting on $266 million —Jennifer Farley⟩
character* *n* : a symbol (as a letter or number) that represents information; *also* : a representation (as in binary form) of such a character that may be accepted by a computer
characteristic* *n* : the smallest positive integer *n* which for an operation in a ring, integral domain, or field yields 0 when any element is used *n* times with the operation and which is arbitrarily denoted by 0 or ∞ if no such integer exists
characteristic equation *n* : an equation in which the characteristic polynomial of a matrix is set equal to 0
characteristic polynomial *n* : the determinant of a square matrix in which an arbitrary variable (as *x*) is subtracted from each of the elements along the principal diagonal
characteristic root *n* : EIGENVALUE *herein*
characteristic value *n* : EIGENVALUE *herein*
characteristic vector *n* : EIGENVECTOR *herein*
char·ac·to·nym \ˈkarəktəˌnim *also* ˈker-\ *n* -s [*character* + *-onym*] : a name esp. for a fictional character (as Mistress Quickly or Caspar Milquetoast) that suggests a distinctive trait of the character
char·broil \ˈchärˌbrȯil, ˈchäˌ-\ *vt* [*charcoal* + *broil*] : to broil on a rack over hot charcoal — **char·broil·er** \ˈ≈ˌbrȯiləˈ(r)\ *n*
cha·ren·tais \ˌsharänˈtā\ *or* **charentais melon** *n, pl* **charentais** *also* **charentaises** \-ˈāz\ *usu cap C* [F *charentais* of Charentes, department in W France] : a small muskmelon with a distinct fragrance and sweet orange flesh that is grown chiefly in France
charge card *n* : CREDIT CARD 1
charge conjugation *n* : an operation in mathematical physics in which each particle in a system is replaced by its antiparticle
charge–coupled device *n* : a semiconductor device that is used esp. as an optical sensor and that stores charge and transfers it sequentially to an amplifier and detector — called also *CCD*
charge nurse *n* : a nurse who is in charge of a health-care unit (as a hospital ward, emergency room, or nursing home)
charismatic* *adj* : of or relating to the religious movement that emphasizes the extraordinary power (as of healing) given a Christian by the Holy Spirit
char·is·mat·ic \ˌkarəzˈmad·ik\ *n* -s : a member of a charismatic religious group or movement
charm* *n* : a quantum characteristic of subatomic particles that accounts for the unexpectedly long lifetime of the J/psi particle, explains various difficulties in the theory of the weak force, is conserved in interactions involving electromagnetism or the strong force, and has a value of zero for most known particles
charmed* *adj* : having the quantum characteristic of charm ⟨a ~ antiquark⟩
char·mo·ni·um \chärˈmōnēəm\ *n, pl* **charmonium** [*charm* (herein) + *-onium* (as in *positronium*)] : any of a group of fundamental particles that are held to consist of a charmed quark-antiquark pair
chart* *n* **1** : a listing by rank (as of sales) — often used in pl. ⟨number one on the ~*s*⟩ **2** : a musical arrangement for an ensemble or a part in such an arrangement
chartbuster \ˈ≈ˌ≈≈\ *n* : BEST SELLER; *esp* : a best-selling recording of a song or album
charter* *n* : a travel arrangement in which transportation (as a bus or plane) is hired by and for a specific group of people
charter school *n* : a tax-supported school established by a charter between a granting body (as a school board) and an outside group (as of teachers and parents) which operates the school without most local and state educational regulations so as to achieve set goals
chartreux* \(ˈ)shärˈtrüs, -ˈäˈt-, -üz *sometimes* -ärˈtrərs *or* -äˈtrəs\ *n, pl* **chartreux** *usu cap* : any of a breed of short-haired domestic cats of French origin having a bluish gray coat and gold or orange eyes
chat* *n* : on-line discussion in a chat room; *also* : an instance of such discussion ⟨participate in computer ~*s*⟩
chat room *n* : a real-time on-line interactive discussion group
chat show *n* : TALK SHOW *herein*
chauvinism* *n* : an attitude of superiority toward members of the opposite sex; *also* : behavior expressive of such an attitude
CHD *abbr* coronary heart disease
cheapo *adj* [alter. of [3]*cheap*] : CHEAP
cheap shot *n* **1** : an act of deliberate roughness against an unprepared opponent esp. in a contact sport that is often intended to cause injury **2** : an unfair statement that takes advantage of a known weakness of the target
cheat sheet *n* **1** : a sheet containing information (as test answers) used illicitly for one's advancement **2** : a written or graphic key or point of reference that helps in understanding or remembering something complex
checkbook journalism *n* : the practice of paying someone for a news story and esp. for granting an interview
check off* *vi* : to change a play at the line of scrimmage in football by calling an audible
checkoff* *n* : designation by a taxpayer of a small amount of income tax to be applied to a special fund (as for financing political campaigns)
checkout** *n* **1** : the process of examining and testing something as to readiness for intended use ⟨the ~ of a spacecraft⟩ **2** : the process of familiarizing oneself with the operation of a mechanical thing (as an airplane) **3** : a counter or area in a store where goods are checked out
check ride *n* : a flight that constitutes the final examination to get or maintain certification as a pilot
che·diak–hi·ga·shi syndrome \shāˈdyäkhēˈgäshē-\ *n, usu cap C&H* [after Moises *Chediak* *fl*1952 Fr. physician and Ototaka *Higashi* *fl*1954 Jap. physician] : a genetic disorder inherited as an autosomal recessive and characterized by partial albinism, abnormal granules in the white blood cells, and marked susceptibility to bacterial infections
cheesesteak \ˈ≈ˌ≈\ *n* : a sandwich consisting of thinly sliced beef topped with melted cheese and condiments (as fried onions or peppers) served on a roll
chef's knife *n* : a large kitchen knife with a curved triangular blade
chef's salad \ˈshefˈsaləd\ *n* : a meal-size salad that includes lettuce, tomatoes, celery, hard-boiled eggs, and julienne strips of meat and cheese
chelation therapy *n* : the use of a chelator to bind with a metal in the body to form a chelate so that the metal loses its toxic effect or physiological activity
che·la·tor \ˈkēˌlād·ə(r)\ *n* -s [[2]*chelate* + [1]*-or*] : a binding agent that suppresses chemical activity by forming chelates
chemical dependency *also* **chemical dependence** *n* : addiction to or dependence on drugs — **chemically dependent** *adj*
chemical peel *n* : PEEL *herein*
chemical vapor deposition *n* : a technique for depositing a usu. thin solid layer of a substance on a surface as the result of vapor-phase chemical reactions in a high temperature gas in close proximity to the surface
chemi·osmotic \ˌkemē+\ *adj* [*chem-* + *osmotic*] : relating to or being a hypothesis that seeks to explain the mechanism of ATP formation in oxidative phosphorylation by mitochondria and chloroplasts without recourse to the formation of high-energy intermediates by postulating the formation of an energy gradient of hydrogen ions across the organelle membranes that results in the reversible movement of hydrogen ions to the outside and is generated by electron transport or the activity of electron carriers
che·mo \ˈkē(ˌ)mō\ *n* -s [by shortening] : CHEMOTHERAPY
che·mo·kine \"+\ *n* -s [*chem-* + *-kine* (as in *cytokine* — herein)] : any of a group of chemotactic cytokines that are produced by various cells (as at sites of inflammation), that are thought to provide directional cues for the movement of white blood cells (as T cells, monocytes, and neutrophils), and that include some playing a role in HIV infection because the cell surface receptors to which they bind are also used by specific strains of HIV for entry into cells
che·mo·nuclear \"+\ *adj* [*chem-* + *nuclear*] : being or relating to a chemical reaction induced by nuclear radiation or fission fragments
che·mo·nucleolysis \"+\ *n* [*chem-* + *nucleolysis*] : treatment of a slipped disk by the injection of chymopapain to dissolve the displaced nucleus pulposus
che·mo·prevention \"+\ *n* [*chem-* + *prevention*] : the use of chemical agents to prevent or slow the development of cancer — **che·mo·preventive** \"+\ *adj or n*
che·mo·sensory \"+\ *adj* [*chem-* + *sensory*] : of, relating to, or functioning in the sensory reception of chemical stimuli ⟨~ hairs⟩ ⟨insect ~ behavior⟩
che·mo·sphere \ˈkēmə, ˈkemə+ˌ\ *n* [*chem-* + *sphere*] : a stratum of the upper atmosphere in which photochemical reactions are prevalent and which begins about 20 miles above the earth's surface

che·mo·sterilant \ˌkēmō, ¦kemo+\ *n* [*chem-* + *sterilant*] : a substance that produces irreversible sterility (as of an insect) without marked alteration of mating habits or life expectancy — **che·mo·sterilization** \"+\ *n* — **che·mo·sterilize** \"+\ *vb*

che·mo·surgery \"+\ *n* [*chem-* + *surgery*] : removal by chemical means of diseased or unwanted tissue — **che·mo·surgical** \"+\ *adj*

che·mo·taxonomy \"+\ *n* [*chem-* + *taxonomy*] : the classification of plants and animals based on similarities and differences in biochemical composition — **che·mo·taxonomic** \"+\ *adj* — **che·mo·taxonomist** \"+\ *n*

che·nin blanc \ˈshenən ˈblaŋk, shənaⁿˈblāⁿ\ *n, pl* **chenin blancs** \-äŋks, -āⁿ\ *often cap C&B* [F, a variety of white grape, the wine made from it, lit., white chenin (a grape variety)] : any of various white wines ranging from dry to sweet made from a grape orig. grown in the Loire valley

cheong·sam \ˈcheu̇ŋ¦säm, ˈchȯŋ-\ *n* -s [Chin (Cant) *chèuhng sàam*, lit., long gown] : a dress of southern Chinese origin with a slit skirt and a mandarin collar

cherry–pick \ˈ==,=\ *vi* : to select the best or most desirable ~ *vt* : to select as being the best or most desirable; *also* : to select the best or most desirable from ⟨*cherry-picked* the art collection⟩ — **cherry picker*** *n* — **cherry picking** *n*

chet·rum \ˈchē·trəm, ˈche-\ *n* -s [Tibetan] **1** : a monetary unit of Bhutan equal to ¹⁄₁₀₀ ngultrum — see MONEY table *in the Dict* **2** : a coin representing one chetrum

chi *or* **ch'i** *also* **qi** \ˈchē\ *n* -s *often cap* [Chin (Pek) *ch'i*⁴ breath, spirit] : vital energy that is held to animate the body internally and is of central importance in some Eastern systems of medical treatment (as acupuncture) and of exercise or self-defense (as tai chi)

chiao \ˈjau̇\ *n, pl* **chiao** [Chin (Pek) *chiao*³] **1** : a monetary unit of China equal to ¹⁄₁₀ yuan **2** : a coin or note representing one chiao

chi·ca·na \chiˈkänə, shi-, -kan-\ *n* -s *cap* [MexSp, fem. of *chicano*] : a female Chicano — **chicana** *adj, usu cap*

chicane* *n* : a series of tight turns in opposite directions in an otherwise straight stretch of a road-racing course

chi·ca·nis·mo \chi¦kä¦niz(ˌ)mō, shi-, -kȧ-, -is(-\ *n* -s *often cap* [MexSp, fr. *chicano* + Sp *-ismo* -ism] : strong ethnic pride exhibited by Chicanos

chi·ca·no \chiˈkän(ˌ)ō, shi-, -kan-\ *n* -s *cap* [MexSp, perh. alter. of *mexicano* Mexican] : an American of Mexican descent — **chicano** *adj, usu cap*

chicken* *n* **1** : any of various contests in which the participants risk personal safety in order to see which one will give up first **2** : a strategy or conflict that involves high risk or brinkmanship ⟨the game of political ~ has reached the moment of truth —Richard Hoppe⟩

chicken–and–egg \ˌchik(ə)nən(d)¦eg, -¦āg\ *adj* [so called fr. the proverbial question "which came first, the chicken or the egg?"] : of, relating to, or being a cause-and-effect dilemma

chicken–fried steak \ˈ==ˈ=-\ *n* : steak coated with batter, fried, and served with gravy

chicken kiev *n, usu cap K* [fr. *Kiev*, Ukraine] : a boneless chicken breast that is stuffed with seasoned butter and deep fried

¹**chick·en·shit** \ˈ==,=\ *adj* **1** : PETTY, INSIGNIFICANT — usu. considered vulgar ⟨jailed . . . on the ~ charge of loitering —Tim Cahill⟩ **2** : lacking courage, manliness, or effectiveness — usu. considered vulgar ⟨too ~ to raise his voice —D.A.Latimer⟩

²**chickenshit** \ˈ==¦=\ *n* **1** : the petty details of duty or discipline — usu. considered vulgar **2** : COWARD, CHICKEN — usu. considered vulgar

chi·com \ˈchi¦käm\ *n* -s *usu cap* [¹*chinese* + *communist*] : a communist Chinese

chief of staff **1 a** : the ranking officer of a staff in the armed forces serving as principal adviser to a commander **b** : the senior official of a staff serving a civilian executive (as the president of the United States) **2** : the commanding officer of the army or air force and a member of the Joint Chiefs of Staff

chien ware \ˈchē'en,-\ *also* **chien yao** \-n¦yau̇\ *n, usu cap C* [Chin (Pek) *ch'ien yao*², fr. *Ch'ien-an*, locality in China where it was first made + Chin (Pek) *yao*² kiln] : a dark Chinese stoneware dating from the Sung period that usu. has a brown-mottled black glaze and is used esp. for tea wares

childproof \ˈ=,=\ *adj* : designed to prevent tampering or opening by children ⟨a ~ door lock⟩

chile relleno *n, pl* **chiles rellenos** *also* **chile rellenos** [Sp, stuffed chili pepper] : a stuffed chili pepper that usu. contains cheese or meat and that is fried or grilled

chili·burger \ˈ==,=\ *n* -s [*chili* + *-burger*] : a hamburger topped with chili

chili dog *n* : a hot dog topped with chili

chill* *vi* **1** : to chill out — often used in the imperative **2** : to hang around

chill factor *n* : WINDCHILL *herein*

chill out *vi* : to calm down : go easy : RELAX — often used in the imperative

chil·te·pin *also* **chil·te·pine** \ˈchiltəpēn\ *n* -s [MexSp *chiltepín*, fr. Nahuatl *chiltecpin*, fr. *chīlli* chili pepper + *tecpin, tecpintli* flea] : a small red wild hot pepper produced by a plant of the genus *Capsicum* (*C. annum glabriusculum* syn. *C. annuum aviculare*) occurring from northern So. America to northern Mexico and the southwestern U.S.; *also* : this plant

chil·tern hundreds \ˌchiltə(r)n-\ *n pl, usu cap C&H* [fr. *Chiltern Hundreds*, three hundreds in the Chiltern hills of England appointment to the stewardship of which is a disqualification for membership in Parliament] : a nominal appointment granted by the British crown that serves as a legal fiction to enable a member of Parliament to relinquish his seat

chi·me·rism \kīˈmi(ə)rˌizəm, kə-; ˈkīməˌriz-\ *n* -s : the state of being a genetic chimera

chi·mi·chan·ga \ˌchimēˈchäŋgə, -mi-, -ˈchaŋ-\ *n* -s [MexSp, trinket] : a tortilla wrapped around a filling (as of meat) and deep-fried

chimney* *n* : a tall column of rock on the ocean floor that is formed by the precipitation of minerals from superheated water issuing from a vent in the earth's crust and rising through the column of rock

chinaman* *n* : an off-break in cricket bowled by a left-handed bowler to a right-handed batsman

china syndrome *n, usu cap C* [so called fr. the notion that a molten reactor's contents could theoretically sink through the earth from No. America to China] : MELTDOWN 1 *herein*

china white *n, usu cap C&W* **1** : a pure potent form of heroin originating in southeast Asia **2** : an illicit analogue of the analgesic fentanyl that resembles heroin in its physical appearance and physiological effects

chin·co·teague \ˈshiŋkə¦tēg, ¦chiŋ-\ *also* **chincoteague oyster** \ˈ==,=-\ *n* -s *usu cap C* [fr. *Chincoteague* Bay on the Maryland-Virginia coast] : an American oyster typically from the Chesapeake Bay

chinese box *n, usu cap C* : something that resembles a set of Chinese boxes esp. in complexity — often used in pl.

chinese fire drill *n, usu cap C* **1** : a state of great confusion or disorder **2** : a prank in which a number of people jump out of an automobile stopped at a red traffic light, run around to the opposite side, and jump back in often in a different seat before the light changes to green

chinese parsley *n, usu cap C* : CILANTRO *herein*

chinese restaurant syndrome *n, usu cap C* : a group of symptoms (as numbness of the neck, arms, and back with headache, dizziness, and palpitations) that is held to affect susceptible persons eating food and esp. Chinese food heavily seasoned with monosodium glutamate

chinese shar–pei *n, usu cap C* : SHAR-PEI *herein*

chip* *n* **1 a** : INTEGRATED CIRCUIT *herein* **b** : a small wafer of semiconductor material that forms the base for an integrated circuit **2 a** : a soft high pass or shot over a defender's head in soccer **b** : a return shot in tennis made by hitting down on the ball to give it backspin

chip* *vt* **1** : to hit (a return in tennis) with backspin **2** : to kick (a soccer ball) in a soft high arc ~ *vi* : to make a chip (as in soccer or tennis)

chi·pot·le *also* **chipotle chili** *or* **chipotle pepper** \chəˈpōtlā, chē-, -ˈpȯt-, -lē; chəˈpōd-ᵊlā\ *n* -s [MexSp *chipotle, chilpotle*, fr. (assumed) Nahuatl *chīlpōctli*, fr. *chīl-* chili pepper, something red (fr. *chīlli* chili pepper) + *pōctli* smoke, something smoked] : a smoked and usu. dried jalapeño

chippy* *adj* [*chip* on one's shoulder] : aggressively belligerent ⟨a ~ hockey player⟩; *also* : marked by much fighting ⟨a ~ game⟩

chi·ral \ˈkī(ə)rəl\ *adj* [*chir-* + ¹*-al*] : of, relating to, or being a molecule that is nonsuperimposable on its mirror image — **chi·ral·i·ty** \kīˈralәd-ē, kəˈ-\ *n* -ES

chi–square distribution *n* : a probability density function that gives the distribution of the sum of the squares of a number of independent random variables each having a normal distribution with zero mean and unit variance, that has the property that the sum of two random variables with such a distribution also has one, and that is widely used in testing statistical hypotheses esp. about the theoretical and observed values of a quantity and about population variances and standard deviations

chit·lin circuit \ˈchitlən-\ *n* [so called fr. the assumption that chitterlings are eaten chiefly by blacks] : a group of theaters and nightclubs that cater to black audiences and feature black entertainers

chlamydia* *n, pl* **chlamydiae** *also* **chlamydias** **1** : a bacterium of the genus *Chlamydia* **2** : an infection or disease (as trachoma or nongonococcal urethritis) caused by chlamydiae — **chlamydial** \-ēəl\ *adj*

chlor–alkali \¦klōr, -ȯr+\ *n* [*chlor-* + *alkali*] : any of a group of chemicals (as chlorine and sodium hydroxide) that are manufactured by the electrolytic decomposition of sodium chloride — usu. used in pl.

chlor·am·bu·cil \klōrˈambyəˌsil, klȯr-\ *n* -s [*chloro*ethyl + *amin-* + *butyric* + *-il*] : an anticancer drug $C_{14}H_{19}Cl_2NO_2$ that is a derivative of nitrogen mustard and is used esp. to treat leukemias, multiple myeloma, some lymphomas, and Hodgkin's disease

chlor·di·az·epox·ide \ˌklōrdīˌazəˈpäkˌsīd, ˌklȯr-\ *n* [*chlor-* + benzo*diazepine* (herein) + *oxide*] : a benzodiazepine $C_{16}H_{14}ClN_3O$ structurally and pharmacologically related to diazepam that is used in the form of its hydrochloride esp. as a tranquilizer and to treat the withdrawal symptoms of alcoholism — see LIBRIUM

chlor·hex·i·dine \klōrˈheksəˌdīn, klȯr-, -ˌdēn\ *n* -s [ISV *chlor-* + *hex-* + *-idine*] : a biguanide derivative $C_{22}H_{30}Cl_2N_{10}$ used as a local antiseptic esp. in the form of its hydrochloride or acetate

chlorine monoxide *n* : a very reactive univalent radical ClO that in the atmosphere is derived esp. from chlorofluorocarbons and plays a major role in stratospheric ozone depletion

chlor·mer·o·drin \klōrˈmerədrən, klȯr-\ *n* -s [*chlor-* + *mercury* + *-o-* + *-hydrin*] : a mercurial diuretic $C_5H_{11}ClHgN_2O_2$ used in the treatment of some forms of edema, ascites, and nephritis

chlo·ro·fluorocarbon \¦klōrə, ¦klȯr-+\ *n* [ISV *chlor-* + *fluorocarbon*] : any of several simple gaseous compounds that contain carbon, chlorine, fluorine, and sometimes hydrogen, that are used as refrigerants, cleaning solvents, and aerosol propellants and in the manufacture of plastic foams, and that are believed to be a major cause of stratospheric ozone depletion — called also *CFC*

chlo·ro·flu·o·ro·methane \¦klōrə¦flu̇(ə)(ˌ)rō, ¦klȯr-, -¦flōr(ˌ)ō, ¦flō(ˌ)rō+\ *n* [ISV *chlor-* + *fluor-* + *methane*] : a chlorofluorocarbon derived from methane

chlo·ro·phy·tum \ˌklōrəˈfīd·əm, ˌklȯr-\ *n* [NL, fr. *chlor-* + Gk *phyton* plant] **1** *cap* : a genus of perennial tropical stemless herbs of the family Liliaceae that are often grown for their foliage **2** -s : a plant of the genus *Chlorophytum*; *esp* : SPIDER PLANT *herein*

chlo·ro·thiazide \¦klōrə, ¦klȯr-+\ *n* [*chlor-* + *thiazide*] : a thiazide diuretic $C_7H_6ClN_3O_4S_2$ used esp. in the treatment of edema and hypertension

chlo·ro·tri·anis·ene \ˌklōrōˌtrīˈanəˌsēn, ˌklȯr-\ *n* -s [*chlor-* + *tri-* + ²*anis-* + *-ene*] : a synthetic estrogen $C_{23}H_{21}ClO_3$ that is administered orally in the treatment of menopause-related conditions (as kraurosis of the vulva), abnormal estrogen deficiency (as in hypogonadism), or in the palliative treatment of some prostate cancers

chlor·phen·ir·amine \-fenˈirəˌmēn, -mən, -fən-\ *n* -s [*chlor-* + *phen-* + *-ir-* (prob. alter. of *pyridine*) + *amine*] : an antihistamine $C_{16}H_{19}ClN_2$ that is usu. administered in the form of its maleate

chlor·prop·amide \-ˈpräpəˌmīd, -prōp-, -ˌməd\ *n* [*chlor-* + *propane* + *amide*] : a sulfonylurea drug $C_{10}H_{13}ClN_2O_3S$ used to reduce blood sugar in the treatment of mild diabetes

chlor·pyr·i·fos \-ˈpirəfäs, -ˈpīr-\ *n* -ES [*chlor-* + *pyrid-* + *-fos*, alter. of *-phos* (as in *coumaphos* — herein)] : a toxic crystalline organophosphate pesticide $C_9H_{11}Cl_3NO_3PS$ that inhibits acetylcholinesterase and is used to control insect pests and ticks

chlor·thal·i·done \klōrˈthaləˌdōn, klȯr-\ *n* -s [*chlor-* + *-thalidone*, fr. *phthalimide* + *ketone*] : a sulfonamide $C_{14}H_{11}ClN_2O_4S$ that is a long-acting diuretic used in the treatment of hypertension and in the treatment of edema associated esp. with congestive heart failure, renal dysfunction, cirrhosis of the liver, or corticosteroid and estrogen therapy

chock* *n* : a metal wedge, nut, or block inserted into a crack in a rock face as an aid to climbing

choc·o·hol·ic *also* **choc·a·hol·ic** \¦chäkə¦hȯlək, ¦chȯ-, -¦hä-, -ēk\ *n* -s [blend of ¹*chocolate* and *alcoholic*] : a person who craves or compulsively consumes chocolate

choc·o·la·tier \ˌchäk(ə)ləˈti(ə)r, ˌchȯ-\ *n* -s [F, fr. *chocolat* chocolate + *-ier* -er] : one that makes or sells chocolate candy

choke* *vi* : to lose one's composure and fail to perform effectively in a critical situation

choke hold *n* **1** : a hold that involves strong choking pressure applied to the neck of another **2** : excessively stringent dominance or control ⟨had a *choke hold* on the city's finances⟩

cho·le·cyst·agogue \¦kōlə¦sistəˌgäg, ¦käl-, -ȯg\ *n* -s [*cholecyst* + *-agogue*] : an agent (as cholecystokinin) that causes the gallbladder to discharge bile

cho·le·cyst·ec·to·mized \ˌkōlə(ˌ)sisˈtektəˌmīzd, ˌkäl-\ *adj* [*cholecystectomy* + *-ize* + ²*-ed*] : having had the gallbladder removed

¹**cho·le·cys·to·kinetic** \¦kōlə¦sistō, ¦käl-+\ *adj* [*cholecyst* + *-o-* + *kinetic*] : tending to cause the gallbladder to contract and discharge bile

²**cholecystokinetic** \"\ *n* -s : CHOLECYSTAGOGUE *herein*

cho·le·sta·sis \ˌkōləˈstāsəs, ˌkäl-\ *n, pl* **cholesta·ses** \-āˌsēz\ [NL, fr. *chol-* + *-stasis*] : a checking or failure of bile flow — **cho·le·stat·ic** \¦kōlə¦stad·ik, ¦käl-\ *adj*

cho·le·styr·amine \ˌkōləˈstīrəˌmēn, kōˈlestirəˌmēn\ *n* [*chol-* + *styrene* + *amine*] : a strongly basic ion-exchange resin that forms insoluble complexes with bile acids and has been used to lower cholesterol levels in hypercholesterolemic patients

cho·li·no·lyt·ic \¦kōlənō¦lid·ik, ¦käl-\ *adj* [ISV acetyl*choline* + *-o-* + *-lytic*] : interfering with the action of acetylcholine or cholinergic agents — **cholinolytic** *n* -s

cho·li·no·mimetic \"+\ *adj* [ISV acetyl*choline* + *-o-* + *mimetic*] : resembling acetylcholine or simulating its physiological action — **cholinomimetic** *n* -s

cho·li·no·receptor \"+\ *n* [acetyl*choline* + *-o-* + *receptor*] : a receptor for acetylcholine in a postsynaptic membrane

chom·skyan *also* **chom·skian** \ˈchäm(p)skēən, -ȯm-, -kyən\ *adj, usu cap* [Avram Noam *Chomsky* b1928 Am. linguist + E *-an*] : of, relating to, based on, or being the linguistic theories of Noam Chomsky

chop* *n, chiefly Brit* : AX 3 ⟨it is the very top men who have got the ~ —*Daily Mirror*⟩

chop block *n* : a dangerous and illegal football block aimed at the legs and esp. knees of another player

chopped liver *n, slang* : one that is insignificant or not worth considering

chopper* *n* **1** : a high-bouncing batted baseball **2** : a customized motorcycle

chop·per \ˈchäpə(r)\ *vb* -ED/-ING/-S [¹*chopper*] : HELICOPTER

chop shop *n* : a place where stolen automobiles are stripped of salable parts

chop–socky \+ˈsäkē\ *adj* [²*chop* + ⁵*sock* + ¹*-y*] : of, relating to, or being a film or video that features martial arts violence — **chop–socky** *n* -ES

chor·do·ma \kȯrˈdōmə, kȯr-\ *n, pl* **chordomas** *or* **chordoma·ta** \-məd-ə, -ətə\ [NL, fr. E noto*chord* + NL *-oma*] : a malignant tumor that is derived from remnants of the embryonic notochord and occurs along the spine attacking esp. the bones at the base of the skull or near the coccyx

chord organ *n* : an electronic or reed organ with buttons for producing simple chords

choreograph* *vt* : to arrange or direct the movement, progress, or details of ⟨clashes with police, ~*ed* to feed the mass media's hunger for sensation —Irving Howe⟩

choreography* *n* : something resembling choreography; *esp* : the movements, progress, or details of a process, activity, or production ⟨a snail-paced ~ of delicate high diplomacy —Wolfgang Saxon⟩

chorionic villus sampling *also* **chorionic villi sampling** *n* : biopsy of the chorion frondosum through the abdominal wall or by way of the vagina and uterine cervix at nine to 12 weeks of gestation to obtain fetal cells for the prenatal diagnosis of genetic disorders — abbr. *CVS*

cho·roi·de·re·mia \¦kȯrˌȯidə¦rēmēə, ¦kȯr-\ *n* -s [NL, fr. E ¹*choroid* + Gk *erēmia* destitution, solitude — more at HERMIT] : progressive degeneration of the choroid that is an X-linked trait chiefly affecting males and that is characterized by night blindness, constriction of the visual field, and eventual blindness

chotchke *var of* TCHOTCHKE *herein*

christmas tree* *n, usu cap C* : a legislative bill under consideration esp. near the end of a session that contains a variety of amendments unrelated to the main purpose of the bill

chroma–key \ˈ==¦=\ *n* [*chroma* (saturation) + ¹*key* (signal operating electronic switch that changes feed from foreground to background cameras)] : a photographic compositing technique based on the separation of colors in the original images; *esp* : BLUE SCREEN *herein*

chromatogram* : a time-based graphic record (as of concentration of eluted materials) of a chromatographic separation

chromatograph* *n* : an instrument for performing chromatographic separations and producing chromatograms

chrome* *n* : something plated with an alloy of chromium

chromium picolinate *n* : a biologically active chromium salt $C_{18}H_{12}CrN_3O_6$ containing three picolinic acid ligands that is used as a dietary supplement

chro·mo·dynamics \¦krōmō+\ *n pl but sing in constr* [*chrom-* + *dynamics*] : QUANTUM CHROMODYNAMICS *herein*

chronic fatigue syndrome *n* : a disorder of uncertain cause that is characterized by persistent profound fatigue usu. accompanied by impairment of short-term memory or concentration, sore throat, tender lymph nodes, muscle or joint pain, and headache unrelated to any preexisting medical condition and that typically has an onset at about 30 years of age

chronic lymphocytic leukemia *n* : lymphocytic leukemia that is marked by an abnormal increase in the number of mature lymphocytes and esp. B cells, that is characterized by slow onset and progression of symptoms which include anemia, pallor, fatigue, appetite loss, granulocytopenia, thrombocytopenia, hypogammaglobulinemia, and enlargement of the lymph nodes, liver, and spleen, and that occurs esp. in older adults — compare ACUTE LYMPHOCYTIC LEUKEMIA *herein*

chronic myelogenous leukemia *also* **chronic myeloid leukemia** *or* **chronic myelocytic leukemia** : myelogenous leukemia that is marked by an abnormal increase in mature and immature granulocytes (as neutrophils, eosinophils, and myelocytes) esp. in bone marrow and blood, that is characterized by fatigue, weakness, loss of appetite, spleen and liver enlargement, anemia, thrombocytopenia, and ultimately a dangerous increase in blast cells and esp. myeloblasts and lymphoblasts, that occurs esp. in adults, and that is associated with the presence of the Philadelphia chromosome — called also *chronic granulocytic leukemia*; compare ACUTE MYELOGENOUS LEUKEMIA *herein*

chronic obstructive pulmonary disease *n* : pulmonary disease (as emphysema or chronic bronchitis) this is characterized by chronic typically irreversible airway obstruction resulting in a slowed rate of exhalation — abbr. *COPD*

chro·no·biology \¦kränə, ¦krō-, -nō+\ *n* [*chron-* + *biology*] : the study of biological rhythms — **chro·no·biologic** \"+\ *or* **chro·no·biological** \"+\ *adj* — **chro·no·biologist** \"+\ *n*

chro·no·therapy \"+\ *n* [*chron-* + *therapy*] **1** : treatment of a sleep disorder (as insomnia) by changing sleeping and waking times in an attempt to reset the patient's biological clock **2** : the administration of medication in coordination with the body's circadian rhythms to maximize effectiveness and minimize side effects

chryso·phyte \ˈkrisəˌfīt\ *n* -s [*chrys-* + *-phyte*] : GOLDEN-BROWN ALGA *herein*

chuffed \ˈchəft\ *adj* [³*chuff* + ¹*-ed*] *Brit* : quite pleased : DELIGHTED

chug \ˈchəg\ *vb* **chugged; chugged; chugging; chugs** [by shortening] : CHUGALUG *herein*

chug·a·lug \ˈchəgəˌləg\ *vb* **chugalugged; chugalugged; chugalugging; chugalugs** [imit.] *vt* : to drink a container of (as beer) without pause; *also* : to drink quickly or copiously : GUZZLE ⟨chain-smoking cigarettes and *chugalugging* tea —Melvin Maddox⟩ ~ *vi* : to drink a container (as of beer) without pause

chump change *n* [¹*chump*] : a relatively small or insignificant amount of money

church key *n* : an implement with a triangular pointed head at one end for piercing the tops of cans (as of beer) and usu. a rounded head at the other end for removing bottle caps

churn* *vt* : to subject (a client's security account) to excessive numbers of purchases and sales primarily to generate additional commissions

churn out *vt* : to produce mechanically or copiously : grind out ⟨orchestras that must *churn out* a different program each week, in week out —Andrew Porter⟩

chur·ro \ˈchu̇rō, ˈchü-\ *n* -s [Sp] : a Spanish and Mexican pastry resembling a doughnut or cruller made from deep-fried unsweetened dough and usu. sprinkled with sugar

chutz·pah *also* **chutz·pa** *or* **hutz·pah** *or* **hutz·pa** \ˈku̇tspə, ˈhu̇-, -(ˌ)spä\ *n* -s [Yiddish *khutspe*, fr. LHeb *ḥuṣpāh*] : supreme self-confidence : NERVE, GALL

chvos·tek's sign \(k)əˌvȯsˌtek(s)-\ *or* **chvostek sign** \-ˌtek-\ *n, usu cap C* [after Franz *Chvostek* †1884 Austrian surgeon] : a twitch of the facial muscles following gentle tapping over the facial nerve in front of the ear that indicates hyperirritability of the facial nerve

chy·lo·mi·cro·ne·mia \ˌkīlōˌmīkrəˈnēmēə\ *n* -s [NL, fr. E *chylomicron* + NL *-emia*] : an excessive number of chylomicrons in the blood ⟨postprandial ~⟩

chy·lo·thorax \¦kīlə+\ *n* [*chyl-* + *thorax*] : an effusion of chyle or chylous fluid into the thoracic cavity

chy·mo·papain \¦kīmō+\ *n* [*chyme* + *-o-* + *papain*] : a proteolytic enzyme from the latex of the papaya that is used in meat tenderizer and has been used medically in chemonucleolysis

chy·mo·tryp·tic \¦kīmō¦triptik\ *adj* [fr. *chymotrypsin*, after such pairs as E *trypsin* : *tryptic*] : of, relating to, produced by, or performed with chymotrypsin ⟨~ peptide mapping⟩

ciao \ˈchau̇\ *interj* [It, fr. It dial. (northern), lit., (I am your) slave, fr. ML *sclavus* slave — more at SLAVE] — used conventionally as an utterance at meeting or parting

Cigarette *trademark* — used for a fast powerful mono-hulled ocean boat

cig·gy *also* **cig·gie** \ˈsigē, -gi\ *n* -s [by shortening & alter.] *chiefly Brit* : CIGARETTE

ci·gua·tox·in \¦sēgwə¦täksən, ¦sig-\ *n* [*ciguatera* + *toxin*] : a potent heat-stable lipid neurotoxin that is produced by a marine dinoflagellate (*Gambierdiscuss toxicus*) and causes ciguatera poisoning in those who eat fish (as barracuda or amberjack) in which toxic levels of it have become concentrated; *also* : any of several related neurotoxins causing ciguatera

ci·lan·tro \sə'läntrō, -län-\ *n* -s [Sp, coriander, modif. of ML *celiandrum*, alter. of LL *coliandrum*, alter. of L *coriandrum* — more at CORIANDER] : leaves of coriander used as a flavoring or garnish; *also* : CORIANDER 1

ci·met·i·dine \sīˈmed·ə,dēn, -etə-\ *n* -s [*ci-* (alter. of *cyan-*) + *meth*yl + *-idin*] : a histamine analogue $C_{10}H_{16}N_6S$ that inhibits gastric acid secretion and is used to treat conditions (as duodenal ulcers) related to such secretion

cine·angiocardiography \¦sinē+\ *n* [*cine-* + *angiocardiography*] : motion-picture photography of a fluoroscopic screen recording passage of a contrasting medium through the chambers of the heart and large blood vessels — **cine·angiocardiographic** \"+\ *adj*

cine·angiography \"+\ *n* [*cine-* + *angiography*] : motion-picture photography of a fluorescent screen recording passage of a contrasting medium through the blood vessels — **cine·an·gio·graph·ic** \¦==,anjēə¦grafik, -ēk\ *adj*

cin·e·ma·theque \¦sinəmə¦tek\ *n* -s [F *cinémathèque* film library, fr. *cinéma* cinema + *-thèque* (as in *bibliothèque* library)] : a small movie theater specializing in avant-garde films

cinema ve·ri·té \¦sinəmə,verə¦tā, -nä,mä,-\ *n* [F *cinéma-vérité*, trans. of Russ *kinopravda*, lit., cinema-truth] : the art or technique of filming a motion picture (as a documentary) so as to convey candid realism

cine·phile \ˈsinə,fīl\ *n* -s [F *cinéphile*, fr. *ciné-* + *-phile*] : a devotee of motion pictures : CINEAST

cine·plex \-,pleks\ *n* -ES [*cine-* + *-plex* (as in *multiplex*)] : a complex that houses several movie theaters

cin·gu·late gyrus \ˈsiŋgyələt-, -,lāt-\ *n* : a medial gyrus of each cerebral hemisphere that partly surrounds the corpus callosum

cin·gu·lec·to·my \,==ˈlektəmē\ *n* -ES [*cingulum* + *-ectomy*] : CINGULOTOMY *herein*

cin·gu·lot·o·my \-ˈläd·əmē, -ätə-\ *n* -ES [*cingulum* + *-o-* + *-tomy*] : surgical destruction of all or part (as the cingulum) of the cingulate gyrus

CIP *abbr* cataloging in publication

cip·ro·flox·a·cin \,siprəˈfläksəsən,-prō-\ *n* -s [prob. fr. ISV *ci-* (alter. of *cycl-*) + *pro*pyl + *fluor-* + *oxa-* + *-mycin*] : a fluorinated derivative of quinolone $C_{17}H_{18}FN_3O_3$ that is often administered in the form of its hydrochloride and is effective esp. against gram-negative bacteria

cir·ca·di·an \(,)sərˈkādēən, ¦sərkə¦dēən\ *adj* [L *circa* about + *dies* day + E *-an* — more at CIRCA, DEITY] : being, having, characterized by, or occurring in approximately 24-hour periods or cycles (as of biological activity or function) ⟨~ oscillations⟩ ⟨~ periodicity⟩ ⟨~ rhythms in activity⟩ ⟨~ leaf movements⟩ — **circa·dianly** *adv*

circ·an·nu·al \(ˈ)sərˈkanyə(wə)l\ *adj* [L *circa* about + E *annual*] : having, characterized by, or occurring in approximately yearly periods or cycles (as of biological activity or function) ⟨~ rhythmicity⟩

circle* *n* : a residential street that curves and typically loops back on itself — used chiefly in the names of streets

circle* *vb* — **circle the wagons** : to assume a collective defensive posture against attack, criticism, or adversity

circuit board *n* : BOARD 3 *herein*

circuit breaker* *n* : a provision (as in an insurance contract or tax law) that limits financial obligations beyond a specified amount for covered individuals

circuitry* *n* : the network of interconnected neurons in the nervous system and esp. the brain; *also* : the neuronal pathways of the brain along which electrical and chemical signals travel

circular dichroism *n* **1** : the property (as of an optically active medium) of unequal absorption of right and left circularly plane-polarized light so that the emergent light is elliptically polarized **2** : a spectroscopic technique that makes use of circular dichroism

circular file *n* : WASTEBASKET

circular polarization *n* : polarization in which the mutually perpendicular components of a transverse wave radiation have equal amplitudes but differ in phase by 90 degrees — **circularly polarized** *adj*

cir·cum·planetary \¦sərkəm+\ *adj* [*circum-* + *planet* + *-ary*] : surrounding and relatively close to a planet ⟨~ space⟩

cir·cum·solar \"+\ *adj* [*circum-* + *solar*] : revolving about or surrounding the sun

cir·cum·stellar \"+\ *adj* [*circum-* + *stellar*] : surrounding or occurring in the vicinity of a star

cir·cum·terrestrial \"+\ *adj* [*circum-* + *terrestrial*] : revolving about or surrounding the earth

cir·cus·iana \,sərkəsēˈāna, -ˈanə\ *n pl* [*circus* + *-ana*] : materials or objects relating to circuses or circus life

cis·lunar \(ˈ)sis+\ *adj* [*cis-* + *lunar*] : of or relating to the space between the earth and the moon or the moon's orbit

cis·plat·in \"+ˈplatən\ *also* **cis–platinum** \"+\ *n* -s [ISV *cis-* + *platinum*] : a platinum-containing antineoplastic drug $Cl_2H_6N_2Pt$ that functions as an alkylating agent, produces cross-links in DNA between and within strands, and is used esp. as a palliative therapy in testicular and ovarian tumors and in advanced bladder cancer

cisterna* *n* : one of the flattened vesicles comprising the Golgi apparatus and the part of the endoplasmic reticulum studded with ribosomes — **cisternal*** *adj*

cis·tron \ˈsi,strän\ *n* -s [*cis-trans* + [2]*-on*] : a segment of DNA that is equivalent to a gene and that specifies a single functional unit (as a protein or enzyme) and within which two heterozygous and closely linked recessive mutations are expressed in the phenotype when on different homologous chromosomes but not when on the same chromosome — **cis·tron·ic** \siˈstränik\ *adj*

citizen's arrest *n* : an arrest made not by a law officer but by a citizen who derives authority from the fact of being a citizen

citizens band *n, sometimes cap C&B* : a range of radio-wave frequencies that in the U.S. is allocated officially for private radio communications

citrus red mite *n* : a comparatively large mite (*Panonychus citri*) that is a destructive pest on the foliage of citrus — called also *citrus red spider*

city* *n, slang* : a thing, event, or situation that is strongly characterized by a specified feature or quality ⟨the movie was shoot-out ~⟩

city·bil·ly \ˈsid·ē,bilē, -d·i,-, -li\ *n* -ES [*city* + hill*billy*] : a musician or singer brought up in a city who performs country music

civilian* *n* : a person who does not belong to a particular group : OUTSIDER ⟨especially effective with the ~s—TV-speak for non-showbiz types —Jack Friedman⟩

CJD *abbr* Creutzfeldt-Jakob disease *herein*

clad *n* -s [[3]*clad*] : CLADDING

clade \ˈklād\ *n* -s [Gk *klados* branch, shoot — more at GLADIATOR] : a group of biological taxa (as species) including all descendants of one common ancestor — compare GRADE *herein*

cla·dism \ˈklādizəm, ˈkla-\ *n* -s : the theory that cladistic methods based on shared characteristics of organisms yield their true evolutionary relationships and provide the basis for a natural biological classification; *also* : CLADISTICS *herein*

cla·dist \ˈklādəst, ˈkla-\ *n* -s : a taxonomist who adheres to the cladistic system of classification

cla·dis·tic \kləˈdistik, klaˈ-\ *adj* [*clade* (herein) + *-istic*] : of, relating to, utilizing, or being cladistics — compare PHENETIC *herein* — **cla·dis·ti·cal·ly** \-tək(ə)lē\ *adv*

cla·dis·tics \-iks\ *n pl but sing in constr* : a system of biological taxonomy that defines taxa uniquely by shared characteristics not found in ancestral groups and uses inferred evolutionary relationships to arrange taxa in a branching hierarchy such that all members of a given taxon have the same ancestors

clado·genesis \¦kladō+\ *n* [NL, fr. G *kladogenese*, fr. *Klado-* clad- + *genese* genesis] : evolutionary change characterized by treelike branching or splitting of a lineage — compare ANAGENESIS *herein* — **clado·genetic** \"+\ *adj* — **clado·genetically** \"+\ *adv*

clado·gram \ˈkladə,gram\ *n* -s [*clad-* + *-gram*] : a branching diagrammatic tree used in cladistic classification to illustrate phylogenetic relationships — compare PHENOGRAM *herein*

claim* *vt* : to assert to be rightfully one's own ⟨~*ed* responsibility for the attack⟩

clam* *n* **1** : DOLLAR ⟨it cost me seventy-five ~*s*, and I wore it only twice —Ethel Merman⟩ **2** : a sour note ⟨hit a ~ during the first few bars —Nat Hentoff⟩

clam·digger \ˈ=,==\ *n* [[5]*clam* + *digger*; fr. the fact that one can wear such a garment while wading without getting it wet] : pants that reach to mid-calf — usu. used in pl.

clang·er \ˈklaŋə(r)\ *n* -s [[2]*clang* + [2]*-er*] *Brit* : a conspicuous blunder — often used in the phrase *drop a clanger*

clapped–out \ˈklapˈdau̇t, -aptˈau̇t\ *adj* [fr. past part. of [1]*clap* + *out*] *chiefly Brit* : WORN-OUT; *also* : TIRED

class* *n* **1** : a group of adjacent and discrete or continuous values of a random variable **2** : a mathematical set; *esp* : a collection of all the sets having a particular property ⟨the ~ of groups includes all possible mathematical groups⟩ — see CATEGORY *herein* **3** : the best of its kind ⟨the ~ of the league⟩ **4** : a data type in object-oriented programming that consists of a group of programming objects with the same properties and behaviors and that is arranged in a hierarchy with other such data types — compare OBJECT *herein*

class action *n* : a legal action undertaken by one or more plaintiffs on behalf of themselves and all other persons having an identical interest in the alleged wrong

classical conditioning *n* : conditioning in which the conditioned stimulus (as the sound of a bell) is paired with and precedes the unconditioned stimulus (as the sight of food) until the conditioned stimulus alone is sufficient to elicit the response (as salivation in a dog)

class·ism \ˈkla,sizəm, -aa,s-, -ai,s-, -ȧ,s-\ *n* -s [[1]*class* + *-ism* (as in *racism*)] : prejudice or discrimination based on class — **class·ist** \-səst\ *adj*

clast \ˈklast, -aas-, -ais-, -ȧs-\ *n* -s [Gk *klastos* broken, verbal of *klan* to break — more at GLADIATOR] : a fragment of rock

clathrate *n* -s [*clathrate*, adj.] : a clathrate compound

claus·tro·phil·ia \,klȯstrəˈfilēə\ *n* -s [NL, fr. L *claustro-* (fr. L *claustrum* bar, bolt) + *-philia* — more at CLOISTER] : an abnormal desire for confinement in an enclosed space

claw back *vt, chiefly Brit* : to get back (as money) by strenuous or forceful means (as taxation) ⟨increases for farm spending . . . will have to be *clawed back*—*Economist*⟩ — **clawback** \ˈ=,=\ *n* -s *chiefly Brit*

clawhammer \ˈ=,==\ *adj* [*claw hammer*, n.] : of or relating to a style of banjo playing using the thumb and one or more fingers picking or strumming in a downward direction

claymore mine *n* [perh. fr. *claymore*] : a usu. electrically fired land mine containing steel fragments that are discharged in a predetermined direction

clean* *adj* **1** *slang* : smartly dressed **2** : free from drug addiction **3** : having no contraband (as drugs) in one's possession

clean* *vb* — **clean one's clock** : to beat or whip one in a fight or competition ⟨she played one of her best matches. . . . She really *cleaned my clock*—Chris Evert⟩

clean room \ˈ=,=\ *n* : a room for the manufacture or assembly of objects (as precision parts) that is maintained at a high level of cleanliness by special means

clean up* *vt* — **clean up one's act** : to behave in a more acceptable manner (as by discontinuing questionable practices)

clear–air turbulence \¦=¦=\ *n* : sudden severe turbulence occurring in cloudless regions that causes violent jarring or buffeting of aircraft passing through

clear–cut \ˈ=¦=\ *n* [*clear-cut*, v.] : CLEAR-CUTTING

clearway \ˈ=,=\ *n, Brit* : FREEWAY

cleaver* *n* : a rock ridge protruding from a glacier or snowfield

cleft sentence *n* : a sentence that emphasizes one part of a simple sentence (as "Kathy likes cognac") typically by transforming it into two clauses with the noun phrase to be emphasized in the first clause if it begins with *it* (as in "It is cognac that Kathy likes" or "It is Kathy who likes cognac") or following a form of *be* if the first clause begins with *what* (as in "What Kathy likes is cognac")

clem·en·tine \ˈklemən,tēn, -tīn\ *n* -s [F *clémentine*, prob. after *Clément* Rodier, Fr. priest who discovered the hybrid near Oran, Algeria, *ab*1902] : a small usu. seedless citrus fruit that is grown chiefly in Spain and No. Africa, has a thin loose orange to red orange skin and slightly acid pink-tinged flesh, and is prob. a hybrid between a tangerine and a sour orange

clergyperson \ˈ==,==\ *n* : a member of the clergy

click* *vi* **1** : to catch on ⟨an issue that ~*ed* with the voters⟩ **2** : to become clear, understandable, or appreciable ⟨for a moment I don't understand, then it ~*s*—Joe Levine⟩; *also* : to produce an understanding or appreciation ⟨something ~*ed* in my mind⟩ **3** : to select, activate, or access an item (as an icon or menu option) on a computer screen by positioning the cursor over the item and depressing a button on the mouse or other input device ⟨~ on the icon to open the file⟩; *also* : to depress a mouse button ⟨~ here⟩ ~ *vt* : to select (an item on a computer screen) by positioning the cursor over the item and depressing a button on the mouse or other input device ⟨~ the icon⟩; *also* : to depress a button of (a mouse) — **click·able** \-əbəl\ *adj*

click* *n* : an instance of clicking ⟨a mouse ~⟩

click *var of* KLICK *herein*

clicker* *n* : REMOTE CONTROL *herein*

client* *n* : a computer in a network that uses the services (as access to files or shared peripherals) provided by a server

client state *n* : a country that is economically, politically, or militarily dependent on another country

clin·da·my·cin \,klindəˈmīsᵊn\ *n* -s [chlor- + *-lindamycin*, alter. (influenced by *deoxy-*) of *lincomycin* (herein)] : a semisynthetic antibiotic $C_{18}H_{33}ClN_2O_5S$ derived from and used similarly to lincomycin

clinical trial *n* : a scientific test of the effectiveness and safety of a therapeutic agent (as a drug or vaccine) using consenting human subjects

clio* *n* -s *usu cap* : any of several statuettes awarded annually by a professional organization for notable achievement in radio and television commercials

clio·met·rics \,klīəˈme·triks\ *n pl but sing in constr* [*Clio*, muse of history + *-metrics* (as in *econometrics*)] : the application of methods developed in other fields (as economics, statistics, and data processing) to the study of history — **clio·met·ric** \-ik\ *adj* — **clio·met·ri·cian** \-me·ˈtrishən, -mə-\ *n* -s

clip art *n* : ready-made usu. copyright-free illustrations sold in books or as part of a software package from which they may be cut and pasted or inserted as artwork

clipboard* *n* : a section of computer memory that temporarily stores data (as text or a graphics image) esp. to facilitate the movement or duplication of the data

clock* *n* **1** : a synchronizing device (as in a computer) that produces pulses at regular intervals **2** : BIOLOGICAL CLOCK *herein* — **kill the clock** *or* **run out the clock** : to use up as much as possible of the playing time remaining in a game (as football) while retaining possession of the ball or puck esp. to protect a lead

clock* *vt, slang* **1** : to hit esp. in the face or on the head **2** *chiefly Brit* : ATTAIN, REALIZE — usu. used with *up* ⟨just ~ up a million . . . paperback sales —*Punch*⟩

clock radio *n* : a combination clock and radio device in which the clock can be set to turn on the radio at a designated time

clo·fi·brate \klōˈfī,brāt, -ˈfib-\ *n* -s [perh. fr. *chlor-* + *fibr-* + propi*onate*] : a synthetic drug $C_{12}H_{15}ClO_3$ used esp. to lower abnormally high concentrations of fats and cholesterol in the blood

cloister* *n* : a place or state of seclusion

clo·mi·phene \ˈklōmə,fēn\ *n* -s [*chlor-* + *amine* + *-phene* (fr. *phenyl*)] : a synthetic drug $C_{26}H_{28}ClNO$ used in the form of its citrate to induce ovulation

clo·mip·ra·mine \klōˈmiprə,mēn\ *n* -s [*chlo-r-* + *imipramine* (herein)] : a tricyclic antidepressant $C_{19}H_{23}ClN_2$ used in the form of its hydrochloride to treat obsessive-compulsive disorder

clone* *n* **1 a** : an individual grown from a single somatic cell of its parent and genetically identical to it **b** : a group of replicas of all or part of a macromolecule and esp. DNA **2** : one that is or appears to be a copy of an original ⟨a ~ of a personal computer⟩

clone *vb* -ED/-ING/-S *vt* **1** : to propagate a clone from ⟨frogs have been successfully *cloned* by transplanting nuclei from body cells to enucleated eggs⟩ **2** : to make a copy of ~ *vi* : to produce a clone

clon·er \ˈklōnə(r)\ *n* -s : a manufacturer of clones (as of a computer system)

clo·ni·dine \ˈklänə,dēn, ˈklōn-, -,dīn\ *n* -s [*chlor-* + phe*n*yl + imi*dazoline*] : an antihypertensive drug $C_9H_9Cl_2N_3$ used esp. to treat essential hypertension, to prevent migraine headache, and to diminish opiate withdrawal symptoms

close* *vt* : to terminate access to (a computer file)

closed* *adj* **1** : traced by a moving point that returns to an arbitrary starting point ⟨~ curve⟩; *also* : so formed that every plane section is a closed curve ⟨~ surface⟩ **2 a** : containing all the limit points of every subset ⟨a ~ set⟩ **b** *of an interval* : containing its endpoints **3** : characterized by mathematical elements that when subjected to an operation produce only elements of the same set ⟨the set of whole numbers is ~ under addition and multiplication⟩ **4** *of the universe* : having enough mass to stop expanding and eventually collapse

closed–captioned \ˈ=¦==\ *adj, of a television program* : broadcast so that captions appear only on the screen of a receiver equipped with a decoder

closed loop *n* : an automatic control system for an operation or process in which feedback in a closed path or group of paths acts to maintain the output at the desired level

closed shop* *n* : an exclusive group or establishment

closely held *adj* : having most stock shares and voting rights in the hands of a few ⟨a *closely held* business⟩

closet* *n* : a state or condition of secrecy, privacy, or obscurity ⟨he comes out of the ~ and unabashedly urges socialism —*New Times*⟩

closet* *adj* : being so in private : SECRET ⟨a ~ racist⟩ ⟨a ~ reader . . . during her years in the limelight as a dancer —John Updike⟩

closet queen *n* : one who secretly engages in homosexual activities while leading an ostensibly heterosexual life — often used disparagingly

closing* *n* : a meeting between parties to a real-estate deal usu. together with their attorneys and interested parties (as a mortgagor) for the purpose of formally transferring title

closing costs *n pl* : expenses (as for appraisal, title search, and title insurance) connected with the purchase of real estate that usu. constitute a charge against the purchaser additional to the cost of the property purchased

closure* *n* **1** : the property that a number system or a set has when it is mathematically closed under an operation **2** : a set that consists of a given set together with all the limit points of that set

clot–buster \ˈ=,==\ *n* : a drug (as streptokinase or tissue plasminogen activator) used to dissolve blood clots — **clot–busting** \ˈ=,==\ *adj*

clothesline \ˈ=,=\ *vt* [*clothesline*, n.] : to knock down (as a football player) by catching by the neck with an outstretched arm — **clothesline** *n*

clo·tri·ma·zole \klōˈtrīmə,zōl, -ōl\ *n* -s [prob. fr. ISV *chlor-* + *trityl* + *imidazole*] : an antifungal agent $C_{22}H_{17}ClN_2$ used to treat candidiasis, tinea, and ringworm

clotting factor *n* : any of several plasma components (as fibrinogen, prothrombin, and thromboplastin) that are involved in the clotting of blood

cloud ear *n* [trans. of Chin (Pek) *yün*[2]*-êrh*[3]] : WOOD EAR *herein*

cloud nine *n* [perh. so called fr. the ninth and highest heaven of Dante's Paradise, whose inhabitants are most blissful because nearest to God] : a feeling of well-being or elation — usu. used with *on* ⟨was on *cloud nine* after his victory⟩

clout* *n* : PULL, INFLUENCE ⟨had a lot of ~ with the governor⟩

clo·vis \ˈklōvəs\ *adj, usu cap* [*Clovis*, New Mexico] : of or relating to a widely distributed prehistoric culture of No. America characterized by leaf-shaped flint projectile points having fluted sides

clox·a·cil·lin \¦kläksə¦silən\ *n* -s [*chlorophenol* + *isoxazole* + *penicillin*] : a semisynthetic oral penicillin $C_{19}H_{17}ClN_3NaO_5S$ effective esp. against staphylococci which secrete penicillinase

clo·za·pine \ˈklōzə,pēn\ *n* -s [ISV *chlor-* + *-zapine*, alter. of *-azepine* (as in *benzodiazepine* — herein)] : an antipsychotic drug $C_{18}H_{19}ClN_4$ with serious side effects that is used in the management of severe schizophrenia

cloze \ˈklōz\ *adj* [by shortening & alter. fr. *closure*] : of, relating to, or being a test of reading comprehension that involves having the person being tested supply words which have been systematically deleted from a text

club* *n* **1** : a group identified by some common characteristic ⟨the nations in the nuclear ~⟩ **2** : CLUB SANDWICH

clue·less \ˈklüləs\ *adj* **1** : having or providing no clue ⟨a ~ case for the police to solve⟩ **2** : completely or hopelessly bewildered, unaware, ignorant, or foolish ⟨~ about what they want⟩ — **clue·less·ly** \-lē\ *adv* — **clu·less·ness** \-nəs\ *n*

clunker* *n* : someone or something that is notably unsuccessful

clunky \ˈkləŋkē\ *adj* -ER/-EST [*clunk* + [1]*-y*] : clumsy in style, form, or execution ⟨a ~ thriller⟩ ⟨~ earrings⟩

cluster* *n* **1** : a group of buildings and esp. houses built close together on a sizable tract in order to preserve open spaces larger than the individual yard for common recreation **2** : a small group of atoms (as of a metal) that are bonded together in usu. polyhedral form

cluster analysis *n* : a statistical classification technique for discovering whether the individuals of a population fall into different groups by making quantitative comparisons of multiple characteristics

cluster bomb *n* : a canister of small fragmentation bombs dropped from an aircraft

cluster college *n* : a small residential college constituting a semiautonomous division of a university and usu. specializing in one branch of knowledge (as history and the social sciences)

cluster headache *n* : a headache that is characterized by severe unilateral pain in the eye or temple, affects primarily men, and tends to recur in a series of attacks

clutch* *vi* : to perform poorly or fail in a critical situation ⟨~*ed* on the final exam⟩

clutch* *n* : CLUTCH BAG *herein*

clutch bag *n* : a woman's small usu. strapless handbag

clut·ton's joints \ˈklətᵊnz-\ *n pl, usu cap C* [after Henry Hugh *Clutton* †1909 Eng. surgeon] : symmetrical hydrarthrosis esp. of the knees or elbows that occurs in congenital syphilis

clyde \ˈklīd\ *n* -s *usu cap* [by shortening] : CLYDESDALE

CMA *abbr* certified medical assistant

CMO \¦sē¦emˈō\ *n* -s : COLLATERALIZED MORTGAGE OBLIGATION *herein*

CMOS \¦sē¦emˈōˈes, ˈsē¦mȯs\ *n, often attrib* [complementary metal-

oxide semiconductor] : a technology for making integrated circuits using metal-oxide semiconductor devices in which flip-flops are made up of pairs of two different types of transistor connected in such a way that power is used only when the state is changed

CMV *abbr* cytomegalovirus *herein*

CN* *abbr* chloroacetophenone

co-adapted \¦kō+\ *adj* [*co-* + *adapted*, past part. of [1]*adapt*] : mutually adapted esp. by natural selection ⟨~ gene complexes⟩

co·ag·u·lop·a·thy \(ˌ)kōˌagyəˈläpəthē\ *n* -ES [*coagulation* + *-o-* + *-pathy*] : a disease or condition affecting the blood's ability to coagulate

coalesce* *vi* : to arise from the combination of distinct elements ⟨an organized and a popular resistance immediately *coalesced*—C.C.Menges⟩

co–anchor \(ˈ)kō+\ *n* [*co-* + *anchor* (herein)] : a newscaster who shares the duties of anchoring a news broadcast — **co–anchor** \"+\ *vt*

co·an·da effect \kō¦andə-, -än-\ *n, usu cap C* [after Henri *Coanda* †1972 Romanian engineer] : the tendency of a jet of fluid emerging from an orifice to follow an adjacent flat or curved surface and to entrain fluid from the surroundings so that a region of lower pressure develops

cobblers \ˈkäblə(r)z\ *n pl* [fr. *cobblers' awls*, rhyming slang for *balls*] *Brit* : NONSENSE, BUNK

co·bol \ˈkōˌbȯl\ *n* -S *usu cap C or all cap* [*common business oriented language*] : a computer programming language designed for business applications

co·chromatograph \¦kō+\ *vb* [*co-* + *chromatograph*] *vi* : to undergo separation out of a mixed sample by cochromatography ~ *vt* : to subject to cochromatography

co·chromatography \"+\ *n* [*co-* + *chromatography*] : chromatography of two or more samples together; *esp* : identification of an unknown substance by chromatographic comparison with a known substance

cock·a·ma·mie *also* **cock·a·ma·my** \ˈkäkəˌmāmē\ *adj* [prob. alter. of earlier *cockamanie* decal, alter. of *decalcomania*] : RIDICULOUS, INCREDIBLE ⟨of all the ~ excuses I ever heard —Leo Rosten⟩

cock·a·poo \ˈkäkəˌpü\ *n* -S [*cocka-*, alter. of *cocker* spaniel + *poodle*; prob. influenced by *cockatoo*] : a dog that is a cross between a cocker spaniel and a poodle

cocks·man \ˈkäksmən\ *n, pl* **cocksmen** [*cock's* (gen. of [1]*cock* penis) + [1]*man*] : a man known for his sexual prowess or promiscuity — usu. considered vulgar

cocksucker \ˈ=ˌ==\ *n* : one who fellates — usu. considered obscene; often used as a generalized term of abuse

cocksucking \ˈ=ˌ==\ *adj* — usu. considered obscene; usu. used as a generalized term of abuse

cocktail* *n* : a mixture of agents usu. in solution that is taken or used esp. for medical treatment or diagnosis ⟨a ~ of three antiviral drugs⟩ ⟨an anesthetic ~⟩

cockteaser \ˈ=ˌ==\ *n* : a female who excites a male sexually and then refuses intercourse — usu. considered vulgar

cock–up \ˈ=ˌ=\ *n* -S [prob. fr. [1]*cock* (penis) + *-up* (as in *balls-up* — herein — or [2]*ballup*)] *Brit* : MESS 5b; *esp* : one caused by bungling or incompetence ⟨the whole thing was a badly-handled *cock-up*—*Punch*⟩

cocooning *n* [fr. gerund of [2]*cocoon*] : the practice of spending leisure time at home in preference to going out

co·cultivation \¦kō+\ *n* [*co-* + *cultivation*] : cultivation of two types of cells or tissue in the same medium — **co·cultivate** \"+\ *vt*

code* *n* **1** : GENETIC CODE *herein* **2** : a set of instructions for a computer program **3** : CODE BLUE *herein*

code* *vt* : to specify the genetic code for ⟨an amino acid *coded* by a nucleotide sequence⟩ ~ *vi* : to specify the genetic code ⟨the DNA sequence of the gene that ~s for that protein —Gina B. Kolata⟩

code blue *n, often cap C&B* [prob. fr. [1]*code* (set of procedures) + [2]*blue* (characteristic color of cyanosis)] : a state of medical emergency or a declaration of such a state along with a call for medical personnel and equipment to attempt to resuscitate a patient esp. when in cardiac arrest or respiratory distress or failure ⟨summoned by emergency *Code Blues*, doctors had brought her back to life more than once —Bill Bryan⟩; *also* : the attempt to resuscitate the patient

co·dec \ˈkōˌdek\ *n* -S [*coder* + *decoder*] : a device that can digitize and often compress an audio or video signal for transmission, as over a telephone line, or can convert an incoming signal to audio or video for reception

co·dependence \¦kō+\ *n* : CODEPENDENCY *herein*

co·dependency \¦kō+\ *n* [*codependent* (herein) + *-ency*] : a psychological condition or a relationship in which a person is controlled or manipulated by another who is affected with a pathological condition (as an addiction to alcohol or heroin)

co·dependent \¦kō+\ *adj* [*co-* + [1]*dependent*] : participating in or exhibiting codependency — **codependent** *n*

code–switching \ˈ=ˌ==\ *n* : the switching from the linguistic system of one language or dialect to that of another

code word* *n* : EUPHEMISM ⟨interpreting "compatibility" as a *code word* for stifling dissent, the faculty denounced the memorandum —Robert Griffith⟩

co·di·col·o·gy \ˌkōdiˈkäləjē, ˌkäd-\ *n* -ES [ML *codic-*, *codex* bound manuscript (fr. L) + E *-ology* (as in *geology*) — more at CODEX] : the study of manuscripts as cultural artifacts for historical purposes — **co·di·co·log·i·cal** \-ˌkəˈläjikəl\ *adj*

codominant* *adj* : being fully expressed in the heterozygous condition ⟨~ alleles⟩

co·don \ˈkōˌdän\ *n* -S [(*genetic*) *code* (herein) + [2]*-on*] : a specific sequence of three consecutive nucleotides that is part of the genetic code and that specifies a particular amino acid in a protein or starts or stops protein synthesis — called also *triplet*

cods·wal·lop \ˈkädzˌwäləp, -wȯl-\ *n* [origin unknown] *chiefly Brit* : NONSENSE, DRIVEL

co·enzymatic \¦kō+\ *adj* [fr. *coenzyme*, after such pairs as E *enzyme* : *enzymatic*] : of or relating to a coenzyme ⟨~ activity⟩ — **co·enzymati·cally** \"+\ *adv*

coenzyme Q *n* [*Q* prob. fr. *quinone*] : UBIQUINONE *herein*

coes·ite \ˈkōˌzīt\ *n* -S [Loring *Coes*, Jr., †1978 Am. chemist + E *-ite*] : a dense crystalline silica formed from quartz under great heat and pressure and found in meteorite craters

co·evolution \ˌkōˌevəˈlüshən, *esp Brit* -ˌēv-\ *n* [*co-* + *evolution*] : evolution involving successive changes in two or more ecologically interdependent species (as of a plant and its pollinators) that affect their interactions — **co·evolutionary** \"+\ *adj* — **co·evolve** \"+\ *vi*

coffee bar *n* : an establishment or counter where coffee and usu. light refreshments are served

coffee lightener *or* **coffee whitener** *n* : a nondairy product used as a substitute for cream in coffee

coffee–table \ˈ==¦=\ *adj* : of, relating to, or being an item (as a book or magazine) intended for display (as on a coffee table); *specif* : of, relating to, or being an expensive lavishly illustrated oversize book

co·generation \¦kō+\ *n* [*co-* + *generation*] : the production of electricity using waste heat (as in steam) from an industrial process or the use of steam from electric power generation as a source of heat — **co·generator** \¦kō+\ *n*

cog·gins \ˈkägənz, ˈkȯ-\ *or* **coggins test** *n, usu cap C* [after Leroy *Coggins* *b*1932 Am. veterinary virologist] : a serological test for the diagnosis of equine infectious anemia

cognitive dissonance *n* : psychological conflict resulting from incongruous beliefs and attitudes (as a fondness for smoking and a belief that it is harmful) held simultaneously

cognitive psychology *n* : a branch of psychology concerned with mental processes (as perception, thinking, learning, and memory) esp. with respect to the internal events occurring between sensory stimulation and the overt expression of behavior — compare BEHAVIORISM *in the Dict* — **cognitive psychologist** *n*

cognitive science *n* : a science that draws on many fields (as psychology, artificial intelligence, linguistics, and philosophy) to develop theories of perception, thinking, and learning

cognitive therapy *n* : psychotherapy esp. for depression that emphasizes the substitution of desirable patterns of thinking for maladaptive or faulty ones — compare BEHAVIOR MODIFICATION *herein*

coherence* *n* : the property of being coherent

co·he·sion·less \kōˈhēzhənləs\ *adj* : composed of particles or granules that tend not to cohere ⟨~ soils⟩

co·housing \¦kō+\ *n, often attrib* [*co-* + [1]*housing*] : semi-communal housing consisting of a cluster of private homes and a shared community space (as for cooking or laundry facilities)

coincident* *or* **coincident indicator** *n* : an economic indicator (as level of personal income or of retail sales) that more often than not correlates directly with the state of the economy

co·infection \ˌkō+\ *n* [*co-* + *infection*] : concurrent infection of a cell or organism with two microorganisms ⟨influenza caused by ~ with two strains of a virus⟩ — **co·infect** \ˌkō+\ *vt*

cokehead \ˈ=ˌ=, ˈkōˌked\ *n* [[3]*coke* + *-head* (as in *hophead*)] *slang* : one who uses cocaine compulsively

COLA *abbr* cost-of-living adjustment

cold* *adj* : low in energy and thus having low velocity ⟨~ neutrons⟩

cold* *n* : a state or condition of having a secret identity, mission, or cover — used in the phrase *in from the cold* ⟨a near-deadly slip . . . made the game too dangerous and the F.B.I. called him in from the ~ —Ralph Blumenthal⟩; *also* : a state of estrangement, isolation, or neglect

cold call *n* : a telephone call soliciting business made directly to a potential customer without prior contact or without a lead — **cold–call** \ˈ=ˌ=\ *vb*

cold dark matter *n* : a form of dark matter theorized to consist of slow-moving elementary particles and to have contributed to the formation of large-scale structure (as galaxies) in the early universe

cold duck *n* [trans. of G *kalte ente*, a drink of mixed wines and lemon juice] : a beverage that consists of a blend of sparkling burgundy and champagne

cold fusion *n* : a hypothetical method for achieving nuclear fusion at low temperature (as room temperature)

cold turkey *adv* [*cold turkey*, n.] : all at once : ABRUPTLY : as **a** : without a period of gradual adjustment, adaptation, or withdrawal ⟨quit smoking *cold turkey*⟩ **b** : without preparation ⟨non-English-speaking students dropped *cold turkey* into English-only classrooms⟩

cold warrior *n, sometimes cap C&W* : an advocate of an aggressively anticommunist cold-war policy ⟨the classic *cold warrior*, wedded to the idea of confrontation with the Soviet Union —Jeff Greenfield⟩

cold weld** *vi* : to adhere on contact without application of pressure or heat — used of metals in the vacuum of outer space

col·i·ci·no·ge·nic \¦käləsənəˈjenik, -ˌsēn-\ *adj* [*colicin* + *-o-* + *-genic*] **1** : producing or having the capacity to produce colicins ⟨~ bacteria⟩ **2** : conferring the capacity to produce colicins ⟨~ genetic material⟩ — **col·i·ci·no·ge·nic·i·ty** \-nəjəˈnis(ə)d-ē\ *n* -ES

col·i·ci·nog·e·ny \ˌ===ˈnäjənē\ *n* -ES [*colicin* + *-o-* + *-geny*] : the capacity to produce colicins

colinear* *adj* : having corresponding parts arranged in the same linear order ⟨good evidence is accumulating that the gene and its polypeptide product are ~ —J.D.Watson⟩ — **co·lin·ear·i·ty** \(ˌ)kōˌlinēˈarəd-ē\ *n* -ES

co·lis·tin \kəˈlistən, kō-\ *n* -S [*colist-* (fr. NL *colistinus*, specific epithet of the bacterium producing it) + *-in*] : a polymyxin antibiotic produced by a bacterium of the genus *Bacillus* (*B. polymyxa* var. *colistinus*) and used against some gram-negative pathogens esp. of the genera *Pseudomonas*, *Escherichia*, *Klebsiella*, and *Shigella*

collage* *n* : a work (as a film) having disparate scenes in rapid succession without transitions

col·lage \kəˈläzh\ *vt* -ED/-ING/-S [*collage*, n.] : to assemble or create a collage from; *also* : to make a collage on

col·la·gen·o·lyt·ic \ˌkäləjənəˈlid-ik, -ˌjen-\ *adj* [*collagen* + *-o-* + *-lytic*] : relating to or having the capacity to break down collagen ⟨~ activity⟩ ⟨~ enzymes⟩

col·lap·sar \kəˈlapˌsär\ *n* -S [[1]*collapse* + *-ar* (as in *quasar* — herein)] : BLACK HOLE 1 *herein*

collateral damage *n* : injury, harm, or death inflicted on something other than an intended target : unintentional secondary damage; *specif* : civilian casualties of a military operation

collateralized mortgage obligation *n* : a bond backed by a pool of mortgages and paid according to the maturity and amortization schedule of its class

collateral ligament *n* : any of various ligaments on one or the other side of a hinge joint (as the knee, elbow, or the joints between the phalanges of the toes and fingers); *esp* : either of two ligaments of the knee that help stabilize it by preventing lateral dislocation

col·lect·ible *or* **col·lect·able** \kəˈlektəbəl\ *n* -S [*collectible* or *collectable*, adj.] : an object that is collected by fanciers; *esp* : one other than such traditionally collectible items as art, stamps, coins, and antiques

collector* *n* : SOLAR COLLECTOR *herein*

collegial* *adj* : marked by camaraderie among colleagues

collegiality* *n* : the participation of bishops in the government of the Roman Catholic Church in collaboration with the pope

col·lid·er \kəˈlīdə(r)\ *n* -S : a particle accelerator in which two beams of particles moving in opposite directions are made to collide at a chosen point

col·li·sion·less \kəˈlizhənləs\ *adj* : of, relating to, or being a plasma in which particles interact through charge rather than collision ⟨a ~ shock wave⟩

colloquial* *adj* : unacceptably informal ⟨considered his writing careless and ~⟩

co·lo·cate \(ˌ)kōˈlōˌkāt, -lōˈkāt\ *vt* [*co-* + *locate*] : to locate together; *esp* : to place (two or more units) close together so as to share common facilities

co·lon·ia \kōˈlōnyä\ *n* -S [MexSp, suburb, fr. Sp, colony, residential development, fr. L — more at COLONY] : an unincorporated settlement (as of Mexican-Americans or Mexicans) in the U.S. usu. near the Mexican border that typically has poor services and squalid conditions

co·lon·ic \(ˈ)kō¦länik, kəˈl-\ *or* **colonic irrigation** *n* -S [*colonic*, adj.] : ENEMA

co·lon·o·scope \kōˈlänəˌskōp, kəˈ-\ *n* [[1]*colon* + *-o-* + *-scope*] : a flexible tube containing a fiberscope for visual inspection of the colon and apparatus for taking tissue samples

co·lo·nos·co·py \ˌkōləˈnäskəpē\ *n* -ES [[1]*colon* + *-o-* + *-scopy*] : endoscopic examination of the colon — **co·lon·o·scop·ic** \ˌkō¦länə¦skäpik, kə-\ *adj*

colony–stimulating factor *n* : any of several glycoproteins that promote the differentiation of stem cells esp. into blood granulocytes and macrophages and that stimulate their proliferation into colonies in culture — abbr. *CSF*; see GRANULOCYTE COLONY-STIMULATING FACTOR *herein*, GRANULOCYTE-MACROPHAGE COLONY-STIMULATING FACTOR *herein*

color* *n* : a hypothetical property of quarks that differentiates each type into three forms that are identical in mass, spin, electric charge, and all other measurable quantities but that have distinct roles in the strong interactions that bind quarks together

color–blind* *adj* : not recognizing differences of race; *esp* : free from racial prejudice

color center *n* : a defect in the lattice structure of a usu. transparent crystal that causes light of only one color to be transmitted by the part of the crystal in which the defect is located

color–code \¦==¦=\ *vt* : to color (as wires or pipes) according to a key designed to facilitate identification

co·lo·rec·tal \¦kōlə¦rektᵊl\ *adj* [[2]*col-* + *rectal*] : relating to or affecting the colon and the rectum ⟨~ cancer⟩ ⟨~ surgery⟩

color–field \¦==¦=\ *n, often attrib* : a style of abstract painting in which color is emphasized and form and surface are correspondingly de-emphasized ⟨*color-field* abstractionists⟩

co·lor·ize \ˈkələˌrīz\ *vt* -ED/-ING/-S : to add color to (a black-and-white film) by means of a computer

colorpoint shorthair \ˈ==¦=-\ *also* **color point** *n* : any of a breed of domestic cats that was developed by crossing a Siamese with an American shorthair and that is of Siamese body type and coat pattern but occurs in different colors and is sometimes considered part of the Siamese breed

col·po·rha·phy \kälˈpȯrəfē, -ȯr-\ *n* -ES [ISV *colp-* + *-rraphy*] : surgical repair of the vaginal wall

column chromatography *n* : chromatography in which the substances to be separated are introduced onto the top of a column packed with an adsorbent (as silica gel or alumina), pass through the column at different rates that depend on the affinity of each substance for the adsorbent and for the solvent or solvent mixture, and are usu. collected in solution as they pass from the column at different times — compare GAS CHROMATOGRAPHY *herein*, PAPER CHROMATOGRAPHY *in the Dict*, THIN-LAYER CHROMATOGRAPHY *herein*

COM *abbr* computer-output microfilm; computer-output microfilmer

combat zone* *n* : a district in which places of pornographic entertainment are concentrated

comb filter *n* : a filter in a signal receiver (as a television set) that passes only distinctly separated narrow ranges of wavelengths

combinatorial* *adj* : of or relating to the arrangement of, operation on, and selection of discrete mathematical elements belonging to finite sets (as the set of possible states making up a digital computer) or making up geometric configurations

combinatorial chemistry *n* : a branch of applied chemistry concerned with the rapid synthesis and screening of large numbers of different but related chemical compounds generated from a mixture of known building blocks in order to recover new substances optimally suited for a specific function

combinatorial topology *n* : a study that deals with geometric forms based on their decomposition into combinations of the simplest geometric figures

com·bi·na·to·rics \ˌkämbənəˈtȯriks, -ȯr- *also* kəmˌbīn-\ *n pl but sing in constr* [*combinatorial mathematics*] : combinatorial mathematics

comb–out* *n* : the combing of hair into a desired hairdo

come* *vb* — **come off*** : to return to a regular activity after (a particular condition, experience, or performance) ⟨an injury-prone wide receiver *coming off* his only good season in five —D.P. Anderson⟩ — **come to** : to be a question of ⟨when it *comes to* pitching horseshoes, I'm the champ⟩ — **come down the pike** : to appear in the normal course of events ⟨the finest piece of classical music journalism to *come down the pike* in quite a while —D.R.Martin⟩

come* *n* **1** : ORGASM — often considered vulgar **2** : SEMEN — often considered vulgar

come·back·er \ˈkəm¦bakə(r)\ *n* -S [*come back* + [2]*-er*] **1** : a grounder in baseball hit directly to the pitcher **2** : a putt back to the hole in golf after a preceding putt has rolled past it

come down* *vi* **1** : to recover from the effects of drugs or alcohol **2** : to go on : HAPPEN

come on* *vi* **1** : to project an indicated personal image ⟨*comes on* gruff and laconic . . . on the telephone —Robert Craft⟩ **2** : to show sexual interest in someone; *also* : to make sexual advances — usu. used with *to* or *with* ⟨didn't get the feeling that [she] was interested in him or that he was *coming on* strong to her —Ellen J. Willis⟩ ⟨in his own inept way was trying to *come on* to her —*East Village Other*⟩ **3** \ˈ=¦=\ — used to express astonishment, incredulity, or recognition of an obvious put-on

come–on* *n* : a usu. sexual advance

come out* *vi* **1** : to openly declare one's homosexuality **2** : to openly declare something about oneself previously kept hidden — used with *as* ⟨blew his cover and *came out* as a CIA agent —William Prochnau⟩

come up* *vi* **1** : to grow up ⟨*coming up* in the early 60s⟩ **2** : to turn out to be ⟨the coin *came up* heads⟩ — **come up empty** : to fail to achieve a desired result ⟨police searched the shopping center and *came up empty* —Craig Horowitz *et al*⟩ — **come up roses** : to turn out far better than expected

comfort food *n* : food prepared in a traditional style having a usu. nostalgic or sentimental appeal

comfort zone *n* **1** : the temperature range within which one is comfortable **2** : the level at which one functions with ease and familiarity ⟨empower a child to take risks within his own *comfort zone* —*Redbook Mag.*⟩

comix \ˈkämiks\ *n pl* [alter. of *comics*] : comic books or comic strips

command* *n* **1** : an electrical or electronic signal that actuates a device (as a control mechanism in a spacecraft or one step in a computer) **2** : the activation of a device in or the control of a vehicle (as a spacecraft) by means of a command

command eocnomy *n* [trans. of G *befehlswirtschaft*] : an economic system in which activity is controlled by a central authority and the means of production are publicly owned

command module *n* : a space vehicle module designed to carry the crew, the chief communication equipment, and the equipment for reentry

commentator* *n* : a layman who leads a congregation in prayer at Mass or explains the rituals performed by the priest

com·mod·i·fy \kəˈmädəˌfī\ *vt* -ED/-ING/-ES [*commodity* + *-fy*] : to turn (as an intrinsic value or a work of art) into a commodity — **com·mod·i·fi·ca·tion** \-ˌmädəfəˈkāshən\ *n* -S

com·mod·i·tize \kəˈmädəˌtīz\ *vt* -ED/-ING/-S : COMMODIFY *herein* — **com·mod·i·ti·za·tion** \ˌmädətəˈzāshən, -d-əˈzā-\ *n* -S

commodity* *n* **1** : a mass-produced unspecialized product ⟨~ chemicals⟩ **2** : one that is subject to ready exchange or exploitation within a market ⟨stars as individuals and as *commodities* of the film industry —*Film Quarterly*⟩

common market *n* : an economic association (as of nations) formed to remove trade barriers among members

common si·tus picketing \-ˈsīd-əs-\ *n* : picketing of an entire construction site by a trade union having a grievance with only a single subcontractor working at the site — compare SECONDARY BOYCOTT *in the Dict*

common trust fund *n* : a fund which is managed by a bank or trust company and in which the assets of many small trusts are handled as a single portfolio with individual beneficiaries receiving returns proportionate to their share of the principal

communication theory *also* **communications theory** *n* : a theory that deals with the technology of the transmission of information (as in the printed word or a computer) between people or people and machines or machines and machines

community antenna television *n* : CABLE TELEVISION *herein*

com·mu·ta·tiv·i·ty \kəˌmyüd-əˈtivəd-ē, ˌkämyəd-əˈti-\ *n* -ES : the property of being commutative ⟨the ~ of a mathematical operation⟩

commutator* *n* : an element of a mathematical group that when used to multiply the product of two given elements either on the right side or on the left side but not necessarily on both sides yields the product of the two given elements in reverse order

commute* *vi* : to yield the same result regardless of order — used of two mathematical elements undergoing an operation or of two operations on elements

com·mute \kəˈmyüt\ *n* -S [*commute*, v.] **1** : an act or instance of commuting ⟨his usual morning ~ to work —*Newsweek*⟩ **2** : the distance covered in commuting ⟨about an hour's ~ from the university —*College Composition & Communication*⟩

co·mor·bid \(ˌ)kō'mȯrbəd\ *adj* [*co-* + *morbid*] **:** existing simultaneously with and usu. independently of another medical condition ⟨laparoscopic surgery for symptomatic gallstones is not usually advisable in patients with ~ cardiopulmonary disease⟩ — **co·mor·bid·i·ty** \-mȯr'bidəd·ē, -ətē\ *n*

¹comp \'kämp, 'kəmp\ *vi* -ED/-ING/-S [short for *accompany*] **:** to play an irregular rhythmic chord accompaniment for jazz

²comp \'kämp\ *n* -S [short for *complimentary*] **:** a complimentary ticket; *broadly* **:** something provided free of charge ⟨flying them here free on charters and supplying them with other ~*s*—a room, meals and liquor —Hal Lancaster⟩

³comp \"\ *vt* -ED/-ING/-S [²*comp* (herein)] **1 :** to provide with something free ⟨being ~*ed* for rooms, meals and beverages —R.A.Aurthur⟩ **2 :** to provide free of charge ⟨meals that are ~*ed*⟩

compact* *adj* **:** being a topological space (as a metric space) with the property that for any collection of open sets which contains it there is a subset of the collection with a finite number of elements which also contains it — **com·pact·ness*** *n*

compact disc *n* **:** a small optical disk usu. containing recorded music or computer data — abbr. *CD*

com·pact·ible \kəm'paktəbəl\ *adj* **:** capable of being compacted ⟨~ soils⟩ — **com·pac·ti·bil·i·ty** \-ˌpaktə-'biləd·ē, -ətē\ *n* -ES

com·pact·i·fi·ca·tion \kəmˌpaktəfə'kāshən\ *n* -S [¹*compact* + *-ification* (as in *saponification*)] **1 :** a compact topological space that contains a given topological space as a subset or that contains a subset homeomorphic to the given topological space **2 :** the application of a topological compactification to a model of the universe (as one involving superstrings) in which the ordinary dimensions of space are held to coexist with several other dimensions too infinitesimal in size to observe

comparable worth *n* **:** the concept that women and men should receive equal pay for jobs calling for comparable skill and responsibility

comparative advertising *n* **:** advertising in which a competitor's product is named and compared with the advertiser's product

comparison shop *vi* **:** to compare prices of competing brands or competing dealers or stores in order to find the best value

com·pas \kōm'pä\ *n* -ES [Haitian Creole *konpa*, lit., beat, rhythm, modif. (influenced by F *compas* compass) of Sp *compás* beat, measure (in music), fr. *compasar* to measure, divide (music) into bars, fr. (assumed) VL *compassare* to measure off by paces — more at COMPASS] **:** a popular music of Haiti that combines Cuban and African rhythms

compass* *n* **:** a guiding, governing, or motivating purpose ⟨ a moral ~⟩

compatible* *adj* **1 :** capable of being used in transfusion or grafting without immunological reaction (as agglutination or tissue rejection) **2 :** designed to work with another device or system without modification; *esp* **:** being a computer designed to operate in the same manner and use the same software as another computer — **compatible** *n* -S

compensatory education *n* **:** educational programs intended to make up for cultural experiences or educational stimulation lacked by disadvantaged children

competence* *n* **1 :** readiness of bacteria to undergo genetic transformation **2 :** the knowledge which enables a person to speak and understand a language — compare PERFORMANCE *herein*

competent* *adj* **:** having the capacity to respond (as by producing an antibody) to an antigenic determinant ⟨immunologically ~ cells⟩

competitive* *adj* **:** depending for effectiveness on the relative concentration of two or more substances ⟨~ inhibition of an enzyme⟩ ⟨~ protein binding⟩

competitive exclusion *or* **competitive exclusion principle** *n* **:** a generalization in ecology: two species cannot coexist in the same ecological niche for very long without one becoming extinct or being driven out because of competition for limited resources

compile* *vt* **:** to run (as a program) through a compiler

compiler* *n* **:** a computer program that translates an entire set of instructions written in a higher-level symbolic language (as Fortran) into machine language before the instructions can be executed — compare INTERPRETER *herein*

complement* *n* **1 :** the set of all elements that do not belong to a given set and are contained in a particular mathematical set containing the given set **2 :** a phrasal category (as a noun phrase or sentence) that is combined with a lexical head (as a verb) or a function word to form a larger constituent

complementarity* *n* **:** the correspondence between complementary strands or nucleotides of DNA or sometimes RNA that permits their precise pairing

complementary* *adj* **:** characterized by molecular complementarity; *esp* **:** characterized by the capacity for precise pairing of purine and pyrimidine bases between strands of DNA and sometimes RNA such that the structure of one strand determines the other

complementary DNA *n* **:** CDNA *herein*

complementation* *n* **1 :** the determination of the complement of a given mathematical set **2 :** production of normal phenotype in an individual heterozygous for two closely related mutations with one on each homologous chromosome and at a slightly different position

com·ple·men·tiz·er \'kämpləmenˌtīzər, -mən-\ *n* -S [¹*complement* + *-ize* + ²*-er*] **:** a function word or morpheme that accompanies a subordinate clause

complete* *adj* **1** *of insect metamorphosis* **:** characterized by the occurrence of a pupal stage between the motile immature stages and the adult — compare INCOMPLETE *herein* **2** *of a metric space* **:** having the property that every Cauchy sequence of elements converges to a limit in the space

complete blood count *also* **complete blood cell count** *n* **:** a blood count that includes separate counts for red and white blood cells — abbr. *CBC*; compare DIFFERENTIAL BLOOD COUNT *in the Dict*

com·plet·ist \kəm'plēd·əst\ *n* -S **:** one who wants to achieve completeness; *specif* **:** one whose collection (as of music) is or aims to be exhaustive ⟨Ella Fitzgerald ~*s* will want this album⟩

complex* *adj* **1 :** of, concerned with, being, or containing complex numbers ⟨a ~ root⟩ ⟨~ analysis⟩ **2** *of wine* **:** having a multiplicity of flavors or aromas — **complexity*** *n*

complex* *n* **:** a building or group of buildings housing related units ⟨an apartment ~⟩ ⟨a sports ~⟩

complex carbohydrate *n* **:** POLYSACCHARIDE; *also* **:** a food (as rice or pasta) composed primarily of polysaccharides

complex conjugate *n* **1 :** CONJUGATE COMPLEX NUMBER **2 :** a matrix whose elements and the corresponding elements of a given matrix form pairs of conjugate complex numbers

complexity theory *n* **:** a field of study shared by mathematics and computer science that is concerned with how the computational complexity of problems increases as the number of cases involved increases and with the classification of the problems according to whether a solution can be found in polynomial time and to the algorithms required for such a solution — compare NP-COMPLETE *herein*, TRAVELING SALESMAN PROBLEM *herein*

com·plex·o·met·ric \kəmˌpleksə'me-trik, (ˌ)käm-\ *adj* [¹*complex* + *-o-* + *-metric*] **:** of, relating to, or being a titration in which a complexing agent (as EDTA) is used as the titrant — **com·plex·om·e·try** \ˌkämˌplek'sämətrē, kəm-\ *n* -ES

com·plic·it \(ˌ)kəm'plisət\ *adj* [back-formation fr. *complicity*] **:** having complicity ⟨who, having abjured killing in revulsion against the war, finds himself guiltily ~ in it in the revolution —C.E.Schorske⟩

com·plic·i·tous \(ˌ)kəm'plisəd·əs, -ətəs\ *adj* [*complicity* + *-ous*] **:** COMPLICIT *herein*

component* *n* **:** a coordinate of a vector; *also* **:** either member of an ordered pair of numbers

com·po·nent·ry \kəm'pōnən·trē, käm-\ *n* -ES [*component* + *-ry*] **:** the parts that make up a system or device

composite* *adj, of a statistical hypothesis* **:** specifying a range of values for one or more statistical parameters — compare SIMPLE *herein*

composite* *n* **1 :** a solid material which is composed of two or more substances having different physical characteristics and in which each substance retains its identity while contributing desirable properties to the whole ⟨dental ~*s*⟩; *esp* **:** a structural material made of plastic within which a fibrous material (as silicon carbide) is embedded **2 :** something made from a composite

composite function *also* **composite*** *n* **:** a function whose values are found from two given functions by applying one function to an independent variable and then applying the second function to the result and whose domain consists of those values of the independent variable for which the result yielded by the first function lies in the domain of the second

composition* *n* **:** the operation of forming a composite function; *also* **:** COMPOSITE FUNCTION *herein*

com·po·si·tion·ist \ˌkämpə'zishənəst\ *n* -S **:** a teacher of writing esp. in a college or university

com·post·a·ble \'kämˌpōstəbəl\ *adj* **:** able to be composted

compromise* *vt* **:** to cause the impairment of ⟨a *compromised* immune system⟩ ⟨a seriously *compromised* patient⟩ ~ *vi* **:** to find or follow a way between extremes

computation* *n* **:** the use or operation of a computer — **com·pu·ta·tion·al·ly** \ˌ==ˈ=shnəlē, -shənᵊlē\ *adv*

computational linguistics *n pl but usu sing in constr* **:** linguistic research carried out by means of a computer

compute* *vt* **:** to determine or calculate by means of a computer ~ *vi* **1 :** to use a computer **2 :** to make sense ⟨that statement does not ~⟩

computed tomographic *adj* **:** using, produced by, or obtained by computed tomography ⟨a *computed tomographic* scan of the abdomen⟩ ⟨*computed tomographic* findings⟩

computed tomography *or* **computerized tomography** *also* **computed axial tomography** *or* **computerized axial tomography** *n* **:** radiography in which a three-dimensional image of a body structure is constructed by computer from a series of plane cross-sectional images made along an axis — see CAT SCAN *herein*

com·put·er·ese \kəmˌpyüd·əˌrēz, -ütə-, -ēs\ *n* -S **1 :** a language designed to be used with or by a computer **2 :** jargon used by computer experts

computerise *Brit var of* COMPUTERIZE *herein*

com·put·er·ist \kəm'pyüd·ərəst, -ütə-\ *n* -S **:** a person who uses or operates a computer

com·put·er·ize \kəm'pyüd·əˌrīz, -ütə-\ *vb* -ED/-ING/-S *vt* **1 :** to carry out, control, or produce by means of a computer ⟨*computerized* typesetting⟩ ⟨*computerized* machines⟩ **2 :** to equip with computers **3 a :** to store in a computer ⟨will soon ~ all available information on the buyers and sellers of property —Ward Morehouse III⟩ **b :** to put into a form that a computer can use ~ *vi* **:** to use computers — **com·put·er·iz·able** \-ˌpyüd·əˌrīzəbəl\ *adj* — **com·put·er·iza·tion** \-ˌpyüd·ərə'zāshən, -ˌrī'z-\ *n* -S

com·put·er·ized \=ˈ==ˌrīzd\ *adj* **:** run or produced as if by computer — used as a generalized term of disapproval ⟨arguments against ~ America with its ~ language —T.L.Gross⟩

computerlike \=ˈ==ˌ=\ *adj* **:** resembling or characteristic of a computer

com·put·er·nik \=ˈ==ˌnik\ *n* -S [*computer* + *-nik* (herein)] **:** a person who works with or has a deep interest in computers

com·put·er·phobe \=ˈ==ˌfōb\ *n* -S [*computer* + *-phobe*] **:** a person who experiences anxiety about computers and esp. about their use — **com·put·er·phobia** \"+\ *n* -S — **com·put·er·phobic** \"+\ *adj*

Com·sat \'kämˌsat\ *service mark* — used for communications services involving an artificial satellite

com·symp \'kämˌsimp\ *n* -S *often cap* [¹*com*munist + *symp*athizer] **:** a person who sympathizes with communist causes — usu. used disparagingly

con* *n* [¹⁰*con*] **:** something (as a ruse) used deceptively to gain another's trust or belief

conative* *adj* **:** of or relating to the function of a message to influence the one receiving it — **conatively** *adv*

concave* *n* **:** a concave line or surface

concealer* *n* **:** a cosmetic used to conceal blemishes esp. under the eyes

conceit* *n* **:** an organizing theme or concept ⟨found his ~ for the film early —Peter Wilkinson⟩

concentrator* *n* **1 :** a mirror or group of mirrors that focus sunlight for use as an energy source **2 :** a device in a computer network that collects data from separate low-volume transmission channels and retransmits it over a single high-volume channel

conceptual* *adj* **:** of, relating to, or being conceptual art

conceptual art *n, sometimes cap C* **:** an art form in which the artist's intent is to convey a concept rather than to create an art object — **conceptual artist** *n*

con·clu·so·ry \kən'klüs(ə)rē, -üz(-\ *adj* [fr. *conclusion*, after such pairs as E *illusion* : *illusory*] **:** relating to, based on, or consisting of a conclusion (sense 8) ⟨we agree plaintiff's petition is ~ and does not adequately state the factual basis for its assertion —*Lavergne v. Western Company of North America*⟩

con·cord \kən'kȯ(ə)rd, kän-\ *vt* -ED/-ING/-S [back-formation fr. *concordance*] **:** to prepare a concordance of

concrete* *adj* **:** of or relating to concrete poetry ⟨~ poet⟩

concrete* *n* **1 :** CONCRETE POETRY *herein* **2 :** a concrete poet

concrete jungle *n* **:** ASPHALT JUNGLE *herein*

concrete poetry *n* **:** poetry in which the poet's intent is conveyed by the graphic patterns of letters, words, or symbols rather than by the conventional arrangement of words

concretism* *n* -S **:** the theory or practice of concrete poetry — **con·cret·ist** \-ēd·əst, -ētə-\ *n* -S

conditional* *adj* **1 :** involving or yielding values that are conditional probabilities ⟨a ~ distribution⟩ **2 :** eliciting a conditional response ⟨a ~ stimulus⟩ **3 :** permitting survival only under special growth or environmental conditions ⟨~ lethal mutations⟩

conditional probability *n* **:** the probability that a given event will occur if it is certain that another event has taken place or will take place

conditioned* *adj* **:** CONDITIONAL 2 *herein*

con·do \'kän(ˌ)dō\ *n* -S [by shortening] **:** CONDOMINIUM

condom* *n* **:** a device that is designed to be inserted into the vagina before coitus and that resembles in form and function the condom used by males

con·dri·eu \kōⁿdrēœ̄\ *n* -S *often cap* [F, fr. *Condrieu*, wine appellation and town in E France] **:** a fragrant white wine made from Viognier grapes grown in the area of Condrieu, France

conduction band *n* **:** the range of permissible energy values which an electron in a solid material can have that allows the electron to dissociate from a particular atom and become a free charge carrier in the material — compare VALENCE BAND *herein*

conference call *n* **:** a telephone call by which a caller can speak with several people at the same time

con·fer·enc·ing \'känfrən(t)siŋ, -fər-\ *n* -S [*conference* + ³*-ing*] **:** the holding of conferences esp. by means of an electronic communications system ⟨computer ~⟩ ⟨video ~⟩

confessional* *adj* **:** of, relating to, or being intimately autobiographical writing or fiction ⟨~ books⟩ ⟨~ journalism⟩

configuration* *n* **:** something (as a figure, contour, pattern, or apparatus) that results from a particular arrangement of parts or components; *esp* **:** a set of interconnected equipment forming a computer system

configure* *vt* **:** to set up for operation or use esp. in a particular way

con·fit \kōn'fē, kōn-, kän-\ *n* -S [F, fr. OF, preparation, preserves, fr. past part. of *confire* to prepare, preserve, soak, fr. L *conficere* to complete, prepare — more at COMFIT] **1 :** meat (as goose, duck, or pork) that has been cooked and preserved in its own fat **2 :** a garnish made usu. from fruit or vegetables that are cooked until tender in a seasoned liquid

conflagration* *n* **:** something like a large disastrous fire; *esp* **:** WAR

conflicted \kən'fliktəd, 'känˌfliktəd\ *adj* [fr. past part. of *conflict*] **:** experiencing or marked by ambivalence or a conflict esp. of emotions ⟨this unhappy and ~ modern woman —John Updike⟩ ⟨~ feelings⟩

con·for·ma·tion·al \ˌkän(ˌ)fō(r)'māshnəl, -ˌfə(r)-, -shənᵊl\ *adj* **:** of, relating to, or being molecular conformation ⟨~ changes in proteins⟩ — **con·for·ma·tion·al·ly** \-nəlē, -lī\ *adv*

con·fron·ta·tion·al \ˌkän(ˌ)frən'tāshənəl\ *adj* **:** relating to or characterized by confrontation

cong \'käŋ, 'kȯŋ\ *n, pl* **cong** *usu cap* [by shortening] **:** VIETCONG

conglomerate* *n* **:** a widely diversified company; *esp* **:** a corporation that acquires other companies whose activities are unrelated to the corporation's primary activity

con·glom·e·ra·teur \kənˌglām(ə)rə'tər; *-R* -'tœ̄\ *n* -S [*conglomerate* + *-eur* (as in *entrepreneur*)] **:** one who forms or heads a conglomerate

con·glom·er·a·tor \kən'glämə̦ˌrād·ə(r)\ *n* -S [*conglomerate* (herein) + ¹*-or*] **:** CONGLOMERATEUR

congresspeople \'==ˌ==\ *n pl* **:** congressmen and congresswomen

congressperson \'==ˌ==\ *n* **:** a member of a congress; *esp, often cap* **:** a member of the U.S. House of Representatives

congruence* *n* **:** a statement that two numbers, mathematical expressions (as polynomials), or geometric figures are congruent

congruent* *adj* **:** related in such a way that the difference is divisible by a given modulus ⟨12 is ~ to 2 (modulo 5) since 12 − 2 = 2·5⟩

conjugate* *adj* **:** relating to or being conjugate complex numbers ⟨complex roots occurring in ~ pairs⟩

conjugate* *n* **1 :** CONJUGATE COMPLEX NUMBER **2 :** an element of a mathematical group that is equal to a given element of the group multiplied on the right by another element and on the left by the inverse of the latter element

conjugated estrogen *n* **:** a mixture of estrogens and esp. of estrone and equilin for oral administration in the form of the sodium salts of their sulfate esters — usu. used in pl. but sing. or pl. in constr.

con·jun·to \kōn'hüntō, -'kün-\ *n* -S [Sp, collection, group, group of musicians, ensemble, fr. *conjunto* joined, joint, fr. L *conjunctus*; fr. the typical performance of such music by small ensembles as opposed to bands or orchestras — more at CONJUNCT] **:** a kind of Mexican-American music that has been influenced by the music of German immigrants to Texas and that features the accordion in addition to Mexican elements

conjugation* *n* **:** the one-way transfer of DNA between bacteria in cellular contact

conk \'käŋk, 'kȯŋk\ *vt* -ED/-ING/-S [prob. by shortening & alter. fr. *congolene*, a preparation for straightening hair, prob. fr. *congolene*, a hydrocarbon produced from Congo copal, fr. *Congolese* + *-ene*] **:** to straighten out (hair) usu. by the use of chemicals — **conk** *n* -S

connected* *adj, of a set* **:** having the property that any two of its points can be joined by a line completely contained in the set; *also* **:** incapable of being separated into two or more closed disjoint subsets — compare SIMPLY CONNECTED *herein* — **con·nect·ed·ness*** *n*

connectivity* *n* **:** the ability to connect to or communicate with another computer or computer system

connect time *n* **:** the amount of time spent by a computer user in being connected to a network (as the Internet)

consciousness–raising \'==ˌ==\ *n* **:** an increasing of concerned awareness esp. of some social or political issue

consensual* *adj* **:** involving or based on mutual consent ⟨~ acts⟩; *also* **:** based on or supported by general or unanimous agreement ⟨~ decisions⟩

con·se·quen·tial·ism \ˌkän(t)sə'kwenchəˌlizəm\ *n* -S [*consequential* + *-ism*] **:** the theory that the value and esp. the moral value of an act should be judged by the value of its consequences — **con·se·quen·tial·ist** \-ˌləst\ *n or adj*

conservation of angular momentum : a principle in physics: the total angular momentum of a system free of external torque remains constant irrespective of transformations and interactions within the system

conservation of baryons : a principle in physics: the number of baryons in an isolated system of elementary particles remains constant irrespective of transformations or decays

conservation of charge : a principle in physics: the total electric charge of an isolated system remains constant irrespective of whatever internal changes may take place

conservation of leptons : a principle in physics: the number of leptons in an isolated system of elementary particles remains constant irrespective of transformations or decays

conserve* *vt* **:** to maintain (a quantity) constant during a process of chemical, physical, or evolutionary change ⟨~ angular momentum⟩ ⟨a DNA sequence that has been *conserved*⟩

con·sig·li·e·re \kōn(ˌ)sil'yere, -rē; kän(ˌ)siglē'yerā, -rē, -'yer\ *n, pl* **con·sig·li·e·ri** \-rē\ *also* **consiglieres** [It, fr. *consiglio* advice, counsel, fr. L *consilium* — more at COUNSEL] **:** COUNSELOR, ADVISER ⟨~ of a Mafia family⟩

consistent* *adj* **:** tending to be arbitrarily close to the true value of the parameter estimated as the sample becomes large ⟨a ~ statistical estimator⟩ — **consistency*** *n*

console* *n* **1 :** a small storage cabinet between bucket seats in an automobile **2 :** the part of a computer used for communication between the operator and the computer

consolidation* *n* **:** a period of backing and filling in a security or commodity market usu. following a strong run-up of prices and typically preceding a further active advance

consolidator* *n* one who buys airline tickets at a discounted bulk rate and sells them to travelers and travel agents

constant region *also* **constant domain** *n* **:** the part of the polypeptide chain of a light or heavy chain of an antibody that ends in a free carboxyl group –COOH and that is relatively constant in its sequence of amino acid residues from one antibody to another — compare VARIABLE REGION *herein*

con·sta·tive \kən'stād·iv, 'känstəd·iv\ *adj* [F *constat*er to assert + E *-ive* — more at CONSTATE] **1** [trans. of G *konstatierend*] **:** of, relating to, or being a verbal form that expresses past completed action **2 :** making an assertion and thus capable of being judged as to truth ⟨~ utterance⟩ — **constative** *n* -S

constituent structure *n* **:** a formal representation of the grammatical structure of a sentence in terms of its individual constituents; *also* **:** the structure which such a representation describes

constitutive* *adj* **1 a :** of, relating to, or being an enzyme or protein produced in relatively constant amounts in all cells of an organism without regard to cell environmental conditions (as the concentration of a substrate) — compare INDUCIBLE 1 *herein* **b :** controlling production of or coding genetic information for a constitutive enzyme or protein ⟨~ genes⟩ ⟨~ mutations⟩ **2 :** being chromatin of a chromosomal region that is condensed into heterochromatin in all cells of an organism rather than just some — **constitutively*** *adv*

construct* *n* **1 :** something produced by human effort ⟨the East bloc was always an unnatural ~ —Walter Isaacson⟩ **2 :** an idea or organization of ideas that is artificial, subjective, or tenuous in its origin or construction

constructivism* *n* **:** a theory of learning based on the assumption that people create knowledge from the interaction between their existing knowledge or beliefs and the new ideas or situations they encounter — **constructivist*** *n or adj*

consult* *vi* **:** to serve as a consultant

con·sul·tan·cy \kən'səltənsē\ *n* -ES [*consultant* + *-cy*] **1 :** CONSULTATION **2 :** an agency that provides consulting services **3 :** the position of a consultant

consumable *n* -s [*consumable*, adj.] : something (as food or fuel) that is consumable — usu. used in pl.

consumer* *n* : an organism requiring complex organic compounds for food which it obtains by preying on other organisms or by eating particles of organic matter — compare PRODUCER *herein*

con·sum·er·ism \kən'sümə,rizəm\ *n* -s **1** : the promotion of the consumer's interests **2** : the theory that an increasing consumption of goods is economically desirable; *also* : a preoccupation with and an inclination toward the buying of consumer goods — **con·sum·er·ist** \-,rəst\ *n* -s — **con·sum·er·is·tic** \¦=¦==¦ristik\ *adj*

consummatory* *adj* : of, relating to, or being a response or act (as eating or copulating) that terminates a period of usu. goal-directed behavior

contact binary *n* : a binary star system in which the two stars are close enough together for material to pass between them

con·tact·ee \,kän,tak'tē\ *n* -s [²*contact* + ¹*-ee*] : a person who has been or is to be contacted; *specif* : one who claims to have been contacted by a being from outer space

contact inhibition *n* : cessation of cellular undulating movements upon contact with other cells with accompanying cessation of cell growth and division

contact language *n* : a language used for communication between groups having different native languages

con·tain·er·iza·tion \kən,tānərə'zāshən, -,rī'z-\ *n* -s [*containerize* (herein) + *-ation*] : a method of shipping whereby a considerable amount of material (as merchandise) is packed in large containers for more efficient handling

con·tain·er·ize \kən'tānə,rīz\ *vt* -ED/-ING/-S [*container* + *-ize*] **1** : to ship by containerization ⟨*containerized* freight⟩ **2** : to pack in containers

containerport \=¦==¦=\ *n* : a shipping port specially equipped to handle containerized cargo

containership \=¦==¦=\ *n* : a ship specially designed or equipped for carrying containerized cargo

con·tem·po \kən'tempō\ *adj* [short for ¹*contemporary*] : CONTEMPORARY, PRESENT-DAY ⟨∼ mainstream youth culture —Richard Gehr⟩

context–free \'=,=¦=\ *adj* : of, relating to, or being a grammar or language based on rules that describe a change in a string without reference to elements outside of the string; *also* : being such a rule

con·tex·tu·al·ize \kən'tekschə(wə),līz, kän-\ *vt* -ED/-ING/-S [*contextual* + *-ize*] : to place (as a word or activity) in a context — **con·tex·tu·al·iza·tion** \=¦==(=)¦lə'zāshən, -,lī'-\ *n*

continental* *adj, often cap* : of, relating to, or being a cuisine derived from the classic dishes of Europe and esp. France

continental* *n* : a person born on the mainland of the United States and living in Puerto Rico or the Virgin Islands

continental seating *n, often cap C* : theater seating with no center aisle and with room enough between rows to allow easy passage

continuing education *n* : formal courses of study for part-time students : ADULT EDUCATION

continuous creation theory *n* : STEADY STATE THEORY *herein*

continuous–tone *adj* : of or relating to artwork (as a photograph) that consists of varying shades of gray — see HALFTONE *in the Dict*

continuum* *n* : a compact set which cannot be separated into two sets neither of which contains a limit point of the other ⟨any closed interval of the real numbers is a ∼⟩

con·toid \'kän,tȯid\ *n* -s [*consonant* + *-oid*] : a speech sound of a phonetic rather than phonemic classification that includes most sounds traditionally treated as consonants and that excludes those (as English \y\, \w\, \r\, and \h\) which like vowels are characterized by the escape of air from the mouth over the center of the tongue without oral friction — compare VOCOID *in the Dict*

con·tra \'kän·trə, 'kōn-, -,trä\ *n* -s *sometimes cap* [AmerSp, short for Sp *contrarrevolucionario* counterrevolutionary] : a member of a guerrilla group opposed to the Sandinista government in Nicaragua

contraceptive pill *n* : BIRTH CONTROL PILL *herein*

contract* *n* : an arrangement whereby an assassin is paid to murder a particular person ⟨the mob put out a ∼ on the man's life —Patricia Burstein⟩

con·tra·cyclical \¦kän·trə+\ *adj* [*contra-* + *cyclical*] : being or acting in opposition to an economic cycle ⟨∼ fiscal policies⟩

con·trar·i·an \kən·'trerēən, (,)kän-\ *n* -s [*contrary* + ¹*-an*] **1** : a person who buys shares of stock when most other investors are selling and sells when they are buying **2** : a person who takes a contrary position or attitude — **contrarian** \"\ *adj* — **con·trar·i·an·ism** \-izəm\ *n* -s

con·tre·fi·let \kōⁿ·trəfēlā; ¦kōn·trəf¦lā, ¦kän-, -'fi(,)lā\ *n* [F *contre-filet*, fr. *contre-* counter- + *filet* fillet] : CLUB STEAK

control chart *n* : QUALITY CONTROL CHART

control freak *n* : one whose behavior indicates a powerful need to control people or circumstances in everyday matters

controlled* *adj* : regulated by law with regard to possession and use ⟨marijuana and cocaine are ∼ substances⟩ ⟨∼ drugs⟩

control rod *n* : a rod of a neutron-absorbing material (as boron carbide) used to regulate the rate of nuclear fission in a reactor

conus med·ul·lar·is \-,medyə'lerəs, -,mejə'-\ *n* [NL, lit., medullary cone] : a tapering lower part of the spinal cord at the level of the first lumbar segment

convection oven *n* : an oven having a fan that circulates hot air uniformly and continuously around food

convenience *adj* [*convenience*, n.] : designed for quick and easy preparation or use ⟨∼ food⟩

convenience store *n* : a small often franchised market that is open long hours

conventional* *adj* : not making use of nuclear weapons : NONNUCLEAR ⟨∼ warfare⟩

conventional wisdom *n* : the generally accepted belief, opinion, judgment, or prediction about a particular matter ⟨the *conventional wisdom* . . . is that in an election year you should forget about tough measures to control spending —*Wall Street Jour.*⟩

convergent lady beetle *also* **convergent ladybug** *or* **convergent** *n* -s [so called fr. the two converging white lines on its prothorax] : a common No. American ladybug (*Hippodamia convergens*) that has red or orange elytra with black spots and feeds on small insects and esp. aphids

convergent thinking *n* : thinking (as in answering a multiple choice question) that weighs alternatives within an existing construct or model in solving a problem or answering a question to find one best solution and that is measured by IQ tests — compare DIVERGENT THINKING — **convergent thinker** *n*

conversation* *n* : an exchange similar to conversation; *esp* : real-time interaction with a computer esp. through a keyboard

conversation pit *n* : a usu. sunken area (as in a living room) with intimate seating that facilitates conversation

converse* *vi* : to carry on an exchange similar to a conversation; *esp* : to interact with a computer

converter* *n* **1** : a device that accepts data in one form and changes it to another ⟨analog-digital ∼⟩ **2** : CATALYTIC CONVERTER *herein*

convex* *adj* **1** : being a continuous function or part of a continuous function with the property that a line joining any two points on its graph lies on or above the graph **2 a** *of a set of points* : containing all points in a line joining any two constituent points **b** *of a geometric figure* : comprising a convex set when combined with its interior ⟨a ∼ polygon⟩

convolution* *n* : a function $h(y)$ that for two given functions f and g is given by

$$h(y) = \int_a^b f(y-x)\, g(x)\, dx$$

where in various applications (as in finding the probability density function of the sum of two independent and continuous random variables) the lower limit of integration is taken as $-\infty$ or 0 and the upper limit is taken as $+\infty$ or the variable y — called also *convolution integral*

cook* *vi* [²*cook*] **1** : to play music extremely well and entertainingly; *specif* : SWING 4b **2** : to go or do well : proceed successfully ⟨the party is ∼*ing*⟩

cookbook* *n* : a book of detailed step-by-step instructions

cookbook \'=,=\ *adj* [*cookbook*, n. (herein)] : characterized by step-by-step procedures ⟨asthma tends to be what we call a ∼ admission; you always ask the same set of questions —Perri Klass⟩; *esp* : using step-by-step procedures to reach a solution without explaining how they work ⟨the ∼ approach does not help the user understand the problem —B.G.Marsden⟩

cooker* *n* : a small and often makeshift container (as a bottlecap) in which a drug (as heroin) is heated and dissolved in water

cookie* *n* : a small file or part of a file stored on the computer of a World Wide Web user, created and subsequently read by a Web site server, and containing personalized user information (as a user identification code, customized preferences, or a record of pages visited)

cookie–cutter \'==¦==\ *adj* [*cookie cutter*, n.] : marked by lack of originality or distinction ⟨*cookie-cutter* shopping malls⟩

cooking top *n* : a built-in cabinet-top cooking apparatus consisting usu. of four heating units for gas or electricity

cook–off \'=,=\ *n* -s [²*cook* + *-off* (as in *runoff*)] : an organized cooking competition

cooktop \'=,=\ *n* [²*cook* + *top*] **1** : the flat top of a range **2** : COOKING TOP *herein*

cool* *adj* : employing understatement and a minimum of detail to convey information and usu. requiring the listener, viewer, or reader to complete the message ⟨another indication of the very ∼ . . . character of this medium —H.M.McLuhan⟩

cool* *vb* — **cool it** : to calm down : go easy

cooldown \'=,=\ *n* [*cool down*, vb.] **1** : a reduction in temperature esp. to cryogenic temperatures **2** : the act or an instance of allowing body activity (as heartbeat and respiration) to return to normal gradually after strenuous exercise by engaging in less strenuous exercise — compare WARM-UP *in the Dict*

cool out* *vi* : RELAX 5

coombs' test \¦kümz-\ *n, usu cap C* [after R.R.A. *Coombs* *b*1921 Brit. immunologist] : an agglutination test used to detect proteins and esp. antibodies on the surface of red blood cells

coon·ass \'kün,as\ *n, sometimes cap* [prob. by folk etymology fr. F *conasse*, term of opprobrium, aug. of *con*, lit., vulva, fr. L *cunnus*] *chiefly in Louisiana* : ACADIAN 2a — often used disparagingly

cooper pair \'küpər-\ *n, usu cap C* [after Leon N. *Cooper* *b*1930 Am. physicist] : a pair of electrons in a superconductor that are attractively bound and have equal and opposite momentum and spin

co–opt* *vt* : to take in and make part of a group, movement, or culture : ABSORB ⟨the students are *co-opted* by a system they serve even in their struggle against it —A.C.Danto⟩; *also* : to take over : APPROPRIATE ⟨many people now view television as a kind of virus, *co-opting* the healthy brain cells of our young —Robert Pattison⟩

co–optation* *n* : the act or action or an instance of co-opting

coordinate* *adj* : of, relating to, or being a system of indexing by two or more terms so that documents may be retrieved through the intersection of index terms

coordinate* *n* **coordinates** *pl* : articles (as of clothing or furniture) designed to be used together and to attain their effect through pleasing contrast (as of color, material, or texture)

coordinated universal time *n, usu cap C&U&T* : the international standard of time that is kept by atomic clocks around the world — abbr. *UTC*

cop* *vt* : PURCHASE ⟨∼ dope⟩ ∼ *vi* **1** *slang* : ADMIT 2b — used with *to* ⟨∼ to the charges⟩ **2** *slang* : to purchase or obtain drugs : SCORE — **cop a feel** *slang* : to touch or fondle another person's body briefly and often surreptitiously

co–parent \¦kō+\ *n* [*co-* + ¹*parent*] : a person (as a noncustodial parent or cohabiting partner) who shares parental duties with a custodial parent

co–pay \¦kō+\ *n* [by shortening] : CO-PAYMENT *herein*

co–payment \¦kō+\ *n* [*co-* + *payment*] : a fixed fee required by a health insurer (as an HMO) to be paid by the patient at the time of each office visit, outpatient service, or filling of a prescription

COPD *abbr* chronic obstructive pulmonary disease *herein*

cop out* *vi* : to back out (as of an unwanted responsibility) : EVADE — often used with *on* or *of* ⟨young Americans who *cop out* on society —*Christian Science Monitor*⟩ ⟨*copping out* of jury duty through a variety of machinations —H.F.Waters⟩

cop–out \'=,=\ *n* -s [*cop out*, v. (herein)] **1** : an excuse for copping out : PRETEXT **2** : the means for copping out **3** : one who cops out **4** : the act or an instance of copping out

copperware \'==,=\ *n* [²*copper* + *ware*] : articles made of copper

cop·ro·antibody \¦käprō+\ *n* [*copr-* + *antibody*] : an antibody whose presence in the intestinal tract can be demonstrated by examination of an extract of the feces

co·processor \¦kō+\ *n* [*co-* + *processor*] : an extra processor in a computer that is designed to perform specialized tasks (as input/output functions or mathematical calculations)

co·produce \¦kō+\ *vt* [back-formation fr. *coproducer* (herein)] : to produce (as a play or movie) in cooperation with another

co·producer \¦kō+\ *n* [*co-* + *producer*] : one who coproduces

copy* *n* — **a copy** *also* **per copy** : APIECE ⟨tickets selling for $15 *a copy*⟩

copycat* *n* : an imitative act or product — often used attributively ⟨∼ board games⟩

coq au vin \,kōkō'vaⁿ, ,käk-, ,kȯk-, -kō'v-, *F* kȯkōvaⁿ\ *n* [F, lit., cock with wine] : chicken cooked in usu. red wine

coquille saint jacques \-saⁿzhäk\ *n, pl* **coquilles saint jacques** *usu cap S&J* [F *coquille Saint-Jacques* scallop, fr. *coquille* mollusk shell + *Saint-Jacques* St. James the apostle, whose identifying token is a scallop shell] : a dish of scallops usu. served with a wine sauce

cor·al·ene \'kȯrə,lēn, 'kär-\ *n* -s [irreg. fr. ¹*coral*] **1** : a raised decoration of glass beading on glassware **2** : glassware with coralene decoration

cord blood *n* : blood from the umbilical cord of a fetus or newborn

cord·less \'kȯ(ə)rdləs, -ō(ə)d-\ *adj* : having no cord; *esp* : powered by a battery ⟨∼ tools⟩ ⟨∼ phone⟩

cordon bleu* *adj, often cap C&B* **1 a** : of, relating to, or being a cook of great skill **b** : of, relating to, or being the food prepared by such a cook **2** : stuffed with ham and Swiss cheese ⟨veal *cordon bleu*⟩

cor·dy·cep·in \,kȯ(r)də'sepən\ *n* -s [*cordyceps* + *-in*] : an adenosine analogue $C_{10}H_{13}N_5O_3$ with antibiotic activity used esp. to study gene regulation because of its ability to inhibit transcription

core* *n* **1** : a tiny doughnut-shaped piece of magnetic material (as ferrite) used in computer memories — called also *magnetic core* **2** *or* **core memory** *or* **core storage** : a computer memory consisting of an array of cores strung on fine wires; *broadly* : the internal memory of a computer

co·repressor \,kō+\ *n* [*co-* + *repressor* (herein)] : a small molecule that activates a particular genetic repressor by combining with it

core temperature *n* : the temperature deep within a living body (as in the viscera)

coriolis effect *n, usu cap C* : the apparent deflection of a moving object that is the result of the Coriolis force

corn chip *n* : a piece of a crisp dry snack food prepared from a seasoned cornmeal batter

corn dog *n* : a frankfurter dipped in cornmeal batter, fried, and served on a stick

cor·neo·scleral \¦kȯ(r)nē(,)ō+\ *adj* [*corne-* + *scleral*] : of, relating to, or affecting both the cornea and the sclera ⟨posterior to the ∼ junction⟩

corner* *adj* : of, relating to, or being a defensive football player who covers one of the flanks ⟨∼ linebacker⟩ ⟨∼ positions⟩

cornerback \'==,=\ *n* [*corner* (herein) + ¹*back*] : a defensive back in football whose duties include defending one side of the formation and covering a wide receiver

cornerman \'==,man\ *n, pl* **cornermen** **1** : CORNERBACK *herein* **2** : a basketball forward **3** : a boxer's second

corn–fed* *adj* : RUSTIC, COUNTRIFIED

cornhole \'=,=\ *vt* [¹*corn* + *hole*] : to perform anal intercourse with : BUGGER — usu. considered vulgar

cor·ni·chon \kȯrnēshōⁿ\ *n* -s [F, gherkin, lit., little horn, dim. of *corne* horn — more at CORNET] : a sour gherkin usu. flavored with tarragon

cornish rex *n, usu cap C & often cap R* : any of a breed of cats with a very short soft wavy coat free of guard hairs, a small head with large ears, and a face that is straight in profile

cornpone \'=,=\ *adj* [*corn pone*, n.; fr. the belief that it is a food typical of the rural South] : DOWN-HOME, *herein*, COUNTRIFIED ⟨∼ humor⟩

cornrow \'=,=\ *vt* [¹*corn* + *row*; fr. the fancied resemblance of the braids to rows of corn] : to style (hair) into a series of tightly braided parallel rows that lie flat to the scalp — **cornrow** *n*

co·ro·na·virus \kə¦rōnə+\ *n* [NL, fr. *corona* + *virus*; fr. their shape as seen under an electron microscope] : any of a family (Coronaviridae) of single-stranded RNA viruses that have a lipid envelope with club-shaped projections and include some causing respiratory symptoms in man

co·rotate \(')kō+\ *vi* [*co-* + *rotate*] : to rotate in conjunction with or at the same rate as another rotating body — **co·rotation** \,kō+\ *n*

cor·po·rat·ize \'kȯrp(ə)rə,tīz\ *vt* -ED/-ING/-S : to subject to corporate ownership or control ⟨argued that health care had been *corporatized*⟩ — **cor·po·rat·i·za·tion** \,=(=)=d·ə'zāshən, -ti'zā-\ *n* -s

cor·pus al·la·tum \,kȯrpəsə'lād·əm, -äd-·\ *n, pl* **cor·po·ra al·la·ta** \,kȯrpərə·ə'lād·ə, -äd-·\ [NL, lit., applied body] : one of a pair of separate or fused bodies in many insects that are sometimes closely associated with the corpora cardiaca and secrete hormones (as juvenile hormone)

corpus car·di·a·cum \-pəskär'dīəkəm\ *n, pl* **cor·po·ra car·di·a·ca** \-pərəkär'dīəkə\ [NL, lit., cardiac body] : one of a pair of separate or fused bodies of nervous tissue in many insects that lie posterior to the brain and dorsal to the esophagus and function in the storage and secretion of brain hormone

corpus spon·gi·o·sum \-,spənjē'ōsəm, -,spän-\ *n* [NL, lit., spongy body] : the median longitudinal column of erectile tissue of the penis that contains the urethra and is ventral to the two corpora cavernosa

correction fluid *n* : a liquid used to paint over typing or writing errors

corresponding angles *n pl* : any pair of angles each of which is on the same side of one of two lines cut by a transversal and on the same side of the transversal

corticotropin–releasing factor *or* **corticotropin–releasing hormone** *also* **corticotrophin–releasing factor** *n* : a substance secreted by the median eminence of the hypothalamus that regulates the release of ACTH by the anterior lobe of the pituitary gland

co–script \'kō+¦\ *vt* [*co-* + *script*] : to collaborate in the preparation of a script for

cosecant* *n* : a trigonometric function csc θ that is the reciprocal of the sine for all real numbers θ for which the sine is not zero and that is exactly equal to the cosecant of an angle of measure θ in radians

co·set \'kō,set\ *n* [*co-* + *set*] : any of the subsets of a mathematical group of which each consists of all the products obtained by multiplying one of the elements of the group on the right side by each of the elements of a subgroup or of the products obtained by such multiplication on the left and which partition the group into subsets of which any two are either identical or disjoint

co·sign \'kō,sīn\ *vb* [*co-* + *sign*] *vi* : to sign a promissory note along with the borrower to guarantee payment should the borrower default ∼ *vt* : to sign (as a note) along with the borrower — **co-sign·er** \"ə(r)\ *n*

cosine* *n* : a trigonometric function cos θ that for all real numbers θ is given by the sum of the alternating series

$$\cos\theta = 1 - \frac{\theta^2}{2!} + \frac{\theta^4}{4!} - \frac{\theta^6}{6!} + \frac{\theta^8}{8!} - \cdots$$

and that is exactly equal to the cosine of an angle of measure θ in radians

cos·me·ceu·ti·cal \,käzmə'süd·əkəl, -süt-\ *n* -s [¹*cosmetic* + ²*pharmaceutical*] : a preparation having both cosmetic and pharmaceutical properties

cosmetic* *n* **cosmetics** *pl* : superficially attractive or impressive features ⟨a poem without rhetorical ∼*s* —Guy Davenport⟩

cosmetic* *adj* **1** : relating to or involving only outward appearance ⟨∼ defects⟩ **2** : lacking depth or substance : SUPERFICIAL ⟨working to make real improvements, not ∼ changes —Andy Rooney⟩

cos·met·i·cize \käz'med·ə,sīz\ *vt* -ED/-ING/-S [²*cosmetic* + *-ize*] : to make (something unpleasant or ugly) superficially attractive

cosmic background radiation *n* : BACKGROUND RADIATION *herein*

cosmic microwave background *n* : BACKGROUND RADIATION *herein*

cosmic string *n* : any of a class of hypothetical supermassive astronomical objects that are extremely thin but are millions of light years long, that are postulated to have formed very early in the history of the universe and to be the cause of the lack of uniformity in mass distribution of the universe, and that have been proposed to act in certain instances as gravitational lenses

cos·mo·drome \'käzmə,drōm\ *n* -S [Russ *kosmodrom*, fr. *kosmonavt* cosmonaut + *-drom* ¹-drome] : a Soviet aerospace center; *esp* : a Soviet spacecraft launching installation

cos·mo·gen·ic \¦käzmə¦jenik\ *adj* [*cosmic* (*ray*) + *-o-* + *-genic*] : produced by the action of cosmic rays ⟨∼ carbon 14⟩

cosmological constant *n* : a constant term used in the relativistic equations for gravity to represent a repulsive force which may account in part for the rate of expansion of the universe

cosmological principle *n* : a principle in astronomy: the distribution of matter in the universe is homogeneous and isotropic except for local irregularities

cos·mo·nau·tics \,käzmə'nȯd·iks, -näd-\ *n pl but usu sing in constr* [*cosmonaut* + *-ics*] : ASTRONAUTICS — **cos·mo·nau·tic** \-d·ik\ *or* **cos·mo·nau·ti·cal** \-d·əkəl\ *adj*

cossack hat *n, often cap C* : an oblong visorless folding cap usu. made of fur or imitation fur

cost–benefit \¦='===\ *adj* : of, relating to, being, or resembling economic analysis that assigns a numerical value to the cost-effectiveness of an operation, procedure, or program

cost–effective \¦=¦==\ *adj* : economical in terms of tangible benefits produced by money spent — **cost–effectiveness** *n*

cost–efficient \¦=¦==\ *adj* : COST-EFFECTIVE *herein*

cost out *vt* **costed out; costed out; costing out; costs out** : to calculate in advance the total cost of (as a project or proposal)

cost–push \¦='=\ *n* : an increase or upward trend in production costs (as wages) that tends to result in increased consumer prices irrespective of the level of demand — compare DEMAND-PULL *herein* — **cost–push** *adj*

cot* *n, Brit* : CRIB 2b

cotangent* *n* : a trigonometric function cot θ that is equal to the cosine divided by the sine for all real numbers θ for which the sine is not equal to zero and is exactly equal to the cotangent of an angle of measure θ in radians

cot death *n, chiefly Brit* : SUDDEN INFANT DEATH SYNDROME *herein*

co·te·chi·no \ˌkōd·āˈkē(ˌ)nō\ *n* -s [It, dim. of *cótica* pigskin, fr. LL *cutica* rind (of a fruit), fr. L *cutis* skin — more at HIDE] : a smoked and dried pork sausage

co·terminal \(ˈ)kō+\ *adj* [*co-* + ¹*terminal*] : having different angular measure but with the vertex and sides identical — used of angles generated by the rotation of lines about the same point in a given line whose values differ by an integral multiple of 2π radians or of 360° ⟨~ angles measuring 30° and 390°⟩

côte rô·tie \ˌkōt·rōˈtē\ *n, pl* **côte rôties** *often cap C&R* [F, fr. *Côte Rôtie*, wine appellation and hilly region on the west bank of the Rhône River in E France] : a red wine produced in the Rhône region

côtes du rhône \ˈkōtdəˈrōn, -dɪ̄-\ *n, pl* **côtes du rhône** *often cap C&R* [F. *Côtes de Rhône*, a wine appellation, lit., hillsides of the Rhône (River)] : a common red wine produced in the Rhône region

co·tin·ine \ˈkōd·ᵊnˌēn, -ˌīn\ *n* -s [prob. anagram of *nicotine*] : an alkaloid $C_{10}H_{12}N_2O$ that is the principal metabolite of nicotine and is widely used as an indicator of recent exposure to nicotine

co·transduction \ˌkō+\ *n* [*co-* + *transduction*] : transduction involving two or more genetic loci carried by a single bacteriophage

cottage industry* *n* **1** : a small and often informally organized industry **2** : a limited but enthusiastically pursued activity or subject ⟨this debate about sex and law became a *cottage industry* for feminist academics —Wendy Kaminer⟩

cotton candy* *n* : something attractive but insubstantial

cou·chette \küˈshet\ *n* -s [F, berth, bunk, dim. of *couche* bed, fr. MF — more at COUCH] **1** : a compartment on a European passenger train so arranged that berths can be provided at night **2** : one of the berths in a couchette

couch potato *n* : a lazy and inactive person; *esp* : one who spends a great deal of time watching television

cou·li·biac \ˌkülēˈbyäk, -ák\ *n* -s [F, fr. Russ *kulebyaka*] : fish rolled in pastry dough and baked ⟨~ of salmon⟩

cou·lis \küˈlē\ *n* -ES [F, fr. OF *couleis*, fr. *couleis*, adj., flowing, fr. *couler* to flow, run — more at COULEE] : a thick sauce made with pureed vegetable or fruit and often used as a garnish ⟨tomato ~⟩ ⟨raspberry ~⟩

cou·lom·bic \(ˈ)küˈlām(b)ik, kəˈl-, -lōm-\ *adj* [ISV *coulomb* + *-ic*] : of or relating to electrostatic coulomb forces

cou·ma·phos \ˈküməˌfäs, -fōs\ *n* -ES [*coumar*in + *phos*phorus] : an organophosphorus systemic insecticide and anthelmintic $C_{14}H_{16}ClO_5PS$ used esp. on cattle and poultry

count·abil·i·ty \ˌkaùn(t)əˈbiləd·ē\ *n* : the quality or state of being countable

count·ably \ˈkaùn(t)əblē\ *adv* : in a way that is countable ⟨a ~ infinite subset⟩

counter* *n* : a football play in which the ballcarrier goes in a direction opposite to the flow of play

counteradvertising \ˈ==ˌ==ˌ==\ *n* [*counter-* + *advertising*] : COUNTERCOMMERCIALS *herein*

countercommercial \ˈ===ˌ==\ *n* [*counter-* + *commercial*] : a commercial that rebuts the claims of another commercial

coun·ter·con·di·tion·ing \ˌ===ˈ=(=)=\ *n* [*counter-* + *conditioning*, gerund of *condition*] : conditioning in order to replace an undesirable response (as fear) to a stimulus (as an engagement in public speaking) by a favorable one

coun·ter·culture \ˈ==ˌ==\ *n* [*counter-* + *culture*] : a culture with values and mores that run counter to those of established society — **coun·ter·cul·tur·al** \ˌ==+\ *adj* — **coun·ter·cul·tur·ist** \ˈ"+\ *n*

coun·ter·electrophoresis \ˌ==+\ *n* [*counter-* + *electrophoresis*] : an electrophoretic method of testing blood esp. for antigens associated with hepatitis

coun·ter·example \ˈ"+\ *n* [*counter-* + *example*] : an example that disproves a theorem or proposition; *broadly* : an example that is inconsistent with or contrary to what is typical or usual

coun·ter·force \ˈ==ˌ=\ *adj* [*counter-* + ¹*force*] : of, relating to, or being an attack directed against enemy military targets rather than civilian targets ⟨~ weapons⟩ ⟨a ~ strategy⟩

coun·ter·institution \ˈ"+\ *n* [*counter-* + *institution*] : an unincorporated group within a college or university that opposes the educational policies of the administration; *broadly* : a group that opposes the traditional ideology or views of an authoritative body

coun·ter·insurgency \ˈ"+\ *n, often attrib* [*counter-* + *insurgency*] : organized activity designed to combat insurgency — **coun·ter·insurgent** \ˈ"+\ *n*

coun·ter·intuitive \ˈ"+\ *adj* [*counter-* + *intuitive*] : contrary to what one would intuitively expect — **coun·ter·intuitive·ly** \-lē\ *adv*

countermeasure* *n* : a military system or device intended to thwart a sensing mechanism (as radar) ⟨electronic ~s⟩

coun·ter·party \ˈ"+\ *n* [*counter* + ¹*party*] : a party to a financial transaction; *esp* : one involved in a derivative contract

coun·ter·phobic \ˈ"+\ *adj* [*counter-* + *phobic*] : relating to or characterized by a preference for or the seeking out of a situation that is feared ⟨~ reaction patterns⟩

coun·ter·productive \ˈ"+\ *adj* [*counter-* + *productive*] : tending to hinder the attainment of a desired goal ⟨violence as a means to achieve an end is ~ —W.E.Brock *b*1930⟩

coun·ter·program \ˈ"+\ *vb* [*counter-* + ²*program*] *vi* : to engage in counterprogramming ~ *vt* : to schedule a television program for broadcast at the same time as (another program)

coun·ter·programming \ˈ==+\ *n* [*counter-* + *programming*] : the scheduling of programs by television networks so as to attract audiences away from simultaneously telecast programs of competitors

coun·ter·pulsation \ˌ==+\ *n* [*counter-* + *pulsation*] : a technique for reducing the work load on the heart by the automatic lowering of systemic blood pressure just before or during expulsion of blood from the ventricle and by the automatic raising of blood pressure during diastole — see INTRA-AORTIC BALLOON COUNTERPULSATION *herein*

coun·ter·shock \ˈ"+\ *n* [*counter-* + ³*shock*] : therapeutic electric shock applied to the heart for the purpose of altering a disturbed rhythm (as in chronic atrial fibrillation)

coun·ter·terrorism \ˈ"+\ *n* [*counter-* + *terrorism*] : the measures taken to combat terrorism — **coun·ter·terrorist** \ˈ"+\ *adj*

coun·ter·trade \ˈ==+ˌ\ *n* [*counter-* + ¹*trade*] : a form of international trade in which goods are exchanged for goods or services instead of for money

coun·ter·trend \ˈ"+\ *n* [*counter-* + ²*trend*] : a trend that is in response or in opposition to another trend

counting number *n* : NATURAL NUMBER

country* *n* : COUNTRY MUSIC

country* *adj* **1** : of, relating to, suitable for, or featuring country music ⟨a ~ singer⟩ ⟨~ fiddling⟩ ⟨~ radio stations⟩ **2** : of or relating to a decorative style associated with life in the country; *also* : possessing a style of rustic simplicity

country and western *also* **country–western** \ˈ==ˈ==\ *n, sometimes cap C&W* : COUNTRY MUSIC — **country and western** *also* **country–western** \ˈ==ˈ==\ *adj, sometimes cap C&W*

country rock *n* : ROCKABILLY *herein*

cou·pon·ing \ˈk(y)üˌpäniŋ\ *n* -s : the distribution or redemption of coupons

cour·gette \kü(ə)rˈzhet, küəˈzhet\ *n* -s [F, dim. of *courge* gourd — more at COURGE] *chiefly Brit* : ZUCCHINI

course·ware \ˈ=ˌ=\ *n* [¹*course* + *-ware* (as in *software* — herein)] : educational software

courtesy light *n* : an interior automobile light that goes on automatically when a door is opened

couth \ˈküth\ *n* -s [²*couth*] : POLISH, REFINEMENT ⟨I expected kindness and gentility and I found it, but there is such a thing as too much ~ —S.J.Perelman⟩

cou·ver·ture \küverˈtu̇r\ *or* **couverture chocolate** *n* -s [F (*chocolat*) *couverture*, lit., chocolate for covering] : chocolate containing considerable cocoa butter used esp. for coating (as candy)

co·variate \ˌkō+\ *n* [*co-* + ²*variate*] : any of two or more random variables exhibiting correlated variation

covary \ˈ"+\ *vi* [back-formation fr. *covariation*] : to exhibit covariation

cover* *vt* : to record or perform a cover of (a song)

cover* *or* **cover version** *n* : a recording or performance of a song orig. done by another performer or aimed at a defferent market

cover–up* *n* **1** : a usu. concerted effort to keep an illegal or unethical act or situation from being made public **2** : a loose outer garment

cow·boy·ing \ˈkaùˌbȯi(-i)ŋ\ *n* -s : the work or occupation of a cowboy

cow pie *n* : a dropping of cow dung

cowshed \ˈ=ˌ=\ *n* : a shed for the housing of cows

coyote* *n, slang* : a person who is paid to smuggle immigrants into the United States illegally

CP \ˈsēˈpē\ *n* -s [charge conjugation (herein) + parity (herein)] : the combination of the theoretical operations of charge conjugation and inversion of parity for all particles involved in a nuclear or electromagnetic interaction that is used as a test of the symmetry of the interaction under the laws of quantum mechanics

CPI *abbr* **1** *usu not cap* characters per inch **2** consumer price index

CPR *abbr* cardiopulmonary resuscitation

CPS* *abbr* **1** certified professional secretary **2** *usu not cap* characters per second

CPU \ˌsē(ˌ)pēˈyü\ *n* -s *often not cap* : the hardware component of a computer system that performs the basic operations of the system including processing of data, exchange of data with memory or peripherals, and management of the system's other components — called also *processor*

crack* *n, often attrib* : a purified potent form of cocaine that is obtained by treating cocaine hydrochloride with sodium bicarbonate to create small chips used illicitly usu. for smoking ⟨~ cocaine⟩

crack baby *n* : an infant born physiologically addicted to crack as a result of continued exposure to the drug in the mother's womb

crackback \ˈ=ˌ=\ *n* [¹*crack* + ¹*back*] : a blind-side block on a defensive player in football by a pass receiver who starts downfield and then cuts back toward the middle of the line

cracker* *n* : HACKER 2 *herein*

crackhead \ˈ=ˌ=\ *n* [*crack* (herein) + *-head* (as in *hophead*)] : one who smokes crack

crack up *vi* : to laugh out loud ~ *vt* : to cause to laugh out loud

craftsman·ly \+lē\ *adj* : of, relating to, or in a manner befitting a craftsman ⟨~ work⟩ ⟨~ writing⟩

craftspeople \ˈ=ˌ==\ *n pl* : workers who practice a trade or a craft

craftsperson \ˈ=ˌ==\ *n* : a craftsman or craftswoman

crambe* *n* : an annual Mediterranean herb of the genus *Crambe* (*C. abyssinica*) cultivated as an oilseed crop

cranberry glass *n* : clear ruby glass usu. with a blue-violet tint

cra·nio·pha·ryn·gi·oma \ˌkrānē(ˌ)ōˌfarənjēˈōmə, -ˌfəˌrin-\ *n, pl* **craniopharyngiomas** *or* **craniopharyngioma·ta** \-məd·ə, -ətə\ [NL, fr. *crani-* + *pharyng-* + *-i-* + *-oma*] : a tumor of the brain near the pituitary gland that develops esp. in children or young adults and is often associated with increased intracranial pressure

crank* *n* : CRYSTAL *herein*

crank* *vt* **1** : to start as if by use of a crank — usu. used with *up* ⟨she *cranked* up the air-conditioner⟩ **2** : to turn up (sense 3) — usu. used with *up* ⟨*crank* up the stereo⟩ ~ *vi* : to gain speed, momentum, or intensity — usu. used with *up* ⟨the campaign is *cranking up*⟩

crankshaft* *n* : a shaft consisting of a series of cranks and crankpins to which the connecting rods of an engine are attached

cranshaw melon *var of* CRENSHAW MELON

crap *adj* [¹*crap*] *slang* : CRAPPY, LOUSY ⟨a ~ movie⟩ ⟨in ~ shape after the game⟩

crap·o·la \ˌkrapˈōlə\ *n* -s [¹*crap* + *-ola*, suffix found in jocular variants of words, prob. fr. It *-ola*, dim. suffix] *slang* : CRAP 4

crapshoot \ˈ=ˌ=\ *n* [⁵*crap* + ²*shoot*] : something (as a business venture) that has an unpredictable outcome

crash* *vi* **1** *slang* : to experience the aftereffects (as dysphoria or depression) of drug intoxication **2** *slang* : SLEEP ⟨sometimes we can't pay the rent and we ~ around town, sleep in yards or at friends' houses —*East Village Other*⟩; *also* : to reside temporarily : STAY ⟨~*ing* with friends for a few days⟩ **3** *of a computer system, component, or program* : to suffer a sudden major failure usu. with attendant loss of data ~ *vt* : to cause (a computer system, component, or program) to crash — **crash*** *n*

crash cart *n* : a cart stocked with emergency medical equipment, supplies, and drugs for use by medical personnel esp. during efforts to resuscitate a patient experiencing cardiac arrest

crash pad* *n* : a place where free temporary lodging is available

crashworthy \ˈ=ˌ==\ *adj* [²*crash* + *-worthy* (as in *seaworthy*)] : resistant to the effects of a collision ⟨~ cars⟩ — **crashworthiness** *n*

crass* *adj* : guided by or indicative of base or materialistic values ⟨~ commercialism⟩ ⟨~ measures of success⟩

cra·ter·iza·tion \ˌkrād·ərəˈzāshən, -ātə-, -rˌīˈz-\ *n* -s [*crater* + *-ization*] : surgical excision of a crater-shaped piece of bone

crawl* *n* : lettering that moves vertically or horizontally across a television or movie screen to give information (as credits or news bulletins)

crawlerway \ˈ==ˌ=\ *n* [*crawler* + *way*; fr. its slow-moving traffic] : a road built esp. for moving heavy rockets and spacecraft

crawlway \ˈ=ˌ=\ *n* : a low passageway (as in a cave) that can be traversed only by crawling

crazy* *adj* — **like crazy** : to an extreme degree ⟨everyone dancing *like crazy*⟩

cra·zy \ˈkrāzē, -zi\ *n* -ES [*crazy*, adj.] : one who is or acts crazy; *esp* : such a one associated with a radical or extremist political cause

c–re·ac·tive protein \ˌ=(ˌ)=ˌ==\ *n, usu cap C* [*C-polysaccharide*, a polysaccharide found in the cell wall of pneumococci and precipitated by this protein, fr. *carbohydrate*] : a protein present in blood serum in various abnormal states (as inflammation or neoplasia)

cream* *vi* **1** : to experience orgasm — usu. considered vulgar **2** : to become rapturously excited — usu. considered vulgar

creamer* *n* : a nondairy product used as a substitute for cream (as in coffee)

cream puff* *n* : a usu. used vehicle (as an automobile) that is in especially good condition

creatine kinase *n* : any of three isoenzymes found esp. in vertebrate skeletal and myocardial muscle and the brain that catalyze the transfer of a high-energy phosphate group from phosphocreatine to ADP with the formation of ATP and creatine and typically occur in elevated levels in the blood following injury to brain or muscle tissue

creatine phos·pho·kinase \-ˌfäsfō+\ *n* [*phosph-* + *kinase*] : CREATINE KINASE *herein*

creation science *n* : CREATIONISM; *also* : scientific evidence or arguments offered in support of creationism

creative* *adj* : managed so as to get around legal or conventional limits ⟨~ financing⟩; *also* : deceptively arranged so as to conceal or defraud ⟨~ accounting⟩

creative *n* -s [*creative*, adj.] **1** : one that is creative; *esp* : one involved in the creation of advertisements **2** : creative activity or the material produced by it esp. in advertising

cred \ˈkred\ *n* -s [by shortening] : CREDIBILITY; *specif* : the ability to gain acceptance as a member of a particular group or class ⟨granted me tremendous street ~ for having had such authentic working-class jobs —*Harper's*⟩

credential* *n* : QUALIFICATION 3a

cre·den·tial \krəˈdenchəl, krē-\ *vt* **credentialed** *also* **credentialled**; **credentialed** *also* **credentialled**; **credentialing** *also* **credentialling** \-ch(ə)liŋ\; **cre·den·tials** [*credential*, n.] : to furnish with credentials

cre·den·tial·ism \krəˈdenchəˌlizəm, krēˈ-\ *n* -s : undue emphasis on credentials (as college degrees) as prerequisites to employment

credibility gap *n* **1 a** : lack of trust ⟨a special *credibility gap* is likely to open between the generations —Kenneth Keniston⟩ **b** : lack of believability ⟨a *credibility gap* created by contradictory official statements —Samuel Ellenport⟩ **2** : DISCREPANCY ⟨the *credibility gap* between the professed ideals . . . and their actual practices —Jeanne L. Noble⟩

creditworthy \ˈ==ˌ==\ *adj* [¹*credit* + *worthy*] : being financially sound enough to justify the extension of credit : having an acceptable credit rating — **creditworthiness** *n*

creeping* *adj* : developing or advancing slowly over a period of time ⟨~ urbanization⟩ ⟨~ senility⟩

creepy* *adj* : of, relating to, or being a creep : annoyingly unpleasant

creepy–crawly \ˌ==ˈ==\ *n* -ES : a small crawling creature (as an insect, spider, or worm) — usu. used in pl.

cre·mains \krəˈmānz, krēˈ-\ *n pl* [blend of *cremated* and *remains*] : the ashes of a cremated human body

crème anglaise \ˌkremäⁿˈglāz, ˌkrēm-, ˌkrām-, -aŋˈ-, -äⁿ-\ *n* [F, lit., English cream] : a vanilla-flavored custard sauce usu. served with desserts

crème brûlée *also* **crème brulée** \ˌ=brüˈlā, -brü-\ *n* [F, lit., scorched cream] : a rich custard topped with caramelized sugar

crème caramel \ˌ=-kärəˈmel, -kar-, -ker-; ˌ=ˈ===\ *n* [F, lit., caramel cream] : a custard that has been baked with caramel sauce

crème fraîche *or* **crème fraiche** \-ˈfresh\ *n* [F, lit., fresh cream] : heavy cream thickened and slightly soured with buttermilk and often served on fruit

cre·mi·ni \kriˈmēnē\ *or* **cremini mushroom** *n* -s [It, pl. of *cremino*, fr. *crema* cream, fr. MF *cresme*; prob. fr. their color — more at CREAM] : a meaty cultivated brown or tan mushroom belonging to the same variety of button mushroom as the larger more mature portobello — called also *crimini*

cren·shaw melon \ˈkrenˌshō-\ *also* **crenshaw** *or* **cran·shaw melon** \ˈkran-\ *n, often cap C* [prob. fr. the name *Crenshaw* or *Cranshaw*] : a winter melon having a smooth green and gold rind and sweet salmon-colored flesh

creosote* *n* : a dark brown or black flammable tar deposited from esp. wood smoke on the walls of a chimney

Crescent *trademark* — used for an adjustable open-end wrench

cresyl violet *n* : an oxazine dye used as a biological stain esp. in histology

creutz·feldt–ja·kob disease *also* **creutz·feld–ja·kob disease** \ˌkrȯitsˌfeltˈyä(ˌ)kōb-, -(ˌ)kȯp-\ *n, usu cap C&J* [after Hans G. *Creutzfeldt* †1964 Ger. psychiatrist and Alfons M. *Jakob* †1931 Ger. psychiatrist] : a rare progressive fatal encephalopathy now usu. considered to be caused by a prion and marked by the development of porous brain tissue, premature dementia in middle age, and gradual loss of muscular coordination — abbr. *CJD*

crew sock *n* [so called fr. its use by rowing crews] : a short bulky usu. ribbed sock

crib death *n* : SUDDEN INFANT DEATH SYNDROME *herein*

¹cri·co·thyroid \ˌkrīkō+\ *adj* [*crico-* + *thyroid*] : relating to or connecting the cricoid cartilage and the thyroid cartilage of the larynx ⟨a ~ muscle⟩

²cricothyroid \ˈ"\ *n* : a cricothyroid muscle that is the principal tensor of the vocal cords

cri du chat syndrome \ˌkrēdüˈshä-, -dəˈ-\ *n* [*cri du chat* fr. F, cry of the cat] : an inherited condition that is characterized by a mewing cry, mental retardation, physical anomalies, and the absence of part of a chromosome

cri·mi·ni \kriˈmēnē\ *or* **crimini mushroom** *n* -s [modif. of It *cremini*] : CREMINI

crisis center *n* : a facility run usu. by nonprofessionals who counsel those who telephone for help in a personal crisis

crisp* *n* : a baked dessert of fruit with a crumb topping ⟨apple ~⟩

crisp·bread \ˈ=ˌ=\ *n* : a plain dry unsweetened cracker made from crushed grain (as wheat or rye)

crista* *n* : any of the inwardly projecting folds of the inner membrane of a mitochondrion

cri·te·ri·um \krīˈtirēəm, kriˈ-\ *n* -s [F *critérium* heat of a race, match, criterion, fr. LL *criterium* criterion, judgment] : a bicycle race of a specified number of laps on a closed course laid out over public roads closed to normal traffic

critical mass *n* [*critical* (capable of sustaining a chain reaction) + ²*mass*] : a size, number, or amount large enough to produce a desired or expected result ⟨wants to achieve the *critical mass* of a major company —*Business Week*⟩ ⟨women may have to reach a point of *critical mass* in any institution to raise that different voice —Betty Friedan⟩

critical path *n* : a path (as in PERT) that connects the tasks in a process which are required to be completed for subsequent work to start or which take the greatest amount of time for completion and that provides an estimate of the duration of the entire process

critical region *n* : the set of outcomes of a statistical test for which the null hypothesis is to be rejected

CRNA *abbr* certified registered nurse anesthetist

crock* *n* [fr. the phrase *crock of shit*] : BUNKUM, BALONEY, BULL — usu. used with *a* ⟨those awards are a ~, a PR stunt —Irma Lipkin⟩

Crockpot \ˈ=ˌ=\ *trademark* — used for an electric cooking pot

crom·o·lyn sodium \ˈkrōməlin-\ *also* **cromolyn** *n* -s [*chrom-* + *glyc-* + *-in*] : a drug $C_{23}H_{14}Na_2O_{11}$ that inhibits the release of histamine from mast cells and is usu. used as an inhalant to prevent bronchial asthma attacks

crop circle *n* : a geometric and esp. circular pattern in a field of grain giving the appearance of having been made by systematically flattening the stalks and now usu. attributed to natural phenomena or to the work of hoaxers or pranksters trying to create the impression of a visit by extraterrestrial beings

crop duster *n* : an airplane used for spraying crops with insecticidal or fungicidal dusts

crop top *n* [*crop* prob. alter. of *cropped*, past part. of ²*crop*] : a short blouse that usu. leaves the midriff bare

cro·quem·bouche \krōkäⁿbüsh\ *n* -s [F, fr. *croque-en-bouche*, lit., crunches in the mouth] : a cone-shaped stack of cream puffs coated with caramelized sugar

cross·court \ˈ=ˌ=\ *adv (or adj)* [⁴*cross* + *court*] : to or toward the opposite side of a court (as in tennis or basketball)

cross–disciplinary \ˌ=ˈ====\ *adj* [³*cross*] : of, relating to, or involving two or more disciplines : INTERDISCIPLINARY

cross–dress \ˌ=ˈ=\ *vi* [⁵*cross*] : to dress in the clothes of the opposite sex — **cross–dresser** \ˌ=ˈ=ə(r)\ *n*

crosslinguistic \ˈ==ˈ==\ *adj* [³*cross* + *linguistic*] : of or relating to languages of different families and types; *esp* : relating to the comparison of different languages — **crosslinguistically** \ˌ==ˈ=(=)=\ *adv*

cross multiply *vi* [back-formation fr. *cross multiplication*] : to find the two products obtained by multiplying the numerator of each of two fractions by the denominator of the other

cross–na·tion·al \ˈ=ˈ===\ *adj* [³*cross*] : of or relating to two or more nations

cross over *vi* : to reach a broader audience ⟨*crossed over* to the pop charts⟩

crossover* *n* **1** : a voter registered as a member of one political party who votes in the primary of the other party **2** : a broadening of the popular appeal of the work of an artist (as a musician) that is often the result of a change of the artist's medium or style; *also* : an artist or artistic work that has achieved such a crossover

crossover* *adj* **1** : CRITICAL 2 ⟨~ point⟩ ⟨~ date⟩ **2** : permitting voting by crossovers ⟨~ primary⟩ **3** : involving or using interchange of the control group and the experimental group during the course of an experiment ⟨a double-blind ~ study⟩

cross–ownership \ˈ=ˌ=ˌ=\ *n* : single ownership of two or more related business enterprises (as a newspaper and a television station) that make the owner able to control competition

cross–pollination* *n* : CROSS-FERTILIZATION 4 — **cross–pollinate*** *vt*

cross product* *n* : either of the two products obtained by multiplying together the two means or the two extremes of a proportion

cross–reactivity \¦=(ˌ)==ˈ===\ *n* [²*cross*] : the capability of undergoing cross-reaction — **cross–react** \"+\ *vi* — **cross–reactive** *adj*

cross–train \¦=¦=\ *vb* [²*cross*] *vt* : to train (a worker) to do more than one specific job ~ *vi* : to engage in different sports or exercises esp. for well-rounded health and muscular development — **cross–training** \ˈ=¦==\ *n*

cross–trainer \ˈ=¦==\ *n* : a sport shoe designed for cross-training

cros·ti·ni \krȯsˈtēnē\ *n pl* [It, pl. of *crostino*, fr. *crosta* crust, rind, fr. L *crusta* shell, crust — more at CRUST] : slices esp. of toasted bread usu. topped with a spread or other food

crow* *vt* : to say with self-satisfaction

crow·die \ˈkraüdē\ *n* -S [alter. (influenced by *crowdy*) of *crud* (curd)] : a Scottish cottage cheese that is partially cooked

crown jewel *n* [*crown jewels*] : the most attractive or valuable one of a collection or group

crown of thorns* *or* **crown–of–thorns starfish** : a starfish (*Acanthaster planci*) of the Pacific region that is covered with long spines and feeds on coral polyps sometimes causing destruction of coral reefs

CRT \ˌsē(ˌ)ärˈtē\ *n* -S [*c*athode-*r*ay *t*ube] : a display device incorporating a cathode-ray tube

crucible* *n* : a place or situation in which concentrated forces interact to cause or influence change or development ⟨conditioned by having grown up within the ~ of Chinatown —Tom Wolfe⟩

cru·ci·ver·bal·ist \ˌkrüsəˈvərbələst\ *n* [L *cruci-*, *crux* cross + *verbum* word + E *-alist* (as in *verbalist*) — more at RIDGE, WORD] : a person skillful in creating or solving crossword puzzles

cru·di·tés \krüˈdētā\ *n pl* [F, pl. of *crudité* raw food, fr. MF, indigestibility, crudity — more at CRUDITY] : pieces of raw vegetables (as celery, carrots, or cauliflower) served as an hors d'oeuvre often with a dip

cruise* *vi* **1** : to search (as in public places) for a sexual partner **2** : to move or proceed speedily, smoothly, or effortlessly ⟨I'll ~ over to her house to see if she's home⟩ ~ *vt* **1** : to search in (a public place) for a sexual partner **2** : to approach and suggest sexual relations to **3** : to explore or search the offerings of; *esp* : SURF *herein* ⟨~ the Internet⟩

cruise control *n* **1** : an electronic device in an automobile that controls the throttle so as to maintain a constant speed **2** : a relaxed and seemingly automatic pace that is easily maintained

cruise missile *n* : a guided missile that has a terrain-following radar system and that flies at moderate speed and low altitude

crumb structure *n* [trans. of G *krümelstruktur*] : a soil condition suitable for farming in which the soil particles are aggregated into crumbs

crunch* *vt* : PROCESS; *esp* : to perform mathematical computations on ⟨~ numbers⟩

crunch* *n* **1** : a tight or critical situation: as **a** : a critical point in the buildup of pressure between opposing elements **b** : a severe economic squeeze (as on credit) **c** : SHORTAGE ⟨energy ~⟩ **2** : a crunchy quality ⟨water chestnuts, walnuts, and other nuts can give ~ and added flavor —Nanalee Clayton⟩ **3** : a conditioning exercise performed from a supine position by raising and lowering the upper torso without reaching the sitting position

crunch time *n* : a critical moment or period (as near the end of a game) when decisive action is needed

cryo·biology \¦krīō+\ *n* [*cry-* + *biology*] : the study of the effects of extremely low temperature on biological systems (as cells or organisms) — **cryo·biological** \"+\ *adj* — **cryo·biologically** \"+\ *adv* — **cryo·biologist** \"+\ *n*

cryo·extraction \"+\ *n* [*cry-* + *extraction*] : extraction of a cataract through use of a cryoprobe whose refrigerated tip adheres to and freezes tissue of the lens permitting its removal

cryo·extractor \"+\ *n* [*cry-* + *extractor*] : a cryoprobe used for removal of cataracts

cryogenic* *adj* **1** : being or relating to a very low temperature ⟨a ~ temperature of –50° C⟩ **2 a** : requiring or involving the use of a cryogenic temperature ⟨~ surgery⟩ **b** : requiring cryogenic storage **c** : suitable for the storage of a cryogenic substance ⟨a ~ container⟩ — **cry·o·gen·i·cal·ly** \-nək(ə)lē\ *adv*

cryo·glob·u·li·ne·mia \¦krīō,glābyələ̇ˈnēmēə\ *n* -S [NL, fr. ISV *cryoglobulin* + NL *-emia*] : the condition of having abnormal quantities of cryoglobulins in the blood

cry·on·ics \krīˈäniks\ *n pl but usu sing in constr* [*cry-* + *-onics* (as in *electronics*)] : the practice of freezing the body of a person who has died from a disease in hopes of restoring life at some future time when a cure for the disease has been developed — **cry·on·ic** \(ˈ)krī¦änik\ *adj*

cryo·precipitate \¦krīō+\ *n* [*cry-* + ²*precipitate*] : a precipitate (as factor VIII) that is formed by cooling a solution (as blood plasma) — **cryo·precipitation** \"+\ *n*

cryo·preservation \"+\ *n* [*cry-* + *preservation*] : preservation (as of cells) by subjection to extremely low temperatures — **cryo·preserve** \"+\ *vt*

cryo·probe \ˈkrīō+ˌ\ *n* [*cry-* + ¹*probe*] : a blunt chilled instrument used to freeze tissues in cryosurgery

cryo·protective \¦krīō+\ *adj* [*cry-* + *protective*] : serving to protect against the deleterious effects of freezing ⟨an intracellular ~ agent⟩ — **cryo·protectant** \"+\ *n or adj*

cryo·pump \ˈkrīō+\ *n* [*cry-* + ¹*pump*] : a vacuum pump whose operation involves the freezing and adsorption of gases on cold surfaces at very low temperatures — **cryopump** *vi*

cryo·sorption \¦krīō+\ *n* [*cry-* + *sorption*] : the adsorption of gases onto the cold surfaces of a cryopump

cryo·surgery \"+\ *n* [*cry-* + *surgery*] : surgery in which usu. diseased or abnormal tissue (as of a tumor or wart) is destroyed or removed by freezing (as by the use of liquid nitrogen) — **cryo·surgeon** \"+\ *n* — **cryo·surgical** \"+\ *adj*

cryp·to·biosis \¦krip(ˌ)tō+\ *n, pl* **cryptobioses** [NL, fr. *crypt-* + *-biosis*] : the reversible cessation of metabolism under extreme environmental conditions (as low temperature)

cryp·to·coc·cal \ˌkriptəˈkäkəl\ *adj* : of, relating to, or caused by cryptococci ⟨~ meningitis⟩

cryp·to·spo·rid·i·o·sis \ˌkriptōspȯrˌidēˈōsəs\ *n, pl* **cryptosporidio·ses** \-ˌsēz\ [NL, fr. *Cryptosporidium*, genus name + *-osis*] : infection with or a disease caused by cryptosporidia

cryp·to·spo·rid·i·um \-spȯrˈidēəm\ *n* [NL, fr. *crypt-* + *spor-* + *-idium*] **1** *cap* : a genus of protozoans of the order Coccidia that are parasitic in the gut of many vertebrates including humans and sometimes cause diarrhea **2** *pl* **cryptospo·rid·ia** \-ēə\ : a protozoan of the genus *Cryptosporidium*

cryp·to·system \¦krip(ˌ)tō+\ *n* [*crypt-* + *system*] : a method for encoding and decoding messages

cryp·to·zoology \¦krip(ˌ)tō+\ *n* [*crypt-* + *zoology*] : the study of the lore concerning legendary animals (as Sasquatch) esp. in order to evaluate the possibility of their existence — **cryp·to·zoologist** \¦krip(ˌ)tō+\ *n*

crystal* *n* : ICE 2 *herein*; *broadly* : methamphetamine in any form when used illicitly

crystal meth *or* **crystal methamphetamine** *n* [*meth* short for *methamphetamine*] : ICE 2 *herein*

CS \ˌsēˈes\ *n* -ES [after Ben B. Corson †1987 and Roger W. Staughton †1957 Am. chemists] : a potent nausea-producing tear gas $C_{10}H_5ClN_2$ used esp. for riot control

c–section \ˈsē,==\ *n, usu cap C* [*C* short for ¹*cesarean*] : CESAREAN

CSF \ˌsē(ˌ)esˈef\ *abbr or n* -S : COLONY-STIMULATING FACTOR *herein*

CT *abbr* computed tomography *herein*; computerized tomography *herein*

ct scan \ˌsēˈtē-\ *n, usu cap C&T* : CAT SCAN *herein* — **ct scanning** *n, usu cap C&T*

ct scanner *n, usu cap C&T* : CAT SCANNER *herein*

c–type \ˈsē,tīp\ *adj, usu cap C* : TYPE C *herein*

cuat·ro \ˈkwä·trō\ *n* -S [AmerSp, fr. Sp, four, fr. L *quattuor*; fr. its four courses of strings] : a Puerto Rican stringed instrument similar to a small guitar

cubic zirconia *also* **cubic zirconium** *n* : a synthetic gemstone of zirconium resembling a diamond

cu·chi·fri·to \ˌküchiˈfrēd·ō, -chē-\ *n* -S [AmerSp, fr. *cuchí* hog, pork (alter. of Sp *cochino* hog) + Sp *frito* fried, past part. of *freir* to fry, fr. L *frigere* — more at FRY] : a deep-fried cube of pork

cued speech *n* : a form of communication for the deaf in which lipreading is enhanced by hand signals that distinguish between similar lip movements

cuff* *n* : a usu. wide metal band worn as a bracelet

cui·se·naire rod \ˌkwēzᵊnˈa(ə)r-, -¦e(-\ *also* **cuisenaire colored rod** *n, usu cap 1st C* [fr. *Cuisenaire*, a trademark] : any of a set of colored rods that are usu. of 1 centimeter cross section and of 10 lengths from 1 to 10 centimeters and that are used for teaching number concepts and the basic operations of arithmetic

cuisine min·ceur \-maⁿˈsœr, -minˈsər\ *n* [F, slimness cooking] : a low-calorie form of French cooking

cui–ui \ˈkwēˌwē\ *n* -S [Northern Paiute *kuyui*] : an endangered sucker (*Chasmistes cujus*) of the family Catostomidae that is found only in Pyramid lake and the Truckee river, Nevada

cul·dot·o·my \(ˌ)kəlˈdäd·əmē, kül-, -ätə-, -mi\ *n* -ES [*culdo-* + *-tomy*] : surgical incision of the pouch of Douglas

cu·li·coi·des \ˌkyüləˈkȯiˌdēz\ *n, cap* [NL, genus name, fr. L *culic-*, *culex* gnat + NL *-oïdes* -oid] : a genus of bloodsucking midges of the family Ceratopogonidae of which some are intermediate hosts of filarial parasites

culprit* *n* : the source or cause of a problem

cul·tur·a·ti \ˌkəlchəˈräd·(ˌ)ē, -ˈrál, |(ˌ)tē, *also* -ˈrāˌtī\ *n pl* [*culture* + *-ati* (as in *literati*)] : people intensely interested in cultural affairs

culture* *n* : the set of shared attitudes, values, goals, and practices that characterize a company or corporation

culture shock *n* : a sense of confusion and uncertainty sometimes with feelings of anxiety that may affect people exposed to an alien culture without adequate preparation

culture–vulture \ˈ==¦==\ *n* : a person who avidly attends cultural events

cumberland sauce *n, usu cap C* [fr. *Cumberland*, former county of England] : a cold sauce flavored with orange, lemon, currant jelly, port wine, and spices that is often served with game

cumulative* *adj* : summing or integrating over all data or values of a random variable less than or less than or equal to a specified value ⟨~ normal distribution⟩ ⟨~ frequency distribution⟩

cumulative distribution function *n* : a function that gives the probability that a random variable is less than or equal to the independent variable of the function

cumulative trauma disorder *n* : REPETITIVE STRAIN INJURY *herein*

cup* *n* : the symbol ∪ indicating the union of two sets — compare CAP *herein*

cup·pa \ˈkəpə\ *n* -S [fr. *cuppa tea*, pronunciation spelling of *cup of tea*] *chiefly Brit* : a cup of tea

cupule* *n* : an outer integument partially enclosing the seed of some seed ferns

cu·rate's egg \¦kyürəts¦=\ *n* [so called fr. a cartoon in the weekly *Punch* depicting a curate who was given a stale egg by his bishop and declared that parts of it were excellent] *chiefly Brit* : something with both good and bad parts or qualities

curb cut *n* : a ramp cut into a street curb at a corner for wheelchair access or at a driveway for vehicular access

curb weight *n* : the weight of an automobile with standard equipment and fuel, oil, and coolant

curl* *n* **1** : a hollow arch of water formed when the crest of a breaking wave spills forward — called also *tube, tunnel* **2** : a body-building exercise in which a weight held at thigh level is raised to chest or shoulder level and then lowered without moving the shoulders or upper arms

cur·sil·lo \kůrˈsē(l)yō\ *n* -S *often cap* [Sp, short course, dim. of *curso* course] : a movement in Roman Catholicism designed to deepen the spiritual life and bring about Christian involvement in daily activities through participation in a 3-day gathering usu. followed by weekly or monthly meetings; *also* : the 3-day gathering

cursor* *n* **1** : a visual cue (as a flashing rectangle) on a video display that indicates position esp. for entry of data or manipulation of information **2** : a usu. transparent movable object with cross hairs used to mark position on a tablet for entry of graphic data into a computer

cushion* *n* : a comfortable lead ⟨a 4–0 ~ in the ninth inning⟩

cusp* *n* : a point of transition (as from one historical period to the next) : TURNING POINT; *also* : EDGE, VERGE ⟨on the ~ of stardom⟩

custard glass *n* : opaque glass of creamy buff color

custom–make \ˈ==¦=\ *vt* [back-formation fr. *custom-made*] : to make to order or to individual specifications

cut* *vt* **1 a** : to sing, play, or act for the studio recording or filming of ⟨~ an album⟩ ⟨~ a commercial⟩ **b** : to sing or play (as a song or a track) for a studio recording ⟨~ a piano roll⟩ **2** : to be able to manage or handle — usu. used in negative constructions ⟨can't ~ that kind of work anymore⟩ ~ *vi* : to make a sudden transition or imaginative leap : pass abruptly (as from one subject, setting, or time to another) ⟨the novel's narrative ~*s* back and forth between Chicago and New York⟩ ⟨~ to 1917⟩ — **cut a deal** : to negotiate an agreement — **cut it** : to manage or perform something successfully — **cut one's losses** : to withdraw (as from an enterprise) and accept current losses in order to prevent further loss — **cut to the chase** : to get to the point

cut* *n* **1** : a single song or musical piece on a phonograph record **2** : the elimination of part of a usu. large field from further competition, participation, or consideration — often used with *miss* or *make* to denote respectively being or not being among those eliminated ⟨played well and made the ~⟩ **3** : an edited version of a film ⟨a director's ~⟩

cutability \ˌ==ˈ===\ *n* -ES [¹*cut* + *-ability*] : the proportion of lean salable meat yielded by a carcass

cut–and–paste \ˈ=¦=\ *n* : a computer software function allowing the user to easily move blocks of information (as text or graphics) within or among documents — **cut and paste** : to remove selected computer data from one location or document and insert it into another

cut–and–paste \¦==ˈ=\ *adj* : pieced together by excerpting and combining fragments from multiple sources ⟨the book was a *cut-and-paste* job⟩

cutaneous t–cell lymphoma *n, usu cap T* : any of several lymphomas (as mycosis fungoides) that are marked by clusters of malignant helper T cells in the epidermis causing skin lesions and eruptions which typically progress to tumors and may spread to lymph nodes and internal organs

cutback* *n* : a surfing maneuver in which a surfboard is turned back toward the crest of the wave

cute *n* [*cute*, adj.] : the quality or state of being cute or cutesy; *also* : an instance of cuteness or cutesyness — usu. used in pl. ⟨a movie suffering from a case of the ~*s*⟩

cute·sy *also* **cute·sie** \ˈkyütsē\ *adj* **cutesier; cutesiest** [²*cute* + *-sy* (as in *folksy*)] : self-consciously or excessively cute ⟨the ~ figures on greeting cards⟩; *esp* : too cute to be taken seriously ⟨the workout program is a gimmick . . . only ~ exercises —Peggy Brawley⟩ — **cute·sy·ness** *also* **cute·si·ness** *n* -ES

cutoff* *n* **cutoffs** *pl* : trousers (as of blue denim) cut off at the knee or higher — **cutoff*** *adj*

cutting edge *n* **1** : the forefront of an art, science, or movement : VANGUARD, FRONTIER ⟨the *cutting edge* of American industrial prowess —P.J.Schuyten⟩ **2** : a sharp effect or quality — **cutting–edge** \¦==ˈ=\ *adj*

CV* *abbr, often not cap* curriculum vitae

CVS *abbr* chorionic villi sampling *herein*; chorionic villus sampling *herein*

cy·a·no·acrylate \¦sīənō+\ *n* [*cyan-* + *acrylate*] : any of several liquid acrylate monomers that readily undergo anionic polymerization and are used as adhesives esp. in industry and in medicine on living tissue to close wounds in surgery

cy·a·no·bacterium \¦sīə(ˌ)nō+\ *n* [NL, fr. *cyan-* + *bacterium*] : BLUE-GREEN ALGA — **cy·a·no·bacterial** \"+\ *adj*

cy·ber- *in pronunciations below*, ¦== = ¦sībər\ *comb form* [*cybernetic*] : computer : computer network ⟨*cyber*space⟩

cy·ber \ˈsībər\ *adj* [*cyber-* (herein)] : of, relating to, or involving computers or computer networks (as the Internet) ⟨the ~ marketplace⟩

cy·ber·cafe \ˈsībə(r)+\ *n* [*cyber-* (herein) + *café*] : a café or coffee shop providing computer terminals for access to the Internet

cy·ber·citizen \"+ˌ\ *n* [*cyber-* (herein) + *citizen*] : NETIZEN *herein*

cy·ber·culture \ˈsībə(r)+\ *n* [*cyber-* (herein) + *culture*] : a society that is served by cybernated industry — **cy·ber·cultural** \¦sībə(r)+\ *adj*

cy·ber·nat·ed \ˈsībə(r)ˌnād·əd, -ātəd\ *adj* [fr. *cybernation* (herein), after such pairs as E *automation : automated*] : characterized by or involving cybernation ⟨a ~ factory⟩ ⟨a ~ society⟩

cy·ber·na·tion \ˌsībə(r)ˈnāshən\ *n* -S [*cyber*netics + *-ation*] : the automatic control of a process or operation (as in manufacturing) by means of computers

cy·ber·naut \ˈsībə(r)+ˌnȯt, -ˌnät\ *n* [*cyber-* (herein) + *-naut* (as in *astronaut*)] : NETIZEN *herein*

cy·ber·porn \ˈsībə(r)+ˌ\ *n* [*cyber-* (herein) + *porn* (herein)] : pornography accessible on-line esp. via the Internet

cy·ber·punk \"+ˌ\ *n* -S [*cyber-* (herein) + ¹*punk*] **1** : science fiction dealing with future urban societies dominated by computer technology **2** : an opportunistic computer hacker

cy·ber·sex \" +ˌ\ *n* [*cyber-* (herein) + ¹*sex*] **1** : on-line sex-oriented conversations and exchanges **2** : sex-oriented material available on the Internet and on CD-ROMs

cy·ber·space \"+ˌ\ *n* [*cyber-* (herein) + ¹*space*] : the on-line world of computer networks

cy·ber·speak \"+ˌ\ *n* [*cyber-* (herein) + *-speak* (as in *newspeak* — herein)] : jargon relating to the Internet; *specif* : jargon used in on-line communications

cy·ber·surfer \"+ˌ\ *n* [*cyber-* (herein) + *surfer*] : one who surfs the Internet

cy·borg \ˈsīˌbȯrg\ *n* -S [*cyb*ernetic + *org*anism] : a bionic human being

cy·ca·sin \ˈsīkəsən\ *n* -S [*cycas* + *-in*] : a glucoside $C_8H_{16}N_2O_7$ that occurs in cycads and results in toxic and carcinogenic effects when introduced into mammals

cy·clan·de·late \ˌsīˈklandᵊlˌāt, -ˌət\ *n* -S [*cyclo*hexyl + m*andelate*] : an antispasmodic drug $C_{17}H_{24}O_3$ used esp. as a vasodilator in the treatment of diseased arteries

cy·clase \ˈsīˌklās, -āz\ *n* -S [*cycl-* + *-ase*] : an enzyme (as adenylate cyclase) that catalyzes cyclization of a compound

cy·claz·o·cine \sīˈklazəˌsēn, -sən\ *n* -S [*cycl-* + *-azocine* (as in *phenazocine* — herein)] : an analgesic drug $C_{18}H_{25}NO$ that inhibits the effect of morphine and related addictive drugs and is used in the treatment of drug addiction

cycle* *n* : a permutation of a set of ordered elements in which each element takes the place of the next and the last becomes first

cycle* *vi* : to undergo the estrous cycle ⟨the mare has begun *cycling*⟩

cy·cle·ry \ˈsīkəl(ˌ)rē, -klə(-\ *n* -ES [¹*cycle* + *-ery*] : a place where bicycles are sold and serviced

cyclic* *adj* **1** : being a mathematical group that has an element such that every element of the group can be expressed as one of its powers **2** *of a polygon* : having all vertices lying on the circumference of a circle ⟨a ~ octagon that does not intersect itself⟩

cyclic adenosine monophosphate *n* : CYCLIC AMP *herein*

cyclic AMP *n* : a cyclic mononucleotide of adenosine that is formed from ATP and is responsible for the intracellular mediation of hormonal effects on various cellular processes (as lipid metabolism, membrane transport, and cell proliferation); adenosine 3′,5′-monophosphate — abbr. *cAMP*

cyclic GMP \-ˌjē(ˌ)emˈpē\ *n* : a cyclic mononucleotide of guanosine that acts similarly to cyclic AMP as a second messenger in response to hormones; guanosine 3′,5′-monophosphate — called also *guanosine monophosphate*

cyclic guanosine mono·phosphate \-ˌmänəˈfäsˌfāt, -ˌmōn-\ *n* [*mon-* + *phosphate*] : CYCLIC GMP *herein*

cy·clin \ˈsīklən, ˈsi-\ *n* -S [¹cycle + -in] : any of a group of proteins active in controlling the cell cycle and in initiating DNA synthesis

cy·clo \ˈsē(ˌ)klō, ˈsik(ˌ)lō\ *n* -S [F, bicycle, moped, fr. *cyclo-* (as in *cyclomoteur* moped, *cyclo-taxi* pedicab), fr. *cycle* two- or three-wheeled vehicle, fr. E] : a 3-wheeled often motor-driven taxi

cy·clo·addition \¦sī(ˌ)klō+, *also* ¦si(ˌ)klō+\ *n* [*cycl-* + *addition*] : a chemical reaction leading to ring formation in a compound

cy·clo·dextrin \"+\ *n* [ISV *cycl-* + *dextrin*] : any of a class of cyclic oligosaccharide sugars that are products of the enzymatic decomposition of starch and that can act as catalysts because they have the form of a rigid cylinder and can hold within their cavities smaller molecules which can then participate in reactions

cy·clo·diene \"+\ *n* -S [*cycl-* + *-diene*] : an organic insecticide (as aldrin, dieldrin, chlordane, or endosulfan) with a chlorinated methylene group forming a bridge across a 6-membered carbon ring

cy·clo·oxygenase \"+\ *n* [*cycl-* + *oxygenase* (herein)] : an enzyme that catalyzes the conversion of arachidonic acid into prostaglandins, that is inactivated by aspirin, and that has two isoforms of which one has been implicated in the cascade of events producing the pain and inflammation of arthritis while the other has not

cy·clo·phos·pha·mide \ˌsīkləˈfäsfəˌmīd, ˌsik-, -ˌməd\ *n* -S [*cycl-* + *phosph-* + *amide*] : an immunosuppressive and antineoplastic drug $C_7H_{15}Cl_2N_2O_2P$ used in the treatment of lymphomas and some leukemias

cy·clo·spo·ra \ˌsīklōˈspōrə, -ˈspȯr-\ *n, cap* [NL, fr. *cycl-* + *-spora*] : a genus of coccidian sporozoans that produce an oocyst containing two sporocysts with each sporocyst containing two sporozoites and that include one (*C. cayetanensis*) causing diarrhea in humans

cy·clo·spo·rine \ˌsīklōˈspȯrən\ *also* **cy·clo·spo·rin** *or* **cyclosporin A** \-ˈā\ *n* -S [ISV *cycl-* + *spor-* + *-ine* or *-in*] : an immunosuppressive drug $C_{62}H_{111}N_{11}O_{12}$ that is a polypeptide obtained from various imperfect fungi (as *Tolypocladium inflatum* syn. *Trichoderma polysporum*) and is used esp. to prevent rejection of transplanted organs

cyclotomic* *adj* : relating to, being, or containing a polynomial of the form $x^{p-1} + x^{p-2} + \cdots + x + 1$ where *p* is a prime number

cyclotron resonance *n* : the absorption of electromagnetic energy by a charged particle orbiting in a magnetic field when the electromagnetic and orbital frequencies are equal

cymric* *n, usu cap* : a long-haired Manx cat that prob. originated as a spontaneous mutation of a short-haired Manx and that is sometimes considered to belong to a separate breed

cy·pro·hep·ta·dine \ˌsīprōˈheptəˌdēn, -ˌdən\ *n* -S [*cycl-* + *propyl* + *hepta-* + *piperidine*] : a drug $C_{21}H_{21}N$ that acts antagonistically to histamine and serotonin and is used esp. in the treatment of asthma

cy·pro·ter·one \sīˈprōd·əˌrōn *also* -ˈpräd-·\ *n* -S [prob. fr. *cycl-* + *progesterone*] : a synthetic steroid $C_{22}H_{27}ClO_3$ used in the form of its acetate to inhibit androgenic secretions (as testosterone)

cys·ta·mine \ˈsistəˌmēn, -ˌmən\ *n* [*cyst*ine + *amine*] : a cystine derivative $C_4H_{12}N_2S_2$

cys·ta·thi·o·nine \ˌsistəˈthīəˌnēn, -ˌnən\ *n* -S [*cyst*eine + connective *-a-* + *methionine*] : a sulfur-containing amino acid $C_7H_{14}N_2O_4S$ formed as an intermediate in the conversion of methionine to cysteine in animals

cys·te·amine \sis'tēə,mēn, -,mən\ *n* [*cysteine* + *amine*] : a cysteine derivative C_2H_7NS used to treat cystinosis and esp. formerly as an antidote for acetaminophen overdose

cys·ti·no·sis \,sistə'nōsəs\ *n, pl* **cystino·ses** \-ō,sēz\ [NL, fr. ISV *cystine* + NL *-osis*] : a recessive autosomally inherited disease characterized esp. by cystinuria and deposits of cystine throughout the body — **cys·ti·not·ic** \-'nād·ik\ *adj*

cys·to·ure·throg·ra·phy \,sistə,yürə'thrägrəfē\ *n* -ES [*cyst-* + *urethrograph* + [2]*-y*] : roentgenography for the purpose of preparing a cystourethrogram — **cys·to·ure·thro·graph·ic** \-,yə,rēthrə'grafik\ *adj*

cy·to·cha·la·sin \,sīd·ōkə'lāsən\ *n* -S [*cyt-* + Gk *chalasis* slackening, relaxation (fr. *chalan* to loosen, relax) + *-in* — more at CHALARA] : any of a group of metabolites isolated from fungi (esp. *Helminthosporium dematioideum*) that inhibit various cell processes

cy·to·chimera \¦sīd·ō+\ *n* [NL, fr. *cyt-* + *chimera*] : an individual (as a plant, an organ, or a tissue) having cells of varied genetic constitution and esp. of various ploidy levels

cy·to·differentiation \"+\ *n* [*cyt-* + *differentiation*] : the development of specialized cells (as muscle, blood, or nerve cells) from undifferentiated precursors

cy·to·kine \'sīd·ō,kīn, -d·ə-\ *n* -S [*cyt-* + *-kine* (as in *lymphokine* — herein)] : any of a class of immunoregulatory proteins (as interleukin, tumor necrosis factor, or interferon) that are secreted by cells esp. of the immune system

cy·to·kinin \¦sīd·ō+\ *n* [*cyt-* + *kinin* (herein)] : any of various plant growth substances (as kinetin) that are usu. derivatives of adenine

cy·to·lyt·ic t cell \,sīd·əl'id·ik-\ *or* **cytolytic t lymphocyte** *n, usu cap T* : CYTOTOXIC T CELL *herein*

cy·to·me·gal·ic \¦sīd·ōmə¦galik\ *adj* [NL *cytomegalia* condition of having enlarged cells (fr. *cyt-* + *-megalia* -megaly) + E *-ic*] : characterized by or causing the formation of enlarged cells

cytomegalic inclusion disease *n* : a severe disease esp. of newborns that is caused by the cytomegalovirus and usu. affects the salivary glands, brain, kidneys, liver, and lungs

cy·to·meg·a·lo·vi·rus \,sīd·ə¦megəlō¦vīrəs\ *n* [NL, fr. E *cytomegalic* (herein) + NL *-o-* + *virus*] : a herpesvirus (genus *Cytomegalovirus*) that causes cellular enlargement and formation of eosinophilic inclusion bodies esp. in the nucleus and that acts as an opportunistic infectious agent in immunocompromised conditions (as AIDS)

cy·to·membrane \¦sīd·ə+\ *n* [*cyt-* + *membrane*] : one of the cellular membranes including those of the plasma membrane, endoplasmic reticulum, nuclear envelope, and Golgi apparatus; *specif* : UNIT MEMBRANE *herein*

cy·tom·e·try \sī'tämə·trē\ *n* -ES [*cyt-* + *-metry*] : a technical specialty concerned with the counting of cells and esp. blood cells — see FLOW CYTOMETRY *herein* — **cy·to·met·ric** \,sīd·ə'me·trik\ *adj*

cy·to·morphology \¦sīd·ō+\ *n* [*cyt-* + *morphology*] : the morphology of cells — **cy·to·morphological** \"+\ *adj*

cy·to·pathogenic \"+\ *adj* [*cyt-* + *pathogenic*] : pathologic for or destructive to cells — **cy·to·pathogenicity** \"+\ *n*

cy·to·photometer \"+\ *n* [*cyt-* + *photometer*] : a photometer for use in cytophotometry

cy·to·photometry \"+\ *n* [*cyt-* + *photometry*] : photometry applied to the study of the cell or its constituents — **cy·to·photometric** \"+\ *adj* — **cy·to·photometrically** \"+\ *adv*

cy·to·physiology \"+\ *n* [*cyt-* + *physiology*] : the physiology of cells — **cy·to·physiological** \"+\ *adj* — **cy·to·physiologically** \"+\ *adv*

cytosine arabinoside *n* : a cytotoxic antineoplastic agent $C_9H_{13}N_3O_5$ that is a synthetic isomer of the naturally occurring nucleoside of cytosine and arabinose and is used esp. in the treatment of acute myelogenous leukemia in adults

cy·to·skeletal \"+\ *adj* [*cyt-* + *skeletal*] : of, relating to, or being the cytoskeleton of a cell

cy·to·sol \'sīd·ə+,\ *n* [*cyt-* + [6]*sol*] : the fluid portion of the cytoplasm exclusive of organelles and membranes — **cy·to·sol·ic** \¦sīd·ə¦sälik, -sōl-, -sȯl-\ *adj*

cy·to·spectrophotometry \¦sīd·ō+\ *n* [*cyt-* + *spectrophotometry*] : the application of spectrophotometry to the study of cells and esp. to the quantitative estimation of their constituents (as DNA)

cy·to·stat·ic \¦sīd·ə¦stad·ik\ *adj* [*cyt-* + *-static* (as in *hemostatic*)] : tending to retard cellular activity and multiplication ⟨~ treatment of tumor cells⟩ — **cytostatic** *n* — **cy·to·stat·i·cal·ly** \-ad·ək(ə)lē\ *adv*

cy·to·tech \'sīd·ə,tek\ *n* -S [by shortening] : CYTOTECHNOLOGIST

cy·to·technologist \¦sīd·ō+\ *also* **cy·to·technician** \"+\ *n* [*cyt-* + *technologist* or *technician*] : a medical technician trained in cytotechnology

cy·to·technology \"+\ *n* [*cyt-* + *technology*] : a specialty in medical technology concerned with the identification of cells and cellular abnormalities (as in cancer)

cy·to·tox·ic t cell \,sīd·ə'täksik-\ *or* **cytotoxic t lymphocyte** *n, usu cap T* : a T cell that usu. bears CD8 molecular markers on its surface and that functions in cell-mediated immunity by destroying a cell (as a virus infected cell) having a specific antigenic molecule on its surface — called also *cytolytic T cell, killer T cell*; compare HELPER T CELL *herein*, SUPPRESSOR T CELL *herein*

cy·to·vi·rin \,sīd·ə'vī(ə)rən\ *n* -S [*cyt-* + *virus* + *-in*] : a compound that is produced by a bacterium of the genus *Streptomyces* (*S. olivochromogenes*) and that is active against some plant viruses (as tobacco mosaic virus)

da* *abbr* deka-

DA \¦dē'ā\ *n* -S [*duck's ass*; fr. its resemblance to the tail of a duck] : DUCKTAIL

DA \,dē'ā\ *abbr or n* -S : a doctor of arts

dab* *n, slang Brit* : FINGERPRINT

DAC \,dē(,)ā'sē\ *n* -S [*digital-to-analog converter*] : an electronic device for converting signals from digital to analog form

dac·quoise \dåkwåz\ *n* -S [F, fr. fem. of *dacquois* of Dax, a town in S France] : a dessert made of layers of baked nut meringue with a filling usu. of buttercream

dac·ryo·cys·to·rhi·nos·to·my \,dakrē(,)ō,sis(,)tōrī'nästəmē\ *n* -ES [*dacryocyst* + *rhin-* + [2]*-stomy*] : surgical creation of a passage for drainage between the lacrimal sac and the nasal cavity

dac·ti·no·mycin \¦daktənō¦mīsən\ *n* -S [alter. of *actinomycin D*] : a toxic antineoplastic drug $C_{62}H_{86}N_{12}O_{16}$ of the actinomycin group — called also *actinomycin D*

daddy* *n* : GRANDDADDY 2

dag·wood \'dag,wu̇d\ *n* -S *often cap* [after *Dagwood* Bumstead, character who made such sandwiches in the comic strip *Blondie* by M.B.Young †1973] : a many-layered sandwich

daisy* *n, usu cap* : a member of a program of the Girl Scouts for girls in kindergarten and first grade

daisy chain* *n* : a group sexual activity in which each person attends to the one in front while being attended to by the one behind

daisy–chain \¦=¦=\ *vt* : to link (computer components) together in series

daisy wheel *n* [so called fr. its resemblance to the flower] : a printing element of an electronic typewriter or printer that consists of a disk with spokes bearing type

dal* *also* **dahl** *or* **dhal*** *n* : a dried legume (as lentils, beans, or peas); *also* : an Indian dish made of simmered and usu. pureed and spiced legumes

dal·a·pon \'dalə,pän\ *n* -S [prob. fr. *di-* + *alpha* + *propionic* acid] : an herbicide $C_3H_4Cl_2O_2$ that kills monocotyledonous plants selectively and is used esp. on unwanted grasses

da·la·si \dä'läsē\ *n, pl* **dalasi** *or* **dalasis** [Wolof, prob. fr. Mandinka (Malinke dial. of Senegambia) *dalasoo*, modif. of W Afr F *dala* five-franc coin, fr. E *dollar*] **1** : the basic monetary unit of Gambia — see MONEY table *in the Dict* **2** : a coin or note representing one dalasi

dal·ton \'dȯltᵊn\ *n* -S [after John *Dalton* †1844 Eng. chemist and physicist] : ATOMIC MASS UNIT — used chiefly in biochemistry

damage control* *n* : measures taken to offset or minimize damage to reputation, credibility, or public image caused by a controversial act, remark, or revelation ⟨people who brought this embarrassment to the institution were attempting to stage a poorly run, last-minute *damage control* operation —G.S.White Jr.⟩

damaged goods *n pl* : a person considered to be flawed or spoiled in character, efficiency, or worth

damsel bug *n* : any of a family (Nabidae) of small brown or black predaceous bugs that feed esp. on pest insects (as aphids and caterpillars)

dan \'dän, 'dan\ *n* -S [Jap, step, grade] : the expert level in Oriental arts of self-defense (as judo and karate) and games (as shogi)

da·na·zol \'dānə,zōl, 'da-, -,zȯl\ *n* -S [*dan-* (perh. anagram of *androgenic*) + isox*azole*] : a synthetic androgenic derivative $C_{22}H_{27}NO_2$ of ethisterone that suppresses hormone secretion by the adenohypophysis and is used esp. in the treatment of endometriosis

D and C *abbr* dilation and curettage

dap·sone \'dap,sōn, -,zōn\ *n* -S [*diaminodiphenyl sulfone*] : DIAMINODIPHENYL SULFONE

dar·ier's disease \där¦yāz, då(r)-\ *n, usu cap 1st D* [after J.F. *Darier* †1938 Fr. dermatologist] : a genetically determined skin condition characterized by patches of keratotic papules — called also *keratosis follicularis*

dark matter *n* : nonluminous matter not yet directly detected by astronomers that is hypothesized to exist because the amount of visible matter in the universe is insufficient to account for various observed gravitational effects

dart* *vt* : to shoot with a dart containing a usu. tranquilizing drug

dar·win's finches \¦därwənz-\ *n pl, usu cap D* [after Charles *Darwin* †1882 Eng. naturalist] : finches (as the ground finches) of a subfamily (Geospizinae) characterized by great variation in bill shape and confined mostly to the Galapagos islands

das *abbr* dekastere *herein*

da·shi \'dåsh(,)ē, dä'shē\ *n* -S [Jap, lit., broth] : a fish broth made from dried bonito

da·shi·ki \dä'shēkē, də'-\ *also* **dai·shi·ki** \dī'-\ *n* -S [modif. of Yoruba *dànṣíkí*] : a usu. brightly colored loose-fitting tunic of African origin worn esp. by black men

DAT \'dat, ,dē(,)ā'tē\ *abbr or n* -S : digital audiotape

data bank *n* **1** : DATABASE *herein* **2** : an institution whose chief concern is building and maintaining a database

database *n* : a collection of data organized esp. for rapid search and retrieval (as by a computer)

dataflow \'=,=\ *n* : a computer architecture that utilizes multiple parallel processors to perform simultaneous operations as data becomes available

data processing *n* : the conversion of raw data to machine-readable form and its subsequent processing (as storing, updating, combining, rearranging, or printing out) by a computer — **data processor** *n*

data structure *n* : any of various methods of organizing data items (as records) in a computer

date* *vi* : to go out on usu. romantic dates; *also* : to be involved in a romantic relationship ⟨they *dated*, and he proposed by telephone —*Time*⟩

date rape *n* : rape committed by someone known to the victim

date–rape *vt* : to commit date rape on

dating bar *n* : SINGLES BAR *herein*

daughterboard \'=,=\ *n* : a secondary circuit board in a computer that is attached to the motherboard

dau·no·my·cin \,dȯnə'mīsᵊn, ,dau̇-\ *n* -S [ISV *dauno-* (fr. L *Daunius* Apulian) + *-mycin*; orig. formed in It as *daunomicina*] : DAUNORUBICIN *herein*

dau·no·ru·bi·cin \,==rübəsən\ *n* -S [ISV *dauno-* (as in *daunomycin* — herein) + *rubidomycin*, a substance found to be identical with daunomycin (fr. L *rubidus* red + ISV *-mycin*)] : an antibiotic that is a nitrogenous glycoside and is used in the form of its hydrochloride $C_{27}H_{29}NO_{10}·HCl$ esp. in the treatment of some leukemias

day care *n* **1** : supervision of and care for children or physically or mentally disabled adults that is provided during the day by a person or organization other than the children's parents or the adults' families **2** : a program, facility, or organization that provides day care

day–care \¦=¦=\ *adj* : of, relating to, or providing day care ⟨*day-care* centers⟩

Day–Glo \'dā,glō\ *trademark* — used for fluorescent materials or colors

day·glow \'dā,glō\ *n* -S [*day* + air*glow*] : airglow seen during the day

day job *n* : one's regular employment as contrasted with an occasional, secondary, or coveted job

day one *also* **day 1** *n, often cap D&O* : the first day of something : the beginning of an activity or enterprise ⟨the trip was great from *day one*⟩

day release *n, chiefly Brit* : a program whereby employees are permitted to spend part of the workday attending courses to develop needed job skills; *also* : a similar program in prisons, jails, and hospitals in which prisoners or patients are permitted to spend part of the day outside their institution of confinement studying, training, or working

daysailer \'=,==\ *n* : a small sailboat without sleeping accommodations

day·side* *n* : the side of a planet in sunlight

day trader *n* : a speculator who seeks profit from the intraday fluctuation in the price of a security or commodity and therefore completes double trades of buying and selling or selling and covering in the course of single sessions of the market — **day–trade** \'=,=\ *n or vb*

day–tripper \'=,==\ *n* : one (as a tourist) who takes a trip that does not last overnight — **day–trip** \'=¦=\ *n or vb*

Db *symbol* dubnium *herein*

DBA *abbr* doctor of business administration

DBCP \,dē,bē(,)sē'pē\ *n* -S [*dibrom-* + *chlor-* + *propane*] : a halocarbon compound $C_3H_5Br_2Cl$ used esp. formerly as an agricultural pesticide that is a suspected carcinogen and cause of male sterility in humans; 1,2-dibromo-3-chloropropane

DBMS \,dē,bē(,)em'es\ *abbr or n* -S [*data base management system*] : software designed to facilitate the creation, update, and retrieval of information in a database

DBS *abbr* direct broadcast satellite

DC *abbr* doctor of chiropractic

ddC \,dē(,)dē'sē\ *n* -S *often all cap* [*dideoxycytidine* (herein)] : a synthetic nucleoside analogue $C_9H_{13}N_3O_3$ that inhibits replication of retroviruses and is used in the treatment of advanced HIV infection — called also *dideoxycytidine, zalcitabine*

DDE \,dē(,)dē'ē\ *n* -S [*dichlorodiphenyldichloroethylene*, fr. *dichlor-* + [1]*diphenyl* + *dichlor-* + *ethylene*] : a persistent organochlorine $C_{15}H_8Cl_4$ that is produced by the metabolic breakdown of DDT

ddI \,dē(,)dē'ī\ *n* -S *often all cap* [*dideoxyinosine* (herein)] : DIDANOSINE

DDVP \,dē,dē(,)vē'pē\ *n* -S [*dimethyl* + *dichlor-* + *vinyl* + *phosphate*] : DICHLORVOS *herein*

de–accession \¦dē+\ *also* **de–ac·cess** \¦dēak'ses\ *vb* [*de-accession* fr. *de-* + *accession*; *de-access* back-formation fr. *de-accession*] *vt* : to remove and sell (a work of art) from an institution's (as a museum's or a library's) collection esp. to raise funds to purchase other works of art ~ *vi* : to de-accession a work of art or part of a collection — **de–accession** *n*

de·acylate \(,)+\ *vt* [*de-* + *acylate*] : to remove an acyl group from (a compound) — **de·acylation** \¦=+\ *n*

dead* *adj* — **dead in the water** **1** : incapable of being effective : STALLED ⟨peace talks were *dead in the water*⟩ **2** : as good as dead : DOOMED ⟨most books are *dead in the water* long before their publication date —Phillip Lopate⟩

dead drop *n* [so called fr. the absence of personal contact between the agents] : a prearranged hiding place for the deposit and pickup of information obtained through espionage

deadhead* *n* : a dull or stupid person

deadhead* *vt* : to remove the faded flowers of (a plant) esp. to keep a neat appearance and to promote reblooming by preventing seed production

dead lift* *n* : a lift in weight lifting in which the weight is lifted from the floor to hip level; *also* : a competitive event involving this lift — **dead–lift** \'=,=\ *vb*

dead meat *n* : one that is doomed ⟨if they catch him, he's *dead meat*⟩

dead–on \¦=¦=\ *adj* [[4]*dead* + [2]*on*] : exactly correct or accurate ⟨*dead-on* timing⟩ ⟨*dead-on* in his contention that effective worker-education programs need firm intellectual . . . underpinnings —Benjamin DeMott⟩

deal* *vt* : SELL ⟨~*s* drugs⟩

deal* *n* **1** : SKINNY, *herein*, EXPLANATION **2** : AFFAIR 2a, d

dear john *n, usu cap D&J* : a letter (as to a soldier) in which a wife asks for a divorce or a girl friend breaks off an engagement or a friendship

death camp *n* : a concentration camp in which large numbers of prisoners are systematically killed

death grip *n* **1** : an extremely tight grip caused esp. by fear **2** : HOLD 3b(1) ⟨maintained their *death grip* on overseas markets⟩

death metal *n* : a type of heavy metal music that is characterized by the use of dark, violent, or gory imagery

death ray *n* : a weapon that generates an intense beam of particles or radiation by which it destroys its target

death sentence **1** : a sentence condemning a convicted defendant to death **2** : an affliction or a situation that is considered to be fatal; *also* : a prognosis of death

death squad *n* : any of various extremist groups whose members kill suspected political adversaries and criminals

deb·by \'debē, -i\ *adj* [*deb* + [1]*-y*] *chiefly Brit* : being, relating to, or resembling a debutante

debit card *n* : a card like a credit card by which money may be withdrawn or the cost of purchases paid directly from the holder's bank account without the payment of interest

de·boost \(')dē, dē+\ *n* [*de-* + [1]*boost*] : the process of slowing down a spacecraft ⟨before ~ into low orbit —C.J.Sitomer⟩

debrief* *vt* : to instruct not to reveal classified information after release from a sensitive position

debug* *vt* **1** : to remove a concealed microphone or wiretapping device from ⟨~ a room⟩ **2** : to make (concealed microphones) ineffective by electronic means

de·bug·ger \(')dē'bəgər\ *n* -S : one that debugs

de·caf \'dē,kaf\ *n* -S [short for *decaffeinated*] : decaffeinated coffee

deca·met·ric \¦dekə¦me·trik\ *adj* [*deca-* + *-metric*; fr. the wavelength range being between 1 and 10 decameters] : of, relating to, or being a radio wave of high frequency

deca·peptide \¦==+\ *n* [*deca-* + *peptide*] : a polypeptide (as angiotensin I) that consists of a chain of 10 amino acids

dec·ath·lete \dē'kath,lēt\ *n* -S [blend of *decathlon* and *athlete*] : an athlete who competes in the decathlon

dec·ca \'dekə\ *n, usu cap* [*Decca* Co., British firm which developed it] : a system of long-range navigation utilizing the phase differences of continuous-wave signals from synchronized ground transmitters

deciding *adj* [fr. pres. part. of *decide*] : having the effect of settling a contest or controversy ⟨the ~ run⟩ ⟨the ~ vote⟩

de·cid·u·o·ma \dē,sijə'wōmə, dē-\ *n, pl* **deciduomas** *or* **de·ciduo·ma·ta** \-məd·ə, -ətə\ [NL, fr. *decidua* + *-oma*] **1** : a mass of tissue formed in the uterus following pregnancy that contains remnants of chorionic or decidual tissue **2** : decidual tissue induced in the uterus (as by trauma) in the absence of pregnancy

dec·i·mal·i·za·tion \,desəməlә'zāshən\ *n* -S [[1]*decimal* + *-ization*] : conversion (as of a currency) to a decimal system — **dec·i·mal·ize** \'===,līz\ *vt* -ED/-ING/-S

decision table *n* : a table that indicates a course of action to be taken for each value or combination of values of one or more variables or parameters

decision theory *n* : a branch of statistical theory that attempts to quantify the process of making choices between alternatives

decision tree *n* : a tree diagram which is used for making decisions in business or computer programming and of which the branches represent choices with associated risks, costs, results, or probabilities

deck* *n* **1** : TAPE DECK *herein* **2** : a layer of clouds — **on the deck** *adj (or adv)* : at very low altitude — used of an airplane

deck shoe *n* [so called fr. the original use of such shoes on boat decks] : a low step-in shoe with a nonslip sole and an upper resembling that of a moccasin but with a broad flat heel

declaratory* *adj* : relating to or being a policy that is formally declared for diplomatic purposes but may in fact not be the real policy ⟨both the ~ and actual policies of the two countries —M.D.Shulman⟩

de·claw \(,)dē, dē+\ *vt* [*de-* + [1]*claw*] : to remove the claws of (a cat) usu. with the nail matrix and all or part of the last bone of the toe

declining–balance method \¦=¦==-\ *n* : a method of calculating periodic depreciation that involves the determining at regular (as annual) intervals throughout the expected life of an asset of equal percentage amounts of a cost balance which is progressively decreased by subtraction of each prior increment of depreciation from the original cost of the asset — compare STRAIGHT-LINE METHOD *in the Dict*

de·clin·ist \dē'klīnəst\ *n* -S : one who theorizes that a particular nation or society is in or is headed for a state of economic, political, or social decline

de·clot \(')dē, dē+\ *vt* [*de-* + [1]*clot*] : to remove blood clots from

deco *n* -S *often cap* : ART DECO *herein*

decoder* *n* : an electronic device that converts a signal from one form to another; *esp* : one that unscrambles a television transmission

decollate* *vt* : to separate the copies of (as a computer printout produced in multiple copies) — **de·collator** \¦dē+\ *n*

de·colonize \(')dē, dē+\ *vb* [*de-* + *colonize*] *vt* : to free from colonial status ~ *vi* : to grant independence to colonies — **de·colonization** \"+\ *n*

de·commitment \¦dē+\ *n* [*de-* + *commitment*] : a dropping or turning away from a prior commitment

decomposer* *n* : any of various organisms (as many bacteria and fungi) that return constituents of organic substances to ecological cycles by feeding on and breaking down dead protoplasm

de·conglomerate \"+\ *vi* [*de-* + [2]*conglomerate*] : to divide a corporate conglomerate into independent companies — **de·conglomeration** \"+\ *n*

de·construct \"+\ *vt* [*de-* + *construct*; trans. of F *déconstruire*] **1** : to discuss (as a work of literature) using the methods of deconstruction **2** : to take apart or examine (as an accepted view) in order to reveal the basis or composition often with the intention of exposing flaws, inconsistencies, or problems in construction; *broadly* : ANALYZE, CRITICIZE — **de·constructor** \"+\ *n*

de·construction \"+\ *n* [F *déconstruction*, fr. *dé-* de- + *construction*] **1** : a method of literary criticism that assumes that language refers only to itself rather than to an extratextual reality, that asserts multiple conflicting interpretations of a text, and that bases such interpretations on the philosophical, political, or social implications of the use of language in the text rather than on the author's intention **2** : the analysis and examination of something (as a theory) often with the intention of revealing its inadequacy **3** : something that deconstructs or that results from the act or process of deconstructing — **de·con·struc·tion·ism** \¦==shə,nizəm\ *n* — **de·con·struc·tion·ist** \-sh(ə)nəst\ *n or adj* — **de·constructive** \"+\ *adj*

de·con·tex·tu·al·ize \ˌdēkənˈtekschəwəˌlīz, -ˌkän-\ *vt* -ED/-ING/-S [*de-* + *contextual* + *-ize*] : to remove from a context

de·convolution \"+\ *n* [*de-* + *convolution*] : simplification of a complex signal (as instrumental data) usu. by removal of instrument noise

decorative art *n* [prob. trans. of F *art décoratif*] **1** : art that is concerned primarily with the creation of useful items (as furniture, ceramics, or textiles) — usu. used in pl. **2** : objects of decorative art

de·cou·page \ˌdākü'päzh, -päzh, ˈ==ˌ=\ *vt* -ED/-ING/-S [*decoupage*, n.] : to decorate the surface of (as a plaque) by the technique of decoupage; *also* : to apply (as cutout pictures) in creating decoupage

de·couple \(ˈ)dē, dė+\ *vt* [*de-* + [1]*couple*] **1** : to reduce or eliminate the coupling of (as circuits or mechanical parts) **2** : to decrease the seismic effect of (a nuclear explosion) by explosion in an underground cavity **3** : SEPARATE — **de·coupler** \"+\ *n*

de·creolization \ˌdē+\ *n* -S [*de-* + *creolization*] : the process of evolving from a creole into a standard language or a variety of a standard language

de·crim·i·nal·ize \(ˈ)dēˈkrimənᵊlˌīz, dəˈ-, -m(ə)nəl-\ *vt* -ED/-ING/-S [*de-* + *criminal* + *-ize*] : to remove or reduce the criminal classification or status of; *esp* : to repeal a strict ban on while keeping under some form of regulation ⟨wanted to ~ the possession of marijuana⟩ — **de·crim·i·nal·iza·tion** \-ˌkrimənᵊlə'zāshən, -līˈ-, -mnəl-, -līˈ-\ *n* -S

de·cumulation \ˌdē+\ *n* [*de-* + *accumulation*] : disposal of something accumulated

DEd *abbr* doctor of education

dedicated* *adj* : given over to a particular purpose ⟨a ~ process control computer⟩

deep* *adj* **1** : LARGE ⟨~ discounts⟩ ⟨~ cuts in the budget⟩ **2** : having many good players ⟨a football team ~ enough to overcome injuries and still win⟩

deep* *adv* : near the outer limits of the normal position of play ⟨the shortstop was playing ~⟩

deep ecology *n, sometimes cap D&E* : a movement or a body of concepts that considers humans no more important than other species and that advocates a corresponding radical readjustment of the relationships between humans and nature — **deep ecologist** *n*

deep focus *n* : a photographic technique or camera setting in which all objects from foreground to background appear in focus

deep pocket *n* **1** : a person or an organization having substantial financial resources **2 deep pockets** *pl* : substantial financial resources — **deep–pock·et·ed** \ˈ=ˈ==\ *also* **deep–poc·ket** \ˈ=ˈ==\ *adj*

deep–sky \ˈ=ˈ=\ *adj* : relating to or existing in space outside the solar system ⟨*deep-sky* objects⟩ ⟨*deep-sky* photography⟩

deep space* *n* : space well outside the earth's atmosphere and esp. that part lying beyond the earth-moon system

deep structure *n* : a formal representation of the underlying semantic content of a sentence; *also* : the structure which such a representation specifies

deer tick *n* : a tick of the genus *Ixodes* (*I. dammini*) that parasitizes mammals including humans and that is a vector of the bacterium causing Lyme disease

de–escalate \(ˈ)dē+\ *vb* [*de-* + *escalate*] *vi* : to decrease in extent, volume, or scope ~ *vt* : LIMIT 3b — **de–escalation** \(ˌ)dē+\ *n*

de–es·ca·la·tor \(ˈ)dēˈeskəˌlād·ə(r), -ātə-, ÷-kyə-\ *n* -S : an advocate of de-escalation

de–es·ca·la·to·ry \-ˌləˌtōrē\ *adj* : of or relating to de-escalation

deet \ˈdēt\ *n* -S [alter. (influenced by [2]*dee*) of *d. t.*, abbr. of *diethyl toluamide*] : a colorless oily liquid insect and tick repellent $C_{12}H_{17}NO$

def \ˈdef\ *adj* [prob. alter. of *death* (fr. the phrase *to death* excessively)] *slang* : COOL 8 ⟨~ music⟩

de·familiarize \ˌdē+\ *vt* [back-formation fr. *defamiliarization*, fr. *de-* + *familiarize* + *-ation*; trans. of Russ *ostranenie*] : to present or render in an unfamiliar form esp. for the artistic or literary purpose of stimulating fresh perception — **de·familiarization** *n*

defang* *vt* : to make harmless or less powerful

default* *vi* : to make an automatic selection esp. in the absence of a choice by a user ⟨since the computer's operating system won't accept such a year, it will ~ to some other date —S.J.Goldman⟩

default* *n* **1** : the absence of a viable alternative — usu. used with *by* ⟨letting the multinationals act as our national planners by ~ —R.J.Barnet⟩ **2** : a selection automatically used by a computer program in the absence of a choice made by the user

defensive* *adj* : of, relating to, or being industries (as foods, utilities, and insurance) which provide essential needs to the ultimate consumer and in which business activity is relatively insensitive to changes in general business activity

defensive medicine *n* : the practice of ordering medical tests, procedures, or consultations of doubtful clinical value in order to protect the prescribing physician from malpractice suits

deferred income* *n* : current income forgone to produce a later higher income (as at retirement)

de·fibrillation \(ˈ)dē, dė+\ *n* [*de-* + *fibrillation*] : restoration (as by electric shock) of the rhythm of a fibrillating heart — **de·fibrillate** \(ˌ)dē, dė+\ *vt* — **de·fi·bril·la·tor** \dēˈfibrəˌlād·ə(r), dė+\ *n* -S

deficit* *n* : a lack or impairment in a functional capacity ⟨cognitive ~*s*⟩ ⟨a hearing ~⟩

[1]**de·focus** \(ˈ)dē, dė+\ *vb* [*de-* + [1]*focus*] *vt* : to cause (as a beam of radiation or a lens) to be out of focus ⟨~*ed* his eye⟩ ⟨a ~*ed* image⟩ ~ *vi* : to lose accuracy of focus : become defocused

[2]**defocus** \"\ *n* : a result of defocusing; *esp* : an image (as on motion-picture film) deliberately blurred for dramatic effect

de·fog \"+\ *vt* [*de-* + [3]*fog*] : to remove fog or condensed moisture from — **de·fog·ger** *n* -S

deform·able \+əbəl\ *adj* : capable of being deformed

de·fragment \ˌdē+\ *also* **de·frag** \"+ˈfrag\ *vt* [*defragment* fr. *de-* + [1]*fragment*; *defrag* short for *defragment*] : to reorganize separated fragments of related data on (a computer disk) into a contiguous arrangement — **de·fragmentation** \"+\ *n*

de·fragment·er \ˌ=ˈ==ə(r)\ *also* **de·frag·ger** \ˌ=ˈ=ə(r)\ *n* -S : software that defragments a computer disk

de·fund \(ˈ)dē, dė+\ *vt* [*de-* + [2]*fund*] : to withdraw funding from (as a government-funded program)

defuse* *vt* : to make less dangerous, potent, or tense

degeneracy* *n* : the coding of an amino acid by more than one codon of the genetic code

degenerate* *adj* **1** : being mathematically simpler (as by having a factor or constant equal to zero) than the typical case ⟨the graph of a second degree equation yielding two intersecting lines is a ~ hyperbola⟩ **2 a** : having two or more states or subdivisions esp. of the same energy or frequency ⟨~ orbital⟩ ⟨~ oscillation⟩ **b** *of a semiconductor* : having a sufficient concentration of impurities to conduct electricity as a semimetal **3** : having more than one codon representing an amino acid; *also* : being such a codon **4** : consisting of degenerate matter ⟨a ~ star⟩

deglaze *vt* -ED/-ING/-S [modif. (influenced by [2]*glaze*) of F *déglacer*, lit., to melt the ice from, fr. *dé-* de- + *glacer* to freeze, fr. *glace* ice — more at GLACIER] : to dissolve the small particles of sautéed meat remaining in (a pan) by adding a liquid and heating

de·grad·able \dəˈgrādəbəl, dē-\ *adj* : capable of being chemically degraded ⟨~ detergents⟩ — **de·grad·abil·i·ty** \ˌ=ˌ==ˈbiləd·ē, -ətē\ *n* -ES

de·granulation \(ˌ)dē, dė+\ *n* [*de-* + *granulation*] : the process of losing granules; *specif* : the process by which cytoplasmic granules (as of mast cells) release their contents

de·hire \"+\ *vt* [*de-* + [2]*hire*] : to dismiss esp. from an executive position

de·hy·drase \dēˈhīˌdrās, -āz\ *n* -S [*dehydr-* + *-ase*] **1** : DEHYDROGENASE **2** : DEHYDRATASE *herein*

de·hy·dra·tase \-ˌdrəˌtās, -āz\ *n* -S [*dehydrate* + *-ase*] : an enzyme that catalyzes the removal of oxygen and hydrogen from metabolites in the proportion in which they form water

de·hy·dro·chlo·ri·nase \(ˌ)dēˌhīdrəˈklōrəˌnās, -lȯr-, -āz\ *n* -S [*dehydrochlorinate* (herein) + *-ase*] : an enzyme that dehydrochlorinates a chlorinated hydrocarbon (as DDT) and is found esp. in some DDT-resistant insects

de·hy·dro·chlo·ri·na·tion \-ˌklōrəˈnāshən, -lȯr-\ *n* [*de-* + *hydr-* + *chlorine* + *-ation*] : the process of removing hydrogen and chlorine or hydrogen chloride from a compound — **de·hy·dro·chlo·ri·nate** \-ˈklōrəˌnāt, -lȯr-\ *vt*

de·hy·dro·epi·androsterone \(ˌ)dēˌhīdrōˌepē+\ *n* [*dehydr-* + *epi-* + *androsterone*] : an androgenic ketosteroid $C_{19}H_{28}O_2$ secreted by the adrenal cortex that is an intermediate in the biosynthesis of testosterone

de·hy·dro·iso·androsterone \-ˌī(ˌ)sō+\ *n* [*dehydr-* + *is-* + *androsterone*] : DEHYDROEPIANDROSTERONE *herein*

de·individualize \(ˈ)dē+\ *vt, see -ize in Explan Notes* [*de-* + *individualize*] : to remove or destroy the individuality of : deprive of individuality — **de·individualization** \"+\ *n*

de·industrialization \ˌdē+\ *n* [*de-* + *industrialization*] : the reduction or destruction of a nation's industrial capacity; *also* : the loss of industrial plants and jobs — **de·industrialize** \"+\ *vb*

dei·non·y·chus \(ˌ)dīˈnänəkəs\ *n* [NL, fr. *din-* + Gk *-onychos* -clawed (fr. *onych-*, *onyx* nail, claw) — more at NAIL] **1** *cap* : a genus of small bipedal carnivorous theropod dinosaurs from the Cretaceous **2** -ES : a dinosaur of the genus *Deinonychus*

de·institutionalization \"+\ *n* [*de-* + *institutionalization*] **1** : the release of institutionalized individuals from institutional care (as in a psychiatric hospital) to care in the community **2** : the reform or modification of an institution to remove or disguise its institutional character — **de·institutionalize** \"+\ *vt*

deix·is \ˈdīksės\ *n* -ES [Gk, lit., display, fr. *deiknynai* to show — more at DICTION] : the pointing or specifying function of some words (as definite articles and demonstrative pronouns)

déjà vu* *n* **1** : a feeling that one has seen or heard something before ⟨a nightmarish *déjà vu* hit us as we sat in on the . . . conference —*Wall Street Jour.*⟩ **2** : something overly or unpleasantly familiar ⟨the appointment seems like a case of *déjà vu*—E.B.Fiske⟩

déjà vu \ˌdā(ˌ)zhäˈvü, -ˌzhä-, -zhə-; *F* dāzhȧvᵫ\ *adj* : so familiar as to be uninteresting : COMMONPLACE ⟨much of what was blasted as revolutionary in 1931 has long since become *déjà vu*—J.J.Lamberts⟩

deka·gram *n* [by alter.] : DECAGRAM

deka·li·ter *n* [by alter.] : DECALITER

deka·me·ter *n* [by alter.] : [2]DECAMETER

deka·met·ric *adj* [by alter.] : DECAMETRIC *herein*

deka·stere *n* [by alter.] : DECASTERE

deke \ˈdēk\ *vb* -ED/-ING/-S [short for [2]*decoy*] *vt* : to fake (an opponent) out of position (as in ice hockey) ~ *vi* : to deke an opponent — **deke** *n* -S

delay* *n* : a play in football in which a ballcarrier or potential receiver delays momentarily as if to block before receiving a handoff or running a prescribed pattern

delayed–stress syndrome \ˌ=ˈ=ˈ=-\ *also* **delayed–stress disorder** *n* : POST-TRAUMATIC STRESS DISORDER *herein*

de·legitimate \ˌdē+\ *vt* [*de-* + [2]*legitimate*] : to diminish or destroy the legitimacy, prestige, or authority of : INVALIDATE — **de·legitimation** \"+\ *n*

de·legitimize \(ˈ)dē+\ *vt* [*de-* + *legitimize*] : DELEGITIMATE *herein* — **de·legitimization** \"+\ *n* -S

deli *also* **del·ly** \ˈdelē, -li\ *n, pl* **del·is** *also* **del·lies** [*deli* by shortening; *delly* by shortening & alter.] : DELICATESSEN

delicacy* *n* : the degree of differentiation between subcategories of linguistic categories ⟨by increase in ~, the primary class is broken down into secondary classes —M.A.K.Halliday⟩

delimiter* *n* : a character that marks the beginning or end of a unit of data (as on a magnetic tape)

deliver* *vt* **1** : to cause (oneself) to produce something as if by giving birth ⟨~*ed* himself of half an autobiography —H.C.Schonberg⟩ **2** : to come through with : PRODUCE ⟨the new car ~*s* high gas mileage⟩ ~ *vi* : to produce the promised, desired, or expected results : come through ⟨failed to ~ on their promises⟩

de·localized \ˌdē+\ *adj* [*de-* + *localized*, fr. past part. of *localize*] : relating to, containing, or being a charge or charge carrier that can reside at any of several locations within a molecule ⟨~ electron⟩

delt \ˈdelt\ *n* -S [by shortening] : DELTOID — usu. used in pl.

delta* *adj, often cap* : of, relating to, or characteristic of the region of the alluvial plain east of the Mississippi River in western Mississippi ⟨~ blues⟩

delta wave *also* **delta*** *or* **delta rhythm** *n* : a high amplitude electrical rhythm of the brain with a frequency of less than 6 cycles per second that occurs esp. in deep sleep, in infancy, and in many diseased conditions of the brain

deltoid tuberosity *n* : a rough triangular bump on the outer side of the middle of the humerus that is the site of insertion of the deltoid muscle

de·magnify \(ˈ)dē, dė+\ *vt* [*de-* + *magnify*] : to reduce the size of (as a photographic image or an electron beam) — **de·magnification** \(ˌ)dē, dė+\ *n*

demagogue* *vb* ~ *vt* : to treat (as an issue) in a demagogic manner

demand* *n* — **on demand*** *adv* : when requested or needed ⟨video *on demand*⟩

demand–pull \ˌ=ˈ=\ *n* [[1]*demand* + [2]*pull*] : an increase or upward trend in spendable money that tends to result in increased competition for available goods and services and a corresponding increase in consumer prices — compare COST-PUSH *herein* — **demand–pull** *adj*

demand–side \ˌ=ˈ=ˈ=\ *adj* [*demand side* (sector of an economy that demands a commodity)] : of, relating to, or being an economic theory that advocates the use of government spending and growth in the money supply to stimulate the demand for goods and services and therefore expand economic activity; *also* : KEYNESIAN

de·marketing \(ˌ)dē, dė+\ *n* [*de-* + *marketing*] : the use of advertising to decrease demand for a product that is in short supply

de·masculinize \"+\ *vt* [*de-* + *masculinize*] : to remove the masculine character or qualities of ⟨~ the behavior of young men⟩ — **de·masculinization** \"+\ *n*

dem·e·ton \ˈdeməˌtän\ *n* -S [prob. fr. ISV *di*ethyl + *mer*capt- + *-thioic* + [2]*-on*] : a mixture of organophosphorus insecticides used as a systemic on plants

demimonde* *n* : a distinctive class, group, or activity that is often an isolated part of a larger class, group, or activity ⟨the pop music ~⟩ ⟨the literary ~⟩; *esp* : one having little reputation or prestige

de min·i·mis \dēˈminəmės, dāˈmēnimis\ *adj* [NL, concerning trifles] : lacking significance or importance : so minor as to merit disregard

demi–pen·sion \ˌdemē(ˈ)pänˈsyōⁿ, -ˌpänsēˈōⁿ\ *n* [F, fr. *demi-* half + *pension* board] : MODIFIED AMERICAN PLAN *herein*

de·mist·er \dēˈmistə(r), dė+\ *n* -S [*de-* + [1]*mist* + [2]*-er*] *Brit* : DEFROSTER

demo* *n* **1** : DEMONSTRATION **2** : DEMONSTRATOR **3** : a recording intended to show off a song or performer to a record producer

demographic* *adj* : of or relating to demographics; *esp* : relating to or intended for a segment of the population identified by demographics ⟨a ~ edition of a magazine⟩ ⟨~ advertising⟩

demographic *n* -S [*demographic*, adj.] **1 demographics** *pl* : statistical characteristics (as age, sex, income, educational level) of a segment of a human population used esp. to identify markets **2** : a market or a segment of the population identified by demographics — sometimes used in pl. ⟨a growing . . . young-female ~ —James Wolcott⟩

demolition derby *n* **1** : a contest in which drivers ram old cars into one another until only one car remains running **2** : something that resembles a demolition derby in destructiveness

de·mothball \(ˈ)dē+\ *vt* [*de-* + [2]*mothball*] : to remove the preservative covering in order to reactivate (as ships)

de·mystify \"+\ *vt* [*de-* + *mystify*] : to eliminate the mystifying features of ⟨his novels . . . ~ death, confronting us with the omnipresent reality of it —Harriet Blodgett⟩ — **de·mystification** \"+\ *n*

demythologize* *vt* : to divest of mythical elements or associations

den·dro·climatic \ˌdendrō+\ *adj* [*dendr-* + *climatic*] : of, relating to, or applying dendroclimatology ⟨~ research⟩

dendro·climatology \ˌdendrō+\ *n* [*dendr-* + *climatology*] : a branch of dendrochronology concerned with constructing records of past climates and climatic events by analysis of tree growth characteristics and esp. annual rings — **dendro·climatological** \"+\ *adj* — **dendro·climatologist** \"+\ *n*

den·dro·dendritic \ˌdendrō+\ *adj* [*dendr-* + *dendritic*] : relating to or being a nerve synapse between a dendrite of one cell and a dendrite of another

de·ni·abil·i·ty \dəˌnīəˈbiləd·ē, dē-\ *n* -ES [*deniable* + *-ity*] : the ability of an official to deny something esp. on the basis of being officially uninformed

denial* *n* : a psychological defense mechanism in which confrontation with a personal problem or with reality is avoided by denying the existence of the problem or reality

density function *n* : PROBABILITY DENSITY FUNCTION

den·som·e·ter \denˈsäməd·ə(r)\ *n* [ISV *dens-* (fr. L *densus* dense) + *-o-* + *-meter*] : an instrument for measuring the porosity of paper by forcing air through it

den·tur·ist \ˈdenchərəst\ *n* -S [*denture* + [1]*-ist*] : a dental technician who makes, fits, and repairs dentures directly for the public

de·nu·cle·ar·ize \(ˈ)dēˈn(y)üklēəˌrīz, ÷-kyələˌrīz\ *vt* -ED/-ING/-S *see -ize in Explan Notes* [*de-* + *nuclear* + *-ize*] : to remove nuclear arms from : prohibit the use of nuclear arms in — **de·nu·cle·ar·iza·tion** \(ˌ)dēˌn(y)üklēərəˈzāshən, ÷-kyələr-, -ˌrīˈz-\ *n*

denver boot *n, usu cap D* [fr. *Denver*, Colo., where it was first used in the U.S.] : a metal clamp that locks onto one of the wheels of an automobile and must be unlocked before a motorist can drive off (as after payment of a fine)

de·orbit \(ˈ)dē+\ *vb* [*de-* + *orbit*] *vi* : to go out of orbit ~ *vt* : to cause to deorbit ⟨~ a spacecraft⟩ — **deorbit** *n*

de·oxy·cytidine \(ˌ)dēˌäksē+\ *n* [*deoxy-* + *cytidine*] : a nucleoside consisting of cytosine combined with deoxyribose that occurs esp. as a component of DNA

de·oxy·ri·bo·nucleotide \(ˌ)dēˌäksēˌrī(ˌ)bō+\ *n* [*deoxyribose* + *nucleotide*] : a nucleotide that contains deoxyribose and is a constituent of DNA

de·part·ee \dəˌpärˈtē, ˌdē-\ *n* -S [[1]*depart* + *-ee*] : one who is departing or has departed

department* *n* : a category consisting esp. of a measurable activity or attribute ⟨lacking in the trustworthiness ~ —Garrison Keillor⟩

dependence* *also* **dependance*** *n* **1** : a drug addiction **2** : HABITUATION 2b

dependent* *adj* **1** : affected with a drug dependence **2 a** : not mathematically or statistically independent ⟨a ~ set of vectors⟩ ⟨~ events⟩ **b** : EQUIVALENT 1 *herein* ⟨~ equations⟩

de·pic·ture \dəˈpikchə(r), dē-, -ksh-\ *vt* [blend of *depict* and [2]*picture*] **1** : DEPICT **2** : IMAGINE — **de·pic·ture·ment** \-mənt\ *n* -S

de·politicize \ˌdē+\ *vt* [*de-* + *politicize*] : to remove the political character from : take out of the realm of politics — **de·po·lit·i·ci·za·tion** \ˌdēpəˌlid·əsəˈzāshən, -ˌsīˈ-\ *n* -S

de·pollute \"+\ *vt* [*de-* + *pollute*] : to remove the pollution from — **de·pollution** \"+\ *n*

dep·re·nyl \ˈdeprəˌnil\ *n* -S [perh. fr. ISV *d*imethyl + *p*ropyne + ph*enyl*] : an optically active compound $C_{13}H_{17}N$ that is an inhibitor of monoamine oxidase usu. administered in the form of its levorotatory hydrochloride esp. in the treatment of Parkinson's disease

depression glass *n, usu cap D* : glassware mass-produced in a variety of colors and patterns during the late 1920s and 1930s

de·pressurize \(ˈ)dē+\ *vt* [*de-* + *pressurize*] : to release pressure from ⟨astronauts ~ the spacecraft before a spacewalk⟩ — **de·pressurization** \"+\ *n*

de·program \"+\ *vt* [*de-* + [2]*program*] : to dissuade or try to dissuade from strongly held convictions (as of a religious nature) or a firmly established or innate behavior pattern ⟨the necessity of countering propaganda and *deprogramming* the indoctrinated —Toni Cade Bambara⟩ — **de·programmer** \"+\ *n* — **de·programming** \"+\ *n*

de·pro·tein·ate \(ˈ)dēˈprōˌtēˌnāt *also* -ˌprōd·ēəˌn- *or* -ōtēəˌn-\ *vt* -ED/-ING/-S [*de-* + *protein* + [4]*-ate*] : DEPROTEINIZE — **de·pro·tein·ation** \(ˈ)dēˌprōˌtēˈnāshən *also* -ˌprōd·ēəˈn- *or* -ōtēəˈn-\ *n* -S

de·quer·vain's disease \dəkerˌvaⁿz-\ *n, usu cap Q* [after Fritz *de Quervain* †1940 Swiss surgeon] : inflammation of tendons and their sheaths at the styloid process of the radius that often causes pain in the thumb side of the wrist

de·rail·leur \dəˈrālə(r), dē-\ *n* -S [F *dérailleur*, fr. *dérailler* to go off the track (fr. *dé-* de- + *rail* rail, fr. E) + *-eur* -or] : a mechanism for shifting gears on a bicycle that operates by moving the chain from one set of exposed gears to another ⟨10-speed ~⟩

de·regulate \(ˈ)dē, dė+\ *vb* [*de-* + *regulate*] *vt* : DECONTROL ⟨proposals to ~ natural-gas prices —*Wall Street Jour.*⟩ ~ *vi* : to remove the rules or restrictions on an industry ⟨latest moves to ~ . . . are working their way through three important sectors of the economy —Susan Lee⟩ — **de·regulation** \(ˌ)dē, dė+\ *n* — **de·regulator** \"+\ *n* — **de·regulatory** \"+\ *adj*

de·repress \ˌdē+\ *vt* [*de-* + *repress*] : to activate (a gene or enzyme synthesis) by releasing from a blocked state — **de·repression** \"+\ *n*

derisory* *adj* : laughably small ⟨land could be bought for a ~ sum⟩

derivative* *n* : a contract or security that derives its value from that of an underlying asset (as another security) or from the value of a rate (as of interest or currency exchange) or index of asset value (as a stock index)

derm·abrasion \ˈdərm+\ *n* [*derm-* + *abrasion*] : surgical removal of skin blemishes or imperfections (as scars or tattoos) by abrasion (as with sandpaper or wire brushes)

dermatitis her·pe·ti·for·mis \-ˌhərpəd·əˈfȯ(ə)rməs, -ȯ(ə)m-\ *n* [NL, skin inflammation resembling herpes] : chronic dermatitis characterized by eruption of itching papules, vesicles, and lesions resembling urticaria typically in clusters

der·mat·o·pathology \(ˌ)dərˌmad·ə, ˌdərməd·ō+\ *n* [*dermat-* + *pathology*] : pathology of the skin — **dermatopathologist** \"+\ *n*

der·ma·toph·a·goi·des \ˌdərməˌtäfəˈgȯi(ˌ)dēz\ *n, cap* [NL, fr. *Dermatophagus*, an arachnid genus (fr. *dermat-* + *-phagus*) + *-oides* -oid] : a genus of mites (family Pyroglyphidae) including several that scavenge shed flakes of human skin and dander and cause allergy

der·mom·e·ter \(ˌ)dərˈmäməd·ər, -ətər\ *n* -S [*derm-* + *-meter*] : an instrument used to measure the electrical resistance of the skin

der·mo·necrotic \ˌdər(ˌ)mō+\ *adj* [*derm-* + *necrotic*] : relating to or causing necrosis of the skin ⟨a ~ toxin⟩ ⟨~ effects⟩

de·romanticize \ˌdē+\ *vt* [*de-* + *romanticize*] : to remove the romance from : make mundane

DES \ˌdē(ˌ)ēˈes\ *n* -ES [*d*iethyl*s*tilbestrol] : DIETHYLSTILBESTROL

de·sa·li·nate \(ˈ)dēˈsaləˌnāt, -sā-\ *vt* -ED/-ING/-S [*de-* + [1]*saline* + [4]*-ate*] : to remove salt from ⟨~ seawater⟩ — **de·sa·li·na·tor** \-ˌnād·ə(r)\ *n* -S

de·salinize \(ˈ)dē+\ *vt* [*de-* + *salinize*] : DESALINATE *herein*

des·a·pa·re·cido \(ˌ)dāsə(ˌ)päːrəˈsēd·ō, (ˌ)de-\ *n* -S [Sp, lit., disappeared, past part. of *desaparecer* to disappear, fr. *des-* [1]dis- (fr. L) + *aparecer* to appear, fr. (assumed) VL *apparescere*, incho. of L *apparēre* to be visible, appear — more at APPEAR] : an Argentine citizen who has been abducted and usu. murdered by right-wing terrorists

descending colon *n* : the part of the large intestine on the left side that extends from the bend below the spleen to the sigmoid flexure — compare ASCENDING COLON *herein*, TRANSVERSE COLON *in the Dict*

de·school \(ˈ)dē+\ *vt* [*de-* + [1]*school*] : to eliminate traditional schools from ⟨the movement to ~ society —John Holt⟩

descriptor* *n* **1** : a word or phrase (as an index term) used to identify an item (as a subject or document) esp. in an information retrieval system; *also* : an alphanumeric symbol so used **2** : something (as a word or phrase or a characteristic feature) that serves to describe or identify

de·select \ˌdē+\ *vt* [*de-* + *select*] : DISMISS, REJECT

de·sert·i·fi·ca·tion \də̇ˌzərd·əfə̇ˈkāshən\ *n* -S [[1]*desert* + *-ification* (as in *saponification*)] : the process of becoming arid land or desert (as from land mismanagement or climate change)

designated driver *n* : a person chosen to abstain from intoxicants (as alcohol) so as to transport others safely who are not abstaining

designated hitter *n* **1** : a baseball player designated at the start of the game to bat in place of the pitcher without causing the pitcher to be removed from the game **2** : REPRESENTATIVE, SUBSTITUTE

de·sign·er \də̇ˈzīnə(r), dēˈ-\ *adj* [*designer*, n.] **1** : of, relating to, or produced by a designer; *esp* : displaying the name, signature, or logo of a designer ⟨~ jeans⟩ **2** : having a distinctive quality intended to reflect the latest in sophisticated taste or fashion ⟨~ ice cream⟩ ⟨a ~ haircut⟩

designer drug *n* [so called fr. the likening of such alterations to the stylistic embellishments of designer apparel] **1** : a synthetic version of a controlled substance (as heroin) that is produced with a slightly altered molecular structure to avoid being classified as an illicit drug **2** : a synthetic drug created (as by genetic engineering) to treat a particular medical condition esp. by producing a specific effect on the body's biochemistry

de·si·pra·mine \də̇ˈziprəˌmēn\ *n* -S [*desmethyl* (fr. *des-* + *methyl*) + imi*pramine* (herein)] : a tricyclic antidepressant $C_{18}H_{22}N_2$ administered in the form of its hydrochloride esp. in the treatment of endogenous depressions (as a bipolar disorder)

[1]**desktop** \ˈ=ˌ=\ *adj* : of a size that can be conveniently used on a desk or table ⟨~ computer⟩

[2]**desktop** *n* **1** : a desktop computer **2** : the top of an office desk simulated by a computer program

desktop publishing *n* : the production of printed matter by means of a desktop computer having a layout program that integrates text and graphics

des·mo·some \ˈdezməˌsōm\ *n* -S [*desm-* + [4]*-some*] : a specialized local thickening of the plasma membrane of an epithelial cell that serves to anchor contiguous cells together — **des·mo·som·al** \-əl\ *adj*

des·mos·ter·ol \dezˈmästəˌrōl, -ˌrōl\ *n* [*desm-* + *sterol*] : a precursor $C_{27}H_{44}O$ of cholesterol that tends to accumulate in blood serum when cholesterol synthesis is inhibited

de·spin \(ˈ)dē+\ *vt* [*de-* + [1]*spin*] : to stop the rotation of or reduce the speed of rotation of (as a satellite)

de–sta·lin·iza·tion \(ˌ)dēˌstälənə̇ˈzāshən, -tal-, -ˌnīˈz-\ *n* -S *usu cap S* [*destalinize* + *-ation*] : the discrediting of Stalin and his policies

de·struct \ˈdēˌstrəkt, də̇ˈs-, dēˈs-\ *n* -S [*destruct*, v.] : the deliberate destruction of a rocket after launching esp. during a test; *also* : destruction of a device or material (as to prevent its falling into enemy hands)

desultory* *adj* : disappointing in progress, performance, or quality ⟨a ~ wine⟩ ⟨a ~ fifth place finish⟩

de·synchronization \(ˈ)dē+\ *n* [*de-* + *synchronization*] : the process or result of getting out of synchronization ⟨~ of circadian rhythms⟩ — **de·synchronize** \"+\ *vt*

deterrence* *n* : the maintaining of vast military power and weaponry in order to discourage war

detonate* *vt* : to set off in a burst of activity : SPARK ⟨programs that *detonated* controversies⟩

[1]**de·tox** \ˈdēˌtäks\ *n* -ES *often attrib* [by shortening] **1** : detoxification from an intoxicating or addictive substance ⟨a unit providing ~ for adolescents⟩ ⟨a ~ program⟩ ⟨~ clinics⟩ **2** : a detox program, ward, or clinic ⟨countless stints in state and private ~*es* —Gail Caldwell⟩

[2]**detox** *vb* -ED/-ING/-ES [by shortening] : DETOXIFY *herein*

detoxify* *vt* **1** : to free (as a drug user or an alcoholic) from an intoxicating or an addictive substance in the body or from dependence on or addiction to such a substance ⟨the clinic started ~*ing* him by gradually lowering his dosage —J.M.Markham⟩ **2** : NEUTRALIZE 2 ⟨~*ing* tensions that arise between people of divergent tastes and goals —M.B.Duberman⟩ **3** : to render (a harmful substance) harmless ~ *vi* : to become free of addiction to a drug or alcohol — **detoxification*** *n*

de·tri·ti·vore \də̇ˈtrīd·əˌvō(ə)r, -ˌvȯr\ *n* -S [ISV *detritus* + *-i-* + *-vore*; orig. formed in G] : an organism (as a small invertebrate animal) that feeds on dead and decomposing organic matter (as leaf litter in a forest or stream) — **de·tri·tiv·o·rous** \ˌdetrə̇ˈtiv(ə)rəs\ *adj*

de·tumescent \ˌdē+\ *adj* : characterized by detumescence

deu·ter·ate \ˈd(y)üd·əˌrāt\ *vt* -ED/-ING/-S [*deuterium* + [4]*-ate*] : to introduce deuterium into (a compound)

developed *adj* [fr. past part. of *develop*] : having a relatively high level of industrialization and standard of living ⟨a ~ country⟩

de·vel·op·ing *adj* [fr. pres. part. of *develop*] : UNDERDEVELOPED 3 ⟨~ nations⟩

developmentally disabled *adj* : having a physical or mental handicap (as of psychosocial or cognitive functioning) which impedes or prevents one's normal development

de·volatilize \(ˈ)dē, də+\ *vt* [*de-* + *volatilize*] : to remove volatile material from (as coal) — **de·volatilization** \"+\ *n*

devon rex *n, usu cap D & often cap R* [fr. *Devon*, county in England] : any of a breed of rex cats with a very short curly coat and a small head with large ears and a strongly marked stop

de·wormer \ˌdē, də+\ *n* [*deworm* + [2]*-er*] : WORMER 1

dex \ˈdeks\ *n* -ES [short for *Dexedrine* (herein)] : the sulfate of dextroamphetamine

dexa·meth·a·sone \ˌdeksəˈmethəˌsōn, -ˌzōn\ *n* -S [*dexa-* (blend of *deca-* and *hexa-*) + *methyl* + *-a-* (perh. fr. *pregnane*) + *-sone* (as in *cortisone*)] : a synthetic glucocorticoid $C_{22}H_{29}FO_5$ used esp. as an anti-inflammatory and antiallergic agent

dex·amphetamine \ˌdeks+\ *n* [alter. of *dextroamphetamine*] *chiefly Brit* : DEXTROAMPHETAMINE

Dex·e·drine \ˈdeksə̇ˌdrēn, -drə̇n\ *trademark* — used for a preparation of the sulfate of dextroamphetamine

dex·fen·flur·a·mine \ˌdeksˈfenflürəˌmēn\ *n* [alter. of *dextrofenfluramine*, fr. *dextr-* + *fenfluramine* (herein)] : the dextrorotatory form of fenfluramine formerly used in the form of its hydrochloride to treat obesity but no longer used due to its association with heart valve disease — see FEN-PHEN *herein*

dex·ies \ˈdeksēz\ *n pl* [*dex* (herein) + *-ie* + [1]*-s*] : tablets or capsules of the sulfate of dextroamphetamine

dex·tran·ase \-strəˌnās, -ˌnāz\ *n* -S [*dextran* + *-ase*] : a hydrolase that prevents tooth decay by breaking down dextran and eliminating dental plaque

dex·tro·me·thor·phan \ˌdekstrōmə̇ˈthȯrˌfan\ *n* -S [*dextr-* + *methyl* + *morphinan* parent substance of morphine alkaloids, fr. *morphine* + [3]*-an*] : a nonaddicting cough suppressant $C_{18}H_{25}NO$ that is widely used esp. in the form of its hydrobromide in over-the-counter cough and cold preparations

dex·tro·propoxyphene \ˌdekstrə+\ *n* [*dextr-* + *propoxyphene* herein] : PROPOXYPHENE *herein*

[1]**DH** *n* -S : DESIGNATED HITTER *herein*

[2]**DH** *vi* -ED/-ING/-S : to play as a DH in a baseball game

DHEA *abbr* dehyroepiandrosterone *herein*

di·a·be·tol·o·gist \ˌdīəbēˈtäləjə̇st, -biˈt-\ *n* -S [*diabetes* + *-ologist* (as in *geologist*)] : a specialist in diabetes

diagnose* *vt* : to diagnose a disease or condition in ⟨let doctors . . . ~ patients electronically —*Washington Post*⟩

di·ag·o·nal·ize \dīˈagənᵊlˌīz, -gnəl-\ *vt* -ED/-ING/-S [[1]*diagonal* + *-ize*] : to convert (a matrix) to a diagonal matrix — **di·ag·o·nal·iz·able** \-ˌīzəbəl\ *adj* — **di·ag·o·nal·iza·tion** \-ˌag(ə)nᵊlə̇ˈzāshən, -gnəl-\ *n* -S

diagonal matrix *n* : a matrix that has all the nonzero elements located along the diagonal from upper left to lower right

dialect* *n* : a version of a computer programming language that differs from other versions of the same language only in minor ways

dialog box *n* : an interactive window on a computer screen for choosing options or inputting information

dialogue* *n* : a discussion between representatives of parties to a conflict that is aimed at resolution

dial–up \ˈ=ˌ=\ *adj* [*dial up*, vb.] : relating to or being a standard telephone line used for computer communications; *also* : accessible via a standard telephone line ⟨a *dial-up* information service⟩

dialysis* *n* : either of two medical procedures to remove wastes or toxins from the blood and adjust fluid and electrolyte imbalances by utilizing the different rates at which substances diffuse through a semipermeable membrane: **a** : the process of removing blood from an artery (as of a kidney patient), purifying it by dialysis, adding vital substances, and returning it to a vein — called also *hemodialysis* **b** : a procedure performed in the peritoneal cavity in which the peritoneum acts as the semipermeable membrane

di·az·e·pam \dīˈazəˌpam\ *n* -S [benzo*diaze*pine (herein) + *-am* (of unknown origin)] : a synthetic tranquilizer $C_{16}H_{13}ClN_2O$ used esp. to relieve anxiety and tension and as a muscle relaxant — see VALIUM *herein*

Di·az·i·non \dīˈazə̇ˌnän\ *trademark* — used for an organophosphate insecticide $C_{12}H_{21}N_2O_3PS$ that is a cholinesterase inhibitor dangerous to human beings if ingested

di·azo·benzenesulfonic acid \(ˌ)dīˌazō, -ˌāzō+ . . .-\ *n* [*diaz-* + *benzene* + *sulfonic*] : a white or reddish crystalline acid derivative $C_6H_4N_2O_3S$ of sulfanilic acid that is used as the reagent in the diazo reaction

di·az·ox·ide \ˌdīˌazˈäkˌsīd\ *n* [*diaz-* + *oxide*] : a drug $C_8H_7ClN_2O_2S$ used in the treatment of hypoglycemia and in the emergency treatment of hypertension

di·ben·zo·fu·ran \(ˈ)dīˌben(ˌ)zō+\ *n* [*dibenz-* + *furan*] : a highly toxic chemical compound $C_{12}H_8O$ that is a derivative of furan, is used in chemical synthesis and as an insecticide, and is a hazardous pollutant in its chlorinated form

di·bro·mo·chlo·ro·pro·pane \(ˌ)dīˌbrōmōˌklōrōˈprōˌpān, -ˌklȯr-\ *n* [*dibrom-* + *chlor-* + *propane*] : DBCP *herein*

dice* *n* : a close contest between two racing-car drivers for position during a race

dice* *vi* : to engage in a dice

di·cen·tric \(ˈ)dīˌsen·trik\ *n* -S [*dicentric*, adj.] : a dicentric chromosome

dic·ey \ˈdīsē\ *adj* **dic·i·er**; **dic·i·est** [[2]*dice* + [1]*-y*] : RISKY, UNPREDICTABLE ⟨consumer loans, which are becoming *dicier* with rising unemployment —*Business Week*⟩

di·chlor·vos \(ˈ)dīˌklō(ə)rˌväs, -lȯ(-, -vəs\ *n* -ES [*dichlor-* + vinyl + ph*os*phate] : an organophosphorus insecticide and anthelmintic $C_4H_7Cl_2O_4P$ used esp. in veterinary medicine; 2,2-dichlorovinyl dimethyl phosphate — called also *DDVP*

di·chot·ic \(ˈ)dīˌkōd·ik, -käd-\ *adj* [*dich-* + [2]*-otic*] : relating to or involving the presentation of a stimulus to one ear that differs in some respect (as pitch, loudness, frequency, or energy) from a stimulus presented to the other ear ⟨~ listening⟩ — **dich·oti·cal·ly** \-d·ək(ə)lē\ *adv*

dichotomy* *n* : something with seemingly contradictory qualities

dictionary* *n* : a list (as of data items or words) stored in a computer for reference (as for information retrieval or word processing)

di·dan·o·sine \dīˈdanəˌsēn\ *n* -S [alter. of *dideoxyinosine* (herein)] : a synthetic nucleoside analogue $C_{10}H_{12}N_4O_3$ that inhibits replication of retroviruses and is used in the treatment of advanced HIV infection — called also *ddI, dideoxyinosine*

diddle* *vi* : FIDDLE, TOY — usu. used with *with* ⟨*diddling* around with the tape machine —Michael Stephens⟩

did·dly \ˈdid(ᵊ)lē\ *n* -ES [by shortening] *slang* : DIDDLY-SQUAT *herein*

did·dly–squat \ˈdid(ᵊ)lē+\ *n* [perh. alter. (influenced by *diddle*) of *doodley-squat* (herein)] *slang* : the least amount : NOTHING ⟨if everyone ignores it, it won't be worth *diddly-squat* —Andrew Tobias⟩

di·de·oxy·cy·ti·dine \ˌdī(ˌ)dēˌäksēˈsid·ədēn, -ˈsīd·ə-\ *n* [*di-* + *deoxy-* + *cytidine*] : DDC *herein*

di·de·oxy·ino·sine \-ˈinəˌsēn, -ˈinə-, -sən\ *n* [*di-* + *deoxy-* + *inosine*] : DIDANOSINE *herein*

die·sel·ing \ˈdēz(ə)liŋ, ˈdēs(-\ *n* -S [[2]*diesel* + [3]*-ing*] : the continued operation of an internal-combustion engine after the ignition is turned off

dietary fiber *n* : ROUGHAGE 2

diethyl tolu·amide \-ˌtäl(ˌ)yü+\ *n* [*tol-* + *amide*] : DEET *herein*

diethyl zinc *n* : a volatile pyrophoric liquid organometallic compound $C_4H_{10}Zn$ used esp. to catalyze polymerization reactions and to deacidify paper

difference* *vt* : to compute the difference between

differently abled *adj* [*differently* + *disabled*] : HANDICAPPED 1 *herein*, CHALLENGED *herein*

di·functional \(ˈ)dī+\ *adj* [*di-* + *functional*] : of, relating to, or being a compound with two highly reactive sites in each molecule — **di·functionality** \(ˌ)dī+\ *n*

di·ge·ra·ti \ˌdijəˈräd·ē, -ˈrāˌtē\ *n pl* [[1]*digital* + *-erati* (as in *literati*)] : persons well versed in computer use and technology

di·ges·tif \dēzhesˈtēf\ *n* -S [F, lit., digestive] : an alcoholic drink (as brandy or a liqueur) usu. taken after a meal

digital* *adj* **1** : providing a readout in numerical digits ⟨a ~ voltmeter⟩ ⟨a ~ clock radio⟩ **2 a** : relating to an audio recording method in which sound waves are represented digitally (as on magnetic tape) with the result that wow and flutter are eliminated and background noise is greatly reduced **b** : of, relating to, or being a medium on which information (as sound) is recorded digitally ⟨~ audiotape⟩

dig·i·tal·ize \ˈdijə̇dᵊlˌīz\ *vt* -ED/-ING/-S [[1]*digital* + *-ize*] : DIGITIZE

digital recording *n* : the process of recording sound usu. on magnetic tape by the digital representation of sound waves as the sum of minute increments in amplitude

digital versatile disc *or* **digital video disc** *n* : DVD *herein*

digitizing tablet *n* : GRAPHICS TABLET *herein*

di·glos·sia \(ˈ)dīˌgläsēə, -lȯs-\ *n* -S [NL, fr. *di-* + *-glossia*] : the use of two languages, dialects, or sociolects in different social contexts — **di·glos·sic** \-sik\ *adj*

di·hy·dro·tes·tos·ter·one \(ˌ)dīˌhīdrō+\ *n* [*dihydr-* + *testosterone*] : a biologically active metabolite $C_{19}H_{30}O_2$ of testosterone having similar androgenic activity and produced in various tissues (as of the skin and prostate)

di·hy·droxy·acetone \ˌdīhīˌdräksē+\ *n* [*dihydroxy-* + *acetone*] : a glyceraldehyde isomer $C_3H_6O_3$ that is used esp. to stain the skin to simulate a tan

di·hy·droxy·cholecalciferol \"+\ *n* [*dihydroxy-* + *cholecalciferol*] : CALCITRIOL *herein*

di·hy·droxy·phenylalanine \"+\ *n* [*dihydroxy-* + *phenylalanine*] **1** : DOPA **2** : L-DOPA *herein*

dike *var of* DYKE *herein*

dil·ti·a·zem \dilˈtīəzem\ *n* [prob. fr. ISV *dil*ator + benzo*thiazepin*, tricyclic compound structurally similar to benzodiazepine (fr. *benz-* + *thi-* + *az-* + *-epin*, alter. of *-epine* (as in *benzodiazepine* — herein) + *-m* (as in *diazepam* — herein)] : a calcium channel blocker $C_{22}H_{26}N_2O_4S$ used esp. in the form of its hydrochloride as a coronary vasodilator

dilute* *vt* : to decrease the per share value of (common stock) by increasing the total number of shares

di·lu·tive \(ˈ)dīˈl(y)üd·iv, dəˈl-\ *adj* [[1]*dilute* + [1]*-ive*] : reducing or involving reduction of per share income of a corporate stock ⟨the ~ effect of stock options and convertible securities⟩

dim bulb *n, slang* : DIMWIT

dime* *n* **1** *slang* **a** : 10 dollars **b** *or* **dime bag** : a packet containing 10 dollars worth of an illicit drug (as marijuana) **2** *slang* : a sentence of 10 years in prison

dimension* *n* : the number of elements in a basis of a vector space

dime–store *adj* [*dime store*, n.] **1** : INEXPENSIVE ⟨*dime-store* perfume⟩ **2** : TAWDRY, SECOND-RATE ⟨what we have here is *dime-store* philosophizing —Jonathan Yardley⟩

di·meth·o·ate \ˌdīˈmethəˌwāt\ *n* -S [*dime*thyl + *-thioic* + [1]*-ate*] : an organophosphorus insecticide and miticide $C_5H_{12}NO_3PS_2$ used esp. on crops and ornamental plants

dimethylhydrazine \ˌ=ˌ=ˌ==ˌ=ˌ=\ *n* [*dimethyl* + *hydrazine*] : either of two flammable corrosive isomeric liquids $C_2H_8N_2$ which are methylated derivatives of hydrazine and of which one is used in rocket fuels

dimethylnitrosamine \ˌ=ˌ=ˌ==(ˌ)nīˈtrōsəˌmēn, -ˌtrōˈsamən\ *n* [*dimethyl* + *nitrosamine*] : a carcinogenic nitrosamine $C_2H_6N_2O$ that occurs esp. in tobacco smoke

dimethyl sulfoxide *n* [*dimethyl* + *sulfoxide*] : a compound C_2H_6SO obtained as a by-product in wood-pulp manufacture and used as a solvent and in medicine esp. as an anti-inflammatory agent (as in the treatment of interstitial cystitis) — called also *DMSO*

dimethyl terephthalate *n* : a chemical $C_{10}H_{10}O_2$ used for making polyester film and fiber

dimethyltryptamine \ˌ=ˌ=ˌ==ˌ=(ˌ)=\ *n* [*dimethyl* + *tryptamine*] : an easily synthesized hallucinogenic drug $C_{12}H_{16}N_2$ that is chemically similar to but shorter acting than psilocybin — called also *DMT*

diminishing returns* *n pl* : benefits that beyond a certain point fail to increase in proportion to extended efforts

dim sum \ˈdimˈsəm\ *n, pl* **dim sums** *also* **dim sum** [Chin (Cant) *dímsām* pastry, brunch consisting of pastry and other light dishes, fr. *dím* dot, speck, refreshment + *sām* heart, center] : traditional Chinese food consisting of a variety of items (as steamed or fried dumplings, pieces of cooked chicken, and rice balls) served in small portions

dinch \ˈdinch\ *vt* -ED/-ING/-ES [origin unknown] : to extinguish by crushing ⟨~ a cigarette⟩

diner–out \ˌ==ˈ=\ *n, pl* **diners–out** [*dine out* + [2]*-er*] : one that dines out ⟨a constant *diner-out*—Thomas Wolfe⟩

ding* *vt* : to cause minor surface damage to

ding* *n* : an instance of minor surface damage (as a dent)

ding–a–ling* *n* : NITWIT, KOOK

dingbat* *n* : DING-A-LING *herein*

dinger* *n* : HOME RUN

dingleberry* *n* : a piece of dried fecal matter clinging to the hair around the anus — often considered vulgar

[1]**dink** \ˈdiŋk\ *n* -S [origin unknown] **1** *slang* : VIETNAMESE — used disparagingly **2** *slang* : FOOL 1 ⟨a witless ~ who doesn't read directions⟩

[2]**dink** *n, often all cap* [*d*ouble *i*ncome, *n*o *k*ids] : a couple with two incomes and no children; *also* : a member of such a couple

dinner theater *n* : a restaurant in which a play is presented after the meal is over

di·no \ˈdī(ˌ)nō\ *n* -S [by shortening] : DINOSAUR

dinosaur* *n* : one that resembles a dinosaur esp. in having been made out-of-date or outmoded by changing conditions

di·ox·in \dīˈäksə̇n\ *n* -S [*di-* + [1]*ox-* + *-in*] : any of several persistent toxic heterocyclic hydrocarbons that occur esp. as by-products of various industrial processes (as pesticide manufacture and paper milling) and waste incineration; *esp* : TCDD, *herein* — see AGENT ORANGE *herein*

dip \ˈdip\ *n* -S [back-formation fr. *dippy*] : a stupid or unsophisticated person

DIP \ˈdip\ *abbr or n* -S [*d*ual *i*n-line *p*ackage] : a usu. rectangular plastic container for an integrated circuit that has two parallel sets of leads and often a row of small switches along the top by which the operation of the circuit can be altered

di·phe·noxy·late \ˌdīˌfēnˈäksəˌlāt, -ˌfen-\ *n* -S [*dipheny*l + car*boxy*lic acid + [1]*-ate*] : an antidiarrheal agent $C_{30}H_{32}N_2O_2$ chemically related to meperidine and administered in the form of its hydrochloride

di·phosphoglycerate \(ˈ)dī+\ *n* [*diphosphoglyceri*c acid (herein) + [1]*-ate*] : an isomeric ester of diphosphoglyceric acid that occurs in human erythrocytes and facilitates release of oxygen by decreasing the oxygen affinity of hemoglobin

di·phos·pho·glyceric acid \(ˈ)dīˌfäsfō+...-\ *n* [*di-* + *phosphoglyceric acid*] : a diphosphate $C_3H_8O_9P_2$ of glyceric acid that is an important intermediate in photosynthesis and in glycolysis and fermentation

di·propionate \(ˈ)dī+\ *n* [*di-* + *propionate*] : an ester containing two propionate groups

dipshit \ˈ=ˌ=\ *n* [*dip* (herein) + [2]*shit*] : a stupid or incompetent person : NITWIT — usu. considered vulgar

dipstick* *n* **1** [prob. euphemism for *dipshit* (herein)] : NITWIT **2** : a chemically sensitive strip of paper used to identify one or more constituents (as glucose or protein) of urine by immersion

di·py·rid·am·ole \ˌdīpiˈridəˌmōl, -ˈpirə̇də,-\ *n* -S [*di-* + *pyrid*ine + *am*ine + [1]*-ole*] : a drug $C_{24}H_{40}N_8O_4$ used as a coronary vasodilator

di·quat \ˈdīˌkwät\ *n* -S [*di-* + [2]*quat*ernary] : a powerful nonpersistent herbicide and plant desiccant $C_{12}H_{12}Br_2N_2$ used esp. to control aquatic weeds (as duckweed) and to desiccate aerial plant parts (as of potatoes) before harvesting

directly proportional *adj* : related by direct variation — compare INVERSELY PROPORTIONAL *herein*

director's chair *n* [so called fr. its use by movie directors] : a lightweight usu. folding armchair with a back and seat usu. of cotton duck

direct product *n* : CARTESIAN PRODUCT *herein*; *esp* : a group that is the Cartesian product of two other groups

direct sum *n* : CARTESIAN PRODUCT *herein*

direct variation *n* **1** : mathematical relationship between two variables that can be expressed by an equation in which one variable is equal to a nonzero constant times the other **2** : an equation or function expressing direct variation — compare INVERSE VARIATION 2 *herein*

dirham* *n* **1 a** : the basic monetary unit of Morocco and the United Arab Emirates — see MONEY table *in the Dict* **b** : a monetary unit of Iraq equal to 1/20 dinar **c** : a monetary unit of Libya equal to 1/1000 dinar — see MONEY table *in the Dict* **2** : a coin or note representing one dirham

di·ri·giste \dērēzhēst\ *adj* [F, fr. *diriger* to direct (fr. L *dirigere*) + *-iste* [2]-ist — more at DRESS] : characteristic of or following a policy of dirigisme

dirtbag \ˈ=ˌ=\ *n, slang* : a dirty, unkempt, or contemptible person

dirt bike *n* : a usu. lightweight motorcycle designed for operation on unpaved surfaces

dirty old man *n* : a lecherous mature man

dirty pool *n* [[3]*pool*] : underhanded or unsportsmanlike conduct

dirty rice *n* [prob. trans. of LaF *riz sale* or Louisiana Creole *diri sal*] : a Cajun dish of white rice cooked with chopped or ground giblets

[1]**dis** *also* **diss** \ˈdis\ *vt* **dissed; dissed; dissing; disses** [short for [1]*disrespect*] **1** *slang* : to treat with disrespect or contempt : INSULT **2** *slang* : to find fault with : CRITICIZE

[2]**dis** *also* **diss** *n, pl* **disses** **1** *slang* : a disparaging remark or act : INSULT ⟨was meant as a tribute, not a ~ —*Vibe*⟩ **2** *slang* : DISRESPECT ⟨no ~ intended —Cathy Maestri⟩

disaggregate* *vb* ~ *vi* : to break up or apart ⟨the molecules of a gel ~ to form a sol⟩ — **dis·aggregative** \(ˈ)dis+\ *adj*

dis·am·big·u·ate \ˌdis(ˌ)amˈbigyəˌwāt\ *vt* -ED/-ING/-S [[1]*dis-* + *ambiguous* + [4]*-ate*] : to establish a single semantic or grammatical interpretation for — **dis·am·big·u·ation** \-ˌbigyəˈwāshən\ *n* -S

disappear* *vb* ~ *vt* : to cause to disappear

dis·arm·er \¦dis'ärmər\ *n* : a person who favors disarmament ⟨a nuclear ~⟩

disastrous* *adj* : extremely bad : TERRIBLE ⟨she was a ~ mother —Garry Wills⟩

dis·benefit \¦dis+\ *n* [[1]*dis-* + [1]*benefit*] : something disadvantageous or objectionable : DRAWBACK ⟨noise nuisance was the main ~ —Philip Howard⟩

dis·bound \(ˈ)dis+\ *adj* [[1]*dis-* + [4]*bound*] : no longer having a binding ⟨a ~ pamphlet⟩

disc brake *n* : a brake that operates by the action of a frictional material pressed against the sides of a rotating disc by a caliper

discharge* *vi* : to release electrical energy by a discharge

disc jockey* *or* **disk jockey*** *n* : one who plays recorded music for dancing at a nightclub or party

disclosing *adj* [fr. pres. part. of *disclose*] : being or using an agent (as a tablet or liquid) that contains a usu. red dye that stains dental plaque

[1]**dis·co** \ˈdis(ˌ)kō\ *n* -S [short for *discotheque*] **1** : a nightclub for dancing to live and recorded music often featuring flamboyant decor, special lighting effects, and disc jockeys **2** : popular dance music characterized by strong steady rhythms, repetitive lyrics, and usu. a predominance of electronically produced sounds

[2]**disco** *vi* -ED/-ING/-S : to dance to disco music

disconnect* *n* [*disconnect*, v.] : a lack of or a break in connection, consistency, or agreement ⟨a ~ between his public image and his private conduct⟩

[1]**dis·co·theque** \ˈdiskəˌtek, ˈdēs-, -kō̜-, ˌ≈≈ˈ≈\ *n* -S [F *discothèque* collection of phonograph records, discotheque, fr. *disque* disk (fr. L *discus*) + *-o-* + *-thèque* (as in *bibliothèque* library, fr. L *bibliotheca*) — more at DISH, BIBLIOTHECA] : a usu. small intimate nightclub for dancing to recorded music; *also* : DISCO 1 *herein*

[2]**discotheque** *vi* -ED/-ING/-S : to dance at a discotheque

discount *adj* [*discount*, n.] **1 a** : selling goods or services at a discount ⟨~ stores⟩ ⟨a ~ broker⟩ ⟨~ airlines⟩ **b** : offered or sold at a discount **2** : reflecting a discount ⟨~ prices⟩

discourse* *n* : a mode of organizing knowledge, ideas, or experience that is rooted in language and its concrete contexts (as history or institutions) ⟨male-dominated ~*s* —Marian M. Sciachitano⟩ ⟨critical ~*s*⟩

discretionary account *n* : a security or commodity market account in which an agent (as a broker) is given power of attorney so as to be able to make independent decisions and buy and sell for the account of the principal

discretionary income *n* : the part of personal income left after payment of basic expenses (as taxes and the cost of food and shelter)

dis·cret·iza·tion \(ˌ)disˌkrēd·əˈzāshən, -ētə-\ *n* -S [*discrete* + *-ization*] : the action of making discrete and esp. mathematically discrete

discriminant function *n* : a function of a set of variables (as measurements of taxonomic specimens) that is evaluated for samples of events or objects and used as an aid in discriminating between or classifying them

diseconomy of scale : an increase in unit costs brought about esp. by increased size of production facilities — usu. used in pl.; compare ECONOMY OF SCALE *herein*

dis·empower \¦dis+\ *vt* [[1]*dis-* + *empower*] : to deprive of power, authority, or influence : make weak, ineffectual, or unimportant — **dis·empowerment** \ˌdis+\ *n*

disengaged* *adj* : DETACHED 2

dish* *n* : GOSSIP ⟨inside ~ about the most powerful book-review medium —Walter Clemons⟩

dish* *vt* **1** : to talk or gossip about esp. disparagingly ⟨at the bar in the lobby, ~*ing* the show —Couri Hay⟩ — often used in the phrases *dish the dirt* or *dish dirt* ⟨~*ing* the dirt about some married friends of ours —Clare B. Luce⟩ ⟨~*ing* some dirt about his rambunctious private life —*Time*⟩ **2** : to pass (a basketball) to a teammate — often used with *off* ~ *vi* **1** : GOSSIP; *also* : to disclose private or personal information **2** : to pass a basketball to a teammate — often used with *off*

dis·habituation \¦dis+\ *n* [[1]*dis-* + *habituation*] : restoration to full strength of a response that has become weakened by habituation — **dis·habituate** \"+\ *vb*

dishware \ˈ≈,≈\ *n* : tableware (as of china) used in serving food

dishy \ˈdishē, -i\ *adj* -ER/-EST [[1]*dish* + [1]*-y*] **1** : ATTRACTIVE **2** : characterized by, full of, or given to gossip or disclosure

dis·information \¦dis+\ *n* [trans. of Russ *dezinformatsiya*] : false information deliberately and often covertly spread (as by the planting of rumors) in order to influence public opinion or obscure the truth

dis·in·hib·it \(ˌ)disᵊnˈhibət\ *vt* [[1]*dis-* + *inhibit*] : to cause the loss or reduction of (an inhibition) ⟨an illicit drug that ~*ed* aggressive behavior⟩

dis·in·sec·tion \ˌdisənˈsekshən, -ˌinˈs-\ *n* -S [[1]*dis-* + *insect* + *-ion*] : DISINSECTIZATION

dis·in·ter·me·di·a·tion \(ˌ)disˌintə(r)ˌmēdēˈāshən\ *n* [[1]*dis-* + *intermediate* + *-ion*; fr. the investor's bypassing of the intermediate institution] : diversion of savings from institutions with governmentally imposed interest ceilings (as savings banks) to direct investment in higher-yielding instruments

dis·intoxicate \¦dis+\ *vt* [*dis-* + [2]*intoxicate*] : DETOXIFY 1 *herein*

disjoint* *adj* : not having all members in common — used of the reference of linguistic expressions ⟨the pronouns *I* and *we* have ~ reference⟩

disjunct* *n* : an adverb or adverbial (as *luckily* in "luckily we had an extra set" or *in short* in "in short, there is nothing we can do") that is loosely connected to a sentence and conveys the speaker's or writer's comment on its content, truth, or matter

disk* *or* **disc*** *n* **1** : a round flat plate (as of metal) coated with a magnetic substance on which data for a computer can be stored — called also *magnetic disk* **2** : a circular grid in a photocomposer **3** *usu disc* **a** : OPTICAL DISK *herein* **b** : COMPACT DISC *herein* **c** : VIDEODISC *herein*

disk drive *n* : a device for reading data on and writing data onto a usu. magnetic disk

disk·ette \ˌdisˈket\ *n* -S [[1]*disk* + *-ette*] : FLOPPY DISK *herein*

disk pack *n* : a storage device for a computer that consists of a stack of magnetic disks mounted on a central hub and their removable protective cover and that can be handled and stored as a unit

dis·ney·esque \¦diznē¦esk\ *or* **dis·ney·ish** \-ish\ *adj, usu cap* [*Disneyesque* fr. Walt *Disney* †1966 Am. film producer + E [1]*-esque; Disneyish* fr. *Disney* + E *-ish*] : resembling or suggestive of the films, television productions, or amusement parks made by Walt Disney or his organization

dis·ney·fi·ca·tion \-fəˈkāshən\ *n* -S *usu cap* [Walt *Disney* + E *-fication*] : the transformation (as of something real or unsettling) into carefully controlled and safe entertainment or an environment with similar qualities ⟨the ~ of a downtown⟩

disodium ino·sin·ate \-iˈnōsəˌnāt, -īˈ-\ *n* [*inosine* + [1]*-ate*] : a salt $C_{10}H_{11}N_4Na_2O_8P$ that is used chiefly as a flavor enhancer in food

dis·par·lure \ˈdispärˌlu̇(ə)r\ *n* [NL *dispar* (specific epithet of *Porthetria dispar*, the gypsy moth) + E *lure*] : a pheromone $C_{19}H_{38}O$ produced by female gypsy moths that has been made synthetically and used to attract males to traps

dispatch* *vt* : to win victory over : DEFEAT ⟨~*ed* the other team easily⟩

displacement* *or* **displacement activity** *or* **displacement behavior** *n* : the substitution of another form of behavior for what is usual or expected esp. when the usual response is nonadaptive

display* *n* : an electronic device (as a cathode-ray tube or a liquid-crystal readout) that presents information in visual form; *also* : the visual information

dis·pos·able \dəˈspōzəbəl\ *n* -S [*disposable*, adj.] : something (as a paper plate) that is disposable

diss *var of* DIS *herein*

dissecting microscope *n* : a low-magnification stereomicroscope used. esp. in examining or dissecting biological specimens

dis·sen·sus \(ˌ)di(s)ˈsen(t)səs\ *n* -ES [[1]*dis-* + *consensus*] : difference of opinion

dissociative identity disorder *n* : MULTIPLE PERSONALITY

dissonance* *n* : inconsistency between the beliefs one holds or between one's actions and one's beliefs — see COGNITIVE DISSONANCE *herein*

dis·tal* *adj* : of, relating to, or being the surface of a tooth that is most distant from the middle of the front of the jaw and is usu. next to the tooth behind it — compare MESIAL *herein*, PROXIMAL *herein* — **dis·tal·ly*** *adv*

distance learning *n* : education that takes place via electronic media linking instructors and students who are not together in a classroom

dis·to·buccal \¦distō+\ *adj* [*dist-* + *buccal*] : relating to or located on the distal and buccal surfaces of a molar or premolar ⟨the ~ cusp of the first molar⟩ — **dis·to·buccally** \"+\ *adv*

dis·to·lingual \"+\ *adj* [*dist-* + *lingual*] : relating to or situated on the distal and lingual surfaces of a tooth ⟨the ~ cusp of a tooth⟩

distracter* *or* **distractor*** *n* : a usu. plausible but incorrect answer given as a choice in a multiple-choice test

distribute* *vt* : to use in or as an operation so as to be mathematically distributive ⟨addition is not *distributed* over multiplication⟩ ~ *vi* : to be mathematically distributive ⟨multiplication ~*s* over addition⟩

dis·trib·ut·ed \-yəd·əd, -yətəd\ *adj* [fr. past part. of *distribute*] **1** : characterized by a statistical distribution of a particular kind ⟨independently ~ random variables⟩ **2** : of, relating to, or being a computer network in which at least some of the processing is done by the individual workstations and information is shared by and often stored at the workstations

distribution* *n* **1** : FREQUENCY DISTRIBUTION **2** : PROBABILITY FUNCTION

distribution function *n* : a function that gives the probability that a random variable is less than or equal to the independent variable of the function

distributive education *n, often cap D&E* : a vocational program in marketing and sales set up between schools and employers in which the student receives both classroom instruction and on-the-job training

di·sul·fo·ton \(ˌ)dīˈsəlfəˌtän\ *n* -S [ISV *di*ethyl + *sulf-* + *-ton* (as in *demeton* — herein)] : an organophosphorus systemic insecticide $C_8H_{19}O_2PS_3$ used esp. on cultivated plants

di·transitive \¦dī¦≈≈\ *adj* [*di-* + *transitive*] *of a verb* : able to take both a direct and an indirect object — **ditransitive** \"\ *n* -S

ditz \ˈdits\ *n* -ES [back-formation fr. *ditzy* (herein)] : a ditzy person

dit·zy *or* **dit·sy** \ˈditsē\ *adj* -ER/-EST [origin unknown] **1** : eccentrically silly, giddy, or inane : DIZZY ⟨she ~ but nice blond who may deserve the guy but seldom gets him —Rebecca Bricker⟩ **2** : overly decorative : FUSSY ⟨a ~ pattern⟩ — **dit·zi·ness** *or* **dit·si·ness** \-nəs\

di·uron \ˈdīyəˌrän\ *n* -S [*di-* + *urea* + [1]*-on*] : a persistent herbicide $C_9H_{10}Cl_2N_2O$ used esp. to control annual weeds

diverge* *vi* : to be mathematically divergent

divergence* *n* : the state of being mathematically divergent

divergent thinking *n* : creative thinking that may follow many lines of thought and that tends to generate new and original solutions to problems — compare CONVERGENT THINKING *herein* — **divergent thinker** *n*

divide* *vt* **1** : to be used as a divisor with respect to (a dividend) ⟨4 ~*s* 16 evenly⟩ **2** : to use as a divisor — used with *into* ⟨~ 14 into 42⟩

divide* *n* : an instance of division performed by a computer; *also* : the means for performing division

division sign *n* **1** : the symbol ÷ used to indicate division **2** : a diagonal / used to indicate a fraction

di·vor·cé \dəˌvȯrˈsā, dē- *also* -ˈsē, ≈ˈ≈ˌ≈\ *n* -S [F — more at DIVORCÉE] : a divorced man

DMA *abbr or n* -S : a doctor of musical arts

DMSO \ˌdēˌem(ˌ)esˈō\ *n* -S [*di*methyl *s*ulfoxide (herein)] : DIMETHYL SULFOXIDE *herein*

DMT \ˌdē(ˌ)emˈtē\ *n* -S [*di*methyl*t*ryptamine (herein)] : DIMETHYLTRYPTAMINE *herein*

DMZ *abbr* demilitarized zone

DNA fingerprinting \ˌdē(ˌ)eˈnā-\ *n* : a technique used esp. for identification (as for forensic purposes) by extracting and identifying the base-pair pattern in an individual's DNA — **DNA fingerprint** *n*

DNA polymerase *n* : any of several polymerases that promote replication or repair of DNA usu. using single-stranded DNA as a template

DN·ase \(ˈ)dēˌenˌās, -ˌāz\ *also* **DNA·ase** \(ˌ)dēˌenˈāˌās, -ˌāz\ *n* -S [*DNase* blend of *DNA* and *-ase; DNAase* fr. *DNA* + *-ase*] : DEOXYRIBONUCLEASE

DNA typing *n* : DNA FINGERPRINTING *herein*

DNA virus *n* : a virus whose genome consists of DNA

DNF *abbr* did not finish

DNR *abbr* do not resuscitate

do* *vt* **1** : to attack physically : BEAT; *also* : KILL **2** : MIMIC; *also* : to behave like ⟨~ a Houdini and disappear⟩ **3** : to consume or take regularly : USE ⟨doesn't ~ cocaine⟩ **4** : to have sexual intercourse with **5** : to partake of : EAT ⟨~ lunch⟩ — **do a number on** **1** : to defeat or confound thoroughly esp. by indirect or deceptive means **2** : MOCK, RIDICULE

do \ˈdü\ *n* -S [by shortening] : HAIRDO

dobra* *n* : the basic monetary unit of Sao Tome and Principe — see MONEY table *in the Dict*

Do·bro \ˈdō(ˌ)brō\ *trademark* — used for an acoustic guitar having a metal resonator

dobson unit *n, usu cap D* [after Gordon M.B. *Dobson* †1976 Brit. physicist] : a unit of atmospheric ozone content above a given spot on earth's surface

dock* *vt* : to join mechanically (as two spacecraft) while in space ~ *vi* **1** : to become docked **2** : to combine with a molecular receptor ⟨the AIDS virus ~*ed* at the T-cell receptor⟩

do·co·sa·hex·a·e·no·ic acid \ˌdōkōsəˌheksəˌēˈnōik-\ *n* [ISV *docosa-* (as in *docosanoic acid*) + *hexa-* + *-ene* + *-oic*] : an omega-3 fatty acid found esp. in cold-water fish — abbr. *DHA*

doctor* *vt* : CASTRATE, SPAY ⟨have your pet cat ~*ed*⟩

docu·drama \ˈdäkyů, -yə+\ *n* [[2]*documentary* + *drama*] : a drama made for television, motion pictures, or theater dealing freely with historical events esp. of a recent and controversial nature; *also* : a book of the same nature

document* *n* : a computer file usu. created with an application (as a word processor) and containing information input by the user of the computer

documentation* *n* : the usu. printed instructions, comments, and other information on the use of a particular piece or system of computer software or hardware

dodge* *vt* — **dodge a bullet** *or* **dodge the bullet** : to avoid a potentially unpleasant outcome ⟨not . . . too late to *dodge the* tax *bullet* on a losing fund —Douglas Armstrong⟩

dodgy* *adj* **1** *chiefly Brit* : not sound, stable, or reliable : QUESTIONABLE ⟨there were thirteen planes, all brand new. And I had to pick the one with the ~ engine —Susan Saggers⟩ **2** *chiefly Brit* : requiring skill or care in handling or coping with ⟨it was a little ~ getting her home and into the parsonage without anyone noticing —R.F.Delderfield⟩; *also* : CHANCY, RISKY ⟨bringing out a restaurant guide is a ~ business, since it has been prepared so far in advance —Alison Mitchell⟩ — **dodg·i·ness** \+nəs\ *n* -ES

dog and pony show *n* : an often elaborate public relations or sales presentation; *also* : an elaborate or overblown affair

doggie bag *or* **doggy bag** *n* [so called fr. the original assumption that such leftovers were destined for the diner's dog] : a container with leftover food to be carried home from a meal eaten at a restaurant

do–good·ing \ˈdüˌgůdiŋ\ *n* -S : the activities of a do-gooder — **do–gooding** *adj*

dogs·body \ˈdȯgzˌbädē *sometimes* ˈdäg-\ *n* [Brit. naval slang, midshipman, fr. slang *dog's body* pease pudding] *chiefly Brit* : one who performs menial tasks : DRUDGE

do–it–your·self \¦düəchə(r)¦self, -ətyə-\ *adj* : of, relating to, or designed for use in construction, repair, or artistic work done by an amateur or hobbyist ⟨a *do-it-yourself* car model kit⟩

do–it–your·self·er \-fə(r)\ *n* -S [*do-it-yourself* (herein) + [2]*-er*] : one who engages in do-it-yourself projects

do·jo \ˈdō(ˌ)jō\ *n* -S [Jap *dōjō*, fr. *dō* way, art + *-jō* place] : a school for training in oriental martial arts

Dol·by \ˈdōlbē, ˈdōl-\ *trademark* — used for an electronic device that eliminates noise from recorded sound or sound broadcast on FM radio

dol·by·ize \ˈdōlbēˌīz, ˈdōl-\ *vt* -ED/-ING/-S *usu cap* [*Dolby* (herein) + *-ize*] : to reduce noise in by the use of a Dolby device

dol·ce vi·ta \ˌdōlchēˈvē(ˌ)tä, -(ˌ)chā-\ *n* [It, lit., sweet life] : a life of indolence and self-indulgence

dollar–cost averaging \ˈ≈≈-\ *n* : DOLLAR AVERAGING

dolly bird *n, Brit* : a pretty young woman

DOM \ˌdē(ˌ)ōˈem\ *n* -S [prob. fr. *d*imethoxy- + *m*ethyl] : STP *herein*

domain* *n* **1** : any of the three-dimensional subunits of a protein that together make up its tertiary structure, that are formed by folding its linear peptide chain, and that are variously considered to be the basic units of protein structure, function, and evolution **2** : the highest taxonomic category in biological classification ranking above the kingdom **3** : a large subdivision of the Internet consisting of computers or sites with a common purpose (as providing commercial, nonprofit, educational, or government information) or a common geographic location (as those in a given country) and denoted in Internet addresses by an abbreviation (as *.com* for commercial sites, *.gov* for government sites, or *.ca* for sites located in Canada); *also* : DOMAIN NAME *herein*

do·maine \dōˈmān, -ˈmen\ *n* -S [F, lit., domain] : a vineyard esp. in Burgundy that makes and bottles wine from its own grapes

domain name *n* : a sequence of usu. alphanumeric characters (as "Merriam-Webster.com") that represents or specifies the resources of a particular entity (as an organization) on the Internet and that forms part of the corresponding World Wide Web addresses, e-mail addresses, or other Internet addresses

dome* *n* : a roofed sports stadium

domestic partner *n* **1** : a company esp. in a developing country that joins in a commercial venture with an international company **2** : either one of an unmarried heterosexual or homosexual cohabiting couple esp. when considered as to eligibility for spousal benefits — **domestic partnership** *n*

domestic prelate *n* : a priest having permanent honorary membership in the papal household and ranking above a papal chamberlain

domestic violence *n* : the inflicting of physical injury by one family member on another; *also* : a repeated or habitual pattern of such behavior

dom·i·na·trix \ˌdäməˈnāˌtriks\ *n, pl* **dominatri·ces** \-ˈnātrəˌsēz, -nəˈtrīˌsēz\ [L, fem. of *dominator* — more at DOMINATOR] : a woman who physically and psychologically dominates and abuses her partner in sadomasochistic sex; *broadly* : a dominating woman

domino effect *n* [so called fr. the fact that if dominoes are stood on end one behind the other with a slight intervening space, a push on the first one will result in the toppling of all the others] : a cumulative effect produced when one event initiates a succession of similar events — compare RIPPLE EFFECT *herein*

domino theory *n* [*domino* (*effect*) (herein)] **1** : the theory that if one nation becomes Communist-controlled the neighboring nations will also become Communist-controlled **2** : the theory that if one act or event is allowed to take place a succession of similar acts or events will follow

do·mo·ic acid \dəˈmōik-\ *n* [part trans. of Jap *dōmoi-san*, fr. *dōmoi*, a name for the alga *Chondria armata* + *san* acid] : a neurotoxic analogue $C_{15}H_{21}NO_6$ of glutamic acid that is produced by some diatoms (esp. genus *Pseudonitzschia*) and has caused poisoning in vertebrates (as whales, birds, and humans) that have consumed diatom-contaminated fish or shellfish

done deal *n* : FAIT ACCOMPLI ⟨thought the trade was a *done deal*⟩

done·ness \ˈdənnəs\ *n* -ES [[2]*done* + *-ness*] : the condition of being cooked to the desired degree ⟨test the meat for ~⟩

dong \ˈdȯŋ\ *n, pl* **dong** [Vietnamese *đồng*] **1** : the basic monetary unit of Vietnam — see MONEY table *in the Dict* **2** : a coin or note representing one dong

doo·bie \ˈdübē\ *n* -S [origin unknown] *slang* : a marijuana cigarette : JOINT

dood·ley–squat \ˈdüd(ᵊ)lē+\ *n* [*doodley* (perh. alter. of *do one's do* to defecate) + [1]*squat*] *slang* : DIDDLY-SQUAT *herein*

doo–doo *also* **do–do** \ˈdü(ˌ)dü\ *or* **doo** *or* **do** \ˈdü\ *n, pl* **doo–doos** *also* **do–dos** *or* **doos** *or* **dos** [baby talk] : EXCREMENT — used as a euphemism

doo·fus *also* **du·fus** \ˈdü(ˌ)fəs\ *n* -ES [perh. alter. of [1]*goof*] *slang* : a stupid, incompetent, or foolish person

dooms·day·er \ˈ≈ˌ≈ə(r)\ *n* -S [*doomsday* + [2]*-er*] : DOOMSAYER

doomsday machine *n, sometimes cap D&M* : a device capable of worldwide destruction (as by automated deployment and detonation of nuclear weapons)

doomy \+ē\ *adj* -ER/-EST : suggestive of doom : DOOMFUL

doorstep* *n* : THRESHOLD — **on one's doorstep** : close at hand; *esp* : too close to be overlooked

doo–wop *also* **do–wop** \ˈdü(ˌ)wäp, dů'wäp\ *n* -S [fr. *doo-wop*, meaningless syllables typical of the style] : a vocal style of popular music characterized by the singing of usu. nonsense syllables in rhythmical support of the melody

do·pa·mine \ˈdōpəˌmēn, -ˌmən\ *n* [blend of *dopa* and *amine*] : a monoamine $C_8H_{11}NO_2$ that is a decarboxylated form of dopa and occurs esp. as a neurotransmitter in the brain and as an intermediate in the biosynthesis of epinephrine

do·pa·min·er·gic \¦dōpəˌmē¦nərjək, -mə¦n-\ *adj* [*dopamine* (herein) + *-ergic* (herein)] : relating to, participating in, or activated by the neurotransmitter activity of dopamine or related substances ⟨a ~ pathway in the nervous system⟩ ⟨~ activity⟩

dop·ant \ˈdōpənt\ *n* -S [[2]*dope* + [1]*-ant*] : an impurity added usu. in minute amounts to a pure substance to alter its properties

doper* *n* : an habitual or frequent drug user

doppelgänger* *n* **1** : DOUBLE 2a(1) **2** : ALTER EGO d **3** : a person who has the same name as another

dopp·ler \ˈdäplə(r)\ *adj, usu cap* **1** : of, relating to, or utilizing a shift in frequency in accordance with the Doppler effect **2** : of or relating to Doppler radar or Doppler navigation **3** : of, relating to, using or produced by Doppler ultrasound ⟨a ~ examination⟩ ⟨~ images⟩

doppler echocardiography *n, usu cap D* : Doppler ultrasound used to measure cardiovascular blood flow velocity for diagnostic purposes (as for evaluating heart valve function)

doppler radar *also* **doppler** *n* -S *usu cap D* : a radar system (as for navigation or weather forecasting) utilizing the Doppler effect for measuring velocity

doppler ultrasound *or* **doppler ultrasonography** *n, usu cap D* : ultrasound that utilizes the Doppler effect to measure movement or flow in the body and esp. blood flow

do–rag \ˈdüˌrag\ *n* [*do* (herein) + *rag*] : a kerchief worn over the hair

dork \ˈdȯrk, ˈdō(ə)k\ *n* -S [perh. alter. of [1]*dick*] **1** : PENIS — usu. considered vulgar **2** *slang* : NERD *herein*; *also* : JERK

dorky \ˈdȯrkē, -i; ˈdō(ə)k-\ *adj* -ER/-EST [*dork* (herein) + [1]*-y*] *slang* : foolishly stupid : CLUELESS

dor·min \ˈdȯrmən\ *n* -S [*dormancy* + *-in*] : ABSCISIC ACID *herein*

dorsal horn *n* : DORSAL COLUMN

DOS *abbr* disk operating system
dosage compensation *n* : the genetic mechanism by which the same effect on the phenotype is produced by a pair of identical sex-linked genes in the sex (as the human female) having the two sex chromosomes of the same type as by a single sex-linked gene in the sex (as the human male) having the two sex chromosomes of different types or having only one sex chromosome (as in the males of some insects)
dot–com \ˌ+ˌkäm\ *n* -S *often attrib* [so called fr. the use of *.com* in the URLs of such companies] : a company that markets its products or services on-line via a World Wide Web site
dot matrix *n* : a pattern of dots in a grid from which alphanumeric characters can be formed ⟨*dot-matrix* printer⟩
double bind *n* : a psychological predicament in which a person receives from a single source conflicting messages that allow no appropriate response to be made; *broadly* : DILEMMA 2
double–blind \ˈ≈ˈ≈\ *adj* : of, relating to, or being an experimental procedure in which neither the subjects nor the experimenters know the identity of the individuals in the test and control groups during the actual course of the experiments — compare SINGLE-BLIND *herein*
double–cover \ˈ≈≈ˈ≈≈\ *vt* : DOUBLE-TEAM
double cream *n, Brit* : an extremely thick and heavy cream; *esp* : cream that contains not less than 48 percent butterfat
double–digit \ˈ≈≈ˈ≈≈\ *adj* : of 10 percent or more ⟨*double-digit* inflation⟩ ⟨*double-digit* price increases⟩
double dip *vi* [[2]*dip* (portion dipped at one time); fr. the likening of the two incomes to a cone with two scoops of ice cream] : to obtain money from two sources at the same time or by two separate accounting methods; *esp* : to draw a pension from one government department while working for another — **double–dipper** \ˌ≈≈ˈ≈≈\ *n*
double dutch* *n, usu cap 2d D* : the jumping of two jump ropes rotating in opposite directions simultaneously
double gloucester *n, usu cap D&G* [fr. *Gloucester*, county in England, where it was first made] : a firm mild orange-colored English cheese similar to cheddar
double helix *n* : a helix or spiral consisting of two strands in the surface of a cylinder that coil around its axis; *esp* : the structural arrangement of DNA in space that consists of paired polynucleotide strands stabilized by cross-links between purine and pyrimidine bases — compare ALPHA-HELIX *herein*, WATSON-CRICK MODEL *herein* — **double–helical** \ˈ≈≈ˈ≈≈≈\ *adj*
double knit *n* : a knitted fabric (as of wool or polyester) made with a double set of needles to produce a double thickness of fabric with each thickness joined by interlocking stitches; *also* : an article of clothing made of such fabric
double–precision \ˈ≈≈ˈ≈≈\ *adj* : using two computer words rather than one to represent a number
double reverse *n* : an offensive play in football consisting of a reverse with an additional handoff so that the ultimate ballcarrier is running in the direction in which the play started
doublespeak \ˈ≈≈ˌ≈\ *n* [*double*think + new*speak* (herein)] **1** : language used to deceive usu. through concealment or misrepresentation of truth ⟨instances of euphemism and ~ displayed by leaders in government —K.G.Wilson⟩ **2** : DOUBLE-TALK 2 — **doublespeaker** \ˈ≈≈ˌ≈≈\ *n*
doublet* *n* **1 a** : a pair of atomic, molecular, or nuclear quantum states that are usu. close together in energy and arise from two possible orientations of spin **b** : a pair of spectral frequencies of light arising from transitions to or from such quantum states **2** : a pair of otherwise similar elementary particles (as a proton and a neutron) with different charge **3** : any of nine pairs of microtubules found in cilia and flagella
double whammy *n* : a combination of two usu. adverse forces, circumstances, or effects
double–wide \ˌ≈≈ˈ≈\ *n* -S : a mobile home consisting of two units that have been fastened together along their length
douche* *n, chiefly British* : an abrupt often chastening shock to the nerves, emotions, or awareness ⟨the icy ~ (what he said about my work) —John Fowles⟩
doug·las bag \ˈdəgləs-\ *n, usu cap D* [after C.G. *Douglas* †1963 Eng. physiologist] : an inflatable bag used to collect expired air for the determination of oxygen consumption and basal metabolic rate
dove* *n* : one who takes a conciliatory attitude (as in a dispute) and advocates negotiations and compromise; *esp* : an opponent of war — compare HAWK *herein* — **dov·ish** \ˈdəvish\ *adj* — **dov·ish·ness** *n* -ES
dowager's hump *n* : an abnormal outward curvature of the upper back with round shoulders and stooped posture caused esp. by bone loss and anterior compression of the vertebrae in osteoporosis
down* *adj* **1** *slang* : COOL 8 ⟨a ~ dude⟩ — often used as a generalized term of approval **2** : being a constituent of nucleons and having the quantum characteristics of an electric charge of −⅓ and a baryon number of ⅓ ⟨~ quark⟩ — compare UP *herein* **3** : being on record ⟨you're ~ for two tickets⟩ **4** *slang* : FRIENDLY, FAVORABLE, SUPPORTIVE ⟨he's ~ with hip-hop⟩
down and dirty *adj (or adv)* **1** : UNVARNISHED ⟨the real *down and dirty* story of the country and the nature of its people —Seymour Krim⟩ **2** : made or done hastily : not revised or polished ⟨delivered a *down and dirty* performance⟩ **3** : marked by or given to fierce often unscrupulous competition : DOG-EAT-DOG ⟨*down and dirty* campaigning⟩ **4** : BAWDY ⟨they exude a leering *down and dirty* sexual energy —Jim Calio⟩ **5** : SEEDY ⟨neglected, *down and dirty* streets —Kurt Anderson⟩
down–and–out* *n* : a pass pattern in football in which the receiver runs straight downfield and then cuts to the outside
downburst \ˈ≈ˌ≈\ *n* [[4]*down* + [2]*burst*] : a powerful downdraft that is usu. associated with a thunderstorm, that strikes the ground and deflects in all directions, and that constitutes a hazard esp. for low-flying aircraft; *also* : MICROBURST *herein*
downer* *n* **1** : a depressant drug; *esp* : BARBITURATE — compare UPPER *herein* **2** : someone or something depressing, disagreeable, or unsatisfactory
downforce \ˈ≈ˌ≈\ *n* [[4]*down* + [1]*force*] : a downward aerodynamic force generated esp. by an airfoil (as a spoiler on a race car)
downhill·er \ˈ≈ˈ≈ə(r)\ *n* **1** : a downhill skier **2** : a putt in golf that must roll down the slope of the green to the cup
downhole \ˈ≈ˈ≈\ *adj* [[3]*down* + *hole*] : of, relating to, or used in a hole in the earth and esp. in a borehole
down–home \ˈ≈ˈ≈\ *adj* [fr. the phrase *down home*] : of, relating to, or having qualities (as informality, simplicity, and earthiness) associated with the common people esp. of the southern U.S.; *broadly* : SIMPLE, UNPRETENTIOUS
[1]**downlink** \ˈ≈ˌ≈\ *n* [[4]*down* + *link*] **1** : a communications channel for receiving transmissions from a spacecraft or satellite; *also* : the transmissions themselves **2** : a facility on earth for receiving transmissions from a spacecraft or satellite — compare UPLINK *herein*
[2]**downlink** *vt* : to transmit (as data) from a spacecraft or satellite to a receiver on earth
[1]**download** \ˈ≈ˈ≈\ *vt* [[2]*down* + *load*] : to transfer (as information, a file, or software) from a usu. large remote computer to the memory of another device (as a smaller computer) — **down·load·able** \ˈ≈ˈ≈əbəl\ *adj*
[2]**download** *n* : an act or instance of downloading something; *also* : the item downloaded
down–market \ˈ≈ˈ≈\ *adj* [[4]*down* + *market*] **1** : of, being, relating to, or appealing to low-income consumers ⟨a *down-market* suburb⟩ **2** : UNFASHIONABLE ⟨associated with more *down-market* corners of the academy —Claude Rawson⟩ — **down–market** \"\ *adv*
downplay \ˈ≈ˌ≈\ *vt* : to play down : DE-EMPHASIZE
downrange \ˈ≈ˈ≈\ *adv (or adj)* [[3]*down* + [1]*range*] : away from a launching site and along the course of a test range
downregulation \ˈ≈ˌ≈≈ˈ≈≈\ *n* [[4]*down* + *regulation*] : the process of reducing or suppressing a response to a stimulus; *specif* : reduction in a cellular response to a molecule (as of insulin) from a decrease in the number of receptors on the cell surface — **down-regulate** *vt*
[1]**downscale** \ˈ≈ˈ≈\ *vt* [[2]*down* + [8]*scale*] : to cut back in size or scope ⟨the recession forced us to ~ vacation plans⟩
[2]**downscale** *adj (or adv)* [[3]*down* + [7]*scale*] : lower in class, income, or quality
downside* *n* : an unappealing, disadvantageous, or negative aspect ⟨the ~ of fame⟩
downsize \ˈ≈ˈ≈\ *vb* [[2]*down* + [1]*size*] *vt* **1** : to reduce in size; *esp* : to design or produce in smaller size **2** : to fire (employees) for the purpose of downsizing a business ~ *vi* : to undergo a reduction in size — **down·siz·ing** *n*
downstream* *adv (or adj)* : in the same direction along a molecule of DNA or RNA as that in which transcription and translation take place and toward the end having a hydroxyl group attached to the position labeled 3′ in the terminal nucleotide ⟨a nucleotide sequence located ~ from the regulatory gene⟩ — compare UPSTREAM 2 *herein*
downstream *adj (or adv)* : of, relating to, in, or toward the later stages of a usu. industrial process ⟨~ products⟩ ⟨improve profits ~⟩
downtick \ˈ≈ˌ≈\ *n* [[4]*down* + [2]*tick*] : a stock market transaction at a price below the last previous transaction in the same security — compare UPTICK *herein*
downtime \ˈ≈ˈ≈\ *n* [[4]*down* + *time*] **1** : time during which production or operation is stopped (as in a factory or on a machine) esp. during setup for an operation, during a breakdown, or when making repairs ⟨few moving parts and, thus, low maintenance costs and ~ —J.C.Friedlander⟩ **2** : time when a person is not at work ⟨spends much of his ~ watching TV —Sue Reilly⟩
downtown* *n* : long range — used esp. of a shot in basketball ⟨known for his shots from ~ —Randy Harvey⟩
downzone \ˈ≈ˌ≈\ *vt* [[2]*down* + [2]*zone*] : to reduce or limit development or the number of buildings permitted on ⟨the county *downzoned* rural land to allow only one home per ten acres instead of one per five acres⟩
dox·e·pin \ˈdäksəˌpin, -ˌpən\ *n* -S [*d*imethyl + *ox-* + *-ep-* (as in *benzodiazepine* — herein) + *-in*] : a tricyclic antidepressant administered in the form of its hydrochloride salt $C_{19}H_{21}NO·HCl$
dox·o·ru·bi·cin \ˌdäksōˈrübəsən\ *n* -S [*deoxy-* + *-rubicin* (as in *daunorubicin* — herein)] : an anthracycline antibiotic with broad antineoplastic activity that is obtained from a bacterium of the genus *Streptomyces* (*S. peucetius*) and is administered in the form of its hydrochloride $C_{27}H_{29}NO_{11}·HCl$
dox·y·cy·cline \ˌdäksēˈsīˌklēn, -ˌklən\ *n* -S [*deoxy-* + tetra*cycline*] : a broad-spectrum tetracycline antibiotic $C_{22}H_{24}N_2O_8$ with potent antibacterial activity that is taken by travelers often as a prophylactic against diarrhea
dozen* *n* **dozens** *pl* : a game that consists of exchanging often obscene insults usu. about the members of the opponent's family — often used in the phrase *play the dozens*
DPI *abbr, usu not cap* dots per inch
DPT *abbr* diphtheria-pertussis-tetanus (vaccine)
draft* *vi* : to stay close behind another racer while racing at high speed in order to take advantage of the reduced air pressure created by the leading racer
draft* *n* : a pocket of reduced air pressure behind a moving object; *also* : the use of such a draft to save energy
drafts·person \ˈdraf(t)s+ˌ\ *n* [*drafts*man + *person*] : a person who makes technical drawings
drag* *n* **1** : one that is boring or impedes the pursuit of enjoyment ⟨their work . . . is a ~ a good deal of the time —Nora Johnson⟩ ⟨knows this sickly kid is going to be a social ~ —Edmund Morris⟩ **2** : COSTUME, OUTFIT, GETUP ⟨dresses hundreds in full clown ~ —Bill Cardoso⟩ **3** : DRAG QUEEN *herein* **4** : man's clothing worn by a woman ⟨a lesbian can also wear ~; that is . . . clothing designed for men —Julia P. Stanley⟩
drag* *vt* **1** : to extract by or as if by pulling **2** : to move (items on a computer display) esp. by means of a mouse
drag *adj* [[1]*drag*] : of, being, involving, or intended for a person in drag ⟨a ~ ball⟩
dragon lady *n* [so called fr. a character with this epithet in the comic strip *Terry and the Pirates* by Milton Caniff †1988 Am. cartoonist] : an overbearing or tyrannical woman; *also* : a glamorous often mysterious woman
drag queen *n* : a male homosexual who dresses as a woman
drag racing *n* [[1]*drag*] : the sport of holding acceleration contests for vehicles over a straight course
drain* *vt* : SINK 14 ⟨snaps his fingers when he ~*s* a long putt —Barry McDermott⟩ ⟨~*ed* two free throws⟩
drain* *n* -S : an electrode in a field-effect transistor to which charge carriers migrate — compare GATE *herein*, SOURCE *herein* — **down the drain** : into a state of decline or of being wasted or irretrievably lost
draize test \ˈdrāz-\ *also* **draize eye test** *n, usu cap D* [after John H. *Draize* †1992 Am. pharmacologist] : a test that is used as a criterion for harmfulness of chemicals to the human eye and that involves dropping the test substance into one eye of rabbits without anesthesia using the other eye as a control
DRAM \ˈdram *also* ˈdēˌram\ *n* -S [*d*ynamic + *RAM* (herein)] : a computer-memory chip that must be continuously supplied with power in order to retain data
dra·me·dy \ˈdrämədē, ˈdra-\ *n* -ES [blend of *drama* and *comedy*] : a comedy (as a film or television show) having dramatic moments
drawdown* *n* **1** : a lowering of the water level (as in a reservoir) **2** : DEPLETION, REDUCTION
dreadlock \ˈ≈ˌ≈\ *n* -S [perh. fr. [3]*dread* + *locks*] **1** : a narrow ropelike strand of hair formed by matting or braiding **2 dreadlocks** *pl* : a hairstyle consisting of dreadlocks — **dreadlocked** \ˈ≈ˌ≈\ *adj*
dreadnought* *n* : one that is among the largest or most powerful of its kind
dream·scape \ˈdrēmˌskāp\ *n* -S [[1]*dream* + *-scape*] : a dreamlike usu. surrealistic scene ⟨seemed greener than he had remembered any jungle to be: a ~ out of neverland —Frank Yerby⟩; *also* : a painting of a dreamscape
dream team *n* : a team whose members are preeminent in a particular field ⟨a legal *dream team*⟩
dress down* *vi* : to dress casually esp. for reasons of fashion
dress–down day \ˈ≈ˈ≈\ *n* [[1]*dress* + [4]*down*] : a day during which employees are allowed to wear casual attire at work
dress rehearsal* *n* : an action, event, or work deemed to be a practice exercise for an ensuing action, event, or work : DRY RUN 2 ⟨the new book might be a *dress rehearsal* for a full-scale autobiography to come⟩
dress up* *vt* : to make more attractive, impressive, or fancy esp. by adding accessories or enhancements ⟨a plain outfit *dressed up* with a gilt mesh belt⟩
DRG \ˌdē(ˌ)ärˈjē\ *n* -S [*d*iagnosis *r*elated *g*roup] : any of the payment categories that are used to classify patients and esp. Medicare patients for the purpose of reimbursing hospitals for each case in a given category with a fixed fee regardless of the actual costs incurred and that are based esp. on the principal diagnosis, surgical procedure used, age of patient, and expected length of stay in the hospital — called also *diagnosis related group*
drill* *vt* [[4]*drill*] : to propel (as a ball) with force or accuracy ⟨~*ed* a single to right field⟩; *also* : to hit with force ⟨~*ed* the batter with the first pitch⟩
drill* *n* [[3]*drill*] : ROUTINE
drillship \ˈ≈ˌ≈\ *n* : a ship equipped for drilling (as for oil) in the ocean floor
drink·er respirator \ˈdriŋkə(r)-\ *n, usu cap D* [after Philip *Drinker* †1972 Am. public health engineer] : IRON LUNG
drive* *vb* — **drive home** : to clarify or make obvious esp. with great impact ⟨if you really want to make a point—*drive* it *home*, make it stick—then you must give examples —E.P.Bailey, Jr.⟩
drive* *n* : a device including an electric motor and heads or a laser for reading or writing on magnetic or optical media (as tapes or disks)
[1]**drive–by** \ˈ≈ˌ≈\ *adj* [fr. the phrase *drive by*] : carried out from a moving vehicle ⟨a *drive-by* shooting⟩
[2]**drive–by** \ˈ≈ˌ≈\ *n* -S : a drive-by shooting
driveline \ˈ≈ˌ≈\ *n* : DRIVETRAIN *herein*
driven* *adj* : propelled or motivated by or for something — used in combination ⟨achievement-*driven*⟩ ⟨a character-*driven* drama⟩
driver* *n* : a piece of computer software that controls input and output operations
[1]**drive–through** *also* **drive–thru** \ˈ≈ˌ≈\ *adj* [fr. the phrase *drive through*] **1** : DRIVE-UP *herein* **2** : designed for viewing by persons riding in a motor vehicle ⟨a *drive-through* zoo⟩
[2]**drive–through** *also* **drive–thru** *n* -S : a drive-through establishment (as a restaurant or bank); *also* : the drive-through window at such an establishment
drive time *n* : the time during rush hour when radio audiences are swelled by commuters listening to car radios
drivetrain \ˈ≈ˌ≈\ *n* : the parts (as the universal joint and the drive shaft) that connect the transmission with the driving axles of an automotive vehicle
drive–up \ˈ≈ˌ≈\ *adj* [fr. the phrase *drive up*] : designed to allow patrons or customers to be served while remaining in their automobiles ⟨two *drive-up* windows at the bank⟩
dro·nab·i·nol \ˌdrōˈnabəˌnōl\ *n* -S [prob. fr. *d*elta + *hydro-* + *cannabinol*] : a prescription preparation of the major physiologically active isomer of THC in soft gelatin capsules that is used to control nausea caused by chemotherapy and to stimulate appetite in cases of AIDS-induced anorexia
drone* *n* : one who does menial, routine, or boring work : DRUDGE
drop* *vt* : to take (a drug) through the mouth : SWALLOW ⟨~ acid⟩ — **drop a dime** : to call and inform authorities (as police) of another's wrongdoing — **drop the ball** : to make a mistake esp. by failing to take timely, effective, or proper action — **drop trou** : to lower one's trousers : remove one's clothing
drop–dead \ˈ≈ˈ≈\ *adj* : sensationally striking, attractive, or impressive ⟨a *drop-dead* evening gown⟩ — **drop–dead** *adv*
drop–down \ˈ≈ˌ≈\ *adj* [fr. the phrase *drop down*] : PULL-DOWN ⟨a *drop-down* menu appears on the screen⟩
drop–in \ˈdräpˌin\ *n* -S [fr. the phrase *drop in*] **1** : one who drops in : a casual visitor **2** : an informal social gathering at which guests are invited to drop in
drop–in center *n* : an establishment designed to provide recreational, educational, or counseling services to a particular group
drop out* *vi* : to withdraw from conventional society because of disenchantment with its values and mores
dropout* *n* **1** : one who drops out of conventional society **2** : a spot on a magnetic tape or disk from which information has disappeared
drop pass *n* : a pass in ice hockey in which the puck carrier skates past the puck leaving it for a teammate following close behind
drown·proof·ing \ˈdrau̇nˌprüfiŋ\ *n* -S [*drown* + *proofing*] : a technique for staying afloat in water for an extended period with minimum effort by using one's natural buoyancy
drug·gie *also* **drug·gy** \ˈdrəgē\ *n, pl* **drug·gies** [[1]*drug* + *-ie*] : one who habitually uses drugs
drug·gy *also* **drug·gie** \ˈdrəgē\ *adj* -ER/-EST [[1]*drug* + [1]*-y*] : relating to, associated with, or affected by drugs or drug use
drug·ola \ˌdrəgˈōlə\ *n* -S [[1]*drug* + *-ola* (as in *payola*)] : payola in the form of illicit drugs
drumbeat* *n* **1** : DRUMBEATING **2** : [2]BARRAGE 2
drum machine *n* : an electronic device producing a repetitive sound like a drumbeat esp. to accompany musical instruments
drunken* *adj* : marinated, cooked, or soaked in beer or wine or in a mixture containing such a beverage ⟨~ chicken⟩
drunk tank *n* : a large detention cell for persons arrested for drunkenness
dry·able \ˈdrīəbəl\ *adj* : capable of being machine dried without damage ⟨machine washable and ~ garments⟩ — **dry·abil·i·ty** \ˌdrīəˈbilədē, -ətē, -i\ *n*
dry eye *or* **dry eye syndrome** *n* : a condition associated with inadequate tear production and marked by redness of the conjunctiva, by itching and burning of the eye, and usu. by filaments of desquamated epithelial cells adhering to the cornea
dry–eyed \ˈ≈ˈ≈\ *adj* **1** : not moved to tears or to sympathy **2** : marked by the absence of sentimentalism or romanticism ⟨an exercise in *dry-eyed* nostalgia —Edith Oliver⟩
dry out *vt* : to subject to withdrawal from the use of alcohol or drugs : DETOXIFY 1 *herein* ~ *vi* : to undergo an extended period of withdrawal from alcohol or drug use esp. at a special clinic : DETOXIFY *herein*
dry sink *n* : a wooden cabinet with a tray top for holding a wash basin
DSP *abbr* digital signal processing; digital signal processor
dual–energy x–ray absorptiometry \ˈ≈≈ˈ≈≈≈-\ *n* : absorptiometry in which the density or mass of a material (as bone or fat) is measured by comparing the amounts of absorption by the material of x-radiation of two different energies generated by an x-ray tube and which is used esp. for determining the mineral content of bone
dual–purpose fund *n* : a closed-end investment company with two classes of shares one of which is entitled to all dividend income and the other to all gains from capital appreciation
dub* *n* [[6]*dub*] : Jamaican popular music in which audio effects and spoken or chanted words are imposed on an instrumental reggae background
dub·ni·um \ˈdübnēəm, ˈdəb-\ *n* -S [NL, fr. *Dubna*, city in Russia where a center for investigation of heavy elements is located] : a short-lived radioactive element of atomic number 105 that is produced artificially — symbol *Db*
du·chenne \düˈshen\ *also* **du·chenne's** \-nz\ *adj, usu cap* : relating to or being Duchenne muscular dystrophy
duchenne muscular dystrophy *also* **duchenne's muscular dystrophy** *n, usu cap 1st D* [after Guillaume Armand *Duchenne* †1875 Fr. neurologist] : a severe progressive form of muscular dystrophy of males that appears in early childhood, affects the muscles of the legs before those of the arms and the proximal muscles of the limbs before the distal ones, is inherited as an X-linked recessive trait, is characterized by complete absence of the protein dystrophin, and usu. has a fatal outcome by age 20 — see BECKER MUSCULAR DYSTROPHY *herein*
duck's ass *n* : DUCKTAIL — often considered vulgar
duct tape *n* : a wide cloth adhesive tape orig. designed for sealing joints in heating or air-conditioning ducts
dude* *n* : FELLOW, GUY — sometimes used as a mode of familiar address ⟨hey, ~, what's up⟩
due diligence *n* : ORDINARY CARE
du·en·de \düˈen(ˌ)dā\ *n* -S [Sp dial., charm, fr. Sp, ghost, goblin, prob. fr. *duen de casa*, fr. *dueño de casa* owner of a house] : the power to attract through personal magnetism and charm
dufus *var of* DOOFUS *herein*
duh \ˈdə, *usu with prolonged* ə\ *interj* **1** — used to express actual or feigned ignorance or stupidity **2** — used derisively to indicate that something just stated is all too obvious or self-evident
DUI \ˌdēˌyüˈī\ *abbr or n* -S **1** : driving under the influence **2** : one who is arrested for or convicted of DUI **3** : an arrest or conviction for DUI
du jour* *adj* : popular, fashionable, or prominent at a particular time ⟨became the Hollywood director *du jour*⟩ ⟨the hysteria *du jour* —James Bovard⟩
duke \ˈdük\ *vb* -ED/-ING/-S [*duke* (fist), prob. fr. *Duke of York*, rhyming slang for *fork* hand, fist] : FIGHT — **duke it out** : to have a fight and esp. a fistfight
dulls·ville \ˈdəlzˌvil, -ˌvəl\ *n* [[1]*dull* + *-s*, formative in place names (fr. *-'s*) + *-ville* (herein)] : something or some place that is dull or boring

dumb* *adj* **1** : not having the capability to process data ⟨a ~ terminal⟩ — compare INTELLIGENT 1 *herein* **2** : being an unguided missile ⟨~ bombs⟩ — compare SMART *herein*

dumb down *vt* : to lower the level of difficulty and the intellectual content of (as a textbook)

dum–dum \ˈdəm¦dəm\ *n* -S [redupl. of *dum*, alter. of [1]*dumb*] : a stupid person : DUMMY

dummy variable *n* : an arbitrary mathematical symbol or variable that can be replaced by another without affecting the value of the expression in which it occurs — compare UMBRAL SYMBOL

dump* *vt* **1** : to copy (data in a computer's internal storage) to an external storage or output device **2** : to lose (a game or match) on purpose : THROW **3** : to throw (as a pass) short and softly ⟨~*ed* the ball to the fullback⟩ — often used with *off* — **dump on** : to treat disrespectfully: as **a** : to take unfair advantage of ⟨feeling overworked and *dumped on* —Joan Sackett⟩ **b** : to abuse verbally : DISPARAGE, BELITTLE ⟨if they want to *dump on* people's work, let them become reviewers —Stephen Sondheim⟩

dump* *n* **1** : an instance of dumping data stored in a computer **2** : a freestanding rack (as of cardboard) used as a promotional display for books

dumping ground *n* : a place to which unwanted people or things are sent ⟨special education classes . . . have too often become the *dumping ground* for those students whom teachers find merely troublesome —Jane Perlez⟩

Dump·ster \ˈdəmpstər\ *trademark* — used for a large trash receptacle

dumpy* *adj* : being in a dirty or shabby condition : GRUNGY *herein* ⟨~ hotel rooms⟩

dune buggy *n* : an off-road motor vehicle with oversize tires for use esp. on sand

dunk* *vt* : to make a dunk shot with ~ *vi* : to make a dunk shot in basketball

dunk* *n* : DUNK SHOT

dun·ny \ˈdənē, -ni\ *n* -ES [alter. of Brit. argot *dunnekin*, of unknown origin] *Austral* : TOILET; *esp* : one outdoors : PRIVY

duplex* *n* : a molecule having two complementary polynucleotide strands of DNA or of DNA and RNA — **duplex** *adj*

duplicate* *vi* : to become duplicate : REPLICATE ⟨DNA in chromosomes ~*s*⟩

duplication* *n* : a part of a chromosome in which the genetic material is repeated; *also* : the process of forming a duplication

durable press *n* : PERMANENT PRESS *herein* — **durable–press** \¦==¦=\ *adj*

dust bunny *n* : an aggregate of dust ⟨swept the *dust bunnies* from under the bed⟩

dust mite *n* : any of various mites (esp. family Pyroglyphidae) implicated in human allergic reactions to dust; *esp* : either of two widely distributed mites of the genus *Dermatophagoides* (*D. farinae* and *D. pteronyssinus*)

dutch cap* *n, usu cap D* [fr. its resemblance to the headgear] : CERVICAL CAP *herein*

duvet* *n* : COMFORTER 3b

DVD \ˌdē(ˌ)vēˈdē\ *n* -S [*d*igital *v*ideo *d*isk] : a high-capacity optical disk format; *also* : an optical disk using such a format and containing esp. a video recording (as a movie) or computer data

dweeb \ˈdwēb\ *n* -S [origin unknown] *slang* : NERD *herein* — **dweeb·ish** \-ish\ *adj* — **dweeby** \-ē\ *adj*

DWI \ˌdēˌdəbəl(ˌ)yəˈwī, -byəˈ-\ *abbr or n* -S **1** : driving while intoxicated **2** : one who is charged with driving while intoxicated **3** : an arrest or conviction for DWI

dye laser *n* : a laser in which light is emitted by a fluorescent organic dye and which can be tuned to radiate at any of a wide range of frequencies

dyke *or* **dike** \ˈdīk\ *n* -S [origin unknown] : LESBIAN; *esp* : one assuming an aggressively masculine role — often used disparagingly — **dyk·ey** *or* **dik·ey** \-kē, -ki\ *adj* **dyk·i·er** *or* **dik·i·er; dyk·i·est** *or* **dik·i·est**

dynamic* *adj, of random-access memory* : requiring periodic refreshment of charge in order to retain data

dynamite *adj* [*dynamite*, n.] : TERRIFIC, WONDERFUL

dy·nein \ˈdīˌnēn, -ˌnēən\ *n* -S [*dyne* + *-in*] : an ATPase that cross-links adjacent microtubules and that by controlling their relative sliding motion regulates the movement of cellular organelles and structures (as the beating of cilia and flagella and the movement of chromosomes to the poles of the spindle)

dyn·or·phin \dīˈnȯrfən\ *n* -S [Gk *dyn*amis power + E end*orphin* (herein) — more at DYNAMIC] : any of a group of potent opioid peptides found in the mammalian central nervous system that have a strong affinity for opiate receptors

dys·au·to·no·mia \(ˌ)disˌȯdəˈnōmēə, -ˌäd-\ *n* -S [NL, fr. *dys-* + E [2]*autonomic* + NL [1]*-ia*] : a disorder of the autonomic nervous system that causes disturbances in all or some autonomic functions and may result from the course of a disease (as diabetes) or from injury or poisoning; *esp* : a familial disorder inherited as an autosomal recessive trait typically affecting individuals of eastern European Jewish ancestry and characterized esp. by multiple sensory deficits (as of taste and pain), excessive sweating and salivation, lack of tears, orthostatic hypotension, motor incoordination, and emotional instability — **dys·autonomic** \(ˈ)dis+\ *adj*

dys·ba·rism \ˈdisbəˌrizəm\ *n* -S [*dys-* + *bar-* + *-ism*] : the complex of symptoms (as bends, headache, or mental disturbance) that accompanies exposure to excessively low or rapidly changing environmental air pressure

dys·cal·cu·lia \ˌdiskalˈkyülēə\ *n* -S [NL, fr. *dys-* + L *calcul*are to compute + *-ia* [1]-ia] : impairment of mathematical ability due to an organic condition of the brain

dys·genesis* \(ˈ)dis+\ *n* : defective development esp. of the gonads (as in Klinefelter's syndrome or Turner's syndrome)

dys·graph·ia \disˈgrafēə\ *n* -S [NL, fr. *dys-* + *-graphia*] : impairment of the ability to write caused by brain damage

dyslexic *n* -S [*dyslexic*, adj.] : a person affected with dyslexia

dys·pro·tein·emia \ˌdisˌprōˌtēˈnēmēə *also* -ōd-ēəˈn- *or* -ōtēəˈn-\ *n* -S [NL, fr. *dys-* + ISV *protein* + NL *-emia*] : any of various abnormalities of the protein content of the blood — **dys·pro·tein·emic** \-ˈnēmik\ *adj*

dysrhythmia* *n* : JET LAG *herein*

dys·to·pia \disˈtōpēə\ *n* -S [*dys-* + *-topia* (as in *utopia*)] **1** : an imaginary place which is depressingly wretched and whose people lead a fearful existence **2** : a work describing a dystopia — **dys·to·pi·an** \-ēən\ *adj*

dys·tro·phin \ˈdistrəˌfin\ *n* -S [*dystrophy* + *-in*] : a protein of high molecular weight that is associated with a transmembrane glycoprotein complex of skeletal muscle cells and is absent in Duchenne muscular dystrophy and deficient or of abnormal molecular weight in Becker muscular dystrophy

e* *symbol, often cap* exponent — used esp. in scientific and floating-point notation (as in a computer display) when a superscript is inconvenient

eames chair \ˈēmz-, ˈāmz-\ *n, usu cap E* [after Charles *Eames* †1978 Am. designer] : any of several chairs designed by Charles Eames to fit the contours of the body and to be made from modern materials (as molded plywood or fiber glass)

ear candy *n* : music that is pleasing to listen to but lacks depth

earl grey \¦=¦grā\ *n, usu cap E&G* [after Charles Grey, 2d *Earl Grey* †1845 Eng. statesman] : a black-tea blend flavored with bergamot oil

earth day *n, usu cap E&D* : a day in April designated for promoting concern for the environment

earth mother* *n* : an embodiment of the female principle of fertility : a nurturing maternal woman

earthrise \=ˌ=\ *n* : the rising of the earth above the horizon of the moon as seen from lunar orbit

earth station *n* : DISH 4d; *esp* : one used primarily for receiving and transmitting television signals

earth tone *n* : any of various rich dark colors containing some brown — **earth–toned** *adj*

east caribbean dollar *n, usu cap E&C* : a basic monetary unit shared by a number of islands of the British West Indies

easy listening *n* : popular vocal and instrumental music that is generally pleasing and that is sometimes considered to be lacking in substance

eat* *vt* **1** : to perform fellatio or cunnilingus on — usu. considered vulgar **2** : to bear the expense of : take a loss on ⟨rather than ~ the loss, most retailers have been insisting that manufacturers offer discounts —James Traub⟩ — **eat alive** : to defeat, conquer, or overwhelm completely : CRUSH — **eat someone's lunch** : to deprive of profit, dominance, or success

eating disorder *n* : any of several psychological disorders (as anorexia nervosa or bulimia) characterized by serious disturbances of eating behavior

eau de toilette \ˌōdətwäˈlet\ *n, pl* **eaux de toilette** \ˌō(z)-\ *or* **eaux de toilettes** \ˌō(z)dətwäˈlet(s)\ *or* **eau de toilettes** \ˌōdətwäˈlet(s)\ [F, lit., water for washing and dressing] : a perfumed liquid containing a lower percentage of fragrant oils than does ordinary perfume — called also *toilet water*

EBCDIC \ˈepsəˌdik, ˈebs-\ *n* [extended *b*inary *c*oded *d*ecimal *i*nterchange *c*ode] : a code for representing alphanumeric information (as on magnetic tape)

ebo·la \ēˈbōlə, i-, e-; ˈēˌbōlə, ˈā-\ *n, usu cap* **1** : EBOLA VIRUS *herein* **2** *also* **ebola fever** *usu cap E* : the hemorrhagic fever caused by the Ebola virus

ebola virus *n, usu cap E* [fr. the *Ebola* River in the Congo (former Zaire), site of an outbreak of the virus in 1976] : any of several filoviruses of African origin that cause an often fatal hemorrhagic fever

ebon·ics \ēˈbäniks, i-, e-\ *n pl but sing or pl in constr, often cap* [blend of [1]*ebony* and *phonics*] : BLACK ENGLISH *herein*

eb·ul·lism \ˈeb(y)əˌlizəm\ *n* -S [L *ebull*ire to come bubbling out + E *-ism* — more at EBULLIENT] : the formation of bubbles in body fluids under sharply reduced environmental pressure

EBV *abbr* Epstein-Barr virus *herein*

EB virus \ˌēˈbē-\ *n* [*E*pstein-*B*arr] : EPSTEIN-BARR VIRUS *herein*

ec-* *or* **eco-*** *comb form* : ecological or environmental ⟨*eco*catastrophe⟩

ec·cle·si·al \əˈklēzēəl, eˈk-, -zhəl\ *adj* [LL *ecclesia* church + E [1]*-al* — more at ECCLESI-] : ECCLESIASTICAL 1a ⟨these differences of ~ belief . . . are not an absolute prohibition of intercommunion —W.W.Bassett⟩

ec·dy·sone \ˈekdəˌsōn\ *n* -S [*ecdys*is + hor*mone*] : any of several arthropod hormones that in insects are produced by the prothoracic gland and that trigger molting and metamorphosis

echo·cardiogram \ˈe(ˌ)kō+\ *n* [[1]*echo* + *cardiogram*] : a visual record made by echocardiography; *also* : the procedure for producing such a record

echo·cardiography \"+\ *n* [[1]*echo* + *cardiography*] : the use of ultrasound to examine and measure structure and functioning of the heart and to diagnose abnormalities and disease — **echo·cardiographer** \"+\ *n* — **echo·cardiographic** \"+\ *adj*

echo·encephalography \"+\ *n* [*echo* + *encephalography*] : the use of ultrasound to examine and measure internal structures (as the ventricles) of the skull and to diagnose abnormalities and disease — **echo·encephalographic** \"+\ *adj*

echog·ra·phy \eˈkägrəfē\ *n* -ES [[1]*echo* + *-graphy*] : ULTRASOUND 1 *herein* — **echo·graph·ic** \ˌekəˈgrafik, ˌe(ˌ)kō-, -ēk\ *adj* — **echo·graph·i·cal·ly** \-ik(ə)lē, -lī\ *adv*

echolocate \¦ekō+\ *vb* [[1]*echo* + *locate*] *vt* : to find by echolocation ⟨a bat ~*s* food⟩ ~ *vi* : to utilize or have the capacity for echolocation

echo·virus \"+\ *n* [*e*nteric *c*ytopathogenic *h*uman *o*rphan + *virus*] : any of several picornaviruses (genus *Enterovirus*) that are found in the gastrointestinal tract, that cause cytopathic changes in cells in tissue culture, and that are sometimes associated with respiratory ailments and meningitis

eco·catastrophe \¦ē(ˌ)kō, ¦e(ˌ)kō+\ *n* [[2]*ec-* + *catastrophe*] : a major destructive upset in the balance of nature esp. when caused by the intervention of humans

eco·cide \ˈēkəˌsīd, ˈek-, -(ˌ)kō,-\ *n* -S [[2]*ec-* + *-cide*] : the destruction of large areas of the natural environment — **eco·cid·al** \¦==¦sīdᵊl\ *adj*

eco·feminism \¦ēkō, ¦ekō+\ *n* [[2]*ec-* + *feminism*] : a movement or theory that applies feminist principles and ideas to ecological issues — **eco·feminist** \"+\ *n or adj*

eco·geographic *or* **eco·geographical** \¦ekō, ¦ēkō+\ *adj* [[2]*ec-* + *geographic* or *geographical*] : of or relating to both ecological and geographical aspects of the environment — **eco·geographically** \"+\ *adv*

e. coli \ēˈkōˌlī\ *n, pl* **e. coli** *also* **e. colis** *usu cap E* [short for NL *Escherichia coli*, species name, lit., Escherichia of the colon] : a straight rod-shaped gram-negative bacterium (*Escherichia coli* of the family Enterobacteriaceae) that is used in public health as an indicator of fecal pollution (as of water or food) and in medicine and genetics as a research organism and that occurs in various strains that may live as harmless inhabitants of the human lower intestine or may produce a toxin causing intestinal illness ⟨one million acid-resistant *E. coli* per gram of feces —John Schwartz⟩ ⟨this *E. coli* can survive . . . longer than all the other *E. colis* —Ed Geldreich⟩

econ·o·box \ēˈkänəˌbäks, -nə,-, əˈk-\ *n* [*econo*my + [2]*box*] : a small economical car

economy *adj* : designed to save money ⟨~ cars⟩

economy of scale : a reduction in the cost of producing something (as a car or a unit of electricity) brought about esp. by increased size of production facilities — usu. used in pl.

eco·physiology \¦ēkō, ¦ekō+\ *n* [[2]*ec-* + *physiology*] : the science of the interrelationships between the physiology of organisms and their enviroment — **eco·physiological** \"+\ *adj* — **eco·physiologist** \"+\ *n*

eco·sphere \ˈēkō, ˈekō+ˌ\ *n* [[2]*ec-* + *sphere*] : the parts of the universe habitable by living organisms; *esp* : BIOSPHERE 1 — **eco·spheric** \¦ēkō, ¦ekō+\ *adj*

eco·tage \ˈē(ˌ)kō,täzh, ˈe-, -tȧl, *sometimes* ¦j *or* ¦==¦\ *n* -S [[2]*ec-* + sab*otage*] : destructive or obstructive action designed to publicize or harass people believed to be harming the environment

eco·terrorism \ˌēkō+, ˌekō+\ *n* [[2]*ec-* + *terrorism*] : sabotage intended to hinder activities that are considered damaging to the environment **2** : political terrorism intended to damage an enemy's natural environment — **eco·terrorist** \"+\ *n or adj*

eco·tour \ˈēkə, ˈekə+\ *n* [[2]*ec-* + [1]*tour*] : a trip that follows the principles of ecotourism

eco·tourism \ˌēkō, ˌekō+\ *n* [[2]*ec-* + *tourism*] : the practice of touring natural habitats in a manner meant to minimize ecological impact — **eco·tourist** \"+\ *n*

eco·toxicology \"+\ *n* [[2]*ec-* + *toxicology*] : a scientific discipline combining the methods of ecology and toxicology in studying the effects of toxic substances and esp. pollutants on the environment — **eco·toxicological** \"+\ *adj* — **eco·toxicologist** \"+\ *n*

ecstasy* *n, often cap* : a synthetic amphetamine analogue $C_{11}H_{15}NO_2$ used illicitly for its mood-enhancing and hallucinogenic properties — called also *MDMA*

ec·to·crine \ˈektəkrən; -ˌkrin, -rīn, -rēn\ *n* -S [*ect-* + *-crine* (as in *endocrine*)] : a metabolite produced by an organism of one kind and utilized by one of another kind

ec·to·hormone \¦ektə+\ *n* [*ect-* + *hormone*] : PHEROMONE *herein* — **ec·to·hormonal** \"+\ *adj*

ECU \ˌē(ˌ)sēˈyü\ *abbr or n* -S *sometimes not cap* [*E*uropean *C*urrency *U*nit (influenced by F *écu* ecu)] : a money of account based on the currency units of members of the European Union from 1979 up to the introduction of the euro in 1999

ecu·me·nop·o·lis \ˌekyəməˈnäpələs, eˌkyüm-\ *n* -ES [NGk *oikoumenopolis*, fr. Gk *oikoumenē* world + *-o-* + *-polis* — more at ECUMENE] : a single city encompassing the whole world that is held to be a possibility of the future

EDB *abbr* ethylene dibromide

edge city *n* : a suburb that has developed its own political, economic, and commercial base independent of the central city

edi·a·car·an \ˌēdēˈak(ə)rən, -əˈkarən\ *also* **edi·a·cara** \-rə\ *adj, usu cap* [*Ediacara* Hills of South Australia, where Precambrian fossils were discovered in 1946 + [2]*-an*] : being or belonging to an assemblage of extinct multicellular soft-bodied marine organisms of the late Precambrian era ⟨~ fauna⟩ — **ediacaran** *n* -S *usu cap*

ed·it \ˈedət\ *n* -S [*edit*, v.] : an instance or the result of editing

editor* *n* : a computer program that permits the user to create or modify data (as text or graphics) esp. on a display screen

EDP *abbr* electronic data processing

edro·pho·nium \ˌedrəˈfōnēəm\ *n* -S [*e*thyl + hy*dro*xy + *phe*nyl + ammo*nium*] : an anticholinesterase $C_{10}H_{16}ClNO$ used esp. to stimulate skeletal muscle and in the diagnosis of myasthenia gravis — called also *edrophonium chloride*

educational television *n* **1** : television that provides instruction esp. for students **2** : PUBLIC TELEVISION *herein*

ed·u·ca·tion·ese \ˌejəˌkāshəˈnēz, -ēs\ *n* -S : the jargonistic language used esp. by educational theorists

ed·u·tain·ment \ˌejəˈtānmənt, ˌedyü-\ *n* -S [*edu*cation + enter*tainment*] : entertainment (as by games, films, or shows) that is designed to be educational

EEO *abbr* equal employment opportunity

EER *abbr* energy efficiency ratio *herein*

effectively* *adv* : in effect : VIRTUALLY ⟨the civil war ~ partitioned Lebanon —J.M.Markham⟩

effector* *n* : a molecule (as an inducer, a corepressor, or an enzyme) that activates, controls, or inactivates a process or action (as protein synthesis or the release of a second messenger)

EFT *abbr* electronic funds transfer *herein*

EFTS *abbr* electronic funds transfer system

EGF *abbr* epidermal growth factor *herein*

egg* *n* — **egg on one's face** : a state of embarrassment or humiliation

egg cream *n* : a sweetened drink made with milk or cream and other ingredients; *esp* : a drink consisting of milk, a flavoring syrup, and soda water

ego–dystonic \¦==disˈtänik\ *adj* [*ego* + *dyston*ia + *-ic*] : incompatible with or unacceptable to the ego ⟨*ego-dystonic* acts or thoughts —J.L.Singer⟩ — compare EGO-SYNTONIC *in the Dict*

ego trip *n* : something that enhances and satisfies one's ego

ego–trip \ˈ==ˌ=\ *vi* : to behave in a self-seeking manner ⟨never overplayed, never *ego-tripped*, never grabbed the spotlight —Bob Palmer⟩ — **ego–tripper** \ˈ=ˌ=ˌ=\ *n* -S

egyptian mau \-ˈmau̇\ *n* -S *usu cap E & often cap M* [*Mau* fr. Egyptian *mȧu*, alternate transliteration of *mìw* cat, of imit. origin] : any of a breed of short-haired domestic cats originating in Egypt and characterized by a spotted coat and light green or amber eyes

eh·lers–dan·los syndrome \ˈālərzˈdan(ˌ)läs-\ *n, usu cap E&D* [after E. *Ehlers* †1937 Dan. dermatologist and H.A. *Danlos* †1912 Fr. dermatologist] : an inherited disorder of connective tissue with several clinical forms characterized esp. by extremely flexible joints, elastic skin, and excessive bruising

EHV *abbr* extra high voltage

ei·co·sa·noid \īˈkōsəˌnȯid\ *n* -S [*eicosa*noic acid + [1]*-oid*] : any of a class of compounds (as the prostaglandins, leukotrienes, or thromboxanes) that are derived from polyunsaturated fatty acids (as arachidonic acid) and that play a role in cellular activity

eigenvalue* *n* : a scalar associated with a given linear transformation of a vector space and having the property that there is some nonzero vector which when multiplied by the scalar is equal to the vector obtained by letting the transformation operate on the vector ⟨if $T(v) = \lambda v$, where T is a linear transformation, v is a nonzero vector, and λ is a scalar, then λ is an ~ of T, and v is an eigenvector of T corresponding to λ⟩; *specif* : a root of the characteristic equation of a matrix

ei·gen·vector \ˈīgən+ˌ\ *n* [ISV *eigen-* (fr. G, peculiar to, characteristic) + *vector* — more at EIGENFREQUENCY] : a nonzero vector that is mapped by a given linear transformation of a vector space onto a vector that is the product of a scalar multiplied by the original vector — called also *characteristic vector*

eightfold way *n* [fr. the *Eightfold Way* Eightfold Path; fr. the fact that the most common grouping contains eight interacting particles] : a unified theoretical scheme for classifying the relationship among elementary particles subject to the strong force on the basis of isospin and hypercharge

800 number \ˌātˈhəndrəd-, -dərd-\ *n* : a toll-free telephone number for long-distance calls (as to a business) that is prefixed by the number 800

eighty–six \¦==¦=\ *or* **86** \"\ *vt* -ED/-ING/-ES [rhyming slang for [4]*nix*] *slang* : to refuse to serve (a customer); *also* : to get rid of : throw out

eis·wein \ˈīsˌwīn, -vīn\ *n* -S [G, fr. *eis* ice (fr. OHG *īs*) + *wein* wine, fr. OHG *wīn* — more at ICE, WINE] : a sweet German wine made from grapes that have frozen on the vine; *also* : a similar wine made elsewhere

ekis·tics \əˈkistiks, ēˈk-\ *n pl but sing in constr* [NGk *oikistikē*, fr. fem. of *oikistikos* of settlement, fr. Gk, fr. *oikizein* to settle, colonize, fr. *oikos* house — more at VICINITY] : a science dealing with human settlements and drawing on the research and experience of professionals in various fields (as architecture, engineering, city planning, and sociology) — **ekis·tic** \-tik\ *adj* — **ekis·ti·cian** \əˌkiˈstishən, (ˌ)ēˌk-\ *n* -S

ek·man dredge \ˈekmən-\ *n, usu cap E* [prob. after V.W. *Ekman* †1954 Swed. oceanographer] : a dredge that has opposable jaws operated by a messenger traveling down a cable to release a spring catch and that is used in ecology for sampling the bottom of a body of water

ekt·exine \(ˈ)ekt+\ *n* [ISV *ekt-* ect- + *exine*] : a structurally variable outer layer of the exine

ekue·le \āˈkwā(ˌ)lā\ *also* **ek·pwe·le** \ekˈpwā(ˌ)lā\ *n, pl* **ekuele** *also* **ekpweles** [Fang, a pre-colonial iron currency] **1** : the basic monetary unit of Equatorial Guinea from 1975 to 1985 **2** : a coin or note representing one ekuele

el cheapo \elˈchē(ˌ)pō\ *adj* [pseudo-Spanish alter. of [3]*cheap*] *slang* : CHEAP 3

eldercare \ˈ==ˌ=\ *n* [[3]*elder* + [1]*care*] : the care of older persons and esp. the care of an older parent by a son or daughter

el·der·ly \ˈeldə(r)lē\ *n, pl* **elderly** *or* **elderlies** : an elderly person

elect·able \əˈlektəbəl, ēˈl-\ *adj* : capable of being elected — **elect·abil·i·ty** \əˌlektəˈbiləd-ē, ēˌl-, -ətē\ *n* -ES

elective* *adj* : beneficial to the patient but not essential for his survival ⟨an ~ appendectomy⟩

electric* *adj* : being or involving a musical performance on electric instruments ⟨loud fast ~ blues⟩

electric broom *n* : a lightweight upright vacuum cleaner

elec·tro·an·ten·no·gram \ə¦lektrōˌanˈtenəˌgram, ē¦l-\ *n* [*electr-* + *antenna* + *-o-* + *-gram*] : a record of electrical activity in an antenna esp. of an insect

elec·tro·cor·ti·cog·ra·phy \=¦=ˌkȯrtəˈkägrəfē, -kȯr-\ *n* -ES [*electr-* + *cortico-* + *-graphy*] : the process of recording electrical activity in the brain by placing electrodes in direct contact with the cerebral cortex — **elec·tro·cor·ti·co·graph·ic** \-təkə¦grafik\ *adj* — **elec·tro·cor·ti·co·graph·i·cal·ly** \-k(ə)lē\ *adv*

electrode* *n* : an element in a semiconductor device (as a transistor) that emits or collects electrons or holes or that controls their movements

elec·tro·dermal \ə¦lektrō, ē¦l-+\ *adj* [*electr-* + *dermal*] : of or relating to electrical activity in or electrical properties of the skin

elec·tro·diagnostic \"+\ *adj* [*electr-* + *diagnostic*] : involving or obtained by the recording of responses to electrical stimulation or of spontaneous electrical activity (as in electromyography) for purposes of diagnosing a pathological condition ⟨~ studies⟩ — **elec·tro·diagnostically** \"+\ *adv*

elec·tro·en·ceph·a·log·ra·pher \ə¦lektrōənˌsefəˈlägrəfər, ē¦l-\ *n* -S [*electroencephalo*graphy + *-grapher*] : one who makes electroencephalograms

elec·tro·fishing \"+\ *n* [*electr-* + *fishing*] : the taking of fish by a system based on their tendency to respond positively to a source of direct electric current

elec·tro·form \"+\ *n* [*electr-* + *form*, n.] : a mold used in electroforming

elec·tro·genesis \"+\ *n* [*electr-* + *genesis*] : the production of electrical activity esp. in living tissue

elec·tro·genic \"+\ *adj* [*electr-* + *-genic*] : of or relating to the production of electrical activity in living tissue ⟨an ~ pump causing movement of sodium ions across a membrane⟩

elec·tro·hydraulic \"+\ *adj* [*electr-* + *hydraulic*] **1** : of, relating to, or involving a combination of electric and hydraulic mechanisms ⟨an ~ elevator⟩ **2** : involving or produced by the action of very brief but powerful pulse discharges of electricity under a liquid resulting in the generation of shock waves and highly reactive chemical species ⟨an ~ effect⟩ — **elec·tro·hydraulically** \"+\ *adv*

elec·tro·less \əˈlektrōləs, -ˌles\ *adj* [*electro*lytic + *-less*] : being or involving chemical deposition of metal instead of electrodeposition

electromagnetic pulse *n* : high-intensity electromagnetic radiation generated by a nuclear blast high above the earth's surface that is held to disrupt electronic and electrical systems

electromagnetism* *n* : a fundamental physical force that is responsible for interactions between charged particles which occur because of their charge and for the emission and absorption of photons, that is about 100 times weaker than the strong force, and that extends over infinite distances but dominates over other forces at atomic and molecular distances — called also *electromagnetic force, electromagnetic interaction*; compare GRAVITY *herein*, STRONG FORCE *herein*, WEAK FORCE *herein*

electronic* *adj* **1** : of, relating to, or being music that consists of sounds electronically generated or modified **2** : of, relating to, or being a medium (as television) in which information is transmitted electronically ⟨~ journalism⟩ **3** : implemented on or by means of a computer : involving a computer ⟨~ food stamps⟩ ⟨~ banking⟩

elec·tron·i·ca \əˌlekˈtränəkə\ *n* -s [prob. fr. *New Electronica*, recording label of the Brit. firm Beechwood Music Ltd.] : dance music featuring extensive use of synthesizers, electronic percussion, and samples of recorded music or sound

electronic funds transfer *n* : the transfer of money from one location or account to another by computerized means

electronic mail *n* **1** : E-MAIL *herein* **2** : mail that is transmitted electronically to a receiving station where it is printed or reproduced as graphic matter and delivered to the addressee (as by messenger or through the postal system)

electronic mailbox *n* : a computer file in which electronic mail is collected

electronic publishing *n* : publishing in which information is disseminated by means of a computer network (as videotex and teletext) or is produced in a format for use with a computer

electron paramagnetic resonance *n* : ELECTRON SPIN RESONANCE *herein*

electron spin resonance *n* : the resonance of unpaired electrons in a magnetic field; *also* : a spectroscopic analytical method based on such resonance

electron transport *n* : the sequential transfer of electrons esp. by cytochromes in cellular respiration from an oxidizable substrate to molecular oxygen by a series of oxidation-reduction reactions

elec·tro·nys·tag·mo·gra·phy \əˌlektrōˌnisˌtagˈmägrəfē, ēˌl-\ *n* -ES [*electr-* + *nystagmus* + *-o-* + *-graphy*] : the use of electrooculography to study nystagmus — **elec·tro·nys·tag·mo·graph·ic** \¦=¦==¦=¦==məˈgrafik\ *adj*

elec·tro·oc·u·lo·gram \¦=¦==¦äkyələˌgram\ *n* [*electr-* + *ocul-* + *-gram*] : a record of the standing voltage between the front and back of the eye that is correlated with eyeball movement (as in REM sleep) and obtained by electrodes suitably placed on the skin near the eye

elec·tro·ocu·log·ra·phy \¦=¦==ˌäkyəˈlägrəfē\ *n* -ES [*electr-* + *ocul-* + *-graphy*] : the preparation and study of electrooculograms — **elec·tro·ocu·lo·graph·ic** \=ˌ==ˌ=yələˈgrafik\ *adj*

electro–optic** *or* **electro–optical**** *adj* **1 a** : relating to or being a change in the refractive index of a material due to an electric field ⟨*electro-optic* effect⟩ **b** : using or being a material that exhibits electro-optic properties ⟨an *electro-optic* crystal⟩ **2** : relating to or being an electronic device for emitting, modulating, transmitting, or sensing light : OPTOELECTRONIC *herein*

elec·tro·pho·rese \əˌlektrəfəˈrēs, ēˌl-, -ˈträfəˌ-, -ēz\ *vt* -ED/-ING/-S [back-formation fr. *electrophoresis*] : to subject to electrophoresis

elec·tro·pho·reto·gram \əˌlektrəfəˈredəˌgram, ēˌl-\ *or* **elec·tro·phero·gram** \=ˌ==ˈferəˌgram\ *n* [*electrophoretogram* fr. *electrophoretic* + *-o-* + *-gram*; *electropherogram* fr. *electr-* + *phero-* (fr. Gk *pherein* to carry) + *-gram* — more at BEAR] : a record that consists of the separated components of a mixture (as of proteins) produced by electrophoresis in a supporting medium (as filter paper)

elec·tro·po·ra·tion \əˌlektrəpȯrˈāshən\ *n* -s [*electr-* + ²*pore* + *-ation*] : the application of an electric current to a living surface (as the skin or the plasma membrane of a cell) in order to open pores or channels through which something (as a drug or DNA) may pass

elec·tro·receptor \ə¦lektrō+\ *n* [*electr-* + *receptor*] : a vertebrate organ found esp. in fish that contains sensory cells capable of detecting electrical fields

elec·tro·ret·i·no·graph \ə¦lektrō¦ret(ə)nəˌgraf, ē¦l-\ *n* [*electr-* + ²*retin-* + *-graph*] : an instrument for recording electrical activity in the retina — **elec·tro·ret·i·no·graph·ic** \-ˌret(ə)nə¦grafik\ *adj* — **elec·tro·ret·i·nog·ra·phy** \-(ə)nˈägrəfē\ *n* -ES

elec·tro·sleep \"+\ *n* [*electr-* + ¹*sleep*] : profound relaxation or a state of unconsciousness induced by the passage of a very low voltage electric current through the brain

electrostatic precipitator *n* : an electrostatic device in chimney flues that removes particles from escaping gases

electrostatic printing *n* : a process (as xerography) for printing or copying in which electrostatic forces are used to form the image (as with powder or ink) directly on a surface

electrotonic* *adj* : of, relating to, or being the spread of electrical activity through living tissue or cells in the absence of repeated action potentials ⟨an ~ junction between cells⟩ — **electrotonically*** *adv*

elec·tro·weak \ə¦lektrō-, ē¦l-\ *adj* [*electr-* + *weak*] : of, relating to, or being the unification of electromagnetism and the weak force ⟨~ theory⟩

el·e·doi·sin \eləˈdȯisᵊn\ *n* -s [irreg. fr. NL *Eledone*, genus name (fr. Gk *eledōnē*, a kind of octopus) + *-in*] : a small protein $C_{54}H_{85}N_{13}O_{15}S$ from the salivary glands of several octopuses (genus *Eledone*) that is a powerful vasodilator and hypotensive agent

elementary particle* *n* : one of the structural units of mitochondrial cristae that are observed by the electron microscope usu. as spheres or stalked spheres and that are prob. sites of fundamental energy-producing reactions

elephant garlic *n* : a wild leek (*Allium ampeloprasum*) of a form having a bulb that resembles that of garlic (*A. sativum*) but is much larger; *also* : the mildly flavored bulb of the elephant garlic used esp. as a seasoning

elevator music *n* : instrumental arrangements of popular songs often piped in (as to an elevator or a retail store)

eleven–plus *or* **11–plus** \=¦==¦=\ *n, Brit* : an examination taken between the ages of 11 and 12 that determines the type of secondary education to which a student is assigned

el·hi \¦elˌhī\ *adj* [*el*ementary school + *hi*gh school] : of, relating to, or designed for use in grades 1 through 12

eli·ot·ian \(ˌ)elēˈōd·ēən, -ātē-\ *or* **eli·ot·ic** \(ˌ)elēˈäd·ək, -ätik\ *adj, usu cap* [T.S. *Eliot* †1965 Brit. (Am.-born) poet + E *-ian* or *-ic*] : of or relating to T.S. Eliot or his works

ELISA \eˈlīsə, -ˈlēs-, -zə\ *n* -s : ENZYME-LINKED IMMUNOSORBENT ASSAY *herein*

elitism* *n* : the selectivity of the elite; *esp* : SNOBBERY ⟨revealed their ~ in choosing new members⟩

elkhorn coral *n* : a reef-building branching coral of the genus *Acropora* (*A. palmata*) of shallow waters of southern Florida and the West Indies

el ni·ño \(ˌ)elˈnēnyō\ *n, pl* **el niños** *cap E&N* [Sp, lit., the child (i.e., the Christ child); fr. the appearance of the flow at the Christmas season] : an irregularly recurring flow of unusually warm surface waters from the Pacific ocean toward and along the western coast of South America that prevents upwelling of nutrient-rich cold deep water and that disrupts typical regional and global weather patterns — compare LA NIÑA *herein*

e–mail \ˈ=ˌ=\ *n, often cap E* [electronic *mail*] **1** : a means or system for transmitting messages electronically (as between terminals linked by telephone lines or microwave relays) **2** : a message sent and received electronically through an e-mail system ⟨sent him an *e-mail*⟩ ⟨checked her *e-mail*⟩ — **e–mail** *vb* — **e–mail·er** \-ər\ *n*

emalangeni *pl of* LILANGENI *herein*

em·battled \əm, em+\ *adj* [ME *embatailled*, fr. past part. of *embatailen* to embattle] **1 a** : ready to fight : prepared to give battle ⟨here once the ~ farmers stood —R.W.Emerson⟩ **b** : engaged in battle, conflict, or controversy ⟨lends psychological support to an ~ president —R.J.Whalen⟩ **2 a** : being a site of battle, conflict, or controversy ⟨defending his ~ capital city —*Wall Street Jour.*⟩ **b** : characterized by conflict or controversy ⟨his highly diversified, often ~ experience as an educator —Nat Hentoff⟩

em·battlement \"+\ *n* -s : the state of being embattled

em·bour·geoise·ment \əmˈbu̇rzhˌwäzmənt, äm-, em-, -ˌmänt, *F* äⁿbürzhwäzmäⁿ\ *n* -s [F, fr. *embourgeoiser* to make bourgeois (fr. *em-* ¹en- + *bourgeois* bourgeois) + *-ment* ¹-ment] : a shift to bourgeois values and practices

embryoid *n* -s [*embryoid*, adj.] : a mass of plant or animal tissue that resembles an embryo

embryo transfer *also* **embryo transplant** *n* : a procedure used esp. in animal breeding in which an embryo from a superovulated female is removed and reimplanted in the uterus of another female

emergency medical technician *n* : EMT *herein*

EMG *abbr* electromyogram; electromyograph; electromyography

emic \ˈēmik\ *adj* [*phonemic*] : of, relating to, or having characteristics which are significant to the structure of a language or other behavioral system ⟨a phonemic transcription . . . is an ~ description of speech —John Algeo⟩ — compare ETIC *herein*

emission line *n* : a bright line in the emission spectrum of a gas or vapor — compare ABSORPTION LINE *in the Dict*

emittance* *n* : the energy radiated by the surface of a body per second per unit area

emo·ti·con \əˈmōd·əˌkän\ *n* -s [*emotion* + *icon*] : a combination of keyboard characters (as :-)) that typically represents a facial expression suggesting the writer's attitude or emotion and that is used esp. in computerized communications (as e-mail)

EMP *abbr* electromagnetic pulse *herein*

em·pa·na·da \ˌempəˈnädə\ *n* -s [Sp, fr. *empanada* breaded, fem. of *empanado*, past part. of *empanar* to bread, fr. *em-* ¹en- + *pan* bread, fr. L *panis* — more at FOOD] : a pastry turnover stuffed esp. with a savory meat filling

empower* *vt* : to promote the self-actualization or influence of ⟨women's movement has been inspiring and *~ing* women —Ron Hansen⟩

empty nester *n* : a parent whose children have grown up and moved away from home

EMS *abbr* emergency medical service; emergency medical services

EMT \ˌē(ˌ)emˈtē\ *n* -s : a specially trained medical technician certified to provide basic emergency services (as cardiopulmonary resuscitation) before and during transportation to a hospital — called also *emergency medical technician*; compare PARAMEDIC 2 *herein*

emulate* *vt* : to imitate (a different computer system) by means of an emulator

emulation* *n* : the use of or technique of using an emulator

emulator* *n* : a hardware device or a combination of hardware and software that permits one computer to run programs designed for another computer or to process data in the same way as another computer

enabler* *n* : one who helps another persist in self-destructive behavior (as substance abuse) by providing excuses or by making it possible to avoid the consequences of such behavior

enal·a·pril \eˈnaləˌpril\ *n* -s [perh. fr. *phenyl* + *alanyl* + *-pril*, alter. of *proline*] : an antihypertensive drug $C_{20}H_{28}N_2O_5$ that is an ACE inhibitor administered orally in the form of its maleate

en·amine \ˈenəˌmēn, ˈēnə-, eˈnaˌm-\ *n* [⁴*en-* + *amine*] : an amine containing the double bond linkage C=C–N

en·cap·su·lant \ənˈkapsələnt, en- *also* -syə-\ *n* -s [*encapsul*ate + *-ant*] : a material used for encapsulating

en·ceph·a·li·to·gen \ənˌsefəˈlīd·əjən, -ˌjen\ *n* -s [*encephalito*genic + *-gen*] : an encephalitogenic agent (as a virus)

en·ceph·a·lo·myocarditis \en¦sefəlō+\ *n* [NL, fr. *encephal-* + *myocarditis*] : an acute febrile virus disease of various vertebrates that is caused by any of several strains of a picornavirus (genus *Cardiovirus*) and that causes a serious condition in swine characterized esp. by degeneration and inflammation of skeletal and cardiac muscle and lesions of the central nervous system

enchilada* *n* : SCHMEAR *herein*, BALL OF WAX *herein* ⟨the whole ~⟩

encode* *vt* : to specify the genetic code for ⟨the gene *~s* a transmembrane protein⟩

encounter* *n* : a coming into the vicinity of a celestial body

encounter group *n* : a usu. leaderless and unstructured group that seeks to develop the capacity of the individual to openly express feelings and to form emotional ties by more or less unrestrained confrontation of individuals — compare T-GROUP

endangered *adj* [fr. past part. of *endanger*] : being or relating to an endangered species ⟨an ~ bird⟩ ⟨put on the ~ list⟩

endangered species *n* : a species threatened with extinction; *broadly* : anyone or anything whose continued existence is threatened

end around *n* : a football play in which an offensive end comes behind the line of scrimmage to take a handoff and attempts to carry the ball around the opposite flank

end·ar·ter·ec·to·my \ˌenˌdärd·əˈrektəmē\ *n* -ES [*endarter*ium + *-ectomy*] : surgical removal of the inner layer of an artery when thickened and atheromatous or occluded (as by intimal plaques)

endemic* *adj* : characteristic of or prevalent in a particular field, area, or environment ⟨problems ~ to translation⟩ ⟨the self-indulgence ~ in the film industry⟩

end·exine \ˌend+\ *n* [ISV *end-* + *exine*] : an inner membranous layer of the exine

endgame** *n* : the final stage of some action or process ⟨the ~ to a long political struggle⟩

en·do·cast \ˈendəˌkast\ *n* [by shortening] : ENDOCRANIAL CAST

en·do·cyt·ic \¦endə¦sid·ək, -ˈsid-\ *adj* [*endo-* + *cyt-* + ¹*-ic*] : of or relating to endocytosis : ENDOCYTOTIC ⟨~ vesicles⟩

en·do·cy·to·sis \ˌendōˌsīˈtōsəs\ *n, pl* **endocyto·ses** \-ōˌsēz\ [NL, fr. ISV *end-* + *cyt-* + NL *-osis*] : incorporation of substances into a cell by phagocytosis or pinocytosis — **en·do·cy·tot·ic** \¦==ˌsī¦täd·ik\ *adj*

end–of–day glass \ˌ=¦=ˌ=\ *n* [so called from its resemblance to objects made by glassblowers at the end of the day's work to use up various odds and ends of glass left over] : glass of various colors mixed together

endogenic* *adj* : ENDOGENOUS ⟨~ growth inhibitors⟩

endomorphism* *n* : a homomorphism that maps a mathematical set into itself — compare ISOMORPHISM *herein*

en·do·nuclease \¦endō+\ *n* [*end-* + *nuclease*] : an enzyme that breaks down a nucleotide chain into two or more shorter nucleotide chains by cleaving the internal phosphodiester bonds — see RESTRICTION ENZYME *herein*; compare EXONUCLEASE *herein*

en·do·nu·cleo·lyt·ic \¦=ˌn(y)üklēōˈlid·ik\ *adj* [*end-* + *nucle-* + *-lytic*] : cleaving a nucleotide chain into two parts at an internal point ⟨~ nicks⟩

en·do·peroxide \"+\ *n* [*end-* + *peroxide*] : any of various biosynthetic intermediates in the formation of prostaglandins

en·do·phil·ic \¦endə¦filik\ *adj* [*end-* + *-philic*] : ecologically associated with humans and their domestic environment ⟨mosquitoes that are ~ vectors of malaria⟩ — compare EXOPHILIC *herein* — **en·doph·i·ly** \enˈdäfəlē\ *n* -ES

endoplasmic reticulum *n* : a system of interconnected vesicular and lamellar cytoplasmic membranes that functions esp. in the transport of materials within the cell and that is studded with ribosomes in some places

en·do·radiosonde \¦endō+\ *n* [*end-* + *radiosonde*] : a microelectronic device introduced into the body to record physiological data

en·dor·phin \enˈdȯrfən\ *n* [*endo*genous + *morphine*] : any of a group of endogenous peptides (as enkephalin and dynorphin) found esp. in the brain that bind chiefly to opiate receptors and produce some of the same pharmacological effects (as pain relief) as those of opiates; *specif* : BETA-ENDORPHIN *herein*

en·do·sul·fan \ˌendōˈsəlfən, -ˌfan\ *n* -s [perh. fr. *endrin* + *-o-* + *sulf-* + ³*-an*] : a brownish crystalline insecticide $C_9H_6Cl_6O_3S$ that is used in the control of numerous crop insects and mites

en·do·testa \¦endō+\ *n* [*end-* + *testa*] : an inner layer of the testa in various seeds — compare SCLEROTESTA *herein*

en·do·the·lin \ˌendōˈthēlən\ *n* -s [*endothe*lial + *-in*] : any of several polypeptides that are powerful vasoconstrictors

endothermy* *n* : physiological regulation of body temperature by metabolic means; *esp* : the property or state of being warm-blooded

endpoint** \ˈ=ˌ=\ *n* : either of two points or values that mark the ends of a line segment or interval; *also* : a point that marks the end of a ray

end–run \ˈ=ˌ=\ *vt* [*end run*, n.] : to avoid artfully ⟨deliberately *end-running* the rules⟩

en·duro \ənˈd(y)u̇(ə)r(ˌ)ō, en-\ *n* -s [pseudo-It or -Sp alter. of *endurance*] : a long race (as for automobiles or motorcycles) stressing endurance rather than speed

end user *n* : the ultimate consumer of a finished product

energetics* *n pl but sing in constr* : the total energy relations and transformations of a physical, chemical, or biological system ⟨the ~ of an ecological community⟩

energizer* *n* : ANTIDEPRESSANT *herein*

energy* *n* : usable power; *also* : the resources for producing such power

energy budget *n* : an accounting of the income, use, and loss of energy esp. in an ecosystem ⟨the sun's contribution to the *energy budget* of the earth —M.K.Hubbert⟩

energy efficiency ratio *n, often cap both Es&R* : a number expressing the relative efficiency of an appliance (as a room air-conditioner) that is obtained by dividing the unit's output in BTUs per hour by its energy requirement in watts

en·flur·ane \enˈflu̇(ə)rˌān\ *n* [²*en-* + tri*fluor-* + eth*ane*] : a liquid inhalational general anesthetic $C_3H_2ClF_5O$ prepared from methanol

enforcer* *n* : an aggressive player (as in ice hockey) known for rough play and fighting

en·ga·gé \ˌäŋgäˈzhā, ˌeŋ-, *F* äⁿgȧzhā\ *adj* [F, fr. past part. of *engager* to engage, pledge] : committed to or supportive of a cause

engine* *n* **1** : a mechanism or object that serves as an energy source ⟨the best candidate for the central ~ of quasars is a black hole —M.J.Rees⟩ **2** : computer software that performs one or more fundamental functions esp. of a larger program ⟨a database ~⟩

engineer* *vt* : to modify or produce by genetic engineering ⟨corn *~ed* to resist crop pests⟩

english cocker spaniel *n, usu cap E* : any of a breed of active friendly spaniels that have square muzzles, wide noses, and heads which are typically half muzzle and half skull with the forehead and skull arched and slightly flattened and that were orig. bred for hunting

english system *n, usu cap E* : the foot-pound-second system of units

enhanced recovery *n* : the extraction of oil from a nearly exhausted well by methods more costly and complex than water-flooding alone

enhancer* *n* : a nucleotide sequence that increases the rate of genetic transcription by preferentially increasing the activity of the nearest promoter on the same DNA molecule

en·keph·a·lin \enˈkefələn, eŋ-\ *n* -s [*enkephal-*, alter. of *encephal-* + *-in*] : either of two pentapeptides with opiate and analgesic activity that occur naturally esp. in the brain and have a marked affinity for opiate receptors — see ENDORPHIN

eno·ki \eˈnōkē, -ˈnäk-, (ˌ)ēˈ-\ *or* **enoki mushroom** *n* -s [Jap *enokitake*, fr. *enoki* Chinese hackberry (*Celtis sinensis*) + *take* mushroom] : a small whitish cultivated mushroom (*Flammulina velutipes* syn. *Collybia velutipes*) of the family Agaricaceae with a long thin stem and a very small cap

ENT *abbr* ear, nose, and throat

en·tero·bacterium \¦entə(ˌ)rō+\ *n* [NL, fr. *enter-* + *bacterium*] : any bacterium of the family Enterobacteriaceae — **en·tero·bacterial** \"+\ *adj* — **en·tero·bacteriologist** \"+\ *n*

en·tero·pathogenic \"+\ *adj* [*enter-* + *pathogenic*] : tending to produce disease in the intestinal tract ⟨~ bacteria⟩

en·ter·op·a·thy \ˌentəˈräpəthē\ *n* [*enter-* + *-pathy*] : a disease of the intestinal tract

en·tero·virus \¦entərō+\ *n* [NL, fr. *enter-* + *virus*] : any of a genus (*Enterovirus*) of picornaviruses (as a Coxsackie virus) that typically occur in the gastrointestinal tract but may be involved in respiratory ailments, meningitis, and neurological disorders — **en·tero·viral** \"+\ *adj*

entitlement* *n* : a government program providing benefits to members of a specified group

entrain* *vt* : to determine or modify the phase or period of ⟨circadian rhythms *~ed* by a light cycle⟩

en·tre·pre·neur·i·al·ism \¦än·trəp(r)ə¦nər·ēəˌlizəm, -n(y)u̇r- *also* -nər-\ *n* -s [*entrepreneurial* + *-ism*] : the policies, practices, or attitudes of an entrepreneur

entry–level \ˈ=ˌ=ˌ=\ *adj* **1** : of, relating to, or being at the lowest level of a hierarchy ⟨*entry-level* jobs⟩ ⟨an *entry-level* computer system⟩ **2** : relating to, being, or priced for the first-time buyer ⟨*entry-level* car buyers⟩ ⟨aiming the . . . computer at the *entry-level* market —*Wall Street Jour.*⟩

envelope* *n* **1** : a set of performance limits (as of an aircraft) that may not be safely exceeded; *also* : the set of operating parameters that exists within these limits **2** : a usu. socially or conventionally accepted limit — **push the envelope** : to test or attempt to move beyond an accepted limit

en·ven·om·ation \ənˌvenəˈmāshən, enˌv-\ *n* -s [*envenom* + *-ation*] : an act or instance of impregnating with a venom (as of a snake or spider); *also* : ENVENOMIZATION *herein* — **en·ven·om·ate** \=ˈ==ˌmāt\ *vt* -ED/-ING/-S

en·ven·om·iza·tion \-ˌməˈzāshən, -(ˌ)mīˈz-\ *n* -s [*envenom* + *-ization*] : a poisoning caused by a bite or sting

en·vi·ro \ənˈvīrō, en-\ *n* -s [by shortening] : ENVIRONMENTALIST *herein*

environment* *n* **1** : the position or characteristic position of a linguistic element in a sequence **2** : an instance of environmental art or theater **3** : a computer interface from which various tasks can be performed ⟨a programming ~⟩

environmental* *adj* : involving or encompassing the spectator ⟨~ art⟩ ⟨~ theater⟩

environmentalism* *n* : advocacy of the preservation, restoration, or improvement of the natural environment; *esp* : the movement to control pollution

environmentalist* *n* **1** : an advocate of environmentalism **2** : one concerned about the quality of the human environment; *specif* : a specialist in human ecology

enzyme immunoassay *n* : an immunoassay (as an enzyme-linked immunosorbent assay) in which an enzyme bound to an antigen or antibody functions as a label

enzyme–linked immunosorbent assay \ˈ≈ˌ≈¦≈-\ *n* : an in vitro method for quantifying an antigen or antibody concentration in which the test material is immobilized on a surface and exposed either to a complex of an enzyme linked to an antibody specific for the antigen or an enzyme linked to an anti-immunoglobulin specific for the antibody followed by reaction of the enzyme with a substrate to yield a colored product corresponding to the concentration of the test material — called also *ELISA*

en·zy·mo·log·i·cal \ˌenzəmə'läjəkəl, -ˌzī-\ *adj* [*enzymology* + *-ical*] : of or relating to enzymology ⟨~ studies⟩

EOE *abbr* equal opportunity employer

EP* *abbr* **1** European plan **2** extended play

ep·a·zote \'epəˌzōt\ *n* -S [MexSp, fr. Nahuatl *epazōtl*] : the fresh or dried pungent smelling leaves of Mexican tea used esp. in Mexican cooking; *also* : MEXICAN TEA

ephemera* *n pl* [²*ephemera*] : paper items (as posters, broadsides, or tickets) that were orig. meant to be discarded after use but have since become collectibles

epi·androsterone \¦epē+\ *n* [*epi-* + *androsterone*] : an androsterone derivative $C_{19}H_{30}O_2$ that occurs in normal human urine — called also *isoandrosterone*

epi·con·dy·li·tis \ˌepəˌkändᵊl'īdəs, -'ītəs\ *n* -ES [NL, fr. ISV *epicondyle* + NL *-itis*] : inflammation of an epicondyle or of adjacent tissues — compare TENNIS ELBOW *in the Dict*

epidermal growth factor *n* : a polypeptide hormone that stimulates cell proliferation esp. of epithelial cells by binding to receptor proteins on the cell surface — abbr. *EGF*

epidural *n* -S [*epidural*, adj.] : an injection of a local anesthetic into the space outside the dura mater of the spinal cord in the lower back region to produce loss of sensation chiefly in the lower part of the body (as of the pelvis or abdomen)

epi·fauna \¦epə, ¦epē+\ *n* [NL, fr. *epi-* + *fauna*] : benthic fauna living on the substrate (as a hard sea floor) or on other organisms — compare INFAUNA *herein* — **epi·faunal** \"+\ *adj*

epi·mor·phism \ˌepə'mȯrˌfizəm\ *n* -S [*epi-* (on) + homo*morphism*] : an onto homomorphism

epiphany* *n* : an illuminating discovery, realization, or disclosure

epi·phyt·ism \ˌepə'fīˌtizəm\ *n* -S : the condition of being epiphytic

episcopal vicar *n* : a bishop assigned to the pastoral supervision of a part of a Roman Catholic diocese

epi·some \'epəˌsōm\ *n* -S [*epi-* + ³*-some*] : a genetic determinant (as the DNA of some bacteriophages) that can replicate either autonomously in bacterial cytoplasm or as an integral part of their chromosomes — compare PLASMID *herein* — **epi·som·al** \¦epə¦sōməl\ *adj* — **epi·som·al·ly** *adv* — **epi·so·mic** \-ōmik\ *adj*

ep·i·tope \'epəˌtōp, 'epē-\ *n* -S [ISV *epi-* + *-tope* (fr. Gk *topos* place) — more at TOPIC] : a molecular region on the surface of an antigen capable of eliciting an immune response and of combining with the specific antibody produced by such a response — called also *antigenic determinant*

EPN \ˌē(ˌ)pē'en\ *n* -S [ethyl *para*-nitro-phenyl] : an organophosphorus miticide and insecticide $C_{14}H_{14}NO_4PS$ used esp. on cotton and orchard crops

ep·oxy \ə'päksē, e'p-, (ˌ)ē'p-\ *vt* **ep·oxied** *or* **ep·oxyed; epoxied** *or* **epoxyed; ep·oxy·ing; epoxies** [*epoxy*, n.] : to glue with epoxy

EPR *abbr* electron paramagnetic resonance *herein*

EPROM \'ēˌpräm\ *abbr or n* -S [erasable programmable *read-only memory*] : a read-only memory that is programmed after manufacture and that can be erased (as by exposure to ultraviolet radiation) and thus reprogrammed

ep·stein–barr virus \ˌepˌstīn'bär-\ *n, usu cap E&B* [after Michael Anthony *Epstein* b1921 Eng. pathologist and Yvonne M. *Barr* b1932 Eng. virologist] : a herpesvirus (genus *Lymphocryptovirus*) that causes infectious mononucleosis and is associated with Burkitt's lymphoma and nasopharyngeal carcinoma — abbr. *EBV*; called also *EB virus*

equal opportunity *n, often attrib* **1** : nondiscrimination in employment esp. as offered by an equal opportunity employer **2** : a context in which there is no discrimination esp. with regard to sex, race, or social standing ⟨alcoholism has become an *equal opportunity* disease —Carol Kitman⟩

equal opportunity employer *n* : an employer who agrees not to discriminate against any employee or job applicant because of race, color, religion, national origin, sex, physical or mental handicap, or veteran status

equilibrium constant *n* : a number that expresses the relationship between the amounts of products and reactants present at equilibrium in a reversible chemical reaction occurring at a given temperature, that is relatively independent of the quantities of the species involved, and that represents the ratio of the mathematical product of the concentrations of the reaction products to the mathematical product of the concentrations of the starting materials

equine infectious anemia *n* : INFECTIOUS ANEMIA

equivalence class *n* : a set for which a given equivalence relation holds between every pair of elements

equivalence relation *n* : a relation (as equality) between elements of a set (as the real numbers) that is symmetric, reflexive, and transitive and for any two elements either holds or does not hold

equivalency* *n* : a level of achievement equivalent to completion of an educational or training program ⟨a high school ~ certificate⟩

equivalent* *adj* **1** : having the same solution set ⟨~ equations⟩ **2** : related by an equivalence relation

ER* *abbr* emergency room

erase* *vt* : to delete from a computer storage device

-er·gic \ə(r)jik, ˌərj-\ *adj comb form* [*-ergy* + ¹*-ic*] : exhibiting or stimulating activity of ⟨dopamin*ergic*⟩

er·go·met·ric \ˌərgə'me-trik\ *adj* [*ergometer* + *-metric*] : relating to, obtained by, or being an ergometer

ergonomics* *n pl but sing or pl in const* : the design characteristics of an object resulting esp. from the application of the science of ergonomics

er·gon·o·mist \(ˌ)ər'gänəməst\ *n* -S [*ergonomic* + ¹*-ist*] : a specialist in ergonomics

er·o·tol·o·gy \ˌerə'täləjē\ *n* -ES [F *érotologie* study of sexual love, fr. Gk *erōt-, erōs* sexual love + F *-o-* -o- + *-logie* -logy — more at EROS] : erotic description or literature — **er·o·to·log·i·cal** \¦erəd·ᵊl¦äjəkəl, eˌrōd·ə-, eˌr-, əˌr-, -ˌräd·ə-\ *adj*

error bar *n* : the estimated uncertainty esp. in data on a graph usu. expressed as the range of values lying between a plotted value plus or minus a value; *broadly* : degree of imprecision

ERT *abbr* estrogen replacement therapy *herein*

erythema in·fec·ti·o·sum \-inˌfekshē'ōsəm\ *n* [NL, lit., infectious erythema] : FIFTH DISEASE *herein*

erythema mi·grans \-'mīgrənz\ *or* **erythema chron·i·cum mi·grans** \-ˌkränəkəm-\ *n* [*erythema migrans* fr. NL, lit., migrating erythema; *erythema chronicum migrans*, fr. NL, lit., chronic migrating erythema] : a red spreading annular skin lesion that is an early symptom of Lyme disease and that develops at the site of the bite of a tick (as the deer tick) infected with the causative spirochete

er·y·thor·bate \ˌerə'thȯrˌbāt\ *n* -S [*erythorbic acid* (herein) + ¹*-ate*] : a salt of erythorbic acid that is used in foods as an antioxidant

er·y·thor·bic acid \¦erə¦thȯrbik-\ *n* [prob. fr. *erythrose* + ascor*bic acid*] : an optical isomer of ascorbic acid

eryth·ro·leukemia \ə¦rithrō+\ *n* [NL, fr. *erythr-* + *leukemia*] : a malignant disorder that is marked by proliferation of erythroblastic and myeloblastic tissue and in later stages by leukemia

eryth·ro·poi·e·tin \əˌrithrə'pȯiətᵊn\ *n* -S [*erythropoietic* + *-in*] : a hormonal glycoprotein that is formed esp. in the kidney and stimulates red blood cell formation

es·bat \'esˌbat\ *n* -S [OF, esbat, diversion, blow, fr. *esbatre* to divert, amuse, beat, fr. (assumed) VL *exbattuere*, fr. L *ex-* + *battuere* to beat] : a meeting of a coven of witches

es·ca·beche \ˌeskə'bāchā\ *n* -S [Sp, prob. fr. Ar *sakbāj* meat cooked in vinegar] : fish or chicken fried in oil then marinated in a spicy sauce and served cold

escalate* *vi* : to increase in extent, volume, number, amount, or scope : EXPAND ⟨any limited nuclear war would rapidly ~ into full-scale disaster —*Sat. Eve. Post*⟩ ~ *vt* : to increase the extent, volume, number, amount, or scope of

escalation* *n* : an increasing in extent, volume, number, amount, or scope — **es·ca·la·to·ry** \'eskələˌtōrē, -ˌtȯr-, ÷-kyə-\ *adj*

escapologist* *n* : ESCAPE ARTIST

es·cap·ol·o·gy \ˌes(ˌ)kā'päləjē, əsˌkā-\ *n* -ES [²*escape* + *-ology* (as in *psychology*)] : the art or practice of escaping

escudo* *n* : the basic monetary unit of Chile between 1960 and 1975

ESL *abbr* English as a second language

ESOP \'ēˌsäp, ˌēˌes(ˌ)ō'pē\ *n* -S [employee stock ownership plan] : a program by which a company's stock is acquired by its employees

esoph·a·go·gastric \ə¦säfə(ˌ)gō, ē¦-+\ *adj* [*esophag-* + *gastric*] : of, relating to, involving, or affecting the esophagus and the stomach ⟨~ anastomosis⟩ ⟨~ ulcers⟩

esoph·a·gos·co·py \əˌsäfə'gäskəpē\ *n* -ES [*esophag-* + *-scopy*] : examination of the esophagus by means of an esophagoscope

ESR *abbr* electron spin resonance *herein*

establishment* *n, often cap* **1** : a group of social, economic, and political leaders who form a ruling class (as of a nation) ⟨by *them* he meant not the English, but the governing classes, the *Establishment* —A.J.P.Taylor⟩ **2** : a controlling group ⟨the Welsh literary *Establishment* . . . kept him out of everything —Keidrych Rhys⟩

es·ter·o·lyt·ic \ˌestərō'lid·ik\ *adj* [*ester* + *-o-* + *-lytic*] : of, relating to, carrying out, or being the splitting of an ester into its component alcohol and acid — **es·ter·ol·y·sis** \ˌ≈≈'äləsəs\ *n*

estimate* *n* : a numerical value obtained from a statistical sample and assigned to a population parameter

estimator* *n* : ESTIMATE *herein*; *also* : a statistical function whose value for a sample furnishes an estimate of a population parameter

es·tro·ge·nic·i·ty \ˌestrəjə'nisəd·ē\ *n* -ES : capacity for estrogenic action or effect

estrogen replacement therapy \'≈≈≈'≈≈-\ *n* : post-menopausal administration of estrogen esp. to prevent osteoporosis and heart disease — abbr. *ERT*

ET* *abbr* **1** elapsed time **2** ephemeris time

eta meson *n* [¹*eta*] : an uncharged elementary particle with zero spin that has a mass 1074 times the mass of an electron and that decays rapidly esp. into pions — called also *eta particle*

eth·a·cryn·ic acid \ˌethəˌkrinik-\ *n* [*eth-* + *acetic* + *butyryl* + *phenol* + ¹*-ic*] : a potent synthetic diuretic $C_{13}H_{12}Cl_2O_4$ used esp. in the treatment of edema

eth·am·bu·tol \eth'ambyùˌtȯl, -ˌtōl\ *n* -S [*ethylene* + *amine* + *butanol*] : a synthetic drug $C_{10}H_{24}N_2O_2$ used esp. in the treatment of tuberculosis

etha·mi·van \e'thaməˌvan, ˌethə'mīvən\ *n* -S [di*ethyl* + *amide* + *vanillic acid*] : an analeptic drug and central nervous system stimulant $C_{12}H_{17}NO_3$ that is related to vanillic acid and is used as a respiratory stimulant for intoxication with depressants of the central nervous system (as barbiturates) and for chronic lung diseases

eth·e·phon \'ethəˌfän\ *n* -S [alter. of chloro*ethyl phosphonic acid*] : a synthetic plant growth regulator $C_2H_6ClO_3P$ that induces flowering and abscission by promoting the release of ethylene and has been used to cause early ripening (as of apples on the tree)

ethid·i·um bromide \e¦thidēəm-\ *n* [*ethyl* + phenanthr*idinium*] : a biological dye that is a phenanthridine derivative used as a trypanocide and to block nucleic acid synthesis (as in mitochondria)

eth·i·on \'ethēˌän\ *n* -S [blend of *eth-* and *thion-*] : an organophosphate $C_9H_{22}O_4P_2S_4$ used esp. as an insecticide and acaricide

eth·i·on·amide \ˌethē'änəˌmīd, ə'thīən-, -ˌmə̇d\ *n* [*eth-* + *thion-* + *amide*] : a compound $C_8H_{10}N_2S$ used against mycobacteria (as in tuberculosis and leprosy)

ethiopian orthodox *adj, usu cap E&O* : ETHIOPIAN 5

ethnic* *n* : a member of an ethnic group; *esp* : a member of a minority group who retains the customs, language, or social views of his group

ethnic cleansing *n* [prob. trans. of Croatian *etničko čišćenje*] : the expulsion, imprisonment, or killing of an ethnic minority by a dominant majority in order to achieve ethnic homogeneity

eth·no·cide \'ethnəˌsīd, -nō-\ *n* -S [*ethno-* + *-cide*] : the deliberate destruction of an ethnic culture

ethnography* *n* : a descriptive work produced from ethonographic research

eth·no·medicine \ˌethnō+\ *n* [*ethno-* + ¹*medicine*] : the comparative study of how different cultures view disease and how they treat or prevent it; *also* : the medical beliefs and practices of indigenous cultures — **eth·no·medical** \"+\ *adj*

eth·no·methodology \¦eth(ˌ)nō+\ *n* [*ethno-* + *methodology*] : a branch of sociology dealing with nonspecialists' commonsense understanding of the structure and organization of society — **eth·no·methodological** \"+\ *adj* — **eth·no·methodologist** \"+\ *n*

eth·no·musicology \"+\ *n* [ISV *ethno-* + *musicology*] : a study of the music chiefly of non-European cultures esp. in relation to the culture that produces it — **eth·no·musicological** \"+\ *adj* — **eth·no·musicologist** \"+\ *n*

eth·no·science \"+\ *n* [*ethno-* + *science*] : the study of a culture's system of classifying knowledge (as its taxonomy of plants and animals); *also* : such a system in a particular culture — **eth·no·scientific** \"+\ *adj* — **eth·no·scientist** \"+\ *n*

etho·gram \'ēthəˌgram\ *n* -S [*etho-* (as in *ethology*) + *-gram*] : a comprehensive list, inventory, or description of the behavior of an organism

eth·o·sux·i·mide \ˌethō'səksəˌmīd\ *n* -S [*eth-* + *-suximide* (by shortening & alter. fr. *succinimide*)] : an anticonvulsant drug $C_7H_{11}NO_2$ derived from succinic acid and used to treat epilepsy

et·ic \'ed·ik\ *adj* [phon*etic*] : of, relating to, or having linguistic or behavioral characteristics considered without regard to their structural significance ⟨a sound spectrogram is a good example of ~ description —John Algeo⟩ — compare EMIC *herein*

et·i·dro·nate \ˌēd·ə'drōˌnāt, ˌed·ə-\ *also* **etidronate disodium** *n* -S [*etidronic* acid, of which etidronate is a salt (perh. fr. *ethylidene* + *hydr-* + phosph*onic acid*) + ¹*-ate*] : a white disodium salt $C_2H_6Na_2O_7P_2$ used to treat osteoporosis and osteitis deformans

etio·cho·lan·o·lone \¦ēd·ē(ˌ)ōkō'lanᵊlˌōn *also* ¦e¦\ *n* -S [*etio-* + *cholane* + ¹*-ol* + *-one*] : a testosterone metabolite $C_{19}H_{30}O_2$ that occurs in urine

etio·pathogenesis \¦ēd·ēō *also* ¦e¦+\ *n* [NL, fr. *etio-* + *pathogenesis*] : the cause and development of a disease or abnormal condition

etor·phine \ē'tȯrˌfēn, ə't-, -ō(ə)-\ *n* -S [*ethene* + *morphine*] : a synthetic narcotic drug $C_{25}H_{33}NO_4$ related to morphine but with more potent analgesic properties

étouf·fée *or* **etouf·fee** \ˌātü'fā, ˌet-\ *n, pl* **étouffées** *or* **etouffees** \-'fāz, -'fā\ [LaF, fr. F *à l'étouffée* braised, lit., in a smothered manner, fr. fem. of *étouffé*, past part. of *étouffer* to smother, fr. OF *estofer*, alter. (influenced by *estofer* to supply amply) of *estoper* to obstruct — more at ESTOP, STUFF] : a Cajun stew of shellfish or chicken served over rice

ETV *abbr* educational television *herein*

eu·phen·ics \yü'feniks\ *n pl but sing in constr* [*eu-* + *phen-* (fr. *phenotype*) + *-ics*; after E *genotype* : *eugenics*] : the therapeutic techniques and procedures (as medical treatment) for amelioration of the deleterious phenotypic effects of a genetic defect esp. without altering the genetic makeup of the germ plasm of the individual — **eu·phen·ic** *adj*

eur-* *or* **euro-*** *comb form, usu cap* : European ⟨*Euro*centric⟩ : western European ⟨*Euro*communism⟩ : of the European Union ⟨*Euro*crat⟩

¹**eu·ro** \'yůr(ˌ)ō\ *adj, usu cap* [*Euro-*] : EUROPEAN

²**euro** *n, pl* **euros** *also* **euro** **1** *pl euros, usu cap* [*Euro-*] : EUROPEAN **2** [short for the equivalent of *Europe* or *European* in the languages of the European Union] : the common basic monetary unit of most countries of the European Union — see MONEY table *in the Dict*

euro–american* *adj, usu cap E&A* **1** : WESTERN 1a, b **2** : WESTERN 3

euro–american *n, usu cap E&A* [*Euro-American*, adj.] **1** : a person of both European and American ancestry **2 a** : ANGLO **b** : WHITE 6

eu·ro·bond \'yůrō+ˌ\ *n, usu cap* [*Eur-* + *bond*] : a bond sold outside its country of origin; *esp* : one of a U.S. corporation that is sold outside the U.S. and that is denominated and paid for in dollars and yields interest in dollars

eu·ro·centric \¦yůrō+\ *adj, usu cap* [*Eur-* + *-centric*] : centered on Europe or the Europeans; *esp* : reflecting a tendency to interpret the world in terms of western and esp. European or Anglo-American values and experiences ⟨many teaching materials are ~ and encourage in students a sense of superiority over the . . . developing world —*Geog. Mag.*⟩ — **eu·ro·cen·trism** \-¦sen-trizəm\ *n* -S *usu cap* — **eu·ro·cen·trist** \-¦sen-trəst\ *n* -S *usu cap*

eu·ro·communism \"+\ *n, usu cap* [*Eur-* + *communism*] : the communism esp. of western European Communist parties that is marked by a willingness to reach power through coalitions and by independence from Soviet leadership — **euro·communist** *n or adj, usu cap*

eu·ro·crat \'yůrəˌkrat\ *n* -S *usu cap* [*Eur-* + *-crat*] : a staff member of the administrative commission of the European Common Market — **eu·ro·cra·cy** \yù'räkrəsē\ *n* -ES *usu cap* — **eu·ro·crat·ic** \¦yůrə¦krad·ik\ *adj, usu cap*

eu·ro·currency \'yůrō+ˌ\ *n, usu cap* [*Eur-* + *currency*] : moneys (as of the U.S. and Japan) held outside their countries of origin and used in the money markets of Europe

eu·ro·dollar \"+ˌ\ *n, usu cap* [*Eur-* + *dollar*] : a U.S. dollar used as Eurocurrency

eu·ro·market \"+ˌ\ *n, usu cap* [*Eur-* + *market*] : a money market in Eurocurrencies

european american *n, usu cap E&A* : EURO-AMERICAN *herein*

european bison *n, usu cap E* : WISENT

european·ist \-əst\ *n* -S *usu cap* **1** : a specialist in European affairs or studies (as of culture, history, or politics) **2** : an advocate for the political and economic unification of Europe

eu·ro·po·centric \yə¦rōpə, ¦yůrəpə+\ *adj, usu cap* [*Europe*, continent + E *-o-* + *-centric*] : EUROCENTRIC *herein* — **eu·ro·po·centrism** \-¦sen-trizəm\ *n* -S *usu cap*

eu·ro·trash \'yůrō+ˌ\ *n, usu cap* [*Eur-* + ¹*trash*] : young well-to-do usu. Europeans who live a trendy lifestyle esp. in the U.S.

eu·social \ˌyü+\ *adj* [*eu-* + ¹*social*] : living in a cooperative group in which usu. one female and several males are reproductively active and the nonbreeding individuals care for the young or protect and provide for the group ⟨~ termites, ants, and naked mole rats⟩ — **eu·sociality** \ˌ≈"+\ *n*

eu·tha·nize \'yüthəˌnīz\ *also* **eu·than·a·tize** \yü'thanəˌtīz\ *vt* -ED/-ING/-S [*euthanize* fr. *euthanasia* + *-ize*; *euthanatize* fr. Gk *euhappy* + *thanatos* death + E *-ize*] : to subject to euthanasia

EVA *abbr* extravehicular activity

even permutation *n* : a permutation that is produced by the successive application of an even number of interchanges of pairs of elements — compare ODD PERMUTATION *herein*

event* *n* : a subset of the possible outcomes of a statistical experiment ⟨7 is an ~ representing 12 possible outcomes in the throwing of two dice⟩

event horizon *n* : the surface of a black hole : the boundary of a black hole at which the escape velocity equals the speed of light and beyond which nothing can escape from within it

ev·er·glade \'evə(r)ˌglād\ *n* -S [fr. the *Everglades*, Fla.] : a swampy grassland esp. in southern Florida usu. containing sawgrass and at least seasonally covered by slowly moving water — usu. used in pl.

everywoman \'≈≈ˌ≈≈\ *n, sometimes cap* [²*every*man + ¹*woman*] : the typical or ordinary woman

evoked potential *n* : an electrical response esp. in the cerebral cortex as recorded following stimulation of a peripheral sense receptor

exa- *comb form* [ISV, modif. of Gk *hexa-* hexa-] : quintillion ⟨*exa*joules⟩

ex·ac·ta \ig'zaktə, eg-\ *n* -S [AmerSp *quiniela exacta* exact quiniela] : PERFECTA *herein*

exceed·ance *also* **exceed·ence** \ik'sēdᵊn(t)s, ek-\ *n* -S : an act or instance of exceeding esp. a limit or amount

ex·cess \ik'ses, 'ekˌses, ek'ses\ *vt* -ED/-ING/-ES [*excess*, n.] : to eliminate the position of ⟨the decline in enrollment has allowed us to ~ about 75 teachers —Stuart Binion⟩

exchange force *n* : a force between two elementary particles (as a neutron and a proton) arising from the continuous interchange between them of other particles (as pions)

ex·ci·mer \'eksə(ˌ)mə(r)\ *n* -S [*excited dimer*] : an aggregate of two atoms or molecules that exists in an excited state

excimer laser *n* : a laser that uses a noble-gas halide to generate radiation usu. in the ultraviolet region of the spectrum

ex·ci·to·tox·ic \ik'sīd-əˌtäksik\ *adj* [*excite* + *-o-* + *toxic*] : being, involving, or resulting from the action of an agent that binds to a nerve cell receptor, stimulates the cell, and damages it or causes its death — **ex·ci·to·tox·ic·i·ty** \≈ˌ≈≈ˌ≈'sisəd-ē\ *n*

ex·ci·to·tox·in \≈ˌ≈≈'≈sən\ *n* [*excite* + *-o-* + *toxin*] : an excitotoxic agent (as kainic acid or glutamate)

exclusionary rule *n* : a legal rule that bars any unlawfully obtained evidence from being used in court proceedings

exclusive disjunction *n* : a compound proposition in logic that consists of two statements and that is true if and only if one and only one of the two statements is true

ex–directory \¦eks+\ *adj* [L *ex* out of — more at EX-] *Brit* : not listed in a telephone directory : UNLISTED

executable* *adj* : containing a program that can be run without using an assembler or compiler ⟨an ~ file⟩ — **executable** *n* -S

execute* *vb* ~ *vi* **1** : to perform properly or skillfully the fundamentals of a sport or a particular play ⟨was blocking and tackling and *executing* just fine —D.S.Looney⟩ **2** *of a computer program or routine* : RUN 8b

executive privilege *n* : exemption from legally enforced disclosure of communications within the executive branch of government when such disclosure would adversely affect that branch's functions and decision-making processes

Ex·er·cy·cle \'eksə(r)ˌsīkəl\ *trademark* — used for a stationary bicycle

exertion·al \+əl\ *adj* : precipitated by physical exertion ⟨~ chest pain⟩

ex·fo·li·ant \(ˌ)eks'fōlēənt, -'fōlyənt\ *n* -S [*exfoliate* + ¹*-ant*] : a mechanical or chemical agent (as an abrasive skin wash or salicylic acid) that is applied to the skin to remove dead cells from the surface

ex·fo·li·at·or \(ˌ)eks'fōlēˌād·ər\ *n* -S [*exfoliate* + ¹*-or*] : EXFOLIANT *herein*

exit* *vb* ~ *vt* **1** : to go away from : LEAVE **2** : to cause (a computer program or routine) to cease running

exit poll *n* : a poll taken (as by news media) of voters leaving the voting place that is usu. used to predict the winners — **exit polling** *n*

exo·biology \"+\ *n* [*exo-* + *biology*] : a branch of biology concerned with the search for life outside the earth and with the effects of extraterrestrial environments on living organisms — **exo·biological** \"+\ *adj* — **exo·biologist** \"+\ *n*

exo·cyclic \¦ek(ˌ)sō+\ *adj* [*exo-* + *cyclic*] : situated outside of a ring in a chemical structure

exo·cy·to·sis \¦ek(ˌ)sōsī¦tōsə̇s\ *n, pl* **exocyto·ses** \-ōˌsēz\ [NL, fr. *exo-* + *cyt-* + *-osis*] : the release of cellular substances (as secretory products) contained in cell vesicles by fusion of the vesicular membrane with the plasma membrane and subsequent release of the contents to the exterior of the cell — **exo·cy·tot·ic** \-sī¦täd·ik\ *adj*

ex·on \ˈekˌsän\ *n* -s [¹*ex-* + ²*-on*] : a polynucleotide sequence in a nucleic acid that codes information for protein synthesis and that is copied and spliced together with other such sequences to form messenger RNA — compare INTRON *herein* — **ex·on·ic** \ekˈsänik\ *adj*

exo·nuclease \ˌeksō+\ *n* [*exo-* + *nuclease*] : an enzyme that breaks down a nucleic acid by removing nucleotides one by one from the end of a chain — compare ENDONUCLEASE *herein*

exo·nu·cleo·lyt·ic \¦==ˌn(y)üklēəˈlid·ik\ *adj* [*exo-* + *nucle-* + *-lytic*] : cleaving a nucleotide chain at a point adjacent to one of its ends

exo·nu·mia \ˌeksəˈn(y)ümēə\ *n pl* [NL, fr. *exo-* + E *numismatic* + NL ²*-ia*] : numismatic items (as tokens, medals, or scrip) other than coins and paper money

exo·nu·mist \(ˌ)egˈzänüməst, (ˌ)ekˈs-\ *n* -s [*exonumia* (herein) + *-ist*] **1** : a specialist in exonumia **2** : a collector of exonumia

exo·phil·ic \¦eksə¦filik\ *adj* [*exo-* + *-philic*] : ecologically independent of man and his domestic environment ⟨an ~ species of mosquito⟩ — compare ENDOPHILIC *herein* — **ex·oph·i·ly** \ekˈsäfəlē\ *n* -ES

exotic* *adj* : of or relating to striptease ⟨~ dancing⟩

exotic* *n* -s : a dancer who performs a striptease

exotic shorthair *also* **exotic*** *n* : any of a breed of stocky short-haired domestic cats developed in the U.S. by crossing American shorthairs and Persians

expansion* *n, often attrib* : the addition of one or more teams to a sports league ⟨an ~ team⟩ ⟨an ~ year⟩

expansion card *n* : a circuit board connecting to a computer motherboard and controlling a peripheral device which expands the capabilities of the computer

expansion slot *n* : an electrical socket on the motherboard of a computer into which an expansion card may be inserted

ex·pat \ˈekˌspat\ *n* -s [by shortening] : EXPATRIATE — **expat** *adj*

ex·pa·tri·a·tism \ekˈspā·trēəˌtizəm *also* -rēəd,iz-, *chiefly Brit* -pa-\ *n* -s : the fact or state of being an expatriate

expert system *n* : computer software that attempts to mimic the reasoning of a human specialist, that usu. has the capability of making inferences, and that can be consulted for advice by a professional (as in medicine or geology)

explosive* *adj* : done by the force of a controlled explosion ⟨~ welding⟩ ⟨~ forming of metal parts⟩

ex·po \ˈek(ˌ)spō\ *n* -s [by shortening] : EXPOSITION 3c

ex·po·nence \ikˈspōnən(t)s, ekˈs-, ˈekˌs-\ *n* -s [fr. *exponent* (herein), after such pairs as E *dependent : dependence*] : the correlation between an abstract linguistic category and its exponents ⟨by moving towards the data within abstractions one is considered to be moving down the scale of ~ —R.H.Robins⟩

exponent* *n* : a specific element of a linguistic category ⟨*eat* is an ~ of the class "verb"⟩

ex·po·nen·ti·a·tion \ˌekspəˌnenchēˈāshən *sometimes* -n(t)sē-\ *n* -s [*exponent* + *-iation* (as in *differentiation*)] : INVOLUTION 2

express* *vt* : to cause (a gene) to manifest its effects in the phenotype ⟨a gene selectively ~*ed* in lung tumors⟩; *also* : to manifest or produce (a character, molecule, or effect) by a genetic process ⟨only a proportion of individuals with the gene ~ symptoms of the disease⟩ ⟨isolation of differentially ~*ed* proteins⟩

ex·pres·so \(ˌ)ekˈspre(ˌ)sō\ *n* [by alter.] *var of* ESPRESSO

extension* *n* : a mathematical set (as a field or group) that includes a given and similar set as a subset

ex·tern·ship \ˈekˌstərnˌship\ *n* [blend of *external* and *internship*] : a period of temporary employment for an advanced student in a professional field (as teaching or engineering) for practical experience outside an educational institution

ex·tra·chromosomal \¦ekstrə+\ *adj* [*extra-* + *chromosomal*] : situated or controlled by factors outside the chromosomes ⟨~ inheritance⟩ ⟨~ DNA⟩

ex·tra·corporeal \"+\ *adj* [*extra-* + *corporeal*] : occurring or based outside the living body ⟨heart surgery employing ~ circulation⟩ — **ex·tra·corporeally** \"+\ *adv*

ex·tra·cranial \"+\ *adj* [*extra-* + *cranial*] : situated or occurring outside the cranium ⟨~ arterial occlusion⟩

ex·tra·linguistic \"+\ *adj* [*extra-* + *linguistic*] : lying outside the province of language or linguistics — **ex·tra·linguistically** \"+\ *adv*

ex·tra·mitochondrial \"+\ *adj* [*extra-* + *mitochondrial*] : situated or occurring in the cell outside the mitochondria

extraneous* *adj* : being a number obtained in solving an equation that is not a solution of the equation ⟨~ roots⟩

extranuclear* *adj* : situated outside the nucleus of an atom

ex·traor·di·naire \ikˌströ(r)dᵊnˈe(ə)r, ˌek-, *also* ˌekstrəˌȯ(r)d-, *F* ekstr(ä)ȯrdēneer\ *adj* [F, extraordinary] : markedly exceptional : EXTRAORDINARY — used postpositively

ex·tra·position \¦ekstrə+\ *n* [*extra-* + *position*] : a transformation in which a syntactic constituent (as a noun phrase or sentence) is moved outside of the constituent that contains it; *esp* : one in which a subject that is a sentence which has itself undergone a transformation is so moved and leaves behind the pronoun *it*

ex·tra·renal \"+\ *adj* [*extra-* + *renal*] : situated or occurring outside the kidneys ⟨~ action of diuretics⟩

ex·tra·solar \"+\ *adj* [*extra-* + *solar*] : originating or existing outside the solar system ⟨~ life⟩

ex·tra·somatic \"+\ *adj* [*extra-* + *somatic*] : of, relating to, or being something that exists external to and distinct from the individual human being or the human body

ex·tra·terrestrial \"+\ *n* : an extraterrestrial being

ex·tra·textual \"+\ *adj* [*extra-* + *textual*] : of, relating to, or being something outside a text ⟨approach the chosen text in its ~ context, that is, the author's life⟩

ex·tra·vehicular \"+\ *adj* [*extra-* + *vehicular*] **1** : taking place outside a vehicle (as a spacecraft) ⟨~ activity⟩ **2** : relating to or used in extravehicular activity ⟨an ~ assignment⟩

extreme* *adj* **1** : of, relating to, or being an outdoor activity or a form of a sport (as skiing) that involves an unusually high degree of physical risk **2** : involved in an extreme sport ⟨~ snowboarder⟩

ex·trem·o·phile \ikˈstrēməˌfīl\ *n* -s [¹*extreme* + *-o-* + ¹*-phile*] : an organism that lives under extreme environmental conditions (as in a hot spring) — **ex·trem·o·philic** \-¦filik\ *adj*

eyeblink \ˈ=ˌ=\ *n* -s **1** : a brief period of time : INSTANT ⟨a marvelously chameleonic actor who can switch in an ~ from sinister Dracula to fawning fop —D.J.Henahan⟩ **2** : BLINK 3

eye candy *n* : something attractive to look at but lacking substance

eye chart *n* : a chart that is read at a fixed distance for purposes of testing sight; *esp* : one with rows of letters or objects of decreasing size

eye contact *n* : visual contact with another person's eyes

eye–lift *n* : BLEPHAROPLASTY *herein*

eyeliner \ˈ=ˌ==\ *n* [¹*eye* + ¹*liner*] : makeup used to emphasize the contour of the eyes

eyes only *adj* [fr. the phrase *for your eyes only*] : to be read only by the person addressed

eyewear \ˈ=ˌ=\ *n* : corrective or protective devices (as glasses or contact lenses) for the eyes

f* *abbr* femto- *herein*

fab \ˈfab\ *adj* [by shortening] *chiefly Brit* : FABULOUS 3b

fabric softener *n* : a product added to laundry during either the washing or drying cycle to make fabrics softer and fluffier

fa·bry's disease \ˈfäbrēz-\ *n, usu cap F* [after Johannes *Fabry* †1930 Ger. dermatologist] : a disorder of lipid metabolism that is inherited as an X-linked recessive trait and is characterized by skin lesions esp. on the lower trunk, severe pain in the extremities, corneal opacities, and vascular disease affecting the kidneys, heart, or brain

face fly *n* : a European fly of the genus *Musca* (*M. autumnalis*) that is similar to the housefly, is widely established in No. America, and causes distress to livestock by clustering about the face

face–off* *n* : a confrontation between opponents

face off *vi* : to have a confrontation ⟨CIA agents *facing off* against drug lords⟩

face time *n* **1** : the amount of time one spends appearing on television **2** : time spent in a face-to-face meeting with someone **3** : time spent at one's place of employment esp. beyond normal work hours

facial·ist \+ə̇st\ *n* -s : a person who gives facials

fac·tion \ˈfakshən\ *n* -s [blend of *fact* and *fiction*] : literary work based on fact but using the narrative techniques of fiction

fac·tion·al·ize \ˈfakshənᵊlˌīz, -shnəˌlīz\ *vt* -ED/-ING/-S [*factional* + *-ize*] : to split into factions

fac·toid \ˈfakˌtȯid\ *n* -s [*fact* + ¹*-oid*] **1** : an invented fact believed to be true because of its appearance in print **2** : a briefly stated and usu. trivial fact

factor* *vt* : to include or admit as a factor — used with *in* or *into* ⟨~ inflation into our calculations⟩

factor VIII \-ˈāt\ *n* : a glycoprotein clotting factor of blood plasma that is essential for blood clotting and is absent or inactive in hemophilia — called also *antihemophilic factor*

factor V \-ˈfīv\ *n* : ACCELERATOR GLOBULIN

factor group *n* : QUOTIENT GROUP *herein*

fade* *n* **1** : a slight to moderate and usu. intentional slice in golf **2** : a hairstyle similar to a crew cut in which the hair on top of the head stands high

fag·got·ry \ˈfagə·trē\ *n* -ES [*faggot* + *-ry*] : male homosexuality

fag·goty *also* **fag·got·ty** \ˈfagəd·ē\ *adj* [*faggot* + ¹*-y*] : resembling or suggesting the manner of an effeminate male homosexual — often used disparagingly

fag hag *n, slang* : a woman who enjoys the company of male homosexuals

fail* *n* : a failure (as by a security dealer) to deliver or receive securities within a prescribed period after a purchase or sale

¹fail–safe \ˈ=ˌ=\ *adj* [¹*fail* + ¹*safe*] **1** : incorporating some feature for automatically counteracting the effect of an anticipated possible source of failure **2** : being or relating to a safeguard that prevents continuing on a bombing mission according to a preconceived plan **3** : having no chance of failure : infallibly problem-free ⟨a written guarantee that your back is in A-1, *fail-safe* condition —Fern Lebo⟩

²fail–safe \"\ *vi* : to counteract the effect of a malfunction automatically ~ *vt* : to equip with a fail-safe device

fair market value *n* : a price at which both buyer and seller are willing to do business

fairness doctrine *n* : a tenet of licensed broadcasting that ensures a reasonable opportunity for the airing of conflicting viewpoints on controversial issues of public concern

fa·ji·ta \fəˈhētə, -d·ə\ *n* -s [AmerSp, dim. of Sp *faja* sash, belt — more at FAJA] : marinated strips of beef or chicken or sometimes shrimp grilled or broiled and served usu. with a flour tortilla and various savory fillings (as sautéed peppers, guacamole, and sour cream)

fake book *n* [³*fake* (to improvise) + *book*] : a book that contains the melody lines of popular copyrighted songs without accompanying harmonies and that is published without the permission of the copyright owners

fakelore \ˈ=ˌ=\ *n* [blend of ⁵*fake* and *folklore*] : imitation folklore (as tales or songs) created to pass as genuinely traditional

fa·laf·el *or* **fe·laf·el** \fəˈläfəl\ \"\ *n, pl* **falafel** *or* **felafel** [Ar *falāfil*] : a mixture of chick-peas or fava beans and spices (as cumin and coriander) formed into balls or patties and then fried; *also* : a sandwich of pita bread filled with falafel and salad

fa·lan·ga \fəˈläŋgə, -aŋ-\ *n* -s [prob. fr. NGk *phalanga*, oblique form of *phalangas* bastinado, modif. (prob. influenced by NGk *phalangi* roller put under a ship) of Turk *falaka* whiffletree, staff and loop for holding the feet of a bastinado victim, bastinado, fr. Ar *falaqa*] : a method of torture in which the soles of the feet are beaten

fallaway \ˈ=ˌ=\ *adj* [*fall away*, v.] : made while moving away from the basket in basketball ⟨a ~ jumper⟩ — **fallaway** *n* -s

fallout* *n* **1** : an incidental result or set of consequences ⟨psychological ~ from this very severe operation —Jim Lehrer⟩ **2** : particulate matter dispersed through the air and landing in a wide distribution

false color *n, often attrib* : color in an image (as a photograph) of an object that does not actually appear in the object but is used to enhance, contrast, or to distinguish details which are evident solely or chiefly from differences in the absorption and reflection of electromagnetic radiation at wavelengths outside the visual spectrum (as in the infrared and ultraviolet regions)

false morel *n* : any fungus of the genus *Gyromitra*

familial adenomatous polyposis *n* : a disease of the large intestine that is marked by the formation esp. in the colon and rectum of numerous glandular polyps of epithelial origin which typically become malignant if left untreated, that may be either asymptomatic or accompanied by diarrhea or bleeding, and that is inherited as an autosomal dominant trait — called also *familial polyposis*

familial hypercholesterolemia *n* : a metabolic disorder that is caused by defective or absent cellular receptors for LDLs, that is marked by an increase in blood plasma LDLs and by an accumulation of LDL cholesterol in the body (as in connective tissue) resulting in xanthomas, atherosclerosis, and an increased risk of myocardial infarction and coronary heart disease, and that is inherited as an autosomal dominant trait

family* *n* **1** : a group constituting a unit of a crime syndicate (as the Mafia) and engaging in underworld activities within a defined geographical area **2** : a set of curves, surfaces, functions, equations, or expressions that differ in mathematical representation only in the values assigned to one or more parameters **3** : any of various social units differing from but regarded as equivalent to the traditional family ⟨a single-parent ~⟩

family* *adj* : designed or suitable for both children and adults ⟨~ restaurants⟩ ⟨~ movies⟩

family doctor* *or* **family physician*** *also* **family practitioner** *n* : a doctor specializing in family practice

family jewels *n pl, slang* : a man's testicles

family leave *n* : a usu. unpaid leave of absence enabling an employee to attend to family concerns (as a serious illness or the care of an infant

family medicine *n* : FAMILY PRACTICE *herein*

family planning *n* : planning intended to determine the number and spacing of one's children through effective methods of birth control

family practice *n* : a medical practice or specialty which provides continuing general medical care for the individual and family

family room *n* : a large room designed as a recreation center for members of a family

family values *n pl* : values esp. of a traditional or conservative kind which are held to promote the sound functioning of the family and the loss or abandonment of which to weaken the fabric of society

fan·co·ni's anemia \fän¦kōnēz-, fan-\ *n, usu cap F* [after Guido *Fanconi* †1979 Swiss pediatrician] : aplastic anemia that is inherited as an autosomal recessive trait and is characterized by progressive pancytopenia, hypoplastic bone marrow, skeletal anomalies (as short stature), microcephaly, hypogonadism, and a predisposition to leukemia

fanconi syndrome *also* **fanconi's syndrome** *n, usu cap F* [after Guido *Fanconi*] : a disorder of reabsorption in the proximal convoluted tubules of the kidney that is characterized esp. by the presence of glucose, amino acids, and phosphates in the urine

fan–jet \ˈ=ˌ=\ *n* **1** : a jet engine having a ducted fan in its forward end that draws in extra air whose compression and expulsion provide extra thrust **2** : an airplane powered by a fan-jet engine

fanny pack *n* [*fanny* (buttocks)] : a pack that straps to the waist and is used for carrying personal articles

fan·tab·u·lous \(ˌ)fanˈtabyələs\ *adj* [blend of *fantastic* and *fabulous*] *slang* : marvelously good

fantasy* *n* : a coin usu. not intended for circulation as currency and often issued by a dubious authority (as a government-in-exile)

FAQ *abbr* frequently asked question; frequently asked questions

faraday rotation *n, usu cap F* **1** : optical rotation of a beam of polarized light due to the Faraday effect **2** : rotation of a beam of polarized microwaves traversing an isotropic medium along the lines of force of a magnetic field

far·fal·le \färˈfä(ˌ)lā, -lē\ *n* -s [It, pl. of *farfalla*, lit., butterfly] : butterfly-shaped pasta

farm* *n* : an area containing a number of similar structures (as radio antennas or storage tanks)

far–out \ˈ=¦=\ *adj* [*far out* (adverbial phrase), fr. ME *fer oute*, fr. *fer* far + *out, oute* out] : marked by a considerable departure from the conventional or traditional ⟨a small, *far-out*, but fervent religious sect —Joseph Alsop⟩ — **far–out·ness** \(ˈ)=ˈ=nə̇s\ *n*

far–red \ˈ=¦=\ *adj* **1** : lying in the part of the infrared spectrum farthest from the red — used of radiations with wavelengths between 30 and about 1000 microns **2** : lying in the part of the infrared spectrum nearest to the red — used of radiations with wavelengths starting at about .8 micron

farsi* *n, cap* : PERSIAN 2b

fart around *vi* : to mess around : waste time — often considered vulgar

fart·lek \ˈfärtˌlek\ *n* -s [Sw, fr. *fart* speed, pace (fr. MLG *vart* journey, pace, alter. of OS *fard*; akin to OE *fierd, fyrd* military expedition, campaign) + *lek* play, game, fr. ON *leikr* — more at FYRD, LAKE] : endurance training in which a runner alternates periods of sprinting with periods of jogging

FAS *abbr* fetal alcohol syndrome *herein*

fastback *n* [¹*fast* + ¹*back*] **1** \ˈ=¦=\ : a back roof on a closed passenger automobile sloping in a long unbroken line toward the rear bumper **2** \ˈ=ˌ=\ : an automobile having a fastback

fast–breeder \ˈ=¦==\ *n* : a breeder reactor that depends on high-energy neutrons to produce fissionable material

fast–food \ˈ=¦=\ *adj* **1** : of, relating to, or specializing in food (as hamburgers or fried chicken) that can be prepared and served quickly ⟨a *fast-food* restaurant chain⟩ **2** : designed for ready availability, use, or consumption and with little consideration given to quality or significance ⟨word processing cranks out *fast-food* prose —Erik Sandberg-Diment⟩ — **fast food** *n*

¹fast–forward \¦=¦=\ *n, often attrib* **1** : a function of a tape player by which the tape is advanced at a higher speed than when it is playing normally **2** : a state or instance of rapid advancement ⟨her career is in *fast-forward*⟩ ⟨the book often reads like a fractured *fast-forward* through the 60's —Annie Gottlieb⟩

²fast–forward *vt* **1** : to advance (a magnetic tape) using the fast-forward of a tape player **2** : to bypass (as a commercial) by fast-forwarding ~ *vi* **1** : to advance a magnetic tape using the fast-forward **2** : to proceed rapidly forward esp. in time ⟨*fast-forward* to the future⟩

fast lane \ˈ=ˌ=\ *n* **1** : a traffic lane intended for vehicles traveling at higher speeds **2** : a way of life marked by a fast pace and usu. the pursuit of immediate gratification **3** : FAST TRACK *herein* — **fast–lane** \ˈ=ˌ=\ *adj*

fast track \ˈ=ˌ=\ *n* **1** : a course leading to rapid advancement **2** : a course of expedited consideration or approval ⟨a regulatory *fast track*⟩ — **fast–track·er** \-ə(r)\ *n*

¹fast–track \ˈ=ˌ=\ *adj* **1** : of, relating to, or moving along a fast track ⟨*fast-track* executives⟩ **2** : of, relating to, or being a construction procedure in which work on a building begins before designs are completed ⟨*fast-track* designs⟩

²fast–track \ˈ=ˌ=\ *vt* : to speed up the processing, production, or construction of in order to meet a goal ⟨*fast-track* the project⟩

fast–twitch \ˈ=ˌ=\ *adj* : of, relating to, or being muscle fiber that contracts quickly esp. during brief high-intensity physical activity requiring strength — compare SLOW-TWITCH *herein*

fatal *n* -s [*fatal*, adj.] : FATALITY 5a

fat city *n, often cap F&C* : an extremely comfortable situation or condition of life

fat depot *n* : ADIPOSE TISSUE

fate* *n* : the expected result of normal development ⟨prospective ~ of embryonic cells⟩

fat farm *n* : a health spa that specializes in weight reduction

fat·wa \ˈfat·wə, ˈfä-, -wä, *Brit* ˈfat·wä\ *n* [Ar *fatwā*] : a legal opinion or decree handed down by an Islamic religious leader

faulk·ner·ian \(ˈ)fȯk¦nirēan, -¦ner-\ *adj, usu cap* [William Cuthbert *Faulkner* †1962 Am. novelist + E ²*-an*] : of, relating to, or suggestive of William Faulkner or his writings

fault line* *n* : something resembling a fault; *esp* : SPLIT, RIFT ⟨a major conceptual *fault line* in foreign policy —Morton Kondracke⟩

faux \ˈfō\ *adj* [F, false, fr. L *falsus* — more at FALSE] : IMITATION, ERSATZ ⟨~ pearls⟩

fa·ve·la *also* **fa·vel·la** \fəˈvelə\ *n* -s [Pg *favela*] : a settlement of jerry-built shacks lying on the outskirts of a Brazilian city

favorite son* *n* : a renowned person (as an artist or celebrity) who is viewed with great favor and affection by the people of his hometown

fax \ˈfaks\ *n* -ES [by shortening & alter.] **1** : FACSIMILE 2 **2** : a machine used to send or receive messages by fax **3** : a message sent or received by fax — **fax** \"\ *vt*

fax modem *n* : a computer peripheral capable of sending data to or receiving data from a fax machine or another computer esp. over telephone lines

FDC* *abbr* fleur de coin *herein*

feature* *n* : any of the properties (as voice or gender) that are characteristic of a grammatical element (as a phoneme or morpheme); *esp* : one that is distinctive

federal case* *n* : a matter or situation that through emphasis or exaggeration takes on disproportionate importance

federal funds *n pl* : reserve funds lent overnight by one member bank of the Federal Reserve to another

feed* *n* **1** : the process of feeding a television program (as to a local station); *also* : the signal being fed **2** : the act or instance of passing a ball or puck to a teammate ⟨scored on a ~ from the right wing⟩

feedback* *n* : the transmission of evaluative or corrective information about an action, event, or process to the original or controlling source; *also* : the information so transmitted

feedback inhibition *n* : inhibition of an enzyme controlling an early stage of a series of biochemical reactions by the end product when it reaches a critical concentration

feeding frenzy *n* : a frenzy of eating; *also* : the excited pursuit of something by a group

feedthrough \ˈ=ˌ=\ *n* -s [*feed through*, v.] : a conductor that connects two circuits on opposite sides of a surface

fee–for–service \ˌ=¦==\ *n, often attrib* : separate payment to a health-care provider for each medical service rendered to a patient

feel–good \ˈ=ˌ=\ *adj* [fr. the phrase *feel good*] **1** : relating to or promoting an often specious sense of satisfaction or well-being ⟨a *feel-good* reform program that makes no basic changes⟩ **2** : LIGHTHEARTED : cheerfully sentimental ⟨a *feel-good* movie⟩

felafel *var of* FALAFEL *herein*
Fel·den·krais \ˈfeldən͵krīs\ *trademark* — used for a system of aided body movements intended to increase body awareness and ease tension
feline leukemia virus *n* : a retrovirus that is widespread in cat populations, is transmitted esp. by direct contact, and in cats causes malignant lymphoma, leukemia, anemia, glomerulonephritis, infertility, and immunosuppression
fel·late \ˈfel͵āt, fəˈlāt, *usu* -ād.+V\ *vb* -ED/-ING/-S [L *fellatus*, past part. of *fellare* to suck — more at FELLATIO] *vt* : to perform fellatio on ~ *vi* : to fellate someone — **fel·la·tor** \ˈfel͵ād·ə(r), fəˈlā-\ *n* -S
fem·i·na·zi \ˈfemə͵nätsē\ *n* [blend of [1]*feminist* and [1]*nazi*] : an extreme or militant feminist — usu. used disparagingly
femme* *n* : a lesbian who plays the female role in a homosexual relationship
fem·to- \ˈfem(p)(͵)tō\ *comb form* [ISV, fr. Dan or Norw *femten* fifteen (fr. ON *fimmtān*) + -o- — more at FIFTEEN] : one quadrillionth (10^{-15}) part of ⟨*femto*second⟩
fem·to·second \"+\ *n* [*femto-* (herein) + [4]*second*] : one quadrillionth of a second
fence–mending \ˈ=͵==\ *n* [[1]*fence* + *mending*] : the rehabilitating of a deteriorated relationship esp. in politics
fender bender *n* : a minor automobile accident
fen·flur·amine \fenˈflürə͵mēn, -͵mən\ *n* [*fen-* (alter. of *phen-*) + *flur-* (alter. of *fluor-*) + *amine*] : an anorectic amphetamine derivative $C_{12}H_{16}F_3N$ with little stimulant effect on the central nervous system formerly used in the form of its hydrochloride to treat obesity but no longer used because of its association with heart valve disease — see FEN-PHEN *herein*; compare DEXFENFLURAMINE *herein*
fen–phen \ˈfen͵fen\ *n* -S [*fen*fluramine (herein) + *phen*termine (herein)] : a former diet drug combination of phentermine with either fenfluramine or dexfenfluramine
fen·ta·nyl \ˈfentᵊn͵il\ *n* -S [alter. of *phenethyl*] : a synthetic opioid narcotic analgesic $C_{22}H_{28}N_2O$ with pharmacologic action similar to morphine that is administered esp. in the form of its citrate
fen·thi·on \fenˈthī͵än, -͵ən\ *n* -S [*fen-* (as in *fenfluramine* — herein) + *thi-* + *-on*] : an organophosphorus insecticide $C_{10}H_{15}O_3PS_2$
fer·mi \ˈfer(͵)mē\ *n* -S [after Enrico *Fermi* †1954 Ital. physicist] : a unit of length equal to 10^{-13} centimeter
fermi level *n, usu cap F* : the energy level of an atom in a solid at a given temperature for which there is a 50 percent probability of occupation of any available state of that energy by an electron
fermi surface *n, usu cap F* : a theoretical geometric surface that consists of points representing the wavelength and direction of propagation of electrons with energies at the Fermi level in an atom of a solid material, that reflects the material's electronic structure, and that is used to characterize or predict the material's physical properties
fern bar *n* : a bar or restaurant that is stylishly decorated esp. with ferns and other green plants
fer·re·dox·in \͵ferəˈdäksən\ *n* -S [L *fer*rum iron + E *redox* + *-in* — more at FARRIER] : any of a group of iron-containing plant proteins that function as electron carriers in photosynthetic organisms and in some anaerobic bacteria
ferricyanide* *n* : the trivalent anion $Fe(CN)_6^{3-}$
fer·ro–cement \ˈfe(͵)rō+\ *n* [*ferro-* + *cement*] : a building material made of thin cement slabs reinforced with steel mesh
ferrocyanide* *n* : the tetravalent anion $Fe(CN)_6^{4-}$
festival seating *n* : a seating arrangement (as in an auditorium) in which unreserved seats are available to the first people to claim them
festoon* *vt* : DECORATE, ADORN; *also* : COVER 4c
FET \͵ef(͵)ēˈtē\ *n* -S : FIELD-EFFECT TRANSISTOR *herein*
FET *abbr* federal excise tax
fetal alcohol syndrome *n* : a highly variable group of birth defects including mental retardation, deficient growth, central nervous system dysfunction, and malformations of the skull and face that tend to occur in the offspring of women who consume large amounts of alcohol during pregnancy — abbr. *FAS*
fetal hemoglobin *n* : a hemoglobin variant that predominates in the blood of a newborn and persists in increased proportions in some forms of anemia (as thalassemia)
fetal position *n* [so called fr. the similar position of the fetus in the womb] : a position (as of a sleeping person) in which the body lies curled up on one side with the arms and legs drawn up toward the chest and the head is bowed forward and which is assumed in some forms of psychic regression
fe·tol·o·gy \fēˈtäləjē\ *n* -ES [*feto-* + *-logy*] : a branch of medical science concerned with the study and treatment of the fetus in the uterus — **fe·tol·o·gist** \-jəst\ *n* -S
fe·to·protein \ˈfēd·ō, -ē(͵)tō+\ *n* [*feto-* + *protein*] : any of several fetal antigens present in the adult in some abnormal conditions; *esp* : ALPHA-FETOPROTEIN *herein*
fe·tos·co·py \fēˈtäskəpē, -pi\ *n* -ES [*feto-* + *-scopy*] : examination of the pregnant uterus by means of a fiber-optic tube — **fe·to·scope** \ˈfēd·ə͵skōp\ *n*
fettuccine al·fre·do *or* **fettucini alfredo** \-(͵)alˈfrā(͵)dō, -ål-, -äl-\ *or* **fettuccine all' alfredo** \-͵al(͵)alˈf-, -͵ål(͵)ål-, -͵äl(͵)äl-\ *n, usu cap Alfredo* [It *fettuccine all' Alfredo* fettuccine in the style of *Alfredo (all'Augusteo)*, restaurant in Rome where the dish originated] : a dish consisting of butter, fettuccine, Parmesan cheese, cream, and seasonings
feul·gen \ˈfȯilgən\ *adj, usu cap* : of, relating to, utilizing, or staining by the Feulgen reaction ⟨positive *Feulgen* mitochondria⟩
fey* *adj* 1 : excessively refined : PRECIOUS 2 : quaintly unconventional : CAMPY
feyn·man diagram *also* **feynman graph** \ˈfīnmən-\ *n, usu cap F* [after Richard *Feynman* †1988 Am. physicist] : a diagram of subatomic particle interactions in which lines represent particles and points where lines meet represent interactions
FG *abbr* field goal
fiber* *n* : ROUGHAGE 2
fiberfill \ˈ==͵=\ *n* : synthetic fibers (as of polyester) used as a filling material (as for cushions)
fiberglass** *n* : a composite structural material of plastic and fiber glass
fiberglass *vt* [*fiberglass*, n.] : to protect or repair by the application of fiberglass
fiber optics *n pl* 1 : thin transparent fibers of glass or plastic that are enclosed by material of a lower index of refraction and that transmit light throughout their length by internal reflections; *also* : a bundle of such fibers used in an instrument (as for viewing body cavities) 2 *sing in constr* : the technique of the use of fiber optics — **fiber–optic** \ˈ==͵==\ *adj*
fi·ber·scope \ˈfībə(r)͵skōp\ *n* [*fiber* + *-scope*] : a flexible instrument utilizing fiber optics and used esp. in medicine for examination of inaccessible areas (as the stomach)
fi·bo·nac·ci number \͵fībəˈnächē-, ͵fēb-\ *n, usu cap F* [after Leonardo *Fibonacci* (Leonardo Pisano) †*ab*1250 Ital. mathematician] : a number in the infinite sequence 1, 1, 2, 3, 5, 8, 13, . . . of which the first two terms are 1 and 1 and each succeeding term is the sum of the two immediately preceding
fibonacci sequence *or* **fibonacci series** *n, usu cap F* : the mathematical sequence consisting of the Fibonacci numbers
fi·branne \ˈfīˈbran\ *n* [F, viscose rayon, fr. *fibre*] : a fabric made of spun-rayon yarn
fi·brino·peptide \ˈfīˈbrinō+\ *n* [ISV *fibrin* + *-o-* + *peptide*] : any of the vertebrate polypeptides that are cleaved from fibrinogen by thrombin during clot formation
fibroblast growth factor *n* : any of several protein growth factors that stimulate the proliferation esp. of endothelial cells and that promote angiogenesis
fi·bro·cystic \ˈfībrō+\ *adj* [*fibr-* + *cystic*] : characterized by the presence or development of fibrous tissue and cysts ⟨~ changes in the pancreas —*Lancet*⟩
fi·bro·elas·to·sis \͵fī(͵)brō͵iˈlasˈtōsəs, -ē͵las-\ *n* [NL, fr. E *fibroelastic* + NL *-osis*] : a condition of the body or one of its organs (as the left ventricle of the heart) characterized by proliferation of fibroelastic tissue
fi·bro·gen·ic \͵fībrəˈjenik\ *adj* [*fibr-* + *-genic*] : promoting the development of fibers ⟨a ~ agent⟩
fi·bro·my·al·gia \(͵)fī͵brō͵mīˈalj(ē)ə\ *n* [NL, fr. *fibr-* + *myalgia*] : any of a group of nonarticular rheumatic disorders characterized by pain, tenderness, and stiffness of muscles and associated connective tissue structures
fib·ro·nec·tin \͵fībrəˈnektən, -(͵)brō-\ *n* -S [*fibr-* + L *nectere* to tie, bind + E *-in* — more at ANNEX] : any of a group of glycoproteins that are present on cell surfaces and in blood plasma and connective tissue and that promote cellular adhesion and migration
fiche \ˈfēsh, *also* ˈfish\ *n, pl* **fiche** *also* **fiches** [by shortening] : MICROFICHE
fick principle \ˈfik-\ *n, usu cap F* [after Adolph Eugen *Fick* †1901 Ger. physiologist] : a generalization in physiology which states that blood flow is proportional to the difference in concentration of a substance in the blood as it enters and leaves an organ and which is used to determine cardiac output from the difference in oxygen concentration in blood before it enters and after it leaves the lungs and from the rate at which oxygen is consumed
fiddle* *vt* : to alter or manipulate fraudulently ⟨accountants *fiddling* the books —Stanley Cohen⟩
fiddle *n* [*fiddle*, v. (herein)] : SWINDLE
fid·dly \ˈfid(ᵊ)lē, -li\ *adj* [[2]*fiddle* + [1]*-y*] *chiefly Brit* : requiring close attention to detail : FUSSY ⟨this method (not difficult—just a bit ~) —Leila Aitken⟩; *esp* : requiring an annoying amount of close attention ⟨the tiny control buttons on the back are ~ — M.J.McNamara⟩
fi·del·ism \ˈfēdᵊl͵izəm; fēˈdel-, fiˈd-, (͵)fiˈdel-\ *n* -S *usu cap* [Sp *fidelismo*, fr. *Fidel* Castro + Sp *-ismo* -ism] : CASTROISM *herein* — **fi·del·ist** \-əst\ *n or adj, usu cap*
fi·del·is·ta \͵fēdᵊlˈēstə, ͵fi-, ͵fī-\ *n* -S *usu cap* [Sp, fr. *Fidel* Castro + Sp *-ista* [1]-ist] : an adherent of Castroism
fi·do \ˈfīd(͵)ō\ *n* -S [*f*reaks + *i*rregulars + *d*efects + *o*ddities] : a coin having a minting error
fiduciary* *adj* : being a mark or set of marks in the reticle of an optical instrument used as a point of reference or for a measurement
field* *n* 1 : a band of horsemen following the leader of a hunt 2 : a particular area (as of a record in a database) in which the same type of information is regularly recorded 3 : a division of a record in computer storage that consists of one or more characters and contains data (as a name or number) to be treated as a unit
field* *vt* 1 : to take care of or respond to (as a telephone call or a request) ⟨~*ed* two bomb threats —Alexander Wolff & Robert Sullivan⟩ 2 : to give an impromptu answer or solution to ⟨~*ed* the questions with ease⟩
field–effect transistor \ˈ==͵=-\ *n* : a nonrectifying transistor in which the output current is controlled by a variable electric field
field ion microscope *n* : a high-magnification microscope in which an image of the atoms of a metal surface is formed on a fluorescent screen by means of usu. helium ions formed in a high-voltage electric field — **field ion microscopy** *n*
field judge *n* : a football official whose duties include covering action on kicks and forward passes and timing intermission periods and time-outs
field–test \ˈ=͵=\ *vt* : to test (as a procedure or product) under conditions of actual use — **field test** *n*
fièvre bou·ton·neuse \fyevrᵊbütónœ̄z\ *n* [F] : BOUTONNEUSE FEVER
fifth disease *n* [prob. trans. of F *cinquième maladie*; so called because it was the fifth of five exanthematous childhood diseases known at the time of its description (1928)] : an acute eruptive disease esp. of children that is caused by a parvovirus (genus *Erythrovirus*) and is first manifested by a blotchy red rash on the cheeks followed by a maculopapular rash on the extremities and that is usu. accompanied by fever and malaise — called also *erythema infectiosum*
figure–ground \ˈ=͵=\ *adj* : relating to or being the relationships between the parts of a perceptual field which is perceived as divided into a part consisting of figures having form and standing out from a part comprising the background and being relatively formless ⟨an ambiguous diagram in which *figure-ground* relationships are easily perceived as reversed⟩
file* *n* 1 : a collection of related data records (as for a computer) 2 : a complete collection of data (as text or a program) treated by a computer as a unit esp. for purposes of input and output
file server *n* : a server esp. for storing files
filigree* *n* : ORNAMENTATION, EMBELLISHMENT ⟨writings . . . heavy with late Victorian ~ —Jack Beatty⟩
fil·i·pin \ˈfiləpən\ *n* -S [NL *filipinensis*, specific epithet of *S. filipinensis* + E *-in*] : an antifungal antibiotic $C_{35}H_{58}O_{11}$ produced by a bacterium of the genus *Streptomyces* (*S. filipinensis*)
fill* *n* : a bit of instrumental music that fills the pauses between phrases (as of a vocalist or soloist)
filler* *n* 1 : an item of poor quality (as a worn coin) kept in a collection until a better specimen can be found to replace it 2 : material of little or no value included in a work (as a book or song collection) just to increase its size 3 : [2]FILL 2a(3)
fil·lo *var of* PHYLLO *herein*
filmcard \ˈ=͵=\ *n* : MICROFICHE
film noir *n, pl* **films noir** *or* **films noirs** [F, lit., black film] : a type of crime film featuring cynical malevolent characters in a sleazy setting and an ominous atmosphere that is conveyed by shadowy photography and foreboding background music; *also* : a film of this type
film·og·ra·phy \filˈmägrəfē, fiüˈm-\ *n* -ES [[1]*film* + *-o-* + *-graphy*] : a list of motion pictures featuring the work of a prominent film figure (as an actor or director) or relating to a particular topic
filmscript \ˈ=͵=\ *n* : a script for a motion picture
filmsetting \ˈ=͵=\ *n* : PHOTOCOMPOSITION — **filmset** \ˈ=͵=\ *adj* — **filmset** *vt* — **filmsetter** \ˈ=͵==\ *n*
filo *var of* PHYLLO *herein*
fi·lo·vi·rus \ˈfīlō͵vīrəs\ *n* [NL, fr. L *fil*um thread + NL *-o-* + *virus* — more at FILE] : any of a family (Filoviridae) of single-stranded chiefly filamentous RNA viruses infecting vertebrates that comprises a single genus (*Filovirus*) characterized by a helical nucleocapsid and glycoprotein envelope and that includes the Marburg virus and the Ebola viruses
final* *n* : the last stage of an aircraft's descent toward a landing place
finance company* *n* : a company that specializes in making loans usu. to individuals
fi·nan·cials \fəˈnanchəlz, (͵)fī-\ *n pl* [*financial*, adj.] : financial statistics ⟨reviewed the company's ~⟩
fi·nas·te·ride \fəˈnastə͵rīd\ *n* -S [*fina-* (of unknown origin) + testos*terone* + am*ide*] : a nitrogenous steroid derivative $C_{23}H_{36}N_2O_2$ that inhibits the enzymatic conversion of testosterone to dihydrotestosterone and is used esp. to treat symptoms of benign prostatic hyperplasia and to increase hair growth in male-pattern baldness
fin·der·scope \ˈfīndər͵skōp\ *n* [*finder* + tele*scope*] : FINDER 3
finder's fee *n* : a fee paid to a financial finder (sense 6) often in the form of a percentage of the sum involved
fine structure *n* 1 : a multiplet occurring in an atomic spectrum as a result of electron interaction 2 : microscopic structure of a biological entity or one of its parts esp. as studied in preparations for the electron microscope — **fine structural** *adj*
fine–structure constant \ˈ=͵==-\ *n* : a dimensionless constant that is a measure of the strength of electromagnetic interactions of subatomic particles and that has an approximate value of 0.0073 or $^1/_{137}$ — symbol α
fine–tune \ˈ=ˈ=\ *vt* 1 a : to adjust precisely so as to bring to the highest level of performance, efficiency, or effectiveness ⟨*fine-tune* a TV set⟩ b : to improve through minor alteration, revision, or modification ⟨*fine-tuning* their policies⟩ 2 : to stabilize (an economy) by small-scale fiscal and monetary manipulations
finger* *n* : BIRD 2 *herein*
finger food *n* : a food (as a chicken wing, carrot, or sandwich) that is meant to be eaten with the fingers
finger–pointing \ˈ==͵==\ *n* : the act of making explicit and often unfair accusations of blame
finger–popping \ˈ==͵==\ *adj* [[1]*finger* + *popping*, pres. part. of [1]*pop*] : characterized by a pronounced beat ⟨*finger-popping*, toe-tapping music⟩
fingerprint* *n* : something that identifies: as **a** : a distinguishing trait or characteristic often indicating origin **b** : analytical evidence (as a spectrogram) that characterizes an object or substance; *esp* : the chromatogram or electrophoretogram obtained by cleaving a protein by enzymatic action and subjecting the resulting collection of peptides to two-dimensional chromatography or electrophoresis **c** : the base-pair pattern in an individual's DNA obtained by DNA fingerprinting
fingerprint* *vt* : to analyze (as spectrographically or chromatographically) in order to determine uniquely the identifying characteristics, origin, or constitution
finicky* *adj* : requiring much care, precision, or attentive effort ⟨a ~ recipe⟩
finish* *n, of a beverage* : the taste left in the mouth after swallowing ⟨a wine with a long dry ~⟩
finite difference *n* : any of a sequence of differences of the general form $f(x + nh) - f(x + (n - 1)h)$ obtained by incrementing successively the dependent variable of the function $f(x)$ by the amount h; *esp* : any of such differences obtained from a polynomial function using successive integral values of its dependent variable
fink* *n* : one who is disapproved of or is held in contempt
fink out *vi* 1 : to fail miserably 2 : to back out : cop out
fin·land·iza·tion \͵finləndəˈzāshən, -͵dīˈz-; (͵)fin͵landəˈz-\ *n* -S *usu cap* [*Finland*, country in northern Europe that pursued such a policy + *-ization*] : a foreign policy of neutrality which made a smaller and weaker non-Communist country susceptible to the influence of the Soviet Union; *also* : the conversion to such a policy — **fin·land·ize** \ˈfinlən(͵)dīz\ *vt* -ED/-ING/-S *usu cap*
fire* *vi* : to transmit a nerve impulse ⟨the rate at which a neuron ~s⟩
firebase \ˈ=͵=\ *n* : a secured site from which field artillery can lay down interdicting fire
fired *adj* [fr. past part. of [2]*fire*] : using a specified fuel — usu. used in combination ⟨an oil-*fired* power plant⟩
firefight** *n* 1 : a hostile confrontation that involves gunfire 2 : SKIRMISH 2
fireflood \ˈ=͵=\ *or* **fireflooding** \ˈ=͵==\ *n* [[1]*fire* + [1]*flood* or *flooding*] : the process of injecting compressed air into a petroleum reservoir and burning some of the oil so as to drive the rest of the oil into producing wells
fire off* *vt* : to write and send usu. in haste or anger ⟨*fired off* a memo⟩
firepot* *n* : HOT POT *herein*
firepower* *n* 1 : effective power or force ⟨intellectual ~⟩ 2 : the scoring ability of a team or player
firestorm** *n* : a sudden or violent outburst ⟨a ~ of public protest⟩
firewall** *n* 1 : something created to prevent the spread of disaster or conflict 2 : a computer or computer program that prevents unauthorized access to private data (as on a company's internal network) by outside computer users
firmament* *n* : the field or sphere of an interest or activity ⟨the international fashion ~⟩
firmware \ˈ=͵=\ *n* [*firm* + *-ware* (as in *software* — herein)] : computer programs or routines contained permanently in a hardware device (as a read-only memory)
first* *adj, usu cap* : of or relating to the family of the president of the U.S. ⟨First Mother⟩ ⟨First Daughter⟩
first blood *n* 1 : the first drawing of blood in a contest (as boxing) 2 : an initial advantage over an opponent
first–line* \ˈ=ˈ=\ *adj* : being the preferred, standard, or first choice ⟨*first-line* treatment of tuberculosis⟩
first strike *n* : a preemptive nuclear attack — **first–strike** \ˈ=ˈ=\ *adj*
first world *n, usu cap F&W* : the highly developed industrialized nations often considered the westernized countries of the world
fiscal court *n* : the executive agency of a county in some states of the U.S.
fish* *vb* — **fish in troubled waters** : to profit or attempt to profit from unsettled or troubled conditions
fish–eye \ˈ=͵=\ *adj* [so called fr. the resemblance of the lens to the protruding eye of a fish] : being, having, or produced by a wide-angle photographic lens that has a highly curved protruding front, that covers an angle of about 180 degrees, and that gives a circular image with barrel distortion ⟨a *fish-eye* view⟩
fish farm *n* : a commercial facility for raising aquatic animals (as fish) for human food — **fish–farm** *vt* — **fish farming** *n*
fish lift *n* : a device resembling an elevator or conveyor belt that transports fish usu. upstream over an obstruction (as a dam)
fishnet* *n, often attrib* : a coarse open-mesh fabric; *also* : an item of clothing (as stockings) made from such fabric
fish protein concentrate *n* : FISH FLOUR
fish sauce *n* [trans. of Vietnamese *nước mắm* or Thai *námplaa*] : a sauce made of fermented anchovies used in Asian cooking
fisting *n* -S : the practice of inserting a hand or clenched fist into the anus or vagina of another person
fitness* *n* : the capacity of an organism to survive and transmit its genotype to reproductively fertile offspring as compared to competing organisms; *also* : the contribution of an allele or genotype to the gene pool of subsequent generations as compared to that of other alleles or genotypes
five* *n* : a slapping of extended right hands by two people (as in greeting or celebration) — usu. used in phrases with *give* or *slap* ⟨so I slapped him *five* and hugged him —J.R.Burke⟩
5–HT \ˈfīv(͵)āchˈtē\ *n* -S [*5-hydroxytryptamine*] : SEROTONIN
five–o'clock shadow *n* [so called fr. the resemblance of a dark beard's stubble to a shadow] : the growth of beard present late in the afternoon on the face of a man who has not shaved since morning
fix* *n* 1 : an accurate determination or understanding especially by observation or analysis ⟨a ~ on the future —Will Manley⟩ 2 : a supply or dose of something strongly desired or craved ⟨a coffee ~⟩ 3 : a solution to a problem : CORRECTION ⟨a short-term ~ to get us through this crisis⟩
fixed–point \ˈ=ˈ=\ *adj* : involving or being a mathematical notation (as in a decimal system) in which the point separating whole numbers and fractions is fixed — compare FLOATING-POINT *herein*
fixer–upper* *n* : something that needs fixing up ⟨the house was a *fixer-upper*⟩ ⟨my first car, a 1950s *fixer-upper*⟩
flack \ˈflak\ *vi* -ED/-ING/-S [[3]*flack*] : to provide publicity : engage in press-agentry
flack·ery \ˈflak(ə)rē, -ri\ *n* -ES [[3]*flack* + *-ery*] : PUBLICITY, PROMOTION, PRESS-AGENTRY
flag* *vt* [[6]*flag*] : to call a penalty on : PENALIZE ⟨a lineman *flagged* for being offsides⟩
fla·gel·lin \fləˈjelən\ *n* -S [*flagell*um + *-in*] : a polymeric protein that is the chief constituent of bacterial flagella, that forms helical chains around the hollow core of the flagellar filament, that determines the specificity of the flagellum in eliciting an immune response by its amino acid sequence, and that within any one serogroup exhibits one of two antigenic states determined by the expression of one or the other of two different genes
flag football *n* : a variation of football in which a player must remove a flag attached to a ballcarrier's clothing to stop the play

flagship* *n* : the finest, largest, or most important one of a series or group ⟨the company's ~ store⟩

flak* *n* **1** : abusive criticism ⟨I've taken ~ from newsmen who think I've sold out —Chet Huntley⟩ **2** : heated discussion : OPPOSITION ⟨this modest proposal ran into ~ —Charles MacDonald⟩ **3** : ³FLACK

flake* *n* [²*flake*] **1** : one that is flaky : SCREWBALL **2** *slang* : COCAINE

flakeboard \ˈ≈,≈\ *n* : a composition board made of flakes of wood bonded with synthetic resin — compare PARTICLEBOARD *herein*

flaky* *also* **flak·ey** *adj* : markedly odd or unconventional : CRAZY ⟨they used to call me ~ . . . but now that I'm a millionaire they'll be calling me an eccentric —Derek Sanderson⟩

flame* *n* **1** : the memory, reputation, or beliefs of a deceased person; *broadly* : MEMORY ⟨keeper of the ~⟩ **2** [*flame*, v. (herein)] : an angry, hostile, or abusive electronic message

flame* *vi* : to send an angry, hostile, or abusive electronic message ~ *vt* : to send an angry, hostile, or abusive electronic message to or about

flame out *vi* : to burn out (sense 2)

flameout* *n* **1** : a sudden downfall, failure or cessation ⟨a business marked by overnight triumph and equally sudden ~*s* —Todd Gold⟩ **2** : a person whose successful career ends abruptly

flame–retardant \ˈ≈,≈≈\ *adj* : made or treated so as to resist burning ⟨*flame-retardant* sleepwear⟩

flame stitch *n* : a needlepoint stitch that produces a pattern resembling flames

flan·ken \ˈflaŋkən, ˈfläŋ-\ *n* -S [Yiddish, pl. of *flank* flank] : flank steak boiled in stock with spices and vegetables

flanker* *or* **flanker back** *n* : a football player stationed wide of the formation; *esp* : an offensive halfback who lines up on the flank slightly behind the line of scrimmage and serves chiefly as a pass receiver

flannel* *n, Brit* : flattering or evasive talk; *also* : NONSENSE, RUBBISH — **flannel*** *vb, Brit*

flap·pa·ble \ˈflapəbəl\ *adj* [back-formation from *unflappable* (herein)] : lacking self-assurance and self-control : easily upset

flare* *n* **1** : a short pass in football thrown to a back who is running toward the sideline **2 flares** *pl* : trousers that flare toward the bottoms **3** : TEXAS LEAGUER

flash* *vi* **1** : to expose one's genitals usu. suddenly and briefly in public **2** : to have a sudden insight — often used with *on* ⟨she just ~*ed* on it: for once in her life, she ought to put her own needs right up front —Cyra McFadden⟩ ~ *vt* : to expose one's genitals usu. suddenly and briefly to ⟨that person *flashed* me⟩

flash* *n* **1** : RUSH *herein* **2** : PIZZAZZ *herein*

flash back** *vi* : to focus one's mind on or vividly remember a past time or incident ⟨*flashes back* on their relationship —Miriam Berkley⟩ ⟨*flashed back* to 1963⟩

flashback* *n* : a brief recurrence of a psychedelic experience

flashcube \ˈ≈,≈\ *n* : a plastic cube containing four flashbulbs that fits into the top of a camera and revolves after each shot

flasher* *n* : an exhibitionist who flashes

flash–forward \ˈ≈,≈≈\ *n* -S [¹*flash*back + ²*forward*] : a literary or theatrical technique used esp. in motion pictures and television that involves interruption of the chronological sequence of events by interjection of events or scenes of future occurrence; *also* : an instance of a flash-forward

flash photolysis *n* : the process of decomposing a chemical with an intense flash of light and observing spectroscopically the transient molecular fragments produced

flash point* *n* : TINDERBOX 2

flat* *adj* **1** : TWO-DIMENSIONAL 2b ⟨~ characters in fiction⟩ **2** : characterized by no significant rise or decline (as in profit, resources, or sales) from one period to another **3** : being or characterized by a horizontal line or tracing without peaks or depressions ⟨a ~ EEG⟩

flat–out* *adv* : to the greatest degree : COMPLETELY — usu. used as an intensive ⟨is just *flat-out* confusing⟩

flatten *vt* : to stabilize esp. at a lower level ⟨the economic boom will ~ interest rates⟩

fla·vi·vi·rus \ˈflävi,vīrəs\ *n* [NL, fr. L *flavus* yellow + NL *-i-* + *virus*; fr. the yellow fever virus, the type species — more at BLUE] : any of a family (Flaviviridae) of single-stranded RNA viruses that are transmitted by ticks and mosquitoes and include the causative agents of dengue, Japanese B encephalitis, and yellow fever

flavor* *n* **1** : a property that distinguishes different types of elementary particles (as quarks or neutrinos); *also* : any of the different types of particles that are distinguished by flavor **2** : VARIETY 3 ⟨always summer here. Days come in two ~*s*: hot and hotter —C.D.May⟩

flavor of the month : one that is very fashionable or popular usu. temporarily

flea collar *n* : a collar for animals that contains insecticide for killing fleas

flea–flicker \ˈ≈,≈≈\ *n* [⁴*flick* (to remove with a light blow) + ²*-er*; prob. fr. the comparison of a quick pass to the action of flicking a flea off one's body] : any of various offensive plays in football involving a combination of hand-offs and forward or lateral passes; *esp* : a play that starts out like a running play (as a double reverse) with the ball coming back to the quarterback who then throws a long pass

fleapit \ˈ≈,≈\ *n, Brit* : a dilapidated building usu. housing a movie theater

fleh·men \ˈflāmən\ *n* -S [G, fr. *flehmen* (of animals) to curl the upper lip] : a mammalian behavior (as of horses, cows, or elephants) in which the animal inhales with the mouth open and upper lip curled to facilitate exposure of Jacobsen's organ to a scent or pheromone — **flehmen** *vi* -ED/-ING/-S

fleur de coin \¦flərdə¦kwaⁿ, ¦flǣd-\ *adj* [F *à fleur de coin*, lit., with the bloom of the die] : being in the preserved mint condition

flex* *vb* — **flex one's muscles** : to demonstrate one's strength ⟨whatever happened to diplomacy where nations talked things out first before *flexing their muscles*? —Art Buchwald⟩

flex·a·gon \ˈfleksə,gän\ *n* -S [¹*flex* + *-agon* (as in *hexagon*)] : a folded paper figure that can be flexed along its folds to expose various arrangements of its faces

flexor ret·in·ac·u·lum \-,retᵊnˈakyələm\ *n* [NL] : any of several bands of fascia that overlie and provide channels for tendons esp. of flexor muscles

flex·time \ˈ≈,≈\ *or* **flexi·time** \ˈfleksə,tīm\ *n* [¹*flex*ible + *time*] : a system that allows employees to choose their own times for starting and finishing work within a broad range of available hours

flick–knife \ˈ≈,≈\ *n* [³*flick* + *knife*] *Brit* : SWITCHBLADE KNIFE

flight* *n* : a selection of wines for tasting as a group ⟨wines are tasted blind and organized into ~*s* by style and region —Jeff Morgan⟩

flight attendant *n* : a person who attends passengers (as by serving food) on an airplane

flight bag *n* **1** : a traveling bag usu. with zippered outside compartments for use esp. in air travel; *esp* : one that fits under an airplane seat **2** : a small thin lightweight canvas satchel decorated with the name of an airline

flight jacket *n* [so called fr. its similarity to aviators' jackets of World War II] : a zippered leather jacket with front pockets and knitted waistband and wristbands

flight recorder *n* : a crashworthy instrument for recording flight data (as airspeed or altitude) — compare BLACK BOX 2 *herein*

flight suit *n* : a usu. one-piece garment esp. of fire-resistant fabric worn esp. by a member of a military aircrew

flip* *vi* **1** : to lose self-control ⟨when he ~*s* it takes three men to hold him —Eddie Krell⟩ — often used with *out* **2** : to become extremely enthusiastic ⟨I *flipped* for that man's music —Melissa Hayden⟩

flip* *n* : an often shoulder-length hair style with the ends of the hair turned upward — compare PAGEBOY *in the Dict*

flip chart *n* : a series of hinged sheets that can be flipped over the top and out of view in presenting information sequentially

flip–flop \ˈ≈,≈\ *n* [²*flip* + ³*flop*] **1** : a rubber sandal loosely fastened to the foot by means of a thong **2** : a sudden reversal (as of policy or strategy) ⟨performed an amazing *flip-flop* . . . that put the plans back in motion —Ed Magnuson⟩ — **flip–flop** \"\ *vi*

flip side *n* [¹*flip* (to turn over)] **1** : reverse side; *specif* : the reverse and usu. less popular side of a phonograph record **2** : OPPOSITE ⟨survival is the *flip side* of profit, or getting rich —Robert Lacville⟩; *esp* : the reverse or opposite aspect or result ⟨the *flip side* of deficient saving . . . is overconsumption —R.S.Gay⟩

flip–top \ˈ≈¦≈\ *n, often attrib* : a top (as of a can) that is opened by pulling a small tab

FLIR *abbr, sometimes not cap* forward-looking infrared

flirt* *vi* : to come close to ⟨the temperature ~*ed* with 100°⟩

flit* *n, slang* : a male homosexual

float* *n* **1** : the time between a transaction (as the writing of a check or a purchase on credit) and the actual withdrawal from funds to cover it **2** : the volume of a company's shares available for active trading in the auction market

float* *vt* : to put forth (as a proposal) for acceptance

floater* *n* **1** : a bit of optical debris (as a dead cell or a cell fragment) in the vitreous humor or lens that may be perceived as a spot before the eye — usu. used in pl.; see MUSCAE VOLITANTES *in the Dict* **2** : a floating security

float fishing *n* **1** : the practice of fishing from a boat or raft allowed to float down a river **2** *chiefly Brit* : the art or practice of fishing usu. with live bait at the end of a line buoyed by a float

float glass *n* : flat glass produced by solidifying molten glass on the surface of a bath of molten tin

floating* *adj* : having no fixed value or rate ⟨~ currencies⟩ ⟨~ interest rates⟩

floating decimal *n* : a system of decimal point placement in an electronic calculator in which the decimal point is free to move automatically across the display in order to allow the maximum number of decimal places in the readout

floating–point \ˈ≈≈¦≈\ *adj* : expressed in, using, or being a mathematical notation in which a number is represented (as in a computer display) by an integer or a decimal fraction usu. with a positive or negative exponent indicating the number of places to move the decimal point to the right or left ⟨a *floating-point* operation⟩ — compare FIXED-POINT *herein*, SCIENTIFIC NOTATION *in the Dict*

floc·cu·lo·nodular lobe \¦fläkyə(,)lō+. . .-\ *n* [*floccul*us + *-o-* + *nodular*] : the posterior lobe of the cerebellum that consists of the nodulus and paired lateral flocculi and is concerned with equilibrium

flog* *vt* **1** *chiefly Brit* : SELL 2a **2** : PROMOTE 4c, PUBLICIZE ⟨using famous personalities to ~ products is not a new idea —Rod Townley⟩

flo·ka·ti \flōˈkätē\ *n* -S [NGk *phlokatē*] : a hand-woven Greek wool rug with a thick shaggy pile

floor exercise *n* : an event in gymnastics competition consisting of various ballet and tumbling movements (as jumps, somersaults, and handstands) performed without apparatus

floor partner *n* : a member of a brokerage firm who owns a seat on an exchange and acts as floor broker for his firm

floor–through \ˈ≈¦≈\ *n* [¹*floor* + *through*] : an apartment that occupies an entire floor of a building

floppy disk *or* **floppy** *also* **floppy diskette** *n* -ES : a small flexible plastic disk coated with magnetic material on which data for a computer can be stored

florentine* *n, sometimes cap* [F *florentin*, prob. short for *gâteau florentin*, lit., Florentine cake] : a thin, crisp cookie made with little or no flour, usu. containing nuts and candied fruit, and coated with chocolate on one side

floret* *n* : a cluster of flower buds separated from the central flower head esp. when used as food ⟨broccoli ~*s*⟩

florid* *adj* : marked by emotional or sexual fervor ⟨a ~ secret life⟩ ⟨a ~ sensibility⟩

florida panther *n, usu cap F* : a highly endangered cougar (*Felis concolor Coryi*) whose range is now limited to southern Florida

floss *vb* -ED/-ING/-ES *vt* : to use dental floss on ⟨the correct way to ~ your teeth⟩ ~ *vi* : to use dental floss to clean between the teeth ⟨everyone knows you should brush, but few know they should ~ —Robert Brackett⟩

flour tortilla *n* : a tortilla made with wheat flour instead of cornmeal

flow cytometry *n* : a technique for identifying and sorting cells and their components (as DNA) by staining with a fluorescent dye, detecting the fluorescence usu. by passing the cells individually in solution through laser beam illumination, and counting or sorting them automatically — **flow cytometer** *n*

flower bond *n* : a U.S. Treasury bond that may be redeemed at face value before maturity if used in settling federal estate taxes

flower bug *n* : any of various small mostly black-and-white predaceous bugs (family Anthocoridae) that frequent flowers and feed on pest insects (as aphids and thrips)

flower child *n* : a hippie who wears or displays flowers; *broadly* : HIPPIE *herein*

flower people *n pl* : FLOWER CHILDREN *herein*

flu·con·a·zole \flüˈkänə,zōl\ *n* -S [*fluor-* + *-conazole* (as in *miconazole* — herein)] : a synthetic triazole antifungal agent $C_{13}H_{12}F_2N_6O$ used orally to treat cryptococcal meningitis and to treat local or systemic infections caused by fungi of the genus Candida

flu·ence \ˈflüən(t)s\ *n* -S [L *fluere* to flow + E *-ence* — more at FLUID] **1** : the number of particles (as photons or neutrons) incident on a sphere divided by the cross-sectional area of the sphere : the total number of particles per unit area with which a material is irradiated ⟨particle ~⟩ **2** : the sum of the energies of the particles of a fluence : the energy per unit area contained in the particles with which a material is irradiated ⟨energy ~⟩

fluidic* *adj* : of, relating to, or being a device (as an amplifier or control) that depends for operation on the pressures and flows of a fluid in precisely shaped channels — **fluidic** \(ˈ)flü¦idik\ *n* -S

flu·id·ics \flüˈidiks\ *n pl but usu sing in constr* [²*fluid* + *-ics*] : the technology of fluidic devices

fluidized bed *also* **fluid bed** *n* : a bed of small solid particles (as in a coal-burning furnace) that are suspended and kept in motion by an upward flow of a fluid (as a gas)

fluk·ish \ˈflükish\ *adj* [⁴*fluke* + *-ish*] : happening or depending on chance; *also* : being out of the ordinary : UNUSUAL

flu·o·cin·o·lone ac·e·to·nide \,flüō¦sinᵊl,ōn,asəˈtō,nīd\ *n* [*fluor-* + *-cinolone* (perh. alter. of *-nisolone*, as in *prednisolone*) + *acetone* + *-ide*] : a glucocorticoid steroid $C_{24}H_{30}F_2O_6$ used esp. as an anti-inflammatory agent in the treatment of skin diseases

fluorescent* *adj* : very bright in color

flu·o·ro·polymer \¦flü(ə)(,)rō, ¦flōr(,)ō, ¦flȯ(,)rō+\ *n* [*fluor-* + *polymer*] : any of various homopolymers or copolymers that consist mainly of fluorine and carbon and that are characterized by chemical inertness, thermal stability, and a low coefficient of friction

flu·o·ro·uracil \"+\ *n* [*fluor-* + *uracil*] : a fluorine-containing pyrimidine base $C_4H_3FN_2O_2$ used to treat some kinds of cancer; 5-fluorouracil

flu·ox·e·tine \,flüˈäksə,tēn\ *n* -S [prob. fr. ISV *fluor-* + *oxy-* + methyl + ami*ne*] : an antidepressant drug $C_{17}H_{18}F_3NO$ administered in the form of its hydrochloride that enhances serotonin activity

flur·az·e·pam \flu̇rˈazə,pam\ *n* -S [*fluor-* + *-azepam* (as in *diazepam* — herein)] : a benzodiazepine $C_{21}H_{23}ClFN_3O$ closely related structurally to diazepam that is used in the form of its hydrochloride as a sleep-inducing agent to treat insomnia — see DALMANE *herein*

flurry* *n* : a sudden occurrence of many things at once : BARRAGE 2

flux·us \ˈfləksəs\ *n, usu cap* [L, lit., flow — more at FLUX] : an avant-garde art movement of the 1950s and 1960s that was heavily influenced by Dada

fly* *vi* [¹*fly*] **1** : to be high (as on drugs or alcohol) **2** : to function successfully : win popular acceptance ⟨a pure human-rights approach would not ~ —Charles Brydon⟩ — **fly at** : to assail suddenly and violently

fly* *n* : a football pass pattern in which the receiver runs straight downfield — **on the fly*** **1** : in a hurry and often without preparation : HASTILY; *also* : SPONTANEOUSLY **2** : simultaneously with a more central task

fly* *adj* [³*fly*] *slang* : impressively good, attractive, or stylish ⟨would have to top myself and really come up with something ~ —John Fuqua⟩

flybridge \ˈ≈,≈\ *n* [prob. short for *flying bridge*] : an open deck on a cabin cruiser located above the bridge on the cabin roof and usu. having a duplicate set of navigating equipment

fly–by–wire \ˈ≈≈,≈(≈)\ *adj* : of, relating to, being, or utilizing a flight-control system in which controls are operated electrically rather than mechanically

fly–in* *n* : a gathering (as at a small airport) of flying enthusiasts who arrive by private plane

fly–off \ˈ≈,≈\ *n* -S [¹*fly* + *-off* (as in *play-off*)] : an exhibition in which competing manufacturers attempt to win government contracts by demonstrating the performance characteristics of their aircraft

FMN \,ef(,)emˈen\ *n* -S [*fl*avin *mono*nucleotide] : FLAVIN MONONUCLEOTIDE

fo·cac·cia \fōˈkäch(ē)ə, fəˈ-\ *n* -S [It, fr. LL *focacia* (neut. pl.), fr. L *focus* hearth — more at FOCUS] : a flat Italian bread typically seasoned with herbs and olive oil

focal ratio *n* : F-NUMBER

focus* *vi* : to concentrate attention or effort ⟨she was already ~*ing* on her next role⟩

focus group *n* : a small group of people whose response to something (as a new product or a politician's image) is studied to determine the response that can be expected from a larger population

foil* *n* : HYDROFOIL

fo·late \ˈfō,lāt\ *n* -S [*fol*ic (acid) + ¹*-ate*] : FOLIC ACID; *also* : a salt or ester of folic acid

folder* *n* : an organizational element of a computer operating system used to group files or other folders together and usu. represented in a graphical user interface by an icon resembling a filing folder

fo·ley \ˈfōlē\ *n, often cap, often attrib* [after Jack D. *Foley* †1967 Am. sound technician] : sound effects (as footsteps or the rustle of clothing) created to match the movements of an actor on film or videotape and later mixed into the sound track

folk guitar *n* : a flat-topped acoustic guitar

¹folk·ie *also* **folky** \ˈfōkē, -ki\ *n, pl* **folkies** [²*folk* + *-ie*] **1** : a folk singer or musician ⟨a quiet-voiced English ~ —Stephen Holden⟩ **2** : a fan of folk music ⟨his fans were the sincere, often politically committed . . . ~*s* of the Kennedy years —*Playboy*⟩

²folkie *or* **folky** \"\ *adj* : of or relating to folk music

folklife \ˈ≈,≈\ *n* : the traditions, activities, skills, and products (as handicrafts) representative of a particular people or group

folk·lor·is·tics \,fōk,lȯrˈistiks\ *n pl but sing or pl in constr* [*folkloristic* + *-ics*] : the study of folklore

folk mass *n* : a mass in which traditional liturgical music is replaced by folk music

folk–rock \ˈ≈,≈\ *n* : folk songs sung to a rock'n'roll background — **folk–rock** \¦≈¦≈\ *adj* — **folk–rocker** \¦≈¦≈ə(r)\ *n*

follow–on \ˈ≈≈¦≈\ *adj* [*follow on*, vb.] : being or relating to something (as an object, technique, or event) held to be a second or later generation in the development of an original ⟨a *follow-on* bomber⟩ — **follow–on**** *n*

fondue* *n* **1** : a dish that consists of small pieces of food (as meat, fruit, or cake) cooked in or dipped into a hot liquid at the table ⟨beef ~⟩ ⟨chocolate ~⟩ **2** : a chafing dish for fondue

fondue fork *n* : a long slender usu. 2-tined fork used in eating or cooking fondue

fon·du·ta \fänˈd(y)üd·ə, -ütə\ *n* -S [It, fr. It dial. (Piedmont) *fondüa*, fr. F *fondue* — more at FONDUE] : a preparation of melted cheese (as fontina) usu. with milk, butter, egg yolks, and sliced white truffles

food chain* *n* : a hierarchical order within a series

food court *n* : an area within a building (as a shopping mall) set apart for food concessions and usu. furnished with tables and chairs

food·ie \ˈfüdē\ *n* -S [*food* + *-ie*] : a person having an avid interest in the latest food fads

food processor *n* : an electric appliance that performs many tasks of food preparation (as slicing, shredding, chopping, or mixing) with one of a set of interchangeable blades revolving inside a container

food pyramid *n* : an ecological hierarchy of food relationships esp. when expressed quantitatively (as in biomass, numbers, or energy) in which a chief predator is at the top, each level preys on the next lower level, and usu. green plants are at the bottom

food stamp *n* : a government-issued stamp that is sold at little cost or given to low-income persons and is redeemable for food

foodways \ˈ≈,≈\ *n pl* [*food* + *-ways* (as in *lifeways*)] : the eating habits and culinary practices of a people, region, or historical period

foos·ball \ˈfüz,bȯl\ *n, often cap* [prob. modif. of G *tischfussball*, fr. *tisch* table (fr. OHG *tisc* dish, table) + *fussball* soccer (trans. of E *football*), fr. *fuss* foot (fr. OHG *fuoz*) + *ball* ball, fr. OHG *bal, balla* — more at DISH, FOOT, BALL] : a table game resembling soccer in which the ball is moved by manipulating rods to which small figures of players are attached — called also *table soccer*

footage* *n* : the material captured on motion-picture film

foot·bag \ˈ≈,≈\ *n* **1** : a small bag usu. made of patches of leather or similar material and stuffed with pellets **2** : any of several games in which a player tries to keep a footbag in the air by striking it chiefly with the foot or leg and usu. passing it on to another player

foot·bed \ˈ≈,≈\ *n* : an insole usu. cushioned and contoured so as to provide orthopedic support

footpad* *n* : a flattish foot on the leg of a spacecraft for distributing weight to minimize sinking into a surface

footprint* *n* : an area of a surface covered by something ⟨automobile tire with a wide ~⟩ ⟨the laser beam's ~ on the ground will be less than half a mile wide —*Science News*⟩

footwork* *n* : MANEUVERING, TACTICS ⟨fancy political ~⟩

force* *n* **1** *usu cap* — used with a number to indicate the strength of the wind according to the Beaufort scale ⟨a *Force* 10 hurricane⟩ **2** : any of the natural influences (as electromagnetism, gravity, the strong force, and the weak force) that exist esp. between particles and determine the structure of the universe

force field* *n* **1** : a special charm, aura, or spirit that can influence anyone in its presence ⟨once out of his magical *force field*, I forgot that all things were possible —Robert Lipsyte⟩ **2** : something resembling a force field esp. in intensity that restricts or impedes movement toward an area or object ⟨soldiers . . . formed an olive-drab *force field* around the launch site ~ —Beth Dickey⟩

force of nature : FORCE 2 *herein*

foreground* *n* : a level of computer processing at which the processor responds immediately to input to a designated high-priority task — compare BACKGROUND *herein*

foreground \ˈ≈,≈\ *vt* [*foreground*, n.] : to place in the foreground; *esp* : to give prominence or emphasis to ⟨in a poem in Scots, a point may be ~*ed* by use of standard English —H.A.Gleason Jr.⟩

foreperson \ˈ≈,≈≈\ *n* [*fore*man + *person*] : a person of either sex serving in the role of foreman (as of a jury)

foreplay* *n* : action or behavior that precedes an event ⟨the ~ of revving his engine before the race⟩

forgiving* *adj* : providing a margin of error for human performance ⟨~ slopes that make a skier feel as though his skills had miraculously sharpened —C.D.May⟩

format* *n* **1** : a particular method of organizing data (as for storage) **2** : the medium upon which data or a recording is stored ⟨the primary ~ was videocassette instead of laserdisc⟩

format *vt* **formatted; formatted; formatting; formats** [*format,* n.] **1** : to arrange (as material to be printed or stored data) in a particular format **2** : to prepare (as a computer disk) for storing data in a particular format ⟨~ a floppy disk⟩ — **for·mat·ter** \ˈfȯrˌmad·ər, -ȯ(ə),m-\ *n* -S

formula *adj* [*formula,* n.] *of a racing car* : conforming to prescribed specifications of size, weight, and engine displacement and usu. having a long narrow body, open wheels, a single-seat open cockpit, and an engine in the rear

formula investing *n* : investing according to a plan under which more funds are invested in equity securities when the market is low and more are put into fixed-income securities when the market advances

for·tran \ˈfȯrˌtran\ *n* -S *usu cap F or all cap* [*for*mula *tran*slation] : a computer programming language that resembles algebra in its notation and is widely used for scientific applications

fortunately* *adv* : it is fortunate that ⟨~ no one was hurt⟩

fortune cookie *n* : a thin folded cookie containing a slip of paper on which a fortune, proverb, or humorous statement is printed

forward contract *n* : an agreement between a buyer and a seller to conclude the sale of an item at a specified time and at a specified price

fos·car·net \fäsˈkärnət\ *n* -S [prob. fr. ISV *fos-* (alter. of *phosph-*) + *carb-* + *-net* (of unknown origin)] : a hydrated sodium salt $Na_3CO_5P{\cdot}6H_2O$ that is an antiviral analogue of pyrophosphate and is administered intravenously to individuals infected with HIV to treat retinitis caused by a cytomegalovirus

fossil fuel *n* : a fuel (as coal, oil, or natural gas) that is formed in the earth from plant and animal remains — **fossil–fueled** \ˌ==ˈ=\ *adj*

fou·caul·di·an \füˈkōdēən\ *adj, usu cap* [F *foucauldien,* fr. Michel *Foucault* †1984 Fr. philosopher] : of, relating to, or characteristic of the philosophy of Michel Foucault

fou·gère \füˈzher\ *n* -S [F, literally, fern (prob. originally in *Fougère Royale,* "Royal Fern," a fragrance introduced by the Paris perfume house Houbigant in 1882), fr. OF *fulgiere,* fr. (assumed) VL *filicaria* fernbrake, fr. L *filic-, filix* fern] : a fragrance that consists of a blend of several oils or scents (as lavender, citrus, or moss)

found object *n* [trans. of F *objet trouvé*] : a natural or discarded object (as a piece of driftwood or an old bathtub) found by chance and held to have aesthetic value

found poem *n* : a poem consisting of words found in a nonpoetic context (as a product label) and usu. broken into lines that convey a verse rhythm

4x4 *also* **four–by–four** \ˈ==ˌ=\ *n* : a four-wheeled automotive vehicle (as a pickup) equipped with four-wheel drive

four–channel \ˈ=ˌ==\ *adj* : QUADRAPHONIC *herein*

fou·ri·er transform *also* **fourier transformation** \ˈfu̇rēˌā-, fu̇rˈyā-\ *n, usu cap F* [after Baron Jean Baptiste Joseph *Fourier* †1830 Fr. geometrician and physicist] : any of various functions (as $F(u)$) that under suitable conditions can be obtained from given functions (as $f(x)$) by multiplying by e^{iux} and integrating over all values of x and that are widely used in analyzing data esp. by computer-driven scientific instrumentation

401(k) \ˌfȯr(ˌ)ō(ˌ)wənˈkā, ˌfȯr-\ *n* -S [fr. *401(k),* section of the U.S. Internal Revenue Code that authorized such accounts] : a retirement account to which employee and employer contribute, on which taxes are deferred until withdrawal, and for which the employee selects the types of investments

fourplex \ˈfō(ə)rˌpleks, -ȯ(ə)r-\ *n* -ES [¹*four* + *-plex* (as in *duplex*)] : a building that contains four separate apartments

fourth market *n* : the private market for the sale of securities by institutional investors — compare THIRD MARKET *herein*

fourth wall *n* : an imaginary wall (as the opening of the proscenium in a theater) that keeps performers from recognizing or directly addressing their audience

fourth world *n, usu cap F&W* : a group of nations esp. in Africa and Asia characterized by extremely low per capita income and an absence of readily exportable natural resources — compare THIRD WORLD *herein*

four–walling \ˈ=ˈ==\ *also* **four–walls contract** \ˈ=ˈ=-\ *n* [so called fr. the fact that the distributor takes over the entire theater] : an arrangement whereby a motion picture distributor rents a theater for the entire run of a film and keeps all the ticket receipts instead of splitting them with the theater owner

4WD *abbr* four-wheel drive

fox* *n* **1** *slang* : an attractive and stylish young woman **2** *slang* : an attractive young man

foxy* *adj* : ATTRACTIVE, SEXY ⟨looking incredibly ~ in a feather boa —Cyra McFadden⟩

FPC* *abbr* fish protein concentrate *herein*

frab·jous \ˈfrabjəs\ *adj* [perh. alter. of *fabulous*] **1** : WONDERFUL **2** : EXTRAORDINARY — **frab·jous·ly** \-lē, -li\ *adv*

frac·tal \ˈfrakt³l\ *n* -S [F *fractale,* fr. L *fractus* broken, uneven (past part. of *frangere* to break) + F *-ale* ²-al — more at BREAK] : any of various extremely irregular curves or shapes for which any suitably chosen part is similar in shape to a given larger or smaller part when magnified or reduced to the same size — **fractal** *adj*

fra di·avo·lo \frädēˈävəlō, -vōlō, -dī-\ *adj, often cap F&D* [It *Fra Diavolo* Brother Devil, nickname of Michele Pezza †1806 Ital. bandit] : prepared with tomato sauce usu. seasoned with garlic, oregano, and hot red pepper ⟨lobster *fra diavolo*⟩

frag \ˈfrag\ *vt* **fragged; fragged; frag·ging; frags** [*frag,* n.] : to deliberately injure or kill (one's military leader) by means of a fragmentation grenade — **frag·ger** \-ə(r)\ *n* -S

fragile x syndrome *also* **fragile x** *n, usu cap x* [so called from a fragile (partially gapped) site at band Xq 27 of the X chromosome in those affected with the disorder] : an X-linked inherited disorder that is caused by a genetic mutation marked by elongation of a normally occurring tandemly repeated trinucleotide sequence, that is characterized by moderate to severe mental retardation, by large ears, chin, and forehead, and by enlarged testes in males, and that often has limited or no effect in heterozygous females

frame* *n* : a unit of programmed instruction calling for a response by the student

frameshift \ˈ=ˌ=\ *adj* [²*frame* + ²*shift*] : relating to, being, or causing a mutation in which a number of nucleotides not divisible by three is inserted or deleted so that some triplet codons are read incorrectly during genetic translation ⟨~ mutations⟩ ⟨~ mutagens⟩ — **frameshift** \"\ *n*

fran·chi·see \ˌfranchəˈzē, -ˌchī-, -raan- *sometimes* -ˌ=ˈsē\ *n* -S [¹*franchise* + ¹*-ee*] : one who is granted a franchise to operate a unit in a chain of business establishments

fran·co–american \ˌfraŋ(ˌ)kō+\ *n, cap F&A* [*Franco-* + *American*] : an American of French or esp. French-Canadian descent — **franco–american** *adj, cap F&A*

¹fran·co·phone \ˈfraŋkəˌfōn\ *adj, often cap* [F, fr. *franco-* Franco- + *-phone* speaking, speaker, fr. Gk *-phonos* -phone] : of, having, or belonging to a French-speaking population esp. in a country where two or more languages are spoken

²francophone \"\ *n* -S *usu cap* : a French-speaking person esp. in a country where two or more languages are spoken

fran·glais \fräⁿˈglā, -äŋˈg-\ *n* -ES *often cap* [F, blend of *français* French and *anglais* English] : French marked by a considerable number of borrowings from English

fratricide* *n* : the hypothetical destruction of incoming missiles aimed at closely spaced targets (as missile silos) by the effects of the first nuclear warhead to detonate

fraud·ster \ˈfrȯdstər\ *n* -S [*fraud* + *-ster*] *chiefly Brit* : one who engages in fraud : CHEAT

fraught* *adj, chiefly Brit* : causing or characterized by emotional distress or tension : UNEASY

freak* *n* **1** : an ardent enthusiast ⟨a film ~⟩ **2** : one who uses illicit drugs **3** : HIPPIE

freak \ˈfrēk\ *vb* [*freak,* n. (herein)] *vi* **1** : to withdraw from reality and society esp. by taking drugs **2** : to experience nightmarish hallucinations as a result of taking drugs : have a bad trip — often used with *out* **3 a** : to behave irrationally or unconventionally under the influence of drugs — often used with *out* **b** : to lose one's composure : react with extreme or irrational distress or excitement — often used with *out* ⟨if I lose my glasses or miss an appointment, I ~ out —Emmylou Harris⟩ ~ *vt* **1** : to put under the influence of a psychedelic drug **2** : to make greatly astonished, distressed, or discomposed : UPSET — often used with *out* ⟨what he saw *freaked* him out so much that he still gets shaken when he remembers it —*Berkeley Barb*⟩ — **freaked** *or* **freaked–out** \ˈ=ˈ=\ *adj*

freak·ery \ˈfrēk(ə)rē\ *n* -ES [¹*freak* + *-ery*] **1** : FREAKINESS *herein* **2** : something that is freaky

freak·i·ness \ˈfrēkēnəs, -kin-\ *n* -ES : the quality or state of being freaky

freak·ing *adj (or adv)* [alter. of *frigging,* pres. part. of *frig* (copulate)] : DAMNED — used as an intensive ⟨it was too ~ much to believe —Chip Crossland⟩

freak–out \ˈ=ˌ=\ *n* -S [*freak out,* v.] **1** : a withdrawal from reality esp. by means of drugs **2 a** : a drug-induced state of mind characterized by terrifying hallucinations : a bad trip **b** : an irrational act by one that freaks out **3** : a gathering of hippies **4** : one who freaks out

free agent *n* : a professional athlete who is free to negotiate a contract with any team — **free agency** *n*

free–associate \ˌ==ˈ==ˌ=\ *vi* [back-formation fr. *free association*] : to engage in free association — **free–associative** \ˌ=ˈsōs(h)ēˌād·iv, -ēəd·iv, -s(h)əd-\ *adj*

¹freebase \ˈ=ˌ=\ *n* [¹*free* + ¹*base* (alkaloid)] : a purified solid form of cocaine (as crack) that is obtained by treating powdered cocaine hydrochloride with an alkaloid base (as sodium bicarbonate) and that can be smoked or heated to produce vapors for inhalation; *specif* : a form derived from treatment of cocaine hydrochloride with ammonia or similar alkaloid solution followed by extraction with a solvent (as ether)

²freebase \"\ *vi* : to prepare or use freebase cocaine ~ *vt* : to prepare or use (cocaine) as freebase — **freebas·er** \-ə(r)\ *n* -S

free·bie *or* **free·bee** \ˈfrēbē, -bi\ *n* -S [by alter. fr. obs. slang *freeby* gratis, irreg. fr. *free*] : something (as a theater ticket) given or received without charge

freedom fighter *n* : one who takes part in a resistance movement against an oppressive political or social establishment

freedom ride *n, often cap F&R* : a ride made by civil rights workers through states of the southern U.S. to ascertain whether public facilities (as bus terminals) are desegregated — **freedom rider** *n, often cap F&R*

free–electron laser \ˈ=ˈ==-\ *n* : a highly efficient laser that can be tuned over a wide range of frequencies and that produces electromagnetic radiation by the motion of electrons moving at relativistic velocities in a specially designed magnetic field

free fall* *n* : a rapid and continuing drop or decline ⟨a *free fall* in stock prices⟩

free–fire zone \ˈ=ˈ=-\ *n* : a combat area where any moving thing is a legitimate target

free–form *adj* : FREE 14b ⟨*free-form* mud wrestling⟩

free lunch* *n* : something given entirely free of charge or obligation ⟨in politics there is no *free lunch*⟩

¹free–range \ˈ=ˈ=\ *vi* : to range and forage with relative freedom ⟨too cold to let hens *free-range*⟩ ⟨*free-ranging* and caged monkey colonies⟩

²free–range *adj* : allowed to range and forage with relative freedom ⟨*free-range* chickens⟩; *also* : of, relating to, or produced by free-range poultry ⟨*free-range* eggs⟩

free–running \ˈ=ˈ==\ *adj* : not involving or subjected to entrainment or resetting periodically by an environmental factor (as photoperiod) ⟨a *free-running* circadian rhythm⟩

free safety *n* : a safetyman in football who has no specific pass receiver to guard in a man-to-man defense and who usu. helps wherever needed on defense

freestanding* *adj* : INDEPENDENT; *esp* : not being part of or affiliated with another organization ⟨a ~ clinic⟩ ⟨a ~ computer store⟩

free university *n* : an unaccredited autonomous free institution established within a university by students to present and discuss subjects not usu. dealt with in the academic curriculum

freeware \ˈ=ˌ=\ *n* [¹*free* + *-ware* (as in *software* — herein)] : software that is available for use at no cost or for a nominal usu. voluntary fee

freeze–etch \ˈ=ˈ=\ *adj* : of, relating to, or used in freeze-etching

freeze–etched \ˈ=ˈ=\ *adj* : having been subjected to or prepared by freeze-etching

freeze–etching \ˈ=ˌ=\ *n* : preparation of a specimen (as of tissue) for electron microscopic examination by freezing, fracturing along natural structural lines, and preparing a replica (as by simultaneous vapor deposition of carbon and platinum)

freeze–fracture \ˈ=ˌ==\ *also* **freeze–fracturing** *n* : FREEZE-ETCHING *herein* — **freeze–fracture** \ˈ=ˈ==\ *vt*

freeze–frame \ˈ=ˌ=\ *n* [²*freeze* + ²*frame*] **1** : a frame of a motion-picture film that is repeated so as to give the illusion of a static picture; *also* : a static picture produced esp. from a videodisc or videotape recording **2** : something having the unchanging quality of a freeze-frame ⟨exist most vividly in the *freeze-frame* of memory —Gioia Diliberto⟩

freight* *n* **1** : COST ⟨wasn't a single sponsor to help pay the ~ —*TV Guide*⟩ **2** : MEANING, SIGNIFICANCE

frequent–flier *also* **frequent–flyer** \ˈ==ˈ==\ *adj* : of, relating to, or being an airline program that offers awards for specified numbers of air miles traveled

frequent·ist \+əst\ *n* -S [*frequent-* (back-derived fr. *frequency*) + ¹*-ist*] : one who defines the probability of an event (as heads in flipping a coin) as the limiting value of its frequency in a large number of trials — compare BAYESIAN *herein*

fret* *vt* : to depress (the strings of a musical instrument) against the frets ~ *vi* : to fret the strings of a musical instrument

fried·man·ite \ˈfrēdmәˌnīt\ *n* -S *usu cap* [Milton *Friedman* b1912 Am. economist + E ¹*-ite*] : a monetarist who adheres to the theory of economist Milton Friedman that economic regulation should be through direct governmental manipulation of the money supply

friendly* *adj* **1** : easy esp. for a nonspecialist to use or understand ⟨the *friendliest* possible introduction to computers —Dan Watt⟩ — often used in combination ⟨reader-*friendly*⟩ **2** : COMPATIBLE 2a — often used in combination ⟨a computer-*friendly* device⟩

frijoles re·fri·tos \-(ˌ)rāˈfrē(ˌ)tōz, -ōs\ *n pl* [Sp, lit., refried beans] : frijoles cooked with seasonings, fried, then mashed and fried again

Fris·bee \ˈfrizbē\ *trademark* — used for a plastic disk several inches in diameter that is sailed between players by a flip of the wrist

fri·sée *also* **fri·sé** \frēˈzā\ *n* [F, short for *chicorée frisée,* lit., curly chicory] : curly endive leaves that have finely dissected edges and are used in salads

frit·ta·ta \frē·ˈtäd·ə\ *n* -S [It, fr. *fritto,* past part. of *friggere* to fry (fr. L *frigere*) + *-ata* -ade — more at FRY] : an unfolded omelet often containing chopped vegetables or meats

fritted *adj* [²*frit*] : being porous glass made of sintered powdered or fiber glass

fritto misto* *n* : small morsels of food typically including seafood, meats, and vegetables that are dipped in batter and fried

frog* *n* : a small holder with perforations or spikes that is placed in a bowl or vase to keep cut flowers in position

front* *vt* **1** : ADVANCE 4b ⟨~*ed* them a loan⟩ **2** : to move (a word or phrase) to the beginning of a sentence **3** *basketball* : to play in front of (an opposing player) rather than between the player and the basket ~ *vi* : BLUFF 2

front* *adj* : acting as a front ⟨~ companies⟩

front and center *adv* : in or to the forefront of activity or consideration

front–end \ˈ=ˈ=\ *adj* : relating to or required at the beginning of an undertaking ⟨take some time for the huge *front-end* investment to be paid off —*Wall Street Jour.*⟩

front end *n* **1** : a unit in a computer system devoted to controlling the data communications link between terminals and the main computer (as by routing messages and checking for errors in transmission) and often to preliminary processing of data **2** : a software interface (as a graphical user interface) that allows user-friendly interaction with a computer

front–end load \ˈ=ˌ=-\ *n* : the part of the total load taken out of early payments under a contract plan for the periodic purchase of investment-company shares

front–end loader *or* **front loader** *n* : a usu. wheeled tractor fitted with a wide scoop in front for excavating and loading loose material (as earth or gravel)

fron·te·nis \ˌfranˈtenəs, (ˈ)frän-\ *n* [AmerSp, blend of Sp *frontón* pelota court and *tenis* tennis, fr. E *tennis* — more at FRONTON] : a game of Mexican origin played with rackets and a rubber ball on a 3-walled court

frontlash \ˈ=ˌ=\ *n* -ES [³*front* + back*lash*] : a counterreaction to a political backlash

front line* *n* : an area of potential or actual conflict or struggle

frontline* *adj* : FIRST-RATE ⟨~ teachers⟩; *also* : FIRST-STRING ⟨a ~ goalie⟩

front money *n* : money that is paid in advance for a promised service or product

frost* *vt* : to make angry or irritated ⟨doesn't that just ~ you when they do that? —Kent Ward⟩

frostbelt \ˈ=ˌ=\ *n, often cap* : the northern and northeastern states of the U.S. — compare SUNBELT *herein*

frosted* *adj* : having undergone frosting ⟨~ hair⟩

frosting* *n* : the lightening (as by chemicals) of small strands of hair throughout the entire head to produce a two-tone effect — compare STREAKING *herein*

fruc·to·kinase \ˌfrəktō, ˌfru̇k-, ˌfrük-+\ *n* [*fructose* + *kinase*] : a kinase that catalyzes the transfer of phosphate groups to fructose

fru·gi·vore \ˈfrüjəˌvō(ə)r, -ˌvȯr\ *n* -S [*frugivorous* + *-vore*] : one that is frugivorous

fruit jar *n* : MASON JAR

fruit leather *n* : a sheet of dried pureed fruit

fruit machine *n* [so called fr. the use of pictures of various fruits as symbols to be matched] *Brit* : SLOT MACHINE 2

fru·se·mide \ˈfrüsəˌmīd\ *n* -S [by alter.] *chiefly Brit* : FUROSEMIDE *herein*

fry* *vi* : to get very hot or burn as if by being fried ⟨sunbathers ~*ing* on the beach⟩ ~ *vt* **1** : to damage or destroy (as one's brain) by overuse or abuse esp. of drugs **2** : to damage (an electronic device or its circuitry) usu. beyond repair by overheating esp. as a result of unusually high voltage

fry bread *n* : bread cooked (as by Navajo Indians) by deep frying

fry–up \ˈ=ˌ=\ *n* -S [fr. *fry up,* v.] *Brit* : a dish or meal of fried food

fs* *abbr* femtosecond *herein*

FSO \ˌef(ˌ)esˈō\ *abbr or n* -S : a foreign service officer

FT* *abbr* Fourier transform *herein*

FTE \ˌef(ˌ)tēˈē\ *abbr or n* -S [*f*ull-*t*ime *e*quivalent] : the statistical equivalent in part-time students or employees of a single full-time student or employee

ftp *abbr* file transfer protocol

¹fuck \ˈfək\ *vb* -ED/-ING/-S [of Gmc origin; akin to MD *fokken* to push, thrust, copulate, Sw dial. *fock* penis] **1** : COPULATE — usu. considered obscene; sometimes used in the present participle as an intensive **2** : to mess around — used with *with*; usu. considered vulgar ~ *vt* **1** : to engage in coitus with — usu. considered obscene; sometimes used interjectionally with an object (as a pronoun) to express anger, contempt, or disgust **2** : to deal with unfairly or harshly — usu. considered vulgar

²fuck \"\ *n* -S **1** : an act of copulation — usu. considered obscene **2** : a sexual partner — usu. considered obscene **3 a** : DAMN 2 — usu. considered vulgar **b** — used esp. with *the* as a meaningless intensive; usu. considered vulgar **4** : FUCKER 2 *herein* — usu. considered vulgar

fucked up *adj* : thoroughly confused or disordered — usu. considered vulgar

fuck·er \ˈfəkə(r)\ *n* -S **1** : one that fucks — usu. considered obscene **2** : an offensive or disagreeable person — usu. considered vulgar

fuck off *vi* **1** : to leave forthwith : go away — usu. used as a command; usu. considered vulgar **2** : to fool around : be idle — usu. considered vulgar

fuckoff \ˈ=ˌ=\ *n* -S : a lazy or unreliable person — usu. considered vulgar

fuck over *vt* : to take advantage of : EXPLOIT — usu. considered vulgar

fuck up *vt* : to ruin or spoil esp. through stupidity, ignorance, or carelessness : BUNGLE — usu. considered vulgar ~ *vi* : to act foolishly or stupidly : BLUNDER — usu. considered vulgar

fuckup \ˈ=ˌ=\ *n* -S **1** : one who fucks up — usu. considered vulgar **2** : BOTCH, BLUNDER — usu. considered vulgar

fudge* *n* : something that is fudged; *esp* : a bending of rules or a compromise ⟨room for ~ in the vague assignment⟩

fudge factor *n* : an arbitrary mathematical term inserted into a calculation in order to arrive at an expected solution or to allow for errors esp. of underestimation; *broadly* : an arbitrary unspecified factor

fuel cell *n* : a device that continuously changes the chemical energy of a fuel (as hydrogen) and an oxidant directly into electrical energy

fueler* *n* : a dragster that uses specially blended fuel

fuel injection *n* : a system of providing atomized fuel to an internal-combustion engine by spraying a precisely metered amount of fuel into the intake manifold or directly into the cylinder in time for it to be ignited with the compressed air — **fuel–injected** \ˈ=ˌ==\ *adj*

fulfillment* *n* **1** : the act or process of delivering a product (as a publication) to consumers **2** : the division of an organization that oversees the fulfilling of customer orders

full–bore \ˈ=ˈ=\ *adj* [*full bore,* adv. (herein)] **1** : FULL-BLOWN 2 ⟨a *full-bore* crisis⟩ **2** : made with maximum effort ⟨a *full-bore* attempt to succeed⟩

full bore *adv* **1** : at maximum engine capacity : at full throttle **2** : with maximum effort or speed ⟨runners sprinting *full bore*⟩

full–court press* *n* : an all-out effort or offensive ⟨campaigned with a *full-court press* —Hays Gorey⟩

full duplex *n* : a mode of communication with a computer via telephone line in which the characters sent to the computer from a remote terminal are echoed back to the terminal for display — compare DUPLEX *in the Dict,* HALF DUPLEX *herein*

ful·ler·ene \ˌfu̇ləˈrēn\ *n* -S [buckminster*fuller*ene (herein)] : any of a class of closed hollow aromatic carbon compounds whose structures are made up of 12 pentagonal and differing numbers of hexagonal faces; *esp* : one having a roughly spherical shape

full–motion video \ˈ=ˈ==-\ *n* : the display of video images at a rate (as thirty frames per second) at which objects appear to move smoothly and continuously

full–service \ˈ=ˈ==\ *adj* : providing comprehensive service of a particular kind ⟨a *full-service* bank⟩

ful·vic acid \ˌfu̇lvik-, ˌfəl-\ *n* [NL *fulvum* (fr. specific epithet of *Penicillium griseofulvum,* a species of fungus) + E *-ic*] : any of various water-soluble organic acids of high molecular weight derived from humus

fu man·chu mustache \ˌfüˌmanˌchü-\ *n, usu cap F & 1st M* [after *Fu Manchu*, Chinese villain in stories by "Sax Rohmer" (A.S. Ward †1955)] : a heavy mustache with ends that turn down to the chin

fun and games *n pl but sing or pl in constr* : light amusement

function* *n* **1** : RESULT ⟨illnesses that are a ~ of stress⟩ **2** : a computer subroutine; *specif* : one that performs a calculation with variables provided by a program and supplies the program with a single result

functional food *n* : NUTRACEUTICAL *herein*

function key *n* : any of a set of keys on a computer keyboard that have or can be programmed to have special functions

functor* *n* **1** : FUNCTION WORD **2** : a rule defined on two mathematical categories that assigns each object and mapping of one category to an object and mapping of the other in such a way as to preserve certain aspects of structure (as identity mappings, composition of mappings, and isomorphism)

fundamental group *n* : a set that is a subset of all paths defined on a set of points each pair of which is joined by a path and that is the quotient group of the group of all paths beginning and ending in the given point

fundamental theorem of algebra : a theorem in algebra: every equation which can be put in the form with zero on one side of the equal-sign and a polynomial of degree greater than or equal to one with real or complex coefficients on the other has at least one root which is a real or complex number

fund–raiser \ˈ=ˌ==\ *n* **1** : a person employed to raise funds (as for a political campaign or charity) **2** : an event or campaign organized to raise funds

fun fur *n* : relatively inexpensive or synthetic fur for casual wear

funk* *n* **1** : music that combines traditional forms of black music (as blues, gospel, or soul) and is characterized by a strong backbeat **2** : the quality or state of being funky ⟨jeans . . . have lost much of their ~ —Tom Wolfe⟩

funky* *adj* -ER/-EST **1** : having an earthy unsophisticated style and feeling; *esp* : having the style and feeling of older black American music (as blues or gospel) or of funk ⟨a slick, heavy beat that is unmistakably contemporary and irresistibly ~ —Jay Cocks⟩ **2 a** : odd or quaint in appearance or feeling ⟨one ~ festival, be it a rattlesnake roundup . . . or even a Rocky Mountain oyster fry —Jay Rosser⟩ **b** : lacking style or taste ⟨a ~ cheap hotel⟩ **c** : unconventionally stylish ⟨lighting gives the . . . shops and streets a ~ prettiness —Pauline Kael⟩

funnel cake *n* [so called because the dough is poured through a funnel] : a small spiral-shaped cake fried in a skillet

funny car *n* : a specialized dragster that has a one-piece molded body resembling the body of a mass-produced car

funny farm *n, slang* : a psychiatric hospital

fu·ra·zol·i·done \ˌfyu̇rəˈzäləˌdōn, -zōl-\ *n* -S [*fur-* + *azole* + *-ide* + *-one*] : an antimicrobial drug $C_8H_7N_3O_5$ used against bacteria and some protozoa esp. in infections of the gastrointestinal tract

fu·ro·se·mide \f(y)əˈrōsəˌmīd\ *also* **fur·se·mide** \ˈfərsə-, ˈfäsə-\ *n* -S [ISV *fur-* + *sulf-* + *-emide*, prob. alter. of *amide*] : a powerful diuretic $C_{12}H_{11}ClN_2O_5S$ used esp. in the treatment of edema

fu·si·coc·cin \ˌfyüsəˈkäksən\ *n* -S [NL *Fusicoccum* (genus name of *Fusicoccum amygdali*) + E *-in*] : a diterpenoid glucoside produced by a pathogenic fungus of the genus *Fusicoccum* (*F. amygdali*) that causes wilting of peach and almond leaves

fu·sil·li \f(y)üˈsilē, -ˈsēlē\ *n* -S [It, pl. of *fusillo*, fr. It dial. (southern Italy), dim. of *fuso* spindle, fr. L *fusus*] : a spiral-shaped variety of pasta

fusion* *n* : popular music combining different styles (as jazz and rock)

fusion cuisine *n* : food prepared by using the techniques and ingredients of two or more ethnic or regional cuisines

fu·ton \ˈfüˌtän\ *n, pl* **futons** *also* **futon** [Jap] : a mattress filled usu. with cotton that is placed on the floor or in a raised frame for use as a bed, a couch, or a chair

future shock *n* : the physical and psychological distress suffered by one who is unable to cope with the rapidity of societal and technological changes

futurism* *n* : FUTUROLOGY *herein*

futurist* *n* : one who studies and predicts the future esp. on the basis of current trends

futurist *adj* [*futurist*, n.] : of or relating to futurism or futurists

fu·tur·is·tics \ˌfyüchəˈristiks\ *n pl but sing in constr* [*futuristic* + *-s*] : FUTUROLOGY *herein*

fu·tu·rol·o·gy \ˌfyüchəˈräləjē\ *n* -ES [G *futurologie*, fr. *futur* future + *-o-* + *-logie* -logy] : a study that deals with future possibilities based on current trends — **fu·tu·ro·log·i·cal** \ˌfyüchərəˈläjəkəl\ *adj* — **fu·tu·rol·o·gist** \ˌ==ˈräləjəst\ *n* -S

futz \ˈfəts\ *vi* -ED/-ING/-ES [perh. part modif., part trans. of Yiddish *arumfartsn*, lit., to fart around] *slang* : FOOL 1 — often used with *around* ⟨~ around without producing any worthwhile music —John Koegel⟩

fuzz tone *or* **fuzz box** *n* : an electronic device (as on an electric guitar) which by distorting the sound gives it a fuzzy quality; *also* : the sound so produced

FWD* *abbr, often not cap* front-wheel drive

FX \ˌefˈeks\ *n pl* [letter names *ef* and *ex* representing *effects*] : SPECIAL EFFECTS

g* *abbr, cap* **1** giga- **2** guanine

G \ˈjē\ *trademark* — used as a rating for a motion picture of such a nature that persons of all ages may be allowed admission; compare NC-17 *herein*, PG *herein*, PG-13 *herein*, R *herein*

GAAP *abbr* generally accepted accounting principles

GABA *abbr* gamma-aminobutyric acid *herein*

ga·ga·ku \gäˈgä(ˌ)kü\ *n, often cap* [Jap, fr. *ga* elegance + *gaku* music] : the ancient court music of Japan

gag order *n* : a court-imposed ruling barring public disclosure or discussion (as by the press) of evidence relating to an ongoing court case; *broadly* : a similar nonjudicial prohibition against the release of confidential information or against public discussion of a sensitive matter

ga·lac·to·kinase \gəˌlaktō+\ *n* [*galactose* + *kinase*] : a kinase that catalyzes the transfer of phosphate groups to galactose

gal·braith·ian \(ˈ)galˈbrāthēən, -thyən\ *adj, usu cap* [John Kenneth *Galbraith* b1908 Am. economist + E *-ian*] : of or relating to the economic theories or programs of John Kenneth Galbraith

ga·le·ro \gəˈle(ə)r(ˌ)ō\ *n* -S [It, fr. L *galerus* cap of skin — more at GALERA] : the flat-crowned wide-brimmed tasseled red hat formerly worn by Roman Catholic cardinals — called also *cardinal's hat*

gal friday *n, usu cap F* : GIRL FRIDAY

gal·le·ria \ˌgaləˈrēə\ *n* -S [It, arcade of shops, gallery, fr. ML *galeria* — more at GALLERY] : a roofed and usu. glass-enclosed promenade or court (as at a shopping mall)

gallium arsenide *n* : a synthetic compound GaAs used esp. as a semiconducting material

gallows humor *n* : humor that makes fun of very serious or terrifying situations

ga·lois theory \(ˈ)galˈwä-\ *n, usu cap G* [after Evariste *Galois* †1832 Fr. mathematician] : a part of the theory of mathematical groups concerned esp. with the conditions under which a solution to a polynomial equation with coefficients in a given mathematical field can be obtained in the field by the repetition of operations and the extraction of nth roots

galvanic skin response *n* : a change in the electrical resistance of the skin that is a physiochemical response to a change in emotional state — abbr. *GSR*

ga·may \gaˈmā, ˈgamˌā\ *n* -S *often cap* [F *Gamay*, a grape variety, wine made from that grape, fr. *Gamay*, village in Burgundy, France] : a light dry red table wine made from the same grape used for French Beaujolais

game* *vt* : to take dishonest advantage of : CHEAT ⟨~ the tax system⟩

game ball* *n* : a ball (as a football) presented by the members of a team to a player or coach in recognition of his contribution to the team's victory

game plan *n* [so called fr. the use of a strategy or plan in a game like football] : a strategy for achieving an objective

gam·er \ˈgāmər\ *n* -S : a player who is game; *esp* : an athlete who relishes competition

gamete in·tra·fal·lo·pi·an transfer \-ˌinˈtrəfəˈlōpēən-, -ˌin(ˌ)trä-\ *also* **gamete intrafallopian tube transfer** *n* : a method of assisting reproduction in cases of infertility in which eggs are obtained from an ovary, mixed with sperm, and inserted into a fallopian tube by a laparoscope — abbr. *GIFT*

gamma–aminobutyric acid \ˌgamə-əˈmē(ˌ)nō, -məˈamə(ˌ)nō+. . .-\ *also* **γ–aminobutyric acid** \"\ *n* [²*gamma* + *amin-* + *butyric acid*] : an amino acid $C_4H_9NO_2$ that is a neurotransmitter that induces inhibition of postsynaptic neurons — abbr. *GABA*

gamma camera *n* : a camera that detects the gamma-ray photons produced by radionuclide decay and is used esp. in medical diagnostic scanning to create a visible record of a radioactive substance injected into the body

gamma hydroxybutyrate *n* : GBH *herein*

gamma interferon *n* : an interferon produced by T cells that regulates the immune response (as by the activation of macrophages and natural killer cells) and is used in a form obtained from recombinant DNA esp. in the control of infections associated with chronic granulomatous disease — called also *interferon gamma*; compare ALPHA INTERFERON *herein*, BETA INTERFERON *herein*

gamma ray* *n* : a high-energy photon

gam·ma–ray astronomy \ˈ==ˌ=-\ *n* : astronomy dealing with the properties of celestial bodies deduced from gamma rays they emit

ga·nache \(ˌ)gäˈnäsh, ˌgə-\ *n* -S [F, lit., jowl, lower jaw, fr. It *ganascia* jowl, modif. of Gk *gnathos* jaw — more at GNATH-] : a sweet creamy chocolate mixture used esp. as a filling or frosting

gan·ci·clo·vir \ganˈsīklə(ˌ)vir\ *n* -S [perh. fr. *guanosine* + *-ciclovir*, alter. of *-cyclovir* (as in *acyclovir* — herein)] : an antiviral drug $C_9H_{13}N_5O_4$ related to acyclovir and used esp. in the treatment of cytomegalovirus retinitis in immunocompromised patients

gang bang *n* **1** : copulation by several persons in succession with the same passive partner **2** : GANG RAPE *herein* — **gang–bang** \ˈ=ˌ=\ *vb*

gang·bang·er \ˈgaŋˌbaŋər\ *n* -S [¹*gang* + ¹*bang* + ²*-er*] : a member of a street gang

gangbuster \ˈ=ˌ==\ *n* [¹*gang* + *buster*] : a person and esp. a law officer engaged in the aggressive breakup of organized criminal gangs — **like gangbusters** : with great force or vigor ⟨knows how to just kind of play things cool—instead of coming on *like gangbusters* —Dave Brower⟩; *also* : at a great rate ⟨buying foreign wheat *like gangbusters* —*Christian Science Monitor*⟩ — often used as a generalized expression of approval ⟨our defense is playing *like gangbusters* —Joe Theismann⟩

gangbusters *adj (or adv)* : doing very well : POPULAR, HOT ⟨in some parts of the country singles are still ~ but in this city they're dead —Perry Ury⟩ ⟨if your company is public and is going ~ —*Esquire*⟩

gan·gle \ˈgaŋgəl, -aiŋ-\ *vi* -ED/-ING/-S [back-formation fr. *gangling*] : to walk or move with or as if with a loose-jointed gait : move like a gangling person — **gangle** \"\ *n* -S

gan·gli·o·si·do·sis \ˌgaŋglēōˌsīˈdōsəs, -ōˌsə-\ *n, pl* **gangliosido·ses** \-ōˌsēz\ [NL, fr. ISV *ganglioside* + NL *-osis*] : any of several inherited metabolic diseases (as Tay-Sachs disease) characterized by an enzyme deficiency which causes accumulation of gangliosides in the tissues

gang rape *n* : rape of one person by several attackers in succession — **gang–rape** *vt*

gang·sa \ˈgäŋ(ˌ)sä\ *n* -S [Indonesian *gambang gangsa*, fr. *gambang* musical instrument consisting of bars struck by hammers + *gangsa* brass] : a Balinese metallophone with bamboo resonators

gang shag *n* [¹*gang* + ⁷*shag*] : GANG BANG 1 *herein*

gang·sta rap \ˈgaŋ(k)stə-\ *n* [*gangsta* gang member, street youth, alter. of *gangster*] : rap music with lyrics explicitly portraying the violence and drug use of urban gang life and typically expressing hostility toward whites, women, and civil authority

gangsta rapper *n* : a performer of gangsta rap

gantry* *n* : a movable scaffold with platforms at different levels for use in erecting and servicing rockets before launching

gap junction *n* : an area of contact between adjacent cells characterized by modification of the plasma membranes for intercellular communication or transfer of low molecular-weight substances — **gap–junctional** \ˈ=ˌ===\ *adj*

garage band *n* [so called fr. the typical use of a garage as a place for rehearsal by such bands] : a young and inexperienced rock and roll band usu. having only a local audience

garage sale *n* : a sale of used household or personal articles (as furniture, tools, or clothing) held on the seller's own premises — called also *tag sale, yard sale*

ga·ra·gist \gəˈräjəst, -ˈäzhə-; *Brit usu* ˈgaˌräzhəst *or* -äj- *or* ˈgarij-\ *n* -S *chiefly Brit* : GARAGEMAN

ga·ram ma·sa·la \gäˈrammə ˈsälə\ *n* [Hindi and Urdu *garam masālā*, lit., hot spices] : a pungent and aromatic mixture of ground spices used in Indian cooking

garbage* *n* : inaccurate or useless data

gar·bol·o·gist \gärˈbäləjəst, gäˈb-\ *n* -S [¹*garbage* + *-ologist* (as in *geologist*)] **1** : a trash or garbage collector **2** : a specialist in garbology

gar·bol·o·gy \-ləjē, -ji\ *n* -ES [¹*garbage* + *-ology* (as in *geology*)] : the study of modern culture through the analysis of what is thrown away as garbage or trash

gar·çon·nière \ˌgärsᵊnˈye(ə)r, -(ˌ)sȯn-\ *n* -S [F, fr. *garçon* boy, bachelor — more at GARÇON] : a bachelor apartment

gar·da \ˈgärdə\ *n, pl* **gar·dai** \ˌgärˈdē\ [IrGael *garda*, *gárda* (pl. *gardaí, gárdaí*), short for *garda síochána*, lit., guardian of the peace] : a policeman in the Republic of Ireland

garment bag *n* : a traveling bag that folds in half and has a center handle for easy carrying

gar·vey·ism \ˈgärvēˌizəm, ˈgȧv-\ *n* -S *usu cap* [Marcus *Garvey* †1940 Jamaican-born black nationalist + E *-ism*] : a 20th century racial and political doctrine advocating black separation and the formation of self-governing black nations in Africa — **gar·vey·ite** \-ēˌīt\ *n* -S *usu cap*

gas* *n* **1** : driving force : ENERGY ⟨the quarter horse runs out of ~ after a quarter mile —Carol Flake⟩ **2** *slang* : one that is very appealing or enjoyable ⟨the party was a ~⟩

GAS *abbr* general adaptation syndrome

gas chromatograph *n* : an instrument used to separate a sample into components in gas chromatography

gas chromatography *n* : chromatography in which the sample mixture is vaporized and injected into a stream of carrier gas (as nitrogen or helium) moving through a column containing a stationary phase comprised of a liquid or a particulate solid and is separated into its component compounds according to the affinity of the compounds for the stationary phase — compare COLUMN CHROMATOGRAPHY *herein*, PAPER CHROMATOGRAPHY *in the Dict*, THIN-LAYER CHROMATOGRAPHY *herein* — **gas chromatographic** *adj*

gasdynamics \ˌ=(ˌ)=ˈ==\ *n pl but sing in constr* [*gas* + *dynamics*] : a branch of dynamics that deals with gaseous fluids including products of combustion and plasmas — **gasdynamic** \ˌ=(ˌ)=ˈ=\ *adj* — **gas·dy·nam·i·cist** \ˌ=(ˌ)dīˈnaməsəst\ *n* -S

gas–guzzler \ˈ=ˌ==\ *n* : a usu. large automobile that gets relatively poor mileage — **gas–guzzling** \ˈ=ˌ==\ *adj*

gas·ket·ed \ˈgaskəd·əd, -aas-, -ais-\ *adj* : furnished with a gasket ⟨a ~ screw-cap can⟩

gas–liquid chromatography \ˌ=ˈ==-\ *n* : gas chromatography in which the stationary phase is a liquid — **gas–liquid chromatographic** \ˌ=ˈ==-\ *adj*

gas·o·hol \ˈgasəˌhȯl *sometimes* -ˌhäl\ *n* -S [blend of *gasoline* and *alcohol*] : a fuel consisting of a blend usu. of 10% ethyl alcohol and 90% gasoline

gastrocolic reflex *n* : the occurrence of peristalsis following the entrance of food into the empty stomach

gas·tro·duo·de·nos·to·my \ˌgastrō,d(y)üəˌdēˈnästəmē, -ˌd(y)üˌädᵊnˈäs-\ *n* -ES [ISV *gastr-* + *duoden-* + ²*-stomy*] : surgical formation of a passage between the stomach and the duodenum

gastroesophageal reflux *n* : backward flow of the gastric contents into the esophagus resulting from improper functioning of a sphincter at the lower end of the esophagus

gate* *n* **1** : an electrode in a field-effect transistor that modulates the current flowing through the transistor according to the voltage applied to the electrode — compare DRAIN *herein*, SOURCE *herein* **2** : a molecule or part of a molecule (as an amino acid sequence in a protein) that acts (as by a change in conformation) in response to a stimulus to permit or block passage through a cell membrane

gate* *vt* : to control passage through a cell membrane by way of (a specific channel) by supplying a specific stimulus ⟨a transmembrane ion channel *gated* by the neurotransmitter acetylcholine⟩ — see LIGAND-GATED *herein*, VOLTAGE-GATED *herein*

-gate \ˌgāt\ *n comb form* -S [Watergate, scandal that arose in 1972 fr. the suppressed investigation of a burglary at Democratic National Committee headquarters in the Watergate office complex in Washington, D.C.] : usu. political scandal often including concealment of wrongdoing ⟨Iran*gate*⟩ ⟨Korea*gate*⟩

gatekeeper* *n* : a person who controls access ⟨family doctors . . . are often used as ~s to advise patients and refer them to specialists —Robert Pear⟩ — **gatekeeping** \ˈ=ˌ==\ *adj*

gateway* *n* **1** : a hardware device or software package that allows communication between computer systems or networks **2** : a city having an airport that provides direct international flights

gaucherie* *n* : gauche quality or behavior ⟨seems now to have lost his early ~ —Peter Evans⟩

gaudy ironstone *n* : a polychrome-decorated mid-19th century English ironstone ware

gauge theory *n* [*gauge* function introduced into a field equation to produce a convenient form of the equation but having no observable physical consequences (trans. of G *masstab*)] : any of several theories in physics that explain the transmission of a fundamental force between two interacting particles by the exchange of an elementary particle

gaussian *adj, usu cap* [Karl Friedrich *Gauss* †1855 Ger. mathematician + E *-ian*] : being or having the shape of a normal curve or Gaussian distribution

gaussian integer *n, usu cap G* : a complex number $a + bi$ where a and b are integers and $i = \sqrt{-1}$

gavel–to–gavel \ˈ===ˈ==\ *adj* : running from start to finish ⟨*gavel-to-gavel* coverage of a political convention⟩

gay* *n* : HOMOSEXUAL; *esp* : a homosexual male

ga·zar \gəˈzär\ *n* -S [origin unknown] : a silk organza

ga·zil·lion \gəˈzilyən\ *n* -S [alter. of *zillion*] : an indeterminately large number — **gazillion** *adj*

ga·zump \gəˈzəmp\ *vt* -ED/-ING/-S [origin unknown] *Brit* : SWINDLE; *specif* : to demand a higher price from (the buyer of a house) than that agreed on

GB \ˌjēˈbē\ *n* -S [U.S. Army code name] : SARIN

GC *abbr* gas chromatograph *herein*; gas chromatography *herein*

G–CSF *abbr* granulocyte colony-stimulating factor *herein*

GDP *abbr* gross domestic product *herein*

gearhead \ˈ=ˌ=\ *n* [¹*gear* + *-head* (as in *hophead*)] **1** : an automobile enthusiast or expert **2** : a computer enthusiast or expert

gear up* *vb* ~ *vi* : to get ready ⟨the team is *gearing up* for the big game⟩

GED *abbr* general education development

geek* *n* **1** : a person often of an intellectual bent who does not fit in socially with others — often used as a generalized term of disapproval **2** : an enthusiast or expert esp. in a technological field or activity ⟨computer ~⟩ ⟨film ~⟩ — **geeky** \+ē\ *adj* -ER/-EST

gee–whiz \(ˈ)jē(h)wiz\ *adj* [*gee whiz*] **1** : designed to arouse wonder or excitement or to amplify the merits or significance of something esp. by the use of clever or sensational language ⟨*gee-whiz* journalism⟩ **2** : marked by spectacular or astonishing qualities or achievement ⟨*gee-whiz* technology⟩ **3** : characterized by wide-eyed enthusiasm, excitement, and wonder ⟨a *gee-whiz* approach to politics that wears a little thin —*Business Week*⟩

gel* *n* **1** : a thin colored transparent sheet used over a stage light to color it **2** : a gelatinous preparation used in styling hair

ge·la·to \jeˈläd·(ˌ)ō, jəˈ-\ *n, pl* **gela·ti** \-d·(ˌ)ē\ **gelatos** [It, ice cream, fr. *gelato*, past part. of *gelare* to freeze, fr. L — more at COLD] : a soft rich ice cream containing little or no air

gel electrophoresis *n* : electrophoresis in which molecules (as proteins and nucleic acids) migrate through a gel and esp. a polyacrylamide gel and separate into bands according to size

gel filtration *n* : chromatography in which the material to be fractionated separates primarily according to molecular size as it moves through a column of a gel and is washed with a solvent so that the fractions appear successively at the end of the column — called also *gel chromatography*

gem·fi·bro·zil \jemˈfībrə(ˌ)zil, -ˈfi-\ *n* -S [origin unknown] : a drug $C_{15}H_{22}O_3$ that regulates blood serum lipids and is used esp. to lower the levels of triglycerides and increase the levels of HDLs in the treatment of hyperlipemia

gemini* *n sing, pl* **geminis** *usu cap* : one born under the astrological sign Gemini

gem·i·ni·an \ˌjeməˈnīən\ *n* -S *usu cap* [*gemini* + E *-ian*] : GEMINI *herein*

ge·müt·lich \gəˈmuētlik\ *adj* [G, fr. MHG *gemüetlich*, fr. *gemüete* spirit, heart (fr. *ge-*, perfective, associative, and collective prefix — fr. OHG *gi-* — + *muot* mood, spirit, mind, fr. OHG) + *-lich* -ly, fr. OHG *-lih* — more at MOOD] : agreeably pleasant : COMFORTABLE ⟨easy, natural and ~ in her writing —*Times Lit. Supp.*⟩

ge·müt·lich·keit \gəˈmuētlikˌkīt\ *n* -S [G, fr. *gemütlich* pleasant + *-keit* -hood, fr. MHG, alter. of *-heit*, fr. OHG] : CORDIALITY, FRIENDLINESS

gender* *n* : the behavioral, cultural, or psychological traits typically associated with one sex

gender bender *n* : a person who dresses and behaves like a member of the opposite sex — **gender–bending** \ˈ==ˌ==\ *adj or n*

gendered *adj* : reflecting the experience, prejudices, or orientations of one sex more than the other; *also* : reflecting or involving gender difference or stereotypical gender roles

gender·less \-ləs\ *adj* **1** : lacking qualities typically associated with either sex **2** : suitable to or for either sex; *also* : not reflective of the experiences, prejudices, or orientations of one sex more than the other ⟨~ language⟩ — **gender·less·ness** \-nəs\ *n* -ES

gene conversion *n* : a genetic process that is sometimes associated with meiotic recombination in heterozygotes if heteroduplex DNA is formed, that involves the selective enzymatic excision of a mismatched DNA sequence from one heteroduplex strand and replacement with a nucleotide sequence complementary to the other strand so that the two DNA strands are genetically identical, that results in aberrant gametic ratios, and that is observed experimentally esp. in ascomycetous fungi (as of the genera *Saccharomyces, Neurospora*, or *Aspergillus*) in which the products of a single meiotic event are retained in one ascus

gene pool *n* : the collection of genes in an interbreeding population that includes each gene at a certain frequency in relation to its alleles : the genetic information of a population of interbreeding organisms ⟨the human *gene pool*⟩

general adaptation syndrome *n* : the sequence of physiological reactions to prolonged stress that in the classification of Hans Selye includes alarm, resistance, and exhaustion

general aviation *n* : the operation of civilian aircraft not under the control of a common carrier; *also* : such aircraft collectively

gen·er·al·iz·abil·i·ty \ˌ=(=)ˌ=əˈbiləd·ē, -ətē, -ti\ *n* : the quality of being generalizable ⟨doubts about the ~ of the test score results⟩

general obligation bond *n* : a municipal bond of which payment of interest and principal is backed by the taxing power and credit of the issuing governmental unit

general relativity *or* **general theory of relativity** *n* : RELATIVITY 3c

general term *n* : a mathematical expression composed of variables and constants that yields the successive terms of a sequence or series when integers are substituted for one of the variables often denoted by *k*

generation xer \+ˈeksər\ *n, pl* **generation xers** *usu cap G&X* : a member of a generation designated X (as the generation of Americans born in the 1960s and 1970s)

generative grammar *n* **1** : a description of a language in the form of a set of rules for producing the grammatical sentences of that language **2** : TRANSFORMATIONAL GRAMMAR *herein*

generative semantics *n pl but usu sing in constr* : a description of a language emphasizing a semantic deep structure that is logical in form, that provides syntactic structure, and that is related to surface structure by transformations

gen·er·a·tiv·i·ty \ˌjenərəˈtivəd·ē, -ətē, -ti\ *n* -ES [*generative* + *-ity*] : a concern for people besides self and family that usu. develops during middle age; *esp* : a need to nurture and guide young people of the next generation — used in the psychology of Erik Erikson

generator* *n* : a mathematical entity that when subjected to one or more operations yields another mathematical entity or its elements; *specif* : GENERATRIX 1

generic* *adj* **1** : not limited to a particular application or to use with a particular device ⟨~ computer software⟩ **2** *of wine* : sold under a broad class name rather than under a specific geographic or varietal name ⟨a ~ burgundy⟩

generic* *n* : a generic product (as a drug) — usu. used in pl.

gene–splicing \ˈ=ˌ==\ *n* : the process of preparing recombinant DNA

gene therapy *n* : the insertion of usu. genetically altered genes into cells esp. to replace defective genes in the treatment of genetic disorders or to provide a specialized disease-fighting function (as the destruction of tumor cells) — **gene therapist** *n*

genetic code *n* : the biochemical basis of heredity consisting of codons in DNA and RNA that determine the specific amino acid sequence in proteins and that appear to be uniform for all known forms of life — **genetic coding** *n*

genetic counseling *n* : guidance provided by a medical professional typically to individuals with an increased risk of having an offspring with a genetic disorder that includes information and advice concerning the probability of producing an offspring with a specific disorder, prenatal diagnostic tests, and available treatments

genetic engineering *n* : the group of applied techniques of genetics and biotechnology used to cut up and join together genetic material and esp. DNA from one or more species of organism and to introduce the result into an organism in order to change one or more of its characteristics — **genetically engineered** *adj* — **genetic engineer** *n*

genetic fingerprinting *n* : DNA FINGERPRINTING *herein* — **genetic fingerprint** *n*

genetic load *n* : the decrease in fitness of the average individual in a population relative to the fittest genotype due to the presence of deleterious genes in the gene pool

genetic map *n* : MAP 1 *herein*

genetic marker *n* : a readily recognizable genetic trait, gene, DNA segment, or gene product used for identification esp. when closely linked to a trait or genetic material that is difficult to identify

genital herpes *also* **genital herpes simplex** *n* : herpes simplex of the type affecting the genitals — called also *herpes genitalis*

gen·na·ker \ˈjenəkə(r)\ *n* -S [blend of *Genoa jib* and *spinnaker*] : a spinnaker sail having an asymmetrical shape

gen·o·gram \ˈjenəˌgram, ˈjē-\ *n* -S [¹*gen-* + *-gram*] : a diagram outlining the emotional and behavioral history of a family's members over several generations in order to recognize and understand past influences on current behavior patterns; *also* : a similar diagram detailing the medical history of a family's members as a means of assessing one's risk of developing disease

ge·noise *also* **gé·noise** \zhānˈwäz\ *n* -S [F *génoise*, fr. fem. of *génois* of Genoa, Italy] : a light cake of sugar, flour, melted butter, and stiffly beaten eggs

ge·no·mics \jēˈnōmiks, jə-\ *n pl but sing in constr* [*genomic* + *-ics*] : a branch of biotechnology and genetics concerned with the genetic mapping and DNA sequencing of sets of genes or the complete genomes of selected organisms using high-speed methods, with organizing the results in databases, and with applications of the data (as in medicine or biology) — compare PROTEOMICS *herein*

gen·ta·mi·cin \ˌjentəˈmīsᵊn\ *n* -S [alter. of earlier *gentamycin*, fr. *gent*ian violet (fr. the color of the organism from which it is produced) + kan*amycin* (herein)] : a broad-spectrum aminoglycoside antibiotic mixture that is derived from an actinomycete (*Micromonospora purpurea* or *M. echinospora*) and is used to treat serious infections (as of the urinary tract and the central nervous system)

gentleperson \ˈ==ˌ==\ *n* : a gentleman or lady

gen·tri·fi·ca·tion \ˌjen·trəfəˈkāshən\ *n* -S [*gentry* + *-fication*] : the process of renewal and rebuilding accompanying the influx of middle-class or affluent people into deteriorating areas (as urban neighborhoods) that often results in the displacement of earlier usu. poorer residents; *also* : any of the aspects of this process

gen·tri·fy \ˈjen·trəˌfī\ *vb* -ED/-ING/-ES [back-formation from *gentrification* (herein)] *vt* **1** : to attempt or accomplish the gentrification of **2** : to raise the social status of; *esp* : to make acceptable to a higher and more affluent level of society ⟨four-wheel-drive utility vehicle was *gentrified* years ago with . . . nicer interiors —John Koten⟩ ~ *vi* : to become gentrified — **gen·tri·fi·er** \-ˌfīə(r)\ *n* -S

gen xer \ˈjenˈeksər\ *n, pl* **gen xers** *usu cap G&X* [short for *Generation Xer* (herein)] : GENERATION XER *herein*

geo·corona \ˈjēō+\ *n* [*ge-* + *corona*] : the outermost part of the earth's atmosphere consisting primarily of hydrogen

geof·froy's cat \zhōˈfrwäz-\ *n, usu cap G* [after Étienne *Geoffroy* Saint-Hilaire †1844 or his son Isidore *Geoffroy* Saint-Hilaire †1861 Fr. zoologists] : a small South American cat of the genus *Felis* (*F. geoffroyi*) that has a silver-gray or ocher coat with small black spots and that inhabits esp. upland forests and scrubland

geology* *n* : the study of the solid matter of a celestial body

geomagnetic storm *n* : MAGNETIC STORM

geo·pres·sured \ˈjēōˈpreshərd\ *adj* [*ge-* + *pressured*, fr. past part. of ²*pressure*] : being under great pressure from geologic forces ⟨~ methane⟩; *also* : of, relating to, or derived from geopressured natural deposits ⟨~ energy⟩

geo·scientist \"+\ *n* [*ge-* + *scientist*] : a specialist in one or more of the geosciences

geo·stationary \ˈjē(ˌ)ō+\ *adj* [*ge-* + *stationary*] : being or having an equatorial orbit at an altitude of about 22,300 miles (35,900 kilometers) and requiring an angular velocity the same as that of earth so that the position of a satellite in such an orbit remains fixed with respect to the surface of the earth

geo·synchronous \"+\ *adj* [*ge-* + *synchronous*] : GEOSTATIONARY *herein* — **geo·synchronously** \"+\ *adv*

geo·technical \"+\ *adj* [*ge-* + *technical*] : of or relating to geotechnical engineering

geotechnical engineering *n* : ENGINEERING GEOLOGY — **geotechnical engineer** *n*

geo·textile \ˈjē(ˌ)ō+\ *n* [*ge-* + *textile*] : a strong synthetic fabric usu. used in civil engineering construction projects (as highway or dam building) that stabilizes loose soil and prevents erosion

geriatric* *adj* **1 a** : OLD, ELDERLY ⟨a ~ writer with literary memories —Michel Lambeth⟩ **b** : of, relating to, or appropriate for elderly people ⟨the ~ set⟩ ⟨slow-tempoed, ~ tunes —John Gruen⟩ **2** : being very old and outmoded ⟨U.S. air travelers probably have no option but to continue riding on ~ planes —Eliot Marshall⟩

geriatric *n* -S [*geriatric*, adj.] : an elderly person

german wirehaired pointer *n, usu cap G* : any of a German breed of liver or liver and white gundogs with a flat-lying wiry coat composed of hairs one and one-half to two inches in length

ge·samt·kunst·werk \gəˈzämtˌkůnstˌverk\ *n* -S *usu cap* [G, fr. *gesamt* whole, entire (fr. MHG *gesamt, gesament*, past part. of *samenen* to gather, assemble, fr. OHG *samanōn*, fr. *saman-* together, in the same place — akin to Goth *samana* together, OE *tōsamne*, ON *samr* same) + *kunst* art + *werk* work, fr. OHG *werc* — more at SAME, KUNSTLIED, WORK] : an art work produced by a synthesis of various art forms (as music and drama)

ges·to·sis \jesˈtōsəs\ *n, pl* **ges·to·ses** \-ōˌsēz\ [NL, fr. E *gestation* + NL *-osis*] : any disorder of pregnancy; *esp* : TOXEMIA OF PREGNANCY

get* *vb* — **get a life** : to stop wasting time on trivial or hopeless matters — often used in the imperative — **get it on 1** : to become enthusiastic, energetic, or excited ⟨when they get with a rock group they just really *get it on* —John Von Ohlen⟩ **2** : to engage in sexual intercourse — **get it together** *or* **get it all together** : to put things in order : get one's act together — **get it up** : to have an erection — **get one's act together 1** *or* **get one's head together** : to put one's life, thoughts, or emotions in order : cease to be confused or misdirected **2** : to begin to function in a skillful or efficient manner ⟨the company finally *got its act together*⟩ — **get one's back up** : to get one's hackles up : make one angry, irritated, or annoyed — **get one's rocks off 1** : to experience orgasm **2** : to become pleasurably excited — **get on the stick** : to start working energetically on something ⟨worrying what might happen if we didn't *get on the stick* pretty fast —Tim Findley⟩ — **get real** : to stop deceiving oneself or fooling around : face reality — often used in the imperative

get–go \ˈgitˌgō, ˈget-\ *also* **git–go** \ˈgit-\ *n* -ES [prob. fr. the phrase *get up and go*] : the very beginning — used in the phrase *from the get-go* ⟨proved irresistible from the *get-go* —Josh Rubins⟩

get off* *vi* **1** : to get high on a drug — usu. used with *on* ⟨*get off* on heroin⟩ **2** : to experience orgasm **3** : to experience great pleasure or satisfaction — usu. used with *on* ⟨*gets off* on the music⟩ ~ *vt* : to cause to get off

GeV *abbr* giga-electron-volt

ge·würz·tra·mi·ner \gəˈvərtsˌtramənər, *Ger* gəˈvɯertstrăˌmēnə(r)\ *n* -S *often cap* [G, fr. *gewürz* spice (fr. *ge-*, collective prefix — fr. OHG *gi-* — + obs. or dial. *wurz* herb, plant, fr. OHG) + *traminer* of or relating to Tramin (Termeno, Italy) — more at WORT] : a light dry Alsatian white wine with a spicy bouquet; *also* : a similar wine made elsewhere

GFCI *abbr* ground fault circuit interrupter

GHB \ˌjē(ˌ)āchˈbē\ *n* -S [gamma *h*ydroxy*b*utyrate] : a metabolite $C_4H_8O_3$ of gamma-aminobutyric acid that is a depressant of the central nervous system and is used illicitly in the form of its synthetic sodium salt to produce sedative and euphoric effects or to stimulate release of growth hormone to increase muscle mass — called also *gamma hydroxybutyrate*

ghetto blaster *n* [so called fr. the stereotypical association of such radios with black inner-city youths] : BOOM BOX *herein*

ghost·ing \ˈgōstiŋ\ *n* [fr. gerund of ²*ghost*] : GHOST 8c; *also* : the formation of ghosts

gi \ˈgē\ *n* -S [Jap] : a garment worn in practice or exhibition of East Asian martial arts (as karate or judo) consisting of loose-fitting pants and a loose jacket held closed by a cloth belt

gibbs free energy \ˈgibz-\ *n, usu cap G* [after J.W. *Gibbs* †1903 Am. physicist] : FREE ENERGY 1 — symbol *G*

GIFT \ˈgift\ *abbr* gamete intrafallopian transfer *herein*; gamete intrafallopian tube transfer *herein*

gig \ˈgig\ *vi* **gigged; gigged; gigging; gigs** [⁷*gig*] : to work as a musician ⟨*gigged* with various bands —*Downbeat*⟩

giga·bit \ˈjigə, ˈgigə+\ *n* [*giga-* + ⁷*bit*] : one billion bits

giga·byte \"+\ *n* [*giga-* + *byte* (herein)] : 1024 megabytes or 1,073,741,824 bytes; *also* : one billion bytes

giga·cycle \"+\ *n* [*giga-* + *cycle*] : GIGAHERTZ

giga·flop \"ˌfläp\ *n* -S [*giga-* + *fl*oating-point *op*eration] : a unit of measure for the speed of calculation of a computer equal to one billion floating-point operations per second

giga·watt \"+\ *n* [*giga-* + *watt*] : a unit of power equal to one billion watts

giggle* *n, chiefly Brit* : someone or something amusing

GI·GO \ˈgīˌgō, ˈgē-\ *abbr* garbage in, garbage out

gilt* *n* : a bond issued by the government of the United Kingdom

gimmickery* *or* **gimmickry*** *n* : use of gimmicks

ginkgo bi·lo·ba \-ˌbīˈlōbə\ *or* **ginkgo*** *n* [*ginkgo biloba* fr. NL *Ginkgo biloba*, species name, lit., bilobate ginkgo] : an extract of the leaves of the ginkgo (*Ginkgo biloba*) that is held to enhance mental functioning by increasing blood circulation to the brain

gi·ro \ˈjī(ˌ)rō, ˈzhi(ˌ)rō *esp Brit* ˈjīˌrō\ *n* -S *often cap* [G, circulation (of currency), fr. It, fr. L *gyrus* circle — more at GYRE] : a system of money transfer in Britain and much of Europe that involves a simple transfer of credits from one account to another without money orders or checks

gi·rolle \zhēˈrōl, -rȯl\ *or* **girolle mushroom** *n* -S [F, perh. modif. of OProv *giroilla* kind of mushroom, fr. *gir* circular movement, whirling, fr. L *gyrus*; fr. the whorl-like form of the centrally depressed cap — more at GYRE] : ¹CHANTERELLE

git \ˈgit\ *n* -S [alter. of *get*, term of abuse, fr. ²*get*] *Brit* : a foolish or worthless person

git–go \ˈgitˌgō\ *var of* GET-GO *herein*

giveback \ˈ=ˌ=\ *n* -S [*give back*, v.] : a previous gain (as an increase in wages or benefits) given back to management by workers (as in a labor contract) ⟨union workers . . . agreed to ~*s* to avoid layoffs —Lawrence Ingrassia⟩

give–up* *n* [*give up*; fr. the giving up by the first broker of part of the commission to the second] **1** : a security or commodity market order which one broker executes for a client of a second broker for a share of the commission **2** : a part of a commission due a broker from a major client (as a mutual fund) that the client directs to be turned over to another broker who has provided special services

¹glam \ˈglam, -aa(ə)m\ *adj* [by shortening] **1** : GLAMOROUS ⟨the slickest and most ~ dude onstage —Vivien Goldman⟩ **2** : of, relating to, or characteristic of glitter rock ⟨~ rockers⟩

²glam *n* -S [by shortening] **1** : GLAMOUR ⟨the glitz and ~ of professional modeling⟩ **2** : GLITTER ROCK *herein*

glam rock *n* : GLITTER ROCK *herein*

glas·nost \ˈgläsˌnōst, ˈglas-, -ˌzˌnō-, -aa(ə)-, -á-\ *n* -S [Russ *glasnost'*, lit., publicity, public airing, fr. *glasnyĭ* public, fr. *glas* voice, fr. OSlav *glasŭ* — more at CALL] : a policy permitting public discourse and expression of opinion on domestic issues formerly forbidden to discussion esp. in the Soviet Union; *also* : a similarly candid approach to affairs long kept secret

glass ceiling *n* : an intangible barrier within the hierarchy of a company that prevents women or members of a minority group from obtaining upper-level positions

glasshouse* *n, Brit* : a military prison : GUARDHOUSE

glatt kosher \ˈglät-\ *adj* [Yiddish *glat kosher*, lit., evenly kosher] : providing, preparing, or being food that conforms stringently to the Jewish kosher laws ⟨a *glatt kosher* restaurant⟩

gleam·er \ˈglēmə(r)\ *n* -S [²*gleam* + ²*-er*] : a cosmetic applied to the face or lips to give the appearance of shine or to accent an area (as the cheekbones)

glitch \ˈglich\ *n* -ES [perh. fr. Yiddish *glitsh* slippery place, fr. *glitshn* (*zikh*) to slide, glide, fr. intensive of MHG *glīten* to glide, fr. OHG *glītan* — more at GLIDE] **1** : an unwanted brief surge of electric power : a false or spurious electronic signal **2 a** : MALFUNCTION ⟨a ~ in the fuel cell of a spacecraft⟩; *also* : BUG 2 **b** : a minor problem that causes a temporary setback : SNAG **3** : a sudden change in the period of rotation of a neutron star

glit·te·ra·ti \ˌglid·əˈräd·(ˌ)ē, ˌglitə-, -ˈrä\, \(ˌ)tē *also* -ˈrāˌtī\ *n pl* [blend of ²*glitter* and *literati*] : BEAUTIFUL PEOPLE *herein*

glitter rock *n* : rock music performed by male musicians who are made up to look grotesquely feminine — **glitter rocker** *n*

¹glitz \ˈglits\ *n* -ES [prob. modif. of G *glitzern* to glitter, fr. MHG *glitzen*; akin to ON *glitra* to glitter] : extravagant showiness : FLASH 4a; *also* : superficial glamour — **glitz·i·ness** \-sēnəs\ *n* -ES — **glitzy** \-sē\ *adj* -ER/-EST

²glitz *vt* -ED/-ING/-ES : to make flashy or extravagant ⟨she got ~*ed* up for the party⟩

global* *adj* **1** : of or relating to a celestial body (as the moon) **2** : of, relating to, or applying to a whole (as a mathematical function or a computer program) ⟨a ~ search of the file⟩

Global Positioning System *n* : GPS *herein*

global village *n* : the world viewed as a community in which distance and isolation have been dramatically reduced by electronic media (as television or the Internet)

global warming *n* : an increase in the earth's atmospheric and oceanic temperatures widely predicted to occur due to an increase in the greenhouse effect resulting esp. from pollution (as from the burning of fossil fuels)

glomus tumor *n* : a painful benign tumor that develops by hypertrophy of a glomus

¹glop \ˈgläp\ *n* -S [prob. imit.] **1 a** : a thick semiliquid food or mixture of foods that is usu. unappetizing in appearance **b** : a thick sticky liquid **2** : tasteless or worthless stuff — **glop·py** \-pē\ *adj* -ER/-EST

²glop \"\ *vt* **glopped; glopped; glopping; glops 1** : to put glop on — often used with *up* ⟨don't ~ up my hamburger with catsup⟩ **2** : to put (something gloppy) on food ⟨~ blue cheese dressing over the delicate leaves —James Villas⟩

gloriosa daisy *n* [*gloriosa* fr. NL, lit., glorious, fr. L, fem. of *gloriosus* — more at GLORIOUS] : a black-eyed Susan (*Rudbeckia hirta*) of either of two tetraploid cultivars with large single or double yellow, orange, maroon, or bicolored flowers

glory hole* *n* : a hole made through the partition of adjoining toilet stalls to enable homosexuals to perform fellatio anonymously

gloss* *n* **1** : a cosmetic preparation for adding shine and usu. color to the lips **2** : bright often superficial attractiveness ⟨show-biz ~⟩

glove box *n* : GLOVE COMPARTMENT

glove leather *n* [so called fr. the use of such leather to make gloves] : a soft lightweight leather

glow plug *n* : a heating element in a diesel-engine cylinder to preheat the air and facilitate starting; *also* : a similar element for ignition in other internal-combustion engines

glu·can \ˈglüˌkan, -ˌkən\ *n* -S [*gluc-* + ³*-an*] : a polysaccharide (as glycogen or cellulose) that is a polymer of glucose

glu·ca·nase \ˈglükəˌnās, -āz\ *n* -S [*glucan* (herein) + *-ase*] : any of various enzymes that digest glucans

glu·co·cer·e·bro·si·dase \ˌglükōˌserəbrōˈsīˌdās, -āz\ *n* -S [*glucocerebroside* (herein) + *-ase*] : an enzyme of mammalian tissue that catalyzes the hydrolysis of the glucose part of a glucocerebroside and is deficient in patients affected with Gaucher's disease

glu·co·cerebroside \ˈglükō+\ *n* [*gluc-* + *cerebroside*] : a lipid composed of a ceramide and glucose that accumulates in the tissues of patients affected with Gaucher's disease

glu·co·gen·ic \ˈ==ˈjenik\ *adj* [*gluc-* + *-genic*] : tending to produce a pyruvate residue in metabolism which undergoes conversion to a carbohydrate (as glucose) and is eventually stored as a complex carbohydrate (as glycogen) ⟨~ amino acids⟩

glucose–6–phosphate dehydrogenase \ˈ=ˌ=ˈ=ˌ=\ *n* : an enzyme found esp. in red blood cells that dehydrogenates glucose phosphate (sense b) in a glucose degradation pathway alternative to the Krebs cycle

glucose tolerance test *n* : a test of the body's ability to metabolize glucose that involves the oral administration of a measured dose of glucose to the fasting stomach and the determination of glucose levels in the blood and urine at measured intervals thereafter and that is used esp. to detect diabetes mellitus

glu·co·sin·o·late \ˌglükōˈsinəˌlāt\ *n* -S [prob. fr. *gluco*side + NL *sin-* (fr. *Sinapis alba*, former species name of white mustard) + E *ole-* + ¹*-ate* — more at SINAPIS] : any of various bitter-tasting sulfur-containing glycosides found esp. in cruciferous plants (as broccoli, cabbage, and mustard) that when hydrolyzed form bioactive compounds (as isothiocyanates)

glucosyltransferase \ˈ=ˌ=ˌ=ˈ=ˌ=\ *n* [*glucosyl* + *transferase*] : an enzyme that catalyzes the transfer of a glucosyl group; *esp* : one implicated in the formation of dental plaque that catalyzes the formation of glucans

glue gun *n* : a usu. gun-shaped electric tool used for melting and applying sticks of adhesive

glue–sniffing \ˈ=ˌ==\ *n* -S [¹*glue* + *sniffing*, fr. gerund of *sniff*, v.] : the deliberate inhalation of volatile organic solvents from plastic glues that may result in symptoms ranging from mild euphoria to disorientation and coma

glu·on \ˈglüˌän\ *n* -S [¹*glue* + ²*-on*] : any of eight hypothetical neutral massless particles that possess color, are thought to bind together quarks to form hadrons (as pions, protons, and neutrons), and are the particles which are exchanged in interactions involving the strong force

glu·tar·aldehyde \ˌglüd·əˈraldəˌhīd\ *n* [*glutaryl* + *aldehyde*] : a compound $C_5H_8O_2$ that contains two aldehyde groups and is used esp. in leather tanning, in the fixation of biological tissues, and as a disinfectant

glute \ˈglüt\ *n* -S [by shortening] : GLUTEUS; *esp* : GLUTEUS MAXIMUS — usu. used in pl.

glu·teth·i·mide \glüˈtethəˌmīd, -ˌməd\ *n* [*glutaryl* + *eth-* + *imide*] : a sedative-hypnotic drug $C_{13}H_{15}NO_2$ that is a derivative of piperidine and has pharmacological properties similar to those of the barbiturates

gly·co·calyx \ˈglīkō+\ *n* [*glyc-* + *calyx*] : a polysaccharide or glycoprotein covering on a cell surface

gly·co·ge·no·sis \ˌglīkōjəˈnōsəs\ *n, pl* **glycogeno·ses** \-ōˌsēz\ [NL, fr. E *glycogen* + NL *-osis*] : GLYCOGEN STORAGE DISEASE *herein*

glycogen storage disease *n* : any of several metabolic disorders that are characterized esp. by abnormal deposits of glycogen in tissue, are caused by enzyme deficiencies in glycogen metabolism, and are usu. inherited as an autosomal recessive trait

gly·cos·ami·no·glycan \ˌglīkōsəˈmē(ˌ)nō, -ōˌsamə(ˌ)nō+\ *n* [*glycose* + *amin-* + *glycan*] : MUCOPOLYSACCHARIDE

gly·co·sphingolipid \ˈglīkō+\ *n* [*glyc-* + *sphingolipid*] : any of various lipids (as a cerebroside or a ganglioside) which are derivatives of ceramides, do not contain the phosphorus or the extra nitrogenous base of the sphingomyelins, and do contain a carbohydrate (as glucose), and some of which accumulate in disorders of lipid metabolism (as Tay-Sachs disease)

gly·co·syl·a·tion \glīˌkōsəˈlāshən\ *n* -S [*glycosyl* + *-ation*] : the process of adding glycosyl groups to a protein to form a glycoprotein — **gly·co·syl·ate** \glīˈkōsəˌlāt\ *vt* -ED/-ING/-S

glyph* *n* [short for *hieroglyph*] : a symbol (as a curved arrow on a road sign) that conveys information nonverbally

glyph·o·sate \ˈglifəˌsāt, ˈglī-\ *n* -S [prob. fr. ISV ¹*glycine* + *phosph-* + ¹*-ate*] : a nonselective organophosphate herbicide $C_3H_8NO_5P$ that is used to control herbaceous and woody weeds esp. on croplands by inhibiting amino acid biosynthesis and is usu. used in the form of a propylamine salt

GM–CSF *abbr* granulocyte-macrophage colony-stimulating factor *herein*

gno·to·biology \ˈnōd·ə+\ *n* [Gk *gnōtos* known + E *biology*] : GNOTOBIOTICS *herein* — **gno·to·biologist** \"+\ *n*

gno·to·bi·ot·ic \ˌnōd·ə(ˌ)bīˈäd·ik *also* -bēˈä-\ *adj* [Gk *gnōtos* known (fr. *gignōskein* to know) + E *biotic* — more at KNOW] : of, relating to, living in, or being a controlled environment containing one or a few kinds of organisms; *also* : AXENIC ⟨~ mice⟩ — **gno·to·bi·ote** \ˌnōd·əˈbīˌōt\ *n* -s — **gno·to·bi·ot·i·cal·ly** \ˌnōd·ə(ˌ)bīˈäd·ək(ə)lē *also* -bēˈä-\ *adv*

gno·to·bi·ot·ics \ˈnōd·ə(ˌ)bīˈäd·iks\ *n pl but sing in constr* [*gnotobiotic* (herein) + *-ics*] : a biological science concerned with the raising and study of animals under gnotobiotic conditions

GnRH *abbr* gonadotropin-releasing hormone *herein*

go* *vi* : to be of advantage ⟨has a lot ~*ing* for her⟩ ~ *vt* **1** *baseball* : PITCH 15b ⟨he *went* 7⅓ innings and gave up no runs —D.S.Looney⟩ **2** : SAY — used chiefly in oral narration of speech ⟨I'm the last person to admit I've achieved anything. . . . But now my friends say it to me, and I ~ "You're right" —Steve Martin⟩ **3** *of a sports team or player* : to have a record of ⟨I *went* 11–0 last season⟩ — **go for it** : to try to attain a goal — **go missing** *chiefly Brit* : to become lost ⟨the file you want *went missing* years ago —John le Carré⟩ — **go public** **1** *of a close corporation* : to offer stock for sale to the general public **2** : to disclose to a much wider audience something not generally known ⟨had *gone public* with his ideas —Al Reinert⟩ — **go with** **1** : CHOOSE 2 ⟨*went with* a 5-iron shot⟩ **2** : to go ahead with — **go with the flow** : CONFORM 2a ⟨it's best to *go with the flow* and keep quiet —B.M.Frolic⟩

go* *n* : permission to proceed : GO-AHEAD ⟨gave the astronauts a ~ for another orbit⟩

go *adj* [[1]*go*] : functioning properly : being in good and ready condition ⟨declared all systems ~⟩

goalmouth \ˈ=ˌ=\ *n* [[1]*goal* + [1]*mouth*] : the area directly in front of the goal (as in soccer or hockey)

goaltending \ˈ=ˌ==\ *n* -s [[1]*goal* + *tending*, fr. gerund of [1]*tend*] **1** : the act of guarding a goal (as in hockey) **2** : a violation of the rules that involves touching or deflecting a basketball on its downward path toward the basket or on or within its rim

gö·del's incompleteness theorem *also* **gödel's theorem** \ˈgœdəlz-\ *n, usu cap G* [after Kurt *Gödel* †1978 Am. mathematician] : a theorem in advanced logic: in any logical system as complex or more complex than the arithmetic of the integers there can always be found either a statement which can be shown to be both true and false or a statement whose truth or falsity cannot be deduced from other statements in the system

godfather* *n* : the leader of an organized crime syndicate

go down* *vi, slang* : to take place : HAPPEN ⟨I'll tell you everythin' that *went down* —V.E.Smith⟩ — **go down on** : to perform fellatio or cunnilingus on — usu. considered vulgar

go·fer *also* **go·pher** \ˈgōfə(r)\ *n* -s [alter. of *go for*] : an employee whose duties include running errands

go–go \ˈgō(ˌ)gō\ *adj* [redupl. of [1]*go* (influenced in sense by *a-go-go* — herein)] **1** : FASHIONABLE, CHIC ⟨will change the name . . . to something more *go-go* —Al Fleming⟩ **2 a** : of, relating to, or being a discotheque or the music or dances performed there **b** : employed as a featured dancer to entertain patrons esp. in a discotheque or bar ⟨a pretty teenage *go-go* girl dances on top of the pedestal —C.D.B.Bryan⟩ **3** : marked by spirited or aggressive action or style ⟨playing *go-go* baseball⟩ ⟨reflects the *go-go* money-chasing mentality of both white-collar types and lowlifes —W.A.Henry III⟩ **4 a** : relating to or dealing in high-yield usu. speculative investments ⟨*go-go* mutual funds⟩ **b** : marked by fast and seemingly unlimited profit from speculative investment or rapid growth ⟨losses, then, of three hundred billion dollars . . . such were the bitter fruits of the *go-go* years —John Brooks⟩

go–go boot *n* [*go-go* (herein)] : a woman's knee-high boot esp. of patent leather or shiny vinyl with a moderate-to-high heel

go–kart *also* **go–cart*** *n* -s [alter. of *go-cart*] : a small motorized vehicle used esp. for racing — **go–kart·ing** *also* **go–cart·ing** *n*

gold* *n* : a medal awarded to the winner of a competition ⟨at the Olympics [she] went on to win the ~ —Joy Duckott Cain⟩; *collectively* : gold medals ⟨has earned him ~ in just about every important . . . competition —Helen Mason⟩

gold* *adj* : qualifying for a gold record ⟨five . . . recordings are certified ~ —Henry Edwards⟩ — **go gold** : to have enough sales to qualify for a gold record ⟨the album *went gold*⟩

gold·en–ag·er \ˌgōldənˈājə(r)\ *n* -s [*Golden Age* (*club*), organization for recreational activities of the elderly + E [2]*-er*] : an elderly person; *esp* : one who has retired

golden–brown alga *n* : any alga of the major group Chrysophyta — called also *chrysophyte, golden alga*

golden handcuff *n* : a set of benefits or perquisites offered to an employee as an inducement to remain in a particular job or with a particular company — usu. used in pl.

golden handshake *n* : a financial settlement given to an employee who retires early at the request of the employer

golden lion tamarin *n* : a lion tamarin (*Leontopithecus rosalia*) having a reddish gold coat and mane that is found in remnants of tropical forest in southeastern Brazil

golden oldie *n* : one (as a song, recording, or television show) that was a hit in the past

golden parachute *n* : a lump-sum bonus and often other valuable considerations guaranteed to a high executive of a corporation to be paid esp. if the corporation is taken over or when the executive leaves the company

gold–plate* *vt* : to add expensive and often unnecessary refinements to ⟨*gold-plate* military weapons⟩

gold point* *n* : a fixed point on the international temperature scale equal to the melting point of gold or 1064.43° C

gold record *n* : a gold phonograph record awarded to a singer or group whose single record has sold at least one million copies or whose album has sold at least 500,000 copies

gold sodium thio·malate \-ˌthīō+\ *n* [*thi-* + *malate*] : a mixture of two gold salts $C_4H_3AuNa_2O_4S$ and $C_4H_4AuNaO_4S$ injected intramuscularly esp. in the treatment of rheumatoid arthritis

gold standard* *n* : something that serves as a standard by which others may be measured or judged : BENCHMARK

golf ball* *n* : the spherical printing element of an electric typewriter or printer

golf cart *n* **1** : a small cart for wheeling a golf bag around a golf course **2** : a motorized cart for carrying a golfer and his equipment around a golf course

go·mor·rah \gəˈmȯrə\ *n* -s *usu cap* [fr. *Gomorrah*, ancient city destroyed by God for its wickedness in Gen. 19] : a place notorious for vice and corruption

gonadotropin–releasing hormone \ˌ=(ˌ)==ˈ===ˈ==-\ *n* : a decapeptide hormone produced by the hypothalamus that stimulates the adenohypophysis to release gonadotropins (as luteinizing hormone and follicle-stimulating hormone) — called also *luteinizing hormone-releasing factor, luteinizing hormone-releasing hormone*

gondola* *n* : an enclosed car suspended from a cable and used for transporting passengers; *esp* : one used as a ski lift

g_1 phase \(ˈ)jēˈwən-\ *n, usu cap G* : the period in the cell cycle from the end of cell division to the beginning of DNA replication — compare G_2 PHASE *herein*, M PHASE *herein*, S PHASE *herein*

gong* *n, Brit* : MEDAL

gonial angle *n* : ANGLE OF THE MANDIBLE

go·ni·ot·o·my \ˌgōnēˈädəmē, -ätə-\ *n* -ES [*goni-* + *-tomy*] : surgical relief of glaucoma used in some congenital types and achieved by opening Schlemm's canal

gon·o·coc·ce·mia \ˌgänəˌkäkˈsēmēə\ *n* -s [NL, fr. *gonococcus* + *-emia*] : the presence of gonococci in the blood — **gon·o·coc·ce·mic** \-mik\ *adj*

go–no–go \ˈgōˈnōˌgō\ *adj* [[1]*go* + [1]*no* + [1]*go*] **1** : being or relating to a required decision to continue or stop a course of action **2** : being or relating to a point at which a go-no-go decision must be made

gon·zo \ˈgän(ˌ)zō, ˈgȯn-\ *adj* [origin unknown] **1** : of or relating to a style of journalism that is a mixture of fact and fiction and is held to be produced under the effect of drugs **2** : FAR-OUT *herein* **3** : ZONKED *herein*

goodness of fit : [6]FIT 1d

good old boy *or* **good ol' boy** *or* **good ole boy** *n* **1** : a typically rural or small-town white Southern man who strongly espouses traditional male values and favors male pursuits; *also* : a man having or assumed to have similar values and tastes **2** : a man whose social position, success, or power is primarily the result of his connections within a select group ⟨there are very few biologists willing to get outside the *good old boy* network —Kenneth Brower⟩

goody–two–shoes \ˌ==ˈ=ˌ=\ *adj or n, often cap G&T&S* [after *Goody Two-Shoes*, heroine of a children's story perh. by Oliver Goldsmith †1774 Brit. author] : GOODY-GOODY

goof–off \ˈ=ˌ=\ *n* -s [*goof off*, v.] : one who evades work or responsibility

goofy–foot \ˈgüfēˌfu̇t\ *or* **goofy–foot·er** \-u̇d·ə(r)\ *n, pl* **goofy–foots** *or* **goofy–footers** : a surfer who rides a surfboard with the right foot forward

goom·bah \ˈgümˌbä, ˈgümbə\ *n* -s [It dial. (Campania, Abruzzo) *cumbà*, voc. form of *cumbar, cumbare, gumbare* respected older man, lit., godfather, fr. ML *compater* — more at COMPEER] **1** : a close friend or associate — used esp. among Italian-American men **2** : a member of a secret chiefly Italian-American crime organization : MAFIOSO *herein*; *broadly* : GANGSTER **3** : a macho Italian-American man

goose* *vt* : to increase the activity, speed, power, amount, or intensity of : SPUR ⟨hired to ~ production in a factory⟩ ⟨the bellows that the pioneers used . . . to ~ recalcitrant fires —John Jobson⟩

go·pik \gōˈpēk, -ˈpik\ *n, pl* **gopik** [Azerbaijani *gəpik* kopeck, fr. Russ *kopeĭka*] : a monetary unit of Azerbaijan equal to ¹⁄₁₀₀ manat — see *manat* at MONEY table *in the Dict*

gor·di·ta \gȯrˈdēd·ə, -ˈdētä\ *n* -s [MexSp, dim. of *gorda* thick tortilla, fr. Sp, fem. of *gordo* fat, thick, fr. LL *gurdus* dull, blunt, fr. L *gurdus*, n., dolt, blockhead] : a deep-fried pocket of cornmeal dough filled with a savory mixture

gorp \ˈgȯ(ə)rp\ *n* -s [origin unknown] : a snack consisting usu. of high-energy food (as raisins and nuts)

gospel* *adj* : of, relating to, or being religious songs of American origin associated with evangelism and popular devotion and marked by simple melody and harmony and elements of folk songs, spirituals, and occas. jazz ⟨~ singer⟩ — **gospel*** *n*

got·cha \ˈgächə\ *n* -s [alter. of *got you*] : an unexpected usu. disconcerting challenge, revelation, or catch

goth* *n* **1** : rock music marked by dark and morbid lyrics **2** : a performer or fan of goth

gothic* *n, often cap* : a novel, film, or play in the gothic style

GPA *abbr* grade point average *herein*

gp120 \ˌjē(ˌ)pēwənˈtwentē\ *n* [*glycoprotein*] : a glycoprotein protruding from the outer surface of the HIV virion that has a molecular weight of 120 and must bind to a CD4 receptor on a T cell bearing such receptors before infection of the cell can occur

g protein *n, usu cap G* [*guanosine triphosphate-binding protein*] : any of a class of cell membrane proteins that are coupled to cell surface receptors and upon stimulation of the receptor by an extracellular signalling molecule (as a hormone or neurotransmitter) bind to GTP to form an active complex which mediates an intracellular event (as activation of adenylate cyclase)

GPS \ˌjē(ˌ)pēˈes\ *n* [*Global Positioning System*] : a navigational system using satellite signals to fix the location of a radio receiver on or above the earth's surface; *also* : a radio receiver so used

grab* *vt* : to seize the attention of : IMPRESS, STRIKE ⟨the technique of *grabbing* an audience —Pauline Kael⟩

grabby* *adj* : having the power to grab the attention

gracile* *adj* : of, relating to, resembling, or being a primitive group of relatively small slender hominids of the genus *Australopithecus* (as *A. africanus*) characterized esp. by molars and incisors of similar size that are adapted to a diet including both plant materials and animal flesh — compare ROBUST *herein* — **gracile** *n* -s

grade* *n* -s : a particular level of organization (as of a morphological trait) characteristic of a group of biological taxa; *also* : a group of taxa (as species) that possess such a level of organization but do not necessarily share a common ancestral lineage — compare CLADE *herein*

grade point *n* : QUALITY POINT

grade point average *n* : the average obtained by dividing the total number of grade points by the total number of credits earned — called also *quality point average*

gradualism* *n* **1** : the evolution of new species by the gradual accumulation of small genetic changes over long periods of time — compare PUNCTUATED EQUILIBRIUM 1 *herein* **2** : a theory or model of evolution emphasizing gradualism — **gradualist*** *n* — **gradualistic*** *or* **gradualist*** *adj*

graffito* *n* : a message or slogan written as or as if a graffito

graft–versus–host *adj* : of or relating to graft-versus-host disease

graft–versus–host disease *n* : a bodily condition that results when T cells from a usu. allogeneic tissue or organ transplant and esp. a bone marrow transplant react immunologically against the recipient's antigens attacking cells and tissues, that affects esp. the skin, gastrointestinal tract, and liver with symptoms including skin rash, fever, diarrhea, liver dysfunction, abdominal pain, and anorexia, and that may be fatal — abbr. *GVHD*

grammar* *n* : a system of rules that defines the grammatical structure of a language

gram·mat·i·cal·i·ty \grəˌmad·əˈkaləd·ē\ *n* -ES : the quality or state of being grammatical

Gram·my \ˈgramē\ *service mark* — used for the annual presentation of a statuette for notable achievement in the recording industry

grand cru \ˌgran(d)ˈkrü, ˌgrä(d)ˈ-, -ˈkrue\ *n* [F, lit., great production (of something grown) — more at CRU] : a wine of the highest rank or reputation within its appellation

grandfather *vt* : to permit to continue under a grandfather clause ⟨existing personnel would be ~*ed* into the present system —*Wall Street Jour.*⟩ ⟨~*ed* water rights⟩

grand·kid \ˈgran(d)ˌkid\ *n* : GRANDCHILD

grand touring car *n* : a usu. 2-passenger coupe

grand unified theory *also* **grand unification theory** *n* : any of several theories that seek to unite in a single mathematical framework the electromagnetic and weak forces with the strong force or with the strong force and gravity

granny dress *n* : a long loose-fitting dress usu. with high neck and long sleeves

granny flat *n* [so called fr. the use of such apartments by one or more older parents of the family living in the house] : an apartment that is adjacent to the main living quarters of a house

granny glasses *n pl* : spectacles with usu. small oval, round, or square lenses and metal frames

gra·no·la \grəˈnōlə\ *n* -s [fr. *Granola*, a trademark] : a mixture of rolled oats and other ingredients (as brown sugar, raisins, coconut, and nuts) that is eaten esp. as a breakfast food and health food

grants·man·ship \ˈgrantsmənˌship\ *n* [*grants* + *-manship* (herein)] : the art of obtaining grants of money (as for research projects) — **grants·man** \-mən\ *n, pl* **grantsmen** \-mən\

granule cell* *n* : one of the small neurons of the cortex of the cerebellum and the cerebrum

granulocyte colony–stimulating factor *n* : a colony-stimulating factor produced by macrophages, endothelial cells, and fibroblasts that acts to promote the maturation of precursor cells into granulocytes (as neutrophils) — abbr. *G-CSF*

granulocyte–macrophage colony–stimulating factor *n* : a colony-stimulating factor produced by T cells, macrophages, endothelial cells, and fibroblasts that promotes the differentiation of bone marrow stem cells, stimulates the maturation of precursor cells into granulocytes and macrophages, and activates mature macrophages — abbr. *GM-CSF*

gra·num \ˈgrānəm, ˈgrä-, ˈgra-\ *n, pl* **gra·na** \-nə\ [NL, fr. L, grain — more at CORN] : one of the lamellar stacks of chlorophyll-containing material in plant chloroplasts

graphic* *n* **1** : a graphic representation displayed by a computer (as on a cathode-ray tube) **2 graphics** *pl but sing or pl in constr* : the process whereby a computer displays graphics and an operator can manipulate them (as with a light pen)

graphical user interface *n* : a computer program designed to allow a computer user to interact easily with the computer typically by using a mouse to make choices from menus or groups of icons

graphic equalizer *n* [so called fr. the graphlike patterns of the visual display or slide controls on such devices] : an electronic device for adjusting the frequency response of an audio system by means of a number of controls each of which adjusts the response for a band centered on a particular frequency

graphic novel *n* : a fictional story for adults that is presented in comic-strip format and published as a book

graphics tablet *n* : a device (as a flat electronic board with an associated stylus) by which graphic data is entered into a computer in a manner similar to drawing

graphite* *n* : a composite material in which carbon fibers are the reinforcing material

GRAS *abbr* generally recognized as safe

grasp* *vb* — **grasp the nettle** : to take positive and decisive steps to deal with a problem : take the bull by the horns

grass* *n* : MARIJUANA

grass carp *n* : an herbivorous cyprinid fish (*Ctenopharyngodon idella*) of eastern Asia that has been introduced elsewhere to control aquatic weeds — called also *white amur*

grasshopper* *n* : a cocktail made with crème de menthe, crème de cacao, and usu. light cream

grass·roots \ˈ=ˌ=\ *adj* [*grass roots*] **1** : BASIC, FUNDAMENTAL ⟨the ~ factor in deciding to buy a house⟩ **2** : being, originating, or operating in or at the basic or local level of society ⟨a ~ organization⟩ ⟨~ political support⟩ **3** : not adapted from or added to an existing facility or operation : totally new ⟨a ~ refinery⟩

gra·vi·tas \ˈgrävē(ˌ)täs, ˈgräwē-, ˈgra-, -vi-\ *n* [L — more at GRAVITY] : high seriousness (as in a person's bearing or the treatment of a subject)

gravitational collapse *n* : the tendency of matter to move toward a common center of gravity (as in the formation of galaxies); *esp* : the rapid collapse of a star at the end of its life cycle

gravitational interaction *also* **gravitational force** *n* : GRAVITY *herein*

gravitational lens *n* : a massive celestial object (as a galaxy) that bends and focuses the light of another more distant object (as a quasar) by gravity in accordance with general relativity and that is usu. detected by the multiple images it forms of the second object

gravitational lensing *n* : the bending and focusing of light and esp. the formation of multiple images of a more distant object by a celestial object acting as a gravitational lens

gravitational radiation *n* : a series of gravitational waves; *also* : the generation of such waves (as by a celestial object)

gravitational wave *n* : a hypothetical wave held to travel at the speed of light and to propagate the gravitational field

grav·i·ti·no \ˌgravəˈtēnō\ *n* -s [*graviton* (herein) + *-ino* (as in *neutrino*)] : a hypothetical fermion that is associated with the graviton in theories of supergravity and is postulated to make up part of the dark matter of the universe

grav·i·ton \ˈgravəˌtän\ *n* -s [ISV *gravity* + [2]*-on*] : a hypothetical particle with zero charge and rest mass that is held to be the quantum of the gravitational field

gravity* *n* : a fundamental physical force that is responsible for interactions between particles, between aggregations of matter (as stars and planets), and between aggregations of matter and particles (as photons) which occur because of mass, that is 10^{39} times weaker than the strong force and is the weakest fundamental physical force, and that extends over infinite distances but because of its weakness is evident only over large distances esp. between aggregations of matter — called also *gravitational force, gravitational interaction*; compare ELECTROMAGNETISM *herein*, STRONG FORCE *herein*, WEAK FORCE *herein*

gravity wave* *n* : GRAVITATIONAL WAVE *herein*

grav·lax \ˈgrävˌläks\ *or* **gravlaks** \"\ *n* [Sw *gravlax* or Norw *gravlaks*, fr. *grav* pit, hole, grave (fr. ON *gröf*) + Sw *lax*, Norw *laks* salmon, fr. ON *lax*; fr. the original custom of burying the salmon while it cured — more at GRAVE, LAX] : salmon usu. cured with salt, pepper, dill, and aquavit

gray* *vi* : AGE; *also* : to contain an increasing percentage of older people ⟨the ~*ing* suburbs⟩

gray \ˈgrā\ *n* -s [after Louis Harold *Gray* †1965 Brit. radiobiologist] : the mks unit of absorbed dose of ionizing radiation equal to an energy of one joule per kilogram of irradiated material — abbr. *Gy*

gray panther *n, usu cap G&P* [*gray* + *panther* (as in *Black Panther* — herein)] : a member of an organization of militant elderly people

graze* *vi* : to eat small portions of food throughout the day instead of three meals — **grazer*** *n*

greaser* *n* : an aggressive swaggering young white male usu. of working-class background

great room *n* : a large room usu. serving several functions (as of a dining room, living room, and family room)

[1]**green*** *adj* **1** *often cap* : relating to or being an environmentalist political movement **2** : concerned with or supporting environmentalism; *also* : tending to preserve environmental quality (as by being recyclable, biodegradable, or nonpolluting)

[2]**green*** *n, often cap* : ENVIRONMENTALIST 1 *herein*; *specif* : a member of an activist political party focusing on environmental and social issues

green beret *n, usu cap G&B* [so called fr. the green beret worn as part of the uniform] : a member of the U.S. Army Special Forces

green card *n* : an identity card attesting the permanent resident status of an alien in the U.S.

green–card·er \ˈ=ˈkärdər, -ˌkädə(r\ *n* -s : a foreign national with permission to work in the U.S.

greener pastures *n pl* : a situation that is better or more promising ⟨leaving their hometowns to look for *greener pastures*⟩

green·field \ˈ=ˌ=\ *n, often attrib* : land (as a potential industrial site) not previously developed or polluted ⟨a new ~ smelter⟩ — compare BROWNFIELD *herein*

green–fingered \ˈ=ˈ=\ *adj, chiefly Brit* : adept at growing plants

green goddess dressing *n* [fr. *The Green Goddess* (1921) play by William Archer †1924 Scot. dramatist and critic] : a green salad dressing consisting of mayonnaise, sour cream, anchovies, chives, parsley, tarragon vinegar, and seasonings

greenhouse \ˈ=ˌ=\ *adj* : of, relating to, or caused by the greenhouse effect ⟨~ warming⟩

greenhouse effect *n* : warming of the surface and lower atmosphere (as of the Earth or Venus) that is caused by conversion of solar radiation into heat in a process involving selective transmission of short wave solar radiation by the atmosphere, its absorption by the planet's surface, and reradiation as infrared which is absorbed and partly reradiated back to the surface by certain atmospheric gases (as carbon dioxide and water vapor) and that tends to increase with increasing amounts of such gases

greenhouse gas *n* : any of various gaseous compounds (as carbon dioxide) that absorb infrared radiation, trap heat in the atmosphere, and contribute to the greenhouse effect

green·ie \ˈgrēnē\ *n* -s : GREEN *herein*, ENVIRONMENTALIST *herein*

greening* *n* **1** : a restoration of freshness or vigor : REVITALIZATION, REJUVENATION **2** : a shift (as of attitudes or policies) toward increased concern with protection of the natural environment

green lacewing *n* : GOLDENEYE 2

green–light \ˈ=ˌ=\ *vt* -ED/-ING/-S [*green light* n.] : to give a green light to ⟨studios grow complacent in good times and *green-light* more iffy films —Anne Thompson⟩

greenmail \ˈ=ˌ=\ *n* [[1]*green* (the color of U.S. paper money) + *-mail* (as in *blackmail*)] : the practice of buying enough of a company's stock to threaten a hostile takeover and reselling it to the company at a price above market value; *also* : the money paid for such stock

greenmailer \ˈ=,==\ *n* : one who engages in greenmail

green paper *n, often cap G&P, Brit* : a government document that discusses proposed approaches to a problem

green revolution *n* : the great increase in production of food grains (as rice, wheat, and maize) due to the introduction of high-yielding varieties, to the use of pesticides, and to better management techniques

green space *n* : community space consisting of land (as parks) rather than buildings

greenwashing \ˈ=,=\ *n* [¹*green* (environmentalist) + brain*washing*] : expression of environmentalist concerns esp. as a cover for products, policies, or activities deleterious to the environment — **greenwash** \ˈ=,=\ *vt or n* — **greenwasher** \ˈ=,==\ *n*

greenway \ˈ=,=\ *n* : a corridor of undeveloped land preserved for recreational use or for environmental protection

grem·mie *also* **grem·my** \ˈgremē, -mi\ *n, pl* **gremmies** [*grem*lin + *-ie*] : a young or inexperienced surfer; *esp* : one whose behavior is objectionable — called also *gremlin*

grem·o·la·ta \ˌgremōˈläd·ə, -tə, -tä\ *or* **grem·o·la·da** \-də, -dä\ *n* -S [It, fr. It dial. (Lombardy) *gremolaa*, fr. *gremolâ*, *gràmolâ* to brake (flax or hemp), mix, knead (flour for dough), fr. *grêmola*, *grâmola* brake for flax or hemp, apparatus for kneading dough] : a seasoning mixture consisting usu. of grated lemon zest, minced garlic, and minced parsley that is used esp. with osso buco

gre·nache \grəˈnäsh\ *n* -S [F, fr. Catal *garnatxa*, *granatxa*, type of grape, fr. It *vernaccia*, fr. *Vernaccia*, *Vernazza*, village in Liguria, Italy] : a widely cultivated sweet red grape used esp. in wine making; *also* : a varietal wine made from this grape

grid* *n* **1** : a network of conductors for the distribution of electric power; *also* : a network of radio or television stations **2** : the starting positions of cars on a racecourse **3** : a device (as of glass) in a photocomposer on which are located the characters to be exposed as the text is composed **4** : something resembling a grid esp. in rigidly organized structure

gridlock \ˈ=,=\ *n* -S [*grid* + dead*lock*] **1** : a traffic jam in which a grid of intersecting streets is so completely congested that no vehicular movement is possible **2** : a situation resembling gridlock (as in congestion or lack of movement) ⟨stumbled toward a nurse amidst a ~ of trauma victims —Peter Noel⟩ ⟨everything that Americans hated about politics—partisan ~, pork-barrel spending —Bill Turque⟩ — **gridlock** \"\ *vt*

grief* *n* : FLAK 1 *herein*

grinch \ˈgrinch\ *n* -ES [so called fr. a character of the same name in the book *How the Grinch Stole Christmas* (1957) by Dr. Seuss, pseudonym of Theodor Seuss Geisel †1991 Am. children's author] : KILLJOY, SPOILSPORT

grinder* *n* **1** : an athlete who succeeds through hard work and determination rather than exceptional skill; *also* : a player (as in hockey) whose actions support the actions of the team's primary playmakers **2** : a crew member on a racing sailboat who is primarily responsible for grinding the winches used to heave the sails

gri·ot \ˈgrē(ˌ)ō\ *n* -S [F] : any of a class of musician-entertainers or storytellers of West Africa whose performances include tribal histories and genealogies; *broadly* : STORYTELLER

grok \ˈgräk\ *vt* **grokked; grokked; grok·king; groks** [coined in the science fiction novel *Stranger in a Strange Land* (1961) by Robert A. Heinlein †1988 Am. author] : to understand esp. profoundly and intuitively : establish deep compassionate rapport with ⟨finally they come to ~ each other in their fullness —Bob Singer⟩

groove* *vb* [fr. the phrase *in the groove*] *vt* **1** : to enjoy appreciatively ⟨~s exciting experiences⟩ **2** : to excite pleasurably ⟨*grooving* their minds with cannabis —Stephen Nemo⟩ ~ *vi* **1** : to enjoy oneself intensely : experience keen pleasure ⟨overachievers who ~ on competition —Barry McDermott⟩ **2** : to interact harmoniously ⟨contemporary minds and rock ~ together —Benjamin De Mott⟩

groove* *n* **1** : an enjoyable, pleasurable, or exciting experience **2** : a pronounced enjoyable rhythm

gross* *adj, slang* : inspiring disgust or distaste ⟨that sandwich looks ~⟩

gross domestic product *n* : the gross national product excluding the value of net income earned abroad — abbr. *GDP*

gross out *vt* [¹*gross*] : to offend, insult, or disgust by something gross

gross–out \ˈ=,=\ *n* -S [*gross out*, v. (herein)] : something inspiring disgust or distaste — **gross–out** *adj*

grot·ty \ˈgrätē, -äd·ē, -i\ *adj* -ER/-EST [origin unknown] *chiefly Brit* : wretchedly shabby : of poor quality ⟨homes which, by the most elementary criteria, are ~ slums —Peter Preston⟩

ground* *vt* : to throw (a football) intentionally to the ground to avoid being tackled for a loss

ground effect* *n* : a down force exerted on a racing car by special design features (as winglike airfoils) that enables it to achieve higher speeds through turns before starting to skid — often used in pl.

ground–effect machine \ˈ=,=-\ *n* : an air-cushion vehicle for traveling over land or water

groundout \ˈ=,=\ *n* -S [*ground out*, v.] : a play in baseball in which a batter is put out after hitting a grounder to an infielder

ground zero* *n* **1** : the center or origin of rapid, intense, or violent activity or change **2** : the very beginning : SQUARE ONE *herein*

group* *n* : a mathematical set that is closed under a binary associative operation (as multiplication or addition) and that has an identity element and an inverse for every element

group a *n, usu cap G&A, often attrib* : the Lancefield group of streptococci that comprises all strains of a species of the genus *Streptococcus (S. pyogenes)* and that includes the causative agents of pharyngitis, scarlet fever, septicemia, some skin infections (as pyoderma and erysipelas), rheumatic fever, and glomerulonephritis ⟨*Group A* streptococcal infections⟩ — compare GROUP B *herein*

group b *n, usu cap G&B, often attrib* : the Lancefield group of streptococci that comprises all strains of a species of the genus *Streptococcus (S. agalactiae)* and that includes the causative agents of certain infections (as septicemia, pneumonia, and meningitis) esp. of newborn infants ⟨affected with *Group B* strep⟩ — compare GROUP A *herein*

grouper* *n* : one of a group of unrelated people who share a rented house (as at the seashore)

group grope *n, slang* : a sex orgy

group home *n* : a residence for individuals (as handicapped persons or foster children) requiring care, assistance, or supervision

group·ie \ˈgrüpē\ *n* -S [¹*group* + *-ie*] **1** : a fan of a rock group; *esp* : one who follows the group on tour **2** : a fan of a celebrity who attends as many of his or her appearances as possible **3** : an enthusiastic follower or supporter ⟨a political ~⟩ ⟨a fashion ~⟩

group theory *n* : a branch of mathematics concerned with finding all mathematical groups and determining their properties — **group–theoretic** \ˈ=,==ˈ=\ *or* **group–theoretical** \ˈ=ˈ=ˈ==\ *adj* — **group theorist** *n*

groupthink \ˈ=,=\ *n* [¹*group* + *-think* (as in *doublethink*)] : conformity to group values and ethics ⟨~ exists that does not make many allowances for individualism —Bruce Newman⟩

groupware \ˈ=,=\ *n* [¹*group* + *-ware* (as in *software* — herein)] : software designed to enable users to work collaboratively on projects or files via a network

growth* *n* : anticipated progressive growth in capital value and income ⟨some investors prefer ~ to immediate income⟩

growth company *n* : a company that grows at a greater rate than the economy as a whole

growth cone *n* : the specialized motile tip of an axon of a growing or regenerating nerve cell

growth industry *n* : a business that has become increasingly popular or profitable; *also* : an interest or activity that is increasingly popular or trendy

growth plate *n* : the region in a long bone between the epiphysis and diaphysis where growth in length occurs

grunge \ˈgrənj\ *n* -S [back-formation fr. *grungy* (herein)] **1** : something that is grungy ⟨public restroom ~⟩ **2** : rock music incorporating elements of punk rock and heavy metal; *also* : the untidy fashions typical of fans of grunge

grun·gy \ˈgrənjē\ *adj* -ER/-EST [origin unknown] **1** : shabby or dirty in character or condition ⟨~ old boots⟩ ⟨~ bars⟩ **2** : characteristic of grunge music or fashion — **grun·gi·ness** \-nəs\ *n* -ES

grunt* *n* **1** : a U.S. army or marine foot soldier esp. in the Vietnam war **2** : one who does routine unglamorous work

GS* *abbr* giant slalom; government service

G6PD *abbr* glucose-6-phosphate dehydrogenase *herein*

GSL *abbr* guaranteed student loan

GSR *abbr* galvanic skin response *herein*

GT \ˌjēˈtē\ *n* -S [grand *t*ouring (car)] : GRAND TOURING CAR *herein*

GTP \ˌjē(ˌ)tēˈpē\ *n* -S [guanosine *t*ri*p*hosphate] : an energy-rich nucleoside triphosphate analogous to ATP that is composed of guanine linked to ribose and three phosphate groups and is necessary for the formation of peptide bonds during protein synthesis — called also *guanosine triphosphate*

g_2 phase \(ˈ)jēˈtü-\ *n, usu cap G* : the period in the cell cycle from the completion of DNA replication to the beginning of cell division — compare G_1 PHASE *herein*, M PHASE *herein*, S PHASE *herein*

gua·neth·i·dine \gwäˈnethə,dēn, -ədən\ *n* -S [*guanidine* + *eth-*] : a synthetic guanidine derivative $C_{10}H_{22}N_4$ used esp. in the form of its sulfate in treating severe high blood pressure

guanosine mono·phosphate \-ˌmä(ˌ)nō, -ˌmō(ˌ)nō, -nə+\ *n* [*mon-* + *phosphate*] : CYCLIC GMP *herein*

guanosine triphosphate *n* : GTP *herein*

gua·nyl·ate cyclase \ˈgwänᵊlˌāt-\ *n* [*guanyl* + ¹*-ate*] : an enzyme that catalyzes the formation of cyclic GMP from GTP

gua·ya·bera \ˌgwīəˈberə\ *n* -S [AmerSp] : a usu. short-sleeved lightweight sport shirt designed to be worn untucked

guerrilla theater *n* : STREET THEATER *herein*

guest worker *n* [trans. of G *gastarbeiter*] : a foreign laborer working on a temporary basis in a country esp. in Europe

GUI \ˈgüē, jē(ˌ)yüˈī\ *abbr or n* -S graphical user interface *herein*

gu·lag \ˈgü,läg\ *n* -S *often cap* [Russ, fr. *G*lavnoe *u*pravlenie ispravitel'no-trudovykh *lag*ereĭ chief administration of corrective labor camps] **1** : the penal system of the U.S.S.R. consisting of a network of labor camps; *also* : such a penal system in other countries **2** : LABOR CAMP 1

gulf war syndrome *n, usu cap G&W* : a syndrome of uncertain cause that includes fatigue, joint pain, memory loss, skin rash, and headache and that has been reported in veterans of the war fought in the Persian Gulf in 1991

gull wing door *n* : an automobile door that is hinged at the top and resembles an airplane gull wing when open

gun* *n* : a long heavy surfboard — called also *big gun* — **under the gun*** : under pressure ⟨I was always *under the gun* to perform —Don Sutton⟩

gunboat diplomacy *n* : diplomacy backed by the use or threat of military force

gun lap *n* : the final lap of a race in track signaled by the firing of a gun as the leader begins the lap

gunn effect \ˈgən-\ *n, usu cap G* [after J.B. *Gunn b*1928 Brit. physicist] : the production of rapid fluctuations of current when the voltage applied to a semiconductor device exceeds a critical value with the result that microwave power is generated

gun patch *n* : a patch so placed on a shirt or jacket as to prevent a rifle butt from slipping

gunship \ˈ=,=\ *n* : a helicopter or cargo aircraft armed with rockets and machine guns

gunslinger* *n* **1** : a money manager who trades high-risk stocks for substantial short-term capital gains or who structures corporate refinancings in the junk bond market **2** : a self-confident or aggressive person considered better than others in a given field, occupation, or situation ⟨overworked lawyers vie for clients and swaggering *gunslingers* carry off the fattest fees —David Luban⟩ — **gunslinging** *adj*

guru* *n* **1** : one who is an acknowledged leader or a chief proponent **2** : EXPERT

gus·sy up \ˈgəsē-\ *vt* **gussied up; gussied up; gussying up; gussies up** [origin unknown] : to dress up : PRETTIFY

gut* *vt* — **gut it out** : PERSEVERE

gut *adj* [¹*gut*] **1** : arising from one's inmost self : VISCERAL ⟨a ~ reaction to the misery he has seen —J.A.Lukas⟩ **2** : having strong impact or immediate relevance ⟨~ issues⟩

GUT \ˈgət; jē(ˌ)yüˈtē\ *abbr or n* -S grand unified theory *herein*

gut course *also* **gut*** *n* [¹*gut*; prob. fr. its being likened in softness to the belly] : a course (as in college) that is easily passed

gut·si·ness \ˈgətsēnəs, -sin-\ *n* -ES [*gutsy* + *-ness*] : the quality or state of being gutsy

guy* *n* **1** : PERSON — used in pl. to refer to the members of a group regardless of sex ⟨saw her and the rest of the ~s⟩ **2** : THING, CREATURE — used of animals and objects ⟨the other dogs in the show will pale in comparison to this little ~⟩ ⟨F-15s take on the ~s above 15,000 ft —Deborah Meyer *et al*⟩

GVHD *abbr* graft-versus-host disease *herein*

gyp·lure \ˈjip,lu̇(ə)r, -u̇ə\ *n* [*gyp*sy (moth) + *lure*] : a synthetic sex attractant used in trapping male gypsy moths

gyp·py tummy \ˈjipē-\ *n* [*gyppy* alter. of *Egyptian*; fr. association of the illness with eating in a foreign country] : DIARRHEA

gypsum board *n* : PLASTERBOARD

gypsy cab *n* : a taxicab licensed only to answer calls; *esp* : such a cab that cruises in search of passengers illegally

gy·ro \ˈyē,rō, ˈzhirō, ÷ˈjī,rō\ *n* -S [NGk *gyros* turn; fr. the rotation of the meat on a vertical spit — more at GYRE] : a sandwich esp. of lamb and beef, tomato, and onion on pita bread

gy·ro·cop·ter \ˈjīrə,käptə(r)\ *n* -S [autogyro + helicopter] : a usu. one-passenger rotary-wing aircraft that is driven forward by a conventional propeller

ha·ba·ne·ro *also* **ha·ba·ñe·ro** \ˌ(h)äbəˈn(y)erō\ *n* -S [AmerSp (*chile*) *habanero*, lit., Havanan chili, fr. *chile* chili + *habanero* Havanan, fr. La *Habana*, Cuba] : a very hot roundish chili pepper (*Capsicum chinense*) that is usu. orange when mature — called also *habanero chili*, *habanero pepper*

habituate* *vi* : to undergo habituation ⟨~ to a stimulus⟩

habituation* *n* : decrease in responsiveness upon repeated exposure to a stimulus

hack* *vi* [¹*hack*] **1** : to write computer programs for enjoyment **2** : to gain access illegally to a computer or the data stored on it

hack* *n* [⁵*hack*] : AMATEUR 3b ⟨a field dominated by ~s, frauds and vulgarians —William Grimes⟩

hack·er* *n* **1** : an expert at programming and solving problems with a computer : computer whiz **2** : a person who illegally gains access to and sometimes tampers with information in a computer system esp. using a home computer

hacking pocket *n* [so called fr. its use on hacking coats] : a slanted coat pocket usu. with a flap

ha·dal \ˈhādᵊl\ *adj* [ISV *had-* (fr. Gk *Hadēs* Hades) + ¹*-al*] : of, relating to, or being the parts of the ocean below 6000 meters

hadley cell *n, usu cap H* [after George Hadley †1768 Eng. scientific writer] : a pattern of atmospheric circulation in which warm air rises near the equator, cools as it travels poleward at high altitude, sinks as cold air near 30° N or S latitude, and warms as it travels equatorward; *also* : a similar atmospheric circulation pattern elsewhere (as at different latitudes or on another planet)

had·ron \ˈha,drän\ *n* -S [ISV *hadr-* + ²*-on*] : any of the subatomic particles that are made up of quarks and are subject to the strong force — **ha·dron·ic** \haˈdränik\ *adj*

haggadah* *n, usu cap* : the book of readings for the seder service

hahn·ium \ˈhänēəm\ *n* [NL, fr. Otto *Hahn* †1968 Ger. chemist + NL *-ium*] : DUBNIUM *herein*

hail mary* *n, usu cap H&M* : a long and chancy football pass made usu. at the end of a quarter or the end of a game

hair spray *n* : a preparation that is sprayed on the hair to keep it in place

hairweaving \ˈ=,==\ *n* : the process of covering a bald spot with human hair and nylon thread woven into the wearer's own hair — **hairweave** \ˈ=,=\ *n* — **hair weaver** *n*

hairy* *adj* : difficult to deal with or comprehend ⟨a ~ math problem⟩

hairy cell leukemia *n* : chronic leukemia usu. of B cell origin that is characterized by malignant cells with a ciliated appearance that replace bone marrow and infiltrate the spleen causing splenomegaly

ha·la·la *also* **ha·la·lah** \həˈlälə\ *n, pl* **halala** *or* **halalas** [Ar] **1** : a monetary unit of Saudi Arabia equal to 1/100 riyal — see MONEY table *in the Dict* **2** : a coin representing one halala

half–and–half* *n* : a mixture of cream and whole milk

half duplex *n* : a mode of communication esp. with a computer via telephone line in which information can be sent in only one direction at a time — compare DUPLEX *in the Dict*, FULL DUPLEX *herein*

half–life* *n* : a period of usefulness or popularity preceding decline or obsolescence ⟨slang has a short *half-life*⟩

half–pipe \ˈ=,=\ *n* -S : a U-shaped high-sided ramp or runway used esp. in snowboarding, skateboarding, or in-line skating

half–space \ˈ=,=\ *n* : the part of three-dimensional euclidean space lying on one side of a plane

halftone* *n* : an image (as one printed on an offset press or laser printer) that renders smooth variations of color in an original by means of dots assigned to areas of the image electronically

halfway house* *n* : a residence for individuals after institutionalization (as for mental disorder, drug addiction, or criminal activity) that is designed to facilitate their readjustment to private life

hallucinate* *vt* : to perceive or experience as an hallucination

hal·lu·ci·na·tor \həˈlüsᵊn,ād·ər\ *n* -S : a person who has hallucinations

hal·lu·ci·no·gen·ic \hə,lüsᵊnəˈjenik, *also* həl,yü-\ *n* -S [*hallucinogenic*, adj.] : HALLUCINOGEN

halo* *n* **1** : a region of space surrounding a galaxy that is sparsely populated with luminous objects (as globular clusters) but is believed to contain a great deal of dark matter **2** *or* **halo brace** : an orthopedic device used to immobilize the head and neck (as to treat fracture of neck vertebrae) that consists of a metal band placed around the head and fastened to the skull usu. with metal pins and is attached by extensions to an inflexible vest

hal·o·bacterium \ˈhalōˈ=+\ *n* [NL, fr. *hal-* + *bacterium*] **1** *cap* : a genus of halophilic rod or disk-shaped gram-negative aerobic primitive bacteria (family Halobacteriaceae) that live in strongly saline pools in red to orange colonies and that at low oxygen levels synthesize the purple-pigmented protein bacteriorhodopsin **2** : a bacterium of the genus *Halobacterium*

hal·o·carbon \ˈ==+\ *n* [*hal-* + ¹*carbon*] : any of various compounds (as a fluorocarbon) of carbon and one or more halogens and sometimes also hydrogen

hal·o·cline \ˈhalə,klīn\ *n* -S [*hal-* + *-cline*] : a usu. vertical gradient in salinity (as of the ocean)

hal·o·per·i·dol \ˌhalōˈperə,dȯl, -,dōl\ *n* -S [*hal-* + *piperidine* + ¹*-ol*] : a depressant $C_{21}H_{23}ClFNO_2$ of the central nervous system used esp. as an antipsychotic drug

hal·o·thane \ˈhalə,thān\ *n* -S [*halogen* + *ethane*] : a nonexplosive inhalational anesthetic $C_2HBrClF_3$

hamate *n* -S [*hamate*, adj.] : HAMATUM

hamiltonian* *n, usu cap* [Sir William R. *Hamilton* †1865 Irish mathematician + E *-ian*] : a function that is used to describe a dynamic system (as the motion of a particle) in terms of components of momentum and coordinates of space-time and that is equal to the total energy of the system when time is not explicitly part of the function — compare KINETIC POTENTIAL *in the Dict*

hamstring* *or* **hamstring muscle** *n* : any of three muscles at the back of the thigh that function to flex and rotate the leg and extend the thigh: **a** : SEMIMEMBRANOSUS **b** : SEMITENDINOSUS **c** : BICEPS b

handedness* *n* **1 a** : the property of an object (as a molecule) of not being identical with its mirror image **b** : either of two configurations of an object that may exist in forms which are nonidentical mirror images **2** : the property of having either a clockwise or counterclockwise structure (as the coiling of a snail shell) or motion (as the corkscrew movement of some microorganisms or their flagella or cilia)

handheld \ˈ=ˈ=\ *adj* **1** : held in the hand; *esp* : designed to be operated while being held in the hand ⟨~ computers⟩ **2** : created by a handheld device (as a camera) ⟨~ photos⟩ — **handheld** \ˈ=,=\ *n* -S

hand–holding \ˈ=,==\ *n* : solicitous attention, support, or instruction (as in the use of new technology)

hand·i·capped \ˈhandē,kapt, -də-\ *adj* **1** : having a physical or mental disability that substantially limits activity esp. in relation to employment or education **2** : of or reserved for handicapped persons ⟨~ parking spaces⟩ ⟨~ access to public buildings⟩

hand job *n, slang* : an act of stimulating the genitals manually usu. to orgasm

handprint \ˈ=,=\ *n* : an impression of a hand on a surface

hands–on \ˈ=ˈ=\ *adj* [*hands-* (as in *hands-off*) + *on*] **1** : relating to, being, or providing direct practical experience (as in the operation or functioning of something) ⟨*hands-on* training with a new computer system⟩; *also* : involving or allowing use of or touching with the hands ⟨*hands-on* health care⟩ ⟨a *hands-on* museum display⟩ **2** : characterized by active and direct personal involvement ⟨a *hands-on* manager⟩

hand up *vt* : to deliver (an indictment) to a judge or higher judicial authority

hand–wringing \ˈ=,==\ *n* -S : an overwrought expression of concern or guilt — **hand–wringer** \ˈ=,==\ *n*

hang* *vt* **1** : to throw (a breaking pitch) so that it fails to break properly **2** : to make (a turn) esp. while driving ⟨*hung* a left into the driveway⟩ ~ *vi* **1** *of a thrown ball* : to fail to break or drop as intended **2** : to spend time idly esp. with a particular person or group of people : hang out — usu. used with *with* **3** : to keep up : stay even (as in a game or race) — often used with *with* — **hang five** : to ride a surfboard with the weight of the body forward and the toes of one foot turned over the front edge of the board — **hang in there** *also* **hang in** : to persist in the face of the adversity : PERSEVERE — **hang it up** : to cease an activity or effort : give up : STOP — **hang loose** : to remain calm and unruffled ⟨decided to *hang loose* and risk it —Cyra McFadden⟩ — **hang out to dry** : to leave stranded in a hopeless or dangerous situation — **hang ten** : to ride a surfboard with the weight of the body forward and the toes of both feet turned over the front edge of the board — **hang tough** : to persist in the face of adversity

hang glider *n* **1** : a kitelike glider from which a harnessed rider hangs while gliding down from a cliff or hill **2** : a person who rides a hang glider — **hang glide** *vi* — **hang gliding** *n*

hang–loose \ˈ=ˈ=\ *adj* [fr. *hang loose* (herein)] : being highly informal, relaxed, unstructured, or uninhibited

hang time *n* : the amount of time a kicked football remains in the air; *also* : the length of time a leaping athlete is in the air

hangtown fry \ˈ=,=-\ *n, usu cap H & often cap F* [fr. *Hangtown*, nickname for Placerville, California] : a scrambled egg dish or omelet containing fried oysters

hang–up* *n* : a source of mental or emotional difficulty; *broadly* : PROBLEM

ha·ni·wa \ˈhänəˌwä\ *n pl, sometimes cap* [Jap] : large hollow baked clay artifacts placed on early Japanese grave mounds and having the form of simple cylinders or in later years of figures (as of people or animals)

hanky–pank \ˈhaŋkēˌpaŋk\ *n* -s [*hanky-pank*, adj.] : any of various carnival games in which contestants may win small prizes for the exercise of simple skills (as dart throwing)

hanky–panky* *n* : sexual dalliance

han·ta·an virus \ˈhantəˌən, ˈhən-, ˈhän-\ *n, usu cap H* [fr. the *Hantaan* River in South Korea near where rodents carrying the virus were collected 1974-78] : a hantavirus that is the causative agent of Korean hemorrhagic fever and related hemorrhagic fevers with renal involvement

han·ta·virus \ˈhantə, ˈhəntə, ˈhäntə+\ *n* [NL, fr. *hanta-* (fr. the *Hantaan* River) + *virus*] : any of a genus (*Hantavirus* of the family Bunyaviridae) of single-stranded RNA viruses that are transmitted by rodent feces and urine and cause a serious pulmonary disease and hemorrhagic fevers marked by renal necrosis

hao \ˈhau̇\ *n, pl* **hao** [Vietnamese *hào*] **1** : a monetary unit of Vietnam equal to 1⁄10 (formerly 1⁄100) dong **2** : a coin representing one hao

hap·ki·do \ˌhäpˈkēdō\ *n* -s [Korean, fr. *hap-* together, joined + *ki* breath, spirit, energy + *to* way, art] : a Korean martial art based on kicking motions and incorporating elements of aikido

haplotype* *n* : a group of alleles of different genes (as of the major histocompatibility complex) on a single chromosome that are closely enough linked to be inherited usu. as a unit

happening* *n* **1** : an event or series of events designed to evoke a spontaneous audience reaction to sensory, emotional, or spiritual stimuli **2** : something (as an event) that is particularly interesting, entertaining, or important ⟨the hearing is a ~, one of those unique events . . . which will be talked about for years —Douglas Kiker⟩

happening *adj* [fr. pres. part. of [1]*happen*] **1** : very fashionable : IN *herein* ⟨a ~ hairstyle⟩ **2** : offering much stimulating activity ⟨a ~ dance club⟩

happy camper *n* : one who is content

happy hour *n* : a period of time during which the price of drinks (as at a bar) is reduced or hors d'oeuvres are served gratis

hap·to·glo·bin \ˈhaptəˌglōbən, ˌ==ˈ==\ *n* -s [Gk *haptein* to fasten, bind + E *-o-* + hemo*globin* — more at APSIS] : any of several forms of a protein found in blood serum that is an alpha globulin that can combine with free hemoglobin in the plasma and thereby prevent the loss of iron into the urine

hard* *adj* **1** : being at once addictive and gravely detrimental to health ⟨such ~ drugs as heroin⟩ **2** : resistant to biodegradation ⟨~ detergents⟩ ⟨~ pesticides like DDT⟩ **3** : being, schooled in, or using the methods of the natural sciences and esp. of the physical sciences ⟨a ~ scientist⟩ **4** : most unyielding or thoroughgoing ⟨the ~ political right⟩

hard–ass \ˈ=ˌ=\ *n* : a tough, demanding, or uncompromising person — often considered vulgar — **hard–assed** \ˈ=ˌ=\ *adj*

hardball* *n* : forceful uncompromising methods employed to gain an end ⟨played political ~ to win the nomination⟩

hard–charging \ˈ=ˌ==\ *adj* : aggressively determined or ambitious ⟨*hard-charging* young executives⟩

hard copy *n* : a copy of textual or graphic information (as from microfilm or computer storage) on paper in normal size

hard–core \ˈ=ˌ=\ *adj* [*hard core*] **1** : of, relating to, or being persons whose economic position and educational background are substandard and who experience chronic unemployment ⟨the *hard-core* unemployed⟩ **2** : CONFIRMED, DIE-HARD ⟨*hard-core* football fans⟩ ⟨a *hard-core* liberal⟩ **3** *of pornography* : containing explicit descriptions of sex acts or scenes of actual sex acts — compare SOFT-CORE *herein* **4** : characterized by or being the purest or most basic form of something : FUNDAMENTAL ⟨a room gussied up in *hard-core* French provincial style —John Canaday⟩ **5** : serious or intense in nature or degree ⟨*hard-core* crime⟩

hardcore** *n* : very loud, fast rock music

hard disk *n* : a rigid metal disk coated with a magnetic material on which data for a computer can be stored; *also* : HARD DRIVE *herein*

hard drive *n* : a high-capacity data-storage device (as for a personal computer) consisting of a drive and one or more hard disks

hard–driving \ˈ=ˈ==\ *adj* : intensely hard-working, competitive, or ambitious

hard–edge \ˈ=ˌ=\ *adj* **1** : of or relating to abstract painting characterized by geometric forms with clearly defined boundaries **2** : HARD-EDGED *herein*

hard–edged \ˈ=ˌ=\ *adj* : possessing a tough, driving, or sharp quality ⟨*hard-edged* reporting of controversial subjects —Av Westin⟩ ⟨the *hard-edged* cold that clears the air —Leona P. Schecter⟩

hardened* *adj* : protected from possible danger from blast or heat by means of concrete or earth or by being situated underground ⟨a ~ missile launching site⟩ ⟨a ~ missile⟩

hard–eyed \ˈ=ˌ=\ *adj* : extremely critical and often skeptical ⟨a ~ realist⟩ ⟨~ scrutiny⟩

hardhat** *n* **1** : a construction worker; *broadly* : a blue-collar worker who wears a hard hat while working **2** : a hard-line conservative

hard–line \ˈ=ˌ=\ *adj* : being, advocating, or pursuing a rigidly uncompromising policy or course of action : UNYIELDING ⟨a *hard-line* policy toward polluters⟩

hard–lin·er \ˈ=ˈlīnər\ *n* : one who advocates or pursues a hard-line policy

hard–pressed \ˈ=ˌ=\ *adj* : hard put; *esp* : being under financial strain

hard rock *n* : rock music marked by a heavy aggressive beat, high amplification, and usu. energetic performances — **hard rocker** *n*

hard ticket *n* : a reserved seat ticket

hardware* *n* : the physical components (as electronic and electrical devices) of a vehicle (as a spacecraft) or an apparatus (as a computer); *broadly* : the equipment employed in an activity or undertaking ⟨educational ~⟩

hardwired \ˈ=ˌ=\ *adj* **1** : implemented in the form of permanent electronic circuits ⟨an instruction repertoire . . . implemented in 400 ~ specifics —*Datamation*⟩; *also* : connected or incorporated by or as if by permanent electrical connections ⟨a ~ phone⟩ ⟨concepts of attractiveness may be universal and ~ into the human brain —Jane E. Brody⟩ **2** : genetically or innately determined : INBORN ⟨creature whose every action is a reflexive, ~ response —Natalie Angier⟩; *also* : genetically or innately predisposed ⟨a human being who is ~ to be sociable —*Forbes*⟩

har·dy–wein·berg \ˌhärdēˈwīnˌbərg\ *adj, usu cap H&W* : of, relating to, or governed by the Hardy-Weinberg law ⟨*Hardy-Weinberg* equilibrium⟩

hardy–weinberg law *n, usu cap H&W* [after Godfrey Harold *Hardy* †1947 Eng. mathematician and Wilhelm *Weinberg* †1937 Ger. physician] : a fundamental principle of population genetics: population gene frequencies and population genotype frequencies remain constant from generation to generation if mating is random and if mutation, selection, immigration, and emigration do not occur — called also *Hardy-Weinberg principle*

ha·re krish·na \ˌhärēˈkrishnə\ *n* [Hindi *harē* invocation of God + *Kṛṣṇa* avatar of the Hindu god Vishnu] **1** *cap H & K* : an ascetic religious movement dedicated to the worship of the Hindu god Krishna **2** *pl* **hare krishnas** *or* **hare krishna** *usu cap H & K* : a member of the Hare Krishna movement

harem pant *n* [so called fr. Western depictions of women wearing such pants in illustrations of harems in SW Asia and N Africa] : women's loose fitting trousers that fit closely at the ankle — usu. used in pl.

har·pac·ti·coid \härˈpaktəˌkȯid\ *n* -s [NL *Harpacticoida*, group name, fr. Gk *harpaktikos* rapacious (fr. *harpaktos* snatched, stolen) + NL *-oida* — more at HARPACTOPHAGOUS] : any of an order or suborder (Harpacticoida) of marine or freshwater usu. bottom-dwelling copepods — **harpacticoid** *adj*

harvest* *vt* : to remove or extract (as living cells, tissues, or organs) from culture or from a living or recently deceased body esp. for transplanting

har·vey wallbanger \ˈhärvēˈ=ˌ==\ *n, pl* **harvey wallbangers** *usu cap H&W* [origin unknown] : a screwdriver with an Italian liqueur floated on top

hash \ˈhash, -aa(ə)sh, -aish\ *n* [by shortening] : HASHISH

ha·shi·mo·to's thyroiditis \ˌhäshēˈmōd·(ˌ)ōz-, -shiˌ-\ *also* **hashimoto's disease** *or* **hashimoto's struma** *n, usu cap H* [after Hakaru *Hashimoto* †1934 Jap. surgeon] : chronic autoimmune thyroiditis characterized by thyroid enlargement, thyroid fibrosis, lymphocytic infiltration of thyroid tissue and the production of autoantibodies that attack the thyroid

has·si·um \ˈhasēəm\ *n* -s [NL, fr. *Hassia* Hesse (German state), location of the laboratory that first produced the element + *-ium*] : a short-lived radioactive element of atomic number 108 that is produced artificially — symbol *Hs*

hassle* *vb* ~ *vt* : to annoy persistently or acutely : HARASS

hatchback \ˈ=ˌ=\ *n* : a back on a closed passenger automobile (as a coupe) having an upward-opening hatch; *also* : an automobile having a hatchback

hate crime *n* : any of various crimes (as assault or defacement of property) motivated by hostility to the victim as a member of a group (as one based on color, creed, gender, or sexual orientation)

hat trick* *n* : a series of three victories, successes, or related accomplishments ⟨scored a *hat trick* when her three best steers corralled top honors —*People*⟩

haul* *vb* — **haul ass** *slang* : to move quickly

haute \ˈōt\ *also* **haut** \ˈōt, ˈō\ *adj* [F, fem. of *haut* superior, lit., high — more at HAUGHT] : FASHIONABLE, HIGH-CLASS ⟨~ interior decorators⟩ ⟨a ~ community of $500,000 mansions —Cable Neuhaus⟩ ⟨from the earthiest peasant cookery to cuisine most loftily ~ —*Publishers' Weekly*⟩

haute cuisine \ˌ(h)ōt-\ *n* [F, lit., high cuisine] : a refined or elaborate style of cooking; *also* : food prepared in this style

havana brown *n, usu cap H & often cap B* [[2]*havana* (cigar)] : any of a breed of short-haired domestic cats developed in England and having a mahogany-brown coat and green eyes

ha·var·ti \həˈvärd·ē\ *n, usu cap* [Dan, fr. *Havarthigård*, farm near Søllerød, Denmark, of Hanne Nielsen †1903 Dan. cheesemaker] : a semisoft Danish cheese with a mild to sharp flavor

haven* *n* : a place offering favorable opportunities or conditions ⟨a tourist's ~⟩

hawaiian shirt *n, usu cap H* : a usu. short-sleeved sport shirt with a colorful pattern

hawk* *n* : one who takes a militant attitude (as in a dispute) and advocates immediate vigorous action — compare DOVE *herein* — **hawk·ish** \ˈhȯkəsh\ *adj* — **hawk·ish·ly** \-lē\ *adv* — **hawk·ish·ness** \-nəs\ *n* -ES

haw·king radiation \ˈhȯkiŋ-\ *n, usu cap H* [after Stephen *Hawking* *b*1942 Brit. physicist] : hypothetical thermal radiation emitted from near the event horizon of a black hole

haw·thorne effect \ˈhȯˌthȯrn-, -ˌthȯ(ə)n-\ *n, usu cap H* [fr. the *Hawthorne* Works of the Western Electric Co., Cicero, Ill., where the effect's existence was established by experiment] : the stimulation to increase output or accomplishment (as in an industrial or educational methods study) that results from the mere fact of being under concerned observation; *also* : such an increase in output or accomplishment

hay·lage \ˈhālij\ *n* -s [[2]*hay* + *silage*] : stored forage that is essentially grass silage wilted to 35 to 50 percent moisture

haz·mat \ˈhazˌmat\ *n* -s *often attrib* [*haz*ardous *mat*erial] : a shipped material (as radioactive, flammable, explosive, or poisonous material) that would be a danger to life or to the environment if released without necessary precautions being taken

HC* *abbr* **1** hard copy *herein* **2** hydrocarbon

HCFC \ˌāch(ˌ)sēˌefˈsē\ *abbr or n* -s : hydrochlorofluorocarbon *herein*

HCG *abbr* human chorionic gonadotropin *herein*

HDL \ˌāch(ˌ)dēˈel\ *n* -s : a lipoprotein of blood plasma that is composed of a high proportion of protein with little triglyceride and cholesterol and that is associated with decreased probability of developing atherosclerosis — called also *high-density lipoprotein*; compare LDL *herein*, VLDL *herein*

HDPE *abbr* high-density polyethylene

HDTV *abbr* high-definition television

head* *n* **1** [short for *pothead* (herein) or *acidhead* (herein)] : one who uses a drug (as LSD or marijuana) **2** : FELLATIO, CUNNILINGUS — usu. used with *give*; often considered vulgar **3** : a devoted enthusiast : AFICIONADO — often used in combination — **on its head** : in such a way that what is normal or expected is reversed ⟨the promised process of stopping the war was stood *on its head* to become one of prolonging it —Barbara W. Tuchman⟩

head·bang·er \ˈhedˌbaŋə(r)\ *n* -s [[1]*head* + [1]*bang* + [2]*-er*; fr. the vigorous rhythmic shaking of the head and body to the beat of such music stereotypically engaged in by its fans during concerts] : one who performs heavy metal or hard rock; *also* : a fan of heavy metal or hard rock

head case *n* : NUT 8b(1), (2); *also* : an athlete whose attitude is disruptive to the team

headcounter \ˈ=ˌ==\ *n* : POLLSTER

head dip *n* : a surfing feat in which a surfer squats on the board, leans forward, and dips his head into the wave

header* *n* **1** : a mounting plate through which electrical terminals pass from a sealed device (as a transistor) **2** : a shot or pass in soccer made by heading the ball **3** : HEAD 17a(1)

headhunt* *vt* : to recruit (personnel and esp. executives) for top-level jobs ~ *vi* : to recruit personnel for top-level jobs

headhunter* *n* **1** : a recruiter of personnel and esp. executives **2** : an athlete who seeks to harm an opponent intentionally

headline* *vb* ~ *vi* : to be featured as a leading performer ⟨~*ing* in all the large halls from coast to coast —Ed McCormack⟩

headliner* *n* : HEADLINING

head restraint *n* : a resilient pad at the top of the back of an automobile seat esp. for preventing whiplash injury

head shop *n* [*head* (herein)] : a shop that specializes in articles of interest to drug users

head–to–head \ˌ==ˈ=\ *adv (or adj)* : in a direct confrontation or encounter usu. between individuals

head trip *n* : an exploration of one's own emotions and ideas

heady* *adj* : intellectually stimulating or demanding ⟨a ~ combination of classics and literature of the counterculture —Elin Schoen⟩

health club *n* : a usu. commercial establishment having members who pay a fee to use its health and fitness facilities and equipment

health food *n* : a food promoted as highly conducive to health

health maintenance organization *n* : HMO *herein*

health spa *n* **1** : SPA 1 *herein*; *esp* : one emphasizing health and fitness **2** : HEALTH CLUB *herein*

heap leaching *n* : a mining process in which metals are leached from a pile of crushed ore by a percolating solution (as of sodium cyanide)

hearing dog *also* **hearing ear dog** *n* : a dog trained to alert its deaf or hearing-impaired owner to sounds (as of a telephone, doorbell, or alarm clock)

heartland* *n* : the central geographical region of the U.S. in which mainstream or traditional values predominate

heart–to–heart *n* [*heart-to-heart*, adj.] : a heart-to-heart conversation

heat* *n* **1** *slang* : POLICE **2** : baseball pitches that are extremely hard and fast **3** *slang* : GUN

heater* *n* : a baseball pitch that is extremely hard and fast

heat island *n* : an urban area in which significantly more heat is absorbed and retained than in surrounding areas

heat pipe *n* : a closed container in which a continuing cycle of evaporation and condensation of a fluid takes place with the heat being given off at the condenser end and which is more effective in transferring heat than a metallic conductor

heat shield *n* : a barrier of ablative material to protect a space capsule from heat on its entry into an atmosphere

heat shock protein *n* : any of a group of proteins that are produced esp. in cells subjected to stressful conditions (as high temperature) and that serve to ensure the proper folding of proteins and are considered to comprise a class of molecular chaperones

heat sink *n* : a substance or device for the absorption or dissipation of unwanted heat (as from a process or an electronic device)

heavy* *adj* **1** : LONG 11 — usu. used with *on* ⟨~ on creative ideas and light on financial plans —Susan Davis⟩ **2** : being or playing hard rock **3** : IMPORTANT, PROMINENT ⟨a ~ star unable to escape his groupies —Garry Wills⟩

heavy* *n* **1** : someone or something influential, serious, or important **2** : MUSCLEMAN, THUG

heavy chain *n* : either of the two larger of the four polypeptide chains that comprise antibodies — compare LIGHT CHAIN *herein*

heavy–duty* *adj* **1** : INTENSIVE ⟨*heavy-duty* interviewing —C.G.Segrè⟩ **2** : IMPORTANT, PROMINENT ⟨a *heavy-duty* gangster —John Schulian⟩

heavy hitter *n* : someone influential or important : BIG SHOT

heavy metal *n* [prob. from the lines "I like smoke and lightning, *heavy metal* thunder" in the song "Born to Be Wild" (1968) by the rock group Steppenwolf] : aggressive highly amplified rock music marked by a heavy beat

heavy weather *n, Brit* : considerable difficulty : HEAVY GOING — often used in the phrase *make heavy weather of*

hedge fund *n* [[1]*hedge*] : an investing group usu. in the form of a limited partnership that employs speculative techniques (as short selling and leverage) in the hope of obtaining large capital gains

hei·an \ˈhēˈän, ˈhāən\ *adj, usu cap* [Jap, lit., tranquility] : of or relating to a period of Japanese history from the late 8th to the late 12th century

height·ism \ˈhītˌizəm, ˈhīd·ˌ-, ˈhītˌth-, ˈhīthˌ-\ *n* -s [[1]*height* + *-ism* (as in *racism*)] : discrimination against short people

heim·lich maneuver \ˈhīmlik-\ *n, usu cap H* [after Henry J. *Heimlich* *b*1920 Am. surgeon] : the manual application of sudden upward pressure on the upper abdomen of a choking victim to force a foreign object from the windpipe

heirloom* *n* : a horticultural variety that has survived for several generations usu. due to the efforts of private individuals ⟨a salad made with ~ tomatoes⟩ ⟨~ seeds⟩

hei·shi *or* **hei·she** \ˈhēshē\ *n* -s [origin unknown] : a bead made usu. by No. American Indians of disk-shaped shells, turquoise, or coral or of silver tubes

he·la cell \ˈhēlə-\ *n, usu cap H & 1st L* [after Henrietta *La*cks †1951 patient from whom the original cells were taken] : a cell of a continuously cultured strain isolated from a human uterine cervical carcinoma and used in biomedical research esp. to culture viruses

he·lic·i·ty \heˈlisəd·ē, hə-\ *n* -ES [*helic-* + *-ity*] **1** : the motion of a particle about an axis parallel to its direction of motion **2** : the component of the spin of a particle in its direction of motion measured in quantum units of spin **3 a** : the quality or state of being helical **b** : the amount or degree of helical curve

hel·i·co·bac·ter \ˈheləkōˌbaktər\ *n* [NL, fr. *helic-* + *-bacter*] **1** *cap* : a genus of bacteria formerly placed in the genus *Campylobacter* and including one (*H. pylori*) associated with gastritis and implicated as a causative agent of gastric and duodenal ulcers and gastric cancer **2** -s : any bacterium of the genus *Helicobacter*

he·li·o·sphere \ˈhēlēəˌsfi(ə)r, -ˌsfiə, -lēōˌ-\ *n* [ISV [1]*heli-* + *sphere*] : the region in space influenced by the sun; *specif* : the region over which the solar wind extends

heli·pad \ˈ==ˌ=\ *n* [[2]*heli-* + [1]*pad*] : HELIPORT

he·li–skiing \ˈhelə, ˈhēlə+\ *n* [[2]*heli-* + *skiing*] : downhill skiing on remote mountains reached by helicopter

helium–4 \ˈ===ˈ=\ *n* [*helium* + *4*, mass number of the isotope] : HELIUM

helium–3 \ˈ===ˈ=\ *n* [*helium* + *3*, mass number of the isotope] : the isotope of helium having the mass number three

hel·la·cious \ˌheˈlāshəs\ *adj* [[1]*hell* + *-acious* (as in *splendacious*)] **1** : exceptionally powerful or violent **2** : remarkably good **3** : extremely difficult **4** : extraordinarily large — **hel·la·cious·ly** \-lē\ *adv*

hell–raiser \ˈ=ˌ==\ *n* [fr. the phrase *raise hell*] : one given to wild, boisterous, or intemperate behavior — **hell–rais·ing** \ˈ=ˌ==\ *n or adj*

he·lo \ˈhē(ˌ)lō\ *n* -s [by shortening + alter.] : HELICOPTER

helper t cell *or* **helper cell** *n, usu cap T* : a T cell that participates in an immune response by recognizing a foreign antigen and secreting lymphokines to activate T cell and B cell proliferation and that is reduced to 20 percent or less of normal numbers in AIDS — called also *T-helper cell*; compare CYTOTOXIC T CELL *herein*, SUPPRESSOR T CELL *herein*

hem·adsorption \ˌhēm+\ *n* [*hem-* + *adsorption*] : adherence of red blood cells to the surface of something (as a virus or cell) — **hem·adsorbing** \"+\ *adj*

hemi·cho·lin·ium \ˌhemēkōˈlinēəm, -mə̇k-\ *n* -s [[1]*hemi-* + *choline* + *-ium*] : any of several blockers of the parasympathetic nervous system that interfere with the synthesis of acetylcholine

hemi·diaphragm \"+\ *n* [[1]*hemi-* + *diaphragm*] : one of the two lateral halves of the diaphragm separating the chest and abdominal cavities in mammals

hem·ing·way·esque \ˌhemiŋˌwāˈesk\ *adj, usu cap* [Ernest Miller *Hemingway* †1961 Am. writer + E [1]*-esque*] : of, relating to, or suggestive of Ernest Hemingway or his writings

hemi·pelagic \ˌhemē+\ *adj* [[1]*hemi-* + *pelagic*] : of, relating to, or comprising deposits or sediments containing the remains of pelagic organisms and material washed down from land

hemlock woolly adelgid *n* : a woolly adelgid (*Adelges tsugae*) of Formosa, Japan, and the northwestern U.S. that has been introduced into the eastern U.S. where it is a serious pest of the eastern hemlock — see WOOLLY ADELGID *herein*

he·mo·dialysis \ˌhēmō, ˌhemō+\ *n* [NL. fr. *hem-* + *dialysis*] : DIALYSIS a *herein*

hemolytic uremic syndrome *n* : any of a group of rare disorders that are characterized by hemolytic anemia caused by red blood cell fragmentation, thrombocytopenia, and varying degrees of kidney failure, that are precipitated by a variety of etiological factors (as infection with toxin-producing bacteria of the genera *Escherichia* or *Shigella*), and that occur esp. in young children

he·mo·phil·ic \ˌhēməˈfilik\ *n* [*hemophilic*, adj.] : HEMOPHILIAC

hemorrhage* *vt* : to lose rapidly and uncontrollably ⟨~ money⟩

hemorrhagic fever *n* : any of a diverse group of virus diseases (as Lassa fever and Ebola) that are usu. transmitted by arthropods or rodents and are characterized by a sudden onset, fever, aching, bleeding in the internal organs (as of the gastrointestinal tract), petechiae, and shock

hepatitis A *n* : INFECTIOUS HEPATITIS 1

hepatitis B *n* : SERUM HEPATITIS

hepatitis B surface antigen *n* : a protein that comprises the envelope of the virus causing hepatitis B and is found circulating in the blood plasma of infected individuals — called also *Australia antigen*

hepatitis C *n* : a hepatitis caused by a flavivirus that is usu. transmitted by parenteral means (as injection of an illicit drug, blood transfusion, or exposure to blood or blood products)

he·pa·to·biliary \hə̇ˌpad·ə, ˌhepəd·ō+\ *adj* [*hepat-* + *biliary*] : of, relating to, situated in or near, produced in, or affecting the liver and bile, bile ducts, and gallbladder ⟨~ disease⟩

he·pa·to·cyte \hə̇ˈpad·əˌsīt, ˈhepəd·ə-\ *n* -s [*hepat-* + *-cyte*] : any of the epithelial parenchymatous cells of the liver that secrete bile

hep·a·top·a·thy \ˌhepəˈtäpəthē\ *n* -ES [*hepat-* + *-pathy*] : an abnormal or diseased state of the liver

hep·a·to·tox·ic·i·ty \ˌhepəd·ō͵täkˈsisəd·ē\ *n* -ES [*hepatotoxic* + *-ity*] **1** : a state of toxic damage to the liver **2** : capacity to cause hepatotoxicity
hep·a·to·toxin \ˌhepəd·ō+\ *n* [*hepat-* + *toxin*] : a substance toxic to the liver
hep·tath·lon \hepˈtath(ə)län, -lən\ *n* -S [*hept-* + *-athlon* (as in *decathlon*)] : a seven-event athletic contest; *specif* : a composite contest for woman athletes that consists of the 100-meter hurdles, the high jump, the shot put, the 200-meter dash, the long jump, the javelin throw, and the 800-meter run
herb* *n, slang* : MARIJUANA
her·biv·o·ry \ˌ(h)ərˈbivərē, -ri\ *n* -ES [*herbivorous* + ²*-y*] : HERBIVORITY
heritability* *n* : the proportion of observed variation in a particular trait (as intelligence) that can be attributed to inherited genetic factors in contrast to environmental ones
heritage *adj* [*heritage*, n.] : of, relating to, or having historic significance ⟨a ~ building⟩; *also* : emphasizing the traditional or nostalgic ⟨~ foods⟩ ⟨~ tourism⟩
he·riz *var of* HEREZ
herky–jerky \ˈhərkēˈjərkē\ *adj* [redupl. of ¹*jerky*] : characterized by sudden, irregular, or unpredictable movement or style ⟨*herky-jerky* dancing⟩ ⟨a *herky-jerky* path⟩
her·ma·typ·ic \ˌhərməˈtipik\ *adj* [Gk *herma* prop, reef + E *typ-* (fr. Gk *typtein* to strike, coin) + *-ic* — more at TYPE] : building reefs ⟨~ corals⟩
her·mi·tian matrix \hərˈmishən-, erˈmēshən-\ *n, usu cap H* [Charles *Hermite* †1901 Fr. mathematician + E *-ian*] : a square matrix having the property that each pair of elements comprised of one in the *i*th row and *j*th column and the other in the *j*th row and *i*th column are conjugate complex numbers
herpes gen·i·tal·is \-ˌjenəˈtaləs\ *n* [NL, genital herpes] : GENITAL HERPES *herein*
herpesvirus \ˈ≈(ˌ)≈+\ *n* [NL, fr. *herpes* + *virus*] : any of a family (Herpesviridae) of DNA viruses (as cytomegalovirus or Epstein-Barr virus) that have a large capsid enveloped by glycoprotein and that include the causative agents of a number of diseases (as herpes simplex, chicken pox, and Marek's disease) characterized esp. by blisters or vesicles on the skin and mucous membranes and often by recurrence sometimes after a long period of latency
her·sto·ry \ˈhərst(ə)rē, ˈhəs-, -ri\ *n* -ES [blend of *her* and *history*] : HISTORY; *specif* : history considered or presented from a feminist viewpoint or with special attention to the experience of women
hertz·sprung–rus·sell diagram \ˈhertˌspru̇ŋˈrəsᵊl-\ *n, usu cap H&R* [after Ejnar *Hertzsprung* †1967 Dan. astronomer and Henry Norris *Russell* †1957 Am. astrophysicist] : SPECTRUM-LUMINOSITY DIAGRAM
he/she \ˈhēˈshē; ˈhē·ər-; ˈhēˈslash-\ *pron* : he or she — used as a pronoun of common gender
het \ˈhet\ *n or adj* -S [by shortening] : HETEROSEXUAL
het·ero \ˈhed·ə(ˌ)rō\ *n* -S [by shortening] : HETEROSEXUAL — **hetero** *adj*
het·ero·atom \ˌhed·ərō+\ *n* [*heter-* + *atom*] : an atom other than carbon in the ring of a heterocyclic compound
het·ero·dimer \"+\ *n* [ISV *heter-* + *dimer*] : a protein composed of two polypeptide chains differing in composition in the order, number, or kind of their amino-acid residues — **het·ero·dimeric** \"+\ *adj*
het·ero·duplex \"+\ *n* [*heter-* + *duplex*] : a nucleic-acid molecule (as DNA) composed of two chains with each derived from a different parent molecule — **heteroduplex** *adj*
het·ero·glos·sia \ˌhed·ərōˈgläsēə, -ˈglōs-\ *n* -S [NL, fr. *heter-* + *-glossia*; trans. of Russ *raznorechie*] : a diversity of voices, styles of discourse, or points of view in a literary work and esp. a novel
het·ero·junction \ˌhed·ərō+\ *n* [*heter-* + *junction*] : an electrical junction between two different materials (as semiconductors)
heterologous* *adj* : characterized by cross-reactivity
het·ero·nym \ˈhed·ərəˌnim, -ə(ˌ)rōˌn-\ *n* -S [*heter-* + *-onym*] : one of two or more homographs that differ in pronunciation and meaning (as a *bass* voice and *bass*, a fish)
het·ero·polysaccharide \ˌhed·ərō+\ *n* [*heter-* + *polysaccharide*] : a polysaccharide consisting of more than one type of monosaccharide
het·ero·sex \"+\ *n* [by shortening] : HETEROSEXUALITY
het·ero·sexism \"+\ *n* [*heter-* + *sexism* (herein)] : discrimination or prejudice by heterosexuals against homosexuals — **het·ero·sexist** \"+\ *adj*
heuristic* *n* : a heuristic method or procedure
hex \ˈheks\ *adj or n* [by shortening] : HEXADECIMAL *herein*
hexa·decimal \ˌheksə+\ *adj* [alter. (influenced by *hexa-*) of *sexadecimal*] : of, relating to, utilizing, or being a system of numbers having 16 as a base — **hexadecimal** *n*
hex·os·a·min·i·dase \ˌhekˌsäsəˈminəˌdās, -āz\ *n* -S [*hexosamine* + ¹*-ide* + *-ase*] : either of two hydrolytic enzymes that catalyze the splitting off of a hexose from a ganglioside and are deficient in some metabolic diseases (as Tay-Sachs disease)
HGH *abbr* human growth hormone
hib \ˈhib, ˌā(ˌ)chīˈbē\ *n* -S *usu cap H* [*Hi-* (fr. the species name *Haemophilus influenzae*) + *Type B*] : a bacterial serotype of the genus *Haemophilus* (*H. influenzae* type B) that causes bacterial meningitis and pneumonia esp. in children
hiccup* *also* **hiccough*** *n* **1** : a slight irregularity, error, or malfunction ⟨a few ~*s* in the computer system⟩ ⟨whatever ~ in the genetic code . . . sets them off from their fellows —Karl Nyren⟩ **2 a** : a usu. short-lived interruption or disruption in a sequence, series, or process ⟨during that ~ in the nation's affairs, when it faced economic disaster —Stephen Fay⟩ **b** : a usu. small and short-lived upturn or downturn ⟨a ~ in the stock market⟩
hickey* *n* : a temporary red mark or bruise produced in lovemaking by biting and sucking the skin
hidden agenda *n* : an ulterior motive ⟨when someone comes in for a physical . . . there is often a *hidden agenda* —John McPhee⟩
hidden tax *n* : INDIRECT TAX
higgs boson \ˈhigz-\ *or* **higgs particle** *n, usu cap H* [after Peter W. *Higgs* *b*1929 Brit. physicist] : a hypothetical elementary particle that has zero spin and large mass and that is required by some gauge theories to account for the masses of other elementary particles
higgs field *n, usu cap H* : a hypothetical physical field that endows elementary particles with mass and is mediated by the Higgs boson
high* *n* : a state of elation or high spirits ⟨the ~ of victory⟩
high–concept \ˈ≈≈\ *adj* : having or exploiting elements (as fast action, glamour, or suspense) that appeal to a wide audience ⟨*high-concept* movies⟩
high–definition \ˌ≈ˌ≈ˈ≈\ *adj* : being or relating to a television system that has approximately twice as many scan lines per frame as a conventional system and a proportionally sharper image ⟨*high-definition* picture⟩ ⟨*high-definition* programming⟩
high–density lipoprotein \ˈ≈ˈ≈≈-\ *n* : HDL *herein*
high–end \ˈ≈ˈ≈\ *adj* **1** : UPSCALE *herein* ⟨*high-end* boutiques⟩ **2** : foremost in rank or quality ⟨*high-end* computers⟩ ⟨*high-end* systems⟩
high–energy \ˈ≈ˈ≈≈\ *adj* **1 a** : having such speed and kinetic energy as to exhibit relativistic departure from classical laws of motion — used esp. of elementary particles whose velocity has been imparted by an accelerator **b** : of or relating to high-energy particles ⟨a *high-energy* reaction⟩ **2** : yielding a relatively large amount of energy when undergoing hydrolysis ⟨*high-energy* phosphate bonds in ATP⟩ **3** : DYNAMIC ⟨*high-energy* music⟩ ⟨a *high-energy* barrage of tales —John Justice⟩
high–energy physics *n* : PARTICLE PHYSICS *herein*
high five *n* [fr. the five fingers of an outstretched hand] : a slapping of upraised right hands by two people (as in celebration) — **high–five** \ˈ≈ˈ≈\ *vb*
highflier* *n* **1** : a stock whose price rises much more rapidly than the market average **2** : a company whose stock is a highflier **3** : someone often willing to take risks in order to achieve success (as in business or politics)
high hat* *or* **hi–hat** \ˈ≈ˌ≈\ *n* : a pair of cymbals operated by a foot pedal
high–level* \ˈ≈ˈ≈≈\ *adj* **1** : of, relating to, or being a computer programming language (as BASIC or Pascal) which is very similar to a natural language (as English) and in which each statement is translated by a compiler usu. into several machine-language instructions **2** : relating to or being nuclear waste that contains highly concentrated radioactive components which are extremely hazardous to the environment
highlight* *vt* : to select or cause (as text or an icon) to be displayed in a way that stands out (as by being of a different color) from other objects on a computer screen esp. prior to editing, movement, or deletion
high·light·er \ˈhīˌlīd·ə(r)\ *n* -S **1** : a cosmetic for highlighting facial features **2** : a pen with a broad felt tip and brightly colored transparent ink for marking selected passages in a text
high–performance liquid chromatography *n* : liquid chromatography in which the degree of separation is increased by forcing a solvent under pressure through a densely packed adsorbent — abbr. *HPLC*; called also *high-pressure liquid chromatography*
¹**high–rise** \ˈ≈ˈ≈\ *adj* **1** : being multistory and equipped with elevators ⟨*high-rise* buildings⟩ **2** : of, relating to, or characterized by high-rise buildings ⟨a *high-rise* district⟩ **3 a** : of, relating to, or being extra-long bicycle handlebars **b** : being a bicycle equipped with high-rise handlebars
²**high–rise** \"\ *n* : a high-rise building
high–riser \-ə(r)\ *n* -S [¹*high-rise* (herein) + ²*-er*] **1** : HIGH-RISE *herein* **2** : a high-rise bicycle
high tech \ˈhīˈtek\ *n* **1 a** : HIGH TECHNOLOGY *herein* **b** : one employing high technology ⟨industry after industry, from agriculture to *high tech*, has felt the impact —C.C.Garvin, Jr.⟩ **2** : a style of interior design featuring industrial products, materials, or designs — **high–tech** \ˈ≈ˈ≈\ *adj*
high technology *n* : technology involving the production or use of advanced or sophisticated methods, materials, or devices esp. in the fields of electronics and computers
high–ticket \ˈ≈ˈ≈≈\ *adj* [¹*ticket* (price tag)] : EXPENSIVE 3
high–top \ˈ≈ˌ≈\ *adj* : extending up over the ankle ⟨*high-top* sneakers⟩ — **high–top** \ˈ≈ˌ≈\ *n*
high–voltage \ˈ≈ˈ≈≈\ *adj* : marked by great energy : ELECTRIC, DYNAMIC ⟨a *high-voltage* performance⟩
high–wire \ˈ≈ˌ≈(ə)\ *adj* [*high wire*, n.] **1** : involving great risk ⟨a financial *high-wire* act⟩ **2** : DARING ⟨*high-wire* prose⟩
hi·jack \ˈhīˌjak\ *n* -S [*hijack*, v.] : an instance of hijacking
hil·bert space \ˈhilbərt-\ *n, usu cap H* [after David *Hilbert* †1943 Ger. mathematician] : a vector space for which a scalar product is defined and in which every Cauchy sequence composed of elements in the space converges to a limit in the space
himalayan* *n, usu cap* : any of a breed of domestic cats developed by crossing the Persian and the Siamese and having the stocky build and long thick coat of the former and the blue eyes and coat pattern of the latter
him/her \ˈhimˈhər, ˈhimər-, ˈhimˈslash-\ *pron, objective case of* HE/SHE *herein*
hindu–arabic \ˈ≈≈ˈ≈≈\ *adj, usu cap H&A* : relating to, being, or composed of Arabic numerals
hip* *n* [⁸*hip*] : HIPNESS *herein*
hip *vt* **hipped; hipped; hipping; hips** [⁸*hip*] : to make aware : TELL, INFORM
hip* *adj* : very fashionable : TRENDY *herein* ⟨the *hippest* nightclub in town⟩ ⟨~ sportswear⟩
hip–hop \ˈhipˌhäp\ *n* [perh. fr. ⁸*hip* + ¹*hop*] **1** : a subculture esp. of inner-city youths whose amusements include rap music, graffiti, and break dancing **2** : the stylized rhythmic music that commonly accompanies rap; *also* : rap together with this music — **hip–hop** \ˈ≈ˌ≈\ *adj*
hip–hop·per \ˈ≈ˌ≈ə(r)\ *n* : a devotee of hip-hop music and culture; *also* : a performer of hip-hop
hip–huggers \ˈ≈ˌ≈≈\ *n pl* : low-slung usu. close-fitting trousers that rest on the hips
hip·ness \ˈhipnəs\ *n* -ES : the quality or state of being hip
hip·pie *or* **hip·py** \ˈhipē\ *n, pl* **hippies** [⁸*hip* + *-ie*] : a usu. young person who rejects the mores of established society and adheres to a nonviolent ethic; *broadly* : a long-haired unconventionally dressed young person — **hip·pie·dom** \-pēdəm, -pid-\ *n* -S
hippie–dippie *or* **hippy–dippy** *also* **hippie–dippy** \ˈ≈≈ˈ≈≈\ *adj* [*hippie* (herein) + *dippy*] : of, relating to, or reflecting the far-out styles and values of hippies
hip–pocket \ˈ≈ˈ≈≈\ *adj* [²*hip* + *pocket*] : of small size or scope
hip·ster·ism \ˈhipstəˌrizəm\ *n* -S **1** : HIPNESS *herein* **2** : the way of life characteristic of hipsters
hire* *n* : one who is hired ⟨met the new ~*s*⟩
hired gun *n* : an expert hired to do a specific and often ethically dubious job ⟨a *hired gun* whose opinion was for sale to the highest bidder⟩
hispanic* *adj, usu cap* : of, relating to, or being a person of Latin-American descent living in the U.S. and esp. one of Cuban, Mexican, or Puerto Rican origin
his·pan·ic \(ˈ)hiˈspanik\ *n* -S *usu cap* [*hispanic*, adj.] : an American of Spanish or esp. Latin-American descent
his·ti·di·ne·mia \ˌhistədəˈnēmēə\ *n* -S [NL, fr. ISV *histidine* + NL *-emia*] : a recessive autosomal metabolic defect that results in an excess amount of histidine in the blood and urine due to a deficiency of histidase — **his·ti·di·ne·mic** \ˌ≈≈≈ˈ≈mik\ *adj*
his·to·compatibility \ˌhi(ˌ)stō+\ *n* [*hist-* + *compatibility*] : a state of mutual tolerance between tissues that allows them to be grafted effectively — see MAJOR HISTOCOMPATIBILITY COMPLEX *herein* — **his·to·compatible** \"+\ *adj*
histocompatibility antigen *n* : any of the antigenic glycoproteins on the surface membranes of cells that enable the body's immune system to recognize a cell as native or foreign and that are determined by the major histocompatibility complex
his·to·incompatibility \"+\ *n* [*hist-* + *incompatibility*] : a state of mutual intolerance between tissues (as of a fetus and its mother or a graft and its host) that normally leads to reaction against or rejection of one by the other — **his·to·incompatible** \"+\ *adj*
his·to·physiological \"+\ *or* **his·to·physiologic** \"+\ *adj* : of or relating to histophysiology
history* *n* **1** : an established record ⟨a prisoner with a ~ of violence⟩ **2** : one that is finished or done for : one consigned or belonging to the past ⟨the winning streak was ~⟩ ⟨you're ~⟩
hit* *vb* ~ *vt* : IMPOSE, LEVY ⟨~ him with a fine⟩ — **hit it big** : to achieve great success — **hit on** : to make esp. sexual overtures to : come on to — **hit the fan** : to have a major usu. undesirable impact — **hit the ground running** : to begin or proceed quickly, energetically, or effectively — **hit the wall 1** : to reach the point of physical exhaustion during strenuous activity **2** : to reach a limiting point or situation at which progress or success ceases
hit* *n* **1** : a quantity of a narcotic drug ingested at one time **2** : a premeditated murder usu. committed by a member of a crime syndicate **3** : an instance of connecting to a particular Website ⟨over a million ~*s* per day⟩
hitch·cock·ian \(ˈ)hichˈkäkēən, -kyən\ *adj, usu cap* [Alfred Joseph *Hitchcock* †1980 Am. (Eng.-born) motion-picture director + E *-ian*] : of, relating to, or suggestive of the cinematic style or technique of Alfred Hitchcock
hitchhike* *vi* : to be carried or transported by chance or unintentionally ⟨destructive insects *hitchhiking* on ships⟩
hi–tech *var of* HIGH-TECH
hit list \ˈ≈ˌ≈\ *n* [*hit* (herein)] : a list of persons or programs to be opposed or eliminated; *broadly* : a list of those targeted for special attention or treatment
hit man *n* [*hit* (herein)] **1** : a professional assassin who works for a crime syndicate **2** : HATCHET MAN
HIV \ˌā(ˌ)chīˈvē\ *n* -S [*h*uman *i*mmunodeficiency *v*irus] : any of several retroviruses (genus *Lentivirus*) and esp. HIV-1 that infect and destroy helper T cells of the immune system causing the marked reduction in their numbers that is diagnostic of AIDS — called also *AIDS virus, human immunodeficiency virus*
hive off* *vb* ~ *vt chiefly Brit* : to make separate: as **a** : to remove from a group ⟨*hived off* a number of girls for special treatment —Barry Hill⟩ **b** : to assign (as assets or responsibilities) to another : relinquish control of ⟨administrative responsibilities . . . have been *hived off* to ad hoc agencies —A.H.Hanson & Malcolm Walles⟩ **c** : to spin off
HIV–1 \ˌā(ˌ)chīˌvēˈwən\ *n* : a retrovirus (genus *Lentivirus*) that is the most prevalent HIV — called also *HTLV-III, LAV*
HIV–2 \-ˈtü\ *n* : a retrovirus (genus *Lentivirus*) that causes AIDS esp. in West Africa, that is closely related in structure to SIV of monkeys and may have crossed over to humans, and that is less virulent and has a longer incubation period than HIV-1
hiz·zon·er \hiˈzänə(r)\ *n, often cap* [alter. of *his honor*] — used as a title for a mayor
HLA \ˌā(ˌ)chelˈā\ *n* -S *often attrib* [*h*uman *l*eukocyte *a*ntigen] **1** : the major histocompatibility complex in humans **2** : a genetic locus, gene, or antigen of the major histocompatibility complex — often used with one or more letters to designate a locus or with such letters and a number to designate an allele at the locus or the antigen of the major histocompatibility complex corresponding to the locus and allele
HMMWV *abbr* high mobility multipurpose wheeled vehicle
HMO \ˌā(ˌ)chemˈō\ *n* -S [*h*ealth *m*aintenance *o*rganization] : an organization that provides comprehensive health care to voluntarily enrolled individuals and families in a particular geographic area by member physicians with limited referral to outside specialists and that is financed by fixed periodic payments determined in advance — compare PPO *herein*
hmong \ˈməŋ\ *n, pl* **hmong** *cap* : MIAO
hoa·gie *also* **hoa·gy** \ˈhōgē\ *n, pl* **hoagies** [origin unknown] : GRINDER 6
hoax·er \ˈ≈ə(r)\ *n* -S : a person who perpetrates a hoax
hobo* *also* **hobo bag** *n* : a large shoulder bag shaped like a pouch
ho·dad \ˈhōˌdad\ *n* -S [origin unknown] : a nonsurfer who frequents surfing beaches and pretends to be a surfer
hog heaven *n* : an extremely satisfying state or situation : FAT CITY *herein* ⟨putting both customers and stockholders in *hog heaven* —Murray Sayle⟩
hoi·sin sauce \ˈhȯiˈs(h)in-\ *n* [part trans. of Chin (Cant) *hóisīn-jeung* seafood sauce] : a thick reddish sauce of soybeans, spices, and garlic used in oriental cookery
hold* *n* : a delay in a countdown (as in launching a missile) — **on hold 1** : into or in a state of interruption during a telephone call that occurs when one party switches to another line without disconnecting the other party **2** : into or in a state or period of indefinite suspension ⟨put our plans *on hold*⟩
holding pattern *n* **1** : a usu. oval course flown (as over an airport) by aircraft awaiting clearance esp. to land **2** : a state of waiting or suspended activity or progress
ho·lid·ic \häˈlidik, hōˈ-\ *adj* [*hol-* + *-idic* (as in *meridic* — herein)] : having the active constituents chemically defined ⟨~ diets⟩ — compare MERIDIC *herein*, OLIGIDIC *herein*
holism* *n* : a holistic study or method of treatment
holistic* *adj* : relating to or concerned with wholes or with complete systems rather than with the analysis of, treatment of, or dissection into parts ⟨~ medicine⟩ ⟨~ ecology⟩
hol·ler·ith \ˈhäləˌrith\ *n* -S *usu cap* [after Herman *Hollerith* †1929 Am. engineer] : a code for representing alphanumeric information on punch cards — called also *Hollerith code*
hollerith card *n, usu cap H* : PUNCH CARD
holocaust* *n* **1** : a great slaughter; *specif, often cap* : a genocidal slaughter (as of European Jews by the Nazis during World War II) **2** : DISASTER ⟨turn an ordinary matrimonial civil war into an explosive do-or-die end-of-the-world ~ —J.A.Ornstein⟩ — **holo·caus·tal** \ˌhäləˈkȯstᵊl, ˌhōl- *also* ˌhȯl- *or* -ˈkäst-\ *adj*
ho·lo·gram \ˈhäləˌgram, ˈhōl-\ *n* -S [*hol-* + *-gram*] : a three-dimensional picture that is made on a photographic film or plate without the use of a camera, that consists of an interference pattern produced by a split coherent beam of radiation and esp. light, and that for viewing is usu. illuminated with coherent light from behind
ho·lo·graph \-af\ *n* -S [*hol-* + *-graph*] : HOLOGRAM *herein*
ho·log·ra·phy \həˈlägrəfē, hō-\ *n* -ES [*hol-* + *-graphy*] : the process of making or using a hologram — **holograph** *vt* -ED/-ING/-S — **ho·log·ra·pher** \hōˈlägrəfər\ *n* — **ho·lo·graph·ic** \ˌ≈≈ˈ≈ik\ *adj* — **ho·lo·graph·i·cal·ly** \-k(ə)lē\ *adv*
ho·lo·mor·phic \ˌhäləˈmȯrfik, ˌhäl-\ *adj* [*hol-* + *-morphic*] *of a function of a complex variable* : ANALYTIC 2 *herein*
hom-* *or* **homo-*** *comb form* : homosexual ⟨*homo*phobia⟩
home-* *or* **homeo-*** *comb form* : containing homeotic genes or their products ⟨*homeo*domain⟩
homeboy \ˈ≈ˌ≈\ *n* **1** : a boy or man from one's neighborhood, hometown, or region — often used as a familiar form of address esp. among inner-city youths; *broadly* : an inner-city youth **2** : a fellow member of a youth gang
homebuilt \ˈ≈ˈ≈\ *adj* : HOMEMADE 1 ⟨~ aircraft⟩ — **homebuilt** \"\ *n*
home computer *n* : a personal computer used in the home
home free *adv* : in a comfortable situation usu. after considerable effort
homegirl \ˈ≈ˌ≈\ *n* **1** : a girl or woman from one's neighborhood, hometown, or region; *broadly* : an inner-city girl or woman **2** : a girl or woman who is a member of one's peer group
homeland* *n* : a state or area set aside to be a state for a people of a particular national, cultural, or racial origin; *specif* : BANTUSTAN *herein*
ho·meo·box \ˈhōmēəˌbäks, -mēō-\ *n* [*home-* (herein) + ²*box*] : a short usu. highly conserved DNA sequence in various genes and esp. homeotic genes that encodes a homeodomain
ho·meo·do·main \ˈhōmēōdōˌmān\ *n* [*home-* (herein) + *domain*] : a domain in a protein that is encoded for by a homeobox, that consists of about 60 amino acid residues which are usu. similar from one such domain to another, and that recognizes and binds to specific DNA sequences in genes regulated by the homeotic gene
homeotic gene *n* : a gene that produces a usu. major shift in the developmental fate of an organ or body part esp. to a homologous organ or part normally found elsewhere in the organism
home page *n* : the page typically encountered first at a Web site and usu. containing hyperlinks to its other pages
homeschool \ˈ≈ˌ≈\ *vi* : to teach school subjects to one's children at home ~ *vt* : to teach (one's children) at home
homeschoo·ler \ˈ≈ˌ≈(r)\ *n* **1** : one that homeschools **2** : a child who is homeschooled
home screen *n* : TELEVISION
home stand *n* : a series of consecutive baseball games played at a team's home field
homestay \ˈ≈ˌ≈\ *n* : a period during which a visiting foreign student lives in the home of a host family; *also* : a stay at a residence by a traveler
home video *n* **1** : prerecorded videocassettes or videodiscs marketed for home viewing **2** : a homemade movie usu. filmed using a camcorder
homey *or* **homie** \ˈhōmē\ *n, pl* **homies**; *or* **homeys** [*homeboy* (herein) + *-ie*] **1** : one who is from one's neighborhood, hometown, or region — often used as a familiar form of address esp. among inner-city youths **2** : a fellow member of a youth gang
hom·i·ni·za·tion \ˌhämənəˈzāshən, -ˌnī-\ *n* -S [F *hominisation*, fr. (*s'*)*hominiser* to acquire human characteristics, tr. L *homin-, homo* man, human being + F *-iser* -ize — more at HOMAGE] **1** : the evolutionary development of human characteristics that differentiate man from his primate ancestors **2** : the process of altering the environment and adapting it to the uses of human beings

hom·i·nized \¦hämə,nīzd\ *adj* [F *hominisé*, past part. of *(s')hominiser*] : characterized by hominization

hommos *var of* HUMMUS *herein*

homo-* — see HOM- *herein*

ho·mo·cys·ti·nu·ria \,hōmə,sistə'n(y)u̇rēə, ,häm-\ *n* [NL, fr. E *homocystine* + NL *-uria*] : a metabolic disorder inherited as a recessive autosomal trait, caused by deficiency of an enzyme important in the metabolism of homocystine with resulting accumulation of homocystine in the body and its excretion in the urine, and characterized typically by mental retardation, dislocation of the crystalline lenses, skeletal abnormalities, and thromboembolic disease

ho·moe·ol·og·ous \,hōmē'äləgəs, ,häm-\ *adj* [*home-* + *-logous* (as in *homologous*)] : of similar genetic constitution — used of chromosomes believed to have been completely homologous in an ancestral form — **ho·moeo·logue** *or* **ho·moeo·log** \'==ə,lȯg, -,läg\ *n* -s

homo erec·tus \-ə'rektəs\ *n, usu cap H* [NL, lit., erect human being] : an extinct large-brained hominid of the genus *Homo* (*H. erectus*) that is known from fossil remains in Africa, Europe, and Asia, is estimated to have flourished from 1.6 million years ago to 250,000 years ago, is thought to be the first hominid to master fire and inhabit caves, and is believed to be the immediate ancestor of modern man

homogeneity* *n* : the state of having identical distribution functions or values ⟨a test for ~ of variances⟩

ho·mo ha·bi·lis \¦hō(,)mō'habələs\ *n, usu cap 1st H* [NL, lit., skillful human] : an extinct hominid of the genus *Homo* (*H. habilis*) that is known from sub-Saharan fossil remains associated with crude stone tools, is estimated to have flourished 1.6 to 2 million years ago, and is believed to be the predecessor of Homo erectus

homology* *n* : similarity of nucleotide or amino acid sequence (as in nucleic acids or proteins)

homomorphism* *n* : a mapping of a mathematical set (as a group, ring, or vector space) on which one or more operations are defined into or onto another set or itself on which one or more corresponding operations are defined in such a way that the result obtained by applying the operations to elements of the first set is mapped onto the result obtained by applying the corresponding operations to their respective images in the second set

ho·mo·phile \'hōmə,fīl\ *adj* [*hom-* + *-phile*] : GAY 8 — **homophile** *n* -s

ho·mo·phobe \¦hōmə¦fōb, -mō-\ *n* -s [*hom-* (herein) + *-phobe*] : one who hates or fears homosexuals

ho·mo·phobia \"+\ *n* [*hom-* (herein) + *phobia*] : irrational fear of, aversion to, or discrimination against homosexuality or homosexuals — **ho·mo·phobic** \"+\ *adj*

homopolar* *adj* : having conductors that move through a unidirectional magnetic flux so that direct current can be used or produced without the use of commutators ⟨a ~ generator⟩

ho·mo·sexy \"+\ *n* [by shortening] : HOMOSEXUALITY

ho·mo·social \"+\ *adj* [*hom-* + ¹*social*] : of, relating to, or involving social relationships between persons of the same sex and esp. between men — **homosociality** \"+\ *n* -ES

hon·cho \'hän(,)chō\ *n* -s [Jap *hanchō* squad leader, fr. *han* squad + *chō* head, chief] : BOSS, LEADER; *also* : HOTSHOT ⟨every other slick guitar ~ in the city was looking to jam with you —Tim Cahill⟩

hone in *vi* [alter. of *home in*] : to move toward or focus attention on an objective — usu. used with *on* ⟨a missile *honing in* on its target —Bob Greene⟩ ⟨*hones in* on the plights and victories of the common man —Lisa Russell⟩

honest broker *n* : a neutral mediator

honey bucket *n* : a bucket for collecting human excrement

honey wagon *n* **1** : a vehicle for transporting human excrement **2** : a portable outdoor toilet

hon·ky *or* **hon·kie** *also* **hon·key** \'hȯŋkē, 'häŋ-, -ki\ *n, pl* **honkies** [prob. alter. of *hunky*] : a white person — usu. used disparagingly

honky–tonk* *n* **1** : a district marked by places of cheap entertainment **2** : country music that has a heavy beat and lyrics dealing usu. with vice or misfortune

hood *or* **'hood** \'hu̇d\ *n* -s [short for *neighborhood*] : a neighborhood and esp. an inner-city neighborhood; *also* : INNER CITY *herein*

hook* *n* **1** : HOOK SHOT **2** : a device esp. in music or writing that catches the attention ⟨trick is to find some sonic ~ that will galvanize dancers on the floor —*Newsweek*⟩ **3** : a selling point or marketing scheme ⟨needed to find a ~ to raise money for the project⟩

hook, line and sinker *adv* : without hesitation or reservation : COMPLETELY

hook up* *vi* : to become associates esp. in a working or social relationship ⟨moved here and *hooked up* with three musicians from the city —Robert Palmer⟩

hoop* *n* : BASKETBALL 1 ⟨college ~⟩ ⟨a ~ fan⟩ — usu. used in pl.

hoot* *n* : something or someone amusing

hootch *or* **hooch** \'hüch\ *n* [shortening of earlier *hoochie*, modif. of Jap *uchi* house] : a thatched hut esp. in Vietnam; *broadly* : HOUSE, DWELLING, BARRACKS

hooter* *n* : BREAST — often considered vulgar

hoo·ver \'hüvə(r)\ *vb* -ED/-ING/-S [fr. *Hoover*, a trademark] *vt, Brit* : to clean with or as if with a vacuum cleaner ~ *vi, Brit* : ³VACUUM *vi* 2

hopefully* *adv* : it is hoped ⟨procedures which would ~ lead to the resolution of the . . . issue —*Amer. Assoc. of Univ. Prof. Bull.*⟩

hormone replacement therapy *n* : the administration of estrogen along with a synthetic progestin to ameliorate the symptoms of menopause and reduce the risk of postmenopausal osteoporosis and heart disease

horror show *n* : something troubling or difficult to deal with or watch ⟨last year's *horror show*, when computer systems failed —Alex Taylor III⟩

horror story *n* : an account of an unsettling or unfortunate occurrence ⟨heard *horror stories* about recent layoffs⟩; *broadly* : something unsettling or unfortunate ⟨his childhood was a *horror story*⟩

horsepower* *n* : effective power ⟨intellectual ~⟩ ⟨computing ~⟩

horse race *n* : a close contest (as in politics)

horse's ass *n* : a stupid or incompetent person : BLOCKHEAD — often considered vulgar

ho scale \(')ā¦chō-\ *n, usu cap H&O* [fr. *HO gage*] : a scale of 3.5 millimeters to one foot used esp. for model toys (as automobiles or trains)

hose* *vt* **1** *slang* : to deprive of something due or expected : TRICK, CHEAT **2** *slang* : to shoot with continuous automatic weapons fire

hosing \'hōziŋ\ *n* -s [fr. gerund of *hose* (herein)] : BEATING, DEFEAT ⟨took a ~ in the stock market⟩

hospice* *n* : a facility or program designed to provide a caring environment for meeting the physical and emotional needs of the terminally ill

hospitality suite *n* : a room or suite esp. in a hotel set aside as a place for socializing usu. in connection with a business meeting or convention

host* *n* **1** : the computer on which a program runs or to which a peripheral (as a monitor) is connected **2** : a computer that controls communications in a network or that administers a database; *also* : SERVER *herein*

hostage* *n* : one that is involuntarily controlled by an outside influence

host plant *n* : a plant upon which an organism (as an insect or mildew) lodges and subsists

hot* *adj* **1** : being full of detail and information and requiring little or no involvement of the listener, viewer, or reader ⟨a ~ medium like radio —H.M.McLuhan⟩ **2** : SEXY

hot* *n* **hots** *pl* : strong sexual desire — used with *the* ⟨about a young girl . . . with the ~s for gypsy-dark men —H.C.Veit⟩

hot button *n* : an emotional and usu. controversial issue or concern that triggers immediate intense reaction

hot comb *n* : a metal comb usu. electrically heated for straightening or styling the hair

hot damn *interj* — usu. used to express pleasant surprise ⟨*hot damn*, that was a good audience out there —Steve Miller⟩

hot dog* *n* : one that hotdogs; *also* : SHOW-OFF

hot·dog \'hät,dȯg *sometimes* -däg\ *vb* **hot·dogged; hot·dogged; hot·dog·ging; hot·dogs** *vi* : to perform in a conspicuous or often ostentatious manner; *esp* : to perform fancy stunts and maneuvers (as when surfing or skiing) ~ *vt* : to perform (as in a sport) in a conspicuous often ostentatious manner — **hot·dog·ger** *n* -s

hotel china *n* [so called fr. its capacity to withstand the hard use typically met with in hotels] : a high-fired well-vitrified American ceramic ware approaching hard-paste porcelain in composition

hot key *n* : a key or combination of keys on a computer keyboard programmed to perform a specific function when pressed

hot line *n* **1** : a direct line of communication between heads of government; *broadly* : any direct line of communication (as between an executive and employees) **2** : a usu. toll-free telephone service available to the public for some specific purpose: as **a** : one by which callers can talk confidentially about personal problems to a sympathetic listener ⟨a suicide *hot line*⟩ **b** : one by which callers can obtain free advice ⟨a legal *hot line*⟩ ⟨a grammar *hot line*⟩ **c** : one by which a citizen can report illegal activities (as to a government agency)

hot pants* *n pl* : very short shorts

hot shit *n* : HOTSHOT; *also* : HOT STUFF — usu. considered vulgar

hot shoe *n* : a receptacle on a camera that provides a point of attachment and electrical contact for an electronic flash lamp

hot spot* *n* **1** : a place in the upper mantle of the earth at which hot magma from the lower mantle upwells to melt through the crust usu. in the interior of a tectonic plate to form volcanic features; *also* : a place in the crust overlying a hot spot **2** : an area of political, military, or civil unrest usu. considered dangerous

hot ticket *n* : someone or something very popular : RAGE

hot tub *n* : a large usu. wooden tub filled with hot water in which bathers soak and usu. socialize; *also* : such a tub with a whirlpool device

hot–wire \'=¦=\ *vt* : to short-circuit the wires of (an automotive vehicle or its ignition system) in order to start the engine without using a key

house* *n* [prob. fr. the *Warehouse*, Chicago dance club opened in 1977 that played such music] : a type of dance music mixed by a disc jockey that features overdubbing with a heavy repetitive drumbeat and repeated electronic melody lines

househusband \'=¦==\ *n* [*housewife* + *husband*] : a husband who does housekeeping usu. while his wife earns the family income

house nigger *n* : UNCLE TOM — usu. used disparagingly

house sitter *n* : a person who occupies a dwelling to provide security and maintenance while the tenant is away — **house–sit** \'=¦=\ *vi* — **house–sitting** \'=¦==\ *n*

hovercraft \'==,=\ *n* [¹*hover* + ¹*craft*] : AIR-CUSHION VEHICLE *herein*

how–to *n, pl* **how–tos** *or* **how–to's** : a practical method or instruction; *also* : something (as a book) that provides such instruction

HPLC *abbr* high performance liquid chromatography *herein*

Hs *symbol* hassium *herein*

HTLV \¦āch,tē(,)el¦vē\ *n* -s [*h*uman *T*-cell *l*eukemia *v*irus] : any of several retroviruses that include one associated with adult T-cell leukemia and a progressive paralyzing myelopathy and that formerly included the original strain of the AIDS virus — often used with a number or Roman numeral to indicate the type; called also *human T-cell leukemia virus*

HTLV–III \-'thrē\ *n* -s : HIV-1 *herein*

HTML \,āch(,)tē(,)em'el\ *abbr or n* -s [*h*yper*t*ext *m*arkup *l*anguage] : a markup language usu. used to create World Wide Web documents incorporating text, graphics, sound, video, and hyperlinks

http *abbr* hypertext transfer protocol

H_2 antagonist \'āch'tü-\ *or* **H_2 blocker** *also* **H_2 receptor antagonist** *n* : a drug (as cimetidine or ranitidine) that reduces or inhibits the secretion of gastric acid by binding competitively with histamine to H_2 receptors on cell membranes

H_2 receptor *also* **H_2 histamine receptor** *n* [*h*istamine] : a receptor for histamine on cell membranes that modulates the stimulation of heart rate and the secretion of gastric acid — see H_2 ANTAGONIST *herein*

hub* *n* : an airport or city through which an airline routes most of its traffic

hub–and–spoke \¦==¦=\ *adj* : being or relating to a system of routing air traffic in which a major airport serves as a central point for coordinating flights to and from other airports

hub·ble constant \¦həbəl-\ *n, usu cap H* [after Edwin P. *Hubble* †1953 Am. astronomer] : a proportionality constant indicative of the rate of expansion of the universe that is used in relating the apparent velocity of recession of a distant galaxy and its distance

hu·go \'(h)yügō\ *n* -s *usu cap* [after *Hugo* Gernsback †1967 Am. (Luxembourg-born) author, inventor, and publisher] : any of several trophies awarded annually by a professional organization for notable achievement in science-fiction writing

human chorionic gonadotropin *n* : a glycoprotein hormone similar in structure to luteinizing hormone that is secreted by the placenta during early pregnancy to maintain corpus luteum function and stimulate placental progesterone production, is found in the urine and blood serum of pregnant women, is commonly tested for as an indicator of pregnancy, is used medically to induce ovulation and to treat male hypogonadism and cryptorchidism, and is produced in certain cancers (as of the testes) — abbr. *HCG*

human ecology* *n* : the ecology of human beings and of human communities and populations esp. as concerned with preservation of environmental quality (as of air or water) through application of conservation and civil engineering practices

human factors *n pl but sing in constr* : ERGONOMICS — called also *human factors engineering*

human growth hormone *n* : the naturally occurring growth hormone of humans or a genetically engineered form that is used to treat children with growth hormone deficiencies and has been used esp. by athletes to increase muscle mass

human immunodeficiency virus *n* : HIV *herein*

human leukocyte antigen *n* : any of various proteins that are encoded by genes of the major histocompatibility complex in humans and are found on the surface of many cell types (as white blood cells); *broadly* : HLA 2 *herein*

human papillomavirus *n* : any of numerous papillomaviruses that cause various human warts (as the common warts of the hands, plantar warts, and genital warts) including some associated with the production of cervical cancer

human resources *n pl* : PERSONNEL 2 ⟨director of *human resources*⟩

human rights *n pl, often attrib* : rights (as freedom from unlawful imprisonment, torture, and execution) regarded as belonging fundamentally to all persons

human t–cell leukemia virus \-'tē,sel-\ *n, usu cap T* : HTLV *herein*

human t–cell lym·pho·tro·pic virus \-¦limfō¦träpik-, -¦trōp-\ *also* **human t–lymphotropic virus** \-'tē¦limfō¦==-\ *n, usu cap T* : HTLV *herein*

hum·mus \'həməs, 'hu̇-\ *also* **hom·mos** \'həm-, 'häm-\ *n* [Ar *ḥummuṣ* chick-pea] : a paste of pureed chick-peas usu. mixed with sesame oil or sesame paste and eaten as a dip or sandwich spread

hu·mon·gous \(h)yü'məŋgəs, -'mäŋ-\ *also* **hu·mun·gous** \-'məŋ-\ *adj* [perh. alter. of *huge* + *monstrous*] *slang* : being very large in size or scope : HUGE

humoral* *adj* : relating to or being the part of immunity or the immune response that involves antibodies secreted by B cells and circulating in bodily fluids — compare CELL-MEDIATED *herein*

Hum·vee \¦həm¦vē\ *trademark* — used for a military automotive vehicle

hu·nan \'hü'nän\ *or* **hunanese*** *adj, usu cap* [fr. *Hunan*, province of China] : of, relating to, or being a hot and spicy style of Chinese cooking

hundreds digit *n* : HUNDRED 4

hundreds place *n* : the place three to the left of the decimal point in a number expressed in the Arabic system of notation

hung \'həŋ\ *adj* [fr. past part. of ¹*hang*] : having a large penis — often considered vulgar

hunger* *n* — **from hunger** : very bad : PATHETIC ⟨they were strictly patchwork and strictly *from hunger* —A.J.Daley⟩

hung up* *adj* **1** : having a hang-up : ANXIOUS ⟨don't know why women have to be so *hung up* about age —Pauline Kael⟩ **2** : being much involved with: as **a** : INFATUATED ⟨they get *hung up* on some fellow here —Jeff Brown⟩ **b** : ENTHUSIASTIC ⟨people who are *hung up* on French Provincial —Walter Goodman⟩ **c** : PREOCCUPIED ⟨*hung up* on winning⟩

hunk* *n* : an attractive well-built man

hunker* *vi* [¹*hunker*] : to settle in or dig in for a sustained period — used with *down* ⟨~ down for a good long wait —*New Yorker*⟩

hunky \'=ē\ *adj* -ER/EST [*hunk* (herein) + ¹*-y*] : muscular and usu. attractive; *also* : having sex appeal ⟨he plays a ~ rancher⟩

huntboard \'=,=\ *n* [fr. its use at hunt breakfasts] : a piece of furniture similar to a sideboard but usu. taller, smaller, and simpler

hunter–gatherer \¦=¦==\ *n* : FOOD-GATHERER

hunting* *n* **1** : a periodic variation in speed of a synchronous electrical machine from that of the true synchronous speed **2** : a self-induced and undesirable oscillation of a variable above and below the desired value in an automatic control system **3** : a continuous attempt by an automatically controlled system to find a desired equilibrium condition

huntington's disease *n, usu cap H* : HUNTINGTON'S CHOREA

hutzpah *or* **hutzpa** *var of* CHUTZPAH *herein*

HVAC *abbr* heating, ventilation, and air-conditioning; heating, ventilating, and air-conditioning

hwyl \'hüil\ *n* -s [W, sail, sheet, journey, course, mood, fervor, fr. OW *huil*; akin to MIr *séol* sail, course, manner, and prob. to OE & ON *segl* sail — more at SAIL] *Brit* : FERVOR, EXCITEMENT

hyaline membrane disease *n* : RESPIRATORY DISTRESS SYNDROME *herein*

hybrid* *n* : something (as a power plant, vehicle, or electronic circuit) that has two different types of components performing essentially the same function — **hybrid*** *adj*

hybrid computer *n* : a computer system consisting of a combination of analog and digital computer systems

hy·bri·do·ma \,hī(,)brid'ōmə\ *n* -s [NL, fr. E *hybrid* + NL *-oma*] : a hybrid cell produced by the fusion of an antibody-producing lymphocyte with a tumor cell and used to continuously culture a specific monoclonal antibody

hy·dra·tase \'hīdrə,tās, -,drād-,ās, -āz\ *n* -s [*hydrate* + *-ase*] : any of several lyases that catalyze the hydration or dehydration of a carbon-oxygen bond

hy·dril·la \hī'drilə\ *n* -s [NL, prob. fr. L *Hydra* mythical water serpent killed by Hercules (fr. Gk) + NL *-illa* -illa — more at HYDRA] : a freshwater aquatic plant (*Hydrilla verticillata*) of the family Hydrocharitaceae native to Asia that resembles elodea and has small narrow serrated leaves with spines on the midrib undersurface that grow in whorls of three to eight around stems which become heavily branched near the water surface and that was introduced into Florida around 1960 for aquarium use and has since become a serious invasive weed

hy·dro·acoustic \¦hī(,)drō+\ *adj* [*hydr-* + *acoustic*] **1** : of or relating to the production of acoustic energy from the flow of fluids under pressure **2** : of or relating to the transmission of sound in water

hy·dro·biologist \"+\ *n* -s : a specialist in hydrobiology

hy·dro·chlorofluorocarbon \¦hīdrō+\ *n* [*hydr-* + *chlor* + *fluorocarbon*] : any of several simple gaseous compounds that contain carbon, chlorine, fluorine, and hydrogen that are used esp. in place of chlorofluorocarbons because they are believed to be less damaging to the ozone layer — compare HYDROFLUOROCARBON *herein*

hy·dro·chlo·ro·thi·a·zide \,hīdrə,klōrə'thīə,zīd\ *n* [*hydr-* + *chlor-* + *thiazide* (herein)] : a diuretic and antihypertensive drug $C_7H_8ClN_3O_4S_2$

hy·dro·crack \¦hī(,)drō+\ *vt* [*hydr-* + *crack*] : to crack (hydrocarbons) in the presence of hydrogen

hy·dro·cracker \"+\ *n* : an apparatus for hydrocracking

hy·dro·dy·nam·i·cist \,hīdrōdī'naməsəst\ *n* -s : one who specializes in hydrodynamics

hy·dro·fluorocarbon \¦hīdrō+\ *n* [*hydr-* + *fluorocarbon*] : any of several simple gaseous compounds that contain carbon, fluorine, and hydrogen that are used esp. in place of chlorofluorocarbons because they are believed to be less damaging to the ozone layer — compare HYDROCHLOROFLUOROCARBON *herein*

hydrofoil* *n* : a boat equipped with hydrofoils

hy·dro·gasification \¦hīdrō+\ *n* [*hydr-* + *gasification*] : the process of reacting hydrogen or a mixture of steam and hydrogen with coal at high temperature and high pressure so that the carbon in the coal reacts directly or indirectly to produce methane fuel — **hy·dro·gasifier** \"+\ *n*

hy·dro·magnetic \"+\ *adj* [*hydr-* + *magnetic*] : MAGNETOHYDRODYNAMIC

hy·dro·magnetics \"+\ *n pl but sing in constr* [*hydr-* + *magnetics*] : MAGNETOHYDRODYNAMICS

hydromagnetic wave *n* : a wave in an electrically conducting fluid (as a plasma) in a magnetic field

hy·dro·naut \'hīdrə,nȯt, -nät\ *n* -s [*hydr-* + *-naut* (as in *astronaut*)] : a member of the crew of a deep-sea vehicle (as a bathyscaphe) other than a submarine

hy·dro·nau·tics \(')hīdrə¦nȯd·iks\ *n pl but sing in constr* [*hydr-* + *-nautics* (as in *aeronautics*)] : the science of constructing and operating marine craft and instruments designed to explore the ocean environment

hy·dron·ic \hī'dränik\ *adj* [*hydr-* + *-onic* (as in *electronic*)] : of, relating to, or being a system of heating or cooling that involves transfer of heat by a circulating fluid (as water or vapor) in a closed system of pipes — **hy·dron·i·cal·ly** \-nək(ə)lē\ *adv*

hy·dron·ics \-niks\ *n pl but usu sing in constr* : a hydronic system

hydroplane* *vi, of a vehicle or tire* : to ride supported by a film of water on a wet surface when a critical speed is reached with a resultant loss of directional stability and braking effectiveness

hy·dro·skimmer \'hīdrō+\ *n* [*hydr-* + *skimmer*] : an air-cushion vehicle for use over water

hy·dro·space \"+,=\ *n* [*hydr-* + *space*] : the regions beneath the surface of the ocean

hydrothermal vent *n* : a fissure in the ocean floor near a midocean ridge that spews forth mineral-rich superheated water which provides the metabolic essentials (as sulfur) for nearby ecosystems containing hyperthermophilic chemosynthetic microorganisms

hy·dro·treat \"+,\ *vt* [*hydr-* + *treat*] : to subject to hydrogenation ⟨~ lube oil⟩ — **hy·dro·treat·er** *n*

hy·dro·trope \'hīdrə,trōp\ *n* -s [back-formation fr. *hydrotropic*] : a hydrotropic substance

hy·droxo·cobalamin \hī¦dräksə, -(,)sō+\ *n* [*hydroxo-* + *cobalamin*] : a member $C_{62}H_{89}CoN_{13}O_{15}P$ of the vitamin B_{12} group used in treating and preventing vitamin B_{12} deficiency

hy·drox·y·lase \hī'dräksə,lās, -,lāz\ *n* -s [*hydroxyl* + *-ase*] : any of a group of enzymes that catalyze oxidation reactions in which one of the two atoms of molecular oxygen is incorporated into the substrate and the other is used to oxidize NADH or NADPH

hy·droxy·lysine \hī¦dräksə+\ *n* [*hydroxy-* + *lysine*] : an amino acid $C_6H_{14}N_2O_3$ that is found esp. in collagen

hy·droxy·urea \(¦)hī,dräksē+\ *n* [*hydroxy-* + *urea*] : an antineoplastic drug $CH_4N_2O_2$ used esp. to treat melanoma, chronic myelogenous leukemia, and malignant tumors (as of the ovary or neck)

¹hype \ˈhīp\ *n* [origin unknown] **1** : DECEPTION, PUT-ON ⟨had come upon some way I could work a ~ on the penal authorities —Malcolm X⟩ **2** : PUBLICITY; *esp* : promotional publicity of an extravagant or contrived kind

²hype \ˈhīp\ *vt* -ED/-ING/-S [*hype*, n. (herein)] **1** : to put on : MISLEAD, DECEIVE **2** : PROMOTE, PUBLICIZE ⟨~ youth-oriented products to young people —Nancy McCarthy⟩

³hype \"\ *vt* -ED/-ING/-S [*hype*, n. (hypodermic injection)] **1** : STIMULATE, JAZZ 2a — usu. used with *up* ⟨his assignment is to ~ up the crowd —J.S.Radosta⟩ **2** : INCREASE ⟨tried to ~ sales with enticing offers⟩ — **hyped–up** \¦hīp¦dəp\ *adj*

hy·per \ˈhīpə(r)\ *adj* [*hyper-*] **1** : HIGH-STRUNG, EXCITABLE; *also* : highly excited **2** : extremely active

hyper-* *prefix* **1** : that is or exists in a space of more than three dimensions ⟨*hyper*cube⟩ ⟨*hyper*space⟩ **2** : bridging points within an entity (as a database or network) non-sequentially ⟨*hyper*link⟩ ⟨*hyper*text⟩

hyperactive *n* [*hyperactive*, adj.] : a hyperactive person

hy·per·activity \¦hīpər+\ *n* -ES : the state or condition of being hyperactive; *also* : ATTENTION DEFICIT DISORDER *herein*

hy·per·aldosteronism \"+\ *n* [*hyper-* + *aldosteronism* (herein)] : ALDOSTERONISM *herein*

hy·per·alimentation \"+\ *n* [*hyper-* + *alimentation*] : the intravenous administration of nutrients esp. to patients who cannot ingest food through the alimentary tract

hyperbaric* *adj* : of, relating to, or utilizing greater than normal pressure esp. of oxygen ⟨~ medicine⟩ ⟨~ chamber⟩ — **hy·per·bar·i·cal·ly** \¦hīpə(r)¦barək(ə)lē\ *adv*

hyperbolic* *adj* : of, relating to, or being a space in which more than one line parallel to a given line passes through a point ⟨~ geometry⟩

hy·per·charge \ˈhīpə(r)+,\ *n* [*hyper-* + ²*charge*] : a quantum characteristic of a closely related group of particles governed by the strong force that is represented by a number equal to twice the average value of the electric charge of the group

hy·per·complex \¦hīpə(r)+\ *adj* [*hyper-* + ¹*complex*] : of, relating to, or being a general form of number that can be expressed as a vector of *n* dimensions in the form $x_1e_1 + x_2e_2 + \ldots + x_ne_n$ where the coefficients $x_1, x_2, \ldots x_n$ range over a given number field and $e_1 = (e, 0, 0, \ldots 0), e_2 = (0, e, 0, \ldots 0), \ldots e_n = (0, 0, \ldots e)$ where *e* is the multiplicative identity of the field ⟨~ variable⟩

hy·per·cube \"+\ *n* [*hyper-* (herein) + ¹*cube*] **1** : a geometric figure in Euclidean space of *n* dimensions that is analogous to a cube in three dimensions in having 2^n vertices each of which is connected to *n* other vertices by mutually perpendicular edges with a total of $n2^{n-1}$ edges **2** : a computer architecture in which each processor is connected to *n* others based on analogy to a hypercube of *n* dimensions

hy·per·diploid \"+\ *adj* [*hyper-* + *diploid*] : having slightly more than the diploid number of chromosomes — **hy·per·diploidy** \"+\ *n*

hy·per·excitability \"+\ *n* [*hyper-* + *excitability*] : the state or condition of being unusually or excessively excitable — **hy·per·ex·citable** \"+\ *adj*

hy·per·extend \"+\ *vt* [*hyper-* + *extend*] : to extend so that the angle between bones of a joint is greater than normal ⟨a ~*ed* elbow⟩; *also* : to extend (as a body part) beyond the normal range of motion ⟨~*ed* her neck⟩ — **hy·per·extension** \"+\ *n*

hy·per·fine structure \"+. . .-\ *n* [*hyper-* + ³*fine*] : a fine structure multiplet occurring in an atomic spectrum that is due to interaction between electrons and nuclear spin

hypergeometric distribution *n* : a probability function of the form

$$f(x) = \frac{\binom{M}{x}\binom{N-M}{n-x}}{\binom{N}{n}} \quad \text{where} \quad \binom{M}{x} = \frac{M!}{x!(M-x)!}$$

that gives the probability of obtaining exactly *x* elements of one kind and *n–x* elements of another if *n* elements are chosen at random without replacement from a finite population containing *N* elements of which *M* are of the first kind and *N–M* are of the second kind

hy·per·inflation \¦hīpər+\ *n* [*hyper-* + *inflation*] : inflation at a very high rate (as in Germany in 1923) — **hy·per·inflationary** \"+\ *adj*

hy·per·ka·le·mia \¦hīpə(r),kāˈlēmēə\ *n* -S [NL, fr. *hyper-* + *kalium* + *-emia*] : the presence of an abnormally high concentration of potassium in the blood

hyperkinetic* *adj* : characterized by fast-paced or frenetic activity : HYPERACTIVE

hy·per·link \ˈhīpə(r)+,\ *n* [*hyper-* (herein) + ²*link*] : an electronic link providing direct access from one distinctively marked place in a hypertext or hypermedia document to another in the same or a different document — **hyperlink** *vt*

hy·per·lip·i·de·mia \¦hīpə(r),lipəˈdēmēə\ *n* -S [NL, fr. *hyper-* + ISV *lipid* + NL *-emia*] : HYPERLIPEMIA — **hy·per·lip·i·de·mic** \-mik\ *adj*

hy·per·li·po·pro·tein·emia \¦=,lipə¦prō,tēˈnēmēə, -,lip- *also* -¦prōd-ēəˈn-\ *n* -S [NL, fr. *hyper-* + E *lipoprotein* + NL *-emia*] : the presence of excess lipoprotein in the blood

hy·per·market \ˈhīpə(r)+,\ *n* [trans. of F *hypermarché*] : a very large store that carries the products found in a supermarket as well as the merchandise commonly found in department stores

hy·per·media \"+\ *n* [*hyper-* (herein) + ¹*media*] : a database format similar to hypertext in which multimedia computer data (as text, sound, or video images) related to text or graphics on a display can be accessed directly from the display (as with a mouse)

hy·per·nucleus \¦hīpə(r)¦n(y)üklēəs\ *n* [*hyper-* + *nucleus*] : an unstable atomic nucleus in which one or more hyperons bind to or replace a proton or neutron

hy·per·pha·gic \,==ˈfājik\ *adj* [*hyperphagia* + ¹*-ic*] : relating to or affected with hyperphagia ⟨~ rats⟩

hy·per·polarize \¦hīpə(r)+\ *vb* [*hyper-* + *polarize*] *vt* : to produce an increase in potential difference across (a biological membrane) or across the membrane of (a nerve cell) ~ *vi* : to undergo or produce an increase in potential difference across something — **hy·per·polarization** \"+\ *n*

hy·per·real \"+\ *adj* [*hyper-* + ¹*real*] : marked by extraordinary vividness ⟨traumatic memories . . . have a ~ quality —Judith Herman⟩

hy·per·realism \"+\ *n* [perh. trans. of F *hyperréalisme*] : realism in art characterized by depiction of real life in an unusual or striking manner — compare PHOTO-REALISM *herein* — **hy·per·real·ist** \"+\ *adj or n* — **hy·per·realistic** \"+\ *adj*

hy·per·reality \"+\ *n* : the state of being hyperreal; *also* : a hyperreal quality

hy·per·sexual \"+\ *adj* [*hyper-* + *sexual*] : exhibiting excessive concern with or indulgence in sexual activity — **hy·per·sexuality** \"+\ *n*

hyperspace* *n* : a fictional space held to support extraordinary events (as travel faster than the speed of light)

hy·per·text \ˈhīpə(r)+,\ *n* [*hyper-* (herein) + ¹*text*] : a database format in which information related to that on a display can be accessed directly from the display (as by selecting a link with a mouse or keyboard); *also* : material (as text) formatted in hypertext

hypertext transfer protocol *n* : an electronic communications protocol governing the exchange of data (as HTML, text, or graphics files) between computers esp. on the World Wide Web — abbr. *http*

hy·per·thermophile \¦hīpər+\ *n* [*hyper-* + ²*thermophile*] : an organism that lives in extremely hot environments (as a hot springs or near a hydrothermal vent) with temperatures around the boiling point of water — **hy·per·thermophilic** \"+\ *adj*

hy·per·tri·glyc·er·i·de·mia \¦hīpə(r),trī¦glisə,rīˈdēmēə\ *n* -S [NL, fr. *hyper-* + E *triglyceride* + NL *-emia*] : the presence of an excess of triglycerides in the blood — **hy·per·tri·gly·cer·i·de·mic** \-mik\ *adj*

hy·per·variable \"+\ *adj* [*hyper-* + ¹*variable*] : relating to or being any of the relatively short polypeptide chain segments in the variable region of an antibody light chain or heavy chain that are extremely variable in the sequence of their amino acid residues and that determine the conformation and specificity of the site which recognizes and combines with an antigen; *also* : relating to, containing, or being a highly variable nucleotide sequence (as in tandemly repeating DNA)

hy·per·velocity \"+\ *n* [*hyper-* + *velocity*] : a high or relatively high velocity; *esp* : one greater than 10,000 feet per second

hy·per·ventilate \"+\ *vb* [back-formation fr. *hyperventilation*] *vi* : to undergo hyperventilation ⟨some swimmers ~⟩ ~ *vt* : to subject to hyperventilation ⟨he *hyperventilated* his lungs by deep breathing⟩

hy·per·vigilance \" +\ *n* [*hyper-* + *vigilance*] : a condition in which an abnormal awareness of environmental stimuli is maintained — **hy·per·vigilant** \"+\ *adj*

hyphenate* *n* : a person who performs more than one function (as a producer-director in filmmaking)

hyp·no·therapist \¦hipnō+\ *n* : a specialist in hypnotherapy

hy·po·center \¦hīpō, -pə+\ *n* [*hypo-* + ¹*center*] : the focus of an earthquake — **hy·po·central** *adj*

hypodermis* *n* : SUPERFICIAL FASCIA

hy·po·diploid \"+\ *adj* [*hypo-* + *diploid*] : having slightly fewer than the diploid number of chromosomes — **hy·po·diploidy** \"+\ *n*

hy·po·gam·ma·glob·u·li·ne·mia \¦hīpə,gamə,gläbyələˈnēmēə, -pō-\ *n* -S [NL, fr. *hypo-* + E *gamma globulin* + NL *-emia*] : a deficiency of gamma globulins and esp. antibodies in the blood; *also* : a state of immunological deficiency characterized by this — **hypo·gam·ma·glob·u·li·ne·mic** \-mik\ *adj*

hypoplastic left heart syndrome *n* : a congenital malformation of the heart in which the left side is underdeveloped resulting in insufficient blood flow

hy·po·ther·mic \¦hīpō¦thərmik, -thəm-\ *adj* : relating to, utilizing, or characterized by hypothermia

hy·po·ventilation \¦hīpō+\ *n* [*hypo-* + *ventilation*] : deficient ventilation of the lungs that results in reduction in the oxygen content or increase in the carbon dioxide content of the blood or both

hy·pox·emic \,hī,päkˈsēmik\ *adj* : relating to, characterized by, or affected with hypoxemia

hys·ter·o·sal·pin·go·gram \¦==,=ˈ=gə,gram\ *n* -S [ISV *hyster-* + *salping-* + *-gram*] : a radiograph made by hysterosalpingography

ibi·zan hound \¦ēbēzən-, ē¦vēthən-\ *n, usu cap I* [*Ibiza*, island in the Balearic group + E *-an*] : any of a breed of slender agile medium-sized hunting dogs developed in the Balearic islands

ibu·pro·fen \,ībyüˈprōfən, -,fen, -,fēn\ *n* -S [*iso-* + *butyl-* + *propionic acid* + *-fen* (alter. of *phenyl*)] : a nonsteroidal anti-inflammatory drug $C_{13}H_{18}O_2$ used in over-the-counter preparations to relieve pain and fever and in prescription strength esp. to relieve the symptoms of rheumatoid arthritis and degenerative arthritis

IC \¦īˈsē\ *n* -S : INTEGRATED CIRCUIT *herein*

ice* *n* **1** : an undercover premium paid to a theater employee for choice theater tickets **2** : methamphetamine in the form of crystals of its hydrochloride salt $C_{10}H_{15}N{\cdot}HCl$ when used illicitly for smoking — called also *crystal meth*

ice* *vt* **1** : to shoot (an ice hockey puck) the length of the rink and beyond the opponents' goal line **2** *slang* : KILL

ice–cream chair *n* [so called fr. its use in ice-cream parlors] : a small armless chair with a circular seat for use at a table

ice dancing *n* : a sport in which ice-skating pairs perform to music routines that are similar to ballroom dances

ice lolly *n, Brit* : a confection made of flavored and colored water frozen on a stick

ice–out \ˈ=,=\ *n* -S [¹*ice* + ¹*out*] : the disappearance of ice from the surface of a body of water (as a lake) as a result of thawing

icing* *n* : an addition that is not essential but adds to the interest, value, or appeal of the main item or event — often used in the phrase *icing on the cake*

icon* *n* : a graphic symbol on a computer display screen that usu. suggests the type of object represented or the purpose of an available function

ICU *abbr* intensive care unit

ID \¦īˈdē\ *n* -S [*identification*] : STATION BREAK

IDDM *abbr* insulin-dependent diabetes mellitus *herein*

idem·po·tent \¦īdəm¦pōtᵊnt, īˈdempədᵊnt\ *adj* [L *idem-* same + *potent-, potens* having power — more at IDENTITY, POTENT] : relating to or being a mathematical quantity which when applied to itself under a given binary operation (as multiplication) equals itself; *also* : relating to or being an operation under which a mathematical quantity is idempotent — **idem·po·ten·cy** \-ənsē, -ᵊnsē\ *n* — **idempotent** *n* -S

identification parade *n, Brit* : a line of persons arranged by the police esp. for the identification of a suspected criminal by a victim or an eyewitness

Iden·ti–Kit \īˈdentə,kit\ *trademark* — used for a method of creating a picture (as of the face of a person wanted by police) by combining several separate images (as of different features)

iden·ti·kit \"\ *adj, sometimes cap* [fr. *Identi-Kit*, a trademark] *chiefly Brit* : produced by or as if by the routine assembly of stock materials : lacking variety or individuality : PREFABRICATED, STEREOTYPED ⟨the type of bland, middlebrow, ~ novel —Quentin Oates⟩

identity crisis *n* : personal psychosocial conflict esp. in adolescence that involves confusion about one's social role and often a sense of loss of the continuity of one's personality; *broadly* : a state of confusion or uncertainty about one's role, function, or goals ⟨both weeklies now seem involved in a sort of middle-aged, corporate *identity crisis*—Dan Wakefield⟩

identity function *n* : a function (as $f(x)$) that is everywhere equal in value to the value of its independent variable (as *x*)

identity matrix *n* : a square matrix with numeral 1's along the principal diagonal and 0's elsewhere

identity politics *n pl but sing or pl in constr* : PARTICULARISM 3

ideo·phone \ˈidēə,fōn *also* ˈīd-\ *n* -S [*ideo-* + *-phone*] : an onomatopoeic element functioning as part of distinct word class esp. in African languages

idiot light *n* : a colored light (as on an automobile instrument panel) designed to give a warning (as of low oil pressure)

idiotproof *adj* : extremely easy to operate or maintain ⟨an ~ VCR⟩

idiot savant* *n* : a person who knows almost everything about some subject but almost nothing about anything else

id·io·type \ˈidēə,tīp\ *n* [*idio-* + *type*] : the molecular structure and conformation in the variable region of an immunoglobulin that confers its antigenic specificity — compare ALLOTYPE *herein*, ISOTYPE *herein* — **id·io·typ·ic** \¦==ˈtipik\ *adj*

IDP *abbr* **1** inosine diphosphate **2** integrated data processing **3** international driving permit

iff \ˈifan(d)ˈōnlēˈif; *sometimes read as* ˈif·f *with a syllabic* f\ *conj* [alter. of *if*] : if and only if ⟨two lines that are not vertical are parallel ~ they have equal slopes⟩

IgA \,ī(,)jēˈā\ *n* [*Immunoglobulin A*] **1** : a class of immunoglobulins including antibodies found in external bodily secretions (as saliva, tears, and sweat) **2** : an immunoglobulin of the class IgA

IgE \-ˈē\ *n* [*Immunoglobulin E*] **1** : a class of immunoglobulins including antibodies that function esp. in allergic reactions **2** : an immunoglobulin of the class IgE

IGF *abbr* insulin-like growth factor *herein* — often used with an identifying number ⟨*IGF-1*⟩

IgG \-ˈjē\ *n* [*Immunoglobulin G*] **1** : a class of immunoglobulins including the most common antibodies circulating in the blood that facilitate the phagocytic destruction of microorganisms foreign to the body, that bind to and activate complement, and that are the only immunoglobulins to cross over the placenta from mother to fetus **2** : an immunoglobulin of the class IgG

IgM \-ˈem\ *n* [*Immunoglobulin M*] **1** : a class of immunoglobulins of high molecular weight including the primary antibodies released into the blood early in the immune response to be replaced later by IgG of lower molecular weight and that are highly efficient in binding complement **2** : an immunoglobulin of the class IgM

ig·nim·brite \ˈignəm,brīt\ *n* -S [L *ignis* fire + *imbr-, imber* rain + E *¹-ite* — more at IGNEOUS, IMBRICATE] : a hard rock formed by solidification of chiefly fine deposits of volcanic ash

ike·ba·na \,ikāˈbänə, ,ēk-, -kēˈ-\ *n* -S [Jap, fr. *ikey-* to make live, caus. of *ik-* live + *-bana*, var. (in compounds) of *hana* flower] : the Japanese art of flower arranging that emphasizes form and balance

IL* *abbr* interleukin *herein* — often used with an identifying number ⟨*IL-6*⟩

il·legal \(ˈ)i(l), ə+\ *n* -S : an illegal immigrant

il·locutionary \,i(l)+\ *adj* [²*in-* + *locutionary* (herein)] : of, relating to, or being an act (as informing, warning, or predicting) performed by a speaker in the course of making an utterance — compare LOCUTIONARY *herein*, PERLOCUTIONARY *herein* — **il·locution** \,i(l)+\ *n* -S

illuminate* *vt* : to subject to radiation

IM* *abbr* **1** intermodulation distortion **2** individual medley

image* *n* **1** : a set of values of a mathematical function (as a homomorphism) that corresponds to a particular subset of the domain **2** : a popular conception (as of a person, institution, or nation) projected esp. through the mass media ⟨promoting a corporate ~ of brotherly love and concern —R.C.Buck⟩

imagery* *n* : pictures produced by an imaging system

im·ag·ing \ˈimijin\ *n* [¹*image* + ³*-ing*] : the action or process of producing an image (as of a planet or a part of the human body) esp. by means other than visible light ⟨acoustic ~⟩ ⟨cardiac ~⟩ — see MAGNETIC RESONANCE IMAGING *herein*

im·bal·anced \(ˈ)im¦balən(t)st\ *adj* [¹*in-* + *balanced*] : not balanced; *esp* : having a disproportionately large number of members of one racial or ethnic group ⟨~ schools⟩

imip·ra·mine \əˈmiprə,mēn\ *n* [*imin-* + *propyl* + *amine*] : a tricyclic antidepressant drug $C_{19}H_{24}N_2$ administered esp. in the form of its hydrochloride

im·mit·tance \iˈmitᵊn(t)s\ *n* -S [*impedance* + *admittance*] : ADMITTANCE; *also* : IMPEDANCE — used of transmission lines, networks, and measuring instruments

immune response *also* **immune reaction** *n* : a bodily response to an antigen that occurs when lymphocytes identify the antigenic molecule as foreign and induce the formation of antibodies and lymphocytes capable of reacting with the antigen and rendering it harmless

immune system *n* : the bodily system that protects the body from foreign substances, cells, and tissues by producing the immune response and that includes esp. the thymus, spleen, lymph nodes, special deposits of lymphoid tissue (as in the gastrointestinal tract and bone marrow), lymphocytes including the B cells and T cells, and antibodies

im·mu·no·adsorbent \¦imyənō, ə¦myünō+\ *n* [*immuno-* + *adsorbent*] : IMMUNOSORBENT *herein* — **immunoadsorbent** *adj*

im·mu·no·assay \"+\ *n* [*immuno-* + *assay*] : a technique or test (as an enzyme-linked immunosorbent assay) used to detect the presence or quantity of a substance (as a protein) through its capacity to act as an antigen or antibody — **immunoassay** *vt* — **im·mu·no·assayable** \"+\ *adj*

im·mu·no·blot \"+\ *n* [*immuno-* + *blot* (herein)] : a blot (as a Western blot) in which a radioactively labeled antibody is used as the molecular probe — **im·mu·no·blotting** \"+\ *n*

im·mu·no·competence \"+\ *n* [*immuno-* + *competence*] : the capacity for a normal immune response ⟨altered the ~ of the lymphocytes⟩ — **im·mu·no·competent** \"+\ *adj*

im·mu·no·compromised \"+\ *adj* [*immuno-* + *compromised*] : having the immune system impaired or weakened (as by drugs or illness) ⟨~ patients⟩

im·mu·no·cyte \ˈimyənə,sīt\ *n* -S [*immuno-* + *-cyte*] : a cell (as a lymphocyte) that has an immunologic function

im·mu·no·cytochemistry \¦imyənō, ə¦myünō+\ *n* [*immuno-* + *cytochemistry*] : the application of biochemistry to cellular immunology — **im·mu·no·cytochemical** \"+\ *adj*

im·mu·no·deficiency \"+\ *n* [*immuno-* + *deficiency*] : inability to produce a normal complement of antibodies or immunologically sensitized T cells esp. in response to specific antigens — see AIDS *herein* — **im·mu·no·deficient** \"+\ *adj*

im·mu·no·depression \"+\ *n* [*immuno-* + *depression*] : IMMUNOSUPPRESSION *herein* — **im·mu·no·depressant** \"+\ *n* — **im·mu·no·depressive** \"+\ *adj*

im·mu·no·diagnosis \"+\ *n* [*immuno-* + *diagnosis*] : diagnosis (as of cancer) by immunodiagnostic methods

im·mu·no·diagnostic \"+\ *adj* [*immuno-* + ¹*diagnostic*] : of, relating to, or being analytical methods using antibodies as reagents ⟨an ~ test for cancer⟩

im·mu·no·diffusion \"+\ *n* [*immuno-* + *diffusion*] : any of several techniques for obtaining a precipitate between an antibody and its specific antigen by suspending one in a gel and letting the other migrate through it from a well or by letting both antibody and antigen migrate through the gel from separate wells to form an area of precipitation

im·mu·no·electrophoresis \"+\ *n, pl* **immunoelectrophore·ses** \-ē(,)sēz\ [*immuno-* + *electrophoresis*] : electrophoretic separation of proteins followed by identification by the formation of precipitates through specific immunologic reactions — **im·mu·no·electrophoretic** \"+\ *adj* — **im·mu·no·electrophoretically** \"+\ *adv*

im·mu·no·fluorescence \"+\ *n* [*immuno-* + *fluorescence*] : the labeling of antigens or antibodies with fluorescent dyes esp. for the purpose of demonstrating the presence of corresponding antibodies or antigens in a tissue preparation or a smear — **im·mu·no·fluorescent** \"+\ *adj*

im·mu·no·geneticist \"+\ *n* : a specialist in immunogenetics

im·mu·no·globulin \"+\ *n* [*immuno-* + *globulin*] : any of the vertebrate serum proteins that are made up of light chains and heavy chains usu. linked by disulfide bonds and include all known antibodies

immunoglobulin A *n* : IGA *herein*

immunoglobulin E *n* : IGE *herein*

immunoglobulin G *n* : IGG *herein*

immunoglobulin M *n* : IGM *herein*

im·mu·no·hematology \"+\ *n* [*immuno-* + *hematology*] : a branch of immunology that deals with the immunologic properties of blood — **im·mu·no·hematologic** \"+\ *or* **im·mu·no·hematological** \"+\ *adj* — **im·mu·no·hematologist** \"+\ *n*

im·mu·no·histochemical \"+\ *adj* [*immuno-* + *histochemical*] : of or relating to the application of histochemical and immunologic methods to chemical analysis of living cells and tissues — **im·mu·no·histochemically** \"+\ *adv* — **im·mu·no·histochemistry** \"+\ *n*

im·mu·no·histology \"+\ *n* [*immuno-* + *histology*] : a branch of immunology that deals with the application of immunologic methods to histology — **im·mu·no·histological** \"+\ *also* **im·mu·no·histologic** \"+\ *adj* — **im·mu·no·histologically** \"+\ *adv*

immunomodulator \"+\ *n* [immuno- + modulator] : a chemical agent (as methotrexate or azathioprine) that modifies the immune response or the functioning of the immune system (as by the stimulation of antibody formation or the inhibition of white blood cell activity) — **immunomodulatory** \"+\ *adj*

im·mu·no·pathology \ˈ+\ *n* [*immuno-* + *pathology*] **1** : a branch of medicine that deals with immune responses associated with disease **2** : the pathology of an organism, organ system, or disease with respect to the immune system, immunity, and immune responses — **im·mu·no·pathologic** \ˈ+\ *or* **im·mu·no·pathological** \ˈ+\ *adj* — **im·mu·no·pathologist** \ˈ+\ *n*
im·mu·no·pharmacology \ˈ+\ *n* [*immuno-* + *pharmacology*] **1** : a branch of pharmacology concerned with the application of immunological techniques and theory to the study of the effects of drugs esp. on the immune system **2** : the immunological effects and significance of a particular drug (as morphine) — **im·mu·no·pharmacologist** \ˈ+\ *n*
im·mu·no·precipitation \ˈ+\ *n* [*immuno-* + *precipitation*] : precipitation of a complex of an antibody and its specific antigen — **im·mu·no·precipitate** \ˈ+\ *n* — **immunoprecipitate** \ˈ+\ *vt*
im·mu·no·prophylaxis \ˈ+\ *n* [*immuno-* + *prophylaxis*] : the prevention of disease by the production of active or passive immunity
im·mu·no·reactive \ˈ+\ *adj* [*immuno-* + *reactive*] : reacting to particular antigens or haptens ⟨~ lymphocytes⟩ — **im·mu·no·reactivity** \ˈ+\ *n*
im·mu·no·regulatory \ˈ+\ *adj* [*immuno-* + *regulatory*] : of or relating to the regulation of the immune system ⟨~ T cells⟩ — **im·mu·no·regulation** \ˈ+\ *n*
¹im·mu·no·sorbent \ˈ+\ *n* [*immuno-* + *sorbent*] : an immunosorbent preparation
²immunosorbent *adj* : relating to or using a substrate consisting of a specific antibody or antigen chemically combined with an insoluble substance (as cellulose) to selectively remove the corresponding specific antigen or antibody from solution — see ENZYME-LINKED IMMUNOSORBENT ASSAY *herein*
im·mu·no·suppression \ˈ+\ *n* [*immuno-* + *suppression*] : suppression (as by drugs) of natural immune responses — **im·mu·no·suppress** \ˈ+\ *vt* — **im·mu·no·suppressant** \ˈ+\ *n or adj* — **im·mu·no·suppressive** \ˈ+\ *adj*
im·mu·no·therapeutic \ˈ+\ *adj* [*immuno-* + *therapeutic*] : of, relating to, or characterized by immunotherapy ⟨~ techniques for treating cancer⟩
impact* *vt* : to have an adverse effect on ⟨imports of stainless steel products continued to ~ . . . profits —*Annual Report Armco Steel Corp.*⟩ ~ *vi* : to have an adverse effect
impacted* *adj* : deeply entrenched : not easily changed or removed ⟨the ~ cynicism about most things American —W.F.Buckley *b*1925⟩
impacted area *n* : an area in which a large number of public school students are from families living or working on nontaxable federal property
impactor* *n* : METEORITE
impaired *adj* [fr. past part. of ¹*impair*] : being in a less than perfect or whole condition: as **a** : handicapped or functionally defective — often used in combination ⟨hearing-*impaired*⟩ **b** : intoxicated by alcohol or narcotics ⟨driving while ~⟩
im·plant·able \(ˌ)imˈplantəbəl\ *adj* : capable of being implanted in the living body ⟨an ~ pacemaker for the heart⟩
implicit differentiation *n* : the process of finding the derivative of a dependent variable in an implicit function by differentiating each term separately, by expressing the derivative of the dependent variable as a symbol, and by solving the resulting expression for the symbol
implode* *vi* **1** : to undergo violent compression **2** : to collapse inward as if from external pressure; *also* : to become greatly reduced as if from collapsing ~ *vt* : to cause to implode
implosion* *n* **1** : an inward collapse; *also* : a reduction or compaction as if from external pressure ⟨a population ~⟩ **2** : the act or action of bringing to or as if to a center; *also* : INTEGRATION ⟨this ~ of cultures makes realistic for the first time the age-old vision of a world culture —Kenneth Keniston⟩
imported fire ant *n* : either of two mound-building So. American fire ants of the genus *Solenopsis* (*S. invicta* and *S. richteri*) that have been introduced into the southeastern U.S., are agricultural pests, and can inflict stings requiring medical attention
impressionist* *n* : an entertainer who does impressions of noted personalities
imprint* *n* : the name under which a publisher issues books
imprinting* *n* : genetic alteration of a gene or its expression that is inferred to take place from the observation that certain genes are expressed differently depending on whether they are inherited from the paternal or maternal parent — called also *genomic imprinting*
im·prov \ˈimˌpräv\ *adj* [short for *improvisation*] : of, relating to, or being improvisation and esp. an improvised comedy routine
imu \ˈēmü\ *n* -S [Hawaiian] : a Hawaiian cooking pit in which hot stones bake the food
in* *adj* **1** : INSIDE 3a ⟨an ~ joke⟩ **2** : extremely fashionable; *broadly* : having widespread popularity ⟨the ~ place to go⟩ **3** : keenly aware of and responsive to what is new and smart ⟨the ~ crowd⟩ — **in–ness** \ˈinnəs\ *n* -ES
-in \ˌin\ *n comb form* -S [²*in* (as in *sit-in*)] **1** : organized public protest by means of or in favor of : demonstration ⟨teach-*in*⟩ ⟨love-*in*⟩ **2** : public group activity ⟨swim-*in*⟩
in–and–out* *adj* : characterized by purchase and sale of the same security within a short period ⟨*in-and-out* trading⟩
inboard *n* [¹*inboard*] : a boat with an inboard motor
inbounds \ˈ≈ˈ≈\ *adj* [fr. the phrase *in bounds*] : of or relating to putting a basketball in play by passing it onto the court from out of bounds ⟨~ pass⟩
inc* *abbr* incomplete
in·ca·pac·i·tant \ˌinkəˈpasətənt, -səd·ə-\ *n* -S : a chemical or biological agent (as tear gas) used to temporarily incapacitate people or animals
incendiary* *adj* : very hot and spicy : FIERY 2a — used of food
in·cen·tiv·ize \inˈsentəˌvīz\ *vt* -ED/-ING/-S : to provide with an incentive
in·clu·siv·i·ty \inˌklüˈsivəd·ē, -ˈzi-, -vətē\ *n* -ES : INCLUSIVENESS
incomplete* *adj, of insect metamorphosis* : having no pupal stage between the immature stages and the adult with the young insect usu. resembling the adult — compare COMPLETE 1 *herein*
inconsistent* *adj* : not satisfiable by the same set of values for the unknowns ⟨~ equations⟩ ⟨~ inequalities⟩
in–country \ˈ≈ˈ≈≈\ *adj or adv* : being or taking place in a country that is the focus of activity (as military operations or scientific research) by the government or citizens of another country ⟨scientists and *in-country* colleagues will carry out field research —*Tropicus Conservation International*⟩ ⟨readied my gear for my first mission *in-country* —Darryl Young⟩
in·cre·men·tal·ism \ˌiŋkrəˈmentᵊlˌizəm, ˌink-\ *n* -S [*incremental* + *-ism*] : a policy or advocacy of a policy of political or social change in small increments — **in·cre·men·tal·ist** \-ᵊləst\ *n* -S
indemnity* *n, often attrib* : FEE-FOR-SERVICE *herein* ⟨~ insurance⟩
independent* *adj* **1** : having linear independence ⟨an ~ set of vectors⟩ **2** : having the property that the joint probability (as of events or samples) or the joint probability density function (as of random variables) equals the product of the probabilities or probability density functions of separate occurrence
independent assortment *n* : formation of random combinations of chromosomes in meiosis and of genes on different pairs of homologous chromosomes by the passage at random of one of each diploid pair of homologous chromosomes into each gamete independently of each other pair
in–depth \ˈ≈ˈ≈\ *adj* [fr. the phrase *in depth*] : COMPREHENSIVE, THOROUGH ⟨an *in-depth* study⟩
index* *vt* : to regulate (as wages or prices) by indexation
in·dex·ation \ˌinˌdekˈsāshən\ *n* -S [²*index* + *-ation*] : a system of economic control in which certain variables (as wages and interest) are tied to a cost-of-living index so that both rise or fall at the same rate and the detrimental effect of inflation is theoretically eliminated — called also *indexing*
index fund *n* : a portfolio made up primarily of stocks listed on a standard index of stock market performance

indicator* *n* : any of a group of statistical values (as level of employment and change in the price of industrial raw materials) that taken together indicate the health of the economy — see COINCIDENT *herein*, LAGGING INDICATOR *herein*, LEADING INDICATOR *herein*
in·din·a·vir \inˈdinəvir\ *n* -S [*indina-* (perh. alter. of *indanyl* univalent radical of indan, fr. *indan* + *-yl*) + *-vir* (as in *acyclovir* — herein)] : a protease inhibitor $C_{36}H_{47}N_5O_4$ used in the form of its sulfate in combination therapy with antiviral drugs (as AZT) to treat HIV infection
indium antimonide *n* : a synthetic compound InSb of indium and antimony that is a semiconducting and photosensitive material and is used esp. in infrared photodetectors
individual retirement account *n* : a savings account in which a person may deposit up to a stipulated amount each year with the deposits deductible from taxable income and both deposits and interest taxable after the person's retirement
in·do·cyanine green \ˈində+. . .-\ *n* [²*ind-* + *cyanine*] : a green tricarbocyanine dye $C_{43}H_{47}N_2NaO_6S_2$ used esp. in testing liver blood flow and cardiac output
indoleamine \ˈ≈ˈ≈(ˌ)≈, ≈ˈ≈≈ˈ≈\ *n* [*indole* + *amine*] : any of various indole derivatives (as serotonin or tryptamine) that contain an amine group
in·do·meth·a·cin \ˌindōˈmethəsən\ *n* -S [*indo*le + *meth-* + *acetic* acid + *-in*] : a nonsteroidal drug $C_{19}H_{16}ClNO_4$ with anti-inflammatory, analgesic, and antipyretic properties used esp. to treat painful inflammatory conditions (as rheumatoid arthritis and osteoarthritis)
inducer* *n* : a substance capable of activating the transcription of a gene by combining with and inactivating a genetic repressor
inducible* *adj* **1** : formed by a cell in response to the presence of its substrate ⟨~ enzymes⟩ — compare CONSTITUTIVE 1a *herein* **2** : activated or undergoing expression only in the presence of a particular molecule ⟨an ~ promoter that turns on its genes only in the presence of lactose⟩
industrial* *adj* : HEAVY-DUTY ⟨an ~ zipper⟩
industrial* *n, often attrib* : highly amplified rock music that is characterized by a fast beat and electronic samples
industrial action *n, Brit* : JOB ACTION *herein*
industrial archaeology *n* : the study of the buildings, machinery, and equipment of the industrial revolution — **industrial archaeologist** *n*
industrial melanism *n* : genetically determined melanism as a population phenomenon esp. in moths in which the proportion of dark individuals tends to increase due to differential predation esp. by birds which more easily find and eat lighter-colored individuals in habitats darkened by industrial pollution
industrial–revenue bond \ˈ≈ˈ≈≈ˈ≈ˈ≈-\ *n* : a revenue bond issued to provide industrial facilities for lease and dependent on the lease revenue for amortization and interest payments
industrial–strength \ˈ≈ˈ≈≈ˈ≈\ *adj* **1** : suitable for industrial use **2** : marked by more than usual power, durability, or intensity ⟨*industrial-strength* cynicism —Joe Klein⟩
in·dy car \ˈ≈-\ *n, usu cap I & sometimes cap C* [*Indy* by shortening & alter. fr. *Indianapolis*, Indiana, site of the Indianapolis 500, a motor race in which cars of this type compete] : a single-seat open-cockpit racing car with the engine in the rear
inertial platform *n* : an assemblage of devices used in inertial guidance together with the mounting
inertial space *n* : a part of space away from the earth assumed to have fixed coordinates so that the trajectory of an object (as a spacecraft or missile) may be calculated in relation to it
infalling \ˈ≈ˌ≈≈\ *adj* [²*in* + *falling*, pres. part. of *fall*] : moving under the influence of gravity toward a celestial object (as a black hole or nascent star)
in·fan·ti·lize \ˈinfantᵊlˌīz *sometimes* inˈfantᵊl-\ *vt* -ED/-ING/-S **1** : to make or keep infantile **2** : to treat as if infantile — **in·fan·ti·li·za·tion** \ˌinfantᵊləˈzāshən, -ᵊlˌīˈz- *sometimes* inˌfantᵊl-\ *n* -S
in·fauna \ˈin+,\ *n* [NL, fr. *in-* ²in- + *fauna*] : benthic fauna living in the substrate and esp. in a soft sea bottom — compare EPIFAUNA *herein* — **in·faunal** \ˈ+\ *adj* — **in·faunally** \ˈ+\ *adv*
infect* *vt, of a computer virus* : to become transmitted and copied to (as a computer)
infectious bovine rhi·no·tracheitis \-ˌrī(ˌ)nō+\ *n* [NL *rhinotracheitis*, fr. *rhin-* + *tracheitis*] : a disease of cattle caused by a herpesvirus (genus *Varicellovirus*) and characterized by inflammation and ulceration of the nasal cavities and trachea
inflammatory bowel disease *n* : an inflammatory disease of the bowel **a** : CROHN'S DISEASE **b** : ULCERATIVE COLITIS
inflation* *n* : a hypothetical extremely brief period of very rapid expansion of the universe immediately following the big bang that accounts for some of the universe's properties (as distribution of energy and matter) — **inflationary*** *adj*
in–flight \(ˌ)≈ˈ≈\ *adj* [fr. the phrase *in flight*] **1** : made or carried out while in flight ⟨*in-flight* calculations⟩ **2** : provided for use or enjoyment while in flight ⟨*in-flight* movies⟩
in·flu·en·tial \ˌinˌflüˈenchəl\ *n* -S [*influential*, adj.] : one that has great influence
in·fo·bahn \ˈin(ˌ)fōˌbän\ *n* [*in*formation + auto*bahn*] : INFORMATION SUPERHIGHWAY *herein*
in·fo·mer·cial \ˈin(ˌ)foˌmərshəl, -fə-\ *n* -S [*info*rmation + ²com*mercial*] : a television program that is an extended advertisement often including a discussion or demonstration
in·for·mat·ics \ˌinfə(r)ˈmad·iks\ *n pl but sing in constr* [ISV *information* + *-ics*; orig. formed as F *informatique* or Russ *informatika*] : INFORMATION SCIENCE *herein*
information* *n* : the attribute inherent in and communicated by one of two or more alternative sequences or arrangements of something (as nucleotides in DNA or binary digits in a computer program) that produce specific effects
information retrieval *n* : the techniques of storing and recovering and often disseminating recorded information esp. through the use of a computerized system
information science *n* : the collection, classification, storage, retrieval, and dissemination of recorded knowledge treated both as a pure and as an applied science — **information scientist** *n*
information superhighway *n* : a telecommunications infrastructure or system (as of television, telephony, or computer networks) used for widespread and usu. rapid access to information; *esp* : INTERNET *herein* — called also *infobahn, information highway*
informed consent *n* : consent to surgery by a patient or to participation in a medical experiment by a subject after achieving an understanding of what is involved
in·fo·tain·ment \ˌin(ˌ)fōˈtānmənt\ *n* -S [*in*formation + enter*tainment*] : media offerings (as television programming) that present information (as news) in a manner intended to be entertaining or lighter material in ways usu. employed for serious information
in·fra·sound \ˈinfrə+\ *n* [*infra-* + ³*sound*] : a wave phenomenon of the same physical nature as sound but with frequencies below the range of human hearing
in·fra·structural \ˈ+\ *adj* : of or relating to an infrastructure
inhalation therapy *n* : the therapeutic use of inhaled gases and esp. oxygen (as in the treatment of respiratory disease) — **inhalation therapist** *n*
inheritance* *n* : a feature of object-oriented programming that allows a class of objects to derive some of its characteristics (as data members or functions) from an existing class through the reuse of code
in·hib·in \inˈhibən\ *n* -S [L *inhibēre* to inhibit + E *-in* — more at INHIBIT] : a glycoprotein hormone that is secreted by the pituitary gland and in the male by the Sertoli cells and in the female by the granulosa cells and that inhibits secretion of follicle-stimulating hormone
in–house \ˈ≈ˈ≈\ *adj* [¹*in* + ¹*house*] : existing, originating, or carried on within a group or organization or its facilities : not outside ⟨*in-house* training⟩ ⟨an *in-house* publication⟩ ⟨a company's *in-house* staff⟩ — **in–house** *adv*

ini·tial·ism \əˈnishəˌlizəm\ *n* -S : an acronym formed from initial letters; *esp* : one (as *RPG*) that is pronounced as separate letters
ini·tial·ize \-ˌlīz\ *vt* -ED/-ING/-S [¹*initial* + *-ize*] : to set to a starting state, position, or value ⟨~ a computer program counter⟩ ⟨~ a diskette⟩ — **ini·tial·iza·tion** \əˌnish(ə)ləˈzāshən\ *n*
initial teaching alphabet *n* [so called because it is used only in the initial stages of teaching reading] : a 44-symbol alphabet designed esp. for children who are learning to read English
in·ject·able \ənˈjektəbəl\ *n* -S [*injectable*, adj.] : an injectable substance (as a drug)
in·jec·tant \ənˈjektənt\ *n* -S : a substance that is injected into something
injection* *n* **1 a** : the placing of an artificial satellite or a spacecraft into an orbit or on a trajectory — called also *insertion* **b** : the time or place at which injection occurs **2** : a mathematical function that is a one-to-one mapping — compare BIJECTION *herein*, SURJECTION *herein*
in·jec·tive \ənˈjektiv, -ēv\ *adj* [*inject* + *-ive*] : being a one-to-one mathematical function
injector razor *n* : a safety razor with a narrow single-edged blade that is forced into place by a blade dispenser
in·je·ra \inˈjerə\ *n* -S [Amharic *ənǰära*] : a flat spongy bread made of fermented teff flour
in–joke \ˈ≈ˌ≈\ *n* [*in* (herein) + *joke*] : a joke for or about a select group of people
ink* *n, slang* : PUBLICITY 2d
in–kind \ˈ≈ˈ≈\ *adj* [fr. the phrase *in kind*] : consisting of something (as goods or commodities) other than money ⟨*in-kind* relief such as food and health care —D.E.Rosenbaum⟩
ink–jet \ˈ≈ˈ≈\ *adj* [¹*ink* + ⁶*jet*] : of, relating to, or being a dot-matrix printer in which electrically charged droplets of ink are projected onto the paper
in–line \(ˈ)≈ˈ≈\ *adj (or adv)* [fr. the phrase *in line*] : having the parts or units arranged in a straight line; *also* : being so arranged
in–line skate *n* : a roller skate whose four wheels are set in-line for greater speed and maneuverability — **in–line skating** *n*
inner child *n* : the childlike usu. hidden part of a person's personality that is characterized by playfulness, spontaneity, and creativity usu. accompanied by anger, hurt, and fear attributable to childhood experiences
inner city *n* : the usu. older, poorer, and more densely populated central section of a city — **inner–city** \ˈ≈ˈ≈≈\ *adj*
inner space *n* **1** : space at or near the earth's surface and esp. under the sea **2** : one's inner self
in·numeracy \(ˈ)in+\ *n* [¹*in-* + *numeracy* (herein)] : the state of being innumerate
in·numerate \ˈ+\ *adj* [fr. *innumeracy* (herein); after such pairs as E *illiteracy* : *illiterate*] : marked by ignorance of mathematics and the scientific approach — **innumerate** \ˈ\ *n* -S
input* *n* : ADVICE, OPINION, COMMENT ⟨there can be nothing worse than ~ from well-meaning family —Sybil Steinberg⟩
input \ˈinˌpu̇t, *usu* d·+V\ *vt* **in·put·ted** *or* **input; in·put·ted** *or* **input; in·put·ting; in·puts** [*input*, n.] : to enter (as data) into a computer or data processing system
insertion* *n* **1** : INJECTION 1 *herein* **2 a** : a section of genetic material inserted into an existing gene sequence **b** : the mutational process producing a genetic insertion — **insertional*** *adj*
in–service* *adj* : of, relating to, or being one that is fully employed ⟨*in-service* teachers⟩ ⟨*in-service* police officers⟩
inside* *n* **1** : the middle portion of a playing area **2** : the area near or underneath the basket in basketball
inside* *adv* : in prison
insider trading *n* : the illegal use of information available only to insiders in order to make a profit in financial trading
instant* *adj* **1** : appearing in or as if in ready-to-use form ⟨~ culture⟩ **2** : produced or occurring with or as if with extreme rapidity and ease ⟨what the technology of communications now offers us — ~ knowledge on the one hand, and ~ boredom . . . on the other —Arlene Croce⟩ ⟨there are always lots of chicks around for ~ sex —Barbara A. Bannon⟩
in·stant·ize \ˈinstənˌtīz\ *vt* -ED/-ING/-S : to make (a food product) instant ⟨*instantized* nonfat milk⟩
instant replay *n* : a videotape recording of an action (as a play in football) that can be played back (as in slow motion) immediately after the action has been completed; *also* : the playing of such a recording
instruction* *n* : a code that tells a computer to perform a particular operation
instrumental* *adj* : OPERANT 2 ⟨~ learning⟩ ⟨~ conditioning⟩
insulin–dependent diabetes \ˈ≈≈≈ˈ≈≈-\ *n* : TYPE 1 DIABETES *herein*
insulin–dependent diabetes mellitus *n* : TYPE 1 DIABETES *herein* — abbr. *IDDM*
insulin–like growth factor \ˌ≈≈≈ˌ≈-\ *n* : either of two polypeptides structurally similar to insulin that are secreted either during fetal development or during childhood and that mediate growth hormone activity; *esp* : INSULIN-LIKE GROWTH FACTOR 1
insulin–like growth factor 1 *n* : the juvenile form of insulin-like growth factor that is produced chiefly by the liver in response to growth hormone with production declining after puberty — abbr. *IGF-1*
in·su·li·no·ma \ˌin(t)səlēˈnōmə\ *n, pl* **insulinomas** \-məz\ *or* **insulinoma·ta** \-məd·ə\ [NL, fr. ISV *insulin* + NL *-oma*] : a usu. benign insulin-secreting tumor of the islets of Langerhans
insulin resistance *n* : reduced sensitivity to insulin by the body's insulin-dependent processes (as glucose uptake, lipolysis, and inhibition of glucose production by the liver) that results in lowered activity of these processes or an increase in insulin production or both and that is typical of type 2 diabetes but often occurs in the absence of diabetes
in·sur·ance \ənˈshu̇r(ə)n(t)s, *chiefly in southern U.S.* ˈinˌ≈(ˌ)\ *adj* : being a score (as a run or goal) that adds to a team's lead so that the opponents cannot tie the game with their next score
integral domain *n* : a mathematical ring in which multiplication is commutative, which has a multiplicative identity element, and which contains no pair of nonzero elements whose product is zero
integrated circuit *n* : a tiny complex of electronic components (as transistors, resistors, and capacitors) and their interconnections produced in or on a single small slice of material (as silicon) — called also *chip, microchip* — **integrated circuitry** *n*
integrated pest management *n* : management of agricultural and horticultural pests that minimizes the use of chemicals and emphasizes natural and low-toxicity methods (as the use of crop rotation and beneficial predatory insects) of pest control — abbr. *IPM*
in·te·gro·differential \ˈintə(ˌ)grō *also* inˌteg-\ *adj* [¹*integral* + *-o-* + *differential*] : involving both mathematical integration and differentiation ⟨~ equations⟩
intellectual property *n* : property that derives from the work of the mind or intellect (as an idea, invention, trade secret, process, program, data, formula, patent, copyright, or trademark); *also* : an application, right, or registration relating to this
intelligence* *n* : the ability to perform computer functions
intelligent* *adj* **1** : guided or controlled by a computer; *esp* : using a built-in microprocessor for automatic operation, for processing of input data, or for achieving greater versatility ⟨an ~ terminal⟩ — compare DUMB *herein* **2** : capable of producing printed material from electronic signals ⟨an ~ office copier⟩
intensive care *adj* : having special medical facilities, services, and monitoring devices to meet the needs of gravely ill patients ⟨an *intensive care* unit⟩ — **intensive care** *n*
interactive* *adj* : of, relating to, or being a two-way electronic communication system (as a telephone, cable television, or a computer) that involves a user's orders (as for information or merchandise) or responses (as to a poll or prompt) — **interactively** *adv*
interception* *n* : an intercepted forward pass
in·ter·crural \ˈintə(r)+\ *adj* [*inter-* + *crural*] : situated or taking

place between two crura and esp. in the region of the groin ⟨~ intercourse⟩

in·ter·disciplinarian \"+\ *n* -S [*interdisciplinary* + *-arian*] : one involved in interdisciplinary studies

in·ter·dis·ci·pli·nar·i·ty \¦==,disəplə'nerəd·ē, -'na(a)r-, -'nār-, -tē, -i\ *n* -ES : interdisciplinary studies; *also* : the diversity produced by such studies

interest* *n* : the profit in goods or money that is made on invested capital

in·ter·ethnic \"+\ *adj* [*inter-* + *ethnic*] : existing or occurring between ethnic groups

interface* *n* **1** : the place at which two independent and often unrelated systems meet and act upon or communicate with each other ⟨the ~ between engineering and science⟩ ⟨the man-machine ~⟩ **2** : the means by which interaction or communication is achieved at an interface ⟨install an ~ between a computer and a typesetting machine⟩

in·ter·face \'intə(r)+,-\ *vt* **1** : to connect by means of an interface ⟨~ a machine with a computer⟩ **2** : to serve as an interface for ~ *vi* **1** : to become interfaced ⟨a system that ~s with a computer⟩ **2** : to interact or coordinate harmoniously ⟨the computer technicians . . . ~ with the flight controllers —H.S.F.Cooper, Jr.⟩

in·ter·fer·on \,intə(r)'fi(ə),rän\ *n* -S [*interference* (prevention of virus development) + [1]*-on*] : any of a group of heat-stable soluble basic antiviral glycoproteins of low molecular weight that are produced usu. by cells exposed to the action of a virus, sometimes to the action of another intracellular parasite (as a bacterium), or experimentally to the action of some chemicals, and that include some used medically as antiviral or antineoplastic agents — see ALPHA INTERFERON *herein*, BETA INTERFERON *herein*, GAMMA INTERFERON *herein*

interferon alpha *n* : ALPHA INTERFERON *herein*

interferon gamma *n* : GAMMA INTERFERON *herein*

in·ter·generational \¦intə(r)+\ *adj* [*inter-* + *generational*] : existing or occurring between generations ⟨~ conflicts⟩

in·ter·individual \"+\ *adj* [*inter-* + *individual*] : involving or taking place between individuals ⟨~ conflicts⟩

in·ter·laboratory \"+\ *adj* [*inter-* + *laboratory*] : of, relating to, or engaged in by more than one laboratory

interlaced* *adj* : of, relating to, or using a method of video scanning (as for a television or computer) in which the odd and even horizontal lines of each frame are drawn on alternating passes

interlanguage* *n* : a language produced by a learner of a second language that often has grammatical features not found in either the learner's native language or the language being acquired

interleave* *vt* : to arrange in or as if in alternate layers

in·ter·leu·kin \,intə(r)'lükən\ *n* -S [*inter-* + *leuc-* + *-in*] : any of various compounds of low molecular weight that are produced by lymphocytes, macrophages, and monocytes and that function esp. in regulation of the immune system and esp. cell-mediated immunity

interleukin–1 \-'wən\ *n* : an interleukin produced esp. by monocytes and macrophages that regulates cell-mediated and humoral immune responses by activating lymphocytes and mediates other biological processes (as the onset of fever) usu. associated with infection and inflammation — abbr. *IL-1*

interleukin–2 \-'tü\ *n* : an interleukin produced by antigen-stimulated helper T cells in the presence of interleukin-1 that induces proliferation of immune cells (as T cells and B cells) and has been used experimentally esp. in treating certain cancers — abbr. *IL-2*

interlock* *n* **1** : a stretchable fabric made on a circular knitting machine and consisting of two ribbed fabrics joined by interlocking **2** : a garment made of interlock

[1]in·ter·media \¦intə(r)+\ *adj* [*inter-* + *media*] : involving the simultaneous use of several media

[2]intermedia \"\ *n* -S [*intermedia*, adj. (herein)] : an art form involving the simultaneous use of several media

intermediate* *n* **1** : an automobile larger than a compact but smaller than a full-sized automobile **2** : a chemical compound synthesized from simpler compounds and usu. intended to be used in later syntheses of more complex products

intermediate filament *n* : any of a class of usu. insoluble cellular protein filaments (as epithelial keratin) composed of various fibrous polypeptides that serve esp. to provide structural stability and strength to the cytoskeleton and are intermediate in diameter between microfilaments and microtubules

intermediate vector boson *n* : any of the three particles that mediate the weak force — see W *herein*, Z 1 *herein*

in·ter·modal \¦intə(r)¦mōd[ə]l\ *adj* [*inter-* + [1]*mode* + *-al*] **1** : being or involving transportation by more than one form of carrier during a single journey **2** : used for intermodal transportation

international system of units *n, usu cap I&S&U* : a system of units based on the metric system and developed and refined by international convention esp. for scientific work — abbr. *SI*; called also *International System*

in·ter·negative \"+\ *n* [*inter-* + [2]*negative*] : a duplicate photographic negative that is made from the original as an intermediate step used esp. for color control

in·ter·net \'intə(r),net\ *n, usu cap* [*inter-* + [1]*net*] : an electronic communications network that connects computer networks and organizational computer facilities around the world

in·ter·operable \"+\ *adj* [*inter-* + *operate* + *-able*] : having or using the same parts or equipment ⟨ammunition ~ in all .50 caliber gun systems⟩ — **in·ter·operability** \"+\ *n*

interpreter* *n* : a computer program that translates an instruction into machine language and executes it before going to the next instruction — compare COMPILER *herein*

in·ter·ro·bang *also* **in·tera·bang** \in'terə,baŋ\ *n* -S [*interrogation* (*point*) + *bang* (printers' slang for *exclamation point*)] : a punctuation mark ‽ designed for use esp. at the end of an exclamatory rhetorical question

interrogate* *vt* : to give or send out a signal to (as a transponder or computer) for triggering an appropriate response

interrupt *n* [*interrupt*, v.] : a feature of a computer that permits the execution of one program to be interrupted in order to execute another; *also* : the interruption itself

in·ter·sensory \¦intə(r)+\ *adj* [*inter-* + *sensory*] : involving two or more sensory systems ⟨~ factors in memory loss⟩

in·ter·state \'intə(r)+,\ *n, often cap* [*interstate*, adj.] : any of a system of expressways connecting most major U.S. cities

in·ter·stimulus \¦intə(r)+\ *adj* [*inter-* + *stimulus*] : of, relating to, or being the interval between the presentation of two discrete stimuli

in·ter·stock \'intə(r)+,\ *n* [*inter-* + [1]*stock*] : a piece inserted between scion and stock in grafting (as to allow union of incompatible varieties or to induce dwarfing)

in·ter·term \"+,\ *n* [*inter-* + *term*] : INTERSESSION

in·ter·tex·tu·al·i·ty \¦intə(r),tekschə'waləd·ē, -lətē, -i\ *n* -ES [F *intertextualité*, fr. *inter-* + *textuel* textual + *-ité* -ity] : the complex interrelationship between a text and other texts taken as being of basic importance to the creation or interpretation of the text — **in·ter·textual** \"+\ *adj*

in·ter·title \'intə(r),tīd·[ə]l, -īt[ə]l\ *n* [*inter-* + *-title* (as in *subtitle*)] : a word or group of words (as dialogue in a silent movie or information about a setting) that appear on-screen during a movie but are not part of a scene

interval* *n* : one of a series of fast-paced exercises interspersed with slower ones or brief rests for training (as of an athlete)

interview* *n* : a person who is interviewed ⟨he was our ~ that morning —Sally Quinn⟩

interview* *vi* : to have an interview (as with a prospective employer) ⟨one of my law school classmates ~*ed* with a . . . law firm in 1967 —Lana Borsook⟩ ⟨~*ing* for admission to graduate school⟩

into* *prep* : involved with or interested in ⟨her two children . . . are both ~ art —*New York*⟩

in·tra–aor·tic balloon counterpulsation \¦in·trə(')ā¦ȯr¦d·ik, -ȯ(ə)¦, ¦tik, -ēk, -trä-\ *n* : counterpulsation in which circulatory assistance is provided by a balloon inserted in the thoracic aorta which is inflated during diastole and deflated just before systole

in·tra–arterial \¦in·trə, ¦in·(,)trä+\ *adj* [*intra-* + *arterial*] : situated or occurring within, administered into, or involving entry by way of an artery ⟨*intra-arterial* chemotherapy⟩ ⟨an *intra-arterial* catheter⟩ — **in·tra–arterially** \"+\ *adv*

in·tra–articular \"+\ *adj* [*intra-* + *articular*] : situated within, occurring within, or administered by entry into a joint — **in·tra–articularly** \"+\ *adv*

in·tra·cardiac \"+\ *also* **in·tra·car·di·al** \¦=(,)=¦kärdēəl\ *adj* [*intracardiac* fr. *intra-* + *cardiac*; *intracardial* fr. *intra-* + *cardi-* + *-al*] : situated or occurring within, introduced into, or involving entry into the heart ⟨~ surgery⟩ ⟨an ~ catheter⟩ — **in·tra·car·di·al·ly** \-ēəlē\ *adv*

in·tra·day \¦==,\ *adj* [*intra-* + *day*] : occurring in the course of a single day ⟨the market showed wide ~ fluctuations⟩

intradermal test *n* : INTRACUTANEOUS TEST

in·tra·fallopian \,in·trə, -in·(,)trä+\ *adj* [*intra-* + *fallopian*] : occurring within a fallopian tube

in·tra·galactic \¦in·trə, ¦in·(,)trä+\ *adj* [*intra-* + *galactic*] : situated or occurring within the confines of a single galaxy

in·tra·gastric \"+\ *adj* [*intra-* + *gastric*] : situated or occurring within the stomach ⟨~ intubation⟩ — **in·tra·gas·tri·cal·ly** \-k(ə)lē\ *adv*

in·tra·generational \"+\ *adj* [*intra-* + *generational*] : occurring or existing between members of one generation ⟨~ spite⟩; *also* : occurring during the span of one generation

in·tra·governmental \"+\ *adj* [*intra-* + *governmental*] : occurring or existing between different branches or departments of government ⟨~ cooperation⟩ ⟨~ competition⟩

in·tra·net \'in·trə,net\ *n* [*intra-* + [1]*net*] : a network operating esp. like the World Wide Web but having access restricted to a limited group of authorized users (as employees of a company)

in·tra·operative \¦in·trə, ¦in·(,)trä+\ *adj* [*intra-* + *operative*] : occurring, carried out, or encountered in the course of surgery ⟨~ radiation⟩ ⟨~ infarction⟩ — **in·tra·operatively** \"+\ *adv*

in·tra·personal \"+\ *adj* [*intra-* + *personal*] : occurring within the individual mind or self ⟨~ concerns of the aged⟩

in·tra·plate \"+\ *adj* [*intra-* + [1]*plate*] : relating to or occurring within the interior of a tectonic plate ⟨an ~ earthquake⟩

in·tra·population \"+\ *also* **in·tra·populational** \"+\ *adj* [*intra-* + *population*; *intrapopulational*, fr. *intra-* + *population* + [1]*-al*] : occurring within or taking place between members of a population ⟨~ allografts⟩

in·tra·pre·neur \¦in·trəp(r)ə¦nər, -¦n(y)u̇(ə)r, -u̇ə, -¦nə̄r, -trä-\ *n* -S [*intra-* + entre*preneur*] : a corporate executive who develops new enterprises within the corporation — **in·tra·pre·neur·ial** \-rēəl\ *adj*

intrauterine device *n* : a device (as a spiral of plastic or a ring of stainless steel) inserted and left in the uterus to prevent effective conception — called also *intrauterine contraceptive device, IUD*

in·tra·vascular \¦in·trə, ¦in·(,)trä+\ *adj* [ISV *intra-* + *vascular*] : situated in, occurring in, or administered by entry into a blood vessel ⟨~ thrombosis⟩ ⟨an ~ injection⟩ — **in·tra·vascularly** \"+\ *adv*

in·tro·gres·sant \,in·trə'gres[ə]nt, -trō-\ *n* -S [*introgression* + [1]*-ant*] : an individual resulting from and exhibiting evidence of introgression — **introgressant** \"\ *adj*

in·tron \'in,trän\ *n* -S [*intervening sequence* + [2]*-on*] : a polynucleotide sequence in a nucleic acid that does not code information for protein synthesis and is removed before translation of messenger RNA — compare EXON *herein*

in·u·it \'inüwət, -nyü-\ *n, pl* **inuit** *or* **inuits** *usu cap* [Inuit, pl. of *inuk* person] **1 a** : an Eskimo people of No. America and Greenland **b** : a member of such people **2 a** : any of the languages of the Eskimo peoples **b** : a group of Eskimo dialects spoken from northwestern Canada to Greenland

inuk·ti·tut \i'nüktə,tüt, -'nu̇ktə,tu̇t\ *n* -S *usu cap* : a group of Eskimo dialects spoken by the Inuit of central and eastern arctic Canada

inu·pi·at \i'nüpē,ät, -'nyü-\ *also* **inu·pi·aq** \-,äk\ *n, pl* **inupiat** *or* **inupiats** *also* **inupiaq** *or* **inupiaqs** *usu cap* [Inupiat *in[y]upiaq* pl. *in[y]upiat*, lit., real person] **1** : a member of an Eskimo people of northern Alaska **2** : the language of the Inupiat people

invasive* *adj* : involving entry into the living body (as by incision or by insertion of an instrument) ⟨~ diagnostic techniques⟩

inverse* *n* : a set element that is related to another element in such a way that the result of applying a given binary operation to them is an identity element of the set — see ADDITIVE INVERSE *herein*, MULTIPLICATIVE INVERSE *herein*

inversely* *adv* : in the manner of inverse variation

inversely proportional *adj* : related by inverse variation

inverse variation *n* **1** : mathematical relationship between two variables which can be expressed by an equation in which the product of two variables is equal to a constant **2** : an equation or function expressing inverse variation — compare DIRECT VARIATION 2 *herein*

investment letter stock *n* : LETTER STOCK *herein*

in vitro fertilization *n* : fertilization of an egg in a laboratory dish or test tube; *specif* : fertilization achieved by the mixture usu. in a laboratory dish of sperm with eggs that have been surgically removed from an ovary followed by implantation of one or more of the resulting fertilized eggs into a female's uterus — abbr. *IVF*

in–your–face \¦==¦=\ *adj* [fr. the phrase *in your face*] : characterized by or expressive of bold and often defiant aggressiveness ⟨*in-your-face* basketball⟩; *also* : aggressively intrusive ⟨*in-your-face* advertising⟩

I/O *abbr* input/output

ion–exchange chromatography \¦==¦=-\ *n* : chromatography in which the separation and deposition of components in the liquid phase is achieved by differences in their rate of migration through a column, layer, or impregnated paper containing an ion-exchange material and by the exchange of ions in solution for those of like charge in the ion-exchange material

ion·o·mer \ī'änəmə(r)\ *n* -S [*ion* + *-o-* + *polymer*] : any of a class of tough synthetic ethylene-based thermoplastic resins consisting of a copolymer containing cross-links formed by ionic bonds

ion·ophore \ī'änə+,\ *n* -S [*ion* + *-o-* + *-phore*] : a compound that facilitates transmission of an ion (as of calcium) across a lipid barrier (as in a plasma membrane) by combining with the ion or by increasing the permeability of the barrier to it

ion·o·sonde \ī'änə,sänd\ *n* [ISV *iono-* (as in *ionosphere*) + *sonde*] : a device for determining and recording the heights of ionized layers in the ionosphere by shortwaves reflected from them

ion propulsion *n* : propulsion of a body by the forces resulting from the rearward discharge of a stream of ionized particles

ion rocket *n* : ION ENGINE

IP address \'ī'pē-\ *n* [*I*nternet *p*rotocol] : the numeric address of a computer on the Internet that consists of four parts separated by dots and containing up to three digits in each part — compare DOMAIN NAME *herein*

IPO *abbr* initial public offering

ipro·ni·a·zid \,iprə'nīəzəd\ *n* -S [blend of *isoniazid* and *propyl*] : a derivative $C_9H_{13}N_3O$ of isoniazid that is a monoamine oxidase inhibitor used as an antidepressant and formerly in treating tuberculosis

IRA \,ī(,)är'ā *also* 'īrə\ *abbr or n* -S : individual retirement account *herein*

IRC *abbr* Internet Relay Chat

ir·i·dol·o·gy \,i(ə)rə'däləjē, -ji\ *n* -ES [*irid-* + *-logy*] : the study of the iris of the eye for indications of bodily health and disease — **ir·i·dol·o·gist** \-əjəst\ *n* -S

iron maiden *n, sometimes cap I&M* : a supposed medieval instrument of torture consisting of an iron frame in human form hinged to admit a victim who was impaled on the spiked interior as the frame closed

irreducible* *adj* : incapable of being factored into polynomials of lower degree with coefficients in some given field (as the rational numbers) or integral domain (as the integers) ⟨~ polynomials⟩ ⟨an ~ equation⟩ — **irreducibility*** *n*

irritable bowel syndrome *n* : a chronic functional disorder of the colon that is characterized esp. by constipation or diarrhea, cramping abdominal pain, and the passage of mucus in the stool : MUCOUS COLITIS — abbr. *IBS*

ISBN *abbr* International Standard Book Number

ISDN \,ī(,)es,dē'en\ *abbr or n* -S [*i*ntegrated *s*ervices *d*igital *n*etwork] : a high-speed digital communications protocol; *also* : a network using this protocol

is·lam·i·cist \is'lämәsəst, iz-\ *n* -S *usu cap* : a specialist in Islamic studies

is·nik \'iznik\ *adj, usu cap* [fr. *İsnik* (now *İznik*), town in Turkey where it was made] : relating to, being, or imitating brilliantly colored pottery or tile originally made in Turkey from the 15th to the 17th centuries

iso·androsterone \¦ī(,)sō *also* ¦izō+\ *n* [*is-* + *androsterone*] : EPIANDROSTERONE *herein*

iso·car·box·az·id \¦==,kär'bäksəzəd\ *n* -S [*is-* + *carb-* + [1]*ox-* + *az-* + [3]*-id*] : a hydrazide monoamine oxidase inhibitor $C_{12}H_{13}N_3O_2$ used as an antidepressant drug

isoelectric focusing *n* : an electrophoretic technique for separating proteins by causing them to migrate under the influence of an electric field through a medium (as a gel) having a pH gradient to locations with pH values corresponding to their isoelectric points

iso·enzyme \¦īsō *also* ¦izō+\ *n* [*is-* + *enzyme*] : any of two or more chemically distinct but functionally similar enzymes — **iso·en·zymatic** \"+\ *or* **iso–enzymic** \"+\ *adj*

isoflavone* *n* : a derivative (as genistein) of isoflavone

iso·form \'īsə,fō(ə)rm, -fȯ(ə)m\ *n* [*is-* + [1]*form*] : any of two or more functionally similar proteins that have a similar but not identical amino acid sequence and are either encoded by different genes or by RNA transcripts from the same gene which have had different exons removed

iso·ge·ne·ic* *adj* : SYNGENEIC *herein* ⟨an ~ graft⟩

iso·la·to \,īsə'lād·ō *also* ,īzə-\ *n* -ES [It, adj., isolated — more at ISOLATED] : one who is physically or spiritually isolated from his fellowman

iso·met·rics \,īsə'me·triks *also* ,īzə-\ *n pl but sing or pl in constr* [[1]*isometric* + *-ics*] : exercise or a system of exercises involving isometric contraction of muscles

isom·e·try \ī'sämə·trē\ *n* -ES [*is-* + *-metry*] : a mapping of a metric space onto another or onto itself so that the distance between any two points in the original space is the same as the distance between their images in the second space ⟨rotation and translation are *isometries* of the plane⟩

isomorphic* *adj* : related by an isomorphism ⟨~ mathematical rings⟩ — **iso·morphically** \-k(ə)lē\ *adv*

isomorphism* *n* -S : a one-to-one correspondence between two mathematical sets; *esp* : a homomorphism that is one-to-one — compare ENDOMORPHISM *herein*

isopycnic* *adj* : being or produced by a technique (as centrifugation) in which the components of a mixture are separated on the basis of differences in density

isosceles* *adj, of a trapezoid* : having the two nonparallel sides equal

iso·spin \'īsə,spin *also* 'īzə-\ *n* [*isotopic spin*] : a quantum characteristic of a group of closely related subatomic particles (as a proton and a neutron) handled mathematically like ordinary spin with the possible orientations in a hypothetical space specifying the number of particles of differing electric charge comprising the group

isotopic spin *n* : ISOSPIN *herein*

iso·tret·i·no·in \,īsō·'tred·ə,nōin, -'tret-\ *n* -S [*is* + *tretinoin* (herein)] : a cis isomer of retinoic acid that is a synthetic derivative of vitamin A, that inhibits sebaceous gland function and keratinization, and that is used in the treatment of severe inflammatory acne but is contraindicated in pregnancy because of implication as a cause of birth defects

isotype* *n* : any of the categories of antibodies determined by their physicochemical properties (as molecular weight) and antigenic characteristics that occur in all individuals of a species — compare ALLOTYPE *herein*, IDIOTYPE *herein* — **isotypic*** *adj*

iso·zyme \'īsə,zīm *also* 'īzə-\ *n* -S [*is-* + *-zyme*] : ISOENZYME *herein* — **iso·zy·mic** \¦īsə¦zimik *also* ¦izə-\ *adj*

ISP \,ī(,)es'pē\ *abbr or n* -S : an Internet service provider

IT* *abbr* information technology

ITA *abbr* initial teaching alphabet *herein*

italian sandwich *n, usu cap I* : GRINDER 6

item* *n* : a couple in a romantic or sexual relationship ⟨they were rumored to be an ~⟩

iteration* *n* **1** : a procedure in which repetition of a sequence of operations yields results successively closer to a desired result **2** : the repetition of a sequence of computer instructions a specified number of times or until a condition is met — compare RECURSION 2 *herein* **3** : one execution of a sequence of operations or instructions in an iteration

iterative* *adj* : relating to or being an iteration

IUD \,ī,yü'dē, ,ī,yü-\ *abbr or n* -S : intrauterine device *herein*

IV \¦ī'vē\ *n* -S [*i*ntra*v*enous] : an apparatus used to administer an intravenous injection or feeding ⟨the patient was hooked up to an ~⟩; *also* : such an injection or feeding

iver·mec·tin \,īvə(r)'mektən\ *n* -S [perh. fr. *dihydr-* + *avermectin* any of the group of agents of which ivermectin is a member, fr. NL *avermitilis* (specific epithet of *Streptomyces avermitilis*, which produces the agents) + E *-ect-* (of unknown origin) + *-in*] : a drug mixture of two structurally similar semisynthetic macrocyclic lactones that is used in veterinary medicine as an anthelmintic, acaricide, and insecticide and in human medicine to treat onchocerciasis

IVF *abbr* in vitro fertilization *herein*

jackboot* *n* : the spirit or policy of militarism or totalitarianism ⟨hurried to completion under threat of Hitler's ~ —*Commonweal*⟩

jackbooted* *adj* : ruthlessly and violently oppressive ⟨~ militarism⟩

jack russell terrier \'jak'rəsəl-\ *also* **jack russell** *n, usu cap J&R* [after *Jack* (John) *Russell* †1883 Eng. clergyman & dog breeder] : any of a breed of small terriers having a white coat with brown, black, or brown and black markings

jack–up \'=,=\ *n* [*jack up*, v.] : a drilling rig used offshore whose platform is a barge from which legs are lowered to the bottom when over the drill site and which is raised above the water and supported on the legs to conduct drilling operations

Ja·cuz·zi \jə'küzē, ja-\ *trademark* — used for a whirlpool bath and a recreational bathing tub or pool

jailhouse lawyer *n* : a prison inmate self-taught in the law who advises fellow inmates on their legal problems or tries to advance his own case

jam* *n* **1** : a round in roller derby in which a jammer from each team attempts to circle the course and pass members of the opposing team in order to score points **2** *slang* : SONG 3

jammer* *n* : a player on a roller derby team who attempts to score during a jam

jam·mies \'jamēz\ *n pl* [by shortening & alter.] : PAJAMAS 2

Jams \'jamz\ *trademark* — used for knee-length loose-fitting swim trunks

JAP \'jap\ *n* -S : JEWISH AMERICAN PRINCESS — usu. used disparagingly

japanese bobtail *n, usu cap J* : a domestic cat of a breed that originated in Japan and is characterized by a short stumpy tail resembling a pompom and a coat often marked with solid patches of black, white, and red

japanese quail *n, usu cap J* : a quail of the genus *Coturnix* (*C. japonica*) of eastern Asia that is sometimes raised for its meat or eggs and is used in laboratory research

ja·pa·nol·o·gist \ˌjapəˈnäləjəst, jəˌpaˈn-\ *n* -s *usu cap* [*Japan* + E *-ologist* (as in *psychologist*)] : a specialist in the study of Japan and the Japanese

jap·lish \ˈjaplish\ *n, usu cap* [*Jap*anese + Eng*lish*] : Japanese marked by a considerable number of borrowings from English

ja·po·nais·erie \zhä,pȯnez(ə)ˈrē\ *n* -s [F, fr. *japonais* Japanese + *-erie* -ery] : a style of art reflecting Japanese qualities or motifs; *also* : a work of art in this style

jarhead* *n, slang* : a member of the U.S. Marine Corps

jawbone \ˈ⸗,⸗\ *vb* [*jawbone*, n.] : to talk to or about in order to gain some end

jawboning *n* -s [fr. gerund of *jawbone* (herein)] : the use of public appeals (as by a president) to influence the actions esp. of business and labor leaders; *broadly* : the use of spoken persuasion

jaw–dropper \ˈ⸗,⸗⸗\ *n* : something that causes extreme surprise or astonishment ⟨the film ends with a *jaw-dropper* of a courtroom scene⟩ — **jaw–dropping** \ˈ⸗,⸗⸗\ *adj* — **jaw–droppingly** *adv*

Jaws of Life *trademark* — used for a hydraulic tool that is used esp. to free victims trapped inside wrecked motor vehicles

jay* *n* [fr. the initial letter of *joint*] : a marijuana cigarette : JOINT

jazz* *n* : similar but unspecified things : STUFF ⟨I *love* sailing . . . that wind, and the waves, and all that ~ —John Updike⟩

jazz–rock \ˈ⸗ˈ⸗\ *n* : a blend of jazz and rock music

jeeves \ˈjēvz\ *n* -ES *usu cap* [after *Jeeves*, valet in the novels of P.G. Wodehouse †1975 Eng. novelist] : a valet or butler esp. of model behavior — **jeeves·i·an** \ˈjēvzēən\ *adj, usu cap*

jerk around *vt* : to treat badly esp. in an underhanded or inconsistent way ⟨the public gets *jerked around* by all this confusing information —Arnold Relman⟩

jerk–off \ˈ⸗,⸗\ *n* -s [*jerk off*, v.] : JERK 5 — usu. considered vulgar

jesus freak *n, usu cap J & often cap F* [after *Jesus* Christ] : a member of a fundamentalist youth group whose life-style includes communal living, Bible study, street preaching, and abstinence from illicit drugs

jet* *vi* : to move or progress by or as if by jet propulsion

jet* *n* **1** : a narrow stream of material (as plasma) emanating or appearing to emanate from a celestial object (as a radio galaxy) **2** : a momentary beam of subatomic particles emitted from the interaction of other usu. high-energy particles

jet boat *n* : a boat propelled by an engine which expels a powerful jet of water

jet lag *n* : a condition that is characterized by various psychological and physiological effects (as fatigue and irritability), occurs following long flight through several time zones, and prob. results from disruption of circadian rhythms in the human body — called also *jet fatigue* — **jet–lagged** \ˈ⸗,⸗\ *adj*

jet set *n* [so called fr. the fact that such people frequently travel by jet] : an international social group of wealthy individuals who frequent fashionable resorts — **jet–set·ter** \ˈjet,sed·ə(r)\ *n* — **jet–setting** \-d·iŋ\ *adj*

Jet·way \ˈjet,wā\ *trademark* — used for a telescoping bridge ramp for loading and unloading passengers between an aircraft and a terminal building

jewel box* *or* **jewel case*** *n* : a clear plastic case for a compact disc

jewel tone *n* : any of various colors (as amethyst, emerald, and ruby) that resemble those of gemstones

jewish princess *n, usu cap J* : a daughter of a well-to-do American Jewish family — usu. used disparagingly; called also *Jewish American princess*

jim·mies \ˈjimēz, -iz\ *n pl* [origin unknown] : tiny rod-shaped bits of variously flavored candy often sprinkled on ice cream and pastry : SPRINKLES

jit *abbr* just-in-time *herein*

jive \ˈjīv\ *adj* [*jive*, n.] *slang* : MISLEADING, DECEITFUL, PHONY ⟨if you are late getting to heaven, you will give Saint Peter some ~ excuse —Langston Hughes⟩

job action *n* : a temporary action (as a slowdown) by workers as a protest and means toward forcing compliance with demands

job bank *n* : a usu. computerized job listing or placement service for the unemployed

job–hopping \ˈ⸗,⸗⸗\ *n* -s : the practice of moving (as for immediate financial gain) from job to job — **job–hopper** \ˈ⸗,⸗⸗\ *n*

jock* *n* [so called fr. the wearing of jockstraps by male athletes] **1** : ATHLETE; *esp* : a school or college athlete **2** : PILOT; *esp* : a fighter pilot **3** : a person devoted to a single pursuit or interest ⟨computer ~*s*⟩

Jock·ey \ˈjäkē, -ki\ *trademark* — used for briefs for men

joe sixpack *n, usu cap J&S* [[4]*joe* + *sixpack*] a six-pack of beer, viewed as a working-class man's beverage] : an ordinary man; *specif* : a blue-collar worker

jogging *n* -s [fr. gerund of *jog*] : running at a slow even pace esp. for exercise

jo·han·nis·berg riesling \yōˈhänəs,berg-, jōˈhanəzbərg-\ *n, usu cap J&R* [fr. *Johannisberg*, castle and village in the Rheingau, Germany] : a Riesling produced in the U.S. (as in California)

john* *n, often cap* : a prostitute's client

john birch·er \ˈjänˈ-\ *n, usu cap J&B* : BIRCHER *herein*

john·son \ˈjän(t)sən\ *n* -s *sometimes cap* [fr. the surname *Johnson*] : PENIS — often considered vulgar

join* *n* : UNION 1 *herein*

joint* *n* **1** *slang* : PRISON **2** : PENIS — usu. considered vulgar

joint* *adj* : being a function of or involving two or more variables and esp. random variables ⟨a ~ probability density function⟩

jo·mon \ˈjō,män\ *adj, often cap* [Jap *jōmon* straw rope pattern; fr. the characteristic method of forming designs on pottery of the period] : of, relating to, or typical of a Japanese neolithic cultural period extending from about the 5th or 4th millennium B.C. or earlier to about 200 B.C. and characterized esp. by elaborately ornamented hand-formed unglazed pottery (**Jomon ware**)

jones \ˈjōnz\ *n* -ES [prob. fr. the name *Jones*] **1** *slang* : HABIT, ADDICTION; *esp* : addiction to heroin **2** *slang* : HEROIN **3** *slang* : an avid desire or appetite for something : CRAVING

jordan curve theorem *n, usu cap J* : a fundamental theorem of topology: every simple closed curve divides the plane into two regions and is the common boundary between them

jo·seph·son effect \ˈjōzəfsən- *also* -ōsə-\ *n, usu cap J* [after Brian D. *Josephson* b1940 Brit. physicist] : the movement of electron pairs through a thin insulator separating two superconductors carrying low current that can be stopped by raising the current in the superconductors above a certain level or by the application of an external voltage

jo·seph·son junction *n, usu cap 1st J* [B.D. *Josephson*] : an electronic fast-switching device that consists of two layers of superconducting metal separated by a thin layer of insulator and that makes use of the Josephson effect

joual \zhüˈäl, ˈzhwäl, *Fr* zhwäl\ *n* -s *often cap* [CanF, rendering of a nonstandard pron. of F *cheval* horse] : spoken Canadian French; *specif* : any of various local forms of the spoken French of Quebec that differ greatly from prescribed standards

jour·no \ˈjərnō, ˈjō-\ *n* -s [*journ*alist + [1]*-o*] *chiefly Brit* : JOURNALIST 1a

joystick* *n* : a manual control for any of various devices (as a computer display) that resembles an airplane's joystick esp. in being capable of motion in two or more directions

jpn *abbr, usu cap* Japan; Japanese

j/psi particle \ˈjāˈsī-\ *n, usu cap J* : an unstable neutral fundamental particle of the meson family that has a mass about 6000 times the mass of an electron, has an unusually long lifetime, and is thought to consist of a charmed quark and antiquark pair — called also *J particle, psi particle*

ju·dez·mo \jüˈdez(,)mō\ *also* **ju·des·mo** \"\ *n* [Judeo-Spanish *džudesmo* Judaism, Judeo-Spanish, fr. *džidyó, džudyó* Jew (fr. L *Judaeus*) + *-esmo* -ism — more at JEW] : JUDEO-SPANISH

ju·do·ist \ˈjü(,)dōəst, -üdəwə-\ *n* -s : one who is trained or skilled in judo

jug band *n* : a band using usu. crude or improvised instruments (as jugs, washboards, and kazoos) to play blues, jazz, and folk music

jug wine *n* : table wine sold in jugs

juice* *n* **1** *slang* : LIQUOR **2** *slang* : exorbitant interest exacted of a borrower under the threat of violence **3** *slang* : INFLUENCE, PULL, CLOUT ⟨a cop may go out of his way to prove that your ~ doesn't influence him —George Frazier⟩ **4** : a motivating, inspiring, or enabling force or factor ⟨when the creative ~*s* were running high —Eudora Welty⟩

juicer* *n* [*juice* (herein) + [2]*-er*] *slang* : a heavy or habitual drinker of alcoholic beverages

ju-ju \ˈjü(,)jü\ *n* [Yoruba *jújú*] : a style of West African music that is characterized by a rapid beat, percussion instruments, and vocal harmonies

juke* *vb* ~ *vi* : to juke someone (as in football or basketball) ~ *vt* : to fake out of position

julienne *vt* -ED/-ING/-S [*julienne*, adj.] : to slice into thin strips the size of matchsticks ⟨~ the carrots⟩

jump* *vi* : to go from one sequence of instructions in a computer program to another ⟨~ to a subroutine⟩ — **jump ship** : to desert a cause or party usu. abruptly : DEFECT

jump* *n* **1** : a transfer from one sequence of instructions in a computer program to a different sequence ⟨conditional ~⟩ **2** : jazz music with a fast tempo

jump cut *n* : a discontinuity or acceleration in the action of a filmed scene brought about by removal of medial portions of the shot; *broadly* : an abrupt transition (as in a narrative) — **jump–cut** \ˈ⸗,⸗\ *vb*

jumper* *n* : JUMP SHOT 3

jumper cables *n pl* : a pair of heavy-duty electrical cables with alligator clips used to make a connection for jump-starting a vehicle — called also *booster cables*

jump hook *n* : a hook shot in basketball in which the player jumps before releasing the ball

jumping gene *n* : TRANSPOSON *herein*

jumping jack* *n* : a conditioning exercise performed while standing by jumping from a position with the feet together and arms at the sides to a position with legs spread and hands touching overhead and then to the original position — called also *side-straddle hop*

jump jet *n* : a military jet aircraft with vertical takeoff and landing capability

jump–start \ˈ⸗,⸗\ *vt* **1** : to start (an engine or vehicle) by temporary connection to an external power source (as another vehicle's battery) **2** : to start or restart rapidly or forcefully : give a sharp stimulus to ⟨attempt to *jump-start* the stalled . . . arms control talks —Walter Friedenberg⟩ — **jump start** \"\ *n*

jumpsuit** \ˈ⸗,⸗\ *n* : a one-piece garment consisting of a blouse or shirt with attached trousers or shorts

jun \ˈjün\ *n, pl* **jun** [Korean *chŏn*] **1** : the chon of North Korea — see MONEY table *in the Dict* **2** : a coin or note representing one jun

junk* *n* **1** : JUNK BOND *herein* **2** : baseball pitches that break or are off-speed (as curve balls or change-ups)

junk art *n* : three-dimensional art made from discarded material (as of metal, mortar, glass, or wood) — **junk artist** *n*

junk bond *n* : a high-risk bond that offers a high yield and is often issued to finance a take-over of a company

junk DNA *n* : a region of DNA that usu. consists of a repeating DNA sequence, does not code for protein, and has no known function

junk food *n* **1** : food high in calories but low in nutritional value **2** : something appealing or enjoyable but of little or no real value ⟨the ultimate in *junk food* for your minds —Cleveland Amory⟩

junkie* *n* : a person who derives great pleasure from or is dependent on something ⟨sports ~*s*⟩ ⟨computer ~*s*⟩ ⟨an ideal book for opera fans and glitter ~*s* —Anthony Burgess⟩

ju·ri·me·tri·cian \ˌju̇rəməˈtrishən\ *n* -s : a specialist in jurimetrics

ju·ri·met·rics \ˌju̇rəˈme·triks\ *n pl but usu sing in constr* [L *juri-, jus* law + E *-metrics* (as in *econometrics*) — more at JUST] : the application of scientific methods to legal problems

ju·ris doctor \ˈju̇rəs-\ *n, usu cap J&D* [NL, doctor of law] : a degree equivalent to bachelor of laws

jury* *n* : one (as the public or test results) that will decide — used esp. in the phrase *the jury is (still) out* ⟨on the question of how well it works, the ~ is still out —Martin Mayer⟩

jury–rig \ˈ⸗⸗,⸗\ *vt* [back-formation fr. *jury-rigged*] : to erect, construct, or arrange in a makeshift fashion

just–in–time \ˈ⸗ˈ⸗ˈ⸗\ *n, often attrib* [fr. the phrase *just in time*] : a manufacturing strategy wherein parts are produced or delivered only as needed

ju·va·bi·one \ˌjüvəˈbī,ōn\ *n* -s [*juv*enile + NL *Abies*, genus name of balsam fir, in which the substance is found + E *-one* (as in *hormone*) — more at ABIES] : PAPER FACTOR *herein*

juvenile diabetes *also* **juvenile–onset diabetes** \ˈ⸗⸗,⸗ˈ⸗⸗-\ *n* : TYPE 1 DIABETES *herein*

juvenile hormone *n* : an insect hormone that is secreted by the corpora allata, inhibits maturation to the imago, controls maturation of eggs and yolk deposition in the imago, and has been used experimentally to control pest insects by disrupting their life cycles

ju·ve·nil·ize \ˈjüvənᵊl,īz, -vnəl-\ *vt* -ED/-ING/-S [*juvenile* + *-ize*] : to restrain from normal development and maturation : prolong the immaturity of ⟨chemicals that ~ insect larvae⟩ — **ju·ve·nil·iza·tion** \ˌjüvənᵊləˈzāshən, -vnəl-, -ᵊl,īˈz-\ *n* -s

jux·ta·glomerular \ˈjəkstə+\ *adj* [*juxta-* + *glomerular*] : situated near a kidney glomerulus ⟨~ cells⟩

k* *n* [*kilo-*] **1** : THOUSAND ⟨a salary of $24*K*⟩ **2** [fr. the fact that 1024 (2^{10}) is the power of 2 closest to 1000] : a unit of computer storage capacity equal to 1024 bytes ⟨uses 120K of disk space⟩

k \ˈkā\ *abbr or n* -s *usu cap* [struck] : strikeout

k* *abbr* **1** kilometer **2** kindergarten

kaf·ka·esque \ˌkäfkəˌesk, ˌkafkə-\ *adj, usu cap* [Franz *Kafka* †1924 Czech-born writer + E *-esque*] : of, relating to, or suggestive of Franz Kafka or his writings; *esp* : having a nightmarishly complex, bizarre, or illogical quality ⟨~ bureaucratic delays⟩

kai·nic acid \ˌkīnik-, ˌkän-\ *n* [Jap *kain*in-sō the alga *Digenia simplex* + E *-ic*] : a neurotoxic pyrrolidine derivative $C_{10}H_{15}NO_4$ from a dried red alga (*Digenia simplex*) that is used as an ascaricide

kai·ro·mone \ˈkīrə,mōn, -rō-\ *n* [Gk *kairos* critical time, opportunity, advantage + E *-o-* + *-mone* (as in *pheromone* — herein) — more at KAIROS] : a chemical substance emitted by one species and esp. an insect or plant that has an adaptive benefit (as a stimulus for oviposition) to another species and either provides no benefit or an unfavorable outcome to the species emitting the substance and that is sometimes used in a natural or synthetic form in the control of certain insect pests

kai·se·ki \ˈkīsekē\ *n* -s *often attrib* [Jap, meeting place, meal of select food served on an individual tray, fr. *kai* meeting, gathering + *seki* seat, place] : a highly ritual Japanese meal characterized by small portions, subtle flavors, artful presentation, and an emphasis on fresh seasonal ingredients

kaiser roll *n* : a round crusty roll often used for sandwiches

ka·la·ma·ta \ˌkäləˈmäd·ə, ˌkal-, -tə\ *also* **ca·la·ma·ta** *n* -s *often cap* [fr. *Kalamata*, port in southern Greece] : a brine-cured black olive grown in Greece

ka·lim·ba \kəˈlimbə, kä-\ *n* -s [of Bantu origin; akin to Bemba *akalimba* zanza, Kimbundu *marimba* xylophone] : an African thumb piano derived from the zanza

kal·li·din \ˈkalədən\ *n* -s [G, fr. *kalli*krein + pept*id* peptide + *-in*] : either of two vasodilator kinins formed from blood plasma globulin by the action of kallikrein: **a** : BRADYKININ *herein* **b** : one that has the same amino acid sequence as bradykinin with a terminal lysine added

kal·li·kre·in \ˌkaləˈkrēən, kəˈlik-\ *n* -s [G, fr. Gk *kallikreas* sweetbread, pancreas (fr. *kalli-* calli- + *kreas* flesh) + G *-in*; fr. its production by the pancreas] : a hypotensive proteinase that liberates kinins from blood plasma proteins and is used therapeutically for vasodilation

ka·na·my·cin \ˌkanəˈmīsᵊn, ˌkän-\ *n* -s [NL *kanamyceticus* (specific epithet of *Streptomyces kanamyceticus*) + E *-in*] : a broad-spectrum antibiotic from a Japanese soil actinomycete of the genus *Streptomyces* (*S. kanamyceticus*)

kan·ban \ˈkän,bän\ *n* -s *often attrib* [Jap, sign, placard, card used on assembly lines to control production and delivery of parts] : JUST-IN-TIME *herein*

kangaroo pocket *n* : a large front pocket (as in a winter jacket)

ka-on \ˈkā,än\ *n* -s [ISV *ka*, a spelling of the name of the letter (fr. *K-meson* — herein) + [2]*-on*] : an unstable meson that occurs in both charged and neutral forms and is about 970 times more massive than an electron

ka·po·si's sarcoma \ka¦pōs(h)ēz-, ¦kapəs(h)ēz-\ *n, usu cap K* [after Moritz *Kaposi* †1902 Austrian (Hung.-born) dermatologist] : a neoplastic disease affecting esp. the skin and mucous membranes, characterized esp. by the formation of pink to reddish-brown or bluish tumorous plaques, macules, papules, or nodules esp. on the lower extremities, and formerly limited primarily to elderly men in whom it followed a usu. benign course but now being a major and sometimes fatal disease associated with immunodeficient individuals with AIDS

ka·ra·oke \ˌkarēˈōkē, kəˈrōkē, ˈkärä¦ōkä\ *n* -s *often attrib* [Jap, fr. *kara* empty + *ōke* (short for *ōkesutora*) orchestra] : a device that plays instrumental accompaniments for a selection of songs to which the user sings along and that records or transmits the user's voice with the music; *also* : a form of entertainment involving the use of a karaoke machine (as in a bar)

ka·ra·tsu ware \kəˈrät(,)sü-\ *n, usu cap K* [fr. *Karatsu*, city in Japan] : a Japanese ceramic ware traditionally made from about the 16th century at Karatsu on Kyushu island that is probably the earliest glazed Japanese ceramic ware, includes both earthenware and stoneware, and comprises chiefly vessels for chanoyu

karma* *n* : VIBRATION 4

kart \ˈkärt\ *n* -s [prob. fr. *GoKart*, a trademark] : GO-KART

kart·ing \ˈkärd·iŋ\ *n* -s [*kart* (herein) + *-ing*] : the sport of racing miniature motorcars

kar·yo·gram \ˈkarēə,gram\ *n* [ISV *kary-* + *-gram*] : KARYOTYPE; *esp* : a diagrammatic representation of the chromosome complement of an organism

karyotype *vt* [*karyotype*, n.] : to determine or analyze the karyotype of ⟨*karyotyped* a newborn infant⟩

kas·se·ri \kəˈserē, kä-\ *n* -s [NGk *kaseri*, fr. Turk *kaşer, kaşar*] : a firm to hard cheese made in Greece from goat's or sheep's milk and in the U.S. from cow's milk

ka·wa·sa·ki disease \ˌkäwəˈsäkē-\ *or* **kawasaki syndrome** *n, usu cap K* [after Tomisaku *Kawasaki* b1925 Jap. pediatrician] : an acute illness of unknown cause affecting esp. infants and children that is characterized by fever, reddish macular rash esp. on the trunk, conjunctivitis, inflammation of mucous membranes (as of the tongue), erythema of the palms and soles followed by desquamation, edema of the hands and feet, and swollen lymph nodes in the neck

kb *abbr* kilobase *herein*

KB* *abbr* kilobyte *herein*

k–band \ˈ⸗,⸗\ *n, usu cap K* : a segment of the radio spectrum that lies between 10.9 GHz and 36.0 GHz and spans the upper super-high-frequency and lower extremely-high-frequency bands and that is used esp. for police radars, satellite communication, and astronomical observation

kbar *abbr* kilobar *herein*

KBPS *abbr, usu not cap B&P&S* kilobits per second

keeper* *n* **1** : a domestic animal considered with respect to how easy it is to care for ⟨horses that are easy ~*s*⟩ ⟨a hard ~⟩ **2** *chiefly Brit* : GOALKEEPER **3** : an offensive football play in which the quarterback runs with the ball **4** : one that is worth keeping : one having genuine or lasting merit ⟨all the songs are ~*s*, perfectly relaxed and wry —Alanna Nash⟩

ke·gel exercises \ˈkāgəl-, ˈkē-\ *also* **ke·gels** \-gəlz\ *n pl, usu cap K* [after Arnold H. *Kegel* †1976 Am. gynecologist] : repetitive contractions by a woman of the pelvic muscles that control the flow in urination in order to strengthen these muscles esp. to control or prevent incontinence or to enhance sexual responsiveness during intercourse

keg·ger \ˈkegər\ *n* -s [*keg* + [2]*-er*] : a party featuring one or more kegs of beer

kel·vin \ˈkelvən\ *n* -s [*Kelvin*, adj.] : the base unit of temperature in the International System of Units that is equal to 1/273.16 of the Kelvin-scale temperature of the triple point of water ⟨a temperature as high as 700 ~*s* —R. Cowen⟩

kennel cough *n* : tracheobronchitis of dogs or cats

ken·te \ˈken,tā, -,te, -ˌtə, ˈkän-; ⸗ˈ⸗\ *n* -s *sometimes cap* [Twi *kenté*] : a cloth made esp. in Ghana and usu. consisting of narrow strips sewn together in geometric patterns — called also *kente cloth*

ken·ya·pi·the·cus \ˌkenyəˈpithəkəs, ˌkēn-, -pəˈthēk-\ *n* [NL, fr. *Kenya*, country in Africa + NL *-pithecus*] **1** *cap* : a genus of extinct ancient primates (*K. africanus* and *K. wickeri* of eastern Africa held to be part of the great ape and human evolutionary lineage of which the primitive form (*K. africanus*) is now sometimes included in another primate genus (genus *Equatorius*) **2** -ES, *usu cap* : a primate of the genus *Kenyapithecus*

keogh plan \ˈkē(,)ō-\ *n, usu cap K* [after Eugene James *Keogh* †1989 Am. politician] : an individual retirement account for the self-employed — called also *Keogh*

ker·a·tec·to·my \ˌkerəˈtektəmē\ *n* -ES [*kerat-* + *-ectomy*] : surgical excision of part of the cornea — see PHOTOREFRACTIVE KERATECTOMY *herein*

ke·rat·in·o·cyte \kəˈrat(ᵊ)nə,sīt\ *n* -s [ISV *keratin* + *-o-* + *-cyte*] : an epidermal cell that produces keratin

ker·a·to·conus \ˌkerəd·ōˈkōnəs\ *n* -ES [NL, fr. *kerat-* + L *conus* cone] : cone-shaped protrusion of the cornea

ker·a·top·a·thy \ˌkerəˈtäpəthē\ *n* -ES [ISV *kerat-* + *-pathy*] : any noninflammatory disease of the eye

keratosis fol·li·cu·lar·is \-ˌfäləkyəˈlerəs\ *n* [NL, follicular keratosis] : DARIER'S DISEASE *herein*

kernel* *n* **1** : a subset of the elements of one set (as a group) that a function (as a homomorphism) maps onto an identity element of another set **2** : a computer program (as in an operating system) that controls low-level functions (as input-output and memory management), is accessed by a user through an intermediary program, and is usu. written specifically for the computer on which it is run

kernel sentence *also* **kernel*** *n* : a sentence (as "John is big" or "John has a book") exemplifying in a language one of a very small group of the grammatically simplest sentence types or patterns (as noun phrase + be + adjective phrase or noun phrase + verb + noun phrase) which in transformational grammar are the basic stock from which all sentences in that language are derived and in terms of which they can all ultimately be described

ke·ta·mine \ˈkēd·ə,mēn, -tə-\ *n* [*ket-* + *amine*] : a general anesthetic that is administered intravenously and intramuscularly in the form of its hydrochloride $C_{13}H_{16}ClNO \cdot HCl$

ke·to·co·na·zole \ˌkēd·ōˈkōnə,zōl\ *n* -s [*ket-* + *-conazole* (as in *miconazole* — herein)] : a synthetic broad-spectrum antifungal agent $C_{26}H_{28}Cl_2N_4O_4$ used to treat chronic internal and cutaneous infections

ke·to·glu·ta·rate \ˌkēd·ō(,)glüˈtā,rāt\ *n* -s [*ketoglutar*ic acid + [1]*-ate*] : a salt or ester of ketoglutaric acid

key* *vb* ~ *vt* : to be essential to : play the most important part in ⟨defense ~*ed* the victory⟩ ~ *vi* **1** : to observe the position or movement of an opposing player in football in order to anticipate the play — usu. used with *on* ⟨the middle linebacker was ~*ing* on the halfback⟩ **2** : KEYBOARD

key \ˈkē\ *n* -s [by shortening & alter. of *kilo*] *slang* : a kilogram esp. of marijuana or heroin

keyboard* *n* : a small usu. portable musical instrument that is played by means of a keyboard like that of a piano and that produces a variety of sounds electronically — often used in pl. — **key·board·ist** \ˈkē,bȯrdəst\ *n* -s

key club *n* [so called because each member is provided with a key to the premises] : an informal private club serving liquor and providing entertainment
key lime *n, often cap K* [[4]key] : a small aromatic lime
keypad \ˈ-ˌ-\ *n* [[1]key + [1]pad] : a small often hand-held keyboard
keyset \ˈ-ˌ-\ *n* [[1]key + [3]set] : KEYBOARD 2
keystone* *n* : a species of plant or animal that produces a major impact (as by predation) on its ecosystem and is considered essential to maintaining optimum ecosystem function or structure
[1]**keystroke** \ˈ-ˌ-\ *n* [[1]key + [2]stroke] : the act or an instance of depressing a key on a keyboard
[2]**keystroke** \"\ *vt* : KEYBOARD
keyword** \ˈ-ˌ-\ *n* : a significant word from a title or document used as an index to content
khoum \ˈküm, ˈküm\ *n* -S [modif. of Ar *khums*, lit., one fifth] **1** : a monetary unit of Mauritania equal to ⅕ ouguiya — see MONEY table *in the Dict* **2** : a coin representing one khoum
ki \ˈkē\ *n* -S *sometimes cap* [Jap and Korean] : CHI *herein*
kick* *vb* ~ *vi* : to run at a faster speed during the last part of a race — **kick ass** : to kick butt — often considered vulgar — **kick butt** : to use bluntly forceful or coercive measures in order to achieve a desired end; *also* : to succeed or win overwhelmingly
kick–ass \ˈ-ˌ-\ *adj* [fr. the phrase *kick ass*] : strikingly or overwhelmingly tough, aggressive, powerful, or effective ⟨*kick-ass* music⟩ ⟨a *kick-ass* managerial style⟩
kick back* *vi* : to assume a relaxed position or attitude; *also* : to spend time relaxing : take it easy ⟨spent two weeks just *kicking back* at home⟩
kick·box \ˈ-ˌ-\ *vi* : to engage in kickboxing — **kick·box·er** \-ə(r)\ *n*
kick·box·ing \ˈ-ˌ-ˌ-\ *n* : boxing in which boxers are allowed to kick with bare feet as in karate
kick in* *vi* : to begin operating or having an effect : get started ⟨waiting for the heater to *kick in*⟩ ⟨a new tax *kicking in* next year⟩
kick out* *vi* : to turn a surfboard around and drive it over the top of a wave by pushing down on the rear of the board with the foot
kick–start \ˈ-ˌ-\ *vt* **1** : to start (as a motorcycle) by means of a kick starter **2** : JUMP-START 2 *herein* ⟨a modest investment . . . could *kick-start* the industry —Andrew Kupfer⟩
kicky* *adj* : providing a kick or thrill : EXCITING ⟨~ violent scenes —Pauline Kael⟩; *also* : excitingly fashionable ⟨~ clothes⟩
kid·nap·pee *or* **kid·nap·ee** \ˌkidˌnaˈpē\ *n* -S [[1]kidnap + -ee] : a person who has been kidnapped
kid·vid \ˈkidˌvid\ *n* -S [[1]kid + *video*] : television programs or videos for children
kill* *vt* : to prevent the opposing hockey team from scoring during ⟨~*ed* two penalties⟩
killer* *n* : one that is extremely difficult to deal with ⟨seems sweet, but she is a ~ at the negotiating table —Calvin Trillin⟩
killer *adj* [*killer*, n.] **1** : strikingly impressive or effective ⟨a ~ smile⟩ ⟨a ~ résumé⟩ **2** : extremely difficult to deal with ⟨a ~ fast ball⟩; *also* : causing death or devastation ⟨a ~ tornado⟩
killer bee *n* : AFRICANIZED BEE *herein*
killer cell *n* : a lymphocyte (as a cytotoxic T cell or a natural killer cell) with cytotoxic activity
killer instinct *n* : an aggressive tenacious urge for domination in a struggle to attain a goal
killer t cell *n, usu cap T* : CYTOTOXIC T CELL *herein*
ki·lo·bar \ˈkēlə, ˈkilə+ˌ\ *n* [ISV *kilo-* + [7]*bar*] : a unit of pressure equal to 1000 bars — abbr. *kbar*
ki·lo·base \"+ˌ\ *n* [ISV *kilo-* + *-base*] : a unit of measure of the length of a nucleic-acid chain (as of DNA or RNA) that equals one thousand base pairs
ki·lo·baud \"+ˌ\ *n* [ISV *kilo-* + *baud* (herein)] : 1000 baud
ki·lo·bit \"+ˌ\ *n* [ISV *kilo-* + [2]*bit*] **1** : 1000 bits **2** : 1024 bits
ki·lo·byte \"+ˌ\ *n* [ISV *kilo-* + *byte* (herein)] : 1024 bytes : K 2 *herein*
ki·lo·joule \"+ˌ\ *n* [ISV *kilo-* + *joule*] : 1000 joules; *also* : a unit in nutrition equivalent to 0.239 calorie
kilo·megacycle \ˈkilə+\ *n* [ISV *kilo-* + *megacycle*] : GIGAHERTZ
ki·lo·oersted \ˈkēlō, ˈkilō+\ *n* [ISV *kilo-* + *oersted*] : 1000 oersteds
ki·lo·pascal \"+\ *n* [ISV *kilo-* + *pascal* (herein)] : 1000 pascals
ki·lo·rad \ˈkēlō, ˈkilō+ˌ\ *n* [ISV *kilo-* + *rad*] : 1000 rads
ki·na \ˈkēnə\ *n, pl* **kina** [Neo-Melanesian, lit., gold lip (used as currency), oyster, clam, fr. Tolai (Austronesian language of the Gazelle Peninsula, New Britain)] **1** : the basic monetary unit of Papua New Guinea — see MONEY table *in the Dict* **2** : a coin or note representing one kina
ki·na·ra \kēˈnärə\ *n* -S [Swahili, candlestick] : a candelabrum with seven candlesticks used in celebrating Kwanzaa
ki·ne·sin \kiˈnēsən\ *n* -S [Gk *kinēsis* movement, motion + E *-in* — more at KINESIS] : an ATPase similar to dynein that regulates the intracellular transport esp. of cell organelles and molecules (as mitochondria and proteins) along microtubules
-kinesis* *n comb form* : production of motion ⟨tele*kinesis*⟩
kinetic art *n* : art in which movement (as of a motor-driven part or a changing electronic image) is a basic element — **kinetic artist** *n*
ki·net·i·cism \kəˈned·əˌsizəm, kīˈ-\ *n* -S : KINETIC ART *herein*
ki·net·i·cist \-səst\ *n* -S **1** : a specialist in kinetics **2** : KINETIC ARTIST *herein*
ki·ne·tin \ˈkīnətən\ *n* -S [*kinet-* + *-in*] : a cytokinin $C_{10}H_9N_5O$ used esp. to stimulate cell division in plant tissue culture
kinetochore* *n* : a specialized structure on the centromere to which the microtubular spindle fibers attach during mitosis and meiosis
ki·neto·some \kəˈned·əˌsōm, kīˈ-\ *n* -S [*kinet-* + [3]*-some*] : BASAL BODY 1
kingside \ˈ-ˌ-\ *n* : the side of a chessboard containing the file on which both kings sit at the beginning of the game
ki·nin \ˈkīnən\ *n* -S [Gk *kinein* to move, stimulate + E *-in* — more at HIGHT] **1** : any of various polypeptide hormones that are formed locally in the tissues and cause dilation of blood vessels and contraction of smooth muscle **2** : CYTOKININ *herein*
ki·ni·nase \ˈkīnəˌnās, -āz\ *n* -S [*kinin* (herein) + *-ase*] : an enzyme in blood that destroys a kinin
ki·nin·o·gen \kīˈninəjən\ *n* -S [*kinin* (herein) + *-o-* + *-gen*] : an inactive precursor of a kinin — **ki·nin·o·gen·ic** \(ˌ)ˌ-ˌ-ˈjenik\ *adj*
kinky* *adj* **1** : relating to, having, or appealing to bizarre or unconventional tastes esp. in sex ⟨every ~ weirdo thing you want to do —Philip Roth⟩; *also* : being sexually deviant ⟨a ~ baron in leg irons, begging for another spanking —Diana Davenport⟩ **2** : OUTLANDISH, FAR-OUT *herein* ⟨~ clothes⟩ — **kinkiness** *n*
kin selection *n* : a theory of natural selection which states that a usu. altruistic behavior or attribute that lowers the fitness of a particular individual is selected for if it increases the probability of survival and reproduction of related kin who possess some or all of the same genes as the altruistic individual
kir \ˈki(ə)r\ *n* -S *often cap* [after Felix *Kir* †1968 Fr. clergyman and politician] : a drink made of dry white wine and crème de cassis
kir·li·an photography \ˌki(ə)rlēən-\ *n, usu cap K* [after Semën D. *Kirlian* †1978 and Valentina Kh. *Kirlian* †1971 Soviet inventors] : a process in which an image is obtained by application of a high-frequency electrical field to an object (as a leaf or metal coin) so that it radiates a characteristic pattern of luminescence that is recorded on photographic film — **kirlian photograph** *n, usu cap K*
ki·run·di \kəˈründē\ *n, usu cap* : RUNDI 2
kiss* *vb* — **kiss ass** : to act obsequiously esp. to gain favor — usu. considered vulgar — **kiss my ass** — used as a contemptuous dismissal or as a term of abuse; usu. considered vulgar — **kiss one's ass** : to act obsequiously toward esp. to gain favor — usu. considered vulgar — **kiss up to** : to curry favor with
kiss–and–tell \ˌ-ˌ-ˈ-\ *adj* : telling details of private matters ⟨*kiss-and-tell* autobiographies⟩ — **kiss–and–tell** *n*
kissing cousin* *n* : one that is closely related in kind to something else ⟨the alcoholic *kissing cousin* of the carbonated soft drinks we love —Nika Hazelton⟩
kissing disease *n* [so called fr. the belief that it is transmitted by kissing] : INFECTIOUS MONONUCLEOSIS
kiss of life **1** *Brit* : artificial respiration by the mouth-to-mouth method **2** *Brit* : something that restores vitality
kissy–face \ˈkisēˌ-\ *n* -S [baby-talk alter. of [1]*kiss* + [1]*face*] : a usu. overt display or expression of affection ⟨don't play *kissy-face* with the clergy —Marney R. Keenan⟩
kis·wa·hi·li \(ˌ)kiˌswäˈhēlē\ *n, usu cap* [Swahili, fr. *ki-* class prefix + *-swahili*, fr. Ar — more at SWAHILI] : SWAHILI 2
kitchen–sink \ˌ-ˈ-\ *adj* **1** *chiefly Brit* : portraying or emphasizing the squalid aspects of modern life ⟨the *kitchen-sink* realism of contemporary British drama —*Current Biog.*⟩ **2** : being or made up of a hodgepodge of disparate elements or ingredients ⟨*kitchen-sink* soup—made with . . . meat, chicken, fish cake, shrimp, mushrooms and greens —Mimi Sheraton⟩
kitschy \ˈ-ē\ *adj* -ER/-EST : of, relating to, or being kitsch : appealing to popular or lowbrow taste
kiwi* *n* : KIWIFRUIT *herein*
kiwifruit \ˈkēwēˌ-\ *n* [*kiwi* (bird symbolic of New Zealand, from where the fruit is exported) + [1]*fruit*] : the edible fruit of the Chinese gooseberry (*Actinidia deliciosa* syn. *A. chinensis*) having a fuzzy brown skin and slightly acidic green flesh — called also *kiwi*
klep·toc·ra·cy \klepˈtäkrəsē\ *n* -ES [*klept-* + *-cracy*] : government conducted by those who seek chiefly status and personal gain at the expense of the governed; *also* : a particular government of this kind — **klep·to·crat** \ˈkleptəˌkrat\ *n* -S — **klep·to·crat·ic** \ˌ-ˈkrad·ik, -at-\ *adj*
klezmer* *n* : the music played by klezmorim
klick *or* **click** \ˈklik\ *n* -S [origin unknown] *slang* : KILOMETER
kline·fel·ter's syndrome \ˌklīnˌfeltə(r)(z)-\ *also* **klinefelter syndrome** *n, usu cap K* [after Harry F. *Klinefelter* *b*1912 Am. physician] : an abnormal condition in a male characterized by two X chromosomes and one Y chromosome, infertility, smallness of the testicles, sparse facial and body hair, and enlarged breasts
kludge *or* **kluge** \ˈklüj\ *n* -S [origin unknown] : a system and esp. a computer system made up of components that are poorly matched or were orig. intended for some other use — **kludgy** \-jē\ *also* **kludgey** *adj*
klutz \ˈkləts\ *n* -ES [Yiddish *klots, kluts*, lit., wooden beam, fr. MHG *kloz* lumpy mass, beam — more at CLOT] : a clumsy and awkward person — **klutz·i·ness** \-tsēnəs, -tsin-\ *n* -ES — **klutzy** \-tsē, -i\ *adj* -ER/-EST
k–meson \ˈkā,-\ *n, usu cap K* [[1]K + *meson*] : KAON *herein*
KMH *or* **KMPH** *abbr, usu not cap* kilometers per hour
kneecapping \ˈ-ˌ-\ *n* -S : the act or practice of maiming a person in the knees esp. by gunshot
knee–jerk \ˈ-(ˌ)-\ *adj* [*knee jerk*, n.] : readily predictable : AUTOMATIC ⟨*knee-jerk* reactions⟩; *also* : reacting in a readily predictable way ⟨*knee-jerk* liberals⟩
knee–slapper \ˈ-ˌ-\ *n* [fr. the phrase *slap one's knee* (to express mirth)] : an extremely funny joke, line, or story
knock* *vb* — **knock one's socks off** : to overwhelm or amaze one ⟨a performance that will *nock your socks off*⟩
knock off* *vt* **1** : to make a knockoff of ⟨*knocks off* popular dress designs⟩ **2** : to make knockoffs of the designs of ⟨*knock off* a well-known designer⟩
knockoff** \ˈ-ˌ-\ *n* : a copy that sells for less than the original; *broadly* : a copy or imitation of someone or something popular or successful
know* *vb* — **know from** [trans. of Yiddish *visn fun*] : to have knowledge of ⟨didn't *know from* sibling rivalry —Penny Marshall⟩
knowledge engineering *n* : a branch of artificial intelligence that emphasizes the development and use of expert systems — **knowledge engineer** *n*
knuckle sandwich *n, slang* : a punch in the mouth
ko·bo \ˈkōˌbō\ *n, pl* **kobo** [alter. of *copper*] **1** : a monetary unit of Nigeria equal to [1]⁄[100] naira — see MONEY table *in the Dict* **2** : a coin representing one kobo
kook \ˈkük\ *n* -S [by shortening & alter. fr. *cuckoo*] : one whose ideas or actions are eccentric, fantastic, or insane
kooky *also* **kook·ie** \ˈkükē\ *adj* **kook·i·er**; **kook·i·est** [*kook* (herein) + [1]*-y* or *-ie*, alter. (influenced by *-ie*) of [1]*-y*] : having the characteristics of a kook : CRAZY, OFFBEAT — **kook·i·ly** \-ilē\ *adv* — **kook·i·ness** \-ēnəs\ *n* -ES
ko·ra \ˈkōr(ˌ)ä, ˈkȯr-, -rə\ *n* -S [Malinke] : a 21-string musical instrument of African origin that resembles a lute
ko·rat \kōˈrät\ *n* -S *usu cap* [fr. *Khorat* plateau, Thailand, where the breed originated] : any of a breed of short-haired domestic cats that originated in Thailand and are characterized by a heart-shaped face, a silver-blue coat, and usu. green eyes
korean hemorrhagic fever *n, usu cap K* : a hemorrhagic fever that is endemic to Asia, is caused by the hantaan virus, and is characterized by acute renal failure in addition to the usual symptoms of the hemorrhagic fevers
kovsh \ˈkȯvsh\ *n, pl* **kovsh** \"\ *or* **kov·shi** \-shē\ [Russ, fr. Lith *kaušas*; perh. akin to Skt *kośa* cask, cupboard] : a ladle or drinking vessel with a boat-shaped bowl and a handle at one end
kPa *abbr* kilopascal
k particle *n, usu cap K* [[1]K] : KAON *herein*
krad \ˈkāˌrad\ *abbr or n, pl* **krad** *also* **krads** : KILORAD *herein*
KREEP \ˈkrēp\ *n* [*K* (potassium) + *Rare-Earth Element* + *P* (phosphorus)] : a type of rock found esp. on the moon that contains potassium, rare-earth elements, and phosphorus
krem·lin·ol·o·gy \ˌkremləˈnäləjē\ *n* -ES *usu cap* [*Kremlin* + *-ology* (as in *psychology*)] : the study of the policies and practices of the Soviet government — **krem·lin·olog·i·cal** \ˌkremlənᵊlˈäjəkəl\ *adj, usu cap* — **krem·lin·ol·o·gist** \ˌ-ˈ-ˌjəst\ *n* -S *usu cap*
krewe \ˈkrü\ *n* -S [alter. of *crew*] : a private organization staging festivities (as parades and balls) during Mardi Gras in New Orleans
krio \ˈkrēō\ *n* -S *usu cap* [Krio, speaker of Krio, Krio language, perh. fr. Yoruba *Kìrìyó* Christian, fr. an African coastal pidgin or creole language, fr. Pg *crioulo* Creole — more at CREOLE] : an English-based creole spoken in Sierra Leone
kro·neck·er delta \ˈkrōˌnekə(r)-\ *n, usu cap K* [after Leopold *Kronecker* †1891 Ger. mathematician] : a function of two variables that is 1 when the variables have the same value and is 0 when they have different values
kru·ger·rand \ˈkrügəˌrand, *in So. Afr. usu* -ˌränd *or* -ˌrȧnt *or* -ˌränt\ *n, usu cap* [S.J.P. *Kruger* †1904 So. African statesman + *rand* (herein)] : a one-ounce gold coin of the Republic of So. Africa
KS *abbr* Kaposi's sarcoma *herein*
k–t \ˈkāˈtē\ *adj, usu cap K&T* : of, relating to, or occurring at the K-T boundary ⟨*K-T* extinctions⟩ ⟨*K-T* sediment⟩
k–t boundary *n, usu cap K&T* [*K* (alternative for *C* as abbr. for *Cretaceous*) + *Tertiary*] : the transition between the Cretaceous and Tertiary periods of geologic time characterized by a mass extinction of many forms of life including the dinosaurs; *also* : a geologic stratum marking this transition
ku·do \ˈk(y)üd(ˌ)ō\ *n, pl* **kudos** [back-formation fr. *kudos* (taken as a pl.)] **1** : AWARD, HONOR ⟨a score of honorary degrees and . . . other ~*s* —*Time*⟩ **2** : COMPLIMENT, TRIBUTE ⟨to all three should go some kind of special ~ for refusing to succumb —Al Hine⟩
ku·fi \ˈküfē\ *n* -S [origin unknown] : a close-fitting brimless cylindrical or round hat
kui·per belt \ˈkīpə(r)-\ *n, usu cap K* [after Gerard P. *Kuiper* †1973 U.S. (Dutch-born) astronomer] : a band of small celestial bodies beyond the orbit of Neptune from which many short-period comets are believed to originate — compare OORT CLOUD *herein*
ku·na \ˈküˌnä, -ˌnə\ *n, pl* **kuna** *or* **ku·ne** \-ˌnā\ [Serbo-Croatian (nom. pl. *kune*, gen. pl. *kunā*), lit., marten (the skin of which was used as currency in medieval Slavic cultures); akin to Lith *kiaunė* marten] **1** : the basic monetary unit of Croatia — see MONEY table *in the Dict* **2** : a coin representing one kuna
kun·da·li·ni \ˌkündᵊlˈēnē, -däˈlē-\ *n* -S *often cap* [Skt *kuṇḍalinī*, fr. fem. of *kuṇḍalin* circular, coiled, fr. *kuṇḍala* ring] : the yogic life-force that is held to lie coiled at the base of the spine until it is aroused and sent to the head to trigger enlightenment
kung fu \ˌkəŋˈfü, ˌküŋ-\ *n, sometimes cap K&F* [Chin (Cant) *gūng-fū* or Chin (Pek) *kung[1]-fu[1]* skill] : any of various Chinese arts of self-defense
kur·ta \ˈkərd·ə, ˈku̇rtä\ *n* -S [Hindi & Urdu *kurtā*, fr. Per *kurta*] : a loose-fitting collarless shirt
ku·ru \ˈkü(ˌ)rü\ *n* -S [Fore (language of eastern highland Papua New Guinea)] : a rare progressive fatal spongiform encephalopathy resembling Creutzfeldt-Jakob disease that occurs among tribesmen in eastern New Guinea, is marked by proliferation of astrocytes in the brain, and is now usu. considered to be caused by a prion
ku·ta·ni \ku̇ˈtänē\ *also* **kutani ware** *n* -S *usu cap K* [fr. *Kutani*, village in Japan] : a Japanese porcelain orig. produced in and about the village of Kutani on Honshu island beginning in the mid-17th century and esteemed for originality of design and coloring
kvell *also* **kvel** \ˈkvel\ *vi* **kvelled; kvelled; kvelling; kvels** [Yiddish *kveln* to be delighted, fr. MHG *quellen* to well, gush, swell, fr. OHG *quellan* — more at DEVIL] : to be extraordinarily proud : REJOICE
[1]**kvetch** \ˈkvech, ˈkfe-, kəˈvech\ *vi* -ED/-ING/-ES [Yiddish *kvetshn*, lit., to squeeze, pinch, fr. MHG *quetschen* — more at QUETSCH] : to complain habitually : GRIPE ⟨~*es* constantly about being 33 years old —H.F.Waters⟩ — **kvetch·er** \-ər\ *n* -S
[2]**kvetch** \"\ *n* -ES **1** : an habitual complainer **2** : COMPLAINT
kwa·cha \ˈkwächə\ *n, pl* **kwacha** [Bemba or Nyanja, lit., it dawns] **1** : the basic monetary unit of Malawi and Zambia — see MONEY table *in the Dict* **2** : a note representing one kwacha
kwan·za \ˈkwänzə\ *n, pl* **kwanza** *or* **kwanzas** [after *Kwanza* (Cuanza), river in Angola] **1** : the basic monetary unit of Angola — see MONEY table *in the Dict* **2** : a note representing one Kwanza
kwanzaa *also* **kwan·za** \ˈkwänzə\ *n* -S *usu cap* [Swahili *kwanza* first (in the phrase *matunda ya kwanza* first fruits)] : an Afro-American cultural festival held from December 26 to January 1
KWIC \ˈkwik\ *n* -S [*key word in context*] : a computer-generated index alphabetized on a keyword that appears within a portion of its context
laa·ri \ˈlä(ˌ)rē\ *n, pl* **laari** *or* **laaris** [prob. fr. Divehi (Indo-Aryan language of the Maldive Islands), fr. Per *lārī* piece of silver wire used as currency, fr. *Lār*, town in S Persia where the currency was first minted] **1** : a Maldivian monetary unit equal to [1]⁄[100] rufiyaa **2** : a coin representing one laari
la·bano·ta·tion \ˌläbənōˈtāshən, ˌlab-; lə̇ˌbän(ˌ)nō-\ *n, usu cap* [Rudolf *Laban* †1958 Hung. dance theorist + E *-o-* + *notation*] : LABAN SYSTEM
labor–intensive \ˈ-ˌ-ˌ-\ *adj* : having high labor costs per unit of output; *esp* : requiring greater expenditure on labor than in capital
labrum* *n* : a ring of fibrous cartilage forming the margin of the glenoid cavity of the shoulder joint that serves to broaden and deepen the cavity and gives attachment to the long head of the biceps brachii ⟨surgery to repair a torn ~⟩
lab·y·rin·thec·to·my \ˌlabə(ˌ)rinˈthektəmē\ *n* -ES [*labyrinth* + *-ectomy*] : surgical removal of the labyrinth of the ear
la·combe \ləˈkōm\ *n* [fr. *Lacombe* Experiment Station, Lacombe, Alta., Canada, where the breed was developed] **1** *usu cap* : a breed of white bacon-type swine developed in Canada from Landrace, Chester White, and Berkshire stock **2** -S *often cap* : a swine of the Lacombe breed
lactate dehydrogenase *n* : any of a group of isoenzymes that catalyze reversibly the conversion of pyruvic acid to lactic acid, are found esp. in the liver, kidneys, striated muscle, and the myocardium, and tend to accumulate in the body when these organs or tissues are diseased or injured
lactic dehydrogenase *n* : LACTATE DEHYDROGENASE *herein*
lac·to–ovo vegetarian \ˌlaktōˌōvō-\ *n* [*lact-* + *ov-* + [1]*vegetarian*] : a vegetarian whose diet includes dairy products, eggs, vegetables, fruits, grains, and nuts — called also *ovo-lacto vegetarian* \ˌōvōˌlakto-\; compare LACTO-VEGETARIAN *herein*
lac·to·peroxidase \ˌlak(ˌ)tō+\ *n* [*lact-* + *peroxidase*] : a peroxidase that is found in milk and saliva and is used to catalyze the iodination of tyrosine-containing proteins (as thyroglobulin)
lac·to–vegetarian \ˌlaktō-\ *n* [*lact-* + [1]*vegetarian*] : a vegetarian whose diet includes dairy products, vegetables, fruits, grains, and nuts — compare LACTO-OVO VEGETARIAN *herein*
la·e·trile \ˈlāəˌtril, -ˌtrəl\ *n* -S *often cap* [*laevorotatory* (levorotatory) + *nitrile*] : a drug derived esp. from apricot pits that contains amygdalin and has been used in the treatment of cancer although of unproved effectiveness
laf·fer curve \ˈlafər-\ *n, usu cap L* [after Arthur *Laffer* *b*1940 Am. economist] : a diagram shaped like a normal curve that is intended to show the relationship between tax rates and tax revenues
lagging indicator *n* : an economic indicator (as spending on new plants and equipment) that more often than not maintains an existent trend for some time after the state of the economy has turned onto an opposite trend — called also *lagger*
lagrangian point *n, usu cap L* [Joseph L. *Lagrange* †1813 Ital.-born geometer and astronomer in France + E *-ian*] : any of five points at which a small object (as a satellite) will be in gravitational equilibrium with and will move in a stable configuration with respect to two large bodies (as the earth and the sun)
laid–back \ˈ-ˈ-\ *adj* : having a relaxed style or character ⟨*laid-back* music⟩ ⟨a *laid-back* attitude⟩ — **laid–backness** \ˈ-ˈ-nəs\ *n* -ES
LAK cell \ˈlak-; ˌel(ˌ)āˈkā-\ *or* **LAK** *n* -S : LYMPHOKINE-ACTIVATED KILLER CELL *herein*
lake effect *n* : a meteorological phenomenon in which warm moist air rising from a body of water mixes with cold dry air overhead resulting in precipitation esp. downwind — often hyphenated when used attrib. ⟨frequent *lake-effect* snows in New York State —D.M.Ludlum⟩
la–la land \ˈläˌlä-\ *n, sometimes cap all 3 Ls* [*la-la* perh. fr. *la-la*, nonsense syllables in the refrains of songs expressing lightheartedness] : a euphoric dreamlike mental state detached from the harsher realities of life
la·maze \ləˈmäz\ *adj, usu cap* [fr. Fernand *Lamaze* †1957 Fr. obstetrician] : relating to or being a method of childbirth that involves psychological and physical preparation by the mother in order to suppress pain and facilitate delivery without drugs
lambda* *or* **lambda particle** *n* : an uncharged unstable subatomic particle that has a mass 2183 times that of an electron and decays typically into a nucleon and a pion
lame* *adj* **1** *slang* : not being in the know : SQUARE **2 a** : INFERIOR ⟨a ~ school⟩ **b** : CONTEMPTIBLE, NASTY ⟨~ racist jokes⟩
lame \ˈlām\ *n* -S *slang* : a person who is not in the know
lam·i·nin \ˈlamənən\ *n* -S [*lamina* + *-in*] : a glycoprotein that is a component of connective tissue basement membrane and that promotes cell adhesion
LAN \ˈlan, ˈel(ˌ)āˈen\ *abbr or n* -S local area network *herein*
landbridge** *n* : an overland route (as by rail) for shipping cargo from a port across a country
lander* *n* : one that lands; *esp* : a space vehicle that is designed to land on a celestial body (as the moon or a planet)
landfill* *n* : a dump where landfill disposal is practiced; *also* : an area built up by landfill disposal
landfill *vt* [*landfill*, n.] : to dispose of by landfill
landmark* *n* : a structure (as a building) of unusual historical and usu. aesthetic interest; *esp* : one that is officially designated and set aside for preservation
lane cake *n* [after Emma Rylander *Lane* †1898 Am. cookbook author] : a white layer cake with a rich filling usu. containing whiskey or wine, pecans, coconut, raisins, and candied fruit
lang·er·hans cell \ˈläŋə(r)ˌhän(t)s-\ *n, usu cap L* [after Paul

Langerhans †1888 Ger. physician] : a cell having slender cytoplasmic projections that is found in the epidermis and functions as an antigen-presenting cell which binds antigen entering through the skin and transports it to the lymph nodes

lan·gos·ti·no \ˌlaŋgəˈstēnō\ *n* -S [Sp, dim. of *langosta* spiny lobster, locust, fr. (assumed) VL *lacusta* — more at LANGOUSTE] : any of several edible crustaceans (as of the genus *Pleuroncodes*) that are or resemble small lobsters or large shrimp; *specif* : NORWAY LOBSTER

lan·gous·tine \ˌlaŋgəˈstēn, lä^ngüstēn\ *n* -S [F, dim. of *langouste* spiny lobster — more at LANGOUSTE] : NORWAY LOBSTER

language* *n* : MACHINE LANGUAGE *herein*

la ni·ña \läˈnēnyə, -nyä\ *n, pl* **la niñas** *usu cap L&N* [Sp, the (female) child (hence a counterpart to the El Niño phenomenon)] : an irregularly recurring upwelling of unusually cold water to the ocean surface along the western coast of South America that often occurs following an El Niño and that disrupts typical regional and global weather patterns esp. in a manner opposite to that of El Niño

lan·tian man \ˈlanˌtyan-\ *also* **lan–t'ien man** \-ˌtyen-\ *n, usu cap L* [fr. *Lant'ien*, district in Shensi province, China] : an extinct hominid known from parts of a skull excavated in China and now classified as a member of the genus *Homo* (*H. erectus*)

lap·a·ro·scope \ˈlap(ə)rəˌskōp\ *n* [ISV *laparo-* (fr. Gk. *lapara* flank, fr. *laparos* slack, loose) + *-scope*] : a slender illuminated optical instrument that is inserted through an incision in the abdominal wall and is used to examine visually the interior of the peritoneal cavity

lap·a·ros·co·py \ˌlapəˈräskəpē\ *n* -ES [ISV *laparo-* + *-scopy*] **1** : visual examination of the interior of the abdomen by means of a laparoscope **2** : an operation (as tubal ligation or gall bladder removal) involving laparoscopy — **lap·a·ro·scop·ic** \-ərəˈskäpik\ *adj* — **lap·a·ro·scop·i·cal·ly** \-k(ə)lē\ *adv* — **lap·a·ros·co·pist** \-əˈräskəpəst\ *n* -S

lap belt *n* : a seat belt that fastens across the lap

lap dancing *n* : dancing in which a semi-nude performer sits and gyrates on the lap of a spectator — **lap dance** *n* — **lap dancer** *n*

lapdog* *n* : a servile dependent or follower : LACKEY

la·place transform \ləˈpläs-, -las-\ *n, usu cap L* [after Pierre Simon de *Laplace* †1827 Fr. astronomer and mathematician] : a transformation of a function *f*(*x*) into the function

$$g(t) = \int_0^\infty e^{-xt} f(x)dx$$

that is useful esp. in reducing the solution of an ordinary linear differential equation with constant coefficients to the solution of a polynomial equation

¹laptop \ˈ=ˌ=\ *adj* [¹*lap* + *-top* (as in *desktop* — herein)] : of a size and design that makes operation and use on one's lap convenient ⟨a ~ personal computer⟩

²laptop *n* : a portable microcomputer having its main components (as processor, keyboard, and display screen) integrated into a single unit capable of battery-powered operation

large–scale integration \ˈ=ˌ=-\ *n* : the process of placing a large number (as hundreds) of circuits on a small semiconductor chip — abbr. *LSI*

lase \ˈlāz\ *vi* -ED/-ING/-S [back-formation fr. *laser*] : to emit coherent light

laser disc *n* : OPTICAL DISK *herein*; *specif* : one containing a video recording (as of a motion picture)

laser printer *n* : a high-resolution xerographic printer for computer output that prints an image (as text or pictures) formed by a laser

LA·SIK \ˈlāsik\ *n* -S [*las*er-assisted *in* situ *k*eratomileusis (surgical reshaping of the cornea, fr. NL, irreg. fr. *kerat-* + Gk *smileusis* carving, fr. *smilē* knife, lancet) — more at SMITH] : a surgical operation to reshape the cornea for correction of nearsightedness, farsightedness, or astigmatism in which the surface layer of the cornea is separated to create a hinged flap providing access to the inner cornea where varying amounts of tissue are removed by an excimer laser followed by replacement of the corneal flap

l–as·par·a·gi·nase \ˌelaˈsparəjəˌnās, -āz\ *n* -S *usu cap L* [*L*-(levorotatory) + *asparagine* + *-ase*] : an enzyme that breaks down the physiologically commoner form of asparagine, is obtained esp. from bacteria, and is used esp. to treat leukemia

las·sa fever \ˈlasə-\ *n, usu cap L* [fr. *Lassa*, village in Nigeria] : a disease esp. of Africa that is caused by an arenavirus (genus *Arenavirus*) and is characterized by a high fever, headaches, mouth ulcers, muscle aches, small hemorrhages under the skin, heart and kidney failure, and a high mortality rate

las·si \ˈläsē\ *n* -S [Hindi *lassī*, fr. (assumed) Skt *lasya* stickiness; akin to Skt *lasīkā* syrup, sugar-cane juice, *rasa* juice — more at ROSEMARY] : a flavored iced yogurt drink that may be either sweet or salted

last hurrah *n* [*The Last Hurrah* (1956) by Edwin O'Connor †1968 Am. novelist] : a final often valedictory effort, production, or appearance ⟨his unsuccessful Senate run was his *last hurrah* —R.W.Daly⟩

lat \ˈlat\ *n* -S [by shortening] : LATISSIMUS DORSI — usu. used in pl.

latchkey child *or* **latchkey kid** *n* [so called because such a child is typically entrusted with a house key] : a school-age child of working parents who spends part of the day at home unsupervised

latent root *n* : an eigenvalue of a matrix

lateral condyle *n* : a condyle on the outer side of the lower extremity of the femur; *also* : a corresponding eminence on the upper part of the tibia that articulates with the lateral condyle of the femur — compare MEDIAL CONDYLE *herein*

lateral thinking *n* : thinking that is not deductive

lath·y·rit·ic \ˌlathəˈrid·ik\ *adj* [*lathyrism* + *-itic*] : of, relating to, affected with, or characteristic of lathyrism ⟨~ rats⟩

lath·y·ro·gen \ˈlathərəˌjen, -jən\ *n* -S [*lathyrism* + *-o-* + *-gen*] : any of a group of nucleophilic compounds that tend to cause lathyrism and inhibit the formation of links between chains of collagen — **lath·y·ro·gen·ic** \ˌ=ˌ=ˈjenik\ *adj*

la·tic·i·fer \lāˈtisəfə(r)\ *n* -S [ISV, fr. *latici-* (fr. NL *latic-*, *latex*) + *-fer*] : a plant cell or vessel that contains latex

la·ti·na \ləˈtēnə, la-\ *n* -S *usu cap* [AmerSp, fem. of *latino* Latino] **1** : a woman or girl who is a native or inhabitant of Latin America **2** : a woman or girl of Latin-American origin living in the U.S. — **latina** *adj, usu cap*

latin americanist *n, usu cap L&A* : a specialist in Latin-American civilization

latino* *n, usu cap* : a person of Latin-American origin living in the U.S. — **latino** *adj, usu cap*

lat·te \ˈlä(ˌ)tā\ *n* -S [by shortening] : CAFFÈ LATTE *herein*

lattice* *n* : a mathematical set that has some elements ordered and that is such that for any two elements there exists a greatest element in the subset of all elements less than or equal to both and a least element in the subset of all elements greater than or equal to both

laugher* *n* : something (as a game or contest) that is easily won or handled

laugh track *n* : recorded laughter that accompanies dialogue or action (as of a television program)

launcher* *n* : LAUNCH VEHICLE *herein*

launching pad* *n* : SPRINGBOARD 2

launch vehicle *n* : a rocket used to launch a satellite or spacecraft

launder* *vt* : to transfer (as illegally obtained money or investments) through an outside party to conceal the true source

laundry list *n* [so called fr. the listing of articles of clothing sent to a laundry] : a usu. long list of items ⟨the *laundry list* of new consumer-protection bills —N.C.Miller⟩

LAV \ˌel(ˌ)āˈvē\ *n* -S [*l*ymphadenopathy-*a*ssociated *v*irus] : HIV-1 *herein*

lavaliere microphone *n* : a small microphone hung around the neck of the user

law of parsimony* : OCKHAM'S RAZOR

law·ren·cium \lóˈren(t)sēəm, lə'-, -nch(ē)əm\ *n* -S [NL, fr. Ernest O. *Lawrence* †1958 Am. physicist + NL *-ium*] : a short-lived radioactive element of atomic number 103 that is produced artificially — symbol *Lr*; see ELEMENT table *in the Dict*

layabout \ˈ=ˌ=ˌ=\ *n* -S [fr. the phrase *lay about*, nonstandard alter. of *lie about*] *chiefly Brit* : IDLER 1

lay–by* *n* : the final operation (as a last cultivating) in the growing of a field crop

layer* *vt* **1 a** : to place as a layer ⟨jackets roomy enough to be *~ed* over sweaters⟩ **b** : to place a layer on top of ⟨pancakes *~ed* with butter and maple syrup⟩ **c** : to form or arrange in layers ~ *vi* : to form out of superimposed layers

laypeople \ˈ=ˌ=ˌ=\ *n pl* : LAYPERSONS *herein*

layperson \ˈ=ˌ=ˌ=\ *n* [⁵*lay* + *person*] : a member of the laity

lazy eye *n* [so called fr. the fact that a person suffering from this condition uses only one eye] : AMBLYOPIA; *also* : an eye affected with amblyopia

lazy eye blindness *n* : AMBLYOPIA

LBO \ˌel(ˌ)bēˈō\ *abbr or n* -S : a leveraged buyout

LCD \ˌel(ˌ)sēˈdē\ *n* -S [*l*iquid *c*rystal *d*isplay] : a constantly operating display (as of the time in a digital watch) that consists of segments of a liquid crystal whose reflectivity varies according to the voltage applied to them

l cell *n, usu cap L* : a fibroblast cell of a strain isolated from mice and used esp. in virus research

LD* *abbr* learning disability; learning disabled *herein*

LDC \ˌel(ˌ)dēˈsē\ *abbr or n* -S : a less developed country

LD50 \ˌelˌdēˈfiftē\ *n* [*l*ethal *d*ose] : the amount of a toxic agent (as a poison, virus, or radiation) that is sufficient to kill 50% of a population of animals usu. within a certain time

LDH *abbr* lactate dehydrogenase; lactic dehydrogenase

LDL \ˌel(ˌ)dēˈel\ *n* -S : a lipoprotein of blood plasma that is composed of a moderate proportion of protein with little triglyceride and a high proportion of cholesterol and that is associated with increased probability of developing atherosclerosis — called also *low-density lipoprotein*; compare HDL *herein*, VLDL *herein*

l–do·pa \(ˈ)elˈdōpə\ *n, usu cap L* [*l-* + *dopa*] : the levorotatory form of dopa that is obtained esp. from broad beans or prepared synthetically, is converted to dopamine in the brain, and is used in treating Parkinson's disease — called also *levodopa*

leading edge *n* : CUTTING EDGE 1 *herein* — **leading–edge** *adj*

leading indicator *n* : an economic indicator (as the level of corporate profits or of stock prices) that more often than not shows a change in direction before a corresponding change in the state of the economy — called also *leader*

leaf·let \ˈlēflət, *usu* -əd-+V\ *vb* **leafleted** *or* **leafletted**; **leafleted** *or* **leafletted**; **leafleting** *or* **leafletting**; **leaflets** [*leaflet*, n.] *vi* : to pass out leaflets ~ *vt* : to pass out leaflets to — **leaf·le·teer** \ˌlēfləˈti(ə)r\ *n* -S

leaky* *adj* : relating to or being a mutant gene that changes the structure of the protein and esp. an enzyme that it determines so that some but not all of its biological activity is lost; *also* : being such a protein with subnormal activity

lean* *vb* — **lean on** : to apply pressure to : COERCE

leap second *n* [*leap* day + ⁴*second*] : an intercalary second added to Coordinated Universal Time to compensate for the slowing of the earth's rotation and keep Coordinated Universal Time in synchrony with solar time

learning curve *n* **1** : PRACTICE CURVE; *esp* : one that graphs the decline in unit costs with cumulative output **2** : the course of progress made in learning something

learning disability *n* : any of various disorders (as dyslexia or dysgraphia) that interfere with an individual's ability to learn and so result in impaired functioning in language, reasoning, or academic skills (as reading, writing, and mathematics) and that are thought to be caused by difficulties in processing and integrating information — **learning disabled** *adj*

leash law *n* : a usu. municipal ordinance requiring dogs to be restrained when not confined to their owners' property

leather* *adj* : relating to, catering esp. to, or being homosexuals exhibiting macho or masochistic behavior ⟨~ bars⟩

¹lech \ˈlech\ *n* -ES **1** : ²LETCH **2** [by shortening] : LECHER

²lech \"\ *vi* -ED/-ING/-ES [¹*lech* 2 (herein)] : to experience sexual desire

LED \ˌel(ˌ)ēˈdē, ˈled\ *n* -S [*l*ight-*e*mitting *d*iode] : a semiconductor diode that emits light when a voltage is applied to it and that is usu. used in an electronic display (as for a pocket calculator or a digital watch)

left brain *n* : the left cerebral hemisphere of the human brain esp. when viewed in terms of its predominant thought processes (as analytic and logical thinking) — **left–brained** *adj*

left field* *n* : a state or position far from the mainstream (as of prevailing opinion) : a source of the unexpected or illogical

leg* *n* **legs** *pl* : long-term appeal or interest ⟨this thing has still got *~s* and it is almost 10 years later —George Stalk, Jr.⟩

legal eagle *n* : LAWYER

legal pad *n* : a writing tablet of usu. 8½ by 14 inch ruled yellow paper

le·gion·el·la \ˌlējəˈnelə\ *n* [NL, fr. E *legionnaire* + NL *-ella*] **1** *cap* : a genus of gram-negative rod-shaped bacteria (family Legionellaceae) that includes the causative agent (*L. pneumophila*) of Legionnaires' disease **2** *pl* **le·gion·el·lae** \-ˈne(ˌ)lē\ *also* **legionellas** : a bacterium of the genus *Legionella*

legionnaires' disease *also* **legionnaire's disease** *n, usu cap L* [so called fr. its first recognized occurrence at a 1976 American Legion convention in Philadelphia] : pneumonia that is caused by a bacterium of the genus *Legionella* (*L. pneumophila*), that is characterized initially by symptoms resembling influenza (as malaise, headache, and muscular aches) followed by high fever, cough, diarrhea, lobar pneumonia, and mental confusion, and that may be fatal esp. in elderly and immunocompromised individuals

leg warmer *n* : a usu. knitted covering for the leg

lei *pl of* LEU

leish·man–don·o·van body \ˈlēshmənˈdänəvən-, -ˈdən-\ *n, usu cap L&D* [after Sir William B. *Leishman* †1926 Eng. army surgeon & Charles *Donovan* †1951 Irish physician] : a protozoan of the genus *Leishmania* (esp. *L. donovani*) in its nonmotile stage that is found esp. in cells of the skin, spleen, and liver of individuals affected with leishmaniasis and esp. kala-azar — compare DONOVAN BODY *in the Dict*

leisure suit *n* : a suit consisting of a shirt jacket and matching trousers for informal wear

lek·var \ˈlekˌvär, -ˌvȧ(r\ *n* -S [Hung *lekvár*] : a prune butter used as a pastry filling

LEM \ˈlem\ *abbr or n* -S lunar excursion module *herein*

lem·ma·tize \ˈleməˌtīz, -əd-,īz\ *vt* -ED/-ING/-S [NL *lemmat-*, *lemma* lemma + E *-ize*] : to sort (words in a corpus) in order to group with a lemma all its variant and inflected forms — **lem·ma·ti·za·tion** \ˌlemədəˈzāshən, -əˌtīˈz-\ *n* -S

lemon law *n* [*lemon* (dud)] : a law protecting car buyers against defects detected during a specified period after purchase

lens* *n* : GRAVITATIONAL LENS *herein*

len·ti·vi·rus \ˈlentəˈvīrəs\ *n* [NL, fr. *lenti-* (fr. L *lentus* slow) + *virus* — more at LITHE] : any of a genus (*Lentivirus*) of retroviruses that cause slowly progressive often fatal human and animal diseases (as equine infectious anemia and AIDS)

leo* *n, usu cap* : one born under the astrological sign Leo

le·one \lēˈōn\ *n, pl* **leones** *or* **leone** [fr. Sierra *Leone*, Africa] **1** : the basic monetary unit of Sierra Leone — see MONEY table *in the Dict* **2** : a note representing one leone

le·oni·an \lēˈōnēən\ *n* -S *usu cap* [L *Leon-*, *Leo* a constellation, lit., lion + E *-ian*] : LEO *herein*

leo·nid \ˈlēənəd\ *n, pl* **leo·nids** *or* **le·on·i·des** \lēˈänəˌdēz\ *usu cap* [L *Leon-*, *Leo* + E ¹*-id*; fr. their appearing to radiate from a point in the constellation Leo] : any of the meteors in a meteor shower occurring every year about November 14

LEP *abbr* limited English proficient

lep·tin \ˈleptən\ *n* -S [Gk *leptos* thin, lean + E *-in* — more at LEPT-] : a peptide hormone that is produced by fat cells and plays a role in body weight regulation by acting on the hypothalamus to suppress appetite and burn fat stored in adipose tissue

lep·ton·ic \(ˈ)lepˈtänik\ *adj* : of, relating to, or producing a lepton ⟨~ decay of a hyperon⟩

lep·to·spire \ˈleptəˌspī(ə)r, -īə\ *n* -S [by alter.] : LEPTOSPIRA 2

lesch–ny·han syndrome \ˈleshˈnīən-\ *also* **lesch–nyhan disease** *n, usu cap L&N* [after Michael *Lesch* *b*1939 Am. cardiologist and William L. *Nyhan* *b*1926 Am. pediatrician] : a rare and usu. fatal genetic disorder of male children that is inherited as an X-linked recessive trait and that is characterized by hyperuricemia, mental retardation, spasticity, compulsive biting of the lips and fingers, and a deficiency of an enzyme that conserves hypoxanthine in the body by limiting its conversion to uric acid

lesion *vt* -ED/-ING/-S [*lesion*, n.] : to produce lesions in

let* *vb* — **let it all hang out** : to reveal one's true feelings : act without dissimulation — **let rip 1** : to utter or release without restraint : let fly ⟨*lets rip* an off-the-cuff attack —Julie Wilson⟩ ⟨the pitcher *let* it *rip* with the first pitch⟩ — often used in the phrase *let her rip* **2** : to do or utter something without restraint : cut loose ⟨*let rip* at the press⟩ — **let the chips fall where they may** : to act knowing that the consequences may prove to be undesirable or disadvantageous

letter bomb *n* : an explosive device concealed in an envelope and mailed to the intended victim

let·ter·boxed \ˈ=ˌ=ˌ=\ *also* **let·ter·box** \ˈ=ˌ=ˌ=\ *adj* [perh. fr. the resemblance of the resulting image on the TV screen or the bands above and below the image to slots in a mailbox] *of a video recording* : formatted so as to display the full rectangular frame of a wide-screen motion picture — compare PAN-AND-SCAN *herein*

letterform \ˈ=ˌ=ˌ=\ *n* : the shape of a letter of an alphabet esp. from the standpoint of design or development

letter quality *n* [¹*letter* (missive)] : printing produced by a computer printer in solid letters similar to or clearer than those produced by a conventional typewriter

let·ter·set \ˈ=ˌ=ˌset\ *n* -S [*letter*press + off*set*] : DRY OFFSET

letter stock *n* [so called fr. the letter signed by the purchaser stating that the stock is acquired for investment and not for public sale] : restricted and unregistered stock that may not be sold to the general public without undergoing registration

leu* *n, pl* **lei** **1** : the basic monetary unit of Moldova — see MONEY table *in the Dict* **2** : a coin or note representing one leu

leu·ke·mic \lüˈkēmik\ *n* -S [*leukemia* + ²*-ic*] : a person suffering from leukemia

leu·ko·dys·tro·phy \ˌlükōˈdistrəfē\ *n* [*leuc-* + *dystrophy*] : any of several genetically determined diseases (as adrenoleukodystrophy) characterized by progressive degeneration of myelin in the brain, spinal cord, and peripheral nerves

leu·ko·tri·ene \ˌlükōˈtrīˌēn\ *n* -S [*leukocyte* + *-triene*; fr. the discovery of the substances in leukocytes] : any of a group of eicosanoids that are generated in basophils, mast cells, macrophages, and human lung tissue by lipoxygenase-catalyzed oxygenation esp. of arachidonic acid and that participate in allergic responses (as bronchoconstriction in asthma)

lev·al·lor·phan \ˌlevəˈlȯrˌfan, -fən\ *n* -S [*lev-* + *allyl* + *morphine* + ³*-an*] : a drug $C_{19}H_{25}NO$ related to morphine that is used to counteract morphine poisoning

le·vam·i·sole \ləˈvaməˌsōl\ *n* -S [perh. fr. *lev-* + *-amisole* (alter. of *imidazole*)] : an anthelmintic drug $C_{11}H_{12}N_2S$ administered in the form of its hydrochloride that also possesses immunostimulant properties and is used esp. in the treatment of colon cancer

level of significance : the probability of rejecting the null hypothesis in a statistical test when it is true — called also *significance level*

leverage* *n* **1 a** : borrowed money or its use to supplement capital or to increase the earning power of a relatively small investment **b** : the ability of a small investment to produce a large return ⟨~ is so great with any options strategy that . . . this portfolio can double in just a few months —M.G.Ansbacher⟩ **c** : the advantage gained by using leverage ⟨it gave business healthy ~: business could do more with less of its own money —Chris Welles⟩ **2** : the ratio of debt to equity ⟨three other critical performance measures: return on assets, ~, and return on equity —*Business Week*⟩

leverage *vt* -ED/-ING/-S [*leverage*, n.] : to provide (as a corporation) or supplement (as money) with leverage ⟨has stretched and *leveraged* capital —*Fortune*⟩; *also* : to enhance as if by supplying with financial leverage ⟨who use tools to ~ personal capabilities to the limit —*advt*⟩

lever·aged \ˈlev(ə)rijd, ˈlēv-\ *adj* **1** : having a high proportion of debt relative to equity ⟨mismanaged, unwisely ~, and highly illiquid corporations —N.A.Bailey⟩ **2** *of the purchase of a company* : made with borrowed money that is secured by the assets of the company bought ⟨a ~ buyout⟩

levo·do·pa \ˌlēvōˈdōpə, ˌlēvə-, ˌlevə-\ *n* : L-DOPA *herein*

lex·i·cal·ist \ˈleksəkələst\ *adj* [*lexical* + ²*-ist*] : of, being, or relating to an approach to grammar in which syntactic structures are derived from properties of lexemes rather than from a large set of transformations

lex·i·cal·iza·tion \ˌleksəkələˈzāshən\ *n* -S [*lexical* + *-ization*] **1** : the realization of a meaning in a single word or morpheme of a language rather than in a grammatical construction **2** : the treatment of a formerly freely composed, grammatically regular, and semantically transparent phrase or inflected form as a formally or semantically idiomatic expression — **lex·i·cal·ize** \ˈ=ˌ=ˌ=ˌlīz\ *vt* -ED/-ING/-S

lex·is \ˈleksəs\ *n, pl* **lex·es** \-kˌsēz\ [Gk, speech, word — more at LEXICON] : VOCABULARY, WORD-STOCK

lez·zie *also* **lez·zy** \ˈlezē\ *n, pl* **lezzies** [by shortening & alter.] : LESBIAN — often used disparagingly

LHRH *abbr* luteinizing hormone-releasing hormone *herein*

lib \ˈlib\ *n* -S [by shortening] : LIBERATION *herein*

lib·ber \ˈlibə(r)\ *n* -S [*lib* (herein) + ²*-er*] : one who advocates liberation ⟨a women's ~⟩

liberation* *n* : a movement seeking equal rights and status for a group ⟨women's ~⟩

liberation theology *n* : a religious movement esp. among Roman Catholic clergy in Latin America that combines political philosophy usu. of a Marxist orientation with a theology of salvation as liberation from injustice — **liberation theologian** *n*

libertarian* *n, usu cap* : a member of a political party advocating libertarian principles

libra* *n, usu cap* : one born under the astrological sign Libra

li·bran \ˈlēbrən, ˈlīb-\ *n* -S *usu cap* [*libra* + E *-an*] : LIBRA *herein*

library* *n* : a collection of cloned DNA fragments that are maintained in a suitable cellular environment and that often represent the genetic material of a particular organism or tissue

Lib·ri·um \ˈlibrēəm\ *trademark* — used for a preparation of chlordiazepoxide

licensed practical nurse *n* : a person trained and licensed (as by a state) to provide routine care for the sick — abbr. *LPN*

licensed vocational nurse *n* : a licensed practical nurse authorized by license to practice in California or Texas — abbr. *LVN*

li·cen·te \ləˈsentē\ *n, pl* **licente** *or* **li·cen·ti** \-tē\ [Sotho, fr. *li-*, class prefix + *-cente* (fr. E *cent*)] : a unit equal to ¹⁄₁₀₀ loti — see MONEY table *in the Dict*

lid* *n* : an ounce of marijuana

li·dar \ˈlīˌdär\ *n* -S [*light* + *radar*] : a device or system for locating an object that is similar in operation to radar but emits pulsed laser light instead of microwaves

lie algebra \ˈlē-\ *n, usu cap L* [after Sophus *Lie* †1899 Norw. mathematician] : a linear algebra which has the multiplicative operation denoted by [,] and is bilinear such that

$$[aA + bB,C] = a[A,C] + b[B,C] \text{ and } [A,aB + bC] = a[A,B] + b[A,C]$$

and satisfies the conditions that

$$[A,A] = 0 \text{ and } [[A,B],C] + [[B,C],A] + [[C,A],B] = 0$$

where *A, B, C* are any vectors in the vector space and *a, b, c* are scalars from the associated field

lie group *n, usu cap L* [Sophus *Lie*] : a topological group for which the coordinates of the product of two elements are functions of the coordinates of the elements themselves and the coordinates of the inverse of an element are functions of the coordinates of the element itself and for which all derivatives of these functions exist and are continuous

life–care \ˈ⸗,⸗\ *adj* : of, relating to, or being a residential complex for elderly people that provides an apartment, personal and social services, and health care for life

life list *n* : a record kept of all birds sighted and identified by a birder

lifer* *n* **1** : a career member of the armed forces **2** : a person who has made a life-long commitment (as to a way of life)

life science *n* : a branch of science (as biology, medicine, and sometimes anthropology or sociology) that deals with living organisms and life processes — usu. used in pl. — **life scientist** *n*

lifestyle \ˈ⸗,⸗(⸗)\ *adj* [*life-style*, n.] : associated with, reflecting, or promoting an enhanced or more desirable lifestyle ⟨~ magazine⟩ ⟨~ product⟩

life–support \ˈ⸗⸗ˈ⸗\ *adj* : providing support necessary to sustain life; *esp* : of, relating to, or being a life-support system

life support *n* : equipment, material, and treatment needed to keep a seriously ill or injured patient alive ⟨asked doctors to withdraw *life support* —*Newsweek*⟩

life–support system *n* : a system that provides all or some of the items (as oxygen, food, water, control of temperature and pressure, disposition of carbon dioxide and body wastes) necessary for maintaining life or health: as **a** : one used to maintain the health of a person or animal in outer space, underwater, or in a mine **b** : one used to maintain the life of an injured or ill person unable to maintain certain physiological processes without artificial support **c** : BIOSPHERE 1

lifetime *adj* [*lifetime*, n.] **1** : LIFELONG ⟨a ~ love affair with books⟩ **2** : of long duration or continuance ⟨~ legislation⟩ **3** : measured or achieved over the span of a career ⟨a baseball player's ~ batting average⟩

life·world \ˈ⸗,⸗\ *n* [trans. of G *lebenswelt*] : the sum total of physical surroundings and everyday experiences that make up an individual's world

lifting body *n* : a maneuverable rocket-propelled wingless vehicle that is capable of travel in aerospace or in the earth's atmosphere where its lift is derived from its shape and that can be landed on the ground

ligand–gated \ˈ⸗⸗ˈ⸗⸗\ *adj* : permitting or blocking passage through a cell membrane in response to a chemical stimulus ⟨a *ligand-gated* ion channel triggered by ATP —J.M.Besson⟩

li·gase \ˈlī,gās, -,gāz\ *n* -s [ISV *lig-* (fr. L *ligare* to bind, tie) + *-ase* — more at LIGATURE] : SYNTHETASE

ligate* *vt* : to join together (as DNA or protein chains) by a chemical process ⟨the DNA fragments were enzymatically *ligated*⟩

ligation* *n* : the process of joining together by a chemical process esp. to form a chain (as of DNA or protein)

light* *or* **lite** *adj* : made with a lower calorie content or with less of some ingredient (as salt or fat) than usual ⟨~ beer⟩ ⟨~ margarine⟩ ⟨~ salad dressing⟩

light–adapt·ed \ˈ⸗ˈ⸗⸗\ *adj* : adjusted for vision in bright light : having undergone light adaptation

light chain *n* : either of the two smaller of the four polypeptide chains that are subunits of antibodies — compare HEAVY CHAIN *herein*

light–day \ˈ⸗ˈ⸗\ *n* : a unit of length in astronomy equal to the distance that light travels in one day in a vacuum or about 26 billion kilometers

light–emitting diode \ˈ⸗⸗ˈ⸗⸗-\ *n* : LED *herein*

lighten up *vi* : to take things less seriously : RELAX

light guide *n* : an optical fiber used esp. for telecommunication with light waves

light–hour \ˈ⸗ˈ⸗\ *n* : a unit of length in astronomy equal to the distance that light travels in one hour in a vacuum or about 1.1 billion kilometers

light pen *n* : a pen-shaped device for a computer that when held to a point on a video screen allows the computer to sense the pen's position and that is used for direct input of data

light pipe *n* : an optical fiber or a solid transparent plastic rod used for transmitting light

light pollution *n* : artificial skylight (as from city lights) that interferes with astronomical observations

light–rail \ˈ⸗ˈ⸗\ *n, often attrib* : a means of urban railway transportation using trolley cars ⟨*light-rail* vehicle⟩

light reaction *n* : the phase of photosynthesis that requires the presence of light and that involves photophosphorylation — compare CALVIN CYCLE *herein*

light show *n* : a kaleidoscopic display of colored lights (as lasers, spotlights, or strobes) usu. accompanied by music

light table *n* : a device that projects even light through a flat translucent surface over which films or tracings may be spread out and viewed

light therapy *also* **light treatment** *n* : PHOTOTHERAPY; *esp* : the use of strong light (as of 10,000 lux intensity) for the treatment of depression and gloom (as in seasonal affective disorder)

light water *n* : WATER 1a, — compare HEAVY WATER *in the Dict*

light–year* *n* : an extremely large measure of comparison (as of distance, time, or quality) ⟨two minutes and yet *light-years* away from the crowded village —Suzanne Patterson⟩

lig·no·caine \ˈlignə,kān\ *n* -s [*lign-* + *-caine*] *Brit* : LIDOCAINE

like \(,)līk\ *interj* [⁵*like*] — used in speech and informal writing to focus attention on a following word, phrase, or clause ⟨terribly upset . . . ~, the most upset I've ever been —Truman Capote⟩ ⟨he was, ~, gorgeous⟩ or to soften or deemphasize a preceding or following word or phrase ⟨I'm ~ the straightest member of my family —Huey Lewis⟩ ⟨I need to, ~, borrow some money⟩ or to suggest approximation ⟨I've been waiting, ~, ten minutes⟩

li·ku·ta \lə̇ˈküd·ə, (ˈ)lēˈk-\ *n, pl* **ma·ku·ta** \(ˈ)mäˈk-\ [prob. fr. Kituba (restructured Kikongo used as a lingua franca), any of various coins of the Belgian Congo, fr. Pg *macuta* Angolan coin, fr. Kikongo *dikuta*, pl. *makuta* palm-leaf cloth bundle used as currency, fr. *-kuta* to gather, bundle] **1** : a monetary unit of Zaire equal to ¹⁄₁₀₀ zaire — see MONEY table *in the Dict* **2** : a coin representing one likuta

li·lan·geni \,lē(,)länˈ(g)enē\ *n, pl* **ema·lan·geni** \,emə-(,)länˈ(g)enē\ [Siswati (Swazi), prob. fr. *emaLangeni* lineage of the Swazi royal family] **1** : the basic monetary unit of Swaziland — see MONEY table *in the Dict* **2** : a coin or note representing one lilangeni

limbic* *adj* : of, relating to, or being the limbic system of the brain

limbic system *n* : a group of subcortical structures (as the hypothalamus, the hippocampus, and the amygdala) of the brain that are concerned esp. with emotion and motivation

lim·bo \ˈlim(,)bō\ *n* -s [E or English Creole of Trinidad & Barbados; akin to Jamaican E *limba* to bend (fr. E ³*limber*)] : a dance or contest that involves bending over backward and passing under a horizontal pole which is lowered slightly for each successive pass

limit point *n* : a point that is related to a set of points in such a way that every neighborhood of the point no matter how small contains another point belonging to the set — called also *point of accumulation*

limo \ˈlim(,)ō\ *n* -s [by shortening] : LIMOUSINE

lim·ou·sin \ˈlimə,zēn, ,⸗⸗ˈ⸗, *F* lēmüzaⁿ\ *n, usu cap* [F, of Limoges, France] **1** : a French breed of medium-sized yellow-red cattle bred esp. for meat **2** -s : an animal of the Limousin breed

limousine liberal *n* : a wealthy political liberal

limp·en \ˈlimpən\ *vi* -ED/-ING/-S [³*limp* + ²*-en*] : to become limp ⟨~*ed* instantly and fell —Carson McCullers⟩

limp–wristed \ˈ⸗ˈristə̇d\ *adj* [¹*limp* + *wrist* + ¹*-ed*] **1** : EFFEMINATE **2** : WEAK, FLABBY

lin·ac \ˈlin,ak\ *n* -s [*linear accelerator*] : LINEAR ACCELERATOR

lin·co·my·cin \,liŋkəˈmīsᵊn\ *n* -s [NL *lincol*nensis (specific epithet of *Streptomyces lincolnensis*, species of actinomycete) + E *-mycin*] : an antibiotic $C_{18}H_{34}N_2O_6S$ obtained from an actinomycete of the genus *Streptomyces* (*S. lincolnensis*) that is effective esp. against gram-positive bacteria

line* *n* **1** : a circuit in an electronic communication system **2** : a telephone connection ⟨tried to get a ~⟩; *also* : an individual telephone extension ⟨a call on ~ 2⟩ **3** : any of the successive horizontal rows of picture elements on a television screen **4** : an amount of cocaine that is arranged in a line to be inhaled through the nose **5** : betting odds set by bookmakers esp. for a sports event **6** : an often numbered section of a computer program containing a single command or a small number of usu. related commands ⟨a ~ of code⟩ **7** : a narrow short sterile synthetic tube (as of plastic) that is inserted approximately one inch into a vein (as of the arm) to provide temporary intravenous access for the administration of fluid, medication, or nutrients — **down the line*** : in the future ⟨going to be trouble *down the line* —Mimi Sheraton⟩ — **on line 1** : in or into operation ⟨base load generating plants take about ten years to bring *on line* —*Resources*⟩ **2** : in line

linear* *adj* **1** : composed of simply drawn lines with little attempt at pictorial representation ⟨~ script⟩ **2 a** : relating to, concerned with, or influenced by the sequential structure of the printed line ⟨~ learning patterns⟩ **b** : arranged or presented in a logical or temporal sequence ⟨~ procedures⟩ ⟨the march of events is strictly ~ —Robert Towers⟩

linear A *n, usu cap L* : a linear form of writing used in Crete from the 18th to the 15th centuries B.C.

linear algebra *n* **1** : a branch of mathematics that is concerned with mathematical structures closed under the operation of addition and scalar multiplication and with their applications and that includes the theory of systems of linear equations, matrices, determinants, vector spaces, and linear transformations **2** : a mathematical ring which is also a vector space with scalars from an associated field and whose multiplicative operation is such that *(aA)(bB)=(ab)(AB)* where *a* and *b* are scalars and *A* and *B* are vectors — called also *algebra*

linear B *n, usu cap L* : a linear form of writing employing syllabic characters and used at Knossos on Crete and on the Greek mainland from the 15th to the 12th centuries B.C. for documents in the Mycenaean language

linear combination *n* : a mathematical entity (as 4x + 5y + 6z) which is composed of sums and differences of elements (as variables, matrices, or functions) whose coefficients are not all zero

linear dependence *n* : the property of one set (as of matrices or vectors) of having at least one linear combination of its elements equal to zero when the coefficients are taken from another given set and at least one of the coefficients is not equal to zero — **linearly dependent** *adj*

linear independence *n* : the property of one set (as of matrices or vectors) of having no linear combination of its elements equal to zero when the coefficients are taken from another given set unless the coefficient of each element is zero — **linearly independent** *adj*

linear motor *n* : a motor that produces thrust in a straight line by direct induction rather than with the use of gears

linear regression *n* : the process of finding a straight line (as by least squares) that best approximates a set of points on a graph

linear space *n* : VECTOR SPACE *herein*

linear transformation *n* **1** : a transformation in which the new variables are linear functions of the old variables **2** : a function that maps the vectors of one vector space onto the vectors of the same or another vector space with the same field of scalars in such a way that the image of the sum of two vectors equals the sum of their images and the image of the product of a scalar and a vector equals the product of the scalar and the image of the vector

line dance *n* **1** : CONTREDANSE 1 **2** : a dance performed by a group usu. in single file **3** : a dance in which the dancers stand in ranks while performing a particular set of steps in unison — **line dancer** *n* — **line dancing** *n*

line item *n* : an appropriation that is itemized on a separate line in a budget — **line–item** \ˈ⸗ˈ⸗⸗\ *adj*

line–item veto *n* : the power of a government executive to veto specific items in an appropriations bill without vetoing the bill altogether

line judge *n* : a football linesman whose duties include keeping track of the official time for the game

line printer *n* : a high-speed printing device (as for a computer) that prints each line as a unit rather than character by character

liner notes *n pl* [²*liner* (text accompanying a recording)] : comments or explanatory notes about a recording printed on its jacket or an insert

line score *n* : a score of a baseball game giving the runs, hits, and errors made by each team

lineup* *n* : a television programming schedule

lin·gui·ca *or* **lin·gui·ça** *also* **lin·gui·sa** \liŋˈgwēsə, lin-, -sä\ *n* -s [Pg *linguiça*] : a spicy Portuguese sausage

lin·gui·ne \liŋˈgwēnē, -(,)nā\ *also* **lin·gui·ni** \-nē, -ni\ *n* -s [It, pl. of *linguina*, dim. of *lingua* tongue, fr. L — more at TONGUE] : pasta in the form of thin flat strings

link* *n* : an identifier attached to an element (as an index term) in a system in order to indicate or permit connection with other similarly identified elements; *esp* : one (as a hyperlink) in a computer file

linked* *adj* : having or provided with links

linksland \ˈ⸗,⸗\ *n* [*links* (sandy land) + ¹*land*] : seaside terrain that is characterized by rolling hills of sand and that is often used as the site of golf courses

lin·u·ron \ˈlinyə,rän\ *n* -s [*lin-* (of unknown origin) + *urea* + ¹*-on*] : a selective herbicide $C_9H_{10}O_2Cl_2N_2$ used esp. to control weeds in crops (as of soybeans or carrots)

lion tamarin *n* : any of three tamarins (*Leontopithecus chrysomelas, L. chrysopygus*, and *L. rosalia*) that have long silky fur and a golden mane and are found in isolated remnants of tropical forests in southeastern Brazil — see GOLDEN LION TAMARIN *herein*

li·pa \ˈlē,pä, -,pə\ *n, pl* **lipa** *also* **lipe** \-,pā\ [Serbo-Croatian (nom. pl. *lipe*, gen. pl. *lipā*), lit., linden tree (of ritual significance in Slavic folk culture); akin to Russ *lipa* linden tree, Czech *lípa*, Lith *liepa*, and prob. to OSlav *prilěpiti* to cleave to, Skt *limpati* he smears — more at LEAVE] : a monetary unit of Croatia equal to ¹⁄₁₀₀ kuna — see *kuna* at MONEY table *in the Dict*

lip cell *n* : one of the narrow thin-walled cells of the sporangia in some ferns that mark the point at which dehiscence begins

li·pid·ic \lə̇ˈpidik\ *adj* [ISV, fr. *lipid* + ¹*-ic*] : of or relating to lipids

li·po·polysaccharide \ˈlipō, ˈlīpō +\ *n* [ISV *lip-* + *polysaccharide*] : a large molecule consisting of lipids and sugars joined by chemical bonds

li·po·some \ˈlīpə,sōm, ˈlip-\ *n* -s [*lip-* + *-some*] : an artificial vesicle that is composed of one or more concentric phospholipid bilayers and is used esp. to deliver microscopic substances (as DNA or drugs) to body cells — **li·po·so·mal** \ˈ⸗ˈsōməl\ *adj*

li·po·suction \ˈlipō, ˈlīpō +\ *n* [*lip-* + *suction*] : surgical removal of local fat deposits (as in the thighs) esp. for cosmetic purposes by applying suction through a small tube inserted into the body

li·po·tro·pin \,lipəˈtrōpə̇n, ,lī-\ *n* -s [*lipotropic* + *-in*] : either of two protein hormones of the adenohypophysis that function in the mobilization of fat reserves; *esp* : BETA-LIPOTROPIN *herein*

li·pox·y·gen·ase \ˈlipˈäksəjə,nās, ˈlīp-, -,nāz\ *n* -s [*lip-* + *oxygen* + *-ase*] : LIPOXIDASE

lip·pes loop \ˈlipəs-, -pēz-\ *n, usu cap 1st L* [after Jack *Lippes* b1924 Am. gynecologist] : an S-shaped plastic intrauterine contraceptive device

lip–smacking \ˈ⸗,⸗⸗\ *adj* **1** : causing the lips to smack in eager anticipation or in delight ⟨*lip-smacking* recipes⟩ ⟨*lip-smacking* desserts⟩ **2** : excitingly sensational or provocative ⟨fervid, *lip-smacking* stuff —Alexandra Jacobs⟩ **3** : markedly gratifying ⟨boasted with *lip-smacking* satisfaction —*Sports Illus.*⟩

lip–synch *or* **lip–sync** *vt* -ED/-ING/-S : to pretend to sing or say in synchronization with something recorded ~ *vi* : to lip-synch something — **lip–synch·er** *or* **lip–sync·er** \ˈ⸗,⸗ə(r)\ *n* -s

lip·tau·er \ˈlip,tau̇(ə)r, -au̇ə(r\ *n* -s *usu cap* [G, fr. *Liptau* former Hung. county in Slovakia] **1** : a soft Hungarian cheese **2** : a cheese spread of Liptauer and seasonings (as paprika); *also* : an imitation of this made with cream cheese or cottage cheese

liquid chromatography *n* : chromatography in which the mobile phase is a liquid; *esp* : HIGH PERFORMANCE LIQUID CHROMATOGRAPHY *herein*

liquid crystal display *n* : LCD *herein*

liquid crystalline *adj* : having the characteristics of a liquid crystal

liquid smoke *n* : a flavoring agent used to simulate the flavor of smoked foods

lisp \ˈlisp\ *n, usu cap L or all cap* [*list processing*] : a computer programming language that is designed for easy manipulation of strings and is used extensively for work in artificial intelligence

lit–crit \ˈlitˈkrit\ *n* -s [by shortening] : literary criticism

lite *adj* [by alter.] **1** : LIGHT 1 *herein* **2** : being, performing, or featuring music in an easy-listening style **3** *sometimes cap* : having less than usual substance or value ⟨ten minutes of ~ news —Margaret Spillane⟩

literary executor *n* : a person entrusted with the management of the papers and unpublished works of a deceased author

lithium niobate *n* : a crystalline material $LiNbO_3$ whose physical properties change in response to pressure or the presence of an electric field and which is used in fiber optics and as a synthetic gemstone

lithography* *n* : the process of producing patterns on semiconductor crystals for use as integrated circuits

lith·o·trip·sy \ˈlithə,tripsē, -thō-, -si\ *n* -ES [ISV *lith-* + *-tripsy* (fr. Gk *tripsis* a rubbing — fr. *tribein* to rub — +ISV ²*-y*) — more at THROW] : the breaking (as by shock waves or crushing with a surgical instrument) of a calculus in the urinary system into pieces small enough to be voided or washed out

lith·o·trip·ter *also* **lith·o·trip·tor** \-,triptər\ *n* -s [alter. of *lithontriptor*, fr. *lithontriptic* breaking up bladder stones, modif. (influenced by Gk *triptos* rubbed, pounded, verbal of *tribein* to rub) of Gk (*pharmaka tōn*) *lithōn thryptika* (drugs) capable of pulverizing stones] : a device for performing lithotripsy; *esp* : a noninvasive device that pulverizes stones by focusing shock waves on a patient immersed in a water bath

litmus test *n* : a test in which a single indicator (as an attitude, event, or fact) is decisive

litter* *n* : material used to absorb the urine and feces of animals

litterbag \ˈ⸗⸗,⸗\ *n* [¹*litter* + *bag*] : a bag used (as in an automobile) for refuse disposal

little guy *n* : LITTLE MAN *herein*

little man *n* : the ordinary individual : COMMON MAN

live \ˈlīv\ *adv* : at the actual time of occurrence : during or at a live performance ⟨the sessions were carried ~ in their entirety by the public television station —Peter Binzen⟩

liveaboard \ˈ⸗⸗⸗\ *n* -s **1** : a person who lives on a boat **2** : a boat suitable for a person to live on

lived–in \ˈ⸗,⸗\ *adj* : of or suggesting long-term human habitation or use : COMFORTABLE; *esp* : showing the effects of age or everyday use ⟨a *lived-in* room⟩ ⟨a *lived-in* voice⟩

live–in \ˈlivˈin\ *adj* **1** : living in one's place of employment ⟨a *live-in* maid⟩ **2** : involving or involved with cohabitation ⟨a *live-in* relationship⟩ ⟨a *live-in* partner⟩ — **live–in** *n*

livery* *n, chiefly Brit* : an identifying design (as on a vehicle) that designates ownership

living will *n* : a document in which the signer requests to be allowed to die rather than be kept alive by artificial means if disabled beyond a reasonable expectation of recovery — see ADVANCE DIRECTIVE *herein*

LM* *abbr or n* -s : lunar module *herein*

LNG *abbr* liquefied natural gas

load* *n* : GENETIC LOAD *herein*

load* *vt* : to copy (as a program or data) esp. from an external storage device (as a disk drive) into a computer's memory

loader* *n* : a computer program that loads a program and readies it for execution

loadmaster \ˈ⸗,⸗⸗\ *n* [¹*load* + *master*] : a crew member of a transport aircraft who is in charge of the cargo

lobotomize* *vt* : to deprive of sensitivity, vitality, or energy ⟨faces wreathed in *lobotomized* smiles —S.J.Perelman⟩

local area network *n* : a network of personal computers in a small area (as an office) that are linked by cable, can communicate directly with other devices in the network, and can share resources — abbr *LAN*

lock* *n* **1** : a controlling hold ⟨had a ~ on the market —L.S.Richman⟩ **2** : someone or something that is assured of success or a favorable outcome ⟨he was a ~ to be elected —Austin Murphy⟩

lockdown** *n* **1** : the confinement of prisoners to their cells for all or most of the day as a temporary security measure **2** : a temporary closing of a school wherein students are kept in locked classrooms for safety during a threat of danger

locked–in* *adj* : unable or unwilling to shift invested funds because of the tax effect of realizing capital gains

locker–room \ˈ⸗⸗,⸗\ *adj* : of, relating to, or suitable for use in a locker room; *esp* : of an earthy or sexual nature ⟨*locker-room* talk⟩

lockstep* *n* : a complete, rigid, and often automatic synchronism, agreement, or conformity — often used with *in* ⟨politicians marching in ~ with the party line⟩ ⟨following a ~ curriculum⟩

locus coe·ru·le·us *also* **locus ce·ru·le·us** \ˌlōkə(s)siˈrülēəs\ *n* [NL, lit., blue place] : a blue area of the brain stem with many norepinephrine-containing neurons

lo·cu·tion·ary \lōˈkyüsh(ə),nerē\ *adj* [*locution* + *-ary*] : of or relating to the physical act of saying something considered apart from the statement's effect or intention — compare ILLOCUTIONARY *herein*, PERLOCUTIONARY *herein*

lo–fi \ˈlōˈfī\ *n* -s [*low fi*delity] : the production or reproduction of audio characterized by an unpolished or rough sound quality — compare HI-FI *in the Dict* — **lo–fi** \ˈ⸗ˈ⸗\ *adj*

logic* *n* : the fundamental principles and applications of truth tables and of the interconnection of circuit elements and gating necessary for computation in a computer; *also* : the circuits themselves

logic bomb *n* : a computer program often hidden within another seemingly innocuous program that is designed to perform usu. malicious actions (as deleting files) when certain conditions have been met (as at a predetermined time or date

lognormal \(ˈ)⸗ˈ⸗⸗\ *adj* [⁴*log* + *normal*] : relating to or being a normal distribution that is the distribution of the logarithm of a random variable; *also* : relating to or being such a random variable — **lognormality** \ˈ⸗(,)⸗ˈ⸗⸗\ *n* — **lognormally** \(ˈ)⸗ˈ⸗⸗\ *adv*

lo·go \ˈlō(,)gō\ *n* -s *usu cap L or all cap* [modif. of Gk *logos* word — more at LEGEND] : a computer programming language that employs simple English commands and is used esp. for introducing schoolchildren to computers

logo·cen·trism \,lōgəˈsen·trizəm, -gō-, ,lä-\ *n* -s [ISV *log-* + *-centric* + *-ism*; orig. formed as F *logocentrisme*] **1** : a philosophy holding that all forms of thought are based on an external point of reference which is held to exist and given a certain degree of authority **2** : a philosophy that privileges speech over writing as a form of communication because the former is closer to an originating transcendental source — **logocentric** *adj*

log off *vi* : to terminate a connection with a time-shared computer or network

log on *also* **log in** *vi* : to establish communication and initiate interaction with a time-shared computer or network — **log–on** \ˈ=,=\ *also* **log–in** \ˈ=,=\ *n*

logotype* *n* : an identifying symbol (as for use in advertising)

loll·er \ˈläl(ə)r\ *n* -S : one that lolls around

lo mein \ˈlō¦män\ *n* -S [Chin (Cant) *lòu-mihn* stirred noodles] : a Chinese dish consisting of sliced vegetables, soft noodles, and usu. meat or shrimp in bite-size pieces stir-fried in a seasoned sauce; *also* : the noodles used in lo mein

lonely hearts *adj* : of or relating to lonely people who are seeking companions or spouses ⟨*lonely hearts* club⟩

lone ranger *n, often cap L&R* [fr. the *Lone Ranger*, hero of an Am. radio and television western] : one who acts alone and without consultation or the approval of others; *broadly* : LONER

look–alike \ˈ==,=\ *n* -S [fr. the phrase *look alike*] : one that looks like another : DOUBLE — **look–alike** \"\ *adj*

look–in* *n* : a quick pass in football to a receiver running diagonally toward the center line of the field

look·ism \ˈlu̇kizəm\ *also* **looks·ism** \ˈlu̇ksizəm\ *n* -S [*looks* + *-ism* (as in *racism*)] : prejudice or discrimination against a group based on physical appearance and esp. physical appearance believed to fall short of societal notions of beauty

lookup \ˈ=,=\ *n* -S [*look up*, v.] : the process or an instance of looking something up; *esp* : the process in which a computer matches data with material stored in memory (as in a table)

loony tune *or* **looney tune** *n, sometimes cap L&T* [fr. *Looney Tunes*, series of short cartoons produced by Warner Bros. 1930–69] : LOONY

loony tunes *or* **looney tunes** *adj, sometimes cap L&T* : LOONY

loop* *n* **1** : a series of instructions (as for a computer) that is repeated usu. until a terminating condition is reached **2** : INTRAUTERINE DEVICE *herein*; *esp* : LIPPES LOOP *herein* **3** : an exclusive group having privileged knowledge or influence ⟨cut dissenters out of the ~⟩ **4** : CYCLE 2a ⟨caught in the ~ of codependency⟩ **5** : a continuously repeated segment of music, dialogue, or images ⟨a drum ~⟩

loose cannon *n* : a dangerously uncontrollable person or thing

loosey–goosey \ˈlüsē¦güsē\ *adj* [fr. the phrase *loose as a goose*] : notably loose or relaxed : not tense

loph·o·phor·ate \ˌlōfəˈfō(ə)rət, -fȯ(ə)r-, ˌlä-\ *n* -S [*lophophore* + [1]*-ate*] : an invertebrate animal (as a brachiopod, bryozoan, or phoronid) having a lophophore

lo·rentz force \(ˌ)lōrˈents-, (ˌ)lȯr-\ *n, usu cap L* [after Hendrik A. *Lorentz* †1928 Du. physicist] : the force exerted on a moving charged particle in electric and magnetic fields

lo·rentz·ian \(ˌ)lōˈrentsēən, (ˌ)lȯˈ-\ *adj, usu cap L* [H.A. *Lorentz* + E *-ian*] : of, relating to, or being a function that relates the intensity of radiation emitted by an atom at a given frequency to the peak radiation intensity, that gives the distribution of the frequencies emitted, that resembles a normal curve but builds up and drops off more gradually, and that has the form

$$I(\nu) = I_0\left(\frac{\gamma}{2\pi}\right)\frac{1}{(\nu-\nu_0)^2+\left(\frac{\gamma}{2}\right)^2}$$

where I is the radiation intensity, ν is the frequency, I_0 is the peak intensity, γ is the width of the distribution, and ν_0 is the frequency of peak intensity

LOS *abbr* **1** line of scrimmage **2** line of sight

lose* *vb* — **lose it 1** : to lose touch with reality; *also* : to go crazy **2** : to become overwhelmed with strong emotion : lose one's composure ⟨so angry I almost *lost it*⟩

loser* *n* : one who is incompetent or unable to succeed ⟨believes that any woman unmarried after the age of twenty-two is a ~ —Lyn Tornabene⟩; *also* : something doomed to fail or disappoint ⟨the breaded and fried veal cutlet Milanese . . . had to be a ~ —Mimi Sheraton⟩

lo·ti \ˈlōtē\ *n, pl* **ma·lo·ti** \mäˈlōtē\ [Sotho, lit., mountain, prob. fr. the *Maloti* Mountains, highest range in Lesotho] : the basic monetary unit of Lesotho — see MONEY table *in the Dict*

lotte \ˈlät, ˈlȯt\ *n* -S [F, fr. MF] : ANGLER 2a

lou geh·rig's disease \ˈlüˈge(ə)rigz-\ *n, usu cap L&G* [after *Lou Gehrig* †1941 Am. baseball player who died of the disease] : AMYOTROPHIC LATERAL SCLEROSIS *herein*

lov·a·stat·in \ˈlōvə¦stat ən, ¦lə-\ *n* -S [*lov-* (perh. by shortening & alter. fr. *mevinolin*, earlier name for the drug) + connective *-a-* + *-stat* + *-in*] : a drug $C_{24}H_{36}O_5$ that decreases the level of cholesterol in the bloodstream by inhibiting the liver enzyme that controls cholesterol synthesis and is used in the treatment of hypercholesterolemia

love beads *n pl* : a necklace of beads; *esp* : beads worn as a symbol of love and peace

lovebug \ˈ=,=\ *n* [so called fr. the fact that it is usually seen copulating] : a small black bibionid fly (*Plecia nearctica*) with a red thorax that swarms along highways in states of the U.S. bordering the Gulf of Mexico

love handles *n pl* : fatty bulges along the sides of the body at the waist

love–in \ˈ=,=\ *n* -S [[2]*love* + *-in* (herein)] : a gathering of people for the expression of mutual love

lowball \ˈ=,=\ *vt* : to give (a customer) a deceptively low price or cost estimate that one has no intention of honoring; *also* : to make (as a cost estimate) deliberately and misleadingly low — **lowball** *n*

low blow* *n* : an unprincipled attack

low–density lipoprotein \ˈ=¦===\ *n* : LDL *herein*

low earth orbit *n, often cap E* : a circular orbit in the approximate range of 90–600 miles above the earth — compare GEOSTATIONARY *herein*

lowest terms *n pl* : the form of a fraction in which the numerator and denominator have no factor in common except 1 ⟨reduce a fraction to *lowest terms*⟩

lowland gorilla *n* : either of two gorillas (*Gorilla gorilla gorilla* or *G. gorilla graueri*) that inhabit lowland rainforests of west central Africa

low–level* *adj* : being or relating to nuclear waste that contains low concentrations of radioactive components

lowlight \ˈ=,=\ *n* [[4]*low* + [1]*light* (as in *highlight*)] : a particularly bad or unpleasant event, detail, or part ⟨the ~*s* of a mediocre performance⟩

low–rent \ˈ=¦=\ *adj* : notably cheap or inferior: as **a** : cheaply made or done ⟨a *low-rent* thriller⟩ **b** : low in character or manner ⟨a *low-rent* thug⟩ **c** : lacking prestige ⟨a decidedly *low-rent* field in those days —Margaret Carlson⟩

lowrider \ˈ=,==\ *n* : a usu. large customized car with a chassis that has been or can be lowered (as by hydraulics) so that it narrowly clears the ground; *also* : a person who drives such a car — **lowriding** \ˈ=¦==\ *n*

low–rise \ˈ=,=\ *adj* [*low* + *rise* (as in *high-rise* — herein)] **1** : being one or two stories and not equipped with elevators ⟨a *low-rise* building⟩; *also* : of, relating to, or characterized by low-rise buildings ⟨a *low-rise* housing development⟩ **2** *of trousers* : having a low waist and usu. close-fitting

low–tech \ˈ=¦=\ *adj* : not relating to, using, or characterized by high technology : technologically simple or unsophisticated ⟨*low-tech* industries⟩

LPM *abbr, often not cap* lines per minute

LPN \ˌel(ˌ)pēˈen\ *n* -S : LICENSED PRACTICAL NURSE *herein*

Lr *symbol* lawrencium *herein*

LSI \ˌelˌesˈī\ *abbr or n* -S **1** : LARGE-SCALE INTEGRATION *herein* **2** : an integrated circuit (as for a computer) employing large-scale integration

LSM* *abbr* letter-sorting machine

LTC *abbr* long-term care

l–tryptophan \ˈ=ˈ==,=\ *n, usu cap L* : the levorotatory form of tryptophan that is a precursor of serotonin and was used formerly as a dietary supplement esp. to promote sleep and relieve depression

lu·ba·vitch·er \ˈlübəˌvichə(r), lüˈbä,v-\ *n* -S *usu cap* [Yiddish *lyubavitsher*, fr. *Lyubavitsh*, town in Belarus, the center of the movement 1813–1915 (fr. Belorussian *Lyubavichi*) + *-er* [2]-er] : a member of a Hasidic sect founded by Schneour Zalman of Lyady in the late 18th century — **lubavitcher** \"\ *adj, usu cap*

luddite* *n, usu cap* : one who is opposed to change and esp. to technological change — **ludd·ite** \ˈlə,dīt\ *adj, usu cap*

lude \ˈlüd\ *n* -S [short for *Quaalude*, a proprietary name for methaqualone] : a pill of methaqualone — usu. used in pl.

lu·dic \ˈlüdik\ *adj* [F *ludique*, fr. L *lud*us play + F *-ique* [1]-ic] : of, relating to, or characterized by play : PLAYFUL ⟨~ behavior⟩ ⟨a ~ novel⟩

lu·mi·nar·ia \ˌlüməˈnerēə\ *n* -S [Sp, festival lamp, fr. LL *luminaria*, pl. of *luminare* lamp — more at LUMINARY] : a traditional Mexican Christmas lantern consisting of a brown paper bag with a lighted candle inside; *also* : a similar lantern of various colors that is displayed with others esp. at ceremonies

lump* *n, Brit* : nonunion construction workers who work as self-employed subcontractors ⟨~ labour⟩

lump·ec·to·my \ˌləmˈpektəmē\ *n* -ES [*lump* + *-ectomy*] : excision of a breast tumor with a limited amount of associated tissue

lum·pen \ˈlu̇mpən, ˈləm-\ *n, pl* **lumpen** *or* **lumpens** [*lumpen*, adj.] : a member of the crude and uneducated lowest class of society

lunar excursion module *or* **lunar module** *n* : a space vehicle module designed to carry astronauts from the command module to the surface of the moon and back

lu·nar·naut \ˈlünə(r)ˌnȯt, -ˌnär,n-, -ät\ *n* [*lunar* + *-naut* (as in *astronaut*)] : an astronaut who explores the moon

lunch* *n* — **out to lunch** *slang* : out of touch with reality

lurker* *n* : a person who reads messages on an Internet discussion forum (as a newsgroup or chat room) but does not contribute — **lurk*** *vi*

luteinizing hormone–releasing hormone *also* **luteinizing hormone–releasing factor** *n* : GONADOTROPIN-RELEASING HORMONE *herein*

LVN \ˌel(ˌ)vēˈen\ *n* -S : LICENSED VOCATIONAL NURSE *herein*

lwei \ləˈwā\ *n, pl* **lwei** *also* **lweis** [prob. after *Lué*, name of several rivers in Angola] **1** : a monetary unit of Angola equal to ¹⁄₁₀₀ kwanza — see MONEY table *in the Dict* **2** : a coin representing one lwei

ly·ase \ˈlīˌās, -āz\ *n* -S [Gk *lyein* to loosen, release + E *-ase* — more at LOSE] : an enzyme (as a decarboxylase) that forms double bonds by removing groups from a substrate other than by hydrolysis or that adds groups to double bonds

lyme disease \ˈlīm-\ *also* **lyme** *or* **lyme borreliosis** *n, usu cap L* [fr. *Lyme*, Connecticut, where it was first reported] : an acute inflammatory disease that is usu. characterized initially by a spreading annular erythematous skin lesion and by fatigue, fever, and chills and if left untreated may later manifest itself in cardiac and neurological disorders, joint pain, and arthritis and that is caused by a spirochete of the genus *Borrelia* (*B. burgdorferi*) transmitted by the bite of an ixodid tick esp. of the genus *Ixodes* (*I. scapularis* syn. *I. dammini* in the eastern and midwestern U.S., *I. pacificus* in the Pacific northwestern U.S., and *I. ricinus* in Europe)

lym·phan·gi·og·ra·phy \ˌlim,fanjēˈägrəfē\ *n* -ES [*lymphangi-* + *-graphy*] : X-ray depiction of lymph vessels and lymph nodes after use of a radiopaque material — called also *lymphography* — **lym·phan·gio·gram** \limˈfanjēə,gram\ *n* — **lym·phan·gio·graph·ic** \=¦==ə¦grafik, ,=,===ˈ=\ *adj*

lym·pho·blast·oid \¦lim(p)fə¦bla,stȯid\ *adj* : resembling a lymphoblast

lym·pho·gran·u·lo·ma·tous \ˌlim(p)fə,granyəˈlōməd·əs\ *adj* [NL *lymphogranulomat-*, *lymphogranuloma* + E *-ous*] : of, relating to, or characterized by lymphogranulomas

lym·phog·ra·phy \limˈfägrəfē\ *n* -ES [*lymph-* + *-graphy*] : LYMPHANGIOGRAPHY *herein* — **lym·pho·gram** \ˈlim(p)fə,gram\ *n* — **lym·pho·graph·ic** \¦==¦grafik\ *adj*

lym·pho·kine \ˈlim(p)fə,kīn\ *n* -S [*lymph-* + *-kine* (fr. Gk *kinein* to set in motion) — more at HIGHT] : any of various substances (as interleukin-2) of low molecular weight that are not immunoglobulins, are secreted by T cells in response to stimulation by antigens, and have a role (as the activation of macrophages or the enhancement or inhibition of antibody production) in cell-mediated immunity

lymphokine–activated killer cell \ˈ==,=ˈ==,==-\ *n* : a lymphocyte (as a natural killer cell) that has been turned into a tumor-killing cell by being cultured with interleukin-2 — called also *LAK*

lym·pho·proliferative \¦lim(p)fə+\ *adj* [*lymph-* + *proliferative*] : of or relating to the proliferation of lymphoid tissue ⟨a ~ response⟩ ⟨~ disorders⟩

lym·pho·reticular \"+\ *adj* [*lymph-* + *reticular*] : RETICULOENDOTHELIAL ⟨~ neoplasms⟩

lym·pho·sarcomatous \"+\ *adj* [NL *lymphosarcomat-*, *lymphosarcoma* + E *-ous*] : being, affected with, or characterized by lymphosarcomas ⟨large ~ masses⟩ ⟨~ cows⟩

ly·oph·i·liz·er \(ˌ)līˈäfə,līzə(r)\ *n* -S [*lyophilize* + [2]*-er*] : a device used to carry out the process of freeze-drying

ly·si·metric \¦līsə+\ *adj* [*lysimeter* + *-metric*] : relating to or involving the use of a lysimeter ⟨~ observations⟩

lysogen* *n* : a lysogenic bacterium or bacterial strain

lysogenic* *adj* : TEMPERATE 1f ⟨~ viruses⟩

ly·sog·e·nize \līˈsäjə,nīz\ *vt* -ED/-ING/-S : to make lysogenic — **ly·sog·e·ni·za·tion** \-,säjənəˈzāshən, -,nī-\ *n* -S

ly·sog·e·ny \līˈsäjənē\ *n* -ES : the state of being lysogenic

ly·so·some \ˈlīsə,sōm\ *n* -S [ISV *lys-* + [3]*-some*; orig. formed in F] : a saclike cellular organelle that contains various hydrolytic enzymes — **ly·so·som·al** \¦līsə¦sōməl\ *adj* — **ly·so·som·al·ly** \,==ˈ=əlē\ *adv*

ly·so·staph·in \ˌlīsəˈstafən\ *n* -S [*lys-* + *staph* + *-in*] : an antimicrobial enzyme that is obtained from a strain of staphylococcus and is effective against other staphylococci

ma–and–pa \ˈ=¦=ˈ=\ *adj, sometimes cap M&P* : MOM-AND-POP *herein*

MABE *abbr* master of agricultural business and economics

mace \ˈmās\ *vt* -ED/-ING/-S : to attack with the Mace liquid

Mace \ˈmās\ *trademark* — used for a temporarily disabling liquid that when sprayed in the face of a person (as a rioter) causes tears, dizziness, immobilization, and sometimes nausea

mâche \ˈmäsh\ *n* -S [F, perh. alter. of F dial. *pomache*, fr. (assumed) VL *pomasca*, fr. L *pomum* fruit] : CORN SALAD

mac·guf·fin *or* **mc·guf·fin** \məˈgəfən\ *n* -S *usu cap M&G* [coined by Alfred Hitchcock †1980 Brit. film director] : an object, event, or person in a film or written narrative that while usu. not intrinsically important or valuable serves to set and keep the plot in motion

machine language *n* **1** : the set of numeric codes usu. in binary form used to represent operations and data in a machine (as a computer) **2** : ASSEMBLY LANGUAGE

machine–readable \=ˈ=¦===\ *adj* : directly usable by a computer

machine translation *n* : automatic translation from one language to another

ma·chis·mo \mäˈchēz(ˌ)mō, mə-, -ˈkē|, -ˈki|, -ˈchi|, |s(-\ *n* -S [Sp, fr. *macho* male + *-ismo* -ism] **1** : a strong sense of masculine pride : an exaggerated masculinity **2** : an exaggerated or exhilarating sense of power or strength ⟨museums which flaunt their directorial ~ —*Time*⟩

[1]**ma·cho** \ˈmä(ˌ)chō\ *adj* [Sp, male, fr. L *masculus* — more at MALE] **1** : having or exhibiting machismo : aggressively virile ⟨all their ~ swagger and bravado —Burr Snider⟩ **2** *of a woman* : having or exhibiting traditionally masculine traits ⟨she wanted . . . to speak with authority and ~ assertion —Carolyn Heilbrun⟩

[2]**macho** \"\ *n* -S **1** : MACHISMO *herein* **2** : one who exhibits machismo

MA·CHO \ˈmä(ˌ)chō\ *abbr or n* -S [*m*assive *c*ompact *h*alo *o*bject] : a hypothetical dark-matter object consisting of a nonluminous astronomical body (as a brown dwarf)

mack·man \ˈmak,man, -,mən\ *n, pl* **mack·men** \-,men, -,mən\ [[2]*mack* + *man*] *slang* : PIMP, MACK

mac·lau·rin's series \məˈklȯrənz-\ *or* **maclaurin series** *n, usu cap M* [after Colin *Maclaurin* †1746 Scot. mathematician] : a Taylor's series of the form

$$f(x) = f(0) + \frac{f'(0)}{1!}\,x + \frac{f''(0)}{2!}\,x^2 + \cdots + \frac{f^{[n]}(0)}{n!}\,x^n + \cdots$$

in which the expansion is about the reference point zero

mc·lu·han·esque \mə¦klüə¦nesk\ *adj, usu cap M&L* [Herbert Marshall *McLuhan* †1980 Canad. educator + E *-esque*] : of, relating to, or suggestive of Marshall McLuhan or his theories

mac·pher·son strut \məkˈfirsᵊn-, -ˈfər-\ *n, usu cap M&P* [after Earle S. *MacPherson* †1960 Am. engineer] : a component of an automobile suspension consisting of a shock absorber mounted within a coil spring

macro* *adj* : of or relating to macroeconomics

mac·ro \ˈmak(ˌ)rō\ *n* -S [short for *macroinstruction* (herein)] : a single computer instruction that stands for a sequence of operations

mac·ro·aggregate \¦makrō+\ *n* [*macr-* + *aggregate*] : a relatively large particle (as of soil or a protein) — **mac·ro·aggre·gated** \"+\ *adj*

mac·ro·benthos \"+\ *n* [*macr-* + *benthos*] : the relatively large organisms living on or in the bottom of bodies of water — **mac·ro·benthic** \"+\ *adj*

macrobiotic* *adj* : of, relating to, or being a diet based on the Chinese cosmological principles of yin and yang that consists of whole cereals and grains supplemented esp. with beans and vegetables and that in its esp. former more restrictive forms has been linked to nutritional deficiencies

macrobiotics* *n pl but sing in constr* : a macrobiotic dietary system

mac·ro·globulin \¦makrō+\ *n* [ISV *macr-* + *globulin*] : a highly polymerized globulin (as IgM) of high molecular weight

mac·ro·glob·u·lin·emia \ˌmakrō,gläbyələˈnēmēə\ *n* -S [NL, fr. ISV *macroglobulin* + NL *-emia*] : a disorder characterized by increased blood serum viscosity and by macroglobulins in the serum — **mac·ro·glob·u·lin·emic** \-nēmik\ *adj*

mac·ro·instruction \¦makrō+\ *n* [*macr-* + *instruction*] : MACRO *herein*

mac·ro·invertebrate \"+\ *n* [*macr-* + *invertebrate*] : any of various invertebrate macroorganisms (as a crayfish or stonefly)

macro lens *n* : a camera lens designed to focus at very short distances with up to life-size magnification of the image

mac·ro·lide \ˈmakrə,līd\ *n* -S [*macro*cyclic + *lact*one + *-ide*] : any of several antibiotics (as erythromycin) containing a macrocyclic lactone ring that are produced by actinomycetes of the genus *Streptomyces* and inhibit bacterial protein synthesis

mac·ro·organism \¦makrō+\ *n* [*macr-* + *organism*] : an organism large enough to be seen by the normal unaided human eye — compare MICROORGANISM *in the Dict*

macular degeneration *n* : a gradual loss of central vision usu. affecting both eyes that occurs esp. in the elderly and that in a slowly progressing form is marked esp. by accumulation of yellow deposits in and thinning of the macula lutea and in a rapidly progressing form by scarring produced by bleeding and fluid leakage below the macula lutea

MAD* *abbr* mutual assured destruction

mad cow disease *n* [so called from the behavioral disturbances in cows symptomatic of the disease] : BOVINE SPONGIFORM ENCEPHALOPATHY *herein*

mafia* *n, often cap* **1** : a group of people of similar interests or backgrounds prominent in a particular field or enterprise ⟨as the little guy in the world of broadcasting, he throws down the gauntlet to the network *Mafia* —Stanley Marcus⟩ **2** : a criminal organization associated with a particular traffic ⟨the cocaine ~⟩

ma·fi·o·so \ˌmäfēˈō(ˌ)sō, -af-, -)zō\ *n, pl* **mafio·si** \-sē, -zē\ *also* **mafiosos** *often cap* [It, fr. *mafioso*, adj., belonging to the Mafia, fr. *Mafia* + *-oso* -ous, fr. L *-osus*] : a member of the Mafia or a mafia

ma·ga·i·nin \məˈgā(ə)nən\ *n* -S [*magain-* (fr. Heb *māghēn* shield) + *-in*; fr. the ability of such peptides to ward off microbial infections on surface wounds of the frogs] : any of a group of antimicrobial peptide substances first isolated from the skin of the African clawed frog

magazine* *n* : a radio or television program presenting usu. several short segments on a variety of topics

magellanic penguin *n, usu cap M* : a penguin (*Spheniscus magellanicus*) of the southern tip of South America and surrounding islands that has a pink mark above the eyes and two broad black bands on the neck and upper chest

magical realism *or* **magic realism** *n* : a literary genre or style associated esp. with Latin America that incorporates fantastic or mythical elements into otherwise realistic fiction — **magical realist** *or* **magic realist** *adj or n*

magic bullet *n* [trans. of G *zauberkugel*] : a substance or therapy that is capable of destroying specific pathogenic agents (as bacteria or cancer cells) or providing an effective remedy for a disease or condition (as Alzheimer's disease or drug addiction) without producing deleterious side effects; *broadly* : something providing an effective solution to a difficult or previously unsolvable problem ⟨a *magic bullet* to stem voter apathy⟩

magic number *n* **1** : one of a set of numbers for which an atomic nucleus exhibits a high degree of stability when either the proton or neutron count is equal to the number **2** : a number that represents a combination of wins for a leader (as in a baseball pennant race) and losses for a contender which mathematically guarantees the leader's winning the championship

mag·i·cube \ˈmajə,kyüb\ *n* [blend of [2]*magic* and [1]*cube*] : a flashcube that for its firing depends only on the mechanical ignition of a primer within the device

mag·lev \ˈmaglev\ *n* -S *often attrib* [*mag*netic *lev*itation] **1** : the use of the physical properties of magnetic fields generated by superconducting magnets to cause an object (as a vehicle) to float above a solid surface **2** : a train utilizing maglev technology

magnetic* *n* : a magnetic substance

magnetic bottle *n* : a magnetic field for confining plasma for experiments in nuclear fusion

magnetic bubble *n* : a tiny magnetized cylindrical volume that is formed in a thin amorphous or crystalline magnetic material, can be moved by a magnetic field, and can be used with other like volumes to represent a bit of information (as in a computer)

magnetic core *n* **1** : CORE 1i **2** : CORE 1 *herein*

magnetic disk *n* : DISK 1 *herein*

magnetic levitation *n* : MAGLEV 1 *herein*

magnetic mirror *n* : a magnetic field that confines a plasma (as in nuclear fusion) by reflecting ions of the plasma back toward the main plasma concentration

magnetic resonance imaging *n* : a noninvasive diagnostic technique that produces computerized images of internal body tissues and is based on nuclear magnetic resonance of atoms within the body induced by the application of radio waves — abbr. *MRI*

mag·ne·to·cardiograph \mag¦nēd·ō, -ed-+\ *n* [*magnet-* + *cardiograph*] : an instrument for recording the changes in the magnetic field around the heart that is used to supplement information given by an electrocardiograph — **mag·ne·to·cardiogram** \"+\ *n* — **mag·ne·to·cardiographic** \"+\ *adj* — **mag·ne·to·cardiog·raphy** \"+\ *n*

mag·ne·to·fluiddynamics \mag¦nēd·ō,==¦==, -ned·-\ *n pl but sing or pl in constr* [*magnet-* + ²*fluid* + *dynamics*] : MAGNETOHYDRODYNAMICS

mag·ne·to·gasdynamics \-,==¦==\ *n pl but sing in constr* [*magnet-* + *gas* + *dynamics*] : MAGNETOHYDRODYNAMICS — **mag·ne·to·gasdynamic** \-¦==¦==\ *adj*

mag·ne·to·pause \mag'nēd·ə,pȯz, -ed·-\ *n* [*magnet-* + *pause*] : the outer boundary of a magnetosphere

mag·ne·to·plasmadynamic \mag¦nēd·ō,==¦==\ *adj* [*magnet-* + *plasma* + ¹*dynamic*] : MAGNETOHYDRODYNAMIC — **mag·ne·to·plasmadynamics** \-,==¦==\ *n pl but sing or pl in constr*

mag·ne·to·sphere \mag'nēd·ə, -ed·ə+,\ *n* [*magnet-* + *sphere*] : a region of space that surrounds a celestial object (as the earth or a star) and is dominated by the object's magnetic field so that charged particles are trapped in it — **mag·ne·to·spheric** \¦==+\ *adj*

mag·ne·to·tail \"+\ *n* [*magnet-* + *tail*] : the region of the magnetosphere of a celestial body (as a planet) that is swept back by the solar wind in the direction away from the sun

magnet school *n* : a public school with superior facilities and often a specialized curriculum designed to attract pupils from throughout a city or school district

mag·no·cellular \¦magnō+\ *adj* [L *magnus* large + E *-o-* + *cellular* — more at MUCH] : being or containing neurons with large cell bodies ⟨motion and depth perception processed by the ~ visual pathway⟩ ⟨neurosecretory ~ neurons of the hypothalamus⟩

mag·non \'mag,nän\ *n* -s [¹*magnetic* + ²*-on*] : SPIN WAVE *herein*

magpie* *n* : one who collects indiscriminately

ma·ha·ri·shi \,mähə'rēshē, -hä-, -'ri-\ *n* -s [Skt *maharṣi*, fr. *mahat* great + *ṛṣi* seer, sage; prob. akin to Lith *aršus* furious, MHG *rāsen* to storm, rage — more at MUCH, RACE] : a Hindu teacher of mystical knowledge

mah·ler·ian \mä'lerēən, -'lir-\ *adj, usu cap* [Gustav *Mahler* †1911 Austrian composer + E *-ian*] : of, relating to, or suggestive of Gustav Mahler or his music

mail* *n* : messages sent electronically to an individual; *specif* : E-MAIL *herein*

mailbox* *n* : ELECTRONIC MAILBOX *herein*

mail cover *n* : a postal monitoring and recording of information about all mail going to a designated addressee

Mail·gram \'mā(ə)l¦gram, -aa(ə)m\ *trademark* — used for a message sent by wire to a post office which delivers it to the addressee

mail·lard reaction \mə'lärd|-, -'yär|-\ *n, usu cap M* [after Louis-Camille *Maillard* †1936 Fr. biochemist] : a nonenzymatic reaction between sugars and proteins that occurs upon heating and that produces browning of some foods (as meat and bread)

mainframe \'=¦=\ *n* [²*main* + *frame*] **1** : a computer with its cabinet and internal circuits; *also* : a large fast computer that can handle multiple tasks concurrently **2** : a skeletal framework into which electronic or instrument modules can be inserted

mainline \¦=¦=\ *adj* [*main line*, n.] **1** : being part of an established group ⟨~ churches⟩ **2** : MAINSTREAM *herein*

main man *n* **1** : best male friend **2** : a man whose character or work is most admired **3** : most significant or important person ⟨he was indisputably college basketball's *main man* —Corry Kirkpatrick⟩; *also* : CHIEF 2 ⟨the Chicago syndicate's reputed *main man* —John McCormick⟩

main squeeze *n, slang* : the principal romantic partner (as a boyfriend or girl friend)

¹**mainstream** \¦=¦=\ *adj* [*mainstream*, n.] **1** : having, reflecting, or being compatible with the prevailing attitudes and values of a society or group ⟨a strictly ~ Christian, Victorian approach toward marriage and morality —Gerda Lerner⟩ **2** : relating to or being tobacco smoke that is drawn directly into the mouth of the smoker and usu. inhaled into the lungs — compare SIDESTREAM *herein*

²**mainstream** \'=,=\ *vt* : to place (as a child with special needs) in conventional school classes — **main·stream·ing** \'=,=\ *n* -s

mai tai \'mī¦tī\ *n, pl* **mai tais** [Tahitian *maitai* good] : a cocktail made with rum, curaçao, orgeat, lime, and fruit juices, shaken with shaved ice, and often garnished with fruit

majolica* *n* : a 19th century earthenware modeled in naturalistic shapes and glazed in bright colors

major depression *n* : an episode of depression characteristic of major depressive disorder; *also* : MAJOR DEPRESSIVE DISORDER *herein*

major depressive disorder *n* : a mood disorder having a clinical course involving one or more episodes of serious psychological depression that last two or more weeks each with no intervening episodes of mania and are characterized esp. by a loss of interest or pleasure in almost all activities and by variable symptoms of depression (as loss of appetite, sleep disturbances, loss of energy, impaired concentration, or suicidal thoughts)

majordomo* *n* : a person who speaks, makes arrangements, or takes charge for another; *broadly* : the person who runs an enterprise ⟨~ of the county fair⟩

major histocompatibility complex *n* : a group of genes that function esp. in determining the histocompatibility antigens found on cell surfaces and that in man comprise the alleles occurring at four loci on the short arm of chromosome 6 — abbr. *MHC*

major–league \'=¦=\ *adj* [*major league*, n.] : BIG-TIME 2 ⟨*major-league* crime fiction⟩ ⟨a *major-league* hypocrite⟩

ma·jor·ly \'mājə(r)lē\ *adv* : in a major way **a** : PRIMARILY 1 ⟨was ~ a poet⟩ **b** : EXTREMELY ⟨was ~ annoyed⟩

major–medical \¦=¦==\ *adj* : of, relating to, or being a form of insurance designed to pay all or part of the medical bills of major illnesses usu. after deduction of a fixed initial sum

make* *vb* — **make it 1** : to be successful ⟨trying to *make it* as writer-in-residence at the university —Gershon Legman⟩ **2** : to have sexual intercourse ⟨one young couple who would . . . *make it* in a rear seat —Thomas Pynchon⟩ **3** : to be satisfactory or pleasing : make the grade ⟨southern cities, with their . . . climates, don't *make it* for me —Bill AuCoin⟩ — **make waves** : to disturb the status quo ⟨unimaginative, traditional career man who does not *make waves* —Henry Trewhitt⟩

make out* *vi* **1** : to engage in sexual intercourse **2** : NECK 1

makeover** *n* : a changing of a person's appearance (as by the use of cosmetics or a different hairstyle

makuta *pl of* LIKUTA *herein*

mal·apportioned \¦mal+\ *adj* [¹*mal-* + *apportioned*, past part. of *apportion*] : characterized by an inequitable or unsuitable apportioning of representatives to a legislative body ⟨one of the country's most ~ legislatures. Eight percent of the population controlled a majority of the Senate seats —*N.Y. Times*⟩

mal·apportionment \"+\ *n* [¹*mal-* + *apportionment*] : the state of being malapportioned

male–pattern baldness \'=¦=-\ *n* : typical hereditary baldness in the male characterized by loss of hair on the crown and temples

mal·i·bu board \'malə,bü-\ *n, usu cap M* [fr. *Malibu* Beach, California] : a lightweight surfboard 9 to 10 feet long

ma·lic \'malək, 'māl-\ *adj* : involved in and esp. catalyzing a reaction in which malic acid participates ⟨~ dehydrogenase⟩

mall* *n* : SHOPPING MALL *herein*

mall rat *n* : a person who habitually spends a lot of time in shopping malls

ma·lo·lactic \¦malō, ¦mälō+\ *adj* [²*mal-* + *lactic*] : relating to or involved in the bacterial conversion of malic acid to lactic acid in wine ⟨~ fermentation⟩

maloti *pl of* LOTI *herein*

MALS *abbr* master of arts in liberal studies; master of arts in library science

ma·ma·li·ga \(,)mämä'lēgə, (,)mämə-, (,)məmə-\ *n* -s [Romanian *mămăligă*] : a Romanian dish of cornmeal mush often garnished with cheese or sour cream

mam·mo·gram \'mamə,gram\ *n* [²*mamma* + *-o-* + *-gram*] : a photograph of the breasts made by X rays; *also* : the procedure for producing a mammogram

mam·mog·ra·phy \ma'mägrəfē\ *n* -ES [²*mamma* + *-o-* + *-graphy*] : X-ray examination of the breasts (as for early detection of cancer) — **mam·mo·graph·ic** \,mamə'grafik\ *adj*

man* *n, usu cap* **1** : POLICE ⟨when I heard the siren, I knew it was the *Man* —*Amer. Speech*⟩ **2** : the white establishment : white society ⟨surprise that any black man . . . should take on so about the *Man* —Peter Goldman⟩

managed care *n* : a system of providing health care (as by an HMO or a PPO) that is designed to control costs through managed programs in which the physician accepts constraints on the amount charged for medical care and the patient is limited in the choice of a physician

ma·nat \mä'nät\ *n, pl* **manat** *or* **manats** [Azerbaijani & Turkmen, ruble, fr. Per *munāt*, fr. Russ *moneta*, *monet* coin, silver ruble coin, fr. Pol *moneta* coin, fr. L — more at MINT] **1** : a monetary unit of Azerbaijan equal to 100 gopik — see MONEY table *in the Dict* **2** : a monetary unit of Turkmenistan equal to 100 tennesi — see MONEY table *in the Dict*

M and A *abbr* mergers and acquisitions

mandate* *vt* : to make mandatory : ORDER ⟨this . . . verdict *mandating* school desegregation —M.L.Abramson⟩; *also* : DIRECT, REQUIRE ⟨people are not *mandated* to wreck their own economic system —Norman Cousins⟩

man·del·brot set \'mandəl,brät-, -,brȯt-, -,brōt-, 'män-\ *n, usu cap M* [after Benoit *Mandelbrot* *b*1924 Am. (Pol.-born) mathematician] : a fractal that roughly resembles a series of heart-shaped disks to which smaller disks are attached and that consists of the set of all points *c* in the complex plane for which the recursive expression $z_{n+1} = z_n^2 + c$ for $n = 0, 1, 2, 3 \ldots$ with the starting value $z_0 = 0$ remains bounded as *n* approaches infinity

mandoline* *also* **mandolin*** *n* : a kitchen utensil with a blade for slicing and shredding

man·eb \'ma,neb\ *n* -s [*manganese* + *ethylene* + *bis-*] : a carbamate agricultural fungicide $C_4H_6MnN_2S_4$

mange–tout \,mänzh'tü, ,män-\ *n, pl* **mange–touts** \-'tü(z)\ [F, lit., eat all — more at MANGER, TUTSAN] : EDIBLE-PODDED PEA

man·hat·tan·iza·tion \,man,hat(ᵊ)nə'zāshən, -n,ī'zā-\ *n* -s *usu cap* [*Manhattan*, borough of New York + E *-ization*] : congestion of an urban area by tall buildings

man·i·cot·ti \,manə'käd·ē\ *n, pl* **manicotti** [It *manicotti* muffs, pl. of *manicotto*, fr. *manica* sleeve, fr. L — more at MANCHE] : tubular pasta shells stuffed with ricotta

manifold* *n* **1** : a mathematical set **2** : a topological space in which every point has a neighborhood that is homeomorphic to the interior of a sphere in euclidean space of the same number of dimensions

-man·ship \mən,ship\ *n suffix* -s [sports*manship*] : art or practice of maneuvering to gain a tactical advantage ⟨games*manship*⟩

mantra* *n* : SLOGAN, WATCHWORD ⟨"quality, not quantity" is their ~⟩

many–valued \¦=¦=\ *adj* : MULTIPLE-VALUED *herein*

mao \'mau̇\ *adj, usu cap* [after *Mao* Tse-tung †1976 Chin. communist leader] : having a long narrow cut and a mandarin collar — usu. used of a jacket

MAO *abbr* monoamine oxidase *herein*

mao·ism \'mau̇,izəm\ *n* -s *usu cap* [*Mao* Tse-tung + E *-ism*] : the theory and practice of Marxism-Leninism developed in China chiefly by Mao Tse-tung — **mao·ist** \'mau̇əst\ *n or adj, usu cap*

mao–tai \'mau̇'dī, -'tī\ *n* [fr. *Mao-Tai*, town in China] : a strong Chinese liquor made from sorghum

map* *n* **1** : the arrangement of genes on a chromosome — called also *genetic map* **2** : FUNCTION 6 — **all over the map** : marked by a high degree of variation — **on the map** : in a position of prominence or fame ⟨had put the fledgling university *on the map* —Lon Tinkle⟩

map* *vt* : to locate (a gene) on a chromosome ⟨mutants which have been genetically *mapped*⟩ ~ *vi, of a gene* : to be located ⟨a repressor ~*s* near the corresponding structural gene⟩

MAP* *abbr* modified American plan

map·ping \'mapiŋ\ *n* -s [fr. gerund of ²*map*] : a relation between the elements of one mathematical or linguistic set and another; *esp* : FUNCTION 6

ma·qui·la·do·ra \mə,kēlə'dōrə, -'thōr-\ *n* -s [MexSp *(planta) maquiladora*, fr. *maquilar* to process (ore or other material) for a fee, fr. *maquila* processing fee, multure, fr. Sp, multure, fr. Ar dial. *makīla* measure of grain] : a foreign-owned factory in Mexico at which imported parts are assembled by lower-paid workers into products for export

mar·ag·ing steel \¦mär,ājiŋ-\ *n* [*martensite* + *aging*] : a strong tough low-carbon martensitic steel which contains up to 25 percent nickel and in which hardening precipitates are formed by aging

mar·burg virus \'märbərg-\ *also* **marburg** *n, usu cap M* [fr. *Marburg*, Germany, where pharmaceutical workers in contact with African green monkeys were infected with the virus in 1967] : a filovirus (genus *Filovirus*) that causes an often fatal hemorrhagic fever and was orig. transmitted to humans from African green monkeys

mar·ek's disease \'maraks-, 'mer-\ *n, usu cap M* [after József *Marek* †1952 Hung. veterinarian] : a highly contagious viral disease of poultry that is characterized esp. by proliferation of lymphoid cells and is caused by a herpesvirus having several serotypes

mar·fan syndrome *or* **mar·fan's syndrome** \¦mär,fan-\ *n, usu cap M* [after Antonin Bernard Jean *Marfan* †1942 Fr. pediatrician] : a disorder of connective tissue that is inherited as a dominant trait, is caused by a defect in the gene controlling the production of a protein in connective tissue, and is characterized by abnormal elongation of the long bones and often by ocular and circulatory defects

mar·ga·ri·ta \,märgə'rēd·ə, -ētə\ *n* -s [fr. the Sp feminine name *Margarita*] : a cocktail consisting of tequila, lime or lemon juice, and an orange-flavored liqueur

marginal* *adj* **1** : excluded from or existing outside of the mainstream of society, a group, or a school of thought **2** : relating to or being a function of a random variable that is obtained from a function of several random variables by integrating or summing over all possible values of the other variables ⟨a ~ probability function⟩ — **marginality*** *n*

mar·gin·al·ize \'märjənə,līz, 'māj-\ *vt* -ED/-ING/-S [*marginal* + *-ize*] : to relegate to an unimportant or powerless position within a society or group : EXCLUDE ⟨factories and big business *marginalized* many of the middle-class breadwinners —Allessandra Comini⟩ — **mar·gin·al·iza·tion** \,===(,)lī'zāshən, -,lə'-\ *n* -s

marginal tax rate *n* : the rate of additional federal income tax to be paid on additional income

mari·culture \'marə+,\ *n* [*mari-* + *culture*] : the cultivation of marine organisms by exploiting their natural environment — **mariculturist** \¦marə+\ *n*

ma·ri·e·li·to \,mārēə'lēd·ō, *Sp* ,mārye'lētō\ *n* -s *cap* [AmerSp, fr. *Mariel*, Cuba] : an emigrant from Cuba to the U.S. who exited Cuba through the port of Mariel during the mass emigration of 1980

mar·i·na·ra \,marə'narə, ,merə'nerə, -när-\ *adj* [It *(alla) marinara* in sailor style, fr. *marinara*, fem. of *marinaro*, dial. form of Tuscan *marinaio* of sailors, fr. *marino* marine — more at MARINATE] : made with tomatoes, onion, garlic, and spices ⟨~ sauce⟩; *also* : served with marinara sauce ⟨spaghetti ~⟩

marker gene *n* : a gene that serves as a genetic marker

market* *n* **1** : the available supply of or potential demand for specified goods or services ⟨the labor ~⟩ ⟨has captured more than two-thirds of the cleaning-agent ~ —Barry Commoner⟩ **2** : a specified category of potential buyers ⟨youth ~⟩

mar·ket·i·za·tion \,märkəd·ə'zāshən\ *n* -s [¹*market* + *-ization*] : the act or process of entering into or participating in a free market or a market economy : the act or process of subjecting (as an economy or industry) to free market forces

market maker *n* : an intermediary in a stock exchange who controls buy and sell orders (as by purchase and resale) for a particular stock or group of stocks

mar·ko·vi·an \mär'kōvēən\ *or* **mar·kov** \'mär,kȯf, -ȯv\ *also* **markoff** \-ȯf\ *adj, usu cap* [*Markov (process)* + *-ian*] : of, relating to, or resembling a Markov process or Markov chain esp. by having probabilities defined in terms of transition from the possible existing states to other states ⟨*Markovian* models⟩

markov process *also* **markoff process** *n, usu cap M* [after Andrei Andreevich *Markov*] : a stochastic process (as Brownian movement) that resembles a Markov chain except that the states are continuous; *also* : MARKOV CHAIN

markup* *n* : the putting of a bill into final form by a U.S. congressional committee; *also* : the session at which this is done

markup language *n* [*markup* fr. *mark up* (to make notations on)] : a system (as HTML or SGML) for marking or tagging a document that indicates its logical structure (as paragraphs) and gives instructions for its layout on the page for electronic transmission and display

marquee *adj* [*marquee*, n.] : having or associated with the name recognition and drawing power of one whose name appears on a marquee : BIG-NAME, STAR

martial art *n* : any of several arts of combat and self-defense (as karate, judo, or kung fu) that are widely practiced as sport — **martial artist** *n*

mar·tin lu·ther king day *R* ,märtᵊn,lüthər'kiŋ-, *-R* ,mätᵊn-,lüthə'k-\ *n, usu cap M&L&K&D* [*Martin Luther King* †1968 Am. civil rights leader] : the third Monday in January observed as a legal holiday in the U.S.

MARV *abbr* maneuverable reentry vehicle

mary gre·go·ry \-'greg(ə)rē, -rāg-\ *n, usu cap M&G* [after *Mary Gregory* †1908 decorator for the Boston & Sandwich Glass Co., Sandwich, Mass.] : colored glassware of a popular 19th century style marked by white enamel decoration usu. including figures of children

mary jane *n, usu cap M&J* [by folk etymology (influenced by Sp *Juana* Jane)] *slang* : MARIJUANA

masa ha·ri·na \-ä'rēnä, -nə\ *n* [MexSp, prob. lit., flour masa (masa in the form of flour)] : corn flour (as for use in making tortillas) made from corn treated with lime water

ma·sa·la \mə'sälə, -lə, mə-\ *n* -s [Hindi & Urdu *masālā* materials, ingredients, spices, fr. Per *maṣāliḥ* affairs, materials, ingredients, spices, pl. of *maṣlaḥat* matter, affair, fr. Ar *maṣlaḥa* matter, requirement, benefit, fr. *ṣalaḥa* to put in order, settle] : a varying blend of spices used in Indian cooking

mas·car·po·ne \,maskär'pō(,)nā\ *or* **mascarpone cheese** *n* -s [It, fr. It dial. (Lombardy) *mascarpón*, aug. of *mascarpa* cream cheese] : an Italian cream cheese

mas·con \'mas,kän\ *n* -s [²*mass* + *concentration*] : any of the high-density regions below the surface of lunar maria that are held to perturb the motion of spacecraft in lunar orbit

¹**mas·cu·lin·ist** \'maskyələnəst, -,lin-\ *n* -s [*masculine* + *-ist* (as in *feminist*)] : an advocate of male superiority or dominance : male chauvinist — **mas·cu·lin·ism** \-,nizəm\ *n* -s

²**masculinist** *adj* **1** : of, relating to, or being a masculinist **2** : marked by a distinctly masculine perspective

mash* *n, Brit* : mashed potatoes

mask* *n* : a pattern of opaque material used to shield selected parts of a photosensitive surface during deposition or etching (as in producing an integrated circuit)

massage* *vt* **1** : to treat flatteringly : BLANDISH ⟨be attentive, ~ my ego, advise me —Sally Quinn⟩ **2** : to alter to suit one's purpose : MODIFY, MANIPULATE ⟨computers to collect and rapidly ~ vast amounts of data —A.L.Robinson⟩

mass·cult \'mas,kəlt\ *n* -s [*mass culture*] : the artistic and intellectual culture associated with and disseminated through the mass media : mass culture

mass driver *n* [²*mass*] : a large electromagnetic catapult designed to hurl material (as from an asteroid) into space — compare RAIL GUN *herein*

massive* *adj* : having mass ⟨a ~ boson⟩

massively parallel *adj* : of, relating to, or being a computer system that uses a large number of separate processors simultaneously to increase power and speed

mass·less \'masləs\ *adj* : having no mass ⟨~ particles⟩ — **mass·less·ness** *n* -ES

mass–market \'=¦=\ *adj* **1** : being a paperback book with a nominal trim size usu. of 4 ³⁄₁₆" x 6 ¾" designed to be sold through non-book retail outlets (as supermarkets and drug stores) as well as through bookstores; *also* : of, relating to, or publishing mass-market books **2** : appealing or sold to a general audience ⟨the uniformity of their principal, *mass-market* brands —Michael Jackson⟩

mass of the resurrection *usu cap M&R* : a mass for the dead in which the celebrant wears white vestments to symbolize the joyous resurrection of the dead

mass spectrometry *or* **mass spectroscopy** *n* : the use of the mass spectrometer — **mass spectrometric** *adj*

master* *n* : a record (as a film, sound recording, or videotape) from which copies can be produced

master* *vt* : to produce a master of (as a sound recording)

master class *n* : a seminar for advanced students (as of music or dance) conducted by a master

mas·to·cy·to·ma \,mastə,sī'tōmə\ *n, pl* **mastocytomas** *or* **mastocyto·ma·ta** \-ōməd·ə, -ətə\ [NL, fr. E *mastocyte* + NL *-oma*] : a tumorous mass produced by proliferation of mast cells

MAT* *abbr* master of arts in teaching

matching *adj* : supplementing by an equal amount funds gotten from other sources by the recipient ⟨~ funds⟩ ⟨a ~ grant⟩

matchstick* *n* : something resembling a matchstick esp. in slenderness ⟨cut a carrot into ~*s*⟩

matchup \'=,=\ *n* -s [*match up*, v.] : ¹MATCH 1, 2

material* *n* **1** : the repertoire of a performer (as a comedian or musician) **2** : a person potentially suited to some pursuit or role ⟨college ~⟩ ⟨husband ~⟩

materials science *n* : the scientific study of the properties and applications of materials of construction or manufacture (as ceramics, polymers, metals, or composites) — **materials scientist** *n*

maternity *adj* [*maternity*, n.] **1** : designed for wear during pregnancy ⟨a ~ dress⟩ **2** : effective for the period close to and including childbirth ⟨~ leave⟩

mathematical biology *n* : a branch of biology concerned with the construction of mathematical models to describe and solve biological problems — **mathematical biologist** *n*

ma·tri·focal \¦ma·trə, ¦mā-+\ *adj* [*matr-* + *focal*] : MATRICENTRIC

matrix algebra *n* : generalized algebra that deals with the operations and relations among matrices

matrix sentence *n* : the one of a pair of sentences joined by means of a transformation that keeps its essential external structure and syntactic status ⟨in "the book that I want is gone", "the book is gone" is the *matrix sentence*⟩

mat·su·ta·ke \,mätsü'täkē, -kā\ *n, pl* **matsutake** *also* **matsutakes** [Jap *matsu-take*, *matsudake*, fr. *matsu* pine tree + *take* mushroom] : a large brownish edible Japanese mushroom (*Tricholoma matsutake*) having firm flesh and a spicy aroma; *also* : a large whitish mushroom (*Tricholoma magnivelare* syn. *T. ponderosum* syn. *Armillaria ponderosa*) of northern North America that is similar to the Japanese matsutake

mature* *adj* : having achieved a low but stable growth rate ⟨~ businesses⟩ ⟨~ products⟩ ⟨~ markets⟩

MATV *abbr* master antenna television

maul* *n* : a tool like a sledgehammer with one wedge-shaped end that is used to split wood

mau–mau \'mau̇¦mau̇\ *vb* **mau–maued; mau–maued; mau–mauing; mau–maus** *sometimes cap both Ms* [*mau-mau*, n.] *vt* : to intimidate (as an official) through hostile confrontation or threats usu. for social or political gain ~ *vi* : to engage in maumauing someone

ma·ven *also* **ma·vin** *or* **may·vin** \ˈmāvən\ *n* -s [Yiddish *meyvn*, fr. LHeb *mēbhīn*, perh. fr. Heb *mēbhī* one who has brought in] : one who is experienced or knowledgeable : EXPERT; *also* : an ardent enthusiast

max* *n* — **to the max** : to the greatest extent possible : TOTALLY, EXTREMELY ⟨enjoyed the evening *to the max*⟩

maxi \ˈmaksē\ *n* -s [*maxi-* (herein)] **1** : a long skirt or coat that usu. extends to the ankle — called also respectively *maxiskirt, maxicoat* **2** : a yacht at least 55 feet long

maxi- \ˈmaksē, -si\ *comb form* [fr. *maximum*, after E *minimum* : *mini-* (herein)] **1** : extra long ⟨*maxi-*dress⟩ ⟨*maxi-*kilt⟩ **2** : extra large ⟨*maxi-*sculpture⟩ ⟨*maxi-*problems⟩

max·il·lo·facial \mak,si(,)lō+\ *adj* [*maxill-* + *facial*] : of, relating to, treating, or affecting the maxilla and the face

maxi·min \ˈmaksə,min\ *n* -s [*maxi*mum + *min*imum] : the maximum of a set of minima; *esp* : the largest of a set of minimum possible gains each of which occurs in the least advantageous outcome of a strategy followed by a participant in a situation governed by the theory of games — compare MINIMAX *herein* — **maximin** *adj*

maximum likelihood *n* : a statistical method for estimating population parameters (as the mean and variance) from sample data that selects as estimates those parameter values maximizing the probability of obtaining the observed data

max out *vb* ~ *vi* : to reach an upper limit or peak ~ *vt* : to push to a limit or extreme; *also* : to use up all available credit on ⟨*maxed out* his credit card⟩

ma·yan·ist \ˈmīənəst\ *n* -s *usu cap* : an expert in the field of Mayan culture and history

ma·yo \ˈmā(,)ō\ *n* -s [by shortening] : MAYONNAISE

MB *abbr* megabyte *herein*

mba·gan·ga \,ůmbäˈkängä, -gə\ *n* -s [Zulu *umbaqanga*, lit. steamed cormeal bread; prob. fr. the association of such bread with the urban working-class milieu in which the music arose] : a South African dance music that combines traditional elements (as chanting and drumming) with elements of modern music (as jazz)

MBD *abbr* minimal brain dysfunction *herein*

mbi·ra \emˈbirə, əm-, -bēr-\ *n* -s [Shona] : an African musical instrument that consists of a gourd resonator, a wooden box, and a varying number of tuned metal or wooden strips that vibrate when plucked with the thumb or fingers

Mbps *abbr* megabits per second

mc- \mək; mə *before forms beginning with* k *or* g\ *prefix, usu cap* [*McDonald's*, chain of fast-food restaurants; fr. the association of the chain with products that are easily available though basic and standardized] : — used to indicate an inexpensive, convenient, or easy but usu. low-quality or commercialized version of something specified ⟨*Mc*Book⟩ ⟨*Mc*Doctor⟩

mcguffin *usu cap M&G, var of* MACGUFFIN

mc·job \məkˈjäb\ *n* -s, *usu cap M&J* [*mc-* (herein) + ¹*job*] : a low-paying job that requires little skill and provides little opportunity for advancement

MCS *abbr* **1** master of commercial science **2** master of computer science **3** missile control system

MD \ˈemˈdē\ *abbr or n* -s : minidisc *herein*

MDMA \,em,dē(,)emˈā\ *n* -s [*m*ethylene + *d*ioxy- + *m*eth*a*mphetamine] : ECSTASY *herein*

meals–on–wheels \ˌ==ˈ=\ *n pl but sing in constr* : a service that delivers daily hot meals to the homes of elderly or disabled people

mean value theorem *n* **1** : a theorem in differential calculus: if a function of one variable is continuous on a closed interval and differentiable on the interval minus its endpoints there is at least one point where the derivative of the function is equal to the slope of the line joining the endpoints of the curve representing the function on the interval **2** : a theorem in integral calculus: if a function of one variable is continuous on a closed interval and differentiable on the interval minus its endpoints, there is at least one point in the interval where the product of the value of the function and the length of the interval is equal to the integral of the function over the interval

meat* *n* : PENIS — usu. considered vulgar

meat–and–potatoes \ˌ===ˈ==\ *adj* **1** : of fundamental importance : BASIC ⟨the *meat-and-potatoes* problems of everyday living and loving —D.J.Heckman⟩; *also* : concerned with or emphasizing the basic aspects of something ⟨*meat-and-potatoes* sports fans⟩ **2** : DOWN-TO-EARTH, SIMPLE ⟨we have the same basic values. We're both *meat-and-potatoes* kids from the Midwest —Marjorie Wallace⟩ **3** : providing or preferring simple food consisting principally of meat and potatoes rather than fancy or exotic fare ⟨a *meat-and-potatoes* crowd⟩

meat and potatoes \"+\ *n pl but sing or pl in constr* [fr. their traditional role as basic dietary items] : the most important or fundamental part : ESSENCE 7

meat market *n* : a depersonalizing environment in which people are treated as sexual or economic resources

mec·a·myl·amine \,mekəˈmilə,mēn, -,mən\ *n* -s [*me*thyl + *cam*phane + *amine*] : a drug that is used orally in the form of its hydrochloride $C_{11}H_{21}N{\cdot}HCl$ as a ganglionic blocking agent to effect a rapid lowering of severely elevated blood pressure

mechanical bank *also* **mechanical*** *n* : a toy bank in which operation of a lever activates a mechanism that goes through some amusing or absurd routine and deposits a coin

mech·a·no·chemical \ˌmekənō+\ *adj* [*mechan-* + *chemical*] : relating to or being chemistry that deals with the conversion of chemical energy into mechanical work (as in the contraction of a muscle) — **mech·a·no·chemically** \"+\ *adv* — **mech·a·no·chemistry** \"+\ *n*

mech·a·no·receptor \ˌmekə(,)nō+\ *n* [*mechan-* + *receptor*] : a neural end organ (as a tactile receptor) that responds to a mechanical stimulus (as a change in pressure) — **mech·a·no·reception** \"+\ *n* — **mech·a·no·receptive** \"+\ *adj*

mech·lor·eth·amine \,me,klōrˈethə,mēn, -lȯr-, -,mən\ *n* [*me*thyl + *chlor*oethyl + *amine*] : a nitrogen mustard $C_5H_{11}Cl_2N$ used in the form of its hydrochloride in the palliative treatment of some neoplastic diseases

mec·li·zine \ˈmeklə,zēn\ *n* -s [*me*thyl + *c*h*l*or- + *-izine* (alter. of *azine*)] : a drug $C_{25}H_{27}ClN_2$ used usu. in the form of its hydrochloride to treat nausea and vertigo

med \ˈmed\ *n* -s [by shortening] : MEDICATION 2 — usu. used in pl. ⟨giving out bedtime ~*s* —Susanna Kaysen⟩

medal* *vb* ~ *vi* : to win a medal ⟨~*ed* in figure skating⟩

¹**med·e·vac** *also* **med·i·vac** \ˈmedə(,)vak, -ē(,)-\ *n* -s [*med*ical *evac*uation] **1** : emergency evacuation of the sick or wounded (as from a combat area) **2** : a helicopter used for medevac

²**medevac** *also* **medivac** *vt* **medevacked** *also* **medevaced** *or* **medivacked** *or* **medivaced; medevacked** *also* **medevaced** *or* **medivacked** *or* **medivaced; medevacking** *also* **medevacing** *or* **medivacking** *or* **medivacing; medevacs** *also* **medivacs** : to transport in a medevac helicopter

media* *n* -s **1** : a medium of cultivation, conveyance, or expression; *esp* : MEDIUM 3c **2 a** *sing or pl in constr* : MASS MEDIA **b** *pl* : members of the mass media

media event *n* : a publicity event staged for coverage by the news media

me·dia·ge·nic \ˌmēdēəˈjenik *also* -jēn-\ *adj* [*media*, pl. of *medium* + *-genic*] : likely to appeal to the audiences of the mass media and esp. television ⟨~ politicians⟩

medial condyle *n* : a condyle on the inner side of the lower extremity of the femur; *also* : a corresponding eminence on the upper part of the tibia that articulates with the medial condyle of the femur — compare LATERAL CONDYLE *herein*

median* *n* **1** : a vertical line that divides the histogram of a frequency distribution into two parts of equal area **2** : a value of a random variable for which all greater values make the distribution function greater than one half and all lesser values make it less than one half

median eminence *n* : a raised area in the floor of the third ventricle of the brain produced by the infundibulum of the hypothalamus

med·ic·aid \ˈmedə,kād, -dē-\ *n, usu cap* [*medical* + *aid*] : a program of medical aid designed for those unable to afford regular medical service and financed by the state and federal governments

med·i·cal·ize \ˈmedəkə,līz\ *vt* -ED/-ING/-S : to view or treat as a medical concern, problem, or disorder ⟨those who seek to dispose of social problems by *medicalizing* them —Liam Hudson⟩ — **med·i·cal·i·za·tion** \ˌ====ləˈzāshən\ *n* -s

medi·care \ˈmedə, -dē+,\ *n, usu cap* [blend of *medical* and *care*] : a government program of medical care esp. for the elderly

med·i·gap \ˈmedə,gap\ *n, often cap, often attrib* [*Medicare* + ¹*gap*] : supplemental health insurance that covers costs (as of medical care or a hospital stay) not covered by Medicare

me·di·og·ra·phy \,mēdēˈägrəfē, -fi\ *n* -ES [*medium* + *-o-* + *-graphy*] : a list of multimedia materials on a given subject

medium* *n* **1** : the tenuous material (as gas and dust) in space that exists outside large agglomerations of matter (as stars) ⟨interstellar ~⟩ **2** : something (as a magnetic disk) on which information may be stored

me·droxy·progesterone acetate \meˌdräksē. . .-\ *also* **medroxyprogesterone** *n* [*medr-*, alter. of *methylhydroxyl* containing a methyl and hydroxyl group + ²*oxy-* + *progesterone*] : hormone $C_{24}H_{34}O_4$ that is a derivative of progesterone and is used esp. in the treatment of amenorrhea and abnormal uterine bleeding, in conjunction with conjugated estrogens to relieve symptoms of menopause and prevent osteoporosis, and as an injectable contraceptive

me·dul·lin \məˈdələn, me-; ˈmedᵊl-, ˈmejəl-\ *n* -s [NL *medulla* + E *-in*; fr. its isolation from the medulla of the kidney] : a renal prostaglandin effective in reducing blood pressure

mef·e·nam·ic acid \,mefə,namik-\ *n* [di*m*ethyl + *fen-* (by shortening & alter. fr. *phenyl*) + *am*inobenzo*ic acid*] : a drug $C_{15}H_{15}NO_2$ used as an anti-inflammatory agent

meg \ˈmeg\ *n* -s [by shortening] : MEGABYTE *herein*

mega \ˈmegə\ *adj* [*mega-*] **1** : HUGE, VAST ⟨a ~ electronics store⟩ **2** : of the highest level of rank, excellence, or importance ⟨a number one hit made her ~⟩

mega-* *comb form* **1** : greatly surpassing others of its kind ⟨*mega*hero⟩ ⟨*mega*polluters⟩ **2** : to a superlative degree ⟨*mega*successful⟩

mega·bar \ˈmegə+,\ *n* [ISV *mega-* + ⁷*bar*] : a unit of pressure equal to one million bars

mega·bit \"+,\ *n* [*mega-* + ⁷*bit*] : one million bits

mega·buck \"+,\ *n, often attrib* [*mega-* + ¹*buck*] : one million dollars ⟨should make it worth 18 ~*s* —*Datamation*⟩; *also* : money in millions — usu. used in pl. ⟨turned an electronic idea into ~*s* —William Stockton⟩; usu. sing. when attrib. ⟨a Hollywood ~ movie⟩

mega·byte \"+,\ *n* [*mega-* + *byte* (herein); fr. the fact that 1,048,576 (2^{20}) is the power of 2 closest to one million] : 1024 kilobytes or 1,048,576 bytes; *also* : one million bytes

mega·city \"+,\ *n* [*mega-* + *city*] : MEGALOPOLIS 1

mega·corporation \"+\ *n* [*mega-* + *corporation*] : a very large corporation

mega·deal \"+,\ *n* [*mega-* + ³*deal*] : a business deal involving a lot of money

mega·death \"+,\ *n* [*mega-* + *death*] : one million deaths — usu. used as a unit in reference to nuclear warfare

mega·dose \"+,\ *n* [*mega-* + ¹*dose*] : a large dose (as of a vitamin)

mega·hit \"+,\ *n* [*mega-* + ²*hit*] : something (as a motion picture) that is extremely successful

mega·machine \"+,\ *n* [*mega-* + ¹*machine*] : a social system that functions impersonally like a gigantic machine

mega·merger \"+,\ *n* [*mega-* + *merger*] : a merger of megacorporations

mega·project \"+\ *n* [*mega-* + ¹*project*] : a major project or undertaking (as in business or construction)

mega·rad \"+,\ *n* [*mega-* + ³*rad*] : one million rads

mega·star \"+,\ *n* [*mega-* + ¹*star*] : SUPERSTAR *herein*

mega·structure \"+,\ *n* [*mega-* + ¹*structure*] : a very large multistory building or complex of buildings

mega·tonnage \"+,\ *n* [*megaton* + *tonnage*] : the destructive capability esp. of a collection of nuclear weapons that is expressed in megatons

mega·unit \"+,\ *n* [*mega-* + ¹*unit*] : one million units

mega·vitamin \ˌmegə+\ *adj* [*mega-* + *vitamin*] : relating to or consisting of very large doses of vitamins ⟨~ therapy⟩

mega·vitamins \ˈmegə+,\ *n pl* [*mega-* + *vitamins*] : a large quantity of vitamins

me·gil·lah *also* **me·gil·la** \məˈgilə\ *n* -s [Yiddish *megile* rigmarole, fr. Heb *mĕgillāh* scroll (used esp. of the Book of Esther, the whole of which is read aloud during Purim)] *slang* **1** : a long involved story or account ⟨the whole ~⟩ ⟨he'd had a lot of stuff patented over the years, but people had robbed him or swiped his ideas; the usual inventor's ~ —Alexander King⟩ **2** : PRODUCTION 1c ⟨a simple matter . . . turns into a big political ~ —Marilyn Stasio⟩

mei·ji \ˈmāˌjē\ *adj, usu cap* [Jap, lit., enlightened rule] : of, relating to, or having the characteristics of the period of the reign of the Japanese emperor Mutsuhito

meio·fauna \ˈmīō+\ *n* [NL, fr. *mi-* + *fauna*] : the mesofauna of the benthos — **meio·faunal** \ˌmīō+\ *adj*

meis·ter \ˈmīstə(r)\ *n* -s [Yiddish *mayster* & G *meister* master, fr. MHG *meister*, fr. OHG *meistar*, fr. L *magister* — more at MASTER] : one who is knowledgeable about something specified — often used in combination ⟨a puzzle-*meister*⟩

meit·ner·i·um \mītˈnirēəm, -ˈner-\ *n* -s [NL, fr. Lise *Meitner* †1968 Ger. physicist + NL *-ium*] : a short-lived radioactive element of atomic number 109 that is produced artificially — symbol *Mt*

melanocyte–stimulating hormone \ˌ===,=ˌ==ˌ==-, ˌ=ˌ=-\ *n* : either of two vertebrate hormones of the pituitary gland that darken the skin by stimulating melanin dispersion to pigment-containing cells — abbr. *MSH*; called also *melanophore-stimulating hormone*

mel·a·no·some \ˈmelənō,sōm\ *n* -s [*melan-* + ³*-some*] : a melanin-producing granule in a melanocyte

mel·a·to·nin \ˌmeləˈtōnən\ *n* -s [prob. fr. *mela*nocyte + sero*tonin*; fr. its power to lighten melanocytes] : a vertebrate hormone $C_{13}H_{16}N_2O_2$ that is derived from serotonin, is secreted by the pineal gland esp. in response to darkness, and has been linked to the regulation of circadian rhythms

meld \ˈmeld\ *n* -s [³*meld*] : BLEND, MIXTURE

mel·lo·tron \ˈmelə,trän\ *n* -s [fr. *Mellotron*, a trademark] : an electronic keyboard instrument programmed to produce the tape-recorded sounds usu. of orchestral instruments

mellow* *adj* **1** *slang* : EXCELLENT, APPEALING, FINE ⟨at first the gig looked ~: $300 for two shows and a supposedly hip crowd —Mark Jacobson⟩ **2** : feeling relaxed and good from smoking marijuana

mel·pha·lan \ˈmelfə,lan\ *n* -s [prob. fr. *me*thanol + *phe*ny*lala*ni*ne*] : an antineoplastic drug $C_{13}H_{18}Cl_2N_2O_2$ that is a derivative of nitrogen mustard and is used esp. in the treatment of multiple myeloma

melt* *n* : a sandwich with melted cheese ⟨a tuna ~⟩

meltdown* *n* **1** : the accidental melting of the core of a nuclear reactor **2** : a rapid or disastrous decline or collapse **3** : a breakdown of self-control (as from fatigue or overstimulation)

mem·bran·al \ˌmemˈbrānᵊl\ *adj* : relating to or characteristic of cellular membranes

meme \ˈmēm\ *n* -s [alter. of *mimeme*, fr. *mim-* (as in *mimesis*) + *-eme*] : an idea, behavior, style, or usage that spreads from person to person within a culture

memory* *n* : capacity for storing information ⟨64 megabytes of ~⟩

memory cell *n* : a long-lived lymphocyte that carries the antibody or receptor for a specific antigen after a first exposure to the antigen and that remains in a less than mature state until stimulated by a second exposure to the antigen at which time it mounts a more rapid effective immune response than a cell which has not been exposed previously

memory lane *n* : an imaginary path through the nostalgically remembered past — usu. used in such phrases as *a walk down memory lane*

men·a·zon \ˈmenə,zän\ *n* -s [perh. fr. di*m*ethyl + diamin*o*- + tri*azine* + thi*on*ate] : an organophosphate insecticide and acaricide $C_6H_{12}N_5O_2PS_2$ used esp. as a systemic in agriculture

me·nin·go·encephalitic \məˌniŋ(,)gō, -in(,)jō+\ *adj* : relating to or characteristic of meningoencephalitis ⟨~ lesions⟩

menopausal* *adj* : relating to or acting as if affected with male menopause — not usu. used technically

meno·taxis \ˌmenə+\ *n* [NL, fr. ²*meno-* + *taxis*] : a taxis involving a constant reaction (as movement at a constant angle to a light source) but not a simple movement toward or away from the directing stimulus

mensch \ˈmench, ˈmensh\ *n* -ES [Yiddish *mentsh* person, human being — more at LUFTMENSCH] : a person of integrity and honor

men·tee \menˈtē\ *n* -s [*mentor* + *-ee*] : one who is being mentored : PROTÉGÉ 1

mentor *vt* -ED/-ING/-S [*mentor*, n.] : to serve as a mentor for

menu* *n* **1** : a list or assortment of offerings ⟨a ~ of television programs⟩ **2** : a list shown on the display of a computer from which a user can select the operation the computer is to perform

me·nu·do \məˈnüdō, *Sp* meˈnüthō\ *n* -s [MexSp, fr. Sp *menudos* innards, giblets, fr. *menudo* small, slight, fine, fr. L *minutus* — more at MINUTE] : a tripe stew seasoned with chili peppers

menu–driven \ˈ==ˌ==\ *adj* : relating to or being a computer program in which options are offered to the user via menus

merc \ˈmərk, ˈmərs\ *n* -s [by shortening & alter.] : MERCENARY 2

mer·cap·to·ethanol \(,)mərˌkaptō+\ *n* [*mercapt-* + *ethanol*] : a reducing agent $HSCH_2CH_2OH$ used to break disulfide bonds in proteins (as for the destruction of their physiological activity)

merciful* *adj* : providing relief ⟨a ~ absence of crowds⟩

mercifully* *adv* : FORTUNATELY *herein* ⟨~ we didn't have to attend the meeting⟩

mercy killing *n* : EUTHANASIA

me·rid·ic \məˈridik\ *adj* [Gk *merid-*, *meris* part + E *-ic*; akin to Gk *meros* part — more at MERIT] : having some but not all active constituents chemically defined ⟨insects reared on a ~ diet⟩ — compare HOLIDIC *herein*, OLIGIDIC *herein*

mer·i·toc·ra·cy \ˌmerəˈtäkrəsē\ *n* -ES [¹*merit* + *-o-* + *-cracy*] **1** : a system or organization in which the talented are chosen and moved ahead on the basis of their achievement **2 a** : leadership by the talented **b** : MERITOCRATS *herein* — **mer·it·o·crat·ic** \ˌmerəd·əˈkrad·ik\ *adj*

mer·it·o·crat \ˈmerəd·ō,krat\ *n* -s [¹*merit* + *-o-* + *-crat*] : one who advances through a meritocratic system

mer·lot \mərˈlō, me(ə)r-\ *n* -s *often cap* [F, a grape variety, fr. *merle* blackbird (fr. the grape's color) — more at MERL] : a dry red varietal wine made from a widely grown grape orig. used in the Bordeaux region of France for blending; *also* : the grape itself

mero·myosin \ˌmerə+\ *n* [³*mer-* + *myosin*] : either of two structural subunits of myosin obtained esp. by tryptic digestion

merry widow *n, often cap M&W* : a strapless corset or bustier usu. having garters attached

mes·clun \ˈmesklən\ *n* -s [F, fr. Prov, lit., mixture, fr. *mescla* to mix, fr. OProv *mesclar*, fr. (assumed) VL *misculare* — more at MEDDLE] : a mixture of young tender greens (as lettuces, arugula, and chicory); *also* : a salad made with mesclun

mesial* *adj* : of, relating to, or being the surface of a tooth that is next to the tooth in front of it or that is closest to the middle of the front of the jaw — compare DISTAL *herein*, PROXIMAL *herein* — **me·si·al·ly*** \-ə-lē\ *adv*

meso·cyclone \"+\ *n* [*mes-* + *cyclone*] : a rapidly rotating air mass within a thunderstorm that often gives rise to a tornado

meso·pelagic \ˌme|zō, ˌmē|, |sō+\ *adj* [*mes-* + *pelagic*] : of, relating to, or inhabiting oceanic depths from about 600 to 3000 feet ⟨~ fish⟩

meso·scale \"+\ *adj* [*mes-* + ⁷*scale*] : of intermediate size; *esp* : of or relating to a meteorological phenomenon approximately 10 to 1000 kilometers in horizontal extent ⟨~ cloud pattern⟩ ⟨~ wind circulation⟩

mesosome* *n* : an organelle of bacteria that appears in electron micrographs as an invagination of the plasma membrane and is a site of localization of respiratory enzymes

messenger* *n* **1** : a substance (as a hormone) that mediates a biological effect — see SECOND MESSENGER *herein* **2** : MESSENGER RNA *herein*

messenger RNA *n* : an RNA produced by transcription that carries the code for a particular protein from the nuclear DNA to a ribosome in the cytoplasm and acts as a template for the formation of that protein — called also *mRNA*; compare TRANSFER RNA *herein*

mess over *vt, slang* : to treat harshly or unfairly : ABUSE

mes·tra·nol \ˈmestrə,nȯl, -,nōl\ *n* -s [*meth-* + *estrogen* + *pregnane* + ¹*-ol*] : a synthetic estrogen $C_{21}H_{26}O_2$ used in oral contraceptives

meta–analysis \ˌmed·ə+\ *n* [*meta-* + *analysis*] : quantitative statistical analysis that is applied to separate but similar experiments or studies of different and usu. independent researchers and that involves pooling the data and using the pooled data to test for statistical significance

meta·centric \"+\ *n* -s [*metacentric*, adj.] : a metacentric chromosome

meta·cognition \"+\ *n* [*meta-* + *cognition*] : awareness or analysis of one's own learning or thinking processes

meta·fiction \"+\ *n* [*meta-* + *fiction*] : fiction which refers to or takes as its subject fictional writing and its conventions — **meta·fictional** \"+\ *adj* — **meta·fictionist** \"+\ *n*

metal* *n, often attrib* : HEAVY METAL *herein*

metal·head \ˈ==,=\ *n* [(*heavy*) *metal* (herein) + *-head* (prob. as in *acidhead*—herein—or *pothead*—herein—with shift of sense from "habitual user" to "devotee")] : a fan or performer of heavy metal music

me·tal·lic \məˈtalik\ *n* -s [*metallic*, adj.] : a fiber or yarn made of or coated with metal; *also* : a fabric made of this

met·al·lide \ˈmed·ᵊl,īd, -etᵊl-\ *vt* -ED/-ING/-S [obs. *metallide*, n., a binary compound of metals, fr. *metall-* + ¹*-ide*] : to diffuse (atoms of a metal or metalloid) into the surface of a metal by electrolysis in order to impart a desired surface property (as hardness) to the bulk metal

me·tal·lo·enzyme \məˌtalō+\ *n* [*metall-* + *enzyme*] : an enzyme consisting of a protein linked with a specific metal

me·tal·lo·protein \"+\ *n* [*metall-* + *protein*] : a conjugated protein in which the prosthetic group is a metal

me·tal·lo·thio·nein \məˌtalōˈthīə,nēn\ *n* -s [*metall-* + ¹*thion-* + *-ein*] : any of various metal-binding proteins involved in the metabolism of copper in the liver and zinc in body tissue (as of the liver) and in the binding of toxic metals (as cadmium)

metal–oxide semiconductor \ˌ==ˌ=ˌ=-\ *n* : a semiconductor device (as a diode or a capacitor) in which a metallic oxide (as silicon dioxide) serves as an insulating layer

metameric* *adj* : of, relating to, or being color metamers ⟨a ~ pair⟩ — **metamerism*** *n*

meta·ram·i·nol \ˌmed·əˈramə,nȯl, -,nōl\ *n* -s [perh. fr. *meta-* + hydroxy- + *amin-* + *-ol*] : a sympathomimetic drug $C_9H_{13}NO_2$ used esp. as a vasoconstrictor to raise or maintain blood pressure

meta·rhodopsin \ˌmed·ə+\ *n* [*meta-* + *rhodopsin*] : either of two intermediate compounds formed in the bleaching of rhodopsin by light

me·te·or·oi·dal \ˌmēd-ēə¦rȯidᵊl\ *adj* : of or relating to meteoroids
me·te·pa \məˈtēpə, meˈ-\ *n* -S [*me*thyl + *tepa* (herein)] : an insect chemosterilant $C_9H_{18}N_3OP$ that is a methyl derivative of tepa
meter maid *n* : a female member of a police force who is assigned to write tickets for parking violations
meth \ˈmeth\ *n* -S [by shortening] : METHAMPHETAMINE
me·than·o·gen \məˈthanəˌjen\ *n* -S [prob. back-formation fr. *methanogenic*, fr. *methane* + *-o-* + *-genic*] : any of various anaerobic microorganisms that produce methane from carbon dioxide and hydrogen, are classified as bacteria (as of the family Methanobacteriaceae) or as archaea, and include some found in the rumina of herbivores (as domestic cattle) that utilize cellulose — **me·than·o·gen·ic** \ˌ-ˌ-ˈ-ik\ *adj*
meth·a·pyr·i·lene \ˌmethəˈpirəˌlēn *also* -ˈpīr-\ *n* -S [di*methyl* + *pyridinyl* + *-ene*] : an antihistamine drug $C_{14}H_{19}N_3S$ formerly used as a mild sedative in proprietary sleep-inducing drugs
metha·qua·lone \ˌmethəˈkwāˌlōn, meˈthakwəˌlōn\ *n* -S [*methyl* + *quinazoline* + *-one*] : a sedative and hypnotic drug $C_{16}H_{14}N_2O$ that is not a barbiturate but is habit-forming and subject to abuse — see QUAALUDE *herein*
meth·e·drine \ˈmethəˌdrēn, -ˌdrən\ *n* [fr. *Methedrine*, a trademark] : METHAMPHETAMINE
meth·i·cil·lin \ˌmethə¦siləñ\ *n* -S [*meth-* + pen*icillin*] : a semisynthetic penicillin $C_{17}H_{19}N_2O_6NaS$ esp. effective against penicillinase-producing staphylococci
me·thi·ma·zole \məˈthīməˌzōl, meˈ-\ *n* -S [*methyl* + *imidazole*] : a drug $C_4H_6N_2S$ used to inhibit activity of the thyroid gland
method* *n, usu cap* : a dramatic technique by which an actor seeks to gain complete identification with the inner personality of the character being portrayed
method of fluxions : DIFFERENTIAL CALCULUS
meth·o·trex·ate \ˌmethəˈtrekˌsāt, -sət\ *n* -S [*meth-* + *-trex-* (arbitrary element) + [1]*-ate*] : a toxic drug $C_{20}H_{22}N_8O_5$ that is an analogue of folic acid and is used to treat certain cancers, severe psoriasis, and rheumatoid arthritis
me·thox·amine \meˈthäksəˌmēn, -mən\ *n* [*methyl* + [1]*ox-* + *amine*] : a sympathomimetic amine $C_{11}H_{17}NO_3$ used in the form of its hydrochloride esp. to raise or maintain blood pressure (as during surgery) by its vasoconstrictor effects
me·thoxy·flu·rane \meˌthäksēˈflü(ə)rˌān\ *n* -S [*meth-* + *oxy-* + *fluor-* + eth*ane*] : a potent nonexplosive inhalational general anesthetic $C_3H_4Cl_2F_2O$
meths \ˈmeths\ *n pl but sing in constr* [short for *methylated spirits*] *Brit* : methylated spirits esp. as an illicit beverage
meth·yl·ase \ˈmethəˌlās, -āz\ *n* -S [*methyl* + *-ase*] : an enzyme that catalyzes methylation (as of RNA or DNA)
methyl chloroform *n* : TRICHLOROETHANE a
methyldopa \¦==¦=\ *n* [*methyl* + *dopa*] : a drug $C_{10}H_{13}NO_4$ used to lower blood pressure
methylisocyanate \¦==¦==(ˌ)=\ *n* [*methyl* + *isocyanate*] : an extremely toxic chemical CH_3NCO that is used esp. in the manufacture of pesticides — abbr. *MIC*
methylmercury \¦==¦==\ *n* [*methyl* + *mercury*] : any of various toxic compounds of mercury containing the complex CH_3Hg– that often occur as pollutants formed as industrial by-products or pesticide residues, tend to accumulate in living organisms (as fish) esp. in food chains, are rapidly and easily absorbed through the human intestinal wall, and cause neurological dysfunction in humans — see MINAMATA DISEASE *herein*
methyl parathion *n* : a potent synthetic organophosphate insecticide $C_8H_{10}NO_5PS$ that is more toxic than parathion
meth·yl·phe·ni·date \ˌmethəlˈfenəˌdāt, -ˈfēn-\ *n* -S [*methyl* + *phenyl* + piper*idine* + *acetate*] : a mild stimulant $C_{14}H_{19}NO_2$ of the central nervous system that is an analogue of amphetamine and is used in the form of its hydrochloride to treat narcolepsy and hyperactivity disorders (as attention deficit disorder) in children — see RITALIN *herein*
methylprednisolone \¦==¦==\ *n* [*methyl* + *prednisolone*] : a glucocorticoid $C_{22}H_{30}O_5$ that is a derivative of prednisolone and is used as an anti-inflammatory agent; *also* : any of several of its salts (as an acetate) used similarly
methyltransferase \¦==¦=ˌ=\ *n* [*methyl* + *transferase*] : any of several transferases that promote transfer of a methyl group from one compound to another
methylxanthine \¦==¦=\ *n* [*methyl* + *xanthine*] : a methylated xanthine derivative (as caffeine, theobromine, or theophylline)
methy·ser·gide \ˌmethəˈsərˌjīd\ *n* -S [*methyl* + *lys*ergic acid + *amide*] : a serotonin antagonist $C_{21}H_{27}N_3O_2$ used as its maleate esp. in the treatment and prevention of migraine headaches
met·i·cal \ˈmetəkəl, ˌmetəˈkal\ *n* -S [Pg, miskal, fr. Ar *mithqāl*] : the basic monetary unit of Mozambique — see MONEY table *in the Dict*
met·o·clo·pra·mide \ˌmedəˈklōprəˌmīd\ *n* -S [*ISV met*hoxy + *chlor-* + *procainamide*; orig. formed as F *métoclopramide*] : an antiemetic drug $C_{14}H_{22}ClN_3O_2$ administered in the form of its hydrochloride
me–too* *adj* : similar or identical to an established product (as a drug) with no significant advantage over it
metric* *n* **1** : a mathematical function that associates with each pair of elements of a set a real nonnegative number constituting their distance and satisfying the conditions that the number is zero only if the two elements are identical, the number is the same regardless of the order in which the two elements are taken, and the number associated with one pair of elements plus that associated with one member of the pair and a third element is equal to or greater than the number associated with the other member of the pair and the third element **2** : METRIC SYSTEM
met·ri·cate \ˈme·trəˌkāt\ *vt* -ED/-ING/-S [[2]*metric* + [4]*-ate*] *Brit* : METRICIZE *herein*
met·ri·ca·tion \ˌme·trəˈkāshən\ *n* -S [[2]*metric* + *-ation*] : the act or process of metricizing
metricize* *vt* : to change into or express in the metric system
metric space *n* : a mathematical set for which a metric is defined for any pair of elements
[1]**met·ro** \ˈme·(ˌ)trō\ *n* -S [fr. the phrase *metropolitan government*] : a metropolitan regional government
[2]**metro** \"\ *adj* [by shortening] : METROPOLITAN 5
met·ro·ni·da·zole \ˌme·trəˈnīdəˌzōl\ *n* -S [*methyl* + *-tron-* (prob. fr. *nitro*) + *imide* + *azole*] : a drug $C_6H_9N_3O_3$ that is effective against various bacteria and protozoans and is used esp. to treat vaginal trichomoniasis, amebiasis, and infections by anaerobic bacteria
met·ro·plex \ˈme·trōˌpleks\ *n* -ES [[2]*metro*politan + *-plex* (herein)] : a large metropolitan area usu. made up of two or more cities along with neighboring heavily populated areas
me·tyr·a·pone \məˈtirəˌpōn\ *n* -S [*meth*yl + *-rapone* (perh. alter. of *propanone*)] : a metabolic hormone $C_{14}H_{14}N_2O$ that inhibits biosynthesis of cortisol and corticosterone and is used to test for normal functioning of the pituitary gland
meur·sault \(ˌ)mərˈsō, mœr-\ *n* -S *usu cap* [F, fr. *Meursault*, commune in France] : a dry white Burgundy wine
me·val·o·nate \məˈvaləˌnāt\ *n* -S [*mevalonic* acid + [4]*-ate*] : a salt of mevalonic acid
MHC *abbr* major histocompatibility complex *herein*
MI *abbr* myocardial infarction
MIA \ˌem(ˌ)īˈā\ *n* -S [*missing in action*] : a member of the armed forces whose whereabouts following a combat mission are unknown and whose death cannot be established beyond reasonable doubt
mic \ˈmīk\ *n* -S [by shortening] : MICROPHONE
mi·chae·lis constant \məˈkāləs-, mə-\ *n, usu cap M* [after Leonor *Michaelis* †1949 Am. biochemist] : a constant that is a measure of the kinetics of an enzyme reaction and that is equivalent to the concentration of substrate at which the reaction takes place at one half its maximum rate
mick·ey–mouse \ˈmikē¦maus, -ki-\ *vt* -ED/-ING/-S [fr. *Mickey Mouse*, a trademark used for a cartoon character] : to provide (a film) with accompanying music that closely describes or mimics the action
[1]**mickey mouse** *adj, usu cap both Ms* **1** : not to be taken seriously ⟨switch to *Mickey Mouse* courses, where you don't work too hard —Willie Cager⟩ ⟨these races are viewed as *Mickey Mouse* events featuring out-of-shape World Cup skiers who come for the appearance money —W.O.Johnson⟩; *also* : not effectual : WORTHLESS ⟨a *Mickey Mouse* lock⟩ ⟨*Mickey Mouse* bookkeeping⟩ **2** : being or performing insipid or corny popular music **3** : of little importance : TRIFLING ⟨*Mickey Mouse* losses⟩ : PETTY ⟨*Mickey Mouse* regulations⟩
[2]**mickey mouse** *n, usu cap both Ms* : something that is Mickey Mouse ⟨eliminating the *Mickey Mouse* from the soldier's routine —L.J.Binder⟩
mi·con·a·zole \mīˈkänəˌzōl, miˈ-\ *n* -S [*micon-* (prob. part blend, part. alter. of *myc-* and NL *Monilia* monilia) + imid*azole*] : an antifungal agent administered esp. in the form of its nitrate $C_{18}H_{14}Cl_4N_2O{\cdot}HNO_3$
MICR *abbr* magnetic ink character recognition
micro* *n* **1** : MICROCOMPUTER *herein* **2** : MICROPROCESSOR *herein*
micro* *adj* **1** : smaller than normal ⟨~ skis⟩ : SMALL-SCALE 1 ⟨~ hydroelectric plants⟩ **2** : concerned with individuals, small units, or small quantities; *also* : involving minute quantities or variations
mi·cro·algae \¦mīkrō+\ *n pl* [*micr-* + *algae*] : algae (as diatoms or chlorellas) not visible to the unaided eye — **mi·cro·algal** \"+\ *adj*
mi·cro·anatomical \"+\ *adj* [*microanatomy* + *-ical*] : HISTOLOGICAL
mi·cro·an·gi·op·a·thy \¦==ˌanjēˈäpəthē\ *n* -ES [*micr-* + *angi-* + *-pathy*] : a disease of very fine blood vessels ⟨thrombotic ~⟩ — **mi·cro·an·gi·o·path·ic** \-jēəˈpathik\ *adj*
mi·cro·beam \ˈmīkrō+ˌ\ *n* [*micr-* + [1]*beam*] : a beam of radiation of small cross section ⟨a focused laser ~⟩ ⟨a ~ of electrons⟩
micro·body \"+ˌ\ *n* [*micr-* + [1]*body*] : PEROXISOME *herein*
micro·brew \"+ˌ\ *n* [*micr-* + [2]*brew*] : a beer produced by a microbrewery — **microbrewed** *adj* — **micro·brewing** \"+ˌ\ *n*
micro·brewery \"+\ *n* [*micr-* + *brewery*] : a small brewery making specialty beer in limited quantities — **micro·brewer** \"+ˌ\ *n*
micro·bubble \"+ˌ\ *n* [*micr-* + [2]*bubble*] : a microscopic bubble
mi·cro·burst \"+ˌ\ *n* [*micr-* + [2]*burst*] : a violent short-lived localized downdraft that creates extreme wind shears at low altitudes and is usu. associated with thunderstorms
mi·cro·capsule \¦mīkrō+\ *n* [*micr-* + [1]*capsule*] : a tiny capsule containing material (as an adhesive or a medicine) that is released when the capsule is broken, melted, or dissolved
mi·cro·cassette \"+\ *n* [*micr-* + *cassette* (herein)] : a small cassette of magnetic tape that is used esp. for dictation
mi·cro·chip \"+ˌ\ *n* [*micr-* + [1]*chip*] : INTEGRATED CIRCUIT *herein*
mi·cro·circuit \"+\ *n* [*micr-* + [1]*circuit*] : INTEGRATED CIRCUIT *herein* — **mi·cro·circuitry** \"+\ *n*
mi·cro·circulation \¦mīkrō+\ *n* [*micr-* + *circulation*] : blood circulation in the microvascular system; *also* : the microvascular system itself — **mi·cro·circulatory** \"+\ *adj*
mi·cro·coccal \"+\ *adj* : relating to or characteristic of micrococci ⟨~ enzymes⟩
mi·cro·code \"+ˌ\ *n* [*micr-* + [1]*code*] : microinstructions esp. for a microprocessor
mi·cro·computer \¦mīkrō+\ *n* [*micr-* + *computer*] **1** : a small computer usu. equipped with a microprocessor; *esp* : PERSONAL COMPUTER *herein* **2** : MICROPROCESSOR *herein*
mi·cro·culture \ˈ==+ˌ\ *n* [*micr-* + [1]*culture*] **1** : the culture of a small group of human beings with limited perspective **2** : a microscopic culture of cells or organisms — **mi·cro·cultural** \¦mīkrō+\ *adj*
mi·cro·distribution \¦mikrō+\ *n* [*micr-* + *distribution*] : the precise distribution of one or more kinds of organisms in a microhabitat or in part of an ecosystem ⟨~ of soil mites⟩
mi·cro·dot \ˈ==+ˌ\ *n* [*micr-* + [1]*dot*] **1** : a photographic reproduction of printed matter reduced to the size of a dot for ease or security of transmittal **2** : a very small pill or capsule of LSD
mi·cro·earthquake \¦==+\ *n* [*micr-* + *earthquake*] : an earthquake of low intensity; *esp* : one of magnitude of less than 3 on the Richter scale
mi·cro·ecology \"+\ *n* [*micr-* + *ecology*] : ecology of all or part of a small community (as a microhabitat or a housing development) — **mi·cro·ecological** \"+\ *adj*
mi·cro·economic \"+\ *adj* [*micr-* + *economic*] : of or relating to microeconomics ⟨~ theory⟩
mi·cro·electronics \¦mīkrō+\ *n pl* [*micr-* + *electronics*] **1** *sing in constr* : a branch of electronics that deals with the miniaturization of electronic circuits and components **2** : devices, equipment, or circuits produced using the methods of microelectronics — **mi·cro·electronic** \"+\ *adj*
mi·cro·emulsion \"+\ *n* [*micr-* + *emulsion*] : an emulsion in which the dispersed phase is in the form of very small droplets usu. produced and maintained with the aid of surfactants and having diameters of from 50 to 500 angstroms
mi·cro·encapsulate \"+\ *vt* [*micr-* + *encapsulate*] : to enclose in a microcapsule ⟨*microencapsulated* aspirin⟩ — **mi·cro·encapsulation** \"+\ *n*
micro·fiber \"+ˌ\ *n* [*micr-* + [1]*fiber*] : a fine usu. soft polyester fiber used esp. in textiles; *also* : a fabric made from such fibers
mi·cro·filament \"+\ *n* [*micr-* + *filament*] : any of the minute actin-containing protein filaments that are widely distributed in the cytoplasm of eukaryotic cells, help maintain their structural framework, and play a role in the movement of cell components
mi·cro·floppy \"+\ *or* **microfloppy disk** *n* [*micr-* + *floppy* (herein)] : a floppy disk smaller than 5¼ inches in diameter
mi·cro·fluorometry \"+\ *n* [*micr-* + *fluorometry*] : the detection and measurement of the fluorescence produced by minute quantities of materials (as in cells) — **mi·cro·fluorometer** \"+\ *n* — **mi·cro·fluorometric** \"+\ *adj*
mi·cro·form* *n* **1** : a process or medium for reproducing printed matter in a much reduced size **2 a** : matter reproduced by microform **b** : MICROCOPY
mi·cro·fungus \¦==+\ *n* [*micr-* + *fungus*] : a fungus (as a mold) with a microscopic fruiting body — **mi·cro·fungal** \"+\ *adj*
mi·cro·gauss \ˈmīkrō+\ *n* [ISV, fr. *micr-* + *gauss*] : one millionth of a gauss
mi·cro·graphics \¦mīkrə+\ *n pl but sing in constr* [*micr-* + *graphics*] : the industry concerned with the manufacture and sale of graphic material in microform; *also* : the production of graphic material in microform — **mi·cro·graphic** \"+\ *adj*
mi·cro·gravity \¦mīkrō+\ *n* [*micr-* + *gravity*] : a condition in space in which only minuscule gravitational forces are experienced : virtual absence of gravity; *broadly* : WEIGHTLESSNESS
mi·cro·heterogeneity \"+\ *n* [*micr-* + *heterogeneity*] : a variation in the chemical structure of a substance (as the amino acid sequence of a protein) that does not produce a major change in its properties
mi·cro·image \¦mīkrō+\ *n* [*micr-* + [1]*image*] : an image (as on a microfilm) that is of greatly reduced size
mi·cro·inject \¦mīkrō+\ *vt* [*micr-* + *inject*] : to subject to or use in microinjection
mi·cro·instruction \¦mīkrō+\ *n* [*micr-* + *instruction*] : a computer instruction that activates the circuits necessary to perform a single machine operation usu. as part of the execution of a machine-language instruction
mi·cro·machining \"+\ *n* -S [*micr-* + *machining*, gerund of [2]*machine*] : the removing (as in drilling, planing, or shaping) of small amounts of material (as metal) by action other than that of a sharp-edged tool ⟨~ done with an electron beam⟩
micro·manage \"+\ *vb* [*micr-* + [1]*manage*] *vt* : to manage esp. with excessive control or attention to details ~ *vi* : to direct or conduct the activities of a group or an enterprise by micromanaging them — **micro·management** \"+\ *n* — **micro·manager** \"+\ *n*
micrometeorite* *n* : a very small particle in interplanetary space — **mi·cro·meteoritic** \¦mīkrō+\ *adj*
mi·cro·meteoroid \¦mīkrō+\ *n* [*micr-* + *meteoroid*] : MICROMETEORITE *herein*
micro·mini \"+\ *n* [*micr-* + [1]*mini* (miniskirt — herein)] : a very short miniskirt
mi·cro·miniature \"+\ *adj* [*micr-* + [2]*miniature*] **1** : MICROMINIATURIZED *herein* **2** : suitable for use with microminiaturized parts
mi·cro·miniaturization \"+\ *n* [*micr-* + *miniaturization*] : the process of producing microminiaturized things
mi·cro·miniaturized \"+\ *adj* [*micr-* + *miniaturized*, past part. of *miniaturize*] : reduced to or produced in a very small size and esp. in a size smaller than one considered miniature ⟨~ electronic circuit⟩
mi·cro·module \"+\ *n* [*micr-* + *module*] : a microminiaturized module
mi·cro·morphology \"+\ *n* [*micr-* + *morphology*] **1** : MICROSTRUCTURE — used esp. with reference to soils **2** : minute morphological detail esp. as determined by electron microscopy; *also* : the study of such detail — **mi·cro·morphologic** \"+\ *or* **mi·cro·morphological** \"+\ *adj* — **mi·cro·morphologically** \"+\ *adv*
mi·cro·particle \"+\ *n* [*micr-* + *particle*] : a very small particle; *esp* : one that is microscopic in size
micro·plate \"+ˌ\ *n* [*micr-* + [1]*plate*] : a small movable segment of the earth's lithosphere much smaller than an ordinary tectonic plate
mi·cro·population \"+\ *n* [*micr-* + *population*] **1** : a population of microorganisms **2** : the population of organisms within a small area
mi·cro·prism \"+\ *n* [*micr-* + *prism*] : a usu. circular area on the focusing screen of a camera that is made up of tiny prisms and causes the image in the viewfinder to blur if the subject is not in focus
mi·cro·probe \ˈmīkrə+ˌ\ *n* [*micr-* + [1]*probe*] : a device for microanalysis that operates by exciting radiation in a minute area or volume of material so that the composition may be determined from the emission spectrum
mi·cro·processor \¦mīkrō+\ *n* [*micr-* + *processor* (herein)] : a computer processor contained on an integrated-circuit chip; *also* : such a processor along with memory and associated circuits on a chip
mi·cro·programming \"+\ *n* [*micr-* + *programming*, gerund of [2]*program*] : the use of routines stored in memory rather than specialized circuits for controlling a device (as a computer) — **mi·cro·program** \"+\ *n or vt*
mi·cro·publication \"+\ *n* [*micr-* + *publication*] **1** : MICROPUBLISHING *herein* **2** : something published in microform
mi·cro·publishing \"+\ *n* [*micr-* + *publishing*] : the publishing of new or previously published material in microform — **mi·cro·publish** \"+\ *vt* — **mi·cro·publisher** \"+\ *n*
mi·cro·puncture \"+\ *n* [*micr-* + *puncture*] : an extremely small puncture ⟨a ~ of the nephron⟩; *also* : an act of making such a puncture
mi·cro·quake \ˈ==+ˌ\ *n* [*micr-* + [2]*quake*] : MICROEARTHQUAKE *herein*
micro·satellite \ˌmīkrō+\ *n* [*micr-* + [1]*satellite*] : any of numerous short segments of DNA that are distributed throughout the genome, that consist of repeated sequences of usu. two to five nucleotides, and that are often useful genetic markers in studies of genetic linkage because they tend to vary from one individual to another
micro·skirt \ˈ==+ˌ\ *n* [*micr-* + [1]*skirt*] : MICROMINI *herein*
microsphere* *n* : a minute sphere ⟨encapsulation of antigens for oral vaccines in biodegradable polymer ~*s* —Bernadine Healy⟩ — **mi·cro·spherical** \¦==+\ *adj*
mi·cro·spo·ran·gi·ate \¦==spə¦ranjēət\ *adj* [*microsporangi*um + [3]*-ate*] : bearing or being microsporangia
mi·cro·state \ˈmīkrō+\ *n* [*micr-* + [1]*state*] : an independent nation that is extremely small in area and population
mi·cro·surgery \¦mīkrō+\ *n* [*micr-* + *surgery*] : minute dissection or manipulation (as by a micromanipulator or laser beam) of living structures (as cells or tissues) for surgical or experimental purposes — **mi·cro·surgeon** \"+\ *n* — **mi·cro·surgical** \"+\ *adj* — **mi·cro·surgically** \"+\ *adv*
mi·cro·teaching \ˈ==+ˌ\ *n* [*micr-* + *teaching*] : practice teaching in which a student teacher's teaching of a small class for a short time is videotaped for subsequent evaluation
mi·cro·tektite \¦mīkrō+\ *n* [*micr-* + *tektite*] : a minute tektite one millimeter or less in diameter found esp. in sediments on the ocean floor
mi·cro·text \ˈ==+ˌ\ *n* [*micr-* + [1]*text*] : text in microform
mi·cro·tubule \¦mīkrō+\ *n* [*micr-* + *tubule*] : any of the minute tubules in eukaryotic cytoplasm that are composed of the protein tubulin and form an important component of the cytoskeleton, mitotic spindle, cilia, and flagella — **mi·cro·tubular** \"+\ *adj*
mi·cro·vascular \"+\ *adj* [*micr-* + *vascular*] : of, relating to, or constituting the part of the circulatory system made up of minute vessels (as venules or capillaries) that average less than 0.3 millimeter in diameter — **mi·cro·vasculature** \"+\ *n*
mi·cro·vessel \"+\ *n* [*micr-* + [1]*vessel*] : a blood vessel (as a capillary, arteriole, or venule) of the microcirculatory system
mi·cro·villus \"+\ *n* [NL, fr. *micr-* + *villus*] : a microscopic projection of a tissue, cell, or cell organelle; *esp* : any of the fingerlike outward projections of some cell surfaces — **mi·cro·vil·lar** \¦vilər\ *adj* — **mi·cro·vil·lous** \-ləs\ *adj*
mi·cro·wav·able *or* **microwave·able** \¦mīkrō¦wāvəbəl, -krə¦-\ *adj* : suitable for preparation in a microwave oven; *also* : capable of being safely used in a microwave oven ⟨~ plates⟩
microwave* *or* **microwave oven** *n* : an oven in which food is cooked by the heat produced as a result of microwave penetration of the food
microwave* *vt* : to cook or heat in a microwave oven
microwave background *n* : BACKGROUND RADIATION *herein*
micro·world \"+\ *n* [*micr-* + [1]*world*] : a small universe; *specif* : the natural universe observed at the microscopic or submicroscopic level
midcourse \¦=¦=\ *adj* [*midcourse*, n., fr. [1]*mid* + [1]*course*] : being or relating to the part of a course (as of spacecraft) that is between the initial and final phases — **midcourse** \¦=¦=\ *n*
mid·cult \ˈmidˌkəlt\ *n* -S [*mid*dlebrow *cult*ure] : the artistic and intellectual culture that is neither highbrow culture nor lowbrow culture : middlebrow culture
middle america *n, often cap M & cap A* : the middle-class segment of the U.S. population; *esp* : the traditional or conservative element of the middle class — **middle american** *n or adj, often cap M & usu cap A*
middle management *n* : management personnel intermediate between operational supervisors and policy-making administrators — **middle manager** *n*
middle–of–the–road·ism \ˌ====ˈrōdˌizəm\ *n* -S : a middle-of-the-road policy or attitude
midi \ˈmidē\ *n* -S [[1]*mid* + *-i* (as in *mini* — herein)] : a dress, skirt, or coat that usu. extends to the mid-calf — called also respectively *midi dress, midi skirt, midi coat*
MIDI \ˈmidē\ *n* -S [*m*usical-*i*nstrument *d*igital *i*nterface] : an electronic standard used for the transmission of digitally encoded music
mid·life crisis \¦=¦=-\ *n* : a period of emotional turmoil in middle age caused by the realization that one is no longer young and characterized esp. by a strong desire for change
mid·ocean ridge \ˈmidˈōshən-\ *n* : an elevated region with a central valley on the ocean floor at the boundary between two diverging tectonic plates where new crust forms from upwelling magma
mid·size \ˈmidˌsīz\ *also* **midsized** \-d\ *adj* : of intermediate size ⟨a *midsize* car⟩
mif·e·pris·tone \ˌmifəˈprisˌtōn, miˈfeprəˌstōn\ *n* -S [perh. fr. ISV

amin- + *fe-* (alter. of *phen-*) + *pri-* (alter. of *prop-*) + estradiol + *-one*; prob. orig. formed as D *mifepriston*] : RU-486 *herein*

mike* *vt* : to supply with a microphone ⟨~ a singer⟩

mil* *n* : THOUSAND ⟨a salinity of 38.4 per ~⟩

mil *or* **mill** \ˈmil\ *n, pl* **mil** *or* **mill** [short for [1]*million*] *slang* : a million dollars

milanese* *adj, usu cap* : coated with flour or bread crumbs, often seasoned with cheese, and sautéed ⟨veal cutlet *Milanese*⟩

mil·i·tar·ia \ˌmiləˈterēə\ *n pl* [*military* + [2]*-ia*] : military objects (as firearms and uniforms) of historical value or interest

military collar *n* : a wide double-pointed collar that lies flat and open esp. on a double-breasted coat

military–industrial complex \ˈ==ˌ===ˈ===-\ *n* : an informal alliance of the military and related government departments with defense industries that is held to influence government policy

millimicro- *comb form* [*milli-* + *micr-*] : [2]NANO-

mil·li·osmol \ˌmilēˈäzˌmōl, -ˈäs-\ *n* [*milli-* + *osmol*] : one thousandth of an osmol

mil·li·radian \ˌmilə+\ *n* [ISV *milli-* + *radian*] : one thousandth of a radian

mil·li·rem \"+\ *n* [*milli-* + *rem*] : one thousandth of a rem

mim·eo \ˈmimēˌō\ *n* -s [short for [1]*mimeograph*] : a mimeographed publication

mim–mem \ˈmimˈmem\ *adj* [*mim*icry + *mem*orization] : of, relating to, or being a drill pattern in which students repeat usu. in chorus a foreign language phrase supplied by their instructor

mimosa* *n* -s : a mixed drink consisting of champagne and orange juice

mina·mata disease \ˌminəˈmätə-\ *n, usu cap M* [fr. *Minamata*, town in Japan where it was first recognized] : a toxic neuropathy caused by the ingestion of methylmercury compounds (as in contaminated seafood) and characterized by impairment of cerebral functions, constriction of the visual field, and progressive weakening of muscles

mi·nau·dière \mēnōdyeer\ *n* -s [F, affected, coquettish, fr. *minauder* to simper, smirk, fr. OF *mine* appearance, perh. fr. Bret *min* beak, snout] : a small decorative case for carrying small articles (as cosmetics or jewelry)

mind–bending \ˈ=ˌ==\ *adj* : MIND-BLOWING *herein*

mind–blowing \ˈ=ˌ==\ *adj* **1** : PSYCHEDELIC 1b *herein* **2** : MIND-BOGGLING *herein* — **mindblower** \ˈ=ˌ=(=)\ *n*

mind–bog·gling \ˈ=ˌ==\ *adj* : mentally or emotionally exciting or overwhelming — **mind–bog·gling·ly** \-lē\ *adv*

mind–expanding \ˈ==ˌ==\ *adj* : PSYCHEDELIC 1a *herein*

mindshare \ˈ=ˌ=\ *n* -s [[1]*mind* + market *share*] : a controlling or predominant hold of one's attention that is gained esp. by marketing ploys ⟨gain ~ with both media and consumers —Barbara Kohn⟩

minefield* *n* : something resembling a minefield; *esp* : a situation or area having many dangers or requiring extreme caution

[1]**mini** \ˈminē, -ni\ *n* -s [*mini-* (herein)] **1** : one that is small of its kind: as **a** : MINICAR **b** : MINISKIRT *herein* **c** : MINICOMPUTER *herein* **2** : MINISERIES *herein*

[2]**mini** \"\ *adj* : small in relation to others of the same kind : smaller than is usual, normal, or standard : SMALL-SCALE

mini- *comb form* [*mini*ature] : smaller or briefer than is usual, normal, or standard

miniature pinscher *n* : a toy dog of a breed that suggests a small Doberman pinscher and measures 10 to 12½ inches in height at the withers

miniature schnauzer *n* : a schnauzer of a breed that is 12 to 14 inches in height and is classified as a terrier

mini·bar \ˈminē+ˌ\ *n* [*mini-* (herein) + [1]*bar*] : a small refrigerator in a hotel room that is stocked with esp. alcoholic beverages and snacks for guests

mini·bike \ˈminē, -nə+ˌ\ *n* [*mini-* (herein) + *bike*] : a small one-passenger motorcycle having a low frame and elevated handlebars — **mini·biker** \"+\ *n*

mini·bus \"+\ *n* [*mini-* (herein) + *bus*] : a small bus

mini·cab \"+\ *n* [*mini-* (herein) + *cab*] : a small car used as a taxicab; *specif, Brit* : one that can be engaged by phone but is not licensed to cruise for customers

Mini·cam \ˈminēˌkam\ *trademark* — used for a portable television camera

mini·camp \"+ˌ\ *n* [*mini-* (herein) + [1]*camp*] : a special abbreviated training camp for football players held usu. in the spring or early summer

mini·computer \ˌminē, -nə+\ *n* [*mini-* (herein) + *computer*] : a computer that is intermediate between a mainframe and a microcomputer in size, speed, and capacity, that can support time-sharing, and that is often dedicated to a single application

mini·course \"+\ *n* [*mini-* (herein) + [1]*course*] : a brief course of study usu. lasting less than a semester

mini·disc \"+\ *n* [*mini-* (herein) + *disc*] : a miniature optical disk

mini·dress \"+ˌ\ *n* [*mini-* (herein) + [2]*dress*] : a short close-fitting dress

mini·floppy \"+\ *n* [*mini-* (herein) + *floppy* (herein)] : a floppy disk that is 5¼ inches in diameter

mini·lab \"+ˌ\ *n* [*mini-* (herein) + [2]*lab*] : a retail outlet offering rapid on-site film development and printing

minimal* *adj, often cap* : of, relating to, or being minimal art

minimal art *n* : abstract art (as painting or sculpture) consisting primarily of simple geometric forms executed in an impersonal style — **minimal artist** *n*

minimal brain dysfunction *also* **minimal brain damage** *n* : ATTENTION DEFICIT DISORDER *herein* — abbr. *MBD*

min·i·mal·ism \ˈminəməˌlizəm\ *n* **1** : MINIMAL ART *herein* **2** : a style or technique (as in music, design, or literature) that is characterized by extreme spareness and simplicity

minimalist* *n* **1** : MINIMAL ARTIST *herein* **2** : an adherent of minimalism

min·i·mal·ist \-ləst\ *adj* **1** : of, relating to, or done in the style of minimalism **2** : MINIMAL ⟨emphasizes individualism . . . and ~ government —Francis Kane⟩

min·i·mal·ity \ˌminəˈmalədē, -ətē, -i\ *n* -ES : the state or quality of being minimal

[1]**mini·max** \ˈminəˌmaks, -nēˌm-\ *n* -ES [*mini*mum + *max*imum] : the minimum of a set of maxima; *esp* : the smallest of a set of maximum possible losses each of which occurs in the most unfavorable outcome of a strategy followed by a participant in a situation governed by the theory of games — compare MAXIMIN *herein*

[2]**minimax** \"\ *adj* : of, relating to, or based on a minimax, the minimax principle, or the minimax theorem

minimax principle *n* : a principle of choice for a decision problem: one should choose the action which minimizes the loss that can be suffered even under the worst circumstances

minimax theorem *n* : a theorem in the theory of games: the lowest maximum expected loss equals the highest minimum expected gain

mini·mill \ˈminē+\ *n* [*mini-* (herein) + [1]*mill*] : a relatively small-scale steel mill that uses scrap metal as starting material

minimum* *n* : the lowest speed allowed on a highway

mini·park \ˌminē, -ni+\ *n* [*mini-* (herein) + [1]*park*] : a small city park

mini·recession \"+\ *n* [*mini-* (herein) + *recession*] : a brief economic downturn of minor proportions

mini·series \"+\ *n* [*mini-* (herein) + [1]*series*] : a television production of a story presented in sequential episodes

mini·ski \ˈminē, -nə+ˌ\ *n* [*mini-* (herein) + [1]*ski*] **1** : a short ski worn esp. by beginners **2** : a miniature ski worn by a skibobber

mini·skirt \ˌminē, -ni+\ *n* [*mini-* (herein) + [1]*skirt*] : a short skirt that usu. extends to the mid-thigh — **mini·skirt·ed** \"+\ *adj*

mini·state \"+\ *n* [*mini-* (herein) + [1]*state*] : MICROSTATE *herein*

mini·sub \"+ˌ\ *n* [*mini-* (herein) + [4]*sub*] : a very small submarine used esp. in research (as on the ocean bottom)

mini·van \"+ˌ\ *n* [*mini-* (herein) + [3]*van*] : a small passenger van

min·ke whale *also* **min·ke** \ˈmiŋkə-\ *n* [Norw *minkehval*, fr. *minke* (perh. fr. *Meincke*, a crewman of Svend Foyn †1894 Norw. whaler) + *hval* whale] : a small baleen whale of the genus *Balaenoptera* (*B. acutorostrata*)

minnesota multiphasic personality inventory *n, usu cap both Ms&P&I* [fr. the University of *Minnesota*, where it was developed] : a test of personal and social adjustment based on a complex scaling of the answers to an elaborate true or false test

minority* *n* : a member of a minority group

min·ox·i·dil \miˈnäksəˌdil\ *n* -s [perh. fr. *amino* + *oxi-* (alter. of *oxy-*) + piper*idine* + *-yl*] : a peripheral vasodilator $C_9H_{15}N_5O$ used orally to treat hypertension and topically in a propylene glycol solution to promote hair regrowth esp. in male-pattern baldness

MIPS *abbr, often not cap* million instructions per second

miracle fruit *n* : MIRACULOUS FRUIT 2a; *also* : its fruit

mi·ran·da \məˈrandə\ *adj, usu cap* [fr. *Miranda v. Arizona*, the U.S. Supreme Court ruling establishing such rights] : of, relating to, or being the legal rights of an arrested person to have an attorney and to remain silent so as to avoid self-incrimination ⟨*Miranda* warnings⟩

mi·ran·dize \məˈranˌdīz\ *vt* -ED/-ING/-S *usu cap* : to recite the Miranda warnings to (a person under arrest)

mi·rex \ˈmīˌreks\ *n* -ES [prob. fr. *mi*smire + *ex*terminator] : an organochlorine insecticide $C_{10}Cl_{12}$ formerly used esp. against ants that is a suspected carcinogen

mir·in \ˈmirin\ *n* -s [Jap] : a sweet Japanese cooking wine made from fermented rice

[1]**MIRV** \ˈmərv\ *n* -s [*m*ultiple *i*ndependently targeted *r*eentry *v*ehicle] : a missile with two or more warheads that are designed to reenter the atmosphere on the way to separate enemy targets; *also* : any of the warheads of such a missile

[2]**MIRV** \"\ *vb, past or past part* **MIRVed**; *pres part* **MIRV·ing** *vt* : to equip with MIRV warheads ⟨both sides would ~ their submarine-borne missiles —Stewart Alsop⟩ ~ *vi* : to arm one's forces with MIRVs

MIS *abbr* management information systems

mis·allocation *n* [[1]*mis-* + *allocation*] : faulty or improper allocation

mis·an·drist \ˈmisˌandrist\ *n* -s [*misandry* + [1]*-ist*] : a person who hates men ⟨a ~ who thinks all men beat family members —J.R.Ryan⟩ — compare MISOGYNIST *in the Dict* — **misandrist** *adj*

mis·communication \"+\ *n* [[1]*mis-* + *communication*] : failure to communicate clearly

mis·diagnose \(ˈ)mis+\ *vt* [[1]*mis-* + *diagnose*] : to diagnose incorrectly — **mis·diagnosis** \ˌmis+\ *n*

mi·so·pros·tol \ˌmīsōˈpräsˌtōl, -ˌtōl\ *n* -s [*miso-* (of unknown origin) + *prost*aglandin + *-ol*] : a synthetic prostaglandin analogue $C_{22}H_{38}O_5$ used to prevent stomach ulcers associated with nonsteroidal anti-inflammatory drug use

mis·orient \"+\ *vt* [[1]*mis-* + *orient*] : to orient improperly or incorrectly — **mis·orientation** \"+\ *n*

mis·sense \ˈmisˌsen(t)s\ *adj* [[1]*mis-* + *-sense* (as in *nonsense*)] : relating to or being a genetic mutation involving alteration of one or more codons so that different amino acids are determined — compare ANTISENSE *herein*, NONSENSE *herein*

missionary position *n* [so called fr. the notion that Trobriand Islanders gave this name to the position] : a coital position in which the female lies on her back with the male on top and with his face opposite hers

mississippian* *adj, usu cap* : of, relating to, or being a prehistoric mound-building culture of American Indians centered in the river valleys of southeast and central North America, characterized by settlement in large villages and dependence on agriculture, and extending from about 800 A.D. until the arrival of European settlers

miss out *vt, Brit* : to leave out : OMIT

mist* *n* : a drink of alcoholic liquor (as Scotch) served over cracked ice and garnished with a twist of lemon peel

mister charlie *n, usu cap M&C* : MR. CHARLIE *herein* — usu. used disparagingly

mist net *n* : a finely woven large mesh net that is erected to entangle and capture birds or bats in flight ⟨birds caught in the *mist net* were banded and released⟩

misty* *adj* : TEARFUL

mitochondrial DNA *n* : an extranuclear double-stranded DNA found exclusively in mitochondria that in most eukaryotes is a circular molecule and is maternally inherited — abbr. *mtDNA*

mi·to·gen \ˈmīd·əjən\ *n* -s [*mit-* + *-gen*] : a substance that induces mitosis

mi·to·genesis \ˌmīd·ō, ˌmītō+\ *n* [NL, fr. *mit-* + *genesis*] : the production of cells mitosis

mi·to·gen·ic \ˌmīd·əˈjenik\ *adj* [*mit-* + *-genic*] : MITOGENETIC — **mi·to·ge·nic·i·ty** \ˌmīd·əjəˈnisəd·ē\ *n* -ES

mi·to·my·cin \ˌmīd·əˈmīsᵊn\ *n* -s [perh. fr. *mit-* + *-mycin*] : a complex of antibiotic substances that is produced by a Japanese streptomyces (*Streptomyces caespitosus*); *esp* : one form $C_{15}H_{18}N_4O_5$ that inhibits DNA synthesis and is used as an antineoplastic agent

mi·to·spore \ˈmīd·ə+ˌ\ *n* [*mit-* + *spore*] : a haploid or diploid spore produced by mitosis

mitral valve prolapse *n* : a valvular heart disorder in which one or both mitral valve flaps close incompletely during systole usu. producing either a click or murmur and sometimes minor mitral regurgitation and which is often a benign symptomless condition but may be marked by varied symptoms (as chest pain, fatigue, dizziness, dyspnea, or palpitations) leading in some cases to endocarditis or ventricular tachycardia

mit·tel·eu·ro·pa \ˌmid·ᵊlyüˈrōpə, *G* ˌmitᵊlȯiˈrōpə\ *adj, usu cap* [G, central Europe, fr. *mittel* middle (fr. OHG *mittil*) + *Europa* Europe] : MIDDLE-EUROPEAN

mix* *vt* : to produce (a recording) by electronically combining or adjusting sounds from more than one source

mix* *n* **1** : a commercially prepared nonalcoholic mixture of ingredients for a mixed drink ⟨mai tai ~⟩ **2** : the combination or adjustment of sounds from different sources in a recording ⟨a record with a good ~⟩

mixed–media \ˈ=ˌ===\ *adj* [*mixed* + *media*, pl. of *medium*] : MULTIMEDIA *herein*

mixed media *n* : MULTIMEDIA *herein*

mixed–use \ˈ=ˌ=\ *adj* : used or suitable for several different functions ⟨sizable *mixed-use* centers, incorporating offices, stores, housing, and parks —Philip Langdon⟩

mixing board *n* : a control panel for combining and adjusting esp. musical sounds for a performance or recording

MLD *abbr* median lethal dose

MMPI *abbr* Minnesota Multiphasic Personality Inventory *herein*

MMR *abbr* measles-mumps-rubella (vaccine)

MNC \ˌem(ˌ)enˈsē\ *n* -s [*m*ulti*n*ational *c*orporation] : MULTINATIONAL *herein*

mobile home *n* : a dwelling structure built on a steel chassis and fitted with wheels that is intended to be hauled to a usu. permanent site — compare MOTOR HOME *herein*

[1]**mod** \ˈmäd\ *adj, often cap* [by shortening] **1** : MODERN; *esp* : bold, free, and unconventional in style or dress **2** : of, relating to, or being the characteristic style of 1960s British youth culture

[2]**mod** \"\ *n* -s *often cap* : one who wears mod clothes

[3]**mod** \"\ *prep* [by shortening] : MODULO

[4]**mod** \"\ *n* -s [short for *module* (herein)] : a class period in a modular schedule

mod con \ˌmädˈkän\ *n* [by shortening] *chiefly Brit* : a modern convenience — usu. used in pl.

model* *n* **1** : a system of postulates, data, and inferences presented as a mathematical description of an entity or state of affairs; *also* : a computer simulation based on such a system ⟨climate ~s⟩ **2** : VERSION, EQUIVALENT **3** : ANIMAL MODEL *herein*

model* *vt* : to produce a representation or simulation of ⟨using a computer to ~ a problem⟩

mo·dem \ˈmōˌdem\ *n* -s [*mo*dulator + *dem*odulator] : a device that converts signals produced by one type of device (as a computer) to a form compatible with another (as a telephone)

moderne* *adj* : of, relating to, or being in the style of art deco

modesty panel *n* : a panel designed to conceal the legs of a person sitting esp. at a desk or table

modified american plan *n, usu cap A* : a hotel rate whereby guests are charged a fixed sum (as by the day or week) for room, breakfast, and lunch or dinner

modular* *adj* **1** : of or relating to a school schedule in which subjects pertinent to more than one course are covered in common class sessions **2** : of, relating to, or being a computer program composed of modules

modular arithmetic *n* : arithmetic that deals with whole numbers where the numbers are replaced by their remainders after division by a fixed number ⟨in a *modular arithmetic* with modulus 5, 3 multiplied by 4 is 2⟩ ⟨5 hours after 10 o'clock is 3 o'clock because clocks follow a *modular arithmetic* with modulus 12⟩

mod·u·lar·i·ty \ˌmäjəˈlarəd·ē, -ler-\ *n* -ES [*modular* + *-ity*] **1** : the use of discrete functional units in building an electronic or mechanical system **2** : a feature of a computer language that allows programs to be composed of modules

mod·u·lar·ized \ˈmäjələˌrīzd\ *adj* [*modular* + *-ize* + [1]*-ed*] : constructed of modules ⟨~ electronic equipment⟩

module* *n* **1** : any in a series of standardized units for use together: as **a** : a unit of furniture or architecture **b** : an educational or instructional unit which covers a single subject or a discrete part of a broad subject **2** : an assembly of components that are packaged or mounted together and constitute a functional unit for an electronic or mechanical system ⟨a ~ for a computer⟩ **3** : an independent unit that constitutes a part of the total structure of a space vehicle ⟨a propulsion ~⟩ **4 a** : a subset of an additive group that is also a group under addition **b** : a mathematical set that is a commutative group under addition and that is closed under multiplication which is distributive from the left or right or both by elements of a ring and for which $a(bx) = (ab)x$ or $(xb)a = x(ba)$ or both where a and b are elements of the ring and x belongs to the set **5** : a usu. semi-independent routine in a computer program that usu. corresponds to one step in the solution of the problem the program was designed to solve

modulus* *n* **1** : the factor by which a logarithm of a number to one base is multiplied to obtain the logarithm of the number to a new base **2** : the number of different numbers used in a system of modular arithmetic

mogul \ˈmōgəl\ *n* -s [G dial.; akin to Viennese dial. *mugl* small hill] : a bump in a ski run

mohawk* *n, usu cap* : a hairstyle with a narrow center strip of upright hair and the sides of the head shaved

mois·tur·ize \ˈmȯischəˌrīz\ *vt* -ED/-ING/-S : to add moisture to ⟨~ the air⟩ — **moisturizer** \-ə(r)\ *n* -s

mojo* *n* [[2]*mojo*] : magical power

moldy fig *n* **1** : a person who prefers the traditional form of a kind of music (as jazz) **2** : one that is old-fashioned

mole* *n* : a spy who establishes a cover long before beginning espionage and who usu. has reached a responsible position in the organization being spied on; *broadly* : one within an organization who passes on inside information

molecular beam epitaxy *n* : a process for manufacturing microelectronic devices by depositing very thin layers of material on a substrate crystal one layer of molecules at a time

molecular clock *n* : a measure of evolutionary change over time at the molecular level that is based on the theory that specific DNA sequences or the proteins they encode spontaneously mutate at constant rates and that is used chiefly for estimating how long ago two related organisms diverged from a common ancestor

molecular genetics *n pl but sing in constr* : a branch of genetics dealing with the structure and activity of genetic material at the molecular level — **molecular geneticist** *n*

molecular mass *n* : MOLECULAR WEIGHT

molecular orbital *n* : a solution of the Schrödinger equation that describes the probable location of an electron relative to the nuclei in a molecule and that thus indicates the nature of any bond in which the electron is involved

mom–and–pop \ˌ=ˌ=ˈ=\ *adj* : being a small owner-operated business ⟨a *mom-and-pop* candy store⟩

moment of truth [trans. of Sp *momento* (or *hora*) *de la verdad*] **1** : the final sword thrust in a bullfight **2** : a moment of crisis on whose outcome much or everything depends ⟨the lift-off of a . . . space vehicle with three men aboard is an awesome *moment of truth* —R.A.Petrone⟩

mommy track *n* : a career path that allows a mother flexible or reduced work hours but tends to slow or block advancement

mon·e·ta·rism \ˈmänətəˌrizəm, ˈmən-, *also* ˈmōn-\ *n* -s [*monetary* + *-ism*] : QUANTITY THEORY — **mon·e·ta·rist** \-rəst, -ˌrist\ *n* -s

monetary aggregate *n* : one of the formal categories of money (as cash and demand deposits or bank credits) in a national economy that is used as a measure in predictions of economic growth

monetize* *vt* : to purchase (public or private debt) and thereby free for other uses money that would have been devoted to debt service

money* *n* — **on the money** : exactly right or accurate

mon·ey \ˈmənē, -ni\ *adj* : being, involving, or reliable in a crucial situation ⟨a ~ situation⟩ ⟨a ~ player⟩ ⟨his ~ pitch⟩

mon·go \ˈmäŋ(ˌ)gō\ *n, pl* **mongo** [Mongolian *möngö*] **1** : a monetary unit of Outer Mongolia equal to $^1/_{100}$ tugrik **2** : a coin representing one mongo

mongolian gerbil *n, usu cap M* : a gerbil of the genus *Meriones* (*M. unguiculatus*) of Mongolia and northern China that has an external resemblance to a rat, has a high capacity for temperature regulation, and is used as an experimental laboratory animal

monitor* *n* : software or hardware that monitors the operation of a system and esp. a computer system

monkey bars *n pl* [fr. their resemblance to the bars provided for monkeys in zoos] : a three-dimensional framework of horizontal and vertical bars from which children can hang and swing

[1]**mono** \ˈmä(ˌ)nō *also* ˈmō(ˌ)-\ *adj* [by shortening] : MONOPHONIC 3 ⟨a ~ broadcast⟩

[2]**mono** *n* -s : monophonic reproduction

[3]**mono** *n* -s [by shortening] : MONONUCLEOSIS

monoamine* *n* : a primary amine (as serotonin or norepinephrine) that is functionally important in neural transmission

monoamine oxidase *n* : an enzyme that deaminates monoamines oxidatively and that functions in the nervous system by breaking down monoamine neurotransmitters

mono·am·i·ner·gic \ˌmänōˌaməˈnərjik, ˌmōn-\ *adj* [*monoamine* (herein) + *-ergic* (herein)] : liberating or involving monoamines (as serotonin or norepinephrine) in neural transmission

mono·cha·sial \ˌmänəˈkāzh(ē)əl, ˌmōn-, -zēəl\ *adj* : of, relating to, or being a monochasium

monochromatic* *adj* : lacking variety, creativity, or excitement : COLORLESS

monochrome* *adj* : BLACK-AND-WHITE 4b

[1]**mono·clo·nal** \ˌmänəˈklōnᵊl, ˌmōn-\ *adj* [*mon-* + *clone* + *-al*] : produced by, being, or composed of cells derived from a single cell ⟨a ~ tumor⟩; *esp* : relating to or being an antibody derived from a single cell in large quantities for use against a specific antigen (as a cancer cell)

[2]**monoclonal** *n* -s : a monoclonal antibody

mono·contaminate \ˌmän(ˌ)ō, ˌmōn-, -nə+\ *vt* [*mon-* + [1]*contaminate*] : to infect (a germ-free organism) with one kind of pathogen — **mono·contamination** \"+\ *n*

mono·crystal \ˌmän(ˌ)ō, ˌmōn-, -nə+\ *n* [*mon-* + *crystal*] : a single crystal — **monocrystal** *adj* — **mono·crystalline** \"+\ *adj*

mono·functional \"+\ *adj* [*mon-* + *functional*] : of, relating to, or being a compound with one highly reactive site in a molecule (as in polymerization) ⟨formaldehyde is a ~ reagent⟩

mono·germ \ˈ=(ˌ)=ˌjərm, -ˌjəm\ *adj* [prob. fr. *mon-* + *germ*inate] : producing or being a fruit that gives rise to a single plant ⟨a ~ variety of sugar beet⟩ — compare MULTIGERM *herein*

mono·hull \ˈ+\ *n* [*mon-* + *hull*] : a vessel (as a sailboat) with a single hull

mono·ki·ni \ˈmänəˈkēnē\ *n* -S [*mon-* + *-kini* (as in *bikini*)] **1** : a topless bikini **2** : extremely brief shorts for men — **mono·ki·nied** \-nēd\ *adj*

monolithic* *adj* **1** : formed from a single crystal ⟨a ~ silicon chip⟩ **2** : produced in or on a monolithic chip ⟨a ~ circuit⟩ **3** : consisting of or utilizing a monolithic circuit or circuits

mono·oxygenase \ˈmän(ˌ)ō, ˈmōn-, -nə+\ *n* [*mon-* + *oxygenase* (herein)] : any of several oxygenases that bring about the incorporation of one atom of molecular oxygen into a substrate

monoploid* *adj* : having or being the basic haploid number of chromosomes in a polyploid series of organisms

mono·pod \ˈmänəˌpäd\ *n* -S [*mon-* + *-pod* (as in [1]*tripod*)] : a one-legged support (as for a camera)

mono·pole \ˈmänəˌpōl, ˈmōn-\ *n* [*mon-* + [4]*pole*] **1** : a single positive or negative electrical charge; *also* : a hypothetical north or south magnetic pole existing alone **2** : a radio antenna in the form of a single often straight radiating element

mono·sexual \ˈmä(ˌ)nō, ˈmō(ˌ)-+\ *adj* [*mon-* + *sexual*] **1** : being or relating to a male or a female rather than a bisexual **2** : composed of or intended for individuals of one sex ⟨~ schools⟩ — **mono·sexuality** \ˈ+\ *n*

monosome* *n* : a single ribosome

mono·specific \ˈ+\ *adj* [*mon-* + [1]*specific*] : specific for a single antigen or receptor site on an antigen — **mono·specificity** \ˈ+\ *n*

mono·therapy \ˈ+\ *n* [*mon-* + *therapy*] : the use of a single drug to treat a particular disorder or disease

mono·unsaturated \ˈ+\ *adj* [*mon-* + *unsaturated*] *of an oil, fat, or fatty acid* : containing one double or triple bond per molecule — compare POLYUNSATURATED *herein* — **mono·unsaturate** \ˈ+\ *n*

mons pubis *n* [NL, pubic eminence] : a rounded eminence of fatty tissue upon the pubic symphysis esp. of the human female

monster* *n* **1** : a roving football linebacker who plays in no set position — called also *monster back, monster man* **2** : one that is highly successful ⟨a box-office ~⟩

monster* *adj* : being or producing a best seller ⟨a ~ hit⟩ ⟨~ bands⟩

montagnard* *n, often cap* : a member of any of various Mon-Khmer and Cham-speaking peoples inhabiting the highlands of central and southern Vietnam — **montagnard** *adj, often cap*

mon·te car·lo \ˌmäntēˈkär(ˌ)lō, -tə̇ˈk-\ *adj, usu cap M&C* [fr. *Monte Carlo*, Monaco, city noted for its gambling casino] : of, relating to, or involving the use of random sampling techniques and often the use of computer simulation to obtain approximate solutions to mathematical or physical problems esp. in terms of a range of values each of which has a calculated probability of being the solution ⟨*Monte Carlo* methods⟩ ⟨*Monte Carlo* calculations⟩

mon·te·zu·ma's revenge \ˌmäntəˈzüməz-\ *n, usu cap M* [after *Montezuma* II †1520 Aztec ruler killed during the Spanish conquest] : diarrhea contracted in Mexico esp. by tourists — compare TRAVELER'S DIARRHEA *herein*

montrachet* *n* -S *usu cap* : a soft goat cheese from the Burgundy region of France

mon·uron \ˈmänyəˌrän, ˈmōn-\ *n* -S [*mon-* + *urea* + [1]*-on*] : a persistent herbicide $C_9H_{11}ClN_2O$ used esp. to control mixed broad-leaved weeds

mood disorder *n* : any of several psychological disorders (as major depressive disorder or bipolar disorder) characterized by abnormalities of emotional state — called also *affective disorder*

mood ring *n* : a ring with a stone made of crystals that change color in response to minute variations in body temperature

Moog \ˈmōg, ˈmüg\ *trademark* — used for a music synthesizer

moon* *n, slang* : the naked buttocks; *also* : an act of exposing the naked buttocks — **moon*** *vt, slang* — **over the moon** : very pleased : in high spirits

mooncraft \ˈ=ˌ=\ *n* : MOONSHIP *herein*

moonflight \ˈ=ˌ=\ *n* : a flight to the moon

moon·ie \ˈmünē\ *n* -s *usu cap* [Sun Myung *Moon b*1920 Korean religious leader + E *-ie*] : a member of the Unification Church founded by Sun Myung Moon

moon·ing \ˈmüniŋ\ *n* -S [fr. gerund of *moon*, v. (herein)] : the practice of exposing one's buttocks (as through the window of a moving vehicle) as a prank

moonport \ˈ=ˌ=\ *n* : a facility for launching spacecraft to the moon

moonroof \ˈ=ˌ=\ *n* : a glass sunroof

moonship \ˈ=ˌ=\ *n* : a spacecraft for travel to the moon

moonshot \ˈ=ˌ=\ *or* **moon shoot** \ˈ=ˌ=\ *n* **1** : the act or an instance of launching a spacecraft on a course to the moon **2** *usu* **moon shot** : a hit or thrown ball with a very high trajectory

[1]**moonwalk** \ˈ=ˌ=\ *n* **1** : an instance of walking on the moon **2** : the dance performed in moonwalking — **moonwalker** \ˈ=ˌ==\ *n*

[2]**moonwalk** *vi* : to dance by gliding backwards while appearing to make forward walking motions

mo·ped \ˈmōˌped\ *n* -S [Sw, fr. *motor* motor + *pedal* pedal] : a lightweight low-powered motorbike that can be pedaled

MOR *abbr* middle of the road

morality play* *n* : something (as a court trial or a political controversy) which involves a direct conflict between right and wrong or good and evil and from which a moral lesson may be drawn

mor·bil·li·virus \mȯrˈbiləˌvīrəs\ *n* [NL, fr. *morbillus* spot on skin, pustule (fr. ML) + *-i-* + *virus* — more at MORBILLI] : any of a genus (*Morbillivirus*) of paramyxoviruses that include the causative agents of measles and canine distemper

mor·gan \ˈmȯrgən, ˈmȯ(ə)g-\ *n* -S [after Thomas Hunt *Morgan* †1945 Am. geneticist] **1** : a unit of inferred distance between genes on a chromosome that is used in constructing genetic maps and is equal to the distance for which the frequency of crossing-over between specific pairs of genes is 100 percent **2** : CENTIMORGAN *herein*

morning-after pill \ˌ==ˈ==-\ *n* [so called fr. its being taken after rather than before intercourse] : an oral drug usu. containing high doses of estrogen that interferes with pregnancy by blocking implantation of a fertilized egg in the human uterus

[1]**morph** \ˈmȯ(ə)rf, ˈmȯ(ə)f\ *n* -S [Gk *morphē* form — more at FORM] **1** : a local population of a species that consists of interbreeding organisms and is distinguishable from other populations by morphology or behavior though capable of interbreeding with them **2** : a phenotypic variant of a species

[2]**morph** *vb* -ED/-ING/-S [short for *metamorphose*] *vi* **1** : to undergo transformation from an image of one object into that of another esp. by means of computer-generated animation **2** : to undergo transformation ~ *vt* : to change the form or character of : TRANSFORM

morph- *or* **morpho-*** *comb form* : form and ⟨*morpho*functional⟩

mor·phac·tin \mȯrˈfaktə̇n\ *n* -S [prob. fr. ISV *morph-* + *act-* (fr. L *actus* motion) + *-in* — more at ACT] : any of several synthetic fluorine-containing compounds that tend to produce morphological changes and suppress growth in plants

mor·pho·gen \ˈmȯrfəjən, -ˌjen\ *n* -S [*morph-* + *-gen*] : a diffusible chemical substance that exerts control over morphogenesis esp. by forming a gradient in concentration

mor·pho·physiological \ˈmȯr(ˌ)fō+\ *adj* [*morph-* + *physiological*] : of, relating to, or concerned with biological interrelationships between form and function — **mor·pho·physiology** \ˈ+\ *n*

MOS *abbr* metal-oxide semiconductor *herein*

MOSFET *abbr* metal-oxide-semiconductor field effect transistor

mosh \ˈmäsh\ *vi* -ED/-ING/-ES [perh. alter. of [2]*mash* or [2]*mush*] : to engage in uninhibited often frenzied activities (as intentional collision) with others near the stage at a rock concert — **mosher** \-ər\ *n*

mosh pit *n* : an area in front of a stage where very physical and rough dancing takes place at a rock concert — called also *pit*

möss·bau·er effect \ˈmə(r)sˌbau̇(ə)r-, ˈmǣs-, ˈmœs-, ˈmōs-\ *n, usu cap M* [after Rudolf L. *Mössbauer b*1929 Ger. physicist] : the emission and absorption of gamma rays without recoil by various radioactive nuclei embedded in solids — compare NUCLEAR RESONANCE *herein*

mössbauer spectroscopy \ˈ+\ *n, usu cap M* : spectroscopy that utilizes the Mössbauer effect

mos·tac·cio·li \ˌmōstätˈchōlē\ *n* -S [It, pl. of *mostacciolo* rhombus, rhomboidal confection flavored with must and raisins, dim. of (assumed) *mostaccio*, fr. L *mustaceus* cake made with must, fr. *mustum* must — more at MUST] : a pasta in the form of a short tube with oblique ends

mother* *n* [by shortening] **1** : MOTHERFUCKER *herein* — usu. used as a generalized term of abuse **2** [trans. of Ar *umm* followed by a genitive noun] : a particularly large, formidable, or extreme example ⟨not just a summer rally, but the ~ of all summer rallies —Alan Abelson⟩

motherboard \ˈ=ˌ=\ *n* : the main circuit board esp. of a microcomputer

motherfucker \ˈ=ˈ==\ *n* [[1]*mother* + *fucker* (herein)] : one that is formidable, contemptible, or offensive — usu. considered obscene; usu. used as a generalized term of abuse — **motherfucking** \ˈ=ˈ==\ *adj*

mother lode* *n* : a principal source or supply

mo·to·cross \ˈmōd·ōˌkrȯs\ *n* -ES [F, fr. *moto* motorcycle (short for *motocyclette*) + *-cross* (as in *cross-country*)] : a closed-course motorcycle race over natural or simulated rough terrain (as with steep inclines, hairpin turns, and mud); *also* : the sport of engaging in motocross races

motor home *n* : a large motor vehicle equipped as living quarters — compare CAMPER *herein*, MOBILE HOME *herein*

motor inn *or* **motor hotel** *n* : MOTEL

motormouth \ˈ=ˌ=\ *n* : a person who talks excessively or rapidly — **motor–mouthed** \ˈ==ˌ=\ *adj*

mou·lin–à–vent \ˌmülanˈävän, *F* mülaⁿnàväⁿ\ *n, pl* **moulin–à–vents** *usu cap M&V* [F, fr. *Moulin-à-Vent*, France] : a Beaujolais from the commune of Moulin-à-Vent

[1]**mountain bike** *n* : an all-terrain bicycle with wide knobby tires, straight handlebars, and typically 18 to 21 gears

[2]**mountain bike** *vi* : to ride a mountain bike — **mountain biker** *n*

mouse* *n* : a small mobile manual device that controls movement of the cursor and selection of functions on a computer display

mous·sa·ka \müˈsäkə, ˈmüˌs-, ˌmüsäˈkä\ *n* -S [NGk *mousakas*, fr. Turk *musakka*] : a dish of ground meat (as lamb) and sliced eggplant or potatoes often topped with a seasoned sauce

mousse* *n* : a foamy preparation used in hair styling

mousse \ˈmüs\ *vt* -ED/-ING/-S : to apply mousse to (hair)

mouthfeel \ˈ=ˌ=\ *n* : the sensation created by food or drink in the mouth

mouth hook *n* : one of a pair of hooked larval mouthparts of some two-winged flies that function as jaws

mover and shaker *n, pl* **movers and shakers** : a person who is active and influential in some field of endeavor

Mov·i·ola \ˌmüvēˈōlə\ *trademark* — used for a device for editing motion-picture film and synchronizing the sound

mox·i·bus·tion \ˌmäksə̇ˈbəschən\ *n* -S [*moxa* + *-i-* + *-bustion* (as in *combustion*)] : medical use of a moxa

MPA *abbr* master of public administration

MPH* *abbr* master of public health

m phase *n, usu cap M* [*m*itosis] : the period in the cell cycle during which cell division takes place — compare G_1 PHASE *herein*, G_2 PHASE *herein*, S PHASE *herein*

MPTP \ˌem(ˌ)pē(ˌ)tēˈpē\ *n* [*1-methyl-4-phenyl-1,2,3,6-tetrahydropyridine* (systematic name of the substance)] : a neurotoxin $C_{12}H_{15}N$ that destroys dopamine-producing neurons of the substantia nigra and causes symptoms (as tremors and rigidity) similar to those of Parkinson's disease

mr. charlie \-ˈchärlē, -äl-, -i\ *n, usu cap M&C* [*Charlie*, fr. *Charles*, proper name] : a white man : white people — usu. used disparagingly

MRE \ˌem(ˌ)ärˈē\ *abbr or n* -S : a meal ready to eat

MRI *n* -S : MAGNETIC RESONANCE IMAGING *herein*; *also* : the procedure in which magnetic resonance imaging is used

mri·dan·ga \mrēˈdəŋgə, ˌmərē-\ *or* **mri·dan·gam** \-gəm\ *n* -S [Skt *mṛdaṅga*, prob. of imit. origin] : a drum of India that is shaped like an elongated barrel and has tuned heads of different diameters

mRNA \ˌemˌär(ˌ)enˈā\ *n* -S [*messenger RNA* (herein)] : MESSENGER RNA *herein*

mr. right *n, usu cap M & 2d R* [[1]*right*] : a man who would make the perfect husband

ms. \(ˈ)miz *sometimes* (ˈ)mis\ *n, pl* **mss.** *or* **mses.** \ˈmizə̇z\ *usu cap* [prob. blend of *miss* and *Mrs.*] — used instead of *Miss* or *Mrs.* (as when the marital status of a woman is unknown or irrelevant) ⟨*Ms.* Mary Smith⟩

MSG* *abbr* master sergeant

MSH *abbr* melanocyte-stimulating hormone *herein*

m16 \ˈemsikˈstēn\ *or* **m16 rifle** *n* -S *usu cap M* [model *16*] : a .223 caliber (5.56 mm.) gas-operated magazine-fed automatic or semiautomatic rifle used by U.S. troops since the mid 1960s

MSLS *abbr* master of science in library science

MSW *abbr* master of social work

Mt *symbol* meitnerium *herein*

mtDNA *abbr* mitochondrial DNA *herein*

mu·co·ciliary \ˈmyükō+\ *adj* [*muc-* + *ciliary*] : of, relating to, or involving cilia of the mucous membranes of the respiratory system ⟨~ transport in the lung⟩

mu·co·peptide \ˌmyükō+\ *n* [*muc-* + *peptide*] : PEPTIDOGLYCAN *herein*

mu·co·poly·sac·cha·ri·do·sis \ˈmyüköˌpälēˌsakə(ˌ)rīˈdōsə̇s\ *n, pl* **mucopolysaccharido·ses** \-ōˌsēz\ [NL, fr. E *mucopolysaccharide* + NL *-osis*] : any of a group of genetically determined disorders of mucopolysaccharide metabolism that are characterized by the accumulation of mucopolysaccharides in the tissues and their excretion in the urine

mud pot *n* : a hot spring filled with mud agitated by venting gases

mues·li \ˈmyüslē, ˈmyüz-\ *n* -S [G dial. (Swiss) *müsli*, dim. of G *mus* soft food, mush, fr. OHG *muos*; akin to OE *mōs* food and prob. to OE *mete* food — more at MEAT] : a breakfast cereal of Swiss origin consisting of rolled oats, nuts, and fruit

MUF* *abbr* material unaccounted for

muf·fu·let·ta *also* **muf·fa·let·ta** \ˌməfəˈled·ə, -tə, -ˈlä-, ˌmü-, ˌmü-\ *n* -S [prob. fr. It dial., fr. It *muffoletta* little muff, dim., of *muffola* muff, fr. F *moufle*, fr. MF — more at MUFF] : a sandwich made of a round loaf of Italian bread and filled usu. with meat, cheese, and olive salad

mug·gee \ˌməgˈē\ *n* -S [[6]*mug* + *-ee*] : a person who is mugged

mug's game *n* [[1]*mug* (fool)] : a profitless or futile activity

mu·ja·hid·een *or* **mu·ja·hed·in** \ˌmüˌjahiˈdēn, mu̇ˌjä-\ *n pl, sometimes cap* [Ar, *mujāhidīn*, pl. of *mujāhid*] : Islamic guerrilla fighters esp. in the Middle East

mule* *n, slang* : a person who smuggles or delivers illicit drugs

mul·ti·band \ˈməltə̇, -tē, -ˌtī+\ *adj* [*multi-* + [1]*band*] : of, relating to, or operable on two or more bands (as of frequencies or wavelengths) ⟨a ~ radio⟩

mul·ti·center \ˈ+\ *adj* [*multi-* + [1]*center*] : involving more than one medical or research institution ⟨a ~ clinical study⟩

mul·ti·centric \ˈ+\ *adj* [*multi-* + *-centric*] : having multiple centers of origin ⟨a ~ tumor⟩ — **mul·ti·centrically** \ˈ+\ *adv* — **mul·ti·centricity** \ˈ+\ *n*

mul·ti·chain \ˈ+\ *adj* [*multi-* + [1]*chain*] : containing more than one chain ⟨~ proteins⟩

mul·ti·col·lin·ear·i·ty \ˈ+kəˌlinēˈarəd·ē, -kä-\ *n* -ES [*multi-* + *collinear* + *-ity*] : the existence of such a high degree of correlation between supposedly independent variables being used to estimate a dependent variable that the contribution of each independent variable to variation in the dependent variable cannot be determined

mul·ti·company \ˈ+\ *n* [*multi-* + [1]*company*] : a large corporate enterprise with interests in two or more separate industries

mul·ti·cul·ti \ˈməltēˈkəltē\ *adj* [by shortening] : MULTICULTURAL *herein*

mul·ti·cultural \ˈ+\ *adj* [*multi-* + *cultural*] : of, relating to, or designed for several or many cultures ⟨~ education⟩ — **mul·ti·cul·tur·al·ism** \ˌ==ˈkəlch(ə)rəlˌizəm\ *n* — **mul·ti·culturalist** \ˈ+\ *n or adj* — **mul·ti·culturally** \ˈ+\ *adv*

mul·ti·disciplinary \ˈ+\ *adj* [*multi-* + *disciplinary*] : INTERDISCIPLINARY

mul·ti·drug \ˈ+\ *adj* [*multi-* + [1]*drug*] : utilizing, consisting of, or relating to more than one drug ⟨~ therapy⟩

mul·ti·enzyme \ˈ+\ *adj* [*multi-* + *enzyme*] : composed of or involving two or more enzymes or subunits similar to enzymes that function in a biosynthetic pathway

mul·ti·ethnic \ˈ+\ *adj* [*multi-* + [2]*ethnic*] : made up of people of various ethnicities ⟨a ~ country⟩; *also* : of, relating to, reflecting, or adapted to diverse ethnicities ⟨~ literature⟩ — **mul·ti·ethnicity** \ˈ+\ *n*

multifactorial* *or* **mul·ti·factor** \ˈ+\ *adj* : having, involving, or produced by a variety of elements or causes ⟨a ~ study⟩

mul·ti·focal \ˈ+\ *adj* [*multi-* + *focal*] **1** : having more than one focal length ⟨~ lenses⟩ **2** : arising from or occurring in more than one focus or location ⟨~ convulsions⟩

mul·ti·function *or* **mul·ti·functional** \ˈ+\ *adj* [*multi-* + [1]*function* or *functional*] : having or performing more than one function ⟨a ~ computer work station⟩

mul·ti·germ \ˈ+\ *adj* [prob. fr. *multi-* + *germinate*] : producing or being a fruit cluster capable of giving rise to several plants ⟨a ~ variety of sugar beet⟩ — compare MONOGERM *herein*

mul·ti·grade \ˈ+\ *adj* [*multi-* + [1]*grade*] *of motor oil* : having a viscosity range that allows use over a wide temperature range

mul·ti·hull \ˈ+\ *n* [*multi-* + [1]*hull*] : a vessel (as a catamaran) with two or more side-by-side hulls

mul·ti–industry \ˈ+\ *adj* [*multi-* + *industry*] : active in or concerned with two or more separate industries

mul·ti·layered \ˈ+\ *or* **mul·ti·layer*** \ˈ+\ *adj* [*multi-* + *layered* or [1]*layer*] : having or involving several distinct layers, strata, or levels — **multilayer*** *n*

[1]**mul·ti·media** \ˈ+\ *adj* [*multi-* + *media*, pl. of [1]*medium*] : using, involving, or encompassing several media

[2]**multimedia** *n pl but sing or pl in constr* : a technique (as the combining of sound, video, and text) for expressing ideas (as in communication, entertainment, or art) in which several media are employed; *also* : something (as software) using or facilitating such a technique

mul·ti·nation \ˈməltə̇, -tē, -ˌtī+\ *adj* [*multi-* + [1]*nation*] : MULTINATIONAL 2 *herein*

[1]**mul·ti·national** \ˈ+\ *adj* [*multi-* + [1]*national*] **1** : of or relating to more than two nationalities ⟨a ~ society⟩ **2 a** : of, relating to, or involving more than two nations ⟨a ~ nuclear force⟩ **b** : having divisions in more than two countries ⟨a ~ corporation⟩

[2]**mul·ti·national** \ˈ+\ *n* : a multinational corporation

mul·ti·nationalism \ˈ+\ *n* : the establishment or operation of multinational corporations

mul·ti·parameter \ˈ+\ *adj* [*multi-* + *parameter*] : of or relating to several parameters

mul·ti·party \ˈ+\ *adj* [*multi-* + [1]*party*] : of, relating to, or involving more than two political parties

mul·ti·photon \ˈ+\ *adj* [*multi-* + *photon*] : involving more than one photon ⟨~ excitation of an atom⟩

mul·ti·player \ˈ+\ *adj* [*multi-* + *player*] : able to be used by more than one player simultaneously ⟨a ~ video game⟩

multiple* *n* **1** : something containing or consisting of more than one or two units of a kind **2** : a mass-produced work of art **3** : a number that expresses the price-earnings ratio of a stock : PRICE-EARNINGS MULTIPLE *herein* **4** *chiefly Brit* : MULTIPLE STORE *herein*

multiple regression *n* : regression in which one variable is estimated by the use of more than one other variable

multiple store *n, chiefly Brit* : CHAIN STORE

multiplet* *n* **1** : any of two or more atomic, molecular, or nuclear quantum states that are usu. close together in energy and that arise from different relative orientations of angular momenta **2** : a group of spectral frequencies arising from transitions to or from a multiplet quantum state **3** : a group of elementary particles different in charge but similar in other properties (as mass)

multiple–valued \ˈ===ˈ=\ *adj* : having at least one and sometimes more of the values of the range associated with each value of the domain — compare SINGLE-VALUED *in the Dict*

multiplex* *n* : a complex housing several movie theaters

multiplication sign *n* : a symbol used to indicate multiplication: **a** : TIMES SIGN *herein* **b** : DOT 2c(2)

multiplicative identity *n* : an identity element (as 1 in the group of rational numbers without 0 under the operation of multiplication) that in a given mathematical system leaves unchanged any element by which it is multiplied

multiplicative inverse *n* : an element of a mathematical set that when multiplied by a given element yields the identity element — called also *reciprocal*

multiplicity* *n* : the number of times a root of an equation or zero of a function occurs when there is more than one root or zero

multiplier effect *n* : the effect of a relatively minor factor in precipitating a great change; *esp* : the effect of a relatively small change in one economic factor (as rate of saving or level of consumer credit) in inducing a disproportionate increase or decrease in another (as gross national product)

mul·ti·ply \ˈməltəˌplī\ *n* -ES [*multiply*, v.] : an instance of multiplication performed by a computer; *also* : the means for performing multiplication

mul·ti·point \ˈməltə̇, -tē, -ˌtī+\ *adj* [*multi-* + [1]*point*] : involving several points; *esp* : of, relating to, or being a computer network having more than two terminals connected by a single communications channel

multipolar* *adj* : characterized by more than two centers of power or interest ⟨a ~ world⟩

mul·ti·potential \ˈ+\ *adj* [*multi-* + [1]*potential*] : having the potential of becoming any of several mature cell types ⟨~ stem cell⟩

mul·ti·processing \ˈ+\ *n* [*multi-* + *processing*, gerund of [2]*process*] : the processing of several computer programs at the same time esp. by a computer system with several processors sharing a single memory — **mul·ti·processor** \ˈ+\ *n*

mul·ti·programming \ˈ+\ *n* [*multi-* + *programming*] : the technique of utilizing several interleaved programs concurrently in a single computer system — **mul·ti·programmed** \ˈ+\ *adj*

mul·ti·pronged \ˈ+\ *adj* [*multi-* + *pronged*] **1** : having several prongs ⟨~ fishing spears⟩ **2** : having several distinct aspects or elements ⟨a ~ attack on the problem⟩

mul·ti·resistant \ˈ+\ *adj* [*multi-* + *resistant*] : biologically resistant to several toxic agents ⟨~ falciparum malaria⟩ — **mul·ti·resistance** \ˈ+\ *n*

mul·ti·screen \ˈ+\ *adj* [*multi-* + [1]*screen*] : having or utilizing more than one screen ⟨~ cinema⟩

mul·ti·sensory \ˈ+\ *adj* [*multi-* + *sensory*] : relating to, having, or involving perception by several sense organs

mul·ti·spectral \ˈ+\ *adj* [*multi-* + *spectral*] : of or relating to two or more ranges of frequencies or wavelengths in the electromagnetic spectrum ⟨~ scanner⟩

mul·ti·tasking \ˈ+\ *n, often attrib* [*multi-* + *tasking*, gerund of [2]*task*] : the concurrent performance of several jobs by a computer — **mul·ti·task** \ˈ+\ *vi*

mul·ti·user \ˈ+\ *adj* [*multi-* + [1]*user*] : able to be used by more than one person simultaneously

mul·ti·variable \ˈ+\ *adj* [*multi-* + [1]*variable*] : MULTIVARIATE

mul·ti·ver·si·ty \ˈməltəˈvərsəd·ē, -tēˈv-, -stē\ *n* -ES [*multi-* + *-versity* (as in *university*)] : a very large university with many component schools, colleges, or divisions, with widely diverse functions, and with a large staff engaged in activities other than instruction and esp. in administration

mun·chau·sen syndrome \ˈmən‚chau̇zən-, ˈmün‚-, -ŋ‚kau̇-, -ŋ‚kau̇-, ‚=ˈ==-\ *or* **munchausen's syndrome** \-zənz-\ *n, usu cap M* [after Baron K.F.H. von *Münchausen* †1797 Ger. soldier and proverbial teller of exaggerated tales] : a psychological disorder characterized by the feigning of the symptoms of a disease or injury in order to undergo diagnostic tests, hospitalization, or medical or surgical treatment

mun·chies \ˈmənchēz\ *n pl* [[1]*munch* + *-ie* + [1]*-s*] **1** : light snack foods **2** : hunger pangs; *esp* : hunger pangs induced by the use of marijuana

munch·kin \ˈmənchkən\ *n* -S [fr. the *Munchkins*, race of diminutive people in *The Wonderful Wizard of Oz* (1900) by L. Frank Baum †1919 Am. writer] : one that is small and charming or weak

mu·ni \ˈmyünē\ *n* -S [by shortening] **1** : MUNICIPAL 3 **2** : a municipal golf course

mu·ni·cip·io \‚myünəˈsipēō\ *n* -S [Sp, fr. L *municipium*] : a chiefly rural territorial unit of local government in many Latin-American countries that includes several villages or barrios

mu·on·ium \m(y)üˈōnēəm, -ˈän-\ *n* -S [NL, fr. ISV *muon* + NL *-ium*] : a short-lived quasi-atom consisting of an electron and a positive muon

mu·ram·ic acid \myu̇‚ramək-\ *n* [*mur-* (fr. L *murus* wall) + glucos*amine* + *-ic*] : an amino sugar $C_9H_{17}NO_7$ that is a lactic acid derivative of glucosamine and is found esp. in bacterial cell walls and in blue-green algae

mu·rein \ˈmyu̇(ə)rēən, ˈmyü(ə)r‚ēn\ *n* -S [*mur*amic acid (herein) + *-ein*] : PEPTIDOGLYCAN *herein*

mur·phy \ˈmərfē\ *or* **murphy game** *n, usu cap M* [fr. Miss *Murphy*, name of the nonexistent prostitute used to lure victims] : a confidence game and esp. one in which the victim believes he is paying for sex

murphy's law \¦mərfēz-, ¦məf-, ¦məif-\ *n, usu cap M&L* [prob. after Edward A. *Murphy* †1990 Am. engineer] : an observation: anything that can go wrong will go wrong

mus·ca·det \‚məskəˈdā, *F* müskȧde\ *n* -S *often cap* [F, grape variety, wine made from this grape, fr. MF, prob. alter (influenced by *-et* -et) of *muscadel* muscatel — more at MUSCATEL] : a dry white wine from the Loire valley of France

muscle car *n* : any of a group of American-made 2-door sports coupes of various makes with powerful engines that are designed for high-performance driving

muslim* *n, usu cap* : BLACK MUSLIM *herein*

must–see \ˈ=ˈ=\ *n* -S : something (as a film) that must or should be seen — **must–see** *adj*

mu·ta·ge·nic·i·ty \‚myüd·əjəˈnisəd·ē\ *n* -ES [*mutagenic* + *-ity*] : the capacity to induce mutations

mu·ta·gen·ize \ˈmyüd·əjə‚nīz\ *vt* -ED/-ING/-S [*mutagen* + *-ize*] : MUTATE

mu·ta·ro·tase \‚myüd·əˈrō‚tās, -āz\ *n* -S [*mutarot*ation + *-ase*] : an isomerase found esp. in mammalian tissues that catalyzes the interconversion of anomeric forms of some sugars

mu·ta·tor gene \¦myü‚tād·ə(r)-\ *also* **mutator** \ˈ=‚==, =ˈ==\ *n* -S [*mutator* fr. [1]*mutate* + [1]*-or*] : a gene that increases the rate of mutation of one or more other genes

mute* *adj* : remaining silent, undiscovered, or unrecognized

mutually exclusive *adj* : being related such that each excludes or precludes the other ⟨*mutually exclusive* events⟩; *also* : INCOMPATIBLE ⟨their outlooks were not *mutually exclusive*⟩

Mu·zak \ˈmyü‚zak\ *trademark* — used for recorded usu. background music

MVP *abbr* most valuable player

MY *abbr, often not cap* million years

my·co·phile \ˈmīkō‚fīl\ *n* -S [*myc-* + *-phile*] : a devotee of mushrooms; *esp* : one whose hobby is hunting wild edible mushrooms

mycoplasma* *n, pl* **my·co·plasmas** *or* **my·co·plas·ma·ta** \¦==¦plazməd·ə\ : PLEUROPNEUMONIA-LIKE ORGANISM — **my·co·plasmal** \"+\ *adj*

my·co·toxin \"+\ *n* [*myc-* + *toxin*] : a poisonous substance produced by a fungus and esp. a mold — compare AFLATOXIN *herein* — **my·co·toxic** \"+\ *adj* — **my·co·toxicity** \"+\ *n* — **my·co·toxicosis** \"+\ *n*

myelin basic protein *n* : a protein that is a constituent of myelin and is often found in higher than normal amounts in the cerebrospinal fluid of individuals affected with some demyelinating diseases (as multiple sclerosis)

myelocytic leukemia *n* : MYELOGENOUS LEUKEMIA

my·elo·fibrosis \¦mīəlō+\ *n* [NL, fr. *myel-* + *fibrosis*] : an anemic condition in which bone marrow becomes fibrotic and the liver and spleen usu. exhibit development of blood cell precursors — **my·elo·fibrotic** \"+\ *adj*

my·elo·peroxidase \"+\ *n* [*myel-* + *peroxidase*] : a peroxidase of phagocytic cells (as neutrophils and monocytes) that is held to assist in bactericidal activity by catalyzing the oxidation of ionic halogen to free halogen

my·e·lo·proliferative \"+\ *adj* [*myel-* + *proliferative*] : of, relating to, or being a disorder (as leukemia) marked by excessive proliferation of bone marrow elements and esp. blood cell precursors

My·lar \ˈmī‚lär\ *trademark* — used for a polyester film

myo·electric \¦mīō+\ *also* **myo·electrical** \"+\ *adj* [*my-* + *electric*] : of, relating to, or utilizing electricity generated by muscle ⟨a ~ prosthesis⟩ — **myo·electrically** \"+\ *adv*

myo·filament \"+\ *n* [*my-* + *filament*] : one of the individual filaments of actin or myosin that make up a myofibril

myotonic dystrophy *n* : an inherited condition that is characterized by delay in the ability to relax muscles after forceful contraction, wasting of muscles, formation of cataracts, premature baldness, atrophy of the gonads, endocrine and cardiac abnormalities, and often mental retardation and that is inherited as an autosomal dominant trait

myotube \"+\ *n* [*my-* + *tube*] : a developmental stage of a muscle fiber composed of a syncytium formed by fusion of myoblasts

Myr *abbr* million years

mythology* *n* : a popular belief or assumption that has grown up around someone or something ⟨defective *mythologies* that ignore masculine depth of feeling —Robert Bly⟩

myxo·virus \¦miksə+\ *n* [NL, fr. *myx-* + *virus*; fr. its affinity for certain mucins] : any of a group of RNA viruses that are now divided into two families (Paramyxoviridae and Orthomyxoviridae) including the paramyxoviruses and influenza-causing viruses — **myxo·viral** \"+\ *adj*

n* *abbr* [2]nano-

NA* *abbr* **1** not applicable **2** not available

naan \ˈnän, ˈnan\ *or* **nan** *n* -S [Hindi + Urdu + Per *nān* bread; Hindi + Urdu *nān*, fr. Per; akin to Baluchi *nayan* bread, Sogdian *nyny*] : a round or oblong flat leavened bread esp. of the Indian subcontinent

nab·o·kov·ian \‚nabəˈkōvēən, -ˈkȯv-, -ˈkȯfēən\ *adj, usu cap* [Vladimir Vladimirovich *Nabokov* †1977 Am. (Russ.-born) novelist & poet + E *-ian*] : of, relating to, or suggestive of Vladimir Nabokov or his writings

nacho \ˈnäch(‚)ō\ *n* -S [AmerSpr, perh. fr. Sp *nacho* flat-nosed] : a tortilla chip topped with cheese and a savory substance (as chili peppers or refried beans) and broiled

NAD \‚e(‚)nāˈdē\ *n* -S [*n*icotinamide *a*denine *d*inucleotide] : DIPHOSPHOPYRIDINE NUCLEOTIDE

nada* *n* NOTHING

na·der·ism \ˈnādə‚rizəm\ *n* -S *usu cap* [Ralph *Nader* b1934 Am. consumer advocate + E *-ism*] : the promotion of consumer interests esp. by public outcry against dangerous or defective goods

NADH \‚e‚nā(‚)dēˈāch\ *n* -S [*h*ydrogen] : the reduced form of NAD

NADP \‚e‚nā(‚)dēˈpē\ *n* -S [*n*icotinamide *a*denine *d*inucleotide *p*hosphate] : TRIPHOSPHOPYRIDINE NUCLEOTIDE

NADPH \‚e‚nā‚dē(‚)pēˈāch\ *n* -S [*h*ydrogen] : the reduced form of NADP

naf·cil·lin \¦nafˈsilən\ *n* -S [*naf-* (alter. of *naphth-*) + *penicillin*] : a semisynthetic penicillin $C_{21}H_{22}N_2O_5S$ that is resistant to penicillinase and is used esp. in the form of its sodium salt as an antibiotic

nail* *vt* : to perform or complete perfectly or impressively ⟨*~ed* a jump shot⟩

nail–biter \ˈ=‚==\ *n* -S : something (as a close contest) that induces tension ⟨a 5–4 12 inning *nail-biter* —Ron Fimrite⟩

nai·ra \ˈnī(ə)rə\ *n* -S [alter. of *Nigeria*, country in West Africa] **1** : the basic monetary unit of Nigeria — see MONEY table *in the Dict* **2** : a coin or note representing one naira

naïve* *or* **naive*** *adj* **1 a** : not previously subjected to experimentation or to a particular experimental situation ⟨experimentally ~ rats⟩ **b** : not having previously used a particular drug (as marijuana) **c** : not having been exposed previously to an antigen ⟨~ T cells⟩ **2 a** : PRIMITIVE 4d(1) **b** : produced by or as if by a self-taught artist ⟨~ murals⟩

naked* *adj* : not backed by the writer's ownership of the commodity contract or security ⟨selling ~ options⟩

naked mole rat *n* : a mole rat (*Heterocephalus glaber*) of the family Bathyergidae found in Ethiopia, Somalia, and Kenya that has pinkish or yellowish nearly hairless wrinkled skin, is practically blind, has an extremely poor capability for thermoregulation, and lives in a complex system of burrows housing an organized colony in which only one female and several males are involved in breeding

na·led \ˈnā‚led\ *n* -S [origin unknown] : a short-lived organophosphate insecticide $C_4H_7Br_2Cl_2O_4P$ used esp. to control crop pests and mosquitoes

na·li·dix·ic acid \‚nālə‚diksik-\ *n* [perh. fr. *naphthyridine* ($C_8H_6N_2$ — fr. *naphth-* + *pyridine*) + carboxy*lic acid*] : an antibacterial agent $C_{12}H_{12}N_2O_3$ that is used esp. in the treatment of genitourinary infections

nal·ox·one \nalˈäk‚sōn\ *n* -S [*N*-*al*lyl + hydr*ox*y- + *-one*] : a synthetic potent antagonist $C_{19}H_{21}NO_4$ of narcotic drugs and esp. morphine that is administered in the form of its hydrochloride

nal·trex·one \nalˈtrek‚sōn\ *n* -S [*N*-*al*lyl + *-trex-* (as in *methotrexate*) + *-one*] : a synthetic opiate antagonist $C_{20}H_{23}NO_4$ that is administered in the form of its hydrochloride esp. to maintain detoxified opiate addicts in a drug-free state

name of the game **1** : the essential or intrinsic quality or nature of a situation ⟨small farms where self-sufficiency was the *name of the game* —*Blair and Ketchum Country Jour.*⟩ **2** : the fundamental goal of an activity ⟨the American businessman is taught early that profits are the *name of the game* —Frank Gibney⟩

[1]**na·mib·i·an** \nəˈmibēən\ *adj, usu cap* [*Namibia*, country in southwest Africa + E *-an*] : of or relating to Namibia or its inhabitants

[2]**namibian** \"\ *n* -S *cap* : a native or inhabitant of Namibia

nam pla \¦nämˈplä\ *n* [Thai *námplaa*, fr. *nám* water + *plaa* fish] : a spicy Thai fish sauce

nan *var of* NAAN

NAND \ˈnand, ˈnaa(ə)nd\ *n* [*not AND* (herein)] : a computer logic circuit that produces an output which is the inverse of that of an AND circuit

nan·no·fossil \¦nanō+\ *n* [*nann-* + *fossil*] : a fossil of nannoplankton

nano·meter \¦nanō+\ *n* [ISV [2]*nano-* + [4]*meter*] : one billionth of a meter — abbr. *nm*

nano·particle \"+\ *n* [[2]*nano-* + *particle*] : a microscopic particle whose size is measured in nanometers

nano·scale \"+\ *adj* [[2]*nano-* + [7]*scale*] : having dimensions measured in nanometers ⟨~ devices⟩

nano·second \"+\ *n* [ISV [2]*nano-* + [4]*second*] : one billionth of a second — abbr. *ns, nsec*

nano·technology \"+\ *n* [[2]*nano-* + *technology*] : the art of manipulating materials on an atomic or molecular scale esp. to build microscopic devices (as robots)

nano·tesla \"+\ *n* [[2]*nano-* + *tesla* (herein)] : one billionth of a tesla

nano·tube \"+\ *n* [[2]*nano-* + [1]*tube*] : a microscopic tube whose diameter is measured in nanometers; *esp* : one of pure carbon : BUCKYTUBE *herein*

nan·tua sauce \nänⁿ(n)ˈtwä-\ *n, usu cap N* [fr. *Nantua*, France] : a cream sauce flavored with shellfish (as crayfish or lobster)

nap* *n* -S [7*nap*] *Brit* : a pick or recommendation as a good bet to win a contest (as a horse race); *also* : one named in a nap

[1]**nap** \ˈnap\ *vt* **napped; napped; napping; naps** [*nap*, n. (herein)] *Brit* : to pick or single out (as a race horse) in a nap

[2]**nap** \"\ *vt* **napped; napped; napping; naps** [F *napper*, lit., to cover with a tablecloth, fr. *nappe* tablecloth, fr. MF — more at NAPKIN] : to pour or spread a sauce over (a prepared dish) ⟨artichokes *napped* with hollandaise sauce⟩

napa cabbage \ˈnapə-\ *n, often cap N* [perh. fr. Jap dial. *nappa* greens] : a Chinese cabbage (*Brassica rapa pekinensis* syn. *B. pekinensis*)

na·prox·en \nəˈpräksən\ *n* -S [*nap*htha + *pro*pionic acid + [2]*oxy-* + *-en* (as in *ibuprofen* — herein)] : an anti-inflammatory analgesic antipyretic drug $C_{14}H_{14}O_3$ that is used esp. to treat arthritis and is often administered in the form of its sodium salt

narc *or* **nark** \ˈnärk\ *n* -S [short for *narcotics agent*] : one (as a government agent) who investigates narcotics violations

narc-* *or* **narco-*** *comb form* **1** : aided by drugs ⟨*narco*diagnosis⟩ ⟨*narco*hypnosis⟩ **2** : of or relating to illegal narcotics ⟨*narco*trafficking⟩

nar·co–terrorism \ˈnär(‚)kō-\ *n* : terrorism financed by profits from illegal drug trafficking — **nar·co–terrorist** \¦när(‚)kō+\ *n*

narcotic* *n* : a drug (as marijuana or LSD) subject to restriction similar to that of addictive narcotics whether in fact physiologically narcotic and addictive or not

nar·ra·tol·o·gy \‚narəˈtäləjē\ *n* -ES [F *narratologie*, fr. *narrat-* (as in *narratif* narrative, *narration* narration) + *-o-* -o- + *-logie* -logy — more at NARRATIVE] : the study of structure in narrative — **nar·ra·to·log·i·cal** \‚==tᵊlˈäjəkəl\ *adj* — **nar·ra·tol·o·gist** \‚==ˈtäləjəst\ *n* -S

narrowband \¦==¦=\ *adj* : operating at, responsive to, or including a narrow range of frequencies — compare BROADBAND 1 *herein*

narrowcast \ˈ=‚=‚=\ *vi* [[1]*narrow* + *-cast* (as in *broadcast*)] : to aim a broadcast at a narrowly defined area or audience

na·so·gastric \¦nāzō+\ *adj* [*nas-* + *gastric*] : of, relating to, being, or performed by intubation of the stomach by way of the nasal passages ⟨a ~ tube⟩ ⟨~ suction⟩

na·ta·lism \ˈnātᵊl‚izəm\ *n* -S [fr. *natalist* (fr. F *nataliste*, fr. *natalité* birthrate), after such pairs as *Communist* : *Communism* — more at NATALITY] : an attitude or policy favoring or encouraging population growth — **na·ta·list** \-ᵊləst\ *n* -S

national seashore *n, sometimes cap N&S* : an area of seacoast maintained by the federal government as a preserve for the natural environment and wildlife and as a public recreation area

native american* *adj, usu cap N&A* **1** : of or relating to Native Americans **2** : of American Indian descent

native american* *n, usu cap N & cap A* : AMERICAN INDIAN

na·tri·ure·sis \¦nā·trē(y)əˈrēsəs, ¦na-\ *also* **na·tru·re·sis** \-trəˈrē-\ *n* [NL, fr. *natrium* or *natr-* + *uresis*] : excessive loss of cations and esp. sodium in the urine — **na·tri·uret·ic** \-trē(y)əˈredik\ *adj or n*

natural* *adj* **1** : relating to or being natural food **2** *of hair* : styled in an Afro — **natural** *n*

natural family planning *n* : a method of birth control that involves abstention from sexual intercourse during the period of ovulation which is determined through observation and measurement of bodily symptoms — abbr. *NFP*

natural food *n* : food that has undergone minimal processing and contains no preservatives or artificial additives

natural gas* *n* : gas manufactured from organic matter (as coal)

natural killer cell *n* : a large granular lymphocyte capable of killing a tumor or microbial cell without prior exposure to the target cell and without having it presented with or marked by a histocompatibility antigen — called also *NK cell*

natural language* *n* : the language of ordinary speaking and writing ⟨fundamental problems of artificial intelligence—teaching computers to understand *natural languages*, such as English —Roger Draper⟩

natural scientist *n* : a specialist in natural science

nature trail *n* : a trail (as through a woods) usu. with natural features identified for better enjoyment or study of nature

Nau·ga·hyde \ˈnȯgə‚hīd, ˈnäg-\ *trademark* — used for vinyl-coated fabrics

NC–17 \‚en‚sē‚sevənˈtēn\ *trademark* — used as a rating for a motion picture of such a nature that admission is denied to persons under the age of 17; compare G *herein*, PG *herein*, PG-13 *herein*, R *herein*

near–infrared \‚==ˈ=\ *adj* : of or relating to the shorter wavelengths of radiation in the infrared spectrum and esp. to those between 0.7 and 2.5 micrometers

near miss** *n* **1** : a near collision (as between aircraft) **2** : CLOSE CALL

near–ultraviolet \‚=‚==ˈ=(=)=\ *adj* : of, relating to, or being the longest wavelengths of radiation in the ultraviolet spectrum and esp. those between 300 and 400 nanometers

neb·bish \ˈnebish\ *n* -ES [Yiddish *nebech* poor thing (used interjectionally), of Slav origin; akin to Czech *nebohý* wretched, Pol *nieboże* poor creature] : a timid, meek, or ineffectual person — **neb·bishy** \-ē\ *adj*

neck* *n* : the part of a tooth between the crown and the root

necklace* *vt* : to execute (a person) by placing and igniting a gasoline-soaked automobile tire around the neck

needle* *n* : a teasing or gibing remark

needleleaf \ˈ==‚=\ *adj* : populated with trees having leaves that are needles ⟨~ evergreen forests⟩; *also* : having leaves that are needles ⟨~ trees⟩

needlestick \ˈ==‚=\ *or* **needlestick injury** *n* : an accidental puncture of the skin with an unsterilized instrument (as a syringe)

needy* *adj* : marked by want of affection, attention, or emotional support ⟨pathetically ~ for affection —N.W. Aldrich Jr.⟩

negative income tax *n* : a system of federal subsidy payments to families with incomes below a stipulated level proposed as a substitute for or supplement to welfare payments

negative option *n* : a provision in a mail-order contract (as of a book club) that requires the customer either to return a refusal card within a specified time or to accept the current selection

negative transfer *n* : the impeding of learning or performance in a situation by the carry-over of learned responses from another situation — compare INTERFERENCE 9, TRANSFER 6b

ne·gri·tude \ˈnēgrə‚tüd, ˈneg-, -rə‚tyüd\ *n* -S [F *négritude*, fr. *nègre* Negro + *-i-* + *-tude* -tude — more at NEGRESS] **1** : a consciousness of and pride in the cultural and physical aspects of the African heritage **2** : the state of being a black person

ne·gro·ness \ˈnē(‚)grōnəs, -grə-\ *n, usu cap* : the quality or state of being Negro : NEGRITUDE

ne·gro·ni \nəˈgrōnē\ *n* -S *often cap* [It, perh. after a marquis *Negroni* who invented the drink in the 1930s] : a cocktail consisting of sweet vermouth, bitters, and gin

neh·ru \ˈne(ə)r(‚)ü, ˈnā(‚)rü\ *adj, usu cap* [after Jawaharlal *Nehru* †1964 Indian nationalist] : MAO *herein*

[1]**nelly*** *or* **nel·lie** \ˈnelē\ *n, pl* **nellies** : an effeminate homosexual — **not on your nelly** *sometimes cap 2d N* [perh. fr. the phrase *not on your Nelly Duff*, rhyming slang for Brit slang *puff* breath, life] *Brit* : certainly not

[2]**nelly** *or* **nellie** \"\ *adj* [[1]*nelly*, n. (herein)] : conspicuously effeminate

neo·colonialism \¦nē(‚)ō+\ *n* [*ne-* + *colonialism*] : the economic and political policies by which a Great Power indirectly maintains or extends its influence over other areas or peoples — **neo·colonial** \"+\ *adj* — **neo·colonialist** \"+\ *n or adj*

neo·con \"+¦kän\ *n* -S [by shortening] : NEOCONSERVATIVE *herein*

neo·conservative \"+\ *n* [*ne-* + *conservative*] : a former liberal espousing political conservatism — **neo·conservatism** \"+\ *n* — **neoconservative** *adj*

neo·cortical \"+\ *adj* [*ne-* + *cortical*] : of or relating to the neocortex

neo–dada \"+\ *n, usu cap D* [*ne-* + *Dada*] : an anti-art movement esp. of the late 1950s and the 1960s based on tenets similar to those of Dada but having more interest in the object than Dada claimed to have; *broadly* : JUNK ART *herein* — **neo–dadaism** \"+\ *n, usu cap D* — **neo–dadaist** \"+\ *adj or n, usu cap D*

neo–expressionism \"+\ *n, often cap N & usu cap E* [*ne-* + *expressionism*] : a revival of expressionism in art characterized by intense colors, dramatic usu. figural forms, and emotive subject matter — **neo–expressionist** *n or adj, often cap N & usu cap E*

neo·liberal \"+\ *n* [*ne-* + [2]*liberal*] : a liberal who de-emphasizes traditional liberal doctrines in order to pursue progress by more pragmatic methods — **neo·liberalism** \-‚lizəm\ *n* — **neo·liberal** \"+\ *adj*

neo·na·tol·o·gy \‚nēōnāˈtäləjē\ *n* -ES [*neonate* + *-ology* (as in *gynecology*)] : a branch of medicine concerned with the care, development, and diseases of newborn infants — **neo·na·tol·o·gist** \-jəst\ *n* -S

neo–nazi \¦nē(‚)ō+\ *n, usu cap 2d N, often attrib* [*ne-* + [1]*Nazi*] : a member of a group espousing the beliefs of the Nazis — **neo–nazism** \"+\ *n, usu cap 2d N*

neo·phil·ia \‚nēōˈfilēə\ *n* -S [NL, fr. *ne-* + *-philia*] : love of or enthusiasm for what is new or novel

neo·phil·i·ac \-ˈfilē‚ak\ *n* -S [fr. *neophilia* (herein), after such pairs as *necrophilia* : *necrophiliac*] : one who has or expresses neophilia

neo·ri·can \¦nēōˈrēkən\ *n* -S *cap* [modif. of AmerSp *neorriqueño* Puerto Rican living in New York City, blend of Sp *neoyorquino* New Yorker, and *puertorriqueño* Puerto Rican] : a Puerto Rican who lives on the U.S. mainland or who has lived there but has returned to Puerto Rico

neo·vascularization \¦nē(‚)ō+\ *n* [*ne-* + *vascularization*] : vascularization esp. in abnormal quantity (as in some conditions of the retina) or in abnormal tissue (as a tumor)

ne·phrit·o·gen·ic \nə‚frid·əˈjenik, ‚nefrid·ōˈ-\ *adj* [*nephritis* + *-o-* + *-genic*] : causing nephritis ⟨~ types of streptococci⟩

ne·phros·to·my \nəˈfrästəmē, ne-\ *n* -ES [ISV *nephr-* + [2]*-stomy*] : the surgical formation of an opening between a kidney pelvis and the outside of the body

nephrotic syndrome *n* : an abnormal condition that is marked by deficiency of albumin in the blood and its excretion in the urine due to altered permeability of the glomerular basement membranes (as by a toxic chemical agent)

nerd *also* **nurd** \ˈnərd, ˈnəd, ˈnəid\ *n* -S [origin unknown] : an unstylish, unattractive, or socially inept person; *esp* : one slavishly devoted to intellectual or academic pursuits ⟨computer ~⟩ — **nerd·ish** \-dish\ *adj* — **nerdy** \-dē\ *adj* -ER/-EST

nerf \ˈnərf, ˈnəf, ˈnəif\ *vt* -ED/-ING/-S [origin unknown] : to bump (another car) in an automobile race

nerf bar *or* **nerfing bar** *n* [fr. *nerf* (herein)] : a usu. tubular steel bumper on some racing cars to keep wheels from touching when cars bump during a race

nerve growth factor *n* : a protein that promotes development of the sensory and sympathetic nervous systems and is required for maintenance of sympathetic neurons — abbr. *NGF*

nest·ed \ˈnestəd\ *adj* [fr. past part. of [2]*nest*] : forming a sequence or hierarchy with each member contained in or containing the next ⟨~ subroutines in computer programming⟩

net* *n, often cap* [by shortening] : INTERNET *herein*

net·i·quette \ˈned·əkət, ˈnet-, -‚ket\ *n* -S *sometimes cap* [blend of [1]*net* (Internet) and *etiquette*] : etiquette governing communication on the Internet

net·i·zen \ˈned·əzən, ˈnet-, *also* -sən\ *n* -S *sometimes cap* [blend of [1]*net* (Internet) and *citizen*] : an active participant in the on-line community of the Internet

network* *n* : a system of computers, terminals, and data bases connected by communications lines

network* *vt* **1** *Brit* : to broadcast (a program) on a radio or television network **2** : to join (computers) in a network ~ *vi* : to meet and exchange information with colleagues, potential business contacts, or like-minded individuals

net·work·ing \ˈ=‚==\ *n* -S **1** : the exchange of information or services among individuals, groups, or institutions **2** : the process of establishing or using a computer network

neural net *or* **neural network** *n* : a computer architecture in which a number of processors are interconnected in a manner suggestive of the connections between neurons in a human brain and which is able to learn by a process of trial and error

neur·amin·i·dase \ˌn(y)u̇rəˈminəˌdās, -āz\ *n* -s [*neuraminic* acid + *-idase* (as in *glucosidase*)] : a hydrolytic enzyme that occurs on the surface of the pneumococcus, influenza-causing viruses, and some paramyxoviruses, and that cleaves terminal acetylated neuraminic acids from sugar residues (as in glycoproteins and mucoproteins)

neu·ris·tor \n(y)u̇ˈristə(r)\ *n* -s [*neuron* + *transistor*; fr. its functioning like a neuron and not requiring the use of transistors] : a usu. electronic device along which a signal propagates with uniform velocity and without attenuation

neu·ro·active \ˌn(y)ürō, -ü- +\ *adj* [*neur-* + [1]*active*] : stimulating neural tissue ⟨~ substances⟩

neu·ro·biology \"+\ *n* [*neur-* + *biology*] : a branch of the life sciences that deals with the anatomy, physiology, and pathology of the nervous system — **neu·ro·biological** \"+\ *adj* — **neu·ro·biologically** \"+\ *adv* — **neu·ro·biologist** \"+\ *n*

neu·ro·chemistry \"+\ *n* [*neur-* + *chemistry*] **1** : the study of the chemical makeup and activities of nervous tissue **2** : chemical processes and phenomena related to the nervous system — **neu·ro·chemical** \"+\ *adj or n* — **neu·ro·chemist** \"+\ *n*

neu·ro·degenerative \"+\ *adj* [*neur-* + *degenerative*] : relating to or characterized by degeneration of nervous tissue

neuroendocrine* *adj* : of, relating to, or functioning in neurosecretion

neu·ro·endocrinology \ˌn(y)ürō, -ü-+\ *n* [*neur-* + *endocrinology*] : a branch of the life sciences dealing with neurosecretion and the physiological interaction between the central nervous system and the endocrine system — **neu·ro·endocrinological** \"+\ *adj* — **neu·ro·endocrinologist** \"+\ *n*

neurofibrillary tangle *n* : a pathological accumulation of paired helical filaments composed of abnormally formed tau protein that is found chiefly in the cytoplasm of nerve cells of the brain and esp. the cerebral cortex and hippocampus and that occurs typically in Alzheimer's disease

neu·ro·genesis \"+\ *n* [NL, fr. *neur-* + *genesis*] : development of nerves, nervous tissue, or the nervous system

neu·ro·he·mal organ *also* **neu·ro·hae·mal organ** \ˌn(y)ürōˌhēməl-, -ü-\ *n* [*neur-* + *hem-* + [1]*-al*] : an organ (as a corpus cardiacum of an insect) that releases stored neurosecretory substances into the blood

neu·ro·hypophyseal *or* **neu·ro·hypophysial** \ˌn(y)ürō, -ü- +\ *adj* [*neur-* + *hypophyseal* or *hypophysial*] : of, relating to, or secreted by the neurohypophysis ⟨~ hormones⟩

neuro·imaging \"+\ *n* [*neur-* + *imaging* (herein)] : a clinical specialty concerned with producing images of the brain by noninvasive techniques (as computed tomography, magnetic resonance imaging, and positron-emission tomography); *also* : imaging of the brain by these techniques

neu·ro·lept·analgesia \ˌn(y)ürōˌlept, -ü- +\ *or* **neu·ro·lep·to·analgesia** \ˌn(y)ürōˌleptō, -ü- +\ *n* [NL, fr. ISV *neurolept-* or *neurolepto-* (fr. *neuroleptic* — herein) + *analgesic* + NL *-ia* (as in *analgesia*)] : joint administration of a tranquilizing drug and an analgesic esp. for relief of surgical pain — **neu·ro·lept·analgesic** \ˌn(y)ürōˌlept, -ü- +\ *adj*

neu·ro·lep·tic \ˌn(y)ürōˈleptik, -ü-\ *n* -s [ISV *neur-* + *-leptic* (as in *psycholeptic*); orig. formed as F *neuroleptique*] : ANTIPSYCHOTIC *herein* — **neuroleptic** \ˌ==ˈ=\ *adj*

neu·ro·peptide \"+\ *n* [*neur-* + *peptide*] : an endogenous peptide (as an endorphin or enkephalin) that influences neural activity or functioning

neu·ro·pharmacology \"+\ *n* [*neur-* + *pharmacology*] **1** : a branch of medical science dealing with the action of drugs on and in the nervous system **2** : the properties and reactions of a drug on and in the nervous system ⟨the ~ of lithium⟩ — **neu·ro·pharmacological** \"+\ *also* **neu·ro·pharmacologic** \"+\ *adj* — **neu·ro·pharmacologist** \"+\ *n*

neu·ro·phy·sin \ˌn(y)ürōˈfīsən, -ür-, -ˈfiz-\ *n* -s [ISV *neurophys-* (fr. NL *neurohypophysis*) + *-in*; orig. formed as F *neurophysine*] : any of several brain hormones that bind with and carry either oxytocin or vasopressin

neu·ro·psychic \ˌn(y)ürō, -ü- +\ *also* **neu·ro·psychical** \"+\ *adj* [*neur-* + *psychic* or *psychical*] : of or relating to both the mind and the nervous system as affecting mental processes

neu·ro·radiology \"+\ *n* [*neur-* + *radiology*] : radiology of the nervous system — **neu·ro·radiological** \"+\ *also* **neu·ro·radiologic** \"+\ *adj* — **neu·ro·radiologist** \"+\ *n*

neu·ro·science \"+\ *n* [*neur-* + *science*] : a branch (as neurology or neurophysiology) of the life sciences that deals with the anatomy, physiology, biochemistry, or molecular biology of nerves and nervous tissue and esp. with their relation to behavior and learning — **neu·ro·scientific** \"+\ *adj* — **neu·ro·scientist** \"+\ *n*

neu·ro·sensory \"+\ *adj* [*neur-* + *sensory*] : of or relating to afferent nerves ⟨~ control of feeding behavior⟩

neu·ros·po·ra* \n(y)u̇ˈräspərə\ *n* -s : a fungus of the genus *Neurospora*

neu·ro·transmission \ˌn(y)ürō, -ü- +\ *n* [*neur-* + *transmission*] : the transmission of nerve impulses across a synapse

neu·ro·transmitter \"+\ *n* [*neur-* + *transmitter*] : a chemical substance (as norepinephrine or acetylcholine) that transmits nerve impulses across a synapse

neu·ter·cane \ˈn(y)üd·ə(r)ˌkān\ *n* -s [L *neuter* neither + E *-cane* (as in *hurricane*); from the difficulty of classifying it as either hurricane or frontal storm] : a subtropical cyclone that is usu. less than 100 miles in diameter and that draws energy from sources common to both the hurricane and the frontal cyclone

neutral current *n* : a weak nuclear interaction between a lepton (as a neutrino) and a hadron (as a neutron) in which the electric charges of the particles remain unchanged

neutron activation analysis *also* **neutron activation** *n* : an analytical method used to determine the chemical elements comprising a material by bombarding it with neutrons to produce radioactive atoms whose emissions are indicative of the elements present

neutron bomb *n* : a nuclear warhead designed to produce lethal neutrons but less blast and fire damage than other nuclear bombs

neutron star *n* : a dense celestial object that consists primarily of closely packed neutrons and that results from the collapse of a much larger stellar body

never–never *adj* [*never-never land*] : characterized by an imaginary, idealistic, or fantastic quality ⟨the *never-never* rhetoric . . . which had to do with perfect justice and perfect harmony —Jane Kramer⟩

never–never land* *n* : an exotic place ⟨a *never-never land* of poodles and chauffeurs —Kathryn Livingston⟩; *also* : an absurd or indeterminate situation ⟨was capital disappearing into an unproductive *never-never land?* —Gregg Easterbrook⟩

[1]**new age** *n* **1** *usu cap N&A* : an eclectic group of cultural attitudes arising in late 20th-century Western society that are adapted from those of a variety of cultures ancient and modern, that emphasize beliefs (as reincarnation, holism, pantheism, and occultism) outside the mainstream, and that advance alternative approaches to spirituality, right living, and health **2** *or* **new age music** *often cap N&A* : a soft soothing form of instrumental music often used to promote relaxation — **new ager** \ˈn(y)üˈājə(r)\ *n, usu cap N&A* — **new agey** \-ˈājē\ *adj, usu cap N&A*

[2]**new age** *adj, sometimes cap N&A* **1** : of, relating to, or being New Age or New Age music **2** : CONTEMPORARY, MODERN ⟨happy *new age* dads expertly diapering their always cheerful babies —Amy Saltzman *et al*⟩

new·bie \ˈn(y)übē\ *n* -s [irreg. fr. [1]*new*] : BEGINNER, NOVICE; *esp* : a newcomer to cyberspace

new drug *n* : a drug that has not been declared safe and effective by qualified experts under the conditions prescribed, recommended, or suggested in the label and that may be a new chemical formula or an established drug prescribed for use in a new way

new economics *n pl but usu sing in constr* : an economic concept that is a logical extension of Keynesianism and that holds that appropriate fiscal and monetary maneuvering can maintain healthy economic growth and prosperity indefinitely

new guard *n, sometimes cap N&G* : a group of persons who have recently gained prominence or power in a particular field (as politics or business); *also* : a group of persons united in an effort to change the status quo

new historicism *n, usu cap N&H* : a method of literary criticism that emphasizes the historicity of a text by relating it to the configurations of power, society, or ideology in a given time — **new historicist** *n or adj, usu cap N&H*

new jack *adj, sometimes cap N&J* [[1]*jack* (man, guy)] **1** : of, relating to, or consisting of new jack swing ⟨*new jack* grooves⟩ **2** : of relating to, or being urban, hip, and usu. black ⟨the *new jack* generation⟩

new jack swing *n, sometimes cap N&J&S* : pop music usu. performed by black musicians that combines elements of jazz, funk, rap, and R and B

new journalism *n, usu cap N&J* : journalism that features the author's subjective responses to people and events and that often employs the techniques of fiction — **new journalist** *n, usu cap N&J*

new left *n, usu cap N&L* : a political movement originating esp. among students in the 1960s, favoring confrontational tactics, often breaking with traditional leftist ideologies, and associated esp. with antiwar, antinuclear, feminist, and ecological issues — **new leftist** *n, often cap N&L*

new math *or* **new mathematics** *n* : mathematics based on set theory esp. as taught in elementary and secondary school

new right *n, usu cap N&R* : a U.S. political movement originating esp. among southern and western Protestant fundamentalists, opposing esp. liberal ideology, and concerned with issues esp. of church and state, gun ownership, pornography, and abortion

newsgroup \ˈ=ˌ=\ *n* : an electronic bulletin board on the Internet that is devoted to a particular topic

newspeak \ˈ=ˌ=\ *n, often cap* [*Newspeak*, a language "designed to diminish the range of thought" in the novel *1984* (1949) by George Orwell †1950 Eng. author, fr. [1]*new* + [2]*speak*] : propagandistic language characterized by euphemism, circumlocution, and the inversion of customary meanings

newsperson \ˈ=ˌ==\ *n* [[1]*news* + *person*] : REPORTER c

new town* *n* : an urban development comprising a small to medium-size city with a broad range of housing and planned industrial, commercial, and recreational facilities

new wave *n, often cap N&W* [trans. of F *nouvelle vague*] **1** : a cinematic movement that is characterized by improvisation, abstraction, and subjective symbolism and that often makes use of experimental photographic techniques **2** : a new movement in a particular field (as art or cooking) ⟨young chefs who call themselves the *New Wave* —R.A.Sokolov⟩ **3** : popular music derived from rock but less raw than punk and typically including unconventional melodies, exaggerated beats, and quirky lyrics **4** : the newest fashion; *esp* : fashion that is strikingly outrageous — **new waver** *n, often cap N&W*

new–wave \ˈ=ˈ=\ *adj* **1** : of or relating to New Wave ⟨*new-wave* filmmakers⟩ **2** : MODERN, CONTEMPORARY ⟨a *new-wave* restaurant⟩

new york minute *n, usu cap N&Y* [*New York* City; fr. the fast pace stereotypically associated with the city] : INSTANT, FLASH ⟨would have done it in a *New York minute*⟩

nexus* *n* : a point of focus or intersection : CENTER ⟨"one little spot on earth" that has served as the ~ of three great religions —John J. O'Connor⟩

ng *abbr* nanogram

n galaxy *n, usu cap N* [*n*uclear] : a galaxy that has a brilliant starlike nucleus surrounded by a much fainter halo or extension

NGF *abbr* nerve growth factor *herein*

NGO *abbr* nongovernmental organization

NGU *abbr* nongonococcal urethritis

ngul·trum \enˈgu̇ltrəm, eŋˈ-\ *n, pl* **ngultrums** *also* **ngultrum** [Tibetan] **1** : the basic monetary unit of Bhutan — see MONEY table *in the Dict* **2** : a coin or note representing one ngultrum

ngwee \enˈgwē, eŋˈ-\ *n, pl* **ngwee** [Bemba, lit., bright] **1** : a monetary unit of Zambia equal to 1/100 kwacha — see MONEY table *in the Dict* **2** : a coin representing one ngwee

ni·al·amide \nīˈaləˌmīd, -məd\ *n* [*ni*cotinic acid + *amyl* + *amide*] : a synthetic antidepressant drug $C_{16}H_{18}N_4O_2$ that is an inhibitor of monoamine oxidase

nibble* *n* **1** : SNACK **2** : a tentative expression of interest

ni·cad \ˈnīˌkad\ *n* -s *sometimes cap N&C* [[1]*ni*ckel + *cad*mium] : a rechargeable storage battery that has a nickel cathode and a cadmium anode

niche* *n, often attrib* : a specialized market

Ni·chrome \ˈnīˌkrōm\ *trademark* — used for an alloy of nickel, chromium, and iron that is commonly used in the heating elements of electrical appliances

nick* *vt* : to produce a nick in (DNA)

nick* *n* **1** *slang Brit* : JAIL; *also* : POLICE STATION **2** : a break in one strand of two-stranded DNA caused by a missing phosphodiester bond

nickel* *n* **1** *slang* : five dollars **2** *or* **nickel bag** *slang* : a packet containing five dollars worth of an illicit drug (as marijuana) **3** : one's own expense ⟨all the exploration is on our ~ —Thomas Kruzshak⟩ — often used in phrases like *it's your nickel* **4** *or* **nickel defense** : a football defensive formation that employs five defensive backs and is used mainly in passing situations

[1]**nickel–and–dime** *adj* **1** : involving or offering only a small amount of money ⟨*nickel-and-dime* insurance claims⟩ ⟨*nickel-and-dime* jobs⟩ **2** : SMALL-TIME ⟨*nickel-and-dime* dealers⟩

[2]**nickel–and–dime** *vt* **nickeled–and–dimed** *or* **nickel–and–dimed; nickeled–and–dimed** *or* **nickel–and–dimed; nickeling–and–diming** *or* **nickel–and–diming; nickels–and–dimes** *or* **nickel–and–dimes** : to impair, weaken, or defeat piecemeal (as through a series of small incursions or excessive attention to minor details) ⟨*nickeled-and-dimed* the Democrats to defeat . . . upstate —*Pittsburgh (Pa.) Press*⟩; *also* : to pester, impoverish, or reduce by small sums ⟨prove their mettle by *nickel-and-diming* your budget —W.G.McDonald⟩ ⟨wanted to *nickel-and-dime* its customers to death —J.C.Dvorak⟩

[1]**ni·coise** *or* **ni·çoise** \nēˈswäz\ *or* **nicoise salad** *n* -s *usu cap N* [F (*salade*) *niçoise* salad in the style of Nice (city in France)] : SALADE NIÇOISE

[2]**nicoise** *or* **niçoise** *adj, usu cap* [F (short for *à la niçoise*, lit., in the style of Nice), fr. fem. of *niçois* of Nice, fr. *Nice*, France] : served with some of the ingredients (as tomatoes and olives) of a nicoise ⟨sole ~⟩

nicotinamide adenine dinucleotide *n* : DIPHOSPHOPYRIDINE NUCLEOTIDE

nicotinamide adenine dinucleotide phosphate *n* : TRIPHOSPHOPYRIDINE NUCLEOTIDE

NICU *abbr* neonatal intensive care unit

NIDDM *abbr* non-insulin-dependent diabetes mellitus *herein*

ni·fed·i·pine \nīˈfedəˌpēn, -ˌpən\ *n* [prob. *nitr-* + *-fe-* (fr. *phenyl*) + *-dipine* (alter. & shortening of *pyridine*)] : a calcium channel blocker $C_{17}H_{18}N_2O_6$ that is a coronary vasodilator used esp. in the treatment of angina pectoris

nig·ga \ˈnigə\ *n, pl* **niggas** *also* **niggaz** [by alter.] : AFRO-AMERICAN — used chiefly among Afro-Americans; usu. taken to be offensive when used by others

nigger* *n* : a member of a socially disadvantaged class of persons ⟨it's time for somebody to lead all of America's ~s . . . all the people who feel left out of the political process —Ron Dellums⟩

nig·gle \ˈnigəl\ *n* -s [*niggle*, v.] *chiefly Brit* : a trifling doubt, objection, or complaint

nightglow \ˈ=ˌ=\ *n* [*night* + *airglow*] : airglow seen at night

nightlife* \ˈ=ˌ=\ *n* : entertainment provided for pleasure-seekers at night (as in nightclubs); *also* : establishments providing nightlife

nightside* *n* : the side of a celestial body not in daylight

nig–nog \ˈnigˈnȯg, -ˈnäg\ *n* -s [redupl. of *nig*] *Brit* : NEGRO — usu. used disparagingly

ni·gro·striatal \ˌnīgrō, ˌnig- +\ *adj* [(*substantia*) *nigra* + *-o-* + *striatal*] : of, relating to, or joining the corpus striatum and the substantia nigra ⟨the ~ dopamine pathway degenerates in Parkinson's disease —S.H.Snyder *et al*⟩

-nik \(ˌ)nik\ *n suffix* -s [Yiddish, fr. Pol & Ukrainian] : one connected with or characterized by being ⟨peace*nik*⟩ ⟨neat*nik*⟩

nil·potent \ˌnil+\ *adj* [L *nil* nothing + *potent-, potens* having power — more at NIL, POTENT] : equal to zero when raised to some power — **nil·potency** \"+\ *n* — **nil·potent** \"+\ *n*

NIMBY \ˈnimbē\ *abbr or n* -s [*not in my backyard*] : the negative reaction to the location of something considered undesirable (as a prison or an incinerator) in one's neighborhood

[1]**nine–to–five** *also* **9–to–5** \ˌ==ˈ=\ *n* : a job with regular daytime hours

[2]**nine–to–five** *or* **9–to–5** *adj* : of, relating to, being, or having a nine-to-five

nine–to–fiver *also* **9–to–5er** \ˌ==ˈfīvə(r)\ *n* : a person who works at a job with regular daytime hours

nin·ja \ˈninjə\ *n, pl* **ninja** *also* **ninjas** *sometimes cap* [Jap, fr. *nin-* persevere, conceal, move stealthily + *-ja* person] : a person trained in ancient Japanese martial arts techniques and employed esp. for espionage and assassinations

nin·jut·su \ninˈju̇tsü, -ˈjət-, -ˈjüt-\ *also* **nin·jit·su** \-ˈjit-\ *n* -s [Jap, fr. *nin-* (as in *ninja* ninja) + *jutsu* art, skill] : ninja techniques taught as a martial art

nit* *n* [[1]*nit*; back-formation fr. *nit-picking*] : a minor shortcoming

[1]**nit** \ˈnit\ *n* -s [ISV, fr. L *nitēre* to shine; orig. formed in F — more at NEAT] : a unit of brightness equal to one candle per square meter of cross section perpendicular to the rays

[2]**nit** *n* -s [by shortening] *chiefly Brit* : NITWIT

ni·ti·nol \ˈnītᵊnˌȯl, -ˌōl\ *n* -s [*Ni* + *Ti* + *-nol* (fr. *N*aval *O*rdnance *L*aboratory, where the alloy was created)] : a nonmagnetic alloy of titanium and nickel that after being deformed returns to its original shape upon being reheated

nit·pick \ˈnitˌpik\ *vb* -ED/-ING/-S *vi* : to engage in nit-picking ~ *vt* : to criticize by nitpicking — **nit·pick·er** *n* -s

nit–picking \ˈ=ˌ==\ *n* -s [[1]*nit* + *picking*, gerund of [1]*pick*] : minute and usu. petty criticism — **nit·pick** \ˈ=ˌ=\ *n* — **nit·picky** \-ē, -i\ *adj*

ni·tro·fu·ran·to·in \ˌnī·(ˌ)trōfyəˈrantəwən\ *n* -s [*nitrofuran* + hydan*toin*] : a nitrofuran derivative $C_8H_6N_4O_5$ that is a broad-spectrum antimicrobial agent used esp. in treating urinary tract infections

ni·tro·ge·nase \ˌnīˈträjəˌnās, ˈnī·trəj-, -āz\ *n* -s [*nitrogen* + *-ase*] : an iron- and molybdenum-containing enzyme of various nitrogen-fixing microorganisms (as some bacteria and blue-green algae) that catalyzes the reduction of molecular nitrogen to ammonia

nitrogen narcosis *n* : a state of euphoria and exhilaration that occurs when nitrogen in normal air enters the bloodstream at approximately seven times atmospheric pressure (as in deep-water diving) — called also *rapture of the deep*

ni·tro·so·dimethylamine \nīˈtrō(ˌ)sō+\ *n* [*nitros-* + *dimethylamine*] : DIMETHYLNITROSAMINE *herein*

ni·tro·so·guanidine \"+\ *n* [*nitros-* + *guanidine*] : an explosive compound CH_4N_4O often used as a mutagen in biological research

ni·tro·so·urea \"+\ *n* [*nitros-* + *urea*] : any of a group of lipid-soluble drugs that function as alkylating agents, have the ability to enter the central nervous system, and are effective in the treatment of some brain tumors and meningeal leukemias

nit·ty–grit·ty \ˌnid·ēˈgrid·ē\ *n* [origin unknown] : what is essential or basic : specific practical details ⟨getting down to the *nitty-gritty*⟩ — **nitty–gritty** *adj*

Nix·ie \ˈniksē\ *trademark* — used for an electronic indicator tube

NK cell \ˌenˈkā-\ *n* : NATURAL KILLER CELL *herein*

nm *abbr* nanometer *herein*

NMDA \ˌen(ˌ)em(ˌ)dēˈā\ *n* -s [*N*-methyl-*D*-*a*spartate] : a synthetic amino acid $C_5H_9NO_4$ that binds selectively to a subset of glutamate receptors on neurons where the binding of glutamate results in the opening of calcium channels

NMR *abbr* nuclear magnetic resonance *herein*

nobble* *vt, Brit* : to get hold of : CATCH, NAB

noble savage *n, sometimes cap N&S* : a mythic conception of people belonging to non-European cultures as having innate natural simplicity and virtue uncorrupted by European civilization; *also* : a person exemplifying this conception

no–brain·er \ˌnōˈbrānə(r)\ *n* -s : something that requires a minimum of thought

no contest *n* : NOLO CONTENDERE

nod* *n* : a drowsy stupefied state caused by or as if by the use of narcotic drugs — used esp. in the phrase *on the nod*

node* *n* **1** : VERTEX 1a(2) **2** : a receiving or transmitting station (as a computer terminal) in an electronic communications network **3** : a point in a linguistic phrase marker that represents a constituent and that usu. bears a category label (as NP)

nod out *vi* : to pass out or fall asleep ⟨parks lined with winos and junkies *nodding out* —Tony Kornheiser⟩

no–fault \ˈ=ˈ=\ *adj* **1** : of, relating to, or being a motor vehicle insurance plan under which an accident victim is compensated usu. up to a stipulated limit for actual losses (as medical bills and lost wages) but not for nuisance claims (as of pain or suffering) by his own insurance company regardless of who is responsible for the accident **2** : of, relating to, or being a divorce law according to which neither party is held responsible for the breakdown of the marriage **3** : being such that individuals are not held responsible for harmful acts or for personal shortcomings ⟨we established a *no-fault* society, a guilt-free age —Eugene Kennedy⟩

no–frills \ˈ=ˈ=\ *adj* : offering or providing only the essentials : not fancy, elaborate, or luxurious ⟨*no-frills* flights⟩

no–good·nik \ˌ=ˈgu̇dnik\ *n* -s [*no good* + *-nik* (herein)] : a person without virtue, honor, or morals : LOWLIFE

noir *n* -s [short for *film noir*] **1** : crime fiction featuring hard-boiled cynical characters and bleak sleazy settings **2** : FILM NOIR *herein* **3** : music having a slow tempo and creating a mood reminiscent of or appropriate for film noir — **noir·ish** \-ish\ *adj*

noise* *n* **1** : electromagnetic radiation (as light or radio waves) that is composed of several frequencies and that involves random changes in frequency or amplitude **2** : something that attracts attention ⟨Utah makes big ~ this year —*Ski*⟩ ⟨the play . . . will make little ~ in the world —Brendan Gill⟩ **3** : something spoken or uttered ⟨when he responded, gave him supportive ~s: "Outasight" —Judson Jerome⟩ ⟨made some encouraging ~s about Britain's good standing in Arab eyes —William Hardcastle⟩ **4** : irrelevant or meaningless output (as from a computer or instrument) occurring along with desired information **5** : a style of rock music that is loud, often discordant, and usu. uses electronic noise (as feedback) **6** : random variation or interference inherent to a system ⟨the seasonal signal . . . is more than ten times the ~ . . . of interannual variability —S.H.Schneider⟩

noise pollution *n* : annoying or harmful noise (as of automobiles or jet airplanes) in the environment

no–knock \ˈ=ˈ=\ *adj* : of, relating to, or being the entry by police into private premises without knocking and without identifying themselves (as to make an arrest) — **no–knock** *n*

no–load \ˈ=ˈ=\ *adj* : charging no sales commission ⟨*no-load* mutual funds⟩ — **no–load** \ˈ=ˌ=\ *n*

nominal* *adj* : being according to plan : falling within a range of acceptable planned limits : SATISFACTORY ⟨everything was ~ during the spacecraft launch⟩ ⟨the satellite had a ~ orbit⟩
nominal* *n* **1** : a linguistic form (as English *boy* or *he*) that inflects for number or case or for both **2** : a word or word group functioning as a noun normally functions
nom·i·nal·iza·tion \ˌnämənᵊlə'zāshən, -mnəl-\ *n* -S [²*nominal* + *-ization*] : the process or result of forming a noun or noun phrase from a clause or a verb — **nominalize*** *vt*
non·addict \ˈnän *sometimes* ¦nən+\ *n* : a person who is not addicted
non·addicting \"+\ *adj* : NONADDICTIVE *herein* ⟨~ painkillers⟩
non·addictive \"+\ *adj* : not causing addiction
non·additive \"+\ *adj* **1** : not having a numerical value equal to the sum of values for the component parts **2** : of, relating to, or being a genic effect that is not additive — **nonadditivity** \"+\ *n*
non·aligned \"+\ *adj* : not allied with other nations and esp. with either the Communist or the non-Communist blocs
non·alignment \"+\ *n* : the condition of a state or government that is nonaligned
¹**no–name** \ˈ=ˌ=\ *n* : a person (as an athlete or actor) whose name is not readily recognized by the public
²**no–name** *adj* : having a name that is not readily recognized by the public ⟨a *no-name* actor⟩ ⟨*no-name* products⟩
non–A, non–B hepatitis \ˈ=ˌā'=ˌbē-\ *n* [*A* fr. *hepatitis A* (herein), *B* fr. *hepatitis B* (herein)] : hepatitis clinically and immunologically similar to infectious hepatitis and serum hepatitis but caused by different viruses; *esp* : HEPATITIS C *herein*
non·bank \ˈ=ˌ=\ *n* : a business that is not an officially established bank but offers many similar services
non·bonding \ˈ=ˌ==\ *adj* : relating to, being, or occupying a molecular orbital that neither promotes nor inhibits bond formation between atoms ⟨a ~ electron⟩
non·book \ˈnän *sometimes* ˈnən +ˌ\ *n* : a book that has little literary merit or factual information and is often a compilation (as of pictures or press clippings)
non·candidate \"+\ *n* : one who is not a candidate; *esp* : one who has declared himself not a candidate for a particular political office — **non·candidacy** \"+\ *n*
non·carcinogenic \"+\ *adj* : not causing cancer
non·chromosomal \ˈnän *sometimes* ¦nən +\ *adj* **1** : not situated on a chromosome ⟨~ DNA⟩ **2** : not involving chromosomes ⟨~ mutations⟩
non·coding \"+\ *adj* : not specifying the genetic code ⟨a ~ DNA sequence⟩
non·com·e·do·gen·ic \"+ˌkämədō'jenik\ *adj* [¹*non-* + *comedo* + *-genic*] : not tending to clog pores (as by the formation of blackheads) ⟨a ~ cosmetic⟩
non·compete \"+\ *n* -S *often attrib* : an agreement or contract not to interfere or compete with a former employer (as by working with a competitor)
non·constant \"+\ *adj* : not constant; *esp* : having a range that includes more than one value ⟨a ~ function⟩
non·crossover \(ˈ)=+\ *adj* : having or being chromosomes that have not participated in genetic crossing-over ⟨~ offspring⟩
non·custodial \¦=+\ *adj* : of or being a parent who does not have sole custody of a child or who has custody a smaller portion of the time
non·dairy \ˈnän *sometimes* ¦nən +\ *adj* : containing no milk or milk products ⟨~ coffee lightener⟩
non·degree \"+\ *adj* : not being, leading to, or required for an academic degree ⟨~ program⟩ ⟨~ courses⟩
non·destructive \"+\ *adj* : not destructive; *specif* : not causing destruction of material being investigated or treated ⟨~ testing of metal⟩ — **non·destructively** \"+\ *adv*
non·diabetic \"+\ *adj* : not affected with diabetes — **non·diabetic** \"+\ *n*
non·diapausing \"+\ *adj* **1** : not having a diapause **2** : not being in a state of diapause
non·discrimination \"+\ *n* : the absence or avoidance of discrimination — **non·discriminatory** \"+\ *adj*
non·dividing \"+\ *adj* : not undergoing cell division
non·drinker \(ˈ)=+\ *n* : one who abstains from alcoholic beverages
non·drinking \ˈnän *sometimes* ¦nən +\ *adj* : abstaining from alcoholic beverages ⟨a ~ family⟩
non·empty \"+\ *adj* : not empty; *specif* : containing at least one element ⟨~ sets⟩
non·enzymatic \"+\ *or* **non·enzymic** \"+\ *also* **non·enzyme** \"+\ *adj* : not involving the action of enzymes ⟨~ cleavage of protein⟩ — **nonenzymatically** \"+\ *adv*
non·event \ˈ=+ˌ\ *n* **1 a** : an event that fails to take place or to satisfy expectations **b** : an often highly publicized event of little intrinsic interest or significance **2** : an occurrence that is officially ignored
nonfiction novel *n* : a book-length factual narrative written in the style of a novel
non·fluency \ˈnän *sometimes* ¦nən +\ *n* **1** : lack of fluency **2** : an instance of nonfluency — **non·fluent** \"+\ *adj*
non·gonococcal \"+\ *adj* : not caused by a gonococcus ⟨~ urethritis⟩
non·graded \"+\ *adj* : having no grade levels ⟨~ schools⟩
non·green \"+\ *adj* : not green; *specif* : containing no chlorophyll ⟨fungi and other ~ saprophytes⟩
non·hero \ˈ=+ˌ\ *n* : ANTI-HERO *herein*
non·hibernating \(ˈ)=+\ *adj* **1** : not being in hibernation **2** : not capable of hibernation ⟨a ~ strain of hamster⟩
non·histone \(ˈ)=+\ *adj* : relating to or being any of the eukaryotic proteins (as DNA polymerase) that form complexes with DNA but are not considered histones
non–hodgkin's lymphoma \¦=+. . .-\ *n, usu cap H* : any of the numerous malignant lymphomas (as Burkitt's lymphoma) that are not classified as Hodgkin's disease and that usu. have malignant cells derived from B cells or T cells
non·host \ˈ=+ˌ\ *n* : a plant that is not attacked or parasitized by a particular organism
non·identical \ˈnän *sometimes* ¦nən +\ *adj* **1** : DIFFERENT **2** : FRATERNAL 2
non·impact \"+\ *adj* : of or relating to a printing process in which the printing element does not strike the paper ⟨a ~ printer⟩
non·insecticidal \"+\ *adj* **1** : lacking an insecticidal action **2** : not involving the use of an insecticide
non–insulin–dependent diabetes \"+\ *n* : TYPE 2 DIABETES *herein*
non–insulin–dependent diabetes mellitus *n* : TYPE 2 DIABETES *herein* — abbr. *NIDDM*
non·interlaced \"+\ *adj* : not interlaced; *specif* : of, relating to, or using a method of video scanning (as for a television or computer) in which the horizontal lines of each frame are drawn consecutively in a single pass
non·invasive \"+\ *adj* **1** : not tending to spread; *specif* : not tending to infiltrate and destroy healthy tissue ⟨~ cancer of the bladder⟩ **2** : not being or involving an invasive medical procedure ⟨~ imaging techniques that do not require the injection of dyes⟩ — **non·invasively** \"+\ *adv*
non·issue \"+\ *n* : an issue of little importance, validity, or concern
non·judgmental \"+\ *adj* : avoiding judgments based on one's personal and esp. moral standards ⟨~ counseling on birth control and abortion —*N.Y. Times*⟩ — **non·judg·men·tal·ly** \-ē\ *adv*
non·minority \"+\ *adj* : of, relating to, or being a person or group that is not a minority
non·negative \"+\ *adj* **1** : being either positive or zero ⟨a ~ integer⟩ **2** : taking on nonnegative values ⟨a ~ function⟩
non·neoplastic \"+\ *adj* : not being or not caused by neoplasms ⟨~ diseases⟩
non·nuclear \"+\ *adj* **1** : not nuclear: as **a** : being a weapon whose destructive power is not derived from a nuclear reaction **b** : not operated by, using, or produced by atomic energy **c** : not using or involving nuclear weapons ⟨~ war⟩ **2** : not having nuclear weapons ⟨a ~ country⟩
no–no \ˈnōˌnō\ *n, pl* **no–no's** *or* **no–nos** **1** : something that is unacceptable or forbidden **2** : NO-HITTER
non–oil \ˈnän *sometimes* ¦nən +\ *adj* **1** : not relating to, containing, involving or being oil **2 a** : being a net importer of petroleum or petroleum products ⟨*non-oil* nations⟩ **b** : not involved in oil production
non·ox·y·nol–9 \nä'näksəˌnȯl, -ōl, nə'-\ *n* [*nonyl* + ²*oxy-* + phe*nol*] : a spermatocide used in contraceptive products that consists of a mixture of compounds having the general formula $C_{15}H_{23}(OCH_2CH_2)_nOH$ but having an average of nine ethylene oxide groups per molecule
non·performing \"+\ *adj* : not producing the expected return ⟨~ loans⟩ ⟨~ assets⟩
non·persistent \"+\ *adj* : not persistent: as **a** : decomposed rapidly by environmental action ⟨~ insecticides⟩ **b** : capable of being transmitted by a vector for only a relatively short time ⟨~ viruses⟩
non·person \ˈ=+¦\ *n* : a person who is regarded as nonexistent: as **a** : UNPERSON *herein* **b** : one having no social or legal status
non·point \ˈ=+ˈ\ *adj* : being a source of pollution (as runoff from farmland or city streets) that is not a point source; *also* : being pollution or a pollutant that does not arise from a single identifiable source
non·polluting \ˈnän *sometimes* ¦nən +\ *adj* : causing little or no pollution ⟨a freely available, ~, renewable source of energy—sunlight —Barry Commoner⟩
non·positive* *adj* **1** : being either negative or zero ⟨a ~ integer⟩ **2** : taking on nonpositive values ⟨a ~ function⟩
non·profit \"+\ *n* [*nonprofit*, adj.] : a nonprofit organization
non·proliferation \"+\ *adj* : providing for the stoppage of proliferation esp. of nuclear weapons ⟨a ~ treaty⟩ — **nonproliferation** *n*
non·psychotic \"+\ *adj* : not psychotic
non·qualified \"+\ *adj* : not meeting government requirements for special tax treatment ⟨~ stock option⟩
non·recombinant \"+\ *adj* : not exhibiting the results of genetic recombination ⟨~ progeny⟩
non·reduction \"+\ *n* : the failure of homologous chromosomes to break apart into separate sets in the reduction division of meiosis with the result that some gametes have the diploid number of chromosomes
non·relativistic \"+\ *adj* **1** : not based on or involving the theory of relativity ⟨~ equations⟩ ⟨~ kinematics⟩ **2** : of, relating to, or being a body moving at less than a relativistic velocity — **non·relativistically** \"+\ *adv*
non·renewable \"+\ *adj* : not renewable; *esp* : not naturally regenerated except over a very long period of time ⟨~ resources⟩
non·reproductive \"+\ *adj* : not reproducing; *esp* : not capable of reproducing — **nonreproductive** *n*
non·responder \"+\ *n* : one (as a person or a cell) that does not respond (as to medical treatment or to an antigen)
non·sedimentable \"+\ *adj* : not capable of being sedimented under specified conditions (as of centrifugation) ⟨~ RNA⟩
non·self \"+\ *n* : material that is foreign to the body of an organism — **nonself** \"\ *adj*
nonsense* *n* : genetic information consisting of one or more codons that do not code for any amino acids and usu. cause termination of the molecular chain in protein synthesis — compare ANTISENSE *herein*, MISSENSE *herein*
nonsense* *adj* : consisting of one or more codons that are genetic nonsense
non sequitur* *n* : a statement (as a response) that does not follow logically from or is not clearly related to anything previously said
non·sexist \ˈnän *sometimes* ¦nən +\ *adj* : not biased or discriminating against persons on the basis of sex; *esp* : not discriminating against women
nonsignificant* *adj* : having or yielding a value lying within limits between which variation is attributed to chance ⟨a ~ statistical test⟩ — **non·significantly** \¦=+\ *adv*
non·starter \"+\ *n* **1** : one that does not start **2** : someone or something that is not productive or effective ⟨his son has been, in politics a ~ —Anthony Lejeune⟩
non·steroidal *also* **non·steroid** \ˈnän *sometimes* ¦nən +\ *adj* : of, relating to, or being a compound and esp. a drug that is not a steroid — see NSAID *herein* — **nonsteroid** *n*
non·stick \"+\ *adj* : allowing of easy removal of cooked food particles ⟨a ~ coating on a frying pan⟩
nonstop \ˈ=ˌ=\ *n* [*nonstop*, adj.] : a nonstop airplane flight
non·system \(ˈ)=+\ *n* : a system that lacks effective organization
non·target \ˈnän *sometimes* ¦nən +\ *adj* : not being the intended object of action by a particular agent
non·terminating \"+\ *adj* : not terminating or ending; *esp* : being a decimal for which there is no place to the right of the decimal point such that all places farther to the right contain 0
non·thermal \"+\ *adj* : not produced by heat ⟨~ radiation⟩; *specif* : of, relating to, or being radiation having a spectrum that does not obey the Planck radiation law ⟨~ emission⟩
non·title \"+\ *adj* : of, relating to, or being an athletic contest in which a title is not at stake
non·trivial \"+\ *adj* **1** : not trivial **2** : having the value of at least one variable or term not equal to zero
non–U \"+\ *adj* [¹*non-* + *U* (herein)] : not belonging to or characteristic of the upper classes ⟨a *non-U* word⟩
non·vanishing \"+\ *adj* : not zero or becoming zero
non·vector \(ˈ)=+\ *n* [¹*non-* + *vector*] : an organism (as an insect) that does not transmit a particular pathogen (as a virus)
non·vocoid \"+\ *n* [¹*non-* + *vocoid*] : CONTOID *herein*
nonvolatile* *adj, of a computer memory* : retaining data when power is shut off
non·voter \"+\ *n* : one that does not vote
¹**noodge** \ˈnůj\ *vt* -ED/-ING/-S [Yiddish *nudyen* to bore, fr. Pol *nudzić*; akin to Pol *nuda* boredom, OSlave *nouditi* to press hard, constrain, *nužda* need — more at NUDNICK] : PESTER, NAG ⟨whose socially ambitious daughter ~*s* him to seek admission to the exclusive Bushwood Country Club —Glenn Collins⟩
²**noodge** *var of* NUDGE *herein*
noog·ie \ˈnůgē\ *n* -S [origin unknown] : the act or an instance of rubbing one's knuckles on a person's head to produce a mildly painful sensation
noo·sphere \ˈnōə+ˌ\ *n* [ISV *noo-* + *sphere*; prob. orig. formed as Russian *noosfera*] : the sphere of human consciousness and mental activity esp. in regard to its influence on the biosphere and in relation to evolution
no·o·tro·pic \ˌnōə'trōpik, -'träp-\ *n* -S [ISV *noo-* + *-tropic*; orig. formed as F *nootrope*] : a substance that enhances cognition and memory and facilitates learning — **nootropic** *adj*
no·pal* \ˈnōpəl; nō'päl, -'pal\ *n, pl* **no·pal·es** \nō'päläs, -'pal-\ : a fleshy young tender stem segment of the prickly pear cactus (genus *Opuntia* and esp. *O. ficus-indica*) or the nopal cactus (genus *Nopalea*) that is used as food
no·pa·li·to \nōpə'lētō\ *n* -S [Amer Sp, dim. of *nopal* nopal] : NOPAL *herein*
NOR \ˈnȯ(ə)r\ *n* [*not OR* (herein)] : a computer logic circuit that produces an output that is the inverse of that of an OR circuit
nor·adrenergic \¦nȯ(ə)r+\ *adj* [*noradren*aline + *-ergic* (herein)] : liberating, activated by, or involving norepinephrine in the transmission of nerve impulses ⟨~ synapses⟩ — compare ADRENERGIC *in the Dict*, CHOLINERGIC *in the Dict*
nordic* *adj, usu cap* : of, relating to, or being competitive ski events consisting of ski jumping and cross-country racing — compare ALPINE *herein*
nor·eth·in·drone \nȯr'ethənˌdrōn, ˌnȯreth'in-\ *n* -S [*nor-* + *ethinyl* + *hydr-* + *-one* (as in *progesterone*)] : a synthetic progestational hormone $C_{20}H_{26}O_2$ used in oral contraceptives often in the form of its acetate
nor·ethisterone \¦nȯ(ə)r+\ *n* [*nor-* + *ethisterone*] *chiefly Brit* : NORETHINDRONE *herein*
nor·ethyn·o·drel \ˌnȯrə'thīnōˌdrel,-'thin-, -'ethən-\ *n* -S [*nor-* + *ethynyl* + *-odr-* (perh. alter. of *hydro-*) + *-el* (of unknown origin)] : a progesterone derivative $C_{20}H_{26}O_2$ used in oral contraceptives and clinically in the treatment of abnormal uterine bleeding and the control of menstruation
nor·ges·trel \nȯr'jes·trəl\ *n* -S [prob. fr. *nor-* + *progest*ogen (herein) + *-rel* (as in *norethynodrel* — herein)] : a synthetic progestogen $C_{21}H_{28}O_2$ having two optically active forms of which the biologically active levorotatory form is used in birth control pills
norm* *n* **1** : a real-valued nonnegative function defined on a vector space and satisfying the conditions that the function is zero if and only if the vector is zero, the function of the product of a scalar and a vector is equal to the product of the absolute value of the scalar and the function of the vector, and that the function of the sum of two vectors is less than or equal to the sum of the functions of the two vectors; *specif* : the square root of the sum of the squares of the absolute values of the elements of a matrix or of the components of a vector **2** : the greatest distance between two successive points of a set of points that partition an interval into smaller intervals **3** : a widespread or usual practice, procedure, or custom
normal* *adj* **1** *of a subgroup* : having the property that every coset produced by operating on the left with a given element is equal to the coset produced by operating on the right with the same element **2** : relating to, involving, or being a normal curve or normal distribution ⟨~ approximation to the binomial distribution⟩ **3** *of a matrix* : having the property of commutativity under multiplication by the transpose of a matrix each of whose elements is a conjugate complex number with respect to the corresponding element of the given matrix
normal divisor *n* : a normal subgroup
normalize* *vt* **1** : to make mathematically or statistically normal **2** : to bring or restore (as relations between countries) to a normal condition — **nor·mal·iz·able** \-ˌlī-zə-bəl\ *adj*
normalizer* *n* **1** : a subgroup consisting of those elements of a group for which the group operation with regard to a given element is commutative **2** : the set of elements of a group for which the group operation with regard to every element of a given subgroup is commutative
normal orthogonal *adj* : ORTHONORMAL *herein*
normed \ˈnȯ(ə)rmd\ *adj* [*norm* (herein) + ¹*-ed*] : being a mathematical entity upon which a norm is defined ⟨a ~ vector space⟩
nor·mo·ther·mia \ˌnȯrmə'thərmēə\ *n* -S [NL, fr. *norm-* + *-thermia*] : normal body temperature — **nor·mo·ther·mic** \¦==¦=mik\ *adj*
nor·te·ño \nȯr'tānyō\ *n* -S [MexSp (prob. short for *conjunto norteño*, lit., northern ensemble) fr. Sp, northern, fr. *norte* north — more at NORTE] : popular music from northern Mexico with a fast tempo and usu. featuring an accordion
north* *n, usu cap* : the industrialized and economically developed nations of the world — compare SOUTH *herein*
northern blot *n, usu cap N* [after *Southern blot* (herein)] : a blot consisting of a sheet of cellulose nitrate or nylon that contains spots of RNA for identification by a suitable molecular probe — compare SOUTHERN BLOT *herein*, WESTERN BLOT *herein* — **northern blotting** *n, usu cap N*
northern corn rootworm *n* : a corn rootworm of the genus *Diabrotica* (*D. longicornis*) often destructive to maize in the northern parts of the central and eastern U.S.
northern oriole *n* : an American oriole (*Icterus galbula*) that is characterized by the black and orange plumage of the male and that includes the Baltimore oriole (*Icterus galbula galbula*) of the eastern U.S. and Bullock's oriole (*Icterus galbula bullockii*) of the western U.S. when they are considered subspecies rather than separate species
northern spotted owl *n* : a rare spotted owl (*Strix occidentalis caurina*) of old forests on the Pacific coast of No. America from northern California to southern British Columbia
nor·trip·ty·line \nȯr'triptəˌlēn\ *n* -S [*nor-* + *-tript-* (perh. fr. *tricyclic* + *heptene*) + *-yl* + ²*-ine*] : a tricyclic antidepressant $C_{19}H_{21}N$ used in the form of its hydrochloride
noseguard \ˈ=ˌ=\ *n* [so called because he plays nose-to-nose against the offensive center] : a defensive lineman in football who plays opposite the offensive center
nose job *n* : RHINOPLASTY
nose–ride \ˈ=ˌ=\ *vi* : to ride or perform stunts on the nose of a surfboard — **nose–rider** \ˈ=ˌ==\ *n*
nose tackle *n* : a noseguard esp. in a 3-man defensive line
¹**nosh** \ˈnäsh\ *vb* -ED/-ING/-ES [Yiddish *nashn*, fr. MHG *naschen* to nibble, fr. OHG *nascōn* — more at NESH] *vi* : to eat a snack ~ *vt* : CHEW, MUNCH — **nosh·er** \-shə(r)\ *n* -S
²**nosh** \"\ *n* -ES **1** : a light snack **2** *chiefly Brit* **a** : MEAL **b** : FOOD
no–show* *n* **1** : a person who buys a ticket (as to a sporting event) but does not attend; *broadly* : a person who is expected but does not show up **2** : failure to show up ⟨was fired . . . for too many *no-shows* —Mary Vespa⟩
no–show \¦=¦=\ *adj* : of, relating to, or being a job (as one obtained through political patronage) for which the incumbent is paid although performing few duties or rarely being present for work
nosh–up \ˈ=ˌ=\ *n* -S [²*nosh* (herein) + *-up* (prob. as in *fry-up* — herein)] *chiefly Brit* : a meal and esp. a large or elaborate meal
nos·tal·gist \nə'staljəst, nä'-\ *n* -S [*nostalgia* + *-ist*] : a person fond of the objects and style of the past
nos·trat·ic \nō'strad·ik, nä-, nə-, -atik\ *n* -S *cap* [modif. of Dan *nostratisk*, fr. L *nostrat-, nostras* native, of our people (fr. *noster* our) + Dan *-isk* -ish — more at NOSTRUM] : a hypothesized family of languages ancestral to several of the established language families of Eurasia and northern Africa and including in some classifications the Indo-European, Uralic, Altaic, Kartvelian, Dravidian, and Afro-Asiatic languages
NOT \ˈnät\ *n* [*not*] : a logical operator that produces a statement that is the inverse of an input statement
notchback \ˈ=ˌ=\ *n* [¹*notch* + ¹*back*] **1** : a back on a closed passenger automobile having a distinct deck — compare FASTBACK *herein* **2** : an automobile having a notchback
notebook* *n* : a portable microcomputer similar to but usu. smaller and lighter than a laptop that is about the size of an ordinary loose-leaf binder
not–for–profit \¦=¦=¦==\ *adj* : NONPROFIT ⟨a *not-for-profit* organization⟩
not·geld \ˈnōtˌgeld, ˈnät-, *G* ˈnōtˌgelt\ *n* -S [G, fr. *not* necessity (fr. OHG *nōt*) + *geld* money (fr. OHG *gelt* income, value) — more at NEED, GELD] : necessity money used in Germany and some eastern European states esp. after World War I
no–till \(ˈ)nō'til\ *n* : NO-TILLAGE *herein*
no–till·age \-ˈəj, -ēj\ *n* : a system of farming that consists of planting a narrow slit trench without tillage and with the use of herbicides to suppress weeds
noun phrase *n, sometimes cap N&P* : a syntactic element (as a word, phrase, or clause) that can be used for a nominal function (as the subject or object of a verb or object of a preposition)
nou·velle \nü'vel\ *adj* [F, fem. of *nouveau* new, fr. MF *novel* — more at NOVEL] **1** : of or relating to nouvelle cuisine **2** : TRENDY *herein*, NOVEL ⟨what's terribly ~ today can be totally passé tomorrow —Robert Masello⟩
nouvelle cuisine *n* [F, lit., new cooking] : a form of French cuisine that uses little flour or fat and stresses light sauces and the use of fresh seasonal produce; *also* : a national or regional cuisine that stresses lightness and freshness in preparation ⟨Mexican *nouvelle cuisine*⟩
nou·velle vague \(ˌ)nüˌvel'väg, -ˈäg\ *n* [F, lit., new wave] : NEW WAVE 1, 2 *herein*

now account \ˈnau̇-\ *n, usu cap N&O&W* [negotiable order of withdrawal] : a savings account on which checks may be drawn
no way** \ˈ=ˈ=\ *adv* — used interjectionally to express emphatic negation
no–win \ˈ=ˈ=\ *adj* : not likely to give victory, success, or satisfaction : that cannot be won ⟨a *no-win* situation⟩ ⟨a *no-win* war⟩
ns *abbr* nanosecond *herein*
NSAID \ˈen,sed *also* -,säd\ *n* [*n*onsteroidal *a*nti-*i*nflammatory *d*rug] : a nonsteroidal anti-inflammatory drug (as ibuprofen)
nsec *abbr* nanosecond *herein*
NTA \ˌen(ˌ)tēˈā\ *abbr or n* -s [*n*itrilo*t*riacetic *a*cid] : a compound $N(CH_2COOH)_3$ used in the form of its sodium salt as a phosphate substitute in detergents
n–type \ˈen‚=\ *adj* [*n*egative + *type*] : relating to or being a semiconductor in which charge is carried by electrons — compare P-TYPE *herein*
nu·buck \ˈn(y)ü,bək\ *n* -s *often attrib* [perh. fr. *nu-* (alter. of [1]*new* + [2]*buck*] : a soft sueded leather
nuclear force *n* : STRONG FORCE *herein*
nuclear·ism \ˈ===,izəm\ *n* -s : dependence on or faith in nuclear weapons as the means for maintaining national security
nuclear magnetic resonance *n* **1** : the magnetic resonance of an atomic nucleus — see MAGNETIC RESONANCE IMAGING *herein* **2** : chemical analysis that uses nuclear magnetic resonance esp. to study molecular structure — abbr. *NMR*
nuclear medicine *n* : a branch of medicine dealing with the use of radioactive materials in the diagnosis and treatment of disease
nuclear resonance *n* **1** : the resonance absorption of a gamma ray by a nucleus identical to the nucleus that emitted the gamma ray — compare MÖSSBAUER EFFECT *herein* **2** : RESONANCE 1a *herein*
nuclear winter *n* : the chilling of climate that is hypothesized to be a consequence of nuclear war and to result from the prolonged blockage of sunlight by high-altitude dust clouds produced by nuclear explosions
nu·cleo·capsid \ˌn(y)üklēō+\ *n* [*nucle-* + *capsid* (herein)] : the nucleic acid and surrounding protein coat of a virus
nu·cleo·genesis \"+\ *n* [NL, fr. *nucle-* + *genesis*] : NUCLEOSYNTHESIS *herein*
nu·cle·o·lo·ne·ma \n(y)ü,klēələˈnēmə\ *also* **nu·cle·o·lo·neme** \-ˈklēələ,nēm\ *n* -s [*nucleolonema* fr. NL, fr. *nucleol-* + *-nema*; *nucleoloneme* fr. *nucleol-* + *-neme*] : a filamentous network consisting of small granules in some nucleoli
nucleon* *n* : a hypothetical single entity with one-half unit of isospin capable of manifesting itself as either a proton or a neutron and of making transitions between these two states
nu·cleo·phile \ˈn(y)üklēō,fīl\ *n* -s [*nucle-* + [1]*-phil*] : a nucleophilic substance (as an electron-donating reagent)
nu·cleo·some \ˈ===,sōm\ *n* -s [ISV *nucle-* + *-some*] : any of the repeating globular subunits of chromatin that consist of a complex of DNA and histone and are thought to be present only during interphase — **nu·cleo·so·mal** \ˌ===ˈsōməl\ *adj*
nu·cleo·synthesis \ˌn(y)üklēō+\ *n* [NL, fr. *nucle-* + *synthesis*] : the production of a chemical element from simpler nuclei (as of hydrogen) esp. in a star — **nu·cleo·synthetic** \"+\ *adj*
nu·cleo·ti·dyl·transferase \ˌn(y)üklēə,tīdˈl+\ *n* [*nucleotide* + *-yl* + *transferase*] : any of several enzymes that catalyze the transfer of a nucleotide residue from one compound to another
nude mouse *n* : a mouse of a hairless strain bred for laboratory use that lacks a thymus and mature T cells and is used esp. in immunological research
nudge *or* **noodge** *also* **nudzh** \ˈnüj\ *n, pl* **nudges** *or* **noodges** *also* **nudzhes** [*noodge*, v. (herein)] : a tedious or excessively persistent person : NAG
[1]**nud·ie** \ˈn(y)üdē\ *n* -s [[1]*nude* + *-ie*] **1** : SKIN FLICK *herein* **2** : a publication that features photographs of nudes
[2]**nudie** \"\ *adj* : featuring nudes ⟨~ films⟩ ⟨~ magazines⟩
[1]**nuke** \ˈn(y)ük\ *n* -s [shortening & alter. of *nuclear*] **1** : a nuclear weapon **2** : a nuclear-powered electric generating station
[2]**nuke** \"\ *vt* -ED/-ING/-S **1** : to attack or destroy with nuclear weapons; *broadly* : DESTROY, DEVASTATE **2** : MICROWAVE *herein*
null* *adj* **1** : having zero as a limit ⟨~ sequence⟩ **2** *of a matrix* : having all elements equal to zero
nullity* *n* : the number of elements in a basis of a null-space
null–space \ˈ=,=\ *n* : a subspace of a vector space consisting of vectors that under a given linear transformation are mapped to zero
number* *n* **1 a** : ROUTINE, ACT **b** : STUNT, TRICK **c** : an act of transforming or impairing ⟨tripped and did a ~ on her knee⟩ **2** *pl* **a** : figures representing amounts of money usu. in dollars spent, earned, or involved **b (1)** : STATISTICS 2; *esp* : individual statistics (as of an athlete) **(2)** : RATING 3
number cruncher \-ˈkrənchə(r)\ *n* **1** : a computer or peripheral designed to perform fast numerical calculations on large amounts of data **2** : a person concerned with the generation, manipulation, or analysis of numerical data
number crunching *n* : the performance of long complex often repetitive mathematical calculations; *also* : statistical analysis — **number crunch** *vb*
number line *n* : a line of infinite extent whose points correspond to the real numbers according to their distance in a positive or negative direction from a point arbitrarily taken as zero
nu·mer·a·cy \ˈn(y)ümərəsē\ *n* -ES [L *numerus* number + *-acy* (as in *literacy*) — more at NIMBLE] : the capacity for quantitative thought and expression — **nu·mer·ate** \-rət\ *adj*
nu·mer·ic \n(y)üˈmerik\ *n* -s [*numeric*, adj.] : NUMBER, NUMERAL
numerical analysis *n* : the study of quantitative approximations to the solutions of mathematical problems including consideration of the errors and bounds to the errors involved
numerical control *n* : automatic control (as of a machine tool) by a digital computer — **numerically controlled** *adj*
numerical taxonomy *n* : taxonomy in which many quantitatively measured characters are given equal weight in the determination of taxa and in the construction of diagrams indicating systematic relationships — **numerical taxonomic** *adj* — **numerical taxonomist** *n*
nu·me·ro uno \ˌn(y)ümə(ˌ)rōˈü(ˌ)nō\ *n or adj* [It or Sp] : NUMBER ONE
nun·cha·ku \ˌnən,chək, nünˈchäk(ˌ)ü\ *n* **nunchakus** *or* **nunchaku** [Jap dial. (Okinawa)] : a weapon of Japanese origin made of two hardwood sticks joined at one end by a short length of rawhide, cord, or chain
nuoc mam \nüˈäkˈmäm, nw-ˈ, -ˈòk-\ *n* [Vietnamese *nu'ó'c mắm*, lit., salted fish sauce] : a sauce made of fish (as anchovies) fermented in brine
nurd *var of* NERD *herein*
nur·i·stani \ˌn(y)ürəˈstänē\ *n* -s *usu cap* [Pers *nūristānī*, fr. *Nūristān*, region of northeastern Afghanistan] **1** : KAFIRI **2** : KAFIR
nurse practitioner *n* : a registered nurse who through advanced training is qualified to assume some of the duties and responsibilities formerly assumed only by a physician
nur·tur·ance \ˈnərchərən(t)s\ *n* -s [[2]*nurture* + *-ance*] : affectionate care and attention — **nur·tur·ant** \-rənt\ *adj*
nut* *n* **1** : a large sum of money **2** *slang* : a bribe given to a policeman
nut case *n* : a foolish, eccentric, or crazy person
nu·tra·ceu·ti·cal *also* **nu·tri·ceu·ti·cal** \ˌn(y)ü·trəˈsüd·əkəl\ *n* -s [*nutraceutical* fr. *nutrition* + [2]*pharmaceutical*; *nutriceutical* fr. *nutrition* + [2]*pharmaceutical*] : a foodstuff (as a fortified food or a dietary supplement) that is held to provide health or medical benefits (as the prevention or cure of disease) in addition to its basic nutritional value ⟨plain bread supplemented with calcium, vitamin D, folate, dietary fiber and a shot of Saint John's wort or whatever becomes a ~ —William Safire⟩
nuts–and–bolts \ˌ=ˈ=ˈ=\ *adj* : of, relating to, or dealing with specific practical details ⟨*nuts-and-bolts* aspects of the job⟩
nuts and bolts *n pl* **1** : the working parts or elements **2** : the practical workings of a machine or enterprise as opposed to theoretical considerations or speculative possibilities
nu·yo·ri·can \ˌnüyòrˈrēkən\ *n* -s *cap* [modif. of AmerSp *nuyorriqueño*, blend of Sp *nuyorquino* New Yorker, and *puertorriqueño* Puerto Rican] : NEORICAN *herein* — **nuyorican** *adj, usu cap*
ny·norsk \ˈn(y)üˈnü(ə)rsk, ˈnüē-\ *n* -s *usu cap* [Norw, lit., new Norwegian, fr. *ny* new (fr. ON *nȳr*) + *norsk* Norwegian — more at NEW, NORSKI] : LANDSMÅL
oaky* *adj* : having the characteristics of being aged in oak casks ⟨an ~ Chardonnay⟩ ⟨an ~ bouquet⟩
oat cell *n* : any of the small round or oval cells with a high ratio of nuclear protoplasm to cytoplasm that resemble oat grains and are characteristic of small-cell lung cancer
ob–gyn \ˌō(ˌ)bēˈjin, -(ˌ)jē(ˌ)wīˈen\ *n* -s [*ob*stetrician + *gyn*ecologist] : a physician who specializes in obstetrics and gynecology
obie \ˈōbē\ *n* -s *usu cap* [*O.B.*, abbr. for *off Broadway* (herein)] : any of several prizes awarded annually by a newspaper for excellence in off-Broadway theater
object* *n* **1** : a set of data, variables, and functions that is created, stored, and manipulated as a discrete basic unit in computer programming **2** : an entity (as an icon or window) esp. as shown on a computer screen that can be manipulated independently of other such entities
ob·ject \ˈäbjikt, -jekt\ *adj* [*object*, n.] : of, relating to, or being object code ⟨run an ~ file⟩
object code *n* : computer code that has been translated from its original programming language into machine language — compare SOURCE CODE *herein*
object language* *n* : TARGET LANGUAGE 1 *herein*
object–oriented \ˌ=(ˌ)=ˈ===\ *adj* : relating to, used in, or implemented by object-oriented programming ⟨an *object-oriented* language⟩ ⟨*object-oriented* databases⟩
object–oriented programming *n* a type of computer programming that uses programming objects as basic building blocks and that allows the creation of new objects which derive characteristics from existing objects
ob·jet trou·vé \ˌòb,zhä(ˌ)trüˈvā\ *n, pl* **objets trouvés** *same*\ [F, lit., found object] : FOUND OBJECT *herein*
obscene* *adj* : so excessive as to be offensive ⟨~ wealth⟩ ⟨~ waste⟩
obsess* *vb* ~ *vi* : to engage in obsessive thinking : become obsessed with an idea ⟨they'll spend hours . . . ~*ing* about how awful we were —Marie Winn⟩
obverse* *n* : a counterpart having the opposite orientation or force ⟨their rise was merely the ~ of the Empire's fall —A.J.Toynbee⟩; *also* : OPPOSITE 3 ⟨joy and its ~, sorrow⟩
oc·ci·tan \ˈäksə,tan\ *n* -s *cap* [F, fr. ML *occitanus*, fr. OProv *oc* yes (contrasted with OF *oïl* yes) + ML *-itanus* (perh. as in *aquitanus* of Aquitaine)] : a Romance language spoken in southern France — compare PROVENÇALE 2 *in the Dict* — **occitan** *adj, usu cap*
OCD *abbr* obsessive-compulsive disorder
ocea·naut \ˈōshə,nòt, -nät\ *n* -s [blend of *ocean* and *-naut* (as in *aquanaut* — herein)] : AQUANAUT *herein*
ocean engineering *n* : engineering that deals with the application of design, construction, and maintenance principles and techniques to the ocean environment
och·ra·toxin \ˌōkrə+\ *n* [*ochra-* (fr. NL *ochraceus* ochraceous, (specific epithet of *Aspergillis ochraceus*) + *toxin*] : a mycotoxin produced by a fungus of the genus *Aspergillus* (*A. ochraceus*)
oci·cat \ˈäsē,kat\ *n* -s *often cap* [blend of *ocelot* and [1]*cat*] : any of a breed of domestic cats that was developed by crossing Siamese, American shorthairs, and Abyssinian cats and that has a short spotted coat with hairs having several bands of color
OCR *abbr* optical character reader; optical character recognition
oc·ta·peptide \ˌäktə+\ *n* [*octa-* + *peptide*] : a protein fragment or molecule (as oxytocin or vasopressin) that consists of eight amino acids linked in a polypeptide chain
oc·to·pamine \äkˈtōpə,mēn, -,mən\ *n* [*octopus* + *amine*; fr. its identification in the salivary glands of an octopus] : an adrenergic biogenic amine $C_8H_{11}NO_2$ acts as a neurotransmitter in invertebrates
oc·to·thorpe *or* **oc·to·thorp** \ˈäktə,thòrp, -tō-\ *n* -s [*octa-* + *-thorp*, of unknown origin; fr. the eight points on its circumference] : the symbol # — called also *number sign, pound sign*
oc·u·lar·ist \ˈäkyələrəst\ *n* -s [[2]*ocular* + *-ist*] : a person who makes and fits artificial eyes
[1]**OD** \ˈōˈdē\ *n* -s [*o*ver*d*ose] **1** : an overdose of a narcotic **2** : one who has taken an overdose of a narcotic
[2]**OD** \"\ *vi* **OD'd** *or* **ODed**; **OD'd** *or* **ODed**; **OD'ing**; **OD's** **1** : to become ill or die from an OD **2** : to have or experience too much of something — *used with on* ⟨OD on television⟩
odd–lot·ter \ˈädˈläd·ə(r)\ *n* -s [*odd lot* + [2]*-er*] : a speculator or an investor who habitually buys and sells stock in less than round lots
odd permutation *n* : a permutation that is produced by the successive application of an odd number of interchanges of pairs of elements — compare EVEN PERMUTATION *herein*
oddsmaker \ˈ=,==\ *n* : one who figures betting odds
odont·o·log·i·cal \(ˌ)ō,däntˀlˈäjəkəl\ *adj* : of or relating to odontology
oem \ˌōˌēˈem\ *n* -s *usu all cap* [*o*riginal *e*quipment *m*anufacturer] : one that produces complex equipment (as a computer system) from components usu. bought from other manufacturers
off* *vt, slang* : KILL, MURDER ⟨wouldn't think no more of ~*ing* a cop than stepping on a roach —Robby Wideman⟩
off broadway *n, often cap O & usu cap B* [so called fr. its usu. being produced in smaller theaters outside of the Broadway theatrical district] : a part of the New York professional theater stressing fundamental and artistic values and formerly engaging in experimentation — **off–broadway** \ˌ=ˈ==\ *adj (or adv), often cap O & usu cap B*
off–camera \ˌ=ˈ=(=)=\ *adv (or adj)* **1** : out of the range of a motion-picture or television camera ⟨chided me *off-camera* during a commercial break —W.H.Manville⟩ **2** : in private life
offering price* *n* : the price at which an open-end mutual fund is sold consisting of its asset value usu. plus a specified load
of·fi·ci·a·lis \ə,fishēˈāləs, -ˈal-\ *n, pl* **of·fi·ci·a·les** \-ˈā(ˌ)lās, -ˈa(ˌ)lēz\ [NL, fr. ML, official — more at OFFICIAL] : the presiding judge of the matrimonial court of a Roman Catholic diocese
off–kilter \ˈ=ˈ==\ *adj* **1** : not in perfect balance : ASKEW ⟨an *off-kilter* smile⟩ **2** : ECCENTRIC, UNCONVENTIONAL ⟨*off-kilter* characters⟩
off–label \ˌ=ˈ==\ *adj* : of, relating to, or being a drug used to treat a condition for which it has not been officially approved
off–limits** \ˈ=ˈ==\ *adj* : not to be interfered with, considered, or spoken of ⟨the subject of sex was *off-limits* in her family⟩
off–line* \ˈ=ˈ=\ *adj (or adv)* : not connected to or served by a system and esp. a computer or telecommunications system; *also* : done independently of a system ⟨*off-line* computer storage⟩
off–off–broadway \ˌ(ˈ)=ˈ=ˈ==\ *n, often cap both Os & usu cap B* [so called fr. its relation to off-Broadway being analogous to the relation of off-Broadway to Broadway] : an avant-garde theatrical movement in New York that stresses untraditional techniques and radical experimentation — **off–off–broadway** *adj (or adv), often cap both Os & usu cap B*
off–price \ˈ=ˈ=\ *adj* : of, relating to, selling, or being discounted merchandise ⟨an *off-price* store⟩ ⟨*off-price* apparel⟩
off–putting \ˈ=ˈ==\ *adj* : that puts one off : REPELLENT, DISAGREEABLE ⟨anything new is always *off-putting* and upsetting —Dwight Macdonald⟩ — **off–put·ting·ly** \ˈ=,==lē, -li\ *adv*
off–ramp \ˈ=,=\ *n* : a ramp by which one leaves a limited-access highway
off–road \ˈ=ˈ=\ *adj* : of, relating to, being, or done with a vehicle designed esp. to operate away from public roads
offshore fund *n* : an investment fund based outside the U.S., not subject to registration with the Security and Exchange Commission, and barred by law from selling its shares within the U.S.
off–site *adj (or adv)* : not located or occurring at the site of a particular activity
off–speed \ˈ=ˈ=\ *adj* : being slower than usual or expected ⟨throwing *off-speed* pitches⟩
off–the–books \ˌ==ˈ=\ *adj* [[1]*book* (record of business transactions)] : not reported or recorded ⟨*off-the-books* transactions⟩ ⟨*off-the-books* covert operations⟩
off–the–peg \ˌ==ˈ=\ *adj, chiefly Brit* : READY-MADE ⟨*off-the-peg* clothes —*The People*⟩
off–the–rack \ˌ==ˈ=\ *adj* : READY-MADE ⟨*off-the-rack* suits⟩
off–the–shelf \ˌ=ˈ=ˈ=\ *adj* : available as a stock item : not specially designed or custom-made
off–the–wall \ˌ=ˈ=ˈ=\ *adj* : highly unusual : BIZARRE ⟨an *off-the-wall* sense of humor⟩
offtrack \ˈ=ˈ=\ *adj (or adv)* : situated or occurring away from a racetrack ⟨~ bookies⟩; *esp* : related to or being pari-mutuel betting that is carried on away from the racetrack
-oholic *n comb form* -s : -AHOLIC *herein*
oil patch *n* **1** : OIL FIELD **2** : the petroleum industry
OJT *abbr* on-the-job training
ok·to·ber·fest \äkˈtōbə(r),fest\ *n* -s *usu cap* [G, fr. *Oktober* October + *fest* festival — more at -FEST] : a fall festival usu. featuring beer drinking
old* *adj* : TIRESOME ⟨doing it the same way all the time will get ~ —Laurie Sue Brockway⟩
old boy* *n* : a man who is a member of a long-standing and usu. influential clique esp. in a professional, business, or social sphere
old lady* *n* : GIRL FRIEND; *esp* : one with whom a man cohabits
old man* *n* : BOYFRIEND; *esp* : one with whom a woman cohabits
old–money \ˈ=ˈ==\ *adj* : possessing wealth that has been inherited through several generations
ole·an·do·my·cin \ˌōlē,andəˈmīsˀn\ *n* -s [*oleandr*ose a sugar derived from oleandrin (fr. *oleandrin* + [2]*-ose*) + *-o-* + *-mycin*] : an antibiotic $C_{35}H_{61}NO_{12}$ produced by a bacterium of the genus *Streptomyces* (*S. antibioticus*)
oles·tra \ōˈlestrə\ *n* -s [prob. by shortening & alter. fr. (*sucrose*) *polyester*] : a noncaloric fat substitute consisting of a series of compounds that are sucrose esters of six to eight fatty acids resistant to absorption by the digestive system because of their large size
o level *n, usu cap O* **1** : the lowest of three levels of standardized British examinations of achievement in a secondary school subject; *also* : the successful completion of an O-level examination in a particular subject — called also *Ordinary level*; compare A LEVEL *herein*, S LEVEL *herein* **2 a** : the level of education required to pass an O-level examination **b** : a course leading to an O-level examination
ol·i·gid·ic \ˌäləˈgidik, ˌōl-, -ˈji-\ *adj* [*olig-* + *-idic* (as in *meridic* — herein)] : having the active constituents with the exception of water undefined chemically ⟨~ growth medium⟩ — compare HOLIDIC *herein*, MERIDIC *herein*
oligo·mer \ōˈligəmə(r), əˈl-\ *n* -s [*olig-* + *-mer*] : a polymer or polymer intermediate that contains relatively few structural units — **oligo·mer·ic** \ˌ=ˌ=ˈmerik, ˌäləgō‚m-, -mir-\ *adj* — **oligo·mer·iza·tion** \=,==,merəˈzāshən, -mir-\ *n* -s
ol·i·go·my·cin \ˌäligōˈmīsˀn, ˌōli-\ *n* -s [*olig-* + *-mycin*] : any of several antibiotic substances produced by a streptomyces (of a species similar to *Streptomyces diastatochromogenes*) and used esp. in biochemical research to inhibit oxidative phosphorylation
ol·i·go·nucleotide \ˌäləgō, əˌligə+\ *n* [*olig-* + *nucleotide*] : a chain of up to 20 nucleotides
olin·go \ōˈliŋ,gō\ *n* -s [origin unknown] : any of a genus (*Bassaricyon*) of slender-bodied carnivores of Central and So. America with long nonprehensile tails that are related to the raccoon
olive ridley *or* **olive ridley sea turtle** *or* **olive ridley turtle** *n* [*ridley*, of unknown origin] : a relatively small sea turtle (*Lepidochelys olivacea*) of the family Cheloniidae that has a uniformly olive-colored carapace and is found along coasts and in the open sea of the tropical parts of the Pacific, Indian and Atlantic oceans
om·buds·man \ˈäm,bu̇dzmən, ˈòm-, -(ˌ)bəd-, ämˈb-, òmˈb-, -,man\ *n, pl* **ombuds·men** \-mən, -,men\ [Sw, lit., representative, commissioner, fr. ON *umbothsmathr*, fr. *umboth* commission (fr. *um* around + *bjōtha* to command) + *mathr* man — more at EMBER DAY, BID, MAN] **1** : a government official (as in Sweden or New Zealand) appointed to receive and investigate complaints made by individuals against abuses or capricious acts of public officials **2** : one that investigates complaints (as from students or customers), reports findings, and helps to achieve equitable settlements — **om·buds·man·ship** \-,mən,ship\ *n*
om·buds·woman \-z,wu̇mən\ *n, pl* **om·buds·women** \-z,wimən\ [*ombuds-* (as in *ombudsman*) + *woman*] : a female ombudsman
omega* *n* **1** *or* **omega minus** *or* **omega particle** : a negatively charged elementary particle that has a mass 3272 times the mass of an electron and that is an unstable baryon with an average lifetime of about 10^{-10} second **2** *or* **omega meson** : a very short-lived unstable meson with mass 1532 times the mass of an electron
omega–3 \ˌ=ˈ==ˈthrē\ *adj* : being or composed of polyunsaturated fatty acids that have the final double bond in the hydrocarbon chain between the third and fourth carbon atoms from the end of the molecule opposite that of the carboxylic acid group and that are found esp. in fish, fish oils, vegetable oils, and green leafy vegetables — **omega–3** \"\ *n* -s
om·ni·cide \ˈämnə,sīd\ *n* [*omn-* + *-cide*] : the destruction of all life esp. by nuclear war
om·ni·focal \ˌämnə, -nē+\ *adj* [*omn-* + *focal*] : of, relating to, or being a bifocal eyeglass that is so ground as to permit smooth transition from one correction to the other
on–air \ˈ=ˈ=\ *adj* [fr. the phrase *on (the) air*] : appearing, used, or done on a radio or television broadcast
onboard \ˈ=ˈ=\ *adj* [fr. the phrase *on board*] : carried within or occurring aboard a vehicle (as a satellite or an automobile) ⟨an ~ computer⟩; *also* : BUILT-IN
on–camera \ˈ=ˈ=(=)=\ *adv (or adj)* : within the range of a motion-picture or television camera ⟨read their lines *on-camera*⟩
on·co·gene \ˈäŋkō,jēn\ *n* [[1]*onco-* + *gene*] : a gene having the potential to cause a normal cell to become cancerous
on·co·genesis \ˌäŋkō+\ *n* [NL, fr. [1]*onco-* + *genesis*] : the induction or formation of tumors
on·co·ge·nic·i·ty \ˌäŋkōjəˈnisəd·ē\ *n* -ES [[1]*onco-* + *-genic* + *-ity*] : the capacity to induce or form tumors
on·cor·na·virus \änˈkòrnə, äŋ-+\ *n* [NL, fr. [1]*onco-* + ISV *RNA* + NL *virus*] : ONCOVIRUS *herein*
on·co·virus \ˈäŋkō+, ˈän-+\ *n* [NL, fr. [1]*onco-* + *virus*] : any of the retroviruses that cause tumor formation and are now placed in several distinct genera but were formerly included in their own subfamily (Oncovirinae)
one–lin·er \ˈ=ˈlīnə(r)\ *n* **1** : a very succinct joke or witticism **2 a** succinct, meaningful, or important and esp. accurate statement ⟨textbook *one-liners* describe him as the discoverer . . . of oxygen —S.J.Gould⟩
one–man band *n* **1** : a musician who plays several instruments during a solo performance **2** : a person who alone undertakes or is responsible for several tasks
one–night stand* *n* : a sexual encounter limited to a single occasion; *also* : a partner in such an encounter
one–note \ˈ=ˈ=\ *adj* : focusing excessively on a single element or aspect ⟨plays the *one-note* role of the dutiful wife⟩
one–off \ˈ=ˈ=\ *adj* [[1]*one* + *off*] *Brit* : limited to a single time, occasion, or instance : ONE-SHOT — **one–off** \"\ *n, Brit*
[1]**one–on–one** \ˌ==ˈ=\ *adj (or adv)* **1** : playing directly against a single opposing player **2** : involving a direct encounter between one person and another
[2]**one–on–one** \ˌ==ˈ=\ *n* : a game or an aspect of a game which pits one offensive player against a single defender; *esp* : an informal basketball game between two players who alternate at offense and defense
ones place *n* : UNITS PLACE *herein*

one–stop \ˈ=ˈ=\ *adj* : providing or offering a comprehensive range of goods or services at one location ⟨a *one-stop* supermarket⟩; *also* : provided or offered at such a location ⟨*one-stop* shopping⟩

one–tailed \ˈ=ˌ=\ *also* **one–tail** *adj* : being a statistical test for which the critical region consists of all values of the test statistic greater than a given value or less than a given value but not both — compare TWO-TAILED *herein*

one–time pad \ˈ=ˌ=-\ *n* [prob. fr. its original form's being a pad of keys whose sheets were torn off and discarded after a single use] : a random-number additive or mixed keying sequence to be used for a single coded message and then destroyed

one–up \ˈ=ˈ=\ *vt* **one–upped; one–upped; one–upping; one–ups** [back-formation fr. *one-upmanship*] : to practice one-upmanship on

one up \ˈ=ˈ=\ *adj* : being in a position of advantage that is usu. attained by one-upmanship — usu. used with *on*

one–way* *adj* : being or containing glass that acts as a mirror when viewed from one direction and as a window when viewed from the opposite direction

one–world·ism \ˌ=ˈwər(ə)lˌdizəm, -ˈwəl-\ *n* -S : a belief in world government

onion dome *n* : a dome (as of a church) having the general shape of an onion — **onion–domed** *adj*

on–line \ˈ=ˈ=\ *adj (or adv)* **1** : connected to, served by, or available through a system and esp. a computer or telecommunications system ⟨an *on-line* database⟩; *esp* : on, connected to, or via the Internet ⟨*on-line* consumers⟩ ⟨went *on-line*⟩ **2** : done while connected to a computer system ⟨*on-line* analysis⟩

on–ramp \ˈ=ˌ=\ *n* : a ramp by which one enters a limited-access highway

on–screen \ˈ=ˈ=\ *adv (or adj)* : in a motion picture or a television program

on–target *adj* : exactly appropriate : ACCURATE ⟨*on-target* advice⟩

on–the–job \ˈ==ˈ=\ *adj* : of, relating to, or being something (as training or experience) learned, gained, or done while working at a job and often under supervision

on–the–scene \ˈ==ˈ=\ *adj* : being at the place of an action or occurrence ⟨an *on-the-scene* witness⟩

onto* *prep* — used as a function word which precedes a word or phrase denoting a set each element of which is the image of at least one element of another set ⟨a function mapping the set *S* ∼ the set *T*⟩

on·to \ˈȯn(ˌ)tü, ˈän-\ *adj* [*onto*, prep. (herein)] : mapping elements in such a way that every element in one set is the image of at least one element in another set ⟨a function that is one-to-one and ∼⟩ — see SURJECTION *herein*

OOB \ˌōˌōˈbē\ *n* -S [*o*ff-*o*ff-*B*roadway (herein)] : OFF-OFF-BROADWAY *herein*

oort cloud \ˈō(ə)rt-, ˈȯrt-\ *n, usu cap O* [after Jan *Oort* †1992 Dutch astronomer] : a spherical shell of cometary bodies which is believed to surround the sun far beyond the orbit of Pluto and from which some are dislodged when perturbed (as by a passing star) to fall toward the sun — compare KUIPER BELT *herein*

[1]**op** \ˈäp\ *or* **op art** *n* -S *sometimes cap O&A* [by shortening] : OPTICAL ART *herein* — **op artist** *n*

[2]**op** \ˈäp\ *n* -S [by shortening] : OPPORTUNITY

op–ed page \ˌäpˈed-\ *n, often cap O&E* [*op*posite + *ed*itorial] : the page usu. opposite the editorial page of a newspaper that features by-lined articles (as by columnists) reflecting individual points of view

open* *adj* **1** : being a mathematical interval that contains neither of its endpoints **2** : being a set each point of which has a neighborhood all of whose points are contained in the set **3** *of a universe* : having insufficient mass to halt expansion gravitationally : expanding forever **4 a** : being an incomplete electric circuit **b** : not allowing the flow of electricity ⟨an ∼ switch⟩ **5** : being an operation or surgical procedure in which an incision is made such that the organs and tissues are fully exposed

open* *vt* : to initiate access to (a computer file) prior to use ∼ *vi* : to provide the opening performance of a show before the feature performance begins ⟨a young singer ∼*ed* for the headliner⟩

open admission *n, pl* **open admissions** *usu sing in constr* : OPEN ENROLLMENT 2 *herein*

open adoption *n* : an adoption that involves contact between the biological and adoptive parents and sometimes between the biological parents and the adopted child

open bar *n* : a bar (as at a wedding reception) at which drinks are served free — compare CASH BAR *herein*

open classroom *n* **1** : an informal flexible system of elementary education in which open discussions and individualized activities replace the traditional subject-centered studies **2** : a classroom in an open classroom system

open dating *n* : the marking of perishable food products with a clearly readable date indicating when the food was packaged or the last date on which it should be sold or used

open enrollment *n* **1** : the voluntary enrollment of a student in a public school other than the one to which assignment would be made on the basis of residence **2** : enrollment on demand as a student in an institution of higher learning irrespective of formal qualifications

open–heart \ˈ=ˈ=\ *adj* : of, relating to, or performed on a heart temporarily relieved of circulatory function and laid open for inspection and treatment ⟨*open-heart* surgery⟩

open loop *n* : a control system for an operation or process in which there is no self-correcting action

open marriage *n* : a marriage in which the partners agree to let each other have sexual partners outside the marriage

open mike *n* [[4]*mike* (microphone)] : a period of time when amateur singers or comics may perform (as at a nightclub) usu. without auditioning first

open reading frame *n* : a reading frame that does not contain a nucleotide triplet which stops translation before formation of a complete polypeptide

open season *n* : a time during which someone or something is the object of strong and continued attack or criticism

open sentence *n* : a statement (as in mathematics) that contains at least one blank or unknown and that becomes true or false when the blank is filled or a quantity is substituted for the unknown

operand* *n* -S : the part of a computer instruction that indicates the quantities to be operated on; *also* : one of these quantities

operatic* *adj* : grand, dramatic, or romantic in style or effect ⟨∼ emotions⟩

operating system *n* : software that controls the operation of a computer and directs the processing of the user's programs (as by assigning storage space in memory and controlling input and output functions)

operation* *n* : a single step performed by a computer in the execution of a program

op·er·a·tion·al·is·tic \ˌäpəˌrāshnəlˈistik, -shənᵊl-\ *adj* : of or relating to operationalism

op·er·a·tion·al·ize \ˌäpəˈrāshnəlˌīz, -shənᵊl-\ *vt* -ED/-ING/-S : to make operational ⟨∼ a program⟩ — **op·er·a·tion·al·i·za·tion** \äp(ə)ˌrāshnələˈzāshən, -shənᵊl-, -(ᵊ)l(ˌ)īz-\ *n* -S

op·er·a·tion·ist \ˌäpəˈrāsh(ə)nəst\ *n* -S : OPERATIONALIST

operator* *or* **operator gene** *n* : a binding site in a DNA chain at which a genetic repressor binds to inhibit the initiation of transcription of messenger RNA by one or more nearby structural genes — compare OPERON *herein*

op·er·on \ˈäpəˌrän\ *n* -S [F *opéron*, fr. *opérer* to bring about, effect (fr. L *operari*) + *-on* [2]-on — more at OPERATE] : a group of closely linked genes that produce a single messenger RNA molecule in transcription and that consists of structural genes and regulating elements (as an operator and promoter)

[1]**opi·oid** \ˈōpēˌȯid\ *adj* [[2]*opiate* + *-oid*] **1** : possessing some properties characteristic of opiate narcotics but not derived from opium **2** : of, involving, or induced by an opioid

[2]**opioid** *n* -S **1** *or* **opioid peptide** : any of a group of endogenous neural polypeptides (as an endorphin or enkephalin) that bind esp. to opiate receptors and mimic some of the pharmacological properties of opiates **2** : a synthetic drug that possesses narcotic properties similar to opiates but is not derived from opium; *broadly* : OPIATE 1

opportunistic* *adj* **1** : of, relating to, or being a microorganism that is usu. harmless but can become pathogenic when the host's resistance to disease is impaired **2** : of, relating to, or being an infection or disease caused by an opportunistic organism

op·son·iza·tion \ˌäpsənəˈzāshən, -ˌnīˈz-\ *n* -S : the process of opsonizing

optical* *adj* **1 a** : VISIBLE 1a ⟨∼ wavelength⟩ **b** : of, relating to, or being objects that emit light in the visible range of frequencies ⟨an ∼ galaxy⟩ ⟨∼ astronomy⟩ **2 a (1)** : of, relating to, or utilizing light esp. instead of another form of energy ⟨∼ microscopy⟩ (2) : using lasers ⟨∼ storage for a computer⟩ **b** : involving the use of light-sensitive devices to acquire information for a computer ⟨∼ character recognition⟩ **3** : of or relating to optical art

optical art *n, sometimes cap O&A* : nonobjective art characterized by the use of straight or curved lines or geometric patterns often for an illusory effect (as of perspective or motion)

optical computer *n* : a computer that uses light rather than electricity to transmit, store, and process data

optical disk *n* : a disk with a plastic coating on which information (as music, visual images, or computer data) is recorded digitally (as in the form of tiny pits) and which is read using a laser

optical fiber *n* : a single fiber-optic strand

optic tectum *n* : the visual projection area of fish and amphibians homologous to the mammalian superior colliculus; *also* : SUPERIOR COLLICULUS

op·to·electronics \ˌäp(ˌ)tō+\ *n pl but sing in constr* [*opt*ical + *-o-* + *electronics*] : a branch of electronics that deals with devices for emitting, modulating, transmitting, and sensing light — **op·to·electronic** \"+\ *adj*

opt out *vi* : to choose not to participate — often used with *of* ⟨*opt out* of the company's insurance plan⟩

OR \ˈȯ(ə)r, ˈō(ə)\ *n* -S [[1]*or*] : a logical operator equivalent to the sentential connective *or* ⟨∼ gate in a computer⟩

OR* *abbr* **1** operational research; operations research **2** own recognizance

or·a·cy \ˈōrəsē, ˈȯr-, ˈär-\ *n* -ES [[1]*oral* + *-acy* (as in *literacy*)] : the capacity for producing and understanding spoken language

oral contraceptive *n* : BIRTH CONTROL PILL *herein*

oral history *n* **1** : tape-recorded historical information obtained in interviews concerning personal experiences and recollections; *also* : the study of such information **2** : a written work based on oral history — **oral historian** *n*

oral sex *n* : oral stimulation of the genitals : CUNNILINGUS, : FELLATIO

orange roughy *n* : a reddish orange fish (*Hoplostethus atlanticus*) of the family Trachichthyidae having firm white flesh that is found in deep waters of the Atlantic Ocean from southern Europe to Africa, the southern Indian Ocean, and the western South Pacific Ocean and that is caught commercially chiefly in the waters off New Zealand

orbiter* *n* : SPACE SHUTTLE *herein*

order* *n* **1** : the number of elements in a finite mathematical group **2** : a class of mutually exclusive linguistic forms any one of which may occur in a fixed definable position in the permitted sequence of items forming a word

ordered* *adj* : having elements succeeding or arranged according to a rule: as **a** : having the property that every pair of different elements is related by a transitive relationship that is not symmetric **b** : having the elements labeled by ordinal numbers ⟨an ∼ triple has a first, second, and third element⟩

ordinal number* *n* : a number assigned to an ordered set that designates both the order of its elements and its cardinal number

ordinary level *n, usu cap O* : O LEVEL 1 *herein*

or·eo \ˈōrē(ˌ)ō, ˈȯr-, ˈär-\ *n* -S *usu cap* [fr. *Oreo*, trademark for a chocolate cookie with a white cream filling] : a black person who adopts the characteristic mentality and behavior of white middle-class society — usu. used disparagingly

organic brain syndrome *n* : any acute or chronic mental dysfunction (as delirium or senile dementia) resulting chiefly from physical changes in brain structure and characterized esp. by impaired cognition

or·ga·no \ˈȯrgə(ˌ)nō, ȯrˈga(-\ *adj* [*organo-*] : of, relating to, or being a chemical compound composed of an organic group bonded to an inorganic element or group

or·gano·chlorine \ȯrˈganə, ˌȯrgənō+\ *adj* [*organ-* + [2]*chlorine*] : of, relating to, or being a chlorinated hydrocarbon and esp. one used as a pesticide (as aldrin, DDT, or dieldrin) — **organochlorine** *n*

or·ga·nol·o·gy \ˌȯrgəˈnäləjē, ˌȯ(ə)g-\ *n* -ES [[1]*organ* + *-ology* (as in *musicology*)] : the study of the structure, history, and use of musical instruments — **or·ga·no·log·i·cal** \ˌ==nəˈläjəkəl\ *adj* — **or·ga·nol·o·gist** \ˌ-==ˈnäləjəst\ *n* -S

or·gano·phosphate \"+\ *n* [*organ-* + *phosphate*] : an organophosphorus compound — **organophosphate** *adj*

or·gano·phosphorus \"+\ *also* **or·gano·phosphorous** \"+\ *adj* [*organ-* + *phosphorus* or *phosphorous*] : of, relating to, or being a phosphorus-containing organic compound and esp. a pesticide (as malathion) that acts by inhibiting cholinesterase — **organophosphorus** *n*

orgasm *vi* -ED/-ING/-S [*orgasm*, n.] : to experience an orgasm

orgy* *n* : a sexual encounter involving many people; *also* : an excessive sexual indulgence

oriental shorthair *also* **oriental** *n, usu cap O* : a slender short-haired domestic cat of a breed resembling the Siamese in conformation but having a solid-colored coat in a wide range of colors

ori·en·teer \ˌ===ˈti(ə)r\ *n* -S [back-formation fr. *orienteering*] : one who engages in orienteering

ori·en·teer·ing \ˌōrēənˈti(ə)riŋ, -ē(ˌ)en-\ *n* -S [prob. modif. (influenced by *-eer*) of Sw *orientering*, fr. *orientera* to orient, fr. F *orienter*] : a cross-country race in which each participant uses a map and compass to navigate his way between checkpoints along an unfamiliar course

oro·so·mucoid \ˌȯrəsōˈmyüˌkȯid\ *n* [irreg. fr. Gk *oros* whey, blood serum + E *-o-* + [2]*mucoid*] : a plasma glycoprotein believed to be associated with inflammation

orphan drug *n* : a drug that is not developed or marketed because its extremely limited use (as in the treatment of a rare disease) makes it unprofitable

orthodromic* *adj* : of, relating to, or inducing nerve impulses along an axon in the normal direction — compare ANTIDROMIC *in the Dict* — **or·tho·drom·i·cal·ly** \ȯrthəˈdräməkᵊ(ə)lē\ *adv*

orthogonal* *adj* **1** : having a sum of products or an integral that is zero or sometimes 1 under specified conditions: as **a** *of real-valued functions* : having the integral of the product of each pair of functions over a specific interval equal to zero **b** *of vectors* : having the scalar product equal to zero **c** *of a square matrix* : having the sum of products of corresponding elements in any two rows or any two columns equal to 1 if the rows or columns are the same and equal to zero otherwise : having a transpose with which the product equals the identity matrix **2** *of a linear transformation* : having a matrix that is orthogonal : preserving length and distance **3** : composed of mutually orthogonal elements ⟨an ∼ basis of a vector space⟩

or·thog·o·nal·iza·tion \ȯ(r)ˌthägənᵊləˈzāshən, -gnəl-, -(ᵊ)lˌīˈz-\ *n* -S [*orthogonalize* + *-ation*] : the replacement of a set of vectors by a linearly equivalent set of orthogonal vectors

or·tho·molecular \ˌȯ(r)thə+\ *adj* [*orth-* + *molecular*] : relating to, based on, using, or being a theory according to which disease and esp. mental disorder may be cured by restoring the optimum amounts of substances normally present in the body ⟨∼ therapy⟩

or·tho·normal \"+\ *adj* [*orth-* + *normal*] **1** *of real-valued functions* : orthogonal with the integral of the square of each function over a specified interval equal to one **2** : being or composed of orthogonal elements of unit length ⟨∼ basis of a vector space⟩

orthosis* *n* : ORTHOTIC *herein*

[1]**or·thot·ic** \ȯrˈthäd·ik\ *adj* **1** : of or relating to orthotics ⟨∼ research⟩ **2** : designed for the support of weak or ineffective joints or muscles ⟨∼ inserts for jogging shoes⟩

[2]**orthotic** *n* -S : an orthotic support or brace

or·thot·ics \ȯrˈthäd·iks\ *n pl but sing in constr* [fr. *orthosis*, after such pairs as E *prosthesis* : *prosthetics*] : a branch of mechanical and medical science dealing with the support and bracing of weak or ineffective joints or muscles — **or·tho·tist** \ˈȯrthətəst\ *n* -S

orthotropic* *adj* **1** : being, having, or relating to properties (as strength, stiffness, and elasticity) that are symmetric about two or three mutually perpendicular planes ⟨a piece of straight-grained wood is an ∼ material⟩ **2** *of a bridge* : designed so that the roadway serves as an orthotropic structural member : constructed with a steel-plate deck as an integral part of the support structure

ORV *abbr* off-road vehicle

or·vie·to \ȯrˈvyā(ˌ)tō, -yed·ō\ *n* -S *usu cap* [It, fr. *Orvieto*, city in central Italy] : a usu. dry Italian white wine

or·well·ian \ȯrˈwelēən\ *adj, usu cap* [George *Orwell* (pseudonym of Eric Blair †1950 Eng. writer) + E *-ian*] : of, relating to, or suggestive of George Orwell or his writings; *esp* : relating to or suggestive of his novel *1984*

or·zo \ˈȯrd(ˌ)zō\ *n* -S [It, lit., barley, fr. L *hordeum* — more at HORDEUM] : rice-shaped pasta

osculating circle *n* : a circle which is tangent to a curve at a given point, which lies in the limiting plane determined by the tangent to the curve and a point moving along the curve to the point of tangency, which has its center situated on the normal to the curve at the given point and, also, on the concave side of the projection of the curve onto the limiting plane, and which has a radius equal to the radius of curvature

oset·ra *also* **os·set·ra** \(ˌ)ōˈse·trə\ *n* -S [modif. (perh. influenced by *sevruga* — herein — and *beluga*) of Russ *osëtr* sturgeon; akin to Czech *jeseter* sturgeon, Serbo-Croatian *jèsetra*, Lith *ašėtras*] : a golden or brownish caviar from a sturgeon of the genus Acipenser (*A. sturio*) with roe smaller than the beluga; *also* : the fish — compare SEVRUGA *herein*

os·mol *or* **os·mole** \ˈäzˌmōl, ˈäs-\ *n* -S [blend of *osmosis* and *mol*] : a standard unit of osmotic pressure based on a one molal concentration of an ion in a solution

os·mo·lal·ity \ˌäzmōˈlaləd·ē, ˌäsm-\ *n* -ES [blend of *osmol* (herein) and *molality*] : the concentration of an osmotic solution esp. when measured in osmols or milliosmols per 1000 grams of solvent — **os·mo·lal** \äzˈmōləl, äs'-\ *adj*

os·mo·lar·i·ty \ˌäzmōˈlarəd·ē, ˌäsm-\ *n* -ES [blend of *osmol* (herein) and *molarity*] : the concentration of an osmotic solution esp. when measured in osmols or milliosmols per liter of solution — **os·mo·lar** \äzˈmōlər, äs'-\ *adj*

osmotic shock *n* : a rapid change in the osmotic pressure (as by transfer to a medium of different concentration) affecting a living system

os·so bu·co *also* **os·so buc·co** \ˌōsōˈbü(ˌ)kō, ˌȯs-, ˌäs-\ *n* [It *ossobuco*, lit., veal shank (Tuscan rendering of Milanese *òs bùs*), fr. *osso* bone (fr. L *ossum*, alter. of *oss-*, *os*) + *buco* pierced, short past part. of *bucare* to pierce, fr. *buca* hole, hollow, prob. fr. (assumed) VL *buca*, by-form of L *bucca* cheek, mouth, cavity — more at OSSEOUS, POCK] : a dish of veal shanks braised with vegetables, white wine, and seasoned stock; *also* : a similar dish made with the shanks of another animal (as a lamb or deer)

osteogenic sarcoma *n* : OSTEOSARCOMA

os·te·on \ˈästēˌän\ *n* -S [Gk, bone — more at OSSEOUS] : HAVERSIAN SYSTEM

ost·mark \ˈȯstˌmärk, ˈäs-\ *n* -S [G, lit., East mark] : the mark of former East Germany (1949-90)

os·to·mate \ˈästəˌmāt\ *n* -S [*ostomy* (herein) + [1]*-ate*] : a person who has undergone an ostomy

os·to·my \ˈästəmē\ *n* -ES [fr. *-ostomy* (as in *colostomy*)] : an operation (as a colostomy) to create an artificial passage for bodily elimination

OTB* *abbr* offtrack betting

OTC *abbr* over-the-counter

oto·rhi·no·laryngologist \ˌōd·əˌrīnō+\ *n* [*otorhinolaryngology* + [1]*-ist*] : OTOLARYNGOLOGIST

oto·toxic \ˌōd·ə+\ *adj* [*ot-* + *toxic*] : producing, involving, or being adverse effects on organs or nerves involved in hearing or balance ⟨an ∼ drug⟩ — **oto·toxicity** \"+\ *n*

ou·gui·ya \üˈg(w)ē(y)ə\ *n, pl* **ouguiya** *or* **ouguiyas** [Ar dial. *ūgiyah*, fr. Ar *ūqīyah*, lit., ounce — more at OKE] **1** : the basic monetary unit of Mauritania — see MONEY table *in the Dict* **2** : a coin or note representing one ouguiya

out* *vt* : to identify publicly as being such secretly ⟨wanted to ∼ pot smokers⟩; *esp* : to identify as being a closet homosexual

out* *adj* **1** : not being in vogue or fashion : not in **2** : publicly known or identified as a homosexual

outcall \ˈ=ˌ=\ *n* : a visit (as by a masseuse or a call girl) to a customer to perform a requested service

outercourse \ˈ==ˌ=\ *n* [[1]*outer* + *intercourse*] : physical sexual activity between individuals that typically includes stimulation of the genitalia but does not involve penetration of the vagina or anus with the penis

out–front \ˈ=ˈ=\ *adj* [fr. the phrase *out front*] : FRANK, OPEN, UNABASHED

outgas* *vb* ∼ *vt* **1** : to remove gases from **2** : to remove (gases) from a material or a space ∼ *vi* : to lose gases

outing* *n* **1** : a usu. public presentation or appearance (as in a particular role) ⟨her first ∼ as a novelist⟩ **2** : the public disclosure of the covert homosexuality of a prominent person often by homosexual advocates

outlet pass *n* : a pass made in basketball by the player taking a defensive rebound to a teammate to start a fast break

out of* *prep* — **out of it*** : in a dazed or confused state

out–of–body \ˌ==ˈ=\ *adj* : relating to or involving a feeling of separation from one's body and of being able to view oneself and others from an external perspective ⟨an *out-of-body* experience⟩

out–of–sight \ˌ==ˈ=\ *adj* **1** *slang* : WONDERFUL **2** : extremely high : EXORBITANT ⟨gasoline prices are *out-of-sight*⟩

out–of–stat·er \ˈ==ˈstād·ə(r), -ātə-\ *n* -S [fr. the phrase *out of state* + [2]*-er*] **1** : a visitor from another state **2** : a person whose legal domicile is in one state but who lives for an extended time in another state (as to attend college)

out–of–town·er \-ˈtaunə(r)\ *n* -S [fr. the phrase *out of town* + [2]*-er*] : a visitor from out of town

outplacement \ˈ=ˌ=\ *n* [[1]*out* + *placement*] : the process of easing unwanted or unneeded executives out of a company by providing them company-paid assistance in finding new jobs

outreach* *n* : the extending of services or activities beyond current or conventional limits; *also* : the extent of such services or activities

outside* *adj* : made or done from the outside or from a distance

outsize* *also* **outsized*** *adj* : exaggerated or extravagant in size or degree

out·sourc·er \ˌau̇tˈsȯrsə(r), -ˈsō(r)s-\ *n* **1** : a company that procures some of its goods or services from usu. smaller specialized companies **2** : a specialized company that provides goods or services to a usu. larger company

out·sourc·ing \ˈau̇tˌsȯrsiŋ, -ˌsō(r)s-\ *n* -S [[3]*out* + *source* + [3]*-ing*] : the procurement by a corporation from outside and esp. foreign or nonunion suppliers of goods or services — **out·source** \ˈ=ˌ=\ *vt*

out–year \ˈ=ˌ=\ *n* : the year beyond a current fiscal year — usu. used in pl. except when attrib.

ovals of cas·si·ni \-kəˈsēnē, -ka-, -kä-\ *usu cap C* [after G.D. *Cassini* †1712 Fr. astronomer] : a curve that is the locus of points of the vertex of a triangle whose opposite side is fixed and the product of whose adjacent sides is a constant and that has the equation $[(x+a)^2+y^2][(x-a)^2+y^2]-k^4=0$ where k is the constant and a is one half the length of the fixed side

ovenproof \ˈ==ˌ=\ *adj* [*oven* + *proof*] : capable of withstanding the heat normally produced in a kitchen oven ⟨~ glass⟩

over·achiev·er \ˌ==əˈchēvə(r)\ *n* -S [¹*over* + *achieve* + *-er*] : one who achieves success over and above a standard or expected level — **overachieve** \ˌ===ˈ=\ *vi* — **over·achievement** \ˌ===ˈ==\ *n*

overbook \ˌ==ˈ=\ *vb* [¹*over* + ²*book*] *vt* : to issue reservations for (as an airplane flight) in excess of the space available ~ *vi* : to issue reservations in excess of the space available

overclass \ˈ==ˌ=\ *n* [³*over* + under*class* (herein)] : the highest social stratum in a society : UPPER CLASS — compare UNDERCLASS *herein*

overdiagnosis \ˌ==ˌ==ˈ==\ *n* [³*over* + *diagnosis*] : the diagnosis of a condition or disease more often than it is actually present — **overdiagnose** \ˌ==ˈ===\ *vt*

overdog* *n* : one that is dominant or victorious

overdominance \ˌ==ˈ===\ *n* [³*over* + *dominance*] : the property of having a heterozygote that produces a phenotype more extreme or better adapted than that of the homozygote — **overdominant** \ˌ==ˈ==\ *adj*

overdose* *vb* ~ *vi* : to take or experience an excess of something — usu. used with *on* ⟨*overdosed* on shopping⟩

overdrive* *n* : a state of heightened activity ⟨going into rhetorical ~⟩

¹**overdub** \ˈ==ˌ=\ *vt* [¹*over* + *dub*] : to transfer (recorded sound) onto a recording that bears sound recorded earlier in order to produce a combined effect

²**overdub** *n* **1** : the act or an instance of overdubbing **2** : recorded sound that is overdubbed ⟨vocal ~*s*⟩

overfatigue \ˌ===ˈ=\ *n* [³*over* + *fatigue*] : excessive fatigue esp. when carried beyond the recuperative capacity of the individual

overground \ˈ==ˌ=\ *n* -S [²*over* + *ground*] : ESTABLISHMENT *herein* ⟨the underground medium as it grows often takes on the characteristics of the ~ —R.J.Glessing⟩ ⟨~ press⟩

overhang* *n* : an excess of something that is left over and not easily disposed of ⟨inventory ~⟩ ⟨an ~ of unemployment⟩

overkill \ˈ==ˌ=\ *n* [¹*over* + *kill*, n.] **1** : a destructive capacity greatly exceeding that required for a given target **2** : an excess of something (as a quantity or an action) beyond what is required or suitable for a particular purpose ⟨promotional ~⟩ ⟨an ~ in weaponry⟩ **3** : killing in excess of what is intended or required — **overkill** \ˈ==ˌ=, ˌ==ˈ=\ *vb*

overnight* *n* : an overnight stay

overnight* *vb* ~ *vt* to send via an overnight delivery service

over·night·er \ˌōvə(r)ˈnīd·ə(r), -ˈnīt-\ *n* -S **1** : OVERNIGHT BAG **2** : an overnight trip **3** : one who stays overnight

overnutrition \ˌ===ˈ==\ *n* [³*over* + *nutrition*] : excessive food intake esp. when viewed as a factor in pathology

overprescribe \ˌ===ˈ=\ *vb* [¹*over* + *prescribe*] *vi* : to prescribe excessive or unnecessary medication ~ *vt* : to prescribe (medication) unnecessarily or to excess

overqualified \ˌ===ˈ==\ *adj* [¹*over* + *qualified*] : having more education, training, or experience than a job calls for

overrespond \ˌ===ˈ=\ *vi* [¹*over* + *respond*] : OVERREACT

overscale \ˈ==ˌ=\ *or* **overscaled** \ˈ==ˌ=\ *adj* [*overscale* fr. ³*over* + ⁷*scale*; *overscaled* fr. ¹*over* + ³*scaled*] : OVERSIZE ⟨an ~ coat⟩ ⟨an ~ sofa⟩

overseed \ˈ==ˌ=\ *vt* [¹*over* + ²*seed*] : to seed (an existing stand) with another type of plant ⟨~*ed* the Bermuda grass with rye grass⟩

overshoot \ˈ==ˌ=\ *n* [*overshoot*, v.] : the action or an instance of overshooting; *esp* : a going beyond an intended point

over–the–top \ˌ===ˈ=\ *adj* [fr. the phrase *over the top*] : extremely or excessively flamboyant or outrageous ⟨an *over-the-top* performance⟩

over–the–transom \ˌ===ˈ==\ *adj* : offered without prior arrangement esp. for publication ⟨an *over-the-transom* manuscript⟩

overwinter \ˌ==ˈ==\ *adj* [²*over* + ¹*winter*] : occurring during the period spanning the winter ⟨~ mortality of small game⟩

overwithhold \ˌ===ˈ=\ *vt* [¹*over* + *withhold*] : to deduct a greater amount of (money) from an employee's pay for withholding tax than the employee is legally required to pay

overwrite* *vt* : to destroy (a computer program or data) by storing other data in the same storage locations

ovi·rap·tor \ˌōvəˈraptər, -tó(ə)r\ *n* [NL, fr. *ov-* + L *raptor* one that plunders, robs — more at RAPTOR] **1** *cap* : a genus (family Oviraptoridae) of bipedal carnivorous theropod dinosaurs of the Late Cretaceous having a toothless muscular beaklike jaw, clawed fingers and toes, and crested skull that is known from fossils of the Gobi desert found in association with nesting sites orig. thought to indicate a behavior of egg predation but now known to be indicative of brooding behavior **2** : a dinosaur of the genus *Oviraptor*

ovo–lac·to vegetarian \ˌ==ˈ==-\ *n* : LACTO-OVO VEGETARIAN *herein*

ovon·ics \ōˈväniks\ *n pl but usu sing in constr, usu cap* [Stanford R. *Ov*shinsky *b* 1923 Am. inventor + electr*onics*] : a branch of electronics that deals with applications of the change from an electrically nonconducting state to a semiconducting state shown by glasses of special composition upon application of a certain minimum voltage — **ovonic** *adj, often cap*

OW* *abbr* one-way

own* *vt* : to have power or mastery over (as in competition) ⟨a pitcher can virtually ~ one team and . . . have so little success against another —*Sport*⟩

ox·a·cil·lin \ˌäksəˈsilən\ *n* -S [*isoxazole* + *penicillin*] : a semisynthetic penicillin $C_{19}H_{19}N_3O_5S$ administered in the form of its sodium salt to treat infections caused by penicillin-resistant staphylococci

ox·az·e·pam \äkˈsazəˌpam\ *n* -S [hydr*oxy*- + di*azepam* (herein)] : a benzodiazepine tranquilizer $C_{15}H_{11}ClN_2O_2$

ox·bridge \ˈäksbrij\ *adj, usu cap* [*Ox*ford University, England + Cam*bridge* University, England] : of, relating to, or characteristic of Oxford and Cambridge universities — compare PLATE-GLASS *herein*, REDBRICK *herein*

oxidative phosphorylation *n* : the synthesis of ATP by phosphorylation of ADP for which energy is obtained by electron transport and which takes place in the mitochondria during aerobic respiration

oxo·trem·o·rine \ˌäksōˈtreməˌrēn, -ˌrən\ *n* -S [¹*ox-* + ¹*tremor* + ²*-ine*] : a synthetic cholinergic agent $C_{12}H_{18}N_2O$ used esp. in pharmacological research (as to induce tremors characteristic of Parkinson's disease)

oxy·acid \ˈäksē+\ *n* [²*oxy-* + *acid*] : an acid (as sulfuric acid) that contains oxygen — called also *oxygen acid*

ox·y·gen·ase \ˈäksəjəˌnās, -ˌnāz\ *n* -S [*oxygen* + *-ase*] : an enzyme that catalyzes the reaction of an organic compound with molecular oxygen

oxygenate *n* -S [*oxygen* + ¹*-ate*] : an oxygen-containing substance (as ethanol) used esp. in gasoline to reduce smog-causing emissions by promoting more complete combustion

oxygen cycle *n* : the cycle whereby atmospheric oxygen is converted to carbon dioxide in animal respiration and regenerated by green plants in photosynthesis

oxygen demand *n* : BIOCHEMICAL OXYGEN DEMAND

oxy·phen·bu·ta·zone \ˌäksēˌfenˈbyüd·əˌzōn, -üt·ə-\ *n* -S [²*oxy-* + *phenylbutazone*] : a phenylbutazone derivative $C_{19}H_{20}N_2O_3$ having anti-inflammatory, analgesic, and antipyretic effects

oysters rocke·fel·ler \-ˈräk(ə)ˌfelə(r)\ *n pl, usu cap R* [after John Davison *Rockefeller* †1937 Am. oil magnate] : a dish of oysters on the half shell cooked with various savory toppings typically including chopped spinach and a seasoned sauce

oz \ˈäz\ *n* -ES *usu cap* [fr. *Oz*, mythical land in a series of books by L. Frank Baum †1919 Am. author] : a seemingly ideal or perfect place ⟨the rationalized, suburbanized *Oz* that is the postwar United States —Verlyn Klinkenborg⟩

ozone hole *n* : an area of the ozone layer (as one near the south pole) that is seasonally depleted of ozone

ozone layer *n* : an atmospheric layer at heights of about 20 to 30 miles (32 to 48 kilometers) which is normally characterized by high ozone content that blocks most solar ultraviolet radiation from entry into the lower atmosphere

ozonesonde \ˈ=ˌ=ˌ=\ *n* [*ozone* + *sonde*] : a balloon-borne instrument that measures the concentration of ozone at various altitudes and broadcasts the data by radio

p* *abbr* **1** *cap* parity **2** pico-

p* *symbol* **1** momentum of a particle **2** *often cap* the probability of obtaining a result as great as or greater than the observed result in a statistical test if the null hypothesis is true

pa* *abbr, usu cap* pascal *herein*

PA* *n* [fr. *PA*, abbr. of *physician's assistant*] : PHYSICIAN'S ASSISTANT *herein*

PA* *abbr* personal assistant

pa·'anga \pä-ˈäŋ(g)ə\ *n, pl* **pa'anga** [Tongan, lit., seed] **1** : the basic monetary unit of Tonga — see MONEY table *in the Dict* **2** : a coin or note representing one pa'anga

pab·lum \ˈpabləm\ *n* -S [fr. *Pablum*, a trademark for an infant cereal] : something (as writing or speech) that is insipid, simplistic, or bland ⟨her half-dozen novels . . . superior to popular ~ —Leslie A. Marchand⟩

PABX \ˌpēˌāˌ(ˌ)bēˈex\ *abbr or n* -S : a private automatic branch exchange

PAC \ˈpak, ˈpēˈāˈsē\ *abbr or n* -S [*p*olitical *a*ction *c*ommittee] : a group formed (as by a corporation, an industry, a union, or an issue-oriented organization) to raise and contribute money to the campaigns of candidates likely to advance the group's interests

pace car *n* : an automobile that leads the field of competitors through a pace lap but does not participate in the race

pace lap *n* : a lap of an auto racecourse by the entire field of competitors before the start of a race to allow the engines to warm up and to permit a flying start

pack* *vt* — **pack it in** : to cease an activity or effort : QUIT ⟨then came disillusionment and he *packed it in* —Richard Crossman⟩

package* *n* : a ready-made computer program or collection of related software

package* *vt* : to present in such a way as to heighten appeal ⟨how to ~ and hype political parties and candidates for the purpose of winning elections —John Lukacs⟩

packet* *n* : a short fixed-length section of data that is transmitted as a unit in an electronic communications network

packet switching *n* : the division of data (as in a message) into packets for transmission in an electronic communications network — **packet–switched** \ˈ==ˌ=\ *adj*

pack journalism *n* [¹*pack* (group)] : journalism practiced (as in following a political candidate) by reporters in a group that is marked by uniformity of news coverage and lack of original thought or initiative

pac·li·tax·el \ˌpakliˈtaksəl\ *n* -S [*Pac*ific yew + *-litax-* (perh. by shortening + alter. fr. NL *Taxus brevifolia*, species name of the Pacific yew) + *-el* (alter. of ¹*-ol* or ³*-ol*)] : an antineoplastic agent $C_{47}H_{51}NO_{14}$ derived esp. from the bark of the Pacific yew and administered intravenously in the treatment of ovarian cancer which has not responded to conventional chemotherapy

pad* *n* **1** : a component of certain brake systems (as disk brakes) consisting of a plate covered with a frictional material that is pressed against the side of a rotating wheel or disk **2** : a horizontal concrete surface (as for parking a mobile home) — **on the pad** *of a police officer* : receiving money in exchange for ignoring illegal activities : taking graft

paddle* *n* : a small hand-held remote control device; *esp* : such a device having a dial used to control linear movement of a visual cue (as a cursor) on a computer display screen

paddle fan *n* : an electric ceiling fan with paddle-shaped vanes

page* *n* : a sizable subdivision of computer memory; *also* : a block of information that fills a page and can be transferred as a unit between the internal and external storage of a computer **2** : the usu. textual information displayed at one time on a video screen **3** : the block of information found at a single World Wide Web address

page* *vi* : to proceed through matter displayed on a video screen as if turning pages

page* *n* : the act or an instance of paging ⟨a ~ came over the loudspeaker⟩

pager* *n* : one having or covering a specified number or kind of pages — usu. used in combination ⟨her final paper was a 15-*pager*⟩

pager *n* [²*page* + ²*-er*] : BEEPER *herein*; *also* : a similar device that signals its user with a flashing light or by vibrating rather than by beeping

page–turner \ˈ=ˌ==\ *n* : an entertaining book

pail·lard \pīˈyär *also* -ärd\ *n* -S [F *paillarde*, fr. *Paillard*, late 19th cent. Fr. restaurateur] : a piece of beef or veal usu. pounded thin and grilled

paint* *n, often attrib* : computer-generated color design ⟨a ~ program⟩

paintball \ˈ=ˌ=\ *n, often attrib* : a game in which two teams try to capture one another's flag while defending their own using compressed-air guns that shoot paint-filled pellets

pair–bond \ˈ=ˌ=\ *n* : an exclusive union with one mate at any one time : a monogamous relationship — **pair–bonding** \ˈ=ˌ==\ *n*

paired–associate learning \ˈ=ˌ===ˈ=-\ *n* : the learning of items (as syllables, digits, or words) in pairs so that one member of the pair evokes recall of the other

pak \ˈpak, ˈpäk, ˈpak\ *n* -S *cap* [by shortening] : PAKISTANI — sometimes taken to be offensive — **pak** \"\ *adj, cap*

paki \ˈpaki, ˈpak-, -ē\ *n* -S *cap* [short for *Pakistani*] *chiefly Brit* : a Pakistani immigrant — usu. used disparagingly

palazzo pants *also* **palazzo pajamas** *n pl* : extremely wide-legged pants for women

pa·leo·bio·geography \ˌpālēōˌbīō+, *chiefly Brit* ˌpal-\ *n* [*pale-* + *bi-* + *geography*] : a science that deals with the geographical distribution of plants and animals of former geological epochs — **pa·leo·bio·geographical** \"+\ *adj*

pa·leo·climate \ˈpālēō, *chiefly Brit* ˈpalēō+\ *n* [*pale-* + *climate*] : the climate during a past geological age

pa·leo·environment \"+\ *n* [*pale-* + *environment*] : an environment of a past geological age — **pa·leo·environmental** \"+\ *adj*

pa·leo·magnetism \"+\ *n* [*pale-* + *magnetism*] **1** : the intensity and direction of residual magnetization in ancient rocks **2** : a study that deals with paleomagnetism — **pa·leo·magnetic** \"+\ *adj* — **pa·leo·magnetically** \"+\ *adv* — **pa·leo·magnetist** \"+\ *n*

pa·leo·pathologist \"+\ *n* : a specialist in paleopathology

pa·leo·temperature \"+\ *n* [*pale-* + *temperature*] : the temperature (as of the ocean) during a past geological age

palestinian* *n, cap* : a usu. Muslim or Christian member of an Arab people living in what was formerly Palestine

palette* *n* : the set of colors available for display on a computer

pal·i·mo·ny \ˈpaləˌmōnē\ *n* -ES [blend of *pal* and *alimony*] : a court-ordered allowance paid by one member of a couple formerly living together out of wedlock to the other

palimpsest* *n* : something having usu. diverse layers or aspects apparent beneath the surface ⟨Egypt has many pasts—the country is a cultural ~ with many layers of civilization —Willis Barnstone⟩

palmtop \ˈ=ˌ=\ *n* [¹*palm* + *-top* (as in *laptop* — herein)] : a small portable computer easily held in the palm of the hand

pal·y·no·morph \ˈpalənəˌmȯrf, -ˌmȯ(ə)f\ *n* -S [*palyn-* (as in *palynology*) + *-o-* + *-morph*] : a microscopic fossil composed esp. of pollen or spores

pan–africanism \ˈpan+, *sometimes* ˈpänˈäfrikənˌizəm\ *n, usu cap P&A* : a movement for the political union of all the African nations — **pan–african** \"+\ *adj, usu cap P&A* — **pan–africanist** \"+\ *n or adj, usu cap P&A*

panama red *n, usu cap P&R* : marijuana of a reddish tint that is of Panamanian origin and is considered very potent

pan·cet·ta \(ˌ)panˈched·ə, -tə\ *n* -S [It, fr. *pancia* belly, paunch (fr. L *pantic-, pantex*) + *-etta*, dim. suffix — more at PAUNCH] : unsmoked bacon used in Italian cuisine

pan·chres·ton \panˈkrestən, -ˌtän\ *n* -S [Gk *panchrēston* panacea, fr. neut. of *panchrēstos* good for all work, fr. *pan-* + *chrēstos* useful — more at CHRESTOMATHY] : a broadly inclusive and often oversimplified thesis that is intended to cover all possible variations within an area of concern

pan·cu·ro·ni·um bromide \ˌpankyəˈrōnēəm-\ *or* **pancuronium** *n* -S [perh. fr. *pan-* + *-cur-* (prob. as in *tubocurarine*) + *-onium*] : a neuromuscular blocking agent $C_{35}H_{60}Br_2N_2O_4$ used as a skeletal muscle relaxant

panda car *n, sometimes cap P* [so called fr. its black and white coloration] *Brit* : a police patrol car

P and H *abbr, usu not cap* postage and handling

pa·neer *also* **pa·nir** \päˈnir\ *n* -S [Hindi & Urdu *panīr*, fr. Pers] : a soft uncured Indian cheese

pan·encephalitis \ˈpan+\ *n* [NL, fr. *pan-* + *encephalitis*] : inflammation of the brain affecting both white and gray matter — see SUBACUTE SCLEROSING PANENCEPHALITIS *herein*

pan·gram \ˈpangrəm, -aŋg-, -ˌgram\ *n* -S [*pan-* + *-gram*] : a short sentence containing all 26 letters of the English alphabet — **pan·gram·mat·ic** \ˌpangrəˈmad·ik, -aŋg-\ *adj*

panic disorder *n* : an anxiety disorder characterized by recurrent unexpected panic attacks accompanied by bodily or cognitive symptoms (as shaking, shortness of breath, or feelings of unreality) followed by a month or more of worry about their recurrence, implications, or consequences or by a change in behavior related to the panic attacks

pannier* *n* : a usu. double pack or basket hung over the rear wheel of a vehicle (as a bicycle)

pantdress \ˈ=ˌ=\ *n* [⁴*pant* + *dress*] **1** : a garment having a divided skirt : CULOTTE 2 **2** : a dress worn over matching shorts

panther* *n, usu cap* : BLACK PANTHER *herein*

pantsuit *or* **pants suit** \ˈ=ˌ=\ *n* [⁴*pant* or *pants* + *suit*] : a woman's ensemble consisting usu. of a long jacket and tailored pants of the same material — **pantsuited** *or* **pants–suited** *adj*

panty hose *also* **panti·hose** \ˈpantēˌhōz\ *n* : a one-piece undergarment for women consisting of hosiery made with a panty-style top — usu. pl. in constr.

panty raid *n* : a raid on a women's dormitory by male college students to obtain panties as trophies

panty stockings *n pl* : PANTY HOSE *herein*

papanicolaou smear *n, usu cap P* [after George N. *Papanicolaou* †1962 Am. medical scientist] : PAPANICOLAOU TEST

pa·pa·raz·zo \ˌpäpəˈrät(ˌ)sō\ *n, pl* **paparaz·zi** \-sē\ [It, fr. *Paparazzo*, the surname of such a photographer in the film *La dolce vita* (1959) by Federico Fellini †1993 It. director & scenarist] : a free-lance photographer who aggressively pursues celebrities in order to take candid photographs

paper factor *n* : a substance orig. isolated from pulpwood of the balsam fir that is a selectively effective insecticide with activity like that of juvenile hormone — called also *juvabione*

paper gold *n* : SDRS *herein*

pa·per·less \ˈpāpə(r)ləs\ *adj* : recording or relaying information by electronic media rather than on paper ⟨~ offices⟩

paper trail *n* : documents (as financial records or published materials) from which a person's actions may be traced or opinions learned

paper–train \ˈ=ˌ=\ *vt* : to train (as a dog) to defecate and urinate on paper in the house

papillomavirus \ˌ==ˈ===ˌ=\ *n* : any of a genus (*Papillomavirus*) of papovaviruses that cause papillomas — see HUMAN PAPILLOMAVIRUS *herein*

pa·po·va·vi·rus \pəˈpōvəˌvīrəs\ *n* [NL, fr. *pa*pilloma + *po*lyoma (herein) + E *va*cuolation + NL, fr. *virus*] : any of a family (Papovaviridae) of viruses that contain a single molecule of circular double-stranded DNA, have a capsid composed of 72 capsomers, that are associated with or are responsible for various neoplasms (as some warts) of mammals, and that include the papillomaviruses and polyoma viruses

pap·par·del·le \ˌpäpärˈdelā\ *n, pl* **pappardelle** [It] : a wide ribbon-like pasta

pap smear *also* **pap test** \ˈpap-\ *n, usu cap P* [*pap* short for *Papanicolaou*] : PAPANICOLAOU TEST

para·cet·a·mol \ˌparəˈsētəˌmȯl, -ˈsēd·ə-\ *n* -S [¹*para-* + *acet*yl + *aminophenol*] *Brit* : ACETAMINOPHEN *herein*

parachute pants *n pl* [prob. so called because the billowiness of such pants suggests a parachute] : baggy casual pants of lightweight fabric often with an elastic or drawstring at the waist and the cuffs

para·crine \ˈparəkrən, -ˌkrīn\ *adj* [¹*para-* + *-crine* (as in *endocrine*)] : of, relating to, promoted by, or being a substance secreted by a cell and acting on adjacent cells ⟨~ stimulation of tumor growth —M.B.Rettig *et al*⟩ — compare AUTOCRINE *herein*

paradigm* *n* : a philosophical and theoretical framework of a scientific school or discipline within which theories, laws, and generalizations and the experiments performed in support of them are formulated

paradigmatic* *adj* **1** : of or relating to the range of elements that may occupy a given position in a linguistic structure **2** : of or relating to a philosophical or theoretical paradigm

par·a·dor \ˌpärä'thȯr\ *n* -S [Sp, inn, fr. *parar* to stop, stay, lodge for the night (fr. L *parare* to provide, prepare) + *-ador* -ator — more at PARE] : a usu. government-operated hostelry found esp. in Spain

paradoxical sleep *n* : REM SLEEP *herein*

para·foil \ˈparəˌfȯil\ *n* [*para-* (as in ¹*parachute*) + *-foil* (as in *airfoil*)] : a self-inflating fabric device that resembles a parachute, behaves in flight like an airplane wing, is maneuverable, is capable of landing a payload at slow speed, and can be launched from the ground in a high wind like a kite

para·gliding \ˈparə+\ *n* -S [*para-* (as in ¹*parachute*) + *gliding*, fr. gerund of ¹*glide*] : the recreational sport of soaring from a slope or a cliff using a modified parachute — **par·glide** \"+\ *vi*

para·glider \ˈparə+\ *n* [*para-* (as in ¹*parachute*) + *glider*] **1** : a triangular device resembling a kite that is deployed from a spacecraft or rocket for recovery **2** : a person who paraglides

para·influenza virus \ˈparə+. . .-\ *or* **parainfluenza** *n* [¹*para-* + *influenza*] : any of several paramyxoviruses (genera *Respirovirus* syn. Paramyxovirus and *Rubulavirus*) associated with or responsible for some respiratory infections esp. in children

para·journalism \"+\ *n* [¹*para-* + *journalism*] : NEW JOURNALISM *herein* — **para·journalist** \"+\ *n* — **para·journalistic** \"+\ *adj*

para·language \ˈparə+\ *n* [¹*para-* + *language*] : optional vocal effects (as tone of voice) that accompany or modify the phonemes of an utterance and may communicate meaning

para·legal \"+\ *adj* [¹*para-* + *legal*] : of, relating to, or being a paraprofessional who assists a lawyer — **paralegal** *n* -S

para·linguistics \ˈparə+\ *n pl but usu sing in constr* [¹*para-* + *linguistics*] : the study of paralanguage — **para·linguistic** \"+\ *adj*

parallel* *adj* **1** : arranged in parallel ⟨a ~ processor⟩ **2** : relating to or being a connection in a computer system in which the bits of a byte are transmitted over separate channels at the same time — compare SERIAL 1 *herein*

parallel* *n* : an arrangement or state that permits several operations or tasks to be performed simultaneously rather than consecutively

parallel port *n* : a port used to connect devices (as a computer and a peripheral) for transmitting information in parallel

para·lym·pics \ˌparəˈlimpiks\ *n pl, usu cap* [*para-* (as in ²*paraplegic*) + *olympics*] : a series of international contests for athletes with disabilities that are associated with and held following the summer and winter Olympic Games — called also *Paralympic Games* — **para·lym·pi·an** \-pēən\ *n* -S *usu cap* — **para·lym·pic** \-pik\ *adj, usu cap*

paralytic shellfish poisoning *n* : food poisoning that results from consumption of shellfish and esp. bivalve mollusks (as clams, mussels, or scallops) contaminated with dinoflagellates causing red tide and that is characterized by paresthesia, nausea, vomiting, abdominal cramping, muscle weakness, and sometimes paralysis which may lead to respiratory failure

paramagnetic resonance *n* : ELECTRON SPIN RESONANCE *herein*

para·medic \¦parə+\ *also* **para·medical** \"+\ *n* [[1]*para-* + *medic, medical*] **1** : one who works in a health field in an auxiliary capacity to a physician (as by taking X rays or giving injections) **2** : a specially trained medical technician certified to provide a wide range of emergency services (as defibrillation and the intravenous administration of drugs) before or during transportation to a hospital — compare EMT *herein*

parameter* *n* **1** : any of a set of physical properties whose values determine the characteristics or behavior of a system ⟨∼*s* of the atmosphere such as temperature, pressure, and density⟩ **2** : something represented by a parameter; *broadly* : CHARACTERISTIC, ELEMENT, FACTOR ⟨political dissent as a ∼ of modern life⟩ **3** : LIMIT, BOUNDARY ⟨working within established ∼*s*⟩ **4** : a variable whose value is input to a procedure or subprogram to be operated on when the procedure or subprogram is called in a computer program

pa·ram·e·ter·ize \pəˈramədˌəˌrīz, ˈpram-\ *or* **pa·ram·e·trize** \-məˌtrīz\ *vt* -ED/-ING/-S : to express in terms of parameters — **pa·ram·e·ter·iza·tion** \-ˌramədərəˈzāshən, ˌpram-, -mətrə-, -ˌīˈz-\ *or* **pa·ram·e·tri·za·tion** \-mətrə-\ *n* -S

parametric amplifier *n* : a high-frequency amplifier whose operation is based on time variations in a parameter (as reactance) and which converts the energy at the frequency of an alternating current into energy at the input signal frequency in such a way as to amplify the signal

parametric equation *n* : any of a set of equations that express the coordinates of the points of a curve as functions of one parameter or that express the coordinates of the points of a surface as functions of two parameters

para·myosin \¦parə+\ *n* [[1]*para-* + *myosin*] : a fibrous protein that is found in molluscan muscle

para·myxovirus \"+\ *n* [NL, fr. [1]*para-* + *myxovirus* (herein)] : any of a family (Paramyxoviridae) of large single-stranded RNA viruses (as a morbillivirus or parainfluenza virus) that have a helical nucleocapsid and lipid-containing envelope and that include the causative agents of measles, mumps, respiratory diseases, and canine distemper

paranoid* *adj* : extremely or unreasonably fearful

para·phyletic \"+\ *adj* [[1]*para-* + *phyletic*] : of, relating to, or being a taxonomic group that does not include all descendants of a common ancestor

para·professional \"+\ *n* [[1]*para-* + *professional*] : a trained aide who assists a professional person (as a teacher or physician) — **para·professional** \"+\ *adj*

para·protein \"+\ *n* [[1]*para-* + *protein*] : any of various abnormal serum globulins with unique physical and electrophoretic characteristics

para·quat \ˈparəˌkwät\ *n* [[1]*para-* + *quat*ernary] : a toxic herbicide containing a salt of a cation [$C_{12}H_{14}N_2$] $^{2+}$ that is used esp. as a weed killer

para·sailing \"+\ *n* [*para-* (as in [1]*parachute*) + *sailing*)] : the recreational sport of soaring in a parachute while being towed usu. by a motorboat — **para·sail** \"+\ *vb* — **para·sailer** *or* **para·sailor** \"+\ *n*

para·sexual \¦parə+\ *adj* [[1]*para-* + *sexual*] : relating to or being reproduction that results in recombination of genes from different individuals but does not involve meiosis and formation of a zygote by fertilization as in sexual reproduction ⟨the ∼ cycle in some fungi⟩ — **parasexuality*** *n*

pa·ra·tha \pəˈrätə\ *n* -S [Hindi *parāṭhā*] : an unleavened Indian wheat bread that is usu. fried on a griddle

par·a·thor·mone \¦parəˈthȯrˌmōn, -ˈthȯ(ə)-\ *n* [*parathy*roid + *hormone*] : PARATHYROID HORMONE *herein*

parathyroid hormone *n* : a hormone of the parathyroid gland that regulates the metabolism of calcium and phosphorus in the body

para·transit \¦parə+\ *n* [[1]*para-* + [1]*transit*] : transportation service that supplements larger public transit systems by providing individualized rides without fixed routes or timetables

para·ventricular nucleus \¦parə+. . .-\ *n* [[1]*para-* + *ventricular*] : a discrete band of nerve cells in the anterior hypothalamus that produce vasopressin and esp. oxytocin and that innervate the neurohypophysis

para·wing \ˈparə+\ *n* [*para-* (as in [1]*parachute*) + *wing*] : PARAGLIDER *herein*

parcel* *n* : a volume of a fluid (as air) considered as a single entity within a greater volume of the same fluid

par·course \ˈpärˌkȯrs, ˈpȧ(r)ˌkȯ(ə)(r)s\ *n* [modif. (influenced by [1]*course*) of F *parcours*, lit., course, circuit, distance covered, fr. MF, animal path, trans. of ML *percursus*, fr. L *percurrere* to move through — more at PERCURRENT] : a trail for jogging that has stations at regular intervals with equipment for calisthenics (as sit-ups or pull-ups)

parent* *vb* ∼ *vi* : to bring up and care for a child ∼ *vt* : to bring up and care for

par·ent·ing \ˈpa(a)rəntiŋ, ˈper-\ *n* -S [fr. gerund of [2]*parent*] : the raising of a child by its parents ⟨felt ∼ was his wife's job more than his —Virginia Satir⟩ **2** : the act or process of becoming a parent **3** : the taking care of someone in the manner of a parent ⟨the ∼ of one's aged parents⟩

par·gy·line \ˈpärjəˌlēn\ *n* [pro*pargyl* + [2]*-ine*] : a monoamine oxidase inhibitor $C_{11}H_{13}N$ that is used in the form of its hydrochloride esp. as an antihypertensive agent

parietal* *n* **parietals** *pl* : the regulations governing the visiting privileges of members of the opposite sex in campus dormitories

parity* *n* **1 a** : the property of an integer with respect to being odd or even ⟨3 and 7 have the same ∼⟩ **b (1)** : the state of being odd or even used as the basis of a method of detecting errors in binary-coded data **(2)** : PARITY BIT *herein* **2** : the property of oddness or evenness of a wave function in quantum mechanics **3** : the symmetry of behavior in an interaction of a physical entity (as a subatomic particle) with that of its mirror image

parity bit *n* : a bit added to an array of bits (as on magnetic tape) to provide parity

parking orbit *n* : an orbit of a spacecraft from which the spacecraft or another vehicle may be launched on a new trajectory

par·kin·son's law \¦pärkənsənz-, ¦pȧk-\ *n, usu cap P&L* [after C. Northcote *Parkinson* †1993 Eng. historian] **1** : an observation in office organization: the number of subordinates increases at a fixed rate regardless of the amount of work produced **2** : an observation in office organization: work expands so as to fill the time available for its completion

parmigiano–reggiano \¦==¦=(ˌ)==ˈ=(ˌ)=\ *n, usu cap P&R* [It, short for *formaggio parmigiano-reggiano*, lit., cheese of Parma and Reggio nell'Emilia — more at PARMIGIANA, REGGIANO] : REGGIANO

par·o·mo·my·cin \ˌparəmōˈmīsᵊn\ *n* -S [prob. fr. Gk *paromoios* closely resembling (fr. *par-* para- + *homoios* like, similar) + E *-mycin* — more at HOME-] : a broad-spectrum antibiotic $C_{23}H_{45}N_5O_{14}$ that is obtained from a bacterium of the genus *Streptomyces* (*S. rimosus paramomycinus*) and is used against intestinal amebiasis esp. in the form of its sulfate

parser* *n* : a computer program that breaks down text into recognized strings of characters for further analysis

par·so·ni·an \pärˈsōnēən, pȧˈs-\ *adj, usu cap* [Talcott *Parsons* †1979 Am. sociologist + E *-ian*] : of or relating to the sociological theories of Talcott Parsons

parsons table *n, usu cap P* [fr. the *Parsons* School of Design, New York City] : a usu. rectangular table having straight legs that form the four corners

partially ordered *adj* : having some or all mathematical elements connected by a relation that is reflexive, transitive, and antisymmetric

partial product *n* : a product obtained by multiplying a multiplicand by one digit of a multiplier with more than one digit

participative* *adj* : of, relating to, or being a style of management in which subordinates participate in decision-making

particleboard \ˈ===ˌ=\ *n* : a composition board made of very small pieces of wood bonded together (as with a synthetic resin) — compare FLAKEBOARD *herein*

particle physics *n* : a branch of physics dealing with the constitution, properties, and interactions of subatomic particles esp. as revealed in experiments using particle accelerators — called also *high-energy physics* — **particle physicist** *n*

partition* *n* **1** : any of the expressions that for a given positive integer consist of a sum of positive integers equal to the given integer ⟨1 + 2 + 3 is a ∼ of 6⟩ **2** : the separation of a set (as the points of a line) into subsets such that every element belongs to one set and no two subsets have an element in common — **partition*** *vt*

par·ton \ˈpärˌtän\ *n* -S [[1]*part* + [2]*-on*] : a hypothetical particle (as a quark or a gluon) held to be a constituent of hadrons

party animal *n* : one who partakes of celebration, revelry, or alcoholic beverages usu. to excess

party·er *also* **parti·er** \ˈ==ə(r)\ *n* -S : one who attends parties; *also* : one who engages in revelry

party poop·er \-¦püpə(r)\ *n* [[7]*poop* + [2]*-er*] : one who refuses to join in the fun at a party; *broadly* : one who refuses to go along with everyone else

parv·albumin \¦pärv, ¦pȧv+\ *n* [*parv-* + *albumin*] : a small calcium-binding protein in vertebrate skeletal muscle

par·vo \ˈpär(ˌ)vō, ˈpȧ-\ *n* -S [by shortening] : PARVOVIRUS *herein*

par·vo·virus \¦pärvō, ¦pȧvō+\ *n* [NL, fr. *parv-* + *virus*] **1** : any of a family (Parvoviridae) and esp. genus *Parvovirus*) of small single-stranded DNA viruses that include the causative agent of fifth disease **2** : a highly contagious febrile disease of dogs that is caused by a parvovirus (genus *Parvovirus*) which may be a mutated form of the virus causing panleukopenia in cats and is marked by loss of appetite, lethargy, often bloody diarrhea and vomiting, and sometimes death

par·y·lene \ˈparəˌlēn\ *n* -S [contr. of *para-xylene*] : any of several thermoplastic crystalline materials that are polymers of para-xylene and are used esp. as electrical insulation coating

pas·cal \pasˈkal, pȧsˈkȧl\ *n* -S [after Blaise *Pascal* †1662 Fr. scientist and philosopher] **1** : a unit of pressure in the mks system equivalent to one newton per square meter **2** *usu cap P or all cap* : a computer programming language developed from Algol and designed to process both numerical and textual data

pas de deux* *n* : an intricate relationship or activity involving two parties or things ⟨every play written for the stage is . . . a *pas de deux* between language and action —Hilton Kramer⟩

pa·sil·la \päˈsēyä, pə-, -yə\ *n* -S [MexSp, prob. dim. of Sp *pasa* raisin, fr. L. *passa* (in *uva passa* raisins, lit., spread of grapes), fem. of *passus*, past part. of *pandere* to spread, unfold — more at FATHOM] : a slender long usu. dried chili pepper that is blackish brown when dried

pas·kha \ˈpäskə\ *n* -S [Russ, fr. *Paskha* Easter, fr. LGk *pascha* — more at PASCH] : a molded Russian dessert that is made of cheese (as cottage cheese), cream, and usu. raisins, candied fruit, and almonds and that is traditionally served at Easter

pa·so fi·no \ˈpä(ˌ)sōˈfē(ˌ)nō\ *n, pl* **paso finos** *usu cap P&F* [AmerSp, short for *caballo de paso fino*, lit., fine-gaited horse] : any of a breed of horses developed in South America and the Caribbean by crossbreeding Andalusian, Barb, and Jennet horses of Spanish stock that are characterized by a smooth lateral 4-beat gait in which the front and hind feet of the same side lift off the ground simultaneously with the hind foot hitting the ground just before the front foot

pass–fail \ˈ=ˈ=\ *n* : a system of grading whereby the grades "pass" and "fail" replace the traditional letter grades — **pass–fail** *adj*

passivate* *vt* : to protect (as a solid-state device) against contamination by coating or surface treatment — **passivation*** *n*

passive* *adj* **1** : not involving expenditure of chemical energy ⟨∼ transport across a cell membrane⟩ **2 a** : exhibiting no gain or control — used of an electronic device (as a capacitor or resistor) **b** : operating solely by means of the power of an input signal ⟨a ∼ communication satellite that reflects television signals⟩ **c** : relating to the detection of or to orientation by means of an object through its emission of energy or sound **3** : of, relating to, or making direct use of the sun's heat usu. without the intervention of mechanical devices ⟨∼ technique⟩ ⟨∼ building design⟩ **4** : of, relating to, or being business activity in which the investor does not have immediate control over income ⟨∼ investment⟩

passive–aggressive \¦===¦==\ *adj* : being, marked by, or displaying behavior characterized by the expression of negative feelings, resentment, and aggression in an unassertive passive way (as through procrastination, stubbornness, and uncommunicativeness) ⟨a *passive-aggressive* personality⟩ — **passive–aggressive** *n* -S

passive immunization *n* : the process of conferring passive immunity

passive restraint *n* : a restraint (as an air bag or self-locking seat belt) that acts automatically to protect an automobile passenger during a crash

password* *n* : a sequence of characters required for access to a computer system

passive smoking *n* : the involuntary inhalation of tobacco smoke (as from another's cigarette) esp. by a nonsmoker — **passive smoker** *n*

pasteurization* *n* : partial sterilization of perishable food products (as fruit or fish) with radiation (as gamma rays)

past·ies \ˈpāstēz\ *n pl* [[2]*paste* + *-ie*] : small round coverings for a woman's nipples worn esp. by a stripteaser

pas·ti·na \päˈstēnə\ *n* -S [It, dim. of *pasta*] : very small bits of pasta used esp. in soup or broth

pas·tis \pȧstēs\ *n* [F, fr. F dial. (Marseilles), lit., jumble, mess, kind of pastry, fr. Prov, fr. OProv *pastitz* cake, fr. (assumed) VL *pasticium*, fr. LL *pasta* dough — more at PASTE] : a French liqueur flavored with aniseed

pas·ti·tsio \päˈstētsē(ˌ)ō, -ˈstē(ˌ)chō\ *also* **pas·ti·tso** \-ˈstēt(ˌ)sō\ *n* -S [NGk *pastitsio, pastitso*, fr. It *pasticcio* pie, baked pasta dish — more at PASTICCIO] : a Greek baked dish made of ground meat layered with pasta and usu. topped with white sauce and cheese

pata·physics \¦pad·ə+\ *n pl but sing in constr* [F *pataphysique*, alter. of *métaphysique* metaphysics] : intricate and whimsical nonsense intended as a parody of science — **pata·physical** \"+\ *adj* — **pata·physician** \"+\ *n*

patch* *n* **1** : a minor usu. temporary correction or modification in a computer program **2** *Brit* : BEAT 7a **3** : a usu. disc-shaped piece of material that is worn on the skin and contains a substance (as a drug) that is absorbed at a constant rate through the skin into the bloodstream ⟨a nitroglycerin ∼⟩

patch* *vt* **1** : to make a patch in (a computer program) **2** : to connect (as circuits) by a patch cord

patchboard \ˈ=ˌ=\ *n* : a plugboard in which circuits are interconnected by patch cords

patch panel *n* : PATCHBOARD *herein*

pâte bri·sée \¦pätbrēˈzā, ¦pȧt-\ *n* [F, lit., broken pastry] : a rich pastry dough used esp. to make flaky tart shells

path* *n* : a sequence of arcs in a network that can be traced continuously without retracing any arc

patho·biology \¦pathō+\ *n* [*path-* + *biology*] : PATHOLOGY 1, 2a

pa·thol·o·gize \pəˈthäləˌjīz, pa-\ *vt* -ED/-ING/-S [*pathology* + *-ize*] : to view or characterize as medically or psychologically abnormal ⟨natural hormonal shifts have been *pathologized* —Joyce C. Mills⟩ ⟨*pathologizing* childhood behavior —Ruth Shalit⟩

patho·morphology \"+\ *n* [*path-* + *morphology*] : morphology of abnormal conditions — **patho·morphological** \"+\ *or* **patho·morphologic** \"+\ *adj*

pâ·tis·sier \(ˌ)pätēˈsyā, -ˌsēˈā\ *n* -S [F, fr. OF *pasticier*, fr. (assumed) *pastitz* cake (fr.—assumed—VL *pasticium*) + *-ier* [2]-er — more at PATISSERIE] : a pastry chef

patriarchy* *n* : a social system or society in which men have more power and control than women; *also* : men viewed collectively as the dominant force in a society

pa·tri·focal \¦pa·trə, ¦pä-+\ *adj* [*patr-* + *focal*] : PATRICENTRIC

patterning* *n* : physical therapy characterized esp. by repeated manipulation of body parts to stimulate normal motor developmental states (as crawling and walking) in order to stimulate the brain to develop specific motor skills lacking in individuals and usu. young children who have neurological deficiencies attributable esp. to brain injury

pat·zer \ˈpätsə(r), ˈpat-\ *n* -S [prob. fr. G *patzer* blunderer, fr. *patzen* to blunder] : an inept chess player

pau·piette \pōˈpyet, -ˌpēˈet\ *n* -S [F, fr. It *polpetta* meat croquette, dim. of *polpa* pulp, flesh, fr. L *pulpa*] : a thin slice of meat or fish wrapped around a filling (as of forcemeat)

pav·lo·va \paˈvlōvə\ *n* -S [after Anna *Pavlova* †1931 Russ. ballerina] : a dessert of Australian and New Zealand origin consisting of a meringue shell topped with whipped cream and usu. fruit (as kiwifruit)

pay* *vb* — **pay one's dues** *also* **pay dues 1** : to experience life's hardships : earn a right or position through experience, suffering, or hard work **2** : to suffer the consequences of or penalty for an act

payback* *n* : REQUITAL

pay–cable \ˈ=ˈ==\ *n* : pay-TV utilizing a cable television system — compare SUBSCRIPTION TV *herein*

payload* *n* : the load carried by an aircraft or spacecraft consisting of things (as passengers or instruments) necessary to the purpose of the flight as opposed to things (as fuel) which are necessary for operation; *also* : the weight of such a load

payout ratio *n* : a ratio relating dividend payout of a company to its earnings or cash flow

pay television *n* : PAY-TV *herein*

pay–TV \ˈ=(ˌ)=¦=\ *n* : a service providing special noncommercial television programming (as recent movies or entertainment specials) by means of a scrambled signal over the air or through a cable system to subscribers who are provided with a signal decoding device — compare PAY-CABLE *herein*, SUBSCRIPTION TV *herein*

pazazz *var of* PIZZAZZ *herein*

PB and J \ˌpēˌbēənˈjā\ *abbr or n* -S : a peanut butter and jelly sandwich

PBB \ˌpē(ˌ)bēˈbē\ *n* -S : POLYBROMINATED BIPHENYL *herein*

pc* *abbr* parsec

PC* *abbr* **1** professional corporation *herein* **2** *sometimes not cap* printed circuit **3** *sometimes not cap* politically correct *herein* **4** political correctness *herein*

PC \ˌpēˈsē\ *n, pl* **PCs** *or* **PC's** : PERSONAL COMPUTER *herein*

PCB \ˌpē(ˌ)sēˈbē\ *n* -S : POLYCHLORINATED BIPHENYL *herein*

PCP \ˌpē(ˌ)sēˈpē\ *n* -S **1** [prob. fr. *p*henyl *c*yclohexyl *p*iperidine] : PHENCYCLIDINE *herein* **2** : PENTACHLOROPHENOL

PCP *abbr* **1** Pneumocystis carinii pneumonia *herein* **2** primary care physician **3** primary care practioner **4** primary care provider

PCR *abbr* polymerase chain reaction *herein*

PCV valve \¦pē(ˌ)sēˈvē-\ *n* [*p*ositive *c*rankcase *v*entilation] : an automotive-emission control valve that recirculates gases (as from blow-by) through the combustion chambers to permit more complete combustion

PDA \ˌpē(ˌ)dēˈā\ *abbr or n* -S : a public display of affection **2** : PERSONAL DIGITAL ASSISTANT *herein*

PDGF *abbr* platelet-derived growth factor *herein*

PE* *abbr* physical education

peaceful coexistence *n* : a living together in peace rather than in constant hostility

peace·nik \ˈpē(ˌ)snik\ *n* -S [*peace* + *-nik* (herein)] : an opponent of war; *specif* : one who participates in antiwar demonstrations

peace sign *n* **1** : a sign made by holding the palm outward and forming a V with the index and middle fingers and used to indicate the desire for peace or as a greeting or farewell **2** : PEACE SYMBOL *herein*

peace symbol *n* : the symbol ☮ used to signify peace

peaches–and–cream \¦===¦=\ *adj* : of, relating to, or having a smooth wholesome complexion

peanut* *n* : a pellet made of usu. polystyrene foam and used chiefly as packing material

pearl* *vi, of a surfboard* : to make a nose dive into the trough of a wave

peatland \ˈ=ˌ=\ *n* : land rich in peat

pec \ˈpek\ *n* -S [short for *pectoral*] : PECTORALIS — usu. used in pl.

peck's bad boy \¦peks-\ *n, usu cap P* [fr. the book *Peck's Bad Boy and his Pa* (1883) by George Wilbur Peck †1916 Am. journalist, humorist, and politician] : one whose bad behavior is a source of embarrassment or annoyance

pedal steel *or* **pedal steel guitar** *n* : a box-shaped musical instrument with legs that has usu. 10 strings which are plucked with metal finger picks and of which the pitch may be adjusted either by sliding a steel bar along them or by using foot pedals to change their tension — compare HAWAIIAN GUITAR *in the Dict*

pedestrianize* *vb* ∼ *vt* : to convert (as a street) into a walkway or mall — **pe·des·tri·an·iza·tion** \pəˌdestrēənəˈzāshən, -ˌnīˈz-\ *n* -S

pe·do·phile \ˈpēdəˌfīl\ *n* -S [fr. *pedophilia*, after such pairs as E *Anglophilia* : *Anglophile*] : a person affected with pedophilia

peek–a–boo* \ˈ=ˌ=ˌ=\ *adj* **1** : of, relating to, or being a document retrieval system in which desired documents are identified by light shining through matching holes in index cards **2** : offering only limited display or disclosure esp. of a teasing sort ⟨engages in some playful *peek-a-boo* nudity —Joe Leydon⟩ ⟨*peek-a-boo* publicity⟩

peel* *vi* : to break away from a group or formation — often used with *off*

peel* *n* : the surgical removal of skin imperfections (as blemishes and wrinkles) by the application of a caustic chemical and esp. an acid to the skin — called also *chemical peel*

peep* *vt, slang* : to have a look at : SEE, WATCH

peer review *n* : a process by which something proposed (as for research or publication) is evaluated by a group of experts in the appropriate field — **peer–review** \ˈ=ˌ=ˈ=\ *vt*

Peg–Board \ˈ=ˌ=\ *trademark* — used for material (as fiberboard) with evenly spaced holes into which hooks may be inserted for the storage or display of articles

peking duck* *n, usu cap P* : a Chinese dish consisting of roasted duck meat and strips of crispy duck skin topped with scallions and sauce and wrapped in thin pancakes

pe·king·ol·o·gy \ˌpē(ˌ)kiŋˈäləjē\ *n* -ES *usu cap* [*Peking*, capital of Communist China + *-ology* (as in *Kremlinology* — herein)] : the study of the policies and practices of Communist China — **pe·king·ol·o·gist** \-jəst\ *n* -S *usu cap*

pel·meni *also* **pel·meny** \pəlˈmenē; pəlʸˈminē, -nʸē\ *n pl* [Russ *pel'meni*, pl. of *pel'men'*, alter. of Russ dial. *pel'nyan'*, fr. Votyak & Zyrian *pel'ńań*, fr. *pel'* ear + *ńań* bread; fr. their shape] : Russian meat dumplings that are often served in broth

peloton* *n* : the main body of riders in a bicycle race

pel·o·ton \ˈpeləˌtän, *F* plȯtōⁿ\ *or* **peloton glass** *n* [F *peloton* ball (of thread); prob. fr. the resemblance of such glass to a ball of multicolored thread — more at PELOTON] : a European ornamental glass often with a variegated metallized and satinized surface and usu. overlaid with strands of contrasting color

pelvic inflammatory disease *n* : infection of the female reproductive tract (as the fallopian tubes and ovaries) that occurs esp. as a result of a sexually transmitted disease, is marked esp. by lower abdominal pain, abnormal vaginal discharge, and fever, and is a leading cause of infertility in women — abbr. *PID*

pem·o·line \ˈpeməˌlēn, -ˌlən\ *n* -S [perh. fr. *p*henyl + *i*mino + oxazolidinone, a derivative of oxazolidine, fr. *oxazolidine* + *-one*] : a synthetic drug $C_9H_8N_2O_2$ that is a mild stimulant of the central nervous system

pen·ne \ˈpen,ā\ *n, pl* **penne** [It, pl. of *penna*, lit., quill, feather, pen, fr. L *pinna* feather & *penna* wing — more at PEN] : short thick diagonally cut tubular pasta

pen·ta·gastrin \¦pentə+\ *n* [*penta*peptide (herein) + *gastrin*] : a pentapeptide $C_{37}H_{49}N_7O_9S$ that stimulates gastric acid secretion

pen·ta·peptide \¦pentə+\ *n* [*penta-* + *peptide*] : a polypeptide that contains five amino acid residues

pen·taz·o·cine \penˈtazə,sēn, -,sən\ *n* -S [*penta-* + *-azocine* (as in *phenazocine* — herein)] : a synthetic, analgesic drug $C_{19}H_{27}NO$ that is less addictive than morphine

pen·to·barbitone \¦pentō+\ *n* [*penta-* + *-o-* + *barbitone*] *Brit* : PENTOBARBITAL

penumbra* *n* : a body of rights held to be guaranteed by implication in a civil constitution ⟨the ~*s* of the Bill of Rights⟩

people meter *n* : an electronic device wired to a television set and used to record the channel selections made by individual viewers

people mover *n* : any of various rapid-transit systems (as of moving sidewalks or automated driverless cars) for shuttling people (as within an airport or to and from it)

people's republic *n, often cap P&R* : a republic usu. organized and controlled by a national Communist or Socialist party

pepper steak *n* **1** : thin-sliced steak cooked with green peppers, onions, tomatoes, and soy sauce **2** : STEAK AU POIVRE *herein*

pep·tid·er·gic \¦peptīd¦ərjik\ *adj* [*peptide* + *-ergic* (herein)] : being, relating to, releasing, or activated by neurotransmitters that are short peptide chains

pep·ti·do·glycan \¦pep,tīdō+\ *n* [*peptide* + *-o-* + *glycan*] : a polymer that is composed of polysaccharide and peptide chains and is found esp. in bacterial cell walls — called also *mucopeptide, murein*

perceive* *vt* : to regard as being such ⟨*perceived* threats⟩ ⟨was *perceived* as a loser⟩

percentile* *n* : a value on a scale of one hundred that indicates the percent of a distribution that is equal to or below it (as in performance) ⟨a score in the 95th ~ is a score equal to or better than 95 percent of the scores⟩

per·cia·tel·li \,perchəˈte(l)lē, ,pər-\ *n* -S [It dial. (southern Italy), fr. *perciato*, past part. of *perciare* to pierce, bore (fr. OF *percier*) + *-elli*, pl. of *-ello*, dim. suffix — more at PIERCE] : long tubular pasta slightly thicker than spaghetti

percolate* *vi* : SIMMER 2a ⟨the feud had been *percolating* for a long time⟩

pe·re·on·ite \pəˈrēə,nīt\ *n* -S [*pereon* (var. of *pereion*) + [1]*-ite*] : any of the segments of a pereion

per·e·stroi·ka \(,)perəˈstrȯikə\ *n* [Russ *perestroĭka*, lit., rebuilding, fr. *perestroit'* to rebuild, fr. *pere-*, prefix denoting repetition (akin to L *per* through) + *stroit'* to build, fr. *stroĭ* system, order; akin to OSlav *stroi* order and prob. to OSlav *prostreti* to extend, L *sternere* to spread out — more at FARE, STREW] **1** : extensive restructuring and reform intended to revitalize the government and economy of the former Soviet Union **2** : a restructuring in another country like that in the Soviet Union; *broadly* : RESTRUCTURING ⟨a ~ of public education —Nancy J. Perry⟩

per·fec·ta \pə(r)ˈfektə\ *n* -S [AmerSp *quiniela perfecta* perfect quiniela] : a betting pool in which the bettor must pick the first and second finishers in a specified race or contest in the correct order — called also *exacta*

performance* *n* : the linguistic behavior of an individual : PAROLE 6; *also* : the ability to speak a certain language — compare COMPETENCE 2 *herein*

performance art *n* : a nontraditional art form that consists of or features a performance by the artist — **performance artist** *n*

per·for·ma·tive \pərˈfȯrməd·iv\ *adj* [*perform* + *-ative* (as in [2]*imperative*)] : being or relating to an expression that serves to effect a transaction or that constitutes the performance of the specified act by virtue of its utterance ⟨~ verbs such as *promise* and *congratulate*⟩ — compare CONSTATIVE *herein* — **performative** *n* -S

per·fu·sion·ist \pə(r)ˈfyüzhənəst\ *n* -S [*perfusion* + [1]*-ist*] : a certified medical technician responsible for extracorporeal oxygenation of the blood during open-heart surgery and for the operation and maintenance of equipment (as a heart-lung machine) controlling it

peri·apsis \¦perē+\ *n* [NL, fr. *peri-* + *apsis*] : the apsis nearest the center of attraction : the low point in an orbit — compare APOAPSIS *herein*

peri·cardio·centesis \¦perə¦kärdēō+\ *n* [NL, fr. *pericardi-* + *centesis*] : surgical puncture of the pericardium esp. to aspirate pericardial fluid

peri·cyn·thi·on \¦perə¦sin(t)thēən\ *n* -S [NL, fr. *peri-* + *Cynthia*, goddess of the moon (fr. Gk *Kynthia*) + *-on* (as in *aphelion*)] : PERILUNE *herein*

peri·lune \ˈperə,lün\ *n* -S [*peri-* + L *luna* moon — more at LUNAR] : the point in the path of a body orbiting the moon that is nearest to the center of the moon

perimenopause \,perē+\ *n* [*peri-* + *menopause*] : the period around the onset of menopause that is often marked by various physical signs (as hot flashes and menstrual irregularity) — **perimenopausal** \"+\ *adj*

perimeter *adj* [*perimeter*, n.] : scoring mostly from the perimeter in basketball ⟨~players⟩; *also* : originating from or centered on the perimeter in basketball ⟨~ shots⟩ ⟨a ~ game⟩

perimeter* *n* : the part of a basketball court outside the three-point line

peri·na·tol·o·gy \,perə,nāˈtäləjē\ *n* -ES [*perinatal* + *-ology* (as in *gynecology*)] : a branch of medicine concerned with perinatal care — **peri·na·tol·o·gist** \-ləjəst\

peri·nuclear \¦perə+\ *adj* [*peri-* + *nuclear*] : situated around or surrounding the nucleus of a cell ⟨~ structures⟩

peripheral* *adj* : AUXILIARY, SUPPLEMENTARY ⟨~ equipment⟩; *also* : of or relating to computer peripherals

peripheral *n* -S [*peripheral*, adj.] : a device connected to a computer to provide communication (as input and output) or auxiliary functions (as additional storage)

peripheral nervous system *n* : the part of the nervous system that is outside the central nervous system and comprises the cranial nerves excepting the optic nerve, the spinal nerves, and the autonomic nervous system

peripheral neuropathy *n* : a disease or degenerative state (as polyneuropathy) of the peripheral nerves in which motor, sensory, or vasomotor nerve fibers may be affected and which is marked by muscle weakness and atrophy, pain, and numbness

peristaltic pump *n* : a pump in which fluid is forced along by waves of contraction produced mechanically on flexible tubing

pe·ri·tus \pəˈrēd·əs\ *n, pl* **peri·ti** \-ēd·ē, -ē,tē\ [NL, fr. L *peritus*, adj., skilled, experienced — more at PERITE] : an expert (as in theology or canon law) who advises and assists the hierarchy (as in the drafting of schemata) at a Vatican council

peri·ventricular \¦perə+\ *adj* [*peri-* + *ventricular*] : situated or occurring around a ventricle esp. of the brain ⟨~ white matter⟩

per·locutionary \¦pər, ¦pə+\ *adj* [*per-* + *locutionary* (herein)] : of or relating to an act (as persuading, frightening, or annoying) performed by a speaker upon a listener by means of an utterance — compare ILLOCUTIONARY *herein*, LOCUTIONARY *herein* — **perlocution** \"+\ *n* -S

[1]**perm** \ˈpərm, ˈpəm, ˈpəim\ *vt* -ED/-ING/-S [[2]*perm*] : to give (hair) a permanent wave

[2]**perm** \ˈpəm, ˈpərm\ *n* -S [short for *permutation*] *Brit* : an arrangement of all possible combinations of a selected number of competitors for wagering on predicted winners (as in a football pool) or the order of finish (as in a horse race)

[3]**perm** \"\ *vt, Brit* : to select for or as if for a betting perm

permanent press *n* [[1]*press*] **1** : the process of treating a fabric with a chemical (as a resin) and heat for setting the shape and for improving resistance to wrinkles **2** : material treated by permanent press **3** : the condition of material treated by permanent press — **permanent-press** *adj*

per·me·ase \ˈpərmē,ās, -āz\ *n* -S [ISV *perme*able + *-ase*; orig. formed as F *perméase*] : an enzyme that catalyzes the transport of another substance across a cell membrane

per·meth·rin \(,)pərˈmethrən\ *n* -S [*per-* + *meth*yl + pyreth*rin*] : a synthetic pyrethroid $C_{21}H_{20}Cl_2O_3$ used esp. as an insecticide

permutation group *n* : a group of which the elements are permutations and in which the product of two permutations is a permutation whose effect is the same as the successive application of the first two

per·oxi·some \pəˈräksə,sōm\ *n* -S [*peroxi*de + [3]*-some*] : a cytoplasmic cell organelle that contains catalytic enzymes (as catalase) which act in oxidative reactions and esp. in the production and decomposition of hydrogen peroxide — **per·oxi·som·al** \-,räksə¦sōməl\ *adj*

per·oxy·ace·tyl nitrate \pə,räksēəˈsēd·əl-, -ˈasəd·əl-, -ˈasə,tēl-\ *n* [*peroxy-* + *acetyl*] : a toxic compound $C_2H_3O_5N$ that is irritating to the eyes and upper respiratory tract and is found esp. in smog

perp \ˈpərp, ˈpə̄p, ˈpəip\ *n* -S [by shortening] : PERPETRATOR

per·phe·na·zine \(,)pərˈfēnə,zēn, -ˈfen-\ *n* -S [blend of *piperazine* and *phen-*] : a phenothiazine tranquilizer $C_{21}H_{26}ClN_3OS$ that is used to control tension, anxiety, and agitation esp. in psychotic conditions

persistent* *adj* **1** : degraded only slowly by the environment ⟨~ pesticides⟩ **2** : remaining infective for a relatively long time in a vector after an initial period of incubation ⟨~ viruses⟩

persona* *n* **1** : a character assumed by an author in a written work **2** : the personality that a person projects in public : IMAGE 2 *herein* ⟨differences between Lafayette as a public ~ and the man at ease with social and intellectual equals —Michael Kammen⟩

personal computer *n* : a general-purpose computer equipped with a microprocessor and designed to run esp. commercial software (as a word processor or World Wide Web browser) for an individual user

personal digital assistant *n* : a small hand-held device equipped with a microprocessor that is used esp. for organization and communication — abbr. *PDA*

personality inventory *n* : any of several tests that attempt to characterize the personality of an individual by objective scoring of replies to numerous questions concerning his or her own behavior and attitudes — compare MINNESOTA MULTIPHASIC PERSONALITY INVENTORY *herein*

personal tax *n* : DIRECT TAX

personhood \ˈ==,=\ *n* : the fact or state of being a person ⟨we recognize them as rights. They are the privileges of ~ —Williard Gaylin & Marc Lappé⟩; *esp* : one's distinctive personal identity ⟨the brave, awkward attempts made . . . to assert their pride and ~ —Dotson Rader⟩

person-hour \ˈ==¦=(ə)\ : a unit of one hour's work by one person

PERT \ˈpərt\ *n* -S [*p*rogram *e*valuation and *r*eview *t*echnique] : a technique for planning, scheduling, and monitoring a complex project esp. by graphically displaying the separate tasks and showing how they are interconnected

perturbation theory *n* : any of various methods of calculating the approximate value of a complex function (as the energy of an electron in quantum mechanics) by first assuming that the dominant influence is the only factor and then making small corrections for additional factors

perv \ˈpərv, ˈpə̄v, ˈpəiv\ *n* -S [by shortening] : PERVERT

pe·se·wa \pəˈsäwə\ *n* -S [Twi *pɛ́sewa*, lit., penny, penny's worth of gold dust] **1** : a monetary unit of Ghana equal to 1/100 cedi — see MONEY table *in the Dict* **2** : a coin representing one pesewa

pesty \ˈpestē, -ti\ *adj* [*pest* + [1]*-y*] : BOTHERSOME, IRRITATING

PET *abbr* **1** positron-emission tomography *herein* **2** polyethylene terephthalate *herein*

peta- \ˈped·ə, ˈpetə\ *comb form* [ISV, modif. of Gk *penta-* penta-] : quadrillion ⟨*peta*-electron volts⟩

peter principle *n, usu cap both Ps* [after Laurence Johnston *Peter* †1990 Am. (Canad.-born) educator] : an observation: in a hierarchy every employee tends to rise to the level of his or her incompetence

petit bourgeois *adj* [*petit bourgeois*, n.] : of, relating to, or characteristic of the petite bourgeoisie

petite si·rah \-səˈrä\ *n, pl* **petite sirahs** *often cap P&S* [modif. of F *petite syrah*, lit. little syrah (grape variety of the Rhône valley in France)] : a dry red varietal wine made esp. in California

pet·nap·ping \ˈpet,napiŋ\ *n* -S [[1]*pet* + *-napping* (as in *kidnapping*)] : the act of stealing a pet (as a cat or dog) usu. for profit

pet·ro·dollar \¦pe·trō+\ *n* [*petr-* + *dollar*] : a dollar's worth of foreign exchange obtained by a petroleum-exporting country through sales abroad and usu. available for foreign investment — usu. used in pl.

pet·ro·politics \"+\ *n pl* [*petr-* + *politics*] : the strategy of controlling petroleum sales as a way of achieving international political goals

PET scan \ˈpet-\ *n* : a sectional view of the body constructed by positron-emission tomography — **PET scanning** *n*

PET scanner *n* : a medical instrument consisting of integrated X-ray and computing equipment that is used for positron-emission tomography

petting zoo *n* : a collection of farm animals (as baby goats) or gentle exotic animals (as llamas) for children to pet and feed

PF* *abbr, usu not cap* personal foul

PFD \,pē(,)efˈdē\ *abbr or n* -S : a personal flotation device

pfie·ste·ria \fēˈstirēə, fisˈtir\ *n, cap* [NL, fr. Lois Ann *Pfiester* Fink †1992 Am. microbiologist + NL *-ia*] : a genus of dinoflagellates including one (*Pfiesteria piscicida*) found in waters esp. along the middle southern Atlantic coast of the U.S. that produces a toxin which causes skin lesions in fish, that feeds upon the lesions sometimes causing large fish die-offs, and that may cause symptoms (as skin lesions and memory loss) in humans exposed to the toxin

p53 \,pē,fiftēˈthrē\ *n* -S [fr. *p53*, the protein made by the gene, fr. *protein* + *53*, the protein's molecular weight] : a tumor suppressor gene that in a defective form tends to be associated with a high risk of certain cancers

pg* *abbr* picogram *herein*

PG \¦pē¦jē\ *trademark* — used as a rating for a motion picture of such a nature that persons of all ages may be allowed admission but parental guidance is suggested; compare G *herein*, NC-17 *herein*, PG-13 *herein*, R *herein*

PG* *abbr* prostaglandin *herein*

PG-13 \¦=¦=¦=¦=\ *trademark* — used as a rating for a motion picture of such a nature that persons of all ages may be admitted but parental guidance is suggested esp. for children under 13; compare G *herein*, NC-17 *herein*, PG *herein*, R *herein*

phago·some \ˈfagə,sōm\ *n* -S [*phag-* + [3]*-some*] : a membrane-bound vesicle that encloses particulate matter taken into the cell by phagocytosis

phallic* *adj* : of, relating to, characterized by, or being the stage of psychosexual development in psychoanalytic theory during which a child becomes interested in his or her own sexual organs — **phal·li·cal·ly** \ˈfalik(ə)lē\ *adv*

phal·lo·cen·tric \¦falə¦sen-trik, -(,)lō-\ *adj* [*phall-* + *-centric*] : centered on or emphasizing the phallus or the male point of view

phal·lo·crat·ic \¦falə¦krad·ik, -at- -(,)lō-\ *adj* [F *phallocratique*, fr. *phallocrate* phallocrat, fr. *phallo-* phall- + *-crate* -crat] : relating to, resulting from, or advocating masculine power and dominance — **phal·loc·ra·cy** \,faˈläkrəsē, fə-\ *n* -ES — **phal·lo·crat** \ˈfalə,krat, -lō-\ *n* -S

phantasmagoria* *n* : a bizarre or fantastic combination, collection, or assemblage

phar·ma·co·genetics \¦färməkō+\ *n pl but sing in constr* [ISV *pharmaco-* + *genetics*] : the study of the interrelation of hereditary constitution and variation in response to drugs — **phar·ma·co·genetic** \"+\ *adj*

phar·ma·co·kinetics \"+\ *n pl but sing in constr* [ISV *pharmaco-* + *kinetics*] **1** : the study of the bodily absorption, distribution, metabolism, and excretion of drugs **2** : the characteristic interactions of a drug and the body in terms of its absorption, distribution, metabolism, and excretion — **phar·ma·co·kinetic** \"+\ *adj*

phasedown \ˈ=,=\ *n* -S [[2]*phase* + *down*] : a gradual reduction (as in size or operation) : a slowing down by phases

phaseout \ˈ=,=\ *n* -S [*phase out*, v.] : a gradual stopping of operations or production : a closing down by phases

phat* *adj, slang* : highly appealing or gratifying ⟨a ~ beat moving through my body —Tara Roberts⟩

phe·naz·o·cine \fəˈnazə,sēn, -sən\ *n* -S [*phen-* + *azocine*, a chemical compound, prob. fr. *az-* + *octa-* + [2]*-ine*] : a drug $C_{22}H_{27}NO$ related to morphine that has greater pain-relieving and slighter narcotic effect

phen·cy·cli·dine \(ˈ)fenˈsiklə,dēn, -ˈsīk-, -,dən\ *n* -S [*phen-* + *cycl-* + *-idin*] : a piperidine derivative $C_{17}H_{25}N$ used esp. as a veterinary anesthetic and sometimes illicitly as a psychedelic drug to induce vivid mental imagery — called also *angel dust, PCP*

phen·el·zine \ˈfenᵊl,zēn\ *n* -S [*phen-* + *ethyl* + hydra*zine*] : a monoamine oxidase inhibitor $C_8H_{12}N_2$ used esp. as an antidepressant drug

phe·neth·i·cil·lin \fə¦nethə¦silən\ *n* -S [*phen-* + *eth-* + peni*cillin*] : a semisynthetic penicillin $C_{17}H_{20}N_2O_5S$ administered orally in the form of its potassium salt and used esp. in the treatment of less severe infections caused by bacteria that do not produce penicillinase

phe·net·ic \fəˈned·ik\ *adj* [*phen*otype + *-etic* (as in *genetic*)] : of or relating to taxonomic analysis that emphasizes the overall similarities of characteristics among biological taxa without regard to phylogenetic relationships — compare CLADISTIC *herein*

phe·net·i·cist \-d·əsəst\ *n* -S : a taxonomist who adheres to the phenetic system of classification

phe·net·ics \-iks\ *n pl but sing in constr* : a system of biological classification based on phenetic methods

phen·met·ra·zine \(ˈ)fenˈme·trə,zēn\ *n* -S [*phen*yl + *me*thyl + *tetra-* + oxa*zine*] : a sympathomimetic stimulant $C_{11}H_{15}NO$ used in the form of its hydrochloride as an appetite suppressant

phe·no·gram \ˈfēnə,gram\ *n* [*phen-* + *-gram*] : a branching diagrammatic tree used in phenetic classification to illustrate the degree of similarity among taxa — compare CLADOGRAM *herein*

phenothiazine* *n* : any of various phenothiazine derivatives (as chlorpromazine) that are used as tranquilizing agents esp. in the treatment of schizophrenia

phe·noxy·ben·za·mine \fə¦näksē¦benzə,mēn\ *n* [ISV *phen-* + [2]*oxy-* + *benz-* + *amine*] : a drug $C_{18}H_{22}ClNO$ that blocks the activity of alpha-receptors and is used in the form of its hydrochloride esp. to produce peripheral vasodilatation

phen·ter·mine \ˈfentər,mēn\ *n* -S [prob. fr. *phen*yl + *ter*t- + butyl*amine*] : an anorectic drug $C_{10}H_{15}N$ used in the form of its hydrochloride to treat obesity

phen·tol·amine \fenˈtälə,mēn, -,mən\ *n* [*phen-* + *tol*uidine + *amine*] : an adrenergic blocking agent $C_{17}H_{19}N_3O$ that is used esp. in the diagnosis and treatment of hypertension due to pheochromocytoma

phenylethylamine \,==+\ *n* [*phenyl* + *ethylamine*] : a neurotransmitter $C_8H_{11}N$ that is an amine resembling amphetamine in structure and pharmacological properties; *also* : any of various derivatives of phenylethylamine

phe·ren·ta·sin \fəˈrentəzən, -əsən\ *n* -S [Gk *pherein* to carry + *entasis* tension, stretching + E *-in* — more at BEAR, ENTASIS] : a pressor amine present in the blood in severe hypertension

phe·re·sis \fəˈrēsəs\ *n, pl* **phe·re·ses** \-,sēz\ [prob. back-formation fr. *plasmapheresis*] : APHERESIS *herein*

pher·o·mone \ˈferə,mōn\ *n* -S [*phero-* (fr. Gk *pherein* to carry) + *-mone* (as in *hormone*); fr. its conveying information from one individual to another — more at BEAR] : a chemical substance that is produced by an animal and serves as a specific stimulus to other individuals of the same species for one or more behavioral responses — **pher·o·mon·al** \,ferəˈmōnᵊl\ *adj* — **pher·o·mo·nal·ly** \-ᵊlē\ *adv*

phil·lips curve \ˈfiləps-\ *n, usu cap P* [after A.W.H. *Phillips* †1975 Brit. (New Zealand-born) economist] : a graphic representation of the relation between inflation and unemployment which indicates that as the rate of either increases the rate of the other declines

phil·lu·men·ist \fəˈlümənəst\ *n* -S [*phil-* + L *lumen* light + E *-ist*] : one who collects matchbooks or matchbox labels

phle·bol·o·gy \fləˈbäləjē\ *n* -ES [ISV *phleb-* + *-logy*] : a branch of medicine concerned with the veins — **phle·bol·o·gist** \-jəst\ *n* -S

phone* *n comb form* -S : speaker of (a specified language) ⟨Franco*phone*⟩

phone *adj comb form* [F, fr. Gk *-phōnos* -sounding, fr. *phōnein* to sound, fr. *phōnē* sound, voice — more at BAN] : of or relating to a population that speaks (a specified language) ⟨Franco*phone*⟩

phone-in \ˈ=¦=\ *n* [*phone in*, v.] : a radio or television program that allows telephone callers to talk on the air with the host or a guest

phone sex *n* **1** : prerecorded sex-oriented telephone messages available to those who call a commercial service **2** : sex-oriented conversations with an operator employed by a commercial service

phone tag *n* : TELEPHONE TAG *herein*

pho·no·cardiograph \¦fōnə+\ *n* [*phon-* + *cardiograph*] : a recording instrument used in phonocardiography

pho·no·cardiographic \"+\ *also* **pho·no·car·dio·graph·i·cal** \"+¦==¦grafəkəl\ *adj* : of, relating to, or involving phonocardiography or a phonocardiogram — **pho·no·car·dio·graph·i·cal·ly** \"+¦==¦=k(ə)lē\ *adv*

pho·no·record \ˈfōnō+,\ *n* [*phono*graph + *record*] : a phonograph record

pho·no·tac·tics \,fōnəˈtaktiks\ *n pl but sing in constr* [*phon-* + *tactics*] : the area of phonology concerned with the analysis and description of the permitted sound sequences of a language — **pho·no·tac·tic** \¦=¦=¦tik\ *adj*

phony-baloney *or* **phoney-baloney** \ˈ===¦==\ *adj* : PHONY

phor·ate \ˈfō(ə)r,āt, ˈfȯ(-\ *n* -S [*phos*phor- + thio*nate*] : a very toxic organophosphate systemic insecticide $C_7H_{17}O_2PS_3$

phor·bol \ˈfȯr,bȯl, -,bōl\ *n* -S [ISV *phorb-* (fr. Gk *phorbē* pasture, fodder) + [1]*-ol*; orig. formed in G — more at PHEOPHORBIDE] : an alcohol $C_{20}H_{28}O_6$ that is the parent compound of tumor-promoting esters occurring in croton oil

phos·pham·i·don \fäsˈfamə,dän\ *n* -S [*phosph-* + *amid-* + [1]*-on*] : a contact and systemic organophosphorus insecticide and miticide $C_{10}H_{19}ClNO_5P$

phosphate* *n* : a trivalent anion PO_4^{3-} derived from phosphoric acid H_3PO_4

phosphatidylcholine \¦==¦==,=¦=,=, =¦==¦=-\ *n* [*phosphatidyl* + *choline*] : LECITHIN

phosphatidylethanolamine \¦==¦==,=¦=,=, =¦==¦=-\ *n* [*phosphatidyl* + *ethanolamine*] : [2]CEPHALIN

phos·pho·diester bond \¦fäs(,)fō+. . .-\ *or* **phosphodiester linkage** *n* : a covalent bond in RNA or DNA that holds a polynucleotide chain together by joining a phosphate group at position 5 in the pentose sugar of one nucleotide to the hydroxyl group at position 3 in the pentose sugar of the next nucleotide

phos·pho·enol·pyr·uvate \¦fäs,fōə,nōlpīˈrü,vāt, -,nōl-, -,pī(ə)rˈyü-\ *n* -S [*phosphoenolpyruv*ic (acid) + [1]*-ate*] : a salt or ester of phosphoenolpyruvic acid

phos·pho·fruc·to·kinase \¦fäs(,)fō,frəktō, -frük-, -frùk-+\ *n* [*phosph-* + *fructose* + *kinase*] : an enzyme that functions in carbohydrate metabolism and esp. in glycolysis by catalyzing the transfer of a second phosphate (as from ATP) to fructose

phos·pho·glyceraldehyde \¦fäs(,)fō+\ *n* [*phosph-* + *glyceraldehyde*] : a phosphate of glyceraldehyde $C_3H_5O_3(H_2PO_3)$ that is formed esp. in anaerobic metabolism of carbohydrates by the splitting of a diphosphate of fructose

phos·pho·kinase \"+\ *n* [*phosph-* + *kinase*] : KINASE 2

phos·pho·pyruvate \"+\ *n* [*phosph-* + *pyruvate*] : PHOSPHOENOLPYRUVATE *herein*

phosphorylcholine \¦==ˈ==\ *n* [*phosphoryl* + *choline*] : a hapten used medicinally in the form of its chloride $C_5H_{15}ClNO_4P$ to treat hepatobiliary dysfunction

phos·pho·transferase \ˌfäs(ˌ)fō+\ *n* [*phosph-* + *transferase*] : any of several enzymes that catalyze the transfer of phosphorus-containing groups from one compound to another

pho·ti·no \fōˈtē(ˌ)nō\ *n* -s [*photon* + *-ino* (as in *neutrino*)] : a hypothetical elementary particle that theories of supersymmetry require to be associated with the photon, to have mass, and to interact only very weakly with ordinary matter and that is postulated to be a constituent of the dark matter of the universe

pho·to·aging \"+\ *n* [*phot-* + *aging*, gerund of ²*age*] : the cumulative detrimental effects (as wrinkles or dark spots) on skin that result from long-term exposure to sunlight and esp. ultraviolet light — **photoaged** *adj*

pho·to·autotroph \¦fōd·ō+\ *n* [*phot-* + *autotroph*] : a photoautotrophic organism

pho·to·biologist \¦fōd·(ˌ)ō+\ *n* : a specialist in photobiology

photo–call \ˈ==ˌ=\ *n, Brit* : an arranged session at which photographs of individuals are taken usu. for publicity

¹**pho·to·chro·mic** \¦fōd·ə¦krōmik\ *adj* [*phot-* + *chrom-* + *-ic*] **1** : capable of changing color on exposure to radiant energy (as light) ⟨~ glass⟩ ⟨~ lenses⟩ **2** : of, relating to, or utilizing the change of color shown by a photochromic substance ⟨a ~ process⟩ — **pho·to·chro·mism** \-ˌmizəm\ *n* -s

²**photochromic** \"\ *n* -s : a photochromic substance — usu. used in pl.

pho·to·coagulation \¦fōd·ō+\ *n* [*phot-* + *coagulation*] : a surgical process of coagulating tissue by means of a precisely oriented high-energy light source (as a laser beam) — **pho·to·coagulator** \"+\ *n*

pho·to·damage \"+\ *n* [*phot-* + ¹*damage*] : damage (as to skin or DNA) caused by exposure to ultraviolet radiation

pho·to·degradable \"+\ *adj* [*phot-* + *degradable* (herein)] : chemically degradable by the action of light ⟨~ plastics⟩

pho·to·detector \"+\ *n* [*phot-* + *detector*] : any of various photoelectric devices for detecting and often measuring the intensity of radiant energy

pho·to·diode \"+\ *n* [*phot-* + *diode*] : a photoelectric semiconductor device for detecting and often measuring radiant energy (as light)

photoelectron spectroscopy *n* : an instrumental method for determining the chemical composition of a material's surface by measuring the energy of electrons freed from the surface by irradiation (as by a laser)

photo–essay \¦==ˈ=ˌ=\ *n* : a group of photographs (as in a book or magazine) arranged to explore a theme or tell a story

pho·to·excitation \"+\ *n* [*phot-* + *excitation*] : the process of exciting the atoms or molecules of a substance by the absorption of radiant energy — **pho·to·excited** \"+\ *adj*

pho·to·fabrication \¦fōd·ˌō+\ *n* [*phot-* + *fabrication*] : a process for manufacturing components (as microcircuits) in which a design is photographed, reduced, and chemically etched on a surface (as of a semiconductor)

pho·to·induced \"+\ *adj* [*phot-* + *induced*, past part. of *induce*] : induced by the action of light

pho·to·isomerization \"+\ *n* [*phot-* + *isomerization*] : the light-initiated process of change from one isomeric form of a compound, radical, or ion to another

photolithography* *n* : a process involving the photographic transfer of a pattern to a surface for etching (as in producing an integrated circuit)

pho·to·mask \"+\ *n* [*phot-* + ²*mask*] : MASK *herein*

pho·to·morphogenesis \"+\ *n* [NL, fr. *phot-* + *morphogenesis*] : plant morphogenesis controlled by radiant energy (as light) — **pho·to·morphogenic** \"+\ *adj*

pho·ton·ics \(ˌ)fōˈtäniks\ *n pl but sing in constr* [*photon* + *-onics* (as in *electronics*)] : a branch of physics that deals with the properties and applications of photons esp. as a medium for transmitting information — compare OPTOELECTRONICS *herein*

photo op *n* [by shortening] : PHOTO OPPORTUNITY *herein*

photo opportunity *n* : a situation or event that lends itself to and is often arranged expressly for the taking of pictures that give favorable publicity to the individuals photographed

photoperiod* *n* : PHOTOPHASE 2 *herein*

pho·to·phase \ˈfōd·ōˌfāz\ *n* [*phot-* + *phase*] **1** : LIGHT REACTION *herein* **2** : the light period of a photoperiodic cycle of light and dark

pho·to·phosphorylation \¦fōd·ō+\ *n* [*phot-* + *phosphorylation*] : the synthesis of ATP from ADP and phospate that occurs in a plant using radiant energy absorbed during photosynthesis

pho·to·pigment \"+\ *n* [*phot-* + *pigment*] : a pigment (as chlorophyll or a compound in the retina) that undergoes a physical or chemical change under the action of light

pho·to·plate \ˈfōd·ō+\ *n* [*phot-* + ¹*plate*] : a photographic plate

pho·to·polarimeter \¦fōd·ō+\ *n* [*phot-* + *polarimeter*] : an instrument used to measure the intensity and polarization of reflected light (as from clouds enveloping a planet)

pho·to·polymer \"+\ *n* [*phot-* + *polymer*] : a photosensitive plastic used esp. in the manufacture of printing plates

pho·to·reactivation \"+\ *n* [*phot-* + *reactivation*] : repair of DNA (as of a bacterium) esp. by a light-dependent enzymatic reaction after damage by ultraviolet irradiation — **pho·to·reactivating** \"+\ *adj*

pho·to–realism \¦fōd·ō+\ *n, sometimes cap P&R* [*phot-* (photographic) + *realism*] : realism in art and animation characterized by extremely meticulous depiction of detail — **pho·to–realist** \"+\ *n or adj, sometimes cap P&R* — **pho·to–realistic** \"+\ *adj*

pho·to·reduce \"+\ *vt* [*phot-* + *reduce*] **1** : to cause to undergo chemical photoreduction **2** : to reduce photographically

pho·to·refractive \"+\ *adj* [*phot-* + *refractive*] : relating to, caused by, or having an index of refraction that changes relative to the intensity of incident light

photorefractive keratectomy *n* [*keratectomy* fr. *kerat-* + *-ectomy*] : surgical removal of part of the corneal surface using an excimer laser in order to correct for myopia — compare RADIAL KERATOTOMY *herein*

pho·to·resist \"+\ *n* [*phot-* + *resist*] : a photosensitive resin that loses its resistance to chemical etching when exposed to radiation and is used esp. in the transference of a circuit pattern to a semiconductor chip during the production of an integrated circuit

pho·to·respiration \"+\ *n* [*phot-* + *respiration*] : a light-dependent process in some higher plants that involves the uptake of molecular oxygen, the synthesis of glycolic acid in chloroplasts, and the subsequent oxidation of glycolic acid in peroxisomes followed by the release of carbon dioxide from mitochondria and that tends to inhibit photosynthesis esp. at higher temperatures, oxygen levels, and light intensities due to competition for a common metabolic substrate — **pho·to·respiratory** \"+\ *adj* — **pho·to·respire** \"+\ *vi*

pho·to·scan \ˈfōd·ō+\ *n* [*photoscan*, v. (herein), fr. *phot-* + ¹*scan*] : a photographic representation of variation in tissue state (as of the kidney) determined by gamma ray emission from an injected radioactive substance — **pho·to·scan** *vb* — **pho·to·scanner** \"+\ *n*

pho·to·system \"+ˌ\ *n* [*phot-* + *system*] : either of two photochemical reaction centers occurring in chloroplasts that consist chiefly of photosynthetic pigments (as chlorophyll) complexed with protein which absorb light energy and convert it to chemical energy in the form of high-energy electrons **a** : one that absorbs light with a wavelength of about 700 nanometers — called also *photosystem I* \-ˈwən\ **b** : one that absorbs light with a wavelength of about 680 nanometers — called also *photosystem II* \-ˈtü\

pho·to·toxic \¦fōd·ō+\ *adj* [*phot-* + *toxic*] **1** : rendering the skin susceptible to damage (as sunburn or blisters) upon exposure to light and esp. ultraviolet light ⟨~ antibiotics⟩ ⟨a ~ topical agent⟩ **2** : induced by a phototoxic substance ⟨a ~ response⟩ — **pho·to·toxicity** \"+\ *n*

pho·to·vol·ta·ics \"+väl'tāiks, -vōl-\ *n pl* [*photovoltaic* + ¹*-s*] : photovoltaic cells or devices

phrase marker *n* : a representation of the immediate constituent structure of a linguistic construction

phrase structure *n* : the arrangement of the constituents of a sentence

phreak·er \ˈfrēkə(r)\ *n* -s [phone *phreak* (herein) + ²*-er*] : one who gains illegal access to the telephone system — called also *phone phreak* — **phreak·ing** \ˈ=iŋ\ *n* -s

phyl·lo \ˈfē(ˌ)lō, ˈfī(-\ *n* -s [NGk, leaf, sheet (of pastry), fr. Gk *phyllon* leaf — more at BLADE] : extremely thin pastry dough that is layered to produce a flaky pastry

phys ed \ˈfizˈed\ *n* [by shortening] : PHYSICAL EDUCATION

physical* *adj* : characterized by forceful physical contact or rough play ⟨a ~ hockey game⟩

phys·i·cal·ize \ˈfizəkəˌlīz\ *vt* -ED/-ING/-S : to give physical form or expression to ⟨she likes to ~ major points of her argument with gestures⟩

physician–assisted suicide \=ˈ===ˈ==-\ *n* : ASSISTED SUICIDE *herein*

physician's assistant *or* **physician assistant** *n* : a person who has received special training and is certified to provide basic medical services usu. under the supervision of a licensed physician — called also *PA*

phy·tane \ˈfīˌtān\ *n* -s [*phyt-* + *-ane*] : an isoprenoid hydrocarbon $C_{20}H_{42}$ that is found esp. associated with fossilized plant remains from the Precambrian and later eras

phy·to·alexin \¦fīd·ō+\ *n* [*phyt-* + *alexin*] : any of various antimicrobial chemical substances produced by plants to combat infection by a pathogen (as a fungus)

¹**phy·to·chemical** \"+\ *adj* [*phyt-* + ¹*chemical*] : of, relating to, or being phytochemistry — **phy·to·chemically** \"+\ *adv*

²**phytochemical** *n* [*phyt-* + ²*chemical*] : a chemical compound (as beta-carotene or isothiocyanate) occurring naturally in plants ⟨promoted the health benefits of ~s⟩

phy·to·chemistry \"+\ *n* [*phyt-* + *chemistry*] : the chemistry of plants, plant processes, and plant products — **phy·to·chemist** \"+\ *n*

phy·to·chrome \ˈfīd·əˌkrōm\ *n* -s [*phyt-* + *-chrome*] : any of a group of proteins bound to light-absorbing pigments in many plants that play a role in initiating floral and developmental processes when activated by red or far-red radiation

phy·to·estrogen \¦fīd·ō+\ *n* [*phyt-* + *estrogen*] : a chemical compound (as genistein) that occurs naturally in plants and has estrogenic properties

phy·to·hemagglutinin *also* **phy·to·haemagglutinin** \"+\ *n* [*phyt-* + *hemagglutinin*] : a proteinaceous hemagglutinin of plant origin used esp. to induce mitosis (as in lymphocytes)

phytolith* *n* : a microscopic siliceous particle that forms in plant cells and is highly resistant to decomposition ⟨ancient plant species revealed by soil ~s⟩

phy·to·sanitary \"+\ *adj* [*phyt-* + *sanitary*] : of, relating to, or being measures for the control of plant diseases esp. in agricultural crops ⟨~ treatments⟩ ⟨a ~ commission⟩

phy·to·tron \ˈfīd·əˌträn\ *n* -s [*phyt-* + *-tron*] : a laboratory with facilities for growing plants under various combinations of strictly controlled environmental conditions

PI* *abbr* programmed instruction *herein*

PI \ˈpēˈī\ *abbr or n* -s : a private investigator

pia·get·ian \pyäˈzhāən, ˌpēəˈjed·ēən, -ˈjet-\ *adj, usu cap* [Jean *Piaget* †1980 Swiss psychologist + E *-ian*] : of, relating to, or dealing with Jean Piaget or his writings, theories, or methods

piano bar *n* : a cocktail bar that features live piano music

pi bond *n* [*pi* perh. after *p* orbital] : a chemical bond between atoms in a molecule having overlapping p orbitals

pi·ca·dil·lo \ˌpikəˈdilō, *Sp* pēkäˈdēyō\ *n* -s [AmerSp, fr. Sp, stew of chopped meat, fr. *picado*, past part. of *picar* to prick, chop, fr. (assumed) VL *piccare* — more at PIKE] : a spicy Latin-American hash or stew of meat and vegetables often with raisins and olives that is commonly used as a filling (as for tacos) or served with rice and beans

pic·ca·ta \pəˈkäd·ə, -ätə\ *n* -s [It, slice of sautéed veal flavored with lemon and parsley, fr. *piccata*, fem. of *piccato*, past part. of *piccare* to lard (meat), prob. fr. F *piquer*, lit., to prick — more at PIKE] : thin slices of meat (as veal) sautéed and served in a lemon and butter sauce

pick* *vt* : to obtain useful information from by questioning — used in such phrases as *pick the brains of*

pick* *n* : a comb with long widely spaced teeth used to give height to a hairstyle

pick–and–roll \ˈ==ˈ=\ *n* : a basketball play in which a player sets a screen and then cuts toward the basket for a pass

picker* *n* **1** : one that picks or plucks the strings of a stringed musical instrument **2** : a person who locates and purchases antiques and collectibles for resale to dealers

pick off* *vt* : INTERCEPT ⟨*picked off* a pass⟩

pick up* *vb* — **pick up on** **1 a** : UNDERSTAND, APPRECIATE **b** : to become aware of : NOTICE **2** : to adopt as one's own

pi·clo·ram \ˈpikləˌram, ˈpīk-\ *n* -s [*picoline* + *chlor-* + *amine*] : a systemic herbicide $C_6H_3Cl_3N_2O_2$ that breaks down only very slowly in the soil

pi·co·curie \¦pēkō+\ *n* [ISV *pico-* + *curie*] : one trillionth of a curie

pi·co·farad \"+\ *n* [ISV *pico-* + *farad*] : one trillionth of a farad

pi·co·gram \"+\ *n* [ISV *pico-* + *gram*] : one trillionth of a gram

pi·co·li·nate \pəˈkäləˌnāt, ˈpik(ə)li-\ *n* -s : a salt or ester of picolinic acid

pi·co·mole \¦pēkō+\ *n* [ISV *pico-* + *mole*] : one trillionth of a mole

pi·cor·na·virus \pəˈkórnə+\ *n* [NL, fr. ISV *pico-* + *RNA* + NL *virus*] : any of a family (Picornaviridae) of small single-stranded RNA viruses that have an icosahedral capsid but lack an envelope and that include the enteroviruses and the rhinoviruses

pi·co·second \¦pēkō+\ *n* [ISV *pico-* + *second*] : one trillionth of a second

pic·to·ri·al·ism \pikˈtōrēəˌlizəm, -ˈtór-\ *n* -s : a movement or technique in photography emphasizing artificial often romanticized pictorial qualities

picture–book \ˈ==¦=\ *adj* : suitable for or suggestive of a picture book: as **a** : PICTURESQUE, FAIRY-TALE ⟨a *picture-book* village⟩ **b** : IDEAL, PERFECT ⟨a *picture-book* landing⟩

picture–perfect \ˈ==ˈ==\ *adj* : completely flawless : PERFECT ⟨a *picture-perfect* day⟩

picture–postcard \¦==¦=ˌ=\ *adj* : PICTURE-BOOK a *herein* ⟨a *picture-postcard* fishing village⟩

PID *abbr* pelvic inflammatory disease *herein*

piece* *n* — **piece of the action** : a share in activity or profit

piece of cake : something easily done : CINCH, BREEZE

piece of work : a complicated, difficult, or eccentric person

piece·wise \ˈpēsˌwīz\ *adv* [¹*piece* + *-wise*] : with respect to a number of discrete intervals, sets, or pieces

pi electron *n* : an electron involved in a pi bond

pie·ro·gi *also* **pirogi** \pəˈrōgē, pi-\ *n, pl* **pierogi** *or* **pierogies** *also* **pirogi** *or* **pirogies** [Pol, pl. of *pieróg*, *pirog* stuffed dumpling; akin to Czech *piroh* filled pastry, Russ *pirog* — more at PIROSHKI] : a case of dough filled with a savory filling (as of meat, cheese, or vegetables) and cooked by boiling and then panfrying

pie safe *n* : a cupboard whose doors have decoratively pierced tin panels for ventilation

pig* *n* : POLICEMAN — usu. used disparagingly

piggyback* *adj* **1** : of, relating to, or being something (as a capsule or package) carried into space as an extra load by a vehicle (as a spacecraft or rocket) **2** : of, relating to, or being a radio or television commercial that is presented in addition to other commercials during one commercial break **3** : SUPPLEMENTAL, ADDITIONAL — **piggyback*** *adv*

piggyback* *vt* : to set up or cause to function in conjunction with something larger or more important ⟨school bus drivers' union is ~*ing* its demand for recognition . . . on the teachers' strike — *New Orleans (La.) Times-Picayune*⟩ ~ *vi* : to function or be carried as if on the back of another

pig out *vi, slang* : to eat greedily : GORGE — **pig–out** *n* -s

PIK *abbr* payment in kind

pike* *n* — **down the pike** **1** : in the course of events ⟨the greatest boxer to come *down the pike* in years⟩ **2** : in the future ⟨today's advances only hint at what's *down the pike*⟩

pileup* *n* **1** : a jammed tangled mass or pile (as of motor vehicles or people) resulting from collision or accumulation **2** : ACCUMULATION

pil·i·pi·no \ˌpiləˈpē(ˌ)nō\ *n, usu cap* [Tag, fr. Sp *filipino* Philippine] : the Tagalog-based official language of the Republic of the Philippines

pill* *n, sometimes cap* : BIRTH CONTROL PILL *herein* — usu. used with *the*

pillhead \ˈ=ˌ=\ *n* [⁴*pill* + *-head* (as in *hophead*)] : a person who takes pills or capsules (as of amphetamines) for nonmedicinal reasons

pillow talk *n* : intimate conversation between lovers in bed

pill pool *n* [⁴*pill*; fr. the drawing of small numbered balls from a bottle to determine which billiard balls the player will try to pocket] : KELLY POOL

pilot* *n* **1** : a television show produced as a sample of a proposed series **2** : PILOT LIGHT

pimpmobile \ˈpimpmōˌbēl, -məˌ *sometimes* -ˌbil\ *n* -s [¹*pimp* + *mobile*] : an ostentatious luxury car that is used by a pimp or looks as if it would be used by a pimp

pin* *n* **1** : something that resembles a pin esp. in slender elongated form ⟨an electrical connector ~⟩ **2** : PITON 2

PIN \ˈpin\ *abbr or n* : a personal identification number

pi·ña co·la·da \¦pēnyəkōˈlädə, ¦pēnə-\ *n* [Sp, lit., strained pineapple] : a tall iced drink made of rum, coconut cream, and pineapple juice

pi·ne·a·lec·to·mize \ˌpinēəˈlektəˌmīz, ˌpī-\ *vt* -ED/-ING/-S : to perform a pinealectomy on

pi·ne·a·lec·to·my \-təmē\ *n* -ES [*pineal (body)* + *-ectomy*] : surgical removal of the pineal body

¹**ping–pong** \ˈ=¦=\ *vb* -ED/-ING/-S [fr. *Ping-Pong*, trademark for table tennis] : SHIFT, BOUNCE ⟨the issue was *ping-ponged* back and forth⟩

²**ping–pong** *n, sometimes cap both Ps* : something resembling a game of table tennis; *esp* : a series of usu. verbal exchanges between two parties ⟨a *ping-pong* of absurdist dialogue — Lawrence O'Toole⟩

pinholder \ˈ=ˌ==\ *n* : a flower holder that consists of a substantial base topped with projecting pins

pink–collar \ˈ=¦=\ *adj* : of, relating to, or constituting a class of employees in occupations (as nursing or clerical jobs) traditionally held by women

pink sheet *n* **1** : a daily listing of over-the-counter stocks and their prices **2** : any of a group of lightly traded over-the-counter stocks

pink–slip \ˈ=ˌ=\ *vt* [*pink slip*, n.] : to give a pink slip to : FIRE

pi·no·cy·tot·ic \¦pinō(ˌ)sī¦täd·ik, ¦pīn-, -ˌsə¦t-\ *or* **pi·no·cyt·ic** \¦==ˈsid·ik\ *adj* [*pinocytosis* + ¹*-otic* or ¹*-ic*] : of, relating to, or being pinocytosis — **pi·no·cy·tot·i·cal·ly** \-ək(ə)lē\ *adv*

pinta \ˈpīntə\ *n* -s [*pint* + *-a* (as in *cuppa* — herein)] *Brit* : a pint of milk

pinteresque \ˌpintəˈresk\ *adj, usu cap* [Harold *Pinter* *b*1930 Eng. dramatist + E *-esque*] : of, relating to, or characteristic of the writings of Harold Pinter; *esp* : characterized by tightly controlled often absurd small talk and tense pauses that mask an underlying menace, fear, or anxiety

pinwheel* *n* : something (as a galaxy) shaped like a pinwheel

pin·yin \ˈpinˈyin\ *n* -s *often cap* [Chin (Pek) *p'in¹ yin¹* to spell phonetically, fr. *p'in¹* to arrange + *yin¹* sound, pronunciation] : a system for romanizing Chinese ideograms in which tones are indicated by diacritics and unaspirated consonants are transcribed as voiced — compare WADE-GILES *herein*

pipeline* *n* — **in the pipeline** : in the process of preparation, production, or completion : in the works

pir·ac·e·tam \pī(ə)rˈasəˌtam\ *n* -s [ISV *pir-* (alter. of *pyrrolidine*) + *acetamide*] : a derivative $C_6H_{10}N_2O_2$ of pyrrolidine that has been used as a nootropic

pirogi *var of* PIEROGI *herein*

pi·sce·an \ˈpīsēən *also* ˈpis-\ *n* -s *usu cap* [*Pisces* + ¹*-an*] : PISCES *herein*

pisces* *n, usu cap* : one born under the astrological sign Pisces

pi·sci·cide \ˈpīsəˌsīd, ˈpisə-, ˈpiskə-\ *n* -s [*pisci-* + *-cide*] : a substance used to kill fish — **pi·sci·ci·dal** \¦==¦sīdᵊl\ *adj*

pi·so \ˈpē(ˌ)sō\ *n* -s [Tag, fr. MexSp *peso* peso] : the peso of the Philippines

pis·sa·la·dière \pēsäläˈdyer\ *n* -s [F, fr. Prov (Nice) *pissaladiero*, fr. *pissala* preserved crushed and salted fish, fr. *pis*, *peis* fish (fr. OProv *peis*, fr. L *piscis*) + *sala*, past part. of *sala* to salt, fr. OProv *salar* — more at FISH, SALAD] : an open-faced pastry topped with olives, onions, and anchovies

piss·er \ˈpisə(r)\ *n* -s [¹*piss* + ²*-er*] : one that is inferior, difficult, or unpleasant — sometimes considered vulgar

piss off *vi, Brit* : to leave immediately : get out — often used as a command; sometimes considered vulgar ~ *vt* : ANGER, IRRITATE — sometimes considered vulgar

pissy \ˈpisē\ *adj* -ER/-EST [¹*piss* + ¹*-y*] **1** *slang* : ANGRY, PISSED OFF ⟨was acting ~⟩ **2** *slang* : IRRITATING, ANNOYING ⟨a ~ bureaucratic hassle⟩ — **piss·i·ly** \ˈpisəlē\ *adv, slang*

pis·tou \pēsˈtü\ *n* -s [F, crushed basil, pesto, fr. Prov, fr. *pista* to crush, fr. OProv *pistar*, fr. LL *pistare* — more at PESTO] : a vegetable soup served with a puree of garlic, herbs, oil, and cheese and often tomatoes

pit* *n* **1 pits** *pl* : something or someone that is the worst — used with *the* **2** : MOSH PIT *herein*

pi·ta \ˈpēd·ə, -ētə\ *also* **pit·ta** \"\ *n* -s [NGk *pita* pie, cake] : a thin flat bread that can be separated easily into two layers — called also *pita bread*

pit bull* *n* **1** : a dog (as an American pit bull terrier or an American Staffordshire terrier) of any of several breeds or a real or apparent hybrid with one or more of these breeds that was developed and is now often trained for fighting and is noted for strength and stamina **2** : an aggressive and tenacious person ⟨a political *pit bull*⟩

pit bull terrier *n* **1** : AMERICAN PIT BULL TERRIER *herein* **2** : PIT BULL *herein*

pitch* *vt* : to attempt to persuade esp. with a sales pitch ⟨~*ed* them on the idea⟩

pitch* *n* : the portion of a route (as in mountain climbing or caving) between belay points

pitch–perfect \ˈ=ˈ==\ *adj* [fr. *perfect pitch* absolute pitch] : DEAD-ON ⟨a *pitch-perfect* rendition⟩

pith helmet *n* : TOPEE

pi·thi·viers \¦pētē¦vyä, -ˌvē¦ā\ *n, pl* **pithiviers** *usu cap* [F, fr. *Pithiviers*, town in north central France] : a usu. round puff pastry with a sweet or savory filling

pit stop *n* **1** : a stop at a pit during an automobile race **2 a** : a stop (as during a trip) for fuel, food, or rest or for use of a rest room **b** (1) : a place where a pit stop can be made (2) : an establishment providing food or drink

pivot* *n* : an offensive player position in basketball that is occupied by a player (as a center) who usu. faces away from the basket to relay passes, shoot, or provide a screen for teammates

pivotman \ˈ=(ˌ)=\ *n, pl* **pivotmen** : one who plays the pivot; *specif* : a center on a basketball team

pix·el \ˈpiksəl, -ˌsel\ *n* -s [²*pix* + *element*] **1** : any of the numerous small discrete elements that together constitute an image (as on a television screen) **2** : any of the detecting elements of a charge-coupled device used as an optical sensor

piz·zazz *or* **pi·zazz** *also* **pa·zazz** \pəˈzaz\ *n* -ES [origin unknown]

: the quality of being exciting or attractive: as **a** : GLAMOUR, APPEAL ⟨bemoans the lack of color and provocative ~ in today's stars —Vernon Scott⟩ **b** : SPIRIT, VITALITY ⟨we had four numbers with ~ and the rest of the show died around them —Gower Champion⟩ **c** : FLASHINESS ⟨pure promotional ~ —Jim Powell⟩

piz·zet·ta \pēt'sed·ə, -'setä\ *or* **piz·zet·te** \pēt'sätä\ *n, pl* **pizzettas** *or* **pizzette** *or* **pizzettes** [It, dim. of *pizza* pizza] : a small pizza

pk* *abbr* pike

PKU *abbr* phenylketonuria

placebo effect *n* : improvement in the condition of a patient that occurs in response to treatment but cannot be considered due to the specific treatment used

place value *n* : the value of the location of a digit in a numeral ⟨in 425 the location of the digit 2 has a *place value* of ten⟩

plain jane *n, usu cap J* [*Jane*, female given name] : one that is plain in appearance

plain–vanilla \'==':=\ *adj* : lacking in special features or qualities : BASIC

¹planeside \'=,=\ *n* [⁴*plane* + ¹*side*] : the area adjacent to an airplane ⟨speaking briefly at ~ —*Christian Science Monitor*⟩

²planeside \'=,=\ *adj* : engaged in or made at planeside ⟨paused first for a ~ interview —*Time*⟩ ⟨his ~ remark —*Newsweek*⟩

planetary science *n* : PLANETOLOGY *herein* — **planetary scientist** *n*

plan·et·ol·o·gy \,planə'täləjē\ *n* -ES [*planet* + *-ology* (as in *cosmology*)] : a science that deals with the condensed matter (as the planets and natural satellites) of the solar system — **plan·et·o·log·i·cal** \-,tᵊl'äjəkəl\ *adj* — **plan·et·ol·o·gist** \-'täləjəst\ *n* -S

plaque* *n* **1** : a visibly distinct and esp. a clear or opaque area in a bacterial culture produced by damage to or destruction of bacterial cells by a virus **2** : a histopathologic lesion of brain tissue that is characteristic of Alzheimer's disease and consists of a dense proteinaceous core composed primarily of beta-amyloid that is often surrounded and infiltrated by a cluster of degenerating axons and dendrites

plasma jet *n* **1** : a stream of very hot gaseous plasma; *also* : a device for producing such a stream **2** *or* **plasma engine** : a rocket engine designed to derive thrust from the discharge of a magnetically accelerated plasma

plasmapause \'==,=\ *n* [*plasma* + *pause*] : the outer boundary of a plasmasphere

plasma physics *n pl but sing in constr* : MAGNETOHYDRODYNAMICS — **plasma physicist** *n*

plasmasphere \'==,=\ *n* [*plasma* + *sphere*] : a region of a planet's atmosphere containing electrons and highly ionized particles that rotate with the planet

plasma torch *n* : a device that heats a gas by electrical means to form a plasma for high-temperature operations (as melting metal)

plas·mid \'plazməd\ *n* -S [*plasm-* + ⁴*-id*] : an extrachromosomal ring of DNA that replicates autonomously and is found esp. in bacteria — compare EPISOME *herein*

plas·mon \'plaz,män\ *n* -S [*plasma* + ²*-on*] : a quantum of energy that propagates through a plasma as a result of charge density fluctuation

plastic* *adj* : having a quality suggestive of objects mass-produced in plastic; *esp* : lacking in vitality, originality, or sincerity ⟨~ smiles⟩ ⟨a ~ marriage⟩ ⟨vilified our skyway-filled downtowns, calling them lifeless and ~ —Brian Lowey⟩

plastic* *n* : credit cards used for payment ⟨the bill was £17.00, the banks were closed, and they don't take ~ —David Coombs⟩

plas·to·cyanin \¦plastō+\ *n* [*plasto-* + *cyanin*] : a copper-containing protein that acts as an intermediary in photosynthetic electron transport

plas·to·quinone \"+\ *n* [*plasto-* + *quinone*] : any of a group of substances that occur mostly in plant chloroplasts, consist of paraquinone with two methyl substituents and a side chain of one or more isoprene units, are related to vitamin K, and play a role in photosynthetic phosphorylation

plate* *n* **1** : LICENSE PLATE **2** : a schedule of matters to deal with ⟨have a lot on my ~ now⟩ **3** : any of the large movable segments into which the earth's crust is divided according to the theory of plate tectonics

plate* *vt* [fr. the crossing of home plate by the scoring runner] **1** : to cause (as a run) to score in baseball **2** : to arrange (food) on a plate

plated amberina *n* : an ornamental glass consisting of an amberina casing over a fiery opalescent or white lining

plateglass \¦=¦=\ *adj, usu cap* [*plate glass*, n.] : of, relating to, or being the British universities founded in the latter half of the twentieth century — compare OXBRIDGE *herein*, REDBRICK *herein*

platelet–derived growth factor \'===,=-\ *n* : a mitogenic growth factor that is found esp. in platelets, consists of two polypeptide chains linked by bonds containing two sulfur atoms each, stimulates cell proliferation (as in connective tissue, smooth muscle, and neuroglia), and plays a role in wound healing

platemaker \'=,==\ *n* : a machine for producing printing plates and esp. offset printing plates — **platemaking** \'=,==\ *n*

plate tectonics *n pl but sing in constr* **1** : a theory that the lithosphere of the earth is divided into a small number of plates which float on and travel independently over the mantle and that much of the earth's seismic activity occurs at the boundaries of these plates as a result of frictional interaction **2** : the process and dynamics of tectonic plate movement; *also* : a similar process on a planet other than the earth — **plate–tectonic** \¦=-=¦==\ *adj*

platform* *n* **1** : a structure on legs used for offshore drilling (as for oil) **2 a (1)** : a vehicle (as a satellite or aircraft) used for a particular activity or purpose or to carry a usu. specified kind of equipment **(2)** : a basic framework (as a chassis) upon which an automobile is constructed **b** : a computer architecture that uses a particular operating system

platform tennis *n* : a variation of paddle tennis that is played on a platform enclosed by a wire fence

platinum* *adj* : qualifying for a platinum record — **go platinum** : to have enough sales to qualify for a platinum record

platinum record : a platinum phonograph record awarded to a singer or group whose album has sold at least 1,000,000 copies

platoon* *n* : two or more players (as in baseball) who alternate playing the same position

platoon* *vt* : to alternate (one player) with another player in the same position ⟨if I can't play him every day, I'll ~ him in left field —Leo Durocher⟩ ~ *vi* **1** : to alternate with another player in the same position **2** : to use alternate players at the same position

platter* *n* : DISK 1 *herein*; *esp* : HARD DISK *herein*

play* *vi* : to gain approval : go over ⟨those issues ~ well in Western Europe —Russell Watson *et al*⟩ ~ *vt* **1** : to catch or pick up (a batted ball) : FIELD ⟨~*ed* the ball bare-handed⟩ **2** : to direct the course of (as a ball) : HIT ⟨~*ed* a wedge shot to the green⟩; *also* : to cause (a ball or puck) to rebound ⟨~*ed* the ball off the backboard⟩ — **play by ear** : to deal with (as a situation) without previous planning or instructions — **play games** : to try to hide the truth from someone by deceptive means — **play one's cards** : to act with the means available to one

play–action pass \¦=¦==-\ *n* : a pass play in football in which the quarterback fakes a hand-off before passing the ball — called also *play-action*

playbook* *n* : a notebook containing diagramed football plays

playdate \'=,=\ *n* [¹*play* + *date*] **1** : an arrangement to have a production (as a movie) shown during a specified period of time **2** : a play session for small children arranged in advance by their parents

player* *n* **1** : a device that reproduces recorded material (as video images or music) from a usu. specified medium **2** : one actively involved esp. in a competitive field or process : PARTICIPANT

playgroup \'=,=\ *n* : an informal gathering of preschool-aged children organized for the purpose of supervised play and companionship

playing field* *n* : a set of conditions for competition (as in business) — usu. used in such phrases as *a level playing field*

playlist \'=,=\ *n* : a list of recordings to be played on the air by a radio station

plaza* *n* **1** : an area adjacent to an expressway which has service facilities (as a restaurant, a filling station, and rest rooms) **2** : an open area usu. located near urban buildings and often featuring pedestrian walkways, trees, places to sit, and sometimes shops

PLC *abbr, Brit* public limited company

plea bargaining *n* : the negotiation of an agreement between a prosecutor and a defendant whereby the defendant is permitted to plead guilty to a reduced charge — **plea–bargain** \'=¦=¦==\ *vb* — **plea bargain** *n*

pleasantry* *n* : a polite social remark ⟨exhanged *pleasantries*⟩

-plex \,pleks\ *n comb form* -ES [partly fr. L *-plex* (as in *duplex* duplex); partly fr. ³*complex*] **1** : a figure having a given power ⟨googol*plex*⟩ **2** : a building divided into an often specified number of spaces (as apartments or movie theaters) ⟨four*plex*⟩ ⟨multi*plex*⟩

PL/1 \,pē(,)el'wən\ *n* -S [*p*rogramming *l*anguage (version) *1*] : a general-purpose language for programming a computer

plot* *vi* : to be located by means of coordinates ⟨the data ~ at a single point⟩

ploughman's lunch *n, sometimes cap P&L* : a cold lunch served esp. in an English pub and typically including bread, cheese, and pickled onions

plug* *vb* — **plug into** : to connect or become connected to by or as if by means of a plug ⟨the entire school is *plugged into* a . . . computer system —Patricia Linden⟩ ⟨pay up to $100 a month to *plug into* these agencies —Elliott McCleary⟩

plug and play *n* : a feature of a computer system by which a new hardware component is automatically detected and configured by the operating system

plug·ola \,plə'gōlə\ *n* -S [¹*plug* + *-ola* (as in *payola*)] : incidental advertising on radio or television that is not purchased like regular advertising

plume* *n* : any of several columns of molten rock rising continuously from the earth's lower mantle that are theorized to be a driving force of plate movement in plate tectonics and to underlie upper-mantle hot spots

plus* *prep* : BESIDES — not often in formal use ⟨~ all this, as a sedative it has no equal —Groucho Marx⟩

plus *conj* **1** : AND — not often in formal use ⟨if you want to make a super investment, ~ you don't happen to be rich —*advt*⟩ **2** : in addition to which — used chiefly in speech and informal writing ⟨it was an achievement. *Plus* I wrote the story and the musical score —Jackie Gleason⟩ ⟨are also fog-proof and impact resistant, ~ they are backed by a lifetime warranty —*Boating*⟩

plyo·met·rics \,plīə'me·triks\ *n pl but sing or pl in constr* [perh. irreg. fr. *plio-* + *-metrics* (as in *isometrics* — herein)] : exercise involving repeated rapid stretching and contracting of muscles (as by jumping and rebounding) to increase muscle power — **plyo·met·ric** \-ik\ *adj*

p marker \'=,==\ *n, usu cap P* [*P*, symbol for *phrase*] : PHRASE MARKER *herein*

PMS \,pē(,)em'es\ *n* : PREMENSTRUAL SYNDROME *herein*

pneu·mo·cys·tis \,n(y)ümə'sistəs\ *n* [NL, fr. *pneum-* + *-cystis*] **1** *cap* : a genus of microorganisms of uncertain affiliation that are usu. considered protozoans or sometimes fungi and that include one (*P. carinii*) causing pneumonia esp. in immunocompromised individuals **2** -ES, *usu cap* : PNEUMOCYSTIS CARINII PNEUMONIA *herein*

pneumocystis ca·ri·nii pneumonia \-kə'rīnē,ē-\ *also* **pneumocystis pneumonia** *n, usu cap 1st P* [NL *Pneumocystis carinii*, species name] : a pneumonia that affects individuals whose immunological defenses have been compromised by malnutrition, by other diseases (as cancer or AIDS), or by artificial immunosuppressive techniques (as after organ transplantation), that is caused by a microorganism of the genus *Pneumocystis* (*P. carinii*), and that attacks esp. the interstitium of the lungs with marked thickening of the alveolar septa and of the alveoli — abbr. *PCP*

poach* *vt* : to attract (as an employee or customer) away from a competitor

po·bla·no \pō'bläno\ *n* -S [MexSp *(chile) poblano*, lit., (chili pepper) of Puebla, fr. Sp. *poblano* of Puebla, fr. *Puebla*, state in central Mexico] : a large usu. mild heart-shaped chili pepper (*Capsicum annuum annuum*) esp. when fresh and dark green — see ANCHO *herein*

pocket* *n* : an area formed by blockers from which a football quarterback attempts to pass

pocket bread *n* : PITA *herein*

pocket door *n* : a usu. interior door that opens by gliding along a track into a recess in the wall

pod* *n* : a detachable compartment (as for personnel, a power unit, or an instrument) on a spacecraft

po–faced \'pō,fāst\ *adj* [perh. fr. *po* chamber pot, toilet, fr. F *pot* pot] *chiefly Brit* : having an assumed solemn, serious, or earnest expression or manner : piously or hypocritically solemn

pogo \'pō(,)gō\ *vi* -ED/-ING/-S [fr. *pogo* stick] : to dance by hopping up and down ⟨punk rockers ~*ing* madly⟩

po·go·noph·o·ran \,pōgə'näfərən\ *n* -S [*Pogonophora* + ¹*-an*] : any marine worm belonging to the phylum or class Pogonophora — **pogonophoran** *adj*

point* *n* **1 a** : a percentage point of the face value of a loan often added as a placement fee or service charge **b points** *pl* : a share of the profits of a business venture **2** : credit accruing from creating a good impression — usu. used in pl. ⟨he gets ~*s* for courage —Sally Quinn⟩

point–and–click \'==¦=\ *adj* : of, relating to, or being a computer interface that allows the activation of a file or function esp. by selection with a pointing device (as a mouse)

point–and–shoot \'==¦=\ *adj, of a camera* : not requiring user adjustment; *esp* : having automatically adjusted controls (as for focus, shutter speed, or flash)

poin·telle \,pȯin'tel\ *n* -S [perh. fr. ¹*point* + *-elle* (as in *dentelle*)] : an openwork design (as in knitted fabric) typically in the shape of chevrons; *also* : a fabric with this design

pointer* *n* : a computer memory address that contains another address (as of desired data)

point estimate *n* : the single value assigned to a parameter in point estimation

point estimation *n* : estimation in which a single value is assigned to a parameter

point guard *n* : a guard in basketball who is chiefly responsible for running the offense

point man* *n* **1** : a soldier who goes ahead of a patrol **2** : one who is in the forefront; *esp* : a principal spokesperson or advocate ⟨establishing himself as *point man* for the new Republican foreign policy —R.L.Strout⟩

point of accumulation : LIMIT POINT *herein*

point of no return **1** : the point in the flight of an aircraft beyond which the remaining fuel will be insufficient for a return to the starting point with the result that the craft must proceed **2** : a critical point (as in development or a course of action) at which turning back or reversal is not possible

point–of–purchase \¦==¦=\ *adj* : of or relating to the place (as a supermarket aisle) where a decision to purchase is made — compare POINT-OF-SALE *herein*

point–of–sale *also* **point–of–sales** \¦==¦=\ *adj* : of or relating to the place (as a check-out counter) where an item is purchased ⟨electronic *point-of-sale* terminals⟩ — abbr. *POS*

point–of–service \¦==¦=\ *adj* : of, relating to, or being a health-care insurance plan that allows enrollees to seek care from a physician affiliated with the service provider at a fixed co-payment fee or to choose a nonaffiliated physician and pay a larger share of the cost ⟨*point-of-service* plan⟩ — abbr. *POS*

point set *n* : a collection of points in geometry or topology

point set topology *n* : a branch of topology concerned with the properties and theory of topological spaces and metric spaces developed with emphasis on set theory

point–slope form \¦=-'=-\ *n* : the equation of a straight line in the form $y - y_1 = m(x - x_1)$ where m is the slope of the line and (x_1, y_1) are the coordinates of a given point on the line — compare SLOPE-INTERCEPT FORM *herein*

point source* *n* an identifiable confined source (as a smokestack or wastewater treatment plant) from which a pollutant is discharged or emitted — see NONPOINT *herein*

point spread *n* : the number of points by which a person who sets odds expects a favorite (as a football or basketball team) to defeat an underdog

poi·sha \'pȯishə\ *n, pl* **poisha** [Bengali *poisa*, prob. fr. Hindi *paisa*, paisa] : the paisa of Bangladesh

poison pill *n* : a financial tactic or provision used by a company to make an unwanted take-over prohibitively expensive or less desirable

pois·son distribution \pwä'sōⁿ-\ *n, usu cap P* [after Siméon D. *Poisson* †1840 Fr. mathematician] : a probability density function that is often used as a mathematical model of the number of outcomes (as traffic accidents, atomic disintegrations, or organisms) obtained in a suitable interval of time and space, that has the mean equal to the variance, that is used as an approximation to the binomial distribution, and that has the form

$$f(x) = \frac{e^{-\mu}\mu^x}{x!}$$

where μ is the mean and x takes on nonnegative integral values

polar* *adj* **1 a** : passing over the north and south poles of a celestial body ⟨a satellite in a ~ orbit⟩ **b** : traveling in a polar orbit ⟨a ~ satellite⟩ **2** : of, relating to, or expressed in polar coordinates ⟨~ equations⟩; *also* : of or relating to a polar coordinate system

polarity therapy *n, often cap P* : a holistic health discipline that seeks to achieve physical and emotional wellness through a system of touch, diet, exercise, and self-awareness designed to balance energy flows in the body

pole* *or* **pole position** *n* [¹*pole*] : the front-row position nearest the infield in the starting lineup of an automobile race

pole* *n* [⁴*pole*] **1** : the point of origin of two tangents to a conic section that determine a polar **2** : a point at which a meromorphic function has infinity as a limit

pole lamp *n* : a lamp that consists of a pole to which light fixtures are attached and that usu. extends from floor to ceiling

po·le·mol·o·gy \(,)pōlə'mäləjē\ *n* -ES [Gk *polemos* war + E *-ology* (as in *psychology*) — more at POLEMIC] : the study of war

police procedural *n, pl* **police procedurals** : a mystery story written from the point of view of the police investigating the crime

po·lio·virus \¦pōlē(,)ō+\ *n* [NL, fr. *polio*myelitis + *virus*] : an enterovirus that occurs in three distinct serotypes of which one is the most frequent cause of human poliomyelitis

political action committee *n* : PAC *herein*

politically correct *adj* : conforming to a belief that language and practices which could offend political sensibilities (as in matters of sex or race) should be eliminated — **political correctness** *n*

politically incorrect *adj* : not politically correct — **political incorrectness** *n*

po·lit·i·ci·za·tion \pə,lid·əsə'zāshən\ *n* -S : the act or process of politicizing ⟨the ~ of art is typical of totalitarian tyranny —B.W.Garfield⟩

poll* *vt* : to test (as several computer terminals sharing a single line) in sequence for messages to be transmitted

po·loi·dal \pō'lȯidᵊl\ *adj* [⁴*pole* + *-oid* + *-al*] : relating to or being a magnetic field that extends between the poles of a magnetic body (as the earth) into surrounding space

po·lo·nia \pə'lōnēə\ *n* -S *cap* [NL, Poland] : people of Polish descent living outside Poland

poly \'pälē\ *n* -S [short for *polymer*] : a polymerized plastic or something made of this; *esp* : a polyester fiber, fabric, or garment

poly(A) \¦pälē'ā\ *n* -S [*poly-* + *a*denylic acid] : RNA or a segment of RNA that is composed of a polynucleotide chain consisting only of adenine-containing nucleotides and that codes for polylysine when functioning as messenger RNA in protein synthesis

poly·acrylamide \¦pälē+\ *n* [*poly-* + *acrylamide*] : a polyamide $(-CH_2CHCONH_2-)_x$ of acrylic acid

polyacrylamide gel *n* : hydrated polyacrylamide that is used esp. to provide a medium for the suspension of a substance to be subjected to gel electrophoresis

poly·ade·nyl·ate \¦pälē,adᵊn'il,āt, -ə'denə,lāt\ *n* -S [*polyadenyl*ic acid (herein) + ¹*-ate*] : POLY(A) *herein* — **poly·ad·e·nyl·ated** \-,ātəd\ *adj* — **poly·ad·e·nyl·a·tion** \-ə,denə'lāshən\ *n* -S

poly·adenylic acid \"+. . .-\ *n* [*poly-* + *adenylic acid*] : POLY(A) *herein*

poly·alcohol \"+\ *n* [ISV *poly-* + *alcohol*] : an alcohol (as ethylene glycol) that contains more than one hydroxyl group

poly·brominated biphenyl \¦pälē, -lə+\ *n* [*poly-* + *brominated*, past part. of *brominate*] : any of several compounds that are similar to polychlorinated biphenyls in environmental toxicity and in structure except that various hydrogen atoms are replaced by bromine rather than chlorine — called also *PBB*

poly·butadiene \"+\ *n* [*poly-* + *butadiene*] : a synthetic rubber that has a high resistance to wear and is used esp. in the manufacture of tires

poly·carbonate \¦pälē, -lə+\ *n* [*poly-* + *carbonate*] : any of various tough transparent thermoplastics characterized by high impact strength and high softening temperature

poly·cen·trism \¦pälē'sen,trizəm, -lə-\ *n* -S [ISV *poly-* + *-centric* + *-ism*; prob. orig. formed as It *policentrismo*] : the existence of a plurality of centers of Communist thought and leadership — **poly·cen·trist** \-,trəst\ *n or adj*

poly·chlorinated biphenyl \¦pälē, -lə+. . .-\ *n* [*poly-* + *chlorinated*, past part. of *chlorinate*] : any of several compounds that are produced by replacing hydrogen atoms in biphenyl with chlorine, have various industrial applications, and are toxic environmental pollutants which tend to accumulate in animal tissues — called also *PCB*

polychromatic* *adj* : being or relating to radiation that is composed of more than one wavelength

poly·cistronic \¦pälē, -lə+\ *adj* [*poly-* + *cistronic* (herein)] : containing the genetic information of a number of cistrons

poly·clo·nal \¦pälē¦klōnᵊl, -lə¦k-\ *adj* [*poly-* + *clone* + ¹*-al*] : produced by, involving, or being cells derived from two or more cells of different ancestry or genetic constitution ⟨~ antibody synthesis⟩ ⟨~ activation of T cells and B cells⟩

poly·culture \¦pälē, -lə+\ *n* [*poly-* + ¹*culture*] : the usu. simultaneous cultivation or growth of two or more compatible plants or organisms and esp. crops or fish in a single area; *also* : a product of such cultivation or growth

polycystic kidney disease *n* : either of two hereditary diseases characterized by gradually enlarging bilateral cysts of the kidney which lead to reduced renal functioning: **a** : a disease that is inherited as an autosomal dominant trait, is usu, asymptomatic until middle age, and is marked by side or back pain, hematuria, urinary tract infections, and nephrolithiasis **b** : a disease that is inherited as an autosomal recessive trait, usu. affects infants or children, and results in renal failure

polycystic ovary syndrome *n* : a variable disorder that is marked esp. by amenorrhea, hirsutism, obesity, infertility, and ovarian enlargement and is usu. initiated by an elevated level of luteinizing hormone, androgen, or estrogen which results in an abnormal cycle of gonadotropin release by the pituitary gland —

called also *polycystic ovarian disease, polycystic ovarian syndrome, polycystic ovary disease*

poly·cytidylic acid \¦pälē, -lə̇+\ *n* [*poly-* + *cytidylic acid*] : RNA or a segment of RNA that is composed of a polynucleotide chain consisting entirely of cytosine-containing nucleotides and that codes for a polypeptide chain consisting of proline residues when functioning as messenger RNA in protein synthesis — see POLY I:C *herein*

poly·drug \ˈpälē, -lə̇+ˌ\ *adj* [*poly-* + ¹*drug*] : of, relating to, or being the abuse of more than one drug esp. when illicit; *also* : engaging in polydrug abuse ⟨~ dependents⟩

poly·es·ter \¦pälē+\ *adj* [*polyester*, n.] **1** : favoring clothes made from polyester fibers ⟨the ~ set⟩ **2** : lacking or tending to repress variety, originality, or good taste ⟨the ~ suburbs⟩

poly·ether \¦pälē+\ *n* [*poly-* + *ether*] : any of a group of polymers in which the repeating unit contains a carbon-oxygen bond derived esp. from an aldehyde or an epoxide and which are used esp. in the manufacture of plastic foams

polyethylene terephthalate *n* : a tough thermoplastic resin used esp. in the manufacture of plastic containers — abbr. *PET*

polyglot* *adj* : widely diverse (as in ethnic or cultural origin) ⟨a ~ cuisine⟩

po·lyg·ra·pher \pəˈligrəfər, ˈpälēˌgrafər, -lə̇ˌ-, -ràf-\ *n* -s : POLYGRAPHIST

poly I:C \ˌpälēˌīˈsē\ *or* **poly I·poly C** \ˌpälēˈīˌpälēˈsē\ *n* [*poly-* + *inosinic acid* + *poly-* + *cytidylic acid*] : a synthetic 2-stranded RNA composed of one strand of polyinosinic acid and one strand of polycytidylic acid that induces interferon formation and has been used experimentally as an anticancer and antiviral agent

poly·imide \¦pälē+\ *n* [*poly-* + *imide*] : any of a class of polymeric synthetic resins resistant to high temperatures, wear, and corrosion and used esp. for coatings and films

poly·inosinic acid \"+. . .-\ *n* [*poly-* + *inosinic acid*] : RNA or a segment of RNA that is composed of a polynucleotide chain consisting entirely of inosinic-acid residues — see POLY I:C *herein*

poly·lysine \"+\ *n* [*poly-* + *lysine*] : a protein whose polypeptide chain consists entirely of lysine residues

poly·mer·ase \pəˈliməˌrās; ˈpäləməˌrās, -āz\ *n* -s [*polymer* + *-ase*] : any of several enzymes that catalyze the formation of DNA or RNA from precursor substances in the presence of preexisting DNA or RNA acting as a template — see DNA POLYMERASE *herein*, RNA POLYMERASE *herein*

polymerase chain reaction *n* : an in vitro technique for rapidly synthesizing large quantitites of a given DNA segment that involves separating the DNA into its two complementary strands, binding a primer to each strand at the end of the segment where synthesis will start, using DNA polymerase to synthesize two-stranded DNA from each single strand, and repeating the process — abbr. *PCR*

poly·metallic \¦pälē+\ *adj* [*poly-* + *metallic*] : containing several metals ⟨~ nodules⟩ ⟨a ~ sulfide⟩

polynuclear aromatic hydrocarbon *n* : POLYCYCLIC AROMATIC HYDROCARBON *herein*

poly·oma virus \ˌpälēˈōmə-\ *or* **polyoma** *n* -s [NL *polyoma*, fr. *poly-* + *-oma*] : any of a genus (*Polyomavirus*) of papovaviruses that affect various vertebrates and includes one that induces tumors in rodents and two that cause an asymptomatic human infection that becomes laten in the kidney and is often reactivated in immunocompromised individuals

poly·ribosome \¦pälē, -lə̇+\ *n* [*poly-* + *ribosome* (herein)] : a cluster of ribosomes linked together by a molecule of messenger RNA and forming the site of protein synthesis — **poly·ribosomal** \"+\ *adj*

poly·semic \"+\ *adj* [*polysemy* + ¹*-ic*] : having many meanings : POLYSEMOUS

poly·silicon \"+\ *n* [*poly-* + *silicon*] : a polycrystalline form of silicon used esp. in electronic devices

poly·some \ˈpälēˌsōm, -lə̇-\ *n* -s [*poly-* + ribo*some* (herein)] : POLYRIBOSOME *herein*

poly·sorbate \¦pälē, -lə̇+\ *n* [*poly-* + *sorbate*] : any of several emulsifiers used in preparing some pharmaceuticals and foods

poly·synaptic \"+\ *adj* [*poly-* + *synaptic*] : involving two or more synapses in the central nervous system ⟨~ reflexes⟩ — **poly·synaptically** \"+\ *adv*

poly(U) *n* -s [*poly-* + *u*ridylic acid] : POLYURIDYLIC ACID *herein*

poly·unsaturated \¦pälē+\ *adj* [*poly-* + *unsaturated*] *of an oil, fat, or fatty acid* : having many double or triple bonds in a molecule — compare MONOUNSATURATED *herein* — **poly·unsaturate** \"+\ *n*

poly·uridylic acid \"+. . .-\ *n* [*poly-* + *uridylic acid*] : RNA or a segment of RNA that is composed of a polynucleotide chain consisting entirely of uracil-containing nucleotides and that codes for a polypeptide chain consisting of phenylalanine residues when functioning as messenger RNA in protein synthesis

pom \ˈpäm\ *n* -s *usu cap* [short for *pommy*] *Austral* : a British person : POMMY — usu. used disparagingly

po·me·rol \¦pōmə¦rōl\ *n* -s *usu cap* [F, fr. *Pomerol*, commune in southwest France] : a dry red Bordeaux wine made chiefly from the merlot grape

pom·mard \pōˈmär(d), *F* pòmàr\ *n* -s *usu cap* [F, fr. *Pommard*, town in eastern France] : a red Burgundy wine

pong \ˈpäŋ\ *n* -s [origin unknown] *Brit* : ODOR; *esp* : an unpleasant odor — **pong** *vi* -ED/-ING/-S

pony car *n* [after the Ford Motor Company's Mustang, the first car of this type] : one of a group of 2-door hardtops of different makes that are similar in sporty styling, high performance characteristics, and price range

pon·zi scheme *also* **ponzi** \ˈpänzē-\ *n*, *usu cap P* [after Charles A. *Ponzi* †1949 Am. (Ital.-born) swindler] : an investment swindle in which some early investors are paid off with the money put up by later ones in order to encourage more and bigger risks

-poo \ˌpü\ *suffix* [origin unknown] — used as a disparaging diminutive ⟨cutesy*poo*⟩ ⟨drink*poo*⟩

poof \ˈpüf, ˈpu̇f\ *also* **poove** \ˈpüv, ˈpu̇v\ *n* -s [prob. alter. of ²*puff*] *Brit* : a male homosexual — usu. used disparagingly

poof·ter *also* **poof·tah** \ˈpüftə, ˈpu̇f-\ *n* -s [alter. of *poof* (herein)] *Brit* : POOF *herein* — usu. used disparagingly

pool* *n* [³*pool*] **1 pools** *pl, often attrib, chiefly Brit* : an organized sports betting system in which a bettor submits predicted outcomes of several contests and pooled money is awarded to those whose predictions were correct **2** : a group of journalists from usu. several news organizations using pooled resources (as television equipment) to produce shared coverage esp. of events to which access is restricted

poop* *vi* [¹*poop*] : DEFECATE — used as a euphemism

poop* *n* [²*poop*] : EXCREMENT — used as a euphemism

poop·er–scoop·er \ˈpüpərˌsküpər\ *n* [rhyming alter. of *poop* (herein) + *scooper*] : a device used for picking up the droppings of a pet (as a dog) for disposal

poo–poo \ˈpüˌpü\ *n* -s [baby talk alter. of ²*poop*] : EXCREMENT — used as a euphemism

poor* *adj* : lacking a normal or adequate supply of something specified — often used in combination ⟨cash-*poor* countries⟩

poorboy \ˈ=ˌ=\ *n* [fr. the phrase *poor boy*; prob. fr. its resemblance esp. in fit to the sort of outgrown sweater a poor child might wear] : a close-fitting ribbed sweater

poo·ri \ˈpürē\ *n, pl* **poori** *or* **pooris** [Hindi + Urdu *pūrī*, fr. Skt *pūra* cake] : an Indian whole wheat bread formed in flat rounds of dough that puff up when deep fried

poor–mouth \ˈ=ˌmau̇th, -t͟h\ *vb* [*poor mouth*, n.] *vi* : to plead poverty as a defense or excuse ⟨usually *poor-mouths* when it's his turn to contribute⟩ ~ *vt* : to speak disparagingly of

pop* *n* [¹*pop*] — **a pop** : for each one : APIECE ⟨tickets at $5 *a pop* —Bob McCoy⟩

pop* *vt* **1** : to take (pills) esp. frequently or habitually ⟨he ~*s* vitamins . . . the way some cowboys gobble jelly beans —P.A.Witteman⟩ **2** *slang* : ARREST **3** : to perform (a wheelie) on a vehicle ⟨*popped* a rambunctious wheelie for two blocks —Robert Cullen⟩ **4** : to open with a pop ⟨~ a cold beer⟩ **5** : to shoot successfully in basketball ⟨~*s* an open jump shot⟩ ~ *vi* : PAY ⟨the house ~*s* for every third beer —Studs Terkel⟩

pop* *adj* **1** : POPULAR ⟨~ fiction⟩; *esp* : of or relating to the popular culture disseminated through the mass media ⟨~ psychology⟩ **2** : of or relating to pop art

pop* *n* [⁶*pop*] **1** : popular music **2** *sometimes cap* : POP ART *herein* **3** : pop culture

POP* *abbr, sometimes not cap* point-of-purchase *herein*

pop art *n, sometimes cap P&A* : art in which commonplace objects (as road signs, hamburgers, comic strips, or soup cans) are used as subjects and often physically incorporated in the work — **pop artist** *n*

popcorn *adj* [*popcorn*, n.] : having widespread appeal but usu. little artistic merit or intellectual stimulation ⟨~ movies⟩

popper* *n, slang* : a vial of amyl nitrite or butyl nitrite used illicitly as an inhalational aphrodisiac

pop·per·ian \päˈperēən, -ˈpir-\ *adj, usu cap* [Karl *Popper* †1994 Brit. (Austrian-born) philosopher + E ²*-an*] : of, relating to, or characteristic of the theories of Karl Popper; *esp* : of or relating to the theory that a hypothesis can be falsified by observed exceptions but never absolutely proven to be true

pop·ster \ˈpäpstə(r)\ *n* -s [*pop* (herein) + *-ster*] : a practitioner of pop

pop–top \¦=¦=\ *n* [¹*pop* + ¹*top*] : a closure that can be pulled to open a container making a special opening device unnecessary

population explosion *n* : a pyramiding of numbers of a biological population; *esp* : the recent great increase in human numbers resulting from both increased survival and exponential population growth

population genetics *n pl but sing in constr* : a branch of genetics concerned with gene and genotype frequencies in populations and considering esp. randomness of mating, immigration, emigration, mutation, and selection — see HARDY-WEINBERG LAW *herein* — **population geneticist** *n*

populist* *adj* **1** : POPULAR 2 **2** : POPULAR 4

pop–up* *adj* : being or appearing in a window overlying the original screen on a computer display ⟨*pop-up* menu⟩

pop wine *n* : an inexpensive sweet wine and esp. a fruit wine

p orbital \ˈpē-\ *n, often ital p* : the orbital of an electron shell in an atom in which the electrons have the second lowest energy

por·ci·ni \pȯrˈchē(ˌ)nē\ *n, pl* **porcini** *also* **porcinis** [It, pl. of *porcino* (short for *fungo porcino*, lit., porcine mushroom), fr. L *porcinus* of a pig — more at PORCINE] : a large wild edible brownish mushroom of the genus *Boletus* (*B. edulis*) : CEPE

por·ci·no \pȯrˈchē(ˌ)nō\ *n, pl* **por·ci·ni** [It] : PORCINI *herein*

pork belly *n* : an uncured side of pork

porn \ˈpȯ(ə)rn, ˈpȯ(ə)n\ *or* **por·no** \ˈpȯr(ˌ)nō, ˈpȯ(ə)(-\ *n* -s [by shortening] : PORNOGRAPHY — **porn** *or* **porno** *adj*

pornography* *n* **1** : material (as a book) that is pornographic **2** : the depiction or portrayal of acts in a sensational manner so as to arouse (as by lurid details) a quick intense emotional reaction ⟨the ~ of violence⟩

porny \ˈpȯrnē, ˈpȯ(ə)n-, -ni\ *adj* -ER/-EST [*porn* (herein) + ¹*-y*] : PORNOGRAPHIC

po·ro·mer·ic \¦pōrə¦merik, ¦pȯr-\ *n* -s [*poro-* + poly*meric*] : any of a class of tough porous synthetic materials used as a substitute for leather (as in shoe uppers)

port* *n* : a hardware interface (as a socket for a cable) by which a computer is connected to a peripheral device (as a printer or mouse); *broadly* : JACK 2l(1)

port *vt* -ED/-ING/-S [perh. fr. *port* (hardware interface — herein) (influence by *portable* and *portability*)] : to translate (a computer program) into a version for another computer or operating system ⟨planned to ~ the program to other computers —John Markoff⟩

portability* *n* : the transferability of a worker's benefits from one pension fund to another when the worker changes jobs

portable* *adj* **1** : characterized by portability ⟨~ pension benefits⟩ **2** : able to be used on any computer with little or no modification ⟨~ software⟩

por·ta·pak *or* **por·ta·pack** \ˈpō(r)d·əˌpak, ˈpȯ(r)-\ *n* -s [¹*portable* + *pak* (alter. of ¹*pack*) or ¹*pack*] : a portable combination of a television camera and videotape recorder

por·to·bel·lo \ˌpȯrd·əˈbe(ˌ)lō, ˌpȯrtə-\ *also* **por·ta·bel·la** \-lə\ *or* **por·ta·bel·lo** \-ˈbe(ˌ)lō\ *n* -s [perh. alter. of It *prataiolo, prataiuolo* or dial. It *pratarolo* meadow mushroom, fr. *prato* meadow, fr. L *pratum* — more at PRAIRIE] : a cultivated mushroom belonging to a large dark meaty variety of the button mushroom

POS *abbr* **1** point-of-sale *herein* **2** point-of-service *herein*

posi·grade \ˈpäzəˌgrād\ *adj* [*positive* + *-grade* (as in *retrograde*)] : relating to, using, or being an auxiliary rocket that imparts additional thrust to a spacecraft in the direction of motion

posit* *vt* : to propose as an explanation : SUGGEST

positional notation *n* : a system of expressing numbers in which the digits are arranged in succession, the position of each digit has a place value, and the number is equal to the sum of the products of each digit by its place value

position paper *n* : a detailed report that recommends a course of action on a particular issue

positive definite *adj* **1** : having a positive value of all values of the constituent variables ⟨*positive definite* quadratic forms⟩ **2** *of a matrix* : having the characteristic roots real and positive

positron–emission tomography \¦==,==¦==\ *n* : tomography in which an in vivo, noninvasive, cross-sectional image of regional metabolism is obtained by a usu. color-coded video representation of the distribution of gamma radiation given off in the collision of electrons in cells with positrons emitted by radionuclides incorporated into metabolic substances that have been administered (as by injection) — abbr. *PET*

post* *vt* [²*post*] : to publish (as a message) in an on-line forum (as an electronic bulletin board)

post* *or* **posting*** *n* [⁴*post*] : something (as a message) that is published on-line

postal* *adj* [fr. a series of incidents during the late 1980s and early 1990s in which disgruntled U.S. postal workers murdered coworkers or supervisors] : insanely or murderously violent — usu. used in the phrase *go postal*

postcard *adj* [*postcard*, n.] : suitable for or suggestive of a picture postcard : PICTURESQUE ⟨a ~ village⟩ ⟨a ~ view⟩

post·code \ˈ=¦=\ *n* : a code (as of numbers and letters) used similarly to the zip code esp. in the United Kingdom and Australia

postcolonial* *adj* : of, relating to, or being a former colony; *also* : of or relating to a period after colonial rule

post–determiner \ˈpōs(t)+\ *n* [*post-* + *determiner*] : a limiting noun modifier (as *first* or *few*) characterized by occurrence after the determiner in a noun phrase

¹**post·doc** \ˈpōs(t)ˌdäk\ *n* -s [short for *postdoctoral*] : one engaged in postdoctoral study or research

²**postdoc** *adj* [by shortening] : POSTDOCTORAL ⟨~ work⟩ ⟨~ mathematicians⟩

poster boy *n* : a male poster child

poster child *n* **1** : a child who has a disease and is pictured in posters to solicit funds for combating the disease **2** : a person or thing having a public image that is identified with something (as a cause or group)

poster girl *n* : a female poster child

pos·ter·iza·tion \ˌpōstərə̇ˈzāshən, -rīˈz-\ *n* -s [²*poster* + *-ization*] : the obtaining of posterlike reproductions having solid tones or colors and little detail from photographs or other continuous-tone originals by means of separation negatives — **pos·ter·ize** \ˈpōstəˌrīz\ *vb* -ED/-ING/-S

post·feminist \¦pōs(t)+\ *adj* [*post-* + ²*feminist*] : of, relating to, occurring in, or being the period following widespread advocacy and acceptance of feminism

postfix notation *n* : REVERSE POLISH NOTATION *herein*

post hoc \ˈpōst ˈhäk\ *adj* [*post hoc*, adv.] **1** : relating to or being the fallacy of arguing from a temporal sequence to a causal relation **2** : formulated after the fact ⟨a *post hoc* rationalization⟩

post·industrial \ˈpōst+\ *adj* [*post-* + ¹*industrial*] : occurring in, existing in, or being a period of social and economic development after the predominance of large-scale industry ⟨a ~ society⟩

post·irradiation \¦pōst+\ *adj* [*post-* + *irradiation*] : occurring after irradiation ⟨mutations in ~ cell divisions⟩

post·literate \¦pōs(t)+\ *adj* [*post-* + ¹*literate*] : relating to or occurring after the introduction of the electronic media

post·marital \"+\ *adj* [*post-* + ¹*marital*] : occurring after a marriage has been terminated

post·modern \"+\ *adj* [*post-* + ¹*modern*] **1** : of, relating to, or being any of several movements (as in art, architecture, or literature) that are reactions against the philosophy and practices of modern movements and that are typically marked by revival of traditional elements and techniques **2** : quintessentially modern : AU COURANT — **post·modernism** \"+\ *n* — **post·modernist** \"+\ *n or adj* — **post·modernity** \"+\ *n*

postoperative* *adj* : having recently undergone a surgical operation ⟨~ patients⟩

post·polio syndrome \"+. .-\ *n* [*post-* + *polio*] : a condition that affects former poliomyelitis patients long after recovery from the disease and that is characterized by muscle weakness, joint and muscle pain, and fatigue

post·production \¦pōs(t)+\ *n* [*post-* + ¹*production*] : the operations (as editing or scoring) following filming by which a motion picture or television show is readied for public presentation

poststructuralism \"+\ *n* [*post-* + *structuralism*] : a movement or theory (as in literary theory or psychoanalysis) that sees inquiry not as the objective exploration of stable structures and categories (as the self) but rather as a relative undertaking shaped by discursive and interpretive practices — **post·structural** \"+\ *adj* — **post·structuralist** \"+\ *n or adj*

post·surgical \"+\ *adj* [*post-* + *surgical*] : POSTOPERATIVE

post·test \ˈpōs(t)+ˌ\ *n* [*post-* + ¹*test*] : a test given to students after the completion of an instructional program to measure their achievement and the effectiveness of the program

post·transcriptional \¦pōs(t)+\ *adj* [*post-* + *transcriptional*] : occurring, acting, or existing after genetic transcription

post·transfusion \"+\ *adj* [*post-* + *transfusion*] **1** : caused by transfused blood ⟨~ hepatitis⟩ **2** : occurring after blood transfusion ⟨induction of ~ shock⟩

post·translational \"+\ *adj* [*post-* + *translational*] : occurring or existing after genetic translation

post–traumatic stress disorder \(ˈ)pōs(t)+. . .-\ *also* **post–traumatic stress syndrome** *n* : a psychological reaction that occurs after a highly stressing event (as wartime combat, physical violence, or a natural disaster) and is usu. characterized by depression, anxiety, flashbacks, recurrent nightmares, and avoidance of reminders of the event — abbr. *PTSD*; called also *delayed-stress syndrome*

post·treatment \(ˈ)pōs(t)+¦\ *adj* [*post-* + *treatment*] : relating to, typical of, or occurring in the stage following treatment ⟨~ examinations⟩ — **posttreatment** *adv*

post up *vt* : to act as a post against (an opponent) in basketball ~ *vi* : to post up an opponent in basketball — **post–up** *adj*

potassium–argon \¦==¦==¦=\ *adj* : of, relating to, or being a method of dating paleontological or geological materials based on the radioactive decay of potassium to argon that has taken place in a specimen

potbellied pig *n* : any of a breed of small pigs originating in southeastern Asia and having a short snout, straight tail, potbelly, swayback, short legs, and black, white, or black and white coat

potential* *n* : POTENTIAL DIFFERENCE

pothead \ˈ=ˌ=\ *n* [¹*pot* + *-head* (as in *hophead*)] : one who smokes marijuana

pot sticker *n* : a crescent-shaped dumpling filled usu. with pork, steamed, and then fried, and usu. served as an appetizer

pouil·ly–fuis·sé \püyēfwʸēˈsā\ *n* -s *usu cap P&F* [F, fr. Solutré-*Pouilly* and *Fuissé*, villages in eastern France] : a dry white Burgundy from an area west of Macon, France

pouilly–fumé \ˈ==füˈmā, -fu̇e-\ *n* -s *usu cap P&F* [F, fr. *Pouilly*-sur-Loire, village in France + *fumé*, past part. of *fumer* to smoke, fr. L *fumare*, fr. *fumus* smoke — more at FUME] : a dry white wine from the Loire valley of France

pound sign *n* **1** : the symbol £ **2** : the symbol # — called also *number sign, octothorpe*

POV *abbr* point of view

powder–puff \¦=¦=\ *adj* : of, relating to, or being a competitive activity or event for women ⟨she played *powder-puff* football —*Sports Illustrated*⟩

power* *n* : the probability of rejecting the null hypothesis in a statistical test when a particular alternative hypothesis is true

power* *vi* : to move with great speed or force

pow·er \ˈpau̇(ə)r, -au̇ə\ *adj* [¹*power*] **1** : of, relating to, or utilizing superior strength ⟨a ~ hitter in baseball⟩ **2** : INFLUENTIAL, IMPORTANT ⟨a ~ critic⟩ **3** : of, relating to, or being a meal at which influential people carry on discussions esp. about business or politics ⟨a ~ restaurant⟩ ⟨a ~ lunch⟩ **4** : characteristic of the style or habits of influential people ⟨blue ~ suits⟩ ⟨a ~ smile⟩

power base *n* : a base of political support

power broker *n* : a person (as in politics) able to exert strong influence through control of votes or individuals — **power brokering** *n*

power forward *n* : a basketball forward whose size and strength are used primarily in controlling play near the basket

power function *n* **1** : a function of a parameter under statistical test whose value for a particular value of the parameter is the probability of rejecting the null hypothesis if that value of the parameter is true **2** : a function (as $f(x) = ax^k$) that equals the product of a constant and a power of the independent variable

powerlifting \ˈ==ˌ==\ *n* : weight lifting in which lifters compete in the squat, bench press, and dead lift — **powerlifter** \ˈ==ˌ==\ *n*

power series *n* : an infinite series whose terms are successive integral powers of a variable multiplied by constants

power strip *n* : an electrical device consisting of a cord with a plug on one end and several sockets on the other

power structure *n* **1** : a group of persons having control of an organization : ESTABLISHMENT **2** : the hierarchical interrelationships existing within a controlling group

power sweep *n* : an end run in football in which one or more linemen pull out and run interference for the ballcarrier

power up *vt* : TURN ON 2 ⟨*power up* the computer⟩ — **power–up** *n*

poxvirus \ˈ=¦==\ *n* [NL, fr. E ¹*pox* + NL *virus*] : any of a family (Poxviridae) of large brick-shaped or ovoid double-stranded DNA viruses (as the causative agent of smallpox) that have a fluffy appearance caused by a covering of tubules and threads

ppb *abbr* parts per billion

PPLO \¦pē(ˌ)pēˌelˈō\ *n, pl* **PPLO** [*p*leuro*p*neumonia-*l*ike *o*rganism] : MYCOPLASMA

PPO \ˌpē(ˌ)pēˈō\ *n, pl* **PPOs** \-ˈōz\ [*p*referred *p*rovider *o*rganization (herein)] : an organization providing health care that gives economic incentives to the individual purchaser of a health-care contract to patronize certain physicians, laboratories, and hospitals which agree to supervision and reduced fees — compare HMO *herein*

pra·der–wil·li syndrome \ˈprädə(r)ˈvilē-\ *n, usu cap P&W* [after Andrea *Prader* b1919 and Heinrich *Willi* †1971 Swiss pediatricians] : a genetic disorder characterized by short stature, mental retardation, hypotonia, abnormally small hands and feet, hypogonadism, and uncontrolled appetite leading to extreme obesity

pragmatics* *n pl but sing or pl in constr* : a branch of linguistics that is concerned with the relationship of sentences to the environment in which they occur

praxis* *n* : practical application of a theory

prayer flag *n* : a flag on which a Buddhist prayer is printed that is flown in the belief that the prayer is wafted continuously as the flag flutters in the breeze

pre·agricultural \ˌprē+\ *adj* [*pre-* + *agricultural*] : existing or occurring before the practice of agriculture

pre·biological \"+\ *also* **pre·biologic** \"+\ *adj* [*pre-* + *biologic*] : PREBIOTIC *herein*

pre·biotic \"+\ *adj* [*pre-* + [1]*biotic*] : of, relating to, or being chemical or environmental precursors of the origin of life ⟨~ molecules⟩; *also* : existing or occurring before the origin of life ⟨~ conditions⟩

pre·born \"+\ *adj* [*pre-* + [1]*born*] : existing but not yet born

pre·calculus \"+\ *adj* [*pre-* + *calculus*] : relating to or being mathematical prerequisites for the study of calculus ⟨~ mathematics⟩ — **precalculus** *n*

pre·capillary \(ˈ)prē+\ *adj* [*pre-* + [2]*capillary*] : being on the arterial side of and immediately adjacent to a capillary

precision* *n* **1** : the accuracy (as in binary or decimal places) with which a number can be represented usu. expressed in terms of the number of computer words available for representation ⟨double ~ arithmetic permits the representation of an expression by two computer words⟩ **2** : RELEVANCE 1 *herein*

pre·ci·sion·ism \=ˈ==ˌizəm\ *n* -s *often cap* [[1]*precision* + *-ism*] : a style of American painting of the 1920s and 1930s characterized by abstracted form, crisp contour, and static composition and usu. depicting industrial or architectural subject matter — **precisionist*** *n or adj, often cap*

pre·coital \(ˈ)prē+\ *adj* [*pre-* + *coital*] : used or occurring before coitus

pre·competitive \"+\ *adj* [*pre-* + *competitive*] : being or resulting from research conducted jointly by usu. competing companies for the purpose of developing new commercially applicable technologies ⟨~ artificial intelligence technology⟩

pre·conference \ˈprē+\ *n* [*pre-* + *conference*] : a conference held before the start of another conference or convention

pre·copulatory \(ˈ)prē+\ *adj* [*pre-* + *copulatory*] : preceding copulation ⟨~ behavior⟩

pre·determiner \ˌprē+\ *n* [*pre-* + *determiner*] : a limiting noun modifier (as *both* or *all*) characterized by occurrence before the determiner in a noun phrase

pre·diabetes \"+\ *n* [*pre-* + *diabetes*] : an asymptomatic abnormal state that precedes the development of clinically evident diabetes — **pre·diabetic** \"+\ *adj or n*

pre·dissociation \"+\ *n* [*pre-* + *dissociation*] : the transition without emission of radiation of a molecule from a stable excited state to an unstable excited state that leads to dissociation

predominantly* *adv* : for the most part : MAINLY ⟨a ~ middle-class neighborhood⟩

pre·emergent \"+\ *adj* [*pre-* + *emergent*] : PREEMERGENCE

preempt* *vt* **1** : to replace with something considered to be of greater value or priority : take precedence over ⟨the busing issue has ~*ed* discussion of more basic problems —William Serrin⟩ **2** : to gain a commanding or preeminent place in ⟨lost the 1970 congressional race . . . but ran so well that he ~*ed* the Democratic field for a rematch two years later —R.M.Williams⟩ **3** : to prevent from happening or taking place : FORESTALL, PRECLUDE ⟨the alcohol completely ~*ed* any kind of dialogue —R.A.Sokolov⟩

preemptive* *adj* : marked by the seizing of the initiative; *esp* : being or relating to a first military strike made to gain an advantage when a strike by the enemy is believed imminent — compare PREVENTIVE *in the Dict*

pre–engineered \ˌprē+\ *adj* [*pre-* + *engineered*, past part. of *engineer*] : constructed of or employing prefabricated modules ⟨*pre-engineered* metal buildings⟩

preferred provider *n* **1** : PPO *herein* — usu. used attrib. **2** : a healthcare provider (as a doctor or hospital) that is part of a PPO

preferred provider organization *also* **preferred provider network** *n* : PPO *herein*

preflight *n* [*preflight*, adj.] : a preflight inspection (of an aircraft)

preg·gers \ˈpregə(r)z\ *adj* [*pregnant* + *-ers* (as in *starkers* — herein)] : PREGNANT — used as a predicate adjective

prehistoric* *adj* **1** : of or relating to a language in a period of its development from which contemporary records of its actual sounds and forms have not been preserved **2** : regarded as being outdated or outmoded ⟨~ attitudes⟩

prehistory* *n* : the prehistoric period of man's evolution

pre·implantation \ˌprē+\ *adj* [*pre-* + *implantation*] : of, involving, or being an embryo before uterine implantation

pre·incubation \"+\ *n* [*pre-* + *incubation*] : incubation (as of a cell, culture, or biochemical) prior to a treatment or process — **preincubate** \"+\ *vt*

prelate nul·li·us \-nüˈlēəs\ *n, pl* **prelates nullius** [part translation of NL *praelatus nullius dioecesis* prelate of no diocese] : a Roman Catholic prelate having ordinary jurisdiction over a district independent of any diocese

pre·launch \ˈprē+\ *adj* [*pre-* + [2]*launch*] : preparing for or preliminary to launch (as of a spacecraft)

pre·meiotic \"+\ *adj* [*pre-* + *meiotic*] : of, occurring in, or typical of a stage prior to meiosis ⟨~ DNA synthesis⟩ ⟨~ tissue⟩

premenstrual syndrome *n* : a varying constellation of symptoms manifested by some women prior to menstruation that may include emotional instability, irritability, insomnia, fatigue, anxiety, depression, headache, edema, and abdominal pain — called also *PMS*

prenatal* *adj* : providing or receiving prenatal medical care

pre–need \"+\ *adj* [*pre-* + [1]*need*] : of, relating to, or being funeral arrangements made before death ⟨*pre-need* selling of cemetery plots⟩

prenuptial agreement *also* **prenuptial** *or* **pre·nup** \ˈprēˌnəp\ *n* -s : an agreement made between a man and a woman before marrying in which they give up future rights to each other's property in the event of divorce or death

pre·oviposition \"+\ *adj* [*pre-* + *oviposition*] : of, relating to, or being the period before oviposition of the first eggs esp. by an insect

pre–owned \ˈ=ˈ=\ *adj* [*pre-* + *owned*] : SECONDHAND, USED ⟨a *pre-owned* luxury car⟩

prepackage* *vt* : to design, prepare, or learn in advance for repeated or ready use ⟨shows are *prepackaged* in New York . . . and shipped on a road tour —Mel Gussow⟩

pre·plant \ˈ=ˌ=, ˌ=ˈ=\ *also* **pre·planting** \ˈ=ˌ==, ˌ=ˈ==\ *adj* [*pre-* + [2]*plant* or [1]*planting*] : occurring or used before planting a crop

pre·polymer \ˌprē+\ *n* [*pre-* + *polymer*] : a stable usu. partially polymerized chemical intermediate that can be fully polymerized at a later time — compare MONOMER

[1]**prep·py** *or* **prep·pie** \ˈprepē\ *n, pl* **preppies** [*prep* + [4]*-y, -ie*] **1** : a student at or a graduate of a preparatory school **2** : a person deemed to dress or behave like a preppy

[2]**preppy** *or* **preppie** *adj* -ER/-EST **1** : relating to, characteristic of, or being a preppy **2** : relating to or being a style of dress characterized esp. by classic clothing and neat appearance — **prep·pi·ly** \ˈprepəlē\ *adv* — **prep·pi·ness** \ˈprepēnəs, -pin-\ *n*

pre·preg \ˈprēˌpreg\ *n* -s [*pre-* + *impregnated*] : a reinforcing or molding material (as paper or glass cloth) impregnated with a synthetic resin before use

pre·press \"+\ *adj* [*pre-* + [1]*press*] : of or relating to the processing of copy preparatory to printing ⟨~ costs⟩ ⟨~ equipment⟩

pre·process \(ˈ)prē+\ *vt* [*pre-* + [2]*process*] : to do preliminary processing of (as data) — **pre·processor** \"+\ *n*

[1]**preproduction** \ˌprē+\ *adj* [*pre-* + [1]*production*] : involving, existing, or taking place in the period before production begins ⟨~ planning⟩; *esp* : relating to or being a prototype ⟨~ models⟩

[2]**preproduction** \"+\ *n* : the period in the development of a play or motion picture prior to staging or filming that usu. involves casting, hiring production crews, constructing sets, and finding a suitable theater or location for filming

pre·program \ˌprē+\ *vt* [*pre-* + [2]*program*] : to program in advance of some anticipated use

pre·punch \(ˈ)prē+\ *vt* [*pre-* + [1]*punch*] : to punch in advance of some anticipated use

pre·quel \ˈprēkwəl\ *n* -s [*pre-* + *-quel* (as in *sequel*)] : a literary or dramatic work whose story precedes that of an earlier work

pre·screen \(ˈ)prē+\ *vt* [*pre-* + [2]*screen*] **1** : to screen beforehand ⟨~ schoolchildren for potential learning and behavior problems —Robert Reinhold⟩ **2** : to view (as a movie or television show) before public release or broadcast

pres·en·tism \ˈprezənˌtizəm\ *n* -s : an attitude toward the past dominated by present-day attitudes and experiences — **pres·en·tist** \-əst\ *adj*

preset \ˈprē+ˌ\ *n* [*preset*, v.] : something (as a radio station) preprogrammed into a device

[1]**pre·soak** \(ˈ)prē+\ *vt* [*pre-* + [1]*soak*] : to soak beforehand

[2]**presoak** \ˈ=ˌ=\ *n* **1** : a cleaning agent used in presoaking clothes **2** : an instance of presoaking

pre·sort \(ˈ)prē+\ *vt* [*pre-* + [2]*sort*] : to sort (outgoing mail) by zip code usu. before delivery to a post office

press* *vb* — **press the flesh** *also* **press flesh** : to greet and shake hands with people esp. while campaigning for political office

press kit *n* : a collection of promotional material for distribution to the press

press secretary *n* : a person officially in charge of press relations for a usu. prominent public figure

pressure point* *n* : a sensitive critical issue or matter that can be exploited for one's advantage ⟨political *pressure points*⟩

pre·stress \ˈprē+\ *n* [*prestress*, v.] **1** : the process of prestressing **2** : the stresses introduced in prestress **3** : the condition of being prestressed

pre·symptomatic \(ˈ)prē+\ *adj* [*pre-* + *symptomatic*] : relating to, being, or occurring before symptoms appear ⟨a ~ diagnosis⟩

pre·synaptic \ˌprē+\ *adj* [*pre-* + *synaptic*] : relating to, occurring in, or being part of a nerve cell by which a nerve impulse is conveyed to a synapse ⟨a ~ nerve ending⟩ ⟨~ inhibition⟩ — **presynaptically** \"+\ *adv*

prêt–à–porter *or* **pret–a–porter** \ˌpret·äpȯrˈtā\ *n, often attrib* [F, ready to wear] : ready-to-wear clothes

pre·tax \(ˈ)prē+\ *adj* [*pre-* + [2]*tax*] : existing before provision for taxes ⟨~ earnings⟩ — **pretax** \"+\ *adv*

[1]**preteen** \"+\ *n* [*pre-* + *teens* (teenagers)] : a boy or girl not yet 13 years old

[2]**pre·teen** \ˌprē+\ *adj* **1** : relating to or produced for children younger than 13 ⟨~ fashions⟩ **2** : being younger than 13 ⟨~ youngsters⟩

pre·term \"+\ *adj* [*pre-* + [1]*term*] : of, relating to, or being premature birth : born prematurely ⟨~ infants⟩ ⟨a ~ delivery⟩

pre·treatment \(ˈ)prē+\ *adj* [*pre-* + *treatment*] : occurring in or typical of the period prior to treatment

prevent defense \ˈprēˌvent'=ˌ=; ˌprēˈvent-, ˌprəˈ-, *also* -ˌ=ˈ=\ *n* : a football defense in which linebackers and backs play deeper than usual in order to prevent the completion of a long pass

preventive detention* *n* : imprisonment of a person under arrest without the right to bail while awaiting trial for a felony because that person is considered a danger to society

pre·writing \ˈprē+ˌ\ *n* [*pre-* + [1]*writing*] : the formulation and organization of ideas preparatory to writing

price–earnings multiple \ˈ=ˈ==-\ *n* : a simple numeral usu. used to express a price-earnings ratio

price–earnings ratio *n* : a measure of the value of a common stock determined as the ratio of its market price to its earnings per share

price point *n* : the standard price set by the manufacturer for its product

primality* *n* : the property of being a prime number

primal scream *n* **1** : PRIMAL SCREAM THERAPY *herein* **2** : a violent verbal outpouring of raw emotion

primal scream therapy *or* **primal therapy** *n* : psychotherapy in which the patient recalls and reenacts a particularly disturbing past experience usu. occurring early in life and expresses normally repressed anger or frustration esp. through spontaneous and unrestrained screams, hysteria, or violence

primary* *adj* **1** : of, relating to, or being the amino acid sequence in proteins ⟨~ protein structure⟩ **2** : of, relating to, involving, or derived from primary meristem ⟨~ tissue⟩ ⟨~ growth⟩ **3** : of, relating to, or involved in the production of organic substances by green plants ⟨~ productivity⟩ **4** : providing primary care ⟨a ~ physician⟩

primary care *also* **primary health care** *n* : health care provided by a medical professional with whom a patient has initial contact and by whom the patient may be referred to a specialist — often used attrib. ⟨*primary care* providers⟩; compare TERTIARY CARE *herein*

primary consumer *n* : a plant-eating organism : HERBIVORE

primary derivative *n* : a word (as *telegram*) whose immediate constituents are bound forms

primary structure *n* : sculpture in the idiom of minimal art — **primary struc·tur·ist** \-ˌstrəkchərəst, -ksh(ə)rəst\ *n*

primary tooth *n* : MILK TOOTH

pri·ma·to·log·i·cal \ˌprīmədᵊlˈäjəkəl\ *adj* : of or relating to primatology ⟨~ research⟩

pri·ma·vera \ˌprēməˈverə\ *adj* [It, short for *alla primavera* in the style of springtime] : served with a mixture of fresh vegetables (as zucchini, snow peas, or broccoli) — usu. used postpositively ⟨pasta ~⟩

primer* *n* : a molecule (as a short strand of RNA or DNA) whose presence is required for formation of another molecule (as a longer chain of DNA)

prime rate *n* : an interest rate formally announced by a bank as the lowest normally available at a particular time to its most creditworthy customers

prime time *n* **1** : the evening period generally from 7 to 11 p.m. during which television has its largest number of viewers; *also* : television shows shown in prime time **2** : the choicest or busiest time — **prime–time** \ˈ=ˈ=\ *adj*

pri·mi·done \ˈprīməˌdōn\ *n* -s [alter. of *pyrimid*inedione (chemical name)] : an anticonvulsant phenobarbital derivative $C_{12}H_{14}N_2O_2$ used esp. to control epileptic seizures

primitive* *n* : a typically rough or simple usu. handmade and antique home accessory or furnishing

pri·mo \ˈprē(ˌ)mō\ *adj* [prob. fr. It, chief, first, fr. L *primus* — more at PRIME] *slang* : of the finest quality : EXCELLENT ⟨a ~ parking spot⟩

primordial soup *n* : a mixture of organic molecules in evolutionary theory from which life on earth originated

principal diagonal *n* : the diagonal in a square matrix that runs from upper left to lower right

principial* *adj* : of, relating to, or based on principle

printhead \ˈ=ˌ=\ *n* [[1]*print* + [1]*head*] : a usu. movable part of a computer printer that contains the printing elements

print out *vt* : to make a printout of

printout \ˈ=ˌ=\ *n* -s [*print out*, v. (herein)] : a printed record produced automatically (as by a computer)

printwheel \ˈ=ˌ=\ *n* : DAISY WHEEL *herein*

pri·on \ˈprēän, ˈprī-\ *n* -s [*pro*teinaceous + *in*fectious + [2]*-on*] : a protein particle that lacks nucleic acid and has been implicated as the cause of various neurodegenerative diseases (as scrapie, Creutzfeldt-Jakob disease, and bovine spongiform encephalopathy)

pri·or·i·tize \ˌprīˈȯrəˌtīz, ˈprīər-\ *vt* -ED/-ING/-S [*priority* + *-ize*] : to list or rate (as projects or goals) in order of priority — **pri·or·i·ti·za·tion** \ˌ=ˈ===tiˈzāshən, ˈ===ti-\ *n* -s

prior restraint *n* : governmental prohibition on expression esp. by publication before the expression actually takes place ⟨official prejudgment is actually a form of *prior restraint* —F.H.Nuessell, Jr.⟩

pri·va·tism \ˈprīvəˌtizəm\ *n* -s [[1]*private* + *-ism*] : the attitude of being uncommitted to or avoiding involvement in anything beyond one's immediate interests — **pri·va·tis·tic** \ˌ==ˈtistik\ *adj*

privatization* *n* : an act or the process of privatizing

pro·abortion \(ˌ)prō+\ *adj* : favoring the legalization of abortion — **pro–abortionist** \"+\ *n*

pro·active \(ˈ)prō+\ *adj* [*pro-* (as in *progress*) + retro*active* or *reactive*] **1** : relating to, caused by, or being interference between previous learning and the recall or performance of later learning ⟨~ inhibition of memory⟩ **2** : acting in anticipation of future problems or needs ⟨a ~ company⟩ — **pro·act·ve·ly** \-lē\ *adv*

probability density *n* : PROBABILITY DENSITY FUNCTION; *also* : a particular value of a probability density function

probability distribution *n* : PROBABILITY FUNCTION; *also* : PROBABILITY DENSITY FUNCTION 2

probe* *n* : a device (as an ultrasound generator) or a substance (as radioactively labeled DNA) used to obtain specific information (as detection of a virus or the location of specific segments of a nucleic acid) for diagnostic or experimental purposes

pro·ben·e·cid \prōˈbenəsəd\ *n* -s [*propyl* + *benzoic* + *-e-* (perh. fr. beneficial) + *acid*] : a drug $C_{13}H_{19}NO_4S$ that acts on renal tubular function and is used to increase the concentration of some drugs (as penicillin) in the blood by inhibiting their excretion and to increase the excretion of urates in gout

prob·lem·at·ic \ˌpräbləˈmad·ik\ *n* -s [*problematic*, adj.] : something that is problematic : a problematic aspect or concern ⟨~s of womanhood, of men and women together —Stephen Koch⟩

pro bono \ˌprōˈbōnō\ *adj* [L *pro bono publico* for the public good] : being, involving, or doing legal work donated esp. for the public good ⟨*pro bono* work⟩ ⟨a *pro bono* lawyer⟩

pro·busing \ˈprō+ˈ\ *adj* [[2]*pro-* + *busing* (herein)] : favoring busing as a means of establishing racial balance in the schools

pro·car·ba·zine \prōˈkärbəˌzēn, -äb-, -əˌzən\ *n* -s [*propyl* + *carb-* + *azine*] : an antineoplastic drug $C_{12}H_{19}N_3O$ that is a monoamine oxidase inhibitor used in the form of its hydrochloride esp. in the palliative treatment of Hodgkin's disease

pro·ce·dur·al \prəˈsējərəl\ *n* -s [*procedural*, adj.] : a realistic crime novel with a specific focus ⟨a courtroom ~⟩; *esp* : POLICE PROCEDURAL *herein*

procedure* *n* : a series of instructions that has a name by which it can be called into action and that is usu. part of a computer program

pro·cess·ible *or* **pro·cess·able** \ˈpräˌsesəbəl, ˈprō-, -ˌsəs-\ *adj* : suitable for processing : capable of being processed — **pro·cess·ibil·i·ty** *or* **pro·cess·abil·i·ty** \ˌ=(ˌ)=əˈbiləd·ē, -ətē\ *n*

processor* *n* **1 a** : COMPUTER **b** : the part of a computer system that operates on data; *specif* : CPU *herein* **2** : a computer program (as a compiler) that puts another program into a form acceptable to the computer

pro–choice \ˌ=ˈ=\ *adj* : PROABORTION *herein* — **pro–choic·er** \ˌprōˈchȯisər\ *n* -s

pro·coagulant \ˌprō+\ *adj* [[1]*pro-* + *coagulant*] : promoting the coagulation of blood ⟨~ activity⟩ — **procoagulant** *n*

producer* *n* : an organism viewed as a source of biomass that can be consumed by other organisms — compare CONSUMER *herein*

productivity* *n* : the rate per unit area or per unit volume at which biomass consumable as food by other organisms is made by producers

product placement *n* : the appearance of a product as a paid advertisement within a television program or film

pro–family \ˌprō+\ *adj* **1** : favoring or encouraging traditional family structures or values **2** : opposing abortion and often birth control

professional corporation *n* : a corporation organized by one or more licensed individuals (as a doctor, lawyer, dentist, or physical therapist) esp. for the purpose of providing professional services and obtaining tax advantages

profile* *n* : degree or level of public exposure ⟨trying to keep a low ~⟩ ⟨a job with a high ~⟩

profit center *n* : a part of a corporation or its product line that is an important source of profits

pro·ges·to·gen *also* **pro·ges·ta·gen** \prōˈjestəjən, -ˌjen\ *n* -s [*progestational* + *-ogen* (as in *estrogen*) or *-agen* (by alter.)] : any of several progestational steroids (as progesterone or norethindrone) — **pro·ges·to·gen·ic** \ˌprōˌjestəˈjenik, -ēk\ *adj*

pro·grade \ˈprōˌgrād\ *adj* [*pro-* (as in *progress*) + *-grade* (as in *retrograde*)] : having or being a direction of rotation or revolution that is counterclockwise as viewed from the north pole of the sky or a planet

program* *n* **1** : a sequence of coded instructions (as genes or behavioral responses) that is part of an organism **2** : what is predominantly desired or expected ⟨get with the ~⟩

program* *vt* **1** : to code in an organism's program ⟨the death of cells and the destruction of tissues, organs, and organ systems are *programmed* as normal morphogenetic events in the development of multicellular organisms —J.W.Saunders, Jr.⟩ **2** : to provide with a biological program ⟨cells *programmed* to synthesize hemoglobin⟩ **3** : to direct or predetermine the thinking or behavior of ⟨those who . . . *programmed* him to kill —Jim Hougan⟩ ⟨children are *programmed* into violence —Lisa A. Richette⟩

[1]**pro·gram·ma·ble** *also* **pro·gram·able** \ˌprōˈgraməbəl\ *adj* : capable of being programmed ⟨a ~ calculator⟩ — **pro·gram·ma·bil·i·ty** \ˌ=ˌ==ˈbiləd·ē\ *n* -ES

[2]**programmable** \"\ *n* -s : a programmable calculator

programmed cell death *n* : APOPTOSIS *herein*

programmed instruction *n* : instruction through information given in small steps with each requiring a correct response by the learner before going on to the next step

programmer* *or* **pro·gram·er** *n* **1** : one that prepares an instructional program **2** : one who plans or prepares entertainment programs ⟨a television ~⟩

programming* *or* **programing*** *n* **1** : the process of instructing or learning by means of an instructional program **2** : the process of preparing an instructional program

programming language *n* : any of various high-level languages used for computer programs — compare ASSEMBLY LANGUAGE *herein*, MACHINE LANGUAGE *herein*, NATURAL LANGUAGE *herein*

program trading *n* : computerized trading of large blocks of stocks in one market against stock index futures in another

progressive rock *n* : rock music characterized by relatively complex phrasings and improvisations and intended for a musically sophisticated audience

prog rock \ˈpräg-\ *n* [by shortening] : PROGRESSIVE ROCK *herein*

pro·gun \(ˈ)prō+\ *adj* : favoring the right to own guns and opposing legislation restricting this right ⟨the ~ lobby⟩

pro·insulin \(ˈ)prō+\ *n* [[1]*pro-* + *insulin*] : a single-chain pancreatic polypeptide precursor of insulin that gives rise to the double chain of insulin by loss of the middle part of the molecule

projection* *n* : the process or technique of reproducing a spatial object upon a plane or curved surface or a line by projecting its points; *also* : a graph or figure so formed

pro·kary·ote *also* **pro·cary·ote** \(ˈ)prōˈkarēˌōt\ *n* -s [NL *Procaryota* or *Procaryotes*, fr. [1]*pro-* + *kary-* + *-ota* or *-otes*, pl. of *-otis* or *-otos*, fr. Gk *-ōtos*] : a typically unicellular organism (as a bacterium or a blue-green alga) that lacks a membrane-bound nucleus — compare EUKARYOTE *in the Dict* — **pro·kary·otic** *also* **pro·cary·otic** \(ˌ)=ˌ==ˈäd·ik\ *adj*

pro–life \prōˈlīf\ *adj* : ANTIABORTION *herein* — **pro–lif·er** \ˈ=ˈ=ə(r)\ *n*

pro·log \ˈprōˌlȯg, -ˌläg\ *n* -s *usu cap P or all cap* [*programming in logic*] : a computer programming language that is designed for easy expression of relationships among objects, is based on the precepts of the predicate calculus of symbolic logic, and is used esp. in artificial intelligence

[1]**pro·mo** \ˈprō(ˌ)mō\ *adj* [by shortening] : PROMOTIONAL ⟨~ leaflets⟩

²promo \"\ *n* -s : a promotional announcement, film, recording, blurb, or appearance

promoter* *n* : a binding site in a DNA chain at which RNA polymerase binds to initiate transcription of messenger RNA by one or more nearby structural genes

prompt* *n* : a symbol or message on a computer display signaling that the computer is awaiting input

pro·nom·i·nal·iza·tion \prō,nämənᵊlə'zāshən, prə,-\ *n* -s [*pronominal* + *-ization*] : the process or fact of using a pronoun instead of another sentence constituent (as a noun or noun phrase) — **pro·nom·i·nal·ize** \prō'nämənᵊ,līz, prə'-\ *vb* -ED/-ING/-S

pro·nuclear \(')prō+\ *adj* [²*pro-* + *nuclear*] : advocating the use of nuclear-powered generating stations

proof* *vt* : to activate (yeast) by mixing with water and sometimes sugar or milk

pro·pa·nil \'prōpə,nil\ *n* -s [*prop-* + *anilide*] : an herbicide $C_9H_9Cl_2NO$ used esp. to control weeds in rice fields

propeller·head \-'==,=\ *n* [so called fr. cartoon images of science fiction fans wearing caps with a propeller protruding from the top, prob. based on the cap worn by the television puppet and cartoon character Beany Boy in the show *Time for Beany* (first aired 1949)] : TECHNOPHILE *herein*

property* *n* **1** : one (as a performer) who is under contract and whose work is esp. valuable **2** : a book or script purchased for publication or production

prophase* *n* : the initial stage of meiosis in which the chromosomes become visible, homologous pairs of chromosomes undergo synapsis and become shortened and thickened, individual chromosomes become visibly double as paired chromatids, chiasmata occur, and the nuclear membrane disappears — compare DIAKINESIS *in the Dict*, DIPLOTENE *in the Dict*, LEPTOTENE *in the Dict*, PACHYTENE *in the Dict*, ZYGOTENE *in the Dict*

pro·pio·phe·none \,prōpēō'fē,nōn, -'fen,ōn, -,ōfə'nōn\ *n* -s [ISV *propio-* + *phenyl* + *-one*] : a flowery-smelling compound $C_9H_{10}O$ used in perfumes and in the synthesis of pharmaceuticals (as ephedrine) and organic compounds

pro·poxy·phene \prō'päksə,fēn\ *n* -s [*propi-* + ²*oxy-* + *phene* (alter. of *phenyl*)] : an analgesic $C_{22}H_{29}NO_2$ structurally related to methadone but less addicting that is administered in the form of its hydrochloride — called also *dextropropoxyphene*

pro·pran·o·lol \prō'pranə,lōl, -,lōl\ *n* -s [*propyl* + *propanol* + ¹*-ol*] : a beta-blocker $C_{16}H_{21}NO_2$ used in the form of its hydrochloride in the treatment of abnormal heart rhythms and angina pectoris

props \'präps\ *n pl but sing in constr* [short for *proper dues*, alter. of *proper due*] **1** *slang* : DUE 1a ⟨give the man his ~⟩ **2** *slang* : RESPECT ⟨teachers have to earn their ~ just like everybody else —Greg Donaldson⟩ **3** *slang* : CREDIT 6b ⟨not eager to give ~ . . . unless prompted —Charles Aaron⟩

pros·e·cu·to·ri·al \,präsəkyü'tōrēəl, -'tȯr-\ *adj* [*prosecutor* + *-ial*] : of, relating to, or being a prosecutor or prosecution

prospective* *adj* : relating to or being a study (as of the incidence of disease) that starts with the present condition of a population of individuals and follows them into the future — compare RETROSPECTIVE *herein*

pross \'präs\ *also* **pros·sie** \'präsē, -si\ *or* **pros·tie** *or* **pros·ty** \'prästē, -ti\ *n, pl* **prosses** *also* **prossies** *or* **prosties** [by shortening & alter.] *slang* : PROSTITUTE

pros·ta·cy·clin \,prästə'sīklən\ *n* -s [*prosta-* (as in *prostaglandin* — herein) + *cycl-* + *-in*] : a prostaglandin that is a metabolite of arachidonic acid, inhibits aggregation of platelets, and dilates blood vessels

pros·ta·glan·din \,prästə'glandən\ *n* -s [ISV ¹*prostate* + E *gland* or F *glande* + ISV *-in*; orig. formed in G; fr. its occurrence in the sexual glands of mammals] : any of various oxygenated unsaturated cyclic fatty acids of animals that are formed chiefly by the action of cyclooxygenase on arachidonic acid and perform a variety of hormonelike actions (as in controlling blood pressure or smooth muscle contraction)

prostate–specific antigen \'==,=='==-\ *n* : a protease that is secreted by the epithelial cells of the prostate and is used in the diagnosis of prostate cancer since its concentration in the blood serum tends to be proportional to the clinical stage of the disease — abbr. *PSA*

protease inhibitor *n* : a substance that inhibits the action of a protease; *specif* : any of various drugs (as indinavir) that inhibit the action of the protease of HIV so that the cleavage of viral proteins into mature functional infectious particles is prevented and that are used esp. in combination with other agents in the treatment of HIV infection

protection* *n* : anchoring equipment placed in cracks for safety while rock climbing

protein kinase *n* : any of a class of enzymes that possess a catalytic subunit which transfers a phosphate from ATP to one or more amino acids (as serine, threonine, or tyrosine) in a protein's side chain resulting in a conformational change affecting protein function, that play a role in regulating intracellular processes, and that include many which are activated by the binding of a second messenger (as cyclic AMP)

protein kinase c *n, usu cap C* : any of a group of isoenzymes of protein kinase that modify the conformation and activity of various intracellular proteins by catalyzing the phosphorylation of specific serine or threonine amino acid residues in the polypeptide chains of the proteins

pro·tein·oid \'prō,tē,nȯid, 'prōtᵊn,ȯid, 'prōd·ēə,nȯid\ *n* -s [*protein* + ¹*-oid*] : any of various polypeptides which can be obtained by suitable polymerization of mixtures of amino acids

proteo·glycan \,prōd·ēō+\ *n* [*prote-* + *glycan*] : any of a class of glycoproteins of high molecular weight that are found in the extracellular matrix of connective tissue, are made up mostly of carbohydrate consisting of various polysaccharide side chains linked to a protein, and resemble polysaccharides rather than proteins in their properties

pro·te·o·mics \,prōd·ē'ōmiks, -tē-\ *n pl but sing in constr* [¹*protein* + *-omics* (as in *genomics* — herein)] : a branch of biotechnology concerned with applying the techniques of molecular biology, biochemistry, and genetics to analyzing the structure, function, and interactions of the proteins produced by the genes of a particular cell, tissue, or organism, with organizing the information in databases, and with applications of the data — compare GENOMICS *herein* — **pro·te·o·mic** \-mik\ *adj*

protestant ethic *n, usu cap P* : an ethic that stresses the virtue of hard work, thrift, and self-discipline

pro·the·tel·ic \,prōthə'telik\ *adj* : of, relating to, or characterized by prothetely ⟨a ~ larva⟩

prothoracic gland *n* : one of a pair of thoracic endocrine organs in some insects that control molting

protocol* *n* : a set of conventions governing the treatment and esp. the formatting of data in an electronic communications system

pro·to·galaxy \¦prōd·(,)ō+\ *n* [*prot-* + *galaxy*] : a hypothetical cloud of gas believed to be the precursor of a galaxy — **proto·galactic** \"+\ *adj*

pro·to–oncogene \"+\ *n* [*prot-* + *oncogene*] : a gene having the potential for change into an active oncogene

pro·to·porcelain \¦prōd·(,)ō+\ *n* [*prot-* + *porcelain*; prob. trans. of G *urporzellan*] : a porcelaneous ware lacking some of the qualities of a true porcelain; *specif* : a hard-fired gray kaolinic Chinese stoneware known since the Han dynasty

pro·to·sun \¦prōd·ō+\ *n* [*prot-* + ¹*sun*] : PROTOSTAR; *esp* : the gaseous cloud that underwent gravitational collapse to form the sun

protract* *vt* : to extend forward or outward ⟨the mandible is ~*ed* and retracted in chewing⟩

pro·vi·ral \prō'vīrəl\ *adj* : of, relating to, or being a provirus ⟨~ DNA⟩

pro·vo \'prō(,)vō\ *n* -s *usu cap* [*Provisional* I.R.A., name of the faction + ¹*-o*] : a member of the extremist faction of the Irish Republican Army

prox·e·mics \präk'sēmiks\ *n pl but sing in constr* [*proximity* + *-emics* (as in *phonemics*)] : the study of the nature, degree, and effect of the spatial separation individuals naturally maintain (as in various social and interpersonal situations) and of how this separation relates to environmental and cultural factors

proximal* *adj* : of, relating to, or being the mesial and distal surfaces of a tooth — **prox·i·mal·ly*** \-mə-lē\ *adv*

ps *abbr* picosecond *herein*

PSA *abbr* **1** prostate-specific antigen *herein* **2** public service announcement

pseud \'süd\ *n* -s [short for *pseudo-intellectual*] *Brit* : a person who is affectedly intellectual

pseu·do·cholinesterase \¦südō+\ *n* [*pseud-* + *cholinesterase*] : CHOLINESTERASE 2

pseudo–event \'südō+\ *n* [*pseud-* + *event*] : an event (as a press conference) that is designed primarily to attract attention

pseu·do·random \"+\ *adj* [*pseud-* + *random*] : being or involving entities (as numbers) that are selected by a definite computational process (as one involving a computer) but that satisfy one or more standard tests for statistical randomness

pseu·do·uridine \"+\ *n* [ISV *pseud-* + *uridine*] : a nucleoside $C_9H_{12}O_6N_2$ that is a uracil derivative incorporated as a structural component into transfer RNA

psi* *or* **psi particle** *n* : J/PSI PARTICLE *herein*

psi·lo·cin \'sīləsən\ *n* -s [ISV *psiloc-* (fr. NL *Psilocybe mexicana*, fungus fr. which it is obtained) + *-in*; orig. formed in G] : a hallucinogenic tertiary amine $C_{12}H_{16}N_2O$ obtained from some fungi (as *Psilocybe mexicana*)

psi·lo·cy·bin \,sīlə'sībən\ *n* -s [ISV *psilocyb-* (fr. NL *Psilocybe mexicana*, fungus fr. which it is obtained) + *-in*; orig. formed in G] : a hallucinogenic indole $C_{12}H_{17}N_2O_4P$ obtained from some fungi (as *Psilocybe mexicana*)

psi·lo·phyt·ic \¦sīlə'fid·ik\ *adj* [*psilophyte* + ¹*-ic*] : of, relating to, or being plants of the order Psilophytales

pso·ra·len \'sōrələn, 'sȯr-\ *n* -s [modif. of NL *Psoralea* psoralea] : a substance $C_{11}H_6O_3$ found in some plants that photosensitizes mammalian skin and is used in conjunction with ultraviolet light to treat psoriasis; *also* : any of various derivatives of psoralen having similar properties

psych* *also* **psyche** \'sīk\ *vt* -ED/-ING/-S **1** : to make (as oneself) psychologically ready esp. for performance — often used with *up* ⟨~*ed* himself up for the race⟩ ⟨getting ~*ed* to paint⟩ **2** : to make psychologically uneasy : INTIMIDATE, SCARE ⟨pressure doesn't ~ me —Jerry Quarry⟩ — often used with *out*

psych *also* **psyche** \"\ *n* -s : the state of being psyched up ⟨spoiled his ~ for the race —Patricia N. Warren⟩; *also* : PSYCH-OUT *herein*

psy·che·de·lia \,sīkə'dēlyə\ *n* [NL, fr. E *psychedelic* (herein) + NL *-ia* ²-ia] **1** : the world of people, phenomena, or items associated with psychedelic drugs **2** : psychedelic music

¹psy·che·del·ic \¦sīkə¦delik *also* -dēl-\ *n* -s **1** : a psychedelic drug (as LSD) **2 a** : a user or an advocate of psychedelic drugs **b** : a person with psychedelic social and cultural interests and orientation

²psychedelic *adj* [irreg. fr. Gk *psychē* soul + *dēloun* to show, reveal (fr. *dēlos* evident) + E *-ic* — more at PSYCHE, ADEL-] **1 a** : of, relating to, or being drugs (as LSD) capable of producing abnormal psychic effects (as hallucinations) and sometimes psychic states resembling mental illness **b** : produced by or associated with the use of psychedelic drugs ⟨a ~ experience⟩ **2 a** : imitating, suggesting, or reproducing the effects (as distorted or bizarre images or sounds) of psychedelic drugs ⟨~ art⟩ **b** (1) : very bright in color ⟨ferryboats soon will take on a ~ look, with an overall coat of international orange and touches of red and yellow —*N.Y. Times*⟩ (2) *of colors* : FLUORESCENT **3** : of or relating to the culture associated with psychedelic drugs ⟨a year ago we couldn't even begin to sell '60s ~ stuff —Paul Glynn⟩ — **psy·che·del·i·cal·ly** \-lək(ə)lē\ *adv*

psychic energizer *n* : ANTIDEPRESSANT *herein*

psy·cho·active \¦sīkō+\ *adj* [*psych-* + *active*] : affecting the mind or behavior ⟨~ drugs⟩

psy·cho·babble \"+\ *n* [*psych-* + *babble*] **1** : a predominantly metaphorical language for expressing one's feelings ⟨a variety of ~, betraying a horror of responsibility and a mindless self-indulgence —Paul Robinson⟩ **2 a** : psychological jargon ⟨listening to the ~ of social workers and therapists —A.S.Regnery⟩ **b** : trite or simplistic language derived from the field of psychotherapy ⟨repeating the usual ~ about self-discovery —Mark Coleman⟩ — **psychobabble** *vb* — **psy·cho·babbler** \"+\ *n*

psy·cho·bil·ly \¦sī(,)kō,bilē\ *n* -ES [²*psycho* + rock*abilly* (herein)] : music that blends punk rock and rockabilly

psy·cho·biography \¦sī(,)kō+\ *n* [*psych-* + *biography*] : a biography written from a psychodynamic or psychoanalytic point of view; *also* : the application of such a point of view to the writing of a biography — **psy·cho·biographer** \"+\ *n* — **psy·cho·biographical** \"+\ *adj*

psy·cho·chemical \¦sīkō+\ *n* [*psych-* + *chemical*] : a psychoactive chemical — **psychochemical** *adj*

psychodrama* *n* **1** : a dramatic work or narrative characterized by psychological overtones **2** : an often ongoing psychological struggle; *also* : an expression of psychological turmoil — **psychodramatic*** *adj*

psy·cho·geriatric \"+\ *adj* [*psych-* + *geriatric*] : of, relating to, caring for, or affected with geriatric mental disorder ⟨a ~ inpatient unit⟩ ⟨~ patients⟩

psy·cho·graphics \"+\ *n pl but sing in const* [*psych-* + *-graphics* (as in *demographics* — herein)] : market research or statistics classifying population groups according to psychological variables (as attitudes, values, or fears); *also* : variables or trends identified through such research — **psy·cho·graphic** \"+\ *adj*

psy·cho·history \¦sīkō+\ *n* [*psych-* + *history*] : historical analysis or interpretation using psychological or psychoanalytical methods; *also* : a work of history using such methods — **psy·cho·historian** \"+\ *n* — **psy·cho·historical** \"+\ *adj*

psy·cho·neu·ro·immunology \¦sīkō¦n(y)ürō, -¦n(y)u̇rō+\ *n* [*psych-* + *neur-* + *immunology*] : a field of medicine that deals with the influence of emotional states (as stress) and nervous system activity on immune function esp. in relation to their effect on the onset and progression of disease

psy·cho·pharmaceutical \¦sīkō+\ *n* [*psych-* + *pharmaceutical*] : a drug having an effect on the mental state of the user

psy·cho·pharmacologist \"+\ *n* [*psych-* + *pharmacologist*] : a specialist in psychopharmacology

psy·cho·quack \'sīkō+,\ *n* [*psych-* + ³*quack*] : an unqualified psychologist or psychiatrist — **psy·cho·quackery** \¦sīkō+\ *n*

psy·cho·surgeon \¦sīkō+\ *n* [*psych-* + *surgeon*] : a surgeon specializing in psychosurgery

psy·chot·o·gen \sī'käd·əjən\ *n* -s [*psychotic* + *-o-* + *-gen*] : a chemical agent (as a drug) that induces a psychotic state — **psy·choto·gen·ic** \(¦)sī,käd·ə¦jenik\ *adj*

psy·choto·mimetic \sī¦käd·ō+\ *adj* [*psychotic* + *-o-* + *mimetic*] : of, relating to, involving, or inducing psychotic alteration of behavior and personality ⟨~ drugs⟩ — **psychotomimetic** *n* -s — **psy·choto·mimetically** \"+\ *adv*

psy·cho·toxic \¦sīkō+\ *adj* [*psych-* + *toxic*] : having or being a detrimental effect on one's mind, personality, or behavior ⟨a ~ chemical⟩

psych–out \'=,=\ *n* -s [fr. *psych out*, v., fr. *psych* (herein)] : an act or an instance of psyching out ⟨in a *psych-out* you always make a show of confidence, while you work to undermine the confidence of your competition —Don Schollander & Duke Savage⟩

PTC \,pē(,)tē'sē\ *n* -s [*phenylthiocarbamide*] : PHENYLTHIOCARBAMIDE

PTFE *abbr* polytetrafluoroethylene

PTO* *abbr* **1** parent-teacher organization **2** power take-off

PTSD *abbr* post-traumatic stress disorder *herein*

PTV *abbr* public television *herein*

p–type \'pē,tīp\ *adj* [*positive* + *type*] : relating to or being a semiconductor in which charge is carried by holes — compare N-TYPE *herein*

public access *n* : the provision of access by the public to television broadcasting facilities (as a cable TV channel) for the presentation of programs

public–key \'==¦=\ *n, often attrib* : a cryptographic element that is the publicly shared half of an encryption code and that can be used only to encode messages

public television *n* : television that provides cultural, informational, and instructional programs for the public and that is financed by a combination of government, private, and corporate sources : noncommercial television

puff* *n* : an enlarged region of a chromosome that is associated with intensely active genes involved in RNA synthesis

pu·gil stick \'pyüjəl-\ *n* [*pugilism*] : a heavy pole with padded ends used in training in the armed services to simulate bayonet fighting

pu·ka \'pükə\ *n* -s [*puka shell*, fr. Hawaiian *puka* hole + E *shell*] : a small usu. perforated wave- and beach-polished shell fragment formed from the spire of a cone (genus *Conus*), found along beaches of Pacific Islands, and used esp. to make necklaces

pu·la \'p(y)ülə\ *n, pl* **pula** [Tswana, lit., rain (used as a greeting or expression of good wishes)] **1** : the basic monetary unit of Botswana — see MONEY table *in the Dict* **2** : a coin or note representing one pula

pull* *vi* **1** *of an offensive lineman in football* : to move back from the line of scrimmage toward one flank to provide blocking for a ballcarrier **2** : to work together to achieve a goal ⟨~*ing* with them to get the bill passed⟩ — **pull one's coat** *slang* : to provide information — **pull out all the stops** *or* **pull out the stops** : to use all one's resources without restraint — **pull the plug 1** : to disconnect a medical life-support system **2** : to withdraw critical and esp. financial support from an organization, undertaking, or person — **pull the rug from under** *or* **pull the rug out from under** : to remove support or assistance from

pull* *n* : an injury resulting from abnormal straining or stretching esp. of a muscle — see GROIN PULL *herein*

pull date *n* : a date stamped on perishable products (as baked goods or dairy products) after which they should not be sold

pull–down \¦=¦=\ *adj* [*pull down*, v.] : being or appearing below a selected item (as an icon) in a window overlaying the original screen on a computer display ⟨a *pull-down* menu⟩

pullman* *n, often cap* : a large suitcase

pullman* *adj, sometimes cap* : being long and square-shaped ⟨a ~ loaf of bread⟩

pull tab* *n* : a metal tab (as on a can) pulled to open the container

pul·mo·nol·o·gist \,pu̇lmə'näləjəst, ,pəl-\ *n* -s [*pulmon-* + *-ologist* (as in *cardiologist*)] : a physician specializing in the anatomy, physiology, and pathology of the lungs

pul·sar \'pəl,sär\ *n* -s [*pulse* + *-ar* (as in *quasar* — herein)] : a celestial source of pulsating electromagnetic radiation (as radio waves) marked by a short relatively constant interval (as .033 second) between pulses that is held to be a rotating neutron star

pulse* *n* : a dose of a substance esp. when applied over a short period of time ⟨~s of colchicine applied to the cells⟩

pulsed–field gel electrophoresis \'=,=-\ *n* : gel electrophoresis that is used esp. to separate large fragments of DNA and that involves changing the direction of the electric current periodically in order to minimize overlap of the spots due to diffusion

pulse oximeter *n* : a device that measures the oxygen saturation of arterial blood in a subject by utilizing a sensor attached typically to a finger, toe, or ear to determine the percentage of oxyhemoglobin in blood pulsating through a network of capillaries

pump* *n* **1** : an energy source (as light) for pumping atoms or molecules **2** : the process of pumping atoms or molecules **3** : a biological mechanism by which atoms, ions, or molecules are transported across cell membranes — see SODIUM PUMP *herein*

pump* *vt* **1** : to transport (as ions) against a concentration gradient by the expenditure of energy **2 a** : to excite (as atoms or molecules) esp. so as to cause emission of coherent monochromatic electromagnetic radiation (as in a laser) **b** : to energize (as a laser) by pumping **3** : PROMOTE 4c ⟨*pumped* his new book in TV and radio interviews⟩ — **pump iron** : to lift weights esp. for exercise or body building

pumped *adj* : filled with energetic excitement and enthusiasm : pumped up *herein* ⟨~ for the football game⟩

pumped storage *n* : a hydroelectric system in which electricity is generated during periods of greatest consumption by the use of water that has been pumped into a reservoir at a higher altitude during periods of low consumption

pump fake *n* : a fake in which a player simulates throwing a pass (as in football) or taking a shot (as in basketball) — **pump–fake** *vb*

pump up* *vt* **1 a** : to fill with enthusiasm and excitement **b** : to fill up as if with air : INFLATE ⟨constant praise *pumped up* his ego⟩ **2** : INCREASE 1 ⟨trying to *pump up* sales⟩

punch out* *vi* : to bail out of an aircraft using an ejection seat ~ *vt* **1** : to beat up **2** : to strike out (a baseball batter)

punch–out* \'=,=\ *n* -s : FISTFIGHT

punctuated equilibrium *n* **1** : a lineage of evolutionary descent characterized by long periods of stability in characteristics of the organism and short periods of rapid change during which new forms appear esp. from small subpopulations of the ancestral form in restricted parts of its geographic range — compare GRADUALISM 1 *herein* **2** *or* **punctuated equilibrium theory** : a theory or model of evolution emphasizing punctuated equilibria

punctuation* *n* : something that contrasts or accentuates ⟨lights that add ~ to the room⟩

pun·ji \'pənjē\ *n* -s *often attrib* [perh. fr. Kachin] : a sharpened stick usu. of bamboo set in the ground esp. in Vietnam as an antipersonnel weapon ⟨~ stick⟩ ⟨~ trap⟩

punk* *n* **1** : PUNK ROCK *herein* **2** : a punk rock musician **3** : one who affects punk styles — **punky** \'pəŋkē\ *adj* -ER/-EST

punk* *adj* **1** : of or relating to punk rock **2** : relating to or being the styles (as of dress or hair) inspired by punk rock — **punk·ish** \-ish\ *adj*

punk·a·bil·ly \'pəŋkə,bilē\ *n* -ES [*punk* rock (herein) + rock*abilly* (herein)] : PSYCHOBILLY *herein*

punk·er \'=ə(r)\ *n* -s **1** : PUNK 2 *herein* **2** : PUNK 3 *herein*

punk rock *n* : a form of rock music characterized by extreme and often deliberately offensive expressions of alienation and social discontent — **punk rocker** *n*

punt \'pu̇nt\ *n, pl* **punt** *or* **punts** [IrGael, lit., pound (weight or money), fr. E *pound*] : the monetary pound of Ireland

puppy dog *n* : a domestic dog; *esp* : one having the lovable attributes of a puppy

puppy mill *n* : a commercial farming operation in which purebred dogs are raised in large numbers often to supply pet retailers

pu·pu \'pü,pü\ *n* -s [Hawaiian *pūpū* appetizer] : an Asian dish often served as an appetizer or main course and consisting of samples of a variety of foods (as fried shrimp, spareribs, egg rolls, and teriyaki) ⟨~ platter⟩

purdah* *n* : a state of seclusion or concealment ⟨in political ~ since losing the election⟩

purse crab* *n* : any of the family Leucosiidae of crabs characterized by a granular carapace and long claws and by an adult female having the abdomen formed into a hemispherical cup that snaps shut against the sternum to form a brood chamber for the eggs; *esp* : one (*Persephona mediterranea*) that occurs in shallow water along the Atlantic coast of Mexico and of the U.S. as far north as New Jersey

pushdown \'=,=\ *n* -s [*push down*, v.] : a store of data (as in a computer) from which the item stored last must be the first retrieved — called also *pushdown list*, *pushdown stack*

pushout \'=,=\ *n* -s [*push out*, v.] : one who is dismissed (as from a school or job)

pussycat* *n* : one that is weak, compliant, or amiable : SOFTY

put* *vb* — **put the make on** : to make sexual advances toward — **put the screws on** *also* **put the screws to** : to exert extreme pressure on ⟨*put the screws on* the small farmers to sell out⟩

put down* *vt* **1 a** : BELITTLE, DISPARAGE ⟨many writers want to *put down* not only their interviews but their critics —Melvin Maddocks⟩ **b** : DISAPPROVE, CRITICIZE ⟨*put down* for the way he dressed⟩ **2** : DEFLATE, SQUELCH ⟨a legendary step-parent: rigid, oppressive, untrue, ever ready to *put down* the honest feeling and sound thought that arise within the individual — R.B.Heilman⟩

put–down \ˈ=,=\ *n* -S [*put down*, v. (herein)] : an act or instance of putting down; *esp* : a deflating remark

put–in \ˈ=,=\ *n* -S [*put in*, v.] : a place where a boat or raft is put into the water

put–on* *n* : an instance of putting someone on ⟨the question might be serious or just a *put-on*⟩; *also* : PARODY, SPOOF ⟨a kind of *put-on* of every pretentious film ever made —C.A.Ridley⟩

put·ta·nes·ca \ˌpü·tä'neskä\ *adj* [It (short for *alla puttanesca*, lit., in the style of a prostitute), fem. of *puttanesco* of a prostitute, fr. *puttana* prostitute, fr. OF *putain* — more at POONTANG] : served with or being a pungent tomato sauce typically containing olives, garlic, capers, hot pepper, and sometimes anchovies — usu. used postpositively ⟨pasta ~⟩

putz \ˈpəts\ *n* -ES [Yiddish *puts*, lit., finery, show, prob. fr. *putsn* to clean, shine; akin to G *putzen* to adorn, clean] **1** *slang* : PENIS **2** *slang* : a stupid, foolish, or ineffectual person : JERK

PV* *abbr* **1** photovoltaic **2** polyvinyl

PWA \ˌpē,dəbəl(,)yü'ā\ *abbr or n* -S : a person affected with AIDS

pygmy chimpanzee *n* : BONOBO *herein*

py·re·throid \pīˈrē,thrȯid, -ˈre,-\ *n* -S [*pyrethrin* + [1]-*oid*] : any of various synthetic compounds related to the pyrethrins and having similar insecticidal properties — **pyrethroid** *adj*

py·ri·meth·amine \ˌpirə'methə,mēn, ˌpīr-\ *n* [*pyrimidine* + *ethyl* + *amine*] : a folic acid antagonist $C_{12}H_{13}ClN_4$ used in the treatment of malaria and toxoplasmosis

qa·tari \kəˈtärē, gə'-, ka'-\ *n* -S *cap* [Ar *qaṭarī*, fr. *Qaṭar*, sheikhdom on the Persian Gulf] : a native or inhabitant of Qatar — **qatari** \"\ *adj, usu cap*

QCD *abbr* quantum chromodynamics *herein*

qi *var of* CHI

qi·vi·ut \ˈkēvēət, -vē,üt\ *n* -S [Esk] : the wool of the undercoat of the musk-ox

QSO \ˌkyü(,)e'sō\ *n* -S [*quasi-stellar object* (herein)] : QUASAR *herein*

quaa·lude \ˈkwā,lüd\ *n* [fr. *Quaalude*, a trademark] : a tablet or capsule of methaqualone

quad* *n* [[6]*quad*] : a ski lift that accommodates four people

[1]**quad** \ˈkwäd\ *n* -S [by shortening] : QUADRAPHONICS *herein*

[2]**quad** \"\ *adj* [by shortening] : QUADRAPHONIC *herein*

[3]**quad** \"\ *n* -S [short for *quadrillion*] : a unit of energy equal to one quadrillion British thermal units

[4]**quad** \"\ *n* -S [by shortening] : QUADRICEPS — usu. used in pl.

qua·dran·tid \kwäˈdrantəd\ *n* -S *usu cap* [NL *Quadrant-, Quadrans* (*Muralis*) mural quadrant, a group of stars in the constellation Draco from which the shower appears to radiate + E [1]-*id*] : any of the meteors in a meteor shower that occurs each year about January 3

quad·ra·phon·ic *also* **quad·ri·phon·ic** \ˌkwädrəˈfänik\ *adj* [*quadra-* (alter. of *quadri-*) + *-phonic* (as in *stereophonic*)] : of, relating to, or using four channels for the transmission, recording, or reproduction of sound

quad·ra·phon·ics *or* **quad·ri·phon·ics** \-niks\ *n pl but sing or pl in constr* [*quadraphonic* (herein) + [1]-*s*] : quadraphonic sound

quadratic form *n* : a homogeneous polynomial of the second degree ⟨$x^2 + 5xy + y^2$ is a *quadratic form*⟩

quality assurance *n* : a program for the systematic monitoring and evaluation of the various aspects of a project, service, or facility to ensure that standards of quality are being met

quality circle *n* : a group of employees who volunteer to meet regularly to discuss and propose solutions to problems (as of quality or productivity) in the workplace

quality point average *n* : GRADE POINT AVERAGE *herein*

quan·go \ˈkwaŋ,gō\ *n* -S [*quasi nongovernmental organization*] *chiefly Brit* : a partly autonomous regulatory agency; *esp* : one in Britain organized outside the civil service but financed and appointed by the government

quan·ta·some \ˈkwäntə,sōm\ *n* -S [prob. fr. *quanta*, pl. of *quantum* + [3]-*some*] : a chlorophyll-containing spherical granule found in the grana of chloroplasts

quantifier* *n* : one that quantifies; *esp* : a person who quantifies data, an activity, or a field of study (as history)

quantum chromodynamics *n pl but sing in constr* : a theory of fundamental particles based on the assumption that quarks are distinguished by differences in color and are held together (as in hadrons) by an exchange of gluons

quantum electronics *n pl but sing in constr* : a branch of physics that deals with the interaction of radiation with discrete energy levels in substances (as in a maser or laser)

quantum field theory *n* : a theory in physics: the interaction of two separate physical systems (as particles) is attributed to a field that extends from one to the other and is manifested in a particle exchanged between the two systems

quantum gravity *n* : a quantum theory of the gravitational field; *specif* : a theory thought by physicists to be possible which would combine general relativity with quantum mechanics

quantum jump* *or* **quantum leap** *n* : an abrupt and usu. significant change or increase

quantum state *n* : any of various states of a physical system (as an electron) that are specified by particular values of attributes (as charge and spin) of the system and are characterized by a particular energy

quark \ˈkwärk, -wȯr-\ *n* -S [coined by Murray Gell-Mann *b*1929 Am. physicist] : any of several elementary particles that are postulated to come in pairs (as of the up and down varieties) of similar mass with one member having a charge of +⅔ and the other a charge of −⅓ and that are held to make up hadrons

quartz heater *n* : a portable electric radiant heater that has heating elements sealed in quartz-glass tubes in front of a reflective backing

quartz–iodine lamp \ˈ=ˈ===-\ *n* : an incandescent lamp that has a quartz bulb and a tungsten filament and that contains iodine which reacts with the vaporized tungsten to prevent excessive blackening of the bulb

qua·sar \ˈkwā,zär *also* -,sär\ *n* -S [*quasi-stellar* radio source (herein)] : any of a class of celestial objects that resemble stars but whose large red shift and apparent brightness imply extreme distance and huge energy output

quasicrystal \ˈ=(,)=,==\ *n* [[2]*quasi* + [1]*crystal*] : a body of solid material that resembles a crystal in being composed of repeating structural units but that incorporates two or more unit cells into a quasiperiodic structure — **quasicrystalline** *adj*

quasiparticle \ˈ=(,)=ˈ==\ *n* [[2]*quasi* + *particle*] : a composite entity (as a vibration in a solid) that is analogous in its behavior to a single particle

quasiperiodic \ˌ=(,)=,=ˈ==\ *adj* [[1]*quasi* + *periodic*] : almost but not quite periodic; *esp* : periodic on a small scale but unpredictable at some larger scale

quasi–stellar object \ˈ=(,)=,==-\ *n* [*quasi-stellar* fr. [1]*quasi* + *stellar*] : QUASAR *herein*

quasi–stellar radio source \ˈ=(,)=ˈ==-\ *n* : QUASAR *herein*

quas·qui·centennial \ˌkwäskwē, -kwō+\ *n* [L *quadrans* quarter or *quartus* fourth + E *sesquicentennial* — more at QUADRANT] : a 125th anniversary — **quasquicentennial** *adj*

queenside \ˈ=,=\ *n* : the side of the chessboard containing the file on which both queens sit at the beginning of the game

queen–size \ˈ=,=\ *adj* **1** : having dimensions of approximately 60 inches by 80 inches — used of a bed **2** : of a size that fits a queen-size bed ⟨a *queen-size* bedspread⟩

queen substance *n* : a pheromone secreted by a queen bee and consumed by worker bees in which it inhibits ovary development; *also* : the same or a similar substance secreted by termites

queue* *n* **1** : a sequence of messages or jobs held in auxiliary storage awaiting transmission or processing **2** : a data structure that consists of a list of records which is added to at one end and removed from at the other

queue* *vt* : to send to or place in a queue

queuing theory *n* : the mathematical and statistical theory of queues and waiting lines (as in heavy traffic or in the use of telephone circuits)

quiche lor·raine \-lə'rān, -lō'-, -lō'-\ *n, often cap L* [F, quiche of Lorraine (region in northwestern France)] : a quiche containing cheese and crisp bacon bits

quick and dirty *adj* : expedient and effective but not without flaws or unwanted side effects ⟨a *quick and dirty* solution⟩

quick fix *n* : an expedient but temporary solution to a problem

quick kick *n* : a punt in football made on first, second, or third down from a running or passing formation and designed to take the opposing team by surprise

quick opener *n* : an offensive play in football in which a back takes a direct handoff and runs straight to a hole in the line

quin·o·lone \ˈkwinᵊl,ōn\ *n* -S [*quinoline* + *-one*] : any of a class of synthetic antibacterial drugs that are derivatives of hydroxylated quinolines and inhibit the replication of bacterial DNA

qui·nu·cli·di·nyl ben·zi·late \kwə̇ˈn(y)üklə̇dēnᵊlˈbenzə,lāt\ *n* -S [*quinuclidine* + *-yl* + *benzil* + [1]-*ate*] : BZ *herein*

quotient group *n* : a group whose elements are the cosets of a normal subgroup of a given group — called also *factor group*

quotient ring *n* : a ring whose elements are the cosets of an ideal in a given ring

q wave \ˈkyü-\ *n, usu cap Q* : the short initial downward stroke of the QRS complex in an electrocardiogram formed during the beginning of ventricular depolarization

QWER·TY \ˈkwərd-ē-\ *or* **QWERTY keyboard** *n, often not cap* [so called fr. the first six letters in the second row of the keyboard] : a standard typewriter keyboard

r* *abbr* **1** *usu cap* radial **2** repeat **3** rerun

r* *symbol* **1** [prob. fr. rate] intrinsic rate of natural increase **2** *cap* the set of all real numbers

R *trademark* — used as a rating for a motion picture of such a nature that admission is restricted to persons over a specified age (as 17) or to younger persons who are accompanied by a parent or guardian; compare G *herein*, NC-17 *herein*, PG *herein*, PG-13 *herein*

rabbit* *n* : a runner in a long-distance race who sets a fast pace in the first part of the race usu. to help a teammate win

rab·bit \ˈrabə̇t, *usu* -əd-+V\ *vi* -ED/-ING/-S [fr. *rabbit-and-pork*, rhyming slang for *talk*] *Brit* : to talk idly or incessantly — often used with *on* ⟨look at the way we go ~*ing* on about our wonderful system of justice —*The People*⟩

rabbit ears *n pl* : an indoor dipole television antenna consisting of two usu. extensible rods connected to a base to form a V shape

race card *n* : the issue of a person's race as it relates to a particular contest (as a political campaign or a court trial) — often used in the phrase *play the race card*

race walking *n* : racing at a fast walk in track-and-field competition with each competitor required to maintain continuous foot contact with the ground and to keep the supporting leg straight — **race–walk** \ˈ=,=\ *vi* — **race walker** *n*

rack car* *n* : a railroad flatcar equipped with a 2-level or 3-level framework for transporting motor vehicles

rac·lette \raˈklet\ *n* -S [F, lit., scraper, fr. F *racler* to scrape, fr. MF, fr. OProv *rasclar*, fr. (assumed) VL *rasiculare*, fr. L *rasus*, past part. of *radere* to scrape — more at RAT] : a dish of Swiss origin consisting of melted cheese traditionally served with tiny boiled potatoes and sour pickles; *also* : a firm cheese suitable for use in this dish

racquetball \ˈ==,=\ *n* : a game similar to handball played on a 4-walled court with a short-handled racket and a ball larger than a handball; *also* : the ball used in this game

rad \ˈrad\ *adj* [short for *radical* (herein)] *slang* : COOL 8

radar astronomy *n* : astronomy dealing with investigations of celestial bodies in the solar system by analyzing radar waves directed toward and reflected from the object being studied

radar gun *n* : a handheld device that uses radar to measure the speed of a moving object (as an automobile or a baseball)

radar telescope *n* : a radar transmitter-receiver with an antenna for use in radar astronomy

radial* *n* : RADIAL TIRE *herein*

radial ker·a·tot·o·my \-ˌkerəˈtäd·əmē\ *n* -ES [ISV *kerat-* + *-tomy*] : a surgical operation on the cornea for the correction of myopia that involves flattening the cornea by making a series of incisions in a radial pattern resembling the spokes of a wheel

radially symmetrical *adj* : of, relating to, or characterized by radial symmetry

radial tire *or* **radial–ply tire** *n* : a pneumatic tire in which the ply cords that extend to the beads are laid at right angles to the center line of the tread

radiation* *n* : transfer of heat by radiation — compare CONDUCTION *in the Dict*, CONVECTION *in the Dict*

radical* *adj, slang* : COOL 8, EXCELLENT

radical* *n* : FREE RADICAL

radical chic *n* : the fashion among socially prominent people of hobnobbing with social inferiors who are usu. left-wing political activists; *broadly* : fashionable and usu. superficial left-wing radicalism — **radical–chic** \ˈ===ˈ=\ *adj*

ra·dic·chio \raˈdikēō, -ˈdē-\ *n* -S [It, chicory, fr. (assumed) VL *radiculus*, alter. of L *radicula* little root — more at RADICLE] : a chicory of a red variety with variegated leaves that is used as a salad green

ra·di·esthesia \ˌrādē+\ *n* [NL, fr. L *radius* ray + NL *esthesia* — more at RAY] **1** : sensitiveness held to enable a person with the aid of divining rod or pendulum to detect things (as the presence of underground water, the nature of an illness, or the guilt of a suspected person); *also* : DOWSING, DIVINING **2** : a study that deals with radiesthesia

ra·dio·al·ler·go·sor·bent \ˌrādē(,)ōˌalərgōˈsȯrbənt\ *adj* [*radio-* + *allergen* + *-o-* + *sorbent*] : relating to or being a blood analysis that tests for allergen-specific antibodies of the immunoglobulin class IgE and is used to detect allergic reactions

radiocarbon dating *n* : CARBON DATING *herein* — **radiocarbon–date** \ˌrādē(,)ō==ˈ=\ *vt*

ra·dio·chromatogram \ˌrādē(,)ō+\ *n* [*radio-* + *chromatogram*] : a chromatogram revealing one or more radioactive substances

ra·dio·chromatography \"+\ *n* [*radio-* + *chromatography*] : the process of making a quantitative or qualitative determination of a radioisotope-labeled substance by measuring the radioactivity of the appropriate zone or spot in the chromatogram — **ra·dio·chromatographic** \"+\ *adj*

radio collar *n* : a collar with an attached radio transmitter that is put on an animal so that its movements in its natural habitat can be remotely monitored — **radio–collar** \ˈ===ˈ=\ *vt*

ra·dio·ecology \"+\ *n* [*radio-* + *ecology*] : the study of the effects of radiation and radioactive substances on ecological communities — **ra·dio·ecological** \"+\ *adj* — **ra·dio·ecologist** \"+\ *n*

radio galaxy *n* : a galaxy that is a strong source of radio waves

ra·dio·immunoassay \ˈrādē,ō+\ *n* [*radio-* + *immunoassay* (herein)] : immunoassay of a substance (as insulin) that has been radioactively labeled — **ra·dio·immunoassayable** \"+\ *adj*

ra·dio·immunological \"+\ *also* **ra·dio·immunologic** \"+\ *adj* [*radio-* + *immunological* or *immunologic*] : of, relating to, or involving radioimmunoassay ⟨~ detection of a hormone⟩

ra·dio·iodinate \ˌrādē(,)ō+\ *vt* [*radio-* + *iodinate*] : to treat or label with radioactive iodine — **ra·dio·iodination** \"+\ *n*

ra·dio·isotopic \ˌrādē(,)ō+\ *adj* : of, relating to, using, or being a radioisotope ⟨~ techniques⟩ — **ra·dio·isotopically** \"+\ *adv*

ra·dio·label \"+\ *vt* [*radio-* + *label*] : to label with a radioactive atom or substance

ra·dio·pharmaceutical \"+\ *n* [*radio-* + [2]*pharmaceutical*] : a radioactive drug used for diagnostic or therapeutic purposes — **radiopharmaceutical** *adj*

ra·dio·protective \"+\ *adj* [*radio-* + *protective*] : serving to protect or aiding in protecting against the injurious effect of radiations ⟨~ drugs⟩ — **ra·dio·protection** \"+\ *n*

ra·dio·protector \"+\ *also* **ra·dio·pro·tec·tor·ant** \ˌrādē(,)ōprəˈtektə(ə)rənt\ *n* [*radio-* + *protector* or *protectorant* (fr. *protector* + *-ant*)] : a radioprotective chemical agent

ra·dio·resistance \ˌrādē(,)ō+\ *n* [*radio-* + *resistance*] : resistance (as of a cell or organism) to the effects of radiant energy

ra·dio·sensitizer \"+\ *n* [*radio-* + *sensitizer*] : a substance or condition capable of increasing the radiosensitivity of a cell or tissue — **ra·dio·sensitization** \"+\ *n* — **ra·dio·sensitizing** \"+\ *adj*

ra·dio·sterilized \"+\ *adj* [*radio-* + *sterilized*] : sterilized by irradiation (as with X rays or gamma rays) ⟨~ mosquitoes⟩ ⟨~ syringes⟩ — **ra·dio·sterilization** \"+\ *n*

ra·dio·telemetry \"+\ *n* [*radio-* + *telemetry* (herein)] **1** : TELEMETRY 1 *herein* **2** : BIOTELEMETRY *herein* — **ra·dio·telemetric** \"+\ *adj*

ra·dio–ulna \"+\ *n* [NL, fr. *radio-* (fr. L *radius*) + *ulna*] : a single bone in the forelimb of an amphibian (as a frog) that represents fusion of the separate radius and ulna of higher forms

radwaste \ˈrad,wāst\ *n* [by shortening] : radioactive waste

ragamuffin* *also* **rag·ga·muf·fin** *n* -S [*raggamuffin* alter. (prob. influenced by *reggae* — herein) of *ragamuffin*] : music distinguished by rap lyrics and a reggae beat

Rag·doll \ˈrag,däl, -,dȯl\ *trademark* — used for a breed of domestic cats

ragg \ˈrəg\ *n* -S *often attrib* [prob. fr. Norw *ragg-* (in *raggsokk* heavy sock made of coarse wool), fr. *ragg* thick, shaggy hair, fr. ON *rögg* tuft, shagginess — more at RUG] : a yarn formed of two strands of dyed wool and one strand of undyed wool often combined with other fibers (as nylon)

rag·ga \ˈragə, ˈrä-\ *n* -S [short for *raggamuffin*] : RAGAMUFFIN *herein*

ragtop \ˈ=,=\ *n* : a convertible automobile

raider* *n* : one that attempts a usu. hostile takeover of a business corporation ⟨corporate ~*s*⟩

rail* *n* : a specialized drag-racing vehicle with very large wide tires in the rear and tiny bicycle tires in the front and with a chassis that consists essentially of two long braced rails

rail gun *n* [[2]*rail*] : an electromagnetic catapult designed to hurl projectiles at extremely high speeds — compare MASS DRIVER *herein*

rainbow* *n, slang* : a combination of the sodium derivatives of amobarbital and secobarbital in a blue and red capsule

rainbow* *adj* : of, relating to, or being people of different races or cultural backgrounds ⟨offered a ~ ticket in the local election⟩

rainbow coalition *n* : a group (as a political coalition) whose members are of different races or of different ethnic, political, or religious backgrounds

rainbow pill *n, slang* : any of a combination of pills (as of amphetamines, laxatives, and thyroid hormones) typically of different colors that were formerly taken to curb appetite and promote weight loss

rain date *n* : an alternative date set aside for use if a scheduled outdoor event must be postponed because of rain

rainmaker* *n* : a person (as a partner in a law firm) who brings in new business; *also* : a person whose influence can initiate progress or ensure success — **rainmaking** *n*

rainsuit \ˈ=,=\ *n* : a suit of waterproof material consisting of pants and a usu. hooded jacket for wear in the rain usu. over ordinary clothes

raised ranch *n* : BI-LEVEL *herein*

rai·ta \ˈrītə, ˈrä·ētä\ *n* -S [Hindi & Urdu *rāytā*, fr. (assumed) Skt *rājikātiktaka*, fr. *rājikā* black mustard + *tiktaka* sharp, pungent, fr. *tikta* verbal adj. of *tejate* it is sharp — more at STICK] : an Indian side dish made of yogurt, usu. diced cucumber, and seasonings

rallymaster \ˈ==,=\ *n* [[2]*rally* + *master*] : one who organizes and conducts an automobile rally

ralph \ˈralf, ˈraůf\ *vb* -ED/-ING/-S [imit.] *slang* : VOMIT

RAM \ˈram\ *abbr or n* -S random-access memory *herein*

raman scattering *n, usu cap R* [after C.V.Raman †1970 Indian physicist] : the scattering of light (as from a laser) by a pure substance that gives rise to a characteristic Raman spectrum

raman spectroscopy *n, usu cap R* : a spectroscopic technique in which the Raman spectrum of a substance is analyzed to determine the properties (as the structure) of the substance

ram disk *n, usu cap R&A&M* : a section of random-access memory in a computer configured to function like a disk drive

ra·men \ˈrämən\ *n* -S [Jap *rāmen*, fr. Chin (Pek) *la*[1] *mien*[4], fr. *la*[1] pull + *mien*[4] noodles] : quick-cooking egg noodles usu. served in a broth with bits of meat and vegetables

ramp* *vt* : to increase or decrease esp. at a constant rate — usu. used with *up* or *down* ⟨~ up production⟩

rancher* *n* : RANCH HOUSE 2

ranch·ette \ˌran'chet\ *n* -S [[2]*ranch* + *-ette*] : a small ranch

rand \ˈrand, *in So. Afr. usu* ˈrȧnd *or* ˈrȧnt *or* ˈränt\ *n, pl* **rand** *or* **rands** [fr. the *Rand* (*Witwatersrand*), gold-producing district in So. Africa] **1 a** : the basic monetary unit of the Republic of So. Africa established in 1961 — see MONEY table *in the Dict* **b** : the former basic monetary unit of Botswana, Lesotho, and Swaziland **2** : a coin or note representing one rand

R and B *abbr or n* : rhythm and blues *herein*

R and D *abbr or n* : research and development

random–access \ˈ=ˈ=,=\ *adj* : permitting access (as to stored information) in any order the user desires ⟨*random-access* capability of a videodisc player⟩

random–access memory *n* : a computer memory that provides the main internal storage available to the user for programs and data — called also *RAM*; compare READ-ONLY MEMORY

ran·dom·iz·er \ˈrandə,mīzə(r)\ *n* -S : a device or procedure used for randomization

ra·nit·i·dine \raˈnid·ə,dēn, -ˈnit-\ *n* -S [prob. fr. *ranit-* (blend of *furan* and *nitr-*) + *-idine* (as in *cimetidine* — herein)] : an analogue $C_{13}H_{22}N_4O_3S$ that is administered in the form of its hydrochloride to inhibit gastric acid secretion (as in the treatment of duodenal ulcers)

rank* *n* **1** : the number of linearly independent rows in a matrix **2** : FACE CORD

[1]**rap** \ˈrap\ *n* -S *often attrib* [perh. by shortening & alter. fr. *repartee*] **1** : TALK, CONVERSATION **2** : [4]SPIEL ⟨the salesman's smooth ~⟩ **3 a** : a rhythmic chanting often in unison of usu. rhymed couplets to a rhythmic accompaniment **b** : a piece so performed

[2]**rap** \"\ *vi* **rapped; rapped; rapping; raps** **1** : to talk freely and frankly ⟨at the corner bar *rapping* —*Newsweek*⟩ **2** : to perform rap music — **rap·per** *n* -S

rapid eye movement *n* : rapid conjugate movement of the eyes associated esp. with REM sleep

rapid eye movement sleep *n* : REM SLEEP *herein*

rap sheet *n* : a police arrest record esp. for an individual

rapture of the deep : NITROGEN NARCOSIS *herein*

ras \ˈras\ *n* -ES *often attrib* [prob. fr. [1]*rat* + sarcoma; fr. the initial isolation of such genes in rat sarcomas] : any of a family of genes that undergo mutation to oncogenes and esp. to some commonly linked to human cancers (as of the colon, lung, and pancreas) ⟨~ oncogenes⟩ ⟨~ proteins⟩

ra·schel \(ˈ)räˈshel\ *n* -S : a fabric made by raschel knitting

ras·ta \ˈrästə, ˈras-\ *also* **ras·ta·man** \-mən, -,man\ *n, pl* **rastas** *also* **ras·ta·men** \-mən, -,men\ *usu cap* [*rasta* by shortening; *rastaman* fr. *rasta* + *man*] : RASTAFARIAN *herein* — **rasta** *adj, usu cap*

ras·ta·fa·ri·an \ˌrästəˈfärēən, ˌras-, -ˈfar-, -ˈfer-\ *n* -s *usu cap* [*Ras Tafari*, name before coronation of Haile Selassie †1975 Ethiopian emperor + E *-an*] : an adherent of Rastafarianism — **rasta·farian** *adj, usu cap*

ras·ta·fa·ri·an·ism \-əˌnizəm\ *n* -s *cap* : a religious cult among black Jamaicans that teaches the eventual redemption of blacks and their return to Africa, employs the ritualistic use of marijuana, forbids the cutting of hair, and venerates Haile Selassie as a god

raster* *n* : a pattern for scanning an area from side to side in lines from top to bottom ⟨an electron beam in a cathode-ray tube scans the phosphor screen in a ∼⟩; *also* : a pattern of closely spaced rows of dots that form the image on a cathode-ray tube (as of a television or computer display)

rat* *n* 1 : a person who spends much time in a specified place ⟨a gym ∼⟩ 2 : a first-year student esp. at a military school

ratchet* *vt* : to cause to move by steps or degrees — usu. used with *up* or *down* ⟨inflation ∼*ing* up the cost of living⟩ ⟨∼*ing* down the debt⟩ ∼ *vi* : to proceed by steps or degrees

rate of change : a value that results from dividing the change of a function of a variable by the change in the variable ⟨velocity is the *rate of change* of distance with respect to time⟩

ratepayer* *n* : one who pays for the consumption of electricity according to established rates

rat fink *n* : FINK *herein*

ratio *vt* -ED/-ING/-S [*ratio*, n.] : to compare esp. numerically or quantitatively with another value or set of values : express in a ratio

rational* *adj* : relating to, consisting of, or being one or more rational numbers

rational expectations *n pl* : an economic theory holding that investors use all available information about the economy and economic policy in making financial decisions and that they will always act in their best interest — **rational ex·pec·ta·tion·ist** \-ˌekˌspekˈtāshənəst\ *n*

rat's ass *n* : a minimum amount or degree of care or interest : HOOT, DAMN — usu. used in the phrase *don't give a rat's ass*; often considered vulgar

raunch \ˈrȯnch, ˈrän-\ *n* -ES [back-formation fr. *raunchy*] : VULGARITY, LEWDNESS

rave* *n* [²*rave*] : a large overnight dance party featuring techno music and usu. involving the taking of mind-altering drugs

raver* *n* : one who frequents raves

rave–up \ˈ=ˌ=\ *n* -s [*rave* (herein) + *-up* (as in *nosh-up* — herein)] 1 *Brit* : a wild party : BASH 2 **a** : the hard-driving sometimes instrumental climactic section of a popular or country music song **b** : a song having a rave-up

raw bar *n* : a restaurant that features raw shellfish usu. served at a counter

ray·naud's phenomenon \(ˈ)rāˈnōz-\ *also* **raynaud's syndrome** *n, usu cap R* [after Maurice *Raynaud* †1881 Fr. physician] : the symptoms associated with Raynaud's disease

razor wire *n* : coiled wire fitted with sharp razor edges and used as an obstacle or a barrier; *also* : CONCERTINA 2

razzle–dazzle *adj* [*razzle-dazzle*, n.] : IMPRESSIVE, DAZZLING, GLITZY ⟨new *razzle-dazzle* fashions⟩

razzmatazz* *n* 1 : DOUBLE-TALK 2 2 : VIM, ZING

RBE *abbr* relative biological effectiveness *herein*

RDA* *abbr, often not cap* recommended daily allowance

read* *vt* 1 **a** : to recognize or interpret as if by reading ⟨a good canoeist ∼*s* the rapids⟩; *also* : ANTICIPATE ⟨the quarterback was able to ∼ the blitz⟩ **b** : to study (a putting green) to predict the movement of the ball; *also* : to predict the movement of (a putt) by observation of the green 2 **a** : to acquire (information) from storage; *esp* : to sense the meaning of (data) in recorded and coded form — used of a computer or data processor **b** : to read the coded information on (as a floppy disk) **c** : to cause to be read and transferred to storage ⟨∼ the contents of a punch card into memory⟩ ∼ *vi* : to admit of interpretation or consideration as specified ⟨the two panels ∼ as one⟩ ⟨that amazing lump of marks and smudges that ∼*s* as "nose" —T.B.Hess⟩

read* *n* 1 : something that is read ⟨an old-fashioned good ∼, bursting with characters and drama and emotion —Jane Clapperton⟩ 2 READING 3

reader·ly \ˈ=ˌlē\ *adj* : of, relating to, or typical of a reader

reader–response criticism \ˈ===ˌ=-\ *n* : a literary criticism that focuses primarily on the reader's reaction to a text

reading frame *n* : any of the three possible ways of reading a sequence of nucleotides as a series of triplets — see OPEN READING FRAME *herein*

read–only memory \ˈ=ˈ==-\ *n* : a usu. small computer memory that contains special-purpose information (as a program) that cannot be altered — called also *ROM*; compare RANDOM-ACCESS MEMORY *herein*

readout* *n* 1 : the process of reading 2 **a** : the process of reading information from an automatic device (as an electronic computer) and displaying it in an understandable form **b** : the information read from such a device and displayed or recorded (as by magnetic tape or printing device) **c** : an electronic device that presents information in visual form 3 : the radio transmission of data or pictures from a space vehicle either immediately upon acquisition or later by playback of a tape recording

readymade \ˈ=ˌ=ˌ=\ *n* -s [F *ready-made*, fr. E, adj.] : a commonplace artifact (as a comb or a pair of ice tongs) selected and displayed as a work of art

re·aggregate \(ˈ)rē+\ *vb* [*re-* + ²*aggregate*] *vt* : to cause to re-form into an aggregate or whole ∼ *vi* : to re-form into an aggregate or whole ⟨the cells *reaggregated* into organized tissue⟩ — **re·aggregate** \"+\ *n* — **re·aggregation** \"+\ *n*

real* *adj* 1 : REAL-VALUED *herein* ⟨functions of a ∼ variable⟩ 2 *of a particle* : DETECTABLE — contrasted with *virtual* 1 *herein*

real* *n* [⁴*real*] 1 : the basic monetary unit of Brazil 2 : a coin or note representing one real

real estate* *n* : SPACE : as **a** : CAPACITY **b** : AREA ⟨desktop *real estate*⟩ ⟨the limited *real estate* on hard drives —Leonard Wiener⟩

reality* *n, often attrib* : television programming that features videos of actual occurrences (as a police chase, stunt, or natural disaster)

reality check *n* : something that clarifies or serves as a reminder of reality often by correcting a misconception

real time *n* : the actual time during which something takes place ⟨here's how it looked in *real time* and in slow motion —J.W.Chancellor⟩ ⟨conversed on-line in *real time* rather than exchanging e-mail⟩ — **real–time** *adj*

real–valued \ˈ=ˌ=\ *adj* : taking on only real numbers for values

ream* *vt* [⁵*ream*] : REPRIMAND — often used with *out* ⟨∼*s* out his players so severely —Alexander Wolff⟩

rear–end \ˈ=ˈ=\ *vt* : to crash into the back of (as an automobile)

re·bar \(ˈ)rē+\ *n* -s [reinforcing *bar*] : a steel rod with ridges for use in reinforced concrete

re·branch \(ˈ)rē+\ *vi* [*re-* + ²*branch*] : to form secondary branches

recall* *n* 1 : a public call by a manufacturer for the return of a product that may be defective or contaminated 2 : the ability (as of an information retrieval system) to retrieve stored material

recamier** *n* [so called fr. its appearance in a well-known portrait of Mme. Récamier by Jacques-Louis David †1825 Fr. painter] : a usu. backless couch with a high curved headrest and low footrest

re·canalization \(ˌ)rē+\ *n* [*re-* + *canalization*] : the process of restoring flow to or reuniting an interrupted channel of a bodily tube (as a blood vessel or vas deferens) — **re·canalize** \(ˈ)rē+\ *vt*

rechargeable \(ˈ)rēˈchärjəbəl, -äj-\ *adj* : capable of being recharged ⟨∼ batteries⟩ — **rechargeable** *n* -s

re·charter \(ˈ)rē+\ *vt* [*re-* + ²*charter*] : to grant a new charter to ⟨∼*ed* the national bank⟩ — **recharter** *n*

reciprocal* *n* : MULTIPLICATIVE INVERSE *herein*

re·cla·ma \rəˈklämə\ *vi* -ED/-ING/-S [perh. short for *reclamation*] : to request the reconsideration of a decision or a change in policy — used esp. in the military

re·clos·able \(ˈ)rēˈklōzəbəl\ *adj* [*re-* + ¹*close* + *-able*] : capable of being tightly closed again after opening

re·com·bi·nant \(ˈ)rēˈkämbənənt\ *adj* [*recombinant*, n.] 1 : relating to or exhibiting genetic recombination 2 **a** : relating to or containing genetically engineered DNA **b** : produced by genetic engineering ⟨∼ bovine growth hormone⟩

recombinant DNA *n* : genetically engineered DNA usu. incorporating DNA from more than one species of organism

reconciliation* *n* : the Roman Catholic sacrament of penance

re·configure \(ˈ)rē+\ *vt* [*re-* + *configure*] : to rearrange into an altered form, figure, shape, or layout — **re·con·fig·ur·able** \-rəbəl\ *adj* — **re·configuration** \(ˈ)rē+\ *n*

re·contextualize \(ˈ)rē+\ *vt* [*re-* + *contextualize* (herein)] : to place (as a literary or artistic work) in a different context

record* *n* : a collection of related items of information (as in a database) treated as a unit

recovered memory *n* : a memory of a traumatic event (as sexual abuse) experienced typically during childhood that is forgotten and then recalled many years later and that is sometimes held to be an invalid or false remembrance generated by outside influence

recovering *adj* [fr. present part. of ¹*recover*] : being one who is trying to overcome a disorder or shortcoming ⟨a ∼ alcoholic⟩ ⟨a still-bookish ∼ academic with a tendency to live in his head —Jon Spayde⟩

recovery* *n, often attrib* : the process of combating a disorder (as alcoholism) or a real or perceived problem ⟨a workaholic in ∼⟩

recreational drug *n* : a drug (as cocaine, marijuana, or methamphetamine) used without medical justification for its psychoactive effects often in the belief that occasional use of such a substance is not habit-forming or addictive

recreational vehicle *n* : a vehicle designed for recreational use (as in camping); *esp* : MOTOR HOME *herein* — called also *RV*

recumbent* *adj* : having the seat positioned so that the rider's legs are extended horizontally forward and the body is reclined ⟨a ∼ bicycle⟩

recursion* *n* 1 : the determination of a succession of elements (as numbers or functions) by operation on one or more preceding elements according to a recursive definition — compare FIBONACCI NUMBER *herein* 2 : the solution of a problem by means of a procedure that uses a copy of itself as one of its steps so that the problem is simplified with each execution of the procedure until a simplest case is reached for which the solution has been defined and the basic solution is applied to complete the solutions of the more complex versions — compare ITERATION 2 *herein*

re·cur·sive \rəˈkərsiv, rē-, -ˈkōs-\ *adj* [²*recursion* + *-ive*] 1 : of, relating to, or involving recursion 2 : of, relating to, or being a procedure that can repeat itself indefinitely or until a specified condition is met ⟨a ∼ rule in a grammar⟩ — **recursively** *adv* — **recursiveness** *n* -ES

re·cycle* *vt* 1 : to process (as liquid body waste, glass, or cans) in order to regain material for human use 2 : to adapt to a new use : ALTER, TRANSFORM ⟨∼ recent real events into prime time entertainment —Karl Meyer⟩ 3 : to bring back : REUSE, REPEAT ⟨a light, chatty tribute that ∼*s* a number of good anecdotes —Larry McMurtry⟩ 4 : to make ready for reuse : RESTORE ⟨the move to ∼ unused gas stations —Robert Frausto⟩ 5 : to reuse (money) by investing esp. in an area or enterprise that will allow the investment to return as new profits ⟨*recycle* petrodollars⟩ ∼ *vi* 1 : to stop the counting and return to an earlier point in a countdown 2 : to return to an original condition so that operation can begin again — used of an electronic device — **re·cy·cla·bil·i·ty** \(ˈ)rēˌsīkləˈbilədē\ *n* -ES — **re·cy·cla·ble** \(ˈ)rēˈsīk(ə)ləbəl\ *adj or n* — **re·cycler** \"+\ *n* -s

recycle* *n* : the process of recycling

red* *n* **reds** *pl, also* **red devils** *slang* : red drug capsules containing the sodium salt of secobarbital

red bean *n* 1 : a red kidney bean 2 : a small dark red seed of the adzuki bean that is often combined with sugar to produce a sweet paste used in cooking

redbrick \ˈ=ˌ=\ *adj, sometimes cap* 1 : built of red brick 2 : of, relating to, or being the British universities founded in the 19th and early 20th centuries — compare OXBRIDGE *herein*, PLATEGLASS *herein*

redefine* *vt* 1 : to reexamine or reevaluate esp. with a view to change 2 : TRANSFORM 1c

re·describe \ˌrē+\ *vt* [*re-* + *describe*] : to describe anew or again; *esp* : to give a new and more complete description to (a biological taxon)

re·description \"+\ *n* [*re-* + *description*] : a new and more complete description esp. of a biological taxon

red–eye* *n* 1 : the phenomenon of a subject's eyes appearing red in color flash photography 2 *or* **red–eye flight** : a late night or overnight flight

red flag *n* 1 : a warning signal 2 : something that attracts usu. irritated attention

red guard *n, usu cap R&G* [trans. of Chin (Pek) *hung² wei⁴ ping¹*] : a member of an activist youth organization in China serving the Maoist cause esp. during the late 1960s

red–hot* *adj* : extremely popular

re·dial \(ˈ)rē+\ *n* -s [*re-* + ²*dial*] : a function on a telephone that automatically repeats the dialing of the last number called; *also* : a button that invokes this function

re·dis·tri·bu·tion·ist \(ˈ)rēˌdistrəˈbyüsh(ə)nəst\ *n* -s [*redistribution* + *-ist*] : WELFARE STATER

redline* *vi* : to withhold home-loan funds or insurance from neighborhoods considered poor economic risks ∼ *vt* : to discriminate against in housing or insurance — **redlining** *n*

redline \ˈ=ˌ=\ *n* : a recommended safety limit : the fastest, farthest, or highest point or degree considered safe; *also* : the red line which marks this point on a gauge

red meat* *n* : something substantial that can satisfy a basic need or appetite ⟨when I started doing serious research, I had to cut through the legends to get to the *red meat* —Barry Clifford⟩

redneck** *n* : a person whose behavior and opinions are similar to those attributed to rednecks — often used disparagingly

redneck *adj* [*redneck*, n.] : of, relating to, characteristic of, or being a redneck ⟨∼ music⟩ ⟨∼ behavior⟩ ⟨∼ bullies⟩

redshirt* *n* [so called fr. the red jersey commonly worn by such a player in practice scrimmages against the regulars] : a college athlete who is kept out of varsity competition for a year in order to extend the period of his eligibility — **redshirt** \ˈ=ˌ=\ *vb* — **redshirting** \ˈ=ˌ=\ *n*

reductionism* *n* : the attempt to explain all biological processes by the same explanations (as by physical laws) that chemists and physicists use to interpret inanimate matter; *also* : the theory that complete reductionism is possible — **reductionist*** *n*

redundancy* *n, chiefly Brit* 1 : dismissal from a job esp. by layoff 2 : duplication of components (as of a computer system) that allows continued functionality despite the failure of an individual component

redundant* *adj* 1 : serving as a duplicate for preventing failure of an entire system (as a spacecraft) upon failure of a single component 2 *Brit* : being out of work : laid off : DISCHARGED ⟨an air hostess who had been made ∼ —A.N.Wilson⟩

re·dux \(ˈ)rēˈdəks\ *adj* [L, lit., brought back, returned, fr. L *reducere* to bring back, fr. *re-* re- + *ducere* lead — more at TOW] : brought back — used postpositively

red zone *n* : the area of a football field inside an opponent's 20-yard line

reel–to–reel \ˈ=ˌ=ˈ=\ *adj* : of, relating to, or utilizing magnetic tape that requires threading on a take-up reel

re·enactor \(ˈ)rē+\ *n* : a person who participates in reenactments of historical events

re·engineer \(ˈ)rē+\ *vt* [*re-* + ²*engineer*] : to reorganize the operations of (an organization) so as to improve efficiency — **re·engineering** \"+\ *n*

referee* *n* : a person who reviews a paper and esp. a technical paper to determine suitability for publication

referee* *vt* : to review (as a technical paper) before publication

reference* *n* : REFERENCE BOOK 1

reference* *vt* : to refer to ⟨a variable in a computer program *references* a location in memory⟩; *also* : to cite as a reference ⟨a frequently *referenced* study⟩

reflate* *vt* : to induce reflation in (as an economy or consumer demand) after an economic recession or a period of deflation

reflection* *n* 1 : a transformation of a figure in which each point is replaced by a point symmetric with respect to a line or plane 2 : a transformation that involves reflection in more than one axis of a rectangular coordinate system

reflexology* *n* : massage of the hands or feet in the belief that pressure applied to specific points on these extremities benefits other parts of the body — **reflexologist** *n* -s

refract* *vt* : to alter or distort as if by refraction ⟨to ∼ that familiar world through the mind and heart of a romantic . . . woman —Anton Myrer⟩

refresh* *vt* : to update or renew (as an image, a display screen, or the contents of a computer memory) esp. by sending a new signal — **refresh** *n*

re·fried beans \(ˈ)rē+. . .-\ *n pl* [trans. of Sp *frijoles refritos*] : FRIJOLES REFRITOS *herein*

re·fuse·nik *also* **re·fus·nik** \rəˈfyüzˌnik, rē-\ *n* [¹*refuse* + *-nik* (herein), part trans. of Russ *otkaznik*, fr. *otkaz* refusal] 1 : a Soviet citizen and esp. a Jew who is refused permission to emigrate 2 : one who refuses or declines something

reg·gae \ˈrā(ˌ)gā, ˈre-; ˈregē\ *n* -s [origin unknown] : popular music of Jamaican origin that combines indigenous styles with elements of rock 'n' roll and soul music and is performed at moderate tempos with the accent on the offbeat

region* *n* : an open connected set together with none, some, or all of the points on its boundary

re·gion·al \ˈrējənᵊl, -jnəl\ *n* -s : something (as a branch of an organization or an edition of a magazine) that serves a region

register* *n* 1 : a device in a computer or calculator for storing small amounts of data; *esp* : one in which data can be both stored and operated on 2 : a variety of a language that a speaker uses in a particular social context

regression analysis *n* : the use of mathematical and statistical techniques to estimate one variable from another esp. by the application of regression coefficients, regression curves, regression equations, or regression lines to empirical data

regulatory gene *or* **regulator gene** *n* : a gene that regulates the expression of one or more structural genes by controlling the production of a protein (as a genetic repressor) which regulates their rate of transcription

re·hab \ˈrēˌhab\ *n* -s *often attrib* [by shortening] 1 : the action or process of rehabilitating : REHABILITATION 2 : a rehabilitated building or dwelling — **rehab** *vt* **rehabbed; rehabbed; re·hab·bing; rehabs** — **re·hab·ber** *n* -s

rei·ki \ˈrāˌkē\ *n* -s *usu cap* [Jap, lit., spirit, fr. *rei* spirit, soul + *ki* vital force, mind] : a system of touching with the hands based on the belief that such touching by an experienced practitioner produces beneficial effects by strengthening and normalizing certain vital energy fields held to exist within the body

re·imagine \ˌrē+\ *vt* [*re-* + *imagine*] : to imagine again or anew; *esp* : to form a new conception of : RE-CREATE

re·industrialization \(ˈ)rē+\ *n* [*re-* + *industrialization*] : a policy of stimulating economic growth esp. through government aid to revitalize and modernize aging industries and encourage growth of new ones — **re·industrialize** \"+\ *vb*

reinforcer* *n* : a stimulus (as a reward or the removal of discomfort) that is effective esp. in operant conditioning because it regularly follows a desired response

re·infuse \ˌrē+\ *vt* [*re-* + *infuse*] : to return (as blood or lymphocytes) to the body by infusion after previous withdrawal — **re·infusion** \"+\ *n*

re·insertion \(ˈ)rē+\ *n* [*re-* + *insertion*] : the action of reinserting something

re·introduction \"+\ *n* [*re-* + *introduction*] : the deliberate return of a plant or animal species to a region in which the endemic population has become severely reduced or eliminated

rejection* *n* : an immune response in which foreign tissue (as of a skin graft or transplanted organ) is attacked by immune system components (as antibodies, T cells, and macrophages) of the recipient organism — **reject*** *vt*

rejective art *n* : MINIMAL ART *herein*

relational* *adj* : relating to, using, or being a method of organizing data in a database so that it is perceived by the user as a set of tables

relative biological effectiveness *n* : the relative capacity of a particular ionizing radiation to produce a response in a biological system — abbr. *RBE*

relatively prime *adj, of integers* : having no common factors except +1 and −1 ⟨12 and 25 are *relatively prime*⟩

relativistic* *adj* 1 : moving at or being a velocity that is a significant fraction of the speed of light such that effects (as change in mass) predicted by the theory of relativity become evident ⟨a ∼ electron⟩ 2 : of or relating to a relativistic particle

relax* *vi* : to attain equilibrium following the abrupt removal of some influence (as light, high temperature, or stress)

relaxed* *adj* : not fitted : somewhat loose-fitting and usu. casual in style ⟨∼ jackets⟩ ⟨∼ jeans⟩

released time* *n* : time off from regular duties (as teaching) granted for a specific activity (as research or committee work)

relevance* *n* 1 : the ability (as of an information retrieval system) to retrieve material that satisfies the needs of the user 2 : practical esp. social applicability : PERTINENCE

relocate* *vi* : to move to a new location

reluctant dragon *n* : a leader (as a politician or military officer) who avoids confrontation or conflict

REM \ˌär(ˌ)ēˈem, ˈrem\ *abbr or n* -s : RAPID EYE MOVEMENT *herein*

re·master \(ˈ)rē+\ *vt* [*re-* + ¹*master*] : to create a new master of esp. by altering or enhancing the sound quality of an older recording

re·me·di·ate \riˈmēdēˌāt\ *vt* -ED/-ING/-S [back-formation fr. *remediation*] 1 : to improve the competence of through remedial instruction 2 : REMEDY, RECTIFY

re·mix \ˈrēˌ+\ *n* -ES [*remix*, v.] : a variant of an original recording (as of a song) made by rearranging or adding to the original

remote* *adj* : acting, acted on, or controlled indirectly or from a distance ⟨time-sharing and other ∼ computing services —*GT&E Annual Report*⟩; *also* : relating to the acquisition of information about a distant object (as by radar or photography) without coming into physical contact with it ⟨∼ sensing instruments⟩

remote control* *or* **remote*** *n* : a remote control device (as for a television)

rem sleep *n, usu cap R&E&M* : a state of sleep that recurs cyclically several times during a normal period of sleep and that is characterized esp. by increased neuronal activity of the forebrain and midbrain, depressed muscle tone, dreaming, and rapid eye movements — called also *paradoxical sleep, rapid eye movement sleep*

renewable* *adj* : capable of being replaced by natural ecological cycles or sound management practices ⟨∼ resources⟩

ren·min·bi \ˈrenˈminˈbē\ *n pl* [Chin (Pek) *jen²min²pi⁴*, fr. *jen²min²* people (fr. *jen²* person + *min²* people) + *pi⁴* currency] : the currency of the People's Republic of China consisting of yuan

re·no·gram \ˈrēnəˌgram\ *n* [*reno-* + *-gram*] : a photographic depiction of the course of renal excretion of a radiolabeled substance — **re·no·graph·ic** \ˌ=ˈgrafik\ *adj* — **re·nog·ra·phy** \rēˈnägrəfē, rəˈ-\ *n* -ES

re·normalization \(ˈ)rē+\ *n* [*re-* + *normalization*] : the replacement of theoretically infinite variables (as the mass and charge of an electron) with experimentally obtained values in the solutions of equations in certain quantum mechanical theories (as quantum electrodynamics) — **re·nor·mal·iz·abil·i·ty** \"ˌnȯ(r)məˌlīzəˈbiləd·ē\ *n* — **re·nor·mal·iz·able** \"ˌnȯ(r)məˈlīzəbəl\ *adj* — **re·nor·mal·ize** \"+\ *vt*

re·no·vascular \¦rēnō+\ *adj* [*reno-* + *vascular*] : of, relating to, or involving the blood vessels of the kidneys

rent boy *n, chiefly Brit* : a usu. young male prostitute

rent strike *n* : a refusal by a group of tenants to pay rent (as in protest against poor service)

reo·vi·rus \¦rēō¦vīrəs\ *n* [NL, fr. E respiratory enteric orphan + NL *virus*] : any of a family (Reoviridae) of double-stranded RNA viruses that include many pathogens of plants or animals, lack a lipoprotein envelope, and usu. have a capsid consisting of two layers of capsomeres and shaped like an icosahedron

rep \ˈrep\ *n* -s [short for *repetition*] : a repetition of a particular movement or exercise (as in weight lifting)

repeat* *n* : a genetic duplication in which the duplicated parts are adjacent to each other along the chromosome

re·perfusion \ˌrē+\ *n* [*re-* + *perfusion*] : restoration of the flow of blood to a previously ischemic tissue or organ

repertoire* *n* : a list or supply of capabilities ⟨the instruction ~ of a computer⟩

repetitive strain injury *or* **repetitive stress injury** *also* **repetitive stress syndrome** *or* **repetitive motion injury** *n* : any of various musculoskeletal disorders (as carpal tunnel syndrome or tendinitis) that are caused by cumulative damage to muscles, tendons, ligaments, nerves, or joints (as of the hand, wrist, arm, or shoulder) from highly repetitive movements and that are characterized chiefly by pain, weakness, and loss of feeling — called also *cumulative trauma disorder*

re·plantation* *n* : reattachment of a bodily part (as a limb) after separation from the body — **replant*** *vt*

rep·li·ca·ble \ˈrepləkəbəl\ *adj* : capable of replication ⟨~ experimental results⟩

rep·li·case \ˈrepləˌkās, -āz\ *n* -s [*replication* + *-ase*] : a polymerase that promotes synthesis of a particular RNA in the presence of a template of RNA — called also *RNA replicase*

replicate* *vi* : to undergo replication : produce a replica of itself

replicate* *n* : something (as a gene, DNA, or a cell) produced by replication

rep·li·ca·tive \ˈrepləˌkād·iv\ *adj* : of, relating to, involved in, or characterized by replication

rep·li·con \ˈrepləˌkän\ *n* -s [*replicate* + [2]*-on*] : a linear or circular section of DNA or RNA which replicates sequentially as a unit

re·po \ˈrē(ˌ)pō\ *n* -s [*re*purchase + [1]*-o*] : REPURCHASE AGREEMENT

re·polarization \¦rē+\ *n* [*re-* + *polarization*] : restoration of the difference in charge between the inside and outside of the plasma membrane of a muscle fiber or cell following depolarization — **re·polarize** \"+\ *vb*

reposition* *vt* : to revise the marketing strategy for (a product or a company) so as to increase sales

repress* *vt* : to inactivate (a gene or formation of a gene product) by allosteric combination at a DNA binding site

re·press·ible \rəˈpresəbəl\ *adj* : capable of being repressed — **re·press·ibil·i·ty** \-ˌpresəˈbiləd·ē\ *n* -ES

repressor* *n* : a protein that is determined by a regulatory gene, binds to a genetic operator, and inhibits the initiation of transcription of messenger RNA

re·pro \ˈrē(ˌ)prō\ *n* -s [by shortening] : REPRODUCTION

re·process \(ˈ)rē+\ *vt* [*re-* + [2]*process*] : to subject to a special process or treatment in preparation for reuse; *specif* : to extract uranium and plutonium from (the spent fuel rods of a nuclear reactor) for use again as fuel

re·program \(ˌ)rē+\ *vb* [*re-* + [2]*program*] *vt* : to program anew; *esp* : to write new programs for (as a computer) ~ *vi* : to rewrite a computer program — **re·programmable** \"+\ *adj*

re·prog·ra·phy \rəˈprägrəfē, rēˈp-\ *n* -ES [ISV *reproduction* + *-graphy*; prob. orig. formed as G *reprographie*] : the facsimile reproduction (as by photocopying) of graphic matter (as books or documents) — **re·prog·ra·pher** \-fə(r)\ *n* -s — **re·pro·graph·ic** \ˈrēprəˈgrafik, ¦rep-, -ēk\ *adj* — **re·pro·graph·ics** \-iks, -ēks\ *n pl but sing in constr*

re–refine \¦rē+\ *vt* [*re-* + [1]*refine*] : to refine (used motor oil) in order to produce a clean usable lubricant — **re–refiner** \"+\ *n*

re·schedule \(ˌ)rē+\ *vt* [*re-* + [2]*schedule*] : to schedule or plan again according to a different timetable; *esp* : to defer required payment of (a debt or loan)

re·segregation \(¦)rē+\ *n* [*re-* + *segregation*] : a return (as of a school) to a state of segregation after a period of desegregation

re·ser·pi·nized \rəˈsərpəˌnīzd, rē-\ *adj* [past part. of *reserpinize*, fr. *reserpine* + *-ize*] : treated or medicated with reserpine or a reserpine derivative — **re·ser·pin·iza·tion** \-ˌsərpənəˈzāshən, -ˌnīˈz-\ *n* -s

reserve* *n* **1** : the lowest price that a seller agrees to accept for an item offered at auction **2** : a wine made from select grapes, bottled on the maker's estate, and aged differently from the maker's other wines of the same vintage

reserve clause *n* : a clause formerly common in contracts of professional athletes reserving for the club the exclusive right automatically to renew the contract and binding the athlete to the club for his entire playing career or until traded or released

re·sid \rəˈzid\ *n* [by shortening] : RESIDUAL OIL *herein*

residence time *n* : the duration of persistence of a substance or mass in a medium or place (as the atmosphere)

residential* *adj* : provided to patients residing in a facility ⟨~ drug treatment⟩; *also* : being a facility providing such treatment ⟨a ~ treatment center⟩

residual* *n* : a payment (as to an actor or writer) for each rerun esp. of a commercial

residual oil *n* : fuel oil that remains after the removal of valuable distillates (as gasoline) from petroleum and that is used esp. by industry — called also *resid*

residual security *n* : common stock or a security convertible into common stock

residue* *n* : the remainder after subtracting a multiple of a modulus from an integer or a power of the integer that can appear as the second of the two terms in an appropriate congruence

residue class *n* : the set of elements (as integers) that leave the same remainder when divided by a given modulus

resilience* *n* : an ability to recover from or adjust easily to misfortune or change

resistance* *n* : RESISTANCE LEVEL *herein*

resistance level *or* **resistance area** *n* : a price level on a rising market at which a security resists further advance due to increased attractiveness of the price to potential sellers

resonance* *n* **1 a** : the enhancement of an atomic, nuclear, or particle reaction or a scattering event by excitation of internal motion in the system **b** : MAGNETIC RESONANCE **2** : an extremely short-lived elementary particle **3** : a synchronous gravitational relationship of two celestial bodies (as moons) that orbit a third (as a planet) which can be expressed as a simple ratio of their orbital periods **4** : a quality of evoking response ⟨how much ~ the scandal seems to be having —*US News & World Report*⟩

respiratory distress syndrome *n* : a respiratory disorder that occurs in newborn premature infants and is characterized by deficiency of the surfactant coating the inner surface of the lungs, by failure of the lungs to expand and contract properly during breathing with resulting collapse, and by the accumulation of a protein-containing film lining the alveoli and their ducts — called also *hyaline membrane disease*; see ADULT RESPIRATORY DISEASE SYNDROME *herein*

respiratory syncytial virus *n* : a paramyxovirus (genus *Pneumovirus*) that forms syncytia in tissue culture and that is responsible for severe respiratory diseases (as bronchopneumonia and bronchiolitis) in children and esp. in infants — abbr. *RSV*

res·pi·ro·met·ric \ˌrespərōˈme-trik, rəˌspīrəˈ-\ *adj* : of or relating to respirometry or to the use of a respirometer ⟨~ studies⟩

respondent* *n* : a reflex that occurs in response to a specific external stimulus ⟨the knee jerk is a typical ~⟩

respondent* *adj* : relating to or being behavior or responses to a stimulus that are followed by a reward ⟨~ conditioning⟩ — compare OPERANT 2 *in the Dict*

res·sen·ti·ment \rəˌsäⁿtēˈmäⁿ\ *n* -s [G, fr. F, resentment — more at RESENTMENT] : deep-seated resentment, frustration, and hostility accompanied by a sense of being powerless to express these feelings directly

re·ste·no·sis \ˌrestəˈnōsəs, ˌrē-\ *n* [*re-* + *stenosis*] : the reoccurrence of stenosis in a blood vessel or heart valve after it has been treated with apparent success

restraining order* *n* : a legal order issued against an individual to restrict or prohibit access or proximity to another specified individual

restriction enzyme *also* **restriction endonuclease** *n* : any of various enzymes that cleave DNA into fragments at specific sites in the interior of the molecule and are often used as tools in molecular analysis

restriction fragment length polymorphism *n* : variation in the length of a DNA fragment produced by a specific restriction enzyme acting on DNA from different individuals that usu. results from a genetic mutation (as an insertion or deletion) and that may be used as a genetic marker

resurface* *vi* : REAPPEAR ⟨fear of inflation *resurfaced*⟩

res·ver·atrol \rezˈvirəˌtrōl, -ˌträl, -ˌtrōl\ *n* -s [origin unknown] : a compound $C_{14}H_{12}O_3$ that is a trihydroxy trans form of stilbene found in some plants, fruits (as the mulberry), and seeds (as the peanut) and esp. in the skin of grapes and certain grape-derived products (as red wine) and that has been linked to a reduced risk of coronary disease and cancer

re·tard \ˈrēˌtärd, rəˈtärd\ *n* -s [*retard*, v.] : a retarded person — often taken to be offensive; *also* : a person held to resemble a retarded person in behavior

rethink *n* [*rethink*, v.] : an act or instance of rethinking ⟨a policy ~⟩

reticent* *adj* : RELUCTANT, HESITANT

ret·i·nal \ˈretᵊnˌal, -ˌȯl\ *n* -s [[2]*retin-* + [3]*-al*] : RETINENE A

retinitis pig·men·to·sa \-ˌpigmənˈtōsə, -(ˌ)men-, -ōzə\ *n* [NL, pigmented retinitis] : any of several hereditary progressive degenerative diseases of the eye marked by night blindness in the early stages, atrophy and pigment changes in the retina, constriction of the visual field, and eventual blindness

ret·i·no·ic acid \¦retᵊn¦ōik-\ *n* [[2]*retin-* + *-oic*] : either of two isomers of an acid $C_{20}H_{28}O_2$ derived from vitamin A and used esp. in the treatment of acne: **a** : TRENTINOIN *herein* **b** : ISOTRETINOIN *herein*

ret·i·noid \ˈretᵊnˌȯid\ *n* -s [[2]*retin-* + [1]*-oid*] : any of various synthetic or naturally occurring analogues of vitamin A

ret·i·nol \ˈretᵊnˌōl, -ˌȯl\ *n* -s [[2]*retin-* + [2]*-ol*] : VITAMIN A_1

ret·i·no·tec·tal \¦retᵊnō¦tektəl\ *adj* [[2]*retin-* + *tectum* + [1]*-al*] : of, relating to, or being the nerve fibers connecting the retina and the tectum of the midbrain ⟨~ pathways⟩

retread* *n* : something made or done again esp. in a slightly altered form ⟨a made-for-TV ~ of the famous film⟩

retro \ˈre·trō\ *adj* [F *rétro*, short for *rétrospective* retrospective] : relating to, reviving, or being the styles or esp. the fashions of the past : fashionably nostalgic or old-fashioned ⟨a ~ look⟩

ret·ro–engine \ˈre·trō *sometimes* ˈrē-+ˌ\ *n* [*retro-* + *engine*] : RETRO-ROCKET

ret·ro·fire \"+\ *vb* [*retro-* + [2]*fire*] *vi, of a retro-engine or retro-rocket* : to become ignited ~ *vt* : to cause to retrofire — **retro·fire** *n*

ret·ro·fit \"+\ *vt* [*retrofit*, n.] : to furnish (as a computer, airplane, or building) with new parts or equipment not available, considered necessary, or in place at the time of manufacture or construction

retrograde* *adj* **1** : being or relating to the rotation of a satellite in a direction opposite to that of the body being orbited **2** : RETRO *herein* ⟨~ fashion⟩

ret·ro·pack \ˈre·trō *sometimes* rē-+ˌ\ *n* [*retro-* + *pack*] : a system of retro-rockets on a spacecraft

ret·ro·reflection \¦re·trō *sometimes* rē-+\ *n* [*retro-* + *reflection*] : the action or use of a retroreflector

ret·ro·reflector \"+\ *n* [*retro-* + *reflector*] : a device that reflects radiation (as light) so that the paths of the rays are parallel to those of the incident rays

retrospective* *adj* : relating to or being a study (as of a disease) that starts with the present condition of a population of individuals and collects data about their past history to explain their present condition — compare PROSPECTIVE *herein*

ret·ro·virology \"+\ *n* [*retrovirus* (herein) + *-ology* (as in *virology*)] : a branch of science concerned with the study of retroviruses — **ret·ro·virologist** \"+\ *n*

ret·ro·virus \"+\ *n* [NL, fr. *retro-* + *virus*] : any of a family (Retroviridae) of single-stranded RNA viruses (as HIV and Rous sarcoma virus) that produce reverse transcriptase by means of which DNA is synthesized using their RNA as a template and incorporated into the genome of infected cells and that include numerous tumorigenic viruses — **ret·ro·viral** \"+\ *adj*

reu·ben sandwich \¦rübən- *in rapid speech also* ¦rübᵊm-\ *or* **reuben** *n, usu cap R* [prob. after *Reuben* Kulakofsky †1960 Am. grocer & reputed inventor of the sandwich] : a grilled sandwich consisting of corned beef, Swiss cheese, and sauerkraut usu. on rye bread

re·uptake \(ˈ)rē+\ *n* [*re-* + *uptake*] : the reabsorption by a neuron of a neurotransmitter following the transmission of a nerve impulse across a synapse

rev* *vt* **1** : INCREASE — used with *up* ⟨*rev* up production⟩ **2** : to drive or operate esp. at high speed — often used with *up* **3** : to make more active or effective — used with *up* ⟨*revving* up the economy⟩ **4** : to stir up or excite esp. in preparation or anticipation — usu. used with *up* ⟨party officials *revved* up the crowd —Suzanne Daley⟩ **5** : [1]JAZZ 2 — used with *up* ⟨combos of black and white . . . *revved* up with vibrant colored accessories —*Christian Science Monitor*⟩ ~ *vi* : to become more excited or active esp. in preparation or anticipation — usu. used with *up* ⟨*revving* up for his turbocharged performance —Paula Chin & T. Kahn⟩

re·vanch·ism \rəˈväⁿˌshizəm\ *n* -s [F *revanchisme*, fr. *revanche* + *-isme* -ism] : REVANCHE ⟨a policy of nationalistic ~ —Bernard Fall⟩

re·vascularization \(¦)rē+\ *n* [*re-* + *vascularization*] : a surgical procedure for the provision of a new, augmented, or restored blood supply to a body part or organ

revenue sharing *n* : the dispensing of a portion of federal tax revenue to state and local governments to assist in meeting their monetary needs

re·verb \rəˈvərb, ˈrē-ˌ, -vəb, -vəib\ *n* -s [short for *reverberation*] **1** : an electronically produced echo effect in recorded music; *also* : a device for producing reverb **2** : REVERBERATION

reverse annuity mortgage *or* **reverse mortgage** *n* : a loan against home equity that provides an annuity to the homeowner and is repayable at the time the home is sold

reverse discrimination *n* : discrimination against whites or males (as in employment or education)

reverse engineer *vt* : to disassemble and examine or analyze in detail (as a product or device) to discover the concepts involved in manufacture usu. in order to produce something similar — **reverse engineering** *n*

reverse osmosis *n* : the flow of fresh water through a semipermeable membrane when pressure is applied to a solution (as seawater) on one side of it

reverse polish notation *n, usu cap P* : a system of representing mathematical and logical operations in which the operands precede the operator and which does not require the use of parentheses ⟨(3 + 5) − (2 + 1) in *reverse Polish notation* is expressed as 3 5 + 2 1 + −⟩ — called also *postfix notation*

reverse tran·scrip·tase \-ˌtranˈskrip(ˌ)tās, -āz\ *n* [*transcription* (herein) + *-ase*] : a polymerase esp. of retroviruses that catalyzes the formation of DNA using RNA as a template

reverse transcription *n* : the process of synthesizing DNA using RNA as a template and reverse transcriptase as a catalyst — compare TRANSCRIPTION *herein*

re·ver·tant \rəˈvərtᵊnt, rē-, -vət-\ *n* -s [[1]*revert* + [1]*-ant*] : a mutant gene, individual, or strain that regains a former capability (as the production of a particular protein) by undergoing further mutation ⟨yeast ~*s*⟩ — **revertant** *adj*

revolving door* *n* : a revolving-door system or process

revolving–door \¦==¦=\ *adj* : characterized by a frequently repeated succession or exchange or by a cycle of leaving and returning ⟨two years of *revolving-door* governments —Tom Buckley⟩ ⟨a *revolving-door* prison system⟩

reward* *n* : a stimulus administered to an organism following a correct or desired response that increases the probability of occurrence of the response — **reward*** *vt*

rex* *n* : any domestic cat of the Cornish rex or Devon rex breeds

reye's syndrome \¦rīz- *also* ¦rāz-\ *also* **reye syndrome** \¦rī- *also* ¦rā-\ *n, usu cap R* [after R.D.K. *Reye* †1977 Australian pathologist] : an often fatal encephalopathy esp. of childhood characterized by fever, vomiting, fatty infiltration of the liver, and swelling of the kidneys and brain

R factor *n* [*resistance*] : a group of genes present in some bacteria that provide a basis for resistance to antibiotics and can be transferred from cell to cell by conjugation

RFP *abbr* request for proposal

rgb \ˌär(ˌ)jēˈbē\ *adj, cap R&G&B* [red-green-blue (colors used in television transmission)] : being or using a video signal in which each component of the signal (as chrominance and luminance) is carried over a separate wire ⟨an *RGB* computer monitor⟩

rhab·do·my·ol·y·sis \¦rabdōmīˈäləsəs\ *n, pl* **-ses** [NL, fr. *rhabd-* + *my-* + *-lysis*] : the destruction or degeneration of skeletal muscle tissue (as from traumatic injury, excessive exertion, or stroke) that is accompanied by the release of muscle cell contents (as myoglobin and potassium) into the bloodstream resulting in hypovolemia, hyperkalemia, and sometimes acute renal failure

rhab·do·virus \¦rabdō+\ *n* [NL, fr. *rhabd-* + *virus*] : any of a family (Rhabdoviridae) of rod- or bullet-shaped single-stranded RNA viruses that are found in plants and animals and include the causative agents of rabies and vesicular stomatitis

rheology* *n* : the ability to flow or be deformed

rheumatoid factor *n* : an autoantibody of high molecular weight that reacts against immunoglobulins of the class IgG and is often present in rheumatoid arthritis

rhi·no·tracheitis \¦rīnō+\ *n* [NL, fr. *rhin-* + *tracheitis*] : inflammation of the nasal cavities and trachea; *esp* : a disease of the upper respiratory tract in cats and esp. young kittens that is characterized by sneezing, conjunctivitis with discharge, and nasal discharges — see INFECTIOUS BOVINE RHINOTRACHEITIS *herein*

rhi·no·virus \"+\ *n* [NL, fr. *rhin-* + *virus*] : any of a genus (*Rhinovirus*) of picornaviruses that are related to the enteroviruses and associated with upper respiratory tract disorders (as the common cold)

RHIP *abbr* rank has its privileges

rho* *or* **rho particle** *n* : a very short-lived unstable meson with mass 1490 times the mass of an electron

rhythm and blues *n* : popular music typically including elements of blues and African-American folk music and marked by a strong beat and simple melody — compare SOUL MUSIC *herein*

RIA *abbr* radioimmunoassay *herein*

ri·ba·vi·rin \ˌrībəˈvīrən\ *n* [perh. fr. *ribonucleic acid* + *virus* + *-in*] : a synthetic broad-spectrum antiviral nucleoside $C_8H_{12}N_4O_5$

ri·bo·nucleoside \¦rī(ˌ)bō+\ *n* [*ribose* + *nucleoside*] : a nucleoside that contains ribose

ri·bo·nucleotide \"+\ *n* [*ribose* + *nucleotide*] : a nucleotide that contains ribose and occurs esp. as a constituent of RNA

ribosomal RNA *n* : RNA that is a fundamental structural element of the ribosome

ri·bo·some \ˈrībəˌsōm\ *n* -s [*ribo*nucleic acid + [3]*-some*] : any of the RNA- and protein-rich cytoplasmic organelles that are sites of protein synthesis — **ri·bo·som·al** \¦=¦sōməl\ *adj*

ri·bo·zyme \ˈrībəˌzīm\ *n* -s [*ribo*nucleic acid + *enzyme*] : a molecule of RNA that functions as an enzyme (as by catalyzing the cleavage of other RNA molecules)

rib–tickler \ˈ=ˌ=(=)=\ *n* : something that provokes laughter

rich·ter scale \¦riktə(r)-\ *n, usu cap R* [after Charles F. *Richter* †1985 Am. seismologist] : an open-ended logarithmic scale for expressing the magnitude of a seismic disturbance (as an earthquake) in terms of the energy dissipated in it with 1.5 indicating the smallest earthquake that can be felt, 4.5 an earthquake causing slight damage, and 8.5 a very devastating earthquake

ricky–tick \¦rikē¦tik\ *n* [imit.] : sweet jazz of a style reminiscent of the 1920s — **ricky–ticky** \-tikē\ *adj*

ride* *vb* — **ride shotgun 1** : to guard someone or something while in transit **2** : to ride in the front passenger seat of a vehicle

ridership *n* : the number of persons who ride a particular system of public transportation

rie·mann integrable \¦rēˌmän-, -ˌmən-\ *adj, usu cap R* [after G.F.B. *Riemann* †1866 Ger. mathematician] : capable of being integrated by a Riemann integral ⟨let the function *f* be *Riemann integrable* on the closed interval from *a* to *b*⟩

riemann integral *n, usu cap R* : a definite integral defined as the limit of sums found by partitioning the interval comprising the domain of definition into subintervals, by finding the sum of products each of which consists of the width of a subinterval multiplied by the value of the function at some point in it, and by letting the maximum width of the subintervals approach zero

riemann surface *n, usu cap R* [after G.F.B. *Riemann*] : a multilayered surface in the theory of complex functions on which a multivalued complex function can be treated as a single valued function of a complex variable

rif·am·pin \ˈrif¦ampən\ *or* **rif·am·pi·cin** \(ˈ)rifˈampəsən\ *n* -s [ISV, alter. of *rifamycin* (herein), with *-pi-* prob. fr. *piperazine*] : a semisynthetic antibiotic $C_{43}H_{58}N_4O_{12}$ that is used esp. in the treatment of tuberculosis and to treat asymptomatic carriers of meningococci

rif·a·my·cin \ˌrifəˈmīsᵊn\ *n* -s [ISV, alter. of earlier *rifomycin*, fr. *rif-* (fr. *Rififi*, title of a Fr. film (1954), name arbitrarily assigned by the drug's It. discoverers to a group of antibacterial substances) + *-o-* + *-mycin*] : any of several antibiotics that are derived from a bacterium of the genus *Streptomyces* (*S. mediterranei*)

riff* *n* **1** : a rapid energetic often improvised verbal tour de force; *esp* : one that is part of a comic performance **2** : a succinct usu. witty comment

riff* *vi* : to deliver or make use of a verbal riff

right brain *n* : the right cerebral hemisphere of the human brain esp. when viewed in terms of its predominant thought processes (as creativity and intuitive thinking) — **right–brained** \¦=¦=\ *adj*

righteous* *adj, slang* : GENUINE, GOOD

right on *interj* — used to express agreement or to give encouragement

right–on \¦=¦=\ *adj* **1** : exactly correct **2** : attuned to the spirit of the times

rightsize \ˈ=ˌ=\ *vt* : to reduce (as a work force) to an optimal size ~ *vi* : to undergo a reduction to an optimal size ⟨the company said it *rightsized* successfully⟩

right–to–life \¦==¦=\ *adj* : opposed to abortion — **right–to–lif·er** \-ˈlīfər\ *n*

right–to–work \¦==¦=\ *adj* : relating to, having, or being a state law banning the closed shop and the union shop ⟨*right-to-work* laws⟩ ⟨a *right-to-work* state⟩

righty \ˈrīd·ē\ *n* -ES [[1]*right*-handed + [1]*-y*] : RIGHT-HANDER

ring* *vi* — **ring off the hook** : to ring frequently or constantly with incoming calls ⟨the phone *rang off the hook* for 20 hours a day —Milt Pappas⟩

ring·git \ˈriŋgət\ *n* -s [Malay] **1** : the basic monetary unit of Malaysia — see MONEY table *in the Dict* **2** : a coin or note representing one ringgit

ringmaster* *n* : a supervisor or moderator esp. of a program, performance, or presentation ⟨the ~ of a late-night talk show⟩

¹rin·ky–dink \ˈriŋkēˌdiŋk\ *adj* [origin unknown] **1** : OLD-FASHIONED **2** : SMALL-TIME

²rinky–dink \"\ *n* **1** : one that is rinky-dink **2** : RICKY-TICK *herein*

rin·ky·tink \ˈ==ˌtiŋk\ *n* [by alter.] : RICKY-TICK *herein* — **rin·ky–tin·ky** \ˈ==ˌtiŋkē\ *adj*

rio·ja \rēˈō(ˌ)hä\ *n* -s *often cap* [fr. La *Rioja*, region of northern Spain] : a wine from the Rioja district

riot grrrl \-ˈgərl, -ˈgər-əl, -ˈgəl\ *n, pl* **riot grrrls** [*grrrl* alter. (influenced by *grrr* representing growling sound) of *girl*] : a girl or woman who participates in a feminist punk subculture

rip* *vt* **1** : to hit sharply ⟨*ripped* a double to left field⟩ **2** : to defeat decisively in a sporting event ⟨*ripped* the visiting team 12 to 1⟩ **3** : CRITICIZE, DISPARAGE **4** : to rip off : ROB, STEAL

ripe* *adj* **1** : SMELLY, STINKING **2** : of a suggestive or indecent character ⟨*riper* video fiction for adults —Les Brown⟩

rip off *vt* **1** : ROB ⟨he *ripped off* a guy for ten grand —G.V.Higgins⟩; *also* : STEAL ⟨$5-million worth of goods *ripped off* at various merchandise-loading . . . spots —*New York*⟩ **2** : to exploit esp. financially : CHEAT ⟨being *ripped off* by . . . bakers who give us zero nutritional value for our money —Mary Daniels⟩ **3** : to copy or imitate blatantly or unscrupulously ⟨*rip off* a movie's plot⟩ **4** : to perform, achieve, or score quickly or easily ⟨*ripped off* ten straight points⟩

rip–off \ˈ=ˌ=\ *n* -s [*rip off*, v. (herein)] **1** : an act or an instance of stealing : THEFT ⟨site of a famous gem theft, among other *rip-offs* —R.R.Lingeman⟩; *also* : an instance of financial exploitation : GYP ⟨don't waste your money on this book . . . it's a *rip-off* —Peter Stollery⟩ **2** : a usu. cheap exploitive imitation ⟨this kaleidoscopic fantasy, a *rip-off* on everything from spy novels to the Oedipus complex —Barbara A. Bannon⟩

ripped \ˈript\ *adj* [fr. past part. of ²*rip*] **1** *slang* : being under the influence of alcohol or drugs : HIGH, STONED **2** *slang* : having high muscle definition ⟨a ~ physique⟩

ripple effect *n* : a spreading, pervasive, and usu. unintentional effect or influence ⟨the whole industry would be forced to close down, which would have a *ripple effect* on other industries —Joe Klein⟩ — compare DOMINO EFFECT *herein*

ripstop \ˈ=ˌ=\ *adj* [³*rip* + *stop*] : of, relating to, or being a fabric that is woven with a double thread at regular intervals so that small tears do not spread ⟨~ nylon⟩

ri·ser·va \rēˈservä\ *n* -s [It, lit., stock, reserve, fr. *riservare* to keep, reserve, fr. L *reservare* to save up — more at RESERVE] : an Italian reserve wine

rise·time \ˈrīz+ˌ\ *n* : the time required for a pulse or signal (as on an oscilloscope) to increase from one specified value (as 10 percent) of its amplitude to another (as 90 percent)

risk* *n* — **at risk** : in a state or condition marked by a high level of risk or susceptibility : in danger ⟨mistakes that put astronauts' lives *at risk* —M.R.Beschloss⟩ ⟨patients *at risk* of infection⟩ ⟨extra attention for *at risk* students⟩

ris·to·ce·tin \ˌristəˈsētᵊn\ *n* -s [*risto-* (of unknown origin) + actinomy*cete* + *-in*] : either of two antibiotics or a mixture of both produced by an actinomycete of the genus *Nocardia* (*N. lurida*)

Ri·tal·in \ˈritələn\ *trademark* — used for a preparation of methylphenidate

river blindness *n* [so called fr. the high incidence of the disease among people living near flowing water, where flies that transmit *Onchocerca* breed] : ONCHOCERCIASIS

RNA polymerase *n* : any of a group of enzymes that promote the synthesis of RNA using DNA or RNA as a template

RNA replicase *n* : REPLICASE *herein*

RNase \ˌä(ˌ)renˈās, -ˈāz; ˌärˌenˌās, -ˌāz\ *or* **RNAase** \ˌä(ˌ)reˈnāˈās, -ˈāz\ *n* -s [*RNA* + *-ase*] : RIBONUCLEASE

road* *n* — **down the road** : in or into the future

roadcut \ˈ=ˌ=\ *n* : CUT 3f; *esp* : one created by blasting that is useful in the geologic study of rock strata

roadholding \ˈ=ˌ==\ *n, chiefly Brit* : the qualities of an automobile that tend to make it respond precisely to the driver's steering

road·ie \ˈrōdē\ *n* -s [¹*road* + *-ie*] **1** : one who manages the activities of entertainers on the road — called also *road manager* **2** : one who works (as by moving heavy equipment) for traveling entertainers

roadkill \ˈ=ˌ=\ *n* **1** : the remains of an animal that has been killed on a road by a motor vehicle **2** : one (as a sports team, political figure, or company) that falls victim to intense competition ⟨the effort became political ~ —Gretchen Morgenson⟩ ⟨left their opposition for ~ early in the tournament⟩

road racing *n* : racing over public roads; *esp* : automobile racing over roads or over a closed course designed to simulate public roads — **road race** *n*

road rage *n* : a motorist's uncontrolled anger that is usu. provoked by another motorist's irritating act and is expressed in aggressive or violent behavior

road show* *n* : a promotional presentation or meeting conducted in a series of locations ⟨put on huge *road shows* to drum up investor interest —Gretchen Morgenson *et al*⟩

roam* *vi* : to travel outside one's local calling area before using a cellular telephone ⟨*roaming* charges⟩

roast* *n* : a banquet honoring a person (as a celebrity) who is subjected to humorous tongue-in-cheek ridicule by friends

rob·ert·son·i·an \ˌräbə(r)tˈsōnēən\ *adj, usu cap* [William R.B. *Robertson* †1941 Am. biologist + E *-ian*] : relating to or being a reciprocal translocation that takes place between two acrocentric chromosomes and that yields one nonfunctional chromosome having two short arms and one functional chromosome having two long arms of which one arm is derived from each parent chromosome

ro·bot·ic \rōˈbäd-ik\ *adj* **1** : of or relating to mechanical robots **2** : having the characteristics of a robot ⟨performs with ~ consistency⟩

ro·bot·i·cist \rōˈbäd-əsəst\ *n* -s : a specialist in robotics

ro·bot·ics \rōˈbäd-iks\ *n pl but sing in constr* : technology dealing with the design, construction, and operation of robots in automation

robust* *adj* [NL *robustus*] : relating to, resembling, or being a specialized group of hominids of the genus *Australopithecus* (as *A. robustus* and *A. boisei*) characterized esp. by heavy molars and small incisors adapted to a vegetarian diet — compare GRACILE *herein*

rock* *n* **1** : a small crystallized mass of crack cocaine **2** *also* **rock cocaine** : CRACK *herein* — **between a rock and a hard place** *or* **between the rock and the hard place** : in a difficult or uncomfortable position with no attractive way out

rock·a·bil·ly \ˈräkəˌbilē, -li\ *n* -ES [*rock* + *-a-* (as in *rockaby*) + hill*billy*] : popular music marked by features of rock and country and western styles

rocker* *n* : a rock performer, song, or enthusiast

rocket scientist *n* : a person who is exceptionally intelligent; *esp* : one who is skilled in technical areas ⟨it didn't take a *rocket scientist* to figure out that this was bad for consumers and the economy —Patrick Sellers⟩

rock·u·men·ta·ry \ˌräkyəˈmentərē, -yü-, -ˈmen-trē\ *n* -ES [blend of ⁴*rock* and ²*documentary*] : a documentary relating to rock music

ro·la·mite \ˈrōləˌmīt\ *n* -s [*roll* + *-amite*, of unknown origin] : a nearly frictionless elementary mechanism consisting of two or more rollers inserted in the loops of a flexible metal or plastic band with the band acting to turn the rollers whose movement can be directed to perform various functions

role model *n* : a person whose behavior in a particular role is imitated by others

role–play \ˈ=ˌ=\ *vt* : to act out ⟨students were asked to *role-play* the thoughts and feelings of each character —R.G.Lambert⟩ ~ *vi* : to play a role — **role–player** \ˈ=ˌ==\ *n*

rolf \ˈrȯlf *also* ˈrȯf\ *vt* -ED/-ING/-S *often cap* : to practice Rolfing on — **rolf·er** \-ə(r)\ *n* -s *often cap*

Rolf·ing \-fiŋ\ *service mark* — used for a system of deep muscle massage intended to serve as both physical and emotional therapy

roll* *n* — **on a roll** **1** : in the midst of a series of successes : on a hot streak **2** — used with a modifier to indicate momentum of a specified kind ⟨swept the . . . doubleheader, 8–3 and 7–1, and, *on a* wild *roll* now, knocked out eighteen hits the next afternoon —Roger Angell⟩ ⟨we've been *on a* bad *roll* —Henry Catto⟩

roll bar *n* : an overhead metal bar on an automobile designed to protect an occupant in case of a rollover

roll cage *n* : a protective framework of metal bars encasing the driver of a vehicle (as a racing car)

Rollerblade \ˈ==ˌ=\ *trademark* — used for an in-line skate

roller hockey *n* : a variation of ice hockey played on roller skates

rolle's theorem \ˈrȯlz-, ˈrōlz-\ *n, usu cap R* [after Michel *Rolle* †1719 Fr. mathematician] : a theorem in mathematics: if a curve is continuous, crosses the x-axis at two points, and has a single tangent at every point between the two intercepts, its tangent is parallel to the x-axis at some point between the intercepts

roll–neck \ˈ=ˌ=\ *n, often attrib, Brit* : TURTLENECK — **roll–necked** \ˈ=ˌ=\ *adj*

roll out* *vi* : to run toward one flank usu. parallel to the line of scrimmage esp. before throwing a pass ⟨the quarterback would either hand off to the fullback or fake to him and *roll out* —Arthur Sampson⟩ ~ *vt* : to introduce (as a new product) esp. for widespread sale to the public

rollout** *n* **1** : a football play in which the quarterback rolls out **2** : the broad public introduction of a new product or service

roll over* *vt* **1** : to renegotiate the terms of (a financial agreement) **2** : to place (invested funds) in a new investment of the same kind : REINVEST ⟨*roll over* IRA funds⟩

rollover \ˈ=ˌ==\ *n* -s [*roll over*, v.] **1** : an act or instance of rolling over **2** : an accident (as of a motor vehicle) in which the vehicle rolls over

ROM *abbr or n* -s : read-only memory *herein*

ro·nin \ˈrōnin\ *n, pl* **ronin** *also* **ronins** [Jap *rōnin*] **1** : a vagrant samurai without a master **2** : a Japanese student who has failed a college entrance examination and is studying to take it again

ron·nel \ˈränᵊl\ *n* -s [fr. *Ronnel*, a trademark] : an organophosphate $C_8H_8Cl_3O_3PS$ insecticide

root canal* *n* : a dental operation to save a tooth by removing the contents of its root canal and filling the cavity with a protective substance

ro–ro \ˈrōˌrō\ *n* -s *usu cap both Rs* [roll on, roll off] : a ship designed and equipped to allow vehicles (as automobiles or tanks) to be driven on or off

rorschach* *or* **rorschach test*** *n, usu cap R* : something that acts like a Rorschach test esp. to reveal personality

ror·schach \ˈrō(ə)r-ˌshäk\ *adj, usu cap* : of, relating to, used in connection with, or resulting from the Rorschach test

rose* *n* : a plane curve which consists of three or more loops meeting at the origin and whose equation in polar coordinates is of the form $\rho = a \sin n\ \theta$ or $\rho = a \cos n\ \theta$ where *n* is an integer greater than 1

rose medallion *n* : a chiefly 19th century enamel-decorated Chinese porcelain with medallions of oriental figures surrounded and separated by panels of flowers and butterflies

rosette* *n* **1** : a rose-shaped cluster of cells **2** : a food decoration or garnish in the shape of a rose ⟨icing *~s*⟩ ⟨carrot *~s*⟩

rotation* *n* : the series of pitchers on a baseball team who regularly start successive games in turn

rotator cuff *n* : a supporting and strengthening structure of the shoulder joint that is made up of part of the capsule of the shoulder joint blended with tendons of the subscapularis, infraspinatus, supraspinatus, and teres minor muscles as they pass to the capsule or across it to insert on the humerus

ro·ta·vi·rus \ˈrōd-əˌvīrəs\ *n* [NL, fr. *rota* wheel (fr. L) + *virus* — more at ROLL] : any of a genus (*Rotavirus*) of reoviruses that have a capsid composed of two layers and cause diarrhea esp. in infants and young children

ro·ti \ˈrō(ˌ)tē\ *n* -s [Hindi & Urdu *roṭī* bread; akin to Prakrit *roṭṭa* rice flour, Skt *roṭika* kind of bread] : a flat unleavened bread; *also* : meat, seafood, or vegetables wrapped in such a bread and eaten as a sandwich

rou·get \rüˈzhā\ *n* -s [F, fr. OF, fr. *rouge* red — more at ROUGE] : any of several food fish of the family Mullidae and esp. of the genus *Mullus* (as *M. surmuletus* and *M. barbatus*) : RED MULLET

rough trade *n* : male homosexuals who are or affect to be rugged and potentially violent; *also* : a homosexual of this sort

rouille \ˈrüe, rüy\ *n* -s [F, lit., rust, fr. OF *reoïlle*, fr. (assumed) VL *robicula*, fr. L *robigo*, *rubigo*; akin to L *ruber* red — more at RED] : a peppery garlic sauce of Mediterranean French origin usu. served with fish soups and stews

round* *adj, of a wine* : being well-balanced in taste with fruit flavors more prominent than tannins — **roundness*** *n*

roundball \ˈ=ˌ=\ *n* -s : BASKETBALL 1

round file *n* : WASTEBASKET

roustabout* *n* : a person with no permanent home or regular occupation : KNOCKABOUT, VAGRANT; *also* : one who stirs up trouble

router* *n* : a device that mediates the transmission and transmission routes of data packets over an electronic communications network (as the Internet)

rover* *n* : a vehicle for exploring the surface of an extraterrestrial body (as the moon or Mars)

RPG \ˌär(ˌ)pēˈjē\ *n* -s [*r*eport *p*rogram *g*enerator] : a computer language that generates programs from the user's specifications esp. to produce business reports

RPV \ˌär(ˌ)pēˈvē\ *abbr or n* -s [*r*emotely *p*iloted *v*ehicle] : an unmanned aircraft flown by remote control and used esp. for reconnaissance

rRNA \ˈärˌär(ˌ)enˌā\ *n* -s : RIBOSOMAL RNA *herein*

rub* *vb* — **rub one's nose in** : to bring forcefully or repeatedly to one's attention ⟨the satirist's business is to *rub our noses in* the mess, without relief —R.B.Heilman⟩

rubber–chicken circuit \ˈ==ˈ==ˌ=\ *n* : a series of social gatherings (as dinners) at each of which a traveling celebrity (as a campaigning politician) gives a speech

rub·bish \ˈrəbish\ *vt* -ED/-ING/-ES [*rubbish*, n.] *Brit* : to express disapproval of : DISPARAGE ⟨in a high good humour that day, *~ing* London and the English with much of his old brio —Salman Rushdie⟩

rub off *vi* : to become transferred — usu. used with *on* ⟨the decorum in [his] narrative voice surely appealed to my grandmother; perhaps she hoped that some of it might *rub off* on me —John Irving⟩

rub–off \ˈ=ˌ=\ *n* -s [*rub off* (herein)] : an instance or result of rubbing off

rubout \ˈ=ˌ=\ *n* -s [*rub out*] : an act or instance of rubbing someone or something out

ruby laser *n* : a laser in which red light is produced by an atomic transition of the chromium contained in a ruby rod

RU–486 \ˈär,yü,fōr,ād-ēˈsiks, -ˌfȯr-\ *n* [Roussel-UCLAF, the drug's Fr. manufacturer + *486*, laboratory serial number] : a drug $C_{29}H_{35}NO_2$ taken orally to induce abortion esp. early in pregnancy by blocking the body's use of progesterone — called also *mifepristone*

ru·go·la \ˈrügələ\ *n* -s [prob. fr. It dial.; akin to It dial. (northern Italy) *ruga* garden rocket, It *ruca* — more at ROCKET] : GARDEN ROCKET 1

rug rat *n* : CHILD, KID ⟨adopt some little *rug rats* —Joseph Wambaugh⟩

rule* *vi, slang* : to be extremely cool or popular — used as a generalized term of praise or approval ⟨for a little attitude at the right price, sneakers ~ —Tish Hamilton⟩

ru·ma·ki *also* **ra·ma·ki** \rəˈmäkē\ *n* -s [perh. modif. of Jap *harumaki*, trans. of Chin *ch'un*¹ *chuan*⁴ spring roll (herein)] : a cooked appetizer consisting of pieces of usu. marinated chicken liver wrapped together with sliced water chestnuts in bacon slices

rumble strip *n* : a strip of corrugated pavement (as along the edge of a highway) that causes vibration and a rumbling sound when driven over

run–and–gun \ˈ=ˌ=ˌ=\ *adj* : relating to or being a fast, freewheeling style of play in basketball that de-emphasizes set plays and defense

runaway* *adj* **1** : highly successful ⟨a ~ bestseller⟩ **2** : gone out of control : being beyond control ⟨a ~ cruise missile⟩ ⟨~ population growth⟩

runner's high *n* : a feeling of euphoria that is experienced by some individuals engaged in strenuous running and that is held to be associated with a release of endorphins by the brain

running dog *n* [trans. of Chin *tsou*² *kou*³ hunting dog, lackey, lit., running dog] : one who does someone else's bidding : LACKEY ⟨charge the missionaries with being *running dogs* for the imperialistic foreign powers — *Living Age*⟩

run–up* *n, chiefly Brit* : a period immediately preceding an action or event ⟨the *run-up* to the country council elections — *Economist*⟩

runway* *n* : a platform along which models walk in a fashion show

rush* *n* **1** : the immediate pleasurable feeling produced by a drug (as heroin or amphetamine) — called also *flash* **2** : a feeling of pleasure or euphoria : THRILL, BANG, KICK

rust belt *also* **rust bowl** *n, often cap R&B* [so called fr. the declining heavy industry taken to be characteristic of the region's economy] : the northeastern and midwestern states of the U.S.

ruth·er·ford·ium \ˌrəthə(r)ˈfō(ə)rdēəm, ˌrəth-\ *n* -s [NL, fr. Ernest *Rutherford* †1937 Brit. physicist + NL *-ium*] : a short-lived radioactive element of atomic number 104 that is produced artificially — symbol *Rf*

RV \ˌärˈvē\ *abbr or n* -s : recreational vehicle *herein*

r–value \ˈ=ˌ=(ˌ)=\ *n, usu cap R* [prob. fr. thermal resistance] : a measure of resistance to the flow of heat through a given thickness of a material (as insulation) with higher numbers indicating better insulating properties — compare U-VALUE *herein*

RVer \ˌärˈvēər\ *n* -s : one who occupies or operates a recreational vehicle

rya \ˈrēə, ˈrīə\ *n* -s [fr. *Rya*, village in southwest Sweden] : a Scandinavian handwoven rug with a deep resilient comparatively flat pile; *also* : the weave typical of this rug

s* *abbr* siemens *herein*

sa·ber·met·rics \ˌsābə(r)ˈme-triks\ *n pl but sing in constr* [*saber*- (fr. *S*ociety for *A*merican *B*aseball *R*esearch) + *-metrics* (as in *econometrics*)] : the statistical analysis of baseball data — **sab·er·me·tri·cian** \ˌ==ˌməˈtrishən\ *n* -s

saccade* *n* : a small rapid jerky movement of the eye esp. as it jumps from fixation on one point to another (as in reading)

sacred mushroom *n* : any of various New World hallucinogenic fungi (as of the genus *Psilocybe*) used esp. in some Indian ceremonies

SAD *abbr* seasonal affective disorder *herein*

saddled prominent *n* [so called fr. the hump or prominence on the back of the larva] : a notodontid moth (*Heterocampa guttivitta*) whose larva is a serious defoliator of hardwood trees in the eastern and midwestern U.S.

safari jacket *n* : a usu. belted shirt jacket with bellows pockets

safari park *n* : a large open reserve stocked with usu. big-game animals (as lions) that visitors driving through can observe in natural surroundings

safari suit *n* : a safari jacket with matching pants

safe house *n* : a place where one may take refuge or engage in secret activities

safe sex *also* **safer sex** *n* : sexual activity and esp. sexual intercourse in which various measures (as the use of latex condoms or the practice of monogamy) are taken to avoid disease (as AIDS) transmitted by sexual contact

safety net *n* : something (as a government program or a prudent precaution) that provides security against misfortune or difficulty

sag·it·tar·ian \ˌsajəˈta(a)rēən\ *n* -s *usu cap* : SAGITTARIUS *herein*

sagittarius* *n, usu cap* : one born under the astrological sign Sagittarius

sag wagon *n* : a vehicle that follows behind bicyclists (as in a race) to pick up those who drop out or to carry gear

sa·hel \səˈhā(ə)l, -ˈhē(ə)l; ˈsähəl\ *n* -s *usu cap* [F, fr. Ar. *sāḥil* coast, shore] : a savanna or steppe region bordering a desert and esp. the Sahara desert — **sa·hel·ian** \-ˈhālēən, -ˈhēl-\ *adj, usu cap*

sailboard \ˈ=ˌ=\ *n* : a small flat sailboat resembling a surfboard — **sailboarding** \ˈ=ˌ==\ *n* — **sailboarder** \ˈ=ˌ==\ *n*

sai·min \ˈsīˈmin\ *n* -s [prob. fr. Chin (Cant) *sai mihn* fine noodles] : an Hawaiian noodle soup

saint emi·lion \ˌsaⁿtāmēˈlyōⁿ\ *n, pl* **saint emilions** \"\ *usu cap S&E* [F, fr. *Saint-Émilion*, wine appellation and village in southwest France] : a red Bordeaux wine

saint john's wort** *n, usu cap S&J* : the dried aerial parts of a Saint-John's-wort (*Hypericum perforatum*) that are held to relieve depression and are used in herbal remedies and dietary supplements

saint vé·ran \ˌsaⁿvāˈräⁿ\ *n, pl* **saint vérans** \"\ *usu cap S&V* [F, fr. *Saint-Véran*, wine appellation, prob. fr. *Saint-Vérand*, village in eastern France] : a white Burgundy wine

salad bar *n* : a self-service counter (as in a restaurant) featuring an array of salad makings and dressings

salade niçoise *also* **salad niçoise** *n* -s *usu cap N* [F *salade niçoise* salad in the style of Nice (city in France)] : a salad that usu. consists primarily of olives, tomatoes, anchovies, tuna, and beans or green vegetables

salamander* *n* : a cooking device with an overhead heat source like a broiler

salaryman \ˈ=(=)=ˌ=\ *n, pl* **salarymen** [Jap *sararī-man*, fr. E ¹*salary* + ¹*man*] : a Japanese white-collar businessman

sal·bu·ta·mol \salˈbyüd-əˌmōl, -ütə-, -ōl\ *n* -s [*sal*icyl- + *but*yl + *am*ino + ¹*-ol*] : ALBUTEROL *herein*

sal·sa \ˈsōlsə, ˈsäl-\ *n* -s [AmerSp, lit., sauce, fr. Sp, fr. L, fem. of *salsus* salted — more at SAUCE] **1** : popular music of Latin-American origin that has absorbed characteristics of rhythm and blues, jazz, and rock **2** : a spicy sauce of tomatoes, onions, and hot peppers

sal·tim·boc·ca \ˌsȯltimˈbä(k)kə, -ˈbō(-, -ˈbō-(-, ˌsal-\ *n* -s [It, lit., something that jumps into the mouth — more at SALTIMBANCO, BOCCA] : scallops of veal prepared with sage, slices of ham, and sometimes cheese and served with a wine sauce

sal·uret·ic \ˌsalyəˈred·ik\ *n* -s [L *sal* salt + E *diuretic* — more at SALT] : a drug that facilitates the urinary excretion of salt and esp. of sodium ion — **saluretic** \ˈ==ˈ==\ *adj* — **sal·uret·i·cal·ly** \-ˈred-ək(ə)lē\ *adv*

SAM \ˈsam, ˌe(ˌ)sāˈem\ *n* -s : SURFACE-TO-AIR MISSILE *herein*

sam·bo* \ˈsam(ˌ)bō, ˈsäm-\ *n* -s [Russ, fr. *samozashchita bez oruzhiya* self-defense without weapons] : an international style of wrestling employing judo techniques

sam·bu·ca \samˈbükə, sämˈbükä\ *n* -s [It, fr. *sambuco* elder bush, fr. L *sambucus*] : an anise-flavored Italian liqueur that is made with the fruit of a Eurasian elder bush (*Sambucus nigra*)

sa·miz·dat \ˈsäməzˌdät\ *n* -s *often attrib* [Russ, fr. *sam* self + *izdatel'stvo* publisher, fr. *izdat'* to publish, fr. *iz* out, from + *dat'* to give; akin to L *dare* to give — more at DATE] : a system in the U.S.S.R. and countries within its orbit by which government-suppressed literature was clandestinely printed and distributed; *also* : such literature

sa·moa time \səˈmōə-\ *n, usu cap S* : the time of the 11th time zone west of Greenwich that includes American Samoa

sa·mo·sa \sə'mōsə\ *n* -S [Hindi *samosā* & Urdu *samosa, sambūsa*, fr. Pers *sambūsa*] : a small triangular pastry filled with spiced meat or vegetables and fried in ghee or oil

sample* *n* : an excerpt from a musical recording that is used in another artist's recording

sample* *vt* : to use a segment of (another's musical recording) as part of one's own recording

sampler* *n* : a synthesizer that reproduces recorded sounds

sampling distribution *n* : the distribution of a statistic (as a sample mean)

san·cerre \säⁿser\ *n* -S *usu cap* [F, fr. *Sancerre*, wine appellation and town in central France] : a dry white wine from the Loire valley of France

san·da ware \'sandə-, 'sän-\ *n, usu cap S* [fr. *Sanda*, city in western Honshu, Japan, where it originated] : a Japanese pottery and esp. porcelain ware produced since the late 17th century and noted for its celadons

sandbag* *vt* : to conceal or misrepresent one's true position, potential, or intent esp. in order to take advantage of ~ *vi* : to hide the truth about oneself so as to gain an advantage over another

san·di·nis·ta \ˌsandə'nēstə, ˌsän-\ *also* **san·di·nist** \'sandənəst\ *n* -S *usu cap* [AmerSp *sandinista*, fr. Augusto César *Sandino* †1933 Nicaraguan rebel leader + Sp *-ista* ¹-ist] : a member of a military and political coalition holding power in Nicaragua from 1979 to 1990

S and L \ˌ==ˌ=\ *n* : SAVINGS AND LOAN ASSOCIATION

S and M *abbr* sadism and masochism; sadist and masochist

sandwich coin *n* : a clad coin

sandwich generation *n* : a generation of people who bear usu. financial and caregiving obligations for both their parents and their children

sandwich shop *n* : LUNCHEONETTE

san·gio·vese \ˌsänjō'vāzā, -'vēz, -'vēs\ *n* -S *usu cap* [It, variety of red grape, a wine made from that grape] : a dry red Italian wine made from a single variety of red grape; *also* : a similar wine made elsewhere (as in California)

san·gria \saŋ'grēə, san-, säŋ-, sän-\ *n* -S [Sp *sangría* — more at SANGAREE] : a punch made of red wine, fruit juice, sugar, and usu. brandy, sliced fruit, and soda water

sanitize* *vt* : to make more acceptable by removing unpleasant or undesired features ⟨~ a document⟩

san·te·ria \ˌsantə'rēə, ˌsän-\ *n* -S *usu cap* [AmerSp *santería*, fr. *santero* practitioner of santeria (fr. *santo* Yoruba deity, lit., saint's image, saint, fr. Sp) + Sp *-ia* — more at SANTO] : a religion practiced originally in Cuba in which Yoruba deities are identified with Roman Catholic saints

sapir–whorf hypothesis \sə¦pi(ə)r'(h)wȯ(ə)rf-\ *n, usu cap S&W* [after Edward *Sapir* †1939 & Benjamin Lee *Whorf* †1941 Am. linguists] : WHORFIAN HYPOTHESIS *herein*

sa·ran·gi \'särənˌgē, -əŋˌg-\ *n* -S [Skt *sāraṅgī*] : a stringed musical instrument of India that is played with a bow and that has a tone similar to that of the viola

sarcoplasmic reticulum *n* : the specialized endoplasmic reticulum of cardiac muscle and skeletal striated muscle that functions esp. as a storage and release area for calcium

SASE *abbr* self-addressed stamped envelope

sas·quatch \'sasˌkwach, -äch\ *n* -ES *usu cap* [Halkomelem (Salishan language of southwest British Columbia) *sésq̓əc*] : a hairy creature like a human being that is reported to exist in the northwestern U.S. and western Canada and is said to be a primate between 6 and 15 feet tall — called also *bigfoot*

sa·tay \'sätā, 'sa-\ *or* **sa·té** *or* **sa·te** *n* -S [Malay *satai, sate*] : small pieces of meat marinated and grilled on a skewer and served with a spicy sauce usu. of peanuts ⟨beef ~⟩

satellite* *n* : a usu. independent urban community situated on the outskirts of a large city

satellite dish *n* : a microwave dish for receiving usu. television transmissions from an orbiting satellite

satellite DNA *n* : a fraction of a eukaryotic organism's DNA that differs in density from most of its DNA as determined by centrifugation, that consists of short repetitive nucleotide sequences, that does not undergo transcription, and is often found in centromeric regions

sat·is·fice \'sad·əˌsfīs\ *vi* -ED/-ING/-S [blend of *satisfy* and *suffice*] : to pursue the minimum satisfactory condition or outcome — **sat·is·fic·er** \-sər\ *n* -S

sat·nav \'satˌnav\ *n* -S [*sat*ellite *nav*igation system] : a satellite-based navigation system for ships

saturated diving *n* : SATURATION DIVING *herein* — **saturated diver** *n*

saturation diving *n* : diving in which a person remains underwater at a certain depth breathing a mixture of gases under pressure for an indefinite period once the body has become saturated with the gases because the decompression time remains the same regardless of how long the diver remains at that depth — **saturation dive** *n*

saturday night special *n, usu cap 1st S* : a cheap easily concealed handgun

saucy* *adj* : served with or having the consistency of sauce

sau·vi·gnon blanc \ˌsōvēˌnyōⁿ'bläⁿ, -äŋk\ *n, pl* **sauvignon blancs** \-äⁿ, -äŋks\ *often cap S&B* [F, white sauvignon (variety of grape)] : a dry white wine made from a grape orig. grown in Bordeaux and the Loire valley

savant* *n* : IDIOT SAVANT

save* *vt* : to store (data) in a computer or on a storage device (as a floppy disk)

saxi·toxin \¦saksə+\ *n* [NL *saxi-* (fr. *Saxidomus giganteus*, species of butter clam from which it is isolated) + E *toxin*] : a potent nonprotein neurotoxin $C_{10}H_{17}N_7O_4·2HCl$ that originates esp. in dinoflagellates of the genus *Gonyaulax* found in red tides and that sometimes occurs in and renders toxic normally edible mollusks which feed on them

s–band \'es-\ *n, usu cap S* [*S*, military code letter] : a radio frequency band that lies between 1550 and 5200 megahertz and is used esp. for aircraft and spacecraft communication and for radar transmission

SBN *abbr* Standard Book Number

scag \'skag, -aa(ə)g, -aig\ *or* **skag*** *n* -S [prob. fr. ²*skag*] *slang* : HEROIN

scalable* *adj, of a computer system* : capable of being easily expanded or upgraded on demand — **scal·abil·i·ty** \ˌskālə'biləd·ē, -ətē\ *n* -ES

scalar* *adj* : of or relating to a scalar or scalar product

scaler* *n* : a dental instrument for removing tartar from teeth

sca·lop·pi·ne \ˌskälə'pēnē, ˌskal-\ *var of* SCALLOPINI

¹scam \'skam, -aa(ə)m, -aim\ *n* -S [origin unknown] : a confidence scheme in which an established business is taken over, merchandise is purchased on credit and quickly sold, and then the business is abandoned or bankruptcy is declared; *broadly* : a fraudulent or deceptive practice ⟨insurance swindles, credit-card rackets, and practically every ~ devised by man —Joe Flaherty⟩

²scam \"\ *vt* **scammed; scammed; scamming; scams** **1** : DECEIVE, DEFRAUD ⟨~*s* his senile grandmother out of $3 million —Jane Clapperton⟩ **2** : to obtain (as money) by a scam — **scam·mer** \-ə(r)\ *n* -S *slang*

scam·pi \'skampē\ *n, pl* **scampi** [It, pl. of *scampo* Norway lobster, fr. It dial. (Venetian), prob. modif. of Gk *kampē* caterpillar — more at -CAMPA] **1** : NORWAY LOBSTER **2** : a usu. large shrimp; *also* : large shrimp prepared with a garlic-flavored sauce

scan* *vt* **1** : to make a scan of (as a human body) **2** : to pass over in the formation of an image ⟨the electron beam ~*s* the picture tube⟩

scan* *n* **1 a** : a depiction (as a photograph) of the distribution of radioactive material in something (as a body organ) **b** : an image of a bodily part produced (as by computer) by combining ultrasonographic or radiographic data obtained from several angles or sections **2** : TRACE 5c

scan line *n* : a horizontal line traced across a cathode-ray tube by an electron beam to form part of an image

scanner* *n* : a device (as a CAT scanner) for making scans of the human body

scanning electron micrograph *n* : a micrograph made by scanning electron microscopy

scanning electron microscope *n* : an electron microscope in which a beam of focused electrons moves across the object with the secondary electrons produced by the object and the electrons scattered by the object being collected to form a three-dimensional image on a cathode-ray tube — called also *scanning microscope*; compare TRANSMISSION ELECTRON MICROSCOPE *herein* — **scanning electron microscopy** *n*

scanning tunneling microscope *n* : a microscope that makes use of the phenomenon of electron tunneling to map the positions of individual atoms in a surface or to move atoms around on a surface — **scanning tunneling microscopy** *n*

scarf \'skärf, 'skȧf\ *vt* -ED/-ING/-S [alter. of ³*scoff*] : to eat or consume esp. rapidly or greedily — often used with *down*

scatter* *n, often attrib* : television advertising time sold after the broadcast season has begun — called also *scatter time*

scattering matrix *n* : S MATRIX *herein*

scenario* *n* : a sequence of events esp. when imagined; *esp* : an account or synopsis of a possible course of action or events ⟨had drawn up a number of possible ~*s* in which nuclear weapons would be used —Martin Mayer⟩

scene* *n* : a sphere of activity : a way of life ⟨the social ~⟩

scene·ster \'sēnstə(r)\ *n* -S [¹*scene* + *-ster*] : a person who frequents a social or cultural scene ⟨London ~*s* can't keep away from the restaurant⟩

schedule* *n, usu cap* : a governmental list of drugs that are all subject to the same legal controls and restrictions — usu. used with a Roman numeral from I to V indicating decreasing potential for abuse or addiction

sche·ren·schnit·te \'shārənˌshnitə\ *n* -S [G, pl. of *scherenschnitt*, lit., scissors cut, fr. *scheren*, pl. of *schere* scissors (fr. MHG *schære*, pl., fr. OHG *skār*) + *schnitt* cut, fr. MHG *snit*, fr. OHG; akin to OE *snid* cut, fr. the Gmc root of *snīthan* to cut — more at SHEAR, SCHNEIDER] : the art of cutting paper into decorative designs — compare SILHOUETTE *in the Dict*

schil·der's disease \'shildə(r)z-\ *n, usu cap S* [after Paul Ferdinand *Schilder* †1940 Austrian psychiatrist] : a demyelinating disease of the central nervous system that is inherited as an X-linked recessive trait affecting males in childhood and that is characterized by progressive blindness, deafness, tonic spasms, and mental deterioration

schizophrenia* *n* : the presence of mutually contradictory or antagonistic parts or qualities

schizy *or* **schiz·zy** \'skitsē\ *adj* [*schizoid* + ¹*-y*] : SCHIZOID

schlepp* *or* **schlep** *or* **shlep** *vi* **schlepped** *or* **shlepped; schlepped** *or* **shlepped; schlepping** *or* **shlepping; schlepps** *or* **schleps** *or* **shleps** **1** : to proceed or move slowly, tediously, or awkwardly **2** : TRAVEL, GO ⟨I ~ to meetings and soccer games —David Ruben⟩

schlepp *or* **schlep** *or* **shlep** \'shlep\ *or* **schlep·per** *or* **shlep·per** \-epə(r)\ *n* -S [modif. of Yiddish *shleper* tramp, bum, fr. *shlepen* to trudge; *schlepper*, fr. Yiddish *shleper* — more at SCHLEPP, v.] : an awkward or incompetent person : JERK

schlock \'shläk\ *also* **schlocky** \-ē\ *or* **shlock** \'shläk\ *or* **shlocky** \-ē\ *adj* [prob. fr. Yiddish *shlak* blow, apoplectic stroke, curse, fr. MHG *slag, slac*, fr. OHG *slag*, fr. *slahan* to strike — more at SLAY] : of low quality or little worth ⟨~ books⟩ ⟨~ merchandise⟩ — **schlock** *n* -S

schlock·meis·ter \'shläkˌmīstə(r)\ *n* -S [*schlock* (herein) + Yiddish *mayster* or G *meister* master] : one who makes or sells schlock products

schlong *also* **shlong** \'shläŋ, 'shlȯŋ\ *n* -S [Yiddish *shlang*, lit., snake, fr. MHG *slange*, fr. OHG *slango* — more at SLANGKOP] *slang* : PENIS 1 — usu. considered vulgar

schm- *or* **shm-** \shm\ *prefix* [Yiddish *shm-*] — used to form a rhyming term of derision by preceding the initial vowel or by replacing the initial consonant or consonant cluster ⟨urban, *schm*urban — *Economist*⟩ ⟨fancy, *shm*ancy⟩

schmear *or* **schmeer** *also* **shmear** \'shmi(ə)r, -iə(r\ *n* -S [Yiddish *shmir* smear, fr. *shmirn* to smear, fr. MHG *smiren, smirwen*, fr. OHG *smirwen* — more at SMEAR] : an aggregate of related things ⟨the whole ~⟩

schmooze* *vb* ~ *vt* : to talk with in a friendly and persuasive manner esp. so as to gain favor or business — **schmooz·er** \'=zə(r)\ *n* -S

schmoozy \'=ē\ *adj* -ER/-EST [¹*schmooze* + ¹*-y*] : of, relating to, or characterized by schmoozing ⟨a ~ patter⟩; *also* : given to schmoozing ⟨a ~ salesclerk⟩

schmuck *or* **shmuck** \'shmək\ *n* -S [Yiddish *shmok*, lit., penis, perh. modif. of Old Pol *smok* snake, dragon] : a stupid, naïve, or foolish person : JERK; *also* : one who is mean or nasty

scholarship level *n, usu cap S* : S LEVEL 1 *herein*

schottky barrier *n, usu cap S* [*Schottky defect*] : a potential barrier that exists at a metal-semiconductor interface (as in a solid-state electronic device)

schtick *var of* SHTICK *herein*

schussboomer \'=ˌ=\ *n* [¹*schuss* + ¹*boomer*] : one who skis usu. straight downhill at high speed

schwarz·schild radius \'shwȯrtˌshild-, 's(h)wȯrtsˌchīld-; 'shvärtˌshilt-\ *n, usu cap S* [after Karl *Schwarzschild* †1916 Ger. astronomer] : the radius of the spherical boundary within which a given mass (as of a star) must collapse to become a black hole; *also* : the distance of the event horizon from the center of a black hole

SCID *abbr* severe combined immunodeficiency *herein*

scientific creationism *n* : a doctrine holding that the biblical account of creation is supported by scientific evidence — **scientific creationist** *n*

sci–fi \¦sī¦fī\ *n* -S *often attrib* [by shortening] : SCIENCE FICTION

scin·ti·scan \'sintəˌskan\ *n* [*scinti*llation + *scan*] : a two-dimensional representation of radioisotope radiation from a bodily organ (as the spleen or kidney) — **scin·ti·scan·ning** \-iŋ\ *n*

scle·ro·testa \¦sklirō, -lerō+\ *n* [NL, fr. *scler-* + *testa*] : the middle stony layer of the testa in various seeds — compare ENDOTESTA *herein* — **scle·ro·tes·tal** \-¦test³l\ *adj*

sclerotherapy \"+\ *n* [*scler-* + *therapy*] : the injection of a sclerosing agent (as saline) into a varicose vein to produce inflammation and scarring which closes the lumen and is followed by shrinkage

sclerotic* *adj* : grown rigid or unresponsive esp. with age ⟨~ institutions⟩

scope* *vt* : to look at a person or a thing often for the purpose of evaluation ⟨*scoped* the dangerous ledge⟩ — often used with *out* ⟨*scoped* her out from across the room —Tim Allis⟩

score* *n, slang* : a purchase or sale of narcotics

score* *vt* **1** : to have sexual relations with ⟨adventuress who . . . ~*s* the dude and splits —Elizabeth Ashley⟩ **2** : to be successful in obtaining ⟨should be able to ~ a ham sandwich —Glenn O'Brien⟩ ~ *vi* : to succeed in having sexual relations ⟨college roommates who . . . ~ with the same girl —L.H.Lapham⟩

scorpio* *n* -S *usu cap* : one born under the astrological sign Scorpio

scorpion* *n, usu cap* : SCORPIO *herein*

s corporation *n, usu cap S* [fr. Subchapter *S* of the Internal Revenue Code, under which taxation of such corporations is described] : a small business corporation that is treated for federal tax purposes as a partnership

scotch bonnet *n, usu cap S* : a small roundish very hot chili pepper that is usu. red or yellow when mature, is related to the habanero, and is grown esp. in the Caribbean

scotch egg *n, usu cap S* : a hard-boiled egg wrapped in sausage meat, covered with bread crumbs, and fried

scottish fold *n, usu cap S* : any of a breed of short-haired domestic cats that originated in Scotland where the breed characteristic of ears folded over at the top occurred as a spontaneous mutation

scouse \'skau̇s\ *n* -S *cap* [back-formation fr. *Scouser* (herein)] **1** : SCOUSER *herein* **2** : a dialect of English spoken in Liverpool

scous·er \'skau̇sə(r)\ *n* -S *cap* [*scouse* (lobscouse) + ²*-er*; fr. the popularity of lobscouse in Liverpool] : a native or inhabitant of Liverpool

scramble* *vi, of a football quarterback* : to run with the ball after the pass protection breaks down

scramble* *n* **1** : a motorcycle race over a rough hilly course **2** : the act or an instance of scrambling by a quarterback

scram·jet \'skramˌjet\ *n* [*s*upersonic *c*ombustion *ramjet*] : a ramjet airplane engine in which thrust is produced by burning fuel in a supersonic airstream after the airplane has attained supersonic speed by other means of propulsion

scratch* *vi* : to produce a rhythmic scratching sound by moving a phonograph record back and forth under a phonograph needle ⟨he cuts and *scratches*, spinning records, giving the crowd something other than the bass to feel —Danyel Smith⟩

scratch* *adj* : made from scratch : made with basic ingredients

scratchpad** *n* : a small fast auxiliary computer memory

screen* *n* : the information displayed on a computer screen at one time

screen·ful \'skrēn(ˌ)fu̇l\ *n, pl* **screenfuls** *also* **screens·ful** \'skrēnz-\ : the amount of information available at one time on a display screen (as of a computer)

screening test *n* : a preliminary or abridged test intended to eliminate the less probable members of an experimental series

screen saver *n* : a computer program that usu. displays various images on the screen of a computer that is on but not in use

screw dislocation *n* : a dislocation in the lattice structure of a crystal in which the atoms are arranged in a helical pattern that is normal to the direction of the stress

screw up* *vb* ~ *vt* **1** : BUNGLE, BOTCH **2** : to cause to act or function in a crazy or confused way : CONFOUND, DISTURB ~ *vi* : to botch an activity or undertaking

screw–up \'=ˌ=\ *n* -S [*screw up* (herein)] **1** : one who screws up **2** : BLUNDER

scrim* *n* : something likened to a theater scrim ⟨the sky was a ~ of creeping mists —Darryl Pinckney⟩ ⟨people perceive bias through the ~ of ideology —Wendy Kaminer⟩

scrimshander* *n* : a person who makes scrimshaw

scrip \'skrip\ *or* **script** \'skript\ *n* -S [by shortening] : PRESCRIPTION 5a (1)

scri·poph·i·ly \skri'päfəlē\ *n* -ES [²*scrip* + *-o-* + *-phily*] : the hobby of collecting old stock and bond certificates; *also* : such a collection — **scri·poph·i·list** *n* -S

script* *vt* : to provide carefully considered details for (as a plan of action) ⟨an event carefully ~*ed* to attract attention⟩

scripture cake *n, usu cap S* : a fruitcake whose recipe refers to biblical passages where the ingredients are mentioned

scroll* *vt* : to cause (text or graphics on a display screen) to move vertically or horizontally usu. one line or column at a time as if by unrolling a scroll ~ *vi* **1** : to move text or graphics across a display screen **2** *of text or graphics* : to move across a screen — **scroll·able** \'skrōləbəl\ *adj*

scroun·gy \'skrau̇njē\ *adj* -ER/-EST [perh. blend of *scraggly* and *grungy* (herein)] : having a shabby, dirty, or unkempt look or quality

scrub nurse *n* : a nurse who assists the surgeon in an operating room

scrum* *n, Brit* : MADHOUSE 2; *also* : a usu. tightly packed or disorderly crowd ⟨made his escape from a ~ of reporters following his postgame press conference —Austin Murphy⟩

scuba diver *n* : one who swims under water with the aid of scuba gear — **scuba dive** *vi* — **scuba diving** *n*

scuffle* *vi* : to struggle (as by working odd jobs) to get by

scumbag \'=ˌ=\ *n* **1** *slang* : CONDOM **2** *slang* : a dirty or unpleasant person — used as a generalized term of abuse

scut work *n* [prob. fr. medical argot *scut* junior intern (of unknown origin)] : routine and often menial work

scuzz·ball \'skəzˌbȯl\ *n* -S [*scuzz-* back-formation fr. *scuzzy* (herein)] *slang* : an unpleasant, dirty, or dangerous person : CREEP, SCUMBAG *herein*

scuz·zy \'skəzē\ *adj* -ER/-EST [perh. alter. of *disgusting*] *slang* : NASTY, SQUALID

SDI *abbr* strategic defense initiative

SDRs \ˌes(ˌ)dē'ärz, -'äz\ *n pl* [special drawing rights] : an international means of exchange created under the auspices of the International Monetary Fund for use by governments in settling their international indebtedness

SE* *abbr* standard English

sea·borg·i·um \sē'bȯrgēəm\ *n* -S [NL, fr. Glenn T. *Seaborg* †1999 Am. chemist + NL *-ium*] : a short-lived radioactive element of atomic number 106 that is produced artificially — symbol *Sg*

seafloor \'=ˌ=\ *n* : SEABED

sea·floor spreading \'=ˌ=-\ *n* : the divergence at midocean ridges of the tectonic plates underlying the oceans that is due to upwelling from the earth's interior of magma which forms new crust

sea–grant college \'=ˌ=-\ *n* : an institution of higher learning that receives federal grants for research in oceanography

seal \'sē(ə)l\ *n* -S *usu all caps* [*se*a, *a*ir, *l*and] : a member of a U.S. Navy special warfare team trained to perform sea, air, and land operations

search engine *n* : computer software used to search data (as text or a database) for specified information; *also* : a site on the World Wide Web that uses such software to find other sites that are related to keywords input by a user

seasonal affective disorder *n* : depression that tends to recur with the shortening length of day during the fall and winter months — abbr. *SAD*

seasonless* *adj* : not restricted to a particular season; *esp* : suitable for wearing in any season ⟨~ fabrics⟩

seat* *n* : a precise or accurate contact between parts or surfaces — **by the seat of one's pants** : using experience and intuition rather than mechanical aids or formal theory ⟨navigating *by the seat of his pants*⟩

secant* *n* : a trigonometric function *sec* θ that is the reciprocal of the cosine for all real numbers θ for which the cosine is not zero and that is exactly equal to the secant of an angle of measure θ in radians

sec·chi disc \'sekē-\ *n, usu cap S* [after Angelo *Secchi* †1878 It. astronomer] : a reflective disc lowered into a body of water to permit measurement of the relative transparency of the water by recording the depth at which the disc is no longer visible

secondary* *or* **secondary offering** *n* : SECONDARY DISTRIBUTION

secondary derivative *n* : a word (as *teacher*) whose immediate constituents are a free form and a bound form

secondary recovery *n* : the process of obtaining oil (as by waterflood) from a well that has stopped producing

secondhand smoke *n* : tobacco smoke that is exhaled by a smoker or is given off by burning tobacco and is inhaled by persons nearby

second messenger *n* : a cellular substance (as cyclic AMP) that mediates cell activity by relaying a signal from an extracellular molecule (as of a hormone or neurotransmitter) bound to the cell's surface

second–strike \¦=¦=\ *adj* : being or relating to a weapons system capable of surviving a nuclear attack and then striking enemy targets

second world *n, often cap S&W* : the Communist nations as a political and economic bloc

sector* *n* : a subdivision of a track on a computer disk

se·cu·ri·tize \sə'kyu̇rəˌtīz\ *vt* -ED/-ING/-S [¹*security* + *-ize*] *banking* : to consolidate and sell (as mortgage loans) to other investors for resale to the public in the form of securities — **se·cu·ri·ti·za·tion** \=ˌ==tī'zāshən, =ˌ==tī-\ *n* -S

security blanket *n* **1** : a blanket carried by a child as a protection against anxiety **2** : a usu. familiar object or person whose presence dispels anxiety
sedimentation coefficient *n* : a measure of the rate at which a molecule (as a protein) suspended in a colloidal solution sediments in an ultracentrifuge usu. expressed in svedbergs
seed money *also* **seed capital** *n* : money used for setting up a new enterprise
seek time *n* : the length of time it takes for a disk drive to locate a given piece of information on a disk
see–through \ˈ=ˌ=\ *adj* : TRANSLUCENT, TRANSPARENT — **see–through** \ˈ=ˌ=\ *n* -S
segue* *vi* : to make a transition from one activity, topic, scene, or part to another as or as if part of a natural progression ⟨time to ~ . . . into the second part of this essay —S.J.Gould⟩ — **segue*** *n*
seismic* *adj* : having a strong or widespread impact : EARTH-SHAKING ⟨~ social changes⟩
selective serotonin reuptake inhibitor *n* : any of a class of antidepressants (as fluoxetine that inhibit the inactivation of serotonin by blocking its reuptake by presynaptic nerve cell endings — abbr. *SSRI*
self* *n* : material that is part of an individual organism ⟨ability of the immune system to distinguish ~ from nonself⟩
self–actualize \ˈ=ˈ==(=)ˌ=\ *vi* : to realize fully one's potential — **self–actualization** \ˈ=ˌ==(=)==ˈ==\ *n* — **self–actualizer** \ˈ=ˈ==(=)ˌ==\ *n* -S
self–administer \ˈ=ˈ===\ *vt* : to administer to oneself
self–assembly \ˈ==ˈ==\ *n* : the process by which a complex macromolecule (as collagen) or a supramolecular system (as a virus) spontaneously assembles itself from its components — **self–assemble** \ˈ==ˈ==\ *vi*
self–concept \ˈ=ˈ=ˌ=\ *n* : the mental image one has of oneself
self–dealing \ˈ=ˈ==\ *n* : financial dealing that is not at arm's length; *esp* : borrowing from or lending to a company by a controlling individual primarily to his own advantage
self–destruct \ˈ==ˈ=\ *vi* : to destroy oneself or itself — **self–destruct** \"\ *adj*
self–fulfilling \ˈ==ˈ==\ *adj* : becoming real or true by virtue of having been predicted or assumed ⟨a *self-fulfilling* prophecy⟩
selfish* *adj* : being a usu. repetitive sequence of nucleic acid that actively replicates within an organism but is not expressed phenotypically and serves no known function ⟨~ DNA⟩
self–medication \ˈ=ˌ==ˈ==\ *n* : medication of oneself esp. without the advice of a physician — **self–medicate** \ˈ=ˈ==ˌ=\ *vb*
self–paced \ˈ=ˈ=\ *adj* : designed to permit the student or subject to learn or proceed at his or her own pace
self–perception \ˈ==ˈ==\ *n* : perception of oneself; *esp* : SELF-CONCEPT *herein*
self–publish \ˈ=ˈ==\ *vt* : to publish (a book) using the author's own resources — **self–publishing** \ˈ=ˈ===\
self–recognition \ˈ=ˌ===ˈ==\ *n* **1** : recognition of one's own self **2** : the process by which the immune system of an organism distinguishes between the body's own chemicals, cells, and tissues and those of foreign organisms and agents — compare SELF-TOLERANCE *herein*
self–referential \ˈ=ˌ==ˈ==\ *adj* : referring to itself; *esp* : concerned with the mental attitudes and creative processes that brought it into existence
self–replicating \ˈ=ˈ==ˌ==\ *adj* : reproducing itself autonomously ⟨DNA is a *self-replicating* molecule⟩ — **self–replication** \ˈ=ˌ==ˈ==\ *n*
self–reproducing \ˈ=(ˌ)=ˈ==\ *adj* : SELF-REPLICATING *herein*
self–serve \ˈ=ˈ=\ *adj* : permitting self-service
self–stick \ˈ=ˈ=\ *adj* : capable of adhering to a surface by application of pressure without the addition of moisture
self–stimulation \ˈ=ˌ==ˈ==\ *n* : stimulation of oneself as a result of one's own activity or behavior ⟨electrical *self-stimulation* of the brain⟩; *esp* : MASTURBATION — **self–stimulatory** \ˈ=ˈ===ˌ==\ *adj*
self–tanner \ˈ=ˈ==\ *n* : a product (as one containing dihydroxyacetone) that when applied to the skin reacts chemically with its surface layer to give the appearance of a suntan — compare BRONZER *herein*
self–tolerance \ˈ=ˈ===\ *n* : the physiological state that exists in a developing organism when its immune system has proceeded far enough in the process of self-recognition to lose the capacity to attack and destroy its own bodily constituents
self–worth \ˈ=ˈ=\ *n* : SELF-ESTEEM
selling climax *n* : a sharp decline in stock prices for a short time on very heavy trading volume followed by a rally
sell–through \ˈ=ˌ=\ *n* -S : the amount or percentage of a product that is sold to consumers relative to the total quantity available in stores ⟨a book with 60% *sell-through*⟩ ⟨methods to improve a magazine's *sell-through*⟩
SEM *abbr* scanning electron microscope *herein*; scanning electron microscopy *herein*
sem·el·pa·rous \(ˈ)semˈelpərəs\ *adj* [L *semel* once (akin to L *simul* together, at the same time) + E *-parous* — more at SAME] : reproducing or breeding only once in a lifetime ⟨~ salmon⟩ ⟨a ~ agave⟩ — **sem·el·par·i·ty** \ˌseməlˈparədē\ *n*
semi–antique \ˈsemē, -ˌmī+\ *adj, of a carpet or rug* : being approximately 50 to 100 years old; *broadly* : being of a quality sufficient to become antique and having had some use but not yet old enough to be considered an antique — **semi–antique** *n*
semi·automated \ˌsemē, -ˌmī, -ˌmi+\ *adj* [*semi-* + *automated*, past part. of *automate*] : partly automated
semi·axis \"+\ *n* [*semi-* + *axis*] : a line segment that has one endpoint at the center of a geometric figure (as an ellipse) and that forms half of an axis
semi·comatose \ˌsemē, -ˌmī, -ˌmə+\ *adj* [*semi-* + *comatose*] : lethargic and disoriented but not completely comatose
semi·conservative \"+\ *adj* [*semi-* + [1]*conservative*] : relating to or being genetic replication in which a double-stranded molecule of nucleic acid separates into two single strands each of which serves as a template for the formation of a complementary strand that together with the template forms a complete molecule — **semi·conservatively** *adv*
semi·dwarf \"+\ *adj* [*semi-* + [1]*dwarf*] : of or being a plant of a variety that is undersized but larger than a dwarf ⟨~ wheats⟩ — **semidwarf** *n*
semi·empirical \"+\ *adj* [*semi-* + *empirical*] : partly empirical; *esp* : involving assumptions, approximations, or generalizations designed to simplify calculation or to yield a result in accord with observation
semi·group \ˈsemē, -mə+ˌ-\ *n* [*semi-* + [1]*group*] : a mathematical set that is closed under an associative binary operation
semi·lethal \ˌsemē, -ˌmī, -ˌmə+\ *n* [*semi-* + *lethal*] : a mutation that in the homozygous condition produces more than 50 percent mortality but not complete mortality — **semilethal** *adj*
semi·nat·u·ral \"+\ *adj* [*semi-* + [1]*natural*] : modified by human influence but retaining many natural features
semi·submersible \"+\ *adj* [*semi-* + [1]*submersible*] : being a floating deepwater drilling platform that is towed to a desired location and then partially flooded for stabilization and usu. anchored — **semisubmersible** \"\ *n*
semi·truck \ˈsemi+ˌ\ *n* : SEMITRAILER 2
sen* *n* [Malay, fr. E *cent*] : a monetary unit of Malaysia equivalent to $^1/_{100}$ ringgit — see MONEY table *in the Dict*
send up* *vt* : to make fun of : SATIRIZE, PARODY
send–up \ˈ=ˌ=\ *n* -S [send up (herein)] : SATIRE, PARODY
sene \ˈsenē\ *n, pl* **sene** *or* **senes** [Samoan, fr. E *cent*] **1** : a monetary unit of Western Samoa equivalent to $^1/_{100}$ tala — see MONEY table *in the Dict* **2** : a coin representing one sene
sen·gi \ˈseŋgē\ *n, pl* **sengi** [Kikongo or Lingala *sengi, senki* five-centime coin of the Belgian Congo, fr. F *cinq* five — more at CINQ-CENTS] : a monetary unit of Zaire equal to $^1/_{100}$ likuta or $^1/_{10,000}$ zaire
senior citizen *n* : an elderly person; *esp* : one who has retired

sen·i·ti \ˈsenətē\ *n, pl* **seniti** [Tongan, fr. E *cent*] **1** : a monetary unit of Tonga equal to $^1/_{100}$ pa'anga — see MONEY table *in the Dict* **2** : a coin representing one seniti
sen·ryu \ˈsenrē(ˌ)ü\ *n, pl* **senryu** [Jap *senryū*, after *Senryū*, pen name of Karai Hachiemon †1790 Jap. poet and practitioner of the form] : a 3-line unrhymed Japanese poem structurally similar to haiku but treating human nature usu. in an ironic or satiric vein
sen·sei \(ˈ)senˈsā\ *n* -S [Jap, teacher, master] : a teacher or instructor usu. of Japanese martial arts (as karate or judo)
sensitive* *adj* : having or showing concern for a specified matter — usu. used in combination ⟨customers are price-*sensitive* —C.J.Balcer⟩
sensitivity training *n* : training in a small interacting group that is designed to increase each individual's awareness of his or her own feelings and the feelings of others and to enhance interpersonal relations through the exploration of the behavior, needs, and responses of the individuals making up the group
sen·so·ri·neural \ˌsen(t)s(ə)rē+\ *adj* [*sensory* + *-i-* + *neural*] : of, relating to, or involving the aspects of sense perception mediated by nerves ⟨~ hearing loss⟩
sentence* *n* : a mathematical or logical statement (as an equation or a proposition) in words or symbols
sen·ti \ˈsentē\ *n, pl* **senti** [Swahili, fr. E *cent*] : the cent of Tanzania
sen·ti·mo \ˈsentəˌmō\ *n* -S [Pilipino, fr. Sp. *céntimo* — more at CENTIMO] **1** : a monetary unit of the Republic of the Philippines equal to $^1/_{100}$ peso : CENTAVO — see MONEY table *in the Dict* **2** : a coin representing one sentimo
separate* *vt* : DISLOCATE 1a ⟨*separated* his left shoulder⟩
septic shock *n* : a life-threatening severe form of sepsis that usu. results from the presence of gram-negative bacteria and their toxins in the bloodstream, that is characterized esp. by decreased blood flow to organs and tissues, hypotension, organ dysfunction (as of the heart, kidneys, or lungs), impaired mental state, and often multiple organ failure, and that typically affects immunocompromised individuals
sequence* *vt* : to determine the sequence of chemical constituents (as amino-acid residues) in
serial* *adj* **1** : relating to or being a connection in a computer system in which the bits of a byte are transmitted sequentially over a single wire — compare PARALLEL 2 *herein* **2 a** : performing a series of similar acts over a period of time ⟨a ~ killer⟩ **b** : occurring in or involving such a series ⟨a ~ murder⟩ ⟨~ monogamy⟩
se·ri·al·ism \ˈsirēəˌlizəm, ˈsēr-\ *n* -S : serial music; *also* : the theory or practice of composing serial music
serial section *n* : any of a series of sections cut in sequence by a microtome from a prepared specimen (as of tissue) — **serially sectioned** *adj* — **serial sectioning** *n*
serious* *adj* : excessive or impressive in quantity, extent, or degree : CONSIDERABLE ⟨making ~ money⟩ ⟨~ drinking⟩
se·ro·conversion \ˌsi(ˌ)rō *sometimes* ˌse(-+\ *n* [*sero-* + *conversion*] : the production of antibodies in response to an antigen — **se·ro·convert** \"+\ *vi*
se·ro·epidemiologic \"+\ *or* **se·ro·epidemiological** \"+\ *adj* [*sero-* + *epidemiologic* or *epidemiological*] : of, relating to, or being epidemiologic investigations involving the identification of antibodies to specific antigens in populations of individuals — **se·ro·epidemiology** \"+\ *n*
se·ro·group \"+\ *n* [*sero-* + [1]*group*] : a group of serotypes having one or more antigens in common
se·ro·negative \"+\ *adj* [*sero-* + [1]*negative*] : having or being a negative serum reaction esp. in a test for the presence of an antibody
se·ro·positive \"+\ *adj* [*sero-* + [1]*positive*] : having or being a positive serum reaction esp. in a test for the presence of an antibody
se·ro·prevalence \"+\ *n* [*sero-* + *prevalence*] : the frequency of individuals in a population that have a particular element (as antibodies to HIV) in their blood serum
se·ro·to·ner·gic \ˌsirətəˈnərjik\ *also* **se·ro·to·nin·er·gic** \ˌsirəˌtōnəˈnərjik, -ˌtän-\ *adj* [*serotonin* + *-ergic* (herein)] : liberating, activated by, or involving serotonin in the transmission of nerve impulses ⟨~ pathways⟩
se·ro·type \ˈsirəˌtīp, ˈser-\ *vt* [*serotype*, n.] : to determine the serotype of
ser·ra·no \səˈrä(ˌ)nō\ *n* -S [MexSp (short for *chile serrano*, lit., mountain chili pepper), fr. Sp, montane, highland, fr. *sierra* jagged mountain range — more at SIERRA] : a small thin very hot Mexican chili pepper (a cultivar of *Capsicum annuum*) that is red when mature
serve* *vt* : PRESENT, PROVIDE — usu. used with *up* ⟨the novel *served* up many laughs⟩
server* *n* : a computer in a network that is used to provide services (as access to files, shared peripherals, or the routing of e-mail) to other computers in the network
service break *n* : a game won on an opponent's serve (as in tennis)
service module *n* : a space vehicle module containing propellant tanks, fuel cells, and the main rocket engine
servicepeople \ˈ==ˌ=\ *n pl* : members of the armed forces
serviceperson \ˈ==ˌ=\ *n* [[2]*service* + *person*] : a member of the armed forces
session man *n* : a studio musician who backs up a performer at a recording session
set–aside* \ˈ=ˌ=\ *n, often attrib* : a program requiring a percentage of opportunities (as for jobs or funding) to be reserved for an underrepresented group
set back* *vt* : COST ⟨how much a diamond would *set* you *back*⟩
set back *n* : an offensive back in football who usu. lines up behind the quarterback
setback* *n* : an automatic scheduled adjustment to a lower temperature setting of a thermostat
SETI \ˈsed·ē *sometimes* ˈsēˌtī\ *abbr* search for extraterrestrial intelligence
se·to ware \ˈsāˌtō-, ˈse-\ *also* **seto** *n* -S *usu cap S* [fr. *Seto*, city in central Honshu, Japan, where it originated] : a Japanese ceramic ware traditionally produced since the 10th century comprising in its earlier period earthenwares often based on contemporaneous Chinese and Korean porcelains, later high-fired stonewares sometimes with notable brown, black, yellow, or celadon glazes, and from the end of the 18th century chiefly porcelain often decorated with underglaze blue
set piece* *n* : a scene, depiction, speech, or event that is obviously designed to have an imposing effect
set point* *n* : the level or point at which a variable physiological state (as body temperature or weight) tends to stabilize
severe combined immunodeficiency *also* **severe combined immune deficiency** *n* : a rare congenital disorder of the immune system that is characterized by inability to produce a normal complement of antibodies and T cells and that results usu. in early death — abbr. *SCID*
Sev·in \ˈsevən\ *trademark* — used for an insecticide consisting of a preparation of carbaryl
sev·ru·ga \seˈvrügə\ *n* -S [Russ *sevryuga* a species of sturgeon] : a light to dark gray caviar from a sturgeon of the genus *Acipenser* (*A. sevru*) that is found in the Caspian Sea and has very small roe; *also* : the fish — compare OSETRA *herein*
sex* *n* : GENITALIA
sex chromatin *n* : BARR BODY *herein*
sex·ism \ˈsekˌsizəm\ *n* -S [[1]*sex* + *-ism* (as in *racism*)] **1** : prejudice or discrimination based on sex; *esp* : discrimination against women **2** : behavior, conditions, or attitudes that foster stereotypes of social roles based on sex — **sex·ist** \ˈseksəst\ *adj or n*
sex kitten *n* : a woman with conspicuous sex appeal
sexless* *adj* : devoid of sexual interest or activity ⟨a ~ relationship⟩
sex object *n* : a person regarded as an object of sexual interest
sex·ploi·ta·tion \ˌsekˌsplȯiˈtāshən\ *n* [blend of *sex* and *exploitation*] : the exploitation of sex in the media and esp. in film

sex shop *n* : a shop selling pornographic and sex-related merchandise
sex symbol *n* : a person noted for conspicuous sex appeal
sexual harassment *n* : uninvited and unwelcome verbal or physical behavior of a sexual nature esp. by a person in authority toward a subordinate (as an employee or a student)
sexually transmitted disease *n* : any of various diseases or infections (as chlamydia, genital herpes, syphilis, and gonorrhea) that are usu. transmitted by direct sexual contact and that include some (as hepatitis B and AIDS) that may be contracted by other than sexual means — called also *STD*
sexy* *adj* : strongly attractive or interesting ⟨colorless benefits, ~ only to economists —Howard Felsher⟩
sey·fert galaxy \ˈsēfə(r)t-, ˈsī-\ *or* **seyfert** *n* -S *usu cap S* [after Carl K. *Seyfert* †1960 Am. astronomer] : any of a class of spiral galaxies that have small compact bright nuclei exhibiting variability in light intensity, emission of radio waves, and spectra which indicate hot gases in rapid motion
Sg *symbol* seaborgium *herein*
sgml \ˌes(ˌ)jē(ˌ)emˈel\ *abbr or n* -S [standard generalized markup language] : a markup language used to define the structure of and manage documents in electronic form
sha·bu–sha·bu \ˈshäbüˈshäbü\ *n* [Jap, of imit. origin] : a Japanese dish consisting of thinly sliced beef and vegetables cooked briefly in simmering broth at the table
shade* *n* **shades** *pl* : SUNGLASSES
shadow mask *n* : a metal plate in a color cathode-ray tube that contains minute apertures permitting passage of the electron beam to specific phosphors on the screen during a scan
shaft* *n* : harsh or unfair treatment — used with *the* ⟨his own mother . . . gave him the ~ —Robert Bloch⟩
shaken baby syndrome *n* : one or more of a group of symptoms (as limb paralysis, epilepsy, vision loss, or mental retardation) that tend to occur in an infant which has been severely shaken but that may also result from other actions (as tossing) causing internal trauma (as hemorrhage, hematoma, or contusions) esp. to the brain region, and that may ultimately result in the death of the infant
shakeout** *n* : a sharp break in a particular industry that usu. follows overproduction or excessive competition and tends to force out weaker producers; *broadly* : a period or process in which the relatively weak or unessential are eliminated
sha·ku·ha·chi \ˌshäküˈhächē\ *n, pl* **shakuhachi** [Jap] : a Japanese bamboo flute
sham·a·teur·ism \ˈshaməˌtərˌizəm, -əd·əˌri-, -əˌt(y)u̇(ə)rˌi-, -əˌchu̇(ə)rˌi-, -əchəˌri-\ *n* -S [blend of [3]*sham* and *amateurism*] : the practice of treating certain athletes as amateurs so that they will be eligible for amateur competition while subsidizing them with illegal payments or with excessive expense money
sham·bol·ic \ˌshamˈbälik, -ˈbȯl-\ *adj* [prob. fr. *shambles* (after E *symbol : symbolic*)] *chiefly Brit* : UNKEMPT, UNTIDY, DISORDERED
shape* *vt* : to modify (behavior) by rewarding changes that tend toward a desired response
shape memory *n* : the ability of a material to resume an original configuration after applied changes (as of temperature or pressure) ⟨*shape memory* alloys⟩
share* *vt* : to tell (as thoughts or experiences) to others — often used with *with* ~ *vi* : to tell insights, thoughts, reflections, or experiences to others — often used with *with*
shareware \ˈ=ˌ=\ *n* [[2]*share* + *-ware* (as in *software* — herein)] : software with usu. limited capability or incomplete documentation which is available for trial use at little or no cost but which can be upgraded upon payment of a fee to the author
shark repellent *n* : any of various measures that a company uses to fend off unwanted takeover attempts
shar–pei \ˈshäˈpā *also* ˈshär-\ *n, pl* **shar–peis** *often cap S&P* [Chin (Cant) *sà* sand + *pèi* fur] : any of an ancient breed of dogs originating in China that have loose wrinkled skin esp. when young, a short bristly coat, blue-black tongue, and wide blunt muzzle
shatter cone *n* : a conical fragment of rock that has striations radiating from the apex and that is formed by high pressure (as from volcanism or meteorite impact)
sha·zam \shəˈzam, -ˈzaa(ə)m\ *interj* [incantation used by the comic-strip hero Captain Marvel, fr. *S*olomon, *H*ercules, *A*tlas, *Z*eus, *A*chilles, and *M*ercury, on whom he called] — used to indicate an instantaneous transformation or appearance
s/he \ˈshēˈhē; ˈshē-ə(r)ˈhē; ˈshēˌslashˈhē\ *pron* : she or he — used in writing as a pronoun of common gender
shell* *n* **1** : a plain usu. sleeveless overblouse **2** *or* **shell company** : a business that exists without assets or independent operation as a legal entity through which another company can conduct certain dealings
shell* *vt* : to score heavily against (as a pitcher in baseball)
shell–shocked \ˈ=ˌ=\ *adj* : mentally confused, upset, or exhausted as a result of excessive stress
sher·got·tite \ˈshərgəˌtīt\ *n* -S [*Shergotty* (Sherghati), town in Bihar state, India, where such a meteorite was collected in 1865 + E *-ite*] : any of a class of achondritic geologically young meteorites of feldspar and pyroxene — compare CHASSIGNITE *in the Dict*
sherpa* *n* : an artificial fiber (as an acrylic fiber) spun to resemble wool fleece and used in many of the same applications
shi·at·su \shēˈät(ˌ)sü\ *n* -S *often cap* [short for Jap *shiatsuryōhō*, lit., finger-pressure therapy, fr. *shi-* finger + *-atsu* pressure + *ryōhō* treatment] : acupressure esp. of a form that originated in Japan
shi·ba inu \ˈshēbäˈēnü\ *n* -S *usu cap S&I* [Jap *shiba-inu*, fr. *shiba* brushwood + *inu* dog] : any of a breed of agile small dogs developed in Japan that have a muscular body and a short straight stiff outer coat and a soft thick undercoat
shield law *n* : a law that protects journalists from forced disclosure of confidential news sources
shift* *n* **1** : a movement of bits in a computer register a specified number of places to the right or left **2** : the act or an instance of depressing the shift key (as on a typewriter)
shih tzu \ˈshēdˈzü, -ˈzü, -tˈsü\ *n, pl* **shih tzus** *also* **shih tzu** *often cap S&T* [Chin (Pek) *shih*[1]*tzŭ kou*[3], fr. *shih*[1]*tzŭ* lion (fr. *shih*[1] lion + *tzŭ*, noun suffix) + *kou*[3] dog] : any of an old Chinese breed of friendly toy dogs that have a square short unwrinkled muzzle, short muscular legs, and a long dense flowing coat
shii·ta·ke *also* **shi·ta·ke** \shēˈtäkē\ *n* -S [Jap *shiitake*, fr. *shiy* the Japanese chinquapin (*Castanopsis cuspidata*) + *take* mushroom] : a large dark Oriental mushroom (*Lentinus edodes*) of the family Agaricaceae widely cultivated esp. on woods of the beech family for its edible flavorful cap
shilingi \ˈshiliŋgē\ *n, pl* **shilingi** [Swahili, fr. E *shilling*] : the shilling of Tanzania
shill* *n* **1** : one who makes a sales pitch or serves as a promoter ⟨a ~ for the food industry —F.J.Prial⟩ **2** : PITCH 9b
shill* *vi* : to act as a spokesperson or promoter
ship* *n* : SPACECRAFT
shiraz* *n, usu cap* **1** : the Syrah grape grown chiefly in Australia and the Republic of So. Africa **2** : a red wine made from the Shiraz grape
shirtdress \ˈ=ˌ=\ *n* : a dress that is patterned after a shirt and has buttons down the front and a collar
shirt–jac \ˈ=ˌjak\ *n* -S [by shortening] : SHIRT JACKET *herein*
shirt jacket *n* : a jacket having an open shirtlike collar and usu. long sleeves with cuffs : a shirt designed to be worn over another shirt or blouse
shirt suit *n* : a clothing ensemble consisting of a shirt or shirt jacket and matching pants
shirt·waist·er \ˈ=ˌwāstə(r)\ *n* -S [*shirtwaist* + *-er*] *Brit* : a shirtwaist dress : SHIRTDRESS *herein*
shit* *n* : any of several intoxicating or narcotic drugs; *esp* : HEROIN — usu. considered vulgar
shithead \ˈ=ˌ=\ *n* : a contemptible person — usu. considered vulgar

shitkicker \ˈ=ˌ==\ *n* **1** *slang* : an unsophisticated person from a rural area **2** *slang* : a fan or performer of country and western music
shit·less \ˈshitləs\ *adv* : to an extreme degree — used as an intensive ⟨scared ~⟩; usu. considered vulgar
shitload \ˈ=ˌ=\ *n* : a very large amount : LOT — usu. considered vulgar
shlep *var of* SCHLEPP *herein*
shlepper *var of* SCHLEPP *herein*
shlock *var of* SCHLOCK *herein*
shlong *var of* SCHLONG *herein*
shlub \ˈshləb\ *n* -S [Yiddish *zhlob, zhlub* yokel, boor, fr. Pol *żłób* blockhead, lit., crib, trough; akin to Serbo-Croatian *žlijeb* gutter, trough, Russ *zhëlob*] : SCHLEMIEL ⟨a sleazy, sad ~ —*People*⟩
shmear *var of* SCHMEAR *herein*
shmuck *var of* SCHMUCK *herein*
shocked *adj* [fr. past part. of [4]*shock*] *of a mineral* : having a crystal structure deformed by exposure to sudden extremely high pressure (as from a meteorite impact or a nuclear blast) ⟨~ quartz⟩
shock jock *n* : a radio personality noted for provocative or inflammatory commentary
shoot* *vt* **1** : to inject (an illicit drug) esp. into the bloodstream **2** *chiefly Brit* : RID 2b — usu. used in the past part. in the phrase *be shot of* or *get shot of* ⟨pared costs ruthlessly and got *shot* of its potentially worst loans —*Economist*⟩ — **shoot from the hip** : to act or speak hastily without consideration of the consequences — **shoot oneself in the foot** : to act against one's own best interests — **shoot the curl** *or* **shoot the tube** : to surf into or through the curl of a wave — **shoot the pier** : to surf between the pilings of an ocean pier
shoot down* *vt* **1** : to put an end to : make ineffective or void : DEFEAT **2** : DEFLATE, RIDICULE; *also* : REPROVE **3** : to expose weakness or inaccuracy in : DISCREDIT ⟨*shoot down* a theory⟩
shootdown \ˈ=ˌ=\ *n* -S [*shoot down*, v.] : an act of shooting something (as an aircraft) down
shoot–'em–up \ˈ==ˌ=\ *n* -S : a movie, television show, or computer game with much shooting and killing
shooter* *n* : a shot of whiskey or whiskey diluted with something (as soda); *also* : a bit of food (as a raw oyster) served in a shot glass
shoot·out** \ˈ=ˌ=\ *n* **1** : a sharp struggle between adversaries ⟨a corporate ~⟩ **2** : a shooting competition in overtime that is used to determine the winner of a game (as in soccer or hockey) tied at the end of regular play
shop* *vt* : to offer for sale — often used with *around* ⟨*shopping* the manuscript around to the smaller publishers⟩
shop·a·hol·ic \ˌshäpəˈhȯlik, -ˈhäl-\ *n* -S [[2]*shop* + *-aholic* (herein)] : one who is extremely or excessively fond of shopping
shopper* *n* : a usu. free paper carrying advertising and sometimes local news
shopping bag *n* : a bag (as of strong paper or plastic) that has handles and is intended for carrying purchases
shopping–bag lady \ˈ===ˌ=\ *n* : BAG LADY *herein*
shopping mall *n* **1** : a pedestrian mall lined with shops **2** : a large usu. suburban building or group of buildings containing various shops with associated passageways
short* *adj* : near the end of one's tour of duty
short* *vt* : to sell (as stocks) short
short fuse *n* : a tendency to get angry quickly : a quick temper
short list *n* : a list of candidates for final consideration (as for a position or a prize)
short–list \(ˈ)=ˌ=\ *vt* [*short list* (herein)] *chiefly Brit* : to place on a short list
short position* *n* : the market position of a trader who has made but not yet covered a short sale
shot* *n* : an act, instance, or result of hitting: **a** : BLOW ⟨the boxer took a hard ~ to the body⟩ **b** : a hard-hit baseball ⟨a three-run ~ over the left-field wall⟩
shot clock *n* : a clock in basketball that displays a countdown of the time within which shooting the ball is required; *also* : the extent of time delimited by a shot clock
shotgun* *n* : an offensive football formation in which the quarterback plays a few yards behind the line of scrimmage and the other backs are scattered as flankers or slotbacks
shotmaking \ˈ=ˌ==\ *n* -S : the ability to make accurate or successful shots (as in golf or basketball)
shoulder belt *or* **shoulder harness** *n* : an automobile safety belt worn across the torso and over the shoulder
show* *vi* : to present an animal (as a dog or horse) for judging in a show or competition
show–and–tell \ˈ==ˈ=\ *n* **1** : a classroom exercise in which children display an item and talk about it **2** : a public display or demonstration
showboat* *n* : one who tries to attract attention by conspicuous behavior
showboat *vi* [*showboat*, n. (herein)] : to show off
show house *n* : a house furnished and decorated for exhibition
showstopper* *n* : something or someone exceptionally arresting or attractive ⟨the gold crown was the ~ of the exhibition⟩ — **showstopping** \ˈ=ˌ==\ *adj*
show trial *n* : a trial (as of political opponents) in which the verdict is rigged and a public confession is often extracted
shrink* *n* **1** [short for *headshrinker*] : a clinical psychiatrist or psychologist **2** : a woman's short usu. sleeveless sweater often worn over a long-sleeved blouse or sweater
shrink–wrap \ˈ=ˈ=\ *vt* : to wrap (as a book or meat) in tough clear plastic film that is then shrunk (as by heating) to form a tightly fitting package — **shrink–wrap** \ˈ=ˌ=\ *n*
shtick *or* **schtick** *also* **shtik** \ˈshtik\ *n* -S [Yiddish *shtik*, lit., piece, fr. MHG *stücke*, fr. OHG *stucki* — more at STOCK] **1** : a show-business routine, gimmick, or gag : BIT **2** : one's special trait, interest, or activity : BAG *herein*, THING *herein*
[1]**shuck** \ˈshək\ *n* -S [origin unknown] : a wily deception : SHAM
[2]**shuck** \ˈ"\ *vi* : to talk or act deceptively ~ *vt* : DECEIVE, TRICK
shun·pik·er \ˈshənˌpīkə(r)\ *n* -S [*shunpike* + [2]*-er*] : one who engages in shunpiking
shun·pik·ing \-kiŋ\ *n* -S [*shunpike* + [3]*-ing*] : the practice of avoiding superhighways esp. for the pleasure of driving on back roads — **shunpike** \ˈ=ˌ=\ *vi*
shunt* *n* **1** *chiefly Brit* : a minor collision esp. in auto racing **2** : a device (as a narrow tube) used to establish an artificial passage by which a bodily fluid is diverted from one vessel or part to another
shuttle* *n* : SPACE SHUTTLE *herein*
shuttle diplomacy *n* : negotiations esp. between nations carried on by an intermediary who shuttles back and forth between the disputants
SI *abbr* [F *Système International d'Unités*] International System of Units *herein*
sibling* *n* : one of two or more things related by a common tie or characteristic ⟨the sun has its starry ~: Alpha Centauri —Philip Morrison⟩
sick building syndrome *n* : a set of symptoms (as headache, fatigue, and eye irritation) typically affecting workers in modern airtight office buildings that is believed to be caused by indoor pollutants (as formaldehyde fumes, particulate matter, or microorganisms)
sick·ie *also* **sick·ee** \ˈsikē\ *n* -S [[1]*sick* + *-ie* or [2]*-ee*] : a person who is morally or mentally sick
sicko \ˈsik(ˌ)ō\ *n* -S [[1]*sick* + [1]*-o*] : SICKIE *herein*
sick–out \ˈ=ˌ=\ *n* -S [[1]*sick* + walk*out*] : an organized absence from work by workers on the pretext of sickness in order to apply pressure to management without an actual strike
sidebar* *n* : a conference between the judge, the lawyers, and sometimes the parties to a case that the jury does not hear — called also *sidebar conference*
sidedress \ˈ=ˌ=\ *n* [*side-dress*, v.] **1** : plant nutrients used to side-dress a crop **2** : the act or process of side-dressing a crop
side effect* *n* : a secondary and sometimes adverse effect ⟨deregulation is having some unpleasant *side effects* —Susan Lee⟩
side–scan sonar \ˈ=ˌ=-\ *n* : a sonar that scans the ocean floor to the side of a ship's track and is used esp. for mapping the ocean bottom
side–straddle hop \ˈ=ˌ==-\ *n* : JUMPING-JACK *herein*
sidestream \ˈ=ˌ=\ *adj* [[1]*side* + main*stream*] : relating to or being tobacco smoke that is emitted from the lighted end of a cigarette or cigar — compare MAINSTREAM 2 *herein*
SIDS *abbr* sudden infant death syndrome *herein*
sie·mens \ˈsēmənz, ˈzē-\ *n, pl* **siemens** [after Werner von *Siemens* †1892 Ger. electrical engineer and inventor] : a unit of conductance in the mks system equivalent to one ampere per volt
sie·vert \ˈsēvərt\ *n* -S [after Rolf Maximilian *Sievert* †1966 Swed. radiologist] : an SI unit for dosage of ionizing radiation equal to 100 rems — abbr. *Sv*
SIG·INT \ˈsigˌint\ *n* -S *sometimes not cap* [*sig*nals *int*elligence] : intelligence obtained through the interception of transmission signals; *also* : an agency engaged in obtaining such information
sigma* *or* **sigma particle** *n* : an unstable subatomic particle of the baryon family existing in positive, negative, and neutral charge states with masses respectively 2328, 2343, and 2333 times the mass of an electron
sigma factor *n* : a detachable polypeptide subunit of RNA polymerase that facilitates the initiation of transcription by recognizing specific DNA promoter sites
sign* *n* : SIGN LANGUAGE
sign·age \ˈsīnij\ *n* -S [[1]*sign* + *-age*] : signs (as of identification, warning, or direction) or a system or design of signs
significance level *n* : LEVEL OF SIGNIFICANCE *herein*
significant other *n* : a person who is important to one's well-being; *esp* : a spouse or one in a similar relationship
signified *n* -S [fr. past part. of *signify*; trans. of F *signifié*] : a concept or meaning as distinguished from a sign through which it is communicated — compare SIGNIFIER 1
signifier* *n* **1** [trans. of F *signifiant*] : a symbol, sound, or image (as a word) that represents an underlying concept or meaning **2** : one who engages in signifying
signify* *vi* : to engage in signifying
sig·ni·fy·ing \ˈsignəˌfīiŋ\ *n* -S [fr. gerund of *signify*] : a good-natured needling or goading esp. among urban blacks by means of indirect gibes and clever often preposterous put-downs; *also* : DOZENS *herein*
sign·ing \ˈsīniŋ\ *n* -S [fr. gerund of [2]*sign*] **1** : SIGNAGE *herein* ⟨highway ~⟩ **2** : SIGN LANGUAGE
sign off* *vi* : to approve or acknowledge something by or as if by a signature — usu. used with *on* ⟨*sign off* on a memo⟩
sign on* *vi* : to announce the start of broadcasting for the day — **sign–on** \ˈ=ˌ=\ *n* -S
si·jo \ˈsē(ˌ)jō\ *n* -S [Korean] : an unrhymed Korean verse form appearing in Korean in 3 lines of 14 to 16 syllables and usu. in English translation in 6 shorter lines
Si·las·tic \sə̇ˈlastik, sī-\ *trademark* — used for a soft pliable plastic
sil·den·a·fil \silˈdenəˌfil\ *n* -S [perh. by alter. and recombination of letters fr. *sulfonyl, phenyl,* and *pyrimidine*] : a drug that is used in the form of its citrate $C_{22}H_{30}N_6O_4S$ to treat erectile dysfunction in males, that by suppressing a phosphodiesterase enzyme also suppresses the enzyme's inhibitory effect on the hormone cyclic GMP, and that enables the cyclic GMP produced during sexual arousal to initiate the muscular and vascular changes which produce an erection
silent* *adj* : having no detectable function or effect ⟨~ DNA⟩ ⟨~ genes⟩
silicon nitride *n* : any of several compounds of silicon and nitrogen; *specif* : a compound Si_3N_4 that is a hard ceramic used in high-temperature applications, as an insulator in semiconductor electronic devices, and in fibrous form in composites
silky terrier *also* **silky** *n* -ES : a low-set toy terrier that weighs 8 to 10 pounds, has a flat silky glossy coat colored blue with tan on the head, chest, and legs, and is derived from crosses of the Australian terrier with the Yorkshire terrier
silly season* *n* : a period marked by frivolous, outlandish, or illogical activity or behavior ⟨the start of the *silly season* on Wall Street —William Gofen⟩
silverback* *n* : an older adult usu. dominant male gorilla having gray or whitish hair on the back
silver bullet *n* : something that acts as a magical weapon; *esp* : one that instantly solves a long-standing problem
sil·vex \ˈsilˌveks\ *n* -ES [prob. fr. L *silva* wood + E *ex*terminator] : a toxic selective herbicide $C_9H_7Cl_3O_3$ formerly in use
sil·vi·chemical \ˈsilvə̇+\ *n* [L *silva* wood + E *-i-* + *chemical*] : any of numerous chemicals derived from wood
sim* *abbr* simulator; simulation
si·ma·zine \ˈsīməˌzēn\ *n* -S [*sim-* (prob. by shortening & alter. fr. *symmetrical*) + tri*azine*] : a selective herbicide $C_7H_{12}N_5Cl$ used esp. to control weeds
simian immunodeficiency virus *n* : SIV *herein*
simple* *adj, of a statistical hypothesis* : specifying exact values for one or more statistical parameters — compare COMPOSITE *herein*
simple closed curve *n* : JORDAN CURVE
simply connected *adj* : being or characterized by a surface divided into two separate parts by every closed curve it contains
simply ordered *adj* : having any two elements connected by a relationship that is reflexive, antisymmetric, and transitive
simulate* *vt* : to make a simulation of (as a physical system) — **sim·u·la·tive** \ˈsimyəˌlād·ə̇v\ *adj*
simulation* *n* **1** : the imitative representation of the functioning of one system or process by means of the functioning of another ⟨a computer ~ of an industrial process⟩ **2** : examination of a problem often not subject to direct experimentation by means of a simulator (as a programmed computer)
sine* *n* : a trigonometric function $\sin \theta$ that for all real numbers θ is exactly equal to the sine of an angle of measure θ in radians and that is given by the sum of the alternating series

$$\sin \theta = \theta - \frac{\theta^3}{3!} + \frac{\theta^5}{5!} - \frac{\theta^7}{7!} + \frac{\theta^9}{9!} - \ldots$$

sing–along \ˈ=ˌ=\ *n* -S [*sing along*, v.] : SONGFEST; *also* : a song appropriate for a sing-along
single* *n* : an unmarried person and esp. one young and socially active — usu. used in pl. ⟨a way of life for young ~*s* —Norman Mailer⟩ ⟨a ~*s* weekend⟩
single–blind \ˈ==ˌ=\ *adj* : of, relating to, or being an experimental procedure in which the experimenters but not the subjects know the makeup of the test and control groups during the actual course of the experiments — compare DOUBLE-BLIND *herein*
single bond* *n* : a chemical bond consisting of one covalent bond between two atoms in a molecule esp. when the atoms can have more than one covalent bond
single–cell protein \ˈ==ˈ=-\ *n* : protein that consists of processed microorganisms (as yeasts or bacteria) grown in culture and that is used as a source of food esp. for livestock
single–hander \ˈ=ˈ==\ *n* : a person who sails single-handed
single·hood \ˈsiŋgəlˌhu̇d\ *n* -S : the state of being single and esp. unmarried
single–lens reflex \ˈ=ˈ=-\ *n* [*single-lens* + *reflex*, short for *reflex camera*] : a camera having a single lens that forms an image which is reflected to the viewfinder or recorded on film — abbr. *SLR*
single–payer \ˈ===\ *adj* : of, relating to, or being a system in which health care providers are paid for their services by the government rather than by private insurers
single photon emission computed tomography *n* : a medical imaging technique that is used esp. for mapping brain function and that is similar to positron-emission tomography in using the photons emitted by the agency of a radioactive tracer to create an image but that differs in being able to detect only a single photon for each nuclear disintegration and in generating a lower-quality image — abbr. *SPECT*
singles bar *n* : a bar that caters esp. to young unmarried men and women
singlet* *n* : an elementary particle not part of a multiplet
singleton* *n* : a mathematical set that contains one element
singular* *adj* **1** *of a matrix* : having a determinant equal to zero **2** *of a linear transformation* : having the property that the matrix of coefficients of the new variables has a determinant equal to zero
singularity* *n* **1** : a point at which the derivative of a given function of a real or complex variable does not exist but every neighborhood of which contains points for which the derivative exists **2** : a point or region of infinite mass density at which space and time are infinitely distorted by gravitational forces that is held to be the final state of matter falling into a black hole
singular point *n* : SINGULARITY 1 *herein*
sin·se·mil·la \ˌsinsəˈmēl(y)ə\ *n* -S [MexSp, fr. *sin semilla* without seed] : highly potent marijuana from female plants that are specially tended and kept seedless by preventing pollination in order to induce a high resin content; *also* : a female hemp plant grown to produce sinsemilla
sin tax *n* : a tax on substances or activities traditionally considered sinful (as tobacco, liquor, or gambling)
sir·ta·ki \sirˈtākē\ *n* -S [NGk *syrtaki*, fr. *syrtos* kind of folk dance, fr. Gk, prob. fr. *syrtos* trailing, verbal of *syrein* to drag, trail behind — more at SWERVE] : a Greek circle dance similar to a hora
sissy bar *n* : a narrow inverted U-shaped bar rising from behind the seat of a motorcycle or bicycle that is designed to support a driver or passenger
sister* *n* **1** : SOUL SISTER *herein* **2** : a member of a sorority
sisterhood* *n* : a relationship of women united by a common cause or motivation ⟨~ of feminists⟩ ⟨gay ~⟩; *also* : women united in a sisterhood
sit·com \ˈsitˌkäm\ *n* -S [*sit*uation *com*edy (herein)] : SITUATION COMEDY *herein*
site* *n* : one or more Internet addresses at which an individual or organization provides information to others; *esp* : WEB SITE *herein*
situation comedy *n* : a radio or television comedy series that involves a continuing cast of characters in a succession of unconnected episodes
situation ethics *or* **situational ethics** *n pl but sing or pl in constr* [trans. of G *situationsethik*] : a system of ethics by which acts are judged within their contexts instead of by categorical principles
SIV \ˌesˌīˈvē\ *n* -S [*s*imian *i*mmunodeficiency *v*irus] : a retrovirus (genus *Lentivirus*) that causes a disease in monkeys similar to AIDS and that is closely related to HIV-2
sixth man *n* : a player in basketball who is regularly used as the first of a team's substitutes in a game
sizzle* *n* **1** : PIZZAZZ *herein* ⟨added a little ~ to a show that had begun to sputter —David Gritten⟩ **2** : EXCITEMENT ⟨conventioneers . . . looking for a bit of ~ —D.A.Lanegran⟩
sjö·gren's syndrome \ˈshœ̄grənz-\ *also* **sjögren syndrome** *or* **sjögren's disease** *n, usu cap 1st S* [after H.S.C. *Sjögren* †1986 Swed. ophthalmologist] : a chronic inflammatory autoimmune disease that affects esp. older women, that is characterized by dryness of mucous membranes esp. of the eyes and mouth and by infiltration of the affected tissues by lymphocytes, and that is often associated with rheumatoid arthritis
ska \ˈskä\ *n* -S [origin unknown] : popular music of Jamaican origin that combines elements of traditional Caribbean rhythms and jazz
skag *var of* SCAG *herein*
skanky \ˈskaŋkē\ *adj* -ER/-EST [origin unknown] **1** *slang* : repugnantly filthy or squalid **2** *slang* : of low or sleazy character
[1]**skate·board** \ˈ=ˌ=\ *n* [[2]*skate* + *board*] : a short board mounted on small wheels that is used for coasting and often for performing athletic stunts
[2]**skateboard** *vi* -ED/-ING/-S : to ride or perform stunts on a skateboard — **skate·board·er** \-ə(r)\ *n* -S — **skate·board·ing** \-iŋ\ *n* -S
skew field *n* : a mathematical field in which multiplication is not commutative
skew lines *n pl* : straight lines that do not intersect and are not in the same plane
skibob \ˈ=ˌ=\ *n* [[1]*ski* + [8]*bob*] : a vehicle that resembles a bicycle with two short skis in place of wheels and that is used for gliding downhill over snow by a rider wearing miniature skis for balance — **ski·bob·ber** \-ə(r)\ *n* — **ski·bob·bing** \-iŋ\ *n* -S
skid* *n* : a losing streak ⟨a five-game ~⟩
skid pad *n* : a large usu. circular area of asphalt that is oiled to make it slick and that is used for testing automobiles and motorcycles with controlled skids and spins
skif·fle \ˈskifəl\ *n* -S [perh. imit.] : American jazz or folk music played entirely or in part on improvised or nonstandard instruments (as jugs, washboards, or jew's harps); *also* : a derivative form of music formerly popular in Great Britain featuring vocals with a simple instrumental accompaniment
skim* *vt* **1** : to remove or conceal (as a portion of casino profits) to avoid payment of taxes **2** : EMBEZZLE 3 ⟨*skimming* money from tax revenues⟩ ~ *vi* : to acquire money by embezzling
ski mask *n* : a knit fabric mask worn esp. by skiers for protection from the cold
skimmer* *n* : a fitted sleeveless usu. flaring sheathlike dress
skin* *n* : a mutual touching or slapping of the palms that takes the place of a handshake — used chiefly in the phrases *give skin* or *give me skin*
skin \ˈskin\ *adj* [[1]*skin*] : involving subjects who are nude ⟨expected to conduct ~ searches for weapons —Diane K. Shah⟩; *specif* : devoted to showing nudes ⟨~ magazines⟩
skin flick *n* : a motion picture characterized by nudity and explicit sexual situations
skinhead* *n* : a usu. white male belonging to any of various sometimes violent youth gangs whose members have close-shaven hair, wear similar clothes (as blue jeans, boots, T-shirts, and leather jackets), and often espouse white-supremacist beliefs
skin·ner·ian \skə̇ˈnirēən, -ˈner-\ *adj, usu cap* [Burrhus Frederick *Skinner* †1990 Am. psychologist + E *-ian*] : of, relating to, or suggestive of the behavioristic theories of B.F. Skinner — **skinnerian** *n* -S *usu cap*
skin·ny \ˈskinē\ *n* [perh. fr. [1]*skin* + [4]*-y*] *slang* : inside information : DOPE ⟨get the straight ~ on what's going on —John Geary⟩
[1]**skin·ny–dip** \ˈskinēˌdip\ *vi* [[1]*skin* + [4]*-y* + [1]*dip*] : to swim nude — **skin·ny–dip·per** \-ə(r)\ *n* — **skin·ny–dip·ping** \-iŋ\ *n*
[2]**skinny–dip** \ˈ"\ *n* : a swim in the nude
skin–pop \ˈ=ˌ=\ *vb* [[1]*skin* + *pop* (herein)] *vi* : to inject a drug subcutaneously rather than into a vein ~ *vt* : to inject (a drug) by skin-popping — **skin–popper** \ˈ=ˌ==\ *n*
skint \ˈskint\ *adj* [perh. alter. of *skinned*, past part. of [2]*skin*] *Brit* : BROKE 2
skirt steak *n* : a narrow boneless strip of tender beef cut from the plate that is usu. broiled
ski touring *n* : cross-country skiing for pleasure — **ski tourer** *n*
skiwear \ˈ=ˌ=\ *n* : clothing for wear while skiing
skosh \ˈskōsh\ *n* -ES [Jap *sukoshi*] : a small amount : [3]BIT 3c, SMIDGEN — usu. used adverbially with *a* ⟨just a ~ bit shook —Josiah Bunting⟩
skunk works *n pl but sing or pl in constr* [fr. Big Barnsmell's *Skonk Works*, illicit distillery in the comic strip *Li'l Abner*, by Al Capp †1979 Am. cartoonist] : a usu. small and often isolated department or facility (as for engineering research and development) that functions with minimal supervision within a company or corporation
skybox \ˈ=ˌ=\ *n* : a roofed enclosure of private seats situated high in

a sports stadium and typically featuring luxurious amenities (as a private bar)

sky·div·ing \ˈskīˌdīviŋ\ *n* -s : the sport of jumping from an airplane at a moderate altitude (as 6000 feet) and executing various tumbles and dives before pulling the rip cord of a parachute — **sky diver** *n*

sky·jack \ˈskīˌjak\ *vt* [¹*sky* + *-jack* (as in *hijack*)] : to commandeer (an airplane in flight) by the threat of violence — **sky·jack·er** \-ə(r)\ *n* -s — **sky·jack·ing** \-iŋ\ *n* -s

sky marshal *n* : an armed federal officer in plainclothes who is assigned to prevent skyjackings

skywalk \ˈ=ˌ=\ *n* : a usu. enclosed aerial walkway connecting two buildings

slacker* *n* : a person and esp. a young person who is perceived to be disaffected, apathetic, cynical, or lacking ambition — **slacker** *adj*

slag* *n, chiefly Brit, slang* : a lewd or promiscuous woman : TRAMP

slam* *n* [²*slam*] **1** : SLAMMER *herein* **2** : a poetry competition performed before judges

slam dance *n* : a type of dance (as to punk rock) in which leaping dancers collide against each other — **slam dance** *vi* — **slam dancing** *n*

slam dunk *n* **1** : DUNK SHOT **2** : SURE THING ⟨the case looks like a *slam dunk* for the plaintiff —Jay Finegan⟩ — **slam–dunk** \(ˈ)=ˈ=\ *vb*

slam·mer \ˈslamə(r), -aa(ə)m-\ *n* -s [³*slam* + ²*-er*] : JAIL, PRISON

slant board *n* : a tiltable usu. padded board on which one lies (as for relaxation or while performing exercises) with the feet elevated

slap shot *n* : a hard usu. long-range shot in ice hockey that is made with a swinging stroke

slash–and–burn* *adj* : ruthlessly destructive ⟨*slash–and–burn* tactics⟩ ⟨*slash–and–burn* criticism⟩

SLBM *abbr or n* -s : a submarine-launched ballistic missile

SLE *abbr* systemic lupus erythematosus

sleaze \ˈslēz\ *n* -s [back-formation fr. *sleazy*] **1** : sleazy quality, appearance, or behavior ⟨bureaucratic ~⟩; *also* : sleazy material ⟨I don't read ~ —Peter Lawford⟩ **2** : a sleazy person : a person of low character ⟨his role as a low-down ~ —John Podhoretz⟩

sleaze·bag \ˈ=ˌ=\ *n, slang* : SLEAZEBALL *herein*

sleazeball \ˈ=ˌ=\ *n, slang* : a sleazy person : SLEAZE *herein*

sleazo \ˈslē(ˌ)zō\ *adj* [*sleazy* + ¹*-o*] *slang* : SLEAZY — **sleazo** *n* -s *slang*

sleazoid \-(ˌ)ȯid\ *adj* [*sleazy* + ²*-oid*] *slang* : SLEAZY — **sleazoid** *n* -s *slang*

sleep apnea *n* : brief periods of recurrent cessation of breathing during sleep that is caused esp. by obstruction of the airway or a disturbance in the brain's respiratory center and is associated esp. with excessive daytime sleepiness

sleep around *vi* : to engage in sex promiscuously

sleeper* *n* **1** *chiefly Brit* : a small usu. gold earring or stud worn esp. in a recently pierced ear to prevent the hole from closing **2** : MOLE *herein*

sleeping pill *n* : a drug and esp. a barbiturate that is taken as a tablet or capsule to induce sleep

sleeping tablet *n, chiefly Brit* : SLEEPING PILL *herein*

sleepover \ˈ=ˌ==\ *n* [*sleep over*, v.] : an overnight stay ⟨a ~ at a friend's home⟩

s level \ˈes-\ *n, usu cap S* [*s*cholarship] **1** : the highest of three levels of standardized British examinations in a secondary school subject used as a qualification for university entrance; *also* : the successful completion of an S-level examination in a particular subject — called also *Scholarship level*; compare A LEVEL *herein*, O LEVEL *herein* **2 a** : the level of education required to pass an S-level examination **b** : a course leading to an S-level examination

slick* *n* : a smooth tire used for racing cars on dry paved surfaces

slide guitar *n* : BOTTLENECK *herein*

slimeball* *n*, *slang* : a repulsive or odious person

slim·mer \ˈslimə(r\ *n* -s [²*slim* + ²*-er*] *chiefly Brit* : DIETER

slim·nas·tics \ˌslimˈnastiks\ *n pl but sing in constr* [blend of ¹*slim* and *gymnastics*] : exercises designed to reduce one's weight

slingshot* *n* **1** : a maneuver in auto racing in which a drafting car accelerates past the car in front by using reserve power **2** : a dragster in which the driver sits behind the rear wheels

slippery slope *n* : a course of action that seems to lead inevitably from one action or result to another with unintended adverse consequences ⟨we are far down the *slippery slope* to the betrayal of the articulate —*Publishers Weekly*⟩

slipstream* *n* **1** : an area of reduced air pressure and forward suction immediately behind a rapidly moving vehicle (as a racing car) **2** *chiefly Brit* : something suggesting a slipstream esp. in exerting a strong pull ⟨came to power in the ~ of his protector —John le Carré⟩

slipstream *vi* : to drive or ride in a vehicle's slipstream

slipway* *n* : a space between docks

slit card *n* : a display card with a slit whereby it is attached to a book

slope* *n* : the slope of the line tangent to a plane curve at a point

slope–intercept form \ˈ=ˌ=ˈ==ˌ=-\ *n* : the equation of a straight line in the form $y = mx + b$ where m is the slope of the line and b is the y-intercept of its graph — compare POINT-SLOPE FORM *herein*

sloppy joe* *n* : ground beef cooked in a seasoned sauce (as chili) and usu. served on a bun

sloshed \ˈsläsht\ *adj* [fr. past part. of ²*slosh*] *slang* : DRUNK

slot* *n* **1** : a gap between an end and a tackle in an offensive line in football **2** : the area directly in front of the goal in ice hockey ⟨scored on a shot from the ~⟩

slotback \ˈ=ˌ=\ *n* : an offensive halfback in football who lines up just behind the slot between an offensive end and tackle

slot car *n* : an electric toy racing automobile that has an arm underneath fitting into a groove for guidance and metal strips alongside the groove for supplying electricity and that is remotely controlled by the operator's hand-held rheostat

slot racing *n* : the racing of slot cars — **slot racer** *n*

slow–pitch *also* **slo–pitch** \ˈslōˌpich\ *n* : softball in which each side has 10 players, each pitch must travel in an arc from 3 to 10 feet high in order to be legal, and base stealing is not permitted

slow–twitch \ˈ=ˈ=\ *adj* : of, relating to, or being muscle fiber that contracts slowly esp. during sustained physical activity requiring endurance — compare FAST-TWITCH *herein*

slow virus *n* : any of various viruses or prions having a long incubation period between infection and the clinical appearance of the slowly progressive serious or fatal disease (as scrapie or Creutzfeldt-Jakob disease) associated with it

slow–wave sleep \ˈ=ˌ=-\ *n* : a state of deep usu. dreamless sleep that occurs regularly during a normal period of sleep with intervening periods of REM sleep and that is characterized by delta waves and a low level of autonomic physiological activity

SLR \ˌes(ˌ)elˈär\ *abbr or n* -s single-lens reflex *herein*

slugging percentage *also* **slugging average** *n* : the ratio of the total number of bases reached on base hits to official times at bat for a baseball player expressed as a 3-place decimal

slumlord \ˈ=ˌ=\ *n* -s [¹*slum* + land*lord*] : a landlord who receives inflated rents from substandard neglected properties

slump·fla·tion \ˌsləmpˈflāshən\ *n* -s [*slump* + in*flation*] : a state or period of combined economic decline and rising inflation

slurb \ˈsləb\ *n* -s [*sl*- (as in *sloppy, sleazy, slovenly, slipshod*) + sub*urb*] : a suburb characterized by wearisomely uniform and usu. poorly constructed houses

slur·vian \ˈslərvēən, -lәv-, -ləiv-\ *n, usu cap* [¹*slur* + *-v-* (as in *Peruvian*) + ¹*-an*] : speech characterized by slurring

slush* *n* **1** : a partially frozen soft drink **2** : unsolicited material submitted to a publisher

smack \ˈsmak\ *n* -s [perh. fr. Yiddish *shmek* sniff, whiff, fr. *shmekn* to smell, reek of, fr. MHG *smecken, smacken* to taste, try, fr. OHG *smecken* — more at SMACK] *slang* : HEROIN

small cap \-ˈkap\ *n* [*cap* short for *capitalization*] : a company with a relatively low stock market capitalization value; *also* the stock of such a company

small–cell lung cancer \ˈ=ˌ=-\ *n* : cancer of a highly malignant form that affects the lungs, tends to metastasize to other parts of the body and is characterized by small round or oval cells resembling oat grains and having little cytoplasm — called also *small-cell carcinoma*

smaller european elm bark beetle *n, usu cap 1st E* : ELM BARK BEETLE b

small forward *n* : a basketball forward who is usu. smaller than a power forward and whose play is characterized by quickness and scoring ability — compare POWER FORWARD *herein*

smarm \ˈsmärm\ *n* -s [back-formation fr. *smarmy*] : smarmy language or behavior

smarmy* *adj* : of low sleazy taste or quality ⟨~ eroticism⟩ — **smarm·i·ly** \ˈsmärməlē\ *adv* — **smarm·i·ness** \ˈsmärmēnəs\ *n* -ES

smart* *n* **smarts** *pl, slang* : INTELLIGENCE, KNOW-HOW ⟨went to show that intellectual heavies could be beautiful in spite of all those ~*s* —Cyra McFadden⟩

smart* *adj* **1** : being a guided missile ⟨a laser-guided ~ bomb⟩ — compare DUMB 2 *herein* **2** : operating automatically or by automation ⟨a ~ machine tool⟩ ⟨~ windows to regulate sunlight⟩ **3** : INTELLIGENT 1 *herein*

smartass \ˈ=ˌ=\ *n* -ES [²*smart* + *-ass* (herein)] : SMART ALECK, WISE GUY — often considered vulgar — **smartass** \ˈ=ˌ=\ *or* **smart-assed** \ˈ=ˌast\ *adj*

smart card *n* : a card that functions as a credit or debit card but also has a built-in microprocessor to store and process data and records (as of bank transactions)

smart drug *n* : NOOTROPIC *herein*

smart–mouth \ˈ=ˌ=\ *n, often attrib* : one given to making remarks that aim for cleverness and wit but that strike others as cocky or annoying : SMART ALECK — **smart–mouth** *vb* — **smart–mouthed** \ˈ=ˌ=\ *adj*

smashed \ˈsmasht\ *adj* [fr. past part. of ¹*smash*] *slang* : DRUNK

smashmouth \ˈ=ˌ=\ *adj* : characterized by brute force and an absence of finesse or trickery : HARD-NOSED ⟨~ football⟩

s matrix *n, usu cap S* [*s*cattering *matrix*] : a unitary matrix in quantum mechanics the absolute values of the squares of whose elements are equal to probabilities of transition between different states — called also *scattering matrix*

smec·tite \ˈsmekˌtīt\ *n* -s [*smectis* fuller's earth (modif. of Gk *smēktris* kind of fuller's earth, fr. *smēchein* to wash off, clean) + ¹*-ite* — more at SMITE] : MONTMORILLONITE — **smec·tit·ic** \(ˈ)smekˈtid·ik\ *adj*

smiley *n* [short for *smiley face* (herein)] : EMOTICON *herein*

smiley face *n* : a line drawing of a smiling face used to show happiness or pleasure

smog* *n* : a photochemical haze caused by the action of solar ultraviolet radiation on atmosphere polluted with hydrocarbons and oxides of nitrogen esp. from automobile exhaust

smog·less \ˈ=ləs\ *adj* **1** : marked by the absence of smog ⟨a ~ city⟩ **2** : emitting no fumes that would contribute to the production of smog ⟨~ cars of the future⟩

smoke* *vt* **1** *slang* : KILL 1a **2** *slang* : to defeat decisively ⟨*smoked* the competition⟩

smoke and mirrors *n pl* [fr. the use of smoke and mirrors in conjuring tricks] : an illusion created (as by public statements) to disguise or draw attention from something potentially embarrassing or unpleasant (as the unworkability of a proposal); *also* : the means of creating such an illusion — **smoke–and–mirrors** \ˈ==ˈ=\ *adj*

smoke detector *n* : an alarm that activates automatically when it detects smoke

smoke–in \ˈ=ˌ=\ *n* -s [²*smoke* + *-in* (herein)] : a large gathering of people publicly smoking marijuana usu. in support of legalizing it

smokeless tobacco *n* : pulverized or shredded tobacco chewed or placed between cheek and gum : SNUFF

smokestack \ˈ=ˌ=\ *adj* : of, relating to, being, or characterized by manufacturing and esp. heavy industry ⟨~ industries⟩

smok·ey \ˈsmōkē, -ki\ *n* -s *usu cap* [after *Smokey* Bear, advertising symbol of U.S. Forest Service who wears a campaign hat like those of state troopers] *slang* : a policeman on highway patrol

smoking gun *n* : something that serves as conclusive evidence or proof (as of a crime or scientific theory)

smooth* *adj, of a curve* : being the representation of a function with a continuous first derivative

smoothy* *or* **smoothie*** *n* : a creamy beverage made of fruit blended with juice, milk, or yogurt

snail darter *n* : a small uncommon freshwater percid fish (*Percina tanasi*) of the Tennessee river drainage system of eastern Tennessee and northern Georgia

snail mail *n* **1** : mail delivered by a postal system **2** : ²MAIL 3a

snake oil* *n* : POPPYCOCK, BUNKUM

snap pea *n* : an edible-podded pea having roundish pods that are easily snapped like beans — called also *sugar snap pea*

snarky \ˈsnärkē, ˈsnȧk-, -ki\ *adj* -ER/-EST [*snark* to find fault with (perh. alter. of ³*nark*) + ¹*-y*] **1** *chiefly Brit* : CROTCHETY, SNAPPISH **2** : marked by a sarcastic, impertinent, or irreverent manner ⟨~ lyrics⟩ ⟨~ commentary⟩

SNF *abbr* skilled nursing facility

SNG *abbr* substitute natural gas; synthetic natural gas

snow* *n, slang* : HEROIN

snowbelt \ˈ=ˌ=\ *n, often cap* : a region that receives an appreciable amount of annual snowfall ⟨a state in the ~⟩

snowbird* *n* : one who goes to a warmer region for the winter

snowblower* *n* : a machine for removing snow (as from a driveway or sidewalk) in which a rotating usu. spiral blade picks up and propels the snow aside

snowboard \ˈ=ˌ=\ *n* [¹*snow* + ¹surf*board*] : a board shorter and wider than a ski that is ridden in a surfing position downhill over snow — **snowboard** *vi* — **snowboarder** *n* — **snowboarding** *n*

snowcat \ˈ=ˌ=\ *n* [alter. of *Sno-Cat*] : a tracklaying vehicle designed for travel on snow

snow cone *n* : SNOWBALL 1b

snow crab *n* : any of several long-legged crabs (genus *Chionoecetes* and esp. *C. opilio* and *C. bairdi*) of the eastern north Pacific ocean and esp. Alaska and western north Atlantic ocean that are used for food

snow machine *n, chiefly Alaska* : SNOWMOBILE

snowmaker \ˈ=ˌ==\ *n* : a device for making snow artificially

snowmaking \ˈ=ˌ==\ *n, often attrib* : the production of snow usu. for ski slopes

snowmobile* *n* : an open vehicle for usu. one or two persons with steerable skis on the front and an endless belt at the rear

snow·mo·bil·ing \ˈsnō(ˌ)mōˌbēliŋ, -ˌmə-\ *n* -s : the sport of driving or racing a snowmobile — **snow·mo·bil·er** \-lə(r)\ *also* **snow·mo·bil·ist** \-ləst\ *n* -s

snow pea *n* : an edible-podded pea having flat pods that are typically harvested when immature

snow thrower *n* : SNOWBLOWER *herein*

snuff \ˈsnəf\ *adj* [²*snuff* (kill)] : characterized by the sensationalistic depiction of violence and esp. violent death ⟨~ television⟩ ⟨a ~ book⟩; *esp* : featuring a real rather than a staged murder ⟨~ movies⟩

soap* *n* **1** : SOAP OPERA **2** : the melodrama and sentimentality characteristic of a soap opera; *also* : something (as a novel) having such qualities

so·a·ve \ˈswävā, səˈw-\ *n* -s *usu cap* [It, fr. *Soave*, village near Verona, Italy] : a dry white wine from the area about Soave, Italy

so·ba \ˈsōbə\ *or* **soba noodle** *n, pl* **soba** [Jap, buckwheat, buckwheat noodles] : a Japanese noodle made from buckwheat flour

so·ca \ˈsōkə, -kä\ *n* -s [*so*ul music (herein) + ²*ca*lypso] : a blend of soul and calypso music

soccer mom *n* : a typically suburban mother who accompanies her children to their soccer games and is considered as part of a significant voting bloc or demographic group

socialist realism *n* [trans. of Russ *sotsialisticheskiĭ realizm*] : a theory of Soviet art, music, and literature that calls for the didactic use of artistic work to develop social consciousness in an evolving socialist state — **socialist realist** *n*

sociobiology* *n* : the comparative study of social organization in animals including humans esp. with regard to its genetic basis and evolutionary history — **sociobiological*** *adj* — **so·cio·bi·ologist** \sōs(h)ē(ˌ)ō+\ *n*

so·cio·demographic \ˈsōs(h)ē(ˌ)ō+\ *adj* [*socio-* + *demographic*] : of, relating to, or involving a combination of social and demographic factors

so·cio·historical \ˈsōs(h)ē(ˌ)ō+\ *adj* [*socio-* + ¹*historical*] : of, relating to, or involving social history or a combination of social and historical factors

so·cio·lect \ˈsōsēəˌlekt, -sē(ˌ)ō-\ *n* -s [*socio-* + *-lect* (as in *dialect*)] : a variety of a language that is used by a particular social group

so·cio·linguistic \ˈsōs(h)ē(ˌ)ō+\ *adj* [*socio-* + *linguistic*] **1** : of or relating to the social aspects of language **2** : of or relating to sociolinguistics

so·cio·linguistics \"+\ *n pl but usu sing in constr* [*socio-* + *linguistics*] : the study of linguistic behavior as determined by sociocultural factors (as social class or educational level) — **so·cio·lin·guist** *n*

so·ci·ol·o·gese \ˌsōsēˌäləˈjēz, -ˈjēs *also* ˌsōshē-\ *n* -s [*sociology* + *-ese*] : a style of writing held to be characteristic of sociologists

so·cio·religious \ˈsōs(h)ēō+\ *adj* [*socio-* + *religious*] : of, relating to, or involving a combination of social and religious factors

sod *vt* **sodded; sodded; sodding; sods** [fr. ⁵*sod*] *chiefly Brit* : DAMN 5

sodium dodecyl sulfate *n* : SODIUM LAURYL SULFATE

sodium pump *n* **1** : a molecular mechanism by which sodium ions are actively transported across a cell membrane; *esp* : one by which a high concentration of potassium ions and a low concentration of sodium ions are maintained within a cell and that is controlled by a specialized plasma membrane protein linking the hydrolysis of ATP to the active transport of intracellular sodium ions out of the cell and extracellular potassium ions into the cell to create an electrical and chemical gradient across the plasma membrane necessary for vital cell functions (as nerve cell excitation and cell volume regulation) **2** : the specialized plasma membrane protein that controls the sodium pump

sodium stearate *n* : a white powdery salt $C_{17}H_{35}COONa$ that is soluble in water, is the chief constituent of some laundry soaps, and is used esp. in cosmetics and toothpaste

soft* *adj* **1** : occurring at such a speed and under such circumstances as to avoid destructive impact ⟨~ landing of a spacecraft on the moon⟩ **2** : not protected against enemy attack ⟨a ~ aboveground launching site⟩ **3** : BIODEGRADABLE *herein* ⟨a ~ detergent⟩ ⟨~ pesticides⟩ **4** *of a drug* : considered less detrimental than a hard narcotic ⟨marijuana is usually regarded as a ~ drug⟩ **5 a** : being low due to sluggish market conditions ⟨~ prices⟩ **b** : SLUGGISH, SLOW ⟨a ~ market⟩ **6** : not firmly committed : IRRESOLUTE, UNDECIDED ⟨~ voters⟩ **7** : SOFT-CORE *herein* ⟨~ pornography⟩ **8 a** : being or based on interpretive or speculative data ⟨~ evidence⟩ ⟨~ data⟩ **b** : utilizing or based on soft data ⟨~ science⟩ **9** : being or using renewable sources of energy (as solar radiation, wind, tides, or biomass conversion) ⟨~ technologies⟩ **10** : being or having keys that are programmable for different functions **11** *of money* : contributed (as by a corporation) to a political party rather than directly to a political candidate

softball* *or* **softball question** *n* : a question requiring only an easy or simple response

softbound \ˈ=ˈ=\ *adj* : not bound in hard covers

soft–coated wheaten terrier \ˈ=ˈ==-\ *n* : any of a breed of compact medium-sized terriers developed in Ireland that have a soft abundant light fawn coat

soft–core \ˈ=ˈ=\ *adj* [¹*soft* + *-core* (as in *hard-core* — herein)] **1** *of pornography* : containing descriptions or scenes of sex acts that are less explicit than hard-core material **2** : relatively mild : MODERATE ⟨*soft-core* support⟩

softgel \ˈ=ˌ=\ *n* [¹*soft* + ¹*gel*] : a pliable soft gelatin capsule containing a liquid preparation (as a medicine)

soft–land \ˈ=ˈ=\ *vb* [back-formation fr. *soft landing*] *vi* : to make a soft landing on a celestial body (as the moon) ~ *vt* : to cause to soft-land — **soft–land·er** \-ə(r)\ *n* -s

soft landing *n* : the averting of a major economic decline through a gradual slowing of the economy

soft–liner \(ˈ)=ˈ==\ *n* -s [¹*soft* + *-liner* (as in *hard-liner* — herein)] : one who advocates or pursues a conciliatory or flexible policy or course of action

soft paste* *n* **1** : a fine-grained opaque Chinese ceramic ware related to true porcelain but having part of the kaolin replaced by pegmatite and usu. being fired twice **2** : a lightweight soft opaque clay body (as of early Staffordshire)

soft rock *n* : rock music that is less driving and gentler sounding than hard rock

soft–top \ˈ=ˌ=\ *n* : an automobile or motorboat having a top that may be folded down

software \ˈ=ˌ=\ *n* [¹*soft* + hard*ware*] : something used or associated with and usu. contrasted with hardware: as **a** : the entire set of programs, procedures, and related documentation associated with a system and esp. a computer system; *specif* : computer programs **b** : materials for use with audiovisual equipment

software engineering *n* : a branch of computer science that deals with the design, implementation, and maintenance of complex computer programs — **software engineer** *n*

soilborne \ˈ=ˌ=\ *adj* [³*soil* + ¹*borne*] : transmitted by or in soil

so·ka gak·kai \ˌsōkəˈgäkī\ *n, usu cap S&G* [Jap *Sōka Gakkai*, lit, value–creation society] : a lay religious organization of Japanese origin that is associated with Nichiren Buddhism and that emphasizes active proselytism and the use of prayer for the solution of all human problems

solar cell *n* : a photovoltaic cell (as one including a junction between two types of silicon semiconductors) that is able to convert light into electrical energy and is used as a power source

solar collector *n* : any of various devices that absorb solar radiation for use in the heating of water or buildings or the production of electricity

solar panel *n* : a battery of solar cells (as in a spacecraft)

solar pond *n* : a pool of salt water heated by the sun and used either as a direct source of heat or to provide power for an electric generator

solar sail *n* : a propulsive device that consists of a flat material (as aluminized plastic) designed to receive thrust from solar radiation pressure and that can be attached to a spacecraft

solar wind *n* : plasma continuously ejected from the sun's surface into and through interplanetary space

soldier* *n* : BUTTON MAN *herein*

solid–state \ˈ=ˈ=\ *adj* **1** : relating to the properties, structure, or reactivity of solid material; *esp* : relating to the arrangement or behavior of ions, molecules, nucleons, electrons, and holes in the crystals of a substance (as a semiconductor) or to the effect of crystal imperfections on the properties of a solid substance ⟨*solid-state* physics⟩ **2 a** : utilizing the electric, magnetic, or optical properties of solid materials ⟨*solid-state* circuitry⟩ **b** : using semiconductor devices rather than electron tubes ⟨a *solid-state* radio⟩

sol·i·ton \ˈsäləˌtän\ *n* -s [*solitary* + ²*-on*] : a solitary wave (as in a gaseous plasma) that propagates with little loss of energy and retains its shape and speed after colliding with another such wave

solution set *n* : the set of values that satisfy an equation; *also* : TRUTH SET *herein*

som \ˈsōm\ *n, pl* **som** [Kirghiz *som* crude iron casting, ruble] : the basic monetary unit of Kyrgyzstan — see MONEY table *in the Dict*

somali* *n, usu cap* : any of a breed of domestic cats that prob. originated as a spontaneous mutation of the Abyssinian and closely resembles it but has a long silky coat and bushy tail

so·mato·me·din \sə͵mad·ə͵mēdᵊn\ *n* -s [*somat-* + *-medin* (perh. as in *intermedin*)] : any of several endogenous peptides produced esp. in the liver that are dependent on and prob. mediate growth hormone activity (as in sulfate uptake by epiphyseal cartilage)

so·mato·sensory \sə͵mad·ə+\ *adj* [*somat-* + *sensory*] : of, relating to, or being sensory activity not having its origin in the special sense organs (as eyes or ears) and conveying information about the state of the body and its immediate environment; *also* : relating to or being either of two regions in the postcentral gyrus that receive and process somatosensory stimuli

so·mato·stat·in \sə͵mad·ə͵statᵊn\ *n* -s [*somat-* + *-stat* + *-in*] : a polypeptide neurohormone that is found esp. in the hypothalamus, is composed of a chain of 14 amino acid residues, and inhibits the secretion of several other hormones (as growth hormone, insulin, and gastrin)

so·mato·therapy \sə͵mad·ə+\ *n* [*somat-* + *therapy*] : therapy for psychological problems that uses physiological intervention (as by drugs or surgery) to modify behavior

somatotropic hormone *n* : GROWTH HORMONE 1

something* *pron* — **something else 1** : something or someone special or extraordinary ⟨the solos . . . were *something else* —Thomas Pynchon⟩ ⟨this guy is *something else* —Claude Brown⟩ **2** : something or someone mystifying, bewildering, or overwhelming ⟨supporting six children . . . got to be *something else* —Flannery O'Connor⟩

son et lumière \sōⁿālümyer\ *n* [F, lit., sound and light] : an outdoor spectacle at an historic site consisting of recorded narration with light and sound effects

sonic* *adj* : of or involving sound and esp. music

son·i·cate \ˈsänə͵kāt\ *vt* -ED/-ING/-S [*sonic* + [4]*-ate*] : to disrupt (as bacterial cells) by exposure to high-frequency sound waves — **son·i·ca·tion** \͵sänəˈkāshən\ *n* -s

so·no·chemistry \͵sänō, ͵sōnō+\ *n* [*son-* + *chemistry*] : a branch of chemistry that deals with the chemical effects of ultrasound — **so·no·chemical** \"+\ *adj*

so·no·gram \ˈsänə͵gram, ˈsōn-\ *n* [*son-* + *-gram*] : an image produced by ultrasound

so·nog·ra·phy \sōˈnägrəfē\ *n* -ES [*son-* + *-graphy*] : ULTRASOUND 1 *herein* — **so·nog·ra·pher** \-fə(r)\ *n* — **so·no·graph·ic** \͵sōnəˈgrafik\ *adj*

so·pai·pil·la \͵sō͵pīˈpē(l)yə\ *also* **so·pa·pil·la** \͵sōpəˈpilə, -ˈpē(l)yə\ *n* -s [Sp *sopaipilla*, dim. of *sopaipa* fritter soaked in honey, fr. *sopa* sop, food soaked in milk, of Gmc origin; akin to OE *sūpan* to swallow; *sopapilla* by modif.] : a usu. puffy piece of deep fried dough often sweetened with honey

sorghum webworm *n* : a noctuid moth (*Celama sorghiella*) whose hairy greenish larva is sometimes a destructive pest of the seed heads of sorghum

sort* *n* : an instance of sorting ⟨an alpha ~⟩

sort out *vt* : to take care of : straighten out ⟨let our problems *sort* themselves *out*⟩; *also* : to figure out : make sense of ⟨I've seen a lot but haven't *sorted* it all *out* yet⟩

sou·kous \ˈsü͵küs\ *n* -ES [African F (of Brazzaville and Kinshasa) *soucous, soukous*, a dance popular in the late 1960s, alter. of F *secousse* jolt, jerk, fr. MF, fr. fem. of *secous*, past part. of *secourre* to shake, fr. OF, fr. L *succutere* to shake from below, jolt — more at SUCCUSSION] : popular guitar-driven dance music created in the Democratic Republic of the Congo under the influence of Cuban rumba

soul* *n* **1** : a strong positive feeling (as of intense sensitivity and emotional fervor) conveyed esp. by black American performers **2** : NEGRITUDE *herein* **3** : SOUL MUSIC *herein* **4** : SOUL FOOD *herein* **5** : SOUL BROTHER *herein*

soul *adj* [*soul*, n. (herein)] **1** : of, relating to, or characteristic of black Americans or their culture ⟨vocals are delivered in a raspy, ~ style —Ellen Sander⟩ **2** : designed for or controlled by blacks ⟨~ radio stations⟩

soul brother *n* : a black male

soul food *n* : food (as chitterlings, hogs' jowls, ham hocks, collard greens, catfish, and cornbread) traditionally eaten esp. by southern black Americans

soul music *n* : music that originated with black American gospel singing, is closely related to rhythm and blues, and is characterized by intensity of feeling and earthiness

soul sister *n* : a black female

sound·alike \ˈsau̇ndə͵līk\ *n* -s [[4]*sound* + *-alike* (as in *lookalike* — herein)] : one (as a person or a word) that sounds like another

sound bite *n* : a brief recorded statement (as by a public figure) broadcast esp. on a television news program; *also* : a brief catchy comment or phrase

sound board *or* **sound card** *n* : a circuit board in a computer system designed to produce or reproduce sound

sounding* *n* : SIGNIFYING *herein*

sound pollution *n* : NOISE POLLUTION *herein*

sound·scape \ˈsau̇n(d)͵skāp\ *n* -s [[2]*sound* + *-scape*] : a mélange of musical and sometimes nonmusical sounds

soundtrack** \ˈ=͵=\ *n* **1** : the sounds (as music and dialogue) recorded on the sound track of a film **2** : an album of music selected from the sound track of a film **3** : accompanying music ⟨walked the runway . . . to a ~ of current rap and R&B —Carol Cooper⟩

soup* *n* : the fast-moving white water that moves shoreward after a wave breaks

source* *n* : an electrode in a field-effect transistor that supplies the charge carriers for current flow — compare DRAIN *herein*, GATE *herein*

source* *vb* ~ *vt* **1** : to obtain from a source ⟨metals *sourced* from outside the U.S.⟩ **2** : to specify the source of (as information) ~ *vi* : to document sources

source \ˈsō(ə)rs, ˈsȯ(ə)rs, ˈsōəs, ˈsȯ(ə)s\ *adj* [[1]*source*] : of, relating to, or being source code ⟨~ listing⟩

source code *n* : computer code in its original programming language — compare OBJECT CODE *herein*

source language *n* : a language which is to be translated into another language — compare TARGET LANGUAGE *herein*

south* *adv* : into a state of decline or ruin ⟨causes the sluggish economy to go ~ —G.F.Will⟩

south* *n, usu cap* : the developing nations of the world : THIRD WORLD 3 *herein*

southern blot *n, usu cap S* [after Edwin M. *Southern* b1938 Brit. biologist] : a blot consisting of a sheet of cellulose nitrate or nylon that contains spots of DNA for identification by a suitable molecular probe — compare NORTHERN BLOT *herein*, WESTERN BLOT *herein* — **southern blotting** *n, usu cap S*

southern–fried \ˈ==ˈ=\ *adj* : SOUTHERN 1

southern oscillation *n, usu cap S&O* : a periodic seesaw fluctuation in sea-level atmospheric pressures over the southern Pacific and Indian oceans that is believed to be linked to El Niño and La Niña events

southern pea *n* : COWPEA

southwestern corn borer *n* : a pyralid moth (*Diatraea grandiosella*) whose larva causes serious damage esp. to corn crops by boring in the stalks

sou·vla·ki \süvˈläkē, -ki\ *or* **sou·vla·kia** \-kēə\ *n* -s [NGk *soublaki*, dim. of *soubla* skewer, fr. MGk, fr. L *subula* awl; *soublakia*, pl. of *souvlaki* — more at SUBULATE] : SHISH KEBAB

soybean cyst nematode *n* : a nematode (*Heterodera glycines*) that is a pest of legumes and esp. soybeans causing stunting and yellowing of the plants and reduction in yield

soy milk \ˈ=͵=\ *n* : a high-protein liquid made from ground cooked soybeans that is usu. fortified (as with calcium and vitamins) and used as a milk substitute

spa* *n* **1** : a commercial establishment (as a resort) providing facilities devoted esp. to health, fitness, weight loss, beauty, and relaxation **2** : a hot tub with a whirlpool device

spa \ˈspä, ˈspȯ, ˈspȧ\ *adj* [*spa*, n.] *of food* : designed to please a gourmet but low in fats, calories, and salt ⟨~ cuisine⟩

space* *n* **1** : a set of mathematical entities (as points or vectors) with a set of axioms of geometric character — compare METRIC SPACE *herein*, TOPOLOGICAL SPACE *herein*, VECTOR SPACE *herein* **2** : the opportunity to assert or experience one's identity or needs freely ⟨we make the ~ that other women will occupy —Marge Piercy⟩

space–age \ˈ=ˈ=\ *adj* : of, relating to, or befitting the age of space exploration : MODERN ⟨*space-age* gadgetry⟩

spaceborne \ˈ=͵=\ *adj* [[1]*space* + [1]*borne*] **1** : carried by a spacecraft ⟨~ radar⟩ **2** : involving the use of spaceborne equipment ⟨~ television⟩

space cadet* *n* : an impractical person who seems unaware of his or her surroundings — called also *space case*

spaced–out \ˈ=ˈ=\ *adj* [fr. past part. of *space out* to become dazed] **1** : dazed or stupefied by or as if by a narcotic substance **2** : of a very strange character : WEIRD ⟨lives with a rather *spaced-out* dog in a stylish penthouse —John Heilpern⟩

spacefaring \ˈ=͵==\ *adj* [*space* + *-faring* (as in *seafaring*)] : of, relating to, or involved in travel in outer space ⟨~ nations⟩ — **spacefarer** \ˈ=͵==\ *n* -s — **spacefaring** *n* -s

space–filling model \ˈ=͵==-\ *n* : a graphic or physical representation of a molecule in which the atoms are partial spheres that have diameters proportional to those of the real atoms and that are joined directly to one another — compare BALL-AND-STICK MODEL *herein*

space frame *n* : a usu. open three-dimensional framework of struts and braces (as in buildings and racing cars) which defines a structure and in which the weight of the structure is evenly distributed in all directions

spacer* *n* : a region of chromosomal DNA between genes that is not transcribed into messenger RNA and is of uncertain function

space shuttle *n* : a reusable spacecraft designed to transport people and cargo between earth and space

space sickness *n* : sickness and esp. nausea and dizziness that occurs under the conditions of sustained spaceflight

spacewalk \ˈ=͵=\ *n* : a period of activity outside a spacecraft by an astronaut in space — **spacewalk** *vi* — **spacewalker** \ˈ=͵==\ *n* — **spacewalking** \ˈ=͵==\ *n*

spacewoman \ˈ==͵=\ *n, pl* **spacewomen** : a woman astronaut

spacy* *or* **spac·ey** \ˈspāsē, -si\ *adj* **spacier; spaciest 1** : SPACED-OUT 1 *herein* **2 a** : DITSY *herein* ⟨her gifted but ~ sister —A.M.Greeley⟩ **b** : OFFBEAT, FAR-OUT *herein* ⟨wild and ~ clothes⟩

spa·ghet·ti·ni \spə͵geˈtēnē\ *n* -s [It, dim. of *spaghetti*] : a pasta thinner than spaghetti but thicker than vermicelli

spaghetti squash *n* : an oval winter squash (*Cucurbita pepo*) with flesh that when cooked separates into strands resembling spaghetti

spaghetti western *n, often cap W* : a western motion picture produced by Italians

[1]**spam** *n* -s [fr. a skit on the British television series *Monty Python's Flying Circus* in which chanting of the word *Spam* (trademark for a canned meat product) overrides the other dialogue] : unsolicited usu. commercial e-mail sent to a large number of addresses

[2]**spam** *vb* **spammed; spammed; spamming; spams** *vt* : to send spam to ~ *vi* : to send spam — **spam·mer** \-ə(r)\ *n* -s

span* *vt* : to be capable under given operations of expressing any element of (a set of vectors that ~*s* a vector space)

spa·na·ko·pi·ta *or* **spa·no·ko·pi·ta** *also* **spa·na·ko·pit·ta** \͵spänəˈkōpēd·ə, -nō'-, -pid-\ *n* -s [NGk *spanakopēta*, fr. *spanaki* spinach (fr. MGk *spanakin*, alter. of *spinakion*, prob. fr. Ar *isbinākh, isbanākh*) + *-o-* -o- + *pēta, pita* pie — more at SPINACH] : a traditional Greek pie of spinach, feta cheese, and seasonings baked in phyllo

span·glish \ˈspaŋ(g)lish\ *n, usu cap* [blend of *Spanish* and *English*] : Spanish marked by numerous borrowings from English

spark chamber *n* : a device usu. used to detect the path of a high-energy particle that consists of a series of charged metal plates or wires separated by a gas (as neon) in which observable electric discharges follow the path of the particle

sparkler* *n* : SPARKLING WINE

spatial summation *n* : sensory summation that involves stimulation of several spatially separated neurons at the same time

spatter glass *n* : END-OF-DAY GLASS *herein*

spaz \ˈspaz\ *n, pl* **spazzes** [by shortening & alter. fr. [2]*spastic*] *slang* : one who is inept : KLUTZ

-speak \͵spēk\ *n comb form* [*newspeak* (herein)] — used to form esp. nonce words denoting a particular kind of jargon ⟨architect*speak*⟩ ⟨California*speak*⟩

speakerphone \ˈ==͵=\ *n* [*speaker* + *-phone*] : a combination microphone and loudspeaker device for two-way communication by telephone lines

speak–out \ˈ=ˈ=\ *n* -s [*speak out*, v.] : an event in which people publicly share their experiences of or views on an issue (as abortion or gay rights)

spear–carrier \ˈ=͵===\ *n* **1 a** : a member of an opera chorus **b** : a bit actor in a play **2** : a person whose actions are of little significance or value in an event or organization

spear·ing \ˈspi(ə)riŋ\ *n* -s [fr. gerund of [3]*spear*] : an illegal check in hockey in which one player jabs another in the body with the blade of a hockey stick

spec \ˈspek\ *vt, past part* **specced** *or* **spec'd**; *pres part* **spec'cing** [by shortening] : to write specifications for

special drawing rights *n pl, often cap S&D&R* : SDRS *herein*

special education *n* : classes or instruction for students with special educational needs (as a learning disability or physical handicap)

special K *n* -s *usu cap S* [*ketamine*, with play on *Special K*, trademark for a breakfast cereal] : the anesthetic ketamine used illicitly usu. by being inhaled in powdered form esp. for the dream-like or hallucinogenic state it produces

special relativity *or* **special theory of relativity** : RELATIVITY 3b

spe·cies·ism \ˈspē(͵)s(h)ē͵zizəm\ *n* -s [[1]*species* + *-ism* (as in *racism*)] **1** : prejudice or discrimination based on species; *esp* : discrimination against animals **2** : the assumption of human superiority on which speciesism is based — **spe·cies·ist** \-ist\ *adj or n* -s

–specific \spə͵sifik\ *comb form* [[1]*specific*] : relating or applying specifically to or intended esp. for ⟨gender-*specific*⟩ ⟨the certification test is Oregon-*specific* —*SYLLABUS*⟩

speckle* *n* : a granular effect in an image that is caused by the scattering of incident wave energy (as laser light or ultrasound) by the uneven surface of the target object

speckle interferometry *n* : interferometry in which a composite image of an object is made by recording individual speckle images over a period of time; *specif* : such a technique used in astronomy to generate a clear image of a celestial body blurred by atmospheric turbulence

SPECT *abbr* single photon emission computed tomography *herein*

spec·ti·no·my·cin \͵spektənōˈmīsᵊn\ *n* -s [*spect-* (fr. NL *spectabilis*, specific epithet of *Streptomyces spectabilis*) + *actinomycin*] : a white crystalline broad-spectrum antibiotic $C_{14}H_{24}N_2O_7$ extracted from a bacterium of the genus *Streptomyces* (*S. spectabilis*) and used clinically esp. in the form of its hydrochloride to treat gonorrhea — called also *actinospectacin*

spectrum* *n* **1** : MASS SPECTRUM **2** : the representation (as a plot) of a spectrum

speed* *n* : METHAMPHETAMINE; *also* : a related stimulant drug and esp. an amphetamine — **up to speed 1** : operating at full effectiveness or potential **2** : INFORMED

speed bump *n* : a low raised ridge laid across a roadway (as in a parking lot) to limit vehicle speed

speedo \ˈspē(͵)dō\ *n* -s [by shortening] *chiefly Brit* : SPEEDOMETER

speed–reading \ˈ=ˈ==\ *n* : a method of reading rapidly by skimming — **speed–read** \ˈ=ˈ=\ *vt* — **speed–reader** \ˈ=ˈ==\ *n*

speed shop *n* : a shop that sells custom automotive equipment esp. to hot rodders

spelling checker *n* : a computer program that identifies possible misspellings in a block of text by comparing the text with a database of accepted spellings — called also *spell check, spell checker*

SPF \͵es(͵)pēˈef\ *n* -s : a number assigned to a sunscreen that is the factor by which the time required for unprotected skin to become sunburned is increased when the sunscreen is used — called also *sun protection factor*

s phase *n, usu cap S* [*synthesis*] : the period in the cell cycle during which DNA replication takes place — compare G_1 PHASE *herein*, G_2 PHASE *herein*, M PHASE *herein*

sphe·ro·plast \ˈsfirə͵plast, ˈsfer-\ *n* -s [*sphaer-* + *-plast*] : a bacterium or yeast cell that has been modified by nutritional or environmental factors or by artificial means (as the use of a lysozyme) and that is characterized by partial loss of the cell wall and by increased osmotic sensitivity

spider hole *n* : a camouflaged foxhole

spider plant* *n* : a plant of the genus *Chlorophytum* (*C. comosum* and esp. *C. comosum variegatum*) that has long narrow green leaves usu. with white or ivory stripes, that produces stems bearing small white flowers at the end of which small tufts of plantlets follow the flowers, and that is widely grown as a houseplant esp. in hanging baskets

spider vein *n* : one or more bluish, purplish, or reddish dilated capillaries, arterioles, or venules just below the surface of the skin (as on the legs or face) that often appear as a central area with outward radiations resembling the legs of a spider

spi·e·di·no \͵spēəˈdē(͵)nō\ *n, pl* **spiedini** \-(͵)nē\ [It, lit., skewer, dim. of *spiedo* spit, spear, fr. OF *espiet* spear, of Gmc origin; akin to OHG *spioz* spear, ON *spjōt*] : a dish of meat rolled around a filling or minced and formed into balls then usu. batter-dipped and cooked on a skewer; *also* : slices of bread and mozzarella prepared in a similar way and served with an anchovy sauce

spike* *n* **1** : a momentary sharp increase and fall in electric potential ⟨voltage ~*s*⟩; *also* : ACTION POTENTIAL *herein* **2** : an abrupt sharp increase (as in prices or rates)

spike* *vt* : to undergo a sudden sharp increase in (temperature or fever) ⟨the patient *spiked* a fever of 103°⟩

spillover* *n* : an extension of something esp. when an excess exists ⟨a ~ of interest from college to high school sports⟩

spin* *n* : a special point of view, emphasis, or interpretation controlling a presentation : ANGLE ⟨put the proper ~ on what took place . . . between their two leaders —Hugh Sidey⟩

spin control *n* : the act or practice of attempting to manipulate the way an event is interpreted by others ⟨organized an elaborate *spin control* to minimize the damage —Colleen O'Connor *et al*⟩

spin doctor *n* : a person (as a political aide) responsible for ensuring that others interpret an event from a particular point of view — **spin–doctor** \ˈ=ˈ==\ *vb*

spinmeister \ˈ=͵==\ *also* **spinmaster** \ˈ=͵==\ *n* -s [*spin* (herein) + *meister* (herein); *spinmaster* fr. *spin* (herein) + [1]*master*] : SPIN DOCTOR *herein*

spin off *vt* : to establish or produce as a spin-off ~ *vi* : to establish or become a spin-off

spin–off* *n* **1** : the distribution by a business to its stockholders of particular assets and esp. of stock of another company; *also* : a new company created by such a distribution **2** : a collateral or derived product or effect : BY-PRODUCT; *also* : a number of such by-products ⟨the *spin-off* from the space program⟩ **3** : something that is imitative or derivative of an earlier work, product, or establishment; *esp* : a television show starring a character who was popular in a secondary role in an earlier show

spinout \ˈ=͵=\ *n* -s [*spin out*, v.] : a rotational skid by an automobile that usu. causes it to leave the roadway

spin·to \ˈspēn(͵)tō, -pin-\ *adj* [It, lit., pushed, fr. past part. of *spingere* to push, fr. (assumed) VL *expingere*, fr. L *ex-* [1]*ex-* + *-pingere* (fr. *pangere* to drive in, fasten) — more at PACT] *of a singing voice* : having both lyric and dramatic qualities — **spinto** *n* -s

spin wave *n* : a wave of quantized energy that propagates through a substance as a result of magnetic field shifts within an atom in response to an outside stimulus (as a variable magnetic field or radio waves) — called also *magnon*

spiny–headed worm \ˈ==͵==-\ *n* : a parasitic worm belonging to the phylum Acanthocephala

spi·ro·no·lactone \spī͵rānə, spə͵rōnō+\ *n* [*spir-* + *-no-* (of unknown origin) + *lactone*] : an aldosterone antagonist $C_{24}H_{32}O_4S$ that promotes diuresis and sodium excretion and is used to treat several conditions (as essential hypertension and edema)

spi·ru·lina \͵spīrəˈlīnə\ *n* -s [NL, fr. *spirula* small coil + *-ina* [2]-ina — more at SPIRULATE] : a microscopic filamentous aquatic photosynthetic bacterium or blue-green alga (genus *Spirulina* and esp. *S. platensis* syn. *Arthrospira platensis*) that is sometimes cultivated for use as a dietary supplement

splashdown \ˈ=͵=\ *n* -s [[1]*splash* + *-down* (as in *touchdown*)] : the landing of a manned spacecraft in the ocean — **splash down** *vi*

splice* *vt* : to combine or insert (as genes) by genetic engineering ⟨researchers *spliced* together DNA from several different organisms⟩ ⟨*spliced* a human gene for insulin into a bacterium⟩ — see GENE-SPLICING *herein*

splicing* *n* : the process that occurs chiefly in eukaryotic nuclei by which introns in an RNA transcript are removed and exons are joined to form functional messenger RNA; *also* : GENE-SPLICING *herein*

spliff \ˈsplif\ *n* -s [origin unknown] : a marijuana cigarette

spline* *also* **spline function** *n* : a function that is defined on an interval, is used to approximate a given function, and is composed of pieces of simple functions defined on subintervals and joined at their endpoints with a suitable degree of smoothness

split* *vt* : LEAVE ⟨~ the scene⟩ ~ *vi* : LEAVE ⟨the women ~ for New York on Tuesday —Linda Francke⟩

split* *n* : the recorded time of an athlete at a specific interval in a race (as of running or swimming)

split–brain \ˈ=ˈ=\ *adj* : of, relating to, concerned with, or having undergone separation of the two cerebral hemispheres by surgical division of the optic chiasma and corpus callosum ⟨behavior in *split-brain* animals⟩ ⟨*split-brain* research⟩

split end *n* : an offensive end in football who lines up usu. several yards to the side of the formation

split–fingered fastball \ˈ=͵==-\ *n* : a fast ball thrown with the ball gripped as for a fork ball so that it drops rapidly as it nears the plate

splitter* *n* : SPLIT-FINGERED FASTBALL *herein*

spo·do·sol \ˈspädə͵sȯl, ˈspōd-\ *n* -s [Gk *spodos* wood ash + *-o-* L *solum* ground, soil — more at SOIL] : any of a group of podzols esp. of cool humid regions that have a horizon below the surface composed of an illuvial accumulation of humus with iron or aluminum or both

spoiler* *n* **1** : an air deflector on an automobile for reducing the tendency to lift off the road at high speeds **2** : one (as a presidential candidate or a baseball team in a pennant race) that has little or no chance of winning but can prevent another's winning

spokes·model \ˈspōks+͵\ *n* : a model who is a spokesperson

spokes·people \"+͵\ *n pl* : people serving as spokesmen or spokeswomen

spokes·person \"+͵\ *n* [*spokes-* (as in *spokesman*) + *person*] : one who speaks as the representative of another

sponge* *n* : an absorbent contraceptive device impregnated with spermatocide that is inserted into the vagina before sexual intercourse to cover the cervix and act as a barrier to sperm

spongeware \ˈ=͵=\ *n* : a typically 19th century earthenware with background color spattered or dabbed (as with a sponge) and usu. a freehand central design

spon·gi·form encephalopathy \ˈspənjəˌfȯrm-\ *n* [*spongiform* resembling a sponge, fr. *spongi-* + *-form*] : any of a group of degenerative diseases of the brain that are characterized by development of brain tissue having a structure like that of a porous sponge and by deterioration in neurological functioning — see BOVINE SPONGIFORM ENCEPHALOPATHY *herein*, TRANSMISSIBLE SPONGIFORM ENCEPHALOPATHY *herein*

spook* *n* : an undercover agent : SPY

spoon·er \ˈspünə(r)\ *n* -S [[1]*spoon* + [2]*-er*] : a container that is designed to hold extra teaspoons and forms part of a 19th century table service

spo·ro·pol·len·in \ˌspōrōˈpälənən, ˌspȯr-\ *n* -S [ISV *spor-* + *pollen* + *-in*] : a relatively chemically inert polymer that makes up the outer layer of pollen grains and spores

sports bar *n* : a bar catering esp. to sports fans and typically containing several televisions and often sports memorabilia

sportswear* *n* : clothing designed for casual or informal wear

sport–utility vehicle \ˈ=ˈ==-\ *n* : a rugged automotive vehicle similar to a station wagon but built on a light-truck chassis

spotted alfalfa aphid *n* : a highly destructive Old World aphid (*Therioaphis maculata*) established in warmer areas of the U.S. that causes yellowing and stunting of infested plants and esp. alfalfa by injecting a toxic saliva while feeding

spotted owl *n* : a rare large dark brown dark-eyed owl of the genus *Strix* (*S. occidentalis*) that has barred and spotted underparts and is found in humid old growth forests and thickly wooded canyons from British Columbia to southern California and central Mexico; *esp* : NORTHERN SPOTTED OWL *herein*

sprang \ˈspraŋ, -aiŋ\ *n* -S [prob. fr. Norw, kind of embroidery — more at SPRAING] : a weaving technique in which threads or cords are intertwined and twisted over one another to form an openwork mesh

spray can *n* : AEROSOL 2b

spray–paint \ˈ=ˌ=\ *vt* **1** : to apply paint from an aerosol to **2** : to write with paint from an aerosol

spread* *n* : POINT SPREAD *herein*

spread end *n* : SPLIT END *herein*

spreadsheet \ˈ=ˌ=\ *n* [fr. *spreadsheet* outsize page used by accountants] : an accounting program for a computer; *also* : the ledger layout modeled by such a program — **spreadsheeting** \ˈ=ˌ==\ *n*

sprech·stim·me \ˈshprek̟ˌshtimə, -ek̟ˌ-\ *n* -S *often cap* [G, fr. *sprech-* (fr. *sprechen* to speak, fr. OHG *sprehhan*) + *stimme* voice, fr. OHG *stimma* — more at SPEAK, STEVEN] : a vocal passage or performance in which a declamation is delivered with rhythmic inflections

spring roll *n* : EGG ROLL; *also* : any of various similar appetizers of oriental cuisine

sprint car *n* : a rugged racing automobile that is midway in size between midget racers and ordinary racers, has about the same horsepower as the larger racers, and is usu. raced on a dirt track

spritz \ˈsprits\ *n* -ES **1** [*spritz*, v.] : SPRAY, SQUIRT, FIZZ **2** [Yiddish *shprits* spray] : an improvised usu. humorous harangue **3** *pl* **spritz** [Sw *spritsbakelse*, part trans. of G *spritzkuchen*, fr. *spritzen* to spray, inject + *kuchen* pastry] : a rich short cookie formed in shapes with a cookie press

spun·bond·ed \ˈspənˌbändəd\ *adj* [fr. the material's being bonded by a substance spun from a spinnerette] : of, relating to, or being a nonwoven polymeric material that resembles cloth or fabric

spy–hop \ˈ=ˌ=\ *vi* [prob. fr. [1]*spy* + [1]*hop*] *of a whale* : to project the head out of the water in a vertical direction

square one *n* : the initial stage or starting point of a process ⟨had to start all over again, from *square one* —H.C.McDonald⟩

square out *n* : a pass pattern in football in which a receiver runs downfield and then breaks sharply for the sidelines

squat* *n* **1** : a lift in weight lifting in which the lifter performs a knee bend while holding a barbell on the shoulders; *also* : a competitive event involving this lift **2** *chiefly Brit* : an empty house or building that is occupied and shared by squatters **3** *slang* : DIDDLY-SQUAT *herein* NOTHING

squeaky–clean \ˈ==ˈ=\ *adj* **1** : completely clean ⟨*squeaky-clean* hair⟩ **2** : completely free from moral taint of any kind ⟨a *squeaky-clean* reputation⟩

squeeze* *n, slang* : MAIN SQUEEZE *herein*

squib kick *n* : a kickoff in football in which the ball bounces along the ground

SQUID \ˈskwid\ *abbr or n* -S *often not cap* [superconducting *qu*antum *i*nterference *d*evice] : an instrument for detecting and measuring very weak magnetic fields

sr* *abbr* steradian

sri lan·kan \(ˈ)srēˈläŋkən, (ˈ)shrē-\ *n, cap S&L* [*Sri Lanka* + E [1]*-an*] : a native or inhabitant of Sri Lanka — **sri lankan** *adj, usu cap S&L*

sRNA \ˌesˌärˌenˈā\ *n* -S [*soluble RNA*] : TRANSFER RNA *herein*

SRO \ˌesˌärˈō\ *n* -S [*single-room occupancy*] : a house, apartment building, or residential hotel in which tenants live in single rooms

SSL *abbr* Licentiate of Sacred Scriptures

SSRI \ˌes(ˌ)es(ˌ)ärˈī\ *abbr or n* -S selective serotonin reuptake inhibitor *herein*

SST \ˌeˌseˈstē\ *n* -S : SUPERSONIC TRANSPORT *herein*

stack* *n* **1** : a memory or a section of memory in a computer for temporary storage in which the last data item stored is the first retrieved; *also* : a data structure that simulates a stack **2** : a computer memory consisting of arrays of memory elements stacked one on top of another

stacked heel *n* [*stacked*, past part. of [2]*stack*] : a heel made of layers of leather and used on shoes

stadium coat *n* : a coat of medium length designed for casual winter wear

staff* *n, pl* **staff** : a member of a staff ⟨employs three full-time ~⟩

stage* *vt* : to determine the phase or severity of (a disease) based on a classification of established symptomatic criteria; *also* : to evaluate (a patient) to determine the phase, severity, or progression of a disease

stage dive *vi* : to leap from the stage into the audience during a rock music performance — **stage dive** *n* — **stage diver** *n*

stag·fla·tion \ˌstagˈflāshən\ *n* -S [blend of *stagnation* and *inflation*] : persistent inflation combined with stagnant consumer demand and relatively high unemployment — **stag·fla·tio·nary** \-shəˌnerē\ *adj*

staging* *n* : the disengaging and discarding of a burned-out rocket unit from a space vehicle during flight

stair climber \ˈ=ˌ==\ *n* : an exercise apparatus that simulates the act of climbing stairs — **stair climbing** \ˈ=ˌ==\ *n*

stand–alone \ˈ=ˈ=ˌ=\ *adj* [fr. the phrase *stand alone*] : SELF-CONTAINED; *esp* : operating or capable of operating independently of a computer system or network ⟨a ~ word processor⟩

standard candle* *n* : an astronomical object (as a star or supernova) of known luminosity that can be used as a gauge of distance

standard–issue \ˈ=ˈ=ˌ=\ *adj* : STANDARD 3, RUN-OF-THE-MILL ⟨wears *standard-issue* business suits and white shirts —Sidney Blumenthal⟩

standard model *n* : a theory in physics: all the particles in nature and their interactions can be described by a combination of quantum chromodynamics and electroweak theory

stand–down* *n* : a relaxation of status of a military unit or force from an alert or operational posture ⟨out there for eighty-three days before we came in for *stand-down* —William Patton⟩

standing crop* *n* : the total amount or number of living things (as an uncut farm crop, the fish in a pond, or organisms in an ecosystem) in a particular area at any given time

standing o *n, usu cap O* [ovation] : a standing ovation

stand–up* *adj* : marked by a high degree of personal integrity or loyalty to one's fellows ⟨a *stand-up* guy⟩

stand–up* *n* **1** : stand-up comedy ⟨worked as the opening act in dinner theatres, doing *stand-up* while the tables were cleared —P.J.Boyer⟩; *also* : a performer of this ⟨began her career as a *stand-up* —Rich Cohen *et al*⟩ **2** : a television broadcast in which the reporter or narrator faces the camera with the scene of the story in the background

stannous fluoride *n* : a white compound SnF_2 of tin and fluorine used in toothpaste to combat tooth decay

sta·pe·dec·to·my \ˌstāpəˈdektəmē, -pēˈd-\ *n* -ES [ISV *staped-* (fr. NL *staped-, stapes* stapes) + *-ectomy*] : surgical removal and prosthetic replacement of the stapes to relieve deafness — **sta·pe·dec·to·mized** \-təˌmīzd\ *adj*

starburst \ˈ=ˌ=\ *n* : a shape or design (as on a piece of furniture, clothing, or jewelry) that resembles a star composition in a fireworks display ⟨~s set in dark floors that were so much the rage of the late thirties and forties —Charlotte Curtis⟩ ⟨a ~ roof ornament in gilded tin —John Richardson⟩

star fruit** *n* : CARAMBOLA 2

stark·ers \ˈstärkərz, -tȧkəz\ *adj* [*stark*-naked + *-ers*, extended form of *-er* (as in *rugger*) used in adjectives] *chiefly Brit* : completely unclothed : NUDE

starquake \ˈ=ˌ=\ *n* [[1]*star* + [2]*quake*] : a hypothetical violent shiver in the crust of a neutron star

starter* *n* : a dish served as an appetizer or first course — **for starters** : to begin with

starter *adj* [*starter*, n.] : of, relating to, or being an item acquired with the expectation that a more elaborate or sophisticated model will be acquired in the future ⟨a ~ home⟩ ⟨stands up well enough to be considered as a ~ VCR —Ron Goldberg⟩

start–up* *n* : a fledgling business enterprise

start–up \ˈ=ˌ=\ *adj* : of or relating to the starting of a new business enterprise ⟨*start-up* costs⟩ ⟨*start-up* activities⟩

statement* *n* **1** : an opinion or message conveyed indirectly usu. by nonverbal means ⟨more than any other garment, the suit makes a ~ —*advt*⟩ **2** : an instruction in a computer program

state of the art : the level of development (as of a device, procedure, process, technique, art, or science) reached at a particular time usu. as a result of modern methods

state–of–the–art \ˈ===ˈ=\ *adj* : involving the most up-to-date methods and technology available ⟨a *state-of-the-art* computer⟩

static* *n* **1** : anything in the surrounding environment that distracts or interferes with communication ⟨sifted out, of all the forest ~, some specific squirrel sound —Chet McCord⟩ ⟨struggles to hear her own voice through the ~ of authoritarian opinion —Sara Neustadtl⟩ **2** : heated opposition or criticism ⟨he takes no ~ from anyone —David Wellman⟩

stat·in \ˈstatᵊn\ *n* -S [fr. *-statin* as final element in *lovastatin* (herein) and the names of other drugs of the group] : any of a group of drugs (as lovastatin) that inhibit the synthesis of cholesterol and promote the production of LDL-binding receptors in the liver resulting in a usu. marked decrease in the level of LDL and a modest increase in the level of HDL circulating in blood plasma

stationary bicycle *also* **stationary bike** *n* : an exercise apparatus that can be pedaled like a bicycle

statistic* *n* : a random variable that takes on the possible values of a statistic

status offender *n* : a young offender (as a runaway or a truant) who is under the jurisdiction of a court for repeated offenses that are not crimes

sta·tusy \ˈstad·əsē, -si\ *adj* : having, showing, or conferring status ⟨luggage with a distinctive ~ logo⟩

stave church *n* [trans. of Norw *stavkirke*] : a church of medieval Nordic origin that is made of wooden staves and has gables, a cupola, and often a series of pitched roofs

staystitching \ˈ=ˌ==\ *n* -S [[5]*stay*] : a line of stitching sewn around an edge (as an armhole) of a garment being made in order to prevent the cloth from stretching — **staystitch** \ˈ=ˌ=\ *vt*

STD \ˌesˌtēˈdē\ *n* -S : SEXUALLY TRANSMITTED DISEASE *herein*

steady state theory *n* : a theory in astronomy: the universe has always existed and has always been expanding with hydrogen being created continuously and spontaneously — compare BIG BANG THEORY *herein*

steak au poivre \-(ˌ)ōˈpwävr(ᵊ), -v(rə)\ *n* [F *au poivre* with pepper] : a steak that has had coarsely ground black pepper pressed into it before cooking, is served with a seasoned sauce, and is often flambéed with cognac

steak diane \-(ˈ)dīˈan\ *n, usu cap D* [prob. fr. the name *Diane*] : a steak that is served with a seasoned butter sauce and is often flambéed with cognac

steak tar·tare \-(ˌ)tärˈtär, -(ˌ)täˈtȧ(r\ *n* [F *tartare* Tartar] : highly seasoned ground beef eaten raw

stealth* *n, often attrib* : an aircraft-design characteristic consisting of oblique angular construction and avoidance of vertical surfaces that is intended to produce a very weak radar return

stealth *adj* [*stealth*, n.] : intended not to attract attention : STEALTHY ⟨a ~ campaign⟩

steamship round *n* : a very large roast of beef consisting of the whole round with rump and heel

steel drum *n* : a musical instrument made by hammering raised and tuned portions on the bottom of an oil drum

steely* *adj* : dry with the acidity predominating over the fruit flavors — used esp. of white wines made to age in the bottle

stel·lar·ator \ˈsteləˌrād·ə(r)\ *n* -S [*stellar* + *-ator* (as in *generator*); fr. its use of temperatures approaching those occurring in some stars] : a toroidal device for producing controlled nuclear fusion that involves the confining and heating of a gaseous plasma by means of an externally applied magnetic field

stellar wind *n* : plasma continuously ejected from a star's surface into surrounding space

stemmy* *adj, of wine* : having a bitter aftertaste

stent* *n* : a short narrow metal or plastic tube often in the form of a mesh that is inserted into the lumen of an anatomical vessel (as an artery or bile duct) esp. to keep a previously blocked passageway open

step* *or* **step aerobics** *also* **step training** *n* : a form of aerobics that involves repeatedly stepping on and off a raised platform

stepfamily \ˈ=ˌ=(ə)=\ *n* [*step-* + [1]*family*] : a family in which there is a stepparent

stepparenting \ˈ=ˌ==\ *n* : the raising of a child by a stepparent

stepper motor *or* **stepping motor** *n* : a motor whose drive shaft rotates in small steps rather than continuously

stepsibling \ˈ=ˌ==\ *also* **stepsib** \ˈ=ˌ=\ *n* [*step-* + *sibling*; *stepsib* fr. *step* + [3]*sib*] : the son or daughter of one's stepparent by a former marriage

ste·re·ol·o·gy \ˌsterēˈäləjē, ˌstir-\ *n* -ES [ISV *stere-* + *-logy*] : a branch of science concerned with inferring the three-dimensional properties of objects or matter ordinarily observed two-dimensionally — **ste·reo·log·i·cal** \-rēəˈläjəkəl\ *also* **ste·reo·log·ic** \-jik\ *adj* — **ste·reo·log·i·cal·ly** \-k(ə)lē\ *adv*

stereophone \ˈ===ˌ=\ *n* [[2]*stereo* + *phone*] : a stereophonic headphone

stereopticon* *n* : STEREOSCOPE

stereotactic* *adj* : involving, being, utilizing, or used in a surgical technique for precisely directing the tip of a delicate instrument (as a needle) or beam of radiation in three planes using coordinates provided by medical imaging (as computed tomography) in order to reach a specific locus in the body (as a tumor in the brain or breast) ⟨a ~ biopsy⟩ — **stereotactically*** *adv*

stereotactic radiosurgery *n* : a surgical technique involving the use of narrow beams of radiation (as gamma rays) that are precisely targeted by stereotactic methods to destroy tumors or lesions esp. of the brain

stereotape \ˈ===ˌ=\ *n* [[2]*stereo* + *tape*] : a stereophonic magnetic tape

ste·reo·tax·ic \ˌsterēəˈtaksik, ˌstir-\ *adj* [*stereotaxis* (herein) + [1]*-ic*] : STEREOTACTIC *herein* — **ste·reo·tax·i·cal·ly** \-k(ə)lē\ *adv*

stereotaxis* *n* : a stereotactic technique or procedure

ste·roido·genesis \stəˌrȯidə-, ˌstirˌȯid- *also* ˌster-+\ *n* [NL, fr. *steroid* + *-o-* + *genesis*] : synthesis of steroids

ste·roido·gen·ic \stəˌrȯidəˈjenik, ˌstirˌȯid- *also* ˌster-\ *adj* [*steroid* + *-o-* + *-genic*] : of, relating to, or involved in steroidogenesis

ste·ven·graph \ˈstēvənˌgraf\ *or* **ste·vens·graph** \-nzˌg-\ *n* -S *usu cap* [Thomas *Stevens*, 19th cent. Am. weaver + E *-graph*] : a picture woven in silk

ste·vens–john·son syndrome \ˌstēvənzˈjänsən-\ *n, usu cap S&J* [after Albert Mason *Stevens* †1945 and Frank Chamblis *Johnson* †1934 Am. pediatricians] : a severe and sometimes fatal form of erythema multiforme that is characterized esp. by purulent conjunctivitis, Vincent's angina, and ulceration of the genitals and anus and that often results in blindness

stew \ˈstü\ *n* -S [short for *steward* and *stewardess*] : an airline flight attendant

stick* *vt* **1** : to execute (a shot) successfully in basketball **2** : to execute (a landing) flawlessly in gymnastics — **stick it to** : to treat harshly or unfairly

sticker price *n* : a manufacturer's suggested retail price that is printed on a sticker and affixed to a new automobile; *broadly* : the stated cost of something

sticker shock *n* [[1]*sticker* (adhesive label printed with an item's cost)] : astonishment and dismay experienced on being informed of a product's unexpectedly high price

stick shift *n* : a manually operated automobile gearshift usu. mounted on the floor

stick–slip \ˈ=ˌ=\ *n, often attrib* : movement of two surfaces relative to each other that proceeds by a series of jerks caused by alternate sticking from friction and sliding when the friction is overcome by an applied force

sticky wicket *n* : a difficult or delicate problem or situation

stic·tion \ˈstikshən\ *n* -S [[1]*static* + [1]*friction*] : STATIC FRICTION

stiff* *vi* : to fail commercially ⟨the movie ~*ed* at the box office⟩ ~ *vt* **1** : STICK 7a ⟨~*ed* us with the bar bill⟩ **2** : SNUB 1 ⟨~*ed* sportswriters after the game⟩

stiletto heel *also* **stiletto*** *n* : a high thin heel on women's shoes that is narrower than a spike heel

still bank \ˈ=ˌ=\ *n* [[1]*still*] : a bank (as in the shape of an animal) with a slot for coins — compare MECHANICAL BANK *herein*

sting* *n* : an elaborate confidence game; *specif* : such a game worked by undercover police in order to trap criminals

[1]**stir–fry** \ˈ=ˈ=\ *vt* [[1]*stir* + [1]*fry*] : to fry quickly over high heat in a lightly oiled pan (as a wok) while stirring continuously

[2]**stir–fry** \ˈ"\ *n* : a dish of something stir-fried

stirrup pants *n pl* : women's pants that have a strap at the hem that goes under the foot

stish·ov·ite \ˈstishəˌvīt\ *n* -S [Sergeĭ M. *Stishov*, 20th cent. Russ. mineralogist + E *-ite*] : a dense tetragonal mineral SiO_2 consisting of silicon dioxide that is a polymorph of quartz and that is formed under great pressure

STM *abbr* scanning tunneling microscope *herein*; scanning tunneling microscopy *herein*

stochastic* *adj* : involving chance or probability : PROBABILISTIC ⟨a ~ model of radiation-induced mutation⟩ — **stochastically*** *adv*

stockholm syndrome *n, usu cap 1st S* [so called fr. a 1973 robbery attempt in *Stockholm*, Sweden, during which four bank employees held hostage for six days developed sympathetic feelings toward their captors] : the psychological tendency of a hostage to bond with, identify with, or sympathize with his or her captor

stoked \ˈstōkt\ *adj* [fr. past part. of [1]*stoke*] *slang* : being in an enthusiastic or exhilarated state

STOL *abbr* short takeoff and landing

stone* *adj* : ABSOLUTE, COMPLETE ⟨a zeal that might be called pure ~ craziness —Edwin Shrake⟩

stone *adv* : ABSOLUTELY, COMPLETELY — used as an intensive ⟨it is a ~ positive fact, a scientific certainty —R.A.Aurthur⟩

stone–faced \ˈ=ˈ=\ *adj* : showing no emotion : EXPRESSIONLESS ⟨a stolid, *stone-faced*, humorless technocrat —E.M.Swift⟩

stoner* *n* : one who habitually uses drugs or alcohol

stonewall* *vi* : to be uncooperative, obstructive, or evasive ⟨the Kremlin will be tempted to ~ . . . until after the election —*Business Week*⟩ ~ *vt* : to refuse to comply or cooperate with ⟨intention to ~ further requests for . . . evidence —*Newsweek*⟩

stone–washed \ˈ=ˌ=\ *adj* : subjected to a washing process during manufacture that includes the use of abrasive stones esp. in order to create a softer fabric ⟨~ denim jeans⟩

stop* *vb* — **stop a stock** : to agree to a later sale or purchase of a number of shares at the price current when the agreement is made

stop out* *vt* : to sell securities of (a shareowner) on a stop order ~ *vi* : to withdraw temporarily from enrollment at a college or university

stop–out \ˈ=ˌ=\ *n* -S [*stop out*, v. (herein)] : a person who stops out of a college or university

storage ring *n* : a device for storing a beam of high-energy particles collected from an accelerator until needed for collision with a second beam

stovepipe \ˈ=ˌ=\ *adj* [*stovepipe*, n.] *of trousers* : having creaseless legs with essentially the same circumference throughout their length

STP \ˌesˌtēˈpē\ *n* -S [fr. *STP*, trademark for a motor fuel additive] : a hallucinogenic drug chemically related to mescaline and amphetamine — called also *DOM*

straight* *adj* **1** : HETEROSEXUAL **2** : not using or under the influence of drugs or alcohol **3** : STRAIGHTBRED

straight* *n* **1** : one who adheres to conventional attitudes and mores **2** : a nonuser of illicit drugs **3** : HETEROSEXUAL

straight–ahead \ˈ=ˈ=ˌ=\ *adj* : relating to or being music performed in an unembellished manner typical of a given idiom or the performer of such music ⟨committed to playing *straight-ahead*, searching jazz with no gimmicks —David Spitzer⟩; *broadly* : STRAIGHTFORWARD, UNADORNED ⟨applauded Hollywood people's *straight-ahead* love for their work —Sheila Weller⟩

straight–arrow \ˌ=ˈ=ˌ=\ *adj* : rigidly proper and conventional — **straight arrow** *n*

straight–leg \ˈ=ˈ=\ *adj, of trousers* : having creased legs with essentially the same diameter throughout their length

straight up** *adj* **1** : served without ice : not on the rocks ⟨a martini *straight up*⟩ **2** : HONEST, STRAIGHTFORWARD

strain·me·ter \ˈstrānˌmēd·ə(r)\ *n* [[1]*strain* + *-meter*] : a mechanical, electrical, or optical instrument for measuring deformation of a body or a change in length under stress

strand·ed \ˈstrandəd, -aa(ə)n-\ *adj* [[4]*strand* + [1]*-ed*] : having a strand or strands esp. of a specified kind or number — usu. used in combination ⟨the double-*stranded* molecule of DNA⟩ — **strandedness** *n*

strange* *adj* : having the quantum characteristic of strangeness ⟨~ quarks⟩

strangeness* *n* **1** : a quantum characteristic of subatomic particles that accounts for the relatively long lifetime of certain particles and is conserved in interactions involving electromagnetism and the strong force **2** *or* **strangeness number** : a quantum number that expresses the strangeness of a particle and has a value of zero for most known particles

strat·e·gize \ˈstrad·əˌjīz\ *vb* -ED/-ING/-S *see -ize in Explan Notes*, *vi* : to devise a plan or strategy ~ *vt* : to devise a plan or strategy for

strategy* *n* : an adaptation or complex of adaptations (as of behavior, metabolism, or structure) that serves or appears to serve an important function in achieving evolutionary success ⟨the reproductive *strategies* of beech and yellow birch —L.K.Forcier⟩

strat·i·fi·ca·tion·al grammar \ˌstrad·əfəˌkāshnəl-, -shənᵊl-\ *n* [*stratification* + [1]*-al*] : a grammar based on the theory that language consists of a series of hierarchically related strata linked together by representational rules

stratified charge engine *n* : an internal-combustion engine in which the fuel charge is divided into two layers with a rich mixture in a small volume close to the spark plug that by its combustion promotes the ignition of a lean mixture in the remainder of the cylinder so that the engine runs on an overall leaner mixture

strato·pause \ˈstrad·əˌpȯz\ *n* [[2]*strato-* + [1]*pause*] : the transition zone between the stratosphere and the mesosphere : the upper boundary of the stratosphere

stra·vin·ski·an *or* **stra·vin·sky·an** \strə'vin(t)skēən\ *adj, usu cap* [Igor Fëdorovich *Stravinsky* †1971 Am. (Russ.-born) composer + E ²-*an*] : of, relating to, or suggestive of Igor Stravinsky or his music

strawberry jar *n* [prob. so called fr. their original use as strawberry planters] : a ceramic planter with pocketed openings in the sides into which small plants can be inserted for growing

straw mushroom *n* [trans. of Chin (Pek) *ts'ao³ku¹*; so called fr. their cultivation on rice straw compost] : a basidiomycetous mushroom (*Volvariella volvacea* of the family Pluteaceae) that has a conical cap and is cultivated in southeastern Asia and used esp. in Chinese cooking

streak* *n* : an act or instance of streaking

streak* *vi* : to run naked through a public place

streak camera *n* : a camera for recording very fast or short-lived phenomena (as fluorescence or shock waves)

streak·er \'strēkə(r)\ *n* -s [*streak* (herein) + ²-*er*] : a person who engages in streaking

streak·ing \'strēkiŋ\ *n* -s [fr. gerund of ²*streak*] **1** : the lightening (as by chemicals) of a few long strands of hair to produce a streaked effect — compare FROSTING *herein* **2** : the act or practice of running naked through a public place

stream* *n, Brit* : ¹TRACK 3c

streaming* *n, Brit* : TRACKING *herein*

street* *n* : the streets of a city seen as an environment of poverty, dereliction, or crime (as prostitution and drug trafficking) ⟨heroin worth about $25,000 on the ~ —Loudon Wainwright⟩

street* *adj* : of, relating to, or characteristic of the street environment ⟨~ drugs⟩ ⟨~ values⟩

street–level \'=,==\ *adj* : of, relating to, or taking place on the street ⟨the *street-level* drug trade⟩ ⟨a *street-level* novel⟩

streetscape \'=,=\ *n* -s [¹*street* + -*scape*] **1** : the appearance or view of a street ⟨the first major high-rise incursion in that cherished ~ —William Marlin⟩ **2** : a work of art depicting a view of a street

street–smart \¦=¦=\ *adj* [²*street* + ²*smart*] : STREETWISE *herein*

street smarts \-¦smä(r)ts, -màt-\ *n pl* [²*smart* + ¹-*s*] : the quality of being streetwise

street theater *n* : drama or mime often dealing with controversial social and political issues usu. performed in an informal setting outdoors — called also *guerrilla theater*

streetwise \¦=¦=\ *adj* [²*street* + ²-*wise*] : having or showing familiarity with the life and attitudes of street people; *esp* : wise and resourceful in surviving and getting what one wants on the street

strep·ta·vi·din \,strep'tavədən, -tə'vīdᵊn\ *n* [NL *strept-* (fr. *Streptomyces*) + E *avidin*] : a protein similar to avidin that is produced by a bacterium of the genus *Streptomyces* (*S. avidinii*), has four identical subunits that each bind tightly to a molecule of biotin, and is used esp. in the detection of molecules (as nucleic acids or antibodies) linked to a biotin label

strep·to·ni·grin \,streptə'nīgrən\ *n* -s [NL *strepto-* (fr. *Streptomyces flocculus*, actinomycete from which it is produced) + L *nigr-, niger* black + E -*in*; prob. fr. its dark color] : a toxic antibiotic $C_{25}H_{22}N_4O_8$ from an actinomycete of the genus *Streptomyces* (*S. flocculus*) that interferes with DNA metabolism and is used as an antineoplastic agent

strep·to·zot·o·cin \¦streptə'zätəsən\ *n* -s [NL *strepto-* (fr. *Streptomyces achromogenes*, bacterium from which it is produced) + E -*zotocin* (perh. fr. *zo-* + toxic + -*mycin*)] : a broad-spectrum antibiotic $C_8H_{15}N_3O_7$ with antineoplastic and diabetogenic properties that has been isolated from a bacterium of the genus *Streptomyces* (*S. achromogenes*)

stressed–out \'=¦=\ *adj* : suffering from high levels of physical and esp. psychological stress

stress fracture *n* : a usu. hairline fracture of a bone that has been subjected to repeated stress

stress·or \'stresə(r), -ó(ə)r, -ó(ə)\ *n* -s [¹*stress* + ¹-*or*] : a stimulus that causes stress ⟨psychological ~*s*⟩

stress test *n* : an electrocardiographic test of heart function before, during, and after a controlled period of increasingly strenuous exercise (as on a treadmill)

stretch* *adj* : longer than the standard size ⟨a ~ car⟩

stretch limo *or* **stretch limousine** *n* : a long limousine able to seat six or more passengers behind the driver

stretch marks *n pl* : striae on the skin (as of the hips, abdomen, and breasts) from excessive stretching and rupture of elastic fibers esp. due to pregnancy or obesity

stretch–out* *n* : a restructuring of a loan repayment schedule over an extended period of time

stretch receptor *n* : MUSCLE SPINDLE

stretch reflex *n* : a spinal reflex involving reflex contraction of a muscle in response to stretching

strewn field *n* [*strewn* fr. past part. of ¹*strew*] : an area in which tektites are found

striation* *n* : one of the alternate dark and light cross bands of a myofibril of striated muscle

stride piano *also* **stride*** *n* [so called fr. the repeated strides taken by the left hand] : a style of jazz piano playing in which the right hand plays the melody while the left hand alternates between a single note and a chord played an octave or more higher

strike* *n* : a perfectly thrown ball ⟨fired a ~ to first base⟩

strike force *n* : a team of federal agents assigned to investigate organized crime in a specific area

strike out* *vi* : FAIL 2e

strike price *also* **striking price** *n* : an agreed-upon price at which an option contract (as a put or call) can be exercised

striker* : a forward in soccer

string* *n* **1** : a sequence of like items: as **a** : a linear sequence of words, morphemes, or symbols **b** : a sequence of characters esp. when treated as text **2** *or* **string bikini** : a very brief bikini **3** : a hypothetical one-dimensional object that is infinitely thin but has a length of 10^{-33} centimeters, that vibrates as it moves through space, and whose mode of vibration manifests itself as a subatomic particle; *esp* : SUPERSTRING *herein* **4** : COSMIC STRING *herein*

string theory *n* : a theory in physics: all elementary particles are manifestations of the vibrations of one-dimensional strings

strip* *vt* : to take (the ball) away from another player

strip* *n* : a commercially developed area esp. along a highway

strip–chart recorder *n* : a device used for the continuous graphic recording of time-dependent data — **strip–chart recording** *n*

strip city *n* : an urban area forming a long narrow strip

strip mall *n* : a long building or group of buildings housing several adjacent retail stores or service establishments

stripped–down \'=¦=\ *adj* : lacking extra or unnecessary features : not fancy ⟨a *stripped-down* model of a car⟩

strip search *n* : a search for something concealed on a person made after removal of the person's clothing — **strip–search** \'=,=\ *vb*

strobe* *or* **strobe light** *n* : a device that uses a flashtube for high-speed illumination (as in photography)

stroke* *vt* : to flatter or treat solicitously esp. in order to reassure or persuade ⟨a gift for *stroking* the . . . bankers to whom he resold those loans —Roy Rowan⟩

stro·mat·o·lite \strō'mad·ᵊl,īt\ *n* -s [alter. of *stromatolith*, fr. NL *stromat-, stroma* + ISV *-o-* + *-lith*; orig. formed in G] : a laminated usu. mounded sedimentary fossil formed from layers of blue-green algae, calcium carbonate, and trapped sediment — **stro·mat·o·lit·ic** \-,mad·ᵊl'id·ik\ *adj*

strong anthropic principle *n* : ANTHROPIC PRINCIPLE b *herein*

strong force *or* **strong interaction** *or* **strong nuclear force** *n* : a fundamental physical force that acts on hadrons and is responsible for the binding together of protons and neutrons in the atomic nucleus and for processes of particle creation in high-energy collisions and that is the strongest known fundamental physical force but that acts only over distances comparable to those between nucleons in an atomic nucleus — compare ELECTROMAGNETISM *herein*, GRAVITY *herein*, WEAK FORCE *herein*

strong safety *n* : a safety in football who plays opposite the strong side of an offensive formation

stro·phoid \'strō,fóid\ *n* -s [F *strophoïde*, fr. Gk *strophos* twisted band (fr. *strephein* to twist) + F *-oïde* ²-oid — more at STROPHE] : a plane curve that is generated by a point whose distance from the y-axis along a variable straight line which always passes through a fixed point is equal to the y-intercept and that has the equation $\rho = \alpha(\sec\theta \pm \tan\theta)$ in polar coordinates

strop·py \'sträpē, -pi\ *adj* [perh. by shortening & alter. fr. *obstreperous*] *Brit* : TOUCHY, CONTRARY, BELLIGERENT ⟨Scotch is the drink but Scots are the people, and very ~ they get about it, too —Leslie Sellers⟩

structural gene *n* : a gene that codes for the amino acid sequence of a protein (as an enzyme) or for a ribosomal RNA or transfer RNA

structuralism* *n* **1** : an anthropological movement associated esp. with Claude Lévi-Strauss that seeks to analyze social relationships in terms of highly abstract relational structures often expressed in a logical symbolism **2** : a method of analysis (as of a literary text or a political system) that is related to cultural anthropology and that focuses on recurring patterns of thought and behavior

structural isomer *n* : a compound that exhibits structural isomerism

structured* *adj* : of, relating to, or being a method of computer programming in which each step of a problem's solution is contained in a separate subprogram having only one entry point and one exit point and in which unconditional branches from one part of a program to another are not permitted

strung out *adj* **1** : addicted to a drug **2** : physically debilitated from or as if from long-term drug addiction **3** : intoxicated or stupefied from drug use **4** *slang* : being in love

student's t distribution *n, often cap S* [*Student*, pseudonym of W.S. Gossett †1937 Brit. statistician] : T DISTRIBUTION *herein*

student union *n* : a building on a college campus that is devoted to student activities and that usu. contains lounges, auditoriums, eating facilities, offices, and game rooms

stuff* *n* : DUNK SHOT

stuff* *vt* **1** : to throw or drive (a ball or puck) into a goal from very close range **2** — used in the imperative to express contempt ⟨if they didn't like it, ~ 'em —Eric Clapton⟩; often used in the phrases *stuff it* and *get stuffed* **3** : to stop (a ballcarrier) abruptly in a football game

stuff shot *n* : DUNK SHOT

stun gun *n* : a weapon designed to stun or immobilize (as by an electric shock) rather than kill or injure the one affected

stunt* *n* : a shifting or switching of positions by defensive players at the line of scrimmage in football to disrupt the opponent's blocking

stylus* *n* : a pen-shaped pointing device used for entering data (as from a graphics tablet) into a computer

Sty·ro·foam \'stīrə,fōm\ *trademark* — used for an expanded rigid polystyrene plastic

subacute scle·ros·ing pan·encephalitis \-sklə¦rōsiŋ¦pan+\ *n* [*sclerosing* (pres. part. of *sclerose*) + *panencephalitis*, fr. *pan-* + *encephalitis*] : a central nervous system disease of children and young adults caused by infection of the brain by the morbillivirus causing measles and marked by intellectual deterioration, convulsions, and paralysis

sub·cellular \¦səb+\ *adj* [*sub-* + *cellular*] **1** : of less than cellular scope or level of organization ⟨~ organelles⟩ ⟨~ studies using synaptosomes⟩; *also* : containing or composed of subcellular elements ⟨recovered ~ fractions by centrifuging homogenized cells⟩ **2** : relating to or being a local or restricted area within a cell ⟨a ~ site of hormonal activity⟩

sub·classification \"+\ *n* [*sub-* + *classification*] **1** : a primary division of a classification **2** : arrangement into or assignment to subclassifications

sub·compact \"+\ *n* [*sub-* + ³*compact*] : an automobile smaller than a compact

sub·discipline \"+\ *n* [*sub-* + *discipline*] : a subdivision of a branch of learning or field of specialization — **sub·disciplinary** \"+\ *adj*

subduction* *n* : the action or process of the edge of one crustal plate descending below the edge of another — **subduct*** *vb*

subdural hematoma *n* : a hematoma that occurs between the dura mater and arachnoid in the subdural space and that may apply neurologically significant pressure to the cerebral cortex

sub·employed \¦səb+\ *adj* [*sub-* + *employed*, past part. of ¹*employ*] : subjected to subemployment

sub·employment \"+\ *n* [*sub-* + *employment*] : inadequate employment including unemployment, part-time employment, and full-time employment that does not provide a living wage

sub·field \'səb+,\ *n* [*sub-* + ¹*field*] **1** : a subset of a mathematical field that is itself a field **2** : a subdivision of a field (as of study)

sub·government \¦səb+\ *n* [*sub-* + *government*] : an informal or unofficial association of persons or institutions that exercises considerable influence on a formal government or organization

sub·graph \'səb+,\ *n* [*sub-* + *graph*] : a graph all of whose points and lines are contained in a larger graph

subgroup* *n* : a subset of a mathematical group that is itself a group

sub·gum \'səb'gəm\ *n* [Chin (Cant) *sahp-gám* lit., assorted, mixed] : a dish of Chinese origin prepared with a mixture of vegetables (as peppers, water chestnuts, and mushrooms)

sub·industry \¦səb+\ *n* [*sub-* + *industry*] : a lesser industry; *esp* : one derived from or dependent on a larger industry

sub·license \¦səb+\ *vt* [*sublicense*, n.] : to grant to another a sublicense for

sub·mandibular gland \"+. . .-\ *also* **submandibular** *n* -s [*sub-* + *mandibular*] : SUBMAXILLARY GLAND

submarine* *vi* : to dive or slide under something ⟨the danger of *submarining* under a seat belt in a crash⟩

sub·metacentric \¦səb+\ *adj* [*sub-* + *metacentric*] : having the centromere situated so that one chromosome arm is somewhat shorter than the other — **submetacentric** *n*

sub·millimeter \"+\ *adj* [*sub-* + *millimeter*] : being less than a millimeter in diameter or wavelength ⟨a ~ radio wave⟩

sub·mitochondrial \"+\ *adj* [*sub-* + *mitochondrial*] : of, relating to, composed of, or being parts and esp. fragments of mitochondria ⟨~ membranes⟩ ⟨~ particles⟩

sub·munition \"+\ *n* [*sub-* + ¹*munition*] : any of a group of smaller weapons carried as a warhead by a missile or projectile and expelled as the carrier approaches its target

sub·notebook \"+\ *n* [*sub-* + *notebook*] : a portable microcomputer similar to but smaller and lighter than a notebook computer

sub·nuclear \"+\ *adj* [*sub-* + *nuclear*] : of, relating to, or being a particle smaller than the atomic nucleus

sub·or·di·na·tor \sə'bórdᵊn,ād·ər, -d·ó(ə)(r)\ *n* -s : one that subordinates; *esp* : a subordinating conjunction

sub·prime \¦səb+\ *adj* [*sub-* + ²*prime*] : of, relating to, or being the issuing of credit to borrowers with poor credit ratings ⟨~ lending⟩ ⟨a ~ borrower⟩

sub·program \'səb+,\ *n* [*sub-* + *program* (herein)] : a semi-independent portion of a program (as for a computer)

sub·ring \"+\ *n* [*sub-* + ¹*ring*] : a subset of a mathematical ring which is itself a ring

sub–saharan \"+\ *adj, usu cap 2d S* [*sub-* + *Saharan*] : of, being, or relating to the part of Africa south of the Sahara desert

sub·satellite \¦səb+\ *n* [*sub-* + *satellite*] **1** : a political entity within the sphere of influence of another entity that is itself a satellite of a stronger power **2** : an object carried into orbit in and subsequently released from an artificial satellite

subscription TV *n* : pay-TV that broadcasts programs directly over the air to customers provided with a special receiver — called also *subscription television*; compare PAY-CABLE *herein*

sub·sequence \'səb+\ *n* [*sub-* + ¹*sequence*] : a mathematical sequence that is part of another sequence

subset* *n* : a smaller part : a particular aspect : PORTION ⟨the science that reaches our newspapers and magazines is a small and biased ~ of the interesting work done by professionals —S.J.Gould⟩ ⟨the business universe is just a ~ of the bigger cosmos —Stanley Bing⟩

sub·shell \'səb+,\ *n* [*sub-* + ¹*shell*] : any of the one or more orbitals making up an electron shell of an atom

sub·specialist \,səb+\ *n* [*sub-* + *specialist*] : an individual and esp. a physician having a subspecialty

subspecies* *n* : a subordinate group whose members usually share some common differential quality : SUBGROUP ⟨video documentaries about famous contemporary artists are mostly a ~ of propaganda film —Hilton Kramer⟩

substance* *n* : something (as drugs or alcoholic beverages) deemed harmful and usually subject to legal restriction ⟨possession of a controlled ~⟩ ⟨has a ~ problem⟩

substance abuse *n* : excessive use of a drug (as alcohol, narcotics, or cocaine) : use of a drug without medical justification

substance P *n* : a neuropeptide that consists of a chain of 11 amino acid residues, that is present in the nervous system and gastrointestinal tract, that causes the contraction of smooth muscle and dilation of blood vessels, and that acts as a potent neurotransmitter esp. in the transmission of signals from pain receptors

sub·stan·tia gel·a·ti·no·sa \(,)səb¦stanch(ē)ə,jelət'ᵊn'ōsə, -'ōzə\ *n* [NL, lit., gelatinous substance] : a mass of gelatinous tissue that lies on the dorsal surface of the dorsal column and extends the entire length of the spinal cord into the medulla oblongata and that functions in the transmission of painful sensory information

sub·text \'səb+,\ *n* [*sub-* + ¹*text*; prob. trans. of Russ *podtekst*] : the implicit or metaphorical meaning (as of a literary text); *broadly* : an underlying or covert message, theme, or idea — **sub·textu·al** \(')səb+\ *adj* — **sub·textually** \"+\ *adv*

sub·tidal \¦səb+\ *adj* [*sub-* + *tidal*] : of, relating to, or being the part of the neritic zone lying below the low-tide mark but still shallow and close to shore ⟨~ kelp beds⟩

sub·til·i·sin \(,)səb'tiləsən *also* ,səbtə'lisən\ *n* -s [NL *subtilis*, specific epithet of *Bacillus subtilis*, species of which *Bacillus amyloliquefaciens* was formerly considered a variant + E -*in*] : an extracellular protease secreted by a soil bacterium of the genus *Bacillus* (*B. amyloliquefaciens*) that has various commercial applications (as in laundry detergent)

sub·to·pia \(,)səb'tōpēə\ *n* -s [*sub*urbs + -*topia* (as in *utopia*)] *chiefly Brit* : the suburbs of a city — **sub·to·pi·an** \-ēən\ *adj, chiefly Brit*

subtopic *n* [*sub-* + *topic*] : a secondary topic : one of the subdivisions into which a topic may be divided

sub·viral \¦səb+\ *adj* [*sub-* + *viral*] : relating to, being, or caused by a piece or a structural part (as a protein) of a virus

sub·vocalization \"+\ *n* [*sub-* + *vocalization*] : the act or process of inaudibly articulating speech with the speech organs — **sub·vo·calize** \"+\ *vb*

sub·woofer \"+\ *n* [*sub-* + *woofer*] : a separate loudspeaker responsive only to the lowest acoustic frequencies that is used for reproducing very low-pitch sounds esp. to supplement the sound produced by standard speakers; *also* : WOOFER

succinate dehydrogenase *n* : SUCCINIC DEHYDROGENASE

succorance* *n* : a dependence on or an active seeking for nurturant care — **suc·cor·ant** \'səkərənt\ *adj*

suck* *vt* : to perform fellatio upon — often used with *off;* usu. considered vulgar ~ *vi, slang* : STINK 2, 4 ⟨charge cards ~ —Reinhold Aman⟩ ⟨as a singer, the truth was, I ~*ed* —Artie Ripp⟩

sucker* *n* — used as a generalized term of reference ⟨see if you can get that ~ working again⟩

sucker–punch *vt* : to punch suddenly, without warning, and often without apparent provocation — **sucker punch** *n*

suck–up \'=,=\ *n* -s [*suck up* (*to*), v.] : one who is ingratiating or fawning ⟨a *suck-up* to the teacher⟩

su·cra·lose \'sükrə,lōs\ *n* -s [prob. fr. *sucrose* + ³-*al* + ²-*ose*] : a white crystalline powder $C_{12}H_{19}Cl_3O_8$ that is derived from sucrose by the chemical substitution of three chlorine atoms for three hydroxy groups and that is used as a low-calorie sweetener having a sweetness of much greater intensity than sucrose

sudden infant death syndrome *n* : death of an apparently healthy infant usu. before one year of age that is of unknown cause and occurs esp. during sleep — abbr. *SIDS*; called also *crib death*

suds·er \'sədzər\ *n* -s [¹*suds* + ²-*er*] : SOAP OPERA

sugar snap pea *n* : SNAP PEA *herein*

suicide pact *n* : an agreement between two or more individuals wherein they commit suicide together or one kills the other or others and then commits suicide

suicide squad *n* [so called fr. the fact that kickoffs are more dangerous than other plays] : a squad used on kickoffs in football

sui·cid·ol·o·gy \,süə,sī'däləjē\ *n* -ES [*suicide* + -*ology* (as in *psychology*)] : the study of suicide and suicide prevention — **sui·cid·ol·o·gist** \-jəst\ *n* -s

suit* *n, slang* : a business executive — usu. used in pl. ⟨meetings with network ~*s*⟩

suitor* *n* : one that seeks to take over a business ⟨negotiations with a corporate ~⟩

sul·fa·meth·oxazole \¦səlfə,meth+\ *n* [*sulfa-* + *meth*yl- + *oxazole*] : an antibacterial sulfonamide $C_{10}H_{11}N_3O_3S$ used alone or in combination with trimethoprim (as in the treatment of urinary tract infections or acute otitis media)

sul·fin·py·ra·zone \,səlfən'pīrə,zōn\ *n* -s [*sulfin*yl + *pyrazole* + -*one*] : a uricosuric drug $C_{23}H_{20}N_2O_3S$ used in long-term treatment of chronic gout

sul·fo·bro·mo·phthalein \¦səlfə,brō(,)mō+\ *n* [ISV *sulf-* + *brom-* + *phthalein*] : a diagnostic material used in the form of its disodium salt $C_{20}H_8Br_4Na_2O_{10}S_2$ in a liver function test

sul·fo·nyl·urea \,səlfə,nil+\ *n* [NL, fr. ISV *sulfonyl* + NL *urea*] : any of several hypoglycemic compounds related to the sulfonamides and used in the treatment of diabetes

sul·fo·raph·ane \,səlfō'raf,ān, -'rāf-\ *n* -s [ISV *sulforaphen*, a chemically similar substance (fr. *sulfo-* + -*raphen*, perh. alter. of *raphanin*, an alternate name, fr. *raphanus* + -*in*) + -*ane*; prob. orig. formed as G *sulforaphan*] : an anticarcinogenic isothiocyanate $C_6H_{11}NOS_2$ found in cruciferous vegetables (as broccoli and cauliflower) that is thought to function by stimulating the production of enzymes in the body that detoxify cancer-causing substances

sulphide* *n* : a ceramic form and esp. a portrait bas-relief enclosed in clear glass where it glitters like silver

sum* *n* : UNION 1 *herein*

su·ma·trip·tan \,sümə'trip,tan, -,tən\ *n* -s [perh. fr. *suma-* (by shortening & alter. fr. *sulfonamide*) + -*triptan* (by shortening & alter. fr. *tryptamine*)] : a triptan $C_{14}H_{21}N_3O_2S$ that is administered either as a nasal spray or in the form of its succinate as an oral tablet or by injection and that is used in the treatment of migraine attacks

su·mi–e \'sümē'ā\ *n* -s [Jap, fr. *sumi* India ink + *e* drawing] : the Japanese art of monochromatic ink painting

sump* *n* : SINK 2a

sum up* *vt, Brit* : ASSESS 4 ⟨that skilled, professional inspection . . . with which we *sum* each other *up* —Doris Lessing⟩

sunbelt \'=,=\ *n, often cap* : the southern and southwestern states of the U.S. — compare FROSTBELT *herein*

sun block *n* : a preparation or its active ingredient (as zinc oxide or PABA) designed to block out more of the sun's rays than a sunscreen; *broadly* : SUNSCREEN

suncatcher \¦=¦==\ *n* : a window ornament esp. of colored glass

sun·choke \'sən,chōk\ *n* -s [¹*sun* + *artichoke*] : JERUSALEM ARTICHOKE

Sunfish \'=,=\ *trademark* — used for a light sailboat with one sail and a footwell that is designed to carry no more than two people

sungrazer \¦=¦==\ *n* : any of a group of comets whose perihelions

are very close to the sun and which are often destroyed by their close approach to it
sun protection factor *n* : SPF *herein*
sunrise \ˈ=ˌ=\ *adj* [*sunrise*, n.] : newly created : being in a period of growth or development ⟨~ industries⟩
sunroof \ˈ=ˌ=\ *n* : a panel in an automobile roof that can be opened
sunseeker \ˈ=ˌ==\ *n* : a person who travels to an area of warmth and sun esp. in winter
sunset \ˈ=ˌ=\ *adj* [*sunset*, n.] **1** : stipulating the periodic review of government agencies and programs in order to continue their existence ⟨~ laws⟩ **2** : being in a period of decline ⟨~ industries⟩
sunshine* *adj* : forbidding or restricting closed meetings of legislative or executive bodies and sometimes providing for public access to records ⟨~ laws⟩
su·per·alloy \¦süpər+\ *n* [*super-* + [1]*alloy*] : any of various high-strength often complex alloys resistant to high temperature
su·per·antigen \"+\ *n* [*super-* + *antigen*] : a substance (as an enterotoxin) that acts as an antigen capable of stimulating much larger numbers of T cells than an ordinary antigen
Super Bowl *service mark* — used for the annual championship game of the National Football League
su·per·city \¦süpə+\ *n* [*super-* + *city*] : MEGALOPOLIS
su·per·cluster \"+\ *n* [*super-* + [1]*cluster*] : a group of gravitationally associated clusters of galaxies
su·per·coil \ˈsüpə(r)+\ *n* [*super-* + [3]*coil*] : a double helix (as of DNA) that has undergone additional twisting either in the same or in the opposite direction as the turns in the original helix — **supercoil** \¦süpə(r)+\ *vb*
su·per·collider \¦süpə(r)+\ *n* [*super-* + *collider* (herein)] : a very large collider capable of accelerating particles to very high energies
su·per·computer \"+\ *n* [*super-* + *computer*] : a large very fast mainframe used esp. for scientific computations — **su·per·com·puting** \"+\ *n* -s
su·per·continent \"+\ *n* [*super-* + [2]*continent*] : a hypothetical former large continent from which other continents are held to have broken off and drifted away
su·per·cool \"+\ *adj* [*super-* + [1]*cool*] : extremely cool: as **a** : showing extraordinary reserve and self-control **b** : being in the latest style or fashion ⟨~ sunglasses⟩
supercritical* *adj* **1** *of an airfoil* : having a flattened upper surface and a trailing edge which is curved downward so that the shock wave that forms at high subsonic speeds is weaker than that of a conventional airfoil and appears farther aft **2** : being or having a temperature above a critical temperature ⟨~ fluid⟩
su·per·current \"+\ *n* [*super-* + [2]*current*] : a current of electricity flowing in a superconductor
su·per·dense \"+\ *adj* [*super-* + *dense*] : of extremely great density; *specif* : relating to or being a highly compact state of matter in which electrons and protons are pressed together to form neutrons ⟨~ neutron star⟩
su·per·fec·ta \¦süpə(r)ˌfektə\ *n* -s [blend of *super-* and *perfecta* (herein)] : a variation of the perfecta in which a bettor must select the first four finishers of a race in the correct order of finish in order to win — compare TRIFECTA *herein*
super g *n, usu cap G* [*super* giant slalom] : an Alpine skiing event combining elements of downhill and giant slalom
su·per·glue \ˈsüpə(r)+\ *n* [*super-* + [1]*glue*] : a very strong glue; *specif* : a glue whose chief ingredient is a cyanoacrylate that becomes adhesive through polymerization rather than evaporation of a solvent
su·per·graphics \¦süpə(r)+\ *n pl but sing or pl in constr* [*super-* + *graphics*] : billboard-sized graphic shapes usu. of bright color and simple design — **sup·er·graphic** \"+\ *adj*
su·per·gravity \"+\ *n* [*super-* + [1]*gravity*] : any of various theories in physics that are based on supersymmetry and attempt to unify general relativity and quantum theory and that state that the principal transmitter of gravity is the graviton
su·per·group \"+\ *n* [*super-* + [1]*group*] : a rock group made up of prominent former members of other rock groups; *also* : an extremely successful rock group
su·per·heated \"+\ *adj* [*super-* + *heated*] : very hot; *also* : exceedingly emotional or intense ⟨some of the most ~ rancorous exchanges yet in the . . . trial —William Carlsen⟩
su·per·heavy \"+\ *adj* [*super-* + [1]*heavy*] : very heavy: as **a** : relating to or being a chemical element with a greater atomic mass than that of any known element **b** : being an atomic nucleus with a higher atomic number than any known — **superheavy** *n*
su·per·heavyweight \"+\ *n* [*super-* + *heavyweight*] : an athlete (as an Olympic weightlifter, boxer, or wrestler) who competes in the heaviest class or division
su·per·helix \"+\ *n* [*super-* + [1]*helix*] : SUPERCOIL *herein* — **su·per·helical** \"+\ *adj* — **su·per·helicity** \"+\ *n*
su·per·hero \"+\ *n* [*super-* + *hero*] : a fictional hero (as in a comic book) having extraordinary or supernatural powers; *also* : an exceptionally skillful or successful person
su·per·jet \"+\ *n* [*supersonic* + [6]*jet*] : a supersonic jet airplane
su·per·majority \"+\ *n* [*super-* + [1]*majority*] : a majority (as two-thirds or three-fifths) greater than a simple majority ⟨treaty ratification requires a ~⟩
su·per·massive \"+\ *adj* [*super-* + *massive*] : having extraordinarily great mass; *esp* : having a mass thousands or usu. millions or billions of times that of the sun ⟨a ~ black hole⟩
su·per·micro \"+\ *n* [*super-* + *micro* (herein)] : a very fast and powerful microcomputer
su·per·mini·computer \¦süpə(r)¦minē, -nə+\ *or* **su·per·mini** \ˈsüpə(r)ˌminē, -nə\ *n* [*super-* + *minicomputer* (herein); *super-* + *mini* (herein)] : a very fast and powerful minicomputer
su·per·model \"+\ *n* [*super-* + [1]*model*] : a famous and successful fashion model
su·per·molecule \"+\ *n* [*super-* + *molecule*] : MACROMOLECULE — **su·per·molecular** \"+\ *adj*
supernova* *n* : one that explodes into prominence or popularity; *also* : SUPERSTAR *herein*
superoxide dis·mut·ase \-disˈmyü(ˌ)tās\ *n* [*dismutase* enzyme catalyzing dismutation, fr. *dismut*ation + *-ase*] : a metal-containing antioxidant enzyme that reduces harmful free radicals of oxygen formed during normal metabolic cell processes to oxygen and hydrogen peroxide
su·per·plastic \"+\ *adj* [*super-* + [1]*plastic*] **1** : capable of plastic deformation under low stress at an elevated temperature — used of metals and alloys **2** : of or relating to superplastic materials ⟨~ forming⟩ — **su·per·plasticity** \"+\ *n*
su·per·potent \"+\ *adj* [*super-* + *potent*] : of greater than normal or acceptable potency — **su·per·potency** \"+\ *n*
supersonic transport *n* : a supersonic transport airplane
su·per·star \ˈsüpə(r)+ˌ\ *n* [*super-* + [1]*star*] **1** : a star (as in sports or the movies) who is considered extremely talented, has great public appeal, and can usu. command a high salary **2** : one that is very prominent or is a prime attraction ⟨a diplomatic ~⟩ ⟨a ~ among growth stocks⟩ — **su·per·stardom** \¦süpə(r)+\ *n*
su·per·station \¦süpə(r)+\ *n* [*super-* + [1]*station*] : a radio or television station whose signal is broadcast nationwide by satellite
su·per·string \ˈsüpə(r)+\ *n* [*super-* + *string* (herein)] : a hypothetical string obeying the rules of supersymmetry whose vibrations manifest themselves as particles existing in ten dimensions of which only four are evident
su·per·symmetry \¦süpə(r)+\ *n* [*super-* + *symmetry*] : the correspondence between fermions and bosons of identical mass that is postulated to have existed during the opening moments of the big bang and that relates gravity to the other forces of nature — **su·per·symmetric** \"+\ *adj*
su·per·title \"+\ *n* [*super-* + [1]*title*] : a translation of foreign-language dialogue displayed above a staged performance (as on a projection screen) ⟨an opera with ~*s*⟩ — compare SUBTITLE 2a *in the Dict*

superwoman* *n* : a woman who is successful in having a career and raising a family at the same time
supply–side \ˈ=ˌ=¦=\ *adj* [[2]*supply* + [1]*side*] : of, relating to, or being an economic theory that recommends the reduction of tax rates esp. in the highest brackets to encourage more earnings, savings, and investment to expand economic activity and therefore the total taxable national income — **supply–sider** \=ˈ=ˌ==\ *n*
support* *vt* : to allow the use of by design ⟨a word processor that ~*s* a variety of printers⟩
support* *n* : SUPPORT LEVEL *herein*
support group *n* : a group of people with common problems and concerns who provide mutual emotional and moral support
support hose *n* : stockings (as elastic stockings) worn to supply mild compression to assist the veins in the legs — usu. pl. in constr.
support level *or* **support area** *n* : a price level on a declining market at which a security resists further decline due to increased attractiveness to traders and investors
support system *n* : a network of people who provide an individual with help and emotional support
suppress* *vt* : to inhibit the genetic expression of ⟨~ a mutation⟩
suppressant *n* -s [*suppressant*, adj.] : an agent (as a drug) that tends to suppress or reduce in intensity rather than eliminate something ⟨a cough ~⟩
suppressor t cell *or* **suppressor cell** *n, usu cap T* : a T cell that suppresses the response of B cells and other T cells to an antigen resulting in tolerance for the antigen by the organism containing the T cell — compare HELPER T CELL *herein*, KILLER CELL *herein*
su·pra·cellular \¦süprə+\ *adj* [*supra-* + *cellular*] : of greater than cellular scope or level of organization
su·pra·chiasmatic nucleus \"+-\ *n* [*supra-* + *chiasmatic*] : either of a pair of neuron clusters in the hypothalamus situated directly above the optic chiasma that receive photic input from the retina via the optic nerve and that regulate the body's circadian rhythms
su·pra·thermal \"+\ *adj* [*supra-* + [1]*thermal*] : being, consisting of, or generated by very energetic particles or ions
suprême* *also* **supreme*** *n* : a skinless and boneless breast esp. of chicken
su·pre·mo \səˈprē(ˌ)mō, süˈp-\ *n* -s *sometimes cap* [Sp & It, fr. *supremo*, adj., supreme, fr. L *supremus*] *Brit* : one who is highest in rank, authority, or prestige
surf* *vi* : to scan a wide range of offerings for something of interest ~ *vt* : to scan the offerings of (as television or the Internet) for something that is interesting or fills a need — **surfer*** *n*
surf·able \ˈsərfəbəl\ *adj* : suitable for surfing
surface–effect ship \ˈ==ˌ=-\ *n* : an air-cushion vehicle that operates over water
surface feeder *n* : DABBLER 2
surface structure *n* : a formal representation of the phonetic form of a sentence; *also* : the structure which such a representation describes
surface–to–air missile \¦==¦=-\ *n* : a usu. guided missile launched from the ground against a target in the air
surf and turf *n* : seafood (as lobster tails or shrimp) and a beefsteak (as filet mignon) served as a single course
surge protector *also* **surge suppressor** *n* : an electrical device that moderates power-line surges to prevent damage to attached electronic devices (as a television or computer)
su·ri·mi \süˈrēmē\ *n* -s [Jap, chopped meat or fish, fr. *suri-* grind, mash + *mi* flesh, meat] : a fish product made from inexpensive whitefish (as pollack) and often processed to resemble more expensive seafood (as crab meat or scallops)
sur·jec·tion \(ˌ)sərˈjekshən\ *n* -s [F, fr. *sur* over, on, onto + *-jection* (as in *projection*) — more at SUR-] : a mathematical function that is an onto mapping — compare BIJECTION *herein*, INJECTION *herein*
sur·jec·tive \-ˈjektiv\ *adj* [F, fem. of *surjectif*, fr. *sur* onto + *-jectif* (as in *projectif* projective)] : ONTO *herein*
sur·re·al·i·ty \(ˌ)sə(r)-rēˈaləd-ē\ *n* -ES [*surreal* + *-ity* (as in *reality*)] : the quality or state of being surreal
surrogacy* *n* : the practice of serving as a surrogate mother
surrogate mother *or* **surrogate*** *n* : a woman who becomes pregnant usu. by artificial insemination or surgical implantation of a fertilized egg for the purpose of carrying the fetus to term for another woman — **surrogate motherhood** *n*
surround sound *n* : sound reproduction that often uses three or more transmission channels to surround the listener with sound and enhance the illusion of a live hearing
sur·veil \(ˌ)sə(r)ˈvā(ə)l\ *vt* **surveilled; surveilled; surveilling; surveils** [back-formation fr. *surveillance*] : to subject to surveillance
survey* *n* : POLL 9a
sur·viv·al·ist \sə(r)ˈvīvələst\ *n* -s : one who views survival as a primary objective; *esp* : one who has prepared to survive in the anarchy of an anticipated breakdown of society — **survivalist** *adj*
su·shi \ˈsüˌshē\ *n* -s [Jap] : a dish of cold rice dressed with vinegar, formed into any of various shapes, and garnished esp. with bits of raw seafood or vegetables
sus·pens·er \səˈspen(t)sə(r)\ *n* -s : a suspenseful film
suss *also* **sus** \ˈsəs\ *vt* **sussed; sussed; sussing; susses** [fr. *suss* to suspect, by shortening & alter. fr. [4]*suspect*] **1** *chiefly Brit* : to inspect or investigate so as to gain more knowledge — usu. used with *out* ⟨arrived in London to *suss out* suitable targets for . . . bomb attacks —Edward Laxton *et al*⟩ **2** *chiefly Brit* : to figure out — usu. used with *out* ⟨when people phone in you've only got five seconds to *suss out* whether they're going to be obscene —Simon Williams⟩
sustainable* *adj* **1** : of, relating to, or being a method of harvesting or using a resource so that the resource is not depleted or permanently damaged ⟨~ techniques⟩ ⟨~ agriculture⟩ **2** : of or relating to a lifestyle involving the use of sustainable methods ⟨~ society⟩
sustained–release \=¦=¦=\ *adj* : designed to release a drug in the body slowly over an extended period of time ⟨*sustained-release* capsules⟩ — compare TIMED-RELEASE *herein*
SUV \ˌesˌyüˈvē\ *abbr or n* -s sport-utility vehicle *herein*
Sv *abbr* sievert *herein*
swamp* *n* : a difficult or troublesome situation or object
SWAT \ˈswät\ *abbr or n* -s *sometimes not cap, often attrib* [special *w*eapons *a*nd *t*actics] : a police or military unit specially trained and equipped to handle unusually hazardous situations or missions
sweat* *vt* **1** *slang* : to worry about ⟨I can't ~ the little things —Johnny Cash⟩ **2** *slang* : HARASS, ANNOY, BOTHER
sweat* *n* **1** **sweats** *pl* : SWEAT SUIT **2** **sweats** *pl* : SWEAT PANTS
sweat equity *n* : equity in a property as a result of labor invested in improvements that increase the value; *also* : the labor so invested
sweater–vest \ˈ==ˌ=\ *n* : a sleeveless pullover or buttoned sweater
sweat test *n* : a test for cystic fibrosis that involves measuring the subject's sweat for abnormally high sodium chloride content
sweep* *n* **1** : a television ratings period during which surveys are taken to determine advertising rates — usu. used in pl. **2** : a wide-ranging or thorough search of an area (as by police)
sweeper* *or* **sweeper back** *n* : a lone back in soccer who plays between the line of the defenders and the goal
sweet spot *n* : the area around the center of mass of a bat, racket, or head of a club that is the most effective part with which to hit a ball
swimmer's ear *n* : inflammation of the canal in the outer ear that is characterized by itching, redness, swelling, pain, discharge, and sometimes hearing loss and that typically occurs when water trapped in the outer ear during swimming becomes infected with a bacterium (as *Pseudomonas aeruginosa* or *Staphylococcus aureus*) or rarely with a fungus
swing* *vi* **1** : to be lively and up-to-date **2** : to engage in sex freely

swing* *also* **swing pass** *n* : a play in football in which a backfield receiver runs to the outside to take a short pass
swingby \ˈ=ˌbī\ *n, pl* **swingbys** : a flight of an interplanetary spacecraft past a celestial body (as Jupiter) close enough to use the gravitational field of the body to alter the course of the craft on its way to another body (as Saturn)
swinger* *n* **1** : a lively and up-to-date person who indulges in what is considered fashionable **2** : one who engages freely in sex
swinging* *n* : the practice of engaging in sex freely; *specif* : the exchanging of sex partners
swinging* *adj* : being lively and up-to-date ⟨~ moderns⟩; *also* : abounding in swingers and swinging entertainment
swing·man* \ˈ=ˌman\ *n* [[3]*swing* + *man*] : a player capable of playing effectively in two different positions and esp. of playing both guard and forward on a basketball team
swing–wing \¦=¦=\ *adj* : having an airplane wing whose outer portion folds back along the fuselage to give the plane an arrowhead planform at high speeds
swipe* *n* : a sharp often critical remark ⟨taking a few ~*s* at the phony model heroes —J.K.Fairbank⟩
swipe* *vt* : to slide (a card with magnetic strip or bar code) through a slot in a reading device so that information stored on the strip can be processed (as in making a purchase) — **swipe*** *n*
switched–on \(ˈ)swicht¦ȯn, -¦än\ *adj* [fr. past part. of *switch on*] : attuned to what is new and exciting
switch–hitter* *n* **1** *slang* : BISEXUAL **2** : one that is flexible or adaptable; *esp* : a person who has more than one skill or capability — **switch–hitting** \ˌ=ˈ==\ *n, slang*
swoopy \ˈswüpē\ *adj* -ER/-EST [[1]*swoop* + [1]*-y*] : having sweeping lines or movement ⟨roads sometimes straight as a laser beam, then sinuous and ~ —Dan Vorderman⟩ ⟨the ~ silhouette of the sports car⟩
sy·li \ˈsēlē\ *n, pl* **syli** *or* **sylis** [Susu *sili*, lit., elephant, a party and national symbol, fr. a nickname of Sékou Touré †1982 Guinean political leader] : the basic monetary unit of Guinea — see MONEY table *in the Dict*
symmetric group *n* : a permutation group that is composed of all of the permutations of *n* things
symmetric matrix *n* : a matrix that is its own transpose
symmetry* *n* **1** : a rigid motion of a geometric figure that determines a one-to-one mapping onto itself **2** : interchangeability of particles and equivalence of interactions existing between forces of nature at very high energies **3** : the property of remaining invariant under certain changes (as of orientation in space, of the sign of the electric charge, of parity, or of the direction of time flow) — used of physical phenomena and of equations describing them
sym·pa·tho·lyt·ic \ˌsimpə(ˌ)thōˈlid-ik\ *n* -s : a sympatholytic agent
sym·pa·tho·mimetic \"+\ *n* -s : a sympathomimetic agent
syn·anthropic \(ˌ)sin, ˌsən+\ *adj* [*syn-* + *anthropic*] : ecologically associated with man ⟨~ flies⟩ — **syn·an·thro·py** \səˈnan(t)thrəpē\ *n* -ES
syn·ap·o·mor·phy \(ˌ)sin¦apə¦mȯrfē\ *n* -ES [ISV *syn-* + *apomorphy* derived evolutionary trait or feature (fr. *apo-* + *-morphy*)] : a character or trait that is shared by two or more taxonomic groups and is derived through evolution from a common ancestral form — **syn·ap·o·mor·phic** \-fik\ *adj*
synaptic cleft *also* **synaptic gap** *n* : the space between neurons at a nerve synapse across which a nerve impulse is transmitted by a neurotransmitter
syn·ap·to·ne·mal complex *or* **syn·ap·ti·ne·mal complex** \sə̇ˌnaptə¦nēməl-\ *n* [*synaptic* + *-o-* or *-i-* + *-nema* + [1]*-al*] : a complex tripartite protein structure that spans the region between synapsed chromosomes in meiotic prophase
syn·ap·to·some \sə̇ˈnaptəˌsōm\ *n* -s [*synaptic* + *-o-* + [3]*-some*] : a nerve ending that is isolated from homogenized nerve tissue (as of the brain) — **sy·nap·to·so·mal** \sə̇ˌnaptəˈsōməl\ *adj*
synchronicity* *n* : the coincidental occurrence of events and esp. psychic events (as similar thoughts in widely separated persons or a mental image of an unexpected event before it happens) that seem related but are not explained by conventional mechanisms of causality — used esp. in the psychology of C.G. Jung
synchronous* *adj* : of, used in, or being digital communication (as between computers) in which a common timing signal is established that dictates when individual bits can be transmitted, in which characters are not individually delimited, and which allows for very high rates of data transfer
synchrotron radiation *n* [so called fr. its having been first observed in a synchrotron] : electromagnetic radiation emitted by high-energy charged relativistic particles (as electrons) when they are accelerated by a magnetic field (as in a nebula)
syndicate* *vt* : to sell (as a series of television programs) directly to local stations
synergism* *n* : interaction of discrete agents, elements, or constituents in such a way that the total effect is greater than the sum of the individual effects
synergy* *n* : a mutually advantageous conjunction or compatibility of distinct business participants or elements (as resources or efforts)
syn·fuel \ˈsinˌ=\ *n* [*synthetic fuel*] : a liquid or gaseous fuel derived esp. from a fossil fuel that is a solid (as coal) or part of a solid (as tar sand or oil shale)
syn·gas \ˈsinˌ=\ *n* [*synthesis gas*] : SYNTHESIS GAS
syn·ge·ne·ic \ˌsinjə¦nēik\ *adj* [*syn-* + *-geneic* (as in *isogeneic*)] : genetically identical esp. with respect to antigens or immunological reactions ⟨~ tumor cells⟩ — compare ALLOGENEIC *herein*, XENOGENEIC *herein*
syntactic foam *n* [*syntactic* fr. Gk *syntaktikos* putting together — more at SYNTACTIC] : a plastic in which preformed cells (as tiny hollow glass spheres) have been incorporated, which can withstand great pressures (as at ocean depths), and which floats
synth \ˈsin(t)th\ *n* -s *often attrib* [by shortening] : SYNTHESIZER *herein*
syn·thase \ˈsinˌthās, -āz\ *n* -s [*synthesis* + *-ase*] : any of various enzymes that catalyze the synthesis of a substance without involving the breaking of a high-energy phosphate bond (as in ATP)
synthesize* *vt* : to produce (as music) by an electronic synthesizer
synthesizer* *n* : a usu. computerized electronic apparatus for the production and control of sound (as for producing music)
synthetic aperture radar *n* : a radar system that uses the motion of the vehicle (as a spacecraft) carrying it to simulate a system having a much larger antenna area and that is used to obtain high-resolution images of a surface (as of a planet)
synthetic division *n* : a simplified method of dividing one polynomial by another of the first degree by writing down only the coefficients of the several powers of the variable and changing the sign of the constant term in the divisor so as to replace the usual subtractions by additions
sy·rah \sēˈrä\ *n* -s *usu cap* [F] **1** *or* **syrah grape** *usu cap S* : a grape grown orig. in the northern valley of the Rhone **2** : a wine made from the Syrah grape
sys·op \ˈsisˌäp\ *n* -s [*sys*tem *op*erator] : an administrator of a computer bulletin board
systems analysis *n* : the act, process, or profession of studying an activity (as a procedure, a business, or a physiological function) typically by mathematical means in order to define its goals or purposes and to discover operations and procedures for accomplishing them most efficiently — **systems analyst** *n*
t* *n, usu cap* **1** : T-SHIRT **2** : TECHNICAL FOUL
t* *abbr, cap* **1** tera- *herein* **2** tesla *herein* **3** thymine **4** : toddler **5** : metric ton
TA *abbr or n* -s : a teaching assistant
TA* *abbr* transactional analysis *herein*
tabard* *n* : a woman's sleeveless outer garment often with side slits
tab·bou·leh *also* **ta·bou·leh** \təˈbülē, -lə\ *or* **ta·bou·li** \təˈbülē\ *n* -s *sometimes cap* [Ar dial. (Levant) *tabbūla*; akin to Ar *taubala* to

spice, season] : a salad of Lebanese origin that usu. includes cracked wheat, onions, parsley, mint, lemon juice, olive oil, and tomatoes

ta·bla \ˈtäblə, ˈtəb-\ *n* -s [Hindi & Urdu *tablā*, fr. Ar *ṭabla*] : a pair of small different-sized hand drums used esp. in music of India

table soccer *n* : FOOSBALL *herein*

tablet* *n* : GRAPHICS TABLET *herein*

ta·can \ˈta,kan\ *n* -s *usu cap T or all cap* [*tactical air navigation*] : a system of navigation employing ultra-high frequency signals to determine the distance and bearing of an aircraft from a transmitting station

tach \ˈtak\ *n* -s [by shortening] : TACHOMETER

tach·e·om·e·try \,takēˈämə·trē, -ri\ *n* -ES [*tacheo-* (as in *tacheometer*) + *-metry*] : TACHYMETRY — **tache·o·met·ric** \¦==¦me·trik\ *adj*

tach·ism \ˈta,shizəm\ *n* -s *often cap* [F *tachisme*, fr. *tache* stain, spot, blob + *-isme* -ism — more at TACHE] : ACTION PAINTING *herein* — **tach·ist** \ˈtashəst\ *adj or n, often cap*

tachy·arrhythmia \¦takē+\ *n* [NL, fr. *tachy-* + *arrhythmia*] : arrhythmia characterized by a rapid irregular heartbeat

tachy·on \ˈtakē,än\ *n* -s [*tachy-* + ²*-on*] : a hypothetical particle held to travel faster than light

tac·rine \ˈta,krēn\ *n* -s [ISV *tetra-* + *acridine*] : an anticholinesterase $C_{13}H_{14}N_2$ administered in the form of its hydrochloride that has a stimulating effect on the central nervous system and is used in the palliative treatment of cognitive deficits (as in memory) associated with Alzheimer's disease

tad* *n* : a small or insignificant amount or degree : BIT ⟨might give him some water and a ~ to eat —C.T.Walker⟩ — **a tad** : SOMEWHAT, RATHER ⟨*a tad* overweight⟩

tae kwon do \ˈtīˈkwänˈdō\ *n, often cap T&K&D* [Korean *t'aekwŏndo*, fr. *t'ae* to kick + *kwŏn* fist + *to* way] : a Korean martial art resembling karate

tag* *n* : a graffito in the form of an identifying name or symbol — **tag*** *vb* — **tagger*** *n*

ta·gine *or* **ta·jine** \täˈzhēn, -ˈjēn\ *n* -s [dial. Ar (Maghreb) *ṭažin*, fr. Ar *ṭājin* frying pan, shallow earthenware pot, fr. MGk *tagēnon* pan, fr. Gk] : a slow-simmered stew of northwestern Africa traditionally cooked in a covered earthenware pot; *also* : the pot in which tagine is cooked

ta·gli·a·tel·le \,tälyäˈtel(,)ā\ *n* -s [It, fr. *tagliato* cut, past part. of *tagliare* to cut, trim, fr. LL *taliare* to split — more at TAILOR] : pasta in the shape of noodles

tag·me·mic \(,)tagˈmēmik\ *adj* [*tagmeme* + ²*-ic*] : of, relating to, or being a grammar that describes language in terms of the relationship between grammatical function and the class of items which can perform that function — **tag·me·mi·cist** \-ˈmēməsəst\ *n* -s — **tag·me·mics** \-ˈmēmiks\ *n pl*

tag question *n* [¹*tag*] : a question (as *isn't it* in "it's fine, isn't it?" or *is it* in "Oh it is, is it?") added to a statement or command (as to gain the assent of or challenge the person addressed); *also* : a sentence ending in a tag question

tag sale *n* : GARAGE SALE *herein*

ta·hi·ni \təˈhē(,)nē, tä-\ *n* -s [Ar dial. *ṭaḥīna*, fr. Ar *ṭaḥana* to grind] : a smooth paste made from sesame seeds

tai chi *or* **t'ai chi** \ˈtīˈjē, -ˈchē\ *or* **tai chi chuan** *or* **t'ai chi ch'uan** \-ˈchüˈän\ *n, often cap T&Cs* [Chin (Pek) *t'ai⁴ chi² ch'üan²*, fr. *t'ai⁴ chi²* the Absolute in Chinese cosmology + *ch'üan²* fist, boxing] : an ancient Chinese discipline practiced as a system of exercises for attaining bodily or mental control and well-being

tailgate* *vi* : to go on a tailgate picnic (as before a football game)

tail·gate \ˈ=¦=\ *adj* [¹*tailgate*] : relating to or being a picnic set up on the tailgate esp. of a station wagon

ta·ka \ˈtäkə\ *n, pl* **taka** *or* **takas** [Bengali *ṭākā* rupee, taka, fr. Skt *ṭaṅka* stamped coin] **1** : the basic monetary unit of Bangladesh — see MONEY table *in the Dict* **2** : a coin or note representing one taka

take* *vb* — **take a bath** : to suffer a heavy financial loss — **take a hike** *or* **take a walk** : to go away : leave the situation : DEPART — **take a position** *of a security dealer* : to hold in his own account stock bought in the course of trading — **take no prisoners** : to be merciless or relentless — **take the mickey** *chiefly Brit* : JOKE, KID — **take the mickey out of** *chiefly Brit* : to make fun of : TEASE

take* *n* : a distinct or personal point of view, outlook, or assessment ⟨was asked for her ~ on recent developments⟩; *also* : a distinct treatment or variation ⟨a new ~ on an old style⟩ — **on the take** : taking money for illegal favors

take–away \ˈ==,=\ *n* -s *often attrib* [*take away*, v.] **1** *chiefly Brit* : CARRYOUT **2** : an act or instance of taking possession of the ball away from an opposing team in football **3** : the first movement of the backswing in golf

take–charge \ˈ=ˈ=\ *adj* [fr. the phrase *take charge*] : having the qualities of a forceful leader ⟨a *take-charge* guy who never let anyone else make a decision —A.H.Raskin⟩

take–home \ˈ=¦=\ *adj* [fr. the phrase *take home*] : that may be worked on without supervision outside the classroom ⟨a *take-home* exam⟩

take off* *vb* ~ *vt, slang* : ROB ~ *vi* : to undergo a rapid increase in growth or popularity ⟨the business *took off* and has been flying high ever since —R.H.Jones⟩

takeoff* *n* : a rapid rise in activity, growth, or popularity ⟨made an economic ~ possible⟩

takeout* *n* **1** : an intensive study or report (as in a newspaper or magazine) **2** : CARRYOUT *herein*

take·out \¦=,=\ *adj* [*take out*, v.] : of, relating to, selling, or being prepared food that is not to be consumed on the premises ⟨*takeout* counter⟩ ⟨a *takeout* sandwich⟩

¹ta·la \ˈtälə\ *n* -s [Skt *tāla* hand-clapping, musical beat, alter. of *tāḍa* beating, fr. *tāḍayati* he beats] : one of the ancient traditional metrical patterns of South Asian music

²tala *n, pl* **tala** [Samoan, fr. E *dollar*] **1** : the basic monetary unit of Western Samoa — see MONEY table *in the Dict* **2** : a coin or note representing one tala

ta·leg·gio \täˈlej(ē,)ō, -ˈlā-, -zh(ē,)-\ *n* -s *often cap* [It, fr. *Taleggio*, commune and valley north of Bergamo, Italy] : a soft creamy cheese made from the whole milk of cows

talking head *n* : the televised image of the head of a person who is talking; *also* a television personality who appears in such shots

talk radio *n* : radio programming made up of call-in shows

talk show *n* : a radio or television program in which usu. well-known persons engage in discussions or are interviewed; *also* : a radio or television call-in program

talk therapy *n* : psychotherapy emphasizing conversation between therapist and patient

tallgrass prairie *n* : PRAIRIE 1a

tall ship *n* : a sailing vessel with at least two masts; *esp* : SQUARE-RIGGER

ta·ma·ri \täˈmärē, tə-, -ri\ *n* -s [Jap] : a high-quality aged soy sauce prepared with little or no added wheat

ta·ma·ril·lo \,taməˈrē(,)yō, -ēl(,)yō\ *n* -s [alter. (prob. influenced by *Tama*, legendary Maori voyager to New Zealand) of *tomatillo*] : TREE TOMATO

tam·ba·la \(,)tämˈbälə\ *n, pl* **tambala** [Nyanja, lit., cockerel] **1** : a monetary unit of Malawi equal to ¹⁄₁₀₀ kwacha — see MONEY table *in the Dict* **2** : a coin representing one tambala

ta·mox·i·fen \təˈmäksi,fen, tə-\ *n* -s [perh. fr. *trans-* + *amin-* + *oxi-* (alter. of *oxy-*) + *-fen* (alter. of *phenyl*)] : an estrogen antagonist $C_{26}H_{29}NO$ used in the form of its citrate esp. to treat postmenopausal breast cancer

T and A *n* [*tits and ass*] : curvaceous and often scantily clothed women; *also* : entertainment featuring such women

tan·door \tänˈdu̇(ə)r\ *n* -s [Hindi & Urdu *tandūr, tannūr*, fr. Pers *tanūr*, fr. Ar *tannūr* — more at TENDOUR] : a cylindrical clay or earthware oven in which food is cooked over charcoal

¹tan·doo·ri \tänˈdu̇(ə)rē\ *adj* [Hindi *tandūrī*, fr. *tandūr*] : cooked in a tandoor ⟨~ chicken⟩

²tandoori *n* -s : food cooked in a tandoor

tangent* *n* : a trigonometric function that is equal to the sine divided by the cosine for all real numbers θ for which the cosine is not equal to zero and is exactly equal to the tangent of an angle of measure θ in radians

tangle* *n* : NEUROFIBRILLARY TANGLE *herein*

tank* *n* : TANK TOP *herein*

tank* *vt* : to make no effort to win : lose intentionally ⟨~*ed* the match⟩ ~ *vi* **1** : to lose intentionally : give up in competition **2** : BOMB *herein*

tank suit *n* : a one-piece bathing suit with shoulder straps

tank top *n* [so called fr. its resemblance to a tank suit] : a sleeveless collarless shirt with shoulder straps and no front opening

tap* *vt* — **tap into** : to make a usu. advantageous connection with ⟨clothing that . . . *taps into* the currents of popular culture —John Duka⟩

tape deck *n* : a device used to play back and often to record on magnetic tape that usu. has to be connected to an audio system

tape player *n* : a self-contained device for the playback of recorded magnetic tapes

ta·phon·o·my \taˈfänəmē, tə-, -mi\ *n* -ES [Gk *taphē* burial (akin to Gk *thaptein* to bury) + E *-o-* + *-nomy* — more at EPITAPH] : the study of the processes (as burial, decay, and preservation) that affect animal and plant remains as they become fossils; *also* : the processes themselves — **taph·o·nom·ic** \,tafəˈnämik, -ēk\ *adj* — **ta·phon·o·mist** \taˈfänəməst, tə-\ *n* -s

tap–in *n* : a very short and easy putt in golf

ta·ra·mo·sa·la·ta \,tärə(,)mōsəˈläd·ə, |tə\ *n* -s [NGk, fr. *taramas* salted fish roe (fr. Turk *tarama*) + *-o-* -o- + *salata* salad] : a Greek dip or spread made from puréed salted fish roe, bread or potato, oil, lemon juice, and seasonings

tar baby \ˈ=,==\ *n* [fr. *Tar-Baby*, doll made of tar in which Brer Rabbit becomes entangled in a story by Joel Chandler Harris †1908 Am. writer] : something from which it is nearly impossible to extricate oneself ⟨the issue become a political *tar baby*⟩

tardive dyskinesia *n* : a central nervous system disorder characterized by twitching of the face and tongue and involuntary motor movements of the trunk and limbs and occurring esp. as a side effect of prolonged use of antipsychotic drugs

tar·dy \ˈtärdē, ˈtȧd-, -di\ *n* -ES [*tardy*, adj.] : an instance of being tardy (as for class)

tar·get·able \ˈtärgəd·əbəl\ *adj* : capable of being aimed at a target ⟨missiles with ~ warheads⟩

target language *n* **1** : a foreign language that is the subject of study **2** : a language into which a translation is made

tar pit *n* : an area in which natural bitumens collect and are exposed at the earth's surface and which tends to trap animals and preserve their hard parts (as bones or teeth)

tarte ta·tin \,tär(t)tȧˈtan, -ˈtaⁿ\ *n, pl* **tarte tatins** *also* **tartes tatin** *often cap 2d T* [F, Tatin tart, after the *Tatin* sisters of Lamotte-Beuvron, France, who served such tarts in their hotel restaurant *ab*1900] : a carmelized apple tart that is baked with pastry on top and then inverted for serving

tart up *vt* [²*tart*] : to dress up : fancy up ⟨*tarted up* pubs and restaurants for the spenders —Arnold Ehrlich⟩

task bar *n* : a strip of icons usu. at the bottom of a computer screen showing the running programs that may be used by selecting their icons

Tas·lan \ˈtas,lan\ *trademark* — used for thread and textured yarn

taste–off \ˈ=,=\ *n* -s [²*taste* + *-off* (as in *runoff*)] : a contest in which similar foods or beverages are compared and rated for taste ⟨a wine *taste-off*⟩

tas·te·vin \ˈtastə¦vaⁿ, -van\ *n* -s [F, lit., wine taster, fr. MF, fr. *taster* to touch, taste (fr. OF) + *vin* wine, fr. L *vinum* — more at TASTE, WINE] : a silver wine-tasting cup traditionally carried by a sommelier

¹tat *n* -s [fr. *tat* rag, perh. back-formation fr. ¹*tatty*] *Brit* : something that is tasteless or of inferior quality : JUNK, RUBBISH

²tat *n* -s [*trans-activating transcriptional regulation*] : a small protein produced by a lentivirus (as HIV) within infected cells that greatly increases the rate of viral transcription and replication and that is also secreted extracellularly where it plays a role in increasing viral replication in newly infected cells and enhancing the susceptibility of T cells to infection; *also* : the viral gene that codes for tat

tau* *n* **1** *also* **tau particle** : a short-lived elementary particle of the lepton family that exists in positive and negative charge states and has a mass about 3500 times heavier than an electron **2** : a protein that binds to and regulates the assembly and stability of neuronal microtubules and that is found in an abnormal form as the major component of neurofibrillary tangles

taurean* *n, usu cap* : TAURUS *herein*

taurus* *n, usu cap* : one born under the astrological sign Taurus

ta·ver·na \täˈve(ə)rnə\ *n* -s [NGk *taberna*, prob. fr. LGk, drinking establishment, fr. L, hut, shop — more at TAVERN] : a Greek café

tax base *n* : the wealth (as real estate or income) within a jurisdiction that is liable to taxation

tax haven *n* : a country or territory in which taxes are low or nonexistent and thus is attractive as a place to live or do business

taxi squad *n* [so called fr. a practice of Arthur B. McBride, an owner of the Cleveland Browns 1945–53, who kept surplus players on the staff of his taxi company] : a group of professional football players under contract who practice with a team but are ineligible to participate in official games

Tax·ol \ˈtak,sȯl\ *trademark* — used for a preparation of paclitaxel

taxon *abbr* taxonomic; taxonomy

tax selling *n* : concerted selling of securities late in the year to establish gains and losses for income-tax purposes

tax shelter *n* : a strategy (as formation of a philanthropic foundation), an investment (as in a venture capital enterprise or tax-free municipal bonds), or a tax code provision (as for a depreciation allowance) that reduces one's tax liability — **tax–sheltered** \ˈ=,==\ *adj*

tay·lor series \ˈtālə(r)\ *also* **taylor's series** \-ə(r)(z)-\ *n, usu cap T* [after Brook *Taylor* †1731 Eng. mathematician] : a power series that gives the expansion of a function *f(x)* in the neighborhood of a point *a* provided a power series exists and converges to the function in the neighborhood and that has the form

$$f(x) = f(a) + \frac{f^{[1]}(a)}{1!}(x-a) + \frac{f^{[2]}(a)}{2!}(x-a)^2 + \cdots + \frac{f^{[n]}(a)}{n!}(x-a)^n + \cdots$$

where $f^{[n]}(a)$ is the derivative of nth order of *f(x)* evaluated at *a*

tay–sachs disease \¦tāˈsaks-\ *also* **tay–sachs** *n, usu cap T&S* [after Waren *Tay* †1927 Eng. physician and Bernard P. *Sachs* †1944 Am. neurologist] : a hereditary disorder of lipid metabolism that typically affects individuals of eastern European Jewish ancestry, that is marked by the accumulation of lipids esp. in nervous tissue due to a deficiency of hexosaminidase, that is characterized by weakness, macrocephaly, red retinal spots, extremely acute hearing, retarded development, blindness, convulsions, paralysis, and death in early childhood, that that is inherited as an autosomal recessive trait

t–ball \ˈ=,=\ *n, usu cap T* [*tee*] : baseball modified for youngsters in which the ball is batted from a support like a golf tee rather than being pitched

t–bill \ˈ=,=\ *n, usu cap T* [*treasury*] : a U.S. treasury note

TCDD \,tē(,)sē(,)dēˈdē\ *n* -s [*tetrachlor-* + *dibenz-* + *dioxin* (herein)] : a carcinogenic dioxin $C_{12}H_4O_2Cl_4$ found esp. as a contaminant in 2,4,5-T

TCE *abbr* trichloroethylene

t cell *n, usu cap T* [*thymus-derived cell*] : any of several lymphocytes (as a helper T cell) that differentiate in the thymus, possess highly specific cell-surface antigen receptors, and include some that control the initiation or suppression of cell-mediated and humoral immunity (as by the regulation of T and B cell maturation and proliferation) and others that lyse antigen-bearing cells — called also *T lymphocyte*; see HELPER T CELL *herein*, CYTOTOXIC T CELL *herein*, SUPPRESSOR T CELL *herein*, T4 CELL *herein*

tchotch·ke \ˈchächkə, -kē; ˈtsätskə\ *n* -s [Yiddish *tshatshke* trinket, fr. obs. Pol *czaczko*] : KNICKKNACK, TRINKET

TCP/IP \,tē(,)sēˈpē,īˈpē\ *n* -s [*transmission control protocol-Internet protocol*] : a set of communications protocols used esp. for the exchange of information over the Internet

t distribution *n* : a probability density function that is used esp. in testing hypotheses concerning means of normal distributions whose standard deviations are unknown and that is the distribution of a random variable

$$t = \frac{u\sqrt{n}}{v}$$

where *u* and *v* are themselves independent random variables and *u* has a normal distribution with mean 0 and a standard deviation of 1 and v^2 has a chi-square distribution with *n* degrees of freedom — called also *student's t distribution*

tea break *n, chiefly Brit* : a short rest period during the working day for the drinking of tea

tea ceremony *n* : CHANOYU

teach–in \ˈ=,=\ *n* -s [*teach* + *-in* (herein)] : an extended meeting usu. held on a college campus for lectures, debates, and discussions to raise awareness of or express a position on a social or political issue

team foul *n* : one of a designated number of personal fouls the players on a basketball team may commit during a given period of play before the opposing team begins receiving bonus free throws

team handball *n* : a game developed from soccer which is played between two teams of seven players each and in which the ball is thrown, caught, and dribbled with the hands

tear* *vb* — **tear a strip off** *Brit* : to bawl out : SCOLD

tear* *n* [⁴*tear*] : a run of unusual success ⟨the team was on a ~⟩

teargas \ˈ=,=\ *vt* : to use tear gas on

tearoom* *n* : a men's room used as a site for homosexual activity

tease* *n* : ¹TEASER 4b

tech·ie \ˈtekē, -ki\ *n* -s [*tech*nician + *-ie*] : TECHNICIAN 1

tech·ne·tron·ic \¦teknə·¦tränik\ *adj* [*technological* + *electronic*] : shaped or influenced by the changes wrought by advances in technology and communications ⟨our modern ~ society⟩

Tech·ni·color \ˈteknə+,\ *trademark* — used for color motion pictures

tech·no \ˈteknō\ *n* -s [*techno-* (as in *techno-pop*—herein—and *techno-rock*, styles of popular music utilizing electronically created sounds)] : electronic dance music that features a fast beat and synthesized sounds usu. without vocals or a conventional popular song structure

tech·no·babble \ˈteknə, ˈteknō+\ *n* [*techno-* + ²*babble*] : technical jargon

tech·nol·o·gize \tekˈnälə,jīz\ *vt* -ED/-ING/-S : to affect or alter by technology

tech·no·phile \ˈteknə,fīl\ *n* -s [*techno-* + *-phil*] : an enthusiast of technology

tech·no·phil·ia \,==ˈfilēə, -ˈfilyə\ *n* -s [*techno-* + *-philia*] : enthusiasm for or preoccupation with technology ⟨from the technophobia of the '50s and '60s to the ~ of the '80s —Tom Shales⟩ — **techno·philic** \,==ˈfilik\ *adj*

tech·no·pho·bia \,==ˈfōbēə\ *n* -s [*techno-* + *phobia*] : fear of advanced technology or complex devices and esp. computers — **tech·no·phobe** \ˈ==,fōb\ *n* -s — **tech·no·pho·bic** \¦==¦fōbik\ *adj*

tech·no–pop \ˈteknō,päp\ *n* -s *often attrib* [*techno-* + *pop* (herein)] : popular music featuring extensive use of synthesizers

tech·no·structure \¦teknō+\ *n* [*techno-* + ¹*structure*] : a large-scale corporation or system of corporate enterprises; *also* : the network of professionally skilled managers (as scientists, engineers, and administrators) that increasingly tends to control the economy both within and beyond individual corporate groups

tech·no–thriller \ˈteknō,thrilə(r), -nə-\ *n* [*techno-* + *thriller*] : a thriller whose plot relies on modern technology

techy \ˈtekē\ *adj* -ER/-EST [*tech*nological + ¹*-y*] : characterized by technological sophistication : TECHNICAL ⟨~ outdoor gear⟩ ⟨~ innovations⟩

teeny \ˈtēnē, -ni\ *n* -ES [*teen* + ⁴*-y*] : TEENAGER

teeny·bop \ˈ==,bäp\ *adj* [back-formation fr. *teenybopper* (herein)] : of, relating to, or being a teenybopper

teenybopper \ˈ==,=\ *n* -s [*teeny* (herein) + *-bopper*, perh. fr. *bop*, v. (herein) + ²*-er*] : a teenager and esp. a teenaged girl; *esp* : one who is enthusiastically devoted to popular music and to current fads

TEFL \ˈtefəl\ *abbr* teaching English as a foreign language

Tef·lon \ˈte,flän\ *trademark* — used for polytetrafluoroethylene used esp. for molding articles and for coatings to prevent sticking (as of food in cookware)

tei·cho·ic acid \tīˈkōik-, tī-\ *n* [*teichoic*, fr. Gk *teichos* wall + E ¹*-ic* — more at DOUGH] : any of a class of strongly acidic polymers found in the cell walls, capsules, and membranes of all gram-positive bacteria and containing residues of the phosphates of glycerol and adonitol

tejano* *n, usu cap, often attrib* **1** : a Texan of Mexican descent **2** [prob. short for *conjunto tejano*, lit., Texan ensemble] : Tex-Mex popular music combining elements of traditional, rock, and country music and often featuring an accordion

tel·co \ˈtel(,)kō\ *n* -s [*telephone company*] : a telecommunications company ⟨a ~ offering long-distance services⟩

tel·e·com \ˈtelə,käm\ *n* -s [by shortening] **1** : TELECOMMUNICATION **2** : the telecommunications industry

tele·commute \ˈtelə+,\ *vi* [¹*tel-* + *commute*] : to work at home by the use of an electronic linkup with a central office — **tele·commuter** \"+\ *n*

tele·con·fer·enc·ing \¦teləˈkänf(ə)rən(t)siŋ\ *n* -s [¹*tel-* + *conference* + ³*-ing*] : the holding of a conference among people remote from one another by means of telecommunication devices (as telephones or computer terminals) — **tele·conference** \"+\ *n*

Tele·copier \ˈtelə,käpēə(r)\ *trademark* — used for transmitting and receiving equipment for producing facsimile copies of documents

tele·diagnosis \¦telə+\ *n* [¹*tel-* + *diagnosis*] : medical diagnosis made by means of telemedicine

tele·facsimile \"+\ *n* [¹*tel-* + *facsimile*] : a system of transmitting and reproducing fixed graphic material (as printing) by means of signals transmitted over telephone lines

tele·marketing \¦telə+\ *n* [¹*tel-* + *marketing*] : the marketing of goods or services by telephone — **tele·marketer** \"+\ *n* -s

tele·medicine \"+\ *n* [¹*tel-* + *medicine*] : the practice of medicine when the doctor and patient are widely separated using two-way voice and visual communication (as by satellite, computer, or closed-circuit television)

te·lem·e·try \təˈleməˌtrē\ *n* -ES [¹*tel-* + *-metry*] **1** : the science or process of telemetering data **2** : data transmitted by telemetry **3** : BIOTELEMETRY *herein*

tele·on·o·my \,telēˈänəmē, ,tēl-\ *n* -ES [*tele-* + *-nomy*] : the quality of apparent purposefulness of structure or function in living organisms due to evolutionary adaptation — **tele·o·nom·ic** \,telēəˈnämik, ,tēl-, -lē-(,)ō-\ *adj*

telephone tag *n* : telephoning back and forth by parties trying to reach each other without success

tele·processing \"+\ *n* [¹*tel-* + *processing*, gerund of ²*process*] : computer processing via remote terminals

Tel·es·tra·tor \ˈtelə,sträd·ə(r), -ātə-\ *trademark* — used for an electronic device which generates drawn video images over a background image

tele·text \ˈtelə+,\ *n* [¹*tel-* + *text*] : a system for broadcasting text over an unused portion of a television signal and displaying it on a decoder-equipped television set — compare VIDEOTEX *herein*

tel·evangelist \,tel+\ *n* [¹*tel-* + *evangelist*] : an evangelist who conducts regularly televised religious programs — **tel·evangelism** \"+\ *n*

¹tel·ex \ˈteˌleks\ *n* -ES [*tel*eprinter + *ex*change] **1** : a communication service involving teletypewriters connected by wire through automatic exchanges; *also* : a teletypewriter used in telex **2** : a message sent by telex

²telex *vt* -ED/-ING/-ES **1** : to send (as a message) by telex ⟨a script would be ~*ed* to New York —V.S.Naipaul⟩ **2** : to communicate with by telex ⟨~*ed* the league office to officially protest the . . . game —Steve Wulf⟩

tel·net \ˈtelˌnet\ *n* [*tel*etype *net*work] : a telecommunications protocol providing specifications for emulating a remote computer terminal so that one can access a distant computer and function on-line using an interface that appears to be part of the user's local system — **telnet** *vi*

tel·o·me·rase \teˈlōməˌrās, -ˌrāz\ *n* -S [*telomere* + *-ase*] : an enzyme that is a ribonucleoprotein catalyzing the synthesis of chromosomal telomeres in eukaryotic cell division and is particularly active in cancer cells

telophase* *n* **1** : the final stage of mitosis and of the second division of meiosis in which the spindle disappears and the nucleus reforms around each set of chromosomes **2** : the final stage in the first division of meiosis that may be missing in some organisms and that is characterized by the gathering at opposite poles of the cell of half the original number of chromosomes including one from each homologous pair

TEM *abbr* transmission electron microscope *herein*; transmission electron microscopy *herein*

temp* *n* : a temporary worker

temp \ˈtemp\ *vi* -ED/-ING/-S : to work as a temporary employee

tem·peh \ˈtemˌpā\ *n* -S [Jav *témpé*] : an Asian food prepared by fermenting soybeans with a rhizopus

template* *n* **1** : a molecule (as of DNA) that serves as a pattern for the synthesis of another macromolecule (as messenger RNA) **2** : something that establishes a pattern : FRAMEWORK 3

temporal summation *n* : sensory summation that involves the addition of single stimuli over a short period of time

temporomandibular joint *n* : the diarthrosis between the temporal bone and mandible that includes the condyloid process below separated by an articular disk from the glenoid fossa above and that allows for the opening, closing, protrusion, retraction, and lateral movement of the mandible — abbr. *TMJ*

temporomandibular joint syndrome *n* : a group of symptoms that may include pain in the temporomandibular joint, headache, earache, neck, back, or shoulder pain, limited jaw movement, or a clicking or popping sound in the jaw and that are caused either by dysfunction of the temporomandibular joint (as derangement of the articular disk) or another problem (as spasm of the masticatory muscles) affecting the region of the temporomandibular joint — called also *temporomandibular disorder, temporomandibular joint disorder, temporomandibular joint dysfunction*

ten·der·om·e·ter \ˌtendəˈrämәd·ə(r)\ *n* [¹*tender* + *-o-* + *-meter*] : a device for determining the maturity and tenderness of samples of fruits and vegetables

-tene \ˌtēn\ *adj comb form* [*-tene*, n. comb. form] : having (such or so many) chromosomal filaments ⟨*polytene*⟩ ⟨*pachytene*⟩

ten·ne·si \ˌte-ne-ˈsē\ *n, pl* **tennesi** [Turkmen *teňňesi*, 3d sing. poss. form of *teňňe*, lit., coin, currency] : a monetary unit of Turkmenistan equivalent to ¹⁄₁₀₀ manat — see *manat* at MONEY table *in the Dict*

ten·nies \ˈtenēz, -iz\ *n pl* [by shortening & alter. fr. *tennis shoes*] : TENNIS SHOES, SNEAKERS

TENS *abbr* transcutaneous electrical nerve stimulation *herein*; transcutaneous electrical nerve stimulator *herein*

tens digit *n* : TEN 8

ten·seg·ri·ty \ten(t)ˈsegrәd·ē\ *n* -ES [*tension* + *integrity*] : the property of a skeletal structure having continuous tension members (as wires) and discontinuous compression members (as metal tubes) so that each member performs efficiently in producing a rigid form

ten·sio·met·ric \ˌten(t)sēǀmeˑtrik\ *adj* [*tension* + *-metric*] : of, relating to, or involving the measurement of tension or tensile strength — **ten·si·om·e·try** \ˌten(t)sēˈämә·trē\ *n* -ES

ten–speed \ˈ=ˌ=\ *n* : a bicycle with 10 gear combinations

tens place *n* : the place two to the left of the decimal point in a number expressed in the Arabic system of writing numbers

tent trailer *n* : a 2-wheeled automobile-drawn trailer having a canvas shelter that can be opened up above the body to provide camping facilities

ten·ured \ˈtenyə(r)d *also* -ˌyù(ə)rd, -ˌyùəd\ *adj* : having tenure ⟨~ faculty members⟩

tenure–track \ˈ=(ˌ)=ǀ=\ *adj* : relating to or being a teaching position that may lead to one's being granted tenure

te·o·na·na·catl \ˌtāōˌnänəˈkätᵊl\ *n* -S [Nahuatl *teōnanacatl*, fr. *teō-, teōtl* god + *nanacatl* mushroom] : any of several New World mushrooms (*Psilocybe* and related genera of the family Agaricaceae) that are sources of hallucinogens

te·pa \ˈtēpə\ *n* -S [*t*ri- + *e*thylene + *p*hosphor- + *a*mide] : a soluble crystalline compound $C_6H_{12}N_3OP$ that is used esp. as a chemosterilant of insects, a palliative in some kinds of cancer, and in finishing and flameproofing textiles

teph·ra \ˈtefrə\ *n* -S [Sw *tefra*, fr. Gk *tephra* ashes — more at DAY] : solid material ejected into the air during a volcanic eruption; *esp* : ³ASH 1c

tep·pan·ya·ki \ˌtepänˈyäkē\ *n* -S [Jap, fr. *teppan* griddle, hot metal plate + *yaki* broiling] : food (as beef or fish) prepared with vegetables and usu. grilled on a large steel plate at the diners' table; *also* : this style of cooking

tequila sunrise *n* : a cocktail consisting chiefly of tequila, orange juice, and grenadine

tera- \ˈterə\ *comb form* [ISV, fr. Gk *teras* monster — more at TERAT-] : trillion ⟨*tera*byte⟩ ⟨*tera*hertz⟩

tera·byte \ˈterəˌbīt\ *n* [*tera-* (herein) + *byte* (herein)] : 1024 gigabytes or 1,099,511,627,776 bytes; *also* : one trillion bytes

ter·a·to·carcinoma \ˌterәd·ō+\ *n* [NL, fr. *terat-* + *carcinoma*] : a malignant teratoma; *esp* : one involving germinal cells of the testis or ovary

ter·a·to·gen \ˈterәd·әjәn, tәˈrad·әjәn, -ˌjen\ *n* -S [*terat-* + *-gen*] : a teratogenic agent (as a drug or virus)

tera·watt \ˈterəˌwät\ *n* [*tera-* (herein) + *watt*] : a unit of power equal to one trillion watts

ter·i·ya·ki \ˌterēˈ(y)äkē\ *n* -S [Jap, fr. *teri* glaze + *yaki* broiling] : a dish of Japanese origin consisting of meat or fish that is grilled or broiled after being marinated in a seasoned soy sauce

terminal* *adj* **1** : approaching or close to death : being in the final stages of a fatal disease ⟨a ~ patient⟩ **2** : extremely or excessively severe ⟨~ boredom⟩

terminal* *n* : a combination of a keyboard and output device (as a video display unit) by which data can be entered into or output from a computer or electronic communications system

terminate* *vt* : ASSASSINATE, KILL ⟨sent to ~ the spy⟩

ter·ra \ˈterə\ *n, pl* **ter·rae** \-r(ˌ)ē, -rˌī\ [NL, fr. L, land — more at TERRACE] : any of the relatively light-colored highland areas on the surface of the moon or a planet

ter·ran \ˈterәn\ *n* -S *usu cap* [*Terra*, the planet Earth (fr. L *terra* earth) + E ¹*-an* — more at TERRACE] : EARTHMAN

territory* *n* — **come with the territory** *or* **go with the territory** : to be a natural or unavoidable aspect or accompaniment of a particular situation, position, or field ⟨criticism *goes with the territory* in this job⟩

tertiary* *adj* **1** : being or relating to the recovery of oil and gas from old wells by means of the underground application of heat and chemicals **2** : being or relating to the purification of wastewater by removal of fine particles, nitrates, and phosphates **3** : providing tertiary care ⟨a ~ medical center⟩

tertiary care *n* : highly specialized medical care usu. over an extended period of time that involves advanced and complex procedures and treatments performed by medical specialists in state-of-the-art facilities — compare PRIMARY CARE *herein*

TESL \ˈtesәl\ *abbr* teaching English as a second language

tes·la \ˈteslə\ *n* -S [ISV, after Nikola *Tesla* †1943 Am. electrician and inventor] : a unit of magnetic flux density in the mks system equivalent to one weber per square meter — abbr. *T*

TESOL *abbr* teachers of English to speakers of other languages; teaching of English to speakers of other languages

tes·sel·la·tion* *n* : a covering of an infinite geometric plane without gaps or overlaps by congruent plane figures of one type or a few types

test* *vb* — **test the waters** *also* **test the water** : to make a preliminary test or survey (as of reaction or interest) before embarking on a course of action

test ban *n* : a self-imposed ban on the atmospheric testing of nuclear weapons that is mutually agreed to by countries possessing such weapons

test–drive \ˈ=ˌ=\ *vt* : to drive (a motor vehicle) in order to evaluate performance — **test–drive** *n*

testosterone* *n* : qualities (as brawn and aggressiveness) usu. associated with males : MANLINESS

tet·ra·ben·a·zine \ǀte·trəǀbenəˌzēn\ *n* [*tetra-* + *benzo*[*a*]quinoli*zine*, fr. *benz-* + *a* (an indicator of position) + *quinoline* + *azine*] : a serotonin antagonist $C_{19}H_{27}NO_3$ that is used esp. in the treatment of psychosis and anxiety

tet·ra·functional \ǀte·trə+\ *adj* [*tetra-* + *functional*] : of, relating to, or being a compound whose molecules have four sites that are highly reactive (as in polymerization)

tet·ra·hy·dro·cannabinol \ˌte·trəˌhīdrə+\ *n* [*tetrahydr-* + *cannabinol*] : THC *herein*

tet·ra·hy·me·na \ˌte·trəˈhīmәnə\ *n* [NL, fr. *tetra-* + Gk *hymēn* membrane] **1** *cap* : a genus of free-living ciliate protozoans much used for genetic and biochemical research **2** -S : a ciliate protozoan of the genus *Tetrahymena*

tet·ra·pyr·role *also* **tet·ra·pyr·rol** \ǀte·trəǀpiˌrōl, -rόl, -əpəǀr-\ *n* [*tetra-* + *pyrrole*] : a chemical group consisting of four pyrrole rings joined either in a straight chain (as in phycobilins) or in a ring (as in chlorophyll)

tet·raz·zi·ni \ˌte·trəǀzēnē\ *adj, usu cap* [after Luisa *Tetrazzini* †1940 Ital. opera singer] : prepared with pasta and a white sauce seasoned with sherry and served au gratin ⟨chicken *Tetrazzini*⟩

texas citrus mite *n, usu cap T* : a red spider (*Eutetranychus banksi*) that causes leaf injury to citrus trees

tex–mex \ǀteksǀmeks\ *adj, usu cap T&M* [*Tex*an + *Mex*ican] : of, relating to, or being the Mexican-American culture or cuisine existing or originating esp. in southern Texas ⟨*Tex-Mex* cooking⟩ ⟨*Tex-Mex* music⟩

text* *n* **1** : matter chiefly in the form of words that is treated as data for processing by computerized equipment **2** : FRAMEWORK 3 ⟨updated to fit the women's lib ~ for consciousness raising —Judith Crist⟩ **3 a** : something (as a story or movie) considered as an object to be examined, explicated, or deconstructed **b** : something resembling a text (as in suitability for analysis) ⟨the surfaces of daily life are ~*s* to be explicated —Michiko Kakutani⟩ ⟨he ceased to be a teacher as he became a ~ —D.J.Boorstin⟩

textbook \ˈ=ˌ=\ *adj* [*textbook*, n.] : of, suggesting, or suitable to a textbook; *esp* : CLASSIC ⟨a ~ example of bureaucratic waste⟩

tex·tu·al·ize \ˈtekschə(wə)ˌlīz\ *vt* -ED/-ING/-S : to put into text : set down as concrete and unchanging ⟨the novel *textualized* complex emotions⟩ — **textualization** \ǀ==(=)ˌlәˈzāshәn, -ˌlīˈ-\ *n* -S

textured vegetable protein *n* : protein obtained from some vegetables and esp. soybeans and used as a substitute for or added to meat

tex·tur·ize \ˈtekschәˌrīz\ *vt* -ED/-ING/-S : ²TEXTURE 2b ⟨the flat thermoplastic yarn . . . is *texturized* as it approaches the knitting needles —*Technical Survey*⟩

t4 cell *also* **t4 lymphocyte** \ˈ=ˈ=-\ *n, usu cap T* : any of the T cells (as a helper T cell) that bear the CD4 molecular marker and become severely depleted in AIDS

TFT *abbr* thin-film transistor

TG* *abbr* **1** transformational-generative **2** transformational grammar *herein*

TGF *abbr* transforming growth factor *herein*

t–group \ˈ=ˌ=\ *n, usu cap T* [*training group*] : a group of people under the leadership of a trainer who seek to develop self-awareness and sensitivity to others by verbalizing feelings uninhibitedly at group sessions — compare ENCOUNTER GROUP *herein*

TGV *abbr* [F *train à grande vitesse*] high-speed train

thalassemia minor *n* [NL, lesser thalassemia] : a mild form of thalassemia associated with the heterozygous condition for the gene involved

thal·as·se·mic \ˌthaləˈsēmik\ *adj* : of, relating to, or affected with thalassemia — **thalassemic** *n*

tha·las·so·therapy \thəˌlasō+\ *n* [*thalass-* + *therapy*] : exposure to seawater (as in a hot tub) or application of sea products (as seaweed or sea salt) to the body for health or beauty benefits

tha·lid·o·mide \thəˈlidəˌmīd, -ˌmәd\ *n* -S [*ph*th*al*ic *imide* + *-o-* + *imide*] : a sedative and hypnotic drug $C_{13}H_{10}N_2O_4$ that has been the cause of malformation in infants born to mothers using it during pregnancy

than·a·tol·o·gist \ˌthanəˈtäləjəst\ *n* : a specialist in thanatology

thankfully* *adv* : thank goodness — used as a sentence modifier ⟨the usual barking dogs, ~ more muted here than in town —Caroline Bates⟩

thatch* *n* : a mat of undecomposed plant material (as grass clippings) accumulated next to the soil in a grassy area (as a lawn)

THC \ˌtē(ˌ)āchˈsē\ *n* -S : either of two physiologically active isomers $C_{21}H_{30}O_2$ from hemp plant resin; *esp* : one that is the chief intoxicant in marijuana and is used medicinally — see DRONABINOL *herein*

the·a·ter \ˈthēәd·ә(r), ˈthiә|, |tә\ *adj* [*theater*, n.] : TACTICAL ⟨~ nuclear weapons⟩

theater of the absurd : theater that seeks to represent the absurdity of man's existence in a meaningless universe by bizarre or fantastic means

the·be \ˈtā(ˌ)bā\ *n, pl* **thebe** [Tswana, lit., shield] **1** : a monetary unit of Botswana equal to ¹⁄₁₀₀ pula — see MONEY table *in the Dict* **2** : a coin representing one thebe

t–help·er cell \ˈ=ǀ==-\ *n, usu cap T* : HELPER T CELL *herein*

the·ma·tize \ˈthēməˌtīz\ *vt* -ED/-ING/-S [L *themat-, thema* theme + E *-ize*] : to make something (as an idea) a theme or framework — **the·ma·ti·za·tion** \ˌ==tәˈzāshәn, -d·әˈz-\ *n* -S

theme \ˈthēm\ *adj* [¹*theme*] : having an often elaborate decor based on a central theme ⟨a ~ restaurant⟩; *also* : featuring activities based on a central theme ⟨a ~ cruise⟩

theme park *n* : an amusement park in which the structures and settings are based on a central theme

theorem* *n* **1** : STENCIL **2** : a painting produced esp. on velvet by the use of stencils for each color

therapeutic index *n* : a measure of the relative desirability of a drug for attaining a particular medical end that is usu. expressed as the ratio of the largest dose producing no toxic symptoms to the smallest dose routinely producing cures

therapeutic touch *n* : a technique considered part of alternative medicine in which the practitioner passes his or her hands over the body of the person being treated and that is held to induce relaxation, reduce pain, and promote healing

thermal* *adj* : designed (as with insulating air spaces) to prevent dissipation of body heat ⟨~ underwear⟩

thermal pollution *n* : the discharge of heated liquid (as wastewater from a factory) into natural waters at a temperature harmful to existing ecosystems

thermal printer *n* : a dot-matrix printer (as for a computer) in which heat is applied to the pins of the matrix to form dots on usu. heat-sensitive paper

ther·mo·form \ˈthərməˌfȯrm\ *vt* [*therm-* + ²*form*] : to give a final shape to (as a plastic) with the aid of heat and usu. pressure — **thermoform** *n* — **ther·mo·form·able** \ǀ==ǀ=əbəl\ *adj*

thermogram* *n* **1** : a photographic record made by thermography **2** : a temperature-weight change graph obtained in thermogravimetry

thermograph* *n* **1** : the apparatus used in thermography **2** : THERMOGRAM *herein*

ther·mo·gravimetry \ǀthər(ˌ)mō+\ *n* [ISV *therm-* + *gravimetry*; prob. orig. formed in F] : the determination (as with a thermobalance) of weight changes in a substance at a high temperature or during a gradual increase in temperature — **ther·mo·gravimetric** \"+\ *adj*

thermoluminescence* *or* **thermoluminescence dating** *n* : the determination of the age of old material (as pottery) by the amount of thermoluminescence it produces

ther·mo·physical \ǀthərmō, -mə+\ *adj* [*therm-* + *physical*] : of, relating to, or being the physical properties of materials as affected by elevated temperatures

ther·mo·regulate \"+\ *vb* [*therm-* + *regulate*] *vt* : to subject to thermoregulation ~ *vi* : to undergo thermoregulation

ther·mo·remanent \"+\ *adj* [*therm-* + *remanent*] : being or relating to magnetic remanence (as in a rock cooled from a molten state or in a baked clay object containing magnetic minerals) that indicates the strength and direction of the earth's magnetic field at a former time — **ther·mo·remanence** \"+\ *n*

ther·mo·sphere \ˈthərmə+ˌ\ *n* [ISV *therm-* + ¹*sphere*] : the part of the earth's atmosphere that begins at about 50 miles (80 kilometers) above the earth's surface, extends to outer space, and is characterized by steadily increasing temperature with height — **ther·mo·spheric** \ǀ==+\ *adj*

theta rhythm *or* **theta wave** *or* **theta*** *n* : a relatively high amplitude brain wave pattern between approximately 4 and 9 hertz that is characteristic esp. of the hippocampus but occurs in many regions of the brain including the cortex

thia·ben·da·zole \ˌthīəˈbendəˌzōl\ *n* -S [*thiazole* + *benzimidazole*] : a compound $C_{10}H_7N_3S$ used in the control of parasitic nematodes and fungus infections and as an agricultural fungicide

thi·a·zide \ˈthīəˌzīd, -ˌzәd\ *n* -S [*thia-* + d*iaz*ine + diox*ide*] : any of a group of drugs used as oral diuretics esp. in the control of high blood pressure

thin film *n* : a very thin layer of a substance on a supporting material; *esp* : a coating (as of a semiconductor) that is deposited in a layer one atom or one molecule thick

thing* *n* : a personal choice of activity : SPECIALTY ⟨sports just aren't my ~⟩ — often used in the phrases *do one's thing* and *do one's own thing* ⟨letting students do their own ~ —*Newsweek*⟩

think tank *also* **think factory** *n* : an institute, corporation, or group organized for interdisciplinary research (as in military strategy or social problems) — **think tank·er** \-ǀtaŋkə(r)\ *n* -S

thin–layer chromatography \ǀ=ǀ=(=)-\ *n* : chromatography in which the solution containing the substances to be separated migrates by capillarity through a thin layer of the adsorbent medium (as silica gel, alumina, or cellulose) arranged on a rigid support — compare COLUMN CHROMATOGRAPHY *herein*, GAS CHROMATOGRAPHY *herein*, PAPER CHROMATOGRAPHY *in the Dict* — **thin–layer chromatogram** \ǀ=ǀ=(=)-\ *n*

thi·o·rid·a·zine \ˌthīəˈridəˌzēn, -ˌzәn\ *n* -S [*thio-* + *piperidine* + phenothi*azine*] : a phenothiazine tranquilizer $C_{21}H_{26}N_2S_2$ used in the form of its hydrochloride for relief of anxiety states and in the treatment of psychotic disorders and severe behavioral problems in children

third market *n* [so called in distinction from the organized exchanges and the market in unlisted securities] : the over-the-counter market in listed securities — compare FOURTH MARKET *herein*

third–stream \ˈ=ǀ=\ *adj* : of, relating to, or being music that incorporates elements of classical music and jazz

third world *n, often cap T&W* [trans. of F *tiers monde*] **1** : a group of nations esp. in Africa and Asia that are not aligned with either the Communist or the non-Communist blocs **2** : an aggregate of minority groups within a larger predominant culture **3** : the aggregate of the underdeveloped nations of the world — **third worlder** \-ǀwər(ə)ldə(r), -ǀwə̄l-\ *n, often cap T&W*

thirtysomething \ˈ==ˌ==ǀ=\ *adj* : of, related to, or being a person who is in his or her thirties ⟨a ~ schoolteacher⟩ ⟨~ parents⟩ — **thirtysomething** *n* -S

ThM *abbr* master of theology

tho·lei·ite \ˈt(h)ōlēˌīt\ *n* -S [*Tholei, Tholey*, village in Saarland, Germany + ISV ¹*-ite*; orig. formed as G *tholeiit*] : a basaltic rock that is rich in aluminum and low in potassium, is found typically in the ocean floor, and is prob. derived from the earth's mantle — **tho·lei·it·ic** \ǀt(h)ōlēǀid·ik\ *adj*

thong* *n* **1** : a sandal held on the foot by a thong between the toes **2** an article of swimwear or underwear consisting of a narrow strip of material passing between the thighs and connecting with another narrow strip passing around the waist — often used attrib.

thoracic gland *n* : PROTHORACIC GLAND *herein*

Tho·ra·zine \ˈthōrəˌzēn, ˈthȯr-\ *trademark* — used for chlorpromazine

thousands digit *n* : THOUSAND 4

thousands place *n* : the place four to the left of the decimal point in a number expressed in the Arabic system of writing numbers

thread* *n* **threads** *pl* : CLOTHES

threatened *adj* [fr. past part. of *threaten*] : having an uncertain chance of continued survival ⟨a ~ species of fowl⟩; *specif* : likely to become an endangered species

three–peat \ˈthrēˌpēt\ *n* -S [blend of ¹*three* and ²*repeat*] : a third consecutive championship

three–point line \ˈ=ǀ=-\ *n* : a line on a basketball court forming an arc at a set distance (as 22 feet) from the basket beyond which a field goal counts for three points

360 \ˈthrēˈsikstē\ *n, pl* **360s** : a 360 degree turn esp. done very rapidly

thrift* *also* **thrift institution** *n* : a mutual savings bank or savings and loan association

thrift shop *n* : a shop that sells secondhand articles and esp. clothes and is often run for charitable purposes

¹throm·bo·lyt·ic \ǀthrämbōǀlid·ik\ *adj* [*thromb-* + *-lytic*] : destroying or breaking up a thrombus ⟨a ~ agent⟩ ⟨~ therapy⟩ — **throm·bol·y·sis** \ˌthrämˈbäləsəs\ *n*

²thrombolytic *n* -S : a thrombolytic drug (as streptokinase or urokinase) : CLOT-BUSTER *herein*

throm·box·ane \thrämˈbäkˌsān\ *n* -S [*thromb-* + ¹*ox-* + *-ane*] : any of several substances that are produced esp. by platelets, are formed from endoperoxides, cause constriction of vascular and bronchial smooth muscle, and promote blood clotting

throttle* *vt* : to increase the speed or intensity of by or as if by adjusting a throttle — used with *up* ⟨~ up the engine⟩ ⟨~*s* up his campaign train —James Bennett⟩ ~ *vi* : to proceed or operate at a speed controlled by or as if by a throttle — used with *up, down*, or *back*

throughput* *also* **thru·put** \ˈthrüˌpu̇t\ *n* : OUTPUT, PRODUCTION ⟨the ~ of a computer⟩

throwaway* *n* **1** : a thing made or done without care or interest **2** : a child who has been forced to leave home or who has run away from indifferent or hostile parents

throwaway \ˈ=ˌ=ˌ=\ *adj* [*throw away*, v.] **1 a** : that may be thrown away : DISPOSABLE ⟨~ containers⟩ **b** : accustomed to or depending on the discarding rather than the reusing or recycling of materials after initial use ⟨our ~ society⟩ ⟨~ economy⟩ **2** : written or spoken (as in a play) in a low-key or unemphasized manner ⟨~ lines⟩ **3** : NONCHALANT, CASUAL ⟨all put together with such style, such ~ chic —Peter Buckley⟩

throw pillow *n* : a small pillow used esp. as a decorative accessory

throw weight *n* : the maximum payload of an ICBM

thrust* *n* **1** : salient or essential element or meaning **2** : principal concern or objective

thrust·er* *also* **thrus·tor** \ˈthrəstə(r)\ *n* -s [*thrustor* fr. [1]*thrust* + [1]*-or*] : REACTION ENGINE

thrust stage *n* [*thrust,* past part. of [1]*thrust*] : a stage surrounded on three sides by the audience; *also* : a forestage that is extended into the auditorium to increase the stage area

thug·gish \ˈthəgish\ *adj* : resembling, suggesting, or being a thug : TOUGH, BRUTISH

thumb piano *n* : any of several musical instruments of African origin (as the kalimba, mbira, or zanza) that consist essentially of a resonator and a set of tuned metal or wooden strips that are plucked with the thumbs or fingers

thumbs–up \ˈ=ˌ=\ *n* -s : an instance or gesture of approval or encouragement

thumb·wheel \ˈ=ˌ=\ *n* : a control for various devices consisting of a partially exposed wheel that can be turned by moving the exposed edge with a finger

thy·la·koid \ˈthīləˌkȯid\ *n* -s [ISV *thylak-* (fr. Gk *thylakos* sack) + *-oid*; orig. formed in G] : any of the membranous lamellae of plant chloroplasts that are composed of protein and lipid and are the sites of the photochemical reactions of photosynthesis

thy·mec·to·mize \thīˈmektəˌmīz\ *vt* -ED/-ING/-S [*thymectomy* + *-ize*] : to excise the thymus of

thy·mi·co·lymphatic \¦thīmə(ˌ)kō+\ *adj* [[2]*thymic* + *-o-* + *lymphatic*] : of, relating to, or affecting both the thymus and the lymphatic system

thymidine kinase *n* : an enzyme that catalyzes the phosphorylation of thymidine in a pathway leading to DNA synthesis, that is active esp. in tissues undergoing growth or regeneration, and that is the key enzyme mediating replication in certain viruses (as the herpesvirus causing herpes simplex)

thy·mo·sin \ˈthīməsən\ *n* -s [Gk *thymos* thymus + E *-in*] : a mixture of polypeptides isolated from the thymus; *also* : any of these

thy·ris·tor \thīˈristə(r)\ *n* -s [*thyratron* + *transistor*] : any of several semiconductor devices that act as switches, rectifiers, or voltage regulators

thy·ro·calcitonin \¦thīrō+\ *n* [*thyr-* + *calcitonin* (herein)] : CALCITONIN *herein*

thyroid–stimulating hormone \¦=ˌ=¦==ˌ==-\ *n* : THYROTROPHIN

thyrotropin–releasing hormone *also* **thyrotropin–releasing factor** *n* : a tripeptide hormone synthesized in the hypothalamus that stimulates secretion of thyrotropin by the anterior lobe of the pituitary gland

TIA \ˌtē(ˌ)īˈā\ *abbr or n* -s transient ischemic attack *herein*

tic* *n* : a frequent usu. unconscious quirk of behavior or speech

ticked \ˈtikt\ *adj* [short for *ticked off,* past part. of *tick off* (herein)] : ANGRY, UPSET ⟨get a little ~ when people give me bad news in a polite way —Will Manley⟩

ticket pocket *n* : a small pocket within or just above the outside pocket of a man's suit jacket

tick off* *vt* : to make angry or indignant

[1]**ticky–tacky** \ˈtikē¦takē\ *also* **ticky–tack** \-¦tak\ *n, pl* **ticky–tackies** *also* **ticky–tacks** [redupl. of *tacky*] : sleazy or shoddy material used esp. in the construction of look-alike tract houses; *also* : something built of ticky-tacky

[2]**ticky–tacky** \"\ *also* **ticky–tack** \"\ *adj* **1** : being of an uninspired or monotonous sameness or commonness **2** : TACKY **3** : built of ticky-tacky

tidal volume *n* : the volume of the tidal air

tie–dye* *n* : a tie-dyed garment or fabric

tiger* *n* : one (as a situation) that is formidable or impossible to control ⟨how the ~ of inflation can be tamed —J.A.Davenport⟩ — often used in the phrases *ride a tiger* and *have a tiger by the tail*

tight* *adj* **1** : marked by friendliness and compatibility : CLOSE ⟨the Men's Alpine Ski Team is a ~ bunch, surprisingly free of backbiting —Herbert Burkholz⟩ **2** : being or performing music in a polished style with precise arrangements ⟨some favor ~ playing, with crisply articulated notes, others open playing, generally faster and more flowing —Eleanor Blau⟩

tight–assed \¦=ˌ=\ *adj, slang* : rigidly proper, conventional, or inhibited

tight end *n* : an offensive end in football who lines up within two yards of the tackle

TIL \ˌtē(ˌ)īˈel\ *abbr or n* -s tumor-infiltrating lymphocyte *herein*

tiling* *n* : TESSELLATION *herein*; *also* : a generalization of this to fill Euclidian space of three or higher dimensions using geometric objects of the same dimension as the space filled

tilt–rotor \ˈ=ˌ==\ *n* : an aircraft that has rotors at the end of each wing which can be oriented vertically for vertical takeoffs and landings, horizontally for forward flight, or to any position in between

time dilation *also* **time dilatation** *n* : a slowing of time in accordance with the theory of relativity that occurs in a system in motion relative to an outside observer and that becomes apparent esp. as the speed of the system approaches that of light

timed–release \¦tīmd-¦=\ *or* **time–release** \¦=¦=\ *adj* : consisting of or containing a drug that is released in small amounts over time (as by dissolution of a coating) usu. in the gastrointestinal tract ⟨*timed-release* capsules⟩

time frame *n* : a period of time esp. with respect to some action or project ⟨mandatory *time frames* within which committees must act —Guy Halverson⟩

time line *n* **1** *usu* **timeline** : a schedule of events or procedures : TIMETABLE ⟨the *timeline* of a space mission⟩ **2** : TIME CHART 2

time–of–flight \¦==¦=\ *adj* : of, relating to, being, or done with an instrument (as a mass spectrometer) that separates particles (as ions) according to the time required for them to traverse a tube of a certain length

time–out* \ˈ=¦=\ *n* : a quiet period used esp. as a disciplinary measure for misbehaving children

time reversal *n* : a formal operation in mathematical physics that reverses the order in which a sequence of events occurs

time reversal invariance *n* : a principle in physics: if a given sequence of events is physically possible the same sequence in the opposite order is also possible

time–sharing \ˈ=ˌ==\ *n* **1** : simultaneous use of a central computer by many users at remote locations **2** *or* **time–share** \ˈ=ˌ=\ : joint ownership or rental of a vacation lodging (as a condominium) by several persons with each occupying the premises in turn for a period — **time–share** \ˈ=ˌ=\ *vt* — **time–sharer** \ˈ=ˌ==\ *n*

times sign *n* : the symbol × used to indicate multiplication — called also *multiplication sign*

timetable* *n* : PROGRAM 4a — **time–table** *vt*

time–tested \ˈ=ˌ==\ *adj* : having effectiveness that has been proved over a long period of time ⟨a *time-tested* formula⟩

time trial *n* : a competitive event (as in auto racing) in which individuals are successively timed over a set course or distance

time–trip *vi* : to experience nostalgia

time warp *n* : an anomaly, discontinuity, or suspension held to occur in the progress of time

ti·mo·lol \ˈtī-mə-ˌlōl\ *n* -s [*tim-* (of unknown origin) + *-olol* (as in *propranolol* — herein)] : a beta-blocker $C_{13}H_{24}N_4O_3S$ used in the form of its maleate salt to treat glaucoma and to reduce the risk of second heart attacks

ting ware \ˈtiŋ-\ *also* **ting yao** \-ˈyau̇\ *or* **ting** *n, often cap T* [*Ting* fr. *Ting Chou,* town southwest of Peking, China, where it was originally made; *Ting yao* fr. *Ting* + Chin (Pek) *yao*[2] pottery] : a Chinese porcelain ware known since Sung times that is typically expertly potted, often decorated with engraved underglaze designs, and characteristically glazed with a milk-white to creamy white or less often an iron-red glaze

Tin·ker·toy \ˈtiŋkə(r)ˌtȯi\ *trademark* — used for a construction toy of fitting parts

tip of the iceberg [fr. the fact that most of an iceberg is submerged] : the earliest, most obvious, or most superficial manifestation of a phenomenon of unknown magnitude or potential

tir·a·mi·su \ˌtirəˈmē(ˌ)sü, -ˈmi-; -mēˈsü\ *n* -s [It *tiramisù,* fr. *tirami su!,* lit., pull me up!] : a dessert made with ladyfingers, mascarpone, and espresso

tissue* *vt* : to remove (as cleansing cream) with a tissue

tissue plasminogen activator *n* : a clot-dissolving enzyme that has an affinity for fibrin, that catalyzes the conversion of plasminogen to plasmin, that is produced naturally in blood vessel linings, and that is used in a genetically engineered form to prevent damage to heart muscle following a heart attack and reduce neurological damage following ischemic stroke — abbr. *TPA*

tissue typing *n* : the determination of the degree of compatibility of tissues or organs from different individuals based on the similarity of histocompatibility antigens esp. on lymphocytes and used esp. as a measure of potential rejection in an organ transplant procedure

tis·su·lar \ˈtish(y)ələ(r)\ *adj* [[1]*tissue* + *-lar* (as in *cellular*)] : of, relating to, or affecting organismic tissue ⟨~ grafts⟩

titer* *n* : the dilution of a serum containing a specific antibody at which the solution just retains a specific activity (as neutralizing or precipitating an antigen) but loses it at any greater dilution

tit·fer \ˈtitfə(r)\ *n* -s [by shortening & alter. fr. *tit for tat,* rhyming slang for *hat*] *Brit* : HAT

TLC *abbr* thin layer chromatography

t lymphocyte *n, usu cap T* [*thymus*-derived *lymphocyte*] : T CELL *herein*

TM* *abbr* transcendental meditation *herein*

TMJ *abbr* temporomandibular joint *herein*; temporomandibular joint syndrome *herein*

TNF *abbr* tumor necrosis factor *herein*

toast* *n* : a rhyming narrative poem existing in oral tradition among black Americans — **toast*** *vi* — **toaster*** *n*

toaster oven *n* : a portable electrical appliance that can function as an oven or a toaster

to·bra·my·cin \ˌtōbrəˈmīsən\ *n* -s [*tobra-* (prob. modif. of NL *tenebrarius,* specific epithet of *Streptomyces tenebrarius*) + *-mycin*] : a water-soluble antibiotic $C_{18}H_{37}N_5O_9$ derived from a soil bacterium of the genus *Streptomyces* (*S. tenebrarius*) and effective esp. against gram-negative bacteria

toea \ˈtȯiə\ *n, pl* **toea** *also* **toeas** [Hiri Motu (pidgin of Papua New Guinea based on Motu), a kind of shell] **1** : a monetary unit of Papua New Guinea equal to 1/100 kina — see MONEY table *in the Dict* **2** : a coin representing one toea

toe loop *n* a jump in figure skating with a takeoff from the back outside edge of one skate followed by a full turn in the air and a landing on the back outside edge of the same skate

toe–to–toe \¦=¦=\ *adj (or adv)* : characterized by direct and aggressive fighting or conflict ⟨a *toe-to-toe* confrontation⟩

together *adj* [*together,* adv.] **1** : appropriately prepared, organized, or balanced ⟨a super-delicious, beautifully ~ album —Clayton Riley⟩ **2** : composed in mind or manner ⟨a warm, sensitive, reasonably ~ girl —*East Village Other*⟩

toggle* *vb* ~ *vi* : to switch between two options esp. of an electronic device usu. by pressing a single button or a simple key combination

to·ka·mak \ˈtōkəˌmak, ˈtäk-\ *n* -s [Russ, fr. *to*roidal'naya *ka*mera s *ma*ksial'nym *ma*gnitnym polem (toroidal chamber with an axial magnetic field)] : a toroidal device for producing controlled nuclear fusion that involves the confining and heating of a gaseous plasma by means of an internal electric current and its attendant magnetic field

[1]**toke** \ˈtōk\ *n* -s [prob. fr. AmerSp, lit., touch, test, fr. *tocar* to touch, fr. (assumed) VL *toccare* — more at TOUCH] *slang* : a puff on a marijuana cigarette or pipe — **toke** *vi* -ED/-ING/-S *slang*

[2]**toke** \"\ *n* -s [perh. fr. *toke* (food, portion of bread)] *slang* : a tip given esp. by a gambler to the dealer at a casino

token* *n* : a member of a group (as a minority) that is included within a larger group through tokenism; *esp* : a token employee

token* *adj* : serving or intended to show by one's position an absence of discriminatory policies ⟨a ~ female employee⟩

to·ken·ism \ˈtōkəˌnizəm\ *n* -s : the policy or practice of making only a token effort (as to desegregate or provide equal employment opportunities) — **to·ken·is·tic** \¦tōkə¦nistik\ *adj*

tok pis·in \ˈtȯkˈpisin\ *n, pl* **tok pisins** *usu cap T&P* [Neo-Melanesian, lit., pidgin talk] : an English-based creole that is a national language of Papua New Guinea

to·lar \ˈtōlär\ *n, pl* **to·lar·jev** \ˈtōlärˌyev\ *or* **tolars** [Slovene (nom. pl. *tolarji,* gen. pl. *tolarjev*), fr. G *taler* taler] : the basic monetary unit of Slovenia — see MONEY table *in the Dict*

to·laz·o·line \tōˈlazəˌlēn\ *n* -s [*tol-* + *azole* + [2]*-ine*] : a weak alpha-adrenergic blocking agent $C_{10}H_{12}N_2$ used in the form of its hydrochloride to produce peripheral vasodilatation

toll–free \¦=¦=\ *adj (or adv)* of, relating to, or being a telephone call that is not charged to the party originating the call

tom* *n, usu cap* : UNCLE TOM

tom *vi* **tommed; tommed; tomming; toms** *often cap* : UNCLE TOM *herein*

tomme *also* **tome** \ˈtȯm\ *n* -s *usu cap* [F *tomme, tome,* fr. F dial. (Savoy, Dauphiné)] : any of several surface-ripened cheeses originating in the Alps

ton* *n* **1** *also* **ton–up** \ˈ=¦=\ *Brit* : a speed of 100 miles per hour — often used in the phrase *do the ton* or *do a ton* ⟨the first cars were doing the ~ barely ten years after Victoria's Diamond Jubilee —*London Times*⟩ **2** *Brit* : a score of 100 runs in cricket : CENTURY — **a ton** : with great force or power ⟨hits the ball *a ton* —Ted Williams⟩

tone block *n* : a rhythm band instrument consisting of a hand-held usu. slotted block of wood struck by a rod or drumstick

toner* *n* **1** : ASTRINGENT b ⟨skin ~*s*⟩ **2** : a substance (as a thermoplastic powder) used esp. in photocopiers and laser printers to develop a latent xerographic image on a piece of paper

tongue–in–cheek \¦==¦=\ *n* [*tongue in cheek*] a manner or attitude of insincerity, irony, or whimsical exaggeration esp. for teasing or comic effect

tonicity* *n* : the osmotic pressure of a solution

tonkinese* *n, pl* **tonkinese** *usu cap* : any of a breed of short-haired cats developed in the U.S. by crossing the Siamese with the Burmese that have a brown, bluish gray, or beige body coat with darker points and blue-green eyes

tonne \ˈtən\ *n* -s [F, fr. *tonne* tun, fr. OF — more at TUNNEL] : METRIC TON

tool* *n* **tools** *pl* : natural ability ⟨has all the ~*s* to be a great pitcher⟩

tool *n* -s [[2]*tool*] : a design (as on the binding of a book) made by tooling

toolbar* *n* : a strip esp. of icons on a computer display providing quick access to certain functions

toot* *vt* [[3]*toot*] *slang* : to take in (as cocaine) by inhalation : SNORT

toot* *n, slang* : COCAINE; *also* : a snort of cocaine

tooth fairy *n* : a fairy believed by children to leave money while they sleep in exchange for a tooth that has come out

toothpick* *n* : a small often elaborate container for a supply of toothpicks at table

top* *adj* : having a quantum characteristic whose existence was postulated on the basis of the discovery of the bottom quark ⟨~ quark⟩ — **over the top*** : beyond the bounds of what is expected, usual, normal, or appropriate

top dollar *n* : the highest amount being paid for a commodity or service ⟨willing to pay *top dollar* to get them —Dean Failey⟩

top–down* *adj* : proceeding by breaking large general aspects (as of a problem) into smaller more manageable constituents : working from the general to the specific ⟨~ programming⟩

[1]**top 40** *n pl, often cap T* : the 40 best-selling audio recordings for a given period

[2]**top 40** *adj* : constituting, playing, or listing the top 40 ⟨*top 40* tunes⟩ ⟨*top 40* stations⟩

top gun *n* : one who is at the top (as in ability, rank, or prestige)

top–heavy* *adj* : oversupplied with one element at the expense of others : lacking balance ⟨a novel *top-heavy* with description⟩

to·po·cen·tric \¦täpə¦sen-trik, ¦tōp-\ *adj* [*top-* + *-centric*] : relating to, measured from, or as if observed from a particular point on the earth's surface : having or relating to such a point as origin ⟨~ coordinates⟩ — compare GEOCENTRIC *in the Dict*

topo·isom·er·ase \ˌtōpōīˈsäməˌrās, -ˌrāz\ *n* -s [*top-* + *isomerase*] : any of a class of enzymes that reduce supercoiling in DNA by breaking and rejoining one or both strands of the DNA molecule

topological* *adj* : being or involving properties unaltered under a homeomorphism

topological group *n* : a mathematical group which is also a topological space, whose multiplicative operation is continuous such that given any neighborhood of a product there exist neighborhoods of the elements composing the product with the property that any pair of elements representing each of these neighborhoods form a product belonging to the given neighborhood, and whose operation of taking inverses is continuous such that for any neighborhood of the inverse of an element there exists a neighborhood of the element itself in which every element has its inverse in the other neighborhood

topologically equivalent *adj* : related by a homeomorphism

topological space *n* : a set with a collection of subsets satisfying the conditions that both the empty set and the set itself belong to the collection, the union of any number of the subsets is also an element of the collection, and the intersection of any finite number of the subsets is an element of the collection

topological transformation *n* : HOMEOMORPHISM 2

topology* *n* **1** : the set of all open sets of a topological space **2** : CONFIGURATION ⟨~ of a molecule⟩ ⟨~ of a computer network⟩

top·onomastic \(ˌ)täp, ˌtəp+\ *adj* [*top-* + *onomastic*] : of or relating to place names ⟨~ study⟩

to·pos \ˈtōˌpōs, ˈtäˌp-\ *n, pl* **to·poi** \-ˌpȯi\ [Gk, place, commonplace, topic — more at TOPIC] : a stock rhetorical theme or topic

tops *adv* [*tops,* adj.] : at the very most ⟨will cost $50, ~⟩

Top–Sid·er \ˈtäpˌsīdə(r)\ *trademark* — used for a low casual shoe having a rubber sole

toque* *n* : a tall brimless usu. white hat worn by a chef — called also *toque blanche*

TOR *abbr* third order regular

tor·chiere \tȯrˈsh(y)e(ə)r, -ˈshē(ə)r\ *also* **tor·chier** *n* -s [by alter.] : TORCHÈRE 2

torpedo* *n* : GRINDER 6

torque *vt* -ED/-ING/-S [[2]*torque*] : to impart torque to : cause to twist (as about an axis) — **torqu·er** \ˈtȯrkər\ *n* -s

tos·yl·ate \ˈtäsəˌlāt\ *n* -s [*tosyl* + [1]*-ate*] : an ester of the para isomer of toluenesulfonic acid

total* *vt* : to make a total wreck of (as a vehicle) : damage so badly that the cost of repairs exceeds the market value of the vehicle : DEMOLISH

total environment *n* : ENVIRONMENT *herein*

tote* *n* : TOTE BAG

tot lot *n* : a small playground for young children

touch* *vb* — **touch base** : to come in contact or communication ⟨coming in from the cold to *touch base* with civilization —Carla Hunt⟩

touch–and–go** *n* : an airplane landing followed immediately by application of power and a takeoff and usu. executed as one of a series for practice at landings

touch pad *n* : a keypad for an electronic device (as a microwave oven) that consists of a flat surface divided into several differently worked areas which are touched to choose options

touch screen *n* : a display screen on which the user selects options (as from a menu) by touching the screen

touchstone* *n* : a fundamental or quintessential part or feature ⟨among the ~*s* of his conversation were terms like "discipline," "craft," "tradition" —H.L.Gates, Jr.⟩ ⟨nor can one possess the work merely by studying the ~ passages —Benjamin De Mott⟩

Touch–Tone \ˈ=¦=\ *trademark* — used for a telephone having push buttons that produce tones corresponding to numbers

touchy–feely \ˌtəchēˈfēlē\ *adj* [[1]*touch* + [1]*-y* + [1]*feel* + [1]*-y*] : characterized by or encouraging interpersonal touching esp. in the free expression of emotions ⟨*touchy-feely* therapy⟩; *also* : openly or excessively emotional and personal ⟨*touchy-feely* management⟩

tough* *adj, slang* : EXCELLENT, SPLENDID, GREAT — used as a generalized term of approval

tou·rette's syndrome \tu̇ˈrets-\ *or* **tou·rette syndrome** \-ˈret-\ *n, usu cap T* [after Georges Gille de la *Tourette* †1904 Fr. physician] : a chronic familial neuropsychiatric disorder that usu. first appears in childhood, that is characterized by multiple tics affecting both bodily movements and vocalizations and often by several psychiatric and behavioral problems (as attention deficit disorder, obsessive-compulsive behavior, and inappropriate or offensive use of language), and that occurs much more often in males than females

touring car* *n* : a usu. 2-door sedan as distinguished from a sports car

tourist trap *n* : a place that exploits tourists

TOW \ˈtō\ *n* -s [*t*ube–launched *o*ptically tracked *w*ire–guided] : an antitank missile that trails a wire by which it is guided in flight

tow–away zone \ˈ==-\ *n* [fr. the phrase *tow away*] : a no-parking zone from which parked vehicles may be towed away

towel·ette \¦tau̇(ə)¦let\ *n* -s [[1]*towel* + *-ette*] : a usu. premoistened small piece of material used for personal cleansing

tower block *n, Brit* : a tall building (as a high-rise apartment building)

town house* *n* : a single-family house of two or sometimes three stories connected to another house by a common sidewall; *also* : ROW HOUSE

toxic shock syndrome *also* **toxic shock** *n* : an acute and sometimes fatal disease that is characterized by fever, nausea, diarrhea, diffuse erythema, and shock, that is associated esp. with the presence of a bacterium of the genus *Staphylococcus* (*S. aureus*), and that occurs esp. in menstruating females using tampons

toy boy *n* : an attractive young man; *esp* : one who is kept by an older lover ⟨the female superstar with her *toy boy*⟩

TPA *abbr* tissue plasminogen activator *herein*

trace fossil *n* : a fossil that shows the existence or activity of an animal or plant but is not formed from the animal or plant itself ⟨*trace fossils* of dinosaur footprints and arthropod burrows⟩

tra·cheo·esophageal \¦trākē(ˌ)ō, trə¦kēō+\ *adj* [*trache-* + *esophageal*] : relating to or connecting the trachea and esophagus

track* *n* **1** : [1]BAND 8; *also* : any of several sections into which a recording medium (as magnetic tape or a floppy disk) may be divided and on which material (as music or information) may be recorded **2** : material recorded esp. on a track : RECORDING 2a ⟨laugh ~⟩ ⟨several exuberant instrumental ~*s*⟩

track* *vt* **1** : to assign (students) to a curricular track **2** : to keep track of (as a trend) : FOLLOW ~ *vi* : to move or progress in accordance with or be consistent with an expected or reasonable pattern

track·ball \ˈ=ˌ=\ *n* [[1]*track* + [1]*ball*] : a ball mounted usu. in a computer console so that only a small portion extends from the surrounding surface and rotated to control the movement of a cursor on a display

track·ing \ˈtrakiŋ\ *n* -s : the policy or practice of assigning students to a curricular track

track lighting *n* : adjustable lamps mounted along an electrified metal track

track record *n* : a record of accomplishments

tracksuit \ˈ=ˌ=\ *n* [[1]*track* + [1]*suit*] : a lightweight suit of clothing consisting usu. of a jacket and pants and often worn by athletes (as runners) when working out or warming up

trackway* *n* : a series of fossilized footprints (as of a dinosaur)

tract house *n* : one of many similarly designed houses built on a tract of land

trade* *n* **1** *slang* : male homosexuals who are prostitutes and often of aggressively masculine manner; *also* : a homosexual of this sort **2** : a publication intended for those in the entertainment business — usu. used in pl.

trade* *adj* : having a larger softcover format than that of a mass-market paperback and usu. sold only in bookstores ⟨~ paperbacks⟩; *also* : of or relating to the publishing of such books
trade·craft \ˈ=,=\ *n* [¹*trade* + ¹*craft*] : the techniques and procedures of espionage
trade–off \ˈ=,=\ *n* -s [*trade off*, v.] **1** : a balancing of desirable considerations or goals all of which are not attainable at the same time ⟨the education versus experience *trade-off* which governs personnel practices —H.S.White⟩ **2** : a giving up of one thing in return for another : EXCHANGE
trail bike *n* : a small motorcycle designed for use off of public thoroughfares
trail·er·able \ˈtrālərəbəl\ *adj* : able to be conveyed by a trailer
trailhead \ˈ=,=\ *n* : the point at which a trail begins
trail mix *n* : a mixture of nuts, seeds, and dried fruits used for a snack esp. by hikers
train·ee·ship \trāˈnē,ship\ *n* : the position or status of a trainee; *specif* : one involving a program of advanced training and study esp. in a medical science and usu. bearing a stipend and allowances (as for travel)
training wheels *n pl* : a pair of small wheels connected to the rear axle of a bicycle to help a beginning bicyclist maintain balance
tramp art *n* : a style of wood carving flourishing in the U.S. from about 1875 to 1930 that is characterized by ornate layered whittling often of cigar boxes or fruit crates; *also* : an object of wood carved in this style
tram·po·lin·ing \¦trampə¦lēniŋ, -raam-, -raim-\ *n* -s : the sport of jumping and tumbling on a trampoline
transactional analysis *n* : a system of psychotherapy involving analysis of individual episodes of social interaction for insight that will aid communication (as by the substitution of constructive mature verbal exchanges for destructive immature ones)
trans·am·i·nate \tran(t)sˈamə,nāt, traan-, -nˈza-\ *vb* -ED/-ING/-S [back-formation fr. *transamination*] *vi* : to induce or catalyze a transamination ~ *vt* : to induce or catalyze the transamination of
trans·axle \ˈtran(t),saksəl, ˈtraan-, -n,za-\ *n* [*trans*mission + *axle*] : a unit consisting of a combination of transmission and front axle used in front-wheel-drive automobiles
trans·car·ba·myl·ase \(,)tran(t)s¦kärbə¦mil,ās, (,)traan-, -nz¦k-, -,āz\ *n* -s [*trans-* + *carbamyl* + *-ase*] : any of several enzymes that catalyze the addition of a carbamoyl radical to a molecule (as ornithine to form citrulline in urea synthesis)
transcendental meditation *n, often cap T&M* : a technique of meditation in which a mantra is chanted in order to foster calm, creativity, and spiritual well-being
trans·cortin \¦tran(t)s, -raan-, -nz+\ *n* [*trans-* + *cortin*] : an alpha globulin produced in the liver that binds with and transports hydrocortisone in the blood
transcribe* *vt* : to cause (as DNA) to undergo genetic transcription
transcript* *n* : a sequence of RNA produced by transcription from a DNA template
tran·scrip·tase \tranˈskrip,tās, -,āz\ *n* -s [*transcription* (herein) + *-ase*] : REVERSE TRANSCRIPTASE *herein*
transcription* *n* : the process of constructing a messenger RNA molecule using a DNA molecule as a template with resulting transfer of genetic information to the messenger RNA — compare REVERSE TRANSCRIPTION *herein*, TRANSLATION *herein* — **transcriptional*** *adj*
transcription factor *n* : any of various proteins that bind to DNA and play a role in the regulation of gene expression by promoting transcription
tran·scrip·tion·ist \tranˈskripsh(ə)nəst, traan-\ *n* -s : one that transcribes (as dictation)
transcutaneous electrical nerve stimulation *n* : electrical stimulation of the skin to relieve pain by interfering with the neural transmission of signals from underlying pain receptors — abbr. *TENS* —**transcutaneous electrical nerve stimulator** *n*
trans·dermal \(,)tran(t)s, -raan-, -nz+\ *adj* [*trans-* + *dermal*] : relating to, being, or supplying a medication in a form for absorption through the skin into the bloodstream ⟨a ~ patch⟩ — **trans·der·mal·ly** \"+ˈdərməlē\ *adv*
trans·disciplinary \"+\ *adj* [*trans-* + *disciplinary*] : INTERDISCIPLINARY
trans·duce \tran(t)sˈd(y)üs, traan-, -nzˈ-\ *vt* -ED/-ING/-S [back-formation fr. *transducer*] **1** : to convert (as energy or a message) into another form **2** : to cause (genetic material) to undergo transduction
trans·duc·tant \-ˈdəktənt\ *n* -s [*transduction* + *-ant*] : a bacterium that has undergone transduction
trans fat *n* : a fat containing trans-fatty acids
trans–fatty acid \ˈ=,==-\ *n* : an unsaturated fatty acid characterized by a trans arrangement of alkyl chains that is formed esp. during the hydrogenation of vegetable oils and has been linked to an increase in blood cholesterol
trans·fec·tion \tran(t)sˈfekshən, traan-, -nzˈf-\ *n* -s [*trans-* + *infection*] : infection of a cell with isolated viral nucleic acid followed by production of the complete virus in the cell; *also* : the incorporation of exogenous DNA into a cell — **trans·fect** \-ˈfekt\ *vt*
transfer factor *n* : a substance that is produced and secreted by a lymphocyte functioning in cell-mediated immunity and that upon incorporation into a lymphocyte which has not been sensitized confers upon it the same immunological specificity as the sensitized cell
transfer RNA *n* : a relatively small RNA that transfers a particular amino acid to a growing polypeptide chain at the ribosomal site of protein synthesis during translation — compare MESSENGER RNA *herein*
transform* *vt* : to cause to undergo genetic transformation
transform* *n* **1** : a mathematical element obtained from another by transformation **2** : a linguistic structure (as a sentence) produced by means of a transformation
trans·for·mant \tranzˈförmənt, -raan-, -n(t)sˈf-\ *n* -s [*transform*, vb. (herein) + *-ant*] : an individual (as a bacterium) that has undergone genetic transformation
transformation* *n* **1 a** : genetic modification of a bacterium by incorporation of free DNA from another ruptured bacterial cell — compare TRANSDUCTION *in the Dict* **b** : genetic modification of a cell by the uptake and incorporation of exogenous DNA **2** : one of a set of rules that specify how to convert the deep structures of a language into surface structures; *also* : the process or relation specified by such a rule
trans·for·ma·tion·al \¦tranzfə(r)¦māshənᵊl, ¦traan-, n(t)sf-, -shnəl\ *adj* : of, relating to, characterized by, or concerned with transformation and esp. linguistic transformation
transformational grammar *n* : a grammar that generates the deep structures of a language and relates these to the surface structures by means of transformations
trans·for·ma·tion·al·ist \,tranzfə(r)ˈmāshənᵊləst, ,traan-, -n(t)sf-, -shnəl-\ *n* -s : an exponent of transformational grammar
transform fault *n* : a strike-slip fault that ends abruptly at a point where its displacement translates into the movement of another feature, that occurs typically between segments of a midocean ridge or other tectonic-plate boundary, and that is characterized by shallow high-magnitude earthquakes
transforming growth factor *n* : any of a group of polypeptides that are secreted by a variety of cells (as monocytes, T cells, or blood platelets) and have diverse effects (as inducing angiogenesis, stimulating fibroblast proliferation, or inhibiting T cell proliferation) on the division and activity of cells — abbr. *TGF*
trans·fu·sion·al \tranzˈfyüzhənᵊl, traan-, -n(t)sˈf-, -zhnəl\ *adj* : of, relating to, or caused by transfusion
trans·gender \(,)tran(t)s, -raan-, -nz+\ *or* **trans·gendered** \"+\ *adj* [*trans-* + ¹*gender*; *transgendered* fr. *trans-* + ¹*gender* + ¹*-ed*] **1** : exhibiting the appearance and behavioral characteristics of the opposite sex **2** : of or relating to transgender people
trans·gene \ˈtran(t)s, -raan-, -nz+\ *n* -s [back-formation fr. *transgenic* (herein)] : a gene that is taken from the genome of one organism and introduced into the genome of another organism by artificial techniques
¹**trans·genic** \¦tran(t)s¦jenək, -raan-, -nz¦-\ *adj* [*trans-* + *-genic*] : being or used to produce an organism or cell of one species into which one or more genes of another species have been incorporated ⟨~ mice⟩ ⟨~ corn plants⟩ ⟨~ techniques⟩; *also* : produced by or composed of transgenic plants or animals ⟨~ foods⟩
²**transgenic** *n* -s **1** : a transgenic plant or animal **2 transgenics** *pl but sing in constr* : a branch of biotechnology concerned with the production of transgenic plants, animals, and foods
trans·historical \"+\ *adj* [*trans-* + ¹*historical*] : transcending historical bounds
transient ischemic attack *n* : a brief episode of cerebral ischemia that is usu. characterized by temporary blurring of vision, slurring of speech, numbness, paralysis, or syncope and that is often predictive of more serious cerebral accidents — abbr. *TIA*
transistor* *or* **transistor radio** *n* : a transistorized radio
transition* *n* : a genetic mutation in RNA or DNA that results from the substitution of one purine base for the other or of one pyrimidine base for the other
transition *vi* -ED/-ING/-S [*transition*, n.] : to make a transition ⟨had a difficult time ~*ing* from a minority to a majority —George Pataki⟩
trans·ke·tol·ase \,tran(t)sˈkēd·ə,lās, -raan-, -nzk-, -āz\ *n* -s [*trans-* + *ketol* + *-ase*] : an enzyme that catalyzes the transfer of the ketonic residue $HOCH_2CO$– from the phosphate of xylulose to that of ribose to form the phosphate of sedoheptulose
translate* *vt* : to subject (as genetic information) to translation in protein synthesis
translation* *n* : the process of forming a protein molecule at a ribosomal site of protein synthesis from information contained in messenger RNA — compare TRANSCRIPTION *herein* — **translational*** *adj*
trans·lunar \(ˈ)tran(t)s, -raan-, -nz+\ *adj* [*trans-* + *lunar*] : of or relating to the entry into or movement along a trajectory between a celestial body (as the earth) and the moon by a spacecraft ⟨~ injection⟩ ⟨~ burn⟩
trans·membrane \"+\ *adj* [*trans-* + *membrane*] : taking place, existing, or arranged from one side to the other of a membrane ⟨a ~ potential⟩ ⟨~ proteins⟩
transmission electron microscope *n* : a conventional electron microscope which produces an image of a cross-sectional slice of a specimen all points of which are illuminated by the electron beam at the same time — compare SCANNING ELECTRON MICROSCOPE *herein* — **transmission electron microscopy** *n*
transmitter* *n* : NEUROTRANSMITTER *herein*
trans·mountain \¦tran(t)s, -raan-, -nz+\ *adj* [*trans-* + ² *mountain*] : crossing or extending over or through a mountain
transmutation* *n* : the effect of controlled reduction firing on certain chiefly oriental copper-containing and/or iron-containing ceramic glazes that is typically a variegation of colors (as purple, blue, and red) and a thick often bubbly consistency
transom* *n* — **over the transom** : without solicitation or prior arrangement ⟨the manuscript arrived *over the transom*⟩
trans·peptidase \¦tran(t)s, -raan-, -nz+\ *n* [*trans-* + *peptidase*] : an enzyme that catalyzes the transfer of an amino acid residue or a peptide residue from one amino compound to another
transpersonal* *adj* : of, relating to, or being psychology or psychotherapy concerned esp. with esoteric mental experience (as mysticism and altered states of consciousness) beyond the usual limits of ego and personality
transport* *n* : a mechanism for moving magnetic tape past a recording head
transposable element *n* : a segment of genetic material that is capable of changing its location in the genome or in some bacteria is capable of undergoing transfer between an extrachromosomal plasmid and a chromosome
transpose* *n* : a matrix that is formed from another matrix by interchanging the rows and columns
trans·pos·on \,tran(t)sˈpō,zän, -raan-, -nz-\ *n* -s [*transpose* + ²*-on*] : a transposable element esp. when it contains genetic material controlling functions other than those related to its relocation
trans·racial \(ˈ)tran(t)s, -raan-, -nz+\ *adj* [*trans-* + *racial*] : involving two or more races ⟨~ adoption⟩
trans·sexual \"+\ *n* -s [*trans-* + *sexual*] : a person with a psychological urge to belong to the opposite sex that may be carried to the point of undergoing surgery to modify the sex organs to mimic the other sex — **transsexual** *adj* — **trans·sexualism** \"+\ *n* — **trans·sexuality** \¦tran(t)(s), -raan-, -nz+\ *n*
trans·thoracic \¦tran(t)s, -raan-, -nz+\ *adj* [*trans-* + *thoracic*] **1** : performed or made by way of the thoracic cavity **2** : crossing or having connections that cross the thoracic cavity ⟨a ~ pacemaker⟩ — **trans·tho·rac·i·cal·ly** \-¦rasək(ə)lē\ *adv*
trans·venous \"+\ *adj* [*trans-* + *venous*] : relating to or involving the use of an intravenous catheter containing an electrode carrying electrical impulses from an extracorporeal source to the heart ⟨~ pacing of the heart⟩
tran·yl·cy·pro·mine \,tranᵊlˈsīprə,mēn, -,mən\ *n* -s [*trans-* + *phenyl* + *cycl-* + *propylamine*] : an antidepressant drug $C_9H_{11}N$ that is an inhibitor of monoamine oxidase and is administered in the form of its sulfate
trap* *n* : a defensive maneuver in basketball in which two defenders converge quickly to block or guard the ball handler in order to steal the ball or force a passing error — **trap*** *vb*
trash* *n* : TRASH TALK *herein* ⟨talk ~⟩
trash* *vt* **1** : VANDALIZE, WRECK ⟨~ a college building⟩ **2** : SMASH, DESTROY ⟨~ store windows⟩ **3** : SPOIL, RUIN ⟨~*ing* the environment⟩ **4** : to subject to criticism or invective; *esp* : to disparage completely **5** : THROW AWAY 1 ⟨standards of reality and truth were ~*ed* —Edwin Diamond⟩ ~ *vi* : to trash something esp. as a form of protest — **trasher** \ˈtrashə(r), -raas-, -rais-\ *n* -s
trashsport \ˈ=,=\ *n* [¹*trash* + *sport*] : an exhibition of sports events which is held solely for the purpose of being televised and in which the participants are celebrities
trash talk *n* : disparaging, taunting, or boastful comments esp. between opponents trying to intimidate each other — **trash–talk** \ˈ=,=\ *vb* — **trash talker** *n*
trauma center *n* : a hospital unit specializing in the treatment of patients with acute and esp. life-threatening traumatic injuries
traveler's diarrhea *n* : intestinal sickness and diarrhea affecting a traveler and typically caused by ingestion of pathogenic microorganisms (as some E. coli) — compare MONTEZUMA'S REVENGE *herein*
travel trailer *n* : a trailer drawn esp. by a passenger automobile and equipped for use as a dwelling
traz·o·done \ˈtrazə,dōn\ *n* -s [prob. fr. ISV *triazo* + *pyrid-* + *-one*] : an antidepressant drug $C_{19}H_{22}ClN_5O$ that is administered in the form of its hydrochloride and inhibits the uptake of serotonin by the brain
treadmill* *n* : a device having an endless belt on which an individual walks or runs in place (as for exercise)
treat·abil·i·ty \,trēd·əˈbiləd·ē\ *n* -ES : the condition of being treatable
tree ear *n* [trans. of Chin (Pek) *mu⁴ erh³*] : WOOD EAR *herein*
tree hugger *n* : ENVIRONMENTALIST *herein* — often used disparagingly
tren·doid \ˈtren,dȯid\ *n* -s [blend of ²*trend* and ¹*android*] : a trendy person
trendsetter \ˈ=,==\ *n* : one that sets a trend
¹**trendy** \ˈtrendē, -di\ *adj* -ER/-EST [²*trend* + ¹*-y*] **1** : very fashionable : UP-TO-DATE, CHIC ⟨he's a ~ dresser —*Sunday Mirror*⟩ **2** : FADDISH ⟨a newspaper of ~ triviality —J.H.Plumb⟩ — **trend·i·ly** \-dəlē, -dᵊlē\ *adv* — **trend·i·ness** \-dēnəs, -dən-\ *n* -ES
²**trendy** *n* -ES : one who slavishly keeps up with trends (as in fashion or culture)
tre·tin·o·in \treˈtinəwən\ *n* -s [perh. fr. *trans-* + *retinoic* acid (herein) + *-in*] : the all-trans isomer of retinoic acid that is applied topically to the skin to treat acne vulgaris and to reduce facial wrinkles, roughness, and pigmented spots and that is administered orally to induce remission of acute myelogenous leukemia in which more than half the cells are malignant premyelocytes
t. rex \ˈtē¦reks\ *n, usu cap T* [NL *T. rex*, short for *Tyrannosaurus rex*, lit., king tyrannosaur] : TYRANNOSAUR
trey* *n* : a shot in basketball that counts for three points if made
triacetate* *n* : a textile fiber or fabric consisting of cellulose that is completely or almost completely acetylated
triage* *n* : the assigning of priority order to projects on the basis of where funds and other resources can be best used, are most needed, or are most likely to achieve success
trial* *n* : one of a number of repetitions of an experiment
tri·am·cin·o·lone \,trīamˈsinᵊl,ōn\ *n* -s [*tri-* + *-amcin-* (by shortening & alter. fr. *American Cyanamid* company, which developed the drug) + ¹*-ol* + *-one*] : a glucocorticoid drug $C_{21}H_{27}FO_6$ that is administered esp. in the form of its acetal and acetate derivatives for its anti-inflammatory and immunosuppressant effects and that is used chiefly in the treatment of skin disorders, asthma, and allergic rhinitis
tri·am·ter·ene \trīˈam(p)tə,rēn\ *n* -s [*triamino-* + *pteridine* + *-ene*] : a diuretic drug $C_{12}H_{11}N_7$ that promotes potassium retention
triangle inequality *n* [so called fr. its application to the distances between three points in a coordinate system] : an inequality stating that the absolute value of a sum is less than or equal to the sum of the absolute value of the terms
tri·ath·lete \trīˈath,lēt\ *n* -s [blend of *triathlon* (herein) and *athlete*] : an athlete who competes in a triathlon
tri·ath·lon \trīˈathlən, -,län\ *n* -s [*tri-* + *-athlon* (as in *decathlon*)] : an athletic contest that is a long-distance race consisting of three phases (as swimming, bicycling, and running)
tri·bol·o·gy \trīˈbäləjē, trə-, -ji\ *n* -ES [*tribo-* + *-logy*] : a branch of mechanical engineering that deals with the design, friction, wear, and lubrication of interacting surfaces in relative motion (as in bearings or gears) — **tri·bo·log·i·cal** \,trībəˈläjəkəl, ,trib-\ *adj* — **tri·bol·o·gist** \trīˈbäləjəst, triˈ-\ *n* -s
tri·bu·tyl·tin \trīˈbyüd·ᵊltən\ *n* [*tri-* + *butyl* + ¹*tin*] : an organic compound of tin used as a biocide esp. in marine antifouling paints
tri·chlor·fon *also* **tri·chlor·phon** \(ˈ)trīˈklō(ə)r,fän, -ˈklȯ(ə)r-\ *n* -s [*tri-* + *chlor-* + *-fon* (irreg. fr. *phosphonate*)] : an organophosphate $C_4H_8Cl_3O_4P$ that is used as a parasiticide in veterinary medicine and as an insecticide in agriculture
tricho·the·cene \,trikəˈthē,sēn, triˈkäthə,sēn\ *n* -s [NL *Tricothecium*, genus name (fr. *trich-* + *-thecium*) + E *-ene*] : any of several mycotoxins that are produced by fungi of the genera *Fusarium* and *Trichothecium* and that include some contaminants of livestock feed and some held to be found in yellow rain
trickle–down \¦==¦=\ *adj* **1** : relating to or working on the principle of trickle-down theory ⟨*trickle-down* economics⟩ **2** : characterized by or being a derived often beneficial effect esp. at a lower level (as in a hierarchy) ⟨political success has had a *trickle-down* effect on the popularity of his books⟩
trickle–down theory *n* : an economic theory that financial benefits given to big business will in turn pass down to smaller businesses and consumers
tri·clo·san \trīˈklō,san\ *n* -s [*trichlor-* + *-san* (of unknown origin)] : a whitish crystalline powder $C_{12}H_7Cl_3O_2$ that is a phenyl ether derivative used esp. as a broad-spectrum antibacterial agent (as in soaps, deodorants, and mouthwash)
tricyclic antidepressant *also* **tricyclic** *n* -s : any of a group of antidepressant drugs (as imipramine and nortriptyline) that contain three fused benzene rings, that potentiate the action of catecholamines (as norepinephrine and serotonin) by inhibiting their uptake by nerve endings, and that do not inhibit the action of monoamine oxidase
tri·fec·ta \(ˈ)trīˈfektə\ *n* -s [*tri-* + *perfecta*] **1** : a variation of the perfecta in which a bettor must select the first 3 finishers of a race in the correct order of finish in order to win — called also *triple*; compare SUPERFECTA *herein* **2** : TRIPLE 1b ⟨achieved a show-business ~ : a platinum record, a hit TV series, and an Oscar nomination⟩
tri·fluo·per·a·zine \¦trī,flüō¦perə,zēn, -,zən\ *n* -s [*tri-* + *fluo-* + *piperazine*] : a phenothiazine tranquilizer $C_{21}H_{24}F_3N_3S$ used esp. to treat psychotic conditions and esp. schizophrenia
tri·flu·ra·lin \trīˈflürələn\ *n* -s [*tri-* + *fluor-* + *aniline*] : an herbicide $C_{13}H_{16}F_3N_3O_4$ used in the control of weeds (as pigweed)
tri·functional \(ˈ)trī+\ *adj* [*tri-* + *functional*] : of, relating to, or being a compound whose molecules have three sites that are highly reactive (as in polymerization)
tri·halo·meth·ane \(,)trī,haloˈme,thān, *Brit usu* -ˈmē-\ *n* [*tri-* + *hal-* + *methane*] : any of various derivatives CHX_3 of methane (as chloroform) that have three halogen atoms per molecule and are formed esp. during the chlorination of drinking water
tri·jet \¦trī+,\ *n* [*tri-* + ⁶*jet*] : an aircraft powered with three jet engines
tri·level \¦=¦==\ *adj* [*tri-* + ¹ *level*] : having three levels or floors ⟨a ~ house⟩ — **tri·level** \"\ *n*
tri·ma·ran \¦trīmə¦ran\ *n* -s [*tri-* + *-maran* (as in *catamaran*)] : a fast pleasure sailboat with three hulls side by side
tri·meth·o·prim \trīˈmethə,prim\ *n* -s [*tri-* + *meth-* + *-prim* (by shortening & alter. fr. *pyrimidine*)] : a synthetic antibacterial drug $C_{14}H_{18}N_4O_3$ used alone or in combination with sulfamethoxazole
trip* *n* **1** : an intense visionary experience undergone by a person who has taken a psychedelic drug (as LSD); *broadly* : an exciting experience ⟨orgasm . . . is the ultimate ~ —D.R.Reuben⟩ **2** : pursuit of an absorbing or obsessive interest : KICK ⟨he's on a nostalgia ~⟩ **3** : SCENE *herein*, LIFE-STYLE ⟨the whole superstar ~ —Joe Eszterhas⟩
trip *vi* **tripped; tripped; tripping; trips** [*trip*, n. (herein)] : to get high on a drug : TURN ON *herein* — often used with *out* — **tripper** \ˈtripə(r)\ *n* -s
trip–hop \ˈ=,=\ *n* [prob. blend of *trip* (herein) and *hip-hop* (herein)] : electronic dance music usu. based on a down-tempo hip-hop beat and incorporating hypnotic synthesized and prerecorded sounds
triple* *n* : TRIFECTA *herein*
triple jump *n* : HOP, STEP, AND JUMP — **triple jumper** *n*
triplet* *n* **1 a** : a group of three elementary particles (as positive, negative, and neutral pions) with different charge states but otherwise similar properties **b** *or* **triplet state** : any state of an elementary particle having one quantum unit of spin **c** : an atom or molecule with an even number of electrons that have a net magnetic moment **2** : CODON *herein*
trip·py \ˈtripē\ *adj* -ER/-EST [*trip* (herein) + ¹*-y*] : of, relating to, or suggestive of a trip on psychedelic drugs or the culture associated with such drugs ⟨~ music⟩ ⟨a ~ experience⟩
trip·tan \ˈtrip,tan, -,tən\ *n* -s [*-triptan* (as in *sumatriptan* — (herein)] : any of a class of drugs (as sumatriptan) that bind to and are agonists of serotonin receptors, that are used to treat migraine attacks, and that are thought to function by producing vasoconstriction of cranial blood vessels, by inhibiting secretion of inflammatory neuropeptides, and by blocking neurotransmission of pain
trip wire* *n* : something (as a small military force) intended to function as a trip wire (as to set a larger military force in motion)
trisomy 21 *n* [so called fr. the occurrence of trisomy in chromosome 21 of individuals with Down's syndrome] : DOWN'S SYNDROME
tri·umph·al·ism \(ˈ)trīˈəm(p)fə,lizəm *also* trīˈəm-\ *n* -s [*triumphal* + *-ism*] : the doctrine, attitude, or belief that one religious creed is superior to all others — **tri·um·phal·ist** \(ˈ)¦==\ *also* \====\ *n or adj*
trivia* *n pl but sing in constr* : a quizzing game involving obscure facts
trivial* *adj* : relating to or being the mathematically simplest case; *specif* : characterized by having all variables equal to zero

triv·i·al·ist \ˈtrivēələst\ *n* -s : one who takes a special interest in trivia or trivial matters

tRNA \ˌtēˌärˌenˈā\ *n* -s [*t*ransfer *RNA* (herein)] : TRANSFER RNA *herein*

trog·lo·bite \ˈträgləˌbīt\ *n* -s [by alter. (influenced by *troglodyte*)] : TROGLOBIONT — **trog·lo·bit·ic** \ˌ≈≈ˈbid·ik\ *adj*

troika* *n* **1** : an administrative or ruling body of three ⟨replaced by a ~ of three coequal secretaries-general —*Newsweek*⟩ **2** : a group of three ⟨astrology, yoga, and poetry are the ~ of humanities that most interest him —A.J.Liebling⟩

trojan horse* *n, usu cap T* : a seemingly useful computer program that contains concealed instructions which when activated at some later time perform an illicit or malicious action (as destroying data files); *also* : the concealed instructions of such a program — compare VIRUS *herein*

trombe wall \ˈtrōmb-, -rämb-, -rōⁿb-\ *n, usu cap T* [after Félix *Trombe* †1985 Fr. designer] : a masonry wall that is usu. separated from the outdoors by a glass wall and is designed to absorb solar heat and release it into the interior of a building

trophic level *n* : one of the hierarchical strata of a food web characterized by organisms which are the same number of steps removed from the primary producers

trophy* *n, often attrib* : one that is prized for qualities that enhance prestige or social status ⟨a ~ wife⟩ ⟨a ~ home⟩

tropical oil *n* : any of several oils (as coconut oil and palm oil) of tropical origin that are high in saturated fatty acids and are used esp. in commercially prepared baked goods, snack products, and confections

tro·po·collagen \ˌträpə, -rōpə+\ *n* [¹*trop-* + *collagen*] : a subunit of collagen fibrils consisting of three polypeptide strands arranged in a helix

tro·po·nin \ˈtrōpənən, ˈträp-, -ˌnin\ *n* -s [by shortening & alter. fr. *tropomyosin*] : a protein of muscle that together with tropomyosin forms a regulatory protein complex controlling the interaction of actin and myosin and that when combined with calcium ions permits muscular contraction

troubleshooter* *n* : a person skilled at solving or anticipating problems or difficulties

trouper* *n* : a person who deals with and persists through difficulty or hardship without complaint ⟨you're a real ~ to wait so long⟩

trouser* *adj* : of or relating to a male dramatic role played by a woman ⟨a ~ character in opera⟩

trouser suit *n, chiefly Brit* : PANTSUIT *herein*

truck* *vi* : to roll along esp. in an easy untroubled way ⟨keep on ~*ing*⟩

true believer *n, sometimes cap T&B* **1** : one who professes absolute belief in something **2** : a zealous supporter of a particular cause

true–blue* *adj* : GENUINE ⟨a *true–blue* romantic⟩

trunk show *n* [prob. fr. ¹*trunk* (luggage) + ²*show*] : a preview of a designer's latest fashion collection at select clothing stores prior to its general distribution

trust fund* *n* : a governmental fund consisting of moneys accepted for a specified purpose (as civil service retirement) that is administered as a trust separately from other funds and is expended only in furthering the specified purpose

truth set *n* : a mathematical or logical set containing all the elements that make a given statement of relationships true when substituted in it

tryp·sin·i·za·tion \ˌtripsənəˈzāshən, trəpˌsin-, -ˌīˈz-\ *n* -s : the action or process of trypsinizing

TSS *abbr* toxic shock syndrome *herein*

T_3 *also* **T–3** \ˈtēˈthrē\ *n* [*T*, abbrev. for *thyronine* + *3*, number of iodine atoms attached to the thyronine nucleus] : TRIIODOTHYRONINE

tubal ligation *n* : ligation of the fallopian tubes that by preventing passage of ova from the ovaries to the uterus serves as a method of female sterilization

tube* *n* **1 a** : CATHODE-RAY TUBE; *esp* : a television picture tube **b** : TELEVISION **2** : CURL *herein* **3** : an article of clothing usu. of knitted material in the shape of a tube ⟨~ top⟩ ⟨~ socks⟩ — **down the tube** *or* **down the tubes** : into a state of collapse, deterioration, or ruin ⟨I know what it means to see a crop go *down the tubes* —B.S.Bergland⟩

tuberous sclerosis *n* : EPILOIA

tube worm* *n* : a pogonophoran and esp. an extremely large one that is found near deep-ocean hydrothermal vents

tu·bu·lin \ˈt(y)übyələn\ *n* -s [*tubule* + *-in*] : a globular protein that polymerizes to form microtubules

'tude \ˈt(y)üd\ *n* -s [short for *attitude*] : a cocky or arrogant attitude

tu·fo·li \t(y)üˈfōlē\ *n, pl* **tufoli** [It dial. (southern Italy), pl. of *tufolo* tube, modif. of L *tubulus* tubule] : a pasta shell large enough for stuffing (as with meat or cheese)

tumble dry *vt* : to dry (as clothes) by tumbling in a dryer — **tumble dryer** *n*

tumm·ler \ˈtümlə(r)\ *n* -s [Yiddish *tumler* one who makes a racket, fr. *tumeln* to make a racket (fr. *tuml* noise, racket, fr. MHG *tumel*) + *-er* -er; prob. akin to OHG *tūmōn* to reel — more at TUMBLE] : a comic entertainer or social director at a Jewish resort; *also* : a loud or brash comedian

tummy tuck *n* : ABDOMINOPLASTY *herein*

tu·mor·i·genesis \ˌt(y)ümərə+\ *n* [NL, fr. *tumor* + *-i-* + *genesis*] : the formation of tumors

tu·mor·i·gen·ic \ˌt(y)üməræˈjenik\ *adj* [*tumor* + *-i-* + *-genic*] : producing or tending to produce tumors; *also* : CARCINOGENIC ⟨~ cells⟩ — **tu·mor·i·ge·nic·i·ty** \ˌ≈≈ˌjəˈnisəd·ē\ *n* -ES

tumor–infiltrating lymphocyte \ˈ≈≈ˈ≈ˌ≈≈-, ˈ≈ˈ≈(ˌ)≈ˌ≈≈-\ *n* : a T cell that is isolated from a malignant tumor, cultured with interleukin-2, and injected back into the patient as a tumor-killing cell and that has greater cytotoxicity than lymphokine-activated killer cells — called also *TIL*

tumor necrosis factor *n* : a protein produced chiefly by monocytes and macrophages in response esp. to endotoxins and that mediates inflammation and induces the destruction of some tumor cells and the activation of leukocytes

tump \ˈtəmp\ *vb* [perh. akin to Brit. dial. *tumpoke* to fall head over heels] *vi, chiefly South* : to tip or turn over esp. accidentally — usu. used with *over* ⟨sooner or later everybody ~*s* over. Nothing to worry about if you don't get caught under the canoe —Don Kennard⟩ ~ *vt, chiefly South* : to cause to tip over : OVERTURN, UPSET — usu. used with *over*

tune* *vt* **1** : to make more precise, intense, or effective **2** : to adjust the output of (a device) to a chosen frequency or range of frequencies; *also* : to alter the frequency of (radiation)

tune out *vt* : to become unresponsive to : IGNORE ⟨the children *tuned out* their mother's commands⟩ ~ *vi* : to dissociate oneself from what is happening

tunnel* *n* : CURL *herein*

tunnel diode *n* : a semiconductor device that has two stable states when operated in conjunction with suitable circuit elements and a source of voltage, is capable of extremely rapid transformations between the two by means of the tunnel effect of electrons, and is used for amplifying, switching, and computer information storage and as an oscillator

tunnel vision* *n* : extreme narrowness of viewpoint; *also* : single-minded concentration on one objective — **tunnel–visioned** \ˈ≈≈ˈ≈≈\ *adj*

-tu·ple \ˌtəpəl, ˌtüp-\ *n comb form* [quin*tuple*, sex*tuple*] : set of (so many) elements — often used of sets with ordered elements ⟨the ordered 2-*tuple* (*a, b*)⟩

tur·bi·dite \ˈtərbəˌdīt\ *n* -s [*turbid*ity current (a current flowing down an underwater slope) + ¹*-ite*] : a sedimentary deposit consisting of material that has moved down the steep slope at the edge of a continental shelf; *also* : a rock formed from this deposit

tur·bo·electric \ˌtərbō+\ *adj* [*turbo-* + *electric*] : using or being a turbine generator that produces electricity usu. for motive power ⟨ships with ~ drive⟩

tur·bo·fan \ˈtərbō+ˌ\ *n* [*turbo-* + ¹*fan*] **1** : a fan that is directly connected to and driven by a turbine and is used to supply air for cooling, ventilation, or combustion **2** : a jet engine having a turbofan

tur·bo·generator \ˌtərbō+\ *n* [*turbo-* + *generator*] : an electric generator driven by a turbine

tur·bo·machinery \"+\ *n* [*turbo-* + *machinery*] : machinery consisting of, incorporating, or constituting a turbine

tur·bo·pump \ˈtərbō+ˌ\ *n* [*turbo-* + ¹*pump*] : a pump that is driven by a turbine

tur·bo·shaft \"+ˌ\ *n* [*turbo-* + ¹*shaft*] : a gas turbine engine that is similar in operation to a turboprop engine but instead of being used to power a propeller is used through a transmission system for powering other devices (as helicopter rotors and pumps)

Tur·bo·train \ˈtərbōˌtrān\ *trademark* — used for a high-speed railroad train powered by a gas-turbine engine

turf* *n* **1** : an artificial substitute for natural turf (as on a playing field) **2** : TERRITORY 2a(1), b; *also* : a sphere of activity or influence ⟨people who could hurt him on his own foreign-policy ~ —*Wall Street Jour.*⟩

turfgrass \ˈ≈ˌ≈\ *n* : any of various grasses (as Kentucky bluegrass or perennial ryegrass) grown to form turf

turf toe *n* [so called because such hyperextension among athletes is associated with play on artificial turf] : a minor but painful usu. sports-related injury involving hyperextension of the big toe that results in spraining or tearing of the ligament of the metatarsophalangeal joint

tu·ring machine \ˈt(y)u̇riŋ-\ *n, usu cap T* [after A.M. *Turing* †1954 Eng. mathematician] : a hypothetical computing machine that has an unlimited amount of information storage

tu·ris·ta \tu̇rˈēstə\ *n* -s [Sp, tourist] : TRAVELER'S DIARRHEA *herein*

turkey* *n* : a stupid, foolish, or inept person

turn* *vt* **1** : to engage in (an act of prostitution) ⟨~ tricks⟩ **2** : to carry to completion ⟨~*ed* a double play⟩

turn* *n* : PERFORMANCE 3a, b

turnaround* *n* : the action of receiving, processing, and returning something ⟨the user's requirement for rapid ~ time —A.B.Veaner⟩

turner's syndrome \ˈtərnər(z)-; ˈtänə(z)-, ˈtəin-\ *or* **turner syndrome** *n, usu cap T* [after Henry Hubert *Turner* †1970 Am. physician] : a genetically determined condition that is typically associated with the presence of only one complete X chromosome and no Y chromosome and with characteristics including a female phenotype underdeveloped, and usu. infertile ovaries, absence of menstrual onset, short stature, excess skin about the neck, aortic coarctation, and a low hairline on the back of the neck

turnkey \ˈ≈ˌ≈\ *adj* : supplied or installed complete and ready to operate ⟨a ~ nuclear plant⟩ ⟨a ~ computer system⟩; *also* : of or relating to a turnkey installation ⟨a ~ contract⟩ ⟨~ vendors⟩

turn off* *vi* : to lose interest : WITHDRAW ⟨the kids *turn off* or drift into another world —Edwin Sorensen⟩ ~ *vt* : to cause to turn off ⟨dropouts who are *turned off* by . . . political phoniness —Hendrik Hertzberg⟩; *also* : to evoke a negative feeling in

turnoff* *n* : one that causes loss of interest or enthusiasm ⟨the music was a ~⟩

turn on* *vt* **1** : to cause to undergo an intense visionary experience esp. by taking a drug; *broadly* : to cause to get high **2** : to excite pleasurably : STIMULATE ⟨the ballet . . . was *turning* the audience *on* like magic —Clive Barnes⟩; *also* : to excite sexually **3** : to cause to gain knowledge or appreciation of something specified ~ *vi* **1** : to undergo an intense visionary experience esp. as a result of taking a drug; *broadly* : to get high **2** : to become pleasurably excited ⟨*turns on* instead with classical music or jazz —Julie M. Heldman⟩ — **turn–on** \ˈ≈ˌ≈\ *n* -s

turn over* *vt* : to cause (an internal-combustion engine) to begin firing

turnover* *n* **1** : the continuous process of loss and replacement of a constituent (as a neurotransmitter, cell, or tissue) of a living system ⟨protein ~ in various pathological states —J.C.Waterlow⟩ ⟨~ of neurons in the hippocampus —B.L.Jacobs *et al*⟩ **2** : the act or an instance of a team's losing possession of a ball through error or a minor violation of the rules (as in basketball or football)

tush \ˈtu̇sh\ *n* -ES [perh. modif. of Yiddish *tokhes*, fr. Heb *taḥath* under, beneath] *slang* : BUTTOCKS

tushy *also* **tush·ie** \ˈtu̇shē\ *n, pl* **tushies** [*tush* (herein) + *-ie*] *slang* : BUTTOCKS

tutorial* *n* : a paper, book, film, or computer program that provides practical information on a specific subject

tut–tut \ˈtətˈtət\ *vi* **tut–tutted; tut–tutted; tut–tutting; tut–tutts** [*tut–tut*, interj.] : to express disapproval or disbelief by or as if by uttering *tut* ⟨busy *tut-tutting* about how unfair and unequal society had become —L.B.Lindsey⟩

TV* *abbr or n* -s : transvestite

tv dinner *n, usu cap T&V* [so called fr. its saving the television viewer from having to interrupt viewing to prepare a meal] : a quick-frozen packaged dinner that requires only heating before it is served

tweak* *vt* **1** : to make small adjustments in; *esp* : FINE-TUNE 1 *herein* **2a** : ANNOY, BOTHER ⟨~*ing* the establishment⟩ **b** : CRITICIZE 2 ⟨~*ed* her for her lack of seriousness⟩ **c** : to poke fun at ⟨a comedian ~*ing* the audience⟩ ~ *vi* : to make small adjustments — **tweak*** *n*

twee \ˈtwē\ *adj* [baby talk alter. of *sweet*] *chiefly Brit* : affectedly or excessively dainty, delicate, cute, or quaint ⟨such a theme might sound ~ or corny —*Times Lit. Supp.*⟩

tween·er \ˈtwēnə(r)\ *n* -s [*tween* + ²*-er*] : a player who has some but not all of the necessary characteristics for each of two or more positions (as in football or basketball)

12–step \ˈ≈ˈ≈\ *adj* : of, relating to, characteristic of, or being a program that is designed esp. to help an individual overcome an addiction, compulsion, serious shortcoming, or traumatic experience by adherence to 12 tenets emphasizing personal growth and dependence on a higher spiritual being

24–7 *or* **24/7** \ˈtwentēˈfō(ə)rˈsevən, -ˈfȯ(ə)r-\ *adv or adj* : for twenty-four hours seven days a week ⟨can now shop *24-7*⟩

20/20* *adj* : marked by keen discernment, judgment, or assessment ⟨hindsight is always *20/20* —Damien Anderson⟩

twilight zone* *n* **1** : TWILIGHT 2a **2** : a world of fantasy, illusion, or unreality

twin double *n* : a system of betting (as on horse races) in which the bettor must pick the winners of four stipulated races in order to win — compare DAILY DOUBLE *in the Dict*

twinset \ˈ≈ˌ≈\ *n* : a combination of a matching pullover and cardigan worn together

twisted *adj* [fr. past part. of ¹*twist*] : mentally or emotionally unsound or disturbed

two–edged sword \ˈ≈ˌejd-, ˌ≈ejəd-\ *n* : something that can produce positive or negative results ⟨public relations appears as a *two-edged sword*—able to enhance or hurt an institution —L.B.Mayhew⟩

twofer* *n* : something that satisfies two criteria or needs simultaneously ⟨her marriage . . . was a ~; it allowed her to accomplish both —Phil Gailey⟩

two–tailed \ˈ≈ˈ≈\ *also* **two–tail** \ˈ≈ˈ≈\ *adj* : being a statistical test for which the critical region consists of all values of the test statistic greater than a given value plus the values less than another given value — compare ONE-TAILED *herein*

ty·iyn \tēˈyēn\ *n, pl* **tyiyn** : a monetary unit of Kyrgyzstan equal to 1/100 som — see MONEY table *in the Dict*

ty·lo·sin \ˈtīləsən\ *n* -s [origin unknown] : an antibacterial antibiotic $C_{45}H_{77}NO_{17}$ from an actinomycete of the genus *Streptomyces* (*S. fradiae*) used in veterinary medicine and as a feed additive

type A *adj* : relating to, characteristic of, having, or being a personality that is marked by impatience, aggressiveness, and competitiveness and that has been implicated by some studies as a factor increasing the risk of cardiovascular disease ⟨*type A* behavior⟩ — **type A** *n*

type B *adj* : relating to, characteristic of, having, or being a personality that is marked by a lack of excessive aggressivenes and tension and that has been implicated by some studies as a factor decreasing the risk of cardiovascular disease ⟨*type B* behavior⟩ — **type B** *n*

type C *adj* : relating to or being any of the oncornaviruses in which the structure containing the nucleic acid is spherical and centrally located ⟨a *type C* RNA virus⟩

typecast* *vt* : STEREOTYPE ⟨administrators . . . fearful of being ~ in the role of autocrats —F.M.Hechinger⟩

type 1 diabetes *also* **type I diabetes mellitus** *n* : a form of diabetes mellitus that usu. develops during childhood or adolescence and is characterized by a severe deficiency in insulin secretion resulting from atrophy of the islets of Langerhans and causing hyperglycemia and a marked tendency toward ketoacidosis — called also *insulin-dependent diabetes mellitus, juvenile diabetes*

type I error \ˌtīpˈwən-\ *n* : rejection of the null hypothesis in statistical testing when it is true

typestyle \ˈ≈ˌ≈(≈)\ *n* : TYPEFACE

type 2 diabetes *also* **type II diabetes mellitus** *n* : a common form of diabetes mellitus that develops esp. in adults and most often in obese individuals and that is characterized by hyperglycemia resulting from impaired insulin utilization coupled with the body's inability to compensate with increased insulin production — called also *adult-onset diabetes, non-insulin-dependent diabetes mellitus*

type II error \ˌtīpˈtü-\ *n* : acceptance of the null hypothesis in statistical testing when it is false

tyrosine hy·drox·y·lase \-hīˈdräksəˌlās, -āz\ *n* -s [*hydroxyl* + *-ase*] : an enzyme that catalyzes the first step in the biosynthesis of catecholamines (as dopamine)

u \ˈyü\ *adj, usu cap* [*u*pper class] : characteristic of the upper classes — usu. used in contrast to *non-U*

u* *abbr, cap* uracil

über– *also* **uber–** \ˈübə(r), ˈtē-\ *prefix, sometimes cap* [G (as in *übermensch* superman), fr. *über* over, beyond the limits of, fr. OHG *ubari* — more at OVER] : being a superlative example of its kind or class ⟨*über*mayor⟩ ⟨*über*thermometer⟩

ubi·qui·none \yüˈbikwəˌnōn; ˌyübəkwəˈn-, -ˈkwiˌn-\ *n* [blend of L *ubique* everywhere and E *quinone*; fr. its occurrence in nature — more at UBIQUITY] : a quinone that contains a long isoprenoid side chain and that functions in the part of cellular respiration comprising oxidative phosphorylation as an electron-carrying coenzyme in the transport of electrons from organic substrates to oxygen esp. along the chain of reactions leading from the Krebs cycle — called also *coenzyme Q*

udon \ˈüˌdän, üˈdōn\ *or* **udon noodle** *n, pl* **udon** [Jap] : a Japanese noodle made from wheat flour

UDP \ˌyüˌdēˈpē\ *n* -s [*u*ridine *d*i*p*hosphate] : a diphosphate of uridine $C_9H_{14}N_2O_{12}P_2$ that functions esp. as a glycosyl carrier in the synthesis of glycogen and starch and is used to form polyuridylic acid

ufol·o·gy \yüˈfäləjē\ *n* -ES *often cap UFO* [*UFO* + *-logy*] : the study of unidentified flying objects — **ufo·log·i·cal** \ˌyüfəˈläjəkəl\ *adj, often cap UFO* — **ufol·o·gist** \yüˈfäləjəst\ *n* -s *often cap UFO*

uil·leann pipe \ˈilən-\ *n* [part trans. of IrGael *píb uilleann; uilleann* fr. IrGael, gen. sing. of *uillinn* elbow, fr. OIr *uilen*; akin to OE *eln* ell — more at ELL] : an Irish bagpipe with air supplied by a bellows held under and worked by the elbow

ULCC \ˌyüˌelˈsēˈsē\ *abbr or n* -s [*u*ltra-*l*arge *c*rude *c*arrier] : a crude-oil tanker with an extremely large capacity

ul·tra·di·an \(ˌ)əlˈtrādēən\ *adj* [*ultra-* + *-dian* (as in *circadian*—herein)] : being, characterized by, or occurring in periods or cycles (as of biological activity) of considerably less than 24 hours ⟨~ pulses of insulin secretion⟩ ⟨an ~ sleep cycle recurring at intervals of about 90 minutes⟩

ul·tra·fast \ˌəltrə+\ *adj* [*ultra-* + ¹*fast*] : extremely fast ⟨an ~ computer⟩

ul·tra·fiche \ˈəltrə+ˌ\ *n* [*ultra-* + *fiche* (herein)] : a microfiche of printed matter reduced 90 or more times

ul·tra·high \ˌəltrə+\ *adj* [*ultra-* + ¹*high*] : very high : exceedingly high ⟨at ~ temperatures⟩

ultrahigh vacuum *n* : a vacuum having a pressure of 10^{-7} pascal or less

¹ul·tra·light \ˌəltrə+\ *adj* [*ultra-* + ⁴*light*] : extremely light in mass or weight ⟨an ~ alloy⟩

²ultralight \ˈəltrə+ˌ\ *n* : a very light recreational aircraft typically for one person that is powered by a small gasoline engine

ul·tra·marathon \"+\ *n* [*ultra-* + ¹*marathon*] : a footrace longer than a marathon — **ul·tra·marathoner** \"+\ *n*

ul·tra·microtome \"+\ *n* [*ultra-* + *microtome*] : a microtome for cutting extremely thin sections for electron microscopy — **ul·tra·microtomy** \"+\ *n*

ul·tra·miniature \"+\ *adj* [*ultra-* + ²*miniature*] : SUBMINIATURE — **ul·tra·miniaturization** \"+\ *n*

ul·tra·pure \"+\ *adj* [*ultra-* + ¹*pure*] : extremely pure

ul·tra·sonogram \"+\ *n* [*ultra-* + *sonogram* (herein)] : SONOGRAM *herein*

ul·tra·so·nog·ra·phy \ˌəltrəsəˈnägrəfē, -sōˈn-\ *n* -ES [²*ultrasonic* + *-o-* + *-graphy*] : ULTRASOUND 1 *herein* — **ul·tra·so·nog·ra·pher** \-səˈnägrəf(r), -sōˈn-\ *n* — **ul·tra·so·no·graph·ic** \-ˌsōnəˈgrafik, -ˌsän-\ *adj*

ultrasound* *n* **1** : the diagnostic or therapeutic use of ultrasound and esp. a noninvasive technique involving the formation of a two-dimensional image used for the examination and measurement of internal body structures and the detection of bodily abnormalities — called also *echography, sonography* **2** : a diagnostic examination using ultrasound

ul·tra·thin \"+\ *adj* [*ultra-* + ¹*thin*] : exceedingly thin

ultraviolet A *n* : UVA *herein*

ultraviolet B *n* : UVB *herein*

uma·mi \üˈmämē\ [Jap, lit., taste, flavor, delicious flavor, fr. *umatasty* + *-mi* flavor, taste] : a taste sensation that is meaty or savory and is produced by several amino acids and nucleotides (as glutamate and aspartate) — **umami** *adj*

umbilical *n* -s : UMBILICAL CORD 2

unak·ite \ˈyünəˌkīt\ *n* -s [*Unaka* mountains, Tenn. & N.C. + E ¹*-ite*] : an altered igneous rock that is usu. opaque with green, black, pink, and white flecks and is usu. used as a gemstone

unanswered* *adj* : scored in succession during a period in which an opponent fails to score ⟨scored twenty ~ points in the last quarter⟩

unary* *adj* : having or consisting of a single element, item, or component : MONADIC

un·bun·dling \ˌənˈbənd(ə)liŋ\ *n* -s [fr. gerund of *unbundle*, fr. ²*un-* + ²*bundle*] : separate pricing of products and services — **un·bundle** *vb*

uncle tom *vi* **uncle tommed; uncle tommed; uncle tomming; uncle toms** *usu cap U&T* : to behave like an Uncle Tom

uncle tom·ism \ˌ≈ˈtäˌmizəm\ *n, usu cap U&T* [*Uncle Tom* + *-ism*] : behavior or attitudes characteristic of an Uncle Tom — **uncle tom·ish** \-ämish\ *adj, usu cap U&T*

un·competitive \ˌən+\ *adj* [¹*un-* + *competitive*] : not competitive : unable to compete

un·conjugated \"+\ *adj* [¹*un-* + *conjugated*] : not chemically conjugated

un·cool \"+\ *adj* [¹*un-* + ¹*cool*] **1** : lacking in assurance, sophistication, or self-control **2** : failing to accord with the mores of a particular group

undead* *n* : ZOMBIE 1c

un·der·achiev·er \ˌəndərəˈchēvə(r)\ *n* -s [¹*under* + *achieve* + ²*-er*] : a person and esp. a student who fails to achieve his or her potential or does not do as well as expected — **underachieve** \ˌ≈≈≈ˈ≈\ *vi* — **underachievement** \ˌ≈≈≈ˈ≈≈\ *n*

underage* *adj* : done by or involving underage persons ⟨~ drinking⟩
underappreciated \ˌ⸗⸗ˈ⸗⸗⸗\ *adj* [[1]*under* + *appreciated*, past part. of *appreciate*] : not duly appreciated
underclass \ˈ⸗⸗ˌ⸗\ *n* [prob. trans. of Sw *underklass*] : the lowest social stratum usu. made up of disadvantaged minority groups — compare OVERCLASS *herein*
undercoating* *n* : a usu. asphalt-based waterproof coating applied to the underside of a vehicle
underfund \ˌ⸗⸗ˈ⸗\ *vt* [[1]*under* + [2]*fund*] : to provide insufficient funds for ⟨Congress has ~*ed* the program⟩
underground* *adj* **1 a** : existing outside the establishment or mainstream ⟨an ~ literary reputation⟩ **b** : existing outside the purview of tax collectors or statisticians ⟨the ~ economy⟩ **2 a** : produced or published outside the establishment esp. by the avant-garde ⟨~ movies⟩ ⟨~ newspapers⟩ **b** : of or relating to the avant-garde underground ⟨an ~ theater⟩
underground* *n* : a usu. avant-garde group or movement that functions outside the establishment
underground \ˌ⸗⸗ˈ⸗\ *vt* [[1]*underground*] : to place underground ⟨~*ing* power lines⟩
underinvest \ˌ⸗⸗⸗ˈ⸗\ *vi* [[1]*under* + [2]*invest*] : to invest insufficient resources ⟨free markets ~ in pure research, so government needs to finance it—Nicholas Lemann⟩ — **underinvestment** \ˌ⸗⸗⸗ˈ⸗⸗\ *n*
underkill \ˈ⸗⸗ˌ⸗\ *n* -S [[3]*under* + *overkill* (herein)] : lack of the force required to defeat an enemy
underperform \ˌ⸗⸗⸗ˈ⸗\ *vb* [[1]*under* + *perform*] *vt* : to do worse than : not do as well as ⟨a mutual fund that ~*ed the market*⟩ ~ *vi* : to fail to do as well as expected ⟨~ on a test⟩ ⟨a stock that ~*s*⟩ — **underperformance** \ˌ⸗⸗⸗ˈ⸗⸗\ *n* — **underperformer** \ˌ⸗⸗⸗ˈ⸗⸗\ *n*
underpopulation \ˌ⸗⸗ˌ⸗⸗ˈ⸗⸗\ *n* [[3]*under* + *population*] : the state of being underpopulated
underpredict \ˌ⸗⸗⸗ˈ⸗\ *vt* [[1]*under* + *predict*] : to predict too small a value for : UNDERESTIMATE ⟨the model also ~*ed* imports and overestimated exports—Anatole Kaletsky⟩ — **underprediction** \ˌ⸗⸗⸗ˈ⸗⸗\ *n*
underserved \ˌ⸗⸗ˈ⸗\ *adj* [[1]*under* + *served*, past part. of [1]*serve*] : provided with inadequate service ⟨rural areas ~ by retailers⟩
understeer \ˈ⸗⸗ˌ⸗\ *n* [[3]*under* + [4]*steer*] : the tendency of an automobile to turn less sharply than the driver intends; *also* : the action or an instance of understeer — **understeer** \ˌ⸗⸗ˈ⸗\ *vi*
underthrow \ˈ⸗⸗ˌ⸗\ *vb* [[1]*under* + [1]*throw*] *vt* : to throw (a ball or pass) short of the intended receiver in football ⟨~ a pass⟩; *also* : to throw a pass short of ⟨the quarterback *underthrew* the receiver⟩ ~ *vi* : to underthrow a pass in football — **underthrow** *n*
underused \ˌ⸗⸗ˈ⸗\ *adj* [[1]*under* + *used*] : not fully used : having more potential than is currently being realized or utilized ⟨~ land⟩ ⟨an ~ actress⟩
underutilize \ˌ⸗⸗ˈ⸗⸗ˌ⸗\ *vt* [[1]*under* + *utilize*] : to utilize less than fully or below the potential use
un·der·whelm \ˌəndə(r)ˈhwelm *also* -ˈw-\ *vt* -ED/-ING/-S [[1]*under* + *overwhelm*] : to fail to impress or stimulate
underwire \ˈ⸗⸗ˌ⸗(ə)\ *n* [[3]*under* + [1]*wire*] : a wire running through the bottom edge of a brassiere to aid in support
undock* *vt* : UNCOUPLE ⟨~ the lunar module from the command module⟩
undulator* *n* : a device consisting of a series of magnetic dipoles of alternating polarity into which a stream of particles (as electrons) moving at relativistic velocity is injected to produce intense essentially monochromatic coherent synchrotron radiation at a very few wavelengths
un·falsifiable \ˌən+\ *adj* : not capable of being proved false
unfazed \ˌ⸗ˈ⸗\ *adj* [[1]*un-* + *fazed*, past part. of *faze*] : not fazed : UNDAUNTED ⟨companies are . . . ~ by the possibility of the economy slowing —Rob Norton⟩
un·flap·pa·ble \ˌənˈflapəbəl\ *adj* [[1]*un-* + [2]*flap* + *-able*] : marked by assurance and self-control : IMPERTURBABLE ⟨the most ~ of politicians —Anthony Lewis⟩ — **un·flap·pa·bil·i·ty** \-ˌflapəˈbilədē\ *n* -ES — **un·flap·pa·bly** \-ˈflapəblē\ *adv*
un·flapped \ˌənˈflapt\ *adj* [[1]*un-* + *flapped*, past part. of [2]*flap*] : UNRUFFLED 1
unforced error *n* : a missed shot or lost point (as in tennis) that is entirely a result of the player's own blunder and not because of the opponent's skill or effort ⟨gave away the final game with three wild *unforced errors* —Sally Jenkins⟩
unforgiving* *adj* : having or making no allowance for error or weakness ⟨lost two friends in avalanches here. The mountains . . . are . . . ~ —Irwin Shaw⟩
un·fussed \ˌən+\ *adj* [[1]*un-* + *fussed*, past part. of [3]*fuss*] **1** *chiefly Brit* : not disturbed or excited : COMPOSED, UNFAZED ⟨whatever the situation . . . remains cool and ~ and in touch with reality—Sue Carroll⟩ **2** *chiefly Brit* : SIMPLE, UNADORNED ⟨evoked in a friendly, ~ prose whose wit is so discreet that we could easily miss it altogether—Michael Wood⟩ ⟨the interior is simple, modern, and ~—Monica Geran⟩
un·glued \ˌənˈglüd\ *adj* [fr. past part. of *unglue*] : being in a confused or agitated state or condition : UPSET, DISORDERED — usu. used with *come* ⟨chief executives came ~ at the thought of a strike —H.E.Meyer⟩
un·hip \ˈ"+\ *adj* [[1]*un-* + [8]*hip*] : not hip : UNCOOL *herein*
uniform* *adj* : relating to or being convergence of a series whose terms are functions in such manner that the absolute value of the difference between the sum of the first *n* terms of the series and the sum of all terms can be made arbitrarily small for all values of the domain of the functions by choosing the *n*th term sufficiently far along in the series — **uniformly*** *adv*
uniform resource locator *n* : URL *herein*
uni·modular \ˌyünə+\ *adj* [*uni-* + *modular*] : represented by, being, or having as each element a square matrix whose determinant has a value of 1 ⟨a ~ group⟩ ⟨a ~ transformation⟩
un·install \ˌən+\ *vt* [[2]*un-* + *install*] : to remove (software) from a computer system esp. by using a program specially designed to do so ⟨~ the browser⟩
un·interruptible \ˌən+\ *adj* [[1]*un-* + *interruptible*] : not able to be interrupted; *also* : serving as a backup source of electricity in the event of an interruption of normal power (as during a blackout) ⟨an ~ power system⟩
union* *n* **1** : the set of all elements belonging to one or more of a given collection of two or more sets — called also *join, sum* **2** : the mathematical or logical operation of converting separate sets to a union
[1]**uni·sex** \ˈyünəˌseks\ *n* [*uni-* + [1]*sex*] : the quality or state of not being distinguishable (as by hair or clothing) as to sex
[2]**unisex** \ˈ"\ *adj* **1** : not distinguishable as male or female ⟨a ~ face⟩ **2** : suitable or designed for both males and females ⟨~ clothes⟩; *also* : being the same for both males and females ⟨~ insurance rates⟩
uni·sexual* *adj* : UNISEX *herein*
uni·tard \ˈyünəˌtärd\ *n* -S [*uni-* + *-tard* (as in *leotard*)] : a close-fitting one-piece garment for the torso, legs, feet, and often the arms
uni·tar·i·ly \ˌyünəˈterəlē\ *adv* : in a unitary manner
uni·tar·i·ty \ˌyünəˈtarəd-ē, -ter-\ *n* -ES : the requirement in quantum mechanics that the S matrix be a unitary transformation between initial and final states of motion
unitary matrix *n* : a matrix that has an inverse and a transpose whose corresponding elements are pairs of conjugate complex numbers
unitary transformation *n* : a linear transformation of a vector space that leaves scalar products unchanged
unit circle *n* : a circle whose radius is one unit of length long
uni·term \ˈyünə+\ *n* [*uni-* + [1]*term*] : a single term used as a descriptor in document indexing
unit investment trust *n* : an investment company that buys a fixed portfolio of securities and holds them for a specified period of time after which cash from their sale or maturity is distributed to shareholders
unit membrane *n* : a 3-layered membrane that consists of an inner lipid layer surrounded by a protein layer on each side
unit pricing *n* [*pricing* fr. gerund of [2]*price*] : the pricing of products (as packaged foods) whereby the unit price is indicated along with the total price
uni·trust \ˈyünə+ˌ\ *n* [*uni-* + [1]*trust*] : a trust from which the beneficiary receives annually a fixed percentage of the fair market value of its assets
units digit *n* : the numeral (as 6 in 456) occupying the units place
units place *n* : the place just to the left of the decimal point in a number expressed in the Arabic system of writing numbers
unit train *n* : a railway train that transports a single commodity directly from producer to buyer
unit trust *n* **1** *Brit* : MUTUAL FUND **2** : an investment company whose portfolio consists of long-term bonds that are held to maturity
universal product code *n, usu cap U&P&C* : a bar code that identifies a product's type and price
universal resource locator *n* : URL *herein*
universal set *n* : a set that contains all elements relevant to a particular discussion or problem : UNIVERSE OF DISCOURSE 2
universal time *n, often cap U&T* : GREENWICH TIME
unleaded* *adj* : not treated or mixed with lead or lead compounds ⟨~ gasoline⟩
un·linked \ˌən+\ *adj* [[1]*un-* + *linked*, past part. of [3]*link*] : not belonging to the same genetic linkage group ⟨~ genes⟩
un·nil·hex·i·um \ˌyünᵊlˈheksēəm\ *n* -S [NL, fr. *unnil-* (fr. L *unus* one + *nil* nothing, zero) + Gk *hex* six + NL *-ium* — more at ONE, NIL, SIX] : SEABORGIUM *herein* — symbol *Unh*
un·nil·pen·ti·um \ˌyünᵊlˈpentēəm\ *n* -S [NL, fr. *unnil-* + Gk *pente* five + NL *-ium* — more at FIVE] : DUBNIUM *herein* — symbol *Unp*
un·nil·qua·di·um \ˌyünᵊlˈkwädēəm\ *n* -S [NL, fr. *unnil-* + *quadri-* + *-ium*] : RUTHERFORDIUM *herein* — symbol *Unq*
un·person \ˈən+\ *n* [[1]*un-* + *person*] : an individual who usu. for political or ideological reasons is removed completely from recognition, consideration, or memory ⟨became an ~ when he was removed from the Lenin Mausoleum —Henry Tanner⟩
unplugged *adj* [fr. past part. of *unplug*] : ACOUSTIC *herein* ⟨recorded several ~ sessions for the record label⟩
unprotected* *adj* : performed without the use of birth control to prevent pregnancy; *also* : performed without the use of a condom to prevent spread of sexually transmitted disease ⟨~ sex⟩
un·put·down·able \ˌənˌpu̇tˈdau̇nəbəl\ *adj* [[1]*un-* + *put down* + *-able*] : unable to be set aside : GRIPPING ⟨one of the most ~ books ever written —*Times Lit. Supp.*⟩
unriddle* *vt* : to make understandable : EXPLAIN ⟨just trying to ~ the man —Helen Dudar⟩
un·slakable *or* **un·slakeable** \ˈ"+\ *adj* [[1]*un-* + [1]*slake* + *-able*] : unable to be slaked : UNQUENCHABLE ⟨an ~ thirst⟩ ⟨an ~ desire for excellence⟩
un·sulfured *also* **un·sulphured** \ˈ"+\ *adj* [[1]*un-* + *sulfured* or *sulphured*, past part. of [3]*sulfur*] : not treated or preserved with sulfur ⟨~ molasses⟩
up* *adj* : being a constituent of nucleons and having the quantum characteristics of an electric charge of +⅔ and a baryon number of ⅓ ⟨~ quark⟩ — compare DOWN *herein*
up* *n* **1** : a feeling of contentment, excitement, or euphoria **2** : UPPER *herein*
UPC *abbr* universal product code *herein*
up·date \ˈəpˌdāt\ *n* -S [*update*, v.] **1** : the act or an instance of updating **2** : current information for updating something ⟨navigational ~ for a spacecraft computer⟩ **3** : an up-to-date version, account, or report
upfield \ˈ⸗ˈ⸗\ *adv (or adj)* [[4]*up* + [1]*field*] : in or into the part of the field toward which the offensive team is headed
up front *adv* **1** : in or at the front or beginning **2** : in advance **3** : FRANKLY, FORTHRIGHTLY
up–front \ˈ⸗ˈ⸗\ *adj* : being or coming in or at the front: as **a** (1) : being in a conspicuous or leading position or role ⟨these are very *up-front* and obvious prejudices —Clive Barnes⟩ ⟨I believe I help the city by being *up-front* and visible —Edward Koch⟩ (2) : OPEN, FORTHRIGHT, FRANK ⟨wishes Hollywood producers would be a bit more *up-front* on the subject —*People*⟩ **b** : playing in a front line (as in football, hockey, or soccer) **c** : paid or incurred in advance or at the beginning ⟨*up-front* interest charges⟩ ⟨offered $2 million in *up-front* cash —Tommy Thompson⟩ **d** *usu* **upfront** : of, relating to, or constituting advertisement sales or acquisitions done shortly before the beginning of a new television season ⟨the ~ market⟩ ⟨~ sales⟩
upgrade* *vt* : to extend the usefulness of (as a device) : IMPROVE ~ *vi* : to improve or replace esp. a device for increased usefulness ⟨you can ~ easily⟩ — **up·grad·abil·i·ty** *or* **up·grade·abil·i·ty** \ˌəpˌgrādəˈbiləd-ē\ *n* — **up·grad·able** *or* **up·grade·able** \ˌ⸗ˈ⸗⸗bəl\ *adj*
up·grade \ˈəpˌgrād\ *n* [*upgrade*, v.] **1** : an instance of upgrading ⟨a system that has been through four ~*s*⟩ **2** : IMPROVEMENT 2b(2)
uplink \ˈ⸗ˌ⸗\ *n* [[2]*up* + [2]*link*] **1** : a communications channel for transmissions to a spacecraft or satellite; *also* : the transmissions themselves **2** : a facility on earth for transmitting to a spacecraft or satellite — compare DOWNLINK *herein*
upload \ˈ⸗ˈ⸗\ *vt* [[1]*up* + [2]*load*] : to transfer (information) from a microcomputer to a remote computer usu. via modem
up·man·ship \ˈəpmənˌship\ *n* [by shortening] : ONE-UPMANSHIP
upmarket \ˈ⸗ˈ⸗⸗\ *adj* [[2]*up* + [1]*market*] : UPSCALE *herein* — **upmarket** *adv*
upper* *n* **1** : a stimulant drug; *esp* : AMPHETAMINE — compare DOWNER *herein* **2** : something that induces a state of good feeling or exhilaration
up·rate \ˈ⸗ˈ⸗\ *vt* [[1]*up* + [3]*rate*] : UPGRADE; *specif* : to improve the power output of (as an engine)
upscale \ˈ⸗ˈ⸗\ *adj* [[2]*up* + [7]*scale*] : of, being, relating to, or appealing to affluent consumers; *also* : of a superior quality — **upscale** *adv or vt*
upside* *n* : a positive aspect
upside \ˈ⸗ˈ⸗\ *prep* [perh. fr. [1]*up* + *-side* (as in *alongside*)] *chiefly dial* : on or against the side of ⟨he turned . . . and I slapped him right ~ the head —Marques Johnson⟩
upsilon* *n* : any of a group of unstable electrically neutral subatomic particles of the meson family that have a mass about 10 times that of a proton and are held to consist of a bottom quark-antiquark pair
upstream* *adv* **1** : in or to a position within the production stream closer to manufacturing processes **2** : in a direction along a molecule of DNA or RNA opposite to that in which transcription and translation take place and toward the end having a hydroxyl group attached to the position labeled 5′ in the terminal nucleotide ⟨a nucleotide sequence located ~ of the initiation codon⟩ — compare DOWNSTREAM *herein*
upstream* *adj* : of or relating to a portion of the production stream closer to basic extraction or manufacturing processes ⟨an ~ chemical manufacturer⟩ ⟨~ profits⟩
uptick \ˈ⸗ˌ⸗\ *n* [[2]*up* + [2]*tick*] **1** : a stock market transaction at a price above the last previous transaction in the same security — compare DOWNTICK *herein* **2** : INCREASE, RISE ⟨a recovery-induced ~ in demand —*Business Week*⟩
uptight \ˈ⸗ˈ⸗\ *adj* [[2]*up* + [3]*tight*] **1** : being in financial difficulties : BROKE ⟨surtax was another blow to an industry already ~ —*Chem. & Engineering News*⟩ **2 a** : showing signs of tension or uneasiness : APPREHENSIVE ⟨I was a little ~ about it at first —Phyllis Craig⟩ **b** : ANGRY, INDIGNANT ⟨I've been doing that voice in Negro theaters for years. Nobody ever got ~ —Flip Wilson⟩ **3** : rigidly conventional ⟨~ and antiseptic white community —J.M.Culkin⟩ — **uptight** *n* -S — **up·tight·ness** *n* -ES
uptime \ˈ⸗ˌ⸗\ *n* [[2]*up* + [1]*time*] : the time during which a piece of equipment (as a computer) is functioning or is able to function
uptown* *adj* : UPSCALE *herein*, FASHIONABLE ⟨an ~ dress⟩
upvalue \ˈ⸗ˈ⸗(ˌ)⸗\ *vt* [[1]*up* + [2]*value*] : to assign a higher value to; *specif* : to officially revalue (a currency) upward — **upvaluation** \ˌ⸗ˌ⸗⸗ˈ⸗⸗\ *n*
upward mobility *n* : the capacity or facility for rising to a higher social or economic class of society — **upwardly mobile** *adj*
up·well·ing \ˌəpˈweliŋ\ *n* -S [fr. gerund of *upwell*] : the process or an instance of rising or appearing to rise to the surface and flowing outward; *esp* : the process of upward movement of marine cold deep usu. nutrient-rich water to the surface near a continental shelf due to offshore drift of surface water (as from the action of winds or the Coriolis force)
ura·nia \yu̇ˈrānēə, -nyə\ *n* -S [NL, fr. *uranium* + *-a*] : URANIUM OXIDE a
uranium dioxide *n* : URANIUM OXIDE a
uranium trioxide *n* : a brilliant orange compound UO_3 that is formed in the course of refining uranium and that has been used as a coloring agent for ceramic wares
uranium 238 *n* : an isotope of uranium of mass number 238 that is the most abundant and stable isotope of uranium, that is not fissionable but can absorb fast neutrons to form a uranium isotope of mass number 239 which then decays through neptunium to form fissionable plutonium of mass number 239, and that has a half-life of 4.51 x 10^9years
ur·ban·ol·o·gist \ˌərbəˈnäləjəst\ *n* -S [*urbanology* (fr. *urban* + *-ology* — as in *psychology*) + *-ist*] : one who specializes in the problems of cities — **ur·ban·ol·o·gy** \-jē\ *n* -ES
urban renewal *n* : a construction program to replace or restore substandard buildings in an urban area
urban sprawl *n* : the spreading of urban developments (as houses and shopping centers) on undeveloped land near a city
urea·plas·ma \yu̇ˈrēəˌplazmə\ *n* [NL, fr. *urea* + *plasma*] **1** *cap* : a genus of mycoplasmas of the family Mycoplasmataceae that are able to hydrolyze urea with the formation of ammonia and that include one (*U. urealyticum*) found in the human genitourinary tract, oropharynx, and anal canal **2** : a mycoplasma of the genus *Ureaplasma*
ureo·tel·ic \yəˌrēəˈtelik, ¦yu̇r-\ *adj* [*ure-* + [2]*tel-* + *-ic*; fr. the fact that urea is the end product] : excreting nitrogen mostly in the form of urea ⟨mammals are ~ animals⟩ — **ureo·te·lism** \-lˌizəm, ˌyu̇rēˈētᵊlˌ-\ *n* -S
uri·co·tel·ic \¦yu̇rəkōˈtelik\ *adj* [*uric-* + [2]*tel-* + *-ic*; fr. the fact that uric acid is the end product] : excreting nitrogen mostly in the form of uric acid ⟨birds are ~ animals⟩ — **uri·co·te·lism** \-lˌizəm, ˌyu̇riˈkätᵊlˌ-\ *n* -S
URL \ˌyü(ˌ)ärˈel, ˈər(ə)l\ *abbr or n* -S [*uniform resource locator*] : the address of a resource (as a document, program, or Web site) on the Internet that consists of a communications protocol followed by the name or address of a computer on the network and that often includes a location (as a directory name) on the computer and an identification (as by a file name) ⟨our Web site's ~ is http://www.Merriam-Webster.com⟩
uro·gynecology \¦yu̇rə+\ *n* [[1]*ur-* + *gynecology*] : a branch of medicine that is concerned with the urological problems (as urinary incontinence) of women — **uro·gynecologic** \ˈ"+\ *or* **uro·gynecological** \ˈ"+\ *adj* — **uro·gynecologist** \ˈ"+\ *n*
uro·kinase \¦yu̇rə+\ *n* [[1]*ur-* + *kinase*] : an enzyme that is produced by the kidney and is found in urine, that activates plasminogen, and that is used therapeutically to dissolve blood clots (as in the heart)
ur·ti·car·io·gen·ic \ˌərd-ə¦ka(a)rēə¦jenik, -¦ker-\ *adj* [*urticaria* + *-o-* + *-genic*] : being an agent or substance that induces or predisposes to urticarial lesions (as wheals on the skin)
use·net \ˈyüzˌnet\ *n, usu cap U* [prob. fr. *Usenix*, an association of computer programmers using the operating system Unix (fr. *users* of *Unix*) + [1]*net* (network)] : the aggregation of all the electronic newsgroups on the Internet
user fee *n* : an excise tax often in the form of a license or supplemental charge levied to fund a public service — called also *user's fee*
user–friendly \ˈ⸗⸗ˈ⸗⸗\ *adj* : easy to learn, use, understand, or deal with — **user–friendliness** \ˈ⸗⸗ˈ⸗⸗⸗\ *n*
UTI \ˌyü(ˌ)tēˈī\ *abbr or n* -S : a urinary tract infection
util·i·dor \yüˈtiləˌdȯ(ə)r, -ˌdȯ(ə), -d(ə)r\ *n* -S [prob. fr. *utility* + *-idor* (as in *corridor*)] : an aboveground insulated conduit used for general utility service esp. in arctic climates
utility* *n* : a program or routine designed to perform or facilitate esp. routine operations (as copying files or editing text) on a computer
utilization review *n* : a critical evaluation (as by a physician or nurse) of health-care services provided to patients that is made esp. for the purpose of controlling costs (as by identifying unnecessary medical procedures) and monitoring quality of care
UVA \ˌyü(ˌ)vēˈā\ *n* [*ultraviolet*] : the region of the ultraviolet spectrum which is nearest to visible light and extends from about 320 to 400 nm in wavelength and from which comes the radiation that causes tanning and contributes to aging of the skin
u–value \ˈ⸗ˌ⸗(ˌ)⸗\ *n, usu cap U* [fr. unit] : a measure of the heat transmission through a building part (as a wall or window) or a given thickness of a material (as insulation) with lower numbers indicating better insulating properties — compare R-VALUE *herein*
UVB \ˌyü(ˌ)vē-ˈbē\ *n* : the region of the ultraviolet spectrum which extends from about 280 to 320 nm in wavelength and from which comes the radiation primarily responsible for sunburn, aging of the skin, and the development of skin cancer
UVC \-ˈsē\ *n* : the region of the ultraviolet spectrum which extends from about 200 to 280 nm in wavelengths and from which comes radiation that is more hazardous than UVB; *also* : such radiation from the Sun that is mostly absorbed by earth's upper atmosphere
vac·ci·nee \ˌvaksəˈnē\ *n* -S [[1]*vaccinate* + *-ee*] : a vaccinated individual
vach·e·rin \ˌvash(ə)ˈran, -ˈraⁿ, ˈ⸗(⸗)ˌ⸗\ *n* -S [F, fr. MF dial. (Franco-Provençal) *vacharin*, a kind of cheese, fr. ML *vaccherinus*, fr. *vaccaria* dairy farm, herd of cows (fr. L *vacca* cow + *-aria* -ary) + L *-inus* -ine — more at VACCINE] **1** : any of several French or Swiss soft cheeses **2** : a dessert consisting of meringue and a filling (as ice cream or fruit)
valence band *n* : the range of permissible energy values that are the highest energies an electron can have and still be associated with a particular atom of a solid material — compare CONDUCTION BAND *herein*
val·in·o·my·cin \ˌvalə(ˌ)nōˈmīsᵊn\ *n* -S [*valine* + *-o-* + *-mycin*] : an antibiotic $C_{54}H_{90}N_6O_{18}$ produced by a bacterium of the genus *Streptomyces* (*S. fulvissimus*)
Val·ium \ˈvalēəm, -lyəm\ *trademark* — used for a preparation of diazepam
valley girl *n, usu cap V & often cap G* : an adolescent girl from the San Fernando Valley; *also* : one whose values, mannerisms, and esp. speech patterns resemble those of such a girl
valorize* *vt* : to assign value or merit to : VALIDATE — **valorization** *n* -S
val·pro·ic acid \(ˈ)valˈprōik-\ *n* [*val*eric (acid) + *pro*pyl + pentano*ic acid*] : a valeric-acid derivative $C_8H_{16}O_2$ used as an anticonvulsant esp. in the form of its sodium salt
value–added tax \ˈ⸗(ˌ)⸗ˈ⸗⸗-\ *n* : an incremental excise that is levied on the value added at each stage of the processing of a raw material or the production and distribution of a commodity and that typically has the impact of a sales tax on the ultimate consumer
value–free \ˈ⸗(ˌ)⸗ˈ⸗\ *adj* : making or having no value judgments ⟨*value-free* distinctions⟩ ⟨*value-free* instruction⟩
vamp* *vi* [[2]*vamp*] : IMPROVISE, EXTEMPORIZE; *also* : to stall for time by improvising or extemporizing
vampy \ˈvampē\ *adj* -ER/-EST [[4]*vamp* + [1]*-y*] : VAMPISH; *also* : RISQUÉ ⟨a ~ minidress⟩
van* *n* **1** : a multipurpose enclosed boxlike motor vehicle having rear or side doors and side panels often with windows **2** : a detachable passenger cabin transportable by aircraft or truck

van·co·my·cin \ˌvaŋkəˈmīsᵊn\ *n* -S [*vanco-* (of unknown origin) + *-mycin*] : an antibiotic $C_{66}H_{75}Cl_2N_9O_{24}$ derived from an actinomycete (*Amycolatopsis orientalis* syn. *Streptomyces orientalis* syn. *Nocardia orientalis*) that is effective against gram-positive bacteria and is used chiefly in the form of its hydrochloride esp. against staphylococci resistant to methicillin

van der waals \ˈvandə(r)ˌwȯlz\ *adj, usu cap W* : of, relating to, or arising from van der Waals forces ⟨*van der Waals* interaction⟩ ⟨*van der Waals* potential⟩

va·nil·la \vəˈnilə, -nelə\ *adj* [*vanilla*, n.; fr. the fact that vanilla ice cream is considered the plainest flavor] : lacking distinction : ORDINARY, PLAIN, CONVENTIONAL ⟨nothing fancy about this design. It's just plain ~ —*Newsweek*⟩ ⟨a plain old ~ terminal —Steven Levy⟩

vanity *adj* [*vanity*, n.] **1** : of, relating to, or being a work (as a book or recording) whose production cost is paid by the author or artist — compare VANITY PRESS **2** : of, relating to, or being a showcase for a usu. famous performer or artist who is often also the project's creator or driving force ⟨write, direct, and star in a ~ film⟩

vanity plate *also* **vanity license plate** *n* : an automobile registration plate bearing letters, numbers, or a combination of these chosen by the owner

vanner* *n* : one who drives a usu. customized van

vanpool \ˈ=ˌ=\ *n* [³*van* + ³*pool*] : an arrangement by which a group of people commute to work in a passenger van — **van·pool·ing** \-ˌpüliŋ\ *n* -S

vaporware \ˈ==ˌ=\ *n* [¹*vapor* + *-ware* (as in *software* — herein)] : a new computer-related product that has been widely advertised but is not yet available

va·rac·tor \vəˈraktər, (ˈ)va(a)|(ə)¦r-, (ˈ)ve|\ *n* -S [*varying* + *reactor*] : a semiconductor device whose capacitance varies with the applied voltage

variable annuity *n* : an annuity contract which is backed primarily by a fund of common stocks and the payments on which fluctuate with the state of the economy

variable rate mortgage *n* : ADJUSTABLE RATE MORTGAGE *herein*

variable region *also* **variable domain** *n* : the part of the polypeptide chain of a light or heavy chain of an antibody that ends in a free amino group $-NH_2$, that varies greatly in its sequence of amino acid residues from one antibody to another, and that prob. determines the conformation of the combining site which confers the specificity of the antibody for a particular antigen — compare CONSTANT REGION *herein*

varietal* *adj* : of, relating to, producing, or characteristic of a varietal wine

var·i·o·la·tion \ˌvarēōˈlāshən\ *n* -S [*variola* + *-ation*] : the deliberate inoculation of an uninfected person with the smallpox virus (as by contact with pustular matter) that was widely practiced before the era of vaccination as prophylaxis against the severe form of smallpox

vas·cu·li·tis \ˌvaskyəˈlīd·əs\ *n, pl* **vas·cu·li·ti·des** \-ˈlīd·əˌdēz\ [NL, fr. *vascul-* + *-itis*] : inflammation of a blood or lymph vessel : ANGIITIS

va·so·active \¦vā(ˌ)zō, ¦vā(ˌ)sō, ¦va(ˌ)sō, ¦va(ˌ)zō+\ *adj* [*vas-* + *active*] : affecting the blood vessels esp. in respect to the degree of their relaxation or contraction — **va·so·activity** \"+\ *n*

vasoactive intestinal peptide *or* **vasoactive intestinal polypeptide** *n* : a protein hormone that consists of a chain of 28 amino acid residues, has been implicated as a neurotransmitter, and has a wide range of physiological activities (as stimulation of secretion by the pancreas and small intestine, vasodilation, and inhibition of gastric juice production)

VAT *abbr* value-added tax

vatican roulette *n, usu cap V, slang* : RHYTHM METHOD

VC* *abbr* Vietcong

v–chip \ˈ=ˌ=\ *n, usu cap V* [*violence*] : a computer chip in a television set that can prevent the viewing of certain programs or channels esp. on the basis of content (as violence)

VCR \ˌvē(ˌ)sēˈär, -ˈä(r)\ *n* -S [*videocassette recorder*] : a videotape recorder and player that uses videocassettes

VDT \ˌvē(ˌ)dēˈtē\ *n* -S [*video display terminal*] : a cathode-ray tube used to display information esp. from a computer

VDU \ˌvē(ˌ)dēˈyü\ *n* -S [*video display unit*] : VDT *herein*

vector* *n* **1** : an element of a vector space **2** : a sequence of genetic material (as a plasmid) into which a DNA segment has been inserted and that can be used to introduce exogenous genes into the genome of an organism

vector space *n* : a set representing a generalization of a system of vectors and consisting of elements which comprise a commutative group under addition, each of which is left unchanged under multiplication by the multiplicative identity of a field, and for which multiplication under the multiplicative operation of the field is commutative, closed, distributive such that both $c(A + B) = cA + cB$ and $(c + d)A = cA + dA$, and associative such that $(cd)A = c(dA)$ where *A*, *B* are elements of the set and *c*, *d* are elements of the field

vee·jay \ˈvēˌjā\ *n* [¹*vee* + ³*jay*; fr. the initial letters of *video jockey*] : an announcer of a program (as on television) that features music videos

vee·na \ˈvēnə\ *n* -S : VINA

ve·gan \ˈvēgən *also* ˈvejən *or* ˈvāg-\ *n* -S [contr. of *vegetarian*] : a strict vegetarian who consumes no animal food or dairy products; *also* : one who abstains from using animal products (as leather)

ve·gan·ism \ˈvēgəˌnizəm *also* ˈvejə- *or* ˈvāg-\ *n* -S : the practices or philosophy of a vegan

vegetable* *n* : a person whose mental and physical functioning is severely impaired and esp. who requires supportive measures (as intravenous feeding or mechanical ventilation) to survive

veg·gie *also* **veg·ie** \ˈvejē\ *n* -S [by shortening & alter.] **1** : VEGETABLE **2** *slang* : VEGETARIAN

veggie burger *n* : a patty chiefly of vegetable protein used as a meat substitute; *also* : a sandwich containing such a patty

veg out \ˈvej-\ *vi* **vegged out; vegged out; vegging out; vegges out** *or* **veges out** [*veg* short for *vegetate*] : to spend time idly or passively

Vel·cro \ˈvel(ˌ)krō\ *trademark* — used for a closure consisting of a piece of fabric of small hooks that sticks to a corresponding fabric of small loops

ve·loc·i·rap·tor \vəˈläsəˌraptər\ *n* [NL, fr. L *veloc-, velox* quick + *raptor* plunderer, predator — more at VELOCITY, RAPTOR] **1** *cap* : a genus of theropod dinosaurs of the late Cretaceous having a long head with a flat snout and a large sickle-shaped claw on the second toe of each foot **2** -S : a dinosaur of the genus *Velociraptor*

ventilate* *vt* : to subject the lungs of (an individual) to ventilation ⟨artificially ~ a patient⟩

ventriculo- *comb form* [NL, fr. L *ventriculus* stomach, ventricle of the heart — more at VENTRICLE] **1** : ventricle ⟨*ventriculo*tomy⟩ **2** : ventricular and ⟨*ventriculo*atrial⟩

ventriloquism* *n* : the expression of one's views and attitudes through another; *esp* : such expression by a writer through a fictional character or literary persona

ve·rap·a·mil \veˈrapəˌmil, və-\ *n* -S [ISV *valer-* + *-apam-* (prob. alter. of *amin-* + *propyl*) + *nitrile*] : a calcium channel blocker $C_{27}H_{38}N_2O_4$ with vasodilating properties that is used esp. in the form of its hydrochloride

ver·di·cchio \(ˌ)vərˈdē(k)kyō, ver-, -kē(ˌ)ō\ *n* -S *often cap* [It, a kind of dry wine, the grape from which it is made, fr. *verde* green, fr. L *viridis*] : a light dry white wine from Italy

ve·ris·mo \vāˈrēz(ˌ)mō, veˈr-, -ˈriz-\ *n* -S [It — more at VERISM] : VERISM

vé·ri·té \ˌverəˈtā\ *n* [F, truth, fr. MF *verité* — more at VERITY] : the quality of candid realism in film or television

vernier* *also* **vernier engine** *n* : any of two or more small supplementary rocket engines or gas nozzles on a missile or rocket vehicle for making fine adjustments in the speed or course or controlling the attitude

vé·ro·nique *also* **ve·ro·nique** \värōnēk\ *adj, usu cap* [F, prob. fr. *Véronique* Veronica] : prepared or garnished with usu. white seedless grapes ⟨chicken ~⟩ ⟨sole ~⟩

vertical integration *n* : the combining of manufacturing operations with source of materials and/or channels of distribution under a single ownership or management esp. to maximize profits

very large scale integration *n* : the process of placing a very large number (as thousands) of circuits on a small semiconductor chip — abbr. *VLSI*

very–low–density lipoprotein *n* : VLDL *herein*

vesico- *comb form* [NL, fr. L *vesica* bladder — more at VESICA] : of or relating to the urinary bladder and ⟨*vesico*ureteral⟩

vest* *n* : an insulated sleeveless waist-length garment often worn under or in place of a coat

ves·tib·u·lo·co·chle·ar nerve \veˌstibyəlō¦kōklēə(r)-, -ˈkäk-\ *n* [*vestibule* + *-o-* + *cochlear nerve*] : AUDITORY NERVE

vest–pocket park *n* : a very small urban park

veto–proof \ˈ==ˌ=\ *adj* : having enough potential votes to be passed over a veto or to override vetoes consistently

vex·il·lol·o·gy \ˌveksəˈläləjē\ *n* -ES [L *vexillum* flag + E *-ology* (as in *psychology*) — more at VEXILLUM] : the study of flags — **vex·il·lo·log·i·cal** \¦veksəlō¦läjəkəl, (¦)vek¦siləˈlä-\ *adj* — **vex·il·lol·o·gist** \ˌveksəˈläləjəst\ *n* -S

VGA \ˌvē(ˌ)jēˈā\ *abbr or n* -S [video graphics array] : a color display format (as for a computer monitor) that has a resolution of 640 pixels by 480 pixels

viable* *adj* : having a reasonable chance of succeeding ⟨a ~ candidate⟩

vi·at·i·cal \vīˈad·əkəl, -ˈatək-\ *adj* [prob. fr. *viaticum* + ¹*-al*] : of, concerned with, or dealing in viatical settlements ⟨adding provisions to the state's ~ law to better protect consumers —J.T.Fakler⟩ ⟨a ~ brokerage firm⟩

viatical settlement *also* **viatical** *n* -S : an agreement by which the owner of a life insurance policy covering a person (as the owner) with a catastrophic or life-threatening illness receives compensation for less than the expected death benefit of the policy in return for an assignment, transfer, sale, devise, or bequest of the death benefit or ownership of the policy to the other party (as a company specializing in such transactions)

vi·a·tor \vīˈād·ə(r), -ˈātə-\ *n* -S [*viatical* (herein) + ¹*-or*] : a person with a catastrophic or life-threatening illness who has a life insurance policy and sells or intends to sell it in a viatical settlement; *broadly* : one who owns and assigns a life insurance policy in a viatical settlement

vibe \ˈvīb\ *n* -S [by shortening] : VIBRATION 4 — usu. used in pl. ⟨the good guy is someone who radiates good ~*s* . . . to others and is not psychotic about doing his own thing —Franklin Chu⟩

vi·bra·harp \ˈvībrəˌhärp, -ˌhäp\ *n* [fr. *Vibra-Harp*, a trademark] : VIBRAPHONE — **vi·bra·harp·ist** \-pəst\ *n*

vi·bron·ic \(ˈ)vīˈbränik\ *adj* [*vibration* + *electronic*] : of or relating to transitions between molecular energy states when modified by vibrational energy

vi·car·i·ance \vīˈkerēən(t)s, və-, -ˈkar-\ *also* **vicariance biogeography** *n* -S [*vicariant* (herein) + *-ance*] : fragmentation of the environment (as by splitting of a tectonic plate) in contrast to dispersal as a factor in promoting biological evolution by division of large continuous populations into isolated populations

vi·car·i·ant \-ēənt\ *adj* [modif. of G *vikariierend*, past part. of *vikariieren* to act as a substitute, fr. *vikar* representative, proxy, fr. MHG *vicar*, fr. L *vicarius* substitute— more at VICAR] : of, relating to, or being the process of vicariance or the organisms that evolved through this process ⟨the possible ~ origin of the Antillean arthropod fauna⟩ — **vicariant** *n* -S

vicious cycle *n* **1** : VICIOUS CIRCLE 1 **2** : VICIOUS CIRCLE 3

vic·tim·less \ˈviktəmləs\ *adj* : having no victim ⟨~ crimes⟩

vic·tim·ol·o·gy \ˌviktəˈmäləjē\ *n* -ES [*victim* + *-ology* (as in *psychology*)] : the study of the ways in which the behavior of crime victims may have led to or contributed to their victimization — **victim·ol·o·gist** \-jəst\ *n* -S

victorian* *n, usu cap* : a typically large and ornate house built during Queen Victoria's reign

vic·to·ri·ana \ˌ(ˌ)vikˌtōrēˈänə, -tór-, -ˈanə, -ˈaa(ə)nə\ *n, usu cap* [Queen *Victoria* †1901 Brit. sovereign + E *-ana*] : materials concerning or characteristic of the Victorian age

vi·da·lia onion \vəˈdālyə-\ *also* **vidalia** *n* -S *usu cap V* [fr. *Vidalia*, town in Georgia, U.S.] : a large mild sweet onion grown in Georgia

video* *n* : VIDEOTAPE *herein*: as **a** : a recording of a motion picture or television program for playing through a television set **b** : a videotaped performance of a popular song often featuring a dramatic interpretation of the lyrics through visual images

vid·eo·cam \ˈvidē(ˌ)ōˌkam\ *n* [short for *videocamera*, fr. ¹*video* + *camera*] : CAMCORDER *herein*

video camera *n* : a usu. stationary camera that transmits images to a remote location for display or recording and is used esp. to monitor (as for security) a specific location (as a doorway or room); *also* : CAMCORDER *herein*

video card *n* : a circuit board in a computer system that is designed to generate output for the system's video display screen

videocassette \ˈ===ˌ=¦=\ *n* [¹*video* + *cassette*] **1** : a case containing videotape for use with a VCR **2** : a recording (as of a movie) on a videocassette

videocassette recorder *n* : VCR *herein*

vid·eo·con·fer·enc·ing \¦==ˌ=¦känfər(ə)n(t)siŋ, -frən-\ *n* -S [¹*video* + *conference* + ³*-ing*] : the holding of a conference among people at remote locations by means of transmitted audio and video signals — **videoconference** *n*

videodisc *also* **videodisk** \¦==(ˌ)=¦=\ *n* [¹*video* + *disc* or *disk*] **1** : a disc similar in appearance and use to a phonograph record on which programs have been recorded for playback on a television set; *also* : OPTICAL DISK *herein* **2** : a recording on a videodisc

video game *n* : an electronic game esp. emphasizing fast action that is played by means of images on a video screen

vi·de·og·ra·phy \ˌvidēˈägrəfē\ *n* -ES [¹*video* + *-graphy*] : the practice or art of recording images with a video camera — **vid·e·og·ra·pher** \-fə(r)\ *n* -S

vid·eo·land \ˈvidē(ˌ)ōˌland\ *n* [²*video* + *land*] : the medium of television or the television industry

vid·eo·phile \-ˌfīl\ *n* -S [²*video* + ¹*-phil*] : one who has a fondness for videos; *esp* : one who is intensely interested in watching or producing videos

vid·eo·phone \-ˌfōn\ *n* [¹*video* + *phone*] : a telephone equipped for transmission of video as well as audio signals so that users can see each other

video recorder *n* : VIDEOTAPE RECORDER *herein*

¹**vid·eo·tape** \-ēəˌtāp, -ēōˌt-\ *n* [¹*video* + ¹*tape*] : a recording of visual images and sound (as of a television production) made on magnetic tape; *also* : the magnetic tape used for such a recording

²**videotape** \"\ *vt* -ED/-ING/-S : to make a videotape recording of

videotape recorder *n* : a device for recording and playing videotapes

vid·eo·tex \ˈvidēəˌteks, -ēōˌt-\ *also* **vid·eo·text** \-ˌtekst\ *n* [¹*video* + *text* or *text*] : an electronic data retrieval system in which usu. textual information is transmitted via telephone or cable-television lines and displayed on a television set or VDT; *esp* : such a system that is interactive — compare TELETEXT *herein*

video vé·ri·té *or* **video ve·ri·té** *or* **video ve·ri·te** \-¦verə¦tā\ *n* [¹*video* + *vérité* or *verité* or *verite* (as in *cinema verité* — herein)] : the art or technique of filming or videotaping a television program (as a documentary) so as to convey candid realism

vi·et·nam·i·za·tion \vēˌetnəməˈzāshən, ˌvyet-, -ˌmīˈz- *also* ˌvēət- *or* ˌvēt-\ *n* -S *usu cap* [*Vietnam*, country in Indochina + *-ization*] : the act or process of transferring war responsibilities from U.S. to Vietnamese hands during the Vietnam War — **vi·et·nam·ize** \vēˈetnəˌmīz, ˈvyet- *also* ˈvēət-, ˈvēt-\ *vb* -ED/-ING/-S *usu cap*

viewdata \ˈ=¦==\ *n* [²*view* + *data*] : a videotex system usu. employing telephone lines

viewer·ship \R ˈvyüərˌship, ˈvyü(ə)r-; -R ˈvyüə-, ˈvyüəˌ-\ *n* [*viewer* + *-ship*] : a television audience

vig \ˈvig\ *n* -S [by shortening] : VIGORISH

-ville \ˌvil *esp South* ˌvəl\ *n suffix* -S [*-ville*, suffix occurring in names of towns, fr. F, fr. OF, fr. *ville* farm, village — more at VILLAGE] : place or category of a specified nature ⟨squares*ville*⟩

VIN *abbr* vehicle identification number

vin·blas·tine \vinˈblaˌstēn, -ˌstən\ *n* -S [contr. of *vincaleukoblastine* (herein)] : an alkaloid $C_{46}H_{58}N_4O_9$ from the Madagascar periwinkle used esp. in the form of its sulfate to treat human neoplastic diseases (as Hodgkin's disease and testicular carcinoma)

vin·ca·leu·ko·blas·tine \ˌviŋkə¦lükə¦blaˌstēn, -ˌstən; -(ˌ)bləˈstēn\ *n* -S [NL *Vinca* + E *leukoblast* + ²*-ine*] : VINBLASTINE *herein*

vin·cris·tine \vinˈkriˌstēn, viŋˈk-, -ˌstən\ *n* -S [*vin*blastine (herein) + leuro*cristine*, an earlier name, perh. fr. *leuko*blast + NL *rosea*, epithet of Madagascar periwinkle + E *-crist-* (alter. of ¹*crystal*) + ²*-ine*] : an alkaloid $C_{46}H_{56}N_4O_{10}$ from the Madagascar periwinkle used esp. in the form of its sulfate to treat human neoplastic diseases (as acute leukemia)

vin·da·loo \ˈvindəˌlü\ *n* -S [prob. fr. Konkani *vindalu*, fr. Indo-Portuguese (Pg creole of India) *vinh d'alho*, lit., wine of garlic, fr. Pg *vinho de alho*] : a curried meat dish made with garlic and wine or vinegar

vine* *n, slang* : an article of clothing; *esp* : a man's suit — usu. used in pl.

vin·i·fy \ˈvinəˌfī, ˈvīn-\ *vt* -ED/-ING/-ES [prob. back-formation fr. *vinification*] **1** : to make wine from (often specified grapes) **2** : to make (wine) from grapes

vi·ol·o·gen \vīˈäləjən\ *n* -S [*violet* + *-o-* + *-gen*] : a chloride of any of several bases used as an oxidation-reduction indicator because color is exhibited in the reduced form

virgin* *n* : a person who is inexperienced in a usu. specified sphere of activity ⟨a ~ in politics⟩

virgo* *n, usu cap* : one born under the astrological sign Virgo

vir·go·an \ˈvərˌgōən, ˈvə̄-\ *n* -S *usu cap* [*Virgo* + E *-an*] : VIRGO *herein*

vi·ri·on \ˈvīrēˌän, ˈvir-\ *n* -S [ISV *viri-* (fr. NL *virus*) + ²*-on*; orig. formed in F] : a complete virus particle that consists of an RNA or DNA core with a protein coat sometimes with external envelopes and that is the extracellular infective form of a virus

viroid* *n* : any of several causative agents of plant disease that consist solely of a single-stranded RNA of low molecular weight arranged in a closed loop or a linear chain

virtual* *adj* **1** : of, relating to, or being a hypothetical particle whose existence is inferred from indirect evidence ⟨~ photon⟩ **2** : of, relating to, or using virtual memory **3** : being on or simulated on a computer or computer network ⟨print or ~ books⟩ ⟨a ~ keyboard⟩ : as **a** : occurring or existing primarily on-line ⟨a ~ library⟩ ⟨~ shopping⟩ **b** : of, relating to, or existing within a virtual reality ⟨a ~ world⟩

virtual memory *n* : external memory (as magnetic disks) for a computer that can be used as if it were an extension of the computer's internal memory — called also *virtual storage*

virtual reality *n* : an artificial environment which is experienced through sensory stimuli (as sights and sounds) provided by a computer and in which one's actions partially determine what happens in the environment; *also* : the technology used to access a virtual reality — abbr. *VR*

virtuoso* *n* : a person who has great skill at some endeavor ⟨a computer ~⟩ ⟨a ~ at public relations⟩

virus* *n* : a computer program that is usu. hidden within another seemingly innocuous program, that produces copies of itself and inserts them into other programs, and that usu. performs a malicious action (as destroying data) — compare TROJAN HORSE *herein*

visionary* *adj* : having or marked by foresight and imagination ⟨a ~ leader⟩ ⟨a ~ invention⟩

visual literacy *n* : the ability to recognize and understand ideas conveyed through visible actions or images (as pictures)

vi·suo·spatial \ˌvizhəwō+\ *adj* [¹*visual* + *-o-* + *spatial*] : of, relating to, or being thought processes that involve visual and spatial awareness ⟨~ problem solving⟩

vital signs *n pl* : signs of life; *specif* : the pulse rate, respiratory rate, body temperature, and often blood pressure of a person

vi·ta·min·i·za·tion \ˌvīd·əmənəˈzāshən, *Brit also* ˌvit-\ *n* -S : the action or process of vitaminizing

vit·rec·to·my \vəˈtrektəmē\ *n* -ES [*vitreous humor* + *-ectomy*] : surgical removal of all or part of the vitreous humor

VJ *abbr* veejay *herein*

VLCC \ˌvēˌel(ˌ)sēˈsē\ *abbr or n* -S [very large crude carrier] : a crude-oil tanker with a very large capacity

VLDL \ˌvē(ˌ)el(ˌ)dēˈel\ *n* -S [*very low-density lipoprotein*] : a plasma lipoprotein that is produced primarily by the liver with lesser amounts contributed by the intestine, that contains relatively large amounts of triglycerides compared to protein, and that leaves a residue of cholesterol in the tissues during the process of conversion to LDL — called also *very low-density lipoprotein*; compare HDL *herein*, LDL *herein*

VLSI \¦vē¦el¦es¦ī\ *abbr or n* very large scale integration *herein*

VOC \ˌvē(ˌ)ōˈsē\ *abbr or n* -S [volatile organic compound] : any of various organic chemical compounds (as formaldehyde) that evaporate quickly esp. from solvents, adhesives, fuels, or industrial wastes and that contribute to photochemical smog in the atmosphere

vocabulary* *n* : a list or collection of terms or codes available for use (as in an indexing system)

vo·ca·lese \ˌvōkəˈlēz, -ˈlēs\ *n* -S [prob. alter. (influenced by ¹*-ese*) of *vocalise*] : a jazz vocal style in which the voice emulates an instrumental part

vogue *vi* **vogued; vogued; vogu·ing** *or* **vogue·ing; vogues** [fr. *Vogue*, a U.S. fashion magazine] : to strike poses in campy imitation of fashion models esp. as a kind of dance — **vogu·er** \ˈvōgə(r)\ *n* -S

voice mail *n* : an electronic communication system in which spoken messages are recorded or digitized and stored for later playback for the intended recipient; *also* : such a message

voice–over \ˈ=ˌ==\ *n* -S : the voice of an unseen narrator heard in a motion picture or television program; *also* : the voice of a visible character indicating his thoughts but without motion of his lips

voiceprint \ˈ=ˌ=\ *n* [¹*voice* + ¹*print*] : an individually distinctive pattern of certain voice characteristics that is spectrographically produced

voi·là *or* **voi·la** \ˌvwäˈlä\ *interj* [F, lit., see there] — used to call attention, to express satisfaction or approval, or to suggest an appearing as if by magic

VOLAR *abbr* volunteer army

volcanogenic \¦välkənə¦jenik, ¦vȯl-\ *adj* [*volcano* + *-genic*] : of volcanic origin ⟨~ sediments⟩

vol·tam·met·ry \vōlˈtaməˌtrē, -ˈtäm-, -ˈri\ *n* -ES [*volt-ammeter* + ²*-y*] : the detection of minute quantities of chemicals (as metals) by measuring the currents generated in electrolytic solutions when known voltages are applied — **vol·tam·met·ric** \ˌvōltəˈmeˑtrik, -ēk\ *adj*

-vol·tine \ˈvōlˌtēn, ˈvȯl-\ *adj comb form* [F, fr. It *volta* time, occasion, lit., turn — more at VOLT] : having (so many) generations or broods in a season or year ⟨multi*voltine*⟩

vol·un·teer·ism \ˌvälənˈti(ə)ˌrizəm\ *n* : the act or practice of doing volunteer work in community service

VOM *abbr* volt-ohmmeter

vomeronasal organ *n* : JACOBSON'S ORGAN

vomitous* *adj* : SICKENING, DISGUSTING

von wil·le·brand's disease \fōn¦viləˌbrän(t)s-\ *n, usu cap W* [after E.A. *von Willebrand* †1949 Finnish physician] : a genetic disorder that is inherited as an autosomal dominant trait and is characterized by deficiency of a plasma clotting factor and by mucosal and petechial bleeding due to abnormal blood vessels

vote* *vb* — **vote with one's feet** : to express one's disapproval or dissatisfaction by leaving

VO$_2$ max \ˌvē(ˌ)ō'tü-\ *n* [volume of *O$_2$ maximum*] : the maximum amount of oxygen the body can use during a specified period of time that depends on body weight and the strength of the lungs

voucher* *n* : COUPON 2g; *specif* : a coupon issued by government to a parent or guardian to be used to fund a child's education in either public or private school

VR *abbr* virtual reality *herein*

vroom \'vrüm, və'rüm\ *vi* -ED/-ING/-S [fr. *vroom*, n. & interj., used to represent the sound of an engine] : to operate a motor vehicle at high speed or with loud engine noise

VSO *abbr* very superior old — usu. used of brandy 12 to 17 years old

VSOP *abbr* very superior old pale — usu. used of brandy 18 to 25 years old

V/STOL \'vē,stōl, -ōl\ *abbr* vertical or short takeoff and landing

VTOL \'vē,tōl, -ōl\ *abbr* vertical takeoff and landing

VVSOP *abbr* very very superior old pale — usu. used of brandy 25 to 40 years old

w* *or* **w boson** *or* **w particle** *n, usu cap W* [*w*eak] : either of two elementary particles about 80 times heavier than a proton that along with the Z particle are transmitters of the weak force and that can have a positive or negative charge

wack *adj* [prob. alter. of *wacky*] *slang* : lacking in quality : INADEQUATE; *also* CORNY

wacked–out \¦wak¦dau̇t\ *var of* WHACKED-OUT

¹wacko \'wak(ˌ)ō\ *adj* [by alter.] *slang* : WACKY

²wacko \"\ *n* -S *slang* : a person who is or who acts wacky

wade–giles \ˌwād'gīlz\ *n, usu cap W&G* [after Thomas F. *Wade* †1895 Brit. diplomat and Herbert A. *Giles* †1935 Brit. sinologist] : a system for romanizing Chinese ideograms in which tones are indicated by superscript numbers and consonantal aspiration is indicated by an apostrophe — compare PINYIN *herein*

wafer* *n* : a thin slice of semiconductor (as silicon) used as a base for an electronic component or circuit

wafer* *vt* **1** : to prepare (as hay or alfalfa) in the form of small compressed cakes suggestive of crackers **2** : to divide (as a silicon rod) into wafers

waffle* *vi* : to talk indecisively or evasively : EQUIVOCATE ⟨has *waffled* miserably in his economic and foreign affairs stances — *Christian Science Monitor*⟩ — **waf·fler** \'wäf(ə)lə(r), 'wȯf-\ *n* -S

waffle *n* -S : empty or pretentious words ⟨a lot of rather vague ~ about how nice he was —Dan Davin⟩

wafflestomper \'=ˌ=ˌstämpə(r)\ *n* -S [¹*waffle* + *stomp* + ²-*er*; fr. the pattern left by the sole] : a hiking boot with a lug sole

wahine* *n* : a girl surfer

wait–list \'=ˌ=\ *vt* [*wait list*, n.] : to put on a waiting list

waitperson \'=ˌ==\ *n* : a person who serves food to others (as in a restaurant) : WAITER, WAITRESS

wait·ron \'wā,trän, -ˌtrən\ *n* -S [blend of *waiter* or *waitress* and *-tron* (suggesting the machine-like impersonality of such work), later (perh. influenced by *neutron*) taken as a gender-neutral term] : WAITPERSON *herein*

wait·staff \'=ˌ=\ *n* : the staff of servers at a restaurant

wa·ka·me \wä'käme\ *n* -S [Jap] : an edible brown seaweed (*Undaria pinnatifida*) of the order Laminariales that is native to Asia

wake·board \'=ˌ=\ *n* [⁴*wake* + ¹*board*] : a short board with foot bindings on which a rider is towed by a motorboat across its wake and esp. up off the crest for aerial maneuvers — **wakeboard·er** \-ər\ *n* — **wakeboard·ing** \-iŋ\ *n*

wake–up call *n* **1** : a telephone call (as from a hotel employee to a hotel guest) that serves to wake one up **2** : something that serves to alert one to a problem, danger, or need ⟨her death was a *wake-up call* that has inspired citizens to action —Mike Sager⟩

walk* *vi* : to avoid criminal prosecution or conviction — **walk one through** : to guide one (as a novice) through an unfamiliar or complex procedure step by step

walk–in* *adj* : being or offering a sevice provided to people who walk in without an appointment or reservation ⟨a *walk-in* medical clinic⟩; *also* : being a person who uses such a service

walk–in* *n* : a person who walks in without an appointment or reservation

walking catfish *n* : an Asian catfish of the genus *Clarias* (*C. batrachus*) that is able to move about on land and has been inadvertently introduced into Florida waters

Walk·man \'wȯkmən, -ˌman\ *trademark* — used for a small portable radio or cassette player listened to by means of headphones or earphones

walk–on* *n* **1** : a minor part or role (as in a novel or a discussion); *also* : one with such a part or role **2** : a college athlete who has not been recruited specifically by the school

walk–up* *adj* : designed to allow pedestrians to be served without entering a building ⟨the *walk-up* window of a bank⟩

wall* *n* — **up against the wall** : in or into a tight or difficult situation ⟨high costs . . . have finally driven a ghastly number of colleges and universities *up against the wall* —G.W.Bonham⟩ — **up the wall** *slang* : into a state of intense agitation, annoyance, or frustration ⟨the steady crunch-crunch drove [him] *up the wall* —Cyra McFadden⟩

wall system *n* : a set of shelves often with cabinets or bureaus that can be variously arranged along a wall

¹wall–to–wall \¦=¦=¦=\ adj **1** : covering the entire floor ⟨*wall-to-wall* carpeting⟩ **2 a** : covering or filling the entire space or time ⟨a disco crammed with *wall-to-wall* bodies —*Women's Wear Daily*⟩ ⟨relying too heavily on *wall-to-wall* action —Karla Kuskin⟩ **b** : occurring or found everywhere : UBIQUITOUS ⟨the *wall-to-wall* comforts that the current affluence made available —W.H.Jones⟩

²wall–to–wall \"\ *n* : a wall-to-wall carpet

wand* *n* : a handheld device used to enter information (as from a bar code) into a computer — **wand** *vt* -ED/-ING/-S

wan·kel engine \¦väŋkəl-, ¦waŋ-\ *n, usu cap W* [after Felix *Wankel* †1988 Ger. engineer] : an internal-combustion rotary engine that has a rounded triangular rotor functioning as a piston and rotating in a space in the engine and that has only two major moving parts

wan·na·be *also* **wan·na·bee** \'wänəˌbē\ *n* -S [fr. the phrase *wanna be*, contr. of *want to be*] **1** : a person who wants or aspires to be someone or something else or who tries to look or act like someone else **2** : something (as a company, city, or product) intended or hoped to rival another of its kind that has been successful; *esp* : one for which hopes have failed or are likely to fail : a pale imitation

warehouse* *vt* : to confine or house (a person) in conditions suggestive of a warehouse ⟨instead of rehabilitating the homeless . . . shelters now simply ~ them —David Whitman⟩

war–game \'=ˌ=\ *vt* : to plan or conduct in the manner of a war game ⟨*war-gamed* an invasion —*Newsweek*⟩ ~ *vi* : to conduct a war game — **war–gamer** \-ˌgāmə(r)\ *n* -S

warm fuzzies *n pl* [*fuzzy*, adj.] : feelings of happiness, pleasure, or contentment ⟨winning the game gave everyone *warm fuzzies*⟩

warning track *or* **warning path** *n* : a usu. dirt or cinder strip around the edge of a grass baseball outfield to warn a fielder running to make a catch that he is nearing a wall or fence

warp speed *n* [fr. the use in science fiction of space-time warps to allow faster-than-light travel] : the highest possible speed

war room* *n* : a room (as in a business headquarters) used for conferences and planning that is often specially equipped (as with computers, maps, or charts)

war story *n* : a story of a memorable personal experience that typically involves an element of danger, hardship, or adventure ⟨politicians swapping *war stories* from past campaigns⟩

wart* *n* : DEFECT, IMPERFECTION — often used in the phrase *warts and all*

wash* *n* : a situation in which losses and gains or advantages and disadvantages balance each other

wash·a·te·ria *also* **wash·e·te·ria** \ˌwäshə'tērēə, ˌwȯsh-, -'tir-\ *n* -S [²*wash* + *-ateria* or *-eteria* (as in *cafeteria*)] *chiefly South* : a self-service laundry usu. with coin-operated machines

wasp \'wäsp, 'wȯsp\ *n* -S *usu cap W or WASP, often attrib* [*w*hite *A*nglo-*S*axon *P*rotestant] : an American of northern European and esp. British stock and of Protestant background; *esp* : a member of the dominant and most privileged class of people in the U.S. — **wasp·dom** \-spdəm\ *n* -S *usu cap W or WASP* — **wasp·ish** \-spish\ *adj, usu cap W or WASP* — **wasp·ish·ness** \-spəshnəs\ *n* -ES *usu cap W or WASP* — **waspy** \-spē, -spi\ *adj* -ER/-EST *usu cap W or WASP*

waste* *vt* : to kill or severely injure

wasted* *adj, slang* : intoxicated from drugs or alcohol

wastewater \'=ˌ==\ *n* : water that has been used (as in a manufacturing process) : SEWAGE

watch* *n* **1** : a notice or bulletin that alerts the public to the possibility of severe weather conditions occurring in the near future ⟨a winter storm ~⟩ **2** : a term as holder esp. of an overseeing or managerial office ⟨the business grew on her ~⟩

water bed *n* : a bed whose mattress is a plastic bag filled with water

water cycle *n* : HYDROLOGIC CYCLE

waterflood \'=ˌ=\ *vi* [¹*water* + ²*flood*] : to pump water into the ground around an oil well nearing depletion in order to force out additional oil — **waterflood** *n*

wa·ter·fowl·er \'wȯd·ə(r)ˌfau̇lə(r), 'wäl, |tə(r)-\ *n* -S : a hunter of waterfowl

wa·ter·fowl·ing \-liŋ\ *n* -S : the occupation or pastime of hunting waterfowl

wa·ter·gate \'wȯ|d·ə(r)ˌgāt, 'wä|, |tə(r)-, *usu* -ād-+V\ *n, usu cap* [fr. *The Watergate*, apartment and office complex in Washington, D.C.; fr. the scandal following the break-in at the Democratic National Committee headquarters there in 1972] : a scandal usu. involving abuses of office and the compounding of wrongdoing through a cover-up

watering hole** *n* : a place (as a bar or restaurant) where people go to eat, drink, and socialize

water park *n* : an amusement park with facilities (as pools and wetted slides) for aquatic recreation

water pill *n* : a diuretic pill

waterslide** \'=ˌ=\ *n* : a continuously wetted chute (as at an amusement park) down which people slide into a pool

wa·ter·zooi \'wȯd·ərˌzüē, 'wäd-, -zōē\ *n* -S [D dial., fr. *water* water (fr. MD *wāter*; akin to OE *wæter* water) + *zooi* quantity of cooked food, lit., act of boiling, contr. of *zode*, fr. MD *sōde*; akin to MD *soot* boiling water, well, OE *sēath* well, *sēothan* to boil — more at WATER, SEETHE] : a stew of chicken or seafood and vegetables in a seasoned stock thickened with cream and egg yolks

wat·son–crick \¦wätsən'krik, *also* ¦wȯt-\ *adj, usu cap W&C* : of or relating to the Watson-Crick model ⟨*Watson-Crick* helix⟩

watson–crick model *n, usu cap W&C* [after James D. *Watson* *b*1928 Am. biologist and Francis H.C. *Crick* *b*1916 Eng. biologist] : a model of DNA structure in which the molecule is a cross-linked double-stranded helix, each strand is composed of alternating links of phosphate and deoxyribose, and the strands are cross-linked by pairs of purine and pyrimidine bases projecting inward from the deoxyribose sugars and joined by hydrogen bonds with adenine paired with thymine and with cytosine paired with guanine — compare DOUBLE HELIX *herein*

wave* *n, often cap* : a display by spectators at a sports event in which they rise in rapid succession, lift their arms overhead, and sit down again quickly so that a continuous swell appears to move through the stands

wave function* *n* : a quantum-mechanical function whose square represents the relative probability of finding a given elementary particle within a specified volume of space

waxing* *n* : the process of removing body hair with a depilatory wax

way–out \'=ˌ=\ *adj* [*way out* (adverbial phrase), fr. ⁴*way* + ¹*out*] : FAR-OUT *herein* — **way–out·ness** \(')=ˌ=nəs\ *n* -ES

wa·zoo \(ˌ)wä'zü\ *n* -S [origin unknown] *slang* : ANUS — **up the wazoo** *also* **out the wazoo** : in excess ⟨we've got lawyers *up the wazoo* —Steve Bochco⟩

weak anthropic principle *n* : ANTHROPIC PRINCIPLE a *herein*

weak force *or* **weak interaction** *also* **weak nuclear force** *n* : a fundamental physical force that governs interactions between hadrons and leptons (as in the emission and absorption of neutrinos) and is responsible for particle decay processes (as beta decay) in radioactivity, that is 10^5 times weaker than the strong force, and that acts over distances smaller than those between nucleons in an atomic nucleus — compare ELECTROMAGNETISM *herein*, GRAVITY *herein*, STRONG FORCE *herein*

weath·er·ize \'weth̲əˌrīz\ *vt* -ED/-ING/-S : to make (as a house) better protected against winter weather esp. by adding insulation and by caulking joints — **weath·er·i·za·tion** \ˌweth̲ərə'zāshən, -əˌrī'z-\ *n* -S

web* *n, usu cap* : WORLD WIDE WEB *herein*

webmaster \'=ˌ=\ *n, usu cap* : a person responsible for the creation or maintenance of a Web site esp. for a company or organization

web site *n, usu cap W* : a group of World Wide Web pages usu. containing hyperlinks to each other and made available on-line by an individual, company, or organization

web·zine \'webˌzēn\ *n* -S *usu cap* [*Web* (herein) + *-zine* (as in *fanzine*)] : a publication usu. in magazine format that exists solely on the World Wide Web

wedding cake* *n* : something (as a large building) resembling a wedding cake esp. in elaborate ornamentation

we·del \'vād³l *also* 'we-\ *vi* -ED/-ING/-S [G *wedeln*] : to ski downhill by means of wedeln

we·deln \'vād³l(ə)n *also* 'we-\ *n, pl* **wedelns** *or* **wedeln** [G, fr. *wedeln*, lit., to fan, wag the tail, fr. OHG *wadalōn*, fr. *wadal* tail; akin to ON *vēli* bird's tail] : a style of skiing in which the skier moves the rear of the skis from side to side making a series of short quick turns while following the fall line

wedg·ie \'wejē\ *n* -S [¹*wedge* + *-ie*] : the condition of having one's clothing wedged between the buttocks usu. from having one's pants or underpants yanked up from behind as a prank — often used with *get* or *give*

weekend warrior *n* : a person who participates in a usu. physically strenuous activity only on weekends or part-time ⟨lunch-hour aerobicizers metamorphosed into *weekend warriors* —Mary Duffy & Maura Rhodes⟩ ⟨nationally ranked athletes as well as *weekend warriors* —Nancy Buck⟩

weenie* *n* **1** *slang* : PENIS **2** : NERD *herein* ⟨computer ~*s*⟩

weep·ie \'wēpē\ *n* -S [¹*weep* + *-ie*] : TEARJERKER

weight training *n* : a system of conditioning involving lifting weights esp. for strength and endurance

weirdo \'wi(ə)r(ˌ)dō, 'wiə(ˌ)dō\ *n* -S [³*weird* + ¹*-o*] : WEIRDIE

weird out *vt* : to make uneasy, bewildered, or discomposed by something considered very strange ⟨it really *weirded* me *out*, and I realized that I wasn't happy —Richard Dreyfuss⟩

well–formed \¦=¦=\ *adj* : produced by the correct application of a set of transformations : GRAMMATICAL 2a ⟨grammar . . . specifies the infinite set of *well-formed* sentences —Jerry Fodor & Jerrold J. Katz⟩ — **well–formed·ness** \ˌwel'fó(r)m(d)nəs\ *n* -ES

well–ordered \¦=¦==\ *adj* : partially ordered with every subset containing a first element and exactly one of the relationships "greater than", "less than", or "equal to" holding for any given pair of elements

well–ordering \¦=¦=(=)=\ *n* -S : an instance of being well-ordered

western black–legged tick \-¦=¦=(=)-\ *n* : a tick of the genus *Ixodes* (*I. pacificus*) that is a vector of Lyme disease and is found esp. in some parts of the Pacific coastal states of the U.S.

western blot *n, usu cap W* [after *Southern blot* (herein)] : a blot consisting of a sheet of cellulose nitrate or nylon that contains spots of protein for identification by a suitable molecular probe and is used esp. for the detection of antibodies — compare NORTHERN BLOT *herein*, SOUTHERN BLOT *herein* — **western blotting** *n, usu cap W*

western omelet *n* : an omelet made usu. with diced ham, green pepper, and onion

western swing *n* : swing music played typically on country-music instruments (as guitar, fiddle, or steel guitar)

west·ie \'westē\ *n* -S *usu cap* [*West* Highland white terrier + *-ie*] : WEST HIGHLAND WHITE TERRIER

west nile encephalitis *n, usu cap W&N* : severe West Nile fever marked by encephalitis

west nile fever *n, usu cap W&N* : illness caused by the West Nile virus

west nile virus *n, usu cap W&N* : a flavivirus (genus *Flavivirus*) that causes an illness marked by fever, headache, muscle ache, skin rash, and sometimes encephalitis or meningitis, that is spread chiefly by mosquitoes, and that is closely related to the viruses causing Japanese B encephalitis and St. Louis encephalitis; *also* WEST NILE FEVER *herein*

wet* *adj* **1** *Brit* : lacking strength of character : NAMBY-PAMBY ⟨we thought him ~ and violence petrified him —William Golding⟩ **2** *Brit* : belonging to the moderate or liberal wing of the Conservative Party ⟨a character called Jeremy Cardhouse, MP, a ~ . . . Conservative —*Times Lit. Supp.*⟩ — **wet behind the ears** : IMMATURE, INEXPERIENCED

wet* *n, Brit* : one who is wet

wet bar *n* : a bar for mixing drinks (as in a home) that contains a sink with running water

wet dream* *n* : an exceedingly pleasurable or exciting experience, situation, or fantasy ⟨statistics on the 747 are either a statistician's nightmare or a trivia freak's *wet dream* —Daniel Grotta-Kurska⟩

wet look *n* **1** : a glossy surface on fabrics that is usu. produced by coating with urethane **2** : the glossy appearance of hair that is treated usu. with a gel

wetware \'=ˌ=\ *n* [²*wet* + *-ware* (as in *software* —herein)] : the human brain or a human being considered esp. with respect to human logical and computational capabilities

WF \¦dəbə(l)yü'ef, -b(ə)yə'(w)ef\ *n* -S [*w*ithdrawn *f*ailing] : a grade assigned by a teacher to a student who withdraws from a course with a failing grade

whack* *vt* : MURDER, KILL ⟨got ~*ed* by the mob⟩

whacked–out \¦(h)wak¦dau̇t\ *adj* **1** : EXHAUSTED, WORN-OUT 2 **2** : WACKY **3** : STONED

whacko \'hwa(ˌ)kō, 'wa-\ *var of* WACKO *herein*

whack off *vb* : MASTURBATE — usu. considered vulgar

what–if \'=ˌ=\ *n* -S : a suppositional question — **what–if** *adj*

wheeler and dealer *n* : WHEELER-DEALER *herein*

wheel·er–dealer \¦hwēlə(r)¦dēlə(r), ¦wē-\ *n* [irreg. fr. *wheel and deal* + ²*-er*] : a shrewd operator esp. in business or politics

wheel·ie \'hwēlē, 'wē-\ *n* -S [¹*wheel* + *-ie*] : a maneuver in which a wheeled vehicle (as a motorcycle, bicycle, or dragster) is balanced momentarily on its rear wheel or wheels

wheels* *n* **wheels** *pl, slang* : a wheeled vehicle; *esp* : AUTOMOBILE

where* *n* — **where it's at** **1 a** : a place of central interest or activity **b** : something (as a topic or field of interest) of primary concern or interest **2** : the true nature of things

whimsy* *n* : WHIMSICALITY ⟨the decor, stylish but with a touch of Lone Star ~, matches the food —Dolly Griffith⟩

whipsawed *adj* [fr. past part. of ²*whipsaw*] : subjected to a double market loss through trying inopportunely to recoup a loss by a subsequent short sale of the same security

whirling disease *n* : an infectious often fatal disease of salmonid fish (as trout and salmon) that is caused by a protozoan of the genus *Myxobolus* (*M. cerebralis*) which attacks cartilage of the head and spinal cord esp. of young fish and that causes the fish to swim in circles and is marked by skeletal deformities

whisker* *n* : a thin hairlike crystal (as of sapphire or copper) of exceptional mechanical strength used esp. to reinforce composite structural material

whistle* *vt* : to charge (as a basketball or hockey player) with an infraction

whistle–blower \'==ˌ==\ *n* : one who reveals something covert or informs on another ⟨a first-class *whistle-blower* whose allegations of fraud and waste threaten to torpedo the powerful Navy bureaucracy —J.S.Kunen⟩ — **whistle–blowing** \'==ˌ==\ *n*

white amur *n* [*amur* fr. *Amur* river] : GRASS CARP *herein*

white backlash *n* : the hostile reaction of white Americans to the advances of the civil rights movement

white–bread \¦=¦=\ *adj* [*white bread*, n.] : being, typical of, or having qualities (as blandness) associated with the white middle class ⟨things *white-bread* America doesn't want to hear about —Mike Pritchard⟩

white–coat hypertension \'=ˌ=-\ *n* [so called fr. the white laboratory coats worn by physicians] : a temporary elevation in a patient's blood pressure that occurs when measured in a medical setting (as a physician's office) and that is usu. due to anxiety on the part of the patient

white flight *n* : the departure of whites from settings (as urban neighborhoods or schools) increasingly or predominately populated by minorities

white hat* *n* [so called fr. the white hats stereotypically worn by the law-abiding characters in movie Westerns] **1** : one who is admirable and honorable **2** : a mark or symbol of goodness ⟨could use a few more guys in *white hats* —Robert Christgau⟩

white hole *n* : a hypothetical extremely dense celestial object that radiates enormous amounts of energy and matter — compare BLACK HOLE *herein*

white knight *n* **1** : one that comes to the rescue; *esp* : a corporation invited to buy out a second corporation in order to prevent an unfriendly takeover by a third **2** : one that champions a cause

white–knuckle \'=¦=\ *also* **white–knuckled** \'=¦==\ *adj* : marked by, causing, or experiencing tense nervousness ⟨a *white-knuckle* ride on a roller coaster⟩ ⟨a *white-knuckle* passenger⟩

white room \'=ˌ=\ *n* : CLEAN ROOM *herein*

whit·ey \'hwīd·ē, 'wī-\ *n, often cap* [¹*white* + *-ie*] : the white man : white society ⟨campaigns of vituperation against ~ that guaranteed violence —Thomas Roeser⟩ — usu. used disparagingly

whiz kid *also* **whizz kid** \'=ˌ=\ *n* [⁴*whiz*] : a person who is unusually intelligent, clever, or successful esp. at an early age

whoa* *v imper* : cease or slow a course of action or a line of thought : pause to consider or reconsider — often used to express a strong reaction (as alarm or astonishment)

whole food *n* : a natural food and esp. one that is organically grown

whole language *n* : a method of teaching reading and writing that emphasizes learning whole words and phrases in meaningful contexts rather than by phonics exercises

wholesale price index *n* : an index measuring the change in the aggregate wholesale price of a large number of commodities in the primary market expressed as a percentage of this price in some base period

whorf–ian hypothesis \'(h)wȯrfēən\ *n, usu cap W* [Benjamin Lee *Whorf* †1941 Am. anthropologist + E *-ian*] : a theory in linguistics: an individual's language determines his conception of the world

who's who* *n* : a listing or grouping of notable persons or things

why·dunit \¦(h)wī'dənət\ *n* -S [¹*why* + *who*dunit] : a mystery having as its primary interest the motivation rather than the identity of the criminal

wic·ca \'wikə\ *n* -S *usu cap* [prob. fr. OE *wicca* wizard — more at WITCH] : a religion influenced by pre-Christian beliefs and practices of western Europe that affirms the existence of supernatural power (as magic) and of both male and female deities who inhere in nature, and that emphasizes ritual observance of seasonal and life cycles — **wic·can** \-kən\ *adj or n, usu cap*

wick* *vt* : to absorb or drain (as fluid or moisture) like a wick ⟨a fabric that ~*s* away perspiration⟩

wicked* *adv* VERY, EXTREMELY

wide area network *n* : a network of personal computers in a large area (as a country or the globe) that are linked (as by cable or satellite) and can communicate directly with other devices in the network

wideband \ˈ=ˌ=\ *adj* : BROADBAND *herein*

wide–body \ˈ=ˌ==\ *n* : a large jet aircraft characterized by a wide cabin

wideout \ˈ=ˌ=\ *n* -S [²*wide* + ¹*out*] : WIDE RECEIVER *herein*

wide receiver *n* : a football receiver who normally lines up several yards to the side of the offensive formation

wig* *vb* ~ *vi* : to lose one's composure : become irrational (as under the influence of drugs) or wildly enthusiastic : FREAK *herein* — usu. used with *out*

wigged–out \ˈ=ˌ=\ *adj* [fr. past part. of *wig out* (herein)] : mentally or emotionally discomposed : UPSET, CRAZY

wiggy* *adj* : WACKY

wig·let \ˈwiglət\ *n* -S [²*wig* + *-let*] : a small wig used esp. to enhance a hairstyle

wild card *n* **1** : one picked to fill a leftover tournament or playoff berth after regularly qualifying competitors have all been determined **2** : an unknown or unpredictable factor

wild·ean \ˈwī(ə)ldēən\ *adj, usu cap* [Oscar *Wilde* †1900 Eng. (Irish-born) writer + E ²*-an*] : of, relating to, or suggestive of Oscar Wilde or his writings

wildly* *adv* : to an extreme extent ⟨~ popular⟩

wil·liams syndrome \ˈwilyəmz-\ *n, usu cap W* [after J.C.P. *Williams b*1922 New Zealand physician] : a rare genetic disorder characterized esp. by hypercalcemia of infants, heart defects, characteristic facial features (as an upturned nose, long philtrum, wide mouth, full lips, and pointed chin), a sociable personality, and a high verbal aptitude, but with mild to moderate mental retardation

willy–nilly* *adv (or adj)* : in a haphazard or spontaneous manner ⟨boxes heaped *willy-nilly*⟩

wil·son's disease \ˈwilsənz-ˌ\ *n, usu cap W* [after Samuel A.K. *Wilson* †1937 Eng. neurologist] : a hereditary disease that is characterized by the accumulation of copper in the body (as in the liver or brain) due to abnormal copper metabolism associated with ceruloplasmin deficiency, that is determined by an autosomal recessive gene, and that is marked esp. by liver dysfunction and disease and neurologic and psychiatric symptoms (as tremors, slowness of speech, inappropriate behaviors, or personality changes)

wimp \ˈwimp\ *n* -S [origin unknown] : one that is weak, cowardly, or ineffectual — **wimp·i·ly** \ˈwimpəlē, -li\ *adv* — **wimp·i·ness** \ˈ-pēnəs, -pi-\ *n* -ES — **wimp·ish** \ˈ-pish\ *adj* — **wimp·ish·ly** \-lē, -li\ *adv* — **wimp·ish·ness** \ˈ-pishnəs\ *n* -ES — **wimpy** \ˈ-pē, -pi\ *adj* -ER/-EST

WIMP \ˈwimp\ *abbr or n* -S [*w*eakly *i*nteracting *m*assive *p*article] : a hypothetical form of dark matter that consists of elementary particles that do not readily interact with normal matter except gravitationally

wimp out *vi* **wimped out; wimped out; wimping out; wimps out** [*wimp*, n. (herein) + ¹*out*] : to behave like a wimp; *esp* : to choose the easiest course of action

win·ches·ter \ˈwinˌchestə(r)\ *adj, usu cap* [fr. the code name used by the original developer] : relating to or being computer disk technology that permits high-density storage by permanently sealing the rigid metal disks within the disk drive mechanism as protection against dust

windblast \ˈ=ˌ=\ *n* **1** : a gust of wind **2** : the injurious effect of air friction on a pilot ejected from a high-speed airplane

windchill** \ˈ=ˌ=\ *or* **windchill factor** *n* : a still-air temperature with the same cooling effect on exposed human flesh as a given combination of temperature and wind speed

wind down \ˈwīn(d)-\ *vt* : to cause a gradual lessening of usu. with the intention of bringing to an end ⟨*wind down* a war⟩ ~ *vi* **1** : to draw gradually toward an end **2** : RELAX, UNWIND — **wind–down** \ˈ=ˌ=\ *n* -S

wind farm *n* : an area of land with a cluster of wind turbines for generating electricity

window* *n* **1** : a range of wavelengths in the electromagnetic spectrum to which a planet's atmosphere is transparent **2 a** : an interval of time within which a rocket or spacecraft must be launched to accomplish a particular mission **b** : a usu. short interval of time during which a certain condition or an opportunity exists ⟨a ~ of vulnerability to Soviet attack⟩ ⟨allowed the race committee a three-day ~ —Robert Sullivan⟩ **3** : an area at the limits of the earth's sensible atmosphere through which a spacecraft must pass for successful reentry **4** : any of the areas into which a computer display may be divided and on which distinctly different types of information may be displayed

windowpane* *n* : TATTERSALL

wind shear *n* : a radical shift in wind speed and direction that occurs over a very short distance

Wind·surfer \ˈ=ˌ==\ *trademark* — used for a sailboard

wind·surf·ing \ˈ=ˌ==\ *n* -S [¹*wind* + ²*surf* + ³*-ing*] : the activity of riding a sailboard — **wind·surf** \ˈ=ˌ=\ *vi* — **wind·surf·er** \-ər\ *n*

wind turbine *n* : a wind-driven turbine for generating electricity

wine bar *n* : an establishment selling wine and usu. food for consumption on the premises

wine cooler *n* : a usu. carbonated beverage that contains a mixture of wine and fruit juice

wing* *vt* : to do or perform without preparation or guidelines : IMPROVISE — usu. used in the phrase *wing it*

winged bean *n* : GOA BEAN

winglet* *n* : a small nearly vertical airfoil at an airplane's wing tip that reduces drag by inhibiting turbulence

winklepicker \ˈ==ˌ==\ *n* [¹*winkle* + *picker*; fr. the notion that the point is sharp enough to be used for picking winkles out of their shells] : a shoe with a sharp-pointed toe

winless \ˈ=ləs\ *adj* : being without a win

win·ter·im \ˈwintəˌrim\ *n* -S [blend of ¹*winter* and *interim*] : an intersession at some colleges and universities chiefly in January

wipe out *vi* **1** : to fall from a surfboard while surfing **2** : to fall while skiing

wipeout \ˈ=ˌ=\ *n* -S [*wipe out*, v. (herein)] **1** : the act or an instance of wiping out **2** : complete or utter destruction **3** : total defeat ⟨a three-game ~⟩

wire* *vt* : to predispose, determine, or establish genetically or innately : HARDWIRE *herein* ⟨the controversy over the extent to which human violence is *wired* biologically⟩

wired* *adj* **1** : feverishly excited or nervous **2** : connected to a telecommunications network and esp. to the Internet

wire fraud *n* : fraud committed using a means of electronic communication (as a telephone or computer)

wishbone* *n* : a variation of the T formation in which the halfbacks line up farther from the line of scrimmage than the fullback

wish list *n* : a list of desired but often not realistically obtainable items

witch of agne·si \-änˈyāzē\ *or* **witch*** *n, usu cap A* [after Maria Gaetana *Agnesi* †1799 Ital. mathematician; *witch*, trans. of It *versiera* cubic curve (modif. of NL *versoria* versed sine) influenced by *versiera* female demon (short for *avversiera*, fr. *avversario* Satan, lit., adversary)] : a plane cubic curve that is symmetric about the y-axis and approaches the x-axis as an asymptote, that is constructed by drawing lines from the origin intersecting an upright circle tangent to the x-axis at the origin and taking the locus of points of intersection of pairs of lines parallel to the x-axis and y-axis each pair of which consists of a line parallel to the x-axis through the point where a line through the origin intersects the circle and a line parallel to the y-axis through the point where the same line through the origin intersects the line parallel to the x-axis through the point of intersection of the circle and the y-axis, and that has the equation $x^2y = 4a^2(2a - y)$

withhold* *vt* : to deduct (withholding tax) from income

with–it \ˈwithət, ˈwith-\ *adj* [fr. the phrase *with it*] : socially or culturally up-to-date ⟨the intelligent, disaffected *with-it* young —Eliot Freemont-Smith⟩

wok \ˈwäk\ *n* -S [Chin (Cant) *wohk*] : a large bowl-shaped cooking utensil used esp. in stir-frying

wolff–par·kin·son–white syndrome \ˌwu̇lfˈpärkənsən'(h)wīt-\ *n, usu cap both Ws&P* [after Louis *Wolff* †1972 Am. cardiologist, John *Parkinson* †1976 Eng. cardiologist, & Paul D. *White* †1973 Am. cardiologist] : an abnormal heart condition characterized by premature activation of the ventricle by atrial impulses and an electrocardiographic tracing with a shortened interval between the P wave and the widened QRS complex

wolf–ra·yet star \ˌwu̇lfrīˈā-\ *n, usu cap W&R* [after Charles *Wolf* †1918 & Georges *Rayet* †1906 Fr. astronomers] : any of a class of stars whose spectra are characterized by very broad bright lines esp. of helium, carbon, nitrogen, and sometimes hydrogen that indicate very hot unstable stars

wom·an·ism \ˈwu̇məˌnizəm\ *n* -S : a form of feminism concerned esp. with the conditions and concerns of black women — **wom·an·ist** \-ˌnəst\ *adj* — **womanist** *n* -S

womanpower \ˈ==ˌ=(=)\ *n* [²*woman* + *-power* (as in *manpower*)] : women available and prepared for service ⟨huge and growing waste of gifted, educated ~ in contemporary American society —*Current Biog.*⟩

womyn *var of* WOMEN — used in some feminist contexts

won \ˈwȯn, ˈwän\ *n, pl* **won** [Korean *wŏn*] **1** : the basic monetary unit of Korea — see MONEY table *in the Dict* **2** : a coin or note representing one won

wonk \ˈwäŋk, ˈwȯ-\ *n* -S [origin unknown] : a person preoccupied with arcane details or procedures in a specialized field; *broadly* : GRIND, NERD *herein* ⟨a policy ~⟩ ⟨a computer ~⟩ — **wonk·ish** \-ish\ *adj* — **wonky** \-ē\ *adj*

wood ear *or* **wood ear mushroom** *n* [trans. of Chin (Pek) *mu*⁴ *erh*³] : any of several ear- or cup-shaped jelly fungi of the genus *Auricularia* that grow on wood: as **a** : an edible brownish fungus (*A. auricula*) of No. America **b** : a cultivated usu. dark brown edible fungus (*A. polytricha*) used in Chinese cooking — called also *cloud ear, tree ear*

wood rose* *also* **wooden rose** *n* : a tropical tuberous climbing woody vine (*Merremia tuberosa* syn. *Ipomoea tuberosa*) of the family Convolvulaceae grown esp. for its hard showy yellow rose-shaped calyx and seed capsule

woody *or* **wood·ie** \ˈwu̇dē, -i\ *n, pl* **woodies** [²*wood* + ¹*-y*] **1** : a wood-paneled station wagon **2** *slang* : ERECTION 2b

woolly adelgid *n* : either of two aphids of the genus *Adelges* that secrete and cover themselves with a white woolly floc and are serious pests of specific coniferous trees esp. in the eastern U.S.: **a** BALSAM WOOLLY ADELGID *herein* **b** : HEMLOCK WOOLLY ADELGID *herein*

word processing *n* : the production of typewritten documents (as business letters) with automated and usu. computerized typing and text-editing equipment — **word process** *vb*

word processor *n* : a keyboard-operated terminal that usu. has a video display and a magnetic storage device and is used in word processing; *also* : software (as for a computer system) to perform word processing

words·man·ship \ˈwərdzmənˌship, ˈwəd-, ˈwəid-\ *n* [¹*word* + *-smanship* (as in *craftsmanship*)] : the art or craft of writing

work* *vt* : to greet and talk with in a friendly way in order to ingratiate oneself or achieve a purpose ⟨politicians ~*ing* the crowd⟩ ⟨~*ed* the room⟩

work·a·hol·ic \ˌwərkəˈhȯlik, ¦wək-, ¦wəik- *sometimes* -ˈhäl-\ *n* -S [¹*work* + *-aholic* (herein)] : a compulsive worker

work·a·hol·ism \ˈ==ˌ=ˌizəm\ *n* -S [*workaholic* (herein) + *-ism*] : an obsessive need to work

work–around \ˈ==ˌ=\ *n* -S [fr. the phrase *work around*] : a plan or method to circumvent a problem (as in computer software) without eliminating it

work ethic *n* : a belief in work as a moral good

work·fare \ˈ=ˌfa(a)|(ə)r, -ˌfe|, |ə\ *n* -S [¹*work* + *welfare*] : a welfare program in which recipients must do usu. public service work

workload** \ˈ=ˌ=\ *n* : the amount of work performed or capable of being performed usu. within a specified period

work release *n* : a corrections program that releases prisoners daily to work at full-time jobs

workstation \ˈ=ˌ==\ *n* **1** : an area with equipment for the performance of a specialized task usu. by a single individual **2 a** : an intelligent terminal or personal computer usu. connected to a computer network **b** : a very powerful microcomputer used esp. for scientific or engineering work

work–to–rule \¦=¦=ˈ=\ *n, chiefly Brit* : the practice of working according to the strictest interpretation of the rules so as to slow down production and force employers to comply with demands — **work–to–rule** \"\ *vi, chiefly Brit*

world–class \¦=ˈ=\ *adj* : of the highest caliber in the world ⟨a *world-class* runner⟩ ⟨*world-class* soccer⟩; *broadly* : FIRST-RATE, OUTSTANDING ⟨a *world-class* symphony⟩

world line *n* : the aggregate of all positions in space-time of any individual particle that retains its identity

world wide web *n, usu cap all 3 Ws* : a part of the Internet designed to allow easier navigation of the network through the use of graphical user interfaces and hypertext links between different addresses — called also *Web*

worm* *n* : a usu. small self-contained computer program that invades computers on a network and usu. performs a malicious action (as taking control of a computer's processor)

wormhole* *n* : a hypothetical connection between universes or different parts of one universe usu. through a pair of singularities

worry beads *n pl* [so called fr. the belief that the fingering releases nervous tension] : a string of beads to be fingered so as to keep one's hands occupied

worse* *adv* : what is worse

worst–case \¦=¦=\ *adj* : involving, projecting, or providing for the worst possible circumstances or the worst outcome of a given situation ⟨a *worst-case* scenario⟩

wo·ven \ˈwōvən\ *n* -S [*woven*, adj., fr. past part. of ¹*weave*] : a woven fabric

WP \¦dəbə(l)yüˈpē, -b(ə)yəˈ-\ *n* -S [*w*ithdrawn *p*assing] : a grade assigned by a teacher to a student who withdraws from a course with a passing grade

WP* *abbr* **1** wettable powder **2** word processing *herein* **3** word processor *herein*

wrap* *vt* : to bring to completion : WRAP UP; *esp* : to finish filming or videotaping ⟨~ a movie⟩ ~ *vi* : to be brought to completion ⟨principal photography is due to ~ soon —*Variety*⟩

wrap* *n* : the completion of filming or videotaping

wraparound \ˈ=ˌ==\ *adj* [fr. *wrap around*, v.] **1** : of or relating to a flexible printing surface wrapped around a plate cylinder **2 a** : shaped to follow a contour; *esp* : made to curve from the front around to the side ⟨~ sunglasses⟩ ⟨~ terraces⟩ **b** : extending laterally to the outermost limits of the field of vision ⟨a ~ movie screen⟩

wrap–up* *n* : the concluding part : FINALE

wrecked \ˈrekt\ *adj* [fr. past part. of ²*wreck*] *slang* : STONED

wrecker's ball *n* : SKULL CRACKER

wrist shot* *n* : a quick usu. short-range shot in ice hockey made while the puck is against the stick's blade by snapping the blade quickly forward

wrist wrestling *n* : a form of arm wrestling in which opponents interlock thumbs instead of gripping hands

write* *vt* : SELL 2a(1) ⟨~ a stock option⟩

writer* *n* : one who writes stock options

writ·er·ly \ˈrīd-ə(r)lē\ *adj* : of, relating to, or typical of a writer ⟨channeled her ~ brilliance into her correspondence —Joyce C. Oates⟩

writer's block *n* : a psychological inhibition preventing a person from proceeding with a piece of writing

wrong–foot \ˈ=ˌ=\ *vt* : to cause (as an opponent in tennis or football) to lean into or step with the wrong foot; *broadly* : to disrupt the equilibrium of ⟨*wrong-footed* three defenders to score⟩ ⟨the sudden deaths of contemporaries *wrong-foot* us —Lorna Sage⟩

wu·shu \ˈwüˈshü\ *n* -S [Chin (Pek) *wu*³*shu*⁴, fr. *wu*³ martial, military + *shu*⁴ art, skill] : Chinese martial arts

wuss \ˈwu̇s\ *n* -ES [origin unknown] : WIMP *herein* — **wussy** \-ē\ *adj*

wu–ts'ai \ˈwüˈtsī\ *n* -S [Chin (Pek) *wu*³*ts'ai*³ five colors] : a 5-colored overglaze enamel decoration used on Chinese porcelain since the Ming period

WWW *abbr* World Wide Web *herein*

wysiwyg \ˈwizēˌwig, -zə-ˌ-\ *n* -S *usu all cap, often attrib* [*w*hat *y*ou *s*ee *i*s *w*hat *y*ou *g*et] : a display generated by word-processing or desktop-publishing software that exactly reflects the appearance of the printed document

x \ˈeks\ *adj, usu cap, of a motion picture* : of such a nature that admission is denied to persons under a specified age (as 17) — used before the adoption of *NC-17*

xan·a·du \ˈzanəˌd(y)ü, -aa(ə)n-\ *n, usu cap* [fr. *Xanadu*, locality in *Kubla Khan* (1798) poem by Samuel T. Coleridge †1834 Eng. poet] : an idyllic, exotic, or luxurious place

xan·than gum \ˈzanthən-\ *also* **xanthan** *n* [*xanth-* (fr. NL *Xanthomonas*, genus name, fr. *xanth-* + *-monas*) + ³*-an*] : a polysaccharide that is produced by fermentation of carbohydrates by a bacterium of the genus *Xanthomonas* (*X. campestris*) and is a thickening and suspending agent used esp. in pharmaceuticals and prepared foods

x band *n, usu cap X* : a segment of the superhigh-frequency radio spectrum that lies between 5.2 GHz and 10.9 GHz and is used esp. for radars and for spacecraft communication

xe·nic \ˈzēnik, ˈzen-\ *adj* [*xen-* + *-ic*] : of, relating to, or employing a culture medium containing one or more unidentified organisms — **xe·ni·cal·ly** \-ik(ə)lē\ *adv*

xe·no·biotic \ˌzenō, ˌzē-+\ *n* [*xen-* + *biotic*] : a chemical compound (as a drug, pesticide, or carcinogen) that is foreign to a living organism — **xenobiotic** \"\ *adj*

xe·no·ge·ne·ic \¦==jəˈnēik\ *also* **xe·no·gen·ic** \¦==ˈjenik\ *adj* [*xen-* + *-geneic* (as in *syngeneic* — herein) or *-genic*] : derived from, originating in, or being a member of another species ⟨a ~ antibody⟩ ⟨~ hosts⟩ — compare ALLOGENEIC *herein*, SYNGENEIC *herein*

xe·no·graft \ˈzenō, ˈzē-+ˌ\ *n* [*xen-* + ²*graft*] : HETEROGRAFT

xe·no·transplantation \ˌzenə, ˌzē-+\ *n* [*xen-* + *transplantation*] : transplantation of an organ, tissue, or cells between two different species — **xe·no·transplant** \"+\ *n or vt*

xe·no·tro·pic \¦zēnəˈträpik, -¦trōp-\ *adj* [*xen-* + *-tropic*] : replicating or reproducing only in cells other than those of the host species ⟨~ viruses⟩

xeri·scape \ˈzirəˌskāp, ˈzer-\ *n, often cap* [*xeri-* (alter. — prob. influenced by *xeric* — of *xero-*) + *-scape*] : a landscaping method developed esp. for arid and semiarid climates that utilizes water-conserving techniques (as the use of drought-tolerant plants, mulch, and efficient irrigation)

xeroderma pig·men·to·sum \-ˌpigmənˈtōsəm, -ˌmenˈ-\ *n* [NL, lit., pigmented xeroderma] : a genetic condition inherited as a recessive autosomal trait that is caused by a defect in mechanisms that repair DNA mutations (as those caused by ultraviolet light) and is characterized by the development of pigment abnormalities and multiple skin cancers in body areas exposed to the sun

Xe·rox \ˈzi(ə)rˌäks, ˈzēˌräks\ *trademark* — used for a xerographic copier

xe·rox \"\ *vt* -ED/-ING/-ES *often cap* [fr. *Xerox* (herein)] **1** : to copy on a Xerox copier **2** : to make (a copy) on a Xerox copier

x–linked \ˈ=ˌ=\ *adj, usu cap X* : located on an X chromosome ⟨an *X-linked* gene⟩; *also* : transmitted by an X-linked gene ⟨an *X-linked* disease⟩

x–rated \ˈ=ˌ=\ *adj, usu cap X* **1 a** : X *herein* **b** : of, relating to, or showing X-rated motion pictures ⟨an *X-rated* theater⟩ **2 a** : relating to or characterized by explicit sexual material or activity ⟨an *X-rated* book⟩ **b** : OBSCENE ⟨an *X-rated* gesture⟩

x–ray astronomy *n, usu cap X* : astronomy dealing with investigations of celestial bodies by means of the X rays they emit — **x–ray astronomer** *n, usu cap X*

x–ray crystallography *n, usu cap X* : an analytical technique in which X-ray diffraction is used to obtain information about the identity or structure of a crystalline substance — **x–crystallographic** *adj, usu cap X*

x–ray diffraction *n, usu cap X* : a scattering of X rays by the atoms of a crystal that produces an interference effect so that the diffraction pattern gives information on the structure of the crystal or the identity of a crystalline substance

x–ray star *or* **x–ray source** *n, usu cap X* : a luminous starlike celestial object emitting a major portion of its radiation in the form of X rays

xu \ˈsü\ *n, pl* **xu** [Vietnamese, fr. F *sou* sou] **1** : a coin formerly used in South Vietnam equivalent to the cent **2** : a unit equal to ¹⁄₁₀₀ dong — see MONEY table *in the Dict*

Xy·lo·caine \ˈzīlōˌkān\ *trademark* — used for a preparation of lidocaine

YA *abbr* young adult

yacht·ie \ˈyäd-ē\ *n* -S [¹*yacht* + *-ie*] : a person who sails or owns a yacht

YAG \ˈyag\ *abbr or n* -S [*y*ttrium *a*luminum *g*arnet] : a synthetic yttrium aluminum garnet of marked hardness and high refractive index that is used esp. as a gemstone and in laser technology

ya·ki·to·ri \ˌyäkiˈtórē\ *n* -S [Jap, grilled chicken, fr. *yaki* roasting, broiling + *tori* bird] : bite-sized marinated pieces of chicken, beef, or seafood grilled on small bamboo skewers

ya·ma·to–e \yäˈmätəˌwā\ *also* **ya·ma–to** \-ˈmä(ˌ)tō\ *n* -S *usu cap* [Jap *Yamato-e*, fr. *Yamato* Japan + *e* picture, painting] : a classical style of Japanese painting marked by shallow spatial illusion, bold colors, surface patterning, and stylized forms

ya·no·ma·mi \ˌyänōˈmämē\ *also* **ya·no·ma·mo** \-mō\ *or* **ya·no·ma·ma** \-mə\ *n, pl* **yanomami** *also* **yanomamis** *or* **yanomamo** *or* **yanomama** *usu cap* [Shirianá *yanomami*, a self-designation] : an indigenous people inhabiting the rain forests of southern Venezuela, and northern Brazil : SHIRIANÁ; *also* : a member of the Yanomani people

yard* *n* — **the whole nine yards** : all of a related set of circumstances, conditions, or details : BALL OF WAX *herein* ⟨who could learn the whole book about making records, about electronics and engineering, *the whole nine yards* —Stephen Stills⟩ — sometimes used adverbially with *go* to indicate an all-out effort

yard sale *n* : GARAGE SALE *herein*

yawn·er \ˈyȯnə(r), ˈyä-\ *n* -S [¹*yawn* + ²*-er*] : one that causes boredom : BORE ⟨the show was a real ~⟩

ya·yoi \(ˈ)yäˈyȯi\ *adj, often cap* [fr. *Yayoi*, site in Tokyo, Japan, where remains of the period were discovered] : of, relating to, or being typical of a Japanese cultural period extending from about 200 B.C., to A.D. 200, being generally neolithic but including the beginning of work in metal, and characterized esp. by unglazed wheel-thrown pottery sometimes with incised surface ornamentation and often of florid shape

yeast infection *n* : an infection of the female genital tract by a yeast of the genus *Candida* (*C. albicans*) and characterized by vaginal discharge and inflammation; *broadly* : an infection (as thrush) caused by a yeast fungus

yech *or* **yecch** \ˈyək, ˈyək\ *interj* [imit.] — used to express rejection or disgust

yellowcake \ˈ=ˌ=\ *n* : a bright yellow compound that consists of uranium oxide U_3O_8 and is an intermediate product in uranium refining

yellow pages *n pl, often cap Y&P* **1** : a telephone directory or section of a telephone directory that lists business and professional firms and people alphabetically by category and includes classified advertising **2** : a directory resembling yellow pages

yellow rain *n* : a yellow substance that has been reported to occur in southeastern Asia as a mist or as spots on rocks and vegetation and that has been held to have been used as a biological warfare agent during the Vietnam war but that appears upon scientific examination to be identical to the pollen-laden feces of bees

yen·ta \ˈyen·tə\ *n* -S [Yiddish *yente* vulgar or sentimental woman, fr. the name *Yente*] : one that meddles; *also* : BLABBERMOUTH, GOSSIP

yer·sin·ia \yərˈsinēə, yer-\ *n* [NL, genus name, after A.E.J. *Yersin* †1943 Fr. bacteriologist] **1** *cap* : a genus of gram-negative bacteria of the family Enterobacteriaceae that includes several important pathogens (as the plague bacterium *Y. pestis*) affecting animals and man and formerly included in the genus *Pasteurella* **2** -s : any bacterium of the genus *Yersinia*

yé–yé \yā(ˌ)yā\ *adj* [F, fr. E *yeah-yeah*, exclamation often interpolated in rock 'n' roll performances] : of, relating to, or featuring rock 'n' roll as it developed in France

yield to maturity : the total rate of return to an owner holding a bond to maturity expressed as a percentage of cost

YIG \ˈyig\ *n* -s [*y*ttrium *i*ron *g*arnet] : a synthetic yttrium iron garnet having ferrimagnetic properties that is used esp. as a filter for selecting or tuning microwaves

yi–hsing ware \ˈyēˈshiŋ-\ *also* **yi–hsing** \ˈ≈ˈ≈\ *or* **yi–hsing yao** \ˈyēˈshiŋˈyau̇\ *n, usu cap 1st Y* [*Yi-hsing* fr. *Yi-hsing* (*Ihing*), town in southern Kiangsu province, China; *Yi-hsing yao* fr. *Yi-hsing* + Chin (Pek) *yao*2 pottery] : BOCCARO

yin and yang *n* : opposite sides, elements, or extremes ⟨cowboys and Indians are the *yin and yang* of America —Richard Rodriguez⟩ ⟨the daily *yin and yang* of the campaign —Steve Lopez⟩

yin·glish \ˈyiŋ(g)lish\ *n* -ES *cap* [blend of *Yiddish* and *English*] : English marked by numerous borrowings from Yiddish

yin–yang \ˈ≈ˌ≈\ *adj* **1** : of, relating to, symbolizing, or being the Chinese principles of yin and yang **2** : being or comprising opposite and esp. complementary elements ⟨*ying–yang* system of good and evil —Diane McWhorter⟩

yip·pie \ˈyipē\ *n* -s *often cap* [*Y*outh *I*nternational *P*arty + *-ie* (as in *hippie* — herein)] : a person belonging to or identified with a politically active group of hippies

yo* *interj* — used esp. to call attention, to indicate attentiveness, or to express affirmation

yob·bo \ˈyäb(ˌ)ō\ *n, pl* **yobbos** *or* **yobboes** [*yob* + 1-*o*] **1** *Brit* : LOUT, YOKEL **2** *or* **yob*** *Brit* : HOODLUM

yock \ˈyək, ˈyäk\ *or* **yuck** \ˈyək\ *or* **yuk** \"\ *vi* **yocked** *or* **yucked** *or* **yukked; yocked** *or* **yucked** *or* **yukked; yocking** *or* **yucking** *or* **yukking; yocks** *or* **yucks** *or* **yuks** [imit.] : to laugh esp. in a boisterous or unrestrained manner

yocto- *comb form* [ISV, prob. blend of *yotta-* (herein) and *octo-*] : one septillionth (10^{-24}) part of ⟨*yocto*second⟩

yo·him·be** \yōˈhimbā, yə-, -bē\ *n* : a preparation of the bark of the yohimbé tree (*Pausinystalia yohimbe* syn. *Corynanthe yohimbe*) that contains the alkaloid yohimbine and in herbal medicine is held to be useful as an aphrodisiac and in treating weakness and feebleness

york·ie \ˈyȯrkē\ *n* -s *usu cap* [*York*shire terrier + *-ie*] : YORKSHIRE TERRIER

yo·se·na·be \ˌyōsəˈnäbā\ *n* -s [Jap, fr. *yose-* to bring near, gather, collect + *nabe* pot] : a soup consisting esp. of seafood and vegetables cooked in a broth

yotta- *comb form* [ISV, alter. of Gk *iōta* (representing *y*, next-to-last letter of the Latin alphabet)] : septillion ⟨*yotta*byte⟩

young turk* *n* : one advocating changes within a group typically in opposition to a dominant usu. conservative element

youthquake \ˈ≈ˌ≈\ *n* [*youth* + earth*quake*] : the impact of the values, tastes, and mores of youth on the established norms of society

yo–yo* *n* **1** : a stupid or foolish person **2** : a condition or situation marked by regular foolish fluctuations from one extreme to another ⟨on the constant diet *yo-yo*—losing weight and gaining it back —William Stockton⟩

yo–yo \ˈyōˌyō\ *vi* **yo–yoed; yo–yoed; yo–yoing; yo–yos** [*yo-yo*, n.] : to move from one position to another repeatedly: as **a** : VACILLATE **b** : FLUCTUATE

1yuck *var of* 4YAK

2yuck \ˈyək, ˈyək\ *also* **yuk*** *interj* [imit.] — used to express rejection or disgust

yucky \ˈyəkē, ˈyəkē\ *adj* -ER/-EST [*yuck* (herein) + 1-*y*] *slang* : REPUGNANT, DISTASTEFUL ⟨not even a decent pool, unless you counted the ~ old bathtub in the phys ed building —W.F.Reed⟩ — **yuck·i·ness** *n* -ES

yup \ˈyəp\ *n* -s [by shortening] : YUPPIE *herein*

yup·pie \ˈyəpē\ *n* -s *sometimes cap, often attrib* [prob. fr. *y*oung *u*rban *p*rofessional + *-ie*; influenced by *yippie* (herein)] : a young college-educated adult who is employed in a well-paying profession and who lives and works in or near a large city

yuppie flu *n* : CHRONIC FATIGUE SYNDROME *herein*

yup·pi·fy \ˈyəpəˌfī\ *vt* -ED/-ING/-ES [*yuppie* (herein) + *-ify* (as in *gentrify* — herein)] : to render appealing to yuppies; *also* : to infuse with the qualities or values of yuppies — **yup·pi·fi·ca·tion** \ˌyəpəfəˈkāshən\ *n* -s

z* *n* **1** *or* **z particle** *usu cap Z* : a neutral elementary particle about 90 times heavier than a proton that along with the W particle is a transmitter of the weak force — called also Z^0 or Z^0 *particle* **2** *often cap* : 2WINK 1a ⟨catch a few *z's* on a quiet graveyard shift —Joseph Wambaugh⟩

zaf·tig *also* **zof·tig** \ˈzäftig, ˈzȯf-\ *adj* [Yiddish *zaftik* juicy, succulent, fr. *zaft* juice, sap, fr. MHG *saf, saft*, fr. OHG *saf* — more at SAP] *of a woman* : having a full rounded figure : pleasingly plump

zai·bat·su \(ˈ)zīˈbät(ˌ)sü\ *n, pl* **zaibatsu** *also* **zaibatsus** [Jap, fr. *zai* money, wealth + *batsu* clique, clan] : a powerful financial and industrial conglomerate of Japan

zaire \zäˈi(ə)r *also* ˈzī(ə)r\ *n* -s [F *zaïre*, fr. *Zaïre*, country in central Africa] **1** : the basic monetary unit of Zaire — see MONEY table *in the Dict* **2** : a note representing one zaire

zair·ian *or* **zair·ean** \zäˈirēən *also* ˈzīr-\ *n* -s *cap* [*Zaire*, central Africa + E *-an*] : a native or inhabitant of Zaire — **zairian** *or* **zairean** *adj, usu cap*

zal·cit·a·bine \zalˈsid·əˌbēn, -ˌbīn\ *n* -s [*zal-* (of unknown origin) + *-citabine* (prob. alter. of *cytidine*)] : DDC *herein*

1zap \ˈzap\ *interj* [imit.] **1** — used to express a sound made by or as if by a gun **2** — used to indicate a sudden or instantaneous occurrence

2zap \"\ *vb* **zapped; zapped; zapping; zaps** *vt* **1 a** : to hit with or as if with a sudden concentrated application of force or energy; *esp* : to shoot with a laser **b** : to get rid of, destroy, or kill esp. with or as if with sudden force **c** : to irradiate esp. with microwaves **2 a** : to propel suddenly or speedily **b** : to transfer or transport instantaneously **3** : to make pungent ⟨a sauce *zapped* with pepper⟩ **4** : to avoid watching (as a television commercial) by changing channels esp. with a remote control or by fast-forwarding a videotape ~ *vi* **1** : to move rapidly and often forcefully **2** : to change television channels using a remote control

3zap *n* -s **1** : a pungent or zestful quality : ZIP **2** : a sudden forceful blow or attack ⟨a ~ or two from a satellite-mounted death ray —Harvey Ardman⟩

zap·per \ˈzapər\ *n* -s : one that zaps: as **a** : an electronic device designed to attract and kill insects **b** : a person who habitually changes channels (as to avoid commercials) **c** : a remote control device used for zapping

za·zen \ˈzäˌzen\ *n* -s *sometimes cap* [Jap, fr. *za* seat + *zen* Zen] : Zen meditation

Z–DNA \ˈ≈ˌ(ˌ)≈ˈ≈\ *n* [zigzag] : the left-handed uncommon form of double helix DNA in which the chains twist up and to the left around the front of the axis of the helix and that has 12 base pairs in each helical turn and one groove on the external surface

ze·atin \ˈzēətən, -tᵊn\ *n* -s [NL *Zea* + E *-tin* (as in *kinetin* — herein)] : a cytokinin first isolated from maize endosperm

zebra* *n, sometimes cap* : a person who officiates a sports contest (as a basketball or football game)

zebra crossing *also* **zebra*** *n, Brit* : a crosswalk marked by a series of broad white stripes

zebra mussel *n* [so called fr. the light and dark stripes on the shell] : a Eurasian lamellibranch mollusk of the genus *Dreissena* (*D. polymorpha*) that inhabits fresh and brackish waters, that was accidentally introduced into the Great Lakes and has spread to other waterways, and that colonizes and clogs water intake pipes and competes with native fish for foods

zeit·ge·ber \ˈtsītˌgābər, ˈzīt-\ *n* [G, fr. *zeit* time (fr. OGH *zīt*) + *geber* (as in *taktgeber* computer clock), lit., giver, fr. *geben* to give, fr. OHG *geban*; akin to OE *giefan* to give — more at TIDE, GIVE] : an environmental agent or event (as the occurrence of light or dark) that provides the stimulus setting or resetting a biological clock of an organism

zelkova* *n* -s : a plant of the genus *Zelkova*; *esp* : a tall widely spreading Japanese tree (*Z. serrata*) resembling the American elm and replacing the latter as an ornamental and shade tree because of its resistance to Dutch elm disease

zen·do \ˈzen(ˌ)dō\ *n* -s *usu cap* [Jap *zendō*, fr. *zen* Zen + *-dō* shrine] : a place used for Zen meditation

ze·ner diode \ˈzēnə(r)-, ˈzen-\ *n, often cap Z* [after Clarence Melvin *Zener* †1993 Am. physicist] : a silicon semiconductor device used esp. as a voltage regulator

zep·po·le \(t)se(p)ˈpōˌlā, ze-, ˈ≈(ˌ)≈\ *also* **zep·po·li** \-(ˌ)lē\ *n, pl* **zeppole** *also* **zeppoli** [It *zeppole*, pl. of *zeppola* fritter, fr. It dial. (southern Italy), perh. fr. LL *zippulae*, a kind of sweet; *zeppoli* fr. It, pl. of *zeppolo*, alter. of *zeppola*] : a doughnut made from cream puff dough

zepto- *comb form* [ISV, blend of *zetta-* (herein) and *hepta-*] : one sextillionth (10^{-21}) part of ⟨*zepto*second⟩

zerk \ˈzərk, ˈzək, ˈzəik\ *n* -s [short for *zerk fitting*, after Oscar U. *Zerk* †1968 Am. (Austrian-born) inventor] : a grease fitting

zero–based \ˈ≈≈ˈ≈\ *or* **zero–base** \ˈ≈≈ˈ≈\ *adj* : having each item justified on the basis of cost or need ⟨*zero-based* budgeting⟩

zero–coupon \ˈ≈≈ˈ≈≈\ *adj* : being a security that is sold at a price significantly below face value, pays no annual interest, and is redeemable at full value at maturity ⟨*zero-coupon* bonds⟩

zero vector *n* : a vector which is of zero length and all of whose components are zero

zest·er \ˈzestə(r)\ *n* -s : a small utensil for peeling zest (as from a lemon)

zetta- *comb form* [ISV, alter. of Gk *zēta* (representing *Z*, last letter of the Latin alphabet)] : sextillion ⟨*zetta*byte⟩

zi·do·vu·dine \zīˈdōvyüˌdēn\ *n* -s [alter. of *azidothymidine* (herein)] : AZT *herein*

zilch \ˈzilch, ˈziu̇ch\ *n* [origin unknown] : ZERO, NIL

zill \ˈzil\ *n* -s [prob. fr. Turk *zil* bell, cymbals, of imit. origin] : a small metallic cymbal used in pairs with one worn on the thumb and the other on the middle finger

zin \ˈzin\ *n* -s *often cap* [by shortening] : ZINFANDEL

zinc finger *n* : any of a class of proteins that typically possess tandem repeats of fingerlike loops of amino acids with each loop containing a zinc-binding site at its base consisting of two molecules of cysteine and two molecules of histidine and that regulates transcription by binding to specific regions of a gene's DNA; *also* : one of the fingerlike loops of such a protein

zine \ˈzēn\ *n* -s [by shortening (influenced by *fanzine*)] : MAGAZINE; *esp* : a noncommercial often homemade or on-line publication usu. devoted to specialized and often unconventional subject matter ⟨a punk ~⟩ ⟨a feminist ~⟩

zing* *vb* ~ *vt* **1** : to hit suddenly : ZAP *herein* ⟨~ you with a . . . service fee every time you step out on the court —Barry Tarshis⟩ **2** : to criticize in a pointed or witty manner ⟨politicians who are ~*ed* in his columns —Ron Nessen⟩ ~ *vi* **1** : ZIP, SPEED ⟨movie ~*s* right along —*Playboy*⟩ **2** : to be alive : bubble over ⟨~*ing* with raw energy and ambition —David Bellamy⟩

zing·er \ˈziŋə(r)\ *n* -s [2*zing* + 2-*er*] **1** : a pointed witty remark or retort **2** : something causing or meant to cause interest, surprise, or shock

zingy \ˈziŋē\ *adj* -ER/-EST [1*zing* + 1-*y*] **1** : enjoyably exciting ⟨a ~ musical⟩ **2** : strikingly attractive or appealing ⟨wore a ~ new outfit⟩ **3** : sharp-flavored : ZESTY ⟨a ~ sauce⟩

1zip \ˈzip\ *n* -s [by shortening] : ZIP CODE *herein*

2zip \"\ *n* -s [prob. fr. 2*zip*] : ZERO, NOTHING ⟨a score of 21–*zip*⟩ ⟨so far we have ~ to show for our efforts —Susan Zirinsky⟩

zip·code \ˈzipˌ-\ *n, often cap Z&I&P* [ZIP fr. *z*one *i*mprovement *p*lan] **1** : a number code that identifies each U.S. postal delivery area **2** : the geographic area identified by such a code ⟨$1,000 contributions from the toniest *zip codes* —J.B. Roskin⟩

zip–code \ˈ≈ˌ≈\ *vt* : to furnish with a zip code

ziplock \ˈ≈ˌ≈\ *adj* : having an interlocking groove and ridge that form a tight seal when pressed together ⟨a ~ plastic bag⟩

zip–out \ˈ≈ˌ≈\ *adj* : attached by means of a zipper ⟨a *zip-out* liner⟩

zip·po \ˈzipō\ *n* -s [2*zip* (herein) + 1-*o*] : ZIP *herein* ⟨have done ~ to reduce the cash crisis —*Wall Street Jour.*⟩

zir·ca·loy *or* **zir·cal·loy** \ˈzərkəˌlȯi\ *n* -s [*zirc*onium + *al*loy] : any of several zirconium alloys notable for corrosion resistance and stability over a wide range of radiation and temperature exposures

zit \ˈzit\ *n* -s [origin unknown] *slang* : PIMPLE

zi·ti \ˈzēd·ē, -ē(ˌ)tē\ *n, pl* **ziti** [It, pl. of *zito*, alter. of *zita* piece of tubular pasta, prob. short for *maccheroni di zita*, lit., bride's macaroni; fr. the custom in southern Italy of serving dishes with such pasta at wedding feasts] : medium-sized tubular pasta

z line *n, usu cap Z* : any of the dark bands across a striated muscle fiber that mark the junction of actin filaments in adjacent sarcomeres

zol·ling·er–el·li·son syndrome \ˈzäliŋərˈeləsən-\ *n, usu cap Z&E* [after Robert M. *Zollinger* †1992 and Edwin H. *Ellison* †1970 Am. surgeons] : a syndrome consisting of fulminating intractable peptic ulcers, gastric hypersecretion and hyperacidity, and hyperplasia of the pancreatic islet cells

zom·bi·fy \ˈzämbəˌfī\ *vt* -ED/-ING/-ES [*Zomb*i + *-ify*] : to turn (as an active alert person) into a zombie — **zom·bi·fi·ca·tion** \ˌzämbəfəˈkāshən\ *n* -s

zone out *vi* [prob. fr. *zone out* (vt.) exclude from a zone, make unaware of] : to become oblivious to one's surroundings esp. in order to relax ⟨*zone out* in front of the TV⟩

zone refining *also* **zone melting** *n* : a technique for the purification of a crystalline material (as a metal or semiconductor) in which a molten region travels through the material to be refined, picks up impurities at its advancing edge, and then allows the purified part to recrystallize at its opposite edge — **zone–refined** *adj*

zon·ian \ˈzōnēən\ *n* -s *cap* [Panama Canal *Zone* + E *-ian*] : a U.S. citizen who lives in the Panama Canal Zone

zonk \ˈzäŋk, ˈzȯŋk\ *vb* -ED/-ING/-S [back-formation fr. *zonked* (herein)] *vt* : STUN, STUPEFY; *also* : STRIKE, ZAP — often used with *out* ~ *vi* : to pass out from or as if from alcohol or a drug — often used with *out*

zonked \ˈzäŋ(k)t, ˈzȯŋ-\ *also* **zonked–out** \ˈzäŋ(k)tˈau̇t, ˈzȯŋ-\ *adj* [origin unknown] : stupefied by or as if by alcohol or a drug

zo·ri \ˈzōrē, -ȯr-\ *n, pl* **zori** *also* **zoris** [Jap *zōri* straw sandals, fr. *zō* grass + *-ri* footwear] : a flat thonged sandal usu. made of straw, cloth, leather, or rubber

zorn's lemma \ˈzȯ(ə)rnz-, ˈtsȯ-\ *n, usu cap Z* [after Max August *Zorn* †1993 Am. (Ger.-born) mathematician] : a lemma in set theory: if S is partially ordered and if each subset for which every pair of elements is related by one of the relationships "less than," "equal to," or "greater than" has an upper bound in S, then S contains at least one element for which there is no greater element in S

zouave pants *n, sometimes cap Z* [so called fr. their resemblance to the baggy trousers worn by Zouaves] : baggy trousers that are gathered at the waist and at the knee, calf, or ankle

zouk \ˈzük\ *n* -s [Lesser Antillean F Creole, lit., dance party, dance, prob. alter. of *mazouk* Fr. Caribbean ballroom and club dance of the earlier 20th cent., alter. of F *mazurka* mazurka] : a form of French West Indian dance music blending African rhythms, reggae, calypso, and electronic dance music

ZPG *abbr* zero population growth

zup·pa in·gle·se \ˈtsüpə·iŋˈglā(ˌ)zā, ˈzü-, -inˈg-, ˈ(ˌ)sā, ˈsē, ˈzē\ *n, often cap I* [It, lit., English soup] : a dessert consisting of sponge cake and custard or pudding that is flavored with rum, covered with cream, and garnished with fruit

zy·de·co \ˈzīdəˌkō\ *also* **zod·i·co** \ˈzädəˌkō\ *n* -s *sometimes cap, often attrib* [perh. modif. of F *les haricots* beans, fr. the Cajun dance tune *Les Haricots Sont Pas Salés*] : popular music of southern Louisiana that combines dance tunes of French origin with elements of Caribbean music and the blues and that is usu. played by small groups featuring guitar, washboard, and accordion

zy·mo·gram \ˈzīməˌgram\ *n* [*zym-* + *-gram*] : an electrophoretic strip (as of starch gel) or a representation of it exhibiting the pattern of separated enzymes and esp. isoenzymes after electrophoresis

Webster's Third New International Dictionary

OF THE ENGLISH LANGUAGE

UNABRIDGED

A DICTIONARY
OF THE ENGLISH LANGUAGE

¹a \ˈā\ *n, pl* **a's** *or* **as** *also* **aes** \ˈāz\ *often cap, often attrib* **1 a :** the first letter of the English alphabet **b :** an instance of this letter printed, written, or otherwise represented **c :** a speech counterpart of orthographic *a* (as the different *a* sounds in *ape, pat, part*) ⟨mouthing out his hollow oes and *aes* —Alfred Tennyson⟩ **2 a :** the keynote of A major or A minor **b :** the tone A **3 :** a printer's type, a stamp, or some other instrument for reproducing the letter *a* **4 :** someone or something arbitrarily or conveniently designated *a*, esp. as the first in order or class ⟨*A* deeded land to B⟩ **5 a :** a grade assigned by a teacher or examiner rating a student's work as excellent, best, first, or superior in quality ⟨receiving an *A* in a science course⟩ **b :** one graded or rated with an A ⟨an *A* student⟩ ⟨those student papers are *A's*⟩ ⟨the movie was an *A*⟩ **6 :** something having the shape of the capital letter A — **from A to Z** *also* **from A to izzard :** from beginning to end **:** with coverage through the whole range or scope involved **:** THOROUGHLY, COMPLETELY

²a \ə, *esp emphatic or hesitating or after a pause* (ˈ)ā\ *indefinite article* [ME, fr. OE *ān* one — more at ONE] **1** — used as a function word before most singular nouns other than proper and mass nouns when the individual in question is undetermined, unidentified, or unspecified, esp. when the individual is being first mentioned or called to notice ⟨there was *a* tree in the field⟩ ⟨*a* man walked past him⟩ ⟨he bought *a* house, but this is not the house he bought⟩; used before words beginning with a consonant sound ⟨*a* man⟩ ⟨*a* union⟩ ⟨*a* one⟩ ⟨*a* heroic effort⟩ and in some dialects also before words beginning with a vowel sound ⟨*a* oak⟩ ⟨*a* apron⟩; used with a plural noun only if *few, very few, good many,* or *great many* is interposed ⟨*a* few hours⟩; used before adjectives modifying a noun to which it refers except that it follows *many, such, what* and any adjective or adjectives preceded by *as* or *how,* and usu. follows any adjective or adjectives preceded by *so* or *too* ⟨*a* long time⟩ ⟨such *a* day⟩ ⟨how good and brave *a* deed⟩ ⟨too long *a* time⟩; compare ¹AN **2 a** — used as a function word before noun and adjective uses of such number collectives as *dozen* and *score* and before such words as *hundred, thousand,* and *million* ⟨*a* gross of candles⟩ ⟨*a* hundred and twenty men⟩ ⟨*a* hundred and fifty thousand⟩ **b** — used as a function word before attributive adjectives expressing number to imply indefiniteness or approximation ⟨*a* twenty men⟩ ⟨*a* twelve hours⟩; now dial. except in constructions given in note following sense 1 ⟨*a* great many men⟩ **3 a :** ONE ⟨swords all of *a* length⟩ ⟨men all of *a* sort⟩ **b** — used as a function word to suggest limitation in number ⟨with only *a* brigade to defend the fort⟩ **c :** the same ⟨birds of *a* feather⟩ **4 a :** a particular illustration of **:** an example of (a named class) ⟨he is *a* man⟩ **b** — used as a function word before a singular noun followed by a restrictive clause or other identifying modifier ⟨*a* man who was here yesterday⟩ **c :** ANY, EACH — used with a following restrictive modifier ⟨*a* man in danger of kidnaping wins scant sympathy⟩ ⟨*a* man who is sick can't work well⟩ **d** — used as a function word before proper nouns to indicate lack of full knowledge concerning what is indicated by them ⟨*a* Mr. Smith called you yesterday⟩ ⟨among the towns of the area there is *a* Smithville, I believe⟩ **e** — used as a function word before proper nouns as a step in commonization, often to designate another having qualities like those of the person or thing named ⟨*a* Shakespeare in his dramatic skill⟩ ⟨*a* new Rome controlling the world⟩ **f** — used as a function word before a mass noun to suggest that a kind or type is under consideration ⟨*a* tobacco that grows well in cold areas⟩ ⟨*a* bronze made in ancient times⟩ **g :** an instance or case of ⟨the patient later developed *a* tonsillitis⟩ **:** a kind of ⟨copper is *a* metal⟩ **h** — used as a function word with form plurals to suggest a unifying notion ⟨*a* falls in the river⟩ ⟨*a* glassworks⟩

³a \ə\ *prep* [ME *a, o,* fr. OE *a-, an, on* — more at ON] **1** *chiefly dial* **:** ¹ON, ¹IN, ¹AT, ¹TO ⟨might get married *a* Christmas —J.H. Stuart⟩ ⟨he that died *a* Wednesday —Shak.⟩ **2 :** in, to, or for each **:** for every — used before words with an initial consonant sound ⟨twice *a* week⟩ ⟨two dollars *a* pound⟩

⁴a *or* **'a** *in senses 1-3* ə, *in sense 4* ə *or* (ˌ)ä\ *pron* [in sense 1, fr. ME *a, ha* he, unstressed var. of *he,* fr. OE *hē;* in sense 2, fr. ME *a, ha,* unstressed var. of *heo, hie, hi,* fr. OE *hēo, hīo, hī,* fem. of *hē;* in sense 3, fr. ME *a, ha,* unstressed var. of *hie, hi,* fr. OE *hie, hī,* pl. of *hē;* in sense 4, fr. ME *a, ha,* unstressed vars. of *he, heo,* used to refer to inanimate objects of masc. or fem. gender; in sense 5, var. of *I* — more at HE, I] **1** *chiefly dial* **:** HE; *sometimes* **:** HIM — usu. used in spoken English in unemphatic positions **2** *dial chiefly Brit* **:** SHE; *sometimes* **:** HER **3** *chiefly dial* **:** THEY; *sometimes* **:** THEM **4** *chiefly dial* **:** IT **5** *chiefly dial* **:** I

⁵a *also* **'a** *or* **a'** \ə, (ˌ)ā\ *or* **ha** *or* **ha'** \hə, (ˌ)ha\ *vb* [ME *a, ha,* contr. of *have* (imper. & pres. subj.), *haven* (infin.)] **:** HAVE ⟨God *'a'* mercy on his soul —Shak.⟩ ⟨I'd *a* done it if I could⟩ — now usu. used as an unstressed auxiliary; often attached without hyphen to the preceding word ⟨could*a*⟩ ⟨might*a*⟩ ⟨would*a*⟩; not often in formal use

⁶a \ə\ *prep* [ME, contr. of *of*] **:** OF ⟨passing the time *a* day⟩ ⟨get it out *a* my locker —James Jones⟩ — often attached without hyphen to the preceding word ⟨kind*a*⟩ ⟨sort*a*⟩ ⟨coupl*a*⟩ ⟨lott*a*⟩; not often now in formal use

⁷a *or* **a'** \ˈȯ\ *adv (or adj)* [ME (northern dial.) *aw,* alter. of *all*] *chiefly Scot* **:** ALL

⁸a *abbr, often cap* **1** about **2** absent **3** absolute **4** academician; academy **5** acceleration **6** accepted **7** accommodation **8** ace **9** acre **10** act; acting; active; activity **11** adjective **12** adjutant **13** administration **14** adult **15** after **16** afternoon **17** age; aged **18** air **19** aircraft **20** airman **21** airplane **22** alto **23** amateur **24** American **25** ampere **26** amphibian; amphibious **27** amplitude **28** ana **29** angstrom unit **30** anna **31 a** [L *anno,* abl. of *annus*] in the year **b** [L *annus* — more at ANNUAL] year **32** anode **33** anonymous **34** answer **35** ante **36** anterior **37** approved **38** aqua **39** arctic **40** are **41** area **42** army **43** article **44** artillery **45** asked **46** assist **47** associate; association **48** asymmetric **49** at **50** atom; atomic **51** atomic weight **52** Australian **53** author **54** automobile **55** [F *avancé,* past part. of *avancer* to advance, be fast (used of a clock), fr. OF *avancier* — more at ADVANCE] fast

⁹a *symbol* **1** *cap* argon **2** [L *ad* — more at AT] at, to — often enclosed in an encircling loop **3** *cap* mass number

¹a- \ə\ *prefix* [ME, fr. OE *a-, an, on*] **1 :** on **:** in **:** at ⟨*a*bed⟩ ⟨*a*foot⟩ ⟨*a*sunder⟩ — sometimes used in dialect speech in locutions not found in standard ⟨he did it *a*-purpose⟩ **2** *obs* **:** at (such) a time ⟨*a*-nights⟩ **3 :** in (such) a state or condition ⟨*a*fire⟩ ⟨*a*sleep⟩ — often used with *with* ⟨acrawl with ants⟩ **4 :** in (such) a manner ⟨*a*loud⟩ **5 :** in the act of **:** in the process of ⟨daddy's gone *a*-hunting⟩ ⟨months later the ship was still *a*-building⟩

²a- \(ˈ)ā, (ˌ)a *also* (ˈ)ä *or* (ˌ)ə; *at individual entries variants other than the first are not shown unless believed to be frequent*\ *or* **an-** \(ˌ)an, ən\ *prefix* [L & Gk; L *a-,* an-, fr. Gk — more at UN-] **:** not **:** without ⟨*a*chromatic⟩ ⟨*a*sexual⟩ — used chiefly with words of Gk or L origin; *a-* before consonants other than *h* and sometimes even before *h, an-* before vowels and usu. before *h* ⟨*a*historical⟩ ⟨*an*esthesia⟩ ⟨*an*hydrous⟩

-a- *comb form* [ISV] **:** replacing carbon esp. in a ring — in initial combining forms as second constituent after a first constituent designating a chemical element ⟨ars*a*-⟩ ⟨az*a*-⟩

-a *n suffix* -s [NL, prob. fr. originally nonsignificant *-a* in *magnesia,* fr. ML *-a* (in *magnesia,* alchemical substance), fr. Gk *-a, -ē* (in *magnēsia, magnēsiē,* alchemical substance, magnet), fr. nom. sing. fem. adjectival ending corresponding to nom. sing. masc. *-os* and nom. sing. neut. *-on*] **:** oxide ⟨ceri*a*⟩ ⟨lanthan*a*⟩ ⟨thori*a*⟩

aa \ˈäˌä, ˈäˈä\ *n* -s [Hawaiian *'a'ā*] **:** rough scoriaceous lava — contrasted with *pahoehoe*

AA \(ˈ)āˈā\ *abbr or n* -s Associate of Arts

AA *abbr* **1** achievement age **2** acting appointment **3** *often not cap* always afloat **4** *often not cap* ana **5** antiaircraft **6** approximate absolute **7** athletic association **8** author's alteration **9** automobile association

AAA *in sense 1 at least,* ˌtäˌāˈā *or* ˌtripəlˈā\ *abbr* **1** amateur athletic association **2** antiaircraft artillery

AAC *abbr* [L *anno ante Christum*] in the year before Christ

aa·chen \ˈäkən, ˈäk-\ *adj, usu cap* [fr. *Aachen,* Germany] **:** of or from Aachen, Germany **:** of the kind or style prevalent in Aachen

aa·lii \äˈlēˌē\ *n* -s [Hawaiian *'a'ali'i*] *Hawaii* **:** a small tree (*Dodonaea viscosa*) with hard dark wood

A and M *abbr* agricultural and mechanical

AAR *abbr, often not cap* against all risks

aard·vark \ˈärdˌvärk\ *also* **erd·vark** \ˈe(ə)rdˌvärk\ *n* -s [obs. Afrik *aardvark* (now *erdvark*), fr. *aard* earth + *vark* pig; akin to OE *eorthe* earth and to OE *fearh* little pig — more at EARTH, FARROW] **:** a burrowing nocturnal African mammal about five feet long that feeds on ants and termites, has a long snout, a snakelike tongue, large ears, and a heavy tapering tail, and is usu. considered to form a single variable species (*Orycteropus afer*) that is the sole recent representative of the obscure mammalian order Tubulidentata — called also *ant bear, anteater, earth pig*

aardvark (*Orycteropus afer*)

aard·wolf \-ˌwu̇lf\ *n, pl* **aard·wolves** \-lvz\ [Afrik, fr. *aard* earth + *wolf;* akin to OE *wulf* wolf — more at WOLF] **:** a hyenalike mammal (*Proteles cristatus*) of southern and eastern Africa that has a striped coat, 5-toed forefeet, and a distinct mane, feeds chiefly on carrion and insects (as termites), and is usu. placed in the Hyaenidae though formerly separated in another family (Protelidae)

aar·hus \ˈȯ(ə)rˌhüs\ *adj, usu cap* [fr. *Aarhus,* Denmark] **:** of or from Aarhus, Denmark **:** of the kind or style prevalent in Aarhus

aa·ron·ic \(ˈ)aˈränik, eˈ-, -aaˈ-, -äˈ-\ *adj, usu cap* [*Aaron fl ab* 1200 B.C. Jewish patriarch & high priest, brother of Moses + E *-ic*] **1 :** of or stemming from Aaron the Levite, the first high priest of the Hebrews **2 :** of, belonging to, or being the lesser order of priesthood in the Mormon church comprising the grades of deacon, teacher, and priest — compare MELCHIZEDEK

aa·ron·ite \ˈarəˌnīt, ˈer-, ˈaar-, ˈär-\ *n* -s *usu cap* **:** a priestly descendant of Aaron

aaron's-beard \ˈ==ˌ=\ *n, pl* **aaron's-beards** *usu cap A* [so called fr. the reference to the patriarch Aaron's beard in Ps 133:2] **:** any of several plants having numerous stamens or threadlike runners: as **a :** GREAT ST.-JOHN'S-WORT **b :** JERUSALEM STAR **c :** STRAWBERRY GERANIUM **d :** KENILWORTH IVY **e** *or* **aaron's-beard cactus :** a cactus (*Opuntia leucotricha*) that has white hairs on its joints

aaron's rod \ˈ==ˌ=\ *n, usu cap A* [so called fr. the reference (Num 17:8) to the patriarch Aaron's rod, which blossomed and yielded almonds] **1 :** any of several plants with tall flowering stems; *esp* **:** GREAT MULLEIN **2 :** an architectural ornament consisting of a rounded molding decorated by a single entwined serpent and sometimes vines and leaves

aas·vo·gel \ˈäsˌfōgəl\ *also* **aas·vo·el** \-ˌfōəl\ *n* -s [obs. Afrik *aasvogel* (now *aasvoël*), fr. *aas* carrion + *vogel* (now *voël*) bird; akin to OE *etan* to eat and to OE *fugol* bird — more at EAT, FOWL] *Africa* **:** VULTURE

AAU *abbr* amateur athletic union

¹ab *or* **av** \ˈäb, ˈäv\ *n* -s *usu cap* [Heb *ābh*] **:** the 11th month of the civil year or the 5th month of the ecclesiastical year in the Jewish calendar — see MONTH table

²ab \ˈab\ *n* -s *often cap* [alternate transliteration of Egypt *'ib*] *Egyptian relig* **:** the spirit of the physical heart and the seat of the will and intentions conceived as proceeding at death to the future world where it gives evidence for or against its possessor

¹ab- *prefix* [ME, fr. OF & L; OF, fr. L, fr. *ab* from — more at OF] **1 :** from **:** departing from ⟨*ab*normal⟩ **2 :** away **:** outside of ⟨*ab*enteric⟩

²ab- *prefix* [¹*absolute*] — used for a cgs electromagnetic unit (as in the following table)

UNIT	NATURE	EQUIVALENT
abampere	current	10 amperes
abcoulomb	charge	10 coulombs
abfarad	capacitance	10^9 farads
abhenry	inductance	10^{-9} henrys
abohm	resistance	10^{-9} ohms
abvolt	potential	10^{-8} volts

ab *abbr* **1** *often cap* abbot **2** about **3** abstract

¹AB \(ˈ)āˈbē\ *abbr or n* -s [abbr. of NL *artium baccalaureus*] Bachelor of Arts

²AB \ˈ"\ *abbr or n* -s able-bodied seaman

AB *abbr* **1** aid to blind **2** airbase **3** airborne **4** *often not cap* at bat

¹aba \ˈabə\ *n* -s [after A. T. d'*Abbadie* †1897 Fr. explorer, its inventor] **:** an altazimuth for astronomical or terrestrial use

²aba *or* **ab·ba** \əˈbä, aˈbä\ *or* **aba·ya** \-ïyə\ *n* -s [Ar *'abā', 'abā'ah*] **1 :** a coarse often striped fabric woven in the Near East from wool or from the hair of camels or goats **2 :** a loose sleeveless outer garment of aba or of fine silk worn chiefly by Arabs

abab·da \əˈbabdə\ *or* **abab·deh** \-de\ *n, pl* **ababda** *or* **ababdas** *or* **ababdeh** *or* **ababdehs** *usu cap* [Ar *'Abābidah*] **1 :** an Arabic-speaking mostly nomadic Beja people of Upper Egypt **2 :** a member of the Ababda people

ab ab·sur·do \ˌabəbˈsərˌdō, ˌaˌbab-, -ˈz-\ *adv (or adj)* [L] **:** from absurdity — used of an argument that an assertion is false because of its absurdity

ab·a·ca \ˌabəˈkä\ *n* -s [Sp *abacá,* fr. Tag *abaká*] **1 :** a fiber obtained from the leafstalk of a banana (*Musa textilis*) native to the Philippines — called also *Manila hemp* **2 :** the plant that yields abaca

aba·ca·te \ˌabəˈkädˌē\ *n* -s [Pg] **:** AVOCADO

aba·ca·xi \ˌabəkəˈshē\ *n* -s [Pg *abacaxi*] **:** a large sweet pineapple grown esp. in Brazil

ab·a·cis·cus \ˌabəˈsiskəs, -ˈki-\ *n, pl* **abacis·ci** \-ˈsˌsī, -ˈkī-, -skē, -ˈkiˌskī\ [NL, fr. LGk *abakiskos,* dim. of Gk *abak-, abax* slab, board] **:** ABACULUS

ab·a·cist \ˈabəsəst, -bək-, əˈbak- *also* əˈbäk- *or* əˈbāk-\ *n* -s [ME, fr. ML *abacista,* fr. L *abacus* + *-ista* -ist] **:** one that uses an abacus

aback \əˈbak\ *adv* [ME *abak,* fr. OE *on bæc,* fr. *on* on, at, towards + *bæc* back — more at ON, BACK] **1** *archaic* **a :** toward or to the back or rear **:** BACKWARD, BACK ⟨all suddenly dismayed . . . he fled ~ —Edmund Spenser⟩ **b :** in the rear **:** BEHIND **2 :** in a position to catch the wind upon the forward surface of a sail — usu. used of a square sail or yard ⟨the ship came up into the wind with all yards ~ —H.A.Chippendale⟩ **3 :** by surprise **:** UNAWARES — used with preceding *take* ⟨completely taken ~ at the question⟩

abacot *var of* BYCOKET

abac·te·ri·al \ˌāˌbakˈtirēəl\ *adj* [²*a-* + *bacterial*] **:** not caused by or characterized by the presence of bacteria ⟨~ urethritis⟩

ab·ac·ti·nal \(ˈ)aˈbaktənᵊl, ˌaˌbakˈtīnᵊl\ *adj* [¹*ab-* + *actinal*] **:** of or relating to the surface or end opposite to the mouth in a radiate animal — **ab·ac·ti·nal·ly** \-nᵊlē\ *adv*

ab·ac·tor \ˈaˌbaktə(r), =ˈ==\ *n* -s [LL, lit., one that drives away, fr. L *abactus* (past part. of *abigere* to drive away, fr. *ab-* ¹ab- + *-igere,* fr. *agere* to drive) + *-or* — more at AGENT] **:** one that steals cattle

a ba·cu·lo \(ˈ)äˈbakyəˌlō, (ˈ)äˈbäkə-\ *adv (or adj)* [NL] **:** by means of the rod — used of an appeal to force rather than reason

abac·u·lus \əˈbakyələs\ *n, pl* **abacu·li** \-ˌlī, -ˌē\ [L, dim. of *abacus*] **:** a tile used in mosaic **:** TESSERA

ab·a·cus \ˈabəkəs, əˈbak- *also* əˈbäk- *or* əˈbāk-\ *n, pl* **aba·ci** \ˈabəˌsī, -ˌkī, -ˌkē, əˈbaˌkī *also* əˈbäˌkī *or* -ˈbā- *or* -ˌkē\ *or* **aba·cus·es** [L, fr. Gk *abak-, abax,* lit., slab] **1 :** a slab that forms the uppermost member or division of the capital of a column and that supports the architrave **2 :** a calculating instrument for performing arithmetical processes by sliding counters by hand on rods or in grooves

1 abacus

aba·dan \ˌabəˈdan, -ˈdän; ˌäbəˈdän\ *adj, usu cap* [fr. *Abadan,* Iran] **:** of or from Abadan, Iran **:** of the kind or style prevalent in Abadan

abad·don \əˈbadᵊn\ *n* -s *usu cap* [fr. *Abaddon* "the angel of the bottomless pit" (Rev 9:11), fr. ME, fr. LL, fr. Gk *Abaddōn,* fr. Heb *'ăbhaddōn,* lit., destruction] **:** a place of destruction **:** an underworld abode of lost souls **:** HELL

abadite *usu cap, var of* IBADITE

ab ae·ter·no \ˌabēˈtər(ˌ)nō, ˌäˌbīˈter-\ *adv* [NL, lit., from forever] **:** from an infinitely remote point of time in the past

¹abaft \əˈbaft, -aa(ə)-, -ai-, -á-\ *adv* [¹*a-* + *baft*] **:** toward or at the stern **:** AFT, ASTERN ⟨ships with square sails sail fairly efficiently with the wind ~ —Elijah Baker⟩

²abaft \ˈ"\ *prep* **:** to the rear of **:** BEHIND ⟨selection by a better-than-average jazz band, taped in a small room ~ the 52d Street night spot —J.M.Conly⟩; *specif* **:** toward the stern from ⟨our deserter stood just ~ the foremast —Vincent McHugh⟩

¹abais·sé \əˈbāˌsā\ *adj* [F, past part. of *abaisser* to lower — more at ABASE] *heraldry* **:** ABASED

²abaisse \əˈbās\ *n* -s [F, fr. *abaisser*] **:** a thin undercrust of pastry

ab·alien·ate \(ˈ)aˈbālyəˌnāt, -lēə-\ *vt* [L *abalienatus,* past part. of L *abalienare,* fr. *ab-* ab- + *alienare* to alienate — more at ALIENATE] **:** to transfer the title of **:** ALIENATE

ab·alien·a·tion \(ˌ)aˌbālyəˈnāshən, -lēə-\ *n* [L *abalienation-, abalienatio,* fr. *abalienatus* + *-ion-, -io* -ion] **:** the act of transferring a legal title

ab·a·lo·ne \ˌabəˈlōnē, -i\ *n* -s [AmerSp *abulón*] **1 :** a gastropod mollusk of the genus *Haliotis* that clings to rocks tenaciously with a broad muscular foot and that has a nacre-lined shell of a flattened, oval, slightly spiral form perforated with a row of apertures for the escape of the water from the gills and covering the animal like a roof **2 :** the edible flesh of certain large abalones

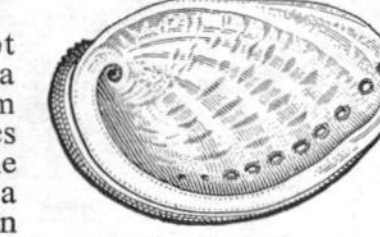
shell of abalone

ab·am·pere \(ˈ)aˈbam,pi(ə)r, -aam-, -iə *also* ˌ==ˈ=\ *n* -s [ISV ²*ab-* + *ampere*] **:** the cgs electromagnetic unit of electric current equaling 10 amperes that flows in a circular path of one centimeter radius and produces a magnetic field of 2 π oersteds at the center of the circle — compare AB- table

¹**aban·don** \əˈbandən, -aand-\ *vt* **abandoned; abandoned; abandoning** \-ndəniŋ, *rapid sometimes* -nniŋ\ **abandons** [ME *abandounen*, fr. MF *abandoner*, fr. *abandon*, n., surrender, abandonment, fr. *a bandon* in one's power, at one's discretion (in the phrase *metre a bandon* to put under someone's jurisdiction or at one's mercy), fr. *a* at, to (fr. L *ad* to) + *banon, bandon* power, authority, discretion, of Gmc origin; akin to OHG *ban* command, prohibition, authority — more at AT, BAN] **1 :** to cease to assert or exercise an interest, right, or title to esp. with the intent of never again resuming or reasserting it **:** YIELD, RELINQUISH ⟨~*ed* the estates when he inherited them —Charles Dickens⟩ **2 :** to give up (as a position, a ship) by leaving, withdrawing, ceasing to inhabit, to keep, or to operate often because unable to withstand threatening dangers or encroachments ⟨the site was ~*ed* after one year because of the number of rattlesnakes —*Amer. Guide Series: Calif.*⟩; *specif* **:** to bail out of (an aircraft about to crash) **3 :** to forsake or desert esp. in spite of an allegiance, duty, or responsibility ⟨endure the ignominy of his ~*ing* her —D.H.Lawrence⟩ **:** withdraw one's protection, support, or help from ⟨a faithful member of the Democratic party, ~*ing* it only once —W.W.Pierson⟩ **4** *obs* **:** to drive or cast out **:** BANISH, EXPEL, REJECT ⟨being all this time ~*ed* from your bed —Shak.⟩ **5 :** to give (oneself) over to or yield (oneself) to without check, restraint, or control ⟨the girl ~*ed* herself without restraint to a delicious wave of voluptuous contentment —J.C.Powys⟩ **6 :** to turn away from, give over, or permit to cease or lapse: as **a :** to desist from maintaining, adhering to, or following ⟨aristocratic families ~*ed* paganism for Christianity —Will Durant⟩ **b :** to desist from practicing, doing, using ⟨they ~*ed* their native speech and adopted the French tongue —T.B.Macaulay⟩ **c :** to turn from or relinquish (some course or action) ⟨he ~*ed* the project with a sigh —Rudyard Kipling⟩ **7 :** to surrender to the insurer the insured's interest in (insured property) and to claim payment for a total loss sometimes permitted only when damage constitutes constructive total loss **syn** see RELINQUISH

²**aban·don** \ˈ", *F* àbäⁿdōⁿ\ *n, pl* **abandons** \-ənz,-ōⁿ(z)\ [F, fr. OF] **:** a yielding to natural impulses **:** freedom from constraint ⟨with childish ~ she gave herself over to grief —Sherwood Anderson⟩ **:** carefree ease or freedom often with disregard for consequences **:** ENTHUSIASM, EXUBERANCE ⟨smashed public property and burned private houses with an ever more ardent ~ —Rose Macaulay⟩

aban·doned \əˈbandənd, -aand-\ *adj* [ME *abandouned*, fr. past part. of *abandounen* to abandon] **1 :** given up **:** DESERTED, FORSAKEN ⟨an ~ child⟩ ⟨an ~ house⟩ **2 :** SELF-ABANDONED **:** given over to vice **:** free from moral restraint ⟨an ~ villain⟩ **3 :** showing abandon **:** free from constraint ⟨an ~ sadness born of grief —Liam O'Flaherty⟩ **4** *of a geological formation* **:** no longer affected by the geologic agent that produced it ⟨an ~ valley⟩ — **aban·doned·ly** \-ndən(d)lē, -i\ *adv*

aban·don·ee \ə,=dəˈnē\ *n* -s **:** one that holds or claims abandoned property; *specif* **:** the person (as the insurer in marine insurance) to whom property or rights are relinquished

aban·don·ment \əˈ=dənmənt\ *n* -s [F *abandonnement*, fr. *abandonner* to abandon (fr. OF *abandoner*) + *-ment* — more at ABANDON] **1 a :** the act of abandoning **:** RELINQUISHMENT, RENUNCIATION ⟨such freedom meant the ~ of many long-cherished phrases —I.M.Price⟩ **b** (1) **:** desertion of a spouse with the intention of creating a permanent separation (2) **:** desertion of a child by its parents **c** (1) **:** such relinquishment by an inventor of his right to secure a patent as will constitute a dedication of the invention to public use (2) **:** an author's relinquishment to the public domain of his copyright **d :** relinquishment by a nonuser for a specified period (as of an easement) **e :** the act of the insured in surrendering all rights to damaged or lost property to the insurer as a total loss **f :** refusal to accept from a delivering carrier a shipment so damaged in transit as to be worthless **g :** permission sought by or granted to a carrier by a state or federal agency to cease operation of all or part of a route or service **2 :** the quality or state of being abandoned **:** freedom from restraint **:** SELF-SURRENDER ⟨in a spirit of utter ~ he carols his simple strain —John Burroughs⟩

aba·ñe·eme \ə,bänyəˈāmē\ *n* -s *usu cap* [Guarani] **:** the southern dialect of the Tupi-Guarani Indians

aban·ic \əˈbanik\ *adj, usu cap* [prob. fr. Ojibwa *Ab-boin-ug* Dakota (Sioux), lit., roasters; fr. their habit of torturing enemies] **:** SIOUAN

ab·ar·thro·sis \ˌa,bärˈthrōsəs\ *n, pl* **abarthro·ses** \-,sēz\ [NL, fr. ¹*ab-* + *arthrosis*] **:** DIARTHROSIS

¹**abas** *or* **abassi** *var of* ABBASI

²**abas** *pl of* ABA

à bas \(ˈ)äˈbä, (ˈ)aˈbä, *F* àbä\ [F] **:** down with ⟨*à bas* the profiteers⟩

abase \əˈbās\ *vt* -ED/-ING/-S [ME *abessen, abassen*, fr. MF *abaisser*, fr. (assumed) VL *abbassiare*, fr. L *ad-* + (assumed) VL *bassiare* to lower, fr. (assumed) VL *bassus* low (whence ML *bassus* fat, short, low)] **1** *archaic* **:** LOWER, DEPRESS **:** cast down ⟨~ the eye⟩ **2 :** to lower or reduce in rank, office, prestige, or esteem **:** HUMBLE ⟨whosoever exalteth himself shall be *abased* —Lk 14:11 (AV)⟩ **:** DEGRADE

abased \əˈbāst\ *adj* **1 :** lowered esp. in rank, office, prestige, or esteem **:** HUMBLED ⟨I shrink ~ and yet aspire to Thee —William Cowper⟩ **2** *heraldry* **a :** borne lower than usual ⟨an ~ fess⟩ — opposed to *enhanced* **b :** turned downward ⟨the ~ tips of a bird's wings⟩ — **abas·ed·ly** \-sədlē, -i\ *adv*

abase·ment \əˈbāsmənt\ *n* -s **1 :** the act of abasing ⟨these may be used for the adornment of life but he believes them more often misused for its ~ —John Baillie⟩ **2 :** the quality or state of being abased ⟨each confession would bring her into an attitude of ~ —H.L.Mencken⟩

abash \əˈbash, -ˈaa(ə)-,-ˈai-\ *vb* -ED/-ING/-ES [ME *abaisen, abaishen, abashen*, fr. (assumed) MF *abaisser* to be astonished, alter. (influenced by *abaisser* to abase) of *esbaiss-*, stem of *esbair* to be astonished, fr. *es-* (fr. L *ex-*) + *bair* to yawn, gape, bark — more at BAY] *vt* **:** to destroy the self-possession of **:** confuse or put to shame (as by arousing suddenly a feeling of guilt or inferiority) **:** DISCONCERT, DISCOMFIT ⟨a man whom no check could ~ —T.B.Macaulay⟩ ~ *vi, obs* **:** to lose self-possession **syn** see EMBARRASS

aba·shev \əˈbäshəf\ *adj, cap* [Russ] **:** belonging to a Bronze Age culture of the Chuvash Republic in the east central Soviet Union

abash·less \əˈ=ləs\ *adj* **:** UNABASHED — **abash·less·ly** *adv*

abash·ment \əˈ=mənt\ *n* -s [ME *abaishment, abashment*, fr. MF *abaissement* astonishment, alter. (influenced by *abaissement* abasing) of *esbaissement*, fr. *esbaiss-* + *-ment*] **:** the quality or state of being abashed

aba·sia \əˈbāzh(ē)ə\ *n* -s [NL, fr. ²*a-* + Gk *basis* step + NL *-ia* — more at BASE (bottom)] **:** inability to walk caused by a defect in muscular coordination — compare ASTASIA — **aba·sic** \əˈbāsik, -āzik\ *adj*

abastardize *vt* -ED/-ING/-S [MF *abastardir* (fr. OF, fr. *a-* — fr. L *ad-* — + *bastart* bastard) + E *-ize* — more at BASTARD] *obs* **:** BASTARDIZE, DEBASE

abat·able \əˈbād·əbəl, -ātə-\ *adj* [¹*abate* + *-able*] **:** capable of being abated

¹**abate** \əˈbāt, *usu* -ād· + V\ *vb* -ED/-ING/-S [ME *abaten*, fr. OF *abatre, abattre* to knock down, fell, slaughter, fr. *a-* (fr. L *ad-*) + *batre, battre* to beat, fr. L *battuere* — more at BAT] *vt* **1** *law* **a :** to bring entirely down **:** DEMOLISH **:** put an end to **:** do away with ⟨~ a nuisance⟩ ⟨~ an action⟩ **b :** NULLIFY **:** make void ⟨~ a writ⟩ **2** *obs* **:** to lower in status **:** HUMBLE **3 a :** to reduce or lessen in degree or intensity **:** DIMINISH, MODERATE ⟨may . . . ~ their zeal and give up their hopes of world conquest —Elmer Davis⟩ **b :** to reduce in value ⟨~ a tax⟩ ⟨the legacies were *abated* pro rata to pay debts⟩ **4 :** DEDUCT, OMIT ⟨~ part of a price⟩ **5 :** to beat down, cut away, or otherwise lower, so as to leave a figure in relief (as in metalwork or stonecutting) **6 :** DEPRIVE ⟨she hath *abated* me of half my train —Shak.⟩ **7** *obs* **:** to turn or dull the edge or point of **:** BLUNT ⟨~*s* my sword's keen edge —Thomas Heywood⟩ ~ *vi* **1 :** to decrease in force, intensity, or violence **:** LESSEN, SUBSIDE ⟨wait for a storm to ~⟩ ⟨the fear of immediate war has measurably *abated*⟩ **2 a :** to become defeated or become null or void (as of a writ or appeal) **b :** to decrease in amount or value ⟨the legacies *abated* proportionately⟩ **syn** see ABOLISH, DECREASE

²**abate** \ˈ"\ *vi* -ED/-ING/-S [AF *abatre*, alter. of *enbatre*, fr. OF *en-* + *batre* to beat] *law* **:** to enter without right upon a tenement after the death of the last possessor and before the heir or devisee takes possession

¹**abate·ment** \əˈ=mənt\ *n* -s [ME, fr. AF, fr. *abatre* to abate + MF *-ment* — more at ABATE] *law* **:** the action of one that abates — compare ²ABATE

²**abatement** \ˈ"\ *n* -s [MF, fr. *abatre* to throw down + *-ment* — more at ABATE] **1 :** the act or process of abating or the state of being abated ⟨laws intended to speed up smoke ~⟩ ⟨the ~, if not the complete disappearance, of some long-standing mutual irritations —*New Yorker*⟩ **2** *heraldry* **:** any of various bearings emblematic of dishonor, degradation, or disgrace which were described by former writers on heraldry but never actually used **3 :** an amount abated **:** DECREASE, DEDUCTION; *esp* **:** a deduction from the full amount of a tax — **in abatement** *law* **:** seeking termination of the proceedings of an action by reason of some formal defect (as misnomer) ⟨a plea *in abatement*⟩

ab·a·tis *or* **ab·at·tis** \ˈabə,tē, -əd·əs; əˈbad·ē, -ad·əs\ *n, pl* **abatis** \-ēz\ *or* **abatises** \-əsəz\ *or* **abattis** *or* **abattises** [F, fr. *abattre* to fell, reduce — more at ABATE] **:** a defensive obstacle usu. formed by felled trees whose butts are secured towards the place defended with the often sharpened branches directed outwards against the enemy but sometimes made of live small trees bent down and often reinforced with barbed wire

ab·a·tised *or* **ab·at·tised** \-ēd,-əst\ *adj* **:** having an abatis

abat-jour \ˌä,bäˈzhü(ə)r, *F* àbàzhüür\ *n, pl* **abat-jours** \-ü(ə)rz, -üür\ [F, fr. *abattre* to throw down + *jour* day, daylight, fr. (assumed) VL *diurnus*, fr. L, daily — more at ABATE, DIURNAL] **1 :** a device for deflecting daylight downward as it enters a window (as a sloping soffit of a lintel or a movable screen) **2 :** SKYLIGHT

¹**aba·tor** \əˈbād·ə(r), -ātə-\ *n* -s [²*abate* + *-or*] *law* **:** one that abates in a tenement

²**abator** \ˈ"\ *n* -s [¹*abate* + *-or*] *law* **:** one that abates a nuisance

abat-sons \ˌä,bäˈsōⁿ, *F* àbàsōⁿ\ *n, pl* **abat-sons** \-ōⁿz, *F* -ōⁿ\ [F, fr. *abattre* + *sons*, pl. of *son* sound — more at SOUND] **:** a device for throwing sound downward (as louver boards in a belfry)

a battery \ˈā,-\ *n, usu cap A* **:** a battery used to heat the filaments or cathode heaters of electron tubes — called also *filament battery*; compare B BATTERY

ab·at·toir \ˈabə,twär, -twä(r,-t(w)ō(ə)r,-t(w)ō(ə), ˌ==ˈ=\ *n* -s [F, fr. *abattre* to slaughter + *-oir* -ory (fr. L *-orium*) — more at ABATE] **:** SLAUGHTERHOUSE

abat-vent \ˌä,bäˈväⁿ, *F* àbàväⁿ\ *n, pl* **abat-vents** \-äⁿz, *F* -äⁿ\ [F, fr. *abattre* to throw down + *vent* wind, fr. L *ventus* — more at ABATE, WIND] **1 :** a series of sloping boards used (as in a belfry light) to break the wind without obstructing the passage of air or sound **2 :** a sloping roof (as of a penthouse) **3 :** a metal chimney cap

abat-voix \ˌä,bävˈwä, *F* àbàvwà *or* -wä\ *n, pl* **abat-voix** \-wäz, *F* -wà *or* -wä\ [F, fr. *abattre* + *voix* voice, fr. OF *vois* — more at VOICE] **:** a device for reflecting sound (as the sounding board over a pulpit or rostrum)

ab·ax·i·al \(ˈ)aˈbaksēəl\ *also* **ab·ax·ile** \-səl,-,sīl\ *adj* [¹*ab-* + *axial* or *axile*] **:** situated outside of or facing away from the axis (as of an organ or organism) **:** DORSAL — opposed to *adaxial*

abaya *var of* ABA

abb \ˈab, ˈaa(ə)b\ *n* -s [(assumed) ME, fr. OE *āb, āweb, ōweb* — more at WOOF] **1 a :** coarse wool from the inferior parts (as the skirtings and edges) of a fleece **b :** a warp yarn made of abb wool **2** *Brit* **:** a filling pick in weaving

abb *abbr* abbess; abbey; abbot

¹**abba** *var of* ABA

²**ab·ba** \ˈabə, aˈbä\ *n* -s *often cap* [ME, fr. LL, fr. Gk, fr. Aram *abbā*] **:** FATHER — a title of honor given variously to the Deity in the New Testament, to bishops and patriarchs in many Eastern churches, and to Jewish scholars in the Talmudic period

ab·ba·cy \ˈabəsē, -i\ *n* -ES [alter. of ME *abbatie*, fr. LL *abbatia* — more at ABBEY] **:** the office, estate, jurisdiction, or term of tenure of an abbot

ab·bad·id \ˈabədəd, -(,)did\ *n* -s *cap* [ʿ*Abbād* ibn-Muḥammad abu-ʿAmr †1042 founder of the dynasty + E *-id*] **:** a member of a Muslim dynasty that ruled at Seville from 1023 to 1091

ab·ba·si \əˈbäsē\ *or* **abas** \əˈbäs\ *also* **abas·si** \əˈbäsē\ *n, pl* **abbasis** *or* **abas** *also* **abassis** [Per ʿ*abbāsī*, lit., of Abbās, fr. *Abbās* I †1628 shah of Persia] **1 :** a Persian silver coin first issued in the late 16th century **2 :** an old Persian unit of weight equivalent to about 0.8 pound **3 :** an Afghan yellow bronze coin equivalent to four shahi issued between 1921 and 1923 **4 :** an Afghan unit of value for postage stamps ⟨one-*abbasi* stamps⟩ ⟨two-*abbasi* stamps⟩

ab·bas·id \əˈbasəd, -ˈä-\ *n* -s *cap* [abu-al-*Abbas* †754 Islamic caliph, founder of the dynasty + E *-id*] **:** a member of a dynasty of caliphs that ruled the Islamic empire (750–1258) from Baghdad and claimed descent from Abbas, the uncle of Muhammad

ab·ba·tial \əˈbāshəl, (ˈ)aˈb-\ *adj* [F, fr. LL *abbatialis*, fr. *abbatia* abbey + L *-alis* -ial — more at ABBEY] **:** of or belonging to an abbot, abbess, or abbey

abbaye *archaic var of* ABBEY

ab·bé \aˈbā, *F* àbā\ *n, pl* **abbés** \-āz, *F* -ā\ [F, fr. LL *abbat-, abbas* — more at ABBOT] **:** a member of the secular clergy of France **:** anyone wearing or entitled to wear the dress of a secular ecclesiastic — used chiefly as a title

ab·be condenser \ˈäbə-, ˈabē-\ *n, usu cap A* [after Ernst *Abbe* †1905 Ger. physicist] **:** an adjustable substage lens used as a condenser for a compound microscope

ab·be refractometer \ˈäbə-, ˈabē-\ *n, usu cap A* [after Ernst *Abbe*] **:** a refractometer in which the critical angle for total reflection at the interface of a film of a liquid between two similar glass prisms is utilized in determining the index of refraction

ab·bess \ˈabəs\ *n* -ES [ME *abbesse*, fr. OF *abbesse, abaesse*, fr. LL *abbatissa*, fem. of *abbat-, abbas* abbot — more at ABBOT] **:** a woman who is the superior of a convent of nuns

ab·bet·din *or* **ab·beth·din** \ˌäv,bätˈdēn\ *n* -s *often cap* [Heb *abh-bēth-dīn*, fr. *abh* chief (of) + *bēth-dīn* court of law, fr. *bēth* house (of) + *dīn* judgment] *in the rabbinical tradition* **:** the vice-president of the Sanhedrin

ab·be·vill·i·an *also* **ab·be·vill·e·an** \(ˈ)abˈvilēən, ˌabəˈv-, -ēl-, -lyən\ *adj, usu cap* [*Abbeville*, town in Somme Dept., France + E *-ian* or *-an*] **:** of or belonging to the earliest epoch of the lower Paleolithic period characterized by the biface stone hand ax

ab·bey \ˈabē, -i\ *n* -s [ME, fr. OF *abeïe, abaïe*, fr. LL *abbatia*, abbacy, abbey, fr. *abbat-, abbas* abbot + L *-ia* — more at ABBOT] **1 :** a monastery ruled by an abbot or a convent ruled by an abbess **2 :** an abbey church ⟨buried in the ~⟩

abbeystead *or* **abbeystede** *n* -s [*abbey* + *stead* or earlier *stede*] *archaic* **:** the seat of an abbey

ab·bot \ˈabət, *usu* -əd·+V\ *n* -s [ME *abbod, abbed*, fr. OE *abbod, abbad*, fr. LL *abbat-, abbas*, fr. LGk *abbas* (also, a title of respect given to monks), fr. Aram. *abbā* father] **:** the superior of an abbey for men

abbot general *n, pl* **abbots general :** the head of a monastic order ⟨the *abbot general* of the Cistercians⟩

abbot nul·li·us \-nüˈlēəs\ *n, pl* **abbots nullius** [part trans. of NL *abbas nullius*, short for *abbas nullius dioecesis*, abbot of no diocese] **:** an abbot who is exempt from diocesan control and under direct papal jurisdiction and who exercises the authority of an ordinary within the district in which his abbey is situated

abbot of misrule *usu cap A&M* [ME *abbot of mysreule*] **:** LORD OF MISRULE 1

abbot of unreason *usu cap A&U* [ME *abbot of unresoun*] **:** an elected leader in old Scottish popular revels — compare LORD OF MISRULE

abbot primate *n, pl* **abbot primates** *or* **abbots primate :** the representative head of all Benedictine congregations

ab·bot·ship \ˈ==,ship\ *n* -s [ME, fr. *abbot* + *-ship*] **:** ABBACY

abbott-miller tube *n, usu cap A&M* **:** MILLER-ABBOTT TUBE

abbozzo *var of* ABOZZO

¹**ab·bre·vi·ate** \əˈbrēvē,āt, aˈb-, *usu* -ad·+V\ *vt* -ED/-ING/-S [ME *abbreviaten*, fr. LL *abbreviatus*, past part. of *abbreviare* — more at ABRIDGE] **:** to make briefer **:** SHORTEN: **a :** to reduce the length of (as a book) by omitting some parts **:** ABRIDGE ⟨~ a novel for very young readers⟩ **b :** to shorten by bringing to an end earlier than that planned or expected **:** cut short ⟨the ceremony, held during the annual Alumni Day, was *abbreviated* by rain —*N. Y. Times*⟩ **c :** to reduce (as an object or a form) in size or complexity by contraction or simplification ⟨in all these systems there was more or less tendency to ~ the pictures, to contract them to a few strokes —A.L.Kroeber⟩ **d :** to reduce (as a word or phrase) to a shorter form intended to stand for the whole ⟨~ *building* as *bldg*⟩ ⟨*United States of America* is commonly *abbreviated* to *U.S.A.*⟩ — compare ABBREVIATION **syn** see SHORTEN

²**ab·bre·vi·ate** \-,ət, -,āt\ *adj* [LL *abbreviatus*] **:** SHORTENED **:** relatively short **:** ABBREVIATED

³**ab·bre·vi·ate** \-,āt\ *n* -s [LL *abbreviatus*, past part.] *Scots law* **:** ABRIDGMENT, ABSTRACT

abbreviated *adj* **1 :** made briefer **:** SHORTENED **2 :** relatively short **:** shorter than others of its kind regarded as normal or conventional ⟨no adornment except an ~ French tower —*Amer. Guide Series: Conn.*⟩ ⟨an ~ dinner dress —*Mademoiselle*⟩

abbreviated number *n* **:** a number from which significant figures are omitted beyond a certain point determined by the degree of approximation desired or of accuracy attainable (as *5.667* for 5⅔ or *93,000,000* for the mean distance in miles to the sun)

ab·bre·vi·a·tion \ə,==ˈāshən\ *n* -s [ME *abreviacioun*, fr. MF *abbreviation*, fr. LL *abbreviation-, abbreviatio*, fr. *abbreviatus* + L *-ion-, -io* -ion] **1 :** the act or result of abbreviating **:** reduction in length or content **:** ABRIDGMENT ⟨our law, which shrinks from any ~ of the span of life —B.N.Cardozo⟩ ⟨~, leading to the omission of essential explanation —*Economist*⟩ **2 a :** a shortened form of a written word or phrase used for brevity in place of the whole made commonly by omission of letters from one or more parts of the whole (as *abbr* for *abbreviation*, *amt* for *amount*, *bldg* for *building*, *doz* or *dz* for *dozen*, *recd* for *received*, *H.E.* for *His Eminence* and *His Excellency*, *N.Y.* for *New York*, *r.p.m.* or *RPM* for *revolutions per minute*) sometimes showing substitution or other alteration in the part or parts retained (as *bbl* for *barrel*, *cwt* for *hundredweight*, *oz* for *ounce*, *Xmas* for *Christmas*) and sometimes doubling of initial letters to show plural form (as *ff* for *folios*, *pp* for *pages*, *SS* for *Saints*) — often extended to include signs and symbols (as ÷ for *divided by*, & for *and*, $ for *dollar*); compare CONTRACTION, SIGN, SYMBOL **b :** a shortened form of a spoken word or phrase (as *Smiffle* for *Smithfield*, *auto* for *automobile*) **3 a :** a device used in a music score as a direction (as *pp.*, *con 8 va*) **b :** a symbol used to shorten music notation by representing repeated notes or groups of notes **4 :** any convenient spoken or written short form or simple substitute for an understood or stipulated whole ⟨the phrase "civil rights" is an ~ for a whole complex of relationships —*Pres. Truman's Committee on Civil Rights*⟩ **5 :** loss in the course of evolution of the final stages of the ancestral ontogenetic pattern — compare ACCELERATION, FETALIZATION

ab·bre·vi·a·tor \əˈ==,ād·ə(r), -ātə-\ *n* -s **:** one that abbreviates

ab·bre·vi·a·ture \-vēə,chü(ə)r\ *n* -s [ML *abbreviatura*, fr. LL *abbreviatus* (past part. of *abbreviare* to abbreviate) + L *-ura* -ure — more at ABBREVIATE] **1** *obs* **:** ABBREVIATION **2 :** ABRIDGMENT, COMPENDIUM, ABSTRACT

abbs *pl of* ABB

abc \ˌā,bēˈsē, ˌābēˈsē\ *n, pl* **abc's** *or* **abcs** \-ˈsēz\ *usu cap A & B & C* **1 a :** ALPHABET ⟨before I knew my *ABC* —A.L. Guérard⟩ — usu. used in pl. ⟨said his *ABC's* over and over —Mark Derby⟩ **b :** the rudiments of reading, writing, and spelling — usu. used in pl. ⟨a worker learned in little more than his *ABC's* —H.A.Overstreet⟩ **2 :** ABECEDARIUS **3** *obs* **:** a primer containing the alphabet and teaching the elements of reading **4 a :** the rudiments of any field of knowledge or practice ⟨the *ABC* of piano playing—H.W.Van Loon⟩ **b :** the first or basic principle ⟨distrust of everybody became the *ABC* of ordinary prudence in daily life —Willi Frischauer⟩ **5** *Brit* **:** an alphabetical guidebook of railway stations and their train service

ABC *abbr* atomic, biological, and chemical

ab·cha·la·zal \ˌabkəˈlāzəl\ *adj* [¹*ab-* + *chalazal*] **:** located or facing away from the chalaza of a seed — compare CHALAZAL

ab·cou·lomb \(ˈ)abˈkü,läm, -lōm\ *n* -s [ISV ²*ab-* + *coulomb*] **:** the cgs electromagnetic unit quantity of electricity equal to 10 coulombs and being the charge that passes in one second through any cross section of a conductor carrying a steady current of one abampere — compare AB- table

abc soil \ˌā,bēˈsē-\ *n, usu cap A & B & C* **:** a soil that has a well-differentiated profile, the A-, B-, and C-horizons being well developed

abd *abbr* abdicated

ab·der·hal·den reaction \ˈäpdə(r),häldən-\ *n, usu cap A* [trans. of G *Abderhaldensche reaktion*, after Emil *Abderhalden* †1950 Swiss chemist & physiologist] **:** the occurrence in body fluids of proteolytic enzymes specific for foreign proteins introduced into the body parenterally

ab·de·ri·an \(ˈ)abˈdirēən\ *adj, usu cap* [*Abdera*, city of ancient Thrace (fr. Gk *Abdēra*) + E *-ian*] **1 :** of or belonging to Abdera or to its inhabitants **2 :** FOOLISH ⟨~ laughter⟩

ab·de·rite \ˈabdə,rīt\ *n* -s *usu cap* [L *Abderita, Abderites*, fr. Gk *Abdēritēs*, fr. *Abdēra*, whose inhabitants were reputedly stupid + Gk *-itēs* -ite] **1 :** a native or inhabitant of Abdera **2 :** SIMPLETON, SCOFFER

ab·di·ca·ble \ˈabdəkəbəl\ *adj* [abdicate + *-able*] **:** that may be abdicated ⟨~ responsibilities⟩

ab·di·cate \ˈabdə,kāt, *usu* -ād·+V\ *vb* -ED/-ING/-S [L *abdicatus*, past part. of *abdicare*, fr. *ab-* ¹ab- + *dicare* to proclaim — more at DICTION] *vt* **1 :** DISOWN, DISINHERIT ⟨a father who ~*s* his son⟩ **2** *obs* **:** to separate (oneself) formally from or divest (oneself) of ⟨the ruler *abdicated* himself from the government⟩ **3 :** to cast off **:** DISCARD ⟨~ an opinion⟩ **4 :** to relinquish formally (as sovereign power) **:** RENOUNCE **:** lay down **:** SURRENDER ~ *vi* **:** to renounce a throne, high office, dignity, or function ⟨leadership that ~*s*⟩

ab·di·ca·tion \ˌabdəˈkāshən\ *n* -s [L *abdication-, abdicatio*, fr. *abdicatus* + *-ion-, -io* -ion] **:** act of abdicating **:** RENUNCIATION, SURRENDER

ab·di·ca·tor \ˈabdə,kād·ə(r), -ātə-\ *n* -s **:** one that abdicates

ab·do·men \ˈabdəmən; abˈdōmən, əb-\ *n, pl* **abdo·mens** \-nz\ *also* **abdom·i·na** \abˈdämənə, əb-\ [MF & L; MF, fr. L; perh. akin to L *abdere* to conceal, fr. *ab-* ¹ab- + *-dere* to put — more at DO] **1 a :** the part of the body, excepting the back, between the thorax and the pelvis or in certain lower vertebrates between the cardiac and caudal regions **:** BELLY **b :** the cavity of this part of the trunk lined by the peritoneum, enclosed by the body walls, the diaphragm, and the pelvic floor, and containing the stomach, intestines, liver, and other visceral organs **c :** the portion of this cavity between the diaphragm and the brim of the pelvis — distinguished from *pelvic cavity* **2 a :** the posterior often elongated region of the body behind the thorax in arthropods consisting of up to 10 segments in insects or of 7 or less in crustaceans and being usu. unsegmented in arachnids — see INSECT illustration **b :** the section of the zooid of a compound ascidian next behind the branchial sac

abdomin- *or* **abdomino-** *comb form* [L *abdomin-, abdomen*] **:** abdomen **:** abdominal ⟨*abdomin*algia⟩ ⟨*abdomino*perineal⟩ ⟨*abdomino*cardiac⟩

ab·dom·i·nal \ab'dämən°l, əb-\ *adj* [F, fr. *abdomin-* + *-al*] **1 :** of or belonging to the abdomen **:** VENTRAL ⟨~ muscle⟩ **2** *of a fish* **:** having the pelvic or ventral fins under the abdomen and behind the pectoral fins
²abdominal \"\ *n* -s **:** an abdominal element (as a vein or muscle)
abdominal fin *n* **:** one of the posterior paired fins of fishes **:** PELVIC FIN
ab·dom·i·nal·ly *adv* **:** in the area of the abdomen
abdominal pore *n* **:** an excretory usu. paired aperture opening within or behind the cloacal region in many fishes and affording communication between the abdominal cavity and the exterior
abdominal pouch *n* **:** MARSUPIUM 1
abdominal region *n* **:** one of the nine areas into which the abdomen is divided by imaginary planes, two vertical through the middle of Poupart's ligament and two horizontal through the junction of the ninth rib and costal cartilage and through the top of the iliac crest — compare EPIGASTRIC, HYPOCHONDRIAC, HYPOGASTRIC, INGUINAL, LUMBAR, UMBILICAL

abdominal regions: *1* epigastric; *2* right hypochondriac; *3* left hypochondriac; *4* right lumbar; *5* umbilical; *6* left lumbar; *7* right iliac; *8* hypogastric; *9* left iliac

abdominal respiration *n* **:** DIAPHRAGMATIC RESPIRATION
abdominal rib *n* **:** any of the riblike structures extending across the abdomen beneath the skin in certain reptiles
abdominal ring *n* **:** either of two external and internal openings in the fasciae of the abdominal muscles on either side, being the outlet and inlet of the inguinal canal, giving passage to the spermatic cord in the male and the round ligament in the female, and constituting a frequent site of hernia formation
ab·dom·i·no·per·i·ne·al resection \ab¦dämə(,)nō,perə¦nēəl-, əb-\ *n* [*abdomin-* + *perineal*] **:** resection of a part of the lower bowel together with adjacent lymph nodes through abdominal and perineal incisions
ab·dom·i·nous \ab'dämənəs, əb-\ *adj* [L *abdomin-*, *abdomen* + E *-ous*] **:** big-bellied
ab·duce \ab'd(y)üs, əb-\ *vt* -ED/-ING/-S [L *abducere* — more at ABDUCT] **:** ABDUCT ⟨*abducing* the forelimb⟩
ab·du·cens nerve \-,senz-\ *also* **abducent nerve** *or* **abducens** *n, pl* **abducen·tes** \,=(,)='sen(,)tēz\ [L *abducent-*, *abducens*, pres. part. of *abducere*] **:** either of the 6th pair of cranial nerves, being a motor nerve arising beneath the floor of the 4th ventricle and supplying the external rectus muscle of the eye
ab·du·cent \(')ab¦d(y)üs°nt, əb'd-\ *adj* [L *abducent-*, *abducens*, pres. part. of *abducere*] *of a muscle* **:** ABDUCTING — opposed to *adducent*
ab·duct \ab'dəkt, əb-\ *vt* -ED/-ING/-S [L *abductus*, past part. of *abducere* lit., to lead away, fr. *ab-* ¹ab- + *ducere* to lead — more at TOW (pull)] **1 :** to carry (a person) off by force **:** lead (a child) away wrongfully — compare ABDUCTION, KIDNAP **2** [back-formation fr. *abduction*] **:** to draw (as a limb) away from a position near or parallel to the median axis of the body ⟨the peroneus longus extends, ~*s*, and everts the foot —C.R.Bardeen⟩ ⟨the deltoid muscle plays a major part in ~*ing* the arm⟩; *also* **:** to separate (similar parts) ⟨~ adjoining fingers⟩
ab·duc·tion \ab'dəkshən, əb-\ *n* -s [in sense 1, fr. F, fr. L *abductus* + F *-ion*; in sense 2, fr. LL *abduction-*, *abductio*, fr. L *abductus* + *-ion-*, *-io* -ion; in sense 3, fr. NL *abduction-*, *abductio* (trans. of Gk *apagōgē*), fr. L *abductus* + *-ion-*, *-io* -ion] **1 :** the action of abducting or condition of being abducted ⟨~ of a limb⟩ **2 :** the unlawful carrying away of a man's wife or child or ward for the purpose of marriage or immoral intercourse — variously defined in statutory law but generally stated to include taking away or detention of a woman under a certain age, usu. 16 or 18, with or without her consent or knowledge of her age; compare KIDNAP **3 :** a syllogism in which the major premise is evident but the minor premise and therefore the conclusion only probable — called also *apagoge*
ab·duc·tive \(')ab¦dəktiv, əb'd-\ *adj* [*abduction* + *-ive*] *logic* **:** involving abduction
ab·duc·tive·ly *adv* **:** in an abductive manner
¹ab·duc·tor \ab'dəktə(r) *also* -,tó(ə)r *or* -,tō(ə)\ *n, pl* **ab·duc·to·res** \,ab,dək'tōr(,)ēz, -'ó-\ *or* **abductors** [NL, fr. L *abductus* + *-or*] **:** a muscle that draws a part away from the median line of the body or from the axis of an extremity
²abductor \"\ *n* -s [*abduct* + *-or*] **:** one that abducts ⟨protecting women from ~*s*⟩
abe \ə'bē\ *vi* [prob. fr. *a-* (in *alone*) + *be*] *dial Brit* **:** BE — used only as infinitive ⟨let ~⟩
abeam \ə'-\ *adv (or adj)* [¹*a-* + *beam*] **:** on a line forming a right angle with a ship's keel **:** opposite the middle of a ship's side ⟨at noon we came ~ of the island⟩ ⟨the tug lay directly ~ of us⟩
abear \ə'ba(ə)(ə)r, -be(ə)r\ *vt* [ME *aberen*, fr. OE *āberan*, fr. *ā-*, *ar-* (perfective prefix) + *beran* to bear; akin to OE *or-* out of, OHG *ir-*, *ur-*, *ur*, ON *ūr-*, *ør-*, *ūr*, Goth *us-*, *us*, and prob. to OE *ūt* out — more at OUT, BEAR] *chiefly dial* **:** ENDURE, ABIDE — usu. used with *can* and negative ⟨I can't ~ a sulk —H.G.Wells⟩
¹abe·ce·dar·i·an \,ābē(,)sē'da(a)rēən\ *n* -s [*abecedary* + *-an*, n. suffix] **1 :** one that is learning the rudiments of something (as the alphabet) **2** *archaic* **:** one that teaches the alphabet and the rudiments of learning **3** *cap* **:** one of a 16th century Anabaptist sect that despised human learning on the ground that the illiterate needed no more than the guidance of the Holy Spirit to interpret Scripture
²abecedarian \¦==(,)=¦===\ *adj* [*abecedary* + *-an*, adj. suffix] **1 :** having reference to the alphabet **:** alphabetically arranged **:** RUDIMENTARY **2 :** of or relating to an abecedarius **:** resembling an abecedarius
abe·ce·dar·i·um \,==(,)='=rēəm\ *n, pl* **abecedar·ia** \-rēə\ [ML] **:** ALPHABET BOOK, PRIMER
abe·ce·dar·i·us \-rēəs\ *n* -ES [NL, fr. LL, adj.] **:** a poem in which the lines or stanzas begin with the letters of the alphabet in regular order (as the 119th Psalm in Hebrew or Chaucer's *A B C*)
¹abe·ce·da·ry \,ā(,)bē'sēdərē\ *n* -ES [ME, fr. ML *abecedarium* alphabet, primer, fr. neut. of LL *abecedarius* of the alphabet, fr. the names of the letters *a* + *b* + *c* + *d* + L *-arius* -ary] **1 :** ABECEDARIUM **2 :** ABECEDARIAN
²abecedary \¦=(,)=¦===\ *adj* **:** ABECEDARIAN
abed \ə'=\ *adv (or adj)* [ME *abedde*, fr. earlier *on bedde*, fr. OE, fr. *on* + *bedde*, dat. of *bedd* bed — more at BED] **:** in bed ⟨sick ~⟩ ⟨~ and asleep⟩
abegg's rule \'ä,begz-, -eks-\ *n, cap A* [after Richard *Abegg* †1910 Ger. chemist] **:** a rule in chemistry: the sum of the hydrogen valence and the maximum oxygen valence of a chemical element is often equal to 8 [as of silicon in SiH_4 (−4) and SiO_2 (+4) or of sulfur in H_2S (−2) and H_2SO_4 (+6)]
abeigh \ə'bēk\ *adv* [prob. ¹*a-* + ON *beigr*, *beygr* fear; akin to ON *beygja* to bend — more at BOW] *Scot* **:** cautiously aloof
abel·am \ə'beləm\ *n, pl* **abelam** *or* **abelams** *usu cap* [native name in New Guinea] **1 :** a Papuan people in the Sepik district, Territory of New Guinea **2 :** a member of the Abelam people
abele \ə'bēl, ə'bāl, 'ābəl\ *n* -s [D *abeel*, fr. MD, fr. ONF *abiel*, irreg. fr. L *albus* white — more at ALB] **:** WHITE POPLAR 1 a
abe·lia \ə'bēlyə, ā'-, -lēə\ *n* [NL, fr. Clarke *Abel* †1826 Eng. botanist + NL *-ia*] **1** *cap* **:** a genus of chiefly eastern Asian shrubs (family Caprifoliaceae) having opposite leaves and white, pink, or reddish flowers in cymes **2** -s **:** a plant of the genus *Abelia*
abel·ite \'ābə,līt\ *n* -s [Sir Frederick *Abel* †1902 Eng. chemist + *-ite*] **:** an explosive consisting essentially of ammonium nitrate and a nitro derivative of some aromatic hydrocarbon
abel·mos·chus \,ābəl'mäskəs, '==,==\ *n, cap* [NL, fr. Ar *abū-l-misk* father (source) of the musk] **:** a genus of tropical coarse herbs (family Malvaceae) having large lobed leaves, a spathelike calyx, and often yellow flowers
abel·mosk \'ābəl,mäsk\ *also* **abel·musk** \-,məsk\ *n* -s [NL *abelmoschus*] **:** a bushy herb (*Hibiscus moschatus*) native to tropical Asia and the East Indies whose musky seeds are used in perfumery and to flavor coffee
abel test \'ābəl-\ *n, usu cap A* [after Sir Frederick *Abel*] **1 :** a test for determining the flash point of a volatile oil by use of a closed cup in which the oil is heated over a fixed flame and by use of a small movable flame that passes at regular intervals of temperature over the surface of the oil **2 :** a test for the stability of smokeless powder and similar explosives in which a ground sample is heated in a test tube with potassium iodide–starch paper, the time required for discoloring the paper being the measure of the stability
abel·tree \'ābəl·,trē\ *n* [part trans., part modif. of D *abeelboom*, fr. *abeel* white poplar + *boom* tree — more at ABELE] **:** WHITE POPLAR 1 a
ab·em·bry·on·ic \¦a,bembrē¦änik\ *adj* [¹*ab-* + *embryonic*] *of an embryonic structure* **:** remote from the embryo proper; *sometimes* **:** VEGETATIVE
abenaki *usu cap, var of* ABNAKI
abend·mu·sik \'äbənt(,)mü,zēk\ *n, pl* **abendmusi·ken** \-kən\ [G, lit., evening music, fr. *abend* evening + *musik* music] **:** an evening performance of music usu. of a religious or semisacred character **:** the music for such a performance
a be·ne pla·ci·to \¦ä,benē'plächə,tō\ *adv* [It] **:** at pleasure **:** ad libitum — used as a direction in music
aben·len \ə'ben,len\ *n, pl* **abenlen** *or* **abenlens** *usu cap* [native name in the Philippines] **1 :** a predominantly pagan Negrito people in the Zambales mountains of western Luzon, Philippines **2 :** a member of the Abenlen people
¹ab·er·deen \¦abə(r)¦dēn\ *adj, usu cap* [fr. *Aberdeen*, city & county in Scotland] **1 :** of or from the city of Aberdeen, Scotland **:** of the kind or style prevalent in the city of Aberdeen **2 :** ABERDEENSHIRE
²aberdeen \"\ *n* -s *usu cap* **1 :** a fishhook of a wide evenly curved pattern — see FISHHOOK illustration **2** *or* **aberdeen terrier :** SCOTTISH TERRIER
aberdeen an·gus \-dē'naŋgəs, -aiŋ-\ *n* [fr. *Aberdeen* & *Angus*, counties in Scotland where the breed originated] **1** *usu cap both As* **:** a breed of black hornless beef cattle originating in Scotland **2** *often cap both As* **:** an animal of the Aberdeen Angus breed
ab·er·deen·shire \,=='=,shi(ə)r, -,shər\ *adj, usu cap* **:** of or from the county of Aberdeen, Scotland **:** of the kind or style prevalent in the county of Aberdeen
ab·er·de·vine *also* **ab·er·da·vine** *or* **ab·er·du·vine** \'abə(r)-də,vīn, ,==='=\ *n* -s [origin unknown] **:** SISKIN 1
¹ab·er·do·ni·an \,abə(r)'dōnyən, -nēən\ *n* -s *cap* [ML *Aberdonia* Aberdeen + E *-an*] **:** a native or resident of Aberdeen, esp. Aberdeen, Scotland
²aberdonian \¦==¦=(=)=\ *adj, usu cap* **:** of or relating to Aberdeen, Scotland
ab·er·ne·thy biscuit \'abə(r),nēthē, -ne-\ *n, usu cap A* [prob. after John *Abernethy* †1831 Eng. surgeon who treated maladies by diet] **:** a hard biscuit containing caraway seeds
ab·er·rance \(')a'berən(t)s\ *or* **ab·er·ran·cy** \-sē, -i\ *n, pl* **aberrances** *or* **aberrancies** [obs. E *aberr* to stray (fr. L *aberrare*) + *-ance* or *-ancy*] **:** DEVIATION
¹ab·er·rant \(')a¦berənt\ *adj* [L *aberrant-*, *aberrans*, pres. part. of *aberrare* to wander from the way, go astray, fr. *ab-* ¹ab- + *errare* to wander, go astray, err — more at ERR] **1 :** straying from the right or normal way **:** deviating from truth, rectitude, propriety **2 :** deviating from the usual or natural type **:** EXCEPTIONAL, ABNORMAL
²aberrant \"\ *n* -s **1 :** an aberrant natural group, individual, or structure; *esp* **:** an individual with a chromosome number atypical for its species **2 :** a person whose behavior departs substantially from the standards for behavior in his group **:** DEVIANT, DEVIATE
ab·er·rant·ly *adv* **:** in an aberrant manner
ab·er·ra·tion \,abə'rāshən\ *n* -s [L *aberratus* (past part. of *aberrare*) + E *-ion*] **1 :** act of wandering away or of going astray **:** deviation from truth or a moral standard, from the natural state, or from a normal type ⟨~*s* of character⟩ ⟨~*s* of structure⟩ **2 :** failure of a mirror, refracting surface, or lens to produce exact point-to-point correspondence between an object and its image **3 :** unsoundness of the mind; *esp* **:** unsoundness insufficient to constitute insanity **4 :** a small periodic change of apparent position in the stars and other heavenly bodies due to the combined effect of the motion of light and the motion of the observer **5 :** an aberrant organ or individual **:** SPORT 6
ab·er·ra·tion·al \¦=='=shən°l, -shnəl\ *adj* **:** characterized by aberration
ab·er·ra·tive \'==,rād·iv\ *adj* [*aberration* + *-ive*] **:** having or showing a tendency to aberration
abert's towhee \'ābə(r)ts-\ *also* **abert's finch** *or* **abert's pipilo** *n, usu cap A* [after J. W. *Abert* †1897 Am. soldier and scientist] **:** a rather large distinctly brown towhee (*Pipilo aberti*) of southwestern No. America
ab·es·sive \(')a¦besiv\ *adj* [L *abesse* to be absent + E *-ive* — more at ABSENT] *of a grammatical case* **:** denoting absence or lack
abet \ə'bet *also* a'-; *usu* -ed· + V\ *vt* **abetted**; **abetted**; **abetting**; **abets** [ME *abetten*, fr. MF *abeter*, fr. OF, fr. *a-* (fr. L *ad-*) + *beter* to bait, of Gmc origin; akin to OHG *beizen* to bait — more at BAIT] **1 :** to incite, encourage, instigate, or countenance — now usu. used disparagingly ⟨~ the commission of a crime⟩ **2 :** to assist or support in the achievement of a purpose ⟨the singer was ably *abetted* by her skillful accompanist⟩ **syn** see INCITE
abet·ment \-tmənt\ *n* -s [ME *abetement*, fr. AF, fr. OF *abeter* + *-ment*] **:** act of abetting ⟨~ of crime⟩
abet·tor *or* **abet·ter** \-ed·ə(r), -etə-\ *n* -s [*abettor* fr. AF *abettour*, fr. OF *abeter* + *-our* -or; *abetter* fr. *abet* + *-er*] **:** one that abets
ab ex·tra \(')a'bekstrə\ *adv* [LL] **:** from without
abey·ance \ə'bāən(t)s\ *n* -s [MF *abeance* desire, expectation, fr. *abaer*, *abair* to desire (fr. *a-* — fr. L *ad-* — + *baer*, *bair* to yawn, gape, stare, desire, fr. ML *batare* to yawn, perh. of imit. origin) + *-ance*] **1 :** a lapse in succession during which there is no person in existence in whom a freehold estate, dignity, or title is vested ⟨a peerage revived after an ~ of many years⟩ — usu. used with *in* ⟨the estate was in ~⟩ **2 :** temporary inactivity or suppression **:** cessation or suspension (as of a customary practice) ⟨statutes fallen into ~⟩ ⟨a rule in ~ since 1935⟩ — used chiefly in the phrases *in abeyance* or *into abeyance*
abey·an·cy \-sē, -i\ *n* -ES **:** ABEYANCE
abey·ant \-ənt\ *adj* [back-formation fr. *abeyance*] **:** in abeyance **syn** see LATENT
ab·far·ad \(')ab'fa,rad, -,rəd\ *n* [ISV ²*ab-* + *farad*] **:** a cgs electromagnetic unit of capacitance equal to one billion farads that measures the capacitance of a condenser that when charged to a potential difference of one abvolt has a charge of one abcoulomb — compare AB- table
ab·ge·sang \'äpgə,zäŋ\ *n* -s *usu cap* [G, fr. *ab-* down, from + *gesang* song] **:** EPISTROPHE; *specif* **:** the concluding section of the medieval bar
ab·hen·ry \(')ab'henrē\ *n* [ISV ²*ab-* + *henry*] **:** a cgs electromagnetic unit of inductance equal to one billionth of a henry that measures the self-inductance of a circuit or the mutual inductance of two circuits in which the variation of current at the rate of one abampere per second results in an induced electromotive force of one abvolt — compare AB- table
abhi·na·ya \ə'binəyə\ *n* -s [Skt, acting, dramatic action] **:** the expressive use of face or hands characteristic of the kathakali dance style of India
abhi·se·ka \ə,bē'shākə\ *n* -s [Skt *abhiseka*, fr. *abhiṣecate* he sprinkles, fr. *abhi* to, toward + *secate* he pours — more at BY, SACK (wine)] *India* **:** LUSTRATION; *also* **:** coronation of a king
abhominable *adj* [alter. (influenced by L *ab homine* from the man, its supposed etymology) of *abominable*] *obs* **:** ABOMINABLE
ab·hor \əb'hō(ə)r, ab-, -ó(ə)r\ *vt* **abhorred**; **abhorred**; **abhorring**; **abhors** [ME *abhorren*, fr. L *abhorrēre*, fr. *ab-* ¹ab- + *horrēre* to bristle, shiver, shudder — more at HORROR] **1 :** to regard with repugnance **:** detest extremely **:** LOATHE ⟨they ~ the thought of going to war⟩ **2** *obs* **:** to fill with horror or disgust ⟨mine own clothes shall ~ me — Job 9:31 (AV)⟩ **3 :** to turn aside or keep away from esp. in scorn **:** AVOID, REJECT ⟨the university should ~ mediocrity —Walter Moberly⟩ **syn** see HATE
ab·hor·rence \-hórən(t)s, -här-\ *n* -s **1 :** the act or state of abhorring **:** the feeling of one who abhors **:** LOATHING ⟨the good man has an ~ of evil —M.H.Weseen⟩ **2 :** one that is abhorred **:** object of loathing ⟨disguise of every sort is my ~ —Jane Austen⟩
abhorrency *n* -ES *obs* **:** ABHORRENCE
ab·hor·rent \-hórənt, -här-\ *adj* [L *abhorrent-*, *abhorrens*, pres. part. of *abhorrēre*] **1 a** *archaic* **:** strongly opposed **:** at variance — used with *from* ⟨a man most ~ from violence⟩ **b :** feeling or showing abhorrence **:** LOATHING, ABHORRING — used with *of* ⟨~ of compromises⟩ **2 :** not in accord **:** not agreeable **:** CONFLICTING, DISCORDANT — used with *to* ⟨a strange notion ~ to their scheme of things⟩ **3 :** DETESTABLE, REPUGNANT ⟨a repugnant, ~, and outrageous procedure for hiring government servants —Wayne Morse⟩ **syn** see HATEFUL
ab·hor·rent·ly *adv* **:** in an abhorrent manner
ab·hor·rer \-hórə(r)\ *n* -s *sometimes cap* **:** one of the signers of an address to Charles II of England in 1679 in which those who had petitioned for the reconvening of Parliament were abhorred and condemned
abib \ä'vēv\ *n* -s *usu cap* [Heb *ābhībh*, lit., ear of grain] **:** the 1st month of the ancient Hebrew calendar coming in the spring and corresponding to Nisan — see MONTH table
abid·ance \ə'bīd°n(t)s\ *n* -s **1 :** a state of abiding or staying **:** CONTINUANCE **2 :** COMPLIANCE ⟨~ by rules⟩
abide \ə'bīd\ *vb* **abode** \-bōd\ *or* **abid·ed** \-bīdəd\ **abode** *or* **abided** *also* **abid·den** \-bid°n\ **abiding**; **abides** [ME *abiden*, fr. OE *ābīdan*, fr. *ā-* (perfective prefix) + *bīdan* to bide, wait — more at ABEAR, BIDE] *vt* **1** *archaic* **a :** to wait for **:** await expectantly **:** watch for **:** EXPECT ⟨I will ~ the coming of my lord —Alfred Tennyson⟩ **b :** to stand ready for **:** AWAIT — used of things awaiting persons ⟨the fate which ~*s* him⟩ **2 a** *obs* **:** to stand up under **:** endure or undergo (a hard trial or task) ⟨material able to ~ hard use⟩ **b :** to endure without yielding **:** await defiantly **:** WITHSTAND, FACE ⟨~ the onrush of the enemy⟩ ⟨~ one's doom⟩ **c :** to endure or bear patiently **:** TOLERATE, STAND — used in negative construction ⟨cannot ~ such people⟩ ⟨can't ~ the taste of caraway⟩ sometimes with *to* and the infinitive ⟨cannot ~ to stay in one position for long —T.B.Costain⟩ **3 :** to await submissively **:** accept without question or objection ⟨unwilling to ~ the decision of the court⟩ **:** submit to ⟨works securely established among the classics have had to ~ the question of a new criticism⟩ **4** [by folk etymology fr. *aby*] **:** to atone for **:** pay for **:** suffer for ⟨dearly I ~ that boast so vain —John Milton⟩ **~** *vi* **1 :** to wait in expectation or before proceeding **:** TARRY, DELAY, STOP ⟨the sawyer did not participate . . . but *abided* at a little distance —Charles Dickens⟩ ⟨we shall ~ till the battle is won —Rudyard Kipling⟩ **2 a :** to be or remain stable or fixed in some state or constant in some relationship **:** CONTINUE ⟨let every man ~ in the same calling wherein he was called — 1 Cor 7:20 (AV)⟩ ⟨a love that ~*s* with him all his days⟩ **b :** to continue to be **:** LAST, ENDURE ⟨though many features were *abiding*, the changes were much felt⟩ **3 :** to be left **:** REMAIN ⟨tho' much is taken, much ~*s* —Alfred Tennyson⟩ **4 :** to continue in a place **:** have one's abode **:** DWELL ⟨I repented my rashness in venturing to ~ in town —Daniel Defoe⟩ **syn** see BEAR, CONTINUE, STAY — **abide by :** to act or behave in accordance with or obedience to (as a rule or promise) ⟨accept a limitation and *abide by* it⟩ **:** conform to **:** acquiesce in ⟨*abide by* a decision⟩
abid·ing \ə'bīdiŋ, -ēŋ\ *adj* [ME, fr. pres. part. of *abiden* to abide] **:** continuing or persisting in the same state without changing or diminishing **:** CONTINUING, ENDURING ⟨the theater has ~ value and importance⟩ **:** great or lasting ⟨music is his ~ passion⟩ — **abid·ing·ly** *adv*
ab·i·djan \¦abə¦jän\ *adj, usu cap* [fr. *Abidjan*, Ivory Coast] **:** of or relating to Abidjan, capital of the Ivory Coast **:** of the kind or style prevalent in Abidjan
ab·i·ence \'abēən(t)s\ *n* -s *psychol* **:** tendency to withdraw from a stimulus object or situation — opposed to *adience*
ab·i·ent \'abēənt\ *adj* [L *abient-*, *abiens*, pres. part. of *abire* to go away, fr. *ab-* ¹ab- + *-ire* to go — more at ISSUE] *psychol* **:** characterized by avoidance or withdrawal ⟨an ~ response⟩ — opposed to *adient*
abi·es \'ābē,ēz, 'ab-\ *n* [NL, fr. L, silver fir] **1** *cap* **:** a genus of north temperate evergreen trees which are the true firs (family Pinaceae) distinguished from spruces by flattish leaves, smooth circular leaf scars, and erect cones — see BALSAM FIR, FIR **2** *pl* **abies :** a tree of the genus *Abies*
ab·i·e·tate \'abēə,tāt\ *n* -s [ISV *abiet-* (fr. *abietic acid*) + *-ate*] **1 :** a salt or ester of abietic acid **2 :** RESINATE — used chiefly commercially
ab·i·e·tene \-,tēn\ *n* -s [*abietic* + *-ene*] **:** the hydrocarbon mixture, chiefly $C_{19}H_{30}$ with two double bonds in the molecule, that results from heating resin acids
ab·i·et·ic acid \¦abē¦ed·ik-\ *n* [ISV *abiet-*, (fr. L *abiet-*, *abies* silver fir) + *-ic*] **:** a colorless crystalline tricyclic acid $C_{19}H_{29}COOH$ with two double bonds that constitutes the major component of rosin, that is formed from certain other resin acids by heat and acid treatment, and that is used chiefly in making esters for plasticizers
ab·i·gail \'abə,gāl\ *n* -s *sometimes cap* [after *Abigail*, serving woman in the play *The Scornful Lady*, by Francis Beaumont †1616 and John Fletcher †1625 English dramatists] **:** a lady's waiting maid
ab·i·lene \'abə,lēn\ *adj, usu cap* [fr. *Abilene*, Tex., near where the artifacts were discovered] **:** of or belonging to a prehistoric culture of central Texas characterized by long slender roughly flaked weapon points and by scrapers and oval grinding stones
abiliment *obs var of* HABILIMENT
abil·i·ty \ə'biləd·ē, -ətē, -i\ *n* -ES [ME *abilite* suitability, aptitude, ability, fr. MF *habilité*, fr. L *habilitat-*, *habilitas* aptness, ability, fr. *habilis* fit, apt, skillful + *-itat-*, *-itas* -ity — more at ABLE] **1 :** the quality or state of being able **:** physical, mental, or legal power to perform **:** competence in doing **:** SKILL ⟨a writer's ~ to interest readers⟩ **2 :** natural talent or acquired proficiency esp. in a particular work or activity **:** APTITUDE — usu. used in pl. ⟨children whose *abilities* warrant higher education⟩
-ability *also* **-ibility** \"\ *n suffix* -ES [ME *-ablete*, *-abilite*, *-iblete*, *-ibilite*, fr. MF *-abileté*, *-abilité*, *-ibileté*, *-ibilité*, fr. L *-abilitas*, *-ibilitas*, fr. *-abilis*, *-ibilis* + *-tas* -ty] **:** capacity, fitness, or tendency to act or be acted on in a (specified) way ⟨ens*ilability*⟩ ⟨wash*ability*⟩
abi·lla \ə'bē(y)ə\ *n* -s [AmerSp] **:** the oily seed of a So. American plant (*Fevillea trilobata*) that is used in making candles
abi·lo \¦abə¦lō\ *or* **abi·lao** \-¦laù\ *n* -s [Tag] **:** BOGO
ab in·con·ve·ni·en·ti \¦a,binkən,venē'entē, -n,tī\ *adv* [NL] **:** from inconvenience or hardship — referring to a rule in law that an argument from inconvenience has great weight
ab in·i·tio \,abə'nishē,ō, -nid·ē,ō\ *adv* [L] **:** from the beginning **:** from the instant of the act ⟨an act outside one's legal competence is void *ab initio*⟩ **:** at the outset (of an inquiry or investigation) ⟨assumes *ab initio* that the idea is worthless⟩
ab in·tra \a'bintrə\ *adv* [NL] **:** from within
abio- *comb form* [²*a-* + *bio-*] **:** whatever is lifeless ⟨*abio*genesis⟩
abio·gen·e·sis \¦ā,bīō'jenəsəs\ *n, pl* **abiogene·ses** \-ə,sēz\ [NL, fr. *abio-* + L *genesis*] **:** the origination of living organisms from lifeless matter — called also *spontaneous generation*
abio·ge·net·ic \¦ā,bīōjə¦ned·ik\ *adj* [fr. NL *abiogenesis*, after E *genesis: genetic*] **:** of or relating to abiogenesis **:** originating by abiogenesis — **abio·ge·net·i·cal·ly** \-ə̇k(ə)lē\ *adv*
abi·og·e·nist \¦ā,bī'äjənəst\ *n* -s [*abiogenesis* + *-ist*] **:** one who believes that life can be produced independently of antecedent life
abi·o·log·i·cal \¦ā,bīə¦läjəkəl, -jēk-\ *adj* [²*a-* + *biological*] **:** not biological; *esp* **:** not involving or produced by organisms ⟨~ synthesis of amino acids⟩ ⟨~ oxidation⟩ — **abi·o·log·i·cal·ly** \-k(ə)lē\ *adv*
abi·ot·ic \¦ā,bī¦äd·ik\ *adj* [²*a-* + *biotic*] **1 :** characterized by the absence of life **2 :** ANTIBIOTIC 1
abio·troph·ic \¦ā,bīə¦träfik, -ōf-\ *adj* **:** relating to or involving abiotrophy ⟨the ~ nature of certain diseases⟩
abi·ot·ro·phy \¦ā,bī'ä·trəfē\ *n* -ES [ISV *abio-* + *-trophy*] **:** degeneration or loss of function or vitality in an organism or in cells or tissues not due to any apparent injury

abi·pón \ˌabəˈpän, ˌ≤≤ˈ≤\ *n, pl* **abi·po·nes** \ˌabəˈpōnēz\ *or* **abipón** *like sing*\ *usu cap* [Sp *abipón*, of AmerInd origin] **1 a :** an extinct people of Paraguay and Argentina **b :** a member of such people **2 :** the Guaicuruan language of the Abipones

abir \əˈbi(ə)r\ *n* -s [Hindi *abīr*] *India* **:** a perfumed red powder used at the Holi festival

ab·i·tibi \ˌabəˈtibē\ *n, pl* **abitibi** *or* **abitibis** *usu cap* [of Algonquian origin; akin to Fox or Ojibwa *abiʹta-bi-g*, lit., halfway across water, fr. *abiʹta* halfway + *bi* water + *-g* (locative suffix)] **1 :** an Algonkian people of the region about Lake Abitibi, Ontario **2 :** a member of the Abitibi people — compare ALGONKIAN

abi·u·ret \(ˈ)āˌbīyəˌret\ *adj* [²*a-* + *biuret*] **:** not giving the biuret reaction

¹ab·ject \ˈabˌjekt *also, esp nonattrib,* ≤ˈ≤\ *adj* [ME, fr. L *abjectus*, fr. past part. of *abicere* to cast off, fr. *ab-* ¹ab- + *-icere* (fr. *jacere* to throw) — more at JET (to spout)] **1 :** sunk to or existing in a low state or condition **2 a :** cast down in spirit **:** without spirit or pride **:** SERVILE ⟨~ knuckling down to the demands of . . . pressure groups —Elmer Rice⟩ **b :** unrelieved by any sign of independence, courage, or originality ⟨~ imitation of foreign ideas⟩ **:** showing utter resignation **:** HOPELESS, HELPLESS ⟨~ surrender⟩ ⟨~ frustration⟩ — **ab·ject·ness** *n* -ES

²abject *vt* -ED/-ING/-S [ME *abjecten*, fr. *abject*, adj.] **1** *obs* **:** to cast off or out **:** REJECT **2** *obs* **:** to cast down **:** ABASE

³ab·ject \ˈabˌjekt\ *n* -s [¹*abject*] **:** one cast off **:** OUTCAST

ab·jec·tion \abˈjekshən\ *n* -s [ME *abjeccioun*, fr. MF or LL; MF *abjection*, fr. LL *abjection-, abjectio*, fr. L *abjectus* cast down + *-ion-, -io* -ion — more at ABJECT] **1 :** a low or downcast state **:** DEGRADATION, HUMILIATION **2 :** the act of making abject: as **a :** HUMBLING ⟨I protest against this vile ~ of youth to age —G.B.Shaw⟩ **b :** a casting out or off **:** REJECTION ⟨the ~ of Satan from heaven⟩ **3 :** the discharge or casting (as of the spores of certain fungi) — compare ABSTRICTION

ab·ject·ive \(ˈ)abˈjektiv\ *adj* [²*abject* + *-ive*] **:** tending to make abject

ab·ject·ly \(ˈ)abˈjek(t)lē, -li\ *adv* [ME, fr. ¹*abject* + *-ly*] **:** in an abject manner

ab·joint \(ˈ)abˈjȯint\ *vb* [¹*ab-* + *joint*] *vt* **:** to form by cutting off (as a protuberance from a mother cell) ~ *vi* **:** to separate by means of a cross wall (as of certain cells and of fungus spores cut off from hyphal tips)

ab·judge \(ˈ)abˈjəj\ *vt* -ED/-ING/-S [¹*ab-* + *judge*; part trans. of L *abjudicare*] **:** to take away by judicial decision — opposed to *adjudge* (sense 3)

ab·junc·tion \(ˈ)abˈjəŋ(k)shən\ *n* -s [¹*ab-* + *junction*] *bot* **:** ABSTRICTION

ab·ju·ra·tion \ˌabjəˈrāshən\ *n* -s [ME *abjuracioun*, fr. ML *abjuration-, abjuratio*, fr. L *abjuratus* (past part. of *abjurare*) + *-ion-, -io* -ion] **1 :** the act of abjuring **2 :** an oath taken on the occasion of abjuring

ab·jure \abˈju̇(ə)r, əb-, -ūə\ *vt* -ED/-ING/-S [ME *abjuren*, fr. MF or L; MF *abjurer*, fr. L *abjurare*, fr. *ab-* ¹ab- + *jurare* to swear — more at JURY] **1 :** to disclaim formally or renounce upon oath ⟨solemnly ~*s* his allegiance to his former country⟩ **:** give up **:** REJECT ⟨~ his old beliefs⟩ **2 :** to take oath to leave (as a realm or country) ⟨the criminal was allowed to claim immunity by *abjuring* the realm⟩ **3 :** to abstain from **:** AVOID ⟨~ extravagant claims for a product⟩

syn RENOUNCE, FORSWEAR, RECANT, RETRACT: ABJURE indicates a firm, final rejecting or abandoning made with measured conviction and, often, signalized by oath or other formality ⟨the friar concluded with beseeching the Peruvian monarch to receive him kindly, to *abjure* the errors of his own faith, and embrace that of the Christians now proffered to him —W.H. Prescott⟩ ⟨Galileo was summoned before the Inquisition at Rome, and there he was made to *abjure* the Copernican theory —S.F.Mason⟩ RENOUNCE indicates a giving up or casting off of something previously believed, practiced, or adhered to, with some spoken or tacit indication of the change of position ⟨abandoning wife and children, home and business, and *renouncing* normal morality and humanity —G.B.Shaw⟩ ⟨he was later to *renounce* impressionism, and to quarrel with most of the impressionists —Herbert Read⟩ ⟨they made a monk of me; I did *renounce* the world, its pride and greed —Robert Browning⟩ FORSWEAR may indicate resolute rejection; it may apply to dishonorable or ill-advised rejection of that to which one should adhere ⟨Mr. Dulles grants by implication that the Peking regime is the government of China. He insists that it *forswear* the use of force in advancing its ambitions —*New Republic*⟩ ⟨support him in an apostasy, in a *forswearing* of honor and principle, for personal power —J.C.Fitzpatrick⟩ RECANT is likely to indicate rejection of a previously adhered-to belief or position accompanied by admission of error and acceptance of a sanctioned belief ⟨Shostakovich, as our newspapers have told us, has suffered from official criticism and been forced to *recant* and rewrite —W.C.Huntington⟩ ⟨if Christians *recanted* they were to be spared, but if they persisted in their faith they were to be executed —K.S.Latourette⟩ RETRACT indicates a withdrawing or calling back, often of a statement or implication to someone's discredit ⟨give the present writer an opportunity of *retracting* criticism from his own pen which he now feels to have been unjust —Richard Garnett⟩ ⟨they . . . *retract* what they have said, and say publicly that they were mistaken —Rose Macaulay⟩

ab·kar \ˈäbˌkär\ *n* -s [Per *ābkār*, fr. *āb* water, liquid (fr. OPer *āpi-*) + *-kār* doer (fr. MPer); akin to Av *āfsh* (acc. sing. *āpəm*) water, Skt *ap-*, Lith *ùpė*, OPruss *ape* river, Gk *Apia* Peloponnesus and to Skt *kāra* doing — more at KARMA] *India* **:** a wine seller **:** DISTILLER; *also* **:** one whose trade is subject to abkari tax

ab·ka·ri *also* **ab·ka·ry** \äbˈkärē\ *n* -s [Per *ābkārī*, fr. *ābkār*] **1** *India* **:** manufacture or sale of intoxicating liquors or drugs **2** *India* **:** an excise or internal revenue tax on the manufacture or sale of intoxicating liquors or drugs

ab·khas \abˈkäs\ *or* **ab·kha·sian** \-ˈkāzhən, -ˈkāzēən\ *n, pl* **abkhas** *or* **abkhasians** *usu cap* [*Abkhas* fr. Russ; *Abkhasian* fr. Russ *Abkhas* + E *-ian*] **1 a :** a Georgian people living on the eastern shore of the Black sea **b :** a member of this people **2 :** the North Caucasic language of the Abkhas people

abl *abbr* ablative

ablach \ˈabläk, ˈä-\ *n* -s [ScGael, mangled carcass, brat; akin to IrGael, carcass, corpse, carrion] *Scot* **:** an insignificant person

ab·lac·ta·tion \ˌaˌblakˈtāshən\ *n* [ME *ablactacioun*, fr. LL *ablactation-, ablactatio*, fr. L *ablactatus* (past part. of *ablactare* to wean, fr. L *ab-* ¹ab- + *lact-, lac* milk) + *-ion-, -io* -ion — more at GALAXY] **:** the act of weaning

ablare \əˈ-\ *adj* [¹*a-* + *blare*, v.] **:** BLARING ⟨with trumpets ~⟩

ablas·te·mic \ˌāˌblaˈstēmik, -em-\ *adj* [²*a-* + *blastemic*] **:** not germinal **:** incapable of blastema formation

ablas·tin \əˈblastən, (ˈ)āˈ-\ *n* -s [Gk *ablastos* not germinating + E *-in*] **:** a substance in the blood of infected animals that inhibits the reproduction of the infecting organism

ablas·tous \(ˈ)āˈblastəs\ *adj* [Gk *ablastos*] **:** having no germ or bud

ab·late \(ˈ)aˈblāt\ *vb* -ED/-ING/-S [L *ablatus* (suppletive past part. of *auferre* to remove), fr. *ab-* ¹ab- + *latus*, suppletive past part. of *ferre* to bear — more at BEAR, TOLERATE] *vt* **:** to carry away **:** remove by cutting or by erosion, melting, or evaporation ~ *vi* **:** to undergo ablation **:** become melted or vaporized and removed at a very high temperature

ab·la·tion \aˈblāshən\ *n* -s [MF & LL; MF, fr. LL *ablation-, ablatio*, fr. L *ablatus* + *-ion-, -io* -ion] **1 :** REMOVAL **2 :** removal of an organ or part by surgery ⟨~ of the appendix⟩ or of an activity by other means ⟨~ of ovarian function by radiation⟩ **3 a :** decrease in volume of ice, névé, or snow in or on a glacier primarily as a result of melting and evaporation — compare ALIMENTATION **b :** lowering of a land surface by wind erosion or weathering agents ⟨the warming of the polar seas leads to ~ of the ice caps⟩ **4 :** the process of ablating

ab·la·ti·val \ˌabləˈtīvəl\ *adj* [*ablative* + *-al*] **:** connected with the ablative case or any of the relations frequently expressed by it **:** of or belonging to the ablative case

¹ab·la·tive \ˈabləd·iv, -ətiv\ *adj* [ME, fr. MF or L; MF *ablatif*, fr. L *ablativus*, fr. *ablatus* + *-ivus* -ive] **1** *of a grammatical case* **:** expressing typically the relations of separation and source (as L *metu* in *liberari metu* "to be freed from fear"; L *ea familia* in *ea familia ortus* "descended from that family") and also frequently esp. in Latin such relations as cause (as L *gaudio* in *exsilire gaudio* "to jump for joy"), instrument (as L *pugnis* in *certare pugnis* "to fight with fists"), time (as L *constituta die* "on the appointed day"), place (as L *media urbe* "in the middle of the city"), accordance (as L *meo modo* "in my fashion"), specification (as L *altero pede* in *claudus altero pede* "lame in one foot"), difference by comparison (as L *Ennio* in *veracior Ennio* "more truthful than Ennius"), difference in measure (as L *annis* in *aliquot ante annis* "several years before"), or price (as L *pecunia* in *regna addicere pecunia* "to sell kingdoms for money") — used esp. in the grammar of Latin, Sanskrit, Hungarian, and Finnish **2 :** of or belonging to the ablative case ⟨an ~ suffix⟩

²ablative \"\ *n* -s **:** the ablative case or a form in it

³ab·la·tive \", (ˈ)aˈblā-\ *adj* [*ablate* + *-ive*] **:** tending to ablate ⟨~ material on a rocket nose cone⟩

ablative absolute *n* **:** a construction in Latin in which a noun or pronoun and its adjunct both in the ablative case form together an adverbial phrase expressing generally the time, cause, or an attendant circumstance of an action (as *acceptis litteris* in *Caesar, acceptis litteris, nuntium mittit* "the letter having been received, Caesar sends a messenger")

ab·laut \ˈäˌplau̇t, ˈaˌbl-\ *n* -s [G, fr. *ab* off, away from, down from (fr. OHG *aba*) + *laut* sound, fr. MHG *lūt*; akin to OE *hlūd* loud — more at OF, LOUD] **:** a systematic variation of vowels in the same root or affix or in related roots or affixes in the Indo-European languages usu. paralleled by differences in use or meaning (as *sing, sang, sung, song;* Gk *petomai* "I fly", *potē* "flight", *ptesthai* "to fly", *pōtaomai* "I fly around"; *-es-* in assumed IE *genesa*, L *genera* "kinds", *-os* in assumed IE *genos*, L *genus* "kind") **:** a similar variation in any language or language family — called also *apophony, gradation*

ablaze \əˈ-\ *adj* [¹*a-* + *blaze*, v.] **1 :** on fire ⟨forests are sometimes set ~ by lightning —John Tyndall⟩ **2 :** radiant with light or bright color ⟨~ with lighted Christmas trees⟩ **3 :** glowing or inflamed esp. with emotion ⟨his face all ~ with excitement —Bram Stoker⟩

¹able \ˈābəl\ *adj* **abler** \-b(ə)lə(r)\ **ablest** \-b(ə)ləst\ [ME, fr. MF, fr. L *habilis* easily managed, apt, skillful, fr. *habēre* to have, hold — more at HABIT] **1 a :** possessed of needed powers (as intelligence or strength) or of needed resources (as means or influence) to accomplish an objective ⟨~ to solve a problem⟩ ⟨~ to buy a house⟩ **b :** designed, constructed, or naturally endowed with the power to perform a task or achieve an end ⟨machines ~ to lift 10 tons⟩ ⟨owls ~ to see in the dark⟩ **c :** having freedom from restriction or obligation or from conditions preventing an action ⟨American women are ~ to vote⟩ ⟨we were ~ to meet her at noon⟩ **d :** constituted or situated so as to be susceptible or readily subjected to some action or treatment ⟨a shoe ~ to be repaired⟩ ⟨a hill ~ to be climbed⟩ **2 a** *obs* **:** having physical strength **:** ROBUST **b** *now dial* **:** WELL-TO-DO, RICH **3** *dial* **:** fit to cope with — usu. used with *for* ⟨~ for four helpings of dessert⟩ **4 :** marked by intelligence, knowledge, skill, or competence ⟨an ~ and rapacious tyrant —H.O.Taylor⟩ ⟨an ~, moving, and fascinating portrait —B.D.Wolfe⟩ **5 :** legally qualified **:** possessed of legal competence ⟨~ to inherit property⟩

syn CAPABLE, COMPETENT, QUALIFIED: placed after the noun modified, ABLE is likely to indicate only the power, strength, skill, or resources needed for an indicated action ⟨some day I would be like one of themselves, *able* to kill animals and catch fish —W.H.Hudson⟩ Placed before the noun modified, it may suggest a combination of superior qualities, esp. as demonstrated in practice ⟨Cleveland was an *able* leader, honest, courageous . . . a fine exponent of Manchester liberalism —Allan Nevins & H.S.Commager⟩ ⟨a priest . . . an *able* one, by all means, not only devoted, but resourceful and intelligent —Willa Cather⟩ CAPABLE is commonly interchangeable with ABLE in this sense. It is more likely than ABLE to be used in situations involving possibilities and potentialities ⟨democracy alone has constructed an unlimited civilization *capable* of infinite progress —F.D.Roosevelt⟩ ⟨a being . . . more *capable* of feeling than even the most gifted of common men —Aldous Huxley⟩ Often it suggests powers of adjustment, adaptability, or resourcefulness adequate for treating satisfactorily whatever matter is under consideration ⟨it was impossible even to recall the house of mourning without a grateful memory of Louisa's *capable* dealing with funerals —Ellen Glasgow⟩ ⟨only people who valued machines more than men were *capable* under these conditions of governing men to their profit and advantage —Lewis Mumford⟩ COMPETENT suggests complete fitness for adequate performance ⟨Tolstoy and Turgenev were quite *competent* in Russian, though they learned English, French, and German in infancy —Bertrand Russell⟩ Sometimes the word connotes special professional or technical training ⟨the associated workers must be *competent* scholars in language and palaeography —F.N.Robinson⟩ Sometimes COMPETENT is used to suggest adequacy but to deny outstanding superiority and hence may be derogatory ⟨the difference between a great dancer and a merely *competent* dancer is in the vital flame, that impersonal and . . . inhuman force which transpires between each of the great dancer's movements —T.S.Eliot⟩ ⟨they were all *competent* practical mechanics, but Gay was an inspired mechanic —John Steinbeck⟩ QUALIFIED suggests either adequate experience and knowledge, satisfactory special training, or formal certification as being especially trained ⟨Poky . . . was . . . my guide . . . no mortal could be better *qualified*; his native country was not large, and he knew every inch of it —Herman Melville⟩ ⟨being a *qualified* doctor, she knew all the facts of life —Upton Sinclair⟩

²able *vt* -ED/-ING/-S [ME *ablen*, fr. *able*, adj.] **1** *obs* **:** to make capable **:** ENABLE, STRENGTHEN **2** *obs* **:** to vouch for

³able \ˈābəl\ *usu cap* — a communications code word for the letter *a*

-able *also* **-ible** \əbəl\ *adj suffix, see Explan Notes* [ME, fr. OF, fr. L *-abilis, -ibilis*, fr. *-a-, -i-* (thematic vowels of various conjugations of verbs) + *-bilis* capable or worthy of (being acted upon)] **1 :** capable of, fit for, or worthy of (being so acted upon or toward) — chiefly in adjectives derived from verbs ⟨break*able*⟩ ⟨connect*ible*⟩ ⟨eat*able*⟩ ⟨lov*able*⟩ **2 :** tending to, given to, favoring, causing, able to, or liable to ⟨agree*able*⟩ ⟨change*able*⟩ ⟨knowledge*able*⟩ ⟨peace*able*⟩ ⟨perish*able*⟩ — **-a·ble·ness** \əbəlnəs\ *n suffix* -ES — **-a·bly** *also* **-i·bly** \əblē, -li\ *adv suffix*

able-bod·ied \ˈ≤≤ˈ≤≤\ *adj* **:** having a sound body **:** not incapacitated for work or service **:** HEALTHY, ROBUST

able-bodied seaman *or* **able seaman** *n* **:** an experienced deck-department seaman qualified to perform routine duties at sea and rated in the British navy and on British and American commercial ships between ordinary seaman and leading seaman or boatswain's mate — abbr. *A.B.*

ableeze \əˈblēz\ *adj* [¹*a-* + *bleeze* (v.)] *Scot* **:** ABLAZE

ab·le·gate \ˈabləgət, -lē-, -ˌgāt\ *n* -s [F *ablégat*, fr. L *ablegatus*, past part. of *ablegare* to send away, fr. *ab-* ¹ab + *legare* to send on a commission, dispatch — more at LEGATE] **:** a papal envoy on a special mission (as the conveying of the insignia of office to a newly named cardinal)

ableph·a·rus \āˈblefərəs\ *n, cap* [NL, irreg. fr. ²*a-* + Gk *blepharon* eyelid] **:** a genus of Old World scincoid lizards with the lower eyelid reduced to a transparent cover fused to the upper lid

abler *comparative of* ABLE

ablest *superlative of* ABLE

ablins \ˈāblənz\ *var of* AIBLINS

abloom \əˈ-\ *adj* [¹*a-* + *bloom*, v.] **:** BLOOMING

¹ablow \əˈ-\ *adj* [¹*a-* + *blow*, v.] **:** BLOWING

²ablow \əˈblō\ *prep* [*a-* (as in *above*) + *blow*, alter. of *below*] *Scot* **:** BELOW

ablush \əˈ-\ *adj* [¹*a-* + *blush*, v.] **:** BLUSHING

ab·lu·tion \əˈblüshən, aˈb-\ *n* -s [ME, fr. MF or L; MF *ablution*, fr. L *ablution-, ablutio*, fr. *ablutus* (past part. of *abluere* to wash away, fr. *ab-* ¹ab- + *-luere*, fr. *lavere* to wash) + *-ion-, -io* -ion — more at LYE] **1 a** *obs* **:** the cleansing of bodies by distillation **b :** the washing of one's body or part of it as a religious rite ⟨historically, the practice of ~*s* is common to many people —W.B.Duckat⟩ **c :** the ceremonial washing of the sacred vessels (as the chalice) and of the priest's thumb and forefinger after communion **d :** the washing of one's body or part of it ⟨he was finished with his ~*s* now —Douglas Woolf⟩ **2 :** the portion of wine or of water used in the ceremonial washing of the sacred vessels after communion **3 ablutions** *pl, Brit* **:** the building housing bathing and toilet facilities on a military base — **ab·lu·tion·ary** \-əˌnerē\ *adj*

ably \ˈāb(ə)lē, -li\ *adv* [ME, fr. *able* + *-ly*] **:** in an able manner **:** with ability

ab·mi·gra·tion \ˌabˌmīˈgrāshən\ *n* -s [¹*ab-* + *migration*] **:** northward summer migration of birds that have not made a corresponding southward journey in the previous autumn

abn *abbr* airborne

ab·na·ki \abˈnäkē\ *also* **ab·e·na·ki** \ˌabəˈnäkē\ *or* **wa·ba·na·ki** \ˌwäbəˈn-\ *n, pl* **abnaki** *or* **abnakis** *usu cap* [of Algonquian origin; akin to Fox and Kickapoo *Wāpanaʹkia*, lit., eastern land, fr. *wāpan* light, dawn, east + *aʹkia* land] **1 a :** an Indian people of Maine and southern Quebec **b :** a member of such people **2 :** an Algonquian language of the Abnaki and Penobscot peoples

ab·ne·gate \ˈabnēˌgāt, -əˌg-\ *vt* -ED/-ING/-S [back-formation fr. *abnegation*] **:** to surrender or relinquish (as a right, belief, or idea) ⟨he asked the assembly to ~ its financial powers⟩ ⟨~ high hope for the sake of barren convenience —A.T. Quiller-Couch⟩ **:** deny or renounce (as desire or self-interest) ⟨communities dedicated to the living of a humble and self-*abnegating* life —Lewis Mumford⟩ **syn** see FORGO

ab·ne·ga·tion \ˌ≤≤ˈgāshən\ *n* -s [LL *abnegation-, abnegatio*, fr. L *abnegatus* (past part. of *abnegare* to refute, deny, fr. *ab-* ¹ab- + *negare* to say no, deny) + *-ion-, -io* -ion — more at NEGATION] **:** renunciation or denial ⟨prepared to move in the direction of early ~ of federal responsibility —D'Arcy McNickle⟩ **:** restraint or denial of desire or self-interest ⟨cold lines, but penned by what heartbroken ~ —George Meredith⟩ **:** SELF-DENIAL, HUMILITY

ab·ne·ga·tor \ˈ≤≤ˌgād·ə(r)\ *n* -s [LL, fr. L *abnegatus* + *-or*] **:** one that abnegates

ab·ney level \ˈabnē-\ *n, usu cap A* [after Wm. de Wiveleslie *Abney* †1920 Eng. scientist] **:** a surveying clinometer consisting of a short telescope, bubble tube, and graduated vertical arc used esp. for measuring tree heights

¹ab·nor·mal \(ˈ)abˈnȯrməl, -ō(ə)m- *also* əbˈ-\ *adj* [alter. (influenced by L *abnormis*) of *anormal*] **1 :** deviating from the normal **:** differing from the typical ⟨the large family is ~ today⟩ **:** IRREGULAR, UNUSUAL **2 :** greater than or superior to the normal **:** EXCESSIVE ⟨~ profits⟩ ⟨~ ambition⟩ **:** EXCEPTIONAL ⟨~ powers of recollection⟩ **3 :** less than or inferior to the normal **:** deficient in intellectual powers **:** characterized by mental defect or disorder ⟨a school for ~ children⟩ **:** SUBNORMAL **4 :** departing from the accepted standards of social behavior — **ab·nor·mal·ly** \-əlē, -i\ *adv*

²abnormal \"\ *n* -s **:** an abnormal person

ab·nor·mal·cy \abˈnȯrməlsē, -ō(ə)m-, -si *also* əb-\ *n* -ES [fr. *abnormal*, after *normal: normalcy*] **:** ABNORMALITY

ab·nor·mal·ism \≤ˈ≤≤ˌlizəm\ *n* -s **:** ABNORMALITY

ab·nor·mal·i·ty \ˌabˌnȯ(r)ˈmaləd·ē, -bnə(r)ˈ-, -ətē, -i\ *n* -ES **1 :** the quality or state of being abnormal **:** IRREGULARITY, DEVIATION **2 :** something abnormal (as a malformation or aberration)

ab·nor·mal·ize \≤ˈ≤≤ˌlīz\ *vt* -ED/-ING/-S **:** to make abnormal

abnormal psychology *n* **:** a branch of psychology that deals with disorders of experience and of behavior (as in neuroses, psychoses, and mental deficiency) or with certain incompletely understood normal phenomena (as dreams and hypnosis)

ab·nor·mi·ty \≤ˈ≤məd·ē, -ətē, -i\ *n* -ES [LL *abnormitas*, fr. L *abnormis* irregular, abnormal (fr. *ab-* ¹ab- + *norma* rule, pattern) + *-itas* -ity — more at NORMAL] *archaic* **:** ABNORMALITY

ab·nor·mous \(ˈ)abˈnȯrməs, -ō(ə)m- *also* əbˈ-\ *adj* [irreg. (influence of *enormous*) fr. L *abnormis*, fr. *ab-* ¹ab- + *norma* rule — more at NORMAL] *archaic* **:** ABNORMAL, IRREGULAR

abo \ˈa(ˌ)bō\ *n* -s [by shortening] *Austral* **:** ABORIGINE, ABORIGINAL

¹aboard \əˈ-\ *adv* [ME *abord*, fr. ¹*a-* + *bord* board, side of a ship — more at BOARD] **1 a :** on board **:** on, onto, or within a ship, a railway car, or a passenger vehicle ⟨all ~⟩ ⟨climb ~⟩ **b :** ASTRIDE ⟨swing ~⟩ ⟨sling a saddle ~⟩ **2 :** ALONGSIDE ⟨another ship close ~⟩

²aboard \"\ *prep* [ME *abord*, fr. *abord*, adv.] **:** on board ⟨go ~ ship⟩ ⟨~ a horse⟩

abococket *var of* BYCOKET

¹abode *past of* ABIDE

²abode \əˈbōd\ *n* -s [ME *abod* waiting, stay, fr. *abod*, past of *abiden* to abide — more at ABIDE] **1** *obs* **:** act of waiting **:** DELAY **:** temporary stay **2 :** continued stay in a place **:** RESIDENCE, SOJOURN ⟨during one's ~ in the country⟩ **3 :** place where one abides or dwells **:** HOME ⟨a cottage became their ~⟩

³abode *vb* -ED/-ING/-S [alter. (influenced by *bode*) of ME *abeden* to announce, fr. OE *ābēodan* to command, proclaim, fr. *ā-* (perfective prefix) + *bēodan* to command, proclaim — more at ABEAR, BID] *vt, obs* **:** FOREBODE, PRESAGE ~ *vi, obs* **:** to be ominous

abo·ga·do \ˌabəˈgäd·(ˌ)ō\ *n* -s [Sp, fr. L *advocatus* — more at ADVOCATE] *Southwest* **:** COUNSEL 6

abo group *n, usu cap A&B&O* **:** ABO SYSTEM

ab·ohm \(ˈ)aˈbōm\ *n* -s [ISV ²*ab-* + *ohm*] **:** the cgs electromagnetic unit of resistance equal to one billionth of an ohm that measures the resistance of a conductor that with a constant current of one abampere flowing through it maintains between its terminals a potential difference of one abvolt — compare AB- table

aboi·deau \ˌábwàdō\ *or* **aboi·teau** \-tō\ *n, pl* **aboi·deaux** \-dō\ *or* **aboi·teaux** \-tō\ [CanF *aboiteau*] *Canad* **:** a tide gate or dam to prevent the overflow of water into marshland

aboil \əˈ-\ *adj* [¹*a-* + *boil*, v.] **:** BOILING

abol·ish \əˈbälish, -ēsh, *esp in pres part* -əsh\ *vt* -ED/-ING/-ES [MF *aboliss-*, stem of *abolir* to abolish, fr. L *abolēre* to abolish, destroy, prob. back-formation fr. *abolescere* to disappear, fr. *ab-* ¹ab- + *-olescere* (as in *adolescere* to grow up) — more at ADULT] **1 :** to do away with wholly **:** ANNUL — used chiefly of laws, customs, institutions, traditions ⟨~ slavery⟩ ⟨~*ed* bedtime during the holidays⟩ **2 :** to destroy completely ⟨a fog . . . ~*ed* the landscape —Aldous Huxley⟩

syn ANNIHILATE, EXTINGUISH, ABATE: ABOLISH indicates the definitive ending or causing a cessation of being or operating; it is used typically but not always with customs, traditions, conditions, conceptions rather than with more tangible items like things or persons ⟨*abolish* racial discrimination⟩ ⟨trying to *abolish* child labor⟩ ⟨*abolishing* a primitive custom⟩ ⟨no plan will be acceptable unless it *abolishes* poverty —G.B.Shaw⟩ ⟨the political liberalism which threatened to *abolish* some of the most flagrant abuses in the Church of England —W.R.Inge⟩ ⟨unfair that the anonymous churl, with an iron tube and some gunpowder and a great slug of lead, could *abolish* a knight —Tom Wintringham⟩ ANNIHILATE indicates utter destruction precluding any chance of re-creation, reforming, revivifying ⟨the events of this week *annihilated* the immature plans of last week —Charles Dickens⟩ ⟨the pollution of the Delaware river and bay by sewage and chemicals has practically *annihilated* the sturgeon —*Amer. Guide Series: Del.*⟩ ⟨the realization that for the first time the homes and cities of the U.S. itself can be *annihilated* by enemy attack —Aidan Crawley⟩ EXTINGUISH may suggest a putting out, choking off, stifling, smothering, as water extinguishes fire ⟨Italy, where the instincts of ancient Rome never were *extinguished* —H.O.Taylor⟩ ⟨a religion of their own which was thoroughly and painfully *extinguished* by the Inquisition —T.S.Eliot⟩ ⟨though the literal extirpation of a nation is an impossibility, there is every reason to believe that the Celtic inhabitants of those parts of Britain which had become English at the end of the sixth century had been as nearly *extinguished* as a nation could be —A.T.Quiller-Couch⟩ ABATE, now almost always a synonym for *lessen* or *decrease*, in legal usage may indicate abolishing or bringing to an end ⟨*abate* a nuisance⟩

abol·ish·ment \-shmənt\ *n* -s [MF *abolissement*, fr. *aboliss-* + *-ment*] **:** ABOLITION

ab·o·li·tion \ˌabəˈlishən\ *n* -s *often attrib* [MF, fr. L *abolition-, abolitio*, fr. *abolitus* (past part. of *abolēre*) + *-ion-, -io* -ion] **:** act of abolishing or state of being abolished **:** ABROGATION ⟨~ of imprisonment for debt⟩; *specif* **:** the abolishing of slavery

ab·o·li·tion·ary \-ə,nerē\ *adj* **:** relating to or favoring abolition

ab·o·li·tion·dom \-əndəm\ *n* -s **:** ABOLITIONISTS; *specif* **:** the northern states in the American Civil War

ab·o·li·tion·ism \-ə,nizəm\ *n* -s **:** the principles or measures favoring abolition (as of slavery or capital punishment) **:** the tenets or practices of abolitionists

ab·o·li·tion·ist \-nəst\ *n* -s *often attrib* **:** an advocate of abolition

ab·o·li·tion·ize \-ə,nīz\ *vt* -ED/-ING/-S **:** to make abolitionists of (the members of a corporate body) ⟨~ Kansas⟩

abo·ma \ə'bōmə\ *n* -s [Pg, F, & AmerSp, prob. modif. of Kongo *mboma* python] **:** any of several large So. American snakes of the genus *Constrictor* or of related genera

ab·o·ma·sal \,abō¦māsəl, -bə-\ *adj* [NL *abomasum* + E *-al*] **:** of, belonging to, or involving the abomasum

ab·o·ma·sum \,=='səm\ *also* **ab·o·ma·sus** \-səs\ *n, pl* **aboma·sa** \-sə\ *also* **aboma·si** \-,sī,-,sē\ [NL, fr. [1]*ab-* + L *omasum* tripe of a bullock] **:** the fourth or true digestive stomach of a ruminant

[1]**a-bomb** \'ā,-\ *n, usu cap A* [by abbr.] **:** ATOM BOMB

[2]**a-bomb** \"\ *vb, usu cap A* **:** ATOM-BOMB

a-bomber \'=,==\ *n, usu cap A* **:** an aircraft capable of delivering a nuclear weapon (as an atom bomb) on a target

abom·i·na·ble \ə'bäm(ə)nəbəl\ *adj* [ME, fr. MF, fr. L *abominabilis*, fr. *abominari* + *-abilis* -able] **1 :** worthy of or causing loathing or hatred **:** revoltingly unnatural **:** DETESTABLE, LOATHSOME **2 :** quite disagreeable or unpleasant ⟨~ weather⟩ — **abom·i·na·bly** \-əblē, -i\ *adv*

abominable snowman *n, often cap A&S* [prob. intended as trans. of Tibetan *mi-te*, lit., man-bear] **:** an animal reported as existing in the high Himalayas and usu. thought to be a bear

[1]**abom·i·nate** \ə'bämə,nāt, *usu* -ād.+V\ *vt* -ED/-ING/-S [L *abominatus*, past part. of *abominari* to deprecate as an ill omen, to detest, fr. *ab-* [1]ab- + *ominari* to forebode, presage, fr. *omin-*, *omen* omen] **:** to hate or loathe intensely **:** ABHOR ⟨~ a crime⟩ **syn** see HATE

[2]**abom·i·nate** \-mənət, -,nāt\ *adj* [L *abominatus*] **:** ABOMINATED

abom·i·na·tion \ə,bämə'nāshən\ *n* -s [ME *abominacioun*, fr. MF *abomination*, fr. LL *abomination-*, *abominatio*, fr. L *abominatus* + *-ion-*, *-io* -ion] **1 :** something that is abominable ⟨guilty of ~s⟩ ⟨a wonderful wooden statue . . . now replaced by the usual metal ~ —Norman Douglas⟩ **2 :** a feeling of extreme disgust and hatred **:** ABHORRENCE, DETESTATION, LOATHING ⟨tobacco . . . was held in ~ —T.B.Macaulay⟩

abom·i·na·tor \ə'bämə,nād·ə(r), -ātə-\ *n* -s **:** one that abominates

abon·go \ə'bäŋ(,)gō\ *n, pl* **abongo** *or* **abongos** *usu cap* **1 :** a Negrillo people on the Ogowe river, Gabon, French Equatorial Africa — called also *Obongo* **2 :** a member of the Abongo people — compare PYGMY

aboon \ə'bün, -'ʊen\ *adj or adv or prep* [ME *abone*, fr. earlier *aboven*, *abuven* — more at ABOVE] *chiefly dial* **:** ABOVE

ab·oospore \(')a'bōə,spō(ə)r\ *n* [[1]*ab-* + *oospore*] **:** an oomycete spore functioning as an oospore but produced without sexual union

abor \'ä,bó(ə)r\ *n, pl* **abor** *or* **abors** *usu cap* **1 :** a primitive people inhabiting the Brahmaputra river region about 100 miles north of the town of Dibrugarh in northern Assam **2 :** a member of the Abor people

ab·orad \(')a'bōr,ad, -ó,r-\ *adv* [[1]*ab-* + *orad*] **:** away from the mouth

ab·oral \(')a¦bōrəl, -ór-, -är-\ *adj* [[1]*ab-* + *oral*] **:** opposite to or away from the mouth — **ab·oral·ly** \-əlē, -i\ *adv*

[1]**abord** *vt* -ED/-ING/-S [ME *aborden*, fr. *abord*, adv., aboard — more at ABOARD] *archaic* **:** APPROACH, ACCOST

[2]**abord** *n* -s *archaic* **:** APPROACH **:** manner of approach

abordage *n* -s [[1]*abord* + *-age*] *archaic* **:** boarding a ship in an attack

[1]**ab·orig·i·nal** \,abə'rijən°l, -jnəl\ *adj* [*aborigine* + *-al*] **1 a :** first according to historical record or scientific analysis **:** INDIGENOUS ⟨~ flora⟩ **b :** PRIMITIVE ⟨~ tribes⟩ ⟨a great safety valve for the ~ human impulses —Lewis Mumford⟩ **2 :** of or belonging to aborigines ⟨~ languages⟩ ⟨~ weapons⟩ **syn** see NATIVE

[2]**aboriginal** \"\ *n* -s **:** ABORIGINE

ab·orig·i·nal·i·ty \,abə,rijə'naləd·ē\ *n* -ES **:** the quality or state of being aboriginal

ab·orig·i·nal·ly \¦==¦=jən°lē, -jnəlē, -i\ *adv* **:** from the beginning **:** from earliest known times

ab·orig·i·ne \,abə'rijə(,)nē, -ənī\ *also* **ab·or·i·gen** \a'bōrəjən, -är-\ *n* -s [back-formation fr. *aborigines*, pl., fr. L, perh. irreg. fr. *ab origine* from the beginning] **1 :** an indigenous inhabitant of a country **:** one of the native people esp. as contrasted with an invading or colonizing people **2 aborigines** *pl* **:** the original fauna and flora of a geographical area

ab orig·i·ne \"\ *adv* [L] **:** from the beginning

abor-miri \,ä,bór'mirē\ *n, usu cap A&M* **:** a language spoken in northern Assam

[1]**aborn·ing** \ə'bórniŋ, -ó(ə)n-, -nēŋ, -nən\ *adv* [[1]*a-* + *borning*] **:** while being born or produced **:** at the moment of birth **:** before coming to completion — used esp. in the phrase *die aborning* ⟨a resolution that died ~⟩

[2]**aborning** \"\ *adj* **:** being born or produced ⟨the ~ social evolution of the girls —Fannie Hurst⟩ ⟨a new world was ~ overseas —B.D.Wolfe⟩

[1]**abort** \ə'bó(ə)rt, -ó(ə)t, *usu* -d.+V\ *vb* -ED/-ING/-S [L *abortare*, fr. *abortus* abortion] *vi* **1 :** to bring forth premature or stillborn offspring ⟨cows with brucellosis often ~⟩ **2 :** to become checked in development so as to remain rudimentary or to shrink away ⟨pollen grains that ~⟩ **3 :** to stop or fail in the early stages ⟨many colds ~ without treatment⟩ ⟨the plans have ~*ed*⟩ ⟨the bomber ~*ed* from its mission⟩ ~ *vt* **1 :** to bring forth (offspring) prematurely ⟨~*ed* a 3-month-old fetus⟩ **:** cause to be delivered of a stillborn or nonviable fetus ⟨~ a malformed patient⟩; *esp* **:** to terminate pregnancy of before term **2 a :** to terminate prematurely ⟨~ a project⟩ **:** stop in the early stages ⟨~ a disease⟩ **b :** to turn back without completion **3 :** to check so as to produce rudimentary development or a shrinking away ⟨~ branches of trees⟩

[2]**abort** \"\ *n* -s [ME, fr. L *abortus*, fr. *abortus*, past part. of *aboriri* to disappear, miscarry, fr. *ab-* [1]ab- + *oriri* to rise, be born — more at ORIENT] **1** *obs* **:** ABORTION **2 :** an abortive flight by an aircraft on a combat or bombing mission; *also* **:** an aircraft making such a flight

abor·ti·cide \ə'bórd·ə,sīd\ *n* -s [[2]*abort* + *-i-* + *-cide*] **1 :** act of destroying a fetus within the uterus **2 :** an agent that destroys the fetus and causes abortion

[1]**abor·ti·fa·cient** \ə'bórd·ə,fāshənt, =,=='==\ *adj* [[2]*abort* + *-i-* + *-facient*] **:** inducing abortion

[2]**abortifacient** \"\ *n* -s **:** a drug or other agent that induces abortion

abort·in \ə'bórt°n\ *n* -s [NL *abortus* (specific epithet of *Brucella abortus*, fr. L, past part.) + E *-in*] **:** an extract made from cultures of a bacterium (*Brucella abortus*) and used in the diagnosis of contagious abortion of cattle

abor·tion \ə'bórshən, -ó(ə)sh-\ *n* -s [L *abortion-*, *abortio*, fr. *abortus* (past part.) + *-ion-*, *-io* -ion] **1 :** the expulsion of a nonviable fetus: **a :** spontaneous expulsion of a human fetus during the first 12 weeks of gestation — compare MISCARRIAGE **b :** induced expulsion of a human fetus **c :** expulsion often due to infection of a fetus by a domestic animal at any time before completion of pregnancy — see CONTAGIOUS ABORTION, VIBRIONIC ABORTION; TRICHOMONIASIS **2 :** a misshapen thing or person **:** MONSTROSITY **3 :** something that fails to attain full development or that ceases to progress before it is matured or perfect ⟨his attempt proved an ~⟩ **4 a :** arrest of development of an organ so that it remains imperfect or is absorbed **b :** the result of such arrest of development (as a fruit that fails to reach maturity or a potential leaf reduced to a scale) **5 :** the arrest of a disease in its earliest stage ⟨~ of a cold⟩

abor·tion·ist \-nəst\ *n* -s **:** one who induces abortions esp. illegally

[1]**abort·ive** \ə'bór¦d·iv, -ó(ə)|, |tiv, -ēv\ *adj* [ME, fr. L *abortivus*, fr. *abortus* (past part.) + *-ivus* -ive] **1** *obs* **:** prematurely born **2 :** failing of purpose or effect **:** MISCARRYING, UNSUCCESSFUL ⟨an ~ enterprise⟩ **3 :** imperfectly formed or developed **:** RUDIMENTARY **4 a :** ABORTIFACIENT **b :** cutting short ⟨~ treatment of pneumonia⟩ **c :** failing to develop completely or typically ⟨an ~ case of poliomyelitis⟩ — **abort·ive·ly** \-əvlē, -li\ *adv* — **abortiveness** \-ivnəs, -ēv-\ *n*

[2]**abortive** \"\ *n* -s [ME, fr. L *abortivus*, adj.] **:** one that is abortive (as a bombing mission)

abor·to·gen·ic \ə¦bórd·ə¦jenik\ *adj* [[2]*abort* + *-o-* + *-genic*] **:** causing abortion **:** ABORTIFACIENT ⟨~ necrosis⟩

abor·tus \ə'bórd·əs\ *n* -ES [NL, fr. L, abortion] **:** an aborted fetus; *specif* **:** a human fetus less than 12 weeks old or weighing at birth less than 17 ounces

abos *pl of* ABO

abo system \¦ā,bē'ō-, ,ābē'ō-\ *n, usu cap A&B&O* **:** the basic system of antigens of human blood behaving in heredity as an allelic unit to produce any of the four blood groups A, B, AB, or O according to the particular antigens passed from parents to child — called also *ABO group*; compare ISOANTIBODY, RH FACTOR

à bouche \ȧbüsh\ *adj* [F, with a bouche] *heraldry, of a shield* **:** having a bouche on the dexter side

abought *past of* ABY

aboulia *var of* ABULIA

abound \ə'baůnd\ *vi* -ED/-ING/-S [ME *abounden*, fr. MF *abonder*, fr. L *abundare* to abound, overflow, fr. *ab-* [1]ab- + *undare* to rise in waves, fr. *unda* wave — more at WATER] **1 :** to be present or available in large numbers or in great quantity ⟨wild animals ~⟩ ⟨iron ore ~*s*⟩ ⟨~*ing* confidence⟩ **2 a** *obs* **:** to be wealthy ⟨feed the poor while he ~*s*⟩ **b :** to be full to overflowing ⟨~*ing* streams⟩ **c :** to be highly productive ⟨~*ing* soil⟩ **3 :** to become copiously supplied — used with *in* or *with* ⟨the city ~*s* in historic remains⟩ ⟨the fields ~ with stones⟩

[1]**about** \ə'baůt, *usu* -d.+V\ *adv* [ME *about*, *abouten*, fr. OE *abūtan*, fr. [1]*a-* + *būtan* outside, without — more at BUT] **1 :** on all sides **:** in every direction **:** AROUND ⟨'tis time to look ~ —Shak.⟩ **2 a :** in rotation **:** ROUND ⟨they go ~ in circles⟩ **b :** around the outside **:** in circumference ⟨the lake is a mile ~ and a half mile across⟩ **c :** in a circuitous way **:** round about ⟨the river . . . is subject to frequent shifts of position, and winds ~ —P.E. James⟩ **3 a :** with some approach to exactness in quantity, number, or time **:** APPROXIMATELY ⟨~ four feet of snow⟩ ⟨~ eight o'clock⟩ **b :** ALMOST **:** NEARLY ⟨~ as serious⟩ **:** little less than ⟨~ starved⟩ **4 :** here and there at random ⟨tools lying ~⟩ **:** from one place to another ⟨carry money ~ with him⟩ **5 :** in the vicinity **:** NEAR ⟨he spoke to the people standing ~⟩ **6 :** in succession **:** one after the other **:** ALTERNATELY ⟨turn ~ is fair play⟩ **7 a :** in the opposite direction ⟨face ~⟩ ⟨bring a ship ~⟩ **:** in reverse order ⟨arranged the other way ~⟩ **:** from the contrary point of view ⟨put the matter the other way ~⟩ **b :** on the opposite tack — see COME ABOUT

[2]**about** \"\ *prep* [ME, fr. OE *abūtan*, fr. *abūtan*, adv.] **1 :** in a circle around **:** AROUND ⟨our thoughts revolve ~ ourselves⟩ **:** on every side of ⟨he found ~ him innumerable flowers⟩ **2 a :** in the immediate neighborhood of **:** NEAR ⟨fish are abundant ~ the reefs⟩ **b :** near or not far from in time ⟨a night ~ midsummer⟩ **c :** by or on (one's person) ⟨secreting money ~ him⟩ **d :** in or as a part of the makeup of ⟨a mature wisdom ~ him⟩ **e :** at the command of **:** in readiness for the use of ⟨he has his wits ~ him⟩ **3 a :** in the act or process of doing **:** engaged in ⟨I put it in the form of a poem while I was ~ it —Eudora Welty⟩ **:** concerned with ⟨no idea of what American music is ~⟩ **b :** on the point or verge of — usu. used with following infinitive ⟨~ to enter the army⟩ ⟨~ to be graduated⟩ **4 a** — used as a function word to indicate that which is dealt with as the object of thought, feeling, or action ⟨resentment ~ this state of affairs⟩ or that to which reference is made ⟨the most exciting thing ~ the adventure⟩ **b :** with regard to **:** CONCERNING **c :** on the subject of ⟨a novel ~ Spain⟩ **5 :** over or in different parts of ⟨he traveled ~ the country⟩ **:** THROUGHOUT ⟨a well-known figure ~ the town⟩ **:** here and there upon ⟨the knife wounded him ~ the face and throat⟩

[3]**about** \"\ *adj* [ME, fr. *about*, adv.] **1 :** stirring or moving from place to place **:** ASTIR ⟨few people were ~ on the streets⟩ **2 :** being in evidence, in existence, or in circulation **:** ABROAD ⟨plenty of money ~⟩ ⟨more reason and less emotion ~ —Herbert Hoover⟩ **3 :** normally active or capable (as after a confining illness) ⟨eager to be up and ~ again⟩

[1]**about-face** \='=,=\ *n* -s [fr. the imper. phrase *about face*, fr. [1]*about* + *face*, v.] **1 :** the act of facing in the opposite direction as a military maneuver ⟨soldiers did an *about-face* and marched away —Dorothy C. Fisher⟩ **2 a :** a reversal of direction ⟨the river does an *about-face*⟩ **b :** a reversal of attitude or point of view ⟨an *about-face* on national policies⟩

[2]**about-face** \"\ *vi* -ED/-ING/-S **:** to execute an about-face

about ship *vi* [fr. the imper. phrase *about ship*, fr. [1]*about* + *ship*, n.] **:** TACK — usu. used as an order

about-turn \=¦=¦=\ *vi* [fr. the imper. phrase *about turn*, fr. [1]*about* + *turn*, v.] **:** ABOUT-FACE

[1]**above** \ə'bəv\ *adv* [ME *above*, *aboven*, fr. OE *abufan*, fr. [1]*a-* + *bufan* above (akin to OS *bi-oban*, MD *bōven*, OFris *bova*, MHG *bobene*), fr. *be-* + *ufan* above — more at OVER] **1 a :** in a higher place **:** OVERHEAD ⟨he lay under the tree and looked at the branches ~⟩ **:** in the sky ⟨the stars ~⟩ **:** in or to heaven ⟨gone ~⟩ **:** UPSTAIRS ⟨a stairway leading ~⟩ **b :** farther up (as on a mountain or river) ⟨the bridge is two miles ~⟩ **c :** on the upper or dorsal surface ⟨these young birds are light brown ~⟩ **2 :** higher on the same page or on a preceding page ⟨except as stated ~⟩ **3 :** higher or superior in rank, position, or power ⟨a vacancy in the rank ~⟩ **:** higher in number ⟨50 and ~⟩ **4** *archaic* **:** in addition **:** BESIDES

[2]**above** \"\ *prep* [ME *above*, *aboven*, fr. *above*, *aboven*, adv.] **1 a :** in or to a higher place than ⟨the house perched ~ the road⟩ **:** directly over ⟨a room ~ the store⟩ **:** higher than **b :** farther up than (as on a mountain or river) ⟨anchored 10 miles ~ the city⟩ **:** on the other side of **:** BEYOND ⟨hunted ~ the farm⟩ **c :** farther north than ⟨the ship sank just ~ the Azores⟩ **d :** on top of — used of clothing ⟨aprons ~ a motley of borrowed . . . raiment —Ellen Glasgow⟩ **2 a :** superior to or surpassing in any respect **:** higher than (as in rank, position, quality, or degree) ⟨filial piety is ~ self-interest⟩ **:** out of reach of **:** not likely to be affected by **:** not exposed to ⟨be ~ suspicion⟩ **:** in preference to **:** over against ⟨preoccupation with design ~ all other elements⟩ **b :** too proud or honorable to stoop or condescend to ⟨~ taking profits for himself⟩ **:** averse to **:** disinclined to ⟨she is not ~ reading her poems⟩ **3 :** exceeding in number, quantity, or size **:** more than ⟨men ~ 50 years old⟩ **4 :** in addition to **:** BESIDES ⟨~ and beyond his good nature⟩ — **above oneself :** showing or feeling self-importance ⟨when he gets a bit *above himself* . . . he inclines to be a nuisance —*Atlantic*⟩

[3]**above** \"\ *n* -s [ME *above*, *aboven*, fr. *above*, *aboven*, adv.] **1 a :** something that is located, written, or discussed higher on the same page or on a preceding page ⟨a diagram like the ~⟩ **b :** a person whose name is written higher on the same page or on a preceding page ⟨the ~ is the owner of this car⟩ **2 a :** higher esp. arbitrary authority ⟨the policy was imposed from ~⟩ **b :** HEAVEN ⟨every perfect gift is from ~ —Jas 1:17 (AV)⟩

[4]**above** \"\ *adj* [[1]*above*] **1 :** being located, written, or discussed higher on the same page or on a preceding page ⟨the ~ chart⟩ **2 :** of heaven **:** HEAVENLY ⟨think on things ~⟩

above all *adv* **:** before every other consideration **:** ESPECIALLY ⟨this *above all*⟩

[1]**above·board** \=¦=¦=\ *adv* [[2]*above* + *board*; fr. the difficulty of cheating at cards when the hands are above the table] **:** in a straightforward manner **:** OPENLY

[2]**aboveboard** \"\ *adj* **:** without concealment or deception **:** in open sight **:** STRAIGHTFORWARD ⟨open and ~ in his opposition⟩

above·ground \=¦=¦=\ *adj* **1 :** located on or above the surface of the ground **2 :** not dead and buried **:** ALIVE

above·proof \=¦=¦=\ *adj* **:** OVERPROOF

[1]**above·stairs** \=¦=¦=\ *adv* **:** in or on an upper story ⟨they sat ~⟩

[2]**abovestairs** \"\ *adj* [[1]*abovestairs*] **:** located on an upper story ⟨a room ~⟩

[3]**abovestairs** \"\ *n pl but sing in constr* [[1]*abovestairs*] **:** the part of a building above the ground floor ⟨a search from ~⟩

above the line *or* **above-line** \ə'bəv,līn\ *adv (or adj)* **1 :** in that part of the score sheet in bridge that is reserved for the scoring of honors, penalties, and premiums — used of any score that does not count toward game; compare CONTRACT BRIDGE **2 :** classified as an ordinary or routine expense or revenue item or as a current expense or asset ⟨an *above-line* surplus⟩

above-wa·ter \=¦=¦==\ *adj* **1 :** above the surface of the water **2 :** above the waterline of a ship

ab ovo \(')a'bō(,)vō\ *adv* [L, lit., from the egg] **:** from the beginning ⟨develops every thought *ab ovo*, leading the reader up to the finest ramifications —Arnold Brecht⟩

abox \ə'bäks\ *adj* [[1]*a-* + *box* (to boxhaul)] **:** braced aback — used of head yards when the headsails only are aback

aboz·zo *also* **ab·boz·zo** \ə'bȯt(,)sō\ *n, pl* **aboz·zi** \-(,)sē\ [It *abbozzo*, fr. *abbozzare* to make a rough sketch or draft, fr. *a-* (fr. L *ad-*) + *bozzare* to make a rough sketch or draft, fr. *bozza* boss, swelling, roughhewn stone, rough sketch or draft — more at BOSS] **:** a rough sketch or draft (as of a picture or a poem)

abp *abbr, often cap* archbishop

abr *abbr* abridged; abridgment

ab·ra·ca·dab·ra \,abrəkə'dabrə\ *n* -s [LL] **1 :** a charm or incantation **:** magical formulas ⟨relied on effigies and ~ to produce results —E.A. Hoebel⟩ — used as a word to ward off calamity esp. when written on an amulet in a mystical design **2 :** confused or unintelligible language **:** JARGON, NONSENSE ⟨pseudoscientific ~⟩

A B R A C A D A B R A
A B R A C A D A B R
A B R A C A D A B
A B R A C A D A
A B R A C A D
A B R A C A
A B R A C
A B R A
A B R
A B
A

abracadabra

[1]**abrad·ant** \ə'brād°nt, a'-\ *n* -s [*abrade* + *-ant*] **:** ABRASIVE

[2]**abradant** \"\ *adj* **:** ABRASIVE

abrade \ə'brād, a'-\ *vb* -ED/-ING/-S [L *abradere* to scrape off, fr. *ab-* [1]ab- + *radere* to scrape — more at RAT] *vt* **1 a :** to rub or wear away esp. by friction **:** ERODE ⟨the waves ~ the rocks⟩ **b :** to irritate by rubbing **:** CHAFE ⟨broad crape . . . *abraded* her soft skin —Arnold Bennett⟩ **c :** to roughen the surface of ⟨*abraded* yarns⟩ **2 :** to wear down or exhaust (as a person or a person's spirit) **:** IRRITATE ⟨the affront to his pride *abraded* him more and more —Robert Shaplen⟩ ~ *vi* **:** to undergo abrasion

abrad·er \-d·ə(r)\ *n* -s **:** one that abrades ⟨a prod, scourge or ~ . . . of the local authorities —Keith Williams⟩: as **a :** a tool or machine for abrading **b** *or* **abrading stone** *archaeol* **:** a primitive stone artifact usu. of sandstone for smoothing, sharpening, or shaping

abra·ham-man \'ābrə,ham,man, -haa(ə)m,maa(ə)n; 'ābrəm,-, 'ābrəhəm,-\ *also* **abram-man** \'ābrəm,-\ *n, pl* **abra·ham-men** *also* **abram-men** *usu cap A* [after *Abraham* or *Abram*, Biblical patriarch of the Jews; prob. fr. the New Testament reference (Lk 16: 19–31) to the beggar Lazarus, who is said to have rested in Abraham's bosom after death] **:** one of a class of beggars who roamed through England esp. in the 16th and 17th centuries usu. feigning lunacy to obtain alms

abraham's bosom *n, usu cap A* [trans. of LL *sinus Abrahae*, trans. of Gk *kolpos Abraam*] **:** the abode of bliss in the other world **:** PARADISE — so called in Jewish writings and in the New Testament, in Lk 16:22 (RSV)

abram *obs var of* [1]AUBURN

ab·ra·mis \'abrəməs\ *n, cap* [NL, fr. Gk, a kind of mullet] **:** a genus of fishes (family Cyprinidae) including the European freshwater bream

abran·chia \(')ā'braŋkēə\ *n pl, cap* [NL, fr. [2]*a-* + *-branchia*] **:** a former division of annelids comprising forms without specialized respiratory structures (as most of the oligochaetes and leeches)

abran·chi·al \(')ā¦braŋkēəl\ *adj* [[2]*a-* + *branchial*] **:** ABRANCHIATE

abran·chi·al·ism \(')=¦===,lizəm\ *n* -s [*abranchial* + *-ism*] **:** the condition of being without gills (as certain mollusks of the genus *Firoloida*)

[1]**abran·chi·a·ta** \¦=,=kē'ād·ə, -ād·ə\ [NL, fr. [2]*a-* + *branchi-* + *-ata*] *syn of* ABRANCHIA

[2]**abranchiata** \"\ *n pl, cap* **:** any of several groups of gill-less animals other than Abranchia

abran·chi·ate \(')=¦=kēət, -ē,āt\ *also* **abran·chi·ous** \-kēəs\ *adj* [[2]*a-* + *branchi-* + *-ate* or *-ous*] **:** lacking gills

abrase \ə'brāz, a'-\ *vt* -ED/-ING/-S [L *abrasus*, past part. of *abradere* — more at ABRADE] **:** to wear down or rub off **:** smooth off **:** ABRADE

abras·er \-zə(r)\ *n* -s **:** ABRADER

abrash \'ä,brəsh, -räsh\ *n* -ES [Ar, mottled] **:** a variation or deviation of a color in Oriental rugs

abra·sin oil \'abrəzə,n-\ *n* [part trans. of F *huile d'abrasin*] **:** TUNG OIL

abra·si·om·e·ter \ə,brāzē'äməd·ə(r), a,-\ *n* -s [*abrasion* + *-meter*] **:** a device for measuring the resistance of surfaces to abrasion

abra·sion \ə'brāzhən, a'-\ *n* -s [ML *abrasion-*, *abrasio*, fr. L *abrasus* (past part. of *abradere* to scrape off) + *-ion-*, *-io* -ion — more at ABRADE] **1 :** wearing, grinding, or rubbing away by friction **2 a :** the rubbing or scraping of the surface layer of cells or tissue from an area of the skin or mucous membrane; *also* **:** a place so abraded **b :** the mechanical wearing away of the tooth surfaces by chewing

abrasion platform *n* **:** the portion of the submerged margin of a continent or island that has been planed off by marine abrasion as distinct from the portion that has been built up to its present level by the deposit of marine sediments

[1]**abra·sive** \-āsiv, -ziv, -ēv\ *adj* [*abrase* + *-ive*] **1 :** tending to abrade **:** producing abrasion **2 :** causing irritation ⟨~ relationships between member nations⟩

[2]**abrasive** \"\ *n* -s **1 a :** any of a wide variety of natural or manufactured substances used to grind, wear down, rub away, smooth, scour, clean, or polish often combined with a binder to make grinding wheels or affixed with glue to the surface of paper or cloth **b :** something made of an abrasive (as sandpaper) **2 :** rock fragments, mineral particles, or sand grains used by running water, wind, waves and currents, and glaciers in abrading a land surface

ab·raum \'ä,praům\ *n* -s [G, lit., rubbish, fr. *ab* off (fr. OHG *aba* away) + *raum* space, fr. OHG *rūm* — more at OF, ROOM] **:** a red ocher used to darken mahogany

abrax·as \ə'braksəs\ *n* [LL *Abraxas*, a god, fr. Gk *Abrasax*, *Abraxas*; perh. regarded as a charm fr. the numerical value of the Greek letters, which is 365] **1** — used as a charm on an amulet or talisman in Europe, Asia Minor, and No. Africa from the 2d century B.C. until the 13th century **2** *also* **abraxas stone** -ES **:** a gem engraved with the word *abraxas*

abra·zo \ə'brä(,)sō, ä'b-\ *n* -s [Sp, fr. *abrazar* to embrace, fr. *a-* (fr. L *ad-*) + *brazo* arm, fr. L *brachium* — more at BRACE] **:** an embrace (as of salutation) employed in Latin America

ab·re·act \¦abrē¦akt\ *vt* -ED/-ING/-S [part trans. of G *abreagieren*, fr. *ab* off, away from, down from (fr. OHG *aba*) + *reagieren* to react — more at OF] **:** to release or express (an emotion previously repressed or forgotten) ⟨~ his resentment over a childhood slight⟩

ab·re·ac·tion \¦abrē'akshən\ *n* -s [part trans. of G *abreagierung*, fr. *ab* + *reagierung* reaction] **:** the discharge of the emotional energy supposed to be attached to a repressed idea esp. by the conscious verbalization of that idea in the presence of a therapist — compare CATHARSIS 3a

ab·re·ac·tive \-ktiv\ *adj* [*abreaction* + *-ive*] **:** relating to or capable of producing abreaction ⟨~ technique⟩

[1]**abreast** \ə'-\ *adv (or adj)* [ME *abrest*, fr. [1]*a-* + *brest* breast] **1 a :** beside one another with bodies in line ⟨four cars standing ~ so as to block the street⟩ ⟨with seats two ~ on each side of the aisle⟩ **b** *naut* **:** in or to a position with the bearing of another object 90 degrees from the bow **:** directly abeam ⟨~ of the tip of the island⟩ **2 :** up to or equal to a particular standard or level (as of performance or development) ⟨kept wages ~ of the rising living costs⟩ **:** in a condition of acquaintance with events or developments in a particular field **:** UP-TO-DATE ⟨the researcher keeps ~ with related work in his field⟩

[2]**abreast** \"\ *prep, naut* **:** abreast of ⟨lying ~ the island⟩

abreed *or* **abreid** \ə'brēd\ *chiefly Scot var of* ABROAD

abrenunciation *n* -s [ML *abrenuntiation-, abrenuntiatio,* fr. LL *abrenuntiatus* (past part. of *abrenuntiare* to renounce), fr. L *ab-* ¹ab- + *renuntiare* to renounce — more at RENOUNCE] *archaic* : RENUNCIATION, REPUDIATION

abri \ȧbrē\ *n, pl* **abris** \-ē(z)\ [F, fr. OF, fr. *abrier* to shelter, fr. LL *apricari* to sun oneself, fr. *apricus* exposed to the sun] : SHELTER; *esp* : a dugout or cavity in a hillside

abri au·dit \,a(,)brē,ō'dē\ *adj, usu cap both As* [fr. F *Abri Audit* (lit., Audit Shelter), a rock shelter in Dordogne dept., France] : of or belonging to a prehistoric culture transitional between late Mousterian and Aurignacian

abridge \ə'brij\ *vt* -ED/-ING/-S [ME *abregen, abriggen,* fr. MF *abregier,* fr. LL *abbreviare,* fr. L *ad-* + *breviare* to shorten, fr. *brevis* short — more at BRIEF] **1 a** *archaic* : DEPRIVE — usu. used with *of* ⟨~ a man of his rights⟩ **b** : to diminish (as a right) by reducing ⟨the danger of *abridging* the liberties of the people —Abraham Lincoln⟩ **2** : to shorten in duration ⟨I have other reasons for *abridging* my stay at Bath —Tobias Smollett⟩ : shorten or cut down in extent ⟨the airplane ~*s* distance⟩ ⟨~ library service during the summer⟩ **3** : to shorten by omission of words without sacrifice of principal meaning : CONDENSE ⟨an *abridged* version of the novel⟩ **syn** see SHORTEN

abridg·er \-jə(r)\ *n* -s : one that abridges

abridg·ment *or* **abridge·ment** \-jmənt\ *n* -s **1** : action of abridging : state of being abridged **2 a** : a shortened form of a work produced by condensation and omission but retaining the general meaning and manner of presentation of the original : COMPENDIUM **3** : a brief statement of a subject : an epitome of general outlines or principles : SYNOPSIS; *specif* : any of various brief statements of case law made before modern reporting of cases

syn ABRIDGMENT, ABSTRACT, BRIEF, SYNOPSIS, CONSPECTUS, EPITOME: these terms all denote a condensation of a larger work or more extended, although often only prospective, treatment. ABRIDGMENT implies reduction in compass yet retention of relative completeness, usu. with the retention too of something of the manner of the original ⟨all *abridgments* of encyclopedic treatments, even when they are the work of their own authors, must inevitably suffer —Paul Radin⟩ ⟨the delivers an *abridgment* of the famous opening soliloquy with little regard for metrical or musical values —Henry Hewes⟩ ⟨a 50-page *abridgment* of a full-length novel⟩ An ABSTRACT is a summary of a document, treatise, or proposed treatment giving the salient points, usu. in the order of presentation, with usu. no claim to independent worth ⟨accounts of ancient and modern political unions . . . He made *abstracts* of them —H.E.Scudder⟩ ⟨this pamphlet contains an *abstract* of the hunting and trapping law as contained in the Biennial Revision —*Maine Hunting & Trapping Laws*⟩ A BRIEF is an abstract of a case or argument, esp. in law ⟨prepared an extended *brief* to support his position —*Amer. Guide Series: Oregon*⟩ ⟨two *briefs* submitted by lawyers —M.R.Cohen⟩ ⟨it became in time the principal *brief* and basic blueprint for the expansion of the Air Force —Gordon Harrison⟩ SYNOPSIS usu. implies a skeletal presentation, esp. of a narrative or proposed narrative, that can be apprehended in a moment or rapidly ⟨a *synopsis* of an argument⟩ ⟨the *synopsis* is an outline of three or four typewritten pages containing the barest summary of character and action . . . made for the convenience of the producer —V.I.Pudovkin⟩ CONSPECTUS implies a quick overall but relatively complete view of something complex or extremely detailed on more leisurely careful examination ⟨a detailed and objective *conspectus* of the ideological background and basis of Soviet communism —*Times Lit. Supp.*⟩ ⟨the book . . . will contain a full *conspectus* of the published treatises —*Mediaeval Academy News*⟩ ⟨a detailed *conspectus* of this society's values —J.J.Spengler⟩ EPITOME suggests the briefest possible condensation yet extreme accuracy in presentation, a complex whole in miniature, usu. with an independent value as a whole ⟨having an *epitome* of all these findings upon a single sheet —L.F.Barker⟩ ⟨*epitomes* of British novels circulated widely —H.R.Warfel⟩ ⟨the title is a neat *epitome* of the contents —*Current Biog.*⟩

abrim \ə'-\ *adj* [¹*a-* + *brim,* v.] : BRIMMING

abrin \'ābrən, 'a-, -(,)brin; ä'brin, a'b-\ *n* -s [ISV *abr-* (fr. NL *Abrus,* genus name of *Abrus precatorius* Indian licorice) + *-in*] : a toxic protein obtained from jequirity

abrine \'ā,brēn, 'a,b-; ⸗'⸗\ *n* -s [alter. of *abrin*] : a toxic crystalline amino acid $C_{12}H_{14}N_2O_2$ obtained from jequirity; *N*-methyltryptophan — distinguished from *abrin*

abris *pl of* ABRI

abris·tle \ə'-\ *adj* [¹*a-* + *bristle,* v.] : BRISTLING

abroach \ə'brōch\ *adv (or adj)* [ME *abroche,* fr. ¹*a-* + *broche* pointed rod, perforation — more at BROACH] **1** *of a cask* : in a condition for letting out liquor : TAPPED ⟨set the cask ~⟩ **2** : in a state to be diffused or propagated ⟨mischiefs that I set ~ —Shak.⟩

¹**abroad** \ə'brȯd\ *adv (or adj)* [ME *abrood,* fr. ¹*a-* + *brood* broad] **1** : over a wide area : at large ⟨a tree spreading its branches ~⟩ : widely apart ⟨flinging his arms wildly ~ —Nathaniel Hawthorne⟩ **2** : out of the house : away from one's home ⟨walk ~ after lunch⟩ : in circulation or movement from place to place : on the street or public ways : here and there ⟨at this hour the few people ~ go quickly on their ways⟩ ⟨the enemy is ~ in the land⟩ : out in the open ⟨insects awakened from torpor and ~ in the spring sun —Walter Pater⟩ **3** : beyond the boundaries of a country ⟨travel ~ in many lands⟩ : in or to foreign countries ⟨a university well known ~⟩ **4** : in circulation throughout society or the world ⟨the idea has got ~⟩ : in evidence : ABOUT ⟨plenty of enthusiasm ~⟩ **5** : wide of the mark : ASTRAY : in confusion ⟨I'm much ~ in my ciphering —Francis Hoover⟩ **6** : contested elsewhere than on the home grounds ⟨the team wears a different uniform for games ~⟩

²**abroad** \"\ *prep* : THROUGHOUT, OVER ⟨and then ~ the world he goes —Emily Dickinson⟩

ab·ro·come \'abrə,kōm\ *n* -s [NL *Abrocoma,* irreg. fr. Gk *habrokomēs* with delicate hair, fr. *habro-* + *komē* hair] : either of two ratlike hystricomorph rodents having fine soft fur and large rounded ears and constituting a genus (*Abrocoma*) restricted to the Andes mountains — called also *rat chinchilla*

¹**abrogate** *adj* [ME *abrogat,* fr. L *abrogatus*] *obs* : ABROGATED

²**ab·ro·gate** \'abrə,gāt, *usu* -ād· + V\ *vt* -ED/-ING/-S [L *abrogatus,* past part. of *abrogare,* fr. *ab-* ¹ab- + *rogare* to ask, propose a law — more at RIGHT] **1** : to abolish by authoritative, official, or formal action : ANNUL, REPEAL ⟨neither a court decision nor a statute can, however, ~ a treaty as an international contract —F.A.Ogg & P.O.Ray⟩ ⟨special legal privileges for foreigners should be *abrogated* —*New Republic*⟩ **2** : to put an end to : do away with : set aside ⟨we are not thereby called upon to ~ the standards of values that are fixed —J.L.Lowes⟩ ⟨he declined to ~ his conscience —Walter H. Page⟩ **syn** see NULLIFY

ab·ro·ga·tion \,abrə'gāshən\ *n* -s [MF or L; MF *abrogation,* fr. L *abrogation-, abrogatio,* fr. *abrogatus* + *-ion-, -io* -ion] : the act of abrogating : definitive repeal

abro·ma \ə'brōmə\ *n, cap* [NL, fr. ²*a-* + Gk *brōma* food; akin to Gk *bibrōskein* to devour — more at VORACIOUS] : a genus of Asiatic and Australian woody plants (family Sterculiaceae) the bark of which yields a strong white fiber — see DEVIL'S-COTTON

abro·nia \ə'brōnēə\ *n* [NL, irreg. fr. Gk *habros* graceful, delicate + NL *-ia* — more at HABRO-] **1** *cap* : a genus of herbs (family Nyctaginaceae) native to western No. America having showy fragrant flowers in bracted heads and with the salver-shaped calyx having a 3-winged base — see SAND VERBENA **2** -s : any plant of the genus *Abronia*

abrood \ə'brüd\ *adv* [ME *abrod,* fr. ¹*a-* + *brod* brood — more at BROOD] *now dial Eng* : on a hatch

abrot·a·num \ə'brät°nəm\ *n* -s [ML, alter. of L *abrotonum,* fr Gk *abrotonon* southernwood, southernwood] : SOUTHERNWOOD

ab·ro·tine \'abrə,tēn\ *n* -s [ISV *abrot-* (fr. ML *abrotanum*) + *-ine;* prob. orig. formed as G *abrotin*] : a colorless crystalline alkaloid $C_{21}H_{22}N_2O$ obtained from southernwood

¹**abrupt** \ə'brəpt, *also* (')a¦b-\ *adj, sometimes* -ER/-EST [L *abruptus,* fr. past part. of *abrumpere* to break off, fr. *ab-* ¹ab- + *rumpere* to break — more at REAVE] **1** : broken off : suddenly terminating as if cut or broken off ⟨short and ~ plant filaments⟩ **2 a** : characterized by or producing the effect of a sharp break or sudden ending ⟨act with ~ decision⟩ : UNEXPECTED ⟨at ~ intervals in the performance⟩ **b** : unceremoniously curt ⟨~ in manner⟩ **c** : lacking transition from one subject to another : DISCONNECTED ⟨an ~ literary style⟩ **3** : rising or dropping sharply as if broken off : PRECIPITOUS, STEEP ⟨an ~ peak rising from the ocean⟩ **syn** see PRECIPITATE, STEEP — **abrupt·ness** *n* -ES

²**abrupt** \"\ *vt* -ED/-ING/-S *archaic* : to break off ⟨let brazen bands ~ their din —W.H.Auden⟩ : SEPARATE

abrup·tion \ə'brəpshən, a'b-\ *n* -s [L *abruption-, abruptio,* fr. *abruptus* (past part.) + *-ion-, -io* -ion] **1** *archaic* : sudden termination or interruption ⟨~ in a narrative⟩ ⟨total ~ of all relations between them⟩ **2** : a sudden breaking off : detachment of portions from a mass ⟨placental ~⟩

ab·rup·tio pla·cen·tae \ə'brəpshē,ōplə'sen,tē, ä'brüptē-,ōplä'ken,tī\ *n, pl* **abruptio pla·cen·ta·rum** \-,plasᵊn'ta(a)rəm, ,plä,ken'tä,rüm\ *or* **abrupti·o·nes placentarum** \-shē-'ō(,)nēz-,-tē'ō,nās-\ [NL, a breaking off of the placenta] : premature detachment of the placenta from the wall of the uterus

abrupt·ly \ə'brəp(t)lē, -li *also* (')a¦b-\ *adv* [¹*abrupt* + *-ly*] : in an abrupt manner

abrus \'ābrəs, 'ā-\ *n, cap* [NL, irreg. fr. Gk *habros* graceful, delicate — more at HABRO-] : a genus of tropical vines (family Fabaceae) having pinnate leaves, purplish flowers with a 4-lobed calyx, and flat pods — see INDIAN LICORICE

abruz·zi ware \ä'brütsē, ə'b-\ *n, usu cap A* [fr. *Abruzzi* e Molise, compartimento of central Italy where it was first made] : an ornate Italian pottery chiefly of the 15th century

abs *pl of* AB

abs *abbr* **1** absent **2** absolute **3** abstract

ab·sa·ro·ka \ab'särəkə\ *or* **ab·sa·ro·ke** *or* **ab·sa·ro·kee** \-särəkē,-sȯrkē\ *n, pl* **absaroka** *or* **absarokas** *or* **absaroke** *or* **absarokes** *or* **absarokee** *or* **absarokees** *usu cap* [Dakota, lit., crow people, bird people] : ¹CROW 8

ab·scess \'ab,ses *also* -səs\ *n* -ES [L *abscessus,* lit., act of going away, fr. *abscessus,* past part. of *abscedere* to go away, fr. *abs-* (var. of *ab-* ¹ab-) + *cedere* to go — more at CEDE] : a localized collection of pus surrounded by an area of inflamed tissue in which hyperemia and infiltration of leukocytes is marked

ab·scessed \-est, -əst\ *adj* : afflicted with an abscess or abscesses

ab·scess·root \'⸗(,)⸗,⸗\ *n* : a perennial herb (*Polemonium reptans*) of the eastern U. S. with compound leaves and blue flowers

ab·scind \ab'sind\ *vt* -ED/-ING/-S [L *abscindere* to cut or tear off, fr. *ab.* ¹ab- + *scindere* to cut, tear — more at SHED (to throw off)] : to cut off

ab·scise \ab'sīz\ *vb* -ED/-ING/-S [L *abscisus,* past part. of *abscidere,* fr. *abs-* (var. of *ab-* ¹ab-) + *-cidere* (fr. *caedere* to cut) — more at CONCISE] *vt* : to cut off by abscission (sense 2) ~ *vi* : to separate (as of a leaf from a twig) by abscission

ab·sciss \ab'sis\ *vb* -ED/-ING/-S [back-formation fr. *abscission*] : ABSCISE

ab·scis·sa \ab'sisə, əb-\ *n* -s [NL, fr. L, fem. of *abscissus,* past part. of *abscindere* — more at ABSCIND] : the horizontal coordinate of a point in a plane Cartesian coordinate system obtained by measuring parallel to the x-axis — compare ORDINATE

AP abscissa of point *P*

ab·scis·sio in·fi·ni·ti \ab'sisē,ō,in-fə'nī,tī\ *n, pl* **abscissi·o·nes infiniti** \-,sisē'ō,nē,zin-\ [NL, abscission of that which is infinite] : a logical process using successive exclusions of the inapplicable for the purpose of determining a true conclusion or the classification of a subject — compare METHOD OF EXCLUSION

ab·scis·sion *also* **ab·sci·sion** \ab'sizhən, əb-, -ish-\ *n* -s [L *abscission-, abscissio,* fr. *abscissus* + *-ion-, -io* -ion] **1** : a cutting off or removal : ABLATION **2** : the natural separation of flowers, fruit, and leaves from plants by the development and subsequent disorganization of the separation layer

abscission layer \"-\ *also* **ab·sciss layer** \'ab,sis-\ *n* : SEPARATION LAYER

abscission zone *n* : the zone in a leaf petiole, fruit stalk, or branch often marked by a constriction within which is developed the separation layer, the vascular bundles in the zone usu. being reduced in diameter, the sclerenchyma being weak or absent, the collenchyma lacking, and the cytoplasm of some of the parenchyma cells being denser than in adjacent cells

ab·scond \abz'kānd, ab'sk-, əb-\ *vb* -ED/-ING/-S [L *abscondere* to hide, fr. *abs-* (var. of *ab-* ¹ab-) + *condere* to found, construct, store up, conceal — more at CONDITE] *vi* **1** : WITHDRAW, FLEE ⟨valleys from which the evil spirits had long ago ~*ed* —Herbert Read⟩ **2** : to depart secretly : withdraw and hide oneself ⟨homesickness which . . . drives so many recruits to ~ —T.B. Macaulay⟩; *specif* : to evade the legal process of a court by hiding within or secretly leaving its jurisdiction ⟨~ from New York⟩ ⟨~ to Canada⟩ ~ *vt, archaic* : CONCEAL **syn** see ESCAPE

ab·scond·ence \-dən(t)s\ *n* -s : fugitive concealment : secret retirement : HIDING

ab·seil \'äp,zīl, -īəl\ *n* -s [G *abseil-,* fr. *abseilen* to descend by a rope, fr. *ab-* down + *seil* rope] : descent in mountaineering by means of a rope looped over a projection above — compare RAPPEL

ab·sence \'absən(t)s\ *n* -s [ME, fr. MF, fr. L *absentia,* fr. *absent-, absens* + *-ia*] **1** : state of being absent or missing from a place or from companionship : failure to be present — opposed to *presence* **2** : failure to be present (as in an accustomed place) or where one is needed, wanted, or normally expected ⟨frequent ~*s* from a job⟩ ⟨drawings executed with ~ of detail⟩ ⟨a noticeable ~ of enthusiasm for his task⟩ : NONATTENDANCE ⟨~ from school⟩ : NONAPPEARANCE ⟨called on to speak in his brother's ~⟩ : DEFICIENCY ⟨the ~ of trained leaders⟩ **3** : inattention to things present ⟨~ of mind⟩ **4** : transient loss or impairment of consciousness beginning and ending abruptly, unremembered afterward, and seen chiefly in mild types of epilepsy **5** : lack of contact between blades in fencing

syn LACK, DEFECT, WANT, PRIVATION: ABSENCE usu. is used to indicate the fact that a thing is not present ⟨absolute liberty is *absence* of restraint —Henry Adams⟩ ⟨in the *absence* of a force strong enough to challenge the Federals, the towns submitted quietly —*Amer. Guide Series: La.*⟩ ⟨the serenity or *absence* of distorting passion in classic art —M.R.Cohen⟩ ⟨a complete *absence* of any thinking on fundamental problems of methodology —René Wellek⟩ LACK, although often interchangeable with ABSENCE, suggests an absence that constitutes a deficiency or falling short ⟨the *lack* of applause seemed a criticism of her work —*Current Biog.*⟩ ⟨he had become impressed by the *lack* of adequate textbooks in the schools —H.E.Starr⟩ ⟨production in other industries was similarly slowed by the power shortage and by a *lack* of raw materials —*Collier's Yr.Bk.*⟩ ⟨the mud and the *lack* of bridges made travel almost impossible —*Amer. Guide Series: Minn.*⟩ DEFECT implies the absence or the lack of something necessary to completeness or perfection ⟨each little fault of temper and each social *defect* —W.S.Gilbert⟩ ⟨*defects* of understanding based on ignorance and unfamiliarity —J.R. Oppenheimer⟩ ⟨those countries which are invaded suffer from the *defects* of the invader's civilization —Stephen Spender⟩ WANT implies the absence of something essential, usu. indispensable, often, however, indicating something only considered essential and, therefore, coming close to signifying something merely desired ⟨a certain *want* of confidence in his superiors⟩ ⟨the country was going to the dogs because of the *want* of education —F.M.Ford⟩ ⟨war production occas. suffered from *want* of hands to tend the machines or harvest the crops —Oscar Handlin⟩ PRIVATION in the sense pertinent here (as opposed to the sense of deprivation or destitution) has a use mainly confined to the fine philosophical definition of a negative state or quality in terms of its opposite ⟨cold is the *privation* of heat⟩ ⟨vice may be called the *privation* of virtue⟩

absence without leave : the military offense of being absent without leave — compare AWOL

¹**ab·sent** \'absənt\ *adj* [ME, fr. MF, fr. L *absent-, absens,* pres. part. of *abesse* to be away, be absent, fr. *ab-* ¹ab- + *esse* to be — more at IS] **1** : not present or not attending ⟨~ committee members⟩ : being elsewhere : MISSING ⟨~ at roll call⟩ : being away ⟨~ from home⟩ ⟨~ friends⟩ **2** : not existing in a place ⟨a species totally ~ in the Great Lakes⟩ : LACKING ⟨danger in a situation where power is ~ —M.H.Trytten⟩ **3** *sometimes* -ER/-EST : INATTENTIVE ⟨his look had grown ~, as if he were calling up memories —William Black⟩ : PREOCCUPIED ⟨drew near to the fireplace, and looked into the flames in an ~ mood —Thomas Hardy⟩ — **ab·sent·ly** *adv*

²**absent** \ab'sent, əb-\ *vt* -ED/-ING/-S [ME *absenten,* fr. MF *absenter,* fr. LL *absentare,* fr. L *absent-, absens*] : to keep away ⟨~*s* himself entirely from all fellowship —R.L.Stevenson⟩

³**ab·sent** \'absənt\ *prep* [¹*absent*] : in the absence of ⟨under this definition, ~ any other facts, there arises an implied contract —*Jour. Amer. Med. Assoc.*⟩

ab·sen·ta·tion \,absən'tāshən, -,sen-\ *n* -s [ML *absentation-, absentatio,* fr. LL *absentatus* (past part. of *absentare* to be absent) + L *-ion-, -io* -ion] : an absenting of oneself

ab·sen·tee \,absən¦tē\ *n* -s *often attrib* **1** : one that is absent or that absents himself (as a pupil from school or a worker from a job) ⟨sick ~*s*⟩; *specif* : a proprietor that lives elsewhere — often used disparagingly ⟨~ landlords⟩ **2** : one that is nonexistent or lacking ⟨trees are notable ~*s* in the perpetually drought-stricken landscape —George Farwell⟩ ⟨in this anthology, these two authors being among the ~*s*⟩

absentee ballot *n* : a ballot cast (as by mail) by a voter unable to be present in person at the polls

ab·sen·tee·ism \,⸗⸗'⸗,izəm\ *n* -s **1** : protracted or permanent absence of an owner from his property ⟨~ of landlords⟩ **2** : continual interruption of attendance ⟨effect of ~ on factory production⟩ ⟨~ of school children⟩ ⟨his record of ~⟩

absentee ownership *n* : ownership esp. of corporation stock by one residing elsewhere than in the locality where income is derived

absentee voter *n* : ABSENT VOTER

ab·sen·te reo \ab¦sentē'rē(,)ō\ [NL] : the defendant being absent

ab·sent-mind·ed \'absənt'mīndəd\ *adj, sometimes* -ER/-EST : preoccupied to the point of failure to respond to ordinary demands on the attention — **ab·sent-mind·ed·ly** *adv* — **ab·sent-mind·ed·ness** *n* -ES

absent over leave *adj* : having failed to return from liberty or leave on time — abbr. *AOL*

absent treatment *n* : treatment that ignores one's presence : SNUB, COLD SHOULDER

absent voter *n* : a qualified voter who is legally permitted to vote by mail because of illness or unavoidable and necessary absence from the voting district

absent without leave *adj* : absent from one's place of duty in the armed forces without authority — abbr. *AWOL*

absidiole *var of* APSIDIOLE

ab·sinthe *or* **ab·sinth** \'ab,sin(t)th *also* -,sən-\ *n* -s [F *absinthe,* fr. L *absinthium* — more at ABSINTHIUM] **1** : WORMWOOD **2** : a green bitter liqueur formerly flavored with wormwood, anise, and other aromatics but now usu. with a substitute for wormwood **3** *or* **absinthe green** : a moderate yellow green that is greener and lighter than average moss green, yellower and less strong than average pea green, and yellower and duller than apple green (sense 1)

absinthe oil *n* : WORMWOOD OIL

absinthe yellow *n* : a grayish greenish yellow that is slightly stronger and very slightly darker than hay, deeper than yellow stone, and greener and duller than dusty yellow

ab·sin·thin \(')ab¦sin(t)thən\ *also* **ab·sin·thi·in** \⸗'⸗thēən\ *n* -s [ISV *absinth-* or *absinthi-* (fr. L *absinthium*) + *-in;* orig. formed as G *absinthin*] : a bitter white crystalline compound $C_{15}H_{20}O_4$ constituting the bitter principle of wormwood

ab·sin·thine \(')ab¦sin(t)thən, 'absən,thīn\ *adj* [*absinthe* + *-ine*] : like absinthe

ab·sin·thism \'absən,thizəm, -,sin-\ *n* -s [F *absinthisme,* fr. *absinthe* + *-isme* -ism] : a diseased condition resulting from habitual excessive use of absinthe that contains oils of wormwood — **ab·sin·this·mic** \¦⸗(,)⸗¦⸗zmik\ *adj*

ab·sin·thi·um \ab'sin(t)thēəm\ *n, pl* **absinthium** [ME, fr. L, fr. Gk *apsinthion*] **1** : WORMWOOD **2 a** : the dried leaves and flowering tops of a common wormwood (*Artemisia absinthium*) once used as a bitter tonic and stomachic **b** : oil of wormwood used as an ingredient of absinthe

ab·sin·thol \'absən,thȯl, -,sin-, -ōl\ *n* -s [ISV *absinthe* + *-ole*] : THUJONE

ab·sit omen \,absəd·'ōmən\ *interj* [L, may (evil) omen be absent, i.e., may what is said not come true] — used as a mild invocation ⟨if he should fail, *absit omen,* all will be lost⟩; compare *God forbid* at ²GOD

¹**ab·so·lute** \'absə,lüt *also* -əl,yüt *or* ,⸗⸗'⸗; *usu* -üd·+V\ *adj, sometimes* -ER/-EST [ME *absolut,* fr. L *absolutus,* fr. past part. of *absolvere* to set free, absolve — more at ABSOLVE] **1** *obs* : ABSOLVED, FREE, DISENGAGED ⟨~ from necessity⟩ **2 a** : free from imperfection or fault : PERFECT ⟨equally ~ is his meticulous taste in choosing the books —Christopher Morley⟩ **b** : free or relatively free from admixture : PURE ⟨~ alcohol contains one percent or less of water⟩ : OUTRIGHT, THOROUGHGOING, UNMITIGATED ⟨~ villainy⟩ ⟨an ~ lie⟩ **3** : marked by freedom from restraint or control by any governing or commanding agent or instrumentality: as **a** : having supreme power effectively or formally without constitutional or other restrictions ⟨an ~ ruler⟩ **b** : marked by extreme concentration of complete power and jurisdiction ⟨an ~ government⟩ ⟨an ~ dictatorship⟩ **c** : proceeding from or characteristic of an absolute ruler or state ⟨~ edicts⟩ ⟨~ power⟩ **d** : possessing or marked by absolute power : in sole control ⟨a ship captain ~ on the high seas⟩ **e** : ABSOLUTIST **4** : characterized by the lack of a particular (as the normal or usual) syntactical connection: **a**(1) *of a case form* : syntactically connected with the rest of its sentence in an atypical manner ⟨a nominative that is not the subject of a finite verb or a genitive that is not dependent on another substantive is an ~ nominative or an ~ genitive⟩ — see ABLATIVE ABSOLUTE, ACCUSATIVE ABSOLUTE, GENITIVE ABSOLUTE, NOMINATIVE ABSOLUTE (2) : standing by itself in loose syntactical connection with the rest of its sentence and qualifying the sentence as a whole rather than any single word in it ⟨*anyhow* in "anyhow, there is still time to catch the train" and *to say the least* in "to say the least, this procedure is unusual" are ~ constructions⟩ **b** *of an adjective or possessive pronoun* : standing alone without a modified substantive ⟨*blind* in "help the blind"; *ours* in "your work and ours" are ~⟩ ⟨*ours* is the ~ form of *our*⟩ **c** *of a comparative or superlative* : expressing a relatively high or an unsurpassed degree without definite comparison to any other under view ⟨*older* in "an older person should be treated with respect"; *greatest* in "I have the greatest confidence in him" are ~⟩ **d** *of a verb* : having no object in the particular construction under consideration though normally transitive ⟨*kill* in "if looks could kill" is an ~ verb⟩ ☞ In this dictionary absolute verbs are treated as intransitive **e** *in Irish and Welsh verb inflection* : belonging to or characteristic of a verb that is not preceded by any of a particular set of particles nor compounded with a preverb ⟨the ~ form⟩ ⟨an ~ ending⟩ — opposed to *conjunct* **5** : free from conditional limitation : operating or existing in full under all circumstances without variation or exception : COMPLETE ⟨an ~ requirement⟩ ⟨an ~ prohibition⟩ ⟨~ agreement⟩ ⟨~ freedom⟩ ⟨experience proved that man's power of choice in action was very far from ~ —Henry Adams⟩ **6** : free from doubt: as **a** *obs* : convinced and certain **b** : POSITIVE, UNQUESTIONABLE ⟨~ proof⟩ ⟨~ facts⟩ ⟨~ standards of righteousness —Rose Macaulay⟩ **c** : PEREMPTORY ⟨an ~ command⟩ **7 a** : independent of arbitrary standards of measurement ⟨an ~ coefficient in an equation⟩ **b** : having reference to or derived in the simplest manner from the fundamental units of length, mass, and time ⟨~ electric units⟩ **c** : relating to the absolute-temperature scale ⟨10° ~⟩ **8** : free from qualification: as **a** : final and not liable to modification or termination : FULL ⟨an ~ denial⟩ ⟨an ~ resignation⟩ ⟨~ divorce⟩ ⟨~ ownership⟩ ⟨rights that even seem ~ have these qualifications —O.W.Holmes †1935⟩ **b** : TOTAL ⟨~ loss⟩ ⟨~ perfection is denied to us humans —M.R.Cohen⟩ ⟨calm and ~ assurance —Arnold Bennett⟩ ⟨~ master of the raciest elements of the vernacular —J.L. Lowes⟩ **c** *of democracy* : ²DIRECT 4b **9 a** : free of relation-

ship or relativity **:** not compared **:** not dependent on or modified or affected by circumstances or by anything outside itself ⟨an ~ term in logic⟩ ⟨truth . . . is no ~ thing, but always relative —John Galsworthy⟩ **b :** FUNDAMENTAL, ULTIMATE, INTRINSIC **:** self-contained and self-sufficient **:** free from the variability and error natural to human perception and human ways of thinking ⟨God's ~ knowledge⟩ **10 :** perfectly realizing or typifying the nature of the thing in question ⟨~ justice⟩ ⟨~ hate⟩ ⟨the abstract of beauty ~ —P.E.More⟩ **11 a :** concerned entirely with the expression of beauty or of pure feeling and devoid of meaningful reference ⟨~ poetry⟩ — see ABSOLUTE MUSIC **b** *of the dance* **:** relying on the medium of the human body for the expression of an idea independent of music, costumes, and stage sets

syn AUTOCRATIC, ARBITRARY, DESPOTIC, TYRANNICAL, TYRANNOUS: ABSOLUTE indicates the fact of having or constituting complete power or authority without external restraint or control ⟨he ruled as an *absolute* monarch⟩ ⟨it was possible for Signor Mussolini to be made *absolute* managing director (Dictator or Duce) of the Italian nation —G.B.Shaw⟩ ⟨they held their subjects with an *absolute* hand as all communistic leaders do —F.M.Brown⟩ AUTOCRATIC and AUTOCRATICAL, likewise designating complete, unchecked power, may be derogatory in implying overwhelming domination or imperious attitudes ⟨*autocratic* prerogatives could be exercised, under the president, by military officers authorized to arrest without warrants, imprison, and mete out penalties at the drumhead —Charles & Mary Beard⟩ ⟨let the emperor turn his nominal sovereignty into a real central and *autocratic* power, subjecting every rebel city and noble —Hilaire Belloc⟩ ARBITRARY is often derogatory in suggesting caprice, unreason, and lack of consideration in exercising power ⟨as absolute a master of all their professional actions as ever was the most *arbitrary* general of the professional actions of his soldiery —W.H.Mallock⟩ ⟨irresponsible in its unrestraint, the majority vote may easily outdo an Oriental despot in *arbitrary* rule —V.L.Parrington⟩ ⟨that *arbitrary* idealism which knows no law —Josiah Royce⟩ DESPOTIC is likely to imply imperious and oppressive misuse of absolute power ⟨a *despotic* government based on fear or blind obedience is a state of slavery —M.R. Cohen⟩ ⟨his manner was imperious, and his administration had been arrogant and *despotic* —Willa Cather⟩ TYRANNICAL and TYRANNOUS, always quite condemnatory, imply cruel, harsh oppression by an absolute ruler or power ⟨the *tyrannical* rule of Porfirio Díaz, who reduced his own people to peonage while he sold out his country to foreign mining and business interests —Allan Nevins & H.S. Commager⟩ ⟨I remember recent instances where *tyrannical* judges sitting in local courts rode roughshod over the civil liberties of defendants charged with crime —W.O.Douglas⟩ **syn** see in addition PURE

²absolute \"\ *n* -s **1 :** something that is absolute: **a :** something that is independent of human perception, valuation, and cognition **b :** something that is not dependent on anything else (as the Spinozistic substance, the first cause, or the primordial) — usu. used with *the* **2** *usu cap* **a :** one of various concepts: as (1) **:** ABSOLUTE EGO (2) **:** the underlying unity of spirit and nature **b :** the whole of reality considered as the final or total fact **:** that totality to which everything may be reduced or which in the estimation of its proponent constitutes the ultimate or final referent — usu. used with *the* **3 :** a concentrated natural flower oil used in perfumery ⟨~ of rose⟩: as **a :** a concentrate prepared by removal of plant waxes from a concrete (sense 5) **b** *also* **absolute of enfleurage :** a concentrate obtained in the enfleurage process by removal of the alcohol from alcoholic extracts of the pomade

absolute altimeter *n* **:** an aircraft altimeter that determines distance to the earth by radio measuring the time needed for an emitted wave to reach the earth and reflect back to the aircraft

absolute altitude *n* **:** the vertical distance between an aircraft and the surface over which it is flying

absolute blocking *n* **:** BLOCK SYSTEM

absolute ceiling *n* **:** the maximum height above sea level at which a particular airplane can maintain horizontal flight under standard air conditions — called also *ceiling*

absolute constant *n* **:** a constant (as π) that has the same value wherever it occurs in mathematics

absolute ego *n* **:** the Fichtean ego that posits its own existence and through the opposition of subject and object thus created dialectically evolves the universe

absolute endorsement *n* **:** an endorsement that binds the endorser to pay only on failure of the prior parties to do so and on due notice thereof to him

absolute fee simple *n* **:** FEE SIMPLE ABSOLUTE

absolute form *n* **1 :** the Platonic form of the supreme idea or unity in which all other ideas participate **2 :** the subject-object relation

absolute humidity *n* **:** the amount of vapor actually present in the air usu. expressed in grams per cubic meter or grains per cubic foot

absolute idealism *n* **:** the Hegelian philosophy of the absolute mind or any one of a group of metaphysical idealisms deriving primarily from Hegel which affirm that fundamental reality is an all-embracing spiritual unity — see IDEALISM; compare HEGELIANISM

absolute impediment *n, canon & civil law* **:** a diriment impediment that makes it impossible for a person to enter into a marriage but does not require punishment or a decree of annulment

ab·so·lute·ly \ˈ⸗⸗ˈ⸗⸗\ *adv* [ME, fr. *absolute* + *-ly*] **:** in an absolute manner or condition **:** INDEPENDENTLY, UNCONDITIONALLY, ENTIRELY, POSITIVELY ⟨~ unmolested inquiry —J.B. Conant⟩ ⟨iron is ~ necessary —Morris Fishbein⟩

absolutely convergent *adj, of an infinite series* **:** remaining convergent even if the signs of negative terms are changed

absolutely privileged communication *n* **:** PRIVILEGED COMMUNICATION 2

absolute magnitude *n* **:** the intrinsic luminosity of a celestial body expressed on a scale for which the distance is arbitrarily established (as of a star observed from a standard distance of 10 parsecs) ⟨the *absolute magnitude* of the sun is about +5 visual⟩

absolute majority *n* **1 :** more than half of the votes: as **a :** more than half of the votes actually cast **b :** more than half of the number of qualified voters **2 :** MAJORITY 3a

absolute music *n* **:** instrumental music independent of the objective suggestion of title, text, or program and dependent on structure alone for its subjective comprehension

ab·so·lute·ness \ˈ⸗⸗ˈ⸗⸗\ *n* -ES **:** the quality or state of being absolute ⟨the ~ of the dictator's decrees⟩

absolute of enfleurage : ²ABSOLUTE 3b

absolute personal equation *n* **:** the deviation between a value obtained by an observer and a standard value assumed as true — compare RELATIVE PERSONAL EQUATION

absolute pitch *n* **1 :** the position of a tone in reference to the whole range of pitch or to a standard scale and independently determined by its rate of vibration — distinguished from *relative pitch* **2 :** the sense or memory of absolute pitch **:** the ability to recognize or sing a given isolated note

absolute pressure *n* **:** total pressure at a point in a fluid equaling the sum of the gage and the atmospheric pressures

absolute privilege *n* **:** a privilege that arises in the law of libel and slander and that protects members of a lawmaking body (as Congress) in their statements made on the floor without regard to whether spoken in good faith — compare QUALIFIED PRIVILEGE

absoluter *comparative of* ABSOLUTE

absolute reality *n* **1 :** ultimate reality as it is in itself unaffected by the perception or knowledge of any finite being **2** *Scholasticism* **:** reality in relation to the divine mind

absolute right *n* **:** an unqualified right **:** a legally enforceable right to take some action or to refrain from acting at the sole discretion of the person having the right

absolutes *pl of* ABSOLUTE

absolute scale *n* **:** a temperature scale that is based on absolute zero and that uses units of measurement equivalent to centigrade degrees on the Kelvin scale or to Fahrenheit degrees on the Rankine scale

absolute space *n* **:** space independent of what occupies it **:** the space in which positions are finally determined

absolutest *superlative of* ABSOLUTE

absolute state *n, in the grammar of the Semitic languages* **:** the form that is characteristic of a noun when it is not linked in a grammatical construction with another noun (as Hebrew *bēn* "son") — compare CONSTRUCT STATE, EMPHATIC STATE

absolute system *n* **:** a system of physical units (as cgs units) based on a unit of force independent of the value of acceleration of gravity

absolute temperature *n* **:** temperature measured on the absolute scale — symbol *T*

absolute term *n, math* **:** the constant term of a polynomial

absolute threshold *n* **:** the smallest magnitude at which a sensory stimulus can reliably evoke a sensation

absolute time *n* **:** empty time apart from the events that occupy it

absolute value *n* **1** *of a real number* **:** the value irrespective of sign **2** *of a complex number* **:** the positive square root of the sum of the squares of the real and imaginary parts of the number

absolute weight *n* **:** the weight of a definite number of seeds used in calculating the average weight of a single seed

absolute zero *n* **:** a hypothetical temperature characterized by complete absence of heat: **a** *on the Kelvin scale* **:** approximately −273.15°C or −459.67°F at which no heat for performance of work could be derived **b** *on the scale of the constant-volume hydrogen thermometer* **:** approximately −273.03°C at which hydrogen pressure would become zero if a linear temperature-pressure relation were maintained **c** *in classical kinetic theory* **:** a point at which mutual linear motions of all the molecules of a substance would cease

ab·so·lu·tion \ˌabsəˈlüshən *also* -lyü-\ *n* -s [ME *absolucioun*, fr. OF *absolution*, fr. L *absolution-, absolutio*, fr. *absolutus* (past part. of *absolvere* to absolve) + *-ion-, -io* -ion — more at ABSOLVE] **1 :** an absolving or setting free from guilt, sin, or penalty **:** forgiveness of an offense **2** *civil law* **:** ACQUITTAL **3 a :** a remission of sins imparted or pronounced by a priest in the sacrament of penance to a person who has confessed his sins **b :** a releasing from religious censure (as from excommunication) **4 :** a rite, ceremony, or form of words in which a remission of sins is pronounced, proclaimed, or prayerfully implored by a priest or minister **syn** see PARDON

ab·so·lut·ism \ˈabsəˌlüˌtizəm, -əlˌyü-, -üd·ˌiz-\ *n* -s **1 :** the doctrine of what is absolute, unconditional, or independent: **a :** the doctrine of God's absolute sovereignty esp. as exhibited in predestination **b :** the political doctrine or practice of unlimited power and absolute sovereignty vested esp. in a monarch, dictator, or oligarchy **c :** a philosophy of an axiological or metaphysical absolute **2 :** ABSOLUTENESS, POSITIVENESS ⟨an ~ of pure aestheticism is artistic and spiritual death —R.W.Stallman⟩

¹ab·so·lut·ist \-üd·əst, -ütə-\ *n* -s **:** one that propounds or advocates a doctrine of absolutism

²absolutist \"\ *or* **ab·so·lu·tis·tic** \ˈ⸗⸗ˌ⸗ˈtistik\ *adj* **:** of, relating to, or in the nature of absolutism **:** ARBITRARY, DESPOTIC ⟨~ principles⟩ — **ab·so·lu·tis·ti·cal·ly** \-ək(ə)lē\ *adv*

ab·so·lut·i·za·tion \ˌabsəˌlüd·əˈzāshən, -əlˌyü-\ *n* -s **:** the process of rendering something absolute or converting it into an absolute

ab·so·lut·ize \ˈabsəˌlüd·ˌīz, -əlˌyü-, -üˌtīz\ *vt* -ED/-ING/-S *see -ize in Explan Notes* [¹*absolute* + *-ize*] **:** to make absolute **:** convert into an absolute

ab·solve \əbˈzälv, ab-, -ˈs-, -ōlv *also* -ä(ù)v *or* -ȯv\ *vt* -ED/-ING/-S [ME *absolven*, fr. L *absolvere*, fr. *ab-* ¹ab- + *solvere* to loosen, release — more at SOLVE] **1 :** to set free or release from some obligation, debt, or responsibility or from the consequences of guilt or from such ties as it would be guilt to violate **:** pronounce free ⟨~ a subject from his allegiance⟩ **2 :** to adjudge or pronounce not guilty **:** ACQUIT ⟨Halifax was *absolved* by a majority of fourteen —T.B.Macaulay⟩ **3 :** to free from a religious penalty **:** PARDON **:** remit (a sin) by absolution **4** *obs* **:** FINISH, ACCOMPLISH **5** *obs* **:** to resolve or explain (as a difficulty) **6 :** to qualify in (an academic requirement) **:** pass or obtain credit for passing (a course or an examination) **syn** see EXCULPATE

ab·solv·er \-və(r)\ *n* -s **:** one that absolves

ab·sol·vi·tor \-älvəd·ər, -ōl-\ *n* -s [L, let him be absolved, 3d pers. sing. pass. imper. of *absolvere* to absolve — more at ABSOLVE] *in Scots law* **:** a dismissal of an action **:** ACQUITTAL — **ab·sol·vi·to·ry** \-vəˌtōri\ *adj*

ab·so·nant \ˈabsənənt\ *adj* [¹*ab-* + *-sonant* (as in *consonant*)] *archaic* **:** DISCORDANT, CONTRARY, UNREASONABLE ⟨~ to nature — Francis Quarles⟩ — compare CONSONANT

ab·sorb \əbˈsȯ(ə)rb, -ˈz-, -ȯ(ə)b *also* ab-\ *vt* -ED/-ING/-S [MF *absorber*, fr. L *absorbēre*, fr. *ab-* ¹ab- + *sorbēre* to suck up, swallow; akin to Gk *rhophein* to sup up, MIr *srub* snout, Lith *srėbti* to sip, and perh. to MHG *sürpfeln* to sip, Norw *slurpe*] **1** *archaic* **:** to swallow up **:** ENGULF ⟨~*ed* by oblivion⟩ **2 :** ASSIMILATE, INCORPORATE ⟨the power of Chinese civilization to ~ new arrivals —G.W.Johnson⟩ **3 a :** to suck up **:** take up by various means (as by capillary, osmotic, solvent, or chemical action) ⟨water ~*ed* by plant roots⟩ ⟨~ ammonia gas in water⟩ — distinguished from *adsorb* **b :** to take in **:** IMBIBE ⟨convictions ~*ed* in youth —M.R.Cohen⟩ ⟨the prudential morality he had ~*ed* from Puritanism —R.H.Gabriel⟩ **4 :** to engage wholly ⟨~*ed* in thoughts of poetry —E.W.H.Lumsden⟩ **:** occupy fully ⟨work ~*s* most of his time⟩ **5 a :** to receive the impact of or undergo the shock of without recoil ⟨~ the vibration of machinery⟩ ⟨capable of ~*ing* punishment⟩ **b :** to receive without repercussion or echo ⟨walls lined with material that ~*s* sound⟩ **c :** to transform (radiant energy) into a different form usu. with a resulting rise of temperature (as when the earth receives energy from the sun) ⟨neutrons ~*ed* by cadmium rods⟩ **6 a :** to take up by purchase ⟨the business being ~*ed* by a competitor⟩ ⟨the market ~*ed* the entire production⟩ **b :** to take over (a cost) ⟨traveling expenses ~*ed* by the employer⟩ **syn** see MONOPOLIZE

ab·sorb·a·bil·i·ty *n* -ES **:** the quality or state of being absorbable

ab·sorb·able *adj* **:** capable of being absorbed

ab·sorb·ate \-bət, -ˌbāt\ *n* -s [*absorb* + *-ate*] **:** an absorbed substance (as a gas absorbed in a liquid)

ab·sorbed \-bd\ *adj* **:** obliviously engaged or occupied ⟨the mere sight of that engrossed look, that ~ and rapt delight —J.C.Powys⟩ ⟨so ~ in the business of his journey —Thomas Hardy⟩ — **ab·sorb·ed·ly** \-bədlē, -li\ *adv*

¹ab·sor·be·fa·cient \⸗ˌ⸗bəˈfāshənt\ *adj* [*absorb* + *-efacient* (as in *rubefacient*)] **:** causing or promoting absorption

²absorbefacient \"\ *n* -s **:** an agent causing or promoting absorption

ab·sorb·en·cy \⸗ˈ⸗bənsē, -si\ *n* -ES **1 :** the quality or state of being absorbent **2** *or* **ab·sorb·ance** \-ən(t)s\ *or* **ab·sorb·an·cy** \-ənsē, -si\ **:** the ability of a layer of a substance to absorb radiation expressed mathematically as the negative common logarithm of transmittance — compare ABSORPTANCE

¹ab·sorb·ent \-bənt\ *adj* [L *absorbent-, absorbens*, pres. part. of *absorbēre* to absorb — more at ABSORB] **:** having power, capacity, or tendency to absorb ⟨as ~ as a sponge⟩

²absorbent \"\ *n* -s **1 :** a substance that absorbs (as starch in pharmaceutical compounds) **:** a means of absorption ⟨surgical dressings used as ~*s*⟩ **2 :** a liquid (as a petroleum oil) used in separating gases or volatile substances (as gasoline) in gas manufacture and petroleum refining

absorbent cotton *n* **:** cotton made absorbent by chemically freeing it from its fatty matter

absorbent paper *n* **:** a soft unsized paper used for absorbing water or other fluids

ab·sorb·er \-bə(r)\ *n* -s **:** a device for absorbing gases or vapors in a liquid (as in an absorption system or a petroleum-refining unit)

ab·sorb·er·man \-ˌman\ *n, pl* **absorbermen :** one that tends an absorber

absorbing *adj* **:** fully taking attention **:** ENGROSSING ⟨an ~ book⟩ ⟨an ~ task⟩ **syn** see INTERESTING

absorbingly *adv* **:** in an absorbing manner

ab·sorp·tance \əbˈsȯrptən(t)s, ab-, -ˈz-\ *n* -s [*absorption* + *-ance*; trans. of G *absorptionsvermögen*] **:** the proportion of radiant energy which is absorbed before it can reach the further boundary of a layer of absorbing matter and which is equal to 1 minus the transmittance — compare ABSORBENCY 2

ab·sorp·ti·om·e·ter \əbˌsȯrpshēˈäməd·ər, (ˌ)ab-, -ˌzō-, -ptē-\ *n* [*absorption* + *-meter*] **1 :** an instrument for measuring the reduction of pressure in a gas as it is absorbed by a liquid to determine the absorption rate **2 :** a colorimeter for transparent fluids usu. employing photoelectric means of comparison — **ab·sorp·ti·o·met·ric** \⸗ˌ⸗⸗ōˈme·trik\ *adj*

ab·sorp·tion \əbˈsȯrpshən, ab-, -ˈz-, -ȯ(ə)p-\ *n* -s [F & L; F, fr. L *absorption-, absorptio*, fr. *absorptus* (past part. of *absorbēre* to absorb) + *-ion-, -io* -ion — more at ABSORB] **1 :** the process of absorbing or of being absorbed: as **a** *obs* **:** a swallowing up or engulfing (as of land due to subterranean movements) **b :** ASSIMILATION, INCORPORATION ⟨~ of immigrants⟩ ⟨~ of one railroad by another⟩ **c :** a taking up by capillary, osmotic, chemical, or solvent action ⟨~ of moisture from the air⟩ ⟨~ of gas by water⟩ ⟨~ of nourishment in the small intestine⟩ ⟨~ by plant roots of nutrients from the soil solution⟩ — distinguished from *adsorption;* compare SORPTION **d :** interception esp. of light or sound waves ⟨the light of an average star in the Milky Way band . . . was dimmed through interstellar ~ —B.J.Bok⟩ ⟨high ~ of certain types of wallboard⟩ **2 :** entire occupation of the mind ⟨~ in his employment⟩ **3 :** the retention of electric polarization by some dielectrics for a measurable time after an exciting field has been removed — called also *dielectric absorption* **4 :** the assumption by a freight carrier of special charges (as for switching) assessed by another carrier usu. without increasing the rate charged the shipper **5 :** reduction of power of radio waves through dissipation (as in the atmosphere) — compare ATTENUATION 4

absorption band *n* **:** a dark band in an absorption spectrum

absorption cell *n* **:** a transparent container in which liquids are placed for the study of their optical absorption

absorption coefficient *n* **1 :** the fraction of incident radiant energy which is absorbed per unit thickness, per unit mass, or per atom of an absorber **2 :** ABSORPTIVITY

absorption dynamometer *n* **:** any of several dynamometers in which the energy measured is absorbed by frictional or electrical resistances — see PRONY BRAKE

absorption edge *n* **:** a clear-cut long-wavelength boundary of an absorption band in an X-ray spectrum

absorption factor *n* **:** ABSORPTIVITY

absorption hygrometer *n* **:** a hygrometer that utilizes the elongation and shrinkage of organic tissue or fiber to indicate increasing or decreasing atmospheric humidity — see HAIR HYGROMETER

absorption line *n* **:** a dark line in the absorption spectrum of a gas or a vapor

absorption pipette *n* **:** a pipette for the absorption of gases

absorption spectrum *n* **:** an electromagnetic spectrum whose intensity distribution has been modified by passage through selectively absorbing substances — compare EMISSION SPECTRUM

absorption system *n* **:** a refrigerating system in which refrigeration is effected by the expansion in evaporating coils of liquid ammonia into gas which is then absorbed by water and used again after the water is evaporated

ab·sorp·tive \⸗ˈ⸗tiv, -ēv\ *adj* [*absorption* + *-ive*] **:** relating to absorption: as **a :** ASSIMILATIVE ⟨problem for several generations was that of maintaining Canada's independence against the ~ powers of the U.S. —B.K.Sandwell⟩ **b :** ABSORBENT

ab·sorp·tiv·i·ty \ˌabˌsȯ(r)pˈtivəd·ē, -ətē, -i *also* əb-\ *n* -ES **:** the fraction of a medium and of its surface that determines what fraction of normally incident radiation or sound flux will penetrate the surface of the medium and be absorbed therein — called also *absorption coefficient, absorption factor*

ab·squat·u·late \abzˈkwächəˌlāt, abˈsk-\ *vi* -ED/-ING/-S [¹*ab-* + *squat* + *-ulate* (as in *speculate*)] **1** *slang* **:** DECAMP ⟨a frontiersman preparing to ~ and head for the wilderness⟩ **2** *slang* **:** ABSCOND ⟨the cashier *absquatulated* with the funds⟩ — **ab·squat·u·la·tion** \(ˌ)⸗ˌ⸗⸗ˈlāshən\ *n* -s *slang*

abs·que im·pe·ti·ti·o·ne va·sti \ˈabzkwēˌimpəˌtishēˈōnēˈvaˌstī\ [NL] *law* **:** without impeachment of waste

ab·stain \əbzˈtān, ab-, -bˈst-\ *vb* -ED/-ING/-S [ME *absteinen, abstenen*, fr. MF *abstenir*, fr. L *abstinēre*, fr. *abs-* (var. of *ab-* ¹ab) + *tenēre* to hold — more at THIN] *vi* **:** to withhold oneself from participation **:** refrain voluntarily **:** withhold oneself deliberately from an action ⟨a vote of nine million in favor, eight million against, and nine million ~*ing* —E.J.Knapton⟩ **:** FORBEAR — often used with *from* ⟨they ~*ed* from comment⟩ ⟨a lifelong pledge to ~ from drinking —M.V.Reidy⟩ **~** *vt*, *obs* **:** WITHHOLD **syn** see REFRAIN

ab·stain·er \-nə(r)\ *n* -s [ME *absteiner*, fr. *absteinen* to abstain + *-er*] **:** one that abstains esp. from the use of intoxicating liquors — used esp. in the phrase *total abstainer*

ab·ste·mi·ous \abzˈtēmēəs, əb-, -bˈst-\ *adj* [L *abstemius*, fr. *abs-* (var. of *ab-* ¹ab-) + *-temius* (fr. *temetum* mead, wine, intoxicating beverage); akin to G *dämlich* stupid, silly, ON *thām* mugginess, OIr *tām* death, Skt *tāmyati* he becomes stunned, exhausted, and perh. to L *tenebrae* darkness — more at TEMERITY] **1 :** sparing in eating and drinking ⟨the pleasures of the table, never of much consequence to one naturally ~ —John Galsworthy⟩ ⟨he was not a teetotaler, but ~ —A.W. Long⟩ **:** generally refraining from indulgence of pleasures and cravings ⟨the most ~ of men . . . he held old-fashioned and rather puritanical views —Virginia Woolf⟩ **:** ABSTINENT **2 :** used with or in conformity with temperance or moderation **:** marked by abstinence ⟨the Roman Empire appropriated far more energy than Greece, with its sparse ~ dietary —Lewis Mumford⟩ — **ab·ste·mi·ous·ly** *adv* — **ab·ste·mi·ous·ness** *n* -ES

ab·sten·tion \əbzˈtenchən, ab-, -bˈst-\ *n* -s [LL *abstention-, abstentio*, fr. L *abstentus*, past part. of *abstinēre* to abstain + *-ion-, -io* -ion — more at ABSTAIN] **1 :** act or practice of abstaining; *specif* **:** withholding of a vote ⟨seven votes in favor, three against, and one ~ —A.W.Rudzinski⟩ **2 :** nonparticipation in political life or (as by a government) in international affairs ⟨cooperation versus isolation in the 'twenties, intervention versus ~ in the late thirties —H.J.Morgenthau⟩ — **ab·sten·tion·ism** \-ˌnizəm\ *n* -s — **ab·sten·tion·ist** \-ˌnəst\ *n* -s

ab·sten·tious \-enchəs\ *adj* [*abstention* + *-ous*] **:** ABSTINENT **:** self-restraining

ab·sterge \abzˈtərj, əb-, -bˈst-\ *vt* -ED/-ING/-S [MF or L; MF *absterger*, fr. L *abstergēre*, fr. *abs-* (var. of *ab-* ¹ab-) + *tergēre* to wipe off — more at TERSE] *archaic* **:** to cleanse esp. by wiping **:** PURGE

¹ab·ster·gent \-jənt\ *adj* [F or L; F, fr. L *abstergent-, abstergens*, pres. part. of *abstergēre*] **:** CLEANSING, DETERGENT

²abstergent \"\ *n* -s **:** a substance used in cleansing **:** DETERGENT ⟨scoured with an ~⟩

ab·ster·sion \-rzhən, -rsh-\ *n* -s [MF, fr. L *abstersus* (past part. of *abstergēre*) + MF *-ion*] *archaic* **:** the action or process of cleansing

¹ab·ster·sive \-rsiv, -rz-\ *adj* [MF *abstersif*, fr. L *abstersus* + MF *-if* -ive] **:** ABSTERGENT

²abstersive *n* -s *obs* **:** ABSTERGENT

ab·sti·nence \ˈabztənən(t)s, -bst-\ *n* -s [ME, fr. OF, fr. L *abstinentia*, fr. *abstinent-, abstinens* + *-ia*] **1 :** the act or practice of abstaining: **a :** self-restraint or self-denial with regard to hunger, pleasure, or craving ⟨after long ~ from the movies —Edmund Wilson⟩ ⟨~ from narcotics⟩ **b :** the abstaining from certain foods (as meat) in obedience to ecclesiastical law or as a matter of religious discipline — distinguished from *fast, fasting* **c :** habitual abstaining from intoxicating liquors — called also *total abstinence* **2 :** postponement of expenditure so as to accumulate capital

abstinence syndrome *n* **:** the physical effects that result from depriving an addict of the drug to which he is habituated

abstinence theory *n* **:** a theory in economics: interest is a reward for economic abstinence

ab·sti·nen·cy \-nənsē\ *n* -ES [L *abstinentia*] *archaic* **:** ABSTINENCE

¹ab·sti·nent \-nənt\ *adj* [ME, fr. MF, fr. L *abstinent-, abstinens*, pres. part. of *abstinēre* to abstain — more at ABSTAIN] **:** practicing abstinence **:** ABSTEMIOUS, CONTINENT, TEMPERATE — **ab·sti·nent·ly** *adv*

²abstinent \"\ *n* -s [ME, fr. *abstinent*, adj.] **1 :** one that abstains **2** *usu cap* **:** one of a 4th century Christian ascetic sect in southwestern Europe that rejected meat eating and held that the relation between the sexes should be purely spiritual — compare PRISCILLIANIST

¹ab·stract \(ˈ)ab¦strakt, əbzˈ-, -ab¦st-, əbˈst-\ *adj, sometimes* -ER/-EST [ME, fr. L *abstractus,* past part. of *abstrahere* to draw away, withdraw, fr. *abs-* (var. of *ab-* ¹ab-) + *trahere* to pull, draw — more at TRACE] **1** *archaic* **:** absent in mind **:** ABSTRACTED 3 ⟨~, as in a trance —John Milton⟩ **2** [ML *abstractus,* fr. L, past part.] **a :** considered apart from any application to a particular object or specific instance **:** separated from embodiment ⟨an ~ entity⟩ ⟨arguments from ~ probability —P.E.More⟩ **b :** difficult to understand **:** ABSTRUSE ⟨more ~ problems involving judgment and ability to reason —*Saturday Rev.*⟩ **c :** IDEAL ⟨to shed tears over ~ justice and generosity . . . and never to know these qualities when you meet them in the street —William James⟩ **d :** insufficiently factual **:** FORMAL ⟨she possessed all civil rights — but these were ~ and empty —H.M.Parshley⟩ ⟨~ and doctrinaire instruction⟩ **e** *of a unit or number* **:** having no reference to a thing or things — opposed to *concrete* **3** *archaic* **:** drawn away **:** REMOVED, SEPARATE **4 :** expressing a property, quality, attribute, or relation viewed apart from the other characteristics inhering in or constituting an object ⟨*honesty, whiteness, triangularity* are ~ words⟩ **5 :** dealing or tending to deal with a subject in the abstract: as **a** *of a science* **:** PURE, THEORETICAL — contrasted with *applied* **b :** IMPERSONAL, DETACHED ⟨I should have remained mainly academic and ~ but for the war —Bertrand Russell⟩ ⟨the ~ compassion of a surgeon —*Time*⟩ **6 a** *of a fine art* **:** presenting or possessing schematic or generalized form frequently suggested by and having obscure resemblance to natural appearances through a contrived ordering of pictorial or sculptural elements — contrasted with *academic;* compare NONOBJECTIVE **b** *music* **:** ABSOLUTE 11a **c** *of dance composition* **:** lacking concrete program or story **7 :** signifying a logical predicate or a class esp. of higher order (as number when conceived of as a class property)

²abstract \" *in sense 2; in other senses usu* ˈ=,=\ *n* -S [ME, fr. L *abstractus,* past part.] **1 :** a summary or an epitome (as of a book, a scientific article, or a legal document) **2 :** an abstract term or idea **:** the result of abstraction **3 :** something that comprises or concentrates in itself the essential qualities of a larger thing or of several things ⟨a man who is the ~ of all faults that all men follow —Shak.⟩ ⟨trial by jury . . . the very ~ and essence of . . . democratic government —W.H. Mallock⟩ **4 :** ABSTRACT OF TITLE **5** *pharmacy* **:** a preparation made by mixing a powdered solid extract of a vegetable substance with sugar of milk in such proportion that one part of the final product represents two parts of the original drug from which the extract was made **6** *fine art* **:** ABSTRACTION 6 **syn** see ABRIDGMENT — **in the abstract :** with reference to theoretical considerations only **:** apart from practical or actual conditions

³ab·stract *in vt senses 3 & 6 usu* ˈ=,= *; in other senses usu like adj*\ *vb* -ED/-ING/-S [¹abstract] *vt* **1 :** to draw away **:** take away **:** REMOVE, SEPARATE ⟨add or ~ baser metal in minting⟩ ⟨a vast cigar-shaped body of gas was raised and eventually ~*ed* from the surface of the sun —W.E.Swinton⟩ **2 :** to separate (as an idea) by the operation of the mind **:** consider (as a quality or attribute) apart from any application to a particular object or instance ⟨~ the notion of dimension from that of space⟩ **3 :** to make an abstract of **:** EPITOMIZE, SUMMARIZE **4 :** to draw away the interest or attention of **:** DIVERT ⟨his imagination had so ~*ed* him that his name was called twice before he answered —James Joyce⟩ **5 :** to take secretly or dishonestly **:** STEAL, PURLOIN ⟨Shaftesbury's son seems to have ~*ed* important documents for Cavour —*Times Lit. Supp.*⟩ **6** *in life insurance* **:** to summarize (an insurance contract) esp. in the effort to induce a policyholder to cancel a policy and substitute another **7** *fine art* **:** to create abstractions suggested by (a concrete or natural object) ~ *vi* **1 :** to perform the process of abstraction or of abstracting something ⟨we naturally ~ when two similar objects are presented to us —Frank Thilly⟩ **2** *fine art* **:** to create abstractions **syn** see DETACH — **abstract from :** to leave out of consideration

abstracta *pl of* **abstractum**

ab·stract·ed \(ˈ)=¦==\ *adj* **1** *archaic* **:** ABSTRACT 2 **2 :** drawn away **:** REMOVED, SEPARATE, APART ⟨the evil one ~ stood from his own evil —John Milton⟩ ⟨possibility is that in which stands achievability, ~ from achievement —A.N.Whitehead⟩ **3 :** withdrawn in mind **:** inattentive to surrounding objects **:** PREOCCUPIED, ABSENTMINDED ⟨sitting silent and ~⟩ ⟨their pallid ~ air of human beings devoted to a difficult ideal —Herman Wouk⟩ — **ab·stract·ed·ly** *adv* — **ab·stract·ed·ness** *n* -ES

abstracter *var of* ABSTRACTOR

abstract expressionism *n* **:** the theory or practice of freely creating (as in painting) abstractions characterized by sinuous linearity, organic shape, and highly decorative surface

ab·strac·tion \abzˈtrakshən, əb-, -bˈst-\ *n* -S [MF or ML; MF, fr. ML *abstraction-, abstractio,* fr. LL, abduction, fr. L *abstractus* (past part. of *abstrahere* to draw away, withdraw) + *-ion-, -io* -ion — more at ABSTRACT] **1 :** the act of drawing or taking away **:** the state of being drawn or taken away **:** REMOVAL, SEPARATION ⟨labels bearing a clearly printed notice of addition or ~⟩ ⟨in search of seclusion, of loneliness, of . . . ~ from the trivial round —*Times Lit. Supp.*⟩ ⟨suspected of the ~ of money from the mail⟩ **2 a :** the act or process of leaving out of consideration one or more qualities of a complex object so as to attend to others (as when the mind considers the form of a tree by itself or the color of the leaves independently of their size or figure) **b :** the act or process of imaginatively isolating or considering apart the common properties or characteristics of distinct objects ⟨~ is necessary for the classification of things into genera and species⟩ **c :** the formation of a concept or an idea by such an act **:** the construction of a class name **3** [prob. fr. ¹*abstract* + *-ion*] **:** the result of a mental process of abstracting **:** an abstract idea or a term expressing such an idea ⟨his style was dense with ~*s*⟩; *sometimes* **:** a visionary or unrealistic idea **4 :** inattention to present objects or surroundings **:** absence of mind ⟨lost in ~⟩ ⟨an air of complete ~⟩ **5 :** abstract quality or character ⟨pantomime with a symbolic ~ that approached ballet⟩ **6** *fine art* **:** an abstract composition or creation **7 :** the merging of two or more streams into a single stream course by the deepening and widening of one valley so that it engulfs a shallower and smaller neighboring valley

ab·strac·tion·ism \-shə,nizəm\ *n* -S **1 :** the creation of abstractions esp. in art **2 :** the principles or ideals of abstract art

¹ab·strac·tion·ist \-sh(ə)nəst\ *n* -S **1 :** one that deals with abstractions rather than with concrete things **:** one that takes abstractions for realities **2 a :** an abstract artist **b :** a supporter of abstractionism in art

²abstractionist \"\ *adj* [¹*abstractionist*] *fine art* **:** showing tendencies toward abstractionism

ab·strac·tive \(ˈ)abz¦traktiv, əbzˈ-, -ab¦st-, əbˈst-, -ēv\ *adj* [ML *abstractivus,* fr. L *abstractus* + *-ivus* -ive] **1 :** having the power of abstracting **:** of an abstracting nature ⟨~ analysis⟩ **2 a :** derived by a process of abstraction ⟨an ~ element⟩ **b :** belonging to or formed by abstraction — **ab·strac·tive·ly** *adv*

ab·stract·ly \(ˈ)=¦==\ *adv* [ME, fr. *abstract,* adj. + *-ly*] **:** in an abstract state or manner **:** SEPARATELY, ABSOLUTELY **:** by itself

abstract music *n* **:** ABSOLUTE MUSIC

ab·stract·ness *n* -ES **:** the quality or state of being abstract

abstract of title : a summary statement of the successive conveyances and other facts upon which a person's title to a piece of land rests

ab·strac·tor *or* **ab·stract·er** \(ˈ)=¦=tə(r)\ *n* -S [³*abstract* + *-or* or *-er*] **:** one that abstracts or makes abstracts (as of records, documents, or scientific articles): as **a :** an accounting clerk who records payroll allotments, deductions, and disbursements **b :** a person who searches out and summarizes information to be used as reference or proof in legal or insurance cases

abstract plant *n* **:** a comprehensive record maintained by a title-insurance company indicating liens, encumbrances, and defects affecting the title to properties located in the community where the company operates as insurer — not often in formal use

abstracts *pl of* ABSTRACT, *pres 3d sing of* ABSTRACT

ab·strac·tum \=ˈ=təm\ *n, pl* **abstrac·ta** \-tə\ [NL, fr. ML, neut. of *abstractus* abstract — more at ABSTRACT] **:** an abstract entity (as a universal, a relation, a class name) ⟨whiteness and virtue are *abstracta*⟩ — contrasted with *concretum*

abstract universal *n* **:** ²UNIVERSAL 2a(1)

ab·strict \abzˈtrikt, abˈst-, əb-\ *vt* -ED/ -ING/ -S [¹*ab-* + L *strictus,* past part. of *stringere* to draw tight — more at STRAIN] **:** ABJOINT

ab·strict·ed \(ˈ)=¦==\ *adj* **:** cut off by abstriction

ab·stric·tion \=ˈ=shən\ *n* [¹*ab-* + LL *striction-, strictio* act of pressing together, fr. L *strictus* + *-ion-, -io* -ion] **:** the formation of spores by the cutting off of usu. successive terminal portions of the sporophore through the growth of septa — see CONIDIUM

ab·struse \əbzˈtrüs, (ˈ)abz¦t-, əbˈst-, -ab¦st-\ *adj, sometimes* -ER/ -EST [L *abstrusus* concealed, fr. past part. of *abstrudere* to push away, conceal, fr. *abs-* (var. of *ab-* ¹ab-) + *trudere* to push, thrust — more at THREAT] **1** *obs* **:** CONCEALED, HIDDEN ⟨the eternal eye whose sight discerns *abstrusest* thoughts —John Milton⟩ **2 :** difficult to comprehend or understand **:** RECONDITE ⟨the ~ calculations of mathematicians⟩ ⟨involved and ~ language⟩

ab·struse·ly *adv* **:** in an abstruse manner

ab·struse·ness *n* -ES **:** ABSTRUSITY

ab·stru·si·ty \=ˈ=sədˌē, -ətē, -i\ *n* -ES **1 :** the quality or state of being abstruse ⟨the intrinsic ~ of the material with which the poem grapples —J.H.Wheelock⟩ **2 :** something abstruse

absume *vt* -ED/ -ING/ -S [L *absumere,* fr. *ab-* ¹ab- + *sumere* to take — more at CONSUME] *obs* **:** to consume gradually

ab·surd \əbˈsərd, ab-, -ˈz-, -əd\ *adj, sometimes* -ER/-EST [MF *absurde,* fr. L *absurdus* harsh-sounding, incongruous, absurd, fr. *ab-* ¹ab- + *surdus* dull-sounding, silent, deaf — more at SURD] **1 :** marked by an obvious lack of reason, common sense, proportion, or accord with accepted ideas **:** ridiculously unreasonable, unsound, or incongruous ⟨the ~ predicament of seeming to argue that virtue is highly desirable but intensely unpleasant —Walter Lippmann⟩ ⟨don't be so ~ as to forget you're a man, and to act like a child —Anthony Trollope⟩ **2 :** SELF-CONTRADICTORY **:** fallacious by reason of contradiction **syn** see FOOLISH

ab·surd·i·ty \-dədˌē, -ətē, -i\ *n* -ES [ME *absurdite,* fr. MF or LL; MF *absurdité,* fr. LL *absurditat-, absurditas,* fr. L *absurdus* + *-itat-, -itas* -ity] **1 :** the quality or state of being absurd ⟨to retain unmarred the sense of the ~ of all life —Rose Macaulay⟩ **2 :** something that is absurd ⟨the *absurdities* of social pretense —T.S.Eliot⟩ **:** a logical contradiction ⟨a new set of inconsistencies, not to say *absurdities* —P.E.More⟩

ab·surd·ly \-lē, -li\ *adv* **1 :** in an absurd manner **2 :** to an absurd degree ⟨an ~ rich young lady⟩

ab·surd·ness *n* -ES **:** the quality or state of being absurd

abt *abbr* about

abt system \ˈäp(t)ˌs-, ˈa-\ *n, usu cap A* [after Roman *Abt* †1933 Swiss railroad engineer who devised it] **:** a system of tracking for mountain railroads in which two or more cog-rails are used and so arranged that the teeth are not opposite on any two of the rails

ab·u·def·duf \ˌabüˈdef(ˌ)dəf\ *n, cap* [NL] **:** a genus of small ovate short-headed marine teleost fishes commonly found about rocks and other submerged objects and usu. included in the percoid family Pomacentridae but sometimes made the type of a separate family (Abudefdufidae)

abuild·ing \əˈbildiŋ, -ēŋ\ *adj* [¹*a-* + *building,* pres. part. of *build*] **:** in the process of building or of being built ⟨formidable discontents, some already strong and some ~ —*N. Y. Times*⟩ ⟨low-cost housing now ~ at the edge of town⟩

ab·u·ku·ma·lite \ˌabəˈküməˌlīt, əˈbükəmə-\ *n* -S [*Abukuma,* river on Honshu Island, Japan + E *-lite*] **:** a mineral (Ca,Y)$_5$(P,Si)$_3$O$_{12}$(OH,F) consisting of a phosphate-silicate of calcium and yttrium sometimes containing uranium or thorium

abu·lia *or* **abou·lia** \(ˈ)āˈb(y)ülēə\ *n* -S [NL, fr. ²*a-* + *-bulia, -boulia*] **:** loss of will power **:** abnormal lack of ability to act or to make decisions characteristic of certain psychotic and neurotic conditions — **abu·lic** *also* **abou·lic** \(ˈ)ā¦b(y)ülik\ *adj*

abu·lo·ma·nia *also* **abou·lo·ma·nia** \¦āˌb(y)üləˈmānēə\ *n* -S [NL, fr. *abulo-, aboulo-* (fr. *abulia, aboulia*) + *-mania*] **:** a form of mental disorder characterized by abulia

abun·dance \əˈbəndən(t)s\ *n* -S [ME *abundaunce, habundaunce,* fr. MF *abundance,* fr. L *abundantia,* fr. *abundant-, abundans* + *-ia*] **1 :** a great quantity or amount **:** large number **:** plentiful supply ⟨an ~ of water power⟩ ⟨illustrated with an ~ of figures and diagrams⟩ — not commonly used of persons **2 :** overflowing fullness **:** great plenty **:** PROFUSION ⟨the ~ that pours from our factories and our farms —*New Republic*⟩ ⟨the whole bucolic ~ of the well-kept country seat —Vicki Baum⟩ **3 :** plentiful supply of means or resources **:** AFFLUENCE, WEALTH ⟨a life of ~⟩ ⟨the economics of the new ~⟩ **4 :** relative quantity or amount (as with respect to an observed or supposed norm) **:** degree of plentifulness ⟨information about the ~ of various species⟩ ⟨measurements on meteorites also indicate very low ~*s* of uranium and thorium —H.C.Urey⟩ **5** *ecol* **:** the relative number of individuals of one kind (as of a species) in an area under consideration

abun·dant \-ənt\ *adj* [ME *abundaunt, habundaunt,* fr. MF *abundant,* fr. L *abundant-, abundans,* pres. part. of *abundare* to abound —more at ABOUND] **1 a :** possessing (as resources) in great quantity **:** having great plenty **:** RICH ⟨a fair and ~ land⟩ ⟨the promise of a more ~ life⟩ **b :** amply supplied **:** ABOUNDING ⟨~ with fly life and other natural trout food —Alexander MacDonald⟩ — used with *in* and *with* **2 :** more than sufficient ⟨~ and well-distributed rainfall⟩ **:** occurring or existing in great quantity **:** AMPLE, PLENTIFUL, COPIOUS ⟨life, in all its forms, is most ~ near water —John Burroughs⟩ ⟨her forthright manner and her ~ common sense —C.G.Bowers⟩ **syn** see PLENTIFUL

abun·dant·ly \-lē, -li\ *adv* [ME *abundauntly, habundauntly,* fr. *abundaunt, habundaunt* + *-ly*] **:** in sufficient or more than sufficient measure **:** FULLY, AMPLY, PLENTIFULLY

abundant number *n* **:** an imperfect number that is less than the sum of all its divisors (as 12)

abundant year *n* **:** PERFECT YEAR

abune \əˈbu̇en\ *chiefly Scot var of* ABOON

abu·ra \əˈb(y)u̇rə\ *n* -S [Yoruba *a¹bu³ra¹*] **:** a medium-sized tropical African tree (*Mitragyne macrophylla*) of the family Loganiaceae having large elliptical leaves, greenish flowers, and soft wood

abu·ra·chan seed \ˌäbərəˈchän-\ *n* [Jap *abura han,* fr. *abura* oil + *chan* pitch] **:** the seed of a Japanese shrub (*Benzoin praecox*) yielding an aromatic medicinal oil

abu·ra·giri \ˌäbərəˈgirē\ *n* -S [Jap *abura-kiri,* fr. *abura* oil + *kiri* paulownia] **:** CANDLENUT 2

aburst \əˈ-\ *adj* [¹*a-* + *burst,* v.] **:** BURSTING

abur·ton \əˈbərtᵊn\ *adv (or adj)* [prob. fr. ¹*a-* + *burton*] **:** with the length athwartship ⟨stowed the barrels and casks ~⟩

abus·a·ble \əˈbyüzəbəl\ *adj* [¹*abuse* + *-able*] **:** capable of being abused

abus·age \əˈbyüsij, -zij\ *n* -S [²*abuse* + *-age*] **:** improper or incorrect use of language **:** bad usage

¹abuse \əˈbyüz\ *vt* -ED/-ING/-S [ME *abusen,* fr. MF *abuser,* fr. *abus,* n., abuse, fr. L *abusus,* past part. of *abuti* to consume, abuse, misuse, fr. *ab-* ¹ab- + *uti* to use — more at USE] **1 a :** to attack or injure with words **:** reproach coarsely **:** DISPARAGE ⟨~ a person in the most violent terms⟩ **b** *obs* **:** to speak falsely of **:** MISREPRESENT ⟨*abused* her to her friends⟩ **2** *obs* **:** to cause to believe the false **:** lead into error **:** DECEIVE ⟨the Moor's *abused* by some most villainous knave —Shak.⟩ **3 a :** to put to a use other than the one intended **:** MISAPPLY ⟨*abusing* the privilege by invoking it for ends not sanctioned by law —Bernard Meltzer⟩ **:** use or apply improperly or to excess ⟨farmers have learned not to ~ the soil⟩ **b :** to put to a bad use **:** PERVERT ⟨*abused* his power by profiting at the expense of others⟩ **:** take unfair or undue advantage of ⟨he has *abused* my confidence in letting this secret become known⟩ **4 :** to use or treat so as to injure, hurt, or damage **:** MALTREAT ⟨~ a horse by overworking it⟩ ⟨~ one's eyes by reading in dim light⟩ **:** treat without consideration or fairness ⟨those left behind felt themselves *abused*⟩ **5 a :** MASTURBATE **b** *archaic* **:** to violate sexually **:** RAPE **c :** to commit indecent assault on — compare ABUSE 5

²abuse \-üs\ *n* -S [ME, fr. MF *abus*] **1 :** a corrupt practice or custom **:** OFFENSE, FAULT ⟨the buying of votes and other election ~*s*⟩ **2 :** improper or incorrect use **:** MISUSE ⟨to call that state a democracy is an ~ of terms⟩ **:** application to a wrong or bad purpose ⟨the arbitrary punishments were an ~ of his power⟩ **3** *obs* **:** a deceitful act **:** DECEPTION, DELUSION ⟨or is it some ~, and no such thing —Shak.⟩ **4 :** language that condemns or vilifies usu. unjustly, intemperately, and angrily ⟨*bolshevist* had become . . . a vague term of ~ —Rose Macaulay⟩ ⟨the political harridans would . . . attack every possible leader with scandal and ~ —H.G.Wells⟩ **5 a :** the act of violating sexually **:** RAPE **b** *under some statutes* **:** rape or indecent assault not amounting to rape — compare CARNAL ABUSE, SELF-ABUSE **6 :** physically harmful treatment **:** MALTREATMENT, ILL-USAGE ⟨to be arrested for ~ of an animal⟩ ⟨~ of one's health⟩

syn INVECTIVE, OBLOQUY, VITUPERATION, SCURRILITY, BILLINGSGATE: ABUSE, the most general word in this list of terms, may frequently indicate a speaker's angry intent to wound; it usually suggests lack of anything that is fair or temperate ⟨now there is one word in the extended vocabulary of barrack-room *abuse* that cannot pass without comment . . . you must not call a man a bastard unless you are prepared to prove it on his front teeth —Rudyard Kipling⟩ INVECTIVE may apply to any denunciatory diatribe, but it often connotes a certain command of cogent language ⟨John Bull stopped at nothing in the way of insult; but its blazing audacity of *invective* never degenerated into dull abuse —Agnes Repplier⟩ ⟨Cicero replied in that masterpiece of *invective* known as the Fifth Philippic —John Buchan⟩ This suggestion is not necessarily present ⟨not the rapier of sarcasm but the bludgeon of *invective* —W.S.Maugham⟩ OBLOQUY may suggest language designed to shame another, language casting shame upon another ⟨those who . . . stood by me in the teeth of *obloquy,* taunt and open sneer, or insult even —Oscar Wilde⟩ ⟨to a symbol of *obloquy,* to an unanswerable epithet of derogation —Bliss Perry⟩ VITUPERATION suggests fluent, ready, and sustained abuse and castigation nastily delivered ⟨hag, nuisance, shrew, termagant let loose, she assailed everybody who violated in the least her prejudices. Presidents were nagged beyond endurance, and senators, and congressmen: no one could escape the vials of her *vituperation* —F.L.Pattee⟩ ⟨avoid reflections on the chastity of your opponent's female relations . . . Once you have gone so far it is impossible to retrace your steps and resort to minor forms of *vituperation* —Robert Graves⟩ SCURRILITY, the most uncomplimentary of these words, implies meanness or viciousness in attack and coarseness or foulness in language ⟨interrupted in his defense by ribaldry and *scurrility* from the judgment seat —T.B.Macaulay⟩ BILLINGSGATE may indicate very ready, easy profanity and obscenity delivered with practiced ease ⟨the *billingsgate* slang they certainly have acquired in perfection, and no white would think of competing with them in abuse or hard swearing —Sidney Baker⟩ ⟨an assortment of *billingsgate* that would have paralyzed a fishwife and brought blushes to a character in a Jim Tully novel or a Eugene O'Neill play —Herbert Asbury⟩

abuse of process *law* **:** the malicious use of a regular judicial proceeding without probable cause

abus·er \-zə(r)\ *n* -S [ME, fr. *abusen* to abuse + *-er*] **:** one that abuses

abusion *n* -S [ME *abusioun,* fr. MF *abusion,* fr. L *abusion-, abusio,* fr. *abusus* (past part. of *abuti* to misuse, abuse) + *-ion-, -io* -ion — more at ABUSE] *obs* **:** ABUSE, MISUSE; *specif* **:** abuse of the truth **:** DECEPTION

abu·sive \əˈbyüsiv, -ēv *also* -üz-\ *adj* [MF *abusif,* fr. LL *abusivus,* fr. L *abusus* + *-ivus* -ive] **1 a :** characterized by wrong or improper use or action **:** constituting an abuse **:** PERVERTED ⟨~ financial practices⟩ **b** *archaic* **:** CATACHRESTIC **c** *obs* **:** tending to deceive **:** FRAUDULENT, CHEATING ⟨an ~ treaty —Francis Bacon⟩ **2 a :** employing harsh insulting language ⟨an ~ spectator⟩ **:** characterized by or serving for abuse **:** SCURRILOUS ⟨~ jibes⟩ **b :** physically injurious **:** tending to damage or weaken **:** ROUGH ⟨tools made for ~ use⟩ — **abu·sive·ly** *adv* — **abu·sive·ness** *n* -ES

abus·tle \əˈ-\ *adj* [¹*a-* + *bustle,* v.] **:** showing great activity **:** stirring busily ⟨a store ~ with crowds⟩

ab·u·sua \ˌabəˈsüə\ *n* -S [Ashanti] **:** a matrilineal exogamous clan among the Ashanti people

abut \əˈbət, *usu* -d-+V\ *vb* **abutted; abutted; abutting; abuts** [ME *abutten,* partly fr. OF *aboter, abouter* to touch at one end, border on (fr. *a-* — fr. L *ad-* — + *bout* end, blow, fr. *boter, bouter* to strike), partly fr. OF *abuter* to come to an end, aim, reach, fr. *a-* + *but* end, aim, purpose, of Gmc origin; akin to ON *butr* piece of wood — more at BUTT (to strike), BUTT (end)] *vi* **:** to touch (as of contiguous estates) along a border or with a projecting part ⟨his land ~*s* on the road⟩ **:** terminate at a point of contact (as with an adjacent structure) **:** lean or rest for support (as upon another structure) — used with *on, upon,* or *against* ~ *vt* **1 :** to border on **:** reach or touch with an end ⟨two lots that ~ each other⟩ **2 :** to cause to abut **:** support by abutment ⟨~ a timber against a post⟩

abu·ta \əˈb(y)üd·ə\ *n, cap* [NL, prob. fr. Sp, a plant of this genus] **:** a genus of tropical American woody vines (family Menispermaceae) — see WHITE PAREIRA, YELLOW PAREIRA

ab uti·li \ab ˈyüd·ᵊlˌī\ [NL] *adv, of an argument* **:** from utility

abu·ti·lon \əˈbyüd·ᵊlˌän, ˌabyəˈtilən\ *n* [NL, fr. Ar *awbūtīlūn,* a plant of this genus] **1** *cap* **:** a large genus of mostly tropical plants (family Malvaceae) having usu. lobed leaves and solitary showy bell-shaped flowers — see FLOWERING MAPLE, INDIAN MALLOW **2** -S **:** any plant of the genus *Abutilon*

abut·ment \əˈbətmənt\ *n* -S **1 :** the place at which abutting occurs ⟨at the ~ of two properties⟩ **2 a :** the part of a structure that directly receives thrust or pressure (as of an arch, vault, beam, or strut) **b :** an anchorage for the cables of a suspension bridge or aerial railway **c :** a tooth to which a denture or other prosthetic appliance is attached for support **3 :** the action of abutting ⟨~ of two braces upon the post⟩ **4 :** a fixed point, surface, or body from which resistance or reaction is obtained (as the cylinder head of a steam engine or the fulcrum of a lever)

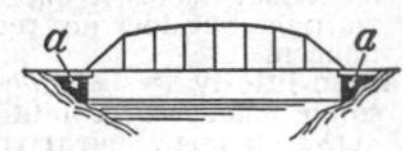

a, a, abutments of a bridge

abut·tals \əˈbəd·ᵊlz, -bətᵊlz\ *n pl* **:** the boundaries of lands with respect to other contiguous lands or highways by which they are bounded

abut·ter \-d·ə(r), -tə-\ *n* -S **:** one that abuts; *specif* **:** the owner of a contiguous property ⟨the ~*s* on a street⟩

abutting *adj* **:** that abuts or serves as abutment **syn** see ADJACENT

abuzz \əˈ-\ *adj* [¹*a-* + *buzz,* v.] **:** buzzing or filled with buzzing **:** filled or resounding with talk and excitement ⟨London was ~ over the new appointment⟩

abv *abbr* above

ab·volt \ˈab,vōlt\ *n* -S [²*ab-* + *volt*] **:** the cgs electromagnetic unit of electrical potential and electromotive force equal to one one-hundred-millionth of a volt and being the potential difference through which transference of one abcoulomb of electricity involves a change of one erg in energy — compare AB- table

ab·wab \əbˈwäb\ *n* -S [Hindi *abwāb,* fr. Ar, doors, sources of public revenue, pl. of *bāb* door] *India* **:** any of various fines, cesses, or imposts levied by a native chief upon a landowner or occupier

aby *or* **abye** \əˈbī\ *vb, past or past part* **abought** \əˈbȯt\ [ME *abien, abiggen,* fr. OE *ābycgan,* fr. *ā-* (perfective prefix) + *bycgan* to buy — more at ABEAR, BUY] *vt* **1** *archaic* **:** to suffer for or pay for (an offense) ⟨lest to thy peril thou ~ it dear —Shak.⟩ **2** *archaic* **:** to pay, suffer, or endure (as a penalty) ~ *vi* **1** *obs* **:** to pay the penalty **:** SUFFER **2** *obs* **:** ENDURE, LAST, CONTINUE ⟨but naught that wanteth rest can long ~ —Edmund Spenser⟩

abysm \əˈbizəm *also* aˈ-\ *n* -S [alter. (influenced by *abyss*) of ME *abime,* fr. OF *abisme,* modif. (influenced by words ending in *-isme* -ism) of LL *abyssus*] **:** ABYSS ⟨the dark backward and ~ of time —Shak.⟩

abys·mal \-zməl\ *adj* **1 :** having the characteristics of an abyss **:** BOTTOMLESS ⟨mountain roads . . . within a few inches of ~ precipices —W.R.Arnold⟩ **:** immeasurably great **:** UNENDING, PROFOUND ⟨~ ignorance⟩ **:** immeasurably low or wretched ⟨~ living conditions of the poor⟩ **2 :** ABYSSAL **syn** see DEEP

abys·mal·ly \-zməlē, -li\ *adv* **:** far down in the scale of acceptability **:** to an extreme degree **:** WRETCHEDLY, DREADFULLY

— used as a pejorative intensive ⟨~ poor⟩ ⟨~ cynical⟩ ⟨~ wretched⟩

abyss \ə'bis *also* a'-\ *n* -ES [alter. of ME *abissus*, fr. LL *abyssus*, fr. Gk *abyssos*, fr. *abyssos*, adj., bottomless, fr. *a-* ²a- + *byssos* depth, fr. *bythos* deep; akin to Gk *bathys* deep — more at BATHY-] **1** : the bottomless gulf, pit, or chaos of the old cosmogonies: as **a** : a confined subterranean body of water that according to the Old Testament was once an ocean surrounding the earth **b** : the infernal regions including the abode of the dead and the place of punishment of the wicked : the abode of the evil powers : HELL **c** : the formless chaos out of which the earth and the heavens were created **2 a** : any vastly or immeasurably deep gulf or great space ⟨a road running close to the ~⟩ ⟨the ~*es* of sky and sea —Joseph Conrad⟩ ⟨the ~ . . . between the artist and the public —Harry Levin⟩ ⟨across the ~ of years⟩ **b** : intellectual or spiritual profundity ⟨in the ~ of his mind he apprehends the world's minuteness —W.L.Sullivan⟩ : moral depths : a condition of vast moral depravity ⟨an ~ of dark impulses⟩ **3** : the bottom water of the deep sea — compare ABYSSAL ZONE

abyss·al \-səl\ *adj* [ML *abyssalis*, fr. LL *abyssus* + L *-alis* -al] **1** *archaic* : having the characteristics of an abyss : UNFATHOMABLE **2 a** : of, relating to, occurring in, or being in the abyssal zone ⟨~ sediments⟩ **b** : resulting from crystallization at a considerable depth within the earth ⟨~ igneous rocks⟩

abys·sal·benthic \ə¦bisəl + ¦-\ *also* **abys·so·benthic** \ə¦bi(,)sō + ¦-\ *adj* [*abyssal* or *abyss* + *-o-* + *benthic*] : of, relating to, or occurring on the sea bottom of the abyssal zone

abys·sal·pelagic \ə¦bisəl + ⸗¦⸗⸗\ *also* **abys·so·pelagic** \ə¦bi(,)sō + ⸗¦⸗⸗\ *adj* [*abyssal* or *abyss* + *-o-* + *pelagic*] : of, relating to, or occurring in the open water of the abyssal zone

abyssal rock *n* : PLUTONIC ROCK

abyssal zone *n* : the biogeographic realm consisting of the deep sea, lacking higher plant life because of the absence of light, and occupied chiefly by carnivorous animals that are often blind or have special luminous organs and are structurally adapted to withstand the great pressures of this level

ab·ys·sin·ia \¦abə¦sinēə, -nyə\ *adj, usu cap* : ETHIOPIAN, ABYSSINIAN

¹ab·ys·sin·i·an \¦abə¦sinēən, -nyən\ *adj, usu cap* [*Abyssinia*, kingdom in eastern Africa + E *-an*] : of or relating to Abyssinia : ETHIOPIAN : ETHIOPIC

²abyssinian \"\ *n* -S *cap* : ETHIOPIAN : ETHIOPIC

abyssinian banana *n, usu cap A* : a banana (*Musa ensete*) having leaves about 20 feet long, inedible fruit, and edible young flower stalks

abyssinian cat *n, usu cap A* : a domestic cat of a breed of African origin comprising small slender cats with short silvery gray or brown hair ticked with darker color and with a black stripe down the spine

abyssinian primrose *n, usu cap A* : a Chinese primrose (*Primula sinensis*) common in cultivation

abyssinian tea *n, usu cap A* : an infusion from the leaves of the kat

abys·so·lith \ə'bisə,lith\ *n* -S [*abyss* + *-o-* + *-lith*] : a deep-seated igneous body lacking a floor of crystalline rock — **abys·so·lith·ic** \⸗¦⸗⸗¦⸗ik\ *adj*

ac- — see AD-

ac *abbr* **1** account **2** acre **3** alicyclic **4** money of account

AC *abbr* **1** absolute ceiling **2** account current **3** after Christ **4** air corps **5** aircraftsman **6** alternating current **7** [L *anno Christi*] in the year of Christ **8** [L *ante Christum*] before Christ **9** *often not cap* [L *ante cibum*] before meals **10** army corps **11** athletic club **12** author's correction **13** automobile club **14** aviation cadet

Ac *symbol* actinium

aca·cat·e·chin \¦akə'kad·əchən, -əsh-,-ək-\ *n* -S [*ac-* (fr. NL *Acacia*, genus name of *Acacia catechu*) + *catechin*] : a crystalline substance that is obtained from acacia catechu, that is held to be a mixture containing catechin, and that is an antioxidant for fatty oils

ac·ac·e·tin \ə'kasət°n, a'k-\ *n* -S [ISV *acacia* (locust) + *acetin*] : a pale yellow crystalline compound $C_{16}H_{12}O_5$ occurring in the form of glycosides esp. in the leaves of the common locust; apigenin 4′-methyl ether

aca·cia \ə'kāshə\ *n* [NL, fr. L, acacia tree, Egyptian thorn, fr. Gk *akakia* shittah] **1** *cap* : a genus of woody plants (family Leguminosae) of warm regions having pinnate leaves and white or yellow flower clusters, the leaves in many Australian members being reduced to phyllodes — see CATECHU, COOBA, WATTLE **2** -S : any plant of the genus *Acacia* **3** -S : LOCUST 3a(2) **4** -S : GUM ARABIC **5** -S : a light to moderate greenish yellow that is redder and less strong than liqueur green — called also *weld*

acacia gum *n* : GUM ARABIC

¹aca·cian \ə'kāsh(ē)ən\ *n* -S *usu cap* [*Acacius* †*ab* A.D. 366 bishop of Caesarea in Palestine + E *-an*] : a follower of Acacius who taught likeness of will alone in the Father and Son in the Christian godhead

²acacian \"\ *adj, usu cap* : of or relating to the Acacians

³acacian \"\ *adj, usu cap* [*Acacius* †A.D. 489 patriarch of Constantinople + E *-an*] : of or relating to a schism occurring 484–519 between Eastern and Western Christian churches

acacia veld *n* : TREE VELD

aca·ci·in \ə'kās(h)ēən, -shən\ *n* -S [ISV *acacia* (locust) + *-in*] : a crystalline glycoside $C_{28}H_{32}O_{14}$ that is found in the leaves of a common No. American locust tree (*Robinia pseudoacacia*) and that yields acacetin on hydrolysis

ac·a·deme \'akə,dēm\ *n* -S [irreg. fr. NL *academia* — more at ACADEMY] **1** *sometimes cap* **a** : a place of study and instruction : SCHOOL **b** : academic environment ⟨the pleasant walks of ~ —R.M.Lovett⟩ **2** : one with a marked leaning toward intellectualism and the academic environment; *esp* : PEDANT

ac·a·de·mia \,akə'dēmyə, -em-\ *n* -S [NL, university — more at ACADEMY] : academic life and interests : academic environment ⟨the complacent paddocks of ~, clubdom, or social status —Lucien Price⟩

¹ac·a·dem·ic \¦akə¦demik, -ēk\ *also* **ac·a·dem·i·cal** \-əkəl *adj* [MF & L; MF *académique* (influenced in meaning by *académie*), fr. L *academicus* of the school of Plato, fr. Gk *akadēmeikos*, fr. *Akadēmeia*, a place where Plato taught + *-ikos* -ic, -ical — more at ACADEMY] **1** *usu cap* : belonging or relating to the philosophy of Plato **2 a** : of, belonging to, or associated with an academy or school esp. of higher learning ⟨the ~ curriculum⟩ ⟨~ interests⟩ **b** : formed by school training or associations : SCHOLARLY ⟨an ~ mind⟩ **c** : very learned but inexperienced in or unable to cope with the world of practical reality : VISIONARY ⟨~ thinkers and schoolmen, men whom the free spaces of thought frightened and who felt safe only behind secure fences —V.L.Parrington⟩ **d** : based on formal study at an institution of learning, esp. of higher learning ⟨though I have no ~ qualifications, I am in fact much more highly educated than most university scholars —G.B. Shaw⟩ **3** : of or belonging to literary or art studies ⟨the state might free the ~ high schools of those who do not belong there, either through an expanded apprentice training program or through vocational guidance —*Amer. Child*⟩ **4 a** : conforming usu. overrigidly to the traditions or rules of a school esp. of literature or art : CONVENTIONAL, FORMALISTIC ⟨I call them ~ because I think the composer's interest in the musical devices he was employing was greater than his effort toward a direct . . . expression of anything in particular —Virgil Thomson⟩ **b** : meeting the standards or deriving from the teachings of an official academy **c** : of a conservative nature : REALISTIC, REPRESENTATIONAL — compare ABSTRACT, MODERN **5 a** : theoretical and not expected to produce an immediate or practical act or result : SPECULATIVE, ABSTRACT ⟨the problem of truth is more than an ~ problem of rational, objective, neutral knowledge —J.L.Hromádka⟩ **b** : of no practical or useful significance **6** : conforming to the architectural theories of Vitruvius (1st century B.C.) and later classical theorists as embodied in the doctrines of the Italian and French academies : marked by conventional use of the classical orders — **ac·a·dem·i·cal·ly** \-mək(ə)lē, -ēk-, -li\ *adv*

²academic \"\ *n* -S **1** *usu cap* **a** : a philosopher of the Academy **b** : one adhering to the philosophy of Plato **2 a** : one (as a professor or student) that is associated with or a member of an institution of learning (as a university) **b** : one that is academic in background, outlook, actions, or procedure

ac·a·dem·i·cals \,⸗⸗'⸗əkəlz\ *n pl* : ACADEMIC COSTUME

academic costume *n* : a costume consisting typically of cap,

academic costume: *1* undergraduate, *2* bachelor, *3* master, *4* doctor

gown, and sometimes hood worn on occasion by students, holders of academic degrees, and faculty of a school, college, or university

academic freedom *n* [trans. of G *akademische freiheit*] **1** : freedom (as of a professor) to teach according to personal convictions about what is or appears to be the truth without fear of hindrance, loss of position, or other reprisal **2** : freedom (as of a student) to learn and inquire fully in any field of investigation without fear of hindrance, dismissal, or other reprisal

ac·a·de·mi·cian \,akədə'mishən, -(,)de'-; ə,kadə'-\ *n* -S [F *académicien*, fr. *académie* academy + *-icien* -ician — more at ACADEMY] **1 a** : a member of an academy **b** : a follower of an artistic or philosophical tradition or a promoter of its ideas **2** : ACADEMIC

ac·a·dem·i·cism \,akə'deмə,sizəm\ *also* **acad·e·mism** \ə'kadə,mizəm\ *n* -S **1** *sometimes cap* : a tenet of Academic philosophy **2** : academic manner, style, or content : FORMALISM, CONVENTIONALITY ⟨writing lacks freshness if it is weighted down with ~⟩ ⟨a modernistic composer who broke away from the fixed norms of musical ~⟩ **3** : purely speculative thoughts and attitudes divorced from immediate or practical effect ⟨he lived in a dreamy, unrealistic world of ~⟩

academic year *n* : the annual period of sessions of an educational institution usu. beginning in September and ending in June — called also *school year*

acad·e·mist \ə'kadəməst\ *n* -S [F *académiste*, fr. *académie* academy + *-iste* -ist] : ACADEMIC

acad·e·my \ə'kadəmē, -mi\ *n* -ES *often attrib* [in sense 1, fr. L *academia*, fr. Gk *Akadēmeia*, *Akadēmia*, fr. the name of the gymnasium near Athens where Plato taught, fr. *Akadēmos* Attic mythological hero + Gk *-eia* or *-ia* -y; in sense 2, partly fr. NL *academia* university, partly fr. F *académie* university, academy, fr. It & NL; It *accademia* university, academy, fr. NL; in senses 3 & 4, fr. F *académie*, fr. NL *academia*, lit., university] **1** *usu cap* : the school of philosophy founded by Plato **2 a** : a school above the elementary level; *esp* : HIGH SCHOOL **b** : a high school or college in which a special art, technical skills, or business courses are taught often to the exclusion of a liberal curriculum in languages and sciences ⟨an ~ of business⟩ ⟨a military ~⟩ **3** : a society of learned individuals united for the advancement of the arts and sciences and literature or of some particular art or science **4** : a body of established opinion in any particular field widely accepted as authoritative and often tending to stifle initiative ⟨the modern movement has been stiffening prematurely into an ~ —Lewis Mumford⟩

academy blue *n* : a moderate greenish blue that is greener, lighter, and stronger than average peacock and greener and deeper than Brittany

academy board *n* [fr. the Royal *Academy* of Painting, Sculpture, and Architecture, England, where it was much used] *n* : a heavy cardboard having a surface prepared for painting in oil

aca·dia·lite \ə'kādēə,līt\ *n* -S [*Acadia* + E *-lite*] : a mineral consisting of a flesh-red chabazite found in Nova Scotia

¹aca·di·an \ə'kādēən; *apparently formerly also* ə'kājən — *compare* CAJUN\ *n* -S *cap* [*Acadia*, Fr. colony of 17th and 18th cent. consisting principally of what is now Nova Scotia (fr. F *Acadie*) + E *-an*] **1** : a native or inhabitant of Acadia **2 a** : a Louisianian descended from French-speaking immigrants from Acadia **b** : a dialect of French spoken by Acadians

²acadian \"\ *adj, usu cap* **1 a** : of or relating to the onetime French colony of Acadia **b** : of or relating to the Acadians **2** : of or relating to the mountain-making movements in No. America in or near the Devonian period

acadian chickadee *n, usu cap A* : a brown-capped chickadee (*Parus hudsonicus littoralis*) of northern New England and Canada

acadian flycatcher *n, usu cap A* : a small No. American flycatcher (*Empidonax virescens*) that is olive-green above and whitish below and tinged with yellow on the belly and sides

acadian owl *n, usu cap A* : SAW-WHET OWL

acae·na \ə'sēnə\ *n, cap* [NL, fr. Gk *akaina* spike, goad, fr. *akē* point — more at EDGE] : a genus of herbs or low shrubs (family Rosaceae) mostly native to south temperate regions and having compound leaves and spiny calyces — see NEW ZEALAND BUR

ac·a·jou \'akə,zhü, -jü\ *n* -S [F, fr. Pg *acajú* — more at CASHEW] **1 a** : CASHEW **b** : CASHEW NUT **1 2** : any of several mahoganies; *esp* : MAHOGANY 1 **3** : LAUREL OAK 2

acal·cu·lia \,ā,kal'kyülēə\ *n* -S [NL, fr. ²*a-* + LL *calculare* to calculate + NL *-ia* — more at CALCULATE] : lack or loss of the ability to perform simple arithmetical tasks

ac·a·leph \'akə,lef\ *n* -S [NL *Acalepha*] : a coelenterate of the group Acalepha

ac·a·le·pha \,akə'lēfə\ *n pl, cap* [NL, alter. of *Acalephae*] *in old classifications* : a class or other group of coelenterates including the jellyfishes, hydroids, and related forms and sometimes the ctenophores

ac·a·le·phae \,akə'lē(,)fē\ [NL, fr. Gk *akalēphai*, pl. of *akalēphē* stinging nettle, sea anemone] *syn of* ACALEPHA

aca·ly·cine \(')ā¦kalə,sīn, -al-\ *or* **aca·lyc·i·nous** \¦ākə¦lis°nəs\ *adj* [*acalycine* fr. ²*a-* + L *calyc-, calyx* + E *-ine*; *acalycinous* fr. *acalycine* + *-ous*] : without a calyx

ac·a·ly·pha \,akə'lifə, ə'kaləfə\ *n, cap* [NL, fr. Gk *akalyphē*, alter. of *akalēphē* nettle] : a genus of herbs and shrubs (family Euphorbiaceae) found in warm regions and having alternate leaves and monoecious apetalous flowers which are showy in cultivated species — see CHENILLE 2

acal·yp·te·rae \,ākə'liptə,rē\ *or* **acal·yp·tra·ta** \¦ā,kaləp'trād·ə, -ād·ə\ [NL, alter. of *Acalyptratae*] *syn of* ACALYPTRATAE

acal·yp·tra·tae \¦ā,kaləp'trād·(,)ē, -ād-\ *n pl, cap* [NL, irreg. fr. ²*a-* + *calypter* + L *-atae* (fem. pl. of *-atus* -ate)] : a group of two-winged flies having the alula small or wanting and including a number of pests (as fruit flies, many leaf miners, frit flies, and the cheese skipper) — **aca·lyp·trate** \¦ākə¦lip,trāt, (')ā¦kaləp,trāt\ *adj*

aca·na \'äkənə, -,nä\ *n* -S [Sp *ácana*, prob. fr. Ciboney or Taino] : either of two West Indian trees (*Manilkara albescens* and *M. bidentata*) of the family Sapotaceae that yield valuable timber

acanth- *or* **acantho-** *comb form* [NL, fr. Gk *akanth-*, *akantho-*, fr. *akantha*; akin to ON *ögn* awn — more at AWN] : thorn : spine ⟨*acantho*carpous⟩ ⟨*Acantho*phis⟩

acan·tha \ə'kan(t)thə\ *n* -S [NL, fr. Gk *akantha* thorn, spine of a fish] : a spine or spinous fin

ac·an·tha·ce·ae \,a,kan'thāsē,ē, ,akən-\ *n pl, cap* [NL, fr. *Acanthus*, type genus + *-aceae*] : a family of widely distributed herbs, shrubs, and trees (order Polemoniales) having opposite leaves and tubular bracted irregular flowers with two or four stamens — **ac·an·tha·ceous** \¦a,kan¦thāshəs, ¦akən-\ *adj* — **acan·thad** \ə'kan(t)thəd, -n,thad\ *n* -S

ac·an·thar·ia \,a,kan'tha(a)rēə, ,akən-\ [NL, fr. *acanth-* + *-aria*] *syn of* ACTIPYLEA

ac·an·thar·i·an \-rēən\ *n* -S [NL *Acantharia* + E *-an*] : a protozoan of the suborder Actipylea

ac·an·thel·la \-'thelə\ *n, pl* **acanthellas** \-ləz\ *also* **acan·thel·lae** \-(,)lē\ [NL, fr. *acanth-* (fr. *Acanthocephala*) + *-ella*] **1** : a transitional larva of the acanthocephalan intermediate between the acanthor and the juvenile infective form — called also *preacanthella* **2** : the juvenile infective form of an acanthocephalan

acanthi *pl of* ACANTHUS

acan·thi·al \ə'kan(t)thēəl\ *adj* [NL *acanthion* + E *-al*] : of or belonging to the acanthion

acan·thine \ə'kan(t)thən, -n,thīn\ *adj* [L *acanthinus*, fr. *acanthus* + *-inus* -ine] **1** : of or relating to the acanthus plant **2** : resembling the leaves of the acanthus plant

acan·thi·on \ə'kan(t)thēən, -ē,än\ *n* -S [NL, fr. Gk *akanthion* thorn, spinous process of the vertebrae, dim. of *akantha* thorn — more at ACANTHA] : a point at the base of the anterior nasal spine — see CRANIOMETRY illustration

acan·thi·sit·ti·dae \ə,kan(t)thə'sid·ə,dē\ *n pl, cap* [NL, fr. *Acanthisitta*, type genus (fr. Gk *akanthis* goldfinch, linnet + *sitta* nuthatch) + *-idae*] : a family (type genus *Acanthisitta*) of passerine New Zealand birds including the rock wren, rifleman bird, and certain related birds

acan·thite \ə'kan,thīt, 'akən,-\ *n* -S [ISV *acanth-* + *-ite*; fr. the thornlike shape of its crystals; orig. formed as G *akanthit*] : a mineral Ag_2S consisting of a silver sulfide like argentite but crystallizing in slender prisms (sp. gr. 7.2–7.3)

acantho- — see ACANTH-

acan·tho·ceph·a·la \ə,kan(t)thə'sefələ\ *n pl, cap* [NL, fr. *acanth-* + *-cephala* (neut. pl. of *-cephalus*)] : a group of elongated unsegmented bilaterally symmetrical parasitic worms that lack a digestive tract, have a hooked proboscis by which as adults they attach themselves to the intestinal wall of various vertebrates, and live out their larval stages as interstitial or digestive parasites, the group being of uncertain systematic position formerly considered a class of Nemathelminthes but now usu. made a separate phylum near Platyhelminthes or associated with or included in Aschelminthes — **acan·tho·ceph·a·lan** \-ələn\ *adj or n* — **acan·tho·ceph·a·lid** \-ləd\ *adj or n*

acan·tho·ceph·a·li \-ə,lī, -,lē\ [NL, alter. of *Acanthocephala*] *syn of* ACANTHOCEPHALA

acan·tho·ce·re·us \-'sirēəs\ *n, cap* [NL, fr. *acanth-* + L *cereus* candle — more at CEREUS] : a genus of tropical American weak often trailing cacti (family Cactaceae) having nocturnal funnel-shaped white flowers and 3-angled spiny stems — see PITAHAYA

acan·tho·chei·lo·ne·ma \ə¦kan(t)thə,kīlə'nēmə\ *n, cap* [NL, fr. *acanth-* + *cheil-* + *-nema*] : a common genus of tropical filarial worms parasitic in man and monkeys

acan·tho·cyb·i·um \ə,kan(t)thə'sibēəm\ *n, cap* [NL, fr. *acanth-* + L *cybium* tunny, fr. Gk *kybion* flesh of the young tunny, fr. *kybos* piece of salted fish, cube] : a genus (sometimes made the type of a separate family Acanthocybiidae though usu. placed in Scombridae) of large predaceous marine fishes that includes the wahoo and other food and game fishes

ac·an·tho·dea \,a,kan'thōdēə, ,akən-\ *or* **ac·an·tho·dei** \-dē,ī\ *or* **ac·an·thod·i·ni** \-'thäd°n,ī\ *syn of* ACANTHODII

ac·an·tho·des \-'thō(,)dēz\ *n, cap* [NL, fr. Gk *akanthōdēs* thorny, spiny, fr. *akanth-* acanth- + *-ōdēs* -ode] : a genus of small slender possibly degenerate fishes having generalized toothless jaws and a single small dorsal fin and found in the Carboniferous and Permian formations

¹ac·an·tho·di·an *also* **ac·an·tho·de·an** \¦a,kan¦thōdēən, ¦akən-\ *adj* [NL *Acanthodii*, *Acanthodei* + E *-an*] : of or belonging to the subclass Acanthodii

²acanthodian *also* **acanthodean** \"\ *n* -S : an animal or fossil belonging to the subclass Acanthodii

ac·an·tho·dii \,a,kan'thōdē,ī, ,akən-\ *n pl, cap* [NL, fr. *Acanthodes*] : a subclass of Placodermi comprising primitive Paleozoic fishes having the anterior margin of each fin supported by a stout spine and often having one or more pairs of spines similar to the fin spines along the lower lateral part of the body between the paired fins of each side

acan·thoid \ə'kan,thȯid\ *adj* [*acanth-* + *-oid*] : shaped like a spine : SPINY, SPINOUS

acan·tho·li·mon \ə,kan(t)thə'lī,män, -mən\ *n, cap* [NL, fr. *acanth-* + *Limonium*] : a genus of stiff oriental herbs (family Plumbaginaceae) having basal leaves and small stalked heads of white or rosy flowers

ac·an·thol·o·gy \,a,kan'thäləjē, ,akən-\ *n* -ES [*acanth-* + *-logy*] : the study of spines (as of sea urchins) esp. as an adjunct of taxonomy

ac·an·thol·y·sis \,a,kan'thäləsəs, ,akən-\ *n, pl* **acantholy·ses** \-ə,sēz\ [NL, fr. *acanth-* + *-lysis*] : atrophy of the prickle-cell layer of the epidermis

ac·an·tho·ma \-'thōmə\ *n, pl* **acanthomas** \-məz\ *or* **acanthoma·ta** \-məd·ə\ [NL, fr. *acanth-* + *-oma*] : a neoplasm originating in the skin and developing through excessive growth of skin cells esp. of the prickle-cell layer

ac·an·thop·a·nax \-'thäpə,naks\ *n, cap* [NL, fr. *acanth-* + *Panax*] : a genus of prickly shrubs and trees (family Araliaceae) native to temperate Asia that have handsome palmate leaves and produce green flowers in much-branched clusters

acan·tho·phis \ə'kan(t)thəfəs\ *n, cap* [NL, fr. *acanth-* + Gk *ophis* snake — more at OPHIDIA] : a genus of venomous Australian snakes (family Elapidae) having a long horny upturned spine at the end of the tail and consisting of the death adder (*A. antarcticus*)

acan·tho·pod \-ə,päd\ *adj* [*acanth-* + *-pod*] : spiny-footed

ac·an·thop·o·dous \¦a,kan¦thäpədəs, ¦akən-\ *adj* [*acanth-* + *-podous*] **1** : spiny-footed **2** : having spiny petioles or peduncles

acan·tho·pore \ə'kan(t)thə,pō(ə)r\ *n* -S [*acanth-* + *-pore*] : a tubular spine in some fossil bryozoans

ac·an·thopt \'a,kan,thäpt, 'akən-\ *n* -S [irreg. fr. NL *Acanthopteri*] : an acanthopterygian fish

ac·an·thop·te·ri \,a,kan'thäptə,rī, ,akən-\ [NL, alter. of *Acanthopterygii*] *syn of* ACANTHOPTERYGII

¹ac·an·thop·te·ryg·i·an \-,thäptə'rijēən\ *or* **ac·an·thop·te·ran** \¦a,kan¦thäptərən, ¦akən-\ *adj* [NL *Acanthopterygii* or *Acanthopteri* + E *-an*] : of or belonging to the Acanthopterygii

²acanthopterygian \"\ *or* **acanthopteran** \"\ *n* -S : ACANTHOPT

ac·an·thop·te·ryg·ii \,a,kan,thäptə'rijē,ī, ,akən-\ *n pl, cap* [NL, fr. *acanth-* + *-pterygii* (fr. Gk *pterygion* fin, small wing)] *in many classifications* : a superorder or other category of teleost fishes containing orig. all those having the anterior rays of the dorsal and anal fins stiff and spiny (as the basses, perches, and mackerels) or now those usu. lacking a duct to the air bladder, having no mesocoracoid bone, and having the pectoral arch suspended from the skull, the ventral fins attached to the clavicular arch, and the gill opening in front of the pectoral fin (as most of the spiny-finned and some soft-finned fishes)

acan·thor \ə'kan,thȯ(ə)r\ *n* -S [NL, fr. *acanth-* (fr. *Acanthocephala*) + *-or*] : the mature embryo of an acanthocephalan just previous to hatching — compare ACANTHELLA

acan·tho·scel·i·des \ə,kan(t)thə'selə,dēz\ *n, cap* [NL, fr. *acanth-* + Gk *skelos* leg + *-ides* (pl. of *-id-, -is*, patronymic suffix)] : a genus of weevils (family Bruchidae) native to America but of cosmopolitan distribution and including the destructive bean weevil

ac·an·tho·sis \,a,kan'thōsəs, ,akən-\ *n, pl* **acanthoses** \-ō,sēz\ [NL, fr. *acanth-* + *-osis*] : a benign overgrowth of the prickle-cell layer of the skin — **ac·an·thot·ic** \¦a,kan-¦thäd·ik, ¦akən-\ *adj*

acanthosis ni·gri·cans \-'nigrə,kanz, -'nīg-\ *n* [NL, lit., blackish acanthosis] : a skin disease characterized by gray-black wartlike patches usu. situated in the axilla or groin or on elbows or knees and sometimes associated with cancer of abdominal viscera

acan·tho·so·ma \ə,kan(t)thə'sōmə\ *n, pl* **acanthosomas** \-ōməz\ *or* **acanthosoma·ta** \-ōməd·ə\ [NL, fr. *acanth-* + *-soma*; fr. its spiny carapace] : a peneid zoea

acan·tho·style \ə'kan(t)thə,stīl\ *n* -S [*acanth-* + *-style*] : a monaxon sponge spicule rounded at one end and bearing tiny spines

acan·thous \ə'kan(t)thəs\ *adj* [*acanth-* + *-ous*] : SPINOUS

acan·thu·ri·dae \ə,kan'th(y)ürə,dē, ,akən-\ *n pl, cap* [NL, fr. *Acanthurus*, type genus + *-idae*] *syn of* TEUTHIDIDAE

ac·an·thu·rus \-rəs\ [NL, fr. *acanth-* + *-urus*] *syn of* TEUTHIS

acan·thus \ə'kan(t)thəs\ *n* [NL, fr. Gk *akanthos* (*Acanthus mollis, Acanthus spinosus*), fr. *akantha* thorn — more at ACANTHA] **1 a** *cap* **:** a genus of prickly herbs (family Acanthaceae) of the Mediterranean region that have spiny-bracted flowers **b** *pl* **acanthuses** \-n(t)thəsəz\ *also* **acan·thi** \-n,thī, -,thē\ **:** any plant of the genus *Acanthus* **2** *pl* **acanthuses** *also* **acanthi :** a usu. sculptured ornamentation representing or suggesting the leaves of the acanthus (as in a Corinthian capital)

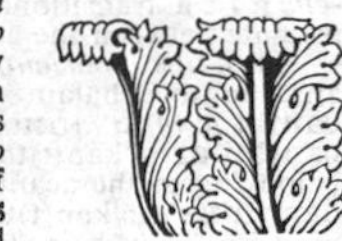

acanthus 2

-a·can·thus \"\ *n comb form* [NL, fr. Gk *akantha* thorn] **:** animal having (such) a spine or (such or so many) spines ⟨Cephal*acanthus*⟩ ⟨Cten*acanthus*⟩ — in generic names esp. of fishes

acanthus family *n, usu cap A* **:** ACANTHACEAE

acap·nia \ā'kapnēə, (')ā'-\ *n* -s [NL, fr. L *acapnos* without smoke, used to mean "without carbon dioxide", which is contained in smoke (fr. Gk *akapnos*, fr. *a-* ²a- + *kapnos* smoke) + NL *-ia* — more at COVET] **:** a condition of carbon dioxide deficiency in blood and tissues — **acap·ni·al** \-ēəl\ *adj*

¹**a cap·pel·la** *also* **a ca·pel·la** \,äkə'pelə, ,ä-\ *adv* [It *a cappella* in chapel or choir style] **1 :** in a style marked by the absence of instrumental accompaniment ⟨sing *a cappella*⟩ **2** *obs* **:** in alla breve time

²**a cappella** *also* **a capella** \"\ *adj* **1 :** unaccompanied by instruments **:** marked by or specializing in unaccompanied singing ⟨an *a cappella* choir⟩ **2** *obs* **:** ALLA BREVE

a ca·pric·cio \,äkə'prē(,)chō, -ri-, -,chē,ō\ *adv* [It, at one's caprice] **:** in any interpretation that appeals to the performer — used as a direction in music

acap·su·lar \(')ā¦kapsələ(r)\ *adj* [²a- + *capsular*] *bot* **:** having no capsule

aca·pu \,äkə'pü\ *n* -s [Pg *acapú*, fr. Tupi] **1 a :** any of several tropical American timber trees of the genus *Andira* (esp. *A. americana*) **b :** the dark chocolate-brown wood of the acapu tree widely used esp. in Brazil for flooring and heavy construction **2 a :** an Amazonian leguminous tree (*Clathrotropis nitida*) **b :** the wood of this tree used for heavy construction

aca·pul·co \,äkə'pül(,)kō\ *n* -s [PhilSp, fr. *Acapulco*, Mexico, its point of export] **:** a Mexican plant (*Cassia alata*) introduced into Guam and the Philippines the leaves of which are used as a folk remedy for ringworm and other skin diseases

acar- *or* **acari-** *or* **acaro-** *comb form* [NL, fr. *Acarus*] **:** mite ⟨*acar*oid⟩ ⟨*acari*cide⟩

aca·ra \,äkə¦rä\ *n* -s [Pg *acará*, fr. Tupi] **:** any of several So. American and Central American fishes (family Cichlidae) that build nests and guard their young — see BLUE ACARA

acar·a·pis \ə'karəpəs\ *n, cap* [NL, fr. *acar-* + L *apis* bee] **:** a genus of minute mites that are chiefly parasitic on insects and include a species (*A. woodi*) that invades the tracheae of honeybees causing Isle of Wight disease

acar·dite \ə'kär,dīt\ *n* -s [origin unknown] **:** a crystalline compound $(C_6H_5)_2NCONH_2$ used as a stabilizer in smokeless powder; 1,1-diphenyl-urea

¹**ac·a·ri** \'akərē, -,rī\ [NL, fr. Gk *akari*, a mite] *syn of* ACARINA

²**acari** *pl of* ACARUS

¹**acar·i·an** \ə'ka(a)rēən\ *adj* [NL *Acari* + E *-an*] **1 :** of or relating to the order Acarina **2 :** of, relating to, caused by, or having the characteristics of a mite or tick

²**acarian** \"\ *n* -s **:** an arachnid of the order Acarina **:** MITE, TICK

ac·a·ri·a·sis \,akə'rīəsəs\ *n, pl* **acaria·ses** \-ə,sēz\ [NL, fr. *acar-* + *-iasis*] **:** infestation with or disease caused by mites

acar·i·cid·al \(,)ə¦karə¦sīdᵊl\ *adj* [*acaricide* + *-al*] **:** that kills mites ⟨an ~ compound⟩

acar·i·cide *also* **acar·a·cide** \ə'karə,sīd\ *n* -s [*acaricide* fr. *acar-* + *-cide; acaracide* alter. of *acaricide*] **:** a substance or preparation that kills mites

¹**ac·a·rid** \'akərəd, -(,)rid\ *adj* [NL *Acarida*] **1 :** ACARIAN **2 :** of or relating to the family Acaridae

²**acarid** \"\ *n* -s **1 :** ACARIAN **2 :** a mite of the family Acaridae

acar·i·da \ə'karədə\ *or* **ac·a·rid·ea** \,akə'ridēə\ [NL, fr. *Acarus* + *-ida* or *-idea*] *syn of* ACARINA

acar·i·dae \ə'karə,dē\ *n pl, cap* [NL, fr. *Acarus*, type genus + *-idae*] **:** a large and widely distributed family of mites that feed on organic substances (as preserved meats, hides, seeds, and grains) and are sometimes responsible for dermatitis in persons exposed to repeated contacts with infested products — see GROCER'S ITCH

¹**acar·i·dan** \ə'karədᵊn, -dən\ *also* **ac·a·rid·e·an** *or* **ac·a·rid·i·an** \¦akə¦ridēən\ *adj* [NL *Acaridae* + E *-an, -ean, -ian*] **:** ACARIAN; *esp* **:** ACARID 2

²**acaridan** \"\ *also* **acaridean** *or* **acaridian** \"\ *n* -s **:** ACARIAN; *esp* **:** ACARID 2

acar·i·dol·o·gist \ə,karə'däləjəst\ *n* -s [*acarid* + *-o-* + *-logist*] **:** ACAROLOGIST

acar·i·form \ə'karə,fȯrm\ *adj* [*acar-* + *form*] **:** shaped like a mite

ac·a·ri·na \,akə'rīnə, -ēnə\ *n pl, cap* [NL, fr. *Acarus* + *-ina*] **:** a cosmopolitan and very large order of Arachnida comprising the mites and ticks most of which lack distinct demarcation into cephalothorax and abdomen and have no book lungs, many of which are parasites of plants, animals, or man, and some of which are vectors of important diseases — compare TEXAS FEVER, TYPHUS

ac·a·ri·nar·i·um \-rə'na(a)rēəm\ *n, pl* **acarinar·ia** \-ēə\ *or* **acarinariums** \-ēəmz\ [NL, fr. *Acarina* + *-arium*] **:** a chamber of the body wall of insects (as wasps) frequently infested by tiny nonparasitic mites

ac·a·rine \'akə,rīn, -,rēn, -,rən\ *adj or n* [NL *Acarina*] **:** ACARIAN

acarine disease *n* **:** Isle of Wight disease of honeybees; *also* **:** any disease caused by ticks or mites

ac·a·ri·nol·o·gy \,akərə'näləjē\ *n* -ES [NL *Acarina* + E *-o-* *-logy*] **:** ACAROLOGY

ac·a·ri·no·sis \-'nōsəs\ *n, pl* **acarino·ses** \-ō,sēz\ [NL, fr. *Acarina* + *-osis*] **:** ACARIASIS

acar·i·o·sis \ə,karē'ōsəs\ *n, pl* **acario·ses** \-ō,sēz\ [NL, by alter.] **:** ACARIASIS

ac·a·ro·ce·cid·i·um \¦akə(,)rōsə'sidēəm\ *n, pl* **acarocecid·ia** \-ēə\ *or* **acarocecidiums** \-ēəmz\ [NL, fr. *acar-* + *cecidium*] **:** a plant gall caused by an acarid

ac·a·roid \'akə,rȯid\ *adj* [*acar-* + *-oid*] **:** resembling a mite

acaroid resin *n* [NL *acaroides*] **:** a red or yellow balsamic alcohol-soluble resin from Australian grass trees used chiefly in varnishes, printing inks, and paper sizes — called also *accroides, gum accroides*

ac·a·rol·o·gist \,akə'räləjəst\ *n* -s [*acarology* + *-ist*] **:** a student of or specialist in acarology

ac·a·rol·o·gy \-jē\ *n* -ES [*acar-* + *-logy*] **1 :** a branch of zoology that treats of mites and ticks **2 :** a treatise on mites and ticks

ac·a·ro·pho·bia \,akərə'fōbēə\ *n* -s [NL, fr. *acar-* + *-phobia*] **1 :** an abnormal dread of skin infestation with small crawling organisms **2 :** a delusion that the skin is infested with small crawling organisms

acar·pel·ous *or* **acar·pel·lous** \(')ā¦kärpələs\ *adj* [²a- + *carpel* + *-ous*] **:** having no carpels

acar·pous \(')ā¦kärpəs\ *adj* [Gk *akarpos*, fr. *a-* ²a- + *-karpos* -carpous] *bot* **:** not producing fruit **:** STERILE

ac·a·rus \'akərəs\ *n* [NL, fr. Gk *akari*, a mite; prob. akin to Gk *keirein* to cut off, shear — more at SHEAR] **1** *cap* **:** a genus of arachnids including a number of small mites and formerly including all mites and ticks **2** *pl* **aca·ri** \-,rī, -,rē\ **:** a mite of the genus *Acarus; sometimes* **:** MITE

¹**acat·a·lec·tic** \¦ā,kad·ᵊl¦ektik\ *adj* [LL *acatalecticus*, fr. *acatalectus* (fr. Gk *akatalēktos*, fr. *a-* ²a- + *-katalēktos*, fr. *katalēgein* to leave off) + L *-icus* -ic — more at CATALECTIC] *prosody* **:** not defective in the last foot **:** complete in the number of syllables ⟨an ~ line of verse⟩

²**acatalectic** \"\ *n* -s **:** a line of verse complete in the number of its syllables

acat·a·lep·sy \(')ā'kad·ᵊl,epsē\ *n* -ES [Gk *akatalēpsia*, fr. *a-* ²a- + *katalēpsis* comprehension, seizing + *-ia* — more at CATALEPSY] **1 :** an ancient Skeptic doctrine that human knowledge amounts only to probability and never to certainty **2 :** real or apparent impossibility of arriving at certain knowledge or full comprehension

¹**acat·a·lep·tic** \¦ā¦==¦eptik\ *adj* [Gk *akatalēptos* incomprehensible (fr. *a-* ²a- + *katalēptos* seized, comprehensible) + E *-ic* — more at CATALEPTIC] **:** relating to or characterized by acatalepsy

²**acataleptic** \"\ *n* -s **:** one that suspends judgment as a matter of principle believing certainty is impossible

acat·a·lex·is \¦ā,kad·ᵊl'eksəs\ *n, pl* **acatalex·es** \-k,sēz\ [LL, fr. Gk *a-* ²a- + *katalēxis* catalexis — more at CATALEXIS] **:** the quality of being acatalectic

acater *n* -s [ME *acatour* — more at CATER] *obs* **:** CATERER

acates *n pl* [ME, pl. of *acat*, lit., purchase — more at CATE] *obs* **:** dainty foods **:** DELICACIES

ac·a·thist hymn \'akəthəst-\ *n, usu cap A* [part trans. of MGk *akathistos hymnos*] **:** ACATHISTUS

ac·a·this·tus \,akə'thistəs\ *or* **aca·thi·stos** \ä'käthē,stȯs\ *also* **ak·a·thist** \'akə,thist\ *or* **aka·thi·stos** \ä'käthē,stȯs\ *n, pl* **ac·a·this·ti** \,akə'thi,stī, -(,)stē\ *or* **aca·thi·stoi** \ä'käthē,stē\ *also* **ak·a·thists** \'akə,this(t)s\ *or* **aka·thi·stoi** \ä'käthē,stē\ *usu cap* [MGk *akathistos* (*hymnos*), lit., standing hymn, fr. *akathistos* standing, fr. *a-* ²a- + *-kathistos* (fr. Gk *kathizein* to seat, set, sit, fr. *kata* down + *-izein* -ize) — more at CATA-] **:** any of several Lenten hymns of the Eastern Orthodox Church sung with the people standing in honor of Christ, the Virgin Mary, or one of the saints

acau·dal \(')ā¦kȯdᵊl\ *or* **acau·date** \(')ā'kȯ,dāt\ *adj* [²a- + *caudal, caudate*] **:** without a tail

acau·les·cence \¦ā(,)kȯ'lesᵊn(t)s\ *n* -s **:** state of being acaulescent

acau·les·cent \¦ā(,)kȯ'lesᵊnt\ *or* **acau·line** \(')ā'kȯ,līn\ *adj* [²a- + *caulescent* or *-cauline* (fr. L *caulis* stem + E *-ine*) — more at COLE] **:** stemless or apparently stemless — opposed to *caulescent*

aca·wai *or* **aka·wai** \'äkə,wī\ *n, pl* **acawai** *or* **acawais** *or* **akawai** *or* **akawais** *usu cap* **1 a :** a Cariban people of northwestern British Guiana **b :** a member of such people **2 :** the language of the Acawai people

aca·xee \ä'käkē\ *n, pl* **acaxee** *or* **acaxees** *usu cap* [Sp *acaxe, acaje*, fr. Nahuatl] **1 a :** a Taracahitian people of western Mexico **b :** a member of such people **2 :** the language of the Acaxee people

acc *abbr* **1** acceleration **2** acceptance; accepted **3** accompanied; accompaniment **4** according **5** account **6** accusative

ac·ca \'akə\ *n* -s [ML, prob. fr. *Acca, Accho*, ancient city of Syria (now *Acre*, Israel), its place of export] **:** a gold and silk brocade of medieval origin

accadian *usu cap, var of* AKKADIAN

acce *abbr* acceptance

ac·ce·das ad cu·ri·am \ä'kādə,säd'k(y)u̇rē,äm\ *n* [ML, lit., that you go to the court] *in English legal practice* **:** a common-law writ to remove a cause from an inferior court not of record to a higher court

ac·cede \ak'sēd, ək-, *chiefly substand* ə's-\ *vi* -ED/-ING/-S [ME *acceden*, fr. L *accedere*, fr. *ad-* + *cedere* to go, yield — more at CEDE] **1** *archaic* **:** to come forward **:** APPROACH **2 a** (1) **:** to become a party (as to an agreement) by associating oneself with others ⟨they were invited to ~ to the covenant⟩ (2) *of a people or territory* **:** to join in political union (as with another country) ⟨Kashmir was said to have *acceded* to India⟩ **b :** to express approval or give consent **:** ASSENT ⟨ready to ~ to his proposal — Jane Austen⟩ **3 :** to assume an office or position **:** attain an honor ⟨he *acceded* to the governorship⟩ **:** come or succeed to the throne ⟨the queen *acceded* in 1918⟩ **4** *law* **:** to become added by way of accession **syn** see ASSENT

¹**ac·ce·le·ran·do** \(,)ä,chelə'ran(,)dō, -än-\ *adv (or adj)* [It, lit., accelerating, fr. L *accelerandum*, gerund of *accelerare*] **:** gradually faster — used as a direction in music

²**accelerando** \"\ *n* -s **:** a gradual increase in tempo ⟨examples of the ~s . . . our metrical ear seems willing to accept —P.F. Baum⟩

ac·cel·er·ant \ik'selərənt, ak- *sometimes* ek-\ *n* -s [*accelerate* + *-ant*] **:** one that accelerates

¹**ac·cel·er·ate** \-lə,rāt, *chiefly substand* ə's-; *usu* -ād- + V\ *vb* -ED/-ING/-S [L *acceleratus*, past part. of *accelerare*, fr. *ad-* + *celerare* to hasten, fr. *celer* swift — more at CELERITY] *vt* **1 :** to bring about at an earlier point of time ⟨anxious to ~ our departure —James Cook⟩ **2 :** to add to the speed of or quicken the motion of ⟨the voice caused me to ~ my steps —W.H.Hudson⟩ **3 :** to hasten the ordinary progress or the development of ⟨war *accelerated* the old trends⟩ ⟨hot weather *accelerated* their efforts to adjourn⟩ **:** increase the rate or amount of ⟨he decided to ~ his advertising⟩ **4 a :** to enable (a student) to complete a course of study more rapidly than usual **b :** to modify (as a course of study) by decreasing the time usu. taken to complete the normal amount of work **5 :** to cause to undergo acceleration; *esp* **:** to increase the velocity of (a body) ~ *vi* **1 a :** to become faster **:** move faster **:** gain speed ⟨a pace that neither ~s nor lags⟩ **b :** to increase in number or amount ⟨the number of newspapers *accelerated*⟩ **c :** to open the throttle or accelerator ⟨the driver *accelerated* gradually on the highway⟩ **2 :** to follow a speeded-up educational program **:** progress from grade to grade more rapidly than usual **:** complete requirements (as for a diploma) more rapidly than usual **syn** see SPEED

²**ac·cel·er·ate** \-lərət, -r,āt, *usu* -d-+V\ *n* -s **:** an accelerated pupil or student

accelerated *adj* **:** beyond one's years in development ⟨~ in intelligence⟩

accelerated amortization *n* **:** a deduction from taxable income in lieu of normal depreciation on qualified facilities based on writing off capital investment over a stated period representing the duration of war or emergency, the higher write-off resulting in a tax advantage

accelerated depreciation *n* **:** depreciation of assets at a higher rate than that normally assigned to cover use and exhaustion

ac·cel·er·a·tion \=,==¦rāshən\ *n* -s [L *acceleration-, acceleratio*, fr. *acceleratus* + *-ion-, -io* -ion] **1 :** the act or process of accelerating ⟨the unusual ~ of economic activity⟩ **:** state of being accelerated **2 :** the time rate of change of velocity (as in speed or direction) **:** the vector derivative of the velocity with respect to time — see ANGULAR ACCELERATION **3 :** gradual appearance in the course of evolution of an ancestral adult character in the immature descendant — compare ABBREVIATION **4 :** advancement in mental growth or achievement beyond the average of one's age

acceleration clause *n* **:** a clause (as in a loan contract) providing for advancement of the date of payment under specified circumstances

acceleration coefficient *n* **:** ACCELERATOR 2

acceleration lane *n* **:** a speed change area or lane consisting of added pavement at the edge of through traffic lanes to permit vehicles to accelerate before merging with the through-traffic flow — compare DECELERATION LANE

acceleration of gravity : acceleration of a body falling in a vacuum under the influence of the earth's gravity expressed as the rate of increase of velocity per unit of time, its value at sea level in latitude 45 degrees being 980.616 centimeters per second per second which is designated as g45 as distinguished from g_0 = 980.665 centimeters per second per second, an arbitrary value adopted in 1901 by the International Committee of Weights and Measures — abbr. *g*

acceleration of the tide : priming of the tide

acceleration principle *n* **:** a principle in economics: an increase or decrease in income induces a corresponding change in investment

ac·cel·er·a·tive \=¦==,rād·iv, -,rə-\ *adj* **:** relating to or tending to cause acceleration **:** ACCELERATING

ac·cel·er·a·tor \-,rād·ə(r), -ātə-\ *n* -s **1 :** one that accelerates: as **a :** any muscle or nerve that speeds the performance of an action ⟨cardiac ~⟩ **b :** a chemical (as an alkali) used in photography for speeding the action of a developer — called also *activator* **c :** any of several devices for increasing the speed of a motor vehicle engine; *esp* **:** a foot-operated throttle that varies the supply of fuel-air mixture to the combustion chamber **d :** an attachment to a dry-pipe valve for accelerating its operation when sprinkler heads are opened **e :** a substance that speeds a chemical reaction; *esp* **:** one that speeds the vulcanization of rubber or the curing of a plastic **f :** a substance added to stucco, plaster, mortar, concrete, or similar materials to hasten the set **g :** an apparatus for imparting high velocities by electromagnetic or electrostatic means to charged particles (as electrons) which are generated in the apparatus, accelerated in controlled paths to a state of high energy, and focused continuously until they emerge as a stream of high-speed projectiles — see CYCLOTRON **2 :** the ratio of increase or decrease in investment to an increase or decrease in income — called also *acceleration coefficient;* compare ACCELERATION PRINCIPLE

accelerator globulin *n* **:** a globulin occurring in inactive form in blood plasma that in its active form is one of the factors accelerating the formation of thrombin from prothrombin in the clotting of blood

ac·cel·er·a·to·ry \-,rə,tōrē\ *adj* **:** ACCELERATIVE

ac·cel·ero·graph \-,rə,graf\ *n* -s [ISV *acceleration* + *-o-* + *-graph;* orig. formed as F *accélérographe*] **1 :** an apparatus for measuring and recording the pressure developed by combustion of an explosive in a closed space **2 :** an instrument for recording the acceleration in velocity of earthquake vibrations

ac·cel·er·om·e·ter \=,==¦rämǝd·ə(r)\ *n* -s [ISV *acceleration* + *-o-* + *-meter;* orig. formed as F *accéléromètre*] **1 :** an instrument for measuring acceleration (as of a moving vehicle) or for detecting and measuring mechanical vibrations (as of machinery) **2 :** an apparatus for measuring the gas pressure at any particular point in a gun

ac·cen·sion \ak'senchən\ *n* -s [LL *accension-, accensio*, fr. L *accensus* (past part. of *accendere* to set on fire, fr. *ad-* + *-cendere*, fr. *candēre* to glow) + *-ion-, -io* -ion — more at CANDID] *archaic* **:** KINDLING, IGNITION, COMBUSTION

¹**ac·cent** \'ak,sent, *Brit usu* -sənt\ *n* -s [MF, fr. L *accentus* (trans. of Gk *prosōidia*), fr. *ad-* + *-centus* (fr. *cantus* song, fr. *cantus*, past part. of *canere* to sing) — more at CHANT, PROSODY] **1 :** a distinctive manner of usu. oral expression: as **a :** the inflection, tone, or choice of words associated with a particular situation, event, emotion, or attitude or taken to be unique in or highly characteristic of an individual — usu. used in pl. ⟨the authoritative ~s of a ruling class —*Time*⟩ ⟨I knew Heathcliff's ~s —Emily Brontë⟩ **b :** speech habits typical of the natives or residents of a region or of any other group (as social, professional, or business) ⟨a heavy foreign ~⟩ ⟨a southern ~⟩ ⟨the staccato ~ of a circus barker⟩ **2 a :** an articulative effort (as an increase of stress or a change of pitch) giving prominence to one syllable of a word or group of words over adjacent syllables **b :** the prominence given a syllable through the use of accent **3 :** rhythmically significant stress on the syllables of a verse usu. at approximately regular intervals **:** ICTUS **4** *archaic* **:** a word or group of words **:** UTTERANCE **5 a :** a mark (as ´, `, ˆ) used in writing or printing to indicate a specific sound value, stress, or pitch, to distinguish words otherwise identically spelled, or to indicate that an ordinarily mute vowel should be pronounced; *broadly* **:** any mark, point, or sign used with a letter whether functional or not — see ACUTE, CIRCUMFLEX, GRAVE; compare DIACRITIC **b :** a letter with a diacritical mark (as é, ç, ä, ñ) — a printers' term; compare PIECE ACCENT **c :** a letter not used in the ordinary alphabet — a printers' term **6 a :** greater stress or emphasis given to one musical tone than to its neighbors **b :** the principle of regularly recurring stresses which serve to distribute a succession of pulses into equal groups or measures — called also *grammatical accent* **c :** special emphasis placed exceptionally upon tones not subject to grammatical accent — called also *rhetorical accent* **d :** the rhythmical principle of grammatical accent operating over such longer spans of time as to mark alternate strong and weak measures or phrase relationships — called also *rhythmical accent* **e :** ACCENT MARK 2 **7 a :** emphasis laid on a part of an artistic design or composition **b :** a detail or area emphasized **:** a striking detail; *esp* **:** a small detail in sharp contrast with its surroundings (as in color or texture) **c :** a substance or object used for emphasis ⟨a plant used for ~ in a landscape design⟩ **8 :** a mark placed to the right of a letter or number and usu. slightly above it: **a :** a mark used singly with letters to distinguish either different mathematical variables (as *x* and *x′*) or singly, doubly, and triply to distinguish different values of the same variable (as *y′* and *y″*) — compare DOUBLE PRIME, PRIME **b :** a mark used singly with numbers to denote minutes and doubly to denote seconds of time (as a 4′3″ interval) or to denote minutes and seconds of an angle or arc **c :** a mark used singly with numbers to denote feet and doubly to denote inches (as 6′3″ tall) **9 :** any distinguishing characteristic or individualizing stamp ⟨his peculiar ~ of wistful naïveté —Edmund Wilson⟩ **10 :** attribution of special importance **:** special concern or attention **:** EMPHASIS — usu. used with *on* ⟨the ~ on air power in the defense program⟩

²**ac·cent** \'ak,sent, =¦=\ *vt* -ED/-ING/-S [MF *accenter*, fr. *accent*, n.] **1 a :** to utter (as a syllable) with accent **:** STRESS ⟨~*ing* the first syllable of each word he spoke⟩ **b :** to mark with a written or printed accent ⟨each word of the list was neatly ~*ed* with a typed stress mark⟩ **2** *archaic* **:** to give voice to **:** ARTICULATE, UTTER, SPEAK ⟨sounds ~*ed* by a thousand voices —Sir Walter Scott⟩ **3 a :** to give prominence to or increase the prominence of **:** make more emphatic, noticeable, or distinct ⟨columns ~ the vertical lines of the building⟩ **:** heighten in effect (as by contrast) **:** bring out **:** set off ⟨a background of mountains ~s the quiet beauty of the landscape⟩ **:** increase in degree **:** INTENSIFY, SHARPEN ⟨hostility that was ~*ed* by inbred antagonism⟩ **b :** to make of special interest or concern **:** give special attention to **:** EMPHASIZE ⟨a defense program ~s air power⟩ ⟨~s the practical utility of science —Frank Thilly⟩

accent mark *n* **1 :** ACCENT 5a, 8 **2 a :** one of several symbols used in music to indicate that stress is to be given to a tone or chord (as > may be used for indicating sforzando) **b :** a mark placed after a letter designating a note of music to indicate in which octave the note occurs (as *a′* indicates A above middle C)

ac·cen·tor \ak'sentə(r), '=,=; =¦=\ *n* -s [NL, fr. ML, one that sings with another, fr. L *ad-* + ML *-centor* (fr. L *cantor* singer) — more at CANTOR] **:** a bird of the genus *Prunella; esp* **:** the European hedge sparrow

accents *pl of* ACCENT, *pres 3d sing of* ACCENT

ac·cen·tu·al \(')ak¦senchəwəl\ *adj* [¹*accent* + *-ual* (as in *manual, visual*)] **:** of, relating to, characterized by, or formed with accent; *specif* **:** based upon accent rather than upon quantity or syllabic recurrence ⟨~ hexameters⟩ — compare QUANTITATIVE — **ac·cen·tu·al·ly** \-wəlē, -li\ *adv*

ac·cen·tu·ate \ak'senchə,wāt, ək-, *usu* -ād-+V\ *vt* -ED/-ING/-S [ML *accentuatus*, past part. of *accentuare*, fr. L *accentus* accent — more at ¹ACCENT] **:** ACCENT

ac·cen·tu·a·tion \=,==¦wāshən\ *n* -s [F, fr. ML *accentuatus* + E *-ion*] **1 :** the act or the result of accentuating **2 a :** the correspondence between the accents of a melody and those of the text to which it is written **b :** the placing of an accent in a musical phrase either coinciding with or independent of the basic meter

ac·cen·tu·a·tor \=¦==,wād·ə(r), -ātə-\ *n* -s **:** one that accentuates

ac·cen·tus \ak'sentəs\ *n, pl* **accentus** [ML, fr. L, accent] **:** the part of the church service sung or recited by the priest and his assistants at the altar usu. in monotone — contrasted with *concentus*

ac·cept \ik'sept, ak- *also* ək- *or* ek-\ *vb* -ED/-ING/-S [ME *accepten*, fr. MF *accepter*, fr. L *acceptare*, freq. of *accipere* to take, receive, accept, perceive, explain, undertake, fr. *ad-* + *-cipere* (fr. *capere* to take) — more at HEAVE] *vt* **1** *obs* **:** to treat with partiality or favoritism ⟨God ~*eth* no man's person —Gal 2:6 (AV)⟩ **2 a :** to receive with consent (something given or offered) ⟨~*ed* the medal⟩ **:** assent to the receipt of ⟨~*ed* lower wages than the native workers⟩ **b :** to be able to take or hold or be designed to take or hold (something applied, affixed, or impressed) ⟨a glazed surface that will not ~ ink⟩ **3 :** to give admittance to (as into one's company or into a particular group) ⟨the town's best families ~*ed* her⟩ **:** give approval to ⟨those people will never ~ abstract sculpture⟩ **4 a :** to take without protest **:** endure or tolerate with patience ⟨queueing is one aspect of English life he will never wholly ~ —*London Calling*⟩ **b :** to regard as proper, suitable, or normal ⟨it came to be ~*ed* that there should be universal education⟩ **:** acknowledge or recognize as appropriate, permissible, or inevitable **:** agree to ⟨refused to ~ the dangerous working conditions —P.E.James⟩ **c :** to regard and hold as true **:** believe in ⟨by ~*ing* the proposition that all men are created equal⟩ **d :** to receive into the mind **:** UNDERSTAND ⟨words mean . . . what we ~ them as meaning —J.L.Lowes⟩ **5 a :** to make an affirmative or favorable response to (as an invitation or offer) ⟨~*ing* an invitation to speak⟩ **:** undertake the responsibility of (as a task or employment) ⟨if he ~*s* a junior partnership in the firm⟩ **b :** to allow (a train) onto the particular section of a line under local control — used of a block operator in the manual block-signal system **6 :** to assume orally, in writing, or by conduct an obligation to pay ⟨~*ing* a bill of exchange⟩ **7** *of a deliberative body* **:** to receive (a report) officially (as from a committee) **8 :** to be sexually responsive to; *esp* **:** to allow to mount and copulate — usu. used of a female domestic mammal **~** *vi* **:** to receive favorably something offered — usu. used with *of* ⟨no person . . . shall . . . ~ of any present —*U. S. Constitution*⟩ **syn** see RECEIVE —**accept service :** to agree that a writ or process shall be considered as regularly served when it has not been

ac·cept·abil·i·ty \\=,==ˈbiləd·ē, -ətē, -i\\ *n* -ES **:** the quality or state of being acceptable

ac·cept·able \\=ˈ=təbəl\\ *adj* [ME, fr. MF, fr. LL *acceptabilis*, fr. L *acceptare* + *-abilis* -able] **1 :** capable or worthy of being accepted ⟨no compromise could ever be ~⟩ **:** SATISFACTORY ⟨~ living conditions⟩ **:** conforming to or equal to approved standards ⟨~ English usage⟩ **2 a :** WELCOME, PLEASING ⟨compliments . . . are always ~ to ladies —Jane Austen⟩ **b :** barely satisfactory or adequate ⟨performances varied from excellent to ~⟩ —**ac·cept·ably** \\-blē, -i\\ *adv*

ac·cept·ance \\=ˈ=tən(t)s\\ *n* -S [MF, fr. *accepter* to accept + *-ance*] **1 :** the act of accepting ⟨~ of an offer⟩ **:** favorable reception ⟨~ by society⟩ **:** APPROVAL ⟨the theory found wide ~⟩ **:** ACQUIESCENCE ⟨passive ~⟩ **2 :** the quality or state of being accepted or acceptable or esp. of being received favorably or with approval **:** ACCEPTABILITY ⟨some men cannot be fools with so good ~ as others —Robert South⟩ **3 :** an agreeing either expressly or by conduct to the act or offer of another so that a contract is concluded and the parties become legally bound — compare CONTRACT, MEETING OF THE MINDS, OFFER **4 a :** the act of accepting a time draft or bill of exchange for payment when due according to the specified terms, the drawee usu. indicating acceptance by writing *accepted* and his signature across the face of the draft or bill **b :** a draft or bill of exchange drawn by the seller either on the purchaser or on a bank in accordance with previous arrangement made with it by the buyer for the purchase price of the goods — see BANK ACCEPTANCE, TRADE ACCEPTANCE **5 :** ACCEPTATION 2 **6 acceptances** *pl, Brit* **:** entries in a horse race the handicap weights for which have been accepted by the owners or their agents **7 :** the period during which the female esp. of a domestic mammal will permit copulation **:** HEAT, ESTRUS

acceptance credit *n* **:** an authorization given by a bank to a specified beneficiary to draw drafts upon the bank up to a specified amount

acceptance for honor *or* **acceptance supra protest :** the action of an acceptor for honor

acceptance house *or* **accepting house** *n* **:** a banking institution in England specializing in financing foreign trade by allowing the use of its name as drawee on bills of exchange and by frequently acting also as fiscal agent and financial adviser (as for foreign nations or municipalities) — compare MERCHANT BANKER

ac·cept·ant \\=ˈ=tənt\\ *adj* [F, fr. pres. part. of *accepter* to accept] **:** willing to accept **:** RECEPTIVE **:** tending to accept passively ⟨an ~ type of mind⟩

ac·cep·ta·tion \\,ak,sepˈtāshən\\ *n* -S [ME *acceptacioun*, fr. MF *acceptation*, fr. *accepter* + *-ation*] **1 :** ACCEPTANCE; *esp* **:** favorable reception or approval **:** BELIEF ⟨a faithful saying and worthy of all ~ —1 Tim 1:15 (AV)⟩ **2 :** the generally accepted meaning of a word or understanding of a concept ⟨the term . . . will be used in its common ~ —H.O.Taylor⟩

accepted *adj* [ME, fr. past part. of *accepten* to accept] **:** generally approved **:** widely used or found ⟨there are three ~ types of pump⟩ **:** generally agreed upon **:** UNCHALLENGED, CONVENTIONAL ⟨~ interpretation of the poem⟩ —**ac·cept·ed·ly** *adv*

ac·cept·er \\ikˈseptə(r), a-,ə-,e-, ˈak,s-\\ *n* -S [ME, fr. *accepten* + *-er*] **1 :** one that accepts **2 :** ACCEPTOR 2

ac·cep·ti·late \\akˈseptə,lāt\\ *vt* -ED/-ING/-S [back-formation fr. *acceptilation*] **:** to discharge (a claim) by acceptilation

ac·cep·ti·la·tion \\(,)ak,septəˈlāshən\\ *n* -S [L *acceptilation-*, *acceptilatio*, fr. *accepti lation-*, *latio*, lit., bringing the receipt, fr. *accepti* (gen. of *acceptum* receipt, fr. neut. of *acceptus*, past part. of *accipere* to accept) + *lation-*, *latio* act of bringing, fr. *latus* (suppletive past part. of *ferre* to bear) + *-ion-*, *-io* -ion — more at ACCEPT, BEAR, TOLERATE] **1** *Roman or civil law* **:** a formal verbal acknowledgment by a creditor or other obligee that his claim has been satisfied with or without payment **2** [ML *acceptilation-*, *acceptilatio*, fr. L] *in the theology of Duns Scotus* **:** the act of God by which the merit of Jesus Christ was accepted as sufficient for man's salvation

accepting *pres part of* ACCEPT

ac·cep·tion \\akˈsepshən\\ *n* -S [ME *accepcioun*, fr. MF or L; MF *acception*, fr. L *acception-*, *acceptio*, fr. *acceptus* + *-ion-*, *-io* -ion] **:** ACCEPTATION

ac·cept·ive \\(ˈ)akˈseptiv\\ *adj* **1 :** RECEPTIVE ⟨~ of every new idea⟩ **2 :** acceptable or appropriate ⟨a psychologically ~ way of living⟩

ac·cep·tor \\ikˈseptə(r), a-,ə-,e-, ˈak,s-\\ *n* -S [L, fr. *acceptus* + *-or*] **1 :** ACCEPTER 1 **2 :** one (as the drawee) that accepts an order or a bill of exchange **3 :** a substance or particle capable of combining with another specified substance or particle ⟨oxygen is a hydrogen ~⟩ ⟨ammonia and bases are proton ~*s*⟩ ⟨a proton is an electron pair ~⟩ ⟨wool is a dye ~⟩ — compare DONOR 2 **4 a :** a circuit that combines inductance and capacitance in series so as to resonate to a given impressed frequency — compare REJECTOR **b :** HOLE 2e(1) **c :** an impurity occurring in a semiconducting material and containing holes that contribute to the conductivity of the material

acceptor for honor *or* **acceptor supra protest :** one who accepts a protested bill of exchange on which he is not already liable for the honor of some party to the bill, the acceptor being liable to the holder and all parties subsequent to the one for whose honor he accepts

accepts *pres 3d sing of* ACCEPT

ac·cess \\ˈak,ses *also* ikˈs- *or* akˈs-\\ *n* -ES *often attrib* [ME, fr. MF & L; MF *acces* arrival, fr. L *accessus* approach, access, admittance, fr. *accessus* past part. of *accedere* to approach — more at ACCEDE] **1** [influenced in meaning by MF *accession* & L *accessio* — more at ACCESSION] **a :** an attack or onset of illness or disease ⟨an ~ of paralysis the afternoon previous —George Ticknor⟩ **b :** a fit or spell of intense feeling ⟨he had such an ~ now —Oliver La Farge⟩ **:** OUTBURST ⟨~*es* of pessimism —S.H.Adams⟩ **2 a** (1) **:** permission, liberty, or ability to enter, approach, communicate with, or pass to and from ⟨~ to every room⟩ ⟨~ to the president⟩ ⟨a country with ~ to the sea⟩ (2) **:** admission to sexual intercourse (3) **:** a landowner's legal right to pass from his land to a highway and to return without being obstructed **b :** freedom or ability to obtain or make use of ⟨give them ~ to jobs of confidence or trust —*N.Y. Times*⟩ **:** ability or means to participate in, work in, or gain insight into ⟨~ to the liberal arts⟩ **c :** a way by which a thing or place may be approached or reached **:** PASSAGEWAY ⟨a lock built to give ~ to the sea⟩ **d** (1) **:** the action of going to or reaching **:** APPROACH, ENTRANCE **:** passage to and from ⟨provide a means of ~ to the lake⟩ ⟨completed plans for ~ tracks to the factory⟩ (2) **:** approach to God through Jesus Christ — used esp. in titles of prayers ⟨the Anglican prayer of humble ~⟩ **3 :** an increase by addition ⟨a sudden ~ of wealth⟩ **4** *obs* **a :** an assembling or meeting esp. of the British Parliament **b :** a coming to office or sovereignty

accessary *var of* ACCESSORY

access clerk *n* **:** a safe-deposit attendant who is responsible for admitting to the vault only properly accredited persons whose signatures he has verified

access control *n* **:** a condition in which the common-law rights of property owners and others to access, light, air, or view in connection with a public road are controlled by public authority by means of physical construction, legal restrictions, toll requirements, or other limitations

ac·ces·si·bil·i·ty \\ik,sesəˈbiləd·ē, (,)ak-,ək-, *chiefly substand* ə,s-\\ *n* -ES **:** the quality or state of being accessible

ac·ces·si·ble \\=ˈ=əbəl\\ *adj* [F, fr. LL *accessibilis*, fr. L *accessus* (past part. of *accedere* to approach) + *-ibilis* -ible — more at ACCEDE] **1 :** capable of being used as an entrance **:** providing access ⟨one ascent ~ from earth —John Milton⟩ **2 a :** capable of being reached or easily approached ⟨a town ~ by rail⟩ **:** easy to meet **b :** easy to get along with, talk to, or deal with **:** APPROACHABLE, COMMUNICATIVE ⟨an ~ and genial man⟩ **3 :** capable of being influenced or affected **:** OPEN ⟨~ to the flattery of this honest praise —Elinor Wylie⟩ **4 :** capable of being used, seen, known, or experienced **:** AVAILABLE ⟨a book ~ to all students⟩ **:** COMPREHENSIBLE ⟨readily ~ to the nonprofessional reader —J.K.Galbraith⟩ —**ac·ces·si·bly** \\-blē, -i\\ *adv* —**ac·ces·si·ble·ness** \\-bəlnəs\\ *n* -ES

[1]ac·ces·sion \\ikˈseshən, ak-,ək-\\ *n* -S [MF, fr. L *accession-*, *accessio*, fr. *accessus* + *-ion-*, *-io* -ion] **1 a :** something added as to a collection or formal group **:** ACQUISITION ⟨new ~*s* in the paintings department of the museum⟩ **b :** a specimen under consideration or study **:** examination sample ⟨all ~*s* of volunteer tomatoes were susceptible⟩ **2 a :** the act of becoming joined (as in a confederacy or union) **:** ADHERENCE ⟨French ~ to the European Defense Community⟩ **b :** the act by which one nation becomes party to engagements already in force between other powers **c :** the mode of acquiring property by which the owner of a corporeal substance (as land or cattle) becomes the owner of an addition by growth, increase, or labor **3 :** increase by something added **:** augmentation from without ⟨the greatest ~ of positive knowledge has come in our own time —W.R.Inge⟩ **4 :** the act of assenting or agreeing ⟨~ to the determination made by Congress —Samuel Williams⟩ **5 a :** a coming near or to **:** APPROACH, ARRIVAL **:** ADMISSION ⟨marriage represents full ~ to adult life —H.M.Parshley⟩ **b :** the act of attaining or coming to high office or a position of honor or power ⟨the ~ of a new queen⟩ **6 :** a sudden fit or spell (as of feeling) **:** OUTBURST ⟨sharp ~*s* of impatience —Mary Austin⟩ **7 :** a hiring or rehiring of an employee

[2]accession \\"\\ *vt* **accessioned; accessioned; accessioning** \\-sh(ə)niŋ\\ **accessions :** to record in the order of acquisition listing essential data (as author, title, and publication date of a book) **:** enter (an accession) in a special record book, list, or file ⟨each book in the library had been carefully ~*ed*⟩ ⟨the art gallery has an efficient way of ~*ing* newly received paintings⟩

ac·ces·sion·al \\-shənᵊl, -shnəl\\ *adj* **:** of or constituting an accession **:** ADDITIONAL

accession book *n* **:** a record book used for accessioning

accession number *n* **:** a number assigned to an acquisition (as a library book) indicating the order of its receipt

accession service *n* **:** a form of service used in the Church of England on the anniversary of the accession of the sovereign to the throne

accessions register *n, Brit* **:** ACCESSION BOOK

ac·ces·sit \\akˈsesət\\ *n* -S [L, he came near, 3d pers. sing. perf. ind. of *accedere* to come near, approach, accede — more at ACCEDE] **:** a distinction awarded in British and other European schools to one who has come nearest to a prize **:** an honorable mention

ac·ces·so·ri·al \\ˈaksəˈsōrēəl\\ *adj* [[2]*accessory* + *-al*] **1 :** of or relating to an accessory ⟨~ guilt⟩ **2 :** relating to an accession or increase **:** SUPPLEMENTARY, ADDITIONAL ⟨~ services included sorting and packing⟩

ac·ces·so·ri·us \\,==ˈ=ēəs\\ *n, pl* **accesso·rii** \\-ē,ī, -ē,ē\\ [NL, fr. ML, accessory] **1 :** a muscle reinforcing the action of another **2 :** ACCESSORY NERVE

ac·ces·so·rize \\ikˈsesə,rīz, ak-, ək-\\ *vt* -ED/-ING/-S [*accessor*ies + *-ize*] **:** to furnish or provide with accessories ⟨dress . . . was *accessorized* for after-dark wear with rhinestone and pearl earrings —*Fashion Accessories*⟩

[1]ac·ces·so·ry *also* **ac·ces·sa·ry** \\ikˈses(ə)rē, ak-,ək-, *chiefly substand* əˈs-\\ *n* -ES [ME *accessorie*, *accessarie*, fr. ML *accessorius*, fr. L *accessus* (past part. of *accedere* to accede) + *-orius* -ory — more at ACCEDE] **1 a :** a thing of secondary or subordinate importance (as in achieving a purpose or an effect) ⟨the pelican's pouch is an ~ to catching fish⟩ **:** an adjunct or accompaniment ⟨some counsel regard the jury as . . . impersonal and inanimate *accessories* of the court —E.M. Lustgarten⟩ **b** (1) **:** an object or device that is not essential in itself but that adds to the beauty, convenience, or effectiveness of something else ⟨spotlights, reflectors, and other auto *accessories* ⟩ ⟨household *accessories* such as small tables and lamps⟩ ⟨the *accessories* of the estate include a putting green and a tennis court⟩ (2) **:** any of several mechanical devices (as pistons or tablets) that assist in operating or controlling the tone resources of an organ (3) **:** any of various articles of apparel (as a scarf, belt, or piece of jewelry) that accent or otherwise complete one's costume **2 :** one that is accessory: as **a :** a person who is not actually or constructively present but contributes as an assistant or instigator to the commission of an offense — called also *accessory before the fact;* compare PRINCIPAL 1d **b :** one who knowing that a crime has been committed aids, assists, or shelters the offender with the intent to defeat justice — called also *accessory after the fact;* compare PRINCIPAL 13c **3 :** a mineral that is accessory

[2]accessory *also* **accessary** \\"\\ *adj* **1** *of a thing* **a :** aiding or contributing in a secondary or subordinate way ⟨~ substances in nutrition⟩ **:** supplementary or secondary to something of greater or primary importance ⟨an ~ function of the tongue⟩ **:** ADDITIONAL ⟨sidewalks lead to ~ buildings⟩ **b :** incidental to a main contract or some other obligation (as by being given as security) ⟨a mortgage is ~ to the main obligation⟩; *specif* **:** constituting a subordinate contract (as a mortgage or pledge) designed to assure the fulfillment of a prior principal contract ⟨an ~ contract⟩ ⟨an ~ obligation⟩ **2** *of a person* **:** assisting or aiding as a subordinate; *esp* **:** uniting in or contributing to a crime, but not as the chief agent ⟨charged . . . with being ~ to the felony —Sir Walter Scott⟩ **3 :** present in a minor amount and not essential as a constituent ⟨an ~ mineral in a rock⟩

accessory body *n* **:** a differentiated structure originating in the Golgi material and included in the neck of the spermatozoon

accessory bud *n* **:** a bud growing near and in addition to a normal axillary bud

accessory cell *n* **:** one of the epidermal cells surrounding and adjacent to the guard cells, differing in configuration from other epidermal cells, and apparently functioning as part of the stomatal apparatus

accessory chromosome *n* **:** a sex chromosome; *specif* **:** an X chromosome that is solitary and unpaired in one sex (as in certain insects)

accessory fruit *n* **:** a fruit (as the apple, strawberry, or fig) of which a conspicuous portion consists of tissue other than that of the ripened ovary — called also *pseudocarp*

accessory gland *n* **:** any of certain glands (as the colleterium) associated with the reproductive organs of insects

accessory nerve *also* **accessory** *n* **:** either of the 11th pair of cranial nerves, being a motor nerve, arising partly from the lateral wall of the medulla and partly from the cervical spinal cord, supplying the pharynx, trapezius, and sternocleidomastoid muscles as well as sending fibers to the vagus nerve in higher vertebrates, and being absent from lower forms

accessory nucleus *n* **:** any of certain small masses or layers of gray matter adjacent to the inferior olivary body, there being typically two on each side — called also *accessory olivary body*

accessory pancreatic duct *n* **:** DUCT OF SANTORINI

accessory scale *n* **:** a modified scale or elongate scalelike projection at the base of the pectoral or pelvic fins of certain bony fishes

accessory shoot *n* **:** a shoot developed from an accessory bud

accessory stop *n* **:** a stop knob used on an organ to control a coupler or other mechanical device rather than a register of pipes

access road *n* **:** a public road affording access to a particular area (as a military establishment or source of raw materials) or to a through highway ⟨the route will have several *access roads* and exits — *N.Y. Times*⟩

ac·ciac·ca·tu·ra \\(,)ä,chäkəˈtu̇rə\\ *n, pl* **acciaccaturas** \\-u̇rəz\\ *or* **acciaccatu·re** \\-u̇,rā, -u̇rē\\ [It, lit., crushing, fr. *acciaccare* to crush (prob. fr. Sp *achacar* to impute falsely, accuse, fr. Ar dial. *ˈatshakka*, 5th form of Ar *shaka* to complain) + *-ura* -ure] **1** *in early keyboard music* **:** a short grace note sounded with a principal note or chord before which it appears and immediately released while the tone of the principal note or chord is sustained **2 :** SHORT APPOGGIATURA

ac·ci·dence \\ˈaksədən(t)s *also* -dᵊn(t)s, *or* -,den(t)s\\ *n* -S [L *accidentia* inflections of words, nonessential qualities or circumstances, pl. of *accident-*, *accidens* nonessential quality or circumstance] **:** the part of grammar that deals with inflections

ac·ci·dens \\ˈaksə,denz; ˈä(t)chē,denz, -nts\\ *n, pl* **acciden·tia** \\,aksəˈdenchēə; ,ä(t)chēˈdentsēə\\ [L] *logic* **:** ACCIDENT

ac·ci·dent \\ˈaksədənt *also* -dᵊnt *or* -,dent\\ *n* -S [ME, fr. MF, fr. L *accident-*, *accidens* nonessential quality or circumstance, accident, chance, fr. pres. part. of *accidere* to happen, fr. *ad-* + *-cidere* (fr. *cadere* to fall) — more at CHANCE] **1 a :** an event or condition occurring by chance or arising from unknown or remote causes ⟨by the ~ that it was observed and noted down —Havelock Ellis⟩ ⟨happenings outside the range of probability which we would term historical ~*s* —M.J. Herskovits⟩ **b :** lack of intention or necessity **:** CHANCE — often opposed to *design* ⟨by ~ rather than with an intention to utilize —Arnold Bennett⟩ **c :** an unforeseen unplanned event or condition ⟨by a charming ~ he had disposed of them to a chance buyer —Arnold Bennett⟩ **2 a :** a usu. sudden event or change occurring without intent or volition through carelessness, unawareness, ignorance, or a combination of causes and producing an unfortunate result ⟨a traffic ~ in which several persons were injured⟩ **b :** an unexpected medical development esp. of an unfavorable or injurious nature occurring in apparently good health or during the course of a disease or a treatment ⟨the paralytic ~ occurred between the 8th and 21st day after the initial injection —*Jour. Amer. Med. Assoc.*⟩ ⟨a cerebral ~⟩ **c :** an unexpected happening causing loss or injury which is not due to any fault or misconduct on the part of the person injured but from the consequences of which he may be entitled to some legal relief **3 :** an adventitious characteristic that is either inseparable from the individual and the species or separable from the individual but not the species; *broadly* **:** any fortuitous or nonessential property, fact, or circumstance ⟨~ of appearance⟩ ⟨~ of reputation⟩ ⟨~ of situation⟩ **4 :** an irregularity of a surface (as of the moon) **syn** see CHANCE, QUALITY

[1]ac·ci·den·tal \\ˈaksəˈdentᵊl\\ *adj* [ME, fr. MF, fr. *accident* + *-al*] **1 :** arising from or produced by extrinsic, secondary, or additional causes or forces **:** not innate, intrinsic, or of the real nature of **:** NONESSENTIAL ⟨some of the colors were mineral, in the rock itself: but others were ~ due to water from the melting snow —T.E.Lawrence⟩ ⟨whether this paralogistic procedure is essential or ~ to his doctrine —T.H.Green⟩ **2 :** occurring sometimes with unfortunate results by chance alone: **a :** UNPREDICTABLE **:** proceeding from an unrecognized principle, from an uncommon operation of a known principle, or from a deviation from normal **b :** happening or ensuing without design, intent, or obvious motivation or through inattention or carelessness ⟨~ collision⟩ ⟨~ shooting⟩ ⟨~ loss⟩ **3 :** having reference to a logical accident **:** not essential **:** CONTINGENT, EXTRINSIC ⟨being dark-haired is an ~ property of a man —Arthur Pap⟩ **4 :** relating to an accidental in music or to its prefixed sign **5** *of a bird* **:** found outside the normal geographic range or season ⟨a common migrant, ~ in winter⟩

syn FORTUITOUS, ADVENTITIOUS, CONTINGENT, CASUAL, INCIDENTAL: when it is used in reference to events, ACCIDENTAL may stress lack of intent or indicate an unusual operation of natural causes ⟨so plain that Thady's presence . . . was *accidental*, and that the attack could not have been premeditated —Anthony Trollope⟩ In reference to qualities, ACCIDENTAL indicates absence of an essential or innate characteristic ⟨their search for the typical and their avoidance of anything that might be considered *accidental* —John Dewey⟩ FORTUITOUS stresses chance and minimizes the idea of definite analyzable cause ⟨I do not look upon public events either as *fortuitous* or absolutely derivable either from the wisdom or folly of man —William Cowper⟩ ADVENTITIOUS stresses the extrinsic, additional, irrelevant, or nonessential ⟨regular repetition of forms, uniformly spaced, the architect depending only upon *adventitious* ornamentation for variety —John Dewey⟩ ⟨in works of imagination and sentiment . . . meter is but *adventitious* to composition —William Wordsworth⟩ CONTINGENT stresses unpredictability and uncertainty, esp. in future events ⟨countless *contingent* difficulties . . . many of which must necessarily arise, though the exact nature of them could not be anticipated —J.A.Froude⟩ It also indicates dependence on something else for existence or occurrence ⟨the resistance that we may meet with is *contingent* on the enemy's continued strength⟩ INCIDENTAL stresses a secondary or minor nature, regardless of manner of origin ⟨war . . . the comprehensive business of the German . . . to the British . . . was an *incidental* adventure —H.G.Wells⟩ CASUAL stresses dependence on chance and lack of prearrangement or predictability ⟨it was no *casual* reencounter. He had been enticed into the place —J.A.Froude⟩ ⟨the *casual* allusion, the chance reference —Henry Adams⟩ CASUAL and INCIDENTAL may indicate occurrences actually planned and intended but presented as if by chance ⟨the pupil must be aroused . . . his curiosity must be awakened by an *incidental* explanation, a *casual* remark —C.H.Grandgent⟩

[2]accidental \\"\\ *n* -S [ME, fr. *accidental*, adj.] **1** *logic* **:** a nonessential property **2 :** NONESSENTIAL **3 a :** a chromatically altered note (as a sharp or flat) in a musical composition that is usu. foreign to the key indicated by the signature **b :** the prefixed sign (as ♯ or ♭) indicating a chromatically altered note **4 :** warp ends not usu. included in the treadling pattern in hand weaving **5 :** a fingerprint showing two or more pattern types or other peculiarities making classification difficult

accidental death *n* **:** death by accidental means usu. sudden and violent; *sometimes* **:** death occurring as the unforeseen and chance result of an intended act — compare DOUBLE INDEMNITY

accidental error *n* **:** an error of observation that cannot be controlled

accidental injury *n* **:** injury occurring as the unforeseen and chance result of a voluntary act

ac·ci·den·tal·ism \\,==ˈ==,izəm\\ *n* -S **:** a theory in philosophy: events can or do occur without cause — compare INDETERMINISM, TYCHISM

ac·ci·den·tal·ist \\-əst\\ *n* -S **:** a believer in accidentalism

ac·ci·den·tal·i·ty \\,aksədənˈtaləd·ē, -(,)den-\\ *n* -ES **:** the quality or state of being accidental ⟨the ~ of history⟩

ac·ci·den·tal·ly \\ˈaksəˈdentlē, -tᵊlē, -li\\ *adv* [ME, fr. *accidental* + *-ly*] **1** *archaic* **:** INCIDENTALLY **2 :** by accident **:** in an accidental manner

accidental means *n* **:** an act or event preceding harm or damage to an insured that is sudden, unexpected, and not intended or designed by any person

accidentary *adj, obs* **:** ACCIDENTAL

ac·ci·dent·ed \\ˈaksə,dentəd\\ *adj* **:** of uneven surface ⟨~ topography⟩

accidentia *pl of* ACCIDENS

accident insurance *n* **:** insurance against loss through accidental bodily injury to the insured — compare DISABILITY INSURANCE

ac·ci·dent·ly \\ˈaksəˈdentlē, -li\\ *adv* [prob. alter. of *accidentally*] **:** ACCIDENTALLY

accident-prone \\ˈ==(,)=ˈ=\\ *adj* **1 :** having a greater number of accidents than would be expected of the average individual under the same conditions ⟨older people are less *accident-prone* than we customarily think —Graenum Berger⟩ **2 :** having personality traits that predispose to accidents ⟨importance of identifying *accident-prone* persons —*Jour. Amer. Med. Assoc.*⟩

accidents *pl of* ACCIDENT

ac·cid·ia \\akˈsidēə\\ *n, pl* **accidias** \\-ēəz\\ *also* **accidi·ae** \\-ē,ē\\ [ML, alter. of LL *acedia* — more at ACEDIA] **:** [2]ACEDIA

ac·ci·die \\ˈaksədē\\ *n* -S [ME *accidie*, *accide*, fr. OF, fr. ML *accidia*, alter. of LL *acedia* — more at ACEDIA] **:** [2]ACEDIA

ac·cinge \\akˈsinj\\ *vt* -ED/-ING/-S [L *accingere*, fr. *ad-* + *cingere* to gird — more at CINCTURE] *archaic* **:** to brace (oneself) up ⟨may ~ ourselves for a supreme effort —A.T.Quiller-Couch⟩

ac·cip·i·ter \\akˈsipəd·ə(r), ÷aˈs-, ÷əˈs-\\ *n* [NL, fr. L, hawk, falcon, prob. by folk etymology (influence of *accipere* to take, accept) fr. (assumed) OL *acupeter*, lit., fast flier, fr. *acu-* fast (akin to L *ocior* faster) + *-peter* flier (akin to Gk *pteron* wing) — more at ACCEPT, FEATHER, OCYPODE] **1** *cap* **:** the type genus of Accipitridae comprising small or medium-sized hawks that have rather short wings and comparatively long legs and tail and that usu. fly low darting in and out among trees **2** -S **:** any hawk of the genus *Accipiter* (as the Cooper's hawk, sharp-shinned hawk, goshawk); *also* **:** any hawk resembling a member of this genus in appearance or habits of flight

ac·cip·i·tral \-pə·trəl\ *adj* [L *accipitr-, accipiter* + E *-al*] **:** resembling that of a hawk

ac·cip·i·tres \-pə,trēz\ [NL, fr. L, pl. of *accipitr-, accipiter* hawk, falcon] **1** *syn of* FALCONIFORMES **2** *syn of* FALCONES

ac·cip·i·trid \-pə·trə̇d\ *n* -S *often attrib* [NL, *Accipitridae*] **:** a bird of the family Accipitridae

ac·ci·pit·ri·dae \,aksə'pi·trə,dē, ÷,asə-\ *n pl, cap* [NL, fr. *Accipitr-, Accipiter*, type genus + *-idae*] **:** a large family (order Falconiformes) of carnivorous birds having comparatively rounded wings, long legs, and an unnotched bill and including the typical hawks and goshawks, the kites, and usu. the eagles — compare FALCONIDAE

¹ac·cip·i·trine \ak'sipə,trīn, -,trən, ÷a's-,÷ə's-\ *adj* [F, fr. L *accipitr-, accipiter* + F *-ine*] **:** of or relating to the genus *Accipiter* or to the typical hawks ⟨the distinctive features of the ~ head⟩ — compare BUTEONINE, CATHARTINE

²accipitrine \"\ *n* -S **:** ACCIPITER 2

accite *vt* -ED/-ING/-S [ME *acciten*, fr. L *accitus*, past part. of *accire* to call, summon, fr. *ad-* + *cire, ciere* to move, rouse, call upon — more at CITE] *obs* **:** CITE, SUMMON

¹ac·claim \ə'klām *also* a'-\ *vb* -ED/-ING/-S [in sense 1, fr. ME *acleimen*, fr. ML *acclamare*, fr. L, to shout at, approve, applaud, fr. *ad-* + *clamare* to shout, call; in senses 2 & 4, fr. L *acclamare;* in sense 3, fr. ML, fr. L — more at CLAIM] *vt* **1** *obs* **:** CLAIM **2 :** PRAISE ⟨a book widely ~*ed* by critics⟩ **:** welcome with praise or applause ⟨~*ed* the guest of honor⟩ **3 :** to declare or proclaim approvingly — usu. used with a complement now usu. preceded by *as* ⟨on the formation of the National Sculpture Society, he was ~*ed* its president —Adeline Adams⟩ ⟨his eyes too openly ~*ed* her a fair woman —Mary Webb⟩ ⟨the hearings have been ~*ed* as something of a model of dignified and fair procedure —*New Republic*⟩ **4** *archaic* **:** to call out loudly **:** SHOUT ⟨~*ing* my joy⟩ ~ *vi* **:** to shout praise **:** APPLAUD

²acclaim \"\ *n* -S **1 :** the act of acclaiming **2 :** PRAISE ⟨deserves the ~ he has received —Lewis Mumford⟩

ac·cla·ma·tion \,aklə'māshən\ *n* -S [L *acclamation-, acclamatio*, fr. *acclamatus* (past part. of *acclamare*) + *-ion-, -io* -ion] **1 :** a loud eager expression of approval, praise, or assent ⟨she was received with ~*s* —Walter Bagehot⟩ **2 :** an overwhelming approving vote by cheering, shouts, or hand clapping rather than by ballot ⟨made a motion to elect the popular candidate to the chairmanship by ~⟩

ac·cli·ma·ta·tion \ə,klīmə'tāshən, (,)a,k-\ *n* -S [F, fr. *acclimater* + *-ation*] **:** ACCLIMATIZATION

ac·cli·mate \ə'klīmə̇t *also* a'-; 'aklə,māt; *usu* -d·+V\ *vt* -ED/-ING/-S [F *acclimater*, fr. *a-* to (fr. L *ad-*) + *climat* climate — more at CLIMATE] **:** ACCLIMATIZE **syn** see HARDEN

ac·cli·ma·tion \,a,klī'māshən, ,aklə'-\ *n* -S [*acclimate* + *-ion*] **1 :** ACCLIMATIZATION **2 :** the usu. physiological adjustment that an individual organism exhibits to a change in its immediate environment — compare ACCLIMATIZATION 2

ac·cli·ma·ti·za·tion \ə,klīməd·ə'zāshən, -əd·,ī'z-, -ətə'z-, -ə,tī'z- *also* a,k-\ *n* -S [*acclimatize* + *-ization*] **1 :** the process of acclimatizing **:** the result of acclimatizing **2** *ecol* **:** adaptation or increased tolerance of a species to a changed environment in the course of several generations — compare ACCLIMATION 2

ac·cli·ma·tize \ə'klīmə,tīz *also* a'-\ *vb* -ED/-ING/-S *see -ize in Explan Notes* [F *acclimater* + E *-ize*] *vt* **1 :** to adapt to a new temperature, altitude, climate, environment, or situation ⟨gradually *acclimatized* to temperatures that prove unsuited . . . under ordinary conditions —*Popular Science Monthly*⟩ ⟨sufficiently *acclimatized* to altitudes of 24,000 feet —*Geog. Jour.*⟩ ⟨American varieties have been *acclimatized* in experimental farms operated by Japanese agriculturists —*Nat'l Geographic*⟩ ⟨the ultimate outcome of this movement to ~ psychical research in the universities —*Jour. of Parapsychology*⟩ ⟨~ the mind to a world of natural beauty —*Times Lit. Supp.*⟩ **2 :** to increase the stability of (a sol) toward a precipitant by adding the latter slowly ⟨yeast *acclimatized* during preparation⟩ ~ *vi* **:** to become acclimatized **syn** see HARDEN

ac·cliv·i·tous \ə'klivəd·əs, (')a¦k-\ *adj* [*acclivity* + *-ous*] **:** sloping upward

ac·cliv·i·ty \ə'klivəd·ē, a'-\ *n* -ES [L *acclivitas*, fr. *acclivus, acclivis* ascending (fr. *ad-* + *clivus* slope) + *-itas* -ity — more at DECLIVITY] **:** an ascending slope (as of a hill) — opposed to *declivity*

ac·cli·vous \ə'klīvəs, (')a¦k-\ *adj* [L *acclivus*] **:** sloping upward — opposed to *declivous*

accloy *vt* -ED/-ING/-S [ME *acloien*, fr. MF *encloer* to drive in a nail, fr. ML *inclavare*, fr. L *in* + *clavare* to nail, fr. *clavus* nail — more at CLAVUS] *obs* **:** CLOY

accoast [MF *accoster* — more at ACCOST] *obs var of* ACCOST

ac·co·lade \'akə,lād, ,==¦= *also* -ḁ̈d *or* -ȧd\ *n* -S [F, fr. *accoler* to embrace (fr. — assumed — VL *accollare*, fr. L *ad-* + *collum* neck) + *-ade* — more at COLLAR] **1 a :** a gesture of greeting; *esp* **:** a ceremonial embrace and kiss on both cheeks ⟨seized me by the hand and, drawing me toward him, gave me the ~ —Frederick O'Brien⟩ **2 a :** a ceremony to mark the conferring of knighthood consisting of an embrace, a kiss, or a tap on each shoulder with the flat of a sword **b :** a ceremony marking the recognition of special merit, distinction, or achievement **3 a :** a mark of acknowledgment ⟨effectively cut short his chances of promotion and the ultimate ~ which might have been his —James Leasor⟩ **b :** AWARD ⟨the Iffland Ring, the highest ~ of the German theater —*Americana Annual*⟩ **c :** a bestowal of praise ⟨receive the ~ of the newspapers⟩ **4 :** a molding in the shape of an ogee arch above a door or window **5 :** a brace or a line used in music to join two or more staffs carrying simultaneous instrumental or voice parts

ac·co·lat·ed \'akə,lād·əd\ *adj* [F *accoler* + E *-ated*] **:** ACCOLLÉ

ac·col·lé *or* **ac·col·lée** \¦akə¦lā\ *adj* [F *accolé*, past part. of *accoler* to embrace] **1** *heraldry* **:** entwined about the neck; *also* **:** COLLARED, GORGED **2** *heraldry* **:** joined or touching at the neck **:** side by side (as sets of arms on a shield or profiles on a coin or medal)

ac·com·mo·da·ble \ə'kämədəbəl *also* a'-\ *adj* [F, fr. *accommoder* to accommodate (fr. L *accommodare*) + *-able*] **:** capable of being accommodated or fitted ⟨anthropologists regard the Upper Paleolithic period as ~ between 25,000 B.C. and 8000 B.C.⟩

¹ac·com·mo·date \-də̇t, -,dāt\ *adj* [L *accommodatus*] *archaic* **:** ADAPTED, SUITABLE, FIT

²ac·com·mo·date \-,dāt, *usu* -ād·+V\ *vb* -ED/-ING/-S [L *accommodatus*, past part. of *accommodare*, fr. *ad-* + *commodare* to make fit, give, lend — more at COMMODATUM] *vt* **1 :** ADAPT ⟨words ~ their meanings to the other words that accompany them —I.A.Richards⟩ **:** make fit, suitable, or congruous ⟨observations had to be *accommodated* to these preconceptions —S.F.Mason⟩ **2 :** to show the correspondence of **:** account for ⟨to ~ the new findings physicists have had to elaborate the theory —*Scientific American Reader*⟩ **:** MATCH ⟨*accommodating* a statement to facts⟩ **3 :** to bring into agreement or concord **:** RECONCILE, ADJUST ⟨he had to ~ his step to hers —Michael Arlen⟩ ⟨~ his religious and cultural life to the culture of the majority while avoiding complete assimilation —F.J.Brown⟩ **4 :** to furnish with something desired, needed, or suited **:** OBLIGE ⟨Rosamond *accommodated* him, taking his picture over and over again to please him —Thomas Barbour⟩: **a :** to grant a loan to esp. without security **b :** to provide with lodgings **:** HOUSE ⟨how are travelers *accommodated* in villages and towns —*Notes & Queries on Anthropology*⟩ **:** make room for ⟨the door was reluctantly opened wide enough to ~ a small brown wet hand —L.C. Douglas⟩ **:** HOLD ⟨the mailbox is huge — obviously designed to ~ packages from mail-order houses —G.R.Stewart⟩ ~ *vi* **:** to adapt oneself ⟨normal and neurotic both ~ to the same situations by different techniques —Abram Kardiner⟩ ⟨try in some way to ~ — morally, intellectually — to the world —Edmund Wilson⟩; *specif, of the eye* **:** to undergo accommodation **syn** see ADAPT, CONTAIN, OBLIGE

accommodating *adj* **:** disposed to be helpful or obliging **:** PLIANT — **ac·com·mo·dat·ing·ly** *adv*

ac·com·mo·da·tion \=,==ˈdāshən\ *n* -S [F or L; F, fr. L *accommodation-, accommodatio*, fr. *accommodatus* + *-ion-, -io* -ion] **1 a :** something that is supplied for convenience or to satisfy a need ⟨huts with no sanitary ~ or running water —S.G.O'Kelly⟩: as (1) **:** ROOM, SPACE ⟨the library ~ is leased —*Library Science Abstracts*⟩ (2) **:** lodging, food, and services (as at a hotel) or seat, berth, or other space occupied together with services available (as on a train) — usu. used in pl. ⟨tourist ~*s* on the boat⟩ ⟨overnight ~*s* for visitors⟩ **b :** a public conveyance (as a railroad train) that stops at all or nearly all points ⟨I drove around the town in a horse-drawn ~ —Mary H. Vorse⟩ ⟨on the ~ local —Bennett Cerf⟩ **2 :** the provision of what is needed or desired for convenience ⟨tables and benches are installed for the ~ of picnickers —*Amer. Guide Series: N. H.*⟩ **3 :** ADAPTATION, ADJUSTMENT ⟨an ~ to transient conditions —W.R.Inge⟩: **a :** application of a writer's language on the ground of analogy to a meaning not orig. referred to or intended ⟨by the very greatest ~ of language —C.M.Crawford⟩ **b :** functional adjustment of an organism to its environment through modification of its habits ⟨a long period of migration, ~, and contest for supremacy among species —C.L.White & G.T.Renner⟩ **c :** a process of functional adjustment of conflict between individuals and groups through change of habits and customs **4 :** an adjustment of differences **:** state of agreement **:** SETTLEMENT ⟨the question of reaching an ~ with Japan —*N.Y.Times*⟩ **5 :** LOAN **6 :** the automatic adjustment of the eye for seeing at different distances effected in the eye of higher animals chiefly by changes in the convexity of the crystalline lens; *also* **:** the range over which such adjustment is possible for a particular eye

ac·com·mo·da·tion·al \=¦==ˈdāshən³l, -shnəl\ *adj* **:** relating to or caused by accommodation of the eye ⟨~ strain⟩

accommodation bill *or* **accommodation paper** *n* **:** a bill, draft, or note made, drawn, accepted, or endorsed by one person for another without consideration to enable that other to raise money or obtain credit thereby

accommodation coefficient *n* **:** the efficiency of a gas in removing heat from a surface expressed as the ratio of the actual heat loss from the surface to the ideal loss

accommodation house *n* **:** a house for boarding and lodging travelers

accommodation ladder *n* **:** a light ladder or similar structure hung over the side of a ship at the gangway for use in ascending from or descending to small boats

accommodation ladder

accommodation line *n* **:** an insurance policy issued on an unsatisfactory risk by a company that wishes to accommodate a particular agent or broker

accommodation train *n* **:** a train that stops at all or nearly all stations **:** a local train

ac·com·mo·da·tive \ə'kämə,dād·iv, a'-, -ātiv, -ēv\ *adj* **:** tending to accommodate **:** relating to accommodation

ac·com·mo·da·tor \-,dād·ə(r), -ātə-\ *n* -S **:** one who substitutes for a regularly employed domestic worker

ac·com·pa·ni·er \ə'kəmp(ə)nēə(r) *also* a'- *or* -käm-\ *n* -S **:** ACCOMPANIST

ac·com·pa·ni·ment \-nēmənt, -nim- *also* -nəm-\ *n* -S [modif. (influenced by *accompany*) of F *accompagnement*, fr. OF *acompaignement* sharing, fr. *acompaignier* to accompany + *-ment*] **1 :** an instrumental or vocal part subordinate to and designed to support, amplify, or complement a principal voice or instrument **2 :** something added to the principal thing to give it completeness or symmetry (as an ornament) **:** COMPLEMENT **3 :** an accompanying situation or occurrence **:** CONCOMITANT ⟨we can no longer live without an ~ of noise —Wynford Vaughan-Thomas⟩ ⟨to the ~ of booming guns —*Amer. Guide Series: Maine*⟩

ac·com·pa·nist \=ˈ=p(ə)nəst\ *also* **ac·com·pa·ny·ist** \-p(ə)nēəst\ *n* -S [*accompany* + *-ist*] **:** one (as a pianist) that plays the accompaniment for a vocalist or instrumentalist; *sometimes* **:** one that sings an accompaniment

ac·com·pa·ny \-p(ə)nē, -ni\ *vb* -ED/-ING/-ES [ME *accompanien*, fr. MF *acompaignier*, fr. *a-* (fr. L *ad-*) + *compaing, compain* companion, fr. LL *companio* — more at COMPANION] *vt* **1 :** to go with or attend as an associate or companion **:** go along with ⟨will you do me the honor to ~ me home for supper? —Laura Krey⟩ ⟨servants came to ~ us to the nobleman's house —Heinrich Harrer⟩ **2 :** to play or sing an accompaniment to or for **3 :** to add or join to, often incidentally or casually ⟨he *accompanied* the advice with a warning⟩ **4 :** to exist or occur in conjunction or association with ⟨the text which *accompanies* these pictures —John Haverstick⟩ ~ *vi* **:** to perform an accompaniment

ac·com·plice \ə'kämplə̇s *also* a'- *or* -əm-\ *n* -S [alter. (resulting from incorrect division of *a complice*, and influenced by *accomplish*) of *complice*] **1 :** one associated with another in wrongdoing **:** one that participates with another in a crime either as principal or accessory ⟨the ~ of the burglar⟩ ⟨an ~ in a robbery⟩ **2 :** an associate in any undertaking

ac·com·plish \ə'kämplish, -ēsh *also* a'- *or* -əm-\ *vt* -ED/-ING/-ES [ME *accomplissen, accomplisshen*, fr. MF *accompliss-*, stem of *acomplir*, fr. (assumed) VL *accomplēre*, fr. L *ad-* + *complēre* to fill up, complete — more at COMPLETE] **1 :** to execute fully **:** PERFORM, ACHIEVE, FULFILL ⟨I have ~*ed* all that God has given me the strength to do —Henry Baerlein⟩ **2 a :** to attain to ⟨I have ~*ed* 92 years of my life —P.B.Kyne⟩ **b :** TRAVERSE ⟨he would starve before ~*ing* half the distance —W.H.Hudson †1922⟩ **3** *archaic* **a :** to equip thoroughly **b :** PERFECT ⟨qualities ~*ing* a proper gentlewoman⟩ **syn** see PERFORM

accomplished *adj* **1 a** *archaic* **:** fully attained **:** COMPLETED ⟨~ term of servitude⟩ **b :** ESTABLISHED ⟨by the 10th century the modern alphabet was an ~ fact —Joseph Blumenthal⟩ **2 :** having or displaying social graces to a marked degree ⟨an ~ hostess⟩ **:** made highly proficient by practice or training ⟨one of Hollywood's most ~ producers —Arthur Knight⟩ **:** marked by proficiency or finish ⟨an ~ dancer⟩

ac·com·plish·ment \-shmənt\ *n* -S [ME, fr. MF *acomplissement*, fr. *acompliss-* + *-ment*] **1 a :** the act of accomplishing **:** COMPLETION, FULFILLMENT ⟨I beheld the ~ of my toils —Mary W. Shelley⟩ **b** *obs* **:** the act of bringing to perfection ⟨the ~ of the soul⟩ **2 :** DEED, ACHIEVEMENT ⟨his force all spent, he counts his small ~ —Amy Lowell⟩ **3 a :** a quality or ability that equips one for society ⟨an ~ of which he was a perfect exponent, the interchange of humorous and agreeable civilities —Agnes Repplier⟩ **b :** a special skill or ability acquired by training or practice ⟨a young lady of the early Victorian period, with china painting as one of her ~*s*⟩

accomplishment quotient *n* **:** the ratio usu. multiplied by 100 of achievement age to mental age

accompt *archaic var of* ACCOUNT

accomptant *archaic var of* ACCOUNTANT

accompting *archaic var of* ACCOUNTING

¹ac·cord \ə'kó(ə)rd, -ó(ə)d *also* a'-\ *vb* -ED/-ING/-S [ME *accorden, acorden*, fr. OF *acorder*, fr. (assumed) VL *accordare*, fr. L *ad-* + *cord-, cor* heart — more at HEART] *vt* **1 :** to bring into agreement **:** RECONCILE, HARMONIZE ⟨the scientists' conclusions seem contradictory but can be ~*ed* by calm reasoning⟩ **2 a :** to grant as suitable or proper **:** render as due ⟨parents have rights which are not ~*ed* to strangers or neighbors —A.I. Melden⟩ ⟨formerly, historians ~*ed* to "justice" less than its due place —J.G.Edwards⟩ **b :** ALLOW, CONCEDE ⟨the law ~*s* them favored status⟩ ⟨he decided to ~ himself the delight of breaking the news —P.B.Kyne⟩ **c :** AWARD ⟨the President ~*ed* him an honorary title⟩ **d :** ALLOT ⟨in spite of the injustices ~*ed* him⟩ ~ *vi* **1** *archaic* **:** to arrive at an agreement **:** come to terms ⟨proceed as we ~*ed* before dinner —Sir Walter Scott⟩ — often used with *with* ⟨the Queen ~*ed* with this view of the matter —Thomas Carlyle⟩ **2** *obs* **:** to give consent — used with *to* ⟨you to his love must ~ —Shak.⟩ **3 :** to be in harmony **:** be consistent — usu. used with *with* ⟨find whether or not the treatment which they have received ~*s* with freedom of speech —Zechariah Chafee b.1885⟩ **syn** see AGREE, GRANT

²accord \"\ *n* -S [ME *accord, acord*, fr. OF *acort, acorde*, fr. *acorder*] **1 a :** agreement (as in opinion, will, or action) ⟨engineers have reached a certain ~ in regard to ethical principles —H.A.Wagner⟩ **:** CONFORMITY ⟨scholars studying human languages in ~ with accepted scientific principles —H.R.Warfel⟩ **b :** a formal act of agreement **:** RECONCILIATION, UNDERSTANDING, TREATY ⟨the Munich ~⟩ **c :** an agreement between parties in controversy by which satisfaction for an injury is stipulated and which when executed bars a lawsuit **2 :** balanced interrelationship (as of ideas, dimensions, colors, or musical tones) **:** PROPORTION, HARMONY ⟨a persuasive ~ in his arguments⟩ ⟨the gentle ~ of rolling plains⟩ ⟨the ~ of voices⟩ **3** *obs* **:** ASSENT ⟨this gentle and unforc'd ~ of Hamlet sits smiling to my heart —Shak.⟩ **4 :** voluntary or spontaneous impulse to act **:** completely free or unprompted will to act ⟨they gave generously of their own ~⟩ — **with one accord** *adv* **:** with unanimity ⟨*with one accord* the crowd shouted its approval⟩

ac·cord·ance \-d³n(t)s\ *n* -S [ME *accordaunce, acordaunce*, fr. MF *acordance*, fr. *acordant*] **1 :** AGREEMENT, ACCORD — now used chiefly in the phrase *in accordance with* ⟨in ~ with their instructions, they took an early plane for New York⟩ **2 :** the act of granting ⟨the ~ of a privilege⟩ **3 :** ACCORDATURA

ac·cord·an·cy \-d³nsē, -si\ *n* -ES **:** ACCORD, ACCORDANCE

ac·cord·ant \-d³nt\ *adj* [ME *accordaunt, acordaunt*, fr. MF *acordant*, fr. pres. part. of *acorder*] **1 a :** AGREEING, CONSONANT, CONFORMABLE — now usu. used with *with* ⟨a place perfectly ~ with man's nature —Thomas Hardy⟩ ⟨more ~ with natural growth than with human planning —W.B.Adams⟩ **b** *obs* **:** of the same mind **:** UNOPPOSED **2 :** correspondent or harmonious ⟨~ tones⟩ **3** *geol* **:** of the same or nearly the same elevation ⟨~ mountain summits⟩ —**ac·cord·ant·ly** *adv*

ac·cor·da·tu·ra \ə,kȯrdə'türə, (,)a,k-\ *n* -S [It, lit., act of tuning, fr. *accordato* (past part. of *accordare* to tune, accord, fr. (assumed) VL) + *-ura* -ure — more at ACCORD] **:** the tuning scheme of a stringed musical instrument ⟨g d′ a′ e″ is the usual ~ of a violin⟩

accorded *past of* ACCORD

¹according *adj* [ME, fr. pres. part. of *accorden* to accord] *archaic* **:** AGREEING, HARMONIOUS ⟨this ~ voice of national wisdom —Edmund Burke⟩

²according *adv, obs* **:** ACCORDINGLY

according as *conj* [²*according*] **1 :** just as **:** proportionately as ⟨you'll receive *according as* you give⟩ **:** depending on how ⟨*according as* this question is answered, there are two suggestions to be made —*Publ's Mod. Lang. Assoc. of America*⟩ **2 :** depending on whether **:** IF ⟨*according as* he gives a favorable answer, you can plan to see him⟩

ac·cord·ing·ly *adv* [ME, fr. ¹*according* + *-ly*] **1 :** in conformity with a given set of circumstances **:** CORRESPONDINGLY ⟨it helps us to understand him and it helps us to act ~ —W.J. Reilly⟩ **2 :** as a consequence **:** CONSEQUENTLY **:** as a logical outcome **:** SO ⟨later the club also accepted amateurs and ~ changed its name⟩

according to *prep* [ME, fr. ¹*according* + *to*] **1 :** in conformity with **:** consistently with ⟨seated *according to* their rank⟩ **2 :** as attested, maintained, or declared by ⟨*according to* the best authorities⟩ ⟨the Gospel *according to* St. Mark⟩ **3** *obs* **:** with regard to ⟨his Son, who was descended from David *according to* the flesh —Rom 1:3 (RSV)⟩ **4 :** contingently upon **:** depending on ⟨we'll go or we won't, *according to* circumstances⟩ —**according to cock·er** \-'käkə(r)\ *usu cap C* [after Edward Cocker †1675 Eng. engraver & teacher, author of *Tutor to Arithmetic* (1664), a much-used textbook] **:** ACCURATE, CORRECT —**according to hoyle** \-'hȯil, -ȯi(ə)l\ *usu cap H* [after Edmond *Hoyle* †1769 Eng. writer and authority on games, whose treatises, esp. on whist (1742), became famous] **:** in agreement with standard practice or rules **:** in conformity with accepted usage or with an accepted procedure or system **:** CONVENTIONALLY ⟨playing the game *according to Hoyle*⟩ ⟨the girl did not behave *according to Hoyle* —Maude Hutchins⟩

¹ac·cor·di·on *also* **ac·cor·de·on** *or* **ac·cor·di·an** \ə'kȯ(r)dēən *also* a'-\ *n* -S [G *akkordion*, fr. *akkord* chord (fr. F *accord*) + *-ion* (as in *melodion*)] **:** a portable keyboard wind instrument in which the wind is forced past free metallic reeds by means of a hand-operated bellows

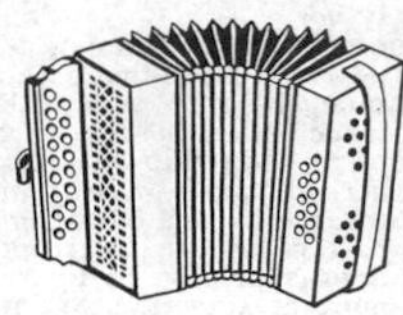

accordion

²accordion \"\ *adj* **:** folding like an accordion **:** creased or hinged so as to fold like an accordion ⟨an ~ pleat⟩ ⟨an ~ map⟩ ⟨an ~ door⟩

accor·di·on·ist \-ə̇st\ *n* -S **:** an accordion player

accords *pres 3d sing of* ACCORD, *pl of* ACCORD

¹ac·cost \ə'kȯst, -äst *also* a'-\ *vb* -ED/-ING/-S [MF *accoster*, prob. fr. OProv *acostar*, fr. LL *accostare*, fr. L *ad-* + *costa* rib, side — more at COAST] *vi, obs* **:** to lie alongside ⟨all the shores which to the sea ~ —Edmund Spenser⟩ ~ *vt* **1 :** to approach and speak to ⟨they were ~*ed* by the immigration officials⟩ **:** speak to without having first been spoken to ⟨the host walked up and ~*ed* the two silent guests⟩ **2 :** to confront, usu. in a somewhat challenging or defensive way ⟨Mrs. Berry, wishing first to see herself as she was, mutely ~*ed* the looking glass —George Meredith⟩ **3 :** to address abruptly (as in a chance meeting) and usu. with a certain degree of impetuosity or boldness ⟨a beggar ~*ed* me in the street⟩ **4 :** to solicit (as a man) for sexual immorality

²accost \"\ *n* -S *archaic* **:** GREETING ⟨she shrunk with fastidious pride from their hail-fellow ~ —Elizabeth C. Gaskell⟩

ac·cost·a·ble \-təbəl\ *adj* [F, fr. *accoster* + *-able*] **:** capable of being approached **:** easily accessible

ac·cost·ed \-təd\ *adj* **1** *heraldry* **:** supported on both sides by other charges **2** *heraldry* **:** side by side

ac·couche \a'küsh, ə'-\ *vt* -ED/-ING/-S [F *accoucher*] **:** to assist during an accouchement

ac·couche·ment \,a,küsh'mäⁿ; a'küsh,mäⁿ, ə'-, -,mənt\ *n* -S [F, fr. *accoucher* to deliver a child, to be delivered of a child (fr. OF *acouchier* to lay down) + *-ment* — more at COUCH] **:** LYING-IN; *esp* **:** PARTURITION

accouchement for·cé \-(,)fȯr'sā\ *n, pl* **accouchements forcés** \-äⁿ(z)(,)f-,-ən(t)s(,)f-\ [F, lit., forced delivery] *med* **:** artificially forced and hastened delivery

ac·cou·cheur \,a,kü'shər(·), a'kü,sh-, -shə(r, ə'=,=\ *n, pl* **accoucheurs** \-ərz,-əz\ [F, fr. *accoucher* + *-eur* -or] **:** one that assists during an accouchement **:** OBSTETRICIAN

¹ac·count \ə'kaůnt *also* a'-\ *n* -S [ME *acount, accompt*, fr. OF *aconte*, fr. *aconter*, v.] **1** *archaic* **:** COUNTING, ENUMERATION, COMPUTATION ⟨a pound good at ~⟩ **2 a :** a record of debit and credit entries chronologically posted to a ledger page from books of original entry to cover transactions involving a particular item (as cash or notes receivable) or a particular person or concern **b :** a statement of transactions during a fiscal period showing the resulting balance **3 :** a collection of items to be balanced — usu. used in pl. **4 :** a statement or explanation of one's activities, conduct, and discharge of responsibilities esp. in financial administration ⟨he could give no satisfactory ~ of what he had done with the money⟩ **5 a :** a periodically rendered reckoning (as one listing charged purchases and credits) ⟨a grocery ~⟩ **b :** the patronage involved in establishing or maintaining an account **:** BUSINESS **:** business relationship ⟨glad to secure that customer's ~⟩; *also* **:** PATRON, CUSTOMER, CLIENT ⟨a salesman with many good ~*s*⟩ **6 a :** value or importance esp. as attributed by others ⟨an official of considerable ~⟩ **b :** ESTEEM, JUDGMENT ⟨he stands high in their ~⟩ **7 :** PROFIT, ADVANTAGE ⟨he turned his wit to good ~⟩ **8 a :** a statement or exposition of underlying or explanatory reasons, causes, grounds, or motives ⟨no satisfactory ~ has been given of these phenomena⟩ **b :** a reason giving rise to an action, decision, opinion, or any other result **:** BASIS ⟨on that ~ he refused the offer⟩ ⟨on all ~*s* you must do it⟩ **c :** ATTENTION, CONSIDERATION **:** careful thought ⟨don't leave that point out of ~⟩ ⟨take ~ of what you are doing⟩ **d :** a usu. mental record based on close observation

⟨keep careful ~ of all you do⟩ **9 a :** a statement of facts or events ⟨a newspaper remarkable for its sober ~s of the theater world⟩ **b :** an informative report or descriptive narration ⟨an ~ of the varieties of tropical vegetation⟩ ⟨the ~ of a battle⟩ **c :** a study or narrative usu. nonfictional and wholly objective ⟨an illuminating ~ of colonial days⟩ **10 :** HEARSAY — usu. used in pl. ⟨by all ~s he is very rich⟩ ⟨he has been quite successful, from all ~s⟩ **11 :** a sum of money or its equivalent deposited in the common cash of a bank and subject to withdrawal at the option of the depositor **12 :** a common-law action for a statement of receipts and disbursements and the recovery of any balance due; *also* **:** the writ by which it was brought **13 :** the fortnightly or monthly settlement between buyers and sellers on the London Stock Exchange; *also* **:** the period from one such settlement to another — usu. used with *the;* compare ACCOUNT DAYS, TERM SETTLEMENT **14 :** performance or rendition (as of a musical composition) ⟨the pianist gave a sensitive ~ of it⟩ **syn** see ²USE — **for account of** *prep* **:** on behalf of — **for the account :** not for settlement until the end of the term-settlement period — **for the account and risk of :** on behalf of and at the hazard of — used by a stock-exchange broker to indicate that he is solely an agent in buying or selling for a customer — **in account with** *prep* **:** in reckoning with **:** in the relationship of creditor or debtor to — **on account of** *prep* **:** for the sake of **:** by reason of **:** because of ⟨*on account of* her love for them, she did all that was possible⟩ — **on one's own account 1 :** for one's own interest or on one's own behalf ⟨I'm doing it *on my own account,* not for anyone else⟩ **2 :** at one's own risk ⟨it's a dangerous plan, one you'll have to follow up *on your own account*⟩ **3 :** on one's own intelligence or strength **:** on one's own motivation **:** by oneself ⟨she left her parents and lived in the city entirely *on her own account*⟩

²**account** \"\ *vb* -ED/-ING/-S [ME *accounten, acounten, accompten,* fr. MF *aconter, acompter,* fr. *a-* (fr. L *ad-*) + *conter, compter* to count — more at COUNT] *vt* **1 a** *obs* **:** to calculate the numerical quantity of **:** COUNT ⟨my father and my mother ~ the days —William Caxton⟩ **b** *obs* **:** to determine or establish by comparison with a fixed point or standard **c** *obs* **:** to include in an enumeration or calculation ⟨~*ing* the Lent season —Thomas Cogan⟩ **d** *archaic* **:** CREDIT, ALLOT **e :** to probe into **:** give an analytical report on **:** take or render account of ⟨the report will be ~*ed* by the finance committee⟩ **2 :** to think of as **:** look upon as **:** rate, regard, or classify as — usu. used passively or reflexively ⟨he was ~*ed* a lawyer of ability —G.S.Bryan⟩ ⟨they ~*ed* themselves fortunate⟩ ~ *vi* **1** *obs* **:** COUNT **2** *archaic* **:** to give or receive a financial account **:** settle an account **3 :** to furnish a justifying analysis or a detailed explanation of one's financial credits and debits or of the discharge of any of one's responsibilities — used with *for* ⟨the broker ~*ed* satisfactorily for his expenditures⟩ ⟨he could not ~ for the time spent away from his post⟩ **4 :** to furnish substantial reasons or a convincing explanation **:** make clear or reveal basic causes — used with *for* ⟨a consistent theory which would ~ for the facts —G.C.Sellery⟩ **5 a :** to be the sole or primary factor in the existence, acquisition, supply, use, or disposal of an indicated thing — used with *for* ⟨the region ~*s* for a large part of usable timber⟩ **b :** to bring about the capture, death, or destruction of an indicated thing — used with *for* ⟨his dog ~*ed* for two of the rabbits⟩ **syn** see CONSIDER, EXPLAIN

ac·count·abil·i·ty \⸗,⸗ə'biləd·ē, -ətē, -i\ *n* -ES **:** the quality or state of being accountable, liable, or responsible

ac·count·able \⸗'⸗əbəl\ *adj* [ME, fr. AF, fr. MF *aconter* to account + *-able*] **1 :** subject to giving an account **:** ANSWERABLE ⟨every sane man is ~ to his conscience for his behavior⟩ **2 :** capable of being accounted for **:** EXPLAINABLE ⟨their apparently strange customs are now ~⟩ **syn** see RESPONSIBLE

ac·count·ably \⸗'⸗⸗blē, -i\ *adv* **:** in an accountable manner

ac·coun·tan·cy \⸗'⸗ᵊnsē, -tən-, -si\ *n* -ES **1 :** the profession of accounting **2 :** the practice of accounting

¹**ac·coun·tant** \-tᵊnt,-tənt\ *n* -S [ME *accountaunt, accomptaunt,* fr. MF *acontant, acomptant,* fr. pres. part. of *aconter, acompter* to account, compute — more at ACCOUNT] **1 a :** one that gives an account **:** one that is accountable **b** *archaic* **:** the defendant in an action of account **2** *archaic* **:** one that counts or calculates **3 :** one that is skilled in the practice of accounting **:** one that has charge of public or private accounts — distinguished from *bookkeeper;* see CERTIFIED PUBLIC ACCOUNTANT, CHARTERED ACCOUNTANT, PUBLIC ACCOUNTANT

²**accountant** *adj* [ME *accountaunt, accomptaunt,* fr. MF *acontant, acomptant,* pres. part.] *obs* **:** liable to account **:** ACCOUNTABLE ⟨~ to the law —Shak.⟩

account book *n* **:** a book in which accounts are kept **:** LEDGER

account current *n, pl* **accounts current :** CURRENT ACCOUNT

account day *n* **:** the final day of the account days **:** SETTLEMENT DAY

account days *n pl* **:** the several days at the end of each term⸗settlement period on the London Stock Exchange when arrangements are made for carrying over the transactions to the next period or for making final settlement

accounted *past of* ACCOUNT

account executive *n* **:** a business executive (as in an advertising agency) responsible for the management of a client's account

accounting *n* -S [ME, fr. gerund of *accounten* to account] **1 a :** the system of classifying, recording, and summarizing business and financial transactions in books of account and analyzing, verifying, and reporting the results **b :** the body of principles, conventions, and procedures underlying accounting — distinguished from *bookkeeping* **2 a :** practical application of accounting — see COST ACCOUNTING, PUBLIC ACCOUNTING **b :** an instance of applying the principles, conventions, and procedures of accounting to the financial condition of an individual or individual organization **3 :** the presenting or stating of accounts ⟨the treasurer rendered his annual ~⟩ **4 :** the process of devising and installing systems of accounts

accounting equation *n* **1 :** the equality of debits and credits as used in the double-entry system **2 :** a statement of net worth as equal to assets minus liabilities

accounting machine *n* **1 :** a key-operated machine which dates, codes, tabulates, adds, subtracts, or totals chiefly in the process of keeping business records (as accounts payable or receivable) **2 :** a business machine that selects information from punched cards fed into it, tabulates, adds, subtracts, or totals in various predeterminable ways, and prints the results

account payable *n, pl* **accounts payable :** the balance due to a creditor on a current account

account receivable *n, pl* **accounts receivable :** a balance due from a debtor on a current account

account render *n* **:** ACCOUNT 12

account rendered *n, pl* **accounts rendered :** an account presented by a creditor to his debtor for examination and settlement

accounts *pl of* ACCOUNT, *pres 3d sing of* ACCOUNT

account sale *or* **account sales** *n* **1 :** a statement showing the net result of a purchase or sale transaction made by one person on another's account or behalf with commission and all other charges included **2 :** a sale on credit

account stated *n, pl* **accounts stated :** an account rendered which by implied or express acceptance has been agreed upon by both parties as correct

accouple *vt* -ED/-ING/-S [ME *acoplen,* fr. MF *accoupler, acopler,* fr. *a-* (fr. L *ad-*) + *cople* couple — more at COUPLE] *obs* **:** JOIN, COUPLE

ac·cou·ple·ment \ə'kəpəlmənt, a'-\ *n* -S [MF, fr. *accoupler* + *-ment*] **1 :** action of joining together **:** COUPLING ⟨proposing an ~ of the two great labor organizations —Edwin Lahey⟩ **2** *archit* **:** placement of two columns very close together or in contact **3 :** something that couples (as a tie or brace)

ac·cou·tre *or* **ac·cou·ter** \ə'küd·ə(r), -ütə- *also* a'k-\ *vt* **accoutred** *or* **accoutered; accoutred** *or* **accoutered; accou·tring** *or* **accou·ter·ing** \-üd·əriŋ, -ütər-,-ü·tr-\ **accoutres** *or* **accouters** [F *accoutrer,* fr. MF *acoustrer,* fr. *a-* (fr. L *ad-*) + *costure* seam, fr. (assumed) VL *consutura,* fr. L *consutus* (past part. of *consuere* to sew together, fr. *com-* + *suere* to sew) + *-ura* -ure — more at SEW] **:** to fit out **:** DRESS **:** provide with equipment or furnishings **:** equip esp. for military service — usu. used passively ⟨they were properly ~*ed* for the trip⟩ ⟨~*ed* for battle⟩ **syn** see FURNISH

ac·cou·tre·ment \-ü·trəmənt; -üd·ə(r)m-, -ütə(-\ *or* **ac·cou·ter·ment** \-ütrə-, -üd·ə(-, -ütə(-\ *n* -S [MF *accoutrement,* fr. *accoutrer* + *-ment*] **1 :** the act of accoutering or state of being accoutered **2 a :** any article of equipment or dress esp. when used merely as an accessory ⟨she carried a pink parasol, a rather startling ~⟩ **b :** OUTFIT, FURNISHINGS, EQUIPMENT, TRAPPINGS, REGALIA; *specif* **:** a soldier's outfit (as a rifle belt, pack, and other accessories) usu. not including clothes and weapons ⟨the ~s of war⟩ — usu. used in pl. **3 a :** an identifying but usu. extraneous characteristic **:** a nonessential but usual accompaniment ⟨political demagoguery accompanied by its unsurprising ~ of prejudice and stupidity⟩ **b :** a typical device or procedure ⟨the lurid ~s employed by the average comic artist —Coulton Waugh⟩

accpt *abbr* accompaniment

¹**ac·cra** \ə'krä, a'-,ä'-\ *adj, usu cap* [fr. *Accra, Akkra,* Ghana] **:** of or from Accra, the capital of Ghana **:** of the kind or style prevalent in Accra

²**accra** *usu cap, var of* AKRA

accra copal *n, usu cap A* **:** a hard resin obtained from certain trees in the coastal forests of western Africa and used in varnishes

accrd *abbr* accrued

ac·cred·it \ə'kredət *also* a'-; *usu* -dəd·+V\ *vt* -ED/-ING/-S [F *accréditer,* fr. *ad-* + *crédit* credit — more at CREDIT] **1 :** to put (as by common consent) into a reputable or outstanding category **:** consider, recognize, or acclaim as rightfully possessing an uncontested status ⟨sages so fully ~*ed* as Mr. Bertrand Russell —C.E.Montague⟩ **2 :** to give official authorization to or approval of: **a :** to order or permit to proceed on an official mission or on one otherwise officially recognized ⟨in the course of service as an air attaché at several capitals . . . governments to which he was ~*ed* gave him medals —J.G. Cozzens⟩ **b :** to vouch for officially **:** recognize or clear officially as bona fide, approved, or in conformity with a standard ⟨only a few counties in the state had been ~*ed* with reference to tuberculosis in cattle —*Jour. Amer. Med. Assoc.*⟩ **c :** to recognize (an educational institution) as maintaining standards that render it eligible for membership in an association of similar institutions and that qualify its graduates for admission to higher or more specialized institutions or for professional practice **3 :** CREDIT **:** to give credit for **:** ascribe or attribute esp. favorably ⟨rare and treasured possessions ~*ed* with magical properties —C.D.Forde⟩ ⟨nobility not generally ~*ed* to him by the coarse world —Bernard DeVoto⟩ **syn** see APPROVE, ASCRIBE, AUTHORIZE

ac·cred·i·ta·tion \⸗,⸗də'tāshən\ *n* -S *often attrib* **:** the act or process of accrediting ⟨recently developed standards for the ~ of junior colleges⟩ ⟨a joint commission on ~ of hospitals⟩ **:** the state or fact of being accredited ⟨ambassador in Rome with concurrent ~ to Italy and Yugoslavia —*Current Biog.*⟩ ⟨the ~ status of an educational institution⟩

accredited *adj* **1 a :** publicly sanctioned or recognized ⟨take it as a personal insult if any of their neighbors break away from ~ custom —W.R.Inge⟩ **b :** officially authorized or recognized **:** provided with credentials ⟨an ~ war correspondent⟩ ⟨~ observers at the United Nations⟩ **c :** accepted as valid or authoritative ⟨theories in keeping with the ~ science of the day⟩ **2 :** officially vouched for or guaranteed as conforming to a prescribed or desirable standard ⟨an ~ hospital⟩: as **a** *of an educational institution* **:** approved by an accrediting agency ⟨an ~ college⟩ **b** *of livestock* **:** guaranteed as free from a usu. specified disease ⟨an ~ herd⟩

ac·cred·i·tee \⸗,⸗də'tē\ *n* -S **:** one that has received accreditation ⟨UN ~s —*Newsweek*⟩

accrediting agency *n* **:** a state-controlled or privately supported agency authorized to grant accreditation to educational institutions

ac·cred·it·ment \⸗'⸗dətmənt\ *n* -S **:** ACCREDITATION

ac·cresce \ə'kres, a'-\ *vi* -ED/-ING/-S [L *accrescere,* fr. *ad-* + *crescere* to grow — more at CRESCENT] **:** ACCRUE *vi* 1

ac·cres·cence \-sᵊn(t)s\ *n* -S [ML *accrescentia,* fr. L *accrescent-, accrescens* (pres. part. of *accrescere*) + *-ia*] **1 :** continuous growth **2 :** ACCRETION

ac·cres·cent \-sᵊnt, 'a,k-\ *adj* [L *accrescent-, accrescens*] **:** growing continuously; *specif* **:** growing larger after flowering — used esp. of a calyx

¹**ac·crete** \ə'krēt, a'-\ *vb* -ED/-ING/-S [back-formation fr. *accretion*] *vi* **1 :** to grow together **:** UNITE, COMBINE **2 :** to become attached by accretion **:** ADHERE ~ *vt* **1 :** to cause to adhere or become attached ⟨a desire to ~ to himself symbols of status —Edward Sapir⟩ **2 :** to gather and attach to oneself or itself ⟨as the story traveled, it *accreted* emotion —E. M.Forster⟩

²**ac·crete** \", 'a,k-\ *adj* [L *accretus*] **1 :** formed by accretion **2** *bot* **:** grown together

ac·cre·tion \ə'krēshən, a'-\ *n* -S [L *accretion-, accretio* increase, increment, fr. *accretus* (past part. of *accrescere* to increase) + *-ion-, -io* -ion — more at ACCRESCE] **1 :** the process of growth or enlargement: **a :** organic growth **:** continued development from within **b :** increase by external addition or accumulation (as by adhesion of external parts or particles) **c** (1) **:** the increase or extension of the boundaries of land or the consequent acquisition of land accruing to the owner by the gradual or imperceptible action of natural forces (as by the washing up of sand or soil from the sea or a river or by a gradual recession of the water from the usual watermark) **:** accession in which the boundaries of land are enlarged by this process; *sometimes* **:** increase in the amount or extent of any kind of property or in the value of any property — compare AVULSION (2) **:** gain to an heir or legatee by failure of a coheir or a colegatee to take his share **2 a :** the result of the process of accretion ⟨every culture is an ~ —A.L. Kroeber⟩ ⟨a complex ~ of rules —Edmund Wilson⟩ **b :** the matter added; *esp* **:** an extraneous addition ⟨~s of grime⟩ ⟨the immense ~ of flesh which had descended on her in middle life —Edith Wharton⟩ **c** *forestry* **:** INCREMENT; *sometimes* **:** increase in diameter as contrasted with increase in volume **3 :** CONCRETION **:** coherence of separate particles

ac·cre·tion·ary \-,nerē\ *adj* **1 :** marked by or involving accretion **2 :** produced by accretion

accretionary hypothesis *n* **:** any explanation of the origin of the earth that involves the hypothesis of gradual growth by the gravitational infall of solid bodies (as asteroids, planetesimals, or meteorites) — compare PLANETESIMAL HYPOTHESIS

accretion borer *n* **:** a hollow auger used for cutting out from a tree a core from which accretion is estimated by counting annual rings

accretion cutting *or* **accretion thinning** *n* **:** thinning of trees in order to secure greater growth in girth of those left standing

ac·cre·tive \ə'krēd·iv, (')a¦k-\ *adj* [*accretion* + *-ive*] **1 :** relating to accretion ⟨made up by a sort of ~ process —*N.Y. Times*⟩ **2 :** growing by accretion

ac·croach \ə'krōch, a'-\ *vt* -ED/-ING/-ES [ME *acrochen* to draw, acquire, fr. MF *acrochier,* fr. *a-* (fr. L *ad-*) + *crochier* to hook, get hold of, fr. *croc* hook, of Gmc origin; akin to ON *krōkr* hook — more at CROOK] **:** ASSUME, APPROPRIATE, USURP ⟨~ to themselves royal power —William Stubbs⟩

ac·croi·des \ə'krȯi(,)dēz, a'-\ *or* **accroides resin** *or* **ac·croides gum** *n* [modif. of NL *acaroides*] **:** ACAROID RESIN

ac·cru·al \ə'krüəl *also* a'-\ *n* -S *often attrib* [¹*accrue* + *-al*] **1 :** the action or process of accruing **2 a :** something that accrues; *esp* **:** an amount of money that periodically accumulates for a specific item (as taxes, interest, or anticipated expenses) **b :** something that has accrued during a specified period

accrual basis *n* **:** the method of keeping accounts that recognizes income when earned and expenses when incurred regardless of when cash is received or disbursed — compare CASH BASIS

¹**ac·crue** \ə'krü *also* a'-\ *vb* -ED/-ING/-S [ME *acreuen, acruwen,* prob. fr. MF *acreue, accreue* increase, fr. fem. of *acreu,* past part. of *acreistre* to increase, grow, fr. L *accrescere,* fr. *ad-* + *crescere* to grow — more at CRESCENT] *vi* **1 :** to come into existence as an enforceable claim **:** vest as a right ⟨a cause of action has *accrued* when the right to sue has become vested⟩ **2 :** to come by way of increase or addition **:** arise as a growth or result — usu. used with *to* or *from* ⟨advantages *accruing* to society from the freedom of the press⟩ **3 :** to be periodically accumulated in the process of time whether as an increase or a decrease ⟨the *accruing* of taxes⟩ ⟨allowing the receivable interest to ~⟩ ~ *vt* **1 :** GATHER, COLLECT, ACCUMULATE ⟨authorized by law to ~ leave . . . in the maximum amount of 120 days —*U.S.Code*⟩ **2 :** to enter in the books as an accrual

²**accrue** \"\ *n* -S [MF *accreue, acreue*] *obs* **:** ACCRUAL, ADDITION

accrued dividend *n* **:** a dividend earned or assumed earned at a specified rate on cumulative preferred stock but not declared or paid

accrued interest *n* **:** interest earned since last settlement date but not yet due or payable

accrued liability *n* **:** the portion of an accruing liability that has become definitely ascertainable and chargeable though actual payment thereof is not yet due

ac·crue·ment \-ümənt\ *n* -S [¹*accrue* + *-ment*] **:** ACCRUAL, INCREMENT

acct *abbr* account; accountant

ac·cul·tur·ate \ə'kəlchə,rāt\ *vb* -ED/-ING/-S [back-formation fr. *acculturation*] *vt* **:** to cause to change through acculturation ⟨enterprises designed to ~ new Americans —Cynthia Ozick⟩ ~ *vi* **:** to become changed through acculturation

ac·cul·tur·a·tion \ə,kəlchə'rāshən, (,)a,k-\ *n* -S [*ad-* + *culture* + *-ation*] **1 a :** a process of intercultural borrowing marked by the continuous transmission of traits and elements between diverse peoples and resulting in new and blended patterns — distinguished from *assimilation;* compare TRANSCULTURATION **b :** modification of a primitive culture resulting from prolonged contact with a more advanced culture **2 :** the process of socialization — compare ENCULTURATION

ac·cul·tur·a·tion·al \-shənᵊl,-shnəl\ *adj* **:** of or relating to the process of acculturation or to the modifications in culture resulting from acculturation

ac·cul·tur·a·tion·ist \-sh(ə)nəst\ *n* -S **:** a student of acculturation

ac·cul·tur·a·tive \ə'kəlchə,rād·iv, a'-\ *adj* **:** of, relating to, or contributing to acculturation

ac·cul·tur·ize \-chə,rīz\ *vt* -ED/-ING/-S [*acculturation* + *-ize*] **:** to cause (a people) to adopt the culture of another

ac·cum·ben·cy \ə'kəmbənsē, a'-\ *n* -ES [L *accumbent-, accumbens* + E *-cy*] **:** the state of being accumbent

ac·cum·bent \ə'kəmbənt, (')a¦k-\ *adj* [L *accumbent-, accumbens,* pres. part. of *accumbere* to lie down, recline at table, fr. *ad-* + *-cumbere* to lie down (akin to *cubare* to lie down) — more at HIP] **1 :** leaning or reclining esp. at meals ⟨the Roman ~ posture in eating⟩ **2** *bot* **:** lying against something — used chiefly of cotyledons having their edges folded against the hypocotyl (as in many crucifers) — compare CONDUPLICATE, INCUMBENT **3** *zool* **:** closely applied to a surface (as of the wing scales of certain insects)

ac·cu·mu·la·ble \ə'kyümyələbəl, ÷-mə- *also* a'-\ *adj* [*accumulate* + *-able*] **:** capable of being accumulated

¹**ac·cu·mu·late** \-,lāt, *usu* -ād·+V\ *vb* -ED/-ING/-S [L *accumulatus,* past part. of *accumulare,* fr. *ad-* + *cumulare* to heap up — more at CUMULATE] *vt* **:** to heap up in a mass **:** pile up ⟨the sands then had their own way, and *accumulated* the barrier which now exists between the two rivers —Douglas Carruthers⟩ ⟨they . . . ~ blame upon the conditions imposed on them by fate —A.C.Benson⟩ **:** AMASS ⟨*accumulated* a fortune as a tea planter⟩ **:** COLLECT, GATHER ⟨true poetry ~s meaning every time it is read —C.D.Lewis⟩ ⟨dismantled the spinning wheel and carried it to the attic to ~ antiquity —John Gould⟩ ~ *vi* **:** to grow or increase in quantity or number ⟨where wealth ~s and men decay —Oliver Goldsmith⟩ ⟨snow *accumulated* to a depth of 10 feet⟩

syn AMASS, HOARD: ACCUMULATE suggests a gradual piling up or increasing so as to make a store or great quantity ⟨to *accumulate* dust⟩ ⟨he who *accumulates* objects of value —Herbert Spencer⟩ ⟨*accumulated* major collections of important Arabic manuscripts —*Amer. Council of Learned Soc. Newsletter*⟩ ⟨to *accumulate* wisdom⟩ AMASS stresses the size, esp. the great size, of the accumulation, usu. of things of value; it may imply rather rapid acquisition ⟨great wealth was *amassed* through steel, railroad, coal, and other industries —*Amer. Guide Series: Pa.*⟩ ⟨scientific knowledge, painstakingly *amassed* by many devotees over an extended period of human history —F.A.Geldard⟩ HOARD always implies a holding or storing up after acquisition, and usu. concealment, sometimes suggesting miserly retention ⟨*hoarding* money is not a safe way of saving —G.B.Shaw⟩ ⟨some delicacy that has been *hoarded* for weeks is brought forth for a guest —Maeanna Cheserton⸗Mangle⟩ ⟨newspapermen, *hoarding* their eloquent comments for their own typewriters —Leonard Lyons⟩

²**ac·cu·mu·late** \-,lət, -,lāt\ *adj* [L *accumulatus*] **:** heaped or piled up **:** ACCUMULATED

accumulated surplus *n* **:** the surplus of a corporation that has been earned or has accrued after incorporation

accumulated temperature *n* **:** CUMULATIVE TEMPERATURE

ac·cu·mu·la·tion \⸗,⸗⸗'lāshən\ *n* -S [F or L; F, fr. L *accumulation-, accumulatio,* fr. *accumulatus* + *-ion-, -io* -ion] **1 :** the action or process of accumulating **:** state of being or having accumulated **:** a collecting together **:** AMASSING ⟨the steady ~ of snow throughout the night⟩ ⟨fabrics subject to the ~ of static electricity⟩ ⟨current theories about the ~ of the sun and stars from dust clouds —H.C.Urey⟩ **2 :** increase or growth by addition esp. when continuous or repeated (as of interest to principal): as **a :** the increase of a fund or property by the continuous addition to it of the interest or income of it, subject in England to a rule analogous to the rule against perpetuities and in the U. S. allowed in many states only during the minority of the person for whom the property is held **b** (1) *in life insurance* **:** retention of dividends for distribution at some later date (2) *in accident insurance* **:** an increase in the principal sum that sometimes takes effect without change of premium upon each renewal of a policy (3) *in marine insurance* **:** an increase in the limit of liability under open-cargo policies to double the normal amount if two or more cargoes at a port are loaded on the same vessel **c :** the gradual purchase of large quantities of securities in anticipation of a rise in price or for investment or control purposes **d :** appreciation between the date of purchase and maturity in the value of a bond bought at a discount **3 :** something that has accumulated or has been accumulated **:** an accumulated mass, quantity, or number ⟨huge ~s of mouse-gray clouds —Ira Wolfert⟩ ⟨clearing away the ~ of centuries from the base of the pyramid —*London Calling*⟩ ⟨the giant ~s of stars known as galaxies —George Gamow⟩ **4 :** the movement of a substance into a cell against a concentration gradient or from a lower to a higher potential for the specific substance — used esp. of movement of ions into plant cells

accumulation factor *n* **:** the factor $(1 + r)^n$ by which any principal must be multiplied to give its amount at compound interest after *n* periods, *r* being the interest for one period ⟨the *accumulation factor* for 10 years at 6 percent compounded quarterly is $(1.015)^{40}$⟩

accumulation of energy *or* **accumulation of power :** the storing of energy by various means (as by weights lifted, masses put in motion, or chemical changes effected)

ac·cu·mu·la·tive \⸗'⸗⸗,lād·iv, -,ləl, |tiv, -ēv\ *adj* **1 :** marked by accumulation **:** produced by accumulation **:** CUMULATIVE ⟨~ toxic effects⟩ ⟨~ rainfall⟩ ⟨to have them in their proper order and thereby to receive their ~ impact —Irving Howe⟩ **2 :** tending to or given to accumulation **:** ACCUMULATING ⟨nations are imperialistic in their ~ stage —D.L.Kemmerer⟩ **3 :** CUMULATIVE 4 — **ac·cu·mu·la·tive·ly** *adv*

ac·cu·mu·la·tor \-,lād·ə(r), -ātə-\ *n* -S **:** one that accumulates: as **a :** an apparatus for storing energy (as a cylinder containing water under the pressure of a weighted piston for hydraulic presses) **b :** a contrivance to take up the force of a sudden strain (as a system of springs or an elastic section in a chain) **c** *Brit* **:** STORAGE CELL **d :** a vessel for collecting a gas or liquid usu. for temporary storage **e :** a part (as in a computer) where numbers are totaled or stored **f** *chiefly Brit* **:** PARLAY 1

ac·cu·ra·cy \'akyərəsē, -si, ÷-k(ə)rəs-\ *n* -ES [*accurate* + *-cy*] **a :** the quality, state, or degree of being accurate: **a :** freedom from mistake or error **:** CORRECTNESS ⟨answers will be marked for neatness as well as for ~⟩ ⟨to achieve ~, errors or their repetition must be avoided —*English Language Teaching*⟩ **b :** conformity to truth or to some standard or model ⟨an account, the general ~ of which could hardly be doubted⟩ ⟨the ~ of a firearm is its ability to deliver a close group of hits on a target⟩ : EXACTNESS ⟨impossible to state with ~ the number of casualties⟩ ⟨a play much admired for the ~ of its idiom⟩ ⟨the highly approximate reconnaissance ~ of the map —*Geog. Rev.*⟩ **c** *of measurement* : the degree of conformity to some recognized standard value : deviation of a result obtained by a particular method from the value accepted as true ⟨elevations have been extended as far as 50 miles across rugged mountainous terrain with an ~ of about 2 feet —*Science*⟩ — contrasted with *precision*

ac·cu·rate \-rət, *rapid* ˈakyərt, *usu* -d·+V\ *adj* [L *accuratus* prepared with care, careful, exact, fr. past part. of *accurare* to take care of, do carefully, fr. *ad-* + *curare* to take care of, heal — more at CURE] **1** : free from error or mistake esp. as the result of care ⟨an ~ estimate of expenses⟩ ⟨new inventions . . . had made it possible to chart and to hold a more ~ course at sea —Lewis Mumford⟩ ⟨sound and ~ observers⟩ ⟨~ methods⟩ : in exact conformity to truth or to some standard : CORRECT, EXACT, PRECISE ⟨the report was dry, factual, painstakingly ~, crabbedly truthful —Carl Sandburg⟩ ⟨a mathematically ~ distribution⟩ ⟨the instruments were sensitive and marvelously ~ —E.K.Gann⟩ **2** *obs* : precisely fixed : executed with care : CAREFUL **syn** see CORRECT

ac·cu·rate·ly \-tlē, -i\ *adv* : in an accurate manner : PRECISELY, EXACTLY

ac·cu·rate·ness \-tnəs\ *n* -ES : the quality or state of being accurate

ac·curse \əˈkərs, -kəs *also* a'-\ *vt* **accursed**; **accursed** *see* ACCURSED\ *or* **accurst**; **accursing**; **accurses** [alter. (influenced by such words as *accord, account*) of ME *acursen*, fr. *a-* (fr. OE *ā-*, perfective prefix) + *cursen* to curse — more at ABIDE, CURSE] : to consign to destruction, misery, or evil by a curse : ANATHEMATIZE — now used chiefly as past part. ⟨looked upon her as a thing *accursed* —Charles Kingsley⟩

ac·cursed \-st,-səd; -səd *usu when a stressed syllable follows without pause*, "-səd breed" *for instance being more frequent than* "-st breed"\ *or* **ac·curst** \-st\ *adj* [ME *acursed*, fr. past part. of *acursen*] **1** : CURSED ⟨this ~ devil —Shak.⟩ **2** : bad enough to be under a curse : DETESTABLE, DAMNABLE ⟨dry, unhealthy, and ~ was the road —Eve Langley⟩ — **ac·curs·ed·ly** \-sədlē, -i\ *adv* — **ac·curs·ed·ness** \-sədnəs\ *n* -ES

ac·cus·a·ble \əˈkyüzəbəl *also* a'-\ *adj* [F, fr. L *accusabilis* blameworthy, fr. *accusare* + *-abilis* -able] : liable to be accused — **ac·cus·a·bly** \-blē\ *adv*

ac·cus·al \-zəl\ *n* -S : ACCUSATION ⟨lurid and rather unlikely scenes of ~, confession, and remorse —*New Yorker*⟩

ac·cus·ant \-zᵊnt\ *n* -S [F, fr. L *accusant-, accusans*, pres. part. of *accusare*] : one that accuses

ac·cu·sa·tion \ˌakyəˈzāshən, -yü'-\ *n* -S [ME *accusacioun*, fr. MF *accusation*, fr. L *accusation-, accusatio*, fr. *accusatus* (past part. of *accusare* to call to account) + *-ion-, -io* -ion — more at ACCUSE] **1** : the act of accusing : the state or fact of being accused ⟨his basic premise that ~ equals proof of guilt —*New Republic*⟩ **2 a** : a charge of wrongdoing, delinquency, or fault : the declaration containing such a charge : ALLEGATION, INDICTMENT ⟨with the calumnies were mingled ~s much better founded —T.B.Macaulay⟩ ⟨~s in the press⟩ **b** : the offense or fault of which one is accused ⟨the ~ was murder⟩

ac·cu·sa·ti·val \əˌkyüzəˈtīvəl *also* aˌ-\ *adj* [²*accusative* + *-al*] : ¹ACCUSATIVE

¹**ac·cu·sa·tive** \əˈkyüzəd·iv, -ətiv, -ēv\ *adj* [ME, fr. MF or L; MF *accusatif*, fr. L *accusativus* (trans. of Gk *aitiatikos*, lit., accusing, causal), fr. *accusatus* (past part. of *accusare*) + *-ivus* -ive] **1 a** *of a grammatical case* : marking typically the direct object of a verb (as Latin *filium* in *mater amat filium* "the mother loves her son"; German *mich* in *er sieht mich* "he sees me") or the object of any of several prepositions (as Latin *eos* in *ad eos* "toward them"; German *den stuhl* in *ohne den stuhl* "without the chair") — used esp. in the grammar of those Indo-European languages that have relatively full inflections **b** *of a word or word group* : being the direct object of a verb or the object of a preposition even when this relation is not marked by any inflectional element (as *Robert* in "John met Robert") — not now used technically **c** : of or belonging to the accusative case ⟨an ~ ending⟩ **2** : ACCUSING, ACCUSATORY ⟨indicating their opponent with ~ forefingers —Stephen Crane⟩ — **ac·cu·sa·tive·ly** *adv*

²**accusative** \"\ *n* -S [ME, fr. MF or L; MF, fr. L *accusativus*, fr. *accusativus*, adj.] : the accusative case of a language or a form in the accusative case

accusative absolute *n* **1** : a construction in German consisting of a noun in the accusative case joined with a predicate that does not include a finite verb and usu. capable of being construed as the modifier of the principal verb in its sentence (as *den hut in der hand* in *den hut in der hand ging er ins haus* "hat in hand he went into the house") **2** : a construction in English, esp. colloquial English, consisting of a pronoun in the accusative case joined with a predicate that does not include a finite verb and otherwise identical with the nominative absolute (as *him being my friend* in "him being my friend, I granted his request")

accusative-dative *adj, of a case of English pronouns* : marking typically the object of a verb (as *me* in "he saw me", *him* in "I gave him the book") or of a preposition (as *us* in "with us")

ac·cus·a·to·ri·al \əˌkyüzəˈtōrēəl, aˌ-, ˌaˌk-\ *adj* [*accusatory* + *-al*] : of or relating to an accuser; *specif* : indicating the form of criminal prosecution in which the alleged criminal is publicly accused of his crime and is tried in public by a judge who is not also the prosecutor — contrasted with *inquisitorial* — **ac·cus·a·to·ri·al·ly** \-ələ\ *adv*

ac·cus·a·to·ry \əˈkyüzəˌtōrē, a'-, -tō-, -ri\ *adj* [L *accusatorius* of an accuser, fr. *accusator* accuser, fr. *accusatus* (past part. of *accusare* to call to account, accuse) + *-or*] **1** : containing or expressing accusation : tending to accusation : ACCUSING ⟨black ~ looks —Corra Harris⟩ ⟨the ~ generalities uttered during the war —R.H.Jackson⟩ **2** *law* : ACCUSATORIAL

ac·cu·sa·trix \ˌakyəˈzātriks, -yü'-\ *n* -ES [L, fem. of *accusator*] : a female accuser

¹**ac·cuse** \əˈkyüz *also* a'-\ *vb* -ED/-ING/-S [ME *accusen, acusen*, fr. OF *acuser*, fr. L *accusare* to call to account, fr. *ad-* + *-cusare* (fr. *causa* cause, lawsuit) — more at CAUSE] *vt* **1 a** : to charge unequivocally with a specified or implied wrong or fault often in a condemnatory or indignant manner ⟨the courtiers *accused* their queen⟩ ⟨the planes were *accused* of spreading cholera, typhus, and bubonic plague — *Current History*⟩ **b** : to charge with an offense judicially or by a public process **c** : to speak censoriously against as culpable or reprehensible ⟨*accused* the brazen corruptions of the capital —Carl Van Doren⟩ ⟨~s a system rather than any specific persons —Bruce Catton⟩ **2** : REVEAL, BETRAY ⟨sometimes, as she passed a high window, the *accusing* light fell for a moment on her oval face —Edith Sitwell⟩ ~ *vi* : to bring an accusation : prefer charges ⟨he *accused* no more, but dumbly shrank before *accusing* throngs of thought —George Eliot⟩ ⟨where thought ~s and feeling mocks —W.H.Auden⟩ ⟨the "war party" fretted and *accused* — *New Republic*⟩

syn CHARGE, INDICT, IMPEACH, ARRAIGN, INCRIMINATE, CRIMINATE: ACCUSE and CHARGE are frequently interchangeable in meaning to declare a person guilty of a fault or offense. CHARGE may suggest a certain formality in the declaration ⟨*charging* him with impiety —J.A.Froude⟩ ⟨suppose the petitioner falsely and unjustly *charged* the judge with having excluded him from knowledge of the facts —O.W.Holmes †1935⟩ ACCUSE may suggest stronger personal feeling or interest ⟨Louvet . . . took his station in the Tribune, saying, "I, Robespierre, *accuse* thee!" —William Wordsworth⟩ INDICT indicates formal accusation in or as if in holding for trial ⟨you are here *indicted* . . . Lord Dudley [and] Lady Jane Grey, of capital and high treason —Thomas Wyatt⟩ IMPEACH implies a charge, esp. one involving corruptness, poor judgment, or malfeasance through duplicity, calling for a defense or answer ⟨any intelligent and noble-minded American can with reason take that side . . . without having either his reason or his integrity *impeached* —Kenneth Roberts⟩ ⟨why should he be *impeaching* the Reverend George Barnard for exceptional futility? —Compton Mackenzie⟩ ARRAIGN suggests formal presentation of charges with a demand for a plea, defense, or explanation ⟨I was carried down to the sessions house, where I was *arraigned* —Daniel Defoe⟩ ⟨Davies's career . . . affords the perfect grounds for *arraigning* both capitalism and socialism —Osbert Sitwell⟩ INCRIMINATE and CRIMINATE once commonly meant to charge with a crime; in today's use they are more likely to mean involving or inculpating in crime, laying open to charges ⟨the answer need not reveal a crime in order to be *incriminating*. It is enough if it might furnish a clue . . . that leads to proof of an illegal act —*New Republic*⟩

²**accuse** *n* -S *obs* : ACCUSATION

accused *n, pl* **accused** : one charged with an offense; *esp* : the defendant in a criminal case ⟨the ~ shall enjoy the right to a speedy and public trial —*U.S.Constitution*⟩ ⟨one of the ~ in a notorious conspiracy case⟩

accusement *n* -S [ME, fr. MF *acusement*, fr. *acuser* + *-ment*] *obs* : ACCUSATION

ac·cus·er \-zə(r)\ *n* -S [ME *accusour, accuser*, fr. MF *acuseor*, fr. *acuser* + *-eor* -or] : one that accuses; *specif* : one that formally accuses another of a crime

accusingly *adv* : in an accusing manner

ac·cus·ive \-ziv, -siv\ *adj* : tending to accuse : ACCUSING ⟨his ~ shoes and telltale trousers —O.Henry⟩

ac·cus·tom \əˈkəstəm *also* a'-\ *vb* -ED/-ING/-S [ME *accustomen*, fr. MF *acustumer, acostumer*, fr. *a-* (fr. L *ad-*) + *costume* custom — more at CUSTOM] *vt* : to make familiar through use or experience : HABITUATE, FAMILIARIZE, INURE ⟨~*ing* one's ears to the din⟩ ⟨opportunity to ~ the girl to sea life —Joseph Conrad⟩ ⟨she would go back to the districts . . . she knew so well, and ~ herself again to the old ways —Israel Zangwill⟩ — usu. used with *to* and an object but sometimes with an infinitive ⟨taught how to ~ themselves to use books and enjoy them —*Library Science Abstracts*⟩ ~ *vi, obs* : to be wont

accustomable *adj* [ME, fr. *accustomen* + *-able*] *obs* : CUSTOMARY — **accustomably** *adv, obs*

accustomary *adj* [obs. *accustom* custom (fr. ME, fr. *accustomen*, v.) + *-ary*] *archaic* : CUSTOMARY

accustomed *adj* [ME, fr. past part. of *accustomen*] **1** : familiar through use or long and repeated experience: **a** : often used or practiced : CUSTOMARY, HABITUAL, USUAL ⟨her ~ cheerfulness⟩ ⟨cut off from its ~ sources of manufactured articles —P.E.James⟩ **b** : HABITUATED, INURED ⟨great wicker baskets balanced easily on ~ heads —Claudia Cassidy⟩ — often used with *to* and an object ⟨eyes not fully ~ to the darkness⟩ ⟨nations become ~ to the use of collective action —Vera M. Dean⟩ **2** : in the habit or custom : established in the practice : USED, WONT — used with *to* and an infinitive or gerund ⟨~ to paint their faces before battle⟩ ⟨~ to making decisions⟩ **3** *archaic* : frequented by customers **syn** see USUAL

ac·cus·tomed·ness \ˈ⸗⸗təm(d)nəs\ *n* -ES : the state of being accustomed

¹**ace** \ˈās\ *n* -S [ME *as*, fr. OF, fr. L *ass-, as* unity, unit, copper coin; akin to L *asser* beam, pole, stake, *assis* board, plank] **1 a** : a die face marked with one spot **b** : a playing card marked in its center with one large pip and usu. having the index *A* in its corners **c** : such a card ranking highest in its suit **d** : a domino end marked with one spot — usu. used in compounds ⟨double-*ace*⟩ ⟨*ace*-blank⟩ **e aces** *pl* (1) : a throw of 2 in craps (2) : a pair of aces in poker; *also* : three aces — used in the phrase *aces full* (3) : honors in no-trump ⟨easy ~s⟩ ⟨150 ~s⟩ (4) : one ace of each suit in pinochle **2** : a very small amount or degree : PARTICLE, BIT ⟨I'll not wag an ~ further —John Dryden⟩ **3** : a score won by a single stroke; *specif* : a point (as in tennis or handball) scored on a shot (as a service) that an opponent fails to touch **4** : a score in golf of one stroke on a hole or a hole made in one stroke **5** : an airplane combat pilot who has brought down at least five enemy airplanes **6 a** : a person who excels at something ⟨a football ~⟩ **b** : an important or outstanding thing or event ⟨speed is the ~ of air transport —*Forum*⟩ — **within an ace of** : on the point of : very near to ⟨*within an ace of* hitting a telephone pole⟩

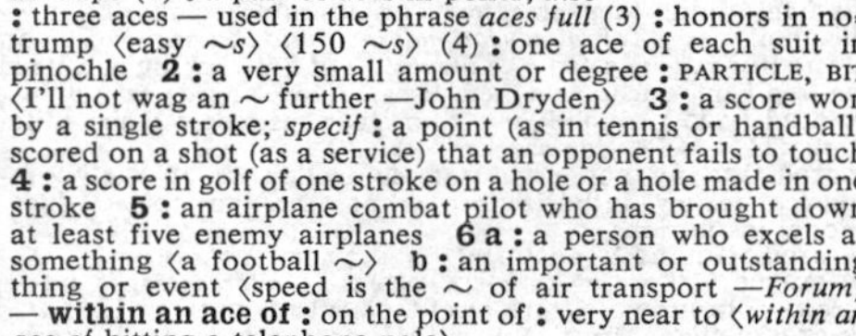
aces 1b

²**ace** \"\ *vt* -ED/-ING/-S **1** : to score an ace against (an opponent) **2** : to make (a hole in golf) in one stroke

³**ace** \"\ *adj* : of first or high rank or quality : OUTSTANDING ⟨an ~ reporter⟩

ace- *comb form* [ISV, fr. *acetic*] : acetic ⟨*acenaphthene*⟩; *specif* : related to acenaphthene ⟨*aceanthrene*⟩

-a·ce \əsē\ *n comb form* -S [LGk *akē* point — more at EDGE] : apex having (so many) faces ⟨hept*ace*⟩⟨tess*arace*⟩

-a·cea \ˈāsh(ē)ə\ *n pl suffix* [NL, fr. L, neut. pl. of *-aceus* -aceous] : animals characterized by : animals of the nature of ⟨Cet*acea*⟩ ⟨Crust*acea*⟩ — in names of zoological divisions larger than a genus, esp. orders and classes

-a·ce·ae \ˈāsēˌē\ *n pl suffix* [NL, fr. L, fem. pl. of *-aceus* -aceous] : plants of the nature of ⟨Acanth*aceae*⟩ ⟨Ros*aceae*⟩ — in names of families of plants; formerly in names of orders of plants

¹**-acean** *adj suffix* [NL *-acea, -aceae* + E *-an*] : -ACEOUS ⟨ros*acean*⟩

²**-acean** *n suffix* -S : organism characterized by : organism of the nature of ⟨crust*acean*⟩ ⟨ros*acean*⟩ — in singular corresponding to plurals in *-acea, -aceae*

¹**ace·dia** \ˌasəˈdēə\ *n* -S [Sp *acedia*] : a flatfish (*Symphurus plagusia*) of the West Indies and the So. American Atlantic coast

²**ace·dia** \əˈsēdēə\ *n* -S [LL, fr. Gk *akēdia, akēdeia*, fr. *a-* ²*a-* + *kēdos* care, anxiety, grief + *-ia, -eia* — more at HATE] **1** : the deadly sin of sloth **2** : spiritual torpor and apathy

ace·di·ast \əˈsēdēˌast, -ˌəst\ *n* -S : one afflicted with acedia

ace-high \ˈ⸗ˈ⸗\ *adj* **1** : having an ace as its highest card — used esp. of a hand of cards **2** : high in esteem or favor ⟨he is *ace-high* with the boss⟩

ace in the hole 1 : an ace when it is a player's hole card in stud poker **2** : an effective or decisive argument or resource held in reserve

acei·tu·na \ˌasēəˈtünə\ *n* -S [Sp, olive, fr. Ar *az-zaytūnah* the olive, fr. *zayt* oil] **1** : a West Indian tree (*Symplocos martinicensis*) having a soft light wood **2** : PARADISE TREE 1

acel·da·ma \əˈseldəmə *also* əˈke-\ *also* **akel·da·ma** \əˈke-\ *n* -S *sometimes cap* [fr. *Aceldama*, field bought with the money received by Judas for betraying Christ (Acts 1: 18-19), fr. Gk *Akeldama*, fr. Aram *ḥăqēl dĕmā*, lit., field of blood] : a field of bloodshed : a place of highly disagreeable associations

acel·lu·lar \(ˈ)āˈselyələ(r)\ *adj* [²*a-* + *cellular*] : not cellular : not made up of cells

acenaphth- *or* **acenaphtho-** *comb form* [ISV, fr. *acenaphthene*] : acenaphthene : acenaphthylene ⟨*acenaphtho*phen-anthrene⟩

ace·naph·thene \ˌasəˈnapˌthēn, -af,th-\ *n* -S [ISV *ace-* + *naphthene*] : a crystalline tricyclic hydrocarbon $C_{12}H_{10}$ obtained esp. from coal tar and used chiefly as a dye intermediate and in biology for inducing polyploidy

ace·naph·the·nyl \-ˌthəˌnil\ *n* -S [*acenaphthene* + *-yl*] : a univalent radical $C_{12}H_9$ formed by removal of one hydrogen atom from acenaphthene

ace·naph·thy·lene \-ˌthəˌlēn\ *n* -S [ISV *acenaphth-* + *-ylene*] : a yellowish crystalline hydrocarbon $C_{12}H_8$ made by dehydrogenation of acenaphthene

-a·cene \əˌsēn\ *n suffix* -S [ISV, fr. *anthracene*] : aromatic polycyclic hydrocarbon containing three or more fused benzene rings in straight linear sequence ⟨naphth*acene*⟩

acenesthesia *var of* ACOENESTHESIA

acen·tric \(ˈ)āˈsen·trik\ *adj* [²*a-* + *-centric*] **1** : lacking a centromere ⟨an ~ chromosome fragment⟩ **2** : ACENTROUS

acen·trous \(ˈ)āˈsen·trəs\ *adj* [²*a-* + *centr-* + *-ous*] *of some primitive fishes* : having the notochord persistent through life and lacking vertebral centra

-a·ceous \ˈāshəs\ *adj suffix* [L *-aceus*] : characterized by ⟨aren*aceous*⟩ ⟨argill*aceous*⟩ : of the nature of ⟨herb*aceous*⟩ : belonging to or connected with a division of animals characterized by or of the nature of ⟨cet*aceous*⟩ ⟨crust*aceous*⟩ : belonging to or connected with a family of plants of the nature of ⟨solan*aceous*⟩ — often in adjectives corresponding to biological classification names in *-acea, -aceae*

aceph·al \(ˈ)āˈsefəl\ *n* -S [NL *Acephala*] : LAMELLIBRANCH

aceph·a·la \(ˈ)āˈsefələ\ [NL, fr. Gk *akephala*, neut. pl. of *akephalos* headless] *syn of* LAMELLIBRANCHIA

aceph·a·lan \(ˈ)āˈsefələn\ *adj or n* [NL *Acephala* + E *-an*] : LAMELLIBRANCH

¹**acephali** *pl of* ACEPHALUS

²**aceph·a·li** \(ˈ)āˈsefəˌlī, əˈ-, -ˌlē\ *n pl, usu cap* [ML, fr. LGk *Akephaloi*, pl. of *Akephalos*, fr. Gk *akephalos* headless — more at ACEPHALOUS] : various groups of 5th century and 6th century Christians that recognized no patriarch; *esp* : Egyptian Monophysites after about A.D. 482

ace·pha·lia \ˌāsəˈfālēə\ *n* -S [NL, fr. Gk *akephalos* + NL *-ia*] : HEADLESSNESS ⟨~ of a fetus⟩

ace·phal·ic \ˌāsəˈfalik\ *adj* [²*a-* + *-cephalic*] : ACEPHALOUS

aceph·a·li·na \(ˌ)āˌsefəˈlīnə, əˌs-, -lē-\ *n pl, cap* [NL, fr. Gk *akephalos* + NL *-ina*] : a tribe or other division of gregarines comprising forms with nonseptate trophozoites that do not undergo schizogony (as earthworm parasites of the genus *Monocystis*) — see MONOCYSTIS — **aceph·a·line** \(ˈ)āˈsefəˌlīn, -əl-, -ˌlən\ *adj*

aceph·a·lo·cyst \(ˈ)āˈsefəlōˌsist, əˈ-\ *n* -S [NL *Acephalocystis*, genus of worms, fr. L *acephalus* + NL *-cystis*] : a hydatid or echinococcus cyst that has not developed a head — **aceph·a·lo·cyst·ic** \ˌāˌsefə(ˌ)lōˈsistik, əˌs-\ *adj*

aceph·a·lous \(ˈ)āˈsefələs, əˈs-\ *adj* [Gk *akephalos*, fr. *a-* ²*a-* + *kephalē* head — more at CEPHALIC] **1 a** : having no head or headlike structure **b** : lacking a distinct head (as in lamellibranch mollusks or amphioxus) or having the head reduced and retracted into the thorax (as in certain larval diptera) **2** : having no governing head or chief ⟨an ~ village⟩ **3** : lacking an expected initial element; *specif* : having the first foot in a line of verse abbreviated or missing — compare TRUNCATION **4** *bot* : having the style issuing from the base instead of from the apex of the ovary

aceph·a·lus \(ˈ)āˈsefələs, əˈ-\ *n, pl* **acepha·li** \-ˌlī, -ˌlē\ [NL, fr. Gk *akephalos* headless] : a headless fetal monster

ace point *n* : the first point in backgammon

acepots \ˈ⸗ˌ⸗\ *n pl but sing in constr* [*ace* + *-pots* (as in *jackpots*)] : draw poker similar to jackpots except that a player is not permitted to open without a pair of aces or better

ace·quia \əˈsākyēə\ *n* -S [Sp, fr. Ar *as-sāqiyah* the irrigation stream, fr. *saqa* to irrigate] *Southwest* : an irrigation ditch or canal

acer \ˈāsər, ˈāˌke(ə)r\ *n, cap* [NL, fr. L, maple tree; akin to OHG, OS, & MLG *ahorn* maple tree, ODan *ær*, Gk *akastos*, a maple tree, *akarna* laurel, and prob. to L *acer* sharp — more at EDGE] : a widely distributed genus of trees and shrubs (family Aceraceae) having simple or compound leaves, polygamous or dioecious flowers, and winged fruits — see BOX ELDER, MAPLE

ac·er·a·ce·ae \ˌasəˈrāsēˌē\ *n pl, cap* [NL, fr. *Acer*, type genus + *-aceae*] : a family of trees and shrubs (order Sapindales) having opposite leaves and small clustered flowers succeeded by fruits consisting of two united samaras — compare MAPLE — **ac·er·a·ceous** \ˌasəˈrāshəs\ *adj*

ac·er·ae \ˈasəˌrē\ [NL, fr. ²*a-* + Gk *keras* horn] *syn of* ACERATA

ac·er·a·ta \ˌasəˈrād·ə, ˌas-, -rā-\ *n pl, cap* [NL, fr. Gk *akeratos* without horns, fr. *a-* ²*a-* + *kerat-, keras* horn — more at HORN] *in old classifications* : a class of arthropods comprising the Merostomata and Arachnida

ac·er·ate \ˈasəˌrāt, -ˌrət\ *or* **ac·er·ose** \-ˌrōs\ *also* **ac·er·ous** \-ˌrəs\ *adj* [L *acer* sharp + E *-ate* or *-ose, -ous* — more at EDGE] **1** : having needlelike leaves **2** *usu acerose* : NEEDLELIKE

acera·there \(ˈ)āˈserəˌthi(ə)r\ *n* -S [NL *Aceratherium*] : a rhinoceros or fossil of the genus *Aceratherium*

acera·the·ri·um \ˌāˌserəˈthirēəm\ *n, cap* [NL, irreg. fr. Gk *akeratos* + NL *-therium*] : a genus of extinct hornless rhinoceroses of the Oligocene, Miocene, and Pliocene

acerb \əˈsərb, a'-, -ēb\ *adj, sometimes* -ER/-EST [F or L; F *acerbe*, fr. L *acerbus*, fr. *acer* sharp — more at EDGE] **1** : acid or sour to the taste ⟨~ apples⟩ **2** : acid in temper, mood, or tone : sharply or bitingly ironic, sarcastic, or critical ⟨an ~ time of it sticking pins in the balloons of his pretensions —*Time*⟩

¹**ac·er·bate** \ˈasə(r)ˌbāt\ *vt* -ED/-ING/-S [L *acerbatus*, past part. of *acerbare*, fr. *acerbus*] : IRRITATE, EXASPERATE

²**acer·bate** \əˈsərbət, -səb-\ *adj* [L *acerbatus*] : IRRITATED, EXASPERATED : HARSH ⟨~ and profane writing⟩

acer·bic \-bik\ *adj* [*acerb* + *-ic*] : ACERB

acer·bi·ty \əˈsərbəd·ē, a'-, -səb-, -ətē, -i\ *n* -ES [MF *acerbité*, fr. L *acerbitat-, acerbitas*, fr. *acerbus* sour + *-itat-, -itas* -ity — more at ACERB] : the quality of being acerb: **a** : acidity of taste **b** : acidity of temper or tone : astringency or sharpness of manner

ace·ria \əˈsirēə\ *n, cap* [NL, fr. L *acer* sharp + NL *-ia*] : a large genus of eriophyid mites including a number of parasites of economic plants — see CITRUS BUD MITE

ac·er·o·la \ˌasəˈrōlə\ *n* -S [AmerSp, fr. Sp, azarole — more at AZAROLE] : BARBADOS CHERRY 1

¹**acerous** *var of* ACERATE

²**ace·rous** \(ˈ)āˈsirəs, -ēr-\ *adj* [Gk *akeros*, fr. *a-* ²*a-* + *keras* horn — more at HORN] **1** : having no horns **2** : having no antennae **3** : having no tentacles

ac·er·tan·nin \ˌasə(r)ˈtanən\ *n* [ISV *acer-* (fr. NL *Acer*, genus name of *Acer ginnala*) + *tannin*; orig. formed in G] : a crystalline tannin $C_{20}H_{20}O_{13}$ found in the leaves of the Amur maple

acer·vate \əˈsərvət, ˈasərˌvāt\ *adj* [L *acervatus*, past part. of *acervare* to heap up, fr. *acervus* heap] : growing in heaps or closely compacted clusters ⟨~ fungous sporophores⟩ — **acer·vate·ly** *adv*

ac·er·va·tion \ˌasə(r)ˈvāshən\ *n* -S [L *acervation-, acervatio*, fr. *acervatus* + *-ion-, -io* -ion] : a heaping up : ACCUMULATION

acer·vu·line \əˈsərvyəlᵊn, -ˌlīn\ *adj* [NL *acervulus* + E *-ine*] : resembling little heaps : HEAPED

acer·vu·lus \-ləs\ *n, pl* **acervu·li** \-ˌlī, -ˌlē\ [NL, dim. of L *acervus* heap] **1** : a fungous fruiting body consisting of a compacted and often saucer-shaped mass of threads lacking a well-developed stromatic base and with the upper surface not tufted — compare SPORODOCHIUM **2** *also* **acervulus cer·e·bri** \-ˈserəˌbrē, -brī\ : BRAIN SAND

aces *pl of* ACE, *pres 3d sing of* ACE

-aces *pl of* -ACE

aces·cen·cy \əˈsesᵊnsē, a'-\ *n* -ES : the quality or state of being acescent

aces·cent \-ᵊnt\ *adj* [F, fr. L *acescent-, acescens*, pres. part. of *acescere* to turn sour, incho. of *acēre* to be sour, fr. *acer* sharp — more at EDGE] **1** : turning sour or tending to turn sour ⟨~ milk⟩ **2** : slightly sour ⟨an ~ flavor⟩

ace-showing \ˈ⸗ˌ⸗⸗\ *n* : the bidding of a suit in contract bridge to show possession of the ace but not necessarily length or other high-card strength in the suit

aces·o·dyne \əˈsesəˌdīn\ *adj* [Gk *akesōdynos*, fr. *akesis* healing, cure + *odynē* pain] : mitigating or relieving pain : ANODYNE

acet- *or* **aceto-** *comb form* [F & L; F *acét-*, fr. L *acet-*, fr. *acetum* vinegar — more at ACETIC] : acetic acid : acetic : acetyl ⟨*acet*aldehyde⟩ ⟨*acet*amide⟩ ⟨*aceto*benzoic⟩

aceta *pl of* ACETUM

ac·e·tab·u·lar \ˌasəˈtabyələ(r)\ *adj* [NL *acetabulum* + E *-ar*] : of or relating to an acetabulum

ac·e·tab·u·lar·ia \ˌasəˌtabyəˈla(a)rēə\ *n, cap* [NL, fr. L *acetabulum* + NL *-aria*] : a genus of delicate more or less calcified green algae (family Dasycladaceae) native to the warmer seas and resembling small mushrooms

acetabular notch *n* : a notch in the rim of the acetabulum through which blood vessels and nerves pass

ac·e·tab·u·late \ˌasəˈtabyələt\ *adj* [NL *acetabulum* + E *-ate*] *anat* : possessing an acetabulum

ac·e·tab·u·lif·era \ˌasəˌtabyəˈlif(ə)rə\ [NL, fr. *acetabulum* + *-i-* + *-fera* (neut. pl. of *-fer*)] *syn of* DIBRANCHIA

ac·e·tab·u·lif·er·ous \ˌasəˌtabyəˈlif(ə)rəs\ *adj* [NL *acetabulum* + E *-i-* + *-ferous*] : ACETABULATE

ac·e·tab·u·lum \ˌasəˈtabyələm\ *n, pl* **acetabulums** \-ləmz\ *or* **acetabu·la** \-lə\ [L, fr. *acetum* vinegar — more at ACETIC] **1** : a little cup used in ancient Rome to hold vinegar or sauce at the table **2 a** : the cup-shaped socket in the hipbone that receives the head of the thigh bone **b** : the cavity into which the leg of an insect is inserted at its articulation with the body **3** [NL, fr. L] : one of the cotyledons or lobes of the placenta in ruminating animals **4** [NL, fr. L] : a sucker of certain invertebrates: as **a** : a ventral sucker of many trematodes **b** : one of the suckers on the scolex of a tapeworm **c** : the posterior sucker of a leech

acetacetic acid *var of* ACETOACETIC ACID

ac·e·tal \ˈasəˌtal\ *n* -S [G *azetal*, fr. *azet-* acet- + *alkohol* alcohol] **1 :** any of a class of organic compounds characterized by the grouping $>C(OR)_2$ and usu. made from aldehydes or ketones by reaction with alcohols; *specif* **:** any acetal derived from acetaldehyde (as by the catalytic addition of an alcohol to acetylene or a vinyl ether) ⟨dimethyl ~ $CH_3CH(OCH_3)_2$⟩ **2 :** a colorless liquid $CH_3CH(OC_2H_5)_2$ made by the reaction of ethyl alcohol with acetaldehyde and used as a solvent

ac·et·al·de·hyd·ase \ˌasəd·ˌaldəˈhīˌdās, -əˌtal-\ *n* -s [*acetaldehyde* + *-ase*] **:** an enzyme that accelerates the oxidation of acetaldehyde to acetic acid

ac·et·al·de·hyde \ˌ=ˌ=ˈ=ˌ=ˌhīd\ *n* -s [ISV *acet-* + *aldehyde*] **:** a colorless volatile water-soluble liquid aldehyde CH_3CHO of pungent odor made usu. by oxidation of ethyl alcohol or by catalytic hydration of acetylene and used chiefly in organic synthesis

acetaldehyde ammonia *n* **:** ALDEHYDE AMMONIA

ac·et·al·dol \-lˌdōl, -ōl\ *n* -s [*acetaldehyde* + *-ol*] **:** ALDOL 1

ac·e·tal·ize \ˈasəˌtaˌlīz\ *vt* -ED/-ING/-S [*acetal* + *-ize*] **:** to convert (as an aldehyde) into an acetal

acet·a·mide \əˈsed·əˌmīd, ˌasəd·ˈaˌm-, -ˌməd\ *n* -s [G *azetamid*, fr. *azet-* acet- + *amid* amide] **:** the white deliquescent crystalline amide CH_3CONH_2 of acetic acid used chiefly as a solvent and in organic synthesis

ac·et·am·i·dine \ˌasəd·ˈaməˌdēn, -əˈtam-, -ˌdən\ *n* -s [ISV *acet-* + *amidine*] **:** the unstable amidine $CH_3C(=NH)NH_2$ of acetic acid that forms crystalline salts with acids

ac·et·ami·do- \ˈasəd·əˈmē(ˌ)dō, -d·ˈaməˌdō\ *comb form* [*acetamide* + *-o-*] **:** containing the univalent radical CH_3CONH- derived from acetamide ⟨*α-acetamido*cinnamic acid⟩

ac·et·ami·no- \ˈasəd·əˈmē(ˌ)nō, -d·ˈaməˌnō\ [*acet-* + *amine* + *-o-*] **:** ACETAMIDO-

Ac·et·am·i·nol \ˌasəd·ˈaməˌnōl, -ōl\ *trademark* — used for an antiseptic powder

ac·et·an·i·lide *or* **ac·et·an·i·lid** \ˌasəd·ˈanᵊlˌīd, -əˈtan-, -ˌəd\ *n* -s [ISV *acet-* + *anilide*; prob. orig. formed as G *azetanilid*] **:** a white crystalline compound $CH_3CONHC_6H_5$ derived from aniline and acetic acid and used chiefly in organic synthesis and in medicine as an analgesic and antipyretic — called also *phenylacetamide*

ac·et·anis·i·dide \ˌasəd·əˈnisəˌdīd, -ˌdəd\ *n* -s [ISV *acet-* + *anisidine* + *-ide*] **:** any of three isomeric crystalline compounds $CH_3CONHC_6H_4OCH_3$ derived from anisidine and acetic acid

ace·tan·nin \ˌasəˈtanən\ *n* -s [*acet-* + *tannin*] **:** ACETYLTANNIC ACID

ac·e·tar·i·ous \ˈasəˈta(a)rēəs\ *adj* [L *acetaria*, pl., salad (fr. *acetum* vinegar + *-aria*, pl. of *-arium* -ary) + E *-ous*] **:** used in salads ⟨~ plants⟩

ac·et·ar·sone \ˌasəd·ˈärˌsōn\ *also* **ac·et·ar·sol** \-sōl, -ōl\ *n* -s [ISV *acet-* + *ars-* + *-one* or *-ol*] **:** a white powder $C_8H_{10}AsNO_5$ sometimes used in the treatment of amebiasis; 3-acetamido-4-hydroxy-benzene-arsonic acid

ac·e·tate \ˈasəˌtāt, ˈaas-, *usu* -ād·+V\ *n* -s [prob. fr. F *acétate*, fr. *acét-* acet- + *-ate*] **1 :** a salt, ester, or acylal of acetic acid **2 :** cellulose acetate or its products: as **a** (1) **:** a textile fiber made from partly hydrolyzed cellulose acetate in filament and staple form and characterized by faster drying properties and better electrical insulating properties than rayon made from viscose and usu. by poorer resistance to softening by heat — called also *acetate fiber*; formerly called *acetate rayon* (2) **:** yarn or fabric made of acetate fiber — formerly called *acetate rayon* **b :** a plastic used esp. in the manufacture of film and phonograph records **3** *or* **acetate disk a :** a phonograph recording disk made of various acetate compounds; *esp* **:** one coated with cellulose acetate **b :** a disk recording consisting of a stiff core (as of aluminum) usu. coated on both sides with cellulose nitrate and used esp. for immediate playback

acetate butyrate *n* **:** a mixed acetate and butyrate; *specif* **:** CELLULOSE ACETATE BUTYRATE

ac·e·ta·tion \ˌasəˈtāshən\ *n* -s [by contr.] **:** ACETIFICATION

ac·e·ta·to- \ˈasəˈtād·(ˌ)ō\ *comb form* [ISV, fr. *acetate* + *-o-*] **:** acetate — in names of minerals and coordination complexes ⟨*acetato*-sodalite⟩ ⟨*acetato*pentamminecobalt(III) nitrate $[Co(NH_3)_5C_2H_3O_2](NO_3)_2$⟩

ac·et·azol·amide \ˌasəd·əˈzōləˌmīd, -ˌməd\ *n* -s [*acet-* + *azole* + *amide*] **:** a white crystalline sulfonamide $CH_3CONHC_2N_2SSO_2NH_2$ derived from thiadiazole and used as a diuretic and antiepileptic drug

acet·e·nyl \əˈsed·əˌnil, -etᵊnəl\ *n* -s [ISV, contr. of *acetylenyl*] **:** ETHYNYL

ac eti·am \(ˈ)akˈed·ēˌam, (ˈ)ä...äm; (ˈ)akˈēshēˌam\ [L] *English law* **:** and also — formerly used in certain actions to introduce a clause stating the real cause of the action after a fictitious cause had been alleged in order to establish jurisdiction

ace·tic \əˈsēd·ik, -ētik, -ēk *also* aˈ- *or* -seˈ-\ *adj* [prob. fr. F *acétique*, fr. L *acetum* sour wine, vinegar, fr. *acēre* to be sour, fr. *acer* sharp — more at EDGE] **:** relating to or producing acetic acid or vinegar

acetic acid *n* **:** a colorless liquid acid CH_3COOH with a pungent odor constituting the chief acid of vinegar, made usu. by oxidation of acetaldehyde, by fermentation of alcohol, or by distillation of wood, and used chiefly in manufacturing cellulose acetate plastics and fibers, in making salts, esters, and other derivatives, in the textile and paint and pigment industries, and occas. in medicine as an astringent and styptic — see GLACIAL ACETIC ACID, PYROLIGNEOUS ACID, VINEGAR; compare KREBS CYCLE

acetic aldehyde *n* **:** ACETALDEHYDE

acetic anhydride *n* **:** a colorless mobile liquid $(CH_3CO)_2O$ with a pungent odor and lacrimatory and vesicant action used in organic synthesis, esp. in making acetyl derivatives (as cellulose acetate and aspirin) and in condensations

acetic ester *n* **:** any ester of acetic acid; *esp* **:** ETHYL ACETATE

acetic ether *n* **:** ACETIC ESTER — not now used scientifically

acetic ferment *n* **:** any microorganism or enzyme capable of producing acetic fermentation

acetic fermentation *n* **:** a process of oxidation in which alcohol is converted into acetic acid by the agency of bacteria of the genus *Acetobacter*, esp. *A. aceti* (as in the production of vinegar from cider or wine)

acetic nitrile *n* **:** ACETONITRILE

ace·ti·fi·ca·tion \əˌsēd·əfəˈkāshən, aˌs-, -ˌse-\ *n* -s [*acet-* + *-i-* + *-fication*] **1 :** a turning sour or into vinegar esp. through the action of bacteria **2 :** the production of acetic acid by acetic fermentation **:** the growth in an alcoholic medium of bacteria that produce acetic and lactic acids

ace·ti·fi·er \=ˈ=ˌ=ˌfī(ə)r\ *n* -s **:** an apparatus in which vinegar is produced (as from wine or cider)

ace·ti·fy \-ˌfī\ *vb* -ED/-ING/-ES [*acet-* + *-ify*] **:** to turn into acetic acid or vinegar

acetimeter *var of* ACETOMETER

ac·e·tin \ˈasətᵊn, -əd·ən, -ətən\ *n* -s [ISV *acet-* + *-in*] **:** any of three liquid acetates formed when glycerol and acetic acid are heated together: **a :** the monoacetate $C_3H_5(OH)_2C_2H_3O_2$ used chiefly in the manufacture of explosives — called also *monoacetin* **b :** the diacetate $C_3H_5(OH)(C_2H_3O_2)_2$ used chiefly as a plasticizer and solvent — called also *diacetin* **c :** the triacetate $C_3H_5(C_2H_3O_2)_3$ used chiefly as a plasticizer and solvent and as a fixative in perfumes — called also *triacetin*

ac·e·tize \ˈasəˌtīz\ *vb* -ED/-ING/-S [*acet-* + *-ize*] **:** ACETIFY

aceto- — see ACET-

ace·to·ac·et·an·i·lide \ˈasə(ˌ)tōˌasəd·ˈanᵊlˌīd, əˈsēd·ō-, -əˈtan-, -ˌəd\ *n* -s [ISV *aceto-* + *acetanilide*] **:** a crystalline compound $CH_3COCH_2CONHC_6H_5$ made by reaction of aniline with acetoacetic ester or with diketene and used as a dye intermediate

ace·to·ac·e·tate \-ˈasəˌtāt\ *n* -s [ISV *acetoacet-* (fr. *acetoacetic acid*) + *-ate*] **:** a salt or ester of acetoacetic acid

ace·to·ace·tic acid \ˈasə(ˌ)tōəˈsēd·ik-, əˈsēd·ō- *also* -ed·ik-\ *also* **ac·et·ace·tic acid** \ˈasəd·əˈ-\ *n* [part. trans. of G *azetessigsäure*, fr. *azet-* acet- + *essigsäure* acetic acid] **:** an unstable acid CH_3COCH_2COOH sometimes found in urine in disease — see KETONE BODY

acetoacetic ester *n* **:** ETHYL ACETOACETATE

ace·to·ace·tyl \ˈasə(ˌ)tōəˈsēd·ᵊl, əˌsēd·ō-, -ōˈasəd·ᵊl\ *n* -s [*acet-* + *acetyl*] **:** the radical CH_3COCH_2CO- of acetoacetic acid

ace·to·ar·se·nite \-ˈärsᵊnˌīt\ *n* -s [*acet-* + *arsenite*] **:** a combined acetate and arsenite — see PARIS GREEN

ace·to·bac·ter \əˈsēd·ōˌbaktə(r)\ *n* [NL, fr. *acet-* + *-bacter*] **1** *cap* **:** a genus of aerobic ellipsoidal to rod-shaped bacteria (family Pseudomonadaceae) growing in the presence of alcohol and securing energy by oxidizing organic compounds to organic acids (as alcohol to acetic acid) **2** -s **:** a bacterium of the genus *Acetobacter*

ace·to·bu·ty·rate \ˈasə(ˌ)tōˈbyüd·əˌrāt, əˌsēd·ō-\ *n* -s [*acet-* + *butyrate*] **:** ACETATE BUTYRATE

ace·to·car·mine \-ˈkärmən, -ˌmīn *also* -ˌmēn\ *n* -s [*acet-* + *carmine*] **:** a saturated solution of carmine in 45 percent acetic acid used esp. for the rapid staining of fresh unfixed chromosomes

ace·to·glyc·er·ide \ˈglisəˌrīd, -ˌrəd\ *n* [*acet-* + *glyceride*] **:** an acetylated glyceride

ace·to·in \əˈsed·əwən\ *n* -s [ISV *acet-* + *-oin*] **:** a colorless liquid hydroxy ketone $CH_3COCHOHCH_3$ formed from various carbohydrates by fermentation — called also *acetylmethylcarbinol*

ace·to·ki·nase \ˈasə(ˌ)tōˈkīˌnās, əˌsēd·ō-, -kiˌn-\ *n* -s [*acet-* + *kinase*] **:** TRANSACETYLASE

ac·e·tol \ˈasəˌtōl, -ōl\ *n* -s [ISV *acet-* + *-ol*] **:** a colorless liquid hydroxy ketone CH_3COCH_2OH obtained indirectly from acetone — called also *acetylcarbinol*

ac·e·tol·y·sis \ˌasəˈtäləsəs\ *n*, *pl* **acetoly·ses** \-əˌsēz\ [NL, fr. *acet-* + *-lysis*] **1 :** any chemical reaction analogous to hydrolysis in which acetic acid plays a role similar to that of water **2 :** simultaneous acetylation and hydrolysis

acet·o·lyze \əˈsed·ᵊlˌīz\ *vt* -ED/-ING/-S [blend of *acetolysis* and *-ize*] **:** to subject to acetolysis

ace·to·me·roc·tol \ˈasə(ˌ)tōməˈräkˌtōl, əˌsēd·ō-, -ōl\ *n* -s [*acetoxymer*curi + *octyl* + *phenol*] **:** a white crystalline mercury derivative $C_{16}H_{24}HgO_3$ of phenol used in solution as a topical antiseptic

ac·e·tom·e·ter \ˌasəˈtämad·ə(r)\ *also* **ac·e·tim·e·ter** \-tim-\ *n* -s [F *acétimètre*, fr. *acét-* acet- + *-i-* + *mètre* meter] **:** an instrument for estimating the amount of acetic acid in any solution of it (as in vinegar)

ac·e·tom·e·try *also* **ac·e·tim·e·try** \-mətrē\ *n* -ES [F *acétimétrie*, fr. *acét-* acet- + *-i-* + *-métrie* -metry] **:** the act or method of ascertaining the amount of acetic acid present esp. in vinegar

ace·to·mor·phine \ˈasə(ˌ)tō-,əˌsēd·ō-\ *n* -s [*acet-* + *morphine*] **:** HEROIN

ace·to·naph·thone \-ˈnapˌthōn, -afˌth-\ *n* -s [ISV *acet-* + *naphth-* + *-one*] **:** either of two isomeric colorless crystalline ketones $C_{10}H_7COCH_3$ — called also *methyl naphthyl ketone*

ace·ton·ate \ˈasə(ˌ)tōˌnāt, -ətəˌn-\ *also* **ac·e·ton·ize** \-ˌnīz\ *vt* -ED/-ING/-S [*acetone* + *-ate* or *-ize*] **:** to combine with acetone

ac·e·tone \ˈasəˌtōn, ˈaas-\ *n* -s [G *azeton*, fr. *azet-* acet- + *-on* -one] **:** a volatile fragrant flammable liquid ketone CH_3COCH_3 occurring in pyroligneous acid, made by dehydrogenation of isopropyl alcohol or by bacterial fermentation (as of molasses or corn mash), and used chiefly as a solvent (as for cellulose acetate or cellulose nitrate) and in organic synthesis — called also *dimethyl ketone, propanone*; see KETONE BODY

acetone body *n* **:** KETONE BODY

acetone chloroform *n* **:** CHLOROBUTANOL 2

acetone cyanohydrin *n* **:** a colorless liquid $(CH_3)_2C(OH)CN$ made from acetone and hydrogen cyanide and used in organic synthesis esp. of esters of methacrylic acid; α-hydroxy-isobutyro-nitrile

ac·e·ton·emia *also* **ac·e·ton·aemia** \ˈasə(ˌ)tōˈnēmēə\ *n* -s [NL, fr. ISV *acetone* + NL *-emia*, *-aemia*] **:** KETONEMIA — **ac·e·ton·emic** *also* **ac·e·ton·aemic** \-ˈnēmik\ *adj*

acetone number *n* **:** the number of grams of acetone that must be added to 100 grams of a thermally treated drying oil in order to cause separation of the acetone-insoluble polymerized phase

acetone oil *n* **:** an oil of complex composition obtained in the distillation of acetone and used as a solvent

ac·e·ton·ic \ˈasəˈtänik, -ōn-\ *adj* [ISV *acetone* + *-ic*] **:** of or related to acetone

ace·to·ni·trile \ˈasə(ˌ)tōˈnīˌtrəl, əˌsēd·ō-, -īˌtrēl, -īl\ *n* -s [ISV *acet-* + *nitrile*] **:** the colorless liquid nitrile CH_3CN of acetic acid usu. made by dehydration of acetamide and used chiefly in organic synthesis and as a solvent — called also *methyl cyanide*

ac·e·ton·uria \ˈasə(ˌ)tōˈn(y)u̇rēə\ *n* -s [NL, fr. ISV *acetone* + NL *-uria*] **:** KETONURIA

ac·e·ton·yl \ˈasə(ˌ)tōˌnil, əˈsed·əˌ-\ *n* -s [ISV *acetone* + *-yl*] **:** the univalent radical CH_3COCH_2 formed by removal of a hydrogen atom from acetone

ac·e·ton·yl·ac·e·tone \-ˈasəˌtōn\ *n* -s [ISV *acetonyl* + *acetone*] **:** a mobile fragrant liquid diketone $(CH_3COCH_2)_2$ obtained by hydrolysis of 2,5-dimethyl-furan and in other ways; 2,5-hexane-dione

ac·e·ton·yl·i·dene \ˌasətōˈniləˌdēn, əˌsed·əˈ-\ *n* -s [*acetonyl* + *-idene*] **:** the bivalent radical $CH_3COCH<$ formed by removal of two hydrogen atoms from the same carbon atom of acetone

ace·to·phe·net·i·dide \ˈasə(ˌ)tōfəˈned·əˌdīd, əˌsēd·ō-\ *also* **ace·to·phen·e·tide** \-ˈfenəˌtīd\ *n* -s [ISV *acet-* + *phenetidine* or *phenetidine* + *-ide*] **:** any of three isomeric compounds $CH_3CONHC_6H_4OC_2H_5$ made by acetylating the three phenetidines — see ACETOPHENETIDIN

ace·to·phe·net·i·din \-fəˈned·ədən\ *also* **ac·et·phe·net·i·din** \ˈasətfə-\ *n* -s [ISV *acet-* + *phenetidin*] **:** a white crystalline compound $C_{10}H_{13}NO_2$ used as an analgesic and antipyretic; *p*-acetophenetidide — called also *phenacetin*

ace·to·phe·none \ˈasə(ˌ)tōfəˈnōn, əˌsēd·ō-\ *n* -s [ISV *acet-* + *-phenone*; prob. orig. formed as F *acétophénone*] **:** a colorless liquid ketone $CH_3COC_6H_5$ found in certain essential oils but prepared synthetically (as from acetic anhydride and benzene in the presence of aluminum chloride) and used chiefly in perfumery — called also *hypnone, phenyl methyl ketone*

ace·to·pro·pi·o·nate \-ˈprōpēəˌnāt, -ˌprəˈpīənət\ *n* -s [*acet-* + *propionate*] **:** a mixed acetate and propionate; *specif* **:** CELLULOSE ACETATE PROPIONATE

ace·to·pur·pu·rine 8B \-ˈpərpyəˌrēn, -ˌrən\ *n*, *usu cap A* [ISV *acet-* + *purpurine*]**:** a direct dye — see DYE table I (under *Direct Red 46*)

ace·to·py·rine \-ˈpīˌrēn, -ˌrən\ *n* -s [ISV *acet-* + *antipyrine*; orig. formed as G *azetopyrin*] **:** a crystalline combination of aspirin and antipyrine used as an analgesic and antipyretic

ace·tose \ˈasəˌtōs, əˈsē-\ *adj* [LL *acetosus* vinegary — more at ACETOUS] **:** ACID, SOUR, ACETOUS

ace·to·sol·u·ble \ˈasə(ˌ)tō-, əˈsēd·ō-\ *adj* [*acet-* + *soluble*] **:** soluble in acetic acid

ace·to·thi·enone \ˈasə(ˌ)tōˈthīəˌnōn, əˌsēd·ō-\ *n* -s [ISV *acet-* + *thienone*] **:** an oily liquid ketone $CH_3COC_4H_3S$ formed by the acetylation of thiophene; methyl 2-thienyl ketone

ace·to·tol·u·i·dide \-təˈlüəˌdīd\ *also* **ac·e·to·tol·u·ide** \-ˈtälyəˌwīd\ *n* -s [ISV *acet-* + *-toluidide* (fr. *toluid-* + *-ide*) or *toluide*] **:** any of three crystalline isomeric compounds $CH_3CONHC_6H_4CH_3$ made by acetylating the toluidines

ace·tous \əˈsēd·əs, ˈasəd-\ *adj* [F *acéteux* vinegary, fr. LL *acetosus*, fr. L *acetum* vinegar — more at ACETIC] **:** having the characteristics of vinegar **:** producing vinegar ⟨~ fermentation⟩ **:** VINEGARY ⟨~ comments⟩

acetous acid *n*, *obs* **:** VINEGAR

ace·to·va·nil·lone \ˈasə(ˌ)tōvəˈniˌlōn, əˌsēd·ō-, -ˈvanᵊlˌōn\ *n* -s [ISV *acet-* + *vanillin* + *-one*] **:** a crystalline ketone $C_9H_{10}O_3$ formed as a by-product in the commercial synthesis of vanillin from lignin; 3-methoxy-4-hydroxy-acetophenone — called also *apocynin*

ace·to·ver·a·trone \-ˈverəˌtrōn\ *n* -s [ISV *acet-* + *veratrole* + *-one*] **:** a white crystalline ketone $CH_3COC_6H_3(OCH_3)_2$ made by acetylating veratrole; 3,4-dimethoxy-acetophenone

ac·et·ox·ime \ˌasəd·ˈäkˌsēm, -ˌsəm\ *n* -s [ISV *acet-* + *oxime*; prob. orig. formed as G *azetoxim*] **:** a colorless crystalline volatile compound $(CH_3)_2C{=}NOH$ formed from acetone by the action of hydroxylamine

ac·e·toxy- \ˈasəˈtäksē\ *comb form* [ISV, fr. *acet-* + *oxy-*] **:** containing the univalent acetate radical CH_3COO- — in names of organic compounds ⟨*acetoxy*naphthoic acid⟩; compare ACETATO-

ac·e·tox·yl \ˌasəˈtäksəl\ *n* -s [*acet-* + *oxyl*] **:** a group or radical derived from acetic acid: as **a** *obs* **:** ACETYL **b :** the acetate group CH_3COO-

ac·e·tract \ˈasəˌtrakt\ *n* -s [*acet-* + *extract*] **:** a powdered extract prepared by exhausting a vegetable drug with an alcoholic menstruum containing 5 to 10 percent of acetic acid ⟨~ of nux vomica⟩

ace·tum \əˈsēd·əm\ *n*, *pl* **ace·ta** \-d·ə\ [L, sour wine, vinegar — more at ACETIC] **1 :** VINEGAR **2 :** a solution of aromatic substances in a mixture of acetic acid, alcohol, and water **3 :** a liquid preparation made by extracting a vegetable drug with dilute acetic acid

ac·e·tu·ric acid \ˈasəˈtyu̇rik-, ˈasəˈtu̇r-\ *n* [ISV *acet-* + *-uric*] **:** a crystalline acid $CH_3CONHCH_2COOH$ — called also *acetylglycine*

ace·tyl \əˈsēd·ᵊl, ˈasəd·ᵊl, ˈasəˌtēl\ *n* -s [ISV *acet-* + *-yl*] **:** the radical CH_3CO- of acetic acid

ace·tyl·ac·e·ton·ate \-ˈasə(ˌ)tōˌnāt, -ətəˌn-\ *n* -s [*acetylacetone* + *-ate*] **:** a metallic derivative of the enol form of acetylacetone

ace·tyl·ac·e·tone \-ˈasəˌtōn\ *n* -s [ISV *acetyl* + *acetone*] **:** a colorless liquid diketone of pleasant odor known in two forms [keto form $CH_3COCH_2COCH_3$ and enol form $CH_3COCHC(OH)CH_3$] made in various ways (as by the reaction of sodium with acetone and ethyl acetate); 2,4-pentanedione

ace·tyl·ami·no- \-əˈmē(ˌ)nō,-ˈaməˌnō\ *comb form* [*acetyl* + *amine* + *-o-*] **:** ACETAMIDO-

acet·y·lase \əˈsed·ᵊlˌās\ *n* -s [*acetyl* + *-ase*] **:** any of a class of enzymes that accelerate the synthesis of acetic esters (as acetylcholine) ⟨choline ~⟩

acet·y·late \-ˌāt\ *or* **acet·y·lize** \-ˌīz\ *vb* -ED/-ING/-S [*acetyl* + *-ate* or *-ize*] *vt* **:** to introduce the acetyl radical into (a compound) by any of various processes (as by the use of a mixture of acetic acid and acetic anhydride) ~ *vi* **:** to become acetylated

acet·y·la·tion \əˌsed·ᵊlˈāshən\ *n* -s **:** the act or process of acetylating ⟨~ of cellulose⟩

acet·y·la·tor \əˈsed·ᵊlˌād·ə(r)\ *n* -s **:** an acetylating apparatus used esp. in making cellulose acetate

acetyl benzoyl peroxide *n* **:** a white crystalline compound $CH_3COO_2COC_6H_5$ that is explosive when pure and is used in germicidal preparations and for initiating polymerization processes

acetyl bromide *n* **:** a liquid CH_3COBr similar to acetyl chloride in properties and use

ace·tyl·car·bi·nol \əˌsēd·ᵊlˈkärbəˌnōl, -nōl; ˈasəd·ᵊl-, -əˌtēl-\ *n* -s [*acetyl* + *carbinol*] **:** ACETOL

acetyl cellulose *n* **:** CELLULOSE ACETATE

acetyl chloride *n* **:** a colorless pungent fuming liquid CH_3COCl made by chlorination of acetic acid or its derivatives (as by distilling a mixture of acetic acid and phosphorus trichloride) and used chiefly in preparing acetyl derivatives

ace·tyl·cho·line \-ˈkōˌlēn, -ˈkä-\ *n* -s [ISV *acetyl* + *choline*] **:** a compound $(CH_3)_3N(CH_2CH_2OOCCH_3)OH$ that is released at many autonomic nerve endings, is believed to have a specific function in the transmission of the nerve impulse, and is formed enzymatically in the tissues from choline with the aid of an acetylase or in vitro by reaction of choline chloride with acetic anhydride

ace·tyl·cho·lin·esterase \"+\ *n* [ISV *acetylcholine* + *esterase*] **:** an enzyme that promotes hydrolysis of acetylcholine

acetyl coenzyme A *n* **:** the coenzyme $C_{21}H_{35}N_7O_{16}P_3SCOCH_3$ of transacetylase that is formed as an intermediate in metabolism and that takes part in various biological acetylations and is oxidized in the Krebs cycle

acet·y·le·na·tion \əˌsed·ᵊləˈnāshən\ *n* -s [*acetylene* + *-ation*] **:** the process of combining with acetylene

acet·y·lene \əˈsed·ᵊlən, -etᵊl-, -lˌēn\ *n* -s [*acetyl* + *-ene*] **1 a :** a colorless gaseous hydrocarbon $HC{\equiv}CH$ containing a triple bond that is explosive when compressed but safe if diluted with nitrogen or acetone, that is made by the action of water on calcium carbide or by pyrolysis or oxidation of other hydrocarbons, and that is used in welding and soldering, for removing paint and for illuminating, and for many organic syntheses — called also *ethyne* **b :** ALKYNE **2 a :** the tetravalent radical $>CHCH<$ **b :** the bivalent radical $-CH{=}CH-$

acetylene black *n* **:** a carbon black characterized by relatively high electrical conductivity, made by decomposing acetylene (as by pyrolysis in a retort or by explosion), and used chiefly as a filler in dry cells, rubber, and plastics

acetylene linkage *n* **:** a carbon-to-carbon triple bond

acetylene series *n* **:** the homologous series of unsaturated aliphatic hydrocarbons C_nH_{2n-2} of which acetylene is the lowest member — compare ALKYNE

acetylene tetrachloride *n* **:** TETRACHLOROETHANE

acet·y·le·nic \=ˌ=ˈ=ˈēnik, -en-\ *adj* [ISV *acetylene* + *-ic*] **:** relating to or derived from acetylene **:** like acetylene esp. in having a triple bond ⟨~ acids⟩

acet·y·le·nyl \əˈsed·ᵊləˈnil\ *n* -s [ISV *acetylene* + *-yl*] **:** ETHYNYL

ace·tyl·gly·cine \əˈsēd·ᵊlˈglīˌsēn, ˈasəd-\ *n* -s [ISV *acetyl* + *glycine*] **:** ACETURIC ACID

acet·y·lide \əˈsed·ᵊlˌīd\ *n* -s [ISV *acetyl* + *-ide*] **:** a carbide derived from acetylene by the replacement of hydrogen by a metal ⟨cuprous ~ C_2Cu_2⟩

acet·y·li·za·tion \əˌsed·ᵊləˈzāshən, -lˌīˈz-\ *n* -s **:** ACETYLATION

acetylize *var of* ACETYLATE

acet·y·liz·er \əˈsed·ᵊlˌīzə(r)\ *n* -s **:** ACETYLATOR

ace·tyl·meth·yl·car·bi·nol \əˈsēd·ᵊlˈmethəlˈkärbəˌnōl, ˈasəd·ᵊl-, -nōl\ *n* -s [*acetyl* + *methyl* + *carbinol*] **:** ACETOIN

acetyl peroxide *n* **:** a low-melting crystalline compound $(CH_3CO)_2O_2$ used esp. for initiating vinyl-type polymerizations

ace·tyl·phen·yl·hy·dra·zine \əˈsēd·ᵊlˈfenᵊlˈhīdrəˌzēn, ˈasəd·ᵊl-, -ˈfēn-\ *n* -s [ISV *acetyl* + *phenylhydrazine*] **:** a white crystalline compound $C_6H_5NHNHCOCH_3$ less toxic than phenylhydrazine and used in the symptomatic treatment of polycythemia

ace·tyl·sa·lic·y·late \-səˈlisəˌlāt, -ˌlət, -ˌsaləˈsi-\ *n* -s [*acetylsalicylic* + *-ate*] **:** a salt or ester of acetylsalicylic acid

ace·tyl·sal·i·cyl·ic acid \-ˈsaləˈsilik-\ *n* [ISV *acetyl* + *salicylic*] **:** ASPIRIN 1

ace·tyl·tan·nic acid \-ˈtanik-\ *n* [*acetyl* + *tannic*] **:** a yellowish white or grayish white powder obtained by the acetylation of tannin and used as an intestinal astringent

ace·tyl·tan·nin \-ˈtanən\ *n* -s [ISV *acetyl* + *tannin*] **:** ACETYLTANNIC ACID

acetyl value *or* **acetyl number** *n* **:** a measure of the free hydroxyl groups in a substance (as a fat or oil) as determined by acetylation, being the number of milligrams of potassium hydroxide required for neutralization of the acetic acid formed by hydrolysis of one gram of the acetylated substance

ac·ey–deuc·ey \ˈāsēˈd(y)üsē\ *n* -s [*acey* (fr. *ace* + *-y*) + *deucey*, fr. *deuce* + *-y*] **:** backgammon in which a roll of 3 entitles the player to name and play any set of doublets he chooses and roll the dice again

acft *abbr* aircraft

ac–glob·u·lin \ˈāˈsē-, ˈakˌ-\ *n*, *often cap A* [by shortening] **:** ACCELERATOR GLOBULIN

[1]**achae·an** \əˈkēən\ *also* **achai·an** \əˈkīən, əˈkā(y)ən\ *adj*, *usu cap* [*Achaea*, *Achaia*, ancient region of the Peloponnesus, Greece (fr. L & Gk; L *Achaea*, fr. Gk *Achaia*) + E *-an*] **:** of or relating to Achaea; *broadly* **:** of or relating to Greece

[2]**achaean** \"\ *also* **achaian** \"\ *n* -s *cap* **:** a native or inhabitant of Achaea; *broadly* **:** GREEK

ach·ae·me·ni·an \ˈakəˈmēnēən, -nyən\ *adj*, *usu cap* [*Achaemenid* + *-an*] **:** of or relating to the Achaemenids or the Persian language of their inscriptions

achae·me·nid \əˈkēmənəd, aˈ-, -kem-, -ˌnid\ *n*, *pl* **achaemenids** \-dz\ *also* **ach·ae·men·i·dae** \ˌakəˈmenəˌdē\ *or* **ach·ae·men·i·des** \ˌakəˈmenəˌdēz\ *usu cap* [Gk *Achaimenidēs*, fr. *Achaimenēs* (Achaemenes), 7th cent. B.C. Persian king, founder of the dynasty + Gk *-idēs* (patronymic suffix)] **:** a member of the ruling house of ancient Persia from 553 B.C. during the reign of Cyrus the Great to the overthrow of Darius III in 330 B.C. — **ach·ae·me·nid·i·an** \ˈakəmə-ˈnidēən\ *adj*, *usu cap*

achae·no·don \əˈkēnəˌdän\ *n*, *cap* [NL, fr. [2]*a-* + Gk *chainein* to yawn + NL *-odon* — more at YAWN] **:** a genus of extinct Eocene piglike mammals related to *Entelodon*

[1]achae·ta \(ˈ)āˈkēd·ə\ [NL, fr. [2]a- + -chaeta] *syn of* SIPUNCULOIDEA 2

[2]achaeta \"\ *n, cap* [NL, fr. [2]a- + -chaeta] **:** a genus of oligochaete worms completely lacking setae

achaetous *also* **achetous** \(ˈ)āˌkēd·əs, əˈk-\ *adj* [[2]a- + Gk *chaitē* hair + E -ous — more at CHAET-] **:** having no setae

acha·gua \əˈchägwə\ *n, pl* **achagua** *or* **achaguas** *usu cap* [Sp, of AmerInd origin] **1 a :** an Arawakan people of the upper valley of the Orinoco **b :** a member of such people **2 :** the Arawakan language of the Achagua people

achak·zai \əˈchäk,zī\ *n, pl* **achakzai** *or* **achakzais** *usu cap* [prob. Pashto] **1 :** a division of the Afghans **2 :** a member of the Achakzai

ach·a·la·sia \ˌakəˈlāzh(ē)ə\ *n* -s [NL, fr. [2]a- + Gk *chalasis* loosening, relaxation (fr. *chalan* to loosen + -sis) + NL -ia] **:** failure of a ring of muscle (as a sphincter) to relax ⟨~ of the esophagus⟩ ⟨~ of the anal sphincter⟩

achang \ˈäˌchäŋ\ *n, pl* **achang** *or* **achangs** *usu cap* **:** a sinicized Shan ethnic group occupying two valleys in the western central frontiers of Yunnan province in southwest China

achar \(ˈ)äˈchär\ *n* -s [Per *āchār*] **:** a pickled article of food as prepared in India **:** a pickle or relish

acha·ra \äˈchärə\ *also* **atsa·ra** \", ätˈsä-\ *n* -s [Tag *atsara*] **:** a pickled article of food as prepared in the Philippines **:** a pickle or relish

achari·ace·ae \əˌkarēˈāsēˌē\ *n pl, cap* [NL, fr. Erik *Acharius* †1819 Swedish botanist + NL -aceae] **:** a family of erect herbs or subshrubs (order Parietales) with palmately lobed leaves and monoecious flowers — **achari·aceous** \əˌkarēˈāshəs\ *adj*

achar·ne·ment \ȧshȧrnəmäⁿ\ *n* -s [F, ardor, relentlessness, ferocity, fr. *acharner* to bait, excite (fr. OF, fr. *a-* — fr. L *ad-* — + *charn-*, stem of *char* meat, fr. L *carn-, caro*) + -ment — more at CARNAL] **:** FEROCITY

achar·ya \äˈchäryə\ *n* -s [Skt *ācārya*, lit., one who knows the rules, fr. *ācāra* custom, rule of conduct, fr. *ācarati* he approaches, proceeds, acts, fr. *ā* towards + *carati* he moves, goes; akin to Gk *o-* (in *okellein* to run aground), Av & OPer *ā* toward, OE *ō-* back, behind, OHG *ā-*, OSlav *ja-* (in *jaskudĭ* ugly) — more at WHEEL] **1 :** a Hindu religious teacher **:** one versed in the sacred writings of the Hindus **2 :** any illustrious or learned person in India

ach·ate \ˈakət\ *or* **acha·tes** \əˈkād·ēz\ *n, pl* **achates** \ˈakəts, əˈkād·ēz\ [ME *achate*, fr. OF, fr. L *achates* — more at AGATE] **:** AGATE 1

achates *var of* ACATES

ach·a·ti·na \ˌakəˈtīnə, -ēnə\ *n* [NL, fr. L *achates* agate + NL -ina — more at AGATE] **1** *cap* **:** a genus (the type of the family Achatinidae) comprising very large air-breathing land snails native to Africa but introduced for food in parts of southeast Asia and the Pacific islands where they have become serious pests of agricultural crops **2** -s **:** a snail of the genus *Achatina* — compare AGATE SNAIL

ach·a·ti·nel·la \ˌakətəˈnelə\ *n* [NL, fr. *Achatina* + -ella] **1** *cap* **:** a genus comprising many species and varieties of air-breathing land snails peculiar to the Hawaiian islands **2** -s **:** a snail of the genus *Achatinella*

a·chat·ter \əˈ-\ *adj* [[1]a- + chatter (v.)] **:** CHATTERING ⟨his teeth ~⟩

[1]**ache** \ˈāk\ *vb* -ED/-ING/-s [alter. (influenced by [2]ache) of ME *aken* to ache, fr. OE *acan*; akin to LG *äken* to hurt, fester, MD *ākel* pain, damage, and perh. to Gk *agos* sin, guilt, Skt *āgas*] *vi* **1 a :** to suffer a usu. dull persistent and sometimes throbbing pain ⟨his muscles *ached* from chopping wood⟩ ⟨*aching* with fatigue⟩ **b :** to become distressed as if with dull persistent pain ⟨~ with the deep sadness of it all —H.A. Overstreet⟩ **:** become disturbed (as with anxiety, remorse, or regret) ⟨~ at the very thought of what may happen⟩ **c :** to feel compassion **:** become moved with pity, sympathy, or grief ⟨her heart *ached* for the homeless children⟩ **2 :** to become filled with persistent desire that is dully painful in intensity ⟨his heart *ached* for her love⟩ **:** desire very strongly **:** YEARN ⟨*aching* to see you again⟩ **3 :** to move with dully painful effort **:** STRAIN ⟨eyes *ached* along the shining rails so as surely not to miss the ... flash of speed —Harriet B. Barbour⟩ ~ *vt, archaic* **:** to cause to ache ⟨snowflakes *aching* my eyes —P.D.Boles⟩

[2]**ache** \ˈāk; *in early Modern Eng the -che was pronounced* -ch\ *n* -s [ME, fr. OE *æce, ece*, fr. *acan* to ache] **:** a usu. dull persistent and sometimes throbbing pain ⟨his loathing of the room became a dull ~ in his brain —Morley Callaghan⟩ **:** a condition marked by aching ⟨an ~ in his heart like the farewell to a dear woman —John Steinbeck⟩ **syn** see PAIN

[3]**ache** *n* -s [ME, fr. OF, fr. L *apium* celery — more at APIUM] *obs* **:** any of several umbelliferous plants (as wild celery or parsley)

ach·e·mon sphinx \ˈakəˌmän-, əˈkēmən-\ *n* [NL *achemon* (specific epithet of *Pholus achemon*), prob. fr. Gk, neut. of *achemōn, acheumōn*, pres. part. of *achein, acheuein* to grieve, annoy, fr. *achos* pain, distress — more at AIL] **:** a large hawk moth (*Pholus achemon*) having a caterpillar that feeds on the grapevine and Virginia creeper

achene *also* **akene** \əˈkēn\ *n* -s [NL *achaenium, achenium*, fr. [2]a- + Gk *chainein* to yawn + NL -ium — more at YAWN] **:** a small dry indehiscent one-seeded fruit developed from a simple ovary and usu. having a thin pericarp attached to the seed at only one point (as in the buttercup) — **ache·ni·al** \əˈkēnēəl\ *adj*

1 a head of buttercup achenes, *2* a single achene, *3* cross section of achene

ach·er·o·ni·an \ˌakəˈrōnēən, -nyən\ *adj, usu cap* [*Acheron*, river in Hades (fr. L, fr. Gk *Acherōn*) + E -ian] **:** dark and gloomy **:** DISMAL ⟨in the depths of an *Acheronian* forest⟩

ach·er·on·tic \ˌakəˈräntik\ *adj, usu cap* [LL *Acheronticus*, fr. L *Acheront-, Acheron* + -icus -ic] **:** ACHERONIAN

ach·e·ta \ˈakəd·ə\ *n, cap* [NL, fr. L, male cicada, fr. Gk (Dor dial.) *acheta, achetas* (Gk *ēcheta, ēchetēs*), lit., chirping one, fr. *acheta, achetas*, adj., shrill, chirping, fr. (Dor dial.) *achein* to sound, ring (Gk *ēchein*) — more at ECHO] **:** a genus of crickets including the common American house crickets and field crickets

achet·i·dae \əˈked·əˌdē\ [NL, fr. *Acheta*, type genus + -idae] *syn of* GRYLLIDAE

achetous *var of* ACHAETOUS

acheu·le·an *also* **acheu·li·an** \əˈshülēən, -ə(r)l-, -ōl-\ *adj, usu cap* [F *acheuléen*, fr. St. Acheul, near Amiens, France, location of the type station + F -éen -ean] **:** of or belonging to the epoch of the Lower Paleolithic period following Abbevillian and characterized by biface tools with cutting edges all around

à che·val \ˌäshəˈväl, F ȧshvȧl\ *adv* [F, lit., on horseback] **1 :** with a part on each side **:** ASTRIDE ⟨climbing a narrow ridge *à cheval*⟩ **2 :** in such a way as to straddle a line on the layout of a game of chance (as roulette) or be split between two numbers, cards, or events

achier *comparative of* ACHY

achiest *superlative of* ACHY

achie·va·ble \əˈchēvəbəl\ *adj* **:** capable of being achieved **:** ATTAINABLE

achieve \əˈchēv\ *vb* -ED/-ING/-s [ME *acheven*, fr. MF *achever* to finish, fr. *a-* (fr. L *ad-*) + *-chever* (fr. *chef, chief* end, head) — more at CHIEF] *vt* **1 a :** to bring to a successful conclusion **:** carry out successfully **:** ACCOMPLISH ⟨*achieving* his purpose⟩ **b** *obs* **:** to cause to end **:** make to cease **:** bring about the end of **:** FINISH **2 :** to get as the result of exertion **:** succeed in obtaining or gaining **:** WIN, REACH, ATTAIN ⟨he *achieved* greatness⟩ ~ *vi* **:** to attain a desired end or aim **:** reach a certain level of performance ⟨pupils who fail to ~ after promotion⟩ **syn** see PERFORM, REACH

achieve·ment \-mənt\ *n* -s [MF *achevement*, fr. *achever* + -ment] **1 :** the act of achieving **:** successful completion **:** ACCOMPLISHMENT, FULFILLMENT ⟨~ of an ambition⟩ **2 a :** a result brought about by resolve, persistence, or endeavor ⟨a major scientific ~⟩ **b :** a great or heroic deed **:** FEAT ⟨the ~ of Christopher Columbus⟩ **3 :** performance by a student in a course **:** quality and quantity of a student's work during a given period ⟨standardized tests to measure ~⟩ **4 :** an escutcheon of arms with the adjuncts (as helm, crest, mantling, motto, and supporters) with which it is displayed

achievement age *n* **:** the level of an individual's educational achievement as measured by an achievement test and related to the norm for his chronological age

achievement quotient *n* **1 :** the ratio usu. multiplied by 100 of achievement age to chronological age **2 :** ACCOMPLISHMENT QUOTIENT

achievement test *n* **:** a standardized test for measuring the skill or knowledge attained by an individual in one or more fields of work or study — compare INTELLIGENCE TEST

achi·la·ry \(ˈ)āˈkīlərē, əˈk-\ *adj* [[2]a- + chil- + -ary] **:** having the labellum or lip of the flower undeveloped or lacking as in some orchids

ach·il·lea \ˌakəˈlēə, əˈkilēə\ *n, cap* [NL, fr. L *achillea, achilleos*, a plant, fr. Gk *achilleios*, a plant supposed to have been used medicinally by Achilles, fr. *achilleios* of Achilles, fr. *Achilleus* Achilles] **:** a large genus of north temperate herbs (family Compositae) having divided leaves, small heads of tubular and ray flowers, and flattened achenes — see SNEEZEWORT, YARROW

ach·il·le·an \ˌakəˈlēən, əˈkilē-\ *adj, usu cap* [*Achilles*, hero of Homer's *Iliad* (fr. L, fr. Gk *Achilleus*) + E -an] **:** like Achilles (as in strength, invincibility, or moody and resentful wrath)

ach·il·le·ine \ˌakəˈlēən, -lēˌēn, əˈkilē-\ *n* -s [ISV *achille-* (fr. NL *Achillea*, genus name of *Achillea millefolium*) + -ine] **:** a brownish red bitter alkaloid $C_{20}H_{38}N_2O_{15}$, found in plants of the genus *Achillea*

achil·les' heel \əˈkilēzˈh-\ *n, usu cap A* [so called fr. the story that Achilles was invulnerable except in the heel] **:** a vulnerable point

achilles tendon *n, usu cap A* **:** the strong tendon formed by the united tendons of the large muscles in the calf of the leg of mammals and inserted into the bone of the heel — compare HAMSTRING

achim·e·nes \əˈkiməˌ(ˌ)nēz\ *n* [NL, alter. of L *achaemenis*, a plant (prob. *Euphorbia antiquorum*) used in magic rites, fr. Gk *achaimenis*] **1** *cap* **:** a genus of tropical American herbs (family Gesneriaceae) commonly cultivated for their gloxinialike flowers **2** *pl* **achimenes :** a plant of the genus *Achimenes*

achi·nese \ˌachəˈnēz, ˌä-, -ēs\ *n, pl* **achinese** *usu cap* [by alter.] **:** ATJEHNESE

aching *adj* [ME *aking*, fr. pres. part. of *aken* to ache] **:** that aches **:** causing pain or distress ⟨what peaceful hours I once enjoyed . . . but they have left an ~ void —William Cowper⟩ ⟨for shade there is only this ~ and hollow waste of rock —Edith Sitwell⟩ **:** VEXATIOUS ⟨a useful work of reference in a field where students have long been conscious of an ~ gap —*Economist*⟩ — **ach·ing·ly** *adv*

achi·o·te \ˌächēˈōd·ē\ *also* **achu·e·te** \ˌächəˈwād·ē\ *n* -s [Sp, fr. Nahuatl *achiotl*] **1 :** the seed of the annatto tree **2 :** ANNATTO 1a **3 :** ANNATTO TREE **4 :** a tropical American tree (*Oncoba laurina*) valued for its hard yellow-brown wood

achi·ra \əˈchirə, -ērə\ *n* -s [AmerSp, fr. Quechua] **:** a canna (*Canna edulis*) with rootstocks bearing edible tubers from which an arrowroot is made

ach·kan \ˈächkən\ *n* -s [Hindi *ackan*] **:** a three-quarter-length coat or tunic worn by men in India

achlam·y·date \(ˈ)āˌklaməˌdāt, -ˌdət\ *adj* [[2]a- + chlamydate] **:** without a mantle — used of gastropods

achla·myd·e·ae \ˌākləˈmidēˌē, ˌakl-\ *n pl, cap* [NL, fr. [2]a- + chlamyd- + -eae] *in some classifications* **:** a group of Apetalae comprising plants with flowers that lack a perianth

achla·myd·e·ous \-ˈmidēəs\ *adj* [[2]a- + chlamyd- + -eous] **:** of, relating to, or characteristic of the Achlamydeae; *often, of flowers* **:** lacking both calyx and corolla

ach–laut \ˈäkˌlau̇t\ *n* -s *sometimes cap A* [G, fr. *ach* ah,alas + *laut* sound, fr. MHG *lūt*; akin to OE *hlūd* loud — more at LOUD] **:** the voiceless velar fricative sound represented by the *ch* of German *ach* or the *ch* of Scottish *loch*, phonemically often allophonic with the ich-laut

achlor·hy·dria \ˌāˌklōrˈhīdrēə\ *n* -s [NL, fr. [2]a- + chlorhydria] **:** absence of hydrochloric acid from the gastric juice — **achlor·hy·dric** \-ˈhīdrik\ *adj*

achlo·ro·phyl·lous \(ˈ)āˈklōrəˌfiləs, ¦≠,≠≠¦≠≠\ *adj* [[2]a- + chlorophyllous] **:** having no chlorophyll ⟨a parasitic ~ plant⟩

achmimic *usu cap, var of* AKHMIMIC

acho·li \əˈchōlē\ *n, pl* **acholi** *or* **acholis** *usu cap* **1 a :** a nomadic pastoral people of northern Uganda **b :** a member of such people **2 :** a Nilotic language of the Acholi people

achol·ic \(ˈ)āˈkälik\ *or* **acho·lous** \(ˈ)āˈkōləs, -ˈäl-, ˈakəl-\ *adj* [[2]a- + chol- + -ic *or* -ous] **:** exhibiting deficiency of bile

achol·uria \ˌāˌkōˈlu̇rēə, ˌāˌkōlˈyü-, -kä-\ *n* -s [NL, fr. Gk *acholos* lacking gall, deficient in bile (fr. *a-* [2]a- + *cholē* gall, bile) + NL -uria — more at GALL] **:** absence of bile pigment from the urine in one type of jaundice — **achol·uric** \¦≠(ˌ)≠¦≠rik\ *adj*

acho·ma·wi \əˈchōməˌwē\ *or* **achu·ma·wi** \-üm-\ *n, pl* **achomawi** *or* **achomawis** *or* **achumawi** *or* **achumawis** *usu cap* [Achomawi, fr. *achóma* river] **1 a :** an Indian people of the Pit river valley in northern California **b :** a member of such people **2 :** a Shastan language of the Achomawi people

achon·drite \(ˈ)āˈkänˌdrīt\ *n* -s [[2]a- + chondrite] **:** a stony meteorite devoid of chondrules — **achon·drit·ic** \ˌāˌkänˈdridˌik\ *adj*

achon·dro·pla·sia \ˌāˌkändrəˈplāzh(ē)ə\ *n* -s [NL, fr. [2]a- + chondr- + -plasia] **:** failure of normal development of cartilage resulting in dwarfism and occurring in many animals including man, cattle, and fowls — called also, in man, *fetal rickets*; compare ATELIOSIS, CREEPER 9, [3]DEXTER — **achon·dro·plas·tic** \-ˈplastik\ *adj*

achor *n* -ES [LL, fr. Gk *achōr* dandruff, scurf] *archaic* **:** PUSTULE

achor·dal \(ˈ)āˈkȯrdᵊl\ *adj* [[2]a- + chordal] **:** ACHORDATE

achor·da·ta \ˌāˌkȯrˈdād·ə, -ȧd·ə\ *n pl, cap* [NL, fr. [2]a- + *Chordata*] **:** an arbitrary subdivision of the animal kingdom including all animals lacking a notochord — opposed to *Chordata* — **achor·date** \(ˈ)āˈkȯrdət, (ˈ)āˈkȯrˌdāt\ *adj or n*

acho·ri·on \əˈkōrēˌän\ *n, cap* [NL, fr. Gk *achor-, achōr* scurf, dandruff + -ion -ium] **:** a genus of imperfect fungi (order Moniliales) that is often regarded as a subgenus of either *Oidium* or *Oospora* and is parasitic on the skin of man, other mammals, and birds

ach·o·ru·tes \ˌakəˈrüd·ēz\ *n, cap* [NL] **:** a genus of springtails (order Collembola) including several destructive to mushrooms, various roots and bulbs, and seedlings, and also including the cosmopolitan snow flea (*A. nivicolus*)

ach·ras \ˈakrəs, -ˌras\ *n* [NL, fr. L, a wild pear tree (prob. *Pyrus amygdaliformis*), fr. Gk; akin to Alb *dardhe* pear tree] **1** *cap* **:** a monotypic genus of tropical American trees (family Sapotaceae) having papery leaves and small white flowers followed by a large one-seeded fruit **2 :** SAPODILLA

achres·tic anemia \əˈkrestik-\ *n* [[2]a- + Gk *chrēstikos* knowing how to use, understanding the use of; fr. the hypothesis that the body of a sufferer from this disease is unable to use the antianemic principle contained in the body] **:** chronic progressive macrocytic anemia characterized by a refractoriness to liver therapy

achro- *or* **achroö-** *comb form* [Gk *achroos*, fr. *a-* [2]a- + -chroos colored — more at -CHROOUS] **:** colorless ⟨*achro*dextrin⟩ ⟨*achroö*cyst⟩

achroa·cyte \(ˈ)āˈkrōəˌsīt\ *n* -s [[2]a- + Gk *chroa* color + E -cyte] *anat* **:** a colorless cell; *specif* **:** LYMPHOCYTE

achrochordidae *syn of* ACROCHORDIDAE

achrodextrin *var of* ACHROÖDEXTRIN

ach·ro·ite \ˈakrəˌwīt\ *n* -s [G *achroit*, fr. *achro-* + -it -ite] **1 :** a colorless variety of tourmaline **2 :** a gem cut from achroite

achroma *var of* ACHROMIA

achro·ma·cyte \(ˈ)āˈkrōməˌsīt\ *n* -s [[2]a- + Gk *chrōma* color + E -cyte] **:** a decolorized red blood cell

achro·ma·sia \ˌākrōˈmāzh(ē)ə, ˌak-\ *n* -s [NL, fr. [2]a- + -chromasia] **1 :** ACHROMIA **2** *of cells or tissues* **:** loss of the usual reaction to stains

ach·ro·mat \ˈakrəˌmat\ *n* -s [prob. fr. G, short for *achromatische linse* achromatic lens] **:** ACHROMATIC LENS

achromat- *or* **achromato-** *comb form* [Gk *achrōmatos* colorless, fr. *a-* [2]a- + -chrōmatos colored, fr. *chrōmat-, chrōma* color — more at CHROMATIC] **:** achromatic ⟨*achromat*uria⟩ **:** something achromatic ⟨*achromato*lysis⟩

ach·ro·mati·ace·ae \ˌakrōˌmad·ēˈāsēˌē, -ˌmāshē-\ *n pl, cap* [NL, fr. *Achromatium*, type genus (fr. *achromat-* + -ium) + -aceae] **:** a family usu. placed in the order Beggiatoales that includes large motile aquatic bacteria containing sulfur or calcium carbonate inclusions but no photosynthetic pigments

ach·ro·mat·ic \ˌakrəˈmad·ik, -rō, -atik, -ēk\ *adj* [Gk *achrōmatos* + E -ic] **1 :** free from color **:** refracting light without dispersing it into its constituent colors **:** giving images practically free from extraneous colors ⟨an ~ telescope⟩ ⟨an ~ microscope objective⟩ **2** *biol* **:** UNCOLORED **:** not readily colored by the usual staining agents ⟨~ part of a cell⟩ — see ACHROMATIC FIGURE **3 a :** possessing no hue **:** totally lacking in saturation **:** NEUTRAL **b :** black, gray, or white **4** *music* **:** without accidentals or modulation **:** DIATONIC — **ach·ro·mat·i·cal·ly** \-ək(ə)lē, -ēk-, -li\ *adv*

achromatic figure *n* **:** the mitotic spindle and associated cell structures that do not stain with the usual microtechnical dyes

ach·ro·ma·tic·i·ty \ˌ≠≠məˈtisəd·ē\ *n* -ES **1 :** the quality or state of being achromatic (as grayness of a color) **2 :** degree of being achromatic

achromatic lens *n* **:** a compound lens made by combining lenses of different material (as flint glass and crown glass) having different focal powers, the light that emerges from the lens forming images practically free from prismatic colors

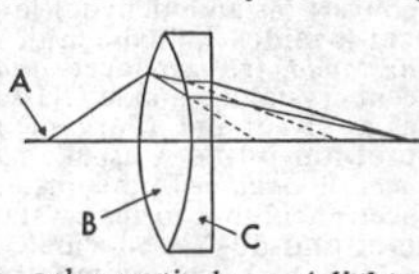

achromatic lens: *A* light source, *B* crown glass, *C* flint glass

achromatic prism *n* **:** a prism made by combining two or more prisms of different refractive index so designed and placed that a ray of white or other nonhomogeneous light passing through the prism is deviated but not dispersed into a spectrum — compare AMICI PRISM

achro·ma·tin \(ˈ)āˈkrōmətən\ *n* -s [achromat- + -in] **:** the part of the cell nucleus that is not readily colored by basic stains — opposed to *chromatin* — **achro·ma·tin·ic** \ˌāˌkrōməˈtinik\ *adj*

achro·ma·tism \(ˈ)āˈkrōməˌtizəm, aˈ-\ *n* -s [achromat- + -ism] **:** the quality or state of being achromatic

ach·ro·ma·ti·um \ˌakrəˈmāshēəm\ *n, cap* [NL, fr. achromat- + -ium] **:** the type genus of the family Achromatiaceae

achro·ma·ti·za·tion \ˌāˌkrōməd·əˈzāshən, (ˌ)aˌk-, -məˌtīˈz-\ *n* -s **:** the act or process of achromatizing

achro·ma·tize \(ˈ)āˈkrōməˌtīz, aˈ-\ *vt* -ED/-ING/-s [achromat- + -ize] **:** to deprive of color **:** make achromatic

achromato- — see ACHROMAT-

achro·mat·o·cyte \ˌākrōˈmad·əˌsīt, ¦ak-; (ˈ)āˈkrōməd·-, aˈ-\ *n* -s [achromat- + -cyte] **:** ACHROMACYTE

achro·ma·tol·y·sis \ˌāˌkrōməˈtäləsəs, aˌ-\ *n, pl* **achromatoly·ses** \-əˌsēz\ [NL, fr. achromat- + -lysis] **:** disorganization of the achromatic part of a cell

[1]**achro·mat·o·phil** \ˌāˈkrōˈmad·əˌfil, ¦ak-; (ˈ)āˈkrōməd·-, aˈ-\ *adj* [achromat- + -phil] *of cells or tissues* **:** having no affinity for stains

[2]**achromatophil** \"\ *n* -s **:** an achromatophil individual

achro·ma·to·phil·ia \ˌāˌkrōməd·əˈfilēə, aˌk-; ¦akrōˌmad·ə-, ˌak-\ *n* -s [NL, fr. achromat- + -philia] *biol* **:** the property of having no affinity for stains

achro·ma·top·sia \ˌāˌkrōməˈtäpsēə\ *n* -s [NL, fr. achromat- + -opsia] **:** a visual defect marked by total color blindness the colors of the spectrum being seen in tones of white-gray-black

achro·mia \(ˈ)āˈkrōmēə\ *also* **achro·ma** \-mə\ *n* -s [achromia, NL, fr. [2]a- + chrom- + -ia; *achroma*, NL, fr. [2]a- + Gk *chrōma* color] **:** absence of normal pigmentation esp. in red blood cells and skin — **achro·mic** \(ˈ)āˈkrōmik\ *adj*

achro·mo·bac·ter \(ˈ)āˈkrōməˌbaktə(r)\ *n* [NL, fr. Gk *achromos* colorless + NL -bacter] **1** *cap* **:** a genus (the type of the family Achromobacteriaceae) of saprophytic usu. gram-negative rod-shaped bacteria that are common in water and soil, form no pigment, cause putrefaction of various organic substrates, and are often active denitrifying bacteria **2** -s **:** any bacterium of the genus *Achromobacter*

achro·mo·trich·ia \ˌāˌkrōməˈtrikēə\ *n* -s [NL, fr. Gk *achromos* + NL -trichia] **:** absence of pigment in the hair

achroö- — see ACHRO-

ach·roö·dex·trin \ˌakrə(ˌ)wōˈdekstrən\ *also* **ach·ro·dex·trin** \ˌakrōˈd-\ *n* -s [ISV *achro-* + *dextrin*] **:** a dextrin that does not give a color with iodine

ach·ter \ˈäktə(r)\ *adj* [obs. Afrik *achter-* (as in *achterveld* interior, backcountry — now *agter, agterveld*), fr. *achter*, adv., behind, after; akin to OE *æfter* — more at AFTER] *Africa* **:** REAR, HINDMOST — often used in combination ⟨*achter*-oxen⟩

achua \äˈchüə\ *n, pl* **achua** *or* **achuas** *usu cap* **1 :** a pygmy people of the Belgian Congo **2 :** a member of the Achua

achuete *var of* ACHIOTE

achumawi *usu cap, var of* ACHOMAWI

achy \ˈākē\ *adj, sometimes* -ER/-EST [[2]ache + -y] **:** afflicted with aches

achy·lia \(ˈ)āˈkīlēə\ *n* -s [NL, fr. [2]a- + -chylia] **:** ACHYLIA GASTRICA — **achy·lous** \(ˈ)āˈkīləs\ *adj*

achylia gas·tri·ca \-ˈgastrikə\ *n* -s [NL, gastric achylia] **1 :** partial or complete absence of gastric juice **2 :** ACHLORHYDRIA

ach·y·ran·thes \ˌakəˈran(ˌ)thēz\ *n* [NL, fr. Gk *achyron* chaff, husk + NL -anthes] **1** *cap* **:** a genus of tropical herbs (family Amaranthaceae) having white or silvery spicate flowers **2** *pl* **achyranthes :** any of several plants of the genera *Iresine* and *Telanthera*

aci- *comb form* [G *azi-*, fr. NL *acidum* acid] acid — in names of acid forms of tautomeric compounds or groups ⟨*aci*-nitro group =NO(OH)⟩

acic·u·la \əˈsikyələ\ *n, pl* **acicu·lae** \-ˌlē, -ˌlī\ *or* **aciculas** [NL, fr. LL, small pin for a headdress, dim. of L *acus* needle — more at ACUTE] **:** a needlelike spine, bristle, or crystal

acic·u·lar \-lə(r)\ *adj* [LL *acicula* + E -ar] **1 a :** like a needle in shape **:** slender and pointed ⟨~ leaves⟩ ⟨~ crystals⟩ **b :** having a sharp needlelike point **2 :** ACICULATE 1

acic·u·late \-lət, -ˌlāt\ *adj* [NL *acicula* + E -ate] **1 a :** furnished with or composed of aciculae **b :** marked with fine irregular streaks like needle scratches **2 :** ACICULAR 1

acic·u·lum \-ləm\ *n, pl* **acicu·la** \-lə\ *or* **aciculums** [NL, alter. of LL *acicula* small pin for a headdress] **:** a needlelike spine or bristle of an animal or plant **:** ACICULA; *specif* **:** one of the stiff setae in the base of a parapodium of an annelid

[1]**ac·id** \ˈasəd, ˈaa-\ *adj* [F or L; F *acide*, fr. L *acidus*, fr. *acēre* to be sour — more at ACUTE] **1 a :** sharp or biting to the taste ⟨~ lemons⟩ **:** SOUR, TART ⟨the ~ juice of unripe grapes⟩ ⟨an ~ apple⟩ **b :** sharp, biting, or sour in manner, disposition, or nature ⟨his ~ way of dealing with people⟩ ⟨an ~ misanthrope⟩ **:** prone to antagonize, wound, or humiliate **:** repellently disagreeable **:** UNPLEASANT, OFFENSIVE ⟨an ~ individual, unable to get along with anyone⟩ **:** CUTTING, CAUSTIC ⟨~ remarks⟩ ⟨~ gibes⟩ **:** CORROSIVE ⟨~ hatred⟩ **c :** sharply clear, discerning, pointed, and usu. more or less mocking or sarcastic ⟨~ criticism⟩ ⟨an ~ analysis of the situation⟩ ⟨~ wit⟩ **:** PENETRATING, TRENCHANT, INCISIVE **:** quick in perception ⟨his cold and ~ intelligence⟩ **:** SHREWD, ACUTE **d :** severe and uncompromising **:** HARSH, RIGID, INFLEXIBLE, UNYIELDING ⟨a censorious and ~ attitude toward freedom of thought⟩ **e :** piercingly intense ⟨the ~ radiance of the bright sunlight⟩ and often jarring ⟨~ splashes of brilliant yellows⟩ or shrill ⟨a singing voice that unfortunately becomes sometimes ~ in the upper register⟩ **2 :** of, relating to, or having the characteristics of an acid: as **a :** having an acid reaction **:** having a pH of less than 7 ⟨~ soil⟩ ⟨a slightly ~ solution⟩ **b** (1) **:** derived from an acid ⟨~ iodide⟩ (2) *of salts and esters* **:** derived by partial exchange of replaceable hydrogen ⟨~ potassium sulfate $KHSO_4$⟩ **c :** containing or involving the use of an acid ⟨~ bath⟩ ⟨~ sludge⟩ ⟨~ hydrolysis⟩ **d :** characterized by or resulting from an abnormally high concentration of acid ⟨~ condition of the stomach⟩ ⟨~ indigestion⟩ — not used technically **e :** relating to or made by an acid process ⟨~ steel⟩ **3 :** rich in silica **:** PERSILICIC ⟨~ rocks⟩ — opposed to *basic* **syn** see SOUR

[2]**acid** \"\ *n* -s [NL *acidum*, fr. L, neut. of *acidus*, adj.] **1 :** a sour substance **2 a :** a compound (as hydrochloric acid, sulfuric acid, or benzoic acid) capable of reacting with a base to form a salt, its aqueous solutions if it is water-soluble tasting sour, reddening litmus, and evolving hydrogen on reaction

with certain metals (as iron, zinc, tin) **:** a compound (HX) containing hydrogen that in aqueous solution yields hydrogen ion (H^+) hydrated to hydronium ion (as H_3O^+), together with the anion (X^-), the degree of ionization in dilute solutions of strong acids (as nitric, hydrochloric, or trichloroacetic acid) being virtually complete, that of weak acids (as acetic or benzoic acid) being possibly one percent, and that of very weak acids (as hydrocyanic or boric acid) being much less than one percent — compare HYDROGEN-ION CONCENTRATION, PH **b** *according to the Brønsted-Lowry system* **:** a hydrogen-containing molecule (as nitric acid) or ion (as hydronium, ammonium, or bicarbonate) that can give up a proton to a base **:** a proton donor ⟨hydrogen chloride is the conjugate ~ of the chloride ion⟩ **c** *according to the G. N. Lewis system* **:** a substance capable of accepting from a base an unshared pair of electrons which then form a covalent chemical bond, many compounds (as boron fluoride, sulfur trioxide, or carbon dioxide) as well as protons and other positive ions being thus included in this class — called also *Lewis acid* **3 :** dilute sulfuric acid used in storage batteries **4 :** something sharp, biting, sour, or corrosive ⟨a social satire dripping with ~⟩ ⟨destroying freedom with the ~ of narrow-mindedness⟩

acid alizarin red B *n, often cap both As & R* **:** an acid chrome monoazo dye that dyes wool Bordeaux red — see DYE table (under *Pigment Red 60*)

ac·i·dan·the·ra \\,asə'danthərə\\ *n* [NL, fr. Gk *akid-, akis* pointed object, needle + NL *-anthera;* akin to Gk *akē* point — more at EDGE] **1** *cap* **:** a genus of African herbs (family Iridaceae) having slender-tubed flowers in loose spikes — see EXOTICA **2** -S **:** any plant of the genus *Acidanthera*

ac·i·das·pis \\,asə'daspəs\\ *n, cap* [NL, fr. Gk *akid-, akis* + NL *-aspis*] **:** a genus of trilobites mostly with long spines found in the Ordovician, Silurian, and Devonian

acid-binding *adj* **:** having the capacity of combining with acids

acid blast *n* **:** a method of etching a photoengraving in which sprays of acid are forced against the face of the plate

acid cell *n* **1** *anat* **:** a gastric parietal cell **2 a :** an electric storage cell with an acid electrolyte (as dilute sulfuric acid) **b :** LEAD-LEAD ACID CELL

acid chloride *n* **:** a chloride (as acetyl chloride, sulfuryl chloride) derived from an acid by replacement of hydroxyl by chlorine and yielding the acid on hydrolysis

acid drop *n, Brit* **:** any tart piece of candy (as one made of sugar flavored with tartaric acid) — compare SOUR BALL

acid dye *or* **acid color** *n* **:** any of a large class of dyes that contain acidic groups (as sulfonic or carboxyl groups) usu. in the form of sodium or potassium salts, that are soluble in water, and that are used in an acid bath for dyeing esp. textile fibers of animal origin and leather or in aqueous or alcoholic solution for staining cytoplasm and various acidophilic structures of cells and tissues — see DYE table I

acid egg *n* **:** a globular or cylindrical receptacle from which acid is forced by compressed air (as in manufacturing sulfuric acid) but which has been largely superseded by centrifugal pumps — called also *blowcase*

ac·i·de·mia \\,asə'dēmēə\\ *n* -S [NL, fr. *acidum* + *-emia*] **:** a condition in which the hydrogen-ion concentration in the blood is increased

acid-fast \\'==,=\\ *adj* **:** not easily decolorized by acids (as when stained or dyed) — used esp. of bacteria and tissues

acid fuchsine *or* **acid magenta** *n, often cap A&F&M* **:** an acid triphenylmethane dye that is now usu. obtained by sulfonation of fuchsine and is used in the form of a salt chiefly in histology as a general cytoplasmic stain and for demonstration of special elements (as mitochondria) and in photographic films as an antihalation dye — see DYE table I (under *Acid Violet 19*)

acid gloss *n* **:** a polish produced (as in stonecutting) with the aid of acids

acid green B *n, usu cap A & G* **:** GUINEA GREEN B

acid halide *n* **:** a halide (as an acid chloride) derived from an acid

acid heat test *n* **:** a test used in petroleum refining for indicating the amount of unsaturated hydrocarbons in gasoline and performed by noting the increase in temperature caused by adding one volume of 93 percent sulfuric acid to five volumes of gasoline in a Dewar flask

acid humus *n* **:** humus with a pH below 7.0

acid·ic \\ə'sidik, (')a's-, -ēk\\ *adj* [²*acid* + *-ic*] **1 :** acid-forming ⟨silicon is the chief ~ element of rocks⟩ ⟨~ oxides⟩ **2 :** ACID

ac·i·dif·er·ous \\,asə'dif(ə)rəs\\ *adj* [²*acid* + *-i-* + *-ferous*] **:** containing or yielding an acid

acid·i·fi·a·ble \\ə'sidə,fīəbəl, a'-\\ *adj* **:** capable of being acidified

acid·i·fi·ant \\ə'==,=ənt\\ *adj* [F, fr. pres. part. of *acidifier* to acidify] **:** ACIDIFYING

acid·i·fi·ca·tion \\ə,sidəfə'kāshən, a,-\\ *n* -S [F, fr. *acidifier* to acidify] **:** the act or process of acidifying

acid·i·fi·er \\ə'==,fī(ə)r, -īə\\ *n* -S [*acidify* + *-er*] **:** one that acidifies: as **a :** a chemical element or group whose presence produces acidity — orig. used of oxygen **b :** a substance (as sulfur or aluminum sulfate) used to increase soil acidity

acid·i·fy \\-,fī\\ *vb* -ED/-ING/-ES [prob. fr. F *acidifier,* fr. *acide* acid + *-ifier* -ify — more at ACID] *vt* **:** to make acid (as by the addition of sufficient quantity of an acid) **:** convert into an acid ~ *vi* **:** to become acid

ac·i·dim·e·ter \\,asə'dimәd·ə(r)\\ *n* -S [²*acid* + *-i-* + *-meter*] **:** an apparatus for measuring the strength or the amount of acid present in a solution

acid·i·met·ric \\ə;sidə;me·trik, a-\\ *adj* **:** relating to or involving acidimetry

ac·i·dim·e·try \\,asə'dimə·trē\\ *n* -ES [²*acid* + *-i-* + *-metry*] **1 :** measurement of the strength of an acid or of the amount of free acid in a solution — compare ALKALIMETRY 2 **2 :** measurement by titration of the amount of alkali in a solution by use of a standard solution of an acid — compare ALKALIMETRY 1

acid·i·ty \\ə'sidəd·ē, a'-, -ətē, -i\\ *n* -ES [F or L; F *acidité,* fr. L *aciditat-, aciditas,* fr. *acidus* acid, sour + *-itat-, -itas* -ity — more at ACID] **1 a :** the quality, state, or degree of being sour or chemically acid **:** SOURNESS, TARTNESS ⟨the ~ of lemon juice⟩ **b :** the quality or state of being abnormally or excessively acid **:** HYPERACIDITY ⟨~ of the stomach⟩ — not used technically **c :** a tartness or sharpness in the taste of wine due to the presence of fruit acids **2 :** the quality, state, or degree of being acid (as in manner) ⟨talking with her usual slightly envious ~ —Mary Deasy⟩

acidity coefficient *n, of rocks* **:** the ratio of the oxygen of the bases to the oxygen in the silica — called also *oxygen ratio*

ac·id·i·za·tion \\,asədə'zāshən, -,dī'z-\\ *n* -S **:** the act or process of acidizing

ac·id·ize \\'asə,dīz\\ *vb* -ED/-ING/-S [²*acid* + *-ize*] *vt* **:** to treat with acid **:** ACIDIFY; *specif* **:** to charge (an oil or gas well) with hydrochloric acid, sometimes with hydrofluoric acid added, for dissolving the lime out of the sand in order to facilitate and increase production ~ *vi* **:** to become acidized

ac·id·iz·er \\-zə(r)\\ *n* -S **:** one that acidizes oil or gas wells

ac·id·ly \\'asədlē, 'aa-, -li\\ *adv* **:** SHARPLY, SARCASTICALLY

acid man *n* **:** a worker who mixes or controls acid solutions used in industrial processes

acid·ness *n* -ES **:** the quality or state of being acid

acid number *n* **:** a measure of the amount of free acids (as fatty acids) in a substance (as an oil or resin) usu. expressed as the number of milligrams of potassium hydroxide required to neutralize one gram of the substance — called also *acid value*

ac·i·do·gen·ic \\,asədō'jenik, ə;sid-\\ *adj* [²*acid* + *-o-* + *-genic*] **:** acid-forming ⟨~ bacteria⟩

¹ac·id·oid \\'asə,dȯid\\ *adj* [²*acid* + *-oid*] *of certain soil substances* **:** like acid **:** potentially acid

²acidoid \\"\\ *n* -S **:** an acidoid substance

ac·i·dol·y·sis \\,asə'dӓləsəs\\ *n, pl* **acidoly·ses** \\-ə,sēz\\ [NL, fr. *acidum* acid + *-o-* + *-lysis*] **:** any chemical reaction analogous to hydrolysis in which an acid plays a role similar to that of water

ac·i·dom·e·ter \\,asə'dӓmәd·ə(r)\\ *n* -S [by alter.] **:** ACIDIMETER

¹acid·o·phile \\ə'sidə,fīl, a'-\\ *or* **acid·o·phil** \\-,fil\\ *adj* [*acid* + *-o-* + *-phile, -phil*] **:** ACIDOPHILIC

²acidophile \\"\\ *or* **acidophil** \\"\\ *n* -S **:** an acidophilic substance, tissue, or organism

ac·i·do·phil·ia \\,asə(,)dō'filēə, ə,sidə'-\\ *n* -S [NL, fr. *acidum* + *-o-* + *-philia*] **:** EOSINOPHILIA

ac·i·do·phil·ic \\,asə(,)dō;filik, ə;sidə;filik\\ *or* **ac·i·doph·i·lous** \\,asə'dӓf(ə)ləs\\ *adj* [²*acid* + *-o-* + *-philic, -philous*] **1** *biol* **:** staining readily with acid stains **2 :** preferring or thriving (as of certain bacteria) in a relatively acid environment — see ACIDURIC

ac·i·doph·i·lus milk \\,asə;dӓf(ə)ləs-\\ *n* [NL *acidophilus* (specific epithet of *Lactobacillus acidophilus,* one of the species of bacteria causing this fermentation), fr. *acidum* + *-o-* + *-philus*] **:** milk fermented by any of several bacteria and used therapeutically to change the intestinal flora

ac·i·do·pro·te·o·lyte \\,asə(,)dō'prōd·ēə,līt\\ *n* -S [back-formation fr. *acidoproteolytic*] **:** any bacterium attacking protein in an acid medium including certain bacteria used for the ripening of cheeses and other dairy products

ac·i·do·pro·te·o·lyt·ic \\'==(,)=;===;lid·ik\\ *adj* [²*acid* + *-o-* + *proteolytic*] **:** of, relating to, or being an action in which there is both acid production and proteolytic digestion (as in the action of certain bacteria on milk)

ac·i·do·sis \\,asə'dōsəs\\ *n, pl* **acido·ses** \\-ō,sēz\\ [NL, fr. *acidum* acid + *-osis*] **:** a condition of decreased alkalinity of the blood and tissues marked by sickly sweet breath, headache, nausea and vomiting, and visual disturbances and usu. a result of excessive acid production — opposed to *alkalosis;* compare KETOSIS 1

ac·i·dot·ic \\,asə'dӓd·ik\\ *adj* [fr. NL *acidosis,* after such pairs as NL *hypnosis:* E *hypnotic*] **:** having or characterized by acidosis

acid phosphate *n* **:** SUPERPHOSPHATE

acid process *n* **:** a process carried on in a furnace lined with acidic or highly siliceous material and under a slag that is predominantly siliceous — used esp. of steelmaking processes; opposed to *basic process*

acid radical *n* **1 :** the negative ion (as the sulfate ion SO_4^{--}) of an acid **:** ANION — now used esp. by analysts **2 :** a radical formed by removal of all hydroxyl or analogous groups (as mercapto) from an acid ⟨benzoyl C_6H_5CO– is the *acid radical* corresponding to benzoic acid C_6H_5COOH⟩ ⟨sulfuryl $>SO_2$ is the *acid radical* of sulfuric acid H_2SO_4⟩ — compare ACYL

acid resist *n* **:** RESIST 2c

acids *pl of* ACID

acid sludge *n* **:** gummy material that separates from a petroleum oil on treatment with sulfuric acid

acid sodium carbonate *n* **:** SODIUM BICARBONATE

acid test *n* [so called fr. the use of nitric acid to determine the gold content of jewelry] **:** a severe or crucial test (as of value, authenticity, or effectiveness) ⟨the *acid test* of our . . . good faith —A.H.Vandenberg⟩ ⟨rationally testing our hypothesis by the *acid test* of seeing how it works —Gardner Murphy⟩ ⟨reading papers is the *acid test* of the teacher —*English Jour.*⟩

acid·u·lant *or* **acid·u·lent** \\ə'sijələnt\\ *n* -S [F *acidulant,* fr. *acidulant,* adj.] **:** an acidulating or acidifying agent ⟨vinegar is an ~⟩

acid·u·late \\-,lāt, *usu* -ād- + V\\ *vt* -ED/-ING/-S [L *acidulus* + E *-ate*] **:** to make acid, esp. slightly acid **:** treat with acid ⟨~ water by adding hydrochloric acid⟩ — **acid·u·la·tion** \\ə,sijə'lāshən\\ *n* -S

acidulated *adj* **:** ACID 1b ⟨a morose ~ individual⟩

acidulated drop *n, Brit* **:** ACID DROP

¹acid·u·lent \\ə'sijələnt\\ *adj* [F *acidulant,* fr. pres. part. of *aciduler* to acidulate, fr. L *acidulus*] **:** ACIDULOUS

²acidulent *var of* ACIDULANT

acid·u·lous \\-ləs\\ *adj* [L *acidulus* sourish, fr. *acidus* sour — more at ACID] **:** acid in taste or manner **:** BITING, CAUSTIC, HARSH ⟨tasting the pungent ~ wood sorrel —John Burroughs⟩ ⟨~ spinsterish pen⟩ ⟨thin ~ voice⟩ **syn** see SOUR

ac·i·du·ric \\,asə'd(y)u̇rik\\ *adj* [²*acid* + L *durare* to endure + E *-ic*] **:** tolerating an environment more acid than the optimum; *also* **:** ACIDOPHILIC

acid value *n* **:** ACID NUMBER

acid wood *n* **:** CHEMICAL WOOD

ac·idy \\'asədē, 'aa-, -di\\ *adj* [²*acid* + *-y*] **:** of a somewhat acid quality ⟨an ~ flavor⟩

ac·id·yl \\'asə,dil, -ēl\\ *n* -S [by alter.] **:** ACYL

acier \\'asē,ā\\ *n* -S [F, steel, fr. (assumed) VL *aciarium,* fr. L *acies* point, sharp edge, fr. *acer* sharp — more at EDGE] **:** QUAKER GRAY

ac·i·er·age \\'asērij\\ *n* -S [F *aciérage,* fr. *acier* + *-age*] **:** the process of coating the surface of a metal plate (as a stereotype plate) with a thin layer of iron by electrolysis, the iron becoming hard like steel **:** STEELING

ac·i·form \\'asə,fȯrm\\ *adj* [L *acus* needle + E *-iform* — more at ACUTE] **:** ACICULAR

acil·i·ate \\(')ā;silēət, -ē,āt\\ *or* **acil·i·at·ed** \\-ē,ād·əd\\ *adj* [²*a-* + *ciliate, ciliated*] **:** without cilia

ac·i·na·ceous \\,asə'nāshəs\\ *adj* [*acinus* + *-aceous*] *bot* **:** containing seeds or kernels

ac·i·nac·i·form \\,asə'nasə,fȯrm\\ *adj* [L *acinaces* short sword (fr. Gk *akinakēs*) + E *-iform*] *bot* **:** shaped like a scimitar — used of a leaf

ac·i·nar \\'asənər, -,nӓr\\ *also* **ac·i·nal** \\'asənəl\\ *or* **acin·ic** \\ə'sinik, a'-\\ *adj* [NL *acinus* + E *-ar* or *-al* or *-ic*] *anat* **:** of or relating to an acinus

ac·i·nar·i·ous \\,asə;na(a)rēəs\\ *adj* [prob. fr. F *acinaire,* fr. L *acinus* berry, grape, grape or berry seed + F *-aire* -arious] **:** covered (as of certain algae) with globose vesicles like grape seeds

¹ac·i·ne·ta \\,asə'nēd·ə, ,akə'nā-\\ *or* **ac·i·ne·tae** \\-nē,tē, -nā,tī\\ [NL, fr. Gk *akinētos* motionless, fr. *a-* ²a- + *kinētos* moving — more at KINETIC] *syn of* SUCTORIA

²acineta \\"\\ *n, cap* [NL, fr. Gk *akinētos*] **:** a widely distributed genus of loricate usu. stalked suctorian protozoa with tentacles in two or three bundles at the anterior end

acing *pres part of* ACE

acin·i·form \\ə'sinə,fȯrm\\ *adj* [L *acinus* + E *-iform*] **1 :** shaped like a cluster of grapes **:** clustered like grapes **2 :** full of small kernels like a grape

acin·o·nyx \\ə'sinə,niks\\ *n, cap* [NL, fr. Gk *akinētos* motionless + NL *-onyx* — more at ACINETA] **:** the genus of cats comprising the cheetahs which are distinguished by the absence of cutaneous sheaths for guarding the claws

ac·i·nose \\'asə,nōs\\ *adj* [L *acinosus*] **:** ACINOUS ⟨an ~ gland⟩

ac·i·no·tu·bu·lar \\;asə(,)nō;-\\ *adj* [NL *acinus* + E *-o-* + *tubular*] **:** of or relating to a gland or other structure made up of tubular acini

ac·i·nous \\'asənəs\\ *adj* [F or L; F *acineux,* fr. L *acinosus,* fr. *acinus* + *-osus* -ous] **:** consisting of or containing acini

ac·i·nus \\'asənəs, ə'sīnəs\\ *n, pl* **aci·ni** \\-,nī\\ [NL, fr. L, berry, grape, berry or grape seed] **1 a :** a small seed or kernel (as of the grape) **b :** an individual drupelet in a multiple fruit (as in the raspberry) **2** *anat* **:** one of the small sacs or alveoli in which the ultimate ramifications of the duct of a racemose gland terminate and which are lined or filled with the secreting cells

ac·i·pen·ser \\;asə'pen(t)sə(r)\\ *n, cap* [NL, fr. L, a fish (prob. sturgeon)] **:** a genus (the type of the family Acipenseridae) of ganoid fishes that includes most sturgeons — **ac·i·pen·ser·id** \\-rəd\\ *n or adj* — **ac·i·pen·ser·ine** \\,==;==,rīn\\ *adj*

ac·i·pen·ser·es \\,asə'pen(t)sə,rēz\\ *or* **ac·i·pen·ser·oi·dei** \\,==,==rō'idē,ī\\ [*Acipenseres,* NL, fr. pl. of *Acipenser; Acipenseroidei,* NL, fr. *Acipenser* + *-oidei*] *syn of* CHONDROSTEI

ac·i·pen·ser·oid \\,==;==,rȯid\\ *adj or n* [NL *Acipenseroidei*] **:** CHONDROSTEAN

ack *abbr* acknowledge; acknowledgment

ack–ack \\'ak-;ak\\ *n* -S *often attrib* [Brit. signalmen's telephone pron. of *AA,* abbr. of *antiaircraft*] **:** an antiaircraft gun or its fire **:** antiaircraft guns or their fire ⟨batteries of *ack-ack*⟩

ackee *var of* AKEE

ack em·ma \\(')ak'emə\\ *adv* [fr. Brit. signalmen's telephone pron. of *A.M.*] *Brit* **:** before noon

ack·er \\'akər, 'a-\\ *n* -S [ME *aker* tidal wave, sea current] *now dial Eng* **:** a ripple or a patch of ruffled water

ack·ey \\'akē\\ *n* -S [alter. of *akee,* the seeds of which were used as weights roughly equivalent to 20 grains of gold dust] **1 :** a silver coin struck in England in 1796 and 1818 for use on the Gold Coast in western Africa **2 :** a unit of value equivalent to one ackey (½-*ackey* and ¼-*ackey* coins were struck)

ackgt *abbr* acknowledgment

acknow *vt* **acknew; acknown; acknowing; acknows** [alter. (influenced by such words as *accord, account*) of ME *aknowen,* fr. OE *oncnāwan* to recognize, confess, fr. *on* + *cnāwan* to know — more at ON, KNOW] *obs* **:** to confess knowledge of

ac·knowl·edge \\ik'nälij, ak-,ək-, -ēj,-əj, *Brit sometimes* -ōl-\\ *vb* -ED/-ING/-S [*ac-* (as in *acknow*) + *knowledge*] *vt* **1 :** to show by word or act that one has knowledge of and agrees to (a fact or truth) ⟨ends generally *acknowledged* to be good —T.B.Macaulay⟩ **:** concede to be real or true ⟨~ that the bombing . . . was a mistake —Norman Cousins⟩ **:** ADMIT **2 a :** to show by word or act that one has knowledge of and respect for the rights, claims, authority, or status of ⟨~ an important contribution to the work⟩ **:** recognize, honor, or respect esp. publicly ⟨*acknowledged* him first citizen of the town⟩ **b :** to take notice of **:** indicate recognition and acceptance of ⟨she *acknowledged* his greeting by a slight inclination of the head⟩ **3 a :** to show by word or act that one has knowledge of and regard for (a duty, obligation, or indebtedness) ⟨~ their moral obligation to the people⟩ **:** express or admit gratitude or obligation for (as a gift, favor, or obligation) ⟨~ his services⟩ **b :** to make known to a sender or giver the receipt of (what has been sent or given) or the fact of (one's having received what has been sent or given) ⟨~ a gift⟩ ⟨~ receipt of a letter⟩ **4 :** to recognize as genuine **:** assent to (as a legal instrument) so as to give validity **:** avow or admit in legal form ⟨~ a deed⟩ ~ *vi* **:** to indicate the receipt and understanding of a message ⟨the pilot *acknowledged* by dipping the plane's wings⟩

syn ADMIT, OWN, AVOW, CONFESS: ACKNOWLEDGE indicates making known to others or recognizing to one's self what might be kept back, suppressed, or left uncertain, esp. under the influence of stress, pressure, or persuasion ⟨I was still smarting at his too candid criticism, all the more because in my heart I *acknowledged* its truth —W.H.Hudson⟩ ⟨with a perversity which he *acknowledged* frankly, he imagined that he had been devoted to her —Jean Stafford⟩ ⟨he started life as the illegitimate son of a Florentine lawyer and a woman of humble origin. His father *acknowledged* him —Stringfellow Barr⟩ ADMIT may be used in situations involving greater reluctance to make known, disclose, grant, or concede and greater stress or pressure ⟨those in whom reason is weak are often unwilling to *admit* this as regards themselves, though all *admit* it in regard to others —Bertrand Russell⟩ ⟨principally because of false pride few people will *admit* being apprehensive or airsick in flight and except in extreme circumstances these cases usually pass unnoticed —H.G.Armstrong⟩ ⟨at last the government at Washington *admitted* its mistake — which governments seldom do —Willa Cather⟩ OWN lacks any special suggestion about the manner or circumstances of an admission or acknowledgment but may apply to admissions having a certain closeness to the personality or individuality of whoever is making them ⟨then let me *own* I'm an aesthetic sham —W.S.Gilbert⟩ ⟨here we *own* to a little private preference —Olin Downes⟩ ⟨I *own* that I had sustained myself through this journey on thoughts of the cheery welcome ahead —Elizabeth Bowen⟩ AVOW suggests not unwilling disclosure but bold, firm declaration, with willingness to repeat or assert in the face of hostility ⟨in a pamphlet defending his political activity, he *avowed* beliefs and displayed a fearlessness that were to make him a national figure thirty years later —F.W.Scott⟩ ⟨let me *avow* at once that I enter this discussion as a layman speaking to laymen —J.S.Dickey⟩ CONFESS may apply to an acknowledgment, often reluctant, of a weakness, failure, omission, guilt, or sin ⟨in his potterings over occultisms he was *confessing* the sterility of intellectual interests —V.L. Parrington⟩ ⟨must I go on weakly *confessing* to you things a woman ought to conceal —Thomas Hardy⟩ ⟨I *confess* myself guilty of this error —J.S.Kenyon⟩ ⟨to *confess* a crime⟩

ac·knowl·edge·a·ble \\-əbəl\\ *adj* **:** capable of being acknowledged

acknowledged *adj* **:** generally known and openly stated to be real or true **:** RECOGNIZED, ACCEPTED, ADMITTED ⟨~ leader of the community⟩ ⟨~ existence of errors⟩ — **ac·knowl·edged·ly** \\-j(ə)dlē, -li\\ *adv*

ac·knowl·edg·ment *also* **ac·knowl·edge·ment** \\-jmənt\\ *n* -S **1 a :** the act of acknowledging **b :** recognition or favorable notice of an act or achievement ⟨received the ~ he deserved as a poet⟩ **2 :** a thing done or given in recognition of something received ⟨an ~ came in the mail⟩ ⟨an author's ~s of assistance⟩ **3 a :** a declaration or avowal of one's act or a fact to give it legal validity; *specif* **:** a declaration before a duly qualified public officer by one who has executed an instrument that the execution was his free act and deed **b :** the formal certificate made by an officer before whom one has acknowledged a deed including as an essential part the signature and seal of the officer

acknown *past part of* ACKNOW

acknows *pres 3d sing of* ACKNOW

ac·le \\'aklē, ə'klā\\ *n* -S [Tag *aklé*] **1 :** a tall Asiatic tree (*Xylia xylocarpa*) **2 :** the very heavy hard durable wood of the acle — called also *pyinkado* **3 :** a Philippine timber tree (*Albizzia acle*) used for cabinetwork and furniture

aclei·di·an \\(')ā;klīdēən, ə'k-\\ *or* **aclid·i·an** \\-id-,-īd-\\ *adj* [F *acléidien, aclidien,* fr. *a-* ²a- + Gk *kleid-, kleis* key, bar, clavicle + F *-ien* -ian] **:** having no clavicles

acli·nal \\(')ā;klīnᵊl\\ *adj* [²*a-* + *-clinal*] **:** having no inclination **:** HORIZONTAL

aclin·ic line \\(')ā;klinik-\\ *n* [²*a-* + *-clinic*] **:** an imaginary line on the earth's surface roughly parallel to the geographical equator and passing through those points where a magnetic needle if suspended freely has no dip or inclination and assumes a horizontal position — called also *magnetic equator;* compare AGONIC LINE, ISOCLINIC LINE

ac·maea \\ak'mēə, 'akmēə\\ *n* [NL, fr. Gk *akmaios* at the height, in full bloom, in the prime, fr. *akmē*] **1** *cap* **:** a cosmopolitan genus (the type of the family Acmaeidae) comprising small conical usu. dark-colored limpets **2** -S **:** a limpet of the genus *Acmaea*

ac·mae·idae \\ak'mēə,dē\\ *n pl, cap* [NL, fr. *Acmaea,* type genus + *-idae*] **:** a family of gastropod mollusks (suborder Docoglossa) comprising the typical limpets with conical shell, fringed mantle, and a single plumelike ctenidium — see ACMAEA

ac·me \\'akmē\\ *n* -S [Gk *akmē* point, highest point, culmination; akin to Gk *akē* point — more at EDGE] **1 :** the highest point or stage (as of growth or development) ⟨reached the ~ of its power⟩ **:** the utmost degree **:** HEIGHT, PEAK, SUMMIT ⟨the ~ of perfection⟩ **2** *archaic* **:** the period of maturity or full growth **3 :** a hypothetical period of maximum evolutionary activity intermediate in the phylogenetic history of a stock between an initial emergent phase and a terminal aging phase

acme harrow *n* **:** a harrow having curved stiff blades attached to a transverse horizontal frame and projecting rearward that crush the clods in front and stir the surface soil in the rear — called also *blade harrow, curved knife-tooth harrow, pulverizer*

ac·mes·the·sia *also* **ac·maes·the·sia** \\,ak,mes'thēzh(ē)ə\\ *n* -S [NL, fr. Gk *akmē* point + NL *esthesia, aesthesia*] *psychol* **:** cutaneous sensation of a sharp point but without pain

acme thread *n* **:** an American screw thread having a section that is a mean between the V threads and square threads

ac·mic \\'akmik\\ *also* **ac·mat·ic** \\(')ak;mad·ik\\ *adj* [*acme* + *-ic* or *-atic* (as in *automatic*)] **:** of or relating to the acme or an acme

ac·mite \\'ak,mīt\\ *n* -S [G *achmit,* fr. Gk *akmē* + G *-it* -ite] **:** a mineral consisting of a brown or green silicate of sodium and iron $NaFe(SiO_3)_2$ belonging to the pyroxene group and often found in long prismatic crystals characteristically pointed (hardness 6–6.5, sp. gr. 3.50–3.55) — called also *aegirite*

ac·mon·i·tal \\ak'mӓnə,tal\\ *n* -S [It, fr. *acciaio monetario italiano* Italian monetary steel] **:** a stainless steel alloy used esp. for low-denomination coins esp. in Italy and Albania

ac·ne \\'aknē\\ *n* -S [Gk *aknē* eruption on the face, MS var. of *akmē,* lit., point — more at ACME] **:** any of several inflammatory diseases involving the oil glands and hair follicles of the skin; *specif* **:** ACNE VULGARIS — compare COMEDO, PIMPLE

ac·ne·form \\'aknē,fȯrm\\ *or* **ac·ne·iform** \\'aknēə,fȯrm, ak'n-\\ *adj* [NL *acne* + E *-form, -iform*] **:** resembling acne

ac·ne ro·sa·cea \ˌaknērōˈzāsh(ē)ə\ *n, pl* **ac·nae rosace·ae** \-(ˌ)nērōˈzās(h)ēˌē\ [NL, rose-colored acne] **:** acne involving the skin of the nose, forehead, and cheeks common in middle age and characterized by congestion, flushing, telangiectasis, and marked nodular swelling of tissues esp. of the nose

ac·ne vul·gar·is \ˌaknē,vəlˈga(a)(ə)rəs\ *n, pl* **ac·nae vulgar·es** \-(ˌ)nē,vəlˈga(a)(ˌ)rēz\ [NL, lit., common acne] **:** a chronic acne involving mainly the face, chest, and shoulders common in adolescent humans and various domestic animals and characterized by the intermittent formation of discrete papular or pustular lesions often resulting in considerable scarring — compare ACNE ROSACEA

ac·ni·da \akˈnīdə\ *n, cap* [NL, fr. ²*a-* + Gk *knidē* nettle — more at CNIDA] **:** a genus of American herbs (family Amaranthaceae) having entire leaves, greenish spicate flowers, and small utricles — see WATER HEMP 1

ac·ni·dar·ia \ˌaknəˈda(a)rēə\ [NL, fr. ²*a-* + Gk *knidē* nettle + NL *-aria*] *syn of* CTENOPHORA

ac·ni·do·spo·rid·ia \akˌnīdəspōˈridēə\ *n pl, cap* [NL, fr. ²*a-* + *cnid-* (fr. Gk *knidē* nettle) + *-sporidia*] **:** a subclass of Sporozoa comprising a number of forms of questionable relationship including the orders Sarcosporidia and Haplosporidia all having simple spores formed in a manner unlike that of the Telosporidia — **ac·ni·do·spo·rid·i·an** \¦=¦===¦=ēən\ *adj or n*

ac·o·as·ma \ˌa(ˌ)kōˈazmə\ *n, pl* **acoasmas** \-məz\ *or* **acoasma·ta** \-mədə\ [NL, by alter.] **:** ACOUSMA

ac·o·can·thera \ˌakōˈkanthərə\ *n, cap* [NL, fr. Gk *akōkē* point, cutting edge (fr. *akē* point) + NL *-anthera* — more at EDGE] **:** a genus of African shrubs or trees (family Apocynaceae) most of them very poisonous having thick leathery leaves and odorous white flowers

acock \əˈ-\ *adj* [¹*a-* + *cock* (to turn up)] **:** turned up or tilted **:** COCKED ⟨with ears ~⟩

acock·bill \əˈkäkˌbil\ *adv (or adj)* [*acock* + *bill* (end of an anchor)] **1** *of an anchor* **:** in place at the cathead or bow and ready to be dropped **2** *of a ship's yards* **:** in a tipped-up position **:** at an angle to the deck

acoel \āˈsēl\ *n* -s [NL *Acoela*] **:** a marine flatworm of the Acoela

acoe·la \(ˈ)āˈsēlə\ *n pl, cap* [NL, fr. ²*a-* + *coeloma* coelom] **:** an order or other division of Turbellaria that is sometimes regarded as a suborder of Rhabdocoela and comprises marine flatworms that lack a digestive cavity with definite walls and that receive food into a porous mass of endodermal tissue

acoe·lo·ma·ta \ˌāsēˈlōmədə\ *n pl, cap* [NL, fr. ²*a-* + *coeloma* + *-ata*] *in some classifications* **:** the Metazoa lacking a true body cavity regarded as a natural group (1) including the sponges and coelenterates and often the lower worms or (2) including only certain worms

acoe·lom·ate \(ˈ)āˈsēləˌmāt; ¦āsēˈlōmət, -sə-\ *also* **acoe·lom·a·tous** \ˌāsēˈlämədəs, -sə-, -ōm-\ *adj* [²*a-* + *coelomate, coelomatous*] **:** without a coelom — compare EUCOELOMATE

acoe·lom·ous \(ˈ)āˈsēləməs\ *adj* [²*a-* + NL *coelom* + E *-ous*] **:** ACOELOMATE

acoe·lous \-ləs\ *adj* [²*a-* + *coelom* + *-ous*] **1 :** lacking a true stomach or digestive tract **2 :** lacking a true body cavity

acoem·e·ti \əˈseməˌtī\ *also* **acoem·e·tae** \-ˌtē\ *n pl, usu cap* [ML, fr. LGk *akoimētoi*, fr. pl. of Gk *akoimētos* sleepless, fr. *a-* ²*a-* + (assumed) *koimētos*, verbal of *koiman* to lull, put to sleep, go to sleep; akin to Gk *keisthai* to lie — more at HOME] **:** monks of large 5th century and 6th century Eastern monasteries who were noted esp. for their choral singing or recitation of the divine office in constant and never interrupted relays

acoe·nes·the·sia *or* **ace·nes·the·sia** \ˌāˌsēnəsˈthēzhə, -en-\ *n* -s [NL, fr. ²*a-* + *coenesthesia, cenesthesia*] **:** loss of awareness of one's own bodily parts or organs **:** absence of coenesthesia

ac·o·ine \ˈakəˌwēn, -ˌwən\ *n* -s [prob. fr. G *akoin*, prob. anagram of *kokain* cocaine — more at COCAINE] **:** a white crystalline derivative $C_{23}H_{26}ClN_3O_3$ of guanidine used as a local anesthetic

ac·o·la·pis·sa \ˌakələˈpisə\ *n, pl* **acolapissa** *or* **acolapissas** *usu cap* [Choctaw *Okla pisa*, lit., watchmen, guardians, spies, fr. *okla* people, tribe + *pisa* one who sees, observer] **1 :** an extinct Muskogean people of Louisiana and Mississippi **2 :** a member of the Acolapissa people

acold \əˈ-\ *adj* [ME, prob. alter. (influenced by *cold*, adj.) of *acoled*, past part. of *acolen* to become cold, fr. OE *ācōlian*, fr. *ā-* (perfective prefix) + *cōlian* to become cold — more at ABEAR, COOL] *archaic* **:** COLD, CHILLED

acol·hua \əˈkōlˌwä\ *n, pl* **acolhua** *or* **acolhuas** *usu cap* [Sp, fr. Nahuatl, lit., strong men, fr. *acollo* shoulder + *hua* having] **1 :** a Nahuatl people of Mexico allied with the Aztec and Tlacopan **2 :** a member of the Acolhua people — **acol·huan** \-ˌwän\ *adj, usu cap*

ac·o·lu·thic \ˌakəˈlüthik\ *adj* [Gk *akolouthos* following + E *-ic* — more at ACOLYTE] **:** following immediately (as a visual afterimage) upon the primary activity aroused by a stimulus

ac·o·lyte \ˈakəˌlīt, *usu* -īd·+V\ *n* -s [ME *acolite, acolyt*, fr. OF & ML; OF *acolite*, fr. ML *acoluthus, acolythus, acolytus, acolitus*, fr. MGk *akolouthos*, fr. Gk, adj., following, fr. *a-* (var. of *ha-* together) + *-kolouthos* (akin to *keleuthos* path); akin to Gk *homos* same and to Gk *kellein* to drive — more at SAME, HOLD] **1 a** *Roman Catholicism* **:** a cleric ordained to the highest of the four minor orders in the Latin Church, his duties being to light and carry candles, prepare the wine and water used at mass, and assist the ministers at mass; *also* **:** one not ordained who performs the duties formerly reserved to an ordained acolyte **:** ALTAR BOY, SERVER **b :** one who assists the celebrant or other officiating ministers in a religious service of any Christian church by the performance of minor duties **2 :** one who attends or assists **:** FOLLOWER ⟨admiring teen-age ~*s* helping him about the depot —Ben Riker⟩

acol·y·thate \əˈkäləˌthāt, -ˌthət\ *n* -s [NL *acolythatus*, fr. ML *acolythatus, acolytatus*, adj., of an acolyte, fr. *acolythus, acolytus* acolyte + L *-atus* -ate] **:** the office or state of an acolyte

acol·y·thist \-ˌthəst\ *n* -s [ML *acolyth*us + E *-ist*] *archaic* **:** ACOLYTE

¹**aco·ma** \ˈäkəˌmō, ˈak-\ *n, pl* **acoma** *or* **acomas** *usu cap* [Sp, fr. Acoma *Akóme*, lit., people of the white rock] **1 :** a Keresan pueblo people of New Mexico **2 :** a member of the Acoma people

²**aco·ma** \əˈkōmə\ *n* -s [AmerSp] **:** MASTIC BULLY

aco·man \ˈäkəmən, ˈak-\ *or* **aco·ma·ni·an** \ˌ==ˈmānēən, -nyən\ *n* -s *usu cap* [¹*Acoma* + *-an, -ian*] **:** ¹ACOMA

acone \ˈāˌkōn\ *adj* [²*a-* + *cone*] *of insect eyes* **:** having ommatidia that lack the crystalline cone of the lens system and that form the image by apposition — compare EUCONE

acon·ic acid \əˈkänik-, aˈ-\ *n* [contr. of *aconitic*] **:** a crystalline lactonic acid $C_4H_3O_2COOH$ formed indirectly from aconitic acid

ac·o·nine \ˈakəˌnēn, -ˌnən\ *n* -s [ISV, contr. of *aconitine*] **:** a colorless alkaloid $C_{25}H_{41}NO_9$ obtained by hydrolysis of aconitine

ac·o·nit·al \ˌakəˈnīdᵊl\ *adj* [*aconite* + *-al*] **:** having the characteristics of aconite

acon·i·tase \əˈkänəˌtās\ *n* -s [*aconitic* + *-ase*] **:** an enzyme occurring in many animal and plant tissues that accelerates the conversion of citric acid first into aconitic acid and then into isocitric acid

acon·i·tate \-ˌtāt\ *n* -s [*aconitic* + *-ate*] **:** a salt or ester of aconitic acid

ac·o·nite \ˈakəˌnīt, *usu* -īd·+V\ *n* -s [MF or L; MF, fr. L *aconitum*, fr. Gk *akoniton*, perh. fr. neut. of *akonitos* without dust, without struggle, fr. *a-* ²*a-* + *-konitos* (fr. *konis* dust) — more at INCINERATE] **1 :** a plant of the genus *Aconitum; esp* **:** the common monkshood (*A. napellus*) — see WINTER ACONITE **2 :** the dried tuberous root of a monkshood (*Aconitum napellus*) formerly much used as a cardiac and respiratory sedative

aconite violet *n* **:** a moderate purple that is redder and duller than heliotrope (sense 4a), bluer, less strong, and slightly darker than average amethyst, and bluer and duller than average lilac (sense 3a)

ac·o·ni·tia \ˌakəˈnish(ē)ə\ *n* -s [NL, fr. *Aconitum* + *-ia*] **:** ACONITINE

ac·o·nit·ic acid \ˌakəˈnid·ik-\ *n* [ISV *aconite* + *-ic*] **:** a white crystalline acid $C_3H_3(COOH)_3$ known in cis and trans forms that occurs in aconite, sugar cane, and beet root and is obtained as a byproduct in sugar manufacture or by dehydration of citric acid; 1,2,3-propene-tricarboxylic acid

acon·i·tine \əˈkänəˌtēn, -ˌtən\ *n* -s [G *akonitin*, fr. *akonit* aconite + *-in* -ine] **:** a white crystalline intensely poisonous alkaloid $C_{34}H_{47}NO_{11}$ from the root and leaves of aconite

ac·o·ni·tum \ˌakəˈnīdəm\ *n* [NL, fr. L] **1** *cap* **:** a genus of poisonous herbs (family Ranunculaceae) found in temperate regions and having palmately divided leaves and very irregular blue, purple, or yellow flowers **2** -s **:** a plant of the genus *Aconitum* — see MONKSHOOD, WOLFSBANE **3** -s **:** ACONITE 2

acon·ti·as \əˈkänchēəs\ *n, cap* [NL, fr. Gk *akontias*, a snake, fr. *akont-*, *akōn* javelin, dart, fr. *akē* point — more at EDGE] **:** a genus of scincoid lizards with the limbs rudimentary or lacking

acon·ti·um \əˈkänchēəm\ *n, pl* **acon·tia** \-ēə\ *or* **acontiums** [NL, fr. Gk *akontion* javelin, dim. of *akont-, akōn*] *zool* **:** one of the free threads continued from the lower ends of the septa of certain actinians, histologically similar to cnidoglandular bands, protruding through the mouth when the animal contracts, and prob. defensive

a con·trar·io \ˌäkənˈtra(a)rēˌō\ *adv* [L] **:** by or from contraries — used of an argument based on contrast

aco·pa \əˈkōpə\ [NL, fr. ²*a-* + Gk *kōpē* oar; fr. the belief that they are without directive organs] *syn of* ASCIDIACEA

acorn \ˈāˌkȯrn, -ˌkō(ə)n *also* ˈākə(r)n\ *n* -s [ME, alter. (influenced by *corn*) of *akern*, fr. OE *æcern*; akin to MHG *ackeran* acorns collectively, ON *akarn* fruit of forest trees, Goth *akran* fruit, produce, IrGael *āirne* sloe, Russ *yagoda* berry] **1 :** the nut of the oak usu. seated in or surrounded by a hard woody cupule of indurated bracts **2 :** a small conical or globular object (as of wood or metal): as **a :** a turned ornamentation commonly used as a finial or pendant in Jacobean furniture **b :** an ornamental piece of wood fixed above the vane of a masthead or a piece of metal used at the top of an upright in a ship's railing **3 :** a grayish yellowish brown that is darker than deer and slightly yellower and lighter than olive wood — called also *meadowlark*

acorns

acorn barnacle *also* **acorn shell** *n* **:** any of numerous conical sessile barnacles (family Balanidae) common on littoral rocks

acorn calf *n* [so called fr. the belief the condition is caused by an excess of acorns in prenatal diet] **:** a calf exhibiting a congenital anomaly involving shortening of the limbs, malformation of the skull, incoordination, and intestinal tympany

acorn cup *n* **:** the cupule of an acorn

acorn disease *n* **:** a virus disease of citrus (as oranges) considered identical with or an expression of stubborn disease and characterized by malformed and more or less acorn-shaped fruit

acorn duck *n* [so called fr. its eating acorns] **:** WOOD DUCK 1

acorn squash *n* **:** a winter squash about four to six inches in width, oval to somewhat acorn-shaped, having a longitudinally grooved and ridged surface, with skin usu. dark green in color but varying to orange yellow esp. at maturity or in storage, and with sweet yellow to orange flesh

acorn tube *n* **:** a very small vacuum tube resembling an acorn in shape and used at extremely high frequencies

acorn weevil *n* **:** any of several long-snouted weevils (genus *Balaninus*) whose larvae feed on acorns

acorn worm *n* [so called fr. the shape of the front part of the body] **:** a worm of the group Enteropneusta

à corps per·du \äkȯ̇rperdüe\ *adv* [F, lit., with lost body] **:** IMPETUOUSLY, DESPERATELY

ac·o·rus \ˈakərəs\ *n, cap* [NL, fr. L, an aromatic plant (perh. sweet flag), fr. Gk *akoros* (*Iris pseudacorus*)] **:** a genus of rushlike herbs (family Araceae) with the flowers in a close spadix — see SWEET FLAG

acos·mic \(ˈ)āˈkäzmik\ *adj* [²*a-* + *cosmic*] **:** denying the objective reality of the temporal world **:** transcendental in a world-negating sense ⟨the Hindu's two aspects of God: cosmic and ~, relative and transcendental⟩

acos·mism *or* **akos·mism** \(ˈ)āˈkäzˌmizəm\ *n* -s [G *akosmismus*, fr. *a-* ²*a-* + *kosmos* cosmos + *-ismus* -ism — more at COSMOS] **:** a theory that denies that the universe possesses any absolute reality or that it has any existence apart from God — compare PANTHEISM

acos·mist \-zməst\ *n* -s [*acosmism* + *-ist*] **:** one who believes in or teaches acosmism — **acos·mis·tic** \ˌāˌkäzˈmistik\ *adj*

acot·y·le·don \ˌāˌkädᵊlˈēdᵊn, ˈā¦==,==, ˈ=,===\ *n* -s [F *acotylédone*, fr. *a-* ²*a-* + *cotylédone* cotyledon] **:** a plant without cotyledons (as the dodder) — **acot·y·le·don·ous** \¦=,==¦==əs, -¦ed-\ *adj*

acou- *or* **acouo-** *comb form* [F *acou-*, fr. Gk *akouein* to hear — more at HEAR] **:** hearing **:** listening ⟨*acou*meter⟩ ⟨*acouo*phonia⟩

acou·chi *also* **acu·chi** \əˈküshē\ *or* **acouchi resin** *n* -s [native name in Guiana] **:** a resin similar in nature and uses to elemi and obtained from various So. American trees of the genus *Protium*

acou·me·ter \əˈkümədə(r), aˈ-, ˈaˌkü,mēd-\ *n* -s [F *acoumètre*, fr. *acou-* + *-mètre* -meter] **:** AUDIOMETER

acou·me·try \əˈkümə·trē, aˈ-\ *n* -ES [F *acoumétrie*, fr. *acou-* + *-métrie* -metry] **:** AUDIOMETRY

-acousia *or* **-acusia** *n comb form, pl* **-acousiae** *or* **-acusiae** [NL, fr. Gk *akousis* (fr. *akouein* to hear + *-sis*) + NL *-ia*] **:** hearing ⟨presby*acousia*⟩ ⟨hyper*acusia*⟩

acous·ma \əˈküzmə, aˈ-\ *n, pl* **acousmas** \-məz\ *or* **acousma·ta** \-mədə\ [NL, fr. Gk, something heard, fr. *akouein* to hear] **1 :** an auditory hallucination of a simple nonverbal character (as a buzzing or ringing) **2** *acousmata pl* **:** exoteric teachings

ac·ous·mat·ic \ˌaˌküzˈmad·ik\ *n* -s [Gk *kousmatikos*, fr. *akousmat-, akousma* + *-ikos* -ic] **:** one who received the exoteric teachings of the Pythagoreans

¹**acous·tic** \əˈküstik, -tēk *also* -kyüs- *or* -kau̇s-\ *or* **acous·ti·cal** \-tə̇kəl, -ēk-\ *adj* [*acoustic* fr. Gk *akoustikos* of hearing, fr. *akoustos* heard, audible (fr. *akouein* to hear) + *-ikos* -ic; *acoustical* fr. *acoustic* + *-al* — more at HEAR] **1 a :** of, relating to, adapted to, or affecting the sense of hearing or the organs of hearing ⟨the ~ apparatus of the human ear⟩ — compare AUDITORY, AURAL **b :** of or relating to sound or sound waves ⟨the ~ intensity of a shrill voice⟩ **:** deriving from sound ⟨~ energy⟩ **c :** controlled or actuated by sound or sound waves ⟨the ship was blown up by an ~ mine⟩ **d :** influencing sound or sound waves (as in direction or speed) ⟨their voices rang back from the ~ barrier of the high cliff before them⟩ **e :** of, relating to, or concerned with acoustics ⟨~ engineering⟩ **:** specializing in acoustics ⟨an ~ contractor⟩ **2 a :** made for, designed for, or having the quality of facilitating or improving the perception of sound ⟨a tiny ~ device very efficient in promoting hearing⟩ **:** designed or serving to produce, carry, or diffuse sound ⟨a highly efficient ~ system⟩ **b :** made for, designed for, or having the quality of controlling sound; *esp* **:** designed to eliminate or lessen noise and other unwanted sound (as reverberations or echoes) **:** noise-absorbent or sound-absorbent ⟨an ~ ceiling⟩ ⟨~ wallboard⟩ ⟨~ tile⟩ **3 a** (1) **:** of, relating to, adapted to, or produced by a method of recording sound by the use of a thin diaphragm vibrated directly by sound waves, the vibrations being in turn transmitted directly by the diaphragm to a recording stylus that cuts corresponding grooves (as in a revolving disc) (2) **:** of, relating to, adapted to, or produced by a method of reproducing sound by the use of a reproducing stylus whose vibrations are transmitted directly to a thin diaphragm, the corresponding vibrations of the diaphragm being directly amplified to produce audible sound ⟨an ~ recording⟩ — compare ELECTRIC 1b **b :** of, relating to, or adapted to measurement of depth (as of the ocean) by means of sonic or ultrasonic vibrations ⟨~ soundings⟩ — **acous·ti·cal·ly** \-k(ə)lē, -ili\ *adv*

²**acoustic** *var of* ACOUSTICS

acoustical feedback *n* **:** a rumbling, whining, or whistling sound resulting esp. from excessive leakage of sound from the output of an electroacoustical system to the input

acoustic area *or* **acoustic center** *n* **:** a sensory area of the temporal lobe of the cerebral cortex receiving afferent projection fibers concerned with the sense of hearing

acoustic bass *n* **:** a 32-foot or 64-foot organ register obtained by the production of resultant tones by smaller pipes — compare COMBINATION TONE

acoustic duct *or* **acoustic meatus** *n* **:** the external auditory meatus

ac·ous·ti·cian \ˌaˌküˈstishən, əˌk- *also* -kyü- *or* -kau̇-\ *n* -s [*acoustics* + *-ian*] **1 :** one versed in the science of acoustics **2 :** one versed in the practice of acoustics **:** one who designs, makes, or repairs acoustic materials, instruments, and apparatus or who sets up or looks after acoustic installations

acoustic impedance *n* **:** the ratio of sound-pressure amplitude to volume-velocity amplitude across a given surface in a medium transmitting sound, the relationship being measured in acoustic ohms and commonly treated as a complex quantity whose components are acoustic reactance and acoustic resistance **:** the acoustic analogue of reactance in alternating-current circuits

acoustic inertance *or* **acoustic mass** *n* **:** the impeding effect of inertia upon the transmission of sound in a conduit, equal in a tubular conduit (as an organ pipe) to the mass of the vibrating medium divided by the square of the cross section **:** the acoustic analogue of alternating-current-circuit inductance — called also *inertance*

acoustic interferometer *n* **:** an instrument similar in principle to the interferometer and adapted to the accurate measurement of sound wavelengths and velocities

acoustic nerve *n* **:** AUDITORY NERVE

acoustic ohm *n* **:** OHM

acous·ti·co·lat·er·al \əˌküstə̇(ˌ)kōˈ-, -stē- *also* -kyüs- *or* -kau̇s-\ *adj* [¹*acoustic* + *-o-* + *lateral*] **:** of or relating to the lateral-line organs and their central connection with the ear

acoustic organ *n* **:** ORGAN OF CORTI

acoustic radiation pressure *n* **:** a feeble net increase in atmospheric pressure experienced by a surface upon which sound waves are incident — compare SOUND PRESSURE

acoustic reactance *n* **:** the imaginary component of acoustic impedance measured in acoustic ohms and concerned with the effects of inertia and elasticity of a medium transmitting sound and differing one-quarter cycle in phase from acoustic resistance **:** the acoustic analogue of reactance in alternating-current circuits

acoustic resistance *n* **:** the real component of acoustic impedance measured in acoustic ohms and involving dissipation of energy through internal friction of a medium transmitting sound and differing one-quarter cycle in phase from acoustic reactance **:** the analogue of resistance in alternating-current circuits

acous·tics \=ˈ=tiks, -ēks\ *n pl but sing or pl in constr* **1 :** a science that deals with the production, control, transmission, reception, and effects of sound and of the phenomena of hearing **2 a** *also* **acoustic :** the aggregate of qualities (as absence of echo or reverberation) of an enclosure (as an auditorium) or other area that affects production, control, transmission, reception, and perception of sound **:** acoustic properties or peculiarities **:** acoustic environment ⟨the ~ of this room are excellent⟩ ⟨in the clear, dead *acoustic* of such halls every musical fault is audible —Virgil Thomson⟩ **b :** the science of planning, building, equipping, or using an enclosure or other area with the object of achieving good acoustics

acoustic tubercle *n* **:** a pear-shaped prominence on the restiform body including the dorsal nucleus of the cochlear nerve

acpt *abbr* acceptance

¹**ac·quaint** \əˈkwānt *also* aˈ-\ *adj* [ME *aquointe, aquainte*, fr. OF *acointe*, fr. LL *accognitus*, past part. of *accognoscere* to know perfectly, fr. L *ad-* + *cognoscere* to know — more at COGNITION] *archaic* **:** ACQUAINTED

²**acquaint** \"\ *vb* -ED/-ING/-S [ME *acoynten, aquainten*, fr. OF *acointier*, fr. ML *accognitare*, fr. LL *acccognitus*] *vt* **1 :** to make known socially **:** INTRODUCE ⟨someone should make them ~*ed*⟩ ⟨I am not ~*ed* with him⟩ ⟨the manager wishes to get ~*ed* with every employee⟩ **2 :** INFORM, APPRISE ⟨~ a new employee with his duties⟩ ⟨we ~*ed* him with our plans⟩ ⟨~ oneself with the facts of a case⟩ **3** *obs* **:** ACCUSTOM, HABITUATE **~** *vi, archaic* **:** to become acquainted — usu. used with *with* **syn** see INFORM

ac·quaint·ance \-tᵊn(t)s, -tən-\ *n* -s [ME *acointaunce, aquaintaunce*, fr. MF *acointance*, fr. *acointier* + *-ance*] **1 a :** personal knowledge ⟨an ~ with all types of men⟩ **:** FAMILIARITY, EXPERIENCE ⟨long ~ with Amazon river Indians⟩ **b :** the quality or state of being acquainted **:** mutual knowledge or familiarity ⟨their ~ was of long standing⟩ **2 a :** persons with whom one is acquainted ⟨let your men-*acquaintance* be of your husband's choice —Jonathan Swift⟩ — sometimes pl. in constr. ⟨the ~ . . . were unworthy of her —Jane Austen⟩ **b :** a not particularly close or intimate friend **:** a person with whom one has had some social contact but for whom one has no strong personal attachment **syn** see FRIEND

ac·quaint·ance·ship \-ānᵊn(t)sˌship, -tən-\ *n* -s **:** ACQUAINTANCE 1b

acquaintant *n* -s [obs. F *acointant*, fr. pres. part. of *acointier*] *obs* **:** ACQUAINTANCE 2

acquainted *adj* [ME *acointed, aquainted*, fr. past part. of *acointen, aquainten*] **1 a :** being known to and having knowledge of ⟨he was here so little, we never really got ~ —Mary Austin⟩ ⟨thoroughly ~ with him⟩ **b** *archaic* **:** personally known **:** FAMILIAR **2 :** having personal knowledge of **:** being somewhat familiar with ⟨reveals herself as not too well ~ with the conditions of women in America —M.F.A.Montagu⟩

ac·quent \əˈkwent\ *adj* [ME *aquente*, var. of *aquainte*] *Scot* **:** ACQUAINTED

ac·quest \əˈkwest, aˈ-\ *n* -s [obs. F (now *acquêt*), fr. (assumed) VL *acquaesitum*, fr. neut. of *acquaesitus*, past part. of *acquaerere* to acquire, alter. of L *acquirere* — more at ACQUIRE] **1** *archaic* **:** the act or action of acquiring **2** *archaic* **:** ACQUISITION **3 :** property acquired through means other than inheritance

ac·qui·esce \ˌakwēˈes\ *vi* -ED/-ING/-S [F *acquiescer*, fr. L *acquiescere* to rest, rejoice in, acquiesce, fr. *ad-* + *quiescere* to be quiet — more at QUIET] **1** *obs* **:** to rest satisfied physically or mentally **2** *obs* **:** to remain submissive — used with *under* **3 :** to accept or comply tacitly or passively **:** accept as inevitable or indisputable — often used with *in*, sometimes with *to*, and formerly with *with* ⟨led by the influence of his upbringing to ~ too much —*Times Lit. Supp.*⟩ ⟨if we ~ in this poorly disguised swindle —Sam Hunter⟩ ⟨political sociologists today are often reluctant to ~ to Michels' law —L.S.Feuer⟩ **syn** see ASSENT

ac·qui·es·cence \ˌakwēˈesᵊn(t)s\ *n* -s [obs. F, fr. (assumed) VL *acquiescentia*, fr. L *acquiescent-, acquiescens* + *-ia*] **1 :** the act or action of acquiescing ⟨his immediate ~ to every demand⟩ — often used with *in*, sometimes with *to*, and formerly with *with* **2 :** the quality or state of being acquiescent **:** passive assent or submission ⟨too great an ~ in American foreign policy —Woodrow Wyatt⟩

acquiescency *n* -ES [obs. F *acquiescence* + E *-y*] *obs* **:** ACQUIESCENCE

ac·qui·es·cent \ˌakwēˈesᵊnt\ *adj* [L *acquiescent-, acquiescens*, pres. part. of *acquiescere*] **:** acquiescing or disposed to acquiesce ⟨they are, if anything, too law-abiding and too ~ —H. S. Commager⟩ — **ac·qui·es·cent·ly** *adv*

ac·quire \əˈkwī(ə)r, -īə *also* aˈ-\ *vt* -ED/-ING/-S [alter. (influenced by L *acquirere*) of earlier *acquere*, fr. ME *aqueren*, fr. MF *aquerre*, fr. L *acquirere*, fr. *ad-* + *-quirere* (fr. *quaerere* to seek, gain, obtain, ask)] **1 :** to come into possession, control, or power of disposal of often by some uncertain or unspecified means ⟨had accumulated for her about as much money as she had herself *acquired* —Arnold Bennett⟩ **2 :** to come to have as a characteristic, attribute, trait, or ability often by sustained effort ⟨he had taken kindly to these languages and had rapidly and easily mastered what many boys take years in *acquiring* —Samuel Butler †1902⟩ **syn** see GET

acquired *adj* **1 :** gained by or as a result of effort or experience ⟨~ wealth⟩ ⟨~ knowledge⟩ ⟨~ response⟩ — compare INNATE, NATIVE **2 :** attained by the individual by or as if by his own efforts: as **a** *of bodily qualities or characters* **:** relating to or being a part of the individual soma **:** caused by environmental forces (as use and disuse) and not subject to transmission from parent to offspring — distinguished from *hereditary* and *genic* **b** *of disease or abnormal states* **:** developed after birth ⟨~ heart disease⟩ — opposed to *congenital*

acquired immunity *n* **:** immunity taken on by a member of a naturally susceptible group (as following an attack of some diseases or as induced by injection of suitable antigens or antibodies) — compare ACTIVE IMMUNITY, NATURAL IMMUNITY

ac·quire·ment \-ī(ə)rmənt, -īəm-\ *n* -S **1 :** the act or action of acquiring **2 :** an attainment of mind or body usu. resulting from continued endeavor and self-cultivation **:** ACHIEVEMENT ⟨our men of the greatest genius have not been most distinguished for their ~s at school or at the university —William Hazlitt⟩

acquisite *adj* [L *acquisitus*] *obs* **:** ACQUIRED

ac·qui·si·tion \ˌakwəˈzishən\ *n* -S [ME *acquisicioun*, fr. MF or L; MF *acquisition*, fr. L *acquisition-, acquisitio*, fr. *acquisitus* (past part. of *acquirere* to acquire) + *-ion-, -io* -ion — more at ACQUIRE] **1 :** the act or action of acquiring ⟨power resulting from the ~ of wealth⟩ ⟨the early ~ of self-control in the matter of fear —Bertrand Russell⟩ **2 :** a thing acquired or gained **:** ACQUIREMENT, GAIN — **ac·qui·si·tion·ist** \-əst\ *n* -S

acquisition cost *n* **:** commissions and other selling expenses in insurance production

acquisititious *adj* [L *acquisitus* + E *-itious*] *obs* **:** ACQUIRED

ac·quis·i·tive \əˈkwizəd·iv, -ətiv *also* aˈ-\ *adj* [*acquisition* + *-ive*] **1 :** capable of acquiring **2 :** strongly desirous of acquiring and possessing **:** GRASPING ⟨in an ~ society the form that selfishness predominantly takes is monetary greed —Edgar Johnson⟩ **syn** see COVETOUS

ac·quis·i·tive·ness *n* -ES **:** the quality or state of being acquisitive

ac·quist \əˈkwist, aˈ-\ *n* -S [ML *acquistum*, alter. of L *acquisitum*, neut. of *acquisitus*, past part. of *acquirere* to acquire — more at ACQUIRE] **:** ACQUISITION 1

¹ac·quit \əˈkwit *also* aˈ-; *usu* -id·+V\ *vt* **acquitted; acquitted; acquitting; acquits** [ME *aquiten*, fr. OF *aquiter*, fr. *a-* (fr. L *ad-*) + *quite* acquitted, free of, tranquil — more at QUIT] **1 a** *archaic* **:** to pay off (as a claim or debt) **b** *obs* **:** to pay back (something done for or to one) **:** REPAY, REQUITE **2 a** *obs* **:** to set free (as by ransoming) **b** *obs* **:** to free or rid (oneself) of anything **c :** to discharge completely (as from an obligation or accusation) ⟨the court *acquitted* the prisoner⟩ ⟨~ a man of liability⟩ **3 :** to perform (one's part) or conduct (oneself) usu. satisfactorily ⟨in their first battle the recruits *acquitted* themselves like veterans⟩ **syn** see BEHAVE, EXCULPATE

²acquit \"\ *adj* [ME, short for *aquited*, past part. of *aquiten*] *archaic* **:** ACQUITTED **:** set free **:** RID ⟨to be ~ fro my continual smart —Edmund Spenser⟩

acquitment *n* -S [F *acquittement*, fr. *acquitter* to acquit (fr. OF *aquiter*) + *-ment*] *obs* **:** ACQUITTAL

ac·quit·tal \əˈkwid·ᵊl, -itᵊl *also* aˈ-\ *n* -S [ME *aquitaille, aquital*, fr. AF *aquitaille*, fr. OF *aquiter* to acquit] **1** *obs* **:** PAYMENT, REQUITAL **2 :** release or discharge from debt or other liability **3 :** a setting free or deliverance from the charge of an offense by verdict of a jury, sentence of a court, or other legal process

¹ac·quit·tance \-itᵊn(t)s\ *n* -S [ME *aquitaunce*, fr. MF *aquitance*, fr. *aquitant* (pres. part. of *aquiter*) + *-ance*] **1** *obs* **:** the settlement of a debt or other obligation **:** REPAYMENT **2** *archaic* **:** ACQUITTAL 2 **3 :** a writing evidencing a discharge **:** a receipt in full — compare RELEASE 2b **4 :** ACQUITTAL 3

²acquittance *vt* -ED/-ING/-S [ME *aquitaunce*n, fr. *aquitaunce*, n.] *obs* **:** ACQUIT, DISCHARGE

acquittance roll *n, Brit* **:** a military payroll

acr- *or* **acro-** *also* **akr-** *or* **akro-** *comb form* [MF or Gk; MF *acro-*, fr. Gk *akr-, akro-*, fr. *akros* topmost, extreme; akin to Gk *akmē* point — more at EDGE] **1 :** beginning **:** end **:** tip ⟨*acrology*⟩ **2 a :** top **:** peak **:** summit ⟨*acropetal*⟩ ⟨*acrocephaly*⟩ **b :** height ⟨*acrophobia*⟩ **c :** extremity of the body, esp. the human body ⟨*acrocyanosis*⟩

acrae·in \əˈkrēən\ *n* -S [NL *Acraeinae* + E *-in*] **:** a self-defensive substance secreted by butterflies of the subfamily Acraeinae that is distasteful to birds and other predators

ac·rae·i·nae \ˌakrēˈī(ˌ)nē\ *n pl, cap* [NL, fr. *Acraea*, type genus (fr. L, fem. of *acraeus* living on the heights, fr. Gk *akraios*, fr. *akron* height) + *-inae*] **:** a subfamily of Nymphalidae consisting of chiefly African butterflies possessing distastefulness to predators and mimicked by many more edible butterflies

ac·ral \ˈakrəl\ *adj* [Gk *akra* end, extremity, highest point + E *-al*] **:** of or belonging to the extremities of peripheral body parts ⟨~ cyanosis⟩

acral·de·hyde \əˈkraldəˌhīd, aˈ-\ *n* -S [L *acr-, acer* sharp + E *aldehyde*] **:** ACROLEIN

¹acra·nia \(ˈ)āˈkrānēə\ *n* -S [NL, fr. ²*a-* + *-crania*] **:** congenital partial or total absence of the skull

²acrania \"\ *n pl, cap* [NL, fr. ²*a-* + *-crania* (fr. Gk *kranion* skull) — more at CRANIUM] *in some classifications* **:** a division of Chordata comprising Hemichordata, Urochordata, and Cephalochordata and including all the chordates without true heads and anterior brains — compare VERTEBRATA

³acrania \"\ [NL, fr. ²*a-* + *-crania* (fr. Gk *kranion* skull)] *syn of* CEPHALOCHORDA

acra·ni·al \(ˈ)ā¦==ēəl\ *adj* [NL ²*Acrania* + E *-al*] **:** ACRANIATE

acra·ni·a·ta \ˌāˌkrānēˈād·ə, -ād·ə\ [NL, fr. ²*a-* + *Craniata*] *syn of* ²ACRANIA

¹acra·ni·ate \(ˈ)ā¦==ēˌāt, -ēˌāt\ *adj* [NL *Acraniata*] **:** of or relating to the major division Acrania

²acraniate \"\ *n* -S **:** a chordate of the major division Acrania

acra·sia \əˈkrāzh(ē)ə\ *n, cap* [NL, prob. fr. Gk *akrasia* bad mixture, fr. *akratos* unmixed + *-ia*] **:** a genus (the type of the family Acrasiaceae) of saprophytic fungi of the order Acrasiales having amoeboid cells produced from spores and aggregated without fusion into a pseudoplasmodium and having a fruiting body, often with a sterile stalklike portion, formed by rounding up and contraction of the pseudoplasmodium

acra·si·a·les \əˌkrāz(h)ēˈā(ˌ)lēz\ *n pl, cap* [NL, fr. *Acrasia* + *-ales*] **:** an order of lower fungi related to the slime molds but having swarm spores without flagella that do not fuse into a true plasmodium — see ACRASIA; compare PSEUDOPLASMODIUM

acras·i·da \əˈkrasədə\ *n pl, cap* [NL, fr. *Acrasia* + *-ida*] *in some classifications* **:** a suborder or order of Mycetozoa equivalent to Acrasiales

acra·si·e·ae \ˌakrāz(h)ēˈēˌē\ *n pl, cap* [NL, fr. *Acrasia* + *-eae*] *in some classifications* **:** Acrasiales regarded as a class distinct from Myxomycetes

acras·pe·da \(ˈ)āˈkraspədə\ *n pl, cap* [NL, fr. Gk *akraspeda*, neut. pl. of *akraspedos* without fringes, fr. *a-* ²*a-* + *kraspedon* edge, border] *in former classifications* **:** a division of coelenterates comprising medusae lacking a swimming velum — compare SCYPHOZOA

acras·pe·dae \-ˌdē\ *syn of* ACRASPEDA

¹acras·pe·dote \(ˈ)ā¦==ˌdōt\ *adj* [NL *Acraspeda* + E *-ote*] **:** of or relating to the division Acraspeda

²acraspedote \"\ *adj* [²*a-* + *craspedote*] *of the segments of a tapeworm* **:** not overlapping

ac·ra·sy \ˈakrəsē, -əzē\ *n* -ES [Gk *akrasia* incontinence, debility, fr. *akratēs* powerless, incontinent, intemperate (fr. *a-* ²*a-* + *kratos* strength) + *-ia* -y] *archaic* **:** EXCESS, INTEMPERANCE

acrawl \əˈ-\ *adj* [¹*a-* + *crawl*, v.] **:** CRAWLING ⟨like young black india-rubber kittens — all ~ —H.G.Wells⟩ ⟨highways ~ with cars⟩

acre \ˈākə(r)\ *n* -S [ME, fr. OE *æcer*; akin to OHG *ackar* field, ON *akr* arable land, Goth *akrs* field, L *ager* field, Gk *agros*, Skt *ajra*, L *agere* to drive — more at AGENT] **1 a :** a field esp. of arable or pasture land — archaic except in proper names or in compounds or phrases ⟨Long *Acre*⟩ ⟨blackacre⟩ **b acres** *pl* **:** LANDS, ESTATE ⟨he commuted between his country ~s and his Madison Avenue office —*Time*⟩ ⟨these skills, like fat flocks or ancestral ~s, were passed from father to son —Harriot B. Barbour⟩ **2 :** any of various units of area based on an old approximate unit equal to the amount of land plowed by a yoke of oxen in a day; *esp* **:** a unit in the U.S. and England equal to 160 square rods ⟨a field of six ~s⟩ ⟨a 10-*acre* field⟩ — see MEASURE table; compare ARPENT **3 :** a broad expanse ⟨smiling valleys were turned into ~s of slums —Gilbert Highet⟩ **:** a large quantity — usu. used in pl. ⟨I have read ~s of source material on European history —H.E.Barnes⟩

acre·age \ˈāk(ə)rij, -ēj\ *n* -S **:** area in acres **:** ACRES

acre-foot \ˈ==¦=\ *n, pl* **acre-feet :** the volume (as of irrigation water) that would cover one acre to a depth of one foot

acre-inch \ˈ==¦=\ *n* **:** the volume (as of water or soil) equivalent to a depth of one inch over an acre of land

acre·man \ˈākə(r)mən\ *n, pl* **acremen** [ME, fr. OE *æcerman*, fr. *æcer* field + *man* — more at ACRE, MAN] **:** the leader of the plow team on a medieval English manor

ac·rid \ˈakrəd\ *adj, usu* -ER/-EST [modif. (influenced by *acid*) of L *acr-, acer* sharp — more at EDGE] **1 :** unpleasantly or irritatingly sharp or strong to the taste ⟨strong brine is ~⟩ ⟨~ alum⟩ or to the smell ⟨~ sulfur fumes⟩ **:** stingingly bitter **:** CAUSTIC **2 :** deeply or violently bitter **:** excessively caustic, rancorous, or acrimonious ⟨an ~ temper⟩ ⟨an ~ denunciation⟩ **syn** see BITTER

ac·ri·dan \ˈakrəˌdan\ *also* **ac·ri·dane** \-ˌdān\ *n* -S [ISV, blend of *acridine* + *-an, -ane*] **:** a colorless crystalline base $C_{13}H_{11}N$ made by reducing acridine

acrid·i·an \əˈkridēən\ *adj* [NL *Acrida* + E *-ian*] **:** of or relating to the family Acrididae

ac·ri·did \ˈakrəˌdid\ *n* -S [NL *Acrididae*] **:** a grasshopper of the family Acrididae

acrid·i·dae \əˈkridəˌdē\ *n pl, cap* [NL, fr. *Acrida*, type genus (fr. Gk *akrid-, akris* grasshopper) + *-idae*] **:** a family of orthopterous insects that includes the true locusts and the grasshoppers with short antennae

ac·ri·di·idae \ˌakrəˈdīəˌdē\ *syn of* ACRIDIDAE

ac·ri·dine \ˈakrəˌdēn, -ˌdən\ *n* -S [*acrid* + *-ine*] **:** a colorless crystalline feebly basic tricyclic compound $C_{13}H_9N$ occurring in crude anthracene fractions from coal tar and important as the parent compound of dyes and pharmaceuticals (as acriflavine and quinacrine) — compare STRUCTURAL FORMULA

acridine

acridine dye *n* **:** any of a small class of basic dyes containing the acridine nucleus, most of them being yellow, orange, red, or brown, that are fluorescent in solution and are used chiefly for dyeing leather and mordanted cotton

acridine orange *n* **:** an orange acridine dye — see DYE table I (under *Basic Orange 14*)

ac·ri·din·i·um \ˌakrəˈdinēəm\ *also* **ac·ri·do·ni·um** \-dōn-\ *n* -S [*acridinium*, NL, fr. ISV *acridine* + NL *-ium*; *acridonium*, NL, fr. ISV *acridone* + NL *-ium*] **:** a univalent radical $C_{13}H_{10}N$ analogous to ammonium derived from acridine

acrid·i·nyl \əˈkridᵊn(ˌ)il, -əl\ *or* **ac·ri·dyl** \ˈakrəˌdil, -dəl\ *n* -S [*acridinyl*, alter. of *acridyl*; *acridyl*, ISV *acridine* + *-yl*] **:** the univalent radical $C_{13}H_8N$ of acridine

acrid·i·ty \aˈkridəd·ē, əˈ-\ *n* -ES **:** the quality or state of being acrid **:** irritating sharpness **:** extreme bitterness ⟨the ~ of alkali⟩ ⟨the ~ of a critic's words⟩

ac·rid·ly \ˈakrədlē, -li\ *adv* **:** in an acrid manner

ac·rid·ness *n* -ES **:** ACRIDITY

ac·ri·dol·o·gy \ˌakrəˈdäləjē\ *n* -ES [Gk *akrid-, akris* grasshopper + E *-o-* + *-logy*] **:** the study of migratory locusts and other grasshoppers

ac·ri·done \ˈakrəˌdōn\ *n* -S [ISV, blend of *acridine* + *-one*; prob. orig. formed as G *akridon*] **:** a yellow crystalline ketone $C_6H_4(CO)(NH)C_6H_4$ yielding acridine on reduction

ac·ri·do·the·res \ˌakrədōˈthi(ˌ)rēz\ *n, cap* [NL, modif. of Gk *akridothēra* locust trap, fr. *akrid-, akris* grasshopper, locust + *-o-* + *thēra* hunt, fr. *thēr* wild beast — more at FIERCE] **:** a genus of chiefly Asiatic passerine birds (family Sturnidae) that include the common myna of southeastern Asia and that are not permitted in the U. S. by private or commercial import because of their destructive feeding habits — compare STARLING

ac·ri·fla·vine \ˌakrəˈflāˌvēn, -ˌvən\ *n* [*acridine* + *flavine*] **:** a yellow acridine dye $C_{14}H_{14}N_3Cl$ obtained by methylation of proflavine as red crystals or usu. in admixture with proflavine as a deep orange powder and used often in the form of its reddish brown hydrochloride as an antiseptic esp. for wounds — called also *neutral acriflavine, trypaflavine*

ac·ri·mo·ni·ous \ˌakrəˈmōnēəs, -nyəs\ *adj* [F *acrimonieux*, fr. ML *acrimoniosus*, fr. L *acrimonia* + *-osus* -ous] **1** *archaic* **:** bitter, irritating, or caustic esp. to the taste **2 :** caustic, biting, or rancorous esp. in feeling, language, or manner **:** BITTER ⟨an ~ dispute⟩ **syn** see ANGRY

ac·ri·mo·ny \ˈakrəˌmōnē, -ni, *US also & Brit usu* -mən-\ *n* -ES [MF or L; MF *acrimonie*, fr. L *acrimonia*, fr. *acr-, acer* sharp — more at EDGE] **1** *archaic* **:** bitterness or sharpness esp. to the taste **2 :** sharpness or rancor esp. in words or manner ⟨timeworn controversies . . . are apt to revive . . . with an ~ undimmed by age — *Times Lit. Supp.*⟩

ac·ri·nyl \ˈakrəˌnil, -nəl\ *n* -S [origin unknown] **:** a univalent radical C_7H_7O; *p*-hydroxy-benzyl

acro- — see ACR-

ac·ro·ama \ˌakrōˈāmə, -ämə\ *n, pl* **acroam·a·ta** \-məd·ə\ [Gk *akroama*, lit., something heard, fr. *akroasthai* to listen; prob. akin to Gk *akros* topmost and to Gk *ous* ear — more at ACR-, EAR] **:** an acroamatic teaching or doctrine

ac·ro·a·mat·ic \¦akrōə¦mad·ik\ *also* **ac·ro·a·mat·i·cal** \-əkəl\ *adj* [Gk *akroamatikos*, fr. *akroamat-, akroama* + *-ikos* -ic] **:** told orally to chosen disciples only **:** ESOTERIC

ac·ro·a·mat·ics \ˌakrōəˈmad·iks\ *n pl* **:** acroamatic doctrines formerly ascribed to Aristotle

ac·ro·ba·cy \ˈakrəbəsē\ *n* -ES [*acrobat* + *-cy*] **:** ACROBATICS

ac·ro·bat \ˈakrəˌbat, *usu* -ad·+V\ *n* -S [F & Gk; F *acrobate*, fr. Gk *akrobatēs* tightrope walker, acrobat, fr. *akrobatos* walking on tiptoe, walking up high, fr. *akros* highest + *-batēs* (fr. *bainein* to go); akin to Gk *akē* point — more at EDGE, COME] **1 :** one that performs (as on a trapeze or bars) gymnastic feats or exercises **2 :** one adept at swiftly changing his position or viewpoint ⟨an intellectual ~⟩

acrob·a·tes \əˈkrābəˌtēz\ *n, cap* [NL, fr. Gk *akrobatēs* acrobat] **:** a genus of very small Australian marsupials having flattened tails and the lateral skin of the body extended into a supporting membrane like that of the flying squirrel and used similarly in gliding — see FLYING PHALANGER

ac·ro·bath·o·lith·ic \¦akrōˌbathə¦lithik\ *adj* [*acr-* + *batholith* + *-ic*] *of ore deposits* **:** located or formed in or near the upward-projecting domes or cupolas of batholiths

¹ac·ro·bat·ic \¦akrə¦bad·ik, -atik, -ēk\ *adj* [F *acrobatique*, fr. *acrobate* + *-ique* -ic] **1 :** relating to or suggestive of an acrobat or acrobatics **2 :** performed with body contortions, back bends, high kicks, somersaults, or tossing of one dancer by a partner — **ac·ro·bat·i·cal·ly** \-ək(ə)lē, -li\ *adv*

²acrobatic \"\ *n* -S **:** an acrobatic trick, performance, or exercise ⟨indulges in every kind of ~ —*Ford Times*⟩

ac·ro·bat·ics \¦==¦=iks, -ēks\ *n pl but sometimes sing in constr* **1 a :** the art, performance, or activity of an acrobat ⟨to perform ~ in a circus⟩ **b :** spectacular, showy, or startling ability esp. in performing something difficult or complex ⟨a politician's mental ~⟩; *also* **:** an instance of such ability ⟨an audience spellbound by a contralto's vocal ~⟩ **2 :** an aircraft maneuver other than that required for normal flight and usu. resulting in an abnormal position, speed, or altitude

ac·ro·bat·ism \ˈakrəˌbad·ˌizəm\ *n* -S **:** ACROBATICS 1

ac·ro·blast \ˈakrəˌblast\ *n* -S [ISV *acr-* + *-blast*] **:** a Golgi remnant that gives rise in spermatogenesis to the acrosome

ac·ro·car·pi \ˌakrəˈkärˌpī\ *n pl, cap* [NL, fr. Gk *akrokarpoi*, pl. of *akrokarpos*] **:** an artificial group of mosses comprising acrocarpous forms (as most members of the orders Dicranales, Pottiales, and Eubryales) — compare PLEUROCARPI

ac·ro·car·pous \¦==¦=pəs\ *adj* [NL *acrocarpus*, fr. Gk *akrokarpos* bearing fruit at the top, fr. *akr-* acr- + *-karpos* -carpous] *of a moss* **:** having the archegonia and hence the capsules terminal on the stem — compare PLEUROCARPOUS

ac·ro·cen·tric \¦akrə¦sen·trik\ *adj* [*acr-* + *centric*] **:** having or relating to a subterminal centromere

ac·ro·ce·phal·ic \¦akrōsə¦falik\ *adj* [ISV *acrocephaly* + *-ic*; orig. formed as F *acrocéphalique*] **:** OXYCEPHALIC

ac·ro·ceph·a·ly \ˌakrəˈsefəlē\ *also* **ac·ro·ce·pha·lia** \ˌakrōsəˈfālyə\ *n, pl* **acrocephalies** *also* **acrocephalias** [*acrocephaly* fr. F *acrocéphalie*, fr. *acr-* + *-céphalie* -cephaly; *acrocephalia*, NL, fr. F *acrocéphalie*] **:** OXYCEPHALY

acroc·e·ra \əˈkräsərə\ *n, cap* [NL, fr. *acr-* + *-cera*] **:** a genus of two-winged flies with very small heads and larvae that feed on spiders or their eggs

acroc·e·rat·i·dae \əˌkräsəˈrad·əˌdē\ [NL, fr. Acrocerat-, *Acrocera*, type genus + *-idae*] *syn of* CYRTIDAE

ac·ro·chor·di·dae \ˌakrəˈkȯrdəˌdē\ *n pl, cap* [NL, fr. *Acrochordus*, type genus (fr. Gk *akrochordōn* wart with a thin neck, fr. *akr-* acr- + *chordē* intestine, catgut) + *-idae* — more at YARN] **:** a small family often considered a colubrid subfamily of aglyphous aquatic snakes of the eastern Asiatic coast comprising the wart snakes

¹ac·ro·clin·i·um \ˌakrəˈklinēəm\ [NL, fr. *acr-* + *-clinium*] *syn of* HELIPTERUM

²acroclinium \"\ *n* -S **:** a plant of the genus *Helipterum*

ac·ro·co·mia \ˌakrəˈkōmēə\ *n, cap* [NL, fr. *acr-* + Gk *komē* hair, foliage + NL *-ia*] **:** a small genus of tall pinnate-leaved Central American and So. American palms with spiny trunk, long pendant clusters of flowers, and nutlike fruits

ac·ro·cra·ni·al \¦akrō¦krānēəl\ *or* **ac·ro·cra·nic** \-nik\ *adj* [*acr-* + *cranial, cranic*] *of a skull* **:** being pyramidal or pointed at the top with a breadth-height index of 98 or above — **ac·ro·cra·ny** \ˈakrōˌkrānē\ *n* -ES

ac·ro·cy·a·no·sis \ˌakrōˌsīəˈnōsəs\ *n, pl* **acrocyanoses** \-ōˌsēz\ [NL, fr. *acr-* + *cyanosis*] **:** blueness or pallor of the extremities usu. associated with pain and numbness and caused by vasomotor disturbances (as in Raynaud's disease); *specif* **:** a disorder of the arterioles of the exposed parts of the hands and feet involving abnormal contraction of the arteriolar walls intensified by exposure to cold and resulting in bluish mottled skin, chilling, and sweating of the affected parts — **ac·ro·cy·a·not·ic** \-¦näd·ik\ *adj*

ac·ro·cyst \ˈakrōˌsist\ *n* -S [*acr-* + *-cyst*] **:** a chitinous cystlike expansion of the gonophore at the top of the gonotheca in certain hydroids

ac·ro·der·ma·ti·tis \¦akrōˌdərmə¦tīd·əs\ *n* -ES [NL, fr. *acr-* + *dermatitis*] **:** inflammation of the skin of the extremities

¹ac·ro·dont \ˈakrəˌdänt\ *adj* [*acr-* + *-odont*] *of teeth* **:** consolidated with the summit of the alveolar ridge without sockets; *also* **:** having such teeth — compare PLEURODONT — **ac·ro·dont·ism** \-nˌtizəm\ *n* -S

²acrodont \"\ *n* -S **:** an acrodont animal

ac·ro·drome \ˈakrəˌdrōm\ *or* **acrod·ro·mous** \əˈkrädrəməs, aˈ-\ *adj* [*acr-* + *-drome, -dromous*] **:** running to a point — used of a form of venation in which the principal veins terminate at the leaf tip (as in plants of the genus *Ziziphus*)

ac·ro·dus \ˈakrədəs\ *n, cap* [NL, fr. *acr-* + *-odus*] **:** a widely distributed genus of Mesozoic sharks (family Hybodontidae) with numerous rounded teeth

ac·ro·dyn·ia \ˌakrōˈdinēə\ *n* -S [NL, fr. F *acrodynie*, fr. *acr-* + *-odynie* -odynia] **:** a disease of unknown cause seen in young children characterized by dusky pink discoloration of hands and feet with local swelling and intense itching and accompanied by insomnia, irritability, and sensitiveness to light — **ac·ro·dyn·ic** \¦==¦=ik\ *adj*

ac·ro·gen \ˈakrəjən\ *n* -S [*acr-* + *-gen*; fr. the growing point's being at the tip of the stem] **:** a plant of the higher cryptogams predominant in the Carboniferous era including ferns, fern allies, mosses, and liverworts and distinguished by growth from a special cell or growing point — compare THALLOGEN, THALLOPHYTE

acrog·e·nous \əˈkräjənəs, aˈ-\ *also* **ac·ro·gen·ic** \¦akrə¦jenik\ *adj* [*acr-* + *-genous, -genic*] **1 :** increasing by growth from the summit or apex **2** [*acrogen* + *-ous* or *-ic*] **:** relating to an acrogen — **acrog·e·nous·ly** *adv*

acrog·y·nae \əˈkräjə(ˌ)nē\ *n pl, cap* [NL, fr. *acr-* + *-gynae* (fr. Gk *gynē* woman) — more at QUEEN] *in some classifications* **:** a group of liverworts including all the leafy members of the Jungermanniaceae — compare ANACROGYNAE

acrog·y·nous \-ˌnəs\ *adj* [*acr-* + *-gynous*] **:** having the archegonia at the apex of the stem and involving the apical cell in their formation resulting in determinate growth of the gametophyte — used of certain liverworts

acro·le·in \əˈkrōlēən\ *n* -S [L *acr-, ocer* sharp + *olēre* to smell + ISV *-in* — more at EDGE, ODOR] **:** a toxic colorless mobile liquid aldehyde $CH_2{=}CHCHO$ with acrid odor and irritating vapors that is obtained by dehydration of glycerol, by destructive distillation of fats, or by oxidation of allyl alcohol, that polymerizes readily into resins, and that is used chiefly in organic synthesis (as of methionine) — called also *acrylaldehyde*

ac·ro·lith \ˈakrəˌlith\ *n* -S [L *acrolithus*, fr. Gk *akrolithos* with ends of stone, fr. *akr-* acr- + *lithos* stone] **:** an acrolithic statue

ac·ro·lith·ic \¦==¦=ik\ *adj, of a statue* **:** having a trunk of wood usu. covered with metal or drapery and extremities of stone

ac·ro·log·ic \¦akrə¦läjik\ *adj* [F *acrologique*, fr. *acrologie* + *-ique* -ic] **:** ACROPHONIC — **ac·ro·log·i·cal·ly** \-jək(ə)lē\ *adv*

acrol·o·gy \əˈkräləjē\ *n* -ES [F *acrologie*, fr. *acr-* + *-logie* -logy] **:** ACROPHONY

ac·ro·ma·nia \ˌakrəˈmānēə\ *n* [NL, fr. Gk. *akros* extreme + *mania* — more at ACR-] **:** crazy top esp. of cotton

¹ac·ro·me·gal·ic \¦akrōmə¦galik\ *adj* [ISV *acromegaly* + *-ic*; orig. formed as F *acromégalique*] **:** exhibiting acromegaly ⟨the oldest human skeleton yet discovered has an ~ skull —C.A.Doan⟩

²acromegalic \"\ *n* -S **:** one affected with acromegaly

ac·ro·meg·a·loid \¦akrō¦megəˌlȯid\ *adj* [*acromegaly* + *-oid*] **:** resembling acromegaly

ac·ro·meg·a·ly \ˌakrōˈmegəlē, -li\ *also* **ac·ro·me·ga·lia** \-ˌməˈgālyə\ *n, pl* **acromegalies** *also* **acromegalias** [*acromegaly* fr. F *acromégalie*, fr. *acr-* + *-mégalie* -megaly; *acromegalia*, NL, fr. F *acromégalie*] **:** a chronic disease of adult life that is characterized by a gradual and permanent enlargement of the flat bones (as the lower jaw) and of the hands and feet, abdominal organs, nose, lips, and tongue, that develops after ossification is complete, and that results from a disorder of the pituitary gland — compare GIGANTISM

acro·mi·al \əˈkrōmēəl\ *adj* [NL *acromion* + E *-al*] **:** of or relating to the acromion

acromial process *n* **:** ACROMION

acromial thoracic artery *n* **:** THORACICOACROMIAL ARTERY

ac·ro·mic·ria \ˌakrōˈmikrēə, -mī-\ *n* -S [NL, fr. *acr-* + *micr-* + *-ia*] **:** abnormal smallness of the extremities

acromio- *comb form* [NL, fr. *acromion*] **:** acromial and ⟨*acromio*deltoid⟩ ⟨*acromio*sternal⟩

acro·mi·on \əˈkrōmēˌän, -ēən\ *or* **acromion process** *n* -S [NL, fr. Gk *akrōmion*, fr. *akr-* acr- + *ōmion* small shoulder, dim. of *ōmos* shoulder — more at HUMERUS] **:** the outer end of the spine of the scapula and in man protecting the glenoid cavity, forming the outer angle of the shoulder, and articulating with the clavicle

ac·ro·mon·o·gram·mat·ic \¦akrōˌmänəgrə¦mad·ik\ *adj* [*acr-* + Gk *monogrammatos* consisting of one letter (fr. *mon-* + *grammat-, gramma* letter) + E *-ic* — more at GRAMMAR] **:** having each verse beginning with the same letter that ends the preceding verse

ac·ro·my·o·di \ˌakrōˌmīˈōˌdī\ *n pl, cap* [NL, fr. *acr-* + *-myodi* (fr. Gk *myōdēs* muscular, fr. *mys* mouse, muscle) — more at MOUSE] *in some classifications* **:** a group of birds nearly equivalent to Passeres having the syringeal muscles attached to the ends of the bronchial half rings

¹ac·ro·my·o·di·an \-¦ōdēən\ *or* **ac·ro·my·o·dic** \-¦ōdik, -äd-\ *or* **ac·ro·my·o·dous** \-¦ōdəs\ *adj* [NL *Acromyodi* + E *-an* or *-ic* or *-ous*] **:** of or relating to the Acromyodi

²acromyodian \"\ *n* -S **:** a bird of the group Acromyodi

ac·ron \ˈaˌkrän, ˈakrən\ *n* -S [NL, fr. Gk *akron* mountain top, end, fr. neut. of *akros* sharp; akin to Gk *akē* point — more at EDGE] **:** the unsegmented preoral part of the body of a segmented animal (as an arthropod) — **ac·ro·nal** \ˈakrənᵊl\ *adj*

¹ac·ro·nar·cot·ic \¦akrə¦==¦=\ *adj* [*acrid* + *-o-* + *narcotic*] **:** possessing both acrid and narcotic properties

²acronarcotic \"\ *n* -S **:** an acronarcotic substance

ac·ro·nym \ˈakrəˌnim\ *n* -S [*acr-* + *-onym*] **:** a word formed from the initial letter or letters of each of the successive parts or major parts of a compound term (as *anzac, radar, snafu*)

ac·ro·nym·ic \¦akrə¦nimik\ *adj* **:** marked by the use of acronyms

ac·ro·pachy \ˈakrōˌpakē, əˈkräpəkē\ *n* -ES [Gk *akropachēs* thick at the end (fr. *akr-* acr- + *-pachēs*, fr. *pachys* thick) + E *-y*] **:** OSTEOARTHROPATHY

ac·ro·par·es·the·sia \¦akrōˌparəs¦thēzh(ē)ə\ *n* -S [NL, fr. *acr-* + *paresthesia*] **:** a condition of burning, tingling, or pricking sensations or numbness in the extremities present on awaking and of unknown cause or produced by compression of nerves during sleep

acrop·e·tal \əˈkräpəd·ᵊl, aˈ-\ *adj* [*acr-* + *-petal*] *bot* **:** from the base toward the apex or from below upward ⟨~ differentiation of an inflorescence⟩ ⟨~ spread of a pathogen in a plant body⟩ — compare BASIPETAL — **acrop·e·tal·ly** \-ᵊlē\ *adv*

ac·ro·pho·bia \\,akrə'fōbēə\ *n* -s [NL, fr. *acr-* + *phobia*] **:** abnormal dread of being at a great height

ac·ro·pho·net·ic \\¦akrə-¦==\ *adj* [*acr-* + *phonetic*] **:** ACROPHONIC

ac·ro·phon·ic \\¦akrə¦fänik\ *adj* **1 :** having to do with acrophony **2 :** instituted or used on the basis of acrophony — **ac·ro·phon·i·cal·ly** \\-nək(ə)lē\ *adv*

acroph·o·ny \\ə'kräfənē, a'-\ *n* -ES [*acr-* + *-phony*] **1 :** the application in the evolution of an alphabet of a pictorial symbol or hieroglyph for the name of an object to the initial sound alone of that name **2 :** the naming of a letter by a word whose initial sound is the same as that which the letter represents

acrop·o·lis \\ə'kräpələs\ *n* -ES [Gk *akropolis*, fr. *akr-* acr- + *polis* city — more at POLICE] **1 :** the upper fortified part of an ancient Greek city (as Athens) **2 :** a height of a city or district fortified or strengthened as a place of refuge ⟨one magnificent photograph of Edinburgh — its ~ in the foreground —Kimon Friar⟩

ac·ro·po·ra \\,akrə'pōrə, ə'kräpərə\ *n, cap* [NL, fr. *acr-* + *-pora*] **:** a genus of corals consisting of the typical madrepores

¹ac·ro·pore \\'akrə,pō(ə)r\ *adj* [NL *Acropora*] **:** of or relating to the genus *Acropora*

²acropore \\"\ *n* -s **:** a coral of the genus *Acropora*

ac·ro·rha·gus \\,akrə'rāgəs\ *n, pl* **acrorha·gi** \\-,jī, -,gī\ [NL, fr. *acr-* + *-rhagus* (irreg. fr. Gk *rhag-, rhax* berry)] **:** one of a series of marginal tubercles found on certain sea anemones each consisting of a local accumulation of nematocysts

ac·ro·scop·ic \\¦akrə¦skäpik\ *adj* [*acr-* + *-scopic*] *bot* **:** facing or on the side toward the apex ⟨a plant with ~ branches⟩ — compare BASISCOPIC

ac·rose \\'a,krōs\ *n* -s [ISV *acrolein* + *-ose*; orig. formed as G *akrose*] **:** either of two sugars $C_6H_{12}O_6$ **: a :** racemic fructose — called also *alpha-acrose* **b :** inactive sorbose — called also *beta-acrose*

ac·ro·some \\'akrə,sōm\ *n* -s [ISV *acr-* + *-some*; orig. formed as G *akrosom*] **:** an anterior cap or hooklike prolongation of a spermatozoon usu. regarded as a derivative of the Golgi apparatus

ac·ro·spire \\-,spī(ə)r\ *n* -s [alter. (influenced by *acr-*) of earlier *akerspire, acherspire*, fr. E dial. *aker, acher* ear of grain (fr. OE *æhher, æcher, ēar*) + *spire* (sprout, blade of grass) — more at EAR (spike of grain)] **:** the spiral plumule in a germinating grain

ac·ro·spore \\'akrə,spō(ə)r\ *n* -s [F, fr. *acr-* + *-spore*] **:** a spore (as a basidiospore) borne at the extremity of the sporophore — **ac·ro·spor·ous** \\¦akrə¦spōrəs, ə'kräspərəs\ *adj*

¹across \\ə'krȯs *also* -ȧs\ *adv* [ME *acrois, acros*, fr. AF *an crois*, fr. *an* in, on (fr. L *in*) + *crois* cross, fr. L *crux* — more at IN, CROSS] **1 :** so as to cross transversely **:** CROSSWISE ⟨boards sawed directly ~⟩ **2 :** to or on the opposite side ⟨a stretch of islandless ocean fully 500 miles ~ —F.C.Lincoln⟩ **3 :** so as to be understandable, acceptable, or successful **:** OVER ⟨a highly individual style which comes ~ even in translation —K.I. Lansner⟩ ⟨failed to get his thoughts ~⟩ ⟨the carefully studied and rehearsed technique for putting himself ~ —T.C.Worsley⟩ **4** *dial Eng* **:** at odds ⟨to get ~ with his friends⟩

²across \\"\ *prep* **1 a :** from one side to the opposite side of **:** OVER ⟨to swim ~ the channel⟩ ⟨to peer ~ the barricade⟩ ⟨to sweep her fingers ~ the strings of a harp⟩ **b :** from one point in time to another ⟨I can remember, ~ the years —W.A.White⟩ **2 a :** so as to intersect or pass at an angle (as a right angle) to **:** crosswise of **:** at an angle with the length, direction, or course of ⟨to lay one stick ~ another⟩ ⟨~ the grain of the wood⟩ ⟨a lake lying ~ the state line⟩ **b :** so as to intrude upon ⟨to flash ~ his mind⟩ **3 :** on the other side of ⟨~ the street⟩

³across \\"\ *adj* **:** CROSSED ⟨with arms ~⟩

across–the–board \\=¦==¦=\ *adj* **1** *of a racing bet* **:** placed in combination to win, place, or show **2 :** embracing all classes or categories without exception **:** BLANKET ⟨an *across-the-board* tax cut⟩ **3** *of a radio or television program* **:** scheduled at the same time on consecutive days (usu. Monday through Friday) each week

acrost \\ə'krȯst *also* -ȧst\ *dial var of* ACROSS

ac·ro·ster·nite \\,akrō'stər,nīt\ *n* -s [*acr-* + *sternite*] **:** the precostal lip of the sternum of a typical segment of an arthropod

¹acros·tic \\ə'krȯstik, -ēk, -ȧs-\ *n* -s [MF & Gk; MF *acrostiche*, fr. Gk *akrostichis*, fr. *akr-* acr- + *-stichis* (fr. *stichos* line); akin to *steichein* to go — more at STAIR] **1 :** a composition usu. in verse in which one or more sets of letters (as the initial, middle, or final letters of the lines) when taken in order form a word, a connected group of words (as a sentence), or the regular sequence of the letters of the alphabet — compare ABECEDARIUS **2 a :** ACRONYM **b :** a word made from any of the letters in the words of a phrase **3 :** a series of words of equal length, the number of words being the same as the number of letters in each word, so arranged that it is the same when read horizontally or vertically

H E A R T
E M B E R
A B U S E
R E S I N
T R E N D

acrostic 3

²acrostic \\"\ *also* **acros·ti·cal** \\-ə̇kəl\ *adj* **:** characterized by, containing, or made up by means of an acrostic ⟨an ~ name⟩ ⟨an ~ poem⟩ ⟨an ~ anagram⟩ — **acros·ti·cal·ly** \\-tə̇k(ə)lē, -li\ *adv*

acros·ti·chal \\ə'krȯstə̇kəl, -ȧs-\ *adj* [*acr-* + *-stich* + *-al*] **:** situated in the highest rank or row — used of certain bristles on the mesonotum of muscoid flies

acros·ti·chum \\-kəm\ *n, cap* [NL, irreg. fr. Gk *akrostichis*; fr. the arrangement of the spores on the leaflets] **:** a genus of tropical ferns (family Polypodiaceae) with varied habit but with the sporangia covering all the underside of the frond

ac·ro·tar·si·al \\¦akrō¦tärsēəl\ *adj* [NL *acrotarsium* + E *-al*] **:** of or relating to the acrotarsium

ac·ro·tar·si·um \\,akrō'tärsēəm\ *n, pl* **acrotar·sia** \\-ēə\ [NL, fr. *acr-* + *tarsus* + *-ium*] **:** the instep of the foot

ac·ro·ter·gite \\-'tər,jīt\ *n* -s [*acr-* + *tergite*] **:** the precostal sector of the typical dorsal plate of a segment of an arthropod

ac·ro·te·ri·al \\¦akrə¦tirēəl\ *adj* [*acroterion* + *-al*] **:** of or like an acroterion

ac·ro·te·ri·on \\,akrə'tirē,än-, -ēən\ *or* **ac·ro·te·ri·um** \\-ēəm\ *or* **ak·ro·te·ri·on** \\-ē,än, -ēən\ *or* **ac·ro·ter** *also* **ak·ro·ter** \\'akrətə(r)\ *n, pl* **acrote·ria** *or* **akrote·ria** \\,akrə'tirēə\ *or* **acroters** *also* **akroters** \\'akrətə(r)z\ [*acroterion, akroterion* fr. Gk *akrotērion*, fr. *akros* topmost, extreme; akin to Gk *akē* point; *acroterium* fr. L, fr. Gk *akrōtērion*; *acroter, akroter* fr. F *acrotère*, fr. L *acroterium* — more at EDGE] **:** a pedestal placed on a pediment to support a statue or other ornamentation; *also* **:** an ornament similarly placed (as on the prow of a galley)

pediment showing three acroteria

ac·ro·tho·rac·i·ca \\¦akrōthə'rasikə\ *n pl, cap* [NL, fr. *acr-* + *Thoracica*] **:** a small order or suborder of barnacles that have the body surrounded by a chitinous mantle and that bore and inhabit cavities (as in mollusk shells or corals)

ac·ro·tre·ta \\¦akrō'trēdə\ *n, cap* [NL, fr. *acr-* + *-treta* (fr. Gk *trētos* perforated)] **:** a genus of brachiopods known from small fossil shells common in Cambrian rocks

ac·ro·troph·ic \\¦akrō¦träfik, -ōf-\ *adj* [*acr-* + *-trophic*] **:** having nutritive cells grouped at the apex of the follicular tube — used of the ovariole of certain insects; compare POLYTROPHIC

ac·ryl·al·de·hyde \\,akrə'laldə,hīd\ *n* [ISV *acrylic* + *aldehyde*] **:** ACROLEIN

ac·ryl·am·ide \\,akrə'la,mīd, ə'krilə,m-, -məd\ *n* -s [*acrylic* + *amide*] **:** the crystalline amide $CH_2{=}CHCONH_2$ of acrylic acid used industrially (as in the manufacture of synthetic textiles) because of its ready polymerization

ac·ry·late \\'akrə,lāt, -lət\ *n* -s [ISV *acrylic* + *-ate*] **1 :** a salt or ester of acrylic acid **2** *or* **acrylate resin :** ACRYLIC RESIN

¹acryl·ic \\ə'krilik, a'-\ *adj* [ISV *acrolein* + *-yl* + *-ic*] **:** relating to acrylic acid or its derivatives ⟨~ polymers⟩

²acrylic \\"\ *n* -s **1 :** ACRYLIC RESIN **2 :** ACRYLIC FIBER

acrylic acid *n* **:** an unsaturated liquid acid $CH_2{:}CHCOOH$ obtainable by oxidation of acrolein, by hydrolysis of acrylonitrile, and otherwise and polymerizing readily to useful products (as water-soluble thickening agents and constituents for varnishes and lacquers) — compare METHACRYLIC ACID

acrylic fiber *n* **:** any of various synthetic textile fibers made by polymerization of acrylonitrile usu. with other monomers that are quick-drying and resistant to the action of weather and moths and that are used esp. in fabrics for clothing and for outdoor exposure

acrylic resin *or* **acrylic plastic** *n* **:** a glasslike thermoplastic made by polymerizing acrylic or methacrylic acid or a derivative of either, esp. an ester (as methyl methacrylate), and used chiefly for cast and molded transparent parts and in solutions or emulsions as coatings (as for textiles and leather) and adhesives

ac·ry·lo·ni·trile \\¦akrə(,)lō'nī·trəl; -,trēl, -īl\ *n* -s [*acrylic* + *-o-* + *nitrile*] **:** a colorless volatile flammable liquid nitrile $CH_2{=}CHCN$ soluble in most organic solvents that is usu. made by reaction of hydrogen cyanide with acetylene or with ethylene oxide with subsequent dehydration of the ethylene cyanohydrin formed and that is used chiefly in organic synthesis (as in cyanoethylation), as an insecticide, and as a raw material for polymerizations esp. to synthetic rubbers (as nitrile rubbers) and acrylic fibers — called also *vinyl cyanide*

acrylo·yl \\ə'krilə,wil, -ēl\ *or* **ac·ry·lyl** \\'akrə,lil\ *n* -s [*acryloyl* fr. *acrylic* + *-o-* + *-yl*; *acrylyl* fr. *acrylic* + *-yl*] **:** the univalent radical $CH_2{=}CHCO{-}$ of acrylic acid

ACS *abbr* **1** antireticular cytotoxic serum **2** autograph card signed

¹act \\'akt\ *n* -s [ME *acte*, partly fr. L *actus* doing, driving, performance, recital, part of a play (fr. *actus*, past part. of *agere* to drive, do), partly fr. L *actum* thing done, public transaction, record, fr. neut. of *actus*, part. — more at AGENT] **1 a :** a thing done or being done **:** DEED, PERFORMANCE ⟨one of the first ~*s* of the new commission⟩ ⟨if some understanding of the ~ is not present, comment on the result may well be irrelevant —Ronald Bottrall⟩ ⟨an ~ of folly⟩ **b** *law* **:** an external manifestation of the will **:** something done by a person pursuant to his volition ⟨the effect may be negative, in which case the ~ is properly described as a "forbearance" —T.E.Holland⟩ **c** *psychol* (1) **:** a motor performance leading to a definite result (2) **:** a dealing with objects (as by moving, perceiving, or desiring them) **d** *sociol* **:** a sequence of human behavior considered as a unit that is directed toward a goal and is regulated by standards of conduct **2** *in Scholasticism* **:** an activity in process of completion; *also* **:** a state of reality or real existence attained — contrasted with *possibility*; compare ACTUS, ENERGY, ENTELECHY **3** *often cap* **:** the formal product of a legislative body **:** the formally declared will of a legislature the final requirement of which is usu. the signature of the proper executive officer **:** STATUTE ⟨an ~ of Congress⟩; *sometimes* **:** a decision or determination of a sovereign, a legislative council, or a court of justice **:** DECREE, EDICT, JUDGMENT, RESOLVE, AWARD — compare ⁴BILL, EX POST FACTO LAW, PRIVATE LAW, PUBLIC LAW **4 :** process of doing **:** ACTION — now used chiefly in the phrase *in the act* ⟨caught in the ~⟩ ⟨they were always on the verge, or in the ~, of civil war —G.L.Dickinson⟩ **5** *often cap* [ME *acte*, fr. MF or L; MF *acte*, fr. L *actum*] **:** a formal record of something done or transacted ⟨given as my free ~ and deed⟩ ⟨*Acts* of the Apostles⟩ ⟨the following section is added to the *Act* of December 22, 1928, supra —*U.S. Code*⟩ **6** [L *actus*] **:** one of the principal divisions of a play or opera — see SCENE **b** (1) **:** one of the successive parts or performances each complete in itself making up an entertainment program (as of a variety show or circus) (2) **:** the performer or performers in such an act ⟨common sense dictates that flying-trapeze ~*s* work over nets⟩ **c** (1) **:** something done for the sake of its intended impression upon others esp. when imitative or suggestive of a theatrical performance ⟨to do the neglected-wife ~⟩ (2) **:** a display of affected esp. insincere behavior **:** PRETENSE ⟨his iconoclasm became a trademark and an ~ —*Time*⟩ ⟨put on an ~ that deceived nobody⟩ **7 :** an exercise formerly required of candidates for a degree at Oxford and Cambridge universities consisting of a thesis to be publicly maintained **8 :** a voluntary inward prayer serving to express such things as faith in God or contrition for one's sins; *also* **:** the expressed form of such prayer — **in act** *archaic* **:** on the point **:** READY, ABOUT — used with *to* and the infinitive ⟨a tiger cat in *act* to spring —Alfred Tennyson⟩ — **into the act** *adv* **:** into an undertaking or situation as an active participant esp. with a view to securing a share in some supposed profit or advantage ⟨many were eager to get *into the act*⟩

²act \\"\ *vb* -ED/-ING/-S *vt* **1** *obs* **:** to move to action **:** ACTUATE, ANIMATE ⟨self-love, the spring of motion, ~*s* the soul —Alexander Pope⟩ **2** *archaic* **:** to carry out into action **:** PERFORM, EXECUTE, DO ⟨had Satan been able to have ~*ed* anything by force —Daniel Defoe⟩ **3 a :** to represent (as an incident or an emotion) by action esp. on the stage ⟨I could have ~*ed* what swept through me then —Mary Austin⟩ ⟨he is handsome and he can ~ neurotic intensity —E.R. Bentley⟩ **b :** to perform (a dramatic work or role) as an actor ⟨beautifully staged and admirably ~*ed*⟩ ⟨~*ing* the part of Ophelia⟩ ⟨every company that ~*s* that operetta has the time of its life —Virgil Thomson⟩ **c :** to make a pretense of **:** FEIGN, COUNTERFEIT, SIMULATE ⟨~ dismay⟩ ⟨~*ed* a reluctance he did not feel⟩ **4 a :** to play the part of (a character in a dramatic work) **:** PERSONATE ⟨~*ed* Desdemona⟩ ⟨~*ing*, as usual, a crotchety octogenarian⟩ **b :** to play the part of as if in a play **:** assume the character of ⟨~ the man of the world⟩ ⟨contentedly ~ a self-sacrificing mother⟩ **c :** to behave in a manner suitable to ⟨~ your age⟩ ~ *vi* **1 a :** to perform on the stage **:** represent a character in the production of a dramatic work ⟨frequently ~*s* in his own plays⟩ ⟨she began ~*ing* as a child of eight⟩ **b :** to behave as if performing on the stage **:** PRETEND, FEIGN, DISSEMBLE ⟨wanted people who would be behaving rather than ~*ing* —*New Yorker*⟩ ⟨watching closely, one had a feeling that she was ~*ing*⟩ **2 :** to carry into effect a determination of the will **:** take action **:** MOVE ⟨to think carefully before ~*ing*⟩ ⟨called on the government to ~ quickly⟩ ⟨in a position to ~ in the light of experience —*London Calling*⟩ ⟨found the truth too unbearable to face, much less to ~ upon —Hamilton Basso⟩ **3 :** to conduct or comport oneself (as in morals or manners or in private life or public office) **:** BEHAVE ⟨to be judged by the way one ~*s*⟩ ⟨~*ed* with becoming modesty⟩ ⟨~ like a fool⟩ ⟨~*ed* as if he felt ill⟩ — often used with an adjective complement ⟨~*ed* tired⟩ ⟨~ superior⟩ **4 :** to discharge the duties of a specified office or post **:** perform a specified function **:** SERVE — used with a prepositional phrase ⟨declaring what officer shall then ~ as President —*U.S.Constitution*⟩ ⟨appointed by the chairman to ~ for him⟩ ⟨~*ed* in this capacity throughout the winter⟩ ⟨trees left standing to ~ as a windbreak⟩ **5 a :** to exert power or influence **:** produce an effect ⟨the gas appears to ~ principally by causing pain —H.G.Armstrong⟩ ⟨forms of magic . . . which are supposed to ~ at a distance —J.G.Frazer⟩ — often used with *on* ⟨caused by acid ~*ing* on metal⟩ ⟨abnormal stimuli, ~*ing* on a neurotic temperament —V.L.Parrington⟩ **b :** to produce a desired effect **:** perform the function for which designed or employed **:** WORK ⟨the brake sometimes ~*s* too quickly⟩ ⟨wait for a medicine to ~⟩ **6** *of a play* **:** to be capable of being performed ⟨this play ~*s* as well as it reads⟩ **7 :** to give a decision or award (as by vote of a deliberative body or by judicial decree) — often used with *on* ⟨adjourned with several important matters still not ~*ed on*⟩

syn BEHAVE, WORK, OPERATE, FUNCTION, REACT: these all have in common the indication of the way in which a person or thing performs, independently or in response to a stimulus. ACT, the most general of this group, stresses the specific nature of the movements or activity or what they indicate in terms of attitude or condition ⟨the child *acted* strangely when his teacher called⟩ ⟨how does the chemical *act* when mixed with water?⟩ ⟨the automobile *acted* all right on the trip⟩ BEHAVE commonly applies to persons and, in that application, commonly implies a standard of what is right, proper, or decorous ⟨*behaved* in a decent and polite way⟩ but has come also to apply more generally as more or less interchangeable with ACT ⟨how does the car *behave* on long trips?⟩ ⟨how the thyroid gland *behaves* under emotional excitement⟩ ⟨a study of how groups *behave* under war conditions⟩ FUNCTION, OPERATE, and WORK agree in meaning to act in a way natural or intended ⟨when the fuse blew, the electric stove ceased to *function*⟩ ⟨under the strain of fatigue his brain refused to *operate*⟩ ⟨the clock no longer *works*⟩ FUNCTION emphasizes the activity itself for which a thing exists or is designed, sometimes also applying to activity that is official or as if official ⟨in order to *function*, man's organism requires a specific temperature, a specific quality of climate, air, light, humidity, and food —Siegfried Giedion⟩ ⟨they have *functioned* as observers rather than participants —J.M.Brown⟩ OPERATE sometimes emphasizes more the degree of efficiency of the activity ⟨the device for lifting heavy objects did not *operate* to anyone's satisfaction⟩ ⟨if the machine is kept oiled, it will *operate* smoothly⟩ WORK emphasizes the degree of success or effectiveness of the activity ⟨the plan for promoting money did not *work* and so was not tried again⟩ ⟨the faucet, partly plugged with rust, did not *work* well⟩ REACT, as the etymology would imply, generally suggests action in response or with reciprocal or counteractive effect ⟨he had found that laboratory animals *reacted* to tests with the chemical by showing various forms of mental disturbances —*Current Biog.*⟩ ⟨we lived there blissfully happy, *reacting* upon one another, stimulating one another —W.A.White⟩ although it has come to be often almost interchangeable with ACT or BEHAVE ⟨at this threat the civil service *reacted* in the way which is always open to any civil service, under any regime —C.P.Fitzgerald⟩ esp. in a desired way ⟨children *react* under kind treatment⟩

— **act a part 1 :** to perform one of the roles in a play **2 :** PRETEND, FEIGN, DISSEMBLE ⟨one would never guess that this paragon of virtue was *acting a part*⟩ — **act the part 1 :** to assume the role **:** perform the function or duties — used with *of* ⟨temporarily *acting the part* of janitor⟩ ⟨has the property of *acting the part* of an acid⟩ **2 :** to exhibit the qualities that characteristically accompany a particular role ⟨now that he's rich he certainly *acts the part*⟩

¹-act \\,akt\ *adj comb form* [Gk *aktis* ray — more at ACTIN-] **:** having (such or so many) rays ⟨polyact⟩ ⟨tetract⟩ — in terms applied to sponge spicules

²-act \\"\ *n comb form* -s **:** one having (such or so many) rays ⟨hexact⟩ ⟨triact⟩ — in names of sponge spicules

act *abbr* **1** acting **2** active **3** actual **4** actuary

ac·ta \\'aktə\ *n pl* [L, pl. of *actum* — more at ACT] **1 :** recorded proceedings **:** official acts **:** TRANSACTIONS ⟨the ~ of the conference⟩ **2 :** narratives of deeds ⟨the Christian ~⟩

act·a·bil·i·ty \\,aktə'bilədē\ *n* -ES **:** the quality or state of being actable

act·a·ble \\'aktəbəl\ *adj* **:** capable of being acted; *esp* **:** suitable for performance on the stage ⟨an ~ scene⟩ ⟨an ~ role⟩

ac·taea \\ak'tēə\ *n, cap* [NL, fr. L, a plant (prob. *Actaea spicata*), fr. Gk *aktaia* baneberry (*Actaea spicata*), elder tree (*Sambucus nigra*)] **:** a small genus of herbs comprising the baneberries (family Ranunculaceae) and having twice-compound leaves, small white racemose flowers, and acrid poisonous berries

ac·tae·on \\ak'tēən\ *n, cap* [NL, fr. *Actaeon*, a hunter in Greco-Roman mythology turned into a stag by Diana and torn to pieces by his own dogs, fr. L, fr. Gk *Aktaiōn*] **:** a genus (the type of the family Actaeonidae) of tectibranchiate mollusks having the viscera twisted to a figure 8 and the shell large and spiral with the spire usu. prominent — compare TECTIBRANCHIA

act curtain *n* **:** a curtain in a theater drawn or lowered between acts

act drop *n* **:** a drop in a theater lowered between acts

acted *past of* ACT

actg *abbr* **1** acting **2** actuating

ACTH *abbr* adrenocorticotropic hormone

ac·ti·as \\'aktēəs, 'akshē-\ *n, cap* [NL] **:** a genus of moths (family Saturniidae) comprising the luna moth and certain Asiatic relatives

Ac·ti·di·one \\,aktə'dī,ōn\ *trademark* — used for cycloheximide

ac·ti·fi·ca·tion \\,aktəfə'kāshən\ *n* -s [fr. *actify*, after such pairs as E *edify*: *edification*] **:** ACTIVATION

ac·ti·fi·er \\'aktə,fī(ə)r\ *n* -s **:** the part of the equipment for liquid purification of gases in which alkaline scrubbing solutions are reactivated (as by use of steam) by driving out hydrogen sulfide — called also *reactivator*

ac·ti·fy \\-,fī\ *vt* -ED/-ING/-S [irreg. fr. *active* + *-fy*] **:** ACTIVATE

ac·tin \\'aktən\ *n* -s [ISV *act-* (fr. L *actus* motion) + *-in*; orig. formed as G *aktin* — more at ACT] **:** a protein in muscle that is active in muscular contraction, is separable from the muscle structure along with myosin by use of strong salt solutions in the presence of adenosine triphosphate, and is known in both globular and fibrous forms

actin- *or* **actini-** *or* **actino-** *comb form* [NL *actin-* ray, fr. Gk *aktin-, aktino-*, fr. *aktin-, aktis*; akin to OE *ūhte* morning twilight, OHG *ūhta*, ON *ōtta*, Goth *ūhtwo*, Skt *aktu* light, night, L *noct-, nox* night — more at NIGHT] **1 a :** having a radiated structure ⟨*Actinopoda*⟩ ⟨*Actinomyces*⟩ **b :** actinian ⟨*actiniform*⟩ ⟨*Actinozoa*⟩ **2 a :** actinic ⟨*actinautography*⟩ **b :** of, relating to, or caused by actinic radiation (as X rays) ⟨*actinotherapy*⟩

ac·ti·nal \\'aktənəl, (')ak¦tīnᵊl\ *adj* [*actin-* + *-al*] **:** belonging to the part of a radiate animal from which the tentacles or arms radiate and where the mouth is situated — often used as an equivalent of *oral* — **ac·ti·nal·ly** \\-əlē, -¦lē\ *adv*

-ac·ti·nal \\¦==\ *adj comb form* [Gk *aktin-, aktis* ray + E *-al*] **:** -ACTINE

ac·ti·nar·ia \\,aktə'na(a)rēə\ [NL, fr. *Actinia* + *-aria*] *syn of* ACTINIARIA

ac·tin·au·to·graph·ic \\¦aktə,nȯdə¦grafik\ *adj* [*actin-* + *autographic*] **:** capable of producing a developable impression on light-sensitive material without contact — used of substances (as zinc) — **ac·tin·au·tog·ra·phy** \\¦aktə,nȯ'tägrəfē\ *n* -ES

ac·tine \\'ak,tīn, -,tən\ *n* -s [Gk *aktin-, aktis* ray — more at ACTIN-] **:** a star-shaped spicule (as of a sponge)

-actine \\¦=(,)=\ *adj comb form* [Gk *aktin-, aktis*] **:** having (such or so many) rays ⟨discoactine⟩ ⟨pentactine⟩ — esp. in terms applied to sponge spicules

¹acting *adj* **1 :** holding a temporary rank or position **:** performing services temporarily ⟨~ president⟩ ⟨served in an ~ capacity⟩ **2 a :** suitable for stage performance ⟨the best ~ play he ever wrote⟩ **b :** prepared with directions for acting or performing ⟨an ~ text of a play⟩

²acting *n* -s **1 a :** the art or practice of representing a character on the stage or in a motion picture or radio or television play ⟨to choose ~ as a career⟩ **b :** a particular mode or style of such representation ⟨the conventions of 19th century ~⟩ **2 :** SIMULATION ⟨his affability is a piece of ~⟩

acting area *n* **:** the area of a stage left visible to the audience by the stage setting and usable by actors in the performance of a scene

actini- — see ACTIN-

ac·tin·ia \\ak'tinēə\ *n* [NL, fr. *actin-* + *-ia*] **1** *cap, in some classifications* **:** a genus of sea anemones nearly coextensive with the order Actiniaria **2** *pl* **actini·ae** \\-ē,ē\ *or* **actinias :** any sea anemone or related animal

¹ac·tin·i·an \\(')ak¦tinēən\ *or* **ac·tin·i·ar·i·an** \\¦ak,tinē¦a(a)rēən, ak¦t-\ *or* **ac·ti·nar·i·an** \\¦aktə¦na(a)r-\ *adj* [NL *Actinia* or *Actiniaria*, *Actinaria* + E *-an*] **:** of or relating to the Actiniaria

²actinian \\"\ *or* **actiniarian** \\"\ *or* **actinarian** \\"\ *n* -s **:** one of the Actiniaria **:** SEA ANEMONE

ac·tin·i·ar·ia \\(,)ak,tinē'a(a)rēə\ *n pl, cap* [NL, fr. *Actinia* + *-aria*] **:** an order or suborder of Anthozoa (subclass Zoantharia) comprising the sea anemones which differ from the corals in forming no hard skeleton and in existing as separate individuals

ac·tin·ic \\(')ak¦tinik\ *adj* [*actin-* + *-ic*] **:** having photochemical properties or effects **:** possessing or exhibiting actinism — **ac·tin·i·cal·ly** \\-nək(ə)lē\ *adv*

actinic focus *n* **:** the focus at which the chemically most effective rays as distinguished from the visually most effective are brought together (as by a lens) — called also *chemical focus*

actinic glass *n* **:** glass that transmits light of high visibility (as green) but reduces the intensity of both infrared and ultraviolet and is often used for protecting the eyes of industrial workers

actinic ray *n* **:** a radiation (as the green, blue, violet, and ultraviolet rays of the spectrum) having marked photochemical action

ac·ti·nide \ˈaktəˌnīd\ *n* -s [ISV *actin-* + *-ide*] **:** a chemical element of the actinide series

actinide series *n* **:** a series of heavy radioactive metallic elements of increasing atomic number considered to be analogous to the lanthanide series and to begin with actinium (89) or thorium (90) and end with element of atomic number 103 — compare ACTINIUM SERIES, PERIODIC TABLE

ac·ti·nid·ia \ˌaktəˈnidēə\ *n, cap* [NL, fr. *actin-* + *-idia* (pl. of *-idium*)] **:** a small genus (the type of the family Actinidiaceae) of Asiatic woody vines having alternate simple leaves, dioecious or polygamous axillary flowers, and many-seeded berries — see SILVERVINE

ac·ti·nid·i·a·ce·ae \ˌaktəˌnidēˈāsēˌē\ *n pl, cap* [NL, fr. *Actinidia*, type genus + *-aceae*] **:** a family of trees, shrubs, or woody vines (order Parietales) with stamens distinct or in fascicles adnate to the petals and a single multiloculate pistil

ac·ti·nif·er·ous \ˌaktəˈnif(ə)rəs\ *adj* [NL *actinium* + E *-ferous*] **:** containing actinium

ac·tin·i·form \akˈtinəˌfȯrm\ *adj* [*actin-* + *-form*] **:** having a radiated form **:** like a sea anemone

ac·ti·nine \ˈaktəˌnēn, -ˌnən\ *n* -s [NL *Actinia* (genus name of *Actinia equina*) + E *-ine*] **:** a base $C_7H_{15}NO_2$ found in a sea anemone (*Actinia equina*)

actinio- *comb form* [*Actinia*] **:** actinian ⟨*actinio*chrome⟩ ⟨*actinio*hematin⟩

ac·tin·i·o·chrome \akˈtinēəˌkrōm\ *n* [ISV *actinio-* + *-chrome*] **:** a reddish pigment found in certain Anthozoa or Actinozoa

ac·tin·i·o·hem·a·tin \akˌtinē(ˌ)ō'-\ *n* -s [*actinio-* + *hematin*] **:** a respiratory pigment obtained from a sea anemone (*Actinia equina*) and now considered to be a mixture of cytochromes

ac·tin·i·o·mor·pha \akˌtinēōˈmȯrfə\ [NL, fr. *actinio-* + *-morpha*] *syn of* ZOANTHARIA

ac·ti·nism \ˈaktəˌnizəm\ *n* -s [*actin-* + *-ism*] **:** the property of radiant energy esp. in the visible and ultraviolet spectral regions by which chemical changes are produced (as in light-sensitive photographic emulsions) — compare ACTINIC RAY

ac·ti·nis·tia \ˌaktəˈnistēə\ *n pl, cap* [NL, fr. *actin-* + *-istia* (fr. Gk *histion* web, cloth, sail); akin to Gk *histos* mast, weaver's beam, web — more at STAMEN] **:** an order (superorder Crossopterygii) of chiefly Mesozoic fishes including the family Coelacanthidae having the interspinous bones supporting each dorsal and anal fin fused into one piece — compare LATIMERIA

ac·tin·i·um \akˈtinēəm\ *n* -s [NL, fr. *actin-* + *-ium*; fr. the darkening effect of light on some zinc sulfide] **1 :** a supposed chemical element once thought to occur in commercial zinc **2 :** a radioactive trivalent metallic element resembling lanthanum in chemical properties formed by alpha radiation from protactinium and found esp. in pitchblende — symbol *Ac;* see ACTINIDE SERIES, ACTINIUM SERIES; ELEMENT table

actinium emanation *n* **:** ACTINON

actinium series *n* **:** a radioactive series beginning with actinouranium, constituting the isotope of uranium of mass number 235, and ending with actinium D, constituting the nonradioactive isotope of lead of mass number 207: actinouranium, at. no. 92 (syn. uranium 235)→ uranium Y, at. no. 90 (syn. thorium 231)→ protactinium 231, at. no. 91→ actinium 227, at. no. 89→ radioactinium, at. no. 90 (syn. thorium 227) [or actinium K, at. no. 87 (syn. francium 223)]→ actinium X, at. no. 88 (syn. radium 223)→ actinon, at. no. 86 (syn. radon 219)→ actinium A, at. no. 84 (syn. polonium 215)→ actinium B, at. no. 82 (syn. lead 211) [or astatine 215, at. no. 85]→ actinium C, at. no. 83 (syn. bismuth 211)→ actinium C, at. no. 84 (syn. polonium 211) [or actinium C, at. no. 81 (syn. thallium 207)]→ actinium D, at. no. 82 (syn. lead 207) — compare ACTINIDE SERIES

ac·tin·i·zoa \(ˌ)akˌtinəˈzōə\ [NL, fr. *actin-* + *-zoa*] *syn of* ANTHOZOA

ac·ti·ni·zo·an \ˌakˌtinəˈzōən, akˌt-\ *adj* [NL *Actinizoa* + E *-an*] **:** ANTHOZOAN

actino- — see ACTIN-

ac·ti·no·bac·il·lary \ˌaktə(ˌ)nōˈbasəˌlerē *also* -ˌbəˈsiləre\ *adj* [*actin-* + *bacillary*] **:** caused by actinobacilli

ac·ti·no·bac·il·lo·sis \-ˌbasəˈlōsəs\ *n, pl* **actinobacilloses** \-ōˌsēz\ [NL, fr. *actinobacillus* + *-osis*] **:** a disease of cattle, swine, and occas. of other domestic animals or man resembling actinomycosis and caused by a true bacterium (*Actinobacillus lignieresi*)

ac·ti·no·bac·il·lot·ic \-ˈläd·ik\ *adj* [fr. NL *actinobacillosis*, after such pairs as NL *psychosis:* E *psychotic*] **:** of or relating to actinobacillosis

ac·ti·no·ba·cil·lus \-bəˈsiləs\ *n* [NL, fr. *actin-* + *bacillus*] **1** *cap* **:** a genus of aerobic gram-negative parasitic bacteria (family Brucellaceae) forming filaments resembling streptobacilli — see ACTINOBACILLOSIS **2** *pl* **actinobacil·li** \-iˌlī\ **:** a bacterium of the genus *Actinobacillus*

ac·tin·o·branch \akˈtinəˌbraŋk\ *or* **ac·ti·no·bran·chia** \ˌaktə(ˌ)nōˈbraŋkēə\ *n* -s [NL *actinobranchia*, fr. *actin-* + *branchia*] **:** a gill-like organ of certain Anthozoa

ac·ti·no·chem·is·try \ˌaktə(ˌ)nō'-\ *n* -ES [*actin-* + *chemistry*] **:** chemistry in its relations to actinism **:** PHOTOCHEMISTRY

ac·ti·no·cri·nite \ˌaktə(ˌ)nōˈkrīˌnīt\ *n* -s [prob. fr. F, fr. NL *Actinocrinus* + F *-ite*] **:** a fossil crinoid of *Actinocrinus* or a related genus

ac·ti·no·cri·nus \-ˈkrīnəs\ *n, cap* [NL, fr. *actin-* + *-crinus*] **:** a genus (the type of the family Actinocrinidae) of crinoids abundant in the Mississippian rocks of America and Europe

ac·tin·o·drome \akˈtinəˌdrōm\ *or* **ac·ti·nod·ro·mous** \ˌaktəˈnädrəməs\ *adj* [*actin-* + *-drome, -dromous*] *of a leaf* **:** palmately veined

ac·ti·no·elec·tric \ˌaktə(ˌ)nō+\ *adj* [*actin-* + *electric*] **:** exhibiting photoconductivity

ac·tin·o·graph \akˈtinəˌgraf\ *n* -s [*actin-* + *-graph*] **:** an instrument operating on the principle of the slide rule and used for calculating suitable exposure time in photography — **ac·ti·nog·ra·phy** \ˌaktəˈnägrəfē\ *n* -ES

ac·ti·noid \ˈaktəˌnȯid\ *adj* [*actin-* + *-oid*] **1 :** resembling a ray esp. of a radially symmetrical animal **2 :** exhibiting radial symmetry

ac·ti·noi·da \ˌaktəˈnȯidə\ *or* **ac·ti·noi·dea** \-dēə\ [NL, fr. *actin-* + *-oida, -oidea*] *syn of* ANTHOZOA

ac·tin·o·lite \akˈtinəˌlīt\ *n* -s [*actin-* + *-lite;* trans. of G *strahlstein*] **:** a mineral consisting of a bright green or grayish green variety of amphibole containing calcium, magnesium, and iron $Ca(Mg,Fe)_5Si_8O_{22}(OH)_2$ and occurring often in fibrous, radiated, or columnar forms (sp. gr. 3–3.2) — **ac·tin·o·lit·ic** \akˌtinəˈlid·ik, akˌt-\ *adj*

ac·tin·o·logue \akˈtinəˌlȯg *also* -äg\ *n* -s [back-formation fr. *actinology*] **:** an organ or part of an actinomere that corresponds to another in a different actinomere — **ac·ti·nol·o·gous** \ˌaktəˈnäləgəs\ *adj*

ac·ti·nol·o·gy \ˌaktəˈnäləjē\ *n* -ES [ISV *actin-* + *-logy*] **1 :** a science that deals with actinism and photochemical effects **2 :** correspondence of similar parts of a radiate animal (as of the different actinomeres) **:** radial homology

ac·tin·o·mere \akˈtinəˌmi(ə)r\ *n* -s [prob. fr. F *actinomère*, fr. *actin-* + *-mère* -mere] **:** one of the radial segments composing the body of a radiate animal — **ac·tin·o·mer·ic** \-ˌtinəˈmerik\ *adj*

ac·ti·nom·e·ter \ˌaktəˈnäməd·ə(r)\ *n* -s [*actin-* + *-meter*] **1 :** an instrument for measuring the direct heating power of the sun's rays **2 :** an instrument for measuring the actinic power of radiant energy usu. by means of light-sensitive paper that darkens on exposure to light; *specif* **:** a photographic instrument for measuring the exposure to be given — compare PHOTOMETER — **ac·ti·no·met·ric** \ˌaktəˌnōˈme·trik\ *adj* — **ac·ti·nom·e·try** \ˌaktəˈnämə·trē\ *n* -ES

ac·ti·no·mor·phic \ˌaktə(ˌ)nōˈmȯrfik\ *also* **ac·ti·no·mor·phous** \-fəs\ *adj* [ISV *actin-* + *-morphic* or *-morphous*] **:** radially symmetrical — used of organisms, organs, or parts capable of division into essentially symmetrical halves by any longitudinal plane passing through the axis; compare ZYGOMORPHIC

ac·ti·no·mor·phy \-fē\ *n* -ES [*actin-* + *-morphy*] **:** the quality or state of being actinomorphic

ac·ti·no·my·ces \ˌ==(ˌ)=ˈmīˌsēz\ *n* [NL, fr. *actin-* + *-myces*] **1** *cap* **:** a genus of filamentous bacteria (family Actinomycetaceae) including numerous soil-inhabiting saprophytes and various disease-producing plant and animal parasites that form a much-branched mycelium which may break up into segments functioning as conidia and which in lesions of the animal body may make up conspicuous rosettes of radiating clavate threads — see ACTINOMYCOSIS **2** *pl* **actinomyces :** a bacterium of the genus *Actinomyces*

ac·ti·no·my·ce·ta·ce·ae \ˌ==(ˌ)=ˌmīsəˈtāsēˌē\ *n pl, cap* [NL, fr. *Actinomycet-, Actinomyces*, type genus + *-aceae*] **:** a family of filamentous bacteria of the order Actinomycetales, often branched, sometimes forming a mycelium that readily breaks up into bacillary elements, and sometimes producing conidia

ac·ti·no·my·ce·tal \-ˌmīˈsēd·ᵊl\ *adj* [NL *Actinomycetales*] **:** of or belonging to the Actinomycetales

ac·ti·no·my·ce·ta·les \-ˌmīsəˈtā(ˌ)lēz\ *n pl, cap* [NL, fr. *Actinomycet-, Actinomyces* + *-ales*] **:** an order of filamentous or rod-shaped bacteria tending strongly to the development of branches and true mycelium and lacking photosynthetic pigment — see MYCOBACTERIACEAE, STREPTOMYCETACEAE

ac·ti·no·my·cete \-ˈmīˌsēt, -ˌmīˈsēt\ *n* -s [ISV *actin-* + *-mycete*] **:** any organism belonging to the order Actinomycetales — **ac·ti·no·my·ce·tous** \-ˌmīˈsēd·əs\ *adj*

ac·ti·no·my·ce·tin \-ˌmīˈsētᵊn\ *n* -s [*actin-* + *mycetin*] **:** an enzymelike antibiotic obtained from a soil actinomycete (*Streptomyces albus*) that lyses various bacteria (as living streptococci or heat-killed colon bacilli)

ac·ti·no·my·cin \ˌ==(ˌ)=ˈmīsᵊn\ *n* -s [NL *Actinomyces* + E *-in*] **:** any of various red or yellow-red mostly toxic crystalline polypeptide antibiotics isolated from various soil bacteria (esp. *Streptomyces antibioticus*) — usu. followed by a distinguishing letter ⟨~ C is one of the less toxic members of the group⟩

ac·ti·no·my·co·ma \ˌ==(ˌ)=ˌmīˈkōmə\ *n, pl* **actinomycomas** \-məz\ *or* **actinomycoma·ta** \-məd·ə\ [NL, fr. *actin-* + *myc-* + *-oma*] **:** the characteristic granulomatous lesion of actinomycosis

ac·ti·no·my·co·sis \-ˌmīˈkōsəs\ *n, pl* **actinomyco·ses** \-ōˌsēz\ [NL, fr. *Actinomyces* + *-osis*] **:** infection with actinomycetes esp. of the genus *Actinomyces:* **a :** a chronic infectious disease of cattle, swine, and man characterized by the formation in mouth and jaw and sometimes also in chest, intestines, skin, mammary tissue, or brain of hard granulomatous masses that may break down and discharge pus containing the causative actinomycetes (usu. *Actinomyces bovis* in domestic animals and presumably *A. israeli* in man) — see ACTINOMYCOMA **b :** POTATO SCAB

ac·ti·no·my·cot·ic \-ˈkäd·ik\ *adj* [fr. NL *actinomycosis*, after such pairs as NL *psychosis:* E *psychotic*] **:** of or relating to actinomycosis

ac·ti·no·myx·i·da \-ˈmiksədə\ *syn of* ACTINOMYXIDIA

ac·ti·no·myx·id·ia \-(ˌ)mikˈsidēə\ *n pl, cap* [NL, alter. of *Actinomyxida*, fr. *actin-* + *myx-* + *-ida*] **:** a small order of cnidosporidian protozoan parasites of worms distinguished by spores with trivalve shells and three polar capsules — **ac·ti·no·myx·id·i·an** \-ˈsidēən\ *adj or n*

ac·ti·no·myx·i·di·i·da \ˌ==(ˌ)=ˌmiksəˈdīədə\ *syn of* ACTINOMYXIDIA

ac·ti·non \ˈaktəˌnän\ *n* -s [NL, fr. *actinium* + *-on*] **:** a heavy radioactive gaseous isotope of the group of inert gases that is isotopic with radon and thoron, is formed from actinium X, emits alpha rays, and lives only a few seconds (mass number 219) — called also *actinium emanation;* see ACTINIUM SERIES

ac·ti·no·ne·ma \ˌaktə(ˌ)nōˈnēmə\ *n, cap* [NL, fr. *actin-* + *-nema*] **:** a form genus of imperfect fungi (order Melanconiales) having hyaline 2-celled spores

ac·tin·o·phage \akˈtinəˌfāj\ *n* -s [*actinomycete* + *-phage*] **:** a phage that develops in and lyses an actinomycete — compare BACTERIOPHAGE

ac·tin·o·phore \-ˌfō(ə)r\ *n* -s [*actin-* + *-phore*] **:** a bony or cartilaginous element supporting the fin rays of fishes

ac·ti·noph·o·rous \ˌaktəˈnäf(ə)rəs\ *adj* [Gk *aktinophoros* ray-bearing, fr. *aktin-* actin- + *-phoros* -phorous] **:** having raylike spines

ac·ti·noph·ry·an \ˌaktəˈnäfrēən\ *adj* [NL *Actinophrys* + E *-an*] **:** of or belonging to *Actinophrys*

ac·ti·noph·rys \ˌaktəˈnäfrəs, akˈtinəf-\ *n* [NL, fr. *actin-* + Gk *ophrys* brow, rim — more at BROW] **1** *cap* **:** a genus of protozoans (order Heliozoa) widely distributed in stagnant water **2** *pl* **actinoph·rys :** a protozoan of the genus *Actinophrys*

actinophrys

ac·ti·no·phy·to·sis \ˌaktə(ˌ)nō(ˌ)fīˈtōsəs\ *n, pl* **actinophyto·ses** \-ōˌsēz\ [NL, fr. *actin-* + *phytosis*] **:** STREPTOTRICHOSIS

ac·tin·o·pod \akˈtinəˌpäd\ *n* -s [NL *Actinopoda*] **:** a protozoan of the subclass Actinopoda

ac·ti·nop·o·da \ˌaktəˈnäpədə\ *n pl, cap* [NL, fr. *actin-* + *-poda*] **1** *in former classifications* **:** an order of holothurians with tentacles arising from radial ambulacral vessels **2 :** a subclass of Sarcodina comprising usu. freely floating protozoans with highly specialized pseudopodia and including the orders Heliozoa and Radiolaria — compare AXOPODIUM — **ac·ti·no·po·di·an** \ˌ==(ˌ)nōˈpōdēən\ *n* -s

ac·ti·nop·te·ran \ˌaktəˈnäptərən\ *n* -s [NL *Actinopteri* + E *-an*] **:** ACTINOPTERYGIAN

ac·ti·nop·te·ri \-təˌrī\ [NL, fr. *actin-* + *-pteri* (pl. of *-pterus*)] *syn of* ACTINOPTERYGII

¹ac·ti·nop·te·ryg·i·an \ˌ==ˌ==ˈrijēən\ *adj* [NL *Actinopterygii* + E *-an*] **:** of or relating to the Actinopterygii

²actinopterygian \"\ *n* -s **:** one of the Actinopterygii

ac·ti·nop·te·ryg·ii \ˌ==ˌ==ˈ=ēˌī\ *n pl, cap* [NL, fr. *actin-* + *-pterygii* (fr. Gk *pteryg-, pteryx* wing); akin to Gk *pteron* feather, wing — more at FEATHER] *in many classifications* **:** a subclass or other division of Teleostomi comprising fishes having the projecting part of the paired fins supported only by dermal rays and being coextensive with the Teleostomi excluding the Choanichthyes — **ac·ti·nop·te·ryg·i·ous** \ˌ==ˌ== ˈ=ēəs\ *adj*

ac·tin·o·some \akˈtinəˌsōm\ *also* **ac·ti·no·so·ma** \ˌaktə(ˌ)nōˈsōmə\ *n* -s [*actinosome* fr. *actin-* + *-some; actinosoma* fr. NL, fr. *actin-* + *-soma*] **:** the entire body of a simple or compound coelenterate

ac·ti·no·sphae·ri·um \ˌaktə(ˌ)nōˈsfirēəm\ *n, cap* [NL, fr. *actin-* + Gk *sphairion* little ball, dim. of *sphaira* ball, sphere — more at SPHERE] **:** a genus of large freshwater protozoans (order Heliozoa)

ac·ti·nost \ˈaktəˌnäst\ *n* -s [*actin-* + *-ost*] **:** one of certain small bones directly supporting the rays of paired fins of teleost and some ganoid fishes — called also *carpal, pterygiophore;* compare HYPERCORACOID

ac·tin·o·stele \akˈtinəˌstēl *also* ˌaktəˌ(ˌ)nōˈstēlē\ *n* -s [*actin-* + *stele*] **:** a vascular core (as in most roots and some stems) having the xylem and phloem in alternating or radial groups within a pericycle — compare STELE

ac·ti·nos·to·mal \ˌaktəˈnästəməl\ *adj* [*actinostome* + *-al*] **:** relating or belonging to an actinostome

ac·tin·o·stome \akˈtinəˌstōm\ *n* -s [*actin-* + *-stome*] **1 :** the mouth of a radially symmetrical animal **2 :** the peristome of an echinoderm

ac·ti·no·ther·a·py \ˌaktə(ˌ)nōˈtherəpē\ *n* -ES [ISV *actin-* + *therapy*] **:** application for therapeutic purposes of the chemically active rays of the spectrum (as ultraviolet light or X rays)

ac·ti·no·trich·i·um \ˌaktə(ˌ)nōˈtrikēəm\ *also* **ac·tin·o·trich** \akˈtinəˌtrik\ *n, pl* **ac·ti·no·trich·ia** \-ˈtrikēə\ *also* **ac·tin·o·trichs** \-ˌtriks\ [NL *actinotrichium*, fr. *actin-* + Gk *trich-, thrix* hair + NL *-ium* — more at TRICH-] **:** any of the hairy threadlike fibers in the fin fold of an embryo fish which fuse and form the base of the rays

ac·ti·not·ro·cha \ˌaktəˈnä·trəkə\ *n, pl* **actinotro·chae** \-ˌkē\ [NL, fr. *actin-* + *-trocha*] **:** the free-swimming larva of the genus *Phoronis*

ac·ti·no·ura·ni·um \ˌaktə(ˌ)nō-\ *n* [ISV *actino-* (fr. NL *actinium*) + *uranium*] **:** the uranium isotope of mass 235

ac·ti·no·zoa \ˌaktə(ˌ)nōˈzōə\ [NL, fr. *actin-* + *-zoa*] *syn of* ANTHOZOA

ac·ti·no·zo·an \ˌ==(ˌ)=ˈzōən\ *or* **ac·ti·no·zo·al** \-əl\ *adj* [NL *Actinozoa* + E *-an* or *-al*] **:** ANTHOZOAN

ac·ti·no·zo·on \ˌ==(ˌ)=ˈzōˌän\ *n* -s [NL, fr. *Actinaria* + *-zoon*] **:** ANTHOZOON

actins *pl of* ACTIN

ac·tin·u·la \akˈtinyələ\ *n, pl* **actinulas** \-ləz\ *or* **actinu·lae** \-ˌlē\ [NL, fr. *actin-* + *-ula*] **:** a creeping larva of the hydroid generation of certain coelenterates (as Tubularia) that finally attaches and develops into a polyp

ac·tio \ˈakshēˌō, ˈäktēˌō\ *n, pl* **acti·o·nes** \ˌakshēˈōˌnēz, ˌäktēˈōˌnās\ [L] *Roman law* **:** an action or right of action — see FORMULA 5

ac·tio ad di·stans \-ˌadˈdiˌstanz, -ˌädˈdiˌstän(t)s\ *or* **actio in distans** \-ˌinˈd-\ *n* [NL] **:** action at a distance or without contact ⟨Leibnitz held that the apparent physical impossibility of *actio ad distans* was an objection to gravitation⟩

actio bo·nae fi·dei \-ˈbōnēˈfīdēˌī, -ˈbōˌnīˈfideˌē\ *n, pl* **actiones bonae fidei** [LL, lit., action of good faith] **:** an action in Roman law giving great power to the trial judge to take all matters of good faith, conscience, and equity into consideration of the whole case — contrasted with *actio stricti juris*

¹ac·tion \ˈakshən\ *n* -s [ME *accioun*, fr. MF *action*, fr. L *action-, actio*, fr. *actus* (past part. of *agere* to do) + *-ion-, -io* -ion — more at AGENT] **1 :** a deliberative or authorized proceeding: **a** (1) **:** a legal proceeding by which one demands or enforces one's right in a court of justice (2) **:** a judicial proceeding for the enforcement or protection of a right, the redress or prevention of a wrong, or the punishment of a public offense — usu. distinguished from *special proceeding* (3) **:** the right to bring or maintain such a legal or judicial proceeding — see SUIT **b** (1) **:** an award by a judicial body (2) **:** an act or decision by an executive or legislative body (as of a government or a political party) or by a supranational agency ⟨the ~ taken by Congress followed a lengthy debate⟩ ⟨strikes organized by ~ committees⟩ **2 a :** the bringing about of an alteration by force or through some natural agency ⟨the ~ of water on rocks⟩ **b :** the process of change or alteration considered as a natural condition **:** ACTIVITY ⟨intervals of ~ and repose⟩ **c :** the progressive alteration of mental states or of mental and physical states coordinately esp. when resulting in an observable effect on the external world — compare BEHAVIOR 1b **d :** a quantity expressed in cgs units of erg seconds relating to the change of a dynamic system from one configuration to another and regarded in classical dynamics as twice the product of the average kinetic energy during the change and the time interval in which the change takes place **e** *ecol* **:** the effect of the environment on the individuals exposed to it as a factor in community formation — see COACTION **3 :** the process of doing **:** exertion of energy **:** PERFORMANCE **:** manner of doing: **a :** the deportment of an actor or speaker or his expression by means of attitude, voice, gesture, and countenance ⟨an actor's words and ~s should agree⟩ **b :** the movement of the feet and legs (of a horse or dog) **c :** a function of the body or of one of its parts or organs; *specif* **:** DEFECATION **4 :** a voluntary act of will that manifests itself externally ⟨an emergency requiring ~⟩ or that may be completed internally (as in contemplation) — contrasted with *passion* **5 a :** a thing done **:** DEED **b actions** *pl* **:** BEHAVIOR, CONDUCT 3c ⟨somber ~s⟩ **c :** INITIATIVE, ENTERPRISE ⟨a man of ~⟩ **6 a** (1) **:** an engagement between troops ⟨two small ~s for control of the hill⟩ or ships ⟨decks cleared for ~⟩ (2) **:** combat in war ⟨he saw ~ on a destroyer⟩ **b** (1) **:** a real or imaginary event or series of events forming the subject of a play, poem, or other composition (2) **:** the unfolding of the events of a drama or work of fiction **:** PLOT (3) **:** the movement of incidents in a plot ⟨*action*-packed drama⟩ ⟨an ~ story⟩ **c :** the combination of circumstances that constitute the subject matter of a painting or sculpture **d** (1) **:** a religious ceremony **:** a sacramental or devotional performance (2) **:** the canon of the mass, the communion service, or the Lord's Supper **7 :** a share of stock **8 a :** an operating mechanism: (1) **:** a mechanism connecting the keys with the sounding or effective part (as strings, pipes, or type faces) of a keyboard instrument or machine (2) **:** a mechanism by means of which a firearm is loaded and fired — compare LOCK; AUTOMATIC, DOUBLE-ACTION, SEMIAUTOMATIC, SINGLE-ACTION **b :** the manner in which a mechanism operates: (1) **:** the response or resistance of keys in a keyboard-operated mechanism to the player's or operator's fingers ⟨a stiff ~⟩ ⟨a sluggish ~⟩ (2) **:** the amount of resiliency and flexibility in a fishing rod in relation to its length and diameter ⟨dry-fly ~⟩ ⟨wet-fly ~⟩ (3) **:** the relationship between the number of turns made by the reel spool in a fishing reel for every turn of the reel handle ⟨a single-*action* reel⟩ **9 a :** the price movement and trading volume of a commodity, security, or market **b :** the entire process of betting including essentially the offering and acceptance of a bet and determination of a winner

²action \"\ *vt* -ED/-ING/-S *archaic* **:** to bring a legal action against

ac·tion·abil·i·ty \ˌaksh(ə)nəˈbiləd·ē\ *n* -ES **:** the quality or state of being actionable

ac·tion·able \ˈaksh(ə)nəbəl\ *adj* **:** subject to or affording ground for an action or suit at law ⟨slander is ~⟩

ac·tion·al \ˈakshənᵊl, -shnəl\ *adj* **1 :** relating to action or an action **2** *of a passive verb form* **:** expressing an action (as *was closed* in "the door was closed at eight o'clock") — contrasted with *statal*

action current *n* **:** an electric current arising from a variation of potential occurring during activity in living tissue (as a muscle or nerve)

actiones *pl of* ACTIO

ac·tion·ing \ˈaksh(ə)niŋ, -ēŋ\ *n* -s **:** the providing of an action to a gun; *also* **:** ACTION 8a(2)

ac·tion·ist \-sh(ə)nəst\ *n* -s **:** an advocate of direct action esp. in politics

action noun *n* **:** a noun denoting action (as *belief, inspection, arrival*) — sometimes used to include verbal nouns (as the infinitive *to believe* or the gerund *believing*)

action on the case 1 : TRESPASS ON THE CASE **2 :** a remedy for recovery of damages for tort in instances where injury was neither immediate nor direct — usu. referring to an action ex delicto but sometimes to assumpsit; compare FORM OF ACTION

action–research *n* **:** the use of techniques of social and psychological research to identify social problems in a group or community coupled with active participation of the investigators in group efforts to solve these problems

action sermon *n* **:** the sermon preached immediately before communion in Scottish Presbyterian churches

action spectrum *n* **:** a graphic representation of a physiological reaction; *specif* **:** physiological activity plotted against light wavelength

action time *n* **:** the time during which a stimulus must act to produce maximum effect — compare PRESENTATION TIME

ac·tio stric·ti ju·ris \-ˈstrikˌtīˈjürəs, -kˌtēˈyürəs\ *n, pl* **actiones stricti juris** [LL, lit., action of strict law] **:** an action in Roman law that the judge was to decide according to the strict legal rules without reference to equitable considerations — contrasted with *actio bonae fidei*

ac·ti·py·laea \ˌaktəˌpīˈlēə\ *or* **ac·ti·py·lar·ia** \-ˈla(a)rēə\ [*Actipylaea* fr. NL, alter. of *Actipylea; Actipylaria* fr. NL, fr. *Actipylea* + *-aria*] *syn of* ACTIPYLEA

ac·ti·py·lea \ˌaktəˌpīˈlēə\ *n pl, cap* [NL, irreg. fr. Gk *aktis* ray + *pylē* gate — more at ACTIN-, PYLON] **:** a suborder of Radiolaria comprising protozoa with skeletons of spicules of strontium sulfate

ac·ti·va·ble \ˈaktəvəbəl\ *adj* [*activate* + *-able*] **:** capable of being activated

ac·ti·vate \ˈaktəˌvāt, *usu* -ād·+V\ *vb* -ED/-ING/-S [*active* + *-ate*] *vt* **:** to make active or more active: as **a** (1) **:** to render (molecules) capable of reaction or to increase the reactivity of (parts of molecules) by the presence of neighboring groups (2) **:** to convert (a compound, as a provitamin or enzyme) into an active form or different compound, esp. into one that has a particular biological action ⟨~ ergosterol by irradiation to vitamin D_2 for use in treating rickets⟩ **b :** to render (a substance) radioactive, luminescent, photosensitive, or photoconductive by treatment (as by radiation or electric oscillation) or by admixture of an impurity **c** (1) **:** to alter the nature of the surface of (specific mineral particles in the flotation of an ore pulp) so that certain reagents will adhere (2) **:** to treat (materials, as carbon, clay, alumina, silica gel) so as to improve esp. adsorptive properties (as for use in removing colors from sugar solutions and other solutions, chemicals from vapor lines, and odors from water) **d :** to treat by prolonged aeration so as to favor the growth of organisms that will decompose (sewage) **e** (1) **:** to start development of (an egg) by fertilization or experimentally by chemicals (2) **:** to stimulate to sexual activity **:** induce heat or rut in **f :** to set up or formally institute (a military unit) with the necessary personnel and equipment ~ *vi* **:** to become active **syn** see VITALIZE

activated alumina *n* **:** a porous highly adsorptive alumina made usu. by heating alumina hydrates and used chiefly in drying gases and liquids

activated carbon *or* **activated charcoal** *n* **:** a highly adsorbent powdered or granular carbon or charcoal made usu. by carbonization of carbonaceous materials (as wood or coconut shells) and chemical activation (as by oxidizing gases) and used chiefly for adsorbing gases, for purifying syrups, for removing undesirable colors and odors, and for solvent recovery — called also *active carbon;* compare BONE BLACK

activated sludge process *n* **:** a sewage treatment procedure in which the decomposition of the raw sewage is hastened by the addition to it of biologically active sewage sludge

ac·ti·va·tion \ˌaktəˈvāshən\ *n* -s **:** the act or process of activating

activation energy *n* **:** the minimum amount of energy required to convert a normal stable molecule into a reactive molecule

ac·ti·va·tor \ˈaktəˌvād·ə(r)\ *n* -s **:** one that activates: as **a :** a substance that renders another substance active in a specific manner: as (1) **:** a chemical (as an ethanolamine) that acts with an accelerator to increase the rate of vulcanization of rubber (2) **:** an impurity (as a metal) present in small amounts in a luminescent solid (as a phosphor) to which the luminescence is attributed (3) **:** a substance (as a chloride ion) that increases the activity of an enzyme — usu. distinguished from *coenzyme* and *kinase* **b** *embryol* **:** a substance given off by developing tissue that stimulates differentiation of adjacent tissue; *also* **:** a structure giving off such a stimulant **c :** ACCELERATOR 1b

¹ac·tive \ˈaktiv, -ēv *also* -əv\ *adj* [ME, fr. MF or L; MF *actif,* fr. L *activus,* fr. *actus* (past part. of *agere* to act) + *-ivus* -ive — more at AGENT] **1 :** characterized by action rather than by contemplation or speculation ⟨an ~ man⟩ **2 :** productive of action or movement ⟨a dog very much awake and filled with ~ antagonism —Jack McLaren⟩ **3 a** *of a verb form or voice* **:** asserting that the person or thing represented by the grammatical subject performs the action represented by the verb ⟨*hits* in "he hits the ball" and *shone* in "the sun shone" are ~⟩ — contrasted with *middle* and *passive* **b :** expressing action as distinct from mere existence or state ⟨"he walks" and "he walked" have ~ verbs⟩ — now used esp. in the grammar of certain American Indian and African languages; compare NEUTER 1b, STATIC, STATIVE **c** *of a grammatical construction* **:** containing an active verb form **4 :** quick in physical movement **:** of agile and vigorous habit **:** NIMBLE, LIVELY ⟨an animal ~ in burrowing⟩ **5 :** requiring vigorous action or exertion ⟨an interest in ~ sports⟩ **6 a :** having practical operation or results **:** EFFECTIVE ⟨an ~ law⟩ **b** *of a volcano* **:** erupting at the present time or at intervals of a few years or having a crater that contains fluid lava — compare DORMANT, EXTINCT **7 a :** disposed to action **:** ENERGETIC, DILIGENT ⟨to take an ~ interest⟩ **b :** engaged in an action or activity **:** PARTICIPATING ⟨an ~ club member⟩ **8 :** engaged in full-time service esp. in the armed forces ⟨ordered to ~ duty⟩ **9 :** marked by present operation, transaction, movement, or use ⟨an ~ coal mine⟩ ⟨an ~ bank account⟩ ⟨~ titles in a publisher's catalog⟩ ⟨a student's ~ vocabulary⟩ **10 a :** capable of acting or reacting esp. in some specific manner or with more than ordinary vigor **:** REACTIVE, ACTIVATED ⟨~ nitrogen⟩ ⟨~ charcoal⟩ **b :** OPTICALLY ACTIVE **c :** RADIOACTIVE ⟨an ~ deposit⟩ **11 :** still eligible to win the pot in poker — used of a player who has not dropped **12 :** moving down the line or visiting in the set — used of couples in contredanses or square dances **13** *of a disease* **:** progressing or retrogressing ⟨~ tuberculosis⟩ — **ac·tive·ly** \-tə̇vlē, -li\ *adv* — **ac·tive·ness** \-ivnə̇s, -ēv- *also* -əv-\ *n* -ES

²active \"\ *n* -s **1 :** one that is active ⟨fraternity alumni and ~s⟩ **2 a :** an active verb **b :** the active voice of a language or a form in it

active amyl alcohol *n* **:** a liquid levorotatory primary alcohol $C_2H_5CH(CH_3)CH_2OH$ occurring in fusel oil; *levo*-2-methyl-1-butanol

active bond *n, Brit* **:** a bond bearing a fixed rate of interest from date of issue

active carbon *n* **:** ACTIVATED CARBON

active component *n* **:** the average power of an alternating electric current divided by the effective voltage in a circuit

active door *n* **:** the one of a pair of doors that is ordinarily used alone

active duty *or* **active service** *n* **:** full-time service in the armed forces with regular duties and pay and subject to appropriate regulations

active immunity *n* **:** immunity commonly long-lasting acquired through production of antibodies within the organism in response to the presence of antigens (as by infection or injection) — see PASSIVE IMMUNITY

active list *n* **:** a list comprising the officers and enlisted personnel of the armed forces who are performing or normally available for military duties and are receiving full pay

active mass *n* **1 :** the concentration of a reacting substance expressed usu. in moles per liter **2 :** the concentration of the portion of a dissolved electrolyte that is dissociated into ions and hence is capable of carrying the electric current

active serum *n* **:** a serum that contains complement

active trust *n* **:** a trust in which the trustee is charged with the performance of some substantial duties in respect to the control, management, and disposition of the trust property

ac·tiv·ism \ˈaktəˌvizəm, -ē,v-\ *n* -s [G *aktivismus,* fr. *aktiv* active (fr. L *activus*) + *-ismus* -ism — more at ACTIVE] **1 :** either of two philosophical doctrines: (1) the mind is active, not passive, in perception or (2) activity is creative or fundamental **:** ACTUALISM — compare PRAGMATISM, VOLUNTARISM **2 :** a doctrine or practice that emphasizes vigorous action (as the use of force for political ends)

¹ac·tiv·ist \-ˌvə̇st\ *n* -s [G *aktivist,* fr. *aktiv* + *-ist*] **:** one that advocates or practices activism

²activist \"\ *also* **ac·tiv·is·tic** \¦≈≈¦vistik, -ēk\ *adj* **:** of or belonging to or having the characteristics of activism or activists **:** advocating or practicing activism

ac·tiv·i·ty \akˈtivəd·ē, -ətē, -i\ *n* -ES [MF *activité,* fr. ML *activitat-, activitas,* fr. L *activus* active + *-itat-, -itas* -ity — more at ACTIVE] **1 :** the quality or state of being active ⟨the sphere of his ~⟩ ⟨solar ~⟩ **2 :** physical motion or exercise of force: as **a :** vigorous or energetic action **:** LIVELINESS ⟨to restrict his ~⟩ **b :** adroit or skillful physical action **:** AGILITY ⟨an athlete's ~⟩ **3 :** natural or normal function or operation ⟨~ on the stock exchange⟩: as **a :** a process (as moving or digesting) that an organism carries on or participates in by virtue of being alive **b :** any similar process (as searching, desiring, learning, or writing) that actually or potentially involves mental function; *specif* **:** an educational procedure designed to stimulate learning by firsthand experience or observation, experiment, inquiry, and discussion ⟨~ program⟩ — compare PROJECT, UNIT **4 a :** an actuating force **b** *sometimes cap* **:** a creative agency or process; *esp* **:** an ultimate or underived cosmic agency **5 a :** an occupation, pursuit, or recreation in which a person is active — often used in pl. ⟨business *activities*⟩ ⟨social *activities*⟩ **b :** a form of organized, supervised, and often extracurricular recreation (as athletic games, dramatics, or dancing) **6** *chem* **a :** the characteristic of acting rapidly or of promoting a rapid reaction ⟨the ~ of adsorbent carbon⟩ ⟨the ~ of a catalyst⟩ **b :** the apparent or effective concentration of a substance esp. in solution as judged by the behavior of the substance under given conditions, such concentration being equal to the actual concentration in very dilute ideal solutions — called also *relative fugacity* **7 :** an organizational unit for performing a specific function; *also* **:** its duties or function ⟨navy supplies procured from the nearest shore ~⟩ ⟨the food-inspection ~ of the health department⟩

activity cage *n* **:** a cage for a small animal with a treadwheel or other device by which it can exercise

activity coefficient *n* **:** the ratio of chemical activity to actual concentration **:** an arbitrary quantity that in the case of solutions is a measure of the deviation of a more or less concentrated solution from an ideal solution

activity group psychotherapy *or* **activity group therapy** *n* **:** group psychotherapy in which the subjects (as children) are permitted to act out their repressed impulses in the presence of a nonparticipating therapist

ac·tiv·ize \ˈaktə̇ˌvīz, -ē,v-\ *vt* -ED/-ING/-S **:** ACTIVATE

act of adjournal *Scots law, usu pl* **:** one of various ordinances issued by the Court of Justiciary for regulating the procedure in that court and the inferior criminal courts

act of bankruptcy *or* **act of insolvency :** an act specified by law as subjecting a person to be proceeded against as an involuntary bankrupt or insolvent

act of faith [trans. of Pg *auto-da-fé*] **:** an act requiring or displaying faith; *specif* **:** AUTO-DA-FÉ

act of god *cap G* **:** an extraordinary interruption by a natural cause (as a severe flood or earthquake) of the usual course of events that experience, prescience, or care cannot reasonably foresee or prevent — compare INEVITABLE ACCIDENT

act of grace : an act extending clemency to offenders before the law (as one at the beginning of a new reign granting pardon or amnesty to numerous offenders)

act of honor : an acceptance or payment for honor of a protested bill of exchange; *also* **:** the instrument reciting such protest and acceptance or payment

act of indemnity 1 : an act passed to relieve persons (as officials) from some penalty to which they have become liable by acting illegally or beyond the limits of their powers **2 :** an act passed to provide compensation for damage incurred in the service of the government or resulting from some public measure

act of law : a change of a person's legal rights, obligations, or liabilities (as in the acquisition of a right or exemption from a liability) arising from the legal effect of some event such as bankruptcy

act of sederunt *Scots law, usu pl* **:** one of various rules of the Court of Session for regulating procedure in that court

ac·to·my·o·sin \ˌaktəˈmīəsə̇n\ *n* [ISV *actin* + *-o-* + *myosin;* orig. formed as G *aktomyosin*] **:** a viscous substance that consists of a complex of actin and myosin, has the property of contractility, and is postulated to be concerned together with adenosine triphosphate in muscular contraction — formerly called *myosin*

ac·ton \ˈaktən\ *n* -s [ME *aketoun,* fr. OF *aketon,* cotton wool, padding, padded jacket, fr. OProv or OSp; OProv *alcoton* cotton, fr. OSp, fr. Ar *al-quṭun* the cotton] **:** a stuffed jacket worn under the mail of medieval body armor; *also* **:** a jacket plated with steel

ac·tor \ˈaktə(r) *also* -ˌtō(ə)r *or* -ˌō(ə)\ *n* -s [ME *actour* doer, pleader, fr. L *actor,* fr. *actus* (past part. of *agere* to drive, do) + *-or* — more at AGENT] **1** *Roman law* **:** one that conducts a legal action **:** PLEADER: **a :** PLAINTIFF — opposed to *reus* **b :** an advocate in civil causes **c :** the officer of a Roman corporation charged with prosecuting lawsuits in its behalf and defending those brought against it **2 a :** one that acts in a stage play, motion picture, radio or television play, or dramatic sketch **b :** a theatrical performer ⟨a professional ~⟩ **c :** one that behaves as if acting a part **3 a :** one that takes part in any affair **:** PARTICIPANT ⟨the papers and memoirs of the leading ~s are shedding new light on the inside story of government —J.A.R.Pimlott⟩ **b :** WRONGDOER, TORT-FEASOR

ac·tor·ish \ˈaktərish\ *adj* **:** having the characteristics of a professional actor; *esp* **:** noticeably histrionic or stagy in appearance or mannerism ⟨much too slick and ~ to be convincing as a cheap hustler —Stuart Byron⟩ — **ac·tor·ish·ly** *adv*

actor-proof \ˈ≈≈¦≈\ *adj* **:** effective no matter how badly acted — usu. used of a play or a part

ac·tory \ˈaktərē\ *adj* **:** ACTORISH

act out *vt* **1 a :** to represent in action ⟨my childhood was spent in reading and *acting out* what I read⟩ **b :** to translate into action ⟨unwilling to *act out* their beliefs⟩ **2** *psychoanalysis* **:** to express (repressed or unconscious impulses) directly in overt behavior without awareness or insight esp. during psychoanalytic investigation

act psychology *n* **:** psychology conceived as the study of the individual act esp. for meaning and intent — called also *intentionalism;* contrasted with *content psychology*

ac·tress \ˈaktrə̇s\ *n* -ES [*actor* + *-ess*] **1** *obs* **:** a woman that takes part in any affair **2 :** a female actor

ac·tressy \-sē\ *adj* **:** having the characteristics of a professional actress; *esp* **:** noticeably histrionic or stagy in appearance or mannerism

acts *pl of* ACT, *pres 3d sing of* ACT

-acts *pl of* -ACT

¹ac·tu·al \ˈakchə(wə)l, -ksh-\ *adj* [ME, active, existing, fr. MF *actuel,* fr. LL *actualis* active, practical, fr. L *actus* act + *-alis* -al — more at ACT] **1** *obs* **:** involving or relating to acts or deeds **:** ACTIVE ⟨her walking and other ~ performances —Shak.⟩ **2 a :** existing in act ⟨our ~ intentions⟩ **:** EXISTENT — contrasted with *potential* and *possible* **b :** existing in fact or reality **:** really acted or acting or carried out — contrasted with *ideal* and *hypothetical* ⟨in ~ life⟩ ⟨the ~ conditions⟩; distinguished from *apparent* and *nominal* ⟨the ~ cost of goods⟩ **3 :** not spurious **:** REAL, GENUINE ⟨an ~ blizzard⟩ ⟨~ falsehood⟩ ⟨hard-pressed but not in ~ poverty⟩ **4 :** in existence or taking place at the time **:** PRESENT, CURRENT ⟨caught in the ~ commission of the crime⟩ **5** *physics* **:** KINETIC; *also* **:** MOTIVE, SENSIBLE — used of energy **syn** see REAL

²actual \"\ *n* -s **1 :** something that is actual or exists in fact **:** REALITY **2 :** something actually received or at hand (as a cash receipt or a market commodity) as distinct from estimated or expected ⟨trading in both ~s and futures in grain⟩

actual cautery *n* **:** an agent (as a hot iron, electrocautery, or moxa) used to destroy tissue by heat — compare POTENTIAL CAUTERY

actual cost *n* **:** cost based on the most factual allocation of historical cost factors — compare ESTIMATED COST, STANDARD COST

actual fraud *n* **:** FRAUD 1a(1)

actual horizon *n* **:** HORIZON 1b(2)

ac·tu·al·ism \ˈakchə(wə)ˌlizəm, -ksh-\ *n* -s [¹*actual* + *-ism*] **1 :** a philosophic doctrine that all existence is active or spiritual, not inert or dead, or that reality is founded on activity or consists of process **2 :** the theory that the self is a bundle of successive perceptions rather than a unified substance or entity

ac·tu·al·ist \-ləst\ *n* -s [¹*actual* + *-ist*] **1 :** one who deals with, aims at, or considers actuality **2 :** an adherent of philosophical actualism — **ac·tu·al·is·tic** \¦≈≈(≈)¦listik\ *adj*

ac·tu·al·i·ty \ˌakchəˈwaləd·ē, -ksh-, -ətē, -i\ *n* -ES [ML *actualitas,* fr. LL *actualis* + L *-itas* -ity] **1 :** the quality or state of being actual **:** FACT, REALITY; *esp* **:** phenomenal reality ⟨by each of these artists emotions and feelings have been given ~ in shape and form —Michael Kitson⟩ ⟨often what seems the most novel is, in ~, merely the revival of something old —R.B.West⟩ **2 :** something that is actual ⟨possible risks which have been seized upon as *actualities* —T.S.Eliot⟩ **3 a** *in Aristotelianism* **:** the being of an existent object insofar as it is not merely potential but is endowed with form — compare ENTELECHY **b** *in Hegelianism* **:** the status of an entity enjoying relative independence and self-sufficiency ⟨the ~ of a commonwealth⟩ **c :** the nature of a thing as realized in existence **d :** something that embodies actuality **4 :** a film record or radio or television broadcast of an event as it actually occurs ⟨~ film⟩ ⟨~ program⟩ — compare DOCUMENTARY

ac·tu·al·iz·a·ble \¦akchə(wə)¦līzəbəl, -ksh-\ *adj* **:** capable of being made actual

ac·tu·al·i·za·tion \ˌakchə(wə)ləˈzāshən, -ksh-, -ˌlīˈz-\ *n* -s **:** the act or process of actualizing **:** REALIZATION

ac·tu·al·ize \ˈakchə(wə)ˌlīz, -ksh-\ *vb* -ED/-ING/-S *see -ize in Explan Notes, vt* **:** to make actual ⟨he was placed in a position calculated to ~ his worst potentialities —F.R.Leavis⟩ ~ *vi* **:** to become actual

ac·tu·al·ly \ˈaksh(ə)lē, ˈakchəl-, -li; ˈakchəwəl-, -chu̇l-, -ksh-; *rap. or chiefly substand* ˈaks(ə)l-\ *adv* [ME, fr. ¹*actual* + *-ly*] **1 :** in act or in fact **:** REALLY ⟨nominally but not ~ independent — Karl Loewenstein⟩ **2 :** at the present moment **:** for the time being ⟨the transmission screen showing the picture that was ~ on the air —Denis Johnston⟩ **3 :** in point of fact **:** in truth — used to imply that one would expect the fact to be the opposite of what is stated ⟨she ~ spoke Latin⟩

actual neurosis *n* **:** a neurosis characterized by hypochondriacal complaints or somatic manifestations believed by Freud to be caused by organic changes resulting from sexual inhibition — distinguished from *psychoneurosis*

actual neurotic *n* **:** one suffering from an actual neurosis

actual sin *n, Roman Catholicism* **:** sin traceable to the personal will of the sinner — distinguished from *original sin*

actual tare *n* **:** tare determined by the actual weight of the container

actual time *n* **:** time taken by an employee to perform a given operation: as **a :** the time recorded for time and motion study before being compared with a normal working pace **b :** the time recorded on a timing device to be compared with a standard time or an allowed time

actual truth *n* **:** EMPIRICAL TRUTH

ac·tu·ar·i·al \ˌakchəˈwerēəl, -ksh-\ *adj* **:** of or relating to actuaries **:** determined by actuaries **:** relating to statistical calculation esp. of life expectancy ⟨a plan based on ~ principles⟩ — **ac·tu·ar·i·al·ly** *adv*

actuaries' table *n* **:** COMBINED EXPERIENCE TABLE

ac·tu·ary \ˈakchəˌwerē, -ksh-, -ri\ *n* -ES [LL *actuarius,* fr. L, shorthand writer, writer of accounts, fr. *actum* public transaction, record + *-arius* -ary — more at ACT] **1** *obs* **:** a clerk or registrar orig. of a law court **2 :** one trained in mathematics and statistics whose business it is to calculate insurance and annuity premiums, reserves, and dividends

ac·tu·ate \ˈakchəˌwāt, -ksh-\ *vb* -ED/-ING/-S [ML *actuatus,* past part. of *actuare,* fr. L *actus* act, deed — more at ACT] *vt* **1 :** to put into mechanical action or motion ⟨most of the hydraulically operated items of equipment are *actuated* by pistons and cylinders —W.R.Sears⟩ **2 :** to move to action ⟨cultural developments which ~ and guide stylistic trends in art —Ralph Wickiser⟩ **:** stir or inspire to activity ⟨motives which ~ religious fanatics —M.R.Cohen⟩ ⟨individuals *actuated* by economic self-interest —Douglas Bush⟩ ~ *vi* **:** to become active **syn** see MOVE

ac·tu·a·tion \ˌ≈≈ˈwāshən\ *n* -s **:** a bringing into action **:** IMPULSION, OPERATION

ac·tu·a·tor \ˈ≈≈ˌwād·ə(r), -ātə-\ *n* -s **:** one that actuates; *specif* **:** any of various electric, hydraulic, or pneumatic mechanisms by means of which something is moved or controlled indirectly instead of by hand (as a motor that turns the rudder of a large ship or moves the elevators of an airplane or an airbrake cylinder operated by a motorman)

act up *vi* **1 :** to act in a way different from that which is natural, normal, usual, or expected: as **a :** to behave in an unruly, recalcitrant, or capricious manner ⟨skittish and inclined to *act up* with an unaccustomed rider⟩ ⟨occasionally the river *acts up*⟩ ⟨I'd advise you not to *act up* with me⟩ **b :** to show off ⟨children *acting up* for the benefit of anyone who cared to notice⟩ **c :** to function improperly ⟨this typewriter is *acting up* again⟩ **2 :** to become active or acute (as of a physical infirmity) after being quiescent ⟨an old injury to his right forefoot began to *act up* again —*New Yorker*⟩

ac·tus \ˈaktəs, *esp in sense 2* ˈäkˌtu̇s\ *n, pl* **actus** [L, lit., driving, doing, act, deed — more at ACT] **1** *Roman law* **:** the right to drive a beast or a vehicle over another's land — distinguished from *iter* and *via* **2** [ML (trans. of Gk *energeia*), fr. L *actus* — more at ENERGY] **:** an act or thing done; *specif* **:** a mental or spiritual act — used in Scholasticism to render Aristotle's terms *energeia* and *entelecheia;* compare ENERGY, ENTELECHY

acu- *comb form* [ML, fr. L *acu,* abl. of *acus* needle; akin to L *acies* edge — more at EDGE] **:** with a needle ⟨*acu*puncture⟩

ac·u·ar·ia \ˌakyəˈwa(a)rēə\ *n, cap* [NL, fr. *acu-* + *-aria*] **:** a genus of spiruroid nematodes that include destructive parasites of the gizzard walls of gallinaceous birds having intermediate stages in grasshoppers or other insects or crustaceans

¹ac·u·ate \ˈakyəˌwāt\ *adj* [ME *acuat,* fr. (assumed) ML *acuatus,* fr. L *acus* needle + *-atus* -ate — more at ACUTE] **:** having a sharp point **:** shaped like a needle **:** SHARPENED

²acuate *vt* -ED/-ING/-S *obs* **:** to make pungent or sharp

acuchi *var of* ACOUCHI

acuer·do \əˈkwer(ˌ)dō, *Sp* äˈkwerthō\ *n, pl* **acuerdos** \-dōz, -thōs\ [Sp, fr. *acordar* to resolve, agree, fr. (assumed) VL *accordare* — more at ACCORD] **1 :** a resolution or decision of a deliberative body or a tribunal in certain Latin American countries **2 :** a session of a tribunal; *also* **:** the members of it

acu·i·ty \əˈkyüəd·ē, aˈ-, -ətē, -i\ *n* -ES [MF *acuité,* alter. (influenced by L *acutus* sharp, pointed) of OF *agüeté,* fr. *agu* sharp (fr. L *acutus*) + *-eté* -ity — more at ACUTE] **:** SHARPNESS, ACUTENESS **:** keenness of sense perception ⟨~ of hearing⟩ or acuteness or perceptiveness of mind ⟨Wordsworth's ~ is exercised on common objects —Herbert Read⟩ — see VISUAL ACUITY

acu·lea \əˈkyülēə\ *n, pl* **acu·le·ae** \-lēˌē\ [NL, alter. of L *aculeus* point, sting] **:** a minute spinous outgrowth on the wing membrane of certain insects

acu·le·a·ta \əˌkyülēˈād·ə, -ädə\ *n pl, cap* [NL, fr. L, neut. pl. of *aculeatus* having stings or prickles, stinging, fr. *aculeus* + *-atus* -ate] **:** a division of Hymenoptera including the bees, ants, and true wasps all characteristically having the ovipositor modified into a sting

¹acu·le·ate \əˈkyülēət, -ˌāt\ *adj* [L *aculeatus*] **1 :** marked by incisiveness ⟨~ language⟩ **:** POINTED, STINGING **2 :** having a sting **3** [NL *Aculeata*] **:** of or belonging to the Aculeata **4** [NL *aculea* + E *-ate*] **:** furnished with spines or aculeae (as of the wings of certain moths)

²aculeate \"\ *n* -s **:** one of the Aculeata

acu·le·i·form \əˈkyülēəˌfȯrm, ¦akyə¦lē-\ *adj* [ISV *acule-* (fr. L *aculeus* prickle, sting) + *-iform*] **:** like a prickle in shape; *specif* **:** resembling an aculeus

ac·u·le·o·late \¦akyə¦lēələt, -ˌlāt\ *adj* [L *aculeolus* small needle (dim. of *aculeus* prickle, sting) + E *-ate*] **:** having very small prickles; *specif* **:** having an aculeolus

ac·u·le·o·lus \ˌakyəˈlēələs\ *n, pl* **aculeo·li** \-ˌlī\ [NL, dim. of *aculeus*] **:** a small aculeus

acu·le·us \əˈkyülēəs\ *n, pl* **acu·lei** \-lēˌī\ [NL, fr. L, point, sting, dim. of *acus* needle — more at ACUTE] *zool* **:** a sharp pointed process; *specif* **:** an insect's ovipositor esp. when modified into a sting

acu·men \əˈkyümən *also* aˈ-; ˈakyəmən *also* -ˌmen\ *n* -s [L, lit., point, fr. *acuere* to sharpen — more at ACUTE] **1 :** acuteness of mind **:** keenness of perception, discernment, or discrimination **:** shrewdness esp. in practical matters ⟨loses confidence in the ~ of reviewers —E.S.McCartney⟩ ⟨business ~ and judicious handling of capital —William McFee⟩ **2** *bot* **:** a tapering point (as of a leaf) **3 :** a short spine on the rostrum of a crayfish or other crustacean

¹acu·mi·nate \əˈkyümənə̇t, -ˌnāt\ *adj* [L *acuminatus,* past part. of *acuminare* to make pointed, sharpen, fr. *acumin-, acumen* point] **:** tapering to a slender point **:** POINTED

²acu·mi·nate \-ˌnāt\ *vb* -ED/-ING/-S [L *acuminatus*] *vt* **:** to make sharp or acute ~ *vi* **:** to taper or come to a point

acu·mi·na·tion \əˌkyüməˈnāshən, ˌa,k-\ *n* -s **:** a sharpening or giving point to; *also* **:** a tapering point

acu·mi·nous \əˈkyümənəs, aˈ-\ *adj* [L *acumin-, acumen* sharp point + E *-ous* — more at ACUMEN] **1 :** characterized by acumen **2 :** ACUMINATE

ac·u·min·u·late \¦akyə¦minyələt, -ˌlāt\ *adj* [blend of ¹*acuminate* and *-ule*] **:** minutely acuminate

acu·punc·ture \ˈakyü +ˌ\ *n*- s [*acu-* + *puncture*] **1 :** the orig. Chinese practice of puncturing the body with special usu. gold or silver needles to cure disease **2 :** puncture of the skin or tissue by a needle (as for vaccination or the removal of fluid) — **acu·punc·tur·ist** \¦≈≈ˈpəŋ(k)chərə̇st, -(k)sh-\ *n* -s

acush·la \əˈku̇shlə, əˈk-\ *n* -s [IrGael *a cuisle* oh darling, fr. *a* oh + *cuisle* darling, lit., pulse, vein, fr. OIr *cusle;* akin to ScGael *cuisle* pulse, vein] *Irish* **:** DARLING

-acusia — see -ACOUSIA
acu·ta \ə'k(y)üd·ə, ä'kü-\ *n* -s *usu cap* [prob. fr. It, fr. *acuta* (fem. of *acuto* sharp), fr. L, fem. of *acutus*] : ACUTE MIXTURE
acut·ance \ə'kyüt°n(t)s\ *n* -s [¹*acute* + *-ance*] : a measure of the steepness or abruptness of an edge in a photographic image
¹**acute** \ə'kyüt, *usu* -üd.+V\ *adj, sometimes* -ER/-EST [L *acutus*, past part. of *acuere* to sharpen, fr. *acus* needle; akin to L *acer* sharp — more at EDGE] **1** : ending in a sharp point : not blunt at the end: as **a** *of an angle* : measuring less than 90 degrees : not right or obtuse ⟨fences . . . so laid out that ~ corners are avoided —Henry Wynmalen⟩ — see ANGLE illustration **b** *of a figure* : marked by or composed of acute angles ⟨an ~ triangle⟩ **c** *of a leaf apex* : abruptly pointed : not tapering **2 a** : marked by keen shrewd discernment or intellectual perception esp. of subtle distinctions : PENETRATING ⟨people of ~ judgment and refined sensibilities —Elinor Wylie⟩ ⟨the fame of an ~ thinker —V.L.Parrington⟩ **b** : sensing or perceiving accurately, clearly, effectively, or sensitively ⟨~ observer⟩ ⟨~ vision, the ability to see sharp instead of blurred, is uncommon . . . in the animal kingdom —A.L. Kroeber⟩ **3** *of a sound* : high in pitch : SHARP, SHRILL ⟨an ~ note⟩ **4** : felt, perceived, or experienced intensely or powerfully ⟨the stench was ~ —Norman Mailer⟩ ⟨the incident . . . seemed to cause . . . ~ distress —Dorothy Sayers⟩ **5 a** *med* (1) : characterized by sharpness or severity ⟨~ pain⟩ ⟨~ infection⟩ (2) *of a pathologic process* : having a sudden onset, sharp rise, and short course ⟨~ disease⟩ ⟨~ inflammation⟩ — opposed to *chronic* (3) : for the treatment of acute diseases ⟨an ~ hospital⟩ **b** : serious, urgent, and demanding attention : intensified or aggravated nearly to a crisis, culmination, or breaking point ⟨there was an ~ shortage of houses after the war⟩ : EXTREME, SEVERE, CRITICAL **6 a** *of an accent mark* : having the form ´ **b** : marked with an acute accent ⟨an ~ *e* in *canapé*⟩ **c** : of the variety indicated by an acute accent ⟨an ~ intonation⟩
syn CRITICAL, CRUCIAL: ACUTE most commonly indicates intensification, sometimes rapid, of a situation demanding notice and showing signs of some definite resolution ⟨intimately associated with Indian affairs was the pressing question of defense. . . . Pontiac's rebellion made the issue *acute* —S.E. Morison & H.S.Commager⟩ ⟨when the food shortage became *acute* in New Haven, the junior class of Yale College was moved to Glastonbury —*Amer. Guide Series: Conn.*⟩ CRITICAL may describe an approach to a crisis or turning point and may imply an imminent outcome or resolution ⟨the war has reached a new *critical* phase . . . we have moved into active and continuing battle —F.D.Roosevelt⟩ ⟨the *critical* lack of rubber in the last war was finally beaten by the development of synthetic rubber plants capable of turning out 1,000,000 tons a year —*Collier's Yr. Bk.*⟩ CRUCIAL applies to an actual crisis situation, often one viewed with fear, worry, or suspense, and implies a speedily ensuing decisive or definitive outcome ⟨a continuous evolution, punctuated by the sudden flaming or flowering of a *crucial* moment now and then —J.L.Lowes⟩ ⟨the next few months are *crucial*. What we do now will affect our American way of life for decades to come —H.S.Truman⟩ **syn** see in addition SHARP
²**acute** \"\ *n* -s : an acute accent used to show that a vowel is pronounced with a rise of pitch (as in ancient Greek), that a vowel has a certain quality (as over *e* in French), that a vowel is long (as in Hungarian), that a syllable has the highest degree of stress (as in Spanish or in phonetic transcription), or that a final *e* in a word in an English context is not silent (as in *maté*)
³**acute** \"\ *vt* -ED/-ING/-S [²*acute*] : to mark with an acute accent : pronounce with higher pitch ⟨~ your inflection⟩
acute abdomen *n* : an acute intra-abdominal condition requiring immediate operation
acute alcoholism *n* : an acute syndrome resulting from intoxication by excessive consumption of alcoholic drinks that is characterized by depression of higher nervous centers with uncontrolled excitement often leading to stupor, incoordination, and impaired motor control and often nausea, dehydration, and other physical symptoms — distinguished from *chronic alcoholism*
acute bisectrix *n* : the bisectrix of the acute angle formed by the axes of a biaxial crystal
acutely *adv* : in an acute manner : KEENLY, INTENSELY
acute mixture *n* : a compound organ stop sounding the higher harmonics and of bright quality — called also *sharp mixture*
acute·ness *n* -ES : the quality or state of being acute ⟨~ of vision —F.A.Geldard⟩ ⟨~ of intellect —Irving Kristol⟩ ⟨~ of sound —Irving Kolodin⟩
acute yellow atrophy *n* : a severe usu. fatal disorder in which the liver degenerates and is reduced in size as a result of toxic chemicals, infection, or other agents
acuti- *comb form* [ML, fr. L *acutus* — more at ACUTE] : sharp-pointed ⟨*acuti*foliate⟩ : sharply angled ⟨*acuti*plantar⟩
acu·ti·plan·tar \ə¦kyüd·ə¦-, -d·ē¦-\ *adj* [*acuti-* + *plantar*] *of certain birds* : having the hinder part of the tarsus sharp angled — opposed to *latiplantar*
acuto- *comb form* [¹*acute*] : acute and ⟨*acuto*-grave⟩ : acutely ⟨*acuto*-nodose⟩
acu·ya·ri palm \,ä,kü'yärē-\ *n* : GRUGRU
acuyari wood *n* [AmerSp *acuyari*, prob. fr. Carib *acaiara*] : a fragrant wood obtained from a tree (*Bursera altissima*) of Guiana
ACW *abbr* **1** aircraftswoman **2** alternating continuous wave
acy·clic \(')ā¦sīklik, -si-\ *adj* [²*a-* + *cyclic*] **1** : not cyclic : not disposed in cycles or whorls : not occurring in cycles **2** *chem* : having an open-chain structure; *esp* : ALIPHATIC **3** *ecol* : lacking regularly recurring population pulses — used esp. of planktonic organisms
acyclic machine *n* : a direct-current dynamo in which there is no reversal of current in the armature and no commutator and which in principle resembles the Faraday disk — called also *homopolar machine*
acyclic motion *n* : irrotational motion in which the velocity potential is single valued (as the rectilinear flow of a fluid)
ac·yl \'asəl, -,sēl\ *n* -s [ISV *acid* + *-yl*; prob. orig. formed as G *azyl*] : a radical derived usu. from an organic acid by removal of the hydroxyl from all acid groups; *esp* : a radical (as benzoyl, adipoyl) derived from a carboxylic acid and having the general formula RCO— in the case of a monobasic acid ⟨~ halides⟩ — compare ACYLOXY
ac·yl·al \'asə,lal\ *n* -s [*acyl* + *aldehyde*] : an acid derivative of an aldehyde or a ketone containing the grouping >C-$(OOCR)_2$ or >C(OR)OOCR
ac·yl·ami·no \,asələ'mē(,)nō, -'lamə,nō\ *adj* [*acyl* + *amino-*] : relating to or containing any radical (as acetamido) formed by removal of one hydrogen atom from nitrogen in an organic acid amide and usu. having the general formula RCONH—
ac·yl·ase \'asə,lās, -āz\ *n* -s [*acyl* + *-ase*] : any of several enzymes (as histozyme) that hydrolyze acylated amino acids — compare CARBOXYPEPTIDASE
¹**ac·yl·ate** \'asə,lāt\ *vt* -ED/-ING/-S [*acyl* + *-ate*] : to introduce acyl into
²**ac·yl·ate** \-,lāt, -lət\ *n* -s [*acyl* + *-ate*] : a salt or ester of an organic acid ⟨titanium ~s⟩
ac·yl·a·tion \,asə'lāshən\ *n* -s : the act or process of acylating
acyl·oin \ə'silәwən, -,wēn; 'asə,lōin, ,asə'lōən\ *n* -s [ISV *acyl* + *benzoin*] : an alpha-hydroxy ketone (as benzoin) of the general formula RCOCH(OH)R
ac·yl·oxy \¦asə¦läksē\ *adj* [*acyl* + *oxy-*] : relating to or containing any radical (as acetoxy) formed by removal of hydrogen from oxygen in an organic acid and usu. having the general formula RCOO-
acys·tic \(')ā¦sistik\ *adj* [²*a-* + *cystic*] : not enclosed in a bladder ⟨~ tapeworm larvae⟩
¹**ad** \'ad, 'aa(ə)d\ *n* -s *often attrib* [by shortening] : ADVERTISEMENT 2b
²**ad** \"\ *n* -s [by shortening] : ADVANTAGE 5 ⟨~ in⟩ ⟨my ~⟩
ad- *or* **ac-** *or* **af-** *or* **ag-** *or* **al-** *or* **ap-** *or* **as-** *or* **at-** *prefix* [*ad-* fr. ME, fr. L, fr. *ad*; *ac-* fr. ME, fr. OF, fr. L, fr. *ad*; *af-* fr. ME, fr. OF, fr. L, fr. *ad*; *ag-* fr. ME, fr. MF, fr. L, fr. *ad*; *al-* fr. ME, fr. MF, fr. L, fr. *ad*; *ap-* fr. ME, fr. MF, fr. L, fr. *ad*; *as-* fr. ME, fr. OF, fr. L, fr. *ad*; *at-* fr. ME, fr. OF, fr. L, fr. *ad* — more at AT] **1** : to : toward — usu. *ac-* before *c*, *k*, or *q* ⟨*ac*culturation⟩ and *af-* before *f* ⟨*af*formative⟩ and *ag-* before *g* ⟨*ag*gradation⟩ and *al-* before *l* ⟨*al*lineation⟩ and *ap-* before *p* ⟨*ap*personation⟩ and *as-* before *s* ⟨*as*self⟩ and *at-* before *t* ⟨*at*tune⟩ and *ad-* before other sounds ⟨*ad*nominal⟩ ⟨*ad*verbial⟩ but sometimes *ad-* even before one of the listed consonants ⟨*ad*pronominal⟩ **2** : near : adjacent to — in this sense always in the form *ad-* ⟨*ad*oral⟩ ⟨*ad*renal⟩
¹**-ad** \,ad, ,aa(ə)d, ,əd\ *n suffix* -s [MF & L; MF *-ade*, fr. L *-ad-*, *-as*, fr. Gk *-ad-*, *-as*, fem. suffix denoting descent from or connection with] **1 a** : period of time ⟨quinquenni*ad*⟩ **b** : group, aggregate, or unit of (so many) parts ⟨quint*ad*⟩ **c** : element, atom, or radical having (such or so great) a chemical valence ⟨arti*ad*⟩ ⟨periss*ad*⟩ ⟨dy*ad*⟩ **2** : epic of : poem celebrating ⟨Columbi*ad*⟩ **3** [prob. fr. NL *-ad-*, *-as* (used as final element in botanical genus names), fr. Gk] : member of (such) a botanical group ⟨magnoli*ad*⟩ ⟨moring*ad*⟩ **4** : kind of plant or animal produced by or associated with ⟨ec*ad*⟩ ⟨vari*ad*⟩ — **-ad·ic** \¦adik, -ēk\ *adj suffix*
²**-ad** \"\ *adv suffix* [L *ad*] *biol* : in the direction of : toward : -WARD ⟨cephal*ad*⟩ ⟨ventr*ad*⟩
ad *abbr* **1** adapted **2** administration **3** adult
AD *abbr* **1** active duty **2** *often not cap* after date **3** air-dried **4** alternate days **5** [L *anno domini*] in the year of our Lord — often printed in small capitals **6** *often not cap* [L *ante diem*] before the day **7** archduke **8** assembly district **9** autograph document **10** average deviation
ad ab·sur·dum \¦adəb'sərdəm\ *adv* [L] : to the point of absurdity ⟨not slavishly imitate it *ad absurdum* —Frank Weitenkampf⟩
adac·tyl·ia \¦ā,dak'tilēə\ *n* -s [NL, fr. ²*a-* + *-dactylia*] : congenital lack of fingers or toes
adac·ty·lous \(')ā¦daktələs\ *adj* [²*a-* + *-dactylous*] **1** : without fingers or without toes **2** : without claws on the feet — used of crustaceans
¹**adad** *interj* [prob. by alter.] *archaic* : EGAD
²**adad** \'ä,däd\ *n* -s [prob. fr. Marshallese *ādād*, a species of *Triumfetta*] : a coarse fiber made from the stems of pilewort
adag *abbr* adagio
¹**ad·age** \'adij, -ēj\ *n* -s [MF, fr. L *adagio*, *adagium*, fr. *ad-* + *-agio*, *-agium* (akin to *aio* I say, fr. — assumed — OL *agio*); akin to Gk *ē* he spoke, Arm *asem* I say] : a saying typically embodying common experience or observation often in metaphorical form (as *it is always darkest before the dawn*)
²**adage** \àdààzh\ *n* -s [F, modif. of It *adagio*] : ADAGIO 2
¹**ada·giet·to** \ə,däjē'ed·(,)ō, ä,-, -äzhē'-, ,adə'je-\ *n* -s [It, dim. of *adagio*] : a short adagio
²**adagietto** \"\ *adv (or adj)* [It, fr. *adagietto*, n.] : less slow than adagio — used as a direction in music
¹**ada·gio** \ə'dä\|(,)jō, ä'dä\|,ə'dà\|,ə'da\|, \|(,)zhō,\|jē,ō,\|zhē,ō\ *adv (or adj)* [It, fr. *ad*, a to, at (fr. L *ad*) + *agio* ease, convenience, fr. Prov. *aize* comfort, fr. L *adjacens*, pres. part. of *adjacēre* to be near — more at AT, EASE] : SLOWLY : in an easy graceful manner : in a tempo between largo and andante — used chiefly as a direction in music
²**adagio** \"\ *n* -s [It, fr. *adagio*, adv.] **1** : a musical composition or a movement or division of a composition in adagio tempo ⟨the ~ of a symphony⟩ **2 a** : a series of sustained and perfectly controlled dance movements (as ballet exercises) displaying balance and grace **b** : a ballet duet by a man and woman or a ballet by a mixed trio displaying difficult feats of balance, lifting, or spinning; *also* : an acrobatic or ballroom duet with similar feats
adagy *n* -ES [L *adagium*] *obs* : ¹ADAGE
adai \ə'dä\,n, pl **adai** \"\ *or* **adaize** \-āz\ *usu cap* [F, prob. fr. Caddo] **1** : a Caddo people of Louisiana **2** : a member of the Adai people
ada·lat \ə'dälət, -äl-\ *or* **adaw·lut** \-ōl-\ *n* -s [Hindi *'adālat*, fr. Ar, *'adālat*, *'adālah* justice, equity] : any of several courts of justice operative in India until the late 18th century
¹**ad·am** \'adəm\ *n* -s *cap* [after *Adam*, the first man of the Bible, who sinned in the Garden of Eden (Gen 2 & 3), fr. ME, fr. LL, fr. Heb *Ādhām*] : the unregenerate nature of man : human frailty — used esp. in the phrase *the old Adam* ⟨a good deal of the old *Adam* in the rascal⟩
²**adam** \"\ *adj, often cap* [after Robert *Adam* †1792 & James *Adam* †1794 Scottish architects and designers] **1** *of furniture* : designed in a late 18th century style resembling Sheraton but differing from it in greater preference for straight lines and decoration of surfaces (as by carving, inlaying, and painting) and in more consistent use of conventional designs (as festooned garlands and medallions) and in occasional employment of superimposed ornaments (as vases and urns) **2** *of architecture* : in a late 18th century style characterized by an ordered use of classic ornament derived from contemporary archaeological discoveries in Italy
ad·a·man·cy \'adəmənsē\ *n* -ES [²*adamant* + *-cy*] : unyielding quality : condition or fact of being adamantine : STUBBORNNESS, OBSTINACY
ad·am-and-eve \¦==ən'(d)ēv\ *n* -s [so called fr. the resemblance of the bulbs to human figures] : any of several plants of the genera *Aconitum*, *Arethusa*, *Corallorhiza*, *Orchis*, and *Pulmonaria*; *esp* : PUTTYROOT
¹**ad·a·mant** \'adəmənt *also* -,mant *or* -,maa(ə)nt\ *n* -s [ME, a fabulous mineral, diamond, lodestone, fr. OF, fr. L *adamant-*, *adamas* hardest iron or steel, diamond, fr. Gk] **1** : an imaginary stone of impenetrable hardness — formerly used of the diamond and other substances of extreme hardness **2** : an unbreakable or extremely hard substance ⟨she became as rigid as ~ —J.C.Powys⟩ ⟨the sharp ~ of fate —Thomas Carlyle⟩
²**adamant** \"\ *adj* : unshakable or immovable esp. in opposition : ADAMANTINE ⟨~ against any . . . game on Sunday —Archibald Marshall⟩ : inflexible or insistent esp. in maintaining a position or opinion ⟨was ~ that he was fit to go —Nevil Shute⟩ — **ad·a·mant·ly** *adv*
ad·a·man·tane \,adə'man,tān\ *n* -s [ISV ¹*adamant* + *-ane*; prob. orig. formed as G *adamantan*] : a crystalline high-melting hydrocarbon $C_{10}H_{16}$ having the carbon atoms of its skeleton in the same tricyclic pattern found in the space lattice of the diamond; symmetrical tricyclo-decane
ad·a·man·tine \,adə'man·,tīn, -ēn, ¦adə¦mant°n\ *adj* [ME, fr. L *adamantinus*, fr. Gk *adamantinos* of steel, like a diamond, fr. *adamant-*, *adamas* steel, diamond] **1** : made of or having the quality of adamant ⟨these ~ gates —John Milton⟩ **2** : rigidly firm : UNYIELDING **3** : resembling the diamond in luster **4** : of or relating to the enamel of the teeth
adamantine drill *n* : a tubular well-drilling bit with hardened steel shot that revolve under the rim of the rotating tube
ad·a·man·ti·no·ma \,adə,mant°n'ōmə\ *n, pl* **ad·a·man·ti·no·mas** \-məz\ *also* **ad·a·man·ti·no·ma·ta** \-məd·ə\ [NL, fr. E *adamantine* (of tooth enamel) + NL *-oma*] : a tumor of the jaw derived from remnants of the embryonic rudiment of tooth enamel — **ad·a·man·ti·nom·a·tous** \¦==,==¦nämәd·əs, -ōm-\ *adj*
adamantive *adj* [¹*adamant* + *-ive*] *obs* : ADAMANTINE
ad·a·man·to·blast \,adə'mantə,blast\ *n* -s [ISV *adamant* + *-o-* + *-blast*] : AMELOBLAST
ad·a·man·to·blas·to·ma \,adə¦mantə,bla'stōmə\ *n* -s [NL, fr. ISV *adamantoblast* + NL *-oma*] : ADAMANTINOMA
adamantoid *n* -s [¹*adamant* + *-oid*] *obs* : HEXOCTAHEDRON
ad·a·ma·wa–east·ern \,adə'mäwə'-, -maùə'-\ *n, usu cap A&E* : a branch of the Niger-Congo language family including Ngbaka, Sango, and Zande spoken from Cameroons eastward across French Equatorial Africa and northern Belgian Congo
¹**ad·am·bu·la·cral** \¦a,dambyə¦lākrəl, -lak-\ *adj* [*ad-* + NL *ambulacrum* + E *-al*] : adjacent to the ambulacra
²**adambulacral** \"\ *n* -s : any of a series of ossicles lying along the ambulacral grooves of starfishes
ad·a·mel·lite \,adə'me,līt\ *n* -s [G *adamellit*, fr. Monte *Adamello*, mountain in Italy, its locality + G *-it* -ite] : any of several minerals: as **a** : an orthoclase-bearing quartz-hornblende-mica-diorite **b** : silica-rich quartz-monzonite **c** : any quartz-monzonite
ad·am·esque \¦adə¦mesk\ *adj, usu cap* [Robert and James *Adam* + E *-esque* — more at ADAM] *of architecture and furniture* : derived from the style of the brothers Adam ⟨attenuated delicacies of Mount Vernon's ~ ceilings —Hugh Morrison⟩
adam·ic \ə'damik, a'-\ *or* **adam·i·cal** \-ə̇kəl\ *adj, usu cap* [*Adam*, the first man of the Bible + E *-ic*, *-ical* — more at ADAM] : of or belonging to the biblical Adam : proceeding from, resembling, or suggestive of Adam ⟨my *Adamic* and fresh daughters —Walt Whitman⟩
¹**ad·am·ite** \'adə,mīt\ *n* -s *usu cap* [*Adam*, the biblical first man + E *-ite*] **1** : a person who imitates Adam in going naked; *specif* : a member of any of various ascetic sects noted for practicing ritual nakedness in secret religious assemblies and dispensing with marriage on the basis of having entered a reborn state of heavenly innocence **2** : a descendant of Adam : a human being
²**adamite** \"\ *adj, usu cap* : of, relating to, or descended from Adam
³**adamite** \"\ *also* **ad·am·ine** \'adə,mēn\ *n* -s [*adamite*, modif. (influenced by *-ite*) of F *adamine*, fr. Gilbert-Joseph *Adam* †1881 Fr. mineralogist + F *-ine*; *adamine* fr. F] : a mineral $Zn_2(OH)AsO_4$ consisting of a basic zinc arsenate (hardness 3.5, sp. gr. 4.34–4.35)
ad·am·it·ic \¦adə¦mid·ik\ *adj, usu cap* [¹*adamite* + *-ic*] : having the characteristics of or resembling Adam or the Adamites ⟨in a state of ~ nudity —Norman Douglas⟩
ad·am·it·ism \'adə,mīd·,izəm\ *n* -s *usu cap* : the practice of going naked : a state of being unclothed
adams *pl of* ADAM
adam's ale *n, usu cap 1st A* [after the biblical *Adam*; fr. its being provided by nature and thus presumably being the only drink in the Garden of Eden] : WATER
¹**adam's apple** *n, usu cap 1st A* **1** : PLANTAIN **2** : CRAPE JASMINE **3** : SHADDOCK 1
²**adam's apple** *n, usu cap 1st A* [trans. of NL *pomum Adami*, trans. of LHeb *tappūah hā ādhām* bodily protuberance on a man, misinterpreted (because of double meanings in Heb) as the apple of Adam] : the projection formed by the thyroid cartilage in the neck particularly prominent in males — compare LARYNX
adam's cup *n, usu cap A* [so called fr. the shape of its leaves] : PITCHER PLANT a
adam's fig *n, usu cap A* : PLANTAIN
adam's flannel *n, usu cap A* [so called fr. the texture of the leaves] : MULLEIN
ad·ams·ite \'adəm,zīt\ *n* -s [Roger *Adams* b1889 Am. chemist + E *-ite*] : a yellow crystalline arsenical $C_{12}H_9AsClN$ similar in action to diphenylchloroarsine — called also *diphenylaminechlorarsine*, *phenarsazine chloride*
adam's needle *also* **adam's needle–and–thread** *n, usu cap A* [so called fr. the shape of the fruits] **1** : any of several species of the genus *Yucca* **2 adam's needles** *pl* : LADY'S-COMB
adam's pitcher *n, usu cap A* : PITCHER PLANT a
ada·na \'äd°n¦ä\ *adj, usu cap* [fr. *Adana*, Turkey] : of or from Adana, Turkey : of the kind or style prevalent in Adana
ad·anal \(')a¦dān°l\ *adj* [*ad-* + *anal*] : near the anus ⟨~ setae⟩
adance \ə'-\ *adj* [¹*a-* + *dance* (v.)] : DANCING
adan·gle \ə'-\ *adj* [¹*a-* + *dangle* (v.)] : DANGLING
ad·an·so·nia \,ad°n'sōnēə, ,a,dan'-, -nyə\ *n, cap* [NL, fr. Michel *Adanson* †1806 Fr. botanist + NL *-ia*] : a genus of trees (family Bombacaceae) having palmately divided leaves, white pendent flowers, and capsular fruits — see BAOBAB, CREAM-OF-TARTAR TREE
adap·i·dae \ə'dapə,dē\ *n pl, cap* [NL *Adapid-*, *Adapis*, type genus + *-idae*] : a family of extinct lemuroid primates widely distributed in the northern hemisphere during the Eocene and generally considered to be ancestral to modern lemurs
ad·a·pis \'adəpə̇s\ *n, cap* [NL] : a genus of primitive crested fossil lemurs from the Eocene of Europe
¹**adapt** \ə'dapt *also* a'-\ *vb* -ED/-ING/-S [F or L; F *adapter*, fr. L *adaptare*, fr. *ad-* + *aptare* to fit, fr. *aptus* fit — more at APT] *vt* **1 a** : to make suitable or fit (as for a particular use, purpose, or situation) : FIT, SUIT ⟨the toughness of the material ~s it for many uses⟩ **b** : to make suitable (for a new or different use or situation) by means of changes or modifications ⟨he ~*ed* the novel for the stage⟩ ⟨~ his instruction to meet individual needs —P.H.Furfey⟩ **2** : to adjust (oneself) to particular conditions or ways : bring (oneself) into harmony with a particular environment : ACCLIMATIZE ⟨I could ~ myself to the isolated life —Ella E. Clark⟩ ⟨a given environment with organisms ~*ing* themselves to it —A.N. Whitehead⟩ ~ *vi* : to become adjusted; *specif* : to bring oneself or esp. one's acts, behavior, or mental state into harmony with changed conditions or environment ⟨man ~s socially to an increasingly complicated . . . culture —J.F.Brown⟩
syn ADJUST, ACCOMMODATE, CONFORM, RECONCILE: TO ADAPT to something or TO ADAPT one thing to another implies a suiting or fitting by alteration or modification ⟨to see men only in terms of the geographical conditions to which they *adapt* themselves —Alfred Kazin⟩ ⟨our plans must change in *adapting* to the new situations —Hugo Wall⟩ ⟨the inside walls are all movable so that the interior can easily be *adapted* to meet new requirements —*London Calling*⟩ TO ADJUST to something or TO ADJUST one thing to another usu. suggests no significant alteration or modification but rather a bringing into a correspondence or harmony, prearranged or clearly possible but not quite achieved previously ⟨the main problem confronting the child is not yet to *adjust* to a cultural milieu but primarily to *adjust* to the rapidly changing phases of his biological growth —Franz Alexander⟩ ACCOMMODATE often suggests the special or transient adaptation of one thing to another or of two things to each other, implying a significant difference overcome in a specially arranged, temporary, or expedient harmony ⟨local building ordinances . . . had been adjusted to *accommodate* the new materials and methods —*Current Biog.*⟩ ⟨a water trough long enough to *accommodate* the noses of a barnful of thirsting cows —*Monsanto Mag.*⟩ ⟨a school auditorium must *accommodate* a large variety of acoustic activities —*Bull. of Amer. Inst. of Architects*⟩ CONFORM implies the achievement of harmony or correspondence by compliance as with a preexisting pattern, form, or principle, sometimes carrying the implication of slavish compliance ⟨to ensure that all work done *conforms* to the highest standards —Ivor Bulmer-Thomas⟩ ⟨certain lies are indulged in to *conform* to etiquette —D.C.Buchanan⟩ ⟨unwilling to *conform* to American ways —Oscar Handlin⟩ TO RECONCILE one thing with another or TO RECONCILE two things, in the sense pertinent to this comparison, is to persuade oneself or others of the fundamental congruity of things that are, or seem to be, incompatible or to adjust the two things so that they are compatible ⟨*reconcile* opposing points of view⟩ ⟨we can *reconcile* naturalism or, if you please, materialism with the piety which has distinguished genuinely spiritualistic views of life —M.R.Cohen⟩ ⟨the critical judgment of those who are suspicious of "best sellers" and unwilling to *reconcile* excellence with public taste —*College English*⟩
²**adapt** *adj, obs* : FITTED, SUITED
adapt·a·bil·i·ty \ə,daptə'bilәd·ē, (,)a,d-, -ətē, -i\ *n* : the quality or state of being adaptable ⟨the ~ of the subject to varied art forms⟩ ⟨youth's ~ to new surroundings⟩
adapt·able \ə'daptəbəl *also* a'-\ *adj* **1** : capable of being adapted or of adapting oneself ⟨a frame ~ to cloth bolts of various widths⟩ ⟨an ~ person⟩ **2** : suitable without change ⟨soil and climate ~ to growth of new crops⟩ **syn** see PLASTIC
adap·tate \ə'dap,tāt, 'a,dap-\ *vt* -ED/-ING/-S [L *adaptatus*, past part. of *adaptare*] : ADAPT
ad·ap·ta·tion \,a,dap'tāshən *also* ,adəp- *or* ə,dap-\ *n* -s [F, fr. ML *adaptation-*, *adaptatio*, fr. L *adaptatus* + *-ion-*, *-io* -ion] **1 a** : the act or process of adapting, fitting, or modifying ⟨his ingenious ~ of the electric cautery knife to . . . surgery —George Blumer⟩ ⟨~ is a basic principle of applied design⟩ **b** : the state or condition of being adapted or adjusted or of adapting or adjusting oneself ⟨the complete ~ of the clergyman to his work⟩ ⟨the characteristic ~ of the emigrant trail to the terrain —G.R.Stewart⟩ **2** : adjustment to environmental conditions: as **a** : adjustment of a sense organ (as the eye) to the intensity or quality of stimulation (as light) prevailing at the moment effected by changes in sensitivity and occurring as a heightened sensitivity ⟨dark ~ of the retina⟩ or as a physical adjustment to meet changed conditions ⟨contraction of pupil or pigment migration in light ~ of the eye⟩ or as decline or loss of sensitivity to a constant stimulus **b** : modification of an organism or of its parts or organs fitting it more perfectly for existence under the conditions of its environment and resulting from the action of natural selection upon variation — compare NATURAL SELECTION, VARIATION 6 **c** : the continuing process through which the organization of groups is modified to meet the requirements of their social and physical environment

3 : something that is adapted: **a** : a modification for a new use : an alteration or change in form or structure ⟨the polar bear's white fur is an ~ which enables it to get food —W.J. Jacobson & Cecilia J. Lauby⟩ **b** : a composition rewritten into a new form ⟨a screen ~ of a novel⟩ — **ad·ap·ta·tion·al** \ˌaˌdapˈtāshənᵊl, -shnəl *also* ˌadəpˈt- *or* əˌdapˈt-\ *adj* — **ad·ap·ta·tion·al·ly** *adv*

adaptation syndrome *n* : the defensive response of the body through the endocrine system to systemic injury evoked by stresses and worked out by an initial stage of shock, a stage of growing resistance or adaptation, and a stage of healing or of becoming exhausted if adaptation fails — see ALARM REACTION

adapt·a·tive \əˈdaptədiv, aˈ-\ *adj* [*adapt* + *-ative* (as in *imitative*)] : ADAPTIVE

adapt·ed \əˈdaptəd *also* aˈd- *or* (*attrib*) ˈaˌd-\ *adj* : suited by nature, character, or design to a particular use, purpose, or situation — used with *to* or *for* ⟨soil well ~ to the growing of wheat⟩ ⟨subjects . . . not well ~ for examinations —W.R.Inge⟩

adapt·er *also* **adap·tor** \əˈdaptə(r) *also* aˈ-\ *n* -s **1** : one that adapts: as **a** : a writer who adapts novels or magazine stories to motion-picture use **b** : a music arranger **2 a** : any of various devices used in adjusting or fitting to each other the separate parts of a machine or apparatus whose design is such that adjustment or fitting would otherwise not be possible (as two pipes of different diameters) **b** : any of several attachments for a camera or other apparatus to fit it for uses for which it was not orig. made (as for a plate camera to permit the use of films) **c** : a fitting usu. of glass or metal that serves to connect one tube to another or to deliver an effluent from a condenser into a receiver in a distillation apparatus **d** : a circuit or circuit element added to change the performance of an electronic apparatus in response to different actuating conditions ⟨a color ~ for black-and-white television sets⟩ **e** : a device (as a bushing) used to obtain proper fit of the fuse for assembly and functioning of a shell or bomb

adap·tion \əˈdapshən, aˈ-\ *n* -s [by contr. (influence of *adoption*)] : ADAPTATION

adap·ti·tude \əˈdaptəˌtüd, -ptə-ˌtyüd, aˈ-\ *n* -s [blend of *adapt* and *aptitude*] : a special fitness : APTITUDE

adapt·ive \əˈdaptiv, -ēv *also* aˈ-\ *adj* : suited to or contributing to adaptation ⟨unfavorable variants would tend to be lost and the ~ favorable variants preserved —W.H.Camp⟩ : showing or having a capacity for or tendency toward adaptation ⟨wolves disappeared and the clever ~ coyotes grew in numbers⟩ — **adapt·ive·ly** *adv*

adaptive radiation *n* : diversification of a group of organisms into subgroups as it evolves in the various directions provided by interaction of its genetic potentialities and the environments it encounters : the evolution of ecologically similar though taxonomically distant organisms to occupy equivalent niches in comparable habitats

ad·ap·tom·e·ter \ˌaˌdapˈtämədə(r)\ *n* -s [ISV *adaptation* + *-o-* + *-meter*] : a device for determining the efficiency of dark adaptation in the human eye — **ad·ap·tom·e·try** \-mə·trē\ *n* -ES

adapts *pres 3d sing of* ADAPT

adar \äˈdär, ˈōdər\ *n* -s *usu cap* [ME, fr. Heb *ădhār*] : the 6th month of the civil year or the 12th month of the ecclesiastical year in the Jewish calendar — see MONTH table

adar sheni \äˌdärshäˈnē, ˌōdərˈshānē\ *n, pl* **adar shenis** *usu cap A&S* [Heb *ădhār shēnī* second Adar] : VEADAR

adat \ˈäˌdät\ *n* -s [Malay, fr. Ar *ʽādah* custom, usage] : local customary law esp. of Islamic-Malay tradition in Indonesia

ad·at·om \ˈaˌdadˌəm\ *n* -s [*adsorbed atom*] : an adsorbed atom

adaw *vt* -ED/-ING/-S [ME *adawen* to put an end to, fr. *adawe*, adv., out of existence, fr. OE *of dagum*, fr. *of*, out of + *dagum*, dat. pl. of *dæg* day — more at OF, DAY] *obs* : SUBDUE, DAUNT

adawlut *var of* ADALAT

ad·ax·i·al \(ˈ)aˈdaksēəl\ *adj* [*ad-* + *axial*] : situated on the same side as or facing the axis of an organ or organism ⟨upper side of a leaf stalk is known as the ~ surface —R.E.Torrey⟩ — opposed to *abaxial*; compare POSTERIOR

a-day \əˈdā, ˈāˌdā\ *n, usu cap A* [¹*a* + *day*] **1** : the day set for launching a particular military operation **2** : the time of a possible enemy attack with atomic bombs

adays \əˈdāz\ *adv* [ME *a dayes*, fr. *a* (on) + *dayes*, gen. of *day*] *archaic* : during the day : in the daytime

adaz·zle \əˈ-\ *adj* [¹*a-* + *dazzle* (n.)] : DAZZLING, GLEAMING, SHINING

ADC *abbr* **1** aide-de-camp **2** aid to dependent children

ad cap·tan·dum *or* **ad captandum vul·gus** \ˌadˌkapˈtandəm(ˈvəlgəs)\ *adj* [*ad captandum*, fr. L, for pleasing; *ad captandum vulgus*, fr. L, for pleasing the crowd] : designed to attract or please the crowd — used often of an argument directed chiefly to the emotions

¹**add** \ˈad, ˈaa(ə)d\ *vb* -ED/-ING/-S [ME *adden*, fr. L *addere*, fr. *ad-* + *-dere* to put — more at DO] *vt* **1 a** : to join, annex, or unite (as one thing to another) so as to bring about an increase (as in number, size, or importance) or so as to form one aggregate ⟨~*ed* music to the list of his interests⟩ ⟨~*s* form to substance and achieves artistic unity⟩ ⟨~*ing* a wing to the house⟩ **b** : to put together mentally : unite or form a single whole in the mind ⟨~ together the ideas of two days —John Locke⟩ **2** : to say or write further : go on to say or write ⟨that, he ~*ed*, was a mistake⟩ **3** *obs* : GIVE, BESTOW ⟨all these things shall be ~*ed* unto you —Mt 6:33 (AV)⟩ **4** : to combine (two or more numbers or quantities or a group or column of numbers or quantities) into one sum : find the total sum of by combining **5** : to join or unite (another thing) to itself ⟨a chemical compound that ~*s* chlorine⟩ **6** : to include (a person) as a member of a group or party : COUNT ⟨don't forget to ~ me in⟩ ~ *vi* **1 a** : to perform the mathematical operation of addition **b** : to come together or unite in or as if in the mathematical process of addition ⟨the facts . . . ~*ed* together to build up a theory which was indisputable —Harvey Graham⟩ **2** : to be or serve as an addition : INCREASE, AUGMENT ⟨the novel ~*ed* to his reputation⟩ : make an addition : ENLARGE ⟨they ~*ed* to the house the next year⟩ — used with *to*

²**add** \"\ *n* -s : copy to be added to a news story ⟨a new ~ on the hurricane story⟩

add *abbr* **1** addendum **2** addition **3** address

ad·da \ˈadə\ *n* -s [Ar dial. (Egypt) *ʽaẓa'*] : the common Egyptian skink (*Scincus officinalis*)

add·a·ble *or* **add·i·ble** \ˈadəbəl, ˈaad-\ *adj* [¹*add* + *-able, -ible*] : capable of being added or added to

ad·dax \ˈaˌdaks\ *n, pl* **addaxes** *also* **addax** [L] : a large light-colored antelope (*Addax nasomaculata*) of No. Africa, Arabia, and Syria

addebted *adj* [ME *adetted*, alter. of *endetted* — more at INDEBTED] *obs* : INDEBTED

added *adj* : ADDITIONAL, FURTHER, SUPPLEMENTARY ⟨takes on ~ significance⟩ ⟨an ~ attraction⟩ — **add·ed·ly** *adv*

added money *n* : money added to stakes by a track or racing association as an additional inducement for entries as distinct from entrance fees or forfeits

added sixth *n* **1** *in classical harmony* : the chord of the subdominant with a major sixth from the root added **2** : a triad with a major sixth from the root added

addax

added value *n* : VALUE ADDED

ad·dend \ˈaˌdend, əˈd-, aˈd-\ *n* -s [short for *addendum*] : a number or quantity to be added to a preceding one or in continued addition to the sum already accumulated

ad·den·dum \əˈdendəm, aˈ-\ *n, pl* **adden·da** *see sense 3* \-də\ [L, neut. of *addendus*, gerundive of *addere* to add — more at ADD] **1** : a thing that is added or is to be added : ADDITION, SUPPLEMENT ⟨as an ~ . . . let me point out one fact —A.C. Eurich⟩ **2 a** : an explanation, comment, or additional item appended to a book ⟨these *addenda* fill six pages⟩ **b** : a list or section consisting of added material; *esp* : a supplement to a book sometimes issued separately ⟨the new edition includes a 10-page ~⟩ — sometimes pl. but sing. in constr. ⟨the *addenda* contains many new words⟩ **3** *pl* **addendums** : the part of a tooth of a gear wheel between pitch line and extreme point of the tooth; *also* : the distance between pitch line and addendum circle — compare DEDENDUM **4** *addenda pl* : ACCESSORIES, APPURTENANCES ⟨a dozen exciting *addenda* to culinary art —*Holiday*⟩

addendum circle *n* : a circle touching the extreme points of the teeth of a circular gear wheel — see PITCH LINE

¹**ad·der** \ˈadə(r)\ *n* -s [ME *addre*, alter. (resulting from incorrect division of *a naddre*) of *naddre*, fr. OE *nǣdre* adder, snake; akin to OHG *nātara* adder, ON *nathr*, Goth *nadrs*, L *natrix* water snake, and prob. to L *nēre* to spin — more at NEEDLE] **1 a** : the common viper (*Vipera berus*) of Europe **b** : any other snake (as a puff adder) of the family Viperidae **2** : KRAIT **3** : any of several harmless No. American snakes: as **a** : HOGNOSE SNAKE **b** : MILK SNAKE

²**add·er** \ˈadə(r), ˈaad-\ *n* -s [¹*add* + *-er*] : one that adds; *esp* : a device (as in a computer) that performs addition

adder's-fern \ˈ==,=\ *n, pl* **adder's-ferns** **1** : the common polypody (*Polypodium vulgare*) **2** : ADDER'S-TONGUE 1

adder's-flower \ˈ==,=\ *n, pl* **adder's-flowers** [prob. so called fr. the spotted leaves] : RED CAMPION

adder's meat *n* [so called fr. their poisonous quality] **1** : CUCKOOPINT **2** : GREATER STITCHWORT

adder's mouth *n* [so called fr. the shape of the leaf] **1** : an orchid of the genus *Malaxis* **2** : SNAKEMOUTH

adderspit \ˈ==,=\ *n* -s [so called fr. the salivalike appearance of the sori] : the common brake (*Pteridium aquilinum*)

adder stone *n* [so called fr. the belief that it is formed by adders and is efficacious against snakebite] : a precious stone formerly believed to be efficacious in drawing out poison; *esp* : a highly absorbent aluminous gem

ad·der's–tongue \ˈ==,=\ *also* **adder tongue** *n, pl* **adder's–tongues** *also* **adder tongues** [so called fr. the shape of its fruiting spike] **1** : a fern of the genus *Ophioglossum* **2** : any of several plants esp. in the genera *Achillea, Arum, Erythronium, Geranium, Orchis*, and *Peramium* having leaves or flower or fruiting spikes suggesting the fruiting spikes of adder's-tongue fern

addible *var of* ADDABLE

¹**ad·dict** \əˈdikt, (ˈ)aˈd-\ *vb* -ED/-ING/-S [L *addictus*, past part. of *addicere* to favor, adjudge, fr. *ad-* + *dicere* to say — more at DICTION] *vt* **1** *obs* **a** : to award or deliver by judicial decree — used in works on Roman law **b** : to give over : give up : SURRENDER **c** : to attach (oneself) as a follower to a person or adherent to a cause ⟨we sincerely ~ ourselves to Almighty God —Thomas Fuller⟩ **2** : to apply or devote (as oneself or one's mind) habitually : give (oneself) up or surrender (oneself) as a constant practice : HABITUATE, DEVOTE ⟨the researches to which your taste ~*s* you —Sir Walter Scott⟩ ⟨such persons . . . will ~ themselves to history or science —J.S.Mill⟩ ⟨to forswear thin potations and to ~ themselves to sack —Shak.⟩ **3** : to cause or induce (a person) to make habitual use of a drug ⟨addicts . . . find it convenient to ~ several other persons —D.W.Maurer & V.H.Vogel⟩ ~ *vi, of a drug* : to bring about or cause habitual use ⟨drugs . . . threaten us because they are . . . ~*ing* —D.W.Maurer & V.H.Vogel⟩

²**ad·dict** \ˈa(ˌ)dikt, ˈadēkt *also* əˈdikt *or* aˈd-\ *n* -s **1** : one who is addicted to a habit; *specif* : one who habitually uses and has an uncontrollable craving for an addicting drug ⟨a morphine ~⟩ ⟨a barbiturate ~⟩ **2** : one showing zealous interest (as in a sport or pastime) : an enthusiastic devotee

addicted *adj* : devoted or given up ⟨~ to wine⟩ ⟨~ to stealing⟩ : strongly disposed or inclined ⟨~ to reading mystery novels⟩ ⟨easygoing as a husband, . . . straightforward as a politician, and as a man, ~ to pleasure —John Galsworthy⟩

ad·dic·tion \əˈdikshən, aˈ-\ *n* -s [¹*addict* + *-ion*] **1** *obs* : INCLINATION, BENT **2 a** : the quality or state of being addicted; *specif* : the compulsive uncontrolled use of habit-forming drugs beyond the period of medical need or under conditions harmful to society ⟨the extent of ~ ranged from 2 months to 10 years⟩ **b** : enthusiastic devotion, strong inclination, or frequent indulgence ⟨his ~ to the comics⟩ ⟨his ~ to vivid metaphors⟩ **3** [L *addiction-, addictio*, fr. *addictus* + *-ion-, -io* -ion] : a formal award or assignment of a person or thing to another; *esp* : an award made by a praetor or other magistrate (as of a debtor to his creditor)

ad·dict·ive \əˈdiktiv, (ˈ)aˈd-\ *adj* : causing or characterized by addiction

adding machine *n* : a usu. key-operated machine that performs arithmetical addition — see CALCULATING MACHINE

ad·dis aba·ba \ˌadəˈsabəbə\ *adj, usu cap both As* [fr. *Addis Ababa*, Ethiopia] : of or from Addis Ababa, the capital of Ethiopia : of the kind or style prevalent in Addis Ababa

¹**ad·di·so·ni·an** \ˌadəˈsōnēən, -nyən\ *adj, often cap* [Joseph *Addison* †1719 Eng. essayist + E *-ian*] **1** : of or resembling Addison or his characteristic writings **2** : clear and polished in literary style

²**addisonian** \"\ *adj, usu cap* [Thomas *Addison* + E *-ian*] : of, relating to, or affected with Addison's disease ⟨~ crisis⟩ ⟨~ patient⟩

addisonian anemia *or* **addisonian pernicious anemia** \"-\ *also* **ad·di·son's anemia** \ˈadəsənz-\ *n, often cap 1st A* [²*Addisonian*] : PERNICIOUS ANEMIA 1

ad·di·son's disease \ˈadəsənz-\ *n, usu cap A* [after Thomas *Addison* †1860 Eng. physician] : a destructive disease marked by deficient secretion of the adrenal cortical hormone and characterized by extreme weakness, loss of weight, low blood pressure, gastrointestinal disturbances, and brownish pigmentation of the skin and mucous membranes

ad·dit·a·ment \əˈdidəmənt, aˈ-\ *n* -s [ME, fr. L *additamentum*, fr. *additus* (past part. of *addere* to add) + connective *-a-* + *-mentum* -ment — more at ADD] : a thing added : ADDITION ⟨the latter verses of the chapter were an ~ of a later age —S.T. Coleridge⟩

ad·di·tion \əˈdishən, aˈ-\ *n* -s [ME *addicioun*, fr. MF *addition*, fr. L *addition-, additio*, fr. *additus* + *-ion, -io* -ion] **1 a** : the result of adding : anything added : INCREASE, AUGMENTATION ⟨the clerk was a recent ~ to the staff⟩ **b** : something added that improves or increases value ⟨that table is certainly an ~ to the room⟩ **2** : the act or process of adding : the joining or uniting of one thing to another ⟨the subject stood in need of correction and ~ —Benjamin Farrington⟩ **3** *obs* : a designation (as of rank or place of residence) added to a person's name ⟨the names of those justices . . . with all their ~*s* and titles —William Penn⟩ **4 a** : the process denoted by the sign + of combining two or more numbers so as to obtain their sum **b** : the part of mathematics that treats of addition **5 a** : a part added to or joined with a building to increase available space **b** : a suburban area marked out into streets and lots as a future residential section **c** *additions pl* : facilities, structures, equipment, or other property added to what is already in service **6** : direct chemical combination of two or more substances to form a single product ⟨the union of ethylene and chlorine to form ethylene dichloride is an ~ reaction: $C_2H_4+Cl_2 \rightarrow C_2H_4Cl_2$⟩ — often contrasted with *substitution* **7 a** : the amalgamation in logic of classes or of terms considered with reference to their denotation ⟨the logical ~ of "white" and "sweet" results in "either white or sweet (or both)"⟩ **b** : ALTERNATION 2 **8** : a material used in the manufacture of portland cement other than water and untreated calcium sulfate that is interground with the clinker in an amount not exceeding two percent **9** : a dice game played with five dice the object being to achieve the highest numerical total in five or fewer casts — **in addition** *adv* : ¹BESIDES 1a — **in addition to** *prep* : over and above

addition agent *n* : ADDITIVE

ad·di·tion·al \əˈdishənᵊl, (ˈ)aˈd-, -shnəl\ *adj* : existing or coming by way of addition : ADDED, FURTHER

additional accompaniment *n* : a musical accompaniment or arrangement of a composition not in the original score but added in a later period

additional insured *n, pl* **additional insureds** : a person other than the one in whose name a policy is issued but who is also protected by that policy

ad·di·tion·al·ly \-ˈlē, -əlē, -li\ *adv* : in or by way of addition : FURTHERMORE ⟨the book is ~ the history of an era⟩

additional tax *n* : SURTAX b

addition axiom *n* : an axiom in mathematics: if equal numbers are added to equal numbers, the results are equal

addition compound *n* : a compound formed by chemical addition; *esp* : MOLECULAR COMPOUND

ad·di·tion la·tente \ädēsyōⁿlätäⁿt\ *n, pl* **additions latentes** \"\ [F, lit., latent addition] : FACILITATION 3

addition polymerization *n* : polymerization without formation of a by-product — distinguished from *condensation polymerization*

addition product *n* : a product formed by chemical addition — see ADDUCT

addition theorem *n* : a formula or rule that expresses algebraically a function of the sum of two arguments in terms of the same or related functions of the separate arguments [as $\sin (x + y) = \sin x \cos y + \sin y \cos x$]

¹**ad·di·tive** \ˈadədiv, -ətiv\ *adj* [LL *additivus*, fr. L *additus* (past part. of *addere* to add) + *-ivus* -ive — more at ADD] **1** : tending to add or be added : admitting, involving, or characterized by addition ⟨the process of cultural development is . . . ~ —A.L.Kroeber⟩ **2** *philos* : having the distinctive character of extensive magnitudes : of the nature of an addition or aggregation rather than an organic union of parts ⟨this pluralistic view of a world of ~ constitution —William James⟩ **3** : having a numeral value equal to the sum of the values for the component parts — used of a property; compare COLLIGATIVE, CONSTITUTIVE 3 ⟨molecular weight may be thought of as an ~ property⟩ **4** : relating to the sum of the pharmacological responses produced by the concurrent administration of two or more drugs capable of producing the same kind of effect **5 a** : relating to the controlled mixing of colored light sources (as red, green, and blue) to form a colored image : formed by superposition or other nondestructive combination of colored lights **b** : relating to a method of making halftone color prints in which the dots for each color are placed beside each other **6** : having a genic effect that is the sum of the individual effects — **ad·di·tive·ly** *adv*

²**additive** \"\ *n* -s **1** : a substance added to another in relatively small amounts to impart or improve desirable properties or suppress undesirable properties: as **a** : a chemical added to a lubricating oil to make it suitable for use at extreme pressures or to prevent corrosion ⟨an extreme-pressure ~⟩ **b** : a chemical (as an antiknock agent or an agent for counteracting deposits on spark plugs) added to gasoline ⟨tetraethyl lead is a gasoline ~⟩ **c** : an agent added to a foodstuff to improve color, flavor, texture, or keeping qualities ⟨gelatin is an ~ in the manufacture of ice cream⟩ **d** : material added to soil or feeds to improve plant or animal growth by indirect action **2** : an arithmetical key for superencipherment esp. when numeral code groups are enciphered by adding to them a numeral keying sequence usu. by noncarrying addition

additive primary *n* : one of a set of the colored lights red, green, and blue by addition of which in varying proportions lights of a maximum number of colors may be produced

ad·di·tiv·i·ty \ˌadəˈtivədē\ *n* -ES : the quality or state of being additive

ad·di·to·ry \ˈadəˌtōrē\ *adj* [*addition* + *-ory*] : tending to add : making an addition

¹**ad·dle** \ˈadᵊl\ *n* -s [ME *adel*, fr. OE *adela;* akin to MLG *adele* liquid manure, Sw dial. *adel* animal urine, and perh. to Gk *onthos* animal dung] *now dial Brit* : stagnant or filthy liquid

²**addle** \"\ *adj* [ME *adel-*, fr. *adel*, n.] **1** *of an egg* : foul smelling and putrid : ROTTEN **2 a** : EMPTY, UNSOUND ⟨I wish him an ounce more wit in his ~ head —William Robertson †1686⟩ **b** : CONFUSED, MUDDLED ⟨the brains of the people growing more and more ~ —Edmund Burke⟩

³**addle** \ˈadᵊl\ *vb* **addled**; **addled**; **addling** \-d(ᵊ)liŋ\ **addles** *vt* : to throw into confusion or disorder : MUDDLE, CONFOUND : make addle ⟨no housing problem . . . to ~ our heads —Irwin Edman⟩ ⟨any thinking . . . is bound to be *addled* by inaccurate language —R.G.Swing⟩ ~ *vi* **1** : to become addle : SPOIL ⟨not one of these eggs ever *addled* —Robert Southey⟩ **2** : to confuse or become confused ⟨the object is to ~ and not to elucidate —G.B.Shaw⟩

⁴**addle** \"\ *vb* -ED/-ING/-S [ME *addlen*, fr. ON *öthlask* (refl. v.) to acquire as property, fr. *ōthal* property — more at ODAL] *vt, now dial Eng* : to earn by labor : GAIN ~ *vi, now dial Eng* : GAIN, THRIVE

addlebrained \ˈ==,=\ *adj* [²*addle* + *brained*] : ADDLEPATED

ad·dle·pate \ˈ==,=\ *n* : one who is addlepated

addlepated \ˈ==,=\ *adj* [²*addle* + *pated*] : stupid and confused, mixed up, or eccentric ⟨blathering like the ~ nincompoop that you are —D.G.Gerahty⟩

ad·dlings *or* **ad·dlins** \ˈadlənz, -liŋz\ *n pl* [pl. of *addling*, gerund of ⁴*addle*] *dial Eng* : EARNINGS, SAVINGS

addn *abbr* addition

ad·dorsed \əˈdȯrst, (ˈ)aˈd-\ *also* **ad·dossed** \-däst, -ȯst\ *adj* [modif. of F *adossé*, past part. of *adosser* to turn the back, set on one's back, fr. *a-* (fr. L *ad-*) + *dos* back, fr. L *dorsum*] : set or turned back to back (as in heraldry)

ad·dra \ˈadrə\ *also* **addra gazelle** *n* -s [prob. native name in Africa] : a large African gazelle (*Gazella dama*); *esp* : a member of the typical race (*G.d.dama*) that is white with reddish hair on the neck and upper back — compare MOHR

¹**ad·dress** \əˈdres *also* aˈd- *or* ˈaˌd-\ *vb* -ED/-ING/-ES [ME *adressen*, fr. MF *adrescer, adresser*, fr. *a-* (fr. L *ad-*) + *drescer, dresser* to straighten, arrange — more at DRESS] *vt* **1** *obs* **a** : to make straight : set in order : ARRANGE ⟨whose stately numbers are so well ~*ed* —Richard Barnfield⟩ **b** : to make right : CORRECT, REDRESS ⟨a parliament being called to ~ many things —John Milton⟩ **2 a** : DIRECT, AIM : make straight (as a course) ⟨the enemy of mankind . . . towards Eve ~*ed* his way —John Milton⟩ **b** : to direct to go : SEND, DISPATCH ⟨he was ~*ed* first to the Earl —Gilbert Burnet⟩ **3** *archaic* **a** : to make ready : PREPARE ⟨he did ~ himself to quit . . . this mountain land —Lord Byron⟩ **b** (1) : to make ready or prepare (as with proper clothing) (2) : CLOTHE, DRESS **c** : to put on : DON ⟨I have ~*ed* a frock of heavy mail —Robert Browning⟩ **4** : to direct the efforts or turn the attention of (oneself) ⟨he ~*ed* himself to the remains of his chicken and salad —C.D.Lewis⟩ ⟨the speakers ~*ed* themselves to a common question⟩ : try to apply (oneself or one's powers) ⟨~ yourself to the task of behaving better —Aldous Huxley⟩ **5 a** : to direct by way of communication : communicate directly ⟨~*ing* his thanks to his host⟩ ⟨they ~*ed* to the governor a plea for clemency⟩ **b** : to direct the words of (oneself) ⟨~*ing* himself to the principal, he defended the students' behavior⟩ **6 a** : to speak, write, or otherwise communicate directly to ⟨~*ing* the chairman, he began his speech⟩ ⟨she ~*ed* the older woman respectfully⟩ **b** : to deliver a prepared or formal speech to ⟨he ~*es* the convention tonight⟩ **7 a** : to write or otherwise mark directions for delivery on : DIRECT ⟨~ a letter for mailing⟩ ⟨~ a package for delivery by messenger⟩ **b** : to consign or entrust to the care of another (as agent or factor) ⟨the ship was ~*ed* to a factor⟩ **8** : to greet directly using a prescribed form either in speech or in writing ⟨many people are uncertain about how to ~ members of the nobility⟩ **9** : to direct one's attentions to (as in courtship) : COURT, WOO ⟨she is too fine and too conscious of herself to repulse any man who may ~ her —J.R.Lowell⟩ **10 a** : to take one's stance and adjust the club preparatory to hitting (a golf ball) **b** : to stand ready to shoot (an arrow) with the body turned at right angles to the target **c** : to bow slightly to (one's square-dancing partner) in preparation for a dance **11** *law* : to unseat or remove (a judge) as unworthy of office by executive order in accordance with a formal petition from the legislature **12 a** : to put information into (a memory or storage device) **b** : to call upon (such a device) for information ~ *vi* **1** *obs* : to prepare oneself : set about ⟨let us ~ to tend on Hector's heels —Shak.⟩ **2** *obs* : to direct one's speech or attentions ⟨my lord of Burgundy, we first ~ toward you —Shak.⟩ **syn** see DIRECT

²**ad·dress** \əˈdres, *in sense 7 usu & in other senses often* ˈaˌd-; *also* aˈdres, *sometimes (esp in sense 7)* ˈadrəs\ *n* -ES **1** *obs* **a** (1) : the act of preparing or making ready (2) : the state of being prepared **b** : something that is prepared; *specif* : DRESS, ATTIRE **2** : the quality or state of being ready or skillful : DEXTERITY, ADROITNESS ⟨to bring the thing off as well as Mike has done requires ~ —Herman Wouk⟩ **3** *obs* : the act or action of addressing oneself or one's words to a person **4 a** : the manner in which one conducts or carries oneself : BEARING, DEPORTMENT ⟨the education and social ~ of the propertied class —G.B.Shaw⟩ **b** : the manner or style of speaking or singing : DELIVERY ⟨a tenor who sang . . . with a remarkable freedom of voice and ease of ~ —Douglas Watt⟩ **5** : courteous or dutiful attention esp. in courtship— usu. used

in pl. ⟨ladies . . . to whom all the polite part of the court . . . paid their ~*es* —Jonathan Swift⟩ **6 :** a formal communication either spoken or written: as **a :** a usu. formal speech or talk esp. as prepared for delivery to a special group ⟨his commencement ~ was subsequently published⟩ **b :** a formal petition esp. by a legislative body to an executive or sovereign **c :** a formal statement of policy or opinion by a sovereign or president to the people or to a legislative body ⟨an ~ by the president to Congress⟩ **7 a :** the designation of a place (as a residence or place of business) where a person or organization may be found or communicated with **:** a part of such a designation ⟨a street ~⟩ **b :** the directions for delivery given on the outside of an object to be delivered (as a letter or package) **c :** the name of the addressee and designation of place of delivery between the heading and the salutation of a business letter — called also *inside address* **8 :** the act of directing or dispatching a ship ⟨the agent at the port being given a commission of ~⟩ **9 :** DIRECTION 11 **10 :** the stance of the player and the position of the club preparatory to hitting a golf ball **11 :** a location (as in the memory of a computer) where particular information is stored; *also* **:** the symbols (as digits or letters) that identify such a location **syn** see TACT

ad·dress·ee \ˌaˌdreˈsē, əˌdreˈsē\ *n* -s **:** one to whom something (as a letter, package, or document) is addressed

ad·dress·er \əˈdresə(r)\ *also* aˈ-\ *n* -s **:** one that addresses: as **a :** a clerk who addresses mail or shipments **b :** a machine for printing addresses for mailing

addressing machine *n* **:** a business machine that automatically imprints names, addresses, or other information on successive envelopes or forms

ad·dres·sor \əˈdresə(r), aˈ-; əˌdreˈsȯ(ə)r, aˌ-, -ō(ə)\ *n* -s **:** ADDRESSER; *esp* **:** one that addresses a letter of credit

adds *pres 3d sing of* ADD, *pl of* ADD

ad·duce \əˈd(y)üs, aˈ-\ *vt* -ED/-ING/-S [L *adducere*, lit., to lead to, fr. *ad-* + *ducere* to lead — more at TOW (pull)] **:** to bring forward (as an example, reason, or proof) for consideration in a discussion, analysis, or contention **:** OFFER, PRESENT, CITE ⟨in the light of the parallels which I have *adduced*, the hypothesis appears legitimate —J.G.Frazer⟩ ⟨let me ~ more pleasing evidence —A.T.Quiller-Couch⟩ **syn** see CITE

ad·du·cent \(ˈ)aˈd(y)üsᵊnt, əˈd-\ *adj* [L *adducent-, adducens*, pres. part. of *adducere*] *physiol* **:** ADDUCTING — opposed to *abducent*

ad·duc·er \əˈd(y)üsə(r), aˈ-\ *n* -s **:** one that adduces

ad·duc·i·ble *also* **ad·duce·a·ble** \-səbəl\ *adj* **:** capable of being adduced

¹ad·duct \əˈdəkt, aˈ-\ *vt* -ED/-ING/-S [L *adductus*, past part. of *adducere*] **:** to draw (as a limb) toward or past the median axis of the body; *also* **:** to bring together (similar parts) ⟨~ the fingers⟩ — compare ABDUCT 2

²ad·duct \ˈaˌdəkt\ *n* -s [G *addukt*, fr. L *adductus*, past part.] **:** a chemical addition product: as **a :** the cyclic product of the addition reaction of a diene with another unsaturated compound (as maleic anhydride) — compare DIELS-ALDER REACTION **b :** a crystalline complex (as one of urea with a straight-chain aliphatic compound)

ad·duc·tion \əˈdəkshən, aˈ-\ *n* -s [F, fr. ML *adduction-, adductio* act of bringing forward, fr. L *adductus* + *-ion-, -io* -ion] **1 :** the action of adducting or the condition of being adducted ⟨prolonged ~ of the arm⟩ **2 :** the act or action of adducing or bringing forward

ad·duc·tive \əˈdəktiv, (ˈ)aˈd-\ *adj* [L *adductus* + E *-ive*] **:** bringing toward or to something **:** ADDUCTING

ad·duc·tor \əˈdəktə(r), (ˈ)aˈd-\ *n* -s [NL, fr. LL, conductor, fr. L *adductus* + *-or*] **1 a :** any of three powerful triangular muscles that contribute to the adduction of the human thigh: (1) **:** one arising from the superior ramus of the pubis and inserted into the middle third of the linea aspera (2) **:** one arising from the inferior ramus of the pubis and inserted into the iliopectineal line and the upper part of the linea aspera (3) **:** one arising from the inferior ramus of the pubis and the ischium and inserted behind the first two into the linea aspera **b :** any of several muscles other than the adductors of the thigh that draw a part toward the median line of the body or toward the axis of an extremity **2 :** a muscle that closes the valves of a bivalve shell (as in the oyster and the scallop) or one of a pair of such muscles (as in other mollusks)

adductor bre·vis \-ˈbrēvəs, -ˈbrev-\ *n* **:** ADDUCTOR 1a (2)

adductor impression *n* **:** one of the scars on the valve of a bivalve shell marking the attachment of the adductors

adductor lon·gus \-ˈlȯŋgəs\ *n* **:** ADDUCTOR 1a (1)

adductor mag·nus \-ˈmagnəs\ *n* **:** ADDUCTOR 1a (3)

addulce *vt* -ED/-ING/-S [alter. (influenced by L *dulcis*) of earlier *addoulce, adoulce*, fr. MF *adoulcer, adoulcier*, lit., to sweeten, fr. *a-* (fr. L *ad-*) + *doulce, douz* sweet, fr. L *dulcis* — more at DULCET] *obs* **:** to bring into harmony or agreement **:** MOLLIFY

add up *vi* **1 a :** to make up or comprise **:** amount to — used with *to* ⟨two and two *add up* to four⟩ ⟨tunes . . . still don't *add up* to a piece —Leonard Bernstein⟩ **b :** SIGNIFY, MEAN — used with *to* ⟨an uneasiness about whether the universe *adds up* to anything —Irwin Edman⟩ **2 a :** to make or come to the expected or correct total ⟨the figures wouldn't *add up* —Charles Dickens⟩ **b :** to form an intelligible pattern **:** be plausible or probable **:** make sense ⟨he was unaccountable, he didn't *add up* —Graham Greene⟩ ~ *vt* **:** to form an opinion or judgment of **:** size up ⟨she could not claim to have *added up* Constance yet —Arnold Bennett⟩

ade \ˈād\ *n* -s [*-ade*] **:** a sweetened drink made from water and fruit juice (as citrus)

-ade \ˌād, ˈād, ˌäd\ *n suffix* -s [ME, fr. MF, fr. OProv *-ada*, fr. LL *-ata*, fr. L, fem. of *-atus* -ate] **1 :** act **:** action ⟨blockade⟩ **2 a :** product ⟨jamrosade⟩ **b :** sweet drink ⟨orangeade⟩

ade·cid·u·ate \ˌādəˈsijəwət, -deˈ-\ *adj* [²*a-* + *deciduate*] **1 :** NONDECIDUATE **2** *bot* **:** not falling **:** EVERGREEN ⟨~ leaves⟩

adeem \əˈdēm, aˈ-\ *vt* -ED/-ING/-S [fr. *ademption*, after such pairs as E *redemption: redeem*] **:** to revoke or satisfy (as a legacy, grant, or donation) by ademption

adel- *or* **adelo-** *comb form* [NL, fr. Gk *adēl-, adēlo-* unseen, fr. *adēlos*, fr. *a-* ²*a-* + *dēlos* visible, evident; akin to OE *tǣtan* to gladden, OHG *zeiz* dear, ON *teitr* glad, Skt *dīdeti* he shines, L *dies* day — more at DEITY] **:** concealed **:** not apparent ⟨*Adelaster*⟩ ⟨*adelopod*⟩

ad·e·laide \ˈadᵊlˌād\ *adj, usu cap* [fr. *Adelaide*, So. Australia] **:** of or from Adelaide, the capital of So. Australia **:** of the kind or style prevalent in Adelaide

ade·lan·ta·do \ˌadᵊlˌänˈtä(ˌ)dō\ *n* -s [Sp, fr. past part. of *adelantar* to put ahead, advance, fr. *adelante* ahead, fr. *a-* (fr. L *ad-*) + *delante* before, in front of, alter. of obs. *denante*, fr. *de* of, from (fr. L) + *enante* before, in front of, fr. LL *in ante*, fr. L *in* + *ante* before] **:** a civil and military governor of a province in Spain or her colonies

ade·lea \əˈdēlēə\ *n, cap* [NL, fr. Gk *adēlos* unseen — more at ADEL-] **:** a large genus of protozoans of the order Coccidia that are parasitic on arthropods and have two sporozoites in each sporocyst

adele balls \əˈdel-\ *n pl but sing or pl in constr, usu cap A* [origin unknown] **:** CONGO RUBBER

adel·ges \əˈdel(ˌ)jēz\ *n, cap* [NL, fr. *adel-* + *-ges* (prob. fr. Gk *gē* earth)] **:** a genus of aphids related to phylloxerans and feeding chiefly on spruce and balsam on which they often cause damaging and unsightly galls — **adel·gid** \-jəd\ *adj or n*

ade·lia \əˈdēlēə, -lyə\ *n, cap* [NL, fr. *adel-* + *-ia*] **:** a genus of tropical American shrubs (family Euphorbiaceae) with toothed leaves and small yellowish flowers

adé·lie penguin *or* **adélie** \əˈdālē\ *n* -s *usu cap A* [fr. *Adélie* Coast, Antarctica] **:** a small Antarctic penguin (*Pygoscelis adeliae*)

ad·e·lite \ˈadᵊlˌīt\ *n* -s [ISV *adel-* + *-ite*] **:** a mineral consisting of a gray or grayish yellow calcium and magnesium arsenate $CaMg(OH)AsO_4$ (hardness 5, sp. gr. 3.74)

ade·lo·chor·da \əˌdēləˈkȯrdə, ˌadᵊl-\ [NL, fr. *adel-* + *chorda*] *syn of* HEMICHORDATA

ade·lo·co·don·ic \əˌdēləkəˈdänik, ˌadᵊl(ˌ)ōk-\ *adj* [*adel-* + Gk *kōdōn* bell + E *-ic*] *zool* **:** remaining attached and developing no umbrella — used of sexual zooids of certain hydroids; opposed to *phanerocodonic*

ade·lo·mor·phic \-ˈmȯrfik\ *or* **ade·lo·mor·phous** \-fəs\ *adj* [*adel-* + *-morphic, -morphous*] **:** of obscure or indefinite form — used of the central cells of the peptic glands

ade·lo·spon·dy·li \əˌdēləˈspändəˌlī, ˌadᵊl(ˌ)ōˈ-\ [NL, fr. *adel-* + *-spondyli*] *syn of* MICROSAURIA

adel·phi·an \əˈdelfēən\ *n* -s *usu cap* [*Adelphi*us, an early leader of the sect + E *-an*] **:** EUCHITE 1

adel·phic \-fik\ *adj* [Gk *adelphikos* brotherly, sisterly, fr. *adelphos* brother + *-ikos* -ic] **:** of or relating to a polygynous marriage in which the wives are sisters or to a polyandrous marriage in which the husbands are brothers

adelpho- *comb form* [Gk, fr. *adelphos*] **:** brother ⟨*adelphogamy*⟩

ad·el·phoc·o·ris \ˌadᵊlˈfäkərəs\ *n, cap* [NL, fr. *adelpho-* + Gk *koris* bug] **:** a widely distributed genus of rather small mirid bugs including a number of species destructive to economic plants (as the alfalfa plant bug)

ad·el·phog·a·my \-ägəmē\ *n* -ES [*adelpho-* + *-gamy*] **1 :** polyandry in which brothers have a wife or wives in common **2** *zool* **:** mating of brothers and sisters (as in some ants) **3 :** union of mother and daughter cells (as in some yeasts)

-adelphous \əˈdelfəs\ *adj comb form* [prob. fr. NL *-adelphus*, fr. Gk *adelphos* brother, fr. *a-* (fr. assumed *ha-*, akin to *heis*, *mia*, *hen* one, *homos* same) + *-delphos* (akin to *delphys* womb) — more at SAME, DOLPHIN] **:** having (such or so many) stamen fascicles ⟨isadelphous⟩ ⟨monadelphous⟩

ademp·tion \əˈdem(p)shən, aˈ-\ *n* -s [L *ademption-, ademptio*, fr. *ademptus* (past part. of *adimere* to take away, fr. *ad-* + *-imere*, fr. *emere* to buy, obtain) + *-ion-, -io* -ion — more at REDEEM] **:** revocation or satisfaction of a property transfer either by disposal (as sale or destruction) of the subject of the property transfer or by some other act (as previous payment) showing such an intention

aden- *or* **adeno-** *comb form* [NL, fr. Gk *adeno-, aden-*, *adēn*; akin to ON *økkr* lump, L *inguen* groin, Gk *nephros* kidney — more at NEPHRITIS] **1 :** gland **:** glandular ⟨*aden*itis⟩ ⟨*adeno*carcinoma⟩ **2 :** glandular and ⟨*adeno*neural⟩

ade·na \əˈdēnə\ *adj, usu cap* [after *Adena*, town in Jefferson co., Ohio, its type station] **:** of or belonging to a prehistoric culture centered in the Mississippi valley marked by large conical burial mounds and thought to precede the Hopewell culture though in some areas it lasted later than Hopewell

ad·e·nan·the·ra \ˌadᵊnˈanthərə\ *n, cap* [NL, fr. *aden-* + *-anthera*] **:** a small genus of Asiatic timber trees (family Leguminosae) with twice-pinnate leaves and racemose flower clusters — see RED SANDALWOOD 2

ad·e·nase \ˈadᵊnˌās\ *n* -s [ISV *adenine* + *-ase*] **:** an enzyme found esp. in animal tissue (as liver) that hydrolyzes adenine to hypoxanthine and ammonia

aden·i·form \əˈdenəˌfȯrm, -ēn-\ *adj* [*aden-* + *-iform*] **:** like a gland

ad·e·nine \ˈadᵊnˌēn\ *n* -s [ISV *aden-* + *-ine*; orig. formed as G *adenin*] **:** a purine base $C_5H_3N_4NH_2$ extracted esp. from many glandular organs and from tea and obtained by hydrolysis of nucleic acids; 6-amino-purine

ad·e·ni·tis \ˌadᵊnˈīdəs\ *n* -ES [NL, fr. *aden-* + *-itis*] **:** inflammation of one or more lymph nodes

ad·e·no·car·ci·no·ma \ˌadᵊn(ˌ)ōˌkärsᵊnˈōmə\ *n, pl* **adenocarcinomas** \-məz\ *also* **adenocarcinoma·ta** \-məd·ə\ [NL, fr. *aden-* + *carcinoma*] **:** a malignant tumor originating in glandular epithelium ⟨~ of the breast⟩ — **ad·e·no·car·ci·nom·a·tous** \-sᵊnˈämədəs, -ōm-\ *adj*

aden·o·chrome \əˈdenəˌkrōm -ēn-\ *n* -s [*aden-* + *-chrome*] **:** an acidic red pigment found in the branchial hearts of the octopus

ad·e·no·dac·tyl \əˈdenəˌdaktᵊl, -ēn-\ *n* -s [*aden-* + Gk *daktylos* finger] **:** one of the penislike supplementary structures in the male reproductive system of certain turbellarians

ad·e·no·fi·bro·ma \ˌadᵊn(ˌ)ōfīˈbrōmə\ *n, pl* **adenofibromas** *or* **adenofibroma·ta** \-məd·ə\ [NL, fr. *aden-* + *fibroma*] **:** a benign tumor of glandular and fibrous tissue

ad·e·no·hy·poph·y·sis \-ˌhīˈpäfəsəs\ *n, pl* **adenohypophyses** \-əˌsēz\ [NL, fr. *aden-* + *hypophysis*] **:** the portion of the pituitary gland that arises from the embryonic pharynx and is predominantly glandular in nature — compare NEUROHYPOPHYSIS

¹ad·e·noid \ˈadᵊnˌȯid, ˈadˌnȯid\ *or* **ad·e·noi·dal** \ˌadᵊnˈȯidᵊl\ *adj* [Gk *adenoeidēs* glandular, fr. *aden-* + *-eidēs* -oid, -oidal] **1 :** of, like, or relating to glands or glandular tissue; *esp* **:** like or belonging to lymphoid tissue **2 :** of or relating to the adenoids ⟨in the ~ region of the pharynx⟩ **3 a :** of, relating to, or affected with abnormally enlarged adenoids ⟨a severe ~ condition⟩ ⟨an ~ patient⟩ **b** *usu adenoidal* **:** typical or suggestive of one affected with abnormally enlarged adenoids: as (1) **:** characterized by mouth breathing **:** GAPING ⟨we can't park here in the driveway like a couple of *adenoidal* tourists —Ellery Queen⟩ (2) **:** nasal, monotonous, or constricted in tone quality **:** BREATHY — used esp. of a singing voice ⟨an *adenoidal* tenor⟩ (3) **:** lacking vivacity esp. in facial expression **:** DULL, APATHETIC ⟨the mumbling of some *adenoidal* moron —Ben Hecht⟩

²adenoid \"\ *n* -s **1 :** an abnormally enlarged mass of lymphoid tissue at the back of the pharynx characteristically obstructing the nasal and ear passages and inducing mouth breathing, nasality, postnasal discharge, and dullness of facial expression — usu. used in pl.; see PHARYNGEAL TONSIL **2 :** PHARYNGEAL TONSIL

adenoids, *A*

ad·e·noid·ec·to·my \ˌadᵊnˌȯiˈdektəmē\ *n* -ES [²*adenoid* + *-ectomy*] **:** surgical removal of the adenoids

ad·e·noid·itis \ˌadᵊnˌȯiˈdīdəs\ *n* -ES [NL, fr. ISV ²*adenoid* + NL *-itis*] **:** inflammation of the adenoids

ad·e·no·ma \ˌadᵊnˈōmə\ *n, pl* **adenomas** *or* **ad·e·no·ma·ta** \-məd·ə\ [NL, fr. *aden-* + *-oma*] **:** a benign tumor of a glandlike structure or of glandular origin ⟨~ of the breast⟩ — **ad·e·nom·a·tous** \-ˈnämədəs, -ōm-\ *adj*

ad·e·no·ma·to·sis \ˌadᵊnˌōməˈtōsəs\ *n, pl* **adenomato·ses** \-ōˌsēz\ [NL, fr. *adenomat-, adenoma* + *-osis*] **:** a condition marked by multiple growths consisting of glandular tissue

ad·e·no·my·o·ma \ˌadᵊn(ˌ)ōˌmīˈōmə\ *n, pl* **adenomyomas** *or* **adenomyoma·ta** \-məd·ə\ [NL, fr. *aden-* + *myoma*] **:** a benign tumor composed of muscular and glandular elements

ad·e·no·my·o·sis \ˌadᵊn(ˌ)ōˌmīˈōsəs\ *n, pl* **adenomyo·ses** \-ōˌsēz\ [NL, fr. *aden-* + *myosis*] **:** ENDOMETRIOSIS

ad·e·no·neu·ral \ˌadᵊn(ˌ)ōˈn(y)u̇rəl\ *adj* [*aden-* + *neural*] **:** of or relating to a gland and nerve ⟨~ junction⟩

ad·e·nop·a·thy \ˌadᵊnˈäpəthē\ *n* -ES [*aden-* + *-pathy*] **:** any disease or enlargement involving glandular tissue; *esp* **:** a disease or enlargement involving lymph glands ⟨cervical ~⟩

ad·e·noph·o·ra \ˌadᵊnˈäfərə\ *n, cap* [NL, fr. *aden-* + *-phora*] **:** a genus of herbs (family Campanulaceae) of Europe and Asia that are distinguished by the cushionlike disk or gland around the base of the style

ad·e·nose \ˈadᵊnˌōs\ *or* **ad·e·nous** \-ˌəs\ *adj* [*aden-* + *-ose*, *-ous*] **1** *biol* **:** like a gland **2** *usu adenose, biol* **:** bearing or full of glands

aden·o·sine \əˈdenəˌsēn, -ˌsən\ *n* -s [ISV, blend of *adenine* and *ribose*; orig. formed as G *adenosin*] **:** a crystalline nucleoside $C_{10}H_{13}N_5O_4$ isolated from various tissues, esp. muscle, and obtained by partial hydrolysis of ribonucleic acid, yielding on hydrolysis adenine and ribose and having a vasodilator effect in the vertebrate system; 6-amino-9-D-ribosyl-purine

adenosine diphosphate *also* **aden·o·sine·di·phos·phor·ic acid** \-ˌdīˌfäˈsfȯrik-\ *n* **:** an ester $C_{10}H_{15}N_5O_3H_3P_2O_7$ of adenosine and pyrophosphoric acid that is formed in living cells as an intermediate between adenosine triphosphate and adenylic acid, its formation from the triphosphate by loss of phosphate leading esp. to a transfer of energy to other compounds in glycolysis, and that reacts in muscle tissue with phosphocreatine or phosphoarginine to regenerate adenosine triphosphate — called also *ADP*

adenosine phosphate *also* **aden·o·sine·phos·phor·ic acid** \-ˌfäˈsfȯrik-\ *n* **:** any of various esters of adenosine and a phosphoric acid; *esp* **:** ADENYLIC ACID

adenosine triphosphatase *n* **:** an enzyme that hydrolyzes adenosine triphosphate, esp. one that hydrolyzes the triphosphate to adenosine diphosphate and inorganic phosphate — compare APYRASE, MYOSIN

adenosine triphosphate *also* **adenosinetriphosphoric acid** *n* **:** an amorphous ester $C_{10}H_{12}N_5O_3H_4P_3O_{10}$ of adenosine and triphosphoric acid that occurs in living cells, esp. in muscle tissue, where its enzymatic hydrolysis to adenosine diphosphate and adenylic acid releases phosphate and available energy for the work of muscular contraction, and that plays a fundamental role in most other biochemical processes that either produce or require energy (as biological oxidations) — called also *adenylpyrophosphate, ATP*

ad·e·nos·to·ma \ˌadᵊnˈästəmə\ *n, cap* [NL, fr. *aden-* + *-stoma*] **:** a small genus of California evergreen shrubs (family Rosaceae) having heathlike leaves and small white panicled flowers and comprising the chamiso and the ribbonwood

ad·e·no·troph·ic \ˌadᵊn(ˌ)ōˈträfik, əˌdenəˈ-, -ōf-\ *adj* [*aden-* + *-trophic*] **:** marked by retention of eggs within the mother until the larvae are hatched and nourished by special nutritive organs in the uterus — used of a form of ovoviviparous development in certain dipterous insects

aden ulcer \ˈādᵊn-, ˈä-,ˈa-,ˈȧ-\ *n, usu cap A* [fr. *Aden*, city and territory in Arabia, where it occurs] **:** TROPICAL ULCER 2

ad·e·nyl \ˈadᵊnˌil\ *n* -s [ISV *aden*ine + *-yl*] **:** a univalent radical $C_5H_4N_5$ derived from adenine

ad·e·nyl·ic acid \ˌadᵊnˌilik-\ *n* [ISV *adenyl* + *-ic*] **:** an amorphous nucleotide $C_{10}H_{12}N_5O_3H_2PO_4$ formed by partial hydrolysis of ribonucleic acid or of adenosine triphosphate, being an ester of adenosine and orthophosphoric acid known in three isomeric forms — called also *adenosine phosphate*; see ADENOSINE DIPHOSPHATE

ad·e·nyl·py·ro·phos·pha·tase \ˈadᵊnˌilˌpīrōˈfäsfəˌtās\ *n* -s [*adenylpyrophosphate* + *-ase*] **:** ADENOSINE TRIPHOSPHATASE

ad·e·nyl·py·ro·phos·phate \-ˌpīrōˈfäˌsfāt\ *n* -s [*adenyl* + *pyrophosphate*] **:** ADENOSINE TRIPHOSPHATE

ad·e·nyl·py·ro·phos·phor·ic acid \-ˌpīrōˌfäˈsfȯrik-\ *n* [ISV *adenyl* + *pyrophosphoric*] **:** ADENOSINE TRIPHOSPHATE

adeph·a·ga \əˈdefəgə\ *n pl, cap* [NL, fr. Gk *adēphaga*, neut. pl. of *adēphagos* gluttonous, fr. *hadēn* enough + *-phagos* -phagous — more at SAD] **:** a suborder of Coleoptera containing certain predaceous beetles (as the tiger beetles, ground beetles, and water beetles) usu. with filiform antennae and the first ventral abdominal segment divided by the hind coxal cavities — **adeph·a·gan** \-gən\ *n* -s

adeph·a·gous \-gəs\ *adj* [NL *Adephaga* + E *-ous*] **:** of or relating to the Adephaga

adeps \ˈaˌdeps\ *n, pl* **adi·pes** \ˈadəˌpēz\ [L — more at ADIP-] **1 :** animal fat **2 :** purified internal abdominal fat of the hog

adeps la·nae \ˌaˌdepˈslā(ˌ)nē, ˈäˌdepˈsläˌnī\ *n, pl* **adi·pes lanae** \ˌadəˌpēzˈlā-, ˈädəˌpāˈslä-\ [NL, lit., wool fat] **:** LANOLIN

¹adept \ˈaˌdept *also* əˈd- *or* aˈd-\ *n* -s [NL *adeptus* alchemist that has attained the knowledge of how to change base metals into gold, fr. *adeptus*, adj., knowing how to change base metals to gold, fr. L, having attained, past part. of *adipisci* to arrive at, attain, fr. *ad-* + *apisci* to reach — more at APT] **1 :** a highly skilled or well-trained individual **:** EXPERT — usu. used with *at* or *in* ⟨an ~ in philosophy⟩ ⟨~*s* at traps and ambushes —Seth Agnew⟩ **2 :** an enthusiastic adherent or devotee (as of a philosophy) — usu. used with *of* **syn** see EXPERT

²adept \əˈdept *also* (ˈ)aˌd-\ *adj, sometimes* -ER/-EST [NL *adeptus* knowing how to change base metals into gold] **1 :** highly skilled **:** well trained **:** thoroughly proficient — usu. used with *at* or *in* ⟨~ at good newswriting⟩ ⟨~ in handicrafts⟩ **2 :** indicative of great skill or proficiency **:** marked by cleverness or aptitude ⟨an ~ save by the goalie⟩ ⟨an ~ transition from comedy to tragedy⟩ **syn** see PROFICIENT

adept·ly \əˈdeptlē, -li *also* (ˈ)aˈd-, *rap.* -pl-\ *adv* **:** in an adept manner

adept·ness \-p(t)nəs\ *n* -ES **:** the quality or state of being adept ⟨showed great ~ at fencing⟩

ad·e·qua·cy \ˈadəkwəsē, -si\ *n* -ES [*adequate* + *-cy*] **:** the quality or state of being adequate **:** sufficiency for a purpose ⟨I do not believe in the ~ of the usual sentimental interpretation of the Golden Rule —M.R.Cohen⟩

¹adequate *vt* -ED/-ING/-S [L *adaequatus*] **1** *obs* **:** EQUAL **2** *obs* **:** to make equal or sufficient **:** EQUALIZE

²ad·e·quate \ˈadəkwət, -ēk-, *usu* -əd·+V\ *adj* [L *adaequatus*, past part. of *adaequare* to make equal, fr. *ad-* + *aequare* to equal — more at EQUATE] **1** *obs* **:** equal in size or scope **2 :** equal to, proportionate to, or fully sufficient for a specified or implied requirement; *often* **:** narrowly or barely sufficient **:** no more than satisfactory — often used with *to* and sometimes with *for* or *with* ⟨public issues are so large and so involved that . . . only a few . . . can hope to have any ~ comprehension of them —G.L.Dickinson⟩ ⟨with only six men covering two million acres, ~ fire prevention is impossible —*Amer. Guide Series: Minn.*⟩ ⟨a solution ~ to the problem⟩ **3 :** legally sufficient **:** such as is lawfully and reasonably sufficient ⟨~ grounds for a lawsuit⟩ **4** *logic* **:** fully representative ⟨an ~ definition⟩ **syn** see SUFFICIENT

adequate idea *n* **:** an idea that is commensurate to its object: as **a** *in Spinoza* **:** an idea having all the intrinsic marks of a true idea **b** *in Leibniz* **:** an idea clearly understood and analyzed into simple components

ad·e·quate·ly *adv* **:** in an adequate manner

ad·e·quate·ness *n* -ES **:** the quality or state of being adequate

adequate stimulus *n* **:** a stimulus that acts only on an esp. adapted end organ ⟨light is an *adequate stimulus* of the rods and cones of the retina⟩

ad·e·qua·tion \ˌ==ˈkwāshən\ *n* -s [LL *adaequation-, adaequatio*, fr. L *adaequatus* + *-ion-, -io* -ion] **1 :** the result of making equal or adequate **:** EQUIVALENCE **2 :** the act of making adequate **:** the act of making equal or commensurate

ad·e·qua·tive \ˈ==ˌkwād·iv\ *adj* **:** EQUIVALENT, ADEQUATE

ader·min \(ˈ)āˈdərmən\ *or* **ader·mine** \", -ˌmēn\ *n* -s [²*a-* + *derm-* + *-in*] **:** VITAMIN B_6

ader wax \ˈädə(r)-\ *n* [prob. part trans. of G *aderwachs*, fr. *ader* vein (fr. MHG *āder*, fr. OHG *ādara*) + *wachs* wax; akin to OE *ǣdre* vein, ON *æthr*, Gk *ētor* heart] **:** OZOKERITE

ad·es·se·nar·i·an \(ˌ)aˌdesᵊnaˈ(a)rēən\ *n* -s *usu cap* [L *adesse* to be present (fr. *ad-* + *esse* to be) + connective *-n-* + E *-arian* — more at IS] **:** one who believes in the real presence of Christ's body in the eucharist but not by transubstantiation

ad·es·sive \(ˈ)aˈdesiv\ *adj* [L *adesse* + E *-ive*] *of a grammatical case* **:** denoting presence at a place — used esp. in Finnish and Hungarian grammar

ad eun·dem *or* **ad eundem gra·dum** \ˌadēˈəndəm(ˈgrādəm), -nˌdem-, -räd-\ *adv (or adj)* [NL] **:** to, in, or of the same rank — used esp. of the honorary granting of an academic standing or degree by a university to one whose actual work for the standing or degree was done elsewhere

¹à deux \äˈdə(r), -dē, *F* àdœ\ *adj* [F] **:** of, for, or between two individuals esp. privately or intimately ⟨a sly whisper of pretty nothings all *à deux* —Sinclair Lewis⟩

²à deux \"\ *adv* [F] **:** with two together ⟨riding along *à deux*⟩; *esp* **:** privately or intimately with only two present ⟨dining *à deux*⟩

ADF *abbr* automatic direction finder

ad fi·lum aq·uae \ădˈfēləˈmäˌkwī\ [L] *law* **:** to the middle of the stream — often used in conveyancing in describing boundaries

ad fin *abbr* [L *ad finem*] at the end; near the end

ad·ha·mant \(ˈ)adˈhāmənt\ *adj* [L *adhamant-, adhamans*, pres. part. of *adhamare* to catch, secure, perh. fr. *ad-* + *hamus* hook] **:** clinging as if by hooks — used esp. of the feet of certain birds (as the swifts)

adhar·ma \əˈdərmə\ *n* -s *sometimes cap* [Skt, fr. *a-* ²*a-* + *dharma* virtue — more at DHARMA] **1** *Hinduism* **:** individual disharmony with the nature of things **:** nonconformity to one's worldly situation — opposed to *dharma* **2** *Jainism* **:** the uncreated and eternal substance that enables souls and matter to be inactive **:** the ontological principle of rest ⟨~ is compared to earth, on which creatures lie and stand —Heinrich Zimmer⟩ — compare DHARMA

ad·here \adˈhi(ə)r, əd-, -iə\ *vb* -ED/-ING/-S [MF or L; MF *adhérer*, fr. L *adhaerēre*, fr. *ad-* + *haerēre* to stick — more at HESITATE] *vi* **1 :** to hold, follow, or maintain loyalty steadily and consistently (as to a person, group, principle, or way) ⟨the agrarian party, to which he *adhered* to the end of his life —V.L.Parrington⟩ **2** *obs* **:** to be consistent or in accord ⟨nor time nor place did then ~ —Shak.⟩ **3 a :** to hold fast or stick by or as if by gluing, suction, grasping, or fusing ⟨paper *adhering* to the wall⟩ **b :** to become joined (as in pathological adhesion) ⟨the lung sometimes ~*s* to the pleura⟩ **4 :** to agree to join : bind oneself to observance (as of a treaty) ⟨other tribes *adhered* to the pact —P.M.Angle⟩ **5** *Scots law* : to cohabit as husband or wife **6** *bot* : to display adhesion ~ *vt* : to cause to stick fast ⟨paper that had been *adhered* to a surface with glue⟩

syn STICK, CLING, CLEAVE, COHERE: ADHERE is a general term somewhat more bookish in suggestion than STICK to indicate any holding to, esp. steadily and over a period of time ⟨the glue *adhering* to the frame⟩ ⟨dried blood still *adhering* to the cloth⟩ ⟨to revise our ideas and not to *adhere* to what passes for respectable opinion —J.H.Robinson⟩ STICK, more familiar and forceful, may more strongly indicate close tenacious holding to, as though fixed in, embedded, glued ⟨the barb *stuck* in the flesh⟩ ⟨the molasses *stuck* to his fingers⟩ ⟨both sides *sticking* obstinately to their old positions —*New Statesman & Nation*⟩ CLING suggests a hanging on or holding to tenaciously as though in danger or fear of losing one's grip ⟨tall spruce, their roots *clinging* tenaciously to the few inches of soil, crown the summit —*Amer. Guide Series: Maine*⟩ ⟨throwing men and women into the sea with a ship to *cling* to and a chance of reaching another country —G.B.Shaw⟩ ⟨hopes which Huxley cherished and to which many still *cling* —J.W.Krutch⟩ CLEAVE, a rather literary word, implies a close sticking or holding of or as if of flat layers glued or plastered together, a very close, lasting, and indissoluble attachment ⟨the soaked shirt *cleaving* to his shoulders⟩ ⟨to love one maiden only, *cleave* to her, and worship her by years of noble deeds —Alfred Tennyson⟩ COHERE may indicate either a physical sticking together in a mass or an abstract common principle or general consistency that facilitates joining or uniting; it applies to the holding together of like things, of parts of a whole ⟨the mortar will *cohere* to the bricks⟩ ⟨the parts of the exposition do not *cohere*⟩

ad·her·ence \-irən(t)s *also* -er- *or* -ēr-\ *n* -s [F or ML; F *adhérence*, fr. ML *adhaerentia*, fr. L *adhaerent-*, *adhaerens* (pres. part. of *adhaerēre*) + *-ia*] : the act, action, or quality of adhering: as **a** : ADHESION ⟨~ of paint to wood⟩ **b** : steady or faithful attachment (as to a party, principle, or cause) : continued observance : FIDELITY ⟨fierce ~ to what seemed true —*Times Lit. Supp.*⟩

ad·her·en·cy \-irənsē\ *n* -ES [ML *adhaerentia*] **1** *archaic* : the act of adhering or the quality of being adherent : ADHERENCE **2** *obs* : a person or thing that adheres

ad·her·end \-ˈhi,rend, ,ad,hiˈr-\ *n* -s [*adhere* + *-end* (as in *addend*)]: the surface to which an adhesive adheres; *also* : one of the bodies held to another by an adhesive

¹ad·her·ent \-ˈhirənt, -er- *also* -ēr-\ *adj* [ME, fr. MF or L; MF *adhérent*, fr. L *adhaerent-*, *adhaerens*, pres. part.] **1** : having the quality of adhering : tending to adhere ⟨an ~ coating of frost⟩ **2** : connected with or related to; *specif* : formally or contractually bound to or associated with ⟨nations ~ to the world organization⟩ **3** *bot* : having usu. separate parts united : ADNATE **4** : modifying a noun and standing before it ⟨*busy* in "a busy street", *tomato* in "tomato soup", *down* in "the down train", *pay-as-you-go* in "a pay-as-you-go plan" are ~⟩ — compare ¹APPOSITIVE 2, ¹ATTRIBUTIVE 1a, ³PREDICATE — **ad·her·ent·ly** *adv*

²adherent \"\ *n* -s [ME, fr. MF *adhérent*, adj., or L *adhaerent-*, *adhaerens*, pres. part.] **1** : one that adheres: as **a** : a follower of a leader, party, or profession ⟨the ~*s* of Charles the First —T.B.Macaulay⟩ ⟨~*s* to the Communist party —J.B.Conant⟩ **b** : a believer in or advocate of a particular thing, idea, or church ⟨~*s* of the respective faiths —B.K.Sandwell⟩ ⟨~*s* to a hostile foreign power —Vannevar Bush⟩ **2** : a person 14 years of age or older who has made the Salvation Army his place of worship and is listed on Army records but has not become a soldier because of reservations or inability to comply with requirements

ad·he·sion \adˈhēzhən, əd-\ *n* -s [F or L; F *adhésion*, fr. L *adhaesion-*, *adhaesio*, fr. *adhaesus* (past part. of *adhaerēre*) + *-ion-*, *-io* -ion] **1** : steady or firm attachment (as to a person, party, principle, or idea) : ADHERENCE ⟨unshakable ~ to one . . . individual —D.W.Brogan⟩ ⟨~ . . . to the federal party —H.E.Scudder⟩ **2** : the action or state of adhering; *specif* : a sticking together of substances (as of glue and wood or of parts united by growth) **3 a** : the abnormal union of surfaces normally separate by the formation of new fibrous tissue resulting from an inflammatory process; *also* : the newly formed uniting tissue ⟨pleural ~*s*⟩ **b** : the union of wound edges esp. by first intention **4** : something that adheres ⟨freeing the concept of executive functions from certain ~*s* sometimes confused with them —Harold Koontz & Cyril O'Donnell⟩ **5** : the act of joining, taking part in, or subscribing to ⟨~ of all countries to a copyright convention⟩ : agreement to join : CONCURRENCE ⟨the country announced its ~ to the pact⟩ **6** : the union of separate plant parts or organs — used chiefly of union between parts of different floral whorls (as between sepals and carpels); compare COHESION **7 a** : a grip or sticking effect produced by friction or the friction itself (as of a smooth locomotive wheel pulling on a smooth rail) **b** : the force that must be developed to overcome this grip before slip occurs **8** : the molecular attraction exerted between the surfaces of bodies in contact —distinguished from *cohesion* **9** : the association of apparently unrelated elements in a culture complex

ad·he·sion·al \-nᵊl\ *adj* : having or showing adhesion

¹ad·he·sive \adˈhēsiv, əd-, -ēz-, -ēv\ *adj* [*adhesion* + *-ive*] **1** : tending to keep close to or in association with ⟨the ~ character of calumny —J.A.Froude⟩ : tending to persist (as in the memory) ⟨an ~ witticism⟩ **2 a** : tending to adhere : STICKY, GLUEY ⟨~ mud⟩ : having the ability to stick things together ⟨powerfully ~ glue⟩ **b** : prepared for adhering (as by having a surface coated with a sticky substance) ⟨~ tape⟩ — **ad·he·sive·ly** *adv*

²adhesive \"\ *n* -s **1 a** : an adhesive substance; *esp* : a substance that bonds two materials together by adhering to the surface of each (as glue, starch paste, mucilage, rubber latex, or a synthetic resin composition) : CEMENT 2 **b** : ADHESIVE TAPE **2 a** : a postage stamp having a gummed back for sticking it onto postal matter as distinguished from one printed directly on a cover **b** : any stamp or seal having a gummed back

adhesive cell *n* : a glandular thread-bearing cell found only in ctenophores and used in capturing prey by adhesion — called also *colloblast, glue cell, lasso cell*

adhesively *adv* : in an adhesive manner : with adhesion

ad·he·sive·me·ter \-,mēd·ə(r)\ *n* -s : an instrument for testing the adhesive qualities of liquids

ad·he·sive·ness \-nəs\ *n* -ES **1** : the quality or state of being adhesive **2** *phrenology* : the propensity to form and maintain attachments to persons

adhesive organ *n* : a transient larval organ situated near the mouth in certain ganoids, African teleosts, and dipnoans and serving for attachment to the sea bottom — called also *cement organ*

adhesive plaster *n* : ADHESIVE TAPE; *sometimes* : a similar material made up in flat sheets

adhesive tape *n* : tape made usu. of woven cotton of various widths coated on one side with an adhesive mixture and used for many purposes in industry, manufacturing, and esp. in surgery to cover and hold dressings, hold wound edges together, or immobilize a limb or joint

ad·hib·it \adˈhibət\ *vt* -ED/-ING/-s [L *adhibitus*, past part. of *adhibēre* to bring to, summon, admit to consultation, apply, fr. *ad-* + *-hibēre* (fr. *habēre* to hold) — more at HABIT] **1** : to let in (as a person or thing) : bring in **2** : AFFIX ⟨~ a label⟩ **3** *archaic* : USE, ADMINISTER ⟨~ medicine⟩ — **ad·hi·bi·tion** \,adəˈbishən, ,adhə-\ *n* -s

¹ad hoc \(ˈ)adˈhäk, -ōk *also* (ˈ)äd-\ *adv* [NL, lit., for this] : for the particular end or purpose at hand and without reference to wider application or employment ⟨a special member appointed *ad hoc* according to the problem being considered⟩

²ad hoc \(ˈ)ˌ=ˌ=\ *adj* : made, established, acting, or concerned with a particular end or purpose ⟨a coordinated policy instead of *ad hoc* decisions⟩ ⟨an *ad hoc* commission of inquiry⟩

ad ho·mi·nem \(ˈ)adˈhämə,nem\ *adj* [NL, lit., to the man] **1** : directed at or appealing to one's hearer's or reader's personal feelings or prejudices rather than his intellect and reason ⟨an *ad hominem* argument⟩ **2** : marked by attack on an opponent's character rather than by answer to his contentions ⟨an *ad hominem* plea that his accuser had been in jail⟩

adhort *vt* -ED/-ING/-s [L *adhortari*, fr. *ad-* + *hortari* to incite — more at YEARN] *obs* : EXHORT

ad·i·a·bat \ˈadēə,bat\ *also* **ad·i·a·bat·ic** \,adēəˈbad·ik, ,ā,dīə-\ *n* -s [*adiabat*, back-formation fr. *adiabatic*, adj.; *adiabatic*, fr. *adiabatic*, adj.] : a curve or line plotted using coordinates selected to represent the pressure and volume or the temperature and entropy of matter during an adiabatic process

ad·i·a·bat·ic \ˌadēəˌbad·ik, ˌā,dīə-\ *adj* [ISV *adiabat-* (fr. Gk *adiabatos* impassable, fr. *a-* ²a- + *diabatos* passable, fr. *diabainein* to go across, fr. *dia-* + *bainein* to go) + *-ic*; orig. formed as G *adiabatisch* — more at COME] *of a process* : occurring without loss or gain of heat by the substance concerned ⟨~ expansion⟩ ⟨~ compression⟩ — opposed to *diabatic*; compare ISENTROPIC— **ad·i·a·bat·i·cal·ly** \-ək(ə)lē\ *adv*

adiabatic chart *n* : a meteorological chart with coordinates usu. given as pressure and temperature on which adiabats have been superposed to assist in evaluating adiabatic energy transformations in the atmosphere

adiabatic gradient *n* : the rate at which the temperature of an ascending or descending body of air is changed by adiabatic expansion or compression, being about 1.6° F. for each 300 feet of change of height; *also* : a curve representing this

adi·ac·tin·ic \ˌā,dī,akˈtinik, -ˈtək-\ *adj* [²*a-* + *diactinic*] : not transmitting actinic rays

adi·ag·nos·tic \ˌā,dīəgˈnästik\ *adj* [ISV ²*a-* + *diagnostic*; orig. formed as G *adiagnostisch*] : having the constituents not distinctly separated but blending together in polarized light under the microscope — used of a rock texture

ad·i·an·tum \,adēˈantəm\ *n, cap* [NL, fr. Gk *adianton* maidenhair, fr. neut. of *adiantos* unwetted, fr. *a-* ²a- + *diantos* capable of being wetted, fr. *diainein* to wet, moisten; prob. akin to Gk *deuein* to drench, steep] : a genus of plants comprising the maidenhair ferns (family Polypodiaceae) having dark and often polished stipes, much-divided fronds, and oblong sori borne on the upper margins of the pinnules, the margins of which are reflexed to form indusia

ad·i·a·phon \ˈadēə,fän\ *n* -s [G, fr. NL *adiaphonon*] : a keyboard instrument resembling the adiaphonon but having tuning forks instead of steel bars

ad·i·aph·o·non \,adēˈafə,nän\ *n* -s [NL, fr. Gk ²*a-* + Gk *diaphōnon*, neut. of *diaphōnos* discordant — more at DIAPHONY] : a keyboard instrument resembling the piano but having steel bars instead of strings

adiaphora *pl of* ADIAPHORON

ad·i·aph·o·rism \,adēˈafə,rizəm\ *n* -s [*adiaphoron* + *-ism*] : indifference concerning religious or theological matters (as points of controversy)

ad·i·aph·o·rist \-,rəst\ *n* -s : one who adheres to adiaphorism — **ad·i·aph·o·ris·tic** \ˌ=ˌ=ˌ=ˈristik\ *adj*

ad·i·aph·o·ron \,adēˈafə,rän, -,rən\ *n, pl* **adiapho·ra** \-rə\ [Gk, fr. neut. of *adiaphoros* indifferent, fr. *a-* ²a- + *diaphora* difference, fr. *diapherein* to carry across, bear to the end, make a difference, fr. *dia-* + *pherein* to bear — more at BEAR] **1** *Stoic philos* : a matter having no moral merit or demerit **2** : a religious ceremonial or ritual observance that is held to be an affair of the individual conscience because it is neither forbidden nor enjoined by the scriptures

ad·i·aph·o·rous \,adēˈaf(ə)rəs\ *adj* [Gk *adiaphoros*] *obs* : INDIFFERENT, NEUTRAL; *esp* : neither right or beneficial nor wrong or harmful

ad·i·ate \ˈadē,āt\ *vt* -ED/-ING/-s [prob. back-formation fr. *adiation*] *Roman Dutch law* : to accept (an inheritance) as heir under a will, taking the liabilities and benefits of the estate

adi·a·ther·man·cy \ˌa,dīəˈthərmənsē\ *n* -ES [²*a-* + *diathermancy*] : imperviousness to infrared radiation

ad·i·a·tion \,adēˈāshən\ *n* -s [modif. of L *adition-*, *aditio* act of entering upon an inheritance — more at ADITIO] : the act of adiating

adi·ba·si \,adəˈbäsē\ *n* -s : a member of one of the aboriginal tribes of India

ad idem \aˈdīdəm\ *adv (or adj)* [L, to the same] *law* : in agreement or at a meeting of minds on a point : at one — used in ref. to the making of a contract ⟨the parties were not *ad idem* —H.L.Robinson⟩

ad·i·ence \ˈadēən(t)s\ *n* -s *psychol* : a tendency to approach or accept a stimulus object or situation — opposed to *abience*

ad·i·ent \-ənt\ *adj* [L *adient-*, *adiens*, pres. part. of *adire* to go to, fr. *ad-* + *ire* to go — more at ISSUE] : characterized by adience : having or showing adience — opposed to *abient*

¹adieu \əˈd(y)ü\ *interj* [ME, fr. MF, fr. *a* to (fr. L *ad*) + *Dieu* God, fr. L *Deus* — more at AT, DEITY] — used to express farewell

²adieu \"\ *n, pl* **adieus** *or* **adieux** \-üz\ [ME, fr. *adieu*, interj.] : a civil or affable expression made upon parting : FAREWELL, LEAVE-TAKING ⟨to make one's ~*s*⟩

adi·ghe \ˌädəˈgā\ *n, pl* **adighe** *or* **adighes** *usu cap* [prob. fr. Circassian] : CIRCASSIAN

ad ig·no·ran·ti·am \ˌa,dignəˈranshē,am\ *adv (or adj)* [L, to ignorance] : by use of unanswerable challenge to disprove rather than by serious attempt to prove ⟨an *ad ignorantiam* argument⟩

ad in·fi·ni·tum \ˌa,dinfəˈnīd·əm, ˌtəm *also* -nē\ *adv (or adj)* [L] : to infinity : without end or limit ⟨talked on and on *ad infinitum*⟩

adin·i·da \əˈdinədə\ *n pl, cap* [NL, fr. ²*a-* + Gk *dinos* act of whirling, whirlpool + NL *-ida*] : a group of primitive flagellate protozoans of the order Dinoflagellata having two flagella but lacking a transverse groove — **adin·i·dan** \-dən\ *adj or n*

ad·i·nole \ˈadᵊn,ōl\ *n* -s [F, fr. Gk *hadinos* close, thick + F *-ole*; akin to Gk *hadēn* enough — more at SAD] : a dense rock composed chiefly of quartz and albite being an alteration product produced by contact metamorphism

¹ad in·ter·im \(ˈ)adˈintərəm *also* -ntə,rim *or* -n·trəm\ *adv* [L] : for the intervening time : TEMPORARILY

²ad interim \(ˈ)ˌ=ˌ(=)ˌ=\ *adj* : made or serving temporarily or for the time being : effective or functioning pending permanent disposition : TEMPORARY ⟨*ad interim* committees for research⟩

ad interim copyright *n* : a temporary copyright valid for five years from the date of first publication abroad of a book or periodical in the English language

ad·ion \ˈa,dīən *also* -ī,än\ *n* -s [*adsorbed ion*] : an ion adsorbed on a surface

adi·os \,adēˈōs, ,ä-, ,ä-\ *interj* [Sp *adiós* (post. trans. of F *adieu*), fr. *a* to (fr. L *ad*) + *Dios* God, fr. L *Deus* — more at AT, DEITY] — used to express farewell

adip- *or* **adipo-** *comb form* [L *adip-*, *adeps*, fr. Gk *aleipha*; akin to Gk *lipos* fat, lard — more at LEAVE] **1** : fat : fatty tissue ⟨*adipic*⟩ ⟨*adipocele*⟩ **2** : connected with adipic acid ⟨*adipamide*⟩ ⟨*adiponitrile*⟩

ad·i·pa·mide \ˈadˈipə,mīd, -,məd\ *n* -s [*adip-* + *amide*] : the crystalline diamide $H_2NCO(CH_2)_4CONH_2$ of adipic acid that is best known in the form of its polymerized hexamethylene derivative — compare NYLON

ad·i·pate \ˈadə,pāt\ *n* -s [ISV *adip-* + *-ate*] : a salt or ester of adipic acid

adipes *pl of* ADEPS

adipes lanae *pl of* ADEPS LANAE

adip·ic acid \əˈdipik-\ *n* [ISV *adip-* + *-ic*] : a white crystalline dicarboxylic acid $HOOC(CH_2)_4COOH$ formed by oxidation of various fats and made usu. by oxidation of cyclohexanol or by hydrolysis of adiponitrile for use esp. in the manufacture of nylon

ad·i·po·cel·lu·lose \ˌadə(,)pōˈselyə,lōs\ *n* -s [*adip-* + *cellulose*] : cellulose associated with suberin in the cell walls of cork tissue

ad·i·po·cere \ˈadəpə,si(ə)r\ *n* -s [modif. of F *adipocire*, fr. *adip-* + *cire* wax, fr. L *cera* — more at CERATED] : a waxy or unctuous brownish substance consisting chiefly of fatty acids and calcium soaps produced by chemical changes affecting dead animal fat and muscle long buried or immersed in moisture — **ad·i·poc·er·ous** \ˌadəˈpäs(ə)rəs, ˌadəpəˈsirəs\ *adj*

ad·i·po·cyte \ˈadəpə,sīt\ *n* -s [*adip-* + *-cyte*] : TROPHOCYTE

ad·i·po·gen·e·sis \ˌadəpōˈjenəsəs\ *n, pl* **adipo·gen·e·ses** \-ə,sēz\ [NL, fr. *adip-* + *genesis*] : the formation of fat or fatty tissue (as in the insect fat body)

ad·i·po·ge·net·ic \ˌadə(,)pōjəˈned·ik\ *or* **ad·i·pog·e·nous** \-ˈpäjənəs\ *adj* [*adip-* + *-genetic* or *-genous*] : fat-producing

ad·i·po·leu·co·cyte \ˌadə(,)pōˈlükə,sīt\ *n* -s [*adip-* + *leucocyte*] : a blood cell typical of certain insects, having the cytoplasm packed with oil globules

ad·i·po·ni·trile \ˌadə(,)pōˈnīˈtrəl; -,trēl, -īl\ *n* -s [*adip-* + *nitrile*] : the high-boiling liquid dinitrile $NC(CH_2)_4CN$ of adipic acid made from 1,4-dichlorobutane and sodium cyanide and used to make the nylon intermediate hexamethylenediamine and adipic acid — called also *tetramethylene cyanide*

¹ad·i·pose \ˈadə,pōs\ *adj* [NL *adiposus*, fr. *adip-* + *-osus* -ose] : of or relating to animal fat : FATTY

²adipose \"\ *n* -s : the fat in the cells of adipose tissue

adipose body *n* : FAT BODY

adipose fin *n* : a soft fleshy rayless modification of the posterior dorsal fin found in certain fishes (as salmons, characins, and typical catfishes)

adipose tissue *n* : animal tissue in which fat is stored, consisting of connective tissue with the cells distended by droplets of fat and constituting the fat of meat

ad·i·po·sis \,adəˈpōsəs\ *n, pl* **adipo·ses** \-ō,sēz\ [NL, fr. *adip-* + *-osis*] **1** : ADIPOSITY, OBESITY **2** : the condition of fatty infiltration or degeneration of single organs (as the heart or liver)

adiposis do·lo·ro·sa \-,dōləˈrōsə\ *n* [NL, lit., painful adiposis] : a condition of generalized obesity characterized by pain in the abnormal deposits of fat

ad·i·pos·i·ty \,adəˈpäsəd·ē\ *n* -ES : the quality or state of being fat : OBESITY

ad·i·po·so·gen·i·tal dystrophy \,adəˌpōsōˌjenəd·ᵊl-\ *n* [*adipose* + *-o-* + *genital*] : a combination of obesity, retarded development of the sex glands, and changes in secondary sex characteristics that results from impaired function or disease of the pituitary gland and hypothalamus — called also *Fröhlich's syndrome*

adipo·yl \əˈdipə,wil, aˈ-\ *or* **ad·i·pyl** \ˈadəpəl\ *n* -s [*adip-* + *-yl*] : the bivalent radical $-OC(CH_2)_4CO-$ of adipic acid

ad·i·ron·dack \,adəˈrän,dak\ *n, pl* **adirondack** *or* **adirondacks** *usu cap* [Mohawk *Hatiróntaks*, lit., they eat trees] **1** : the Algonkian people formerly north of the St. Lawrence river **2** : a member of the Adirondack people

adirondack blackfly *n, usu cap A* : a common blackfly (*Prosimulium hirtipes*) widespread in eastern No. America

adirondack chair *n, often cap A* [prob. so called fr. its popular use in the Adirondack resort area] : a wooden slant-back lawn chair the seat of which usu. is higher at the front than at the back

Adirondack chair

ad·it \ˈadət\ *n* -s [L *aditus* approach, entrance, fr. *aditus*, past part. of *adire* to go to, approach, fr. *ad-* + *ire* to go — more at ISSUE] **1** : a nearly horizontal opening by which a mine is entered, drained, or ventilated — called also *tunnel*; compare DRIFT 6, GALLERY, INCLINE, LEVEL, SHAFT **2** : the act of coming to : APPROACH, ADMISSION, ACCESS ⟨gain ~ to the throne⟩

adi·tio \əˈdishē,ō\ *n* -s [LL, fr. L, approach, fr. *aditus* (past part.) + *-io* -ion] *Roman law* : the informal acceptance by an outsider of heirship; *broadly* : the vesting of the inheritance in an heir to a testate or intestate estate or the entering into the inheritance

ad·i·tus \ˈadəd·əs\ *n, pl* **aditus** *or* **adituses** [L] : a passage or opening for entrance

adive \əˈdēv\ *n* -s [F] : CORSAC

adj *abbr* **1** adjacent **2** adjective **3** adjourned **4** adjudged **5** adjunct **6** adjustable; adjusted; adjustment **7** *often cap* adjutant

ad·jab \ˈa,jab\ *n* -s [prob. native name in Africa] : NJAVE

ad·ja·cence \əˈjāsᵊn(t)s\ *n* -s [LL *adjacentia*] : ADJACENCY 2

ad·ja·cen·cy \-ᵊnsē, -si\ *n* -ES [ML *adjacentia*, fr. LL, state of being adjacent, fr. L *adjacent-*, *adjacens* + *-ia* -y] **1 a** : whatever is adjacent in space **b** : nearby or neighboring places — usu. pl. **2** [LL] : the quality or state of being adjacent : CONTIGUITY **3** : a radio or television program or announcement immediately following or preceding another ⟨his 9:30 program was helped by a popular ~ at 9:45⟩

adjacency effect *n* : a change in size, density, or other property of a photographic image sometimes observed when small adjacent images are close enough to influence each other and when such a change is not to be expected from the normal sensitometric properties of the material — compare BORDER EFFECT, EBERHARD EFFECT, MACKIE LINE

ad·ja·cent \-ᵊnt\ *adj* [ME, fr. MF or L; fr. L *adjacent-*, *adjacens*, pres. part. of *adjacēre* to lie near, border on, fr. *ad-* + *jacēre* to lie, fr. *jacere* to throw — more at JET (to spout)] **1 a** : not distant or far off ⟨the city square and the ~ streets⟩ : nearby but not touching ⟨the islands and the ~ mainland coast⟩ **b** : relatively near and having nothing of the same kind intervening : having a common border : ABUTTING, TOUCHING : living nearby or sitting or standing relatively near or close together ⟨hills . . . composed of oyster shells . . . the ~ inhabitants burn them —Mark van Doren⟩ **c** : immediately preceding or following with nothing of the same kind intervening **2** *of two angles* : having the same vertex and one side in common

syn ADJOINING, ABUTTING, CONTIGUOUS, CONTERMINOUS, COTERMINOUS, JUXTAPOSED: ADJACENT is sometimes merely a synonym for *near* or for *close to* ⟨the heavy lands *adjacent* to Paris —Charles Dickens⟩ ⟨Indian Pass, Mount Marcy, and the *adjacent* mountains —John Burroughs⟩ ⟨the safety of the western hemisphere and of the seas *adjacent* thereto —F.D. Roosevelt⟩ Applied to things of the same type, it indicates either side-by-side proximity or lack of anything of the same nature intervening ⟨the doors of the *adjacent* apartment were opened, and Egmont saw himself surrounded —J.L.Motley⟩ ADJOINING is quite similar to ADJACENT in meaning and suggestion but may more strongly indicate existence of common bounding lines or lines or points of junction ⟨in upstate New York and the *adjoining* counties of Pennsylvania —Hans Kurath⟩ ⟨the grayish white stone building and the *adjoining* graveyard —*Amer. Guide Series: Pa.*⟩ ABUTTING most strongly predicates actual contact at a bounding or dividing line ⟨*abutting* lots⟩ ⟨the state of Utah and the *abutting* state of Idaho —W.L.Sperry⟩ ⟨the north wall, to which *abutting* rooms were added —Christopher Hussey⟩ CONTIGUOUS shows variable usage but is likely to suggest touching along a dividing line; it may indicate an unbroken continuity ⟨Marsh and McDunn were each alone in *contiguous* labs, and McDunn attests that Marsh was still at the telephone when he entered his lab —Edith C. Rivett⟩ ⟨Tompkinsville and Stapleton are *contiguous* localities, virtually indistinguishable from each other —*Amer. Guide Series: N. Y. City*⟩ ⟨adjacent events need not be *contiguous*; just as there may be stretches of a string which are not occupied by beads, so the child may experience uneventful periods of time —James Jeans⟩ CONTERMINOUS may apply to a boundary strip in common; often it and COTERMINOUS indicate that all boundaries for two areas are the same and consequently that the two are practically identical ⟨*conterminous* with Philadelphia county, the Quaker City lies along the west bank of the Delaware river —*Amer. Guide Series: Pa.*⟩ ⟨the city and county of Philadelphia are *coterminous* —*American Yr. Bk.*⟩ ⟨the mythology of early man was not *conterminous* with the religion of early man —F.B.Gummere⟩ ⟨the history of Zionism, in fact, is *coterminous* with the history of Jewry —H.E.Wedeck⟩ JUXTAPOSED indicates placement face to face and may suggest likelihood of contrast or opposition ⟨opulence wildly *juxtaposed* to unbelievable poverty —Virginia A. Oakes⟩ ⟨disputes about water rights were almost inevitable between closely *juxtaposed* communities with expanding populations —V.G.Childe⟩

ad·ja·cent·ly *adv* : so as to be adjacent

ad·jag \ˈa,jag\ *n* -s [prob. native name in Java] : a wild dog (*Cuon javanicus*) found in Java

ad·ject \əˈjekt, aˈ-\ *vt* -ED/-ING/-s [ME *adjecten*, fr. L *adjectus*, past part. of *adicere* to throw to, add to, fr. *ad-* + *-icere* (fr. *jacere* to throw) — more at JET (to spout)] *archaic* : to add or annex : JOIN — **ad·jec·tion** \-kshən\ *n* -s *archaic*

ad·jec·ti·val \ˌajəkˈtīvəl, -ek-\ *adj* [²*adjective* + *-al*] **1** : of or belonging to an adjective : functioning as an adjective : ADJECTIVE ⟨~ phrase⟩ **2** : given to using adjectives ⟨an ~ poet⟩ : characterized by the use of numerous adjectives ⟨an ~ style⟩ ⟨~ language⟩ — **ad·jec·ti·val·ly** \-əlē, -li\ *adv*

¹ad·jec·tive \ˈajəktiv, -ēk-, *rapid sometimes* ˈajəd·iv\ *adj* [ME, fr. MF or LL; MF *adjectif*, fr. LL *adjectivus*, fr. L *adjectus* + *-ivus* -ive] **1 :** being an adjective ⟨an ~ word⟩ **:** functioning as an adjective ⟨an ~ clause⟩ **:** fitting or suitable to an adjective ⟨~ uses of nouns⟩ ⟨~ inflections⟩ **2 a :** not standing by itself **:** DEPENDENT, DERIVATIVE **b :** QUALIFYING, LIMITING **:** ACCIDENTAL — contrasted with *essential* and *substantive* **3 :** relating to dyes that require a mordant or to the processes in which they are employed ⟨~ colors or dyes⟩ ⟨~ dyeing⟩ — opposed to *substantive* — **ad·jec·tive·ly** *adv*

²adjective \"\ *n* -s [ME, fr. MF or LL; MF *adjectif*, fr. LL *adjectivum*, fr. neut. of *adjectivus*] **1 :** a word belonging to one of the major form classes in any of a great many languages, typically used as a modifier of a noun to denote a quality of the thing named (as *brave* in "a brave man" or "the man is brave", *new* in "the new dress" or "the dress is new"), to indicate its quantity or extent (as *five* in "five cows", *every* in "every word"), or to specify or designate a thing as distinct from something else (as *these* in "these wheels") and in many languages declined for gender, number, and case and agreeing in all these respects with the noun it modifies but in English having no such inflections (except for *this*, plural *these*, and *that*, plural *those*) **2 :** something that has only dependent or qualifying status or existence ⟨a perceptual object is a true Aristotelian ~ of some event which is its situation —A.N. Whitehead⟩ **:** something that cannot stand alone **:** DEPENDENT

³adjective \"\ *vt* -ED/-ING/-S **1 :** to make an adjective of **:** furnish with an adjective or adjectives **2 :** to express or describe using many adjectives ⟨slick, glowingly *adjectived* phrases —Andy Logan⟩

adjective equivalent *n* **:** a word or word group that is not an adjective but has the noun-modifying function of an adjective (as *music* in "music teacher", *dancing* in "dancing teacher", *John's* in "John's dog", *on the wall* in "the picture on the wall", *the doctor* in "my friend the doctor", *who plays golf* in "a man who plays golf")

adjective law *n* **:** the portion of the law that deals with the rules of procedure governing evidence, pleading, and practice

ad·jec·tiv·ize \-tə,vīz\ *vt* -ED/-ING/-S [²*adjective* + *-ize*] **:** to make an adjective of **:** form an adjectival derivative from

ad·join \əˈjȯin *also* aˈ-\ *vb* -ED/-ING/-S [ME *ajoinen*, *adjoinen*, fr. MF *ajoindre*, fr. L *adjungere*, fr. *ad-* + *jungere* to join — more at YOKE] *vt* **1 a :** to join or attach physically ⟨it is forbidden to ~ to a postcard any sample of merchandise —*Bahamas Official Gazette*⟩ **b :** to add, attach, or append esp. as a supplement ⟨he ~s the remark that God was . . . reconciling the world to himself —P.L.Holmer⟩ **2 :** to lie next to **:** be in contact with **:** abut upon ⟨his land ~s the sea —F.D.Smith & Barbara Wilcox⟩ **3 :** to add to a domain of numbers (a number not orig. belonging to it) thereby deriving a larger domain ⟨$x^2 - 2$ can be factored by ~*ing* $\sqrt{2}$ to the domain of rational numbers⟩ ~ *vi* **:** to be close, next to, or in contact with one another ⟨the two lots ~⟩

adjoining *adj* [ME *ajoining*, *adjoining*, fr. pres. part. of *ajoinen*, *adjoinen*] **:** touching or bounding at some point or on some line **:** near in space ⟨islands . . . formed by owners living on the ~ shores —*Amer. Guide Series: N. H.*⟩ **syn** see ADJACENT

ad·journ \əˈjərn, -ən, -əin\ *vb* -ED/-ING/-S [alter. (influenced by such words as *adjoin*, *adjure*) of ME *ajornen*, *ajournen*, fr. MF *ajorner*, *ajourner*, fr. *a-* (fr. L *ad-*) + *jour* day, fr. LL *diurnum*, fr. L, neut. of *diurnus* daily — more at DIURNAL] *vt* **1 :** to suspend continuance of or action or decision on **:** put off **:** DEFER ⟨the simple plea that partisanship and selfishness be ~*ed* —F.D.Roosevelt⟩ **2 :** to put off further proceedings of either indefinitely or until a later stated time **:** disband with or without an understanding about a future meeting **:** close formally ⟨~*ing* the session⟩ ~ *vi* **1 :** to suspend a session or meeting till another time or indefinitely **:** suspend formal business or procedure and disband ⟨the group ~*ed* at 10 o'clock⟩ ⟨the congress will ~ next month⟩ **2 :** to move to another place ⟨we ~*ed* to the library beside the fire —A.N. Whitehead⟩

ad·journ·al \-nᵊl\ *n* -S **:** ADJOURNMENT, POSTPONEMENT

adjourned summons *n*, *English law* **:** an originating summons that has been adjourned from chambers for a hearing in court

ad·journ·ment \-nmənt\ *n* -S [F *ajournement*, fr. *ajourner* + *-ment*] **1 :** the act of adjourning or state of being adjourned ⟨a motion for ~ of the meeting⟩ **2 :** the interval for which a body adjourns ⟨after the summer ~⟩

adjt *abbr*, *often cap* adjutant

ad·judge \əˈjəj *also* aˈ-\ *vt* -ED/-ING/-S [alter. (influenced by such words as *adjoin*, *adjure*) of ME *ajugen*, fr. MF *ajugier*, *ajuger*, fr. L *adjudicare*, fr. *ad-* + *judicare* to judge — more at JUDGE] **1 a :** to decide or rule upon as a judge or with judicial or quasi-judicial powers **:** ADJUDICATE ⟨~ a lawsuit⟩ ⟨~ a labor controversy⟩ **b :** to pronounce judicially **:** FIND, RULE ⟨he was *adjudged* insane⟩ ⟨*adjudging* that the defendant owns the land⟩ **2** *archaic* **:** to sentence or condemn (a person) to some punishment ⟨*adjudged* to death —John Milton⟩ ⟨*adjudged* to die⟩ **3 :** to regard, hold, or pronounce to be **:** JUDGE, DEEM ⟨studies . . . *adjudged* standard works in their field —A.D.H.Smith⟩ — opposed to *abjudge* **4 :** to award or grant judicially in a case of controversy ⟨the difficulty of *adjudging* the prize⟩ **5** *Scots law* **:** to award to a creditor by adjudication

ad·ju·di·ca·taire \əˌjüdəkəˈta(a)(ə)r\ *n* -S [F, fr. L *adjudicatus* + F *-aire* -ary] *Canadian law* **:** a purchaser at a judicial sale

ad·ju·di·cate \əˈjüdəˌkāt, -ē,k-, *usu* -ād-+V\ *vb* -ED/-ING/-S [L *adjudicatus*, past part. of *adjudicare* — more at ADJUDGE] *vt* **1 a :** to settle finally (the rights and duties of the parties to a court case) on the merits of issues raised **:** enter on the records of a court (a final judgment, order, or decree of sentence) **b :** to decide (as an interlocutory matter) arising prior to a final decision **c :** to make (a decision) final or interlocutory in the course of quasi-judicial proceedings — compare ADJUDGE **2 :** to pass judgment on **:** settle judicially **:** JUDGE ⟨*adjudicating* a dispute⟩ ~ *vi* **:** to come to a judicial decision **:** act as judge ⟨the court *adjudicated* upon the case⟩

ad·ju·di·ca·tio \əˌjüdəˈkādēˌō\ *n* -S [LL] **1 :** the part appearing at the end of the formula or written order of reference in an action in Roman law for partition of property held by common or joint owners that empowered the judge to adjudge the ownership of the property and to make the actual partition **2** *Roman & civil law* **:** a court decree awarding or establishing ownership; *also* **:** acquisition by operation of law

ad·ju·di·ca·tion \əˌjüdəˈkāshən, -ēˈk-\ *n* -S [F or LL; F *adjudication*, fr. LL *adjudication-*, *adjudicatio*, fr. L *adjudicatus* + *-ion-*, *-io* -ion] **1 :** the act or process of adjudicating ⟨the commission for the ~ of the interstate dispute —*Current Biog.*⟩ **2 :** a determination, decision, or sentence esp. without imputation of guilt (as a decree in bankruptcy or the disposition of a juvenile delinquent) **3** *Scots law* **:** an attachment of heritable estate (as for security or for a debt) **4** *Roman law* **:** the part of a formula that directed the judge to apportion shares in property — **ad·ju·di·ca·to·ry** \=ˈ==ˌkə,tōrē, -ȯr-, -ri\ *adj*

ad·ju·di·ca·tive \əˈjüdəˌkādiv, -,kā-\ *adj* **:** tending to adjudicate or concerned with adjudication

ad·ju·di·ca·tor \ˌkād-ə(r), -ātə-\ *n* -S **:** one that adjudicates

ad·ju·di·ca·ture \-ˌkə,chu̇(ə)r, -kəchər, -,kāchər\ *n* -S [*adjudicate* + *-ure*] **:** ADJUDICATION

¹ad·junct \ˈa,jəŋ(k)t\ *n* -S [L *adjunctum*, fr. neut. of *adjunctus*] **1 a :** something joined or added to another thing but not essentially a part of it ⟨meter and rhyme are not mere ~s of poetry —Samuel Alexander⟩ **:** an accompaniment or auxiliary to another thing ⟨road building . . . bridge building became necessary ~s of warfare —Lewis Mumford⟩ **b :** a valuable individual quality or attribute ⟨temperance is an ~ only of the wise⟩ **2** *logic* **:** an accidental or nonessential quality or characteristic (as the particular color of a body) **3 :** a word or word group that qualifies, amplifies, or completes the meaning of another word or other words and is not itself one of the principal structural elements in its sentence ⟨in the sentence "most children eat heartily", *most* is an ~ to the subject *children*, and *heartily* is an ~ to the predicate verb *eat*⟩ **4 :** a person associated with or assisting another in some duty or service **:** ASSOCIATE **5 :** ADJUVANT b

²adjunct \"\ *adj* [L *adjunctus*, past part. of *adjungere* to add, join — more at ADJOIN] **1 :** added or joined as an accompanying object or circumstance ⟨though that my death were ~ to my act, by heaven, I would do it —Shak.⟩ **2 :** added or accompanying in a subordinate capacity; *specif* **:** attached to a faculty or staff as a temporary member having for the time of his appointment the duties, privileges, and remuneration indicated by his rank ⟨~ psychiatrist⟩ ⟨~ associate professor⟩ — see ADJUNCT PROFESSOR — **ad·junct·ly** *adv*

adjunct accusative *n* **:** OBJECTIVE COMPLEMENT

ad·junc·tion \əˈjəŋ(k)shən *also* aˈ-\ *n* -S [L *adjunction-*, *adjunctio*, fr. *adjunctus* + *-ion-*, *-io* -ion] **1 :** a joining on or adding of a person or thing ⟨improve a sentence by ~ of a word⟩ **2 :** *Roman, civil, & Scots law* **:** a species of accession brought about by the activity or work of man as distinguished from that occurring in nature — compare INDUSTRIAL ACCESSION **3** *math* **:** the process of adjoining to a field a number not in it

ad·junc·tive \əˈjəŋ(k)tiv, (ˈ)aˈj-\ *adj* [LL *adjunctivus*, fr. L *adjunctus* + *-ivus* -ive] **1 :** having the quality of joining **:** forming an adjunct **2 :** involving the medical use of an adjunct ⟨~ therapy⟩

adjunct professor *n*, *in some colleges and universities* **:** a teacher ranking next below a professor

ad·ju·ra·tion \ˌajəˈrāshən\ *n* -S [F or L; F *adjuration*, fr. L *adjuration-*, *adjuratio*, fr. *adjuratus* (past part. of *adjurare*) + *-ion-*, *-io* -ion] **1 :** a solemn charging on oath or under penalty of a curse ⟨an ~ by the living God⟩ **2 :** an earnest or solemn urging or charging (as in command, advice, or appeal) ⟨his father's ~ to him to work harder⟩

ad·jur·a·to·ry \əˈju̇rə,tōrē, ˈajər-\ *adj* [LL *adjuratorius*, fr. L *adjuratus* + *-orius* -ory] **:** having the characteristics of an adjuration **:** containing a solemn charge or appeal **:** suited to adjuration ⟨~ terms⟩

ad·jure \əˈju̇(ə)r, -üə\ *vt* -ED/-ING/-S [ME *adjuren*, fr. MF & L; MF *ajurer*, fr. L *adjurare*, fr. *ad-* + *jurare* to swear — more at JURY] **1** *obs* **:** to put on oath **:** induce by the penalty of a curse **2 :** to charge or command solemnly as if under oath or penalty of a curse ⟨*adjuring* him by his belief in God to tell the truth⟩ **3 :** to entreat or advise earnestly **:** CHARGE ⟨these columns are *adjured* to have some bearing on literary matters —*Saturday Rev.*⟩ **syn** see BEG

ad·jur·er *also* **ad·ju·ror** \əˈju̇rə(r)\ *n* -S [ME *adjurer*, fr. *adjuren* to adjure + *-er*] **:** one that adjures

ad·just \əˈjəst\ *vb* -ED/-ING/-S [F *ajuster* (formerly also *adjuster*), fr. *a-* (fr. L *ad-*) + *juste* right, exact — more at JUST] *vt* **1 a** (1) **:** to bring to a more satisfactory state ⟨will not ~ their immigration policies for the empire —D.W.Brogan⟩ **:** SETTLE, RESOLVE ⟨orderly ways of ~*ing* conflicts⟩ **:** RECTIFY ⟨~*ing* the error⟩ (2) **:** to determine the amount to be paid under an insurance policy in settlement of (a loss) ⟨agents who ~ losses⟩ **b** (1) **:** to make correspondent or conformable **:** ADAPT ⟨~ the books to include these unrecorded data —R.B.Kester⟩ ⟨he ~*ed* his argument to meet the opposition⟩ (2) **:** to achieve an orientation of (oneself or itself) **:** ACCUSTOM ⟨writers ~*ing* themselves to the demands of the "new order" —*Times Lit. Supp.*⟩ ⟨plants ~ themselves to many influences —*Encyc. Americana*⟩ **:** satisfy mental and behavioral needs of (oneself) ⟨characters who . . . ~ themselves better . . . in the army —Robert Lowry⟩ **2 :** to put in order **:** reduce to a system **:** REGULATE ⟨~ one's daily schedule to leave time for everything⟩ **3 a** (1) **:** to bring to a true or effective relative position (as the parts of a device) ⟨~ a carburetor⟩ (2) **:** to rearrange the relationship of components of (a watch movement) after complete assembly for improving performance with respect to temperature, positional, or balance-arc variations — distinguished from *regulate* **b :** to change the position of (as for better fit or appearance) ⟨~*ing* his hat on his head⟩ ⟨~*ing* the pillows on the couch⟩ **4 a :** to change the range and direction of (as an artillery piece) so as to move the center of impact of fire onto the target **b :** to send to (the firing unit) the information necessary to make changes in range and direction ~ *vi* **1 :** to come into conformity **:** adapt itself ⟨these groups . . . ~ freely to the opportunities of American life —Oscar Handlin⟩ **:** resolve itself **:** become settled ⟨differences have ~*ed* easily —R.H.Jackson⟩ **2 :** to achieve a harmonious mental and behavioral balance between one's own personal needs and strivings and the demands of other individuals and of society **syn** see ADAPT

ad·just·a·ble \-əbəl\ *adj* **:** capable of being adjusted

adjustable-pitch \=ˈ===ˈ=\ *adj*, *of an airplane propeller* **:** having means of pitch adjustment of the blades while at rest but incapable of such adjustment while in motion

adjustable spanner *n*, *Brit* **:** MONKEY WRENCH

adjustable square *n* **:** a try square having a sliding connection between the two arms so that it may take the form of T as well as L — called also *double square*

adjustable wrench *n* **:** a wrench similar to an open end wrench but having one fixed jaw and one adjustable jaw

adjusted *adj* **1 a :** accommodated, altered, or revised to suit a particular set of circumstances or requirements **b :** having achieved a harmonious relationship with the environment or with other individuals (as by accommodation of physical characteristics or of personal desires) ⟨the ideally ~ plant form⟩ ⟨the well-*adjusted* school child⟩ **2** *of a river system or drainage pattern* **:** having the larger stream courses located for considerable distances in belts of relatively weak rocks

ad·just·er *also* **ad·jus·tor** \əˈjəstə(r)\ *n* -S **1 :** one that sets up or inspects and tunes machines, fits and assembles parts of furniture or electrical equipment, or inspects and adjusts completed products (as typewriters) **2 :** one that investigates claims for personal or property damage or complaints of unsatisfactory service, defective or damaged merchandise received, or improper billing and makes estimates for effecting settlement **3 :** any of various devices for adjusting the position of a part or object esp. with relationship to another part in a machine or apparatus (as one for attaching the rods of an oil-well pump to the walking beam and for adjusting the position of the rods) **4** *usu adjustor* **:** one of a set of muscles in some brachiopods that attach the peduncle to the shell and serve to raise the animal erect

ad·just·ive \əˈjəstiv\ *adj* **:** conducive or contributory to adjustment

ad·just·ment \əˈjəs(t)mənt\ *n* -S [F *ajustement* (formerly also *adjustement*), fr. *ajuster*, *adjuster* + *-ment*] **1 :** the act or process of adjusting: as **a :** the bringing into proper, exact, or conforming position or condition ⟨~ of a river to the underlying rock structure⟩ **b :** a harmonizing or settling ⟨the ~ of variant views —I.A.Richards⟩ ⟨the orderly ~ of disputes —F.A.Ogg & P.O.Ray⟩ **c** *ecol* **:** functional and often transitory alteration by which an organism is better adapted to its immediate environment — compare ADAPTATION 2b **2 :** a settlement of a claim or debt in a case in which the amount involved is uncertain or in which full payment is not made **3 :** the state of being adjusted: as **a :** a satisfactory or desirable solution or arrangement ⟨a series of emotional ~s —H.G. Armstrong⟩ ⟨the ~ of the boundary question —*Amer. Guide Series: Maine*⟩ **b :** a harmonized or balanced condition ⟨the nice ~ on either side of the scale —J.L.Lowes⟩ **4 :** a means (as a mechanism) by which things are adjusted one to another ⟨an ~ for focusing a microscope⟩ **5 a :** a correction or modification of an account to reflect the actual condition at the close of a given period by means of actual journal entries recording accruals, correction of errors, and depreciation **b :** an increase or decrease ⟨an ~ in his salary⟩; *sometimes* **:** a decrease in business activity **:** a mild depression **6** *psychol* **a :** the process by which one becomes adjusted **b :** the extent to which one is able to adjust — **ad·just·men·tal** \əˌjəs(t)ˈmentᵊl, ˌa,jə-\ *adj*

adjustment bond *n* **:** a bond issued in settlement of a prior obligation as part of a reorganization and on which interest payments are usu. contingent upon earnings

ad·ju·tage *or* **aj·u·tage** \ˈajəd-ij, əˈjüd-\ *n* -S [alter. (influenced by *ad-*) of earlier *ajutage*, lit., adjustment, fr. MF *ajustage*, fr. *ajuster* to adjust + *-age* — more at ADJUST] **:** a tube or nozzle attached to facilitate or regulate the discharge of water (as in a fountain) or other fluids

ad·ju·tan·cy \ˈajəd·ənsē, -ətən-, -si *also* -tᵊn-\ *n* -ES [¹*adjutant* + *-cy*] **:** the office or rank of an adjutant

¹ad·ju·tant \ˈajəd·ənt, -ətənt *also* -tᵊnt\ *n* -S [L *adjutant-*, *adjutans*, pres. part. of *adjutare* to help — more at AID] **1 :** a staff officer acting as a general assistant to the commanding officer **2 :** a staff officer in charge of and responsible for all official correspondence except combat orders, all returns and records of personnel, strength reports, and the preparation and distribution of orders **3 :** one that helps **:** ASSISTANT ⟨sensibility, refinement, good taste, breeding: all are . . . ~*s* —Raymond Williams⟩ **4 :** ADJUTANT BIRD

²adjutant \"\ *adj* [L *adjutant-*, *adjutans*] **:** giving help **:** ASSISTING ⟨the regular army was aided by ~ irregular troops⟩

adjutant bird *or* **adjutant stork** *also* **adjutant crane** *n* [prob. so called fr. its fancied resemblance to a military figure pacing a parade ground] **:** any of several large upright storks (genus *Leptoptilos*) having the head and neck bare of feathers and feeding on carrion or on small aquatic animals or snakes: as **a :** an Indian stork (*L. dubius*) that attains a height of seven feet **b :** a smaller Indian stork (*L. javanicus*)

adjutant general *n*, *pl* **adjutants general** **1 :** the chief administrative officer of the Army of the U. S. with the rank of major general who is head of the adjutant general's department and office and is responsible for the procedures affecting personnel procurement and for the administration and preservation of records of all army personnel **2 :** the chief administrative officer of a major military unit (as a division or corps)

adjutant's call *n* **:** a bugle call signaling a military unit to form for a ceremony

ad·ju·ta·tor \ˈajəˌtād·ə(r)\ *n* -S *usu cap* [by folk etymology (influence of *adjutant*)] **:** AGITATOR 1

ad·ju·van·cy \ˈajəvənsē\ *n* -ES **:** the action of assisting **:** HELP

¹ad·ju·vant \-vənt\ *adj* [F or L; F, fr. L *adjuvant-*, *adjuvans*, pres. part. of *adjuvare* to aid — more at AID] **1 :** serving to aid or contribute **:** AUXILIARY ⟨an ~ discipline to . . . forms of mysticism —Havelock Ellis⟩ **2 :** involving the use of or functioning as a medical adjuvant ⟨the ~ action of certain bacteria⟩

²adjuvant \"\ *n* -S [F *adjuvant*, adj., or L *adjuvant-*, *adjuvans*, pres. part.] **:** one that helps or facilitates: as **a :** an ingredient (as in a prescription or solution) that facilitates or modifies the action of the principal ingredient ⟨an ~ that dries paint⟩ ⟨the beneficial activity of the spray is enhanced by ~*s*⟩ **b :** a method, drug, or other means that enhances the effectiveness of medical treatment ⟨X rays and antibiotics are ~*s* to surgery⟩

ad·lay *also* **ad·lai** \ˈad,lī\ *n* -S [Bisayan] **:** any of several soft-shelled Job's tears (esp. *Coix lachryma-Jobi mayuen*) cultivated for food and for forage and fodder esp. in southeastern Asia, Japan, and the Philippines

adle *obs var of* ADDLE

ad·le·ri·an \(ˈ)adˈlirēən\ *adj*, *usu cap* [Alfred *Adler* †1937 Austrian psychologist & psychiatrist + E *-ian*] **:** having to do with a theory of character, conduct, and neurosis and with a technique of psychotherapy that emphasize the importance of feelings of inferiority, a will to power, and overcompensation as a denial of personal weakness or inadequacy

ad·less \ˈadləs, ˈaad-\ *adj* [¹*ad* + *-less*] **:** without an advertisement **:** lacking advertising material ⟨an ~ newspaper⟩

¹ad lib \(ˈ)adˈlib\ *adv* [modif. of NL *ad libitum*] **:** in accordance with one's wishes ⟨the skirt is . . . to be belted in *ad lib* —Lois Long⟩ **:** without restraint or imposed limit ⟨the animals were given water *ad lib* —*Science*⟩

²ad lib \(ˈ)=ˈ=\ *n*, *pl* **ad libs** [²*ad-lib*] **:** something ad-libbed ⟨the entire program was an *ad lib*⟩

¹ad–lib \(ˈ)=ˈ=\ *adj* **1 :** spoken or composed extempore ⟨free and easy *ad-lib* questioning —*N. Y. Times*⟩ **2 a :** available for free or spontaneous use or consumption ⟨dinner, with wine *ad-lib* —Bernard Smith⟩ **b :** made or done spontaneously **:** not controlled by a schedule ⟨*ad-lib* feeding of animals⟩

²ad–lib \(ˈ)=ˈ=\ *vb* **ad–libbed; ad–libbed; ad–libbing; ad–libs** *vt* **1 a :** to improvise as a part of something (as lines not in the script or music not in the score) **b :** to improvise all of (as a speech or a dance) **2 :** to devise (something) impromptu **:** employ offhand (as a makeshift) ⟨without spare parts the repairmen had to *ad-lib* material⟩ ~ *vi* **:** to improvise or deliver extempore esp. for filling in during a break in a program

ad–lib·ber \(ˈ)=ˈ=ə(r)\ *n* -S [²*ad-lib* + *-er*] **:** one that ad-libs

¹ad lib·i·tum \(ˈ)adˈlibəd·əm\ *adv* [NL, in accordance with one's wishes] **:** ad lib

²ad libitum \(ˈ)=ˈ===\ *adj* **:** variable according to a performer's pleasure **:** OMISSIBLE — abbr. *ad lib;* used esp. of music; distinguished from *obbligato*

ad li·tem \(ˈ)adˈlī,tem\ [L] *adv* (*or adj*) **:** for the suit or action ⟨guardian *ad litem*⟩

ad·lit·to·ral \(ˈ)ad;-\ *adj* [*ad-* + *littoral*] **:** of, relating to, occurring in or being the shallow water adjacent to a shore ⟨~ mollusks⟩

ad lo·cum \(ˈ)adˈlōkəm\ *adv* [L] **:** to or at the place

ad·lu·mia \adˈlümēə\ *n*, *cap* [NL, fr. John *Adlum* †1836 Am. pioneer in viticulture + NL *-ia*] **:** a genus of climbing herbs (family Fumariaceae) with a spongy persistent corolla

ad·lu·mi·dine \-mə,dēn\ *n* -S [blend of *adlumine* and *-id*] **:** an alkaloid $C_{19}H_{15-17}NO_6$ found in the climbing fumitory

ad·lu·mine \-,mēn, -mən\ *n* -S [NL *adlumia* (genus name of *Adlumia fungosa*) + E *-ine*] **:** an alkaloid $C_{21}H_{21}NO_6$ found in the climbing fumitory

adm *abbr* **1** administration; administrative; administrator **2** *often cap* admiral; admiralty **3** admission

ad·man \ˈad,man, -mən, -maa(ə)n\ *n*, *pl* **admen** [¹*ad* + *man*] **1 :** one that writes, solicits, or places advertisements **2 :** a compositor who sets advertisements

ad ma·num mor·tu·am \adˈmānəmˈmȯrchə,wäm\ [ML, lit., to a dead hand] *adv* **:** in mortmain

ad·max·il·lary \(ˈ)adˈmaksə,lerē\ *adj* [*ad-* + *maxillary*] **:** near or connected with the maxilla

ad·mea·sure \adˈmezhə(r), -äzh-\ *vt* -ED/-ING/-S [alter. (influenced by such words as *administer*, *admit*) of ME *amesuren*, fr. MF *amesurer*, fr. *a-* (fr. L *ad-*) + *mesurer* to measure — more at MEASURE] **:** to determine the proper share of **:** APPORTION ⟨~ land among heirs⟩ **:** mete out ⟨the ally of the judge in the business of *admeasuring* the sentence —B.N. Cardozo⟩

ad·mea·sure·ment \=ˈ==mənt\ *n* -S **1 :** determination and apportionment of shares ⟨~ of common lands for pasturage⟩ **2 :** application of a measure to determine or compare dimensions ⟨land consisting of two acres by ~⟩ **3 :** DIMENSIONS, SIZE ⟨a ship of considerable ~⟩

ad·me·di·al \(ˈ)adˈmēdēəl\ *or* **ad·me·di·an** \-ēən\ *adj* [*ad-* + *medial* or *median*] *biol* **:** near the median plane

ad·mi \ˈadmē\ *n* -S [Berber (Touareg) *édemi*] **:** a gazelle (*Gazella cuvieri*) found in northeastern Africa

ad·min·i·cle \adˈminəkəl, əd-\ *n* -S [L *adminiculum* support, prop, perh. fr. *ad-* + *-miniculum* (fr. *minae* pinnacle of a wall + *-iculum*, dim. suffix)] **1 :** SUPPORT, AUXILIARY ⟨to serve as an ~ of the senate⟩ ⟨the ~*s* of modern culture⟩ **2** [ML *adminiculum*, fr. L] **a :** *law* **:** corroborative or explanatory proof **b** *Scots law* **:** any writing tending to establish the existence or terms of a lost document

ad·mi·nic·u·lar \ˌadməˈnikyələ(r)\ *also* **ad·mi·nic·u·lary** \-,lerē\ *adj* [L *adminiculum* + E *-ar* or *-ary*] **:** supplying help **:** AUXILIARY, CORROBORATIVE ⟨~ evidence⟩

ad·min·is·ter \ədˈminəstə(r) *also* ad-\ *vb* **administered; administered; administering** \-st(ə)riŋ\ **administers** [ME *aministren*, *administren*, fr. MF *aministrer*, *administrer*, fr. L *administrare* to attend, manage fr. *ad-* + *ministrare* to serve — more at MINISTER] *vt* **1 a** (1) **:** to manage the affairs of ⟨a government that is badly ~*ed* can never be expected to last long —C.J.Friedrich⟩ (2) **:** to direct or superintend the execution, use, or conduct of ⟨~*ed* the regulations governing interstate travel —W.M.Emery⟩ ⟨in many Japanese homes the funds are ~*ed* by the wife —D.C.Buchanan⟩ ⟨vocational interest tests are ~*ed* to all students⟩ **b :** to act in lieu of an executor in settling (an intestate estate) **2 a :** to mete out **:** DISPENSE ⟨~ relief⟩ ⟨she was able to ~ a more piquant flattery —Ellen Glasgow⟩ ⟨~ justice⟩ ⟨disclaiming any intention to ~ any official rebuke —W.A.Slade⟩ ⟨~*ed* a public thrashing to the landlord who had mistreated his brother —C.V.Woodward⟩ **b :** to give ritually ⟨~ the last rites of the church⟩ **c :** to give remedially (as medicine) ⟨the amount of the antitoxin ~*ed* is determined by the doctor —Morris Fishbein⟩ **3 :** TENDER ⟨the following questions were first ~*ed* by the Archbishop of Canterbury —*Whitaker's Almanack*⟩ — often used with *to* ⟨the formal oath of office was ~*ed* to him —*Current Biog.*⟩ ~ *vi* **1 :** to perform the office of administrator — sometimes used with *upon* ⟨A ~*s* upon the estate of B⟩ **2 :** to give or furnish a real or assumed benefit **:** MINISTER — used with *to* ⟨~*ing* to the last wants of his friend⟩ **3 :** to manage or conduct affairs ⟨the government ~*s* when it appoints an officer —F.J.Goodnow⟩

administered price *n* **:** a price determined by the conscious price policy of a seller rather than by impersonal competitive market forces

ad·min·is·te·ri·al \əd¦minə¦stirēəl, ad-, ¦ad,mi-\ *adj* **:** ADMINISTRATIVE

ad·min·is·tra·ble \əd'minəstrəbəl, ad-\ *adj* [*administrate* + *-able*] **:** capable of being administered

ad·min·is·trant \-strənt\ *n* -s [*administer* + *-ant*] **:** one that administers

ad·min·is·trate \-nə,strāt\ *vt* -ED/-ING/-S [L *administratus*, past part. of *administrare* — more at ADMINISTER] **:** ADMINISTER

ad·min·is·tra·tion \əd,minə'strāshən *also* (,)ad,m-\ *n* -s [ME *administracioun*, fr. MF or L; MF *administration*, fr. L *administration-, administratio*, fr. *administratus* + *-ion-, -io* -ion] **1 :** an act of administering: **a :** a furnishing or tendering according to a prescribed rite or formula ⟨~ of the sacraments⟩ ⟨~ of an oath⟩ **b :** a meting out ⟨~ of justice⟩ ⟨~ of discipline⟩ **c :** APPLICATION, DOSAGE ⟨~ of a medicine⟩ ⟨~ of sensory stimuli⟩ **2 a** *archaic* **:** performance of a service in any capacity **b :** performance of executive duties **:** MANAGEMENT, DIRECTION, SUPERINTENDENCE ⟨achieved a more businesslike ~⟩ ⟨engage in the ~ of public affairs⟩ ⟨~ of a relief fund⟩ — compare LOGISTICS **3 a :** the management and disposal under legal authority of the estate of an intestate or of a testator having no competent executor **b :** the management of an estate of a deceased person by an executor **c :** the management of an estate (as of an infant) by a trustee or guardian legally appointed to take charge of it **4 a :** the total activity of a state in the exercise of its political powers including the action of the legislative, judicial, and executive departments **:** GOVERNMENT 2 **b :** the management of public affairs as distinguished from the executive or political function of policy making **5 a :** the principles, practices, and rationalized techniques employed in achieving the objectives or aims of an organization **b :** administrative management **:** the phase of business management that plans, organizes, and controls the activities of an organization for the accomplishment of its objectives in the long run often as distinguished from operative management **6 a :** a body of persons who are responsible for managing a business or institution **b** *usu cap* **:** a group constituting the political executive in a presidential system ⟨even a supposedly friendly Congress may flout the *Administration's* program —F.A.Ogg & P.O.Ray⟩ — compare GOVERNMENT 8 c(1) **c :** a governmental agency or board **7 :** the term during which an administrative officer or body holds office; *specif* **:** the term or terms of office of a president of the U.S. — **ad·min·is·tra·tion·al** \əd¦minə¦strāshən°l, -shnəl *also* ¦ad,m-\ *adj*

ad·min·is·tra·tive \əd'minə,strā|d·iv, -,strə|, |tiv, -ēv *also* ad- *or* -əv\ *adj* [L *administrativus*, fr. *administratus* + *-ivus* -ive] **:** of, belonging to, proceeding from, or suited to administration or an administration **:** EXECUTIVE — **ad·min·is·tra·tive·ly** *adv*

administrative county *n* **:** a territorial division in Great Britain often not coincident with the older county and to which the administrative functions but not the judicial and political ones of the older counties have been transferred

administrative law *n* **:** law dealing with the establishment, duties, and powers of and available remedies against authorized agencies in the executive branch of government

administrative unit *n* **1 :** a military unit (as a company or regiment) whose headquarters is directly responsible for administration and supply of the unit **2 :** a geographic area having a single school administration over several schools

ad·min·is·tra·tor \-,strād·ə(r), -ātə-, -ā,tō(ə)r, -ā,tō(ə)\ *n* -s [L, manager, fr. *administratus* + *-or*] **1 :** a person legally vested by a probate court with the right of administration of an estate — compare EXECUTOR **2 :** one that administers: as **a :** an officer appointed to govern (as a colony or dependency) **b :** an officer that directs or superintends affairs (as of a business, school, or government agency) **c :** a priest appointed to administer temporarily a diocese, parish, or ecclesiastical institution

administrator ad litem *n* [NL, administrator for the action] **:** a special administrator appointed to represent an estate in an action in which it must be represented when there is no executor or the executor for some reason cannot act

administrator with the will annexed : one appointed to administer an estate where the testator has appointed no executor or where his appointment of an executor has failed (as through death, incompetency, or refusal to act)

ad·min·is·tra·trix \əd¦minə¦strā·triks, ad-\ *n, pl* **adminis·tratri·ces** \-,-ˌ-'strā·trə,sēz, -,strə·'trī(,)sēz\ [ML, fem. of L *administrator*] **:** a female administrator esp. of an estate

¹**ad·mi·ra·ble** \'adm(ə)rəbəl\ *adj* [MF, fr. L *admirabilis*, fr. *admirari* to admire + *-abilis* -able — more at ADMIRE] **1** *obs* **:** worthy of being marveled at **:** WONDERFUL, SURPRISING ⟨it seemeth equally ~ to me, that holy king Henry the Sixth should do any wrong, or harsh Edward the Fourth do any right to the muses —Thomas Fuller⟩ **2 :** capable of exciting wonder united with approbation **:** deserving the highest esteem ⟨a record of a long, varied, and ~ career in the Foreign Service —R.H.Rovere⟩ **3 :** EXCELLENT 3 ⟨he is in many ways an ~ and even estimable figure —Irving Howe⟩ ⟨his taste was impeccable, his health ~ —Virginia Woolf⟩ — **admirableness** *n* -ES — **admirably** *adv*

²**admirable** *adv, obs* **:** ADMIRABLY

ad·mi·ral \'adm(ə)rəl\ *n* -s [ME *admiral, amiral*, fr. ML *admiralis* emir & OF *amiral* emir & MF *amiral* naval officer of high rank; ML *admiralis*, prob. by folk etymology (influence of L *admirabilis* admirable) fr. Ar *amīr* commander, *amīr-al-* commander of the (in such phrases as *amīr-al-baḥr* commander of the sea); OF & MF *amiral* fr. Ar *amīr, amīr-al-*] **1** *archaic* **:** the commander in chief of a navy **2 a :** a naval officer of high rank **:** FLAG OFFICER — see ADMIRAL OF THE FLEET, FLEET ADMIRAL, REAR ADMIRAL, VICE ADMIRAL **b :** a flag officer who is junior only to a fleet admiral, wears 4 stars and flies a 4-starred flag, and ranks with a four-star general in the army **3 :** a commander or officer having a certain general control of a fishing or merchant fleet; *specif* **:** a fisherman appointed to preserve order and decide differences in a fishing fleet **4** *archaic* **:** the chief ship of a fleet **:** FLAGSHIP **5 :** any of several brightly colored butterflies of the family Nymphalidae — see RED ADMIRAL **6 :** LOGWOOD 2

admiral of the fleet : the highest-ranking officer of the British navy corresponding to fleet admiral in the U. S. navy

¹**ad·mi·ral·ty** \'adm(ə)rəltē, -ti\ *n* -ES [alter. (influenced by *admiral*) of ME *amiralte*, fr. MF *amiralté*, fr. *amiral* admiral + *-té* -ty] **1** *archaic* **:** the office or jurisdiction of an admiral **2** *Brit, usu cap* **:** the executive department or officers having authority over naval affairs generally **3 :** the court having jurisdiction of maritime questions and civil and criminal maritime offenses, in the U. S. such jurisdiction being vested in the federal district court and in England in the probate, divorce, and admiralty division of the High Court of Justice; *also* **:** the system of law administered by admiralty courts

²**admiralty** \"\ *adj* **1 :** relating to maritime law ⟨~ jurisdiction⟩ ⟨~ practice⟩ **2** *usu cap* **:** of or belonging to British naval affairs or officials ⟨an *Admiralty* lord⟩ ⟨the *Admiralty* buildings⟩

admiralty bond *n* **:** a bond furnished by vessel or cargo owners in admiralty proceedings as security for the payment of legal claims to other vessel or cargo owners

admiralty brass *n* [*Admiralty Metal*] **:** a corrosion-resistant alloy containing about 71 percent copper, 28 percent zinc, and 1 percent tin

admiralty flag *n, usu cap A* [so called fr. its being flown on boats carrying members of the Board of *Admiralty*] **:** a British sea flag of red with an anchor and cable in yellow in the center

Admiralty Metal *trademark* — used for a corrosion-resistant alloy

admiralty mile *n, often cap A* **:** NAUTICAL MILE a

ad·mi·ra·tion \,admə'rāshən\ *n* -s [ME *admiracioun*, fr. MF or L; MF *admiration*, fr. L *admiration-, admiratio*, fr. *admiratus* (past part. of *admirari*) + *-ion-, -io* -ion] **1** *archaic* **:** WONDER, ASTONISHMENT **2 :** the object or source of wonder, astonishment, or esteem ⟨Poe was one of his greatest ~s —Amy Lowell⟩ **3 :** a feeling of mingled wonder, esteem, approbation, and delight ⟨my respect for him increased, and I looked on him almost with ~ —George Borrow⟩ ⟨there is perhaps a disproportionate ~ for the man who can produce original and good results —A.W.Haslett⟩ **4 :** act of viewing or contemplating with wonder, esteem, or approbation ⟨guided not by the giddy ~ of the shining accomplishments, but by the sober esteem of modesty —Adam Smith⟩ ⟨his persistence and courage won ~ even from those who thought him a madman —W.C.Ford⟩ ⟨he wagged his head and looked about for ~ —Pearl Buck⟩ **syn** see REGARD

admirative *adj* [F *admiratif*, fr. *admiration* + *-if* -ive] *archaic* **:** expressing admiration — **admiratively** *adv*

ad·mire \əd'mī(ə)r, -īə *also* ad-\ *vb* -ED/-ING/-S [MF *admirer*, fr. L *admirari*, fr. *ad-* + *mirari* to wonder — more at SMILE] *vt* **1** *archaic* **:** to regard with wonder or astonishment **:** view with surprise **:** marvel at ⟨how can we sufficiently ~ the stupidity and madness of these persons? —Joseph Addison⟩ **2 :** to regard with wondering esteem accompanied by pleasure and delight **:** regard with an elevated feeling of pleasure ⟨~ the beauty of the scene⟩ **3 :** to esteem or regard highly ⟨~ one's efficiency⟩ **4** *dial* **:** to take pleasure in **:** LIKE, ENJOY — usu. used with an infinitive ~ *vi* **:** WONDER, MARVEL — sometimes used with *at* ⟨his friends *admired* at his sudden success⟩

admired *adj* **:** regarded with admiration ⟨the most ~ single phrase that Shakespeare ever wrote —C.D.Lewis⟩ ⟨I was much about with a beautiful, ~ woman —W.B.Yeats⟩

ad·mir·er \-īrə(r)\ *n* -s **:** one that admires ⟨an ~ of the president⟩ ⟨among the ~s of his preaching⟩; *specif* **:** LOVER, BEAU ⟨one of the young lady's ~s⟩

admiring *adj* **:** feeling or showing admiration ⟨~ friends⟩ ⟨~ glances⟩ — **ad·mir·ing·ly** *adv*

admis *pl of* ADMI

ad mi·se·ri·cor·di·am \,admə,zerə'kȯrdē,am, -ēəm\ *adv* (*or adj*) [L] **:** to compassion or pity — used of an argument

ad·mis·si·bil·i·ty *also* **ad·mis·sa·bil·i·ty** \əd,misə'biləd·ē, (,)ad,-, -ətē, -i\ *n* -ES **:** the quality or state of being admissible

ad·mis·si·ble *also* **ad·mis·sa·ble** \əd'misəbəl *also* ad-\ *adj* [*admissible* fr. F, fr. ML *admissibilis*, fr. L *admissus* + *-ibilis* -ible; *admissable*, alter. of *admissible*] **1 a :** capable of being allowed or conceded **:** ALLOWABLE ⟨retelling the story, if done by a gifted writer, was felt to be ~ —N.A.McQuown⟩ ⟨a kind of speculation that was ~ in cosmology but inadmissible in medicine —Benjamin Farrington⟩ ⟨Buddhism, Taoism, and Confucianism are all ~ philosophies —C.P.Fitzgerald⟩ ⟨the difficulty would be lessened if entries in books of account were ~ as prima-facie evidence —B.N.Cardozo⟩ **b** *of a logical or mathematical value* **:** capable of producing a meaningful expression when substituted for a variable ⟨in the sentence "*X* is tall", *John* is an ~ substitute for *X* but *two* is not⟩ **2 :** entitled or worthy to be admitted ⟨handicapped persons ~ to industrial employment⟩ ⟨foreign products ~ to the domestic market⟩ ⟨hearsay evidence is not ordinarily ~ in court⟩

ad·mis·sion \əd'mishən *also* ad-\ *n* -s [in sense 1, fr. ME *admissioun*, fr. ML *admission-, admissio*, fr. L, admittance to an audience with a prince, fr. *admissus* (past part. of *admittere*) + *-ion-, -io* -ion; in other senses, fr. L *admissus* + E *-ion*] **1 a** *archaic* **:** acceptance into an office or position **b :** formal approval of a presentee to a benefice by a bishop of the Church of England; *sometimes* **:** the institution of such a presentee **2 a :** the granting of an argument or position not fully proved **:** the act of acknowledging something asserted **:** acquiescence or concurrence in the truth of an allegation **b** *in criminal law* **:** a concession that a fact or allegation is true without implying any acknowledgment of criminal intent — distinguished from *confession* **c :** a revealing statement (as of acknowledgment or fact) ⟨this ~ had the effect of an electric shock upon my older sister —Sidney Lovett⟩ **3 a :** an act of admitting **:** the fact of being admitted **:** permission or right to enter (as a place or a membership) **:** ACCESS **b** (1) **:** the act of admitting the working fluid (as steam) to the engine cylinder (2) **:** the point in the cycle of operations or on the corresponding indicator diagram at which this act occurs (3) **:** the period from this point to the completion of the cutoff **4 :** price of entrance **:** fee paid at or for entering

admission day *n, usu cap A&D* **:** the anniversary of the admission of a state to the U. S.

ad·mis·sive \-isiv\ *adj* [L *admissus* + E *-ive*] **:** characterized by or allowing admission ⟨an Elizabethan tragedy ~ of comic scenes —Rene Wellek & Austin Warren⟩

ad·mit \əd'mit *also* ad-; *usu* -id.+V\ *vb* **admitted**; **admitted; admitting; admits** [ME *admitten*, fr. L *admittere*, fr. *ad-* + *mittere* to send — more at SMITE] *vt* **1 a :** PERMIT ⟨the geological vocabulary ~s a less satisfactory treatment than does that of some of the other sciences —T.H.Savory⟩ **b :** to accept as true or valid **:** ACKNOWLEDGE ⟨Brunel was compelled to ~ failure —O.S.Nock⟩ ⟨*admitting* the possibility that the bomb might wipe out civilization —*Current Biog.*⟩ ⟨a reluctance to ~ any of the ample evidence —J.G.Cozzens⟩ ⟨another troublesome problem was settling a date after which no evidence would be *admitted* —W.O.Aydelotte⟩ — compare ADMISSION 2a **2 :** to allow entry (as to a place, membership, or privilege) ⟨this ticket ~s one person⟩ ⟨he was *admitted* a fellow of the Royal Society —Ella Lonn⟩ — often used with *to* or *into* ⟨he was *admitted* to the university⟩ ⟨*admitted* to candidacy⟩ ⟨states *admitted* to the Union⟩ ~ *vi* **1 :** to give entrance or access — used with *to* ⟨a gate that ~s to a yard⟩ **2 a :** ALLOW, PERMIT — often used with *of* ⟨indeterminate situations which ~ of answers —J.J.O'Connor⟩ ⟨many crucial dilemmas simply do not ~ of analysis on one page —Dorothy Fosdick⟩ **b :** to make acknowledgment — used with *to* ⟨they dare not publicly ~ to these doubts —Hessell Tiltman⟩ **syn** see ACKNOWLEDGE, RECEIVE

ad·mit·tance \-t°n(t)s\ *n* -s **1 a :** permission to enter (a place) **:** ENTRANCE **b :** ADMISSION 3a **2** *English law* **:** the act of giving possession of a copyhold **3 :** the reciprocal of the impedance of a circuit

ad·mit·ta·tur \,admə'tād·ə(r)\ *n* -s [L, let him be admitted (often the first word on such a certificate)] **:** a certificate of admission formerly given by a college or university

admitted *adj* **:** received as true or valid **:** CONCEDED, ACKNOWLEDGED — **ad·mit·ted·ly** *adv*

admitted asset *n* **:** any asset of an insurer allowed by state regulations to be reckoned in determining the financial condition of an insurance company

admitted company *n* **:** an insurance company that having complied with the laws is authorized to transact business within a certain state or country

¹**ad·mix** \(ˈ)ad¦miks, əd'm-\ *vt* -ED/-ING/-ES [back-formation fr. obs. *admixt* mingled with, fr. ME, fr. L *admixtus*] **:** MINGLE, MIX, BLEND — often used with *with* ⟨a saturated hydrocarbon that cannot be vulcanized unless ~*ed* with a little isoprene —J.W.McBain⟩

²**ad·mix** \'ad,miks\ *n* [by shortening] **:** ADMIXTURE 2b

admix *abbr* administratrix

ad·mix·ture \(ˈ)ad¦mikschə(r), əd'm-\ *n* [L *admixtus* (past part. of *admiscēre* to mix with, fr. *ad-* + *miscēre* to mix) + E *-ure* — more at MIX] **1 a :** the act of mixing ⟨a favorable result will be obtained only by careful ~ of ingredients⟩ **b :** the fact of being mixed ⟨repeated sifting is necessary to secure complete ~⟩ **2 a :** an element or substance added by mixing ⟨comic verses with an occasional ~ of mild bawdry —Alexander Cowie⟩ **b :** a substance other than cement, aggregate, or water that is mixed with concrete **3 :** a compound formed by mixing ⟨by using wool, silk, cotton, and linen fibers in various ~s —A.C.Morrison⟩

adml *abbr, often cap* admiral

ad·mon·ish \əd'mänish, -ēsh *also* ad-\ *vb* -ED/-ING/-ES [ME *admonesen, admonisshen*, alter. (*amonest-, admonest-* being taken as past & past part.) of *amonesten, admonesten*, fr. MF *amonester, admonester*, fr. (assumed) VL *admonestare*, alter. of L *admonēre* to remind, warn, fr. *ad-* + *monēre* to warn — more at MIND] *vt* **1 :** to indicate duties, obligations, or requisite action to (a person) **:** express warning or disapproval to about remissness or error esp. gently, earnestly, and solicitously in urging duty, caution, or amendment ⟨necessary to the decorum of her character that she should ~ her erring children —T.B.Macaulay⟩ **2 :** to express a direction or explanation or give advice or encouragement to esp. in friendly earnest counsel ⟨someone has ~*ed* you not to miss Brandon —E.W. Smith⟩ ~ *vi* **:** to give admonition **syn** see REPROVE

ad·mon·ish·ing·ly *adv* **:** in an admonishing manner

ad·mon·ish·ment \-mənt\ *n* -s [alter. of ME *admonestement, amonestement*, fr. OF, fr. *amonester* to admonish + *-ment*] **:** ADMONITION

ad·mo·ni·tion \,admə'nishən\ *n* -s [alter. (influenced by *admonish*) of ME *amonicioun*, fr. MF *amonition*, fr. L *admonition-, admonitio*, fr. *admonitus* (past part. of *admonēre*) + *-ion-, -io* -ion] **1 :** gentle or friendly reproof, warning, or reminder ⟨admirably took a middle key between ~ and philosophizing —Mary Austin⟩ ⟨a silent ~ to the guests to enjoy life while it lasted —T.L.Peacock⟩ **2 :** counsel against a fault, error, or oversight ⟨~s against the oversimplification, overdramatization, and lurking distortion of historiography —Ephraim Fischoff⟩ **3 :** expression of authoritative advice or warning esp. in ecclesiastical censure ⟨pressure is exerted largely through precept and ~ —Catherine H. Berndt⟩

ad·mon·i·to·ri·ly \əd¦mänə¦tōrəlē, ad-, ¦ad,m-\ *adv* **:** in an admonitory manner

ad·mon·i·to·ry \əd'mänə,tōrē, ad-, -ȯr-, -ri\ *adj* [ML *admonitorius*, fr. L *admonitus* + *-orius* -ory] **:** expressing admonition **:** WARNING, REPROVING ⟨the low, ~ growl of a fierce old dog —P.B.Kyne⟩ ⟨keep an ~ eye on the school children —Dorothy Sayers⟩ ⟨the king and queen received ~ letters from Pope Boniface V —F.M.Stenton⟩

admor *abbr* administrator

admr *abbr* administrator

admrx *abbr* administratrix

adms *or* **admstr** *abbr* administrator

admx *abbr* administratrix

ad·nate \'ad,nāt\ *adj* [L *adnatus*, past part. of *adnasci*, alter. of *agnasci* to be born in addition to — more at AGNATE] **1** *biol* **:** grown together — used esp. of unlike parts ⟨a coral zooid ~ to the stem⟩ ⟨a calyx ~ to the ovary⟩; compare CONNATE **2** *biol* **:** growing with one side adherent to a stem ⟨an ~ anther⟩

ad·na·tion \(ˈ)ad¦nāshən\ *n* -s **:** the state of being adnate — compare ADHESION 6

ad nau·se·am \ad'nȯzē,am *also* äd- *or* aad- *or* ȧd- *or* -s| *or* -zh| *or* -sh| *or* |ā *or* a(ə)d . . . ,a(aə)m *or* äd . . . ,äm *or* ȧd . . . ,ȧm; äd'nau̇sä,ām, ȧd . . . ,ȧm *also* -zä- *or* a(ə)d'nau̇zēəm\ *adv* [L] **:** to a sickening degree **:** so as to disgust

ad·nexa \ad'neksə\ *also* **an·nexa** \ə'n-,a'n-\ *n pl* [NL, fr. L *adnexa, annexa*, neut. pl. of *adnexus, annexus*, past part. of *adnectere, annectere* to bind to — more at ANNEX] *anat* **:** conjoined, subordinate, or associated parts **:** APPENDAGES ⟨the fallopian tubes and ovaries are ~ of the uterus⟩; *specif* **:** the embryonic membranes and other temporary structures of the embryo — **ad·nex·al** \(ˈ)ad¦neksəl\ *also* **an·nex·al** \ə'neksəl, (ˈ)a¦n-\ *adj*

ad·nexed \(ˈ)ad¦nekst\ *adj* [L *adnexus* + E *-ed*] *bot* **:** reaching to the stem, but not attached to it — used of the gills of some agarics

ad·nex·i·tis \,ad,nek'sīd·əs\ *n* -ES [NL, fr. *adnexa* + *-itis*] **:** inflammation of adnexa, esp. those of the uterus

ad·nom·i·nal \(ˈ)ad¦nämən°l\ *adj* [*ad-* + *nominal*] **:** modifying a noun ⟨*hot* in "hot soup" or "this soup is hot", *John's* in "John's hat", *city* in "city limits", *for action* in "the time for action", *that Jack built* in "the house that Jack built" are ~⟩ **:** ¹ADJECTIVE 1 — **adnominally** *adv*

ad non ex·e·cu·ta \(,)ad¦nän,eksə'kyüd·ə\ *adv* [L] *law* **:** for the things not executed by an executor

ado \ə'dü\ *n* -s [ME, fr. *at do*, fr. *at* to, at + *do*, *don* to do — more at AT, DO] **1 a :** fussy excitement **:** TO-DO **b :** bustling about ⟨the annoying ~ of a political campaign⟩ **c :** confusing and wearying turmoil ⟨loath to plunge into the holiday ~⟩ **2 :** time-wasting bother over trifling details ⟨he answered the letter without much ~⟩ **3 :** difficulty esp. of a sort that makes special resourcefulness and stamina necessary ⟨in spite of the unexpected competition, he won the race without ~⟩ **syn** see STIR

ado·be \ə'dōbē\ *n* -s *often attrib* [Sp, fr. Ar *aṭ-ṭūb* the brick, fr. Copt *tōbe* brick] **1 :** a brick of sun-dried earth and straw **:** building material of sun-dried earth and straw **2 :** a heavy-textured clay soil (as that of the semiarid southwestern U.S.) used in making sun-dried bricks **:** alluvial or playa clay in desert or arid regions **3 :** a house or other structure made of adobe bricks **4 :** MUDCAP

adobe brown *n* **:** a moderate yellowish brown that is slightly paler than Bismarck brown, duller and very slightly yellower than maple sugar, and slightly yellower and paler than cinnamon brown

adobe bug *n* [so called fr. its distribution in areas where adobe is common] **:** a hemipterous insect pest (*Haematosiphon inodora*) of poultry in arid southwestern U.S. and adjacent Mexico — called also *coruco, Mexican chicken bug*

adobe lily *n* [so called fr. the typical soil of its locality] **:** a Californian bulbous herb (*Fritillaria pluriflora*) having pinkish purple flowers

adobe tick *n* [so called fr. its distribution in areas where adobe is common] **:** CHICKEN TICK

ad·o·les·car·ia \,ad°l,es'ka(a)rēə\ *n, pl* **adolescariae** \-rē,ē\ *or* **adolescarias** [NL, fr. L *adolescere* + *-aria* (fem. of *-arius* -ary)] **:** a late larval trematode or a developing trematode not yet attained to sexual maturity — compare MARITA, PARTHENITA — **ad·o·les·car·i·al** \¦--,-¦-ēəl\ *adj*

ad·o·lesce \,ad°l¦es\ *vi* -ED/-ING/-S [back-formation fr. ¹*adolescent* & *adolescence*] **:** to grow toward maturity **:** pass through adolescence ⟨it is a young nation, still *adolescing*⟩

ad·o·les·cence \,ad°l'es°n(t)s\ *n* -s [ME, fr. MF, fr. L *adolescentia*, fr. *adolescent-, adolescens* (pres. part. of *adolescere* to grow up) + *-ia* — more at ADULT] **1 :** the state or process of growing up **:** the period of life from puberty to maturity terminating legally at the age of majority **2 :** the transition from youth to maturity in the cycle of stream erosion, valley development, or regional sculpture by running water **syn** see YOUTH

ad·o·les·cen·cy \-°nsē\ *n* -ES [ME *adolescencie*, fr. L *adolescentia*] *archaic* **:** ADOLESCENCE

¹**ad·o·les·cent** \,ad°l'es°nt\ *n* -s [F, fr. L *adolescent-, adolescens*] **:** one that is in the state of adolescence

²**adolescent** \¦--¦--\ *adj* **1 :** in the state or process of adolescence **2 :** peculiar to, suggestive of, or relating to adolescence or an adolescent ⟨~ instability⟩ **:** developing during adolescence ⟨~ goiter⟩ — **adolescent·ly** *adv*

adolescent stream *n* **:** a stream in transition from the stage of youth to that of maturity in the erosion cycle characterized by a smoothly graded course without waterfalls or rapids and with only a very narrow valley flat

ado·nai *also* **ado·nay** \,ädə'nȯi, -'nä,ē, -'nī, ,ad- *also* ,adə'nā-,ī\ *n* -s *cap* [Heb *'ădhōnāy*] **:** GOD — a Hebrew word usu. translated in the Old Testament by *Lord*; see TETRAGRAMMATON

¹**adon·ic** \ə'dänik\ *also* **ado·ni·an** \ə'dōnēən\ *adj, often cap* [*Adonis*, mythological personage + E *-ic* or *-ian*] **1 :** of, relating to, or like Adonis; *esp* **:** exceptionally handsome ⟨the youth's ~ features⟩ **2 :** having a rhythm consisting of a dactyl followed by a spondee or by a trochee ⟨~ verse⟩

²**adonic** \"\ *n* -s *often cap* **:** a verse having adonic rhythm

adon·i·din \ə'dänədən\ *n* -s [ISV *adon-* (fr. NL *Adonis*, genus name of *Adonis vernalis*) + *-id* + *-in*; orig. formed in G] **:** a mixture of glucosides obtained from an adonis (*Adonis vernalis*) and used esp. formerly as a cardiac stimulant

adon·in \ə'dänən, -dō-\ *n* -s [ISV *adon-* (fr. NL *Adonis*, genus name of *Adonis autumnalis*) + *-in*; orig. formed in G] **:** a bitter gumlike glucoside $C_{24}H_{40}O_9$ found in the root of plants of the genus *Adonis*

¹**adon·is** \ə'dänəs, -dō-\ *n* [NL, after *Adonis*, in Greco-Roman mythology a beautiful youth beloved by Aphrodite and killed by a wild boar, fr. L, fr. Gk *Adōnis*; fr. the legend that a plant sprang forth from his blood] **1** *cap* **:** a small genus of herbs (family Ranunculaceae) having alternate finely dissected leaves and solitary red or yellow flowers **2** -ES *pharm* **:** the herbage of a plant (*Adonis vernalis*) formerly used like digitalis in dropsy

²**adonis** \"\ *n* -ES [after *Adonis*, mythological personage] **1** *usu cap* **:** an exceptionally handsome young man **2 :** an 18th century wig

adon·i·tol \ə'dänə,tōl, -ōl\ *n* -s [ISV *adon-* (fr. NL *Adonis*, genus name of *Adonis vernalis*) + *-itol*; orig. formed in G] **:** a crystalline pentahydroxy alcohol $HOCH_2(CHOH)_3CH_2OH$ occurring in a plant (*Adonis vernalis*) and obtainable by reduction of ribose — called also *ribitol*

ad·o·nize \'ad°n,īz\ *vb* -ED/-ING/-S [F *adoniser*, fr. *Adonis*, mythological personage + F *-iser* -ize] **:** BEAUTIFY — usu. used of a man

adoors *adv* [earlier *a doors*, fr. ³*a* and/or *a* (fr. *at*) + *doors*] *obs* **:** at the door **:** of the door ⟨run in ~ quickly —R.B. Sheridan⟩

adopt \ə'däpt\ *vt* -ED/-ING/-S [MF or L; MF *adopter*, fr. L *adoptare*, fr. *ad-* + *optare* to choose, desire — more at OPINE] **1 :** to take by free choice into a close relationship previously not existing esp. by a formal legal act ⟨a country glad to have them as ~*ed* citizens⟩; *specif* **:** to take voluntarily (a child of other parents) to be in the place of or as one's own child ⟨they ~*ed* him as their sole heir⟩ **2 a :** to take up or accept esp. as a practice or tenet often evolved by another: as (1) **:** to come to believe in **:** MAINTAIN, SUPPORT ⟨one no longer ~*s* an idea unless it is driven in with hammers of statistics and columns of figures —Henry Adams⟩ (2) **:** to accept formally **:** acknowledge or enact as true, wise, fitting, germane ⟨no proposal for curtailment of the Supreme Court power over legislation has ever been ~*ed* —Felix Frankfurter⟩ (3) **:** to use as wonted or accustomed **:** EMPLOY, PRACTICE ⟨she had ~*ed* a blend of sisterly authority and business brusqueness —William McFee⟩ ⟨a precaution which . . . he had ~*ed* whenever he carried more than two or three shillings —Thomas Hardy⟩ **b :** to take over (a loanword) esp. with little or no change in form **3** *of a deliberative body* **:** to endorse and assume official responsibility for (a resolution of a committee) **4 :** to choose (a textbook) for required study in a school subject

syn EMBRACE, ESPOUSE agree in indicating an accepting, taking, or receiving as a belief to be held or practice to be followed. ADOPT may stress the fact that the belief or practice is not of one's own invention but is voluntarily taken from another's example ⟨none seem to have yet *adopted* the utterly abominable European hat — Lafcadio Hearn⟩ ⟨Turkey . . . has *adopted* a Latin alphabet⟩ ⟨gave up old customs reluctantly, but once they had *adopted* a new one they found it impossible to understand why everyone else did not immediately do likewise —Edith Wharton⟩ It may refer to an attitude or gesture taken or to a bill or measure passed or accepted formally ⟨he noticed that now, far from looking glum, she had *adopted* a winning manner —Edith Sitwell⟩ ⟨Calhoun's address was *adopted*, the Whigs voting against it —R.P.Brooks⟩ EMBRACE may suggest ready, willing, or happy acceptance or reception of a belief or practice ⟨born on Manhattan's poverty-ridden East Side, they *embraced* the Communist movement in their teens —*N.Y.Times*⟩ ⟨"I hate inversions", declared Tennyson — a statement which, I fear, will lead some of the modernists forthwith to *embrace* them —J.L.Lowes⟩ ESPOUSE may indicate either genuine depth of attachment or lasting and participating acceptance and alliance ⟨when . . . Gobineau's *Essay* was resuscitated from comparative oblivion and its dogmas passionately and popularly *espoused* —Ruth Benedict⟩ ⟨the spirit of uncompromising individualism that would eventually *espouse* the principle of democracy in church and state —V.L. Parrington⟩

adopt·a·bil·i·ty \ə,däptə'bilәd·ē\ *n* -ES **:** capability of being adopted

adopt·a·ble \ə'däptəbəl\ *adj* **:** capable of being adopted

adop·tee \ə,däp'tē, ə¦däp¦tē\ *n* -S **:** one that is adopted

adop·tian \ə'däpshən\ *adj, sometimes cap* [ML *adoptianus*, fr. L *adoptare* + *-ianus* -ian] **:** of, relating to, or forming the doctrine of adoptionism

adop·tion \ə'däpshən\ *n* -S [ME *adopcioun*, fr. MF or L; MF *adoption*, fr. L *adoption-, adoptio*, fr. *ad-* + *option-, optio* choosing — more at OPTION] **1 :** act of adopting or state of being adopted **2 :** the taking of an outsider into a family, clan, or tribal group usu. by investing him with the rights and responsibilities of a member by birth but occas. by giving him only a subservient status

adop·tion·ism *also* **adop·tian·ism** \-shə,nizəm\ *n* -S *often cap* [*adoption* or *adoptian* + *-ism*] **:** the doctrine that Jesus of Nazareth became son of God by exaltation to a status that was not his by birth: as **a :** any of various theories in the first three centuries A.D. holding that Jesus was adopted to sonship at the time of his baptism or resurrection **b :** an 8th century doctrine of dual sonship holding that Christ as God is son by generation and nature but as man is son by adoption and grace

adop·tion·ist *also* **adop·tian·ist** \-,nəst\ *n* -S *often cap, often attrib* **:** one that adheres to adoptionism

adop·tive \-ptiv, -ēv *also* -əv\ *adj* [ME, fr. MF & L; MF *adoptif*, fr. L *adoptivus*, fr. *adoptare* to adopt + *-ivus* -ive — more at ADOPT] **1 :** of or relating to adoption **2 :** made or acquired by adoption ⟨an ~ father⟩ ⟨an ~ country⟩ **3 :** tending or inclined to adopt ⟨a gentle ~ matron⟩ — **adop·tive·ly** \-tәvlē, -li\ *adv*

adoptive arms *n* **:** ARMS OF ADOPTION

adopts *pres 3d sing of* ADOPT

ador·a·bil·i·ty \ə,dōrə'bilәd·ē, -ȯr-, -ətē, -i\ *n* -ES **:** the quality of being adorable

ador·a·ble \ə'dōrəbəl, -ȯr-\ *adj* [F, fr. L *adorabilis*, fr. *adorare* to adore + *-abilis* -able — more at ADORE] **1 :** worthy of being adored **2 :** inviting adoration **:** extremely charming or lovable **:** DELIGHTFUL ⟨an ~ child⟩ ⟨an ~ home⟩ — **ador·a·ble·ness** *n* -ES — **ador·a·bly** \-blē, -li\ *adv*

¹ad·oral \(')a¦dōrəl\ *adj* [*ad-* + *oral*] **:** near the mouth ⟨~ cilia⟩ — **ad·oral·ly** \- əlē\ *adv*

²adoral \"\ *n* -S **:** an adoral plate, ossicle, or other part

¹ador·ant \ə'dōrənt\ *adj* [L *adorant-, adorans*, pres. part. of *adorare* to adore — more at ADORE] **:** ADORING

²adorant \"\ *n* -S **:** one that adores

ad·o·ra·tion \,adə'rāshən\ *n* -S [MF or L; MF, fr. L *adoration-, adoratio*, fr. *adoratus* (past part. of *adorare*) + *-ion-, -io* -ion] **1 :** the act or state of adoring or of being adored **2 :** the object or recipient of the act of adoring ⟨she was his life, his ~⟩ **3 a :** worship given to God alone **:** LATRIA — distinguished from *veneration* **b :** HYPERDULIA **c :** DULIA **4 a :** a method of electing a pope by the obeisance to a candidate of two thirds of the cardinals in conclave

ador·a·to·ry \ə'dōrə,tōrē\ *n* -ES [ML *adoratorium*, fr. L *adoratus* + *-orium*] **:** a place of adoration ⟨a pagan ~⟩

adore \ə'dō(ə)r, -d(ə)r, -ōə, -ȯ(ə)\ *vb* -ED/-ING/-S [MF *adorer*, fr. L *adorare*, fr. *ad-* + *orare* to speak, pray — more at ORATION] *vt* **1 :** to worship with profound reverence **:** pay divine honors to **:** honor as a deity or as divine **:** offer worship to **2 :** to regard with reverent admiration and devotion prompted by veneration, esteem, or love often with an accompanying outward expression of such regard ⟨he so *adored* his mother —Elizabeth Goudge⟩ **3 :** to be extremely fond of **:** be deeply attached to often to the point of excess ⟨to dance, to ride, she had *adored* all that —Virginia Woolf⟩ ~ *vi* **:** to become filled with a spirit of profound reverence (as toward a deity) often with an accompanying outward expression of such a spirit ⟨to bend, to tremble, and ~ —P.B.Shelley⟩ **syn** see REVERE

ador·er \ə'dōrə(r), ə'dȯr-\ *n* -S **:** one that adores

adoring *adj* **:** marked by, motivated by, or manifesting adoration — **ador·ing·ly** *adv*

adorn \ə'dō(ə)rn, -ȯ(ə)n\ *vt* -ED/-ING/-S [ME *adornen*, fr. MF *adorner*, fr. L *adornare*, fr. *ad-* + *ornare* to furnish, embellish — more at ORNATE] **1 a :** to make pleasing or attractive **b :** to add to the pleasantness, attractiveness, splendor, or beauty of ⟨a competence . . . ~*ed* by an unexcelled brilliance of vivid expression —A.H.Johnson⟩ **c :** to point up, highlight, or set off to advantage the pleasantness, attractiveness, splendor, or beauty of ⟨the simplicity with which great composers ~ their works —Warwick Braithwaite⟩ **2 :** to decorate with or as if with external ornamentation ⟨as a bride ~*s* herself with her jewels —Isa 61:10 (RSV)⟩ **3 :** to deck out or dress up esp. with a resultant sham splendor ⟨garish gin palaces that ~ all the suburbs —S.P.B.Mais⟩

syn DECORATE, ORNAMENT, EMBELLISH, BEAUTIFY, DECK, BEDECK, GARNISH: to ADORN signifies to give a certain attractiveness or beauty to (esp. to something already quite attractive) by being associated with, physically or otherwise, or by adding something beautiful to ⟨the painters who *adorned* the Minoan palaces with lovely frescoes —V.G.Childe⟩ ⟨her feet, stockingless, and *adorned* rather than clad in blue-satin slippers —Scott Fitzgerald⟩ To DECORATE, often interchangeable with ADORN, generally implies the adding of something of color or interest to relieve plainness or monotony ⟨the music was brief, gracefully *decorated* with trills and curlicues —*Time*⟩ ⟨pathways, *decorated* with ornamental trees and shrubs —Tom Marvel⟩ To ORNAMENT implies a decorating by means of something extraneous, as an adjunct or accessory ⟨columns *ornament* the front entrance —*Amer. Guide Series: Maine*⟩ To EMBELLISH, stressing more the act of an agent than an effect, suggests strongly the adding of superfluous or adventitious ornamental elements ⟨Gothic cathedrals . . . *embellished*, both inside and out, with grinning gargoyles —Lytton Strachey⟩ To BEAUTIFY is to make relatively beautiful, esp. by neutralizing, masking, or transforming a certain plainness or ugliness ⟨salt cedars and oleanders have been planted to *beautify* the highway —*Amer. Guide Series: Texas*⟩ To DECK or BEDECK implies the addition of something which contributes to gaiety, interest, splendor, or sometimes gaudiness ⟨*deck* the halls with boughs of holly⟩ ⟨he was as fine as any prince, ablaze with jewels, *bedecked* with yards of snowy lace and fine embroidery — Frank Yerby⟩ ⟨*bedecked* with cheap finery⟩ To GARNISH implies a decorating with something small but bright and attractive as a final touch in preparation for use or service ⟨a steak *garnished* with parsley⟩ ⟨the old-fashioned polemical sermon . . . *garnished* with quotations in Greek —Van Wyck Brooks⟩

adorned *adj* **1** *heraldry* **:** decorated with a specified accessory charge ⟨a double tressure ~ with roses⟩ **2** *heraldry* **:** ornamented in a specified tincture ⟨an antique shield azure ~ gold⟩

adorn·ment \ə'dȯrnmənt, -dō(ə)n-\ *n* -S [MF *adornement*, fr. *adorner* + *-ment*] **1 :** the action of adorning or state of being adorned **2 :** something with which one is adorned ⟨her hair was a lovely ~⟩

ador·no \ə'dȯr(,)nō\ *n* -S [Sp, ornament, ornamentation, back-formation fr. *adornar* to adorn, fr. L *adornare*] **:** an appliqué ornamentation; *esp* **:** a modeled or molded ornamentation appliquéd to pottery

ados *pl of* ADO

ad·os·cu·la·tion \(,)a,däskyə'lāshən\ *n* -S [LL *adosculatus* (past part. of *adosculari* to kiss, fr. L *ad-* + *osculari* to kiss) + E *-ion* — more at OSCULATE] **:** impregnation by external contact without intromission

¹adown \ə'-\ *adv* [ME *adoun, adoune*, fr. OE *adūne, of dūne*, fr. *a-* (fr. *of*) or of off, from + *dūne*, dat. of *dūn* hill — more at OF, DOWN] *archaic* **:** DOWN

²adown \"\ *prep* [ME *adoun, adoune*, fr. *adoun, adoune*, adv.] **:** DOWN ⟨~ the long years —G.B.Shaw⟩

adoxa \ə'däksə\ *n, cap* [NL, fr. Gk *adoxos* without glory, fr. *a-* ²a- + *doxa* glory; fr. the lack of showy flowers] **:** a genus (the type of the family Adoxaceae) of perennial rhizomatous herbs having berrylike fruit

ad·ox·a·ce·ae \,a,däk'sāsē,ē\ *n pl, cap* [NL, fr. *Adoxa*, type genus + *-aceae*] **:** a family of herbs (order Rubiales) by some included in the Caprifoliaceae but distinguished by having flowers without a calyx and with the stamens inserted in pairs on the tube of the corolla

ADP \¦ā,dē'pē\ *abbr or n* -S adenosine diphosphate

adpressed *var of* APPRESSED

ad·pro·mis·sion \,adprō'mishən\ *n* -S [*adpromissor* + *-ion*] **:** a legal contract or relation of suretyship

ad·pro·mis·sor \,adprō'misər, -,sȯr\ *n, pl* **adpromissors** \-rz\ *also* **ad·prom·is·so·res** \,ad,prämə'sōr(,)ēz\ [LL *adpromissor, appromissor* one who gives bail, bail, fr. *ad-* + *promissor* promiser — more at PROMISSOR] **:** SURETY, BAIL

ad quod damnum \,ad,kwäd'damnəm, ,äd,kwōd'däm,nům\ [L, to what damage] **:** a writ issued in proceedings (as of condemnation) to assess damages for land seized for public use

adrad *adj* [ME *adrad, adred*, fr. past part. of *adreden, adraden* to be afraid, fr. OE *adrǣdan, ondrǣdan* (fr. ¹a-, on + *drǣdan* to fear, dread) & *ofdrǣdan*, fr. *of-* (akin to OE *ofer* over) + *drǣdan* — more at DREAD] *archaic* **:** put in dread **:** AFRAID

ad·ra·di·al \(')ad¦rādēəl\ *adj* **:** of or relating to the adradius in coelenterates — **ad·ra·di·al·ly** \-əlē\ *adv*

ad·ra·di·us \(')ad-¦rādēəs\ *n, pl* **adra·dii** \-ē,ī\ *or* **adradi·uses** [*ad-* + *radius*] **:** a radius of the third order in coelenterates

adream \ə'-\ *adj* [¹*a-* + *dream*, v.] **:** DREAMING ⟨old people motionless and ~⟩

adreamed *past part* [prob. fr. *a-* (perfective prefix) + *dreamed*, past part. of *dream* — more at ABEAR] *obs* **:** visited by a dream ⟨I was ~ that I sat all alone —John Bunyan⟩

ad·rec·tal \(')ad-¦rektᵊl\ *adj* [*ad-* + *rectal*] **:** adjacent to the rectum — used esp. of a gland in certain mollusks that secretes a fluid which turns purple on exposure to light; see TYRIAN PURPLE

¹ad rem \(')ad-'rem, (')ä-\ *adv* [L, to the affair] **:** in a way that is marked by strict attention to essential points **:** without digression ⟨she seems incapable of speaking *ad rem*⟩

²ad rem \(')⸗¦⸗\ *adj* **:** pertinent to the matter at issue or under consideration **:** relevant or vital to the point or purpose ⟨a persuasive *ad rem* argument⟩

adren- *or* **adreno-** *comb form* [¹*adrenal*] **1 :** adrenal glands ⟨*adreno*cortical⟩ ⟨*adreno*medullary⟩ ⟨*adreno*tropic⟩ **:** adrenal and ⟨*adreno*genital⟩ **2 :** adrenaline ⟨*adren*ergic⟩

¹ad·re·nal \ə'drēnᵊl, (')a¦d-\ *adj* [*ad-* + *renal*] **1 :** adjacent to the kidneys; *specif* **:** relating to or derived from adrenal glands **2 :** having an effect like that of the secretion of adrenaline **:** stimulating anger or energetic action

²adrenal \"\ *n* -S **:** ADRENAL GLAND

adrenal corticotrophic hormone *n* **:** ADRENOCORTICOTROPIC HORMONE

ad·re·nal·ec·to·mize \ə,drēnᵊl'ektə,mīz, a-\ *vt* -ED/-ING/-S **:** to excise the adrenal glands of

ad·re·nal·ec·to·my \-təmē\ *n* -ES [²*adrenal* + *-ectomy*] **:** surgical removal of either adrenal gland or both

adrenal gland *n* **:** either of a pair of complex endocrine glands located near the anterior medial border of the kidney and comprising a yellowish lipoid-rich cortex of mesodermal origin and a darker highly vascular medulla of ectodermal origin, the hormone adrenaline being produced by specialized chromaffin cells of the medulla while the cortex forms several hormones significant in control of salt and water balance, sodium and potassium metabolism, and utilization of glucose and certain steroids related to or identical with sex hormones — called also esp. in man *suprarenal gland*

Adren·a·lin \ə'drenᵊlən\ *trademark* — used for a preparation of levorotatory epinephrine

adren·a·line \-ən *also* -,ēn\ *n* -S [¹*adrenal* + *-ine*] **:** EPINEPHRINE — used esp. in physiology

adren·a·lone \-,ōn\ *n* -S [ISV *adrenaline* + *-one*] **:** a crystalline ketone $(HO)_2C_6H_3COCH_2NHCH_3$ that yields racemic epinephrine on hydrogenation; 3,4-dihydroxy-α-methylamino⸗acetophenone

adren·er·gen \ə'drenərjən\ *n* -S [*adren-* + *-ergen* (fr. Gk *ergon* work) — more at WORK] **:** a drug having a physiologic action resembling that of adrenaline

ad·re·ner·gic \¦adrə¦nərjik\ *adj* [*adren-* + Gk *ergon* work + E *-ic*] **1** *of autonomic nerve fibers* **a :** liberating adrenaline or a substance like adrenaline **b :** activated by adrenaline — compare CHOLINERGIC **2** *of drugs and their action* **:** like or like that of adrenaline

adre·nin \ə'drēnən, -ren-\ *or* **adre·nine** \", ə'dre,nēn\ *n* -S [*adren-* + *-in, -ine*] **:** EPINEPHRINE

adreno·chrome \ə'drenə,krōm, -ēn-\ *n* -S [*adren-* + *-chrome*] **:** a red-colored mixture of quinones derived from epinephrine by oxidation and yielding a melaninlike product on further oxidation

adre·no·cor·ti·cal \ə¦drēnō¦kȯrd·əkəl, -en-\ *also* **ad·re·nal·cor·ti·cal** \ə¦drēnᵊl¦-, (')a¦d-\ *adj* [*adren-* or ¹*adrenal* + *cortical*] **:** of, belonging to, or derived from the cortex of the adrenal glands ⟨~ hormones⟩

adre·no·cor·ti·co·trop·ic \ə'drē(,)nō¦kȯrd·əkō¦träpik, -e(,)n-\ *or* **adre·no·cor·ti·co·troph·ic** \-rāfik, -ōf-\ *adj* [*adren-* + *cortico-* + *-trophic* or *-tropic*] **:** acting on or stimulating the adrenal cortex

adrenocorticotropic hormone *n* **:** a protein produced by the anterior lobe of the pituitary gland that has a stimulatory effect on the adrenal cortex and a diabetogenic action — compare CORTICOTROPHIN

adre·no·gen·i·tal syndrome \ə¦drēnō¦jenəd·ᵊl-, -dren-\ *n* [*adren-* + *genital*] **:** CUSHING'S DISEASE

adre·no·lyt·ic \ə¦drēnᵊl¦id·ik, -en-\ *adj* [*adren-* + *-lytic*] **:** adrenaline-destroying — used of substances that check the release or action of adrenaline at nerve endings

adre·no·ste·rone \ə¦drēnōstə,rōn, -dren-; ,adrə'nästə,r-\ *n* -S [ISV *adren-* + *-sterone* (fr. *steroid* + *-one*); orig. formed as G *adrenosteron*] **:** a crystalline steroid $C_{19}N_{24}O_3$ obtained from the adrenal cortex and having androgenic activity

adre·no·sym·pa·thet·ic \ə¦drēnō,simpə¦thed·ik, -en-\ *adj* **1 :** of or relating to the adrenergic portion of the autonomic nervous system **2 :** of or involving interaction of the sympathetic nervous system and the adrenal gland

adre·no·troph·ic \ə¦drēnō¦träfik, -en-, -ōfik\ *or* **adre·no·trop·ic** \-äpik\ *adj* [*adren-* + *-trophic* or *-tropic*] **:** ADRENOCORTICOTROPIC

ad·re·nox·ine \,adrə'näk,sēn\ *n* -S [*adren-* + *ox-* + *-ine*] **:** a cardiac inhibitor formed by enzymatic oxidation of either dextrorotatory or levorotatory epinephrine or of tyramine

adret \a'drā\ *n* -S [F, fr. F dial., lit., good side, obverse, fr. *a-* (fr. L *ad-*) + *dret* straight, direct, fr. L *directus* — more at DRESS] **:** a mountain slope so oriented as to receive considerable light and warmth from the sun during the day — used chiefly of the Alps

adri·a·no·ple red \¦ādrēə¦nōpəl- *also* ¦a-\ *n, often cap A* [fr. *Adrianople* (now *Edirne*), Turkey] **:** TURKEY RED

adri·at·ic \¦ādrē¦ad·ik, -atik, -ēk *also* ¦adr-\ *adj, usu cap* [L *Adriaticus, Hadriaticus*, fr. *Adria, Hadria*, ancient Etruscan settlement & seaport in northeast Italy] **:** of or relating to the sea that lies east of Italy

adriatic fig *n, usu cap A* **:** a cultivated fig that does not mature the first crop without caprification

adriatic oak *n, usu cap A* **:** TURKEY OAK

adrift \ə'-\ *adv (or adj)* [¹*a-* + *drift*, v.] **1 :** without motive power and without anchor or mooring **:** DRIFTING ⟨~ for three days on the open ocean⟩ ⟨cut the boat ~⟩ **2 :** without guidance or means of orientation ⟨give to a people morally ~ a code and a belief —Elspeth Huxley⟩ **:** without ties, relations, or security or without a fixed place in society ⟨young men were ~ in a lawless society —Willa Cather⟩ **3 :** in or into a state of being free from restraint or freed from fastenings or supports **:** LOOSE ⟨poorly secured barrels came ~ in the storm⟩

adrip \ə'-\ *adj* [¹*a-* + *drip*, v.] **:** DRIPPING ⟨he was ~ with perspiration⟩

ad·ro·gate \'adrō,gāt\ *vt* -ED/-ING/-S [L *adrogatus*, var. of *arrogatus*, past part. of *arrogare* to appropriate — more at ARROGATE] **:** ARROGATE 3

ad·ro·ga·tion \,adrō'gāshən\ *n* -S **:** ARROGATION 2

adroit \ə'drȯit\ *adj, sometimes* -ER/-EST [F, fr. *à droit* properly, fr. *à* to, at (fr. L *ad*) + *droit* right, fr. L *directus* straight, direct — more at AT, DRESS] **1 :** dexterous in the use of the hands **2 :** marked by shrewdness, craft, resourcefulness, readiness at devising, or physical skill and address so that one is enabled to cope with difficulty or danger ⟨one of the most ~ technicians ever to have employed the English language —John Mason Brown⟩ ⟨~ leadership⟩ ⟨an ~ tennis player⟩ ⟨his ~ replies to hecklers soon won him a large following⟩ **syn** see CLEVER, DEXTEROUS

adroitly *adv* **:** in an adroit manner

adroitness *n* -ES **:** the quality or state of being adroit **:** skill and readiness **:** DEXTERITY

adroop \ə'-\ *adj* [¹*a-* + *droop*, v.] **:** DROOPING

adrop *n* -S [ME] **1** *obs* **:** a substance (as lead) believed essential to evolving the philosophers' stone **2** *obs* **:** PHILOSOPHERS' STONE 1

ad·ros·tral \(')ad-¦rästrəl\ *adj* [ISV *ad-* + *rostral*; orig. formed as F *adrostrale*] *zool* **:** near the rostrum

adry \ə'drī\ *adj* [¹*a-* + *dry*, adj.] **1** *archaic* **:** THIRSTY **2** *archaic* **:** DRY

ads *pl of* AD

-ads *pl of* -AD

ads *abbr* [L *ad sectam*] at the suit of

ADS *abbr* autograph document signed

ad·sci·ti·tious \¦adsə¦tishəs\ *also* **as·ci·ti·tious** \,asə-\ *adj* [L *adscitus, ascitus* derived, assumed, foreign (fr. past part. of *adsciscere, asciscere* to approve, receive, admit, appropriate, fr. *ad-* + *sciscere* to accept, approve, incho. of *scire* to know) + E *-itious* — more at SCIENCE] **1 :** originating, derived, or acquired from something extrinsic **:** ADVENTITIOUS ⟨an ~ habit rather than an inherent taste⟩ **2 :** SUPPLEMENTAL, ADDITIONAL ⟨~ remarks⟩ — **ad·sci·ti·tious·ly** *adv*

¹ad·script \'adz,kript, -d,sk-\ *adj* [L *adscriptus, ascriptus*, past part. of *adscribere, ascribere* to ascribe, add to — more at ASCRIBE] **1** [influenced in meaning by ML *adscriptitius, adscripticius*] **:** bound to a tract of land so that the right to exact service is transferable from one owner to another ⟨men ~ to their overlord's lands⟩ **2 :** written after ⟨iota ~⟩ **:** printed or written immediately to the right of another letter or character and aligning with it ⟨in the pronunciation transcription \lu:t\ *u* bears an ~ diacritic⟩ — distinguished from *subscript* and *superscript*

²adscript \"\ *n* -S **:** an adscript serf

ad·script·ed \(')⸗¦⸗əd\ *adj* **:** ADSCRIPT 1

ad·scrip·tion \(')⸗¦⸗pshən\ *n* -S [L *adscription-, adscriptio, ascription-, ascriptio* written addition (influenced in meaning by ML *adscriptitius*) — more at ASCRIPTION] **:** the quality or state of being added, annexed, or bound ⟨~ of serfs⟩ ⟨~ of an estate⟩

ad·scrip·ti·tious \¦⸗,⸗p¦tishəs\ *adj* [ML *adscriptitius, adscripticius* (in *adscriptitius glebae* attached to the soil), fr. LL *adscripticius* enrolled, fr. L *adscriptus, ascriptus*] **:** ADSCRIPT 1

ad·scrip·tive \(')⸗¦⸗ptiv\ *adj* [²*adscript* + *-ive*] **:** ADSCRIPT 1

ad·ses·sor \(')ad¦sesə(r)\ *n* -S [by alter.] **:** ASSESSOR

ad·smith \'⸗,⸗\ *n* -S [¹*ad* + *smith*] **:** an advertising-copy writer

ad·sorb \ad'sȯrb, -'z-\ *vt* -ED/-ING/-S [*ad-* + *-sorb* (as in *absorb*)] **:** to take up and hold by adsorption — distinguished from *absorb*

ad·sorb·a·bil·i·ty \(,)⸗,⸗ə'biləd·ē\ *n* -ES **:** the ability to be adsorbed

ad·sorb·a·ble \⸗'⸗bəbəl\ *adj* **:** capable of being adsorbed

ad·sorb·ate \-bət, -,bāt\ *n* -S [ISV *adsorb* + *-ate*] **:** an adsorbed substance

¹ad·sorb·ent \(')⸗¦⸗bənt\ *adj* [*adsorb* + *-ent*] **:** having power, capacity, or tendency to adsorb

²adsorbent \"\ *n* -S **:** a solid or liquid substance that takes up and holds another substance by adsorption

ad·sorp·tion \ad'sȯrpshən, -'z-\ *n* -S [fr. *adsorb*, after E *absorb: absorption*] **:** a taking up by physical or chemical forces of the molecules of gases, of dissolved substances, or of liquids by the surfaces of solids or liquids with which they are in contact — distinguished from *absorption*; compare CHEMISORPTION, SORPTION

adsorption compound *n* **:** a more or less stable combination of varying chemical composition formed between an adsorbing surface and the substance adsorbed — compare ³COMPOUND 2a

adsorption isotherm *n* **:** a curve obtained by plotting at constant temperature the quantity of adsorbate against the concentration of the substance in the original gas or solution

ad·sorp·tive \(')⸗¦⸗tiv\ *adj* **:** relating to adsorption **:** ADSORBENT — **ad·sorp·tive·ly** \-tәvlē\ *adv*

ad·stip·u·late \ad'stipyə,lāt\ *vi* -ED/-ING/-S [L *adstipulatus*, past part. of *adstipulari*, fr. *ad-* + *stipulari* to stipulate — more at STIPULATE] **:** to act as an adstipulator — **ad·stip·u·la·tion** \(,)⸗,⸗⸗'lāshən\ *n* -S

ad·stip·u·la·tor \⸗'⸗⸗,lād·ə(r)\ *n* -S [L, fr. *adstipulatus* + *-or*] **:** an additional party made accessory to a promise or contract in order to provide an agent or attorney or to enable a man to make an agreement that would take effect after his death

adsuki bean *var of* ADZUKI BEAN

ad·sum \'ad,səm, 'äd,sům\ *interj* [L, I am present, 1st pers. sing. pres. ind. of *adesse* to be present — more at ADESSENARIAN] — used to indicate one's presence usu. in answer to a roll call

a due \ä'dü,ā\ *adv* [It, lit., by two] **1 :** TOGETHER — used as a direction in music to two performers to play or sing the same part in unison **2 :** SEPARATELY — used as a direction in music to a group of performers to divide into two parts; compare DIVISI

ad·u·la·res·cence \,ajələ'resᵊn(t)s, -,lā'-\ *n* -S [*adularia* + *-escence* (as in *luminescence*)] **:** the changeable white to pale bluish luster of an adularia cut cabochon

ad·u·lar·ia \,ajə'la(a)rēə\ *also* **ad·u·lar** \'ajə,lär\ *n* -S [*adularia* fr. It, modif. of F *adulaire*, fr. *Adula*, mountain group in Switzerland + F *-aire* -ary; *adular*, modif. of It *adularia*] **:** a transparent or translucent variety of orthoclase of pseudo⸗orthorhombic crystal habit some specimens of which have pearly internal reflections — see MOONSTONE

ad·u·late \'ajə,lāt *also* 'adyə,l- *or* 'adᵊl,-\ *vt* -ED/-ING/-S [back-formation fr. *adulation*, fr. ME *adulacioun*, fr. MF *adulation*, fr. L *adulation-, adulatio*, fr. *adulatus* (past part. of *adulari* to flatter, to wag a tail, perh. fr. *ad-* + a root akin to Skt *vāla, vāra* tail, Lith *valaĩ* horse's tail) + *-ion-, -io* -ion] **1 a :** to praise effusively and slavishly **:** flatter excessively **:** fawn upon ⟨sheepish fools that ~ every decision of their leaders⟩ **b :** to pay homage to without exercising a critical sense of values ⟨a man who respects science without *adulating* it⟩ **2 :** to admire or be devoted to abjectly and excessively ⟨teen-agers *adulating* the newest movie star⟩

ad·u·la·tion \,==ˈāshən\ *n* -S **:** the act of adulating ⟨feasted his self-esteem on their ~ —Aldous Huxley⟩

ad·u·la·tor \'==,ād·ə(r), -atə-\ *n* -S [L, fr. *adulatus* + *-or*] **:** one that adulates

ad·u·la·to·ry \-ə,tōrē, -ōrē, -ri\ *adj* [L *adulatorius*, fr. *adulatus* + *-orius* -ory] **:** characterized by or given to adulation ⟨an ~ speech⟩

adul·lam·ite \ə'dələ,mīt\ *n* -S *usu cap* [*(Cave of) Adullam* + E *-ite* — more at CAVE OF ADULLAM] **:** one of a small group of seceders from a particular political or intellectual position; *esp* **:** one who withdraws to join with others in forming a new group

¹**adult** \ə'dəlt, 'a,dəlt *also* a'd- *or* 'adᵊlt\ *adj* [L *adultus*, past part. of *adolescere* to grow up, fr. *ad-* + *-olescere* (fr. *alescere* to grow, incho. of *alere* to nourish) — more at OLD] **1 :** fully developed (as in size, strength, or intellectual capacity) **:** fully mature **:** GROWN-UP ⟨an ~ man⟩ ⟨an ~ lion⟩ ⟨an ~ plant⟩ **2 :** of or belonging to adults ⟨the standards of the ~ world —*Saturday Rev.*⟩ **3 :** evidencing the maturity (as the intellectual maturity) usu. associated with an adult ⟨his ~ approach to the problem⟩ **4 a :** on a par with the maturity usu. associated with an adult ⟨a thoroughly ~ comedy of manners⟩ **b :** designed for or restricted to adults ⟨~ murder mysteries that children wouldn't like⟩ — **adult·ness** *n* -ES

²**adult** \"\ *n* -S **1 :** one that has arrived at full development esp. in size, strength, or intellectual capacity **:** one that has reached full maturity **2 a** *civil law* **:** a human male after the age of 14 or a human female after the age of 12 **b** *common law* **:** a human male or female after a specific age (as 21)

adult education *n* **:** lecture or correspondence courses for adults usu. not otherwise engaged in formal study

¹**adul·ter·ant** \ə'dəltərənt, -l·trənt\ *n* -S [L *adulterant-, adulterans*, pres. part. of *adulterare*] **:** an adulterating substance or agent

²**adulterant** \"\ *adj* **:** ADULTERATING

¹**adul·ter·ate** \ə'dəltə,rāt, *usu* -ād·+V\ *vb* -ED/-ING/-S [L *adulteratus*, past part. of *adulterare* to pollute, defile, commit adultery, fr. *ad-* + *-ulterare* (fr. *alter* different, other) — more at ELSE] *vt* **1 a :** to corrupt, debase, or make impure by the addition of a foreign or a baser substance **:** prepare (as for sale) with one or more ingredients included that are not part of the alleged substance ⟨*adulterated* food⟩ **b :** to alter or treat (as an article) esp. deceptively in order to give a false value or to hide defects through some method or process not involving the addition of a spurious substance: (1) **:** to remove a valuable or necessary ingredient from ⟨*adulterating* milk by removing the cream⟩ (2) **:** to sell (a commodity) under the name of another commodity (3) **:** to offer as acceptable (what is in reality diseased, infected, or tainted) (4) **:** to conceal artificially the defects of (5) **:** to cause to simulate a better article **2 :** to lessen the full intensity of (as a state of happiness) through the addition of extraneous, incongruous, or discordant elements or through the removal of a vital element **:** lessen the purity of **:** make spurious ~ *vi, obs* **:** to commit adultery

²**adul·ter·ate** \-lterət,-l·trət,-tə,rāt\ *adj* [L *adulteratus*] **1 :** tainted with adultery **:** ADULTEROUS ⟨a perverse and ~ generation —H.M.Jones⟩ **2 :** ADULTERATED, SPURIOUS

adul·ter·a·tion \ə,dəltə'rāshən\ *n* -S [L *adulteration-, adulteratio*, fr. *adulteratus* + *-ion-, -io* -ion] **1 :** the process of adulterating **:** the condition of being adulterated; *esp* **:** the partial substitution of one substance for another without acknowledgment **2 :** an adulterated product

adul·ter·a·tor \ə'dəltə,rād·ə(r), -ātə-\ *n* -S [*adulterate* + *-or*] **1 :** one that adulterates **2** [LL, fr. L *adulteratus* + *-or*] *law* **:** COUNTERFEITER

adul·ter·er \ə'dəltərə(r)\ *n* -S [alter. (influenced by *adultery* & L *adulter*) of ME *advouterer, avouterer*, alter. (influenced by L *adulter* & E words ending in *-er*) of MF *avoutre*, fr. L *adulter* — more at ADULTERY] **:** one that commits adultery; *esp* **:** a man who commits adultery

adul·ter·ess \ə'dəltərəs, -l·trəs\ *n* -ES [alter. of earlier *advoutresse*, alter. of ME *avoutresse*, fr. MF, fr. *avoutre* + *-esse* -ess] **:** a woman who commits adultery

adul·ter·ine \-ltə,rīn, -,rēn, -,rən\ *adj* [L *adulterinus*, fr. *adulterare* + *-inus* -ine] **1 :** relating to or marked by adulteration **:** SPURIOUS ⟨~ drugs⟩ **2 :** without the support of law **:** ILLEGAL ⟨an ~ guild⟩ **3 :** born of adultery ⟨an ~ child⟩

adul·ter·ize \-ltə,rīz\ *vi* -ED/-ING/-S [obs. *adulter* adulterer (fr. L) + *-ize*] *archaic* **:** to commit adultery

adul·ter·ous \-ltərəs,-l·trəs\ *adj* [alter. of ME *advoutrous*, fr. *advoutrie* + *-ous*] **1 :** of, characterized by, or given to adultery ⟨she lived in what was legally an ~ relation —M.R.Cohen⟩ **2** *archaic* **:** ADULTERATED ⟨an ~ mixture, brewed up of nauseous ingredients —Tobias Smollett⟩ — **adul·ter·ous·ly** *adv*

adul·tery \ə'dəltərē, -l·trē, -ri\ *n* -ES [ME *adulterie*, alter. (influenced by L *adulterium*) of *advoutrie, avoutrie*, fr. MF *avoutrie*, alter. of OF *avoutire*, fr. L *adulterium*, fr. *adulter* adulterer, back-formation fr. *adulterare* to pollute, defile, commit adultery — more at ADULTERATE] **1 :** voluntary sexual intercourse between a married man and someone other than his wife or between a married woman and someone other than her husband ⟨if a man commits ~ with the wife of his neighbor, both the adulterer and the adulteress shall be put to death —Lev 20:10 (RSV)⟩ — compare FORNICATION **2 a :** unchastity of thought or act ⟨every one who looks at a woman lustfully has already committed ~ with her in his heart —Mt 5:28 (RSV)⟩ **b :** religious infidelity; *esp* **:** IDOLATRY ⟨she polluted the land, committing ~ with stone and tree —Jer 3:9 (RSV)⟩

adult·hood \ə'dəl,tu̇d, -lt,hu̇d\ *n* -S **:** the state or time of being an adult

adult·i·ci·dal \ə¦dəltə¦sīdᵊl\ *adj* **:** of, relating to, or being an adulticide

adult·i·cide \ə'dəltə,sīd\ *n* -S [*adult* + *-i-* + *-cide*] **:** an insecticide used to kill adult insects — compare LARVICIDE

adult·ly \ə'dəltlē, 'a,d-, a'd-, -li\ *adv* **:** in a manner typical of an adult ⟨you're too ~ serious —Aldous Huxley⟩ ⟨~ uncompromising⟩

adult·ness \-tnəs\ *n* -ES **:** the quality or state of being adult; *esp* **:** intellectual maturity usu. associated with an adult ⟨an ~ in the quality of his dialogue —R.A.Cordell⟩

adult·oid \ə'dəl,tȯid\ *n* -S *biol* **:** an immature individual that resembles an adult

ad·um·brate \'adəm,brāt, a'd-,ə'd-\ *vt* -ED/-ING/-S [L *adumbratus*, past part. of *adumbrare*, fr. *ad-* + *umbra* shadow — more at UMBRAGE] **1 a :** to foreshadow, symbolize, or prefigure esp. in a not altogether conclusive or not immediately evident way ⟨social unrest *adumbrated* the French Revolution⟩ **b :** to suggest, indicate, or point out in advance ⟨an invention that *adumbrated* automation⟩ **c :** FORESEE, PREDICT **2 a :** to give a sketchy representation of **:** outline broadly, omitting details ⟨there was only time to ~ the plan⟩ **b :** to suggest, indicate, or disclose partially and with a purposeful avoidance of precision ⟨the meaning of the poem is *adumbrated* in its title⟩ **3 a :** SHADE **b :** to cast a shadow over **:** DARKEN **:** throw a gloomy pall upon ⟨bubbling optimism, not at all *adumbrated* by difficulties⟩ **c :** to conceal partially **:** OBSCURE

ad·um·bra·tion \,a(,)dəm'brāshən\ *n* -S [L *adumbration-, adumbratio*, fr. *adumbratus* + *-ion-, -io* -ion] **1 :** the action of adumbrating or state of being adumbrated **2 a :** a faint sketch **:** an imperfect portrayal or representation **:** OUTLINE **b** *heraldry* **:** the shadow or outlines of a figure **3 :** a vague foreshadowing **4 :** OVERSHADOWING, SHADE

adum·bra·tive \a'dəmbrəd·iv, ə'd-, 'adəm,brād-\ *adj* **:** ADUMBRATING — **adum·bra·tive·ly** *adv*

Ad·u·rol \'adə,rōl, 'ajə-, -ōl\ *trademark* — used for either of two white crystalline photographic developing agents

¹**adust** \ə'dəst, (')a¦d-\ *adj* [ME, fr. L *adustus*, past part. of *adurere* to set fire to, inflame, fr. *ad-* + *urere* to burn — more at EMBER] **1 :** dried up with heat **:** BURNED, SCORCHED, PARCHED ⟨a vast desert all ~⟩ **2** *archaic* **:** of a burned or esp. sunburned appearance ⟨a tall, thin man, of an ~ complexion —Sir Walter Scott⟩ **3 :** of a gloomy appearance or disposition ⟨a wizened ~ old servant⟩

²**adust** \"\ *n* -S **:** LEATHER 4

adus·ti·o·sis \ə,dəstē'ōsəs, (,)a,d-, -dəschē-\ *n, pl* **adustioses** \-ō,sēz\ [NL, fr. L *adustus* + *-i-* + *-osis*] **:** a physiological breakdown of the rind of citrus fruit (as lemons) causing a reddish discoloration — called also *red blotch*

adv *abbr* **1** ad valorem **2** advance **3** *usu cap* advent **4** adverb; adverbial **5** advertisement; advertising **6** advice **7** advise; advisory **8** *often cap* advocate

advai·ta \əd'vīd·ə\ *n, usu cap* [Skt, fr. *a-* ²a- + *dvaita* duality, fr. *dvi* two — more at TWO] **:** Vedantic nondualism that denies the separateness of any aspect of reality from the impersonal oneness of Brahma

ad va·lo·rem \¦advə¦lōrəm, -ȯr-, -,rem\ *adj* [L, according to the value] **1** *of a tax on goods* **:** imposed at a rate percent of the value as stated in an invoice rather than as a specific sum for a given quantity or number **2** *of a property tax* **:** levied according to assessed value — abbr. *ad val.*

¹**ad·vance** \əd'van(t)s, -aa(ə)n-,-ain-,-ȧn- *also* ad-\ *vb* -ED/-ING/-S [ME *advauncen*, alter. (influenced by L *ad-*) of *avauncen*, fr. OF *avancier*, fr. (assumed) VL *abantiare*, fr. L *abante* before, from before, fr. *ab-* + *ante* before — more at ANTE-] *vt* **1 :** to move forward along a course or toward a terminus or goal **:** make to proceed or to progress ⟨preparing to ~ his pawn⟩ **:** FORWARD ⟨finding ways to ~ the job more rapidly⟩: **a :** to accelerate the progress or hasten the development of ⟨~ the ripening of fruit⟩ **b :** to help on or aid the success or improvement of **:** FURTHER ⟨volunteers soliciting funds to ~ the work of the society⟩ ⟨used propaganda to ~ their cause⟩ ⟨*advancing* his own interests at the expense of his friend's⟩ **2 :** to raise in rank or position **:** PROMOTE ⟨the rank of lieutenant, to which he was *advanced* in 1940⟩ ⟨was *advanced* to the priesthood⟩ ⟨*advanced* him over the heads of his seniors⟩ **:** raise in importance ⟨in *advancing* the husband in the office, the corporation is quite likely to ~ him socially —W.H.Whyte⟩ **3** *obs* **:** EXTOL, MAGNIFY, LAUD ⟨greatly *advancing* his gay chivalry —Edmund Spenser⟩ **4 :** to supply or provide ahead of time: **a** *law* **:** to furnish by way of an advancement **b :** to supply (as money or other value) beforehand in expectation of repayment or other future adjustment ⟨~ an employee a week's pay as a loan⟩ ⟨to farmers willing to raise soybeans, seed is *advanced* by the company —*Amer. Guide Series: Mich.*⟩ **5** *archaic* **:** to lift up **:** RAISE, ELEVATE ⟨*advanced* their eyelids —Shak.⟩ **6 :** to bring forward in time: **a :** to make earlier (as an event or date) **:** HASTEN ⟨first scheduled for Nov. 1, then *advanced* to Oct. 15⟩ **b :** to bring or set forward to a later time **:** make or place later ⟨modern scholarship has *advanced* the date of composition from the first to the second century A.D.⟩ **c :** to readjust (the timing of an ignition spark) so that ignition occurs earlier with reference to top dead center in the piston stroke **7 a :** to set, push, or thrust forward, ahead, or to or toward the front **:** cause to go on ⟨cautiously *advancing* one foot⟩ ⟨*advanced* the tunnel 10 feet a day⟩ ⟨~ the hands of a clock⟩ **b** *phonetics* (1) **:** to move (the tongue) further forward (2) **:** FRONT **8 :** to bring forward for notice, consideration, or acceptance **:** bring to view **:** OFFER, PROPOSE ⟨~ an opinion⟩ ⟨explanations were *advanced* and rejected⟩ ⟨those *advancing* a claim to the vacant throne⟩ **9 :** to raise in rate **:** INCREASE ⟨measures to keep landlords from *advancing* rents unfairly⟩ ⟨*advancing* the price of gasoline twice in one week⟩ ~ *vi* **1 :** to move forward **:** go or come forward **:** PROCEED ⟨opened the door and *advanced* into the room⟩ ⟨saw in the distance another lantern *advancing* toward them —Anne D. Sedgwick⟩ ⟨the infantry *advanced* to the attack⟩ ⟨the physicist, accustomed to . . . *advancing* from certainty —*Amer. Scholar*⟩ **2 :** to increase or make progress ⟨a question on which knowledge is *advancing*⟩ ⟨as he *advanced* in age and stature he *advanced* in knowledge⟩ ⟨their children are *advancing* toward maturity⟩ ⟨sagebrush and juniper are *advancing* at the expense of grass —G.R.Stewart⟩ **3 :** to rise in rank, position, or importance ⟨at 30 he had already *advanced* to colonel⟩ ⟨the family has *advanced* to a position of influence in the community⟩ ⟨the self-made man . . . who *advanced* through his own unaided efforts —R.B.Morris⟩ ⟨have a fair chance to ~⟩ **4 :** to rise in rate or price ⟨as wages *advanced*, so did the cost of living⟩ ⟨government securities *advanced* steadily⟩ **5** *of a color* **:** to seem to come forward toward the viewer **:** stand out to the eye ⟨deep colors ~⟩ — contrasted with *recede*

syn FORWARD, FURTHER, PROMOTE: these four verbs signify in common to help to move ahead. ADVANCE, FORWARD, and FURTHER are virtually interchangeable. If a distinction exists it is perhaps that ADVANCE more than the others lays stress on the movement forward or the effectiveness of the assistance to that end ⟨these policies had been considerably *advanced* during the preceding year —*Americana Annual*⟩ ⟨ever alert to *advance* the cause of the freedom —W.H.Allison⟩ FORWARD is seldom applied to persons and perhaps stresses a little more than ADVANCE the activity or moral force intended to achieve the movement forward ⟨the high school as a means of *forwarding* the education of all youth —T.H.Briggs⟩ ⟨his military operations were successful, *forwarding* the Union cause —T.M. Spaulding⟩ FURTHER may be said, in comparison to ADVANCE and FORWARD, to put the least stress upon the movement forward and a great deal on the activity or force ⟨*furthering* no special school of art, the institute seeks to make the museum a compendium of the evolution and history of art as a whole —*Amer. Guide Series: Minn.*⟩ ⟨to *further* his selfish ends, he kept Monica from marrying the young man of her choice —Ann F. Wolfe⟩ PROMOTE, in the sense pertinent here, usu. implies nothing about a movement forward; it stresses solely the activity of assisting, encouraging, or fostering advancement, esp. openly ⟨she decided to *promote* a crusade to the Holy Land in a specially chartered liner —Carey McWilliams⟩ ⟨a sound forest economy *promotes* the prosperity of agriculture and rural life —A.F.Gustafson⟩ **syn** see in addition CITE

²**advance** \"\ *n* -S **1 :** a moving forward ⟨the ~ of the infantry⟩ ⟨the ~ of the polar caps⟩ ⟨the frontier ~ followed a well-defined pattern —R.A.Billington⟩ **2 a :** forward movement on a course of action or development **:** PROGRESS, IMPROVEMENT ⟨mistaking material ~ for spiritual enrichment —H.J. Laski⟩ ⟨the ~ of farm techniques⟩ ⟨recent ~s in social legislation⟩ **b :** a manifestation of progress or improvement **:** a step forward or beyond ⟨far from being an ~ on its predecessor, his new play is a regression⟩ ⟨a method which was a definite ~ over earlier practices⟩ **3 :** a rise or increase (as in price, value, or amount) **:** addition to the price ⟨during the year many workers won wage ~s⟩ ⟨a year-long ~ in stock prices⟩ **4 :** a first step toward the attainment of a result **:** an approach made (as to gain favor, form an acquaintance, adjust a difference) **:** OVERTURE, TENDER, OFFER ⟨an attitude that discouraged all ~s⟩ ⟨she would certainly misunderstand the most guarded words, the most careful ~s —Joseph Conrad⟩ **5 :** a furnishing of something (as money or goods) before a return is received **:** payment beforehand **:** the money or goods thus furnished **:** money or value supplied beforehand ⟨offered him an ~ to complete the book⟩ ⟨may also make cash ~s to the packers before shipment is made —E.A.Duddy⟩ **6 a :** the translational movement of a body in helical motion (as the forward motion of a screw) **b :** the interval by which an event in a cycle precedes a reference datum **7 :** a story written for a news medium before the actual event ⟨a Halloween ~ written early in October⟩ **8 :** the distance made parallel to the original course of a turning ship from the time of putting the rudder over until the ship is on the new course — **in advance** *adv* **:** BEFORE, AHEAD, BEFOREHAND ⟨the heavy luggage had been sent on *in advance*⟩ ⟨registered for the examination well *in advance*⟩ **:** before receiving an equivalent ⟨to pay *in advance*⟩ — **in advance of** *prep* **:** ahead of **:** BEFORE, BEYOND ⟨a thinker well *in advance of* his time⟩ ⟨designed to persuade customers *in advance of* their visit to the store —A.S.Igleheart⟩

³**ad·vance** \əd'v-,(')ad¦v-\ *adj* [²*advance*] **1 :** given, made, sent, issued, furnished, or received ahead of time or of need ⟨~ payment⟩ ⟨an ~ copy of a book⟩ ⟨~ information⟩ **2 :** going or situated before ⟨sent out an ~ party of soldiers **3 :** forward of major bases of supply ⟨an ~ depot⟩ ⟨~ base⟩

ad·vance·able \-səbəl\ *adj* **:** capable of being advanced

advance agent *also* **advance man** *n* **:** a business representative (as of a theatrical company or a lecturer) who travels ahead in order to make necessary arrangements for the public appearance of his employer

ad·vanced \əd'v- *also* (')ad¦v-\ *adj* [ME *avaunced*, fr. past part. of *avauncen*] **1 :** far on in time or course ⟨a man ~ in years⟩ ⟨an ~ state of exhaustion⟩ ⟨the night was well ~⟩ **2 :** moved or set forward or in the front **:** ADVANCE ⟨~ air bases⟩ ⟨captured by an ~ unit of the infantry⟩ ⟨established a new ~ post⟩ **3 a :** beyond the elementary or introductory **:** carrying on from that which precedes ⟨an ~ course⟩ ⟨~ chemistry⟩ **b :** in front of or beyond others as regards progress or ideas ⟨the most ~ artists and critics⟩ ⟨believed himself to be very ~ in his views⟩ **c :** greatly developed beyond the initial stage ⟨a technologically ~ world⟩ ⟨turbines of an ~ construction⟩ **4 :** having altered from a presumed ancestral state ⟨he regards the jaw as more ~ than those of the Rhodesian group —R.W.Murray⟩ **syn** see LIBERAL

advanced charge *n* **:** a transportation service charge passed on by one carrier to another to be collected from the consignee

advanced credit *n* **:** academic credit allowed by an educational institution to students entering with higher than first-year standing for courses taken elsewhere usu. at a comparable institution

advanced degree *n* **:** a university degree higher than a bachelor's (as a master's or doctor's degree)

advanced fry *n* **:** young fishes having the yolk sac absorbed but not yet being developed into fingerlings

ad·vanc·ed·ly \=ˈ=sədlē\ *adv* **:** in an advanced manner or to an advanced degree

advanced score *n* **:** a partial score in the game of bridge

advanced standing *n* **1 :** the standing of a student who has been granted advanced credit **2 :** ADVANCED CREDIT

advance guard *n* **1 :** a detachment usu. divided into point, advance party, support, and reserve preceding a body of troops on the march to protect it and secure its uninterrupted advance **2 :** AVANT-GARDE — **advance guardist** *n*

ad·vance·ment \=ˈ=smənt\ *n* -S [alter. (influenced by L *ad-*) of ME *avauncement*, fr. OF *avancement*, fr. *avancier* to advance + *-ment* — more at ADVANCE] **1 :** the action of advancing or the state of being advanced: **a :** promotion or elevation to a higher rank or to a position of greater personal dignity or importance ⟨they came, not for personal ~ . . . but literally to establish a New France —B.K.Sandwell⟩ ⟨positions offering excellent opportunities for professional ~⟩ ⟨his ~ to captain came the following year⟩ **b :** furtherance or progression esp. toward perfection or to a higher stage of development **:** a helping or moving forward **:** IMPROVEMENT ⟨programs for the ~ and diffusion of knowledge⟩ ⟨leadership in the ~ of political and economic democracy —Vera M. Dean⟩ ⟨contributed greatly to the ~ of the new organization⟩ **2 :** property given usu. by a parent to a child in advance of a future distribution **:** an irrevocable gift by an intestate during his life of part or all of the donee's anticipated share in the donor's estate upon distribution, differing from an absolute gift in that it is charged against the donee's future share in the estate and from an advance in that the donee cannot be called upon to account for or repay it except by this charging of it **3 :** an advance of money or value

advance note *n* **:** a draft on owners or agents of a ship drawn by the master for the benefit of a seaman usu. for one month's advance wages

ad·vanc·er \=ˈ=sə(r)\ *n* -S **1 :** one that advances **2** [ME *avauncer*, fr. *avauncen* + *-er*] **:** a second branch of a buck's antler **3 :** PHASE ADVANCER

advances *pres 3d sing of* ADVANCE, *pl of* ADVANCE

advance track *n* **:** a track in a railroad yard for receiving a train as soon as made up

advancing *pres part of* ADVANCE

advancing color *n* **:** any of certain colors (as the yellows and colors closely related to yellow) that tend to appear nearer to the eye than other colors lying in the same plane

ad·van·cive \=ˈ=siv *also* 'ad,v-\ *adj* **:** tending to advance

¹**ad·van·tage** \əd'vantij, -aan-,-ain-,-ȧn-,-ēj *also* ad-\ *n* -S [alter. (influenced by L *ad-*) of ME *avauntage*, fr. MF *avantage*, fr. *avant* before (fr. L *abante*) + *-age* — more at ADVANCE] **1 :** the quality or state of being superior **:** a more favorable or improved position or condition **:** SUPERIORITY ⟨control of the higher ground gave them an ~ over their opponents⟩ ⟨at the end of an hour's play the ~ lay definitely with the challenger⟩ ⟨our present ~ in the air⟩ ⟨gained the ~ by skillful maneuvering⟩ **2 a :** benefit, profit, or gain of any kind ⟨you will be given information to your ~⟩; *esp* **:** benefit resulting from some course of action ⟨a mistake which ironically turned out to his ~⟩ ⟨that can be done with ~ to all of us⟩ ⟨a manuscript that could be cut with ~⟩ **b** *obs* (1) **:** profit or gain in money **:** INTEREST ⟨you neither lend nor borrow upon ~ —Shak.⟩ (2) **:** excess quantity or number **:** SURPLUS ⟨it is but an ~ to the dozen —John Milton⟩ **3** *obs* **a** (1) **:** a place giving superiority **:** vantage ground (2) **:** high or higher ground **:** ELEVATION **b :** a favorable time or occasion **:** OPPORTUNITY **4 :** a factor or circumstance that gives superiority to its possessor or that puts him or it in a favorable or improved position ⟨among the ~s of a small college is its campus life⟩ ⟨a plan whose only ~ was its simplicity⟩ ⟨with none of the ~s of birth, wealth, or good health, he nevertheless rose quickly to the top⟩ ⟨a reputation that he later regarded as more of a handicap than an ~⟩ **5 :** the first point won in tennis after deuce; *also* **:** the score for it — called *advantage in* if won by the server, *advantage out* if won by the receiver **syn** see USE — **have the advantage of :** to have superiority over; *specif* **:** to have or profess a personal knowledge of (someone) that is not reciprocal — often used as a polite disclaimer of acquaintanceship ⟨I'm afraid you *have the advantage of* me⟩ — **to advantage** *adv* **:** so as to produce a favorable impression or effect **:** FAVORABLY, ADVANTAGEOUSLY ⟨shelves arranged to display the books *to advantage*⟩ ⟨a mountain seen *to advantage* in the morning light⟩

²**advantage** \"\ *vb* -ED/-ING/-S [alter. (influenced by L *ad-*) of ME *avauntagen*, fr. MF *avantager*, fr. *avantage*, n.] *vt* **:** to give an advantage to **:** be of benefit to **:** FURTHER, PROMOTE, PROFIT ⟨our present law of libel greatly ~s financial sharks —*Economist*⟩ ⟨considerably *advantaged* by his biological heritage —M.F.A.Montagu⟩ ~ *vi* **:** to derive advantage **:** BENEFIT ⟨the forces that would ~ —V.H.Burnstein⟩

ad·van·ta·geous \¦ad,van¦tājəs, -,van- -,vaan-, -,vȧn-\ *adj* [*advantage* + *-ous*] **:** giving an advantage or the advantage **:** FAVORABLE, PROFITABLE, BENEFICIAL ⟨trade agreements ~ to both countries⟩ ⟨politically ~ to keep the other side guessing⟩ ⟨an unusually ~ financial settlement⟩ **syn** see BENEFICIAL

ad·van·ta·geous·ly *adv* **:** in an advantageous manner

advantage position *n* **:** a position in amateur wrestling in which a contestant has control of his opponent — compare NEUTRAL POSITION

ad·vec·tion \(')ad¦vekshən\ *n* -S [L *advection-, advectio* act of bringing, transportation, fr. *advectus* (past part. of *advehere* to carry to, fr. *ad-* + *vehere* to convey) + *-ion-, io* -ion — more at WAY] **:** the horizontal movement of a mass of air which causes changes in temperature or in other physical properties of air — compare CONVECTION — **ad·vec·tion·al** \-shənᵊl, -shnəl\ *adj*

ad·vec·tive \-ktiv\ *adj* **1 :** causing advection **2 :** relating to advection

ad·ve·hent \(')ad¦vēənt; 'advəhənt, -,hent\ *adj* [L *advehent-, advehens*, pres. part. of *advehere*] **:** AFFERENT

ad·vene \(')ad¦vēn\ *vb* -ED/-ING/-S [L *advenire* to come to, fr. *ad-* + *venire* to come — more at COME] *vi* **:** to become added to something or become a part of it ~ *vt* **:** to come to or reach

ad·ve·nient \(')ad¦vēnyənt, -ēnēənt\ *adj* [L *advenient-, adveniens*, pres. part. of *advenire*] **:** coming from outward causes **:** SUPERADDED, ADVENTITIOUS

ad·vent \'ad,vent, *esp Brit* -,vənt; *sometimes* əd'vent\ *n* -S [ME, fr. ML *adventus*, fr. L, arrival, fr. *adventus*, past part. of *advenire* to come to] **1** *usu cap* **:** the period beginning four Sundays before Christmas and observed by many Christians as a season of prayer and fasting **2** *usu cap* **:** the coming of Christ: **a :** INCARNATION **b :** the coming of Christ as judge on the last day — called also *Second Advent, Second Coming* **3** [L *adventus*] **:** any coming or arrival ⟨the ~ of spring⟩ ⟨changes

that followed the ~ of the railroad and the telegraph⟩ ⟨was watched in his ~ and departure —Mary Webb⟩ ⟨his ~ to the presidency was greeted by the guns of Fort Sumter —Edmund Wilson⟩ ⟨the ~ of the Cold War —*New Yorker*⟩
advent christian *n, usu cap A&C* **:** a member of the Advent Christian Church organized in 1861 under the original name of the Advent Christian Association
ad·ven·tial \(ˈ)ad¦venchəl\ *adj* [L *adventus* (past part.) + E *-ial*] **:** ADVENTITIOUS
ad·vent·ism \ˈad,ven,tizəm, -,vən-; əd'ven-, ad'-\ *n* -s *usu cap* **:** the doctrine that the second coming of Christ and the end of the world are near at hand; *specif* **:** the millenarian doctrine preached by William Miller and followers from 1831 on
[1]**ad·vent·ist** \ˈad,ventəst, -,vən-; əd'ven-, ad'-\ *n* -s *usu cap* [*advent* + *-ist*] **:** a believer in the doctrine of Adventism **:** a member of any of various religious bodies emphasizing this doctrine — called also *Second Adventist*
[2]**adventist** \"\ *adj, usu cap* **:** of or relating to the Adventists or Adventism
ad·ven·ti·tia \,advən'tish(ē)ə, -,ven-\ *n* -s [NL, alter. of L *adventicia*, neut. pl. of *adventicius* coming from outside, fr. *adventus* + *-icius* -icious] **:** an external covering or investment of an organ chiefly derived from the surrounding connective tissue; *esp* **:** the external coat or layer of a blood vessel consisting mostly of fibroelastic connective tissue
ad·ven·ti·tial \¦≈(,)≈¦tishəl\ *adj* [NL *adventitia* + E *-al*] **:** of or relating to an adventitia
adventitial cell *n* **:** MACROPHAGE
ad·ven·ti·tious \-shəs\ *adj* [L *adventicius*] **1 :** coming from another source **:** added or appended extrinsically and not sharing original, essential, and intrinsic nature **:** not inherent or innate ⟨we distinguish between borrowed, ~ energy in verse, and its natural energy —C.D.Lewis⟩ ⟨a disengagement of its own proper ideas from the ~ notions which have crept into it —A.N.Whitehead⟩ ⟨the ~ paraphernalia of 20th century living —*Time*⟩ **2** *biol* **a :** arising sporadically or in other than the usual location ⟨an ~ part in embryonic development⟩ **b :** occurring spontaneously or accidentally in a country or region to which it is not native ⟨~ weeds⟩ ⟨an ~ insect⟩ **3 :** ADVENTITIAL **4 :** not congenital **:** ACQUIRED ⟨~ deafness⟩ **syn** see ACCIDENTAL
adventitious bud *n, bot* **:** a bud arising in other than the normal position (as where elongation has ceased) and lacking a vascular trace — compare TRACE BUD
ad·ven·ti·tious·ly *adv* **:** in an adventitious manner
adventitious membrane *n* **:** a membrane connecting parts not usu. connected or of a different texture from the ordinary connection
ad·ven·ti·tious·ness *n* -ES **:** the quality or state of being adventitious
adventitious root *n* **:** a root that arises from any point other than the radicle or the root axis (as the prop roots of corn arising from the lower stem) — compare AERIAL ROOT; see ROOT illustration
adventitious vein *n* **:** a vein appearing irregularly between the accessory and intercalary veins of the wings of certain insects
[1]**ad·ven·tive** \(ˈ)ad¦ventiv, əd'v-\ *adj* [L *adventus* (past part.) + E *-ive*] **1 :** not native **:** imperfectly naturalized **:** IMMIGRANT ⟨an ~ weed⟩ **2 :** arising in an unusual position **:** ADVENTITIOUS — **ad·ven·tive·ly** *adv*
[2]**adventive** \"\ *n* -s **:** an exotic (as a plant) that is introduced often accidentally and imperfectly naturalized (as in being unable to bear fully mature fruit)
adventive crater *n* [[1]*adventive*] **:** a small volcanic cone or crater on the flanks of a major volcanic cone
advents *pl of* ADVENT
advent sunday *n, usu cap A&S* **:** the first Sunday in Advent
[1]**ad·ven·ture** \əd'venchə(r) *also* ad-\ *n* -s [alter. (influenced by L *ad-*) of ME *aventure*, fr. OF, fr. (assumed) VL *adventura*, fr. L *adventus* (past part. of *advenire* to arrive, happen) + *-ura* -ure — more at ADVENE] **1** *obs* **a :** CHANCE, FORTUNE ⟨wished me fair ~ for the year —John Dryden⟩ **b :** a chance occurrence **:** an unplanned event **2 a** *chiefly marine insurance* **:** chance of loss **:** RISK, JEOPARDY, PERIL **b** *obs* **:** TRIAL, TEST **3 a :** a dangerous or risky undertaking **:** an enterprise or performance involving the uncertain or unknown ⟨an ~ in mountain climbing⟩ ⟨the time had come for drastic changes and bold ~*s* —Drew Middleton⟩ **b :** the encountering of risks **:** hazardous or exciting enterprise or experience ⟨the spirit of ~⟩ ⟨~ was gone from life in Mandalay —F.T. Jesse⟩ ⟨for the sake of the ~⟩ **4 :** a novel, exciting, or otherwise remarkable event or experience ⟨I found delightful ~*s* in the woods —W.B.Yeats⟩ ⟨long-forgotten childhood ~*s*⟩ ⟨hardly a day passed without its ~*s*⟩ **5 a :** an undertaking, enterprise, or venture involving financial risk or speculation esp. in mercantile or mining affairs; *also* **:** the risk incurred **b :** a shipment by a merchant on his own account
[2]**adventure** \"\ *vb* **adventured; adventured; adventuring** \-ch(ə)riŋ\ *vb* **adventures** [alter. (influenced by L *ad-*) of ME *aventuren, auntren*, fr. OF *aventurer*, fr. *aventure*] *vt* **1 :** to expose to possible danger or loss **:** RISK, VENTURE ⟨~ their capital in foreign trade⟩ ⟨so far had he *adventured* himself that I began to be afraid there might be no recovery —Hugh McCrae⟩ ⟨it is usual to ~ the very considerable cost of "wildcat" trial wells —W.G.Fearnsides⟩ ⟨~ himself gingerly into the water —Archibald Marshall⟩ **2 :** to venture upon **:** run the risks of **:** CHANCE, TRY ⟨durst not ~ such unknowen ways —Edmund Spenser⟩ ⟨the last volume I have *adventured* is a very amusing book —H.J.Laski⟩ ⟨invites unbelievers . . . to retrace their steps and ~ Christianity —*Times Lit. Supp.*⟩ **3 :** to suggest venturesomely ⟨~ an opinion⟩ ~ *vi* **1 :** to proceed despite danger or risk **:** venture or hazard oneself (as in a dangerous or unknown region or risky undertaking) **:** DARE ⟨leaps at chances and . . . ~*s* to the shores washed with the farthest sea —J.L.Lowes⟩ ⟨only a madman would have *adventured* down the declivity —W.J.Locke⟩ ⟨David there *adventuring* in the blue, in the Middle Heaven —Mary Austin⟩ **2 :** to take the chance or risk **:** VENTURE ⟨I would ~ for such merchandise —Shak.⟩ ⟨wondering why the English theater is so slow to ~ with his last plays —*Irish Digest*⟩ — **ad·ven·ture·ment** \-mənt\ *n* -s
ad·ven·tur·er \-chərər, -ch(ə)rə\ *n* -s **1 :** one that adventures or seeks or engages in adventures: as **a :** a mercenary fighter **:** a free-lance volunteer **:** SOLDIER OF FORTUNE ⟨reported that the rebel command consisted largely of foreign ~*s*⟩ **b** (1) **:** one that engages or shares in commercial enterprises of considerable risk for profit esp. in foreign countries — compare MERCHANT ADVENTURER (2) *chiefly Brit* **:** a shareholder in a mining company **2 :** a person of uncertain qualifications seeking to attain unmerited wealth or position by sharp practice and dubious methods esp. by playing on the credulity or prejudices of others **:** one that lives by his wits ⟨if he had . . . no aim except to live at my expense, then I should regard him as an ~ —G.B.Shaw⟩ ⟨there were no courtesans . . . there were no ~*s* —F.L.Allen⟩ ⟨ring of political ~*s* —D.D.Martin⟩
ad·ven·ture·some \-chə(r)səm\ *adj* **:** given to incurring risks **:** ADVENTUROUS, VENTURESOME ⟨the risks — and gains — of an ~ economy —*Time*⟩ **syn** see ADVENTUROUS
ad·ven·ture·some·ly *adv* **:** in an adventuresome manner
ad·ven·tur·ess \-ch(ə)rəs\ *n* -ES [*adventurer* + *-ess*] **:** a female adventurer; *esp* **:** a woman who seeks position or livelihood by questionable means ⟨you just sit there . . . and let an ~ ruin your son's life —Josephine Pinckney⟩ ⟨a mercenary ~ who thought only of her 2000 guineas —Max Peacock⟩
ad·ven·tu·rine \əd'vench-\ *n* -s [by folk etymology] **:** AVENTURINE
ad·ven·tur·ism \-chə,rizəm\ *n* -s **1 :** the actions or attitudes of an adventurer **:** disregard of accepted standards of behavior **2 :** adventurous, dangerous, capricious, or haphazard improvisation or experimentation **:** ill-considered or rash adoption of expedients in the absence or in defiance of consistent plans or principles ⟨a personal ~ which is using the whole labor situation as a stamping ground for his own hatreds —*New Republic*⟩ ⟨a policy of sheer ~⟩
ad·ven·tur·ist \-chərəst\ *n* -s **:** one that adheres to adventurism — **ad·ven·tur·is·tic** \≈¦≈chə¦ristik\ *adj*
ad·ven·tur·ous \≈'≈ch(ə)rəs\ *adj* [alter. (influenced by L *ad-*) of ME *aventurous*, fr. MF *aventureos*, fr. *aventure* adventure + *-eos* -ous — more at ADVENTURE] **1 :** having, enjoying, or seeking adventures **:** disposed to encounter dangers or risks or to cope with the new and unknown ⟨Caesar, the most skillful and prudent of generals, was yet as ~ as a knight-errant —J.A.Froude⟩ ⟨encouraged ~ Portuguese captains to push out into the Atlantic —G.C.Sellery⟩ **2 :** characterized by dangers and risks or by new or unknown situations ⟨an ~ period of river history⟩ ⟨my most ~ whaling voyage up to that time —H.A.Chippendale⟩ ⟨regions where life is still somewhat ~⟩
syn ADVENTURESOME, VENTURESOME, VENTUROUS, DARING, DAREDEVIL, TEMERARIOUS, FOOLHARDY, RECKLESS, RASH **:** ADVENTUROUS and the less common ADVENTURESOME may apply to a disposition to encounter danger or to explore the new and unknown ⟨the Dyaks . . . ferocious and *adventurous*, who had no equals in daring either in battles with rivers or in battles with enemies —Agnes N. Keith⟩ ⟨to be *adventurous* — to explore and discover in life as in art —Malcolm Cowley⟩ ⟨Admiral Byrd's *adventuresome* expeditions⟩ ⟨*adventuresome*, I sent my herald thought into a wilderness —John Keats⟩ VENTURESOME and VENTUROUS, the latter now somewhat uncommon, may imply greater willingness to chance danger or risk ⟨in 1919 Alcock and Brown undertook the first and highly *venturesome* crossing of the Atlantic by air —*Manchester Guardian*⟩ ⟨a faint pathway blazed through the wilderness by *venturesome* scouts and trappers from 1827 on —*Amer. Guide Series: Calif.*⟩ ⟨among these rocks that *venturous* feet could reach —William Wordsworth⟩ ⟨emancipation had some interest for *venturous* spirits —T.S.Eliot⟩ DARING may indicate fearlessness or boldness in greater dangers or most extreme ventures ⟨a *daring* and crafty captain, as careless of his own life as of other folk's —Charles Kingsley⟩ ⟨*daring* burglaries by armed men, and highway robberies, took place in the capital itself every night —Charles Dickens⟩ DAREDEVIL may imply the ostentatious, sensational, or bizarre in courting uncommon danger ⟨*daredevil* feats sometimes performed in the sperm-whale fishery —Herman Melville⟩ TEMERARIOUS, FOOLHARDY, RECKLESS, and RASH are mainly uncomplimentary. TEMERARIOUS, relatively uncommon in situations involving physical danger, may refer to actions or efforts ill-advised and overambitious ⟨summaries . . . more *temerarious* and experimental than the body of the book —George Saintsbury⟩ FOOLHARDY usu. describes the needless tempting or incurring of unnecessary dangers with virtually no chance of success ⟨the perfectly *foolhardy* feat of swimming the flood —Sinclair Lewis⟩ RECKLESS may apply to lack of concern about or consideration of the consequences of probable disaster and defeat ⟨he had frightfully dissipated his little capital. How wild and *reckless* he had been —W.M.Thackeray⟩ ⟨a *reckless*, devil-may-care individual who is ready for trouble, even looking for it, his advent into town is usually heralded by pistol shots and the splintering of glass —*Amer. Guide Series: Ariz.*⟩ RASH indicates imprudent haste and lack of thought ⟨like a *rash* exorcist, I was appalled by the spirit I had raised —L.P.Smith⟩ ⟨is it true that you were *rash* enough, mad enough, to speak to these men about murdering Keegan? —Anthony Trollope⟩
ad·ven·tur·ous·ly *adv* **:** in an adventurous manner
ad·ven·tur·ous·ness *n* -ES **:** the quality or state of being adventurous ⟨the insatiable ~ of man's imagination —H.G.Wells⟩
[1]**ad·verb** \ˈad,vərb, -əb\ *n* -s [MF *adverbe*, fr. L *adverbium* (translation of Gk *epirrhēma*, lit., that which is said afterwards), fr. *ad-* + *-verbium* (fr. *verbum* word, verb) — more at EPIRRHEMA, WORD] **1 :** a word belonging to one of the major form classes in any of a great many languages typically used as a modifier of a verb, an adjective, another adverb, a preposition, a phrase, a clause, or a sentence and typically expressing some relation of manner or quality (as *well* in "she sings well", *surprisingly* in "surprisingly slow"), place (as *here* in "sit here"), time (as *now* in "now under consideration"), degree (as *too* in "too hastily", *rather* in "rather near us"), number (as *triply* in "triply bound"), cause (as *therefore* in "therefore the statement is true"), opposition (as *however* in "if however this proves impossible"), affirmation (as *certainly* in "he certainly did"), or denial (as *not* in "he did not"), sometimes having degrees of comparison expressed by affixation (as *soon, sooner, soonest*), suppletion (as *well, better, best*), or periphrasis (as *happily, more happily, most happily*) but otherwise uninflected, and frequently formed with a characteristic derivative affix (as *-ward, -wards* in "homeward", "homewards", *-wise* in "clockwise", and *-ly* in "aptly"), this last being esp. frequent since it is the principal means of forming adverbs from adjectives **2 adverbs** *pl but sing or pl in constr* **:** a game whose object is to guess an adverb by interpreting verbal or pantomimic answers given in the manner of the adverb chosen
[2]**adverb** \"\ *adj* **:** of or belonging to an adverb **:** functioning as an adverb usu. by modifying a verb or adjective ⟨an ~ phrase⟩ ⟨an ~ clause⟩
ad·verb·al \(ˈ)ad¦vərbəl, -əb-\ *adj* [*ad-* + *verb* + *-al*] **:** modifying a verb
adverb equivalent *n* **:** a word not otherwise an adverb or a word group that has one of the typical functions of an adverb (as *months* in "we have waited months for this", *without leave* in "absent without leave", *in the corner* in "stand it there in the corner", *when I can* in "I'll write when I can")
ad·verb·i·al \(ˈ)ad¦vərbēəl, əd'v-, -əb-\ *adj* [LL *adverbialis*, fr. L *adverbium* + *-alis* -al] **1 :** being an adverb (in some sentences the word *likely* is ~ rather than adjectival) **:** of or belonging to an adverb ⟨the ~ suffix *-ly*⟩ **2 :** having one of the typical functions of an adverb ⟨an ~ phrase⟩ ⟨an ~ clause⟩ ⟨the ~ noun *months* in "to wait months"⟩ — **ad·verb·i·al·ly** \-əlē, -li\ *adv*
ad ver·bum \(ˈ)ad'vərbəm, -er-\ [L] **:** to a word **:** VERBATIM
ad ve·re·cun·di·am \¦ad,verə'kəndē,am -ēəm\ [L] **:** to modesty — used of an argument
ad·ver·sar·ia \,advə(r)'sa(a)rēə\ *n pl but sing or pl in constr* [L, journal, memorandum, fr. neut. pl. of *adversarius* turned toward] **1 :** commentaries or notes (as on a text or document) **2 :** a miscellaneous collection of notes, remarks, or selections **:** COMMONPLACE BOOK
[1]**ad·ver·sary** *R* 'advə(r),serē, *-R* -və,s-; -ri\ *n* -ES [ME, fr. MF & L; ME *adversere*, fr. MF *adversier*, fr. L *adversarius*; ME *adversarie*, fr. L *adversarius*, fr. *adversarius*, adj., turned toward, antagonistic toward, fr. *adversus* (past part. of *advertere* to turn to) + *-arius* -ary — more at ADVERT] **1 :** one that contends with, opposes, or resists **:** ANTAGONIST, OPPONENT, ENEMY, FOE ⟨do as *adversaries* do in law, strive mightily but eat and drink as friends —Shak.⟩ ⟨powers of sarcasm that made him feared as an ~⟩ ⟨the sea powers have repeatedly succeeded in defeating their continental *adversaries* —G.H.Miller⟩ **2 a :** an opponent in a game **b :** an opponent of the declarer in the game of bridge or of the player who plays the dummy
[2]**adversary** \"\ *adj* [ME, fr. L *adversarius*] **1** *archaic* **:** OPPOSED, ADVERSE, ANTAGONISTIC **2 :** having or involving opposing antagonistic parties or interests **:** involving the Anglo-American system of procedure for conducting trials under strict rules of evidence with the right of cross-examination and argument, one party with his witnesses striving to prove the facts essential to his case and the other party striving to disprove those facts or to establish an affirmative defense **:** CONTESTED, LITIGATED
ad·ver·sa·tive \əd'vərsəd·iv, -əs-, -əis-, ad-\ *adj* **:** expressive or indicative of antithesis, opposition, adverse circumstance, reservation, or contrary suggestion ⟨an ~ proposition⟩ ⟨the ~ conjunctions *but, only, still, yet*⟩ ⟨an ~ clause such as *although it was raining* in "although it was raining, the race started"⟩ — **ad·ver·sa·tive·ly** \-d·əvlē\ *adv*
[1]**ad·verse** \(ˈ)ad¦vərs, -əs, -əis *also* əd'v-\ *adj* [ME, fr. MF *advers*, fr. L *adversus* (past part. of *advertere* to turn to) — more at ADVERT] **1 :** acting against or in a contrary direction **:** OPPOSING ⟨~ winds⟩ ⟨hindered by ~ forces⟩ **:** HOSTILE, OPPOSED, ANTAGONISTIC ⟨her feelings were still ~ to any man save one —Jane Austen⟩ ⟨a spirit ~ to class distinctions⟩ **2 a :** in opposition to one's interests **:** DETRIMENTAL, UNFAVORABLE ⟨an ~ balance of trade⟩ ⟨circumstances ~ to success⟩ ⟨~ fortune⟩ ⟨an ~ verdict⟩ **b :** tending to stress faults and withhold praise **:** CONDEMNATORY, CRITICAL ⟨irritated by ~ reviews of his play⟩ ⟨overheard several ~ comments⟩ **3 a :** opposite in position **:** CONFRONTING ⟨Calpe's ~ height —Lord Byron⟩ ⟨the two ~ carriages would therefore, to a certainty, be traveling on the same side —Thomas De Quincey⟩ **b** *bot* **:** turned toward the stem or axis ⟨~ leaves⟩ — opposed to *averse* **4** *law* **:** having opposing interests **:** having interests for the preservation of which opposition is essential
syn INIMICAL, ANTAGONISTIC, COUNTER, COUNTERACTIVE **:** ADVERSE describes what is unfavorable, harmful, difficult, detrimental; it may refer to opposition, often decisive or fateful opposition ⟨what very small things in *adverse* circumstances suffice to make people happy — a little food, warmth, and something to look forward to —Hervey Allen⟩ ⟨an *adverse* wind had so delayed him that his cargo brought but half its proper price —Amy Lowell⟩ INIMICAL may describe strongly adversative or prejudicial tendencies or effects or determinedly hostile persons, sometimes malevolent ⟨the fact of universal elementary education is *inimical* to poetry —C.D.Lewis⟩ ⟨nor was Miss Briggs, although forced to adopt a hostile attitude, secretly *inimical* to Rawdon —W.M.Thackeray⟩ ANTAGONISTIC, more frequently applied to persons than to things, may suggest incompatibility, antipathy, irreconcilability, or hostile opposition ⟨the West Indian planters, upon whom the successful working of the system largely depended, were not merely unsympathetic but violently *antagonistic* to it —*Times Lit. Supp.*⟩ ⟨the *antagonistic* principles of aristocracy and democracy —V.L.Parrington⟩ COUNTER may be applied to opposition, to action or tendency in an opposing direction, sometimes to parrying, retaliation, or reprisal ⟨as I reached the limit of my swing and prepared to rush back on the *counter* swing —Jack London⟩ ⟨currents and *counter* currents⟩ ⟨a *counter* threat that the interdict would be followed by the banishment of the clergy —J.R.Green⟩ COUNTERACTIVE refers to opposition tending to check, nullify, or destroy ⟨*counteractive* measures against the epidemic⟩
[2]**adverse** \"\ *vt* -ED/-ING/-S **:** OPPOSE ⟨~ a land patent⟩
ad·verse·ly \-lē, -li\ *adv* **1 :** in an adverse or hostile manner **:** with hostile effect **2 :** UNFAVORABLY, DISADVANTAGEOUSLY
adverse possession *n* **:** a possession that is hostile, under a claim or color of title, actual, open, notorious, exclusive, and continuous, continued for the required period of time (generally 20 years) thereby giving an indefeasible right of possession or ownership to the possessor by operation of the limitation of actions
adverse witness *n, law* **:** a hostile witness
ad·ver·si·ty \ad'vərsəd·ē, əd'v-, -əs-, -əis-, -sətē, -i\ *n* -ES [ME *adversite* (also, opposition), fr. OF *adversité, aversité*, fr. LL *adversitat-, adversitas*, fr. L, opposition, fr. *adversus* + *-itat-, -itas* -ity] **1 :** a state of adverse fortune **:** a condition of suffering, destitution, or affliction often implying previous prosperity or well-being ⟨what fairy palaces we may build of beautiful thought — proof against all ~ —John Ruskin⟩ ⟨showed unexpected courage in ~⟩ **2 :** a stroke of ill fortune **:** a calamitous or disastrous experience — usu. used in pl. ⟨a period marked by *adversities* and misfortunes⟩
ad·ver·sive \(ˈ)ad¦vərsiv, əd'v-\ *adj* [[1]*adverse* (opposite) + *-ive*] *anat* **:** OPPOSITE
[1]**ad·vert** \ad'vərt, əd'v-, -ət, -əit, *usu* -d·+V\ *vb* -ED/-ING/-S [ME *averten, adverten*, fr. MF & L; MF *avertir, advertir*, fr. L *advertere*, fr. *ad-* + *vertere* to turn — more at WORTH] *vi* **1 :** to turn the mind or attention **:** pay heed or attention — used with *to* ⟨surely our present-day positivists can never indicate what is good for man without ~*ing* to his nature —J.A.McWilliams⟩ ⟨cosmologies that Freud, when he ~*ed* to them at all, regarded as too highbrow to be given the name of religion —David Riesman⟩ **2 :** to direct or call attention in the course of speaking or writing **:** REFER, ALLUDE — used with *to* ⟨will be ~*ed* to here, but will be dealt with more fully in other chapters —T.E.May⟩ ⟨~*ed* briefly to the circumstances of their first meeting⟩ ~ *vt* **1** *obs* **:** to turn the attention to **:** OBSERVE, CONSIDER **2 :** to give warning of **:** make aware **:** WARN
[2]**ad·vert** \ˈad,vərt, -ət\ *n* -s [by shortening] *chiefly Brit* **:** ADVERTISEMENT
ad·vert·ence \ad'vərtᵊn(t)s, əd-, -ət-, -əit-\ *n* -s [ME, fr. MF *avertence, advertence*, fr. *avertir, advertir* + *-ence*] **1 :** the action or process of adverting **:** ATTENTION, NOTICE, REFERENCE ⟨to this difference it is right that ~ should be had in regulating taxation —J.S.Mill⟩ ⟨selected samples with no ~ to the usefulness of controls in a scientific study —W.A.Harvey⟩ **2 :** ADVERTENCY 1
ad·vert·en·cy \-nsē, -i\ *n* -ES **1 :** the quality or state of being advertent **:** HEEDFULNESS **2 :** ADVERTENCE 1
ad·vert·ent \(ˈ)ad¦vərtᵊnt, əd'v-, -ət-, -əit-\ *adj* [L *advertent-, advertens*, pres. part. of *advertere* to advert — more at ADVERT] **:** giving attention **:** HEEDFUL — **ad·vert·ent·ly** *adv*
ad·ver·tis·a·ble \¦advə(r)¦tīzəbəl\ *adj* **:** capable of being effectively advertised
ad·ver·tise \ˈadvə(r),tīz *also* ,≈≈'≈\ *also* **ad·ver·tize** \"\ *vb* -ED/-ING/-S [ME *avertisen, advertisen*, fr. MF *avertiss-, advertiss-*, stem of *avertir, advertir* — more at ADVERT] *vt* **1 a :** to make known to (someone) **:** give notice to **:** INFORM, NOTIFY ⟨one does not need to ~ the squirrels where the nut trees are —J.R.Lowell⟩ ⟨the translators . . . were careful to ~ the reader that what they offered was Le Clerc's *Moreri* —*Times Lit. Supp.*⟩ — often used with *of* ⟨of which we have been *advertised* by the same authority —Jane Austen⟩ ⟨it seemed to Nathan as if the entire neighborhood were being *advertised* of the fact —Mary S. Watts⟩ **b** *obs* **:** WARN, ADMONISH — used with the infinitive ⟨St. Paul *advertised* all women to give a good ensample of . . . godliness —Hugh Latimer⟩ **2 :** to make generally known **:** call attention to **:** give notice of: **a :** to give publicity to ⟨extravagantly *advertised* by Swinburne —T.S.Eliot⟩ ⟨this renowned establishment, widely *advertised* in . . . works of fiction —N.F.Busch⟩ ⟨began deliberately *advertising* his willingness to make concessions —*Time*⟩ ⟨that higher *advertising* of England which has employed so many distinguished pens —F.R.Leavis⟩ **b :** to make conspicuous ⟨no tall man can be a successful pickpocket, because he must bend to his work, and so ~ it to every beholder —Arthur Morrison⟩ ⟨unrecognizable save by their fragrance and lean stamens, *advertised* neither by color nor form of blossom —William Beebe⟩ **c** (1) **:** to give public notice of **:** announce publicly esp. by a printed notice or through a radio or television broadcast ⟨the return of Sir Victor with Lady Pandolfo . . . had been officially *advertised* —W.J.Locke⟩ ⟨*advertised* him as their jail editor —Walter Lippmann⟩ ⟨a poster *advertising* forthcoming events⟩ ⟨enlist the aid of disc jockeys in *advertising* a rummage sale⟩ (2) **:** to call public attention to esp. by emphasizing desirable qualities so as to arouse a desire to buy or patronize ⟨~ a breakfast food⟩ ⟨spent a fortune *advertising* their filter-tip cigarettes⟩ ~ *vi* **:** to issue a public statement (as through printed notices, radio or television broadcasts) of something offered or wanted ⟨~ in the lost-and-found column⟩ ⟨~ for a stenographer⟩ ⟨business increased soon after they began to ~ on the radio⟩ **syn** see DECLARE, INFORM
ad·ver·tise·ment \,advə(r)'tīzmənt *also* '≈≈,≈≈; əd'vər\d·əz-, ad-, -vəl,-vəi|, -|tə-, -əs-\ *also* **ad·ver·tize·ment** \"\ *n* -s [ME, fr. MF *avertissement, advertissement*, fr. *avertiss-, advertiss-* + *-ment*] **1 :** the action of advertising **:** a calling attention to or making known: as **a** *obs* **:** WARNING, ADMONITION **b** *obs* **:** an informing or notifying **:** NOTIFICATION **c :** a calling to public attention **:** PUBLICITY ⟨the limitations we have imposed will receive wide ~ in other parts of colonial Asia —*Atlantic*⟩ ⟨an unwarranted amount of ~ for an unattractive group —W.E.Swinton⟩ **2 a** *archaic* **:** a statement calling attention to something **:** NOTICE ⟨the publisher's ~ to the reader⟩ **b :** a public notice; *esp* **:** a paid notice or announcement published in some public print (as a newspaper, periodical, poster, or handbill) or broadcast over radio or television ⟨a full-page ~⟩ ⟨the classified ~*s*⟩ — compare COMMERCIAL
advertisement curtain *n* **:** a theater curtain covered with the advertisements of local businesses
ad·ver·tis·er \ˈadvə(r),tīzə(r) *also* ,≈≈'≈≈\ *also* **ad·ver·tiz·er** \"\ *n* -s **:** one that advertises
advertising *also* **advertizing** *n* -s *often attrib* **1 :** the action of calling something (as a commodity for sale, a service offered or desired) to the attention of the public esp. by means of printed or broadcast paid announcements **2 :** ADVERTISEMENTS ⟨a magazine containing a great deal of ~⟩ ⟨the ~ pages of the Sunday paper⟩ **3 :** the business or profession

of designing and preparing advertisements for publication or broadcast ⟨an ~ firm⟩ ⟨a career in ~⟩ ⟨began to work for the ~ department of a small insurance firm —*Current Biog.*⟩
ad·ver·to·ri·al \ˌadvə(r)ˈtōrēəl\ *n* -s [blend of *advertisement* and *editorial*] **:** a report in the form of a paid advertisement intended to provide information to the public esp. about some aspect of business activity and usu. sponsored by a commercial or industrial organization or a group of allied organizations
adverts *pres 3d sing of* ADVERT, *pl of* ADVERT
ad·vice \ədˈvīs *also* ad-\ *n* -s [alter. of ME *avise, advise,* fr. OF *avis, advis* opinion, judgment, prob. fr. *a vis* apparent (as in *ce m'est a vis* that appears to me), fr. *a* to, at, in (fr. L *ad*) + *vis* view, opinion, fr. L *visus* appearance, probability, fr. *visus,* past part. of *vidēre,* to see — more at AT, WIT] **1** *obs* **:** the way in which one regards something **:** VIEW, OPINION ⟨with power to make known their ~ —Thomas Hobbes⟩ **2** *obs* **:** careful thought **:** CONSIDERATION, DELIBERATION ⟨consider of it, take ~, and speak your minds —Judg 19:30 (AV)⟩ **3 :** recommendation regarding a decision or course of conduct **:** COUNSEL ⟨among strangers, remote from the eye and ~ of my father —Benjamin Franklin⟩ ⟨the leader's commands, the priest's exhortations, and the philosopher's ~ —Alan Gregg⟩ ⟨my ~ to you is — don't do it⟩ ⟨to seek medical ~⟩ **4 :** information or notice given **:** INTELLIGENCE, NEWS ⟨and at last ~ had gone on a hunger strike —*Canadian Forum*⟩ — usu. used in pl. ⟨the latest ~s from our Paris correspondent⟩ ⟨had ~s that Casale was sufficiently provisioned to last for many months —Hilaire Belloc⟩ **5 :** a formal or official notice sent by one person or office to another concerning a business transaction ⟨a remittance ~⟩ ⟨shipping ~s⟩: as **a :** a letter by which the drawer of a bill of exchange notifies the drawee that the bill has been issued — called also *letter of advice* **b** (1) **:** a descriptive notice sent by a post office issuing an international money order to the post office which is to make payment (2) **:** a notice concerning a postal shipment (as one to the sender informing him of delivery to the addressee)
advice boat *n, archaic* **:** DISPATCH BOAT
adviceful *adj* **1** *obs* **:** THOUGHTFUL, ATTENTIVE **2** *obs* **:** skillful in giving advice
ad·vis·a·bil·i·ty \əd,vīzəˈbilədē, -ətē, -i *also* ad,v-\ *n* -ES **:** the quality of being advisable **:** DESIRABILITY, EXPEDIENCY
ad·vis·a·ble \-ˈzəbəl\ *adj* **1 :** proper to be advised or to be done **:** EXPEDIENT, PRUDENT ⟨neither necessary nor ~⟩ ⟨extreme caution is ~⟩ **2 :** ready to receive advice **:** open to advice **syn** see EXPEDIENT
ad·vis·able·ness *n* -ES **:** the quality of being expedient
ad·vis·a·bly \-əblē, -li\ *adv* **:** in an advisable manner **:** EXPEDIENTLY, PRUDENTLY
ad·vis·a·to·ry \-ə,tōrē\ *adj* **:** of or belonging to an adviser or to advice **:** ADVISORY
ad·vise \ədˈvīz *also* ad-\ *vb* -ED/-ING/-S [ME *avisen, advisen,* partly fr. OF *aviser, adviser* to give an opinion, inform, consider (fr. *avis* opinion), partly fr. OF *aviser, adviser* to observe, recognize, perceive, fr. *a-* (fr. L *ad-*) + *viser* to aim, fr. (assumed) VL *visare,* fr. L *visus,* past part. of *vidēre* to see] *vt* **1** *obs* **:** to look at **:** OBSERVE, CONSIDER ⟨abashed that her a stranger did ~ —Edmund Spenser⟩ **2** *obs* **:** BETHINK ⟨~ you what you say —Shak.⟩ **3 a :** to give advice to **:** COUNSEL ⟨among those *advising* the president⟩ ⟨was *advised* to try a warmer climate⟩ **b :** CAUTION, WARN ⟨*advised* him of the danger⟩ ⟨against which a solemn trespass board *advised* us —Mary Austin⟩ **c :** RECOMMEND ⟨~ going slow⟩ ⟨*advised* prudence⟩ **4 :** to give information or notice to **:** INFORM, APPRISE ⟨had not *advised* his friends of his marriage —Willa Cather⟩ ⟨a note on the flyleaf *advised* that this was a limited edition —*Discovery*⟩ ⟨a stone guidepost *advised* him that Gaza was still eight miles distant —L.C.Douglas⟩ ~ *vi* **1** *obs* **:** to take thought **:** CONSIDER, DELIBERATE **2 :** to give advice **:** offer counsel ⟨an article written to inform, not to ~⟩ ⟨knowledge enabling them to ~ on actions designed to improve the well-being of people —Fritz Machlup⟩ **3 :** to take counsel **:** hold a consultation **:** CONSULT — used with *with* ⟨~ with friends⟩ ⟨by cooperating and *advising* with voluntary . . . nonprofit organizations —*U. S. Code*⟩ ⟨inspects their farms and ~s with them on the best farming methods —*Banking*⟩ **syn** see INFORM
ad·vised \-zd\ *adj* [ME *avised, advised,* fr. past part. of *avisen, advisen*] **:** characterized by or resulting from deliberation or reflection **:** thought out **:** CONSIDERED ⟨badly ~ conduct⟩ — used chiefly in the phrases *ill-advised, well-advised* **syn** see DELIBERATE
ad·vis·ed·ly \-zədlē, -li\ *adv* [alter. (influenced by *advised*) of ME *avisily, advisily,* fr. *avisy, advisy* well-advised, circumspect (fr. MF *avisé,* fr. past part. of *aviser*) + *-ly*] **:** with or after forethought or consideration **:** DELIBERATELY, INTENTIONALLY ⟨a strong term, but one used ~ and only after careful thought⟩
ad·vis·ee \əd¦vīˈzē, (ˌ)ad-\ *n* -s **:** one that is advised; *specif* **:** a student assigned to a faculty member for counseling
ad·vise·ment \ədˈvīzmənt *also* ad-\ *n* -s [ME *avisement, advisement,* fr. MF, partly fr. *aviser, adviser* to give an opinion, inform + *-ment,* partly fr. *aviser, adviser* to observe, recognize, perceive + *-ment*] **1 :** the process of observing or considering **:** CONSIDERATION, DELIBERATION ⟨take a matter under ~⟩ **2 a :** ADVICE, COUNSEL ⟨both ~ and aid are given to physically handicapped students⟩ **b :** the action or process of advising **:** the giving of advice or counsel ⟨a center for the vocational testing and ~ of veterans⟩
ad·vis·er *also* **ad·vi·sor** \-zə(r)\ *n* -s **1 :** one that gives advice ⟨served as special ~ to the American delegation⟩ ⟨the president's medical ~s⟩ ⟨a firm of investment ~s⟩; *specif* **:** one designated to advise students (as in the choice of studies, vocational preparation, or the conduct of research) or to supervise a student organization or activity ⟨the senior English teacher is ~ to the yearbook⟩ **2 :** an adult leader of a group of horizon clubbers — compare GUARDIAN, LEADER
ad·vis·er·ship \-,ship\ *n* -s **:** the office of an adviser
adviso *n* -ES [modif. (influenced by E *advice*) of Sp *aviso,* back-formation fr. *avisar* to advise, inform, fr. F *aviser* — more at ADVISE] **1** *obs* **:** ADVICE 4 **2** *obs* **:** ADVICE 3 **3** *obs* **:** DISPATCH BOAT
ad·vis·o·ri·ly \ədˈvīz(ə)rəlē, -li *also* ad-\ *adv* **:** in an advisory manner or capacity
¹ad·vis·o·ry \-z(ə)rē, -ri\ *adj* [*advise* + *-ory*] **1 :** having or exercising power to advise ⟨an ~ council⟩ ⟨accompanied the president in an ~ capacity⟩ **2 :** containing or giving advice **:** intended to advise ⟨an ~ bulletin⟩ ⟨an ~ speed sign⟩
²advisory \"\ *n* -ES **:** a report giving information (as one issued by a weather bureau on the progress of a hurricane) ⟨the latest ~ from Miami⟩ ⟨after two days he emerges, receives an ~ on his battery-powered radio —R.E.Lapp⟩
advisory opinion *n* **:** a formal opinion by a judge, a court, or a law officer upon a question of law submitted by a legislative body or a governmental official but not presented in a concrete case at law and having no binding force
ad vi·tam aut cul·pam \ädˈwē,täm·,aùtˈkùl,päm\ [L] **:** for life or until misbehavior — used to qualify orig. a feudal tenure and later an appointment to office
ad·vo·caat \ˌadvō¦kät\ *n* -s [D, short for *advocatenborrel,* fr. *advocaat* lawyer (fr. MD *advocaet,* fr. L *advocatus* one summoned to another) + *borrel* drink, bubble, fr. *borrelen* to bubble, alter. of MD *bordelen, bortelen,* of imit. origin; fr. its throat-soothing effect, esp. helpful for irritations caused by the traditional eloquence of lawyers — more at ADVOCATE] **:** an eggnog chiefly mixed and bottled in Holland made from eggs, sugar, and brandy with vanilla and coffee flavoring
ad·vo·ca·cy \ˈadvəkəsē, -si\ *n* -ES [ME *advocacie,* fr. MF *advocacie,* fr. ML *advocatia,* fr. L *advocatus* + *-ia*] **1 :** the profession or work of an advocate **2 :** the action of advocating, pleading for, or supporting ⟨devoted a lifetime to the ~ of economic reforms⟩ ⟨a success of his moving ~ —W.O. Douglas⟩
¹ad·vo·cate \-kət, -,kāt, *usu* -d·+V\ *n* -s [ME *avocat, advocat,* fr. MF, fr. L *advocatus,* fr. past part. of *advocare* to summon, call to one's aid, fr. *ad-* + *vocare* to call — more at VOICE] **1 :** one that pleads the cause of another **:** DEFENDER ⟨we have an ~ with the Father, Jesus Christ —1 Jn 2:1 (AV)⟩ ⟨accepted the responsibility of acting as a personal ~ for his chief⟩; *specif* **:** one that pleads the cause of another before a tribunal or judicial court **:** COUNSELOR ⟨never a close student of the law, his success was won as an ~⟩ — used as the technical name in Scotland, France, and various other countries whose legal system is based on the Roman law and in the English ecclesiastical courts and various other special courts; compare ATTORNEY, BARRISTER, COUNSEL **2 :** one that argues for, defends, maintains, or recommends a cause or proposal ⟨its warmest ~s agree in this with its severest critics —W.C. Brownell⟩ ⟨the ~s of classical education⟩ ⟨an ~ of air power⟩
²ad·vo·cate \-,kāt, *usu* -d·+V\ *vb* -ED/-ING/-S *vt* **:** to plead in favor of **:** defend by argument before a tribunal or the public **:** support or recommend publicly ⟨~ a permanent corps of civil servants⟩ ⟨~s changes be made⟩ ~ *vi* **:** to act as advocate
ad·vo·cate·ship \-kət,ship, -,kāt-\ *n* -s **:** the office or duty of an advocate
ad·vo·ca·tion \ˌadvəˈkāshən\ *n* -s [L *advocation-, advocatio* act of calling, summoning, legal assistance, fr. *advocatus* + *-ion-, -io* -ion] **1 a :** SUMMONING **b** *Scots law* **:** the process whereby a superior court formerly reviewed cases brought in inferior courts **2 :** the act of advocating or pleading **:** PLEA
ad·vo·ca·tor \ˈadvə,kād·ə(r)\ *n* -s **:** ¹ADVOCATE 2
ad·voc·a·to·ry \(ˈ)ad¦väkə,tōrē, ˈadvə,kād·ərē\ *adj* **:** of or relating to an advocate
ad·vo·ca·tus dei \ˌadvə¦kād·əsˈdē,ī; ¦advə¦käd·əsˈdā,ē, ¦ädvō¦kä,tüs-\ *n, usu cap D* [LL] **:** an official of the Roman Catholic Congregation of Rites whose duty is to refute the objections raised by the advocatus diaboli against the beatification or canonization of a person
advocatus di·a·bo·li \-kä...,dīˈabə,lī, -sdē-; -kä...sdēˈäbə-(,)lē\ *n* [ML] **:** DEVIL'S ADVOCATE
ad·vo·lu·tion \ˌadvəˈlüshən\ *n* -s [L *advolutus* (past part. of *advolvere* to roll to, fr. *ad-* + *volvere* to roll) + E *-ion* — more at WELL] **:** a rolling toward something **:** growth or development toward — contrasted with *evolution*
ad·vow·ee \ˌad¦vaùˈē, (ˌ)ad¦-\ *n* -s [*advowson* + *-ee*] **:** one that holds an advowson
ad·vow·son \ədˈvaùzᵊn, ad-\ *n* -s [ME, *avoweson, advouson,* fr. OF *avoeson, avoueson,* fr. ML *advocation-, advocatio,* fr. L, act of summoning — more at ADVOCATION] *English law* **:** the right of presenting a nominee to a vacant ecclesiastical benefice
advt *abbr* advertisement
advtg *abbr* **1** advantage **2** advertising
ady·nam·ia \ˌāˌdīˈnamēə, -ām-, ˌadə-\ *n* -s [NL, fr. Gk, fr. *a-* ²a- + *-dynamia*] **:** asthenia caused by disease
ady·nam·ic \ˌā,dī¦namik, ˌadə¦-\ *adj* [NL *adynamia* + E *-ic*] **1 :** characterized by or relating to adynamia **2** *physics* **:** characterized by the absence of force
ad·y·tum \ˈadətəm\ *or* **ad·y·ton** \-,tän\ *also* **ad·yt** \-ət\ *n, pl* **ad·y·ta** \-ətə\ *also* **adyts** [L *adytum,* fr. Gk *adyton,* neut. of *adytos* not to be entered, fr. *a-* ²a- + *-dytos* (fr. *dyein* to enter, dive in, sink); akin to Gk *deielos* evening, Skt *upā-du-* to put on, and perh. to Skt *dosā* evening, dark, Av *daoshatara-* toward the west] **:** the innermost sanctuary or shrine in ancient temples which was open only to priests and from which oracles were given **:** a private chamber **:** SANCTUM, HOLY OF HOLIES
¹adz *or* **adze** \ˈadz *also* ˈaa(ə)-\ *n, pl* **adz·es** [ME *adse, adese,* fr. OE *adesa*] **:** a cutting tool that has a thin arched blade sharpened on the concave side and set at right angles to the handle and is used principally for rough-shaping wood
²adz *or* **adze** \"\ *vt* **adzed; adzed; adzing; adzes :** to cut or shape with an adz
adz block *n* **:** the block in a wood-planing machine in which the cutters are fixed
adz-eye hammer *n* **:** a hammer having an extended eye for the handle

1 2 3

1 carpenter's adz with flat head, *2* ship carpenter's adz with spur head, *3* cooper's adz

adzhar \ˈä,jär\ *n, pl* **adzhar** *or* **adzhars** *usu cap* [Russ] **1 a :** a Georgian people of the southern Caucasus region — compare GURIAN, IMERITIAN **b :** a member of such people **2 :** the language of the Adzhar people
¹adzhar·i·an \əˈjärēən\ *adj, usu cap* [*Adzhar, Adzharia,* autonomous Soviet Socialist Republic (fr. Russ *Adzhar, Adzhariya*) + E *-ian*] **1 :** of, relating to, or characteristic of the Adzhar Republic **2 :** of, relating to, or characteristic of the people of the Adzhar Republic
²adzharian \"\ *n* -s *cap* **:** a native or inhabitant of the Adzhar Republic
ad·zu·ki bean \adˈzükē-\ *or* **ad·su·ki bean** \", -ˈs-\ *n* [Jap *azuki*] **:** an annual bushy bean (*Phaseolus angularis*) widely grown in Japan and China for the flour made from its seeds
ae \ˈā\ *adj* [ME (north dial.) *a,* alter. (before consonants) of *an,* fr. OE *ān* — more at ONE] *chiefly Scot* **:** ONE
ae *abbr* [L *aetatis,* gen. of *aetas* age — more at AGE] of age; aged
AE \(ˈ)āˈē\ *abbr or n* -s **1** aeronautical engineer **2** agricultural engineer
ae·ae·an \ēˈēən\ *adj, usu cap* [*Aeaea,* island in the Tyrrhenian sea, legendary abode of Circe, fr. L, fr. Gk *Aiaia*] **:** of or belonging to the island of Aeaea
aeb·le·ski·ve \ˈebləˌskivə\ *n, pl* **aebleski·ver** \-və(r)\ [Dan *æbleskive,* lit., apple slice, fr. *æble* apple + *skive* slice; akin to ON *epli* apple and to ON *skīfa* slice — more at APPLE, SHEAVE] **:** a muffin-shaped pastry made of yeast-leavened batter baked in a special pan
ae·cial \ˈēsh(ē)əl, -sēəl\ *adj* [NL *aecium* + E *-al*] **:** of or belonging to an aecium
ae·cid·i·al \(ˈ)ē¦sidēəl\ *adj* [NL *aecidium* + E *-al*] **:** of or relating to an aecidium
ae·cid·i·o·spore \ēˈsidēə,spō(ə)r\ *n* [ISV *aecidio-* (fr. NL *aecidium*) + *spore*] **:** AECIOSPORE
ae·cid·i·um \ēˈsidēəm\ *n* [NL, fr. Gk *aikia* + NL *-idium*] **1** *pl* **aecidia :** AECIUM; *esp* **:** a cup-shaped or spheroidal aecium with a peridial layer **2** *cap* **:** a form genus of rust fungi having only an aecial stage with toothed cup-shaped peridia
ae·ci·o·spore \ˈēs(h)ēə,spō(ə)r\ *n* [NL *aecium* + E *-o-* + *spore*] **:** one of the spores in chainlike series within an aecium — **ae·ci·o·spor·ic** \¦ₑₑₑ¦spȯrik\ *adj*
ae·ci·um \ˈēs(h)ēəm\ *n, pl* **ae·cia** \-ēə\ [NL, irreg. fr. Gk *aikia* torture, assault, fr. *aikēs, aeikēs* unseemly, shameful (fr. *a-* ²a- + *-eikēs* seemly, akin to *eoikōs, eikōs* fitting, apt) + *-ia;* akin to Gk *eikōn* picture, image — more at ICON] **:** the fruiting body of rust fungi sometimes flat and lacking peridial cells and in which the first binucleate spores are usu. produced — see CAEOMA; compare TELIUM, UREDINIUM
aecology *var of* ECOLOGY
ae·de·a·gal \¦ēdē¦agəl, ēˈdēg-\ *adj* [NL *aedeagus* + E *-al*] **:** of or relating to an aedeagus
ae·de·agus *also* **ae·doe·agus** \-gəs\ *n, pl* **aede·agi** *also* **aedoe·agi** \-,gī, -,jī\ [NL, fr. Gk *aidoia* genitals + *agos* leader, fr. *agein* to lead — more at EDE-, AGENT] **:** the intromittent organ of a male insect **:** PHALLUS; *sometimes* **:** the distal part of this structure
ae·des \āˈē(,)dēz\ *n, cap* [NL, fr. Gk *aēdēs* distasteful, nauseous] **:** a large cosmopolitan genus of mosquitoes distinguished from *Anopheles* by the trilobate scutellum and short palpi of the female and from *Culex* by the pointed abdomen of the female and including a number of species (as the yellow-fever mosquito) important as vectors of diseases of man and animals
ae·dic·u·la \ēˈdikyələ\ *also* **aed·i·cule** *or* **ed·i·cule** \ˈedə,kyül, ˈēd-\ *n, pl* **aedicu·lae** \-ə,lē\ *also* **aedicules** *or* **edicules** \-ülz\ [L *aedicula,* dim. of *aedes* temple, building — more at EDIFY] **:** a small structure used as a shrine **:** a niche for a statue — usu. used in pl.
ae·dic·u·lar \ēˈdikyələ(r)\ *adj* **:** of or relating to an aedicula **:** having niches ⟨an ~ façade⟩
ae·dile *also* **edile** \ˈē,dīl, -īəl\ *n* -s [L *aedilis,* fr. *aedes* temple, pl. building + *-ilis* -ile — more at EDIFY] **:** an official in ancient Rome charged with policing the city, superintending public works and the grain supply, and providing for the public games — **ae·di·li·tian** \ˌēdᵊl¦ishən, ¦ē,dī¦li-\ *adj*
ae·dil·i·ty *also* **edil·i·ty** \ēˈdiləd·ē\ *n* -ES [L *aedilitas,* fr. *aedilis* + *-itas* -ity] **1 :** the office of an aedile **2 :** the superintendence of public buildings and works
ae·dine \āˈē,dīn, -ēn\ *adj* [NL *Aedes* + E *-ine*] **:** of, related to, or involving the genus *Aedes* or mosquitoes of this genus
AeE *abbr or n* -s **:** aeronautical engineer
ae·ga·grop·i·la \ˌēgəˈgräpələ\ *n* [NL, fr. Gk *aigagros* + L *pila* ball, fr. *pilus* hair — more at PILE] **1** *also* **ae·gag·ro·pile** *or* **egag·ro·pile** \ēˈgagrō,pīl\ *pl* **aegagropilas** \ˌēgəˈgräpələz\ *or* **aegagropilae** \-,lē\ *also* **aegagropiles** *or* **egagropiles** \ēˈgagrōpīlz\ **:** a ball of hair or a concretion found in the stomach of the goat and other ruminants **2** *pl* **aegagropilas** *or* **aegagropilae :** a ball-shaped mass of hairlike filaments formed by some algae (as certain species of the genus *Cladophora*) **3** *cap, in some classifications* **:** a genus of algae comprising all forms forming aegagropilas — **ae·ga·grop·i·lous** \ˌēgə¦gräpələs\ *adj*
ae·gag·rus \ēˈgagrəs\ *n, pl* **aegag·ri** \-,grī\ [NL, fr. Gk *aigagros,* fr. *aig-, aix* goat + *agrios* wild] **:** the wild goat (*Capra aegagrus*) of Asia Minor
ae·ge·an \ēˈjēən\ *adj, usu cap* [L *Aegaeus* (fr. Gk *Aigaios*) + E *-an*] **1 :** of or relating to the arm of the Mediterranean sea east of Greece **2 :** of or relating to the prehistoric civilization of the islands of the Aegean sea and the countries adjacent to it esp. in the Bronze Age (3000–1100 B.C.) — see MINOAN, MYCENAEAN; CYCLADIC, HELLADIC
¹ae·ge·ri·id \ēˈjirēəd\ *adj* [NL *Aegeriidae*] **:** of or relating to the Aegeriidae
²aegeriid \"\ *n* -s **:** CLEARWING MOTH
ae·ge·ri·i·dae \ˌējəˈrīə,dē\ *n pl, cap* [NL, fr. *Aegeria, Egeria,* type genus (fr. *Aegeria, Egeria,* a nymph, fr. L, fr. Gk *Ēgeria*) + *-idae*] **:** a family of small bright colored moths that resemble wasps and bees — see CLEARWING MOTH
ae·gi·lops \ˈējə,läps, ˈej-\ *n, cap* [NL, fr. Gk *aigilōps* haver-grass, Turkey oak (*Quercus cerris*) — more at OAK] *in some classifications* **:** a genus of grasses sometimes used to include the presumed wild ancestors of domestic wheat which are now usu. placed in the genus *Triticum*
¹ae·gi·ne·tan \ˌējə¦nētᵊn\ *adj, usu cap* [L *Aegineta* native of Aegina (fr. *Aegina,* island in the Saronic gulf off the SE coast of Greece, fr. Gk *Aigina*) + E *-an*] **:** of or relating to the island or ancient Greek state of Aegina or its inhabitants
²aeginetan \"\ *n* -s *cap* [L *Aegineta* inhabitant of Aegina (fr. Gk *Aiginētēs,* fr. *Aigina*) + E *-an*] **:** a native or inhabitant of the island or ancient Greek state of Aegina
aegir *var of* EAGRE
ae·gir·ite \ˈāgə,rīt, ˈējə-\ *also* **ae·gir·ine** \-,rēn\ *or* **aegirine-augite** *n, pl* **aegirites** *also* **aegirines** *or* **aegirine-augites** [*aegerite,* modif. (influenced by *-ite*) of G *aegerin; aegirine* fr. G *aegirin,* fr. *Aegir,* ancient Scand. sea god (fr. ON *Ægir*) + G *-in* -ine] **:** ACMITE
ae·gis *also* **e·gis** \ˈējəs\ *n, pl* **aegises** *also* **egises** [L, fr. Gk *aigis* goatskin, shield of Zeus, perh. fr. *aig-, aix* goat; akin to Arm *aic* goat, Av *izaēna* leathern] **1 :** a shield or breastplate emblematic of majesty that was orig. associated chiefly with the god Zeus but later, bordered with serpents and set with a Gorgon's head, associated mainly with the goddess Athena **2 a :** PROTECTION, DEFENSE ⟨the unfailing ~ of the law⟩ **b :** a set of favorable circumstances ⟨to live under the ~ of complete toleration and understanding⟩ **c :** controlling or conditioning influence ⟨literary activity under the ~ of symbolism —Carlos Lynes⟩ **3 a :** patronage, backing, or sponsorship esp. when afforded by a notable or authoritative organization, group, or individual **:** AUSPICES **b :** LEADERSHIP ⟨the country rallying under the ~ of the prince⟩ **c :** control, guidance, or direction esp. as afforded by an organization, group, individual, system, or doctrine of notable or authoritative influence ⟨under the ~ of the government —R.A.Tybout⟩
ae·gi·tha·los \ˌējəˈthä,läs, -ləs\ *n, cap* [NL, fr. Gk *aigithallos, aigithalos* titmouse] **:** a genus of titmice with very long tail feathers — see LONG-TAILED TIT
ae·gi·thin·i·dae \ˌējəˈthinə,dē\ *n pl, cap* [NL, fr. *Aegithina,* type genus (fr. Gk *aigithos,* a kind of bird, perh. the linnet + NL *-ina*) + *-idae*] **:** a family of brightly colored passerine birds of the Oriental region that have stocky legs and curved bills and feed on fruits or insects — see IRENA
ae·gle \ˈē(,)glē, ˈe-\ *n, cap* [NL, prob. fr. L, one of the Hesperides (nymphs who guarded the golden apples), fr. Gk *Aiglē,* lit., brightness; prob. fr. the apple-shaped fruit] **:** a genus of thorny trees (family Rutaceae) of tropical Asia and western Africa with compound leaves, greenish white flowers, and orangelike fruits — see BEL
ae·go·li·us \ēˈgōlēəs\ *n, cap* [NL, fr. L *aegolios,* an owl, fr. Gk *aigōlios*] **:** a genus of small northern owls including the saw-whet owl
aegophony *var of* EGOPHONY
ae·go·po·di·um \ˌēgəˈpōdēəm\ *n, cap* [NL, fr. Gk *aig-, aix* goat + NL *-o-* + *-podium;* prob. fr. the shape of the leaflets] **:** a small genus of herbs (family Umbelliferae) native to the north temperate zone with compound leaves, white flowers, and smooth 5-angled fruits — see GOUTWEED
ae·gro·tat \ēˈgrō,tat, ˈēgrō-\ *n* -s [L, he is ill, 3d pers. sing. pres. indic. act. of *aegrotare* to be ill, fr. *aegr-, aeger* ill; akin to Toch A *ekro* ill, Toch B *aikre, aikare,* and perh. to OE *ācol* dismayed, Norw *eikja, eikla* to plague, pester, Alb *kë-ëk* evil, and perh. to OE *inca* suspicion, doubt, quarrel — more at INKLING] **1** *Brit* **:** a medical certificate testifying that a student is ill and unable to attend his lectures or examinations **2** *Brit* **:** the unclassified university degree granted to a candidate who is prevented by illness from attending examinations
ae·gy·pi·i·dae \ˌējəˈpīə,dē\ *n pl, cap* [NL, fr. *Aegypius,* type genus (fr. Gk *aigypios* vulture) + *-idae*] *in some classifications* **:** a family (order Falconiformes) comprising the Old World vultures all with naked heads and longer wings and smaller tails than the typical eagles
ae·gyp·tia·nel·lo·sis \ē,jipshə(,)neˈlōsəs\ *n, pl* **aegyptianel·lo·ses** \-ō,sēz\ [NL, fr. *Aegyptianella* (genus name of *Aegyptianella pullorum*), irreg. fr. L *Aegyptius* Egyptian + NL *-ella*) + *-osis* — more at EGYPTIAN] **:** a disease of domestic fowls marked by fever, anemia, jaundice, and typhoidlike symptoms and caused by a protozoan (*Aegyptianella pullorum*) related to the piroplasms and transmitted by the chicken tick esp. in the Mediterranean region
ae·gyp·til·la \ˌējəpˈtilə\ *n* -s [L, a gem formerly found in Egypt, fr. *Aegyptus* Egypt + L *-illa,* dim. suffix] **:** a gem produced from a 2-layered agate usu. cut so that one color is encircled by the other
aelodicon *var of* AEOLODICON
aelur- *or* **aeluro-** — see AILUR-
ae·lu·roid \ēˈlü,rȯid\ *n* -s *often cap* [NL *Aeluroidea*] **:** one of the Aeluroidea
ae·lu·roi·dea \ˌēl(y)əˈrȯidēə, ˌelyə-\ *n pl, cap* [NL, fr. *aelur-* + *-oidea*] **:** a superfamily of Carnivora comprising the cats, civets, hyenas, and related carnivorous mammals all distinguished from related forms by skull formations and by the absence or great reduction of the penis bone and Cowper's glands
aelurophile *var of* AILUROPHILE
aelurophobia *var of* AILUROPHOBIA
ae·lu·rop·o·dous \¦ēl(y)ə¦räpədəs, ¦elyə-\ *adj* [*aelur-* + *-podous*] **:** having feet with retractile claws (like those of a cat)
ae·lu·ro·pus \ēˈlürəpəs\ [NL, fr. *aelur-* + *-pus*] *syn of* AILUROPODA
ae·lu·rus \-rəs\ *syn of* AILURUS
-aemia — see -EMIA
ae·mu·la·tio vi·ci·ni \ˌīmüˈläd·ē,ōwəˈkē(,)nē\ *n, pl* **aemula·ti·o·nes vicini** \-,läd·ēˈō(,)nāsw-\ [L, malevolence or jealousy of a neighbor] *civil & Scots law* **:** the exercise of a legal right only to cause annoyance, harm, or injury to another
aen *abbr* [L *aeneus, aenus*] made of copper or bronze
aen·ach *or* **aon·ach** \ˈānək, -ək\ *n* -s [IrGael, fr. OIr *ōenach,* lit., reunion, fr. *ōen* one; akin to OE *ān* one — more at ONE] **:** an assembly in ancient Ireland for the promulgation of laws and for athletic contests
a end \ˈā,end\ *n, usu cap A* **:** the end of a railway freight or passenger car opposite the end where the handbrake is located
ae·ne·o·lith·ic \ā¦nēō¦lithik\ *or* **ene·o·lith·ic** \¦ēn-\ *adj, usu cap* [L *aeneus* of copper or bronze + E *-o-* + *-lithic*] **:** of or belonging to a transitional period between the Neolithic and Bronze ages in which some copper was used
ae·ne·ous *also* **ae·ne·us** \āˈēnēəs\ *adj* [L *aeneus* of bronze, of copper, alter. of *aenus,* fr. *aes* bronze, copper — more at ORE] **:** like brass in color and luster **:** greenish gold ⟨~ beetles⟩
aenigma *var of* ENIGMA
aenigmatite *var of* ENIGMATITE
¹ae·o·li·an \ēˈōlēən, -lyən\ *adj, usu cap* [*Aeolis, Aeolia,* ancient country in Asia Minor (fr. L, fr. Gk *Aiolis*) + E *-an*] **1 :** of or relating to Aeolis or Aeolia, colonized by the Aeolians **2 :** of or relating to the inhabitants of Aeolis or Aeolia
²aeolian \"\ *n* -s *cap* **1 :** a member of a group of Greek

peoples that in early prehistoric times was settled in Thessaly and Boeotia, occupied some parts of the Peloponnesus before the Achaeans, and colonized Lesbos and the adjacent coast of Asia Minor **2 :** AEOLIC

³aeolian \"\ *adj* [*Aeolus*, god of the winds (fr. L, fr. Gk *Aiolos*) + E *-ian*] **1** *often cap* **:** of or relating to Aeolus **2 :** giving forth or marked by a soughing sound or musical tone produced by or as if by the wind ⟨trees with voices ~ —Richard Realf⟩

⁴aeolian *var of* EOLIAN

aeolian attachment *n* [³*Aeolian*] **:** a contrivance attached to a piano that prolongs vibrations and increases volume of sound by forcing a stream of air upon the strings

aeolian harp *n, sometimes cap A* [³*Aeolian*] **:** a box-shaped musical instrument having stretched strings usu. tuned in unison on which the wind produces varying harmonics over the same fundamental tone

ae·o·li·an·ly *adv* [³*Aeolian* + *-ly*] **:** with a soughing sound or musical tone produced by or as if by the wind ⟨distant voices humming ~ in the summer night⟩

aeolian minor scale *n, sometimes cap A* [¹*Aeolian*] **:** NATURAL MINOR SCALE

aeolian mode *n, sometimes cap A* [¹*Aeolian*] **:** an authentic ecclesiastical mode consisting of a pentachord and an upper conjunct tetrachord represented on the white keys of the piano by an ascending diatonic scale from A to A — see MODE illustration

¹ae·ol·ic \ē'älik\ *adj, usu cap* [L *Aeolicus*, fr. Gk *Aiolikos*, fr. *Aiolis* Aeolia + Gk *-ikos* -ic] **:** ¹AEOLIAN

²aeolic \"\ *n* -s *cap* **:** a group of dialects of ancient Greek used by the Aeolians

³aeolic \"\ *adj, usu cap* [L *Aeolicus*, lit., of Aeolia] **:** of or relating to lyric rhythms marked by isosyllabic balance and combination of dactyls and trochees with frequent variation or of tetrasyllabic units (as choriambs) — compare LOGAOEDIC, POLYSCHEMATIST DIMETER

ae·o·lid \'ēəlәd\ *n* -s [NL *Aeolid-, Aeolis*] **:** a nudibranch mollusk of the genus *Aeolis*

ae·o·lid·i·dae \,ēə'lidə,dē\ *n pl, cap* [NL, fr. *Aeolid-, Aeolis*, type genus + *-idae*] **:** a family that is made up of nudibranchs that have many nematocysts obtained from the hydroids on which they feed and that is sometimes placed with related families in a superfamily (Aeolidoidea)

aeo·light \'ēə,līt\ *n* [perh. fr. Gk *aiolos* quick-moving, glittering + E *light*] **:** a gas-discharge glow lamp which is used in optical sound recording and the luminous intensity of which can be varied by varying the terminal voltage

ae·o·line \'ēə,lēn\ *also* **ae·o·li·na** \,ēə'lēnə, -lē-\ *n* -s [*Aeolus*, god of winds + E *-ine, -ina* — more at AEOLIAN] **1 a :** a very soft organ stop of mild string quality — called also *aeolodicon* **b :** a soft free-reed stop in a European organ **2 :** a mouth harmonica

ae·ol·i·pile *also* **ae·ol·i·pyle** *or* **eol·i·pile** \ē'älə,pīl\ *n* -s [L & Gk; L *aeolipila*, by folk etymology (influence of L *pila* ball) fr. Gk *aiolipylē*, *Aiolon pylē*, fr. *aioli-* (fr. *Aiolos*, god of wind) or *Aiolon* (gen. of *Aiolos*) + *pylē* gate — more at PYLON] **:** an apparatus that was invented in the 2d century B.C. and is often called the first steam engine and that consisted essentially of a closed vessel (as a globe or cylinder) with one or more projecting bent tubes out of which steam is made to pass from the vessel, the action of the steam jets causing it to revolve

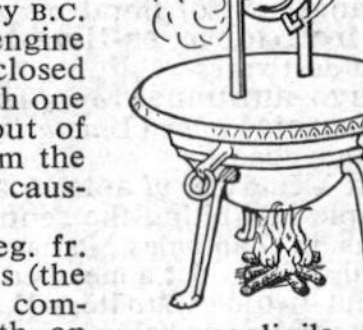

aeolipile

ae·o·lis \'ēələs\ *n, cap* [NL, irreg. fr. Gk *aiolos* quick-moving] **:** a genus (the type of the family Aeolididae) comprising nudibranch mollusks with an elongated sluglike body and a series of tufts of fingerlike gills, often brightly colored, along each side of the back

ae·o·lism \'ēə,lizəm\ *also* **ae·ol·i·cism** \ē'älə,sizəm\ *n* -s *usu cap* [²*Aeolian* or *Aeolic* + *ism*] **:** an idiom or peculiarity of the Aeolic dialect

ae·o·lod·i·con \,ēə'lädəkən\ *also* **ae·lod·i·con** \ē'lä-\ *or* **ae·o·lo·di·on** \,ēə'lōdēən\ *n* -s [*Aeolus* + *melodicon* or *melodion*] **1 :** a keyboard wind musical instrument similar to the harmonium **2 :** AEOLINE

ae·o·lo·me·lod·i·con \,ēə(,)lōmə'lädəkən\ *n* -s [*aeolo-* (fr. *Aeolus*) + *melodicon*] **:** an aeolodicon with tube resonators attached to the reeds

ae·o·lo·so·ma \,ēələ'sōmə\ *n, cap* [NL, fr. Gk *aiolos* quick-moving, glittering + NL *-soma*] **:** a nearly cosmopolitan genus (the type of the family Aeolosomatidae) comprising minute aquatic oligochaete worms with large prostomia and usu. with bright-colored oil globules in the integument — **ae·o·lo·so·ma·tid** \¦===¦sōmətәd\ *adj or n* — **ae·o·lo·so·mid** \¦===¦sōməd\ *adj or n*

ae·o·lo·trop·ic *also* **eo·lo·trop·ic** \¦ēəlō¦träpik\ *adj* **:** ANISOTROPIC 1

ae·o·lot·ro·py *also* **eo·lot·ro·py** \,ēə'lä·trəpē\ *n* -ES [Gk *aiolos* + E *-tropy*] **:** ANISOTROPY

ae·on *or* **eon** \'ēən, 'ē,än\ *n* -s [L *aeon*, fr. Gk *aiōn* age, lifetime — more at AYE] **1 :** an immeasurably or indefinitely long period of time **:** AGE ⟨the obscure ~s of prehistory⟩ **2** *in Gnosticism esp as taught by the Valentinians* **:** one of the group of eternal beings that together form the fullness of the supreme being from whom they emanate and between whom and the world they are intermediaries **3** *usu* **eon :** any large part of geological time usu. longer than an era **syn** see PERIOD

ae·o·ni·an *also* **eo·ni·an** \ē'ōnēən, -nyən\ *or* **ae·o·ni·al** \-ēəl, -yəl\ *or* **ae·on·ic** \(')ē¦änik\ *adj* **:** lasting for an immeasurably or indefinitely long period of time ⟨the ~ ages preceding our present universe⟩

ae·pi·or·nis \,ēpē'ȯrnəs\ *syn of* AEPYORNIS

ae·pyc·er·os \ē'pisərəs\ *n, cap* [NL, fr. MGk *aipykerōs* high-horned, fr. Gk *aipys* high + *-kerōs* (fr. *keras* horn)] **:** a genus of large African antelopes having the horns lyrate in the male — see IMPALA

ae·py·or·nis \,ēpē'ȯrnəs\ *n* [NL, fr. Gk *aipys* + NL *-ornis*] **1** *cap* **:** a genus (the type of the family Aepyornithidae coextensive with the order Aepyornithiformes of the superorder Palaeognathae) of gigantic ratite birds known only from remains found in Madagascar though believed to have survived into historic times and to have been the source of legends about the roc **2** -ES **:** a bird of the genus *Aepyornis* or the order Aepyornithiformes

aeq *abbr* [L *aequalis* — more at EQUAL] equal

aequator *archaic var of* EQUATOR

ae·qui \'ē,kwī, 'ī,kwē\ *or* **ae·quic·u·li** \ē'kwikyə,lī\ *n pl, cap* [L] **:** a people of ancient Latium east of Rome

aequi- — see EQUI-

¹ae·qui·an \'ēkwēən\ *adj, usu cap* [*Aequi* + *-an*] **1 :** of, relating to, or characteristic of the Aequi people **2 :** of, relating to, or characteristic of the Aequian language

²aequian \"\ *n* -s *usu cap* **1 :** a member of the Aequi people **2 :** the language of the Aequi people

ae·qui·dens \'ēkwə,denz, 'ek-\ *n, cap* [NL, fr. *aequi-* + L *dens* tooth — more at TOOTH] **:** a genus of small bright-colored So. American cichlid fishes including several species popular in the tropical aquarium — see BLUE ACARA

ae·quo·rea \ē'kwōrēə\ *n, cap* [NL, fr. L, fem. of *aequoreus* of the sea, fr. *aequor* sea, even surface, fr. *aequus* even, equal — more at EQUAL] **:** a cosmopolitan genus (the type of the family Aequoridae) of brilliantly luminescent hydrozoan jellyfish of moderate size

aer \'āə(r)\ *n* -s [MGk *aēr*, fr. Gk, air — more at AIR] **:** a large veil used in the Eastern Church to cover either the chalice or the paten

aer- *or* **aero-** *comb form* [ME *aero-*, fr. MF, fr. L, fr. Gk *aer-*, *aero-*, fr. *aer-*, *aēr* — more at AIR] **1 a :** air **:** atmosphere **:** aerial ⟨*aerate*⟩ ⟨*aerenchyma*⟩ ⟨*aerobic*⟩ **b :** aerial and ⟨*aero*hydrous⟩ **2 :** gas ⟨*aero*metry⟩ ⟨*aero*sol⟩ **3 :** aviation ⟨*aero*drome⟩ ⟨*aero*technical⟩

aera *archaic var of* ERA

aer·ate \'a(ə),rāt, 'e(ə),-, 'aa(ə),-, 'āə,-; *chiefly substand* 'arē,āt *or* ,erē- *or* 'aarē- *or* 'ärē-; *usu* -ād+V\ *vb* -ED/-ING/-S [*aer-* + *-ate*] *vt* **1 :** to supply (the blood) with oxygen by respiration **2 a :** to expose to air by passing air through (as an aquarium) **:** AERIFY **:** cause air to bubble through **b :** to introduce air into (a liquid) by stirring, spraying, or some similar method **c :** to supply or impregnate with air (as soil or sand) **d :** to expose to or as if to fresh air **:** VENTILATE, AIR ⟨a well-*aerated* room⟩ **3 a :** to combine or charge with gas, sometimes carbon dioxide **:** cause a gas to bubble through **b :** to make effervescent or sparkling ⟨*aerated* his writing with a persuasive colloquialism —H.T.Moore⟩ ⟨a kind of purposely clumsy charm, set off by *aerated* lyricism —*Atlantic*⟩ ~ *vi* **:** to be in a situation or condition that permits sufficient exposure to or adequate circulation of air ⟨the potatoes were set outside to ~⟩

aerated bread *n* **:** bread raised by introducing carbon dioxide into the water used for the dough

aerated water *n, chiefly Brit* **:** any water artificially impregnated with a large amount of gas (as carbon dioxide)

aer·a·tion \a(ə)'rāshən *etc* (*see* AERATE); *chiefly substand* ,arē'ā- *etc*\ *n* -s **1 :** the act or process of aerating or the state of being aerated **:** exposure to air **2 :** the process of discharging hot milk or cream through one or more vacuum chambers of a vacuum pasteurizer for elimination of undesirable flavors followed by passage over a surface cooler

aer·a·tor \'a(ə),rād·ə(r) *etc* (*see* AERATE), -ātə-; *chiefly substand* 'arē,ā- *etc*\ *n* -s **:** one that aerates: as **a :** any specialized apparatus for aerating a liquid, esp. water or milk **b :** a fumigator used to bleach grain, destroying fungi and insects **c :** a device with a roller equipped with hollow tines that remove cores of soil from turf

aerator c

aer·en·chy·ma \,(')a(ə)'reŋkəmə, |e(ə)-,|aa(ə)-,|āə-, -enk-\ *n* -s [NL, fr. *aer-* + *-enchyma*] **:** any of various tissues with large intercellular spaces; *specif* **:** the spongy modified cork tissue characteristic of many aquatic plants that develops large intercellular spaces as a result of elongation of certain cells and that facilitates gaseous exchange and maintains buoyancy

aeri- *comb form* [LL *aeri-*, fr. L *aer* — more at AIR] **:** air ⟨*aeri*form⟩ ⟨*aeri*fy⟩

¹aer·i·al \'a|rēəl, 'e|,'aa|,'ā| *also* ā'i| *or* ā'ē| *or* ā'e|\ *adj* [L *aerius* (fr. Gk *aerios*, fr. *aer-*, *aēr* air) + E *-al* — more at AIR] **1 a :** of or belonging to the air or atmosphere ⟨vast ~ gulfs —J.C.Powys⟩ **b :** consisting of air ⟨~ particles⟩ **c** (1) **:** existing in the air **:** moving through the air ⟨~ spirits⟩ (2) **:** existing, forming, or growing in the air rather than in the ground or in water ⟨~ plants⟩ **d :** found, placed, or suspended in the air ⟨an ~ supply of oxygen⟩ ⟨~ germicides⟩ **e :** produced by or performed in the air ⟨~ oxidation⟩ ⟨a hummingbird moving about in an ~ dance among the flowers—W.H.Hudson †1922⟩ **f :** rising high in the air **:** LOFTY ⟨~ spires⟩ **g :** operating or operated overhead on elevated cables or rails ⟨~ conveyors for transportation of raw materials⟩ ⟨an ~ railway⟩ **2 a :** resembling or suggestive of air: as (1) **:** THIN, ATTENUATED **:** lacking substance ⟨fine and ~ distinctions⟩ (2) **:** IMAGINARY, ETHEREAL, IDEAL ⟨visions of ~ joy —P.B.Shelley⟩ (3) **:** clear as air **:** LUCID ⟨compare the ~ texture of his essay with the . . . darkness of the original sources —John Russell⟩ **b :** representative of the effect of atmosphere **:** ATMOSPHERIC ⟨the principal charm of all Italian scenery, its graceful outlines and much of its delicate ~ tints —Norman Douglas⟩ **3 a :** of or relating to aircraft ⟨~ navigation⟩ **b :** designed for use in, taken from, or operating from or against aircraft ⟨~ camera⟩ ⟨~ photo⟩ ⟨~ gun⟩ **c :** by means of aircraft ⟨documents . . . for ~ transmission to the headquarters —*Punch*⟩ **4 :** using or resulting from a forward pass in football ⟨some fine ~ work⟩ ⟨an ~ attack that led . . . to their 27–20 victory —*N.Y. Times*⟩ — **aer·i·al·ly** \-ēəlē, -i\ *adv*

²aerial \"\ *n* -s **1 :** ANTENNA 3 **2 :** AERIAL LADDER **3 :** FORWARD PASS

aerial blue *n* **:** a delicate monochrome faïence ware having blue designs on a grayish ground

aerial bomb *n* **:** a bomb designed to be dropped from an aircraft

aerial cascade *n* **:** a swift wind passing down the side of a hill or mountain above surface eddies roughly following the major contours of the land

aerial drainage *n* **:** the downslope flow of surface air caused by its relatively high density produced by contact cooling, esp. prevalent on still clear nights in hilly or mountainous terrain

aerial farming *n* **:** the use of aircraft for seeding or for applying chemicals for weed or pest control

aerial funicular *n* **:** FUNICULAR RAILWAY; *esp* **:** one in which the cars are suspended from pulleys that run on an overhead cable

aerial gunner *n* **:** a gunner on an airplane **:** one qualified to fly as a gunner on a combat flight crew

aer·i·al·ist \-ləst\ *n* -s [¹*aerial* + *-ist*] **:** one that performs feats in the air or above the ground; *specif* **:** an entertainer on the flying trapeze

aer·i·al·i·ty \,e'ēal·əd·ē, ¦s'ē-\ *n* -ES **:** the quality or state of being aerial **:** UNSUBSTANTIALITY

aerial ladder *n* **:** a mechanically operated extensible fire ladder usu. mounted on a truck

aerial mine *n* **1 :** a mine designed to be dropped from the air esp. into water **2 :** a large light-case bomb dropped by parachute — called also *land mine*

aerial observation *n* **:** AIR OBSERVATION

aerial perspective *n* **1 :** the expression of space in painting by gradation of color or distinctness **2 :** the diminution of clarity of outline and intensity of color in a distant object as distance increases **:** the optical effect produced by diffusion of light whereby objects appear lighter in tone the farther away they are viewed

aerial photograph *n* **:** a photograph taken from an aircraft — **aerial photography** *n*

aerial potato *n* **:** a small tuber produced in the axil of a potato leaf

aerial root *n* **:** any root exposed to the air; *esp* **:** one of the roots found in epiphytes and climbers not in contact with the soil but usu. anchoring the plant to its support and often functioning in photosynthesis — compare PROP ROOT; see ROOT illustration

aerial survey *n* **:** a survey utilizing aerial photographs

aerial torpedo *n* **1 :** an explosive projectile fired from a trench mortar **2 :** a torpedo designed for launching from an airplane **3 :** a heavy aerial bomb **4 :** a guided missile capable of powered flight

aer·i·an \ä'irēən\ *n* -s *usu cap* [*Aerius* of Pontus, 4th cent. A.D. presbyter in Asia Minor + E *-an*] **:** one of a 4th century A.D. Arian sect that believed in the equality of bishops and priests and repudiated prayers for the dead and compulsory fasts

aer·i·des \'a(ə)rə,dēz, ā'er-\ *n, cap* [NL, fr. *aer-* + L *-ides* (patronymic suffix) — more at -IDAE] **:** a genus of epiphytic orchids natives of tropical Asia having stiff 2-ranked leaves and white flowers in lateral clusters

ae·rie \'a(ə)(ə)rē, 'e(ə)-,'i(ə)-,'a(ə)-, 'ērē, -rī\ *or* **ey·rie** \", 'īr-\ *or* **aery** *like* AERIE\ *n, pl* **aeries** *or* **eyries** [ML *aeria, aerea*, fr. OF *aire*, fr. L *area* open space, feeding place for animals — more at AREA] **1 :** the nest of a bird (as an eagle or hawk) on a cliff or a mountaintop **2** *obs* **:** a brood of birds, esp. birds of prey **3 :** a room or a dwelling or other quarters placed high up

aer·if·er·ous \(')a(ə)¦rif(ə)rəs, -e(ə)-,-aa(ə)-,-ā-\ *adj* [*aer-* + *-i-* + *-ferous*] **:** containing or conveying air

aer·i·fi·ca·tion \,arəfə'kāshən, ,er-, ,aar-, ,är- *also* ā,er-\ *n* -s **1 :** the act of aerifying or of aerating **:** the state of being aerified or aerated **2 :** atomization of fuel oil

Aer·i·fi·er \'arə,fī(ə)r *etc* (*see* AERIFY)\ *trademark* — used for a machine used to dig or punch holes in sod to permit free movement of air

aer·i·form \-,fȯrm\ *adj* [*aer-* + *-iform*] **1 :** having the nature of air **:** GASEOUS **2 :** lacking substance or real existence **:** INTANGIBLE ⟨figures light and ~ come unlooked for and melt away —Thomas Carlyle⟩

aer·i·fy \'a(ə)rə,fī, 'er-,'ā(ə)r-,'ā'er-\ *vt* -ED/-ING/-ES [*aer-* + *-ify*] **1 :** to infuse or force air into **:** AERATE 2 **2 :** to change into an aeriform state **:** VAPORIZE

aer·i·ly \'a(ə)rəlē, 'er-,'är-, -li\ *adv* [*aery* + *-ly*] **:** in an aery manner

aero \'a(ə)(,)rō, 'e(ə)-,'aa(ə)-,'āə-, *chiefly substand* 'arē(,)ō *or* 'erē- *or* 'aarē- *or* 'ärē-\ *adj* [*aer-*] **:** of or relating to aircraft or aeronautics ⟨~ club⟩ ⟨~ engine⟩ **:** designed for aerial use esp. in aerial photography ⟨~ lens⟩

aero- *in pronunciations below*, ¦=(=)= = ¦arə *or* ¦erə *or* ¦aarə *or* -rō *also* ¦aərə *or* ¦eə- *or* ¦aaə- *or* ¦āə- *or* -ə(,)rō, *chiefly substand* ¦arēə *or* ¦erēə *or* ¦aarēə *or* ¦ärēə *or* -rē(,)ō; =(=)= = (,)a(ə)¦rä *or* (,)e(ə)- *or* (,)aa(ə)- *or* ,āə-, *chiefly substand* ,arē¦ä *or* ,erē- *or* ,aarē- *or* ,ärē-\ — see AER-

aero·ba·cil·lus \¦=(=)=-\ *n, cap* [NL, fr. *aer-* + *bacillus*] *in some classifications* **:** a genus of bacteria (family Bacillaceae) including forms usu. placed in *Bacillus* but in some morphological and physiological characters resembling members of *Clostridium*

aero·bac·ter \'=(=)=,baktə(r)\ *n* [NL, fr. *aer-* + *-bacter*] **1** *cap* **:** a genus of aerobic gram-negative bacteria (family Enterobacteriaceae) producing acid and gas from many sugars (as dextrose and lactose), forming acetylmethylcarbinol, and being widely distributed in nature (as in feces, soil, water, and the contents of human and animal intestines) and often concerned in the natural souring of milk **2** -s **:** a bacterium of the genus *Aerobacter*

aero·bac·te·ri·ol·o·gy \¦=(=)=-\ *n* [*aer-* + *bacteriology*] **:** the branch of aerobiology that is concerned with the bacteria of the air

aero·bal·lis·tics \¦=(=)=-\ *n pl but sing in constr* [*aer-* + *ballistics*] **:** the study of the effects of aerodynamic forces upon the flight of missiles and projectiles

aero·bat·ic \,=(=)=¦bad·ik\ *adj* [prob. back-formation fr. *aerobatics*] **:** of or relating to aerobatics **:** marked by, engaging in, or suitable for aerobatics

aero·bat·ics \,=(=)=¦=iks\ *n pl but sing in constr* [blend of *aer-* and *acrobatics*] **:** spectacular flying feats and evolutions (as rolls and dives); *also* **:** flying specializing in such performances

aer·obe \'a(ə),rōb, 'e(ə)-,'aa(ə)-,'āə-\ *n* -s [F *aérobie*, fr. *aér-* aer- + *-bie* (fr. Gk *bios* life) — more at QUICK] **:** an organism that lives only in the presence of oxygen; *esp* **:** one of certain bacteria — compare ANAEROBE

aerobia *pl of* AEROBIUM

aero·bic \¦=(=)¦rōbik, -ēk\ *adj* [*aer-* + *bi-* + *-ic*] **1 :** living or active only in the presence of oxygen **2 :** taking place in the presence of oxygen **:** OXIDATIVE ⟨~ glycolysis⟩ **3** [*aerobe* + *-ic*] **:** of, relating to, or induced by aerobes ⟨~ fermentation⟩ — **aer·o·bi·cal·ly** \-ək(ə)lē, -ēk-, -li\ *adv*

aero·bi·o·log·i·cal \¦=(=)=,bīə¦l-\ *also* **aero·bi·o·log·ic** *adj* **:** belonging to, relating to, or for the purposes of aerobiology — **aero·bi·o·log·i·cal·ly** *adv*

aero·bi·ol·o·gy \¦=(=)=¦-\ *n* [*aer-* + *biology*] **:** the branch of biology that deals with the occurrence, transportation, and effects of airborne microorganisms or biological objects (as viruses, pollen, or plant spores)

aero·bi·o·scope \¦=(=)='bīə,skōp\ *n* [*aer-* + *bi-* + *-scope*] **:** an apparatus used to collect air for determination of its bacterial count

aero·bi·o·sis \¦=(=)=,bī'ōsəs\ *n, pl* **aerobioses** \-ō,sēz\ [NL, fr. *aer-* + *-biosis*] **:** life in the presence of air or oxygen

aero·bi·ot·ic \¦=(=)=,bī¦ä-\ *adj* [*aer-* + *-biotic*] **:** living only in the presence of free oxygen — **aero·bi·ot·i·cal·ly** *adv*

aer·o·bi·um \(,)a(ə)'rōbēəm, 'e(ə)-,-aa(ə)-,-āə-\ *n, pl* **aero·bia** \-bēə\ [NL, modif. of F *aérobie* — more at AEROBE] **:** AEROBE

aero·cam·era \¦=(=)=¦-\ *n* [*aer-* + *camera*] **:** a camera specially designed for aerial photography

aero·car·to·graph \¦=(=)=-\ *n* [*aer-* + *cartograph*] **:** an apparatus for making contour maps from aerial photographs

aero·chem·i·cal \¦=(=)=¦-\ *adj* [*aer-* + *chemical*] **:** utilizing the projection of chemical warfare agents by aircraft ⟨an ~ attack⟩

aero·chlo·rin·a·tion \¦=(=)=-\ *n* [*aer-* + *chlorination*] **:** the treatment of sewage with compressed air and chlorine gas for removal of fatty matter

aero·craft \'=(=)=,-\ *n* [by alter.] **:** AIRCRAFT

Aero·crete \'=(=)=,krēt\ *trademark* — used for a lightweight concrete

aer·odon·tal·gia \¦a(ə),rō,dän'talj(ē)ə, ¦e(ə)-,¦aa(ə)-,¦āə-\ *n* -s [NL, fr. *aer-* + *odontalgia* toothache, fr. *odont-* + *-algia*] **:** the toothache resulting from atmospheric decompression (as in high-altitude flying or confinement in decompression chambers) — **aer·odon·tal·gic** \-¦taljik\ *adj*

aer·odon·tia \-rō'dänch(ē)ə\ *n* -s [NL, fr. *aer-* + *-odontia*] **:** the branch of dentistry associated with dental problems arising in connection with flying

aero·drome \'=(=)=,drōm\ *n* -s [*aer-* + *-drome*] *Brit* **:** AIRFIELD, AIRPORT

aero·drom·ics \,=(=)='drämiks\ *n pl but sing in constr* [obs. *aerodrome* airplane (fr. Gk *aerodromos* traversing the air, fr. *aer-* + *-dromos* -drome) + *-ics*] **:** the science or art of flying aircraft

aero·dy·nam·ic \¦=(=)=(,)=¦==\ *adj* [back-formation fr. *aerodynamics*] **:** of or relating to aerodynamics — **aero·dy·nam·i·cal·ly** *adv*

aero·dy·nam·i·cist \-,dī'naməsəst, -,də'n-\ *n* -s **:** one who specializes in aerodynamics

aero·dy·nam·ics \¦=(=)=-\ *n pl but sing in constr* [*aer-* + *dynamics*] **:** the branch of dynamics that treats of the motion of air and other gaseous fluids and of the forces acting on bodies in motion relative to such fluids

aero·dyne \'=(=)=,dīn\ *n* -s [*aer-* + *-dyne* (fr. Gk *dynamis* power) — more at DYNAMIC] **:** a heavier-than-air aircraft that derives its lift in flight from aerodynamic forces — compare AEROSTAT

aero·elas·tic \¦=(=)==¦==\ *adj* [*aer-* + *elastic*] **:** subject to stretching or deformity under aerodynamic forces **:** relating to distortion through aerodynamic forces — **aero·elas·tic·i·ty** *n*

aero·em·bo·lism \¦=(=)=-\ *n* [*aer-* + *embolism*] **1 :** a gaseous embolism **2 :** a condition equivalent to caisson disease caused by rapid ascent to high altitudes and resulting exposure to rapidly lowered air pressure — called also *air bends*

aero·fil·ter \'=(=)=,-\ *n* [*aer-* + *filter*] **:** a sewage filter bed that employs coarse material and is operated at relatively high speed often with recirculation

aero·foil \'=(=)=,-\ *chiefly Brit var of* AIRFOIL

aero·gel \¦=(=)=,-\ *n* [*aer-* + *gel*] **:** a highly porous solid formed by replacement of liquid in a gel with a gas so that there is little shrinkage — see SILICA AEROGEL; compare XEROGEL

aero·gen·er·a·tor \¦=(=)=¦-\ *n* [*aer-* + *generator*] **:** a wind-driven electric generator designed for utilization of wind power on a commercial scale

aero·gen·ic \¦=(=)=¦jenik\ *or* **aer·og·e·nous** \¦=(=)'=jənəs\ *adj* [*aer-* + *-genic, -genous*] **:** forming gas — **aero·gen·i·cal·ly** \¦=(=)=¦jenək(ə)lē\ *adv*

aero·ge·og·ra·phy \¦=(=)=-\ *n* [*aer-* + *geography*] **1 :** the geography of air bases and air routes **2 :** the study of geographic features by aerial observation and aerophotography

aero·ge·ol·o·gist \¦=(=)=¦-\ *n* **:** a specialist in aerogeology

aero·ge·ol·o·gy \¦=(=)=-\ *n* [ISV *aer-* + *geology*] **:** the study of geological features by aerial observation and aerophotography

aero·gram \'=(=)=,gram\ *n* [*aer-* + *-gram*] **1 :** a message sent by wireless telegraphy, aircraft, or radio **2** *or* **aero·gramme** \"\ **:** AIR LETTER

aero·graph \'=(=)=,graf\ *n* [*aer-* + *-graph*] **:** METEOROGRAPH 1

¹aer·og·ra·pher \=(=)'=grəf=(r)\ *n* -s [*aer-* + *-grapher*] **:** one that sprays with an airbrush

²aerographer \"\ *n* -s [*aerography* + *-er*] **:** a warrant officer in the U.S. Navy whose duties include the observation of weather and the preparation of weather and surf forecasts

aerographer's mate *n* **:** a petty officer in the U.S. Navy assisting or performing the duties of the aerographer

aer·og·ra·phy \=(=)'=grəfē\ *n* -ES [*aer-* + *-graphy*] **:** METEOROLOGY

aero·hy·drous \¦=(=)=¦-\ *adj* [*aer-* + *hydrous*] *of minerals* **:** containing both air and water

aer·oi·des \(,)a(ə)'rȯi(,)dēz, -e(ə)-,-aa(ə)-,-āə-\ *n, pl* **aeroides** [Gk *aeroeidēs* like the air or sky, cloudy, fr. *aer-* + *-eidēs* -oid] **:** a pale blue beryl

aero·lite \'=(=)=,līt\ *also* **aero·lith** \'=(=)=,lith\ *n* [*aer-* + *-lite, -lith*] **:** a stony meteorite — **aero·lit·ic** \¦=(=)=¦lid·ik\ *adj*

aero·lith·ol·o·gy \ˌ⸗(⸗)⸗(ˌ)li'thäləjē\ *n* -ES [*aerolith* + *-o-* + *-logy*] : the science that deals with meteorites
aero·lit·ics \ˌ⸗(⸗)⸗'lid·iks\ *n pl but sing in constr* [*aerolite* + *-ics*] : the science that deals with aerolites
aero·log·i·cal \ˌ⸗(⸗)⸗ˌläjəkəl\ *adj* : of or relating to aerology
aer·ol·o·gist \-ə(ˌ)⸗ləjəst\ *n* -S : a specialist in aerology
aer·ol·o·gy \-əjē\ *n* -ES [*aer-* + *-logy*] **1** : METEOROLOGY **2** : the branch of meteorology that deals esp. with the description and discussion of the phenomena of the free air as revealed by kites, balloons, airplanes, and clouds
aero·mag·net·ic \ˌ⸗(⸗)⸗ˌmag'n-\ *adj* [*aer-* + *magnetic*] : of, relating to, or derived from a study of the terrestrial magnetic field esp. from the air ⟨an ~ survey⟩ ⟨an ~ map⟩
aero·man·cy \'⸗(⸗)⸗ˌman(t)sē\ *n* -ES [ME *aeromancie*, alter. (influenced by MF *aeromancie* or ML *aeromantia*) of *aeromaunce*, fr. (assumed) MF *aeromance*, fr. ML *aeromantia*, fr. L *aer-* + *-mantia* -mancy] : divination from the state of the air or from atmospheric substances; *also* : weather forecasting
aero·ma·rine \ˌ⸗(⸗)⸗mə¦rēn\ *adj* [*aer-* + *marine*] : of or relating to aerial navigation above sea or ocean ⟨under the conditions of ~ combat —Fletcher Pratt⟩
aero·me·chan·ic \ˌ⸗(⸗)⸗⸗¦⸗⸗\ *n* -S [*aer-* + *mechanic*] : an aircraft mechanic
aero·me·chan·ics \ˌ⸗(⸗)⸗⸗¦⸗⸗\ *n pl but sing in constr* [*aer-* + *mechanics*] : the branch of mechanics that deals with the equilibrium and motion of gases and of solid bodies immersed in them — compare AERODYNAMICS, AEROSTATICS, PNEUMATICS
aero·med·i·cal \ˌ⸗(⸗)⸗¦-\ *adj* [*aer-* + *medical*] : of or relating to aeromedicine ⟨~ research⟩ ⟨~ laboratory⟩ ⟨~ historical museum⟩
aero·med·i·cine \ˌ⸗(⸗)⸗¦-\ *n* -S [ISV *aer-* + *medicine*] : the branch of medicine that deals with the diseases and disturbances arising from present-day flying and involves the study and solution of resulting physiologic, psychologic, pathologic, and epidemiologic problems
aero·me·te·or·o·graph \ˌ⸗(⸗)⸗-\ *n* -S [*aer-* + *meteorograph*] : METEOROGRAPH; *esp* : one adapted for use on an aircraft
aer·om·e·ter \ˌa(ˌ)⸗'rämȯd·ə(r)\ *n* -S [prob. fr. F *aéromètre*, fr. *aér-* + *-mètre* -meter] : an instrument for ascertaining the weight or density of air or other gases
aero·met·ric \ˌ⸗(⸗)⸗¦me·trik\ *adj* [*aer-* + *-metric*] : relating to measurement of the properties or contaminants of air ⟨~ survey⟩
aero·mo·tor \'⸗(⸗)⸗ˌ-\ *n* [*aer-* + *motor*] : an aircraft motor
aero·naut \'⸗(⸗)⸗ˌnȯt, -ät, *usu* -d·+V\ *n* -S [F *aéronaute*, fr. *aéro-* aer- + Gk *nautēs* sailor — more at NAUTICAL] : one that operates or travels in an airship or balloon
aero·nau·ti·cal \-əkəl, -ēk-\ *or* **aero·nau·tic** \ˌ⸗(⸗)⸗¦nȯd·ik, -näl, \|tik, -ēk\ *adj* [*aeronautical* fr. *aeronautic* + *-al*; *aeronautic* back-formation fr. *aeronautics*] : of or relating to aeronautics — **aero·nau·ti·cal·ly** \-ək(ə)lē, -ēk-, -li\ *adv*
aeronautical station *n* : a radio transmitting station usu. on the ground for communication with aircraft — compare AIRCRAFT STATION, LAND STATION
aero·nau·tics \ˌ⸗(⸗)⸗¦⸗iks, -ēks\ *n pl but sing in constr* [modif. (influenced by *-ics*) of NL *aeronautica*, fr. *aer-* + L *nautica*, neut. pl. of *nauticus* nautical — more at NAUTICAL] **1** *archaic* : the art or practice of sailing (as in lighter-than-air craft) through the air **2** : the science that deals with the operation of aircraft **3** : the art or science of flight
aero·na·val \ˌ⸗(⸗)⸗¦-\ *adj* [*aer-* + *naval*] : of or involving combined air and naval forces ⟨an ~ base⟩ ⟨~ war⟩
aero·neu·ro·sis \ˌ⸗(⸗)⸗-\ *n* [NL, fr. *aer-* + *neurosis*] : a functional nervous disorder of airmen caused by emotional stress and characterized by physical symptoms (as restlessness, pains in the abdomen, and diarrhea)
aero–oti·tis me·dia \ˌ⸗(⸗)⸗ō'tīd·ə'smēdēə\ *also* **aero–otitis** *or* **aer·oti·tis** \-rō'tīd·əs\ *n* [NL] : the traumatic inflammation of the middle ear resulting from differences between atmospheric pressure and pressure in the tympanic cavity and occurring in high-altitude flyers, caisson or tunnel workers, and deep-sea divers
aero·pause \'⸗(⸗)⸗ˌpȯz\ *n* -S [*aer-* + *pause*] : the level above the earth's surface where the atmosphere becomes ineffective for human and aircraft functions
aero·pha·gia \ˌ⸗(⸗)⸗'fāj(ē)ə\ *also* **aer·oph·a·gy** \ˌ⸗(⸗)'⸗fəjē\ *n, pl* **aerophagias** *also* **aerophagies** [NL *aerophagia*, fr. *aer-* + *-phagia* -phagy] : the swallowing of air esp. in hysteria
aer·oph·a·gist \ˌ⸗(⸗)⸗'fəjəst\ *n* -S : one that swallows air
aero·phane \'⸗(⸗)⸗ˌfān\ *n* -S [prob. fr. F *aérophane*, fr. *aér-* aer- + *-phane*] : a fine silk gauze
aero·phil·a·tel·ic \ˌ⸗(⸗)⸗ˌ⸗⸗¦⸗⸗\ *adj* : of or relating to airmail stamps and flown covers
aero·phi·lat·e·list \ˌ⸗(⸗)⸗-\ *n* : a specialist in aerophilately
aero·phi·lat·e·ly \ˌ⸗(⸗)⸗-\ *n* -ES [*aer-* + *philately*] : the collection and study of airmail stamps and flown covers
aero·phile \'⸗(⸗)⸗ˌfīl\ *n* -S [*aer-* + *-phile*] : a lover of aviation
aero·pho·bia \ˌ⸗(⸗)⸗'fōbēə\ *n* -S [NL, fr. *aer-* + *-phobia*] : abnormal or excessive fear of drafts or of fresh air — **aero·pho·bic** \ˌ⸗(⸗)⸗¦fōbik *also* -äb-\ *adj*
aero·phone \'⸗(⸗)⸗ˌfōn\ *n* -S [*aer-* + *-phone*] : a musical instrument (as a trumpet or flute) in which sound is generated by a vibrating column or eddy of air : WIND INSTRUMENT — **aero·phon·ic** \ˌ⸗(⸗)⸗¦fänik\ *adj*
aero·phor \'⸗(⸗)⸗ˌfō(ə)r\ *also* **aero·phore** \-ˌfō(ə)r, -ȯ(-\ *n* -S [G *aerophor*, fr. *aer-* + *-phor* -phore] : a device employing a foot bellows by means of which a tone may be sustained on a wind instrument for an indefinite period
aero·pho·to \'⸗(⸗)⸗ˌ-\ *n* -S [*aer-* + *photo*] : AERIAL PHOTOGRAPH
aero·pho·tog·ra·phy \ˌ⸗(⸗)⸗-\ *n* -ES [*aer-* + *photography*] : photography from aircraft
aero·phys·i·cal \ˌ⸗(⸗)⸗¦-\ *adj* : of or relating to aerophysics
aero·phys·ics \ˌ⸗(⸗)⸗¦-\ *n pl but sing in constr* [*aer-* + *physics*] **1** : the physics of the air **2** : physics dealing with the design, construction, and operation of devices that move rapidly through the air (as projectiles, guided missiles, rockets, and aircraft)
aero·plane \'⸗(⸗)⸗ˌplān, *or like* AIRPLANE\ *chiefly Brit var of* AIRPLANE
aero·pol·i·tics \ˌ⸗(⸗)⸗¦-\ *n pl but sing in constr* [*aer-* + *politics*] : politics as conditioned by considerations of air power ⟨the air future, a primer of ~ —Burnet Hershey⟩
aero·pulse \'⸗(⸗)⸗ˌ-\ *or* **aero·res·o·na·tor** \ˌ⸗(⸗)⸗'-\ *n* -S [*aer-* + *pulse* or *resonator*] : PULSE-JET ENGINE
aero·scep·sis \ˌ⸗(⸗)⸗'skepsəs\ *also* **aero·scep·sy** \'⸗(⸗)⸗ˌ⸗sē\ *n, pl* **aeroscep·ses** \-p(ˌ)sēz\ *also* **aeroscepsies** \-psēz\ [*aeroscepsis*, NL, fr. *aer-* + Gk *skepsis* perception, consideration; *aeroscepsy*, modif. of NL *aeroscepsis*] : the power possessed by certain animals of observing the quality of the air by means of special organs
aero·sid·er·ite \ˌ⸗(⸗)⸗-\ *n* -S [*aer-* + *siderite*] : a meteorite composed chiefly of iron : SIDERITE
aero·sid·er·o·lite \ˌ⸗(⸗)⸗-\ *n* -S [*aer-* + *siderolite*] : a meteorite composed of both stone and iron : SIDEROLITE
aero·si·nus·i·tis \ˌ⸗(⸗)⸗-\ *n* [NL, fr. *aer-* + *sinusitis*] : the traumatic inflammation of the nasal sinuses resulting from the difference between atmospheric pressure and the pressure within the sinus cavities and occurring in high-altitude flyers, caisson or tunnel workers, or deep-sea divers
aero·sol \'⸗(⸗)⸗ˌsȯl, -ōl\ *n* -S [*aer-* + *sol*] **1** : a suspension of ultramicroscopic solid or liquid particles in air or gas (as smoke, fog, or mist) **2 a** : a substance and a propellant (as compressed gas) in a container with a valve through which the substance is dispensed as an aerosol; *esp* : a liquid containing an active agent (as an insecticide, germicide, medicine, or cosmetic) **b** : a container for this
aerosol bomb *n* : a small container for dispensing an aerosol usu. by release of pressure
aero·sol·i·za·tion \ˌ⸗(⸗)⸗ˌsȯlə'zāshən, -sōl-, -säl-, -(ˌ)lī'z-\ *n* -S : dispersal (as of a medicine) in the form of an aerosol ⟨~ of penicillin⟩
aero·sol·ize \'⸗(⸗)⸗ˌsȯˌlīz, -sō-, -sä-\ *vt* -ED/-ING/-S : to disperse (as a medicine, bactericide, or insecticide) as an aerosol ⟨possible to ~ salt solutions, acids, bases, suspensions and emulsions —*Swiss Industry & Trade*⟩ — **aero·sol·izer** \-zə(r)\ *n* -S
aerosol therapy *n* : inhalation treatment using medicated aerosols
aero·sphere \'⸗(⸗)⸗ˌ-\ *n* -S [F *aérosphère*, fr. *aér-* aer- + *-sphère* -sphere] : the body of air around the earth : ATMOSPHERE
aero·stat \'⸗(⸗)⸗ˌstat\ *n* -S [F *aérostat*, fr. *aér-* aer- + *-stat*] **1** : an aircraft (as a balloon or airship) that embodies one or more containers filled with a gas lighter than air and that is supported chiefly by buoyancy derived from the surrounding air — compare AERODYNE **2** : either of a pair of pouches located at the base of the abdomen in dipterous flies
¹aero·stat·ic \ˌ⸗(⸗)⸗¦stad·ik\ *also* **aero·stat·i·cal** \-d·əkəl\ *adj* [*aer-* + *static*, *statical*] : of or relating to aerostatics : PNEUMATIC
²aerostatic *also* **aerostatical** \"\ *adj* [F *aérostatique*, fr. *aérostat* + *-ique* -ic, -ical] : of or relating to aerial navigation
aero·stat·ics \ˌ⸗(⸗)⸗'⸗iks\ *n pl but sing in constr* [modif. of NL *aerostatica*, fr. *aer-* + *-statica* -statics] : the branch of statics that deals with the equilibrium of gaseous fluids and of solid bodies immersed in them
aero·sta·tion \ˌ⸗(⸗)⸗¦stāshən\ *n* -S [F *aérostation*, irreg. fr. *aérostat* + *-ion*] : the art or science of operating lighter-than-air aircraft — compare AVIATION
aero·tac·tic \ˌ⸗(⸗)⸗¦taktik\ *adj* [fr. NL *aerotaxis*, after such pairs as NL *chemotaxis*: E *chemotactic*] : of or relating to aerotaxis
aero·tax·is \ˌ⸗(⸗)⸗'taksəs\ *n* [NL, fr. *aer-* + *-taxis*] : a taxis in which air or oxygen is the directive factor
aero·tech·ni·cal \ˌ⸗(⸗)⸗¦-\ *adj* [*aer-* + *technical*] : of or relating to aeronautics
aero·ther·a·peu·tics \ˌ⸗(⸗)⸗-\ *n pl but sing in constr* [*aer-* + *therapeutics*] : the treatment of disease by varying pressure or composition of air breathed by the patient
aero·ther·a·py \ˌ⸗(⸗)⸗¦-\ *n* -ES [*aer-* + *therapy*] : AEROTHERAPEUTICS
aero·ther·mo·dy·nam·ics \ˌ⸗(⸗)⸗-\ *n pl but sing in constr* [*aer-* + *thermodynamics*] : the thermodynamics of gases and esp. air
aerotitis *var of* AERO-OTITIS
aer·ot·ro·pism \ˌ⸗(⸗)'⸗trəˌpizəm\ *n* -S [*aer-* + *tropism*] : response usu. by change in direction of growth of roots or other plant structures to changes in oxygen tension
aers *pl of* AER
ae·ru·gi·nous \ē'rüjənəs, i'-,ī'-\ *also* **e·ru·gi·nous** \ē'-, ē'-, i'-\ *adj* [L *aeruginosus*, fr. *aerugin-*, *aerugo* + *-osus* -ous] : having the characteristics of or the color of verdigris
ae·ru·go \ē'rü(ˌ)gō, i'-,ī'-\ *n* -S [L, fr. *aer-*, *aes* copper, bronze, brass — more at ORE] : the rust of a metal and esp. brass or copper : VERDIGRIS
¹aery \'a\|(ə)rē, 'e\|,'aa\|,'ā\|, -ri\ *adj* [L *aerius*, fr. *aer* air — more at AIR] : having an aerial quality : ETHEREAL ⟨in ~ vision wrapped —James Thomson †1748⟩
²aery *var of* AERIE
aes *pl of* ¹A
AE's *pl of* AE
aesch·na \'eskna\ *n, cap* [NL, alter. of *Aeshna*] : a genus of large often bright-colored dragonflies including the blue darners
aes·chy·le·an \ˌeskə¦lēən\ *adj, usu cap* [*Aeschyl*us †456 B.C. Greek tragic poet (fr. L, fr. Gk *Aischylos*) + E *-ean*] : of, relating to, or suggestive of Aeschylus
aes·chy·nan·thus \ˌeskə'nan(t)thəs\ *n* [NL, fr. Gk *aischynē* shame + NL *-anthus*; fr. the red flowers, thought of as blushing] **1** *cap* : a genus of East Indian ornamental woody epiphytic plants (family Gesneriaceae) having red or orange flowers and seeds that bear one bristle or hair at the apex and one or more at the base **2** -ES : a plant of the genus *Aeschynanthus*
aeschynite *var of* ESCHYNITE
aes·chy·nom·e·ne \ˌeskə'nämə(ˌ)nē\ *n, cap* [NL, fr. Gk *aischynomenē* sensitive plant, fr. *aischynē* shame + *-menē* (fr. *menos* mind); fr. the fact that the leafstalks droop when touched] : a genus of shrubs and herbs (family Leguminosae) widely distributed in warm regions and having jointed pods and pinnate and often sensitive leaves — see SENSITIVE JOINT VETCH, SOLA
aes·cu·la·ce·ae \ˌeskyə'lāsēˌē\ *n pl, cap* [NL, fr. *Aesculus*, type genus + *-aceae*] *in some classifications* : a family of shrubs and trees of the order Sapindales that are usu. made a tribe of the family Hippocastanaceae or placed among the Sapindaceae — compare AESCULUS — **aes·cu·la·ceous** \ˌ⸗⸗¦⸗shəs\ *adj*
aes·cu·la·pi·an \ˌeskyə¦lāpēən\ *adj, usu cap* [*Aesculapi*us, the god + E *-an*] : of or belonging to Aesculapius or the healing art : MEDICAL, MEDICINAL
aesculapian staff *n, usu cap A* : STAFF OF AESCULAPIUS
aes·cu·la·pi·us \ˌeskyə'lāpēəs\ *n* -ES *usu cap* [after *Aesculapius*, Greco-Roman god of medicine, fr. L, fr. Gk *Asklēpios*] : PHYSICIAN
aesculapius' snake \-ēəs'sn-\ *or* **aesculapian snake** *n, usu cap A* [fr. *Aesculapius*, god of medicine] : a harmless European snake (*Coluber*, or *Elaphe*, *longissimus*) believed to have been held sacred to Aesculapius by the Romans
aesculetin *var of* ESCULETIN
aesculin *var of* ESCULIN
aes·cu·lus \'eskyələs\ *n, cap* [NL, fr. L, an oak — more at OAK] : a genus of trees and shrubs (family Hippocastanaceae) found in north temperate regions with palmately divided leaves, showy flowers in ample panicles, and large shiny seeds — see BUCKEYE, HORSE CHESTNUT
aes gra·ve \'īs'grä,vā\ *n* [L, lit., heavy bronze] : a cumbersome bronze coinage used by the Romans and other Italic peoples and based on the as as unit of value
ae·sir \'asir, 'aa-, 'ī-\ *n pl, usu cap* [ON *Æsir*, pl. of *āss* god; akin to OE *ōs* god (name of a rune), OS *ās-*, *ōs-* & OHG *ans-* (in proper names), (assumed) Goth *ans* (whence ML *ansis*, acc. pl., demigods), and prob. to Skt *asu* life, vital strength, *asura*, adj. & n., mighty, lord, demon, Av *ahurō* lord] : the chief gods of pagan Scandinavia
ae·so·pi·an \ē'sōpēən, -äp-\ *also* **ae·sop·ic** \ē'säpik\ *adj, usu cap* [*Aesop* fr. L *Aesopus*, fr. Gk *Aisōpos*), legendary 6th cent. B.C. Greek author of fables + E *-ian* or *-ic*] : conveying an innocent meaning to an outsider but a concealed meaning to an informed member of a conspiracy or underground movement ⟨*Aesopian* language⟩
ae·sop prawn \'ē,säp-, -ˌsəp- *sometimes* 'ā-\ *n, usu cap A* [NL *aesopius*, lit., Aesopian (specific epithet of *Periclimenes aesopius*), fr. L *Aesopus*; fr. the belief that Aesop was humpbacked] **1** : a small decapod crustacean of the genus *Hippolyte* **2** *Austral* : a small humpbacked prawn (*Periclimenes aesopius*)
aes ru·de \'īs'rü,dā\ *n* [L, lit., crude bronze] : ancient money of Rome and Italy having as units rude uncoined masses of bronze
aes sig·na·tum \-ˌsig'näd·əm\ *n* [L, lit., marked bronze] : ancient money of Rome and Italy having as unit of exchange a bronze bar and usu. stamped with an animal figure
aesthacyte *var of* ESTHACYTE
aesthesia *var of* ESTHESIA
aesthesio- — see ESTHESIO-
aesthesis *var of* ESTHESIS
aes·thete *also* **es·thete** \'es,thēt, *usu* -ēd·+V; *Brit usu* 'ēs-\ *n* -S [fr. *aesthetics*, after such pairs as E *athletics*: *athlete*] : one professing devotion to the beautiful : one having or affecting artistic perception or judgment of or sensitivity to the beautiful esp. in art
aes·thet·ic *or* **es·thet·ic** \es'thed·ik, is-,əs-, -etik, -ēk, *sometimes* 'es,th-, *Brit usu* ēs'-\ *or* **aes·thet·i·cal** *or* **es·thet·i·cal** \-əkəl, -ēk-\ *adj* [G *ästhetisch*, fr. NL *aestheticus*, fr. Gk *aisthētikos* of sense perception — more at AESTHETICS] **1** : relating to or dealing with aesthetics or its subject matter ⟨~ theories⟩ ⟨~ philosophers⟩ **2 a** : relating to the beautiful as distinguished from the merely pleasing, the moral, and esp. the useful and utilitarian ⟨a purely ~ reaction⟩ ⟨~ criteria⟩ **b** : ARTISTIC ⟨the illustrations made the book an ~ success⟩ : BEAUTIFUL **3** : appreciative of, responsive to, or zealous about the beautiful ⟨an ~ person⟩ ⟨he lived in an ~ age⟩ : having a sense, real or affected, of beauty or fine culture **4** : relating to sensuous cognition : **a** : involving pure feeling or sensation esp. in contrast to ratiocination ⟨the ~ component of knowledge⟩ **b** : based on or derived from immediate esp. sensuous experience ⟨gustatory and tactile ~ delights⟩ ⟨~ feeling⟩ **syn** see ARTISTIC
aes·thet·i·cal·ly *or* **es·thet·i·cal·ly** \-k(ə)lē, -li\ *adv* : in an aesthetic way ⟨a happy ending is morally and ~ satisfying —J.C.Bushman⟩
aesthetic distance *n* : the frame of reference that an artist creates by the use of technical devices in and around the work of art to differentiate it psychologically from reality
aes·the·ti·cian *also* **es·the·ti·cian** \ˌesthə'tishən, *Brit usu* ˌēs-\ *or* **aes·thet·i·cist** \es'thed·əsəst, is-,əs-, -etə-, *Brit usu* ēs-\ *n* -S : a specialist in aesthetics
aes·thet·i·cism *also* **es·thet·i·cism** \es'thed·əˌsizəm, is-,əs-, -etə-, *Brit usu* ēs-\ *n* -S **1 a** : the doctrine that the principles of beauty are basic and that other principles (as of the good or the right) are derived from them **b** : the advocacy of artistic and aesthetic autonomy, esp. of freedom of art from any interference on political, religious, social, or moral grounds **2** : an extensive, singular, or excessive devotion to or emphasis on aesthetic experiences or the search for beauty esp. as evidenced by a cultivation of the arts to the neglect of other human interests
aes·thet·i·cize *also* **es·thet·i·cize** \-ˌsīz\ *vt* -ED/-ING/-S : to make aesthetic ⟨remodeled and *aestheticized* the old railroad station⟩
aes·thet·ics *also* **es·thet·ics** \-iks,-ēks\ *n pl but usu sing in constr, also* **aesthetic** *or* **esthetic** [G *ästhetik*, fr. NL *aesthetica*, fr. Gk *aisthētikē*, fem. of *aisthētikos* of sense perception, fr. *aisthanesthai* to perceive — more at AUDIBLE] **1** : a branch of philosophy dealing with beauty and the beautiful esp. with judgments of taste concerning them : **a** : the science of sensuous knowledge whose goal is beauty — compare LOGIC **b** : TRANSCENDENTAL AESTHETIC **c** : a particular philosophical theory or conception of art ⟨a forward-looking ~⟩ ⟨an ~ of his own⟩ **2** : the philosophy or science of art; *specif* : the science whose subject matter is the description and explanation of the arts, artistic phenomena, and aesthetic experience and includes the psychology, sociology, ethnology, and history of the arts and essentially related aspects
aesthetic truth *n* : NORMATIVE TRUTH
aes·thi·ol·o·gy \ˌesthē'äləjē, *Brit usu* ˌēs-\ *n* -ES [irreg. fr. Gk *aisthanesthai* to perceive + E *-logy* — more at AESTHETICS] : ESTHESIOPHYSIOLOGY
aes·tho–physiology \ˌes(ˌ)thō-, *Brit usu* ¦ēs-\ *n* -ES : ESTHESIOPHYSIOLOGY
aes·ti·val *or* **es·ti·val** \'estəvəl, (')es¦tīvəl, *Brit usu* -ēs-\ *adj* [ME *estival*, fr. MF or L; MF, fr. L *aestivalis*, fr. *aestivus* of summer (fr. *aestas* summer + *-ivus* -ive) + *-alis* -al; akin to L *aedes* temple — more at EDIFY] : of or belonging to the summer ⟨the sky was a burnished ~ blue —*Irish Statesman*⟩
aes·ti·vate *or* **es·ti·vate** \'estəˌvāt, *usu* -äd-+V; *Brit usu* 'ēs-\ *vi* -ED/-ING/-S [L *aestivatus*, past part. of *aestivare* to spend the summer, fr. *aestivus*] **1** : to spend the summer usu. at one place and sometimes in relative inactivity ⟨*aestivating* at his mountain lodge⟩ **2** : to pass the summer in a state of torpor — used esp. of animals ⟨crabs *aestivating* in the sand⟩; compare HIBERNATE
aes·ti·va·tion *or* **es·ti·va·tion** \ˌ⸗⸗'vāshən\ *n* -S [L *aestivatus* + E *-ion*] **1** : the state or condition of torpidity or dormancy induced by heat and dryness of summer (as in certain snails) — opposed to *hibernation* **2** : the disposition or method of arrangement of floral parts in a bud — compare VERNATION
aes·ti·va·tor *or* **es·ti·va·tor** \'⸗⸗ˌvād·ə(r)\ *n* -S : an animal that aestivates
aestivo–autumnal *var of* ESTIVO-AUTUMNAL
aet *or* **aetat** *abbr* [L *aetatis*, gen. of *aetas* age — more at AGE] of age; aged
ae·ta \'ed·ə\ *n, pl* **aeta** *or* **aetas** *usu cap* [Tag] **1** : a Negrito people inhabiting the central and southern Zambales mountains in Zambales, Papanga, and Bataan provinces of the Philippines **2** : a member of the Aeta people
ae·tha·li·oid \ē'thālēˌȯid\ *adj* [NL ¹*aethalium* + E *-oid*] : resembling or belonging to an aethalium
¹ae·tha·li·um \-lēəm,lyəm\ *n, pl* **ae·tha·lia** \-ēə,-yə\ [NL, fr. Gk *aithalos* thick smoke, soot (fr. *aithein* to burn) + NL *-ium* — more at EDIFY] : a sessile flat encrusted fruiting body in several genera of the slime molds (class Myxomycetes) formed by the fusion of many plasmodia
²aethalium \"\ [NL] *syn of* FULIGO
aetheling *often cap, var of* ATHELING
aether *var of* ETHER
aethereal *or* **aetherial** *var of* ETHEREAL
aetheria *syn of* ETHERIA
aetheric *var of* ETHERIC
aetherin *var of* ETHERIN
aetherophone *var of* ETHEROPHONE
ae·thi·o·ne·ma \ˌēthēō'nēmə\ *n, cap* [NL, fr. *aethio-* (fr. Gk *aēthēs* strange) + *-nema*] : a genus of herbs (family Cruciferae) found in the Mediterranean region that have sessile glaucous leaves, some being cultivated for their white or rose-colored flowers
aethiopian *usu cap, var of* ETHIOPIAN
aethiops *var of* ETHIOPS
ae·thri·o·scope \'ēthrēəˌskōp, 'e-\ *n* [Gk *aithrios* clear + E *-scope*] : an instrument consisting in part of a differential thermometer for measuring changes of temperature produced by different conditions of the sky
aetio- — see ETIO-
aetiology *var of* ETIOLOGY
aetioporphyrin *var of* ETIOPORPHYRIN
ae·ti·tes \ˌāə'tīd·(ˌ)ēz\ *n, pl* **aetites** [L, fr. Gk *aetitēs*, fr. *aetitēs*, adj., of an eagle, fr. *aetos*, *aietos* eagle — more at AVIARY] : EAGLESTONE
aeto- *comb form* [NL, fr. Gk *aetos*; akin to L *avis* bird — more at AVIARY] : eagle ⟨*aeto*morph⟩ ⟨*Aeto*saurus⟩ — esp. in names of taxonomic groups in zoology
aeto·bat·i·dae \āˌed·ə'bad·əˌdē, āˌē-\ [NL, fr. *Aetobatus*, type genus (fr. *aeto-* + Gk *batos*, a fish, prob. a skate) + *-idae*] *syn of* MYLIOBATIDAE
ae·to·li·an \ē'tōlēən, -lyən\ *adj, usu cap* [*Aetolia*, ancient district of Greece (fr. L, fr. Gk *Aitōlia*) + E *-an*] **1** : of, relating to, or characteristic of Aetolia **2** : of, relating to, or characteristic of the people of Aetolia
aeto·sau·rus \āˌed·əˌsȯrəs, āˌē-\ *n, cap* [NL, fr. *aeto-* + *-saurus*] : a genus of small extinct crocodiles of the Triassic period
-a·e·tus \ā'ēd·əs, 'ātəs\ *n comb form* [NL, fr. Gk *aetos* — more at AETO-] : eagle — in generic names of birds ⟨*Circaetus*⟩
aex \'eks\ *syn of* AIX
af- — see AD-
Af *abbr* Afghani
AF *abbr* **1** [L *actum fide*] done in faith **2** [L *ad finem*] at the end; to the end **3** admiral of the fleet **4** air force **5** [It *al fine*] to the end **6** audio frequency
afaint \ə'-\ *adj* [¹*a-* + *faint* (v.)] : FAINTING
afa·lou man \'afəˌlü-\ *n, usu cap A* [fr. *Afalou* bou Rummel, near Bougie, Algeria, where remains were found] : one of an Upper Paleolithic people of northern Africa closely related to Cro-Magnon man but having a broader nose, a sloping forehead, and heavy brow ridges
¹afar \ə'fär, -ä(r\ *adv* [ME *afer*, fr. *on fer* at a distance and *of fer* from a distance — more at FAR] : from or at a great distance : far away ⟨the world of books is something ~ —S.G. Shaw⟩ — often used with *off* ⟨I saw him ~ off⟩
²afar \"\ *n* -S : a great distance — usu. used with *from* ⟨saw him from ~⟩
³afar \'ä,fär\ *n, pl* **afar** \"\ *or* **afa·ra** \ə'färə\ *usu cap* **1** : DANAKIL **2** : the Cushitic language of the Danakil people — see AFRO-ASIATIC LANGUAGES table
afa·ra \ə'färə\ *n* -S [Yoruba *a²fa³ra³*] : ²LIMBA
AFB *abbr* air force base
AFC *abbr* **1** automatic flight control **2** automatic frequency control
¹afear \ə'fi(ə)r\ *vt* [ME *aferen*, fr. OE *āfǣran*, fr *ā-* (perfective prefix) + *fǣran* to frighten — more at ABEAR, FEAR] *now dial Eng* : FRIGHTEN
²afear \"\ *conj* [ME *afere*, adv., in fear, fr. ¹*a-* + *fere* fear] *now dial Brit* : for fear
afeard *or* **afeared** \-i(ə)rd\ *adj* [ME *afered*, fr. OE *āfǣred*, past part. of *āfǣran*] *now dial* : AFRAID
afebrile \(')ā+¦-\ *adj* [²*a-* + *febrile*] : free from fever : not marked by fever
af·er·nan \'afə(r)ˌnan\ *n* -S [Ar *al-farnān* the afernan] : a desert shrub (*Euphorbia balsamifera*) native to the Canary

islands that has leaves at the ends of the branches and inconspicuous yellow flowers

aff \ˈaf\ *Scot var of* OFF

aff *abbr* **1** affectionate **2** affirmative

af·fa·bil·i·ty \ˌafəˈbilәd·ē, -ətē, -i\ *n* -ES [MF *affabilité*, fr. L *affabilitat-, affabilitas*, fr. *affabilis* + *-itat-, -itas* -ity] **:** the quality or state of being affable **:** SOCIABILITY

af·fa·ble \ˈafəbəl\ *adj* [MF, fr. L *affabilis*, fr. *affari* to speak to (fr. *ad-* + *fari* to speak) + *-abilis* -able — more at BAN] **1 a :** pleasant and at ease in talking to others ⟨an ~ person⟩ **b :** characterized by ease and friendliness ⟨on ~ terms with his neighbors⟩ **2 :** BENIGN ⟨an ~ smile⟩ **:** PLEASANT ⟨more of this composer's ~ music —Arthur Berger⟩ **syn** see GRACIOUS

af·fable·ness *n* -ES **:** the quality or state of being affable

af·fa·bly \-blē, -i\ *adv* **:** in an affable manner **:** COURTEOUSLY, PLEASANTLY

af·fair \əˈfa(a)(ə)r, -e(ə)r, -a(a)ə, -eə\ *n* -S [ME & MF; ME *afere, affaire*, fr. MF, fr. *a faire* to do, fr. *a* to (fr. L *ad*) + *faire* to do, fr. L *facere* — more at AT, DO] **1 a affairs** *pl* **:** commercial, professional, or public business ⟨the Federal Republic agrees to conduct its ~*s* in conformity with the principles stated in the charter —*Current History*⟩ ⟨a well-known man of ~*s*⟩ **b :** MATTER, CONCERN ⟨religion is also an ~ of the imaginative life —Roger Fry⟩ ⟨they don't want to get mixed up in it because it isn't their ~ —Brad Sebstad⟩ **2 a :** any procedure, action, or occasion not clearly distinguished or only vaguely specified ⟨an ~ of honor⟩ ⟨one of the most brilliant social ~*s* of the season⟩ ⟨public life had become so discreditable an ~ —F.M.Ford⟩ ⟨the whole ~ from start to finish did not occupy more than thirty seconds —S.H.Holbrook⟩ ⟨if he knew anything about rain, this was going to be an all-day ~ —Hamilton Basso⟩ — sometimes used in pl. ⟨an attempt to end this sad state of ~*s*⟩ **b** [F *affaire*] *also* **af·faire :** a romantic or passionate attachment typically of limited duration **:** an illicit sexual relationship **:** LIAISON, INTRIGUE ⟨a series of ~*s* before her marriage⟩ **c** [F *affaire*] *or* **affaire :** a matter or episode occasioning public anxiety or dispute or giving rise to scandalous report and speculation **:** CASE — used often with proper names ⟨the Doe ~⟩ ⟨the ~ Roeville⟩ **d :** any object or collection of objects not clearly distinguished or only vaguely specified ⟨a black-and-white checked wool ~ with a double collar —Lois Long⟩ ⟨the orchestra has arrived, no thin five-piece ~, but a whole pitful of oboes and trombones and saxophones —Scott Fitzgerald⟩

af·faire d'a·mour \ˈdəˈmü(ə)r, -üə\ *n, pl* **affaires d'amour** \-(z)də-\ [F, love affair] **:** AFFAIR 2b

affaire de coeur \-dəˈkər, -kə\ *n, pl* **affaires de coeur** \-(z)də-\ [F *affaire de cœur*, lit., affair of the heart] **:** AFFAIR 2b

affaire d'hon·neur \-dəˈnər, -ˌdȯˈ-, -nə\ *n, pl* **affaires d'honneur** \-(z)də-, -(z)ˌdȯ-\ [F, lit., affair of honor] **:** a matter involving honor; *specif* **:** DUEL

affamish *vb* -ED/-ING/-ES [modif. (influenced by *famish*) of MF *affamer, afamer* — more at FAMISH] *vt, obs* **:** to cause to hunger **:** STARVE ~ *vi, obs* **:** to suffer or die from hunger **:** STARVE

¹af·fect \ˈaˌfekt, aˈf-,əˈf-\ *n* -S [L *affectus* disposition, affection, desire, fr. *affectus*, past part. of *afficere*] **1** *obs* **:** FEELING, EMOTION **2** [G *affekt*, fr. L *affectus*] *psychol* **:** the conscious subjective aspect of an emotion considered apart from bodily changes

²af·fect \əˈfekt, (ˈ)aˈf-\ *vb* -ED/-ING/-S [MF & L; MF *affecter*, fr. L *affectare*, freq. of *afficere* to exert an influence, to bestow, apply oneself, fr. *ad-* + *-ficere* (fr. *facere* to do) — more at DO] *vt* **1** *archaic* **:** to aim at **:** aspire to **:** try to attain ⟨this proud man ~*s* imperial sway —John Dryden⟩ **2 a** *archaic* **:** to have affection for (a person or object) ⟨as for Queen Katharine, he rather respected than ~*ed*, rather honored than loved her —Thomas Fuller⟩ **b :** to be given to **:** FANCY ⟨~ a precise way of speaking⟩ ⟨~ brightly colored clothing⟩ **3 :** to make a display of liking or using **:** cultivate or profess ostentatiously ⟨it was the habit of the moment at Oxford to ~ irreverence —T.B.Costain⟩ **4 :** to assume the character or appearance of **:** put on a pretense of **:** PRETEND, FEIGN, COUNTERFEIT ⟨~ indifference⟩ ⟨youthfulness is something she has to ~ —E.R. Bentley⟩ ⟨Lewis at first ~*ed* to receive these propositions coolly —T.B.Macaulay⟩ **5 :** to tend toward ⟨drops of water ~ roundness⟩ **6 :** to be frequently or habitually found in **:** FREQUENT ⟨swallows that ~ chimneys⟩ ⟨she was employed far away from the table which I ~*ed* —Arnold Bennett⟩ ~ *vi, obs* **:** INCLINE 2 **syn** see ASSUME

³affect \"\ *vt* -ED/-ING/-S [L *affectus*, past part.] **1 :** to act upon: **a :** to produce an effect (as of disease) upon ⟨a condition ~*ing* the heart⟩ **b** (1) **:** to produce a material influence upon or alteration in ⟨rainfall ~*s* plant growth⟩ ⟨areas to be ~*ed* by highway construction⟩ (2) **:** to have a detrimental influence on — used esp. in the phrase *affecting commerce* **c :** to make an impression on (as the mind or the feelings) ⟨the physical details that had once ~*ed* her so deeply —Ellen Glasgow⟩ **:** INFLUENCE ⟨the only law on the books ~*ing* the conduct of the individual —Zechariah Chafee⟩ **2 :** ASSIGN, ALLOT ⟨endowment funds ~*ed* to the provision of scholarships⟩

syn INFLUENCE, TOUCH, IMPRESS, STRIKE, SWAY: AFFECT applies to a stimulus strong enough to bring about a reaction, sometimes emotional, or bring about some modification, usu. without total change ⟨a sentence about the weather, and how it *affected* her joints —Floyd Dell⟩ ⟨I was more than a little unstrung. Those long weeks of solitude had *affected* my nerves —Jack McLaren⟩ ⟨the crop in China would have been larger had not flood damage adversely *affected* the yields —*Collier's Yr. Bk.*⟩ INFLUENCE applies to a force that brings about a change or determines a course or stand ⟨the general political views of John Quincy Adams strongly *influenced* him, though he was not attracted by the example and methods of the older man —W.C.Ford⟩ ⟨the British expressed views still strongly *influenced* by nineteenth-century concepts of diplomacy and imperialism —Vera M. Dean⟩ ⟨she *influenced* profoundly the history of her people by her political acumen as minister without portfolio —*Americana Annual*⟩ TOUCH, similar to AFFECT but more vivid, may suggest forceful or emotional arousing, stirring, or impinging on ⟨they do care! their hearts are *touched*. We can do anything with them now —Hugh Walpole⟩ ⟨a small object whose exquisite workmanship has *touched* me with its intimate charm —Jean S. Untermeyer⟩ IMPRESS may suggest a deep lasting effect ⟨the populace was *impressed* because the president in person had heeded the call of a poor farmer —H.F.Wilkins⟩ ⟨his appeal was to fear, and he so *impressed* his hearers that frequently they fell to the floor or shrieked in terror —H.E.Starr⟩ STRIKE is more likely to suggest sudden sharp perception or reaction ⟨with a note in her voice that *struck* them all awake and fearful —Grace Campbell⟩ ⟨she was *struck* silent by her love —Ethel Wilson⟩ ⟨we may be *struck* with a sense of otherness, of unfamiliarity, and we seek orientation in terms of what we already know —A.C.Danto⟩ SWAY often applies to influences that are either not resisted or have such force that resistance is overcome, with resulting change in the subject's nature or course ⟨capricious deities, *swayed* by human passions and desires —G.L.Dickinson⟩ ⟨it is generally conceded that phrasing can *sway* opinions most easily when those opinions are not strongly held —S.L.Payne⟩ ⟨the elemental forces which *sway* the spirit with immortal hopes and infinite terrors —Roger Fry⟩

af·fect·a·bil·i·ty *or* **af·fect·i·bil·i·ty** \əˌfektəˈbilәd·ē, (ˌ)aˌf-\ *n* -ES **:** ability or readiness to be affected

af·fect·a·ble *or* **af·fect·i·ble** \əˈfektəbəl, (ˈ)aˈf-\ *adj* **:** able to be affected **:** easily affected ⟨a material very ~ by sudden changes in temperature⟩

affectate *vt* -ED/-ING/-S [L *affectatus*] *obs* **:** ²AFFECT 4

af·fec·ta·tion \ˌaˌfekˈtāshən *also* -ˌfik-, -ˌfēk-\ *n* -S [MF & L; MF *affectation*, fr. L *affectation-, affectatio* act of striving, conceit, fr. *affectatus* (past part. of *affectare* to aim) + *-ion-, -io* -ion — more at AFFECT] **1** *obs* **:** a striving after **:** aspiration toward **2** *obs* **:** FONDNESS, AFFECTION **3 :** the act of taking up or esp. displaying a feeling, attitude, opinion, or desire not natural to oneself or not genuinely felt ⟨his love of music was mere ~⟩ ⟨his ~ of righteous indignation fooled nobody⟩ **4 :** manner of speech or behavior not natural to one's actual personality or capabilities **:** artificiality of behavior esp. in display of feelings ⟨was there nothing in beautiful manners but foppery, prudery, starch, and ~, with false pride overtopping all? —Van Wyck Brooks⟩

affected *adj* [fr. past part. of ²*affect*] **1 :** attached to **:** inclined or disposed toward ⟨the house of Gonzaga was already well ~ to the Spanish cause —J.A.Symonds⟩ ⟨events causing him to be differently ~ toward his brother⟩ **2 a** *obs* **:** deliberately chosen **b** *obs* **:** aimed at **:** sought after **:** wished for **c** *obs* **:** regarded with affection or liking **d :** FANCIED ⟨a republication of a diluted medical work much ~ by laymen —G.F. Whicher⟩ **3 a :** given to false show **:** assuming or pretending to possess what is not natural or real ⟨an ~ person⟩ ⟨too ~ in his manner to be convincing⟩ **b :** assumed artificially or falsely **:** not natural **:** PRETENDED ⟨with all the marks, real or ~, of intoxication —J.G.Frazer⟩ ⟨a sound and healthy revolt against an ~ and citified diction —J.L.Lowes⟩ ⟨titles for some of these paintings are ~ — closer to poetry than need be —H.D.Walker⟩ — **af·fect·ed·ly** *adv* — **affectedness** *n* -ES

af·fect·er \əˈfektə(r), aˈ-\ *n* -S [²*affect* + *-er*] **1** *obs* **:** one that affects or loves **2 :** one that strives after or pretends to something ⟨an ~ of unusual words⟩

affecting *adj* [fr. pres. part. of ²*affect*] **1** *obs* **:** AFFECTED 3a **2** *obs* **:** IMPRESSING, ARRESTING **3 :** moving the emotions **:** TOUCHING, PATHETIC ⟨the scenes of disappointment are quite as ~ —Walt Whitman⟩ ⟨mounts . . . toward an extraordinarily ~ climax —Dan Wickenden⟩ **syn** see MOVING

affectingly *adv* **:** in an affecting manner **:** MOVINGLY

¹af·fec·tion \əˈfekshən *also* aˈ-\ *n* -S [ME *affeccioun*, fr. OF & MF *affection*, fr. L *affection-, affectio*, fr. *affectus* (past part. of *afficere* to exert an influence, bestow, apply oneself) + *-ion-, -io* -ion — more at AFFECT] **1 :** any moderate feeling or emotion ⟨that serene and blessed mood in which the ~*s* gently lead us on —William Wordsworth⟩ **2 :** kind feeling **:** tender attachment **:** LOVE, GOOD WILL ⟨the young man warmly reciprocated her ~ —Elinor Wylie⟩ ⟨music played with ~ and understanding —Irving Kolodin⟩ ⟨you had some ~ for him —George Meredith⟩ — sometimes used in pl. ⟨he had been endowed with powerful family ~*s* that were progressively frustrated —Allen Tate⟩ ⟨the dearest object of their ~*s* —H.T. Buckle⟩ ⟨a powerful rival for the ~*s* of the working class —J.G.Colton⟩ **3** *obs* **a :** a strong emotion or passion (as anger, fear, or hatred) **b :** PARTIALITY, PREJUDICE ⟨'tis the curse of service, preferment goes by letter and ~, and not by old gradation, where each second stood heir to the first —Shak.⟩ **4** *psychol* **a :** the feeling aspect of consciousness (as in pleasure, displeasure) — distinguished from *conation*; compare COGNITION **b :** ¹AFFECT 2 **5 a :** bent of mind **:** feeling or natural impulse swaying the mind **:** PROPENSITY, DISPOSITION, INCLINATION ⟨my lawyer is bound by all his ~*s* to encourage me in litigation —G.B.Shaw⟩ **b** *archaic* **:** AFFECTATION 3, 4 ⟨they might discover themselves mock'd in these monstrous ~*s* —Ben Jonson⟩ **syn** see ATTACHMENT, FEELING

²affection \"\ *vt* -ED/-ING/-S [MF *affectionner*, fr. *affection*, n.] **:** to have affection for **:** LOVE

³affection \"\ *n* -S [MF, fr. L *affection-, affectio*] **1 :** action of affecting or state of being affected ⟨the reciprocal ~ of moving bodies⟩ **2 a** (1) **:** a bodily condition (2) **:** DISEASE, MALADY ⟨a pulmonary ~⟩ **b** (1) *archaic* **:** an alterable or nonessential state or mode of being ⟨veins that produce an accidental ~ of granite⟩ (2) **:** ATTRIBUTE, PROPERTY ⟨shape and weight are ~*s* of bodies⟩ **3 :** ¹UMLAUT 1 — used esp. in the grammar of the Celtic languages

af·fec·tion·al \-shənᵊl, -shnəl\ *adj* [¹*affection* + *-al*] **:** belonging or relating to the affections — **af·fec·tion·al·ly** \-nᵊlē, -nəlē\ *adv*

¹af·fec·tion·ate \-sh(ə)nət\ *adj* [¹*affection* + *-ate*] **1** *obs* **:** mentally or emotionally affected: **a :** PREJUDICED, BIASED **b :** favorably disposed **:** FRIENDLY **c :** governed by passion **:** HEADSTRONG **d :** AMBITIOUS, EARNEST **2 :** having affection or warm regard **:** LOVING, FOND ⟨he watched the boy's quick descent with an ~ eye —T.B.Costain⟩ ⟨he flung an ~ arm around Hector's neck —Dorothy Sayers⟩ ⟨as ~ a pet as any you will find, the coati tends to be a devoted one-man animal —C.A.Nicholson⟩ **3 :** proceeding from affection **:** indicating love **:** TENDER ⟨Lafayette's ~ remembrance of the life there —H.E.Scudder⟩ ⟨his ~ care for his people was winning him love —John Buchan⟩ — **af·fec·tion·ate·ly** *adv*

²af·fec·tion·ate \-shəˌnāt\ *vt* -ED/-ING/-S **1** *obs* **:** to feel or acquire affection for **2 :** to make affectionate ⟨he *affectionated* himself to the child⟩

affectionated *adj* **1** *obs* **:** favorably inclined **2** *obs* **:** AFFECTIONATE

affectioned *adj* [¹*affection* + *-ed*] **1 a** *obs* **:** kindly disposed **:** well-affected **b** *archaic* **:** DISPOSED ⟨be kindly ~ one to another —Rom 12:10 (AV)⟩ **2** *obs* **a :** AMBITIOUS, ZEALOUS **b :** WILLFUL, OBSTINATE

af·fec·tive \(ˈ)aˈfektiv, əˈf-, -ēv\ *adj* [MF *affectif* (fr. L *affectus* disposition, affection + MF *-if* -ive) & G *affektiv*, fr. *affekt* emotion (fr. L *affectus*) + G *-iv* -ive — more at AFFECT] **1 :** relating to, arising from, or influencing feelings or emotions **:** EMOTIONAL ⟨sacrificing physical life and ~ life to mental life —Aldous Huxley⟩ **2 :** expressing emotion ⟨~ language⟩ ⟨the ~ force of a diminutive suffix⟩

af·fec·tiv·i·ty \ˌaˌfekˈtivәd·ē *also* əˌf-\ *n* -ES **:** ability to feel emotions **:** the division of mental life and activity relating to the emotions **:** EMOTION

affects *pres 3d sing of* AFFECT, *pl of* AFFECT

affectuous *adj* [ME, fr. MF or LL; MF *affectueux*, fr. LL *affectuosus*, fr. L *affectus* disposition, affection, desire + *-osus* -ous — more at AFFECT] *obs* **:** ARDENT, AFFECTIONATE

affectuously *adv* [ME, fr. *affectuous* + *-ly*] *obs* **:** ARDENTLY, AFFECTIONATELY

af·feer \əˈfi(ə)r\ *vt* -ED/-ING/-S [ME *afferen, affuren*, fr. MF *affeurer, afforer*, fr. *a-* (fr. L *ad-*) + *feur, fuer* market price, tax, fr. ML *forum* market price, fr. L, market place — more at FORUM] **1** *law* **:** to fix the amount of (an amercement) **:** ASSESS **2** *obs* **:** CONFIRM, ASSURE ⟨the title is ~*ed* —Shak.⟩

af·feer·er *or* **af·feer·or** \-irər\ *n* -S [ME *affurer*, fr. *affuren* + *-er* or *-or*] **:** one that affeers

af·feer·ment \-i(ə)rmənt\ *n* -S **:** the act of affeering

af·feir·ing \əˈfiriŋ\ *adj* [fr. pres. part. of obs. E *affeir* to pertain, be proper, fr. ME *afferen, affieren*, fr. MF *afferir, aferir*, fr. (assumed) VL *afferire*, alter. of L *afferre*] *Scot* **:** PERTAINING, BEFITTING

af·fen·pin·scher \ˈafənˌpinchə(r), ˈäf-\ *n* -S [G, fr. *affe* monkey (fr. OHG *affo*) + *pinscher*; fr. its monkeylike face] **:** a small dog of a breed related to the Brussels griffon having a stiff red, gray, or black coat, pointed ears, and bushy eyebrows, chin tuft, and mustache

af·fer·ence \ˈaf(ə)rən(t)s\ *n* -S **:** afferent activity

af·fer·ent \-nt\ *adj* [L *afferent-, afferens*, pres. part. of *afferre* to bring to, fr. *ad-* + *ferre* to bear — more at BEAR] *physiol* **:** bearing or conducting inward to a part or an organ; *specif* **:** conveying nervous impulses from a peripheral part toward a nerve center (as the brain or spinal cord) — opposed to *efferent* — **af·fer·ent·ly** *adv*

af·fet·tu·o·so \(ˌ)aˌfechəˈwō(ˌ)sō, -fed·əˈ-, -zō\ *adj* (*or adv*) [It, fr. LL *affectuosus* — more at AFFECTUOUS] **:** tender or affecting — used as a direction in music

¹af·fi·ance \əˈfīən(t)s, aˈ-\ *n* -S [ME *affiaunce*, fr. MF *affiance, afiance*, fr. *affier, afier* to trust (fr. ML *affidare*, fr. L *ad-* + *fidare* to trust) + *-ance*; akin to L *fides* faith, *fidere* to trust — more at BIDE] **1** *archaic* **:** TRUST, RELIANCE, FAITH, CONFIDENCE **2** *archaic* **:** plighted faith **:** marriage contract or promise **3** *obs* **:** close or intimate relationship

²affiance \"\ *vt* -ED/-ING/-S [MF *afiancer*, fr. *afiance*, n.] **:** to pledge one's faith to for marriage **:** solemnly promise (oneself or another) in marriage **:** BETROTH, ENGAGE ⟨the king *affianced* his daughter to the ruler of a neighboring principality⟩ ⟨the *affianced* couple will marry next month⟩

af·fi·ant \-nt\ *n* -S [MF *affiant, afiant*, fr. pres. part. of *affier, afier*] *law* **:** one that swears to an affidavit; *broadly* **:** DEPONENT

af·fiche \aˈfēsh, əˈ-\ *n* -S [F, fr. *afficher* to affix, fr. *a-* (f. L *ad-*) + *ficher* to drive in, fr. (assumed) VL *figicare*, fr. L *figere* to fasten, thrust in — more at DIKE] **:** POSTER, PLACARD

afficionado *var of* AFICIONADO

af·fi·da·vit \ˌafəˈdāvət\ *n* -S [ML, he has made oath, 3d pers. sing. perf. indic. act. of *affidare* — more at AFFIANCE] **:** a sworn statement in writing made esp. under oath or on affirmation before an authorized magistrate or officer; *specif* **:** such a statement under oath made ex parte and without cross-examination — compare DEPOSITION

affidavit of merits : an affidavit made by a party to an action (as to prevent the automatic entry of judgment against that party) setting forth that the party has a substantial and genuine ground of action or defense and that the complaint or plea filed is not sham or dilatory

affidavit of verification : a short affidavit taking oath to the truth of the allegations in an instrument (as a petition or complaint) instead of including the allegations in extenso in a separate affidavit

af·fi·da·vy \-vē\ *n* -ES [by shortening & alter.] *dial* **:** AFFIDAVIT

af·fied *past of* AFFY

affies *pres 3d sing of* AFFY

¹af·fil·i·ate \əˈfilēˌāt *also* aˈ-; -ād·+V\ *vb* -ED/-ING/-S [ML *affiliatus*, past part. of *affiliare* to adopt as a son, fr. L *ad-* + *filius* son — more at FEMININE] *vt* **1 a :** to attach as a member or branch **:** bring or receive into close connection ⟨the university would assist in organizing and *affiliating* high schools —*Amer. Guide Series: Texas*⟩ ⟨the number of *affiliated* schools or institutes varies from one university to another —R.J. Matthew⟩ ⟨a number of loose national federations with which the local bodies *affiliated* —Oscar Handlin⟩ ⟨everyone should be *affiliated* to the religious customs prevalent in his country —George Santayana⟩ **b :** to join as a member **:** ASSOCIATE ⟨detached in the sense of being neither politically *affiliated* nor yet antipathetic —Muriel Howlett⟩ ⟨*affiliated* himself with the social and literary circles —H.P.Willis⟩ ⟨lumbering and its *affiliated* activities form the city's chief industry —*Amer. Guide Series: Oregon*⟩ **2 :** to fix the paternity of (an illegitimate child) — used with *to* ⟨sufficient grounds for *affiliating* the child to its alleged father⟩; *broadly* **:** to connect in the way of descent **:** trace the origin of ⟨~ Shakespeare's *Hamlet* to earlier plays⟩ ~ *vi* **:** to connect or associate oneself **:** COMBINE — usu. used with *with* ⟨he refused to ~ with a political party⟩ ⟨these phenomena ~ with certain beliefs⟩

²af·fil·i·ate \-ēət *also* -ēˌāt; *usu* -d·+V\ *n* -S **1 :** an affiliated person **:** ASSOCIATE ⟨~*s* and nonmembers attended the public ceremony⟩ **2 a :** a branch or unit of a larger organization ⟨the regional ~ of the national association⟩ **b** (1) **:** a company effectively controlled by another or associated with others under common ownership or control (2) **:** SUBSIDIARY

af·fil·i·a·tion \əˌ==ˈāshən\ *n* -S [F, fr. ML *affiliation-, affiliatio*, fr. L *affiliatus* + *-ion-, -io* -ion] **:** the act of affiliating **:** the state or relation of being affiliated

affinage *n* -S [F, fr. *affiner* to refine + *-age* — more at AFFINE] *obs* **:** act of refining (a metal)

af·fi·nal \(ˈ)aˈfīnᵊl, əˈf-\ *adj* [L *affin*is neighboring on, related by marriage + E *-al* — more at AFFINITY] **:** related by, based on, or involving marriage ⟨~ relatives⟩ ⟨~ relationships⟩ — distinguished from *consanguineous*

af·fi·na·tion \ˌafəˈnāshən, ˌaˌfīˈ-\ *n* -S [²*affine* + *-ation*] **:** the treatment of raw sugar crystals with a heavy sugar syrup to remove the film of adhering molasses

¹af·fine \aˈfīn, əˈ-\ *n* -S [MF *affin*, fr. *affin*, adj.] **:** a relative by marriage (as one's wife's brother)

²af·fine \"\ *vt* -ED/-ING/-S [F *affiner*, fr. *a-* (fr. L *ad-*) + *fin* fine, refined — more at FINE] **:** to subject (raw sugar) to affination

³affine \"\ *adj* [F *affin*, akin, connected, fr. L *affinis* related by marriage — more at AFFINITY] *math* **:** preserving finiteness [as in the transformation $y = ax + b$ (a not zero), where to every finite value of the variable x there corresponds a finite value of the variable y, and vice versa] — **af·fine·ly** *adv*

af·fined \-nd\ *adj* [MF *affin* + E *-ed*] **1 :** joined in a close relationship **:** CONNECTED ⟨syllable to blessed syllable ~ —Wallace Stevens⟩ **2** *obs* **:** bound by obligation ⟨be judge yourself whether I in any just term am ~ to love the Moor —Shak.⟩

af·fin·i·tive \əˈfinəd·iv, aˈ-\ *adj* [*affinity* + *-ive*] **:** closely related ⟨a situation ~ to his own⟩

af·fin·i·ty \əˈfinəd·ē, -ətē, -i *also* aˈ-\ *n* -ES [ME *affinite, affinitie*, fr. MF or L; MF *afinité*, fr. L *affinitas*, fr. *affinis* bordering on, related by marriage (fr. *ad-* + *finis* border) + *-itas -ity* — more at FINAL] **1 :** relationship by marriage (as between a husband and his wife's blood relatives) — distinguished from *consanguinity* ⟨his kinsman, by blood, or by ~ —Lev 25:49 (DV)⟩ ⟨that grim friendliness which at last arises in all such cases of undesired ~ —Thomas Hardy⟩; *broadly* **:** any familial relationship ⟨every creature that bears any ~ to my mother is dear to me —William Cowper⟩ **2 a :** sympathy esp. as marked by community of interest **:** KINSHIP ⟨the strange *affinities* and hostilities of temperament —A.C.Benson⟩ — often used with *with* or *between* ⟨odd *affinities* she had with people she had never spoken to —Virginia Woolf⟩ ⟨her temperamental ~ with the stage —S.L.Gulick⟩ ⟨the mysterious ~ between them —Zane Grey⟩ **b :** attraction to or liking for ⟨metals without magnetic ~⟩ ⟨the special ~ of a virus for the nervous system⟩ ⟨he soon developed an ~ for politics⟩; *specif* **:** the attractive force exerted in different degrees between substances or particles that causes them to enter into and remain in chemical combination — usu. used with *for* ⟨basic dyes have an ~ for wool and silk⟩ ⟨hemoglobin has a greater ~ for carbon monoxide than for oxygen⟩ ⟨the tungsten surface has high electron ~ —V.K.Zworykin & E.G.Ramberg⟩ **c :** a person esp. of the opposite sex having a particular attraction for one ⟨she became his ~⟩ **3** *obs* **:** ASSOCIATION, ALLIANCE ⟨should we again break thy commandments, and join in ~ with the people of these abominations —Ezra 9:14 (AV)⟩ **4 :** causal connection or relationship **:** RESEMBLANCE ⟨reveals his Scandinavian *affinities* —Havelock Ellis⟩ ⟨a recognizable stylistic ~ between the extremes —Herbert Read⟩ ⟨essays arranged in groups by ~ of topic —H.W. Odum⟩ ⟨whatever bears ~ to cunning is despicable —Jane Austen⟩ ⟨this highly individual work of art bears ~ with diverse sources —Elizabeth Janeway⟩: **a** (1) **:** possession of common features as a result of descent from the same ancestral language ⟨the ~ of Dutch with English⟩ (2) **:** possession of common features not resulting from descent from the same ancestral language (as the uvular *r* which French shares with German but not with the other Romance languages) **b** *biol* **:** a relation between species or higher groups dependent on resemblance in the whole plan of structure and indicating community of origin

af·firm \əˈfərm, -ə̄m, -əim *also* aˈ-\ *vb* -ED/-ING/-S [alter. (influenced by L *affirmare*) of ME *affermen*, fr. MF *afermer*, fr. L *affirmare*, fr. *ad-* + *firmare* to make firm, fr. *firmus* firm — more at FIRM] *vt* **1 a :** VALIDATE, CONFIRM ⟨he was ~*ed* as a candidate⟩ **b :** to state positively or with confidence **:** declare as a fact **:** assert to be true ⟨science has become too complex to ~ the existence of universal truths —Henry Adams⟩ ⟨we cannot ~ that this is the later play —T.S.Eliot⟩ — opposed to *deny* **c :** to assert as valid or confirmed (as a judgment, decree, or order brought before an appellate court for review) — compare MODIFY, REVERSE **d :** to testify to or declare by affirmation — distinguished from *swear* ~ *vi* **1 a :** to declare or assert positively ⟨we must work and ~, but we have no guess of the value of what we say or do —R.W.Emerson⟩ **b :** to testify or declare by affirmation ⟨a court ruling that atheists may ~⟩ **2 :** to uphold a judgment or decree of a lower court ⟨the Court of Appeals ~*ed* —*N.Y. Certified Public Accountant*⟩ **syn** see ASSERT, SWEAR

af·firm·a·ble \-məbəl\ *adj* **:** capable of being affirmed — often used with *of* ⟨a quality ~ of every member of his family⟩

af·firm·ance \-mən(t)s\ *n* -S [MF *afermance*, fr. *afermer* + *-ance*] **:** a strong declaration **:** AFFIRMATION: **a :** an affirming of or assent to the existence, truth, or validity (as of a statement) **b :** a decision by a person to deal with an unauthorized act as though authorized **c :** a confirmation by a superior court of the validity and correctness of a judgment, decree, or order of a lower court

af·fir·ma·tion \ˌafə(r)ˈmāshən\ *n* -S [MF, fr. L *affirmation-, affirmatio*, fr. *affirmatus* (past part. of *affirmare* to affirm) + *-ion-, -io* -ion — more at AFFIRM] **:** act of affirming, asserting as true, or confirming **:** a positive assertion ⟨~ of human dignity —*Time*⟩ ⟨~ by the vendor of the quality of goods⟩: **a** *logic* **:** an affirmative proposition, statement, or judgment **b :** a solemn declaration made under the penalties of perjury by a person who conscientiously declines taking an oath

affirmation of the consequent : the logical fallacy of inferring the truth of the antecedent of an implication from the truth of the consequent (as in, "if it rains, then the game is cancelled and the game has been cancelled, therefore it has rained") — called also *assertion of the consequent*

[1]**af·fir·ma·tive** \ə'fərməd·iv, -əm-, -əim-, -ətiv *also* a'-\ *adj* [MF *affirmatif*, fr. L *affirmativus*, fr. *affirmatus* + *-ivus* -ive] **1** *obs* : CONFIRMATIVE, RATIFYING **2** *logic* : asserting a predicate of a subject or of a part of a subject; *also* : asserting the truth or validity of a statement ("All A is B", "Some A is B", and "It is true that A is B" are ~ propositions) — contrasted with *negative* **3 a** : asserting that the fact is so : declaratory of what exists (~ proof that he was in fact a danger to public safety —David Fellman) **b** : affirming the existence of certain facts or a particular state of things at the time a contract of insurance is made —used of representations and warranties; compare IMPLIED CONTRACT, PROMISSORY **4** : ASSERTIVE, POSITIVE (an ~ approach to the problem) — **af·firm·a·tive·ly** *adv*

[2]**affirmative** \"\ *n* -s [ME, fr. MF *affirmatif*, fr. *affirmatif*, adj.] **1** : an expression (as the word *yes* or the phrase *that's so*) of affirmation or assent — often used adverbially esp. in radiotelephone communication ("Is his wingman still with him?" "Affirmative." —J.A.Michener) **2** *logic* : AFFIRMATION a **3 a** : the side of a question that affirms or maintains the proposition stated — opposed to *negative* (40 votes were in the ~) **b** (1) : the speaker or speakers on the affirmative side in a debate (2) : the party in a legal proceeding upon whom falls the burden of proof

affirmative defense *n* : a defense setting up new matter that provides a defense against the plaintiff's case, assuming the complaint to be true

affirmative easement *or* **affirmative servitude** *n* : POSITIVE EASEMENT

affirmative pregnant *n, in pleading* : an affirmative allegation implying or not excluding some negative in favor of the adverse party

af·firm·a·to·ry \-mə,tōrē\ *adj* [*affirmation* + *-ory*] : giving affirmation (an ~ gesture)

[1]**af·fix** \ə'fiks, (')a¦f-\ *vt* -ED/-ING/-ES [ML *affixare*, fr. L *affixus*, past part. of *affigere* to fasten to, fr. *ad-* + *figere* to fasten — more at DIKE] **1** : to attach physically (as by nails or glue) : FASTEN — usu. used with *to* (the king's seal dangled from the ribbon which ~*ed* it to the proclamation) (~ the label to the package) **2** : to attach in any way : connect with : ADD, SUBJOIN — usu. used with *to* (a penalty ~*ed* to hasty, superficial thinking —A.N.Whitehead) (a title of honor ~*ed* to a person's name) (~ your signature to the letter) **3** : IMPRESS (dropping a blob of wax upon the parchment, he ~*ed* his seal) **4** *obs* : to fix upon : settle upon : FIX **syn** see FASTEN

[2]**af·fix** \'a,fiks\ *n* -ES [F *affixe*, fr. L *affixus*, past part.] **1 a** : a sound or sequence of sounds or, in writing, a letter or sequence of letters occurring as a bound form attached to the beginning or end of a word, base, or phrase or inserted within a word or base and serving to produce a derivative word (as *un-* in *untie*, *-ate* in *chlorate*, *-ish* in *morning-after-ish*) or an inflectional form (as *-s* in *cats*) or the basis of part or all of a paradigm (as L *-n-* in *vinco* "I conquer", *vincit* "he conquers" as contrasted with the perfect tense forms *vici* "I have conquered", *vicit* "he has conquered") — compare [2]INFIX, PREFIX, SUFFIX 1 **b** *among animal breeders* : a registered generic or common name combined with the individual name of purebred animals to indicate the particular breeding or strain **2** : APPENDAGE, ADDITION **3** : a small decorative figure (as a flower) added to ceramic or bronze ware or to an architectural detail — **af·fix·al** \'a,fiksəl\ *or* **af·fix·i·al** \(')a¦fiksēəl\ *adj*

af·fix·a·tion \,a,fik'sāshən\ *n* -s **1** : the action or process of affixing **2** : the use of an affix

affix-clipping *n* : METANALYSIS

af·fix·ion \ə'fikshən, a'-\ *n* -s [LL *affixion-*, *affixio*, fr. L *affixus* (past part. of *affigere* to fasten to) + *-ion-*, *-io* -ion — more at AFFIX] : the act of affixing : the state of being affixed

af·fix·ture \-kschə(r)\ *n* -s [[1]*affix* + *-ture* (as in *fixture*)] : state of being affixed

af·flat·ed \ə'flād·əd, a'-\ *adj* [obs. *afflate* to blow on, fr. L *afflatus* + E *-ed*] : INSPIRED

af·fla·tion \-āshən\ *n* -s [L *afflatus* + E *-ion*] : a breathing into : INSPIRATION

af·fla·tus \-ād·əs,-ātəs\ *n* -ES [L *afflatus*, lit., act of blowing or breathing on, fr. *afflatus*, past. part. of *afflare* to blow on, fr. *ad-* + *flare* to blow — more at BLOW] : a divine imparting of knowledge or power : supernatural or overmastering impulse : INSPIRATION (we imagine that a great speech is caused by some mysterious ~ that descends into a man from on high —Max Eastman)

af·flict \ə'flikt\ *vt* -ED/-ING/-S [ME *afflicten*, fr. L *afflictus*, past part. of *affligere* to cast down, deject, fr. *ad-* + *fligere* to strike — more at PROFLIGATE] **1** *obs* **a** : HUMBLE (that we might ~ ourselves before our God —Ezra 8:21 (AV)) **b** : to strike down : OVERTHROW (in hope to find better abode, and my ~*ed* powers to settle here on earth —John Milton) **2 a** : to distress severely so as to cause continued suffering (cutting off the food supply and ~*ing* the people with dearth —J.G. Frazer) (strife between the Emperors and Popes which ~*ed* the Middle Ages —Herbert Agar) **b** : TROUBLE (the mummers themselves were not ~*ed* with any such feeling for their art —Thomas Hardy) : INJURE, DAMAGE (that debasement of the verbal currency which ~*s* terms used in advertising —*Times Lit. Supp.*)

syn TORTURE, TORMENT, RACK, GRILL, TRY: AFFLICT is a general term that is applicable to most situations involving distress or difficulty. It is often interchangeable with the following words although it lacks their more specific suggestions and stresses the fact of affliction rather than the manner. TORTURE is the strongest word in the group in suggesting most extreme infliction of pain, suffering, anguish, strain (until his eye be *tortured* out with fire —P.B.Shelley) (and laid the strips and jagged ends of flesh even once more, and slacked the sinew's knot of every *tortured* limb —Robert Browning) Although the two may be interchangeable, TORMENT may have a less extreme suggestion than TORTURE and may imply greater continuity or customary practice (it was inevitable that the older boys should become mischievous louts; they bullied and *tormented* and corrupted the younger boys —H.G.Wells) (other epochs had been *tormented* by the misery of the existence and the terror of the unknown —*Humanist*) RACK is likely to suggest a straining or wrenching with stress, duress, disease, pain, or emotion (Thucydides' world was a place *racked* and ruined and disintegrated by war —Edith Hamilton) (a lean and nameless phantom *racked* by a consumptive cough —*Amer. Scholar*) Although GRILL orig. suggested the torment of being broiled, it has weakened and is likely to suggest less pain than the preceding words; it is usu. used in situations involving stringent cross-examination or, in the present participle, in situations involving much vexation and agitation (representatives of Intelligence . . . they gave his lordship a respectful but thorough *grilling* —Upton Sinclair) (a *grilling* afternoon trying to work despite confusions and interruptions) TRY implies that which tests one's endurance, stamina, control (other men were *tried* by puny ailments, were not searched and shaken by one tremendous shock —George Meredith) (it *tried* her that he gave her no encouragement —Willa Cather)

afflicted *adj* : grievously affected or troubled esp. by disease : mentally or physically impaired

afflictedness *n* -ES : AFFLICTION

af·flic·tion \-kshən\ *n* -s [ME *afflicciouN*, fr. MF *affliction*, fr. L *affliction-*, *afflictio*, fr. *afflictus* + *-ion-*, *-io* -ion — more at AFFLICT] **1** *obs* : act of afflicting; *specif* : SELF-MORTIFICATION **2** : the state of being afflicted; a state of pain, distress, or grief (some virtues are seen only in ~ —Joseph Addison) **3** : the cause of continued pain or distress of body or mind (as illness or losses); *also* : the pain, distress, or grief resulting from such a cause (the dark and senseless ~*s* of a nightmare —Kenneth Roberts) **syn** see TRIAL

af·flict·ive \-ktiv\ *adj* [F *afflictif*, fr. L *afflictus* + F *-if* -ive] : giving pain : causing affliction : DISTRESSING — **af·flict·ive·ly** *adv*

aff loof \(')a'flüf\ *adv* [*aff* (alter. of *off*) + *loof*] *Scot* : without preparation : OFFHAND

af·flu·ence \'a,flüən(t)s, 'afləwən-\ *n* -s [ME, fr. MF, fr. L *affluentia*, fr. *affluent-*, *affluens* + *-ia*] **1 a** : an abundant flow or supply (as of words or feelings) : PROFUSION (from the various falls and cataracts there is an ~ and variety of iris bows —John Muir) **b** : abundance of property : WEALTH (the heirs reduced from ~ to destitution —G.B.Shaw) **2 a** : a flowing to or toward a point : INFLUX (looking at the . . . constant ~ of newcomers —T.E.Lawrence)

[1]**af·flu·ent** \-nt\ *adj* [ME, fr. MF, fr. L *affluent-*, *affluens*, pres. part. of *affluere* to flow abundantly, fr. *ad-* + *fluere* to flow — more at FLUID] **1 a** : flowing in abundance : ABUNDANT, COPIOUS (his florid and ~ fancy was greatly admired —Van Wyck Brooks) **b** : having an abundance of goods or riches : WEALTHY (nor did the bankbook show that Mr. Oldacre was in such very ~ circumstances —A. Conan Doyle) **2** : flowing toward (~ breezes stirred the water) **syn** see RICH

[2]**affluent** \"\ *n* -s [F, fr. L *affluent-*, *affluens*, pres. part] **1** : a stream or river flowing into a larger river or into a lake : a tributary stream — compare EFFLUENT **2** : the raw sewage entering a disposal plant

af·flu·ent·ly *adv* : with abundance : RICHLY

af·flux \'a,fləks\ *n* -ES [F or L; F, fr. L *affluxus*, past part. of *affluere* to flow to, flow abundantly] : AFFLUENCE 2 (an ~ of blood to the head) (a regular ~ of laborers has been set up —James Bryce)

af·flux·ion \a'flәkshən, ə'-\ *n* -s [L *affluxus* + E *-ion*] : AFFLUX

affly *abbr* affectionately

af·force \ə'fō(ə)rs, ə'-\ *vt* -ED/-ING/-S [ML *afforciare*, fr. OF *aforcier* to strengthen, increase, fr. *a-* (fr. L *ad-*) + *forcier*, *forcer* to force — more at FORCE] : to strengthen (as a court or jury) by adding specially qualified members

af·force·ment \-mənt\ *n* -s : an afforcing (as of a court or jury)

af·ford \ə'fō(ə)rd, -ó(ə)rd,-ōəd,-ó(ə)d\ *vt* -ED/-ING/-S [ME *aforthen*, fr. OE *geforthian* to carry out, accomplish, further, fr. *ge-* (perfective prefix) + *forthian* to carry out, fr. *forth* forth, forward — more at CO-, FORTH] **1 a** : to manage to bear without serious detriment — used with infinitive (a dictionary of an ancient language can ~ to embrace everything that can be called a word —R.W.Chapman) (you can't ~ to get out of balance —Lou Smyth) (most of us, however, can well ~ to look critically at our writing —Milton Hall) (she could ~ to be generous with Irene —Louis Auchincloss) **b** : to manage to pay for or incur the cost of (no country, however rich, can ~ the waste of its human resources —F.D. Roosevelt) (people who can ~ leisure sit in cafés by the hour —W.P.Webb) (our failure to recognize and foster promising students who cannot ~ college —Douglas Bush) (we can ~ only those threats that we are ready to carry out —*New Republic*) **2 a** : GIVE, FURNISH (history ~*s* us a wealth of examples —John Strachey) (an old building with grillwork elevators ~*ing* passengers a view of the cable —J.F.Powers) — sometimes used with *to* (their business is not to praise their age, but to ~ to the men who live in it the highest pleasure which they are capable of feeling —Matthew Arnold) (the bill was a measure necessary to ~ protection to labor as well as industry —*Current Biog.*) **b** : to furnish or offer typically or as an essential concomitant (apartments are small and ~ very little living space —D.P.O'Mahony) (by the great distribution ~*ed* by the printing press —R.A.Hall b.1911) **3** *archaic* : to sell at a particular price

af·for·est \ə'fórəst, a'-, -är-\ *vt* -ED/-ING/-S [ML *afforestare*, fr. L *ad-* + ML *forestis*, *foresta* forest — more at FOREST] **1** *English law* : to convert into a forest (sense 1) **2** : to establish forest cover on (as land not previously forested) — compare REFOREST

af·for·es·ta·tion \(,)a,fórəs'tāshən, ə,f-, -är-\ *n* -s : the act or process of afforesting

[1]**af·form·a·tive** \a'fó(r)məd·iv, ə'-\ *n* -s [*ad-* + *formative*] : SUFFIX 1 — used esp. in Semitic grammar; contrasted with *preformative*

[2]**afformative** \(')a¦f-, ə'f-\ *adj* : characterized by the use of suffixes (the ~ conjugation) : being an afformative (an ~ element)

af·fran·chise \ə'-,ə'-\ *vt* -ED/-ING/-S [modif. (influenced by *-ise*) of MF *afranchiss-*, stem of *afranchir*, fr. *a-* (fr. L *ad-*) + *franchir* to free — more at FRANCHISE] : ENFRANCHISE 1 **syn** see FREE

[1]**af·fray** \ə'frā, a'f-, 'a,f-\ *n* -s [ME *afray*, *affray*, fr. MF *esfrei*, *effray*, *affray*, fr. *esfreer*, *effreer*, *affreer*, v.] **1** *obs* : ALARM, FRIGHT, TERROR **2 a** : a tumultuous assault : a violent engagement or action : FRAY, BRAWL, QUARREL (the walls themselves were torn down in the fury of the ~ —M.J. O'Kelly) (European crises, diplomatic ~*s* —C.E.Montague); *specif* : the fighting of two or more persons in a public place so as to frighten others, the offense under the law consisting in the disturbance of the public peace **syn** see CONTEST

[2]**affray** \"\ *vt* -ED/-ING/-S [ME *afraien*, *affraien*, fr. MF *esfreer*, *effreer*, *affreer*, fr. (assumed) VL *exfridare*, fr. L *ex-* + (assumed) VL *-fridare* (of Gmc origin; akin to OHG *fridu* peace) — more at FRITHBORH] **1** *archaic* : STARTLE, ALARM **2** *archaic* **a** : SCARE **b** : to frighten away **syn** see FRIGHTEN

af·freight \a'frāt, ə'-\ *vt* -ED/-ING/-S [modif. (influenced by *freight*) of F *affréter*, fr. *a-* (fr. L *ad-*) + *fréter* to freight or charter a ship, fr. *fret* freight, fr. OF, fr. MD *vrecht*, *vracht* — more at FREIGHT] : to hire or charter (a ship) for the transportation of goods or freight — **af·freight·er** \-ād·ə(r)\ *n* -s

af·freight·ment \-mənt\ *n* -s [modif. of F *affrètement*, fr. *affréter* + *-ment*] : a mercantile lease of a vessel under which it remains in charge of the owners; *also* : the act of hiring a vessel under such a lease — compare CHARTER 5

af·fret·tan·do \,afrə'tän(,)dō, ¦äf-\ *adj* [It, lit., hastening, verbal of *affrettare* to hasten, fr. *a-* (fr. L *ad-*) + *fretta* haste, fr. *frettare* to rub, fr. (assumed) VL *frictare*, fr. L *frictus*, past part. of *fricare* to rub — more at BRINE] : becoming faster, as if excited — used as a direction in music

af·fri·cate \'afrəkət, -ēk-, *usu* -əd·+V\ *n* -s [prob. fr. G *affrikata*, fr. L *affricata*, fem. of *affricatus*, past part. of *affricare* to rub against, fr. *ad-* + *fricare* to rub — more at BRINE] *phonetics* : a stop and its immediately following release through the articulatory position for a continuant nonsyllabic usu. homorganic consonant (as the \t\ and \sh\ that are the constituents of the \ch\ in *why choose* and that are different from the \t\ and \sh\ of *white shoes*)

af·fri·cat·ed \-,kād·əd\ *adj, phonetics* : changed in character from a simple stop into an affricate

af·fri·ca·tion \,==='kāshən\ *n* -s : conversion (of a simple stop sound) into an affricate

[1]**af·fric·a·tive** \a'frikəd·iv, ə-; 'afrə,kād-\ *adj* [*affricate* + *-ive*] : having the articulation of an affricate or a fricative

[2]**affricative** \"\ *n* -s **1** : AFFRICATE **2** : FRICATIVE

[1]**affright** *adj* [ME *afright*, alter. of *afyrht*, fr. OE *āfyrht*, past part. of *āfyrhtan* to frighten, fr. *ā-* (perfective prefix) + *fyrhtan* to fear — more at ABEAR, FRIGHT] *obs* : AFFRIGHTED

[2]**af·fright** \a'frīt, ə'-, *usu* -īd·+V\ *vt* -ED/-ING/-S **1** : to impress with sudden fear : FRIGHTEN, ALARM (a strange wild country that began a little to ~ us —Daniel Defoe) (~*ing* cycle of reincarnation —J.R.Ullman) **2** : to make frightful (casques that did ~ the air at Agincourt —Shak.) (these birds from their secret haunts ~ the quiet of the night —Sheridan Le Fanu) **syn** see FRIGHTEN

[3]**affright** \"\ *n* -s [[2]*affright*] **1** : sudden and great fear approaching terror (he looks behind him with ~ and forward with despair —Oliver Goldsmith) **2** *archaic* : a cause of terror

affrighted *adj* : seized with affright : FRIGHTENED — **af·fright·ed·ly** *adv*

af·fright·en \-t[ə]n\ *vt* -ED/-ING/-S [[1]*affright* + *-en*] : AFFRIGHT

af·fright·ful \-tfəl\ *adj* [[3]*affright* + *-ful*] *archaic* : FRIGHTFUL — **af·fright·ful·ly** *adv*

af·fright·ment \-tmənt\ *n* -s [[2]*affright* + *-ment*] *archaic* : the act of affrighting : the state of being affrighted

[1]**af·front** \ə'frənt, a'-\ *vt* -ED/-ING/-S [ME *afronten*, *afrounten*, fr. MF *afronter*, *affronter*, fr. (assumed) VL *affrontare*, fr. L *ad-* + *front-*, *frons* forehead — more at FRONT] **1 a** : to insult esp. to the face by behavior or language (those who now smile upon and embrace would ~ and stab each other if managers did not interpose —Earl of Chesterfield) **b** : to offend esp. by showing disrespect (the prince ~*ed* his father by embarking on a love affair —Geoffrey Bruun) **2 a** : to face in defiance : CONFRONT (~ death) **b** *archaic* : to meet in hostile encounter **c** *obs* : to meet or encounter face to face **3** : to appear directly before (the still fresh scar on the hillside which ~*s* the traveler's eye —Norman Douglas) **4** *archaic* : to front upon : border upon **syn** see OFFEND

[2]**affront** \"\ *n* -s [MF, back-formation fr. *affronter*] **1 a** : a deliberately offensive act or utterance (in this heat every extra gesture was an ~ to the common store of life —Scott Fitzgerald) **b** : an offense to one's self-respect (for the Greeks, the Roman Empire was a necessity of life and at the same time an intolerable ~ —A.J.Toynbee) **2** *obs* : a hostile encounter

syn INSULT, INDIGNITY: AFFRONT is a deliberate indication of disrespect calculated to offend (an old *affront* will stir the heart through years of rankling pain —Jean Ingelow) (my determination to break this educational lockstep was an *affront* to their pride as schoolmasters —Sidney Lovett) INSULT refers to a personal attack intended to rankle and humiliate (the *insults* offered to the Federal troops by the women of New Orleans —W.C.Ford) (he suffered the greatest *insult* ever offered to a man in the House of Commons: when he entered with the Liberal party, the Conservatives rose to a man and left the House —O.S.J.Gogarty) INDIGNITY indicates an outrageous or contemptuous offense to one's personal dignity (that after all which had passed he should be compelled to accept his pardon at Caesar's hands was an *indignity* to which he could not submit —J.A.Froude) (to nearly all men serfdom was, without qualification, a degrading thing, and they found trenchant phrases to describe the *indignity* of the condition —R.W.Southern)

af·fron·té *or* **af·fron·tee** \¦a,frən¦tā; ə'frəntē, a'f-\ *adj* [F *affronté*, fr. past part. of *affronter* to confront, affront — more at AFFRONT] **1** *also* **af·fronty** \ə'frəntē, a'-\ *of two heraldic figures* : facing each other — compare COMBATANT, RESPECTANT **2** *of a heraldic figure* : facing to the front : full-faced : GARDANT

affrontedly *adv* [*affronted* (past part. of [1]*affront*) + *-ly*; intended as trans. of F *effrontément*] *obs* : IMPUDENTLY

af·front·ive \ə'frəntiv, a'-\ *adj, archaic* : OFFENSIVE

afft *abbr* affidavit

af·fuse \a'fyüz, ə'-\ *vt* -ED/-ING/-S [L *affusus*, past part.] *archaic* : POUR

af·fu·sion \-üzhən\ *n* -s [LL *affusion-*, *affusio* act of pouring on, fr. L *affusus* (past part. of *affundere* to pour on, fr. *ad-* + *fundere* to pour) + *-ion-*, *-io* -ion — more at FOUND (melt & pour)] : act of pouring a liquid upon (as in baptism)

affy *vb* -ED/-ING/-ES [ME *afien*, *affien*, fr. OF *afier* — more at AFFIANCE] *vt* **1** *obs* : CONFIDE, TRUST **2 a** *obs* : (1) : ESPOUSE (2) : AFFIANCE, BETROTH **b** *archaic* : to join closely (as in bonds of faith) (souls *affied* by sovereign destinies —R.W. Emerson) ~ *vi, obs* : CONFIDE, TRUST

[1]**af·ghan** \'af,gan, -aa(ə)n *also* -,gən\ *n* -s [Pashto *afghānī*] **1** *cap* : a native or inhabitant of Afghanistan, in western Asia **2** *cap* : PASHTO **3** : a blanket or shawl of colored wool, knitted or crocheted in strips or squares which are joined by sewing or crocheting **4** : a Turkoman carpet of large size and long pile woven in geometric designs and predominantly wine red in color **5** *often cap* : CHIPPENDALE 2 **6** *usu cap* : AFGHAN HOUND

[2]**afghan** \"\ *adj, usu cap* : of, relating to, or like that of Afghanistan, its people, or its language

afghan fox *n, usu cap A* : CORSAC

afghan hound *n, usu cap A* : a swift greyhoundlike hunting dog of an ancient breed native to the Near East with a coat of silky thick hair of very fine texture, a head surmounted by a long silky topknot, and being about 26 inches tall

af·ghani \af'ganē, -änē\ *n* -s [Pashto *afghānī*, lit., Afghan] **1 a** : the basic monetary unit of Afghanistan — see MONEY table **b** : a silver coin no longer in active circulation representing the basic monetary unit of Afghanistan **2** *cap* : [1]AFGHAN 2

af·ghan·i·stan \af'ganə,stan, -taa(ə)n\ *adj, usu cap* [fr. *Afghanistan*, country in western Asia] : of or from Afghanistan : of the kind or style prevalent in Afghanistan

afi·brin·o·gen·emia \¦ā,=\ *n* -s [NL, fr. [2]*a-* + E *fibrinogen* + NL *-emia*] : an abnormality of the blood-clotting mechanism caused by usu. congenital absence of fibrinogen in the blood and marked by a tendency to prolonged bleeding

afi·ci·o·na·da \ə,fisēə'nädə, ə,fēsēə'-,ə,fishə'-, a,f-, -ädə; -,fēthēə'nä<u>th</u>ə, -nä-\ *n* -s [Sp, fr. fem. of *aficionado*, past part.] : a female aficionado

afi·ci·o·na·do *also* **af·fi·ci·o·na·do** \-ä(,)dō, -ä(-, -)<u>th</u>ō\ *n* -s [Sp *aficionado*, fr. *aficionado*, past part. of *aficionar* to inspire devotion or affection (as in *aficionarse* to be fond of), fr. *afición* fondness, affection, fr. L *affection-*, *affectio* — more at AFFECTION] **1** : an enthusiastic follower of bullfighting (the most important single thing for the beginning ~ to concentrate on is the matador's feet —Barnaby Conrad) **2** : an ardent follower, supporter, or enthusiast : FAN (an ~ of science fiction) (~*s* of progressive education argue that this has a frustrating effect on the children —Richard Joseph)

afield \ə'-\ *adv* (*or adj*) [ME *afelde*, fr. OE *on felda*, *on felde*, fr. *on* + *felda*, *felde*, dat. of *feld* field — more at FIELD] **1 a** : upon a field of battle (the armies were ~, challenging the enemy's advance) **b** : out to a field of battle (fierce warriors rushing ~) **2** : into or in a field : in or into the countryside (unlawful to carry hunting rifles ~ until the open season) (~, too, he had a quick eye for scenery —*Times Lit. Supp.*) **3 a** : away from home, usual surroundings, or native country : ABROAD (looking ~ for new lands to conquer —R.A.Hall b.1911) **b** : to or at a distance : away from a given point — used esp. with *far* or *farther* (they were at work far ~ —Russell Lord) (he did not want to go any farther ~) **4 a** : outside the circle of one's immediate family, usual associates, or ordinary activities (always looking ~ for new friends, new interests) (she did not go ~ for those who affected art and advanced ideas —Willa Cather) **b** : beyond one's ordinary methods of procedure or patterns of behavior : out of the way : to extreme lengths (an artist who has rarely gone ~ for his striking effects) **5 a** : beyond the point at issue : off the subject : away from the line of reasoning or interest : ASTRAY — used esp. with *far* or *farther* (inane remarks that were completely ~) (such a digression would lead us too far ~ —R.W. Murray) **b** : beyond evident causes, reasons, or circumstances — usu. used with *farther* (a social upheaval that can be understood only by going farther ~) **c** : beyond the fundamental limitations or boundaries (difficult problems that, so far as psychiatry is concerned, are quite ~)

afi·ko·men \¦äfē'kōmən\ *n* -s [Heb *āphīqōmān*] : a piece broken from the middle one of the three matzoth used by Jews at the Passover Seder service and set aside to be eaten at the end of the meal

afire \ə'-\ *adj* [ME *afire*, *afure*, fr. [1]*a-* + *fire*, *fure*, dat. of *fir*, *fur* fire] : on fire : BLAZING, FLAMING (the building was ~)

afla·gel·lar \¦āflə¦jelə(r)\ *also* **aflag·el·late** \(')ā¦flajələt, -,lāt, ¦āflə¦jelət\ *adj* [[2]*a-* + *flagellar*, *flagellate*] *zool* : without a flagellum

aflame \ə'-\ *adj* [[1]*a-* + *flame*, n.] : AFIRE

aflare \ə'-\ *adj* [[1]*a-* + *flare*, v.] : FLARING, FLAMING (~ with burning coals —Roderick Cameron)

a flat \'=¦=\ *n, usu cap A* **1** : the keynote of A-flat major or A-flat minor **2** : the tone a half step below A

a-flat major \'=,='==\ *n, usu cap A* : the major musical key having a signature of four flats

a-flat minor \'=,='==\ *n, usu cap A* : the minor musical key having a signature of seven flats

aflick·er \ə'-\ *adj* [[1]*a-* + *flicker*, v.] : FLICKERING

afloat \ə'flōt, *usu* -ōd·+V\ *adv* (*or adj*) [ME *aflote*, *afflot*, fr. OE *on flote*, *on flot*, fr. *on* + *flote*, *flot*, dat. & acc. respectively of *flot* deep water, sea; akin to OE *flēotan* to float — more at FLOAT] **1 a** : borne on the water : not aground : FLOATING (though badly battered, the boat remained ~) **b** : at sea : away from port (all the ships are still ~) **c** : buoyed up, floating, or suspended on, in, or as if on or in water, air, or any similar medium (water lilies placidly ~) (her hair ~ in the summer breeze) (~ on a tide of happiness —Marcia Davenport) **d** : on shipboard — used of persons or goods (preference for duty ~ —Louis Auchincloss) (a large quantity of wheat still ~) **2** : free of difficulties, esp. financial ones or those requiring the intervention of outside assistance : self-sufficient (the inheritance kept them ~ for years) **3 a** : circulating about from one individual or place to another : RU-

MORED ⟨a story was ~ that they faced bankruptcy⟩ **b :** moving about haphazardly without guide or control **:** ADRIFT ⟨they were confused, ~, unable to plan for the future⟩ **4 :** flooded with or submerged under water **:** AWASH ⟨the ship's main deck was ~⟩ **5 :** actively functioning **:** fully operating ⟨a neat publishing venture, set ~ at the right time⟩

aflow \ə'-\ *adj* [¹*a-* + *flow*, v.] **:** FLOWING ⟨their founts ~ with tears —Robert Browning⟩

aflow·er \ə'-\ *adj* [¹*a-* + *flower*, v.] **:** FLOWERING ⟨meadows ~ in the warm sun⟩

aflut·ter \ə'-\ *adj* [¹*a-* + *flutter*, v.] **1 :** FLUTTERING ⟨with white wings ~⟩ **2 :** in a flutter **:** nervously excited ⟨all ~ at the thought of her return⟩ **3 :** filled with or marked by the presence of fluttering things ⟨the woods were ~ with unknown birds —Van Wyck Brooks⟩

afoam \ə'-\ *adj* [¹*a-* + *foam*, v.] **:** FOAMING ⟨brimming tankards all ~⟩

afo·cal \(ˈ)ā¦-\ *adj* [²*a-* + *focal*] *physics* **:** having focal points infinitely distant ⟨an ~ lens⟩

à fond \äfōⁿ\ *adv* [F, lit., to the bottom] **1 :** THOROUGHLY ⟨he knows his subject *à fond*⟩ **2 :** to the fullest extent **:** to the utmost ⟨supporting their party's principles *à fond*⟩

afoot \ə'-\ *adv (or adj)* [ME *afote*, fr. ¹*a-* + *fote*, dat. of *fot* foot — more at FOOT] **1 :** on foot ⟨traveling ~⟩ ⟨quail are hunted either ~ or on horseback —*Amer. Guide Series: Tenn.*⟩ **2 :** up and about **:** not bedridden ⟨she is ~ again, after her short illness⟩ **3 a :** on the move **:** in action **:** ASTIR ⟨there's trouble ~⟩ ⟨he knew that something out of the ordinary was ~ —Hamilton Basso⟩ **b :** under way **:** in progress ⟨there was much work ~ everywhere⟩ ⟨a plan to set ~ a new network of highways⟩

afore \ə'fō(ə)r, -ō(ə)r,-ōə,-ō(ə)\ *adv or conj or prep* [ME *aforen, aforn, afore*, fr. OE *onforan*, fr. *on* + *foran* before — more at BEFORE] *chiefly dial* **:** BEFORE

¹**afore·hand** \=ˈ=,=\ *adv* [ME, fr. *afore* + *hand*] *chiefly dial* **:** BEFOREHAND

²**aforehand** \"\ *adj, chiefly dial* **:** ready for the future ⟨sagacity that is ~ with events —Samuel Richardson⟩

afore·men·tioned \=ˈ=¦== *sometimes* ¦a,fōr¦- *or* ¦a,fōə¦- *or* ¦a,fō(r)¦- *or* ¦afə(r)¦-\ *adj* [*afore* + *mentioned*] **:** mentioned previously

afore·said \=ˈ=¦= *sometimes* ¦a,fōr¦- *or* ¦a,fōə¦- *or* ¦a,fō(r)¦- *or* ¦afə(r)¦-\ *adj* [ME *aforneseid*, fr. *aforn* afore + *seid* said] **:** AFOREMENTIONED

¹**afore·thought** \=ˈ=¦= *sometimes* ¦a,fōr¦- *or* ¦a,fōə¦- *or* ¦a,fō(r)¦- *or* ¦afə(r)¦-\ *adj* [*afore* + *thought*, past part. of *think*; prob. after *prepense*] **:** PREMEDITATED **:** previously in mind **:** DELIBERATE — usu. used postpositively ⟨with malice ~⟩ ⟨sheer falsehood, idle fables, allegory ~ —Thomas Carlyle⟩

²**afore·thought** \=ˈ=,=\ *n* -s [*afore* + *thought*, n.] **:** PREMEDITATION, DELIBERATION ⟨doing nothing without ~⟩

¹**afore·time** \=ˈ=,=\ *adv* [ME, fr. *afore* + *time*] *archaic* **:** FORMERLY

²**aforetime** \"\ *adj, archaic* **:** FORMER

a formation \ˈā-\ *n, usu cap A* [¹*a*] **:** an offensive football formation in which the line is unbalanced to one side and the backfield strong to the other — compare FORMATION

¹**a for·ti·o·ri** \¦ä,fō(r)d·ēˈōr,ī, ¦ä...ōr(,)ē,¦ä...ōr(,)ē, -fōr¦-fōə¦, ¦tē-,¦shē-, -ēˈō-\ *adv* [L] **:** all the more certainly **:** with greater reason **:** with still more convincing force — used in drawing a reasoned conclusion which as compared with some other reasoned conclusion or recognized fact is inferred to be even more certain or inescapable ⟨the man of prejudice is, *a fortiori*, a man of limited mental vision⟩ ⟨if no major country has the resources for the enterprise, *a fortiori* neither has any lesser power⟩

²**a fortiori** \¦=,==¦=(,)=\ *adj* **1 :** marked by a certainty inferred from and taken to be even more conclusive than another reasoned conclusion or recognized fact ⟨*a fortiori* proof⟩ **2 :** making use of conclusions inferred from and taken to be even more conclusive than another reasoned conclusion or recognized fact ⟨*a fortiori* argumentation⟩

afoul \ə'-\ *adj* [¹*a-* + *foul* (entangled)] **:** FOULED, TANGLED ⟨a ship with its sails ~⟩

afoul of *prep* **:** in or into conflict with **:** in or into opposition to ⟨he fell *afoul of* the law⟩ **:** in or into collision or entanglement with ⟨one ship ran *afoul of* the other⟩

afr- *or* **afro-** *comb form, usu cap* [L *Afr-, Afer* African] **:** African ⟨*Afr*americans⟩ **:** African and ⟨*Afro*-Asiatic⟩

afraid \ə'frād, *in S often* -re(ə)d\ *adj* [ME *affraied, afraied*, fr. past part. of *affraien* to frighten — more at AFFRAY] **1 :** FRIGHTENED **:** filled with fear, alarm, or apprehension ⟨running because they were ~⟩ ⟨~ of the dark⟩ ⟨~ he wouldn't live⟩ ⟨the author was ~ that he would lose his prestige⟩ ⟨to say bluntly what everyone else is ~ to say —T.S.Eliot⟩ — usu. used predicatively **2 :** filled with concern, regret, or sorrow over a situation that is or seems to be inescapable ⟨they said they were ~ they couldn't accept the invitation⟩ ⟨we have witnessed, I am ~, only the first phase of a basic conflict —J.B.Conant⟩ — often used to express a polite depreciation of one's own opinion or importance ⟨he told her he was ~ she was quite wrong⟩ **3 :** filled with annoyed expectation of an unwanted contingency ⟨he seemed ~, if he were kind, he might be ridiculed —E.A.Peeples⟩ **4 :** DISINCLINED, RELUCTANT, AVERSE ⟨he's ~ of even a little work⟩ ⟨~ to let his emotions seize upon his speech —V.L.Parrington⟩ ⟨not ~ of being declamatory in his fervor —Leslie Rees⟩

syn ANXIOUS, FEARFUL, AFRAID, FRIGHTENED, SCARED, TERRIFIED, and AGHAST all imply effects of apprehension, fear, or terror upon the one so described and form a roughly ascending order of intensity in the symptoms of such effects. ANXIOUS usu. suggests a mild fear amounting often to little more than a fretful though usu. persistent worry or mild apprehensiveness about possible misfortune ⟨your letter is a great relief to my mind for I still was *anxious* —O.W.Holmes †1935⟩ ⟨*anxious* for her own safety against dangers threatening from the Mediterranean —A.S.Esmer⟩ ⟨Cicero, *anxious* for his own safety, knowing now that he had made enemies of half the Senate, watching how the balance of factions would go —J.A.Froude⟩ FEARFUL, though often the same as ANXIOUS, usu. suggests a somewhat stronger and more generalized apprehensiveness stemming often rather from a natural timidity than particular objective causes and implying reactions of fear but fear usu. strongly mingled with shyness, uncertainty, and a more general tendency to foreboding and worry ⟨I was *fearful* lest we should strike the timbered edge of the plain —Francis Birtles⟩ ⟨they have been *fearful* of the unorthodox —S.E.Harris⟩ ⟨the average individual is somewhat *fearful* of high speeds —H.G.Armstrong⟩ ⟨it is timorous and *fearful* of challenge —H.L.Mencken⟩ ⟨now that he had these and a dozen other distinctions, he was *fearful* and insecure —Walter O'Meara⟩ AFRAID, FRIGHTENED, and SCARED are often interchangeable in meaning in common use; AFRAID, however, is the most general of the three and usu. implies a deep-seated though not necessarily outwardly apparent reaction of fear manifest in a strong sense of personal insecurity or danger or in a strong and usu. uncontrollable desire to avoid or evade the cause of the reaction ⟨*afraid*, in her extreme perturbation, of the loneliness of the deserted rooms, and of half-imagined faces peeping from behind every open door in them —Charles Dickens⟩ ⟨I was too *afraid* of her to shudder, too afraid of her to put my fingers to my ears —Joseph Conrad⟩ ⟨ten thousand regular soldiers of his wonderful army that everybody in the world was *afraid* of —Dorothy C. Fisher⟩ FRIGHTENED implies a fear that usu. gives rise to an inner disorder and temporary loss of self-command bordering on and often involving paralysis of muscle and will ⟨the men were *frightened* by the sudden and unexpected attack on the fort but they defended it valiantly⟩ ⟨*frightened* at the prospect of failure⟩ ⟨a child *frightened* by stories of the boogeyman⟩ ⟨*frightened* so that he broke out in a cold sweat and could hardly stand⟩ SCARED is the same as FRIGHTENED in intensity but suggests a more all-inclusive usu. childlike reaction as that of running away, trembling, or acting in ways that for adults would be foolish and irrational ⟨run like *scared* rabbits all the way down the hill to the Charles Street elevated station —Joseph Dever⟩ ⟨many of the houses here were still occupied by *scared* inhabitants, too frightened even for flight —H.G.Wells⟩ TERRIFIED and AGHAST, in this sense, suggest total paralysis of action and will. TERRIFIED implies the total reign of terror over the person resulting in stupefaction or in a total incapacity to act or think in any rational way ⟨a child *terrified* into screaming by the idea of going to the dentist⟩ ⟨*terrified* by the very sound of a plane after several months of steady bombings⟩ ⟨the mind, indeed, in its first blank outlook on life is *terrified* by the demoniac force of nature and the swarming misery of man —G.D.Brown⟩ AGHAST, a somewhat older use in this sense, puts strong emphasis on an immobility resulting from a terror or more usu. a horror or horrified disbelief esp. over the fate of someone or something other than oneself ⟨were *aghast* that in their own midst there were men capable of such barbarism —Ruth Gruber⟩ ⟨many who are *aghast* at the type of world which we are now entering, in which a war could cause obliteration —Vannevar Bush⟩ ⟨I stood *aghast*, unable to move, while the gravediggers uncovered a skeleton, cleaned the bones, laid them alongside the grave —J.A.Lomax⟩ ⟨an intelligent woman, remembering her own childhood, must stand *aghast* at the utter disregard of the children's ordinary human rights —G.B.Shaw⟩

a-frame \ˈ=,=\ *n, cap A* [¹*A* + *frame*] **:** a 3-piece frame put together like the lines of a capital A and used to support or hold in position a heavy weight, a hoist, a shaft, or a pipe

aframerican *cap, var of* AFRO-AMERICAN

af·ra·sian \(ˈ)a¦frāzhən, -āsh-\ *adj, usu cap* [*Afr-* + *Asian*] **:** of or belonging to both Africa and Asia

afreet *or* **afrit** *also* **afrite** \ˈa,frēt, əˈf-\ *or* **efreet** \ˈe,f-, əˈf-\ *n* -s [Ar *ʻifrīt*, prob. fr. Per *āfrīda* created being] **:** a powerful evil jinni, demon, or monstrous giant in Arabic mythology

afresh \ə'-\ *adv* [ME, fr. ¹*a-* + *fresh*] **1 :** ANEW **:** with fresh or unabated vigor, force, or impetus ⟨at every word her sobbing broke out ~⟩ **2 :** AGAIN **:** over again ⟨translation is a labor that must be done ~ for each succeeding age —J.C. Swaim⟩ **3 :** from a totally fresh beginning ⟨it is difficult to organize a school ~ in a primitive country⟩

¹**af·ric** \ˈafrik\ *adj, usu cap* [L *Africus*, fr. *Afr-, Afer* African (perh. back-formation fr. *Africa*) + *-icus* -ic] **:** AFRICAN

²**afric** \"\ *n* -s *cap* [L *Africus*] **:** AFRICAN

af·ri·ca \-rəkə, -rē-\ *adj, usu cap* [fr. *Africa*, the continent, fr. L] **:** of or from the continent of Africa **:** of the kind or style prevalent in Africa **:** AFRICAN

¹**af·ri·can** \-kən\ *adj, usu cap* [ME, fr. L *Africanus*, adj. & n., fr. *Africa* + L *-anus* -an] **1 :** of, relating to, or characteristic of Africa or its people **2 a :** being or constituting the biogeographic subregion that comprises Africa south of the Sahara; *broadly* **:** ²ETHIOPIAN 3 **b :** of, relating to, or native to the African subregion

²**african** \"\ *n* [ME, fr. OE, fr. L *Africanus*] **1** -s **a** *cap* **:** a native or inhabitant of Africa **b** *usu cap* **:** an individual of immediate or remote African ancestry; *esp* **:** NEGRO **2** -s *often cap* **:** a nearly neutral slightly brownish black that is darker than lava **3** *usu cap* **:** a breed of medium-sized ashy-brown geese with knobbed black bill, dewlap, and orange shanks possibly derived from the Chinese goose

african blackwood *n, usu cap A* **:** a tropical African tree (*Dalbergia melanoxylon*) with hard purple wood used esp. in the manufacture of musical instruments

african bladdernut *n, usu cap A* **:** a small evergreen tree (*Royena lucida*) of southern Africa with downy shoots, solitary pale yellow or white flowers, and small somewhat fleshy red or purple fruits

african bowstring hemp *n, usu cap A* **:** a bowstring hemp (*Sansevieria guineensis*) of tropical Africa

african boxthorn *n, usu cap A* **:** a tall shrub (*Lycium tetrandrum*) with spiny branchlets, rather thick leaves, and orange-red berries

african boxwood *n, usu cap A* **:** CAPE BOX

african breadfruit *n, usu cap A* **:** TRECULIA

african brown *n, often cap A* **1 :** a dark grayish brown that is very slightly redder, lighter, and stronger than average chocolate brown and paler and very slightly redder than Chippendale **2** *Brit* **:** a very dark chocolate brown

african buffalo *n, usu cap A* **:** CAPE BUFFALO

african cane *n, usu cap A* **:** PEARL MILLET 1

african cherry orange *n, usu cap A* **1 :** any of several small spiny central African citrus trees (genus *Citropsis*) with leathery unequally pinnate leaves and small sweet bright orange fruits growing in clusters **2 :** a fruit of the African cherry orange

african coast fever *n, usu cap A&C* **:** EAST COAST FEVER

african copaiba *n, usu cap A* **:** a copaibalike oleoresin supposedly derived from an African tree (*Hardwickia manii*)

african corn lily *n, usu cap A* **:** a plant of the genus *Ixia*

african cubeb *n, usu cap A* **:** the fruit of a tropical African shrub (*Piper clusii*) tasting like black pepper and used to adulterate it

african cypress *n, usu cap A* **:** any of several cypress pines of southern Africa that vary in size from moderate shrubs to tall trees and include some that produce a fragrant yellowish to brown wood suitable for cabinetwork and a resin that is used locally

african daisy *n, usu cap A* **1 :** a shrub (*Lonas inodora*) of the family Compositae having daisylike heads of flowers **2 :** any of several annual or perennial composite herbs (genus *Arctotis*); *esp* **:** a bushy perennial (*A. stoechadifolia*) with white or violet rays **3 :** DIMORPHOTHECA 2

¹**af·ri·can·der** *or* **af·ri·kan·der** \,afrəˈkandə(r), -rē-, -aan- *also* -ān- *or* -ən-\ *n* -s *cap* [Afrik *Afrikaander*, alter. (prob. influenced by *Hollander*) of *Afrikaner*] **:** AFRIKANER

²**africander** *or* **afrikander** \"\ *n* -s *usu cap* [Afrik *Afrikaner, Afrikaander*, prob. short for *Afrikanerbees, Afrikaanderbees*, lit., African cattle, fr. *Afrikaner, Afrikaander* African + *bees* head of cattle — more at AFRIKANER] **1 :** a breed of tall red large-horned humped southern African cattle used chiefly for meat or draft **2 :** a breed of fat-rumped mutton-type southern African sheep

africanderism *var of* AFRIKANDERISM

african dominoes *n pl, usu cap A* [so called fr. the stereotypical popularity of dice games among American Negroes] **1** *slang* **:** DICE **2** *sing in constr, slang* **:** CRAPS

african elephant *n, usu cap A* **:** the very tall large-eared elephant (*Loxodonta africana*) that is widely distributed in tropical Africa — compare ASIATIC ELEPHANT

african fleabane *n, usu cap A* **:** any of several shrubby composite plants (genus *Tarchonanthus*) having stalked leathery leaves, small flower heads in axillary or terminal clusters, and usu. an odor like that of balsam

african ginger *n, usu cap A* **:** WHITE GINGER

african golf *n, usu cap A* [see AFRICAN DOMINOES] *slang* **:** CRAPS

african goose *n, usu cap A* **:** a goose of the African breed

african gray *n, usu cap A* **:** a parrot (*Psittacus erithacus*) that is native to equatorial Africa, has gray plumage, red tail, black primaries, and whitish face, and is very commonly domesticated esp. because of its aptness in learning to talk

african ground squirrel *n, usu cap A* **:** any of several large coarse-furred ground-dwelling squirrels of *Xerus* and related genera often conspicuously marked with white and widely distributed in drier parts of Africa

african hair *n, usu cap A* **:** a fiber obtained from the leaves of hemp palm and used for mattress stuffing and also made into a fabric resembling haircloth

african hemp *n, usu cap A* **1 :** AFRICAN BOWSTRING HEMP **2 :** a southern African shrub (*Sparmannia africana*) with white flowers

african holly *n, usu cap A, in California* **:** an arborescent woolly-stemmed biennial herb (*Solanum giganteum*) that is native to India but is grown in many warm regions as an ornamental for its large leaves with silky-white undersurface, clusters of showy blue or lilac flowers, and bright red fruits resembling holly berries

african horse sickness *n, usu cap A* **:** a serious and commonly fatal virus disease of horses endemic in parts of central and southern Africa, characterized by fever, edematous swellings, and internal hemorrhage, and transmitted by certain biting flies

african hunting dog *n, usu cap A* **:** a powerful doglike mammal (*Lycaon pictus*) brightly marked in black, white, and reddish yellow formerly abundant in southern and eastern Africa where it hunted in large packs but now becoming rare in settled areas

african incense *or* **african elemi** *n, usu cap A* **:** a fragrant oleoresin that is obtained from an Arabian tree (*Boswellia freeriana*)

af·ri·can·ism \ˈafrəkə,nizəm, -ēk-\ *n* -s *usu cap* **:** something that is characteristically African: as **a :** a characteristic feature of the Latin used by early Christian writers of northern Africa **b :** the theological doctrines of early Christian writers of northern Africa (as St. Augustine of Hippo †430) **c :** a characteristic feature of an African language occurring in a non-African language ⟨~s in the Gullah dialect —L.D. Turner⟩

af·ri·ca·nist \-nəst\ *n* -s *usu cap* **:** a specialist in African languages or cultures

af·ri·can·i·za·tion \,==kənəˈzāshən, -,nīˈz-\ *n* -s *often cap* **:** the action of africanizing esp. by bringing under the influence or domination of Negroes

af·ri·can·ize \ˈ==kə,nīz\ *vt* -ED/-ING/-S *often cap* **1 :** to cause to acquire a trait regarded as distinctive of Negroes **2 :** to bring under the control or the cultural or civil supremacy of Africans, esp. Negroes

african juniper *n, usu cap A* **:** a tall evergreen tree (*Juniperus procera*) of the mountains of eastern Africa

african latin *n, cap A&L* **:** Latin of the style and idiom found in the earliest Latin version of the Bible

african lethargy *n, usu cap A* **:** SLEEPING SICKNESS 1

african lily *n, usu cap A* **1 :** AGAPANTHUS 2 **2 :** BLOOD LILY

african locust *n, usu cap A* **:** a plant of the genus *Parkia*; *esp* **:** a tree (*P. africana*)

african lynx *n, usu cap A* **:** CARACAL

african marigold *n, usu cap A* **:** a stout branching annual herb (*Tagetes erecta*) with flower heads two to four inches across and yellow to orange in color

african milkbush *n, usu cap A* **:** a shrub (*Synadenium grantii*) of the family Euphorbiaceae that is cultivated for its red flowers

african millet *n, usu cap A* **1 :** a tall form of kafir **2 :** RAGI **3 :** PEARL MILLET 1

african mustard *n, usu cap A* **:** an Old World weedy annual plant (*Erysimum repandum*) that is related to the mustards, has bright yellow flowers, and is an adventive weed in much of No. America

african oak *n, usu cap A* **1 a :** an African timber tree (*Oldfieldia africana*) of the family Euphorbiaceae that yields a very heavy hard teaklike reddish brown or purplish brown timber **b :** the wood of this tree — called also *African teak* **2 :** EKKI

af·ri·can·oid \ˈafrəkə,nȯid, -rēk-\ *adj, usu cap A* **:** resembling or having characteristics of the peoples of Africa or their artifacts or cultures ⟨a long-headed member of the *Africanoid* races —W.Z.Ripley⟩

african oil palm *n, usu cap A* **:** a tall pinnate-leaved palm (*Elaeis guineensis*) with fruits yielding palm oil

african orthodox *adj, usu cap A&O* **:** of or relating to the African Orthodox Church, an independent church of Negro Episcopalians formed in 1921 under the leadership of the Rev. George A. McGuire

african padauk *n, usu cap A* [modif. of F *padouk*, fr. a native name in western Africa] **1 :** an African tree (*Pterocarpus soyauxii*) that yields a close-grained reddish brown wood important esp. as a source of red dyestuff — compare REDWOOD **2 :** the wood of African padauk — called also *barwood*

african pepper *n, usu cap A* **1 :** AFRICAN CUBEB **2 :** CAYENNE PEPPER

african polecat *n, usu cap A* **:** MUISHOND

african rosewood *n, usu cap A* **1 :** an African tree (*Lingoum erinaceum*) **2 :** the close-grained fine-textured smooth and quite lustrous hard wood of the African rosewood **3 :** BUBINGA

african rue *n, usu cap A* **:** an African plant (*Peganum harmala*) yielding harmine and harmaline

africans *pl of* AFRICAN

african saffron *n, usu cap A* **1 :** a product formed by adulterating the true saffron with the flowers of other plants (as *Carthamus tinctorius* and *Calendula officinalis*) **2 a :** a shrub (*Lyperia crocea*) of southern Africa **b :** an orange dye obtained from the flowers of this shrub

african satinbush *n, usu cap A* **:** a southern African shrub (*Podalyria sericea*) grown for its silvery foliage and rosy purple pealike flowers

african scented mahogany *n, usu cap A* **:** MAHOGANY 1b(2)

african school *n, usu cap A* **:** an early ante-Nicene school of patristic philosophy developed in northern Africa of which Tertullian and Arnobius were chief representatives

african snail *n, usu cap A* **:** a large pulmonate land mollusk (*Achatina fulica*) introduced from the western coast of Africa into Ceylon, the East Indian region, and the Pacific islands — compare ACHATINA

african swallowwort *n, usu cap A* **:** a plant of the genus *Stapelia*

african tea *n, usu cap A* **:** KAT

african teak *n, usu cap A* **1 :** AFRICAN OAK **2 :** BUBINGA **3 :** IROKO

african tea tree *n, usu cap A* **:** an African shrub (*Lycium afrum*) having spiny branches, small linear leaves, and solitary purple flowers

af·ri·can·thro·pus \,afrəˈkan(t)thrəpəs, -,kanˈthrōpəs\ *n, cap* [NL, fr. *Africa* + *-anthropus* (as in *Pithecanthropus*)] *in some classifications* **:** a genus of primitive hominids from the Upper Pleistocene of Africa known from partial reconstruction of several shattered skulls found near Lake Eyasi in Tanzania, considered in some respects intermediate between Neanderthal man and pithecanthropus, and by some held congeneric with Florisbad man and Rhodesian man

african trypanosomiasis *n, usu cap A* **:** SLEEPING SICKNESS 1

african tulip *n, usu cap A* **1 :** BLOOD LILY **2 :** AGAPANTHUS 2

african valerian *n, usu cap A* **:** an herb (*Fedia cornucopiae*) of the family Valerianaceae cultivated for its red flowers or for use as a salad

african violet *n, usu cap A* **:** a tropical African plant (*Saintpaulia ionantha*) with long-petioled fleshy leaves in a basal cluster that is very popular as a house plant in color varieties of purple, pink, and white

african walnut *n, usu cap A* **1 :** a tropical African timber tree (*Lovoa klaineana*) of the family Meliaceae **2 :** the yellowish wood of the African walnut having the grain and figure of mahogany

africs *pl of* AFRIC

afri·di \əˈfrēdē, aˈ-\ *n, pl* **afridis** *or* **afridi** *usu cap* [Pashto, prob. fr. Per *āfrīda* man, created being] **1 :** Pathan people occupying the hilly country about the Khyber Pass and found on both sides of the frontier between Pakistan and eastern Afghanistan **2 :** a member of the Afridi people

af·ri·kaans \ˈafrə,kän(t)s, -ān-, -nz, -anz,-aa(ə)nz, ,==ˈ=\ *n, cap* [Afrik, fr. *afrikaans*, adj., African, fr. obs. Afrik *afrikanisch*, fr. L *africanus* African + obs. Afrik *-isch* (now *-s*) -ish — more at AFRICAN] **:** a language that developed in southern Africa from 17th century Dutch and is one of the official languages of the Union of So. Africa — called also *Cape Dutch, Taal*; see INDO-EUROPEAN LANGUAGES table

afrikander *usu cap, var of* AFRICANDER

af·ri·kan·der·ism *or* **af·ri·can·der·ism** \,afrəˈkandə,rizəm, -rē-, -aan- *also* -än- *or* -ən-\ *n* -s **1** *usu cap* **:** the principles, policies, or practices of Afrikaners **2** *often cap* **:** a characteristic feature of Afrikaans occurring in another language esp. in So. Africa

af·ri·ka·ner \,afrəˈkänə(r), -rē-, -an-,-än- *also* ,äf- *or* ,af-\ *n* -s *cap, often attrib* [Afrik, lit., African, fr. L *Africanus* + Afrik *-er*] **:** a So. African native of European descent; *esp* **:** an Afrikaans-speaking descendant of the 17th century Dutch settlers who colonized Cape Province and neighboring regions of southern Africa

af·ri·ka·ner·dom *also* **af·ri·kan·der·dom** *or* **af·ri·can·der·dom** \-dəm\ *n* -s *cap* [Afrik *Afrikanerdom, Afrikaanderdom*, fr. *Afrikaner, Afrikaander* + *-dom*] **:** the Afrikaner section of the population of the Union of So. Africa

afrit *also* **afrite** *var of* AFREET

afro- *in pronunciations below*, ¦== = ¦a(,)frō\ — see AFR-

¹**af·ro-amer·i·can** \¦===¦===\ *or* **af·ra·mer·i·can** \¦afrə¦===\ *adj, usu cap initial As* [*Afr-* + *American*] **:** of or relating to Americans of African and esp. of Negroid descent

²**afro-american** \"\ *or* **aframerican** \"\ *n, cap initial As* **:** an American of African and esp. of Negroid descent

AFRO-ASIATIC LANGUAGES

SUBFAMILY	BRANCH	DIVISION	SUBDIVISION	GROUP	SUBGROUP	LANGUAGES AND DIALECTS[1]	CHIEF LOCALITIES
SEMITIC	East Semitic					*Akkadian* (*Old Akkadian, Old Assyrian* or *Cappadocian, Assyrian, Old Babylonian, Middle Babylonian, Neo-Babylonian, Nuzi*)	Ancient Mesopotamia
	West Semitic	Northwest Semitic	Aramaic		Eastern Aramaic	*Babylonian Aramaic, Talmudic, Mandaean, Harranian,* Syriac	Ancient Mesopotamia and Syria, northwestern Iran, northeastern Turkey, northern Iraq, modern Syria and Lebanon
					Western Aramaic	*Old Aramaic, Biblical Aramaic, Jewish Palestinian Aramaic, Christian Palestinian Aramaic, Samaritan, Palmyrene, Nabataean, Sinaitic Aramaic,* Modern Western Aramaic	Ancient Syria, Palestine, and Sinai Peninsula, the Anti-Lebanon
			Canaanitic		Canaanite-Phoenician	*Canaanite, Phoenician, Punic, neo-Punic, Ugaritic*	Ancient Syria, Phoenicia, Carthage, ancient Palestine
					Hebraic	Hebrew (*Biblical, Mishnaic, Rabbinic, Medieval,* Modern), *Moabite, Ammonite, Edomite*	Ancient Palestine, Babylonia, modern Palestine
		Southwest Semitic	North Arabic			*Lihyanic, Thamudic, Safaitic, Nabataean Arabic,* classical Arabic, Modern Arabic (Maltese)	Arabia, Iraq, Syria, Lebanon, Palestine, North Africa, medieval Andalusia, Zanzibar, Madagascar, Malta
			Southeast Semitic	South Arabic	Old South Arabic	*Minaean, Sabaean, Qatabanian, Himyaritic, Hadhramautic*	Ancient Hejaz, Yemen, and Hadhramaut
					Modern South Arabic	Mahri, Sokotri, Qarawi, Shkhauri	Southern Arabia, Socotra
				Ethiopic	North Ethiopic	*Ethiopic* or *Geez*, Tigre, Tigrinya	Ethiopia, Eritrea
					South Ethiopic	Amharic, Argobba, Harari, *Gafat*, Gurage	Ethiopia
EGYPTIAN[2]						*Old Egyptian, Middle Egyptian, Late Egyptian, Demotic Egyptian, Coptic* (*Sahidic, Akhmimic, Subakhmimic, Fayumic, Memphitic, Bohairic*)	Egypt
BERBER[2]				Libyan		*Libyan*	Ancient North Africa and Canary islands
				Saharan		*Saharan*	Ancient Sahara
				Berber	Western Berber	Shluh (Shluh proper, Beraber, Draa), Tamashek, Zenaga, Kabyle	Morocco, central Sahara, southwestern Mauritania, Great Kabylia and Little Kabylia in Algeria
					Zenete	Zenete proper, Rif, Shawia, Siwi	In scattered areas of northern Africa from the Siwa oasis in Egypt west into Morocco
					Guanche	*Guanche*	Canary islands
CUSHITIC[2]	North Cushitic					Beja	Southeastern Egypt, northeastern Sudan, northwestern Eritrea
	Northeast Cushitic					Saho-Afar	Eritrea, French Somaliland, northeastern Ethiopia
	Central Cushitic					Agau (Bilin, Khamir, Quara, Awiya), Galla	Ethiopia, Kenya
	East Cushitic					Somali	French Somaliland, British Somaliland, Italian Somaliland, southeastern Ethiopia
	South Cushitic					Burji-Sidamo (Burji, Darasa, Kambatta; Alaba, Sidamo, Qabena), Konso-Geleba	Southern Ethiopia
	Southwest Cushitic					Ometo (Wolamo, Zala, Gofa, Basketo, Haruro, and other dialects), Janjero, Kafa, Gimira-Maji	Southwestern Ethiopia
CHAD						Hausa and numerous others	West and south of Lake Chad

[1]Parentheses denote dialects and periods; italics denote dead languages. [2]The Egyptian, Berber, and Cushitic subfamilies are often called collectively the Hamitic languages.

af·ro–asi·at·ic languages \ˌ==ˌ==ˌ==-\ *n pl, usu cap both As* **:** a family of languages widely distributed over southwestern Asia and northern Africa, comprising the Semitic, Egyptian, Berber, Cushitic, and Chad subfamilies — see HAMITIC LANGUAGES

af·ro–cu·ban \ˌ==ˌ-\ *adj, usu cap A & C* [*Afr-* + *Cuban*] **:** of or relating to Cubans of African, esp. Negroid, descent

af·ro–eu·ro·pe·an \ˌ==,==ˌ==\ *adj, usu cap A & E* [*Afr-* + *European*] **:** of or relating to Africa and Europe

af·ro·gae·an \ˌ==ˌjēən\ *adj, usu cap* [NL *Afrogaea* the Ethiopian region of Africa (fr. *Afr-* + *-gaea*) + E *-an*] **:** ETHIOPIAN — used in biogeographic description

afront *adv* [ME, fr. [1]*a-* + *front*, n.] *obs* **:** ABREAST

af·ro·pa·vo \ˌ=='pā(ˌ)vō, -pä-\ *n* [NL, fr. *Afr-* + L *pavo* peacock] **1** *cap* **:** a genus of bronzy green and brown African birds that are about the size of the ring-necked pheasant but closely related to the peacocks though lacking the distinctive tail of the latter **2** -s **:** a bird of the genus *Afropavo* — called also *Congo peacock*

af·ro·pla·nor·bis \ˌ==plə'nȯrbəs\ *n, cap* [NL, fr. *Afr-* + *Planorbis*] **:** a genus of African pulmonate freshwater snails (family Planorbidae) including important intermediate hosts of the blood fluke (*Schistosoma mansoni*)

af·shar \'afˌshär\ *n* -s **1** *cap* **:** AISSOR **2** *usu cap* **:** a Shiraz rug of coarse weave

[1]**aft** \'aft, 'aa(ə)-,'ai-,'å-\ *adv* [ME *afte* back, fr. OE *æftan* behind, from behind (akin to OHG *aftan*, ON *aptan*, Goth *aftana*), fr. the root of OE *æft* behind + *-an* (suffix denoting place from which) — more at AFTER, HENCE] **:** near, toward, or in the stern of a ship or the tail of an aircraft **:** ABAFT ⟨the captain would call all hands ~ —N.D.Ford⟩ ⟨midwing monoplane with a large vertical fin and rudder ~ —A.R.Weyl⟩; *broadly* **:** BEHIND ⟨a few trams were running, policemen posted fore and ~ —Christopher Isherwood⟩ ⟨a cloth Sherlock Holmes cap pulled down fore and ~ —Richard Joseph⟩ — sometimes used with *of* ⟨along the fairing ~ of the engines —Howard Nemerov⟩

[2]**aft** \"\ *adj* **:** REARWARD, REAR ⟨motion in the ~ direction⟩ **:** [4]AFTER 2 ⟨orders came for our unit to assemble on the ~ deck —H.D.Skidmore⟩

[3]**aft** \'aft\ *Scot var of* OFT

aft *abbr* afternoon

af·ten \'afən\ *Scot var of* OFTEN

[1]**af·ter** \'aftə(r), 'aa-,'ai-,'å-, +V *sometimes* -ftr *as in* 'aftrim *for "after him"*\ *adv* [ME *after, efter*, fr. OE *æfter;* akin to OHG *aftar* after, ON *eptir* after, *aptr* back, Goth *aftaro* from behind, *aftra* backwards, and perh. to Skt *apataram* farther away, OPer, elsewhere, and perh. to OE *of* of, from, off — more at OF] **:** following in time or place **:** AFTERWARD, BEHIND ⟨we arrived shortly ~⟩ ⟨in Chaucer's day and for long ~ —G.M.Trevelyan⟩ ⟨along came a fox with the hounds following ~⟩

[2]**after** \"\ *prep* [ME *after, efter*, fr. OE *æfter*, fr. *æfter*, adv.] **1** — used as a function word to indicate the object or goal of a stated or implied action ⟨my soul thirsteth ~ thee —Ps 143:6 (AV)⟩ ⟨women go ~ causes harder than men do —Paul Engle⟩ ⟨he was too greedy ~ the treasures —Van Wyck Brooks⟩ ⟨it's serious work I'm ~ —Maurice Hewlett⟩ **2 a :** behind in place or time ⟨men in line one ~ another⟩ ⟨wave ~ wave beat on the shore⟩ ⟨the rains continued day ~ day⟩ **b :** below in rank **:** next in order to ⟨the richest and most splendid church in England ~ Westminster Abbey —Henry Riddell⟩ ⟨~ money, the biggest problem is personnel —*Time*⟩ **3 a** (1) **:** later than a particular time or period of time **:** following the expiration of ⟨20 minutes ~ 4⟩ ⟨at a quarter ~ 8⟩ ⟨it's half ~ 6⟩ ⟨events occurring ~ 1940⟩ ⟨~ three days⟩ ⟨condition of roads ~ the snow storm⟩ (2) **:** immediately following but not necessarily including the day, period, or date of event named ⟨thirty days ~ April 1⟩ ⟨two months ~ July⟩ ⟨ten days ~ sight of a draft⟩ **b** (1) **:** subsequent to and in consequence of ⟨~ what you have told me, I'll be careful⟩ ⟨net income ~ taxes⟩ (2) **:** subsequent to and notwithstanding ⟨even ~ the policeman's warning, the driver continued to speed⟩ **4 :** so as to resemble in some respect: **a :** in accordance with ⟨make me ~ thy will —Adelaide Pollard⟩ ⟨his ways are not ~ our expectations —Gilbert Kilpack⟩ ⟨Napoleon himself she admired as a man ~ her own heart —G.H.Genzmer⟩ **b** *obs* (1) **:** with reference to **:** in correspondence to **:** in proportion to (2) **:** at the rate of **c :** with the name of or by a name derived from that of ⟨John was named ~ his father⟩ ⟨called poinsettia ~ Joel R. Poinsett⟩ **d :** in imitation of **:** in the characteristic manner of **:** on the pattern of ⟨a great military power ~ the Western pattern —Ruth Benedict⟩ ⟨portrait of Charles I ~ Van Dyck —S.P.B. Mais⟩ ⟨he was built ~ his father —Conrad Richter⟩ **e :** derived from and shaped like ⟨malachite is a pseudomorph ~ cuprite⟩ **5** *chiefly Irish* **:** having just **:** in the act of **:** at the point of **:** given to — used with gerund ⟨it's a queer thing you wouldn't care to be hearing it and them girls ~ walking four miles to be listening to me now —J.M.Synge⟩ ⟨a pot of water they were ~ boiling potatoes in —Augusta Gregory⟩ ⟨you won't be ~ putting curses on people —Lucy M. Montgomery⟩ — **after a fashion** *adv* **:** in a careless, hasty, or perfunctory way **:** HAPHAZARDLY ⟨the house had been cleaned *after a fashion*⟩ ⟨cared for the children *after a fashion*⟩

[3]**after** \"\ *conj* [ME, short for *after that*, fr. *after*, prep. + *that*, conj.] **1 :** subsequently to the time when ⟨~ arrangements are made, we will follow⟩ **2** *obs* **:** in proportion as **:** just as

[4]**after** \"\ *adj* ['after] **1 :** NEXT **:** later in time **:** SUBSEQUENT, SUCCEEDING ⟨in ~ years⟩ ⟨during his ~ life⟩ **2** [ME, prob. fr. *afte* aft + *-er*] **:** HINDER **:** nearer the rear **:** toward the stern of a ship or tail of an aircraft — used esp. of any object abaft midships ⟨~ cabin⟩ ⟨~ hatchway⟩

[5]**after** \"\ *n* -s [by shortening] **:** AFTERNOON

after all *adv* **:** in spite of considerations to the contrary **:** NEVERTHELESS ⟨they decided to go by the overland route *after all* —G.F.Hudson⟩ ⟨Asia, *after all*, is rich in raw materials —D.G.Bridson⟩

afterbath \'==ˌ=\ *n* [[4]*after* + *bath*] **:** a solution for special treatment of photographic negatives or prints after fixation

afterbay \'==ˌ=\ *n* -s [[4]*after* + *bay*] **:** TAILRACE; *also* **:** a reservoir into which it empties

afterbeat \'==ˌ=\ *n, often attrib* [[4]*after* + *beat*] **:** a musical note or tone falling on a weak beat or on a weak portion of a beat

afterbirth \'==ˌ=\ *n* [[4]*after* + *birth*] *in viviparous mammals* **:** the placenta and that part of the fetal membranes that are discharged from the uterus after the birth of offspring

afterblow \'==ˌ=\ *n* [[4]*after* + *blow* (heat)] **:** the continuation of the blow after the complete oxidation of the carbon in the Bessemer process in order to oxidize and separate the phosphorus

afterbody \'==ˌ==\ *n* [[4]*after* + *body*] **:** the after part of a body: as **a :** the part of a ship abaft midships **b :** the bottom portion of a seaplane hull or float aft of the main step

after–born \ˌ==ˌ=\ *adj* [[1]*after* + *born*] **1 a :** born after the father's death **:** POSTHUMOUS **b :** born after the making and publishing of the father's last will **2 :** born later **:** YOUNGER

afterbrain \'==ˌ=\ *n* [[4]*after* + *brain*] **:** the posterior subdivision of the hindbrain **:** MYELENCEPHALON

afterburner \'==ˌ==\ *n* [[4]*after* + *burner*] **:** an auxiliary burner attached to the tail pipe of a turbojet engine for injecting fuel into the hot exhaust gases and burning it to provide extra thrust — called also *tail-pipe burner*

afterburning \'==ˌ==\ *n* [[4]*after* + *burning*] **1 :** the combustion that proceeds in an internal-combustion engine after the maximum pressure of explosion has occurred **2 :** the use of an afterburner — called also *reheat*

after–burthen *or* **after–burden** *n* [[4]*after* + *burthen, burden*] *obs* **:** AFTERBIRTH

aftercare \'==ˌ=\ *n* [[4]*after* + *care*] **1 :** the care, nursing, or treatment of a convalescent patient (as the postoperative treatment of a surgical patient or the puerperal treatment of a mother after childbirth) **2 :** rehabilitative services for juvenile and adult offenders on parole or after release

aftercastle \'==ˌ==\ *n* [[4]*after* + *castle*] **:** a ship's castle located at the stern — called also *sterncastle*

[1]**afterchrome** \'==ˌ=\ *adj* [[4]*after* + *chrome*] **:** relating to a method of dyeing (as wool) by applying a chromium mordant after a dye **:** TOPCHROME

[2]**afterchrome** \"\ *vt* -ED/-ING/-S **:** to dye by the afterchrome method

afterclap \'==ˌ=\ *n* [ME, fr. [1]*after* + *clap*] **:** an unexpected usu. untoward event resulting from or following a supposedly closed affair

aftercooler \'==ˌ==\ *n* [[4]*after* + *cooler*] **1 :** an apparatus for cooling the discharge air from air compressors in order to remove its condensed moisture **2 :** a device for cooling the fuel mixture heated by compression in a supercharger

aftercrop \'==ˌ=\ *n* [[4]*after* + *crop*] **:** a later crop of the same year from the same soil

afterdamp \'==ˌ=\ *n* [[4]*after* + *damp*] **:** a toxic gas mixture remaining after an explosion of firedamp in mines and consisting principally of carbon dioxide, carbon monoxide, and nitrogen

afterday \'==ˌ=\ *n* [[4]*after* + *day*] **:** a later day or period ⟨in this ~ these encounters and developments . . . appear to have made astonishingly little impression —A.B.Guthrie⟩ — often used in pl. ⟨he was known for his good works in his ~*s*⟩

afterdeath \'==ˌ=\ *n* [[2]*after* + *death*] **:** an existence following death

afterdeck \'==ˌ=\ *n* [[4]*after* + *deck*] **:** the part of a deck abaft midships

afterdinner *n* [ME *afterdiner*, fr. [2]*after* + *diner* dinner] *obs* **:** AFTERNOON

after–dinner cup *n* **:** DEMITASSE

afterdischarge \'==ˌ=ˌ=, '===ˌ=\ *n* [[4]*after* + *discharge*] **:** discharge of neural impulses (as by a ganglion cell) after termination of the initiating stimulus

aftereffect \'===ˌ=\ *n* [[4]*after* + *effect*] **1 :** an effect that follows its cause after an interval **2 :** a secondary result esp. in the action of a drug coming on after the subsidence of the first effect **syn** see EFFECT

after–feather \'==ˌ==\ *n* [[4]*after* + *feather*] **:** AFTERSHAFT

afterfeed \'==ˌ=\ *n* [[4]*after* + *feed*] **:** aftergrass used for grazing

aftergame \'==ˌ=\ *n* [ME, fr. [1]*after* + *game*] **:** a subsequent scheme or expedient undertaken to afford a chance of retrieval or improvement

afterglow \'==ˌ=\ *n* [[4]*after* + *glow*] **1 a :** the light esp. in the western sky after sunset **b :** ALPENGLOW **2 :** a glow continuing after the disappearance of flame (as of a match) or electric discharge (as in a rarefied gas) and sometimes regarded as a type of phosphorescence **3 :** a reflection of past splendor, success, or emotion ⟨Budmouth still retained sufficient ~ from its Georgian gaiety and prestige —Thomas Hardy⟩ ⟨the mellow ~ of the septuagenarian —R.L.Strout⟩ ⟨the ~ of holidays spent in Europe —George Santayana⟩

aftergrass \'==ˌ=\ *n* [[4]*after* + *grass*] **:** grass that grows after the first hay crop has been cut or among the stubble after harvest

aftergrowth \'==ˌ=\ *n* [[4]*after* + *growth*] **:** a second growth or crop

afterguard \'==ˌ=\ *n* [[4]*after* + *guard*] **1 :** the division composed usu. of ordinary seamen and apprentices stationed on the poop or after part of a ship to attend the after sails **2 :** the owner and other amateurs of a yacht's crew

after·hend \'==ˌhend\ *adv* [ME *efterhend*, fr. *efter, after*, prep. + *hend*, pl. of *hand*] *chiefly dial* **:** AFTERWARD

after–hours \ˌ==ˌ=\ *adj* **1 :** engaged in after closing time ⟨they suddenly realized that there must be a great charm in *after-hours* drinking —Donagh MacDonagh⟩ **2 :** operating after a legal or conventional closing time ⟨a district notorious for *after-hours* clubs⟩

afterhouse \'==ˌ=\ *n* [[4]*after* + deck*house*] **:** the deckhouse nearest the stern of a ship

afterimage \'==ˌ==\ *n* [[4]*after* + *image;* trans. of G *nachbild*] **:** a usu. visual sensation occurring after the external stimulus causing it has ceased to operate — see COMPLEMENTARY AFTERIMAGE, HERING IMAGE, HESS IMAGE, NEGATIVE AFTERIMAGE, POSITIVE AFTERIMAGE, PURKINJE AFTERIMAGE

afterimpression \'===ˌ==\ *n* [[4]*after* + *impression*] **:** AFTERIMAGE

af·ter·ings \'aft(ə)riŋz, -rənz\ *n pl* [[1]*after* + *-ings*] **1** *dial* **:** STRIPPING 2a **2 :** COLOSTRUM

afterlife \'==ˌ=\ *n* [[4]*after* + *life*] **1 :** an existence after death ⟨it is doubtful whether the Egyptian conception of the ~ really enters into the background of Hebrew religion —S.H. Hooke⟩ **2 :** a later period in one's life ⟨he then laid a good foundation for his great work in that field in ~ —*World's Work*⟩

afterlifetime \'=='=ˌ=\ *n* [[4]*after* + *lifetime*] **:** duration of life of an insured person subsequent to a specified age

afterlight \'==ˌ=\ *n* [[4]*after* + *light*] **1 :** AFTERGLOW, TWILIGHT **2 :** RETROSPECT

aftermarket \'==ˌ==\ *n* [[4]*after* + *market*] **:** the market for parts and accessories for a manufactured article (as an automobile) for repair and replacement as distinguished from the use of such parts as original components

aftermast \'==ˌ=\ *n* [[4]*after* + *mast*] **:** the mast nearest the stern

af·ter·math \'==ˌmath, -aa(ə)th,-åth\ *n, pl* **aftermaths** \-ths,-thz\ [[4]*after* + *math* (mowing)] **1 :** a second-growth mowing **:** the crop of grass cut, grazed, or plowed under after the first crop of the season from the same soil **:** ROWEN ⟨the clover ~ being turned under —A.F.Gustafson⟩ **2 :** CONSEQUENCE, RESULT ⟨as a gratifying ~ of the recent aeronautical exposition —*N.Y.Times*⟩ **syn** see EFFECT

af·ter·most \'==ˌmōst, *esp Brit also* -ˌməst\ *adj* [[4]*after* + *-most*] **:** nearest the stern of a ship **:** farthest aft

af·ter·nan \'aftə(r)ˌnan\ *n* -s [origin unknown] **:** a desert shrub (*Euphorbia balsamifera*) native to the Canary islands having leaves at the ends of the branches and inconspicuous yellow flowers

afternight \'==ˌ=\ *n* [[2]*after* + *night* (nightfall)] *chiefly dial* **:** EVENING

[1]**afternoon** \ˌ==ˌ=\ *n* [ME *afternon*, fr. [2]*after* + *non* noon]

1 : the part of day between noon and sunset ⟨we were forced to make camp that ~ while it was still light —Kenneth Roberts⟩ ⟨during the late ~ and early evening —Frank Yerby⟩ **2 :** the part of the day between noon and midnight ⟨keeping open until after 10 in the ~⟩ — chiefly in legal use; abbr. *p.m.* **3 :** a relatively late period (as of time or life) ⟨a story that carries us through four wars, through the long Victorian ~ —Clifton Fadiman⟩ — compare EVENING 2

²afternoon \"\ *adj* **:** of, relating to, or intended primarily for use in the afternoon ⟨~ tea⟩ ⟨~ papers are issued from about 10:30 a.m. until about 5 p.m. —Bruce Westley⟩ ⟨~ dress⟩

af·ter·noon·er \,==ˈ=(r)\ *n* -s **:** an afternoon newspaper

afternoon lady *n* **:** FOUR-O'CLOCK

af·ter·noons \,==ˈnünz\ *adv* **:** in the afternoon repeatedly **:** on any afternoon ⟨~ he'd drop off to sleep —Helen Eustis⟩

afternoon watch *n* **:** the watch on a ship from noon to 4 p.m.

afterpain \ˈ==,=\ *n* -s [⁴*after* + *pain*] **1 :** pain that follows an exciting cause only after a distinct interval ⟨the ~ of a tooth extraction⟩ **2 afterpains** *pl* **:** pains that follow the termination of labor and are associated with contraction of the uterus towards its nonpregnant size

afterpart \ˈ==,=\ *n* [ME, fr. ⁴*after* + *part*] **:** the stern area of a ship

afterpeak \ˈ==,=\ *n* [⁴*after* + *peak*] **:** the extreme after compartment in a ship's hold where the ship narrows toward the sternpost

afterpiece \ˈ==,=\ *n* [⁴*after* + *piece*] **:** a short usu. comic entertainment performed after a play

afterpotential \ˈ===ˈ==\ *n* [⁴*after* + *potential*] **:** the sequence of electrical events that follows the spike potential of nerve activity and that usu. takes the form of a negative followed by a positive potential with both being of much smaller amplitude than the spike potential

afterpressure \ˈ==,==\ *n* [⁴*after* + *pressure*] **:** AFTERTOUCH

afterripen \ˈ==ˈ==\ *vb* [¹*after* + *ripen*] *vi* **:** to undergo afterripening ~ *vt* **:** to subject to afterripening

afterripening \ˈ==ˈ=(=)=\ *n* **:** a complex enzymatic process occurring in seeds, bulbs, tubers, and fruits after harvesting and often necessary for subsequent germination or palatable consumption

af·ters \-tə(r)z\ *n pl* [¹*after* + *-s*] *Brit* **:** DESSERT

aftersensation \ˈ==(,)=,==\ *n* [⁴*after* + *sensation*] **:** AFTERIMAGE

aftershaft \ˈ==,=\ *n* [⁴*after* + *shaft*] **:** an accessory plume arising from the posterior side of the stem of the feathers of many birds — **af·ter·shaft·ed** \ˈ==,==\ *adj*

aftershock \ˈ==,=\ *n* [⁴*after* + *shock*] **:** a minor or accessory shock following the main shock of an earthquake

aftershow \ˈ==,=\ *n* [⁴*after* + *show*] **:** a short entertainment (as a band concert) presented in the main tent of a circus after the regular performance

aftersupper *n* [ME *aftersoper*, fr. ²*after* + *soper* supper] *obs* **:** the period of time after supper

afterswarm \ˈ==,=\ *n* [⁴*after* + *swarm*] **:** a swarm of honeybees that leaves a hive after the prime or first swarm

aftertack \ˈ==,=\ *n* [⁴*after* + *tack*] **:** residual tackiness or stickiness of a film (as of a varnish) after drying is complete

aftertaste \ˈ==,=\ *n* [⁴*after* + *taste*] **1 :** persistence of a sensation of flavor after the stimulating substance has passed out of contact with the sensory end organs for taste — used esp. of unpleasant flavors ⟨the powder leaves no bitter ~ —*Scientific Monthly*⟩ **2 :** a remnant or recurrence (as of an emotion) ⟨the ~ of hot anger⟩

afterthought \ˈ==,=\ *n* [⁴*after* + *thought*] **1 :** an idea or notion occurring later ⟨left space on every page for ~s⟩ **2 :** a part, feature, or device not present in a whole as first planned or made ⟨the porch was added as an ~⟩

aftertime \ˈ==,=\ *n* [⁴*after* + *time*] **:** time after the present **:** FUTURE

aftertouch \ˈ==,=\ *n* [⁴*after* + *touch*] **:** the sensation of pressure persisting for a time after actual pressure has ceased

aftertreat \ˈ==,trēt\ *vt* [back-formation fr. *aftertreatment*] **:** to subject to aftertreatment

aftertreatment \ˈ==,==\ *n* [⁴*after* + *treatment*] **:** a secondary treatment to which a material (as film or dyed goods) is subjected after the primary treatment is finished

afterturn \ˈ==,=\ *n* [⁴*after* + *turn*] **:** the twist of the strands composing a rope — compare FORETURN

afterwale \ˈ==,=\ *n* [⁴*after* + *wale* (ridge of a horse collar)] **:** the body or pad of a horse collar that rests on the horse's shoulders

afterwar \ˈ==ˈ=\ *adj* [²*after* + *war*] **:** POSTWAR

¹af·ter·ward *R* ˈstə(r)wərd, *-R* -təwəd\ *or* **af·ter·wards** \-dz\ *adv* [ME *afterward, afterwardes*, fr. OE *æfterweard*, fr. *æfter* behind + *-weard* -ward, -wards — more at AFTER] **:** at a later or succeeding time **:** SUBSEQUENTLY

²afterward \"\ *or* **afterwards** \"\ *n, pl* **afterwards :** FUTURE

afterwash \ˈ==,=\ *n* [⁴*after* + *wash*] **:** BACKWASH 2

afterwelt \ˈ==,=\ *n* [⁴*after* + *welt*] *in women's stockings* **:** the narrow strip between the welt and the leg knitted of medium-weight yarn

¹afterwhile \ˈ==ˈ=\ *adv* [²*after* + *while* (n.)] **:** after a while **:** by and by **:** later on

²afterwhile \ˈ==,=\ *n* [⁴*after* + *while*] **:** AFTERTIME

afterwisdom \ˈ==,==\ *n* [⁴*after* + *wisdom*] **:** wisdom after the event **:** wisdom arrived at when it is too late

afterwit *n* [⁴*after* + *wit*] **1** *obs* **:** later knowledge **2 :** wisdom or perception that comes after it can be of use

afterword \ˈ==,=\ *n* [⁴*after* + *word*; prob. translation of G *nachwort*] **:** EPILOGUE 1

afterwork \ˈ==,=\ *or* **afterworking** \ˈ==,==\ *n* [⁴*after* + *work, working*] **:** ELASTIC AFTERWORK

afterworld \ˈ==,=\ *n* [⁴*after* + *world*] **:** a future world **:** a world after death

afteryears \ˈ==,=\ *n pl* [⁴*after* + *years*] **:** subsequent years **:** later times

aftn *abbr* afternoon

af·to·ni·an \(ˈ)afˈtōnēən\ *adj, usu cap* [*Afton*, town in Iowa + E *-ian*] **:** belonging to the first interglacial interval during the glacial epoch in No. America

af·to·sa \afˈtōsə, -ōzə\ *n* -s [AmerSp, short for Sp. *fiebre aftosa* aphthous fever, fr. *fiebre* fever + *aftosa*, fem. of *aftoso* aphthous, fr. *afta* aphtha (fr. L *aphtha*) + *-oso* -ous — more at APHTHA] **:** FOOT-AND-MOUTH DISEASE

a·func·tion·al \(ˈ)āˈf-\ *adj* **:** lacking a normal function ⟨the ~ vestigial teeth of certain snakes⟩ ⟨having a stiff ~ knee⟩

af·wil·lite \ˈafwə,līt\ *n* -s [Alpheus Fuller Williams *b*1874 Am. mining engineer + E *-ite*] **:** a mineral $Ca_3Si_2O_4(OH)_6$ consisting of a hydrous calcium silicate and occurring in colorless monoclinic crystals (sp. gr. 2.6)

ag \ˈag, ˈaa(ə)g, ˈaig\ *adj* [short for *agriculture* & *agricultural*] **:** of or relating to agriculture ⟨~ school⟩

ag- — see AD-

ag *abbr* angolar

AG *abbr* **1** accountant general **2** adjutant general **3** agent-general **4** attorney general

Ag *symbol* [L *argentum*] silver

aga *also* **agha** \ˈägə, ˈa-\ *n* -s *often cap* [Turk *ağa* lord, master] **:** a man of authority who bears a title of respect: as **a :** a military or civil officer in the Ottoman Empire ⟨a vast body of dragoons . . . under . . . their great ~ —Jonathan Swift⟩ **b :** a Turkish chief ⟨the khans . . . and ~s . . . are probably the oldest landed aristocracy of the world —Harold Lamb⟩ **c :** a religious leader ⟨the *Aga* Khan . . . claims descent from Fatima —H.G.Rawlinson⟩

agaces *pl of* AGAZ

¹again \əˈgen *also* -ān *or* (*less often in stand than in substand speech*) -in\ *adv* [ME *again, agen, ayen*, fr. OE *ongēan, ongeagn, ongēn* towards, against, back (akin to OS *angegin*, OHG *ingagan, ingegin*), fr. *on* + (assumed) *gēan, geagn, gēn* against, toward (whence OE *gēan-, geagn-, gēn-*); akin to OHG *gegin, gagan* against, toward, ON *gegn* against, direct, OFris *jēn* against, toward] **1 a :** BACK; *specif* **:** in the opposite direction ⟨let us turn ~ and go home —John Bunyan⟩ **b** (1) **:** in return or in response **:** BACK ⟨soft eyes looked love to eyes which spake ~ —Lord Byron⟩ (2) **:** as a result or consequence ⟨the wind blowing . . . till every timber of the old house creaked ~ —Charles Dickens⟩ **2 :** another time **:** once more **:** ANEW ⟨I shall not look upon his like ~ —Shak.⟩ **3 :** as another point, fact, or instance: **a :** on the other hand ⟨he might go and ~ he might not⟩ **b :** in the next place **:** FURTHER ⟨~, these cases would not go to court —S.H.Hofstadter⟩ **4 a :** in addition **:** BESIDES ⟨that's something else ~⟩ **b :** by as much more ⟨his house is as big ~ as mine⟩ ⟨he has half ~ as much land as I do⟩

²again \"\ *prep* [ME *again, agen, ayen* toward, opposite, against, fr. OE *ongēan, ongeagn, ongēn*, fr. *ongēan, ongeagn, ongēn*, adv.] *now dial* **:** AGAINST ⟨sitting up with pillows behind her, leaning ~ them —Richard Llewellyn⟩

³again \"\ *conj* [ME *again, agen, ayen*, fr. *again, agen, ayen*, prep.] *now dial* **:** by the time that **:** AGAINST ⟨~ I got there, he was gone⟩

again and again *adv* **:** time after time **:** OFTEN, REPEATEDLY

¹against \əˈgen(t)st, -nzt *also* -ān- *or* (*less often in stand than in substand speech*) -in-\ *prep* [ME *against, agenst, ayenst*, alter. of *againes, agenes, ayenes*, fr. *again, agen, ayen*, prep. + *-es* -'s] **1 a :** directly opposite **:** in front of **:** FACING ⟨America seems to stand ~ it with a fire extinguisher and . . . gets burned —E.A.Mowrer⟩ — often used with preceding *over* **b** *obs* **:** in the presence of **:** exposed to **:** WITH ⟨those boughs which shake ~ the cold —Shak.⟩ **2 a :** from an opposite direction and into contact with **:** UPON ⟨the fighter was knocked back ~ the ropes⟩ **b :** in contact with **:** TOUCHING ⟨~ the walls of . . . the houses . . . were pear trees —Ernest Hemingway⟩ **c :** close to **:** BESIDE, NEAR ⟨ships lay ~ the walls —Daniel Defoe⟩ **3 :** in a direction opposite to the course or motion of **:** counter to ⟨they sailed ~ the wind⟩ ⟨a ground swell running ~ the new education —Paul Woodring⟩ **4 a :** in opposition or hostility to ⟨stood steadfast ~ alumni pressure —J.B. Conant⟩ ⟨a successful campaign ~ the enemy⟩ **b :** not in conformity with **:** contrary to ⟨offenses ~ the law⟩ ⟨forced to act ~ his conscience⟩ **c :** in spite of **:** NOTWITHSTANDING ⟨succeeded ~ many handicaps⟩ **d :** in competition with ⟨a race run ~ the clock⟩ **5 a :** as a defense or protection from **:** in resistance to ⟨puffed his cigar ~ the mosquitoes —Claud Cockburn⟩ ⟨at wit's end what to do ~ the inexorable ticking of the clock —G.J.Nathan⟩ **b :** in the face of **:** FROM ⟨to protect their native subjects ~ the rapacity of some . . . business communities —W.T.Stace⟩ **6 :** compared with or contrasted to ⟨the importance of space as ~ time and of time as ~ space —A.N.Whitehead⟩ ⟨net profits of 80 cents a share ~ 70 cents last year⟩ **7 :** in preparation or provision for **:** in anticipation of ⟨silver coins hoarded ~ a day of need —W.P.Webb⟩ **8 :** with respect to **:** relating to **:** TOWARD ⟨customs which had the force of law ~ both lord and tenant —E.C.Smith⟩ **9 a :** in the opposite scale to **:** as a counterbalance to ⟨his pride in his own prestige is set ~ his kindness to younger writers —P.M. Fulcher⟩ **b :** in exchange for **:** in return for ⟨the free-market rate ~ dollars was 302 francs⟩ **c :** as a charge upon **:** to the debit of ⟨to make today's purchases ~ tomorrow's earnings⟩ **10 :** having as background: as **a :** before the surface or expanse of ⟨the rain is dark ~ the white sky —Amy Lowell⟩ ⟨~ this background the developments of the last two . . . years are . . . easy to grasp —Barbara Ward⟩ **b :** above the sound of ⟨talking ~ the music⟩ **11** *dial* **:** not later than **:** by the time of ⟨to leave ~ noon⟩ — **against the grain** *adv* **1 :** across the fiber of the wood **2 :** counter to one's inclination, disposition, or feelings ⟨the check he had imposed upon himself in the chapel, *against the grain* —Margery Bailey⟩ — **against the sun** *adv* **:** in a direction opposite to that of the sun's motion as it appears to one facing south in the northern hemisphere **:** COUNTERCLOCKWISE — opposed to *with the sun* — **against time** *adv* **1 :** in an attempt to approach, equal, or surpass a record or a previously recorded time ⟨they raced, not against each other, but *against time*⟩ **2 :** in an effort to complete an action before a certain time ⟨he wrote the essay hurriedly, as if *against time*⟩ ⟨were working *against time* to repair the levees⟩ **3 :** with the intention of effecting a delay by using up time ⟨the legislator was merely talking *against time*⟩

²against \"\ *conj* [ME *against, agenst, ayenst*, fr. *against, agenst, ayenst*, prep.] **1** *now chiefly dial* **:** BEFORE **:** by the time that **2** *now chiefly dial* **:** in readiness for the time when

agal \əˈgäl\ *n* -s [Ar *ʿiqāl* bond, rope] **:** a cord usu. of goat's hair that Arabs (as the Bedouins) wind around their heads to hold down the kerchieflike headdress

ag·a·lac·tia \ˌāgəˈlaksh(ē)ə, -ktēə\ *n* -s [NL, fr. Gk *agalaktia* lack of milk, fr. *agalaktos* giving no milk (fr. *-a-* ²*a-* + *galakt-, gala* milk) + *-ia*] **:** the failure of the secretion of milk in mammals from any cause other than the normal ending of a lactation period — **aga·lac·tic** \ˈ==ˈ=tik\ *adj* — **aga·lac·tous** \ˈ==ˈ=təs\ *adj*

agal-agal \ˈä,gäˈlä,gäl\ *n* -s [of Indonesian origin; akin to Malay *agar-agar*] **:** AGAR 1a

ag·a·lax·ia \ˌāgəˈlaksēə\ *or* **ag·a·laxy** \ˈagə,laksē\ *n, pl* **agalaxias** *or* **agalaxies** [NL *agalaxia*, fr. Gk *agalax* giving no milk (fr. *a-* ²*a-* + *-galax*, fr. *gala* milk) + NL *-ia*] **:** AGALACTIA

ag·a·le·na \ˌagəˈlēnə\ *n, cap* [NL, fr. ²*a-* + Gk *galēnē* stillness, fr. fem. of *galēnos* calm, gentle] **:** a genus (the type of the family Agalenidae) of spiders that spin concave webs ending in a funnel-shaped tube where the spider hides — see GRASS SPIDER

ag·a·li·nis \ˌagəˈlīnəs\ *n, cap* [NL, irreg. fr. Gk *aga, agē* wonder + L *linum* flax] **:** a genus of flaxlike American herbs (family Scrophulariaceae) with opposite sessile leaves and irregular tubular mostly purple flowers

ag·a·lite \ˈagə,līt\ *n* -s [prob. fr. Gk *aga, agē* + E *-lite*] **:** a fine fibrous variety of talc

agal·lia \əˈgalēə\ *n, cap* [NL, fr. ²*a-* + LGk *gallia* guts] **:** a genus of leafhoppers that includes some species implicated as vectors of a virus disease of So. American sugar beets resembling curly top

agal·loch \əˈgalək, ˈagə,läk\ *also* **agal·lo·chum** \əˈgaləkəm\ *n* -s [*agalloch* fr. LL or Gk; LL *agallochon*, fr. Gk, prob. by folk etymology (influence of *agallein* to adorn) fr. a word of Dravidian origin; akin to Tamil *akil* agalloch; *agallochum*, NL, fr. LL *agallochon*] **:** the soft resinous wood of an East Indian tree (*Aquilaria agallocha*) of the family Thymelaeaceae that is burnt as a perfume by the Orientals — called also *agalwood, agilawood, aloeswood, eaglewood*

agal·lop \əˈ-\ *adv* [¹*a-* + *gallop*, v.] **:** at a gallop

agal·ma \əˈgalmə\ *n, pl* **agalma·ta** \-mədə\ [Gk, fr. *agallein* to adorn; prob. akin to Gk *megas* large, great — more at MUCH] **:** MEMORIAL; *specif* **:** a primitive Greek statue of a god

ag·al·mat·o·lite \ˌagəlˈmad·əl,īt, əˌgal'-, ˌaˌgal'-\ *n* -s [NL *agalmatolithus*, fr. Gk *agalmat-, agalma* + NL *-lithus* -lite] **:** a soft compact stone of a grayish, greenish, or yellowish color, sometimes stained, carved into images or miniature pagodas by the Chinese — called also *figure stone, pagodite*

ag·al·wood \ˈagəl,-\ *or* **ag·a·la·wood** \ˈagələ,-\ *n* [*agal-* or *agala-* (fr. *agalloch*) + *wood*] **:** AGALLOCH

agam- *or* **aga·mo-** *comb form* [NL, fr. LL *agamus* unmarried, fr. Gk *agamos*, fr. *a-* ²*a-* + *gamos* marriage — more at BIGAMY] **:** asexual ⟨*agamic*⟩ ⟨*agamogenesis*⟩

¹aga·ma \ˈägəmə, ˈagəmə\ *n* [NL] **1** *cap* **:** a genus (the type of the family Agamidae) of Old World terrestrial lizards including many that are of bright and changeable colors **2** -s **:** a lizard of the genus *Agama*

²aga·ma \ˈägəmə\ *n* -s [Skt *āgama*, lit., arrival, acquisition of knowledge, fr. *āgacchati* he comes, arrives, fr. *ā* towards + *gacchati* he goes; akin to *gamati* he goes — more at ACHARYA, COME] **:** one of a class of tantric treatises accepted as scripture within Hinduism and Buddhism — compare TANTRA

ag·a·mae \ˈagə(,)mē\ *n pl* [NL, fr. ²*a-* + *-gamae*] *syn of* CRYPTOGAMIA

aga·mete \ˌāgəˈmēt, (ˈ)āˈga,mēt, ˈagə,mēt\ *n* -s [ISV, fr. Gk *agametos, agamētos* unmarried, fr. *a-* ²*a-* + *-gametos, -gamētos* married (fr. *gametēs* spouse, fr. *gamos* marriage) — more at BIGAMY] **:** an asexual reproductive cell (as a spore or a merozoite)

agam·ic \(ˈ)āˈgamik\ *adj* [*agam-* + *-ic*] **:** ASEXUAL, PARTHENOGENETIC — **agam·i·cal·ly** \-ək(ə)lē\ *adv*

¹ag·a·mid \ˈagəməd, -(,)mid\ *adj* [NL *Agamidae*] **:** of or relating to the Agamidae

²agamid \"\ *n* -s **:** a lizard of the family Agamidae

agam·i·dae \əˈgaməˌdē\ *n pl, cap* [NL, fr. *Agama*, type genus + *-idae*] **:** a widely distributed family of Old World lizards related to the New World iguanas but distinguished by acrodont dentition and including arboreal, terrestrial, and semiaquatic forms most of which are insectivorous (as the frilled lizard, the flying dragon, and the Australian moloch)

agam·ma·glob·u·li·ne·mia \ˌā,gaməˈgläbyələˈnēmēə\ *n* -s [NL, fr. ²*a-* + E *gamma globulin* + NL *-emia*] **:** a pathological condition in which the body forms no gamma globulins or antibodies or forms them only in minute amounts

aga·mo·gen·e·sis \ˌā,gaməˈjenəsəs, ˈagəmō'-\ *n* [NL, fr. *agam-* + L *genesis*] **1 :** PARTHENOGENESIS **2 :** asexual reproduction — **aga·mo·ge·net·ic** \ˌā,gaməjəˈned·ik, ˈagəmōj-\ *adj* — **aga·mo·ge·net·i·cal·ly** \-ək(ə)lē\ *adv*

ag·a·moid \ˈagə,mȯid\ *adj* [NL *Agama* + *-oid*] **:** of or resembling *Agama* or lizards of this genus

aga·mog·o·ny \ˌāgəˈmägənē, ˌag-\ *n* -ES [*agam-* + *-gony*] **:** asexual reproduction; *specif* **:** SCHIZOGONY

ag·a·mo·mer·mid \ˌagəmōˈmərməd\ *n* -s [irreg. fr. NL *Agamomermith-, Agamomermis*] **:** a worm of the genus *Agamomermis*

ag·a·mo·mer·mis \-məs\ *n, cap* [NL, fr. *agam-* + Gk *mermis* cord, string — more at MERMIS] **:** a genus of nematode worms (family Mermithidae) that are normally free living as adults and larval parasites of insects and that may accidentally parasitize man

agam·ont \(ˈ)āˈga,mänt\ *n* -s [²*a-* + *gam-* + *-ont*] **:** SCHIZONT

aga·mo·spe·cies \ˌāgəmō̇ˈ-\ *n* [*agam-* + *species*] **:** a group of obviously related asexually reproducing biotypes regarded as a group equivalent to a species

agamo·sperm·ic \(ˈ)āˌgaməˈspərmik, ˈagəmō'-\ *also* **agamo·sperm·ous** \-məs\ *adj* [*agam-* + *-spermic, -spermous*] **:** exhibiting or reproducing by agamospermy

agamo·sper·my \(ˈ)āˈgamə,spərmē, ˈagəmō,-\ *n* -ES [*agam-* + *-spermy*] **:** APOGAMY 2; *specif* **:** apogamy in which sexual union is not completed because of abnormal development of both embryo sac and pollen, embryos being produced from the innermost layer of the integument of the female gametophyte — compare APOMIXIS 1

aga·mo·spore \(ˈ)āˈgamə,spō(ə)r, ˈagəmə,-\ *n* -s [*agam-* + *spore*] **:** an asexual spore

ag·a·mous \ˈagəməs\ *adj* [Gk *agamos* unmarried, fr. *a-* ²*a-* + *-gamos* (fr. *gamos* marriage) — more at BIGAMY] **1 :** of or relating to agamy **2 :** AGAMIC

ag·a·my \ˈagəmē\ *n* -ES [Gk *agamia* celibacy, fr. *agamos* + *-ia*] **1 :** absence, nonregulation, or nonrecognition of marriage **2 :** AGAMOGENESIS

agan·gli·on·ic \(ˈ)āˈ==ˈ==\ *adj* [²*a-* + *ganglionic*] **:** lacking ganglia

ag·a·on·i·dae \ˌagāˈänə,dē\ [NL, fr. *Agaon*, type genus + *-idae*] *syn of* AGAONTIDAE

ag·a·on·ti·dae \ˌagāˈäntə,dē\ *n pl, cap* [NL, alter. of *Agaonidae*] **:** a family of small chiefly tropical chalcid wasps having the fore and hind pairs of legs heavier than the middle pair and the male usu. wingless — see FIG WASP

ag·a·pan·thus \ˌagəˈpan(t)thəs\ *n* [NL, fr. Gk *agapē* love + NL *-anthus*] **1** *cap* **:** a small genus of southern African herbs (family Liliaceae) having radical leaves and scapose umbels of showy blue or purple flowers **2** -ES **:** a plant of the genus *Agapanthus* (esp. *A. africanus*) — called also *African lily, African tulip*

¹agape \əˈgāp *sometimes* -ap\ *adj* [¹*a-* + *gape*, v.] **1 :** wide open **:** GAPING ⟨his mouth was ~ in yokel fashion —Stephen Crane⟩ **2 :** being in an attitude or state of wonder, expectation, or eager attention ⟨leaving him alone and ~ upon his feet —Dorothy Sayers⟩

²aga·pe \äˈgä,pā, ˈägə,-, ˈagə,-; ˈagə,pē\ *n, pl* **aga·pae** \-,pī; -,pē\ *or* **aga·pai** \-,pī\ *also* **agapes** *sometimes cap* [LL, fr. Gk *agapē*, lit., love, back-formation fr. *agapan* to welcome, love; perh. akin to *agallein* to adorn — more at AGALMA] **1 :** a love feast or common meal of fellowship originating among the early Christians and including prayers, songs, the reading of Scripture, and offerings for the poor **2 :** spontaneous self-giving love expressed freely without calculation of cost or gain to the giver or merit on the part of the receiver: **a :** the love of God for man **b :** Christian brotherly love in its highest manifestation

ag·a·pem·o·ne \ˌagəˈpemə(,)nē\ *n* -s *often cap* [fr. *Agapemone*, a communistic establishment that was founded *ab*1849 at Spaxton, England, and had a reputation for immoral behavior, irreg. fr. Gk *agapē* love + *monē* stopping place, fr. *menein* to remain — more at MANSION] **:** a free-love institution ⟨allow Christopher to run an *Agapemone* in what was after all her own house —F.M.Ford⟩

aga·pe·tae \ˌägəˈpä,tī, ˌagə-; ˌagəˈpē,tē\ *n pl* [LL, fr. LGk *agapētai*, pl. of *agapētē*, fr. Gk, fem. of *agapētos* beloved, desirable, to be acquiesced in, fr. *agapan* to welcome, love] **:** women of the early church who lived under a pledge of spiritual love in the same house with men bound to strict celibacy

ag·a·pe·ti \ˌagəˈpä,tē, -ˈpē,tī\ *n pl* [LGk *agapētoi*, pl. of *agapētos*, fr. *agapētos*, adj., beloved] **:** Christian monks of the early church who lived under vows of celibacy in the same house with nuns

ag·a·por·nis \ˌagəˈpȯrnəs\ *n, cap* [NL, fr. Gk *agapē* love + NL *-ornis*] **:** a genus of small short-tailed African parrots — see LOVEBIRD

agar \ˈägə(r)\ *or* **agar-agar** \ˌ==ˈ==\ *n* -s [Malay *agar-agar*] **1 a :** any of various colloidal extractives of certain red algae (as of the genera *Gelidium, Gracilaria*, and *Eucheuma*) that are similar products both in appearance, being usu. in the form of translucent strips or flakes or a white powder, and in other physical properties (as ability to swell in cold water and to dissolve in hot water); that may differ in chemical structure, a common type being thought to be essentially a sulfuric acid ester of a linear galactan occurring as salts in the cell walls of the algae; and that are used chiefly in culture media, as bases for dental impression materials, as bulk producers in treating chronic constipation, and as gelling and stabilizing agents in foods (as jellies, dairy products, and canned meat and fish) — called also *Chinese gelatin, Chinese isinglass, Japanese gelatin, Japanese isinglass* **b :** any of the plants from which agar is obtained **2 :** any of various culture media having agar as a solidifying agent ⟨nutrient ~⟩ ⟨blood ~⟩

¹ag·a·ric \ˈagərik, ˈaig-; əˈgarik, -ēk *also* -ˈger-\ *n* -s [L *agaricum*, a fungus, fr. Gk *agarikon*] **1 :** a fungus of the family Agaricaceae and esp. of the genus *Agaricus* **2 :** any of several species of the genus *Fomes* (esp. *F. igniarius*) used in the preparation of punk **3 :** the dried fruit body of a mushroom (*Fomes officinalis* or *Polyporus officinalis*) formerly used in the treatment of excessive perspiration (as in the night sweats of tuberculosis)

²agaric \"\ *adj* **:** of or relating to agarics **:** like a fungus

agar·i·ca·ce·ae \əˌgarəˈkāsē,ē\ *n pl, cap* [NL, fr. *Agaricus*, type genus + *-aceae*] **:** a large family of fungi (order Agaricales) including many familiar mushrooms with the sporophore usu. consisting of a central stalk and an umbrellalike cap on the lower surface of which are numerous lamellae bearing the hymenium — **agar·i·ca·ceous** \ˈ==ˈ=ˈshəs\ *adj*

agaric acid *or* **ag·a·ric·ic acid** \ˌagəˈrisik-\ *n* **1 :** a white powdery tribasic acid $C_{22}H_{40}O_7$ constituting the active principle of agaric — called also *agaricinic acid* **2 :** AGARINIC ACID

agar·i·ca·les \əˌgarəˈkā(,)lēz\ *n pl, cap* [NL, fr. *Agaricus* + *-ales*] **:** an extensive order of basidiomycetous fungi that includes the typical gilled mushrooms and a number of related forms all having the basidia produced in a distinct hymenial fruiting layer usu. spread over the surface of a definite but transitory fruiting body which may be flat or be supinate, simply or compoundly club-shaped, or with the surface increased by pores, gills, or spines

ag·a·ric·i·form \ˌagəˈrisə,fȯrm\ *adj* [ISV ¹*agaric* + *-iform*] **:** having the form of an agaric

agar·i·cin \əˈgarəsən\ *n* -s [¹*agaric* + *-in*] **:** an impure form of the active principle of agaric (sense 3)

agar·i·cine \-,sēn,-,sən\ *n* -s [ISV ¹*agaric* + *-ine*] **:** CHOLINE

agar·i·cin·ic acid \əˌgarəˌsinik-\ *n* [*agaricine* + *-ic*] **:** AGARIC ACID 1

agaric mineral *n* **:** a light chalky deposit of calcium carbonate formed in caverns or fissures of limestone — called also *rock milk*

agar·i·coid \əˈgarə,kȯid\ *adj* [ISV ¹*agaric* + *-oid*] **:** resembling an agaric ⟨~ fungi⟩

agar·i·cus \-kəs\ *n, cap* [NL, alter. of L *agaricum*, a fungus — more at AGARIC] **:** a genus (the type of the family Agaricaceae) comprising gill fungi which have brown spores and including several members which are edible — see HORSE MUSHROOM, MEADOW MUSHROOM

ag·a·rin·ic acid \ˌagəˌrinik-\ *n* [*agar* + *-in* + *-ic*] **:** the free acid that is held to occur in agar — called also *agaric acid*

ag·a·ris·ti·dae \ˌagəˈristəˌdē\ *n pl, cap* [NL, fr. *Agarista*, type genus (perh. after *Agariste fl* 6th cent. B.C. daughter of Cleisthenes, tyrant of Sicyon, fr. Gk *Agaristē*) + *-idae*] **:** a family of mostly diurnal and brightly colored moths having the antennae thickened toward the tip and including the Australian whistling moths — see FORESTER

ag·a·ri·ta \ˌagəˈrēd·ə, ˌäg-\ *also* **agri·to** \əˈgrēd·(ˌ)ō\ *n* -s [MexSp *agrito*, prob. fr. Sp *agrio* sour, fr. OSp *agro*, fr. L *acr-*, *acer* — more at EAGER] **:** a shrub (*Mahonia trifoliata*) of Texas, New Mexico, and adjacent Mexico that yields a yellow dye, a tanning extract, and an ink and produces a bright red berry that is used to make jelly — compare OREGON GRAPE

ag·a·roid \ˈagəˌrȯid\ *n* -s **:** a substance similar to agar in properties that is obtained from certain red algae (as of the genus *Phyllophora*)

agar·o·phyte \əˈgarəˌfīt\ *n* -s [*agar* + *-o-* + *-phyte*] **:** an agar-yielding seaweed

ag·a·rum \ˈagərəm\ *n, cap* [NL, fr. E *agar*] **:** a genus of kelps (family Laminariaceae) inhabiting the colder oceans and having a branched holdfast, a brief stipe, and a lamina with smooth perforated margins

agar·wal \ˈəgərˌwäl, ˈag-\ *n* -s [Hindi *aggarwāl*] **:** a mercantile caste of central India

ag·as·siz·o·cri·nus \ˌagəˌsē(z)əˈkrīnəs\ *n, cap* [NL, fr. Alexander *Agassiz* + NL *-o-* + *-crinus* (fr. L *crinis* hair) — more at CRINAL] **:** a genus of fossil crinoids known chiefly from Mississippian formations of No. America and characterized by a thick-walled ovoid cup

ag·as·siz trawl \ˈagə(ˌ)sē-\ *n, usu cap A* [after Alexander *Agassiz* †1910 Am. zoologist] **:** a dredge that consists of a heavy rectangular iron frame to which is fitted the mouth of a bag of stout netting and that is used in collecting plankton

agas·ta·che \əˈgastə(ˌ)kē\ *n, cap* [NL, irreg. fr. Gk *agan* very much + *stachys* ear of grain — more at STING] **:** a genus of No. American herbs (family Labiatae) having opposite toothed leaves and dense terminal spikes of 2-lipped flowers — see GIANT HYSSOP

agas·tric \(ˈ)āˌgastrik\ *adj* [²*a-* + Gk *gastr-*, *gastēr* stomach + E *-ic*] *zool* **:** having no stomach or distinct digestive canal ⟨the tapeworm is ~⟩

ag·a·ta \ˈagəd·ə\ *n* -s [It, agate, fr. L *achates*] **:** a late 19th century American glassware characterized by a mottled finish

¹**ag·ate** \ˈagət, ˈaig-\ *n* -s [MF, fr. L *achates*, fr. Gk *achatēs*] **1 :** a fine-grained chalcedony frequently mixed with opal and having various colors arranged in stripes or bands, blended in clouds, or showing mosslike forms — see FORTIFICATION AGATE, MOSS AGATE **2** *obs* **:** a very small person ⟨I was never manned with an ~ till now —Shak.⟩ **3 :** something made of or fitted with agate: as **a :** a drawplate having a drilled eye of agate used by gold-wire drawers **b :** a bookbinder's burnisher with an agate tip **c :** a playing marble of agate or of glass resembling agate **4 :** a size of type between pearl and nonpareil, approximately 5½ point — called also *ruby;* compare POINT SYSTEM **5 :** IRON-OXIDE RED

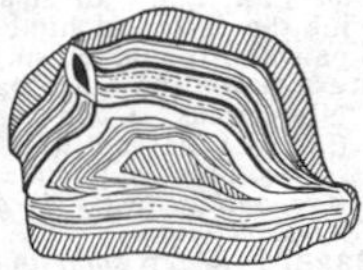
agate 1

²**agate** \"\ *adj* **:** of or resembling agate; *esp* **:** of the color of agate ⟨his brown ~ eyes —Oscar Wilde⟩

³**agate** \əˈgāt\ *adv* (*or adj*) [¹*a-* + *gate* (way)] **1** *dial Brit* **:** on the way **:** in motion **2** *dial Brit* **a :** going on **:** ASTIR **b :** AMISS, WRONG ⟨what's ~ now⟩

agate glass *n* **:** glass made by blending two or more colored glasses or by rolling transparent glass into powdered glass of various colors during the melting

agate gray *n* **:** a nearly neutral slightly yellowish medium gray that is lighter than flint gray, gull (sense 2 a), or old silver

agate jasper *n* **:** a chalcedonic quartz consisting of jasper and agate

agate line *n* **:** a space one column wide and ¹⁄₁₄ inch deep used as a unit of measurement in publication advertising — see ¹AGATE 4

agate opal *n* **:** opalized agate

agate shell *n* **1 :** the shell of the agate snail **2 :** AGATE SNAIL

agate snail *n* [so called from the variegated colors] **:** a member of the African family Achatinidae which includes the largest known land mollusks, some reaching 9 or 10 inches in length — compare ACHATINA

ag·ate·ware \ˈ==ˌ=\ *n* **1 :** pottery veined and mottled to resemble agate **2 :** an enameled iron or steel ware for household utensils

agath- *or* **agatho-** *comb form* [Gk, fr. *agathos;* perh. akin to OE *gōd* good — more at GOOD] **:** good ⟨*Agath*osma⟩ ⟨*agatho*logy⟩

ag·a·thau·mas \ˌagəˈthȯməs\ *n, cap* [NL, irreg. fr. Gk *agan* very much + *thaumasios* marvelous, fr. *thauma* marvel] **:** a genus of herbivorous dinosaurs related to and possibly not distinct from *Triceratops*

agath·ic acid \əˈgathik-\ *n* [NL *Agathis* + E *-ic*] **:** a crystalline diterpenoid dibasic acid $C_{18}H_{28}(COOH)_2$ obtained from Manila copal and from kauri

Ag·a·thin \ˈagəthən\ *trademark* — used for a yellow crystalline compound formerly used to relieve neuralgia and rheumatism

ag·a·this \ˈagəthəs\ *n, cap* [NL, fr. Gk *agathis* ball of thread; perh. akin to Skt *gadh-* to cling to, hang on to] **:** a small genus of evergreen timber trees (family Pinaceae) chiefly of Australasia and the Philippines that are distinguished from members of the genus *Araucaria* by having larger leaves with flat stalks and the seed free from the cone scale and are valued for their wood and fragrant resins

ag·a·thism \ˈagəˌthizəm\ *n* -s [*agath-* + *-ism*] **:** the doctrine that all things tend toward ultimate good — compare OPTIMISM

ag·a·thist \-ˌthəst\ *n* -s **:** an adherent of agathism

ag·a·tho·dae·mon *or* **ag·a·tho·de·mon** \ˌagə(ˌ)thōˈdēmən\ *n, often cap* [Gk *agathodaimōn*, fr. *agath-* + *daimōn* spirit, daemon — more at DEMON] **:** a good genius or beneficent divinity

ag·a·tho·kak·o·log·i·cal \ˌ==(ˌ)=ˌkakəˌläjəkəl\ *adj* [*agath-* + *kako-* (var. of *cac-*) + *-logical*] **:** composed of both good and evil

ag·a·thol·o·gy \ˌagəˈthäləjē\ *n* -ES [ISV *agath-* + *-logy*] **:** the science or doctrine of the good

ag·a·thos·ma \-ˈthäzmə\ *n* [NL, fr. *agath-* + *-osma*] **1** *cap* **:** a genus of southern African shrubs (family Rutaceae) having heathlike foliage from which a sulfur-containing oil used in folk medicine is obtained and numerous small flowers in dense heads **2** -s **:** any plant of the genus *Agathosma*, several of which are cultivated in the cool greenhouse

ag·a·tif·er·ous \ˌagəˌtif(ə)rəs\ *adj* [ISV ¹*agate* + *-i-* + *-ferous*] **:** bearing agate ⟨~ rocks⟩

ag·a·ti·form \ˈagəd·əˌfȯrm\ *adj* [¹*agate* + *-iform*] **:** like agate in form

ag·at·ine \ˈagəd·ˌīn, -əˌtīn, -ēn\ *adj* [ISV ¹*agate* + *-ine*] **:** of, relating to, or resembling agate

ag·at·ize \-d·ˌīz, -ˌtīz\ *vt* -ED/-ING/-S [ISV ¹*agate* + *-ize*] **:** to change into agate or give the appearance of agate to ⟨*agatized* wood⟩

ag·aty \-əd·ē, -ətē\ *adj* **:** resembling or containing agate ⟨a large piece of ~ flint⟩

agau *also* **agaw** \əˈgau̇\ *n* -s *usu cap* **1 a :** a Cushitic-speaking Negroid peasant people of the northern highlands of Ethiopia **b :** a member of such people **2 :** the Cushitic language of the Agau people

ag·a·va·ce·ae \ˌagəˈvāsēˌē\ *n pl, cap* [NL, fr. *Agave*, type genus + *-aceae*] *in some classifications* **:** a family of the order Liliales that comprises chiefly tropical and xerophytic plants with fibrous linear leaves arranged in a basal rosette, rhizomatous rootstock, and usu. with flowers in large panicles, that includes species usu. divided between the families Liliaceae and Amaryllidaceae, and that has as its type the genus *Agave*

aga·ve \əˈgävē *also* -āvē\ *n* [NL, fr. Gk *agauē*, fem. of *agauos* noble, illustrious, brilliant] **1** *cap* **:** a genus of plants (family Amaryllidaceae) native to tropical America and to the southwestern U.S. having heavy stiff often spiny persistent leaves mostly in basal rosettes and tall panicles or spikes of flowers like candelabras and including some members that are cultivated for their fiber (as sisal), for other economic products (as mescal), or for ornament — see AGAVACEAE, CENTURY PLANT, MAGUEY, PULQUE **2** -s **:** a plant of the genus *Agave*

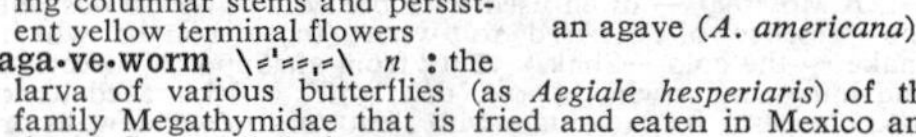
an agave (*A. americana*)

agave cactus *n* **:** a cactus (*Leuchtenbergia principis*) having columnar stems and persistent yellow terminal flowers

aga·ve·worm \=ˈ==ˌ=\ *n* **:** the larva of various butterflies (as *Aegiale hesperiaris*) of the family Megathymidae that is fried and eaten in Mexico and the U.S. — called also *maguey worm*

aga·vose \-ˌvōs\ *n* -s [ISV *agav-* (fr. NL *Agave*) + *-ose*] **:** a sugar $C_{12}H_{22}O_{11}$ obtained from the stalks of the century plant

agaz \əˈgäs\ *n, pl* **agaz** \"\ *or* **aga·ces** \əˈgäˌsās\ *usu cap* [Sp, of AmerInd origin] **1 :** an Indian people formerly living in southern Paraguay **2 :** a member of the Agaz people

agaze \əˈgāz\ *adj* [ME *a gase*, fr. ³*a* + *gasen* to gaze — more at GAZE] **:** GAZING

agazed *adj* [prob. alter. (influenced by *gaze*) of *aghast*] *obs* **:** struck with astonishment **:** AMAZED

ag·ba \ˈagbə\ *n* -s [native name in Africa] **:** a large African tree (*Gossweilerodendron balsamiferum*) having wood used for furniture and interior finish

AGC *abbr* automatic gain control

ag·chy·los·to·ma \ˌagkəˈlästəmə, ˌaŋk-\ *syn of* ANCYLOSTOMA

agcy *abbr* agency

agd *abbr* agreed

¹**age** \ˈāj\ *n* -s [ME, fr. OF *aage*, *eage*, fr. (assumed) VL *aetaticum*, fr. L *aetat-*, *aetas*, fr. OL *aevitas*, fr. *aevum* lifetime, age + *-itat-*, *-itas* -ity — more at AYE] **1 a** (1) **:** the length of time during which a being or thing has lived or existed **:** the length of life or existence from birth or beginning to the time spoken of or referred to ⟨the ~ of the student was 20⟩ ⟨the ~ of the wood was determined by measuring its radioactivity⟩ ⟨what is the ~ of your car⟩ (2) *of the moon* **:** the time that has elapsed since the last new moon **b :** the complete duration of the life or existence of a being or thing **:** LIFETIME ⟨the ~*s* of the Old Testament patriarchs were astonishingly long⟩ ⟨the normal ~ of a dog is reckoned as 12 years⟩ **c :** any one of the periods or stages of life ⟨Jaques' analysis of the seven ~*s* of man is one of the most familiar passages in Shakespeare⟩ **d** (1) **:** the time of life at which one becomes naturally or conventionally qualified or disqualified for something ⟨he was past the ~ for military service⟩ (2) **:** MATURITY; *specif* **:** the time of life at which one attains full legal rights and responsibilities ⟨last week he came of ~⟩ **e** (1) **:** an advanced stage of life **:** the latter part of life ⟨the child of his parents' ~ —Alan Paton⟩ ⟨the feebleness of ~⟩ (2) **:** the quality or state of being old ⟨~ cannot wither her, nor custom stale her infinite variety —Shak.⟩ **f :** a measure of the development, capacity, condition, or quality of an individual or of one of his traits or parts (as mentality or the skeleton) that tends to alter with age, expressed as the chronological age at which such state is mean or average ⟨a child of 7 with a mental ~ of 10⟩ ⟨X radiation revealed a bone ~ of 8 years and 5 months⟩ **g** *of a railroad employee* **:** seniority or time in service **2 a :** the period contemporary with a person's lifetime or with his active life ⟨the leading poet of his ~⟩ ⟨his ideas, considered radical in his own ~, seem almost reactionary in ours⟩ **b :** the period equal to the average span of human life **:** GENERATION ⟨actions of the last ~ are like almanacs of the last year —John Denham⟩ ⟨the mystery hidden for ~*s* and generations but now made manifest to his saints —Col 1: 26 (RSV)⟩ **c :** a period of 100 years **:** CENTURY ⟨be true to yourselves and this new 19th ~ —J.R. Lowell⟩ **d :** an indefinite but relatively long period of time in human affairs ⟨in that ~ before printing —G.F. Hudson⟩ ⟨the argument can continue on through the ~*s* —Deems Taylor⟩ **e :** a long time **:** many years ⟨it seemed an ~ though it was . . . only a few minutes —Sheila Kaye-Smith⟩ ⟨you haven't taken me to a nightclub in ~*s* —Louis Auchincloss⟩ ⟨the frames . . . stay smart for ~*s* —*Punch*⟩ — see COON'S AGE, DOG'S AGE **3 a :** a period of time in history or in the development of man esp. with reference to cultural evolution ⟨the golden ~⟩ ⟨the ~ of exploration⟩ ⟨the atomic ~⟩ **b :** a period of time in prehistory characterized by the use of artifacts made from a distinctive material — compare BRONZE AGE, IRON AGE, STONE AGE **4 a :** a period of time in the history of the earth often characterized by its dominant type of life **b :** the time during which a particular geologic event or series of events occurred — see ICE AGE **c :** one of the divisions of geologic time usu. included in an epoch ⟨the Lockport ~ of the Niagara epoch⟩ **5 a :** EDGE 7 **b :** the poker player having the edge **syn** see PERIOD — **act one's age** *or* **be one's age :** to behave in a reasonable manner

²**age** \"\ *vb* **aged** \ˈājd\ **aged** \"\ **aging** *or* **ageing** \ˈājiŋ\ **ages** [ME *agen*, fr. *age*, n.] *vi* **1 a :** to grow older **:** become old **:** show the effects of or undergo change with the passage of time ⟨no two people ~ alike⟩ ⟨his mind did not ~ —R.W. Firth⟩ **b :** to suffer with the passage of time a diminution of essential qualities or forces ⟨a car battery ~*s* during a severe winter⟩ **2 a :** to acquire a desirable quality by standing undisturbed for some time ⟨carbon paper . . . would easily pass the test if given time to ~ —C.E.Waters⟩ ⟨after flour is milled it ~*s* —S.C.Prescott⟩ **b :** to become mellow or mature **:** RIPEN ⟨this cheese has *aged* for nearly two years⟩ **c** *of metal* **:** to remain undisturbed at atmospheric temperature or at some higher temperature so that crystalline changes may occur ⟨an alloy ~*s*⟩ ~ *vt* **1 a :** to make old **:** cause or allow to grow old ⟨grief ~*s* a man⟩ **b :** to give the appearance of age to ⟨the painter sprayed the movie set with brown paint in order to ~ it⟩ **c :** to bring about with the passage of time a diminution of essential qualities or forces of ⟨excessive driving at night ~*s* a car battery⟩ **2 a :** to bring to a state fit for use ⟨the logwood chips had been properly *aged*⟩ **b :** to bring to a state of maturity or ripeness **:** MELLOW ⟨it's the tannic acid contained in . . . oak . . . that ~*s* the brandy —P.E.Deutschman⟩ **c :** to cause (an alloy) to remain at an appropriate temperature for a predetermined period of time in order to induce certain changes in structure and physical or mechanical properties ⟨~ duralumin alloys⟩ **d :** to develop (as a dye) by passage through or by hanging in warm moist air or by the use of steam ⟨*aged* aniline black⟩ **3 :** to determine the age of ⟨the forester is able to ~ trees —Wendell Lalime⟩ ⟨*aging* deer by dentition⟩ **4 :** to analyze (a customer's account) to rate entries as not yet due or as due for various given periods of time **syn** see MATURE

-age \ij, ēj *also* əj\ *n suffix* -s [ME, fr. OF, fr. L *-aticum*] **1 :** aggregate **:** collection ⟨cellar*age*⟩ ⟨surplus*age*⟩ ⟨track*age*⟩ ⟨word*age*⟩ **2 a :** action **:** process ⟨cover*age*⟩ ⟨haul*age*⟩ ⟨stopp*age*⟩ **b :** cumulative result of ⟨break*age*⟩ ⟨shrink*age*⟩ **c :** rate of ⟨dos*age*⟩ ⟨leak*age*⟩ ⟨out*age*⟩ ⟨slipp*age*⟩ **3 :** house or place of ⟨orphan*age*⟩ ⟨parson*age*⟩ **4 :** state **:** rank ⟨bond*age*⟩ ⟨peon*age*⟩ **5 :** charge for (an act or service) ⟨post*age*⟩ ⟨tow*age*⟩ ⟨wharf*age*⟩

age·a·ble \ˈājəbəl\ *adj* [¹*age* + *-able*] *chiefly Midland* **:** advanced in years **:** OLD

age and area concept *or* **age and area hypothesis** *n* **:** a principle of the diffusion of culture traits according to which those lying close to or at the center of distribution are considered relatively new and those lying farthest from it relatively old

age-area *adj* **:** of or relating to the age and area concept

age-class \ˈ=ˌ=\ *n* **1 :** a group of persons of the same sex and approximately the same age who have been initiated together or have passed through other social experiences together **2 :** an age-grade or a subdivision thereof

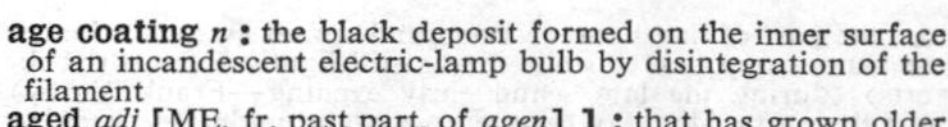

age coating *n* **:** the black deposit formed on the inner surface of an incandescent electric-lamp bulb by disintegration of the filament

aged *adj* [ME, fr. past part. of *agen*] **1 :** that has grown older or become old: **a** (1) \ˈājəd *also* ˈājd\ **:** having lived or existed long ⟨~ men⟩ ⟨an ~ oak⟩ (2) \ˈājəd\ **:** belonging to or characteristic of old age ⟨the ~ wrinkles in my cheeks —Shak.⟩ **b** \ˈājd\ **:** having lived **:** of or at the age of ⟨a man ~ 40 years⟩ **c** \ˈājd\ **:** having attained an age that is fixed for particular animals (as usu. 7 for horses, 3 or 4 for cattle, 2 for swine, 1 for sheep) **d** \ˈājəd\ **:** well advanced toward reduction to base level — used of topographic features **2** \ˈājd\ **:** having acquired a desirable quality or undergone an expected and desired change with the passage of time ⟨~ wine⟩ ⟨~ cheese⟩ — **ag·ed·ly** \ˈājədlē, -li\ *adv*

agee \əˈjē\ *adv* [¹*a-* + E dial. *gee*, *jee* to move to one side, turn, tilt] *dial Brit* **:** out of line **:** ASKEW, OBLIQUELY ⟨he wore his hat ~⟩

¹**age-grade** \ˈ=ˌ=\ *n* **1 :** a group of persons of the same sex and approximately the same age having certain definite duties and privileges in common and constituting a division of a tribe or society **2 :** a stage (as boyhood, adolescence, or manhood) through which an age-grade passes

²**age-grade** \"\ *vt* [¹*age-grade*] **:** to grade by age or organize by age-grades ⟨an *age-graded* tribe⟩

age-group \ˈ=ˌ=\ *n, chiefly Brit* **:** AGE-GRADE

age-harden \ˈ=ˌ==\ *vb* **:** to harden by aging

ageing *pres part of* AGE

ag·e·la·cri·ni·tes \ˌajələkrəˈnīd·ēz\ *n, cap* [NL, fr. Gk *agelē* herd + *krinon* lily + *-itēs* -ite] **:** a genus (the type of the family Agelacrinitidae) of saclike Devonian echinoderms with five covered food grooves on the oral side

ag·e·la·ius \ˌajəˈlā(y)əs\ *n, cap* [NL, fr. Gk *agelaios* gregarious, fr. *agelē* herd] **:** a genus of birds (family Icteridae) comprising the red-winged blackbirds

age·less \ˈājləs\ *adj* **1 :** not growing old or showing the effects of age ⟨a tall ~ . . . woman —Richard Wright⟩ **2 :** having no limits in time **:** ETERNAL ⟨the ~ theme of man and society —T.V.Smith⟩ — **age·less·ly** *adv* — **age·less·ness** *n* -ES

agel·i·cism \əˈjeləˌsizəm\ *n* -s [Gk *agelikos* of the herd, fr. *agelē* herd (fr. *agein* to lead) + E *-ism* — more at AGENT] **:** the doctrine that holds that society completely determines the thoughts, feelings, and acts of individuals

age·long \ˈ=ˌ=\ *adj* **:** lasting for an age **:** EVERLASTING, UNENDING ⟨man's ~ struggle for freedom⟩

age-mate \ˈ=ˌ=\ *also* **age-fellow** \ˈ=ˌ=(ˌ)=\ *n* **:** one who is a member of the same age-class as another

agen·cy \ˈājənsē, -si\ *n* -ES [²*agent* + *-cy*] **1 :** the capacity, condition, or state of acting or of exerting power **:** action or activity **:** OPERATION ⟨I have no intention to dispute her free ~ —Tobias Smollett⟩ **2 :** a person or thing through which power is exerted or an end is achieved **:** INSTRUMENTALITY, MEANS ⟨through the ~ of Benjamin Rush he renewed relations with Jefferson —W.C.Ford⟩ ⟨example is still . . . the greatest ~ by which men help each other —G.F.Kennan⟩ **3 a :** the office or function of an agent **b :** the relationship between a principal and his agent **4 a :** an establishment engaged in doing business for another ⟨an advertising ~⟩ ⟨an employment ~⟩ **b :** the place of business or the district of such an agency **5 a :** a department or other administrative unit of a government ⟨the War Department, the only ~ equipped to administer occupied areas —E.J.Hayward⟩ ⟨the independent *agencies* are generally regulatory in nature —H.M.Somers⟩ **b :** the office or headquarters of a government agent (as of an Indian agent) ⟨the house had once been used as an Indian ~⟩ **c :** the district administered by a government agent (as by a former British agent in India)

agency shop *n* **:** a shop in which the union serves as the agent for and receives dues and assessments from all employees in the bargaining unit regardless of union membership

agency tariff *n* **:** a tariff issued on behalf of two or more carriers by an authorized agent

agen·da \əˈjendə\ *n* -s [L, neut. pl. of *agendum*, gerundive of *agere* to drive, do — more at AGENT] **1 :** a memorandum book ⟨dragged a small ~ from his pocket and began flicking the pages —Monica Stirling⟩ **2 a :** a list or outline of things to be done, subjects to be discussed, or business to be transacted ⟨he sent out an ~ before each meeting⟩ **b :** a plan of procedure **:** PROGRAM ⟨military aggression was . . . on the ~ of international Communism —E.S.Furniss b.1890⟩ ⟨a brisk ~ of calisthenics —E.J.Kahn⟩

agen·dum \-dəm\ *n, pl* **agendums** *or* **agen·da** \-də\ [L] **1** *agenda pl* **a :** the forms and ceremonies of church liturgy **:** the ritual or order of worship ⟨the church constitutions and ~ of this period —G.C.Rietschel⟩ — used in Protestant Christianity **b :** matters of practical duty ⟨the ~ of a Christian —Ephraim Chambers⟩ — distinguished from *credenda* **2 :** AGENDA 2a ⟨the ~ for the conference was agreed upon⟩

ag·ene \ˈāˌjēn\ *n* -s [fr. *Agene*, a trademark] **:** commercially produced nitrogen trichloride for use in bleaching and aging flour

agen·e·sis \(ˌ)āˈjenəsəs\ *n, pl* **agene·ses** \-əˌsēz\ [NL, fr. ²*a-* + *genesis*] **1** *biol* **:** lack of development **:** faulty or incomplete development ⟨cerebral ~⟩ **2** *also* **age·ne·sia** \ˌājəˈnēzh(ē)ə\ -s *med* **:** the complete absence of an organ or part due to the absence of or a defect in its embryologic anlage — compare APLASIA

age·net·ic \ˌājəˌned·ik\ *adj* [²*a-* + *genetic*] **:** NONGENETIC

ag·en·ize \ˈājəˌnīz\ *vt* -ED/-ING/-S [*agene* + *-ize*] **:** to treat (flour) with nitrogen trichloride

age norm *n* **:** the norm (as for height, weight, or intellectual achievement) of individuals of a given chronological age

¹**agent** \ˈājənt\ *n* -s [in sense 1, fr. ME, fr. ML *agent-*, *agens*, fr. L, pres. part.; in senses 2, 3 & 4, fr. F or L; F, fr. L, pres. part.; in sense 5, fr. LL & ML, fr. L, pres. part.] **1 a :** something that produces or is capable of producing a certain effect **:** an active or efficient cause **:** a force effecting or facilitating a certain result ⟨the . . . emergence of the Christian church as the civilizing ~ of the western world —Helen Sullivan⟩ **b :** a substance capable of producing a chemical reaction or a physical or biological effect **:** an active principle ⟨chromic acid is an oxidizing ~⟩ ⟨detergents are surface-active ~*s* or wetting ~*s*⟩ **2 a :** one that acts or exerts power (as by driving, inciting, or setting in motion) **:** a moving force ⟨the distinction between ~ and patient, between something which acts and some other thing which is acted upon —Francis Bowen⟩ **b :** a person who originates a telepathic impulse or message — compare PERCIPIENT **3 :** one that acts or performs an act (as an act involving reason, conscience, and free will) **:** a person responsible for his act or acts ⟨for that same deed now at Lorenzo's church both ~*s*, conscious and inconscious, lie —Robert Browning⟩ **4 :** a means or instrument by which a guiding intelligence achieves a result **:** a person governed, guided, or instigated by another in some action ⟨where the heads of departments are the political or confidential ~*s* of the executive, merely to execute the will of the president —John Marshall⟩ **5 :** one that acts for or in the place of another by authority from him: as **a :** a representative, emissary, or official of a government ⟨a crown ~⟩ ⟨an Indian ~⟩ ⟨a secret-service ~⟩ **b :** a special representative sent from one military organization to another to establish and maintain liaison **c :** a field worker from a welfare bureau **d :** a paid party worker who manages the financial and other affairs of a British political party during an election and is legally responsible for any corrupt practices **e :** a business representative: as (1) **:** a manager of an assigned territory or a branch office or plant of an industry (2) **:** one that sells and rents real estate on a commission basis (3) **:** an independent sales or service representative of an insurance company usu. paid on a commission basis **syn** see MEAN

²**agent** \"\ *adj* [L *agent-*, *agens*, pres. part. of *agere* to drive, lead, act, do; akin to ON *aka* to travel in a vehicle, Gk *agein* to lead, drive, OIr ad-*aig* to drive, Skt *ajati* (he) goes, drives] *archaic* **:** acting or exerting power — opposed to *patient*

agent cipher *n* **:** a cipher adapted for use in espionage

agent code *n* **:** a code adapted for use in espionage

agent de change \äzhäⁿtshäⁿzh\ *n, pl* **agents de change** \"\ [F, agent of the exchange] **:** a member of the board of licensed brokers who form the official bourse in France and some other European countries

agent-general \ˌājəntˌ=(=)=\ *n, pl* **agents-general :** a chief agent; *specif* **:** the representative in England of a British dominion acting in behalf of the political, economic, and commercial interests of the dominion

agen·tial \(ˈ)āˈjenchəl\ *adj* [ˡ*agent* + *-ial*] **:** of, relating to, or expressive of an agent or agency — **a·gen·tial·ly** \-əlē\ *adv*

agent·ing \ˈājəntiŋ\ *n* -s **:** the work or activities of an agent ⟨the business of literary ~⟩

agent intellect *n* [trans. of ML *intellectus agens*, trans. of Gk *nous poiētikos*] **:** INTELLECT 1d(2)

agen·ti·val \ˌājənˈtīvəl\ *or* **agent·ive** \ˈājəntiv\ *adj* [ˡ*agent* + *-ival*, *-ive*] **:** expressive of an agent or of agency **:** denoting the performer of an action ⟨*agentive* nouns⟩ ⟨an *agentive* suffix⟩

agent middleman *n* **:** a middleman who negotiates purchases or sales on an agency basis

agent noun *n* **:** a noun denoting the performer of an action (as *writer, inspector, patron, hanger-on*)

agent officer *n* **:** a military officer appointed to disburse funds

agent pro·vo·ca·teur \ȧzhäⁿprōvȯkätœr; ˈājəntprəˌväkəˌtər, -tü(ə)r\ *n, pl* **agents provocateurs** \-äⁿp...œr; -ntsp...-ər(z), -ü(ə)r(z)\ [F, lit., provoking agent] **:** one employed to associate himself with members of a group or with suspected persons and by pretended sympathy with their aims or attitudes to incite them to some illegal or harmful action that will make them liable to apprehension and punishment **:** a secret agent or undercover man ⟨a city overrun with spies and *agents provocateurs*⟩

agent·ry \ˈājəntrē, -ri\ *n* -ES **:** the office, duties, or activities of an agent

agents *pl of* AGENT

age of consent : the age at which one is legally competent to give consent esp. to marriage or to unlawful sexual intercourse

age of copper *usu cap A&C* **:** the Aeneolithic period

age of discretion : the age at which the law imputes to a person the possession of sufficient knowledge for him to become responsible for certain acts or competent to exercise certain powers

age of fishes *usu cap A&F* **:** DEVONIAN

age of gold : GOLDEN AGE

age of mammals *usu cap A&M* **:** CENOZOIC

age of man *usu cap A&M* **:** QUATERNARY

age of reason : a period characterized by the dominance of reason and common sense; *esp* **:** the 18th century in England and France

age of reptiles *usu cap A&R* **:** MESOZOIC

age-old \ˈ=ˈ=\ *adj* **:** having existed for ages **:** ANCIENT ⟨an *age-old* problem⟩

ag·er \ˈājə(r)\ *n* -s **:** one that ages: as **a :** a chamber usu. containing rollers for aging material with steam **b :** one that inspects electric lamps in process **c :** a worker who puts radio tubes in an aging machine that passes current through them to stabilize their quality

ag·er·a·tum \ˌajəˈrādəm, -ātəm\ *n* [NL, fr. L *ageraton*, a plant, fr. Gk *ageraton*, fr. neut. of *agēratos* ageless, fr. *a-* ²a- + *-gēratos* (fr. *gēras* old age) — more at GERIATRICS] **1** *cap* **:** a genus of tropical American herbs (family Compositae) having opposite leaves and small heads of blue or white flowers in terminal cymes **2** -s **:** a plant of the genus *Ageratum* (esp. *A. houstonianum*) **3** -s **:** any of several blue-flowered plants of the genus *Eupatorium*

ageratum blue *n* **:** FLOSSFLOWER BLUE

ages *pl of* AGE, *pres 3d sing of* AGE

-ages *pl of* -AGE

age score *n* **:** a test score translated into terms of a scale of age norms

age-set \ˈ=ˌ=\ *n, chiefly Brit* **:** AGE-CLASS

age-society \ˈ=ˌ=ˌ==\ *n* **:** AGE-GRADE 1

ageu·sia \əˈgyüzēə, (ˈ)āˈg-\ *n* -s [NL, fr. ²*a-* + Gk *geusis* taste (fr. *geuesthai* to taste) + *-ia* — more at CHOOSE] **:** the absence or impairment of the sense of taste—**ageu·sic** \(ˈ)=ˈ=zik\ *adj*

agg *abbr* aggregate

aggada *usu cap, var of* HAGGADA

ag·gag \ˈäˌgäg\ *n* -s [Chamorro] **1 :** a screw pine (*Pandanus tectorius*) with prop roots and sword-shaped spiny leaves covered with a whitish bloom **2 :** an article (as a mat or bag) made from the split leaves of the aggag

ag·ger \ˈajə(r)\ *n* -s **1** [L] **:** EARTHWORK: as **a :** MOUND, RAMPART **b :** a military or public road usu. raised and with sloping drainage embankments **2** [NL, fr. L] *anat* **:** PROMINENCE **3** [NL, fr. L] **:** a double tide: **a :** a high tide with two maxima separated by a slight lowering of water **b :** a low tide with two minima separated by a slight rise of water

ˡ**ag·gie** \ˈagē, ˈaig-, -gi\ *n* -s [alter. (influenced by *-ie*) of ˡ*agate*] **:** a playing marble; *specif* **:** an agate marble

²**aggie** \ˈ"\ *n* -s *often cap* [*ag-* (as in *agricultural college, agricultural school*) + *-ie*] **1 :** a student at an agricultural school or college **2 :** an agricultural school or college

ag·glom·er·ant \əˈglämərənt, a-\ *n* -s [L *agglomerant-, agglomerans*, pres. part. of *agglomerare*] **:** something that causes agglomeration

ˡ**ag·glom·er·ate** \-ˌrāt\ *vb* -ED/-ING/-S [L *agglomeratus*, past part. of *agglomerare* to heap up, join, fr. *ad-* + *glomerare* to wind into a ball, to assemble, fr. *glomus* ball — more at CLAM] *vt* **1** *obs* **:** to wind or collect into a ball **2 :** to gather into a mass or cluster ⟨~ dust particles⟩ ~ *vi* **:** to collect or come together in a mass ⟨caused the oxide film to ~⟩

²**ag·glom·er·ate** \-ˌrət\ *adj* [L *agglomeratus*] **:** collected into a ball, heap, or mass; *specif* **:** clustered or growing together but not coherent ⟨an ~ head of flowers⟩

³**agglomerate** \ˈ"\ *n* -s **1 :** a confused or jumbled mass, heap, or collection ⟨this fine ~ of duchies —Thomas Carlyle⟩ **2 a :** a rock composed of volcanic fragments of various sizes and degrees of angularity; *esp* **:** a rock in which the constituent fragments were produced by explosions in the throat of a volcano — compare CONGLOMERATE

ag·glom·er·at·ic \=ˌ==ˈrad·ik\ *adj* [³*agglomerate* + *-ic*] **:** having the characteristics of an agglomerate ⟨~ lavas⟩

ag·glom·er·a·tion \=ˌ==ˈrāshən\ *n* -s **1 :** the action or process of collecting in a mass **:** an agglomerated condition ⟨protection against caking and ~⟩ **2 :** an indiscriminately formed mass **:** a cluster of disparate elements ⟨the ~ of buildings which somehow made up this town —Elizabeth Bowen⟩

ag·glom·er·a·tive \=ˈ==ˌrād·iv, ˌrəd·iv\ *adj* **:** tending to agglomerate **:** AGGLOMERATING

ag·glom·er·a·tor \-ˌrād·ə(r)\ *n* -s **:** one that agglomerates ⟨sonic ~s⟩

ag·glu·ti·na·bil·i·ty \əˌglütᵊnəˈbiləd·ē, aˌ-\ *n* -ES [²*agglutinate* + *-ability*] **:** capacity (as of red blood cells, bacteria, or virus particles) to be agglutinated — **ag·glu·ti·na·ble** \=ˈ===bəl\ *adj*

ˡ**ag·glu·ti·nant** \-ˈ==nənt\ *adj* [L *agglutinant-, agglutinans*, pres. part. of *agglutinare* to glue to, fr. *ad-* + *glutinare* to glue, fr. *glutin-, gluten* glue — more at CLAY] **:** uniting closely **:** causing or tending to cause adhesion

²**agglutinant** \ˈ"\ *n* -s **:** an agglutinating substance

ˡ**ag·glu·ti·nate** \-ət\ *adj* [L *agglutinatus*, past part. of *agglutinare*] **1 :** joined with or as if with glue ⟨~ spores⟩ **2 :** AGGLUTINATIVE 2

²**ag·glu·ti·nate** \-ˌāt, *usu* -ād.+V\ *vb* -ED/-ING/-S *vt* **1 :** to cause to adhere **:** UNITE, FASTEN ⟨the town ~s them all to its own atmosphere —Waldo Frank⟩ **2 :** to combine (words) into a compound **:** attach (a linguistic form) to a base as an affix **3 :** to cause (as blood cells) to undergo agglutination ~ *vi* **1 :** to unite or combine into a group or mass ⟨groups . . . coalesced, fragmented, *agglutinated* again —John Hersey⟩ **2 :** to form words by agglutination **:** be agglutinative ⟨*agglutinating* languages⟩ ⟨the *agglutinating* state of language⟩ **3 :** to undergo agglutination

³**ag·glu·ti·nate** \-ət\ *n* -s **:** a clump of material (as blood cells or bacteria) that has undergone agglutination

ag·glu·ti·na·tion \=ˌ==ˈāshən\ *n* -s **1 :** the action or process of uniting or adhering **:** an agglutinated condition ⟨the ~ of foreign bodies⟩ **2 :** a mass or group formed by the union of separate elements ⟨a boundless ~ of streets, dramshops, and low buildings —A.J.Liebling⟩ **3 :** the formation of derivative or compound words by putting together constituents of which each expresses a single definite meaning (as in Wishram, a Chinook dialect, in which *ačimlúda* "he will give it to you" has the constituents *a-* "future", *-č-* "he", *-i-* "him", *-m-* "thee", *-l-* "to", *-ud-* "give", and *-a* "future", as contrasted with Latin, in which the *-o* of *amo* "I love" expresses the meanings of first person, singular number, present tense, active voice, and indicative mood) **4 :** a reaction in which particles (as red blood cells, bacteria, virus particles, or rickettsiae) suspended in a liquid collect into clumps or floccules with loss of motility in the case of flagellated or ciliated organisms and which occurs when the suspension is treated with certain substances that combine with the surface of the particles — see AGGLUTINATION TEST, CROSS AGGLUTINATION

agglutination test *n* **:** any of several tests based on the ability of a specific serum to cause agglutination of a suitable system and used in the diagnosis of infections, the identification of microorganisms, and in blood grouping — compare WIDAL TEST

ag·glu·ti·na·tive \=ˈ==ˌād·iv, -ˌəd·iv\ *adj* **1 :** causing or produced by agglutination **:** ADHESIVE **2 :** characterized by agglutination ⟨an ~ language⟩ — distinguished from *inflectional* and *isolating*

ag·glu·ti·nin \=ˈ==nən\ *n* -s [ISV *agglutination* + *-in*; prob. orig. formed in G] **:** a substance producing agglutination; *specif* **:** any antibody capable of effecting the agglutination of the agglutinogen that stimulated its production — see HEMAGGLUTININ

ag·glu·tin·o·gen \ˌa(ˌ)glüˈtinəjən\ *n* -s [ISV *agglutinin* + *-o-* + *-gen*] **:** any substance that acting as an antigen stimulates the production of an agglutinin — **ag·glu·tin·o·gen·ic** \ˌ=(ˌ)=ˌ==ˈjenik, əˌglütᵊnəˈ-\ *adj*

ag·glu·ti·noid \əˈglütᵊnˌȯid, aˈ-\ *n* -s [ISV *agglutinin* + *-oid*] **:** an agglutinin that has lost or never had the power to agglutinate but can still unite with its agglutinogen — compare ANTIBODY, BLOCKING ANTIBODY

ag·gra·da·tion \ˌagrəˈdāshən\ *n* -s [*aggrade* + *-ation*] **:** a modification of or the process of modifying the earth's surface in the direction of uniformity of grade or slope by deposition (as of detrital material in a river bed) — compare DEGRADATION

ag·gra·da·tion·al \ˌ==ˈ=shənᵊl, -shnəl\ *adj* **:** relating to, characterized by, or formed by aggradation

ag·grade \əˈgrād, aˈ-\ *vb* -ED/-ING/-S [*ad-* + *grade*] *vt* **:** to fill with detrital material ⟨silt has *aggraded* the river bed and waterlogged it for a hundred miles —Erna Fergusson⟩ ~ *vi* **:** to build up by aggradation ⟨meltwater streams were *aggrading* beyond the moraines —R.J.Lougee⟩

ag·gran·dize \əˈgranˌdīz, -aan-; ˈagran-, ˈaig-\ *vt* -ED/-ING/-S [modif. (influenced by *-ize*) of F *agrandiss-* stem of *agrandir*, fr. *a-* (fr. L *ad-*) + *grandir* to increase, fr. L *grandire*, fr. *grandis* great — more at GRAND] **1 :** to make great (as in degree, number, or size) **:** INCREASE, AUGMENT ⟨all he desired was to ~ his estate —Hilaire Belloc⟩ **2 :** to make great or greater (as in power, honor, or wealth) ⟨to ~ his family and his favorites Sixtus caused wars —R.A.Hall b. 1911⟩ **3 :** to make appear great or greater **:** EXALT ⟨in *aggrandizing* the one, he necessarily depreciated the other⟩ **syn** see EXALT

ag·gran·dize·ment \əˈgrandəzmənt, -aan- *also* əˈgra(a)n,dīz-; *also* ˈagran,dīz- *or* ˈaig- *or* ˌ=ˈ=ˈ==\ *n* -s [modif. (influenced by *-ize*) of F *agrandissement*, fr. *agrandiss-* + *-ment*] **:** the act, action, or result of aggrandizing **:** ADVANCEMENT ⟨their ~ from low estate to social prominence⟩ **:** ENLARGEMENT ⟨critics of his ~ of federal power —B.N.Cardozo⟩

ag·gran·diz·er \əˈgra(a)nˌdīzə(r), ˈa(i)grən,-\ *n* -s **:** one that aggrandizes

aggrate *vt* -ED/-ING/-S [It *aggratare*, alter. of *aggradare*, fr. Prov *agradar*, fr. *a-* (fr. L *ad-*) + *grat* pleasing, agreeable (fr. L *gratus*) — more at GRACE] *obs* **:** to gratify or express gratitude to

ag·gra·vate \ˈagrəˌvāt, ˈaig-, *usu* -ād.+V\ *vt* -ED/-ING/-S [L *aggravatus*, past part. of *aggravare* to make heavier, fr. *ad-* + *gravare* to burden, fr. *gravis* heavy — more at GRIEVE] **1** *obs* **a :** to make heavy **:** weigh down **:** BURDEN ⟨a great grief *aggravateth* the heart that suffers it —Bartholomew Young⟩ **b :** to add weight to **:** INCREASE, MAGNIFY ⟨then, soul, live thou upon thy servant's loss and let that pine to ~ thy store —Shak.⟩ **2** *archaic* **:** to give an exaggerated representation of **:** EXAGGERATE ⟨I have not . . . *aggravated* your sense or words —Andrew Marvell⟩ **3 :** to make worse, more serious, or more severe **:** INTENSIFY ⟨such a defense only *aggravated* the offense —R.W.Southern⟩ ⟨the war . . . had *aggravated* the confusions and social disasters of rapid industrial change —J.H.Plumb⟩ **4 a :** to arouse the displeasure, impatience, or anger of **:** PROVOKE, ANNOY ⟨nothing so ~s an earnest person as a passive resistance —Herman Melville⟩ **b :** to produce inflammation in **:** IRRITATE ⟨the operation *aggravated* the ulnar nerve⟩ **syn** see INTENSIFY, IRRITATE

aggravated assault *n* **:** an assault regarded as more heinous than a common assault: as **a :** an assault combining an intent to commit a crime other than that involved in the mere assault itself **b :** any of various assaults so defined by statute

aggravated larceny *n* **:** larceny attended with aggravating circumstances (as when the theft is from the person)

aggravating *adj* **1 :** making worse **:** INTENSIFYING **2 :** arousing displeasure, impatience, or anger **:** EXASPERATING, IRRITATING — **ag·gra·vat·ing·ly** \ˈ==ˌ===lē\ *adv*

ag·gra·va·tion \ˌ=ˈ=ˈvāshən\ *n* -s [ML *aggravation-, aggravatio*, fr. L *aggravatus* + *-ion-, -io* -ion] **1 :** the act, action, or result of aggravating; *esp* **:** an increasing in seriousness or severity ⟨in order to prevent an ~ of the problem⟩ **2 :** an act or circumstance that intensifies or makes worse ⟨an ~ to a person in slavery to reflect that he was sold by his parent —Thomas Paine⟩ **3** *obs* **:** an exaggerated statement or representation ⟨I from ~s will forbear —George Wither⟩ **4 :** the act or action of irritating or annoying **:** PROVOCATION ⟨~s between people South and North were getting worse —Carl Sandburg⟩

ag·gra·va·tor \ˈ==ˌvād·ə(r)\ *n* -s **:** one that aggravates

ag·gre·ga·ble \əˈgrəgəbəl, ˈaig-, -rē-\ *adj* [²*aggregate* + *-able*] **:** that may be aggregated ⟨property ~ with other property⟩

ˡ**ag·gre·gate** \-gət *also* -ˌgāt; *usu* -d·+V\ *adj* [ME *aggregat*, fr. L *aggregatus*, past part. of *aggregare* to add to, fr. *ad-* + *greg-, grex* flock — more at GREGARIOUS] **1 :** formed by the collection of units or particles into a body, mass, or amount **:** COLLECTIVE ⟨the ~ sentiments of mankind —J.F.Byrnes⟩: **a** (1) *of a flower* **:** clustered in a dense mass or head (2) *of a fruit* **:** formed from the several separate or fused ovaries of a single flower — distinguished from *multiple*; see FRUIT illustration **b** *of a rock* (1) **:** composed of mineral crystals of one or more kinds (2) **:** composed of mineral or rock fragments **c** (1) *of a colonial animal* **:** united in a somewhat continuous mass (2) *of a hibernating animal* **:** gathered into a compact mass **d :** formed into clusters or groups of lobules **2 :** AGGREGATIVE 2 — **aggregately** *adv* — **aggregateness** *n* -ES

²**ag·gre·gate** \-ˌgāt, *usu* -ād.+V\ *vb* -ED/-ING/-S *vt* **1 :** to collect or gather into a mass or whole **:** bring together ⟨wealth *aggregated* by their industrial and commercial skill —Will Durant⟩ **2 :** to make a part of the aggregate **:** unite as a constituent member ⟨these people are now *aggregated* with us —Thomas Jefferson⟩ **3 :** to amount in the aggregate to **:** form an aggregate of ⟨audiences *aggregating* a million people⟩ ~ *vi* **:** to come together **:** ASSEMBLE ⟨people . . . abandon their normal occupations, ~ in predesignated places —Anatol Rapoport⟩

³**ag·gre·gate** \-gət *also* -ˌgāt; *usu* -d.+V\ *n* -s **1 :** a mass or body of units or parts somewhat loosely associated with one another ⟨an ~ of individuals actuated by economic self-interest —Douglas Bush⟩ **2 :** the whole sum or amount **:** SUM TOTAL ⟨the ~ of knowledge . . . is greater than ever before —C.H.Grandgent⟩ **3 a :** an aggregate rock **b :** any of several hard inert materials used for mixing in various-sized fragments with a cementing material to form concrete, mortar, or plaster **c :** a clustered mass of individual soil grains or particles varied in shape, ranging in size from a microscopic granule to a small crumb, and usu. considered the basic structural unit of soil **4 a :** a total comprising all the elements or individuals in a particular category or a group of categories in an economy **b** *Brit* **:** the sum total of grades made by a student **5 :** a set of mathematical elements having some property in common ⟨the ~ of rational numbers⟩ **syn** see SUM — **in the aggregate :** considered as a whole **:** COLLECTIVELY ⟨dividends for the year amounted *in the aggregate* to $60,000⟩

aggregated *adj* **1 :** gathered into a whole **:** AGGREGATE ⟨the ~ masses in . . . the cells —C.R.Darwin⟩ **2 :** containing aggregates ⟨a highly ~ soil⟩

aggregate mortality table *n* **:** an insurance mortality table based on both newly medically selected lives and lives from which the effect of selection has been eliminated

aggregate polarization *n* **:** polarization by a rock section in which the constituent minerals cannot be individually recognized

aggregate ray *n* **:** a group of rays in certain woods appearing at low magnification as a single vascular ray but consisting of smaller rays, fibers, and sometimes vessels — called also *compound ray*

ag·gre·ga·tion \ˌagrəˈgāshən, ˌaig-, -rē-\ *n* -s [MF or ML; MF *agregation*, fr. ML *aggregation-, aggregatio*, fr. L *aggregatus* + *-ion-, -io* -ion] **1 a :** the action or process of aggregating **:** the collection of units or parts into a mass or whole ⟨learning is . . . the ~ of many men's sentences —William Baldwin⟩ **b :** the state or condition of being aggregated or of having aggregates ⟨in most soils . . . there is only a partial ~ of the various particles —L.D.Baver⟩ **2 :** a group, body, or mass composed of many distinct parts **:** ASSEMBLAGE ⟨one of the world's largest ~s of industry⟩ ⟨a musical ~ touring the small towns⟩: as **a :** a collection of individuals gathered together in response to the same external conditions **b :** an assemblage of animals of one or more species usu. come together in response to an external stimulus (as drought) **3** *patent law* **:** the bringing together of two or more separate parts without changing their function or producing any result other than the sum of the results of the separate operation of the parts **4 :** the condensation or movement of the contents of cells, esp. those of tentacles or tendrils of insectivorous or sensitive plants, in response to stimuli **5** *ecol* **a :** ASSOCIATION 8 **b :** SOCIETY

ag·gre·ga·tive \ˈ==ˌgād·iv, -ātiv, -ēv\ *adj* **1 :** of, relating to, or tending toward aggregation ⟨an ~ process⟩ **2 :** of or relating to aggregates, specif. economic aggregates ⟨~ terms⟩

aggrege *vt* -ED/-ING/-S [ME *aggreggen*, fr. MF *agregier*, fr. (assumed) VL *aggraviare*, *aggreviare*, alter. of L *aggravare* to make heavier — more at AGGRAVATE] *obs* **:** to make graver **:** AGGRAVATE

ag·gress \əˈgres *also* aˈ-\ *vb* -ED/-ING/-S [LL *aggressus* attack, fr. L *aggressus*, past part. of *aggredi* to approach, attack, undertake, fr. *ad-* + *-gredi* (fr. *gradi* to step, go) — more at GRADE] *vi* **:** to make an attack **:** commit aggression ⟨westerners even ~*ed* against one another —A.E.Stevenson b. 1900⟩ ~ *vt* **:** to set upon **:** ATTACK ⟨lions . . . seeking whom they may ~ —*Saturday Rev.*⟩

ag·gres·sin \-sᵊn\ *n* -s [ISV *aggress-* (fr. LL *aggressus*) + *-in*; orig. formed in G] **:** a hypothetical substance held to contribute to the virulence of pathogenic bacteria by paralyzing the defensive mechanisms of the host, esp. the leukocytes, and held to be produced by the bacteria in the body of the host

ag·gres·sion \əˈgreshən *also* aˈ-\ *n* -s [F & L; F *agression*, fr. L *aggression-, aggressio*, fr. *aggressus* + *-ion-, -io* -ion] **1 a :** an offensive action or procedure; *esp* **:** a culpable unprovoked overt hostile attack ⟨we have borne with their ~s —Thomas Jefferson⟩ **b :** the practice of making attacks or encroachments **:** offensive tactics ⟨a war of ~⟩ **2 :** the action of a nation in violating the rights, esp the territorial rights, of another nation (as by unprovoked attack, invasion, or other unfriendly military action or sometimes by serious threat of or preparation for such action) ⟨that country was said to be guilty of ~⟩ **3 :** a form of psychobiologic energy, either innate or arising in response to or intensified by frustration, which may be manifested by (1) overt destruction, fighting, infliction of pain, sexual attack, or forcible seizure, (2) covert hostile attitudes, covetousness, or greed, (3) introjection into one's self (as self-hate or masochism), (4) sublimation into play or sports, or (5) healthy self-assertiveness or a drive to accomplishment or to mastery esp. of skills

ag·gres·sive \-esiv, -ēv\ *adj* **1 a :** tending toward, characterized by, or practicing aggression ⟨her ~ behavior⟩ ⟨an ~ nation⟩ **b :** marked by combative readiness or bold determination **:** not conciliatory **:** MILITANT ⟨an ~ fighter⟩ **2 a :** marked by driving forceful energy, ambition, or initiative **:** ENTERPRISING ⟨an ~ salesman⟩ ⟨~ leadership⟩ **b :** marked by obtrusive energy and self-assertiveness **:** demanding or attracting attention **:** SELF-CONFIDENT ⟨swaggering, blatant, and idiotically ~ vulgarity —George du Maurier⟩ **3 a :** promoting or accessory to aggression in predaceous animals (as insects) esp. by concealment or disguise ⟨an ~ trait⟩ **b** *bot* **:** spreading with vigor ⟨~ weeds⟩ **c :** chemically active ⟨~ waters⟩ **d :** tending or able to utilize a variety of habitats **:** able to encroach on occupied areas **:** variable and adaptable — used of organisms and taxa ⟨an extremely ~ subspecies⟩

syn MILITANT, ASSERTIVE, SELF-ASSERTIVE, PUSHING, PUSHFUL: AGGRESSIVE may apply either to zealous loyalty to causes or to personal ambitions and aims; it suggests forceful and confident procedures and attitudes, sometimes truculent contentiousness or cavalier treatment of others ⟨positive in his convictions, *aggressive* and imperious, he became a zealot in any cause he embraced —F.L.Hise⟩ ⟨as intolerant and *aggressive* as any of the traditional satirists —C.D.Lewis⟩ MILITANT, complimentary except for suggestions of doctrinaire intractability, applies to fervent, resolute, devoted furthering of a cause ⟨the *militant* suffragist nuisance —Rose Macaulay⟩ ⟨*militant* in fighting to get for workers a larger share of the national income —*Time*⟩ ASSERTIVE suggests bold self-confidence and determination in expression of opinion ⟨an *assertive*, opinionated, likable fellow, ready to fight, drink, dance, shoot, or brag —V.L. Parrington⟩ ⟨to say, with some challenging *assertive* people, that trees are more beautiful than flowers —E.V.Lucas⟩ SELF-ASSERTIVE, usu. uncomplimentary, generally connotes obtrusive, crass forwardness or brash self-confidence ⟨the social and political revolt beginning in the new middle class against the Tory aristocracy found more vigorous expression in the *self-assertive* and ubiquitous energy of Henry Brougham —G.M.Trevelyan⟩ ⟨*self-assertive* and ill-bred bourgeois —Edmund Wilson⟩ PUSHING and PUSHFUL may praise by indicating ambition, energy, and enterprise ⟨an energetic, *pushing* youth, already intent on getting on in the world —Sherwood Anderson⟩ ⟨the *pushful* energetic man of business —Aldous Huxley⟩ or blame by indicating snobbish or crude intrusiveness ⟨a *pushing* sort, forever exposing themselves to the slights arising from their own undesirability —Mary Austin⟩ ⟨ignorant, *pushful*, impatient of restraint and precedent —H.L.Mencken⟩

aggressively *adv* **:** in an aggressive manner

ag·gres·sive·ness *or* **ag·gres·siv·i·ty** \əˌgreˈsivəd·ē, ˌaˌg-\ *n* -ES **:** the quality or state of being aggressive **:** AGGRESSION

ag·gres·sor \əˈgresə(r), aˈ- *also* -ˌsȯ(ə)r *or* -ō(ə)\ *n* -s [LL, fr. L *aggressus* + *-or*] **1 :** one that commits or practices aggression; *esp* **:** a nation that commits an act of aggression ⟨economic insecurity and poverty . . . breed conflict and give ~s their chance —E.R.Stettinius⟩ **2 a :** a military force organized, trained, and deployed to act as the enemy during a field problem or in maneuvers **b :** a member of such a force

ag·griev·ance \əˈgrēvən(t)s *also* aˈ-\ *n* -s [ME *agrevaunce*, fr. MF *agrevance*, fr. *agrever* + *-ance*] **:** GRIEVANCE

ag·grieve \əˈgrēv *also* aˈ-\ *vt* -ED/-ING/-S [ME *agreven*, fr. MF *agrever*, fr. L *aggravare* to make heavy — more at AGGRAVATE] **1 :** to give pain, sorrow, or trouble to **:** GRIEVE, DISTRESS ⟨I was *aggrieved* it did not include so notable a plant —Andrew Young⟩ **2 :** to inflict injury upon **:** OPPRESS, WRONG ⟨provisions should be made for recourse to the courts by parties who may be *aggrieved* by such orders —S.T.Powell⟩ **syn** see WRONG

aggrieved *adj* [ME *agreved*, fr. past part. of *agreven*] **1 :** troubled or distressed in spirit ⟨he spoke like one ~⟩ **2 a :** showing grief, injury, or offense ⟨did not understand the ~ attitude of the mate —Joseph Conrad⟩ **b :** having a grievance; *specif* **:** suffering from an infringement or denial of legal rights ⟨compensation paid to the ~ party⟩ — **ag·griev·ed·ly** \-vədlē, -li\ *adv*

ag·group \əˈgrüp, aˈ-\ *vt* -ED/-ING/-S [F *agrouper*, fr. *a-* (fr. L *ad-*) + *groupe* group — more at GROUP] **:** to arrange in a group ⟨were ~*ed* near the center of the square⟩ — **ag·group·ment** *n* -s

ag·gry bead *also* **ag·gri bead** \ˈagrē-\ *n* [of African origin; akin to Hausa *gori* snail shell used as an ornament, Twi *agyiratwefā*, a weight of gold, *gyirapaw*, a charm] **:** a variegated glass bead found buried in the earth in Ghana and in England

agha *often cap, var of* AGA

aghan \ə'gän\ *n* -s *usu cap* [Skt *Agrahāyaṇa*] **:** a month of the Hindu year — see MONTH table

aghast \ə'gast, -aa(ə)st, -aist. -äst\ *adj* [alter. (prob. influenced by Sc *ghast*, var. of E *ghost*) of ME *agast*, fr. past part. of *agasten* to frighten, be frightened, fr. *a-* (perfective prefix) + *gasten* to frighten — more at ABEAR, GAST] **1 :** seized with fear or terror **:** FRIGHTENED, TERRIFIED ⟨with shuddering horror pale and eyes ~ —John Milton⟩ **2 :** struck with amazement, bewilderment, disgust, or surprise **:** SHOCKED ⟨the trustees, ~ when he allowed pupils to study out-of-doors, demanded stricter discipline —E.W.Parks⟩ — usu. used predicatively ⟨he was ~⟩ but sometimes prepositively ⟨thousands of ~ Britons whose rage is concentrated on their government —Mollie Panter-Downes⟩ **syn** *see* AFRAID

agh·lab·ite \'aglə,bīt. ag'la,-\ *also* **agh·lab·id** \-,bəd\ *n* -s, *cap* [Ibrāhīm ibn- al- *Aghlab* (Ibrahim I) †A.D. 812 African sultan, founder of the dynasty + E *-ite* or *-id*] **:** a member of an Arab dynasty ruling at Kairouan, northern Africa, A.D. 800–909

ag·i·la·wood *also* **ag·ui·la·wood** \'agələ,wu̇d\ *n* [Pg *aguila* (fr. Tamil *akil*) + E *wood*] **:** AGALLOCH

ag·ile \'ajəl, *US also & Brit usu* 'a,jīl *or* -īəl\ *adj* [MF, fr. L *agilis*, fr. *agere* to move, act + *-ilis* -ile — more at AGENT] **1 :** characterized by ready ability to move quickly and easily with suppleness and grace ⟨as bright-eyed and ~ as the hares and slim gazelles —Elinor Wylie⟩ **2 :** characterized by quickness or liveliness of mind, resourcefulness, or adaptability in coping with new and varied situations ⟨the work of a . . . sympathetic intelligence, ~, humane, and . . . persuasive —A.D.Culler⟩

syn NIMBLE, BRISK, SPRY: AGILE suggests ease in quick motion along with smooth coordination and dexterous performance of sudden or difficult actions ⟨I saw her bounding down the rocky slope like some wild, *agile* creature possessed of padded hoofs and an infallible instinct —W.H.Hudson⟩ ⟨Silver, *agile* as a monkey, even without leg or crutch, was on the top of him next moment —R.L.Stevenson⟩ Applied to mental or intellectual matters it suggests ready adaptability and ability to change and adjust ⟨in a flow of racy comment, skimming from one topic to another with an *agile* irrelevance —Rose Macaulay⟩ NIMBLE stresses lightness and ease of sudden physical motion and suggests ability to dart, dash, or skip; applied to matters mental it suggests quick comprehension and ready responsiveness to change ⟨out ran the two maidens, their frocks flying, *nimble* feet scudding over the springy turf —Mary Webb⟩ ⟨the mind and the body have in this respect a striking resemblance of each other. In childhood they are both *nimble*, but not strong; they can skip and frisk about with wonderful agility —William Cowper⟩ BRISK suggests lively energetic activity or vivacity; it often applies to manner or attitude rather than physical capability or dexterity ⟨a *brisk* wind sending small white clouds scudding across the vast East Anglian sky —Osbert Lancaster⟩ ⟨that *brisk*, managing, lively, imperious woman —W.M.Thackeray⟩ SPRY indicates an ability for quick easy activity, esp. among the old or infirm in whom such ability may be unexpected ⟨I'm a little lame, I ain't as *spry* as I used to be —J.K.Jerome⟩ ⟨poor Canon Bonnyboat could only limp . . . whereas Reverend Mother was still as *spry* as a sparrow —Bruce Marshall⟩

agile gibbon *n* [*agile*, trans. of NL *agilis*, specific epithet of *Hylobates agilis*] **:** a gibbon (*Hylobates agilis*) of Malaysia and Sumatra that occurs in two color phases, one blackish brown, the other buffy brown, both with white brow and black face

ag·ile·ly \-əl(l)ē,-īllē, -i\ *adv* **:** in an agile manner

agil·i·ty \ə'jiləd·ē, -ətē, -i *also* a'-\ *n* -ES [ME *agilite*, fr. MF *agilité*, fr. L *agilitat-, agilitas*, fr. *agilis* + *-itat-, -itas* -ity] **:** the quality or state of being agile: **a :** quickness and dexterity of movement ⟨a monkeylike ~⟩ **b :** quickness and resourcefulness of mind ⟨his ~ in debate⟩

agil·men·te \,ajəl'mentē, *It* äjēl'män·tä\ *adv* [It, fr. *agile*, adj., fr. L *agilis*] **:** with agility — used as a direction in music

¹agin \ə'gin\ *dial var of* AGAIN

²agin \"\ *dial var of* AGAINST

aging *pres part of* AGE

agio \'a(,)jō, 'ajē,ō, 'ä(,)jō\ *n* -s [It *aggio*, *agio*, alter. (by false word division, *l* being taken as the def. article) of It dial. *lajjē*, fr. MGk *allagion* exchange, fr. Gk *allagē* change, exchange, fr. *allos* other — more at ELSE] **1 a :** a premium or percentage paid for the exchange of one currency for another (as where gold is given for silver or metallic for paper currency) **b :** the premium or discount on foreign bills of exchange **2 :** MONEY CHANGING

agio·tage \'ajəd·ij, -ətij\ *n* -s [F, fr. *agioter* to practice stockjobbing (fr. *agio* stockjobbing, fr. It *aggio, agio*) + *-age*] **1 :** exchange business **2 :** speculative buying or selling of stocks **:** STOCKJOBBING

agist \ə'jist\ *vb* -ED/ -ING/ -S [MF *agister*, fr. *a-* (fr. L *ad-*) + *gister* to give lodging, fr. *giste* lodging, abode, fr. (assumed) VL *jacita*, fr. L *jacēre* to lie, fr. *jacere* to throw — more at JET] *vt* **1 :** to take in (livestock) for feeding or grazing and to collect the amount due therefor **2 :** to tax (land or owner) with a share of any public charge or burden ~ *vi* **:** to graze and feed for a specified period at a fixed rate

agist·er *or* **agis·tor** \-tə(r)\ *n* -s [ME *agister*, fr. AF *agistour*, fr. MF *agister* + *-our* -or] **:** one that agists livestock; *specif* **:** an officer of the royal forests in England who has the care of livestock agisted

agist·ment \-mənt\ *n* -s [MF *agistement*, fr. *agister* + *-ment*] **1 a :** the taking in of livestock for feeding at a specified rate **b :** the opening of a forest to livestock for a specified period **2 a :** the price paid for or the profit made from agisting livestock **b :** a charge or rate against lands

ag·i·ta·ble \'ajəd·əbəl\ *adj* [L *agitabilis*, fr. *agitare* + *-abilis* -able] **:** capable of being agitated

agi·ta·na·do \,ä,hētə'nä(,)thō\ *n* -s [Sp, gypsylike, fr. *a-* (fr. L *ad-*) + *gitano* gypsy (fr. — assumed — VL *Aegyptanus* Egyptian, fr. L *Aegyptius* + *-anus* -an) + *-ado* -ate — more at EGYPTIAN] **:** nonflamenco heelwork in dancing or a nonflamenco dance using heelwork

ag·i·tate \'ajə,tāt, *usu* -ād·+V\ *vb* -ED/ -ING/ -S [L *agitatus*, past part. of *agitare* to drive, agitate, turn over in the mind, freq. of *agere* to drive, do — more at AGENT] *vt* **1 a** *obs* **:** to give action or motion to **:** ACTUATE ⟨who fills, surrounds, informs, and ~s the whole —James Thomson⟩ **b :** to move to and fro **:** give regular motion to ⟨the ladies sigh and ~ their fans —J.E.Cooke⟩ **c :** to move with a brisk irregular action **:** shake or move rapidly or violently ⟨the convulsions and tremors which had *agitated* the body . . . were fewer —P.J.Phelan⟩ **2 :** to excite or trouble the mind or feelings of ⟨a discussion which has *agitated* thinkers —A.N.Whitehead⟩ **:** stir up **:** DISTURB ⟨questions which ~ modern states —G.L.Dickinson⟩ **3 :** to discuss or debate excitedly and earnestly ⟨the child and woman labor issues were *agitated* —H.M.Diamond⟩ **4** *obs* **:** to turn over in the mind **:** CONTRIVE, PLOT ⟨statesmen *agitating* new plans⟩ ~ *vi* **:** to attempt to arouse public feeling or influence public opinion (as by constant discussion) ⟨they were *agitating* for schools and the vote —V.G.Heiser⟩ **syn** see DISCOMPOSE, DISCUSS, SHAKE

agitated *adj* **1 :** moving to and fro **:** QUIVERING, SHAKING ⟨his ~ hand always gliding over the network of fine nerves about his mouth —Charles Dickens⟩ **2 :** troubled in mind **:** DISTURBED, EXCITED ⟨Wickham's alarm now appeared in a heightened complexion and ~ look —Jane Austen⟩ **3 :** kept before the public by extended discussion or debate ⟨the long ~ plan for a new high school⟩ — **ag·i·tat·ed·ly** \-ād·ədlē, -li\ *adv*

agitated depression *n* **:** a psychotic state characterized by restlessness, overactivity, anxiety, and despair but not accompanied by gross disorganization or deterioration — compare INVOLUTIONAL MELANCHOLIA

ag·i·tat·ing·ly \-ād·iŋlē, -ēŋ-, -li\ *adv* **:** in an agitating manner

ag·i·ta·tion \,ajə'tāshən\ *n* -s [MF or L; MF, fr. L *agitation-, agitatio*, fr. *agitatus* + *-ion-, -io* -ion] **1 a :** the action of moving **:** MOTION, ACTIVITY ⟨by exercise . . . I understand all . . . ~ of the body —Francis Fuller⟩ **b :** a moving back and forth **:** SHAKING, SWIRLING ⟨the ~ of milk can lead to a decrease in its keeping quality⟩ **c :** the state or condition of being moved to and fro violently, steadily, or with a fluttering effect ⟨a trifling ~ of the curtains —George Meredith⟩ **2 :** mental excitement or emotional perturbation **:** a tremulous and disturbed state ⟨in spite of his ~ his voice was low and quiet —Sherwood Anderson⟩ **3 :** earnest and thoughtful consideration **:** DISCUSSION, DEBATE ⟨this design was in ~ —Francis Parkman⟩ **4 :** the persistent and sustained attempt to arouse public feeling or influence public opinion (as by appeals, discussions, or demonstrations) ⟨no sudden revolt, but the culmination of a long ~ for national independence —W.R.Inge⟩ **syn** see COMMOTION

ag·i·ta·tion·al \,ajə¦tāshənᵊl, -shnəl\ *adj* **:** of or concerned with agitation

ag·i·ta·tive \'ajə,tād·iv, -ātiv, -ēv\ *adj* **:** causing or tending to cause agitation

agi·ta·to \,ajə'täd·(,)ō, ,äjē'tä,tō\ *adj* (*or adv*) [It, lit., agitated, fr. L *agitatus*] **:** restless and agitated — used as a direction in music

ag·i·ta·tor \'ajə,tād·ə(r) *also* ¦ajə¦tä,tō(ə)r *or* -tō(ə)\ *n* -s [*agitate* (meaning also, in 17th cent., to administer, manage) + *-or*] **1** *usu cap* **:** an agent appointed by the Parliamentary army in Cromwell's time to look after the interests of the private soldiers — called also *Adjutator* **2 :** one that agitates: as **a :** one who stirs up political, economic, religious, or other social agitation ⟨an ~ for the rights of the common people⟩ **b :** an implement or apparatus (as one utilizing a propeller on a shaft) for mixing, stirring, or shaking — **ag·i·ta·to·ri·al** \,ajətə¦tōrēəl\ *adj*

agitator 2b

agitator feed *n* **:** a device consisting of adjustable holes and rotating wheels used to prevent clogging in implements for broadcasting seed or fertilizer

¹ag·it·prop \'ajət¦präp\ *n* -s [in sense 1, fr. Russ, fr. *agitatsiya-propaganda* agitation propaganda, fr. *agitatsiya* agitation (fr. F *agitation*) + *propaganda*, fr. G; in sense 2, Russ, a department of the Communist party, short for *Agitpropbyuro* Department of Agitprop — more at AGITATION, PROPAGANDA] **1 :** propaganda and agitation esp. in behalf of communism ⟨disillusioned ex-Communists who blame politics itself for their own earlier susceptibility to ~ —David Riesman⟩ **2 a :** a department or bureau in charge of agitprop ⟨he could no more be imagined cringing before a witch-hunting demagogue than taking orders from an ~ —*Nation*⟩ **b :** a person who engages in agitprop ⟨slogans chalked on walls by ~s⟩

²agitprop \"\ *adj* **:** of, relating to, or serving as a vehicle of agitprop ⟨~ officers⟩ ⟨the ~ drama⟩

ag·it·prop·ist \¦==¦=əst\ *n* -s **:** an agitprop agent

ag·it·punkt \'==,pu̇ŋ(k)t\ *n* -s [Russ, fr. *agitatsiya-punkt*, fr. *agitatsiya* + *punkt* point, place, fr. Pol or G; Pol, fr. G, fr. LL *puncta* — more at POINT] **:** an indoctrination and political propaganda center in the Soviet Union

ag·kis·tro·don \ag'kistrə,dän, aŋ'k-\ *n, cap* [NL, irreg. fr. Gk *ankistron* fishhook + NL *-odon*] **:** a genus of pit vipers including the American copperhead and water moccasin — used generally instead of the technically preferable *Ancistrodon*

ag·lao·ne·ma \,aglēō'nēmə\ *n, cap* [NL, fr. Gk *aglaos* shining, bright + NL *-nema*] **:** a genus of Indo-Malayan climbing herbs of the arum family having thick fleshy oblong leaves and naked unisexual flowers on a spadix shorter than the spathe — see CHINESE EVERGREEN

ag·lao·zo·nia \,aglēə'zōnyə, -nēə\ *n* [NL, fr. Gk *aglaos* + *zōnē* belt + NL *-ia*] **1** -s **:** the asexual stage of any brown alga of the genus *Cutleria* **2** *cap, in former classifications* **:** a genus of brown algae comprising those having aglaozonia stages

aglare \ə'-\ *adj* [¹*a-* + *glare* (v.)] **:** GLARING ⟨with eyes ~⟩

aglas·pis \ə'glaspəs\ *n, cap* [NL, fr. Gk *aglaos* + NL *-aspis*] **:** a genus of extinct Cambrian Xiphosura related to the modern king crab

agleam \ə'-\ *adj* [¹*a-* + *gleam* (v.)] **:** GLEAMING ⟨his face ~ in the sunlight⟩

ag·let \'aglət, 'aig-\ *or* **ai·glet** \'āg-\ *n* -s [ME *aglet*, fr. MF *aguillette*, dim. of *aguille* needle, fr. LL *acucula* ornamental pin, alter. of *acicula*, dim. of L *acus* needle, pin — more at ACUTE] **1 a (1) :** the plain or ornamental tag covering the ends of a point (sense 10a) **(2) :** an ornamental tag used for decoration on costumes **b :** any of various ornamental studs, cords, or pins worn on clothing **2 a :** HAWTHORN **b :** HAZEL 1a

agley \ə'glā, -lē,-lī, *Scot usu* -lē *or* -ləi\ *also* **aglee** \-lē\ *adv* [Sc, lit., squintingly, fr. E ¹*a-* + Sc & dial. E *gley, glee* to squint, fr. ME (northern dial.) *gleyen*] *chiefly Scot* **:** against hope, expectation, or plan **:** AWRY, WRONG ⟨the best-laid schemes o' mice an' men gang aft ~ —Robert Burns⟩

aglim·mer \ə'-\ *adj* [¹*a-* + *glimmer*, v.] **:** GLIMMERING ⟨a city ~ with light⟩

aglint \ə'-\ *adj* [¹*a-* + *glint*, v.] **:** GLINTING ⟨an island ~ in the sun⟩

¹ag·li·pay·an \,aglə'pīən\ *n* -s *usu cap* [Gregorio *Aglipay* †1940 Philippine archbishop + E *-an*] **:** a member of the independent church of the Philippines organized on a national Catholic basis in 1902

²aglipayan \¦==¦==\ *adj, usu cap* **:** of or relating to Aglipayans

ag·li·pay·an·ism \,==ˈ==,nizəm\ *n* -s *usu cap* **:** the doctrines, principles, and practices of Aglipayans

aglis·ten \ə'-\ *adj* [¹*a-* + *glisten*, v.] **:** GLISTENING ⟨the garden ~ with dew⟩

aglit·ter \ə'-\ *adj* [¹*a-* + *glitter*, v.] **:** GLITTERING ⟨a coronet ~ with diamonds⟩

aglo·mer·u·lar \¦ā+\ *adj* [²*a-* + *glomerular*] **:** lacking glomeruli ⟨the ~ toadfish⟩

aglos·sa \ā'gläsə, -ōsə\ *n pl, cap* [NL, fr. ²*a-* + *-glossa*] **1** *in some classifications* **:** a suborder of amphibians including frogs or toads that have no tongue and have a common pharyngeal opening for the Eustachian tubes and comprising the families Pipidae and Xenopodidae **2** *in some classifications* **:** a division of mollusks having neither radula nor head coextensive with Lamellibranchia

¹aglos·sate \(')ā'gläsət, (')ā'glä,sāt, -lō-\ *or* **aglos·sal** \(')=¦=əl\ *adj* [Gk *aglōssos* (fr. *a-* ²*a-* + *glōssa* tongue) + E *-ate* or *-al*] **1** *zool* **:** having no tongue **2** [NL *Aglossa* + E *-ate* or *-al*] **:** of or relating to the Aglossa

²aglossate \(')=¦=(,)ə\ *n* -s **:** one of the Aglossa

aglow \ə'-\ *adj* [¹*a-* + *glow*, v.] **:** GLOWING ⟨a student ~ with liberalism⟩

aglu·con *or* **aglu·cone** \-lü-\ *n* -s [ISV *a-* (fr. Gk *a-, ha-* together) + *gluc-* + *-on, -one*] **:** AGLYCON; *esp* **:** one combined with glucose in a glucoside

agly·con \a'glī,kän, ä'-,a'-\ *or* **agly·cone** \-ōn\ *n* -s [ISV *a-* (fr. Gk *a-, ha-* together) + *glyc-* + *-on, -one*] **:** an organic compound, usu. a phenol or an alcohol, combined with the sugar portion of a glycoside and obtainable by hydrolysis ⟨quercetin is the ~ of quercitrin⟩

ag·ly·pha \'agləfə\ *n pl, cap* [NL, fr. Gk *aglypha*, neut. pl. of *aglyphos* unhewn, fr. *a-* ²*a-* + *-glyphos* (fr. *glyphein* to cut, hew) — more at CLEAVE (to cut)] **:** a primary division of the family Colubridae, in its widest sense nearly or exactly coextensive with the Aglyphodonta of other classifications

aglyph·o·don·ta \ə,glifə'däntə\ *n pl, cap* [NL, fr. *Aglypha* + *-odonta*] **:** a group of snakes without grooved fangs or venom glands and without limb vestiges, comprising the families Amblycephalidae, Acrochordidae, Colubridae (sensu stricto) and including the majority of common nonpoisonous snakes which are sometimes all placed in the family Colubridae

aglyph·o·don·tia \-nch(ē)ə\ *syn of* AGLYPHODONTA

ag·ly·phous \'agləfəs\ *adj* [NL *Aglypha* + E *-ous*] **1 :** of or relating to the Aglypha **2** *zool* **:** having solid teeth

ag·ma \'agmə\ *n* -s [LGk, fr. Gk, fragment] **1 :** the sound \ŋ\ in Greek or Latin **2 :** the Greek letter gamma (γ) when used to represent the sound \ŋ\ **3 :** ENG

ag·ma·tine \-,tēn\ *n* -s [ISV *agmat-* (fr. Gk *agmat-, agma* fragment) + *-ine*] **:** a base $C_5H_{14}N_4$ formed from arginine in putrefaction; (δ-amino-butyl)-guanidine

ag·mi·nate \'agmənət, -,nāt\ *or* **ag·mi·nat·ed** \-,nād·əd\ *adj* [L *agmin-, agmen* motion, march, troop + E *-ate, -ated*] **:** grouped together ⟨*agminated* glands are called Peyer's patches⟩

agn *abbr* again

ag·nail \'ag,nāl, 'aig-\ *n* -s [ME, fr. OE *angnaegl* corn, fr. *ang-* (akin to *enge* tight, painful) + *naegl* nail (of iron) — more at ANGER, NAIL] **1** *obs* **:** a corn on the foot or toe **2 :** a sore or inflammation about a fingernail or toenail **3 :** HANGNAIL

¹ag·nate \'ag,nāt, 'aig-, *usu* -ād·+V\ *n* -s [L *agnatus*, fr. *agnatus*, past part. of *agnasci* to be born in addition to, fr. *ad-* + *nasci* to be born — more at NATION] **1 :** a relative whose kinship is traceable exclusively through males **2 :** any paternal kinsman — compare COGNATE, ENATE

²agnate \"\ *adj* [L *agnatus*] **1 :** related through male descent or on the father's side **2 :** having a kindred nature **:** ALLIED, AKIN

ag·na·tha \'agnəthə\ *n pl, cap* [NL, fr. ²*a-* + *-gnatha*] **1 :** a superclass or other division of Vertebrata comprising those without jaws — compare GNATHOSTOMATA **2 :** a group of carnivorous air-breathing snails without jaws

ag·nath·ia \ag'nathēə, (')ā'n-, -āth-\ *n* -s [NL, fr. ²*a-* + Gk *gnathos* + NL *-ia*] **:** the congenital complete or partial absence of one or both jaws

ag·na·tho·sto·ma·ta \,agnəthə'stōməd·ə, ¦ā,nath-\ [NL ²*a-* + Gk *gnathos* jaw + NL *-stomata*] *syn of* AGNATHA

ag·na·tho·stom·a·tous \¦===¦stäməd·əs, ¦=,==-, -ōm-\ *adj* [NL *Agnathostomata* + E *-ous*] **:** AGNATHOUS 2

ag·na·thous \'agnəthəs\ *also* **ag·nath·ic** \(')ag¦nathik, (')ā¦n-\ *adj* [²*a-* + Gk *gnathos* + E *-ous* or *-ic*] **1 :** having no jaws **2** [NL *Agnatha* + E *-ous* or *-ic*] **:** of or relating to the Agnatha

ag·nat·ic \(')ag¦nad·ik\ *adj* [¹*agnate* + *-ic*] **:** of or relating to agnates **:** akin through male descent or on the father's side

ag·nat·i·cal·ly \-ək(ə)lē\ *adv* **:** in an agnatic manner

ag·na·tion \ag'nāshən\ *n* -s [F or L; F, fr. L *agnation-, agnatio*, fr. *agnatus* (past part. of *agnasci* to be born in addition to) + *-ion-, -io* -ion — more at AGNATE] **:** the relationship of agnates

ag·ne·an \'ägnēən\ *n* -s *cap* [*Agni*, ancient kingdom in Turkestan + E *-an*] **:** TOCHARIAN A

agnel \an'yel\ *n, pl* **agneaux** \-yō\ [F, fr. MF, lit., lamb, fr. L *agnellus* little lamb, dim. of *agnus* lamb — more at YEAN] **:** a gold coin of France, issued in the 13th to 16th centuries, bearing the figure of a lamb

ag·ni \'agnē\ *n, pl* **agni** *or* **agnis** *usu cap* **1 a :** a people of western Africa ethnologically allied to the Ashanti **b :** a member of such people **2 :** a Kwa language of the Agni people

ag·ni·fi·ca·tion \,agnəfə'kāshən\ *n* -s [L *agnus* lamb + E *-i-* + *-fication*] **:** the representation (as in painting) of persons as sheep or lambs

agnition *n* -s [L *agnition-, agnitio*, fr. *agnitus* (past part. of *agnoscere* to recognize, acknowledge, fr. *ad-* + *gnoscere* to know) + *-ion-, -io* -ion — more at KNOW] *obs* **:** RECOGNITION, ACKNOWLEDGMENT

ag·nize \(')ag¦nīz\ *vt* -ED/-ING/-S [fr. L *agnoscere*, after *recognoscere*: E *recognize*] *archaic* **:** RECOGNIZE, ACKNOWLEDGE ⟨I do ~ a natural and prompt alacrity —Shak.⟩

ag·no·e·tae \,ag(,)nō'ē,tē\ *n pl, usu cap* [LL *Agnoetae, Agnoitae*, fr. LGk *Agnoētai*, lit., ignorant ones, fr. Gk *agnoein* to be ignorant, fr. *a-* ²*a-* + *-gnoein* (fr. *gignōskein* to know) — more at KNOW] **1 :** a 4th century A.D. sect of Arians that considered God's omniscience limited to the present **2 :** a 6th century sect of Severian Monophysites that denied the omniscience of Jesus Christ

ag·no·ete \'ag(,)nō,ēt\ *or* **ag·no·ite** \-,īt\ *n* -s *usu cap* [LL *Agnoetae, Agnoitae*, pl.] **:** one of the Agnoetae

ag·no·e·tism \,ag(,)nō'ē,tizəm, 'ag(,)nō,ēd·,iz-\ *n* -s *usu cap* **:** the doctrinal principles of the Agnoetae

ag·no·gen·ic \¦agnō¦jenik\ *adj* [²*a-* + Gk *gnōmē* means of knowing + E *-genic*] *med* **:** of unknown cause ⟨~ metaplasia⟩

ag·no·men \(')ag¦nōmən\ *n, pl* **ag·nom·i·na** \-nämənə, -nōm-\ *or* **agnomens** [L, irreg. (influence of *agnoscere* to acknowledge, fr. *ad-* + *noscere* to know) fr. *ad-* + *nomen* name — more at NAME] **:** an additional name or epithet; *specif* **:** an additional cognomen given to a person by the ancient Romans (as in honor of some achievement) — compare NOMEN, PRAENOMEN

ag·nom·i·na·tion \(,)ag,nämə'nāshən\ *n* -s [L *agnomination-, agnominatio*, fr. *ad-* + *nomination-, nominatio* naming; trans. of Gk *paronomasia* — more at NOMINATION] **1 :** the echoing of a sound of one word in another in close relationship with it (as in the same sentence) **2 :** the repetition of a word but in different senses often for purpose of wit (as in punning) or for emphatic contrast

ag·no·sia \ag'nōzh(ē)ə\ *n* -s [NL, fr. Gk *agnōsia* ignorance, fr. *a-* ²*a-* + *-gnōsia* -gnosia] **:** the partial or complete loss of the ability to recognize familiar objects esp. by seeing, hearing, or touching and usu. as a result of brain damage

ag·no·sis \ag'nōsəs\ *n, pl* **agno·ses** \-ō,sēz\ [NL, fr. ²*a-* + *-gnosis*] **:** AGNOSIA

ag·nos·te·rol \ag'nästə,rōl, -ōl\ *n* -s [L *agnus* lamb + E *-o-* + *-sterol*] **:** a crystalline tetracyclic triterpenoid alcohol $C_{30}H_{47}OH$ obtained from wool fat

¹ag·nos·tic \ag'nästik, əg-,aig-, -ēk\ *n* -s [modif. (influenced by E *Gnostic*) of Gk *agnōstos* unknown, unknowable, not knowing, fr. *a-* ²*a-* + *gnōstos* known, fr. *gignōskein* to know — more at KNOW] **:** one who professes agnosticism; *broadly* **:** one who maintains a continuing doubt about the existence or knowability of a god or any ultimates ⟨~ . . . came into my head as suggestively antithetic to the gnostic of church history who professed to know so much —T.H.Huxley⟩

syn AGNOSTIC, FREETHINKER, and ATHEIST can all apply to one who does not take an orthodox religious position. AGNOSTIC is the most neutral; it usu. implies only an unwillingness on available evidence to affirm or deny the existence of God or subscribe to tenets that presuppose such existence. FREETHINKER is broader; it can apply to one of no determinable religious position or to one who feels truth is made more available by not committing oneself to any orthodoxy, esp. a belief in God's existence. Often it can suggest a reprehensible and dangerous license of opinion. ATHEIST can apply strictly and neutrally to one who denies the existence of God or tenets presupposing it. More frequently than FREETHINKER, however, it has carried ideas of reprehensible license of opinion and menacing godlessness.

²ag·nos·tic \(')a(i)g¦n-, əg'n-\ *also* **ag·nos·ti·cal** \-təkəl, -ēk-\ *adj* **1 :** relating to or involving agnosticism; *esp* **:** professing ignorance or uncertainty about the ultimates usu. on the ground of unknowability ⟨so far as faith in God is concerned they are ~ rather than atheistic —W.L.Sperry⟩ **2 :** characterized by tolerance **:** UNDOGMATIC — **ag·nos·ti·cal·ly** \-ək(ə)lē, -ēk-, -li\ *adv*

³ag·nos·tic \(')ag¦nästik\ *adj* [Gk *agnōstos* + E *-ic*] **:** of, relating to, or characterized by agnosia ⟨~ symptoms⟩

⁴agnostic \"\ *n* -s **:** one who is a subject of agnosia

ag·nos·ti·cism \ag'nästə,sizəm, əg-\ *n* -s **1 a :** the doctrine that the existence or nature of any ultimate reality is unknown and probably unknowable or that any knowledge about matters of ultimate concern is impossible or improbable; *specif* **:** the doctrine that God or any first cause is unknown and probably unknowable **b :** a doctrine affirming that the existence of a god is possible but denying that there are any sufficient reasons for holding either that he does or does not exist — compare ATHEISM, SKEPTICISM **2 :** SKEPTICISM 1b **3 :** an agnostic attitude or disposition

ag·nos·tid \ag'nästəd\ *adj* [NL *Agnostus* + E *-id*] **:** of or belonging to the genus *Agnostus*

ag·nos·tus \-təs\ *n, cap* [NL, fr. Gk *agnōstos* unknown] **:** a genus of small blind Cambrian and Ordovician trilobites that with a number of related forms in which the cephalon and pygidium are almost indistinguishable constitute an order (Agnostida) of highly specialized forms

ag·no·to·zo·ic \ag¦nōd·ə¦zōik, ¦ag,n-\ *n or adj, usu cap* [ISV *agnoto-* (fr. Gk *agnōtos* unknown) + *-zoic*] **:** ALGONKIAN, PROTEROZOIC

agnus *n* -ES [ME, short for *Agnus Dei*] **:** AGNUS DEI

ag·nus cas·tus \¦agnə'skastəs\ *n, pl* **agnus castuses** [ME, fr. L, by folk etymology (influence of L *agnus* lamb & *castus* chaste) fr. Gk *agnos* (confused with *hagnos* chaste, holy), perh. of Sem origin; akin to Heb *'āghan* to remain closed in or hidden — more at CASTE] **:** an ornamental shrub (*Vitex agnus-castus*) having blue or white flowers and fruit that has been used as a stimulant and carminative — called also *chaste tree*

ag·nus dei \ˌäg,nu̇sˈdā,ē, -ˌnəs-, ˈän,yüs-, -yu̇s-; *sometimes, when not sung,* -ˈdā; ˌagnəsˈdē,ī\ *n, usu cap A&D* [ME, fr. LL, lamb of God, trans. of Gk *Amnos tou Theou*] **1 :** an image of a lamb, often with a halo and bearing a banner or a cross, symbolizing Jesus Christ **2** *Roman Catholicism* **a :** a small cloth-covered disk of wax stamped with the figure of a lamb, blessed by the pope, and carried or worn through devotion **b :** a prayer in the ordinary of the mass beginning with the words "Agnus Dei" **3** *Anglicanism* **:** a liturgical prayer or anthem beginning "O Lamb of God"

Agnus Dei 1

ago \əˈgō\ *also* **agone** \əˈgȯn *also* -än\ *adj (or adv)* [ME *ago, agon,* fr. past part. of *agon* to go away, pass by, fr. OE *āgān* to pass away, fr. *ā-* (perfective prefix) + *gān* to go — more at ABEAR, GO] **:** gone by **:** PAST ⟨two days~⟩ ⟨he lived here long ~⟩

agog \əˈgäg *also* -ȯg\ *adj* [MF *en gogues* merry, lively, lit., in mirth] **:** full of intense interest, ardent anticipation, or extreme excitement ⟨the abrupt announcement . . . left everybody . . . ~ —Bennett Cerf⟩ **:** EAGER ⟨always ~ for news —Virginia Woolf⟩ **syn** see EAGER

ago·ge \əˈgōjē, -ōgē, ˌägōˈgā\ *n* -s [Gk *agōgē*, lit., act of carrying away, fr. *agein* to lead — more at AGENT] *Greek music* **:** rate of speed **:** TEMPO

agog·ic \əˈgäjik, -gōgik\ *adj* [G *agogisch*, fr. Gk *agōgē* + G *-isch* -ish] **:** of or relating to agoge or agogics esp. to variations in tempo within a piece or movement ⟨tempos and ~ indications of an operatic score⟩

agogic accent *n* **:** stress secured through relative prolongation of the tones to be emphasized — compare AGOGICS

agog·ics \-iks\ *n pl but usu sing in constr* [G *agogik*, fr. Gk *agōgē* + G *-ik* -ics] **1 :** the musical theory that rhetorical emphasis involves not only dynamic stress but also the emphasis implied in the greater relative length of the tones to be emphasized — compare RUBATO **2 :** the quantitative aspect of musical nuances involving all variations from the rigid basic meter (as of retard, pause, accelerando)

-a·gogue \ə,gäg *also* -ȯg\ *also* **-a·gog** \"\ *n comb form* -s [F & NL; F *-agogue*, fr. LL *-agogus* promoting the expulsion of, fr. Gk *-agōgos*, fr. *agōgos* leading, drawing forth, fr. *agein* to lead; NL *-agogon*, neut. of *-agogos* promoting the expulsion of, fr. Gk *-agōgos* — more at AGENT] **:** substance that promotes the secretion or expulsion of ⟨chol*agogue*⟩ ⟨lymph*agogue*⟩

ago·ho *or* **ago·jo** \əˈgō,hō\ *n* -s [*agoho* fr. Tag *agohó; agojo* fr. PhilSp, fr. Tag *agohó*] **:** HORSETAIL TREE

ag·on \ˈä,gän, äˈgōn, ˈa,ˈgän, ˈā,gän\ *n, pl* **agons** \-nz\ *also* **ago·nes** \äˈgō,nes, əˈgō(,)nēz\ [Gk *agōn*, lit., gathering, assembly, contest — more at AGONY] **:** a struggle or contest: as **a :** a contest in athletics, chariot or horse racing, music, or literature at a public festival in ancient Greece **b :** the dramatic conflict between the chief characters in a Greek play **c :** the struggle between protagonist and antagonist in a literary work ⟨the central ~ of the novel⟩

ag·o·nal \ˈagənᵊl\ *adj* [*agony* + *-al*] **:** of, relating to, or associated with agony, esp. the death agony or period of dying ⟨the ~ state⟩ ⟨~ leukocytosis⟩

ago·ni·a·da \ə,gōnēˈädə, -adə\ *or* **agoniada bark** *n* -s [Pg *agoniada*] **:** the bark of a tropical So. American shrub (*Plumieria lancifolia*) yielding plumieride

ago·ni·a·ti·tes \(ˌ)ā,gōnēəˈtīd·(,)ēz, ə,g-\ *n, cap* [NL, fr. ²*a-* + *Goniatites*] **:** a genus of Devonian ammonoid mollusks (family Goniatitidae)

ag·on·ic \(ˌ)āˈgänik, əˈg-\ *adj* [Gk *agōnos* without angle (fr. *a-* ²a- + *gonia* angle, corner) + E *-ic*] **:** not forming an angle

agonic line *n* **:** an imaginary line on the earth's surface connecting the north and south magnetic poles and passing through those points where there is no magnetic declination and where a freely suspended magnetic needle indicates true north — compare ACLINIC LINE, ISOGONIC LINE

agon·i·dae \əˈgänə,dē\ *n pl, cap* [NL, fr. *Agonus*, type genus + *-idae*] **:** a family of small slender fishes (order Scleroparei) having the body covered with overlapping striated often spiny plates

ag·o·nist \ˈagənəst\ *n* -s [LL *agonista*, fr. Gk *agōnistēs* combatant, fr. *agōnizesthai* to contend, fr. *agōn* gathering, assembly, contest — more at AGONY] **1 :** one that is engaged in a struggle: as **a :** a leading character (as the protagonist) in a literary work ⟨the chief interest of the novel . . . is an analysis of the nature and moods . . . of the four ~*s* —Iris Barry⟩ **b :** one that is beset by intellectual or spiritual conflicts ⟨an ~, a self-tormentor who ran to meet suffering halfway —John Buchan⟩ **2** [back-formation fr. *antagonist* "a muscle"] **:** a muscle that on contracting is automatically checked and controlled by the opposing simultaneous contraction of another muscle — see ANTAGONIST 2a; compare SYNERGIST

ag·o·nis·tic \ˌagəˈnistik\ *also* **ag·o·nis·ti·cal** \-təkəl\ *adj* [LL *agonisticus* of a contest, fr. Gk *agōnistikos* fit for combat, contentious, fr. *agōnistēs* + *-ikos* -ic, -ical] **1 :** of or relating to the athletic contests of ancient Greece ⟨~ inscriptions⟩ **2 :** seeking to overcome in discussion or debate **:** ARGUMENTATIVE ⟨a dialectical and ~ approach to knowledge⟩ **3 :** striving for effect **:** STRAINED ⟨~ poses⟩ — **ag·o·nis·ti·cal·ly** \-tək(ə)lē\ *adv*

ag·o·nize \ˈagə,nīz, ˈaig-\ *vb* -ED/-ING/-S *see -ize in Explan Notes* [MF *agoniser* to be in agony, fr. LL *agonizare*, fr. Gk *agōnizesthai*, fr. *agōnia* agony — more at AGONY] *vt* **:** to cause to suffer agony **:** TORTURE ⟨he *agonized* himself with the thought —Aldous Huxley⟩ ~ *vi* **1 :** to suffer agony or torture **:** be in great pain or anguish ⟨who *agonized* and prayed and yet could not secure release from their guilt —Lillian Smith⟩ **2 :** to try desperately **:** STRUGGLE ⟨strive to do and ~ to do and fail in doing —Robert Browning⟩ **syn** see WRITHE

agonized *adj* **:** characterized by, suffering, or expressing agony ⟨an ~ search⟩ ⟨an ~ father⟩ ⟨an ~ cry⟩ — **ag·o·niz·ed·ly** \-zədlē, -lī\ *adv*

agonizing *adj* **:** causing agony **:** PAINFUL ⟨an ~ reappraisal of the role and the future of the French Empire —D.W.Brogan⟩ — **ag·o·niz·ing·ly** *adv*

ag·o·nos·to·mus \ˌagəˈnästəməs\ *n, cap* [NL, fr. Gk *agōnos* without angle + NL *-stomus*] **:** a genus of tropical freshwater mullets of the East and West Indies and Mexico much used as food

agon·o·thete \əˈgänə,thēt\ *n, pl* **agonothetes** \-ēts\ *or* **ag·o·noth·e·tae** \ˌagəˈnäthə,tē, -,tī\ [LL *agonotheta*, fr. Gk *agōnothetēs*, fr. *agōn* + *-thetēs* (fr. *tithenai* to appoint, make, do) — more at DO] **:** the judge or director of public games in ancient Greece

ag·o·ny \ˈagənē, ˈaig-, -ni\ *n* -ES [ME *agonie*, fr. MF & LL; MF *agonie*, fr. LL *agonia*, fr. Gk *agōnia* contest, struggle, anguish, fr. *agōn* gathering, assembly at games, contest for a prize, fr. *agein* to lead, celebrate — more at AGENT] **1 a :** intense pain of mind or spirit **:** extreme distress **:** ANGUISH ⟨the ~ of being found wanting and exposed to the disapproval of others —Margaret Mead⟩ **b** *often cap* **:** the sufferings of Jesus in the garden of Gethsemane ⟨and being in an ~ he prayed more earnestly —Lk 22:44 (AV)⟩ **2 a :** intense pain of body **:** extreme torment **:** TORTURE ⟨left arm twisted upward behind him . . . in slow, deliberate ~ —Kay Boyle⟩ **b :** the throes of death **:** death struggle ⟨his final ~⟩ **3 :** a violent struggle, conflict, or contest ⟨the world is convulsed by the *agonies* of great nations —T.B.Macaulay⟩ **4 :** a strong sudden and often uncontrollable display (as of joy or delight) **:** OUTBURST ⟨my cousin . . . in an ~ of mirth —Edith Wharton⟩ **syn** see DISTRESS

agony column *n* **:** a newspaper column of personal advertisements relating esp. to lost objects, missing relatives or friends, and marriage separations

agood [¹*a-* + *good* (adj.)] *obs* **:** in earnest **:** HEARTILY

ag·o·ra \ˈagərə\ *n, pl* **agoras** \-rəz\ *or* **ago·rae** \-,rē, -ī\ [Gk, fr. *ageirein* to assemble — more at GREGARIOUS] **:** a gathering place or assembly; *esp* **:** the market place in ancient Greece

ag·o·ra·pho·bia \ˌagərəˈfōbēə\ *n* -s [NL, fr. Gk *agora* + NL *-phobia*] **:** abnormal fear of crossing or of being in the midst of open spaces — contrasted with *claustrophobia* — **ag·o·ra·pho·bic** \ˌ≈≈≈ˈfōbik *also* -äb-\ *adj*

agoua·ra *also* **agua·ra** \ˌagwəˈrä\ *n* -s [Pg *aguara* & Sp *aguará*, fr. Guarani *aguará*] **1 :** any of several So. American wild dogs (genus *Chrysocyon*) **2 :** CRAB-EATING RACCOON

¹**agou·ti** *also* **agou·ty** \əˈgüd·ē, -ütē, -i\ *n, pl* **agoutis** *also* **agouties** [F *agouti*, fr. Sp *agutí*, fr. Guarani *acutí, agutí*] **1 :** a rodent of the genera *Dasyprocta* and *Myoprocta* being about the size of a rabbit and brownish or grizzled in color and peculiar to So. and Central America and the West Indies **2 a :** a grizzled color of the fur or hair of many rodents (as wild guinea pigs, rats, mice, and squirrels) consisting of the barring of each hair in several alternate dark and light bands blackish blue or brown at the base and yellowish at the tip **b :** an agouti-coated animal

²**agouti** \"\ *adj* **:** characterized by or bearing the color agouti

ag·pa·ite \ˈagpə,īt\ *n* -s [*Agpa*, locality in southern Greenland + E *-ite*] **:** any of a group of feldspathoid rocks (as naujaites, lujauvrites, or kakortokites) from Ilimausak, Greenland, which differ from normal nephelite-syenites in having alumina in excess of the alkalies — **ag·pa·it·ic** \ˌ≈≈ˈid·ik\ *adj*

agr *abbr* agriculture

¹**agra** \əˈgrȯ\ *n* -s [IrGael *a grādh*, fr. *a* oh + *grādh* love, fr. MIr *grād*; akin to L *gratus* beloved, dear — more at GRACE] *Irish* **:** my dear **:** SWEETHEART

²**agra** \ˈägrə\ *adj, usu cap* [fr. *Agra*, India] **:** of or from the city of Agra, India **:** of the kind or style prevalent in Agra

³**agra** \"\ *n* -s *usu cap* [fr *Agra*, India, where it is made] **:** a carpet usu. distinguished by thick pile and heavy knotting

-ag·ra \ˈagrə, ˈaig- *sometimes* ˈäg-\ *n comb form, pl* **-ag·rae** \-,grē\ *also* **-agras** [ME, fr. L, fr. Gk, fr. *agra* hunting, catch; akin to W *aer* war, L *agere* to drive — more at AGENT] **:** seizure of pain ⟨cardi*agra*⟩ ⟨mel*agra*⟩

agrafe *or* **agraffe** \əˈgraf\ *n* -s [F *agrafe*, fr. *agrafer* to hook, fasten, fr. MF, fr. *a-* (fr. L *ad-*) + *grafer* to hook, fr. *grafe* hook, fr. OHG *krāpfo*; akin to OHG *krampfo* hook — more at CRAMP] **1 :** a hook-and-loop fastening; *esp* **:** an ornamental clasp used on armor or costumes ⟨an ~ set with pearls⟩ **2 :** a hook, eyelet, or other device by which a piano wire is so held as to prevent the section between the pin and the bridge from vibrating **3 a :** a cramp used in building to hold stones together **b :** relief sculpture put upon the head of an arch **4 :** the iron clamp used to secure the cork in a champagne bottle or the closure in any jug, bottle, or carboy

agrafe 1

agra gauze \ˈägrə-\ *n, usu cap A* [fr. *Agra*, India, where it was made] **:** a silk gauze with stiff finish used for trimming

agram·ma·tism \(ˈ)āˈgramə,tizəm\ *n* -s [ISV *agrammat-* (fr. Gk *agrammatos* illiterate, fr. *a-* ²a- + *grammat-, gramma* letter) + *-ism*; orig. formed as G *agrammatismus* — more at GRAMMAR] **:** the pathologic inability to use words in grammatical sequence

agran·u·lo·cyte \(ˈ)āˈgranyəlō,sīt\ *n* -s [ISV ²*a-* + *granulo-* + *-cyte*] **:** a leukocyte without cytoplasmic granules **:** a lymphocyte or monocyte — compare GRANULOCYTE

agran·u·lo·cyt·ic angina \ˌ≈,≈≈≈ˈsid·ik\ *n* **:** GRANULOCYTOPENIA

agranulocytosis \ˌ≈,≈≈≈,sīˈtōsəs\ *n, pl* **agranulocyto·ses** \-ō,sēz\ [NL, fr. ²*a-* + E *granulocyte* + NL *-osis*] **1 :** GRANULOCYTOPENIA **2** *Brit* **:** PANLEUCOPENIA

ag·ra·pha \ˈagrəfə\ *n pl* [Gk, neut. pl. of *agraphos* unwritten, fr. *a-* ²a- + *-graphos* (fr. *graphein* to write) — more at CARVE] **:** sayings of Jesus unrecorded in the canonical gospels but found in other parts of the New Testament or in early Christian writings

agraph·ia \(ˈ)āˈgrafēə\ *n* -s [NL, fr. ²*a-* + *-graphia* -graphy] **:** the pathologic loss of the ability to write — **agraph·ic** \(ˈ)āˈgrafik\ *adj*

¹**agrar·i·an** \əˈgrerēən, -ra(a)r-, -rār-\ *adj* [L *agrarius* (fr. *agr-*, *ager* field + *-arius* -ary) + E *-an* — more at ACRE] **1 :** of or relating to the land or landed property ⟨a policy of ~ redistribution was sketched out —G.A.Craig⟩ **2 a :** of, by, or characteristic of the farmer or his way of life ⟨the application of ~ virtues to . . . industrial economy —Lloyd Morris⟩ **b :** organized or designed to promote agricultural interests ⟨an ~ party drawing its original impulse from the grain growers and dairymen —H.R.Penniman⟩ **3 :** growing wild in fields **:** CAMPESTRAL — **agrarianly** *adv*

²**agrarian** \"\ *n* -s *often cap* **:** one who favors agrarianism; *esp* **:** a member of an agrarian party or movement

agrar·i·an·ism \-,nizəm\ *n* -s **1 a :** the doctrine of an equal division or equitable redistribution of landed property **b :** a social or political movement designed to bring about land reforms or to improve the economic status of the farmer **2 :** the way of life associated with a farm economy and country towns in contrast to that associated with an industrial economy

agré·a·tion \ˌagrāäsyōⁿ\ *n* -s [F, lit., approval, fr. *agréer* to agree + *-ation*] **:** a diplomatic procedure by which a state determines in advance whether a proposed envoy will be acceptable to the receiving state — compare AGRÉMENT

agree \əˈgrē\ *vb* **agreed; agreed; agreeing; agrees** [ME *agreen*, fr. MF *agreer*, fr. *a-* (fr. L *ad-*) + *gré* will, pleasure, fr. L *gratum*, neut. of *gratus* beloved, dear, agreeable — more at GRACE] *vt* **1 a :** to concur in (as an opinion) **:** ADMIT ⟨all *agreed* that he was a man of stature⟩ **b :** to indicate willingness **:** CONSENT ⟨~ to abide by the interpretation of the court —M.R.Cohen⟩ **2** *chiefly Brit* **a :** to settle upon by arrangement **:** ARRANGE ⟨the following articles were *agreed* —Sir Winston Churchill⟩ **b :** to bring into settlement ⟨they have *agreed* their quarrel⟩ ~ *vi* **1 :** to give assent **:** express approval **:** ACCEDE — usu. used with *to* or *with* and sometimes with *in* ⟨~ to a plan⟩ ⟨~ with an opinion⟩ ⟨I ~ . . . in . . . what you say —Benjamin Jowett⟩ **2 a :** to achieve harmony (as of opinion, feeling, or purpose) **:** become of one mind ⟨no two of his admirers would . . . ~ in their selection of characteristic passages —Bliss Perry⟩ ⟨~ with classical antiquity in deeming a figure of speech to be worth frequent use —C.E. Montague⟩ **b :** to live or act together harmoniously **:** get along together ⟨the two managed to ~ fairly well and the next month passed very pleasantly —Elinor Wylie⟩ **c :** to reach a harmonious understanding **:** come to terms — usu. used with *on* or *upon* ⟨~ on a fair division of the profits⟩ ⟨the means of settling the dispute were finally *agreed* upon⟩ **3 a :** to be similar **:** CORRESPOND — used with *with* ⟨the photographs ~ exactly with the originals⟩ **b :** to resemble one another **:** correspond to each other ⟨the accounts of the wreck did not ~⟩ **c :** to be consistent or consonant **:** HARMONIZE — used with *with* ⟨popular poetry . . . *agreed* with the favorite fiction . . . in attitude —J.D.Hart⟩ **4 a** *obs* **:** to react suitably, pleasingly, or healthfully — used with *with* ⟨your appetites and your digestions do not ~ with it —Shak.⟩ **b :** to be fitting, pleasing, or healthful **:** SUIT — used with *with* ⟨a dry climate will ~ with the patient⟩ ⟨onions don't ~ with everyone⟩ **5 :** to have an inflectional form denoting either identity or some regular correspondence other than identity in such grammatical categories as gender, number, case, or person ⟨the German verb ~*s* with its subject in person and number⟩ ⟨the Latin adjective ~*s* with its noun in gender, number, and case⟩ ⟨in classical Greek a verb in the third person singular ~*s* with a neuter plural subject⟩

syn CONCUR, COINCIDE: AGREE suggests an accord, harmony, or compatibility arrived at by a settling of differences, as in the making of a truce, or by acquiescence where there was or might have been opposition or contention ⟨*agree* upon a price⟩ ⟨I will presume that Mr. Murry and myself can *agree* that for our purposes these counters are adequate —T.S.Eliot⟩ CONCUR suggests a thinking, acting, or functioning cooperatively or harmoniously toward a given end or for a given purpose ⟨for the creation of a masterwork of literature two powers must *concur*, the power of the man and the power of the moment —Matthew Arnold⟩ ⟨all those who have been concerned in the administration of our finances have *concurred* in representing its importance or necessity —John Marshall⟩ COINCIDE emphasizes the identity or precise accord of nature, function, opinion, or attitude in much the same way that, applied to historical events, it signifies their occurrence at precisely the same time or place. It is infrequently used of persons ⟨private groups whose interests did not *coincide* with national defense —T.W.Arnold⟩ ⟨the hearty tones natural when the words demanded by politeness *coincide* with those of deep feeling —Thomas Hardy⟩

syn TALLY, SQUARE, CONFORM, CORRESPOND, HARMONIZE, ACCORD, JIBE: AGREE is a general term indicating a going, fitting, or matching together without significant difference, contradiction, or conflict ⟨in general, the two accounts *agree*⟩ ⟨their findings *agree* with his⟩ TALLY suggests an agreement like that between two correct sets of accounts or records matching in both itemized details and overall conclusions ⟨one thing must match another or representation must *tally* with thing represented, like items in a tradesman's account —R.M. Weaver⟩ SQUARE suggests an exact agreeing, as if one item could perfectly fit with the form or shape of another ⟨these two assertions *square* with orthodox tradition —T.S.Omond⟩ ⟨the facts of history exist; but they hardly trouble us. We select and interpret our documents till they *square* with our theories —Aldous Huxley⟩ CONFORM suggests an essential agreement in form or in action, nature, or import making differences or deviations unimportant ⟨a widely diffused popular story of a fairy wife or husband which *conforms* to the type known as the Swan Maiden, or Beauty and the Beast, or Cupid and Psyche —J.G.Frazer⟩ ⟨and since theology was philosophy's queen, medieval philosophy *conformed* to that system which Augustine employed in his theology —H.O.Taylor⟩ CORRESPOND may be used to indicate the matching of far-apart or dissimilar things in falling into the same category or in being analogous, as well as to apply to closely similar items ⟨remind ourselves that ideas and images and thoughts are merely the objects that *correspond* to certain impulses and conations of our own —Samuel Alexander⟩ ⟨conjurers, who *correspond* to the Siberian shamans, affect the usual mystery of the priestly craft —Edward Clodd⟩ HARMONIZE suggests a matching, juxtaposing, or combining agreeably or pleasurably without jarring or grating ⟨the advantage of the Ptolemaic scheme, complicated though it was, was that it *harmonized* fairly well with the observable phenomena of the heavens —G.C.Sellery⟩ ⟨such mortal impulses were so very difficult to *harmonize* with the eternal beatitude which consisted in the cognition and love of God —H.O.Taylor⟩ ACCORD suggests a general compatibility, a capacity for fitting, matching, or accompanying without friction, discord, difficulty ⟨the common doctrine of liberty *accorded* with the passions released by the Revolution —V.L. Parrington⟩ ⟨the splendid moving ritual, with a Queen who so perfectly *accorded* with its spirit, lifted the people of Britain out of their normal selves —*Britain Today*⟩ JIBE is more colloquial than the preceding; it suggests matching, fitting, or accord without serious difficulty or contradiction ⟨that the attempts at "reconciliation" were futile, that common sense and science simply wouldn't *jibe*, was not Mill's fault —Gail Kennedy⟩ **syn** see in addition ASSENT

agree·a·bil·i·ty \ə,grēəˈbiləd·ē, -ətē, -i\ *n* -ES **:** the quality or state of being agreeable

¹**agree·a·ble** \əˈgrēəbəl\ *adj* [ME *agreable*, fr. MF, fr. *agreer* + *-able*] **1 a :** pleasing to the mind or senses **:** to one's liking **:** PLEASANT ⟨an ~ manner⟩ ⟨an ~ garden⟩ ⟨~ people⟩ ⟨an occupation ~ to his tastes⟩ **b** *of an odor* **:** FRAGRANT **2 :** ready or willing to agree or consent **:** favorably disposed ⟨~ to the plan⟩ **3 :** in harmony or keeping **:** CONSISTENT, CONSONANT ⟨the theory . . . was ~ to the general evolutionary conceptions of the period —S.F.Mason⟩ **syn** see PLEASANT

²**agreeable** \"\ *n* -s **:** an agreeable person or thing — usu. used in pl. ⟨superficial advantages and outside ~*s* —S.T.Coleridge⟩

agree·a·ble·ness *n* -ES **:** AGREEABILITY

agreeable to *prep* **:** in accordance with the requirements of **:** as provided by **:** according to ⟨chose officers *agreeable to* the laws of that province —*Amer. Guide Series: Vt.*⟩

agree·a·bly \-blē, -li\ *adv* [ME *agreablely, agreably*, fr. *agreable* + *-ly*] **1 :** in an agreeable manner **:** PLEASANTLY **2** *obs* **:** in the same way **:** SIMILARLY

agreeably to *prep* **:** in conformity with **:** as provided by **:** according to ⟨disobedience of orders in not attacking the enemy . . . *agreeably to* repeated instructions —H.E.Scudder⟩

agreed *past of* AGREE

agreed case *n* **:** CASE STATED

agreed rate *n* **:** an esp. low rate granted by a carrier to a shipper in return for the allocation of a high proportion of the shipper's freight to that carrier

agreed valuation *n* **:** the value of articles or shipments agreed upon by shipper and carrier in order to obtain a specific rating or limited liability — compare RELEASED VALUATION

agreed weight *n* **:** the weight per package or unit agreed upon by shipper and carrier to avoid weighing each package or unit

agreeing *pres part of* AGREE

agreeingly *adv* **:** in an agreeing manner

agree·ment \əˈgrēmənt\ *n* -s [ME *agrement*, fr. MF, fr. *agreer* to please, agree + *-ment* — more at AGREE] **1 a :** the act of agreeing or coming to a mutual arrangement ⟨never any solemn ~ amongst themselves —John Locke⟩ **b :** oneness of opinion, feeling, or purpose **:** harmonious understanding **:** CONCORD ⟨with which religious tradition . . . must come to some sort of ~ —W.R.Inge⟩ **c :** the state of agreeing or being in accord **:** HARMONY, CORRESPONDENCE ⟨~ between the measured ionospheric data and the indications of practical communication experience —*London Calling*⟩ **2 a :** an arrangement (as between two or more parties) as to a course of action ⟨entered into an ~ . . . to assist in planting a colony —R.J.Stanley⟩ **b :** a compact entered into by two or more persons or heads of nations **:** COVENANT, TREATY **3 a :** a contract duly executed and legally binding on the parties entering into it — see CONTRACT, MEETING OF THE MINDS **b :** the written or oral phraseology embodying reciprocal promises **c :** the written instrument that is the evidence of an agreement **4 :** the fact of agreeing grammatically ⟨the ~ of the English personal pronoun with its antecedent in gender and number⟩

agrees *pres 3d sing of* AGREE

agré·ga·tion \ˌagrāgäsyōⁿ\ *n, pl* **agrégations** \"\ *n* -s [F, lit., admittance, fr. ML *aggregation-, aggregatio* act of collecting, fr. L *aggregatus* (past part. of *aggregare*) + *-ion-, -io* -ion] **:** a competitive examination given at French universities which must be passed for admission to the rank of agrégé

agré·gé \ˌagrāzhā, -rezhā\ *n, pl* **agrégés** \"\ [F, fr. past part. of *agréger* to admit (influenced in meaning by *agrégation*), fr. L *aggregare* to add to — more at AGGREGATE] **:** an academic rank conferred by a French university on one who has passed a rigidly competitive examination and who is therefore entitled to appointment to the highest teaching post in a lycée or in one of the faculties of a university

agré·mens \ˌagrāmäⁿ\ *or* **agré·ments** *n pl* [F *agréments* (formerly also spelled *agrémens*), pl. of *agrément* pleasure, ornament, agreement, approval — more at AGREEMENT] **:** AMENITIES ⟨the ~ of social life⟩

agré·ment \ˌagrāmäⁿ\ *n, pl* **agréments** \"\ [F] **1 :** GRACE NOTE, ORNAMENT **2 :** the approval of a diplomatic representative by the state to which he is to be accredited — compare AGRÉATION

agres·tal \əˈgrestᵊl\ *or* **agres·tial** \-es(h)chəl\ *adj* [L *agrestis* (fr. *agr-, ager* field) + E *-al*] **:** dwelling or growing wild in the fields **:** WILD

agres·tic \-stik\ *adj* [L *agrestis* + E *-ic*] **:** of or relating to the fields or country **:** RUSTIC

ag·ri·business \ˈagrə, ˈaigrə+,-\ *n* [blend of *agriculture* and *business*] **:** a combination of the producing operations of a farm, the manufacture and distribution of farm equipment and supplies, and the processing, storage, and distribution of farm commodities

ag·ri·cere \ˈagrə,si(ə)r\ *n* -s [L *agri* (gen. of *ager* field) + *-cere* (fr. *cera* wax) — more at ACRE, CERE] **:** a waxy or resinous coating of organic matter on soil particles

agric·o·lite \əˈgrikə,līt\ *n* -s [G *agricolit*, fr. Georgius *Agricola* (Georg Bauer) †1555 Ger. mineralogist + G *-it* -ite] **:** monoclinic bismuth silicate **:** EULYTITE

ag·ri·cul·tur·al \ˌagrəˈkəlch(ə)rəl, ˌaig-\ *adj* **1 a :** of, relating to, or used in agriculture ⟨~ production⟩ ⟨~ equipment⟩ **b :** characterized by or engaged in farming as the chief occupation ⟨an ~ community⟩ **c :** founded or designed to promote the interest or study of agriculture ⟨an ~ college⟩ ⟨an ~ magazine⟩ **2 :** of or having the characteristics of the farmer or his way of life ⟨the ~ life⟩ — **ag·ri·cul·tur·al·ly** \-rəlē, -li\ *adv*

agricultural agent *n* **1** : COUNTY AGENT **2** : an expert employed by a business organization (as a railroad) to promote agriculture in its trade territory

agricultural ant *n* [so called fr. its habit of clearing away all plants about its nest except those which provide its food] : HARVESTER ANT

agricultural dance *n* : a solo or group dance sometimes with mime of planting and harvesting that is related to the maturing of cultivated food plants and found in primitive cultures

agricultural economics *n* : the scientific study of methods, practices, conditions, and policies affecting agriculture

agricultural engineer *n* : an engineer specializing in agricultural engineering

agricultural engineering *n* : the branch of engineering that deals with the design of farm machinery, the location and planning of farm structures, farm drainage, soil management and erosion control, water supply and irrigation, rural electrification, and the processing of farm products

agricultural geology *n* : the branch of geology that deals with the character and origin of soils, the occurrence of mineral fertilizers, and the behavior of underground water

agricultural lien *n* : a lien securing a loan made esp. on the strength of growing crops

agricultural meteorology *n* : the branch of meteorology that deals with the relationship of weather and climate to crop and livestock production and soil management

agricultural paper *n* : negotiable paper created in granting loans for agricultural purposes

ag·ri·cul·ture \ˈagrə,kəlchə(r), ˈaig- *also* ,==ˈ==\ *n* -s [F, fr. L *agricultura*, fr. *agri* (gen. of *ager* field) + *cultura* cultivation — more at ACRE, CULTURE] **1 a** : the science or art of cultivating the soil, harvesting crops, and raising livestock : HUSBANDRY, FARMING **b** : the science or art of the production of plants and animals useful to man and in varying degrees the preparation of these products for man's use and their disposal (as by marketing) **2** : FARMERS

ag·ri·cul·tur·ist \,==ˈ=ch(ə)rəst\ *or* **ag·ri·cul·tur·al·ist** \,==ˈ=ch(ə)rələst\ *n* -s **1** : one trained in the theory or science of agriculture **2** : FARMER, HUSBANDMAN

ag·ri·lus \ˈagrələs\ *n, cap* [NL] : a genus of slender beetles (family Buprestidae) having larvae that bore in or girdle twigs and wood and the stems of semiwoody plants

ag·ri·mo·nia \,agrəˈmōnēə, -nyə\ *n* [NL, fr. L, agrimony] **1** *cap* : a genus of herbs (family Rosaceae) found chiefly in north temperate regions that have pinnately compound leaves, yellow flowers, and bristly fruits **2** -s : a plant of the genus *Agrimonia*

ag·ri·mo·ny \ˈagrə,mōnē\ *n* -ES [ME *egrimoigne, agrimonie*, fr. MF & L; MF *aigremoine*, fr. L *agrimonia*, alter. of *argemonia*, fr. Gk *argemōnē, argemōnia*, a plant (prob. *Papaver argemone*), prob. fr. Heb *argāmān* red purple] : any of various plants: as **a** : a plant of the genus *Agrimonia* **b** : a plant of the genus *Bidens* **c** : HEMP AGRIMONY

ag·ri·mo·tor \ˈagrə,mōd·ə(r)\ *n* -s [*agricultural* + *motor*] : an agricultural tractor

agrin \əˈ-\ *adj* [ˡ*a-* + *grin* (v.)] : GRINNING ⟨his face all ~⟩

agrio- *comb form* [Gk & NL; NL, fr. Gk, fr. *agrios*, fr. *agros* field — more at ACRE] : wild ⟨*agriology*⟩

ag·ri·o·choe·rus \,agrēōˈkirəs\ *n, cap* [NL, fr. *agrio-* + *-choerus*] : a genus (the type of the large family Agriochoeridae) of extinct Oligocene ungulates resembling pigs but with teeth like those of camels

ag·ri·o·ecol·o·gy \ˈagrē(,)ō-\ *or* **ag·ro·ecol·o·gy** \,agrō-\ *n* -ES [*agrio-* or *agro-* + *ecology*] : the ecology of cultivated plants esp. with respect to the relation of varietal characteristics to environmental adjustment and adaptation

ag·ri·o·li·max \,agrēˈōlī,maks\ *n, cap* [NL, fr. *agrio-* + L *limax* snail] : a genus of slugs (family Limacidae) including a common garden pest (*A. agrestis*) and several forms that serve as intermediate hosts for worm parasites of vertebrates

ag·ri·ol·o·gy \,agrēˈäləjē\ *n* -ES [*agrio-* + *-logy*] : the comparative study of the customs of nonliterate peoples

ag·ri·on·i·dae \,agrēˈänə,dē\ *n pl, cap* [NL, fr. *Agrion*, type genus (fr. Gk, neut. of *agrios* wild) + *-idae*] : a family of slender-bodied usu. brilliantly colored damselflies

agri·o·tes \əˈgrīə,tēz\ *n, cap* [NL, fr. Gk *agriotēs* wildness, fr. *agrios* wild] : a large cosmopolitan genus of beetles (family Elateridae) including several with larvae that are serious pests of the roots of crop plants — compare WIREWORM

ag·ri·o·type \ˈagrēə,tīp\ *n* -s [*agrio-* + *type*] : a wild form regarded as ancestral to a domesticated one ⟨an ~ of the domestic cat⟩

agrise *vt* -ED/-ING/-S [ME *agrisen*, fr. OE *āgrīsan* to shudder, fr. *ā-* (perfective prefix) + *-grīsan* — more at ABEAR, GRISLY] *obs* : TERRIFY, AFFRIGHT

agrito *var of* AGARITA

agrl *abbr* agricultural

agro- *comb form* [F, fr. Gk, fr. *agros* field — more at ACRE] **1** : of or belonging to fields or soil : agricultural ⟨*agronomy*⟩ ⟨*agrosterol*⟩ **2** : agricultural and ⟨*agroindustrial*⟩

ag·ro-anal·o·gous \ˈa(,)grō+\ *adj* [*agro-* + *analogous*] : having a similar climate and a suitability for similar crops

ag·ro·bac·te·ri·um \,agrō,bakˈtirēəm\ *n, cap* [NL, fr. *agro-* + *bacterium*] : a genus of small usu. gram-negative and motile bacterial rods (family Rhizobiaceae) including soil forms that vigorously reduce nitrates and several pathogens of cultivated plants that typically cause galls on stems — compare CROWN GALL

ag·ro·bi·o·log·ic \ˈa(,)grō,=ˈ==\ *or* **ag·ro·bi·o·log·i·cal** *adj* : of or relating to agrobiology — **ag·ro·bi·o·log·i·cal·ly** *adv*

ag·ro·bi·ol·o·gist \ˈa(,)grō-\ *n* -s : a specialist in agrobiology

ag·ro·bi·ol·o·gy \ˈa(,)grō-\ *n* -ES [*agro-* + *biology*] : the study of plant nutrition and growth and crop production in relation to soil management

ag·ro-city \ˈa(,)grō,-\ *n* [part trans. of Russ *agrogorod* — more at AGROGOROD] : AGRO-TOWN

ag·ro·cli·mat·ic \ˈa(,)grō,=ˈ==\ *adj* [*agro-* + *climatic*] **1** : of or relating to the relationship between crop adaptation and climate ⟨~ studies⟩ **2** : characterized by similar agroclimatic status ⟨~ analogues in the New and Old Worlds⟩

ag·ro·cli·ma·to·log·i·cal \ˈa(,)=,===ˈ===\ *adj* : of or relating to agroclimatology

ag·ro·cli·ma·tol·o·gy \ˈa(,)=-\ *n* -ES [*agro-* + *climatology*] : the branch of climatology concerned esp. with agroclimatic factors and effects

ag·ro·eco·type \ˈa(,)grōˈekə,tīp\ *n* [blend of *agrotype* and *ecology*] : a crop-plant type adapted to a particular environment

ag·ro·ge·o·log·i·cal \ˈa(,)grō,==ˈ==\ *adj* : of or relating to agrogeology — **ag·ro·ge·o·log·i·cal·ly** *adv*

ag·ro·ge·ol·o·gist \ˈa(,)grō-\ *n* -s : one trained in the structure, origin, and uses of soil

ag·ro·ge·ol·o·gy \ˈa(,)grō-\ *n* -ES [*agro-* + *geology*] : AGRICULTURAL GEOLOGY

ag·ro·go·rod \,agrōˈgȯrəd\ *n* -s [Russ, fr. *agro-* agro- + *gorod* city, town] : a group of amalgamated collective farms in the U.S.S.R.

ag·ro·log·ic \ˈagrəˈläjik\ *or* **ag·ro·log·i·cal** \-jəkəl\ *adj* : of or relating to agrology — **ag·ro·log·i·cal·ly** \-jək(ə)lē\ *adv*

agrol·o·gist \əˈgräləjəst, aˈ-\ *n* -s : a specialist in agrology

agrol·o·gy \-əjē\ *n* -ES [ISV *agro-* + *-logy*; orig. formed as F *agrologie*] : the branch of agriculture that deals with the origin, structure, analysis, and classification of soils esp. in their relation to crop production

ag·ro·me·te·o·rol·o·gy \ˈa(,)grō-\ *n* -ES [*agro-* + *meteorology*] : AGRICULTURAL METEOROLOGY

ag·ro·my·za \,agrōˈmīzə\ *n, cap* [NL, fr. *agro-* + *-myza*] : the type genus of Agromyzidae including economically important leaf miners and certain flies that cause galls on wild and cultivated plants — see BEAN FLY

ag·ro·my·zid \ˈagrōˈmīzəd\ *adj* [NL *Agromyzidae*] : of or relating to the Agromyzidae

ag·ro·my·zi·dae \,agrōˈmīzə,dē, -miz-\ *n pl, cap* [NL, fr. *Agromyza*, type genus + *-idae*] : a family of small or minute acalyptrate two-winged flies having phytophagous larvae many of which are leaf miners on cultivated plants

ag·ro·nom·ic \ˈagrəˈnämik\ *or* **ag·ro·nom·i·cal** \-məkəl\ *adj* [*agronomy* + *-ic, -ical*] : of, relating to, or designed to promote agronomy

agron·o·mist \əˈgränəməst, aˈ-\ *n* -s : a specialist in agronomy

agron·o·my \-əmē, -mi\ *n* -ES [prob. fr. F *agronomie*, fr. *agro-* + *-nomie* -nomy] : the branch of agriculture that deals with field-crop production and soil management

ag·ro·py·ron \,agrōˈpī,rän\ *also* **ag·ro·py·rum** \-,rəm\ *n, cap* [NL, fr. *agro-* + *-pyron*, *-pyrum* (fr. Gk *pyros* wheat) — more at FURZE] : a widely distributed genus of chiefly perennial grasses with erect spikes of usu. solitary several-flowered sessile spikelets — see COUCH GRASS

ag·ro·stem·ma \,agrōˈstemə\ *n, cap* [NL, fr. *agro-* + Gk *stemma* wreath, garland — more at STEMMA] : a genus of herbs (family Caryophyllaceae) with calyx lobes that are leaflike and extend far beyond the petals

agros·tis \əˈgrästəs\ *n, cap* [NL, fr. L, couch grass, fr. Gk *agrōstis*, a grass] : a large and widely distributed genus of grasses having an open or contracted panicle with small one-flowered spikelets and including important pasture, hay, and lawn grasses — see BENT 2d, REDTOP

ag·ros·tog·ra·pher \,agrəˈstägrəfə(r), ,a,gräˈ-, ə,gräˈ-\ *n* -s [*agrostography* + *-er*] : a specialist in agrostography

agros·to·graph·ic \əˈgrästəˈgrafik\ *or* **agros·to·graph·i·cal** \-əkəl\ *adj* [*agrostography* + *-ic, -ical*] : of or relating to agrostography

ag·ros·tog·ra·phy \,agrəˈstägrəfē, ,a,gräˈ-, ə,gräˈ-\ *n* -ES [Gk *agrōstis* + E *-o-* + *-graphy*] : a description of the grasses

agros·to·log·ic \əˈgrästəˈläjik\ *or* **agros·to·log·i·cal** \-əkəl\ *adj* : of or relating to agrostology

ag·ros·tol·o·gist \,agrəˈstäləjəst, ,a,gräˈ-, ə,gräˈ-\ *n* -s : a specialist in agrostology

ag·ros·tol·o·gy \-ləjē\ *n* -ES [Gk *agrōstis* + E *-o-* + *-logy*] : the branch of systematic botany that deals with the grasses

ag·ro·tech·ny \ˈagrō,teknē\ *n* -ES [*agro-* + *-techny*] : the branch of agriculture that deals with the conversion of agricultural products into manufactured articles on or close to the farm

agrot·i·dae \əˈgräd·ə,dē\ [NL, fr. ²*Agrotid-, Agrotis*, type genus] *syn of* NOCTUIDAE

ˡ**agro·tis** \əˈgrōd·əs\ [NL, fr. Gk *agrotēs* wild, fr. *agros* field — more at ACRE] *syn of* EUXOA

²**agrotis** \"\ [NL] *syn of* NOCTUA

ag·ro-town \ˈa(,)grō,-\ *n* [part trans. of Russ *agrogorod* — more at AGROGOROD] : a group of collective farms in the U.S.S.R. that operate as a unit

ag·ro·type \ˈagrō,tīp\ *n* -s [*agro-* + *type*] **1** : any of various soils used in agriculture **2** : a cultivar esp. of an agricultural field crop

aground \əˈ-\ *adv (or adj)* [ME, fr. ˡ*a-* + *ground*] **1** : in or into a stranded condition esp. with the bottom lodged on the ground or on the shore ⟨ran his boat ~⟩ **2** : on the ground ⟨enemy air power aloft and ~ —G.R.Wilson⟩

agryp·nia \əˈgripnēə, aˈ-\ *n, pl* **agrypni·ai** \-ē,ī\ [LGk, fr. Gk, sleeplessness, time of watching, fr. *agrypnos* wakeful, sleepless + *-ia*] : a vigil before certain feasts (as Easter) in the Eastern Church

agst *abbr* against

agt *abbr* **1** agent **2** agent **3** agreement

ag·ter \ˈäktə(r)\ *var of* ACHTER

agua \ˈägwə\ *or* **agua toad** *n* -s [AmerSp *agua*, prob. fr. Tupi] : the largest known toad (*Bufo marinus*) reaching a length of eight inches and being native to Central America but introduced into Argentina, Hawaii, and the West Indies where its voracious habits make it a valuable destroyer of insect pests

agua·ca·te \,ägwəˈkäd·ē\ *n* -s [Sp — more at AVOCADO] : AVOCADO

agua·ca·tec \əˈgwäkə,tek\ *n, pl* **aguacatec** *or* **aguacatecs** *usu cap* [Sp *aguacateca*, of AmerInd origin] **1 a** : an Indian people living in the region of Aguacatan, Guatemala **b** : a member of such people **2** : the Mayan language of the Aguacatec people

agua·ji \ˈägwəˈhē\ *n, pl* **aguaji** [Sp *aguají*, prob. fr. Taino] : any of several marine fishes (as the black grouper, the gag, or the rock hind) of the warmer parts of the western Atlantic

agua·miel \ˈägwəmˈyel\ *n* -s [MexSp, fr. Sp, honey water, fr. *agua* water (fr. L *aqua*) + *miel* honey, fr. L *mel* — more at ISLAND, MELLIFLUOUS] : the unfermented freshly gathered juice of any of several Mexican plants of the genus *Agave* that becomes pulque when fermented

ˡ**agua·no** \əˈgwä(,)nō\ *n, pl* **aguano** *or* **aguanos** *usu cap* [Sp, of AmerInd origin] **1 a** : an Indian people of Brazil **b** : a member of such people **2** : the language of the Aguano people

²**aguano** \"\ *n* -s [Pg] : a mahogany (*Swietenia macrophylla*)

aguara *var of* AGOUARA

aguar·di·en·te \ˈä,gwärdēˈentē, -dˈyen(,)tā\ *also* **aguar·dien·te** \ˈä,kw-\ *n* -s [Sp *aguardiente*, fr. *agua* water + *ardiente* burning, fr. L *ardent-, ardens*, pres. part. of *ardēre* to burn — more at ARDOR] : any of several distilled alcoholic beverages: as **a** : a coarse brandy made in Spain and Portugal **b** : a liquor that is usu. made from sugarcane and is common in So. America, Central America, and the southwestern U.S.

agua·ru·na \ˈä,gwəˈrünə\ *n, pl* **aguaruna** *or* **aguarunas** *usu cap* [Sp, of AmerInd origin] **1 a** : an Indian people of Peru **b** : a member of such people **2** : the Jivaroan language of the Aguaruna people

ˡ**ague** \ˈā(,)gyü, *chiefly dial or old-fash* ˈāgə(r); ˈāg *by many to whom it is only a book word*\ *n* -s [ME, fr. MF *ague* (trans. of ML *acuta*, short for *febris acuta*, lit., sharp fever), fr. fem. of *agu* sharp, fr. L *acutus* — more at ACUTE] **1** : a fever of malarial character marked by paroxysms of chills, fever, and sweating that recur at regular intervals **2** : a fit or spell of shaking or shivering (as with cold) : CHILL ⟨people shaking with the ~ of the terrorized —W.L.Sullivan⟩

²**ague** \"\ *vt* -ED/-ING/-S : to affect with or as if with ague

ague bark *n* : HOP TREE

ague cake *n* : the enlarged hard spleen of chronic malaria

ague drop *n* : FOWLER'S SOLUTION

ague grass *or* **ague root** *n* : a colicroot (*Aletris farinosa*) with a scurfy or granuliferous perianth

ague tree *n* : SASSAFRAS

ague·weed \ˈā(,)gyü,wēd\ *n* **1** : BONESET **1** **2** : FIVE-FLOWERED GENTIAN

agui·lar·ite \,ägəˈlä,rīt\ *n* -s [P. *Aguilar fl* 1892 Mexican mine superintendent + E *-ite*] : a mineral consisting of silver selenide-sulfide Ag_4SeS (hardness 2, sp. gr. 7.59)

aguilawood *var of* AGILAWOOD

agui·nal·do \,ägəˈnäl(,)dō\ *n* -s [Sp (also, gift given on festive occasions, esp. Christmas and New Year's Day), alter. of earlier *aguilando, aguinando*, perh. fr. L *hoc in anno* in this year (a phrase common in the refrain of old popular songs sung on New Year's Day)] **1** : any of several ornamental plants of the morning-glory family native to Puerto Rico **2** : a Spanish-American Christmas carol

aguise *vt* -ED/-ING/-S [ˡ*a-* + *guise* (v.)] *obs* : DRESS, ARRAY

agu·ish \ˈāgyəwish, ˈā(,)gyüish\ *adj* [ˡ*ague* + *-ish*] **1** : productive of, subject to, or resulting from ague ⟨an ~ climate⟩ ⟨an ~ man⟩ ⟨~ pains⟩ **2** : somewhat chilly or quivering : SHAKY ⟨one candle with a small ~ beam shaking in the cold —Edith Sitwell⟩ — **agu·ish·ly** *adv*

agu·nah \,ägüˈnä, äˈgünə\ *n* -s [Heb *ʽăghūnāh* prevented, restrained (from remarrying)] *Jewish law* : a woman whose husband has deserted her or has disappeared and who may not remarry until she gives proof of his death or obtains a bill of divorce

agust \əgəst\ *n* -s [Hindi *agast*, fr. Skt *agasti*] : a bast fiber derived from a southern Indian plant (*Sesbania grandiflora*)

ah \ˈä(ä), ˈá(á); *when expressing displeasure, often* ˈō\ *interj* [ME *a, ah*] — used to express various emotions (as delight, relief, regret, or contempt)

AH *abbr* **1** *often not cap* ampere-hour **2** [ML *anno hegirae*] in the year of the hegira — often printed in small capitals

aha \äˈhä, áˈhá, əˈ-\ *interj* [ME] — used to express surprise, triumph, or derision

aha·ai·na \ˈä,häˈīnə\ *n* -s [Hawaiian, fr. *ʼaha* company + *ʼaina* meal] *Hawaii* : a banquet or feast

ahan·ka·ra \ə,həŋˈkärə\ *n* -s [Skt *ahaṁkāra*, fr. *aham* I + *kāra* act of making, fr. *karoti* he makes — more at I, KARMA] : the principle of individuation in Hinduism and Jainism; *specif* : the activity of attributing objective existence to the ego on the basis of subjective consciousness

ahantch·u·yuk \əˈhänchə,yük\ *n, pl* **ahantchuyuk** *or* **ahantchuyuks** *usu cap* [Kalapooia] **1 a** : a Kalapooian people of the Pudding river valley, Oregon **b** : a member of such people **2** : the language of the Ahantchuyuk people

ahau \äˈhau\ *n* -s *often cap* [Maya] : the last of the 20 day names of the Maya calendar that with its associated numbers 1 to 13 in a peculiar order (13, 11, 9, 7, 5, 3, 1, 12, 10, 8, 6, 4, 2) designated the 13 katuns of a series ⟨13 ~ the first⟩

ˡ**ahead** \əˈhed\ *adv* [ˡ*a-* + *head*] **1** : in or toward a position in advance ⟨set the clock ~⟩ : farther in the direction in which a person or thing is going ⟨send your dog ~ —Corey Ford⟩ ⟨the road stretches straight ~⟩ : FORWARD, ONWARD ⟨the propeller is turning ~⟩ **2** : at or toward a point of time before another ⟨he moves the spring starting of chicks ~ to late fall —*New England Homestead*⟩ : in advance ⟨plan ~⟩ **3** : in or toward a position of advantage ⟨facilities for pushing ~ talented students —*Saturday Rev.*⟩

²**ahead** \"\ *adj* **1** : farther in the direction in which a person or thing is going : farther forward in time — used postpositively ⟨advance to the next job ~ —W.J.Reilly⟩ **2** : leading toward a position of advantage — used postpositively ⟨a way ~ for aspiring youths⟩

ahead of *prep* **1** : in or into a position of advantage over ⟨helping to keep our country's weapons *ahead of* the rest of the world's⟩ **2** : in advance of : BEFORE ⟨*ahead of* the times⟩ ⟨a few days *ahead of* the German disclaimer —F.L.Paxson⟩ **3** : in excess of : ABOVE ⟨output had been *ahead of* estimates —*New Republic*⟩

aheight *adv* [ˡ*a-* + *height*] *obs* : AHIGH

ahem *a throat-clearing sound; often read as* əˈhem, *sometimes as* ˈā,hem\ *interj* [imit.] — used esp. to attract attention often as a humorously exaggerated warning to a minor social error or oversight

aher·ma·typ·ic \ˈā,hərməˈtipik\ *adj* [²*a-* + Gk *herma* reef, prop + E *-typic*] *of corals* : not building reefs

ahey \əˈhā\ *interj* [*a* (as in *aha*) + *hey*] — used esp. to attract attention

ahi \ˈä,hē\ *n* -s [Hawaiian *ʼahi*] *Hawaii* : TUNA; *esp* : the Pacific yellowfin tuna

ahigh *adv* [ME, fr. ˡ*a-* + *high*] *obs* : on high : ALOFT

ahim·sa \əˈhim,sä, -iŋ,sä\ *n* -s *sometimes cap* [Skt *ahiṁsā* noninjury, fr. *a-* ²*a-* + *hiṁsā* injury, fr. *hiṁsati* he injures; akin to Skt *hinvati* he throws, urges on — more at GOAD] *Jainism, Hinduism, and Buddhism* : the doctrine of refraining from the harming of others or the taking of life

ahind \əˈhint, -in(d),-īn(d)\ *or* **ahint** \-int\ *prep* [ˡ*a-* + *hind*, adj.] *dial* : BEHIND

ahir \əˈhi(ə)r\ *n* -s *usu cap* [Hindi *Ahīr*, fr. Skt *Ābhīra*] : a member of a cattle-breeding and cattle-herding caste of India

ahis·tor·ic \ˈā=ˈ==\ *or* **ahis·tor·i·cal** \ˈā==ˈ===\ *adj* [²*a-* + *historic, historical*] **1** : free from or without regard for the temporal or finite world **2** : not concerned with or related to history, historical development, or tradition ⟨figures . . . born without a sense of the past . . . the *ahistorical* man —Clifton Fadiman⟩ : concerned only with the present and the immediately perceptible

ahl \ˈäl\ *n* -s [Ar] : the group of kinsmen of an Arabian consisting of three ascending and three descending generations

ah·med·abad *or* **ah·mad·abad** \ˈämədə,bäd\ *adj, usu cap* [fr. *Ahmedabad, Ahmadabad*, India] : of or from the city of Ahmedabad, India : of the kind or style prevalent in Ahmedabad

ahn·felt·ia \änˈfeltēə, ˈ=,===\ *n, cap* [NL, fr. Nils O. *Ahnfelt* †1837 Swed. botanist + NL *-ia*] : a small genus of dark-colored cartilaginous red algae (family Gigartinaceae) with tufted stemlike branchlets

ˡ**ahold** *adv* [ˡ*a-* + *hold*, v.] *obs* : near the wind

²**ahold** \əˈhōld, -lt\ *also* **aholt** \-lt\ *n* -s [prob. fr. ²*a* + *hold*, n.] *dial* : a hold ⟨take ~ of⟩ ⟨get ~ of⟩

aho·le·ho·le \ə,hōlēˈhōlē\ *or* **aho·le** \əˈhōlē\ *n* -s [Hawaiian] : a small percoid food fish (*Kuhlia marginata*) widely distributed in brackish tropical waters

ahom \ˈä,hōm\ *n, pl* **ahom** *or* **ahoms** *usu cap* **1 a** : a people of the Tai race who settled in Assam **b** : a member of such people **2** : the now extinct Thai language of the Ahom people

a-horizon \ˈā===\ *n, usu cap A* [ˡ*A* + *horizon*] : the outer dark-colored light-textured layer of a soil profile consisting typically of undeveloped soil rich in organic debris in varied stages of disintegration — see B-HORIZON, C-HORIZON

ahorse \əˈ-\ *adv (or adj)* [ˡ*a-* + *horse*] : AHORSEBACK

ahorse·back \əˈ-\ *adv (or adj)* [ˡ*a-* + *horseback*] *archaic* : on horseback

ahou·saht \əˈhau,sät\ *n, pl* **ahousaht** *or* **ahousahts** *usu cap* [Nootka] **1** : a Nootka people of Vancouver Island **2** : a member of the Ahousaht people

ahoy \əˈhȯi\ *interj* [*a-* (as in *aha*) + *hoy*, interj.] — used in hailing ⟨ship ~⟩

aht \ˈät\ *n, pl* **aht** *or* **ahts** *usu cap* [Nootka] : NOOTKA

ah·te·na \ˈätᵊnə\ *n, pl* **ahtena** *or* **ahtenas** *usu cap* [Ahtena, lit., ice people] **1 a** : an Athapaskan people of the Copper river valley in southeastern Alaska **b** : a member of such people **2** : the language of the Ahtena people

ˡ**ahu** \ˈä,hü\ *n* -s [Per *āhū*, fr. MPer *āhūk*] : the common gazelle (*Gazella subgutturosa*) of central Asia

²**ahu** \"\ *n* -s [Hawaiian, Maori, Tahitian, & Marquesan] **1** *Polynesia* : a mound or stone heap serving as a boundary, waymark, or memorial **2** : a sacred Polynesian burial place

ahuat·le \ˈä,wätlē\ *n* [MexSp *ahuatle, ahuautle*, fr. Nahuatl *ahuautli*, fr. *atl* water + *huautli* wild amaranth] : water-insect eggs dried and used as food by Mexicans

ahue·hue·te \ˈä,wēˈwād·ē\ *n* -s [Sp, fr. Nahuatl *ahuehueton*, lit., old man of the water, fr. *atl* water + *huehueton* old man, fr. *huehue* old] : a Mexican cypress (*Taxodium mucronatum*) of great girth

ahull \əˈ-\ *adv* [ˡ*a-* + *hull*] : with sails furled and helm lashed alee — used in the phrase *lie ahull*

ahum \əˈ-\ *adj* [ˡ*a-* + *hum*, v.] : HUMMING

ahung \ˈä,hüŋ\ *n* -s [Chin *a⁴-hong⁴*, fr. Per *ākhūn* theologian, preacher] **1** : a Chinese mosque official **2** — used in China as a term of deference or esteem

ahun·gered \əˈhəŋgə(r)d\ *adj* [ME *ahungred, anhungred*, fr. ˡ*a-*, *an-* + *hungred* hungered] *archaic* : made hungry : very hungry

ahunt \əˈ-\ *adj* [ˡ*a-* + *hunt*, v.] : HUNTING

ahu·ula \,ähəˈülə, ,ä,hüˈü·lə\ *n* -s [Hawaiian, fr. *ʼahu* garment + *ʼula* red, regal] : a feather cloak or cape made of minute red or yellow bird feathers occas. trimmed with black or green and formerly worn in Hawaii by high chiefs and kings

ˡ**ai** \ˈī\ *or* **aie** \ˈīē\ *or* **ai·ee** \ˈīē\ *interj* [ME] — used to express grief, despair, or anguish

²**ai** \ˈī, ˈä,ē, äˈē\ *n* -s [Pg *aí* or Sp *aí*, fr. Tupi *ai*] : a three-toed sloth of the genus *Bradypus* of So. America

³**ai** *var of* AYU

AI *abbr* **1** active ingredient **2** *often not cap* ad interim **3** air interception **4** artificial insemination

ai·blins \ˈāblənz\ *adv* [earlier *ablins*, fr. *able* + *-lins* (alter. of *-lings*)] *chiefly Scot* : PERHAPS

ˡ**aid** \ˈād\ *vb* -ED/-ING/-S [ME *eyden*, fr. MF *aider*, fr. L *adjutare*, freq. of *adjuvare* to help, fr. *ad-* + *juvare* to help] *vt* : to give help or support to : FURTHER, FACILITATE, ASSIST ⟨he ~*ed* the cause⟩ ⟨the . . . Committee ~*ed* veterans in their applications for pensions —*Current Biog.*⟩ : contribute to ⟨finances are ~*ed* by rummage sales⟩ ~ *vi* : to give assistance : be of use : HELP ⟨he ~*ed* in the attempt⟩ **syn** see HELP

²**aid** \"\ *n* -s [ME *aide*, fr. MF, fr. *aider*, v.] **1** : a subsidy granted to the king by the English parliament until the 18th century for an extraordinary purpose **2** : the act of helping or the help given : ASSISTANCE, SUPPORT, RELIEF ⟨~ extended to Confederate privateers —Eleanor M. Sickels⟩ ⟨a rescue party sent to their ~⟩ **3 a** : a person who gives assistance : HELPER ⟨accepted the position of ~ in the U.S. Naval Observatory —W.J.Humphreys⟩ — compare AIDE **b** : something by which assistance is given (as in achieving an end) ⟨visual ~*s* in teaching⟩ **c** : an organization auxiliary to another organization; *esp* : a woman's local auxiliary church group (as a ladies' aid society) **4** : a tribute paid by a vassal to his lord for the lord's ransom from captivity, for knighting his eldest son, and for dowry of his eldest daughter **5** *English law* : assistance in defending an action that the defendant may or should legally claim from another having a joint interest

in the defense **6 :** directive signals conveyed to a horse (as through the use of the hands, legs, shift of body weight, or voice)

aid·ance \'ād°n(t)s\ *n* -s [MF, fr. *aider* + *-ance*] **:** a means of help **:** AID

aid·ant \'ād°nt\ *adj* [ME, fr. MF, pres. part. of *aider*] **:** of service or assistance **:** HELPFUL ⟨I would gladly be ~, as far as my poor mite of judgment will enable me —S.T.Coleridge⟩

ai·da trumpet \ä,ēdə-\ *n, usu cap A* [after *Aida*, opera by Giuseppe Verdi †1901 Ital. composer, for which it was designed] **:** a long straight trumpet

aide \'ād\ *n* -s [short for *aide-de-camp*] **:** a person who acts as an assistant; *specif* **:** a military officer acting as assistant to a superior

aide-de-camp *also* **aid-de-camp** \ˌāddə¦kamp, -aa(ə)mp, -aimp, -äⁿ\ *n, pl* **aides-de-camp** *also* **aids-de-camp** \ˌādz-də-\ [F *aide de camp*, lit., camp assistant] **:** a military aide

aided school *n* **:** a usu. denominational voluntary English school receiving one half of its maintenance costs from public funds but retaining control over appointments and religious instruction — compare CONTROLLED SCHOOL

aide-mé·moire \ˌād(ˌ)mām'wär, -(ˌ)mem-, -wå(r\ *n, pl* **aide-mémoire** [F, fr. *aider* to aid + *mémoire* memory, fr. L *memoria* — more at MEMORY] **1 :** an aid to the memory (as a mnemonic device) **2 :** a written summary or outline of important items of a proposed agreement or diplomatic communication **:** MEMORANDUM

aid·er \'ādə(r)\ *n* -s [prob. fr. MF *aider* to aid] **:** an act of aiding — used esp. in pleading in the phrase *aider by verdict*

aider by verdict : the presumption after a verdict that all facts necessary to the verdict were proved

aid·ful \'ādfəl\ *adj, archaic* **:** abounding in aid **:** HELPFUL

aid·le \'ād°l\ *chiefly Scot var of* ADDLE

aid·less \'ādləs\ *adj* **:** devoid of help **:** HELPLESS ⟨it is not meet . . . to leave thee thus, ~, alone —Alfred Tennyson⟩

aid–major *n, obs* **:** the adjutant of a regiment

aid·man \'ād,man, -ˌman\ *n, pl* **aidmen** [(*first*) *aid* + *man*] **:** a medical-corps enlisted man attached to a unit in the field to give first aid — compare HOSPITAL CORPSMAN

aid prayer *n, English law* **:** a defendant's appeal for aid

aids *pres 3d sing of* AID, *pl of* AID

aid station *n* [(*first*) *aid*] **:** an establishment for giving emergency medical treatment; *specif* **:** a forward medical installation where wounded receive emergency treatment

aie *or* **aiee** *var of* ¹AI

ai·el \'ā(ə)l\ *n* -s [ME, grandfather, fr. MF *ael, aiuel*, fr. (assumed) VL *aviolus*, dim. of L *avus* grandfather — more at UNCLE] **:** a writ by which an heir entered into his grandfather's estate and dispossessed the third person who had attempted to gain possession

aiery *obs var of* AIRY

ai·ga \ä'ēŋə, ä'ēgə\ *n* -s [Samoan *'āiga*] *Samoa* **:** FAMILY

ai·gi·a·lo·saur \ī'jīə(ˌ)lō,sȯ(ə)r\ *n* -s [NL *Aigialosaurus*] **:** an animal or fossil of the genus *Aigialosaurus* or family Aigialosauridae

ai·gi·a·lo·sau·rus \ˌī,jīə(ˌ)lō'sȯrəs\ *n, cap* [NL, fr. Gk *aigialos* seashore + NL *-saurus*] **:** a genus (the type of the family Aigialosauridae) of fossil prob. semiaquatic lizards of the Lower Cretaceous

aiglet *var of* AGLET

ai·grette \(ˈ)ā¦gret\ *n* -s [F — more at EGRET] **1 :** EGRET 1 **2 a :** a spray of feathers orig. those of the egret **b :** a spray of gems often worn on a hat or in a woman's hair **3 :** something resembling a plume or tuft (as a cluster of rays in the sun's corona seen during total eclipses) **4 :** a sharp point attached to an electrical conductor (as a lightning rod) to facilitate the formation of a corona discharge

aigue-marine *n* [F, trans. of (assumed) Prov *aiga marina*] *obs* **:** AQUAMARINE

aigues mortes *n pl* [F, lit., dead waters] *obs* **:** stagnant waters left by a river when it changes its channel — compare CUTOFF 4

ai·guière \(ˈ)ā¦gye(ə)r\ *n* -s [F, fr. MF, fr. OProv *aiguiera*, fr. (assumed) VL *aquaria*, fr. L, fem. of *aquarius* of water — more at EWER] **:** a decorative pitcher-shaped usu. tall and slender vessel with a handle and spout

ai·guille \(ˈ)ā¦gwēl, -ēəl, *F* äg(wʸ)ēēy\ *n* -s [F, lit., needle — more at AGLET] **1 :** a sharp-pointed pinnacle of rock commonly found in glaciated mountains **2 :** an instrument for boring holes in stone or other masonry materials or holes used in blasting

ai·guill·esque \ˌā(ˌ)gwē¦lesk\ *adj* **:** having the shape of an aiguille

ai·guil·lette \ˌāgwə¦let\ *n* -s [F — more at AGLET] **1 :** AGLET; *specif* **:** a shoulder cord worn by a military aide to the president of the U.S. and to high-ranking officers — compare FOURRAGÈRE **2 :** long narrow strips of cooked food (as meat or fowl)

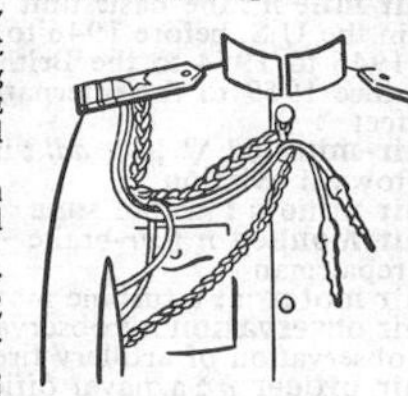

dress aiguillette of a presidential aide

ai·ka·ne \ī'kānē\ *n* -s [Hawaiian *aikāne*] *Hawaii* **:** a good friend **:** CHUM

ai·kin·ite \'ākə,nīt\ *n* -s [Arthur *Aikin* †1854 Eng. chemist + E *-ite*] **:** a mineral $PbCuBiS_3$ consisting of lead, copper, bismuth, and sulfur occurring massive and in lead-gray needle-shaped orthorhombic crystals (hardness 2, sp. gr. 7.07)

¹**ail** \'āl, 'āəl\ *vb* -ED/-ING/-S [ME *eilen*, fr. OE *eglan* to trouble, afflict; akin to OE *egle* hideous, loathsome, MLG *egelen* to annoy, Goth *usagljan* to oppress and perh. to MIr *ālad* wound, Skt *agha* evil and perh. to OE *ege* fear, OHG *egī*, ON *agi*, Goth *agis* fear, Gk *achos* pain, OIr *ad-āgor* I fear; basic meaning: fearing] *vt* **:** to affect with an unnamed disease or physical or emotional pain or discomfort **:** trouble or interfere with **:** be the matter with — used only of unspecified causes ⟨can the doctor tell what ~*s* the patient⟩ ⟨he will not concede that anything ~*s* his business⟩ ⟨what ~*s* that naughty boy⟩ ~ *vi* **:** to become affected with pain or discomfort **:** have something the matter ⟨he ~*ed* throughout his childhood⟩ ⟨the business is ~*ing*⟩ ⟨was ~*ing* from a cold⟩

²**ail** \"\ *n* -s [ME *eil*, fr. *eilen*, v.] **:** INDISPOSITION, AILMENT ⟨wild herbs that were . . . counted upon to ease their winter ~*s* —Sarah O. Jewett⟩

³**ail** \'ī(ə)l\ *n* -s [ME *eile*, fr. OE *egl*; akin to OE *ecg* edge, sword — more at EDGE] *now dial Eng* **:** the beard of grain — usu. used in pl.

ai·lan·thus \ā'lan(t)thəs, ī'-\ *n* [NL, fr. Amboinese *ai lanto*, lit., tree (of) heaven] **1** *cap* **:** a small genus of East Indian and Chinese trees (family Simaroubaceae) with odd-pinnate leaves and terminal panicles of greenish flowers succeeded by oblong twisted samaras **2** -ES **:** a tree of the genus *Ailanthus* (esp. *A. altissima*) — see TREE OF HEAVEN

ailanthus silkworm *n* **:** a large green silkworm (*Samia cynthia* or *S. walkeri*) native to eastern Asia but introduced into the U.S. that feeds on ailanthus leaves and has been used experimentally for the commercial production of silk — compare CYNTHIA MOTH

ai·lan·to \ī'lan,tō\ *n* -s [Amboinese *ai lanto*] **:** AILANTHUS 2

ai–lao \'ī,lau\ *n, pl* **ai–lao** *or* **ai–laos** *usu cap A* **1 :** a Westa Yunnan people of the Tai group who formed the Nan-chao kingdom in southwestern China from the 8th to 13th centuries **2 :** a member of the Ai-lao people

ai·la·va·tor *or* **ai·le·va·tor** \'ālə,vād·ə(r)\ *n* -s [blend of *aileron* and *elevator*] **:** ELEVON

aild \'ā(ə)ld\ *vi* -ED/-ING/-S [by alter.] *dial* **:** AIL ⟨nothin' ~*ed* me —Marjorie K. Rawlings⟩

aile *obs var of* AISLE

ai·le·ron \'ālə,rän\ *n* -s [F, bird's pinion, aileron, dim. of *aile* wing, fr. L *ala* — more at AISLE] **1 :** a half gable or wing wall (as at the end of the aisle of a church) **2 :** a movable portion of an airplane wing or a movable airfoil external to the wing that is usu. located at the trailing edge near the wing tips and whose function is to impart a rolling motion to the airplane and thus provide lateral control

aileron roll *n* **:** a flight maneuver in which an airplane is rotated about its longitudinal axis through a full 360 degrees by means of the ailerons without altering its flight path

ailes de pi·geon \eldəpēzhōⁿ\ [F, lit., pigeon wings] **:** PIGEON-WING 3

ai·lette \'ā'let\ *n* -s [F, fr. OF *ailette, alette, elette* small wing, dim. of *ele* wing — more at AISLE] **:** a plate of forged iron or steel worn over a coat of mail to protect the shoulder

aillettes, A

ail·ing *adj* **:** having or suffering from an ailment

aillt \'īlt\ *n* -s [W] **:** one of a semiservile class among the early Cymry; *also* **:** TENANT FARMER

ail·ment \'ālmənt\ *n* -s **1 :** a bodily sickness, disorder, or chronic disease ⟨always complaining of some ~ or other⟩ ⟨patients suffering from minor ~*s* were infected with all manner of diseases —A.C.Morrison⟩

ails *pres 3d sing of* AIL, *pl of* AIL

ail·syte \'āl,sīt\ *n* -s [*Ailsa* Craig, island off the coast of Scotland, its locality + E *-yte* (var. of *-ite*)] **:** a rock composed of an alkalic microgranite containing considerable riebeckite

ailur- *or* **ailuro-** *or* **aelur-** *or* **aeluro-** *comb form* [NL, fr. Gk *ailouro-*, fr. *ailouros*] **:** cat ⟨*ailur*odon⟩ ⟨*ailuro*phobia⟩

ai·lu·roi·dea \ˌīlyə'rȯidēə, ˌāl-\ *syn of* AELUROIDEA

ai·lu·ro·phile \ī'lürə,fīl, ā'-\ *or* **ae·lu·ro·phile** \ē'-\ *n* -s [*ailur-, aelur-* + *-phile*] **:** a cat fancier **:** a lover of cats

ai·lu·ro·phobe *or* **ae·lu·ro·phobe** \-,fōb\ *n* -s [*ailur-, aelur-* + *-phobe*] **:** one that hates or fears cats **:** one suffering from ailurophobia

ai·lu·ro·pho·bia *or* **ae·lu·ro·pho·bia** \ˌ=ˌ==ˈfōbēə\ *n* -s [NL, fr. *ailur-, aelur-* + *-phobia*] **:** abnormal fear of cats

ai·lu·rop·o·da \ˌīlyə'räpədə, ˌāl-\ *n, cap* [NL, fr. *ailur-* + *-poda*] **:** a genus of Procyonidae including only the giant panda

ai·lu·ro·pus \ī'lürəpəs, ā'\ [NL, fr. *ailur-* + *-pus*] *syn of* AILUROPODA

ai·lu·rus \-rəs\ *n, cap* [NL, fr. Gk *ailouros* cat] **:** a genus of mammals (family Procyonidae) comprising the panda and formerly regarded as the type of a separate family

¹**aim** \'ām\ *vb* -ED/-ING/-S [ME *aimen, amen* to guess, estimate, aim, fr. MF *aesmer* & *esmer*; MF *aesmer* fr. OF, fr. *a-* (fr. L *ad-*) + *esmer*, fr. L *aestimare* to estimate — more at ESTEEM] *vi* **1 :** to direct a course: as **a :** to point in a particular direction or at a particular object ⟨that gun is ~*ing* straight at me —V.C.Aldrich⟩ **b :** to channel efforts toward a goal ⟨officer-candidate schools toward which men . . . can ~ —J.J.O'Donnell⟩ ⟨the monastic scholars did not ~ high —R.W.Southern⟩ **2** *obs* **:** to guess with intent to discover meaning or truth ⟨~ at another man's speech⟩ ⟨~ at suspected enmity⟩ **3 :** to have as a purpose **:** PLAN, INTEND — used only with infinitive ⟨he ~*s* to encourage mutual understanding —*Saturday Rev.*⟩ ⟨this book ~*s* to effect a partial remedy of this situation —E.A. Maziarz⟩ ⟨I ~ to finish up this job —I.S.Cobb⟩ ~ *vt* **1** *obs* **:** GUESS, CONJECTURE **2 a :** to direct or point (as a weapon or a missile) at or so as to hit an object ⟨on the lawn a small cannon was ~*ed* into space⟩ ⟨a camera was ~*ed* at the scene⟩ ⟨he ~*ed* the rock at the dog⟩ **b :** to direct (as an act or proceeding) at or toward a specified object or attainment ⟨the study was ~*ed* at developing a comparative picture —*N. Y. Times*⟩ ⟨the haphazard transcription inevitable in work ~*ed* solely at vocabulary collecting —Stanley Newman⟩ **c :** to intend for ⟨a new printing press ~*ed* at medium and small-sized newspapers —*Wall Street Jour.*⟩ ⟨radio and TV shows ~*ed* at juvenile audiences —*Current Biog.*⟩

²**aim** \"\ *n* -s [ME *aime, ame*, fr. *aimen, amen*, v.] **1** *obs* **:** the point intended to be hit (as by an arrow) **:** MARK, TARGET **2 :** the pointing of a weapon (as a gun) at an object intended to be hit ⟨to take ~ at the target⟩: **a :** the ability to hit a target ⟨his ~ was deadly⟩ **b :** effectiveness of a weapon ⟨the ~ is accurate up to 75 feet⟩ **3** *obs* **a :** CONJECTURE, GUESS ⟨a man may prophesy, with a near ~, of the main chance of things —Shak.⟩ **b :** the directing of effort toward an object in order to affect it **c :** direction or guidance as to a course or procedure to be followed **4 :** the object intended to be attained **:** PURPOSE, DESIGN ⟨his ~ being the translation of certain religious and devotional writings —Edward Clodd⟩ ⟨the ~ of the Elizabethans was to attain complete realism —T.S.Eliot⟩ ⟨the only fault I find in the book is a certain lack of ~ —Geoffrey Boumphrey⟩ ⟨such exaggeration is purely impressionistic in ~ —R.M.Weaver⟩ **syn** see INTENTION

ai·mak \'ī,mak, 'ā,-\ *n* -s [Mongolian, clan] **1 :** a clan or tribal band among Mongolian peoples **2 :** a province or administrative district of Outer Mongolia

aimara *usu cap, var of* AYMARA

aiming circle *n* **:** an instrument for measuring horizontal and vertical angles and magnetic azimuths in determining gunnery data and laying guns and in artillery surveying

aiming point *n* **:** the point at which the line of sight is directed when sighting (as for the dropping of bombs) or when a firing piece is being laid for direction

aiming stake *also* **aiming post** *n* **:** a stake used as an aiming point for laying mortars and artillery pieces for direction

aim·less \'āmləs\ *adj* [²*aim* + *-less*] **:** without aim or purpose ⟨living an ~ existence⟩ — **aim·less·ly** *adv* — **aim·less·ness** *n* -ES

ai·mo·re \ˌīmə¦rā\ *n, pl* **aimore** *or* **aimores** *usu cap* [Pg & Sp *aimoré*, of AmerInd origin] **:** BOTOCUDO

¹**ain** \'ān\ *adj or n* [ME (northern dial.) *an*, fr. OE *ān* — more at ONE] *chiefly Scot* **:** ONE

²**ain** \"\ *adj* [prob. fr. ON *eiginn* — more at OWN] *dial Brit* **:** OWN

³**ain** *var of* AYIN

'ain *or* **ain** *var of* 'AYN

aince \'ān(t)s\ *adv* [ME (northern dial.) *anes* — more at ONCE] *chiefly Scot* **:** ONCE

ai·nhum \ī'nyüm, -üⁿ\ *n* -s [Pg, fr. Yoruba *eʸyun³*] **:** a tropical disease of unknown cause that results in increasing fibrous constriction and ultimately in spontaneous amputation of the toes and esp. the little toes

ai·ni \'īnē\ *n* -s [Quechua *áyni*, lit., recompense] **:** a Quechuan system of exchange of assistance usu. in the form of labor; *also* **:** a group that lends such assistance

ai·noi \'ānē\ *n pl* [MGk, fr. Gk, pl. of *ainos* praise, tale — more at ENIGMA] **:** a part of the divine office concluding the orthros in the service of the Eastern Church

ai·noid \'ī,nȯid\ *adj, usu cap* [*Ainu* + *-oid*] **:** resembling the Ainu

ain't \'ānt\ *also* **an't** \" *also* 'ant *or like* AREN'T\ [prob. contr. of *are not, is not, am not, & have not*] **1 a :** are not ⟨you ~ going⟩ ⟨they ~ here⟩ ⟨things ~ what they used to be⟩ **b :** is not ⟨it ~ raining⟩ ⟨he's here, ~ he⟩ **c :** am not ⟨I ~ ready⟩ — though disapproved by many and more common in less educated speech, used orally in most parts of the U. S. by many cultivated speakers esp. in the phrase *ain't I* **2** *substand* **a :** have not ⟨I ~ seen him⟩ ⟨you ~ told us⟩ **b :** has not ⟨he ~ got the time⟩ ⟨~ the doctor come yet⟩

ai·nu \'ī,nü *sometimes* -,nyü\ *also* **ai·no** \-,nō\ *n, pl* **ainu** *also* **ainus** *or* **ainos** *usu cap* [Ainu, lit., man] **1 a :** an indigenous Caucasoid people of Japan formerly occupying all or most of the archipelago but now confined to part of Hokkaido, Sakhalin, and parts of the Kurile islands **b :** a member of such people **2 :** the language of the Ainu people

¹**air** \'ā(ə)r\ *var of* ¹ERE

²**air** \"\ *adj* -ER/-EST [ME (northern dial.) *ar, are*, fr. *ar*, adv. — more at ERE] *Scot* **:** EARLY

³**air** \a(a)(ə)r, 'e(ə)r, 'a(a)ə, 'eə\ *n* -s *often attrib* [ME, fr. OF, fr. L *aer*, fr. Gk *aēr* air, mist; prob. akin to Gk *aētes* wind, gale — more at WIND] **1 a :** the element described by early natural philosophers as having the qualities of moisture and heat **b :** a mixture of invisible odorless tasteless compressible elastic sound-transmitting and liquefiable gases composed chiefly of nitrogen and oxygen nearly in the ratio of four volumes to one together with 0.9 percent argon, about 0.03 percent carbon dioxide, varying amounts of water vapor, and minute quantities of helium, krypton, neon, and xenon, that surrounds the earth, half its mass being within four miles of the earth's surface, its pressure at sea level being about 14.7 pounds per square inch, and its weight being 1.293 grams per liter at 0°C and 760 mm. pressure **c :** the portion of the earth's atmosphere that immediately surrounds us and affects the senses ⟨the tang of wood smoke is in the ~ —Corey Ford⟩ ⟨the open ~⟩ ⟨the ~ was not so stale and sultry in the room as it was downstairs —Carson McCullers⟩ **d** *obs* **:** scent given off by exhalation into the atmosphere **:** ODOR ⟨the ~ of rotting vegetation⟩ **e :** ATMOSPHERE 8 ⟨canvases with much light and ~ and color⟩ **f :** air in motion **:** a gentle breeze ⟨we moved onward in light ~*s* to the Narrows and dropped anchor —Kenneth Roberts⟩ **g** *archaic* **:** soft or faint breathing **:** BREATH ⟨the least ~ of suspicion⟩ **h** *archaic* **:** GAS ⟨the generation of ~*s* by explosions⟩ **i** (1) **:** empty space ⟨needle in ~, I stopped what I was making —Eudora Welty⟩ ⟨the victim of the hanging danced on ~⟩ (2) **:** NOWHERE ⟨the figure of 10 billion dollars . . . was a nice round amount taken out of the ~ —J.P. Warburg⟩ (3) *slang* **:** an obvious snub or a sudden severance of relations — usu. used with *the* ⟨I got the ~ last night —Gwethalyn Graham⟩ ⟨she threatened to give me the ~ —Robert Graves⟩ **j :** air as a working fluid (as in ventilation systems, measuring and testing, fuel combustion, and pressure-operated devices) **:** COMPRESSED AIR ⟨mine ~ shafts⟩ ⟨~ barometer⟩ ⟨~ adapters located between the compressor outlets and the combustion chambers⟩ ⟨borings made with an ~ drill⟩ **k** (1) **:** air as a field of operation for aircraft ⟨the battle of the ~⟩; *also* **:** travel or transportation by aircraft ⟨European editions which reached me by ~ —Marcia Davenport⟩ ⟨~ parcel post⟩ (2) **:** AIRCRAFT ⟨~ attack⟩ ⟨~ patrol⟩ (3) **:** AVIATION ⟨~ safety⟩ (4) **:** AIR FORCE **l :** the medium of transmission of radio waves; *also* **:** RADIO, TELEVISION ⟨advertisers who use the ~ as a means for selling goods —C.A.Siepmann⟩ — often used in the phrase *on the air* ⟨he went on the ~ with the first of a series of Saturday-night broadcasts —*Atlantic*⟩ **2 :** public utterance usu. oral **:** PUBLICITY ⟨he gave ~ to his opinion⟩ **3** [F, fr. OF] **a** (1) **:** the look, appearance, or bearing of a person **:** attitude or action peculiar to or expressive of some personal quality or emotion **:** DEMEANOR ⟨sat rigidly erect with the ~ of a man accustomed to brief parleys —L.C.Douglas⟩ (2) **:** an artificial or affected manner **:** show of style or vanity **:** HAUGHTINESS ⟨to put on ~*s*⟩ ⟨to give oneself ~*s*⟩ (3) **:** the artificial motion or carriage of a horse **b :** outward appearance of a thing **:** apparent character **:** MANNER, STYLE ⟨my work may have an ~ of fiction —Van Wyck Brooks⟩ ⟨a pioneer town with broad dusty streets, that has not yet acquired an ~ of permanence —Ivor Jones⟩ **c :** a surrounding or pervading influence or condition **:** ATMOSPHERE ⟨the controversy which has been troubling the ~ about us —Victor Riesel⟩ ⟨the place had a little of the ~ of a college dormitory after the final exams —John Dos Passos⟩ ⟨steps it could take to clear the ~ considerably and give evidence before the world of its good intentions —*N.Y.Times*⟩ **4** *or* **ayre** [prob. trans. of It *aria*] **a** *Elizabethan & Jacobean music* **:** an accompanied song or melody in strophic form **b :** the chief voice part or melody in choral or other part music **c :** TUNE, MELODY **d :** a separate instrumental composition or one of the optional movements of the classical suite typically of a lyric character **5** [trans. of NGk *aēr*] **:** AER **6 :** an airmail stamp — **in the air :** not protected by some substantial obstacle (as a river, mountain, or fortification) against flank attacks or turning movements — **on air** *adv* **:** in a state of elation **:** BUOYANTLY ⟨walking *on air*⟩ ⟨treading *on air*⟩ — **up in the air :** in a state of confusion, perturbation, or disorder **:** not yet settled or decided **:** in suspense ⟨the question was still *up in the air*⟩

⁴**air** \"\ *vb* -ED/-ING/-S *vt* **1 a** (1) **:** to expose to the air for the purpose of drying or purifying **:** VENTILATE ⟨~ damp clothing⟩ ⟨stench of whiskey and of things that were never ~*ed* —Ellen Glasgow⟩ ⟨~ the house⟩ (2) *archaic* **:** to expose to heat so as to expel dampness or to warm ⟨a brisk fire will soon ~ the room⟩ **b :** to expose to the air for the purpose of cooling or refreshing **:** exercise in the open air ⟨she left the overheated room to ~ herself⟩ ⟨take the dog out and ~ him⟩ **2 a :** to display ostentatiously **:** to expose to public view ⟨~ the latest fashions⟩ ⟨he constantly ~*s* his stupidity⟩ **b :** to expose for the sake of public notice **:** make open to the public ⟨he did not ~ his politics in the pulpit —K.B. Murdock⟩ ⟨the issue will be thoroughly ~*ed* —*Newsweek*⟩ **3 :** to transmit by radio or television **:** BROADCAST ⟨programs which will be ~*ed* in the future —*Musical Digest*⟩ ~ *vi* **1 :** to become exposed to the open air ⟨your suit is ~*ing* on the line⟩ **2 :** to become broadcast ⟨the program ~*s* daily⟩ **syn** see EXPRESS

⁵**air** \'är\ *n* -s [ME (northern dial.) *are, ar*, fr. OE & ON *ār* — more at OAR] *Scot* **:** OAR

⁶**air** *Scot var of* EYRE

⁷**air** \'är\ *n* -s [ON *eyrr* gravelly bank; akin to OE *ēar* earth, OHG *ōrah* gravelly, ON *aurr* sand, Goth *aurahjons* graves, and perh. to OIr *ūr* earth] *Scot* **:** SANDBANK, BEACH

⁸**air** *like* ³AIR\ *dial var of* ARE

⁹**air** \"\ *var of* ARY

ai·ra \'īrə\ *n, cap* [NL, fr. Gk, darnel] **:** a genus of delicate annual grasses with 2-flowered spikelets

air alert *n* **1 :** the period during which military and civilian agencies are required to be in readiness for an enemy air attack; *also* **:** the warning signal that begins such a period **2 :** combat or standby status of the aircraft, aircrew, and ground communications system that may have to repel the enemy air attack

ai·ram·po \ī'räm(ˌ)pō\ *n* -s [Sp, fr. Quechua *ayrampu*] **:** a prostrate cactus (*Opuntia soehrensii*) whose dried seeds yield a substance used in the Andes for coloring jellies red

ai·ran \ī'rän\ *n* -s [Turk *ayran*] **:** an Altaic and Turkish drink prepared from fermented milk

air–atomic \¦=¦=¦=\ *adj* **:** capable of sending atomic weapons through space ⟨*air-atomic* power —Carl Spaatz⟩

air base *n* **:** a base of operations for military aircraft and for the housing and repairing of the craft, the storage of munitions, the housing of aviation personnel, and the administrative center of control over the operations of the aircraft

air bath *n* **1 :** a hygienic exposure of the body to the open air **2 :** a bath of air; *also* **:** a receptacle (as a small oven heated from below) containing such a bath

air bell *n* **1 :** an air bubble **2 :** an undeveloped spot on a negative or print caused by the adherence of an air bubble to the film surface during development

air bends *n pl* **:** AEROEMBOLISM

airbill *var of* AIRWAYBILL

air billow *n* **:** a wave at the interface of two horizontal layers of air caused by their difference in velocity

air bladder *n* **:** a bladder containing gas, esp. air: as **a :** a hydrostatic organ present in most fishes that consists of a gas-filled sac lying dorsal to the alimentary canal and sometimes being connected with the organ of hearing and that serves also as an accessory respiratory organ in dipnoans and some ganoids — called also *swim bladder*; compare LUNG **b :** FLOAT 4h

air bleed *n* **:** a slow escape or admission of air provided for in a mechanical system (as for equalizing pressure)

air blue *n* **:** AZURITE BLUE

airboat \'=,=\ *n* **1 :** SEAPLANE **2 :** a shallow-draft boat driven by an airplane propeller and steered by an airplane rudder

airborne \'=,=\ *adj* **1 :** supported wholly by aerodynamic and aerostatic forces ⟨an airplane is ~ after attaining flying speed in takeoff⟩ **2 :** transported or designed to be transported by air ⟨~ infantry⟩ ⟨~ bacteria⟩ **3 :** employing forces (as paratroops) that are transported by air ⟨an ~ attack⟩

air–bound \'=,=\ *adj* **:** obstructed or inoperative because of air in a space normally filled with liquid ⟨an *air-bound* pipe⟩

air brake *n* **1 :** a brake operated by a piston driven by compressed air from reservoirs connected to brake cylinders by triple valves which upon reduction of air pressure in the brake pipe automatically admit air from the reservoirs into the brake cylinder **2 :** a surface (as an aileron) that may be projected into the airstream for increasing the resistance and lowering the speed of an airplane

Air·bra·sive \'=,brāsiv, -ziv\ *trademark* — used for an apparatus designed to abrade surfaces by means of a jet of gas carrying abrasive powder under pressure

air–break switch *n* **:** an electrical switch that breaks the circuit in air — compare OIL-BREAK SWITCH

air brick *n* **:** a hollowed or perforated brick or a metal box of brick size with grated sides used for ventilation

[1]air·brush \'ˌ\ *n* **:** an often pencil-shaped atomizer for applying by compressed air a fine spray of paint, protective coating, or liquid color (as in shading drawings or retouching photographs)

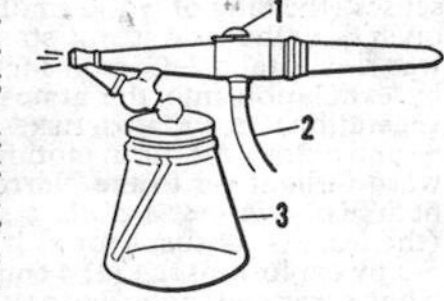

airbrush: *1* valve, *2* tube for compressed air, *3* color cup

[2]airbrush \"\ *vt* **1 :** to treat with an airbrush ⟨~ the print with gray paint to achieve a soft, high-key effect —*Popular Photography*⟩; *specif* **:** to take out (as a blemish in a photograph) — used with *out* ⟨freckles and awkward angles are ~*ed* out —*Time*⟩ **2 :** to paint (as a picture or a detail in a photograph) with an airbrush — often used with *on* or *in* ⟨orchids ~*ed* on towels⟩

air·burst \'ˌ\ *n* **:** the burst of a shell or bomb in the air

air cargo *n* **:** express, freight, or mail carried by aircraft

air carrier *n* **1 :** an organization transporting passengers and cargo by aircraft **:** AIRLINE **2 :** an aircraft certificated by a designated governmental agency to carry persons or cargo for hire

air casing *n* **1 :** a casing (as of sheet iron) surrounding a pipe or reservoir with an air space between to prevent transmission of heat **2 :** the coaming around the stack of a ship at the weather deck serving to ventilate the boiler room

air castle *n* **:** CASTLE IN THE AIR

air cell *n* **:** a cavity or receptacle for air: **a :** the air sac of a bird **b :** a dilation of a trachea of an insect **c :** a pulmonary alveolus **d :** the space between the membranes of an egg usu. at the large end that increases in size with age

air chamber *n* **:** a cavity filled with air: as **a :** a cavity containing air to act by its elasticity as a spring for equalizing the flow of a liquid in a pump or other hydraulic machine — see HYDRAULIC RAM illustration **b :** one of the chambers in the nautilus or other chambered cephalopods

air check *n* **:** a recording esp. of a radio broadcast

air chief marshal *n* **:** an officer of the British Royal Air Force equivalent in rank to a general in the army

air cleaner *n* **:** any of various devices for removing impurities (as suspended particles) from air (as by filtering, washing, or electrostatic precipitation)

air coach *n* **:** a passenger airliner offering service at less than first-class rates usu. with curtailed accommodations (as in space per passenger)

air command *n* **:** a unit of the highest echelon in the U. S. Air Force usu. composed of two or more air forces

air commodore *n* **:** an officer in the British Royal Air Force equivalent in rank to a brigadier in the army

air condenser *n* **:** a surface condenser in which steam or other vapor is cooled by contact with air-cooled surfaces

air-condition \ˈˌˌ\ *vt* [back-formation fr. *air conditioning*] **:** to equip with an apparatus for washing, humidifying, dehumidifying, and controlling the temperature of air ⟨*air-condition* a building⟩; *also* **:** to subject (air) to the process of washing, humidifying, and dehumidifying — **air–conditioned** *adj* — **air conditioning** *n* -s

air–conditioner *n* **:** one that air-conditions

air controller *n* **:** a military officer responsible for coordinating and directing close-support attacks of combat aircraft against enemy ground forces and installations

air controlman *n, pl* **air controlmen :** a petty officer in the U. S. Navy having as a specialty the control and coordination of air traffic on airfields, seadromes, and carriers

air–cool \'ˌ\ *vt* [back-formation fr. *air-cooled* & *air cooling*] **:** to cool by means of air; *specif* **:** to cool the cylinder or cylinders of (an internal-combustion engine) by air without the use of any intermediate medium (as water or oil) — **air-cooled** *adj* — **air cooling** *n*

air–cooled storage *n* **:** COMMON STORAGE

air–core \'ˌ\ *also* **air–cored** \'ˌ\ *adj* **:** having no magnetic material (as iron) in its magnetic circuit — used esp. of certain coils, solenoids, or transformers

air cover *n* **:** a screen of fighter aircraft provided for a ground, sea, or air unit for protection esp. against enemy aircraft

aircraft \'ˌ\ *n* [[3]air + *craft* (vessel)] **:** a weight-carrying machine or structure for flight in or navigation of the air that is designed to be supported by the air either by the buoyancy of the structure or by the dynamic action of the air against its surfaces — used of airplanes, balloons, helicopters, kites, kite balloons, orthopters, and gliders but chiefly of airplanes or aerostats

aircraft carrier *n* **:** a warship equipped with a flight deck on which airplanes can be launched and landed and with a hangar deck for servicing airplanes

aircraft division *n* **:** a subdivision of a squadron of U.S. naval aircraft containing usu. from four to six planes

aircraft observer *n* **:** a person holding a rating in the U. S. Air Force for any aircrew position except that of pilot

aircraft section *n* **:** a subdivision of U.S. naval aircraft containing usu. two planes of the same type

air·crafts·man \-f(t)smən\ *also* **air·craft·man** \-f(t)mən\ *n, pl* **aircraftsmen** *also* **aircraftmen** *chiefly Brit* **:** an airplane mechanic who is a noncommissioned member of an air-force ground crew

aircraft station *n* **:** a radio transmitting station aboard an aircraft — compare AERONAUTICAL STATION

air·crafts·wom·an \-f(t)s·+,-\ *also* **air·craft·wom·an** \-f(t)+,-\ *n, pl* **aircraftswomen** *also* **aircraftwomen** *chiefly Brit* **:** a woman who is a noncommissioned member of the air force

aircrew \'ˌ\ *n* **:** the crew manning an aircraft

air·crew·man \-mən\ *n, pl* **aircrewmen :** a member of an aircrew often as distinguished from the pilot or other officers

air crossing *n* **:** a passage in a mine by which one airway crosses another — compare OVERCAST, UNDERCAST

air cushion *n* **1 :** an airtight inflatable cushion **2 :** a mechanical device using confined air for arresting motion without shock

air cylinder *n* **:** a cylinder in which air is compressed by a piston, in which compressed air is stored, or in which a piston is driven by air pressure

air defense *n* **:** the means, techniques, and organizations devoted to preventing or minimizing the effects of attack by enemy aircraft or guided missiles

Air·dent \'ˌdent\ *trademark* — used for an instrument designed to grind tooth surfaces by means of a jet of carbon dioxide carrying abrasive powder under pressure

air division *n* **:** a unit of that echelon of the U. S. Air Force that is higher than a wing and lower than an air force and is composed of a headquarters and usu. from two to five wings

airdock \'ˌ\ *n* **:** HANGAR

air drainage *n* **:** AERIAL DRAINAGE

air·drau·lic \(ˈ)ˈdrolik\ *adj* [[3]air + *hydraulic*] **:** combining pneumatic and hydraulic operation ⟨an ~ machine employing both air and oil in the same pressure enclosure⟩

air drill *n* **:** a drill driven by compressed air

air·drome \'ˌdrōm\ *n* [alter. (influenced by [3]*air*) of *aerodrome*] **:** AIRPORT

air–drop \'ˌ\ *vt* **:** to drop (troops or supplies) from an aircraft by parachute

airdrop \"\ *n* **:** delivery of cargo or personnel by parachute from an aircraft in flight

air–dry \'ˌ\ *adj* **:** dry to such a degree that no further moisture is given up on exposure to air

air duct *n* **1 :** a duct or pipe for conveying air (as to the rooms of a house or ship for ventilation or to a furnace) **2 :** the duct connecting the air bladder and alimentary canal of certain fishes

ai·re \'ărə\ *n, pl* **ai·rig** \-rik, -ik\ [IrGael, nobleman, chief, fr. OIr — more at ARYAN] **:** a person of any of various ranks in early Irish society above the common freeman and below the king

aired *past of* AIR

aire·dale \"\ *n* -s [*airedale (terrier)* (influenced in meaning by [3]*air*)] **1** *slang* **:** a naval airplane pilot or aircrewman **2** *slang* **:** an airplane handler on a naval aircraft carrier

airedale terrier \'a(ə)(ə)r,dāl-, 'e(ə)r-,'a(a)ə-,'eə-\ *or* **airedale** *n* -s *often cap A* [fr. *Airedale*, valley of the Aire river, Yorkshire, England] **:** a large terrier with hard and wiry coat of a breed supposedly produced by crossing the black-and-tan terrier, bullterrier, and otterhound being about 22 inches high, weighing from 35 to 45 pounds, and having a coat black or dark-grizzled on back and sides and tan elsewhere

air ejector *n* **1 :** a device that removes air and other gases from steam condensers through the suction action of a stream jet **2 :** a small jet pump (as a filter pump)

air embolism *n* **:** obstruction of the circulation by air that has gained entrance to veins usu. through wounds — compare AEROEMBOLISM

air engine *n* **1 :** an engine built like a steam engine but driven by compressed air **2 :** HOT-AIR ENGINE

air entrainment *n* **:** the incorporation in concrete or mortar of minute air bubbles (as by addition of soap or grease) to increase resilience and resistance to wear and weathering

air equivalent *n* **:** the absorbency of a layer of material in terms of the thickness of a layer of air that would have the same absorbency for the same radiation

airer *comparative of* AIR

airest *superlative of* AIR

air explorer *n* **:** a boy at least 14 years old who is enrolled in the air exploring program of the Boy Scouts of America

air express *n* [fr. *Air Express*, a service mark] **:** package transport service using airlines but distinct from airfreight because of special scheduling, handling, billing, pickup, and delivery; *also* **:** the packages so shipped

airfield \'ˌ\ *n* **1 :** the landing field of an airport **2 :** AIRPORT

air fleet *n* **:** a group or assemblage of aircraft (as of military aircraft under a single command); *also* **:** the military aircraft of a nation

air float *n* **:** an air vesicle

airflow \'ˌ\ *n* **:** the motion of air relative to the surface of a body immersed in it (as the wind passing an obstruction or the streamline flow of air around parts of an airplane in flight)

Airfoam \'ˌ\ *trademark* — used for a fine-grained sponge rubber cushioning material

airfoil \'ˌ\ *n* [[3]air + *foil*] **:** a body (as an airplane wing or propeller blade) designed to provide a desired reaction force when in motion relative to the surrounding air

air force *n* **1 :** one of the armed services of a state analogous to or part of the military and naval services and having the primary missions of gaining control of the air, interdicting the enemy lines of communication, supporting surface forces (as by bombing and strafing), and accomplishing strategic bombing objectives **2 :** a unit of that echelon of the U.S. Air Force that is higher than an air division and lower than an air command and is usu. composed of two or more air divisions

air force blue *often cap A&F* **:** an ultramarine blue

airframe \'ˌ\ *n* [*aircraft* + *frame*] **:** the complete structure of an aircraft (as an airplane or rocket) without the power plant

[1]airfreight \'ˌ\ *n* **:** forwarding service by air for freight in volume **:** freight forwarded by a cargo-carrying airplane; *also* **:** the money charged or paid for this service

[2]airfreight \"\ *vt* [[1]*airfreight*] **:** to ship by airfreight

airfreighter \'ˌˌ\ *n* **1 :** an aircraft for transporting freight **2 :** a carrier operating airfreight service

air furnace *n* **:** a furnace that depends on a natural draft (as a reverberatory furnace) and not on blast

air gap *n* **1 :** an air-filled gap in a magnetic or electric circuit (as the space between the field-magnet poles and the armature in a dynamo or motor) **2 :** WIND GAP **3 :** the vertical distance between the point where water enters a plumbing fixture (as a tub) and the level at which it would overflow

air gas *n* **1 :** a combustible gas made by charging air with the vapor of some volatile hydrocarbon mixture (as gasoline) and used for lighting and heating **2 :** a producer gas consisting chiefly of carbon monoxide and nitrogen and made by blowing air into a producer

air gauge *n* **1 :** a gauge for measuring air pressure **2 :** a comparator in which the rate of escape of air between the surface under test (as that of a gun bore) and one of known curvature nearly fitting it (as that of a spindle inserted in the bore) is used as a measure of the difference between the two

airglow \'ˌ\ *n* **:** light that is observed esp. during the night, that originates in the high atmosphere, and that is associated with photochemical reactions of gases caused by solar radiation

air·graph \'ˌgraf, -àf\ *n* -s [*air* + tele*graph*] *Brit* **:** V-MAIL

air group *n* **:** the two or more squadrons composing all of an aircraft carrier's airplanes

air gun *n* **1 :** a gun from which a projectile is propelled by compressed air **2 :** AIR HAMMER; *esp* **:** one held in the hand like a pistol and controlled by a trigger **3 :** AIRBRUSH

air gunner *n* **:** AERIAL GUNNER

air hammer *n* **:** a portable tool in which a chisel, rivet set, or other tool is driven percussively by compressed air — called also *pneumatic hammer*

air harbor *n* **:** a landing place for seaplanes

air–hardening steel *n* **:** an alloy steel that can be hardened by cooling from a temperature higher than the transformation range either in air or or by quenching in a liquid — called also *self-hardening steel*

airhead \'ˌ\ *n* [[3]air + *-head* (as in *beachhead*)] **1 :** an area in hostile territory secured usu. by airborne troops for further use in bringing in troops and materiel by air **2 :** an advance air base

air hoist *n* **:** a hoist operated by compressed air

air hole *n* **1 a :** a hole to admit or discharge air **b :** water not frozen over esp. because of a spring or current in a river or pond **2 :** a discontinuity produced in a foundry casting by a bubble of gas **:** BLOWHOLE **3 :** AIR POCKET 1

air horn *n* **1 :** a carburetor main air intake **2 :** a pneumatic horn (as on a motor vehicle or diesel locomotive)

air hostess *n* **:** a stewardess on an airplane

air hunger *n* **:** deep labored breathing at an increased or decreased rate (as in acidosis and other conditions)

airier *comparative of* AIRY

airiest *superlative of* AIRY

air·i·fied \'a(ə)rə,fīd, 'er-\ *adj* **1 :** fashioned in an airy style **2 :** affecting airs

airig *pl of* AIRE

air·i·ly \-rəlē, -li\ *adv* **:** in an airy manner **:** JAUNTILY, LIGHTLY, THINLY ⟨dismissed the idea ~⟩ ⟨~ graceful⟩

air·i·ness \-rēnəs, -rin-\ *n* -ES **:** the quality or state of being airy **:** SPRIGHTLINESS, DELICACY

airing *n* -s [fr. gerund of [4]*air*] **1 :** exposure to air or heat for drying or freshening **:** VENTILATION ⟨give the clothes an ~⟩ ⟨this room needs an ~⟩ **2 :** exposure to or exercise in the open air esp. to promote health or fitness ⟨relief that this backyard had turned out to be as good a place for John's ~*s* as it had —Marcia Davenport⟩ ⟨she must take the dogs for an ~ —Arnold Bennett⟩ **3 :** exposure to public view or notice ⟨tolerant of his father's incessant ~ of his views —L.C. Douglas⟩ ⟨to get a congressional ~ soon —*Newsweek*⟩ **4 :** a radio or television broadcast ⟨series that have been booked for regular weekly ~*s* —Saul Carson⟩

air injection *n* **:** the injection of atomized fuel oil into the combustion chamber of a diesel engine by means of a jet of compressed air — compare SOLID INJECTION

air·ish \'a(a)rish, 'er-, -ēsh\ *adj* [ME, fr. *air* + *-ish*] **:** CHILLY, COOL

air knife *n* **:** a blade in a papermaking machine for removing excess coating from newly coated paper by means of an air blast

air–lance \'ˌ\ *vt* **:** to remove (as clinkers from a boiler wall) by means of a stream of air under pressure

air lance *n* **:** a device (as a nozzle) used in air-lancing

airland \'ˌ\ *vt* **:** to land (troops or materiel) in an area

air lane *n* **:** a path customarily followed by airplanes; *esp* **:** one made easy for navigation by steady winds

air–launch \'ˌ\ *vt* **:** to launch (a rocket or missile) from a flying air vehicle

air law *n* **:** that part of the law dealing with air transport

air layer *n* **:** a plant propagated by air layering

air layering *n* **:** vegetative propagation of a plant (as one difficult or impossible to graft or bud) by enclosing a branch or shoot often after wounding or girdling in a moist medium (as sphagnum or soil) until roots have formed, the branch or shoot then being severed to form an independent plant — compare MARCOTTAGE

airle–pen·ny \'er(ə)l,-\ *n* [older Sc *arlis-penny*, fr. *arlis* (alter. of *arles*) + *penny* — more at ARLES] **:** ARLES

air·less \'a(a)(ə)rləs, 'e(ə)rl-,'a(a)l-,'el-\ *adj* **1 :** lacking air **2 :** lacking fresh air or movement of air ⟨a dusty ~ attic⟩

air letter *n* **1 :** an airmail letter **2 :** a letter sheet esp. for airmail

air lift *n* **:** a pumping device consisting of two different-sized pipes, one within or adjacent to the other, compressed air or gas being forced down through the smaller pipe causing the fluid which is to be pumped to rise through the larger

[1]airlift \'ˌ\ *n* **1 :** a supply line operated by aircraft **2 :** air transportation esp. as improvised apart from regular schedules

[2]airlift \"\ *vt* [[1]*airlift*] **:** to transport by means of an airlift

air line *n* **1 :** a straight line through the air between two points that disregards irregularities of the intervening ground or space **:** BEELINE; *also* **:** a great-circle arc between two points on the earth's surface **2 :** a pipe or hose used to supply air under pressure (as to a pneumatic tool or to a diver under water) **3** *usu* **airline** \'ˌ\ **:** an established system of aerial transportation, its equipment, or the organization owning or operating it

airline hostess *n* **:** AIR HOSTESS

airliner \'ˌˌ\ *n* **:** an aircraft belonging to or operating over an airline

air load *n* **:** the aerodynamic load on a moving airfoil

air lock *n* **1 :** an air space with two airtight doors or openings for permitting entrance to or exit from a sealed-off space under pressure (as a ship's stokehole) or vacuum: as **a :** an intermediate chamber between the outer air and the working chamber of a pneumatic caisson **b :** the chamber in an electron microscope between outer air and inner vacuum **c :** the entrance chamber to a gas-proof shelter **2 :** a stoppage of flow (as in a pumping device) caused by air being in a part where liquid ought to circulate — compare VAPOR LOCK

air–lock \'ˌ\ *vt* [*air lock*] **:** to stop (a flow) by an air lock

air locking *n* **:** materials (as weather stripping) and devices used in building construction for making enclosed spaces airtight

air log *n* **:** an instrument that records the distance traveled by an aircraft relative to the air through which it moves, the average true airspeed being computable from the distance traveled and the time elapsed

[1]airmail \'ˌ\ *n* [[3]air + *mail*] **1 :** the system of transporting mail by aircraft **2 :** mail transported or to be transported by air **3 :** an airmail stamp

[2]airmail \'ˌ\ *adj* **:** relating to, for use with, or intended for airmail ⟨~ service⟩ ⟨~ stamp⟩ ⟨~ letter⟩

[3]airmail \'ˌ\ *vt* **:** to send by airmail

airmail field *n* **:** an airport having a transfer office for sorting, distributing, dispatching, and transferring airmail; *also* **:** the office at such airport — abbr. *A.M.F.*

air·man \'ˌmən, -ˌman, -ˌmaa(ə)n\ *n, pl* **airmen 1 :** BRATTICER **2 :** an icehouse worker who freshens the water in the cores of partially frozen blocks of ice to remove impurities and make the ice clear **3 :** one engaged in the operation, navigation, or maintenance of aircraft: as **a :** an enlisted man or woman in the U.S. Air Force; *specif* **:** one of any of four ranks below a staff sergeant **b :** an enlisted man in the U.S. Navy who performs general duties concerned with the operation of aircraft **c :** a civilian or military person who is a pilot or is associated with aviation

airman basic *n* **:** an enlisted man of the lowest rank in the air force

air·man·ship \-ˌmən,ship\ *n* **:** skill in piloting or navigating an aircraft

air map *n* **:** a map made up of a series of photographs taken from an aircraft

airmark \'ˌ\ *vt* **:** to mark out (as a town) with ground location signs visible from the air as an aid to aerial navigation — **airmarker** \'ˌˌ\ *n*

air marshal *n* **:** an officer of the British Royal Air Force equivalent in rank to a lieutenant general in the army

air mass *n* **:** a body of air extending hundreds or thousands of miles horizontally and sometimes as high as the stratosphere and maintaining during transcontinental or transoceanic movements approximately uniform conditions of temperature and humidity at any given level ⟨a polar continental *air mass*⟩

air mass weather *n* **:** weather within an air mass in distinction from that occurring at its front

air mile *n* **:** the basic unit of distance in air navigation equal in the U.S. before 1946 to the statute mile of 5280 feet, from 1946 to 1954 to the British nautical mile of 6080 feet, and since 1959 to the international nautical mile of 6076.11549 feet

air–mind·ed \'ˌˌ\ *adj* **:** interested in or favorably disposed toward aviation

air mine *n* **:** AERIAL MINE

air monkey *n* [*air*-brake + (*grease*) *monkey*] **:** an air-brake repairman

air motor *n* **:** a turbine motor powered by compressed air

air observation *n* **:** observation from an aircraft; *specif* **:** such observation of artillery fire

air officer *n* **:** a naval officer who heads the air department of an aircraft carrier and is responsible for all aircraft operations

airpark \'ˌ\ *n* **:** a small airport

air philately *n* **:** AEROPHILATELY

air photograph *n* **:** AERIAL PHOTOGRAPH — **air photography** *n*

air pistol *n* **:** a pistol that uses compressed air to propel shot or a slug

[1]air·plane \'ˌplān\ *n* [alter. (influenced by [3]*air*) of *aeroplane*, prob. fr. LGk *aeroplanos* wandering in air, fr. Gk *aer-* + *planos* wandering, fr. *planasthai* to wander — more at PLANET] **1 :** a fixed-wing aircraft heavier than air that is driven by a screw propeller or by a high-velocity jet and supported by the dynamic reaction of the air against its wings — commonly used of a landplane as distinguished from a seaplane; see MONOPLANE, BIPLANE **2 :** a piece of paper folded in three dimensions to be thrown (as by children) and made to swoop briefly through the air **3 :** pinochle in which partners may exchange certain cards

[2]airplane \"\ *vi* **:** to fly, glide, or soar in or as if in an airplane **:** travel by airplane ⟨*airplaning* across the continent⟩

airplane cloth *or* **airplane fabric** *n* **1 :** a cotton or linen fabric of firm plain weave doped for use on airplane parts **2 :** a shirting fabric resembling airplane cloth

airplane hostess *n* **:** AIR HOSTESS

airplane spin *n* **:** a professional-wrestling maneuver in which the opponent is picked up in a crotch-and-head hold, lifted onto the back, whirled about in the air, and thrown forward to the mat

air plant *n* **1 :** EPIPHYTE **2 :** any of several plants of the genus *Kalanchoe* (esp. *K. pinnata*) that propagate new plants from the leaves — called also *life plant*

air plot *n* **:** the room on an aircraft carrier from which all air operations are directed

air plug *n* **:** a removable plug screwed into a watertight manhole or scuttle cover

air pocket *n* **1 :** a condition of the atmosphere (as a local down current or an abrupt change of wind velocity in the direction of travel) that causes an airplane to drop suddenly **2 :** an air-filled section (as of a pipe) normally completely filled with liquid **3 :** a situation in the security market in which there is no nearby bid for an issue or for securities generally and which results in acute price weakness

air police *n* **:** an organized force in an air unit that exercises the function of police among air personnel and is responsible esp. for the security of the base, for prisoners, and for road traffic control — abbr. *A.P.*

air port *n* [[3]air + *port* (opening in a ship's side)] **:** an opening to release or admit air

airport \'ˌ\ *n* [[3]air + *port* (harbor)] **:** a tract of land or water that is adapted and maintained for the landing and takeoff of aircraft and at which facilities for their shelter, supply, and repair are provided **:** a terminal point for air passengers and cargo — compare AIRFIELD

airport of entry : a port of entry for aircraft

airpost \'ₛ,ₛ\ *n* [prob. trans. of G *luftpost*] **:** AIRMAIL
air potato *n* **:** an Asiatic yam (*Dioscorea bulbifera*) sometimes cultivated for its large axillary potatolike tubers
air power *n* **:** the force that a nation is able to apply by military aviation to gain and secure its political and military ends **:** AIR FORCE
air pressure *n* **:** ATMOSPHERIC PRESSURE
¹airproof \'ₛ¦ₛ\ *adj* [³*air* + *proof*] **1 :** AIRTIGHT **2 :** made impervious to air
²airproof \"\ *vt* **1 :** to make airtight **2 :** to protect from the injurious action of air
air propeller *n* **:** a rotary fan for circulating air
air pump *n* **:** a pump for exhausting air from a closed space or for compressing air or forcing it through other apparatus — compare VACUUM PUMP
air raid *n* **:** an attack by armed aircraft (as bombers) on a surface target
air receiver *n* **:** a storage tank for compressed air
air rifle *n* **1 :** a rifle from which a projectile is propelled by air or carbon dioxide compressed usu. by a lever and pump system **2 :** BB GUN
air right *n* **:** a property right to the space above a plane fixed a specified distance above the ground esp. when owned separately from the right to use the ground itself and the space immediately above it and usu. with a right to support from the ground below
air ring *n* **:** an inflatable rubber ring used as a cushion to relieve pressure on prominent bony points (as in helping to prevent bedsores)
air room *n* **:** a high-security room in an air headquarters displaying the latest air intelligence and estimates of the situation and used for the briefing of authorized personnel
air root *n* **:** AERIAL ROOT
airs *pl of* AIR, *pres 3d sing of* AIR
air sac *n* **1 :** a cavity in the pollen grain of pines **2 a :** one of the spaces in different parts of the bodies of birds that are air-filled and connected with the air passages of the lungs and usu. with cavities in the bones and that serve to reduce the specific gravity of the body and assist respiration by the great increase of surface thus exposed to the air as well as by providing a space for the residual air so that the lungs may be completely filled with fresh air at each respiration **b :** paired bladderlike backward extensions of the branchial cavity of certain Indian fishes that are lined with vascular tissue and serve as accessory breathing organs **c :** the internal subumbrellar portion of the specialized inverted pneumatophore in siphonophores that contains air and keeps the colony afloat **3 :** a thin-walled dilation of a trachea occurring in many insects **4 :** a pulmonary alveolus
air-sac disease *n* **:** a serious inflammatory condition of the air sacs of poultry
air-sac mite *n* **:** a small pale oval nearly hairless mite (*Cytoleichus nudus*) having the legs ending in suckers and parasitizing the respiratory passages and air sacs of various wild and domesticated birds
air·scape \'ₛ,skāp\ *n* -s [³*air* + -*scape*] **:** a view or a picture taken from a position in an aircraft or on a height
air scoop *n* **:** an air-duct inlet or cowl that projects from an outer surface of an aircraft or automobile in such a way as to utilize the dynamic pressure of the airstream in maintaining a flow of air (as to a power plant or a ventilating system)
air scout *n* **1 :** an airplane used for reconnaissance **2 :** AIR EXPLORER
airscrew \'ₛ,ₛ\ *n* **1 :** a screw or screw propeller designed to operate in air **2** *Brit* **:** an airplane propeller
air seal *n* **:** a seal to prevent passage of air or vapor
air service *n* **1 :** the air arm of a nation **2 :** mail, passenger, and freight service provided by the operation of aircraft
air-set \'ₛ¦ₛ\ *vi* **:** to set in air at normal temperatures and pressures ⟨allowing mortar to *air-set*⟩
air shaft *n* **:** AIR WELL
airsheet \'ₛ,ₛ\ *n* **:** an air-letter sheet
airship \'ₛ,ₛ\ *n* **:** a lighter-than-air aircraft having a propelling system and a means for controlling the direction of motion
air shower *n* **:** cosmic rays formed into a shower by passage through the atmosphere
airsick \'ₛ,ₛ\ *adj* **:** affected with airsickness
airsickness \'ₛ,ₛₛ\ *n* **:** motion sickness associated with flying and the modifying factors of high speed and altitude characterized by dizziness, nausea, headache, muscular weakness, faintness, anxiety, pallor, cold sweats, tremor, and vomiting — compare ALTITUDE SICKNESS
air-slake *also* **air-slack** \'ₛ,ₛ\ *vt* **:** to slake (lime) by exposure to the air
air sleeve *or* **air sock** *n* **:** WIND SOCK
air space *n* **1 :** an enclosed space for or containing air: as **a :** space (as in a room) available for air for respiration **b :** a space between walls or in a wall to protect against dampness or to provide thermal insulation **c :** AIR SAC 2a **d :** the space between the powder charge and projectile in a firearm **e :** a cavity containing air in the cellular tissue of a plant **2** *usu* **airspace :** the space lying above the earth or above a certain area of land or water; *esp* **:** the space lying above a nation and considered as under its jurisdiction
airspace reservation *n* **:** a sector of airspace in which aerial navigation is restricted or prohibited by governmental authority
airspeed \'ₛ,ₛ\ *n* **:** the speed of an aircraft with relation to the air as distinguished from speed relative to the earth — compare GROUND SPEED
airspeed head *n* **:** a device mounted in the airstream and used to measure the airspeed of an aircraft — compare PRESSURE NOZZLE
airspeed indicator *or* **airspeed meter** *n* **:** a dial gauge showing the airspeed of an aircraft
air spot *n* **:** spotting and reporting from aircraft the fall of missiles in relation to a target; *also* **:** the aircraft and pilot assigned to this duty
air-spray \'ₛ¦ₛ\ *adj* **:** applied or used to apply in the form of a spray by means of air under pressure ⟨*air-spray* lacquer⟩ ⟨*air-spray* equipment⟩
air stack *n* **:** planes circling at different assigned altitudes above an airport while waiting their turn to land
air stage *n, Canad* **:** the carrying of supplies to northern settlements by regularly scheduled airplane flights
air station *n* **:** a stopping place for aircraft equipped with facilities for receiving and servicing the craft — compare AIR BASE, AIRFIELD, AIRPORT
airstream \'ₛ,ₛ\ *n* **1 :** AIRFLOW **2 :** a current of air **:** WIND; *esp* **:** a high-velocity wind at high altitude
airstream engine *or* **airstream motor** *n* **:** a jet engine that unlike a rocket depends upon the oxygen in the surrounding atmosphere for combustion
air strike *n* **:** an air attack
airstrip \'ₛ,ₛ\ *n* [³*air* + *strip*] **:** a paved or unpaved runway that lacks normal airbase or airport facilities (as taxi strips, hangars)
air support *n* **:** air operations esp. in direct support of ground forces, naval forces, or other air forces
air surveillance *n* **:** the systematic scanning of a portion of the airspace esp. by electronic or visual means to detect and track flying aircraft or missiles
air survey *n* **:** AERIAL SURVEY
air system *n* **:** a system of mechanical refrigeration in which cold air is compressed, cooled, and permitted to expand and thus act as the refrigerating agent
¹airt \'ārt, 'e-\ *n* -s [ME *art*, fr. ScGael *āird* point of the compass, promontory; akin to OIr *aird* point, height — more at ARDISIA] *chiefly Scot* **:** point of the compass **:** DIRECTION
²airt \"\ *vb* -ED/-ING/-s *vt, chiefly Scot* **:** DIRECT, GUIDE ~ *vi, chiefly Scot* **:** to make one's way
airtight \'ₛ¦ₛ\ *adj* **1 :** so tight as to be impermeable or nearly so to air ⟨~ stove⟩ **2 :** impenetrable esp. by an opponent; *also* **:** permitting no opportunity for an opponent to score ⟨an ~ argument⟩ ⟨an ~ defense⟩ — **air·tight·ness** *n* -ES
air-to-air \'ₛₛ¦ₛ\ *adv (or adj)* **:** from one aircraft to another while in flight ⟨*air-to-air* rockets⟩ ⟨refueling *air-to-air*⟩
air tourist *n* **:** air-coach service
air train *n* **:** SKY TRAIN
air transport *n* **1 :** air transportation **2 :** an aircraft designed for use in transporting esp. military personnel and cargo
air trap *n* **1 :** a device for shutting off foul air or gas from drains or sewers **2 :** AIR POCKET
air trumpet *n* **:** one of a pair of short breathing tubes that project from the thorax of mosquitoes and related insects
air twist *n* **:** a decorative spiral of air in the stem of a glass vessel formed during blowing and manufacture
air vehicle *n* **:** a man-made object that propels itself through the air (as an aircraft or a guided missile)
air vice-marshal *n* **:** an officer of the British Royal Air Force equivalent in rank to a major general in the army
airview \'ₛ,ₛ\ *n* **:** AERIAL PHOTOGRAPH
air volcano *n* **:** an eruptive sometimes volcanic opening in the earth from which large volumes of gas are discharged along with mud and stones — compare MUD VOLCANO
air war *n* **:** war waged by an air force or between opposing air forces
air warden *n* **:** a local civilian officer who supervises defensive measures against air raids during a war

air twist

air washer *n* **:** the part of an air-conditioning system in which the air is freed from dust and given the desired humidity by means of a spray of water
airwave \'ₛ,ₛ\ *n* **1 :** the medium of radio and television transmission — usu. used in pl. **2 :** AIRWAY 5 — not used technically
airway \'ₛ,ₛ\ *n* **1 :** a passage for a current of air often underground (as in a mine) **2 :** a designated route along which aircraft fly from airport to airport; *esp* **:** such a route equipped with navigational aids **3 :** AIR LINE 3 **4 :** a passageway for air into or out of the lungs; *specif* **:** a device passed into the trachea by way of the mouth or nose or through an incision to maintain a clear respiratory passageway (as during anesthesia, convulsions, or in obstructive laryngitis) **5 :** a channel of a designated radio frequency for broadcasting or other radio communication
airway beacon *n* **:** a revolving beacon light of high intensity marking the course of an airway
airwaybill \'ₛ,ₛ,ₛ\ *also* **airbill** \'ₛ,ₛ\ *n* **:** a bill of lading issued by an air carrier
airway distance *n* **:** the distance by air between two points over a course chosen with due regard to airway aids and regulations, available equipment, and known hazards
air well *n* **:** a court enclosed within walls and open at the top for supplying air to windows — called also *air shaft*
air wing *n* **:** an organizational unit of military aircraft that may number up to 75 airplanes
air-wise \'ₛ,ₛ\ *adj* **:** skillful or experienced in aviation
airworthiness \'ₛ,ₛₛₛ\ *n* -ES **:** the quality or state of being airworthy
airworthy \'ₛ,ₛₛ\ *adj, of an aircraft* **:** fit for operation in the air **:** able to bear the strains of flight and to withstand storms
airy \'a(ə)rē, 'er-, -ri\ *adj* -ER/-EST [ME, fr. ³*air* + -*y*] **1 a :** relating or belonging to air **:** ATMOSPHERIC ⟨the ~ clouds⟩ **b :** high in the air **:** LOFTY ⟨~ regions⟩ **c :** performed in air **:** AERIAL ⟨~ flight⟩ **2 :** consisting of air ⟨~ phantoms⟩ **3 a :** resembling air in its immaterial character **:** without reality or solid foundation **:** EMPTY: (1) **:** TRIFLING, FLIPPANT (2) **:** VISIONARY **b :** resembling air in elasticity or lightness **:** AIRLIKE: (1) **:** light in movement or manner **:** SPRIGHTLY, VIVACIOUS (2) **:** delicate and graceful as air **:** ETHEREAL **4 :** open to the free circulation of air **:** exposed to the air **:** BREEZY ⟨~ hillside⟩ **5 :** having an affected manner **:** being in the habit of putting on airs **:** affectedly grand ⟨~ condescension⟩ **6** *of a sign of the zodiac* **:** having a hot and moist complexion
airy disk *n, usu cap A* **:** the bright central spot in the system of diffraction rings formed by an optical system with light from a point source (as a star)
airy-fairy \'ₛₛ¦ₛₛ\ *adj* **1 :** FAIRYLIKE, DELICATE ⟨*airy-fairy* beings⟩ **2 :** VISIONARY ⟨*airy-fairy* notions⟩
¹ais \'äs\ *n, pl* **ais** *usu cap* **1 a :** a people in the Indian river valley, Florida, thought to have been Muskogean **b :** a member of such people **2 :** the language of the Ais people
²ais *pl of* AI
ais·chro·la·treia \,īskrōlə'trīə\ *n* -s [Gk *aischros* shameful, ugly (fr. *aischos* disgrace) + -*latreia* -latry; prob. akin to OE *ǣwisc*, *ǣwisce* disgrace, shame, *ǣwan* to despise, MHG *eisch* ugly, MLG *eichelen*, *ēchelen* to disgust, Goth *aiwiski* disgrace] **:** worship of filth **:** cult of the obscene
aise·weed \'āz,wēd\ *n* [perh. fr. F *aise* ease (fr. OF, comfort) + E *weed* — more at EASE] **:** GOUTWEED
aisle \'īl, 'īəl\ *n* -s [alter. (influenced by F *aile* wing, aisle) of earlier *isle*, alter. (influenced by *isle* "island") of ME *ile*, alter. (influenced by ME *ile* isle, island) of *ele*, *eile*, fr. MF *ele*, *aile* wing, wing of a building, fr. L *ala* wing, armpit; akin to OE *eaxl* shoulder, ON *öxl*, OHG *ahsala*, L *axilla* armpit — more at AXIS] **1 :** the side of a church nave separated by piers from the nave proper — see BASILICA illustration **2** [influenced in meaning by *alley*] **:** a passage between sections of seats **3 :** a long high narrow passage in a cave
aisle seat *n* **:** a seat on or next to an aisle
aisle·way \'ₛ,ₛ\ *n* **:** a cleared passageway (as in a store or warehouse) for inside traffic
ais·ling \'ishliŋ\ *n, pl* **aislings** \-ŋz\ *or* **ais·lingi** \-ŋē\ [IrGael, dream, vision, fr. OIr *aislinge*] **:** a poetical or dramatic description or representation of a vision
aissawa *usu cap, var of* ISAWA
ais·sor \'īsə(r)\ *n, pl* **aissor** *or* **aissors** *usu cap* **1 :** a people in parts of Asiatic Turkey and in Persia calling themselves Syrians and believed to be descended from the Chaldeans **2 :** a member of the Aissor people
¹ais·to·pod \'ā'istə,päd\ *adj* [NL *Aistopoda*] **:** of or relating to the Aistopoda
²aistopod \"\ *n* -s **:** an amphibian or fossil of the Aistopoda
ais·top·o·da \,āə'stäpədə\ *n pl, cap* [NL, fr. Gk *aïstos* unseen + NL -*poda*] **:** an order or other group of extinct Carboniferous and Permian lepospondylous amphibians having a snakelike body and no limbs
¹ait \'āt\ *n* -s [ME *ait*, *eit*, fr. (assumed) OE *ēget*, alter. of OE *īegoth*, *īgeth*, *īget*, fr. *īeg*, *īg*, *ēg* — more at ISLAND] *dial chiefly Brit* **:** a little island
²ait \"\ *n* [ME (northern dial.) *ate*, fr. OE *āte* — more at OAT] *Scot* **:** OAT
aitch \'āch\ *n* -ES [earlier *ache*, fr. F *hache*, fr. (assumed) VL *hacca*] **:** the letter *h*
aitch·bone \'āch,bōn\ *also* **edge·bone** \'ej,-\ *n* [ME *hachboon*, (assumed) *achebon*, alter. (resulting from incorrect division of *a nachebon*) of (assumed) *nachebon*, fr. *nache*, *nage* buttock (fr. MF, fr. LL *natica*, fr. L *natis*) + *bon* bone — more at NATES] **1 :** the hipbone esp. of cattle **2 :** the cut of beef containing the aitchbone
ait·en \'āt³n\ *adj* [²*ait* + -*en*] *Scot* **:** OATEN
aith \'āth\ *n* [ME (northern dial.) *ath*, fr. OE *āth* — more at OATH] *chiefly Scot* **:** OATH
ai·thoch·roi \ī'thäkrə,wī\ *n pl* [NL, fr. Gk *aithos* reddish brown + NL -*chroi* (fr. Gk *chrōa* color)] **:** people having dark red-brown skin
aitio- — see ETIO-
aitiology *var of* ETIOLOGY
ai·ti·on \'īd-ē,än\ *n, pl* **ai·tia** \-ēə\ *or* **aiti·ons** [Gk *aition* cause, fr. neut. sing. of *aitios* responsible; akin to Gk *aitia* cause — more at EMULATE] **:** a tale devised to explain the origin of a religious observance
ait·ken·ite \'āt,kə,nīt, 'ākə-\ *n* -s *usu cap* [Robert *Aitken* †1873 Scot. clergyman + -*ite*] **:** a follower of Aitken in desiring to introduce into the Anglican Church certain Methodist practices and views esp. in regard to conversion
ait·meal \'āt,-\ *n* -s [²*ait* + *meal*] *Scot* **:** OATMEAL
ai·toff projection \'ī,tȯf-\ *or* **ai·toff's projection** \-fs-\ *n, usu cap A* [after David *Aitoff* †1933 Russ. geographer] **:** an equal-area projection similar in appearance to the Mollweide projection but with curved parallels
ai·tu \'ī,tü\ *n* -s [Samoan *āitu*] *Samoa* **:** SPIRIT, DEMON
¹ai·tu·ta·ki·an \,īd-ə¦täkēən\ *adj, usu cap* [*Aitutaki*, one of the Cook islands, So. Pacific ocean + E -*an*] **:** of or concerning Aitutaki Island
²aitutakian \"\ *n* -s *usu cap* **:** a native or inhabitant of Aitutaki Island
ai·ver *or* **aver** \'āvər\ *n* -s [ME *aver*, *aveyr* property, goods, fr. MF *aver*, *aveir*, fr. OF, fr. *aver*, *aveir* to have, fr. L *habēre* — more at HABIT] *now chiefly Scot* **:** a draft animal; *esp* **:** an old workhorse
aiwain *var of* AJOWAN
aix \'īks\ *n, cap* [NL, fr. Gk, a water fowl] **:** a genus of short-legged perching ducks having brilliant multicolored plumage in the male and including the mandarin duck and the wood duck (sense 1)
ai·zle \'āzəl, 'aiz-\ *n* -s [ME *isel*, fr. OE *ysel*, *ysle* — more at EMBER] *chiefly Scot* **:** a glowing coal **:** SPARK, EMBER
ai·zo·a·ce·ae \ā,īzə'wāsē,ē\ *n pl, cap* [NL, fr. *Aizoon*, type genus + -*aceae*] **:** a family of herbs or small shrubs (order Caryophyllales) with solitary or cymose flowers and capsular fruit (as the carpetweed and the fig marigolds) — **ai·zo·a·ceous** \ā¦īzə¦wāshəs, ¦ā,ī-\ *adj*
ai·zo·on \,ā,ī'zō,än\ *n, cap* [NL, fr. Gk *aei* always + NL -*zoon*] **:** a small genus (the type of the family Aizoaceae) of low-growing evergreen spreading plants found in Africa, Australia, and the Mediterranean region having fleshy entire leaves and containing some species that are cultivated for their yellow flowers or silvery foliage
AJ *abbr* associate justice
ajan·gle \ə'-\ *adj* [¹*a-* + *jangle*, v.] **:** JANGLING ⟨you can hear the chains ~ —R.L.Stevenson⟩
¹ajar \ə'jä(r), -ā(r\ *adv (or adj)* [earlier *on char*, fr. *on* + *char* turn — more at CHARE] **:** slightly open ⟨the door stood ~⟩
²ajar \"\ *adj* [¹*a-* + *jar* (discord)] **:** in a state of discord ⟨~ with the world⟩
aja·ri \¦äzhə¦rē\ *n* -s [prob. modif. of Pg *ajará*, fr. Tupi] **:** ¹TIMBO 1
ajax powder \'ā,jaks-,-\ *n, usu cap A* [after *Ajax*, one of the Greek heroes in Homer's *Iliad*, possessed of great stature and strength, fr. L, fr. Gk *Aias*] **:** an explosive used in coal mining consisting chiefly of nitroglycerin, potassium perchlorate, ammonium oxalate, and wood flour
ajee \ə'jē\ *var of* AGEE
aji \ä'hē\ *n* -s [AmerSp *ají*, fr. Taino *axí*] *in Spanish America* **:** a plant of the genus *Capsicum*
aji·mez \äkē'māth, -äs\ *n* -ES [Sp, fr. Ar *ash-shammis* the ajimez] **:** a twin window derived from Arab architecture consisting usu. of two narrow windows separated by a slim mullion
ajin·gle \ə'-\ *adj* [¹*a-* + *jingle*, v.] **:** JINGLING
ajit·ter \ə'-\ *adj* [¹*a-* + *jitter*, v.] **:** JITTERY ⟨all ~ with fear —*Harper's*⟩
aji·va \ə'jēvə\ *n* -s *sometimes cap* [Skt *ajīva* lifeless, fr. *a-* ²*a-* + *jīva* living] *Jainism* **:** inanimate matter — opposed to *jiva*
ajivika \ə'jēvəkə\ *n* -s [Skt *ājīvika*, lit., following special rules with regard to livelihood, fr. *ājīva* livelihood, fr. *ājīvati* he lives on, fr. *ā* toward + *jīvati* he lives, fr. *jīva* living — more at ACHARYA, QUICK] **:** a member of a nontheistic religious sect greatly resembling Jainism that was founded by the Indian teacher Maskarin Gosala, a contemporary of the Buddha and Mahavira, and that flourished from the 6th to the 3d centuries B.C. as a rival of Buddhism and Jainism
aj·ma·line \'ajmə,lēn\ *n* -s [origin unknown] **:** an amber crystalline alkaloid $C_{20}H_{26}N_2O_2$ obtained from trees or shrubs of the genus *Rauwolfia*, esp. from an Asiatic shrub (*R. serpentina*)
aj·mer \'əj,me(ə)r, -mi(ə)r\ *adj, usu cap* [fr. *Ajmer*, India] **:** of or from the city of Ajmer, India **:** of the kind or style prevalent in Ajmer
ajo \'ä,hō\ *n* -s [Sp, fr. L *allium*, *alium* — more at ALLIUM] *chiefly Southwest* **:** GARLIC 1
ajoint \ə'-\ *adj* [¹*a-* + *joint*] **:** twisting about as though on a pivot
ajon·jo·li \äkōŋkō'lē\ *n* -s [Sp *ajonjolí*, fr. colloq. Ar *jonjolīl* (classical Ar *juljulān*)] **:** SESAME 1
a jour \ä'zhu(ə)r\ *or* **ajou·ré** \¦ä,zhü¦rā\ *adj* [*a jour* fr. F *à jour*, lit., toward day; *ajouré* fr. F, fr. *ajour* perforation (fr. *à jour*) + -*é* (fr. L -*atus* -ate)] **:** pierced, cut away, or made translucent in such a way as to form a design **:** having figured openwork **:** decorated with translucent, pierced, or openwork designs — used of carving, metalwork, lace, drawnwork, or cutwork
ajou·ri·sé \(')ä¦zhürə¦zā\ *adj* [F, fr. *ajour* + -*isé* -ized] **:** OPEN-WORKED
aj·o·wan \'ajə,wän\ *also* **ai·wain** \'ī,wīn\ *n* -s [origin unknown] **:** the fruit of a plant (*Carum copticum*) used both as a medicine and as a condiment
ajowan oil *n* **:** an almost colorless essential oil containing thymol obtained from ajowan
aju·ga \'ajəgə\ *n, cap* [NL, fr. ²*a-* + -*juga* (fr. L *jugum* yoke) — more at YOKE] **:** a large genus of herbs (family Labiatae) having verticillate flowers and a corolla with a short upper lip — see ¹BUGLE
ajutage *var of* ADJUTAGE
aka \'äkə\ *n* -s [Maori] *NewZeal* **:** any of several species of woody vines of the genus *Metrosideros*
aka·akai \ä,kä-ä'kī\ *n* -s [Hawaiian] **:** a stout European bulrush (*Scirpus lacustris*) adventive in Hawaii and used for making mats and baskets
akal \ə'käl\ *n, usu cap* [Panjabi *Akāl*, fr. Skt *akāla* timeless, fr. *a-* ²*a-* + *kāla* time; perh. akin to Skt *carati* he moves, goes — more at WHEEL] *Sikhism* **:** the immortal or timeless one — an epithet of the Deity
aka·la \ə'kälə\ *also* **ake·la** \ə'kälə\ *n* -s [Hawaiian] **:** a shrub or climber (*Rubus macraei*) of Hawaii with very large red or purplish raspberrylike edible fruit
aka·li \ə'kälē\ *n* -s *usu cap* [Panjabi *Akālī*, fr. *Akāl*] **:** one of a militant sect of Sikhs
aka·mai \äkä'mī\ *adj* [Hawaiian] *Hawaii* **:** SMART, INTELLIGENT
aka·ma·tsu \,äkə'mät(,)sü\ *n* -s [Jap, fr. *aka* red + *matsu* pine] **:** JAPANESE RED PINE
aka·mu·shi mite \¦äkə¦müshē-\ *n* [Jap, fr. *aka* red + *mushi* bug] **:** TSUTSUGAMUSHI MITE
akan \'ä,kän\ *n, pl* **akan** *or* **akans** *cap* **1 :** a Kwa language spoken over a wide area in Ghana and extending into the Ivory Coast — see FANTI, TWI **2 :** the Akan-speaking peoples including the Akim, Akwapim, Ashanti, and Fanti
aka·roa \,äkə'rōə\ *n* -s [Maori] **:** RIBBON TREE
akar·y·ote \(')ā'karē,ōt\ *n* -s [modif. of NL *akaryoton*, fr. ²*a-* + *karyoton* nucleated cell, fr. Gk *karyōton*, neut. of *karyōtos* nut-shaped, fr. *karyon* nut — more at KARY-] **:** a cell lacking a nucleus
akathist *or* **akathistos** *usu cap, var of* ACATHISTUS
akawai *usu cap* [Carib] *var of* ACAWAI
¹ake (āk) *obs var of* ACHE
²ake \'äkä\ *adv* [Maori] *Austral* **:** FOREVER
ake·ake \,äkē'äkē\ *or* **ake** \'äkē\ *n* -s [Maori] **1 :** a small tropical tree (*Dodonaea viscosa*) with young twigs compressed or triangular and viscid **2 :** either of two New Zealand trees (*Olearia avicenniaefolia* and *O. traversii*)
ake·bi \'äkəbē\ *n* -s [Jap] **:** an eastern Asiatic vine (*Akebia quinata*) valued for its oily seeds and as material for basket-making
ake·bia \ə'kēbēə\ *n, cap* [NL, fr. Jap *akebi*] **:** a small genus of woody vines (family Lardizabalaceae) of eastern Asia having racemose purple-brown flowers and an oblong purple-violet bananalike berry — see AKEBI
akee *or* **ack·ee** \'a,kē, a'kē\ *n* -s [Kru *ā-kee*] **:** a tree (*Blighia sapida*) of the family Sapindaceae native to tropical West Africa and grown throughout the tropics for the white or yellowish spongy flesh of the aril which is attached to each of the many shiny black seeds and which is edible when cooked although other parts of the fruit esp. when fallen, unripe, or discolored and the seeds have been reported as deadly poisonous
ake·ki \'äkə,kē\ *n* -s [Jap] **:** HIBA ARBORVITAE
¹a·ke·la *var of* AKALA
²ake·la \ə'kēlə\ *n* -s [after *Akela*, wolf-pack leader in Rudyard Kipling's *Jungle Book*] **:** a leader of a cub scout pack
akeldama *sometimes cap, var of* ACELDAMA
ake·ley \'a'kēlē\ *n* -s [modif. of NL *aquilegia*, *aquileia*] **:** any of several plants of the genus *Aquilegia*

akene *var of* ACHENE

ak·e·no·be·ite \ˌakəˈnōbēˌīt\ *n* -s [*Akenobe* district, Japan, its locality + E *-ite*] **:** a crisscross-granular leucocratic differentiation rock composed of oligoclase, orthoclase, a little biotite, and in the interstices considerable quartz

ake·pi·ro \ˌäkəˈpi(ˌ)rō\ *n* -s [Maori] **:** a showy New Zealand tree (*Olearia furfuracea*) with silvery leaves

aker·i·dae \əˈkerəˌdē\ *n pl, cap* [NL, fr. *Akera*, type genus + *-idae*] **:** a family of gastropod mollusks comprising typical bubble shells — see HAMINOEA

aker·ite \ˈōkəˌrīt, ˈak-\ *n* -s [G *åkerit*, fr. *Åker*, former district near Oslo, Norway + G *-it* -ite] **:** a quartz-syenite rock containing oligoclase and augite besides soda-microcline

aker·man·ite \ˈōkə(r)məˌnīt, ˈak-\ *n* -s [G *åkermanit*, fr. Richard *Åkerman*, 19th cent. Swedish mineralogist + G *-it* -ite] **:** a mineral $Ca_2MgSi_2O_7$ that consists of calcium magnesium silicate and is an end-member of the melilite series

akh \ˈäk\ *n* -s *often cap* [alternate transliteration of Egypt *ʾḫ(w)*] *Egyptian relig* **:** the spirit of a deceased person conceived as gloriously transfigured so as to reflect the deeds of the person in life

akha \ˈäkə\ *n, pl* **akha** *usu cap* **:** the most southerly group of Lolo-speaking Tibeto-Burman people forming a large part of the hill tribes of Shan State, Burma, and scattered in adjoining sections of southern Yunnan province of southern China, Laos, and northern Thailand

ak·his·sar \ˌäk(h)iˈsär\ *n* -s *usu cap* [after *Akhisar*, town in W Turkey near Izmir (Smyrna)] **:** a kind of heavy modern carpet made at Akhisar, near Izmir, Turkey

akh·mim·ic *also* **ach·mim·ic** \äkˈmimik\ *n* -s *usu cap* [Ar *Akhmīm* (of Hamitic origin; akin to Copt *Shmīm* Akhmimic, Egypt *hnty-mn*) + E *-ic*] **:** an Upper Egyptian dialect of Coptic

akhrot \əˈkrōt\ *n* -s [Hindi *akhroṭ*; akin to Skt *akṣoṭa* walnut, Sindhi *akhiroṭu*] *India* **:** the English walnut tree

akhund·za·da \ˌäˌkünˈzädə\ *n* -s [Hindi *ākhūndzāda*, fr. Per, fr. *ākhūnd* teacher + *zāda* son] *India* **:** the son of a head officer — used as a title

akia \äˈkēə\ *n* -s [Hawaiian] **:** any of several shrubs of the genus *Wikstroemia* with bark that is used as a fish poison

akim \ˈäˌkim, ˈäˌchim\ *n, pl* **akim** *or* **akims** *usu cap* [Akan] **1 :** an African Negro Akan-speaking people of Ghana **2 :** a member of the Akim people

¹akim·bo \əˈkim(ˌ)bō\ *adv* [ME *in kenebowe*] **:** in or into a position in which the hand is placed usu. on or near the hip so that the elbow projects outward at an angle ⟨to stand ~ surveying their little plots of land —John Galsworthy⟩ ⟨her arms went ~ on her hips —Donn Byrne⟩

²akimbo \"\ *adj* **1 :** placed akimbo ⟨with one elbow ~⟩ ⟨she stood with arms ~⟩ — usu. used postpositively **2 :** set in a bent position ⟨a tailor sitting with legs ~⟩ ⟨his hands folded under his head, his elbows ~⟩

akin \əˈkin\ *adj* [¹*a-* + *kin*] **1 a :** related by blood **:** of the same kind or family ⟨they discovered that they were ~ — cousins, in fact⟩ — used postpositively or predicatively **b :** descending from a common ancestor or prototype ⟨the dog and fox are closely ~⟩ **c :** ¹COGNATE 2 **2 :** showing the same nature **:** marked by similarity of essential characteristics suggesting a close relationship ⟨palsied by a feeling ~ to terror —Sheridan Le Fanu⟩ ⟨a state of feverish disorder ~ to that of a disturbed anthill —P.A.Sorokin⟩ **3 :** related and compatible, sympathetic, or close ⟨consanguinity there may have been . . . but the two were never spiritually ~ —Elinor Wylie⟩ **syn** see LIKE

aki·ne·sia \ˌāˌkīˈnēzh(ē)ə, -kə'-\ *n* -s [NL, fr. Gk *akinēsia* absence of motion, fr. *a-* ²a- + *-kinēsia* -kinesia] **:** loss or impairment of voluntary activity (as of a muscle or a death-feigning animal) — called also *akinesis*

aki·ne·sis \-ˈnēsəs\ *n, pl* **akine·ses** *also* **akyne·ses** \-ēˌsēz\ [NL, fr. ²*a-* + *-kinesis*] **1 :** AKINESIA **2 :** AMITOSIS **3 :** a state of rest or nervous inhibition of muscular activity brought on by contact stimuli to or experimental removal of the antenna of an insect

ak·i·nete \(ˈ)āˈkīˌnēt, ˈakə,-\ *n* -s [Gk *akinētos* motionless, fr. *a-* ²a- + *kinētos* moving, fr. *kinein* to move; akin to Gk *kiein* to go — more at HIGHT] *in certain algae* **:** a thick-walled single-celled nonmotile asexual resting spore formed by the thickening of the parent cell wall, corresponding to the chlamydospore of many fungi, and usu. germinating directly into a new filament — see APLANOSPORE

aki·net·ic \ˌāˌkīˈnedˌik, -kə'-\ *adj* [²*a-* + *kinetic*] **1 :** of, relating to, or affected by akinesia **2 :** AMITOTIC

¹aki·ta \äˈkēd·ə\ *n* -s [Jap] **:** a Japanese breed of spitzlike dogs

²aki·ta \"\ *adj, usu cap* [fr. *Akita*, Japan] **:** of or from the city of Akita, Japan **:** of the kind or style prevalent in Akita

ak·ka \ˈäkə, ˈa-\ *n, pl* **akka** *or* **akkas** *usu cap* **1 :** a Pygmy people of the Vele basin in the Belgian Congo **2 :** a member of the Akka people

¹ak·ka·di·an \əˈkādēən, aˈ-, äˈ-, -käd-\ *or* **accadian** *adj, usu cap* [*Akkad*, northern division of ancient Babylonia + E *-ian*] **1 :** of or relating to Akkad, the Accad of Gen 10: 10, identified by some with Agade, near Sippar, north of Babylon **2** *archaic* **:** SUMERIAN **3 :** of or belonging to the Semitic inhabitants of central Mesopotamia before 2000 B.C. — compare ASSYRIAN, BABYLONIAN, SUMERIAN **4 :** of or relating to Akkadian

²akkadian \"\ *n* -s *cap* **1** *archaic* **:** SUMERIAN **2 :** one of the Semitic inhabitants of central Mesopotamia before 2000 B.C. **3 a :** an ancient Semitic language of Mesopotamia used from about the 28th to the 1st century B.C. as the vehicle of a widely varied literature in cuneiform writing — see ASSYRIAN, BABYLONIAN **b :** the earliest known stage of this language, used by the Akkadians **:** old Akkadian

ak·kum \ˈäkəm\ *n* -s [Heb *ʿakkum*, an acrostic (its details obscured by transliteration) of *ʿōbhedh kōkhābhīm ūmazzālōth* worshiper of stars and constellations] **1 :** a Chaldean star worshiper **2** *in the Talmud* **:** HEATHEN, IDOLATER

aklan \ˈäˌklän\ *also* **akla·non** \ˈäkləˌnän\ *n, pl* **aklan** *or* **aklans** *also* **aklanon** *or* **aklanons** *usu cap* [Aklan] **1 a :** a predominantly Christian Bisayan people on Panay Island, Philippines **b :** a member of such people **2 :** the Austronesian language of the Aklan people

akle *n* -s [var. of *acle*] **:** ACLE 3

ako·lu·thia *or* **ako·lou·thia** \ˌäkə(ˌ)lüˈthēə\ *n* -s [MGk *akolouthia*, fr. Gk, sequence, fr. *akolouthos* following, fr. *ha-*, *a-* together + *keleuthos* path; akin to Gk *homos* same and to Lith *keliáuti* to travel and perh. to Gk *kellein* to drive — more at SAME, HOLD] **1 :** a set order or traditional arrangement of a religious service in the Eastern Church **2 :** DIVINE OFFICE

akon·tae \əˈkänˌtē\ *n pl, cap* [NL, fr. ²*a-* + *-kontae* (fr. Gk *kontos* punting pole)] *in former classifications* **:** a division of algae coextensive with the order Zygnematales

ako·ri \ˈäkərē\ *n* -s [prob. native name in western Africa] **1 :** a porous coral formerly used for ornaments by West African Negroes and Samoans **2 :** any one of several baser substitutes for akori

akosmism *var of* ACOSMISM

akr- *or* **akro-** — see ACR-

akra *also* **ac·cra** \əˈkrä, aˈ-,äˈ-\ *n, pl* **akra** *or* **akras** *also* **accra** *or* **accras** *usu cap* [Akra] **:** GA

ak·ro·chor·dite \ˌakrōˈkȯrˌdīt\ *n* -s [Gk *akrochordōn* wart + E *-ite*] **:** a mineral $MgMn_4(AsO_4)_2(OH)_4.4H_2O$(?) consisting of a hydrous basic manganese magnesium arsenate occurring in reddish brown rounded aggregates (hardness 3, sp. gr. 3.2)

ak·ron \ˈakrən\ *adj, usu cap* [fr. *Akron*, Ohio] **:** of or from the city of Akron, Ohio ⟨*Akron* factories⟩ **:** of the kind or style prevalent in Akron

ak·ro·po·di·on \ˌakrəˈpōdēən, -ēˌän\ *n* -s [NL, fr. Gk, dim. of *akropous* extremity of the leg, foot, fr. *akr-* acr- + *pous* foot — more at FOOT] **:** the most prominent point on the back of the heel

akroter *or* **akroterion** *var of* ACROTERION

aksumite *usu cap, var of* AXUMITE

ak·to·graph \ˈaktəˌgraf\ *n* -s [G, fr. L *actus* (past part. of *agere* to do, drive) + G *-graph* — more at AGENT] **:** a device for recording the movements of a caged but not restrained experimental animal

aku \ˈä(ˈ)kü\ *n* -s [Hawaiian] *Hawaii* **:** OCEANIC BONITO

akua *var of* ATUA

aku·am·mine \ˌaˌküˈaˌmēn\ *n* -s [Tshi *akuamma* owala + E *-ine*] **:** a crystalline alkaloid $C_{22}H_{26}N_2O_4$ found in the seeds of a West African tree (*Picralima nitida*) of the dogbane family

aku·le \äˈkülē\ *also* **atu·le** \äˈt-\ *n* -s [Hawaiian] **:** BIG-EYED SCAD

akund \ˈäˌkünd\ *n* -s [Hindi] **:** MUDAR

akvavit *var of* AQUAVIT

akwa·'ala \ˌäkwəˈälə\ *n, pl* **akwa·'ala** *or* **akwa·'alas** *usu cap* **1 a :** an Indian people of Lower California, Mexico **b :** a member of such people **2 :** the Yuman language of the Akwa'ala people

akwa·pim \ˈäkwəˌpim\ *n, pl* **akwapim** *or* **akwapims** *usu cap* [Akwapim *aˈkuaˈpemə*] **1 :** an African Negro Akan-speaking people of Ghana **2 :** a member of the Akwapim people

akynesis *var of* AKINESIS

al \ˈäl\ *n* -s [Hindi *āl*] **:** INDIAN MULBERRY 1

al- — see AD-

¹-al \əl,ᵊl\ *adj suffix* [ME *-al*, *-el*, fr. OF & L; OF *-al*, *-el*, fr. L *-alis*] **:** of, relating to, or characterized by ⟨direction*al*⟩ ⟨fiction*al*⟩ ⟨hormon*al*⟩ ⟨organization*al*⟩ ⟨spectr*al*⟩ ⟨tid*al*⟩

²-al \"\ *n suffix* -s [ME *-aille*, fr. OF, fr. L *-alia*, neut. pl. of *-alis*] **:** action or process ⟨bestow*al*⟩ ⟨rehears*al*⟩ ⟨withdraw*al*⟩

³-al \ˌal, ˌȯl, əl, ᵊl; *in sense 2* " *or* -ˌȯl *or* -ˌäl\ *n suffix* -s [F, fr. *alcool* alcohol, fr. ML *alcohol*] **1 a :** aldehyde ⟨butan*al*⟩ ⟨salicyl*al*⟩ — compare GENEVA SYSTEM **b :** acetal ⟨butyr*al*⟩ **2 :** pharmaceutical product ⟨barbit*al*⟩

al *abbr* **1** alias **2** alley

AL *abbr* **1** air letter **2** all lengths **3** [L *anno lucis*] in the year of light **4** autograph letter

Al *symbol* aluminum

a la *or* **à la** \ˈä(ˌ)lä, ˈa(ˌ)lä, -lə *or, esp in some of the most frequently used phrases so beginning*, ˌalə *or* ˈä(ˌ)la\ [F *à la*] **:** after the fashion of **:** in the manner of — used freely with English nouns regardless of gender or number ⟨dangling from the rafters *a la* Douglas Fairbanks⟩ ⟨publicity shots *a la* Hollywood⟩ ⟨reciter of . . . "The Happy Prince", done *a la* Emlyn Williams and Dickens — Lewis Nichols⟩

¹ala \ˈālə\ *n, pl* **alae** \ˈāˌlē\ [L — more at AISLE] **1 :** a wing ⟨an insect ~⟩ or a winglike process or part ⟨the *alae* of the nose⟩ ⟨the lateral *alae* of a nematode worm⟩ **2 :** one of the two side petals in a papilionaceous corolla **3 :** the membranous expansion found in some seeds **4 :** the basal lobes in the leaves of mosses

²ala \ˈä(ˌ)lä\ *or* **alal** \ˈäˌläl\ *n* -s [Sumerian *a-lal*] **:** a large ancient Sumerian drum

al·a·ba·do \ˌaləˈbä(ˌ)dō\ *n* -s [MexSp, fr. Sp, past part. of *alabar* to praise, fr. LL *alapari* to boast, perh. fr. L *alapa* slap on the cheek] **:** a Mexican hymn

¹al·a·bama \ˌaləˈbamə *sometimes* -ämə *or* -ȧmə *esp in places distant from the state of Alabama; attrib* ˈ==ˌ=\ *also* **al·i·ba·mu** \-(ˌ)mü\ *n, pl* **alabama** *or* **alabamas** *also* **alibamu** *or* **alibamus** *usu cap* [prob. fr. Choctaw *alba ayamule* I make a clearing] **1 a :** a Muskogean people of central Alabama and of the Creek confederacy **b :** a member of such people **2 :** the language of the Alabama people

²alabama \"\ *adj, usu cap* [fr. *Alabama*, state in the southern U.S., prob. fr. the *Alabama* river, prob. fr. the *Alabama* people] **:** of or from the state of Alabama ⟨*Alabama* highways⟩ **:** of the kind or style prevalent in Alabama **:** ALABAMIAN

³alabama \"\ *n, cap* [NL, fr. *Alabama*, state] **:** a genus of moths (family Noctuidae) including a species of which the larva is the destructive cotton leafworm

alabama terrapin *or* **alabama turtle** *also* **alabama slider** *n, usu cap A* **:** a freshwater tortoise (*Pseudemys alabamensis*) having a range extending from the Gulf coast of Florida to Louisiana

¹al·a·bam·i·an \ˌ==ˈ=mēən\ *also* **alabaman** *adj, usu cap* [*Alabama* + E *-ian* or *-an*] **1 :** of, relating to, or characteristic of the state of Alabama **2 :** of, relating to, or characteristic of Alabamians

²alabamian \"\ *also* **alabaman** *n* -s *cap* **:** a native or resident of Alabama

al·a·bam·ine \ˌ==ˈ=ˌmēn, -mən\ *n* -s [*Alabama* (state) + *-ine*] **:** chemical element 85 — a name now superseded by *astatine*

al·a·ban·dite \ˌaləˈbanˌdīt\ *n* -s [G *alabandit*, fr. *Alabanda*, town in Turkey, its locality + G *-it* -ite] **:** manganese sulfide MnS usu. in iron-black massive form with cubic cleavage

al·a·barch \ˈaləˌbärk\ *n* -s [L *alabarches*, fr. Gk *alabarchēs*, alter. of *arabarchēs*, fr. *Arabia* + Gk *-archēs* -arch] **:** the chief magistrate of the Jews at Alexandria under the Ptolemies and the Roman Empire

¹al·a·bas·ter \ˈaləˌbastə(r), -aas-,-ais-,-ȧs- *also* ˌ==ˈ==\ *n* -s [ME *alabastre*, fr. MF, fr. L *alabaster*, *alabastrum*, fr. Gk *alabastros*, *alabastron* alabaster, vase made of alabaster] **1 a :** a compact variety of fine-textured gypsum usu. white and translucent but sometimes yellow, red, or gray that is carved into objects (as vases and mantel ornaments) **b :** a hard compact variety of calcite or aragonite that is translucent and sometimes banded — called also *Mexican onyx*, *onyx marble*, *oriental alabaster* **2 :** a pale yellowish pink to yellowish gray — called also *tilleul buff*, *white jade*

²alabaster \"\ *adj* **:** of or resembling alabaster; *specif* **:** having a nearly white color and a light-diffusing surface

alabaster tint *n* **:** a bluish white

al·a·bas·trine \ˌ==ˈ=strən\ *adj* [*alabaster* + *-ine*] *archaic* **:** of or like alabaster

al·a·bas·trum \ˌ==ˈ=strəm\ *or* **al·a·bas·tron** \-ˌsträn,-ˌstrən\ *or* **al·a·bas·tos** \-ˌstäs,-stəs\ *n, pl* **alabas·tra** \-strə\ *or* **alabastrums** *or* **alabastrons** [L & Gk; L *alabastrum*, fr. Gk *alabastron*, *alabastos* — more at ALABASTER] **:** an ancient Greek or Roman jar for oils, ointments, or perfumes having a flattened lip with narrow orifice and an elongated body rounded at the bottom

alabastrum

alablaster *obs var of* ALABASTER

ala·ca·luf *or* **ala·ka·luf** *also* **ali·ku·luf** \ˌaləkəˈlüf, ˈäl-\ *n, pl* **alacaluf** *or* **alacalufs** *or* **alakaluf** *or* **alakalufs** *usu cap* [Sp & Yahgan; Sp *alacaluf*, prob. fr. Yahgan (*Innalum*) *Aala Kaluf*, lit., western men with mussel-shell knives] **1 a :** a people of Tierra del Fuego **b :** a member of such people **2 :** a language of the Alacaluf people

a la carte \ˌ=(ˌ)=ˈkärt, -kȧt; *see* A LA\ *adj* [F *à la carte*] **:** by the card **:** by the bill of fare — used of a meal that is ordered dish by dish each of which has a separate price ⟨an *a la carte* dinner⟩

alack \əˈlak\ *interj* [ME *alacke*, prob. fr. *a* ah! + *lack* fault, loss — more at LACK] *archaic* — used to express sorrow or regret or formerly reproach ⟨of reading, ~, but little —H.J.Laski⟩

alack·a·day \əˈlakəˌdā\ *also* **alack the day** *interj, archaic* — used to express sorrow or deprecation

al·a·cre·a·tine \ˌaləˈkrēəˌtēn\ *n* -s [ISV *alanine* + *creatine*] **:** a white crystalline acid $C_4H_9N_3O_2$ formed from alanine and cyanamide; α-guanidino-propionic acid

alacrious *adj* [L *alacr-*, *alacer* swift, eager + E *-ious*] *obs* **:** BRISK, LIVELY — **alacriously** *adv, obs*

alac·ri·tous \əˈlakrəd·əs\ *adj* [*alacrity* + *-ous*] **:** characterized by alacrity

alac·ri·ty \əˈlakrəd·ē, -ətē, -i\ *n* -ES [L *alacritas*, fr. *alacr-*, *alacer* quick, lively, eager, happy + *-itas* -ity; akin to OE & OHG *ellen* zeal, courage, ON *eljan* power, Goth *aljan* zeal and perh. to L *adolēre* to burn up— more at ALTAR] **:** a promptness in responding **:** cheerful readiness **:** BRISKNESS, EAGERNESS ⟨to accept with ~⟩ ⟨the ~ with which he sprang from the vehicle —T.L.Peacock⟩

alac·ta·ga \əˈlaktəgə\ *syn of* ALLACTAGA

alae *pl of* ALA

al·a·gui·lac \ˌaləgwēˈläk\ *n, pl* **alaguilac** *or* **alaguilacs** *usu cap* [Sp, of AmerInd origin] **1 a :** a Nahuatlan people in eastern Guatemala **b :** a member of such people **2 :** the Uto-Aztecan language of the Alaguilac people

alai·mus \əˈlīməs, aˈ-\ *n, cap* [NL, fr. ²*a-* + Gk *laimos* throat, gullet] **:** a nearly cosmopolitan genus of soil nematodes

al·a·ite \ˈaləˌīt\ *n* -s [F *alaïte*, fr. *Alai* mountains, Kirgiz S.S.R., U.S.S.R., Asia + F *-ite*] **:** a mineral $V_2O_5·H_2O$ consisting of a hydrous vanadium pentoxide occurring in blood-red mossy aggregates

alakaluf *usu cap, var of* ALACALUF

alake \əˈläk\ *chiefly Scot var of* ALACK

a la king \-ˈkiŋ; *see* A LA\ *adj* [*a la* + *king*] **:** in a cream sauce with mushrooms and pimiento or green peppers ⟨chicken *a la king*⟩ — used after the noun

alal *var of* ALA

ala·lau·wa \ˌäləˈlau̇wə\ *n* -s [Hawaiian] **:** any of several food fishes (genus *Pocacanthus*) widely distributed in tropical seas

ala·lia \(ˈ)āˈlālēə, əˈ-, -lal-\ *n* -s [NL, fr. ²*a-* + *-lalia*] **:** MUTISM, APHASIA

al·a·lite \ˈaləˌlīt\ *n* -s [F, fr. *Ala*, town & valley in northwestern Italy + F *-lite*] **:** a light-green variety of diopside from the Ala valley

al·a·lon·ga \ˌaləˈlōŋgə\ *also* **al·a·lun·ga** \-ləŋgə\ *or* **al·i·long·hi** \-lōŋgē\ *n* -s [It; *alalonga*, *alalunga* fr. *ala* fin, wing (fr. L *ala* wing) + *longa*, *lunga*, fem. of *longo*, *lungo* long, fr. L *longus*; *alilonghi* fr. *ali* (pl. of *ala*) + *longhi*, pl. of *longo* — more at AISLE, LONG] **:** an albacore (*Thunnus germo*)

al·a·lus \ˈaləlǝs; (ˈ)āˈlāləs, -ˈlal-\ *n, pl* **al·a·li** \-ˌlī\ *or* **al·a·loi** \-ˌlȯi\ [NL, fr. Gk *alalos* speechless, fr. *a-* ²a- + *lalos* loquacious] **:** a hypothetical lower order of man lacking the faculty of speech

al·a·man·dine \ˌaləˈmanˌdēn, -ˌdən,-ˌdīn\ *n* -s [alter. of earlier *alabandine* — more at ALMANDINE] **:** GARNET — compare ALMANDINE

alamanni *usu cap, var of* ALEMANNI

alamannian *or* **alamannic** *usu cap, var of* ALEMANNIC

al·a·me·da \ˌaləˈmēdə, -ˈmädə\ *n* -s [Sp, fr. *álamo* poplar] **:** a public walk or promenade; *esp* **:** one with trees on each side

al·a·mi·qui \ˌaləməˈkē\ *n* -s [AmerSp *almiquí*] **:** a furry long-snouted Cuban insectivore (*Solenodon cubanus*) related to the tenrecs; *also* **:** a closely related Haitian form

al·a·mo \ˈaləˌmō, ˈäl-\ *n* -s [Sp *álamo*] *Southwest* **:** a tree of the genus *Populus*; *esp* **:** ASPEN

a la mode \-ˈmōd; *see* A LA\ *adj* [F *à la mode*] **1 :** according to the fashion **:** in fashion **:** FASHIONABLE ⟨costumes which are *a la mode* in the rest of Europe —Ernest Barker⟩ **2 :** topped or accompanied by a serving of ice cream — used of an individual portion of dessert (as pie)

ala·mode \"\ *n* -s **:** a thin glossy silk fabric (as for hoods and scarfs)

ala·mort \-ˈmȯ(ə)rt; *see* A LA\ *adj* [MF *a la mort* to the death] **:** AMORT

al·a·mos·ite \ˈalə(ˌ)mōˌsīt, ˌ==ˈ=ˌ=\ *n* -s [*Álamos*, Sonora, Mexico, its locality + E *-ite*] **:** a monoclinic lead silicate $PbSiO_3$ occurring in white or colorless radiating fibers (hardness 4.5, sp. gr. 6.5)

alamo vine *n* **:** a white-flowered morning-glory (*Ipomoea dissecta*) of the southeastern U. S.

alan *or* **alaunt** *also* **alant** *or* **alaun** *or* **alaund** *n* -s [ME *alaunt*, fr. MF *alant*, *alan*, fr. OSp *alán*, *alano*] **1** *archaic* **:** a large dog used to hunt wild animals **2** *heraldry* **:** a short-eared dog

aland *adv* [ME *aland*, *alande*, fr. ¹*a-* + *land*, acc. & dat. & *lande*, dat. of *land*] **1** *obs* **:** in the land or country **2** *obs* **:** on the land **3** *archaic* **:** to the land **:** ASHORE

alane \əˈlān\ *adj (or adv)* [ME (northern dial.) *alan*, var. of *alon*, *alone* — more at ALONE] *Scot* **:** ALONE

alang \əˈlaŋ\ *Scot var of* ALONG

alang–alang \ˈäˌläŋˈäˌläŋ\ *n* -s [Java & Malay] **:** COGON

alán·gan \əˈlaŋˌgän\ *n, pl* **alángan** *or* **alángans** *usu cap* [Tag] **1 :** a pagan people inhabiting the mountainous interior of northern Mindoro Island, Philippines **2 :** a member of the Alángan people

alang grass \ˈäˌläŋ-\ *n* [short for *alang-alang*] **:** COGON

alan·gi·um \əˈlanjēəm\ *n, cap* [NL, fr. Kanarese *aḷaṅgi*] **:** a genus (the type of the family Alangiaceae of the order Umbellales) of shrubs and trees found in warm regions of the Old World and having alternate leaves, axillary flowers, and one-seeded drupaceous fruit

al·a·nine \ˈaləˌnēn\ *n* -s [G *alanin*, irreg. fr. *aldehyd* aldehyde + *-in* -ine] **1 :** a white crystalline amino acid $CH_3CH(NH_2)COOH$ that is known in three optically different forms, that is formed by the hydrolysis of proteins and made synthetically, and that takes part in transamination reactions in the living organism; α-amino-propionic acid **2 :** a white crystalline amino acid $NH_2CH_2CH_2COOH$ found in muscle in the form of carnosine and anserine, made synthetically, and used in making pantothenic acid; β-amino-propionic acid — used with an initial Greek beta ⟨β-*alanine*⟩

alans \ˈalənz, -ˌlanz\ *also* **ala·ni** \əˈlāˌnī, əˈlä(ˌ)nē\ *n pl, cap* [L *Alani*, fr. Gk *Alanoi*] **:** a Scythian people in pre-Slavic Russia and the Black sea regions

al·ant \ˈalənt, əˈlant\ *n* -s [G, fr. OHG, fr. (assumed) VL *iluna*, alter. of L *inula* — more at INULA] **:** SNEEZEWEED 1a

alan·tic acid \əˈlantik-\ *n* [ISV *alantic* (fr. *alant* + *-ic*) + *acid*; orig. formed as G *alantsäure*] **:** a crystalline acid $C_{15}H_{22}O_3$ obtained from alantolactone by hydration

alan·tin \əˈlantᵊn\ *n* -s [prob. fr. G *alant* + *-in*] **:** INULIN

alan·to·lac·tone \əˌlan(ˌ)tōˈlakˌtōn\ *n* -s [ISV *alant* + *-o-* + *lactone*; prob. orig. formed as G *alantolakton*] **:** a white crystalline lactone $C_{15}H_{20}O_2$ obtained from elecampane root

al·an·tol·ic acid \ˌalənˈtälik-\ *n* [*alantol*, liquid derived from alant (fr. *alant* + *-ol*) + *-ic*] **:** ALANTIC ACID

al·a·nyl \ˈaləˌnil\ *n* -s [ISV *alanine* + *-yl*] **1 :** the acyl radical $CH_3CH(NH_2)CO–$ of alanine **2 :** the acyl radical $NH_2CH_2CH_2CO–$ of beta-alanine — used with an initial Greek beta ⟨β-*alanyl*⟩

al·a·ouite *also* **al·a·wite** \ˌaləˈwēt\ *n* -s *usu cap* [F] **:** one of a Muslim people living in Syria along the Turkish border

a la pou·pee \-ˌpüˈpā; *see* A LA\ *adj* [F *à la poupée* in the ink-pad (lit., doll) manner] *of an engraving or etching* **:** having several areas of the plate inked in different colors by separate cloth pads for a single multicolor impression

alar \ˈālə(r)\ *adj* [L *alaris*, fr. *ala* wing + *-aris* -ar — more at AISLE] **1 :** of or resembling a wing or wings **2** *bot* **:** belonging to the axil **:** AXILLARY

alar cartilage *n* **:** one of the pair of lower lateral cartilages of the nose

ala·re \əˈla(a)(ˌ)rē, əˈlā(-\ *n* -s [NL, fr. L, neut. sing. of *alaris*] **:** the most lateral point on the ala of the nose

¹alar·ia \əˈla(a)rēə\ *n, cap* [NL, fr. L *ala* wing + NL *-aria*] **:** a genus (the type of the family Alariaceae) of olive-brown to black seaweeds found in northern seas, characterized by an elongate strap-shaped lamina, and having the sori restricted to tongue-shaped sporophylls borne at or near its apex — see BADDERLOCKS

²alaria \"\ *n, cap* [NL] **:** a genus of trematode worms (family Strigeidae) that is parasitic as adults in the intestines of carnivorous mammals but requires several intermediate hosts to complete the life cycle

alar ligament *n* **1 :** CHECK LIGAMENT **2 :** either of two fringe-like folds of the synovial membrane of the knee

¹alarm \əˈlärm, -ȧm\ *also* **alar·um** \-ä(ə)rəm, -er-,-ār-,-ȧr-\ *n* -s [*alarm* fr. ME *alarme*, fr. MF, fr. OIt *all' arme* to arms, lit., to the weapon, fr. *all'* to the (fr. *alla*, fr. L *ad illam* to that, fr. *ad* to + *illam*, accus. fem. of *ille* that, prob. alter. — influenced by *is* he, that — of OL *olle*, *ollus* that, akin to L *uls* beyond) + *arme* weapon, fr. L *arma* weapons; *alarum* fr. ME *alarom*, alter. of *alarme* — more at AT, ITERATE, ALL, ARM] **1** *usu alarum*, *obs* **:** a call to arms (as on the approach of an enemy) **2** *often alarum* **:** a disturbing noise **:** DISTRACTION, DIN — usu. used in pl. ⟨all is quiet, no *alarms* —A.E.Housman⟩ **3 a :** a sound or signal giving notice of danger or calling attention to some event or condition ⟨the whole village heard the ~⟩ ⟨only one fire company will respond to the first ~⟩ **b :** a device that warns or signals by means of a noise (as a bell or siren) or visual effect (as a flashing light) ⟨set the ~ to wake me at seven⟩ ⟨a burglar set off the ~ at the bank⟩ **4** *obs* **:** a surprise attack **:** ASSAULT **5 a :** fear or terror resulting from a sudden sense of danger ⟨could not but observe with ~ the quickened motion of our horses —Thomas De Quincey⟩ **b :** apprehension of an unfavorable outcome, of failure, or of dangerous consequences ⟨viewed with ~ the growing power of the central government⟩ **c :** an occasion of excitement or apprehension ⟨the anxieties of common life began soon to succeed to the ~s of romance —Jane Austen⟩ **6 :** a notice, warning, or announcement calling attention to a circumstance or event ⟨police put out a two-state ~ for the missing car⟩ ⟨the dog's barking gave the ~ and the intruders were routed⟩ — see ALARUMS AND EXCURSIONS **syn** see FEAR

²alarm \"\ *also* **alarum** \"\ *vb* -ED/-ING/-S *vt* **1** *often alarum*, *obs* **:** to rouse to action **:** urge on ⟨I needed not the shout that should *alarm* all Asia militant —Thomas De Quincey⟩ **2** *often alarum, obs* **:** to call to arms **3** *sometimes alarum* **:** to arouse to a sense of danger **:** put on the alert ⟨before the battle of Trenton he crossed the river and *alarmed* the Hessians —E.M.Coulter⟩ **4 :** to strike with fear **:** fill with anxiety as to threatening danger or harm ⟨~*ed* by the sudden rumbling in the earth⟩ **5 :** to keep in excitement or commotion **:** DISTURB ⟨heavy trucks ~*ed* one all night —Glenway Wescott⟩ **~** *vi* **1 :** to sound an alarm ⟨when one or both clocks ~ the trigger spring releases —W.F.Cloud⟩ **2 :** to serve as an alarm — used of a sound **syn** see FRIGHTEN

alarm·a·ble \ə'lärməbəl, -ām-\ *adj* **:** tending or disposed to become alarmed **:** EXCITABLE

alarm bird *n* **:** KOOKABURRA

alarm clock *n* **:** a clock that can be set to give an alarm

alarm·ed·ly \-mədlē, -li\ *adv* **:** with alarm **:** in an alarmed manner ⟨Britons . . . who ~ believe that too many leaders spoil a party —Mollie Panter-Downes⟩

alarm·ing·ly \-miŋlē, -ēŋ-, -li\ *adv* **:** in a manner or to a degree that excites alarm

alarm·ism \-,mizəm\ *n* -S **:** the practice of the alarmist **:** the needless raising or exciting of alarms

¹alarm·ist \-,məst\ *n* -S [¹*alarm* + *-ist*] **:** one inclined to raise or excite alarms esp. needlessly

²alarmist \"\ *adj* **:** characteristic of an alarmist **:** needlessly raising or exciting alarms

alarm reaction *n* **1 :** the first stage of the adaptation syndrome during which the anterior pituitary gland is stimulated to increased secretory activity **2 :** a series of muscular movements frequently repeated according to a regular pattern that certain birds exhibit when disturbed

¹al·a·ro·di·an \,alə'rōdēən\ *n* -S *usu cap* [Gk *Alarodios* + E *-an*] **1 :** a member of an Asian people mentioned in historical accounts by Herodotus who were predecessors and neighbors of the ancient Armenians and who are linguistically related to the contemporary Georgians of the Caucasus **2 :** the language of the Alarodians

²alarodian \¦==¦===\ *adj, usu cap* **1 :** of, relating to, or characteristic of Alarodians **2 :** of, relating to, or characteristic of the language of the Alarodians

alar septum *n* **:** one of the pair of lateral primary septa in the Paleozoic Tetracoralla from each of which the septa of one quarter of a corallite arise

alarum *var of* ALARM

alarum clock *chiefly Brit var of* ALARM CLOCK

alarums and excursions *n pl* **1 :** martial sounds and the movement of soldiers across the stage — used as a stage direction in Elizabethan drama **2 :** clamor, excitement, and feverish or disordered activity ⟨the *alarums and excursions* of the uneasy Manchu empire —*N.Y. Herald Tribune*⟩

ala·ry \'ālərē, 'al-, -ri\ *adj* [L *alarius*, fr *ala* wing + *-arius* -ary — more at AISLE] **1 :** relating to a wing **2 :** wing-shaped or fan-shaped ⟨the ~ muscles of an insect⟩

¹alas \ə'las, -aa(ə)s,-ais,-ȧs\ *interj* [ME, fr. OF, fr. *a* ah + *las* weary, wretched, fr. L *lassus* weary — more at LET] — used to express unhappiness, sorrow, pity, or concern ⟨~ for their sad fate⟩ ⟨~ the heavy day⟩

²alas \'ä,läs\ *n, pl* **alas** *usu cap* **1 :** an Indonesian people of northern Sumatra **2 :** a member of the Alas people

ala·sas \¦alə¦säs\ *n* -ES [Tag *alasás*] **:** any of several Philippine plants of the genus *Pandanus*

alas·can \ə'laskən, -aas-\ *n* -S *usu cap* [Johannes *a Lasco* (Jan Laski) †1560 Polish religious reformer in charge of foreign Protestants in London (*ab* 1550) + E *-an*] **:** a foreign Protestant in England during the reign of Edward VI

¹alas·ka \ə'laskə, -laas-\ *adj, usu cap* [fr. *Alaska*, state of the U.S., fr. Russ *Alashka*, fr. Aleut *alakshak* peninsula] **:** of or from the territory or state of Alaska **:** of the kind or style prevailing in Alaska **:** ALASKAN

²alas·ka \"\ *n* -S *sometimes cap* **:** a storm rubber having a rubberized cloth vamp

alaska blackfish *n, usu cap A* **:** BLACKFISH 1f

alaska cedar *or* **alaska cypress** *n, usu cap A* **:** YELLOW CEDAR 1a

alaska cod *n, usu cap A* **:** a cod (*Gadus macrocephalus*)

alaska day *n, usu cap A&D* **:** October 18, the anniversary of the formal transfer of the territory of Alaska in 1867 by Russia to the U.S., celebrated as a legal holiday in Alaska

alaska goose *n, usu cap A* **:** LESSER SNOW GOOSE

alaska grayling *n, usu cap A* **:** a northern arctic grayling

alaska longspur *n, usu cap A* **:** a longspur (*Calcarius lapponicus alascensis*) of northwestern No. America

¹alas·kan \ə'laskən, -aas-\ *adj, usu cap* [*Alaska* + E *-an*] **1 :** of, relating to, or characteristic of the territory or state of Alaska **2 :** of, relating to, or characteristic of the people of Alaska

²alaskan \"\ *n* -S *cap* **:** a native or resident of Alaska

alaskan malamute *n* **1** *usu cap A&M* **:** a breed of powerful heavy-coated deep-chested dogs that were developed from native Alaskan sled dogs and have erect ears, heavily cushioned feet, and plumy tail and are usu. colored wolf gray or black and white **2** *usu cap A & sometimes cap M* **:** a dog of the Alaskan Malamute breed

alaska pine *n, usu cap A* **:** a valuable timber hemlock (*Tsuga heterophylla*) of northwestern No. America

alaska pollack *n, usu cap A* **:** WALLEYE POLLACK

alaska time *or* **alaska standard time** *n, cap A* **:** the time of the 10th time zone west of Greenwich that includes most of Alaska and is four hours slower than eastern time

alas·kite \ə'la,skīt, -aa,s-\ *n* -S [*Alaska*, its locality + E *-ite*] **:** a leucocratic granite of medium or fine grain composed chiefly of quartz and alkali feldspars

ala spu·ria \¦ālə'spyu̇rēə\ *n* [NL, lit., false wing] **:** BASTARD WING

alas·tor \ə'lastər, -aas-, -,stȯ(ə)r\ *n* -S *usu cap* [Gk *alastōr*, fr. *a-* ²a- + *-lastōr* (prob. fr. *lan* to look); akin to Skt *lasati* he shines] **:** any of certain avenging deities or spirits esp. in Greek antiquity

alas·trim \¦alə¦strim\ *n* -S [Pg, fr. *alastrar* to spread, cover, fr. *lastro* covering, ballast, fr. F *laste*, a weight used in shipping, fr. D *last* load; akin to OHG *hlast* load — more at LAST] **:** a mild form of smallpox of low mortality

¹alate \ə'lāt\ *adv* [ME, fr. ¹*a-* + *late*] *archaic* **:** of late **:** LATELY

²alate \'ā,lāt, usu -ād·+V\ *also* **alat·ed** \'ā,lād·əd\ *adj* [L *alatus*, fr. *ala* wing + *-atus* -ate — more at AISLE] **1 :** having wings **:** WINGED ⟨an ~ horse in mythology⟩ **2 :** furnished with winglike expansions ⟨certain stems and fruits are ~⟩ **3 a :** having a broad expanded lip — used of shells **b :** having winged forms — used of certain insects (as ants and aphids) **c :** of or relating to alates

³alate \"\ *n* -S **:** a winged individual of a kind of insect (as ant or aphid) that has both winged and wingless forms

ala·tion \ā'lāshən\ *n* -S [²*alate* + *-ion*] *biol* **:** the state of having wings

alau·da \ə'lȯdə, -lau̇də\ *n, cap* [NL, fr. L, lark, fr. Gaulish] **:** the type genus of Alaudidae comprising the skylark

alau·di·dae \-də,dē\ *n pl, cap* [NL, fr. *Alauda*, type genus + *-idae*] **:** a family of usu. brownish terrestrial gregarious passerine birds comprising the larks and having the hind claw elongated and more or less straight

alaun *or* **alaund** *or* **alaunt** *var of* ALAN

alawite *usu cap, var of* ALAOUITE

alb \'alb\ *n* -S [ME *albe*, fr. OE, fr. ML *alba*, fr. L, fem. of *albus* white — more at ELF] **1** *also* **albe :** a liturgical vestment worn by priests and certain other ecclesiastics consisting of a full-length close-sleeved tunic usu. of linen and usu. gathered at the waist with a cincture, now uniformly white in Western churches but of any of various colors in Eastern churches **2 :** a flat or gently inclined shelf high in a glaciated mountain valley

alb

alb- *or* **albo-** *comb form* [L, fr. *albus*] **:** white ⟨*albite*⟩ ⟨*albocinereous*⟩

¹al·ba \'älbə\ *n* -S [OProv, lit., dawn, fr. (assumed) VL *alba* dawn, fr. L, fem. of *albus*] **1 :** an often Provençal love lyric usu. dealing with a parting of lovers at dawn **2 :** the musical accompaniment of an alba

²al·ba \'albə\ *n* -S [NL, fr. L, fem. of *albus*] **:** the white matter of the brain and spinal cord

al·ba·cea \,albə'sāə\ *n* -S [Sp, fr. Ar *al-waṣīyah* the thing designated in a will, fr. *waṣā* to entrust, make a will] *Spanish law* **:** the person designated by a testator to fulfill and execute the directions of the will **:** EXECUTOR

al·ba·co·ra \,albə'kōrə\ *n, pl* **albacoras** *or* **albacora** [Sp, fr. Ar *al-bakūrah*] **1 :** ALBACORE **2 :** SWORDFISH

al·ba·core *or* **al·bi·core** \'albə,kō(ə)r, -ȯ(ə)r, -ōə, -ȯ(ə)\ *n, pl* **albacores** *or* **albacore** *or* **albicores** *or* **albicore** [Pg *albacor*, fr. Ar *al-bakūrah* the albacore, perh. fr. *bākūr* precocious] **1 :** a large pelagic tuna of the genus *Thunnus* (*T. alalunga*) having long pectoral fins and noted for its fine flesh which is the source of most canned tuna **2 :** BLUEFIN TUNA **3 :** any of several smaller fishes related to the albacore (as a bonito) **4 :** any of several fishes of the family Carangidae

al·ba·da finder \al'bädə-\ *n, usu cap A* [after L.E.W. von *Albada fl* 1924, its inventor] **:** a camera viewfinder for use at eye level in which a white field-limiting frame is made to appear very distant by reflection at the rear surface of the front lens — called also *sport finder*

al·ba fir·ma \¦albə'fərmə\ *n* [ML, lit., white rent] **:** rent payable in silver in accordance with early English law

alba graeca *pl of* ALBUM GRAECUM

al·ba·ha·ca \,albə'häkə, -akə\ *n* -S [Sp, fr. Ar *al-habaqah* the basil] **:** any of several aromatic plants of the family Labiatae esp. of the genus *Ocimum*

al·bam \äl'bäm, 'al,bam\ *n* -S [Heb] **:** a cipher used in Jewish mystical and allegorical writing in which each letter of the first half of the Hebrew alphabet is replaced by or replaces the letter occupying the corresponding position in the second half of the alphabet — compare ATHBASH

al·ba·nen·ses \,albə'nen,sēz\ *n pl, usu cap* [ML, pl. of *Albanensis*, lit., inhabitant of *Alba*, irreg. fr. *Alba*, Italy + L *-ensis* -ese] **:** members of a 12th century dualistic Catharistic sect closely related to the Albigenses — **al·ba·nen·sian** \¦==¦nenchən, -nen(t)sēən\ *adj, usu cap*

al·ba·nia \(')al¦bānēə, -nyə *sometimes* (')ȯl-\ *adj, usu cap* [fr. *Albania*, country in Balkan peninsula] **:** of or from Albania **:** of the kind or style prevalent in Albania **:** ALBANIAN

¹al·ba·nian \-nēən,-nyən\ *adj, usu cap* [*Albania*, country in the Balkan peninsula + E *-an*] **1 a :** of, relating to, or characteristic of Albania **b :** of, relating to, or characteristic of the Albanians **2 :** of, relating to, or characteristic of the Albanian language

²albanian \"\ *n* -S *cap* **1 :** a native or inhabitant of Albania **2 a :** the language of the Albanian people **b :** a branch of the Indo-European language family containing only the Albanian language

³al·ba·ni·an \ȯl'bānēən, -nyən\ *n* -S *cap* [*Albany*, N.Y. + E *-an*] **:** a native or resident of Albany, N. Y.

albanian church *n, cap A & usu cap C* [¹*Albanian*] **:** the autocephalous Church of Albania, a branch of the Orthodox Church

al·ban·ite \'ȯlbə,nīt, 'al-\ *n* -S [*Alban* hills near Rome, Italy, its locality + E *-ite*] **:** a melanocratic leucitite

al·ba·ny \'ȯlbənē, -ni\ *adj, usu cap* [fr. *Albany*, N.Y.] **:** of or from Albany, the capital of New York ⟨*Albany* stores⟩ **:** of the kind or style prevalent in Albany

albany beef *n, usu cap A* [fr. *Albany*, N.Y.; fr. its former use as a food in and near Albany] **:** the flesh of the sturgeon

albany slip *n, usu cap A* [fr. *Albany*, N.Y.] **:** a clay slip rich in natural fluxes that is used as a brown to black glaze on high-fired ceramic wares (as stoneware)

al·bar·co \al'bär(,)kō\ *n* -S [modif. of AmerSp *abarco*] **:** COLOMBIAN MAHOGANY

al·ba red \'albə-\ *n, usu cap A&R* [fr. (assumed) VL *alba* dawn — more at ALBA] **:** an organic pigment — see DYE table I (under *Pigment Red 100*)

al·ba·rel·lo \,albə're(,)lō\ *n, pl* **albarel·li** \-(,)lē\ *or* **albarellos** [It *alberello* bottle, phial, prob. dim. of *albero* poplar, fr. (assumed) VL *albarus* white poplar, fr. L *albus* white — more at ELF] **:** a majolica jar more or less cylindrical in form but with concave sides used orig. as a container esp. of drugs

al·bar·i·um \al'ba(a)rēəm\ *n* -S [L, fr. neut. of *albarius* of the whitening of walls, fr. *albus* + *-arius* -ary] **:** a thin white stucco

albas *pl of* ALBA

albas·pi·din \al'baspədən\ *n* -S [ISV *alb-* (fr. L *albus* white) + NL *Aspidium* + ISV *-in*; orig. formed in G] **:** a white crystalline compound $C_{25}H_{32}O_8$ extracted from aspidium

al·ba·tross \'albə-,trȯs, -äs\ *n, pl* **albatrosses** *or* **albatross** [prob. alter. (prob. influenced by L *albus* white) of *alcatras*, fr. Pg or Sp *alcatraz* pelican, prob. fr. Ar *al-ghaṭṭās* the white-tailed sea eagle (*Haliaeetus albicilla*), fr. *al-* the + *ghaṭṭās* white-tailed sea eagle] **1 :** any of a number of large web-footed seabirds that are related to the petrels, that form a family (Diomedeidae) of the order Procellariiformes, and that include the largest of seabirds, being capable of long-continued flight and often appearing at great distances from land chiefly over southern seas — see BLACK-BROWED ALBATROSS, LAYSAN ALBATROSS, SOOTY ALBATROSS, WANDERING ALBATROSS **2 a :** a fine thin worsted fabric with a crepy surface made in various weaves **b :** a plainwoven cotton cloth with a soft nap similar to cotton bunting **3 a :** something that causes persistent deep concern or anxiety **b :** something that makes accomplishment particularly difficult **:** ENCUMBRANCE, HANDICAP

¹albe *var of* ALB

²al·be \(')al¦bē, (')ȯl-\ *conj* [ME — more at ALBEIT] *archaic* **:** ALBEIT

al·be·do \al'bē(,)dō\ *n* -S [LL, whiteness, fr. L *albus* white — more at ELF] **1 :** reflective power **2 a :** the fraction of incident light or electromagnetic radiation that is reflected by a surface or body (as the moon, a planet, a cloud, the ground, or a field of snow) **b :** the fraction of incident neutrons that are reflected by a surface **3 :** the whitish inner portion of the rind of citrus fruits that is a source of pectin used esp. in jelly and jam — compare FLAVEDO

al·be·dom·e·ter \,albə'dämed·ə(r)\ *n* -S [*albedo* + *-meter*] **:** a device for measuring the reflection of light (as by snow)

al·be·it \(')ȯl¦bēət, (')al-\ *conj* [ME, lit., completely though it be, fr. *al* completely + *be* (3rd pers. sing. pres. subj. of *been* to be) + *it* — more at ALL, BE] **:** even though **:** ALTHOUGH ⟨destined to pass his fortieth year before fame saluted him — ~ his was a special genius —*Fashion Digest*⟩

Al·be·rene \'albə,rēn\ *trademark* — used for a soapstone used to make acid-resistant or alkali-resistant surfaces

al·bers projection \'älbə(r)z-, -)s-\ *n, usu cap A* [after Heinrich C. *Albers* †1833 Ger. cartographer] **:** an equal-area projection with straight-line meridians and two standard parallels of true scale

al·bert \'albə(r)t\ *n* -S [after *Albert* †1861 prince consort of England] **:** a watch chain worn across the front of a vest

al·ber·ta \(')al¦bərd·ə\ *adj, usu cap* [fr. *Alberta*, province of Canada] **:** of or from the province of Alberta

¹al·ber·tan \(')al¦bərtᵊn\ *adj, usu cap* [*Alberta*, province of Canada + E *-an*] **1 :** of or relating to Alberta **2 :** of or relating to a subage and substage of the Cambrian period

²albertan \"\ *n* -S *cap* **:** a native or resident of the province of Alberta

al·ber·ti bass \al'bərd·ē, äl'ber-\ *n, usu cap A* [after Domenico *Alberti* †*ab* 1740 It. musician] **:** a bass part in keyboard music consisting of broken chords in close position

al·ber·tist \al'bərd·əst, 'albər-\ *n* -S *usu cap* [*Albert*us Magnus (Albert, Count von Bollstädt) †1280 Ger. scholastic philosopher + E *-ist*] **:** a follower of Albertus Magnus, who adapted Aristotle's philosophy to Christian theology

al·bert·ite \'albərd·,īt\ *n* -S *sometimes cap* [*Albert* county, New Brunswick, Canada, its locality + E *-ite*] **:** a bituminous mineral resembling asphaltum (hardness 1-2, sp. gr. 1.097)

al·ber·tus·ta·ler \al'berd·əs,tälər\ *n, pl* **albertustaler** *or* **albertustalers** [G, fr. D *albertusdaalder*, fr. Albert VII (*Albertus*) †1622 archduke of Austria and regent of the Netherlands, its coiner + D *daalder* taler, fr. G *taler* — more at DOLLAR] **:** a silver coin worth three gulden

al·ber·type \'albər(t),tīp\ *n* -S *sometimes cap* [part trans. of G *albertypie*, *albertypie*, fr. Joseph *Albert* †1886 Ger. photographer, its inventor + G *-typie* -type] **:** COLLOTYPE

al·be·spine \'albə,spīn\ *n* -S [ME, fr. MF, fr. (assumed) VL *albispina*, fr. L *alba* (fem. of *albus* white) + *spina* thorn — more at ELF, SPINE] **1 :** a European hawthorn (*Crataegus oxycantha*) **2 :** the wood of the albespine

al·be·tad \'albə,tad\ *n* -S [prob fr. Ar *al-birzad*] **:** GALBANUM

¹al·bi·an \'albēən\ *adj, usu cap* [*Alb-* (prob. fr. *Aube*, department of France, its type station) + E *-ian*] **:** of or relating to the lowest division of the Upper Cretaceous esp. in western Europe and the Mediterranean basin — see GEOLOGIC TIME table

²albian *n* -S *usu cap* **:** the Albian series or epoch

albicore *vi of* ALBACORE

al·bi·gen·ses \,albə'jen,sēz\ *n pl, usu cap* [ML, pl. of *Albigensis*, lit., inhabitant of Albi, fr. *Albiga* (Albi), France + L *-ensis* -ese] **:** members of a Catharistic sect of southern France that arose in the 11th century and was exterminated in the 13th century through the influence of Pope Innocent III and the Inquisition — **al·bi·gen·sian** \¦albə¦jenchən, -en(t)sēən\ *adj or n, usu cap*

al·bi·gen·sian·ism \-,nizəm\ *n* -S *usu cap* **:** the principles and practices of the Albigenses

al·bi·nism \'albə,nizəm\ *also* **al·bi·no·ism** \al'bī(,)nō,izəm, -bē-\ *n* -S [F or G; F *albinisme*, fr. *albino* + *-isme* -ism; G *albinismus*, fr. *albino* + *-ismus* -ism] **1 :** the state or quality of being an albino **2 :** complete inability to produce pigment, a recessive genetic condition of wide occurrence esp. in respect to coat, skin, and eye color of mammals — compare CHINCHILLA, HIMALAYAN, WILD TYPE

al·bi·nis·tic \¦albə¦nistik\ *also* **al·bi·nic** \(')al¦binik\ *or* **al·binal** \'albənᵊl\ *adj* [*albino* + *-istic* or *-ic* or *-al*] **:** of, relating to, or affected with albinism

al·bi·no \al'bī,nō, *Brit usu & US sometimes* -bē-\ *n* -S *often attrib* [Pg, fr. Sp, fr. *albo* white, fr. L *albus* — more at ELF] **1 :** any organism exhibiting deficient pigmentation: as **a :** a human being or other animal affected with albinism and typically having a milky or translucent skin, white or nearly colorless hair, and eyes with pink or blue iris and deep-red pupil; *sometimes* **:** an albinotic individual **b :** a member of a strain (as of mice or rabbits) developed by selectively breeding for pigment deficiency **c :** a plant lacking normal pigment or chromatophores: (1) **:** a plant that is pathologically deficient in chlorophyll and yellow leaf pigments (2) **:** an etiolated plant (3) **:** a plant whose flowers are white because of undeveloped chromoplasts **2 :** an impression of an embossed stamp (as on an envelope) made without ink

al·bi·not·ic \¦albə¦näd·ik\ *adj* [*albino* + *-tic* (as in *melanotic*)] **1 :** ALBINIC **2 :** tending toward albinism

al·bite \'al,bīt\ *n* -S [Sw *albit*, fr. L *albus* white + Sw *-it* -ite — more at ELF] **:** a triclinic usu. white feldspar consisting of a sodium aluminum silicate $NaAlSi_3O_8$, occurring massive or in crystals, and forming a common constituent of granite and of various igneous rocks — **al·bit·ic** \(')al¦bid·ik\ *adj*

al·bi·tite \'albə,tīt\ *n* -S [*albite* + *-ite*] **:** a granular dike rock consisting essentially of albite

al·bi·ti·za·tion \,albəd·ə'zāshən\ *n* -S [*albite* + *-ization*] **:** a process in which albite replaces the plagioclase feldspar of an igneous rock

al·bit·o·phyre \al'bid·ə,fī(ə)r\ *n* -S [ISV *albite* + *-o-* + *-phyre*; orig. formed in F] **:** a porphyritic rock containing phenocrysts of albite in a groundmass usu. of albite and a little quartz and chlorite

al·biz·zia \al'bizēə\ *n* [NL, after Filippo degli *Albizzi fl*1749 It. naturalist who introduced it into Italy] **1** *cap* **:** a large genus of unarmed trees (family Leguminosae) found in warm regions of the Old World and having twice-pinnate leaves, solitary or panicled globelike clusters of flowers, and long flat pods — see SILK TREE **2** -S **:** a tree of the genus *Albizzia*

albo- — see ALB-

al·bo·ci·ne·re·ous \¦al(,)bō¦====\ *adj* [*alb-* + *cinereous*] *anat* **:** composed of white and gray matter

al·bo·lite \'albə,līt\ *or* **al·bo·lith** \-,lith\ *n* -S *often attrib* [ISV *alb-* + *-lite*, *-lith*] **:** a plastic cement consisting chiefly of magnesia and silica

al·bo·ra·da \,albə'rädə\ *n* -S [Sp, fr. *alba* dawn, fr. fem. of *albo* white, fr. L *albus* — more at ELF] **:** an instrumental serenade usu. played on a bagpipe or oboe to the accompaniment of a small drum **:** AUBADE

al·bo·ran·ite \,albə'ra,nīt\ *n* -S [G *alboranit*, fr. *Alborán* island, Spain, its locality + G *-it*, -ite] **:** a hypersthene-basalt having a porphyritic texture and containing phenocrysts of labradorite but no olivine

al·bright \'ȯl,brīt\ *n* -S *usu cap* [after Jacob *Albright* †1808 Am. preacher, founder of the association] **:** a member of a 19th century evangelical association now merged into the Evangelical United Brethren Church

al·bu·ca \al'byükə\ *n, cap* [NL, fr. L, asphodel] **:** a genus of bulbous plants (family Liliaceae) native to southern Africa and having pale yellow flowers in large clusters

al·bu·gi·na·ce·ae \(,)al,byüjə'nāsē,ē\ *n pl, cap* [NL, fr. *Albugin-*, *Albugo*, type genus + *-aceae*] **:** a family of fungi (order Peronosporales) that produce whitish blisterlike conidial sori on certain flowering plants and that reproduce by forming conidia in chains within the sori or by producing oospores within the affected host tissue — compare WHITE RUST

al·bu·gi·na·les \-'nā(,)lēz\ *n pl, cap* [NL, fr. *Albugin-*, *Albugo* + *-ales*] *in some classifications* **:** an order of fungi coextensive with the family Albuginaceae

al·bu·go \al'byü(,)gō\ *n, cap* [NL, fr. L, white spot, fr. *albus* white — more at ELF] **:** a genus of fungi (the type of the family Albuginaceae) causing the white rusts

al·bu·la \'albyələ\ *n, cap* [NL, fr. L, fem. of *albulus* whitish, fr. *albus* white] **:** a genus (coextensive with the family Albulidae) of silvery marine fishes widely distributed in warm seas and prob. including only a single species (*A. vulpes*) — see BONEFISH

al·bum \'albəm, *rapid* 'albᵊm *or* 'au̇bᵊm\ *n* -S [L, tablet on which edicts were written, list of names, fr. neut. of *albus* white — more at ELF] **1 a :** a bound or loose-leaf book usu. with mostly blank pages or some other volume or packet designed or used for making a collection (as of autographs, stamps, photographs, drawings, or specimens) usu. according to a selected theme, subject, or pattern — compare SCRAPBOOK **b :** a rigid or semirigid envelopelike, booklike, or boxlike container usu. made of strong paperboard and designed to hold and protect one or more phonograph records **c :** one or more phonograph records or tape recordings carrying either the whole of a long recording (as of a complete opera) or a grouped selection of shorter recordings (as of excerpts from a film score) **2 :** a usu. representative collection (as of literary selections, musical compositions, or pictures) **:** ANTHOLOGY; *esp* **:** a published collection of this kind usu. in book form

al·bum·blatt \'älbəm,blät, 'albəm,blat\ *n, pl* **albumblät·ter** \-led·ə(r)\ *or* **albumblatts** *usu cap* [G, lit., album leaf, fr. *album* (fr. L) + *blatt* leaf, fr. OHG *blat* — more at BLADE] **:** a short instrumental composition usu. for piano

album board *n* **:** a thick album paper often consisting of two layers of album paper pasted together

al·bu·men \al'byümən *sometimes* -,men *or* 'albyə-\ *n* -S [L, fr. *albus* white — more at ELF] **1 a :** the white of an egg — see EGG illustration **b :** EGG ALBUMIN 2 **2** *archaic* **:** ENDOSPERM **3 :** ALBUMIN

albumen paper *n* **:** a light-sensitive paper prepared by coating with white of egg and a salt (as ammonium chloride) and sensitized by an after-treatment with a solution of silver nitrate

albumen plate *n* **:** a plate coated with bichromated albumen used in photolithography

al·bum grae·cum \¦albəm'grēkəm, -rīk-\ *n, pl* **al·ba grae·ca** \-bə...kə\ *usu cap G* [NL, lit., Greek white; fr. the fact that it becomes white when exposed to air] **:** dried dung of dogs or hyenas sometimes used in dressing leather

al·bu·min \al'byümən, -,min *sometimes* 'albyə-\ *n* -S [ISV *album-* (fr. L *albumen*) + *-in*; orig. formed as F *albumine*] **:** any of a large class of simple proteins that are characterized by their solubility in pure water, dilute salt solutions, and half-saturated ammonium sulfate or sodium sulfate solutions, that are coagulable by heat, thereby carrying colloidal matters and impurities along with them, that form important constituents of human or animal blood plasma or serum and are found also in muscle, the whites of eggs, milk, and other animal substances and in many vegetable tissues and fluids, and that are used esp. for clarifying liquids, in photography, and in textile printing — see LACTALBUMIN, OVALBUMIN, SERUM ALBUMIN

al·bu·min- *or* **albumini-** *or* **albumino-** *comb form* [prob. fr. F, fr. L *albumin-, albumen*] **:** albumen **:** albumin ⟨*albumin*oid⟩ ⟨*albumini*ferous⟩ ⟨*albumino*lysis⟩

al·bu·mi·nate \alˈbyüməˌnāt, -ˌnət, *usu* -d·+V\ *n* -s [*albumin-* + *-ate*] **:** a compound derived from an albumin (as by the action of acids or alkalies or by combination with another substance)

al·bu·mi·nize *or* **al·bu·me·nize** \-ˌnīz\ *vt* -ED/-ING/-S [*albumin-* or *albumen* + *-ize*] **:** to cover or saturate with albumen **:** coat or treat with an albuminous solution

¹al·bu·mi·noid \-ˌnȯid\ *adj* [ISV *albumin-* + *-oid*] **:** resembling albumin in properties **:** PROTEIN

²albuminoid \"\ *n* -s **1 :** PROTEIN **2 :** SCLEROPROTEIN

al·bu·mi·nom·e·ter \alˌbyüməˈnäməd·ə(r)\ *also* **al·bu·mi·nim·e·ter** \-ˈnim-\ *n* -s [*albumin-* + *-meter*] **:** an instrument, usu. a graduated tube, for determining the presence and amount of protein (esp. albumin) in a liquid (as urine)

al·bu·mi·nous \alˈbyümənəs\ *adj* [*albumin-* + *-ous*] **1 :** relating to or containing albumin **:** having the properties of albumen or albumin **2 :** ENDOSPERMOUS

albuminous cell *n* **:** one of the parenchyma cells adjacent to the sieve cells in gymnosperm wood, distinguished by staining deeply with cytoplasmic stains, and apparently associated physiologically with the sieve cells and joined to them by sieve areas

albumin tannate *n* **:** a yellowish white powder used as an astringent in diarrhea

al·bu·min·uria \(ˌ)alˌbyüməˈn(y)u̇rēə\ *n* -s [NL, fr. *albumin-* + *-uria*] **:** the presence of albumin in the urine, usu. a symptom of disease of the kidneys but sometimes a response to other diseases or physiologic disturbances of benign nature — **al·bu·min·uric** \(ˈ)==ˌ==ˈn(y)u̇rik\ *adj*

al·bu·mose \ˈalbyəˌmōs\ *n* -s [F, fr. *albumine* albumin + *-ose*] **:** any of various protein derivatives formed by the action of hydrolytic enzymes, esp. pepsin, on proteins — compare PROTEOSE

album paper *n* **:** a plain usu. black or gray cover paper commonly used for the leaves of photograph albums

albums *pl of* ALBUM

al·bu·quer·que·an \ˌalbəˈkərkēən *also* -byə-\ *n* -s *cap* [*Albuquerque*, New Mexico + E *-an*] **:** a native or resident of Albuquerque, N. Mex.

al·bur·num \alˈbərnəm\ *n* -s [L, fr. *albus* white — more at ELF] **:** SAPWOOD

al·bus \ˈalbəs\ *n, pl* **albuses** [G, fr. ML, fr. L, white] **:** a minor billon coin of Germany and the Low Countries of the 13th and 14th centuries — compare BLANC

al·bu·tan·nin \ˌalbyəˈtanən\ *n* -s [*albumin* + *tannin*] **:** ALBUMIN TANNATE

alc *abbr* alcohol

al·ca \ˈalkə\ *n, cap* [NL, fr. Sw *alka* auk, fr. Norw *alk, alka* — more at AUK] **:** the type genus of Alcidae usu. including solely the razor-billed auk

al·ca·de \älˈkädē\ *n* -s [obs. Sp (now *alcalde*) — more at ALCALDE] **:** ALCALDE

al·cae \ˈalˌsē\ *n pl, cap* [NL, fr. *Alca*] **:** a suborder of Charadriiformes coextensive with the family Alcidae and including the auks, murres, and puffins

alcahest *var of* ALKAHEST

¹al·ca·ic \(ˈ)alˈkāik\ *adj, often cap* [LL *Alcaicus* of Alcaeus, fr. Gk *Alkaikos*, fr. *Alkaios* (Alcaeus) *fl ab* 600 B.C. Greek lyric poet who used such verse forms + Gk *-ikos* -ic] **:** relating to or written in verse or strophe marked by complicated variation of a dominant iambic pattern by initial anacrusis and by spondees, trochees, and dactyls used mostly in medial or final positions

²alcaic \"\ *n* -s *often cap* **:** alcaic meter **:** an alcaic verse or strophe

al·cai·de *also* **al·cay·de** \älˈkīdē, al-\ *n* -s [Sp *alcaide*, fr. Ar *al-qāʼid* the captain, fr. *qād* to command] **:** a commander of a castle or fortress (as among Spaniards, Portuguese, or Moors)

al·cal·de \älˈkäldē, al-\ *n* -s *sometimes cap* [Sp, fr. Ar *al-qāḍī* the judge, fr. *qaḍā* to judge] **:** an administrative and judicial officer in villages, towns, or districts in Spain and regions under Spanish influence

al·ca·lig·e·nes \ˌalkəˈlijəˌnēz\ *n* [NL, fr. F *alcali* alkali + Gk *-genēs* -gen — more at ALKALI] **1** *cap* **:** a genus of usu. aerobic and gram-negative bacteria that are related to the achromobacters, do not ferment carbohydrates and are aerobes or facultative anaerobes, occur in the intestines of man and animals and in dairy products, and are probably all nonpathogenic though one species (*A. viscosum*) is economically important as a cause of a ropy condition of milk **2** *pl* **alcaligenes :** an organism of the genus *Alcaligenes*

al·ca·mine \ˈalkəˌmēn\ *n* -s [ISV *alcohol* + *amine*; orig. formed as G *alkamin*] **:** AMINO ALCOHOL

al·can·na \alˈkanə\ *n* -s [Sp *alcana* henna (shrub) — more at ALKANNA] **:** HENNA 3

al·cap·ton *var of* ALKAPTON

alcaptonuria *var of* ALKAPTONURIA

al·car·ra·za \ˌalkəˈräzə\ *n* -s [Sp, fr. Ar *al-karrāz* the jar] **:** a jug or similar container made of porous earthenware

al·ca·tras \ˈalkəˌtras, -az\ *n, pl* **alcatras** *or* **alcatrases** [Pg or Sp *alcatraz* pelican — more at ALBATROSS] **:** a large water bird (as the pelican or frigate bird)

al·ca·zar \alˈkäzər, alˈka-, älˈkä-, ˌalkəˈzär\ *n* -s [Sp *alcázar*, fr. Ar *al-qaṣr* the castle, fr. *al* the + *qaṣr* castle, fr. L *castrum* — more at CASTLE] **:** a Spanish fortress or palace

al·ce·din·i·dae \ˌalsəˈdinəˌdē\ *n pl, cap* [NL, fr. *Alcedin-, Alcedo*, type genus + *-idae*] **:** a large family of large-headed short-bodied birds comprising the kingfishers and constituting a suborder (Alcedines) of the order Coraciiformes

al·ce·do \alˈsē(ˌ)dō\ *n, cap* [NL, fr. L, kingfisher] **:** the type genus of Alcedinidae comprising Old World kingfishers including the small brightly colored European kingfisher

al·cel·a·phine \alˈseləˌfīn\ *adj* [NL *Alcelaphus* + E *-ine*] **:** of or belonging to the genus *Alcelaphus*

al·cel·a·phus \-fəs\ *n, cap* [NL, fr. L *alces* elk + Gk *elaphos* deer] **:** a genus of African antelopes including the hartebeest, bubalis, and related animals

al·ces \ˈalˌsēz\ *n, cap* [NL, fr. L, elk, of Gmc origin; akin to ON *elgr* elk — more at ELK] **:** the genus of mammals (order Artiodactyla) comprising the moose and the European elk

al·chem·ic \(ˈ)alˈkemik, -ēk\ *or* **al·chem·i·cal** \-əkəl, -ēk-\ *adj* [*alchemy* + *-ic, -ical*] **:** of, relating to, marked by, or concerned with alchemy — **al·chem·i·cal·ly** \-ək(ə)lē, -ēk-, -li\ *adv*

al·che·mil·la \ˌalkəˈmilə\ *n* [NL, perh. fr. ML *alchymia* alchemy; fr. the belief that the dew on the leaves of the plants is efficacious in alchemy] **1** *cap* **:** a genus of widely distributed perennial herbs (family Rosaceae) with compound serrate leaves and inconspicuous flowers — see LADY'S-MANTLE **2** -s **:** a plant of the genus *Alchemilla*

al·che·mist \ˈalkəməst *sometimes* -ˌkem-\ *n* -s [ME *alkamist, alkamistre*, prob. fr. ML *alchymista*, fr. *alchymia* alchemy + L *-ista* -ist] **:** one that studies or practices alchemy

al·che·mis·tic \ˌalkəˈmistik, -ēk\ *also* **al·che·mis·ti·cal** \-əkəl, -ēk-\ *adj* **:** ALCHEMIC

alchemistry *n* -ES [*alchemist* + *-ry*] *archaic* **:** ALCHEMY

al·che·mize *or* **al·che·mise** \ˈalkəˌmīz\ *vt* -ED/-ING/-S **:** to change by or as if by alchemy **:** TRANSMUTE ⟨trying to ~ a base metal into gold⟩ ⟨pity *alchemized* her feeling —Richard Llewellyn⟩

al·che·my \ˈalkəmē, -mi\ *n* -ES [ME *alkamie, alquemie*, fr. MF or ML; MF *alquemie*, fr. ML *alchymia, alchimia*, fr. Ar *al-kīmiyāʼ* the philosopher's stone, the alchemy, fr. *al* the + *kīmiyāʼ*, fr. LGk *chēmeia*, prob. alter. of *chymeia*, prob. fr. Gk *chyma* fluid, fr. *chein* to pour — more at FOUND (to melt)] **1 :** the medieval chemical science and speculative philosophy whose aims were the transmutation of the base metals into gold, the discovery of a universal cure for diseases, and the discovery of a means of indefinitely prolonging life **2 a :** a great or magic power of transmutation ⟨no . . . dishonest candidate could, by an ~ of election, be converted into an honest president —A.E.Stevenson †1965⟩ **3 a** *archaic* **:** a golden-colored alloy **b** *obs* **:** a golden-colored trumpet ⟨put to their mouths the sounding ~ —John Milton⟩ **syn** see MAGIC

al·che·ra \ˈalchəˌrä\ *or* **al·che·rin·ga** \ˌalchəˈriŋgə\ *n* -s [native name in Australia] **:** DREAMTIME

al·chor·nea \alˈkȯrnēə\ *n* [NL, fr. Stanesby *Alchorne* †*ab* 1799 Eng. botanist] **1** *cap* **:** a genus of tropical trees and shrubs (family Euphorbiaceae) with alternate leaves and small unisexual apetalous flowers in spikes or racemes **2** -s **:** a plant of the genus *Alchornea*

alchymie *obs var of* ALCHEMY

al·cian blue 8GX \ˈalsh(ē)ən-\ *n, usu cap A&B* [*Alcian* of unknown origin] **:** an ingrain dye — see DYE table I (under *Ingrain Blue 1*)

al·ci·cor·ni·um \ˌalsəˈkȯrnēəm\ [NL, fr. L *alces* elk + NL *-i-* + L *cornu* horn + NL *-ium*] *syn of* PLATYCERIUM

al·ci·dae \ˈalsəˌdē\ *n pl, cap* [NL, fr. *Alca*, type genus + *-idae*] **:** a family of diving birds (order Charadriiformes) having short wings and tail, webbed feet, a large head and heavy body, and thick compact plumage, being confined to the northern parts of the northern hemisphere, and including the auks, puffins, guillemots, murres, and related forms

al·clad \ˈalˌklad\ *n* -s [fr. *Alclad*, a trademark] **:** a duplex metal product made by cladding an aluminum alloy core with surface layers of pure aluminum or aluminum alloy usu. for giving increased resistance to corrosion

¹alc·ma·ni·an \(ˈ)alkˈmānēən\ *or* **alc·man·ic** \-manik\ *adj, usu cap* [*Alcmanian* fr. *Alcman* 7th cent. B.C. Greek lyric poet (fr. Gk *Alkman*) + E *-ian*; *Alcmanic* fr. Gk *Alkmanikos*, fr. *Alkman* + Gk *-ikos* -ic] **:** of or relating to Alcman or to verse composed wholly or partly of Alcmanians

²alcmanian \"\ *n* -s *usu cap* **:** a metrical line of four dactyls

al·co \ˈal(ˌ)kō\ *n* -s [Sp, fr. Quechua *álkko, álkkho* dog] **:** a small long-haired dog with pendulous ears that is native to and sometimes domesticated in tropical America

alco- *or* **alcoo-** *comb form* [*alcohol*] **:** alcohol ⟨*alco*gel⟩ ⟨*alco*sol⟩ ⟨*alcoo*meter⟩

al·cock's canal \ˈalˌkäks-, ˈȯl-\ *n, usu cap A* [after Benjamin *Alcock fl* 1836 Irish anatomist] **:** a fascial compartment on the lateral wall of the ischiorectal fossa containing the pudendal arteries, veins, and nerves

alcock spruce *n, usu cap A* [after Sir Rutherford *Alcock* †1897 English diplomat] **:** a Japanese pyramidal evergreen tree (*Picea bicolor*) that has stiff branches and slightly flattened leaves and is cultivated for ornament

al·co·gel \ˈalkəˌjel\ *n* -s [*alco-* + *-gel* (fr. *gelatin*)] **:** a gel formed by the coagulation of an alcosol

al·co·hol \ˈalkəˌhȯl, ˈau̇k- *sometimes* -ˌhäl\ *n* -s [NL & ML; NL, liquid produced by distillation, fr. ML, finely pulverized antimony used by women to darken the eyelids, fr. OSp, fr. Ar *al-kuḥul, al-kuḥl* the powdered antimony] **1** *obs* **:** a fine powder of varying ingredients; *often* **:** KOHL **2** *obs* **:** the essence or spirit obtained by distillation **3 :** a colorless volatile flammable liquid C_2H_5OH formed by vinous fermentation and contained in wine, beer, whiskey, and the other fermented and distilled liquors of which it is the intoxicating principle, that is manufactured principally by fermentation of carbohydrate materials (as blackstrap molasses, various grains, esp. corn, and potatoes) and by hydration of ethylene, being obtained usu. by fractional distillation in a concentration of about 95 percent with about 5 percent water, and that in addition to its use in beverages and in medicines is used chiefly as a solvent (as for fats, oils, and resins), as an antifreeze, as a fuel (as for internal-combustion engines and rockets and for heating on a small scale), and as a raw material for many organic chemicals (as acetaldehyde, butadiene, ethers, and esters) — called also *ethanol, ethyl alcohol, grain alcohol*; see INDUSTRIAL ALCOHOL **4 :** any of a class of compounds analogous to ethyl alcohol in constitution and regarded as hydroxyl derivatives of hydrocarbons, being classed according to the number of hydroxyl groups (as monohydric, dihydric, trihydric, polyhydric) or according to structure — see GLYCOL 2, PRIMARY ALCOHOL, SECONDARY ALCOHOL, TERTIARY ALCOHOL; compare PHENOL **5 :** liquor (as whiskey) containing alcohol

al·co·hol·ate \-ˌlāt, -lət, ˌ==ˈ=(ˌ)=\ *n* -s [ISV *alcohol* + *-ate*] **1 a :** a crystallizable compound of a substance with alcohol in which the alcohol plays a part analogous to that of water of crystallization ⟨chloral ~ $CCl_3CHO.C_2H_5OH$⟩ **b :** ALKOXIDE ⟨a sodium ~⟩ **2** *pharmacy* **:** a preparation made by dissolving a volatile oil in alcohol or by distilling with alcohol the medicament containing a volatile principle — called also *spirit*

al·co·hol·a·ture \ˌ==ˈ=ˌləˌchu̇(ə)r\ *n* -s [F *alcoolature*, fr. *alcool* alcohol, fr. MF *alcohol* liquid produced by distillation, fr. NL — more at ALCOHOL] **:** an alcoholic tincture prepared from a fresh vegetable drug

¹al·co·hol·ic \ˌ==ˈhȯlik, -ˈäl-, -ēk\ *adj* [*alcohol* + *-ic*] **1 a :** of, relating to, or having the characteristics of alcohol ⟨an ~ odor⟩ **:** having to do with alcohol ⟨~ propensities⟩ **b :** composed of or containing alcohol ⟨an ~ solution⟩ **:** INTOXICATING ⟨an ~ drink⟩ **c :** derived from alcohol **:** caused by or showing the effects of alcohol ⟨suffering from ~ depression⟩ **d :** preserved in or treated with alcohol ⟨an ~ specimen⟩ **2 :** marked by the use of alcohol; *esp* **:** addicted to the usu. excessive use of alcoholic drinks ⟨~ expatriates in Paris —Carl Van Doren⟩ — **al·co·hol·i·cal·ly** \-ək(ə)lē, -ēk-, -li\ *adv*

²alcoholic \"\ *n* -s **1 :** one who is addicted esp. compulsively to the excessive use of alcoholic drinks **:** one who suffers from alcoholism **2 :** a biological specimen preserved in alcohol

alcoholic fermentation *n* **:** a process in which certain kinds of sugar (as glucose) are converted into alcohol and carbon dioxide by the action of various yeasts, molds, or bacteria on carbohydrate materials (as dough or sugar solutions) some of which do not themselves undergo fermentation but can be hydrolyzed into fermentable substances (as in the production of alcohol and alcoholic beverages)

al·co·hol·ism \ˈ==ˌhȯˌlizəm, -ˌhəˌl- *sometimes* -ˌhä- *or* ˈ==ˌliz-\ *n* -s [NL *alcoholismus*, fr. NL *alcohol* + L *-ismus* -ism] **1 :** continuous and usu. excessive use of alcoholic drinks; *usu* **:** addiction esp. when compulsive to excessive use of alcoholic drinks **2 :** the state of being poisoned by alcohol; *specif* **:** the pathologic results of excessive use of alcoholic drinks — see ACUTE ALCOHOLISM, CHRONIC ALCOHOLISM

al·co·hol·ist \-ˌləst\ *n* -s **:** ALCOHOLIC

al·co·hol·iza·tion \ˌ==ˌhȯləˈzāshən *sometimes* -ˌäl-\ *n* -s **:** the act or process of alcoholizing or the condition of being alcoholized

al·co·hol·ize \ˈ==ˌ=ˌlīz\ *vt* -ED/-ING/-S **1 a :** to treat or saturate with alcohol **b :** to subject to the influence of alcohol **2 :** to convert into alcohol

alcohol of crystallization : alcohol, usu. ethyl alcohol, combined in a manner analogous to that of water of crystallization — see ALCOHOLATE 1a

al·co·hol·om·e·ter \ˌ==ˌhȯˈläməd·ə(r) *sometimes* -äˈl-\ *also* **al·co·hol·me·ter** \ˌ==ˌhȯlˌmēd·ə(r) *sometimes* -äl-\ *or* **al·co·hol·im·e·ter** \ˌ==ˌhȯˈliməd·ə(r) *sometimes* -äˈl-\ *n* -s [F *alcoolomètre*, fr. *alcool* alcohol + *-o-* + *-mètre* -meter] **:** a device for determining the alcoholic strength of liquids

al·co·hol·om·e·try \ˌ==ˌhȯˈläməˌtrē *sometimes* -äˈl-\ *n* -ES [*alcohol* + *-o-* + *-metry*] **:** the determining of the alcoholic strength of liquids

al·co·hol·y·sis \-ˈhäləsəs, -ȯl-\ *n, pl* **alcoholy·ses** \-əˌsēz\ [NL, blend of *alcohol* and *-lysis*] **:** any chemical reaction analogous to hydrolysis in which an alcohol plays a role similar to that of water ⟨~ of an ester to a different ester⟩

al·co·hol·yt·ic \ˌ==ˌhȯˈlid·ik, -ˌhäˈl-\ *adj* **:** of, relating to, or productive of alcoholysis

al·co·o- — see ALCO-

al·co·ran \ˌalkəˈran\ *n* -s *usu cap* [ME *alcoran, alkaron*, fr. MF or ML; MF *alcoran* & ML *alcoranum, alcoranus*, fr. Ar *al-qurʼān*, lit., the recitation, the reading — more at KORAN] *archaic* **:** KORAN

al·cor·no·que \ˌal(ˌ)kȯrˈnōkē\ *n* -s [Pg (also, cork tree) & AmerSp *alcornoque*, both fr. Sp, cork tree, prob. fr. a 12th cent. Ar dial. (Spain) word formed fr. Ar *al* the + ML *quernus* oak tree (fr. L, oaken, fr. *quercus* oak tree) + ML *-occus* (dim. & pejorative suffix) — more at FIR] **:** any of several tropical American trees felt to resemble the cork oak

alcos *pl of* ALCO

al·co·sol \ˈalkəˌsȯl, -ōl\ *n* -s [*alco-* + *-sol* (fr. *solution*)] **:** a sol in which the liquid is alcohol

al·cove \ˈalˌkōv\ *n* -s [F *alcôve*, fr. Sp *alcoba*, fr. Ar *al-qubbah* the arch, vault] **1 a :** a recessed part (as a breakfast nook) of a room or a small room opening into a larger one (as in a library) **b :** a niche or similar arched opening (as in a wall) **:** a vaulted space (as a small clearing) **2 :** a small ornamental building usu. with seats (as in a park or garden) **:** SUMMERHOUSE

al·cres·ta ipecac \(ˈ)alˈkrestə-\ *n* [fr. *Alcresta*, a trademark] **:** a preparation of ipecac in which the alkaloids have been adsorbed on hydrous aluminum silicate

alcumy *obs var of* ALCHEMY

al·cy·on \ˈalsēən\ *n* -s [NL *Alcyonium*, genus of soft corals, fr. Gk *alkyoneion, alkyonion*, a zoophyte, fr. neut. of *alkyoneios* of a kingfisher, fr. *alkyōn* kingfisher; fr. its resemblance to a kingfisher's nest] **:** a soft coral of *Alcyonium* or a related genus

al·cy·o·na·cea \ˌalsēəˈnāsh(ē)ə\ *n pl, cap* [NL, fr. *Alcyonium* + *-acea*] **:** an order or other division of Alcyonaria comprising the soft corals — **al·cy·o·na·cean** \ˌ====ˈ=shən\ *adj or n* — **al·cy·on·ic** \ˌ==ˈänik\ *adj* — **al·cy·on·i·form** \ˌ==ˈänəˌfȯrm\ *adj*

al·cy·o·nar·ia \-ˈna(a)rēə\ *n pl, cap* [NL, fr. *Alcyonium* + *-aria*] **:** a subclass or order of Anthozoa including chiefly compound coelenterates having polyps with 8-branched tentacles and eight septa and comprising the Stolonifera, Alcyonacea, Gorgonacea, and Pennatulacea — **al·cy·o·nar·i·an** \ˌ====ˈrēən\ *adj or n*

al·cy·o·nes \alˈsīə(ˌ)nēz\ *n pl, cap* [NL, fr. Gk *alkyōn* kingfisher] *in some classifications* **:** a group of birds consisting of the kingfishers

al·cy·o·ni·a·ce·ae \ˌalsēˌōnēˈāsēˌē\ *syn of* ALCYONACEA

al·cy·o·ni·o·mor·pha \-nēōˈmȯrfə\ [NL, fr. *Alcyonium* + *-morpha*] *syn of* ALCYONARIA

al·cy·o·noid \ˈalsēəˌnȯid\ *n* -s [NL *Alcyonoidea*] **:** one of the Alcyonaria

al·cy·o·noi·dea \ˌalsēəˈnȯidēə\ [NL, fr. *Alcyonium* + *-oidea*] *syn of* ALCYONARIA

ald \ˈȯl(d), ˈō-\ *adj* [ME, var. of *old*] *now dial Brit* **:** OLD

ald- *or* **aldo-** *comb form* [prob. fr. F *ald-*, fr. *aldéhyde*, fr. G *aldehyd* — more at ALDEHYDE] **1 :** containing the aldehyde group — in names of classes of compounds ⟨*aldo*hexose⟩; compare ALDEHYDO- **2 :** related to an aldehyde ⟨*ald*imine⟩

ald *abbr* alderman

al·da·zine \ˈaldəˌzēn\ *n* -s [ISV *ald-* + *azine*] **:** an azine RCH=NN=CHR formed from an aldehyde

al·de·hyde \ˈaldəˌhīd\ *n* -s [G *aldehyd*, fr. NL *al dehyd*, abbr. of *alcohol dehydrogenatum* dehydrogenated alcohol] **1 :** ACETALDEHYDE **2 :** any of a class of very reactive organic compounds typified by acetaldehyde and characterized by the group —CHO that are intermediate in state of oxidation, having two fewer hydrogen atoms in the molecule than primary alcohols and one less oxygen atom than carboxylic acids — **al·de·hyd·ic** \ˌaldəˈhīdik\ *adj*

aldehyde ammonia *n* **:** any compound formed by the union of an aldehyde with ammonia; *specif* **:** a crystalline compound $CH_3CH(OH)NH_2$ derived from acetaldehyde — called also *acetaldehyde ammonia*

aldehyde collidine *n* **:** METHYLETHYLPYRIDINE

aldehyde hydrate *n* **:** any compound (as chloral hydrate) formed by the union of an aldehyde with water and having the general formula $RCH(OH)_2$

aldehyde resin *n* **1 :** any resin produced from one or more aliphatic aldehydes by a condensation reaction brought about by concentrated alkali solutions **2 :** any resinous product made by interaction of an aldehyde (as formaldehyde or furfural) with another substance (as phenol or urea)

al·de·hyd·ine \ˈaldəˌhīˌdēn, ˌ==ˈ=ˌ=\ *n* -s [ISV *aldehyde* + *-ine*; orig. formed as G *aldehydin*] **1 :** METHYLETHYLPYRIDINE **2 :** any of a class of solid bases containing the imidazole ring formed by condensing aldehydes with aromatic *ortho*-diamines

al·de·hy·do \ˌaldəˈhī(ˌ)dō\ *adj* [*aldehydo-*] **:** of or relating to an aldehyde **:** containing the group —CHO **:** ALDEHYDIC

aldehydo- *comb form* [ISV, fr. *aldehyde* + *-o-*] **1** *usu ital* **:** containing the aldehyde group — in names of open-chain aldehydic forms of specific sugars ⟨*aldehydo*-D-galactose⟩; compare ALD- **2 :** formyl ⟨*aldehydo*benzoic acid⟩

al·der \ˈȯldə(r)\ *n* -s [ME *alder, aller*, fr. OE *alor, aler*; akin to OHG *elira, erila* alder, ON *ǫlr*, (assumed) Goth *alisa* (whence Sp *aliso*), L *alnus*, LGk (Maced dial.) *aliza* white poplar, Lith *al̃ksnis* alder] **1 :** a tree or shrub of the genus *Alnus* **2 :** any of several shrubs resembling the alder

alder blight *n* **:** WOOLLY ALDER APHID

alder buckthorn *also* **alder dogwood** *n* [so called fr. its occurrence in the neighborhood of alders] **:** a common European tree (*Rhamnus frangula*) with flowers in sessile umbels

alder flea beetle *n* **:** a small metallic-colored beetle (*Altica ambiens*) feeding on alders and sometimes causing defoliation

alderfly \ˈ==ˌ=\ *n* **:** any of numerous insects (order Megaloptera) of the genus *Sialis* or related genera having aquatic larvae that are used for bait — compare DOBSONFLY

alder flycatcher *n* **:** a small greenish flycatcher (*Empidonax traillii*) with a dull white breast frequenting alder swamps and other moist secluded spots in much of eastern No. America

alder-leaved buckthorn *n* **:** either of two American shrubs (*Rhamnus alnifolia* or *R. caroliniana*)

alder-leaved dogwood *n* **:** a shrubby dogwood (*Cornus rugosa*) native to eastern No. America

alderliefest *adj* [ME *alderlevest*, fr. *alder-, aller-, alre-* (fr. OE *alra*, gen. pl. of OE *all, eall* all) + *levest*, superl. of *leef* dear — more at ALL, LIEF] *obs* **:** most beloved

al·der·man \ˈȯldə(r)mən\ *n, pl* **aldermen** \-mən\ [ME, fr. OE *aldorman, ealdorman*, fr. *aldor, ealdor* parent, head of a family (fr. *ald, eald* old) + *man* — more at OLD] **1 :** a person of rank, dignity, or authority; *specif* **:** one governing a former kingdom, a district, or a shire as the permanent representative of an Anglo-Saxon king **2** *obs* **:** a headman of a guild **3 a** *in England and Ireland* (1) **:** a magistrate ranking next to the mayor in cities and boroughs from medieval times until modern municipal reorganization (2) **:** a member of the smaller of the two classes composing the borough or county council — compare BAILIE 2b **b :** one of the 26 chief officers chosen for life who heads a ward of the City of London **c :** a member of a legislative body of a city ⟨a board of *aldermen*⟩

al·der·man·ic \ˌ==ˈmanik, -ēk\ *adj* **:** of, relating to, or like an alderman

alderman lizard *n* [so called fr. its large belly] **:** CHUCKWALLA

al·der·man·ly \ˈȯldə(r)mənlē\ *adj* **:** like or appropriate to an alderman ⟨~ decorum⟩

al·der·man·ry \-rē\ *n* -ES [ME *aldermanrie*, fr. *alderman* + *-rie* -ry] **1 :** a kingdom, district, or shire in Anglo-Saxon England **2 a :** a district of an alderman **b :** the office or rank of an alderman

al·der·ney \ˈȯldə(r)nē, -ni\ *n* -s [fr. *Alderney*, one of the Channel islands in Guernsey bailiwick, England] **1** *usu cap* **:** an animal of any Channel island breed of cattle (as a Jersey or a Guernsey) **2** *often cap* **:** a moderate yellowish brown that is paler than Bismarck brown and less strong and very slightly yellower than maple sugar

al·der·wom·an \-ˌwu̇mən\ *n, pl* **alderwomen** [*alderman* + *woman*] **:** a woman with the office and rank of an alderman

al·di·mine \ˈaldəˌmēn\ *n* -s [*ald-* + *imine*] **:** any Schiff base of the general formula RCH=NH or RCH=NR′ formed by condensation of an aldehyde with ammonia or a primary amine

¹al·dine \ˈȯlˌdīn, -ˌdēn *sometimes* ˈal-\ *adj, usu cap* [It *aldino*, fr. *Aldo* Manuzio or Manucci (Aldus Manutius) †1515 It. printer and scholar + It *-ino* -ine] **:** printed or published by Aldus Manutius of Venice or his family in the 16th century who produced fine editions of chiefly Greek, Latin, and Italian classics, each book usu. bearing an anchor and dolphin emblem ⟨an *Aldine* book⟩ ⟨an *Aldine* edition⟩

anchor and dolphin of Aldus

²aldine \"\ *n* -s *usu cap* **:** an Aldine book or edition

³al·dine \ˈalˌdēn\ *n* -s [ISV *ald-* + *-ine*] **:** PYRAZINE

Al·dis \ˈȯldəs\ *trademark* — used for a hand-carried signal lamp used to flash messages esp. from ships and aircraft

al·di·tol \ˈaldəˌtȯl, -ōl\ *n* -s [*aldose* + *-itol*] **:** a polyhydroxy alcohol (as mannitol) formed by reducing an aldose (as mannose)

aldm *abbr* alderman

al·do- — see ALD-

al·do·bi·on·ic acid \ˌal(ˌ)dō,bīˈänik-\ *n* [blend of *aldonic* and *bi-* (two)] **:** an aldonic acid (as lactobionic acid) formed by simple oxidation of a reducing disaccharide (as lactose)

al·do·bi·u·ron·ic acid \-,bīyəˈränik-\ *n* [*ald-* + *bi-* + *-uronic*] **:** a disaccharide of acid nature in which one of the two sugar constituents is a uronic acid joined as a glycoside to a hexose or pentose unit

al·do·fu·ran·o·side \-fyüˈranə,sīd\ *n* -s [*ald-* + *furan* + *-oside*] **:** a glycoside containing a 5-member ring and hydrolyzable to an aldose

al·do·hex·ose \ˌaldōˈhek,sōs\ *n* -s [ISV *ald-* + *hexose*] **:** a hexose (as glucose or mannose) of an aldehyde nature

al·do·ke·tene \-ˈkē,tēn\ *n* -s [*ald-* + *ketene*] **:** any ketene having the general formula RHC:CO

al·dol \ˈal,dȯl, -ōl\ *n* -s [ISV *ald-* + *-ol;* orig. formed in F] **1 :** a colorless liquid $CH_3CH(OH)CH_2CHO$ obtained by condensation of two molecules of acetaldehyde and used in organic synthesis and in denaturing alcohol; β-hydroxy-butyraldehyde — called also *acetaldol* **2 :** any of a class of beta-hydroxy aldehydes typified by acetaldol

al·dol·ase \ˈaldə,lās\ *n* -s [*aldol* + *-ase*] **:** a crystalline enzyme that occurs widely in animal tissues (as muscle) and plant cells (as of bacteria and yeasts) and that accelerates both the cleavage of the 1,6-diphosphoric ester of fructose into two triose phosphates and the reverse reaction

al·dol·i·za·tion \ˌal,dōləˈzāshən, -dōl-\ *n* -s **:** conversion into an aldol

al·dol·ize \ˈaldə,līz\ *vb* -ED/-ING/-S [*aldol* + *-ize*] *vt* **:** to convert into an aldol ~ *vi* **:** to undergo aldolization

aldon- *or* **aldono-** *comb form* [ISV, fr. *aldonic* (in *aldonic acid*)] **:** related to or derived from an aldonic acid ⟨*aldon*amide⟩ ⟨*aldono*lactone⟩

al·don·ic acid \(ˈ)alˈdänik-\ *n* [*ald-* + *-onic*] **:** any of a class of acids (as gluconic acid) formed from aldoses (as glucose) by oxidizing the aldehyde group to a carboxyl group

al·do·py·ran·o·side \ˌal(ˌ)dō,pīˈranə,sīd\ *n* -s [*ald-* + *pyran* + *-oside*] **:** a glycoside containing a 6-member ring and hydrolyzable to an aldose

al·dose \ˈal,dōs\ *n* -s [ISV *ald-* + *-ose*] **:** a sugar (as xylose, glucose, mannose) containing one aldehyde group per molecule — contrasted with *ketose;* see MONOSACCHARIDE

al·do·side \ˈaldə,sīd\ *n* -s [*ald-* + *-oside*] **:** any glycoside derived from an aldose

al·dos·ter·one \alˈdästə,rōn, ˌaldōstəˈrōn\ *n* -s [*ald-* + *sterol* + *-one*] **:** a steroid hormone $C_{21}H_{28}O_5$ extracted from the adrenal cortex that is very active in regulating the salt and water balance in the body

al·dox·ime \alˈdäk,sēm, -,səm\ *n* -s [ISV *ald-* + *oxime*] **:** any oxime of an aldehyde

al·drin \ˈȯldrən\ *n* -s [Kurt *Alder* †1958 Ger. chemist + E *-in*] **:** a white crystalline insecticide consisting chiefly or entirely of a chlorinated tetracyclic derivative $C_{12}H_8Cl_6$ of naphthalene obtained by the Diels-Alder reaction

al·dro·van·da \ˌaldrōˈvandə\ *n, cap* [NL, fr. Ulisse *Aldrovandi* †1605 It. naturalist] **:** a genus of floating aquatic plants (family Droseraceae) found from southern Europe to Australia having small white flowers and whorls of leaves that act as traps for insects

ale \ˈāl, ˈāəl\ *n* -s [ME, fr. OE *alu, ealu;* akin to MHG *al*schaf vessel for beer, OS *alo*fat, ON *öl* beer, ale, and perh. to L *alumen* alum, Gk *alydimos* bitter] **1 :** a malted and hopped beverage that is usu. higher in alcoholic content than beer, heavier in body, and more bitter and is brewed by top fermentation **2 :** a country festival at which ale was the principal beverage ⟨at wakes and ~s —Ben Jonson⟩ — **in ale** *obs* **:** drunk with ale

aleak \əˈ-\ *adj* [¹*a-* + *leak* (v.)] **:** LEAKING ⟨hills ~ with thousands of cascades —Stephen Graham⟩

ale·a·to·ry \ˈālēə,tōrē, -ȯr-, -ri\ *adj* [L *aleatorius* of a gambler, fr. *aleator* gambler, dice player, fr. *alea,* a dice game] **1** *civil law* **:** depending on an uncertain event or contingency as to both profit and loss ⟨an ~ contract⟩ **2 :** relating to good or bad luck and esp. the risks of bad luck ⟨the ~ element in life⟩

alebench \ˈ=,=\ *n* **:** a bench in or before an alehouse

alec·i·thal \(ˈ)āˈlesəthəl\ *also* **ale·cith·ic** \ˌāləˈsithik\ *adj* [²*a-* + Gk *lekithos* yolk + E *-al* or *-ic*] **:** without yolk — used of eggs with little or no food yolk embedded in their protoplasm (as those of placental mammals)

aleconner \ˈ=,==\ *n* -s [*ale* + *conner*] **:** an English town official formerly charged with tasting and testing ale and beer and still a titular official in some communities

ale·cost \ˈā(ə)l,käst\ *n* -s [*ale* + obs. E *cost* costmary — more at COSTMARY] **:** COSTMARY

¹al·ec·to·ria \ˌaləkˈtōrēə\ *or* **al·lec·to·ry** \əˈlektərē\ *or* **al·ec·to·ri·an** \ˌaləkˈtōrēən\ *or* **al·ec·to·ri·us** \-ōrēəs\ *n, pl* **alectori·ae** \ˌaləkˈtōrē,ē\ *or* **allectories** *or* **alectorians** *or* **alecto·rii** \-ōrē,ī\ [*alectoria, allectory* fr. ML *alectoria,* short for L *alectoria gemma,* lit., cock's gem, fr. *alectoria* (fem. of *alectorius* of a cock, fr. Gk *alektōr* cock) + *gemma* gem; *alectorian* fr. L *alectorius* + E *-an; alectorius* fr. L, adj.] **:** a talismanic stone that is supposedly found in the crop of a cock and is believed to be magical

²al·ec·to·ria \ˌaləkˈtōrēə\ *n, cap* [NL, fr. Gk *alektōr* cock (prob. fr. *Alektōr,* a name) + NL *-ia*] **:** a genus of lichens (family Usneaceae) characterized by a dark brown erect or pendulous much-branched thallus of cylindrical form

alec·to·ris \əˈlektərəs\ *n, cap* [NL, fr. Gk *alektōr* cock] **:** a genus of Old World partridges including the chukars

alec·tri·on \əˈlektrē,än\ *n* [NL, perh. fr. Gk *alektryōn* cock] *syn of* NASSARIUS

alec·try·o·man·cy \əˈlektrēō,man(t)sē\ *or* **alec·to·ro·man·cy** \-tərō,-\ *n* -ES [Gk *alektryōn* or *alektōr* cock + E *-mancy*] **:** divination by means of a cock encircled by grains of corn placed on the letters of the alphabet which are then put together in the order in which the grains were eaten

alec·try·on \əˈlektrē,än\ *n, cap* [NL, fr. Gk *alektryōn* cock, fr. *Alektryōn,* a name] **:** a monotypic genus of New Zealand trees of the family Sapindaceae with alternate compound leaves and showy paniculate flowers — see TITOKI

aledraper *n* [*ale* + *draper* (as in *linen draper*)] *obs* **:** an alehouse keeper

alee \əˈlē\ *adv (or adj)* [ME, fr. ¹*a-* + *lee*] **1 :** on or toward the lee **:** to leeward ⟨put the helm ~⟩ ⟨with helm ~⟩ — opposed to *aweather* **2 :** ahead or in the direction of movement (as of a glacier or a current) ⟨sand is deposited ~ of the course base —*Jour. of Geol.*⟩

alef *var of* ALEPH

aleft \əˈ-\ *adv* [ME, fr. ¹*a-* + *left*] **:** to or on the left

ale gallon *n* **:** an old English unit of liquid capacity equal to 282 cubic inches or 4.62 liters — called also *beer gallon*

al·e·gar \ˈaligə(r), ˈāl-\ *n* -s [*ale* + *vinegar*] **:** sour ale **:** vinegar made of ale

al·e·gria \ˌaləˈgrēə\ *n* -s [MexSp *alegria,* fr. Sp, happiness, gaiety, fr. *alegre* happy, gay, fr. (assumed) VL *alecrus* — more at ALLEGRO] *Southwest* **:** any of certain herbs of the genus *Amaranthus* the red juice of which is sometimes used locally as a cosmetic

ale·gri·as \ˌaləˈgrēəs, ˌäl-\ *n pl but sing or pl in constr* [Sp *alegrias,* pl. of *alegria,* lit., gaiety, happiness] **:** a solo flamenco dance performed by a woman and marked by many intricate heelwork variations

alehouse \ˈ=,=\ *n* [ME *alehous,* fr. OE *ealahūs,* fr. *ealu* ale + *hūs* house — more at ALE, HOUSE] **:** a place where ale is sold to be drunk on the premises

aleknight *n* [*ale* + *knight*] *obs* **:** TIPPLER

al·e·man·ni *or* **al·a·man·ni** \ˌaləˈman,ī, -manē\ *n pl, usu cap* [LL, of Gmc origin; akin to Goth *alamans* totality of people] **:** a predominantly Suevian coalition of Germanic peoples first mentioned in the 3d century A.D. that settled in the area between the Main and Danube rivers and whose descendants are German-speaking inhabitants of Alsace, Switzerland, and southwestern Germany

¹al·e·man·nic *or* **al·a·man·nic** \ˌaləˈmanik\ *also* **al·e·man·ni·an** *or* **al·a·man·ni·an** \-nēən\ *n* -s *usu cap* [*Alemanni, Alamanni* + E *-ic* or *-an*] **:** the group of dialects of German spoken in Alsace, Switzerland, and southwestern Germany

²alemannic *or* **alamannic** *also* **alemannian** *or* **alamannian** *adj, usu cap* [*Alemanni, Alamanni* + E *-ic* or *-an*] **1 :** of, relating to, or characteristic of the Alemanni **2 :** of, relating to, or characteristic of the Alemannic dialects

alem·bert \ˌaləmˈbe(ə)r\ *n* -s *usu cap* [after Jean Le Rond d'*Alembert* †1783 Fr. mathematician] **:** a system of betting in gambling games whereby the player increases his stake by one unit each time he loses a bet and decreases it by one unit each time he wins one — called also *progressive system*

alem·bic \əˈlembik\ *n* -s [ME *alambic, alembic,* fr. MF & ML; MF *alambic* & ML *alembicum,* fr. Ar *al-anbiq* the still, fr. *al* the + *anbiq* still, fr. LGk *ambik-, ambix* alembic, fr. Gk, spouted cup, cap of a still] **1 :** an apparatus usu. made of glass or metal formerly much used in distillation **2 :** something that refines or transmutes as if by a process of distillation ⟨intellect as an ~ for the refinement of sensation —*Listener*⟩ ⟨philosophy of Asia and Greece as filtered through the ~ of Plato's mind —*Amer. Scholar*⟩

alembic: *a* head, *b* cucurbit, *c* receiver, *d* lamp

alem·bi·cate \-bə,kāt, *usu* -ād+V\ *vt* -ED/-ING/-S **:** to distill as if in an alembic **:** refine to an essence

alembicated *adj* **:** overrefined as if by excessive distillation **:** excessively subtle **:** PRECIOUS ⟨highly sophisticated and ~ poetry —Richard Aldington⟩ ⟨the ~, the etiolate, the highly elaborated —Eric Partridge⟩

alem·bi·ca·tion \ə,lembəˈkāshən\ *n* -s **1 :** the action of alembicating or the state of being alembicated **:** DISTILLATION ⟨the ~ of a lifetime's thought and experience —Olin Downes⟩ **2 :** OVERREFINEMENT, PRECIOSITY

alem·broth \əˈlem,brȯth, ˈaləm,-\ *n* -s [ME *alembroth, alembroke, albrot*] **:** a double chloride of ammonium and mercury believed by the alchemists to be a universal solvent — called also *key of art, salt of wisdom*

alem·mal \(ˈ)āˈleməl\ *adj* [²*a-* + neuri*lemmal*] *of a nerve fiber* **:** without neurilemma

alen·çon \əˈlen,sän, -en(t)sən *also* ˌalənˈsōⁿ\ *or* **alençon lace** *n* -s *usu cap A* [*Alençon* fr. F *alençon,* short for *point d'Alençon* Alençon lace, fr. *Alençon,* France, where it is made; *Alençon lace,* trans. of F *point d'Alençon*] **:** a delicate orig. handmade needlepoint lace characterized by the cordonnet outlining the floral designs on a fine mesh ground

alençon diamond *n, usu cap A* [fr. *Alençon,* France] **:** a smoky quartz sometimes valued as a jewel

aleph *also* **alef** \ˈä,lef, -ləf\ *n* -s [Heb *āleph,* prob. var. of *eleph* ox] **1 :** the first letter of the Hebrew alphabet — symbol א; see ALPHABET table **2 :** the letter of the Phoenician or of any of various other Semitic alphabets corresponding to Hebrew aleph **3 :** any transfinite cardinal number

aleph–null \ˈ=(ˌ)=ˈ=\ *also* **aleph–zero** \ˈ=(ˌ)=ˈ=(ˌ)=\ *n* **:** the smallest transfinite cardinal number **:** the power of the aggregate of all the finite integers

¹alep·i·dote \(ˈ)āˈlepə,dōt\ *adj* [Gk *a-* ²*a-* + *lepidōtos* covered with scales, fr. *lepid-, lepis* scale — more at LEPID-] *zool* **:** without scales

²alepidote \"\ *n* -s **:** a fish without scales

alep·i·sau·rus \ˌā,lepəˈsȯrəs\ *n, cap* [NL, fr. Gk *alepis* without scales (fr. *a-* ²*a-* + *lepis* scale) + NL *-saurus*] **:** a genus (order Iniomi) of large slender scaleless active and predaceous deep-sea fishes comprising the handsaw fishes

¹alep·pine \əˈlepən, -,pēn *also* -,pīn\ *adj, usu cap* [*Aleppo,* Syria + E *-ine*] **1 :** of, relating to, or characteristic of the city of Aleppo, Syria **2 :** of, relating to, or characteristic of the people of Aleppo

²aleppine \"\ *n* -s *cap* **:** a native or resident of Aleppo

alep·po \əˈle(ˌ)pō\ *adj, usu cap* [fr. *Aleppo,* Syria] **:** of or from the city of Aleppo, Syria **:** of the kind or style prevalent in Aleppo

aleppo boil *n, usu cap A* **:** ORIENTAL SORE

aleppo gall *n, usu cap A* **:** a hard brittle spherical body that is about the size of a hickory nut and is produced on the twigs of an oak (*Quercus infectoria*) by a gall wasp (*Cynips tinctoria*)

aleppo grass *n, usu cap A* **:** JOHNSON GRASS

aleppo pine *n, usu cap A* **:** a pine (*Pinus halepensis*) of southern Europe and the Levant that is of graceful habit, has usu. two leaves in each persistent sheath, and yields a wood that is much used for shipbuilding

aleppo stone *n, usu cap A* [so called fr. its use as a remedy for Aleppo boils] **:** an old oriental gem made by cutting an agate so that it suggests an eye — called also *eye agate*

aler·ce *or* **aler·se** \əˈlərsə\ *n* -s [Sp *alerce* larch, fr. Ar *al-arz* the larch] **1 :** the wood of the sandarac tree of Morocco **2 :** an irregularly branched Patagonian timber tree (*Fitzroya patagonica*)

alerion *var of* ALLERION

¹alert \əˈlərt, -ōt, -əit, *usu* -d· + V\ *adj, sometimes* -ER/-EST [It *all'erta* on the watch, lit., on the ascent] **1 a :** marked by careful zealous watchfulness and promptness to counter threats and dangers and to cope with emergencies ⟨silent and ~, like a sentinel on duty —J.G.Frazer⟩ ⟨the ~ Washington who guided Braddock's army —Allan Nevins & H.S.Commager⟩ **b :** marked by ready perception and recognition and by promptness in perceiving, evaluating, or responding ⟨~ to the script's theatrical possibilities —John Mason Brown⟩ ⟨~ to urge favorable legislation by Congress —Louis Pelzer⟩ **2 :** marked by ready activity, brisk liveliness, or quick reactions ⟨an ~ birdlike movement —Ellen Glasgow⟩ ⟨light, ~ step and a certain gamesome assurance of manner —G.B. Shaw⟩ **syn** see INTELLIGENT, WATCHFUL

²alert \"\ *n* -s **1 a :** an alarm or other signal to warn of danger (as from hostile aircraft or a violent storm) **b :** the period during which an alert is in effect **2 :** the state of readiness of those warned by an alert ⟨sirens brought the whole street to the ~⟩ — see BLUE ALERT, RED ALERT, WHITE ALERT, YELLOW ALERT — **on the alert :** on the lookout for or watch against attack or danger **:** ready to act

³alert \"\ *vb* -ED/-ING/-S *vt* **1 :** to call to a state of readiness: as **a :** to make watchful **:** put on guard **:** WARN ⟨hurricane warning systems for ~*ing* island residents⟩ ⟨vigilantes who could ~ each community to the threatened danger —*Atlantic*⟩; *esp* **:** to call to a state of readiness for an air raid ⟨sirens ~*ing* the cities long before the bombers arrived⟩ **b :** to give warning or notice to (as troops or their commanders) to prepare for movement or action ⟨~*ed* the division for shipment overseas⟩ **2 :** to make clearly perceptive to or aware of **:** AWAKEN, AROUSE ⟨~*ed* a community to the need for better schools⟩ ⟨a matter of ~*ing* teachers to their responsibility —*Educational Leadership*⟩ ~ *vi* **:** to give a warning signal esp. in the presence of an enemy — used chiefly of dogs employed in scouting ⟨after proceeding several hundred yards . . . the patrol's scout dog ~*ed*⟩ ⟨dogs ~ on all human beings, not the enemy alone —*Infantry Jour.*⟩

alert·ly *adv* **:** in an alert manner ⟨much enjoyment may be gained from listening to music ~ —Charles Johnson⟩

alert·ness *n* -ES **:** the quality or state of being alert

ales *pl of* ALE

-a·les \ˈā(ˌ)lēz\ *n pl suffix* [NL, fr. L, pl. of *-alis* -al] **:** plants belonging to or related to ⟨Chytridi*ales*⟩ ⟨Ros*ales*⟩ — in the names of orders of plants; in some classifications in the names of other superfamilial groups of plants (as alliances or cohorts)

al·e·san \ˈalə,san\ *n* -s [F *alezan,* fr. Sp *alazán*] **:** a light brown that is less strong and slightly yellower and lighter than blush, paler and slightly redder than French beige, and redder and paler than cork — called also *café au lait, French nude*

aleth·ic \əˈlethik, -ēth-\ *adj* [Gk *alēthikos,* fr. *alētheia* truth (fr. *alēthēs* true, fr. *a-* ²*a-* + *-lēthēs,* fr. *lēthē* forgetfulness) + *-ikos* -ic — more at LETHE] **:** of or relating to truth ⟨~ mode⟩

al·e·thop·ter·is \ˌaləˈthäptərəs\ *n, cap* [NL, fr. Gk *alēthēs* (fr. *alēthēs* true) + NL *-pteris*] **:** a genus of large fossil seed ferns represented by abundant remains in Carboniferous coal measures and having large bipinnate to tripinnate fronds with the thick pinnules being inserted on the rachis by a broad decurrent base — **al·e·thop·ter·oid** \ˌaləˈthäptə,rȯid\ *adj*

al·e·tris \ˈalə·trəs\ *n, cap* [NL, fr. Gk, female slave who ground meal, noble Athenian maiden who prepared offering cakes, fr. *alein, aletreuein* to grind; fr. the floury appearance of the blossoms] **:** a small genus of bitter-rooted herbs (family Liliaceae) found in eastern No. America and Asia and having basal leaves and small white or yellow bracted racemose flowers — see COLICROOT

alette *or* **al·lette** \əˈlet, aˈ-\ *n* -s [F *alette,* fr. OF *alette, elette* small wing, dim. of *ele* wing — more at AISLE] **1** *Roman & neoclassic archit* **:** the pilasterlike abutment of an arch that is seen on either side of the large engaged column and that carries the entablature **2 :** a wing of a building

aleu·ke·mia *also* **aleu·kae·mia** \ˌā(ˌ)-\ *n* [NL, fr. ²*a-* + *leukemia, leukaemia*] **:** leukemia in which the circulating leukocytes are normal or decreased in number

aleu·ke·mic *also* **aleu·kae·mic** \ˌā(ˌ)=ˈ==\ *or* **aleu·ce·mic** *or* **aleu·cae·mic** \-ˈsē-\ *adj* [ISV ²*a-* + *leukemic, leukaemic, leucemic, leucaemic*] **:** not marked by increase in circulating white blood cells

aleukemic leukemia *also* **aleukemic myelosis** *n* **:** leukemia resulting from changes in the leukocyte-forming tissues and characterized by a normal or decreased number of leukocytes in the circulating blood

aleu·ri·o·spore \əˈlu̇rēə,spō(ə)r\ *also* **aleu·ro·spore** \əˈlu̇rə,-\ *n* -s [*aleurio-* or *aleuro-* (fr. Gk *aleuron*) + *spore*] **:** an asexual spore in certain fungi produced terminally by septation but remaining attached until disintegration of the mycelium **:** a nondeciduous chlamydospore

al·eu·ri·tes \ˌalyəˈrīd·(ˌ)ēz\ *n, cap* [NL, fr. Gk *aleuritēs* of flour, fr. *aleuron* flour + *-itēs* -ite] **:** a genus of Asiatic trees (family Euphorbiaceae) having a milky juice, small white flowers, and rich oily seeds in drupes — see CANDLENUT

al·eu·rit·ic acid \ˌalyəˈrid·ik-\ *n* [NL *Aleurites* + E *-ic*] **:** a crystalline acid $C_{15}H_{28}(OH)_3COOH$ occurring in shellac; 9,10,16-trihydroxy-palmitic acid

aleuro- *comb form* [F, fr. Gk, fr. *aleuron* wheat flour, flour; akin to Arm *alam* I grind] **:** flour ⟨*aleuro*meter⟩

al·eu·ro·bi·us \ˌalyəˈrōbēəs\ *n, cap* [NL, fr. *aleuro-* + *-bius*] **:** a genus of mites (family Tyroglyphidae) including a species (*A. farinae*) common in flour and stored cereals and implicated as a cause of enteritis and dysentery in animals feeding on such contaminated grain products

aleu·ro·did \əˈlu̇rədəd, -,did\ *n* -s [NL *Aleurodidae*] **:** ALEYRODID

al·eu·rod·i·dae \ˌalyəˈrädə,dē\ [NL, alter. of *Aleyrodidae*] *syn of* ALEYRODIDAE

aleu·ro·man·cy \əˈlu̇rə,man(t)sē\ *n* -ES [F *aleuromancie,* fr. Gk *aleuromanteion,* fr. *aleuro-* + *manteion* divination, oracle] **:** divination by means of flour

al·eu·rom·e·ter \ˌalyəˈrämed·ə(r)\ *n* -s [*aleuro-* + *-meter*] **:** an instrument for determining the expansive properties or the quality of gluten in flour

aleu·ro·nat \əˈlu̇rə,nat\ *n* -s [G *aleuronat,* fr. *aleuron* aleurone + *-at* -ate] **:** a flour with a high gluten content

al·eu·rone \ˈalyə,rōn\ *also* **al·eu·ron** \-,rän\ *n* -s [G *aleuron,* fr. Gk *aleuron* flour — more at ALEURO-] **:** ergastic protein matter in the form of minute granules or grains produced by crystallization or solidification of the protein content of certain vacuoles, often associated with other substances (as calcium oxalate), and occurring chiefly in endosperm and in some seeds (as cereal grains) concentrated in a special peripheral layer of endodermal cells — **al·eu·ron·ic** \ˌalyəˈränik\ *adj*

¹aleut \ˌaleˈüt, ˈalē,üt, aˈlüt, aˈl- *also* alˈyüt *or* alˈy-\ *also* **aleu·tian** \əˈlüshən *also* əlˈyü-\ *n* -s *cap* [Russ, prob. fr. a native name in Asia] **1 a :** a people of the Aleutian and Shumagin islands and the western part of Alaska peninsula **b :** a member of such people **2 :** an Eskimo-Aleut language of the Aleut people

²aleut \"\ *adj, usu cap* **:** of or belonging to an early, middle, or late period of a prehistoric Aleutian culture of about 100 B.C. to A.D. 1750

aleu·tian \əˈlüshən *also* əlˈyü-\ *adj, usu cap* **:** of or relating to the Aleutian islands

al·e·vin \ˈaləvən\ *n* -s [F, fr. OF, fr. *alever* to lift up, rear (offspring), fr. L *allevare* to lift up, fr. *ad-* + *levare* to raise — more at LEVER] **:** a young fish; *esp* **:** the newly hatched salmon when still attached to the yolk mass

¹ale·wife \ˈāl,wīf\ *n, pl* **alewives** \-,wīvz\ [ME *alewif,* fr. *ale* + *wif* wife] **:** a woman who keeps an alehouse

²ale·wife \"\, *sometimes* ˈel-\ *n, pl* **alewives** \-,wīvz\ [prob. so called fr. its big belly] **1 a :** a food fish (*Pomolobus pseudoharengus*) of the herring family (Clupeidae) very abundant on the Atlantic coast **b :** any of several related fishes: as (1) **:** MENHADEN (2) **:** a pilchard (*Harengula pensacolae*) of the Florida coast (3) **:** ALLICE SHAD **2 :** ROUND POMPANO

¹al·ex·an·der \ˌaligˈzandə(r), ˌel-, -lēg- *sometimes* -ān-; *attrib* ˌ=ˌ=ˈ=\ *or* **al·i·san·der** \ˌaləˈsa- *also* -sä-\ *n* -s [ME *alexaundre, alisaundre,* fr. ML & OF; ME *alexaundre* fr. OF *alexandre,* fr. ML *alexandrum,* prob. by folk etymology (influence of L *Alexander* Alexander the Great †323 B.C. king of Macedonia) fr. L *holus atrum,* fr. *holus* vegetable (akin to L *helvus* light bay) + *atrum,* neut. of *ater* black; ME *alisaundre* fr. OF, fr. ML *alexandrum* — more at ATROCIOUS, YELLOW] **:** any of various plants of the family Umbelliferae: as **a :** a European plant (*Smyrnium olusatrum*) that somewhat resembles celery and was formerly cultivated as a potherb — usu. used in pl. **b :** COW PARSNIP — usu. used in pl.

²alexander \"\ *n* -s *usu cap* [by shortening & alter. fr. *Alexandrine silk*] **:** a striped silk of the 14th to 16th centuries

³alexander \"\ *also* **alexander cocktail** *n* -s *often cap A* [prob. fr. the name *Alexander*] **:** an iced cocktail made from crème de cacao, sweet cream, and gin or brandy

al·ex·an·dra palm \ˌaligˈzandrə-, ˌel-, -lēg- *sometimes* -än-\ *n, usu cap A* [after *Alexandra* †1925 Danish princess, queen of England] **:** a lofty Australian pinnate-leaved palm (*Archontophoenix alexandrae*)

al·ex·an·dria \ˌ==ˈ=drēə\ *adj, usu cap* [fr. *Alexandria,* Egypt] **:** of or from the city of Alexandria, Egypt **:** of the kind or style prevalent in Alexandria **:** ALEXANDRIAN

¹al·ex·an·dri·an \-ēən\ *adj, usu cap* [*Alexandria,* Egypt + E *-an*] **1 :** of, relating to, or characteristic of Alexandria and esp. Alexandria, Egypt **2 :** of, relating to, or characteristic of the people of Alexandria **3** [so called from the cultural prominence of Alexandria in the Hellenistic period] **:** HELLENISTIC **4 a :** of, relating to, or resembling the Alexandrian school **b** *of a writer or literary work* (1) **:** overly recondite, derivative, or artificial ⟨an *Alexandrian* devotion to elaborate complexity⟩ (2) **:** concerned primarily with the technical perfection of language or literary form

²alexandrian \"\ *n* -s **1** *cap* **:** a native or resident of Alexandria **2** *usu cap* **:** a member of the Alexandrian school

³alexandrian \"\ *adj* [*Alexander* the Great †323 B.C. king of Macedonia + E *-ian*] **1 a** *usu cap* **:** of or relating to Alexander the Great **b** *often cap* [by alter.] **:** ALEXANDRINE **2** *usu cap* [*Alexander,* the name + E *-ian*] **:** of or relating to the name Alexander or any individual so named; *esp* **:** of or relating to Pope Alexander VI (about 1431–1503)

⁴alexandrian \"\ *n* -s *often cap* [by alter.] **:** ALEXANDRINE

alexandrian clover *n, usu cap A* [¹*Alexandrian* + *clover*] **:** BERSEEM

al·ex·an·dri·an·ism \ˌ==ˈ===,nizəm\ *n* -s *often cap* [¹*Alexandrian* + *-ism*] **:** the teachings or tenets of the Alexandrian culture or theology — compare ALEXANDRIAN SCHOOL, PATRISTIC PHILOSOPHY

alexandrian laurel *n, usu cap A* [¹*Alexandrian* + *laurel*] **1 :** a leafless shrub (*Danaë racemosa*) of the Levant **2 :** ᵖPOON

alexandrian philosophy *n, usu cap A* [¹*Alexandrian*] **:** the philosophy that flourished at Alexandria in the early centuries of the Christian era and that was chiefly concerned with attempts to interpret oriental and esp. Hebrew religious beliefs in the light of Greek philosophy — compare NEOPLATONISM, NEO-PYTHAGOREANISM

alexandrian school *n, usu cap A* [¹*Alexandrian*] **1 :** the school of literature, science, and philosophy that flourished at Alexandria while that city was ruled by the Greeks and the Romans **2 :** an ante-Nicene school of patristic philosophy developed slightly later than the African school, taking its rise from Pantaenus, including Clement and Origen, and centered in Alexandria **3 :** a succession of Alexandrine Christian theologians who, in the 5th century and later, in the Christological debates against the theologians of Antioch, stressed the divinity and unity of Jesus Christ

al·ex·an·dria senna \ˌ==ˌ-drēə-\ *n, usu cap A* [fr. *Alexandria,* Egypt, its chief place of export] **:** senna from a cassia (*Cassia acutifolia*)

¹**al·ex·an·drine** \ˌalig¦zandrən, ˌel-, -lēg-, -drīn, -ˌdrēn *sometimes* -zän-\ *adj, often cap* [MF *alexandrin,* fr. *Alexandre* Alexander the Great †323 B.C. king of Macedonia + MF *-in* -ine; fr. its use in an Old French poem on Alexander] **:** of, relating to, or having the structure of an alexandrine

²**alexandrine** \"\ *n* -s *often cap* **:** a verse of 12 syllables or of 13 syllables when with feminine rhyme consisting regularly of 6 iambics with a caesura after the 3d iambic — compare HEROIC VERSE

³**alexandrine** \"\ *adj, often cap* [L *Alexandrinus,* fr. *Alexandria,* Egypt + L *-inus* -ine] **:** ALEXANDRIAN

alexandrine rat *n, usu cap A* [³*Alexandrine;* fr. its original habitat; trans. of NL *rattus alexandrinus*] **:** ROOF RAT

al·ex·an·drite \ˌ==ˈ=ˌdrīt\ *n* -s [G *alexandrit,* fr. *Alexander I* †1825 Russ. emperor + G *-it* -ite] **:** a grass-green variety of chrysoberyl that shows a columbine-red color by transmitted or artificial light

alex·ia \əˈleksēə, (ˈ)āˈ-\ *n* -s [NL, fr. ²*a-* + Gk *lexis* speech (fr. *legein* to speak, but influenced in meaning by L *legere* to read) + NL *-ia* — more at LEGEND] **:** aphasia characterized by loss of ability to read

alex·ian \əˈlekshən, -ksēən\ *n* -s *usu cap* [St. *Alexius,* 5th cent. Roman Christian founder of the order + E *-an*] **:** a member of a Roman Catholic order devoted to care of the sick

alex·in \əˈleksən\ *also* **alex·ine** \", -ˌsēn\ *n* -s [G *alexin,* fr. Gk *alexein* to ward off, protect + G *-in* -in, -ine; akin to OE *ealh* temple, OS *alah,* Primitive Norse (Runic) *aluh* amulet, Goth *alhs* temple, Gk *alkar* protection, Skt *rakṣati* he protects, guards] **:** COMPLEMENT 10 — **al·ex·in·ic** \ˌaˌlek¦sinik\ *adj*

alexipharmac *n* -s *obs* **:** ALEXIPHARMIC

¹**alex·i·phar·mic** \əˌleksəˈfärmik\ *n* -s [alter. of earlier *alexipharmac,* fr. Gk *alexipharmakos,* fr. *alexein* + *pharmakon* poison, drug, remedy — more at PHARMACY] **:** an antidote against poison or infection

²**alexipharmic** \=¦==¦==\ *or* **alex·i·phar·mi·cal** \-əkəl\ *adj* **:** expelling or counteracting poison **:** ANTIDOTAL

ale yard *n* **:** a tall slender flaring drinking glass used also as a measure for liquids — compare YARD OF ALE

al·ey·ro·des \ˌaləˈrō(ˌ)dēz\ *n, cap* [NL, irreg. fr. Gk *aleurōdēs* like flour, fr. *aleuron* flour — more at ALEURO-] **:** the type genus of Aleyrodidae including several pests of cultivated plants

¹**aley·ro·did** \əˈlārədəd, -ˌdid\ *n* -s [NL *Aleyrodidae*] **:** an insect of the family Aleyrodidae **:** WHITEFLY

²**aleyrodid** \"\ *adj* **:** of or relating to the Aleyrodidae

al·ey·rod·i·dae \ˌaləˈrädəˌdē\ *n pl, cap* [NL *Aleyrodes,* type genus + *-idae*] **:** a family of minute homopterous insects winged as adults with the body and wings covered with a white powdery wax, the larvae being initially motile but after the first molt resembling unarmored scales and, like these, feeding on plant juices — compare CITRUS WHITEFLY, GREENHOUSE WHITEFLY

¹**al·fa** \ˈalfə\ *or* **alfa grass** *n* -s [Ar *ḥalfā'*] *Africa* **:** ESPARTO

²**alfa** \"\ *usu cap* — a communications code word for the letter *a*

al·fal·fa \alˈfalfə, *attrib* (ˈ)=¦==\ *n* -s [Sp., modif. of Ar dial. (Spain) *al-fasfaṣah* the alfalfa, alter. of *al-fisfisah*] **:** an important European leguminous forage plant (*Medicago sativa*) with trifoliate leaves and bluish purple flowers grown widely and principally for hay, capable of surviving dry periods because of its extraordinarily long root system, and adapted to widely varying conditions of climate and soil — called also *lucerne*

alfalfa butterfly *n* **:** an orange butterfly (*Colias eurytheme*) that is the adult form of the alfalfa caterpillar — compare CLOUDED SULPHUR

alfalfa caterpillar *n* **:** the green larva of the alfalfa butterfly that feeds on the foliage of alfalfa through most of No. America and is esp. abundant and destructive in the southwestern U. S.

alfalfa dwarf *n* **:** a virus disease of alfalfa that appears also as Pierce's disease of grapes and is characterized by dwarfing and usu. by darker color of leaves

alfalfa looper *n* **:** the caterpillar of a noctuid moth (*Autographa californica*) sometimes injurious to alfalfa

alfalfa meal *n* **:** ground alfalfa hay

alfalfa plant bug *n* **:** an Old World mirid bug (*Adelphocoris lineolatus*) accidentally introduced into Minnesota where it seriously damages flowering clover and alfalfa

alfalfa snout beetle *n* **:** a parthenogenetic wingless Old World weevil (*Brachyrhinus ligustici*) that attacks clovers, alfalfa, and other legumes and is esp. destructive to alfalfa since the larvae feed on the taproot while the adults consume the leaves

alfalfa webworm *n* **:** the small greenish or blackish larva of a pyralid moth (*Loxostege commixtalis*) that feeds on and webs together the leaves of various succulent plants and is esp. destructive on sugar beet and alfalfa

alfalfa weevil *n* **:** a small dark-brown European weevil (*Hypera postica*) now widely established in No. America having a yellowish or greenish white-striped larva that feeds on the foliage of alfalfa

al·fe·rez \alˈferəs, -ir-\ *n, pl* **alfere·ces** \ˌaləˈrāsēz, -səz\ *also* **alferez** [Sp *alférez,* fr. Ar *al-fāris* the horseman, fr. *faras* horse] **:** ENSIGN, STANDARD-BEARER — used as a military title

al·fil·a·ria *or* **al·fil·e·ria** *also* **al·fil·e·ri·lla** \(ˌ)alˌfiləˈrēə\ *n* -s [modif. of AmerSp *alfilerillo,* fr. Sp, dim. of *alfiler* pin, modif. of Ar *al-khilāl* the thorn, the pin] **:** a European weed (*Erodium cicutarium*) grown for forage in the dry regions of the southwestern U. S. — called also *pin grass*

al·fil·e·ri·llo \-ˈrē(ˌ)(y)ō\ *n* -s [AmerSp, alfilerillo, alfilaria] **:** a Mexican cactus (*Pereskiopsis diguetii*) used for hedges

al·fin \ˈalfən\ *adj* [*alcohol* + *olefin*] **:** of or relating to any of various catalysts made from sodium derivatives of alcohols (as isopropyl alcohol) and olefins (as propylene) and used in certain polymerizations (as of butadiene alone or with styrene and a high-viscosity oil) yielding synthetic rubbers

al·fi·o·na \ˌalfēˈōnə\ *or* **al·fi·o·ne** \-ōnē\ *n* -s [perh. fr. MexSp] **:** RUBBERLIP PERCH

al·for·ja \alˈfȯrhə\ *n* -s [Sp, fr. Ar *al-khurj* the saddlebag, the wallet] *West* **:** SADDLEBAG

al·fre·di·an \alˈfrēdēən\ *adj, usu cap* [*Alfred* the Great †899 king of the West Saxons + E *-ian*] **:** belonging or relating to or originating with Alfred the Great ⟨the *Alfredian* Gospels⟩

¹**al·fres·co** \alˈfre(ˌ)skō\ *adv* [It, lit., in the open] **1** *of painting* **:** in the fresco manner **2 :** in the open air ⟨what Paris . . . offered in its cloistered salons . . . Venice presented ~ amid its marble-walled canals —Janet Flanner⟩

²**alfresco** \(ˈ)al¦f-\ *adj* **1** *of a painting* **:** executed in fresco **2 :** OPEN-AIR ⟨an ~ dinner⟩

al·fur \ˈalˌf(y)u̇(ə)r\ *also* **al·fu·ro** \alˈf(y)u̇(ˌ)rō\ *n* -s *usu cap* [Sp *alfur, alfor,* fr. Pg *alforro,* of Malayo-Indonesian origin; akin to Indonesian *alifuru*] **1 :** any one of a group of aboriginal peoples of mixed ancestry inhabiting interior regions of the Moluccas and parts of the Celebes **2 :** a member of an Alfur people

¹**al·fu·rese** \ˌalf(y)ə¦rēz, -ēs\ *n, usu cap* [*Alfur* + *-ese*] **:** the language of the Alfuros esp. those of the Celebes

²**alfurese** \"\ *adj, usu cap* **:** of or belonging to an Alfur people

alg- *or* **algo-** *comb form* [NL, fr. Gk *alg-, fr. algos*] **:** pain ⟨*alg*esthesia⟩ ⟨*alg*anesthesia⟩ ⟨*algo*phobia⟩

alg *abbr* algebra

al·ga \ˈalgə\ *n, pl* **al·gae** \ˈal(ˌ)jē\ *also* **algas** [L, seaweed] **:** a plant of the group Algae or of the divisions Chlorophyta, Euglenophyta, Pyrrophyta, Chrysophyta, Phaeophyta, Cyanophyta, and Rhodophyta

al·gae \ˈal(ˌ)jē\ *n pl, cap* [NL, fr. L, pl. of *alga*] *in some classifications* **:** a major group of lower plants that is often included in Thallophyta, that comprises usu. photosynthetic plants of extremely varied morphology and physiology, and that is now commonly considered to be a heterogeneous assemblage — see ALGA, FUNGI

algaecide *var of* ALGICIDE

al·gal \ˈalgəl\ *adj* **:** relating to, consisting of, or resembling an alga or algae

al·gal–al·gal \ˈalgəˈlalgəl\ *n* -s [alter. of *agar-agar*] **:** AGAR; *esp* **:** agar produced in the Malay archipelago from red algae of the genus *Eucheuma*

algal disease *n* **:** RED RUST 3a

algal fungus *n* **:** any fungus of the class Phycomycetes

algal layer *n,* **:** GONIDIAL LAYER

algaroth *n* -s *usu cap* **:** POWDER OF ALGAROTH

al·gar·ro·ba *also* **al·ga·ro·ba** *or* **al·gar·ro·bo** *or* **al·ga·ro·bo** *or* **al·ge·ro·ba** \ˌalgəˈrōbə\ *n* -s [Sp, *algarroba,* fr. Ar *al-kharrūbah* the carob] **1 :** CAROB 1a **2** *or* **algarroba bean :** CAROB 1b **3** [MexSp *algarroba,* fr. Sp] **:** MESQUITE 1a **4** [MexSp *algarroba,* fr. Sp] **:** the sweet pulpy pods of the mesquite **5** [AmerSp, fr. Sp] **:** WEST INDIAN LOCUST **6** [AmerSp, fr. Sp] **:** RAIN TREE

al·gar·ro·bi·lla *or* **al·ga·ro·bi·lla** \ˌalgə(ˌ)rōˈbē(y)ə\ *or* **al·ga·ro·bel·lo** \-ˈbe(ˌ)lō\ *also* **al·ga·ro·vi·lla** \-ˈvē(y)ə\ *n* -s [AmerSp *algarrobilla,* fr. Sp, carob tree, dim. of *algarroba*] **:** the seeds and pods of certain leguminous trees and shrubs (esp. of *Pithecolobium parvifolium, Caesalpinia brevifolia,* and *Prosopis juliflora*) having astringent properties and used for tanning and dyeing

al·gar·ro·bin \ˌalgəˈrōbən\ *n* -s [*algarroba* + *-in*] **:** a brown dyestuff and mordant of Argentina said to be obtained from the wood of the carob tree

al·gates \ˈȯlˌgāts\ *adv* [ME *algate, algates* always, in all ways, entirely, fr. *al* all + *gate* (way), or *gates,* prob. pl. of *gate;* perh. influenced by ON *alla götu* always, throughout — more at GATE] **1** *now dial Brit* **:** WHOLLY, COMPLETELY **2** *obs* **:** NEVERTHELESS, NOTWITHSTANDING, YET

algazel *n* -s [Pg] *obs* **:** a gazelle or other antelope of Africa

al·ge·bra \ˈaljəbrə\ *n* -s [ML, algebra, bonesetting, fracture (whence ME, bonesetting, fracture), fr. Ar *al-jabr* the algebra, the bonesetting, lit., the reduction] **1 :** a branch of mathematics in which arithmetic relations are generalized and explored by using letter symbols to represent numbers, variable quantities, or other mathematical entities (as vectors and matrices), the letter symbols being combined, esp. in forming equations, in accordance with assigned rules **2** *logic* **:** a process of reasoning by the use of symbols — used esp. with reference to 19th century formulations in symbolic logic or the areas then dealt with; compare BOOLEAN ALGEBRA, SYMBOLIC LOGIC **3 :** a treatise on the science of algebra

al·ge·bra·ic \ˌaljə¦brāik\ *also* **al·ge·bra·i·cal** \-əkəl\ *adj* **1 :** of, relating to, involving, or according to the laws of algebra **2** *of a mathematical expression or equation* **:** involving only a finite number of algebraic operations — opposed to *transcendental* — **al·ge·bra·i·cal·ly** \-ək(ə)lē, -li\ *adv*

algebraic arithmetic *n* **:** the part of the theory of numbers in which the methods of algebra are used to yield relations between integers

algebraic curve *n* **:** a curve the Cartesian coordinates of whose points are related by an algebraic equation

algebraic equation *n* **:** an equation obtained by equating to zero a sum of a finite number of terms each one of which is a product of positive integral powers (including the zero power) of the variables

algebraic expression *n* **:** an expression obtained by a finite number of the fundamental operations of algebra upon symbols representing numbers

algebraic form *n* **:** a homogeneous rational integral function of two or more variables

algebraic function *n* **:** a function whose dependence on the independent variable or variables is determined by an algebraic equation

algebraic geometry *n* **:** analytic geometry in which the graphs or curves considered can be represented by algebraic equations

algebraic logic *n* **:** ALGEBRA 2

algebraic number *n* **:** a root of an algebraic equation whose coefficients are rational

algebraic operation *n* **:** any combination of a finite number of the operations of addition, multiplication, subtraction, and division

algebraic sum *n* **:** the aggregate of two or more numbers or quantities taken with regard to their signs (as + or −) according to the rules of addition in algebra ⟨the *algebraic sum* of −2, 8, and −1 is 5⟩ — compare ARITHMETICAL SUM

algebraic surface *n* **:** a surface expressible analytically through an algebraic equation connecting its Cartesian coordinates

al·ge·bra·ist \ˈaljəˌbrāəst, ˌ==ˈ==\ *n* -s **:** a specialist in algebra

al·ge·bra·i·za·tion \ˌaljəˌbrāəˈzāshən\ *or* **al·ge·bri·za·tion** \-ˌbrəˈz-, -ˌbrīˈz-\ *n* -s **:** the act or process of algebraizing

al·ge·bra·ize \ˈaljəbrəˌīz, -rāˌīz\ *vt* -ED/-ING/-s **:** to perform by algebra **:** reduce (a verbal or numerical statement) to algebraic form

algebra of classes : a branch of symbolic logic sometimes regarded as an independent discipline that deals with classes and has as its main operations the forming of logical products, sums, and complements — called also *calculus of classes;* compare INCLUSION, MEMBERSHIP

algebra of relations : a branch of symbolic logic dealing with relations analogously to the manner in which classes are dealt with in the algebra of classes — called also *calculus of relations*

al·ge·do·nic \ˌaljə¦dänik\ *adj* [Gk *alg-* + *hēdonikos* pleasant — more at HEDONIC] **:** characterized by or relating to pain esp. as associated with pleasure ⟨~ aesthetics⟩

al·ge·don·ics \ˌ==ˈ=niks\ *n pl but sing in constr* **:** HEDONICS 2

al·ge·ria \(ˈ)alˈjirēə, -ēr-\ *adj, usu cap* [fr. *Algeria,* country in NW Africa] **:** of or from the country of Algeria **:** of the kind or style prevalent in Algeria

¹**al·ge·ri·an** \(ˌ)al¦jirēən, -ēr-\ *adj, usu cap* [F *algérien,* fr. *Algérie* Algeria, Africa] **1 :** of, relating to, or characteristic of Algeria or the former Barbary State of Algiers **2 :** of, relating to, or characteristic of the Algerians

²**algerian** \"\ *n* -s **1** *cap* **:** a native or inhabitant of Algeria or of the former Barbary State of Algiers **2** *usu cap* **:** a dialect of modern Arabic **3** *often cap* **:** TANBARK 2

algerian fir *n, usu cap A* **:** an evergreen tree (*Abies numidica*) having ornamental dark green white-banded leaves

algerian ivy *n, usu cap A* **:** a trailing or climbing vine or shrub (*Hedera canariensis*) resembling English ivy but having reddish twigs and petioles and thin, comparatively large, sometimes variegated leaves

algerian stripe *n, usu cap A* **:** a usu. cream-colored coating fabric with alternate stripes of coarse cotton and fine silk

¹**al·ge·rine** \ˌaljə¦rēn\ *adj, usu cap* [*Algeria* + *-ine*] **:** ALGERIAN

²**algerine** \"\ *n* -s **1** *cap* **:** a native or inhabitant of Algeria or of the former Barbary State of Algiers; *esp* **:** one of a native race **2 :** one with piratical characteristics ⟨~s of the black market⟩ **3** [fr. *Algerine,* British minesweeper, the first ship in this class] **:** a British or Canadian minesweeper of about 1000 tons displacement **4** *or* **al·ge·ri·enne** \(ˌ)alˌjirēˈen\ [F *algérienne,* fr. fem. of *algérien* Algerian] **:** a soft woolen fabric with bright weftwise stripes used for shawls; *also* **:** this fabric in a heavier weight used in northern Africa for tents and awnings

al·ge·ri·ta \ˌaljəˈrēd·ə\ *n* -s [MexSp, alter. of *agarita,* alter. of *agrita, agrito*] **:** AGARITA

algeroba *var of* ALGARROBA

al·ge·sia \alˈjēzēə, -ēzhə\ *n* -s [NL, fr. Gk *algēsis* sense of pain, fr. *algein* to feel pain, fr. *algos* pain] **:** sensitiveness to pain — **al·ge·sic** \-ēzik, -ēs-\ *adj*

al·ge·sim·e·ter \ˌaljəˈsimәd·ə(r)\ *n* -s [NL *algesia* + E *-meter*] **:** an instrument used in determining acuteness of pain perception — **al·ge·sim·e·try** \-mə·trē\ *n* -ES

al·get·ic \alˈjed·ik\ *adj* [ISV *alg-* + *-etic*] **:** relating to or causing pain

-al·gia \ˈalj(ē)ə\ *n comb form* -s [Gk *-algia,* fr. *algos*] **:** pain **:** painful condition ⟨*cephalalgia*⟩ ⟨*podalgia*⟩ — **-al·gic** \ˈaljik, -ēk\ *adj comb form*

al·gic acid \ˈaljik-\ *n* [*alga* + *-ic*] **:** ALGINIC ACID

al·gi·cide \ˈaljəˌsīd\ *or* **al·gae·cide** \", -jē,-\ *n* -s **:** a chemical (as copper sulfate) used to kill algae

al·gid \ˈaljəd\ *adj* [L *algidus,* fr. *algēre* to feel cold; akin to Icel *elgur* slush] **1 :** CHILL, COLD ⟨the river . . . grew colder . . . compressing their . . . lower limbs in an ~ vise —A.J. Cronin⟩ **2 :** marked by prostration, cold and clammy skin, and low blood pressure — used chiefly of a severe form of malaria — **al·gid·i·ty** \alˈjidəd·ē\ *n* -ES

al·giers \(ˈ)alˈjī(ə)rz, -iəz\ *adj, usu cap* [fr. *Algiers,* Algeria] **1 :** of or from Algiers, the capital of Algeria **:** of the kind or style prevalent in Algiers **2 :** of or relating to the former Barbary State of Algiers

-algies *pl of* -ALGY

al·gin \ˈaljən\ *n* -s [*alga* + *-in*] **:** any of various colloidal substances that occur in or are extracted from marine brown algae, esp. giant kelp: as **a :** a naturally occurring mixture held to contain alginic acid and certain of its salts **b :** ALGINIC ACID **c :** any soluble salt of alginic acid; *esp* **:** the sodium salt that forms a viscous solution with cold or hot water, that is obtained in the form of a white to brown powder by extraction from kelp with a soda solution, and that is used chiefly as a stabilizing, emulsifying, thickening, coating, or water-holding agent in foods (as ice cream), pharmaceuticals, cosmetics, and cold-water paints, in sizing textiles, in creaming rubber latex, and as a base for dental-impression materials

al·gi·nate \ˈaljəˌnāt, -ˌnət\ *n* -s [ISV *algin* + *-ate*] **:** a salt of alginic acid

alginate fiber *n* **:** any of various fibers made from alginates (as calcium alginate) that are characterized by nonflammability and in some cases by solubility in water or dilute alkaline solutions and are used in making yarns and textiles

al·gin·ic acid \(ˈ)al¦jinik-\ *n* [ISV *algin* + *-ic*] **:** an insoluble colloidal acid $(C_6H_8O_6)_n$ that in the form of salts is a constituent of the cell walls of marine brown algae and that is hard and horny when dry and is capable of absorbing large amounts of water when moist — called also *algic acid, algin*

al·giv·o·rous \(ˈ)al¦jiv(ə)rəs\ *adj* [*alga* + *-i-* + *-vorous*] **:** feeding on algae

algo- — see ALG-

al·go·cy·an \ˌalgōˈsīˌan, -ˌən\ *n* -s [*alga* + *-o-* + *-cyan*] **:** PHYCOCYANIN

al·go·don·ci·llo \ˌalgaˌdänˈsē(ˌ)(y)ō\ *n* -s [AmerSp, fr. Sp, milkweed, dim. of *algodón* cotton, fr. Ar dial. (Spain) *al-quṭun* the cotton] **:** MAJAGUA a

al·go·do·nite \ˌalgəˈdōˌnīt\ *n* -s [*Algodones* mine, Coquimbo prov., Chile, its locality + E *-ite*] **:** a copper arsenide mineral Cu_6As allied to domeykite (sp. gr. 7.62)

¹**al·go·gen·ic** \ˌalgō¦jenik\ *adj* [*alg-* + *-genic*] **:** producing pain

²**algogenic** \"\ *adj* [L *algor* cold + E *-genic*] **:** reducing body temperature

al·goid \ˈalˌgȯid\ *adj* [ISV *alga* + *-oid*] **:** of the nature of or resembling an alga

al·go·lag·nia \ˌalgōˈlagnēə\ *n* -s [NL, fr. *alg-* + *-lagnia*] **:** the finding of sexual pleasure in inflicting or suffering pain — compare MASOCHISM, SADISM

al·go·lag·nic \¦==¦=nik\ *adj* **:** of or relating to algolagnia

al·go·lag·nist \ˈ==¦=nəst\ *n* -s **:** one who practices algolagnia

al·go·log·i·cal \ˌalgə¦läjəkəl\ *adj* **:** of or relating to algology

al·gol·o·gist \alˈgäləjəst\ *n* -s **:** one that studies algology

al·gol·o·gy \-jē\ *n* -ES [*alga* + *-o-* + *-logy*] **:** the study or science of algae

al·gol variable \ˈalˌgäl-, -ȯl-\ *n, usu cap A* [fr. *Algol,* an eclipsing binary star, fr. Ar. *al-ghūl,* lit., the ghoul, ogre] **:** a variable star with light variations resembling those of the binary star Algol

al·go·man *also* **al·go·mi·an** *or* **al·go·mic** *adj, usu cap* [*Algoma,* district in Ontario, Canada + E *-an* or *-ian* or *-ic*] **:** of or relating to the mountain-making movements and granitic intrusion commonly referred to the middle of the Proterozoic era

al·gom·e·ter \alˈgämәd·ə(r)\ *n* [*alg-* + *-meter*] **:** an instrument for measuring the smallest pressure upon the skin that will arouse a sensation of pain

al·gom·e·try \-mə·trē\ *n* -ES [*alg-* + *-metry*] **:** the measurement of pain sensitivity (as by an algometer)

¹**al·gon·ki·an** \alˈgäŋkēən\ *or* **al·gon·kin** \-ŋkən\ *or* **al·gon·qui·an** \-ŋkwēən, -äŋkwē-,-äŋkē-\ *or* **al·gon·quin** \-äŋkwən,-äŋkwən *sometimes* -ŋkən\ *n, pl* **algonkian** *or* **algonkians** *or* **algonkin** *or* **algonkins** *or* **algonquian** *or* **algonquians** *or* **algonquin** *or* **algonquins** *usu cap* [*Algonkian, Algonquian,* blend of *Algonkin, Algonquin* + E *-ian; Algonkin, Algonquin* fr. CanF *Algonquin* (recorded by Champlain as *Algoumequin*), perh. fr. Micmac *algoomaking,* lit., at the place for spearing fish] **1 a :** an Indian people in the Ottawa river valley of Ontario and Quebec, Canada **b :** a member of such people **2** *usu algonquin* **:** a dialect of Ojibwa **3** *usu algonquian* **:** a stock of languages spoken from Labrador to Carolina and westward to the Great Plains, consisting of Cree, Ojibwa, Menomini, Fox, Potawatomi, Illinois, Shawnee; Pamlico, Powhatan, Nanticoke, Delaware; Mahican, Massachuset, Abnaki, Malecite, Micmac; Blackfoot; Cheyenne; Arapaho **4** *usu algonquian* **:** a member of any of the Indian peoples speaking Algonquian languages **5** *algonkian, geol* **:** the Algonkian era or system or group of systems

²**algonkian** \"\ *adj, usu cap* **:** of or relating to a geological era between the Archean and the Paleozoic, from both of which it is usu. separated by unconformities **:** PROTEROZOIC — used by the U.S. Geological Survey — see GEOLOGIC TIME table

al·goph·a·gous \alˈgäfəgəs\ *adj* [*alga* + *-o-* + *-phagous*] **:** feeding on algae ⟨~ insects⟩

al·go·phil·ia \ˌalgōˈfilēə\ *n* -s [NL, fr. *alg-* + *-philia*] **:** a morbid pleasure in the pain either of oneself or of others

al·goph·i·list \alˈgäfələst\ *n* -s **:** one who is subject to algophilia

al·go·pho·bia \ˌalgəˈfōbēə\ *n* -s [NL, fr. *alg-* + *-phobia*] **:** morbid fear of pain

al·go·rism \ˈalgəˌrizəm\ *n* -s [ME *augrim, algorisme,* fr. OF & ML; OF *augorisme,* fr. ML *algorismus,* fr. Ar *al-khuwārizmi* after abu-Ja'far Mohammed ibn-Mūsa *al-Khuwārizmi fl* 825 A.D. Persian mathematician] **1 a :** the system of Arabic numerals **b :** the art of calculating by means of nine figures and zero **:** ARITHMETIC **2 :** the art of calculating with any species of notation ⟨the ~ of fractions⟩ — **al·go·ris·mic** \ˌ==¦rizmik\ *adj*

al·go·rist \ˈalgərəst\ *n* -s [*algorism* + *-ist*] **:** one of a school of medieval mathematicians who made use of the algorismic notation — opposed to *abacist* — **al·go·ris·tic** \ˌ==¦ristik\ *adj*

al·go·rithm \ˈalgəˌrith̲əm, -th-\ *n* -s [alter. (influenced by *arithmetic*) of *algorism*] **:** ALGORISM — **al·go·rith·mic** \ˌ==¦rith̲mik, -th-\ *adj*

al·gous \ˈalgəs\ *adj* [L *algosus,* fr. *alga* + *-osus* -ous] **:** relating to, of the nature of, or full of algae

al·gra·phy \ˈalgrəfē\ *n* -ES [*aluminum* + *-graphy*] **:** a lithographic process in which an aluminum plate is used instead of a stone

al·gua·cil \¦algwə¦sēl, -il\ *or* **al·gua·zil** \-ə¦z-\ *n, pl* **alguacils** \-lz\ *or* **alguaci·les** \ˌ==ˈsē(ˌ)lās\ *or* **alguazils** \-lz\ [Sp *alguacil* (formerly *alguazil*), fr. Ar *al-wazīr* the vizier] **1 :** an officer of justice in Spain, formerly of high rank, now of inferior rank **2 :** a sheriff or constable in Latin-American countries or in regions under Spanish influence

al·gum \ˈalˌgəm *also* ˈȯl-\ *also* **al·mug** \-ˌməg\ *n* -s [fr. (assumed) Heb *algōm, almōg* (attested only in pl. as *algummīm, almuggīm*)] **1 :** a tree mentioned in the Old Testament, prob. cypress, perhaps sandalwood or walnut **2 :** RED SANDALWOOD

-al·gy \ˌaljē, -ji\ *n comb form* -ES [Gk *-algia*] **:** -ALGIA

al·ha·gi \alˈhājē, -häˌjī\ *n, cap* [NL, fr. Ar *al-ḥāj* camel thorn] **:** a small genus of desert shrubs (family Leguminosae) found in northern Africa and Asia Minor having simple leaves, spiny branches, and tough pods — see CAMEL THORN

al·ham·bresque \ˌalˌhamˈbresk\ *or* **al·ham·bra·ic** \-¦brāik\ *adj, usu cap* [*Alhambra,* palace of the Moorish kings at Granada, Spain, erected in the 13th & 14th cents. (fr. Sp, fr. Ar *al-ḥamrā'* the red house) + E *-esque* or *-ic*] **:** made or decorated after the fanciful style of the ornamentation in the Alhambra

ali- *comb form* [L, fr. *ala* — more at AISLE] **1 :** wing ⟨*ali*form⟩ ⟨*ali*trunk⟩ **2 :** relating to the side parts of (a specified organ or structure) ⟨*ali*ethmoid⟩ ⟨*ali*nasal⟩

-a·lia \ˈālēə, -lyə\ *n comb form* [NL, fr. Gk *halia* assembly & Gk *hal-, hals* sea; Gk *halia* akin to Gk *eilein* to compress, OSlav *veliků* great, and perh. to L *vulgus* common people; Gk *hals* sea akin to Gk *hals* salt — more at VULGAR, SALT] **:** realm of marine animal life — in names of biogeographic realms ⟨*Arctalia*⟩ ⟨*Bassalia*⟩ — **-a·li·an** \ˈālēən, -lyən\ *adj comb form*

¹**ali·as** \ˈālēəs, -lyəs\ *adv* [L, otherwise, at another time, fr.

alius other — more at ELSE] **1 :** otherwise called **:** otherwise known as — used esp. in legal proceedings to connect the different names of anyone who has gone by or been known by two or more names ⟨Smith, ~ Simpson⟩ **2 :** at another time

²alias \"\ *n* -ES **1 :** another name **:** an assumed name ⟨masquerading under an indeterminate number of ~*es* —A.E. Wier⟩ **2 :** ALIAS WRIT

alias writ *n* [L *alias* at another time, otherwise; fr. the occurrence in the writ (in its Latin form) of the phrase *sicut alias praecipimus* as we at another time command] *law* **:** a second writ issued after an earlier writ has been returned without action having been taken as commanded

alibamu *usu cap, var of* ALABAMA

al·i·bi \'alə,bī\ *adv* [L] **:** in another place **:** ELSEWHERE ⟨the defendant was able to prove himself ~⟩

²alibi \"\ *n* -s **1** *law* **:** the plea of having been at the time of the commission of an act elsewhere than at the place of commission; *also* **:** the fact or state of having been elsewhere at the time **2 :** a plausible excuse esp. for failure or negligence **:** any excuse ⟨this sounds a little like the ~ which some editors make in defending . . . oversensational stories —F.L.Mott⟩ **syn** see APOLOGY

³alibi \"\ *vb* -ED/-ING/-ES [²*alibi*] *vi* **:** to offer an excuse ⟨*~ed* for not giving money to the teachers' organization —Victor Boesen⟩ ~ *vt* **:** to exonerate by an alibi **:** furnish an excuse for ⟨*~ed* themselves and accused other men —C.W.M.Hart⟩

al·i·ble \'aləbəl\ *adj* [L *alibilis*, fr. *alere* to nourish + *-ibilis* -ible — more at OLD] *archaic* **:** affording nourishment **:** NOURISHING

ali·can·te \¦alə¦käntē\ *adj, usu cap* [fr. *Alicante*, Spain] **:** of or from the city of Alicante, Spain **:** of the kind or style prevalent in Alicante

al·ice blue \'aləs-\ *n, often cap A* [after *Alice* Roosevelt Longworth *b*1884 daughter of Theodore Roosevelt] **:** a pale blue to grayish blue that is redder and stronger than forget-me-not (sense 2b)

alice clover \"-\ *usu cap A, var of* ALYCE CLOVER

alice's fern *n, usu cap A* [prob. fr. the name *Alice*] **:** CLIMBING FERN

al·i·cole \'alə,kōl\ *n* -s [*ali-* + *-cole* (fr. NL *-cola*)] *bot* **:** SPIKE, SPIKELET

al·i·cy·clic \¦alə¦-\ *adj* [ISV *ali*phatic + *cyclic;* orig. formed as G *alizyklisch*] **:** combining the properties of aliphatic and cyclic substances — used of organic compounds (as cycloparaffins and cycloolefins) containing a ring of carbon atoms but not belonging to the aromatic series — called also *cycloaliphatic;* see CARBOCYCLIC

al·id \'aləd, 'ä-\ *n* -s *usu cap* [prob. fr. (assumed) ML *Alides*, fr. *'Alī ibn-abi-Ṭālib* †661 Arab caliph + L *-ides* -id — more at -IDAE] **:** one that claims descent from the caliph Ali and Fatima, son-in-law and daughter respectively of Muhammad

al·i·dade \'alə,dād\ *also* **al·i·dad** \-,dad\ *n* -s [alter. (influenced by F *alidade*) of ME *allidatha*, fr. ML *alhidada*, fr. Ar *al-'iḍādah* the revolving radius of a circle] **:** a rule equipped with simple or telescopic sights and used for determination of direction: as **a :** a part of an astrolabe **b :** the ruler of a plane table **c :** a part of a surveying instrument (as a transit) consisting of the telescope, the telescope standards, the plate levels, the vernier and associated magnifiers, and the spindle **d :** a telescope mounted on a compass repeater and used as part of a ship's navigational equipment for taking bearings

¹alien \'ālyən, -lēən\ *adj* [ME, fr. OF, fr. L *alienus*, fr. *alius* other — more at ELSE] **1 a :** belonging or relating to another person or place **:** STRANGE ⟨followed the crops north and back again year after year, ~ and set apart —Marjory S. Douglas⟩ **b :** relating, belonging, or owing allegiance to another country, land, or government **:** FOREIGN ⟨the government's attempt to expel all ~ agents⟩ **2 :** different in nature or character **:** far removed — used with *from* ⟨with an effect entirely ~ from the one intended⟩ **3 a :** of a foreign character or origin **:** belonging to something else ⟨a statement ~ to the topic under consideration⟩ **b :** repugnant in nature **:** HOSTILE, OPPOSED — used with *to* ⟨a political philosophy ~ to democracy⟩ **syn** see EXTRINSIC

²alien \"\ *n* -s [ME, fr. *alien*, adj.] **1 :** a person of another family, race, or place **:** STRANGER **2 :** one owing allegiance to another country **:** a foreign-born resident who has not been naturalized and is still a subject or citizen of a foreign country; *broadly* **:** a foreign-born citizen **3** *archaic* **:** one excluded from certain privileges **:** one alienated or estranged

³alien \"\ *vt* -ED/-ING/-s [ME *alienen*, fr. L *alienare*, fr. *alienus*] **1 :** ALIENATE, ESTRANGE ⟨*~ed* from all thoughts of . . . the marriage —Edward Hyde⟩ **2 :** to make over (as property or ownership)

alien·a·bil·i·ty \,ā(ē)ənə'bilәd.ē\ *n* -ES **:** the capability of being transferred to other ownership ⟨~ of property⟩

alien·a·ble \'ā(ē)ənəbəl\ *adj* [prob. fr. F *aliénable*, fr. *aliéner* to transfer property, estrange (fr. L *alienare*) + *-able*] **:** that may be transferred to the ownership of another ⟨~ lands⟩

al·ien·age \-nij\ *n* -s [¹*alien* + *-age*] **:** the status of an alien ⟨the government had sufficiently borne the burden of proving ~ to warrant deportation —*Amer. Labor Yr. Bk.*⟩

¹alienate *adj* [ME *alienat*, fr. L *alienatus*, past part. of *alienare* to alienate, fr. *alienus* strange — more at ALIEN] *obs* **:** made unfriendly, hostile, or indifferent **:** ESTRANGED

²alien·ate \'ālyə,nāt, -lēə,-, *usu* -ād.+V\ *vt* -ED/-ING/-s **1 :** to convey or transfer to another (as title, property, or right) **:** part voluntarily with ownership of **:** ALIEN — usu. used of the transfer of the title to property by act of the owner as distinguished from a transfer entirely by operation of law (as in case of descent) **2 :** to cause to be estranged **:** make unfriendly, hostile, or indifferent esp. where attachment formerly existed ⟨her children are *alienated* from her —Ann F. Wolfe⟩ ⟨would ~ potential supporters among the faculty and student body —Sylvan Fox⟩ **3 :** to cause to be withdrawn or transferred ⟨~ capital from its natural channels⟩ **syn** see ESTRANGE

alien·a·tion \,ā(ē)ə'nāshən\ *n* -s [ME *alienacioun*, fr. L *alienation-, alienatio*, fr. *alienatus* + *-ion-, -io* -ion] **1 :** the act of alienating: as **a :** a transfer of ownership of title **:** a conveyance of property to another **b :** a withdrawing or separation of a person or his affections from an object or position of former attachment **:** ISOLATION, EXILE ⟨his ~ from the mainstream of American life —*Times Lit. Supp.*⟩ **2 :** the state of being alienated or diverted from normal function; *specif* **:** mental derangement

alienation of affection : the diversion of a person's affection from someone who has certain rights or claims to such affection to a third person who is held to be the instigator or cause of the diversion

alienation office *n* **:** an office in London where fees had to be paid upon the writs used in fine and recovery

alien corporation *n* **:** a corporation created and existing under the laws of some nation or state other than that wherein it is doing business

aliened *past of* ALIEN

al·ien·ee \¦ā(ē)ə¦nē\ *n* -s [³*alien* + *-ee*] **:** one to whom the title of property is transferred

alien enemy *n* **:** a person owing allegiance to an enemy state

alien·ic·o·la \,ā(ē)ə'nikələ\ *n, pl* **alienico·lae** \-,lē\ [NL, fr. L *alienus* foreign + *-i-* + *-cola* (fr. *colere* to cultivate, dwell)] **:** a foreign inhabitant; *specif* **:** an aphid of a seasonally migrating species (as *Aphis rumicis*) that is developed and lives on the secondary or summer host plant, producing living young asexually

ali·e·ni ju·ris \,alē'ē,nī'jürəs, ,ällē'ā(,)nē'yü-\ *adj* [L, of another's law] *law* **:** subject to the authority of another — opposed to *sui juris*

aliening *pres part of* ALIEN

alien·ism \'ālyə,nizəm, -lēə,-\ *n* -s **:** the status of an alien

alien·ist \-,nəst\ *n* -s [F *aliéniste*, fr. *aliéné* insane, made insane (fr. L *alienatus*, lit., estranged, past part. of *alienare* to estrange) + *-iste* -ist — more at ALIEN] **:** one that treats diseases of the mind; *esp* **:** a physician specializing in legal problems of psychiatry

al·ien·or \¦ā(ē)ə¦nó(ə)r, 'ā(ē)ənər\ *n* -s [fr. (assumed) AF *alienour*, fr. MF *aliener* to transfer property (fr. OF, fr. L *alienare* to transfer property, estrange) + AF *-our* -or — more at ALIEN] **:** one that transfers property to another

alien property custodian *n* **:** the person appointed in time of war to take charge of the property of alien enemies

aliens *pl of* ALIEN, *pres 3d sing of* ALIEN

¹ali·eth·moid \¦alē¦-, ¦al-\ *or* **ali·eth·moi·dal** \¦==¦=¦==\ *adj* [*ali-* + *ethmoid, ethmoidal*] **:** relating to or indicating the lateral expansions of the ethmoid bone or cartilage of certain birds

²aliethmoid \"\ *or* **aliethmoidal** \"\ *n* -s **:** an aliethmoid bone or cartilage

alif \'äləf\ *n* -s [Ar] **:** the first letter of the Arabic alphabet consisting of a simple vertical stroke — see ALPHABET table

alife *adv* [¹*a-* + *life*] *obs* **:** DEARLY

alif·er·ous \ā'lif(ə)rəs, a'-,ə'-\ *adj* [*ali-* + *-ferous*] **:** having wings

ali·form \'alə,fórm, 'al-\ *adj* [*ali-* + *-form*] **:** having winglike extensions **:** wing-shaped

ali·garh \'alə,gär\ *adj, usu cap* [fr. *Aligarh*, India] **:** of or from the city of Aligarh, India **:** of the kind or style prevalent in Aligarh

¹alight \ə'līt, *usu* -d.+V\ *vi* **alighted** \-īd.əd,-ītəd\ *or sometimes* **alit** \ə'lit\ **alighted; alighting; alights** [ME *alighten* to alight, alighten, fr. OE *ālīhtan*, fr. *ā-* (perfective prefix) + *līhtan* to alight, lighten — more at ABEAR, LIGHT] **1 :** to spring down, get down, or descend (as from horseback or from a vehicle) **:** DISMOUNT **2 :** to descend and settle after falling or flying **:** LODGE, LAND ⟨a bird ~s on a twig⟩ ⟨snow *~ing* on a roof⟩ **3** *archaic* **:** FALL **:** come down and strike **4** *archaic* **:** to come by chance — used with *upon* ⟨~ upon a solution⟩ **syn** see DESCEND

²alight \"\ *adj* [ME, alter. of *alighted*, past part. of *alighten* to light up, fr. OE *alīhtan*, fr. ¹*a-* + *līhtan* to light — more at LIGHT] **:** lighted up **:** in a flame **:** LIGHTED ⟨the sky ~ with stars⟩ ⟨his face ~ with inspiration⟩

alighten *vt* -ED/-ING/-s [irreg. fr. ME *alighten* — more at ALIGHT] *obs* **:** to make lighter (as a boat) **:** relieve of care

align *also* **aline** \ə'līn\ *vb* -ED/-ING/-s [F *aligner*, fr. OF, fr. *a-* (fr. L *ad-*) + *ligne* line, fr. L *linea* — more at LINE] *vt* **1 :** to adjust or form to a line **:** range or form in line ⟨the tents were *aligned* in two rows —Norman Mailer⟩ **:** bring into line or alignment ⟨~ set type⟩ **2 :** to put (two or more parts of a machine or structure, esp. parts that should be parallel or in line with each other) into proper relative position or orientation ⟨~ the wheels⟩ **3 :** to make semipermanent adjustments in (a piece of electronic or radio equipment) in order to obtain optimum performance **4 :** to array on the side of or against a party or cause ⟨~ the nations of the world against warfare⟩ ~ *vi* **1 :** to get or fall into line ⟨~ with your friends against a common enemy⟩ **2 :** to be in or come into precise adjustment or correct relative position ⟨the wheels should ~ with the frame⟩ **3 :** to be in alignment (as of one printed character with another)

align·er *also* **alin·er** \-nə(r)\ *n* -s **:** one that aligns: as **a :** a device (as a telescope) for sighting an angle-measuring instrument used in surveying **b :** a sighter of small arms **c :** one that aligns type for use in typewriters

align·ment *also* **aline·ment** \-nmənt\ *n* -s [F *alignement*, fr. MF, fr. *aligner* + *-ment*] **1 :** the act of aligning or state of being aligned **2 a :** a forming in line (as of troops) **b :** the line thus formed; *specif* **:** an arrangement of soldiers in a line or lines **3 :** the ground plan (as of a railroad or fieldwork) in distinction from the profile **4 a :** the condition of being properly aligned **:** the condition of being in satisfactory adjustment or of having the parts in proper relative position **b :** the correct positioning of printed characters in horizontal lines and vertical columns **5** *dancing* **:** the reference of body movement to a vertical axis or directive horizontal line

alignment chart *n* **:** NOMOGRAM

al·i·greek \'alə,grēk\ *n* -s [modif. of It *alla greca* in the Greek manner] **:** a Greek ornamental fret

alii \ä'lē,ē\ *or* **ari·ki** \ä'rē(,)kē\ *or* **arii** \ä'rē,ē\ *n, pl* **alii** *or* **ariki** *or* **arii** [Hawaiian & Samoan *ali'i*, Maori & Rarotongan *ariki*, Tahitian *ari'i*] **:** a Polynesian chief, noble, or king

al·i·poe \ä,lē(,)ē'pō,ā\ *n* -s [Hawaiian] *Hawaii* **:** INDIAN SHOT

¹alike \ə'līk\ *adj* [ME *ilik, alik*, alter. (influenced by ON *ālīkr*) of *ilich*, fr. OE *gelīc* fr. *ge-* — collective prefix — + *līc* body) and *onlīc*, fr. *on* + *līc* — more at CO-, LIKE] **1 :** showing strong resemblance, likeness, or accord ⟨the two cars are much ~⟩ **2 :** showing no difference or no salient difference **:** ⟨the two dresses were quite ~⟩ ⟨the twins, ~ in face and manners —Charles Kingsley⟩ **syn** see LIKE

²alike \"\ *adv* [ME *ilike*, alter. (influenced by ON *ālīka*) of *iliche*, fr. OE *gelīce* and *onlīce*, fr. *gelīc*, adj., and *onlīc*, adj., respectively] **:** in the same manner, form, or degree **:** in common **:** EQUALLY ⟨we are all ~ concerned with religion⟩

alike·ness \-nəs\ *n* -ES [ME *aliknesse*, fr. *alik* + *-nesse* -ness] **:** the quality or state of being alike **:** mutual resemblance ⟨the ~ of mother and daughter was startling⟩

alikuluf *usu cap, var of* ALACALUF

alilonghi *var of* ALALONGA

alim \'ä,lim\ *n* -s [Ar *'ālim*] **:** a Muslim learned in religious matters

al·i·ma \'aləmə\ *n* -s [NL, fr. L. *Alima*, in older classifications a genus of crustaceans, irreg. fr. Gk *halimos* of the sea, fr. *hals* sea] **:** the newly hatched larva of certain stomatopod crustaceans

¹al·i·ment \'aləmənt\ *n* -s [ME, fr. L *alimentum*, fr. *alere* to nourish + *-mentum* -ment — more at OLD] **1 :** something that nourishes **:** FOOD, NUTRIMENT **2 a :** a necessity for life **:** means of support ⟨luxuries are not an ~⟩ **3** *chiefly Scot* **:** an allowance for maintenance

²aliment \-,ment,-,mənt — *see* ²-MENT\ *vt* -ED/-ING/-s [MF *alimenter*, fr. *aliment*, n.] **:** to give aliment to ⟨raise money to ~ a cause⟩ ⟨force a man to ~ his wife⟩

al·i·men·tal \¦alə¦mentᵊl\ *adj, obs* **:** having the quality of nourishing **:** furnishing the materials for natural growth

al·i·men·ta·ry \¦alə¦mentərē, -n·trē, -ri\ *adj* [L *alimentarius*, fr. *alimentum* + *-arius* -ary] **1 :** of, concerned with, or relating to nourishment or to the function of nutrition **:** NUTRITIVE ⟨~ processes of the body⟩ **2 :** having to do with sustenance or maintenance **:** furnishing maintenance ⟨that great ~ thoroughfare of the blossomed desert —A.B.Guthrie⟩

alimentary canal *n* **:** the tubular and in part sacculated passage that serves the functions of digestion, absorption of food, and elimination of residual waste products, being in man about 30 feet long and comprising the mouth, pharynx, esophagus, stomach, small intestine, and large intestine

alimentary castration *n* **:** inhibition of sexual development associated with nutritional deficiencies (as in worker bees)

alimentary paste *n* [trans. of It *pasta alimentaria*] **:** a shaped and dried dough (as macaroni, spaghetti, and vermicelli) prepared from semolina, farina, or wheat flour or a mixture of these with water or milk and with or without egg or egg yolk

alimentary system *n* **:** the organ system devoted to the ingestion, digestion, and assimilation of food and the discharge of residual wastes and consisting of the alimentary canal and those glands or parts of complex glands that secrete digestive ferments

al·i·men·ta·tion \,aləmən'tāshən, -(,)men-\ *n* -s [ML *alimentation-, alimentatio*, fr. LL *alimentatus* (past part. of *alimentare* to nourish, fr. L *alimentum* food) + L *-ion-, -io* -ion — more at ALIMENT] **1 :** the supplying with the necessities of life **:** MAINTENANCE **2 :** the process of giving nourishment ⟨intravenous ~ —M. S. Dunn⟩ **3 :** the act or process of receiving nourishment **4 :** an accumulation of snow (as from wind-blown drifts or avalanches) that tends to increase the volume of a glacier — compare ABLATION

al·i·men·ta·tive \¦alə¦mentəd·iv\ *adj* **:** having to do with the supply of aliment **:** NUTRITIVE — **al·i·men·ta·tive·ly** *adv*

al·i·men·ter \'alə,mentə(r)\ *n* -s **:** one that aliments; *specif* **:** a worker who feeds material into a machine

al·i·men·to·ther·a·py \,alə¦mentō'therəpē\ *n* [¹*aliment* + *-o-* + *therapy*] **:** the treatment of disease by dietetic methods

al·i·mo·ny \'alə,mōnē, -ni, *US also & Brit usu* -,mən-\ *n* -ES [L *alimonia* sustenance, fr. *alere* to nourish — more at OLD] **1 :** the means of living **:** MAINTENANCE **2 :** an allowance made to a woman for her support out of the estate or income of her husband (or to a husband from the property of the wife) or of him who was her husband upon her legal separation or divorce from him or during a suit for the same

alimony pendente lite *n* [L *pendente lite* pending suit] **:** alimony granted pending a suit for divorce or separation to include a reasonable allowance for the prosecution of the suit — called also *temporary alimony*

alims *pl of* ALIM

ali·na·sal \¦alə¦-, ¦al-\ *adj* [*ali-* + *nasal*] **:** relating to the lateral portions of the nose

aline *var of* ALIGN

alineation *var of* ALLINEATION

ali·no·tum \,alə'nōd·əm, ,al-\ *n, pl* **alino·ta** \-d·ə\ [NL, fr. *ali-* + *notum*] **:** the dorsal plate of the thoracic exoskeleton of a winged insect to which the wings are attached

alin·ta·tao \¦älintä¦taù\ *n* -s [PhilSp, fr. Tag *alintatáw*] **1 :** a tree (*Diospyros pilosanthera*) **2 :** the hard dark wood of the alintatao

ali·pa·ta \¦aləpə¦tä\ *n* -s [Sp, fr. Bisayan *alipatá*] **:** BLIND-YOUR-EYES

al·i·pat·ric \¦alə¦pa·trik\ *adj* [by alter.] **:** ALLOPATRIC

ali·ped \'alə,ped, 'al-\ *adj* [*ali-* + *-ped*] **:** wing-footed ⟨the ~ bat⟩

al·i·phat·ic \¦alə¦fad·ik\ *adj* [ISV *aliphat-* (fr. Gk *aleiphat-, aleiphar* oil, fat, fr. *aleiphein* to smear) + *-ic*] **:** of, relating to, or derived from fat **:** FATTY, ACYCLIC — used of a large class of organic compounds characterized by an open-chain structure and consisting of the paraffin, olefin, and acetylene hydrocarbons and their derivatives (as the fatty acids); distinguished from *alicyclic, aromatic, heterocyclic* ⟨~ terpenes⟩

¹al·i·quant \'alə,kwänt, -,kwənt\ *adj* [fr. (assumed) ML or NL *aliquantus* (as in — assumed — *pars aliquanta* aliquant part), fr. L, some, moderate, fr. *alius* some, other + *quantus* how great, how much — more at ELSE, QUANTITY] **:** being a part of a number or quantity but not dividing it without leaving a remainder ⟨5 is an ~ part of 16⟩ — opposed to *aliquot*

²aliquant \"\ *n* -s **:** an aliquant part

¹al·i·quot \'alə,kwät, -,kwət\ *adj* [ML *aliquotae* (as in *partes aliquotae* aliquot parts), fr. L *aliquot* some, several, fr. *alius* + *quot* how many — more at QUOTA] **1 :** contained an exact number of times in something else — used of a divisor or part ⟨5 is an ~ part of 15⟩; opposed to *aliquant* **2 :** FRACTIONAL ⟨an ~ portion of a chemical solution⟩ ⟨an ~ part of an estate⟩

²aliquot \"\ *n* -s **:** an aliquot part

³aliquot \"\ *vt* -ED/-ING/-s **:** to divide (a number or quantity) into equal parts

aliquot scaling *n* **:** a method of strengthening the tone of the upper notes of the piano by providing an extra sympathetic string for each note

aliquot tone *n, music* **:** a partial tone **:** HARMONIC

alisander *var of* ALEXANDER

ali·sep·tal \¦alə¦-, ¦al-\ *adj* [*ali* + *septal*] *anat* **:** relating to or designating lateral expansions of the nasal septum

ali·si·er \ə'lēzē,ā\ *n* -s [F, service tree, fr. *alise* sorb apple, of Gmc origin; akin to MD *else* alder, OHG *erila* — more at ALDER] **1 :** BLACK HAW 1 **2 :** SHEEPBERRY 1a

alis·ma \ə'lizmə\ *n* [NL, fr. L, water plantain, fr. Gk] **1** *cap* **:** a small genus (the type of the family Alismataceae) of aquatic or semiaquatic herbs with long-petioled often floating leaves and white flowers — see WATER PLANTAIN **2** -s **:** a plant of the genus *Alisma*

al·is·ma·ce·ae \,a(,)liz'māsē,ē\ *syn of* ALISMATACEAE

al·is·ma·les \,aləz'mā(,)lēz\ *or* **alis·ma·ta·les** \ə,lizmə'tā-(,)lēz\ *n pl*, *cap* [NL, fr. *Alisma* + *-ales*] *syn of* NAIADALES

alis·ma·ta·ce·ae \ə,lizmə'tāsē,ē\ *n pl, cap* [NL, fr. *Alismat-, Alisma*, type genus + *-aceae*] **:** a family of monocotyledonous aquatic or marsh herbs (order Naiadales) having regular perfect monoecious flowers

ali·so \ə'lē(,)zō, -sō\ *n* -s [Sp] **1 :** any of several shrubs or trees of the genus *Alnus* **2 :** the wood of an aliso

al·i·son \'aləsən\ *n* -s [by folk etymology (influence of name *Alison*)] **:** ALYSSUM

¹ali·sphe·noid \¦alə¦-, ¦al-\ *or* **ali·sphe·noi·dal** \¦===¦==, ¦==¦==\ *adj* [*ali-* + *sphenoid, sphenoidal*] **:** belonging or relating to or forming the wings of the sphenoid or the pair of bones that becoming fused with other sphenoidal elements form in adult man the greater wings of the sphenoid

²alisphenoid \"\ *or* **alisphenoidal** \"\ *n* -s **:** an alisphenoid bone

alist \ə'-\ *adv (or adj)* [¹*a-* + *list* (to incline)] *of a ship* **:** LISTED **:** in a list

alit *past of* ALIGHT

alite \'ä,līt\ *n* -s [¹*a* + *-lite*] **:** a constituent of portland-cement clinker now identified as a calcium silicate approximately Ca_3SiO_5 containing small but essential amounts of aluminum and magnesium in substitution for silicon and empty holes in the crystal structure

al·i·ter \'alətər, -əd·ər, -ə,te(ə)r\ *adv* [L, fr. *alius* other — more at ELSE] **:** OTHERWISE

ali·trunk \'alə,trəŋk, 'al-\ *n* -s [*ali-* + *trunk*] **:** the portion of the insect thorax that bears the wings, in the Hymenoptera including also the first abdominal segment

ali·tur·gic *also* **ali·tur·gi·cal** \¦ā=¦-, ¦a=¦-\ *adj* [²*a-* + *liturgic, liturgical*] *of a specified day* **:** marked by the omission of the celebration of the Christian liturgy or a portion of it ⟨an ~ day⟩

al·i·un·de \¦alē¦ən(,)dē\ *adv (or adj)* [L, fr. *alius* other + *unde* whence; akin to *ubi* where — more at ELSE, UBIQUITY] **:** from another source **:** from elsewhere

alive \ə'līv\ *adj* [ME *alive, on live*, fr. OE *on līfe*, fr. *on* + *līfe*, dat. of *līf* life — more at LIFE] **1 a :** having life **:** not dead or inanimate **:** LIVING; *esp* **:** marked by a state in which the organs perform their vital functions ⟨so good to be ~⟩ ⟨a large number were still ~ after the explosion⟩ — usu. used predicatively or postpositively **b :** LIVING — used for emphasis after the noun ⟨he was the proudest boy ~⟩ ("Man ~!" he said. "You don't really mean that") ⟨sakes ~⟩ **2 a :** still in existence, force, or operation **:** effective at least to a degree **:** not dead, defunct, or extinct **:** EXISTENT, ACTIVE ⟨small farms kept ~ by judicious husbanding of the lake waters —*Amer. Guide Series: Calif.*⟩ ⟨keep ~ the conception of morals he preached —Havelock Ellis⟩ **b :** still in use **:** current to a degree **:** still exerting force or influence ⟨neither of these works is much ~ today —*Times Lit. Supp.*⟩ **c** *bowls* **:** in play **:** not dead **3 a :** marked by ready perception of **:** knowing or realizing the existence of **:** comprehending and vigilant about or appreciative of ⟨becoming ~ to the folly of what he had been doing —Samuel Butler⟩ ⟨consciousness of this danger . . . made her . . . ~ to the risks of an undesirable marriage —John Galsworthy⟩ **b :** quick to note or feel **:** readily impressed or influenced by **:** notably aware of, susceptible or sensitive to ⟨dreadfully ~ to nervous terrors —Charles Lamb⟩ ⟨veterans are as fully ~ to the romance . . . of newspaper work as any cub —Stanley Walker⟩ **4 a :** marked by alertness, activity, vitality, energy, animation, or briskness **:** not static, torpid, sluggish, or lifeless ⟨not sufficiently ~ to feel the tang of sense nor yet to be moved by thought —John Dewey⟩ ⟨the ~ promise of spring —H.D.Skidmore⟩ **b :** communicating a feeling of life, esp. of blended verisimilitude, activity, verve, and interestingness ⟨making the commonplaces of American culture . . . come ~ through his plain words —Babette Deutsch⟩ **5 :** FILLED, THRONGED, TEEMING **:** marked by much pulsating, stirring life, animation, or activity ⟨the sea was ~ with large whales —Herman Melville⟩ ⟨this decade was ~ with controversy and intellectual combat —*Amer. Guide Series: Ind.*⟩ **6 a :** electrically connected to a source of voltage or electrically charged **:** having a potential different from that of the earth or of the conducting ground of a radio or automobile **b :** not inactive, inactivated, shut off, or dead **:** operating and functioning **:** TRANSMITTING, BROADCASTING, RECORDING ⟨despite the hurricane the phone was still ~⟩ **7 :** LIVE 10 **syn** see AWARE

alive·ness *n* -ES **:** the quality or state of being alive

ali·vin·cu·lar \¦alə¦viŋkyələ(r), ¦al-\ *adj* [*ali-* + *vinculum* + *-ar*] **:** having a short ligament with its longer axis transverse to the hinge line — used of certain bivalves

ali·yah \ä'lē(,)yä, ə'lēyə, ¦äle¦yä\ *n, pl* **aliyahs** \-äz,-əz\ *or* **ali·yoth** *or* **ali·yot** \¦älē¦yōs, -ōt\ [Heb *'aliyāh* ascent, act of going up] **:** the action of going up or of being called to the reading desk of the synagogue to read from the scriptures

al·i·zan·threne navy blue R \,alə'zan,thrēn-\ *n, usu cap A &N&B* [*alizanthrene* fr. alizarin + *-anthrene*] **:** a vat dye — see DYE table I (under *Vat Blue 18*)

al·i·za·ri \,alə'zärē\ *also* **li·za·ri** *or* **li·za·ry** \lə'zärē\ *n, pl* **alizaris** *also* **lizaris** *or* **lizaries** [F & Sp; F, *alizari*, fr. Sp] **:** the madder of the Levant

aliz·a·rin \ə'lizərən\ *also* **aliz·a·rine** \", -,rēn\ *n* -s [prob.

fr. F *alizarine*, fr. *alizari* (fr. Sp, prob. fr. Ar *al-'aṣārah* the juice, fr. *'aṣara* to squeeze) + *-ine*] **1 :** an orange or red crystalline compound $C_{14}H_6O_2(OH)_2$ formerly prepared from madder and now made synthetically from anthraquinone that with different mordants produces on cotton the Turkey reds and other shades (as pink and chocolate) but that is used now more in making red pigments than in dyeing; 1,2-dihydroxy-anthraquinone — see DYE table I (under *Mordant Red 11*) **2 :** any of a group of acid, mordant, and solvent dyes derived like alizarin proper from anthraquinone and used to produce various hues — see DYE table I **3 :** any of various dyes not derived from anthraquinone but somewhat similar to alizarin in dyeing properties

alizarine blue *n, often cap A&B* **:** any of various blue acid, mordant, and solvent dyes most of which are derived from anthraquinone — see DYE table I (under *Acid Blue* and *Solvent Blue*)

alizarine brown *n, often cap A&B* **:** ANTHRAGALLOL

alizarine carmine *n, often cap A&C* **:** ALIZARINE RED b

alizarine cyanine green *n, often cap A&C&G* **:** an acid anthraquinone dye derived from quinizarin that dyes wool and mordanted silk yellowish green to bluish green — see DYE table I (under *Acid Green 25* and *Solvent Green 3*)

alizarine lake *n, often cap A&L* **:** an organic pigment made from alizarin — see DYE table I (under *Pigment Red 83*)

alizarine red *n, often cap A&R* **:** any of various red mordant or acid dyes most of which are derived from anthraquinone: as **a :** TURKEY RED 1a **b :** an orange-yellow crystalline compound $C_{14}H_7NaO_7S$ used chiefly for dyeing and printing aluminum-mordanted wool scarlet red, as a biological stain, and as an analytical reagent (as for detecting aluminum); sodium 3-alizarin-sulfonate — called also *Alizarine Carmine, Alizarine Red S, Alizarine S;* see DYE table I (under *Mordant Red 3*)

alizarine S *n, often cap A* **:** ALIZARINE RED b

alizarine saphirol *n, often cap A&S* **:** either of two acid anthraquinone dyes — see DYE table I (under *Acid Blue 43 & 45*)

alizarine yellow *n, often cap A&Y* **:** any of various mordant dyes not related chemically to alizarin but applicable by similar methods: as **a :** a monoazo dye made by coupling diazotized *m*-nitroaniline with salicylic acid — called also *Alizarine Yellow 2G;* see DYE table I (under *Mordant Yellow 1*) **b :** a monoazo dye made by coupling *p*-nitroaniline with salicylic acid and used chiefly as an acid-base indicator — called also *Alizarine Yellow R;* see DYE table I (under *Mordant Orange 1*) **c :** GALLACETOPHENONE — called also *Alizarine Yellow C*

al·ja·ma \äl'hämə\ *n* -S [Sp, fr. Ar *al-jamā'ah* the assembly, congregation of people — more at AMALGAM] **:** a Jewish congregation or community in medieval Spain; *esp* **:** a Jewish (sometimes Moorish) quarter, school, or synagogue

al·ja·ma·do \,älhä'mä(,)thō\ *n, pl* **aljamados** [Sp, fr. *aljama* + *-ado*, n. & adj. suffix (fr. L *-atus* -ate)] **:** an inhabitant of an aljama

al·ja·mia *or* **al·ja·mi·ah** \,ălhä'mēə\ *n* -S [Sp *aljamía*, fr. Ar *al-'ajamīyah* the non-Arab, barbarian] **1 :** Spanish written in Hebrew or esp. Arabic characters **2 :** the Arabic alphabet as adapted for writing Spanish

¹al·ja·mi·a·do \¦äl,häme¦ä(,)thō\ *adj* [Sp, fr. *aljamía* + *-ado*] **:** written in Spanish with Arabic characters ⟨an ~ text⟩

²aljamiado \"\ *n* -S [Sp, fr. *aljamiado*, adj.] **:** a work written in Spanish with Arabic characters

alk \'alk\ *or* **alk gum** *n* -S [Ar *'ilk* resin] **:** resin of Chian turpentine

alk- *comb form* [*alkyl*] **:** alkyl ⟨*alk*acrylic⟩ ⟨*alk*iodide⟩

alk *abbr* alkaline

alka- *comb form* [*alkane*] **:** alkane ⟨*alka*diyne⟩ ⟨*alka*polyene⟩

al·ka·di·ene \,alkə'dī,ēn\ *n* -S [*alkali* + *di-* + *-ene*] **:** DIOLEFIN

al·ka·di·en·yl \,alkə'dī,ēnᵊl\ *n* -S [*alkadiene* + *-yl*] **:** a univalent aliphatic hydrocarbon radical containing two double bonds

al·ka·hest *also* **al·ca·hest** \'alkə,hest\ *n* -S [NL *alchahest*] **:** the universal solvent supposed by the alchemists to exist — **al·ka·hes·tic** \¦=='=tik\ *adj*

alkakengi *var of* ALKEKENGI

al·ka·le·mia \,alkə'lēmēə\ *n* -S [NL, fr. ML *alkali* + NL *-emia*] **:** a condition in which the hydrogen ion concentration in the blood is decreased

al·ka·les·cence \,alkə'lesᵊn(t)s\ *also* **al·ka·les·cen·cy** \-ᵊnsē\ *n* -S **:** alkaline property **:** quality or degree of being alkaline

al·ka·les·cent \¦==¦=ᵊnt\ *adj* [*alkali* + *-escent*] **:** tending to the properties of an alkali **:** slightly alkaline

al·ka·li \'alkə,lī\ *n, pl* **alkalies** *or* **alkalis** \-īz\ *often attrib* [ME, fr. ML *alcali*, *alkali*, fr. Ar *al-qili* the ashes of the plant saltwort] **1 a :** a soluble salt obtained from the ashes of plants and consisting largely of potassium carbonate or (as from sea plants) of sodium carbonate **b :** a substance having marked basic properties like the above salts; *esp* **:** a hydroxide or carbonate of an alkali metal (as sodium or potassium) or less often of an alkaline-earth metal (as calcium) — see CAUSTIC ALKALI; compare BASE 8 **2 :** ALKALI METAL — used esp. in names of compounds ⟨~ cyanides⟩ **3 a :** a soluble salt or a mixture of soluble salts (as the sulfates and chlorides of sodium, potassium, and magnesium and the carbonates of sodium and potassium) present in some soils of arid or semiarid regions in quantity detrimental to ordinary agriculture ⟨~ soils⟩ **b :** a region in which the soil abounds in alkali

alkali bee *n* **:** a common solitary bee (*Nomia melanderi*) important as a pollinizer of alfalfa in the western U.S.

alkali blue *n* **1 :** any of various alkali-soluble triphenylmethane dyes that are essentially sodium salts of monosulfonic acids of phenylated pararosaniline and are used chiefly in making pigments — see DYE table I (under *Acid Blue 110*) **2 :** any of the fairly permanent pigments made from an alkali blue dye and used chiefly in printing inks

al·kal·ic \(')al¦kalik\ *adj* [*alkali* + *-ic*] *of igneous rocks* **:** containing a comparatively large proportion of the alkalies sodium and potassium

alkali cellulose *n* **:** a compound of cellulose with an alkali (as sodium hydroxide) formed during the mercerization of cotton and as the first step in the manufacture of viscose and cellulose ethers

alkali chlorosis *n* **:** a yellowing of the foliage of a plant caused by an excess of soluble salts in the soil

alkali disease *n* [so called fr. the belief that it was caused by alkaline water] **1 :** trembles of cattle — compare MILK SICKNESS **2 :** botulism of ducks — compare DUCK SICKNESS **3 :** chronic selenosis

al·ka·lied \-,līd\ *adj* **1 :** affected with alkali disease **2** *of grain or hay* **:** containing selenium

alkali fast green 10 G *n, usu cap A&F&G* **:** an acid dye — see DYE table I (under *Acid Green 22*)

alkali feldspar *n* **:** feldspar containing alkali metals (as sodium or potassium or both) but little calcium

alkali flat *n* **:** a level area in an arid or semiarid region that is encrusted with salt or alkali (as the dried bed of an evaporated pond or lake)

al·kal·i·fy \al'kalə,fī, 'alkə-\ *vb* -ED/-ING/-ES [*alkali* + *-fy*] *vt* **:** to convert or change into an alkali **:** make alkaline ~ *vi* **:** to become alkaline

alkali grass *n* [so called fr. its growth in alkaline soil] **1 :** a grasslike plant (*Zygadenus elegans*) with flowers in a loose cylindrical raceme **2 :** SALT GRASS a **3 :** any of several grasses of the genus *Puccinellia* that grow in saline situations

alkali heath *n* [so called fr. its growth in alkaline soil and fr. its heathlike leaves] **:** a California undershrub (*Frankenia grandifolia*) with revolute leaves, pinkish flowers in small terminal clusters, and linear many-seeded capsules

alkali lake *n* **:** a saline lake containing large amounts of sodium and potassium carbonates in solution as well as sodium chloride, commonly found in arid regions — called also *soda lake*

alkali mallow *n* **:** a low whitish scurfy perennial herb (*Sida hederacea*) having roundish or kidney-shaped leaves and cream-colored flowers

alkali metal *n* **:** any of the univalent mostly basic metals of group I of the periodic table comprising lithium, sodium, potassium, rubidium, cesium, and francium

al·ka·lim·e·ter \,alkə'limәd·ə(r)\ *n* -S [F *alcalimètre*, fr. *alcali* alkali (fr. ML) + *-mètre* -meter] **1 :** an apparatus for measuring the strength or the amount of alkali in a mixture or solution **2 :** an apparatus for measuring the amount of carbon dioxide (as that liberated from a weighed sample of carbonate-containing material by reaction with acid)

al·ka·li·met·ric \¦alkələ¦me·trik\ *adj* **:** relating to or involving alkalimetry

al·ka·lim·e·try \-'limə·trē\ *n* -ES **1 :** the measurement of the strength of an alkali or of the amount of alkali in a mixture or solution — compare ACIDIMETRY 2 **2 :** the measurement by titration of the amount of acid in a solution by use of a standard solution of an alkali — compare ACIDIMETRY 1

alkali mustard *n* [so called fr. its growth in alkaline soil] **:** JACKASS CLOVER 2

al·ka·line \'alkələn, -,līn\ *adj* [*alkali* + *-ine*] **1 :** of, relating to, or having the properties of an alkali: as **a :** having an alkaline reaction **:** having a pH of more than 7 ⟨an ~ soil⟩ ⟨a strongly ~ solution⟩ **b :** containing or involving the use of alkali ⟨~ bath⟩ ⟨~ fusion⟩ — see BASIC 3, CAUSTIC 1 **2 :** of or relating to the alkali metals

alkaline detergent *n* **:** DETERGENT b

alkaline earth *n* **1 :** the oxide of any of a group of bivalent strongly basic metals comprising calcium, strontium, and barium and, according to some, magnesium, radium, and less often beryllium **2 :** ALKALINE-EARTH METAL

alkaline–earth metal *n* **:** any of the metals of group II of the periodic table whose oxides are the alkaline earths

alkaline metal *n* **:** ALKALI METAL

alkaline tide *n* **:** the period or condition of increased alkalinity of the body fluids and urine during digestion associated with the loss of acid by secretion of gastric juice

al·ka·lin·i·ty \,alkə'linəd·ē, -ətē, -i\ *n* -ES [*alkaline* + *-ity*] **:** the quality, state, or degree of being alkaline

al·ka·lin·i·za·tion \,alkə,linə'zāshən, -,lən-, -,līn-, -,lə,nī'z-\ *n* -S **:** the act or process of alkalinizing

al·ka·lin·ize \'alkələ,nīz\ *vt* -ED/-ING/-S [*alkaline* + *-ize*] **:** to make alkaline ⟨*alkalinized* the body by using sodium citrate as the agent⟩

alkali orange RT *n, usu cap A&O* **:** a direct dye — see DYE table I (under *Direct Orange 10*)

alkali sacaton *n* **:** a dropseed (*Sporobolus airoides*) that is abundant in dry alkali soils esp. in the southern U.S.

al·ka·li·troph·ic \¦alkələ¦träfik, -ōf-\ *adj* [*alkali* + *-trophic*] **:** exhibiting the alkaline state characteristic of lakes in arid regions — **al·ka·lit·ro·phy** \,alkə'li·trəfē\ *n* -ES

alkali weed *n* [so called fr. its growth in alkaline soil] **:** YERBA MANSA

al·ka·li·za·tion \,alkələ'zāshən, -,lī'z-\ *n* -S **:** ALKALINIZATION

al·ka·lize \'alkə,līz\ *vt* -ED/-ING/-S [F *alcaliser*, fr. *alcali* alkali (fr. ML) + *-iser* -ize] **:** ALKALINIZE

al·ka·loid \'alkə,lȯid\ *n* -S *often attrib* [G, fr. *alkali* + *-oid*] *chem* **:** any of a very large group of organic bases containing nitrogen and usu. oxygen that occur esp. in seed plants for the most part in the form of salts with acids (as citric, oxalic, or sulfuric acid), most of the bases being colorless and well crystallized, bitter tasting, complex in structure with at least one nitrogen atom in a ring (as a pyrrole, quinoline, or indole ring), and optically and biologically active, many of the bases or their salts being used as drugs (as morphine and codeine) ⟨ergot contains a number of closely related ~s⟩ — **al·ka·loi·dal** \¦==¦=dᵊl\ *adj*

al·ka·lom·e·try \,alkə'lämə·trē\ *n* -ES [ISV *alkaloid* + *-metry*] **1 :** the quantitative determination of alkaloids by chemical or other methods **2 :** the administration of alkaloids according to an exact system of dosage

al·ka·lo·sis \,alkə'lōsəs\ *n, pl* **alkalo·ses** \-ō,sēz\ [NL, fr. ML *alkali* + NL *-osis*] **:** a condition of increased alkalinity of the blood and tissues caused by excessive alkali intake or excessive loss of acid and resulting in muscular irritability and sometimes convulsions — opposed to *acidosis*

al·ka·lot·ic \¦alkə¦läd·ik\ *adj* **:** marked by the presence of or tendency toward alkalosis

al·ka·mine \'alkə,mēn, -,mən\ *n* -S [G *alkamin*, fr. *alk*ohol alcohol + *amin* amine] **:** AMINO ALCOHOL

al·ka·nal \'alkə,nal\ *n* -S [*alkane* + *al*dehyde] **:** any aliphatic aldehyde (as decanal) regarded as derived from an alkane and containing the same number of carbon atoms as the alkane

al·kane \'al,kān\ *n* -S [*alkyl* + *-ane*] **:** any of a series of saturated aliphatic hydrocarbons C_nH_{2n+2} (as methane) **:** PARAFFIN 2

al·ka·net \'alkə,net\ *n* -S [ME, fr. OSp *alcaneta*, dim. of *alcana*] **1 a :** a European plant (*Alkanna tinctoria*) **b :** the root of this plant **2 :** a red dyestuff prepared from alkanet root and used similarly to alkannin **3 :** BUGLOSS 1 **4 :** PUCCOON 1b

al·kan·na \al'kanə\ *n* [NL, fr. Sp *alcana* henna (shrub), fr. ML *alchanna*, fr. Ar *al-ḥinnā'* the henna] **1** *cap* **:** a genus of herbs (family Boraginaceae) native to southern Europe with funnel-shaped flowers and pitted or wrinkled nutlets **2** *also* **al·ken·na** \-ke-\ -S **:** HENNA 1

al·kan·nin \al'kanən\ *n* -S [ISV *alkann-* (fr. NL *Alkanna*) + *-in*] **:** a red crystalline coloring matter $C_{16}H_{16}O_5$ obtained from alkanet and used chiefly in coloring beverages and fatty and oily pharmaceutical and cosmetic preparations

al·ka·no·ic acid \¦alkə¦nōik-\ *n* [*alkane* + *-oic*] **:** an aliphatic acid (as hexanoic acid) regarded as derived from an alkane and containing the same number of carbon atoms as the alkane

al·ka·nol \'alkə,nōl, -ōl\ *n* -S [ISV *alkane* + *-ol*] **:** an aliphatic alcohol (as methanol) regarded as derived from an alkane

al·ka·nol·a·mine \,==¦=ə¦mēn\ *n* -S [*alkanol* + *amine*] **:** a compound (as ethanolamine) that is both an alkanol and an amine

al·kap·ton *or* **al·cap·ton** \al'kap,tän, -,tən\ *n* -S [ISV *alkali* + Gk *kaptein* to gulp + ISV *-on*, orig. formed as G *alkapton*] **:** HOMOGENTISIC ACID

al·kap·ton·u·ria *or* **al·cap·ton·u·ria** \(,)al,kaptə'n(y)u̇rēə\ *n* -S [NL, fr. ISV *alkapton*, + *alcapton* + NL *-uria*] **:** a rare recessive metabolic anomaly in man marked by inability to complete the degradation of tyrosine and phenylalanine resulting in the presence of alkapton in the urine — **al·kap·ton·u·ric** \¦=,==¦rik\ *adj*

al·ka·ryl \'alkə,ril, -ēl\ *n* -S [*alkyl* + *aryl*] **:** an alkyl-substituted aryl radical (as ethyl-phenyl)

al·ka·ver·vir \,alkə'vər,vi(ə)r, al'kavə(r),-\ *n* -S [*alk*aloid + *vervir*, abbr. of NL *Veratrum viride*] **:** a preparation containing ester alkaloids obtained from a hellebore (*Veratrum viride*) and used in treating hypertension

al·ke·ken·gi *also* **al·ka·ken·gi** \,alkə'kenjē\ *n* -S [ME *alkenkengy*, fr. ML *alkekengi*, fr. Ar *al-kākanj* the ground-cherry, fr. Per *kākunaj*] **:** CHINESE LANTERN PLANT

al·kene \'al,kēn\ *n* -S [ISV *alkyl* + *-ene*] **:** any of a series of aliphatic hydrocarbons C_nH_{2n} (as ethylene) containing a double bond **:** OLEFIN

al·ke·nyl \'alkə,nil, -ēl\ *n* -S [*alkene* + *-yl*] **:** any univalent aliphatic hydrocarbon radical C_nH_{2n-1} (as 2-butenyl $CH_3CH{:}CHCH_2$–) derived from an alkene by removal of one hydrogen atom

al·ker·mes \al'kərmēz, -məs; ,alkər'mes\ *n* -ES [F *alkermès*, fr. Sp *alkermes* (now usu. *alquermes*), fr. Ar *al-qirmiz* the alkermes — more at CRIMSON] **1** *obs* **:** the kermes insect **2 :** an orig. Italian liqueur made of brandy flavored with bay leaves, mace, nutmeg, cloves, and cinnamon and colored a brilliant red with the kermes insect or with cochineal

alk gum *var of* ALK

al·kide \'al,kīd, -,kəd\ *n* -S [*alkyl* + *-ide*] **:** a binary compound of an alkyl esp. with a metal ⟨diethyl-zinc $(C_2H_5)_2Zn$ is an ~ of zinc⟩

alk·i·o·dide \al'kīə,dīd, -,dəd\ *n* -S [*alkyl* + *iodide*] **:** a compound (as a methiodide) with an alkyl iodide (as methyl iodide)

alk·ox·ide \al'käk,sīd, -,səd\ *n* -S [*alkoxy-* + *-ide*] **:** a binary compound (as a methoxide) of an alkoxyl; *esp* **:** a base formed from an alcohol by replacement of the hydroxyl hydrogen with a metal

alk·oxy \(')al¦käksē\ *adj* [fr. ISV *alkoxy-*, fr. *alkoxyl*] **:** of, relating to, or containing alkoxyl ⟨~ groups⟩

alk·ox·yl \al'käksəl\ *n* -S [blend of *alkyl* and *oxy-*] **:** an univalent radical RO (as methoxyl) composed of an alkyl group united with oxygen

alk·ox·yl·ate \al'käksə,lāt\ *vt* -ED/-ING/-S [*alkoxyl* + *-ate*] **:** to introduce alkoxyl into (a compound)

alk·ox·yl·a·tion \(,)=,==lāshən\ *n* -S **:** the act or process of alkoxylating

al·ky \'alkē\ *n* -ES [by shortening & alter.] **1** *slang* **:** ALCOHOL **2** *slang* **:** ALCOHOLIC

al·kyd \'alkəd\ *or* **alkyd resin** *n* -S *often attrib* [blend of *alkyl* and *acid*] **:** any of a large group of thermoplastic or thermosetting synthetic resins that are essentially polyesters made by heating polyhydric alcohols (as glycerol, ethylene glycol, or pentaerythritol) with polybasic acids or their anhydrides (as phthalic anhydride, maleic anhydride, or sebacic acid) and used chiefly in making protective coatings characterized in general by their gloss, flexibility, and good weathering properties

al·kyl \'alkəl\ *n* -S [prob. fr. G, fr. *alkohol* alcohol (fr. ML *alcohol*) + *-yl*] **1 a :** a univalent aliphatic radical C_nH_{2n+1} (as methyl, ethyl) derived from an alkane by removal of one hydrogen atom **b :** any univalent aliphatic, aromatic-aliphatic, or alicyclic hydrocarbon radical **2 :** a compound of one or more alkyl radicals with a metal ⟨sodium ~s⟩

al·kyl·a·mine \¦alkələ¦mēn, ,==¦lamən, -'la,mēn\ *n* -S [ISV *alkyl* + *amine*] **:** an amine (as methylamine) containing alkyl attached to amino nitrogen

al·kyl·a·mi·no \¦alkələ¦mē(,)nō, -kə¦lamə,nō\ *adj* [*alkylamino-*, fr. *alkylamine*] **:** of, relating to, or containing an alkylamine

alkyl aryl sulfonate *n* **:** a salt of an alkyl-substituted aromatic sulfonic acid — used chiefly commercially; see ANIONIC DETERGENT 2

¹al·kyl·ate \'alkə,lāt\ *vt* -ED/-ING/-S [*alkyl* + *-ate*] **:** to introduce one or more alkyl groups into (a compound)

²alkylate \", -lət\ *n* -S **:** a product of alkylation; *esp, in petroleum refining* **:** a mixture of liquid paraffins (as isooctane) of high antiknock value used as a blending agent for gasoline (as aviation gasoline)

al·kyl·a·tion \,alkə'lāshən\ *n* -S **:** the act or process of alkylating; *esp, in petroleum refining* **:** a process in which gaseous paraffins (as isobutane) are converted into higher liquid branched-chain paraffins (as iso-octane) by reaction with gaseous olefins (as butylenes)

al·kyl·ene \'alkə,lēn\ *n* -S [ISV *alkyl* + *-ene*] **1 :** a bivalent saturated aliphatic radical (as ethylene) regarded as derived from an alkene by opening of the double bond or from an alkane by removal of two hydrogen atoms from different carbon atoms **2 :** ALKENE

alkyl halide *n* **:** a compound (as methyl iodide, ethyl bromide) of an alkyl group with a halogen

al·kyl·ic \(')al¦kilik\ *adj* [*alkyl* + *-ic*] **:** of or relating to an alkyl

al·kyl·i·dene \al'kilə,dēn\ *n* -S [ISV *alkyl* + *-idene*] **:** a bivalent aliphatic radical (as ethylidene) derived from an alkane by removal of two hydrogen atoms from the same carbon atom

al·kyl·ize \'alkə,līz, -,ki,-\ *vt* -ED/-ING/-S [*alkyl* + *-ize*] **:** ALKYLATE

al·kyl·o·gen \al'kiləjən, -,jen\ *n* -S [*alkyl* + *halogen*] **:** ALKYL HALIDE

al·kyl·ol \'alkə,lōl, -ōl\ *n* -S [*alkyl* + *-ol*] **:** a hydroxy derivative of an alkyl radical **:** hydroxy-alkyl

al·kyl·ol·a·mine \,==¦=ə¦mēn\ *n* -S [*alkylol* + *amine*] **:** ALKANOLAMINE

al·kyne *also* **al·kine** \'al,kīn\ *n* -S [*alkyl* + *-yne*, *-ine*] **:** any of a series of aliphatic hydrocarbons C_nH_{2n-2} (as acetylene) containing a triple bond

al·ky·nyl \'alkə,nil, -ēl\ *n* -S [*alkyne* + *-yl*] **:** a univalent aliphatic hydrocarbon radical containing a triple bond

¹all \'ȯl\ *adj* [ME *all, al*, fr. OE *all, eall;* akin to OHG *al* all, ON *allr*, Goth *alls*, and perh. to OIr *oll* large, beyond, L *uls* beyond, OSlav *lani* in the preceding year, Skt *araṇa* foreign; basic meaning: beyond] **1 a :** that is the whole amount or quantity of ⟨~ rubbish should be cleared out of cellars⟩ ⟨needed ~ the courage he had⟩ ⟨it ~ began one rainy afternoon⟩ **:** that is the whole extent or duration of ⟨~ the year round⟩ ⟨sat up ~ night⟩ ⟨one of the greatest victories in ~ history⟩ **b :** as much as possible **:** the greatest possible ⟨wished them ~ happiness⟩ ⟨traveled with ~ speed⟩ ⟨was told in ~ seriousness⟩ **2 a :** every member or individual component of **:** each one of — used distributively with a plural noun or pronoun to mean that a statement is true of every individual considered ⟨~ things to ~ men⟩ ⟨~ my friends were there⟩ ⟨a film suitable for ~ ages⟩ ⟨refugees ~, from one thing or another —*Punch*⟩ ⟨they ~ came late⟩ **b** *of members of a class* **:** each and every one of — used in logic as a verbalized equivalent of the universal quantifier **3 :** the whole number or sum of — used collectively with a plural noun or pronoun to mean that a statement is true of the sum of the individuals considered ⟨~ the angles of a triangle are equal to two right angles⟩ ⟨~ these together are not worth 10 dollars⟩ ⟨after ~ these years⟩ **4 :** EVERY — used chiefly in the phrases *all manner of, all kind of* ⟨endured ~ manner of hardship⟩ **5 :** any whatever ⟨beyond ~ doubt⟩ ⟨denied ~ responsibility⟩ **6 :** nothing but **:** ONLY, ALONE ⟨I was born to speak ~ mirth and no matter —Shak.⟩ **:** **a :** completely taken up with, given to, or absorbed by ⟨found him ~ gratitude⟩ ⟨suddenly became ~ attention⟩ **b :** having or seeming to have (some physical feature) in conspicuous excess or prominence ⟨a body ~ legs⟩ ⟨a face ~ pimples⟩ **c :** marked by acute or eager concentration on full perception by **:** paying full attention with ⟨at the mention of bicycles the boy was ~ ears⟩ **7** *dial* **:** used up **:** entirely consumed — used esp. of food and drink ⟨the keg of beer was ~⟩ **8 :** being more than one person or thing — used chiefly in speech esp. after interrogative and plural personal pronouns ⟨who ~ was there⟩ ⟨what ~ do you have to do⟩; often written with hyphen between pronoun and *all* ⟨we-*all* had better wait⟩; see YOU-ALL **syn** see WHOLE — **all the :** as much of . . . as **:** as much of a . . . as **:** the only ⟨*all the* home I ever had⟩ — **all two** *now dial* **:** all of two **:** BOTH ⟨walking hand in hand, *all two* of them⟩

²all \"\ *adv* [ME *al, all*, fr. OE *all, eall*, fr. *all, eall*, adj.] **1 :** WHOLLY, ALTOGETHER, QUITE ⟨sat ~ alone⟩ ⟨a statement that was not ~ true⟩ ⟨~ gone⟩ ⟨arrived ~ too late to be of service⟩ ⟨he was ~ for the racy phrase —W.S.Maugham⟩ — often used before other words and phrases or (chiefly in speech) after interrogative adverbs to intensify meaning ⟨dealers ~ across the country⟩ ⟨ran into the house ~ covered with mud⟩ ⟨could hear moaning ~ around him⟩ ⟨~ too few⟩ ⟨that's ~ very human and would harm nobody —Deems Taylor⟩ ⟨where ~ have you been⟩; often used in compounds to indicate representation of a whole area ⟨an *all*-British soccer team⟩ or selection of the best ⟨an *all*-girl team⟩ **2** *obs* **:** EXCLUSIVELY, ONLY ⟨I shall never marry like my sisters, to love my father ~ —Shak.⟩ **3** *archaic* **:** JUST **:** quite as indicated ⟨a damsel lay deploring, ~ on a rock reclined —John Gay⟩ — often merely intensive **4 :** by that amount **:** so much **:** very much — used with *the* and an adverb or adjective in the comparative degree ⟨~ the better for a night's sleep⟩ ⟨from private sources and therefore ~ the more revealing⟩ **5 :** for each side **:** APIECE, EACH ⟨the score is two ~⟩ — **all of 1 :** QUITE, FULLY ⟨a man *all of* 6 feet tall⟩ ⟨arrived *all of* 15 minutes ago⟩ ⟨this building cost *all of* five million dollars —Lewis Mumford⟩ **2 :** with marked signs of — used with *a* ⟨*all of a* flutter⟩ ⟨*all of a* tremble⟩ — **all the** *chiefly dial* **:** as . . . as — used with an adverb or adjective usu. comparative in form ⟨*all the* higher⟩ ⟨*all the* high⟩ but with the meaning of the positive (as high as) ⟨*all the* farther he could go was up to that fence⟩

³all \"\ *pron* [ME *al, all* (fr. *al, all*, adj.) & *alle*, pl. of *al, all*] **1 :** the whole number, quantity, or amount **:** TOTALITY — often used with a following relative clause ⟨~ that I have⟩ and with *of* and a pronoun and in recent usage with *of* and a noun ⟨~ of us⟩ ⟨~ of the books⟩ **2 :** EVERYBODY, EVERYTHING **:** everything in a particular scene or sequence of events ⟨through ~ he sat immovable⟩ ⟨sacrificed ~ for love⟩ ⟨to make it plain to one and ~⟩ ⟨that is ~⟩ ⟨when ~ is said and done⟩ — **and all :** and everything else esp. of a kind suggested by a previous context ⟨there he sat, pipe *and all*⟩ ⟨exhausted *and all* as he was —Gerrard MacDermott⟩ — often used merely to emphasize a previous context ⟨her friends was a queer lot, *and all* —Richard Llewellyn⟩

⁴all \"\ *n* -S [ME *all*, fr. *al, all*, adj.] **1 a :** the whole of one's possessions or of what one holds dear ⟨to lose one's

~⟩ **b alls** *pl, now chiefly dial* : BELONGINGS : personal possessions **2** *usu cap* **a** : WHOLE, TOTALITY **b** : the universe

all- *or* **allo-** *comb form* [Gk, fr. *allos* other, different — more at ELSE] **1** : other : different : dissimilar : extraneous ⟨*al*lergy⟩ ⟨*allo*pathy⟩ ⟨*allo*sematic⟩ **2** *allo-* : isomeric form, close relative, or variety of (a specified chemical compound) ⟨*allo*ocimene⟩ ⟨*allo*telluric acid⟩: as **a** : the more stable form (of two geometrical isomers) ⟨*allo*cinnamic acid⟩ **b** : TRANS- 3 — esp. in names of stereoisomeric compounds containing two fused saturated rings ⟨*allo*cholanic acid⟩ ⟨*allo*pregnane⟩ **3** *usu allo-* : having dissimilar genomes ⟨*allo*heteroploid⟩ ⟨*allo*ploid⟩ ⟨*allo*triploid⟩ — opposed to *aut-*

1al·la breve \ˌaləˌbrev(ə), ˌäl-, -re(ˌ)vā\ *adv (or adj)* [It, lit., according to the breve] : in duple or quadruple time, the beat being represented by the half note

2alla breve \"\ *n, pl* **alla breves** : the sign C marking a piece or passage to be played alla breve; *also* : a passage so marked — called also *cut time*

al·lac·ta·ga \ə'laktəgə\ *n, cap* [NL] : a genus of small Asiatic jerboas having five toes on the hind feet

al·lac·tite \ə'lak,tīt\ *n* -s [ISV *allact-* (irreg. fr. Gk *allag-*, stem of *allassein* to change, fr. *allos* other) + *-ite;* orig. formed as Sw *allaktit* — more at ELSE] : a mineral consisting of a brownish red basic manganese arsenate $Mn_7(AsO_4)_2(OH)_8$

al·la·ha·bad \ˌaləhəˌbad, -bäd\ *adj, usu cap* [fr. *Allahabad*, India] : of or from the city of Allahabad, India : of the kind or style prevalent in Allahabad

al·la·man·da \ˌalə'mandə\ *n* [NL, after Jean N.S. *Allamand* †1787 Swiss naturalist and physicist] **1** *cap* : a genus of tropical American woody vines (family Apocynaceae) having funnel-shaped flowers **2** -s : a plant of the genus *Allamanda*

al·la mar·cia \ˌälə'mär,chä; ˌalə'märchə, ˌäl-\ *adv (or adj)* [It] : in march style : like a march — used as a direction in music

1all-amer·i·can \ˌ==ˌ===\ *adj, cap 2d A* **1** : composed wholly of American elements ⟨played an *all-American* program⟩ **2** : thought of as representative of the U.S. as a whole ⟨the tales are not sectional or provincial in spirit; they are *all-American* —*Nation*⟩ ⟨a real *all-American* boy⟩; *esp* : selected (as by vote or nomination) as the best in the U.S. at a given time ⟨the *all-American* football team for the year⟩ ⟨suggested names for an all-time *all-American* relay team⟩ **3** : entirely within the U.S. ⟨access to the sea by an *all-American* system of waterways⟩ **4** : of or relating to the American nations collectively ⟨*all-American* research projects in Uruguay and Mexico⟩

2all-american \"\ *n, cap 2d A* [1*all-American*] **1** : a team or other unit composed of performers rated as best in the U.S. according to a vote or expert's choice **2** : a player or performer named to an all-American team

all-a-mort *adj* [by folk etymology (influence of 2*all*) fr. MF *a la mort* to the death] *archaic* : AMORT

allanerly *var of* ALLENARLY

al·lan·ic acid \ə'lanik-\ *n* [ISV *allan*toin + *-ic*] : a crystalline acid $C_4H_5N_5O_5$ formed by the action of fuming nitric acid on allantoin

al·lan·ite \'alə,nīt\ *n* -s [Thomas *Allan* †1833 Eng. mineralogist, its discoverer + E *-ite*] : a mineral consisting of a brown or black monoclinic silicate allied to epidote and containing cerium, thorium, and other rare metals — **al·lan·it·ic** \ˌaləˌnid·ik\ *adj*

allant- *or* **allanto-** *comb form* [NL, fr. Gk, sausage, fr. *allant-*, *allas*, prob. of Italic origin; akin to L *alium* garlic — more at ALLIUM] **1** : allantoic : allantoid ⟨*allanto*chorion⟩ ⟨*allanto*in⟩ **2** : sausage ⟨*allant*iasis⟩

al·lan·to·am·ni·on·ic *or* **al·lan·to·am·ni·ot·ic** \əˌlan(ˌ)tō-ˌ==ˌ==\ *adj* [*allant-* + *amnionic* or *amniotic*] : relating to the allantois and amnion esp. when fused into a single membrane — compare CHORIOALLANTOIS

al·lan·to·ic \ˌalən·ˌtōik, ˌa,lan·-\ *adj* [ISV *allant-* + *-ic*] : relating to or contained in the allantois : characterized by an allantois

allantoic acid *n* : a crystalline acid $C_4H_8N_4O_4$ obtained by hydrolysis of allantoin; di-ureido-acetic acid

allantoic bladder *n* : a urinary bladder derived (as in certain vertebrates) from the allantois

allantoic vesicle *n* : the cavity of the allantois

1al·lan·toid \ə'lan,tȯid, -ntəwəd\ *adj* [F *allantoïde* allantois] : of or relating to the allantois

2allantoid \"\ *n* -s [F *allantoïde*, fr. Gk *allantoeidēs* sausage-shaped, fr. *allant-* + *-eidēs* -oid] : ALLANTOIS

3allantoid \"\ *adj* [Gk *allantoeidēs*] : shaped like a sausage

al·lan·toi·dal \ˌalən·ˌtȯidᵊl, ˌa,lan·-, -tōədᵊl\ *adj* [2*allantoid* + *-al*] : ALLANTOID

al·lan·toi·dea \ˌalən·'tȯidēə, ˌa,lan·-; ə,lantə'widēə\ *n pl, cap* [NL, fr. *allantoid-*, *allantois*] *in some classifications* : a division of Vertebrata comprising all forms in which the embryo develops a complete allantois

1al·lan·toi·de·an *or* **al·lan·toi·di·an** \ˌalən·ˌtȯidēən, ˌa,lan·-; əˌlantəˌwid-\ *adj* [NL *allantoid-*, *allantois* + E *-ean*, *-ian*] : of, relating to, or derived from the allantois

2allantoidean \"\ *adj* [NL *Allantoidea* + E *-an*] : of or relating to the Allantoidea

al·lan·to·in \ə'lantəwən\ *n* -s [prob. fr. G, fr. NL *allantois* + G *-in*] : a crystalline oxidation product $C_4H_6N_4O_3$ of uric acid found in the allantoic liquid of cows, in the urine of most mammals, and in many plants (as sugar beets) and used in the treatment of wounds and ulcers

al·lan·to·in·ase \-,nās\ *n* -s [*allantoin* + *-ase*] : an enzyme occurring esp. in animals other than mammals that hydrolyzes allantoin

al·lan·to·is \ə'lantəwəs, -n·,tȯis\ *n, pl* **allanto·i·des** \ˌalən-'tōə,dēz, ˌa,lan·-, -tȯi,dēz\ [NL, irreg. fr. MF *allantoide* — more at ALLANTOID] : a vascular fetal membrane of reptiles, birds, or mammals arising as a pouch or sac from the hindgut, in reptiles and birds expanding greatly between the amnion and chorion to serve as a respiratory organ while its cavity stores the fetal excretions and in placental mammals intimately associated with the chorion in formation of the placenta to which it contributes blood vessels and usu. a part of the cellular stroma

al·lant·ox·a·idin \ˌa,lan,täk'sāədᵊn\ *n* -s [ISV *allantoxa*nic + *-idin*] : a crystalline compound $C_3H_3N_3O_2$ derived from allantoxanic acid by decarboxylation; 5-imino-hydantoin

al·lant·ox·an·ic acid \ˌa,lan,täk'sanik-\ *n* [ISV *allant-* + *oxanic*] : a crystalline acid $C_4H_3N_3O_4$ formed by the oxidation of allantoin or of uric acid — called also *oxonic acid*

al·lan·tu·ric acid \ˌalənˌtu̇rik-, ˌa,lan-, -tyu̇-\ *n* [ISV *allant-* + *-uric*] : an acid $C_3H_4N_2O_3$ obtained as a deliquescent mass by the oxidation of allantoin and in other ways; (carboxymethylene)-urea

al·la po·lac·ca \ˌäləpə'läkə, ˌaləpə'la-\ *adv (or adj)* [It, lit., in the Polish manner] : in the manner of a polonaise — used as a direction in music

al·la pri·ma \ˌälə'prēmə, ˌal-\ *n* [It, at once] : a method of painting in which pigments are laid on in a single application instead of being built up by repeated paintings

al·lar·gan·do \ˌä,lärˌgän(ˌ)dō\ *adj (or adv)* [It, making slow, widening, verbal of *allargare* to make slow, widen, fr. *al-* (fr. L *ad-*) + *largare* to widen, fr. LL, to widen, loosen, fr. L *largus* abundant, generous — more at LARD] : becoming gradually broader with the same or greater volume — used as a direction in music

all-around \ˌ==ˌ=\ *also* **all-round** \(')=ˌ=\ *adj* [2*all*] **1** : not limited or specialized: as **a** : marked by competence in many fields ⟨an *all-around* athlete⟩ ⟨an *all-around* man of letters producing fiction, drama, poetry, and criticism⟩ **b** : marked by general utility : serviceable in various situations ⟨an *all-around* tool⟩ : meritorious for various reasons ⟨the best *all-around* breed⟩ **2 a** : INCLUSIVE, COMPREHENSIVE : not narrowly particularized ⟨taking an *all-around* view⟩ ⟨an *all-around* reduction in value⟩ **b** : comprising all charges including extras ⟨the *all-round* cost of the project⟩ **syn** see VERSATILE

all around *var of* ALL ROUND

al·lasch \'ä,läsh\ *n* -ES *usu cap* [G, fr. *Allasch* (*Allaži*), town near Riga, Latvia, where it originated] : a sweet kümmel prepared with flavoring agents not usu. found in kümmel (as bitter almonds, angelica root, anise, and orange peel)

al·las·so·ton·ic \əˌlasəˌtänik\ *adj* [ISV *allass-* (fr. Gk *allassein* to change) + *-o-* + *tonic* — more at ALLACTITE] *of the movements of mature plant organs* : temporarily induced by stimulus — opposed to *auxotonic;* compare IRRITOMOTILITY

al·la te·des·ca \ˌälətə'deskə, ˌal-, -tā'-\ *adv (or adj)* [It, in the German manner] **1** : in the style of the allemande **2** : in the style of the ländler or the waltz

1al·la·tive \'aləd·iv\ *adj* [L *allat*us carried to (suppletive past part. of *afferre* to carry to; *allatus* fr. *ad-* + *latus*, suppletive past part. of *ferre* to bear) + E *-ive* — more at BEAR, TOLERATE] *of a grammatical case* : denoting motion to or toward

2allative \"\ *n* -s : the allative case of a language or a form in the allative case

al·la tur·ca \ˌälə'tu̇rkə, ˌal-; ˌalə'tər-\ *adv (or adj)* [It, in the Turkish manner] : in the style of the Turkish military band

1al·lay \ə'lā, a'-\ *vb* -ED/-ING/-S [ME *alayen*, *aleggen*, fr. OE *ālecgan*, fr. *ā-* (perfective prefix) + *lecgan* to lay — more at ABEAR, LAY] *vt* **1** *obs* : OVERTHROW, SUBDUE ⟨~ this thy abortive pride —Shak.⟩ **2** : to subdue or reduce in intensity or severity : ALLEVIATE, RELIEVE, ABATE ⟨this ration is palatable, very rapidly ~*s* hunger —H.G.Armstrong⟩ ⟨widely used in our community to ~ aches —Ben Riker⟩ ⟨sought . . . to catch every river breeze to ~ the summer heat —Maxwell Mays⟩ **3** : to put at rest (as disquiet, fear, or suspicion) : make quiet : PACIFY, APPEASE, QUELL, CALM ⟨some answer to ~ all his anxieties —Norman Kelman⟩ ⟨the turmoil that had been partly ~*ed* returned —Elizabeth M. Roberts⟩ ⟨competition was embittered rather than ~*ed* —*Times Lit. Supp.*⟩ **4 a** : to limit the pleasurable or good effect of : moderate by something unpleasant ⟨the victors' joy was ~*ed* by the death of their prince⟩ **b** : WEAKEN, DIMINISH, QUALIFY ~ *vi, obs* : to diminish in strength : SUBSIDE ⟨when the rage ~*s* —Shak.⟩ **syn** see RELIEVE

2allay *n* -s **1** *archaic* : ALLEVIATION, ABATEMENT **2** *obs* : CHECK, STOPPAGE

3allay *vt* -ED/-ING/-S [ME *alayen*, fr. MF *alayer*, *aleier*, *aloier*, *alier* to combine, fr. L *alligare* to bind, bind to — more at ALLY] *archaic* : ALLOY

4allay *n* -s [ME *alay*, fr. MF *alay*, *aloi*, fr. *alayer*, *aloier*, v.] *archaic* : ALLOY

al·lay·ment \ə'lāmənt, a'-\ *n* -s [1*allay* + *-ment*] : the action of quieting or alleviating : the state of being quieted or alleviated : MITIGATION

al·la zin·ga·ra \ˌälə'tsiŋgərə, ˌal-; ˌalə'zi-\ *adv (or adj)* [It] : in gypsy style — used as a direction in music

al·la zop·pa \ˌälətˌsäpə, ˌal-, -ȯpə; ˌaləˌzäpə\ *adv (or adj)* [It, in a limping manner] : in syncopated style — used as a direction in music

all but *adv* : very nearly : ALMOST ⟨makes travel *all but* impossible⟩ ⟨*all but* fell in love with him⟩ ⟨marched forward *all but* unopposed⟩ ⟨the pain that is *all but* a pleasure —W.S. Gilbert⟩

all clear *n* : a signal that enemy aircraft have left

all-commodity rate *n* : a freight rate applied to all goods in a particular shipment regardless of particular classifications

all-court press *n* : FULL-COURT PRESS

all-day \'=ˌ=\ *adj* : lasting for, occupying, or appearing throughout an entire day ⟨an *all-day* picnic⟩ ⟨an *all-day* trip⟩ — used esp. of a newspaper that puts out editions throughout the day as contrasted with a morning or evening paper ⟨an *all-day* daily⟩

all-day sucker *n* : a piece of hard candy on a stick : a large lollipop

allectory *var of* ALECTORIA

alledge *obs var of* ALLEGE

al·lée \(')aˌlā\ *n* -s [F, fr. OF *alee* action of going, journey, fr. fem. of *alé*, past part. of *aler* to go — more at ALLEY] **1** : WALK; *specif* : a walk or path between two rows of formally planted trees or shrubs that are at least twice as high as the width of the walk or path **2** : a formal avenue or mall

al·lée cou·verte \(ˌ)a,lā,kü'vert\ *n, pl* **allées couvertes** \-ā(z),k-\ [F, lit., covered passage] : a passage like a tunnel leading to a neolithic tomb

allegany *usu cap, var of* ALLEGHENY

al·le·ga·tion \ˌalə'gāshən, -ē'-\ *n* -s [ME *allegacioun*, fr. MF *allegation*, fr. L *allegation-*, *allegatio*, fr. *allegatus* (past part. of *allegare* to send on an errand, cite, adduce, fr. *ad-* + *legare* to send with a commission or charge, depute) + *-ion-*, *-io* -ion — more at LEGATE] **1** : the act of alleging or asserting positively often before a court **2** : something asserted or declared : a positive assertion : formal averment ⟨suffered dismissal . . . after unproved ~*s* of "pro-Germanism" —*Amer. Guide Series: Minn.*⟩; *specif* : a statement by a party to a legal action of what he undertakes to prove — usu. applied to each separate averment; see CHARGE, COUNT **3** : an assertion unsupported and by implication regarded as unsupportable ⟨the absurd and familiar ~ —*Encounter*⟩ ⟨there were several ~*s* . . . none of them creditable —Audrey Barker⟩ ⟨vague ~*s* of misconduct⟩

al·le·ga·tor \'==,gād·ə(r)\ *n* -s [*allegat*ion + *-or*] : one that alleges

al·le·ga·tum \ˌ=='gād·əm\ *n, pl* **allega·ta** \-d·ə\ [NL, fr. L, neut of *allegatus*, past part. of *allegare*] : ALLEGATION 2

1al·lege \ə'lej *also* a'-\ *vt* -ED/-ING/-S [ME *alleggen*, modif. (influenced by OF *alegier* to acquit, fr. LL *allegare* to free from servitude by adducing reasons, fr. L, to cite, adduce) of OF *alleguer*, fr. L *allegare* to cite, adduce] **1** *archaic* : to state under oath : plead in court **2 a** : to state or declare as if under oath positively and assuredly but without offering complete proof **b** : to assert, affirm, state without proof or before proving (*alleged* that the suspect is a kidnaper) ⟨the newspaper ~*s* the mayor's guilt⟩ **3** *archaic* : to adduce or bring forward (as a source or authority) esp. for or against ⟨his Muse can ~ most of "the apologies of Aristophanes" —T. L. Peacock⟩ **4** : to bring forward as a cause or reason esp. for excusing oneself from blame, reproach, or dislike ⟨when she turned to him for help . . . he perhaps justly *alleged* that he had troubles of his own —Gamaliel Bradford⟩ **syn** see CITE

2al·lège \a'lezh\ *n* -s [F, fr. MF *alege* alleviation, fr. OF *alegier* to alleviate, lighten, fr. LL *alleviare* — more at ALLEVIATE] : a part of a wall that has been thinned (as the spandrel under a window)

al·lege·able \ə'lejəbəl *also* a'-\ *adj* : capable of being alleged or affirmed

al·leged \-jd *also* -jəd\ *adj* **1** : asserted to be true or to exist ⟨an ~ miracle⟩ ⟨~ abuses of housing benefits —*Wall Street Jour.*⟩ ⟨ordering seizure of the steel mills under ~ "inherent" rights —*Current Biog.*⟩ **2** : questionably true or of the kind specified : SUPPOSED, SO-CALLED ⟨a program of ~ descriptive music⟩ ⟨another glass of that ~ brandy⟩ — **al·leg·ed·ly** \-jədlē, -li\ *adv*

al·lege·ment \-jmənt\ *n* -s [1*allege* + *-ment*] : ALLEGATION

al·le·gha·ny·ite \ˌalə'gānē,īt\ *n* -s *usu cap* [*Alleghany* county, N. C. + E *-ite*] : a mineral consisting of a pink basic silicate of manganese $Mn_5Si_2O_8(OH)_2$

al·le·ghe·ni·an *also* **al·le·gha·ni·an** \ˌaləˌgānēən, -nyən, -ˌgen-\ *adj, usu cap* [*Alleghany*, *Alleghany* mts. + E *-an*] **1** : ALLEGHENY 1 **2** : relating to or constituting the humid division of the biogeographic Transition zone that extends across the northern U. S. from New England to eastern No. and So. Dakota and includes also most of Pennsylvania and the mountainous region as far south as northern Georgia

al·le·ghe·ny *also* **al·le·gha·ny** *or* **al·le·ga·ny** \ˌaləˌgānē, -ni *also* -ˌgen-\ *adj, usu cap* [fr. *Allegheny*, *Allegheny* mts., ranges of the Appalachian system in eastern U. S.] **1** : of or relating to the Allegheny mountains or the region where they are situated **2** : relating to or included in a subdivision of the Pennsylvanian coal measures

allegheny barberry *n, usu cap A* : AMERICAN BARBERRY

allegheny spurge *or* **allegheny mountain spurge** *n, usu cap A* : a low herb or subshrub (*Pachysandra procumbens*) with white or pinkish flowers in basal or axillary spikes native to southern U. S. but grown also elsewhere as a ground cover — compare JAPANESE SPURGE

allegheny vine *or* **allegheny fringe** *n, usu cap A* : CLIMBING FUMITORY

al·le·giance \ə'lējən(t)s *also* a'-\ *also* **al·le·gian·cy** \-nsē, -si\ *n* -s [ME *alligeaunce*, *allegeaunce*, modif. (influenced by ME *alleggeaunce* allegation, fr. *alleggen* to allege + *-aunce* -ance) of MF *ligeance*, fr. OF, fr. *lige* liege + *-ance* — more at LIEGE] **1 a** : the relation or obligation of a feudal vassal to his liege lord — compare FEALTY **b** (1) : the duty of fidelity owed by a subject or citizen to his sovereign or government (2) : the obligation of an alien to the government under which he resides — see LOCAL ALLEGIANCE, NATURAL ALLEGIANCE; compare EXPATRIATE *vi* **2** : devotion or loyalty esp. to a person, group, or cause entitled to obedience or service and respect ⟨wandered between . . . his ~*s* to political democracy and Marxist economics —*Time*⟩ ⟨the ~ of a poet to a specific philosophy —René Wellek⟩ ⟨rival powers compete for our ~; we are forever straining to serve two masters —Herbert Agar⟩ **syn** see FIDELITY

1al·le·giant \-jənt\ *adj* [*allegi*ance + *-ant*] : giving allegiance : LOYAL ⟨it is impossible to be ~ to two opposing forces —*Christian Science Monitor*⟩

2allegiant \"\ *n* -s : one that owes allegiance

alleging *pres part of* ALLEGE

al·le·gor·i·cal \ˌaləˌgȯrəkəl, -lēˌ-, -är-\ *also* **al·le·gor·ic** \-ik,-ēk\ *adj* [ME *allegorik*, fr. LL *allegoricus*, fr. Gk *allēgorikos*, fr. *allēgoria* allegory + *-ikos* -ic — more at ALLEGORY] **1** : of, relating to, or having the characteristics of allegory or an allegory : occurring in, constituting, or containing an allegory ⟨~ poetry⟩ ⟨~ figures⟩ ⟨an ~ interpretation⟩ **2** : stressing a hidden spiritual meaning transcending the literal sense of the text of sacred books — **al·le·gor·i·cal·ly** \-ək(ə)lē, -i\ *adv* — **al·le·gor·i·cal·ness** *n* -ES

al·le·go·rism \'==,gōr,izəm, -,gȯ,ri-,-_gə,ri-\ *n* -s [fr. *allegorize*, after such pairs as E *baptize: baptism*] : the process or result of allegorizing : the allegorical method of literary interpretation

al·le·go·rist \-_rəst\ *n* -s [*allegory* + *-ist*] : one that allegorizes; *esp* : a writer of allegory

al·le·go·ri·za·tion \ˌ==,gōrə'zāshən, -ȯr-,-är-; -_gərə'z-, -,rī'z-\ *n* -s **1** : allegorical representation **2** : allegorical interpretation

al·le·go·rize \'==,gōr,īz, -,gȯ,rīz,-_gə,r-\ *vb* -ED/-ING/-S [ME *allegorisen*, fr. LL *allegorizare*, fr. L *allegoria* + *-izare* -ize] *vt* **1** : to make into allegory ⟨~ the history of a people⟩ **2** : to treat or explain as allegory ⟨their symbolic content can be *allegorized* for purposes of analysis —*Accent*⟩ ⟨*allegorizing* the ancient stories of their people⟩ ~ *vi* **1** : to give allegorical explanations **2** : to compose or use allegory ⟨the poets liked to ~ on the story⟩

al·le·go·riz·er \-zə(r)\ *n* -s : one that allegorizes

al·le·go·ry \'alə,gōrē, -ē,g-, -ȯr-, -ri\ *n* -ES [ME *allegorie*, fr. L *allegoria*, fr. Gk *allēgoria*, fr. *allēgorein* to speak figuratively, prob. fr. *alla* (neut. pl. of *allos* other) + *-agorein* to speak publicly, fr. *agora* assembly — more at ELSE, GREGARIOUS] **1 a** : the written, oral, or artistic expression by means of symbolic fictional figures and actions of truths or generalizations about human conduct or experience (as in Bunyan's *Pilgrim's Progress* and Spenser's *Faerie Queene*) **b** : an instance of such expression ⟨a poetic ~⟩ **2** : something resembling or suggestive of an allegory in its effect : symbolic representation : EMBLEM ⟨an organization that stands as an ~ of cooperation⟩

syn ALLEGORY, PARABLE, MYTH, FABLE, APOLOGUE: these five words apply in this comparison to literary forms typically telling a story for the sake of presenting a truth, a moral. ALLEGORY, the most general, applies to fiction in which action and character, usu. of a certain complexity, are symbolic or figurative, the characters usu. typical, the whole by its analogy to real-life situations or actual moral facts presenting a moral or spiritual truth or a normative generalization or a series of them. A PARABLE is a short, allegorical tale, usu. simple and homely, typically illustrating or reenforcing a single spiritual truth. MYTH in this application applies chiefly to Platonic myth, which was a brief explanation of a difficult philosophic truth by means of a short allegorical analogy. A FABLE or APOLOGUE is an allegorical tale, usu. a beast fable, that points up in its analogy the weaknesses or follies of man for the sake of a moral or normative generalization usu. formulated and appended at the end of the tale

1al·le·gret·to \ˌaləˌgred·(ˌ)ō, -e(ˌ)tō, ˌäl-\ *adv (or adj)* [It, fr. *allegro*] : faster than andante but not so fast as allegro — used as a direction in music

2allegretto \"\ *n* -s : a piece or movement in allegretto tempo

1al·le·gro \ə'le(ˌ)grō, -lā-, ä'-\ *adv (or adj)* [It, merry, gay, fr. (assumed) VL *alecrus* lively, alter. of L *alacr-*, *alacer* — more at ALACRITY] : in a brisk lively manner — used as a direction in music

2allegro \"\ *n* -s **1** : a piece or movement or division of a movement in allegro tempo **2 a** : ballet steps (as leaps, jumps, and turns) performed in a lively fast tempo **b** : rapid exercises and steps terminating a ballet class

allegro form *n* : a linguistic form shortened as a result of frequent occurrence in rapid speech (as *Miss* for *Mistress*)

al·lele \ə'lē(ə)l\ *also* **al·lel** \-lel\ *n* -s [G *allel*, short for *allelomorph*] **1** : either of a pair of alternative Mendelian characters (as smooth or wrinkled seed in the pea) — compare MENDEL'S LAW, MULTIPLE ALLELE **2** : GENE, FACTOR — used chiefly of a gene considered as the vehicle of an allele — **al·lel·ic** \-'lēlik, -lel-\ *adj* — **al·lel·ism** \-'lē,lizəm, -le,-\ *n* -s

allelo- *comb form* [Gk *allēlo-* each other, fr. *allēlōn* of each other, fr. *allos . . . allos* one . . . the other, fr. *allos* other — more at ELSE] **1** : alternative ⟨*allelo*morph⟩ **2** : of or for each other : reciprocal : reciprocally ⟨*allelo*catalytic⟩ ⟨*allelo*tropism⟩

al·lelo·ca·tal·y·sis \əˌle(ˌ)lō, -ē(ˌ)-\ *n, pl* **allelocatalyses** [NL, fr. *allelo-* + *catalysis*] : the mutually stimulating effect on the rate of growth and reproduction of two or more microorganisms in a volume of medium as compared to the rate of a single microorganism in a like volume of the same medium — **al·lelo·cat·a·lyst** *n* -s — **al·lelo·cat·a·lyt·ic** \=ˌ=(ˌ)=,==ˌ==\ *adj*

al·lelo·morph \ə'lēlə,mȯrf, -lel-\ *n* -s [ISV *allelo-* + *-morph*] : ALLELE — **al·lelo·morph·ic** \=ˌ==ˌ=fik\ *adj* — **al·lelo·morph·ism** \='==,=,fizəm\ *n*

al·le·lop·a·thy \əˌlēləˌpathē, -ˌlel- *also* ˌalə'läpəthē\ *n* -s [ISV *allelo-* + *-pathy*; orig. formed as G *allelopathie*] : the reputed baneful influence of one living plant upon another due to secretion of toxic substances

1al·le·lu·ia *or* **al·le·lu·iah** *or* **al·le·lu·ja** \ˌaləˌlüyə\ *interj* [ME *alleluya*, fr. LL *alleluia*, fr. Gk *allēlouia*, fr. Heb *halălūyāh* praise ye Jehovah] : HALLELUJAH — used frequently in liturgies and hymns of praise and thanksgiving; used also as an expression of humble mourning in the Eastern Orthodox Church

2alleluia *or* **alleluiah** *or* **alleluja** \"\ *n* -s [ME *alleluia*, *alleluya*, fr. ML *alleluia*, fr. LL *alleluia*, interj.] *often cap* **1** : a responsory chant in various Christian liturgies **2** : the part of the Roman mass consisting of two or more alleluias and a verse usu. from a psalm and usu. sung or said after the gradual and before the gospel

3alleluia *also* **alleluja** \"\ *n* -s [1*alleluia*, repeatedly sung at Easter, when it blooms] **1** : a wood sorrel (*Opalis montana*) **2** : WOODWAXEN

al·le·lu·iat·ic \ˌalə,lüˌyad·ik\ *adj* [ML *alleluiaticus*, fr. *alleluia* (chant) + *-aticus* (as in LL *dramaticus*)] : of or relating to a religious alleluia

1al·le·mande \'alə,mand, -änd,-aa(ə)nd, ˌ=='=; 'alәmən(d)\ *n* -s *often cap* [F, fr. fem. of *allemand* German, fr. LL *Alamannus* member of the Alamanni, sing. of *Alamanni*] **1 a** : a 17th century and 18th century court dance developed in France from a German folk dance and characterized by elaborate intertwinings of a couple's arms with joined hands **b** : a step with arms interlaced **c** : a quadrille figure in which each man turns his corner, then his partner, then usu. proceeds to a grand right and left **d** : a change of places by the first and second couples in Scottish country dancing **2 a** : music for the allemande **b** : a dance movement in moderate tempo and duple time (as in the classical suites of Bach and Handel)

2allemande \"\ *vi* -ED/-ING/-S : to perform an allemande

3allemande \"\ *also* **allemande sauce** *n* -s *often cap A* [F (*sauce*) *allemande*, lit., German sauce] : a rich yellow sauce made by adding egg yolks to velouté — compare BÉCHAMEL, BROWN SAUCE

all-embracing \ˌ==ˌ==\ *adj* : taking in or including everybody or everything : COMPLETE, UNQUALIFIED, SWEEPING ⟨explain in one grand *all-embracing* formula —*N. Y. Times Mag.*⟩

al·le·mont·ite \ˌalə'män,tīt, '==,=,=\ *n* -s [F, fr. *Allemont*, *Allemond*, Isère dept., France, its locality + F *-ite*] : a mineral consisting of an arsenic antimony compound SbAs occurring in metallic-looking reniform masses

al·len·ar·ly \ə'lenərlī\ *also* **al·an·er·ly** \-ăn-\ *adv* [ME (northern dial.) *allanerly, allaneli*, var. of *allonely, allonly*, fr. *all* + *onely, only* solely, only — more at ONLY] *Scot* **:** SOLELY, ONLY

al·lene \'a,lēn\ *n* -s [ISV, contr. of *allylene*] **1 :** a gaseous hydrocarbon $CH_2=C=CH_2$ — called also *propadiene, sym-allylene* **2 :** a diolefin with its two double bonds in adjacent positions

al·len·ic \a'lēnik, ə'-, -en-\ *adj* **:** relating to or derived from allene **:** like allene esp. in having two double bonds in adjacent positions ⟨~ alkadienes⟩ — often distinguished from *conjugated*

al·len screw \'alən-\ *n* [fr. *Allen*, a proper name] **:** a screw with a hexagonal recess in the head

allen's hummingbird *n, usu cap A* [after Joel A. *Allen* †1921 Am. zoologist] **:** a hummingbird (*Selasphorus sasin*) of western No. America, the male being metallic green above with bright red throat and whitish breast, the female being variably marked with reddish brown, gray, and white

allen's rule *n, usu cap A* [after Joel A. *Allen*] **:** a statement in zoology: protruding body parts (as ears, tail, legs, bill) of warm-blooded animals are relatively shorter in cooler than in warmer parts of the range

al·len·tan·do \¦alən¦tän(,)dō, ¦al-, ¦alən¦ta-\ *adv* (*or adj*) [It, making slack, making slow, fr. (assumed) VL *allentandum*, gerund of (assumed) VL *allentare* to make slack, make slow, fr. L *ad-* + *lentare* to bend, prolong, fr. *lentus* flexible, slow, sluggish — more at LITHE] **:** in a manner becoming relaxed in tempo — used as a direction in music

¹al·len·ti·ac \ə'lentē,ak\ *also* **al·len·ti·a·can** \¦alən¦tiəkən\ *adj, usu cap* [*Allentiac* fr. Sp, of AmerInd origin; *Allentiacan* fr. Sp *allentiac* + E *-an*] **:** of, relating to, or characteristic of a people of the San Juan province of western Argentina

²allentiac \"\ *n* -s *usu cap* **1 a :** a people of the San Juan province of western Argentina **b :** a member of such people **2 :** the language of the Allentiac people

al·len·town \'alən,taùn\ *adj, usu cap* [fr. *Allentown*, Pa.] **:** of or from the city of Allentown, Pa. **:** of the kind or style prevalent in Allentown

al·len wrench \'alən-\ *n* [fr. *Allen*, a proper name] **:** an L-shaped hexagonal bar of hardened steel either end of which fits the socket of a screw or bolt

al·ler·gen \'alə(r)jən\ *n* -s [G, fr. *allergie* allergy + *-gen*] **:** a substance that induces allergy — **al·ler·gen·ic** \¦=¦jenik\ *adj* — **al·ler·gen·ic·i·ty** \,==jə'nisəd·ē\ *n* -ES

al·ler·gic \ə'lərjik, -ōj-,oij-, -ēk *also* a'-\ *adj* [ISV *allergy* + *-ic*] **1 :** of, relating to, characterized by, or affected by allergy ⟨~ diseases⟩ ⟨an ~ reaction⟩ ⟨~ to actinic rays⟩ **2 :** disagreeably sensitive (as to a person, thing, or idea) **:** responding with a feeling of irritation or annoyance **:** feeling antipathy, aversion, or repugnance ⟨deaf, if not ~, to ambitious music —John Mason Brown⟩ ⟨ ~ to work⟩ ⟨unmoved by oratory and ~ to double talk —*New Republic*⟩

al·ler·gin \'alə(r)jən\ *n* -s [alter. of *allergen*] **1 :** ALLERGEN **2 :** REAGIN

al·ler·gist \-jəst\ *n* -s **:** a specialist in allergy

al·ler·gol·o·gy \,alə(r)'jäləjē, -'gä-\ *n* -ES [ISV *allergy* + *-o-* + *-logy*] **:** the scientific study of allergy

al·ler·gy \'alə(r)jē, -ji, *sometimes* -,lərj-, -,lōj-, -,loij-\ *n* -ES [G *allergie*, fr. *all-* + *-ergie* -ergy] **1 :** altered bodily reactivity to an antigenic substance in response to a first exposure ⟨an ~ to bee venom so severe that a second sting may be fatal⟩ **2 :** exaggerated or pathological reaction marked by sneezing, respiratory embarrassment, itching and skin rashes, or other symptoms to substances (as germs, pollens, food, or drugs), situations (as mental or emotional excitement or exposure to sunlight), or physical states (as coldness) that are without comparable effect on the average individual ⟨sneezing follows inhalation of pollens by persons having an ~ to them⟩ ⟨*allergies* due to foods often cause hives⟩ — compare HYPERSENSITIVE **3 :** medical practice concerned with the diagnosis and treatment of allergy ⟨he has practiced ~ for 15 years⟩ **4 :** a feeling of antipathy or repugnance ⟨a reputation of having an ~ to books —R.J.Crohn⟩

al·ler·i·on *also* **ale·ri·on** \ə'lirēən, -ē,än\ *n* -s [F *alérion*] **:** an eagle depicted in heraldry with expanded wings but without beak or feet

al·le·thrin \'aləthrən\ *n* -s [*allyl* + *pyrethrin*] **:** a light yellow viscous oily synthetic insecticide $C_{19}H_{26}O_3$ used esp. in household aerosols

allette *var of* ALETTE

al·le·vi·ant \ə'lēvēənt *also* a'-\ *n* -s [*alleviate* + *-ant*] **:** an alleviating agent **:** PALLIATIVE

al·le·vi·ate \ə'lēvē,āt *also* a'-; *usu* -ād·+V\ *vt* -ED/-ING/-S [LL *alleviatus*, past part. of *alleviare* to lighten, relieve, fr. L *ad-* + *levis* light — more at LIGHT] **1 :** LIGHTEN, LESSEN **:** RELIEVE, MODERATE: as **a :** to make easier to be endured (as physical or mental suffering) ⟨does not cure but ~s the disease⟩ ⟨a lotion for *alleviating* the itching of poison ivy⟩ ⟨little can be done for the sufferer beyond *alleviating* his agony —V. G. Heiser⟩ ⟨helped slightly to ~ his sorrow⟩ **b :** to remove or correct in part (as a troublesome condition or state of mind) ⟨measures for *alleviating* the critical labor shortage⟩ ⟨could ~ the causes of conflicts among nations —Vera M. Dean⟩ ⟨efforts which do nothing to ~ that hate —*New Republic*⟩ — opposed to *aggravate* ⟨how these problems are aggravated or *alleviated* by advances in technical knowledge —Clyde Kennedy⟩ **2** *archaic* **:** EXTENUATE ⟨~s his fault by an excuse —Samuel Johnson⟩ **syn** see RELIEVE

al·le·vi·a·tion \=,=='āshən\ *n* -s [ML *alleviation-, alleviatio*, fr. LL *alleviatus* + L *-ion-, -io* -ion] **1 :** the action of alleviating or of being alleviated ⟨beyond correction or ~⟩ ⟨seeking ~ of his distress⟩ **2 :** something that alleviates ⟨all the humane ~s of brutal violence . . . were disregarded —W.R. Inge⟩

al·le·vi·a·tive \=¦==,ā|d·iv, -,əl, |tiv, -ēv\ *or* **al·le·vi·a·to·ry** \-,ə,tōrē, -ór-, -ri\ *adj* **:** tending to alleviate **:** PALLIATIVE

al·le·vi·a·tor \-,ād·ə(r), -ātə-\ *n* -s **:** one that alleviates ⟨the ~s, the doctors and nurses —Cyril Connolly⟩ ⟨snow can be a great ~ of the American restlessness —J.W.Krutch⟩; *specif* **:** a shock absorber in a hydraulic system

all-expense \'==¦=\ *adj* **:** involving the payment of all costs by the sponsor or the assessment of a fixed single charge for all costs (as of transportation, meals, hotels, and entertainment) ⟨winners of the contest will be awarded an *all-expense* trip⟩ ⟨railroads offering *all-expense* tours this summer⟩

¹al·ley \'alē, -li\ *n* -s [ME *aley*, fr. ML *aleia* passage & MF *alee* action of going, journey, passage, fr. OF *alee* action of going, journey, passage, fr. fem. of *alé*, past part. of *aler* to go, prob. fr. (assumed) VL *amlare*, alter. of L *ambulare* to walk — more at AMBLE] **1 :** a garden or park walk or passage bordered by trees or bushes **2 a** (1) **:** a grassed enclosure for bowling or skittles (2) **:** a hardwood lane at the end of which pins are set up for bowling and down which a ball is bowled (3) **:** the bowling unit consisting of surface lane, gutter, and backstop (4) **:** the building housing a group of such units **b :** the space on each side of a tennis doubles court between the sideline and the service sideline — see TENNIS illustration **c :** the strip of a field-hockey area between the 5-yard line and the sideline **3 a :** a passageway between buildings **b :** a lane wide enough only for persons on foot **:** a narrow street wide enough for only one vehicle **c :** a thoroughfare through the middle of a square or block giving access to the rear of lots or buildings **d :** a passage or covered way into or to a house or building **4 :** a blank or open space between rows of any kind: as **a** *chiefly dial* **:** a passageway between rows of pews in a church **:** AISLE **b :** the floor space between the long sides of two parallel rows of compositors' stands **c :** the space between each two rows of a crop — **up one's alley** *also* **down one's alley :** adapted or suited esp. to one's abilities or tastes ⟨the . . . fund-raising business is right *up his alley* —John Brooks⟩

²alley *also* **al·ly** \"\ *n* -s [by alter. and shortening fr. *¹alabaster*] **:** a superior playing marble; *esp* **:** one made of alabaster, glass, or marble

alley cat *n* **1 :** a stray cat **2 :** a domestic short-haired cat esp. when of uncertain ancestry

al·leyed \'alēd, -id\ *adj* [ME *aleyed*, fr. *aley* + *-ed*] **:** furnished with alleys **:** forming an alley

alleyway \'==,=\ *n* -s **:** a narrow alley or passageway (as between houses or between rows of cabins on a ship)

all-father \'=,==\ *n* -s *usu cap A* **:** father of all — used of a deity — **all-fatherly** \(')=¦===\ *adj*

¹all-fired \'=,=\ *adj, superlative often* **all-firedest** [euphemism for *hell-fired*] **:** INFERNAL, EXTREME, EXCESSIVE — used as a mild imprecation ⟨had the *all-fired* cheek to take my money away —Dorothy Sayers⟩ — **all-fired·ly** \-,fī(ə)rdlē, -īrəd-\ *adv*

²all-fired \"\ *adv* **:** EXTREMELY, EXCESSIVELY — used as a mild imprecation ⟨don't be so *all-fired* sure about it⟩ ⟨*all-fired* hot⟩

all fives *n pl but usu sing in constr* **1 :** a form of all fours in which the five of trumps has a scoring value of five points **2 :** MUGGINS 1b

all fools' day *n, usu cap A&F&D* **:** APRIL FOOLS' DAY

all fours *n pl* **1 :** all four legs of a quadruped or the two legs and two arms of a person ⟨he explored it on *all fours* —John Buchan⟩ ⟨jumped and landed heavily on *all fours*⟩ **2** *sing in constr* **:** any of various card games whose essential feature is that points are scored for winning high, low, jack, and the game — see HIGH-LOW-JACK — **on all fours** *adv* (*or adj*) **:** in exact correspondence **:** on the same footing ⟨it is not easy to make a simile go *on all fours* —T.B.Macaulay⟩ — often used with *with* ⟨this principle is *on all fours* with that of the real-estate bloc —Stuart Chase⟩

all get-out \,ȯl(,)gid·'aùt, -,ged-·,(')='=,=\ *n, slang* **:** the extreme (as of extent, degree, quality, or condition) encountered or conceivable — used in comparisons to suggest something superlative ⟨a handbag big as *all get-out* —*New Yorker*⟩ ⟨stubborn as *all get-out*⟩

allgood \'=,=\ *n* -s **:** GOOD-KING-HENRY

all hail *interj* [ME *al hail*, fr. *al* all + *hail* (healthy)] — used to express greeting or welcome or sometimes acclamation

all-hail *vt* -ED/-ING/-S *archaic* **:** to greet with *all hail* ⟨who *all-hailed* me "Thane of Cawdor" —Shak.⟩

allhallond *usu cap, obs var of* ALLHALLOWS

allhallowmas *n* -ES *usu cap* [ME *Alhalwemesse, Alhalowmesse*, fr. OE *ealra halgena mæsse*, lit., all saints' mass] *archaic* **:** the feast of All Saints

allhallown *adj, usu cap* [*Allhallown-* (as in *Allhallowntide* & *Allhallownmas*, earlier variants of *Allhallowtide, Allhallowmas*)] *obs* **:** occurring at or near the time of Allhallows ⟨*Allhallown* summer —Shak.⟩

all·hal·lows \(')ȯl'ha(,)lōz, -,lə\ *also* **all·hal·low** *n, pl* **allhallows** *usu cap* [short for *All Hallows' Day, All Hallow Day*, fr. ME *Alhalwenday, Alhalowday, All Hallows Day*] **:** ALL SAINTS' DAY

allhallowtide *n* -s *usu cap* [ME *All Halewentid, All Halowtid*, lit., all saints' season] *archaic* **:** the time at or near All Saints' Day

all hands *n pl* **1 :** an entire ship's company **2 :** everybody engaged in the same pursuit

allheal \'=,=\ *n* -s **1 :** VALERIAN **2 :** SELF-HEAL **3 :** MISTLETOE **4 :** WOUNDWORT **5 :** YARROW

all hours *n pl* **1 :** an hour or time that one likes or that suits one's convenience ⟨he comes home to lunch at *all hours*⟩ **2 :** the very late hours of the night ⟨stay up till *all hours*⟩

al·li·a·ble \ə'līəbəl *also* a'-\ *adj* [*¹ally* + *-able*] **:** capable of being allied **:** able to enter into an alliance

al·li·a·ce·ae \,alē'āsē,ē\ *n pl, cap* [NL, fr. *Allium*, type genus + *-aceae*] *in some classifications* **:** a family of monocotyledonous plants comprising chiefly the genus *Allium* which is now usu. included in the family Liliaceae

al·li·a·ceous \,alē¦āshəs\ *adj* [L *allium* garlic + E *-aceous* — more at ALLIUM] **1 :** having the smell of garlic or onions **2** [NL *Alliaceae* + E *-ous*] **:** of or relating to the genus *Allium* or the family Alliaceae

al·li·ance \ə'līən(t)s *also* a'-\ *n* -s [ME *alliaunce*, fr. OF *aliance*, fr. *alier* to ally + *-ance* — more at ALLY] **1 :** the state of being allied or the action of allying or uniting ⟨toleration at home and ~ with Protestantism abroad —Hilaire Belloc⟩ ⟨the two great men of letters stood in ~ —*Time*⟩ **:** union or connection esp. between families, states, parties, or individuals ⟨any ~ between church and state⟩ ⟨the dowry was small and the honor of the ~ great —Robert Graves⟩ ⟨a closer ~ between government and industry⟩ ⟨went through three marriages and several ~s of more doubtful character⟩ **2 :** an association or union formed for the furtherance of the common interests and aims of the members ⟨an ~ among the independent unions⟩ ⟨a world ~ of interested groups⟩; *esp* **:** an association, confederation, or union of two or more independent states or nations that is created by a formal agreement (as a treaty or compact) in their common interest esp. for mutual assistance and protection ⟨~s and cooperative associations of states —C.K.Streit⟩ ⟨the ~ of western nations⟩ **3 :** union by relationship in qualities **:** AFFINITY ⟨an indefinable sense of ~ draws one to books as to people —Allan McMahon⟩ ⟨between aesthetic and religious rapture there is a family ~ —Clive Bell⟩ **4 :** a group of related botanical or zoological families; *esp* **:** a group of plants intermediate between a class and an order **5 :** a treaty of alliance

alliance ring *n* **:** a wedding ring composed of two interlocking bands bearing the initials of the bride and groom and the date of the wedding

al·li·ar·ia \,alē'a(a)rēə\ *n, cap* [NL, fr. L *allium, alium* garlic + NL *-aria* — more at ALLIUM] **:** a genus of Old World herbs (family Cruciferae) having broad undivided leaves, white flowers, and long siliques — see GARLIC MUSTARD

al·lice shad \'aləs(h),sh-\ *also* **al·lice** *or* **al·lis** \'aləs\ *n* -s [alter. of earlier *allowes*, fr. F *alose*, fr. LL *alausa*, fr. Gaulish] **:** a European shad (*Alosa alosa*) of the Severn and other rivers

alliciency *n* -ES [ML *allicientia* fr. L *allicient-, alliciens* (pres. part. of *allicere* to allure, fr. *ad-* + *-licere*, fr. *lacere* to entice) + *-ia* -y — more at DELIGHT] *obs* **:** the quality or power of attracting **:** ATTRACTIVENESS

al·li·cin \'aləsən\ *n* -s [*alliin* + *-cin*] **:** a liquid compound $C_6H_{10}OS_2$ with a garlic odor and antibacterial properties formed from alliin by enzymatic action

al·lied \ə'līd, a'-; *freq in all senses & most freq in sense 2b* 'a,l-\ *adj* [ME, fr. past part. of *allien* to ally — more at ALLY] **1 :** JOINED, CONNECTED ⟨closely ~ to his pride was his very strict sense of justice —R.A.Hall b.1911⟩ **2 a :** joined in alliance by compact or treaty ⟨all the ~ powers⟩ ⟨a party of ~ soldiers⟩ ⟨flags of the ~ nations⟩ **b** *usu cap* **:** of, by, or relating to the nations united against the Central European powers in World War I or those united against the Axis powers in World War II ⟨the largest *Allied* naval exercise ever held⟩ ⟨a unified *Allied* theater was created under British direction —R.M.Leighton⟩ **3 a :** related esp. by common properties or similar characteristics ⟨geography and ~ sciences⟩ ⟨agricultural and ~ workers⟩ **b :** genetically related; *specif* **:** presumed to share common ancestors ⟨~ groups of plants or animals⟩

allies *pl of* ALLY, *pres 3d sing of* ALLY

al·li·ga·tion \,alə'gāshən\ *n* -s [L *alligation-, alligatio* tying, band, fr. *alligatus* (past part. of *alligare* to tie to, fr. *ad-* + *ligare* to tie) + *-ion-, -io* -ion — more at LIGATURE] **1 :** the action of attaching or the state of being attached **2 :** a process or rule for the solution of problems concerning the compounding or mixing of ingredients differing in price or quality either (1) when a definite mixture is required or (2) when the price or quality of the mixture is to be determined — called also respectively (1) *alligation alternate*, (2) *alligation medial*

¹al·li·ga·tor \'alə,gād·ə(r), -ē,g-, -ātə-\ *n* [alter. of earlier *aligarto, alagarto*, fr. Sp *el lagarto* the lizard, fr. *el* the (fr. L *ille* that) + *lagarto* lizard, fr. (assumed) VL *lacartus*, fr. L *lacertus, lacerta* — more at LIZARD] **1** -s **a :** either of two loricates comprising the genus *Alligator* having broad heads not tapering to the snout and a special pocket in the upper jaw for reception of the enlarged lower fourth tooth and being in general much more sluggish than the typical crocodiles (genus *Crocodylus*) **b :** CAIMAN **c :** LORICATE **2** [NL, fr. E] *cap* **:** the genus of Crocodylidae comprising the American and Chinese alligators **3** -s **:** any of various animals that resemble alligators (as an alligator lizard, a hellbender, or a hellgramite) **4** -s **:** leather made from alligator's hide ⟨a handbag of ~⟩ **5** -s **:** a machine with strong jaws (as a crocodile squeezer or rock breaker) one of which opens like the movable jaw of an alligator ⟨~ squeezer⟩ **6** -s **a :** a boat used in handling floating logs and provided with a windlass and cable for being drawn overland **b :** a small sled often made from the fork of a tree and used as an aid in skidding logs — called also *crotch, go-devil, lizard, travois* **7** -s **:** a devotee of swing music

²alligator \"\ *adj* **1 :** of, relating to, or like an alligator; *specif* **:** marked with a design resembling that of the skin of an alligator ⟨~ cloth⟩ **2 :** opening like an alligator's jaws ⟨~ forceps⟩

³alligator \"\ *vi* -ED/-ING/-S **:** to develop intersecting cracks and ridges — used of films of paint, varnish, and similar coatings

alligator apple *n* [so called fr. the gnarled appearance of the fruits and its growth in the habitat of alligators] **:** POND APPLE

alligator bonnet *n* [so called fr. the appearance of the blossoms and its growth in the habitat of alligators] **1 :** either of two water plants of the genus *Nymphaea*: **a :** a yellow pond lily (*N. sagittaefolia*) **b :** a fragrant water lily (*N. odorata*) **2 :** the flower or fruit of alligator bonnets

alligator button *n* [so called fr. the appearance of the seeds and its growth in the habitat of alligators] **1 :** WATER CHINQUAPIN **2 :** the flower or fruit of the water chinquapin

alligator cacao *n* [so called fr. the resemblance of the pod to alligator hide] **:** a cacao (*Theobroma pentagona*) cultivated in Central America

alligator clip *n* **:** a wire or cable terminal having jaws resembling an alligator's and used for making temporary electrical connections — called also *crocodile clip*

alligator fish *n* [so called fr. its covering of bony plates] **:** a sea poacher (as *Podothecus acipenserinus*) of the Pacific coast of No. America

alligator gar *n* [so called fr. its size] **:** a large freshwater gar (*Lepisosteus spatula*) of the central U. S. that attains a length of over 7 feet and a weight in excess of 150 pounds; *also* **:** any of certain related Cuban and Central American fishes that are all valueless as food or game fishes and considered destructive of aquatic life and waterfowls

al·li·ga·tor·i·dae \,aləgə'tōrə,dē\ *n pl, cap* [NL, fr. *Alligator*, type genus + *-idae*] *in some classifications* **:** a family of crocodilians comprising the alligators and the caimans

alligator juniper *n* [so called fr. the ridged appearance of its bark] **:** an evergreen shrub or small tree (*Juniperus deppeana*) of the southwestern U. S. and adjacent Mexico having an edible sweet fruit

alligator lizard *n* **:** any of various small American lizards that resemble an alligator (as members of the genera *Anolis, Sceloporus*, or in the western U. S. *Gerrhonotus*)

al·li·ga·tor·oid \'alə,gād·ə,rȯid\ *adj* [*¹alligator* + *-oid*] **1 :** resembling an alligator **2 :** relating to alligators

alligator pear *n* [*alligator* by folk etymology fr. Sp *abbogada, aquacato* avocado, fr. Nahuatl *ahuacatl* — more at AVOCADO] **:** AVOCADO

alligator shears *n pl* [so called fr. its resemblance to an alligator's jaws] **:** LEVER SHEARS

alligator snapper *also* **alligator turtle** *or* **alligator terrapin** *n* **1 :** a voracious snapping turtle (*Macrochelys temminckii*) of the rivers of the Gulf states differing from the common snapping turtle in its larger size which in old age reaches nearly 150 pounds in weight and 5 feet in length, its scaly head, and its numerous small scales beneath the tail **2 :** a snapping turtle (*Chelydra serpentina*)

alligator tree *n* [so called fr. the ridged appearance of its bark] *South* **:** SWEET GUM

alligator weed *or* **alligator grass** *n* [so called fr. its long narrow leaves] **:** a prolific herbaceous weed (*Alternanthera phylloxeroides*) having opposite entire linear-lanceolate leaves and flowers in short headlike spikes and being esp. troublesome in irrigation canals and waterways which it clogs with a dense floating mass

alligatorwood \'===,=,=\ *n* -s [*alligator* (*tree*) + *wood*] **1 :** SWEET GUM **2 :** GUARAGUAO

alligator wrench *n* [so called fr. its resemblance to an alligator's jaws] **:** a wrench having a flaring jaw with teeth on one side

alligator wrench

al·lihn condenser \(')a¦lēn-\ *n, usu cap A* [fr. the name *Allihn*] **:** a condenser similar to a Liebig condenser with an inner tube consisting of a series of bulbs

allihn filter tube *n, usu cap A* [fr. the name *Allihn*] **:** a glass filtering funnel the top part of which is a cylindrical tube into which is sealed a fritted glass disk as a filter

al·li·in \'alēən\ *n* -s [ISV *alli-* (fr. NL *Allium*, genus name of the garlic *Allium sativum*) + *-in*] **:** a crystalline amino acid $C_6H_{11}NO_3S$ occurring in garlic oil

al·li·klik \'alə,klik\ *n, pl* **alliklik** *or* **allikliks** *usu cap* [Chumash] **1 :** a Shoshonean people in the upper Santa Clara river valley, California **2 :** a member of the Alliklik people

all-important \¦=¦=¦==\ *adj* **:** of greatest or very great importance or significance ⟨the last and *all-important* bit of evidence⟩ ⟨discussing the *all-important* subject of disarmament⟩

all-in \'=¦=\ *adj* [short for *all-inclusive*] **1** *chiefly Brit* **:** ALL-INCLUSIVE ⟨*all-in* health insurance⟩ ⟨an *all-in* 10-day tour⟩ ⟨*all-in* cost⟩ ⟨*all-in* weight⟩ **2 :** completely determined **:** sparing nothing ⟨an *all-in* effort⟩ **3** *of wrestling* **:** without restriction **:** having almost no holds barred

all in \(')=¦=\ *adj* [*²all* + *in* (adj.)] **:** completely tired **:** EXHAUSTED ⟨by evening he was *all in*⟩ — used predicatively

¹all in all : something that represents all things regarded as having value, significance, or importance **:** EVERYTHING ⟨the craft that was *all in all* to her —Rudyard Kipling⟩

²all in all *adv* **1 :** as a whole **:** ALTOGETHER ⟨*all in all*, each article undergoes 20 inspections before leaving the plant⟩ ⟨take it *all in all*, this has been a hard week⟩ **2 :** on the whole **:** all things considered **:** generally speaking ⟨*all in all*, the chautauqua was a tremendous force in American life —Russell Potter⟩ ⟨*all in all*, it might have been worse⟩

all-inclusive \¦=¦==\ *adj* **:** including everything **:** fully or broadly comprehensive ⟨a survey that was selective rather than *all-inclusive*⟩ ⟨the *all-inclusive* whole of our vast industrial machine —F.D.Roosevelt⟩ ⟨a broader and more nearly *all-inclusive* view⟩

al·lin·eate \ə'linē,āt, a'-\ *vt* -ED/-ING/-S [back-formation fr. *allineation*] **:** ALIGN

al·lin·eation *also* **alin·eation** \=,=='āshən\ *n* -s [*ad-* + *-lineation* (as in *delineation*)] **:** ALIGNMENT

all-in-one \¦=¦=\ *n* -s **:** ²CORSELET

al·li·o·nia \,alē'ōnēə, -nyə\ *n, cap* [NL, fr. Carlo *Allioni* †1804 Ital. physician and botanist + NL *-ia*] **:** a genus of chiefly American herbs (family Nyctaginaceae) having opposite entire leaves and small panicled flowers

al·li·o·ni·a·ce·ae \,alē,ōnē'āsē,ē\ *n* [NL, fr. *Allionia*, type genus + *-aceae*] *syn of* NYCTAGINACEAE

allis *var of* ALLICE SHAD

al·li·sion \ə'lizhən, a'-\ *n* -s [LL *allision-, allisio*, fr. L *allisus* (past part. of *allidere* to strike against, fr. *ad-* + *-lidere*, fr. *laedere* to hurt) + *-ion-, -io* -ion — more at LESION] **1** *obs* **:** the action of dashing against or striking upon **2 :** the running of one ship upon another ship that is stationary — distinguished from *collision*

al·li·son tuna \'aləsən-\ *or* **allison tunny** *n, usu cap A* [after James A. *Allison fl* 1920 Am. ichthyology enthusiast] **:** YELLOWFIN TUNA

al·lit·er·al \a'lid·ərəl, ə'-, -itər-, -li·trəl\ *adj* [*alliterate* + *-al* (as in *literal*)] **:** ALLITERATIVE

¹al·lit·er·ate \ə'lid·ə,rāt, -itər- *also* a'-; *usu* -ād·+V\ *vb* -ED/-ING/-S [back-formation fr. *alliteration*] *vi* **1 :** to form an alliteration ⟨a sentence in which four of the six words *alliterated*⟩ **2 :** to write or speak alliteratively ~ *vt* **:** to arrange or place so as to make alliteration ⟨with the stress falling on the *alliterated* syllables⟩

²al·lit·er·ate \a'lid·ə·rət, -itər-, -,rāt *also* ə'-\ *adj* [back-formation fr. *alliteration*] **:** characterized by alliteration **:** ALLITERATED

al·lit·er·a·tion \ə,lid·ə'rāshən, -itə'- *also* a,-\ *n* -s [*ad-* + L *litera, littera* letter + E *-ation* — more at LETTER] **:** the repetition usu. initially of a sound that is usu. a consonant in two or more neighboring words or syllables (as wild and woolly, threatening throngs)

al·lit·er·a·tion·al \ə¦==¦=shən°l, -shnəl\ *adj* **:** ALLITERATIVE

al·lit·er·a·tive \ə'==,rād·iv, -,rəl, ¦tiv, -ēv\ *adj* [*alliteration* + *-ive*] **:** of, related to, or marked by alliteration ⟨an ~ line⟩ — **al·lit·er·a·tive·ly** *adv*

alliterative verse *n* **:** verse usu. unrhymed having alliteration as a structural element ⟨Old English *alliterative verse*⟩

al·lit·er·a·tor \ə'==,rād·ə(r), -ātə-\ *n* -s [*alliteration* + *-or*] **:** one that alliterates esp. extensively or characteristically

al·lit·ic \ə'lid·ik, (')a¦l-\ *adj* [ISV *aluminum* + *-litic*] **:** lacking silica but having a high proportion of aluminum and iron compounds

al·li·um \'alēəm\ *n* [NL, fr. L *allium, alium* garlic; perh. akin to Skt *āluka* edible root of an aroid plant (*Amorphophallus campanulatus*)] **1** *cap* **:** a genus of bulbous herbs (family Liliaceae) distinguished by the characteristic odor, sheathing, mostly basal leaves, and umbellate white, yellow, or red flowers — see CHIVES, GARLIC, LEEK, ONION **2** -s **:** a plant of the genus *Allium*

al·li·va·lite \'aləvə,līt\ *n* -s [*Allival* Hill, Isle of Rum, Inner Hebrides, Scotland, its locality + E *-ite*] **:** a plutonic rock composed of anorthite and olivine in approximately equal amounts

all kinds of *adj* **:** many or much **:** plenty of ⟨*all kinds of* time to spend⟩ ⟨they say he has *all kinds of* money⟩ ⟨*all kinds of* opportunities to play golf⟩

allmouth \'=,=\ *n* -s [so called fr. its large mouth] **:** ANGLER 2

all·ness \'ȯlnəs\ *n* -ES *sometimes cap* **:** the quality or state of being complete or universal ⟨to learn it not in a specialized way but . . . in its relation to the ~ of things —D.C.Peattie⟩ ⟨he seemed at the center of the vast ~ —Irwin Edman⟩ **:** TOTALITY, COMPLETENESS, UNIVERSALITY

all-night *adj* **1 :** lasting throughout an entire night ⟨an *all-night* sitting of the House of Commons⟩ ⟨an *all-night* card game⟩ **2 :** open throughout the night ⟨an *all-night* lunch counter⟩

al·lo \'a(,)lō\ *adj* [*all-*] **:** isomeric or closely related — used esp. of one of two stereoisomers; sometimes contrasted with *normal;* compare ALL- 2

¹allo- — see ALL-

²al·lo- *in pronunciations below,* ¦== = ¦alō *or* ¦alə\ *comb form* [Gk *allos . . . allos* one . . . the other, fr. *allos* other — more at ELSE] **:** being one of a group whose members together constitute a structural unit esp. of a language ⟨allophone⟩ ⟨allomorph⟩ — compare -EME

allo *abbr* allegro

al·lo·bar \'==,bär\ *n* -s [*all-* + *-bar* (as in *isobar*)] **1 :** barometric pressure change **2 :** ISALLOBAR

al·lo·bar·bi·tal *also* **al·lo·bar·bi·tone** \¦==-\ *n* -s [*all-* + *barbital, barbitone*] **:** DIALLYLBARBITURIC ACID

al·lob·ro·ges \ə'läbrə,jēz\ *n pl, cap* [L, pl. of *Allobrox*] **:** a people of Gaul inhabiting the region now known as Savoy and Dauphiné

al·lo·ca·bil·i·ty \,aləkə'biləd·ē, -lōk-\ *n* -ES **:** the quality or state of being allocable or assigned

al·lo·ca·ble \'==kəbəl\ *or* **al·lo·cat·a·ble** \-,kād·əbəl\ *adj* [*allocable,* contr. of *allocatable; allocatable* fr. *allocate* + *-able*] **1 :** capable of being allocated **2** *in accounting* **:** assignable to a particular account or to a particular period of time

al·lo·cate \'==,kāt, *often* -ād·+V\ *vt* -ED/-ING/-S [ML *allocatus,* past part. of *allocare* to place, grant, fr. L *ad-* + *locare* to place fr. *locus* place — more at STALL] **1 :** to apportion for a specific purpose or to particular persons or things ⟨if blame were to be *allocated* it must be apportioned elsewhere —F.W. Crofts⟩: as **a :** to give (a share of money, land, or responsibility) to a person **b :** to distribute or to divide and distribute according to relative contribution to an objective whether on an equal, proportional, or judiciously calculated basis ⟨~ a fortune to charitable foundations⟩ **c :** to apportion and distribute (as costs or revenues) among accounts according to some predetermined ratio or agreed measure of involvement (as degree of responsibility or benefit received) **d :** to deal out (something limited in supply) according to an allowance schedule established esp. by a public authority or major producer **:** RATION ⟨under a mobilization program metals may be *allocated* among manufacturers⟩ **2 :** to set apart and earmark or designate **:** ASSIGN ⟨~ materials or facilities for a project⟩ ⟨government of the conscience is *allocated* to the clergy —*New Republic*⟩ **syn** see ALLOT

al·lo·ca·tee \'==kə¦tē\ *n* -s **:** one to whom material is allocated

al·lo·ca·tion \,==¦kāshən\ *n* -s [ML *allocation-, allocatio,* fr. *allocatus* + L *-ion-, -io* -ion] **1** *archaic* **:** the action of putting or adding one thing to another **2 :** the action of apportioning **:** apportionment for specific purposes or to particular persons or organizations: as **a** *in accounting* **:** the apportionment of costs and expenses to accounts according to some arbitrary rule **b :** apportionment as a governmental or economic control measure ⟨the ~ of resources in a war economy⟩ **3 :** a governmental or economic apportioning schedule or an assignment in it ⟨materials now on ~⟩ **4 :** the amount allocated to one sharer

al·lo·ca·tive \'==,kād·iv, -ātiv\ *adj* **:** serving to allocate ⟨an ~ analysis⟩ ⟨determination of ~ efficiency —Julius Margolis⟩

al·lo·ca·tor \-,kād·ə(r), -ātə-\ *n* -s **:** one that allocates

al·lo·ca·tur \,=='kād·ər, -ā,tər\ *n* -s [ML, it is allowed, 3d pers. sing. pres. indic. pass. of *allocare*] **:** an order or writ of a court or of an assessor of damages or costs in a court granting something requested (as an order allowing an appeal, writ of certiorari, or a bill of costs or approving an assessment of damages)

al·lo·cen·tric \¦==¦-\ *adj* [*all-* + *-centric*] **:** having one's interest and attention centered on other persons — compare EGOCENTRIC

al·lo·chet·ite \,alə'ked·,īt\ *n* -s [G *allochetit,* fr. *Allochet* valley, Tyrol, Austria + G *-it* -ite] **:** a porphyritic dike rock containing phenocrysts of labradorite, orthoclase, titanaugite, and nepheline in a dense groundmass of feldspar, augite, and hornblende

al·lo·chi·ria *also* **al·lo·chei·ria** \,=='kīrēə\ *n* -s [NL, fr. *all-* + Gk *cheir* hand + NL *-ia* — more at CHIR-] **:** a confusion or transference of sides in the localization of sensation in which a person suffering from a central nervous lesion refers irritation of one point on the skin to some other point usu. corresponding to it on the other side of the body

al·lo·chlo·ro·phyll \¦==-\ *n* -s [ISV *all-* + *chlorophyll*] **:** an isomer of chlorophyll easily formed from the latter

al·lo·chro·mat·ic \¦===¦==\ *adj* [*all-* + *chromatic*] **1 :** accidentally rather than inherently pigmented **:** variable in color — used of certain minerals that are without pigmentation when pure **2 :** having or relating to photoelectric properties due to the presence of an impurity or as a result of irradiation

al·lo·chron·ic \¦==¦kränik\ *adj* [*all-* + *chronic*] *of taxa* **:** occurring in different segments of geologic time **:** not contemporaneous — compare SYNCHRONIC

al·loch·ro·ous \ə'läkrəwəs, a'-\ *adj* [Gk *allochroos* changed in color, fr. *all-* + *chroa, chroia* color, skin; akin to Gk *chrōs* skin — more at GRIT] **:** changing color

al·loch·thon \ə'läkthən, a'-, -,thän\ *or* **al·loch·thone** \-,thōn\ *n* -s [back-formation fr. *allochthonous*] **:** an overthrust block of rocks that have been moved along a fault for a great distance from their place of origin

al·loch·tho·nous *also* **al·loc·tho·nous** \-,thənəs\ *adj* [*all-* + *-chthonous* (as in *autochthonous*)] **1 a :** of or relating to the rocks of an allochthon **b** *of coal* **:** formed elsewhere than in situ and hence not autochthonous **c** *of limestone* **:** composed largely of organic debris moved far from the place where the base organisms lived **2** *biol* **:** of foreign origin **:** INTRODUCED — compare AUTOCHTHONOUS

al·lo·co·chick \'aləkə,chik\ *n* -s [Yurok *otl we-tsik,* fr. *otl* human beings + *we-tsik* their dentalium shells] **:** Indian shell money of northern California

al·lo·cor·tex \,==-\ *n* [NL, fr. *all-* + L *cortex*] **:** ARCHIPALLIUM

al·lo·cryp·tic \¦==¦==\ *adj* [*all-* + *cryptic*] **:** imitating other objects for concealment by a covering of extraneous things ⟨an ~ hermit crab in a sponge⟩

al·lo·cute \'alə,kyüt\ *vi* -ED/-ING/-S [back-formation fr. *allocution*] **:** to pronounce an allocution

al·lo·cu·tion \,alə'kyüshən\ *n* -s [L *allocution-, allocutio,* fr. *allocutus* (past part. of *alloqui* to speak to, fr. *ad-* + *loqui* to speak) + *-ion-, -io* -ion] **1 :** the act of addressing or exhorting ⟨a period eminently suited to exhortatory ~ —F.S.Crafford⟩ **2 :** ADDRESS; *esp* **:** an authoritative or hortatory address ⟨a trio of centenary ~s —*Times Lit. Supp.*⟩ ⟨that other ~ delivered 15 years later, when he was pleading with the Americans for a loan —R.F.Harrod⟩ **3 :** an address delivered by a pope in secret consistory and often later published

allod *var of* ALOD

al·lo·der·ma·nys·sus \¦==,dərmə'nisəs\ *n, cap* [NL, fr. *all-* + *derma-* + *-nyssus* (fr. Gk *nyssein* to prick)] **:** a genus of bloodsucking mites parasitic on rodents including a species (*A. sanguineus*) that has been implicated as a vector of rickettsialpox in man

allodial *var of* ALODIAL

allodium *var of* ALODIUM

al·loe·o·coe·la \ə,lēə'sēlə\ *syn of* ALLOIOCOELA

al·loe·os·tro·pha \,alē'ästrəfə\ *n pl* [NL, fr. Gk, neut. pl. of *alloiostrophos* of irregular strophes, fr. *alloios* of another sort (fr. *allos* other) + *strophe* strophe — more at ELSE, STROPHE] **:** irregular strophes or stanzas

al·lo·erot·ic \¦alō¦==\ *adj* [*all-* + *erotic*] **:** of or relating to alloerotism ⟨~ impulses⟩

al·lo·er·o·tism *also* **al·lo·erot·i·cism** \,alō-\ *n* -s [*all-* + *erotism, eroticism*] **:** sexual feeling or activity finding its object in another person — contrasted with *autoerotism*

al·log·a·mous \ə'lägəməs, a'-\ *adj* [*all-* + *-gamous*] **:** reproducing by cross-fertilization

al·log·a·my \-mē\ *n* -ES [ISV *all-* + *-gamy*] **:** CROSS-FERTILIZATION

al·lo·ge·ne·i·ty \,==jə'nēəd·ē\ *n* -ES **:** difference in nature or kind

al·lo·ge·ne·ous \¦alə¦jēnyəs, -nēəs\ *adj* [*all-* + *-geneous* (as in *heterogeneous, homogeneous*)] **:** different in nature or kind

al·lo·ge·net·ic \¦alōjə¦ned·ik\ *adj, of plankton* **:** produced elsewhere

al·lo·gen·ic \-¦jenik\ *adj* [*all-* + *-genic*] **1 :** ALLOTHIGENIC **2** *of an ecologic succession* **:** resulting from factors (as a prolonged drought) that arise external to a natural community and alter its habitat ⟨~ changes in the vegetation⟩ — **al·lo·gen·i·cal·ly** *adv*

al·log·e·nous \ə'läjənəs, a'-\ *adj* [*all-* + *-genous*] **:** RELICT **:** persisting from an earlier floral and environmental situation — used of floras and their components

al·lo·gnath·o·su·chus \,alə,nathə'sükəs, ,a,läg,n-\ *n, cap* [NL, fr. *all-* + *gnath-* + *-suchus* (irreg. fr. Gk *sychnos* long, large)] **:** a genus of Eocene crocodilians sometimes regarded as ancestral to the true alligators

al·lo·graph \'==,graf\ *n* -s [*all-* + *-graph*] **1 :** a writing or signature made for a person by another — contrasted with *autograph* **2 a :** a letter of an alphabet in a particular shape (as A or a) **b :** any letter or combination of letters that is one of a number of ways of representing one phoneme (as *pp* in *hopping* representing the phoneme p) — compare GRAPH, GRAPHEME — **al·lo·graph·ic** \¦==¦=ik, -ēk\ *adj*

al·loi·o·bi·o·gen·e·sis \ə¦lȯi(,)ō-\ *n* [NL, fr. Gk *alloios* different + NL *biogenesis*] **:** alternation of generations esp. of a sexual and an asexual generation — compare ALLOIOGENESIS

al·loi·o·coe·la \ə,lȯiə'sēlə\ *n pl, cap* [NL, fr. Gk *alloios* different, of another sort + NL *-coela* (irreg. fr. Gk *koilia* cavity of the body)] **:** an order of Turbellaria sometimes regarded as a suborder of Rhabdocoela comprising aquatic flatworms with a saclike intestine

al·loi·o·gen·e·sis \ə¦lȯiō'jenəsəs\ *n* [NL, fr. Gk *alloios* + NL *genesis*] **:** alternation of sexual and parthenogenetic generations esp. in certain flatworms

al·lo·isom·er·ism \,alō,ī's-\ *n* -s [*all-* + *isomerism*] **1 :** isomerism not explainable by the ordinary structural formulas **2 :** CIS-TRANS ISOMERISM a

al·lo·ki·ne·sis \,==kə'nēsəs, -,kī-\ *n, pl* **allokine·ses** \-ē,sēz\ [NL, fr. *all-* + *kinesis*] **:** passive or reflex movement — **al·lo·ki·net·ic** \¦==(,)=¦ned·ik\ *adj*

al·lo·lo·boph·o·ra \¦==lō'bäfərə\ *n, cap* [NL, fr. *all-* + *lobo-* + *-phora*] **:** a common and widely distributed genus of earthworms (family Lumbricidae) not readily distinguished from *Lumbricus* and including one of the commonest earthworms (*A. caliginosa*) of temperate regions

al·lom·er·ism \ə'lämə,rizəm, a'-\ *n* -s [*all-* + *-merism*] **:** variability in chemical constitution without variation in crystalline form — **al·lom·er·ous** \-rəs\ *adj*

al·lo·met·ric \¦alə¦me·trik\ *also* **al·loi·o·met·ric** \ə¦lȯiō¦-\ *adj* **:** of or relating to allometry **:** exhibiting or marked by allometry

al·lom·e·tron \ə'lämə,trän, a'-\ *n* -s [*all-* + Gk *metron* measure, rule] **:** quantitative alteration in the course of evolution of the proportional relation of body parts

al·lom·e·try \ə'lämə·trē, a'-\ *also* **al·loi·om·e·try** \,alȯi'äm-\ *n* -ES [*all-* or Gk *alloios* different + E *-metry*] **:** relative growth of a part in relation to an entire organism; *also* **:** the measure and study of such growth

¹al·lo·morph \'alə,mȯrf, -ō(ə)f\ *n* -s [ISV *all-* + *-morph*] **1 :** any of two or more distinct crystalline forms of the same substance ⟨calcium carbonate occurs in the ~s calcite and aragonite⟩ **2 :** a pseudomorph that has undergone partial or complete change or substitution of material ⟨limonite is frequently an ~ after pyrite⟩ — **al·lo·mor·phic** \¦==¦=fik, -ēk\ *adj* — **al·lo·morph·ism** \'==,=,fizəm\ *n* -s

²allomorph \"\ *n* -s [²*allo-* + *morpheme*] **:** one of two or more forms that a morpheme has at different points in the language ⟨the *slep-* \slep\ of *slept* and the *sleep* \slēp\ of *sleep well, sleeping,* and *sleeper* are ~s of the same morpheme⟩ ⟨the *-es* \əz\ of *dishes,* the *-s* \z\ of *dreams,* the *-s* \s\ of *traps,* the *-en* \ən\ of *oxen,* the vowel modification distinguishing *teeth* from *tooth,* and the zero suffix of *sheep* in *those sheep* are ~s of the same morpheme⟩ — compare MORPH, MORPHEME 2 — **al·lo·mor·phic** \¦==¦=fik, -ēk\ *adj* — **al·lo·morph·ism** \'==,=,fizəm\ *n* -s

al·lo·mor·phite \,=='mȯr,fīt\ *n* -s [G *allomorphit,* fr. Gk *allomorphos* of strange shape (fr. *all-* + *-morphos* -morphous) + G *-it* -ite] **:** a mineral consisting of barite that resembles anhydrite

al·lo·mor·pho·sis \-'mȯrfəsəs *sometimes* -,mȯr'fōsəs\ *n, pl* **allomorpho·ses** \-,sēz\ [NL, fr. *all-* + *morphosis*] **:** biological evolution marked by rapid increase of specialization **:** evolutionary allometry — compare AROMORPHOSIS

all one *adj* **:** of such a nature that no one possible outcome or course of events is more desirable than another ⟨it is *all one* to me what he does⟩

¹al·longe \a'lōⁿzh\ *n, pl* **allonges** \-zhəz\ [F, lit., lengthening, fr. OF *alonge,* fr. *alongier* to make long, fr. (assumed) VL *allongare,* fr. L *ad-* + LL *longare* to make long, fr. L *longus* long — more at LONG] **:** a slip of paper attached to a bill of exchange or similar document to provide space for additional endorsements **:** RIDER

²al·lon·gé \,alōⁿ¦zhā\ *adj* [F, fr. past part. of *allonger* to extend (an arm or leg), make long, fr. OF *alongier* to make long] *ballet* **:** with arms and one leg extended to form a long line ⟨an arabesque ~⟩

al·lo·nym \'alə,nim\ *n* -s [F *allonyme,* fr. *all-* + *-onyme* -onym] **1 :** a name that is assumed by an author but that actually belongs to another person **2 :** a work published under the name of a person other than the author

al·lo·pal·la·di·um \¦==-\ *n* -s [*all-* + *palladium*] **:** palladium that is found in hexagonal tables with gold

al·lo·path \'alə,path, -aa(ə)th,-aith\ *n* -s [G, fr. *all-* + *-path*] **:** one who practices allopathy

al·lo·path·ic \¦==¦pathik, -ēk\ *also* **al·lo·path·i·cal** \-ȯkəl, -ēk-\ *adj* [G *allopathisch,* fr. *all-* + *-pathisch* -pathic, -pathical] **:** of or relating to allopathy — **al·lo·path·i·cal·ly** \-ək(ə)lē, -ēk-, -li\ *adv*

al·lop·a·thy \ə'läpəthē, a'-, -thi\ *n* -ES [G *allopathie,* fr. *all-* + *-pathie* -pathy] **1 :** a system of medical practice that aims to combat disease by use of remedies producing effects different from those produced by the special disease treated **2 :** a system of medical practice making use of all measures that have proved of value in treatment of disease

al·lo·pat·ric \¦alə¦pa·trik, -pā-\ *adj* [*all-* + Gk *patra* fatherland (fr. *patēr* father) + E *-ic* — more at FATHER] **:** biologically relating to or taking place in different areas — used esp. of speciation in which isolated populations evolve into good species; compare SYMPATRIC — **al·lo·pat·ri·cal·ly** \-ək(ə)lē\ *adv* — **al·lop·a·try** \ə'läpə·trē, 'alə,pa·t-\ *n* -ES

al·lo·pe·lag·ic \¦===¦==\ *adj* [ISV *all-* + *pelagic;* orig. formed as G *allopelagisch*] **:** of or relating to marine organisms occurring irregularly at the surface or at varying depths in response to influences other than temperature

all–operator \'=,==,==\ *n* **:** a universal quantifier

al·lo·phan·a·mide \,alə'fanə,mīd, -,məd\ *n* -s [*allophanic* + *amide*] **:** BIURET

al·loph·a·nate \ə'läfə,nāt\ *n* -s [*allophanic* + *-ate*] **:** a salt or ester of allophanic acid

al·lo·phane \'alə,fān\ *n* -s [Gk *allophanēs* appearing otherwise, fr. *all-* + *-phanēs* (fr. *phainesthai* to appear)] **:** an amorphous translucent mineral of various colors often in incrustations or stalactite forms consisting of a hydrous aluminum silicate (hardness 3, sp. gr. 1.85–1.89)

al·lo·phan·ic acid \¦alə¦fanik-\ *n* [ISV *allophan-* (after G *allophansäure* allophanic acid, fr. Gk *allophanēs* appearing otherwise + G *säure* acid) + *-ic*] **:** an acid $NH_2CONHCOOH$ known only in the form of derivatives (as esters)

al·lo·phone \'alə,fōn\ *n* -s [²*allo-* + *phone*] **:** one of two or more articulatorily and acoustically different forms of the same phoneme ⟨the aspirated *p* of *pin* and the nonaspirated *p* of *spin* are ~s of the phoneme *p*⟩ — compare PHONE, PHONEME — **al·lo·phon·ic** \¦alə¦fänik, -ēk\ *adj*

al·lo·phore \,==fō(ə)r\ *n* -s [*all-* + *-phore*] **:** a chromatophore containing an alcohol-soluble red pigment that occurs in the skins of fishes, amphibia, and reptiles

al·lo·phyl·i·an \¦==¦filēən, -lyən\ *adj* [LL *allophylus* + E *-ian*] *archaic* **:** Asiatic or European but neither Indo-European nor Semitic ⟨an ~ language⟩ **:** Asiatic or European but speaking a language that is neither Indo-European nor Semitic ⟨an ~ people⟩

al·lo·phy·lus \,=='fīləs\ *n, cap* [NL, fr. LL, of another tribe, foreign, fr. Gk *allophylos,* fr. *all-* + *phylē* tribe] **:** a genus of tropical trees (family Sapindaceae) with trifoliolate or rarely unifoliolate leaves and small white racemose tetramerous flowers

al·lo·plasm \,==,plazəm\ *n* -s [ISV *all-* + *-plasm;* prob. back-formation fr. *alloplasmatic,* fr. *all-* + *plasmatic;* orig. formed as G *alloplasmatisch*] **:** differentiated active protoplasm (as myofibrils, tonofibrils, and cilia); *also* **:** certain protoplasmic derivatives (as cell walls or intercellular substances) — **al·lo·plas·mat·ic** \-,plaz¦mad·ik\ *adj* — **al·lo·plas·mic** \¦==¦plazmik\ *adj*

al·lo·plas·tic \¦==¦plastik\ *adj* [*all-* + *-plastic*] **:** molding or molded by external factors (as environment) ⟨man's evolution . . . is through ~ experiments with objects outside his own body —Weston La Barre⟩ — contrasted with *autoplastic* — **al·lo·plas·ti·cal·ly** \-ək(ə)lē\ *adv*

al·lo·plas·tic·i·ty \,==,pla'stisəd·ē\ *or* **al·lo·plas·ty** \¦==,plastē\ *n* -ES [*all-* + *plasticity* or *-plasty*] **:** the capacity for being molded or modified by the external world — contrasted with *autoplasticity*

¹al·lo·pol·y·ploid \,=='päla,plȯid\ *n* -s [*all-* + *polyploid*] **:** an individual or strain exhibiting allopolyploidy

²al·lo·pol·y·ploid \¦==¦==,=\ *adj* **:** exhibiting allopolyploidy **:** being an allopolyploid

al·lo·poly·ploi·dy \,=='==,=dē\ *n* -ES **:** the state of having more than two genomes more or less dissimilar and derived from two or more different ancestral species — compare AUTOPOLYPLOIDY

al·lo·psy·chic \¦alō¦sīkik\ *adj* [*all-* + *psychic*] **:** related mentally to the outside world ⟨~ adjustment⟩ — contrasted with *autopsychic*

all–or–none \¦==¦=\ *adj* **:** occurring either completely or not at all **:** marked either by entire, complete, inclusive, or unqualified operation or effect or by none at all ⟨in unequal degrees, rather than in *all-or-none* fashion —Walter Firey⟩ ⟨an *all-or-none* reaction⟩ ⟨a nerve cell has . . . an *all-or-none* response, like the trigger of a gun —C.E.Berkeley⟩

all–or–none law *n* **:** a principle in physiology: in any single nerve or muscle fiber the response to a stimulus above threshold level is maximal and independent of the intensity of the stimulus

all–or–nothing \¦==¦==\ *adj* **1 :** ALL-OR-NONE **2 a :** accepting no less than everything ⟨an *all-or-nothing* attitude⟩ ⟨an *all-or-nothing* choice⟩ **b :** risking everything ⟨playing an *all-or-nothing* game⟩

al·lo·sau·rus \,alə'sȯrəs\ *n, cap* [NL, fr. *all-* + *-saurus*] **:** a genus of No. American Jurassic carnivorous dinosaurs having hind feet with three functional toes and sometimes being over 20 feet long

al·lose \'a,lōs\ *n* -s [ISV *all-* + *-ose;* orig. formed in G] **:** a sugar $C_6H_{12}O_6$ obtained synthetically as a syrup that is stereoisomeric with glucose and epimeric with altrose

al·lo·se·mat·ic \¦==sə¦mad·ik\ *adj* [*all-* + *sematic*] **:** having protective coloration that imitates the coloration of some dangerous or inedible animal

al·lo·some \'==,sōm\ *n* -s [*all-* + *-some*] **:** an atypical chromosome; *esp* **:** SEX CHROMOSOME — compare AUTOSOME

al·lo·sy·nap·sis \,==sə'napsəs\ *n, pl* **allosynap·ses** \-p,sēz\ [NL, fr. *all-* + *synapsis*] **:** ALLOSYNDESIS

al·lo·syn·de·sis \,=='sindəsəs\ *n, pl* **allosynde·ses** \-ə,sēz\ [NL, fr. *all-* + *syndesis*] **:** pairing at meiosis of nonhomologous chromosomes from the diverse sets of an allopolyploid individual — compare AUTOSYNDESIS — **al·lo·syn·det·ic** \¦==(,)sin¦ded·ik\ *adj* — **al·lo·syn·det·i·cal·ly** \-ək(ə)lē\ *adv*

al·lot \ə'lät *also* a'-; *usu* -äd·+V\ *vb* **allotted; allotted; allotting; allots** [ME *alotten,* fr. MF *aloter,* fr. *a-* (fr. L *ad-*) + *-loter* (fr. *lot,* of Gmc origin; akin to OE *hlot* lot) — more at AT, LOT] *vt* **1 :** to assign as a portion or lot ⟨the right of society to ~ to each the work . . . that he should do —J.A. Hobson⟩: as **a :** to prescribe as one's lot (as in life) **:** ORDAIN, APPOINT ⟨man's *allotted* life span according to the psalmist⟩ ⟨nature . . . propels us like children through the role she has *allotted* us —D.C.Peattie⟩ ⟨each in his *allotted* place⟩ **b :** to assign as a share or portion to a particular person or thing or for a particular purpose **:** ALLOCATE ⟨business began to encroach upon the time *allotted* to rest —S.M.Crothers⟩ ⟨*allotted* to the civilian economy what was left over —*Current History*⟩ ⟨exceeded his *allotted* time by 15 minutes⟩; *specif* **:** to assign to a subscriber (his proportionate share of an issue of securities) **2 :** to distribute by lot or as if by lot **:** parcel out in parts or portions or to each individual concerned **:** apportion esp. without regard to the choice or wishes of the recipients ⟨the council should not waste time on *allotting* blame between him and his junior officers⟩ ⟨some fairly good-sized parts to ~ among all those people who are coming to the tryout —Robertson Davies⟩ **3 :** to assign as due or deriving **:** ATTRIBUTE ⟨~ diverse sets of instincts to the biological ego —P.A.Sorokin⟩ ~ *vi, North* **:** INTEND, RECKON, ANTICIPATE — usu. used with *on* or *upon* ⟨I ~ upon going⟩

syn ASSIGN, APPORTION, ALLOCATE: ALLOT may imply more or less arbitrary distribution ⟨*allotted* a task of vital importance —Sir Winston Churchill⟩ ⟨you will probably be *allotted* your seat for meals —Agnes M. Miall⟩ ⟨had been *allotted* a small sitting room —Compton Mackenzie⟩ ASSIGN may stress authoritative, usu. fixed, allotment suggesting no necessarily equitable distribution ⟨*assigns* to different departments their respective powers —John Marshall⟩ ⟨antiaircraft guns had been *assigned* the mission of protecting the bridge —P.W. Thompson⟩ ⟨an attic *assigned* to me as a playroom —R.M. Lovett⟩ APPORTION suggests a more or less equitable or proportionate distribution ⟨the duty of husbanding and *apportioning* the meager food stores of the party —W.J.Ghent⟩ ⟨works in which the violin and a keyboard instrument are *apportioned* equal musical interest —A.E.Wier⟩ ⟨to *apportion* the judicial power between the supreme and inferior courts —John Marshall⟩ ALLOCATE, chiefly applied to money, materiel, authority, or responsibility, implies appropriation to a particular person, group, or purpose ⟨various sums *allocated* to the different sciences —S.F.Mason⟩ ⟨*allocate* only part of the supply of the metals in order to affect civilian economy as little as possible —*Current Biog.*⟩ ⟨the Marine Corps would be *allocated* primary responsibility for amphibious development and doctrine pertaining to landing forces —*Collier's Yr. Bk.*⟩

al·lot·ee *var of* ALLOTTEE

al·lo·tet·ra·ploid \¦==¦==,=\ *n* -s [*all-* + *tetraploid*] **:** AMPHIDIPLOID — **al·lo·tet·ra·ploi·dy** \-,dē\ *n* -ES

al·lo·the·ism \'==(,)thē,izəm\ *n* -s [*all-* + *-theism*] **:** the worship of foreign or unsanctioned gods ⟨commandments against ~ and polytheism⟩

al·lo·the·ria \ˌ=ˈthirēə\ *n pl, cap* [NL, fr. *all-* + *-theria*] **:** a subclass of Mammalia comprising small primitive forms extinct since the early Cenozoic, being usu. considered coexistensive with the Multituberculata but sometimes extended to include the Protodonta and Triconodonta

al·lo·thig·e·nous \ˌ==ˈthijənəs\ *adj* [G *allothigen* + E *-ous*] **:** ALLOTHOGENIC

al·loth·i·morph \əˈlathəˌmȯrf\ *n* -s [ISV *allothi-* (fr. Gk *allothi* elsewhere, old loc. of *allos* other) + *-morph;* orig. formed in G — more at ELSE] **:** any constituent of a metamorphic rock that in the new rock still possesses its original crystal boundaries — **al·loth·i·mor·phic** \=ˌ==ˈ=fik\ *adj*

al·lo·to·gen·ic \ˌaləthəˈjenik\ *also* **al·lo·thog·e·nous** \ˌaləˈthäjənəs\ *adj* [irreg. (influenced by E *-o-*) fr. G *allothigen* allothogenic (fr. Gk *allothi* elsewhere — fr. *allos* other — + *-genēs* born) + E *-ic* or *-ous* — more at ELSE, -GEN] **:** formed elsewhere **:** derived from preexisting rocks ⟨clastic rocks or their mineral particles formed elsewhere and transported to their present position are ~⟩ **:** ALLOGENIC — opposed to *authigenic*

al·lot·ment \əˈlätmənt *also* aˈ-\ *n* -s [MF *alotement,* fr. *aloter* to allot + *-ment*] **1 :** the act of allotting ⟨funds available and ready for ~⟩: as **a :** APPORTIONMENT **b :** assignment to a particular person or thing or for a particular use **2 :** something that is allotted **:** a part or portion distributed or assigned: as **a :** something that is assigned by or as if by lot or by destiny ⟨possessing a generous ~ of common sense —*Saturday Rev.*⟩ ⟨receiving . . . their varying ~*s* of discomfort and disappointment and discouragement —J.G.Cozzens⟩ **b :** something set apart by distribution or assignment for special use or for a distinct party: as (1) *chiefly Brit* **:** a small piece of land let or assigned to an individual (as by the town council) for cultivation as a family garden ⟨a disused railway siding that was turned into ~*s* —Anthony Powell⟩ ⟨an ~ garden⟩ (2) **:** a portion of range land, esp. of national forest, allotted to the use of a particular grazier or herd or flock of grazing animals (3) **:** a portion of a serviceman's salary paid, esp. with additional contributions, to a designated party at his request or to a bank for his account (4) **:** the portion of a newly issued security received by a subscriber **3 :** acceptance of an order to purchase or subscribe to securities of a new offering in part or whole

al·lo·top·o·type \ˌ==ˈtäpəˌtīp\ *n* -s [blend of *allotype* and *topotype*] *biol* **:** an allotype obtained from the type locality

al·lot·ri·og·na·thi \əˌlä·trēˈägnəˌthī\ *n pl, cap* [NL, fr. Gk *allotrio-* (fr. *allotrios* strange) + *gnathoi,* pl. of *gnathos* jaw] **:** an order or suborder of oceanic teleost fishes comprising the opah, the dealfishes, ribbonfishes, and related forms

al·lot·ri·o·mor·phic \əˌlä·trēōˈmȯrfik\ *adj* [Gk *allotrio-* + E *-morphic*] **:** marked by a form different from the normal or expected because of development in special circumstances — used esp. of mineral grains of igneous rocks whose mutual growths have prevented the assumption of outward crystal form; contrasted with *idiomorphic*

al·lot·ri·oph·a·gy \əˌlä·trēˈäfəjē\ *also* **al·lot·ri·o·pha·gia** \-əˈfāj(ē)ə\ *n, pl* **allotriophagies** *also* **allotriophagias** [*allotriophagy* fr. G *allotriophagie,* fr. Gk *allotrio-* + G *-phagie* -phagy; *allotriophagia,* NL, fr. G *allotriophagie*] *med* **:** PICA

al·lo·trope \ˈaləˌtrōp\ *n* -s [ISV, back-formation fr. *allotropy*] **:** a form showing allotropy

al·lo·troph·ic \ˌ==ˈträfik, -ōf-\ *adj* [ISV *all-* + *-trophic*] **1 :** having an altered, esp. lowered, nutritive value ⟨~ foods⟩ **2 :** HETEROTROPHIC

al·lo·trop·ic \ˌ==ˈträpik\ *adj* [ISV *allotropy* + *-ic*] **1 :** of, relating to, or exhibiting allotropy ⟨~ chemical changes⟩ ⟨sulfur is known in a number of ~ forms⟩ **2 :** showing a variation of form **:** existent in a different form ⟨dialects with ~ developments⟩

al·lot·ro·pize \əˈlä·trəˌpīz\ *vt* -ED/-ING/-S [*allotropy* + *-ize*] **:** to change from one allotropic form to another

al·lot·ro·py \əˈlä·trəpē\ *also* **al·lot·ro·pism** \-ˌpizəm\ *n, pl* **allotropies** *also* **allotropisms** [*all-* + *-tropy, -tropism*] **:** the phenomenon of the existence of a substance, esp. an element, in two or more different modifications usu. in the same phase (as different crystalline forms of carbon, iron, and phosphorus or as different kinds of molecules of oxygen and ozone) — compare POLYMORPHISM

allots *pres 3d sing of* ALLOT

al·lot·ta·ble \əˈläd·əbəl, -ätə- *also* aˈ-\ *adj* **:** capable of being allotted

all' ot·ta·va \ˌälōˈtävə ˌal-\ *adv (or adj)* [It, at the octave] **:** OTTAVA

allotted *past of* ALLOT

al·lot·tee *or* **al·lot·ee** \əˌläˈdē, -äˈtē, ˌaˌläˈtē\ *n* -s **:** one that receives an allotment ⟨divided among the original ~*s* or their heirs —E.E.Dale⟩

allotting *pres part of* ALLOT

al·lo·type \ˈaləˌtīp\ *n* -s [*all-* + *type*] **1 :** a type specimen of opposite sex to the holotype; *esp* **:** one designated by the original author **2 :** PARATYPE 1 — **al·lo·typ·ic** \ˌaləˈtipik\ *adj*

all out *adv* **:** with full vigor, determination, or enthusiasm or with full use of one's powers, ingenuity, and influence, esp. in an effort or a cause — used chiefly in the phrase *go all out* ⟨went *all out* for excess-profits legislation —*New Republic*⟩ ⟨go *all out* to complete a job⟩ ⟨prevented them from going *all out*⟩

all-out \ˈ=ˈ=\ *adj* [*all out*] **:** exerting every energy and employing every resource (as military, economic, and political) ⟨an *all-out* offensive⟩ **:** thoroughgoing and unreserved ⟨the *all-out* support of the press⟩ ⟨*all-out* reformers⟩ **:** without reservation

all-out·er \ˈȯlˈaùdə(r), -autə-\ *n* -s **:** one that advocates an all-out policy or measure **:** EXTREMIST ⟨*all-outers* for "unconditional surrender" and "total victory" —J.R.Chamberlain⟩

all over *adv* [ME *alover,* fr. *al* all + *over*] **1 a :** over the whole extent ⟨decorated *all over* with a pattern of flowers⟩ ⟨felt tired *all over*⟩ **b :** EVERYWHERE ⟨looked *all over* for it⟩ **2 :** in every respect **:** THOROUGHLY, COMPLETELY ⟨she is her mother *all over*⟩ **3 :** everywhere on the outside ⟨he is *all over* dirt⟩ ⟨ragged and *all over* bruises⟩ — not often in formal use

¹allover \ˈ=ˌ==\ *adj* **:** covering the whole extent of anything ⟨variations in solar radiation or some other ~ effect —*Time*⟩; *esp* **:** covering the entire surface (as of a fabric) — used esp. of designs or figuration ⟨~ quilting⟩ ⟨an ~ marbleized appearance⟩

²allover \"\ *n* -s **1 :** an embroidered, printed, or lace fabric with a design covering most of the surface **2 :** a pattern or design in which a single unit is repeated along two or more intersecting systems of lines so as to cover an entire surface

all-o·ver·ish \(ˈ)ȯlˈōv(ə)rish\ *adj* [¹*allover* + *-ish*] **1 :** vaguely uneasy **:** APPREHENSIVE **2 :** slightly indisposed

all-o·vers \ˈȯˈlōvə(r)z\ *n pl* [*all over* + *-s*] *chiefly South & Midland* **:** FIDGETS, CREEPS ⟨it gives me the *all-overs* just to think of it⟩

al·low \əˈlau̇\ *vb* -ED/-ING/-S [ME *allowen,* fr. MF *aloer, alouer* to place, use, grant (fr. ML *allocare*) & *allouer* to approve, fr. L *adlaudare* to extol, fr. *ad-* + *laudare* to praise — more at ALLOCATE, LAUD] *vt* **1** *archaic* **a :** PRAISE **b :** APPROVE, SANCTION, ACCEPT ⟨truly ye bear witness that ye ~ the deeds of your fathers —Lk 11:48 (AV)⟩ **2 a** *obs* **:** to give or recognize as a right **b** (1) **:** to give or assign as a share or suitable amount (as of time or money) to a particular person or for a particular purpose ⟨~ an hour for lunch⟩ ⟨~*ed* each child one dollar a week as spending money⟩ (2) **:** to allot or assign as a deduction or an addition ⟨~ a gallon for leakage⟩ **3 :** to accept as true or as represented **:** ADMIT, CONCEDE, ACKNOWLEDGE ⟨a people of whom this is true must be ~*ed* to be musical —Wyn Griffith⟩ ⟨he will not ~ that we have eliminated these evils⟩ ⟨played a more important part in his life than his biographer ~*s*⟩ **4 :** PERMIT ⟨a pipe to ~ the heated air to escape⟩ ⟨occasional gaps ~ passage through the mountains⟩ ⟨pulled to the side to ~ us to pass⟩: as **a :** to permit by way of concession ⟨no smoking ~*ed*⟩ ⟨he ~*s* himself many luxuries⟩ ⟨children too young to be ~*ed* out at night⟩ **b :** to permit by neglecting to restrain or prevent ⟨~ a garden to become overgrown with weeds⟩ ⟨conditions which should never have been ~*ed* to develop⟩ ⟨she had ~*ed* herself to become very fat⟩ **5** *dial* **a :** to be of the opinion **:** THINK, SUPPOSE ⟨we ~*ed* it was too late to start⟩ **b :** INTEND, PLAN — usu. used with an infinitive ⟨I ~ to go fishing tomorrow⟩ ~ *vi* **1 :** to make a possibility **:** provide opportunity or basis **:** ADMIT, PERMIT — used with *of* ⟨evidence that ~*s* of only one conclusion⟩ ⟨underbrush too dense to ~ of shooting⟩ **2 :** to give consideration **:** make allowance — used with *for* ⟨a distance, ~*ing* for detours, of about 10 miles⟩ **3** *dial* **:** SUPPOSE, CONSIDER **syn** see LET

al·low·a·bil·i·ty \əˌlau̇əˈbiləd·ē\ *n* -ES **:** the quality or state of being allowable

¹al·low·a·ble \əˈlau̇əbəl\ *adj* [ME, fr. MF *allouable,* fr. *allouer* to approve + *-able*] **1** *obs* **:** worthy of praise **:** LAUDABLE **2 :** PERMISSIBLE **:** not forbidden **:** not unlawful or improper ⟨the ~ rate of continuous descent of commercial airliners —H.G.Armstrong⟩ ⟨~ income tax deductions⟩ ⟨a degree of freedom ~ among friends⟩ — **al·low·a·ble·ness** *n* -ES

²allowable \"\ *n* -s **:** the amount of oil that an oil-well operator is permitted by law to take from a given well in any one day

al·low·a·bly \-əblē, -li\ *adv* **:** in an allowable manner

¹al·low·ance \əˈlau̇ən(t)s\ *n* -s [ME *allowance,* fr. MF *allouance* approbation (fr. *allouer* to approve + *-ance* -ance) & *alouance* action of leasing, fr. *aloer, alouer* to place, use, grant + *-ance* -ance] **1 a** *archaic* **:** APPROVAL, APPROBATION **b** *obs* **:** ACKNOWLEDGMENT **2 :** something that is allowed **:** a share or portion allotted or granted ⟨an ~ of time for stopovers⟩ ⟨~*s* for depreciation⟩: **a** (1) **:** a sum granted as a reimbursement or a bounty or as appropriate for such purposes as personal or household expenses ⟨an officer's pay and ~*s*⟩ ⟨a schoolboy's weekly ~⟩ ⟨per diem ~*s* in lieu of subsistence —*U.S.Code*⟩ ⟨cost-of-living ~*s*⟩ ⟨spending the winter in California on the ~ he gets —Hamilton Basso⟩ (2) *law* **:** a sum in addition to the regular taxable costs awarded by court to a party in a difficult case — called also *extra allowance* **b :** a fixed amount allowed ⟨a sailor's daily ~ of grog⟩ ⟨the 66-pound free-luggage ~ granted by transatlantic air lines⟩ **c** (1) **:** a customary deduction from the gross weight of goods, different in different countries (2) **:** a reduction from a list price or stated price (as one granted on used products turned in or because of a previous credit) ⟨a trade-in ~⟩ **d :** a concession or privilege accorded a contestant to make his chances more nearly equal to his competitors': as (1) **:** an allowed deduction from the weight a racehorse is required to carry ⟨maidens were given special ~*s*⟩ (2) **:** a deduction from the actual elapsed time of a racing yacht computed against a scratch boat's elapsed time **e :** nonproductive time added in time study to the actual or base time of an operation to allow for fatigue, personal needs, and delays — compare BASE TIME, STANDARD TIME **f :** clearance in founding **g :** an allowed dimensional difference between mating parts of a machine (as between a shaft and a bearing in which it turns) — compare TOLERANCE 3 **3 :** the act of allowing **:** AUTHORIZATION, PERMISSION, SANCTION ⟨without the king's will or the state's ~ —Shak.⟩ ⟨no newspaper was suffered to appear without his ~ —T.B.Macaulay⟩ **4 :** the taking into account of circumstances (as mitigating circumstances) or of contingencies — often used with the verb *make* and the preposition *for* ⟨make ~*s* for the inexperience of youth⟩ ⟨~ must be made for what was then the fashionable pose —R.B.Merriman⟩ ⟨regional differences must be recognized and ~ made for them in any generalizations —C.R.Woodward⟩

²allowance \"\ *vt* -ED/-ING/-S **1 :** to put upon a fixed allowance (as of provisions and drink) ⟨the captain *allowanced* his crew⟩ **2 :** to supply in a fixed and limited quantity

allowance account *n* **:** RESERVE ACCOUNT 1

allowed *adj* **:** in accordance with selection principles in physics **:** PERMITTED — used of electron-energy states and transitions or spectrum lines

al·low·ed·ly \əˈlau̇ədlē, -li\ *adv* **:** by allowance **:** ADMITTEDLY

allowed time *n* **1** *industrial engin* **:** STANDARD TIME **2 :** the amount of time an employee is permitted to spend per work cycle for attending to personal needs — called also *time allowance*

allowing *pres part of* ALLOW

allows *pres 3d sing of* ALLOW

allox- *comb form* [ISV, fr. *alloxan*] **:** alloxan

al·lox·an \əˈläksən\ *n* -s [G, fr. *all*antoin + *ox*alsäure oxalic acid + *-an*] **:** a crystalline compound $C_4H_2N_2O_4$ or its monohydrate $C_4H_4N_2O_5$ formed by oxidation of uric acid and causing diabetes mellitus when injected into experimental animals

al·lox·an·ate \-səˌnāt, -ˌnət\ *n* -s [ISV *alloxan* + *-ate*] **:** a salt or ester of alloxanic acid

al·lox·an·ic acid \ˌaˌläkˈsanik-\ *n* [ISV *alloxanic* (fr. *alloxan* + *-ic*) + *acid;* orig. formed as G *alloxansäure*] **:** a crystalline acid $C_4H_4N_2O_5$ formed by hydrolysis of alloxan; 4-hydroxy= 4-hydantoin-carboxylic acid

al·lox·an·tin \əˈläksənˈtən\ *n* -s [ISV *alloxan* + connective *-t-* + *-in;* orig. formed in G] **:** a crystalline compound $C_8H_6N_4O_8 2H_2O$ formed by oxidation of uric acid and by reaction of alloxan and dialuric acid

al·lox·a·zine \əˈläksəˌzēn\ *n* -s [*allox-* + *azine*] **:** either of two acidic compounds $C_{10}H_6N_4O_2$ containing a pyrimidine ring fused to quinoxaline: **a :** a grayish green powder obtained by reaction of alloxan with *ortho*-phenylenediamine **b :** ISOALLOXAZINE

al·lox·u·ric \ˌaˌläkˈsu̇rik, -ksˈyu̇-\ *adj* [ISV *allox-* + *uric*] **:** related to alloxan and urea

alloxuric base *n* **:** PURINE BASE

¹al·loy \ˈaˌlȯi, əˈl-, ˈaˈl-; =ˈ= *is prob more freq for noun senses 4 & 5, and for the verb, than for noun senses 2 & 3*\ *n* -s [MF *aloi,* fr. *aloier*] **1** *obs* **:** essential quality or character **:** STANDARD **2 :** degree of mixture with base metals **:** comparative purity (as of gold or silver) **:** FINENESS **3 a :** a substance composed of two or more metals intimately mixed and united usu. by being fused together and dissolving in each other when molten ⟨brass is an ~ of copper and zinc⟩; *also* **:** the state of union of the components **b :** a similar substance with metallic properties, sometimes with limited malleability and conductivity, formed by union of a metal and a nonmetal ⟨steel is an ~ of iron and carbon⟩ **c** *archaic* **:** an inferior metal mixed with a more valuable one ⟨coins made of silver and ~⟩ **4 a :** an admixture that lessens value or detracts from quality **b :** an impairing alien element or part ⟨no happiness is without ~⟩ ⟨had his ~, like other people, of ambition and selfishness —Rose Macaulay⟩ **5 :** any compound, mixture, or union of different things **:** AMALGAM ⟨an ethnic ~ of many peoples⟩

²alloy \"\ *vb* -ED/-ING/-S [obs. F *aloyer,* fr. OF *aleier, aloier, alier* to combine, fr. L *alligare* to bind, bind to — more at ALLY] *vt* **1 :** to reduce the purity of by mixing with a less valuable metal ⟨~ gold with copper⟩ **2 :** to mix with another metal or metals (as by melting together) **:** use as the constituent or constituents of an alloy **:** mix so as to form an alloy **3 :** to lower, impair, or debase by mixture ⟨~*ing* the splendor of the sight⟩ **:** ALLAY, MODERATE, TEMPER ⟨mercy should ~ our stern resentment —W.S.Gilbert⟩ ~ *vi* **:** to mix to form an alloy **:** lend itself readily to being alloyed ⟨iron ~*s* well⟩

al·loy·age \əˈlȯi-ij, aˈl-, ˈaˌl-\ *n* -s [obs. F *aloyage,* fr. *aloyer* + *-age*] **:** the act or art of alloying

alloy steel *n* **:** a steel with modified properties made by incorporating with iron one or more elements in addition to carbon — contrasted with *carbon steel*

al·lo·zo·oid \ˌaləˈzōˌȯid\ *n* -s [*all-* + *zooid*] **:** a zooid differing from its parent — opposed to *isozooid*

all-points \ˈ=ˌ=\ *adj* **:** directed to all points **:** sent in all directions **:** GENERAL — used esp. of police messages ⟨an *all-points* alarm⟩ ⟨broadcast an *all-points* bulletin⟩

all-possessed \ˌ==ˈ=\ *adj* **:** as if dominated by an evil spirit **:** DEMONIAC ⟨ran down the street like *all-possessed*⟩

all-powerful \(ˈ)ȯlˈ-\ *adj* **:** having complete power or sole power ⟨perhaps dictators are not so *all-powerful* as they seem —Bertrand Russell⟩ ⟨an *all-powerful* arbiter —John Gunther⟩

all-purpose \ˈ=ˈ==\ *adj* **:** for all or many purposes **:** suited or adapted to various uses, including those uses ordinarily requiring special adaptations **:** not specialized ⟨an *all-purpose* wardrobe⟩ ⟨military *all-purpose* gasoline⟩ ⟨*all-purpose* emergency kits⟩

all-purpose flour *n* **:** flour made from a blend of hard or soft wheats suitable for all cookery except the finest cakes

all red *adj, usu cap A&R* [so called fr. the color of British territory on British official maps] **:** wholly within the British Commonwealth — used of connections between Britain and her overseas territories ⟨an *All Red* route⟩

¹all right \ȯ(l)ˈrīt, *esp in senses 2 & 3* ˈ=ˌ=; *usu* -īd·+V\ *adv* [ME *alright, alriht,* fr. *al* all + *right, riht* right — more at RIGHT] **1 :** SATISFACTORILY ⟨doing *all right*⟩ ⟨getting along *all right*⟩ **2 :** YES, AGREED **:** very well ⟨*all right,* let us suppose your plan is sound⟩ — often used as a generalized expression of assent ⟨*all right,* I'll meet you at 10 o'clock⟩; sometimes used in irritation by children ⟨*all right* for you. I'm going⟩ **3 :** beyond doubt **:** CERTAINLY ⟨the element has been conquered, *all right,* but it still hits back —*New Yorker*⟩ — often added as an expression of emphasis ⟨you've started *all right.* Right at the bottom —Louis Auchincloss⟩

²all right *nonattrib usu* =ˈ=, *attrib usu* ˈ=ˌ=\ *adj* **1 :** SATISFACTORY: as **a :** AGREEABLE ⟨that is *all right* with me⟩ **b :** CORRECT ⟨checked his work and found it *all right*⟩ **c :** ADEQUATE ⟨not very good in his first role but *all right* in the second⟩ ⟨*all right* for the last century⟩ **d :** SUITABLE, PROPER ⟨a picture that is *all right* for children⟩ **2 :** SAFE, WELL ⟨he was ill but he is *all right* again⟩ **3** *slang* **:** GOOD, HONEST, DEPENDABLE — usu. used attributively as a generalized expression of approval ⟨an *all right* guy⟩ ⟨an *all right* party after it got started⟩

³all right \ˈ=ˈ=\ *n, chiefly Brit* **:** a signal (as a blue flag) raised over the number board to indicate that results of a horse race are official and that winning bets may be paid out

all risk *or* **all risks** *adj* **:** covering loss from all hazards insured against except those specif. excluded from coverage — compare BROAD FORM

all-round *var of* ALL-AROUND

all round *also* **all around** *adv* [*all-round*] **:** INCLUSIVELY **:** without concentration on one area or aspect **:** concerning or considering all members, units, parts, or phases ⟨some will fail *all round;* others will succeed in part⟩ ⟨our best athlete, if taken *all round*⟩

all-round·er \ˈȯlˈrau̇ndə(r)\ *n* -s **:** one that is all-around **:** a person (as a workman or an athlete) or an animal (as a dog or horse) excelling or capable in many fields or in many departments of the same field ⟨he was an *all-rounder* at school (classics, science, history, languages) —Brian Dowling⟩ ⟨the working horse kept by the Irish farmer was a good *all-rounder* —Stanislaus Lynch⟩: as **a** *chiefly Brit* **:** an athlete, esp. a cricketer, who excels in several departments of play **b :** a show-dog judge considered capable of judging dogs of several different breeds

alls *pl of* ALL

all saints' cherry *n, usu cap A & S* [so called fr. its alleged blooming on All Saints' Day] **:** an ornamental horticultural variety (*Prunus cerasus semperflorens*) of the sour cherry blooming in spring and autumn

all saints' day *n, usu cap A & S & D* **:** a feast observed in various Christian churches on November 1 in honor of all the saints or all the blessed in heaven

all saints' summer *n, usu cap A & 1st S* **:** INDIAN SUMMER

allseed \ˈ=ˌ=\ *n* -s **:** any of several many-seeded plants: as **a :** KNOTWEED **b :** a goosefoot (*Chenopodium polyspermum*)

all-sliming \ˈ=ˈ==\ *n* -s **:** grinding to the fineness of slime so that practically all material will pass through a 200-mesh screen — used of a common method of treating gold ores

all souls' day *n, usu cap A & S & D* **:** a day observed in the medieval Western church and in the modern Roman Catholic and some Anglican churches, usu. on November 2, by the solemn commemoration of and supplicatory prayers for the dead

all·spice \ˈȯlˌspīs\ *n* -s [so called fr. the belief that it combines the flavor of cinnamon, nutmeg, and cloves] **1 :** the berry of the allspice tree yielding a pungent and aromatic spice; *also* **:** the spice prepared from this berry **2** *also* **allspice tree :** a West Indian tree (*Pimenta dioica*) of the family Myrtaceae that yields allspice **3 :** any of several aromatic shrubs: as **a :** CAROLINA ALLSPICE **b :** JAPAN ALLSPICE

allspice oil *n* **:** PIMENTO OIL

all standing *adv* **1 :** with all sail set — used of a ship brought suddenly to a stop while all sail is set ⟨to bring up *all standing*⟩ **2 :** in a fully clothed state ⟨to turn in *all standing*⟩

¹all-star \ˈ=ˈ=\ *adj* **:** composed wholly or chiefly of stars or of outstanding performers or participants ⟨an *all-star* team⟩ ⟨an *all-star* cast⟩ ⟨an *all-star* television program⟩ **:** participated in by stars ⟨an annual *all-star* game⟩

²all-star \"\ *n* -s [¹*all-star*] **:** a member of an all-star team — usu. used in pl. ⟨major league *all-stars*⟩

all that *n* **:** everything of or related to the kind specified ⟨one last fling and he would put *all that* behind him⟩ ⟨believed in the stiff upper lip and *all that*⟩

all there *adj* **1 :** in full possession of one's mental faculties **:** SANE ⟨behaved in such a way as to make one wonder if he was quite *all there*⟩ — not often in formal use **2** *slang* **:** alert and well informed **:** QUICK-WITTED ⟨wide-awake, alert, *all there;* he knows just where he is and what he means and where he is going —*Times Lit. Supp.*⟩

all the same *adv* **:** NEVERTHELESS

all the world *n* **:** everybody or everything in existence; *esp* **:** everybody or everything regarded as of account ⟨convinced that *all the world* was against him⟩ — **for all the world 1 :** for the sake of gaining everything **:** for any consideration **2 :** in every respect **:** WHOLLY, EXACTLY ⟨whose posy was *for all the world* like cutler's poetry —Shak.⟩ ⟨with his father's pipe in his mouth and looking *for all the world* like him⟩

allthing *adv* [obs. *allthing* everything, fr. ME *althing,* fr. *alle thing* all things, fr. OE *ealle thing*] *obs* **:** ALTOGETHER

allthorn \ˈ=ˌ=\ *n* -s **:** a spiny much-branched shrub (*Koeberlinia spinosa*) found in the southwestern U.S. and adjacent Mexico

all threes (thrēz) *n pl, but usu sing in constr* **:** a variety of muggins in which multiples of three are counted

all-time \ˈ=ˌ=\ *adj* **1 :** FULL-TIME **2 a :** for or of all time up to and including the present ⟨an *all-time* average⟩; *esp* **:** exceeding all others of all time ⟨an *all-time* record⟩ ⟨receipts are expected to reach an *all-time* high⟩ **b :** the best, or hypothetically the best, in recorded sports history ⟨an *all-time* baseball team⟩

all to *adv* [ME *al to-* completely apart, completely to pieces, fr. OE *eall tō-,* fr. *eall* completely + *tō-, te-* apart, to pieces — more at ALL, DIS-] *obs* **:** all to pieces **:** THOROUGHLY, COMPLETELY ⟨a certain woman cast a piece of a millstone upon Abimelech's head, and *all to* brake his skull —Judg 9:53 (AV)⟩

all told *adv* **:** everything counted **:** in all **:** ALTOGETHER ⟨a town of perhaps 5000 people *all told*⟩ ⟨6 pounds of beef and 4 of lamb, 10 pounds *all told*⟩ ⟨*all told,* it had been one of the most frustrating experiences imaginable⟩

all-turned \ˈ=ˈ=\ *adj, of a piece of furniture* **:** having all the supporting members (as legs) shaped by turning in a lathe

al·lu·au·dite \ˌalyəˈwōˌdīt\ *n* -s [G *alluaudit,* fr. François *Alluaud* †1865, Fr. mineralogist + G *-it* -ite] **:** a rare mineral $(Na,Fe,Mn)PO_4$ consisting of sodium-iron-manganese phosphate

al·lude \əˈlüd *sometimes* əlˈyüd *or* aˈ- *or* alˈ-\ *vi* -ED/-ING/-S [L *alludere* to play with, jest, refer to, fr. *ad-* + *ludere* to play — more at LUDICROUS] **:** to have or make indirect reference (as in passing or by suggestion) **:** refer indirectly — used with *to* ⟨proposals . . . always *alluded* to slightingly as innovations —Compton Mackenzie⟩ ⟨though any reference to his deformity annoyed him, there were times when she felt obliged to ~ to it —Ellen Glasgow⟩ ⟨a letter *alluding* to some unspecified family difficulties⟩

al·lu·lose \ˈalyəˌlōs\ *n* -s [*all-* + *-ulose*] **:** a syrupy ketohexose sugar $C_6H_{12}O_6$ found in the unfermentable residue from cane molasses and related stereochemically to allose and altrose — called also *psicose*

all' uni·so·no \ˌä(ˌ)lüˈnēsəˌnō\ *adv (or adj)* [It, lit., in unison] **:** in unison — used as a direction in music that several performers regularly grouped in parts are to play or sing a single part in unison

all up *adj* [²*all* + *up,* adj.] **1 :** at or very near an end **:** with death, defeat, or failure hopelessly or unalterably approaching — used predicatively and in impersonal constructions with *it* ⟨by night it was *all up* for the trapped miners⟩ **2 :** total inclusive of the weight of machine, necessary flight accessories, crew, passengers, and cargo ⟨a plane with an *all up* weight of 50,000 pounds⟩ **:** total inclusive of weight of oil, coolant, and necessary accessories ⟨the *all up* weight of the motor⟩ **3 :** paid for at first-class surface rates but carried by air ⟨*all up* mail to larger cities⟩ **:** of or relating to such carriage arrangements ⟨*all up* systems being planned⟩

¹al·lure \əˈlu̇(ə)r, -u̇ə *also* əlˈyü- *or* aˈl- *or* alˈ-\ *vt* -ED/-ING/-S

[ME *aluren*, fr. MF *alurer, aleurrer*, fr. OF, fr. *a-* (fr. L *ad-*) + *loire, loirre* lure — more at LURE] **:** to influence, sway, or entice with some tempting appeal, some offered or suggested benefit or pleasure, genuine or specious ⟨ancient fables of men *allured* by beautiful forms and melodious voices to destruction —W.H.Hudson †1922⟩ **syn** see ATTRACT

²allure \"\ *n* -s **:** power of attraction or fascination **:** ALLUREMENT ⟨about the legends of the islands there is a glowing, haunting ~⟩ ⟨the neat ~ in mathematical formulae —Harlow Shapley⟩; *esp* **:** the power to entice or attract through personal charm ⟨is neatly made, has a cobra-cold ~ . . . and dances with the unerring grace of a cat —*Time*⟩ ⟨a female performer with no particular ~ —*New Yorker*⟩

al·lure·ment \-mənt\ *n* -s **1 :** a means of alluring **:** something that attracts or entices ⟨the social ~*s* of the city⟩ ⟨she had discarded forever the ~*s* of youth —Ellen Glasgow⟩ **2 :** the act of alluring **3 :** the power or quality of alluring **:** ALLURE, FASCINATION, CHARM ⟨the fatal gift of ~ —Idwal Jones⟩

al·lur·er \-ùrə(r)\ *n* -s **:** one that allures

alluring *adj* **:** marked by allure **:** ATTRACTIVE, ENTICING, TEMPTING ⟨not an ~ prospect⟩ ⟨declines any path, however ~, that does not commend itself to his intellect —Brand Blanshard⟩ ⟨a land of mystery, remote and ~⟩ — **al·lur·ing·ly** *adv* — **al·lur·ing·ness** *n* -ES

al·lu·sion \ə'lüzhən, a'- *sometimes* əl'yü- *or* al'yü-\ *n* -s [ML *allusion-, allusio*, fr. LL, playing with, fr. L *allusus* (past part. of *alludere* to play with, jest, refer to) + *-ion-, -io* -ion — more at ALLUDE] **1** *obs* **:** a figurative or symbolical reference **2 :** an implied indication or indirect reference **:** ALLUDING ⟨the English habit of understatement, of ~ —D.W.Brogan⟩ **3 a :** a reference usu. by indirection or implication or in passing esp. as utilized in literature ⟨with historical ~*s* on every page⟩ ⟨Pope's ~*s* to Horace⟩ **b :** the use of such reference esp. in poetry

al·lu·sive \-siv,-sēv *also* -z- *or* -əv\ *adj* [L *allusus* (past part. of *alludere* to allude) + E *-ive* — more at ALLUDE] **1** *archaic* **:** FIGURATIVE, SYMBOLICAL **2 a :** of, having the character of, or marked by allusion **b :** containing allusions ⟨~ writing⟩ **3 :** PUNNING — **al·lu·sive·ly** *adv* — **al·lu·sive·ness** *n* -ES

alluvia *pl of* ALLUVIUM

¹al·lu·vi·al \ə'lüvēəl, -vyəl *also* a'- *or* əl'yü- *or* al'yü-\ *also* **al·lu·vi·an** \-ən\ *adj* [*alluvium* + *-al* or *-an*] **1 :** relating to or composed of alluvium ⟨~ soil⟩ ⟨an ~ divide⟩ **2 :** found in alluvium ⟨~ diamonds⟩

²alluvial \"\ *n* -s **1 a :** alluvial soil **b** *Austral* **:** gold-bearing alluvial soil **2 :** a mineral occurring in placer deposits

alluvial cone *n* **:** an alluvial fan with steep slopes

alluvial deposit *n* **:** ALLUVIUM

alluvial fan *n* **:** the fanlike deposit of a stream where it issues from a gorge upon a plain or of a tributary stream near or at its junction with its main stream

alluvial plain *n* **1 :** a level or gently sloping flat or a slightly undulating land surface resulting from extensive deposition of alluvial materials by running water **2 :** a plain formed by lateral coalescence of alluvial fans **:** a piedmont *alluvial plain* — compare BAJADA

alluvial terrace *n* **:** a river terrace composed of alluvium rather than carved in solid rock, resulting from a change in the regimen of the stream from alluviation to downcutting

al·lu·vi·ate \-vē,āt, *usu* -ād·+V\ *vb* -ED/-ING/-S [*alluvium* + *-ate*] *vt* **:** to cover with alluvium ⟨an *alluviated* valley⟩ ~ *vi* **:** to deposit alluvium

al·lu·vi·a·tion \ˌ==ˈāshən\ *n* -s **:** the process that results in deposits of clay, silt, sand, or gravel at places in rivers or estuaries, or along the shores of lakes or seas, where stream velocity is decreased

al·lu·vio \=ˈ==ˌō\ *n, pl* **alluvi·o·nes** \=ˌ==ˈō(ˌ)nēz\ [L] *Roman law* **:** ALLUVION

al·lu·vi·on \=ˈ==ən, -ˌän\ *n* -s [L *alluvion-, alluvio*, fr. *alluere* to wash against (fr. *ad-* + *-luere*, fr. *lavere* to wash) + *-ion-, -io* -ion — more at LYE] **1 :** the wash or flow of water against the shore or bank **2 :** an overflowing **:** INUNDATION, FLOOD **3 :** ALLUVIUM **4 :** an accession to land by the gradual addition of matter by the action of water or sometimes by the gradual reliction of the water from its bank, the land so added belonging to the owner of the land to which it is added; *also* **:** the land so added — compare ACCESSION 2c, ACCRETION 1c

al·lu·vi·ous \-vēəs\ *adj* [LL *alluvius*] **:** ALLUVIAL

al·lu·vi·um \-vēəm\ *n, pl* **alluviums** \-ēəmz\ *or* **allu·via** \-ēə\ [LL, neut. of *alluvius* alluvial, fr. L *alluere*] **:** clay, silt, sand, gravel, or similar detrital material deposited by running water esp. during recent geologic time, the deposits ordinarily occurring on the floodplains of streams or as alluvial fans or cones at places where streams issuing from mountains lose velocity and deposit their contained sediment on a valley floor

all-weather \ˈ=ˈ==\ *adj* **:** of or for all kinds of weather **:** usable, operative, or practiced in all kinds of weather ⟨a good *all-weather* highway⟩ ⟨*all-weather* flying⟩

allwhere *adv* [ME *al wher*, fr. *al* all + *wher* where] *archaic* **:** EVERYWHERE

allwhither \ˈ=ˈ==\ *adv* [²*all* + *whither*] **:** in all directions

¹al·ly \ə'lī, a'lī, 'a,lī; ˈ=ˌ= *is most freq for the form "allied"* — *see* ALLIED\ *vb* -ED/-ING/-S [ME *allien*, fr. OF *alier*, fr. L *alligare* to bind to, fr. *ad-* + *ligare* to bind — more at LIGATURE] *vt* **1 :** to unite or form a connection between (as one family and another by marriage or two or more states by treaty) **:** join in association or alliance — usu. used with *with* or *to* ⟨has *allied* herself to the West to attain certain economic aspirations —*New Republic*⟩ ⟨were so closely *allied* by prewar economic agreements —Alan Valentine⟩ ⟨the powerful family with which he had *allied* himself by marriage⟩ **2 :** to connect or form a relation between (as by likeness, resemblance, or compatibility) **:** ASSOCIATE, RELATE — usu. used with *with* or *to* ⟨the song of the kinglet is the only characteristic that *allies* it to the wrens —John Burroughs⟩ ⟨fear is an unbecoming affliction, *allied* to boasting—Herbert Agar⟩ ⟨functions which are complementary and closely *allied*⟩ ⟨sentiments are *allied* to the desire to achieve new goals —George Wythe⟩ ~ *vi* **:** to form or enter into an alliance ⟨a completely independent country free to choose with whom she would ~⟩ ⟨persuade the nation to ~ with the other democracies⟩ ⟨he again *allied* with his friends —S.L.A.Marshall⟩

²al·ly \'a,lī, ə'lī, a'lī; ˈ=ˌ= *is much more freq than* =ˈ= *for the pl, & somewhat more freq than* =ˈ= *for the sing*\ *n* -ES [ME *allie*, fr. *allien*, v.] **1 a** *obs* **:** KINSMAN, RELATIVE **b :** a plant or animal linked to another by natural genetic or evolutionary relationship ⟨the honey bees and *allies* as well as the more distantly related ants⟩ ⟨ferns and their *allies*⟩ **2 a :** one usu. a sovereign or state united, banded, or associated with another in a common cause or by treaty or league ⟨the duke and his *allies*⟩ ⟨an eastern empire with strong western *allies*⟩ **:** one of the subjects or citizens so united **b allies** *pl, usu cap* **:** the nations allied against the Central Powers in World War I or against the Axis in World War II **3 :** someone or something associated with another as a helper **:** AUXILIARY, SUPPORTER ⟨let the teacher appear always the ~ of the pupil, not his natural enemy —Bertrand Russell⟩ ⟨gained an ~ in organized labor —D.E.Clark⟩ ⟨time is at once the enemy and the ~ of life —F.B.Millett⟩

³ally *var of* ALLEY

-al·ly \(ə)lē, (ə)li\ *adv suffix* [¹*-al* + *-ly*] **:** ²-LY ⟨semantic*ally*⟩ — in adverbs formed from adjectives in *-ic* with no alternative form in *-ical*

all-year \ˈ=ˈ=\ *adj* **:** lasting, available, or suitable throughout the year **:** the whole year round ⟨a healthful *all-year* climate⟩ ⟨an *all-year* resort community⟩

al·lyl \'aləl\ *n* -s [ISV *all-* (fr. L *allium* garlic) + *-yl* — more at ALLIUM] **1 :** an unsaturated univalent radical $CH_2{=}CHCH_2-$ derived from allyl alcohol by removal of the hydroxyl group **2 :** ISOPROPENYL — used with an initial Greek beta ⟨β-*allyl*⟩ — **al·lyl·ic** \ə'lilik, a'-\ *adj*

allyl alcohol *n* **:** a colorless pungent liquid $CH_2{=}CHCH_2OH$ made chiefly by hydrolysis of allyl chloride and polymerized to a viscous substance by heating in the presence of oxygen

allyl aldehyde *n* **:** ACROLEIN

al·lyl·amine \ˌaləl'amēn, ˌalə'la,mēn, ə'liləˌmēn\ *n* -s [ISV *allyl* + *amine*] **:** a pungent strongly basic liquid $CH_2{=}CHCH_2NH_2$ formed variously (as by hydrolysis of allyl isothiocyanate)

al·lyl·ate \'alə,lāt\ *vt* -ED/-ING/-S [*allyl* + *-ate*] **:** to introduce allyl into

al·lyl·a·tion \ˌalə'lāshən\ *n* -s **:** the act or process of allylating

allyl chloride *n* **:** a volatile pungent toxic flammable liquid $CH_2{=}CHCH_2Cl$ made by high-temperature chlorination of propylene and used chiefly in making glycerol and allyl derivatives (as allyl alcohol and allyl resins)

al·lyl·ene \'alə,lēn\ *n* -s [ISV *allyl* + *-ene*] **1 :** METHYLACETYLENE **2 :** ALLENE 1

allylic rearrangement *n* **:** the migration of an ion or radical from one end of a 3-carbon allyl sequence to the other with concurrent shifting of the position of the double bond (as $CH_2{=}CHCHRX{\rightarrow}XCH_2CH{=}CHR$)

allyl isothiocyanate *or* **allyl mustard oil** *n* **:** a colorless pungent irritating liquid ester $CH_2{=}CHCH_2NCS$ that is the chief constituent of mustard oil (sense 1b) and is used as a flavoring agent and as a medical counterirritant

al·lyl·nor·mor·phine \ˌaləlˌnȯr'mȯrˌfēn\ *n* -s [*allyl* + *nor-* + *morphine*] **:** a white crystalline compound $C_{19}H_{21}NO_3$ derived from morphine and used as a respiratory stimulant in poisoning by morphine and similar narcotic drugs — called also *N-allylnormorphine, nalorphine*

allyl resin *or* **allyl plastic** *n* **:** any of a group of thermosetting transparent abrasion-resistant synthetic resins or plastics made usu. from esters derived from allyl alcohol or allyl chloride and used chiefly in making cast products (as sheets) and low-pressure laminated products

allyl starch *n* **:** any of various allyl ethers of starch made from starch and allyl chloride for use in coatings, printing inks, and plastics

al·lyl·thi·ou·rea \ˌaləl,-\ *n* -s [NL, fr. ISV *allyl* + NL *thiourea*] **:** a white crystalline compound $C_3H_5NHCSNH_2$ made from allyl isothiocyanate and ammonia and used in photography esp. as a sensitizing agent — called also *allylthiocarbamide, thiosinamine*

al·ma-ata \ˌalmə·ə'tä\ *adj, usu cap both As* [fr. *Alma-Ata*, U.S.S.R.] **:** of or from Alma-Ata, a city of Soviet Central Asia, U.S.S.R. **:** of the kind or style prevalent in Alma-Ata

almacantar *var of* ALMUCANTAR

al·ma·ci·ga \al'mäsēgə, -ˌgä\ *n* -s [Sp *almáciga* mastic, fr. Ar *al-maṣṭakah* the mastic, fr. Gk *mastichē* — more at MASTIC] **1 :** a tall Philippine timber tree (*Agathis alba*) yielding a dammar resin **2 :** the resin yielded by the almaciga tree

al·ma·ci·go \-ˌgō\ *n* -s [AmerSp *almácigo*, fr. Sp, mastic tree, fr. *almáciga*] *in the West Indies* **:** GUMBO-LIMBO 1

al·ma·gest \'alməˌjest\ *n* -s *sometimes cap* [ME *almageste*, fr. MF & ML, fr. Ar *al-majusṭī* the almagest, fr. *al* the + Gk *megistē* (*syntaxis*) greatest (composition), fem. of *megistos*, superl. of *megas* great — more at MUCH] **:** any of several great early medieval treatises on a branch of knowledge (as the 9th century Arabic translation of Ptolemy's Greek work on astronomy)

almain *sometimes cap, obs var of* ALLEMANDE

al·main rivets \'al,mān-, 'ȯl-\ *n pl* [obs. *Almaine* Germany, fr. ME, fr. MF, fr. LL *Alamannia* land of the Alamanni, fr. *Alamannus* member of the Alamanni + L *-ia*] *archaic* **:** a flexible light armor of overlapping plates sliding on rivets

al·ma ma·ter \ˌalmə'mäd·ə(r), -'mā|, |tə- *also* ˌäl- *or* -mä-\ *n, pl* **alma maters** \-ə(r)z\ *also* **al·mae ma·tres** \ˌal,mī-ˌmä·,trās, ˌäl-, -mā-; ˌal(ˌ)mēˌmā·(ˌ)trēz\ [L, fostering mother (applied as a title to such goddesses as Ceres and Cybele)] **1 :** a school (as a college or university) which one has attended and usu. from which one has graduated **2 :** the song or hymn of a school or college

alman *often cap, obs var of* ALLEMANDE

al·ma·nac *also* **al·ma·nack** \'ȯlməˌnak, 'al- *also* 'äl- *or* -ˌnik\ *n* -s [ME *almenak*, fr. ML *almanach*, prob. fr. Ar *al-manākh* the almanac, calendar] **1 a :** a publication containing astronomical and meteorological data arranged according to the days, weeks, and months of a given year and often including a miscellany of other information **b :** a publication containing statistical, tabular, and general information (as on world events, an individual society, or a religious body) related to a given calendar period, usu. a year ⟨*Nat'l Catholic Almanac*⟩ ⟨*Information Please Almanac*⟩ **c :** a publication containing a collection of useful or otherwise interesting facts or statistics usu. in the form of tables and often covering the period of a given year ⟨*The World Almanac*⟩ **2 :** a publication containing data on royal and titled families of Europe

al·man·dine \'almənˌdēn, -ˌdīn\ *n* -s [alter. (influenced by ML *alamandina*, alter. of *alabandina*, or G *almandin*, fr. ML) of earlier *alabandine*, fr. ME, fr. ML *alabandina, alabandinus*, fr. *Alabanda*, ancient city in Asia Minor where gems were cut and sold + L *-ina, -inus* -ine] **1 :** ALMANDITE **2 :** a violet variety of the ruby spinel or sapphire **3 :** the purple Indian garnet

al·man·dite \'almən,dīt\ *n* -s [alter. (influenced by E *-ite*) of *almandine*] **:** a deep red variety of garnet consisting of an iron aluminum silicate $Fe_3Al_2(SiO_4)_3$

almc *abbr* almanac

al·me·mar \al'mēˌmär\ *or* **al·me·mor** \-ō(ə)r\ *n* -s [Heb *almēmār*, fr. Ar *al-minbar* the pulpit] **:** a platform in a Jewish synagogue bearing the reading desk from which are read the Pentateuch and the Prophets — called also *bema, bimah*

al·men·dro \al'men(ˌ)drō, äl-\ *n* -s [AmerSp, fr. Sp, almond tree, modif. of (assumed) VL *amyndulus*, alter. of L *amygdalus*, fr. Gk *amygdalos*, fr. *amygdalē* almond] **:** MALABAR ALMOND

al·me·ri·an \ˌalmə'rēən\ *adj, usu cap A* [*Almería*, province of Spain + E *-an*] *archaeol* **:** of or relating to Neolithic and Aeneolithic cultures of Almería province, Spain

al·me·ri·ite \ˌalmə'rēˌīt\ *n* -s [Sp *almeriita*, fr. *Almería*, city and province in Spain, its locality + Sp *-ita* -ite] **:** NATROALUNITE

alm·ery \'ämərē, 'alm-\ *n* -ES [ME *almerie, almarie* — more at AMBRY] **:** AMBRY 1a

al·mi·core \'almə,kō(ə)r\ *n* -s [origin unknown] **:** AMBERJACK 1

al·might·i·ly \(ˈ)ȯlˈmīd·əlē, -ītᵊl-, -ᵊli\ *adv* **:** in an almighty manner

al·might·i·ness \-d·|ēnəs, -t|, |i-\ *n* -ES **:** the quality of being almighty

¹al·mighty \(ˈ)ȯlˈmīd·ē, -ītē; *in "God Almighty"* *sometimes* ᵊlˈm-\ *adj* [ME (akin to OHG *alamahtig*, ON *almáttigr*), fr. OE *ælmihtig, ealmihtig*, fr. *æl-, eal-* all (akin to OE *eall* all) + *mihtig* mighty — more at ALL, MIGHTY] **1 a** *often cap* **:** having absolute power over all — used esp. of God **b :** relatively unlimited in power ⟨~ armies swept over the country⟩ **2** *slang* **:** very bad **:** EXTREME ⟨he's in one ~ fix⟩

²almighty \"\ *n* -ES *cap* **:** GOD — used with *the*

³almighty \"\ *adv, slang* **:** EXTREMELY ⟨~ cold⟩ ⟨took an ~ long time to make up his mind⟩

al·mi·que \ˌalmə'kē\ *n* -s [modif. of AmerSp *almiquí*] **:** an acana (*Manilkara albescens*) with hard compact heavy deep red wood

al·mi·rah \al'mīrə\ *n* -s [Hindi *almārī*, fr. Pg *almario, armario*, fr. L *armarium* — more at AMBRY] *India* **:** CABINET, WARDROBE

al·mo·had \'alməˌhad\ *or* **al·mo·hade** \"·,-ˌhād, ˌalmə'hādē\ *n* -s *usu cap* [Ar *al-muwaḥḥid* the Almohad] **:** a member of a Muslim Berber sect and dynasty that established its rule in No. Africa and Spain in the 12th and 13th centuries, opposed anthropomorphic theology, and taught the absolute unity of God

al·moign *or* **al·moin** \(ˈ)alˈmȯin\ *n* -s [ME *almoyn*, fr. AF *almoigne*, fr. (assumed) VL *alemosina* alms — more at ALMONER] **:** FRANKALMOIGN

al·mon \'alˌmōn\ *n* -s [Bisayan] **:** a tall Philippine timber tree (*Shorea eximia*) with soft yellowish white wood — called also *Philippine mahogany*

al·mond \'ämənd, 'a(l)m-,'ȧm- *also* 'älm- *or* 'ȧlm- *sometimes* 'ȯ(l)m-\ *n* -s *often attrib* [ME *almande*, fr. OF, fr. LL *amandula*, alter. of L *amygdala*, fr. Gk *amygdalē*] **1 :** the drupaceous fruit of a small tree (*Prunus amygdalus* syn. *Amygdalus communis*); *esp* **:** the ellipsoidal slightly compressed nutlike stone or kernel of this tree differing from the peach in having a dry instead of pulpy epicarp so that the nut or kernel is really the stone of the fruit — see ALMOND MEAL, AMYGDALIN **2 :** any tree that bears almonds **3 :** the fruit of any one of several trees in shape or flavor somewhat resembling the almond **4 :** any plant that bears almonds (sense 3) — usu. used with a descriptive attributive ⟨Malabar ~⟩ **5 :** an almond flavoring **6 a** *or* **almond brown :** a light grayish yellowish brown that is stronger and slightly redder and darker than gravel — called also *doe, pawnee, wood* **b :** a pale to moderate orange yellow

almond cake *n* **:** the residue of almonds from which the oil has been expressed

almond extract *n* **:** an alcoholic extract of macerated kernels (as of almonds, apricots, or peaches) used for flavoring

almond eye *n* **:** a somewhat triangular obliquely set eye ⟨a beautiful dark-skinned girl with the *almond eyes* of a Mongolian⟩; *specif, of dogs* **:** a slit-shaped eye (as in the bull-terrier) with the outer corner pointing toward the ear

almond green *n* **:** a variable color averaging a moderate yellowish green that is greener and less strong than tarragon, duller than malachite green, and duller and slightly yellower than verdigris

almond-leaved willow \ˈ==ˌ=-\ *n* **:** PEACHLEAF WILLOW

almondlike \ˈ==ˌ=\ *adj* **:** resembling an almond

almond meal *n* **1 :** a powder obtained by grinding or pounding blanched almonds and used as an ingredient of various cosmetics and perfumes **2 :** ground almond cake

almond milk *n* **:** an emulsion (as from blanched almonds, acacia, sugar, and water) used as a demulcent

almond moth *n* **:** a small grayish brown-marked moth (*Cadra cautella*) having a larva that feeds on and mats together with webbing a variety of stored products of vegetable origin — called also *fig moth*

almond oil *n* **1 a :** a colorless or pale yellow bland and nearly odorless nondrying fatty oil expressed from sweet or bitter almonds and used as an emollient in pharmaceuticals and cosmetics and as a lubricant for delicate mechanisms (as in watches) — called also *expressed almond oil, sweet almond oil* **b :** a colorless to yellow essential oil owing its characteristic odor and flavor to benzaldehyde and its toxicity to hydrocyanic acid that is obtained from bitter almonds by steam distillation of almond cake or almond meal after decomposition of the amygdalin present and that is used in medicine (as for certain skin disorders) and after removal of the hydrocyanic acid as a flavoring agent — called also *bitter almond oil* **2 :** any of certain essential oils very similar in properties and uses to bitter almond oil and obtained from kernels other than almonds that contain amygdalin (as apricot and peach kernels) — called also *bitter almond oil* **3 :** BENZALDEHYDE

almond pink *or* **almond blossom** *n* **:** a pale pink

almonds *pl of* ALMOND

almond willow *n* **1 :** an Old World willow (*Salix amygdalina*) that has light green leaves and is cultivated for use in basketry — called also *black Hollander* **2 :** PEACHLEAF WILLOW

almondwood \ˈ==ˌ=\ *n* **:** a dark brown close-textured chittagong wood (*Chickrassia tabularia*) with lustrous surface

al·mondy \-dē\ *adj* **:** like an almond

al·mo·ner \'almənə(r), 'äm-\ *n* -s [ME *aumener*, fr. OF *aumosnier, almosnier*, fr. *aumosne, almosne* alms, fr. (assumed) VL *alemosina*, alter. of LL *eleemosyna* — more at ALMS] **1 :** one that distributes alms **2 :** a onetime official of a monastery or almshouse charged with distributing alms; *also* **:** one that dispenses alms for another ⟨the ~ of a king⟩ **3** *Brit* **:** a social-service worker in a hospital

al·mo·ning \-niŋ\ *n* -s [*almoner* + *-ing*] *Brit* **:** medical social work

al·mon·ry \-nrē\ *n* -ES [MF *almosnerie*, fr. OF, fr. *almosnier* + *-ie* -y] **:** a usu. ecclesiastical building set aside for the distribution of alms

almons *pl of* ALMON

al·mo·ra·vid \ˌalmə'rävəd, al'mȯrəv-\ *or* **al·mo·ra·vide** \ˌ==ˈ=vəd, =ˈ==ˌvīd\ *n* -s *usu cap* [Ar *al-murābiṭ* lit., the inhabitant of a fortified convent] **:** a member of a Muslim dynasty of No. African natives that flourished 1049–1145, led a religious reform along orthodox Islamic lines, and established political dominance over northwestern Africa and Spain

¹al·most \(ˈ)ȯlˈmōst, -ō(ü)ˈm- *also* ˈ=ˌməst\ *adv* [ME *almost, almest*, fr. OE *ealmǣst, ealmǣst*, fr. *al-, eal-* all (akin to OE *eall*) + *mǣst* most — more at ALL, MOST] **1 a :** close to the total of ⟨~ all the warriors were heathens⟩ **:** with few exceptions ⟨~ every man⟩ **b :** by far the greater part of ⟨~ the entire book⟩ **:** excepting only a small or minor section ⟨fire destroyed ~ the whole town⟩ **2 a :** not actually but very close to being **:** not really but deceptively near ⟨a creature ~ human⟩ **b :** what would amount to being ⟨he was after all ~ a failure⟩ **:** what would essentially approximate ⟨he paid ~ nothing for it⟩ **3 :** more than just approximately ⟨~ identical plans of attack⟩ **:** lacking by very little in being exactly ⟨~ half of the money⟩ **:** all but absolutely or utterly ⟨~ unique⟩

²almost \"\ *adj* **:** very close to being a ⟨an ~ bullseye⟩ **:** nearly a ⟨an ~ failure⟩ **:** NEAR

al·mous \'äməs, 'ō-\ *n, pl* **almous** [ME (northern dial.) *almouse, almus, awmus*, fr. ON *almusa, ǫlmusa*, fr. OS *almôsa* or OHG *alamuosan* — more at ALMS] *dial Brit* **:** ALMS

alms \ˈä|mz, ˈà| *also* |lmz; *sporadic & old-fash* ˈamz\ *n, pl* **alms** [ME *almesse, almes*, fr. OE *ælmesse, ælmes*; akin to OS *alamôsa*, MD *aelmoese*, OHG *alamuosan*; all fr. a prehistoric WGmc word borrowed fr. LL *eleemosyna*, fr. Gk *eleēmosynē* pity, alms, fr. *eleos* pity] **1** *archaic* **a :** CHARITY ⟨such virtues as ~ and mercy⟩ **b :** charitable deeds ⟨when thou doest ~, let not thy left hand know what thy right hand doeth —Mt 6:3 (AV)⟩ **2 :** anything given freely to relieve the poor (as money, food, or clothing) **:** a charitable gift — usu. pl. in constr. **3 :** an offering of money received from the congregation during an Anglican religious service and usu. presented at the altar by the minister

alms basin *n* **:** a large plate on which the total offering received at a church service is presented at the altar

alms chest *n* **:** a box with a hole for alms and with three locks

alms·deed \ˈ=ˌ=\ *n* [ME *almesdede*, fr. *almes, almesse* + *dede* deed] **1** *archaic* **:** an act of giving alms ⟨this woman was full of good works and ~*s* —Acts 9:36 (AV)⟩ **2** *obs* **:** habitual practice of giving alms

alms dish *n* **1 :** a dish in which alms are collected **2 :** ALMS BASIN

alms fee *n* [trans. of OE *ælmesfēoh*, fr. *ælmes, ælmesse* alms + *fēoh* fee] **:** PETER'S PENCE

almsgiving \ˈ=ˌ==\ *n* **:** the giving of alms esp. as an habitual practice ⟨remarkably generous in his ~⟩

almshouse \ˈ=ˌ=\ *n* [ME *almeshous*, fr. *almes, almesse* + *hous* house] **1 :** a section of medieval religious houses set aside for distribution of alms **2 a** *Brit* **:** a privately financed home for the poor **b** *archaic* **:** POORHOUSE, WORKHOUSE

alms·man \-zmən\ *n, pl* **alms·men** [ME *almesman*, fr. OE *ælmesman*, fr. *ælmes, ælmesse* + *man*] **:** a recipient of alms

al·mu·can·tar \ˌalmyü'kantə(r)\ *also* **al·ma·can·tar** \-mə-\ *n* -s [alter. (prob. influenced by ML *almucantarath*) of earlier *almicanter*, fr. ME *almicanteras* (pl.), fr. MF *almicantarath*, fr. ML *almicantarath, almucantarath*, fr. Ar *al-muqanṭarāt* the almucantars, fr. *al-* the + *muqanṭarāt*, pl. of *muqanṭarah* almucantar, sundial, fr. *qanṭarah* bridge, arch] **1 :** a small circle of the celestial sphere parallel to the horizon and connecting all points of equal altitude ⟨two stars on the same ~⟩ **2 :** a telescope mounted on a mercurial float and used for observing the heavenly bodies as they cross a given almucantar

almucantar staff *n* **:** an ancient instrument having an arc of 15 degrees and used at sea to take observations of the sun's amplitude and to find the variation of the compass

al·muce \'al,myüs\ *n* -s [MF *almuce, aumuce* — more at AMICE] **:** an ecclesiastical hood lined with fur worn commonly in the pre-Reformation era by canons and also by various other ecclesiastics

al·mud \(ˈ)alˈmüd\ *or* **al·mu·de** \al'müdə\ *n* -s [Sp *almud* & Pg *almude*, fr. Ar *al-mudd*, a dry measure] **:** any of various old Portuguese and Spanish units of capacity varying as a dry measure from about 2 to 21 quarts and as a liquid measure from about 5 to 32 quarts

al·muer·zo \äl'mwer(ˌ)sō\ *n* -s [Sp, fr. (assumed) VL *admordium*, fr. L *admordēre* to bite into, fr. *ad-* + *mordēre* to bite — more at SMART] *Southwest* **:** the first substantial meal of the day taken usu. just before noon

almug *var of* ALGUM

alnage *n* -s [ME *aulnage*, fr. MF, fr. *aulner* to measure by the ell (fr. *aulne* ell, of Gmc origin, akin to OHG *elina* ell) + *-age* — more at ELL] *old Eng law* **:** measurement of cloth by the ell esp. with official inspection and certification; *also* **:** a fee for such measurement

alnager *n* -s [*alnage* + *-er*] **:** a onetime officer in England whose duty it was to inspect and attest the measure and quality of woolen cloth

al·ni·co \'alnə,kō, -nē-; al'ni(,)kō\ *n* -ES [*al*uminum + *ni*ckel + *co*balt] **:** a powerful permanent-magnet alloy containing iron, nickel, aluminum, and one or more of the elements cobalt, copper, and titanium

al·no·ite \'alnə,wīt\ *n* -S [G *alnöit,* fr. *Alnö,* island of Sweden, its locality + G *-it* -ite] **:** a rare basaltic dike rock of the composition of a melilite-basalt having phenocrysts of biotite, augite, and olivine in a groundmass of melilite and augite

al·nus \'alnəs\ *n* [NL, fr. L, alder — more at ALDER] **1** *cap* **:** a genus of alders (family Betulaceae) found in the north temperate zone and the Andes and having toothed leaves, a 4-parted calyx, and a woody conelike fruit **2** -S **:** any plant of the genus *Alnus*

al·o·ca·sia \,alə'kāzh(ē)ə\ *n* [NL, alter. of *Colocasia*] **1** *cap* **:** a genus of tropical Asiatic herbs (family Araceae) with basal long-petioled often showy leaves, a glaucous boat-shaped spathe, and reddish berries **2** -S **:** a plant of the genus *Alocasia*

al·o·cin·ma \,alə'sinmə\ *n, cap* [NL] **:** a genus of Asiatic pulmonate snails (family Helicidae) including a species (*A. longicornis*) which may serve as an intermediate host of the Chinese liver fluke

al·od *or* **al·lod** \'a,läd, 'aləd\ *n* -S [prob. fr. F *alode, allode,* fr. ML *alodium, allodium*] **:** ALODIUM

¹alo·di·al *or* **al·lo·di·al** \ə'lōdēəl, a'-\ *adj* [ML *allodialis,* fr. *allodium* + L *-alis* -al] **:** of or relating to alodium

²alodial *or* **allodial** \"\ *n* -S **:** land or property held in alodium

alo·di·al·ism *or* **al·lo·di·al·ism** \-,lizəm\ *n* -S **:** the alodial system

alo·di·al·ist *or* **al·lo·di·al·ist** \-,ləst\ *n* -S **:** a proprietor holding an alodium

alo·di·al·i·ty *or* **al·lo·di·al·i·ty** \ə,lōdē'alədē, (,)a,l-\ *n* -ES **:** the quality or state of being alodial

alo·di·al·ly *or* **al·lo·di·al·ly** \ə'lōdēəlē, a'-\ *adv* **:** by alodial tenure

alo·di·ary *or* **al·lo·di·ary** \-dē,erē\ *n* -ES [ML *allodiarius,* fr. *allodium* + L *-arius* -ary] **:** one that holds an alodium

alod·i·fi·ca·tion *or* **al·lod·i·fi·ca·tion** \ə,lädəfə'kāshən, (,)a,l-\ *n* -S [*alodium, allodium* + *-fication*] **:** the change in the title to lands from feudal tenure to complete ownership

alo·di·um *or* **al·lo·di·um** \ə'lōdēəm, a'-\ *n* -S [ML, fr. OHG (Franconian) *alōd,* fr. *al* all + *-ōd* property (akin to OE *ēad* property, OS *ōd,* OHG *ōtac* rich, ON *authr* property, Goth *audags* blessed)] **1 :** a form of estate among 11th century Anglo-Saxons in which absolute possession and control were vested in the holder — opposed to *feodum* **2** *usu* *allodium* **:** land that is the absolute property of the owner **:** real estate held in absolute independence without being subject to any rent, service, or acknowledgment to a superior

al·oe *in sense 2* 'al,wē, *in other senses* 'a(,)lō, *pl* 'a(,)lōz *or* 'aləz\ *n* [ME, agalloch, fr. LL, fr. L, dried juice of aloe leaves, fr. Gk *aloē* dried juice of aloe leaves, agalloch, prob. fr. a Sem word akin to Heb *ăhālīm, ăhālōth,* perh. fr. Skt *agaru,* prob. of Dravidian origin; akin to Tamil *akil* agalloch] **1 aloes** *pl* **:** AGALLOCH **2** [NL, fr. ML, aloe plant, fr. L, dried juice of aloe leaves] *cap* **:** a genus of succulent chiefly southern African plants (family Liliaceae) having basal leaves with a hemplike fiber and spicate often showy flowers **3** [ME, fr. ML, fr. L, dried juice of aloe leaves] -S **:** a plant of the genus *Aloe* **4** [ME, fr. L] -S **:** the dried bitter juice of the leaves of a plant of the genus *Aloe* used as a purgative, tonic, and emmenagogue — usu. pl. but sing. in constr. **5** -S **:** any of several plants of the genus *Furcraea* **6** *or* **aloes** *or* **aloes green :** a pale green that is stronger and slightly bluer than celadon gray, yellower and darker than spray green, and yellower, stronger, and slightly lighter than bayberry gray

1 2

an aloe (*Aloe succotrina*): *1* entire plant, *2* single flower

al·oe-em·o·din \,alō'wemədən, ,alō'e-, -dᵊn\ *n* -S **:** an orange-yellow crystalline compound $C_{15}H_{10}O_5$ derived from anthraquinone and obtained from many species of aloes, rhubarb, and senna leaves

aloe hemp *n* **1 :** any plant of the genus *Agave* that yields a hemplike fiber **2 :** BOWSTRING HEMP

al·oe·root \'=(,)=,=\ *n* **:** COLICROOT

al·oes·wood \'=(,)=,=\ *n* **:** AGALLOCH

al·o·et·ic \,alə'wed·ik\ *adj* [*aloe* + *-etic* (as in *diuretic*)] **:** using, consisting of, containing, or belonging to aloes ⟨~ medicines⟩

al·oe·wood \'=(,)=,=\ *n* **:** GEIGER TREE

¹aloft \ə'lȯft *also* -äft\ *adv* [ME *aloft, alofte* fr. ON *ā lopt, ā lopti,* fr. *ā* on, in + *lopt, lopti,* acc. & dat. respectively of *lopt* air, sky — more at ON, LOFT] **1 a :** in the higher atmosphere above the earth ⟨weather conditions ~ are poor⟩ **b :** at a relatively great height **:** high up ⟨huge black buzzards hovered ~ —H.E.Rieseberg⟩ **2 a :** up into the air **:** away from or off the ground ⟨the air is filled with dust whirled ~ —P.E. James⟩ **b :** upward from an inferior position or from a depressing mood ⟨this happy news sent their spirits soaring ~⟩ **c :** in the air; *esp* **:** in flight (as of an airplane) ⟨an airline famous for the wonderful meals served ~⟩ **3** *naut* **:** at, on, or to the masthead or the higher rigging ⟨going ~ to unfurl the lighter sails —H.A.Chippendale⟩ **4** *archaic* **:** on or at the top ⟨a ladder with a man ~⟩

²aloft *prep* [ME *alofte,* fr. *alofte,* adv.] **1** *obs* **:** on the top of **2** *obs* **:** ABOVE, OVER ⟨they bear her still ~ men's heads —George Chapman⟩

alo·gi \(')ā'lō,gī, -lä-,-lō-\ *n pl, usu cap* [ML, fr. LGk *Alogoi,* pl. of *Alogos* (after Gk *alogos* absurd, speechless), fr. Gk *a-* ²a- + *logos* word of God, word, reason — more at LEGEND] **:** the early opponents of the Logos doctrine expressed in the Gospel of John and in the book of Revelation

alo·gia \(')ā'lōj(ē)ə\ *n* -S [NL, fr. LL, fr. Gk, fr. *alogos* speechless, absurd (fr. *a-* ²a- + *logos* word, reason) + *-ia*] **:** inability to speak esp. when caused by a brain lesion

alo·gi·an \(')ā'lāgēən, -lō-,-lō-\ *n* -S *usu cap* **:** one of the Alogi

alog·i·cal \(')ā'läjəkəl, -ēk-\ *adj* [²a- + *logical*] **:** outside the bounds of that to which logic can apply — **alog·i·cal·ly** \-k(ə)lē, -li\ *adv*

al·o·gism \'alə,jizəm\ *n* -S [LL *alogia* unreasonableness (fr. Gk, fr. *a-* ²a- + *-logia* -logy) + E *-ism*] **1 :** anything that is contrary or indifferent to logic; *specif* **:** an irrational statement or piece of reasoning **2 :** a view that denies to thought a place in the valid and final apprehension of reality

alo·ha \ə'lōə, ä'-,ə'-,ä'-; ä'lō,hä, ä'lō,hä, ə'-, a'-\ *n* -S [Hawaiian] **:** LOVE, AFFECTION, KINDNESS — often used to express greeting or farewell

aloha party *n* **:** a farewell party (as in Hawaii); *also* **:** a party to welcome newcomers or visitors (as to Hawaii)

aloha shirt *n* **:** a loose brightly colored Hawaiian sport shirt

al·o·in \'aləwən\ *n* -S [*aloe* + *-in*] **:** a bitter yellow crystalline cathartic obtained from the aloe and containing one or more glycosides (as barbaloin and isobarbaloin) and used for the same purposes as aloes

alo·isi·ite \,alə'wi,shīt, -wis(h)ē,īt\ *n* -S [Prince Luigi (*Aloisius*) Amedeo †1933 duke of the Abruzzi + E *-ite*] **:** a mineral consisting of a hydrous subsilicate of calcium, ferrous iron, magnesium, and sodium occurring in amorphous brown-to-violet masses

alo·ma \ə'lōmə\ *n* -S [origin unknown] **:** a light brown to yellowish brown that is darker than bran and duller than pablo

alombrado *usu cap, var of* ALUMBRADO

¹alone \ə'lōn\ *adj* [ME *alon, alone,* fr. *al* all + *on, one* one] **1 a :** separated esp. physically from all other individuals or groups **:** ISOLATED ⟨the girl, intently listening, was ~ with her fear —G.D.Brown⟩ — usu. used predicatively or postpositively **b :** away from others of one's own kind ⟨~ except for his new gun and Ned, the setter —S.V.Benét⟩ **2 a :** exclusive of anyone or anything else **:** without anyone or anything else **:** ONLY ⟨Jack ~ arrived⟩ ⟨learning ~ produces not a university but a research institute —J.B.Conant⟩ **b :** considered apart and without reference to anyone or anything else ⟨in that country ~ 20 million bushels were produced⟩ **c :** lacking relative, friend, or helper ⟨a widow ~ in the world⟩ **d :** lacking the presence or support of those that are congenial to one's interests, temperament, viewpoint, or way of life ⟨~ in a crowded room⟩ **e :** lacking those that share one's situation ⟨he was not ~ in his ignorance⟩ **3 a :** lacking an equal or rival **:** INCOMPARABLE ⟨Hercules stood ~ in strength⟩ **b :** possessing radically distinctive qualities not found in others **:** UNIQUE ⟨of all the suggestions advanced, this theory is altogether ~ in its penetration of the problem⟩ **c :** acting without the influence or contribution of other factors ⟨that job ~ will take all your time⟩

syn SOLITARY, LONELY, LONESOME, LONE, LORN, FORLORN, DESOLATE may all refer to situations of being apart from others or emotions experienced while apart. In addition to indicating the physical fact of being apart, ALONE, less rich in suggestion than the other words, may connote feelings of isolation from others ⟨the captain of a ship at sea is a remote, inaccessible creature, something like a prince of a fairy tale, *alone* of his kind —Joseph Conrad⟩ SOLITARY may indicate a state of being apart that is desired and sought for ⟨Netta loved these *solitary* interludes . . . she could dream things there and tell herself stories there, untroubled —J.C.Powys⟩ It may lack connotation ⟨being *solitary* he could only address himself to the waiter —Virginia Woolf⟩ It may be used in indicating sadness at a lack of close intimate connections ⟨an only child, he was left *solitary* by the early death of his mother, Susan Sturgis, whose loss he felt severely —J.F.Fulton⟩ Sometimes LONELY simply indicates the fact of being alone ⟨he was *lonely,* but not in an unhappy sense . . . it was no hardship for him to be alone —H.S.Canby⟩ Sometimes it indicates a sense of isolation, often from intimate relatives or friends ⟨his grim look, his pride, his silence, his wild outbursts of passion, left William *lonely* even in his court —J.R.Green⟩ It may apply to feelings of deep sorrow and bereavement ⟨he felt more *lonely* and forsaken than at any time since his father's death —Archibald Marshall⟩ LONESOME, often more poignant, suggests sadness after a separation or bereavement ⟨you must keep up your spirits, mother, and not be *lonesome* when I'm not at home —Charles Dickens⟩ ⟨her flight . . . yet smote my *lonesome* heart more than all misery —P.B.Shelley⟩ LONE may indicate the mere fact of being alone ⟨in his *lone* course the shepherd oft will pause —William Wordsworth⟩ It may indicate a lack of close relatives ⟨the mother's dead and I reckon it's got no father; it's a *lone* thing —George Eliot⟩ LORN, now humorous or literary, suggests recent separation or bereavement ⟨when *lorn* lovers sit and droop —W.M.Praed⟩ FORLORN indicates dejection, woe, and listlessness at separation from someone dear ⟨as *forlorn* and stupefied as I was when my husband's spirit flew away —Thomas Hardy⟩ ⟨as *forlorn* as King Lear at the end of his days —G.W.Johnson⟩ DESOLATE is most extreme in suggesting inconsolable grief at loss or bereavement ⟨fatherless, a *desolate* orphan —S.T.Coleridge⟩ ⟨for her false mate has fled and left her *desolate* —P.B.Shelley⟩ SOLITARY, LONELY, LONESOME, and DESOLATE are applied to places and locations more than the other words are. SOLITARY may be applied either to that which is apart from things similar or to that which is uninhabited or unvisited by human beings ⟨a *solitary* chamber, or rather a cell, at the top of the house, and separated from all the other apartments by a gallery and staircase —Mary W. Shelley⟩ LONELY may be applied to what is either far apart from things similar and seldom visited or to that which is inhabited by only one person or group and conducive to loneliness ⟨heard not only in the towns but even in *lonely* farmhouses —Sherwood Anderson⟩ LONESOME has much the same suggestion. DESOLATE indicates either that a place is abandoned by people or that it is so barren and wild as never to have attracted them ⟨as if nothing had life by day, in that lifeless *desolate* spot —Anthony Trollope⟩

²alone \"\ *adv* [ME *alon, alone,* fr. *al* all + *on, one* one] **:** SOLELY, SIMPLY, EXCLUSIVELY; *often* **:** without the aid or support of another ⟨the proof does not rest ~ on that statement⟩ ⟨he said he could do it ~⟩

alonely *adv* [ME *alonly,* fr. *al* all + *only*] *obs* **:** ²ALONE

alone·ness *n* -ES **:** the state of being alone

¹along \ə'lȯŋ *also* -äŋ\ *prep* [ME, fr. OE *andlang, ondlang,* fr. *and-, ond-* against + *lang* long — more at ANTE-, LONG] **1 :** over the length of (a surface) ⟨he crawled ~ the fence until he reached the gate⟩ ⟨halfway ~ the street they stopped⟩ **2 :** in the course of (as time or distance) ⟨somewhere ~ the years —Ben Riker⟩ **3 :** in a line parallel with the length or direction of ⟨a ship sailing ~ the coast⟩ or on a line through the center or central axis of ⟨the boundary runs ~ the road⟩ — distinguished from *across* **4 :** in accordance with **:** IN ⟨research ~ certain specific lines —R.E.Barnaby⟩

²along \"\ *adv* [ME, fr. *along,* prep] **1 a :** onward with progressive movement **:** FORWARD, AHEAD, ON ⟨hurrying their education ~⟩ ⟨you'll see the hill as you ride ~⟩ ⟨rushing ~ through the speech⟩ — see COME ALONG, GET ALONG, GO ALONG **b :** on the way **:** OFF ⟨send a gift ~ to a friend⟩ **2 a :** in a line parallel with the length or direction — usu. used with *by* ⟨cottages ~ by the river⟩ **b :** down the line **:** from one to another ⟨word was passed ~ that the attack was coming⟩ **3 a** *obs* **:** at full length **:** LENGTHWISE ⟨Saul fell straightway all ~ on the earth —1 Sam 28:20 (AV)⟩ ⟨there lay he stretched ~ like a wounded knight —Shak.⟩ **b :** for the whole length — used with *all* ⟨the wall had crumbled all ~⟩; *specif* **:** with the thread stitches of a book passed direct from two opposed kettle stitches — used with *all* ⟨to handsew a book or section all ~⟩ **4 a :** in company or as company **:** as a companion ⟨he brought his wife ~⟩ — often used with *with* ⟨walking the fields ~ with his dog⟩ **b :** in association or accord — used with *with* ⟨working ~ with his colleagues⟩ **5 a :** at a loosely fixed point within a specified or implied extent of time, distance, or development — usu. used with *about* ⟨~ about the time the first leaves fall —*Saturday Rev.*⟩ ⟨~ about July 25⟩ **b :** at or to an advanced point; *esp* **:** at or to a point marked by a notable passage of time, increase of distance, or furtherance of development ⟨the morning was well ~⟩ ⟨farther ~ toward the goalpost⟩ ⟨plans are now far ~⟩ **c :** during the whole period **:** all the time — used with *all* ⟨the police knew all ~ who was guilty⟩ **6 :** in addition **:** ALSO ⟨food was sent to them and clothing went ~ in the package⟩ — often used with *with* ⟨a bill came ~ with the merchandise⟩ **7 :** in possession **:** at hand **:** as part of the equipment **:** as a necessary item, part, or feature ⟨the sheriff had his gun ~⟩ — often used with *with* ⟨a plane carrying heavy radar equipment ~ with full fuel tanks⟩ **8 :** in company **:** on hand **:** THERE ⟨sorry you weren't ~⟩ ⟨tell him I'll be ~ to see him⟩

along of *prep* [ME *along* (construed with *on*), alter. of *ilong* (construed with *on*), fr. OE *gelang* (construed with *on, æt*), fr. *ge-,* associative prefix + *lang* long — more at CO-, LONG] **1** *dial* **:** because of **:** on account of ⟨it's all *along of* mother leaving us like this —Joseph Conrad⟩ **2** *dial* **a :** WITH ⟨you come in here *along of* me —Richard Llewellyn⟩ **b :** TO ⟨they belong *along of* Snug here —G.A.Chamberlain⟩

¹alongshore \=¦=¦=\ *adv (or adj)* [¹*along* + *shore*] **:** along the shore or coast ⟨~ currents⟩ ⟨there are many trees ~⟩

²alongshore \=¦=¦=\ *n* -S **:** WATERFRONT

¹alongside \=¦=¦=\ *adv* [¹*along* + *side*] **1 :** along the side **:** in parallel position ⟨a small cabin with logs piled ~⟩ **2 :** in company **:** at the side **:** close to ⟨a guard with his prisoner ~⟩

²alongside \"\ *prep* **1 a :** along the side of **:** at the side of or parallel to ⟨the tug drew up ~ the freighter⟩ **b :** in combination or company with **:** along with ⟨a pleasure to work ~ such men⟩ **2 :** in a position or manner comparable with ⟨a new writer who takes his place ~ the best⟩

alongside of *prep* **1 a :** side by side with **:** parallel to ⟨a car parked *alongside of* the curb⟩ **b :** in company with **:** at the side of ⟨the son fought *alongside of* his father⟩ **2 :** in comparison with ⟨a player who can stand up well *alongside of* the best⟩

alongst \ə'lȯŋ(k)st, -äŋ-, -ŋzt\ *adv or prep* [ME *alongest,* alter. of *alonges,* alter. (influenced by *-es* -s) of *along*] *dial* **:** ALONG

alon·soa \ə'länzəwə, -n(t)sə-\ *n, cap* [NL, fr. Zanoni *Alonso* *fl* 1798 Sp. official at Bogotá, Colombia] **:** a genus of often shrubby tropical American plants (family Scrophulariaceae) with showy red flowers in terminal racemes

¹aloof \ə'lüf\ *adv* [¹*a* + *loof,* var. of *luff* (side of a ship)] **1** *obs* **:** to windward ⟨keeping the ship ~⟩ **2** *archaic* **a :** from a distance ⟨barely visible, the mountains loomed up ~⟩ **b :** at a distance ⟨trying to keep failure ~⟩

²aloof \"\ *adj* **:** removed or distant either physically or spiritually and usu. by choice and with indifference to the feelings, opinions, or interests of others **:** APART, REMOTE ⟨he stood ~ from worldly success —John Buchan⟩ ⟨holding herself ~ in chosen loneliness —P.E.More⟩ ⟨a severe, ~ building —Green Peyton⟩ ⟨the ~ composer neither worried nor cared about public opinion —Mary Jane Matz⟩ **syn** see INDIFFERENT

³aloof *prep, obs* **:** away from **:** clear from

aloofly *adv* **:** in an aloof manner

aloof·ness *n* -ES **:** the quality or state of being aloof

al·o·pe·cia \,alə'pēsh(ē)ə\ *n* -S [alter. of ME *allopicia, allopucia* baldness, leprosy, fr. L *alopecia* baldness, fr. Gk *alōpekia* baldness, mange on foxes, fr. *alōpek-, alōpēx* fox + *-ia* — more at VULPINE] **:** loss of the hair, wool, or feathers **:** BALDNESS — **al·o·pe·cic** \¦==¦=sik\ *adj*

alopecia ar·e·a·ta \-,arē'ād·ə, -ē'ä-\ *n* [NL, circumscribed baldness] **:** sudden loss of hair in circumscribed patches accompanied by little or no inflammation

alop·e·coid \ə'läpə,kȯid\ *adj* [Gk *alōpekoeidēs,* fr. *alōpek-, alōpēx* fox + *-oeidēs* -oid] **:** like a fox **:** VULPINE

alop·e·cu·rus \ə,läpə'kyürəs, ,alәpə-\ *n, cap* [NL, fr. Gk *alōpekouros* beard grass (*Polypogon monspeliensis*), fr. *alōpek-, alōpēx* fox + *-ouros* -urous] **:** a genus of grasses found in temperate regions and having slender culms, flat leaves, and soft spikes — see MEADOW FOXTAIL

alo·pex \ə'lō,peks, 'alə,p-\ *n, cap* [NL, fr. Gk *alōpēx* fox — more at VULPINE] **:** a genus (family Canidae) comprising the arctic foxes

alo·pi·as \ə'lōpēəs\ *n, cap* [NL, modif. of Gk *alōpekias* thresher shark] **:** a monotypic genus of elasmobranch fishes that comprises the thresher sharks and is usu. included in the Lamnidae but sometimes made the type and sole representative of a separate family

al·o·rese \¦alə¦rēz, -ēs\ *n, pl* **alorese** *cap* [*Alor* island, Indonesia + E *-ese*] **:** an Indonesian native or resident of Alor Island in the Lesser Sundas, Indonesia

alo·sa \ə'lōsə\ *n, cap* [NL, fr. LL *alosa, alausa*] **:** a genus of fishes (family Clupeidae) comprising the shads

al·ou·at·ta \,alə'wad·ə\ *n, cap* [NL, fr. F *alouate*] **:** a genus of monkeys comprising the howler monkeys

al·ou·atte \¦alə¦wat\ *n* -S [F *alouate,* of Cariban origin; akin to Galibi *aluáta,* Cumanagoto *araguata*] **:** HOWLER MONKEY

aloud \ə'laud\ *adv* [ME, fr. ¹*a-* + *loud*] **1** *archaic* **:** LOUDLY ⟨singing ~ with joy⟩ **2 :** not in a whisper or undertone **:** with the distinctly audible normal speaking voice ⟨say it ~ — nobody will hear you⟩; *specif, of reading* **:** with visual scanning of words accompanied by their distinctly audible vocal utterance

aloun-aloun *var of* ALUN-ALUN

à l'outrance *var of* À OUTRANCE

¹alow *or* **alowe** \ə'lō\ *adv* [¹*a* + *low* (blaze)] *dial Brit* **:** AFIRE

²alow \"\ *adv* [ME, fr. ¹*a* + *low*] **:** in or to a lower part **:** BELOW ⟨work ~ and aloft was to my liking —Roland Barker⟩

alo·ys·ia \,alə'wish(ē)ə\ *n* -S [NL, after María Luisa (*Aloysia*) Teresa †1819 wife of Charles IV of Spain] **:** LEMON VERBENA

¹alp \'alp\ *n* -S [ME *alpe*] *dial Eng* **:** BULLFINCH

²alp \'alp, 'aùp\ *n* -S [back-formation fr. *Alps,* mountain system of Europe, fr. ME *Alpes,* fr. L] **1 :** a high rugged mountain resembling topographically those in the Alps of Europe **2 :** something comparable to or suggesting comparison with an alp in height, size, or ruggedness ⟨intellectual ~s⟩ **3** [G, fr. MHG *albe,* pl. *alben,* fr. OHG *albūn, Alpūn* alps, fr. L *Alpes*] **:** a mountain pasture or mountain meadowland

al·paca \al'pakə, *attrib* (')al¦p-\ *n* -S [Sp, fr. Aymara *allpaca*] **1 :** an animal like a llama with fine long woolly hair domesticated in Peru and adjacent countries being possibly a variety of the guanaco **2 a :** the usu. brown or black or sometimes white woolly undercoat of the alpaca used in yarns and fabrics **b :** shearlings of alpaca **3 a :** a fine lightweight cloth of plain weave made of the hair of the alpaca often mixed with other fibers; *also* **:** any of various cotton or rayon imitations of this cloth **b :** a garment (as a coat) made of this cloth

alpaca 1

al·par·ga·ta \,alpə(r)'gäd·ə\ *n* -S [Sp, alter. of *alpargate,* fr. Ar dial. (Spain) *al-parghāt,* pl. of *al-parghah* the sandal, fr. Ar *al* the + *parghah* sandal, fr. Sp *abarca*] **:** ESPADRILLE

al·peen \'alpēn, əl-\ *n* -S [IrGael *ailpīn*] *Irish* **:** CUDGEL

al·pen·glow \'alpən,glō\ *n* -S [prob. part trans. of G *Alpenglühen,* fr. *Alpen* Alps + *glühen* glow] **:** a reddish glow or sometimes the entire series of light phenomena seen near sunset or sunrise on the summits of mountains; *specif* **:** a reillumination sometimes observed after the summits have passed into shadow and supposed to be due to a refraction of the light rays from the west resulting from the cooling of the air

al·pen·horn \'alpən,hȯrn, -ō(ə)n\ *or* **alpine horn** *n* -S [G, fr. *Alpen* Alps (fr. OHG *Albūn,* fr. L *Alpes*) + *horn* — more at HORN] **:** a straight wooden horn 7 to 15 feet in length with an upturned bell and a cupped mouthpiece used by Swiss herdsmen

alpenhorn

al·pen·stock \'alpən,stäk\ *n* -S [G, fr. *Alpen* Alps + *stock* staff, fr. OHG *stoc* — more at STOCK] **:** a long iron-pointed staff used in mountain climbing

al·pes·trine \(')al¦pestrən\ *adj* [ML *alpestris* mountainous (fr. L *Alpes* Alps) + E *-ine*] **:** growing at high elevations but not above the timber line **:** SUBALPINE

¹al·pha \'alfə, 'aùf-\ *n* -S [ME, fr. L, fr. Gk, fr. a Phoenician word akin to Heb *āleph,* lit., ox] **1 :** the first letter of the Greek alphabet — symbol Α or α; see ALPHABET table **2 :** the first (as in sequence, order, classification) **:** BEGINNING ⟨the *Alpha* and the Omega, the first and the last, the beginning and the end —Rev 22:13 (RSV)⟩ — compare OMEGA **3 :** an alpha particle or alpha ray

²alpha *or* **α-** \"\ *adj* **1 :** of or relating to one of two or more closely related chemical substances ⟨α-yohimbine⟩ — used somewhat arbitrarily to specify ordinal relationship or to specify a particular physical form, esp. an allotropic modification (as in α-iron), or an isomeric or sometimes polymeric or stereoisomeric form (as in α-D-glucose); abbr. sometimes *a-* **2 :** first in position from or closest in the structure of an organic molecule to a particular group or atom or having a structure characterized by such a position ⟨the ~ positions of furan⟩ ⟨α-amino acids⟩ ⟨α-naphthol⟩ **3 :** producing green pigment when grown on blood media — used of certain hemolytic streptococci **4 :** first in order of brightness — used of a star in a constellation

alpha and omega *n* [so called with reference to Rev 1:8, fr. alpha and omega's being respectively the first and last letter of the Greek alphabet] **1 :** the beginning and ending **2 :** the principal element **:** the most important feature ⟨wheat is the *alpha and omega* of their diet —T.H.Fielding⟩

¹al·pha·bet \'alfə,bet, 'aùf- *also* -,bət; *often* -d·+V\ *n* -S [ME *alphabete,* fr. LL *alphabetum,* irreg. fr. Gk *alphabētos,* fr. *alpha* + *bēta,* the first two letters of the Gk alphabet — more at BETA] **1 a :** any particular set of letters with which one or more languages are written; *esp* **:** such a set of letters arranged in a customary order — see LETTER **b :** any set of characters with which one or more languages are written whether these characters are letters (sense 1a), the signs of a syllabary, or other basic units of writing **c :** a set of the letters of an alphabet written, engraved, printed, or otherwise represented in some particular form or style, usu. one in which the characters are considered to have an artistic uniformity with one another

ALPHABET TABLE

Showing the letters of five non-Roman alphabets and the transliterations used in the etymologies

HEBREW[1,4]

Letter	Name	Transliteration
א	aleph	ʼ [2]
ב	beth	b, bh
ג	gimel	g, gh
ד	daleth	d, dh
ה	he	h
ו	waw	w
ז	zayin	z
ח	heth	ḥ
ט	teth	ṭ
י	yodh	y
כ ך	kaph	k, kh
ל	lamedh	l
מ ם	mem	m
נ ן	nun	n
ס	samekh	s
ע	ayin	ʻ
פ ף	pe	p, ph
צ ץ	sadhe	ṣ
ק	qoph	q
ר	resh	r
שׂ	sin	ś
שׁ	shin	sh
ת	taw	t, th

ARABIC[3,4]

Alone	Joined to preceding	Joined to both	Joined to following	Name	Transliteration
ا	ـا	[5]		alif	
ب	ـب	ـبـ	بـ	bā	b
ت	ـت	ـتـ	تـ	tā	t
ث	ـث	ـثـ	ثـ	thā	th
ج	ـج	ـجـ	جـ	jīm	j
ح	ـح	ـحـ	حـ	ḥā	ḥ
خ	ـخ	ـخـ	خـ	khā	kh
د	ـد			dāl	d
ذ	ـذ			dhāl	dh
ر	ـر			rā	r
ز	ـز			zāy	z
س	ـس	ـسـ	سـ	sīn	s
ش	ـش	ـشـ	شـ	shīn	sh
ص	ـص	ـصـ	صـ	ṣād	ṣ
ض	ـض	ـضـ	ضـ	ḍād	ḍ
ط	ـط	ـطـ	طـ	ṭā	ṭ
ظ	ـظ	ـظـ	ظـ	ẓā	ẓ
ع	ـع	ـعـ	عـ	ʻayn	ʻ
غ	ـغ	ـغـ	غـ	ghayn	gh
ف	ـف	ـفـ	فـ	fā	f
ق	ـق	ـقـ	قـ	qāf	q
ك	ـك	ـكـ	كـ	kāf	k
ل	ـل	ـلـ	لـ	lām	l
م	ـم	ـمـ	مـ	mīm	m
ن	ـن	ـنـ	نـ	nūn	n
ه	ـه	ـهـ	هـ	hā	h[6]
و	ـو			wāw	w
ى	ـى	ـيـ	يـ	yā	y

GREEK[7]

Letter	Name	Transliteration
Α α	alpha	a
Β β	beta	b
Γ γ	gamma	g, n
Δ δ	delta	d
Ε ε	epsilon	e
Ζ ζ	zeta	z
Η η	eta	ē
Θ θ	theta	th
Ι ι	iota	i
Κ κ	kappa	k
Λ λ	lambda	l
Μ μ	mu	m
Ν ν	nu	n
Ξ ξ	xi	x
Ο ο	omicron	o
Π π	pi	p
Ρ ρ	rho	r, rh
Σ σ ς	sigma	s
Τ τ	tau	t
Υ υ	upsilon	y, u
Φ φ	phi	ph
Χ χ	chi	ch
Ψ ψ	psi	ps
Ω ω	omega	ō

RUSSIAN[8]

А а	a
Б б	b
В в	v
Г г	g
Д д	d
Е е	e
Ж ж	zh
З з	z
И и Й й	i, ĭ
К к	k
Л л	l
М м	m
Н н	n
О о	o
П п	p
Р р	r
С с	s
Т т	t
У у	u
Ф ф	f
Х х	kh
Ц ц	ts
Ч ч	ch
Ш ш	sh
Щ щ	shch
Ъ ъ[9]	”
Ы ы	y
Ь ь[10]	’
Э э	e
Ю ю	yu
Я я	ya

SANSKRIT[11]

अ	a	ञ	ñ
आ	ā	ट	ṭ
इ	i	ठ	ṭh
ई	ī	ड	ḍ
उ	u	ढ	ḍh
ऊ	ū	ण	ṇ
ऋ	ṛ	त	t
ॠ	ṝ	थ	th
ऌ	ḷ	द	d
ॡ	ḹ	ध	dh
ए	e	न	n
ऐ	ai	प	p
ओ	o	फ	ph
औ	au	ब	b
ं[12]	ṁ	भ	bh
ः[13]	ḥ	म	m
क	k	य	y
ख	kh	र	r
ग	g	ल	l
घ	gh	व	v
ङ	ṅ	श	ś
च	c	ष	ṣ
छ	ch	स	s
ज	j	ह	h
झ	jh		

1 See HEBREW ALPHABET and ALEPH, BETH, etc., in Vocab. Where two forms of a letter are given, the second one is the form used at the end of a word. 2 Not represented in transliteration when initial. 3 See ARABIC ALPHABET. In this table the first form given for each letter is used when it stands alone, the second when it is joined to the preceding letter, the third when it is joined to both the preceding and the following letter, and the fourth when it is joined to the following letter only. Many of the letters also have other forms which are used only in certain combinations; the number and nature of these differ from one style of handwriting or font of type to another. 4 The Hebrew and Arabic letters are all primarily consonants; a few of them are also used secondarily to represent certain vowels, but full indication of vowels, when provided at all, is by means of a system of dots or strokes adjacent to the consonantal characters. 5 Alif represents no sound in itself, but is used principally as a bearer of the hamza (transliterated ʼ medially and finally; not represented in transliteration when initial) and as the sign of a long *a*. 6 When ه has two dots above it (ة), it is called *tā marbūta* and, if it immediately precedes a vowel, is transliterated *t* instead of *h*. 7 See ALPHA, BETA, GAMMA, etc., in Vocab. The letter gamma is transliterated *n* only before velars; the letter upsilon is transliterated *u* only as the final element in diphthongs. 8 See CYRILLIC ALPHABET in Vocab. 9 This sign indicates that the immediately preceding consonant is not palatalized even though immediately followed by a palatal vowel. 10 This sign indicates that the immediately preceding consonant is palatalized even though not immediately followed by a palatal vowel. 11 The alphabet shown here is the Devanagari. When vowels are combined with preceding consonants they are indicated by various strokes or hooks instead of by the signs here given, or, in the case of short *a*, not written at all. Thus the character क represents *ka;* the character का, *kā;* the character कि, *ki;* the character की, *kī;* the character कु, *ku;* the character कू, *kū;* the character कृ, *kṛ;* the character कॄ, *kṝ;* the character के, *ke;* the character कै, *kai;* the character को, *ko;* the character कौ, *kau;* and the character क्, *k* without any following vowel. There are also many compound characters representing combinations of two or more consonants. 12 See ANUSVARA. 13 See VISARGA.

⟨a script ~⟩ ⟨a book printed in an old style ~⟩ **d :** the set of speech sounds that any particular language employs — not in technical use **e :** a series of words, paragraphs, stanzas of verse, or other units of composition the successive members of which have as their initial letters the letters of the alphabet in order or which deal with topics of which the initial letters of the names correspond to the letters of the alphabet in order; *specif* **:** an alphabetic acrostic poem **f :** the alphabetic system of writing as distinguished from syllabic, ideographic, and other systems — used with *the* ⟨the birthplace of the ~⟩ **g :** a series of words, phrases, names, or other units arranged in alphabetical order ⟨the entries in this dictionary are all in one ~⟩ **h :** any system of signs or signals, visual, auditory, or tactile, that serve as equivalents for the usual written letters of an alphabet ⟨the ~ used in spelling words for the deaf⟩ ⟨the dots and dashes of the telegraphic ~⟩ **i :** a particular set of names used to designate the various letters of an alphabet ⟨the pronouncing ~ used in civil aviation⟩ **j** *cryptology* **:** a set of one-to-one equivalences between a sequence of plaintext letters and the sequence of their cipher substitutes; *sometimes* **:** one of these sequences — called also *substitution alphabet;* see VIGENÈRE CIPHER **2 :** the simplest rudiments **:** ELEMENTS, ABC ⟨the very ~ of our law —T.B.Macaulay⟩ **3** *obs* **a :** an index alphabetically arranged **b :** a complete or long series

²alphabet \"\ *vt* -ED/-ING/-S **:** ALPHABETIZE

al·pha·be·tar·i·an \\ˌ==ˌbə'ta(a)rēən\ *n* -S **:** a learner or student of the alphabet **:** ABECEDARIAN

alphabet block *n* **:** a cubical block of wood, plastic, or other material having letters of the alphabet on some of the sides, a set of which constitutes a toy for young children

alphabet book *n* **:** a book for teaching the alphabet

al·pha·bet·ic \\¦==¦bed·ik, -etik, -ēk\ *or* **al·pha·bet·i·cal** \-ə̇kəl, -ēk-\ *adj* **1 :** of or belonging to an alphabet or alphabets in general **2 :** written in an alphabet **:** employing an alphabet ⟨an ~ inscription⟩ ⟨an ~ language⟩ **3 :** employing letters that by and large represent single phonemes ⟨an ~ system of writing⟩ **4 :** arranged, subdivided, or proceeding according to the order of the letters of the alphabet ⟨an ~ sequence⟩ **5 a :** fulfilling the function of a letter of an alphabet ⟨an ~ character⟩ **b :** characteristic of a letter of an alphabet ⟨a sign having ~ value⟩ **6 :** frequently designated esp. in informal and unofficial use by a shortened name consisting of the initial letters of the several words that constitute the full official name ⟨~ government agencies⟩

alphabetical code *n* **:** ONE-PART CODE

al·pha·bet·i·cal·ly \-ə̇k(ə)lē, -ēk-, -li\ *adv* **1 :** according to an arrangement or procedure based on alphabetical order **2 :** in an alphabetic method

al·pha·bet·i·co-classed catalog \\¦==¦=ə̇ˌkō,-\ *n* **:** a subject catalog in which main divisions are ordinarily arranged in some logically progressive order and subdivisions alphabetically

al·pha·bet·ics \\ˌ==¦=iks, -ēks\ *n pl but sing in constr* **:** the science dealing with the representation of spoken sounds by means of letters

al·pha·bet·i·form \\¦==¦=əˌfȯrm\ *adj* [*alphabet* + *-iform*] **:** having the form of an alphabet **:** resembling letters — used specif. of certain figures on rocks of the cave period in Europe

al·pha·bet·ism \'==ˌbəˌtizəm, -ˌbəd·ˌiz-, -ˌbed·ˌiz-\ *n* -S **:** the use of letters as symbols: **a :** the representation of speech sounds by vowel and consonantal rather than syllabic signs **b :** the use of groups of letters (as ABC or XYZ) as a signature or nom de plume

al·pha·bet·ist \-ˌbed·ə̇st *also* -ˌbəd-·\ *n* -S **:** one that studies or invents alphabets

al·pha·bet·i·za·tion \\ˌ==ˌbed·ə'zāshən, -etə'- *also* -ˌbəd-- *or* -bət- *or* -bəd·ˌī'z- *or* -bəˌtī'-\ *n* -S **1 :** the act or action of arranging alphabetically **2 :** an alphabetically arranged series, list, or file

al·pha·bet·ize \'==ˌbəˌtīz, -bəd·ˌīz\ *vt* -ED/-ING/-S **1 :** to furnish with or express by an alphabet ⟨the revised system of *alphabetizing* Japanese —Cornelius Osgood⟩ **2 :** to arrange alphabetically ⟨~ a list of words⟩

alphabet length *n* **:** the total width of the 26 single lower-case unspaced letters of the alphabet in a particular font usu. given in points and used as an indicator of relative face width

al·pha·be·tol·o·gist \\ˌ==ˌbə'täləjə̇st\ *n* -S **:** one that engages in alphabetology

al·pha·be·tol·o·gy \-ləjē\ *n* -ES [¹*alphabet* + *-o-* + *-logy*] **:** the study of alphabetic systems of writing

alphabets *pl of* ALPHABET, *pres 3d sing of* ALPHABET

alphabet soup *n* **:** a soup containing macaroni paste cut in the shapes of letters

alpha brass *n* **:** brass composed of a solid solution of zinc in copper and containing up to 39 or formerly 36 percent zinc

alpha cell *n* **:** an acidophile glandular cell (as of the pancreas or the adenohypophysis)

alpha cellulose *n* **:** CELLULOSE 2b

alpha globulin *n* **:** any of several globulins of human or animal plasma or serum that have at alkaline pH the greatest electrophoretic mobility next to albumin — compare BETA GLOBULIN, GAMMA GLOBULIN

al·pha·gram \'alfəˌgram\ *n* -S [¹*alpha* + *-gram* (as in *cryptogram*)] **:** a puzzle that consists in the defining of one phrase with another phrase made up of rhyming words that are spelled alike except for the first letters ⟨*boy toy* is an ~ for *male doll*⟩ ⟨*funny bunny* is an ~ for *amusing little rabbit*⟩

alpha hemolysis *n* **:** a greenish discoloration and partial hemolysis of the red blood cells immediately surrounding colonies of certain streptococci on blood agar plates

al·pha–hy·poph·a·mine \¦alfə-\ *n* **:** OXYTOCIN

alpha iron *n* **:** the form of iron stable below 910°C and characterized by a body-centered cubic crystal structure — compare BETA IRON

al·pha·mer·ic \¦alfə¦merik\ *or* **al·pha·mer·i·cal** \-rə̇kəl\ *adj* [*alpha*bet + nu*meric, numerical*] **:** ALPHANUMERIC

al·pha–naph·thol \ˌalfə-\ *n* [²*alpha* + *naphthol*] **:** NAPHTHOL 1a

al·pha–naph·thyl \ˌalfə-\ *n* [²*alpha* + *naphthyl*] **:** NAPHTHYL a

al·pha–naph·thyl·thio·urea \¦alfə¦n-\ *n* [NL, fr. ISV *alpha-naphthyl* + NL *thiourea*] **:** ANTU

¹al·pha·nu·mer·ic \¦alf(ə)=¦==\ *also* **al·pha·nu·mer·i·cal** \-rə̇kəl, -rēk-\ *adj* [*alpha*bet + *numeric, numerical*] **1 :** consisting of both letters and numbers and often other symbols (as punctuation marks and mathematical symbols) as well ⟨an ~ code⟩; *also* **:** being a character in an alphanumeric system **2 :** capable of using alphanumeric characters ⟨an ~ computer⟩ — **al·pha·nu·mer·i·cal·ly** \-rə̇k(ə)lē, -rēk-, -li\ *adv*

²alphanumeric \"\ *n* -S **:** an alphanumeric character

alpha particle *n* **:** a positively charged nuclear particle identical with the nucleus of a helium atom, consisting of 2 protons and 2 neutrons, having atomic mass 4 and atomic number 2, ejected at high speed in certain radioactive transformations

alpha privative *n* [trans. of MGk *alpha sterētikon*] **1 :** the Greek prefix *a-* or usu. before vowels *an-* expressing negation (as in Gk *abatos* "impassable" from *batos* "passable") **2 :** the English prefix *a-* expressing negation

alpha pulp *n* **:** chemical pulp that has been given a further chemical treatment to remove impurities and thus increase its alpha cellulose content

alpha quartz *n* **:** quartz with trigonal-trapezohedral symmetry **:** the stable form of quartz below about 573°C

alpha radiator *n* **:** a radioactive substance which radiates alpha rays

alpha ray *n* **1 :** an alpha particle moving at high speed (as in radioactive emission) **2** *or* **alpha radiation :** a stream of alpha particles

alpha test *n* **:** a group intelligence test used esp. by the U.S. Army in World War I

al·pha–to·coph·er·ol \¦alfə-\ *n* **:** TOCOPHEROL a

alpha wave *or* **alpha rhythm** *n* **:** an electrical rhythm of the brain that can be recorded by an electroencephalograph, occurs 8 to 13 cycles per second, and is often associated with a state of wakeful relaxation

al·phi·to·mor·phous \al¦fid·ə¦mȯrfəs, ¦alfə(ˌ)tō¦-\ *adj* [prob. fr. F *alphitomorphe*, fr. Gk *alphiton* barley meal + F *-morphe* -morphous] **:** resembling barley meal — used of certain parasitic fungi

al·phonse and gas·ton \'alˌfänz...'gastən, 'aùˌf-, -än(t)s-, -aast-\ *n, pl* **alphonses and gastons** *usu cap 1st A&G* [after *Alphonse* and *Gaston*, characters displaying excessive politeness and often uttering the phrases "after you, my dear Gaston" and "after you, my dear Alphonse" that appeared in the comic strip *Alphonse and Gaston* by Frederick B. Opper †1937 Amer. illustrator and cartoonist] **:** a pair of persons exhibiting an excessive usu. exaggerated politeness or deference to each other esp. about not taking precedence

al·phon·sine \(')al¦fän(t)sə̇n, -änzə̇n\ *adj, usu cap* [Sp *alfonsino*, fr. *Alfonso* X †1284 king of Castile and León + Sp *-ino* -ine] **:** relating to the set of astronomical tables prepared in 1252 by order of Alfonso X, king of León and Castile

alphorn *var of* ALPENHORN

¹al·pine \'alˌpīn *also* -ˌpə̇n\ *adj* [ME, fr. L *Alpinus*, fr. *Alpes* Alps + *-inus* -ine] **1** *often cap* **:** resembling or relating to the Alps or any lofty mountain or mountain system ⟨~ scenery⟩ ⟨~ winter⟩ **2** *usu cap* **:** of or relating to the mountain-making movements in Europe in the Tertiary period — see GEOLOGIC TIME table **3 a** *usu cap* **:** of, relating to, or being the biogeographic zone made up of elevated slopes above timber line and characterized by the presence of rosette-forming herbaceous plants and low shrubby slow-growing woody plants **b** *often cap* **:** growing in this zone ⟨~ plants⟩ **c** *often cap* **:** of, relating to, or made up of alpine plants ⟨an ~ forest⟩ **4** *usu cap* **:** of or relating to a broadheaded medium-statured brown-eyed or brown-haired white man of stocky build who is often regarded as representative of one of the three physical types of the white race ⟨a pure *Alpine* type⟩ — compare MEDITERRANEAN, NORDIC **5** *often cap* **:** devoted to mountaineering activities ⟨an ~ club⟩ — **al·pine·ly** *adv*

²alpine \"\ *n* -S **1 :** a plant native to mountain summits or boreal regions that is often grown in alpine or rock gardens **2** *sometimes cap* **:** a goat of a breed of large hardy milch goats originated in the Swiss Alps — see BRITISH ALPINE **3 :** any of several predominantly dark-brown or blackish butterflies (genus *Erebia*) of northern regions **4** *usu cap* **:** a person possessing Alpine physical characteristics

alpine anemone *n* **:** a silky-foliaged herb (*Anemone tetonensis*) of the Rocky mountains with bluish white flowers

alpine ash *n* **:** a tall Australian timber tree (*Eucalyptus gigantea*) having the lower part of the trunk covered with thick woolly gray bark

alpine aster *n* **:** a Rocky mountain herb (*Aster meritus*) with violet-purple flowers

alpine azalea *n* **:** a low-branching prostrate shrub (*Loiseleuria procumbens*) of the heath family found in high mountain regions in the northern hemisphere

alpine bartsia *n* [part trans. of NL *Bartsia alpina*] **:** a hemiparasitic herb (*Bartsia alpina*) of arctic America and northern Europe with opposite leaves and showy irregular purple flowers in a leafy spike

alpine bearberry *n* **:** a tufted or prostrate bearberry (*Arctostaphylos alpina*) of the mountainous regions of northeastern No. America

alpine beardtongue *n* **:** a common Rocky mountain perennial herb (*Pentstemon ellipticus*) with a partly woody stem and violet-purple flowers

alpine birch *n* **:** a low shrub (*Betula nana*) native in high northern regions

alpine bistort *n* **:** a slender perennial herb (*Bistorta vivipara*) with oblong leaves and reddish white flowers found in northern regions

alpine brook saxifrage *n* [¹*brook*, prob. part trans. of NL *Saxifraga rivularis*] **:** a white-flowered herb (*Saxifraga rivularis*) found on mountain summits and in arctic regions of the northern hemisphere

alpine campion *n* **:** a low tufted herb (*Lychnis alpina*) with pink flowers found throughout the north temperate zone esp. at high altitudes

alpine catchfly *n* **:** a European white-flowered herb (*Silene alpestris*) that is sometimes cultivated

alpine chough *n* **:** a small yellow-billed chough (*Pyrrhocorax graculus*) of mountainous parts of Europe

alpine clover *n* **:** a European mountain clover (*Trifolium alpinum*) with heads of pink flowers

alpine combined *n, usu cap A* **:** a competitive ski event consisting of both downhill racing and slalom — compare NORDIC COMBINED

alpine cress *n* **:** a low white-flowered perennial herb (*Cardamine bellidifolia*) found on mountain summits and in arctic regions of the north temperate zone

alpine currant *n* **:** a spreading dense European shrub (*Ribes alpinum*) often used as an ornamental or hedge plant esp. in shady locations — called also *mountain currant*

alpine dock *n* **:** a tall coarse rough-leaved dock (*Rumex alpinus*) of the Alps with drooping flowers and fruits in large branching clusters

alpine eyebright *n* **:** a showy New Zealand perennial herb (*Euphrasia monroi*) with yellow and white flowers

alpine fir *n* **:** a tall Rocky mountain evergreen timber tree (*Abies lasiocarpa*) having flat blue-green leaves and upright cones

alpine fireweed *n* **:** a perennial herb (*Epilobium latifolium*) with reddish white flowers found in arctic America and south through the Rocky mountains to Colorado

alpine forget-me-not *n* **:** a Rocky mountain perennial herb (*Eritrichium howardi*) with ashy yellowish foliage and dark blue flowers

alpine garden *n* **:** a garden on rock ledges or among rocks in the alpine zone or one (as in certain cool damp locations) intended to simulate such a garden; *broadly* **:** ROCK GARDEN

alpine glacier *n* **:** a glacier formed among summits and descending a mountain valley

alpine hemlock *n* **:** a valuable timber tree (*Tsuga mertensiana*) found in the northern Rocky mountains

alpine horn *var of* ALPENHORN

alpine lady fern *n* **:** a fern (*Athyrium americanum*) with deeply cut leaf segments found in the Rocky mountains

alpine larch *n* **:** a larch (*Larix lyallii*) growing in the higher mountains of the northwestern U.S. and British Columbia

alpine lift *n, often cap A* **:** T-BAR LIFT

alpine lousewort *n* **:** a white-flowered perennial herb (*Pedicularis contorta*) found on mountains of western No. America

alpine parnassia *n* **:** a white-flowered herb (*Parnassia kotzebuei*) found in Siberia, Greenland, and the Rocky mountains

alpine pine *n* **:** SWISS PINE

alpine poppy *n* **1 :** ICELAND POPPY **2 :** a tiny yellow-flowered Rocky mountain poppy (*Papaver pygmaeum*)

alpine rose *n* **1 :** any of various European and Asiatic alpine rhododendrons **2 :** EDELWEISS 1

alpine salamander *n, usu cap A* **:** an ovoviviparous tailed amphibian (*Salamandra atra*) occurring in the Alps that retains its one or two young in the uterus until metamorphosis is completed

alpine sedge *n* **:** a Rocky mountain sedge (*Carex scopulorum*) with sharply triangular culms

alpine spring beauty *n* **:** a fleshy perennial herb (*Claytonia megarrhiza*) found on summits of the Rocky mountains

alpine strawberry *n* **:** a variety (*Fragaria vesca monophylla*) of the wood strawberry with unifoliolate leaves

alpine structure *n, usu cap A* [so called fr. its prevalence in the Swiss Alps] **:** rock structure characterized by extensive overthrust faults and overturned folds

alpine totara *n* **:** a dense New Zealand shrub (*Podocarpus nivalis*) often low and widely spreading with leaves closely and irregularly arranged

alpine umbrella plant *n* **:** a Rocky mountain perennial herb (*Eriogonum androsaceum*) with white foliage and yellowish white flowers

alpine vole *n* **:** any of numerous European upland voles (genus *Microtus*)

alpine whitebark pine *n* **:** a timber tree (*Pinus albicaulis*) found in the Rocky mountains and in California

alpine woodsia *n* [part trans. of NL *Woodsia alpina*] **:** a slender fern (*Woodsia alpina*) of northern No. America with shining chestnut-colored stipes, bipinnate fronds, and usu. distinct marginal sori — called also *flower-cup fern*

al·pin·ia \al'pinēə\ *n* [NL, fr. Prospero *Alpini* †1617 Ital. botanist + NL *-ia*] **1** *cap* **:** a large genus of herbs (family Zingiberaceae) found in Asia, Australia, and Polynesia with showy very irregular flowers and large aromatic rootstocks — see GALINGALE **2** -S **:** a plant of the genus *Alpinia*

al·pin·ism \'alpəˌnizəm\ *n* -S *often cap* **:** mountain climbing in the Alps or other high mountain ranges

al·pin·ist \'alpənə̇st, -ˌpīn-\ *n* -S *often cap* **:** a mountain climber specializing in high difficult ascents

al·pi·no \al'pē(ˌ)nō\ *n, pl* **alpi·ni** \-(ˌ)nē\ *usu cap* [It, fr. *alpino* of the Alps, fr. L *alpinus* — more at ALPINE] **:** a member of an Italian army unit trained to fight in mountainous terrain

al·pin·oid \'alpəˌnȯid\ *adj, usu cap* [¹*alpine* + *-oid*] **:** resembling or related to the Alpine race

al·pist \'alpə̇st, (')al¦pēst\ *also* **al·piste** \", al'pēstə\ *n* -S [Sp *alpiste*, fr. Mozarabic *al-bishī* the alpist, fr. *al-* the (fr. Ar) + *bishī* alpist, fr. ML *pistum*, fr. L, neut. of *pistus*, past part. of *pinsere* to pound, crush — more at PESTLE] **1 :** the seed of canary grass **2 :** the seed of any of various species of *Phleum*

alp·land \'alˌpland, -ˌplənd\ *n* **:** an area resembling the Alps in its topography

al·pu·jar·ra \ˌalpü'härə\ *n* -S *usu cap* [*Las Alpujarras*, region of Spain where it is made] **:** an antique or modern Spanish rug embroidered in woolen or silken loops on canvas

al·raun \'alˌraùn, ='=\ *n* -S [G, fr. MHG *alrūn*, alter. of OHG *alrūna* (perh. a fem. proper name), fr. *al-*, *all* all + *rūna* secret — more at ALL, RUNE] **:** MANDRAKE 1

al·ready \(')ȯl¦redē, -di\ *adv* [ME *al redy*, fr. *al redy*, adj., wholly ready, prepared, fr. *al* all + *redy* ready — more at ALL, READY] **1 :** prior to some specified or implied past, present, or future time **:** by this time **:** PREVIOUSLY — usu. used to refer to time that is past with respect to the verb modified ⟨if you stop to think, you'll find you ~ know the answer⟩ or to a condition that has been reached prior to the time of observation ⟨an ~ noticeable decrease⟩ **2 a :** so soon **:** so early ⟨is it time to go home ~?⟩ **b :** NOW ⟨give me my money ~⟩

alright *adv or adj* [ME *alright*, *alriht* — more at ALL RIGHT] **:** ALL RIGHT — in reputable use although *all right* is more common

al·root \'äl,r-\ *n* -S [Hindi *āl* + E *root*] **:** INDIAN MULBERRY 1

al rovescio *var of* A ROVESCIO

¹als *obs var of* ¹ALSO

²als *pl of* AL

-als *pl of* -AL

ALS *abbr* autograph letter signed

al·sace-lor·rain·er \\ˌalsaslə'rānə(r), -ˌsās-\ *n* -S *cap A&L* [*Alsace-Lorraine*, frontier region between Germany, France, Belgium, and Switzerland + E *-er*] **:** a native or inhabitant of Alsace-Lorraine

al·sa·tia \al'sāsh(ē)ə\ *n* -S *usu cap* [*Alsatia* (slang name for Whitefriars, a section of London that was a sanctuary for lawbreakers in the 17th cent.), fr. ML *Alsatia* Alsace, Rhenish province long in dispute between France and Germany] **:** any asylum or refuge for criminals **:** a region without law ⟨an *Alsatia* of dives, dance halls, and depravity —Herbert Asbury⟩

¹al·sa·tian \al'sāshən\ *n* -S *usu cap* [ML *Alsatia* Alsace + E *-an*] **1 :** a native or inhabitant of Alsatia or of Alsace **2** *also* **alsatian dog :** GERMAN SHEPHERD

²alsatian \(')=¦==\ *adj, usu cap* **:** relating to, situated in, inhabiting, or coming from Alsatia or Alsace

alsatian clover *n, usu cap A* [by folk etymology] **:** ALSIKE CLOVER

als·bach·ite \'ȯlzˌbäˌkīt, 'älz-,'äls-\ *n* -S [G *alsbachit*, fr. *Alsbach*, village in Germany, its locality + G *-it* -ite] **:** a porphyritic aplite sometimes containing garnets

al·sea \al'sēə\ *n, pl* **alsea** *or* **alseas** *usu cap* [Alsea *Alsé*] **1 a :** an Indian people of the Pacific coast of Oregon **b :** a member of such people **2 :** the Yakonan language of the Alsea people

¹al sec·co \al'seˌkō\ *adj* [It, in the secco manner] *of a painting* **:** executed in the secco manner ⟨an *al secco* mural⟩ — compare ALFRESCO

²al secco \"\ *adv, of painting* **:** in the secco manner

al se·gno \äl'sān,yō, al-\ *adv* [It, to the sign] **1 :** to the sign — used as a direction in music for the performer to continue as far as the sign :S: **2 :** DAL SEGNO

al·si·film \'alsəˌfilm\ *n* -S [*al*uminum *si*licate + *film*] **:** an oil-resistant and heat-resistant material produced in sheets from a gel of bentonite and used esp. for electrical insulation

al·sike clover *also* **alsike** \'alˌsak, -īk *also* 'ȯlˌsīk\ *n* -S [fr. *Alsike*, Sweden, its locality] **:** a European perennial clover (*Trifolium hybridum*) much used as a forage plant and characterized by pinkish flowers that early become deflexed in the head

al·si·na·ce·ae \ˌalsə'nāsēˌē\ *n pl, cap* [NL, fr. *Alsine*, type genus + *-aceae*] *in some classifications* **:** a family of herbs having opposite entire leaves and small mostly perfect flowers with distinct sepals, clawless petals, and capsular fruits, often included in the Caryophyllaceae

al·si·na·ceous \¦alsə¦nāshəs, -ˌsī¦-\ *adj* [NL *Alsinaceae* + E *-ous*] **:** of or relating to the family Alsinaceae or genus *Alsine*

al·si·ne \al'sīnē\ *n, cap* [NL, fr. L, a plant (perh. chickweed), fr. Gk *alsinē* (*Parietaria lusitanica*)] *in some classifications* **:** a genus (the type of the family Alsinaceae) of herbs that includes the chickweeds and stitchworts and is equivalent to *Stellaria* or to a combination of *Stellaria* and *Arenaria* of other classifications

al si·rat \ˌalsə'rät\ *n, usu cap A&S* [Ar *al-sirāṭ* the road] **:** SIRAT

¹al·so \'ȯl(ˌ)sō, 'ȯlt(-\ *adv* [ME *also, alswa*, fr. OE *alswā, ealswā, ælswā* just as, likewise, fr. *al-, eal-, æl-* (akin to OE *eall* all) + *swā* so — more at ALL, SO] **1 :** in the same manner as something else **:** LIKEWISE ⟨another fallen prince, who is ~ not unknown to the students of literature —R.D.Altick⟩ ⟨they ~ serve who only stand and wait —John Milton⟩ **2 :** in addition **:** as well **:** BESIDES, TOO ⟨had immense dignity and reserve, but he ~ was self-sufficient —Harry Hansen⟩

²also \"\ *conj* [ME *also, alswa*, fr. *also, alswa*, adv.] **1** *obs* **:** as if **:** AS **2 :** AND ⟨his speech was tedious, ~ absurd⟩

als ob \äls'ʔōp\ *n, pl* **als obs** [G, fr. *als ob* as if] **:** ASSUMPTION; *esp* **:** one made so that action, thought, or further assumption is possible

al·soph·i·la \al'säfələ\ *n* [NL, fr. Gk *alsos* grove + NL *-phila*; akin to Gk *aldēskein* to grow — more at OLD] **1** *cap* **:** a large genus of tree ferns (family Cyatheaceae) found in tropical mountainous regions having ample finely divided fronds bearing naked sori **2** -S **:** a fern of the genus *Alsophila* **3** *cap* **:** a genus of geometrid moths having wingless females and green-striped larvae that are loopers and include the common destructive fall cankerworm

also–ran \'=(ˌ)=ˌ=\ *n* -S **1 a :** a racehorse or racing dog that finishes behind the first three contestants or out of the money **b :** a contestant in any actual or presumed competition that is not among the prize or point winners, is only moderately successful, or is a failure **c :** a failing or only moderately successful entry in any actual or presumed competition ⟨the book was an *also-ran* on the publisher's list⟩ **2 :** a person of little or no importance

al·sto·nia \ȯlz'tōnēə, ȯl'st-\ *n, cap* [NL, fr. Charles *Alston* †1760 Scottish botanist + NL *-ia*] **:** a genus of trees or shrubs (family Apocynaceae) found in tropical Asia, Australia, and Polynesia having white funnel-shaped flowers and seeds comose at both ends

al·sto·nine \'ȯlztəˌnēn, -lst-\ *n* -S [ISV *alston-* (fr. NL *Alstonia*, genus name of *Alstonia constricta*) + *-ine;* orig. formed as G *alstonin*] **:** an alkaloid $C_{21}H_{20}N_2O_4$ found in the bark of a tree (*Alstonia constricta*) — called also *chlorogenine*

al·ston·ite \'ȯlztəˌnīt, -lst-\ *n* -S [*Alston*, Cumberland, England + E *-ite*] **:** BROMLITE

al·stroe·me·ria \ˌalztrə'mirēə, -lst-\ *n* [NL, fr. Baron Klas von *Alstroemer* †1794 Swedish botanist + NL *-ia*] **1** *cap* **:** a genus of showy So. American herbs (family Amaryllidaceae) having leafy stems **2** -S **:** a plant of the genus *Alstroemeria*

alt *abbr* **1** alteration **2** alternate; alternating; alternative **3** altitude **4** alto

al·ta fescue \'altə-\ *n* [prob. fr. Mount *Alta*, peak in Kittitas co., central Wash.] **:** a variety (*Festuca elatior arundinacea*) of meadow fescue used esp. as a late hay and forage grass

al·tai \'alˌtī\ *n* [fr. *Altai* Mts., range in central Asia] **1** -S *usu cap* **:** a Turkic dialect of Kirghiz, U.S.S.R. **2** *usu cap* **:** an Asiatic breed of small shaggy sturdy horses **3** -S *often cap* **:** an animal of the Altai breed

[1]**al·ta·ic** \(ˈ)alˈtāik\ *or* **al·ta·ian** \(ˈ)alˈtā(y)ən, -tīən\ *adj, usu cap* **1 :** of or belonging to the Altai mountains of central Asia **2 :** of or relating to the Altaic peoples or languages

[2]**altaic** \"\ *or* **altaian** \"\ *n* -s *usu cap* **1 :** a language family comprising the Turkic, Tungusic, and Mongolic subfamilies **2 :** a member of the peoples belonging to the Altaic language group

al·ta·ist \alˈtāəst\ *n* -s *usu cap* [[1]*altaic* + *-ist*] **:** a specialist in Altaic languages or cultures

al·ta·ite \alˈtāˌīt, ˈalˌtīt\ *n* -s [G *altait*, fr. *Altai* Mts., Asia, its locality + G *-it* -ite] **:** a mineral consisting of lead telluride PbTe tin-white when untarnished and usu. occurring massive with cubic cleavage

al·tar \ˈȯltə(r)\ *n* -s [alter. (influenced by L *altare*) of ME *alter, auter;* ME *alter*, fr. OE *altar*, fr. L *altare* altar, materials for burning on an altar; ME *auter*, fr. OF, fr. L *altare;* akin to L *adolēre* to burn up, and perh. to Sw dial. *ala* to flame, burn, Skt *alāta* firebrand, coal] **1 :** a raised structure (as a block, pile of blocks, pillar, or stand) on which sacrifices are offered or incense burned (as in the worship of a deity or of the spirit of a deceased ancestor); *broadly* **:** any structure or place serving as a place of sacrifice or worship **2 a :** a tablelike construction used in the Christian church in celebrating the Eucharist **:** COMMUNION TABLE — called also *Lord's table, Holy Table* **b** *in the Eastern Church* **:** SANCTUARY 1a(2) **3 :** a piece of furniture resembling an altar and used in ritual and ceremonial practices in the Masonic and other fraternal societies **4 :** any of the steps, ledges, or offsets the flights of which form the inner sides of a graving dock or dry dock

al·tar·age \-rij\ *n* -s [alter. (influenced by *altar*) of ME *awterage*, fr. AF *auterage*, fr. OF *auter, alter* altar (fr. L *altare*) + *-age*] **1 :** the offerings made upon an altar or to a church **2 :** the honorarium received by a priest for services at the altar **3 :** endowments for masses for deceased persons

altar boy *n* **:** a boy who is or functions as an acolyte

altar brass *n* **:** a set of brass furnishings (as candlesticks, cross, and flower vases) for use on a Christian altar

altar bread *n* **:** bread or a piece of bread to be used in the Eucharist

altar call *n* **:** a general appeal issued by a preacher from the pulpit in evangelistic worship services inviting worshipers to come forward to the front of the church or meeting area to signify their decision to commit their lives to Jesus Christ

altar card *n* **:** one of three printed cards containing certain eucharistic prayers placed on the altar during Roman Catholic mass as an aid to the celebrant's memory

altar cloth *n* **:** a cloth used as a covering for an altar

altar desk *n* **:** MISSAL STAND

altar facing *or* **altar front** *n* **:** FRONTAL 2

altar girl *n* **:** a girl acting as a lay assistant in church services

al·tar·ist \ˈȯltərəst\ *n* -s [ML *altarista*, fr. L *altare* altar + *-ista* -ist] **:** one that attends at an altar; *specif* **:** VICAR

altar ledge *n* **:** a raised ledge at the back of an altar for candles, flowers, cross, or ornaments

altar mound *n* **:** an Indian mound built over an altar on which sacrifices had been burned

altar of repose *often cap A&R* **:** REPOSITORY 1d

altarpiece \ˈ==,=\ *n* **:** a work of art to decorate the space above and behind an altar

altar plate *n* **:** plate used in the Eucharist

altar rail *n* **:** a railing in front of an altar separating the chancel from the body of the church

altars *pl of* ALTAR

altar screen *n* **:** a screen at the back of a church altar **:** REREDOS

altar slab *n* **:** MENSA 1

altar stone *n* **1 :** a stone slab serving as the top of an altar and often (as in the Roman Catholic Church) specially consecrated **2 :** a small rectangular consecrated stone used as an altar by the Roman Catholic Church

altar wine *n* **:** SACRAMENTAL WINE

altarwise \ˈ==,=\ *adv* **:** as an altar is usu. placed

alt·az·i·muth \alˈtazəməth\ *n* -s [ISV *alt*itude + *azimuth*] **:** an instrument consisting of a telescope mounted so that it can swing horizontally and vertically and used for observing the altitude and azimuth of a celestial body; *also* **:** any of several other instruments (as a theodolite) mounted so that it swings in the same way

[1]**al·ter** \ˈȯltə(r)\ *vb* **altered; altered; altering** \ˈȯlt(ə)riŋ, ˈȯl·triŋ\ **alters** [ME *alteren*, fr. MF *alterer*, fr. ML *alterare*, fr. L *alter* other (of two); akin to L *alius* other — more at ELSE] *vt* **1 :** to cause to become different in some particular characteristic (as measure, dimension, course, arrangement, or inclination) without changing into something else ⟨the extent of a monosyllable the text has here been *~ed* —J.B. Cabell & A.J.Hanna⟩ ⟨preserve it as it is or . . . ~ it out of all recognition —Aldous Huxley⟩ **2** *archaic* **:** to affect mentally **:** AGITATE ⟨the *~ed* mood of terror⟩ **3 :** to castrate or spay (as a domestic mammal) ~ *vi* **:** to become different in some respect **:** undergo change usu. without resulting difference in essential nature ⟨the old witch had not *~ed* by a wrinkle in twenty years —Compton Mackenzie⟩ ⟨people themselves ~ so much that there is something new to be observed in them for ever —Jane Austen⟩ ⟨customs that must ~ with every new invention —Herbert Agar⟩ **syn** see CHANGE

[2]**al·ter** \ˈȯltə(r) *also* ˈäl- *sometimes* ˈal-\ *or* **al·te·rum** \-tərəm, -ˌrům\ *adj* [L] **:** OTHER — used of something that is distinguished from the ego or esp. of other persons as contrasted with the ego

al·ter·abil·i·ty \ˌȯltərəˈbiləd·ē, ˌȯl·tr-\ *n* -ES **:** the quality or state of being alterable

al·ter·able \ˈȯltərəbəl, ˈȯl·tr-\ *adj* **:** capable of being altered — **al·ter·ably** \-blē\ *adv*

al·ter·ant \ˈȯltərənt\ *n* -s [LL *alterant-, alterans* pres. part. of *alterare*] **:** something that alters

al·ter·a·tion \ˌȯltəˈrāshən\ *n* -s [ME *alteracioun*, fr. MF & ML; MF *alteration*, fr. ML *alteration-, alteratio*, fr. *alteratus* (past part. of *alterare*) + L *-ion-, -io* -ion] **1 a :** the act or action of altering **b :** the quality or state of being altered **2 :** the result of altering: as **a :** a change in a legal instrument that changes its legal effect either in the obligation it imports or its force as legal evidence — distinguished from *spoliation* **b :** a change made in fitting a new or old garment ⟨no charge for *~s*⟩ **c :** a change marked on a proof that does not accord with the copy or with a previous proof — distinguished from *correction* **d :** a change or modification made on a building that does not increase its exterior dimensions

☞ In this dictionary the abbreviation "alter." for "alteration" is used in etymologies with reference only to changes occurring within a language

[1]**al·ter·a·tive** \ˈȯltəˌrād·iv, -ˌrəd-, ȯlˈterəd-\ *n* -s [ME, fr. MF or ML; MF *alteratif*, fr. ML *alterativus*, fr. *alteratus*, adj.] **:** any drug used empirically to alter favorably the course of an ailment and to restore healthy body functions — now rarely used technically

[2]**alterative** \"\ *adj* [ME, fr. MF or ML; MF *alteratif*, fr. ML *alterativus*, fr. LL *alteratus* (past part. of *alterare*) + L *-ivus* -ive] **:** causing alteration

al·ter·cate \ˈȯltə(r)ˌkāt\ *vi* -ED/-ING/-S [L *altercatus*, past part. of *altercari*, fr. (assumed) *altercus* contending, fr. *alter* other — more at ALTER] **:** to contend wordily **:** dispute with zeal, heat, or anger **:** WRANGLE

al·ter·ca·tion \ˌȯltə(r)ˈkāshən\ *n* -s [ME *altercacioun*, fr. MF *altercation*, fr. L *altercation-, altercatio*, fr. *altercatus* + *-ion-, -io* -ion] **:** warm contention **:** dispute carried on with feeling (as anger) **:** noisy controversy **:** wordy strife **syn** see QUARREL

altered *past of* ALTER

altered chord *n* **:** a chord in music having one or more tones that are chromatic or foreign to the key of the passage

al·ter ego \ˌȯltəˈrē(ˌ)gō *also* ˌäl- *or* -ˈre- *or* -təˈē *or* -təˈe- *sometimes* ˌal-\ *n, pl* **alter egos** [L, lit., second I] **1 :** a second self: **a :** a trusted friend ⟨John became his *alter ego*⟩ **b :** a confidential representative ⟨his political *alter ego*⟩ **c :** a guardian spirit often represented in So. and Central American Indian carvings by the figure of an animal on the head, back, or shoulders of a human being **d :** the opposite side of a personality **e :** COUNTERPART 3

al·ter·er \ˈȯltərə(r)\ *n* -s **:** one that alters ready-made clothing to fit the customer

altering *pres part of* ALTER

al·ter·i·ty \ȯlˈterəd·ē *also* al-\ *n* -ES [LL *alteritat-, alteritas* (trans. of Gk *heterotēs*), fr. L *alter* other + *-itat-, -itas* -ity — more at ALTER] **:** the quality or state of being other **:** OTHERNESS

al·tern \ȯlˈtərn, al-, ˈ=(ˌ)=\ *adj* [L *alternus* interchangeable, alternate, fr. *alter*] *archaic* **:** acting by turns **:** ALTERNATE

al·ter·na·cy \ˈȯltərnəsē *also* ˈal-; =ˈ===\ *n* -ES [[1]*alternate* + *-acy*] **:** ALTERNATENESS, ALTERNATION

al·ter·na·men·te \(ˌ)älˌternəˈmentē\ *adv* [It, fr. *alterno* alternate, fr. L *alternus*] **:** ALTERNATELY — used as a direction in music

al·ter·nance \ˈȯltərnən(t)s *also* ˈal-; *chiefly Brit* =ˈ==\ *n* -s **:** ALTERNATION ⟨the sun marks the ~ of day and night —S.L.Terrien⟩

[1]**al·ter·nant** \ˈȯltə(r)nənt *also* ˈal-; *chiefly Brit* ȯlˈtən- *also* alˈt-\ *adj* [L *alternant-, alternans*, pres. part. of *alternare* to alternate — more at ALTERNATE] **:** ALTERNATING

[2]**alternant** \"\ *n* -s **1** *math* **:** a determinant the constituents of whose different rows are (in order) the same set of functions of different variables, the same variable appearing in each row and the same function in each column, the terms row and column here being interchangeable **2 :** one of the statements in logic composing an alternation **3 :** any of the nonsignificant variants (as an allomorph or allophone) that together constitute a significant linguistic category

al·ter·nan·the·ra \ˌȯltə(r)ˈnanthərə *also* ˌal-\ *n* [NL, fr. L *alternus* + NL *-anthera*] **1** *cap* **:** a genus of low herbs (family Amaranthaceae) chiefly of tropical America and Australia with inconspicuous flowers — see ALLIGATOR WEED **2** -s **:** a plant of the genus *Telanthera*

al·ter·nar·ia \-ˈna(a)rēə\ *n, cap* [NL, fr. L *alternus* + NL *-aria*] **:** a genus of imperfect fungi (family Dematiaceae) producing chains of dark muriform conidia that taper at the upper end — compare EARLY BLIGHT, LEAF SPOT, MACROSPORIUM

al·ter·nat \älternä\ *n, pl* **alternats** \-nä(z)\ [F, lit., alternation, prob. fr. NL *alternatus*, fr. L *alternatus*, past part. of *alternare*] **:** the practice among diplomats of regulating precedence among powers of equal rank by lot or in a certain regular order; *esp* **:** the practice in the signing of treaties and conventions of giving each power the copy on which it appears at the head of the list of signatories

[1]**al·ter·nate** \ˈȯltə(r)nət *also* ˈal-; *chiefly Brit* ȯlˈtərn- *or* -ˈtən- *also* alˈt-; *usu* -əd·+V\ *adj* [L *alternatus*, past part. of *alternare*, fr. *alternus* interchangeable, alternate — more at ALTERN] **1 :** occurring or succeeding by turns **:** one following the other in time **:** by turns first one and then the other ⟨~ gain and loss⟩ ⟨~ periods of working and unemployment⟩ **:** changing back and forth by turns **:** RECIPROCATING ⟨~ favors between friends⟩ **2 a :** arranged first on one side and then on the other at different levels or points along an axial line **:** not side by side ⟨stems with ~ leaves⟩ ⟨~ pitting in cell walls⟩ — see PHYLLOTAXY; compare OPPOSITE **b :** disposed at intervals **:** arranged one above or alongside the other ⟨~ stamens and petals⟩ ⟨~ layers of brick and stone⟩ **3 :** composed of members that occur or succeed by turns ⟨recurring figures in an ~ pattern⟩ **4 :** belonging to a series in which the members regularly intervene between or follow by turns the members of another series (as the odd or even members of the numerals) **:** every other **:** every second ⟨the ~ members 1, 3, 5, and 7⟩ ⟨the ~ verses of a responsive reading⟩ ⟨a maid who works on ~ days⟩ **5 :** ALTERNATIVE, SUBSTITUTE ⟨this highway is an ~ route⟩ ⟨copper may be used as an ~ material⟩ ⟨make an ~ selection⟩ — **al·ter·nate·ly** *adv*

[2]**al·ter·nate** \ˈȯltə(r)ˌnāt *also* ˈal-; *usu* -ād·+V\ *vb* -ED/-ING/-S *vt* **:** to perform by turns or in succession **:** cause to perform or succeed by turns **:** interchange regularly ⟨~ the melodies⟩ ⟨~ endurance tests⟩ ⟨~ pipe and cigar⟩ ~ *vi* **1 :** to vary by turns ⟨gravel and macadam ~ along the route⟩ **:** take turns ⟨singers who ~ in the leading role⟩ — often used with *between* ⟨the weather *alternated* between sunshine and storms⟩ ⟨~ between study and writing⟩ **2 :** to happen, succeed, or act by turns **:** follow reciprocally — used with *with* ⟨the flood and ebb tides ~ with each other⟩ **syn** see ROTATE

[3]**al·ter·nate** *like adj*\ *n* -s **1 :** a choice between two or among more than two objects or courses **:** ALTERNATIVE ⟨the port is the ~ to New York as a shipping terminus⟩ ⟨several basic *~s* to expansion of the building⟩ **2 :** one that takes the place of another **:** one that alternates with another: as **a :** an extra person appointed to take the place of another who is unable to perform his duty **:** SUBSTITUTE ⟨delegates to the convention and their *~s*⟩ **b :** a person that takes his turn often at regular intervals with another of equal rank in an occupation or in performing a duty ⟨appointed ~ to the chief of staff⟩

alternate angle *n* **:** either angle of a pair of nonadjacent angles that a transversal forms with two lines, the angles being on opposite sides of the transversal, two pairs lying within and two without the two lines

c d a b b' a' d' c'

alternate interior angles a, a' and b, b'; alternate exterior angles c, c' and d, d'

alternate bearing *n* **:** biennial bearing (as in some varieties of apples)

alternate consciousness *n* **:** a conscious state dissociated from a person's usual state and not remembered when he has returned to the latter

alternate host *n* **:** a host belonging to a species different from the one usu. inhabited by a parasite

alternate proportion *n, math* **:** a proportion derived from another proportion by interchanging the means

alternate straight *n* **:** SKIP STRAIGHT

alternating *pres part of* ALTERNATE

alternating current *n* **:** an electric current that reverses its direction at regularly recurring intervals the frequency being determined by the frequency of the alternator supplying the current and the successive half waves being similar in shape and area — abbr. *A.C.*

alternating-current resistance *n* **:** the ratio of the average power dissipated to the square of the effective current in a conductor carrying an alternating current — called also *effective resistance*

alternating function *n, math* **:** a function in which the interchange of two variables changes only the sign of the function

al·ter·nat·ing·ly *adv* **:** ALTERNATELY

alternating personality *n* **1 :** MULTIPLE PERSONALITY **2 :** multiple personality in which the several conscious states are not present simultaneously but follow each other consecutively

alternating psychosis *n* **:** MANIC-DEPRESSIVE PSYCHOSIS

alternating series *n* **:** a series in mathematics whose terms are alternately positive and negative

al·ter·na·tion \ˌȯltə(r)ˈnāshən *also* ˌal-\ *n* -s [ME *alternacioun*, fr. LL *alternation-, alternatio*, fr. L *alternatus* + *-ion-, -io* -ion] **1 a :** the act or action of alternating or effecting alternate succession ⟨intelligent ~ of crops⟩ **b :** alternating occurrence **:** SUCCESSION ⟨the ~ of day and night⟩ **2 a :** a statement in logic of the form *p* v *q*, idiomatically rendered "*p* or *q*" and meaning "*p* or *q* or both" **b :** the sentential connective v or *or* used in logic in the inclusive sense **c :** the truth-function or operation symbolized or signified in logic by *or* or v **3 :** the occurrence of different allomorphs or allophones

alternation of generations : the occurrence of two or more forms differently produced in the life cycle of a plant or animal usu. involving the regular alternation of a sexual with an asexual generation but not infrequently consisting of alternation of a dioecious generation with one or more parthenogenetic generations, the alternative forms differing greatly in appearance (as in the gametophyte and sporophyte of higher plants or the hydroid and medusa of certain coelenterates) or being distinguished with difficulty (as the dioecious and parthenogenetic females of some aphids or the sexual and asexual generations of certain algae and fungi) — compare HETEROGENESIS, METAGENESIS

[1]**al·ter·na·tive** \ȯlˈtərnəd·iv, -tən-,-tərn-, -nətiv *also* al-\ *adj* [[1]*alternate* + *-ive*] **1 :** offering a choice of two or more things **:** offering for choice a second thing or proposition or other things or propositions ⟨a means of transportation ~ to the railroad⟩ ⟨several ~ plans⟩ **:** expressing a choice or choices ⟨~ proposition⟩ **2** *of a conjunction* **:** indicating that the terms connected are to be taken not together but one in place of the other (as *or* in "for dessert you may have cake or pie") **3 :** ALTERNATE — **al·ter·na·tive·ly** *adv*

[2]**alternative** \"\ *n* -s **1 a :** a proposition or situation offering a choice between two things wherein if one thing is chosen the other is rejected ⟨a government facing the ~ of high taxes or poor highways⟩ **b :** an opportunity or necessity for deciding between two courses or propositions either of which may be chosen but not both ⟨the ~ of going by train or by plane⟩ **2 a :** either of two paired or contrasted things, courses, or propositions offered for one's choice in a situation in which taking either necessarily entails rejecting the other ⟨that humanism is the ~ to religion —T.S.Eliot⟩ **b :** a counter case matched with one expressed or accepted and characterized by implicit or explicit unreality or implausibility ⟨if the states had any power, it was assumed that they had all power and that the necessary ~ was to deny it altogether —O.W.Holmes †1935⟩ **3 a :** one of a number of things or courses offered for choice ⟨a third ~⟩ ⟨certain customs in our culture are *~s*⟩; *specif* **:** one of the subsidiary statements preceded or followed by *or* in an alternation **:** ALTERNANT **b :** a choice or an opportunity or necessity for choice among three or more things **syn** see CHOICE

alternative cost *n* **1 :** the determination of cost and value by comparison with the best alternative product rather than by totaling factor inputs **2 :** OPPORTUNITY COST

alternative denial *n* **:** the complex proposition that denies that both of two propositions are true ⟨the *alternative denial* "not both *p* and *q*" is true if either or both of *p* and *q* are false⟩ — compare JOINT DENIAL

alternative tariff *n* **:** a schedule of transportation rates each section of which provides that the rates in some other section may be used if they are lower

alternative title *n* **:** SUBTITLE 1a

alternative vote *n* **:** PREFERENTIAL VOTING

alternative writ *n* **:** a writ in the nature of an order to show cause commanding the person to whom it is addressed to perform some duty or show cause why a peremptory or final writ should not issue

al·ter·na·tiv·i·ty \(ˌ)ȯlˌtərnəˈtivəd·ē *also* (ˌ)al-\ *n* -ES **:** the power to choose between two courses of action

al·ter·na·ti·vo \(ˌ)älˌternəˈtē(ˌ)vō\ *n, pl* **alternati·vi** \-(ˌ)vē\ [It, alternative, fr. ML *alternativus* — more at ALTERNATIVE] **1** *music* **:** a contrasting middle section of a movement in the 18th century suite — compare TRIO **2 :** a second trio section played or to be played between repetitions of the first trio in 19th century music

al·ter·na·tor \ˈȯltə(r)ˌnād·ə(r), -nātə- *also* ˈal-\ *n* -s **:** an electric generator for producing alternating current

alternats *pl of* ALTERNAT

al·terne \ˈalˌtərn\ *n* -s [F, fr. *alterne*, adj., alternate, fr. L *alternus* — more at ALTERN] **:** one of a group of adjoining plant communities usu. sharply differentiated from one another ⟨a grass ~ on the southward-facing slope of a ridge contrasted with forest ~ on the northward-facing slope⟩

alterni- *comb form* [NL, fr. L *alternus* alternate — more at ALTERNATE] **:** alternate **:** alternately ⟨*alterni*foliate⟩ ⟨*alterni*petalous⟩ ⟨*alterni*pinnate⟩

al·ter·o·cen·tric \ˌȯltə(ˌ)rōˈsen·trik *also* ˌal-\ *adj* [L *alter* other + E *-o-* + *-centric*] **:** ALLOCENTRIC

alters *pres 3d sing of* ALTER

alterum *var of* ALTER

al·thaea \alˈthēə\ *n* [NL, fr. L, marsh mallow, fr. Gk *althaia*] **1** *cap* **:** a genus of Old World herbs (family Malvaceae) with terminal spikelike clusters of showy flowers each with 6 to 9 bracteoles below the calyx — see HOLLYHOCK, MARSHMALLOW **2** *or* **althea** -s [L *althaea*] **a :** ROSE OF SHARON 3 **b :** a plant of the genus *Althaea* **c :** the dried root of the marsh mallow deprived of the brown corky layer and small roots and used as a demulcent and emollient

al·thae·in *or* **al·the·in** \alˈthēən\ *n* -s [ISV *althae-, althe-* (fr. NL *Althaea*, genus name of *Althaea rosea*) + *-in;* orig. formed as G *althein*] **:** a crystalline pigment obtained from the hollyhock having a bronze luster but being blue in alkaline solution

alt hor *abbr* [L *alternis horis*] every two hours

alt·horn \ˈalˌtȯrn, ˈaltˌhȯ-, -ō(ə)n\ *n* -s [G *althorn*, fr. *alt* alto (fr. It *alto*) + *horn*, fr. OHG — more at ALTO, HORN] **:** the alto member of the saxhorn family used most frequently in bands where it often replaces the French horn — called also *alto, alto saxhorn;* see BALLAD HORN

althorn

al·though *also* **al·tho** \(ˈ)ȯlˈthō\ *conj* [ME *although, although*, fr. *al* all + *thogh, though* — more at ALL, THOUGH] **:** granting or supposing that **:** even if **:** even though **:** in spite of the fact that **:** notwithstanding that **:** THOUGH ⟨~ he is hungry, he will not eat⟩

alti *pl of* ALTUS

alti- *comb form* [ME, fr. L, fr. *altus* — more at OLD] **1 :** high ⟨*alti*sonant⟩ **2 :** altitude ⟨*alti*graph⟩ ⟨*alti*meter⟩

al·ti·ca \ˈaltikə\ *n, cap* [NL, prob. irreg. fr. Gk *haltikos* good at leaping, fr. *hallesthai* to leap — more at SALLY] **:** a genus of flea beetles usu. of blue or green color

al·ti·ca·me·lus \ˌaltəkəˈmēləs\ *n, cap* [NL, fr. *alti-* + *Camelus*] **:** a genus of large long-necked American Miocene camels

al·ti·graph \ˈaltəˌgraf\ *n* -s [*alti-* + *-graph*] **:** an altimeter equipped with a recording mechanism

al·ti·lik \ˈaltəˌlik\ *n* -s [Turk *altılık*] **:** a coin, orig. of silver and equivalent to 6 piasters, formerly used in Turkey

al·tim·e·ter \alˈtiməd·ə(r), ˈaltəˌmēd·ə(r), |tə-\ *n* -s [*alti-* + *-meter*] **:** an instrument for measuring height (as above sea level or ground level) usu. in the form of an aneroid barometer designed to register changes in atmospheric pressure accompanying changes in altitude and calibrated in feet, yards, or meters

airplane altimeter, reading an indicated altitude of 500 feet: *1* barometer scale, reading 29.92 inches of mercury; *2* setting knob

al·tim·e·try \alˈtimə·trē\ *n* -ES [*alti-* + *-metry*] **:** the science of measuring altitudes

al·tin·gi·a·ce·ae \(ˌ)alˌtinjēˈāsēˌē\ [NL, fr. *Altingia*, type genus (fr. W. A. *Alting* †1800 governor-general of the Netherlands East Indies + NL *-ia*) + *-aceae*] *syn of* HAMAMELIDACEAE

al·tin·gi·a·ceous \ˌ=ˌ==ˈāshəs, =ˈ=ˈ=-\ *adj* [NL *Altingiaceae* + E *-ous*] **:** HAMAMELIDACEOUS

al·ti·pla·na·tion \ˌaltəplāˈnāshən, -pləˈ-\ *n* -s [*alti-* + *planation*] **:** the erosion process that produces extensive flat surfaces at high altitudes

al·ti·pla·no \ˌaltəˈplä(ˌ)nō\ *also* **al·ti·pla·ni·cie** \-pləˈnēsēˌā\ *n* -s [*altiplano* fr. AmerSp, fr. Sp *alti-* (fr. L) + *plano* plane, fr. *plano*, adj., fr. L *planus* level, flat; *altiplanicie* fr. Sp, fr. *alti-* + *planicie* plain, fr. L *planities*, fr. *planus* — more at FLOOR] **:** a high plateau or plain **:** TABLELAND

al·tis·o·nant \(ˈ)alˈtisənənt\ *adj* [*alti-* + *sonant*] *archaic* **:** lofty or pompous **:** HIGH-SOUNDING

al·ti·ther·mal \ˌaltəˈthərməl\ *adj* [*alti-* + *thermal*] **:** of or belonging to a time during which the climate is relatively warm — often used of a part of postglacial time

al·ti·tude \ˈaltəˌtüd, -əˌtyüd\ *n* -s [ME, fr. L *altitudo*, fr. *alti-* + *-tudo* -tude] **1 a :** the angular elevation of a celestial object above the horizon measured by the arc of a vertical circle intercepted between the object and the horizon **b :** the vertical elevation of an object above a given level (as a foundation, the ground, or sea level) ⟨a city with an ~ of 2547 feet⟩ **c** (1) **:** a perpendicular line segment from a vertex of a geometric figure (as a triangle or pyramid) to the opposite side or the opposite side extended or from a side or face to a parallel side or face or the side or face extended (2) **:** the length of an altitude (3) **:** a line that is an extension of an altitude **2 :** the height or an extremity of some quality or degree of excellence ⟨the ~ of passion⟩ ⟨standards in the College have been rising, and . . . despite their present ~, they continue to rise —N.M.Pusey⟩ **3 a :** vertical distance or extent **:** height or depth ⟨~ of the fluid in the tube⟩ **b** (1) **:** position at a height ⟨the plane lost ~

rapidly⟩ (2) **:** exalted position (as in rank or power) ⟨a command issued from the ~ of the general staff⟩ **c :** an elevated region **:** EMINENCE — usu. used in pl. ⟨mountain ~s⟩ **4 altitudes** *pl, archaic* **:** haughty airs **:** POMPOSITY

altitude chamber *n* **:** a chamber having an interior that can be so controlled as to simulate the air pressure, humidity, and temperature encountered at various altitudes

altitude sickness *n* **:** the effects (as headache, lassitude, palpitation, nosebleed, nausea) of oxygen deficiency in the blood and tissues developed in rarefied air at high altitudes

al·ti·tu·di·nal \¦==¦=d(ᵊ)nəl\ *adj* [L *altitudin-, altitudo* + E *-al*] **:** of or relating to altitude — **al·ti·tu·di·nal·ly** \-əlē\ *adv*

al·ti·tu·di·nous \¦==¦=d(ᵊ)nəs\ *adj* [L *altitudin-, altitudo* + E *-ous*] **:** LOFTY, HIGH

al·ti·us non tol·len·di \'ältēəs·,nōn·tə'len(,)dē\ *n* [L, of not raising higher] **:** the right to restrain another from building higher than a certain limit

alt·mann's granules \'öltmənz-, 'ält,männz-\ *n pl, usu cap A* [trans. of G *Altmannsche granula,* after Richard *Altmann* †1901 Ger. histologist, their discoverer] **:** minute granules in protoplasm once regarded as its ultimate formative units but now physically equated with mitochondria

altn *abbr* **1** alteration **2** alternate

al·to \'al(,)tō\ *n* -s *often attrib* [It, lit., high, fr. L *altus* — more at OLD] **1 a :** the part sung by the highest men's voices — compare COUNTERTENOR, FALSETTO **b :** the second highest of the four voice parts of the mixed chorus or choir or the lower part or parts in a women's chorus **2 :** a singer of alto parts; *esp, Brit* **:** a male alto singer (as in a cathedral choir) **3 :** the second highest member of a family of musical instruments ⟨the viola is the ~ of the violin family⟩ **4** *or* **alto horn :** ALTHORN

alto clarinet *n* **:** a large clarinet pitched a fifth below the standard B-flat clarinet

alto clef *n* **:** the C clef placed so as to designate the middle line of the staff in musical notation as middle C — called also *viola clef;* see CLEF illustration

al·to·cumulus \¦al(,)tō+\ *n, pl* **altocumuli** [NL, fr. L *altus* high) + NL *-o-* + *cumulus*] **:** a fleecy cloud or cloud formation consisting of large whitish or grayish globular cloudlets with shaded portions often grouped in flocks, rows, or layers and similar to cumulus clouds but at higher altitudes — see CLOUD illustration

altocumulus cas·tel·la·tus \-,kastə'lād·əs, -äd-\ *n, pl* **altocumuli castella·ti** \-'läd·,ī, -'läd·(,)ē\ [NL, fr. *altocumulus* + ML *castellatus* past part. of *castellare* to fortify — more at CASTELLATED] **:** an altocumulus shaped like a tower

alto flute *n* **:** a large flute pitched a fourth lower than the ordinary flute — called also *bass flute*

¹al·to·geth·er \¦öltə¦ge<u>th</u>ə(r)\ *adv* [ME *altogedere, al togedere,* fr. *al* all + *togedere* together] **1 :** WHOLLY, COMPLETELY, THOROUGHLY ⟨not ~ a fool⟩ ⟨~ stupid notions⟩ ⟨the evening was ~ pleasant⟩ **2 :** in all **:** all told ⟨losses amounting ~ to nearly a hundred dollars⟩ **3 :** on the whole **:** in the main **:** as a whole ⟨~ the institution compares favorably with others in the city⟩ — **al·to·geth·er·ness** *n* -ES

²altogether \,==¦==\ *n* **:** NUDE — used with *the* ⟨swimming in the ~⟩

al·to·ist \'al,tōəst, 'altəwəst\ *n* -s **:** a player of the alto saxophone — called also *alto man*

al·to-re·lie·vo *or* **al·to-ri·lie·vo** \¦al(,)tōrē'lē(,)vō; ¦äl(,)tōrēl'yā-, -ye-\ *n, pl* **alto-relievos** \-vōz\ *or* **alto-rilie·vi** \¦äl(,)tōrēl'yā(,)vē, -ye-\ [It *alto rilievo*] **1 :** HIGH RELIEF ⟨adorned with columns and trophies in *alto-relievo* —Tobias Smollett⟩ **2 :** a sculpture executed in high relief; *esp* **:** a relief sculpture in which anatomical details (as arms or legs) are undercut so that, in part, they are detached from the background ⟨an *alto-relievo* by an unknown sculptor⟩ — opposed to *basso-relievo*

alto saxhorn *n* **:** ALTHORN

alto saxophone *or* **alto sax** *n* **:** the second highest member of the saxophone family pitched in F or E flat

al·to·stratus \¦al(,)tō+\ *n, pl* **altostrati** [NL, fr. L *altus* + NL *-o-* + *stratus*] **:** a cloud formation similar to cirrostratus but darker and at a lower level — see CLOUD illustration

alto tenor *n* **:** a boy's voice during the changing period which, while encompassing a limited tenor range, is neither alto nor tenor in tone quality and range

al·tri·ces \al'trī(,)sēz\ *n pl, often cap* [L, pl. of *altric-, altrix* female nourisher, fr. *altor* male nourisher (fr. *altus,* past part. of *alere* to nourish + *-or* -or) + *-ic-, -ix* -trix — more at OLD] **:** altricial birds

al·tri·cial \(')al·'trishəl\ *adj* [*altrices* + *-ial*] **:** having the young hatched in a very immature and helpless condition so as to require care for some time ⟨~ birds⟩ — compare PRECOCIAL

al·tri·gen·der·ism \,al·trə'jendə,rizəm\ *n* -s [*altri-* (fr. L *alter* other, other of two) + *gender* + *-ism*] **:** the state or the period of development in which one becomes interested in or attracted to members of the opposite sex

al·tro·hep·tu·lose \¦al·(,)trō-\ *n* -s [*altrose* + *heptulose*] **:** SEDOHEPTULOSE

al·trose \'al·,trōs, -ōz\ *n* -s [*altr-* (fr. L *alter* other) + *-ose* — more at ALTER] **:** a sugar $C_6H_{12}O_6$ obtained synthetically as a syrup that is stereoisomeric with glucose and epimeric with allose

al·tru·ism \'al·trə,wizəm, -,trü,iz-\ *n* -s [F *altruisme,* fr. *altrui-* (alter. — influenced by L *alter* — of F *autrui* someone else, fr. OF, oblique case form of *autre* other, another, fr. L *alter* other) + *-isme* -ism] **:** uncalculated consideration of, regard for, or devotion to others' interests sometimes in accordance with an ethical principle ⟨Christianity, which is a religion of extreme ~ —R.M.Weaver⟩ ⟨the conflict is between selfishness and ~ —Estes Kefauver⟩ — compare EGOISM, EGOTISM

al·tru·ist \-rəwəst, -rüə-\ *n* -s **:** one that adheres to or practices altruism

al·tru·is·tic \¦al·trə¦wistik, ¦al·,trü¦is-, -ēk\ *adj* [*altruism* + *-istic*] **:** relating to or given to altruism **:** UNSELFISH — **al·tru·is·ti·cal·ly** \-ək(ə)lē, -ēk-, -li\ *adv*

alts *pl of* ALT

al·tus \'altəs\ *n, pl* **al·ti** \-,tī\ *or* **altuses** [NL, fr. L, high — more at OLD] **:** ALTO

alu·chi resin \ə'lüchē-\ *n* [native name in Guiana] **:** ACOUCHI RESIN

al·u·del \'alyə,del\ *n* -s [MF *alutel, aludel,* fr. Sp & ML; Sp *aludel* & ML *allutel,* fr. Ar *al-uthāl* the vessel] **:** one of the pear-shaped or bottle-shaped pots open at both ends so that the neck can be fitted into the bottom of another similar pot in succession used to form a condenser in sublimation processes

al·u·la \'alyələ\ *n, pl* **alu·lae** \-,lē,-,lī\ [NL, fr. L, dim. of L *ala* wing — more at AISLE] **1 :** BASTARD WING **2 a :** a scalelike structure between the base of the wing and the halter of a two-winged fly — called also *calypter, squama* **b :** a small basal posterior lobe of the wing of a two-winged fly; *also* **:** a similar lobe of the elytron of certain water beetles — **al·u·lar** \-ələ(r)\ *adj*

al·u·let \-,let,-,lət\ *n* -s [irreg. fr. NL *alula* + E *-let*] **:** ALULA 2

¹al·um \'aləm\ *n* -s [ME, fr. MF *alum, alun,* fr. L *alumen* — more at ALE] **1 :** either of two colorless or white isomorphous crystalline double sulfates of aluminum having a sweetish-sourish astringent taste and used chiefly in medicine internally as emetics and locally as astringents and styptics: **a :** the potassium double sulfate $KAl(SO_4)_2.12H_2O$ occurring naturally and also made commercially (as by treating bauxite with sulfuric acid and then potassium sulfate) **:** potassium aluminum sulfate — called also *potash alum, potassium alum;* compare ALUNITE, KALINITE **b :** the ammonium double sulfate $NH_4Al(SO_4)_2.12H_2O$ made commercially (as from ammonium sulfate and aluminum sulfate) — called also *ammonia alum, ammonium alum* **2 :** any of a series of double salts isomorphous with potash alum that may contain analogous elements in place of the potassium, aluminum, and sulfur ⟨soda ~⟩ ⟨chrome ~⟩ ⟨selenium ~⟩ — compare PSEUDOALUM **3 :** ALUMINUM SULFATE — used chiefly commercially

²alum \ə'ləm\ *n* -s [by shortening] **:** an alumnus or alumna

al·um·bloom \'aləm,blüm\ *n* -s **:** ALUMROOT 1

alum·bra·do *also* **alom·bra·do** \,aləm'brä(,)<u>th</u>ō, -ä(,)dō\ *n* -s *usu cap* [Sp *Alumbrado,* lit., illuminated one, fr. *alumbrado* illuminated, fr. (assumed) VL *alluminatus,* past part. of *alluminare* to illuminate, fr. L *ad-* + *luminare* to illuminate, fr. *lumin-, lumen* light — more at LUMINARY] **:** a member of a 16th century mystical Spanish sect striving for spiritual illumination and union with God — called also *Perfectibilist*

alum cake *n* **:** a product of the action of sulfuric acid on clay consisting chiefly of silica and aluminum sulfate

alum carmine *n* **:** a red staining fluid composed of alum, carmine, ammonia, and water

alum cochineal *n* **:** a red staining fluid composed of alum, cochineal, and water

alu·men \ə'lümən\ *n, pl* **alumens** \-mənz\ *or* **alumi·na** \-mənə\ [L — more at *alum*] **:** ALUM

alumen us·tum \-'əstəm, -'üs-\ *n, pl* **alumi·na us·ta** \-mənə'əstə, -'üs-\ [NL] **:** BURNT ALUM

alum flower *n* **:** powdered burnt alum

alum hematoxylin *n* **:** a staining fluid composed of hematoxylin, alum, alcohol, and water

al·u·mif·er·ous \¦alyə¦mif(ə)rəs\ *adj* [*alum* or *aluminum* + *-i-* + *-ferous*] **:** ALUMINIFEROUS

alumin- *or* **alumino-** *comb form* [MF *alumin-,* fr. L, fr. *alumin-, alumen* — more at ALUM] **1 :** alum ⟨*alumin*iform⟩ **2 :** aluminum ⟨*alumino*graphy⟩

alu·mi·na \ə'lümənə\ *n* -s [NL, fr. L *alumin-, alumen*] **:** the oxide of aluminum Al_2O_3 that occurs native as corundum and in hydrated forms, that is made, usu. from bauxite, in various forms (as a white powder obtained by calcination or a hard crystalline substance resembling natural corundum obtained by heating calcined aluminum oxide almost to the fusion point), and that is used chiefly as a source of metallic aluminum, as an abrasive and refractory, as a catalyst and catalyst carrier, and as an adsorbent (as in drying gases and liquids and in chromatography) — see ALUMINUM HYDROXIDE

alumina cement *n* **:** hydraulic cement having a higher alumina content, developing strength more rapidly, and being more resistant to heat and chemicals than portland cement

alumina porcelain *n* **:** a porcelain composed chiefly of alumina and used in spark plugs

¹alu·mi·nate \ə'lümə,nāt\ *vt* -ED/-ING/-S [*alumin-* (alum) + *-ate*] **:** to treat or combine with alum or alumina

²alu·mi·nate \-,nət, -,nāt\ *n* -s [*alumin-* + *-ate*] **:** a compound of alumina with a metallic oxide often regarded as a salt of an aluminum hydroxide⟨magnesium ~ $MgAl_2O_4$⟩—compare SPINEL

al·u·min·ic \¦alyə¦minik\ *adj* [ISV *alumin-* + *-ic*] **:** of or relating to aluminum

alu·mi·nif·er·ous \ə¦lümə¦nif(ə)rəs\ *adj* [*alumin-* + *-i-* + *-ferous*] **:** containing alum or aluminum

alu·mi·nite \ə'lümə,nīt\ *n* -s [G *aluminit,* fr. *alumin-* + *-it* -ite] **:** a hydrous aluminum sulfate $Al_2SO_4(OH)_4.7H_2O$ usu. occurring in white compact reniform masses

al·u·min·i·um \,alyə'minēəm, -nyəm\ *n* -s [NL, by alter.] *chiefly Brit* **:** ALUMINUM

alu·mi·nize \ə'lümə,nīz\ *vt* -ED/-ING/-S [*alumin-* + *-ize*] **1 :** to treat (as a metal) with aluminum or an aluminum compound to form a protective surface alloy ⟨~ steel⟩ **2 :** ALUMINATE **3 :** to coat (as glass) with a film of aluminum

alumino- — see ALUMIN-

alu·mi·nog·ra·phy \ə,lümə'nägrəfē\ *n* -ES [*alumin-* + *-graphy*] **:** ALGRAPHY

alu·mi·non \ə'lümə,nän\ *n* -s [*aluminum ion*] **:** a precipitant for aluminum ion used in analytical work; ammonium aurintricarboxylate

alu·mi·no·sil·i·cate \ə¦lümə(,)nō-\ *n* -s [ISV *alumin-* + *silicate*] **:** a combined silicate and aluminate; *specif* **:** a silicate in which aluminum occurs in the crystalline structure in positions analogous to those of silicon, with four oxygen atoms as closest neighbors

alu·mi·no·sis \ə,lümə'nōsəs\ *n, pl* **alu·mi·no·ses** \-ō,sēz\ [NL, fr. *alumin-* + *-osis*] **:** a lung disease caused by the inhalation of dusts of certain aluminum compounds

alu·mi·no·ther·mic \ə¦lümə(,)nō¦thərmik\ *adj* [*alumin-* + *thermic*] **:** of or relating to aluminothermy

alu·mi·no·ther·mics \=,==(,)=¦=miks\ *n pl but sing in constr* **:** ALUMINOTHERMY

alu·mi·no·ther·my \='==(,)=,=mē\ *n* -ES [ISV *alumin-* + *-thermy;* orig. formed as G *aluminothermie*] **:** a process of producing great heat and strong chemical reduction by oxidizing finely divided aluminum with oxygen taken from another metal, this metal being thus reduced from its oxide (as molten iron is obtained from iron oxide in welding by the Thermit process)

alu·mi·no·type \-,tīp\ *n* -s [*alumin-* + *type*] **:** a relief-surface printing plate made by forcing molten aluminum alloy into a plaster-of-paris mold made from the surface to be duplicated

alu·mi·nous \ə'lümənəs\ *adj* [MF *alumineux* containing alum, fr. L *aluminosus,* fr. *alumin-, alumen* alum + *-osus* -ose] **:** relating to or containing alum or aluminum

aluminous cake *n* **:** ALUM CAKE

¹alu·mi·num \ə'lümənəm *sometimes* əl'yü-\ *n* -s [NL, alter. of *alumium,* fr. *alumina* + *-ium*] **1 :** a bluish silver-white trivalent metallic element, very malleable, ductile, and sonorous and noted for its lightness, good electrical and thermal conductivity, high reflectivity, and resistance to oxidation, that is the most abundant metal in the earth's crust, of which it forms over seven percent, always occurring in combination (as in bauxite, cryolite, corundum, alunite, diaspore, turquoise, spinel, kaolin, feldspar, mica), that is manufactured by electrolysis of a solution of alumina in molten fluorides, followed sometimes by electrolytic refining, that is used usu. in the form of alloys for structural purposes (as in the construction of aircraft, automobiles, and buildings), in the chemical and food-processing industries, in cooking utensils, and in electrical conductors, and that is used in the form of powder or flakes in pigments, pyrotechnic compositions, and explosives — symbol *Al;* see ELEMENT table **2 :** a nearly neutral medium-to-light gray

²aluminum \"\ *adj* **:** relating to, made of, or containing aluminum ⟨an ~ kettle⟩ ⟨~ earth⟩

aluminum brass *n* **:** an alloy containing about 76 percent copper, 22 percent zinc, and 2 percent aluminum

aluminum bronze *n* **:** a pale gold-colored alloy composed of copper and usu. five to ten percent aluminum with iron, nickel, and tin usu. being present in amounts less than one percent each and used esp. for corrosion-resistant parts, for wear-resistant bearings, bushings, gears, and dies, and for ornamental articles

aluminum chloride *n* **:** a deliquescent crystalline compound $AlCl_3$ or Al_2Cl_6 white when pure, that fumes in air and reacts explosively with water, that is obtained by chlorination (as of aluminum or a mixture of bauxite and carbon), and that is used in the anhydrous form chiefly as a catalyst — see CHLORALUM

aluminum hydrate *n* **:** the trihydrate of alumina — used chiefly commercially

aluminum hydroxide *n* **:** any of several white gelatinous or crystalline hydrates $Al_2O_3.nH_2O$ of alumina found in nature, esp. in bauxite, or obtained as precipitates by treating solutions of aluminum salts with hydroxides **:** hydrated alumina; *esp* **:** the trihydrate $Al_2O_3.3H_2O$ or $Al(OH)_3$ of alumina, regarded as acting both as a weak base and as a weak acid, that occurs as gibbsite and is used chiefly in ceramics, in pigments, and as a reinforcing agent for rubber

aluminum oxide *n* **:** ALUMINA

aluminum paint *n* **:** a paint composed of powdered aluminum and varnish

aluminum paper *n* **:** a paper of silvery appearance coated with powdered aluminum

aluminum soap *n* **:** any of various aluminum salts of higher carboxylic acids (as fatty acids) including aluminum stearate and aluminum resinate that are amorphous solids insoluble in water but soluble in hydrocarbon solvents and that are used chiefly in lubricating greases, in protective coatings, and in waterproofing compositions

aluminum sulfate *n* **:** a salt $Al_2(SO_4)_3$ colorless when pure that crystallizes with 18 molecules of water (as in alunogen) but is commonly desiccated to about 14 H_2O, that is usu. made by treating bauxite with sulfuric acid, and that is used chiefly in papermaking, in water purification, in sewage treatment, in tanning, in dyeing as a mordant, and in flameproofing — called also *alum, filter alum, papermakers' alum*

aluminum trihydrate *n* **:** the trihydrate of alumina — used chiefly commercially

alumite *var of* ALUNITE

alum leather *n* **:** leather tanned by the use of such substances as alum, egg yolk, and salt

alum·na \ə'ləmnə\ *n, pl* **alum·nae** \-(,)nē *also* -,nī\ [L, fem. of *alumnus*] **1 :** a girl or woman who has attended or has graduated from a particular school, college, or university **2 :** a woman who is a former member (as of an organization), employee (as in an office), or contributor (as to a magazine)

alum·nal \-nəl\ *adj* [*alumnus* or *alumna* + *-al*] **:** of or relating to alumni or alumnae

alum·nor \-nər, -,nō(ə)r\ *n* -s [*alumni* + *-or*] **:** a person employed to work with alumni and their organizations

alum·nus \ə'ləmnəs\ *n, pl* **alum·ni** \-,nī *sometimes* -(,)nē\ [L, pupil, nursling, foster son, fr. *alere* to nourish — more at OLD] **1 :** one that has attended or has graduated from a particular school, college, or university ⟨a Harvard ~⟩ ⟨an ~ of my college⟩ — usu. used of a man in the sing. but often of men and women in the pl. **2 :** one that is a former member (as of an organization), employee (as in an office), contributor (as to a magazine), or inmate (as of a penitentiary)

alu·mo·hy·dro·cal·cite \ə¦lümō,hīdrō'kal,sīt, ¦alyə(,)mō-\ *n* [ISV *alumo-* (fr. *aluminum*) + *hydr-* + *calcite*] **:** a mineral consisting of a hydrous calcium aluminum carbonate $CaAl_2(CO_3)_2(OH)_4.2H_2O$ and occurring as white chalky radiating masses

alum rock *n* **:** ALUNITE

al·um·root \'==,=\ *n* [¹*alum* + *root*] **1 :** any of several herbs of the genus *Heuchera; esp* **:** a No. American plant (*H. americana*) **2 :** SPOTTED CRANESBILL

alums *pl of* ALUM

alum shale *or* **alum slate** *also* **alum schist** *n* **:** a shale or clay slate orig. containing pyrite and after weathering containing aluminum sulfate formed by the action of sulfuric acid from the decomposition of the pyrite on the aluminous materials of the rock

al·um·stone \'==,=\ *n* **:** ALUNITE

alun–alun *also* **aloun–aloun** \'a¦lü'nä,lün\ *n* -s [Malay] **:** the public square in a Malaysian town usu. consisting of a grassplot surrounded by trees

Alun·dum \ə'ləndəm\ *trademark* — used for a material made by fusing alumina in an electric furnace and used chiefly as an abrasive and refractory

al·u·nite \'al(y)ə,nīt\ *also* **al·um·ite** \'alə,mīt\ *n* -s [F *alunite,* fr. *alun* alum (fr. L *alumen*) + *-ite* — more at ALE] **:** a mineral consisting of a hydrous potassium aluminum sulfate $KAl_3(SO_4)_2(OH)_6$ and occurring in massive form or in rhombohedral crystals

alu·no·gen \ə'lünəjən\ *n* -s [F *alunogène,* fr. *alun* + *-gène* -gen] **:** a mineral consisting of a white fibrous aluminum sulfate $Al_2(SO_4)_3.18H_2O$ frequently found on the walls of mines and quarries — called also *feather alum, hair salt*

alu·pag \¦ä,lü¦päg\ *n* -s [Tag *alupág*] **:** a common Philippine timber tree (*Euphoria didyma*) with sweet edible fruit, the wood being used esp. for making combs

alur \'ä,lü(ə)r, ä'l-\ *n, pl* **alur** *or* **alurs** *usu cap* **1 a :** a cattle-breeding Negro people north of Lake Albert **b :** a member of such people — called also *Luri* **2 :** the Nilotic language of the Alur people

al·ure *n* -s [ME *alour, alure,* fr. OF *aleor, aleoir* passage (fr. *aler* to go) & *aleure, alure* gait, course, gallery, fr. *aler* to go — more at ALLEY] *archaic* **:** PASSAGE, GALLERY, AMBULATORY

alur·gite \ə'lər,jīt, 'alər-\ *n* -s [ISV *alurg-* (fr. Gk *halourgēs* genuine purple dye, lit., wrought in or by the sea, fr. *hals* salt, sea + *-ourgēs,* fr. *ergon* work) + *-ite;* orig. formed as G *alurgit* — more at SALT, WORK] **:** a manganese mica of purplish color

alush·tite \ə'ləsh,tīt, 'aləsh-\ *n* -s [Russ *alushtit,* fr. *Alushta,* town in the Crimea, its locality + Russ *-it* -ite] **:** a mineral consisting of a hydrous aluminum silicate and occurring in bluish or greenish claylike crusts and veins

alu·ta \ə'lüd·ə\ *n* -s [L] **:** a soft tawed leather

al·u·ta·ceous \¦alyə¦tāshəs\ *adj* [irreg. (influence of *-aceous*) fr. LL *alutacius,* fr. L *aluta* soft leather, fr. *alumen* alum (used in tanning) — more at ALUM] **:** having the quality or color of tawed leather

¹al·var \'al,vär, 'äl-\ *n* -s *usu cap* [Tamil *Āḷvār,* fr. *āḷ-* to sink, be immersed in meditation] **:** one of a group of southern Indian Vaishnava saints and devotional writers of the 7th to 9th centuries A.D.

²al·var \'öl,vär\ *n* -s [Sw *ålvar*] **:** the plant community consisting typically of mosses and calciphilous herbaceous plants that grows on steppelike shallow alkaline soils overlying Scandinavian limestones

alvei *pl of* ALVEUS

al·ve·loz *also* **al·ve·los** \¦alvə¦lōz\ *n* -ES [Pg *alveloz*] **:** the milky sap of a Brazilian plant (*Euphorbia heterodoxa*) used by the natives in the treatment of cancerous ulcers

alveol- *or* **alveolo-** *comb form* [L, fr. *alveolus*] **1 :** alveolus ⟨*alveol*ectomy⟩ **2 :** alveolar and ⟨*alveolo*labial⟩

al·ve·o·la \al'vēələ\ *n, pl* **alveo·lae** \-,lē,-,lī\ [NL, alter. of L *alveolus* small cavity — more at ALVEOLUS] **1 :** a small depression or pit: as **a :** one of the pits in the naked receptacle of composite plants **b :** a pore of such fungi as *Polyporus* **c :** the pitted perithecium in certain fungi **2 :** ALVEOLUS

¹al·ve·o·lar \al'vēələ(r) *also* -,lär *or* -,lȧ(r *or* ¦alvē¦ōl- *or* 'alvēəl-\ *adj* [prob. fr. F *alvéolaire,* fr. *alvéole* alveolus (fr. L *alveolus*) + *-aire* -ar] **1 :** of, relating to, resembling, made up of, or having an alveolus or alveoli **2 a :** of, relating to, or taking the form of a small pit or sac **b :** of or relating to the part of the jaw where the teeth arise, the air cells of the lungs, or glands in which the secretory cells are gathered about a central space **3 :** articulated with the tip of the tongue touching or near the teethridge (as the English consonant sounds \t\, \d\, \n\, \s\, and \z\) — **al·ve·o·lar·ly** *adv*

²alveolar \"\ *n* -s **1 alveolars** *pl* **a :** the alveolar processes in which the teeth are set **b** *or* **alveolar arch :** that part of the upper jaws in which the teeth are set; *esp* **:** the inner surface of such a part that is involved in the formation of certain speech sounds **2 a :** an alveolar consonant (as English \t\, \d\, \n\, \s\, or \z\) **b :** an alveolar sound

alveolar artery *n* **:** the branch of the internal maxillary artery that supplies the upper molar and bicuspid teeth

alveolar canals *n pl* **:** the canals in the jawbones for the passage of the dental nerves

alveolar ducts *also* **alveolar passages** *n pl* **:** the somewhat enlarged terminal sections of the bronchioles that branch into the terminal alveoli

al·ve·o·lar·i·form \¦alvē¦larə,fȯrm\ *adj* [ISV *alveolar* + *-iform*] **:** ALVEOLIFORM

alveolar index *n* **:** GNATHIC INDEX

alveolar point *n* **:** a point on the alveolar process midway between the median upper incisor teeth — see CRANIOMETRY illustration

alveolar process *or* **alveolar ridge** *n* **:** the ridge or raised thickened border of the mandible and superior maxillary bones that contains the sockets of the teeth

alveolar surface *n* **:** a flat surface lying just within the cutting margin of the jaw of a turtle and functioning in mastication

alveolar theory *n* **:** a now discarded cytological theory that held protoplasm to be essentially an emulsion in which the apparent ground substance is the discontinuous phase

al·ve·o·lary \al'vēə,lerē, 'alvē-\ *adj* [*alveolar* + *-y*] **:** ALVEOLAR

al·ve·o·late \-ələt, -ə,lāt\ *adj* [L *alveolus* + *-ate*] **:** pitted like a honeycomb

al·ve·o·la·tion \al,vēə'lāshən, ,alvē-\ *n* -s **:** the quality or state of being alveolate

al·ve·ole \'alvē,ōl\ *n* -s [F *alvéole,* fr. L *alveolus*] **:** ALVEOLUS

al·ve·o·lec·to·my \al,vēə'lektəmē, ,alvē-\ *n* -ES [*alveol-* + *-ectomy*] **:** the excision of a portion of the alveolar process usu. as an aid in fitting dentures

al·ve·o·li·form \al'vēələ,fȯrm, ¦alvē¦ōl-\ *adj* [*alveol-* + *-iform*] **:** shaped like an alveolus

al·ve·o·lite \al'vēə,līt, 'alvē-\ *n* -s [NL *Alveolites*] **:** a fossil coral of *Alveolites* or a related genus

al·ve·o·li·tes \,alvēə'līd·ēz, (,)al,vē-\ *n, cap* [NL, fr. L *alveolus* small cavity + NL *-ites* -ite] **:** a genus of fossil corals of the Silurian and Devonian rocks having massive or branching bodies with compressed thin-walled corallites

alveolo- — see ALVEOL-

al·ve·o·lo·con·dyl·e·an \al¦vēə,lō(,)kän¦dilēən, -,kändə¦lēən\ *adj* [*alveol-* + *condyle* + *-an*] **:** of or relating to the plane which passes through the occipital condyles and the alveolar point — see CRANIOMETRY illustration

al·ve·o·lo·na·sal \-¦nāzəl\ *adj* [*alveol-* + *nasion* + *-al*] **:** of or relating to the alveolar point and the nasion

al·ve·o·lus \al'vēələs\ *n, pl* **al·ve·o·li** \-,lī, -,lē\ [L, small hollow, tray, dim. of *alveus* tub, cavity, hollow, fr. *alvus* belly, hollow; akin to ON *hvannjōli* stalk of angelica, Gk *aulos* reed instrument like an oboe, OSlav *ulica* street, Arm *ul, uli* path; basic meaning: tube, long cavity] **1 :** a small cavity or pit: as **a :** a socket for a tooth **b :** an air cell of the lungs **c :** an acinus of a compound gland **d :** a cell or compartment of a honeycomb **e :** any of the pits in the wall of the stomach into which the glands open **2 :** the conical cavity in the anterior end of the guard of a belemnite **3 :** TEETHRIDGE **4 :** any of the converging tooth-bearing ossicles about the mouth of a sea urchin

al·ve·on \'alvē,än\ *n* -s [*alveola* + *-on* (as in *prosthion, nasion*)] **:** ALVEOLAR POINT

al·ve·o·pal·a·tal \¦alvē(,)ō¦-\ *or* **al·ve·o·lo·pal·a·tal** \al-¦vēə(,)lō-\ *adj* [*alveol-* + *palatal*] **:** being in the more palatal of two positions between alveolar and palatal — compare PALATO-ALVEOLAR

al·ve·us \'alvēəs\ *n, pl* **al·vei** \-ē,ī, -ē,ē\ [NL, fr. L, tub, cavity, hollow] **:** a thin layer of medullary nerve fibers on the ventricular surface of the hippocampus major

al·way \'ȯl(,)wā, ⸗'⸗\ *adv* [ME *alwey, alway*] *archaic* **:** ALWAYS

al·ways \'ȯlwēz, 'ȯuw-, -wəz, -(,)wāz, *before some consonants sometimes* -wəs\ *adv* [ME *alweyes, alwayes*, alter. (influenced by *-es* -s) of *alwey, alway*, fr. OE *ealne weg*, lit., all the way, fr. *ealne* (acc. of *eal, æl, al* all) + *weg* (acc.) way — more at ALL, WAY] **1 :** on every occasion **:** at all times **:** INVARIABLY, CONSTANTLY ⟨medieval spelling was ~ flexible —R.D.Altick⟩ **2 :** throughout all time **:** FOREVER, PERPETUALLY ⟨the cult of the superman will . . . ~ be with us —J.C.Wyllie⟩ **3 a :** in every circumstance or contingency **:** without exception ⟨an observed regularity will ~ hold —Edgar Zilsel⟩ **b :** at any rate **:** in any event **:** ANYHOW ⟨as a last resort one can ~ work⟩

al·yce clover *also* **al·ice clover** \'aləs-\ *n, usu cap A* [prob. by folk etymology fr. NL *Alysicarpus* (genus name of *Alysicarpus vaginalis*), fr. Gk *halysis* chain + NL *-carpus*] **:** a low spreading annual Old World legume (*Alysicarpus vaginalis*) of warm climates that is used in southern U.S. as a cover crop in citrus and tung orchards and for hay and pasturage

alyp·ia \ə'lipēə\ *n, cap* [NL, perh. fr. Gk, freedom from pain or grief, fr. *alypos* + *-ia*] **:** a genus of diurnal moths having black wings with brilliant white spots and including the eight-spotted forester

al·y·pin \'aləpən\ *also* **al·y·pine** \"", -,pēn\ *n* -s [fr. *Alypin*, a trademark] *pharmacy* **:** amydricaine or its hydrochloride

alys·sum \ə'lisəm\ *n* [NL, fr. Gk *alysson* plant believed to cure rabies, fr. neut. of *alyssos* curing rabies, fr. *a-* ²a- + *-lyssos* (fr. *lyssa* rage, rabies) — more at LYSSA] **1** *cap* **:** a genus of European and Asiatic herbs (family Cruciferae) having small usu. yellow racemose flowers **2** -s **a :** a plant of the genus *Alyssum* **b :** SWEET ALYSSUM

al·y·tes \'alə,tēz\ *n, cap* [NL, prob. irreg. fr. Gk *alytos* not to be loosed or broken, fr. *a-* ²a- + *lytos* capable of being loosed, fr. *lyein* to loose; prob. fr. the chainlike strings of eggs fastened to the male — more at LOSE] **:** a genus of toads (family Discoglossidae) comprising the obstetrical toads of southwestern Europe

alz·hei·mer's disease \'älts,hīmə(r)z-\ *n, usu cap A* [trans. of G *Alzheimersche krankheit*, after Alois *Alzheimer* †1915 Ger. physician] **:** senile dementia occurring at an early age

am [ME, fr. OE *eom, am;* akin to ON *em* am, Goth *im*, L *sum*, Gk *eimi*, OIr *am*, Skt *asmi* am, *asti* is — more at IS] *pres 1st sing of* BE

-am \,am, ,aa(ə)m\ *n comb form* -s [prob. fr. G, prob. fr. NL *ammonia*] **:** chemical compound related to ammonia ⟨*lactam*⟩ ⟨*phospham*⟩

am *abbr* **1** ammeter; amperemeter **2** ammunition **3** amplitude

AM *abbr or n* -s [ML *artium magister*] Master of Arts

AM *abbr* **1** airmail **2** air marshal **3** amplitude modulation **4** [L *anno mundi*] in the year of the world — often printed in small capitals **5** *often not cap* [L] ante meridiem **6** associate member **7** Ave Maria

Am *symbol* americium

¹ama \'ämə, 'a-, 'ā-\ *n* -s [LL *ama, hama*, fr. L, water bucket, fr. Gk *amē;* akin to L *sentina* bilge water, OIr to-eks-*sem* to pour out, Lith *sémti* to draw up water] **:** AMULA

²ama \'ämə, 'ä,mä\ *n* -s [Hawaiian, Tahitian, Marquesan, Samoan, & Maori] **:** CANDLENUT 2

³ama \"\ *n, pl* **ama** *or* **amas** [Jap] **:** a Japanese woman diver who works usu. without diving gear

⁴ama \"\ *n* -s [Hawaiian] **:** the float of a Hawaiian outrigger canoe

amaas \'ä,mäs\ *n* -ES [Afrik] **:** ALASTRIM

ama·bi·le \ä'mäbə,lā, ə'-, -lē\ *adj* [It, lovable, fr. L *amabilis*, fr. *amare* to love + *-bilis* capable or worthy of (being so acted upon) — more at AMATEUR, -ABLE] **:** TENDER, GENTLE — used as a direction in music

ama·bi·lis fir \ə'mäbələs-\ *n* [part trans. of NL *Abies amabilis*] **:** a fir (*Abies amabilis*) of western No. America having deeply grooved leaves with a prominent midrib and a silvery-white lower surface — called also *white fir*

amability *n* -ES [L *amabilitat-, amabilitas*, fr. *amabilis* + *-tat-, -tas* -ty] *obs* **:** LOVABLENESS

am·a·crine \'amə,krīn, ā'ma,k-\ *adj* [²a- + *macr-* + Gk *in-, is* fiber, muscle, strength] **:** of, relating to, or being an amacrine cell ⟨~ synapses⟩

amacrine cell *n* **:** a unipolar nerve cell found in the retina, in the olfactory bulb, and in close connection with the Purkinje cells of the cerebellum

ama·dan \'ämə,thȯn\ *var of* OMADHAUN

amadavat *var of* AVADAVAT

am·adel·phous \¦amə¦delfəs\ *adj* [irreg. fr. Gk *hama* together with + *adelphos* brotherly, fr. *adelphos* brother — more at SAME, -ADELPHOUS] **:** GREGARIOUS

am·a·dou \'amə,dü\ *n* -s [F, fr. Prov, amadou, lover, fr. L *amator* lover — more at AMATEUR] **:** ³PUNK 2

ama·ga·sa·ki \,ämə̄gə¦säkē\ *adj, usu cap* [fr. *Amagasaki*, Japan] **:** of or from Amagasaki, Japan **:** of the kind or style prevalent in Amagasaki

ama·gat unit \¦amə¦gä-\ *n, usu cap A* [after Emile-Hilaire *Amagat* †1915, Fr. physicist] **1 :** a unit of the density of a substance (as gas or vapor) at 0°C and standard atmospheric pressure **2 :** a unit of the specific volume of a substance (as gas or vapor) at 0°C and standard atmospheric pressure

amag·mat·ic \¦ā,mag¦mad·ik\ *adj* [²a- + *magmatic*] **:** not related to or involved in magmatic activity

amah \'ämə, 'ä(,)mä, ä'mä\ *n* -s [Pg *ama* wet nurse, governess, fr. ML *amma* wet nurse, prob. of imit. origin] **:** an Oriental female servant; *esp* **:** a Chinese nurse ⟨Shanghai people . . . whole big families along with their cooks and ~s —Christopher Rand⟩

ama·hua·ca *or* **ama·wa·ca** \,ämə'wäkə, ,am-\ *n, pl* **amahuaca** *or* **amahuacas** *or* **amawaca** *or* **amawacas** *usu cap* [Sp, of AmerInd origin] **1 a :** a Panoan people of Brazil and Peru **b :** a member of such people **2 :** the Panoan language of the Amahuaca people

¹amain \ə'mān\ *adv* [¹a- + *main* (strength)] **1 :** with all one's might **:** with full force **:** VIOLENTLY ⟨he tugged and toiled ~ —Nathaniel Hawthorne⟩ **2 a :** at full speed ⟨they on the hill . . . came down ~ —John Milton⟩ **b :** in great haste **:** SUDDENLY ⟨left ~ their broken tasks —Joanna Baillie⟩ **3 :** to a high degree **:** GREATLY, EXCEEDINGLY ⟨pleased ~ —John Keats⟩

²amain *vi* -ED/-ING/-S [MF *amener* to lower, lead up (3d pers. sing. pres. indic. *ameine*) — more at AMENABLE] *obs* **:** to lower the topsail as a sign of surrender **:** YIELD

a ma·io·re \¦ä(,)mä'yōrē, ¦ä,mī'ō-\ *adj* [L *a majore* from the larger] **:** of or relating to an ionic foot beginning with two long syllables

amaist \ə'māst, a'-\ *adv* [ME (northern dial.) *almast*, alter. of *almost*] *Scot* **:** ALMOST

a major \'ā-\ *n, usu cap A* ['a] **:** the major musical key having a signature of three sharps

amakosa *pl of* XHOSA

ama·la \'äməlа\ *also* **am·lah** \'ämlə\ *n* -s [Hindi *'amala*, *'amla*, fr. Ar *'amalah*, pl. of *'āmil* official] *India* **:** a minor official of a lawcourt

ama·la·ka \ä'mələkə\ *n* -s [Skt *āmalaka* myrobalan] **:** a bulbous or melonlike ornament terminating the shikaras of medieval Indian temples

am·a·lek·ite \'amə,le,kīt, ə'malə,-\ *n* -s *usu cap* [Heb *'Ămālēqī*, after *'Ămālēq* (Amalek), grandson of Esau (Gen 36:12), from whom they were said to be descended] **:** a member of a powerful nomadic people living in the region around Kadesh south of Canaan by the time of the Exodus and wiped out by the Jews in the time of Hezekiah

¹amal·gam \ə'malgəm\ *n* -s [ME *amalgame, malgame*, fr. MF *amalgame*, fr. ML *amalgama*, prob. modif. of Ar *al-jamā'ah* the assembly] **1 :** an alloy of mercury with another metal being made with most of the well-known metals except iron and platinum by merely bringing mercury and the other metal into contact, being solid or liquid at room temperature according to the proportion of mercury present, and being used esp. in making tooth cements; *specif* **:** a native alloy of mercury and silver occurring in isometric crystals or in massive form **2 :** a combination or mixture of different elements ⟨an ~ of wisdom and nonsense⟩ ⟨an ~ of peasants and businessmen —*N.Y. Times*⟩

²amalgam \"\ *vb* -ED/-ING/-S [ME *amalgamen*, fr. MF *amalgamer*, fr. *amalgame*] *vt* **1 :** AMALGAMATE **2 :** to cover with amalgam ~ *vi* **:** to unite, combine, or alloy — used with *with* ⟨mercury ~*ing* with an alloy⟩ — **amal·ga·ma·ble** \-gəməbəl\ *adj*

amalgama *n* -s [ML] *obs* **:** AMALGAM

¹amal·ga·mate \-gəmət, -,māt\ *adj* **:** AMALGAMATED ⟨two ~ natures⟩

²amal·ga·mate \-,māt, *usu* -ād·+V\ *vb* -ED/-ING/-S *vt* **1 :** to compound or mix together **:** COMBINE, ALLOY ⟨silver *amalgamated* with mercury⟩ **2 a :** to unite or combine into a uniform and independent whole **:** INTEGRATE ⟨scattered fragments of humanity had never shown any desire to be *amalgamated* with the social structure —Edith Wharton⟩ **b :** to unite or combine with an already existing whole **:** ABSORB, ANNEX ⟨policy of conciliating and *amalgamating* conquered nations —Agnes Repplier⟩ **3 :** to merge (as two societies) in a single body ⟨the two colleges were *amalgamated* to constitute a university⟩ ~ *vi* **1 :** to become amalgamated **:** become one **:** enter into close or intimate relations ⟨never united or *amalgamated* with man —*Commonweal*⟩ **2 :** to enter into a union (as by marriage) **:** INTERMARRY ⟨a tendency to ~ with the natives —C.W. Spencer⟩ **syn** see MIX

amalgamated union *n* **:** a union of smaller unions or of related crafts or occupations

amal·ga·ma·tion \ə,malgə'māshən\ *n* -s [*amalgam* + *-ation*] **1 a :** the action or process of amalgamating **:** UNITING ⟨an opportunity for the ~ of Wales with England —G.M.Trevelyan⟩ **b :** the quality or state of being amalgamated ⟨in the 14th century the ~ of the races was all but complete —T.B. Macaulay⟩ **2 :** the result of amalgamating **:** AMALGAM ⟨an ~ of parishes to provide a workhouse for . . . the poor —G.E. Fussell⟩ **3 :** a consolidation or merger (as of two corporations) ⟨formed in 1844 by ~ of three smaller companies —O.S.Nock⟩ **4 :** a biological process of race mixture

amal·ga·ma·tion·ist \-ə̇st\ *n* -s **:** an advocate of racial amalgamation

amalgamation process *n* **:** a process of extracting metals (as native gold and silver) from their ores by the addition of small quantities of mercury to the stamping or grinding unit so that the resulting amalgam is caught on mercury-coated copper plates from which it is then scraped, the precious metals in it being recovered by distilling off the mercury

amal·ga·ma·tive \ə'malgə,mād·iv\ *adj* **:** characterized by or tending to amalgamation

amal·ga·ma·tor \-,mād·ə(r)\ *n* -s **1 :** one that amalgamates ⟨henceforth Christianity was to be the prime ~ —H.O.Taylor⟩ **2 a :** a machine for use in the amalgamation process **b :** a person who tends such a machine

amal·ga·mize \-,mīz\ *vt* -ED/-ING/-S **:** AMALGAMATE

am·al·ri·cian \,aməl'rishən\ *n* -s *usu cap* [*Amalric* of Bena †*ab*1204 Fr. theologian and philosopher + E *-ian*] **:** a member of a sect of pantheists founded by the French philosopher Amalric of Bena

amal·tas \ə'məl,täs\ *n, pl* **amaltas** [Hindi *amaltās* drumstick tree] **1 :** CASSIA FISTULA **2 :** a tanning extract derived from the drumstick tree

ama·mau \¦ämə¦mau̇\ *n* -s [Hawaiian *ama'uma'u*] **:** a small Hawaiian tree fern (*Sadleria cyatheoides*) of the family Cyatheaceae having petioles which yield soft hairs used for the same purposes as pulu

aman \'ämən\ *n* -s [Hindi *āman*] **:** long-stemmed rice grown in the rainy season in India

ama·na·yé \,ämənə¦yā\ *n, pl* **amanayé** *or* **amanayés** *usu cap* [Pg, of AmerInd origin] **1 a :** a Tupi-Guaranian people of the state of Maranhão in northeastern Brazil **b :** a member of such people **2 :** the language of the Amanayé people

amand *vt* -ED/-ING/-S [L *amandare*, fr. *a-* (fr. *ab-* ¹ab-) + *mandare* to send — more at MANDATE] *obs* **:** to send away **:** DISMISS

am·an·din \'amənd ən, 'am-; ə'man-\ *n* -s [F *amandine*, fr. *amande* + *-ine* -ine, -in] **:** the typical protein of sweet almonds and peach kernels with the properties of a globulin

aman·dine \¦ämən¦dēn, ¦am-\ *adj* [F, fr. *amande* almond (fr. OF *almande*) + *-ine* — more at ALMOND] **:** prepared or served with almonds

amang \ə'maŋ\ *prep* [ME (northern dial.), alter. of *among*] *chiefly Scot* **:** AMONG

¹ama·ni \ə'mänē\ *n* -s [Hindi & Per *amānī*, fr. Ar *amānah* security] **1 :** Indian government estates or other sources of revenue not leased or farmed out — compare ZAMINDARI **2 :** Indian government lands paying rent in kind instead of in money

²ama·ni \'ämənē\ *n* -s [Pashto, after *Aman*ullah Khan †1960, amir of Afghanistan, 1919–29] **1 :** a gold coin of Afghanistan issued by Amanullah 1919–26 **2 :** a unit of value equivalent to one afghani

aman·ist \ə'manəst\ *n* -s *usu cap* [*Amana* Society (prob. trans. of G *Amana-Gesellschaft*, fr. *Amana*, biblical name — Song of Sol 4:8 — for a range of the Lebanon mts.) + E *-ist*] **:** a member of the religious communal Amana Society organized in Germany in 1714, located at Amana, Iowa, in 1855, and known to the members as the Community of True Inspiration

am·a·ni·ta \,amə'nīd·ə, -ēd·ə\ *n, cap* [NL, prob. fr. Gk *amanitai* (pl.), a kind of fungus] **:** a genus of widely distributed white-spored agarics having an annulus and a volva that is separate from the pileus and with a few exceptions being poisonous

aman·i·top·sis \ə,manə'täpsə̇s\ *n, cap* [NL, fr. *Amanita* + *-opsis*] **:** a genus of agarics distinguished by the absence of an annulus and being with a few exceptions poisonous

ama·no·ri \,ämə'nōrē\ *n* -s [Jap] **:** an alga or a product prepared from algae of the genus *Porphyra* comprising purple gelatinous seaweeds that are dried and pressed and are important as food in Japan — called also *laver, nori*

am·a·nous \'amənəs, (')ā¦man-\ *adj* [²a- + L *manus* hand — more at MANUAL] **:** having no hands ⟨~ bipeds⟩

am·a·nu·en·sis \ə,manyə'wen(t)sə̇s\ *n, pl* **amanuen·ses** \-n,sēz\ [L, fr. *a-* (fr. *ab-* ¹ab-) + *manus* hand, handwriting (as in *servus a manu* clerk) + *-ensis* -ese — more at MANUAL] **:** one who is employed to write from dictation or to copy what another has written **:** SECRETARY

ama·pa \ə'mäpə\ *n* -s [MexSp] **1 :** either of two Mexican timber trees (*Tabebuia chrysantha* and *T. palmeri*) used for veneering **2 a :** a large tree (*Parahancornia amapa*) of the family Apocynaceae of the Amazon valley **b :** a gum of this tree resembling chicle

am·a·ra \'amərə\ *n, cap* [NL, fr. Gk, trench; akin to Gk *amē* shovel, *diaman* to dig, OSlav *jama* pit] **:** a large genus of phytophagous ground beetles (family Carabidae) of oblong-ovate form, medium size, and usu. bronze color

am·a·ranth \'amə,ran(t)th, -aa(ə)n-\ *n* -s [in sense 1, alter. (prob. influenced by Gk *anthos* flower) of Gk *amaranton*, fr. neut. of *amarantos* immortal, fr. *a-* ²a- + *-marantos* (fr. *marainein* to waste, wither, quench); in other senses, fr. NL *Amaranthus*, alter. (prob. influenced by Gk *anthos*) of L *amarantus*, a flower (prob. *Celosia cristata*), modif. of Gk *amaranton* — more at SMART] **1 :** an imaginary flower supposed never to fade ⟨beds of ~ and moly —Alfred Tennyson⟩ **2 a :** a plant of the genus *Amaranthus* **b :** PURPLEHEART **3 :** a dark reddish purple that is redder and less strong than patriarch and bluer and stronger than auricula purple or raisin purple **4 :** a red acid azo dye $C_{20}H_{11}N_2Na_3O_{10}S_3$ that is used chiefly in coloring foods, beverages, and pharmaceutical preparations and in dyeing wool and silk — see DYE table 1 (under *Acid Red 27*)

am·a·ran·tha·ce·ae \,amə,ran'thāsē,ē\ *n pl, cap* [NL, fr. *Amaranthus*, type genus + *-aceae*] **:** a cosmopolitan family of herbs and low shrubs (order Caryophyllales) having bracteate flowers in dense clusters for which many members are cultivated

amaranth family *n* **:** AMARANTHACEAE

am·a·ran·thine \¦amə¦ran(t)thən, -n,thīn\ *adj* [*amaranth* + *-ine*] **1 a :** of or relating to amaranth ⟨~ bowers —Alexander Pope⟩ **b :** FADELESS, UNDYING ⟨the only ~ flower on earth is virtue —William Cowper⟩ **2 :** of the color amaranth

amaranth pink *n* **:** a deep purplish pink that is bluer and stronger than average orchid rose

amaranth purple *n* **:** a deep purplish red that is bluer and stronger than American beauty, redder and less strong than magenta (sense 2a), and redder, lighter, and slightly stronger than hollyhock

am·a·ran·thus \,amə'ran(t)thəs\ *n* [NL — more at AMARANTH] **1** *cap* **:** a large and widely distributed genus (the type of the family Amaranthaceae) of mostly coarse annual herbs having alternate leaves and small flowers with a 5-parted calyx and 2-celled anthers **2** -s **:** a plant of the genus *Amaranthus* — see PIGWEED

am·a·ran·tite \-ran,tīt\ *n* -s [ISV *amarant-* (fr. L *amarantus* amaranth) + *-ite;* orig. formed as G *amarantit* — more at AMARANTH] **:** a hydrous ferric sulfate $FeSO_4(OH).3H_2O$ of amaranth color

am·a·relle \¦amə¦rel\ *n* -s [G, fr. ML *amarellum*, fr. L *amarus* bitter, sour — more at AMAROID] **:** any of several cultivated cherries derived from the sour cherry (*Prunus cerasus*) and distinguished from the morellos by their colorless juice

ama·re·vo·le \,ämə'revəlē\ *adv (or adj)* [It *amaro* bitter (fr. L *amarus*) + *-evole* -able (fr. L *-ibilis*)] **:** with bitterness **:** POIGNANTLY — used as a direction in music

amar·go·so \,ämər'gō(,)sō, -sə\ *also* **amar·go·sa** \-sə\ *n* -s [MexSp *amargoso* goatbush, fr. Sp, bitter, fr. (assumed) VL *amaricosus*, fr. L *amarus*] **1 :** the bark of the goatbush **2** [PhilSp, fr. Sp, bitter] **:** the balsam apple of the Philippines

am·a·ril·lite \,amə'ri,līt\ *n* -s [prob. fr. F, fr. Tierra *Amarilla*, Atacama province, Chile + F *-ite*] **:** a mineral $NaFe(SO_4)_2.6H_2O$ consisting of a hydrous sodium ferric sulfate

ama·ril·lo \,amə'ri(,)lō, ,amə'rē(,)(y)ō, ,äm-\ *n* -s [AmerSp, fr. Sp, yellow, fr. ML *amarellus* yellowish, pale, fr. L *amarus* bitter; perh. fr. association of the yellow skin color of jaundice with the bitterness of bile] **:** any of several tropical American timber trees: as **a :** a Venezuelan tree (*Aspidosperma vargasii*) **b :** either of two widely distributed Brazilian trees (*Terminalia obovata* and *Lafoensia punicifolia*) **c :** FUSTIC 1a

amar·na \ə'märnə\ *adj, usu cap* [fr. Tell el *'Amarna*, ancient station on the Nile river bet. Thebes and Memphis, Egypt] **:** of or belonging to the period of time about 1375–1360 B.C. that is described on the ancient Egyptian Tell el'Amarna tablets discovered 1887 and written in cuneiform characters containing the Asiatic correspondence of Amenhotep IV and his father Amenhotep III

am·a·roid \'amə,rȯid\ *n* -s [L *amarus* bitter + E *-oid;* akin to OE *ampre* sorrel, OHG *ampfaro*, ON *apr* sharp, Gk *ōmos* raw, cruel, Skt *amla, ambla* sour] **:** any bitter vegetable extractive of definite chemical composition other than an alkaloid or glucoside

am·a·roi·dal \¦amə¦rȯidᵊl\ *adj* **:** relating to bitters or having a bitter taste

am·a·ryl·lid \,amə'riləd\ *n* -s [NL *Amaryllid-, Amaryllis*] **:** a plant of the family Amaryllidaceae — **am·a·ryl·lid·e·ous** \¦amə(,)ri¦lidēəs\ *adj*

am·a·ryl·li·da·ce·ae \,amə,rilə'dāsē,ē\ *n pl, cap* [NL, fr. *Amaryllid-, Amaryllis*, type genus + *-aceae*] **:** a family of plants (order Liliales) found mostly in tropical regions and having perfect showy flowers with the tube of the perianth adnate to the ovary

am·a·ryl·li·da·ceous \¦amə,rilə¦dāshəs\ *adj* [NL *Amaryllidaceae* + E *-ous*] **:** of or relating to the family Amaryllidaceae

am·a·ryl·lis \,amə'riləs\ *n* [NL, prob. fr. L, the name of a shepherdess in Virgil] **1** *cap* **:** a genus (the type of the family Amaryllidaceae) of bulbous southern African plants having umbellate flowers with a corona of scales between the filaments — see BELLADONNA LILY **2** -ES **:** a plant of the genus *Amaryllis* or of any of several related genera formerly united with it (as *Hippeastrum, Sprekelia*, or *Vallota*)

amaryllis family *n* **:** AMARYLLIDACEAE

amas *pl of* AMA

amass \ə'mas, -aa(ə)s, -ais\ *vb* -ED/-ING/-ES [MF *amasser*, fr. OF, fr. *a-* (fr. L *ad-*) + *masser* to gather into a mass, fr. *masse* mass — more at MASS] *vt* **1 :** to collect for oneself **:** gather as one's own **:** ACCUMULATE ⟨~*ed* a large fortune⟩ **2 :** to collect into a mass **:** bring together **:** GATHER ⟨~*ing* daily trifles, writing down what came into her head —Virginia Woolf⟩ ~ *vi* **:** to come together **:** ASSEMBLE ⟨ivy . . . ~*ed* in bushes above . . . the porch —Elizabeth Bowen⟩ **syn** see ACCUMULATE

amas·sette \¦amə¦set\ *n* -s [F, fr. *amasser* + *-ette*] **:** a scraping instrument used in ancient and medieval painting for gathering on a slab colors intended to be ground

amass·ment \ə'masmənt, -aas-, -ais-\ *n* -s **:** the act or result of amassing **:** ACCUMULATION

amas·tia \(')ā'mastēə\ *n* -s [NL, fr. ²a- + Gk *mastos* breast + NL *-ia* — more at MAMMA] **:** the absence or underdevelopment of the mammary glands

¹amate *vt* -ED/-ING/-S [ME *amaten*, fr. MF *amatir*, fr. OF, fr. *a-* (fr. L *ad-*) + *matir* to overcome, fr. *mat* defeated, overcome — more at MAT] *archaic* **:** to cast down **:** DISHEARTEN, SUBDUE

²amate *vt* -ED/-ING/-S [*a-* (perfective prefix) + *mate* (to couple, match) — more at ABEAR] *obs* **:** to be a mate to **:** MATCH

³ama·te \ä'mäd·ē\ *n* -s [Sp, fr. Nahuatl *amatl*, short for *amacuahuitl*, lit., paper tree, fr. *amatl* paper + *cuahuitl* tree] **:** a Central American timber tree (*Ficus glabrata*) with lustrous foliage and edible fruits

¹am·a·teur \'amə,tər (+V -ər-), -,tə̄r (*also* ,⸗'⸗); -,d·ə(r), -,tə(r); -,tü(ə)r, -,tüə, -,tyü(ə)r, -,tyüə (*also* ,⸗⸗'⸗); -,chü(ə)r, -,chüə, -,chə(r)\ *n* -s [F, fr. L *amator* lover, fr. *amatus* (past part. of *amare* to love) + *-or;* prob. akin to OHG *amma* mother, nurse, ON *amma* grandmother, L *amita* father's sister, Gk *amma* nurse, Phrygian *adamnein* to love] **1 :** one that has a marked fondness, liking, or taste **:** DEVOTEE, ADMIRER ⟨~s of this splendid wine will surely rejoice to learn that a limited quantity . . . will be available —*New Yorker*⟩ **2 a :** one that engages in a particular pursuit, study, or science as a pastime rather than as a profession ⟨the professional historians . . . have again let an ~ make off with a theme of real significance —T.H.Williams⟩ **b :** one that competes in sports or athletics for pleasure rather than for financial gain — compare PROFESSIONAL **3 a :** one that follows an art or science in a superficial way **:** DILETTANTE, DABBLER ⟨affected the pose of the gentleman ~ of the arts —F.H.Ellis⟩ **b :** one that engages in an activity in an inexperienced or incompetent manner ⟨the ~s, the green beginners . . . are naturally appalled by the shelffuls our curiosity persuades us to tackle —John Mason Brown⟩

²amateur \"\ *adj* **1 :** of, relating to, or having the status of an amateur ⟨football on an ~ basis⟩ ⟨an ~ writer⟩ **2 :** engaged in or performed by or as if by an amateur **:** NONPROFESSIONAL ⟨~ acting⟩

amateur band *n* **:** one of the bands of frequencies used by radio amateurs for communication

am·a·teur·ish \¦⸗⸗¦tər·ish, -¦türi-, -¦tyüri-, '⸗⸗,chüri-, -ēsh\ *adj* **:** having the characteristics of an amateur **:** lacking professional finish ⟨an ~ actor⟩ — **am·a·teur·ish·ly** *adv*

am·a·teur·ism \'⸗⸗(,)⸗,izəm\ *n* -s **:** the practice, characteristics, or status of an amateur **:** NONPROFESSIONALISM ⟨~ in athletics⟩ ⟨a staff notable for its ~⟩

am·a·tho·pho·bia \,aməthə'fōbēə\ *n* -s [NL, fr. Gk *amathos* sand + NL *-phobia*] **:** fear of dust

ama·ti \ä'mäd·ē, ə'-\ *n* -s *usu cap* [after *Amati*, 16th & 17th cent. Ital. family of violin makers] **:** a violin made by a member of the Amati family of Cremona

am·a·tive \'amədiv\ *adj* [ML *amativus*, fr. L *amatus*, past part. of *amare* to love + *-ivus* -ive — more at AMATEUR] **:** disposed or disposing to love **:** AMOROUS — **am·a·tive·ly** *adv*

am·a·tol \'amə,tōl, -ȧl\ *n* -s [ISV *ammonium* + connective *-a-* + trinitro*toluene*] **:** an explosive consisting of ammonium nitrate and trinitrotoluene

am·a·to·ry \'amə,tōrē, -ōr-, -ri\ *or* **am·a·to·ri·ous** \¦==¦rēəs\ *also* **am·a·to·ri·al** \¦==¦=əl\ *adj* [*amatory, amatorious* fr. L *amatorius*, fr. *amatus* (past. part. of *amare* to love) + *-orius* -ory; *amatorial* fr. L *amatorius* + E *-al*] **:** of, relating to, or expressing sexual love ⟨the ~ affairs of youth⟩ ⟨an anthology of ~ poems⟩

ama·trice \ə'mā·trəs, (')a¦m-\ *n* -s [blend of *American* and *matrice*] **:** a gem cut from variscite and its surrounding matrix

am·a·tun·gu·la \,amə'taŋg(y)ələ\ *n* -s [Zulu *amatungulu*, pl.] **:** NATAL PLUM

am·au·ro·sis \,a,mȯ'rōsəs\ *n, pl* **amauro·ses** \-ō,sēz\ [Gk *amaurōsis*, lit., dimming, fr. *amauroun* to dim (fr. *amauros* dark, dim) + *-sis* -sis] **:** a partial or total loss of sight from disease of the optic nerve, retina, or brain without any perceptible external change in the eye — **am·au·rot·ic** \,a,mȯ¦räd·ik\ *adj*

amaurotic idiocy *or* **amaurotic family idiocy** *n* **:** a recessive genetic defect manifested by mental deficiency associated with impaired vision or blindness

amau·ta \ə'mau̇d·ə\ *n* -s *often cap* [Sp, fr. Quechua] **:** an Inca wise man and professional teacher

amawaca *usu cap, var of* AMAHUACA

amax·o·pho·bia \ə,maksə'fōbēə\ *n* -s [NL, fr. Gk *amaxo-, hamaxo-* (fr. *amaxa, hamaxa* wagon) + NL *-phobia*] **:** fear of being in or riding in a vehicle

amaxosa *or* **amaxhosa** *pl of* XHOSA

¹amaze \ə'māz\ *vb* -ED/-ING/-S [ME *amasen*, fr. OE *āmasian*, fr. *ā-* (perfective prefix) + (assumed) *masian* to confuse — more at ABEAR, MAZE] *vt* **1** *obs* **a :** to fill with bewilderment **:** PERPLEX **b :** to fill with terror or alarm **:** CONFOUND **2 :** to fill with wonder **:** ASTONISH, ASTOUND ⟨proportions which continually ~ foreign observers —F.L.Mott⟩ ~ *vi* **:** to show or cause astonishment ⟨means by which they might astound or ~ —A.E.Wier⟩ **syn** see SURPRISE

²amaze \"\ *n* -s **1** *obs* **a :** mental confusion **b :** PANIC **2 :** AMAZEMENT ⟨with unfeigned wonder and ~ —J.L.Lowes⟩

amazed \-zd\ *adj* [ME *amased*, fr. past part. of *amasen*] **:** filled with wonder or astonishment **:** ASTOUNDED ⟨more and more ~ and not a little perplexed —T.L.Peacock⟩ — **amazed·ly** \ə'māz(ə)dlē, -li\ *adv*

amazeiner *n* -s [origin unknown] **:** a worker who feeds strips of shoe leather through a skiving machine to ensure thinner seams when strips are joined

amaze·ment \ə'māzmənt\ *n* -s **1** *obs* **a :** FRENZY, MADNESS **b :** BEWILDERMENT, PERPLEXITY **c :** CONSTERNATION, TERROR **2 :** the quality or state of being amazed ⟨left the squire staring after him in perfect ~ —Samuel Lover⟩ **:** great wonder or astonishment ⟨to her utter ~ she saw Mr. Darcy walk into the room —Jane Austen⟩ **3 :** something that amazes ⟨the wonders, the ~s of New York —H.H.Johnston⟩

¹amazing *adj* [fr. pres. part. of ¹*amaze*] **:** causing amazement, great wonder, or surprise **:** ASTONISHING — **amaz·ing·ly** *adv*

²amazing *adv, dial* **:** in a remarkable manner **:** EXCEPTIONALLY, WONDERFULLY ⟨the snow was ~ deep⟩

am·a·zon \'amə,zän *also* -,zən\ *n* -s [ME, fr. L, fr. Gk *Amazōn*] **1 a** *usu cap* **:** one of a race or nation of female warriors usu. associated with Scythia or Asia Minor with whom the ancient Greeks of mythology repeatedly warred **b :** a female warrior **c :** a tall strong masculine woman **:** VIRAGO **2 :** a member of a species or strain of animals known only as parthenogenetic females **3 :** a woolen dress goods in a satin or twill weave with the nap raised and shorn for softness **4** [NL *Amazona*] *sometimes cap* **a :** any of numerous parrots of *Amazona* and related genera of Central and So. America **b :** any of several brilliantly colored hummingbirds **c :** AMAZON ANT

am·a·zo·na \,amə'zōnə\ *n, cap* [NL, fr. *Amazon* river (Pg *Amazonas*)] **:** a large genus of tropical American parrots

amazon ant *n, usu cap 1st A* [so called fr. the legend that the Amazons captured children from other tribes and reared them as their own] **:** an ant of a genus (*Polyergus*) of slave-making ants of Europe and America which carry away and rear in their own nests the larvae and nymphs of other species

¹am·a·zo·ni·an \¦amə¦zōnēən, -nyən\ *adj* [*Amazon* + *-ian*] **1 a** *usu cap* **:** of, like, or befitting an Amazon **b** *of a woman* **:** having masculine characteristics **:** WARLIKE **2** *usu cap* **:** of or relating to the Amazon river or its valley

²amazonian \"\ *n* -s *usu cap* [*Amazonia*, regions about the *Amazon* river in So. America + E *-an*] **:** an Indian of the Amazon region in So. America

am·a·zon·ism \'amə,zä,nizəm, -,zə,-\ *n* -s *often cap* **:** the assumption by women of habits and occupations usu. regarded as masculine

am·a·zon·ite \-,nīt\ *or* **am·a·zon·stone** \'==(,)=,=\ *n* -s [*Amazon* river + E *-ite* or *stone;* fr. the mistaken belief that it is found near the Amazon] **:** an apple-green or verdigris-green microcline

amazon lily *n, usu cap A* **:** a plant of the genus *Eucharis*

amazon sword *or* **amazon swordplant** *n, usu cap A* [fr. *Amazon* river] **:** an aquatic or marsh herb (*Echinodorus intermedius*) used as a table centerpiece and in aquariums

amazon terrapin *n, usu cap A* [fr. *Amazon* river] **:** a large tropical American river terrapin (*Podocnemis expansa*) whose eggs are a valuable source of oil

amazon water lily *n, usu cap A* [fr. *Amazon* river] **:** ROYAL WATER LILY

amb *abbr* **1** ambassador **2** ambulance

¹am·ba *var of* ANBA

²am·ba \'ambə, 'äm-\ *n, pl* **amba** *or* **ambas** *usu cap* **1 :** a Bantu-speaking people of southwestern Uganda of small stature and supposed to be of mixed Pygmy descent **2 :** a member of the Amba people

ambach *var of* AMBATCH

am·bage \'ambij\ *n, pl* **amba·ges** \am'bā,jēz, 'ambijəz\ [back-formation fr. ME *ambages*, fr. MF or L; MF, fr. L, roundabout way, circumlocution, ambiguity, fr. *amb-* (var. of *ambi-*) + *-ages* (fr. *agere* to drive, lead, act, do) — more at AGENT] **1** *archaic* **:** a roundabout way of speaking **:** AMBIGUITY, CIRCUMLOCUTION — usu. used in pl. **2** *ambages pl, archaic* **a :** winding or circuitous paths **b :** indirect ways or proceedings **c :** secret or mysterious ways of action

am·ba·gious \(')am¦bājəs\ *adj* [L *ambagiosus*, fr. *ambages* + *-osus* -ous] *archaic* **:** ROUNDABOUT, CIRCUITOUS — **am·ba·gious·ly** *adv*

am·ba·lam \'əmbələm\ *n* -s [Sinhalese *ambalama*] **:** a Ceylonese resthouse for travelers; *also* **:** a village meeting place in Ceylon

am·ba·ree *also* **am·ba·ri** \(,)əm'bärē\ *n* -s [Hindi *'ambārī*, *'amārī*, fr. Per *'amārī*, fr. Ar] *India* **:** a canopied howdah

am·ba·rel·la \,ambə'relə\ *n* -s [Sinhalese *æmbarælla*, fr. Skt *āmravāṭaka* (*Spondias mangifera*), fr. *āmra* mango (fr. *amla* sour) + *vāṭaka* enclosure, garden, fr. *vaṭa* surrounded; akin to Skt *valate* he turns — more at AMAROID, VOLUBLE] **:** OTAHEITE APPLE

am·ba·ri \am'bärē, ,əm-\ *or* **ambari hemp** \(')am¦b-, ¦əm¦b-\ *n* -s [Hindi *ambāṛā, ambāṛī*] **:** KENAF

am·bash·tha \(,)əm'bəshtə\ *n* -s *usu cap* [Skt *Ambaṣṭha*] **:** a member of a caste in India formed by persons descended from Brahman fathers and Vaisya mothers and having the practice of the art of healing as its prerogative

am·bas·sade \¦ambə¦säd, -ād\ *also* **em·bas·sade** \¦em-\ *n* -s [ME *ambassade, ambassiat*, fr. MF *ambassade, ambassiate*, fr. OIt *ambasciata* — more at EMBASSY] *archaic* **:** the mission of an ambassador or those sent on a mission

am·bas·sa·dor *also* **em·bas·sa·dor** \am'basədə(r), əm-, aam'baas- *also* em- *or* -sə,dō(ə)r *or* -sə,dȯ(ə) *or* -sdə(r) *or*, *rap.*, -stə(r)\ *n* -s [ME *ambassadour, embassadour, ambassatour, embassatour, ambassiatour, embassiatour*, fr. MF *ambassadeur, embassadeur, ambassateur, embassateur, ambassiateur*, fr. OIt *ambasciatore*, fr. OProv *ambaisador*, fr. (assumed) *ambaisa* mission — more at EMBASSY] **1** *sometimes cap* **:** an official representative of a sovereign or state: as **a :** a minister of the highest rank accredited to a foreign government or sovereign as the resident representative of his own government or sovereign **b :** a minister of the highest rank appointed for a special and often temporary diplomatic assignment **2 a :** an authorized or appointed representative or messenger ⟨the association . . . sends ~s to the state and national capitals to promote its interests —W.P.Webb⟩ **b :** an unofficial representative ⟨an effective ~ of American culture⟩

ambassador–at–large *n, pl* **ambassadors–at–large** *sometimes cap 1st A & L* **:** a minister of the highest rank not accredited to a particular foreign government or sovereign ⟨the *ambassador-at-large* . . . could assist . . . in important international negotiations —G.H.Stuart⟩

am·bas·sa·do·ri·al \(,)am,basə'dōrēəl, əm-, (,)aam-, -aas-, -ōr- *also* em-\ *adj* **:** of or relating to an ambassador or ambassadors — **am·bas·sa·do·ri·al·ly** \-əlē, -li\ *adv*

am·bas·sa·dor·ship \='===,ship\ *n* -s **:** the office, position, or function of an ambassador

am·bas·sa·dress *also* **em·bas·sa·dress** \am'basədrəs, əm-, aam'baas- *also* em-\ *n* -ES [*ambassador, embassador* + *-ess*] **1 :** a female ambassador **2 :** the wife of an ambassador

am·bas·sage *var of* EMBASSAGE

am·batch *also* **am·bach** \'am,bach\ *n* -ES [prob. of Ethiopic origin; akin to Tigrinya *ambasha, ambatcha*, Amharic *ambatcho*, names of various plants] **:** a rapidly growing thorny tree (*Aeschynomene elaphroxylon*) of the Nile valley valued for its white pithlike wood

am·ba·to·ar·i·nite \,ambə(,)tō'arə,nīt\ *n* -s [F, fr. *Ambatoarina*, town near Ambositra, Madagascar, its locality + F *-ite*] **:** a mineral $5SrCO_3.4(Ce,La,Di)_2(CO_3)_3.(Ce,La,Di)_2O_3$ consisting of an orthorhombic carbonate of the cerium metals and strontium

am·bay \'am,bī\ *n* -s [modif. of AmerSp *ambaiba*, fr. Tupi] **:** an Argentine timber tree (*Cecropia adenopus*) with light soft wood

am·beer \'am,bi(ə)r, -iə\ *n* -s [prob. alter. of *amber;* fr. its color] *chiefly South & Midland* **:** TOBACCO JUICE

¹am·ber \'ambə(r), 'aam-\ *n* -s [ME *ambra, ambre*, fr. MF & ML; MF *ambre*, fr. ML *ambra, ambar*, fr. Ar *'anbar* ambergris] **1** *obs* **:** AMBERGRIS **2 a :** a very hard yellowish to brownish translucent fossil resin that is found in alluvial soils, in beds of lignite, or on some seashores, that takes a fine polish, and that is used chiefly in making ornamental objects (as beads and pipe mouthpieces) **3 a :** a variable color averaging a dark orange yellow that is yellower, lighter, and stronger than topaz **b :** the variable color of amber that averages the color lime **c :** AMBER YELLOW **4 a :** KLAMATH WEED **b :** SWEET GUM 1a

²amber \"\ *adj* **1 :** consisting of amber **2 :** resembling amber; *esp* **:** having the color amber ⟨on a special ~ afternoon of late November —Gladys B. Stern⟩

³amber \"\ *vt* **ambered; ambered; ambering** \-b(ə)riŋ\ **ambers** [²*amber*] **:** to make amber in color

⁴amber *n* -s [OE *amber, ambor, ember* vessel, pail, a dry measure; akin to OS *ēmbar* pail, OHG *ambar;* all fr. a prehistoric WGmc word borrowed fr. L *amphora* vessel with two handles — more at AMPHORA] **:** an Anglo-Saxon unit of capacity for dry or liquid measure

amber brown *n* **:** a brownish orange that is less strong and slightly yellower and lighter than spice, slightly yellower and lighter than prairie brown, Windsor tan, or Titian, and slightly redder and darker than gold pheasant

ambercane \'==,=\ *n* -s [so called fr. its color] **:** a sorghum (*Sorghum dochna*) used esp. in southern Africa as a fodder and grain crop

amberfish \'==,=\ *n* [so called fr. its color] **:** any of numerous tropical or subtropical fishes of *Seriola* or related genera (family Carangidae) — compare AMBERJACK, YELLOWTAIL

amber forest *n* **:** a forest whose trees yielded the resin that fossilized into amber

am·ber·gris \'ambə(r),gris, 'aam-, -,grēs, -,grəs *sometimes* -,grē\ *also* **am·ber·grease** \-,grēs\ *n, pl* **ambergrises** *also* **ambergreases** [*ambergris* fr. ME *ambregris*, fr. MF *ambre gris*, fr. *ambre* ambergris, amber + *gris* gray; *ambergrease* by folk etymology fr. *ambergris* — more at AMBER, GRIZZLE] **:** a white, ash-gray, yellow, or black and often variegated substance having a characteristic odor and the consistency of wax, found floating in or on the shores of the Indian ocean and other tropical waters, believed to originate as an accumulation in the intestines of the sperm whale, and used in perfumery as a fixative

am·ber·i·na \,=bə'rēnə\ *n* -s [fr. *Amberina*, a trademark] **:** a late 19th century American clear glassware of graduated color that shades from ruby to amber

am·ber·jack \'=bə(r),jak\ *n* -s [¹*amber* + *jack* (fish); fr. its color] **1 :** AMBERFISH: as **a :** a large vigorous sport fish (*Seriola zonata* or *dumerili*) of the western Atlantic from Massachusetts to Brazil **b :** a yellowtail (*S. dorsalis*) **2 :** SPHALERITE

am·ber·lite \-,līt\ *n* -s [prob. fr. *Amberlite*, a trademark (for certain resins)] **:** a light yellowish brown that is redder, lighter, and stronger than khaki, lighter, stronger, and slightly redder than walnut brown, and lighter and stronger than cinnamon

amber malt *n* **:** malt cured at a high temperature in the kiln, the diastase being greatly restricted

amber mica *n* **:** PHLOGOPITE

am·ber·oid \'=bə,rȯid\ *also* **am·broid** \-,brȯid\ *n* -s [¹*amber* + *-oid*] **:** a material consisting of small pieces of amber or sometimes other resins united by heat and pressure

amber oil *n* **1 :** a pale yellow to brownish essential oil of empyreumatic odor and acrid taste made by destructive distillation of amber **2 :** a light essential oil obtained by destructive distillation of rosin

amber seed *n* **:** the seed of the abelmosk resembling millet and having a musky flavor — called also *ambrette, musk seed*

amber shell *or* **amber snail** *n* **:** a pulmonate land snail of the family Succineidae

amber tree *n* **1 :** a fossil tree (*Pinites succinifer*) **2 :** a southern African shrub of the genus *Anthospermum*

amber white *n* **:** a pale yellow green that is yellower, lighter, and stronger than smoke gray, yellower, stronger, and slightly lighter than oyster gray, and yellower, lighter, and slightly stronger than average Nile

amber yellow *n* **:** a light to moderate yellow that is greener and stronger than buff (sense 4b) and greener than snapdragon — called also *Venetian yellow*

ambi- *prefix* [L *ambi-, amb-* both, on both sides, around; akin to L *ambo* both, Gk *amphō* both, *amphi* around — more at BY] **:** both ⟨*ambi*lateral⟩ ⟨*ambi*parous⟩

am·bi·col·or·ate \ambē¦kələrət, -,rāt\ *adj* [*ambi-* + *colorate*] **:** exhibiting ambicoloration

am·bi·col·or·a·tion \¦==,=='rāshən\ *n* -s [*ambi-* + *coloration*] **:** an abnormal development of color or pigmentation on the eyeless and ordinarily whitish side of any flatfish of the families Pleuronectidae and Soleidae

¹am·bi·dex·ter \¦ambə¦dekstə(r), ¦aam-\ *n* -s [in sense 1, fr. ME, fr. ML, fr. *ambidexter*, adj., fr. LL, skillful with both hands; in sense 2, fr. LL, fr. *ambidexter*, adj.] **1 a :** one that takes bribes or fees from both sides **b** *archaic* **:** one that practices duplicity **2** *obs* **:** one that uses both hands with equal facility

²ambidexter \"\ *adj* [ML & LL; ML, double-dealing, fr. LL, skillful with both hands (trans. of Gk *amphoterodexios*), fr. *ambi-* + *dexter* on the right, skillful — more at DEXTER] *archaic* **:** AMBIDEXTROUS

am·bi·dex·ter·i·ty \,==,dek'sterəd·ē, -ətē, -i\ *n* -s **:** the quality or state of being ambidextrous

am·bi·dex·trous \¦=¦dekstrəs\ *adj* [LL & ML *ambidexter* + E *-ous*] **1 :** capable of using both hands with equal ease ⟨~ tennis players are rare⟩ **2 :** unusually skillful **:** VERSATILE, FACILE ⟨completely ~ . . . completely able to express himself in verse or prose —T.S.Eliot⟩ **3 :** characterized by duplicity **:** DOUBLE-DEALING ⟨unordained, uneducated, and theologically . . . ~ —G.H.Genzmer⟩ — **am·bi·dex·trous·ly** *adv*

am·bi·ence *or* **am·bi·ance** \äⁿbyäⁿs\ *n, pl* **ambi·ences** *or* **ambi·ances** \"\ [F *ambiance*, fr. *ambiant* surrounding (after such pairs as *confiant* confident: *confiance* confidence), fr. L *ambient-, ambiens* — more at AMBIENT] **:** a surrounding or pervading atmosphere **:** ENVIRONMENT, MILIEU ⟨moves out of provincial society and out of the ~ of exclusively female friendships —Lionel Trilling⟩

am·bi·ens \'ambē,enz\ *n, pl* **ambien·tes** \,=='en,tēz\ [NL, fr. L, pres. part. of *ambire*] **:** a thigh muscle of certain birds having the tendon passing over the knee and connecting with the tendon of a muscle that bends the toes so that the body weight on perching causes the knee to bend and the feet to clasp the perch on which the bird sits

¹am·bi·ent \'ambēənt, 'aam-\ *adj* [L *ambient-, ambiens*, pres. part. of *ambire* to go around, surround, encompass, fr. *ambi-* around + *ire* to go — more at AMBI-, ISSUE] **:** surrounding on all sides **:** ENCOMPASSING, ENVELOPING ⟨to exist in the ~ matter of space, to envelop him like a peculiar fragrance —Joseph Conrad⟩ ⟨~ temperature⟩

²ambient \"\ *n* -s **1 :** an encompassing sphere; *esp* **:** ATMOSPHERE **2 :** an encompassing atmosphere **:** ENVIRONMENT, AMBIENCE ⟨the re-creation of the various ~s in which Unamuno moved —Dudley Fitts⟩

am·bi·en·te \am'byentē, aam-; ,ambē'en-\ *n* -s [It & Sp, fr. L *ambient-, ambiens*, pres. part.] **:** surrounding atmosphere **:** MILIEU, ENVIRONMENT ⟨expert at portraying the spiritual ~ of Chile —Francis Herron⟩

am·bi·gu·i·ty \,ambə'gyüəd·ē, ,aam-, -ətē, -i\ *n* -ES [ME *ambiguite*, fr. MF *ambiguité*, fr. L *ambiguitat-, ambiguitas*, fr. *ambiguus* + *-itat-, -itas* -ity] **1** *obs* **:** intellectual uncertainty **:** DOUBT ⟨resolve me of all *ambiguities* —Christopher Marlowe⟩ **2 a** (1) **:** the condition of admitting of two or more meanings, of being understood in more than one way, or of referring to two or more things at the same time ⟨their very ~ is one source of their use in defense of any measure —John Dewey⟩ (2) **:** looseness of signification or reference ⟨the technical writer must rigorously avoid all ~ —C.E.Kellogg⟩ **2 b** (1) **:** uncertainty of meaning or significance or of position in relation to something or somebody else ⟨a sufficiently detailed account . . . to remove all ~ —P.E.More⟩ ⟨the social ~ of his parents —Lionel Trilling⟩ (2) **:** mystery or mysteriousness arising esp. from a vague knowledge or understanding ⟨there was an ~ about this young lady —Nathaniel Hawthorne⟩ **3 :** the intellectual or emotional interplay or tension resulting from the opposition or contraposing of apparently incompatible or contradictory elements or levels of meaning in a poem or other literary work; *esp* **:** the opposition or contraposition of two or more meanings inherent in one word or symbol or in a consistent set of metaphoric or symbolic words **4 :** the maintaining of two or more logically incompatible beliefs or attitudes at the same time or alternately **:** inconsistency resulting from vacillation between two opposing views ⟨the inner ~ in each of us between reason and coercion —T.V.Smith⟩ **5 :** an ambiguous word or expression ⟨a poetical ~ depends on the reader's weighting the possible meanings according to their probability —William Empson⟩

am·big·u·ous \am'bigyəwəs, aam-\ *adj* [L *ambiguus*, fr. *ambigere* to wander about, waver, dispute, fr. *ambi-* around, about + *-igere* (fr. *agere* to drive, lead, act, do) — more at AMBI-, AGENT] **:** characterized by, suggestive of, or exhibiting ambiguity ⟨the ~ wording of a message⟩ ⟨an ~ smile⟩ ⟨an ~ position⟩; *specif* **:** capable of being classified in two or more categories ⟨an ~ insect⟩ **syn** see OBSCURE

ambiguous figure *n* **:** a picture of a subject which the viewer may see as either of two different subjects or as the same subject from either of two different viewpoints depending on his interpretation of the total configuration

am·big·u·ous·ly *adv* **:** in an ambiguous manner

ambiguous middle *n* **:** the fallacy of using the middle term of a syllogism in two different meanings **:** UNDISTRIBUTED MIDDLE

am·big·u·ous·ness *n* -ES **:** AMBIGUITY

am·bil·anak \¦ambə¦länə(k)\ *adj* [Malay *ambil-anak*, fr. *ambil* taking over + *anak* child] **:** of or relating to a form of Malayan marriage esp. in Sumatra where the husband in lieu of a bride-price enters the wife's family, has no property right in children or wife, and may be dismissed by her father

am·bi·lat·er·al \¦ambə¦-, -bē¦-\ *adj* [*ambi-* + *lateral*] **:** relating to or affecting both sides **:** BILATERAL — **am·bi·lat·er·al·i·ty** \-,lad·ə'ralǝd·ē\ *n* -ES — **am·bi·lat·er·al·ly** *adv*

am·bil·i·an \(')am¦bilyən, -lēən\ *adj* [Malay *ambil*-anak + E *-ian*] **:** AMBILANAK

am·bi·o·pia \,ambē'ōpēə\ *n* -s [NL, fr. *ambi-* + *-opia*] **:** DIPLOPIA

¹ambisexual *var of* AMBOSEXUAL

²am·bi·sex·u·al \¦==¦=\ *n* **:** an ambosexual person

am·bi·sex·u·al·i·ty \¦==,=\ *n* -ES [*ambi-* + *sexuality*] **:** partial hermaphroditism — used esp. of behavioral conditions

am·bi·syl·lab·ic \¦===¦==\ *adj* [*ambi-* + *-syllabic*] *of a sound or cluster of sounds* **:** partly in the first and partly in the second or not assignable to one only of two consecutive syllables ⟨the *n* in *cynic* is ~⟩

am·bit \'ambət\ *n* -s [ME, fr. L *ambitus* going around, circuit, circular edge, fr. *ambitus*, past part. of *ambire* to go round — more at AMBIENT] **1 :** CIRCUIT, COMPASS, CIRCUMFERENCE ⟨everywhere within an ~ of four feet —*Punch*⟩ **2 a :** the space surrounding a house, a castle, or a town **:** PRECINCTS **b :** the bounds or limits of a place or district **3 :** the sphere of action, expression, or influence **:** EXTENT, SCOPE ⟨going far outside his proper ~ as secretary —R.F.Harrod⟩ ⟨ranges freely throughout the entire ~ of universal history —Morris Watnick⟩

am·bi·tend·en·cy \'ambē,-, 'aam-\ *n* -ES [*ambi-* + *tendency*] **:** a tendency to act in opposite ways or directions **:** the presence of opposing behavioral drives

¹am·bi·tion \am'bishən, aam-\ *n* -s [ME *ambicioun*, fr. MF or L; MF *ambition*, fr. L *ambition-, ambitio* solicitting of votes, desire for honor or power, lit., going around, fr. *ambitus* (past part. of *ambire* to go around, solicit, strive for) + *-ion-, -io* -ion — more at AMBIENT] **1 a :** an ardent desire for rank, fame, or power ⟨his ruin was that ~ . . . had laid hold of him —Thomas Carlyle⟩ **b :** the will or desire to succeed or achieve a particular goal or end **:** ASPIRATION ⟨it was her ~ for me which proved the deciding factor — David Fairchild⟩ **2 :** the object of one's desire ⟨accomplished its curious ~ of breaking into and robbing the state prison —Dixon Wecter⟩ **3 :** a desire for activity or exertion **:** INITIATIVE, ENERGY ⟨I felt no ~ when I was under the weather for a few days —S.T. Byington⟩ **4** *chiefly Midland* **:** ILL WILL, SPITE, MALICE

²ambition \"\ *vt* **ambitioned; ambitioned; ambitioning** \-sh(ə)niŋ\ **ambitions :** to have as one's ambition **:** DESIRE ⟨I never ~ed it —Augusta Gregory⟩

am·bi·tion·less *adj* **:** having little or no ambition

am·bi·tious \am'bishəs, aam-\ *adj* [ME *ambicious*, fr. L *ambitiosus*, fr. *ambitio* + *-osus* -ous] **1 a :** having or controlled by ambition **:** eager for rank, fame, or power ⟨~ Rome —Edmund Spenser⟩ **b :** having a desire to succeed or to achieve a particular goal **:** ASPIRING ⟨~ youths . . . turned to the law as a congenial career —V.L.Parrington⟩ **2** *obs* **:** RISING, TOWERING ⟨the ~ ocean —Shak.⟩ **3 :** resulting from, characterized by, or showing ambition: as **a :** EXTENSIVE, ELABORATE ⟨the most ~ life of Washington . . . began appearing in 1948 —Walter Trohan⟩ **b :** PRETENTIOUS, SHOWY ⟨in a hard-cover book where I expect something more ~ —Marston Bates⟩ — **am·bi·tious·ly** *adv*

am·bi·ty \(')am¦bid·ē\ *adj* [prob. fr. F *ambité*] **:** DEVITRIFIED — used in glass manufacture of glass in the pot during manipulation

am·bi·tus \'ambətəs\ *n, pl* **ambitus** [L — more at AMBIT] **1 :** the exterior edge or periphery (as of a leaf, a bivalve shell, or the test of a sea urchin) **2 :** DENOTATION 4 **3 :** the compass of a melody in a Gregorian chant

am·biv·a·lence \am'bivələn(t)s, aam-\ *also* **am·biv·a·len·cy** \-nsē, -si\ *n, pl* **ambivalences** *also* **ambivalencies** [ISV *ambi-* + *valence, valency;* orig. formed as G *ambivalenz*] **1 :** contradictory emotional or psychological attitudes esp. toward a particular person or object and often with one attitude inhibiting the expression of another ⟨a heightened ~ which is expressed in behavior by alternating obedience and rebellion, followed by self-reproach —G.S.Blum⟩; *specif* **:** simultaneous attraction toward and repulsion from an object, person, or action ⟨Apache ~ in attitude and behavior toward death —C.K.Kluckhohn⟩ **2 a :** continual oscillation (as between one thing and its opposite) **:** FLUCTUATION ⟨Thackeray's major novels are vitiated by an ~ between satire and sentimentalism —J.L.Davis⟩ **b :** uncertainty as to which approach, attitude, or treatment to follow ⟨the English film . . . because of a nervous ~ toward its subject matter . . . fails to produce the chuckles —John McCarten⟩

am·biv·a·lent \-lənt\ *adj* [ISV *ambi-* + *valent;* orig. formed in G] **:** characterized by, suggestive of, motivated by, or exhibiting ambivalence ⟨an ~ nature⟩ ⟨~ feelings⟩ ⟨an ~ position toward religion⟩ ⟨the ~ aspects of the American spirit are reconciled —Louis le Fevre⟩ — **am·biv·a·lent·ly** *adv*

am·bi·ver·sion \ˌambēˈvərzhən, -bə- *also* -rsh-\ *n* -s [*ambi-* + *-version* (as in *introversion, extroversion*)] **:** the personality configuration of an ambivert **:** a state of balance between introversion and extroversion — **am·bi·ver·sive** \ˌ==ˈ=siv, -ziv\ *adj*

am·bi·vert \ˈ==ˌvərt\ *n* -s [*ambi-* + *-vert* (as in *introvert, extrovert*)] **:** a type of person intermediate between the extrovert and the introvert

¹**am·ble** \ˈambəl, ˈaam-\ *vi* **ambled; ambled; ambling** \b(ə)liŋ\ **ambles** [ME *amblen,* fr. MF *ambler,* fr. L *ambulare* to walk, fr. *amb-* around + *-ulare* (verb base prob. akin to L *-ilium* in *exilium* exile); prob. akin to Gk *alasthai* to wander, Latvian *aluôt* to wander around — more at *ambi-*] **1 a :** to go at an amble ⟨the pony *ambled* down the lane⟩ **b :** to walk or move in an easygoing or leisurely manner **:** SAUNTER ⟨time to ~ back to the office⟩ **2 :** to go or proceed smoothly or easily ⟨the interpretation ~*s* on —H.O.Taylor⟩

²**amble** \"\ *n* -s **1** *of a horse* **a :** an easy 4-beat gait with lateral motion **b :** ⁷RACK **b 2 :** an easy gait **3 :** an easygoing or leisurely walking movement ⟨the aimless ~ of the . . . holiday crowd —L.C.Douglas⟩

am·bler \-b(ə)lə(r)\ *n* -s [ME, fr. *amblen* + *-er*] **:** one that ambles; *esp* **:** an ambling horse

am·bling \-b(ə)liŋ\ *adj* **:** moving at an easy pace ⟨~ carriages⟩ ⟨an ~ light novel⟩ — **am·bling·ly** *adv*

am·blop·li·tes \ˌam,bläpˈlīd·ēz\ *n, cap* [NL, fr. Gk *amblys* blunt + *hoplitēs* hoplite] **:** a genus of sunfishes (family Centrarchidae) including the rock bass of the central U.S. and Great Lakes region

ambly- *or* **amblyo-** *comb form* [LL *ambly-,* fr. Gk, fr. *amblys;* akin to L *mollis* soft, *molere* to grind — more at MEAL] **1 :** blunt **:** obtuse ⟨*Ambly*cephalus⟩ **2 :** dulled **:** dimmed ⟨*ambly*acousia⟩ **3 :** connected with amblyopia ⟨*amblyo*scope⟩

am·bly·ce·phal·i·dae \ˌambləsəˈfaləˌdē\ *n pl, cap* [NL, fr. *Amblycephalus,* type genus (fr. *ambly-* + *-cephalus*) + *-idae*] **:** a small family of tropical nonvenomous broad-headed snakes with extremely large eyes and very long delicate teeth occas. considered a colubrid subfamily Amblycephalinae — see BLUNTHEAD

am·bly·chro·mat·ic \ˌamblē;==ˈ==, -lə-\ *adj* [ISV *ambly-* + *chromatic*] **:** lightly staining ⟨certain marrow cells are ~⟩

am·bly·dac·ty·la \ˌambləˈdaktələ\ [NL, fr. *ambly-* + *-dactyla* (fr. Gk *daktylos* finger, toe)] *syn of* AMBLYPODA

am·blyg·o·nite \amˈbligəˌnīt\ *n* -s [G *amblygonit,* fr. Gk *amblygōnios* obtuse-angled (fr. *ambly-* + *-gōnios,* fr. *gōnia* angle) + G *-it* -ite] **:** a mineral $(Li,Na)AlPO_4(F,OH)$ consisting of basic lithium aluminum phosphate commonly containing sodium and fluorine and occurring in white cleavable masses

am·bly·om·ma \ˌambleˈäməə\ *n, cap* [NL, fr. *ambly-* + *-omma*] **:** a genus of ixodid ticks including the lone star tick of the southern U.S. and the African bont tick

am·bly·o·pia \-ˈōpēə\ *n* -s [NL, fr. Gk *amblyōpia* dimness of sight, fr. *ambly-* + *-ōpia* -opia] **:** dimness of sight without apparent change in the eye structures associated esp. with the toxic effects of certain drugs or chemicals or with dietary deficiencies — **am·bly·op·ic** \ˌ==;ˈäpik, -ōp-\ *adj*

am·bly·op·sis \ˌ==ˈäpsəs\ *n, cap* [NL, fr. *ambly-* + *-opsis*] **:** a genus (the type of the family Amblyopsidae) of small blanched sightless fishes related to the killifishes and including the blindfish of Mammoth Cave

am·bly·o·scope \ˈambleəˌskōp\ *n* -s [ISV *amblyo-* (fr. NL *amblyopia*) + *-scope*] **:** an instrument for training amblyopic eyes to function properly

am·bly·pod \ˈambləˌpäd\ *n* -s [NL *Amblypoda*] **:** an ungulate of the order or suborder Amblypoda

am·blyp·o·da \amˈblipədə\ *n pl, cap* [NL, fr. *ambly-* + *-poda*] *in some classifications* **:** an order or suborder of extinct ungulates found in the Eocene rocks chiefly of No. America having very small smooth brains and some of them resembling the elephants in size and in the structure of their limbs but having horns as well as long tusks

am·blyp·o·dous \-dəs\ *adj* [NL *Amblypoda* + E *-ous*] **:** of or relating to the Amblypoda

am·bly·rhyn·chus \ˌambləˈriŋkəs\ *n, cap* [NL, fr. *ambly-* + *-rhynchus*] **:** a genus of iguanid lizards containing only one species (*A. cristatus*) of the Galápagos islands

am·bly·si·pho·nel·la \ˌ==ˌsīfəˈnelə\ *n, cap* [NL, fr. *ambly-* + L *siphon-, sipho* + NL *-ella*] **:** a genus of thin-walled extinct calcareous sponges including important index fossils of Pennsylvanian age

am·blys·te·gite \amˈblistəˌjīt\ *n* -s [ISV *ambly-* + Gk *stegos* roof + ISV *-ite;* orig. formed as G *amblystegit*] **:** a variety of hypersthene

am·blys·to·ma \-təmə\ [NL, alter. (influenced by *ambly-*) of *Ambystoma*] *syn of* AMBYSTOMA

¹**am·bo** \ˈam,bō\ *n, pl* **ambos** \-bōz\ *or* **ambo·nes** \amˈbō(ˌ)nēz\ [ML *ambon-, ambo,* fr. LGk *ambōn,* fr. Gk, edge, rim] **:** a large pulpit or reading desk in early churches and in contemporary Greek and Balkan churches standing on the gospel side of the nave and often having its counterpart on the epistle side

²**ambo** \"\ *var of* AMBON

³**am·bo** \", ˈäm-\ *n, pl* **ambo** *or* **ambos** *usu cap* **1 :** a Bantu people of the northern part of southwestern Africa **2 :** the language of the Ambo people

am·bo·cep·tor \ˈamboˌseptə(r)\ *n* -s [ISV *ambo-* (alter. of *ambi-*) + *receptor;* orig. formed as G *ambozeptor*] **1 :** an intermediary body or antibody acting as a detached receptor **2 :** the lytic antibody used in complement-fixation tests

am·bo·coe·lia \ˌamboˈsēlēə\ *n, cap* [NL, prob. fr. Gk *ambōn* rim, edge + *koilia* cavity, fr. *koilos* hollow + *-ia*] **:** a genus of small smooth or spinose plano-convex fossil brachiopods characteristic of Devonian and Carboniferous rocks

am·boi·na button \(ˈ)amˈbȯinə-\ *n, usu cap A* [fr. *Amboina,* town, island, and division of the Moluccas] **:** YAWS

amboina pine *or* **am·boy·na pine** \"\ *n, usu cap A* **:** a tall tree (*Agathis alba*) native to the Moluccas and the Philippines and the chief source of dammar resin

¹**am·boi·nese** \ˌam,bȯiˈnēz, -ēs, amˈbȯi,n-\ *also* **am·bo·nese** \ˌambəˈn-\ *adj, usu cap* [*Amboina, Ambon* + E *-ese*] **1 :** of, relating to, or characteristic of the island of Amboina **2 :** of, relating to, or characteristic of the people of Amboina

²**amboinese** \"\ *also* **ambonese** \"\ *n, pl* **amboinese** *also* **ambonese** *usu cap* **1 :** a native or inhabitant of Amboina **2 :** the language of the Amboinese people

am·bo·mal·le·al \ˌam(ˌ)bōˈmalēəl\ *adj* [*ambos* + *malleal*] **:** relating to the ambos and malleus ⟨the ~ articulation⟩

am·bon \ˈam,bän\ *also* **am·bo** \-bō\ *n, pl* **ambo·nes** \amˈbō(ˌ)nēz\ [NL, fr. Gk *ambōn* edge, rim] **:** the fibrocartilaginous ring around an articular cavity

am·bon·ite \ˈambəˌnīt\ *n* -s [D *amboniet,* fr. *Ambon,* its locality + D *-iet* -ite] **:** a mineral consisting of cordierite-bearing hornblende-biotite-andesite

am·bos \ˈam,bäs\ *n* -ES [G *amboss* anvil, fr. OHG *anabōz,* fr. *ana* on + *bōz* blow; akin to OHG *bōzzan* to beat] **:** INCUS

am·bo·sex·u·al \ˈam(ˌ)bō;-\ *also* **am·bi·sex·u·al** \ˈambē;-, -bə;-\ *adj* [L *ambo* both or E *ambi-* + *sexual* — more at AMBI-] **:** exhibiting or constituting sexual traits or characters common to male and female ⟨axillary hair is an ~ trait⟩

am·boy·na *or* **am·boi·na** \amˈbȯinə\ *n* -s [fr. *Amboina,* town, island, & division of the Moluccas, Indonesia] **1 :** a mottled curly-grained wood of a tree (*Pterocarpus indicus*) of India and the Malay archipelago — called also *Andaman redwood, rosewood* **2 :** the tree that yields amboyna

am·brein \ˈam,brān, -ˌbrə,in\ *n* -s [F *ambréine,* fr. *ambre* amber (fr. L *ambra*) + *-ine* -in] **:** a crystalline triterpenoid alcohol $C_{30}H_{51}OH$ obtained from ambergris

am·brette \(ˈ)amˈbret\ *n* -s [F, fr. OF, fr. *ambre* amber + *-ette*] **1 :** a French dessert pear having a musky odor **2 :** AMBER SEED **3 a :** an extract of amber seeds having a strong musky odor and used in perfumery as a fixative **b :** MUSK AMBRETTE

am·brite \ˈam,brīt\ *n* -s [ISV *amber* + *-ite;* orig. formed as G *ambrit*] **:** a fossil resin occurring in large masses in New Zealand

am·broid *var of* AMBEROID

am·bro·sia \amˈbrōzh(ē)ə, aam-, *attrib* (ˈ)=;=(=)=\ *n* [L, fr. Gk, lit., immortality, fr. *ambrotos* immortal (fr. *a-* ²*a-* + *-mbrotos* — assumed — Gk *mbrotos* mortal — whence Gk *brotos*) + *-ia* — more at MURDER] **1** -s **a :** the food of the Greek and Roman gods ⟨a table where the heaped ~ lay —W.C.Bryant⟩ **b :** the ointment or perfume of the gods ⟨his dewy locks distilled ~ —John Milton⟩ **2** -s **:** something extremely pleasing to taste or smell ⟨with sweet ~ all besprinkled —Edmund Spenser⟩ **3** [NL, fr. L] *cap* **:** a genus of mostly American monoecious herbs (family Compositae) distinguished by the united involucre of the staminate heads of flowers and by the single row of spines on the involucre of the pistillate heads — see RAGWEED **4** -s **:** JERUSALEM OAK 1 **5** -s **:** a dessert of a fruit or of mixed fruits topped with shredded coconut **6** -s **:** a moderate reddish brown that is yellower and paler than roan and paler than mahogany

ambrosia beetle *n* [*ambrosia (fungus)*] **:** any of certain small semisocial beetles (family Ipidae or Scolytidae) that bore deeply in dead or dying wood and tend and cultivate ambrosia fungus on which they feed and raise their larvae

am·bro·si·ac \=ˈ=zhēˌak\ *adj* [L *ambrosiacus,* fr. *ambrosia*] **:** AMBROSIAL ⟨an ~ odor⟩

am·bro·si·a·ce·ae \am,brōz(h)ēˈāsēˌē\ *n pl, cap* [NL, fr. *Ambrosia,* type genus + *-aceae*] *in some classifications* **:** a family of herbs comprising all the composites (as ragweeds) that have the flower head subtended by an involucre of separate or united bracts and the stamens separate or merely connivent — see COMPOSITAE

am·bro·si·a·ceous \=;==ˈāshəs, ;=,==;-\ *adj* [NL *Ambrosiaceae* + E *-ous*] **:** of or relating to Ambrosiaceae

ambrosia fungus *also* **ambrosial fungus** *n* **:** a fungus upon which ambrosia beetles feed

am·bro·si·al \(ˈ)amˈbrōzh(ē)əl, (ˈ)aam-\ *or* **am·bro·si·an** \-(ē)ən\ *adj* [L *ambrosia* + E *-al* or *-an*] **1 a :** consisting of or like ambrosia ⟨fed by fair Iris with ~ food —Alexander Pope⟩ **b :** relating to or worthy of the gods or paradise **:** DIVINE ⟨these pure ~ weeds —John Milton⟩ **2 :** extremely pleasing to the senses esp. of taste or smell **:** DELICIOUS, FRAGRANT ⟨the ~ islands of the South Seas —Dixon Wecter⟩ ⟨an afternoon of warm ~ May weather —Elinor Wylie⟩ — **am·bro·si·al·ly** \-(ē)əlē, -li\ *adv*

¹**am·bro·si·an** \-(ē)ən\ *adj, usu cap* [LL *Ambrosianus,* fr. St. Ambrose (*Ambrosius*) †397 bishop of Milan and church father + L *-anus* -an] **1 :** of, relating to, established by, or ascribed to St. Ambrose ⟨the *Ambrosian* rite⟩ **2 :** characterized by the style of St. Ambrose ⟨the *Ambrosian* type of hymn is written in iambic tetrameter⟩

²**ambrosian** \"\ *n* -s *usu cap* [ML *Ambrosianus,* fr. LL, of St. Ambrose] **:** a member of a religious order (as of the Congregation of the Brethren of St. Ambrose founded by Crivelli in Milan in 1375, of the Oblates of St. Ambrose founded by Carlo Borromeo in 1578, or of the Sisterhood of St. Ambrose founded by Catherine Morigia in 1474)

ambrosian chant *n, usu cap A* **:** the plainsong associated with the liturgy of the church of Milan including antiphonal psalm chants ascribed to St. Ambrose

am·bro·sin \ˈambrəˌzin, -ēn\ *n* -s [ML *Ambrosinus* (*nummus*), lit., Ambrosian coin, fr. St. Ambrose (*Ambrosius*) + L *-inus* -ine] **:** a Milanese gold or silver coin of the late 13th and early 14th centuries having as device a figure of St. Ambrose

am·bro·sine \-ˌzēn\ *n* -s [¹*amber* + *-rosine* (alter. of *rosin*)] **:** a resinous hydrocarbon mineral that is a variety of amber

am·bro·type \-ˌtīp\ *n* -s [Gk *ambrotos* immortal (fr. *a-* ²*a-* + *-mbrotos* — akin to *brotos, mortos* mortal —) + E *type* — more at MURDER] **:** a positive picture made by the collodion process on glass and viewed against a dark background

am·bry \ˈambrē, -ri, *dial Brit* " *or* ˈämr- *or* ˈȯm(b)r-\ *n* -ES [earlier *aumbry, armorie,* fr. ME *almerie, almarie, awmerie, armarie,* fr. OF *almarie, aumaire, armarie,* fr. ML *almarium* & L *armarium;* ML *almarium* fr. L *armarium,* fr. *arma* weapons, tools + *-arium* -ary — more at ARM] **1 :** a place for keeping things: as **a :** a recess in a church wall for holding sacramental vessels, vestments, or books **b** *dial chiefly Brit* (1) **:** PANTRY (2) **:** a cupboard or chest in which food is kept **2** *obs* **:** ALMONRY

ambs·ace *also* **ames·ace** \ˈām,zās, ˈam-\ *n* -s [ME *ambes as,* fr. OF, fr. *ambes* both (fr. L *ambo*) + *as* aces, pl. of *as* ace — more at AMBI-, ACE] **:** the lowest throw at dice; *also* **:** something worthless or unlucky — **within ambsace of** *archaic* **:** within an ace of

ambulacra *pl of* AMBULACRUM

am·bu·lac·ral \ˌambyəˈlakrəl *also* -āk-\ *adj* [NL *ambulacrum* + E *-al*] **:** of or relating to an ambulacrum

ambulacral brush *n* **:** a modified oral or anal ambulacral foot in heart urchins expanded into appendages resembling tentacles

ambulacral foot *n* **:** a tube foot of an echinoderm

ambulacral system *n* **:** the water-vascular system of echinoderms

am·bu·lac·ri·form \ˌambyəˈlakrəˌfȯrm\ *adj* [NL *ambulacrum* + E *-iform*] **:** like an ambulacrum in shape

am·bu·lac·rum \ˌambyəˈlakrəm *also* -āk-\ *n, pl* **ambulac·ra** \-rə\ [NL, fr. L, alley, covered way, fr. *ambulare* to walk — more at AMBLE] **1 :** one of the radially disposed areas of echinoderms along which run the principal nerves, blood vessels, and water tubes and which usu. bear rows of locomotive suckers or tentacles that protrude from regular pores **2 :** one of the suckers on the feet of mites

am·bu·lance \ˈambyələn(t)s, ˈaam-, *chiefly substand* -bəl-\ *n* -s *often attrib* [F, field hospital, fr. *ambulant* itinerant, traveling (esp. as used in the term *hôpital ambulant* field hospital, lit., traveling hospital), fr. L *ambulant-, ambulans,* pres. part. of *ambulare* to walk — more at AMBLE] **1 :** a vehicle equipped for transporting wounded, injured, or sick persons or animals **2 :** a passenger vehicle formerly used in the western U.S.

ambulance chaser *n* **:** a lawyer or lawyer's agent who incites accident victims to bring suit for damages

am·bu·lant \-byələnt\ *adj* [L *ambulant-, ambulans,* pres. part. of *ambulare* to walk — more at AMBLE] **1 :** walking or in a walking position; *specif* **:** AMBULATORY ⟨an ~ patient⟩ **2 :** moving or capable of being moved from place to place ⟨an ~ radio station⟩ **:** ITINERANT ⟨an ~ blacksmith⟩

am·bu·late \-ˌlāt, *usu* -ād·+V\ *vi* -ED/-ING/-S [L *ambulatus,* past part. of *ambulare*] **:** to move from place to place **:** WALK ⟨the patient was allowed to ~ in his room⟩

am·bu·la·tion \ˌ==ˈlāshən\ *n* -s [L *ambulation-, ambulatio,* fr. *ambulatus* + *-ion-, -io* -ion] **:** the act or action of moving about or walking ⟨most surgeons encourage early ~⟩

am·bu·la·to·ri·al \ˌ==ˌləˈtōrēəl\ *adj* [¹*ambulatory* + *-al*] **1 :** AMBULATORY **2** *of a forest animal* **:** adapted to progression by walking rather than by running, leaping, or crawling

¹**am·bu·la·to·ry** \ˈambyələˌtōrē, ˈaam-, -ōr-, -ri\ *adj* [L *ambulatorius,* fr. *ambulatus* (past part. of *ambulare* to walk) + *-orius* -ory — more at AMBLE] **1 a :** of or relating to walking ⟨~ exercise⟩ **b :** capable of, adapted to, or occurring while walking ⟨an ~ animal⟩ ⟨an ~ confession⟩ **2 a :** moving from place to place **:** ITINERANT, PERIPATETIC ⟨an ~ teacher⟩ **b :** having no fixed headquarters ⟨an ~ business⟩ **3 :** not yet fixed legally or settled past alteration **:** ALTERABLE ⟨a will is ~ until the testator's death⟩ **4 a :** able to walk about **:** not bedfast **:** AMBULANT ⟨the ~ clinic patient⟩ **b :** of, for, or involving an individual who is able to walk about ⟨~ treatment of tuberculosis⟩

²**ambulatory** \"\ *n* -ES [ML *ambulatorium,* fr. L, neut. of *ambulatorius*] **1 :** a sheltered place to walk in: as **a :** the gallery portion of a cloister **b :** the apse aisle of a church **c :** a passageway in some churches in back of the altar and behind the chancel used as an uninterrupted processional path **2 :** an appendage used for or adapted to walking (as a tube foot or one of the segmental abdominal appendages of a crustacean)

am·bu·lia \amˈbyülēə\ *n* -s [modif. of Malabar *amuli*] **:** any of several aquatic plants of the genus *Limnophora* (family Scrophulariaceae) having finely dissected submerged and peltate floating leaves and being often grown as an aquarium plant

¹**am·bus·cade** \ˈambəˌskād, ˈaam-, ˌ==ˈ=\ *n* -s [MF *embuscade,* modif. (influenced by MF *embuschier* to place in ambush) of OIt *imboscata,* fr. fem. of *imboscato,* past part. of *imboscare* to place in ambush, fr. *in* (fr. L) + *-boscare,* fr. *bosco* forest, perh. of Gmc origin; akin to OHG *busc* forest — more at IN, BUSH, AMBUSH] **:** AMBUSH 1

²**ambuscade** \"\ *vt* -ED/-ING/-S **:** to attack from an ambuscade

am·bus·ca·do \ˌ==ˈskā(ˌ)dō\ *n* -s [alter. (influenced by *-ado,* as in *bastinado, bravado*) of *ambuscade*] *archaic* **:** AMBUSCADE

¹**am·bush** \ˈam,bu̇sh, ˈaam-\ *vb* -ED/-ING/-ES [ME *embushen, abushen,* fr. OF *embuschier* to place in ambush, fr. *en* in (fr. L *in*) + *-buschier,* fr. *busche* stick of firewood, prob. of Gmc origin; akin to MHG *būsch* cudgel — more at IN, BOAST] *vt* **1 :** to station in ambush ⟨he ~*ed* his force in a canebrake —J.F.H.Claiborne⟩ **2 :** to lie in wait for and attack by surprise **:** WAYLAY ⟨units in superior strength had ~*ed* . . . the 2d and 19th regiments —R.C.Cameron⟩ ~ *vi* **:** to lie in wait **:** LURK ⟨imaginary persons ~*ed* in the fog —Marguerite Young⟩

²**ambush** \"\ *n* -ES [MF *embusche,* fr. OF, fr. *embuschier,* v.] **1 a :** a hidden or concealed station of troops lying in wait to attack an enemy by surprise ⟨attempt of a . . . boy to warn them of an ~ over the brow of the hill —Mary Gregoire⟩ **b :** the body of troops lying in wait for an enemy **2 a :** a hidden or concealed position ⟨trapped, baited, and shot from ~ like a criminal —D.C.Peattie⟩ **b :** a person occupying a concealed position **3 :** the act of lying in wait in or of attacking by surprise from a concealed position

ambush bug *n* **:** any of numerous carnivorous bugs that constitute the family Phymatidae, conceal themselves in flowers, and prey on other insects

am·bush·ment \-mənt\ *n* -s [ME *embushement,* fr. MF *embuschement,* fr. *embuschier* + *-ment*] **:** AMBUSH

am·bys·to·ma \amˈbistəmə\ *n* [NL, irreg. fr. *ambly-* + *-stoma*] **1** *cap* **:** a genus (the type of the family Ambystomidae) of common salamanders confined to America and characterized by amphicoelous vertebrae, short prevomers, and internal fertilization **2** -s **:** a salamander of the genus *Ambystoma* — see AXOLOTL — **am·bys·to·mid** \-məd, ˌ=ˌmid\ *adj or n*

am·bys·to·moi·dea \(ˌ)am,bistəˈmȯidēə\ *n pl, cap* [NL, fr. *Ambystoma* + *-oidea*] **:** the suborder of caudate amphibians that comprises the single family Ambystomidae — compare AMBYSTOMA

AMDG *abbr* [L *ad majorem Dei gloriam*] to the greater glory of God

amdt *abbr* amendment

ameba *var of* AMOEBA

am·e·bel·o·don \ˌaməˈbeləˌdän\ *n, cap* [NL, fr. Gk *amē* shovel + *belos* missile, dart + NL *-odon*] **:** a genus of No. American Pliocene mastodonts having an elongated lower jaw and lower tusks flattened into broad scoops

am·e·bi·a·sis *or* **am·oe·bi·a·sis** \ˌamēˈbīəsəs\ *n, pl* **amebiases** *or* **amoebia·ses** \-əˌsēz\ [NL, fr. *ameba, amoeba* + *-iasis*] **:** infection with or disease caused by amoebas; *specif* **:** infection of the human colon with amoebas — see AMEBIC DYSENTERY

amebic *or* **ameban** *or* **amebous** *var of* AMOEBIC

amebic abscess *n* **:** a specific purulent invasive lesion commonly of the liver caused by parasitic amoebas esp. of the common species (*Endamoeba histolytica*)

amebic dysentery *n* **:** acute intestinal amebiasis of man caused by infection with the amoeba (*Endamoeba histolytica*) and marked by frequent passage of thin mucus-filled and blood-filled stools, griping pain, and more or less severe erosion of the intestinal wall and esp. the colon

ame·bi·ci·dal *also* **ame·ba·ci·dal** \əˌmēbəˈsīdᵊl\ *adj* **:** of, relating to, or being an amebicide

ame·bi·cide *also* **amoe·bi·cide** *also* **ame·ba·cide** \əˈmēbəˌsīd\ *n* -s [NL *ameba, amoeba* + E *-i-* + *-cide*] **:** a substance used to kill or capable of killing amoebas (as parasitic amoebas)

amebid *var of* AMOEBID

amebiform *var of* AMOEBIFORM

amebocyte *var of* AMOEBOCYTE

ameboid *var of* AMOEBOID

amebula *var of* AMOEBULA

âme dam·née \ˈämdänā\ *n, pl* **âmes damnées** \-nā(z)\ [F, lit., damned soul] **:** a willing and devoted tool or slave of another ⟨a writer who is the *âme damnée* of certain interests⟩

ameen *or* **amin** \əˈmēn\ *n* -s [Hindi *amīn,* fr. Ar] *India* **:** a confidential agent; *esp* **:** a minor official of the judicial and revenue departments

ameer *var of* EMIR

ame haarez *pl of* AM HAAREZ

amei·o·sis \ˌā,mīˈōsəs\ *n, pl* **ameio·ses** \-ōˌsēz\ [NL, fr. ²*a-* + *meiosis*] **:** suppression of one of the meiotic divisions resulting in nonreduction of chromosomes (as in parthenogenesis)

amei·ot·ic \ˌ=;=ˈäd·ik\ *adj* [²*a-* + *meiotic*] **:** without meiosis

am·ei·u·rus \ˌa,mīˈyu̇rəs\ *n, cap* [NL, fr. ²*a-* + Gk *meiouros* tapering (used of a fish's snout), alter. (influenced by *meioun* to diminish) of *myouros,* lit., mouse-tailed, fr. *mys* mouse + *-ouros* (fr. *oura* tail)] **:** a genus of freshwater catfishes comprising the No. American bullheads

amei·va \əˈmävə, -īvə\ *n, cap* [NL, fr. Pg, lizard, fr. Tupi] **:** a genus of New World lizards (family Teiidae)

am·el \ˈaməl\ *n* -s [ME *amal, amel,* fr. MF *esmal, asmol, emal* — more at ENAMEL] *archaic* **:** ENAMEL

am·e·lan·chi·er \ˌaməˈlaŋkēə(r)\ *n, cap* [NL, fr. F *amélanchier* shadbush, shadberry, of Celt origin; akin to Gaulish *avallo* apple, OIr *ubull* — more at APPLE] **:** a genus of shrubs and trees (family Rosaceae) with showy usu. racemose white flowers and sweet edible pomes resembling small berries — see JUNEBERRY

am·el·corn \ˈaməl,kȯrn\ *n, pl* **amelcorn** [G *amelkorn,* fr. L *amylum* starch + *korn* grain, fr. OHG — more at AMYL-, CORN] **:** EMMER

ameli *pl of* AMELUS

ame·lio·rant \əˈmēlyərənt, -lēə-\ *n* -s [*ameliorate* + *-ant*] **:** a substance that aids plant growth primarily by improving the physical condition of the soil

ame·lio·rate \-ˌrāt, *usu* -ād·+V\ *vb* -ED/-ING/-S [alter. (influenced by F *améliorer,* alter. — influenced by L *melior* — of *ameilleurer,* fr. OF *ameillorer,* fr. *a-* — fr. L *ad-* — + *-meillorer,* fr. *meillor* better, fr. L *melior*) of *meliorate* — more at MELIORATE] *vt* **:** to make better **:** IMPROVE ⟨~ conditions⟩ ~ *vi* **:** to grow better **:** IMPROVE ⟨the situation *ameliorated*⟩ **syn** see IMPROVE

ame·lio·ra·tion \=,=(=)=ˈrāshən\ *n* -s [F *amélioration,* fr. *améliorer* + *-ation*] **1 :** act of ameliorating or state of being ameliorated **:** IMPROVEMENT ⟨the ~ of human affairs —J.S. Mill⟩ **2** *Canadian law* **:** BETTERMENT 1a

ame·lio·ra·tive \=ˈ=(=)=ˌrād·iv, -rə|, |tiv, -ēv\ *also* **ame·lio·ra·to·ry** \-rəˌtōrē, -ōr-, -ri\ *adj* **:** tending to ameliorate

ame·lio·ra·tor \-ˌrād·ə(r), -ātə-\ *n* -s **:** one that ameliorates **:** AMELIORANT

am·e·lo·blast \ˈaməlōˌblast\ *n* -s [*amel* + *-o-* + *-blast*] **:** one of the columnar cells of the inner layer of the enamel organ that produce and deposit enamel on the surface of a developing tooth — **am·e·lo·blas·tic** \ˌ===ˈblastik\ *adj*

am·e·lo·blas·to·ma \ˌ==(ˌ)=ˌblaˈstōmə\ *n* -s [NL, fr. E *ameloblast* + NL *-oma*] **:** ADAMANTINOMA

am·e·lo·den·tin·al \ˌ==(ˌ)=ˈden,tēnᵊl, -ˌdenˈt-, *attrib often* ˈ==(ˌ)=ˌ==ˌ==\ *adj* [*amel* + *-o-* + *dentinal*] **:** of or relating to enamel and dentine ⟨the ~ junction of a tooth⟩

am·e·lo·gen·e·sis \ˌ==(ˌ)=ˈjenəsəs\ *n* [NL, fr. E *amel* + NL *-o-* + *genesis*] **:** the forming of tooth enamel

am·e·lung glass \ˈaməliŋ-, -ləŋ-\ *n, usu cap A* [after John F. *Amelung* fl 1784 Am. glass manufacturer] **:** a rare late 18th century American glassware often similar to fine engraved Stiegel glass

am·e·lus \ˈaməlәs, (ˈ)āˈmel-\ *n, pl* **ame·li** \-ˌlī, -ē\ [NL, fr. ²*a-* + Gk *melos* limb] **:** a limbless fetus

¹**amen** *in religious use,* (ˈ)äˈmen *or* (ˈ)ä- *when sung,* (ˈ)ä- *or* (ˈ)äˈ- *or* (ˈ)ā- *when not sung; in nonreligious use usu* (ˈ)āˈ-\ *interj* [ME, fr. OE, fr. LL, fr. Gk *amēn,* fr. Heb *āmēn*] — used to express solemn ratification (as of an expression of faith, a prayer, or an invocation) or hearty approval (as of an assertion)

²**amen** \" *also* ˈ=,=\ *n* -s [ME, fr. *amen*, interj.] **:** a response esp. of ratification, approval, conclusion, or termination ⟨as a sort of ~ to that, nine nations quickly recognized the new regime —*Time*⟩ ⟨he paused for a response of ~s —M.L. Bach⟩ ⟨responses including chants, doxologies, and ~s —Dwight Weldy⟩

ame·na·bil·i·ty \ə,mēnəˈbiləd·ē, -ətē, -i *also* -en-\ *n* -ES **:** the quality or state of being amenable **:** TRACTABLENESS

ame·na·ble \ə'mēnəbəl\ *adj* [prob. fr. (assumed) AF *amenable*, fr. MF *amener* to lead up, bring (fr. OF, fr. *a-* — fr. L *ad-* — + *mener* to lead, fr. L *minare* to drive, fr. *minari* to threaten) + *-able* — more at MOUNT] **1 a :** liable to be brought to account or judgment **:** liable to the legal authority of **:** ANSWERABLE, ACCOUNTABLE ⟨is it to be contended that the heads of departments are not ~ to the laws —John Marshall⟩ ⟨offenses ~ to the ecclesiastical judicature —Herman Melville⟩ **b :** liable to a claim or charge ⟨was ~ to the accusation⟩ **2 a :** capable of submission (as to a judgment or test) ⟨~ to the comparatively small-scale form of enquiry —K.E.Read⟩ ⟨~ data⟩ **b :** readily brought to yield or submit **:** RESPONSIVE, TRACTABLE ⟨a personality ~ to our desires —Mary Austin⟩ ⟨an ~ view on matters of mutual concern —Robert Trumbull⟩ **syn** see OBEDIENT, RESPONSIBLE

ame·na·bly \-blē, -i\ *adv* **:** in an amenable manner

amenance *n* -s [AF, action of bringing, fr. MF *amener* + *-ance*] *obs* **:** BEHAVIOR, BEARING

amen corner \ˈā,men- *sometimes* ˈä,- *or* ˈā,-\ *n* **:** a corner in a church near the pulpit formerly occupied by those leading in the responsive amens **:** a conspicuous corner occupied by fervent worshipers

amend \əˈmend\ *vb* -ED/-ING/-S [ME *amenden*, fr. OF *amender*, modif. (influenced by L *ad-*) of L *emendare*, fr. *e*, *ex* out + *-mendare* (fr. *menda* fault); akin to L *mendax* lying, false, *mendicus* beggar, Skt *mindā* physical defect] *vt* **1** *obs* **:** to reform, convert, or make better esp. in character ⟨may God ~ these sinful people⟩ **2** *archaic* **:** REPAIR, RESTORE, MEND **3 a :** to put right **:** CORRECT, RECTIFY ⟨~ such flaws⟩; *specif* **:** to make emendations in (as a text) **b** *archaic* **:** HEAL, CURE **c** (1) **:** to change or modify in any way for the better **:** IMPROVE, BETTER ⟨~ our situation⟩ (2) **:** to change or alter in any way esp. in phraseology ⟨~ a remark⟩; *specif* **:** to alter (as a motion, bill, or law) formally by modification, deletion, or addition ⟨~ the constitution⟩ **4** *obs* **:** to make amends or reparation for ~ *vi* **1 :** to reform oneself **:** become better by rectifying manners or morals ⟨when will you ~⟩ **2** *obs* **:** to recover from illness **3** *obs* **:** to become better **:** IMPROVE **syn** see CORRECT

amend·a·ble \-dəbəl\ *adj* **:** capable of being amended

amend·a·to·ry \-ə,tōrē, -ōr-, -ri\ *adj* [*amend* + *-atory* (as in *emendatory*)] **:** designed or serving to amend **:** effecting amendment **:** CORRECTIVE

amende ho·no·ra·ble \àmäⁿdònòràblᵊ, -b(lə)\ *n, pl* **amendes honorables** \"\ [F, lit., honorable reparation] **:** reparation for a crime or injury formerly consisting in such a formal and humiliating acknowledgment of offense and apology as will restore the injured or offended honor of the one wronged; *broadly* **:** a full acknowledgment of error with apology

amend·ment \əˈmenmənt *also* -ndm-\ *n* -s [ME, fr. OF *amendement*, fr. *amender* to amend + *-ment* — more at AMEND] **1 :** act of amending esp. for the better **:** correction of a fault or faults **:** reformation (as of one's life) **2 :** a substance (as lime) that aids plant growth indirectly by improving the chemical condition of the soil (as by neutralizing soil acidity) **3 a :** the process of amending (as a motion, bill, act, or constitution) ⟨a well-drawn constitution will provide for its own ~ —C.J.Friedrich⟩ **b :** an alteration proposed or effected by such process ⟨the prohibition ~⟩

¹**amends** \əˈmen(d)z\ *pres 3d sing of* AMEND

²**amends** \"\ *n pl but usu sing in constr* [ME *amendes*, fr. OF, pl. of *amende* reparation, fr. *amender*] **1 :** compensation for a loss or injury **:** RECOMPENSE, REPARATION ⟨gesture which one hopes is the beginning of some fuller ~ —Virgil Thomson⟩ — rarely in sing. ⟨pay an *amend* of 50 pounds to the injured person⟩; often used with *make* ⟨he is ashamed and wants to make ~ —Glenway Wescott⟩ **2** *obs* **:** IMPROVEMENT **:** AMENDMENT

amene \əˈmēn\ *adj* [ME, fr. L *amoenus*, perh. akin to *amare* to love — more at AMATEUR] *archaic* **:** AGREEABLE, PLEASING

¹**amen·i·ty** \əˈmenəd·ē, -ēn-, -ətē, -i\ *n* -ES [ME *amenite*, fr. L *amoenitat-, amoenitas*, fr. *amoenus* pleasant + *-itat-, -itas* -ity; prob. akin to L *amare* to love — more at AMATEUR] **1 a :** the quality of being pleasant or agreeable (as in situation or climate or in manners or disposition) ⟨the ~ of the countryside⟩ ⟨large houses are divided up into smaller rooms with a lower standard of ~ —Stuart Piggott⟩ ⟨his ~ of temper⟩ **b** (1) **:** the attractiveness and aesthetic or nonmonetary value of real estate or of any structure for purely residential use ⟨woods . . . of which a good deal is capable of immediate realization without in the least detracting from the ~ —*Financial Times*⟩ (2) **:** a feature (as architectural distinction or desirability of location) conducive to such attractiveness and value ⟨the speculative builder who wants to put up a house regardless of its effect on the *amenities* —*Manchester Guardian Weekly*⟩ **2 a :** a feature, trait, or characteristic that makes for pleasantness ⟨the *amenities* of literature⟩ **b :** something that conduces to physical or material comfort or convenience or to a pleasant and agreeable life ⟨*amenities* like shops and community centers⟩ ⟨every ~ . . . including . . . showers, central heating, and first-class cuisine —Hugh G. Smith⟩ **c :** an area or location that provides comforts, conveniences, or attractive surroundings to residents or visitors ⟨a small . . . house in a choice ~ with clear bright sunny outlook —*Scotsman*⟩ ⟨preserving the region and . . . developing it as an ~ —*African Wild Life*⟩ **3** *usu pl* **a :** manner, civility, or relationship usu. expressive of or conducive to pleasantness or smoothness of social intercourse ⟨the *amenities* of diplomacy⟩ **b :** an act or form conventionally observed esp. in social intercourse ⟨the visitor got the *amenities* over quickly and got down to business⟩ ⟨one of the *amenities* which . . . lawyers have recognized . . . is the obligation to refrain from deliberately stealing each other's clients —H.S.Drinker⟩

²**amenity** \"\ *adj* **:** of, relating to, or providing an amenity ⟨~ values of the countryside —Hugh G. Smith⟩ ⟨an ~ tree for streets and parks⟩

amen·or·rhea *also* **amen·or·rhoea** \(ˌ)ā,menəˈrēə\ *n* -s [NL, fr. ²*a-* + Gk *mēn* month + NL *-o-* + *-rrhea, -rrhoea* — more at MOON] **:** absence or suppression of menstruation from any cause other than pregnancy or the menopause — **amen·or·rhe·al** *also* **amen·or·rhoe·al** \-ˌrēəl\ *adj* — **amen·or·rhe·ic** *also* **amen·or·rhoe·ic** \-ik\ *adj*

a men·sa et tho·ro \äˈmen(t)sə,et't(h)ōr(,)ō, ä'm-\ *adj* [NL, lit., from table and bed] **:** relating to a separation in which the parties remain husband and wife but without cohabitation

amen seat \ˈā,men *sometimes* ˈä,- *or* ˈā,-\ *n* **:** a seat in the amen corner of a church

¹**am·ent** \ˈamənt, ˈām-, -,ment\ *n* -s [NL *amentum*, fr. L *amentum, ammentum* thong, strap, prob. fr. *apere* to fasten + *-mentum* -ment — more at APT] **:** an indeterminate spicate inflorescence bearing scaly bracts and apetalous unisexual flowers (as in the willow) — called also *catkin*

aments: *a* staminate, *b* pistillate

²**ament** \ˈā,ment, ˈāmə-\ *n* -s [L *ament-, amens* mad, fr. *a-* (fr. *ab-* ab-) + *ment-, mens* mind — more at MIND] **:** a person mentally deficient from birth (as an idiot, imbecile, or moron)

am·en·ta·ceous \ˌamənˈtāshəs, ˌām-, -,men-\ *adj* [¹*ament* + *-aceous*] **1 a :** resembling an ament **b :** consisting of aments ⟨an ~ inflorescence⟩ **2 :** AMENTIFEROUS

¹**am·ent·al** \ˈaməntᵊl, ˈāmə-, ā,men-\ *adj* [¹*ament* + *-al*] **:** AMENTACEOUS

²**amen·tal** \(ˈ)āˈmentᵊl\ *adj* [²*a-* + *mental*] **:** devoid of mind ⟨a practically ~ hospital patient⟩

amen·tia \(ˈ)āˈmench(ē)ə, -nsh-\ *n* -s [NL, fr. L, madness, fr. *ament-, amens* + *-ia*] **:** mental deficiency; *specif* **:** a condition characterized by a primary lack of development of intellectual capacity — contrasted with *dementia*

am·en·tif·er·ae \,amənˈtifə,rē, ,ām-\ *n pl, cap* [NL, fr. *amentum* ament + *-i-* + *-ferae* (fem. pl. of *-fer*) — more at AMENT] *in some classifications* **:** a group, class, or other category including the dicotyledonous plants that bear aments

am·en·tif·er·ous \ˌ==ˈ=f(ə)rəs\ *adj* [ISV ¹*ament* + *-i-* + *-ferous*] **:** bearing aments

amen·ti·form \aˈmentə,fȯrm, āˈ-, əˈ-\ *adj* [¹*ament* + *-iform*] **:** having the shape of an ament

amen·tum \əˈmentəm\ *n, pl* **amen·ta** \-tə\ [L — more at AMENT] **:** a thong or cord attached to a javelin for aid in casting

amer- *or* **amero-** *comb form, cap* [*American*] **:** American ⟨*Amerophile*⟩ **:** American and ⟨*Amerasian*⟩

am·era \ˈamərə\ *n pl, cap* [NL, fr. ²*a-* + *-mera* (fr. Gk *meros* part)] *in certain classifications* **:** a major division of invertebrate animals comprising unsegmented more or less wormlike forms (as Platyhelminthes, Nemathelminthes, and certain Bryozoa) — compare OLIGOMERA, POLYMERA

amerce \əˈmərs, -ōs,-əis\ *vt* -ED/-ING/-S [ME *amercien*, fr. AF *amercier*, fr. OF *a merci* at (one's) mercy, fr. *a-* (fr. L *ad-*) + *merci* mercy — more at MERCY] **:** to punish by a pecuniary penalty the amount of which is not fixed by law but is left to the discretion of the court ⟨the court *amerced* the criminal in the sum of $100⟩; *broadly* **:** PUNISH

amerce·ment \-mənt\ *n* -s [ME *amerciment, amerciament*, fr. AF, fr. *amercier* + OF *-ment*] **:** the infliction of a penalty at the discretion of the court; *also* **:** a mulct or penalty thus imposed — compare AFFEER

amer·ci·a·ble \əˈmərsēəbəl, -shəb-\ *adj* [alter. (influenced by *amerciament*) of earlier *amerceable*, fr. *amerce* + *-able*] **:** punishable by amercement

amer·ci·a·ment \-sēəmənt, -shəm-\ *n* -s [ME — more at AMERCEMENT] *archaic* **:** AMERCEMENT

amer·i·ca \əˈmerəkə *also* -rē-\ *adj, usu cap* [fr. *America*, the continental region, fr. NL, after *Americus* Vespucius, Latinized form of Amerigo Vespucci †1512 Ital. navigator once believed to be its discoverer] **1 :** of or from No. America or So. America **:** of the kind or style prevalent in No. America or So. America **:** AMERICAN 1 **2 :** of or from the U.S. **:** of the kind or style prevalent in the U.S. **:** AMERICAN 2

¹**amer·i·can** \-kən\ *n* -s *cap* [*America*, the continental region + E *-an*] **1 :** an Indian of No. America or So. America **2 :** a native or inhabitant of No. America or So. America — usu. used with a qualifying adjective ⟨Latin *Americans*⟩ ⟨North *Americans*⟩ of all except inhabitants of the U.S. **3 :** a citizen of the U.S. **4 :** AMERICAN ENGLISH

²**american** \"\ *adj, usu cap* **1 :** belonging to, inhabiting, coming from, or forming part of America ⟨*American* waters⟩ ⟨an *American* people⟩ ⟨*American* products⟩ ⟨the *American* land masses⟩ **2 :** belonging to, inhabiting, coming from, or forming part of the U.S., its possessions, or original territory ⟨*American* air bases⟩ ⟨the first *American* colonists⟩ ⟨*American* soldiers⟩ ⟨a typical *American* city⟩ **3 :** relating or belonging to the division of mankind that comprises the Indians of No. America and So. America now regarded as an offshoot of the Mongolian

amer·i·cana \ə,merəˈkanə, -ˈänə,-ánə *also* -ānə\ *n pl, usu cap* [*America* + E *-ana*] **:** materials (as literary or historical documents and relics) distinctively bearing on, concerning, or characteristic of America, its civilization, or its culture; *also* **:** a collection of such materials ⟨has collected Western *Americana*, especially old books and early firearms —*Current Biog.*⟩

american alder *n, usu cap 1st A* **:** SPECKLED ALDER

american alligator *n, usu cap 1st A* **:** the alligator (*Alligator mississipiensis*) of the southeastern U.S. occas. reaching 16 feet in length with a tough hide much sought for leather

american allspice *n, usu cap 1st A* **:** CAROLINA ALLSPICE

american aloe *n, usu cap 1st A* **:** CENTURY PLANT

american arborvitae *n, usu cap 1st A* **:** an evergreen tree (*Thuja occidentalis*) of eastern No. America having branchlets in horizontal planes — compare ORIENTAL ARBORVITAE

american ash *n, usu cap 1st A* **:** WHITE ASH 1a

american aspen *n, usu cap 1st A* **:** a slender tree (*Populus tremuloides*) with quaking leaves native to eastern No. America

american badger *n, usu cap A* **:** a badger (*Taxidea taxus*) of western No. America

american baptist *n, usu cap A&B* **:** a member of a body of Baptist churches in northern and western U.S. which was organized in 1907 as the Northern Baptist Convention and renamed American Baptist Convention in 1950

american barberry *n, usu cap A* **:** a shrub (*Berberis canadensis*) of the southeastern U.S. with brown branches and flowers in short umbelliform clusters — called also *Allegheny barberry*

american basement *n, usu cap A* **:** a basement story above the ground level containing the principal entrance to the building

american basswood *n, usu cap A* **:** an American tree of the genus *Tilia* (esp. *T. americana*)

american beauty *n, usu cap A* **:** a deep purplish red that is redder and paler than hollyhock, redder and less strong than magenta (sense 2a), and less strong and slightly redder and darker than Harvard crimson (sense 2)

american beech *n, usu cap A* **:** a forest tree (*Fagus grandifolia*) having smooth gray bark, light green leaves, and edible nuts

american bison *or* **american buffalo** *n, usu cap A* **:** the bison (*Bison bison*) of No. America that formerly ranged in great herds over much of temperate No. America but is now nearly extinct

american bittern *n, usu cap A* **:** a large No. American marsh bird (*Botaurus lentiginosus*) that is related to the herons and has a brown body, dark gray outer wings, and a black stripe down each side of the neck — called also *stake driver, thunder pumper*

american bladdernut *n, usu cap A* **:** a shrub or small tree (*Staphylea trifolia*) of eastern No. America with trifoliolate leaves, drooping clusters of white flowers, and a bladdery capsule

american blight *n, usu cap A, Brit* **:** WOOLLY APPLE APHID

american bond *n, usu cap A* **:** a masonry bond in which the headers recur every 5th or 6th course, the stretcher courses that come together being laid so as to break joints — called also *common bond*

American bond

american boneset *n, usu cap A* **:** a boneset (*Eupatorium hyssopifolium*) with narrow leaves and white flowers found in sandy areas of the eastern U.S.

american brant *n, usu cap A* **:** a small dark short-necked goose (*Branta bernicla hrota*) that winters along the middle Atlantic coast and breeds in northwest Greenland and adjacent islands

american brown rot *n, usu cap A* **:** brown rot of stone and pome fruits caused by a fungus (*Sclerotinia fructicola*)

american catholic *adj, usu cap A&C* **:** of or relating to a church organized in 1885 for the purpose of bringing together American Catholics interested in the Old Catholic movement

american centaury *n, usu cap A* **:** either of two pink-flowered marsh plants (*Sabbatia angularis* and *S. stellaris*) of the eastern U.S. resembling the true centaury

american chameleon *n, usu cap A* **:** a lizard (*Anolis carolinensis*) of the southeastern U.S.

american cheese *n, usu cap A* **1 :** cheddar cheese made in America **2 :** a process cheese made from American cheddar

american cherry *n, usu cap A* **:** BLACK CHERRY 2

american chinaroot *n, usu cap A* **:** a greenbrier (*Smilax pseudo-china*) with large tuberous roots

american class *n, usu cap A* **:** a group of breeds of domestic fowls originated or developed chiefly in No. America — compare MEDITERRANEAN CLASS

american cloth *n, usu cap A, Brit* **:** a sturdy enameled oilcloth

american cockroach *n, usu cap A* **:** a free-flying cockroach (*Periplaneta americana*) that is a common pest infesting ships or buildings (as homes, warehouses, or bakeries) in the northern hemisphere

american columbo *n, usu cap A* **1 :** a perennial herb (*Frasera caroliniensis*) — called also *American gentian, columbo;* see DEER'S-EAR **2 :** the dried root of the American columbo formerly used as a bitter tonic

american coot *n, usu cap A* **:** a common American marsh bird (*Fulica americana*) having the bill, edge of wings, and upper tail coverts white, the rest of the plumage slaty and darker on the back than below — called also *blue peter, mudhen;* compare COOT 1

american copper *n, usu cap A* **:** a common copper butterfly (*Lycaena hypophlaeas*) widely distributed in central and eastern No. America north of the Gulf coast

american cotton *n, usu cap A* **:** UPLAND COTTON

american cowslip *n, usu cap A* **:** SHOOTING STAR

american crab apple *n, usu cap A* **:** a medium-sized tree (*Malus coronaria*) of the eastern U. S. with pink flowers and small hard yellow fruit — called also *garland crab*

american cranberry *n, usu cap A* **:** a trailing red-fruited cranberry (*Vaccinium macrocarpon*) with leaves oblong and obtuse, flowers in lateral clusters, and fruit ⅓ to ¾ inches in diameter — called also *large cranberry;* compare EUROPEAN CRANBERRY

american cranberry bush *n, usu cap A* **:** CRANBERRY BUSH 2

american crawl *n, usu cap A* **:** CRAWL 2; *specif* **:** a 6-beat crawl

american crocodile *n, usu cap A* **:** a tropical American crocodile (*Crocodylus acutus*) whose range extends to Florida

american dewberry *n, usu cap A* **:** a prostrate dewberry (*Rubus hispidus*) found in eastern No. America having persistent trifoliolate leaves, white flowers, and small reddish black fruit

american dog tick *n, usu cap A* **:** a common No. American tick (*Dermacentor variabilis*) attacking dogs, man, and other mammals and being an important vector of spotted fever and tularemia in man — called also *wood tick*

american dog violet *n, usu cap A* **:** a leafy-stemmed violet (*Viola conspersa*) with pale flowers found in moist woods

american dwarf birch *n, usu cap A* **:** a shrub (*Betula glandulosa*) of the colder parts of No. America with short aments and roundish glandular leaves

american eagle *n, usu cap A* **1 :** BALD EAGLE **2 :** a figure of a bald eagle with extended wings similar to that in the coat of arms of the U. S.

american ebony *n, usu cap A* **:** GRANADILLA TREE

american egret *n, usu cap A* **:** the common egret of No. America usu. being considered a variety (*egretta*) of the Old World egret (*Casmerodius alba* or *Egretta alba*)

american elder *n, usu cap A* **:** an elder (*Sambucus canadensis*) of eastern No. America with pale yellow branches, leaves with usu. seven leaflets, flat-topped flower clusters, and purplish black fruit about ¼ inch in diameter

american elm *n, usu cap A* **:** a large and well-known ornamental tree (*Ulmus americana*) common in eastern No. America with gradually spreading branches and pendulous branchlets

american empire *n, usu cap A* **:** a style of furniture of the second quarter of the 19th century influenced by contemporary French style, characterized by simple often heavy forms, and usu. finished in mahogany veneers

american english *n, cap A&E* **:** the native language of most inhabitants of the U. S. — used esp. with the implication that it is a variety of English clearly distinguishable from that used in Great Britain and not deriving its standards of usage from it, yet not so divergent as to be a separate language; compare AUSTRAL ENGLISH, AUSTRALIAN ENGLISH, BRITISH ENGLISH

amer·i·can·ese \əˌmerəkəˈnēz, -ēk-, -ēs\ *n* -s *cap A* **:** English speech or writing containing a high proportion of Americanisms — usu. used disparagingly

amer·i·can·ess \=ˈ===,nəs\ *n* -ES *usu cap A* **:** an American woman

american featherfoil *n, usu cap A* **:** an aquatic herb (*Hottonia inflata*) of the eastern U. S. with a spongy submerged stem, finely divided leaves, and white flowers

american feverfew *n, usu cap A* **:** a stout herb (*Parthenium integrifolium*) of the southeastern U. S. with whitish flowers resembling those of the feverfew

american fingering *n, usu cap A* **:** marking of piano music that uses the letter X to indicate the thumb and the figures 1, 2, 3, and 4 to indicate the other fingers — compare GERMAN FINGERING

american flag fish *n, usu cap A* **:** a small cyprinodont fish (*Jordanella floridae*) native to Florida swamps and mottled in blue and brown with white sides striped with red

american fluke *n, usu cap A* **:** the large liver fluke (*Fascioloides magna*) of cattle and related game mammals — compare LIVER FLUKE

american foulbrood *n, usu cap A* **:** foulbrood of the honeybee caused by a bacterium (*Bacillus larvae*) and characterized by a ropy or gummy condition of affected larvae

american foxhound *n, usu cap A* **:** a foxhound of a breed developed in America largely from English stock being slightly smaller than the English foxhound with longer ears, a dense hard glossy coat usu. of black, tan, and white, straight strong forelegs, and very powerful hindquarters

american fried potatoes *n pl, usu cap A* **:** HASHED BROWN POTATOES

american frog's-bit *n, usu cap A* **:** FROGBIT 2

american gentian *n, usu cap A* **:** AMERICAN COLUMBO 1

american germander *n, usu cap A* **:** an herb (*Teucrium canadense*) with serrate leaves, flowers in spikelike racemes, and calyx with a feltlike coat

american goldeneye *n, usu cap A* **:** a duck of the No. American subspecies (*americana*) of the goldeneye being stocky, medium sized, and large headed with the male chiefly black and white, the female brown and gray

american gooseberry *n, usu cap A* **:** any of several tropical American shrubs constituting a genus *Heterotrichum* of the family Melastomaceae and being often cultivated in warm regions for their showy panicles of white or pink flowers

american gooseberry mildew *n, usu cap A* **:** a powdery mildew (*Sphaerotheca mors-uvae*) of the gooseberry

american gray birch *n, usu cap A* **:** a medium-sized tree (*Betula populifolia*) of No. America having grayish or white bark, triangular leaves, and nearly valueless wood and occurring very commonly as a second-growth forest tree

american great valerian *n, usu cap A* **:** an herb (*Polemonium reptans*) of the eastern U. S. with pinnate leaves and blue flowers

american green *n, usu cap A* **:** a moderate yellowish green that is greener and duller than tarragon and yellower and duller than malachite green or verdigris — called also *jadesheen*

american gromwell *n, usu cap A* **:** a rough perennial herb (*Lithospermum latifolium*) of eastern No. America with hairy ovate leaves and axillary yellowish white flowers

american heather *n, usu cap A* **:** a beach heather (*Hudsonia tomentosa*)

american hellebore *n, usu cap A* **1 :** a white hellebore (*Veratrum viride*) of the eastern U. S. with dense spikelike flower clusters and rootstock that is the source of veratrum **2 :** the roots and rhizomes of the American hellebore

american hemp *n, usu cap A* **1 :** INDIAN MALLOW 1 **2 :** INDIAN HEMP 1

american holly *n, usu cap A* **:** a tree (*Ilex opaca*) of moist woodlands in the eastern U. S. having duller and less spiny leaves than the European holly

american hookworm *n, usu cap A* **:** a man-infesting hookworm (*Necator americanus*) discovered in No. America though probably native to Africa

american hornbeam *n, usu cap A* **:** a hornbeam (*Carpinus caroliniana*) of No. America with toothed leaves, winged fruit, and very hard durable wood

american horse chestnut *n, usu cap A* **:** OHIO BUCKEYE

american·i *or* **amer·i·ka·ni** \ə,merəˈkänē\ *n* -s *often cap* [Swahili, fr. E ²*American*] **:** unbleached cotton sheeting orig. made in America and used in Africa and the Far East

american indian *n, cap A&I* **:** a member of any (except usu. the Eskimos) of the aboriginal peoples of the western hemisphere constituting one of the divisions of the Mongoloid stock **:** RED INDIAN, AMERIND

american ipecac *n, usu cap A* **:** INDIAN PHYSIC 1

amer·i·can·ism \əˈmerəkə,nizəm, -ēk-\ *n* -s *usu cap* **1 :** a characteristic feature of American English esp. as contrasted with British English (as *hydrant, lynch, cookie, prairie, frame house, woodchuck, I guess, catercorner, store* meaning "shop", *corn* meaning "maize") **2 :** attachment or allegiance to the traditions, interests, or ideals of the U.S. or of democracy as practiced in the U. S. **3 a :** a custom peculiar to the U. S. or to America **b :** an American attitude or trait ⟨his frankness was considered an *Americanism*⟩ **c :** a socio-political principle or practice essential to American national culture ⟨the Declaration of Independence and the U. S. Constitution are fundamental to *Americanism*⟩ **4 :** HECKERISM

amer·i·can·ist \-ˌnəst\ *n* -s *usu cap* **1 :** a specialist in the languages or cultures of the aboriginal inhabitants of America **2 :** a member of a nation other than the U. S. who is favorable to the policies of the U. S. or to cooperation with the U. S.

amer·i·can·is·tic \=ˈ===ˈnistik, -tēk\ *adj, usu cap* **:** relating to America as a subject of study

amer·i·can·ite \=ˈ===ˌnīt\ *n* -s *sometimes cap* [[2]*American* + *-ite*] **:** a glassy meteoritic mineral found in a large area of western So. America

amer·i·can·itis \=ˌ===ˈnīd·əs\ *n* -ES *usu cap* **1 :** excessive nervous tension **2 :** enthusiastic or aggressive advocacy of Americanism

american ivy *n, usu cap A* **:** VIRGINIA CREEPER

amer·i·can·i·za·tion \=ˌ===nəˈzāshən, -ˌnīˈz-\ *n* -s *usu cap* **1 :** the act or process of americanizing **2 :** instruction of foreigners (as immigrants) in the English language, in U. S. history and government, and in other studies to prepare them for life in the U. S. or to familiarize them with U. S. culture, institutions, and ideals

amer·i·can·ize \=ˈ===ˌnīz\ *vb* -ED/-ING/-S *often cap* [[2]*American* + *-ize*] *vt* **1 :** to make American: **a :** to cause to acquire traits or characteristics distinctively or conceived as distinctively American **b :** to bring into close conformity with American national customs and institutions **:** change in behavior and attitude to suit the American way of life **2 :** to bring into conformity with characteristically American spelling or pronunciation **3 :** to bring (an area) under the political, cultural, or commercial influence of the U. S. ~ *vi* **:** to acquire American traits **:** integrate with or assimilate in spirit and culture to life in the U. S.

amer·i·can·iz·er \-zə(r)\ *n* -s *usu cap* **1 :** one entrusted with or engaged in americanizing immigrants or resident aliens in the U. S. **2 :** an ardent advocate of Americanism

american jade *n, usu cap A* **:** CALIFORNITE

american joy *n, usu cap A* **:** VIRGINIA CREEPER

american judas tree *n, usu cap A&J* **:** REDBUD

american jute *n, usu cap A* **:** INDIAN MALLOW 1

american language *n, usu cap A* **:** AMERICAN ENGLISH — usu. used with *the*

american lanner *n, usu cap A* **:** PRAIRIE FALCON

american larch *n, usu cap A* **:** a tamarack (*Larix laricina*)

american laurel *n, usu cap A* **:** MOUNTAIN LAUREL

american licorice *n, usu cap A* **:** WILD LICORICE 1

american lion *n, usu cap A* **:** COUGAR

american lobster *n, usu cap A* **:** the common lobster (*Homarus americanus*) of the northeastern coast of No. America

american lotus *n, usu cap A* **:** an aquatic plant (*Nelumbo lutea*) of the eastern U. S. with large usu. emerged leaves, very large yellow flowers, and deeply pitted fruits

amer·i·can·ly \=ˈ===lē\ *adv, usu cap* **:** in a distinctively American way ⟨so able to meet anything that might come . . . so *Americanly* capable and sure of the event —Booth Tarkington⟩

american mandrake *n, usu cap A* **:** MAYAPPLE

american merganser *n, usu cap A* **:** a common No. American diving duck usu. considered a variety (*Mergus merganser americanus*) of the European goosander

american milk pea *n, usu cap A* **:** a prostrate herbaceous vine (*Galactia regularis*) of the southeastern U. S. having trifoliolate leaves and reddish purple racemose flowers

american mint *n, usu cap A* **1 :** PEPPERMINT 1a **2 :** CANADA MINT

american mistletoe *n, usu cap A* **1 :** a small scaly leafless herb (*Arceuthobium pusillum*) that is parasitic on spruce and larch and has reddish brown stems, minute flowers, and berrylike fruits **2 :** MISTLETOE 2a

american morse code *n, cap A & usu cap M* **:** the Morse code used on telegraphic landlines in the U.S. and Canada — see MORSE CODE table

american moss *n, usu cap A* **:** SPANISH MOSS

american mountain ash *n, usu cap 1st A* **:** a mountain ash (*Sorbus americana*) with leaves that become glabrous beneath, sticky winter buds, and fruit about ¼ inch in diameter

american nettle tree *n, usu cap A* **:** HACKBERRY 1

american nightshade *n, usu cap A* **1 :** POKEWEED **2 :** DITCH STONECROP

amer·i·ca·no \əˌmerəˈkä(ˌ)nō\ *also* **americano cocktail** *n* -s *usu cap A* [Sp *americano* American, fr. *América* + Sp *-ano* -an] **:** a cocktail made from sweet vermouth, bitters, and soda water

amer·i·can·oc·ra·cy \əˌmerəkəˈnäkrəsē\ *n* -ES *usu cap* [*American* + *-o-* + *-cracy*] **:** political and economic control of a country by the U. S.

amer·i·can·oid \=ˈ===ˌnȯid\ *adj, usu cap* **:** resembling or having the form of something American; *specif* **:** showing certain lexical or structural affinities with the American Indian languages — used of certain languages of northeastern Asia (as Yukaghir, Chukchi, and Koryak); compare PALEO-ASIATIC

american olive *n, usu cap A* **:** DEVILWOOD

american organ *n, usu cap A* **:** a reed organ in which the air is drawn in through the reeds by a suction bellows

american orpine *n, usu cap A* **:** a succulent herb (*Sedum telephioides*) of the eastern U. S. with thick fleshy leaves and pink flowers

american ostrich fern *n, usu cap A* **:** an ostrich fern (*Pteretis pennsylvanica*)

american pansy *n, usu cap A* **:** BIRD'S-FOOT VIOLET

american pasqueflower *n, usu cap A* **:** any of several American plants of the genus *Anemone*; *esp* **:** a hirsute perennial (*A. ludoviciana*) with long-petioled leaves and persistent plumose styles

american pellitory *n, usu cap A* **:** an alternate-leaved weed (*Parietaria pennsylvanica*) of eastern No. America having axillary green flowers

american perch *n, usu cap A* **:** YELLOW PERCH

american pintail *n, usu cap A* **:** a dabbling duck breeding in northwestern No. America and wintering along the southern part of both coasts southward to Panama usu. being considered indistinguishable from the Old World pintail

american plan *n, usu cap A* **1 :** a hotel rate whereby guests are charged a fixed sum by the day, week, or other period for room and meals combined — contrasted with *European plan* **2 :** the principle of direct dealing between employers and employees without the intervention of labor unions or their officials or through a company union

american plane *or* **american plane tree** *n, usu cap A* **:** SYCAMORE 3a

american plum *n, usu cap A* **:** any of various cultivated plums derived chiefly from native American plums (as from *Prunus americana*) — compare EUROPEAN PLUM

american pondweed *n, usu cap A* **:** WATERWEED

american poplar *n, usu cap A* **1 :** AMERICAN ASPEN **2 :** TULIP TREE

american redstart *n, usu cap A* **:** a fly-catching warbler (*Setophaga ruticilla*) chiefly of eastern No. America, the male being largely black with white belly and bright orange on sides, wings, and tail, the female being olivaceous with pale yellow markings

american robin *n, usu cap A* **:** ROBIN 1c

american rock brake *n, usu cap A* **:** a rock-inhabiting fern (*Cryptogramma acrostichoides*) of northern No. America

american ruby *n, usu cap A* **:** a garnet cut from pyrope found in Arizona and New Mexico

american russia leather *n, usu cap A&R* **:** calfskin or cowhide leather finished to resemble Russia leather

american sable *n, usu cap A* **:** a pine marten (*Martes americana*) or its fur — compare SIBERIAN SABLE

american saddle horse *n, usu cap A* **:** a 3-gaited or 5-gaited saddle horse of a breed developed chiefly in Kentucky from Thoroughbreds and native stock and distinguished by their slender clean-cut build, high clean action, and alert carriage of head and tail

american saffron *n, usu cap A* **:** SAFFLOWER 1

american saibling *n, usu cap A* **:** SUNAPEE TROUT

american sanicle *n, usu cap A* **:** either of two hairy greenish flowered herbs (*Heuchera americana* and *H. villosa*) of eastern No. America

american school *n, usu cap A* **:** the economists that adhered to the American system; *specif* **:** the American economists who rejected the Ricardian doctrine of rent and the Malthusian doctrine, advocated a protective tariff, accepted the labor theory of value but not its implication of a subsistence wage, and held that labor's lot continuously improves

american scoter *n, usu cap A* **:** a large No. American scoter (*Oidemia americana*), the male being coal black with a bright yellow protuberance at the base of the upper mandible, the female being dusky brown with whitish cheeks

american sea rocket *n, usu cap A* **:** a fleshy herb (*Cakile edentula*) with purplish flowers and jointed pods found on seabeaches

american senna *n, usu cap A* **:** a wild senna (*Cassia marilandica*)

american service tree *n, usu cap A* **:** MOUNTAIN ASH 1

american shad *n, usu cap A* **:** a shad (*Alosa sapidissima*)

american shield fern *n, usu cap A* **:** a woodland fern (*Dryopteris spinulosa intermedia*) of eastern No. America with pinnae bearing glandular hairs

american snowball *n, usu cap A* **:** a shrub (*Styrax grandifolia*) of the southeastern U. S. with large leaves and racemose white flowers appearing before or with the leaves

american spindle tree *n, usu cap A* **:** [2]WAHOO a

american star grass *n, usu cap A* **:** a low grasslike herb (*Hypoxis hirsuta*) of eastern No. America with villous narrow leaves and yellow umbellate flowers

american sumac *n, usu cap A* **1 :** STAGHORN SUMAC **2 :** DIVI-DIVI 1

american surra *n, usu cap A* **:** INFECTIOUS ANEMIA

american system *n, cap A* **:** the policy of promoting industry in the U. S. by adoption of a high protective tariff and of developing internal improvements by the federal government (as advocated by Henry Clay from 1816 to 1828)

american tiger *n, usu cap A* **:** JAGUAR

american trotter *n, usu cap A* **:** a Standardbred horse

american trypanosomiasis *n, usu cap A* **:** CHAGAS' DISEASE

american valerian *n, usu cap A* **:** any of several American species of *Cypripedium*

american vegetable-tallow tree *n, usu cap A* **:** WAX MYRTLE

american vermilion *n, usu cap A* **1 :** vermilion or a color resembling it (as imitation vermilion) **2 :** a pigment usu. consisting of a lead molybdate or a basic lead chromate (as chrome red)

american vessel *n, usu cap A* **:** a vessel registered under the laws of the U. S. **:** a vessel owned by or chartered to Americans

american vetch *n, usu cap A* **:** a vetch (*Vicia americana*) with trailing or climbing stems, compound leaves, and racemose bluish purple flowers — called also *buffalo pea*

american walnut *n, usu cap A* **:** BLACK WALNUT 1

american watercress *n, usu cap A* **:** a weak perennial herb (*Cardamine rotundifolia*) found in cold springs in the eastern U. S. having undivided leaves and thin pods

american water spaniel *n, usu cap A* **:** a medium-sized spaniel of American origin with a thick curly chocolate or liver-colored coat

american wayfaring tree *n, usu cap A* **:** HOBBLEBUSH

american white avens *n, usu cap A* **:** a woodland herb (*Geum canadense*) of eastern No. America with hairy trifoliolate leaves, small white flowers, and bristly fruits

american white hellebore *n, usu cap A* **:** AMERICAN HELLEBORE

american white ipecac *n, usu cap A* **:** IPECAC SPURGE

american widgeon *n, usu cap A* **:** BALDPATE 2

american wine *n, usu cap A* **:** a U.S. wine made from grapes developed from or containing blood of an American wild grape (*Vitis labrusca*) and grown chiefly in the eastern or middle western part of the U. S.; *broadly* **:** any wine made in the U. S. — compare CALIFORNIA WINE

american wistaria *n, usu cap A* **:** a native woody vine (*Wisteria frutescens*) resembling the cultivated Japanese wistaria

american witch alder *n, usu cap A* **:** a shrub (*Fothergilla gardeni*) of the southeastern U. S. with hairy foliage and fruits and catkinlike spikes of apetalous flowers

american wormseed *n, usu cap A* **:** MEXICAN TEA

american wormseed oil *n, usu cap A* **:** CHENOPODIUM OIL

american yellow *n, usu cap A* **:** a variety of chrome yellow in the preparation of which alum and barium sulfate are used

american yew *n, usu cap A* **:** GROUND HEMLOCK

am·er·i·ci·um \ˌaməˈris(h)ēəm\ *n* -s [NL, fr. *America* + NL *-ium*] **:** a radioactive metallic element produced by bombardment of plutonium with high-energy neutrons — symbol *Am*; see ELEMENT table

americo- *comb form, cap* [*America*] **1 :** relating to America or Americans ⟨*Americomania*⟩ **2 :** American and ⟨*Americo-Liberian*⟩

amer·i·co-li·be·ri·an \əˈmerəˌkōˌlīˈbirēən\ *n, cap A&L* **:** a Liberian of American origin or descent

amerikani *often cap, var of* AMERICANI

am·er·ind \ˈaməˌrind\ *n* -s *cap* [*American Ind*ian] **:** an individual of one of the native peoples of America **:** an American Indian or Eskimo — **am·er·in·di·an** \ˌ==ˈ===\ *adj, usu cap* — **am·er·in·dic** \-dik\ *adj, usu cap*

am·er·ism \ˈaməˌrizəm, (ˈ)āˈme,r-\ *n* -s [*ameristic* + *-ism*] **:** the quality or state of being ameristic

am·er·is·tic \ˌaməˈristik, ˌāˌmeˈr-\ *adj* [Gk *ameristos* undivided (fr. *a-* [2]a- + *meristos* divided) + E *-ic* — more at MERISTEM] **:** UNDIFFERENTIATED — used of certain ferns having the prothallia not fully developed and lacking in meristematic tissue thus failing to produce archegonia

amero- — see AMER-

am·er·toy \ˈamə(r)ˌtȯi\ *n* -s [*Amer-* + *toy (terrier)*] **:** a small terrierlike dog of a breed of American origin having a short sleek satiny coat and attaining a weight of 6 to 10 pounds

amesace *var of* AMBSACE

ames·ite \ˈāmˌzīt\ *n* -s [alter. (influenced by *-ite*) of earlier *amesine*, fr. James *Ames* †1883 Am. mineralogist + E *-ine*] **:** an apple-green chlorite mineral $(Mg,Fe)_4Al_4Si_2O_{10}(OH)_8$ occurring in foliated hexagonal plates

ame·tab·o·la \ˌāməˈtabələ\ *n pl, cap* [NL, fr. Gk *ametabolos* unchanged] **:** a group of insects that includes certain primitive orders (as Thysanura) that undergo an inconspicuous metamorphosis — **amet·a·bo·li·an** \ˌāˌmed·əbōlēən\ *adj*

amet·a·bo·lia \ˌāˌmed·əˈbōlēə\ *syn of* AMETABOLA

amet·a·bol·ic \ˌāˌmed·əˌbälik\ *or* **ame·tab·o·lous** \ˌāməˌtabələs\ *adj* [[2]a- + *metabolic, metabolous*] **:** lacking metamorphosis

ame·tab·o·lism \ˌāməˈtabəˌlizəm\ *n* -s [Gk *ametabolos* + E *-ism*] **:** development without or with minimal metamorphosis (as in the Ametabola) — compare HOLOMETABOLISM

ameth·o·caine \əˈmethəˌkān\ *n* -s [perh. fr. Gk *amethystos* not intoxicating + *-ocaine* (as in *cocaine*)] **:** TETRACAINE

am·e·thyst \ˈaməthəst, -(ˌ)thi-\ *n* -s [ME *amatist, ametist*, fr. OF & L; OF *amatiste, ametiste*, fr. L *amethystus*, fr. Gk *amethystos* remedy against drunkenness, amethyst (so considered), fr. *amethystos* not drunk, not intoxicating, fr. *a-* [2]a- + *-methystos* drunk (fr. *methyskein* to make drunk, fr. *methyein* to be drunk, fr. *methy* wine) — more at MEAD] **1 a :** a clear purple or bluish violet variety of crystallized quartz much used as a jeweler's stone **b :** a deep purple variety of corundum — called also *Oriental amethyst* **2** *or* **amethyst violet :** a variable color averaging a moderate purple that is redder and duller than heliotrope (sense 4a) or manganese violet, bluer and duller than cobalt violet, and darker and slightly stronger than average lilac (sense 3a)

am·e·thys·tine \ˌ==ˈthistən, -ˌtīn, -ˌtēn\ *adj* [L *amethystinus*, fr. Gk *amethystinos*, fr. *amethystos* + *-inos* -ine] **1 :** resembling, composed of, or containing amethyst **2 :** of the color amethyst

am·e·trope \ˈaməˌtrōp\ *n* -s [back-formation fr. *ametropic*] **:** an ametropic person

am·e·tro·pia \ˌaməˈtrōpēə\ *n* -s [NL, fr. Gk *ametros* without measure (fr. *a-* [2]a- + *-metros*, fr. *metron* measure) + NL *-opia* — more at MEASURE] **:** an abnormal condition of the eye (as myopia, hypermetropia, or astigmatism) in which visual images do not come to a focus upon the retina — **am·e·tro·pic** \ˌaməˌträpik, -ˈäp-\ *adj*

AMF *abbr* airmail field

amg *abbr* among

am·garn \ˈamˌgärn\ *n* -s [W, ferrule, fr. *am-* around + *carn* handle; akin to L *ambi-* on both sides, around and to Corn *karn* handle — more at AMBI-] **:** an ancient stone implement supposed to have served as a guard or ferrule for the shaft or butt of a spear

am ha·a·rez \ˌäm(ˌ)häˈäˌrets\ *n, pl* **am·me haarez** *or* **ame haarez** \ˌämə(-\ [Heb *ʿam hāʾāreṣ* the people of the land] **1** *cap A* **:** the inhabitants of Palestine as distinguished from the Israelites; *also* **:** the country people as distinguished from the inhabitants of Jerusalem **2** *often cap A, in rabbinic literature* **:** the Jews not ritually as strict as the Pharisees **3** *sometimes cap A* **:** IGNORAMUS **:** one who is ignorant of Jewish custom, law, or ethics

am·hara \amˈharə, -ärə\ *n, pl* **amharas** *or* **amhara** *usu cap* **1 :** a Semitic-speaking people of northern Ethiopia **2 :** a member of the Amhara people

[1]**am·har·ic** \-ik\ *n* -s *cap* **:** the Semitic language of the central part of the Abyssinian plateau in Ethiopia that as the official language of Ethiopia is also used in government, education, and trade throughout the country

[2]**amharic** *adj, usu cap* **:** of, relating to, characteristic of, or composed in Amharic

am·herst·ia \amˈhərstēə, aˈmər-\ *n, cap* [NL, fr. Sarah, Countess *Amherst* †1838 & Sarah Elizabeth *Amherst* †1876 British amateur naturalists + NL *-ia*] **:** a genus of leguminous trees of India and Burma containing a single species (*A. nobilis*) of trees with immense pinnate leaves and pendent clusters of yellow-spotted vermilion flowers

am·herst·ite \ˈamərˌstīt\ *n* -s [*Amherst* co., Va., its locality + E *-ite*] **:** a plutonic syenodiorite rock whose feldspar is andesine-antiperthite

amherst pheasant *n, usu cap A* **:** LADY AMHERST'S PHEASANT

ami *or* **amy** \aˈmē, äˈ-\ *n, pl* **amis** *or* **amies** [ME, fr. OF *ami*, fr. L *amicus*] *law* **:** FRIEND — see PROCHEIN AMI

[1]**amia** \ˈamēə, ˈam-\ *n, cap* [NL, fr. Gk, a tunny] **:** a genus of ganoid fishes (order Cycloganoidei) including only the bowfin and helping the type of a small otherwise extinct family

[2]**amia** \"\ [NL, fr. Gk, a tunny] *syn of* APOGON — a prior use that has been ruled invalid by the International Commission for Zoological Nomenclature

ami·a·bil·i·ty \ˌāmēəˈbiləd·ē, -ətē, -i *also* -myəˈ-\ *n* -ES **1 :** the quality of being amiable **:** genial disposition ⟨made everyone happy by his unfailing ~⟩ **2 :** a manifestation or instance of being amiable ⟨the natives showed them every courtesy and ~⟩

ami·a·ble \ˈāmēəbəl *also* -myəb-\ *adj, sometimes* **amia·bler** \-b(ə)lə(r)\ **amia·blest** \-b(ə)ləst\ [ME, fr. MF, fr. LL *amicabilis* friendly, fr. L *amicus* friend + *-abilis* -able; akin to L *amare* to love — more at AMATEUR] **1** *archaic* **:** PLEASING, LOVELY, ATTRACTIVE ⟨how ~ are thy tabernacles —Ps 84:1 (AV)⟩ **2 a** *obs* **:** AMOROUS ⟨lay an ~ siege to the honesty of this Ford's wife —Shak.⟩ **b :** generally agreeable **:** devoid of anything contentious or offensive **:** good-natured and well-intentioned ⟨he has no improper pride. He is perfectly ~ —Jane Austen⟩ **c :** friendly, sociable, and congenial **:** civil and urbane **:** not stiff, cold, haughty, or stubborn ⟨an ~ friend⟩ ⟨an ~ gathering⟩ **d :** praiseworthy esp. as mild, lovable, socially beneficent, or unaggressive ⟨an ~ character⟩ ⟨so ~ a virtue as moral honesty —Laurence Sterne⟩ **e :** ENJOYABLE **:** affording ready easy pleasure ⟨a genial comic swagger . . . very ~ to behold —Hilaire Belloc⟩

syn GOOD-NATURED, OBLIGING, COMPLAISANT: AMIABLE may suggest an easy congenial good humor, socially pleasant and unaggressive smoothness, or gracious acquiescence ⟨an *amiable* neighborhood character⟩ ⟨the women . . . seemed to find a great deal of time for *amiable* empty gabbling —Edna Ferber⟩ ⟨their manners were more engaging, their tempers more *amiable* —T.B.Macaulay⟩ ⟨he considered a passive attitude in love more feminine and preferred an *amiable* softness to a tragic intensity —Ellen Glasgow⟩ GOOD-NATURED suggests a good-humored willingness to help or cooperate, sometimes an undue compliance ⟨the crowd was *good-natured* and civil . . . all seemed desirous to welcome me with every sign of pleasure —C.B.Nordhoff & J.N.Hall⟩ ⟨"If you're sick of the job, I'll take her off your hands", said the *good-natured* Fred —Anthony Trollope⟩ ⟨when he is *good-natured* . . . he will often pay her more than he is legally obliged to —G.B.Shaw⟩ OBLIGING suggests ready accommodation of others' wishes, usu. with civility or friendliness ⟨Dr. Armstrong, whose name the *obliging* young lady at the office allowed me to read upon the counterfoil of Staunton's urgent message —A. Conan Doyle⟩ ⟨he always had the courtesy to answer me, for he was a most *obliging* fellow —Agnes N. Keith⟩ COMPLAISANT, less common than the others, suggests courteous amiability and willingness to accede, sometimes because of a weak lack of resistance ⟨even if Mrs. Smith had been *complaisant*, Andrew's plan could not have been carried out —Margaret Deland⟩ ⟨her importunity prevailed with me and I am extremely glad I was so *complaisant* —Mary W. Montagu⟩

ami·able·ness *n* -ES **:** the quality or state of being amiable

ami·a·bly \-blē, -li\ *adv* **:** in an amiable manner ⟨~ talkative —Jean Stafford⟩

am·i·an·thine \ˌamēˈan(t)thən, ˌthīn\ *adj* [*amianthus* + *-ine*] **:** of, relating to, or like amianthus

am·i·an·thoid \ˌ==ˈanˌthȯid\ *or* **am·i·an·thoid·al** \ˌ==ˌ=ˈthȯidəl, ˌ==ˈ=ˌ==\ *adj* [*amianthus* + *-oid, -oidal*] **:** resembling amianthus

am·i·an·thus \ˌamēˈan(t)thəs\ *or* **am·i·an·tus** \-ntəs\ *n* -ES [L *amiantus*, fr. Gk *amiantos*, fr. *amiantos* unpolluted, pure, fr. *a-* [2]a- + *-miantos* (fr. *miainein* to pollute) — more at MIASMA] **:** fine silky asbestos

am·i·ca·bil·i·ty \ˌaməkəˈbiləd·ē, -mēk-, -ətē, -i\ *n* -ES **1 :** the quality of being amicable ⟨constant ~ existed between the two nations⟩ **2 :** a manifestation or instance of amicableness ⟨much impressed by all these *amicabilities*⟩

am·i·ca·ble \ˈ==kəbəl\ *adj* [ME, fr. LL *amicabilis* — more at AMIABLE] **:** characterized by or as if by friendship and goodwill **:** PEACEABLE **:** not quarrelsome ⟨consistently ~ discussions —F.D.Roosevelt⟩

syn NEIGHBORLY, FRIENDLY: AMICABLE stresses lack of quarreling, contention, bitterness, or hostility ⟨at the precise time when the feeling between the two countries was friendliest, and an *amicable* settlement of differences seemed likeliest —V.L.Parrington⟩ ⟨after more than thirty-two years of trading, *amicable* relations with the Indians were severed by the Indian wars —*Amer. Guide Series: Maine*⟩ NEIGHBORLY suggests either complete goodwill or sociable helpfulness and interest befitting a neighbor ⟨the only encirclement sought is the encircling bond of good old-fashioned *neighborly* friendship —F.D.Roosevelt⟩ ⟨a lover of men, the most *neighborly* soul in the world, mingling freely with all classes, and although quite properly proud of a visit from the governor or other great person, never above chatting with the carpenter, or doing a kindness to an old nurse —V.L.Parrington⟩ FRIENDLY may suggest warm intimacy, kindly benevolence, or amiable lack of ill will ⟨continually thanking Father John for his *friendly* visit, saying how kind it was of him to come and sit with an old man like him —Anthony Trollope⟩ Sometimes it indicates only an appearance of these qualities ⟨we must keep smiling faces and be *friendly* with him no matter how repulsive it may be —Jack London⟩

amicable action *n* **:** an action commenced and prosecuted by amicable consent of the parties for the purpose of obtaining a decision of the court on some matter of law ⟨*amicable action*, in the sense in which these words are used in courts of justice, presupposes that there is a real dispute between the parties concerning some matter of right . . . The amity consists in the manner in which it is brought to issue before the court. And such *amicable actions*, so far from being objects of censure, are always approved and encouraged—49 U.S. 251, 255⟩

am·i·cable·ness *n* -ES **:** the quality or state of being amicable

amicable number *n* **:** either of two numbers each of which is equal to the sum of all the submultiples of the other

am·i·ca·bly \-kəblē, -li\ *adv* **:** in an amicable manner ⟨a Presbyterian elder and a Methodist parson who rode in ~ together one April afternoon —Green Peyton⟩

am·ic acid \ˈamik-\ *n* [*amide* + *-ic*] **:** a compound (as carbamic acid) that is both an amide and an acid

am·i·cal \ˈaməkəl\ *adj* [L *amicalis*, fr. *amicus* friend + *-alis* -al] **:** FRIENDLY

1**am·ice** \'amės\ *n* -s [ME *amyse*, prob. fr. MF *amis* amices, pl. of *amit* amice, fr. ML *amictus*, fr. L, cloak, fr. *amictus*, past part. of *amicire* to wrap around, clothe, fr. *am-*, *amb-* around + *-icire* (fr. *jacere* to throw) — more at AMBI-, JET] **:** a liturgical vestment consisting of an oblong piece of cloth usu. of white linen, worn about the neck and shoulders and partly under the alb

1 amice

2**amice** \"\ *n* -s [ME *amisse*, fr. MF *aumuce*, fr. ML *almucia*, *almutia*] **:** ALMUCE

ami·ci prism \ə'mēchē-\ *n*, *usu cap A* [after G. B. *Amici* †*ab*1863 It. astronomer] **:** a composite prism used in direct-vision spectroscopes and made by combining alternate flint and crown glass components with their refracting edges in opposite directions and with prism angles so chosen that nonhomogeneous light passing through the prism is dispersed into a spectrum, the beam as a whole undergoing no net deviation — compare ACHROMATIC PRISM

ami·cron \(ˈ)ā'mī,krän *sometimes* -mi- *or* -,krən\ *n* -s [ISV ²*a-* + *micron*, orig. formed as G *amikron*] **:** one of the smallest particles detectable with the ultramicroscope (about 1×10^{-7} cm in diameter)

ami·cro·nu·cle·ate \¦ā¦=¦=-\ *adj* [²*a-* + *micronucleate*] **:** lacking a micronucleus

amic·tic \ə'miktik, (')ā¦-\ *adj* [Gk *amiktos* unmixed (fr. *a-* ²*a-* + *miktos* mixed) + E *-ic*] **1 :** incapable of being fertilized **:** PARTHENOGENETIC **:** producing eggs that develop without fertilization — used of female rotifers **2 :** produced by an amictic female **:** capable of developing without fertilization

ami·cus cu·ri·ae \ə¦mēkə'skyůrē,ī\ *n*, *pl* **ami·ci curiae** \-ē(,)kē'ky-\ [NL, lit., friend of the court] **:** a bystander that suggests or states some matter of law for the assistance of a court; *specif* **:** a lawyer that files a printed brief or makes an oral argument before an appellate court on behalf of a person affected by or interested in a pending case but not actually a party to it

amid \ə'mid\ *or* **amidst** \-idzt,-idst,-itst\ *prep* [*amid* fr. ME *amidde*, fr. OE *onmiddan*, fr. *on* + *middan*, dat. sing. masc. of *midde*, adj., middle, mid; *amidst* fr. ME *amiddes*, fr. *amidde* + *-s* — more at MID] **1 a :** in or into the middle of ⟨burst like a bombshell *amidst* the contemporary complacency —Isaac Goldberg⟩ ⟨*amid* such a world, if anywhere, our ideals henceforth must find a home —Bertrand Russell⟩ **b :** surrounded or encompassed by **:** AMONG ⟨*amidst* a patch of snow-covered firs, a sixth cart waited —F.V.W.Mason⟩ ⟨*amid* bulging wicker and pasteboard suitcases and bundles done up in cloth sat elderly men —Andy Logan⟩ **2 a :** in the course of **:** DURING ⟨*amidst* all the fighting there still remained a steady hope for peace⟩ **b :** with the accompaniment of — used to indicate that two or more specified conditions or occurrences are linked in time, cause, or circumstance ⟨he completed the feat *amidst* cheers —*Time*⟩ ⟨the buffaloes, who reproduced so rapidly *amidst* the favorable environment —R.A.Billington⟩

amid- *or* **amido-** *comb form* [ISV, fr. *amide*] **1 :** containing the group NH_2 characteristic of amides united to a radical of acid character ⟨*amido*sulfuric⟩ — distinguished from *amin-* **2 :** AMIN- ⟨*amido*phenol⟩ **3 :** containing the radical –CONH– characteristic of polyamides, peptides, and proteins

ami·dah \ə'mē(,)dä, ä'-, -(,)dä; ,ämē'dō\ *n*, *pl* **ami·doth** *or* **ami·dot** \-,dōs, -,dōt; -'dōt\ *or* **amidahs** *usu cap* [Heb *'ămīdhāh* standing] **:** a benediction recited while standing during the main section of the daily Jewish liturgy and at the additional service on Sabbaths and holy days

am·i·dase \'amə,dās, -āz\ *n* -s [ISV *amid-* + *-ase*] **:** an enzyme that hydrolyzes acid amides usu. with the liberation of ammonia

am·i·date \-,dāt\ *vt* -ED/-ING/-S [*amid-* + *-ate*] **1 :** to convert into an amide **2 :** AMINATE — **am·i·da·tion** \,amə'dāshən\ *n* -s

am·ide \'a,mīd, 'amėd, *in compounds often* ə,mīd *or* ,əmėd\ *n* -s [G *amid* (fr. *ammoniak* ammonia — fr. F or L— + *-id* -ide) or F *amide*, fr. *ammoniaque* ammonia + *-ide* — more at AMMONIAC] **1 :** any of a class of crystalline compounds derived from ammonia by replacement of one hydrogen atom by a metal ⟨lithium ~ $LiNH_2$⟩ ⟨calcium ~ $Ca(NH_2)_2$⟩ — called also *metallic amide* **2 :** any of a class of compounds (as acetamide, sulfamide) derived from ammonia or an amine by replacement of ammoniacal hydrogen by an acid radical (as an acyl radical) — called also *acid amide;* compare IMIDE; see SULFONAMIDE

amid·ic \ə'midik, a'-\ *adj* [*amid-* + *-ic*] **:** of or relating to an amide

am·i·dine \'amə,dēn, -,dən\ *n* -s [ISV *amid-* + *-ine*] **:** any strong monobasic compound containing an amino and an imino group attached to the same carbon atom, having the general formula $RC(=NH)NH_2$, and formed by the action of ammonia on nitriles or by reaction of ammonia with imido esters

am·i·di·no \,amə'dē(,)nō\ *adj* [*amidino-*] **:** containing the group $-C(=NH)NH_2$

amidino- *comb form* [ISV, fr. *amidine* + *-o-*] **:** containing the univalent group $-C(=NH)NH_2$ characteristic of an amidine ⟨*amidino*pyridine⟩

am·i·dism \'amə,dizəm\ *n* -s *usu cap* [Jap *Amida* the Buddha Amitabha (fr. Chin *a*⁴ *-mi*² *-t'o*² *-fu*², fr. Skt *Amitābha*, a Mahayana Buddha, worshiped as the Buddha of boundless light, life, and mercy, lit., of boundless light, fr. *amita* boundless, unmeasured — fr. *a-* ²a- + *mita* measured — + *ābhā* light, fr. *ā* towards + *-bhā*, akin to *bhāti* it shines) + E *-ism;* akin to Skt *māti* he measures — more at ACHARYA, FANCY, MEASURE] **:** the Buddhist cult of Amitabha that promises rebirth in paradise to its followers and emphasizes salvation by faith — see PURE LAND

1**am·i·dist** \-,dėst\ *adj*, *usu cap* [Jap *Amida* + E *-ist*] **:** of or relating to Amidism

2**amidist** \"\ *n* -s *usu cap* **:** a member of the cult of Amitabha

ami·do \ə'mē(,)dō, 'amə,dō\ *adj* [*amid-*] **1 :** relating to or containing the group NH_2 or a substituted group NHR or NR_2 united to a radical of acid character — distinguished from *amino* **2 :** AMINO — now less used than formerly

amido black green B *n*, *often cap A&B&G* **:** an acid azo dye — see DYE table I (under *Acid Green 20*)

ami·do·gen \ə'mēdəjən, -,jen\ *n* -s [*amid-* + *-gen*] **:** the radical NH_2 derived from ammonia esp. as detected in the free state — compare AMIDO, AMINO

am·i·dol \'amə,dōl, -ōl\ *n* -s [G, fr. *Amidol*, a trademark] **:** a colorless crystalline salt $C_6H_3(NH_2)_2OH.2HCl$ used chiefly as a photographic developer; the dihydrochloride of 2,4-diamino-phenol

ami·do naph·thol red \ə¦mēdō¦=,=-, ¦amə,dō¦-\ *n*, *often cap A&N&R* [*amid-* + *naphthol*] **:** either of two acid azo dyes — see DYE table I (under *Acid Red 1* and *Acid Violet 7*)

am·i·done \'amə,dōn\ *n* -s [ISV dimethyl*amino-* + *d*iphenyl + hept*anone;* prob. orig. formed as G *amidon*] **:** METHADONE

ami·do·phos·phor·ic acid \ə¦mēdō¦=¦==-, ¦amə,dō¦-\ *n* [*amid-* + *phosphoric*] **:** an acid $PONH_2(OH)_2$ derived from phosphoric acid by replacement of one hydroxyl group by an amido group — called also *phosphamic acid, phosphoramidic acid*

ami·do·py·rine \ə,mēdō'pī,rēn, ,amə,dō'-, -,rən\ *n* -s [*amid-* + *pyrine*] **:** AMINOPYRINE

am·i·dos·to·mum \,amə'dästəməm\ *n*, *cap* [NL, fr. Gk *amid-, amis* chamber pot + NL *-o-* + *-stomum*] **:** a genus of strongyloid nematodes including destructive parasites of the gizzard wall of ducks and geese

amidoth *or* **amidot** *pl of* AMIDAH

am·i·dox·ime \,amə'däk,sēm, -,səm\ *n* -s [ISV *amid-* + *oxime;* orig. formed as G *amidoxim*] **:** the oxime of an amide having the general formula $RC(=NOH)NH_2$

amido yellow E *n*, *often cap A&Y* **:** an acid dye — see DYE table I (under *Acid Orange 3*)

1**amidships** *also* **amidship** \ə'=,=\ *adv* [*amidships* fr. *amid* + *ship* + *-s* (gen. ending); *amidship*, alter. of *amidships*] **1 a :** in or toward that part of a ship midway between the bow and the stern **b :** in or toward that part of a ship midway between the sides **2 :** in or toward the middle

2**amidships** *also* **amidship** \"\ *adj* **:** of, relating to, or situated in the middle part of a ship ⟨an ~ cabin⟩

amidst *var of* AMID

amidstream \ə'=,=\ *adv* **:** in midstream

amies *pl of* AMY

ami·go \ə'mē(,)gō, ä'-\ *n* -s [Sp, fr. L *amicus;* akin to L *amare* to love — more at AMATEUR] **:** FRIEND

amil \'amȯl, -,mil\ *var of* AUMIL

amil·dar \'amȯl,där\ *var of* AUMILDAR

amil·le·nar·i·an \¦ā-\ *n* -s [²*a-* + *millenarian*] **:** one who holds the doctrine of amillennialism

amil·len·ni·al \¦ā¦=-\ *adj* **1 :** of or relating to amillennialism **2** [²*a-* + *millenial*] **:** not expecting a literal millennium

amil·len·ni·al·ism \¦ā-\ *n* -s [²*a-* + *millenialism*] **:** the denial that an earthly millennium of universal righteousness and peace will either precede or follow the second advent of Jesus Christ — compare POSTMILLENNIALISM, PREMILLENNIALISM

amil·len·ni·al·ist \¦ā-\ *n* -s **:** AMILLENARIAN

amim·ia \(')ā'mimēə\ *n* -s [NL, fr. ²*a-* + Gk *mimos* actor, mime + NL *-ia* — more at MIME] **1 :** loss or impairment of the power of communicating thought by gestures, due to cerebral disease or injury **2 :** loss of the power to give facial expression to emotion (as the inability to smile) because of paralysis of the facial muscles

a·min *var of* AMEEN

amin- *or* **amino-** *comb form* [ISV, fr. *amine*] *now usu amino-* **:** containing the group NH_2 characteristic of primary amines united to a radical other than an acid radical ⟨*amino*acetanilide⟩ ⟨*amino*guanidine⟩ — distinguished from *amid-*

am·i·nase \'amə,nās\ *n* -s [*amin-* + *-ase*] **:** any of a group of enzymes capable of promoting assimilation of ammonia

1**am·i·nate** \-,nāt\ *n* -s [*amin-* + *-ate*] **:** a compound with an amine

2**aminate** \"\ *vt* -ED/-ING/-S [*amin-* + *-ate*] **:** to introduce the amino group into **:** convert into an amine — **am·i·na·tion** \,amə'nāshən\ *n* -s

amine \ə'mēn, 'amėn\ *n* -s [ISV *ammonium* + *-ine*] **1 :** any of a class of basic compounds derived from ammonia by replacement of hydrogen by one or more univalent hydrocarbon radicals or other nonacidic organic radicals, being classed as primary, secondary, or tertiary according as one, two, or three atoms of ammoniacal hydrogen have been replaced — distinguished from *imine;* compare QUATERNARY AMMONIUM COMPOUND **2 :** a compound (as a chloramine) containing one or more halogen atoms attached to nitrogen

amin·ic \ə'mēnik, -in-, a'-\ *adj* [*amin-* + *-ic*] **:** of or relating to an amine or the amino group

am·in·ize \'amə,nīz; ə'mē-, a'-\ *vt* -ED/ -ING/ -S [*amin-* + *-ize*] **:** AMINATE

ami·no \ə'mē(,)nō, a'-; 'amə,nō\ *adj* [*amin-*] **:** relating to or containing the group NH_2 or a substituted group NHR or NR_2 united to a radical other than an acid radical — distinguished from *amido*

ami·no·ace·tic acid \=¦===¦==-, ¦==,=¦==\ *n* [*amin-* + *acetic*] **:** GLYCINE

amino acid *n* **:** an organic acid in which a portion of the nonacid hydrogen has been replaced by one or more amino groups and which therefore shows both basic and acidic properties; *esp* **:** one of the more than 20 alpha-amino acids, most of which have the general formula $RCH(NH_2)COOH$, that are synthesized in plant and animal tissues, that are considered the building blocks of proteins, from which they can be obtained by hydrolysis, and that play an important role in metabolism, growth, maintenance, and repair of tissue — see ESSENTIAL AMINO ACID, PEPTIDE

amino alcohol *n* **:** a compound (as ethanolamine) that is both an alcohol and an amine — called also *alcamine, hydroxy amine*

ami·no·azo \=¦==a(,)zō, ¦==,=-\ *adj* [*aminoazo-*] **:** containing both the amino and azo groups

aminoazo- *comb form* [ISV, fr. *amin-* + *az-*] **:** containing both the amino and azo groups esp. in compounds formed by rearrangement of diazoamino compounds

ami·no·azo·benzene \"+\ *n* [ISV *aminoazo-* + *benzene*] **:** a solvent dye $C_6H_5N{=}NC_6H_4NH_2$ — see DYE table I (under *Solvent Yellow 1*)

ami·no·azo·toluene \"+\ *n* [*aminoazo-* + *toluene*] **:** a solvent dye — see DYE table I (under *Solvent Yellow 3*)

ami·no·ben·zo·ate \=,=='-, ¦==,='-\ *n* -s [*amin-* + *benzoate*] **:** a salt or ester of an aminobenzoic acid, esp. of the para isomer

ami·no·ben·zo·ic acid \=¦==¦=¦==-, ¦==,=¦==-\ *n* [ISV *amin-* + *benzoic*] **:** any of three crystalline monoamino derivatives $NH_2C_6H_4COOH$ of benzoic acid: as **a :** the colorless or yellowish para-substituted acid that is found as a component of the vitamin B complex and of the folic acids but is usu. made synthetically, that is antagonistic to many sulfa drugs in their action on bacteria, and that is used in local anesthesia in the form of some of its esters (as butacaine, procaine) — called also *PABA, p-aminobenzoic acid, para-aminobenzoic acid* **b :** ANTHRANILIC ACID

am·i·nol·y·sis \,amə'näləsės\ *n*, *pl* **aminoly·ses** \-ə,sēz\ [NL, fr. *amin-* + *-lysis*] **1 :** ammonolysis or any analogous decomposition in which an amine takes the place of ammonia **2 :** hydrolytic deamination (as the conversion of an amino acid into a hydroxy acid) — **ami·no·lyt·ic** \ə¦mēnō¦lid-ik, a¦-; ¦amə,nō¦-\ *adj*

ami·no·meth·yl·a·tion \ə¦mēnō,methə'lāshən, a¦-; ¦amə,nō,-\ *n* -s [*aminomethyl* (fr. *amin-* + *methyl*) + *-ation*] **:** introduction of the amino-methyl group NH_2CH_2- into a compound

amino nitrogen *n* **:** nitrogen occurring as a constituent of the amino group

ami·no·pep·ti·dase \=,=¦pepṭə,dās, ¦==='-\ *n* -s [*amin-* + *peptide* + *-ase*] **:** an enzyme (as an enzyme found in the duodenum) that hydrolyzes peptides, esp. polypeptides, by splitting off the amino acids containing free amino groups

ami·no·phe·nol \-'=,=\ *n* -s [ISV *amin-* + *phenol;* orig. formed in G] **1 :** any of three crystalline compounds $NH_2C_6H_4OH$ derived from phenol, distinguished as *ortho*-aminophenol, *meta*-aminophenol, and *para*-aminophenol, and used as dye intermediates, the para compound being also used as a fur and hair dye and as a photographic developer **2** *usu* **amino phenol :** an amino derivative of a phenol

am·i·noph·er·ase \,amə'näfə,rās\ *n* -s [*amin-* + *pher-* + *-ase*] **:** TRANSAMINASE

ami·no·phyl·line \ə,mēnō'fi,lēn, ¦amə,nō'-; ,amə'näfə,-\ *n* -s [*amin-* + theo*phylline*] **:** a white or slightly yellow granular compound $(C_7H_8N_4O_2)_2.C_2N_4(NH_2)_2.2H_2O$ of theophylline and ethylenediamine that has an ammoniacal odor and bitter taste and is used in medicine similarly to theophylline

ami·no·plast \=¦==,plast, '==,=-\ *n* -s [by shortening] **:** AMINO PLASTIC

amino plastic *or* **amino resin** *n* **:** a plastic or synthetic resin (as a urea-formaldehyde resin) made from amino or amido compounds usu. excluding the polyamides

ami·no·poly·pep·ti·dase \=¦==,päle'peptə,dās, ¦==,=-\ *n* -s [*amin-* + *polypeptide* + *-ase*] **:** an aminopeptidase that acts on polypeptides

am·i·nop·ter·in \,amə'näptərėn\ *n* -s [*aminopteroylglutamic* + *-in*] **:** a yellow crystalline compound $C_{19}H_{20}N_8O_5.2H_2O$ used clinically as an antagonist to folic acid in the treatment of certain leukemias — called also *4-aminopteroylglutamic acid*

ami·no·py·rine \ə,mēnō'pī,rēn, a,-, -,rən; ,amə,nō'-\ *n* -s [ISV dimethyl*amin-* + anti*pyrine*] **:** a white crystalline compound $C_{13}H_{17}N_3O$ derived from pyrazolone and used as an anodyne and antipyretic — called also *amidopyrine*

a minor \'ā'mīnə(r)\ *n*, *usu cap A* **:** the minor musical key having neither sharps nor flats in its signature

a mi·no·re \,ä,mė'nōrė, ,äm-; ¦ā,mī'-\ *adj* [L, from the lesser] **:** of or relating to an ionic foot beginning with two short syllables

ami·no·sal·i·cyl·ic acid \=¦==¦==¦==-, ¦==,=¦==¦==-\ *n* [*amin-* + *salicylic*] **:** any of four isomeric monoamino derivatives $NH_2C_6H_3(OH)COOH$ of salicylic acid; *esp* **:** the white crystalline para-substituted acid made synthetically and used in the treatment of tuberculosis usu. as an adjunct to streptomycin or dihydrostreptomycin

ami·no·thi·a·zole \=¦==-, ¦==¦='-\ *n* -s [*amin-* + *thiazole*] **:** a light yellow crystalline heterocyclic amine $H_2NC_3H_2NS$ made by condensing thiourea and chloro-acetaldehyde and used esp. in the manufacture of sulfathiazole — called also *2-aminothiazole*

am·i·oi·dei \,amē'ȯidē,ī\ [NL, fr. ¹*Amia* + *-oidei*] *syn of* CYCLOGANOIDEI

amir *var of* EMIR

amis *pl of* AMI

1**amish** \'ämish, -ēsh *also* 'am- *sometimes* 'ām-\ *adj*, *usu cap* [prob. fr. G *amisch*, fr. Jacob Amman or *Amen fl* 1693 Swiss Mennonite bishop, the founder of the sect + G *-isch* -ish] **:** of, belonging, or relating to a strict sect of Mennonite followers of Amman that settled in America

2**amish** \"\ *n*, *cap* **:** the Amish people

amish·go \ə'mish(,)gō\ *n*, *usu cap* **:** AMUSGO

am·ish·man \'ämishmən, 'am-,'ām-, -ēsh-\ *n*, *pl* **amishmen** *cap* **:** an Amish Mennonite

1**amiss** \ə'mis\ *adv* [ME *amis*, fr. ¹*a-* + *mis* mistake, wrong — more at MISS] **1 a :** in a mistaken way **:** WRONGLY ⟨if you think he is guilty, you judge ~⟩ **b :** out of the right way **:** ASTRAY ⟨something had gone ~ —Van Wyck Brooks⟩ **2 :** in a faulty way **:** IMPERFECTLY ⟨Miss Bennet would not play at all ~ if she practiced more —Jane Austen⟩ **3 a :** in a reprehensible way ⟨no doubt he got his money ~⟩ **b :** in an uncalled-for way ⟨a crude fellow, forever speaking ~⟩

2**amiss** \"\ *adj* [ME *amis*, fr. *amis*, adv.] **1 :** not in accordance with right order **:** WRONG ⟨undue provincialism is ~ —D.G. Mandelbaum⟩ **2 :** FAULTY, IMPERFECT ⟨whether his general health had been previously at all ~ —Charles Dickens⟩ **3 a :** deserving blame **:** REPREHENSIBLE ⟨could prove nothing ~ —Hartzell Spence⟩ **b :** out of place under given circumstances **:** uncalled for — usu. used with a negative ⟨a few expurgated excerpts may not be ~ —R.B.Merriman⟩; usu. used predicatively

3**amiss** *n* -ES [ME *amis*, fr. *amis*, adj. & adv.] *obs* **:** FAULT, MISDEED

amis·si·bil·i·ty \ə,misə'bilәd-ē\ *n* -ES [prob. fr. NL *amissibilitas*, fr. LL *amissibilis* amissible + L *-itas* -ity] **:** capability of being lost **:** likelihood of being lost

amis·si·ble \ə'misəbəl\ *adj* [LL *amissibilis*, fr. L *amissus* (past part. of *amittere* to lose, send away, fr. *a*, *ab* from + *mittere* to send) + *-ibilis* -able — more at OF, SMITE] **:** capable of being lost **:** likely to be lost

amission *n* -s [F or L; F, fr. L *amission-*, *amissio*, fr. *amissus* + *-ion-*, *-io* -ion] *obs* **:** LOSS

amit *vt* [L *amittere*] *obs* **:** LOSE ⟨a loadstone fired doth presently ~ its proper virtue —Sir Thomas Browne⟩

am·i·tate \'amə,tāt -,tət\ *n* -s [L *amita* paternal aunt + E *-ate*] **1 :** a special relationship obtaining among some peoples between a niece and her brother's children and the rights and responsibilities associated therewith — compare AVUNCULATE

ami·to·sis \¦ā,mī'tōsės, ,amə'-\ *n*, *pl* **amito·ses** \-ō,sēz\ [NL, fr. ²*a-* + *mitosis*] **:** cell division in which there is first a simple cleavage of the nucleus without differentiation (as of chromosomes or spindle) followed by the division of the cytoplasm — called also *direct cell division;* opposed to *mitosis*

ami·tot·ic \¦ā,mī¦täd-ik, ¦amə'-\ *adj* [fr. NL *amitosis*, after such pairs as NL *hypnosis*: E *hypnotic*] **:** of, relating to, or involving amitosis — **ami·tot·i·cal·ly** \-ək(ə)lē\ *adv*

am·i·ty \'aməd-ē, -ətē, -i\ *n* -ES [ME *amite*, fr. MF *amité*, *amitié*, fr. ML *amicitas*, fr. L *amicus* friend, friendly + *-itas* -ity; akin to L *amare* to love — more at AMATEUR] **:** friendship and goodwill esp. as characterized by mutual acceptance and toleration of potentially antagonistic standpoints or aims ⟨so the two women kept up an elaborate pretense of warm ~ —Scott Fitzgerald⟩; *specif* **:** friendly relations between large groups ⟨nations striving for lasting ~⟩

am·i·u·rus \,a,mī'yůrəs\ *syn of* AMEIURUS

amix·ia \(')ā'miksēə\ *n* -s [NL, fr. Gk, purity, lack of intercourse, fr. *amiktos* unmixed, pure, unsociable (fr. *a-* ²*a-* + *miktos* mixed, fr. *meignynai* to mix) + *-ia* — more at MIX] *biol* **:** absence of interbreeding (as that resulting from geographical isolation)

am·i·zil·ia \,amə'zilyə\ *n*, *cap* [NL] **:** a genus of large hummingbirds chiefly of Central America of which two species (*Amizilia tzacal* and *A. yucatanensis chalconota*) range as far north as southern Texas

am·la \'ämlə\ *n* -s [Hindi *āmlā*, fr. Skt *āmalaka*] **:** EMBLIC

amlah *var of* AMALA

amm- *or* **ammo-** *comb form* [*ammo-*, fr. Gk, fr. *ammos* sand — more at SAND] **:** sand ⟨*ammo*philous⟩

am·man \'a,man, 'ä,män\ *adj*, *usu cap* [fr. *Amman*, Jordan] **:** of or from Amman, the capital of Jordan **:** of the kind or style prevalent in Amman

am·man·ite \'amə,nīt\ *n* -s *usu cap* [Jacob *Ammann* or *Amen fl* 1693 Swiss Mennonite bishop + E *-ite*] **:** an Amish Mennonite

amme haarez *pl of* AM HAAREZ

am·me·ter \'a(m),mēd-ə(r), -ētə- *sometimes* 'amə-\ *n* -s [*ampere* + *-meter*] **:** an instrument for measuring electric current in amperes by an indicator activated by the movement of a coil in a magnetic field or by the longitudinal expansion of a wire carrying the current — compare GALVANOMETER, MICROAMMETER, MILLIAMMETER, VOLTAMETER

am·mi \'a,mī\ *n*, *cap* [NL, fr. L *ammi*, *ami*, a plant (prob. *Carum copticum*), fr. Gk] **:** a small genus (the type of the family Umbelliferae) of branched annual herbs of the Mediterranean region and the No. Atlantic islands with pinnate or pinnatifid leaves and compound umbels — see BISHOP'S WEED

am·mi·a·ce·ae \,amē'āsē,ē\ *n pl*, *cap* [NL, fr. *Ammi*, type genus + *-aceae*] *in some classifications* **:** a family of plants coextensive with Umbelliferae — **am·mi·a·ceous** \¦amē¦āshəs\ *adj*

am·mine \'a,mēn, 'amən; ə'mēn, a'-\ *n* -s [ISV *ammonia* + *-ine*] **1 :** a molecule of ammonia as it exists in a coordination complex ⟨hex-*ammine*-cobalt chloride $[Co(NH_3)_6]Cl_3$⟩ **2 :** any compound with ammonia or sometimes with an amine regarded as a coordination complex ⟨metal ~*s*⟩ — compare AMMONIATE

am·mi·no \'amə,nō; ə'mē(,)nō, a'-\ *adj* [*ammino-*] **:** of, relating to, or characteristic of an ammine

ammino- *comb form* [prob. fr. G, fr. *ammin* ammine] **:** ammine ⟨*ammino*chloride⟩

am·mo \'a(,)mō\ *n* -s [by shortening & alter.] **:** AMMUNITION ⟨a GI carrying enough ~ to fight a week⟩

am·mo·bi·um \ə'mōbēəm, a'-\ *n* [NL, fr. *amm-* + *-bium* (fr. Gk *bios* life)] **1** *cap* **:** a small genus of Australian herbs (family Compositae) with yellow flowers and silvery foliage — see WINGED EVERLASTING **2** -s **:** a plant of the genus *Ammobium*

am·mo·coe·tes \,amə'sēd-ēz\ *also* **am·mo·coete** \'amə,sēt\ *n*, *pl* **am·mo·coetes** \,amə'sēd-ēz, 'amə,sēts\ [NL *Ammocoetes*, former genus consisting of the ammocoetes, fr. *amm-* + *-coetes* (fr. Gk *koitē* bed, fr. *keisthai* to lie) — more at CEMETERY] **:** the larva of any of various lampreys — **am·mo·coe·tid** \¦amə¦sēd-əd\ *n or adj* — **am·mo·coe·toid** \-¦sē,tȯid\ *adj*

am·mo·dyte \'amə,dīt\ *n* -s [NL *Ammodytes*] **:** SAND LAUNCE

am·mo·dy·tes \,amə'dīd-ēz\ *n*, *cap* [NL, fr. Gk *ammodytēs*, a snake, lit., sand burrower, fr. *amm-* + *dytēs* diver, fr. *dyein* to enter, get into, sink] **:** a genus (the type of the family Ammodytidae) of percomorph fishes containing the typical sand launces — **am·mo·dy·toid** \¦amə¦dī,tȯid\ *adj*

am·mo·nal \'amə,nal\ *n* -s [ISV *ammonium* + *aluminum;* prob. orig. formed in G] **:** an explosive containing chiefly ammonium nitrate, trinitrotoluene, and powdered aluminum

1**am·mo·nate** \'amə,nāt\ *vb* -ED/-ING/-S [*ammonia* + *-ate*] **:** to combine with ammonia to form only one product without decomposition (as in ammonolysis) of the ammonia — **am·mo·na·tion** \,amə'nāshən\ *n* -s

2**ammonate** *var of* AMMONIATE

am·mo·nea \,amə'nēə\ [NL, by shortening] *syn of* AMMONOIDEA

ammoni- *or* **ammonio-** *comb form* [ISV, fr. *ammonium*] **:** containing ammonia or ammonium ⟨*ammonio*cupric sulfate⟩

am·mo·nia \ə'mōnyə *also* -nēə\ *n* -s [NL, fr. L (*sal*) *ammoniacus* sal ammoniac, lit., salt of Ammon, fr. *ammoniacus* of Ammon, fr. Gk *ammōniakos*, fr. *Ammōn*, an Egyptian deity identified by the Greeks with Zeus, fr. Egypt *Amōn;* fr. its having been prepared near a temple of Ammon in Egypt] **1 :** a colorless gaseous alkaline compound of nitrogen and hydrogen NH_3 that is lighter than air, of extremely pungent smell and taste, and very soluble in water, that can easily be condensed by cold and pressure to a liquid and for this reason is much used in producing artificial cold by the absorption of heat that takes place when the liquid ammonia evaporates, that was formerly made from nitrogenous organic matter (as horn, hoofs) but is now produced as a by-product of the gas and coke industry, that forms ammonium salts by combination with acids and forms many organic derivatives (as amines, amino acids, amides, alkaloids), and that is used both free and combined in medicine, the arts, and industry (as in making fertilizers and explosives) — see LIQUID AMMONIA, SYNTHETIC AMMONIA PROCESS **2 :** AMMONIA WATER

ammonia alum *n* **:** ALUM 1b

am·mo·ni·ac \ə'mōnē,ak\ *or* **am·mo·ni·a·cum** \,amə'nīəkəm\ *n* -S [ME & L; ME *ammonyak*, fr. L *ammoniacum* ammoniac, fr. Gk *ammōniakon*, fr. neut. of *ammōniakos* of Ammon; prob. fr. its occurrence in plants growing near a temple of Ammon in Egypt] **1 :** the aromatic gum resin of the ammoniac plant that occurs in commerce in the form of yellowish tears or lumps with a bittersweet somewhat nauseous and acrid taste and that is used as an expectorant and stimulant and in the formation of certain plasters — called also *gum ammoniac, Persian ammoniac* **2 :** a dark-colored gum resin derived from a northern African plant (*Ferula brevifolia*) — called also *African ammoniac*

am·mo·ni·a·cal \¦amə'nīəkəl\ *or* **am·mo·ni·ac** \ə'mōnē,ak\ *adj* [*ammoniacal* fr. *ammoniac*, n. + *-al*; *ammoniac* fr. ME (*sal*) *ammoniac*, fr. L *sal ammoniacus* — more at AMMONIA] **:** of or relating to ammonia **:** containing or having the properties of ammonia

ammoniac plant *n* **:** a tall Persian herb (*Dorema ammoniacum*) of the family Umbelliferae whose milky juice yields ammoniac

ammonia dynamite *n* **:** DYNAMITE 1c

ammonia gelatin *n* **:** an explosive of the gelatin dynamite class containing ammonium nitrate

ammonia liquor *or* **ammoniacal liquor** *n* **:** AMMONIA WATER; *esp* **:** the impure solution obtained as a by-product in destructive distillation (as of coal, tar, and bones)

am·mo·ni·an \ə'mōnēən, -nyən\ *adj, usu cap* [*Ammonius*, 3d cent. Alexandrian Christian philosopher + E *-an*] **:** of or relating to Ammonius of Alexandria, reputed author of a harmony of the Gospels and a work on the agreement of the teachings of Moses and Jesus

ammonia nitrogen *n* **:** nitrogen combined in the form of ammonia or ammonium

ammonia soda *n* **:** soda made by the ammonia soda process

ammonia soda process *n* **:** a process for making soda from common salt by using ammonia and carbon dioxide; *specif* **:** SOLVAY PROCESS

¹am·mo·ni·ate \ə'mōnē,āt, *usu* -ād·+V\ *vt* -ED/-ING/-S [*ammonia* + *-ate*] **1 :** to combine or impregnate with ammonia or an ammonium compound ⟨*ammoniated* superphosphate⟩ **2 :** AMMONIFY

²ammoniate \"\ *also* **am·mo·nate** \'amə,nāt\ *n* -S [*ammonia* + *-ate*] **1 :** a compound with ammonia regarded as analogous to a hydrate ⟨calcium chloride hexa-*ammoniate* $CaCl_2.6NH_3$⟩ — compare AMMINE **2 :** any organic material (as tankage or hoof and horn) from which nitrogen can be obtained in the form of ammonia — used chiefly commercially

ammoniated mercury *n* **:** a heavy white odorless amorphous compound NH_2HgCl obtained by treating a solution of mercuric chloride with excess of ammonia and used in external treatment of skin diseases and to destroy lice — called also *white precipitate*

am·mo·ni·a·tion \ə,mōnē'āshən\ *n* -S **:** the act or process of ammoniating

am·mo·ni·a·tor \ə'mōnē,ād·ə(r)\ *n* -S **:** an apparatus for introducing ammonia into a compound or for impregnating a substance with ammonia

ammonia water *or* **ammonia solution** *n* **:** a solution of ammonia in water — called also *aqua ammonia, aqueous ammonia, spirit of hartshorn;* compare AMMONIUM HYDROXIDE, HOUSEHOLD AMMONIA

am·mo·ni·fi·ca·tion \ə,mōnəfə'kāshən, -mä-\ *n* -S [*ammonia* + *-ification*] **1 :** AMMONIATION **2 :** decomposition with production of ammonia or ammonium compounds esp. by the action of bacteria on nitrogenous organic matter (as in soils)

am·mo·ni·fi·er \=ˈ==,fī(ə)r\ *n* -S **:** a bacterium that produces ammonia from organic matter containing nitrogen

am·mo·ni·fy \ə'mōnə,fī, -mä-\ *vb* -ED/-ING/-ES [*ammonia* + *-fy*] *vt* **:** to subject to ammonification ~ *vi* **:** to produce or undergo ammonification

ammonio- — see AMMONI-

am·mo·ni·o·bo·rite \ə,mōnē(,)ō-\ *n* -S [*ammoni-* + *borite*] **:** a mineral consisting of hydrous ammonium borite $(NH_4)_2B_{10}O_{16}.5H_2O$ found at Larderello, Italy

am·mo·ni·o·ja·ro·site \=ˈ==(,)=-\ *n* -S [*ammoni-* + *jarosite*] **:** a member of the jarosite group of minerals in which ammonium replaces potassium

¹am·mo·nite \'amə,nīt, *usu* -īd·+V\ *n* -S [NL *ammonites*, fr. *ammon-* (fr. L *cornu Ammonis* ammonite, lit., horn of Ammon, Egyptian deity represented with ram's horns, fr. *cornu* horn + *Ammonis*, gen. of *Ammon*, fr. Gk *Ammōn*) + *-ites* -ite — more at AMMONIA] **1 :** any of numerous fossil shells of cephalopods of the order Ammonoidea having the form of a flat spiral similar to that of the nautilus and esp. abundant in the Mesozoic age, some being 3 feet or more in diameter **2 :** one of the Ammonoidea — **am·mo·nit·ic** \¦amə¦nid·ik\ *adj*

²am·mo·nite \"\ *n* -S [*ammon-* (in *ammonium nitrate*) + *-ite*] **:** a nitrogenous animal product of rendering works consisting largely of dried meat residues and used as a fertilizer

³am·mon·ite \"\ *n* -S *usu cap* [LL *Ammonites*, fr. Heb *'Ammōn*, people of the Ammonites + L *-ites* -ite] **1 :** a member of a people who in Old Testament times lived east of the Jordan between the Jabbok and the Arnon **2 :** the Semitic language of the Ammonites, closely allied to Hebrew

⁴am·mon·ite \"\ *adj, usu cap* **:** of or relating to the Ammonites

am·mo·ni·tes \,amə'nīd·ēz\ *n, cap* [NL, fr. *ammonites* ammonite] **1** *in former classifications* **:** a genus of ammonites **2 :** a group of ammonites comprising forms known only from fragments too imperfect to allow accurate identification — used as a generic name

am·mo·ni·ti·cone \,amə'nīd·ə,kōn, -ni-\ *n* -S [¹*ammonite* + *-i-* + *cone*] **:** ¹AMMONITE 1

am·mo·ni·ti·da \,amə'nīd·ədə\ [NL, fr. *Ammonites* + *-ida*] *syn of* AMMONOIDEA

am·mo·nit·if·er·ous \¦amə,nīd·'if(ə)rəs\ *adj* [¹*ammonite* + *-i-* + *-ferous*] **:** containing ammonites

¹am·mon·it·ish \'amə,nīd·ish\ *adj, usu cap* [³*Ammonite* + *-ish*] **:** ⁴AMMONITE

²ammonitish \"\ *n, usu cap* **:** ³AMMONITE 2

am·mo·nit·oid \¦amə¦nīd·,ȯid, ə'mänə,tȯid\ *adj* [¹*ammonite* + *-oid*] **:** resembling an ammonite

am·mo·ni·toi·dea \,amə,nīd·'ȯidēə\ [NL, fr. *Ammonites* + *-oidea*] *syn of* AMMONOIDEA

am·mo·ni·um \ə'mōnēəm, -nyəm\ *n* -S [NL, fr. *ammonia* + *-ium*] **:** an ion NH_4^+ or radical NH_4 derived from ammonia by combination with a hydrogen ion or atom and known in compounds (as salts formed by reaction of dry or aqueous ammonia with acids) that resemble in properties the compounds of the alkali metals and known also in organic compounds (as quaternary ammonium compounds) in which one or more of the hydrogen atoms attached to the nitrogen are substituted by organic radicals

ammonium alum *or* **ammonium aluminum sulfate** *n* **:** ALUM 1b

ammonium bicarbonate *n* **:** a white crystalline salt NH_4HCO_3 made by passing carbon dioxide through an aqueous ammonia solution and used chiefly in baking powders and in fire-extinguishing compositions — called also *ammonium acid carbonate, ammonium hydrogen carbonate*

ammonium bromide *n* **:** a colorless crystalline salt NH_4Br used in photography and in medicine as a sedative

ammonium carbamate *n* **:** a salt NH_2COONH_4 found in commercial ammonium carbonate and formed as an intermediate in the manufacture of urea by reaction of ammonia and carbon dioxide

ammonium carbonate *n* **:** a ammonium salt of carbonic acid: as **a :** the normal carbonate $(NH_4)_2CO_3$ that readily decomposes into the bicarbonate and ammonia **b :** AMMONIUM BICARBONATE **c :** a white crystalline mixture of ammonium bicarbonate and ammonium carbamate obtained commercially by subliming an ammonium salt with calcium carbonate and used chiefly in medicine, in smelling salts, in baking powders, in fire-extinguishing compositions, and in scouring and dyeing preparations

ammonium chloride *n* **:** a white crystalline volatile salt NH_4Cl that occurs naturally esp. as a product of volcanic action or is manufactured and that is used chiefly as an electrolyte in dry cells and as an expectorant for bronchitis — called also *sal ammoniac*

ammonium cyanate *n* **:** a white crystalline salt NH_4OCN that changes into urea on standing or on heating in an aqueous solution

ammonium hydrosulfide *n* **:** AMMONIUM SULFIDE b

ammonium hydroxide *n* **:** a weak base NH_4OH formed when ammonia dissolves in water and existing only in solution

ammonium molybdate *n* **:** a white crystalline salt used in analytical chemistry as a precipitant of phosphoric acid with which it forms a yellow precipitate of ammonium phosphomolybdate

ammonium nitrate *n* **:** a colorless crystalline salt NH_4NO_3 made usu. by the union of ammonia and nitric acid and used chiefly in explosives and fertilizers

ammonium perchlorate *n* **:** a crystalline salt NH_4ClO_4 used chiefly as an oxidizer in explosives, in fireworks, and solid propellant systems for rockets

ammonium persulfate *n* **:** a colorless crystalline salt $(NH_4)_2S_2O_8$ used as an oxidizing agent and for improving dense photographic negatives

ammonium phosphate *n* **:** a phosphate of ammonium made by reaction of ammonia and phosphoric acid: as **a :** the white crystalline primary phosphate $NH_4H_2PO_4$ or sometimes a commercial mixture of this with ammonium sulfate, used chiefly as a fertilizer and as a fire retardant — called also *ammonium dihydrogen phosphate, monoammonium phosphate, monobasic ammonium phosphate* **b :** the white crystalline secondary phosphate $(NH_4)_2HPO_4$ similarly used — called also *diammonium phosphate, dibasic ammonium phosphate*

ammonium picrate *n* **:** a yellow or red salt of picric acid $NH_4OC_6H_2(NO_3)_3$ used as an explosive, its resistance to impact, shock, and friction permitting its use in armor-piercing projectiles

ammonium sulfamate *n* **:** a white crystalline salt $NH_4SO_3NH_2$ used chiefly as a fire retardant and as a weed killer

ammonium sulfate *n* **:** a colorless crystalline salt $(NH_4)_2SO_4$ occurring in nature as mascagnite and made usu. by reaction of sulfuric acid with ammonia and used chiefly as a fertilizer

ammonium sulfide *n* **:** a sulfide of ammonium: as **a :** the unstable colorless to yellow crystalline normal sulfide $(NH_4)_2S$ **b :** the white crystalline hydrosulfide NH_4HS used in aqueous solution chiefly in the textile industry

ammonium thiocyanate *n* **:** a colorless crystalline salt NH_4SCN made by reaction of ammonia and carbon disulfide and used chiefly in textile printing, as a rust inhibitor, and as a weed killer and defoliant

ammonium thioglycolate *n* **:** a colorless crystalline salt NH_4OOCH_2SH used in setting cold waves

am·mo·no \ə'mō(,)nō\ *adj* [*ammono-*] **:** of or relating to compounds considered as bearing to ammonia relations analogous to those that certain other compounds bear to water ⟨lithium amide $LiNH_2$ is an ~ base⟩ — compare AQUO

ammono- *comb form* [ISV, fr. *ammonia*] **1 :** ammonia ⟨*ammonolysis*⟩ **2 :** derived from ammonia — in names of chemical compounds ⟨*ammono*carbonic acid $HN{=}C(NH_2)_2$⟩ — compare AQUO- 2

am·mo·noid \'amə,nȯid\ *n* -S [NL *Ammonoidea*] **:** one of the Ammonoidea **:** AMMONITE

am·mo·noi·dea \,amə'nȯidēə\ *n pl, cap* [NL, irreg. fr. *Ammonites* + *-oidea*] **:** an order of extinct chiefly Mesozoic Tetrabranchia comprising cephalopods having an external chambered shell that is either straight or variously curved or coiled — see ¹AMMONITE — **am·mo·noi·de·an** \¦amə¦nȯidēən\ *adj or n*

am·mo·nol·y·sis \,amə'näləsəs\ *n, pl* **ammonoly·ses** \-ə,sēz\ [NL, fr. *ammono-* + *-lysis*] **:** any chemical reaction analogous to hydrolysis in which ammonia plays a role similar to that of water, one or more atoms of hydrogen in the ammonia being replaced by other atoms or radicals ⟨the ~ of organic esters yields acid amides⟩ — often distinguished from *ammonation* — **am·mo·no·lyt·ic** \ə¦mōnə¦lid·ik, a¦-; ¦amənō¦-\ *adj*

am·mo·no·lyze \ə'mōnᵊl,īz, a'-\ *vt* -ED/-ING/-S [fr. NL *ammonolysis*, after such pairs as E *analysis: analyze*] **:** to subject to ammonolysis

am·mon's law \'amənz-, 'am-; 'ä,mōnz-\ *n, usu cap A* [after Otto *Ammon* †1916 Ger. anthropologist] **:** a generalization in anthropology: the cephalic index varies inversely as the stature

¹am·moph·i·la \ə'mäfələ, a'-\ *n, cap* [NL, fr. *amm-* + *-phila*] **:** a small genus of coarse perennial grasses growing on sandy shores and dunes and having awnless flowers crowded into a long spikelike panicle — see BEACH GRASS, MARRAM GRASS

²ammophila \"\ [NL, fr. *amm-* + *-phila*] *syn of* SPHEX

³ammophila \"\ *n* -S **:** a sand wasp of the genus *Sphex*

am·moph·i·lous \-ləs\ *adj* [*amm-* + *-philous*] **:** living or growing in the sand or in dry sandy places ⟨~ grasses⟩

ammos *pl of* AMMO

¹am·mu·ni·tion \,amyə'nishən, *chiefly in substand speech* ,amə'-\ *n* -S [obs. F *amunition*, *amonition*, fr. MF, alter. (influenced by MF *amonition* admonition) of *munition*] **1** *obs* **:** general military supplies **2 a :** the various projectiles together with their fuzes, propelling charges, and primers that are fired from guns **b :** explosive military items (as grenades, bombs, and pyrotechnical matériel) **c :** any item or material that is thrown in fight or play (as spears or snowballs) **3 :** resources for attack or defense often in a contention or struggle in which one must engage ⟨~ to support sweeping changes —T.W.Arnold⟩

²ammunition \"\ *vb* -ED/-ING/-S **:** to supply with ammunition **:** LOAD ⟨the gunners were fast in firing and ~*ing*⟩

ammunition scuttle *n* **:** an opening through a ship door or bulkhead to permit the passing of ammunition

amn *abbr* ammunition

am·ne·sia \am'nēzhə, aam-\ *n* -S [NL, fr. Gk *amnēsia* forgetfulness, prob. alter. of *amnēstia*] **1 :** loss of memory sometimes including the memory of personal identity due to brain injury, shock, fatigue, repression, or illness or sometimes induced by anesthesia ⟨suffering from ~ and unable to identify himself⟩ ⟨a period of ~ after the wreck⟩ **2 :** a gap in one's memory ⟨an ~ concerning his high-school years⟩

am·ne·si·ac \-z(h)ē,ak\ *also* **am·ne·sic** \-zik, -sik, -ēk\ *n* -S [*amnesia* + *-ac* (as in *maniac*, n.) or *-ic*] **:** a sufferer from amnesia

am·ne·sic \(')am¦nēzik, -aam-, -sik, -ēk\ *also* **am·ne·si·ac** \-z(h)ē,ak\ *adj* [NL *amnesia* + E *-ic* or *-ac* (as in *maniac*, adj.)] **:** of or relating to amnesia **:** suffering from or caused by amnesia ⟨an ~ patient⟩ ⟨an ~ trauma⟩

am·nes·tic (')a¦nestik, -ēs-\ *adj* [Gk *amnēstia* forgetfulness + E *-ic*] **:** AMNESIC

¹am·nes·ty \'amnəstē, 'aam-, -ti *also* -,nes-\ *n* -ES [Gk *amnēstia* forgetfulness, amnesty, fr. *amnēstos* forgotten (fr. *a-* ²a- + *-mnēstos*, fr. *mnasthai* to remember) + *-ia* -y — more at MIND] **1** *archaic* **:** the voluntary overlooking of an offense by the one offended **2 :** the act of an authority (as a government) by which general pardon of an offense is granted often before trial or conviction esp. to a large group of individuals ⟨an ~ for war criminals⟩ **syn** see PARDON

²amnesty \"\ *vt* -ED/-ING/-ES **:** to grant amnesty to

amnia *pl of* AMNION

am·ni·ac \'amnē,ak\ *adj* [*amnion* + *-ac* (as in *cardiac*)] **:** AMNIOTIC

am·ni·col·i·dae \,amnə'käləˌdē\ [NL, fr. *Amnicola*, type genus (fr. L, that dwells by a river, fr. *amnis* river + *-cola*, fr. *colere* to dwell) + *-idae*] *syn of* BULIMIDAE

am·ni·o- *comb form* [NL, fr. *amnion*, fr. Gk] **1 :** amnion ⟨*amniotome*⟩ **2 :** amniotic and ⟨*amnio*allantoic⟩

am·nio·car·di·ac vesicle \¦amnē(,)ō¦-\ *n* **:** one of the paired infolding portions of the vertebrate embryonic coelom that give rise to the pericardial cavity

am·ni·o·cho·ri·on \¦==(,)=ˈ-\ *n* -S [NL, fr. *amnio-* + *chorion*] **:** the amnion and chorion acting as a functional unit

am·ni·o·gen·e·sis \,==(,)=ˈ-\ *n* [NL, fr. *amnio-* + L *genesis*] **:** amnion formation

am·ni·on \'amnē,än, -ən\ *n, pl* **amnions** \-nz\ *or* **am·nia** \-ēə\ [NL, fr. Gk, caul, prob. fr. dim. of *amnos* lamb — more at YEAN] **1 :** a thin membranous fluid-filled sac surrounding the embryo (of reptile, bird, or mammal) that is typically formed together with the chorion through growth about the embryo of the amniotic folds, these folds completely enclosing the embryo, fusing at their line of final contact, and then splitting across the line of fusion to separate an inner amnion immediately enclosing the embryo and an outer chorion **2 :** a membrane resembling an amnion and enclosing the embryos of many insects and other invertebrates

am·ni·on·ic \¦amnē¦änik\ *also* **am·nic** \'amnik\ *adj* [NL *amnion* or *amnion* + E *-ic*] **:** AMNIOTIC

am·ni·os \'amnē,äs\ *n, pl* **amnios** [NL, fr. Gk, alter. of *amnion*] **:** AMNION

am·ni·o·ta \,amnē'ōd·ə\ *n pl, cap* [NL, irreg. fr. *amnion*] **:** the group of vertebrates that develop an amnion in embryonic life — **am·ni·ote** \'amnē,ōt\ *adj or n*

am·ni·ot·ic \¦amnē¦äd·ik\ *adj* [*amnio-* + *-otic*] **1 :** of or relating to the amnion **2 :** characterized by the development of an amnion

amniotic band *n* **:** a band of fibrous tissue extending between the embryo and amnion and often associated with faulty development of the fetus

amniotic fluid *n* **:** the serous fluid in which the embryo is suspended within the amnion

amniotic fold *n* **:** one of the folds consisting of ectoderm and the outer layer of mesoderm that arises from the extraembryonic blastoderm first at the head, then at the tail, and finally on each side and that gives rise to the amnion and much of the chorion

amn't \'ànt *sometimes* 'a(a)nt *or* 'amənt *or* 'a(a)m(p)t\ [by contr.] *dial* **:** am not

am·o·bar·bi·tal \,a(,)mō'-\ *n* -S [*amyl* + *-o-* + *barbital*] **:** a crystalline compound $C_{11}H_{18}N_2O_3$ used as a sedative and hypnotic with its sodium salt being used similarly; 5-ethyl-5-isoamyl-barbituric acid

am·o·di·a·quin \-'dīə,kwin\ *also* **am·o·di·a·quine** \-,kwēn\ *n* -S [*amino-* + *dihydrochloride* + connective *-a-* + *-quin* (fr. *quinoline*) or *-quine*] **:** a compound $C_{20}H_{22}ClN_3O$ derived from quinoline and used in the form of its dihydrochloride as an antimalarial

amoe·ba \ə'mēbə\ *n* [NL, fr. Gk *amoibē* change, fr. *ameibein* to change — more at MIGRATE] **1 a** *cap* **:** a large genus of naked rhizopod protozoans with lobose and never anastomosing pseudopodia and without permanent organelles or supporting structures and that are widely distributed in fresh and salt water and moist terrestrial situations **b** *also* **ameba** \"\ *pl* **amoebas** \-bəz\ *or* **amoe·bae** \-(,)bē\ **:** any protozoan of this or a related genus **c** *also* **ameba** *pl* **amoebas** *or* **amoebae :** an amoeboid unicellular individual (as the amoeboid stage of a flagellate or of a sporozoan) **2** -S **:** a contour (as of a table top) of irregular curves

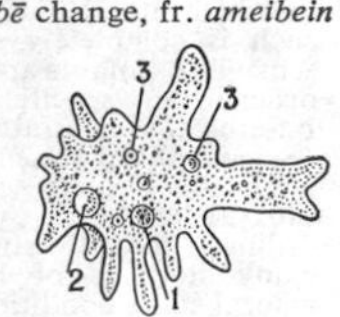

amoeba (magnified) showing *1* nucleus, *2* contractile vacuole, *3* food vacuole

amoeba disease *n* **:** a disease of adult honeybees caused by an amoeba (*Vahlkampfia mellifica*)

¹am·oe·baea \,amē'bēə, -mə'-\ *n pl, cap* [NL, fr. *Amoeba*] *in some classifications* **:** a subclass of Sarcodina comprising the Amoebina and Testacea

²amoebaea \"\ [NL, fr. *Amoeba*] *syn of* AMOEBINA

am·oe·be·an verse \¦amē¦bēən-, -mə¦-\ *n* [L *amoebaeus* alternate, fr. Gk *amoibaios* interchanging (fr. *amoibē* change) + E *-an*] **:** poetry written in the form of a dialogue between two speakers — compare STICHOMYTHIA

amoebiasis *var of* AMEBIASIS

amoe·bic *also* **ame·bic** \ə'mēbik, -ēk\ *or* **amoe·ban** *or* **ame·ban** \-bən\ *or* **amoe·bous** *or* **ame·bous** \-bəs\ *adj* [NL *amoeba*, *ameba* + E *-ic* or *-an* or *-ous*] **1 :** resembling or relating to an amoeba or amoebalike organisms **2** *usu amebic* **:** caused by amoebas or amoebalike organisms

amoebicide *var of* AMEBICIDE

amoe·bid *also* **ame·bid** \-bəd\ *n* -S [NL *amoeba*, *ameba* + E *-id*] **:** an amoeba or amoebalike animal

amoe·bi·form \-bə,fȯrm\ *adj* [NL *amoeba*, *ameba* + E *-iform*] **1** *also* **ame·bi·form** \"\ **:** AMOEBOID **2 :** having an amoeba contour ⟨an ~ swimming pool⟩

am·oe·bi·na \,amē'bīnə, -mə'-, -ēnə\ *n pl, cap* [NL, fr. *Amoeba* + *-ina*] **:** an order of naked rhizopods that are commonly clearly differentiated into endoplasm and ectoplasm, form lobopodia, and include the common amoebas of soil and water and some parasitic forms — see ENDAMOEBIDAE

amoe·bo·bac·ter \ə'mēbō,baktə(r)\ *n* [NL, fr. *Amoeba* + *-o-* + *-bacter*] **1** *cap* **:** a genus of purple sulfur bacteria (family Thiorhodaceae) having spherical or elongated cells that are aggregated in amoeboid colonies without an enclosing capsule and that occur in mud and stagnant water **2** -S **:** any organism of the genus *Amoebobacter*

amoe·bo·cyte *also* **ame·bo·cyte** \ə'mēbə,sīt\ *n* -S [NL *amoeba*, *ameba* + E *-o-* + *-cyte*] **:** a cell having amoeboid form or movements: as **a :** a wandering cell of blood or tissues of many invertebrate animals that acts as a phagocyte and aids in assimilation and excretion **b :** LEUKOCYTE

amoe·bo·ge·ni·ae \ə,mēbō'jēnē,ē\ [NL, fr. *Amoeba* + *-o-* + *-gen* + *-iae* (pl. of *-ia*)] *syn of* NEOSPORIDIA

amoe·boid *also* **ame·boid** \ə'mē,bȯid\ *adj* [ISV *amoeb-*, *ameb-* (fr. NL *amoeba*, *ameba*) + *-oid*] **1 :** like an amoeba specif. in moving or changing in shape by means of protoplasmic flow brought about by sequential changes in the protoplasmic colloidal system **2 :** AMOEBIFORM 2

amoe·bo·tae·nia \ə,mēbō'tēnēə\ *n, cap* [NL, fr. *amoeba* + *-o-* + *Taenia*] **:** a genus of tapeworms (family Dilepididae) parasitic in the intestines of poultry

amoe·bu·la *also* **ame·bu·la** \ə'mēbyələ\ *n, pl* **amoebulas** \-ləz\ *or* **amoebu·lae** \-,lē\ [NL, dim. of *amoeba*, *ameba*] **1 :** a small amoeba **2 :** any small organism or cell resembling an amoeba in form (as certain stages in the life cycles of myxomycetes or of gregarines)

¹amok \ə'mək *also* -äk\ *or* **amuck** \ə'mək\ *n* -S [Malay *amok* furious attack, charge (as in *měngamok* he runs amok, *pěngamok* one that runs amok)] **1** *archaic* **:** a Malay that goes into a murderous frenzy and attacks people at random **2 :** a murderous frenzy that occurs chiefly among Malays ⟨an inflexible, confined, and unpermissive environment is the essence of ~ —J.M.Van der Kroef⟩

²amok \"\ *or* **amuck** \"\ *adv* [Malay *amok*] **1 :** in a murderously frenzied manner **2 a :** in a violently raging manner ⟨the North Sea ran ~ —Joseph O'Connor⟩ **b :** in an undisciplined manner **:** NEEDLESSLY ⟨an era which seems to have run ~ with its love for the strange —E.P.Hanson⟩

³amok \"\ *or* **amuck** \"\ *adj* [Malay *amok*] **:** possessed with a murderous or violently uncontrollable frenzy ⟨an ~ soldier⟩

amol·der·ing \ə'mōld(ə)riŋ\ *adj* [¹*a-* + *moldering*, gerund of *molder*] **:** in a decaying condition ⟨~ in the grave⟩

amo·le \ə'mōlē, -,lā\ *n* -S [Sp, fr. Nahuatl *amolli* soap, prob. fr. *atl* water + *molli* stew, confection] **1 :** any part of a plant possessing detergent properties and used as a substitute for soap **2 :** any of a number of plants utilized as a source of soap: as **a :** SOAP PLANT a **b :** any of various Mexican amaryllidaceous plants of the genera *Manfreda* (as *M. brachystachys*), *Agave* (as *A. heteracantha*), and *Prochnyanthes* whose rootstock when pounded to a pulp readily produces a lather when moistened

amo·mis \ə'mōməs\ *n, cap* [NL, fr. L, a plant similar to amomum, fr. Gk *amōmon*] **:** a genus of aromatic tropical American trees (family Myrtaceae) with large leathery leaves and small axillary flowers

amo·mum \ə'mōməm\ *n* [NL, fr. L, an aromatic shrub, fr. Gk *amōmon*] **1** *cap* **:** a large genus of herbs (family Zingiberaceae) found in tropical regions of the Old World and differing from members of the genus *Zingiber* only in having the anther cells divergent and the connective between them not long-spurred **2** -s **:** a plant of the genus *Amomum* **3** -s **:** the fruit or seed of an amomum plant

among \ə'məŋ\ *or* **amongst** \-ŋzt,-ŋ(k)st\ *prep* [*among* fr. ME, fr. OE *on gemang, on gemange,* fr. *on* + *gemonge, gemange,* dat. of *gemong, gemang* mingling, crowd, fr. *ge-* (collective prefix) + *-mong, -mang* (akin to OE *mengan* to mix, mingle]; *amongst,* alter. of ME *amonges,* fr. *among* + *-es* -s — more at CO-, MINGLE] **1 a :** surrounded by **:** in the midst of **:** intermingled with ⟨~ the celebrity-packed audience at each opening were seven men —*Time*⟩ **b :** through the midst of ⟨he passed ~ the crowd⟩ **2** *among, obs* **:** DURING **:** in the course of **3 a :** in or to the locality of ⟨he lived ~ us for a few days⟩ **b :** in company with **:** in association with **:** WITH ⟨living ~ a group of artists⟩ **4 a :** with or by the generality of ⟨a characteristic activity ~ pioneer Norwegian congregations —*Amer. Guide Series: Minn.*⟩ — used to indicate the group agent of an activity or the group source of an attribute **b :** in a widening circle throughout ⟨discontent spreads ~ the ignorant⟩ **c :** in the opinion or estimation of ⟨an author held, ~ a large part of our reading public, as superior⟩ **5 :** outstanding in the category of ⟨an actor ~ actors⟩ **6 :** in the number or class of ⟨~ their good qualities is a high regard for tolerance⟩ **:** in or from the group of **:** from the number of ⟨~ so many only a few can survive⟩ ⟨choose ~ us⟩ **7 a :** in separate and usu. equal shares to each of ⟨the property was divided ~ the four survivors⟩ **b :** for distribution to **:** to be shared by ⟨there's not enough food ~ a crowd like this⟩ ⟨that leaves five dollars ~ us⟩ **8 a :** through the reciprocal acts of ⟨fighting ~ themselves⟩ **b :** by the joint action of esp. so as to produce a separable effect ⟨they earned a fortune ~ themselves⟩

amon·til·la·do \ə,mäntə'lä(,)dō, -tə(l)'yä(,)thō\ *n* -s [Sp, fr. *a-* (fr. L *ad-*) + *montilla* + *-ado* (fr. L *-atus* -ate) — more at MONTILLA] **:** a pale dry sherry

amor \'ä,mó(ə)r\ *n* -s [L, fr. *amare* to love — more at AMATEUR] **:** CUPID, CHERUB 3

amo·ra \ə'mōrə\ *n, pl* **amo·ra·im** \,ämō'rä,im\ *often cap* [Heb *āmōrā'* (pl. *āmōrā'īm*) speaker, interpreter, fr. Aram *āmōrā*] **:** one of a group of rabbis (A.D. 250–500) who discussed the Mishnaic law in the law schools of Palestine and Mesopotamia and whose discussions are recorded in the Palestinian and Babylonian Talmuds — compare SABORA, TANNA

amo·ra·ic \,ämō'rāik\ *adj, often cap* **:** of or relating to the amoraim ⟨the ~ period⟩

amor·al \(')ā¦-, (')a¦-\ *adj* [*a-* + *moral*] **1 a :** neither moral nor immoral **:** NONMORAL; *specif* **:** outside the bounds of that to which moral distinctions or judgments apply ⟨science as such is completely ~ —W.S.Thompson⟩ **b :** without moral sensibility ⟨infants are ~⟩ **2 a :** outside or beyond the moral order or any specific traditional code of morals ⟨~ customs⟩ **b :** ethically neutral **:** not entailing moral norms or ideals ⟨~ metaethical statements⟩ **3 :** refraining from making value judgments **:** OBJECTIVE ⟨an ~ historian⟩ — **amor·al·ly** *adv*

amor·al·ism \(')ā'-, (')a'-\ *n* -s **1 :** a doctrine that repudiates ordinary moral distinctions as invalid ⟨the ~ professed by many students of human affairs —Ernest Nagel⟩ **2 :** an amoral state, condition, or attitude **:** AMORALITY

amor·al·ist \(')ā'-, (')a'-\ *n* -s **1 :** one who professes the doctrine of amoralism **2 :** one who lives amorally

amor·al·is·tic \¦=,=¦==\ *adj* **:** of, relating to, or professing amoralism

amo·ral·i·ty \,ā-, ,a-\ *n* -ES **:** the state of being amoral **:** amoral procedure ⟨power politics in an atmosphere of ~⟩

amo·ret·to \,amə'red·(,)ō, ,äm-\ *n, pl* **amor·et·ti** \-d·(,)ē\ *or* **amorettos** *also* **amorettoes** [It, dim. of *amore* cupid] **:** CUPID, CHERUB 3

am·o·reux·ia \,amə'rüksēə, -zh(ē)ə\ *n, cap* [NL, fr. Pierre Joseph *Amoreux* †1824 Fr. physician + NL *-ia*] **:** a genus of herbs or undershrubs (family Cochlospermaceae) of the southwestern U.S. and Mexico having palmate leaves and large flowers

amo·ri·no \,amə'rē(,)nō, ,äm-\ *n, pl* **amori·ni** \-(,)nē\ *or* **amorinos** [It, dim. of *amore* cupid, fr. L *Amor,* god of love, fr. *amor* love] **:** CUPID, CHERUB 3

am·or·ist \'amərəst\ *also* **am·our·ist** \", ə'mùr-, a'-,ä-\ *n* -s [L *amor* + E *-ist*] **1 :** a devotee of love, esp. sexual love **:** GALLANT **2 :** one that writes romantically about love — **am·or·is·tic** \¦amə¦ristik\ *adj*

¹am·o·rite \'amə,rīt, *usu* -īd·+V\ *n* -s *usu cap* [Heb *ĕmōrī* + E *-ite*] **1** *in the Bible* **a :** a member of a pre-Israelite people of Palestine that dwelt in the hill country of Canaan and also east of the Jordan between the Moabites and the Ammonites — distinguished from *Canaanite* **b :** any pre-Israelite inhabitant of Palestine **:** CANAANITE **2 a :** a member of an ancient Semitic people that settled in Mesopotamia, Syria, and Palestine as early as the 3d millennium B.C. and established a kingdom, with its capital at Mari on the middle Euphrates, which was at the height of its power approximately from 2200 to 1700 B.C. **b :** the Semitic language spoken by this people, known only from proper names in Akkadian texts **3 :** ¹CANAANITE 3

²amorite *adj, usu cap* **:** of or belonging to any of the peoples known as Amorites

¹am·o·rit·ic \¦amə¦rid·ik\ *adj, usu cap* [¹*Amorite* + *-ic*] **1 :** ²AMORITE **2 :** of, belonging to, or characteristic of the language Amorite **3 :** ¹CANAANITIC 2—compare ¹AMORITE 2b

²amoritic *n, usu cap* **1 :** ¹AMORITE 2b **2 :** ²CANAANITIC

¹am·o·rit·ish \¦amə¦rid·ish\ *adj, usu cap* [¹*Amorite* + *-ish*] **:** ²AMORITE

²amoritish *n* -ES *usu cap* **1 :** ¹AMORITE 2b **2 :** ¹CANAANITE 3

amornings *adv* [ME *amorninges,* fr. ¹*a-* + *morninges,* gen. of *morning*] *obs* **:** in the morning

am·o·ros·i·ty \,amə'räsəd·ē\ *n* -ES [ME *amorouste, amorositie,* fr. *amorous* + *-te* -ty, *-itie* -ity] **:** AMOROUSNESS

am·o·ro·so \,ämə'rō(,)sō, ,am-\ *adv* (*or adj*) [It, amorous, fr. ML *amorosus*] **:** with tenderness — used as a direction in music

am·o·rous \'am(ə)rəs, 'aamr-\ *adj* [ME, fr. MF, fr. ML *amorosus,* fr. L *amor* love (fr. *amare* to love) + *-osus* -ose — more at AMATEUR] **1 :** strongly moved by love, esp. sexual love **:** given to lovemaking ⟨a prey for ~ women —H.S.Canby⟩ **2 :** in love **:** ENAMORED — usu. used with *of,* formerly with *on* ⟨he is ~ of the girl⟩ ⟨naturally ~ of all that is beautiful —Sir Thomas Browne⟩ **3 a :** manifesting love **:** indicative of love ⟨black swans on the lake twine their necks in ~ play —James McAuley⟩ **b :** produced by or productive of love **c :** of or relating to love ⟨an ~ novel⟩ **4 a :** warmly affectionate **:** FOND, LOVING ⟨the ~ care with which Tom drew a volume from the bookcase —Arnold Bennett⟩ **b :** characterized by warmth and passion ⟨~ music or poetry⟩ ⟨an ~ outburst of lyricism⟩ — **am·o·rous·ly** *adv* — **am·o·rous·ness** *n* -ES

amorph \'ā,mȯrf, ə'mȯ(ə)rf\ *n* -s [*a-* + *-morph*] **:** a gene without detectable effect

amorph- *or* **amorpho-** *comb form* [Gk *amorph-,* fr. *amorphos*] **:** amorphous ⟨*amorph*ism⟩ ⟨*amorpho*phyte⟩

amor·pha \ə'mȯrfə\ *n* [NL, fr. Gk *amorphē,* fem. of *amorphos* shapeless] **1** *cap* **:** a genus of American herbs or shrubs (family Leguminosae) with odd-pinnate leaves and purplish spicate flowers, the corolla being reduced to one petal — see FALSE INDIGO, LEADPLANT **2** -s **:** a plant of the genus *Amorpha*

amor·phic \-fik\ *adj* [*a-* + *-morphic*] **:** AMORPHOUS

amor·phin·ism \(')ā'-\ *n* -s [*a-* + *morphinism*] **:** the condition caused by depriving an addict of morphine

amor·phism \ə'mȯr,fizəm\ *n* -s [G *amorphismus,* fr. *amorph* amorphous + *-ismus* -ism] **:** the quality or state of being amorphous

amor·pho·phal·lus \ə,mȯrfə'faləs\ *n* [NL, fr. *amorph-* + *phallus*] **1** *cap* **:** a genus of tropical East Indian aroids having a mottled flowering spathe in advance of the large compound leaf and often attaining a height of several feet — see KRUBI **2** -ES **:** a plant of the genus *Amorphophallus*

amor·pho·phyte \ə'==,fīt\ *n* -s [ISV *amorph-* + *-phyte*] **:** a plant producing irregular or anomalous flowers

amor·phous \ə'mȯrfəs, -ó(ə)f-\ *also* **amor·phose** \-,fōs\ *adj* [Gk *amorphos,* fr. *a-* ²*a-* + *morphē* form — more at FORM] **1 a :** without definite form or shape **:** FORMLESS ⟨an ~ cloud of dust⟩ ⟨an ~ mass⟩ **b :** without clearly drawn limits **:** not precisely indicated or established ⟨an ~ boundary⟩ **c :** without definite nature or character **:** not allowing clear classification or analysis **:** UNCLASSIFIABLE ⟨cities have swollen into ~ agglomerations —Siegfried Giedion⟩ ⟨that indefinite ~ thing called the consuming public —John Dewey⟩ **d :** without organization **:** without cohesion **:** lacking unity ⟨an ~ mass of frightened fugitives —J.W.Aldridge⟩ ⟨an ~ style of writing⟩ **e :** without a clearly defined direction, purpose, or controlling influence ⟨lifeless and ~ routine —Phyllis Ackerman⟩ ⟨growth is not ~, but restricted by a limited number of physical laws —Herbert Read⟩ **2 a (1) :** without real or apparent crystalline form **:** UNCRYSTALLIZED — used esp. of supercooled liquids (as glasses) and colloidal substances ⟨~ sulfur⟩ ⟨~ wax⟩ **(2) :** without crystal structure ⟨an ~ mineral⟩ **b :** without division in parts such as that effected by stratification or cleavage **c :** without developed organization — used chiefly of the lower forms of life — **amor·phous·ly** *adv* — **amor·phous·ness** *n* -ES

amor·phus \-fəs\ *n, pl* **amor·phi** \-,fī, -,fē\ *or* **amorphuses** [NL, fr. Gk *amorphos,* adj.] **:** a fetus without head, heart, or limbs

amor·phy \'ā,mȯrfē, ə'm-\ *n* -ES [Gk *amorphia* shapelessness, fr. *amorph-* + *-ia* -y] **:** AMORPHISM

amors *pl of* AMOR

amort \ə'mȯrt\ *adj* [short for *all-a-mort,* taken as an adjectival phrase beginning with ²*all*] **1** *archaic* **:** at the point of death ⟨I felt benumbed, ~ —Llewelyn Powys⟩ **2** *archaic* **:** OBLIVIOUS ⟨all ~ save to St. Agnes —John Keats⟩ **3** *archaic* **:** utterly cast down with discouragement **:** DEJECTED

amor·tis·seur \ə¦mȯrdə¦sər, +V -ər-\ *or* **amortisseur winding** *n* -s [F *amortisseur,* fr. *amortir* to deaden — more at AMORTIZE] **:** DAMPER WINDING

am·or·tiz·a·ble \'amə(r),tīzəbəl, *sometimes* ə'mȯr,- *or* 'a,mȯr,- *or* -mó(ə),-\ *adj* **:** capable of being amortized

am·or·ti·za·tion \,amə(r)d·ə'zāshən, -)tə'- *also* ə,mó(r)- *or* ,a,mó(r)- *or* -)d·,ī'z- *or* -),tī'z-\ *n* -s [ML *admortization-, admortizatio,* fr. *admortizatus* (past part. of *admortizare*) + L *-ion-, -io* -ion] **1 :** the act or process of amortizing **2 :** the result of amortizing

am·or·tize \'amə(r),tīz *sometimes* ə'mȯr,- *or* 'a,mȯr,- *or* -mó(ə),-\ *also* **am·or·tise** \"\ *vt* -ED/-ING/-S [ME *amortisen,* modif. (influenced by ML *amortizare* to amortize, fr. OF *amortir* + LL *-izare* -ize) of MF *amortiss-,* stem of *amortir,* fr. (assumed) VL *admortire* to deaden, fr. L *ad-* + (assumed) VL-*mortire,* fr. *mort-, mors* death — more at MURDER] **1** *law* **:** to alienate in mortmain ⟨*amortized* the estate⟩ **2** *accounting* **a :** to provide for the gradual extinguishment of (an obligation, as a mortgage or bond issue) by payment of a part of the principal or by contribution to a sinking fund usu. with or at the time of each periodic interest payment **b :** to write down gradually to extinguishment the cost of (an asset) by periodic charges to expense or profit and loss — usu. applicable to intangible assets (as patents, bond premiums)

am·or·tize·ment \¦amə(r)¦tīzmənt; ə'mó(r)d·əzm-, -əsm-\ *n* -s [modif. (influenced by *amortize*) of F *amortissement,* fr. OF, fr. *amortiss-* (stem of *amortir*) + *-ment*] **1 :** AMORTIZATION **2 a :** the sloping top of a projecting pier (as a buttress) **b :** a crowning architectural member in an edifice

am·o·site \'amə,sīt, -,z-\ *n* -s [*A*sbestos *M*ine of *S*outh Africa + E *-ite*] **:** a mineral that is an iron-rich variety of anthophyllite occurring in long fibers and much used as a type of asbestos

amo·tion \a'mōshən, ə'-\ *n* -s [L *amotion-, amotio* removal, fr. *amotus* (past part. of *amovēre* to remove) + *-ion-, -io* -ion — more at AMOVE] **1 a :** removal of a specified object from a place or position **b :** OUSTING; *specif* **:** removal of a corporate officer from his office — distinguished from *disfranchisement* **2 :** deprivation of possession of property

¹amount \ə'maùnt\ *vi* -ED/-ING/-S [ME *amounten,* fr. OF *amonter, amounter,* fr. *amont* upward, fr. *a-* (fr. L *ad-*) + *mont* mountain — more at MOUNT] **1** *obs* **:** ASCEND **2 :** to add up **:** reach a total — used with *to* ⟨the bill ~*ed* to 10 dollars⟩ ⟨total casualties ~*ing* to over a thousand⟩ **3 :** to be really or practically equivalent **:** attain in effect or significance — used with *to* ⟨anxiety that almost ~*ed* to agony —Mary W.Shelley⟩ ⟨an act that ~*ed* to treason⟩

²amount \"\ *n* -s **1 a :** the total number or quantity **:** AGGREGATE ⟨the ~ of the fine is doubled⟩ **:** SUM, NUMBER ⟨add the same ~ to each column⟩ ⟨the ~ of the policy is 10,000 dollars⟩ **b :** the sum of individuals ⟨the unique ~ of worthless IOUs collected during each day's business —R.L.Taylor⟩ **c :** the quantity at hand or under consideration ⟨only a small ~ of trouble involved⟩ ⟨a surprising ~ of patience⟩ **2 :** the whole or final effect, significance, or import ⟨the ~ of his remarks is that we are hopelessly beaten⟩ **3** *accounting* **:** a principal sum and the interest on it **syn** see SUM

amount at risk : the difference between the face amount of a life-insurance policy and its reserve value

amount limit *n* **:** a fixed quantity of work assigned in a test with the object of measuring either the time required by an individual to finish that amount or the total he can do in unlimited time — contrasted with *time limit*

amount subject *n* **:** any value estimated by an underwriter to be the expected loss as a result of a fire or casualty, variable according to the risk involved

amour \ə'mù(ə)r, a'-,ä'-, -ùə\ *n* -s [ME, fr. OF *amour, amor,* fr. OProv *amor,* fr. L., fr. *amare* to love — more at AMATEUR] **1** *obs* **:** close attachment **:** intimate friendship **2 a :** LOVEMAKING, COURTSHIP — usu. used in pl. ⟨passing the hours in tender ~*s*⟩ **b :** a love affair esp. when illicit ⟨rushing from one ~ to another⟩ **3 :** LOVE; *esp* **:** sexual love ⟨the film explores various aspects of ~⟩ ⟨an almost endless chain of exploits in ~ —H.L.Mencken⟩ **4 a :** one that is loved **b :** MISTRESS **:** LOVER ⟨she was his newest ~⟩

am·ou·rette \¦amə¦ret\ *n* -s [F, fr. OF, fr. *amour* + *-ette*] **1 :** a trifling or ephemeral love affair **2 :** a woman involved in a trifling love affair

am·ou·rist *var of* AMORIST

amour pro·pre \¦a,mù(ə)r'prōp(rᵊ), ¦ä,-, -ùə'p-, -rōp-\ *n* [F *amour-propre,* lit., love of oneself, fr. *amour* love + *propre* own, proper — more at PROPER] **1 :** self-love characterized by sensitive regard for one's rights, dignity, and honor as an individual and in relationship with one's fellows **:** SELF-RESPECT, SELF-ESTEEM ⟨offensive to a wife's *amour propre* —H.L.Mencken⟩ **2 :** exaggerated self-love **:** VANITY ⟨his *amour propre* would not tolerate criticism⟩ **syn** see CONCEIT

amov·a·bil·i·ty \(,)a,müvə'biləd·ē, ə,m-\ *n* -ES **:** capability of being removed from a given position; *specif* **:** liability to amotion

amov·a·ble \ə'==bəl\ *adj* [alter. of earlier *amovible,* fr. F, fr. L *amovēre* to remove + F *-ible*] **:** REMOVABLE; *specif* **:** liable to amotion

¹amove *vt* -ED/-ING/-S [ME *amoven, ameven,* fr. MF *amovoir* to incite (fr. L *admovēre* to bring to, put to, apply to, fr. *ad-* + *movēre* to move) & *esmovoir* to set in motion, stir up emotionally (fr. L *exmovēre, emovēre* to move away, remove, fr. *ex,* e out of, from + *movēre* to move) — more at EX-, MOVE] *obs* **:** to cause to be agitated (as with excitement); *specif* **:** to stir up emotionally

²amove \a'müv, ə'-\ *vt* -ED/-ING/-S [ME *amoven, ameven,* modif. (influenced by ME *amoven, ameven* to stir up emotionally) of L *amovēre,* fr. *a-* (fr. *ab-*) + *movēre* to move — more at MOVE] **:** REMOVE; *esp* **:** to dismiss from an office or position

¹amoy \(')ä¦mȯi, (')a¦-\ *adj, usu cap* [fr. *Amoy,* China] **:** of or from Amoy, China **:** of the kind or style prevalent in Amoy

²amoy \=¦=\ *n, usu cap* **:** the dialect of Chinese spoken in and near Amoy in southeastern China

amoy·ese \¦ä,mȯi¦ēz, ¦a,-, -ēs, =¦=,=\ *n, pl* **amoyese** *usu cap* **1 :** a native or inhabitant of Amoy, China **2 :** AMOY

amp \'amp, 'aa-,'ai-\ *abbr or n* -s amperage; ampere

am·pa·la·ya \¦ämpəlä¦yä\ *n* -s [Tag *ampalayá*] *Philippines* **:** BALSAM APPLE

am·pan·ga·be·ite \,äm,päŋ'gäbē,īt\ *n* -s [F *ampangabéite,* fr. *Ampangabé,* Madagascar, its locality + F *-ite*] **:** a mineral consisting of a tantalo-niobate (as of yttrium, erbium, or uranium) occurring in reddish brown rectangular prisms

am·pa·ro \äm'pä(,)rō\ *n* -s [Sp, lit., protection, fr. *amparar* to protect, fr. (assumed) VL *anteparare,* fr. L *ante* before + *parare* to prepare — more at ANTE-, PARE] **1** *Spanish law* **:** a preliminary certificate issued to a claimant of land as a protection to his claim until a survey can be had and the full title vested **2** *Spanish law* **:** a proceeding analogous to habeas corpus

amparo blue \"-\ *n* **:** a strong blue to brilliant purplish blue

amparo purple *n* **:** a moderate purple that is redder and paler than heliotrope (sense 4a) and bluer, lighter, and stronger than average amethyst or cobalt violet

ampel- *or* **ampelo-** *comb form* [NL *ampel-,* fr. Gk *ampel-, ampelo-,* fr. *ampelos*] **:** grapevine ⟨*ampel*opsis⟩ ⟨*ampelog*raphy⟩

am·pe·lite \'ampə,līt\ *n* -s [L *ampelitis,* fr. Gk, fr. *ampelos* vine] **1 :** a black earth rich in pyrites used by the ancients to kill insects on vines **2 :** carbonaceous schist **:** CANNEL COAL — **am·pe·lit·ic** \¦ampə¦lid·ik\ *adj*

am·pe·lop·sis \,ampə'läpsəs\ *n* [NL, fr. *ampel-* + *-opsis*] **1** *cap* **:** a genus of woody climbers (family Vitaceae) closely related to *Vitis* and distinguished by the separate petals and the absence of adhesive disks on the tendrils **2** *pl* **ampelopsis a :** a plant of the genus *Parthenocissus:* as **a :** BOSTON IVY **b :** VIRGINIA CREEPER

am·per \'ampə(r)\ *n* -s [ME *ampre,* fr. OE *ompre* swelling, varicose vein] **1** *now dial Eng* **:** SWELLING, BLOTCH **2** *now dial Eng* **:** PUS, MATTER

am·per·age \'amp(ə)rij, 'aam-, -ēj *also* -,pir-\ *n* -s [ISV *ampere* + *-age*] **:** the strength of a current of electricity expressed in amperes

am·pere \'am,pi(ə)r, 'aam-, -iə\ *n* -s [after André M. *Ampère* †1836 Fr. physicist] **1 :** the practical mks unit of electric current that is equivalent to a flow of one coulomb per second or to the steady current produced by one volt applied across a resistance of one ohm and that is taken as the standard in the U.S. **:** ¹⁄₁₀ abampere **2 :** a unit of electric current equal to .99985 ampere and formerly taken as the standard — called also *international ampere*

ampere–hour \'==¦=\ *n* **:** a unit quantity of electricity, being the quantity carried past any point of a circuit in one hour by a steady current of one ampere, one ampere-hour equaling 3600 coulombs

am·pere·me·ter \-,mēd·ə(r)\ *n* [ISV *ampere* + *-meter*] **:** AMMETER

ampere's law *n, usu cap A* **:** either of two laws in electromagnetism: (1) the magnetic field resulting from an electric current in a circuit element is at any point perpendicular to the plane passing through the circuit element and the point, appears clockwise to an observer looking along the element in the direction of the current flow, is directly proportional to the product of the current multiplied by the length of the component of the element perpendicular to the line joining it to the point, and is inversely proportional to the square of the length of this line; or (2) the work done in carrying a magnetic pole around any closed path is proportional to the electric current flowing through the area bounded by the closed path

ampere–turn \'=,=¦=\ *n* **:** the mks unit of magnetomotive force equal to the magnetomotive force around a path that links with one turn of wire carrying an electric current of one ampere, one ampere-turn being equal to 0.4π or 1.257 gilberts

am·per·o·met·ric \¦am,pirə¦me·trik\ *adj* [*ampere* + *-o-* + *-metric*] *of chemical titration* **:** based on the measurement of the electric current that flows when a potential is applied between two electrodes in a solution for the purpose of detecting the end point — compare POLAROGRAPHIC

am·per·om·e·try \,ampə'rämə·trē, -,pi'r-\ *n* -ES [*ampere* + *-o-* + *-metry*] **:** the process of performing an amperometric titration

am·per·sand \'ampə(r),sand, 'aam-, -aand *also* -,z-\ *also* **am·per·zand** \-,z-\ *n* -s [alter. of *and* (&) *per se and,* lit., (the character) & by itself (is the word) *and*] **:** a single character (typically & or &) standing for the word *and* — called also *short and*

amph *abbr* amphibian; amphibious

am·phe·rot·o·kous \,amfə'räd·əkəs\ *adj* [*ampherotoky* + *-ous*] **:** of or relating to ampherotoky

am·phe·rot·o·ky \,amfə'räd·əkē\ *or* **am·phit·o·ky** \am'fid·əkē\ *also* **am·phot·er·ot·o·ky** \(,)am,fäd·ə'räd·əkē\ *n* -ES [*ampherotoky* irreg. fr. Gk *amphoteros* both + *tokos* offspring + E *-y; amphitoky* fr. *amphi-* + Gk *tokos* + E *-y; amphoterotoky* fr. Gk *amphoteros* + *tokos* + E *-y*] **:** parthenogenesis in which both male and female offspring are produced — compare ARRHENOTOKY, THELYTOKY

am·phet·a·mine \am'fed·ə,mēn, -,mən\ *n* -s [ISV *alpha-methyl-phenethyl* + *amine*] **:** a substance $C_9H_{13}N$ used as an inhalant and in solution as a spray in head colds and hay fever or in the form of its sulfate or phosphate as a stimulant for the central nervous system; racemic alpha-methyl-phenethyl-amine

amphi- *or* **amph-** *prefix* [L *amphi-* around, on both sides, fr. Gk *amphi-, amph-,* fr. *amphi* — more at AMBI-] **1 :** around ⟨*amphi*spermous⟩ **2 :** on both sides **:** of both kinds **:** both ⟨*amphi*carpic⟩ ⟨*amphi*vorous⟩ **3** *usu amphi-, chem, usu ital* **:** having substituents in positions 2 and 6 in two fused 6-membered rings (as in naphthalene)

am·phi·ap·o·mict \¦amfē'apə,mikt\ *n* -s [*amphi-* + *apo-* + Gk *miktos* blended] **:** an organism reproducing both sexually and asexually

am·phi·ar·thro·di·al \,amfē,är¦thrōdēəl\ *adj* [*amphi-* + *arthrodial*] **:** characterized by amphiarthrosis

am·phi·ar·thro·sis \,==,=¦=sə̇s\ *n* [NL, fr. *amphi-* + *arthrosis*] *anat* **:** articulation admitting slight motion and including symphysis and syndesmosis

am·phi·as·ter \'==,astə(r)\ *n* -s [NL, fr. *amphi-* + *-aster*] **1 :** a spicule stellate at both ends (as in some sponges) **2 :** the achromatic figure, esp. of animal cells, in which well-defined asters are commonly formed — compare MITOSIS — **am·phi·as·tral** \¦=¦=trəl\ *adj*

am·phib \(')am¦fib, -aam-\ *n* -s [by shortening] **1 :** ²AMPHIBIAN 3 **2 amphibs** *pl* **:** amphibious forces

am·phib·a·lus \am'fibələs\ *n, pl* **amphiba·li** \-,lī, -,lē\ [ML, fr. LL *amphibalus, amphibalum* cloak, prob. irreg. fr. Gk *amphiballein* to put around, throw around — more at AMPHIBOLE] **:** CHASUBLE; *also* **:** a vestment resembling the chasuble worn by the Gallican clergy prior to the 9th century

am·phib·ia \am'fibēə, aam-\ *n, pl, cap* [NL, fr. *amphibia,* pl. of *amphibium* amphibious being, fr. Gk *amphibion,* fr. neut. of *amphibios* leading a double life, amphibious — more at AMPHIBIOUS] **1 :** a class of Vertebrata comprising forms (as the frogs, toads, newts, and salamanders) that are intermediate in many respects between fishes and reptiles, all being cold-blooded with nucleated red blood cells and a 3-chambered heart; having limbs that, when present, terminate in digits that are unlike fins, two occipital condyles, ribs not attached to the sternum, and a moist skin without scales, feathers, or hair; developing without forming either amnion or allantois; being in most cases oviparous, passing through an aquatic larval stage in which they are provided with gills, afterwards undergoing a more or less marked metamorphosis usu. losing the gills and breathing by means of lungs or, when these are lacking, as in certain salamanders, through the skin or mucous membrane of the mouth; and feeding chiefly on insects and other small invertebrates, some forms being important destroyers of insects — see CAUDATA, GYMNOPHIONA, SALIENTIA **2 :** the members of the class Amphibia **:** AMPHIBIANS

¹am·phib·ian \(')=¦=ēən\ *adj* [Gk *amphibios* + E *-an*] **1 :** AMPHIBIOUS **2** [NL *Amphibia* + E *-an*] **:** of, relating to, or belonging to the class Amphibia **3** [²*amphibian* (vehicle)] **:** of or relating to an amphibian (sense 3)

²amphibian \"\ *n* -s **1 a :** an animal or plant accustomed or adapted to life both on land and in the water (as certain snakes) **b :** any animal of the class Amphibia (as a frog or newt) **2 :** an airplane designed to take off from and land on either land or water ⟨an ~ . . . is perhaps the most difficult of all airplane types to build and design —T.A.Dickinson⟩ **3 :** a flat-bottomed vehicle that moves on tracks having finlike extensions by means of which it is propelled on land or water and that is typically used for landing assault troops

am·phi·bich·nite \,amfə'bik,nīt\ *n* -s [*amphibian* + *ichnite*] **:** the fossil track of an extinct amphibian

am·phi·bi·e·ty \,amfə'bīəd·ē\ *n* -ES **:** the quality or state of being amphibious

am·phib·i·o·log·i·cal \am¦fibēə¦läjəkəl\ *adj* **:** of or relating to amphibiology

am·phib·i·ol·o·gist \am,fibē'äləjəst\ *n* -s **:** a specialist in amphibiology

am·phib·i·ol·o·gy \-jē\ *n* -ES [NL *Amphibia* + E *-o-* + *-logy*] **:** the branch of zoology that deals with the Amphibia

am·phib·i·on \⸗ˈ⸗ēən, -ē,än\ *n* -S [Gk, amphibious being, fr. neut. of *amphibios* leading a double life, amphibious] **:** an amphibian aircraft

am·phib·i·on·tic \am¦fibē¦äntik, ¦am,f-\ *adj* [Gk *amphibiont-, amphibion* + E *-ic*] **:** LITTORAL a, b

am·phi·bi·ot·ic \¦amfə,bī¦äd·ik\ *adj* [ISV *amphi-* + *-biotic*] **:** terrestrial in the adult stage but aquatic as a larva or nymph

am·phib·i·ous \(ˈ)am¦fibēəs, -aam-\ *adj* [Gk *amphibios* leading a double life, amphibious, fr. *amphi-* + *bios* life — more at QUICK] **1 :** able to live both on land and in water ⟨frogs, crocodiles and beavers are ~⟩ ⟨~ plants⟩ **2 a :** belonging to, adapted for, or consisting of both land and water ⟨the ~ character of an island people⟩ ⟨~ activities in a lakeside village⟩ ⟨an ~ swampy country⟩ **b** (1) **:** executed by coordinated action of land, sea, and air forces organized for invasion from the sea, usu. employing warships, assault boats, landing barges, assault troops, aircraft carriers, and covering aircraft (2) **:** trained or organized for participation in such action ⟨skill in ~ warfare⟩ ⟨an ~ corps⟩ **3 :** having or combining two lives, positions, or qualities ⟨an ~ existence, both mental and physical⟩ — **am·phib·i·ous·ly** *adv* — **am·phib·i·ous·ness** *n* -ES

am·phi·blas·tic \¦amfə¦blastik\ *adj* [*amphi-* + *-blastic*] **:** segmenting unequally — used of telolecithal eggs with complete segmentation

am·phi·blas·tu·la \¦amfə-\ *n, pl* **amphiblastu·lae** [NL, fr. *amphi-* + *blastula*] **:** a free-swimming larva of certain sponges that is essentially a blastula with small flagellated cells in one hemisphere and large nonflagellated cells in the other

am·phib·o·la \amˈfibələ\ *n, cap* [NL, fr. LL, fem. of *amphibolus*] **:** a genus of marine snails common in New Zealand having a rough turbinate shell and being unique among Pulmonata in possessing a well-developed operculum

am·phi·bole \ˈamfə,bōl\ *n* -S [F, fr. LL *amphibolus* fr. Gk *amphibolos* ambiguous, doubtful, fr. *amphiballein* to throw round, doubt, fr. *amphi-* + *ballein* to throw; fr. its many varieties — more at DEVIL] **1 :** HORNBLENDE **2 :** a mineral or mineral variety belonging to the amphibole group

amphibole group *n* **:** a group of minerals (as anthophyllite, tremolite, actinolite, and hornblende) with essentially like crystal structures involving a silicate chain $[OH(Si_4O_{11})]n$ and generally containing three groups of metal ions, the large ions being sodium and calcium, the intermediate being chiefly bivalent iron, magnesium, and manganese, and the small ions chiefly silicon with some aluminum and rarely ferric iron, the general formula for the group being $A_2B_5(Si,Al)_8O_{22}(OH)_2$

am·phi·bo·lia \,amfəˈbōlēə, -lyə\ *n, pl* **amphiboli·ae** \-ōlē,ē\ [LL — more at AMPHIBOLOGY] **:** AMPHIBOLOGY

am·phi·bol·ic \¦amfə¦bälik\ *adj* [*amphiboly* + *-ic*] **1 :** AMPHIBOLOGICAL **2** *zool* **:** capable of being directed either forward or backward ⟨the ~ outer toe of a fish hawk or owl⟩ **3** *med* **:** UNCERTAIN, IRREGULAR — used of stages in fevers or the critical period of disease when prognosis is uncertain

am·phi·bol·if·er·ous \-(,)bō¦lif(ə)rəs\ *adj* [*amphibole* + *-i-* + *-ferous*] **:** containing or producing amphibole

am·phib·o·lips \amˈfibə,lips\ *n, cap* [NL, fr. Gk *amphibolos* ambiguous, doubtful + *ips* woodworm — more at AMPHIBOLE] **:** a genus of gall wasps including forms responsible for many of the large oak-apple galls

am·phib·o·lite \amˈfibə,līt, ˈamfə,bō,l-\ *n* -S [F, fr. *amphibole* + *-ite*] **:** a usu. metamorphic rock consisting essentially of amphibole — **am·phib·o·lit·ic** \am,fibə¦lid·ik, am¦f-, ¦amfə(,)bō¦l-\ *adj*

am·phib·o·li·tize \amˈfibələ,tīz, ,amfəˈbōlə-\ *vt* -ED/-ING/-S **:** to convert (rock) to amphibolite

am·phib·o·li·za·tion \am,fibələˈzāshən, ,amfə,bōlə-\ *n* -S [*amphibole* + *-ization*] **:** a metasomatic process whereby a preexisting dark mineral has been converted to amphibole

am·phib·o·log·i·cal \¦am,fibə¦läjəkəl, am¦f-\ *adj* **:** characterized by the ambiguity found in an amphibology **:** AMBIGUOUS **:** EQUIVOCAL — **am·phib·o·log·i·cal·ly** \-k(ə)lē\ *adv*

am·phi·bol·o·gy \,amfəˈbäləjē\ *n* -ES [ME *amphibologie*, fr. LL *amphibologia*, alter. (influenced by L *-logia* -logy) of *amphibolia*, fr. Gk, fr. *amphibolos* ambiguous + *-ia* -y — more at AMPHIBOLE] **1 :** ambiguity in language **2 :** a phrase or sentence susceptible of more than one interpretation by virtue of an ambiguous grammatical construction — contrasted with *equivocation*

am·phib·o·lous \(ˈ)amˈfibələs\ *adj* [LL *amphibolus*, fr. Gk *amphibolos*] **:** capable of two meanings; *specif* **:** manifesting amphibology

am·phib·o·ly \amˈfibəlē\ *n* -ES [LL *amphibolia*] **:** AMPHIBOLOGY

am·phi·brach \ˈamfə,brak\ *n* -S [L *amphibrachys*, fr. Gk, lit., short at both ends, fr. *amphi-* + *brachys* short — more at BRIEF] **:** a trisyllabic foot consisting of a long syllable between two short syllables in quantitative verse or of a stressed syllable between two unstressed syllables in accentual verse ⟨the word *romantic* is an accentual ~⟩ — **am·phi·brach·ic** \¦⸗⸗¦brakik\ *adj*

amphibs *pl of* AMPHIB

am·phi·car·pa \,amfəˈkärpə\ *n, cap* [NL, fr. *amphi-* + *-carpa* (fr. Gk *karpos* fruit)] **:** a genus of No. American and Asiatic vines (family Leguminosae) having trifoliate leaves and small white or violet flowers and bearing both aerial and hypogeous pods

am·phi·car·pic \¦⸗⸗¦pik\ *or* **am·phi·car·pous** \-pəs\ *adj* [*amphi-* + *-carpic* or *-carpous*] **:** producing fruit of two kinds, either as to form or time of ripening

am·phi·car·pi·um \,⸗⸗ˈ⸗pēəm\ *n, pl* **amphicar·pia** \-ēə\ [NL, fr. *amphi-* + Gk *karpos* + NL *-ium*] **:** an archegonium that persists after fertilization to form a fruit envelope

am·phi·car·pog·e·nous \¦amfə,kär¦päjənəs\ *adj* [*amphi-* + *carpogenous*] **:** producing fruit aboveground which becomes buried before the time of ripening ⟨the peanut is ~⟩

am·phi·cen·tric \¦amfə¦-\ *adj* [*amphi-* + *-centric*] **:** converging at both ends — used of a plexus of blood vessels having one afferent and one efferent trunk

am·phi·chrome \ˈamfə,krōm\ *n* -S [*amphi-* + *-chrome*] **:** a plant that produces flowers of different colors on the same stalk (as certain of the sweet williams) — **am·phi·chro·my** \-mē\ *n* -ES

am·phi·coe·lia \,amfəˈsēlēə\ *n pl, cap* [NL, fr. LGk *amphikoilos* + NL *-ia*] *in some classifications* **:** an order of extinct crocodilians comprising Mesozoic forms with amphicoelous or amphiplatyan presacral vertebrae

am·phi·coe·li·an \¦amfə¦sēlēən\ *adj* [LGk *amphikoilos* + E *-ian*] **:** AMPHICOELOUS

am·phi·coe·lous *also* **am·phi·ce·lous** *or* **am·phy·coe·lous** \-¦sēləs\ *adj* [LGk *amphikoilos* doubly concave, fr. Gk *amphi-* + *koilos* hollow — more at CAVE] **:** BICONCAVE — used of vertebrae (as those of certain reptiles) having both the anterior and posterior surfaces of the centrum concave

am·phi·con·dy·lous \-¦kändələs\ *adj* [*amphi-* + *condyle* + *-ous*] **:** provided with two condyles

am·phi·cra·nia \,amfəˈkrānēə\ *n* -S [NL, fr. *amphi-* + *-crania*] **:** pain affecting both sides of the head — opposed to *hemicrania*

am·phi·crib·ral \¦⸗⸗¦kribrəl\ *adj* [*amphi-* + *cribral*] **:** having the phloem surrounding the xylem — used of certain concentric vascular bundles; compare AMPHIVASAL

am·phic·ty·on \amˈfiktēən, -ē,än\ *n* -S [back-formation fr. *Amphictyons*, pl., fr. L *Amphictyones*, fr. Gk *Amphiktyones*, *Amphiktiones*, lit., neighbors, fr. *amphi-* + *-ktyones*, *-ktiones* (fr. *ktizein* to found); akin to Skt *kṣeti* he dwells, *kṣiti* abode, Av *shitish* dwelling, Arm *šen* inhabited, cultivated] **:** a deputy to an amphictyonic council

am·phic·ty·on·ic \am,fiktē¦änik, am¦f-\ *adj* [Gk *amphiktyonikos, amphiktionikos*, fr. *Amphiktyones, Amphiktiones* + *-ikos* -ic] **:** relating to an amphictyony or to the amphictyons

am·phic·ty·o·ny \amˈfiktēənē\ *n* -ES [Gk *amphiktyonia, amphiktionia*, fr. *Amphiktyones, Amphiktiones* + *-ia* -y] **:** an association of neighboring states or tribes in ancient Greece orig. established to defend a common religious center and later developing into a league with certain legislative and judicial functions; *broadly* **:** any association of neighboring states banded together for their common protection and interest

am·phic·y·on \amˈfisē,än, -ēən\ *n, cap* [NL, fr. *amphi-* + Gk *kyōn* dog] **:** a genus (the type of the family Amphicyonidae) of Miocene and Pliocene Carnivora intermediate between the dogs and the bears — see BEAR DOG

am·phi·cyr·tic \¦amfə¦sərd·ik\ *adj* [LL *amphicyrtos* (fr. Gk *amphikyrtos*—fr. *amphi-* + *kyrtos* curved, bent—) + E *-ic*; akin to Gk *korōnos* curved — more at CROWN] **:** having both sides convex — used of angles between curves

am·phi·cyt·u·la \,amfəˈsichələ\ *n, pl* **amphicytu·lae** \-,lē\ [NL, fr. *amphi-* + *cytula* fertilized egg cell, fr. *cyt-* + *-ula*] *embryol* **:** a zygote capable of holoblastic unequal cleavage

am·phid \ˈamfəd\ *n* -S [Gk *amphidea* anything that is bound around] **:** one of a pair of circular depressions situated laterally at the anterior end of aquatic nematodes and believed to be chemoreceptors

am·phi·des·mous \¦amfə¦dezməs\ *adj* [*amphi-* + Gk *desmos* bond + E *-ous* — more at DIADEM] **:** provided with two ligaments

am·phi·det·ic \¦⸗⸗¦ded·ik\ *adj* [Gk *amphidetos* tied all around (fr. *amphidein* to tie around, fr. *amphi-* + *dein* to tie) + E *-ic* — more at DIADEM] **:** extending both before and behind the beak — used of the ligament of certain bivalves; compare OPISTHODETIC, PROSODETIC

am·phid·i·al \(ˈ)am¦fidēəl\ *adj* **:** of or relating to an amphid

¹am·phi·dip·loid \¦amfə¦di,plȯid\ *adj* [*amphi-* + *diploid*] *of an interspecific hybrid* **:** having a complete diploid chromosome set from each parent strain as a result of chromosome doubling in the first hybrid generation — **am·phi·dip·loi·dy** \¦amfə¦di,plȯidē\ *n* -ES

²amphidiploid \"\ *n* -S **:** an amphidiploid individual or strain

am·phi·dis·coph·o·ra \¦amfə(,)diˈskäfərə\ *n pl, cap* [NL, fr. *Amphidiscus*, genus of sponges (fr. *amphi-* + *-discus*) + *-o-* + *-phora*] **:** an order of Hyalospongiae comprising sponges with an anchoring root tuft and with amphidisks but no hexasters among the spicules

am·phi·disk *or* **am·phi·disc** \ˈamfə,disk\ *n* -S [*amphi-* + *disk, disc*] **:** a spicule having a stellate disk at each end found in the reproductive bodies of freshwater sponges of the genus *Spongilla* and in some of the Hyalospongiae

am·phi·drom·ic \¦⸗⸗¦drämik\ *adj* [Gk *amphidromos* running both ways (fr. *amphi-* + *dromos* course, racecourse) + E *-ic* — more at DROMEDARY] **:** relating to a system of tidal action in which the tide wave progresses around a point or center of little or no tide ⟨~ point⟩ ⟨~ region⟩

am·phid·ro·mous \(ˈ)amˈfidrəməs\ *adj* [*amphi-* + *-dromous*] *of fishes* **:** migrating from fresh to salt water or from salt to fresh water at some stage of the life cycle other than the breeding period

am·phi·erot·ic \¦amfē+\ *adj* [*amphi-* + *erotic*] **:** of, relating to, or manifesting amphierotism

am·phi·erotism \¦amfē+\ *n* -S [*amphi-* + *erotism*] **:** capacity of erotic reaction toward either sex

¹am·phi·gae·an *or* **am·phi·ge·an** \¦amfə¦jēən\ *adj, often cap* [*amphi-* + *-gaean*, *-gean* (fr. Gk *gaia* earth + E *-an*)] **1** *of a plant or animal* **:** found in both hemispheres **:** COSMOPOLITAN **2** *of a plant* **:** having flowers arising from the rootstock

²amphigaean *also* **amphigean** \"\ *adj, often cap* [NL *Amphigaea* (fr. *amphi-* + *-gaea*) temperate So. America + E *-an*] **:** occurring in temperate parts of So. America

am·phi·gas·tri·um \-ˈgastrēəm\ *n, pl* **amphigas·tria** \-rēə\ [NL, fr. *amphi-* + *gastr-* + *-ium*] **:** one of the small appressed stipulelike leaves on the ventral side of the stem in certain liverworts — compare JUNGERMANNIALES

am·phi·gas·tru·la \,amfə-\ *n, pl* **amphigastru·lae** [NL, fr. *amphi-* + *gastrula*] *embryol* **:** a gastrula developed from an amphicytula

am·phi·gene \ˈamfə,jēn\ *n* -S [F *amphigène*, fr. *amphi-* + *-gène* -gene] **:** LEUCITE

am·phi·gen·e·sis \,amfə-\ *n, pl* **amphigene·ses** [NL, fr. *amphi-* + *genesis*] **:** AMPHIGONY — **am·phi·ge·net·ic** \¦⸗⸗⸗-¦⸗⸗\ *adj*

am·phig·e·nous \(ˈ)amˈfijənəs\ *adj* [*amphi-* + *-genous*] **1 a** *of the fruiting bodies of parasitic fungi* **:** occurring on both surfaces of the leaves of an infected plant **b** *of the oogonium of fungi of the family Pythiaceae* **:** growing through an encircling antheridium **2 :** given to or marked by sexual attraction to members either of the same or of the opposite sex — **am·phig·e·nous·ly** *adv*

am·phi·gon·ic \¦amfə¦gänik\ *or* **am·phig·o·nous** \(ˈ)amˈfigənəs\ *adj* **:** reproducing sexually — used esp. of female insects

am·phig·o·ny \amˈfigənē\ *n* -ES [*amphi-* + *-gony*] **:** sexual reproduction

am·phi·go·ry \ˈamfə,gōrē, amˈfigərē\ *also* **am·phi·gou·ri** \,amfə,güˈrē\ *n, pl* **amphigories** *also* **amphigouris** [F *amphigouri*] **:** a nonsense verse or composition **:** a rigmarole with apparent meaning which proves to be meaningless

am·phi·kar·y·on \,amfəˈkarē,än, -ēən\ *n* -S [ISV *amphi-* + *karyon*; orig. formed in G] **:** a cell nucleus containing two haploid groups of chromosomes — opposed to *hemikaryon*; compare DIPLOKARYON — **am·phi·kar·y·ot·ic** \¦⸗⸗,⸗⸗¦äd·ik\ *adj*

am·phil·i·na \amˈfilənə\ *n, cap* [NL, fr. Gk *amphilinos* bound with flaxen thongs] **:** a genus (the type of the family Amphilinidae) comprising the cestodarian worms with flat leaflike body and an anterior extensible proboscis — compare GYROCOTYLE — **am·phil·i·nid** \-nəd, -,nid\ *adj or n*

am·phim·a·cer \amˈfiməsə(r), ˈamfə,mās-\ *n* -S [L *amphimacrus*, fr. Gk *amphimakros*, lit., long at both ends, fr. *amphi-* + *makros* long — more at MEAGER] **:** a trisyllabic foot consisting of a short syllable between two long syllables in quantitative verse or of an unstressed syllable between two stressed syllables in accentual verse ⟨the word *runaway* is an accentual ~⟩ — called also *cretic*

am·phi·mict \ˈamfə,mikt\ *n* -S [*amphi-* + Gk *miktos* blended, fr. *mignynai* to mix — more at MIX] **:** an individual produced by or reproducing by sexual means

am·phi·mic·tic \¦⸗⸗¦miktik\ *or* **am·phi·mic·ti·cal** \-təkəl\ *adj* [ISV *amphi-* + Gk *miktos* + ISV *-ic, -ical*] **:** capable of interbreeding freely and of producing fertile offspring — **am·phi·mic·ti·cal·ly** \-tək(ə)lē\ *adv*

am·phi·mix·is \,⸗⸗ˈmiksəs\ *n, pl* **amphimix·es** \-k,sēz\ [NL, fr. *amphi-* + Gk *mixis* mingling, fr. *mignynai*] **1 :** the union of germ cells in sexual reproduction — compare AUTOMIXIS **2 :** INTERBREEDING **3 :** the combining of pregenital, anal, and urethral eroticism in the development of genital sexuality

am·phi·neu·ra \-ˈn(y)u̇rə\ *n pl, cap* [NL, fr. *amphi-* + *-neura*] **:** a class of bilaterally symmetrical marine mollusks sometimes considered an order of Gastropoda, comprising the chitons and their related forms, having two lateral and two ventral nerve cords, and being commonly divided into the Polyplacophora and the Aplacophora — **am·phi·neu·ran** \-rən\ *n* -S — **am·phi·neu·rous** \¦⸗⸗¦⸗rəs\ *adj*

am·phi·nu·cle·us \,amfə-\ *n* [NL, fr. *amphi-* + *nucleus*] **:** a cell nucleus that contains a large karyosome

amph·ion \ˈam(p),fīən *also* -ī,än\ *n* -S [*amphi-* + *ion*] **:** DIPOLAR ION — **amph·ion·ic** \¦⸗,⸗¦änik\ *adj*

am·phi·ox·ea \,amfēˈäksēə, -ē(,)äkˈsēə\ *n* -S [NL, fr. *amphi-* + *oxea*] **:** a slightly curved needlelike sponge spicule

am·phi·oxi \-ˈäk,sī\ [NL, pl. of *amphioxus*] *syn of* CIRROSTOMI

am·phi·ox·i·dae \-ˈäksə,dē\ [NL, fr. *Amphioxus*, type genus + *-idae*] *syn of* BRANCHIOSTOMIDAE

am·phi·ox·i·des \-,dēz\ *n, cap* [NL, fr. ¹*Amphioxus* + Gk *-idēs* (patronymic suffix)] **:** a formerly recognized genus of pelagic lancelets mistakenly based on larvae of the genus *Asymmetron*

am·phi·ox·id·i·dae \-(,)äkˈsidə,dē\ [NL, fr. *Amphioxides*, type genus + *-idae*] *syn of* BRANCHIOSTOMIDAE

¹am·phi·ox·us \-ˈäksəs\ [NL, irreg. fr. *amphi-* + Gk *oxys* sharp] *syn of* BRANCHIOSTOMA

²amphioxus \"\ *n, pl* **am·phi·oxi** \-ˈäk,sī\ *or* **amphioxuses** **:** a lancelet of the genus *Branchiostoma*, typically being a small transparent marine animal pointed at both ends, having an oral opening just below the anterior end surrounded by cirri, dorsal and anal fins but no limbs, a notochord, a dorsally situated nerve cord but no definite brain, a system of blood vessels but no heart, eyes represented by a medium pigment spot, and an olfactory but no auditory organ

am·phi·phlo·ic \¦amfə¦flōik\ *adj* [*amphi-* + *phloem* + *-ic*] **:** having phloem both internal and external to the xylem — used of the siphonostele of certain vascular plants; compare ECTOPHLOIC

am·phi·plat·y·an \-ˈplad·ēən\ *adj* [*amphi-* + Gk *platys* flat + E *-an*] **:** flat at both ends — used of vertebrae having both anterior and posterior surfaces of the centrum flat

am·phi·pleu·ra \,amfəˈplu̇rə\ *n, cap* [NL, fr. *amphi-* + *-pleura*] **:** a genus of diatoms (family Naviculaceae) that includes one species (*A. pellucida*) which is distinguished by a finely striate and punctate frustule often used to test the resolving power of microscope lenses

¹am·phi·ploid \ˈ⸗⸗,plȯid\ *adj* [*amphi-* + *-ploid*] *of an interspecific hybrid* **:** having at least one complete diploid set of chromosomes derived from each ancestral species — compare AMPHIDIPLOID — **am·phi·ploi·dy** \-ȯidē\ *n* -ES

²amphiploid \"\ *n* -S **:** an amphiploid individual or strain

am·phi·pneus·tic \¦amfə¦n(y)üstik, -,fip¦n-\ *adj* [*amphi-* + Gk *pneustikos* of or for breathing, fr. (assumed) Gk *pneustos* (verbal of Gk *pnein* to breathe) + Gk *-ikos* -ic — more at SNEEZE] **1** *of some amphibians* **:** having both gills and lungs throughout life **2** *of an insect larva* **:** having the first and last pair of spiracles functional

am·phip·no·us \amˈfipnəwəs\ *n, cap* [NL, irreg. fr. *amphi-* + Gk *pnoē* breath, fr. *pnein* to breathe] **:** a genus of teleost fishes (order Symbranchii) comprising the cuchia

¹am·phi·pod \ˈamfə,päd\ *or* **am·phip·o·dal** \(ˈ)am¦fipəd°l\ *or* **am·phip·o·dan** \-ədən\ *or* **am·phip·o·dous** \-ədəs\ *adj* [*amphipod* fr. NL *Amphipoda*; *amphipodal, amphipodan, amphipodous* fr. NL *Amphipoda* + E *-al* or *-an* or *-ous*] **:** of or relating to the Amphipoda

²amphipod \"\ *or* **amphipodan** \"\ *n* -S **:** one of the Amphipoda

am·phip·o·da \amˈfipədə\ *n pl, cap* [NL, fr. *amphi-* + *-poda*] **:** a large group, usu. an order, of malacostracan crustaceans (division Peracarida) comprising the beach fleas and related forms; being mostly of small size with laterally compressed body, four anterior pairs of thoracic limbs directed forward, and three posterior pairs directed backward and upward, the thoracic limbs bearing gills; being usu. aquatic in fresh or salt water, and a few (as the whale louse) being parasitic

am·phi·pod·i·form \¦amfə¦pädə,fȯrm\ *adj* **:** resembling an amphipod

¹am·phi·pro·style \,amfəˈprō,stī(ə)l\ *adj* [L *amphiprostylos*, fr. Gk, fr. *amphi-* + *prostylos* having pillars in front — more at PROSTYLE] **:** marked by columniation consisting of free columns in porticoes at both ends of the structure and across the full ends — see COLUMNIATION illustration

²amphiprostyle \"\ *n* -S **:** an amphiprostyle building

am·phi·pro·tic \¦amfə¦pröd·ik\ *adj* [*amphi-* + *proton* + *-ic*] **:** AMPHOTERIC

am·phi·rhi·na \,amfəˈrīnə\ *n pl, cap* [NL, fr. *amphi-* + *-rhina* (fr. Gk *rhin-, rhis* nose)] *in some classifications* **:** a primary division of Vertebrata having double nasal chambers and including all vertebrates except the lancelets and cyclostomes — **am·phi·rhi·nal** \¦⸗⸗¦rīn°l\ *adj* — **am·phi·rhine** \ˈ⸗⸗,rīn\ *adj*

am·phi·sar·ca \,⸗⸗ˈsärkə\ *n* -S [NL, fr. *amphi-* + *-sarca* (fr. Gk *sark-, sarx* flesh) — more at SARCASM] **:** a many-celled and many-seeded indehiscent fruit that is pulpy within and has a hard or woody rind (as the melon or the calabash)

am·phis·bae·na \,amfəsˈbēnə\ *n* [L, fr. Gk *amphisbaina*, fr. *amphis* on both sides (fr. *amphi* around) + *-baina* (fr. *bainein* to walk, go) — more at BY, COME] **1** *pl* **amphisbae·nae** \-(,)nē\ *or* **amphisbaenas :** a serpent in classical mythology having a head at each end and being capable of moving in either direction **2** *cap* [NL, fr. L] **:** a genus (the type of the family Amphisbaenidae) of harmless limbless lizards having concealed eyes and ears and short blunt tail and living in warm or tropical countries — **am·phis·bae·ni·an** \¦⸗⸗¦nēən\ *adj or n* — **am·phis·bae·nic** \-nik\ *adj* — **am·phis·bae·noid** \-,nȯid\ *adj* — **am·phis·bae·nous** \-,nəs\ *adj*

am·phis·ci·ans \amˈfish(ē)ənz\ *or* **am·phis·cii** \-shē,ī\ *n pl* [*amphiscians* fr. LL *amphiscius* one who dwells in the tropics (fr. Gk *amphiskios*, fr. the adj., throwing a shadow both ways, fr. *amphi-* + *skia* shadow) + E *-an* + *-s*; *amphiscii* fr. LL, pl. of *amphiscius* — more at SCENE] *archaic* **:** the inhabitants of the tropics

am·phi·sex·u·al \¦amfə¦-\ *adj* [*amphi-* + *sexual*] **:** possessing the potentiality for development of the characters specific to each sex

am·phis·i·le \amˈfisə,lē\ [NL] *syn of* CENTRISCUS

am·phi·sil·i·dae \,amfəˈsilə,dē\ [NL, fr. *Amphisile*, type genus + *-idae*] *syn of* CENTRISCIDAE

am·phi·spore \ˈ⸗⸗,-\ *n* -S [ISV *amphi-* + *spore*] **:** a modified urediniospore that is characteristic of certain rusts of arid regions and that functions as a resting spore

am·phi·sto·ma·ta \,amfəˈstōməd·ə\ *n pl, cap* [NL, fr. *amphi-* + *-stomata*] *in some classifications* **:** a suborder of Digenea comprising trematodes somewhat conical in form with a highly developed posterior acetabulum — **am·phis·to·mate** \amˈfistə,māt, -mət\ *adj* — **am·phi·stome** \ˈamfə,stōm\ *adj or n*

am·phi·sto·mat·ic \¦amfəstō¦mad·ik\ *adj* [*amphi-*+*stomatic*] **:** having stomata on both surfaces ⟨~ leaves⟩

am·phis·to·mous \(ˈ)am¦fistəməs\ *adj* [NL *amphistomus*, fr. Gk *amphistomos* with a double mouth, fr. *amphi-* + *-stomos* (fr. *stoma* mouth) — more at STOMACH] *zool* **:** having a sucker at each extremity

am·phi·sty·lar \¦amfə¦stīlə(r)\ *adj* [*amphi-* + *-stylar*] **:** marked by columniation consisting of free columns in porticoes either at both ends or at both sides of the structure and across the full ends or sides — see COLUMNIATION illustration

am·phi·sty·lic \-lik\ *adj* [*amphi-* + *-stylic*] **:** having the upper jaw partly free from the brain case and braced by the hyomandibular cartilage (as in certain primitive sharks) — compare AUTOSTYLIC, HYOSTYLIC

am·phi·tene \ˈamfə,tēn\ *n* -S [ISV *amphi-* + *-tene*; orig. formed as F *amphitène*] **:** ZYGOTENE

am·phi·the·a·ter \ˈam(p)fə,-, ˈaam-, ÷-mpə-, ,⸗⸗ˈ-\ *n* -S [L *amphitheatrum*, fr. Gk *amphitheatron*, fr. *amphi-* + *theatron* theater — more at THEATER] **1 :** an oval, circular, or semicircular building with rising tiers of seats about a central open space used in ancient Rome for spectacles and contests ⟨Marcus Aurelius could sit for hours in the ~, bored and distrait . . . but with unmoved serenity—Agnes Repplier⟩ **2 :** something felt to resemble an amphitheater: **a :** a large auditorium used esp. for conventions, stock shows, sports events, and indoor circuses ⟨an exposition held in the International *Amphitheater* in Chicago⟩ **b :** a large room (as in a hospital) with a rising gallery of seats from which doctors and medical students may observe surgical operations **c :** a semicircular rising gallery in a modern theater **d :** a land form characterized by steep slopes rising abruptly from a somewhat semicircular flat or gently sloping area ⟨laid out the prisoners' camp in a sort of ~ among knolls—Kenneth Roberts⟩ **3 :** a place of public contests or games **:** ARENA

am·phi·the·a·tral \¦⸗⸗thē·trəl\ *adj* [L *amphitheatralis*, fr. *amphitheatrum* + *-alis* -al] **:** AMPHITHEATRIC

am·phi·the·at·ric \¦⸗⸗thē¦a·trik\ *or* **am·phi·the·at·ri·cal** \-trəkəl\ *adj* [L *amphitheatricus*, fr. *amphitheatrum* + *-icus* -ic, -ical] **1 :** performed in an amphitheater **2 :** resembling an amphitheater or its arrangement of seats — **am·phi·the·at·ri·cal·ly** \-ək(ə)lē\ *adv*

am·phi·the·cial \¦amfə¦thēsh(ē)əl, -sēəl\ *adj* [NL *amphithecium* + E *-al*] **:** of or relating to the amphithecium

am·phi·the·ci·um \,⸗⸗ˈsē(h)ēəm\ *n, pl* **amphithe·cia** \-ēə\ [NL, fr. *amphi-* + *-thecium*] **1 :** the external layer of cells surrounding the sporogenous tissue in the sporangium of a moss **2 :** the inner layer of the perithecium next to the hymenium in certain lichens

am·phith·y·ron \amˈfithə,rän\ *n, pl* **amphithy·ra** \-ərə\ [LGk, fr. Gk, hall, fr. neut. of *amphithyros* having a door on both sides, fr. *amphi-* + *thyra* door — more at DOOR] **:** a veil or curtain before the doors of the iconostasis in the Eastern Church

am·phit·o·ky *var of* AMPHEROTOKY

am·phi·tri·aene \,amfəˈtrī,ēn\ *n* -S [*amphi-* + *triaene*] **:** a sponge spicule with three divergent rays at each end — see TRIAENE

am·phit·ri·chous \(ˈ)amˈfi·trəkəs\ *adj* [*amphi-* + *-trichous*] **:** having flagella at both ends

am·phi·tri·te \ˌamfəˌtrīd·ē, ˌ==ˈ==\ *n, cap* [NL, fr. L *Amphitrite*, wife of Neptune and goddess of the sea, fr. Gk *Amphitritē*] **:** a genus of tube-inhabiting marine annelid worms having branching gills and many tentacles anterior to the mouth

am·phit·ro·pous \(ˈ)amˈfi·trəpəs\ *adj* [*amphi-* + *-tropous*] **:** having the ovule inverted but with the attachment near the middle of one side — compare ANATROPOUS

am·phi·uma \ˌamfēˈyümə\ *n, cap* [NL, prob. irreg. fr. *amphi-* + Gk *pneuma* breath, fr. *pnein* to breathe] **:** a genus (coextensive with the family Amphiumidae) of amphibians including only the congo snakes

am·phi·va·sal \ˌamfə;-\ *adj* [*amphi-* + *vasal*] **:** having the xylem surrounding the phloem — used of certain concentric vascular bundles; compare AMPHICRIBRAL

am·phiv·o·rous \(ˈ)amˈfiv(ə)rəs\ *adj* [*amphi-* + *-vorous*] **:** eating both animal and vegetable food

ampho- *comb form* [NL, fr. Gk *amphō* — more at AMBI-] **:** both ⟨*ampho*philic⟩

am·pho·gen·ic \ˌamfəˈjenik\ *adj* [*ampho-* + *-genic*] **:** producing approximately equal numbers of male and female offspring — **am·phog·e·ny** \amˈfäjənē\ *n* -ES

am·pho·lyte \ˈamfəˌlīt\ *n* -S [*ampho*teric + electro*lyte*] **:** an amphoteric electrolyte — **am·pho·lyt·ic** \ˌamfəˈlid·ik\ *adj*

am·pho·phil·ic \ˌ==ˈfilik\ *also* **am·pho·phil** \ˈ==ˌfil\ *or* **am·phoph·i·lous** \(ˈ)amˈfäfələs\ *adj* [*ampho-* + *-philic, -phil, -philous*] **:** staining with both acid and basic dyes **:** NEUTROPHILIC

am·pho·ra \ˈamfərə, ˈaam-\ *n, pl* **ampho·rae** \-ˌrē\ *or* **amphoras** [L, modif. of Gk *amphoreus* jar with two handles, alter. of *amphiphoreus*, fr. *amphi-* + *phoreus* bearer, fr. *pherein* to bear — more at BEAR] **1 a :** an ancient Greek jar or vase having a large oval body, narrow cylindrical neck, and two handles that rise almost to the level of the mouth: (1) **:** a jar usu. undecorated and pointed at the bottom, used esp. for holding or storing wine, oil, honey, or grain (2) **:** a decorated vase with a disk-shaped base, used esp. as an ornament or a prize (as in athletic contests) **b :** a 2-handled vessel shaped like an amphora **2 :** an ancient unit of capacity: **a :** a Greek unit equal to 10.3 gal (39 liters) **b :** a Roman unit equal to 6.7 gal (25.5 liters)

amphora 1a (1)

am·phor·ic \(ˈ)amˈfȯrik\ *adj* [NL *amphoricus*, fr. L *amphora* + *-icus* -ic] **:** resembling the sound made by blowing across the mouth of an empty bottle ⟨~ breathing⟩ — **am·pho·ric·i·ty** \ˌamfəˈrisəd·ē\ *n* -ES

am·pho·ris·kos \ˌamfəˈriskəs\ *n, pl* **amphoris·koi** \-ˌkȯi\ [Gk, dim. of *amphoreus* jar with two handles — more at AMPHORA] **:** a small amphora typically four inches high

am·pho·ter·ic \ˌamfəˈterik\ *adj* [ISV *amphoter-* (fr. Gk *amphoteros* each of two, fr. *amphō* both) + *-ic* — more at AMBI-] **:** partly one and partly the other; *specif* **:** capable of reacting chemically either as an acid or as a base

am·phot·er·ism \amˈfäd·əˌrizəm\ *n* -S **:** the property of being amphoteric

am·phot·er·ite \-ˌrīt\ *n* -S [Gk *amphoteros* + E *-ite*] **:** a meteorite consisting essentially of olivine and bronzite with minor amounts of iron sulfide and metal

amphoterotoky *var of* AMPHEROTOKY

amphycoelous *var of* AMPHICOELOUS

am·ple \ˈampəl, ˈaam-, ˈaim-\ *adj* **ampler** \-p(ə)lə(r)\ **amplest** \-p(ə)ləst\ [MF, fr. L *amplus*; prob. akin to L *ampla* handle and perh. to Skt *amatra* vessel, drinking bowl; basic meaning: grasping] **1 :** marked by extensive or more than adequate size, volume, space, or room ⟨two celebrated palaces, each with an ~ garden —T.B.Macaulay⟩ ⟨it is doubtful that the Fathers in 1783 contemplated expansion across the empty continent beyond the ~ boundaries set down —S.F.Bemis⟩ **2 a :** marked by more than adequate measure in strength, force, scope, effectiveness, or influence ⟨the light they yielded was more than ~ for the purpose —Thomas Hardy⟩ ⟨a government entrusted with such ~ powers —John Marshall⟩ **b :** marked by more than adequate measure in number or amount ⟨possessing ~ means they entertained generously —C.A.Dinsmore⟩ ⟨supplies were ~ for three days —Dorothy Sayers⟩ **3 a :** marked by generous plenty or by abundance **:** more than adequate **:** not scant or niggard ⟨an ~ picnic basket —Dixon Wecter⟩ **b :** COPIOUS, VOLUMINOUS, FULL ⟨an ~ biography⟩ **4 :** satisfying wants or desires more than adequately ⟨~ comfort⟩ **5 :** BUXOM, PORTLY ⟨an imposing creature, tall and stout, with an ~ bust —W.S.Maugham⟩

syn SPACIOUS, CAPACIOUS, COMMODIOUS: AMPLE always means considerably more than adequate or sufficient. Applied to what can be measured or counted, it suggests size, scope, space, or fullness and contrasts with *scant, sparse*, or *narrow* ⟨an *ample* sun—one sufficient to supply those wants of hers —Thomas Hardy⟩ ⟨"Do you want me to miss this train?" But he knew that the margin of time was *ample* —Arnold Bennett⟩ ⟨the plan, which Julius had designed for a lengthy campaign and *ample* forces, failed when it was put into execution in a hurry with inadequate troops —John Buchan⟩ Applied to persons' figures it suggests stoutness ⟨a plump, maternal-looking woman, with an *ample* figure, which did not conform to the wasp waist of the period —Ellen Glasgow⟩ ⟨genial clergy of *ample* girth, stuffed with the buttered toast of a refectory tea —S.B.Leacock⟩ In other matters it may indicate unstinted copiousness or generosity ⟨the work . . . is of *ample* proportions. There will be six volumes altogether —Dumas Malone⟩ SPACIOUS stresses great space, area, or scope ⟨white villas, gray convents, church spires, villages, towns . . . were scattered upon this *spacious* map —Nathaniel Hawthorne⟩ ⟨the great chilly unused drawing room whose *spacious* ceremoniousness seemed to embrace and envelope her —J.C. Powys⟩ In more figurative senses it may suggest breadth, expanse, and freedom from constriction ⟨in his lordly way — for he always talked, and unfortunately acted, in a *spacious* manner —Osbert Sitwell⟩ ⟨ frequent visits to Europe, with grouse shooting in Scotland and swimming on the Riviera, were part of the *spacious* life of the wealthy —H.W.Baehr⟩ CAPACIOUS suggests ability to hold or contain a great deal, a wealth of freely available space ⟨a *capacious* old house with big rooms⟩ It is often used with humorous suggestion ⟨was very stout . . . he wore a *capacious* waistcoat —Samuel Butler⟩ ⟨a man of *capacious* mind, seeing that he could draw much wider conclusions without evidence than could be expected of his neighbors —George Eliot⟩ COMMODIOUS stresses roominess and freedom from constriction, being limited or pent in ⟨we passed a large inlet . . . it appeared to be the entrance to a safe and *commodious* harbor —C.B.Nordhoff & J.N.Hall⟩ It may have added suggestions of convenience and comfort ⟨my mother's room is very *commodious* . . . large and cheerful looking . . . the most comfortable apartment in the house —Jane Austen⟩ **syn** see in addition PLENTIFUL

am·plec·tic \(ˈ)amˈplektik\ *adj* [L *amplecti* to embrace, surround + E *-ic*] **:** of or relating to amplexus

am·pleness *n* -ES **:** the quality or state of being ample

am·plex·i·cau·date \ˌamˌpleksə;-, amˌp-\ *adj* [ISV *amplexi-* (fr. L *amplexus*, past part. of *amplecti*) + *caudate*] **:** having the whole tail included in the interfemoral web — used of various bats

am·plex·i·caul \amˈpleksəˌkȯl\ *adj* [NL *amplexicaulis*, fr. L *amplexus* (past part. of *amplecti* to entwine, embrace) + *-i-* + *caulis* stem, cabbage — more at COLE] *of a leaf* **:** sessile with the base or with stipules surrounding the stem from which it arises — compare PERFOLIATE

am·plex·i·fo·li·ate \ˌamˌpleksə;-, amˌp-\ *adj* [ISV *amplexi-* (fr. L *amplexus*, past part. of *amplecti*) + *foliate*] **:** having amplexicaul leaves

am·plex·us \amˈpleksəs\ *n, pl* **amplexus** \"\ [L, lit., embrace, fr. *amplexus*, past part. of *amplecti*] **:** the mating embrace of the frog or toad during which eggs are shed into the water and there fertilized

am·pli·ate \ˈamplēət, -ēˌāt\ *adj* [L *ampliatus*, past part. of *ampliare* to make wider, enlarge, fr. *amplior*, compar. of *amplus* wide, large — more at AMPLE] **1 :** WIDENED, ENLARGED **2 :** having the outer edge prominent — used of insects' wings

am·pli·a·tion \ˌampləˈāshən\ *n* -S [MF, fr. LL *ampliation-*, *ampliatio*, fr. L, postponement of the decision of a cause, fr. *ampliatus* (past part of *ampliare* to enlarge, postpone the decision of) + *-ion-*, *-io* -ion] **1** *archaic* **:** ENLARGEMENT, AMPLIFICATION **2** [L *ampliation-*, *ampliatio*] **:** a postponement of the decision of a cause in civil law

am·pli·a·tive \ˈamplēˌād·iv\ *adj* [ML *ampliativus*, fr. L *ampliatus* + *-ivus* -ive] *logic* **:** adding in the predicate something not contained in the meaning of the subject term **:** SYNTHETIC ⟨an ~ proposition⟩ — opposed to *explicative*

ampliative inference *n* **:** BACONIAN INDUCTION

am·pli·dyne \ˈampləˌdīn\ *n* -S [*amplifier* + *-dyne* (fr. Gk *dynamis* power) — more at DYNAMIC] **:** a direct-current generator that by the use of compensating coils and a short circuit across two of its brushes precisely controls a large power output whenever a small power input is varied in the field winding of the generator

am·pli·fi·ca·tion \ˌampləfəˈkāshən, ˌaam-\ *n* -S [L *amplification-, amplificatio*, fr. *amplificatus* (past part. of *amplificare* to amplify, enlarge) + *-ion-*, *-io* -ion — more at AMPLIFY] **1 :** an act, example, or product of amplifying **:** ENLARGEMENT, EXTENSION ⟨a few final remarks may be added in defense and ~ of this account —R.J.Hirst⟩ ⟨~ of radio signals⟩ **2 a :** matter by which a statement or idea is expanded **b :** an expanded statement ⟨he offered no ~ of his pleasure —Clemence Dane⟩

amplification factor *n* **:** the ratio of the changes in plate and grid voltage that cause equal changes in the plate current of an electron tube

am·pli·fi·er \ˈ==ˌfī(ə)r, -īə\ *n* -S **:** one that amplifies; *specif* **:** an electronic circuit usu. employing vacuum tubes and used to obtain amplification of voltage, current, or power

am·pli·fy \ˈampləˌfī, ˈaam-\ *vb* -ED/-ING/-ES [ME *amplifien*, fr. MF *amplifier*, fr. L *amplificare*, fr. *amplus* ample + *-ficare* -fy — more at AMPLE] *vt* **1 :** to enlarge, expand, or extend (a statement or other expression of ideas in words) by addition of detail or illustration or by logical development **2 a** *obs* **:** to enlarge in size or capacity **b :** to increase or extend (as in amount, importance, or intensity) ⟨~ knowledge⟩ ⟨~ the jurisdiction of a court⟩ **c** *archaic* **:** OVERSTRESS, EXAGGERATE **3 :** to utilize (an input of voltage, current, or power) so as to obtain an output of greater magnitude through the relay action of a transducer ~ *vi* **:** to explain in greater detail or expand or extend one's remarks or ideas ⟨~ on his remarks⟩ **syn** see EXPAND

am·pli·stat \ˈampləˌstat\ *n* -S [*amplifier* + *-stat*] **:** a magnetic amplifier for the regulation of voltage

am·pli·tude \ˈampləˌtüd, ˈaam-, -lə-ˌtyüd\ *n* -S [L *amplitudo*, fr. *amplus* + *-tudo* -tude] **1 :** the quality or state of being ample **:** extent esp. of surface or space **:** largeness of dimensions **:** SIZE **2 :** largeness of mental scope **:** BREADTH, ABUNDANCE, FULLNESS: **a :** extent of mental capacity or intellectual power **b :** extent esp. of means, resources, dignity, or splendor **3** *navigation* **a :** the arc of the horizon between the true east or west point and the foot of the vertical circle passing through any star or object — compare AZIMUTH **b :** the arc of the horizon between the magnetic east or west point and a heavenly body — called also *magnetic amplitude* **4 :** the extent of a vibratory movement or of an oscillation **:** the maximum numerical value of a periodically varying quantity (as an alternating current, a radio wave, the air pressure in a sound-wave field, or the angular displacement of a pendulum) measured from its normal or equilibrium value taken as zero **5 :** ARGUMENT 6b **6 :** the range of ecological adaptability of a kind or group of organisms (as of a species, genus, or family)

amplitude–modulated \ˈ==,=;==,==\ *adj* **:** operating by amplitude modulation

amplitude modulation *n* **:** modulation of the amplitude of a radio carrier wave in accordance with the strength of the audio or other signal; *also* **:** a broadcasting system using such modulation — abbr. *AM*; compare FREQUENCY MODULATION

amplitude of accommodation : the difference between the refracting power of the eye when adjusted for vision at the far point and when adjusted for vision at the near point

am·plo·some \ˈampləˌsōm\ *n* -S [L *amplus* large, ample + E *-o-* + *-some* — more at AMPLE] **:** a body of endomorphic build **:** an endomorphic or pyknic individual

am·ply \ˈamp(ə)lē, ˈaam-, ˈaim-, -li\ *adv* **:** in an ample manner

am·pongue \ˈamˌpȯŋ\ *n* -S [native name in Madagascar] **:** WOOLLY LEMUR

amps *pl of* AMP

am·pul \ˈamˌpyül, ˈaam- *sometimes* -ˌpu̇l *or* -ˌpəl\ *also* **am·pule** \-ˌpyü(ə)l\ *or* **am·poule** \-ˌpül\ *sometimes* -ˌpül\ *n* -S [*ampul* fr. ME *ampulle* flask, fr. OE & OF; OE *ampulle* & OF *ampole, ampoule*, fr. L *ampulla*; *ampule, ampoule* fr. F *ampoule*] **1 :** a small bulbous glass vessel hermetically sealed and used to hold a solution for hypodermic injection **2 :** a vessel or vial resembling an ampul

am·pul·la \amˈpu̇lə, -ˈpə-, aam-\ *n, pl* **ampul·lae** \-ˌlē, -ˌī\ [ME, fr. OE, fr. L, dim. of *amphora* — more at AMPHORA] **1 :** a flask of glass or earthenware having a somewhat globular body and two handles and used esp. by the ancient Romans to hold ointment, perfume, or wine **2 a :** a vessel in which holy oil is kept ⟨the ~ ordered for the coronation of Charles II —L.G.W.Legg⟩ **b :** a cruet in which wine or water for ecclesiastical use is kept **3** [NL, fr. L] **a :** one of the small bladders attached to the submerged parts of plants of *Utricularia* and related genera **b :** one of the flask-shaped swellings on the hyphae of certain fungi **4** [NL, fr. L] **:** a flasklike dilatation or sac: as **a :** the dilatation containing a patch of sensory epithelium at one end of each semicircular canal of the ear **b :** one of the muscular vesicles of the water vascular system of echinoderms by the contraction of which the suckers are protruded **c :** one of the dilatations of the lactiferous tubules of the mammary glands that serve as reservoirs for milk **d :** the middle portion of the fallopian tube

ampulla 1

am·pul·la·ceous \ˌ=pəˈlāshəs, -ˌpu̇-, -ˌpə-\ *adj* [L *ampullaceus*, fr. *ampulla* + *-aceus* -aceous] **:** resembling an ampulla **:** shaped like a flask or bladder

ampulla of va·ter \-ˈfätə(r), -ät-\ *usu cap V* [trans. of G *Vatersche ampulle*, after Abraham *Vater* †1751 Ger. anatomist] **:** a trumpet-mouthed dilatation of the duodenal wall at the opening of the fused pancreatic and common bile ducts

am·pul·lar \(ˈ)amˈpu̇lə(r), -ˈpə-\ *also* **am·pul·la·ry** \-ləré; ˈampəˌlerē\ *adj* **:** resembling or relating to an ampulla

am·pul·lar·ia \ˌampəˈla(a)rēə\ [NL, fr. L *ampulla* + NL *-aria*] *syn of* PILA

ampullar sense *n* **:** the sense for rotation for which the end organs are in the ampullae of the semicircular canals

am·pul·late \(ˈ)amˈpu̇lət, -ˈpə-; ˈampəlāt, -ˌlāt\ *or* **am·pul·lat·ed** \ˈampəˌlād·əd\ *adj* **:** having an ampulla **:** shaped like a flask

am·pul·li·form \amˈpu̇ləˌfȯrm, -ˈpə-\ *adj* **:** shaped like a flask **:** DILATED

am·pul·lu·la \amˈpu̇lyələ, -ˈpə-\ *n, pl* **ampullu·lae** \-ˌlē, -ˌlī\ [NL, fr. LL, dim. of L *ampulla*] *anat* **:** a minute ampulla (as of the lymphatics or lacteals)

am·pu·tate \ˈampyəˌtāt, ˈaam-, *usu* -ād·+V\ *vt* -ED/ -ING/ -S [L *amputatus*, past part. of *amputare* to cut around, prune, fr. *am-, amb-* around + *putare* to cut, prune — more at AMBI-, PAVE] **1 :** to cut or lop off **:** PRUNE ⟨*amputating* data from its cultural context —S.E.Hyman⟩ ⟨a dimension has been *amputated* from man's political existence —Irving Kristol⟩ **2 :** to cut off (a limb or portion of a limb or a projecting part of the body) — compare EXCISE

am·pu·ta·tion \ˌ==ˈtāshən\ *n* -S [L *amputation-, amputatio*, fr. *amputatus*, + *-ion-*, *-io* -ion] **1 a :** a cutting, pruning, or lopping off ⟨bare thorny stumps and slanting marks of ~ —Kathleen Fruman⟩ ⟨a deliberate ~ of freedom —*Time*⟩ **b :** excision (as of letters, words, or sentences) from writing ⟨confusion follows too drastic an ~ —Creighton Peet⟩ **2 :** an act, process, or instance of amputating a body part whether occurring immediately after an injury or delayed until inflammation and suppuration are present — called also respectively *primary amputation, secondary amputation;* see CONGENITAL AMPUTATION, SPONTANEOUS AMPUTATION

am·pu·ta·tor \ˈ==ˌtād·ə(r), -ātə-\ *n* -S **:** one that amputates

am·pu·tee \ˌ==ˈtē *also* -tā\ *n* -S [prob. modif. of F *amputé*, fr. past part. of *amputer*, fr. L *amputare*] **:** one that has had a limb amputated ⟨a quadruple ~⟩

am·pyx \ˈam(ˌ)piks\ *n, cap* [NL, fr. Gk, woman's diadem, prob. fr. *am-* (fr. *ana-*) + *-pyx* (akin to Gk *pykazein* to cover closely, surround, crown); akin to Av *pusā-* diadem] **:** a genus of small blind Ordovician trilobites with a long spine at the anterior end of the head

am·ra \ˈəm(ˌ)rä, ˈämrə\ *n* -S [Hindi *amrā, amṛā, ambāṛā* — more at AMBARELLA] **:** a hog plum (*Spondias mangifera*) of India

am·rad gum \ˈämˌräd-\ *n* [Bengali *āmrāt* hog plum] **:** an inferior usu. colored gum arabic obtained chiefly in India from the babul

am·ra·tian \(ˈ)amˈrāshən\ *adj, usu cap* [El-*Amra*, site near Abydos, Egypt, its type station + E *-atian* (as in *Alsatian*)] **:** of or belonging to an aeneolithic culture of Upper Egypt characterized by semisubterranean dwellings, working of raw gold, the use of copper and ivory, and the wearing of linen

am·ri \ˈäm(ˌ)rē\ *adj, usu cap* [fr. *Amri*, town in Sind province, Pakistan, its type station] **:** of or belonging to the earliest known stone-using and shell-using culture of the Indus river system which extends also into the Sind and southern Baluchistan and is characterized by a special kind of decorated pottery

am·rit \ˈamrət\ *or* **am·ri·ta** \amˈrēd·ə\ *n* -S [Panjabi & Skt; Panjabi *amrt*, lit., immortal, fr. Skt *amrta*, fr. *a-* ²a- + *mrta* dead, death — more at MURDER] **:** a sweetened water used by the Sikhs as a sacred drink and as baptismal water

¹am·rit·sar \(ˈ)amˈritsə(r), ˌəm;-\ *adj, usu cap* [fr. *Amritsar*, India] **:** of or from Amritsar, India **:** of the kind or style prevalent in Amritsar

²amritsar \"\ *n* -S *usu cap* [fr. *Amritsar*, where it is made] **:** a large-sized machine-made Indian carpet

AMs *pl of* AM

-ams *pl of* -AM

am·sinck·ia \amˈsiŋkēə\ *n, cap* [NL, fr. Wilhelm *Amsinck* †1831 Ger. botanist + NL *-ia*] **:** a genus of rough annual herbs (family Boraginaceae) with oblong leaves and scorpioid-spicate yellow flowers, at least the lowest being leafy-bracted — see FIDDLE-NECK 2

am·so·nia \amˈsōnēə, -nyə\ *n* [NL, fr. Charles *Amson fl* 1760 Am. physician + NL *-ia*] **1** *cap* **:** a genus of herbs (family Apocynaceae) having a milky juice, alternate entire leaves, and showy bluish flowers in terminal cymes, one species (*A. tabernaemontana*) being common in the southeastern U.S. **2** -S **:** an herb of the genus *Amsonia*

am·ster·dam \ˈamztə(r)ˌdam, -mstə-, ˈaam...daa(ə)m\ *adj, usu cap* [fr. *Amsterdam*, Netherlands] **:** of or from Amsterdam, the capital of the Netherlands **:** of the kind or style prevalent in Amsterdam

am·ster·dam·er *or* **am·ster·dam·mer** \-mə(r)\ *n* -S *cap* [D, *Amsterdammer*, fr. *Amsterdam* + D *-er*] **:** a native or inhabitant of Amsterdam

amt \ˈam(p)t, ˈä-\ *n* -S [Dan, fr. G, fr. OHG *ambaht* service — more at EMBASSY] **:** a magistracy or administrative district in some countries of Teutonic origin

amt *abbr* amount

am·trac *or* **am·track** \ˈam·ˌtrak\ *n* -S [*amphibious* + *tractor*] **:** AMPHIBIAN

AMU *abbr, often not cap* atomic mass unit

amuck *var of* AMOK

amue·sha \ämˈwāshə\ *n, pl* **amuesha** *or* **amueshas** *usu cap* [Sp, of AmerInd origin] **1 a :** a people of central Peru **b :** a member of such people **2 :** a language of the Amuesha people of uncertain but perhaps Arawakan affinity

amu·guis *also* **amu·gis** \äˈmü(ˌ)gēs\ *n* -ES [Tag *amugis*] **1 :** a timber tree (*Koordersiodendron pinnatum*) of the family Anacardiaceae found in the Philippines, Celebes, and New Guinea **2 :** the light-colored reddish water-resisting and ant-resisting wood of the amuguis

am·u·la \ˈamyələ\ *n, pl* **amu·lae** \-ˌlē, -ī\ *or* **amulas** [LL *amula, hamula*, fr. L, water bucket, dim. of *ama, hama* bucket — more at AMA] **:** a vessel for eucharistic wine offered by the people in the early Christian church

am·u·let \ˈamyələt *also* -ˌlet, *usu* -d·+V\ *n* -S [L *amuletum*] **:** a charm (as an ornament, gem, or relic) often inscribed with a spell, magic incantation, or symbol and believed to protect the wearer against evil (as disease or witchcraft) or to aid him (as in love or war)

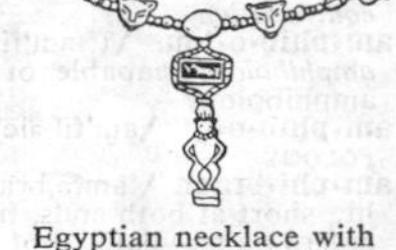

Egyptian necklace with amulets

am·u·let·ic \ˌamyəˈled·ik\ *adj* **:** functioning as an amulet

amur cork \(ˈ)äˈmu̇(ə)r-, əˈm-\ *n, usu cap A* [fr. *Amur* river, NE Asia, where it grows] **:** a medium-sized tree (*Phellodendron amurense*) with corky bark and pinnate leaves native to eastern Asia but used as an ornamental elsewhere

amur maple *n, usu cap A* [fr. *Amur* river] **:** a graceful shrub (*Acer ginnala*) of eastern Asia used in cultivation and having 3-lobed leaves and yellow paniculate flowers

amur privet *or* **amur river privet** *n, usu cap A* [fr. *Amur* river] **:** a shrub (*Ligustrum amurense*) of eastern Asia cultivated for its persistent foliage, white flowers, and black fruit

amuse \əˈmyüz\ *vb* -ED/-ING/-S [MF *amuser* to cause to waste time, amuse, bemuse, deceive, fr. OF, fr. *a-* (fr. L *ad-*) + *muser* to muse — more at MUSE] *vt* **1** *archaic* **:** to divert the attention of (as from the truth or one's real intent) **:** DECEIVE, DELUDE, BEMUSE **2** *obs* **a :** to occupy or engage the attention of **:** plunge in deep thought **:** ABSORB **b :** DISTRACT, BEWILDER **3 a :** to entertain or occupy in a pleasant manner **:** DIVERT ⟨he ~*s* himself by reading⟩ ⟨~ the child with a story⟩ ⟨~ his friends⟩ **b :** to while away ⟨~ leisure time⟩ ~ *vi, obs* **:** MUSE

syn DIVERT, ENTERTAIN, RECREATE: AMUSE means to engage the attention in a way to keep one interested or engrossed esp. in a laugh-provoking, usu. light or frivolous way ⟨I write because it *amuses* me —Rose Macaulay⟩ ⟨he has something to say that will either *amuse* or help his audience —W.J.Reilly⟩ DIVERT, in this comparison, stresses the distraction of the attention, esp. from worry and routine occupations, and usu. the inducing of relaxation or gaiety ⟨a series of *diverting* and some mildly harrowing adventures —*Current Biog.*⟩ ⟨when idle moments occur during the day, fill them in quickly by *diverting* yourself with an absorbing book —*Better Homes & Gardens*⟩ ⟨only men of leisure have the need for beautiful women to *divert* them —Pearl Buck⟩ ENTERTAIN implies the activity of others to provide amusement or diversion and usu. suggests formal or specially contrived methods ⟨his prose has been described as lucid, *entertaining*, and, at times, inspired —*Current Biog.*⟩ ⟨the radio keeps them informed and *entertained* —Harold Griffin⟩ ⟨a party of Frenchmen . . . *entertained* the friendly natives aboard their boats —*Amer. Guide Series: La.*⟩ RECREATE, an infrequent verb in this sense, implies a change of occupation or an indulgence in diversions for the sake of relaxation or refreshment of mind or body ⟨*recreating* herself in the company of her sisters —Jane Austen⟩

amused *adj* **1 :** pleasantly diverted ⟨~ spectators⟩ **2 :** expressing amusement ⟨an ~ look on his face⟩ — **amus·ed·ly** \-zədlē, -li\ *adv*

amuse·ment \-zmənt\ *n* -S *often attrib* [F, fr. MF, fr. *amuser* + *-ment*] **1** *obs* **a :** BEWILDERMENT **b :** diversion of the attention (as from the truth or one's real intent) **:** DISTRACTION **2 a :** a means of amusing or entertaining ⟨what are your favorite ~*s*⟩ **b :** the condition of being amused ⟨his ~ knew no bounds⟩ **c :** pleasurable diversion **:** ENTERTAINMENT ⟨he plays the piano for his own ~⟩

amusement park *n* **:** a commercially operated park having various devices for entertainment (as a merry-go-round and roller coaster) and usu. booths for the sale of food and drink

amuses *pres 3d sing of* AMUSE

am·u·sette \ˌamyəˈzet\ *n* -S [F, lit., plaything, diversion, fr. *amuser* + *-ette*] **:** an obsolete light rifled fieldpiece

amus·go \əˈmüsˌgō, -üz-\ *n, pl* **amusgo** *or* **amusgos** *usu cap* [Sp, of AmerInd origin] **1 a :** a people of the coast of Oaxaca and Guerrero, Mexico **b :** a member of such people **2 :** a Mixtecan language of the Amusgo people

1

amu·sia \(ˈ)āˈmyüzēə\ *n* -s [NL, fr. Gk *amousia* lack of harmony, fr. *amousos* without song (fr. *a-* ²a- + *mousa* muse, music) + *-ia*] **:** a condition marked by an inability to produce music or to comprehend it — called also respectively *motor amusia, sensory amusia;* compare APHASIA

amusing *adj* **:** giving amusement **:** pleasantly entertaining **:** DIVERTING ⟨an ~ story⟩ — **amus·ing·ly** *adv*

amus·ive \əˈmyüziv, -siv\ *adj* **:** tending to amuse or to tickle the fancy or excite mirth **:** AMUSING — **amus·ive·ly** *adv*

amy *var of* AMI

am·y·da \ˈaməda\ [NL, fr. ²*a-* + *-myda* (fr. Gk *mydos* dampness)] *syn of* TRIONYX

amyd·ri·caine \əˈmidrə,kān\ *n* -s [²*a-* + *mydr*iatic + *-caine* (as in *cocaine*)] **:** a local anesthetic $C_{16}H_{26}N_2O_2$ that is usu. administered in the form of its bitter crystalline hydrochloride and that unlike cocaine is not mydriatic

amy·e·lin·ic \ˌā,mīəˈlinik, ā¦m-\ *adj* [²*a-* + *myelinic*] **:** NONMEDULLATED — used of nerve fibers

amy·e·lon·ic \-ˈlänik\ *adj* [²*a-* + *myelonic*] **1 :** lacking a spinal cord **2 :** lacking marrow

amygdal- *or* **amygdalo-** *comb form* [L *amygdal-*, fr. *amygdala*] **1 :** almond **:** almond family ⟨*amygdal*ase⟩ ⟨*amygdal*iferous⟩ **2** [NL, fr. *amygdala*] **a :** tonsil ⟨*amygdal*otomy⟩ **b :** tonsillar and ⟨*amygdalo*-uvular⟩

amyg·da·la \əˈmigdələ\ *n, pl* **amygda·lae** \-,lē, -ī\ [NL, fr. L, almond — more at ALMOND] **1 :** one of the tonsils of the pharynx **2 :** one of the rounded prominences of the lower surface of the lateral hemispheres of the cerebellum **3 :** the one of the four basal ganglia in each cerebral hemisphere that consists of an almond-shaped mass of gray matter in the roof of the lateral ventricle

amyg·da·la·ce·ae \ə¦=ˈlāsē,ē\ *n pl, cap* [NL, fr. *Amygdalus*, type genus + *-aceae*] *in some esp. former classifications* **:** a family of trees and shrubs comprising those plants of the family Rosaceae (as the plum, peach, and almond) that have a single pistil with united carpels and a characteristic drupe — **amyg·da·la·ceous** \ə¦=¦=¦shəs\ *adj*

amyg·da·lin \əˈ==lən\ *n* -s [*amygdal-* + *-in*] **:** a white crystalline glucoside $C_6H_5CH(CN)OC_{12}H_{21}O_{10}$ that occurs in the kernels of the bitter almond and certain other plants of the genus *Prunus* and that on complete hydrolysis yields benzaldehyde, hydrogen cyanide, and glucose

amyg·da·line \", -,līn\ *adj* [L *amygdalinus* of almonds, fr. Gk *amygdalinos*, fr. *amygdalē* almond + *-inos* -ine] **1 :** of, relating to, or resembling an almond **2 :** of or relating to a tonsil

amyg·da·loid \-,lȯid\ *n* -s [*amygdal-* + *-oid*] **:** an igneous and usu. volcanic rock orig. containing small cavities produced before solidification by expansion of steam and afterward filled with deposits of different minerals (as chalcedony, quartz, calcite, or zeolites)

amyg·da·loi·dal \ə¦=¦=ˈdȯidᵊl\ *also* **amyg·da·loid** \əˈ==,=\ *adj* **:** having the characteristics of amygdaloid

amygdaloid nucleus *also* **amygdaloid body** *n* **:** AMYGDALA 3

amyg·da·lus \əˈ==ləs\ *n, cap* [NL, fr. LL, almond tree, fr. Gk *amygdalos*] *in some esp. former classifications* **:** a small genus of Asiatic trees and shrubs including those plants of the genus *Prunus* (as the peach and almond) that have numerous stamens, an often velvety exocarp, and a deeply grooved stone

amyg·dule \əˈmig,d(y)ül, ˈamig-\ *also* **amyg·dale** \-,dā(ə)l\ *n* -s [irreg. fr. *amygdal-* + *-ule*] **:** one of the rounded nodules occurring in an amygdaloid

am·yl \ˈaməl *also* ˈām-\ *n* -s [blend of *amyl-* and *-yl*] **1 :** PENTYL **2 :** either of two mixtures of pentyl radicals: **a :** the radicals derived from amyl alcohol (sense 2a) — called also *isoamyl* **b :** the radicals derived from amyl alcohol (sense 2b)

amyl- *or* **amylo-** *comb form* [LL *amyl-*, fr. L *amylum*, fr. Gk *amylon*, fr. neut. of *amylos* not ground at the mill, fr. *a-* ²a- + *mylos, mylē* mill — more at MEAL] **:** starch ⟨*amyl*ase⟩ ⟨*amyl*emia⟩ ⟨*amylo*meter⟩

am·y·la·ceous \ˌamə¦lāshəs\ *adj* [*amyl-* + *-aceous*] **:** of, relating to, or having the characteristics of starch **:** STARCHY

amyl acetate *n* **:** an acetic ester $CH_3COOC_5H_{11}$ of pentyl alcohol: as **a :** the ester obtained from a commercial amyl alcohol as a water-insoluble liquid with a strong fruity odor and used as a solvent (as for cellulose nitrate lacquers) and in artificial fruit essences and perfumes — called also *banana oil, pear oil* **b :** ISOAMYL ACETATE

amyl alcohol *n* **1 :** PENTYL ALCOHOL **2 :** either of two commercially produced mixtures of pentyl alcohols used chiefly in making esters and as solvents: **a :** the optically active mixture consisting of isopentyl alcohol and active amyl alcohol obtained from fusel oil — called also *fermentation amyl alcohol, isoamyl alcohol* **b :** the optically inactive mixture consisting of seven pentyl alcohols obtained by chlorination of pentanes from natural-gas gasoline or petroleum followed by hydrolysis — called also *synthetic amyl alcohol*

am·y·lase \ˈamə,lās\ *n* -s [ISV *amyl-* + *-ase*] **1 :** any of the enzymes that accelerate the hydrolysis of starch and glycogen or their intermediate products of hydrolysis — called also *diastase* **2 a :** an enzyme that is found esp. in malt, in certain molds and bacteria, and in saliva and pancreatic juice and that acts chiefly on starch and glycogen with the formation of dextrins as intermediate products and sugars as final products — called also *alpha-amylase, dextrinogenic enzyme* **b :** an enzyme that is found esp. in grains, malt, and vegetables (as sweet potatoes) and that acts on starch, glycogen, and some dextrins with the formation of maltose — called also *beta-amylase, saccharifying enzyme*

am·yl·ene \-,lēn\ *n* -s [ISV *amyl* + *-ene*] **:** any of several low-boiling olefin hydrocarbons C_5H_{10}: as **a :** a flammable liquid $CH_3CH{=}C(CH_3)_2$ obtained from fusel oil by dehydration; 2-methyl-2-butene — called also *beta-isoamylene, trimethylethylene* **b :** PENTENE

amylene hydrate *n* **:** TERTIARY AMYL ALCOHOL — used chiefly in pharmacy

amyl ether *n* **:** any symmetrical ether $(C_5H_{11})_2O$ derived from amyl alcohol; *esp* **:** a mixture of normal pentyl ether and isopentyl ether obtained as a by-product in the preparation of amyl alcohol (sense 2a) and used as a solvent

amyl·i·dene \əˈmilə,dēn, aˈ-\ *n* -s [ISV *amyl* + *-idene*] **:** PENTYLIDENE

am·y·lif·er·ous \ˌamə¦lif(ə)rəs\ *adj* [*amyl-* + *-i-* + *-ferous*] **:** bearing or producing starch

amyl nitrate *n* **:** the nitric ester $C_5H_{11}ONO_2$ of commercial amyl alcohol used as a liquid additive to diesel fuel for raising the cetane number

amyl nitrite *n* **:** a pale yellow pungent flammable liquid ester $C_5H_{11}ONO$ of commercial amyl alcohol and nitrous acid that is used chiefly in medicine as a vasodilator esp. in angina pectoris — called also *isoamyl nitrite*

am·y·lo \ˈamə,lō\ *adj* [*amyl-*] **:** of or relating to starch

amylo- — see AMYL-

am·y·lo·dex·trin \ˌ==(ˌ)=ˈdekstrən\ *n* -s [ISV *amyl-* + *dextrin*] **:** an intermediate product of the hydrolysis of starch that is soluble in water and gives a blue color with iodine — compare LIMIT DEXTRIN

am·y·lo·gram \ˈamələ,gram\ *n* -s [*amyl-* + *-gram*] **:** the record made by an amylograph

am·y·lo·graph \-,graf\ *n* -s [*amyl-* + *-graph*] **:** an instrument that measures and records the gelatinization temperature and viscosity of pastes of starch and flour

¹am·y·loid \ˈamə,lȯid\ *or* **amy·loi·dal** \¦=ˈ=¦dᵊl\ *adj* [ISV *amyl-* + *-oid, -oidal*] **1 :** resembling or containing amylum **:** resembling starch **2 :** relating to or marked by the production of amyloid (sense 3)

²amyloid \"\ *n* -s **1 :** a nonnitrogenous starchy food **:** a starchlike substance **2 a :** a gelatinous hydrated cellulose produced by the action of moderately concentrated sulfuric acid on cellulose (as in making parchment paper) **b :** a gummy substance found in the seeds of the nasturtium and other plants **3 :** a waxy translucent substance related to protein and deposited in some animal organs under abnormal conditions probably involving a disturbance of protein metabolism

amyloid degeneration *n* **:** AMYLOIDOSIS

am·y·loi·do·sis \ˌamə,lȯiˈdōsəs\ *n, pl* **amyloido·ses** \-ō,sēz\ [NL, fr. ISV ²*amyloid* + NL *-osis*] **:** a condition characterized by the deposition of amyloid in organs or tissues of the animal body either as a primary disease of unknown cause or secondary to chronic disease (as tuberculosis or osteomyelitis)

am·y·lo·leu·cite \ˌamə(ˌ)lōˈlü,sīt\ *n* -s [ISV *amyl-* + *leucite*] **:** LEUCOPLAST

am·y·lol·y·sis \ˌaməˈläləsəs\ *n, pl* **amyloly·ses** \-ə,sēz\ [NL, fr. *amyl-* + *-lysis*] **:** the conversion of starch into soluble products (as dextrins and sugars) esp. by the action of enzymes — **amy·lo·lyt·ic** \ˌamə(ˌ)lō¦lid·ik\ *adj*

am·y·lo·pec·tin \ˌamə(ˌ)lōˈpektən\ *n* -s [ISV *amyl-* + *pectin*] **:** a component of starch that comprises about four fifths of cornstarch, that is separated from amylose by precipitation of the amylose from a dilute starch solution, and that is characterized by the lack of tendency of its aqueous solutions to gel, by the red color it gives with iodine, and by its high molecular weight and branched structure made up in some cases of as many as 2000 glucose units

am·y·lo·plast \ˈ==(ˌ)=,plast\ *also* **am·y·lo·plas·tid** \ˌ==(ˌ)=-ˈplastəd\ *or* **am·y·lo·plas·tide** \", -,stīd\ *n* -s [ISV *amyl-* + *-plast, plastid, plastide*] **:** a starch-forming leucoplast

am·y·lop·sin \ˌaməˈläpsən, ˌ=ˈ==\ *n* -s [*amyl-* + *-psin* (as in *trypsin, pepsin*)] **:** the amylase of the pancreatic juice

am·y·lose \ˈamə,lōs\ *n* -s [ISV *amyl-* + *-ose*] **1 :** any of various polysaccharides (as starch or cellulose) **2 :** a component of starch that comprises about one fifth of cornstarch, that is separated from amylopectin by precipitation from a dilute starch solution with butyl or amyl alcohol, and that is characterized by the tendency of its aqueous solutions to set to a stiff gel at room temperature, by the blue color it gives with iodine, and by its moderately high molecular weight and linear structure made up of hundreds of glucose units **3 :** any of various compounds (as dextrin) $(C_6H_{10}O_5)_x$ obtained by the hydrolysis of starch

amyl salicylate *n* **:** the salicylic ester $C_6H_4(OH)COOC_5H_{11}$ of commercial amyl alcohol that is a liquid of lasting pleasant odor used chiefly as an ingredient of perfumes and soaps — called also *isoamyl salicylate*

am·y·lum \ˈaməlәm\ *n* -s [L — more at AMYL-] **:** STARCH

amylum body *n* **:** a starch grain

amylum center *n* **:** PYRENOID

amylum grain *n* **:** a laminated starch body formed by the leucoplasts

amylum star *n* **:** a star-shaped propagative body densely filled with starch and formed about the lower nodes of certain stoneworts

amyn·o·don \əˈminə,dän\ *n, cap* [NL, fr. Gk *amynein* to ward off + NL *-odon*] **:** a genus of Eocene perissodactyls related to the rhinoceros but hornless and having the canines developed into curved tusks —**amyn·o·dont** \-nt\ *n or adj*

amy·o·to·nia \ˌā,mīəˈtōnēə\ *n* -s [NL, fr. ²*a-* + *myotonia*] **:** deficiency of muscle tone

amyotonia con·gen·i·ta \-kənˈjenəd·ə\ *n* [NL, congenital amyotonia] **:** a congenital disease of infants characterized by flaccidity of the skeletal muscles resulting in an inability to move freely or maintain upright posture

amy·o·tro·phia \ˌā,mīəˈtrōfēə\ *or* **amy·ot·ro·phy** \-īˈä·trəfē\ *n, pl* **amyotrophias** *or* **amyotrophies** [NL *amyotrophia*, fr. ²*a-* + *my-* + *-trophia*] **:** atrophy of a muscle

amy·o·troph·ic \ˌā,mīə¦träfik, ā¦m-, -ōf-\ *adj* **:** relating to or marked by amyotrophia

am·y·ral·dism \ˌaməˈral,dizəm\ *n* -s *usu cap* [Moses *Amyraldus* (Moïse Amyraut) †1664 Fr. Protestant theologian + E *-ism*] **:** a liberal form of Calvinism distinguished by its doctrines of universal atonement and universal salvation

am·y·rin \ˈamərən\ *n* -s [ISV *amyr-* (fr. NL *Amyris*) + *-in*] **:** either of two crystalline isomeric triterpenoid alcohols $C_{30}H_{49}OH$ found esp. in Manila elemi and dandelion roots and distinguished as alpha-amyrin and beta-amyrin

am·y·ris \ˈamərəs\ *n, cap* [NL, prob. irreg. fr. Gk *amyros* not watery, prob. fr. *a-* (akin to *hama* together) + *myron* sweet oil, unguent; fr. the oily quality of the plant] **:** a genus of tropical American trees and shrubs (family Rutaceae) with compound leaves and white flowers

amyris oil *n* **:** an oil distilled from the wood of a torchwood (*Amyris balsamifera*) and used in perfumery

amy·root \ˈāmē,-\ *n* -s [origin unknown] **:** INDIAN HEMP 1

An·y·tal \ˈamə,tȯl *also* -al\ *trademark* — used for amobarbital

¹an \ ən, *after some consonants often* ᵊn, *esp emphatic or hesitating or after a pause* (¦)an; *see usage note below*\ *indefinite article* [ME, fr. OE *ān* one — more at ONE] **:** ²A — used (1) usu. in speech and writing before words beginning with a vowel sound ⟨*an* oak⟩ ⟨*an* hour⟩ ⟨*an* X ray⟩; (2) usu. in speech and often in writing before *h*-initial words beginning with an unstressed or lightly stressed syllable in which \h\ may or may not be pronounced ⟨*an* historian⟩ ⟨*an* heroic⟩; (3) sometimes (less often now than formerly) before words whose initial letter is a vowel and whose initial sounds are \yü\ or \yu̇\ or \w\ in *one* ⟨*an* European⟩ ⟨*an* unique⟩ ⟨such *an* one⟩; (4) sometimes in speech and writing and regularly in the Old Testament (AV) before a stressed syllable in *h*-initial words ⟨*an* hundred⟩ ⟨*an* heritage⟩

²an \ ən, ˌan\ *prep* **:** ³A 2 — usu. used before words with an initial vowel sound ⟨once *an* afternoon⟩ ⟨earns three dollars *an* hour⟩

³an *or* **an'** *conj* [ME *an*, alter. of *and*] **1** *the spelling without "d" is substand but the pronunciation without* d *is not — see* ¹AND\ *substand* **:** AND ⟨he would sit ~ let on to be learning —Wright Morris⟩ **2** \(ˌ)an, ən, ᵊn\ *archaic* **:** IF ⟨~ thou dalliest, then I am thy foe —Ben Jonson⟩

an- — see ²A-

¹-an *or* **-ian** *also* **-ean** *n suffix* -s [*-an* & *-ian* fr. ME *-an, -ian, -ien*, fr. OF & L; OF *-ien*, fr. L *-ianus*, fr. *-i-* + *-anus*, fr. *-anus*, adj. suffix; *-ean* fr. such words as *Mediterranean, European*] **1 :** one that is of or belonging to ⟨Americ*an*⟩ ⟨Boston*ian*⟩ **2 :** one skilled in or specializing in — esp. in derivatives from nouns ending in *-ic* or *-ics*, in the latter case with loss of *-s* ⟨dialectic*ian*⟩ ⟨phonetic*ian*⟩ ⟨statistic*ian*⟩ **3 :** one belonging to a (specified) zoological group ⟨crustace*an*⟩ ⟨mammal*ian*⟩ ⟨crocodil*ian*⟩

²-an *or* **-ian** *also* **-ean** *adj suffix* [*-an* & *-ian* fr. ME *-an, -ian, -ien*, fr. OF & L; OF *-ien*, fr. L *-ianus*, fr. *-i-* + *-anus; -ean* fr. such words as *Mediterranean, European*] **1 :** of or belonging to ⟨Americ*an*⟩ ⟨Florid*ian*⟩ ⟨Wesley*an*⟩ **2 :** characteristic of **:** resembling ⟨Mozart*ean*⟩ ⟨Shav*ian*⟩ **3 :** of or belonging to a (specified) geologic period, epoch, or series ⟨Cambr*ian*⟩

³-an *n suffix* -s [ISV *-an, -ane*, alter. of *-ene, -ine, & -one*] **1 :** unsaturated carbon compound ⟨tol*an* $C_6H_5C{\equiv}CC_6H_5$⟩ ⟨ureth*an*⟩ — esp. in names of heterocyclic compounds ⟨fur*an*⟩ ⟨allox*an*⟩; compare -ANE **2 a :** anhydride representing a polymer of a carbohydrate — usu. replacing final *-ose* of the carbohydrate name ⟨xyl*an*⟩ ⟨dextr*an*⟩, less often replacing final *-e* ⟨pentos*an*⟩ **b :** intramolecular anhydride of a carbohydrate — replacing final *-e* of the carbohydrate name ⟨β-glucos*an*⟩

an *abbr* **1** animate **2** [L *anno*] in the year; [L *annum; annus*] year **3** anonymous

AN *abbr* **1** *often not cap* above-named **2** army-navy **3** arrival notice

¹ana \ˈanə\ *adv* [ME, fr. ML, fr. Gk, to the amount of, at the rate of, lit., up] **:** of each an equal quantity — used in prescriptions ⟨wine and honey ~ two ounces⟩; usu. written ĀĀ or Ā

²ana \ˈanə, ˈä-,ˈȧ- *also* ˈā-\ *n, pl* **ana** *or* **anas** [*-ana*] **1 a :** collection of the memorable sayings or table talk of a person ⟨his chatty autobiographic sketches are a notable ~⟩ **b :** a collection of anecdotes or interesting or curious information about a person or a place ⟨the ~ of the graduate dormitories⟩ **2 :** an item in or suitable for a collection of table talk or anecdotes ⟨a secretarial corps was employed to examine and list the ~ —S.H.Adams⟩

³ana *var of* ANNA

ana- *or* **an-** *prefix* [ML, fr. L *ana-* & LL *an-*, fr. Gk *ana-, an-*, fr. *ana* up, on — more at ON] **1 :** up **:** upward ⟨*an*ode⟩ ⟨*Ana*cardium⟩ **2 :** back **:** backward ⟨*ana*nym⟩ **3 :** again **:** anew ⟨*ana*genesis⟩ **4** *usu* **ana-**, *chem, usu ital* **:** having substituents in positions 1 and 5 in two fused 6-membered rings (as in naphthalene, quinoline)

-ana \ˈanə, ˈä-,ˈȧ- *also* ˈā-\ *or* **-i·ana** \ēˈ-\ *n pl suffix* [NL, collected quotations from, fr. L, neut. pl. of *-anus* -an & *-ianus* -ian] **:** collected items of information esp. anecdotal or bibliographical concerning ⟨American*a*⟩ ⟨Johnson*iana*⟩ ⟨Burns*iana*⟩ ⟨college*iana*⟩ — chiefly in derivatives from persona names and place names

an'a \əˈnȧ, -nȯ\ [by alter.] *Scot* **:** and all

an·a·bae·na \ˌanəˈbēnə\ *n* [NL, fr. Gk *anabainein* to go up, shoot up, fr. *ana-* + *bainein* to go — more at COME] **1** *cap* **:** a genus of freshwater blue-green algae (family Nostocaceae) having cells in beadlike filaments and often contaminating reservoirs **2** -s **:** an alga of the genus *Anabaena*

an·a·ban·tid \ˌanəˈbantəd\ *adj* [NL *Anabantidae*, fr. *Anabant-, Anabas*, type genus + *-idae*] **:** of or relating to the genus *Anabas* or the family Anabantidae

an·a·bap·tism \ˌanə¦-\ *n* -s [NL *anabaptismus*, fr. LGk *anabaptismos* rebaptism, fr. *anabaptizein* + Gk *-ismos* -ism] **1** *usu cap* **:** the doctrine or practices of the Anabaptists **2 :** REBAPTISM; *esp* **:** the baptism of adults formerly baptized as infants practiced by Anabaptists

¹an·a·bap·tist \ˌanə¦-\ *n* -s *usu cap* [NL *anabaptista*, fr. LGk *anabaptizein* + L *-ista* -ist] **:** a Protestant sectarian associated with a radical movement which made its appearance in the 16th century rejecting infant baptism and insisting on believer's baptism and advocating complete religious liberty, the separation of church and state, opposition to military service, and religious communalism

²anabaptist \"\ *or* **an·a·bap·tis·tic** \¦==,=¦=\ *adj, usu cap* **:** of, relating to, or characteristic of the Anabaptists or their doctrine and practice — **an·a·bap·tis·ti·cal·ly** \-tək(ə)lē\ *adv*

an·a·bap·tize \ˌ==,=ˈ=, ˌ==ˈ=,=, ˈ==,=¦=\ *vt* -ED/-ING/-S [LGk *anabaptizein* to rebaptize, fr. *ana-* + *baptizein* to baptize — more at BAPTIZE] **:** to baptize over again **:** RECHRISTEN

an·a·bas \ˈanəbəs, -,bas\ *n, cap* [NL, fr. Gk, aorist part. of *anabainein*] **:** a genus (the type of a family Anabantidae) comprising small perchlike freshwater spiny-finned fishes of southeastern Asia and Africa and often being placed with a few related fishes in a separate suborder of the Percomorphi — see CLIMBING PERCH

anab·a·sine \əˈnabə,sēn, -sən\ *n* -s [NL *Anabasis* (genus name of *Anabasis aphylla*) + E *-ine*] **:** an insecticidal liquid alkaloid $(C_5H_4N)\ C_5H_{10}N$ related to nicotine and found in tobacco and in a nearly leafless subshrub (*Anabasis aphylla*) of southeastern Russia; 2-(3-pyridyl)-piperidine

anab·a·sis \əˈnabəsəs\ *n* [Gk, act of going up, expedition up from the coast into Asia, increasing period of a disease, fr. *anabainein* to go up, to go up from the coast — more at ANABAENA] **1** *pl* **anaba·ses** \-ə,sēz\ **:** a going or marching up **:** ADVANCE ⟨~ of the Slum —Wallace Stevens⟩; *esp* **:** a military advance ⟨the Russian ~ and katabasis of Napoleon —Thomas De Quincey⟩ **2** [NL, fr. L, a plant, fr. Gk] *cap* **:** a genus of small woody or herbaceous perennials (family Chenopodiaceae) native to the Caucasus and nearby regions and having jointed stems and opposite fleshy often reduced leaves **3** [so called fr. the fact that a famous retreat of Greek mercenaries from the Euphrates to the Black sea is described in the *Anabasis*, historical work by Xenophon †*ab*355 B.C. Greek historian & essayist] *pl* **anabases :** a difficult and dangerous military retreat

anab·a·ta \əˈnabəd·ə\ *n* -s [NGk, fr. ML *anabata, anabala*, prob. modif. of Gk *anabolē* cloak, fr. *anaballein* to put on (also, to lift or throw up, delay), fr. *ana-* + *ballein* to throw — more at DEVIL] **:** a hooded cope worn esp. in outdoor processions in the Eastern Church

ana·bath·mos \ˌänəˈbäthˈmȯs\ *n, pl* **anabath·moi** \-ˈmē\ [MGk, fr. Gk, flight of steps, "song of steps", fr. *anabainein* to go up — more at ANABAENA] **:** one of the gradual psalms in the Eastern Church

an·a·bat·ic \ˌanə¦bad·ik\ *adj* [LGk *anabatikos* (influenced in meaning by Gk *anabasis* going up, ascension), fr. Gk, skilled in mounting, fr. *anabainein* to go up, mount, ascend] **:** upward-moving ⟨an ~ wind⟩

an·a·be·ro·ga \ˌanəbəˈrōgə\ *n* [Malay *anabiroga*, fr. *anak* child + (*ayam*) *biroga* jungle fowl] **:** a root disease and collar rot of the areca palm attributed to a pore fungus (*Fomes lucidus*)

an·a·bib·a·zon \ˌanəˈbibə,zän\ *n* -s [Gk *anabibazōn*, pres. part. act. of *anabibazein* to raise, mount, fr. *ana-* + *bibazein* to lift, fr. *bainein* to go — more at COME] **:** the ascending node of the moon's orbit with the ecliptic

ana·bi·o·sis \ˌanə,bīˈōsəs\ *n, pl* **anabio·ses** \-ō,sēz\ [NL, fr. Gk *anabiōsis* return to life, fr. *anabioun* to return to life, fr. *ana-* + *bioun* to live, fr. *bios* life — more at QUICK] **:** a state of suspended animation induced in organisms (as rotifers) by desiccation and ending on return of moisture in resumption of normal life

ana·bi·ot·ic \ˌanə,bī¦äd·ik\ *adj* [fr. NL *anabiosis*, after such pairs as E *narcosis: narcotic*] **:** of or related to anabiosis

an·a·blep·id \ˌanə¦blepəd\ *adj* [NL *Anablepidae*, family of fishes, fr. *Anableps*, type genus + *-idae*] **:** of or belonging to *Anableps* or to the four-eyed fishes

an·a·bleps \ˈanə,bleps\ *n, cap* [NL, fr. Gk *anableps-*, stem of *anablepein* to look up, fr. *ana-* + *blepein* to look] **:** a genus of tropical American saltwater and freshwater fishes comprising the four-eyed fishes, being closely related to the topminnows but constituting a separate family, and having the eyes divided into an upper and lower division by the growth of two processes of the iris across the pupil and a band of conjunctiva across the cornea, the upper part serving to see objects in the air, the lower part to see objects under water

an·a·bo·hit·site \ˌanəbōˈhit,sīt\ *n* -s [F *anabohitsite*, fr. *Anabohitsy*, Madagascar, its locality + F *-ite*] **:** a variety of olivine-pyroxenite rock containing hypersthene, hornblende, and about 30 percent of ilmenite and magnetite

an·a·bol·ic \ˌanə¦bälik\ *adj* [ISV *ana-* + *-bolic* (as in *metabolic*)] **1 :** relating to, characterized by, or promoting anabolism ⟨~ steroids taken by athletes to increase muscular size temporarily⟩ **2 :** of, relating to, or exhibiting anaboly

anab·o·lism \əˈnabə,lizəm, aˈ-\ *n* -s [ISV *ana-* + *-bolism* (as in *metabolism*)] **:** constructive metabolism — opposed to *catabolism*

anab·o·lite \-,līt\ *also* **anab·o·lin** \-lən\ *n* -s [*anabolism* + *-ite* or *-in*] **:** a product of an anabolic process — **anab·o·lit·ic** \ə¦nabə¦lid·ik\ *adj*

anab·o·lize \əˈ==,līz\ *vi* -ED/-ING/-S [fr. *anabolism*, after such pairs as E *hypnotism: hypnotize*] **:** to perform anabolism

anab·o·ly \əˈnabəlē\ *n* -ES [modif. of Gk *anabolē* anything thrown up, prelude, act of delaying, ascent, fr. *anaballein* to throw or lift up, delay, put on — more at ANABATA] **:** evolutionary differentiation involving the addition of new terminal stages to the ancestral pattern of morphogenesis

an·a·branch \ˈanə,branch\ *n* -ES [*ana-* + *branch*] **:** a diverging branch of a river which reenters the main stream or which loses itself in sandy soil

ana·ca·hui·ta \ˌanəkəˈwēd·ə\ *or* **ana·ca·hui·te** \", -ē,tā\ *n* -s [Sp, fr. Nahuatl *amacuahuitl* — more at AMATE] **:** a small aromatic tree (*Cordia boissieri*) found in Texas and Mexico, having yellowish white flowers, and used medicinally

an·a·can·thine \ˌanə¦kan(t)thən, -n,thīn\ *adj* [NL *Anacanthini*] **:** of or belonging to the Anacanthini

an·acan·thi·ni \ˌanəˈkan(t)thə,nī\ *n pl, cap* [NL, fr. Gk *anakanthos* without a spine, without thorns (fr. *an-* + *akanthos* spine, thorn) + NL *-ini*] **:** an order or suborder of teleost fishes having all the rays of the median and pelvic fins soft and jointed, the pelvic fins thoracic or jugular in position, and the air bladder, when present, usu. without a duct, and comprising the codfishes, hakes, and their related forms and formerly sometimes including the flounders and soles — **an·acan·thous** \¦=¦=thəs\ *adj*

an·a·car·di·a·ce·ae \ˌanə,kärdēˈāsē,ē\ *n pl, cap* [NL, fr. *Anacardium*, type genus + *-aceae*] **:** a widely distributed family of trees and shrubs (order Sapindales) comprising the sumacs, cashews, and related plants and having compound leaves, small regular dioecious or perfect flowers, and drupaceous fruits — **an·a·car·di·a·ceous** \¦=¦=,=¦=¦āshəs\ *adj*

an·a·car·dic acid \ˌanə¦kärdik-\ *n* [ISV *anacardic* (fr. NL *Anacardium* + ISV *-ic*) + *acid*; orig. formed as G *anakardsäure*] **:** a brown crystalline vesicant phenolic acid found as the principal constituent of cashew nutshell liquid, held to consist of a mixture of unsaturated derivatives of salicylic acid, and converted to cardanol by decarboxylation

an·a·car·di·um \ˌanəˈkärdēəm\ *n* [NL, fr. *ana-* + Gk *kardia* heart + NL *-ium;* fr. the heartlike shape of the top of the fruit stem] **1** *cap* **:** a small genus of tropical American trees (the type of the family Anacardiaceae) having kidney-shaped fruit borne at the apex of a fleshy receptacle — see CASHEW **2** *pl* **anacar·dia** \-dēə\ **:** a plant of the genus *Anacardium*

anacardium nut *n* **:** CASHEW NUT

anach·a·ris \ə'nakərəs\ [NL, fr. *ana-* + Gk *charis* grace] *syn of* ELODEA

an·a·chop·ter·is \,anə'käptərəs\ *n, cap* [NL, fr. LGk *anachoē* eruption + NL *-pteris*] **:** a genus (the type of the family Anachopteridaceae) of fossil ferns characterized by pinnately divided leaves having all leaflets in the same plane and sporangia on the flattened margins of the ultimate segments

anachoret *var of* ANCHORITE

an·a·chro·ma·sis \,anə'krōməsəs\ *n, pl* **anachroma·ses** \-ə,sēz\ [NL, fr. *ana-* + *chrom-* + connective *-a-* + *-sis*] **:** the mitotic nuclear transformations leading to formation of the metaphase plate — compare KATACHROMASIS

an·a·chron·ic \¦anə¦kränik\ *or* **an·a·chron·i·cal** \-nəkəl\ *or* **anach·ro·nous** \ə'nakrənəs\ *adj* [*anachronism* + *-ic, -ical, or -ous*] **:** ANACHRONISTIC — **an·a·chron·i·cal·ly** \¦anə¦krän-ək(ə)lē\ *adv* — **anach·ro·nous·ly** \ə'nakrənəslē\ *adv*

anach·ro·nism \ə'nakrə,nizəm\ *n* -s [prob. fr. MGk *anachronismos*, fr. *anachronizesthai* to be an anachronism, fr. LGk *anachronizein* to be late, fr. Gk *ana-* + *chronizein* to spend time, continue, linger, fr. *chronos* time + *-izein* -ize] **1 :** an error in chronology; *esp* **:** a chronological misplacing of persons, events, objects, or customs in regard to each other ⟨two of the rulers mentioned . . . are otherwise unknown but there is no glaring ~ in the names that can be tested —F.M.Stenton⟩ **2 :** a person or a thing that is chronologically out of place; *esp* **:** one that belongs to a former age and is incongruous if found in the present ⟨born a thousand years . . . too late and an ~ in this culminating century of civilization —Jack London⟩ ⟨felt . . . that an absolute monarchy was an ~ for a civilized country —Kenneth Lawson⟩

anach·ro·nis·tic \ə¦nakrə¦nistik, -ēk\ *also* **anach·ro·nis·ti·cal** \-təkəl, -ēk-\ *adj* [*anachronism* + *-istic, -istical*] **:** characterized by or involving anachronism **:** chronologically out of place — **anach·ro·nis·ti·cal·ly** \-tək(ə)lē, -ēk-, -li\ *adv*

an·acid·i·ty \¦anə'sidəd·ē\ *n* -ES [*an-* + *acidity*] **:** ACHLORHYDRIA

anac·la·sis \ə'naklәsәs\ *n, pl* **anacla·ses** \-ə,sēz\ [NL, fr. Gk *anaklasis* act of bending back, reflection, fr. *anaklan* to bend back, reflect (fr. *ana-* + *klan* to break) + *-sis* — more at GLADIATOR] **:** an exchange of place between a short syllable and a preceding long one that is frequent in ionic rhythms

an·a·clas·tic \¦anə¦klastik\ *adj* [Gk *anaklastos* bent back, reflected (fr. *anaklan* to bend back, reflect, fr. *ana-* + *klan* to break, deflect) + E *-ic*] **1 :** capable of springing back ⟨the bottom of an ~ glass springs out or in when air is forced into or drawn from the glass⟩ **2 :** relating to or constituting anaclasis

an·a·cli·nal \¦anə¦klīnᵊl\ *adj* [*ana-* + *-clinal*] **:** descending in a direction opposite to that of the dip of the strata ⟨an ~ river⟩ — opposed to *cataclinal*

an·a·clit·ic \¦anə¦klid·ik\ *adj* [Gk *anaklitos* for reclining (fr. *anaklinein* to lean upon, fr. *ana-* + *klinein* to lean) + E *-ic* — more at LEAN] **:** characterized by dependence: **a :** characterized by dependence of libido on a nonsexual instinct (such as the hunger drive) **b :** of, relating to, or characterized by the direction of libido toward a pregenital love object (as the mother)

an·a·co·lu·thia \,anəkə'lüthēə\ *n* -s [NL, alter. of LL *anacoluthon*] **:** ANACOLUTHON

an·a·co·lu·thic \¦anəkə¦lüthik\ *adj* [*anacoluthon* + *-ic*] **:** of or relating to anacoluthon — **an·a·co·lu·thi·cal·ly** \-thək(ə)lē\ *adv*

an·a·co·lu·thon \,anəkə'lü,thän\ *n, pl* **anacolu·tha** \-,thə\ *or* **anacoluthons** [LL, fr. LGk *anakolouthon* inconsistency in logic, fr. Gk, neut. of *anakolouthos* inconsistent, fr. *an-* + *akolouthos* following — more at AKOLUTHIA] **:** syntactical inconsistency or incoherence within a sentence; *esp* **:** the shift from one construction, left incomplete, to another, sometimes for rhetorical effect (as "you really ought — well, do it your own way")

an·a·con·da \,anə'kändə\ *n* -s [prob. modif. of Singhalese *henakandayā* green whip snake (*Dryophis mycterizans*), understood to be a name for the python, lit., lightning stem, fr. *hena* lightning + *kanda* stem (prob. fr. Skt, bulbous root, perh. of Dravidian origin; akin to Tamil *kaṇṭa* bulbous root, Tulu *kaṇde*) + *-yā* (nominal suffix)] **1** *archaic* **:** a python of Ceylon **2 :** a large arboreal snake (*Eunectes murinus*) of the boa family of tropical So. America having a double row of large black spots along the back, being semiaquatic in its habits, capturing its food by lying in wait in trees at watering places chiefly at night for animals that come to drink, and being powerful enough to crush in its coils a small deer though subsisting mostly on smaller animals and waterfowl **3 :** any large constricting snake other than an anaconda

¹anac·re·on·tic \ə,nakrē'äntik\ *n* -s *sometimes cap* [L *Anacreonticus*, adj.] **1 :** a poem in imitation of or in the manner of Anacreon **:** a drinking song or light lyric **2** *in Greek prosody* **:** a verse having the cadence analyzed as two ionics a minore with anaclasis and supplement or as iambic dimeter catalectic with anapestic opening

²anacreontic \=¦==¦==\ *adj, usu cap* [L *Anacreonticus*, fr. *Anacreont-, Anacreon* †ab488B.C. Greek poet noted for his gay songs of love and drinking (fr. Gk *Anakreont-, Anakreōn*) + L *-icus* -ic] **1 a :** of or relating to Anacreon **b :** like the poetry of Anacreon in structure, style, or theme **2 :** relating to the praise of love and wine **:** gay, convivial, or amatory in tone or theme ⟨Adrian waxed now and then *Anacreontic* in his compliments —George Meredith⟩ — **anacreontically** *adv*

an·a·cri·sis \,anə'krīsəs\ *n, pl* **anacri·ses** \-ī,sēz\ [Gk *anakrisis* examination of the parties concerned in a lawsuit, fr. *anakrinein* to examine, interrogate, fr. *ana-* + *krinein* to choose, determine, separate — more at CRISIS] **:** an investigation of truth in a civil law case in which the interrogation and inquiry are often accompanied by torture

an·a·crog·y·nae \,anə'kräjə(,)nē\ *n pl, cap* [NL, fr. *an-* + *Acrogynae*] *in some classifications* **:** a group of liverworts including all the thalloid members of the Jungermanniaceae — compare ACROGYNAE

an·a·crog·y·nous \¦anə¦kräjənəs\ *adj* [ISV *an-* + *acrogynous*] **1 :** having the archegonia arising below the apex of the stem and not involving the apical cell **2 :** having indeterminate growth of the gametophyte

anac·ro·my·o·di·an \¦a,nakrō,mī¦ōdēən, a¦n-\ *adj* [*ana-* + *acromyodian*] **:** having the intrinsic syringeal muscles inserted on the dorsal ends of the bronchial semirings

an·a·cru·sis \,anə'krüsəs\ *n, pl* **anacru·ses** \-ü,sēz\ [NL & Gk; NL *anacrusis*, fr. Gk *anakrousis* act of pushing back, beginning of a song, fr. *anakrouein* to push back, begin a song (fr. *ana-* + *krouein* to strike, push) + *-sis* — more at RUE] **1** *also* **an·a·krou·sis** \-'krüsəs\ **:** one or more syllables at the beginning of a line of poetry that are regarded as preliminary to and not a part of the metrical pattern of that line **2** *also* **anakrousis :** UPBEAT; *specif* **:** one or more notes or tones preceding the first downbeat of a musical phrase — called also *pickup* **3 :** a preparatory gesture leading into an accented or climactic dancing movement

an·a·cul·ture \'anə,-\ *n* -s [ISV *ana-* + *culture*; prob. orig. formed in F] **:** a mixed bacterial culture; *esp* **:** a culture containing various strains of pathogenic bacteria used in the preparation of autogenous vaccines

an·a·cyc·lus \,anə'sikləs, -īk-\ *n, cap* [NL, fr. *ana-* + Gk *kyklos* ring, circle] **:** a small genus of annual herbs (family Compositae) of the Mediterranean region having dissected leaves and white or yellow flowers

an·a·dem \'anə,dem, -,dəm\ *n* -s [L *anadema*, fr. Gk *anadēma*, fr. *anadein* to wreathe, fr. *ana-* + *dein* to bind — more at DIADEM] *archaic* **:** a wreath for the head **:** GARLAND, CHAPLET

an·a·di·plo·sis \,anədə'plōsəs\ *n, pl* **anadiplo·ses** \-ō,sēz\ [LL, fr. Gk *anadiplōsis*, lit., repetition, fr. *anadiploun* to double, reduplicate (fr. *ana-* + *diploun* to double) + *-sis* — more at DIPLOMA] **:** repetition of a prominent word, usu. the last in a phrase, clause, sentence, or verse, at the beginning of the next phrase, clause, sentence, or verse (as "rely on his honor — honor such as his?")

anad·ro·mous \ə'nadrəməs, a'n-\ *adj* [Gk *anadromos* running upward, fr. *anadramein* to run upward, fr. *ana-* + *dramein* to run — more at TREAD] **1** *of fish* **:** ascending rivers from the sea at certain seasons for breeding ⟨salmon and shad are ~⟩ — compare CATADROMOUS **2** *also* **an·a·drom·ic** \¦anə¦drämik\ [*anadromic* fr. Gk *anadromos* + E *-ic*] **:** having the first set of veins arising on the upper side of the midrib toward the tip — used of the pinnae of a fern frond

anaemia *var of* ANEMIA

an·aer·obe \'anə,rōb; (')a'na(a)(ə),rōb, -ne(ə),-, -nā̈ə,-\ *n* -s [ISV *an-* + *aerobe*; orig. formed as F *anaérobie*] **:** an organism (as a bacterium) that does not require air or free oxygen for maintaining life — compare AEROBE; FACULTATIVE, OBLIGATE

¹an·aer·o·bi·an \¦anə¦rōbēən; ¦a,na(a)(ə)¦r-, ¦a,ne(ə)¦r-, ¦a,nā̈ə¦r-\ *adj* [*anaerobe* + *-ian*] **:** ANAEROBIC

²anaerobian \"\ *n* -s **:** ANAEROBE

an·aer·o·bic \¦anə¦rōbik; ¦a,na(a)(ə)¦r-, ¦a,ne(ə)¦r-, ¦a,nā̈ə¦r-\ *also* **an·er·o·bic** \¦anə¦r-\ *adj* [*anaerobe* + *-ic*] **1 :** living or active in the absence of free oxygen **2 :** relating to or induced by anaerobes — **an·aer·o·bi·cal·ly** \-bək(ə)lē\ *adv*

an·aer·o·bi·on \,==¦=bē,än, ,=,=(=)ə-b-, -ēən\ *n, pl* **anaero·bia** \-bēə\ [NL, fr. ISV *anaerobe* + NL *-ion*] **:** ANAEROBE

an·aer·o·bi·ont \-bē,änt, ¦anə¦rō'bī,ä-, ¦a,na(a)rō'bī,ä-\ *n* -s [blend of *anaerobe* and *-biont*] **:** ANAEROBE

an·aer·o·bi·o·sis \,anə,rō,bī'ōsəs, ¦a,na(a)rō,b-\ *n, pl* **anaerobio·ses** \-ō,sēz\ [NL, fr. *an-* + *aer-* + *biosis*] **:** life in the absence of air or free oxygen

an·aer·o·bi·ot·ic \¦anə,rō,bī¦äd·ik, ¦a,na(a)rō,b-\ *adj* **:** ANAEROBIC — **an·aer·o·bi·ot·i·cal·ly** \-ək(ə)lē\ *adv*

an·aer·o·bi·um \,anə'rōbēəm, ,a,na(a)'r-\ *n, pl* **anaero·bia** \-ēə\ [NL, fr. ISV *anaerobe* + NL *-ium*] **:** ANAEROBE

an·aes·the·si·a *var of* ANESTHESIA

anaesthetic *var of* ANESTHETIC

anag *abbr* anagram

an·a·ga·lac·tic \¦anəgə¦laktik\ *adj* [Gk *ana-* (alter. of *an-*) + E *galactic*] **:** EXTRAGALACTIC

an·a·gal·lis \,anə'galəs\ *n* [NL, fr. L, a plant (prob. pimpernel or chickweed), fr. Gk, pimpernel] **1** *cap* **:** a genus of 15 species of chiefly Old World herbs (family Primulaceae) having mostly opposite leaves and small axillary 5-parted rotate flowers — see PIMPERNEL 2 **2** -ES **:** a plant of the genus *Anagallis*

an·a·gen·e·sis \,anə'-\ *n, pl* **anageneses** [NL, fr. *ana-* + L *genesis*] **:** REPRODUCTION, REGENERATION ⟨~ of tissue⟩ — **an·a·ge·net·ic** \¦anə¦==¦==\ *adj*

an·a·gig·nos·kom·e·na \,anə,gignə'skämənə\ *n pl* [NGk *anagignōskomena*, fr. Gk, neut. pl. of pres. pass. part. of *anagignōskein*, to know, acknowledge, read, fr. *ana-* + *gignōskein* to know, recognize — more at KNOW] *Eastern Church* **:** the Old Testament Apocrypha

an·a·glyph \'anə,glif\ *n* -s [LL *anaglyphus* wrought in low relief, embossed, fr. Gk *anaglyphos*, fr. *anaglyphein* to emboss, fr. *ana-* + *glyphein* to carve — more at CLEAVE] **1 :** any sculptured, chased, or embossed ornament worked in low relief (as a cameo) **2 :** a stereoscopic motion or still picture in which the right component of a composite image usu. red in color is superposed upon the left component in a contrasting color (as bluish green) to produce a three-dimensional effect when viewed through correspondingly colored filters in the form of spectacles

an·a·glyph·ic \¦==¦=ik\ *also* **an·a·glyph·i·cal** \-əkəl\ *adj* **:** relating to anaglyphs or anaglyphy — opposed to *diaglyphic*

an·a·glyph·ics \,anə'glifiks\ *n pl but sing in constr* [*anaglyph* + *-ics*] **:** ANAGLYPHY 1

an·a·glyph·o·scope \-fə,skōp\ *n* -s [ISV *anaglyph* + *-o-* + *-scope*] **:** a pair of spectacles for viewing an anaglyph

anag·ly·phy \ə'nagləfē, 'anə,glifē\ *n* -ES [*anaglyph* + *-y*] **1 :** art of carving, chasing, or embossing in relief **2 :** work done in relief

an·a·glyp·tic \¦anə¦gliptik\ *also* **an·a·glyp·ti·cal** \-tәkəl\ *adj* [LL *anaglypticus*, fr. L *anaglyptus* wrought in bas-relief (fr. Gk *anaglyptos, anaglyphos*) + *-icus* -ic — more at ANAGLYPHIC] **:** ANAGLYPHIC

an·a·glyp·tics \,==¦=tiks\ *n pl but sing in constr* **:** ANAGLYPHY

an·a·glyp·to·graph \-ptə,graf\ *n* -s [Gk *anaglyptos* + E *-graph*] **:** an instrument for the mechanical execution from any embossed object of an engraving giving the proper appearance of relief — **an·a·glyp·tog·ra·phy** \-,glip'tägrəfē\ *n* -ES

an·a·glyp·ton \,anə'glip,tän, -,tən\ *n* -s [Gk, neut. of *anaglyptos*] **:** ANAGLYPH

an·ag·no·ri·sis \,a,nag'nōrəsəs\ *n, pl* **anagnori·ses** \-ə,sēz\ [Gk *anagnōrisis*, fr. *anagnōrizein* to recognize, fr. *ana-* + *gnōrizein* to make known, become acquainted (fr. *gnōrimos* well-known) + *-sis* — more at GNORIMOSCHEMA] **:** RECOGNITION 1g

an·ag·nost \'a,nag,näst\ *or* **an·ag·nos·tes** \,=,='nä,stēz\ *n, pl* **anagnosts** \-sts\ *or* **anagnos·tae** \-,stī, -ē\ [LGk *anagnōstēs*, fr. Gk, reader, slave trained to read, secretary, fr. *anagignōskein* to read, fr. *ana-* + *gignōskein* to know — more at KNOW] **:** a cleric in the first of the minor orders of the Eastern Church who reads lessons aloud from the Epistles or the Old Testament in the liturgy

an·a·go·ge \'anə,gōjē *sometimes* -gäjē *or* ,==¦==\ *or* **an·a·go·gy** \'==,=\ *n, pl* **anagoges** *or* **anagogies** [LL *anagoge*, fr. LGk *anagōgē*, fr. *anagein* to spiritualize, fr. Gk, to lead up, bring up, lift up, fr. *ana-* + *agein* to lead, drive — more at AGENT] **1 :** an uplifting of the mind to spiritual things **2 :** literary interpretation that seeks to extract from language a spiritual significance; *specif* **:** exegesis that stresses what is taken to be a secret heavenly meaning in scriptural texts or a hidden reference to a future life in heaven

an·a·gog·ic \¦anə¦gäjik, -ēk\ *or* **an·a·gog·i·cal** \-jəkəl\ *adj* [*anagogic* fr. ME, fr. ML *anagogicus*, fr. LL *anagoge* + L *-icus* -ic; *anagogical* fr. *anagogic* + *-al*] **1 :** of, exemplifying, or based on anagoge; *specif* **:** having a spiritual meaning or a sense referring to the heavenly life ⟨the final or ~ meaning that transformed the symbolic object into a spiritual truth — Malcolm Cowley⟩ **2 a :** relating to or arising from the striving of inner psychic forces toward progressive or lofty ideals ⟨an ~ image⟩ **b :** relating to the psychotherapeutic interpretation of dreams and with emphasis on anagogic striving ⟨~ methods⟩ — **an·a·gog·i·cal·ly** \-jək(ə)lē, -ēk-, -li\ *adv*

¹an·a·gram \'anə,gram, -aa(ə)m\ *n* -s [prob. fr. MF *anagramme*, fr. NL *anagramma*, modif. of Gk *anagrammatismos*, fr. *anagrammatizein* to transpose letters, fr. *ana-* + *grammat-, gramma* letter + *-izein* -ize — more at GRAMMAR] **1 a :** the change of one word or phrase into another by the transposition of its letters **b :** the word or phrase made by transposing the letters of another word or phrase ⟨*rebate* is an ~ of *beater*⟩ **2** *obs* **:** MUTATION, TRANSPOSITION **3 anagrams** *pl but sing in constr* **:** a game in which words are formed by rearranging the letters of other words or by arranging letters taken at random (as printed blocks from a stock)

²anagram \"\ *vt* **anagrammed; anagrammed; anagramming; anagrams 1 :** ANAGRAMMATIZE **2 :** to rearrange (the letters of a text) in order to discover a hidden message **3 :** to attack (a transposition cipher) by moving a set of letters presumed to have related encipherments (as successive letters presumed to be from the same column of the transposition rectangle, or the letters from the same position in a number of messages) into position next to another such set, forming a tentative set of plaintext polygraphs, a promising juxtaposition being recognized by the formation of many common polygraphs and a probably wrong juxtaposition by the formation of improbable polygraphs

an·a·gram·mat·ic \¦anəgrə¦mad·ik, -atik, -ēk\ *or* **an·a·gram·mat·i·cal** \-ad·əkəl, -atək-, -ēk-\ *adj* [*anagram* + *-matic, -matical* (as in *grammatic, grammatical*)] **:** of, relating to, containing, or making an anagram — **an·a·gram·mat·i·cal·ly** \-ək(ə)lē, -ēk, -li\ *adv*

an·a·gram·ma·tism \,anə'gramə,tizəm\ *n* -s [F *anagrammatisme*, fr. Gk *anagrammatismos* — more at ANAGRAM] **:** the formation of anagrams

an·a·gram·ma·tist \-məd·əst, -mətə-\ *n* -s **:** a maker of anagrams

an·a·gram·ma·tize *or* **anagrammatise** \-mə,tīz\ *vt* -ED/-ING/-S [Gk *anagrammatizein* — more at ANAGRAM] **:** to transpose (as letters in a word) so as to form an anagram

an·a·gy·ris \,anə'jīrəs\ *n, cap* [NL, fr. Gk, alter. of *anagyros* bean trefoil, fr. *ana-* + *gyros* ring] **:** a small genus of shrubs (family Leguminosae) of the Mediterranean region having trifoliolate leaves, yellow flowers, and narrow compound pods — see BEAN TREFOIL 1

ana·hau *also* **ana·hao** \ä'nä,hau̇\ *n* -s [Tag & Hiligaynon *anahaw*] **:** a tall Philippine palm (*Livistona rotundifolia*) yielding a valuable wood used for golf clubs, a fiber used for bowstrings, and leaves used for thatching and for hats and fans

an·a·heim disease \'anə,hīm-\ *n, usu cap A* [fr. *Anaheim*, Calif.] **:** PIERCE'S DISEASE

an·a·kim \'anə,kim\ *n pl, usu cap* [Heb *'ănāqīm*, pl. of *'ănāq*] **:** aboriginal giants reported in the Old Testament to have inhabited southern Palestine before the Hebrews entered the land and virtually annihilated them

anakrousis *var of* ANACRUSIS

¹anal \'ānᵊl\ *adj* [*anus* + *-al*] **1 :** of, relating to, or situated near the anus **2 a :** of, relating to, or characterized by the phase of psychosexual development following the oral stage and during which a child is largely concerned with the products of alimentation, and his parents with his toilet training **b :** of, relating to, or characterized by those personality traits that are believed to develop from overconcentration on this phase of maturation — see ANAL CHARACTER — **anal·i·ty** \ā'nalәd·ē\ *n* -ES — **anal·ly** \-ᵊlē,-ᵊli\ *adv*

²anal \"\ *n* -s **:** an anal structure (as an anal fin or plate)

anal *abbr* **1** analogous; analogy **2** analysis; analytic

an·a·la·bos \ä'nälə,bȯs\ *n* -ES [LGk, fr. Gk *ana-* + *-labos* (fr. *lambanein* to take) — more at LATCH] **:** a cloak decorated with crosses worn by monks in the Eastern Church

anal angle *n* **:** the angle between the outer and inner margins of an insect's wing

anal area *n* **:** the posterior part of usu. the hind wing of many insects that bears the anal veins

anal canal *n* **:** the terminal section of the rectum

anal character *n* **:** a personality type characterized by a predilection for anal eroticism or by its symbolic manifestations (as excessive neatness, acquisitiveness, miserliness, self-discipline, pedantry, and obstinacy)

anal·cime \ə'nal,sēm, -īm\ *n* -s [F, fr. Gk *analkimos* weak, fr. *an-* + *alkimos* strong, fr. *alkē* strength, defense] **:** a white or slightly colored zeolite $NaAlSi_2O_6.H_2O$ occurring in certain igneous rocks massive or in isometric crystals

analcime basalt *n* **:** a variety of basalt consisting of augite, olivine, magnetite, analcite, and usu. a little feldspar

anal·ci·mite \-sə,mīt\ *n* -s [It, fr. *analcimo* analcime (fr. F *analcime*) + *-ite*] **1 :** a rock occurring in the Cyclades that orig. was probably a nephelite-syenite but is now altered and contains over 50 percent of analcime **2 :** ANALCITITE

anal·cite \ə'nal,sīt\ *n* -s [alter. (influenced by *-ite*) of *analcime*] **:** ANALCIME

anal·ci·tite \-sə,tīt\ *n* -s [*analcite* + *-ite*] **:** olivine-free analcime basalt — called also *analcimite*

an·a·lects \'anᵊl,ek(t)s\ *also* **an·a·lec·ta** \,anə'lektə\ *n pl* [L *analecta*, fr. Gk *analekta*, neut. pl. of *analektos* select, choice, fr. *analegein* to collect, fr. *ana-* + *legein* to gather, speak — more at LEGEND] **1 :** leftovers from a feast ⟨I delight in the *analecta* . . . of the preceding day's dinner —Sir Walter Scott⟩ **2 :** selected miscellaneous written passages **:** literary gleanings **:** COLLECTANEA ⟨the *Analects* of Confucius⟩

an·a·lem·ma \,anə'lemə\ *n, pl* **analemmas** \-məz\ *or* **analemma·ta** \-məd·ə\ [L, sundial on a pedestal, showing latitude and meridian, fr. Gk *analēmma* sundial, construction, support, fr. *analambanein* to take up, fr. *ana-* + *lambanein* to take — more at LATCH] **1 :** an archaic astronomical instrument of wood or brass on which an orthographic projection of the sphere is made with a movable horizon or cursor **2 :** a graduated scale shaped like a figure 8 and showing the sun's declination and the equation of time for each day of the year usu. constituting part of a sundial and often shown on terrestrial globes

an·a·lep·sis \,anə'lepsəs\ *n, pl* **analep·ses** \-(,)sēz\ [LGk *analēpsis*, fr. Gk, act of taking up, fr. *ana-* + *lēpsis* act of taking, fr. *lambanein* to take — more at LATCH] *Eastern Church* **:** the feast of Christ's ascension into heaven

¹an·a·lep·tic \¦anə¦leptik\ *adj* [Gk *analēptikos* restorative, fr. (assumed) *analēptos* (verbal of *analambanein* to take up, regain, fr. *ana-* + *lambanein* to take, seize) + *-ikos* -ic] **:** of, relating to, or acting as an analeptic

²analeptic \"\ *n* -s **:** a restorative agent; *esp* **:** a drug that acts as a stimulant on the central nervous system

anal erotic *adj* **:** marked by or related to anal eroticism

anal eroticism *or* **anal erotism** *n* **:** the experiencing of pleasurable sensations or sexual excitement associated with or symbolic of stimulation of the anus — compare ANAL CHARACTER

anal fin *n, in fishes* **:** a median unpaired fin on the lower posterior part of the body behind the vent and sometimes confluent with the caudal fin—see FISH illustration

an·al·ge·sia \,anᵊl'jēzēə, -jēzhə\ *n* -s [NL, fr. Gk *analgēsia*, fr. *an-* + *algēsis* sense of pain + *-ia*] **:** insensibility to pain without loss of consciousness

¹an·al·ge·sic \¦anᵊl¦jēzik, -ēs- *sometimes* -es-\ *adj* [ISV *analges-* (fr. NL *analgesia*) + *-ic*] **:** relating to, characterized by, or producing analgesia

²analgesic \"\ *n* -s **:** an agent for producing analgesia

analgesic balm *n* **:** an ointment containing methyl salicylate and menthol used as a rubefacient

¹an·al·ge·sid \ə'naljəsəd, ¦anᵊl¦jesəd\ *adj* [NL *Analgesidae*] **:** of or relating to the Analgesidae

²analgesid \"\ *n* -s **:** a mite of the family Analgesidae

an·al·ges·i·dae \,anᵊl'jesədē\ *n pl, cap* [NL, fr. *Analges*, type genus (fr. Gk *analgēs* painless, fr. *an-* + *-algēs*, fr. *algos* pain) + *-idae*] **:** a large family of small soft-bodied blind mites that live on birds esp. on the feathers

an·al·get·ic \¦anᵊl¦jed·ik\ *n or adj* [Gk *analgētos* without pain (fr. *an-* + (assumed) *algētos*, verbal of *algein* to suffer pain) + E *-ic* — more at ALGESIA] **:** ANALGESIC

anal gland *n* **:** any of numerous glands, occurring solitary or in pairs or groups, near the anus and sometimes opening into the rectum: as **a :** either of the paired glands of a skunk that produce an offensive secretion **b :** a gland in mollusks of the genus *Murex* that secretes a purple substance used in dyeing **c :** INK SAC

an·al·lan·to·ic \¦a,nalən-¦tōik, -a,lan-, a¦na-\ *adj* [*an-* + *allantoic*] **:** not having or not developing an allantois

an·al·lan·toi·dea \¦a,nalən'tȯidēə, -na,lan'-\ *n pl, cap* [NL, fr. *an-* + *allantois* + *-idea*] **:** the division of Vertebrata, including amphibians, fishes, and cyclostomes, in which no allantois, or at most a rudimentary one, is developed — compare AMNIOTA — **an·al·lan·toi·de·an** \-¦tȯidēən\ *adj or n*

an·al·lo·bar \(')a'nalə,bär\ *n* -s [*ana-* + *allobar*] **:** an area over which barometric pressure has increased

anal margin *n* **:** the inner margin of an insect's wing

anal membrane *n* **:** the membranous partition occluding the fetal anus **:** PROCTODAEUM

analog *var of* ANALOGUE

anal·o·gate \ə'nalə,gāt, -,gət\ *n* -s [*analogue* + *-ate*] **:** a thing, term, or concept analogized **:** ANALOGUE ⟨the First Being is the prime ~⟩

analog computer *also* **analogue computer** *n* **:** a computer that operates with numbers represented by directly measurable quantities (as voltages or rotations)

an·a·log·i·cal \¦anᵊl¦äjəkəl, -ēk-\ *also* **an·a·log·ic** \¦=¦=ik, -ēk\ *adj* [*analogy* + *-ical, -ic*] **1 a :** of, relating to, or based on analogy ⟨~ reasoning⟩ **b :** expressing or implying analogy ⟨when a country which has . . . colonies is termed the mother country the expression is *analogical* —J.S.Mill⟩ **2** *archaic* **:** having analogy **:** ANALOGOUS — **an·a·log·i·cal·ly** \-jək(ə)lē, -ēk-, -li\ *adv*

ana·lo·gi·on \,änə,lō'yē,ȯn, -ə'lō,yȯn\ *n, pl* **analo·gia** \-,lō'yē-,ä,-'lō,yä\ *or* **analogions** [Gk *analogeion* reading desk, fr. *analegesthai* to read through, fr. *ana-* + *legein* to gather, speak — more at LEGEND] **:** a stand on which choir singers in the Eastern Church keep their books

anal·o·gism \ə'nalə,jizəm\ *n* -s [*analogy* + *-ism*] **:** reasoning by analogy ⟨investigates the philosophies of Aristotle and . . . rejects it as ~ —L.A.Foley⟩

anal·o·gist \-,jəst\ *n* -s [*analogy* + *-ist*] **1 :** one who searches for or reasons from analogies **2 :** an adherent of the view held by certain Greek grammarians of the 2d century B.C. that language is based on correspondence between word and idea — opposed to *anomalist*

anal·o·gize \-,jīz\ *vb* -ED/-ING/-S [*analogy* + *-ize*] *vi* **1 :** to make use of analogy esp. in reasoning ⟨~s effectively in debate⟩ **2 :** to show analogy ~ *vt* **:** to make analogous **:** bring into analogy ⟨~s nature to the crafts —Austin Warren⟩

anal·o·gon \-ˌgän, -ˌgən\ *n, pl* **analo·ga** \-ˌgə\ [Gk, fr. neut. of *analogos*] **:** ANALOGUE

anal·o·gous \əˈnaləgəs\ *adj* [L *analogus*, fr. Gk *analogos* according to a due ratio, proportionate, fr. *ana-* + *logos* ratio, thought, word, fr. *legein* to gather, speak — more at LEGEND] **1 :** showing an analogy or a likeness permitting one to draw an analogy **:** susceptible of comparison either in general or in some specific detail ⟨the doctrines of symbolism were . . . ~ to the doctrines of romanticism —Edmund Wilson⟩ **2 a :** having a similar function but differing in structure and origin ⟨the wings of a bird and those of an airplane are ~⟩ **b** *in commerce* **:** showing similar characteristics (as bulk, weight, or value) ⟨~ articles likewise given special handling⟩ **3** *of colors* **:** having a close relationship with respect to hue **syn** see LIKE

analogously *adv* **:** by or according to analogy

analogous pole *n* **:** the pole of a crystal that becomes positively electrified when the crystal is heated

an·a·logue \ˈanᵊlˌóg *also* -äg\ *also* **an·a·log** \"\ *n* -S [F *analogue*, fr. *analogue* analogous, fr. Gk *analogos*] **1 :** anything that is analogous or similar to something else **:** PARALLEL ⟨he would relate the poem to earlier sources and ~*s* —C.W. Shumaker⟩ **2 a :** an organ similar in function to an organ of another animal or plant but different in structure and origin ⟨the gill of a fish is the ~ of the lung of a cat⟩ — distinguished from *homologue* **b :** a species in one group corresponding in some particular characters with a member of another group **c :** a species or genus in one country that is closely related to a species of the same genus or a genus of the same group in another country **3 :** a previous weather chart that in its main features resembles the current weather chart

analogue computer *var of* ANALOG COMPUTER

anal·o·gy \əˈnaləjē, -ji\ *n* -ES [prob. fr. Gk *analogia* mathematical proportion, correspondence, fr. *analogos* proportionate + *-ia* -y] **1 a :** mathematical proportion or ratios (as in a statement of the form $a \times b = c \times d$ where the values of *a*, *b*, and *c* are given, so that *d* may be calculated) **b :** a proposition or a statement that embodies such an analogy **2 a :** similarity of ratios or of properties **b :** inference that if two or more things agree with one another in one or more respects they will prob. agree in yet other respects ⟨scholasticism distinguished between *analogies* of proportionality, *analogies* by attribution, and *analogies* by metaphor⟩ **3 :** resemblance in some particulars between things otherwise unlike **:** SIMILARITY, CORRESPONDENCE, PARALLELISM ⟨mathematicians have . . . appealed to the arts in order to find some ~ to their own work —Havelock Ellis⟩ ⟨enameled bowls . . . show *analogies* . . . with late twelfth century English illumination —O. Elfrida Saunders⟩ **4 a :** ANALOGUE **b :** a figure of speech embodying an extended or elaborate comparison between two things or situations **:** SIMILITUDE **5 :** correspondence between the members of pairs or sets of linguistic forms that is taken as a basis for the creation of another form (as *reindeers*, plural of *reindeer*, created on the basis of such pairs as *bear, bears* or *dog, dogs; cows*, plural of *cow*, replacing earlier *kine* and *kye*, on the basis of such pairs as *bough, boughs; glided*, past tense of *glide*, replacing earlier *glode* and *glid*, on the basis of such pairs as *guide, guided; a deck of cigarettes*, standing in the same synonymous relationship to *a pack of cigarettes* as *a deck of cards* does to *a pack of cards*) **6** [F *analogie*, fr. Gk *analogia*] **:** correspondence in function between organs or parts of different structure and origin — distinguished from *homology*

analogy test *n* **:** a reasoning test requiring a person examined to supply a final term in a proportion (as to supply *darkness* in the proportion *day: light:: night:* . . .)

an·al·pha·bet \(ˈ)aˈnalfəˌbet *also* -ˌbət\ *n* -S [Gk *analphabētos* not knowing the alphabet, fr. *an-* + *alphabētos* alphabet — more at ALPHABET] **:** one who cannot read **:** ILLITERATE

¹an·al·pha·bet·ic \ˌaˌnalfəˈbed·ik, aˈn-\ *adj* [*analphabet* + *-ic*] **1 :** ILLITERATE **2** [*an-* + *alphabetic*] **:** not alphabetic; *specif, of a system of phonetic transcription* **:** representing each sound by a set of three symbols indicating respectively the articulating organs, place of articulation, and size and form of aperture

²analphabetic \"\ *n* -S **:** one who cannot read **:** ILLITERATE ⟨these . . . humble ~*s* . . . have left us no record —Norman Douglas⟩

an·al·pha·bet·ism \(ˈ)aˈnal-\ *n* -S **:** an analphabetic phonetic system

anal pit *n* **:** the posterior terminal depression of the primitive streak of the embryo

anal plate *n* **1 a :** one of the posterior plates of the plastron of a turtle **b :** the large scale in front of the anus of most snakes **2 :** the fused plate of early embryonic ectoderm and endoderm through which the anus later ruptures

anal proleg *n* **:** either of the pair of false legs occurring on the 10th abdominal segment of caterpillars

anals *pl of* ANAL

anal sadism *n* **:** a level of personality development characterized by preoccupation with pleasant sensations arising from fecal retention or by its symbolic manifestations (as power and cruelty) — compare ANAL CHARACTER

anal–sadistic \ˌ≈≈≈ˈ≈≈\ *adj* **:** relating to anal sadism ⟨see such grotesque behavior as a fierce perversion of the life instincts into *anal-sadistic* aggressiveness —Theodore Roszak⟩

anal sphincter *n* **:** either of two sphincters controlling the closing of the vertebrate anus: **a :** an outer sphincter of striated muscle extending from the coccyx to the central tendinous part of the perineum and surrounding the anus immediately beneath the skin — called also *external anal sphincter* **b :** an inner sphincter formed by thickening of the circular smooth muscle of the rectum — called also *internal anal sphincter*

anal vein *n* **:** one of the three posterior veins of the wing of a primitive insect

anal·y·sand \əˈnaləˌsand, -ˌza-\ *n* -S [*analyse* + *-and* (as in *multiplicand*)] **:** one that is analyzed; *specif* **:** one who is undergoing psychoanalysis

anal·y·san·dum \≈,≈≈ˈ≈əm\ *n, pl* **analysan·da** \-ə\ [NL, fr. *analysis* + L *-andum* (gerundive suffix)] **:** something that is to be analyzed or defined

anal·y·sans \≈ˈ≈≈,sanz, -ˌza-\ *n, pl* **analysans** [NL, fr. *analysis* + L *-ans* (part. suffix)] **:** something that serves to analyze or define

¹an·a·lyse *chiefly Brit var of* ANALYZE

²analyse *n* -S [F, fr. Gk *analysis*] *obs* **:** ANALYSIS

anal·y·sis \əˈnaləsəs\ *n, pl* **analy·ses** \-əˌsēz\ [NL, fr. Gk, fr. *analyein* to dissolve (fr. *ana-* + *lyein* to loosen, dissolve) + *-sis* — more at LOSE] **1 :** separation or breaking up of a whole into its fundamental elements or component parts ⟨his problem defied ~⟩ **2 a :** a detailed examination of anything complex (as a novel, an organization, a race) made in order to understand its nature or to determine its essential features **:** a thorough study ⟨the ~ . . . of the structure of a poem can be a form of literary criticism —James Thorpe⟩ **b :** the presentation, usu. in writing, of such an analysis ⟨each chapter of the book is an ~ of a well-known painting⟩ **3 :** the use of function words (as prepositions, pronouns, and auxiliary verbs) instead of inflectional forms as a highly frequent and characteristic device in the structure of a language (as English *I have seen* contrasted with Latin *vidi* or English *of the room* tending to replace *the room's* or *does he know that?* replacing *knows he that?*) — contrasted with *synthesis* **4 a :** the separation of compound substances into their constituents by chemical processes **b :** the determination, which may or may not involve actual separation, of one or more ingredients of a substance either as to kind or amount; *also* **:** the tabulated result of such a determination — see GRAVIMETRIC ANALYSIS, PROXIMATE ANALYSIS, QUALITATIVE ANALYSIS, QUANTITATIVE ANALYSIS, ULTIMATE ANALYSIS **c :** a statement of the amount or percent of each functional ingredient present in a mixture (as a vitamin solution or an animal feed); *often* **:** a statement of the percentage of nitrogen expressed as N, phosphoric acid as P_2O_5, and potash as K_2O in a fertilizer — called also *fertilizer analysis, fertilizer grade* **5 a :** the practice of proving a mathematical proposition by assuming the result and reasoning back to the data or to already established principles **b :** the investigation of a problem by the methods of algebra **c :** any proof based on considerations of number and the theory of limits, as opposed to geometric intuition **d :** the differential and integral calculus **6 a :** the resolution of knowledge into its fundamental factors or original principles and the tracing or reduction of physical, phenomenal, or abstract entities to their source or elements **b :** the elucidation, clarification, and explication of expressions and statements through a determination of their meaning or logical use **7 :** the process of ascertaining the name of a species in biology or its place in a system of classification by means of an analytical table or key **8 :** PSYCHOANALYSIS **9 :** BOWLING ANALYSIS — **in the final analysis** *or* **in the last analysis :** everything having been taken into consideration ⟨it is the individual who is responsible, *in the last analysis*, for all additions to culture —L.A.White⟩ ⟨the lower grades of glue, while they may give satisfactory results, may not always be the cheapest *in the final analysis —Bindery Glues*⟩

analysis si·tus \-ˈsīd·əs, -ˈsē-\ *n* [NL, analysis of situation] **:** TOPOLOGY 3

an·a·lyst \ˈanᵊləst\ *n* -S [prob. fr. *analyze*, after such pairs as E *Latinize: Latinist*] **:** a person who analyzes or who is skilled in analysis: as **a :** one whose occupation is the making of analyses of the chemical, physical, or other properties of a substance or product **b :** a columnist or commentator who specializes in interpreting social and political developments **c :** PSYCHOANALYST **d :** STATISTICIAN

¹an·a·lyt·ic \ˌanᵊlˈid·ik, -itik, -ēk\ *adj* [LL *analyticus*, fr. Gk *analytikos*, fr. (assumed) *analytos* (verbal of *analyein*) + *-ikos* -ic] **1 :** of or relating to analysis or analytics; *esp* **:** separating or breaking up a whole or a compound into its component parts or constituent elements ⟨an ~ experiment⟩ ⟨~ reasoning⟩ **2 :** skilled in or using analysis ⟨a keenly ~ man⟩ **3** *logic* **:** of or relating to a truth, a proposition, or a statement that is true in all possible worlds, that is true independently of any facts by reference to meanings alone, or that is logically true or definitionally reducible to logical truth **4 :** characterized by analysis (sense 3) rather than inflection ⟨English is an ~ language⟩ — contrasted with *synthetic;* compare ISOLATING **5 :** PSYCHOANALYTIC **6 :** treated by the methods or represented by the symbolism of algebra or calculus ⟨~ statics⟩ — distinguished from *graphic*

²analytic \"\ *n* -S **1 :** something that is analytic **2 :** ANALYTICAL ENTRY

an·a·lyt·i·cal \-ə̇kəl, -ēk-\ *adj* [LL *analyticus* + E *-al*] **1 :** ANALYTIC **2** *of cubist art* **:** involving the breakdown of a natural subject into component planes and geometric forms — **an·a·lyt·i·cal·ly** \-ə̇k(ə)lē, -ēk-, -li\ *adv*

analytical balance *n* **:** a balance of precision used esp. in quantitative chemical analysis

analytical chemistry *n* **:** the branch of chemistry that deals with analysis

analytical entry *n* **:** an entry in a library catalog that locates a specific part of a more general work or collection (as the treatment of one specific subject in a book)

analytical jurisprudence *n* **:** the study and examination of law in terms of its logical structure

analytical note *n* **:** the information at an analytical entry that locates the source of that analytical entry

analytical table *n* **:** KEY 3c

analytic geometry *n* **:** a branch of mathematics that studies geometric properties by means of arithmetic and algebraic operations upon symbols defined in terms of a coordinate system — called also *coordinate geometry*

4 2 3 4 1 5 6 6

analytical balance: *1* handle to move rider, *3*, on beam, *2; 4, 4* knife edges; *5* pointer; *6, 6* scalepans

an·a·ly·tic·i·ty \ˌanᵊlə̇ˈtisəd·ē\ *n* -ES **:** the nature, character, or property of being analytic

analytic judgment *n, logic* **:** a judgment in which what is predicated is already implied in the subject of the predication — opposed to *synthetic judgment*

analytic mechanics *n* **:** theoretical mechanics esp. as treated by the methods of infinitesimal calculus

analytic psychology *n* **1 :** the analysis and classification of mental data (as sensations and feelings) esp. by introspection — contrasted with *experimental psychology* **2 :** a modification of psychoanalysis that adds to the concept of the personal unconscious by postulating a racial or collective unconscious, that objects to a narrowly sexual interpretation of libido, and that advocates that psychotherapy be conducted in terms of the patient's present-day conflicts and maladjustments rather than in terms of his early psychosexual development

an·a·lyt·ics \ˌanᵊlˈid·iks, -iti-\ *n pl but sing in constr* **:** the science of analysis esp. as a subdivision of logic

analytic trigonometry *n* **:** the branch of trigonometry that treats of the relations and properties of the trigonometrical functions

an·a·lyz·a·ble \ˈanᵊlˌīzəbəl\ *adj* **:** admitting or capable of being analyzed ⟨the . . . data into which he believed things are ~ —Ernest Nagel⟩

an·a·ly·za·tion \ˌanᵊləˈzāshən, -ˌīˈz-\ *n* -S **:** ANALYSIS

an·a·lyze \ˈanᵊlˌīz\ *vb* -ED/-ING/-S *see -ize in Explan Notes* [prob. irreg. fr. *analysis* + *-ize*] *vt* **1 a :** to ascertain the components of or separate into component parts **:** determine carefully the fundamental elements of (as by separation or isolation) for close scrutiny and examination of constituents or for accurate resolution of an overall structure or nature ⟨in the laboratory . . . we were required to ~ specimens —V.G. Heiser⟩ **:** subject to analysis **b :** to determine by mental discernment the nature, significance, and relationship of the various parts, elements, aspects, or qualities of (whatever is under consideration) ⟨Balzac . . . *analyzed* a society in which human existence was no longer possible —P.F.Drucker⟩ **2 :** to weigh or study (various aspects, factors, or elements) in order to arrive at an answer, result, or solution ⟨constantly tries to ~ the motives for his own behavior —*Midwest Jour.*⟩ **3 a :** to determine one or more chemical ingredients of **:** examine by chemical analysis ⟨~ cast iron for phosphorus⟩ **b :** to show or yield on chemical analysis ⟨a slag that ~*s* 25 percent silica⟩ **4 :** to divide (as a sentence) into parts and indicate the relation of each part to the other parts or to the whole **5 :** to make an analytical entry for **6 :** PSYCHOANALYZE ~ *vi* **:** to engage in analysis

syn RESOLVE, BREAK (*down*), DISSECT, ANATOMIZE: ANALYZE is likely to suggest ascertainment of components, sometimes by physical separation of those components, in the interests of determining a thing's nature or structure or the relationship of its parts ⟨he would make a plate or a fork or a bell, set it to ringing by a blow, and *analyze* the combination of musical notes which it emitted —K.K.Darrow⟩ It may suggest a scientific or objective attitude ⟨a cultured person, therefore, regards Nature with what might be called a Goethean, rather than a Newtonian, eye. He trains himself to see and to feel, rather than to *analyze* or to explain —J.C.Powys⟩ In more complex matters it involves ascertainment and individual scrutiny of aspects, traits, characteristics, qualities ⟨Gard was much struck. It never occurred to him to *analyze* the people that he loved —Mary Austin⟩ RESOLVE is likely to stress the fact of change of form, of metamorphosis, rather than necessarily indicating division into components, through some process or chain of effects ⟨one inseparable drop, crystallized beyond change . . ., nor *resolved* by any alchemy —W.H. Hudson⟩ ⟨labor measures the value not only of that part of price which *resolves* itself into labor, but of that which *resolves* itself into rent, and of that which *resolves* itself into profit —Adam Smith⟩ ⟨nothing but death was strong enough to shatter that inherited restraint and *resolve* it into tenderness —Ellen Glasgow⟩ BREAK (*down*) suggests classifying, itemizing, subgrouping, or other treatment of specific, individual component items for clarity or convenience ⟨an overall figure of 1,623,404. There was no attempt to *break* this *down* into dead, wounded, and missing —*N.Y.Times*⟩ DISSECT suggests laying bare parts, pieces, or relationships under consideration or actually severing them for individual scrutiny, as with a scalpel ⟨when I speak of *dissecting* atoms or *dissecting* matter, I refer to the fact that we can draw negative electricity out of every substance which there is —K.K.Darrow⟩ ⟨to understand Elizabethan drama it is necessary to study a dozen playwrights at once, to *dissect* with all care the complex growth —T.S.Eliot⟩ ⟨a complicated record must be *dissected*, the narratives of witnesses, more or less incoherent and unintelligible, must be analyzed —B.N.Cardozo⟩ ANATOMIZE differs from DISSECT chiefly in suggesting even more meticulous innate scrutiny, often of character traits ⟨his colleagues also are vividly described and *anatomized* — with a few brush strokes to show us their outsides, and a few scalpel thrusts to expose their insides —Robert Halsband⟩ ⟨Thoreau could *anatomize* the professional reformer as amusingly as Dickens —Laurence Stapleton⟩

an·a·lyz·er \-zə(r)\ *n* -S **:** one that analyzes: as **a :** the part of a polariscope that receives the light after polarization and exhibits the properties of light **b :** a combined ammeter, voltmeter, and ohmmeter designed for testing electronic equipment **c :** the part of an absorption or gas refrigeration apparatus in which the ammonia vapor escapes from the recently heated solution and passes on to be liquefied in the condensing coils — compare ABSORPTION SYSTEM

an·a·mir·ta \ˌanəˈmərd·ə\ *n, cap* [NL, prob. fr. *an-* + Skt *amṛtā*, a plant (slightly different from *Anamirta*), fr. *amṛta* immortal] **:** a genus of East Indian woody vines (family Menispermaceae) having dioecious flowers and very numerous stamens — see COCCULUS INDICUS

an·a·mite \ˈanəˌmīt\ *n* -S [origin unknown] **:** TWINE 5

an·am·ne·sis \ˌanəmˈnēsə̇s, ˌaˌnam-\ *n, pl* **anamne·ses** \-ēˌsēz\ [NL, fr. Gk *anamnēsis*, fr. *anamimnēskein* to remind (fr. *ana-* + *mimnēskein* to remind) + *-sis* — more at MIND] **1 :** a recalling to mind **:** REMINISCENCE ⟨in only one sense is *B.F.'s Daughter* a departure from the author's previous *anamneses* —John Woodburn⟩ **2 :** information concerning a medical or psychiatric patient and his background for use in analyzing his condition — compare CATAMNESIS, FOLLOW-UP **3** *often cap* **:** the eucharistic prayer recalling the sacrifice of Christ and ending with the words "Do this in remembrance of me"

an·am·nes·tic \ˌ≈≈ˈnestik\ *adj* [Gk *anamnēstikos* easily recalled, fr. *anamnēstos* capable of being recalled (fr. *anamimnēskein*) + *-ikos* -ic] **:** of or relating to anamnesis — **an·am·nes·ti·cal·ly** \-tə̇k(ə)lē\ *adv*

anamnestic reaction *n* **:** renewed rapid production of an antibody following second or later contact with the provoking antigen or with related antigens

an·am·ni·on·ic \(ˌ)aˌnamnēˈänik, aˌn-\ *adj* [*an-* + *amnionic*] **:** not developing an amnion

an·am·ni·o·ta \-nēˈōd·ə\ *also* **an·am·nia** \(ˈ)aˈnamnēə\ *or* **an·am·ni·a·ta** \ˌaˌnamnēˈäd·ə, aˌn-, -ˈād·ə\ *or* **an·am·ni·o·na·ta** \-nēəˈnäd·ə, -ād·ə\ *n pl, cap* [*Anamniota*, NL, fr. *an-* + *Amniota; Anamnia*, NL, fr. *an-* + *amnia*, pl. of *amnion; Anamniata, Anamnionata*, NL fr. *an-* + *amnion* + *-ata*] **:** vertebrates that develop no amnion regarded as a natural group — **an·am·ni·ote** \(ˈ)aˈnamnēˌōt\ *adj or n* — **an·am·ni·ot·ic** \ˌaˌnamnēˈäd·ik, aˌn-\ *adj*

an·a·mor·pha \ˌanəˈmȯrfə\ *n pl, cap* [NL, fr. *ana-* + *-morpha*] **:** a division (commonly considered a subclass) of Chilopoda comprising the centipedes whose number of body segments increases as the animals mature, the young hatching with 7 pairs of legs and the adults having 15 pairs — compare EPIMORPHA, NOTOSTIGMA, PLEUROSTIGMA

an·a·mor·phic \ˌ≈≈ˈfik\ *adj* [*anamorph*ism + *-ic*] **1 :** characterized by progressive complexity or changing to a form of greater complexity **:** exhibiting or relating to anamorphosis **2 :** producing or having different magnification of the image in each of two perpendicular meridians — used of an optical device or the image formed by one

anamorphic zone *n* **:** the zone within the earth in which simple mineralogical compounds become changed by silication, decarbonization, and deoxidation to more complex ones

an·a·mor·phism \ˌ≈≈ˈfizəm\ *n* -S [*ana-* + *-morphism*] **1 :** ANAMORPHOSIS 2 **2 :** the group of changes that rocks undergo in the anamorphic zone or the group of processes that effect the change — compare KATAMORPHISM, METAMORPHISM

an·a·mor·pho·scope \-ˌfəˌskōp\ *n* -S [*anamorphosis* + *-scope*] **:** an optical device consisting usu. of a cylindrical mirror or lens that restores to its normal proportions an image distorted by anamorphosis

an·a·mor·phose \-ˌfōz, -ōs\ *vt* -ED/-ING/-S [back-formation fr. *anamorphosis*] **:** to represent by anamorphosis

an·a·mor·phos·er \-ˌfōzər, -ˌfōs-, -ˌfə-\ *n* -S **:** an optical device used to form a sharply defined image having a different magnification in each of two perpendicular meridians, usu. vertical and horizontal

an·a·mor·pho·sis \ˌanəˈmȯrfəsə̇s *sometimes* -ˌmȯrˈfō-\ *n, pl* **anamorpho·ses** \-ˌsēz\ [MGk *anamorphōsis*, fr. LGk *anamorphoun* to transform (fr. Gk *ana-* + *morphoun* to form, fr. *morphē* shape) + Gk *-sis* — more at FORM] **1 a :** an image produced by a distorting optical system or by some other method that renders the image unrecognizable unless viewed by the proper restoring device **b :** the process of making such distorted images **2 :** a gradually ascending progression or change of form from one type to another in the evolution of a group of animals or plants; *esp* **:** the acquisition in certain arthropods of additional body segments after hatching

an·a·mor·phote lens \ˌanəˌmȯrˌfōt-\ *n* [LGk *anamorphōtēs* transforming, fr. *anamorphoun* to transform] **:** a distorting lens used to produce anamorphosis — compare ANAMORPHOSCOPE

an·a·mor·phot·ic \-ˌmȯrˈfäd·ik\ *adj* [LGk *anamorphōtēs* transforming + E *-ic*] **:** ANAMORPHIC

anan \əˈnan\ *dial var of* ²ANON

ana·nas *in sense 1* ˈanəˌnas, əˈnanəs; *in sense 2* ˌanəˈnäs *or* ˈän-\ *n* [F or Sp: F, fr. Sp *ananás*, fr. Pg. modif. of Guarani *naná*] **1** *cap* **:** a small genus of tropical American plants (family Bromeliaceae) having basal sword-shaped leaves, terminal racemose flowers, and large syncarpous fruits — see PINEAPPLE **2** *also* **ana·na** \ˌanəˈnä, ˈän-\ *pl* **ananas** \"\ *n* -S **:** any of several plants of the family Bromeliaceae: as **a :** PINEAPPLE **b :** PINGUIN

an·a·ni·as \ˌanəˈnīəs\ *n* -ES *usu cap* [after *Ananias*, an early Christian who, according to Acts 5:1-11, was struck dead for lying to the Apostle Peter] **:** LIAR

ana·ni·no \əˈnänyēˌnō, -ˈnäˌnə-\ *adj, usu cap* [fr. *Ananino*, town in the Kirov region, U.S.S.R., its type station] **:** of or belonging to a culture of east central Europe transitional between the Bronze and Iron ages and possibly ancestral to the culture of the early Volga Finns

an·an·ism \ˈanəˌnizəm, əˈnäˌn-\ *n* -S *usu cap* [*Anan* ben David, 8th cent. Jewish religious leader in Persia + E *-ism*] **:** Karaism as taught by Anan ben David

an·an·kas·tic *also* **an·an·cas·tic** \ˌananˈkastik, ˌaˌnanˈ-, ˌaˌnanˈ-\ *adj* [Gk *anankastikos* compulsory, fr. *anankastos* forced (fr. *anankē*) + *-ikos* -ic] **:** of, relating to, or arising from compulsion esp. in an obsessive or compulsive neurosis

anan·ke \əˈnaŋ(ˌ)kē, -anˌkē\ *n* -S *usu cap* [Gk *Anankē*, fr. *anankē* necessity; akin to OIr *écen* necessity, need, W *angen*, Corn & Bret *anken*] *Greek relig* **:** a personification of compelling necessity or ultimate fate to which even the gods must yield

an·a·nym \ˈanəˌnim\ *n* -S [*ana-* + *-nym* (as in *anonym*)] **:** a pseudonym consisting of the real name written backwards ⟨*Elberp* is the ~ of *Preble*⟩

anapa·ite \əˈnapəˌīt\ *n* -S [G *anapait*, fr. *Anapa*, seaport on Black sea, U.S.S.R., its locality + G *-it* -ite] **:** a calcium ferrous iron hydrous phosphate occurring in pale-green transparent triclinic crystals and in columnar massive forms (hardness 3–4, sp. gr. 3.81)

an·a·pest *or* **an·a·paest** \ˈanəˌpest, *esp Brit* -ēst\ *n* -S [L *anapaestus*, fr. Gk *anapaistos*, lit., struck back (a dactyl reversed), fr. (assumed) *anapaiein* to strike back (whence LGk *anapaiein*), fr. *ana-* + *paiein* to strike] **1 :** a metrical foot of three syllables the first two being unstressed and the last being stressed (as in Lord Byron's "and his cohorts were gleaming in purple and gold") or the first two being short and the last being long (as in classical prosody) **:** a trisyllabic rising cadence — symbol ⌣ ⌣ – or oó6; compare DACTYL **2 :** a verse written in anapests

[1]**an·a·pes·tic** *or* **an·a·paes·tic** \¦==¦=tik\ *adj* [LL *anapaesticus*, fr. Gk *anapaistikos*, fr. *anapaistos* + *-ikos* -ic] **:** relating to or consisting of anapests — **an·a·pes·ti·cal·ly** \-tək(ə)lē\ *adv*

[2]**anapestic** *or* **anapaestic** *n* -s **:** an anapestic foot or line

anaph·a·lis \ə'nafələs\ *n, cap* [NL] **:** a genus of herbs (family Compositae) of north temperate regions having canescent foliage and small discoid heads of dioecious flowers — see PEARLY EVERLASTING

an·a·phase \'anə,fāz\ *n* -s [ISV *ana* + *phase;* orig. formed in G] **:** the stage of mitosis in which the chromosome halves move towards the poles of the spindle — **an·a·phas·ic** \¦==¦=zik\ *adj*

anaph·o·ra \ə'naf(ə)rə, *in sense 2* " *or* ,änəfə'rä\ *n* -s [LL, fr. LGk, fr. Gk, act of carrying up, ascent, offering, fr. *anapherein* to carry up, fr. *ana-* + *pherein* to carry — more at BEAR] **1 a :** repetition of a word or words at the beginning of two or more successive clauses or verses esp. for rhetorical or poetic effect **b :** use of a grammatical substitute to refer to a preceding word or group of words (as use of *does* in place of *dances* in "Mary dances better than June does") **2** [LGk, fr. Gk, offering] *often cap, Eastern Church* **a :** a eucharistic prayer of consecration in the divine liturgy **b :** the portion of the liturgy in which the eucharistic elements are offered as an oblation **c :** the eucharistic oblation — **anaph·o·ral** \ə'naf(ə)rəl\ *adj*

an·a·phor·ic \¦anə¦fórik, -är-\ *adj* [*anaphora* + *-ic*] **:** referring to a preceding word or group of words ⟨the ~ pronoun *one* in "I prefer a big bun to a little one"⟩ ⟨the ~ verb *do* in "act as we do"⟩ — **an·a·phor·i·cal·ly** \-rək(ə)lē\ *adv*

anaph·o·thrips \ə'nafə,thrips\ *n, cap* [NL] **:** a widely distributed genus of thrips including species destructive to many wild and cultivated grasses

an·aph·ro·di·sia \¦a,nafrə'dizh(ē)ə, a,n-\ *n* -s [NL, fr. *an-* + *aphrodisia*] **:** absence or impairment of sexual desire

[1]**an·aph·ro·dis·i·ac** \¦a,nafrə¦dizē,ak, a¦n-\ *adj* [*an-* + *aphrodisiac*] **:** of, relating to, or causing anaphrodisia

[2]**anaphrodisiac** \"\ *n* -s **:** an anaphrodisiac agent

an·a·phy·lac·tic \¦anəfə¦laktik\ *adj* [fr. NL *anaphylaxis*, after such pairs as NL *prophylaxis:* E *prophylactic*] **:** of, relating to, affected by, or accompanying anaphylaxis — **an·a·phy·lac·ti·cal·ly** \-tək(ə)lē\ *adv*

anaphylactic shock *n* **:** a state of shock in an anaphylactic animal resulting from injection or more rarely ingestion of sensitizing antigen or hapten and due mainly to contraction of smooth muscle and increased capillary permeability caused by release in the tissues and circulation of histamine, heparin, and perhaps acetylcholine and serotonin

an·a·phy·lac·tin \,anəfə'laktən\ *n* -s [*anaphylactic* + *-in*] **:** an antibody held to produce anaphylaxis — called also *sensibilisin*

an·a·phy·lac·to·gen \-təjən\ *n* -s [ISV *anaphylactic* + *-o-* + *-gen*] **:** any substance capable of producing a condition of anaphylaxis — **an·a·phy·lac·to·gen·ic** \¦===,=tə¦jenik\ *adj*

an·a·phy·lac·toid \¦===¦=,tóid\ *adj* [ISV *anaphylactic* + *-oid*] **:** resembling anaphylaxis

an·a·phyl·a·tox·in \,anə,filə'täksən\ *n* -s [ISV *anaphyla-* (fr. NL *anaphylaxis*) + *toxin*] **:** a hypothetical substance formerly regarded as responsible for the symptoms of anaphylaxis

an·a·phy·lax·is \,anəfə'laksəs\ *n, pl* **anaphylax·es** \-k,sēz\ [NL, fr. *ana-* + *-phylaxis* (as in *prophylaxis*)] **1 :** hypersensitivity (as to foreign proteins or drugs) that is marked by a tendency to intense systemic reaction and that results from specific sensitization following one or more usu. parenteral contacts with a sensitizing agent and seen chiefly in experimental animals but manifested in man in acute serum sickness and in severe or fatal reactions to second or later administrations of certain drugs (as penicillin) **2 :** ANAPHYLACTIC SHOCK

an·a·pla·sia \,anə'plāzh(ē)ə\ *n* -s [NL, fr. *ana-* + *-plasia*] **:** reversion of cells or tissues to a more primitive, embryonic, or undifferentiated form often with increased capacity for multiplication (as in a malignant tumor) — **an·a·plas·tic** \¦==¦plastik\ *adj*

an·a·plasm \'anə,plazəm\ *n* -s [NL *anaplasma*] **:** ANAPLASMA 2; *specif* **:** a marginal body

an·a·plas·ma \,anə'plazmə\ *n* [NL, fr. *ana-* + *-plasma*] **1** *cap* **:** a genus of microorganisms that are found in the red blood cells of ruminants, resemble small masses of chromatin without cytoplasm, are transmitted by ticks and other biting arthropods, cause anaplasmosis, and are now usu. considered to constitute a family of rickettsias though sometimes esp. formerly considered sporozoans related to *Babesia* **2** *pl* **anaplasma·ta** \-məd·ə\ *or* **anaplasmas :** an organism of the genus *Anaplasma*

an·a·plas·mo·sis \,==,='mōsəs\ *n, pl* **anaplasmo·ses** \-ō,sēz\ [NL, fr. *Anaplasma* + *-osis*] **:** infection with organisms of the genus *Anaplasma; specif* **:** a disease of cattle transmitted by ticks and showing symptoms like those of Texas fever except that blood does not tinge the urine

an·a·pol·y·sis \,anə'päləsəs\ *n, pl* **anapoly·ses** \-ə,sēz\ [NL, fr. *an-* + *apolysis*] **:** the retention of ripe proglottids throughout life (as in most pseudophyllidean tapeworms) — compare APOLYSIS — **an·apo·lyt·ic** \(')a¦napə¦lid·ik, ¦anəp-\ *adj*

an·ap·o·phys·i·al \¦a,napə¦fizēəl, a¦n-\ *adj* [NL *anapophysis* + E *-al*] **:** of or relating to an anapophysis

an·a·poph·y·sis \,anə'päfəsəs\ *n, pl* **anapophy·ses** \-ə,sēz\ [NL, fr. *ana-* + *apophysis*] **:** a small process arising at the dorsal side of the base of the transverse process of the lumbar vertebrae in man and many other mammals

an·a·pro·tas·pis \,anəprō'taspəs\ *n, pl* **anaprotas·pes** \-ta,spēz\ [NL, fr. *ana-* + *protaspis*] **:** an early protaspis with but six segments all of which are incorporated in the cephalon of the adult trilobite

an·ap·sid \ə'napsəd\ *adj* [NL *Anapsida*] **:** of, belonging to, or like that of the Anapsida

an·ap·si·da \-sədə\ *n pl, cap* [NL, fr. *an-* + *-apsida* (fr. Gk *apsid-, apsis* mesh, loop, net)] **:** a subclass of Reptilia comprising primitive forms in which the skull lacks temporal openings and including chiefly Permian forms with the turtles as its only present representatives

an·ap·to·mor·phus \ə,naptə'mórfəs, a,-\ *n, cap* [NL, fr. *an-* + Gk *haptein* to bind + NL *-o-* + *-morphus* -morphous] **:** a genus (the type of the family Anaptomorphidae) of extinct short-skulled large-eyed lemurs from the Eocene of No. America sometimes regarded as near the ancestral line of the anthropoids

an·ap·tyc·tic \¦anəp¦tiktik, ¦a,nap-\ *also* **an·ap·tyc·ti·cal** \-ktəkəl\ *adj* [fr. NL *anaptyxis*, after such pairs as LL *syntaxis* syntax: E *syntactic, syntactical*] **:** relating to or resulting from anaptyxis ⟨development of an ~ vowel⟩

an·ap·tyx·is \,a,(,)ə'tiksəs\ *n, pl* **anaptyx·es** \-k,sēz\ [NL, fr. Gk *anaptyxis* act of unfolding, fr. *anaptyssein* to unfold, fr. *ana-* + *ptyssein* to fold] **:** vowel epenthesis

ana·qua \ə'näkwə\ *n* -s [MexSp *anacua, anagua*] **:** a tree (*Ehretia elliptica*) of Mexico and southern Texas that is sometimes planted for shade

an·ar·ces·tes \,anər'se,stēz, ,a,när-\ *n, cap* [NL, fr. *an-* + *Arcestes*, genus of mollusks] **:** a genus of primitive early Devonian ammonoids from central Europe

an·arch \'a,närk, -äk *sometimes* 'anə(r)k\ *n* -s [back-formation fr. *anarchy*] **1 :** a leader or advocate of revolt **:** REBEL, ANARCHIST **2 :** DESPOT, TYRANT ⟨imperial ~s doubling human woes — Lord Byron⟩

anarch- *or* **anarcho-** *comb form* [ML *anarch-*, fr. Gk, fr. *anarchos*] **1 :** without government ⟨*anarchical*⟩ **2 a :** anarchism and ⟨*anarcho*pacifism⟩ **b :** anarchist and ⟨*anarcho*-individualist⟩

an·ar·chic \(')a¦närkik, ə'n-, -näk-, -kēk\ *also* **an·ar·chi·cal** \-kəkəl, -ēk-\ *or* **an·ar·chi·al** \-kēəl\ *adj* [*anarchy* + *-ic, -ical* or *-ial*] **:** of, relating to, or tending towards anarchy **:** LAWLESS, REBELLIOUS ⟨thought is ~ and lawless, indifferent to authority — Bertrand Russell⟩ — **an·ar·chi·cal·ly** \-kək(ə)lē, -kēk-, -li\ *adv*

an·ar·chism \'anə(r),kizəm *also* -,när,- *or* -,nä,-\ *n* -s [*anarchy* + *-ism*] **1 :** a political theory opposed to all forms of government and governmental restraint and advocating voluntary cooperation and free association of individuals and groups in order to satisfy their needs — compare NIHILISM **2 :** the advocacy or practice of anarchistic principles ⟨stood for the divine character of established authority against the ~ of free and critical thought — A.L.Guérard⟩

an·ar·chist \'anə(r)kəst\ *n* -s *often attrib* [*anarchy* + *-ist*] **1 :** one who rebels against any authority, established order, or ruling power ⟨the drawing-room ~, the literary rebel, the artistic iconoclast lay down the law for all of us — C.H.Grandgent⟩ **2 :** one who believes in, advocates, or promotes anarchism or anarchy; *esp* **:** one who uses violent means to overthrow the established order ⟨I feel like an ~! I want to blow up the whole town — Sinclair Lewis⟩

an·ar·chis·tic \¦anə(r)¦kistik, -tēk\ *adj* **:** of, relating to, or tending toward anarchism or the acts or principles of anarchists ⟨an almost ~ distrust of government — J.H.Plumb⟩

an·ar·cho–syn·di·cal·ism \a¦när(,)kō'-, ə¦n-, ¦anər,kō'-\ *n* **:** SYNDICALISM

an·ar·cho–syn·di·cal·ist \"-\ *n* **:** SYNDICALIST

an·ar·chy \'anə(r)kē, -ki *sometimes* -,närk-, -,näk-\ *n* -ES [ML *anarchia*, fr. Gk, fr. *anarchos* rulerless (fr. *an-* + *archos* ruler) + *-ia* -y — more at ARCHI-] **1 a :** absence of government ⟨society finds its highest perfection in the union of order with ~ — B.R.Tucker⟩ **b :** a state of lawlessness or political disorder due to the absence of governmental authority ⟨an ~ as absolute as that . . . during the terror — W.C.Brownell⟩ **c :** a Utopian society having no government and made up of individuals who enjoy complete freedom ⟨looks forward to the establishment of ~ . . . the absence of a master and the rule of law — J.H.Hallowell⟩ **2 a :** absence or denial of any authority, established order, or ruling power ⟨for our people liberty so often means only license and ~ — C.L.Sulzberger⟩ **b :** absence of order **:** CONFUSION ⟨have managed to achieve complete ~ in their electrical fixtures — Richard Joseph⟩ **3 :** ANARCHISM ⟨society defending itself against heretical ~ from within — Hilaire Belloc⟩

an·ar·gy·ros \ä'närgē,rōs\ *n, pl* **anargy·roi** \-(,)rē\ [LGk, fr. Gk, adj., without money, not accepting money, fr. *an-* + *argyros* silver, money — more at ARGENT] *Eastern Church* **:** one of thirteen saints who were mostly physicians said to have assisted the suffering and needy without accepting payment

an·a·rith·mia \,anə'rithmēə, -ith-\ *n* -s [NL, fr. *an-* + Gk *arithmos* number + NL *-ia* — more at ARITHMETIC] **:** loss of the ability to count (as resulting from a brain lesion)

an·ar·thria \a'närthrēə\ *n* -s [NL, fr. Gk *anarthros* inarticulate + NL *-ia*] **:** inability to articulate remembered words as a result of brain lesion — compare APHASIA — **an·ar·thric** \(')a¦närthrik\ *adj*

an·ar·throus \(')a¦närthrəs\ *adj* [Gk *anarthros* not differentiated, strengthless, inarticulate, without the article, fr. *an-* + *arthron* joint, article — more at ARTHR-] **1** *of a Greek substantive* **:** used without the article **2** *zool* **:** without distinct joints — **an·ar·throus·ly** *adv*

[1]**an·ar·ya** \(,)ə'näryə\ *adj* [Skt *anārya*, fr. *an-* + *ārya* Aryan — more at ARYAN] *India* **:** not Aryan

[2]**anarya** \"\ *n* -s [Skt *anārya*] *India* **:** one that is not Aryan

[1]**anas** *pl of* ANA

[2]**an·as** \'anəs\ *n, cap* [NL, fr. L, duck; akin to OE *æned* duck, OS *anad*, OHG *enit, anut*, ON *önd*, Lith *ántis*, and perh. to Gk *nassa, nēssa* duck, and perh. to Skt *āti* aquatic bird] **:** the type genus of Anatidae comprising a large number of widely distributed freshwater ducks (as the mallard and black duck)

an·a·sa \'anəsə\ *n, cap* [NL] **:** a genus of coreid bugs including the squash bugs

an·a·sar·ca \,anə'särkə\ *n* -s [NL, fr. *ana-* + *-sarca* (fr. Gk *sark-, sarx* flesh) — more at SARCASM] **:** edema characterized by the accumulation of serum in the connective tissue of the body — called also *dropsy*

an·a·sar·cous \¦==¦=kəs\ *adj* [NL *anasarca* + E *-ous*] **:** characterized or affected by anasarca **:** DROPSICAL

[1]**ana·sa·zi** \,änə'säzē, ,an-\ *n, pl* **anasazi** *or* **anasazis** *usu cap* [Navaho *'a-naa-sází* alien ancient one] **:** one of the people who produced the Anasazi culture **:** a Basket Maker or a Pueblo

[2]**anasazi** \¦==¦==\ *adj, usu cap* **:** of or belonging to the Basket Maker-Pueblo culture of the plateau area of northern Arizona, New Mexico, and adjacent areas of Colorado and Utah contemporaneous with the Hohokam to the south

an·a·schist·ic \¦anə¦shistik, -¦ski-\ *adj* [*ana-* + *schistic*] **:** dividing longitudinally — used esp. of normal meiotic chromosomes; compare DIASCHISTIC

anas·pa·lin \ə'naspələn\ *n* -s [origin unknown] *pharmacy* **:** a mixture of wool fat and petrolatum; *also* **:** impure wool fat

an·as·pid \ə'naspəd\ *n* -s [NL *Anaspida*] **:** one of the Anaspida

an·as·pi·da \-pədə\ *n pl, cap* [NL, fr. *an-* + *-aspida* (fr. Gk *aspid-, aspis* shield)] **:** a class or other division of primitive fishlike ostracoderms having a heterocercal tail and a covering of small elongated scales and known from Silurian-Devonian transition beds of Europe and America

an·as·pi·da·cea \ə,naspə'dāshēə, (,)a,n-\ *n pl, cap* [NL, fr. *Anaspides*, genus of crustaceans (fr. *an-* + *-aspides*, fr. Gk *aspid-, aspis* shield) + *-acea*] **:** an order of crustaceans (Malacostraca) like shrimp that have mostly biramous thoracic limbs and deposit their eggs among water plants or under stones

an·a·state \'anə,stāt\ *n* -s [*anabolism* + *-state*] **:** ANABOLITE

an·a·stat·ic \¦anə¦stad·ik\ *adj* [*ana-* + Gk *statikos* causing to stand — more at STATIC] **1 :** relating to a process of printing from a zinc plate on which a transferred design is left in relief by the etching out of the rest of the surface **2** [*anastate* + *-ic*] **:** ANABOLIC

an·a·stat·i·ca \,==¦=ikə\ *n, cap* [NL, fr. *ana-* + *-statica* (fr. Gk *statikos*)] **:** a genus of Arabian herbs (family Cruciferae) having a taproot, a disklike crown, and axillary white flowers

an·as·tig·mat \(')a'nastig,mat, ,anə'stig,-\ *n* -s [G, back-formation fr. *anastigmatisch* anastigmatic] **:** an anastigmatic lens

an·a·stig·mat·ic \¦anə(,)stig¦mad·ik, ¦a,nast-, a¦nast-, -naast-, -a(a)stēg-, -matik, -ēk\ *also* **an·as·tig·mat** \(')a¦nastig,mat, ¦anə¦stig,-\ *adj* [*anastigmatic*, ISV, fr. *an-* + *astigmatic; anastigmat* fr. *anastigmat*, n.] **:** not astigmatic — used esp. of lenses that are able to form approximately point images of object points

anas·to·mose \ə'nastə,mōz, -ōs\ *vb* -ED/-ING/-S [prob. fr. F, anastomosis, fr. Gk *anastomōsis*] *vt* **:** to connect or join by anastomosis ~ *vi* **1 :** to communicate by anastomosis **:** INOSCULATE **2 :** to divide, subdivide, and reunite repeatedly ⟨an *anastomosing* stream⟩

anas·to·mo·sis \ə,nastə'mōsəs, ,anəs-\ *n, pl* **anastomo·ses** \-ō,sēz\ [LL, fr. Gk *anastomōsis* opening, fr. *anastomoun* to furnish with a mouth, to open (fr. *ana-* + *stoma* mouth, opening) + *-sis* — more at STOMACH] **1 :** an act or instance of joining, intercommunicating, or inosculating: **a :** the union of artery and vein or the rejoining of branches of a common vascular trunk to form a network by which the circulation of a part is maintained when the usual channel is obstructed (as by ligature or a thrombus) **b :** similar joining of the parts of other branched systems (as the veins of a leaf or streams in a swamp) **c :** the surgical union of parts, esp. of hollow tubular parts ⟨~ of the ureter and colon is surgically practicable⟩ **2 :** a product of anastomosis; *esp* **:** a network (as of channels or branches) produced by anastomosis

anas·to·mot·ic \ə¦nastə¦mäd·ik, ¦anəs-\ *also* **anas·to·mat·ic** \-mad·ik\ *adj* [*anastomosis* + *-otic* or *-atic*] **:** of, relating to, or exhibiting anastomosis

an·as·tral \(')a¦nastrəl\ *adj* [*an-* + *astral*] **:** lacking asters — used of achromatic figures

anas·tre·pha \ə'nastrəfə\ *n, cap* [NL, fr. Gk *anastrephein* to turn upside down, fr. *ana-* + *strephein* to turn — more at STROPHE] **:** a genus of tropical American fruit flies (family Trypetidae) including a number of destructive pests of citrus

anas·tro·phe \ə'nastrə(,)fē\ *n* -s [ML, fr. Gk *anastrophē*, lit., turning back, fr. *anastrephein* to turn back, fr. *ana-* + *strephein* to turn — more at STROPHE] **:** inversion of the usual syntactical order of words for rhetorical effect

an·a·stro·phia \,anə'strōfēə\ *n, cap* [NL, fr. Gk *anastrophē* + NL *-ia*] **:** a genus of costate subglobular Silurian and Devonian brachiopods

an·a·sty·lo·sis \,anə,stī'lōsəs\ *n, pl* **anastylo·ses** \-ō'sēz\ [NL, fr. *ana-* + Gk *stylōsis* colonnade, fr. *styloun* to prop with pillars (fr. *stylos* pillar) + *-sis* — more at STEER] **:** the reconstruction of a monument from fallen parts

anat *abbr* anatomical; anatomy

an·a·tase \'anə,tās\ *n* -s [F, fr. Gk *anatasis* extension, fr. *anateinein* to extend, fr. *ana-* + *teinein* to stretch — more at THIN] **:** a tetragonal form of titanium dioxide used esp. as a white pigment in paints and printing inks

an·a·tec·tic \¦anə¦tektik\ *adj* [fr. NL *anatexis*, after such pairs as LL *syntaxis* syntax: E *syntactic*] **:** of or relating to anatexis

an·a·tex·is \,anə'teksəs\ *n, pl* **anatex·es** \-k,sēz\ [NL, fr. Gk *anatēxis* act of melting, thawing, fr. *anatēkein* to melt, thaw (fr. *ana-* + *tēkein* to thaw) + *-sis* — more at THAW] **:** any process by which plutonic rocks are dissolved and again converted into magmas

[1]**an·a·the·ma** \,anə'thēmə, ə'nathəmə\ *n, pl* **anathemas** \-məz\ *or* **anathem·a·ta** \,anə'themәd·ə, -ēm-\ [LL, fr. Gk *anathēma*, lit., anything set up, fr. *anatithenai*] **:** a thing consecrated to divine use **:** a votive offering

[2]**anath·e·ma** \ə'nathəmə\ *n* -s [LL, fr. Gk, anything devoted, anything devoted to evil, curse, fr. *anatithenai* to set up, dedicate, fr. *ana-* + *tithenai* to place, set — more at DO] **1 a :** a ban or curse solemnly pronounced by ecclesiastical authority and accompanied by excommunication ⟨the third letter to Nestorius . . . contained the ~s — R.M.French⟩ **b :** the denunciation of anything as accursed ⟨continued openly . . . to flaunt their beauties in spite of the ~s from the pulpits — P.I.Wellman⟩ **c :** a vigorous denunciation **:** IMPRECATION, CURSE ⟨the direst critical ~s — James Hinton⟩ **2 a :** one that is cursed by ecclesiastical authority ⟨the encyclical . . . declared the society ~ — C.W.Ferguson⟩ **b :** one that is intensely disliked or loathed ⟨he was ~ to the moderates — S.H.Adams⟩ ⟨changing a law is ~ to many people — S.L.Payne⟩

anath·e·mat·ic \ə¦nathə¦mad·ik\ *or* **anath·e·mat·i·cal** \-əkəl\ *adj* [Gk *anathemat-, anathema* + E *-ic, -ical*] **:** HATEFUL, LOATHSOME ⟨however *anathematic* the principle may be — *Life*⟩ — **anath·e·mat·i·cal·ly** \-ək(ə)lē\ *adv*

anath·e·ma·tism \ə'==mə,tizəm\ *n* -s [LL, fr. LGk *anathematismos*, fr. Gk *anathematizein* + *-ismos* -ism] **:** [2]ANATHEMA

anath·e·ma·ti·za·tion \ə,==məd·ə'zāshən, -mə,tī'z-\ *n* -s [ML *anathematisation-, anathematisatio*, fr. LL *anathematizatus* (past part. of *anathematizare*) + L *-ion-, -io* -ion] **:** [2]ANATHEMA

anath·e·ma·tize *also* **anathematise** \ə'==mə,tīz\ *vt* -ED/-ING/-S [LL *anathematizare*, fr. Gk *anathematizein*, fr. *anathemat-, anathema* anything devoted to evil + *-izein* -ize — more at ANATHEMA] **:** to pronounce an anathema upon **:** CURSE, DENOUNCE ⟨*anathematized* the leader of the Kentist insurgents — F.M.Stenton⟩ **syn** see EXECRATE

anath·e·mize \-,mīz\ *vt* -ED/-ING/-S [[2]*anathema* + *-ize*] **:** ANATHEMATIZE

an·a·tid \'anətəd, ə'nad·əd\ *n* -s [NL *Anatidae*] **:** one of the Anatidae

anat·i·dae \ə'nad·ə,dē\ *n pl, cap* [NL, fr. *Anat-, Anas*, type genus + *-idae*] **:** a large family of chiefly aquatic birds (order Anseriformes) having relatively heavy bodies, short legs, webbed feet, a bill with a hard horny nail at the tip and transverse toothlike ridges on the biting edges and including the ducks, geese, swans, and related forms

an·a·ti·na·cea \,anətə'nāshēə\ *n pl, cap* [NL, fr. *Anatina*, genus of mollusks (fr. L *anat-, anas* duck + NL *-ina*) + *-acea*] **:** a suborder of Eulamellibranchia of worldwide distribution comprising mollusks that have separate orifices for the ovaries and testes, a small foot, and the hinge of the shell without teeth

an·a·tine \'anə,tīn\ *adj* [L *anatinus* of a duck, fr. *anat-, anas* duck + *-inus* -ine] **:** of or belonging to the surface-feeding ducks of *Anas* and closely related genera

anat·i·pes·ti·fer infection \ə¦nad·ə¦pestəfə(r)-\ *n* [NL *anatipestifer*, fr. L *anat-, anas* duck + NL *-i-* + L *pestifer* pestiferous — more at PESTIFEROUS] **:** an acute infectious disease of domestic ducks caused by a bacterium (*Pasteurella anatipestifer* or *Pfeifferella anatipestifer*) and marked by sluggishness, greenish diarrhea, and respiratory symptoms with death commonly resulting in 6 to 12 hours

anatman *var of* ANATTA

anato *var of* ANNATTO

anat·o·cism \ə'nad·ə,sizəm\ *n* -s [L *anatocismus*, fr. Gk *anatokismos*, fr. *ana-* + *tokismos* usury, fr. *tokizein* to lend on interest (fr. *tokos* interest, offspring, fr. *tiktein* to beget) + *-ismos* -ism — more at THANE] **:** COMPOUND INTEREST **:** the taking of compound interest

[1]**an·a·to·li·an** \,anə¦tōlēən, -lyən\ *adj, usu cap* [*Anatolia* Asia Minor + E *-an*] **1 :** of, relating to, or characteristic of Anatolia, the country east of the Bosporus, roughly coincident with Asia Minor **2 :** of, relating to, or characteristic of the inhabitants of Anatolia or their languages **3 :** ARMENIAN

[2]**anatolian** \"\ *n* -s *cap* **1 :** a native or inhabitant of Anatolia, specif. of the western plateau lands of Turkey in Asia **2 a :** a southern dialect or group of dialects of Turkish **b :** a group of extinct languages of ancient Anatolia sometimes considered a branch of the Indo-European language family — see INDO-EUROPEAN LANGUAGES table **3 :** any rug or carpet woven in Anatolia

an·a·tol·ic \¦anə¦tälik\ *adj, usu cap* [*Anatolia* + E *-ic*] **:** ANATOLIAN

an·a·tom·ic \¦anə¦tämik, -ēk\ *or* **an·a·tom·i·cal** \-əkəl, -ēk-\ *adj* [*anatomic* fr. F *anatomique*, fr. MF, fr. LL *anatomicus*, fr. Gk *anatomikos*, fr. *anatomē* dissection + *-ikos* -ic; *anatomical* fr. MF *anatomique* + E *-al* — more at ANATOMY] **1 :** of or relating to anatomy ⟨*anatomical* knowledge⟩ **2 :** STRUCTURAL 2 ⟨an *anatomic* obstruction⟩ — opposed to *functional* — **an·a·tom·i·cal·ly** \-ək(ə)lē, -ēk-, -li\ *adv*

anatomical age *n* **:** the age of an individual in terms of his anatomical development

anatomical dead space *n* **:** the air-bearing portion of the respiratory system in which no significant gaseous exchange takes place and which includes the air-conveying ducts from the nostrils to the terminal bronchioles

anatomical position *n* **:** the normal position of activity ⟨the upright posture is man's *anatomical position*⟩

an·a·tom·i·co·path·o·log·ic \,anə'tämə,kō¦==¦==\ *or* **an·a·tom·i·co·path·o·log·i·cal** \-¦==¦===\ *adj* [*anatomic* + *-o-* + *pathologic* or *pathological*] **:** of or relating to anatomy and pathology or to pathological anatomy

anat·o·mist \ə'nad·əməst, -atəm-\ *n* -s [MF *anatomiste*, fr. *anatomie* + *-iste* -ist] **1 :** a student of anatomy; *specif* **:** one skilled in the art of dissection **2 :** one who examines and analyzes minutely and critically ⟨an ~ of urban society⟩

anat·o·mi·za·tion \ə,==mə'zāshən, -,mī'z-\ *n* -s **:** DISSECTION

anat·o·mize *also* **anatomise** \ə'==,mīz\ *vt* -ED/-ING/-S [MF *anatomiser*, fr. *anatomie* anatomy (fr. LL *anatomia*) + *-iser* -ize] **1 :** to cut (an animal or plant body) in pieces in order to display or examine the structure and use of the several parts **:** DISSECT **2 :** to separate minutely or thoroughly the parts, aspects, or components of in order to permit detailed scrutiny or meticulous examination **:** ANALYZE ⟨the novel . . . written to ~ adequately this moment of our history — R.P. Warren⟩ **syn** see ANALYZE

anat·o·my \ə'nad·əmē, -atəm-, -mi\ *n* -ES [LL *anatomia* dissection, fr. Gk *anatomē* dissection (fr. *anatemnein* to dissect, fr. *ana-* + *temnein* to cut) + L *-ia* -y — more at TOME] **1 a :** the branch of morphology that deals with the structure of animals — see HISTOLOGY **b :** the branch of morphology that deals with the structure of plants, esp. the internal structure as revealed by the microscope **:** PHYTOTOMY **2 :** a treatise on anatomic science or art **3 :** the art of artificially separating the different parts of an animal or plant in order to ascertain their position, relations, structure, and function **:** DISSECTION **4** *obs* **a :** a body dissected or to be dissected **b :** a representation of a dissected body (as in plaster) **5 :** the structural makeup, esp. of an organism or any of its parts ⟨the peculiar ~ of the duckbill⟩ **6 :** a separating or dividing into parts, aspects, or components in order to make a thorough study **:** detailed examination **:** ANALYSIS ⟨an attempt at an ~ of modern . . . conservatism — Clinton Rossiter⟩ ⟨the ~ of melancholy⟩ **7 a :** one that has been or appears to have been anatomized or dissected: (1) **:** SKELETON (2) **:** a corpse dried to skin and bone (3) **:** a withered or emaciated person **b :** the human body ⟨in what vile part of this ~ doth my name lodge — Shak.⟩

an·a·to·no·sis \,anətə'nōsəs\ *n, pl* **anatono·ses** \-ō,sēz\ [NL, fr. *ana-* + Gk *tonōsis* strengthening] **:** the process of adjustment of intracellular osmotic pressure of plant cells by variation of the sugar content of the vacuolar sap

an·a·tox·in \,anə'täksən\ *n* -s [ISV *ana-* + *toxin*] **:** TOXOID

an·a·tri·aene \,anə'trī,ēn\ *n* -s [*ana-* + *triaene*] **:** a triaene with downcurved cladi

anat·ro·pous \ə'na·trəpəs\ *adj* [*ana-* + *-tropous*] **:** having the ovule inverted at an early period in its development so that the micropyle is bent down to the funiculus to which the body of the ovule is united — compare AMPHITROPOUS, CAMPYLOTROPOUS, ORTHOTROPOUS

1an·at·ta \ˌənəˈtä\ *or* **an·at·man** \(ˌ)əˈnätmən\ *n* -s [Pali & Skt; Pali *anatta*, fr. Skt *anātman*, lit., having no soul] **:** a basic Buddhist doctrine affirming the nonexistence of a soul, essence, or any other enduring substantial entity underlying any form of phenomenal existence

2anatta *or* **anatto** *var of* ANNATTO

an·au·dia \aˈnȯdēə, əˈ-\ *n* -s [NL, fr. Gk, fr. *anaudos* without voice (fr. *an-* + *audē* voice) + *-ia*; akin to Gk *audein* to sing — more at ODE] **:** loss of voice **:** inability to articulate

an·aun·ters \əˈnantə(r)z\ *conj* [ME *anaunter* (fr. *an* — fr. OE, var. of *on* — + *aunter*, var. of *aventure* adventure) + *-s* — more at ADVENTURE] *now dial Eng* **:** on the chance that **:** LEST

an·aux·ite \əˈnȯkˌsīt\ *n* -s [G *anauxit*, fr. Gk *anauxēs* not increasing (fr. *an-* + *-auxēs*, fr. *auxein* to increase) + G *-it* -ite] **:** a mineral consisting of hydrous aluminum silicate, occurring as interstratified layers of silica Si_8O_{16} and kaolin $Al_4Si_4O_{10}(OH)_8$ with the latter predominant, and being a constituent of certain clays

an·ax·ag·o·re·an \ˌaˌnakˌsagəˈrēən, ¦anȯk-\ *adj, usu cap* [*Anaxagoras* †428 B.C. Greek philosopher + E *-ean*] **:** of or relating to the philosophy of Anaxagoras who taught that the world is composed of many qualitatively different substances that developed from homogeneous particles under the impetus of nous

an·ax·i·al \(ˈ)a¦naksēəl\ *adj* [*an-* + *axial*] **:** having no distinct axis or axes **:** irregular in form

anax·i·man·dri·an \ə¦naksə¦mandrēən\ *adj, usu cap* [*Anaximander* †547 B.C. Greek astronomer and philosopher + E *-ian*] **:** of or relating to the philosophy of Anaximander who taught that the first principle is an infinite indeterminate matter out of which arise the elemental contraries, warm and cold, moist and dry, that evolve the universe

an·ax·o·nia \ˌaˌnakˈsōnēə\ *n pl, usu cap* [NL, fr. *an-* + *Axonia*] **:** the organisms that have no distinct axis regarded as a group — opposed to *Axonia*

an·ba \ˈambə\ *or* **am·ba** \"\ *n* -s [Ar, fr. Copt *apa, abba*, fr. Syr *abbā* father] **:** FATHER — used as a title of a Coptic clergyman or saint

an·bury \ˈanbərē, ˈam-, -ˌbe-\ *n* -ES [prob. alter. of (assumed) earlier E *angberry*, fr. *ang-* (fr. OE *ange*, narrow, painful) + *berry* — more at AGNAIL] **1 :** ANGLEBERRY **2 :** CLUBROOT

anc *abbr* ancient

ance \ˈan(t)s\ *adj or adv or conj or n* [ME (northern dial.) *anes*, var. of *ones* — more at ONCE] *chiefly Scot* **:** ONCE

-ance \ən(t)s, ᵊn(t)s\ *n suffix* -s [ME, fr. OF, fr. L *-antia*, fr. *-ant-, -ans* -ant + *-ia* -y] **1 :** action or process ⟨attend*ance*⟩ ⟨deliver*ance*⟩ ⟨further*ance*⟩ **:** instance of an action or process ⟨appear*ance*⟩ ⟨perform*ance*⟩ **2 :** quality or state ⟨resembl*ance*⟩ ⟨temper*ance*⟩ **:** instance of a quality or state ⟨protuber*ance*⟩ **3 :** amount or degree ⟨conduct*ance*⟩ ⟨transmitt*ance*⟩

an·ce·ra·ta \ˌansəˈrädə, -ādə\ [NL, irreg. fr. *an-* + Gk *kerat-, keras* horn — more at CEREBRAL] *syn of* TYLOPODA

1an·ces·tor \ˈanˌsestə(r), ˈaan-, *Brit usu & US sometimes* -ˌsəs-\ *n* -s [ME *ancestre, ancessour*, fr. OF *ancestre* (fr. LL *antecessor*, nom.), *ancessour* (fr. LL *antecessorem*, acc.), fr. LL *antecessor* predecessor, fr. L, one that goes in front, fr. *antecessus* (past part. of *antecedere* to go before, fr. *ante-* ante- + *cedere* to go) + *-or* — more at CEDE] **1 :** one from whom a person is descended and who is usu. more remote in the line of descent than a grandparent; *specif* **:** one from whom an estate has descended, at the common law being orig. only a person in the line of ascent and later also of descent, but under the statutes including any person of lineal or collateral relationship from whom the property has been derived by descent — compare HEIR **2 :** something belonging to a relatively early developmental period of a contemporary or fully developed object or phenomenon **:** FORERUNNER, PROTOTYPE ⟨modern scholarly ideas and their classic Greek ~s⟩ ⟨the ~s of today's station wagon —Mildred B. Smith⟩ **3 :** a progenitor (as one living in an earlier geological period) of a more recent or existing species or group ⟨species descended from a 5-chromosome ~ —E.B.Babcock⟩

syn PROGENITOR, FOREFATHER, FOREBEAR (or FORBEAR): ANCESTOR implies lineal descent through father or mother but may apply to kinship through collaterals or race, never, however, being applied except humorously to a relation within family memory ⟨have *ancestors* in British royal families⟩ ⟨generation after generation adding its part . . . to what their *ancestors* had begun —Manès Sperber⟩ ⟨we have a better chance of living far beyond 55, and even well beyond 65, than our *ancestors* had —W.J.Reilly⟩ PROGENITOR can include parents or grandparents as well as ancestors though it generally involves no family or racial feeling, usu. suggesting a reference to heredity or the transmission of characters ⟨the Finlayson family, whose *progenitors* came to America from Scotland in 1800 —*Amer. Guide Series: Fla.*⟩ ⟨the wild relatives of the goat include the pasang [which is] generally regarded as the true *progenitor* of all our modern domesticated breeds —V.A. Rice & F.N.Andrews⟩ FOREFATHER is more common than ANCESTOR in rhetorical or poetic context, usu. emphasizing family feeling or family group unity ⟨political beliefs for which our *forefathers* gladly fought and died⟩ FOREBEAR is interchangeable with though more neutral than ANCESTOR, being generally devoid of associations with feeling ⟨one of his *forebears* fought under Washington in the Revolutionary War —*Current Biog.*⟩ ⟨carnivals, in which the members impersonate their primal *forbears* —*Amer. Guide Series: Oregon*⟩ ⟨this male specialization in strength must indeed . . . have been inherited from our ape *forebears* —Weston La Barre⟩

2ancestor \"\ *vt* -ED/-ING/-s **:** to provide with ancestors ⟨the biographer finally gets his subject ~*ed* and born⟩ **:** be the ancestor of ⟨the man who ~*ed* many of the residents of this place⟩

ancestor cult *n* **:** a ritualistic system of veneration, honor, and propitiation of the spirits of dead ancestors for the purpose of avoiding evil consequences and securing good fortune

an·ces·to·ri·al \ˌanˌse¦stōrēəl, ¦aan-, -ˌsə¦-, -ȯr-\ *adj* **:** ANCESTRAL — **an·ces·to·ri·al·ly** \-ēlē\ *adv*

an·ces·tral \(ˈ)an¦sestrəl, -aan-\ *adj* [earlier *auncestrell*, fr. MF *ancestrel*, fr. *ancestre* + *-el* -al] **1 a :** of or belonging to an ancestor or ancestors ⟨~ portraits⟩ ⟨~ ideas no longer valid⟩ **b :** inherited or derived from an ancestor or ancestors ⟨~ estates⟩ **2 :** being, serving as, or of the nature of a forerunner, prototype, or precursor ⟨an ~ language⟩ ⟨a second pre-Phoenician alphabet is clearly not ~ to the Phoenician —A.L. Kroeber⟩ — **an·ces·tral·ly** *adv*

an·ces·tress \ˈanˌsestrəs, ˈaan-, -ˌsəs-\ *n* -ES **:** a female ancestor

an·ces·tri·al \(ˈ)an¦sestrēəl\ *adj* [by alter.] *archaic* **:** ANCESTRAL

an·ces·tri·an \-ēən\ *adj* [*ancestry* + *-an*] *archaic* **:** ANCESTRAL

an·ces·tru·la \anˈsestrələ, aan-\ *n, pl* **ancestru·lae** \-ˌlē\ *or* **ancestrulas** [NL, fr. E *ancestor* + NL *-ula*] **:** the primary or first zooid of a bryozoan colony from which secondary individuals are formed by budding — **an·ces·tru·lar** \(ˈ)=¦==lə(r)\ *adj*

an·ces·try \ˈanˌsestrē, ˈaan-, -ri, *Brit usu & US sometimes* -ˌsəs-\ *n* -ES [ME *ancestrie*, modif. (influenced by ME *ancestre* ancestor) of MF *ancesserie*, fr. OF, fr. *ancessour* ancestor + *-ie* -y — more at ANCESTOR] **1 a :** line of descent **:** genealogical succession **:** LINEAGE ⟨a Mexican proud of his pure Spanish ~⟩; *specif* **:** good birth **:** honorable, noble, or aristocratic descent ⟨an upstart society without breeding or ~⟩ **b :** persons initiating or comprising a line of descent **:** ANCESTORS ⟨farmers still using methods employed by their colonial ~⟩ **2 a :** material inception (as of an object or phenomenon) ⟨a mountain of volcanic ~⟩ **b :** developmental process **:** HISTORY ⟨radical politics has a far longer ~ than most people had thought —*Times Lit. Supp.*⟩

syn ANCESTRY, LINEAGE, PEDIGREE are often used interchangeably to designate one's progenitors or their total quality or character, often distinguished or notable. ANCESTRY, however, usu. connotes the treelike family branchings and ramifications as symbolized on a chart showing one's relation to progenitors through parental lines ⟨came of distinguished Scotch, Welsh, and Huguenot *ancestry* settled in the Carolinas before the Revolution —Allan Westcott⟩ LINEAGE stresses descent in line, suggesting an order of persons descending from a single ancestor, though each may have a different ancestry ⟨a family which traced its *lineage* from a Cavalier who came to America —*Americana Annual*⟩ ⟨his mother . . . traced her *lineage* to Miles Standish, John and Priscilla Alden, and George Soule, of the Mayflower group —C.J.Kraemer⟩ PEDIGREE implies a known and recorded ancestry, usu. distinguished or notable ⟨accustomed when making his marriage alliances to seek out *pedigree* as well as fortune in his wives —L.G.Pine⟩ ⟨son of a local baronet with a bank balance that makes up for lack of *pedigree* —Richard Harrison⟩ ⟨a champion show dog with a champion's *pedigree*⟩

an·chi·e·tea \ˌaŋkēˈēshēə, ˌanchē-, -ˈēd-ēə\ *n, cap* [NL, after José de *Anchieta* †1597 Port. Jesuit missionary in Brazil] **:** a genus of So. American climbing shrubs (family Violaceae) with white clustered flowers and thin capsules

an·chi·eu·tec·tic \¦aŋkēyü¦tektik\ *adj* [ISV *anchi-* (fr. Gk *anchi* near) + *-eutectic* (fr. Gk *eutēktos* easily melted + ISV *-ic*); orig. formed as G *anchi-eutektisch*] **:** having minerals in practically eutectic proportions

an·chi·mono·min·er·al \-ˌmänō¦min(ə)rəl\ *adj* [ISV *anchi-* + *mono-* + *mineral*; orig. formed as G *anchi-monomineralisch*] **:** composed essentially of a single-mineral species

an·chis·tea \ˌaŋkiˈstēə, aŋˈkis-\ *n, cap* [NL, fr. Gk *anchisteia* close kinship, fr. *anchistos* nearest, superl. of *anchi* near; fr. its relationship with another genus (*Woodwardia*); akin to Gk *anchein* to strangle — more at ANGER] *in some classifications* **:** a genus of ferns (family Polypodiaceae) of eastern No. America including only the chain fern — see WOODWARDIA

an·chi·there \ˈaŋkəˌthi(ə)r\ *n* -s [NL *Anchitherium*] **:** a member of the genus *Anchitherium*

an·chi·the·ri·um \ˌaŋkəˈthirēəm\ *n, cap* [NL, fr. Gk *anchi* near + NL *-therium*] **:** a genus of extinct Miocene and Pliocene perissodactyl mammals related to the modern horse from which they differ in dentition and esp. in the limbs, having a complete ulna and fibula and three functional toes of which the middle one is much the largest

1an·chor \ˈaŋkə(r), ˈaiŋ-\ *n* -s *often attrib* [ME *anker, ancre*, fr. OE *ancer, ancor*, fr. L *ancora, anchora*, fr. Gk *ankyra*; akin to Gk *ankos* bend, hollow, glen — more at ANGLE] **1 a :** a device usu. of metal (as steel) attached to a ship or boat by a cable and cast overboard to hold the vessel in a particular place by means of a fluke that digs into the bottom ⟨the trawler dropped ~ in the inner harbor⟩ — see 1STOCK 6a **b :** any device (as a stone or piece of concrete) used in the manner of an anchor to hold a boat in place **2 :** a reliable support (as in danger) **:** a source of confidence ⟨we have this as a sure and steadfast ~ of the soul — Heb 6:19 (RSV)⟩ **3 :** something that serves to hold an object firmly: **a :** a contrivance to hold the end of a bridge cable **b :** an arrangement of timber for holding a dam fast **c :** an escapement piece on which the pallets of a timepiece are formed or to which they are attached **d :** CHAPLET 4 **e** (1) **:** a device (as a metal tie) for giving stability to one part of a structure by making it fast to another (as a beam to a wall, one wall to another, or a stone facing to rough masonry behind it) (2) **:** a tie rod with visible ends, decorated or plain **f :** the loop of a rope used by mountain climbers that is made fast to some fixed object (as a piton or tree) **g :** a boss to which one end of each brake shoe in an internal brake is pivoted to prevent its being dragged around by the drum **4 :** an object shaped like a ship's anchor: as **a :** the dart an egg-and-dart molding **b :** SPICULE ⟨the ~s in certain holothurians⟩ **5 a :** the rear man on either side in a tug-of-war contest **b** *or* **anchor man :** the member of a team who competes last ⟨the ~ on a relay team⟩ ⟨the ~ of a bowling team⟩ — **at anchor :** being anchored (as to the bottom by an anchor or to a buoy secured to the bottom) ⟨a ship riding *at anchor* in the bay⟩ — used also in law of a vessel moored to a dock

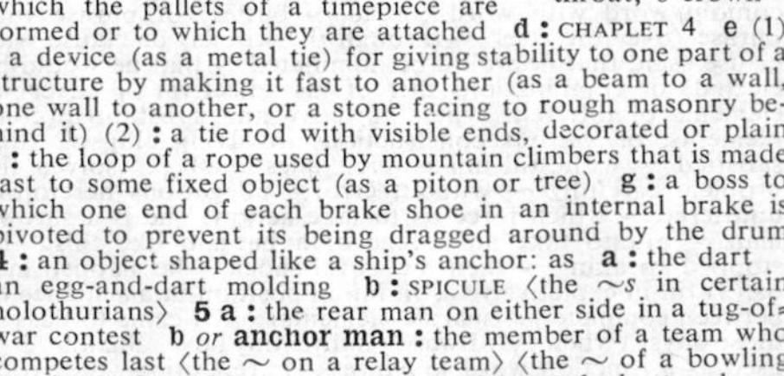

anchor 1a: *1* ring; *2* stock; *3* shank; *4* bill; *5* fluke, or palm; *6* arm; *7* throat; *8* crown

2anchor \"\ *vb* **anchored; anchored; anchoring** \-k(ə)riŋ\ **anchors** [ME *ancren*, prob. fr. *anker, ancre*, n.] *vt* **1 :** to hold in place in the water by an anchor ⟨~ a dinghy with a grapnel⟩ — compare MOOR 1 **2 :** to secure firmly **:** fasten in a stable condition **:** FIX ⟨~ a post in concrete⟩ ⟨~ the roof of a house⟩ ⟨~ papers on a desk by a paperweight⟩ ⟨the railroad car on the siding was ~*ed* when the hand brakes were set⟩ ⟨he was ~*ed* to his home⟩ **3 :** to serve or act as an anchor for ⟨the loveliness of the Loire Valley might fail to ~ the attention of the hurried traveler —Isolde Farrell⟩ ⟨~*ed* the Japanese women's relay team —*Time*⟩ **4** *psychol* **:** to relate to a point or frame of reference (as to a person, a situation, an object, or a conceptual scheme) ~ *vi* **1 :** to cast anchor **:** come to anchor ⟨the ship ~*ed* in the stream⟩ **2 :** to become fixed **:** FIX, REST, STOP ⟨his attention ~s on his friend⟩

3anchor *n* -s [ME *anker, ancre*, fr. OE *ancor, ancra*, fr. OIr *anchara*, fr. LL *anachoreta* — more at ANCHORITE] *obs* **:** ANCHORITE, HERMIT

4anchor *n* -s *obs* **:** ANKER

1an·chor·age \ˈaŋk(ə)rij, ˈaiŋ-, -ēj\ *n* -s [1*anchor* + *-age*] **1** *obs* **:** a toll or duty for anchoring a ship (as in a harbor) **2** *obs* **:** the set of anchors used to hold a ship **3 a :** the act or action of anchoring a ship **b :** condition of lying at anchor ⟨room for the ~ of many ships⟩ ⟨pay duty for ~⟩ **c** *also* **anchorage ground :** a place where vessels anchor or a place suitable for anchoring ⟨the inner harbor is an ~ used only in the hurricane season⟩ **d :** bottom for holding a ship's anchor ⟨fine sand offers poor ~ in rough weather⟩ **4 :** a means of security **:** a ground of trust **:** a resting place for the mind or feelings **:** a source of emotional reassurance ⟨this ~ of Christian hope —T.O.Wedel⟩ ⟨a deep and healing sense of ~ —Adria Langley⟩ **5 :** the provision of a secure hold for something **:** that which provides a secure hold ⟨~ supplied for a dental plate⟩ ⟨~ for the second coat of paint⟩ ⟨erosion caused by lack of forest ~⟩ ⟨the importance of roof ~ during hurricanes⟩ ⟨~s for suspension cables⟩ **6** *psychol* **:** a point or frame of reference

2anchorage \"\ *n* -s [3*anchor* + *-age*] **:** the dwelling place of an anchorite

anchor and collar *n* **:** a hinge (as for heavy gates or doors) having the socket attached to or made with an anchor which is embedded in the masonry

an·chor·ate \-kərət, -ˌrāt\ *adj* [1*anchor* + *-ate*] *of a sponge spicule* **:** having one or more processes like the fluke of an anchor

anchor ax *n* **:** a crescent-shaped stone weapon once used in Brazil

anchor ball *n* **1 :** a projectile with grappling hooks attached used in the lifesaving service to fire into the rigging of wrecked vessels **2 :** a black ball displayed in the rigging between bow and foremast by a vessel at anchor in or near a channel

anchor bar *n* **:** a handspike with an ironshod wedge-shaped end used in prying (as an anchor into or out of its place)

anchor bed *n* **:** 1BILLBOARD

anchor bend *n* **:** FISHERMAN'S BEND

anchor bolt *n* **:** a bolt for securing a machine, structure, or part to masonry or other material — called also *anchor rod*

anchor box *n* **:** ANCHOR SPACE

anchor buoy *n* **:** a buoy attached to or marking the position of an anchor

anchor chock *n* **1 :** a reinforcing piece of wood let into an anchor stock where worn **2 :** a chock or a wooden block used to hold a stowed anchor steady

anchor dart *n* **:** the arrowhead part of an egg-and-dart molding

anchor drag *n* **:** DRAG 3a(1)

anchored *adj, of the object balls in billiards* **:** situated so close together (as on the rail or in a corner of the table) that a number of caroms can be made with little or no disturbance of position

anchor escapement *n* **:** a clock escapement employing an anchor-shaped pallet piece which causes the escape wheel to recoil slightly upon the locking action of each arm of the anchor

an·cho·ress \ˈaŋk(ə)rəs, ˈaiŋ-\ *or* **an·cress** \-kr-\ *n* -ES [ME *ankeresse, ancresse*, fr. *anker, ancre* hermit + *-esse* -ess — more at ANCHOR] **:** a female anchorite

1anchor-hold \ˈ==ˌ=\ *n* [1*anchor* + *hold* (grasp)] **1 a :** the grip of an anchor **b :** the bottom that an anchor grips **2 :** firm hold **:** SECURITY

2anchor-hold \"\ *n* [3*anchor* + *hold* (shelter)] **:** the cell of an anchorite

anchor hoy *n* **:** a lighter equipped for raising or handling anchors and chains

anchor ice *n* **:** ice formed below the surface of a body of water (as a stream or lake) and attached to the bottom or to submerged objects — called also *ground ice*

anchoring *pres part of* ANCHOR

1an·cho·rite \ˈaŋkəˌrīt, ˈaiŋ-\ *also* **an·cho·ret** \-ˌret\ *n* -s [ME *ancorite*, fr. ML *anchorita*, alter. (prob. influenced by L *anchora* anchor) of LL *anachoreta*, (assumed) LL *anachorita*, fr. LGk *anachōrētēs*, fr. Gk *anachōrein* to withdraw, retire, fr. *ana-* + *chōrein* to make room, give way, fr. *chōros* place; akin to Gk *chēros* left, bereaved — more at HEIR] **:** one that renounces the world to live in seclusion usu. for religious reasons **:** HERMIT, RECLUSE

2an·chor·ite \"\ *n* -s [fr. *Anchor* Inn, Caldecote, Nuneaton, England, its locality + E *-ite*] **:** a variety of diorite mottled with dark mafic segregations and light feldspathic veins

an·cho·rit·ess \ˌ-ˌrīd·əs\ *n* -ES [1*anchorite* + *-ess*] **:** ANCHORESS

an·cho·rit·ic \¦==¦rid·ik\ *also* **an·cho·ret·ic** \-red·ik\ *adj* [1*anchorite* + *-ic*] **:** relating to, belonging to, or suggestive of an anchorite ⟨~ devotions⟩

an·cho·rit·ism \ˈ==ˌrīd·ˌizəm\ *n* -s [1*anchorite* + *-ism*] **:** the practice or mode of life of an anchorite

an·chor·less \ˈaŋkə(r)ləs, ˈaiŋ-\ *adj* [1*anchor* + *-less*] **:** UNSETTLED, DRIFTING ⟨~ people perpetually riding the crest of their emotions —William Phillips b.1907⟩

anchor lift *n* **:** a grappling device to raise a grouser

anchor light *n* **:** the light shown at night by a vessel at anchor

anchor lining *n* **:** a protection of planks or sheathing on a ship's side to prevent the anchor from injuring the side

anchor log *n* **:** a wooden, concrete, or metal bar buried in the earth to hold a guy rope firmly — called also *deadman*

anchor man *n* **:** 1ANCHOR 5b

anchor nurse *n* **:** a nurse in billiards in which the two object balls are kept anchored

anchor plant *n* [so called fr. the shape of the branches] **:** a So. American shrub (*Colletia cruciata*) with flattened branches and creamy-white flowers

anchor plate *n* **:** a wooden or metal plate attached to or embedded in a support and used as an anchor (as for supporting cables)

anchor point *n* **:** a point on an archer's face (as the chin) up to which he brings his drawing hand in order to stabilize his aim before release of the arrow

anchor ring *n* **:** the surface formed by rotating a circle around a line that lies in the plane of the circle but does not intersect the circle — called also *torus*

anchor rocket *n* **:** a rocket with flukes like an anchor used in the lifesaving service in carrying a line to a wrecked vessel

anchor rod *n* **:** ANCHOR BOLT

anchors *pl of* ANCHOR, *pres 3d sing of* ANCHOR

anchor shackle *n* **:** a shackle to secure a chain to the ring of an anchor **:** BENDING SHACKLE

anchor shot *n* **1 :** GRAPPLE SHOT **2** *or* **anchor stroke :** a shot in billiards made with the object balls anchored

anchor space *n* **:** any of eight spaces in balkline billiards seven inches square lying along a cushion and bisected transversely by a balkline in which object balls are treated as in balk — called also *anchor box*

anchor tooth *n* **:** ABUTMENT 2c

anchor watch *n* **:** a detail of one or more men who keep watch on deck at night when a vessel is at anchor

anchor well *n* **:** a well for anchors in the forward overhang of a ship

an·chory \-k(ə)rē, -ri\ *adj* [prob. modif. (influenced by 1*anchor*) of F *ancré*] **:** ANCRÉE

an·cho·veta *or* **an·cho·vet·ta** \ˌanchōˈved·ə\ *n* -s [Sp *anchoveta*, dim. of *anchova*] **:** a small anchovy (*Cetengraulis mysticetus*) common along the Pacific coast of No. America and often used as bait

an·cho·vy \ˈanˌchōvē, ˈanˈchō-, ˈancha-, (ˈ)aan-, -vi\ *n, pl* **anchovies** *or* **anchovy** [Sp *anchova, anchoa*, prob. fr. It dial. (Genoa) *ancioa*, fr. (assumed) VL *apjua*, fr. Gk *aphyē* small fry (of any of several fishes)] **:** any of a number of small herringlike fishes (family Engraulidae); *esp* **:** a common Mediterranean form (*Engraulis encrasicholus*) esteemed for its rich and peculiar flavor and caught in vast numbers for preserving and for making sauces and relishes

anchovy pear *n* [so called fr. its use as an hors d'oeuvre] **1 :** the fruit of a West Indian tree (*Grias cauliflora*) of the family Lecythidaceae often eaten as a pickle **2 :** the tree that bears anchovy pears

an·chu·sa \aŋˈkyüsə, -üzə\ *n* [NL, fr. L, alkanet, fr. Gk *anchousa*] **1** *cap* **:** a large genus of rough-hairy Old World herbs (family Boraginaceae) with one-sided clusters of trumpet-shaped flowers — see BUGLOSS **2** -s **:** a plant of the genus *Anchusa*

anchyl- *or* **anchylo-** — see ANKYL-

anchylose *var of* ANKYLOSE

anchylosis *var of* ANKYLOSIS

anchylostomiasis *var of* ANCYLOSTOMIASIS

anchylotic *var of* ANKYLOTIC

anciency *n* -ES [alter. of ME *anciente*, fr. MF *ancienté*, fr. *ancien* + *-té* -ty] *archaic* **:** ANTIQUITY

an·cien ré·gime \äⁿsyaⁿrāzhēm\ *n, pl* **anciens régimes** \-m(z)\ [F, lit., old regime] **1 :** the political and social system of France before the Revolution of 1789 **2 :** a system or mode no longer prevailing

1an·cient \ˈānshənt, ˈānch- *also* ˈāŋ(k)sh-\ *adj, often* -ER/-EST [ME *ancien*, fr. MF, fr. (assumed) VL *anteanus*, fr. L *ante* before + *-anus* -an — more at ANTE-] **1 :** having had an existence of many years **:** OLD: **a :** AGED ⟨a strangely dressed ~ man⟩ **b** *archaic* **:** of long standing in some capacity or relation ⟨an ~ champion still defending his title⟩ **c :** existing from a long-past date or period **:** of early origin ⟨an ~ landmark⟩ ⟨the ~ rights of freemen⟩ **d :** having had an uninterrupted existence of 20 or 30 or more years — used of various things the continued existence of which for such a period gives rise to a presumption of legal validity in the face of the defect in proof due to lapse of memory, absence of witnesses, or loss of documents **2 :** belonging or relating to a remote period, to a time early in history, or to those who lived in such a period or time; *specif* **:** belonging or relating to the historical period beginning with the earliest known civilizations and extending to the fall of the western Roman Empire A.D.476 — compare MEDIEVAL, MODERN **3 :** having the qualities of age or long existence: **a** *of a person* (1) **:** VENERABLE (2) **:** adept by reason of long experience **:** WISE **b :** OLD-FASHIONED, ANTIQUE ⟨dressed in ~ garb⟩ **4** *obs* **:** FORMER, BYGONE, SOMETIME **syn** see OLD

2ancient \"\ *n* -s **1 :** an aged living being: **a :** a patriarchal or venerable man or woman ⟨a dignified ~⟩ **b** (1) *obs* **:** one older in age **:** SENIOR — usu. used with the possessive (2) *archaic* **:** an elder in his capacity as dignitary **2** *obs* **:** ANCESTOR **3 :** one who lived in ancient times: **a ancients** *pl* **:** the civilized peoples of antiquity; *esp* **:** those of the classical nations — usu. used with *the* ⟨the religions of the ~*s*⟩ **b :** one of the classical authors ⟨Plutarch and other ~*s*⟩ **4** *archaic* **:** one of the senior members forming the governing body of the Inns of Court or of Chancery **5 :** an ancient coin

3ancient \"\ *n* -s [alter. (influenced by 1*ancient*) of *ensign*] **1** *archaic* **:** an ensign, standard, or flag **2** *or* **ancient bearer** *obs* **:** the bearer of an ensign ⟨my ~, a man he is of honesty and trust —Shak.⟩

ancient demesne *n* **:** demesne held from ancient times; *specif* **:** the demesne belonging to the English crown at the time of the settlement of the Norman Conquest as recorded in the Domesday Book

ancient history *n* **:** knowledge or information (as of something in the recent past) that is widespread and has lost its initial freshness or importance **:** common knowledge ⟨this

may be *ancient history*, but it still makes fascinating reading —Leland Stowe〉
ancient light *n* **:** a window or other opening that has been used 20 or more years without interruption and is therefore protected at common law against obstruction by an adjoining holder
an·cient·ly *adv* **1 :** in ancient times **:** long ago **2** *obs* **:** FORMERLY
ancient murrelet *n* [so called fr. its having a form known fr. the Pleistocene] **:** a murrelet (*Synthliboramphus antiquum*) of the No. Pacific that is chiefly dark slate above and white below
ancientness *n* -ES **1 :** the quality or state of being ancient **2** *obs* **:** PRIORITY, SENIORITY
ancient regime *prond as English*\ *n* [part trans.] **:** ANCIEN RÉGIME
an·cient·ry \-rē\ *n* -ES **1** *obs* **:** old people **:** ELDERS **2 a :** ANCIENTNESS, ANTIQUITY 〈a custom drawn from the ~ of the East —John Buchan〉 **b :** old-fashioned style 〈married with great state and ~ —Rudyard Kipling〉 **3** *obs* **:** ancient lineage **:** ANCESTRY **4 :** ancient times 〈legends of ~〉
-ancies *pl of* -ANCY
an·ci·le \ˈäŋˈkē,lä, anˈsīlē\ *n, pl* **ancil·ia** \äŋˈkilēə, anˈsi-\ [L, prob. fr. *ancidere* to cut around, fr. *an-* (var. of *ambi-* around) + *-cidere* (fr. *caedere* to cut) — more at AMBI-, CONCISE] **:** any of 12 sacred shields of the ancient Romans that were thought to guarantee the preservation of the city
an·cil·la \anˈsilə\ *n, pl* **ancil·lae** \-i(,)lē\ [L, female servant, dim. of (assumed) *ancula* (whence *Ancula*, a goddess who ministered to the gods), fem. of (assumed) *anculus* (whence *Anculus*, a ministering god), fr. *an-* (var. of *ambi-* around) + *-culus* circulating (akin to *colere* to cultivate, dwell — formerly, to circulate) — more at AMBI-, WHEEL] **1 :** an adjunct esp. to something large or significant **:** ACCESSORY 〈a mere ~ to architecture〉 **2 :** an aid in achieving or mastering something difficult, complex, or obscure **:** HELPER 〈a most necessary ~ to literary appreciation —George Saintsbury〉
¹an·cil·lary \ˈansə,lerē, ˈaan-, -nts-, -ri, *US also & Brit usu* anˈsilər- *or* aan-\ *adj* [L *ancillaris* of a maidservant, fr. *ancilla* + *-aris* -ar] **:** SUBORDINATE, SUBSIDIARY 〈the main factory and its ~ plants〉 **:** AUXILIARY 〈surgery and ~ treatment〉 **:** RELATED 〈mathematics and ~ subjects〉 **:** SUPPLEMENTARY 〈the need for ~ evidence〉; *specif* **:** subordinate or auxiliary to a primary or principal legal document, proceeding, office, or officer 〈~ letters of administration〉 〈~ action〉 〈~ administrator〉
²ancillary \"\ *n* -ES **1** *Brit* **:** one who assists or serves another person 〈the bill proposed no more than a three-year experiment in training and employing *ancillaries* under the direction of the General Dental Council —*Lancet*〉 **2** *Brit* **:** APPURTENANCE, ACCESSORY 〈development of aircraft, aircraft engines, and *ancillaries* —*Manchester Guardian Weekly*〉
an·cip·i·tal \(ˈ)anˈsipəd·ᵊl\ *or* **an·cip·i·tous** \-d·əs\ *adj* [L *ancipit-, anceps* two-headed, two-edged (fr. — assumed — *ambicipit-, ambiceps*, fr. *ambi-* + *-ceps*, fr. *caput* head) + E *-al* or *-ous* — more at HEAD] **:** DOUBLE-EDGED — used of flattened stems (as of certain grasses)
an·ci·pi·tis usus \anˈsipəd·əsˈyüsəs, äŋˈkipəd·əˈsüsəs\ *adj* [L] **:** of twofold use — used esp. of an article (as coal) that can be utilized for commercial as well as belligerent purposes and hence raises the question of whether or not it is justifiable contraband of war
an·cis·troc·la·dus \,an,siˈsträkləd·əs\ *n, cap* [NL, fr. Gk *ankistron* fishhook + *klados* branch; akin to Gk *ankos* glen — more at ANGLE, GLADIATOR] **:** a genus of climbing shrubs (order Parietales) of the East Indies and Africa constituting a distinct family and having hooked branches and panicled flowers with 10 stamens and a single pistil that are followed by nutlike fruits
an·cis·tro·don \anˈsistrə,dän\ *syn of* AGKISTRODON
an·cis·troid \anˈsi,strȯid, ˈansi,s-\ *adj* [Gk *ankistroeidēs*, fr. *ankistron* fishhook + *-eidēs* -oid] **:** shaped like a hook **:** resembling a hook
an·cis·tro·syrinx \an¦sistrō +\ *n* [NL, fr. Gk *ankistron* fishhook + *syrinx* shepherd's pipe — more at SYRINX] **1** *cap* **:** a small genus (family Turritidae) of gastropod mollusks that occur in warm deep seas and have delicate steeply shouldered pale shells ringed with upward-curving spines **2** *pl* **ancistrosyringes :** any mollusk or shell of the genus *Ancistrosyrinx*
an·cle *Brit var of* ANKLE
an·co·bar \ˈaŋkō,bär\ *n* -s *usu cap* [*Ancona* + *barred* Plymouth Rock] **:** any of an autosexing strain or breed of chickens developed by crossing Anconas and barred Plymouth Rocks
an·co·dont \-,dänt\ *n* -s [NL *Ancodonta*] **:** an animal or fossil of the division Ancodonta
an·co·don·ta \,aŋkōˈdäntə\ *n pl, cap* [NL, fr. Gk *ankos* bend, hollow + NL *-odonta*] **:** a division of Artiodactyla comprising the hippopotamuses and extinct related forms and with the Suina and certain extinct related forms forming the suborder Suiformes
¹an·con \ˈaŋ,kän\ *also* **an·cone** \-kōn\ *n, pl* **an·cones** *as pl of* "ancon", aŋˈkōnēz; *as pl of* "ancone", ˈaŋ,kōnz\ [L *ancon*, fr. Gk *ankōn* elbow] **:** a bracket, elbow, or console used as an architectural support (as for the cornice over a doorway) **:** CROSSETTE 1, MODILLION
²ancon *usu cap, var of* ANCON SHEEP
³an·con \ˈaŋ,kōn, -än, (ˈ)äŋ¦kōn\ *adj, usu cap* [fr. *Ancón*, near Lima, Peru, its type station] **:** of or belonging to an early, middle, or late period of the Chavin civilization of Peru characterized by distinct pottery types
¹an·co·na \aŋˈkōnə\ *n* -s *usu cap* [fr. *Ancona*, Italy] **:** a domestic fowl of a breed of the Mediterranean class resembling the Leghorns in build and having mottled black-and-white plumage
²ancona \"\ *n, pl* **anco·ne** \-nē\ *or* **anconas** [It, prob. modif. (prob. influenced by *Ancona*, seaport on Adriatic coast, Italy) of Gk *eikona*, acc. of *eikon-, eikōn* image — more at ICON] **:** ALTARPIECE; *specif* **:** one composed of one or more paintings in an elaborate architectural framework
an·co·nal \(ˈ)aŋ¦kōnᵊl\ *also* **an·co·ne·al** \-nēəl\ *adj* [NL *ancon* elbow (fr. Gk *ankōn*) + E *-al, -eal*] **:** of, relating to, or belonging to the elbow 〈~ pain〉
an·co·ne·us \aŋˈkōnēəs\ *n, pl* **anco·nei** \-ē,ī\ [NL, fr. *ancon* + L *-eus* -eous] **:** a small triangular extensor muscle superficially situated behind and below the elbow joint
an·co·noid \ˈaŋkə,nȯid\ *adj* [NL *ancon* + E *-oid*] **:** resembling an elbow
an·con sheep \ˈaŋkən-, -,kän-\ *also* **ancon** *n* -s *usu cap A* [NL *ancon*; fr. their short, crooked legs] **:** a short-legged achondroplastic sheep; *esp* **:** such a sheep of an extinct strain or breed formerly maintained in Massachusetts
ancony *n* -ES [origin unknown] *archaic* **:** a piece of iron wrought into the shape of a bar in the middle and left rough at the ends
an·cred \ˈaŋkə(r)d\ *adj* [prob. modif. of F *ancré*] **:** ANCRÉE
an·crée \äŋ·krā\ *adj* [F *ancré*, fr. *ancre* anchor (fr. L *ancora, anchora*) + *-é* (fr. L *-atus* -ate) — more at ANCHOR] *of a cross* **:** having the end of each arm divided into two recurving points like the flukes of an anchor — usu. used postpositively; often distinguished from *moline*
ancress *var of* ANCHORESS
anct *abbr* ancient
-an·cy \ənsē, -si\ *n suffix* -ES [L *-antia* — more at -ANCE] **1 :** quality or state 〈*buoyancy*〉 〈*pliancy*〉 **2 :** instance of a quality or state 〈*expectancy*〉
ancyl- *or* **ancylo-** — see ANKYL-
an·cyl·i·dae \aŋˈkilə,dē, anˈsi-\ *n pl, cap* [NL, fr. *Ancylus*, type genus + *-idae*] **:** a cosmopolitan family of small thin-shelled conical pulmonate snails related to the Planorbidae — compare FRESHWATER LIMPET
an·cy·lite \ˈansə,līt\ *n* -s [prob. fr. Dan *ankylit*, fr. *ankyl-* + *-it* -ite] **:** a mineral $Sr_3Ce_4(CO_3)_7(OH)_3.3H_2O$ consisting of hydrous basic carbonate of strontium and cerium
an·cy·loc·er·as \,ansəˈläsərəs\ *n, cap* [NL, fr. *ankyl-* + *-ceras*] **:** a genus of ammonoids having a partly uncoiled shell and the aperture of the living chamber directed toward the coiled part
an·cy·loc·la·dus \-ˈäkləd·əs\ [NL, fr. *ankyl-* + Gk *klados* branch] *syn of* WILLUGHBEIA
an·cy·lo·dac·ty·la \¦ansə(,)lōˈdaktələ\ [NL, fr. *ankyl-* + *-dactyla* (fr. Gk *daktylos* finger)] *syn of* ANCYLOPODA
an·cy·lop·o·da \,ansəˈläpəd·ə\ *n pl, cap* [NL, fr. *ankyl-* + *-poda*] *in some classifications* **:** a division of fossil Miocene and Pliocene ungulates of both the Old and the New World having clawed feet resembling those of the edentates
ancylose *var of* ANKYLOSE
ancylosis *var of* ANKYLOSIS
an·cy·los·to·ma \,aŋkəˈlästəmə, -kēˈ- *also* ,ansəˈ-\ *n, cap* [NL, fr. *ankyl-* + *-stoma*] **:** the type genus of Ancylostomatidae comprising hookworms that have buccal teeth resembling hooks and are parasites in the intestines of man and various mammals — compare NECATOR
an·cy·lo·sto·mat·i·dae \¦==(,)lōstōˈmad·ə,dē, ,==,lästəˈm-\ *n pl, cap* [NL, fr. *Ancylostomat-, Ancylostoma*, type genus + *-idae*] **:** a family of strongyloid nematodes containing the hookworms
an·cyl·o·stome \aŋˈkilə,stōm *also* anˈsi-\ *or* **an·kyl·o·stome** \aŋˈki-\ *n* -s [NL *Ancylostoma*] **:** a hookworm of the genus *Ancylostoma*
an·cy·lo·sto·mi·a·sis \¦aŋkə(,)lōstōˈmīəsəs, -kē-, ,==,lästəˈm- *also* ¦ansə- *or* ,ansə-\ *also* **an·ky·lo·sto·mi·a·sis** *or* **an·chy·lo·sto·mi·a·sis** \¦aŋk-, ,aŋk-\ *n, pl* **ancylostomia·ses** \-ə,sēz\ [NL, fr. *Ancylostoma* + *-iasis*] **:** infestation with or disease caused in man or animals by hookworms; *specif* **:** a condition in man marked by lethargy, severe anemia, and relative eosinophilia due to loss of blood through the feeding of hookworms in the small intestine — called also *hookworm disease*
an·cy·lo·stom·i·dae \¦aŋkō(,)lōˈstäm·ə,dē, -kē- *also* ¦ansə-\ [NL, fr. *Ancylostoma*, type genus + *-idae*] *syn of* ANCYLOSTOMATIDAE
an·cy·los·to·mum \,==ˈlästəməm\ [NL, fr. *ankyl-* + *-stomum*] *syn of* ANCYLOSTOMA
ancylotic *var of* ANKYLOTIC
an·cy·lus \ˈaŋkələs, -kē-, ˈansəl-\ *n, cap* [NL, fr. Gk *ankylos* curved — more at ANKYL-] **:** the type genus of Ancylidae
ancyroid *var of* ANKYROID
¹and \ən(d), (ˈ)an(d); *usu* ᵊn(d) *after* t, d, s, *or* z *as in* "*hit and run*", *often* ᵊm *after* p *or* b *as in* "*up and down*", *sometimes* ᵊŋ *after* k *or* g *as in* "*lock and key*"; *in rapid speech sometimes* n (*as in one pronunciation*, ,bəd·ə(r)ˈnegz, *of* "*butter and eggs*") *or sometimes* m (*as in one pronunciation*, bīmˈbī, *of* "*by and by*"); *sometimes* (ˈ)aa(ə)n(d); *sporadically* (ˈ)en(d)\ *conj* [ME, fr. OE *and, ond, end;* akin to OFris *anda, enda* and, OHG *anti, enti, unti, inti*, ON *enn* and, but, and perh. to Oscan *ant* up to, Toch B *entwe* then, therefore, and perh. to OE *in* — more at IN] **1 a :** along with or together with 〈he ~ his son were here〉 **b :** added to or linked to 〈a thousand ~ one nights〉 〈I have a hundred ~ one things to do〉 〈cream ~ sugar with your coffee〉 **c :** as well as 〈he took aspirin ~ bicarbonate of soda〉 **d :** again then again 〈the dog barked ~ barked〉 **e :** also at the same time 〈they walked ~ talked〉 **f :** THEN 〈they drove five miles ~ stopped to eat〉 **g :** in addition to being 〈secretary ~ treasurer〉 **h :** but not less truly **:** YET 〈an entertaining ~ scholarly book〉 — symbol *&;* used as a function word to (1) express the general relation of connection or addition, esp. accompaniment, participation, combination, contiguity, continuance, simultaneity, sequence or (2) conjoin word with word 〈bread ~ butter〉 or phrase with phrase 〈over the river ~ through the woods〉 or clause with clause 〈said that he would be nominated ~ that he would be elected〉 or combinations thereof (as adjectival or adverbial elements of different types, adjective and substantive complements, or various constructions involving ellipsis) 〈dissatisfied ~ with still unanswered questions〉 〈he solved the problem carefully ~ without error〉 〈allegations heretofore unuttered ~ which force us to take action〉 〈he is a shrewd man ~ apt to take advantage of a bargain like this〉 〈he stopped speaking ~ then the awful shock — he slapped me〉 or (3) fill in expletively (as in initial position in a sentence or between completely disparate elements) 〈~ it came to pass in those days〉 〈when that I was ~ a little tiny boy —Shak.〉 **2** — used as a function word to express (1) repetition 〈they rode two ~ two〉 〈hundreds ~ hundreds〉 or (2) variation or difference 〈there are women ~ women〉 or (3) logical or semantic modification of one notion by another as when (a) two elements are joined so that the second logically qualifies the first 〈your fair ~ outward character〉 〈in poverty ~ distress〉 or (b) two adjectives are joined so that the first becomes equivalent to an adverb modifying the second 〈nice ~ warm〉 〈good ~ ready〉 or (c) one finite verb (as *go, come, try, write*) is joined with another so that it becomes logically equal to an infinitive of purpose 〈go ~ call him〉 〈come ~ see me〉 〈try ~ stop me〉 〈write ~ tell me〉 or (d) two verbs are joined so that the first represents a position or state and the second represents an attendant action that may also be expressed by a participle 〈he sat ~ smoked〉 〈to sit ~ wait〉 or (4) a consequence or sequel 〈I said go ~ he went〉 〈one step further ~ he is a dead man〉 or (5) contrary action, incongruous outcome, or antithesis 〈he promised to come ~ didn't〉 〈he sailed for Florida ~ landed in Cuba〉 or (6) reference to either or both of two alternatives 〈choose between him ~ me〉 esp. in legal language when also plainly intended to mean *or* 〈bequeathed to a person ~ her bodily issue〉 〈property taxable for state ~ county purposes〉 or (7) supplementary explanation or restriction often with climactic emphasis in an appended phrase 〈he ~ he alone could control it〉 〈living in one room ~ that room a cellar〉 or (8) at the point of junction or intersection 〈Main Street ~ First Avenue〉 **3** *obs* **:** as if **:** IF, THOUGH 〈they will set an house on fire, ~ it were but to roast their eggs —Francis Bacon〉 — see ²AN **4** — used in logic as a sentential or propositional connective that produces a compound proposition true only if both compounds are true 〈symbolically *p·q* is true if ~ only if neither *p* nor *q* is false〉 — see CONJUNCTION — **and how** \(ˈ)an(d)ˈhau̇\ — used to emphasize the preceding idea 〈Congress is fully restored to its position as a separate branch of the government — *and how* —*Barron's*〉 — **and interest :** with an amount equal to all interest accrued to the date of payment to be added to the price of a bond being purchased — compare ³FLAT 4 — **and so forth** \=ˈ=,= *also* =ˈ=ˈ=\ **:** and others or more of the same or similar kind 〈pamphlets, books, *and so forth*〉 **:** further in the same or similar manner 〈afterward she screamed and cried *and so forth*〉 **:** and the rest 〈he moved his furniture, clothes, *and so forth*〉 **:** and other things (as ingredients) 〈milk, eggs, flour, *and so forth*〉 — **and so on** \=ˈ=,= *also* =ˈ=ˈ=\ **:** and so forth
²and *conj* [ME, prob. modif. (influenced by ¹*and*) of ON *an, enn*, fr. Runic Norse *than* — more at THAN] *obs* **:** ¹THAN 1a
³and \ˈand *sometimes* ˈaa(ə)nd, *sporadically* ˈend\ *n, pl* **ands** \-n(d)z\ [¹*and*] **:** an added particular or condition 〈I want to hear no ifs or ~*s* about it〉
and *abbr* andante
an·da \anˈdä\ *or* **an·da–as·su** \anˈdä(,)sü\ *n* -s [*anda* fr. Pg, fr. Tupi; *anda-assu* fr. Pg, fr. Tupi *andá-açu*, fr. *anda* + *açu* big] **:** a Brazilian timber tree (*Joannesia princeps*) of the family Euphorbiaceae having light soft wood
an·da·ki *or* **an·da·qui** \¦ändä¦kē, ¦an-\ *n, pl* **andaki** *or* **andakis** *or* **andaqui** *or* **andaquis** *usu cap* [Sp *andaqui*, of AmerInd origin] **1 a :** a Chibchan people of southern Colombia **b :** a member of such people **2 :** the language of the Andaki people — **an·da·qui·an** \-ēən\ *adj, usu cap*
¹an·da·lu·sian \¦andə¦lüzhən, ¦aan-\ *adj, usu cap* [*Andalusia* (Sp *Andalucía*), region of southern Spain + E *-an*] **1 :** of, relating to, or characteristic of Andalusia 〈*Andalusian* music〉 **2 :** of, relating to, or characteristic of the people of Andalusia
²andalusian \"\ *n* -s **1** *usu cap* **:** a native or inhabitant of Andalusia **2** *often cap* **:** a domestic fowl of a Mediterranean breed similar to the Leghorn **3** *cap* **:** the dialect of Spanish spoken in Andalusia
an·da·lu·site \,==ˈ=,sīt\ *n* -s [F *andalousite*, fr. *Andalousie* Andalusia, region in Spain where it was discovered + F *-ite*] **:** a silicate of aluminum Al_2SiO_5 usu. in thick nearly square orthorhombic prisms of various colors used in making refractory porcelains
an·da·man \ˈandəmən, -,man\ *also* **an·da·man·ese** \¦andəmə¦nēz, -ēs\ *adj, usu cap* [*Andaman* fr. *Andaman* islands, Bay of Bengal, India; *Andamanese* fr. *Andaman* islands + E *-ese*] **1 a :** of, relating to, or characteristic of the Andaman islands **b :** of, relating to, or characteristic of the people of the Andaman islands **2 :** of, relating to, or characteristic of the Andamanese language
andamanese \"\ *n, pl* **andamanese** *usu cap* **1** *or* **an·da·man** \ˈandəmən, -,man\ *usu cap* **:** a Negrito native to the Andaman islands — called also *Andaman Islander* **2 :** an agglutinative language of the Andamanese which is unconnected with any known language family
andaman marble *or* **andaman marblewood** *n, usu cap A* **:** MARBLEWOOD
andaman padauk *n, usu cap A* **1 :** a tree (*Pterocarpus dalbergioides*) of the Andaman islands with reddish or red-brown wood like mahogany **2 :** the wood of the Andaman padauk tree
andaman redwood *n, usu cap A* **:** AMBOYNA
¹an·dan·te \(ˈ)an¦dantē, -aan¦daa-; än¦dän,tā, ȧnˈdȧn-, (ˈ)=¦=,tē\ *adv* (*or adj*) [It, lit., going, pres. part. of *andare* to go, prob. fr. (assumed) VL *amlare* — more at ALLEY] **1** *in 18th century musical notation* **:** in strict time **2 :** moderately slow and in tempo between larghetto and allegretto 〈a cello passage in an ~ section〉 — often used as a direction in music
²andante \"\ *n* -s **:** a musical piece or movement in andante tempo
¹an·dan·ti·no \,=,=ˈtē(,)nō\ *adj* (*or adv*) [It, fr. *andante* + *-ino* -ine (fr. L *-inus*)] **:** rather quicker in tempo than andante; *sometimes* **:** somewhat slower than andante — often used as a direction in music
²andantino \"\ *n* -ES **:** a musical piece or movement in andantino tempo; *also* **:** a short andante
an·de·an \ˈandēən, ˈaan-, =ˈ==\ *adj, usu cap* [*Andes* + E *-an*] **:** of, relating to, or characteristic of the Andes mountain system 〈the Andean wolf〉 〈*Andean* Indians〉
-an·der \,andə(r), ,aan-\ *n comb form* -s [NL *-andrus*, fr. Gk *-andros* having (such or so many) men — more at -ANDROUS] **:** one having (such or so many) stamens — in words denoting members of Linnaean botanical classes in *-andria* 〈*hexander*〉
an·der·son·ite \ˈandə(r)sə,nīt\ *n* -s [Charles A. *Anderson* *b*1902 Am. geologist + E *-ite*] **:** a mineral consisting of a secondary hydrous sodium calcium uranium carbonate $Na_2Ca(UO_2)(CO_3)_3.6H_2O$ found in the uranium districts of the western U.S.
an·des berry \ˈan(,)dēz-, ˈaan-\ *n, usu cap A* [fr. *Andes* mts.] **:** a bramble (*Rubus glaucus*) of tropical American highlands having dark purple fruit like raspberries
an·de·sine \ˈandə,zēn\ *n* -s [G *andesin*, fr. *Andes*, mountain system in So. America, where it is found + G *-in* -ine] **:** a triclinic feldspar intermediate between albite and anorthite that is an ingredient of andesite — **an·de·sin·ic** \¦andə¦zinik\ *adj*
an·de·si·nite \ˈandəzə,nīt\ *n* -s [*andesine* + *-ite*] **:** a leucocratic rock composed essentially of andesine
an·de·site \ˈandə,zīt\ *n* -s [G *andesit*, fr. *Andes*, its locality + G *-it* -ite] **:** an extrusive usu. dark grayish rock consisting essentially of oligoclase or andesine feldspar with augite, hornblende, hypersthene, or biotite — **an·de·sit·ic** \¦andə¦zid·ik\ *adj*
an·dhra \ˈändrə\ *n* -s *usu cap* [fr. *Andhra*, India] **:** the Dravidian language of the Andhra region of southern India
an·dhran \ˈändrən\ *n* -s *usu cap* [fr. *Andhra*, India + E *-an*] **:** a native or inhabitant of the Andhra region or of Andhra Pradesh, southern India
an·di \ˈändē\ *n* -s *usu cap* **:** a north Caucasic language — **an·di·an** \-ēən\ *adj, usu cap*
an·dine \ˈan,dēn, -,dīn\ *adj, usu cap* [Sp *andino*, fr. *Andes* mountains + Sp *-ino* (fr. L *-inus* -ine)] **:** ANDEAN
¹an·di·no \anˈdē(,)nō\ *n* -s *usu cap* [Sp, adj. & n.] **:** a native or inhabitant of the Andes
²andino \"\ *adj, usu cap* [Sp, Andean] **:** of or belonging to the middle period of the ancient Tiahuanaco culture of coastal Peru
an·di·ra \anˈdērə, -dīrə\ *n, cap* [NL, fr. Pg, angelim, fr. Tupi] **:** a genus of tropical American trees (family Leguminosae) characterized by large odd-pinnate leaves, fragrant showy rose to purplish flowers in terminal clusters, and a fruit resembling a drupe
an·di·ro·ba \,andəˈrōbə\ *n* -s [AmerSp *andiroba* or Pg *andiroba, jandiroba*, fr. Tupi *andiróba, nandiroba*] **:** ¹CRABWOOD
and·iron \ˈan,dī(ə)rn, ˈaan-, -īən\ *n* -s [ME *aundiren*, modif. (influenced by ME *iren* iron) of OF *andier*, fr. (assumed) Gaulish *anderos* young bull; akin to W *anner* heifer, MIr *ainder* young woman; fr. the figures used as ornamentation] **:** one of a pair of metal supports for firewood used on a hearth and consisting of a horizontal bar mounted on short legs, one in the rear and two in front, an often ornamented vertical shaft usu. surmounting the front end

andirons

an·do·ke \ˈan¦dōkē\ *n, pl* **andoke** *or* **andokes** *usu cap* **1 a :** a people of southern Colombia **b :** a member of such people **2 :** the language of the Andoke people, of uncertain relationship
and/or \ˈan¦dȯr, -ō(ə)\ *conj* — used as a function word to indicate that words are to be taken together or individually 〈men *and/or* women means men *and* women or men *or* women〉
an·dor·ite \ˈandə,rīt\ *n* -s [G *andorit*, fr. *Andor* von Semsey †1923 Hungarian nobleman + G *-it* -ite] **:** a mineral consisting of a compound of silver, lead, antimony, and sulfur $PbAgSb_3S_6$ occurring in dark gray or black prisms
an·dor·ra \(ˈ)an¦dȯrə, -ärə\ *adj, usu cap* [fr. *Andorra*, state in the Pyrenees between France and Spain] **:** of or from the republic of Andorra **:** of the kind or style prevalent in Andorra **:** ANDORRAN
¹an·dor·ran \-rən\ *adj, usu cap* [*Andorra* + *-an*] **:** of, relating to, or characteristic of Andorra
²andorran \"\ *n* -s *cap* **:** a native or inhabitant of Andorra
an·do·ver green \ˈan,dōvə(r)-, ˈaan-, -dəv-\ *n, often cap A* [prob. fr. *Andover*, Mass.] **:** a grayish olive green that is greener and paler than average ivy green and yellower and paler than bronze green
andr- *or* **andro-** *comb form* [MF *andro-*, fr. L *andr-, andro-*, fr. Gk, fr. *andr-, anēr* man (male person); akin to OIr *nert* strength, Oscan *ner* man (male person), Skt *nr*] **1 :** man 〈*androcentric*〉 〈*androphagous*〉 **:** of or belonging to a man or men 〈*androcracy*〉 〈*androphobia*〉 **:** having the characteristics of a man and 〈*androtauric*〉 **2 :** male 〈*androgenesis*〉 **:** male and 〈*androgynous*〉 **3 :** stamen **:** anther 〈*androecium*〉
-an·dra \ˈandrə, ˈaan-\ *n comb form* [NL, fem. of *-andrus* -androus] **:** one having (such) a stamen — in generic names of plants 〈*Calliandra*〉 〈*Pachysandra*〉
an·dra·dite \anˈdrä,dīt\ *n* -s [José B. de *Andrada* e Silva †1838 Brazilian geologist and statesman + E *-ite*] **:** a garnet $Ca_3Fe_2(SiO_4)_3$ of any of various colors ranging from yellow and green to brown and black
an·dre·ae·a·les \,andrēˈēə,lēz\ *n pl, cap* [NL, fr. *Andreaea* genus of mosses (after G. R. *Andreae* Ger. botanist) + *-ales*] **:** an order of Musci comprising a single genus of brown or blackish alpine mosses with a capsule that dehisces by four longitudinal slits
an·drea·sen method \ˈan·drāzᵊn-\ *n, usu cap A* [fr. the name *Andreasen*] **:** a method of estimating particle size of ceramic clay by sedimentation
an·dre·na \anˈdrēnə\ *n, cap* [NL, prob. irreg. fr. Gk *anthrēnē* hornet, wasp — more at ATHEROMA] **:** a genus (the type of the family Andrenidae) of burrowing solitary short-tongued bees including important pollinators of economic plants
an·dre·nid \-ēnəd\ *n* -s [NL *Andrenidae*] **:** a bee of the family Andrenidae
an·dren·i·dae \-renə,dē, -ēn-\ *n pl, cap* [NL, fr. *Andrena*, type genus + *-idae*] **:** a large family of short-tongued bees which are solitary in habit and most of which burrow in the ground
an·drews·ite \ˈan(,)drü,zīt\ *n* -s [Thomas *Andrews* †1885 Ir. chemist + E *-ite*] **:** a mineral consisting of a hydrous phosphate of copper and iron $(Cu,Fe^{II})_3Fe_6^{III}(PO_4)_4(OH)_{12}$
-an·dria \ˈandrēə, ˈaan-\ *n pl comb form* [NL, fr. Gk, fact or condition of having (such or so many) men — more at -ANDRY] **:** plants having (such or so many) stamens — in names of Linnaean botanical classes 〈*Polyandria*〉
an·dri·as \ˈandrēəs\ *n, cap* [NL, fr. Gk, image of a man, fr. *andr-, anēr* man; fr. the fact that the first specimen found was

believed to be the remains of a man destroyed by the Deluge] : a genus of large fossil Miocene salamanders scarcely distinct from the recent genus *Cryptobranchus*

an·dric \'andrik\ *adj* [Gk *andrikos*, fr. *andr-* + *-ikos* -ic] : of or belonging to a male person — contrasted with *gynic*

an·dri·cus \an'drīkəs\ *n, cap* [NL] : a genus of cynipid gall wasps chiefly affecting various oaks

-andries *pl of* -ANDRY

an·drite \'an,drīt\ *n* -s [origin unknown] : a meteorite composed essentially of augite with a little olivine and troilite

andro- *in pronunciations below*, ¦== = ¦andrə *or* ¦aan- *or* -drō *sometimes* -,drō\ — see ANDR-

an·dro·cen·tric \¦==¦==\ *adj* [*andr-* + *-centric*] : centering or centered on or in the male : dominated by or emphasizing masculine interests or point of view ⟨an ~ society⟩ — contrasted with *gynecocentric*

an·dro·co·ni·um \,==ˈkōnēəm\ *n, pl* **an·dro·co·nia** \-ēə\ [NL, fr. *andr-* + Gk *konis* dust + NL *-ium* — more at INCINERATE] : any of certain modified scales associated with glandular structures on the fore wings of the male of some butterflies and moths and concerned with the production of an odor attractive to members of the opposite sex

an·droc·ra·cy \an'dräkrəsē\ *n* -ES [*andr-* + *-cracy*] : political and social supremacy of men — contrasted with *gynecocracy; compare* PATRIARCHY — **an·dro·crat·ic** \¦andrə¦krad·ik\ *adj*

an·dro·cyte \'==,sīt\ *n* -s [*andr-* + *-cyte*] : a cell in bryophytes that by modification becomes a sperm cell — compare SPERMATID, SPERMATOCYTE

an·dro·di·oe·cious *or* **an·dro·di·ecious** \¦==,=¦==\ *adj* [*andr-* + *dioecious, diecious*] : having perfect and staminate flowers on different plants — **an·dro·di·oe·cism** \-,dī'ē,sizəm\ *n* -s

an·droe·ci·um \an'drēs(h)ēəm\ *n, pl* **androe·cia** \-)ēə\ [NL, fr. *andr-* + Gk *oikion*, dim. of *oikos* house — more at VICINITY] **1** : the aggregate of microsporophylls in the flower of a seed plant : stamens and their appendages **2** : the male inflorescence of a liverwort

an·dro·gam·one \,=='ga,mōn\ *n* -s [*andr-* + *gamone*] : a gamone in a male cell

an·dro·gen \'==jən, -,jen\ *n* -s [ISV *andr-* + *-gen*] : a sex hormone (as androsterone or testosterone) produced esp. in the testes and adrenal cortex and usu. characterized by its ability to stimulate the development of sex characteristics in the male; *also* : a synthetic compound (as methyltestosterone) having similar biological activity — compare ESTROGEN — **an·dro·gen·ic** \¦==¦jenik\ *adj*

an·dro·gen·e·sis \,==ˈjenəsəs\ *n* [NL, fr. *andr-* + *-genesis*] : male parthenogenesis : development in which the embryo contains only paternal chromosomes due to failure of the egg nucleus to participate in fertilization — compare GYNOGENESIS — **an·dro·ge·net·ic** \¦===¦==\ *adj* — **an·dro·ge·net·i·cal·ly** *adv* — **an·drog·e·nous** \(')an¦dräjənəs\ *adj*

an·dro·gen·ic·i·ty \¦==jə'nisəd·ē\ *n* -ES [*androgen* + *-icity*] : the property of producing physiological reactions similar to those produced by androgens

an·drog·e·ny \an'dräjənē\ *n* -ES [*andr-* + *-geny*] : ANDROGENESIS

androgen zone *or* **androgenic zone** *n* : the portion of the adrenal cortex believed to secrete male hormones or steroids resembling male hormones

an·dro·gone \'==,gōn\ *n* -s [*andr-* + *gone*] : ANDROGONIUM

an·dro·go·ni·al \¦==¦gōnēəl\ *adj* [NL, fr. *androgonium* + E *-al*] : of or relating to an androgonium

an·dro·go·nid·i·um \,==gō'nidēəm\ *n, pl* **androgonid·ia** \-ēə\ [NL, fr. *andr-* + *gonidium*] **1** : one of the male cells whose subsequent divisions produce spermatozoids in members of the genus *Volvox* **2** : ANDROSPORE 1

an·dro·go·ni·um \-'gōnēəm\ *n, pl* **androgo·nia** \-ēə\ [NL, fr. *andr-* + *-gonium*] : one of the group of cells that divide to produce androcytes and eventually spermatozoids (as in mosses and ferns)

an·drog·ra·phis \an'drägrəfəs\ *n, cap* [NL, fr. *andr-* + Gk *graphis* stylus, pencil, paintbrush, fr. *graphein* to write; fr. the form of the filaments — more at CARVE] : a genus of Indian plants (family Acanthaceae) with entire leaves, small tubular flowers, and dry capsular fruits — see CREAT

an·dro·gyne \'==,jīn\ *also* **an·dro·gyn** \-,jin\ *n* -s [MF, fr. L *androgynus*, fr. Gk *androgynos*, fr. *andr-* + *-gynos* -gynous] **1** : HERMAPHRODITE **2** *archaic* : an effeminate man

an·dro·gy·ne·i·ty \¦==jə'nēəd·ē, -jī'-\ *n* -ES [*androgyne* + *-ity*] : ANDROGYNY

an·drog·y·nism \an'dräjə,nizəm\ *n* -s [*androgynous* + *-ism*] : the quality or state of being androgynous : HERMAPHRODITISM

an·drog·y·nous \(')an¦dräjənəs\ *adj* [*androgyne* + *-ous*] **1** : having the characteristics of both sexes : being at once both male and female : HERMAPHRODITIC **2** *archaic* : sometimes hot and sometimes cold — used of planets **3** *a* : bearing both staminate and pistillate flowers in the same cluster with the male flowers uppermost — compare GYNAECANDROUS *b of fungi* : bearing both antheridium and oogonium on the same hypha

an·drog·y·ny \an'dräjənē\ *n* -ES [*androgynous* + *-y*] : the quality or state of being androgynous : HERMAPHRODITISM, EFFEMINACY

[1]**an·droid** \'an,drȯid\ *also* **an·droi·des** \an'drȯi(,)dēz\ *n, pl* **androids** *or* **androides** [LGk *androeidēs* manlike, fr. Gk *andr-* + *-oeidēs* -oid] : an automaton of human form

[2]**android** \"\ *adj* [LGk *androeidēs* manlike] *of the pelvis* : having the angular form and narrow outlet typical of a well-built man ⟨a disproportionate number of difficult labors occur in women with ~ pelves⟩ — compare GYNECOID

an·drom·eda \an'drämədə\ *n* [NL, fr. *Andromeda*, mythological Ethiopian princess (daughter of Cepheus) fastened to a rock for a sea monster to devour but rescued by Perseus, fr. L, fr. Gk] **1** *cap* : a small genus of low evergreen boreal or arctic shrubs (family Ericaceae) with revolute coriaceous leaves and drooping white or pinkish flowers in terminal umbels — see BOG ROSEMARY **2** -s : a plant of the genus *Andromeda* **3** -s : JAPANESE ANDROMEDA

an·drom·edo·tox·in \an¦drämə(,)dō'täksən\ *n* [ISV *andromed-* (fr. NL *Andromeda*) + *-o-* + *toxin*; orig. formed in G] : a toxic crystalline compound $C_{31}H_{50}O_{10}$ that exists in various ericaceous plants (as members of the genus *Andromeda*) and that taken in small doses lowers the blood pressure of animals

an·dro·me·rog·o·ny \¦an(,)drōmə'rägənē\ *n* -ES [*andr-* + *merogony*] : development of an embryo from a fertilized enucleated egg or egg fragment which shows only male characters : ANDROGENESIS

an·dro·mi·met·ic \¦==,=¦==\ *adj* [*androgen* + *mimetic*] : simulating the effect of androgen

an·dro·mo·noe·cious *also* **an·dro·mo·ne·cious** \¦===¦==\ *adj* [*andr-* + *monoecious, monecious*] : having perfect and staminate flowers on the same plant — **an·dro·mo·noe·cism** \-'nē,sizəm\ *n* -s

an·dro·phil·ic \¦=='filik\ *adj* [*andr-* + *-philic*] : showing preference for males or for men as distinguished from animals ⟨an ~ mosquito⟩

an·dro·pho·bia \,=='fōbēə\ *n* -s [NL, fr. *andr-* + *-phobia*] : an abnormal dread of men : repugnance to the male sex — **an·dro·pho·bic** \¦==¦fōbik *also* -äb-\ *adj*

an·dro·phore \'==,fō(ə)r\ *n* -s [F, fr. *andr-* + *-phore*] **1** : the stalk or column supporting the stamens in certain flowers **2** : a branch bearing antheridia in fungi **3** : a generative bud or modified medusa in coelenterates in which only male elements are developed : a male gonophore

an·droph·o·rous \(')an¦dräf(ə)rəs\ *adj* [*andr-* + *-phorous*] : bearing male sexual organs or zooids

an·dro·po·gon \,=='pō,gän\ *n, cap* [NL, fr. *andr-* + *-pogon*] : a large and important genus of almost cosmopolitan grasses with spikelike racemes having the flowers in pairs, one sterile and one fertile — see BLUESTEM, BROOM SEDGE

an·dros·a·ce \an'dräsə,kē, -ə,sē\ *n, cap* [NL, alter. of L *androsaces*, a plant or zoophyte, fr. Gk *androsakes*, a sea plant (prob. a species of *Acetabularia*)] : a genus of usu. tufted herbs (family Primulaceae) native to the northern hemisphere having basal tufted leaves, small terminal white or pink flowers, and capsular fruits — see ROCK JASMINE

an·dro·sin \'andrəsən, -,sin\ *n* -s [ISV *andros-* (fr. NL *androsaemifolium* — specific epithet of *Apocynum androsaemifolium* —, fr. *andr-* + *saemi-* semi- + L *folium* leaf) + *-in*] : a crystalline glucoside $C_{15}H_{20}O_8$ that is found in an herb (*Apocynum androsaemifolium*) and that yields glucose and acetovanillone on hydrolysis

an·dro·spo·ran·gi·um \¦==+\ *n, pl* **androsporan·gia** [NL, fr. *andr-* + *sporangium*] : a sporangium for androspores

an·dro·spore \'==,spō(ə)r\ *n* -s [NL *androsporus*, fr. *andr-* + *spora* spore] **1** : a zoospore characteristic of members of the algal family Oedogoniaceae that gives rise to a small male plant that produces true spermatozoids — called also *androgonidium* **2** : MICROSPORE

an·dro·stane \'==,stān\ *n* -s [*androsterone* + *-ane*] : a crystalline saturated steroid hydrocarbon $C_{19}H_{32}$ obtainable from androsterone by reduction

an·dros·te·rone \an'drästə,rōn, aan-\ *n* -s [ISV *andr-* + *sterol* + *-one*; orig. formed as G *androsteron*] : an androgenic hormone that is much less active than testosterone and that is a hydroxy ketone $C_{19}H_{30}O_2$ found esp. in human male urine and obtained synthetically from cholesterol

an·drot·o·my \an'dräd·əmē\ *n* -ES [*andr-* + *anatomy*] : ANTHROPOTOMY

an·dro·type \'==,tīp\ *n* -s [*andr-* + *type*] : a designated male type specimen

-an·drous \¦andrəs, ¦aan-\ *adj comb form* [NL *-andrus*, fr. Gk *-andros* having (such or so many) men, fr. *andr-*, *anēr* man (male person) — more at ANDR-] : having (such or so many) stamens ⟨mon*androus*⟩

-an·dry \,andrē, ,aan-, -ri\ *n comb form* -ES [NL *-andria*, fr. Gk, fact or condition of having (such or so many) men, fr. *-andros* + *-ia* -y] : possession of (such or so many) stamens ⟨hetero*andry*⟩

an·dry·a·la \an'drīələ\ *n, cap* [NL] : a genus of hardy perennial composite herbs with milky sap and alternate leaves that are native to the Mediterranean region and occas. cultivated for their heads of bright yellow ligulate flowers

ands *pl of* AND

andy over *var of* ANTONY OVER

ane \'ān\ *adj or n or pron* [ME (northern dial.) *an*, fr. OE *ān* — more at ONE] *chiefly Scot* : ONE

-ane \,ān\ *n suffix* -s [ISV *-an*, *-ane*, alter. of *-ene*, *-ine*, & *-one*] **1** : [3]-AN 1 ⟨ureth*ane*⟩ **2** : saturated or completely hydrogenated carbon compound — in names of hydrocarbons and some parent heterocyclic compounds ⟨meth*ane*⟩ ⟨cholest*ane*⟩ ⟨diox*ane*⟩; distinguished from *-ene*, *-yne*

[1]**anear** \ə'-\ *vt* [[1]*a-* + *near*, v.] *archaic* : to come near to : NEAR

[2]**anear** \"\ *adv* [[1]*a-* + *near*, adv.] **1** *archaic* : NEARLY, ALMOST ⟨the lady shrieks and well ~ does fall —Shak.⟩ **2** *archaic* : CLOSE, NEAR ⟨timidly the women drew ~ —William Morris⟩

[3]**anear** \"\ *prep, now chiefly dial* : NEAR : close to ⟨sat ~ me⟩

aneath \ə'nēth, -neth\ *prep* [[1]*a-* + *beneath*] *dial Brit* : BENEATH

an·ec·dot·age \'anik,dōd·ij\ *n* -s **1** : ANECDOTES ⟨something of the interest in ~ common to the time —Bernard Smith⟩ **2** [blend of *anecdote* and *dotage*] : advanced age that is accompanied by a strong tendency to reminisce and tell anecdotes ⟨some kindly, garrulous old gentleman who was in his ~ —*Amer. Jour. of Pub. Health*⟩ — compare DOTAGE

an·ec·dot·al \¦anik¦dōd·ᵊl, -ōtᵊl\ *adj* **1** : relating to, characteristic of, or containing anecdotes ⟨~ conversation⟩ **2** *of a painting or sculpture* : representing an incident that implies earlier or later action or dramatizes a situation of human interest ⟨an ~ painting of a dejected girl leaving a post office⟩ — **an·ec·dot·al·ism** \-,lizəm\ *n* -s — **an·ec·dot·al·ist** \-ləst\ *n* -s — **an·ec·dot·al·ly** \-ᵊlē, -i\ *adv*

an·ec·dote \'anik,dōt *also* -nək-; *usu* -ōd·+V\ *n, pl* **anecdotes** \-ts\ *or* **anecdo·ta** \,=='dōd·ə, -ōtə\ *see numbered senses* [F & Gk; F, fr. Gk *anekdotos* unpublished, fr. *an-* + *ekdotos* given out, fr. *ekdidonai* to give out, publish, fr. *ek* out, out of + *didonai* to give — more at EX-, DATE] **1** *pl* **anecdota** *also* **anecdotes** : items of unpublished or secret history or biography **2** *pl* **anecdotes** : a usu. short narrative of an interesting, amusing, or curious incident often biographical and generally characterized by human interest — **an·ec·dot·ism** \'==,dōd·,izəm,-ō,tiz-\ *n* -s — **an·ec·dot·ist** \-ōd·əst, -ōtə-\ *n* -s

an·ec·dot·ic \¦anik¦däd·ik, -ätik, -ēk\ *or* **an·ec·dot·i·cal** \-ə̇kəl, -ēk-\ *adj* [prob. fr. F *anecdotique*, fr. *anecdote* + *-ique* -ic] **1** : ANECDOTAL **2** : given to or ready at telling anecdotes ⟨at his most ~⟩ — **an·ec·dot·i·cal·ly** \-ə̇k(ə)lē, -ēk-,-li\ *adv*

an·echo·ic \¦anə¦kōik, -(,)ne-\ *adj* [*an-* + *echoic*] : free from echoes and reverberations — used of rooms with sound-absorbent walls esp. designed for acoustic measurements; compare DEAD 10

an·ei·le·ma \,a,nī'lēmə, ,anə'-\ *n, cap* [NL, fr. Gk *aneilēma* act of rolling up, fr. *aneilein* to roll up, fr. *ana-* + *eilein* to roll, wind; akin to Gk *eilyein* to enfold, enwrap — more at VOLUBLE] : a large genus of widely distributed chiefly tropical trailing or creeping perennial herbs (family Commelinaceae) that have slender evergreen leaves and blue flowers usu. in small panicles and are sometimes cultivated in the cool greenhouse

an·elas·tic \¦an+\ *adj* [*an-* + *elastic*] : having no single-valued relation between stress and strain in the elastic region of the stress-strain curve — **an·elas·tic·i·ty** \¦an-\ *n* -ES

anele \ə'nē(ə)l\ *vt* -ED/-ING/-s [ME *anelen*, fr. *an* (fr. OE, var. of *on*) + *elen* to anoint, fr. *ele* oil, fr. OE *ele*, fr. L *oleum* — more at OIL] *archaic* : to anoint esp. in giving extreme unction

an·elec·tro·ton·ic \¦anə¦lektrə¦tänik\ *adj* : relating to anelectrotonus

an·elec·trot·o·nus \¦anə¦lek'trätᵊnəs\ *n* -ES [NL, fr. *ana-* + *electrotonus*] : the condition of decreased irritability of a nerve in the region of a positive electrode or anode on the passage of a current of electricity through it — compare CATELECTROTONUS

an·el·y·trous \(')a¦ne-\ *adj* [*an-* + *elytrous*] : without elytra

anem- *or* **anemo-** *comb form* [prob. fr. F *anémo-*, fr. Gk *anem-*, *anemo-*, fr. *anemos* — more at ANIMATE] **1** : wind ⟨*anemosis*⟩ ⟨*anemometer*⟩ **2** : inhalation ⟨*anemopathy*⟩

ane·ma·tize \ə'nēmə,tīz\ *vt* -ED/-ING/-s : to affect with anemia : induce anemia in

anemi *var of* ANIMÉ

[1]**ane·mia** *also* **anae·mia** \ə'nēmēə, *esp Brit* -myə\ *n* -s [NL, fr. Gk *anaimia*, fr. *an-* + *-aimia* -emia] **1** *a* : a condition in which the blood is deficient in red blood cells, hemoglobin, or both or deficient in total volume (as from hemorrhage) — see HYPOCHROMIC ANEMIA, PERNICIOUS ANEMIA *b* : ISCHEMIA **2** : lack of vitality : BLOODLESSNESS, LIFELESSNESS, EMPTINESS ⟨intellectual ~ —John Fischer⟩ ⟨the New England tradition had died of ~ —Malcolm Cowley⟩

[2]**anemia** \"\ *n, cap* [NL, fr. Gk *aneimōn* unclad (fr. *an-* + *-eimōn* clad, fr. *heima* garment) + NL *-ia*; fr. the naked sporangia; akin to Gk *hennynai* to clothe — more at WEAR] : a genus of ferns (family Schizaeaceae) found in warm regions having pinnatifid almost skeletonlike fronds with sporangia borne in a close single row on either side of the pinnules

ane·mic *also* **anae·mic** \ə'nēmik, -mēk\ *adj* [ISV *anem-*, *anaem-* (fr. NL *anemia, anaemia*) + *-ic*] **1** : relating to or affected with anemia **2** : lacking vitality : BLOODLESS ⟨pale and ~ interpretations of Mozart —A.E.Wier⟩ — **ane·mi·cal·ly** \-ə̇k(ə)lē, -ēk-, -li\ *adv*

an·e·mo·bi·a·graph \¦anə(,)mō'bīə,graf\ *n* -s [*anem-* + Gk *bia* force + E *-graph*] : a pressure-tube anemometer that records wind speed

anem·o·chore \ə'nemə,kō(ə)r\ *n* -s [*anem-* + *-chore*] : a plant that has seeds or spores adapted (as by pappi) to distribution by wind — **anem·o·cho·ry** \-ōrē\ *n* -ES

an·e·mo·clas·tic \¦anəmō¦klastik\ *adj* [*anem-* + *clastic*] : formed by wind action — used of clastic rocks

ane·mo·gen·ic \ə¦nemə¦jenik\ *adj* [*anem-* + *-genic*] : causing anemia

anem·o·gram \ə'nemə,gram\ *n* -s [*anem-* + *-gram*] : a record made by an anemograph

anem·o·graph \-,graf\ *n* -s [*anem-* + *-graph*] : a recording anemometer — **anem·o·graph·ic** \=¦==¦ik\ *adj* — **anem·o·graph·i·cal·ly** \-ə̇k(ə)lē\ *adv*

an·e·mo·log·i·cal \¦anəmə¦läjəkəl\ *adj* : of or relating to anemology

an·e·mol·o·gy \,anə'mäləjē\ *n* -ES [*anem-* + *-logy*] : the study of winds

an·e·mom·e·ter \,anə'mämәd·ə(r), -ətə(r)\ *n* -s [*anem-* + *-meter*] : an instrument for measuring and indicating the force or speed of the wind : WIND GAUGE

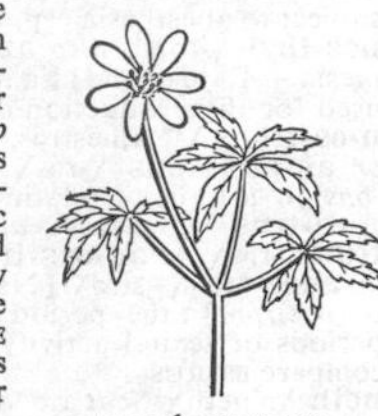

anemometer

an·e·mo·met·ric \¦anəmō¦me·trik\ *also* **an·e·mo·met·ri·cal** \-rə̇kəl\ *adj* : of or relating to anemometry

an·e·mo·met·ro·graph \,anəmō'me·trə,graf\ *n* -s [*anemometer* + *-o-* + *-graph*] : ANEMOGRAPH; *esp* : one that records simultaneously the pressure, speed, and direction of the wind — **an·e·mo·met·ro·graph·ic** \¦anəmō,me·trə¦grafik\ *adj* — **an·e·mo·met·ro·graph·i·cal·ly** \-ə̇k(ə)lē\ *adv*

an·e·mom·e·try \,anə'mämə·trē\ *n* -ES [*anem-* + *-metry*] : the act or process of ascertaining the force, speed, and direction of wind

anem·o·ne \ə'nemənē, -ni *also* -,nē\ *n* [L, fr. Gk *anemōnē*, perh. by folk etymology (influence of *anemos* wind) fr. a word of Sem origin; akin to Heb *Na'ămān*, epithet of Adonis] **1** -s : a plant or flower of the genus *Anemone* **2** *cap* [NL, fr. L] : a genus of herbs (family Ranunculaceae) widely distributed in temperate and subarctic regions that have lobed or divided often involucral leaves and showy flowers that lack petals but have showy sepals **3** -s : SEA ANEMONE **4** -s : a pale reddish purple that is redder, stronger, and slightly lighter than dusty orchid

wood anemone

anemone dahlia *n* : any of a class of dahlias having flower heads with only one row of rays and with the disk flowers elongated and forming an effect like a pincushion

anem·o·nin \ə'nemənən\ *n* -s [G, fr. NL *Anemone* (genus name of *Anemone pulsatilla*) + G *-in*] : an acrid poisonous crystallizable dilactone obtained from certain plants esp. of the genera *Ranunculus* and *Anemone*

anemony *n* -ES [by alter.] *archaic* : ANEMONE

an·e·moph·i·lous \¦anə¦mäfələs\ *adj* [*anem-* + *-philous*] : normally wind-pollinated ⟨~ flowers⟩ — compare ENTOMOPHILOUS — **an·e·moph·i·ly** \,anə'mäfəlē\ *n* -ES

an·e·mop·sis \,anə'mäpsə̇s\ *n, cap* [NL, fr. *anem-* (fr. *Anemone*) + *-opsis*; fr. its resemblance to an anemone] : a small genus of herbs (family Saururaceae) found in southwestern No. America having long-stalked entire leaves and minute flowers in a terminal bracted spike

anem·o·scope \ə'nemə,skōp\ *n* -s [prob. fr. F *anémoscope* (fr. *anémo-* anem- + *-scope*)] : a contrivance for indicating or for indicating and recording the direction of the wind; *also* : a device intended to foretell changes in the weather

an·e·mo·sis \,anə'mōsə̇s\ *n, pl* **anemo·ses** \-ō,sēz\ [NL, fr. *anem-* + *-osis*] : WIND SHAKE

an·e·mo·tax·is \,anəmō'taksə̇s\ *n, pl* **anemotax·es** \-k,sēz\ [NL, fr. *anem-* + *-taxis*] : ANEMOTROPISM

an·e·mo·trop·ic \¦anəmō¦träpik\ *adj* [*anem-* + *-tropic*] : relating to anemotropism

an·e·mot·ro·pism \,anə'mä·trə,pizəm\ *n* -s [*anem-* + *tropism*] : a tropism in which a current of air is the orienting factor (as in flies poised facing the wind)

an·en·ce·pha·lia \¦a,nensə'fālyə\ *n* -s [NL, fr. *an-* + *-encephalia*] : ANENCEPHALY

an·en·ce·phal·ic \¦a,nensə¦falik\ *or* **an·en·ceph·a·lous** \¦anən'sefələs, ¦a,nen-\ *adj* [*anencephalic* fr. *an-* + *encephalic*; *anencephalous* fr. Gk *anenkephalos* having no brain, fr. *an-* + *-enkephalos* -encephalous] : characterized by partial or total absence of the brain

an·en·ceph·a·lus \,anən'sefələs, ,a,nen-\ *n, pl* **anencepha·li** \-,lī\ [NL, fr. *an-* + *-encephalus*] : a fetus characterized by anencephaly

an·en·ceph·a·ly \-,lē\ *n* -ES [*an-* + *-encephaly*] : congenital absence of all or a major part of the brain

an end *adv* [ME *an ende*, *on ende*, fr. *an* (alter. of *on*), *on* + *ende* end] **1** *archaic* : to the end : CONTINUOUSLY **2** *obs* : UPRIGHT, ENDWAYS **3** : directly ahead : LENGTHWISE

anenst \ə'nenzt, -en(t)st\ *prep* [ME, alter. of *anentes*, alter. (influenced by *-es* -s, adv. ending) of *anent*] *dial chiefly Brit* : ANENT

anent \ə'nent\ *prep* [ME *anent*, *onevent*, fr. OE *onemn*, *on efen* alongside, together (akin to OS *an eban*), fr. *on* + *efen* even — more at EVEN] **1** *now dial Brit* : on a line or level with : BESIDE **2** *archaic* : TOWARD, AGAINST **3** *chiefly dial* : over against : OPPOSITE : close to ⟨the house is ~ the church⟩ **4** : in reference to : ABOUT, CONCERNING ⟨thoughts ~ the proper dissemination of religion —F. Tennyson Jesse⟩

an·en·ter·ous \(')a¦nentərəs\ *adj* [*an-* + *enterous*] : having no stomach or intestine

aner \'ānər, ä'ne(ə)r\ *n* -s [Gk *anēr* man, male animal — more at ANDR-] : a male insect; *esp* : a male ant

an·er·gic \(')a¦nərjik\ *adj* : exhibiting or marked by anergy

an·er·gy \'a,nərjē, 'anər-\ *n* -ES [NL *anergia*, fr. *an-* + Gk *ergon* work + NL *-ia* — more at WORK] : a condition in which the body fails to react to an injected allergen or antigen (as tuberculin)

anerobic *var of* ANAEROBIC

an·er·oid \'anə,rȯid\ *adj* [F *anéroïde*, fr. *a-* [2]*a-* + LGk *nērōn* water (fr. Gk *nearon*, neut. of *nearos* fresh, new) + F *-oïde* -oid; akin to L *noverca* stepmother, Arm *nor* new, Gk *neos* new — more at NEW] : containing no liquid or actuated without the use of liquid ⟨an ~ mechanism⟩ ⟨a ~ manometer⟩

aneroid barometer *also* **aneroid** *n* -s : a barometer in which the action of atmospheric pressure in bending the thin corrugated top of a closed and partially exhausted metallic box or in distorting a thin-walled bent tube of metal is made to move a pointer

aneroid barometer: *1*, exhausted box; *2*, spring attached to box and connected by lever, *3*, with rocking bar, *4*, which is connected by chain, *5*, with spindle of pointer, *6*

an·er·oid·o·graph \¦==ˈ=də,graf\ *n* -s [*aneroid* + *-o-* + *-graph*] : an aneroid barometer with a mechanism for recording automatically and continuously the atmospheric pressure

[1]**anes** \'ān(t)s, 'änz\ *adv* [ME (northern dial.), var. of *ones* — more at ONCE] *chiefly Scot* : ONCE

[2]**anes** *pl of* ANE

-anes *pl of* -ANE

an·e·sone \'anə,sōn\ *n* -s [origin unknown] : an anise-flavored liqueur often added to black coffee

an·es·the·sia *also* **an·aes·the·sia** \,anəs'thēzhə\ *n* -s [NL, fr. Gk *anaisthēsia* insensibility, fr. *an-* + *aisthēsis* feeling, perception (fr. *aisthanesthai* to perceive, feel) + *-ia* — more at AUDIBLE] **1** *a* : loss of sensation esp. to touch usu. resulting from a lesion in the nervous system or from some other abnormality — see GLOVE ANESTHESIA *b* : loss of sensation and usu. of consciousness without loss of vital functions artificially produced by the administration of one or more agents that block the passage of pain impulses along nerve pathways to the brain **2** : temporary dullness of perception or sensitiveness ⟨feeling the ~ of exhaustion —Norman Mailer⟩

Anes·the·sin \ə'nesthəsən, a'-\ *trademark* — used for benzocaine

an·es·the·si·ol·o·gist \,anəs,thēzē'äləjəst *also* -thēsē-\ *n* -s : ANESTHETIST; *specif* : a physician specializing in anesthesiology

an·es·the·si·ol·o·gy \-jē, -ji\ *n* -ES [ISV *anesthesio-* (fr. NL *anesthesia*) + *-logy*] : a branch of medical science dealing with anesthesia and anesthetics

[1]**an·es·thet·ic** *also* **an·aes·thet·ic** \¦anəs¦thed·ik, -etik, -ēk\ *adj* [Gk *anaisthētos* without sense or feeling, unfelt, imper-

ceptible (fr. *an-* + *aisthētos* sensible, perceptible, fr. *aisthanesthai* to perceive, feel) + E *-ic* — more at AUDIBLE] **1 a :** capable of producing anesthesia ⟨~ agents⟩ **b :** involving or connected with anesthesia ⟨~ effect⟩ ⟨~ symptoms⟩ **2 a :** lacking perceptive sensitiveness ⟨the young girls are in a state of possession, blind, deaf, and ~ —Joyce Cary⟩ **b :** OBTUSE — used with *to* ⟨persons ~ to new ideas⟩ — **an·es·thet·i·cal·ly** *adv*

²**anesthetic** *also* **anaesthetic** \"\ *n* -s **1 :** a substance that produces anesthesia **2 :** something that brings relief (as from pain, worry, uneasiness) : PALLIATIVE ⟨Vienna's most effective mass ~ against our time is the coffeehouse —Frederic Morton⟩

anes·the·tist *also* **anaes·the·tist** \ə'nesthədəst, a'-, -thətə-, *Brit usu* -nēs-\ *n* -s [*anesthetize, anaesthetize* + *-ist*] **:** one who administers anesthetics — compare ANESTHESIOLOGIST

anes·the·ti·za·tion *also* **anaes·the·ti·za·tion** \⸗,⸗thəd·ə'zāshən, -ətə'-, -ə,tī'z-\ *n* -s **:** the process of anesthetizing or state of being anesthetized

anes·the·tize *also* **anaes·the·tize** \ə'nesthə,tīz, a'-, *Brit usu* -nēs-\ *vt* -ED/-ING/-s [²*anesthetic, anaesthetic* + *-ize*] **:** to subject to anesthesia esp. by the use of an anesthetic

anes·thyl \-thəl\ *also* **anes·tile** \-tᵊl, -,tīl\ *n* -s [NL *anesthesia* + E *-yl* or *-ile*] **:** a mixture of ethyl and methyl chlorides used for the production of local anesthesia by spraying

an·es·trous \(')a¦nestrəs, *esp Brit* -ēs-\ *also* **an·es·tric** \-rik\ *or* **an·oes·trous** \-rəs\ *adj* [NL *anestrus, anoestrus* + E *-ous* or *-ic*] **:** of or relating to anestrus

an·es·trus \(')⸗'⸗trəs\ *also* **an·es·trum** \-rəm\ *or* **an·oes·trus** \-rəs\ *or* **an·oes·trum** \-rəm\ *n, pl* **anes·tri** \-,strī\ *or* **anes·tra** \-strə\ [NL, fr. *an-* + *estrus, estrum, oestrus*, or *oestrum*] **:** the period of sexual quiescence between two periods of sexual activity in cyclically breeding mammals — compare ESTRUS

aneth \ə'neth\ *Scot var of* ANEATH

an·e·thole \'anə,thōl\ *also* **an·e·thol** \-ōl,-ōl\ *n* -s [ISV *aneth-* (fr. L *anethum*) + *-ole, -ol;* prob. orig. formed as G *anethol*] **:** an ether $CH_3OC_6H_4C_3H_5$ obtained esp. from the oils of anise and fennel in the form of soft shining scales and used in flavoring and in cosmetics **:** *para*-propenyl-anisole — called also *anise camphor*

ane·thum \ə'nēthəm\ *n* [NL, fr. L, dill, fr. Gk *anēthon*] **1** *cap* **:** a small genus of Asiatic herbs (family Umbelliferae) with dissected foliage and yellow flowers — see DILL **2** *pl* **ane·tha** \-thə\ *or* **anethums :** the dried ripe fruit of an herb (*Anethum graveolens*) that is used in medicine as a carminative and stomachic

aneuch \ə'n(y)ük\ *adj or adv or n* [ME, var. of *enogh* — more at ENOUGH] *Scot* **:** ENOUGH

¹**an·eu·ploid** \'a(,)nyü,plȯid, 'anyə,-, (')a'nyü,-\ *adj* [*an-* + *euploid*] **:** having or being a chromosome number that is not a multiple of the monoploid number — compare EUPLOID, HETEROPLOID, HYPERPLOID — **an·eu·ploidy** \'a(,)nyü,plȯidē, 'anyə,-\ *n* -ES

²**aneuploid** \"\ *n* -s **:** an organism having an aneuploid chromosome number

aneu·ri·lem·mic \¦a,⸗⸗¦⸗⸗\ *adj* [²*a-* + NL *neurilemma* + E *-ic*] **:** having no neurilemma

an·eu·rin \'anyərən, (')ā'nyür-\ *also* **an·eu·rine** \-,rēn\ *n* -s [ISV ²*a-* + *neur-* + *-in*] **:** THIAMINE

aneu·ro·gen·ic \¦ā,nu̇rə¦jenik, -ür-\ *adj* [²*a-* + *neur-* + *-genic*] *of embryonic parts* **:** developing without the normal neural component ⟨a grafted limb bud is ~⟩

an·eu·rysm *also* **an·eu·rism** \'anyə,rizəm\ *n* -s [Gk *aneurysma*, fr. *aneurynein* to dilate, fr. *ana-* + *eurynein* to stretch, fr. *eurys* wide — more at EURY-] **:** a localized abnormal dilatation of a blood vessel (as an artery) filled with fluid or clotted blood, usu. forming a pulsating tumor, and resulting from disease of the vessel wall

an·eu·rys·mal *also* **an·eu·ris·mal** \¦anyə¦rizməl\ *adj* **:** relating to or affected by an aneurysm ⟨an ~ dilatation⟩ — **an·eu·rys·mal·ly** \-məlē\ *adv*

anew \ə'n(y)ü\ *adv* [ME *anewe, of newe*, fr. OE *of nīwe*, fr. *of* + *nīwe* new — more at NEW] **1 :** for an additional time ⟨each day raises ~ the possibility —*N.Y.Times*⟩ **:** as if a new start were being made and without reference to or observance of past acts or actions **:** AFRESH ⟨men chosen ~ on each occasion —S.G.Morley⟩ **2 :** in a new form

ane·zeh *or* **aney·ze** \ə'näzə\ *n, pl* **anezeh** *or* **anezehs** *or* **aneyze** *or* **aneyzes** *usu cap* **1 :** an Arab people of the Syrian desert **2 :** a member of the Anezeh people

an·frac·tu·os·i·ty \(,)an,frakchə'wäsəd·ē\ *n* -ES [MF *anfractuosité*, fr. LL *anfractuosus* + MF *-ité* -ity] **1 :** the quality or state of being anfractuous **2 :** a winding channel, course, or passage; *esp* **:** an intricate path or process (as of the mind) ⟨the history of mathematics . . . is one of quirks and *anfractuosities* —Norbert Wiener⟩

an·frac·tu·ous \(')an¦frachəwəs\ *adj* [F *anfractueux*, fr. LL *anfractuosus*, fr. L *anfractus* coil, crook (fr. *anfractus* crooked, fr. *an-* — fr. *ambi-* around — + *fractus*, past part. of *frangere* to break) + *-osus* -ose — more at AMBI-, BREAK] **:** full of windings and esp. intricate turnings **:** TORTUOUS, SINUOUS ⟨~ cliffs —T.H.White b. 1906⟩ ⟨these ~ times —Richard Eberhart⟩

ang- *comb form, usu ital* [*angular*] **:** angular (sense 5)

ang *abbr* angular

an·gai·té \,äŋ,gī'tā\ *n, pl* **angaité** *or* **angaités** *usu cap* [Sp, of AmerInd origin] **1 :** an Indian people of Paraguay **2 :** a member of the Angaité people

an·ga·kok *also* **an·ge·kok** \'aŋgə,käk\ *n, pl* **angakoks** *also* **angekoks** \-,käks\ [Esk] **:** an Eskimo medicine man or shaman

an·ga·mi \an'gämē\ *also* **angami–na·ga** \-'nägə\ *n, pl* **angami** *or* **angamis** *also* **angami–naga** *or* **angami–nagas** *usu cap A&N* **1 a :** a people of Assam, India **b :** a member of such people **2 :** the language of the Angami

an·gar·a·lite \an'garə,līt\ *n* -s [G *angaralith*, fr. *Angara* river, U.S.S.R., its locality + G *-lith* -lite] **:** a mineral $Mg_2(Al,Fe)_{10}Si_6O_{29}$ consisting of a magnesium aluminum iron silicate and occurring in thin black plates (sp. gr. 5.6)

an·gar·ia \aŋ'ga(a)rēə, an'-\ *n* [LL, fr. Gk *angareia*, fr. *angaros* royal (Persian) courier — more at ANGEL] **1** *in Roman and civil law* **:** a compulsory service exacted by the government, a lord, or the church **2** *in maritime law* **:** the forcible seizure of a ship for public service **3** *in international law* **:** ANGARY **4** *in feudal law* **:** a troublesome or vexatious service exacted by a lord of his tenant

an·ga·ry \'aŋgərē\ *n* [LL *angaria*] **:** the right in international law of a belligerent to seize, use, or destroy property of neutrals, or to take over use of neutral ships in case of necessity

-ange \,anj, ,aa(ə)nj\ *n comb form* -s [NL *-angium*] **:** -ANGIUM

¹**an·gel** \'ānjəl\ *n* -s [ME *angel*, fr. OF *angele*, fr. LL *angelus*, fr. Gk *angelos* (trans. of Heb *mal'ākh*), lit., messenger, prob. of Iranian origin; akin to the source of Gk *angaros* imperial Persian courier; perh. akin to Skt *aṅgiras* one of a group of luminous divine beings] **1 a :** a supernatural spirit esp. in Persian, Jewish, Christian, and Islamic theologies that is commonly depicted as being winged and serving as God's messenger and divine intermediary and as special guardian of an individual or nation **b :** a member of any order of the heavenly hierarchy, esp. of the lowest order — see CELESTIAL HIERARCHY **2** *obs* **:** one of the fallen spirits regarded as former angels of God **3 :** one bearing a divine message (as a preacher or prophet) **4 :** BISHOP, PASTOR ⟨to the ~ of the church in Ephesus —Rev 2:1 (RSV)⟩ **5 :** an attendant spirit or guardian — often used without implication of belief in its supernatural character ⟨my good ~⟩ **6 :** a person deceased and regarded as received into heaven **7 a** *or* **angel–noble** \⸗'⸗¦⸗⸗\ **:** an English gold coin issued 1465–1634 that was similar in device to the Anglo-Gallic angelot and at first valued at 6*s* 8*d*, but later at 7*s* 6*d*, then at 8*s*, and after 1553 at 10*s* **b :** a corresponding unit of value ⟨half an ~⟩ **c** *obs* **:** a bill of public credit for 10 shillings issued in the Massachusetts Colony in 1713 **8 :** a white-robed winged figure of human form in fine art **9 :** MESSENGER, HARBINGER ⟨the ~ of the spring, the nightingale —Ben Jonson⟩ **10 :** a person (as a woman or a child) felt to resemble an angel (as in innocence or loveliness) **11** *Christian Science* **:** a message originating from God in his aspects of Truth and Love **12** *slang* **:** one who aids or supports with money or influence (as a backer of a theatrical venture) — sometimes used derogatively to refer to a wealthy man easily separated from his money **13 :** ANGELFISH ⟨a black ~⟩ **14 :** a member of a religious cult called Father Divine's Peace Mission

²**angel** \"\ *vt* -ED/-ING/-s *slang* **:** to support or back with contributions of money ⟨~*ed* several musicals⟩

angel bed *n* [trans. of F *lit d'ange*] **:** a bed without posts but with a small canopy

angel cake *or* **angel food** *or* **angel food cake** *n* [so called fr. its pure white color] **:** a white sponge cake made of flour, sugar, and whites of eggs

an·ge·le·no *also* **an·ge·le·ño** \,anjə'lē(,)nō *also* -lān(,)yō\ *n* -s *cap* [AmerSp *angeleño*, fr. Los *Angeles*, Calif. + Sp *-eño* (suffix added to place names to form names of inhabitants)] **:** a native or resident of Los Angeles, Calif.

an·gel·et \¦anjə¦let\ *n* -s [ME, fr. MF, fr. OF, little angel, fr. OF *angele* angel + *-et* — more at ANGEL] **:** an English gold coin issued 1470–1619 that was worth half an angel

angeleyes \'⸗⸗,⸗\ *n pl* **:** BLUETS

angelfish \'⸗⸗,⸗\ *n* [so called fr. its appearance, suggesting in sense 1 the wings, in other senses the splendor and delicacy, of an angel] **1 :** MONKFISH 1 **2 :** any of several compressed bright-colored teleost fishes of warm seas of the family Chaetodontidae — called also *butterfly fish;* see BLACK ANGELFISH, BLUE ANGELFISH **3 :** SPADEFISH **4 :** SCALARE

an·gel·hood \-,hu̇d\ *n* **1 :** the nature or status of an angel **2 :** an angelic being

an·gel·ic \(')an¦jelik, -aan-, -ēk\ *or* **an·gel·i·cal** \-əkəl, -ēk-\ *adj* [*angelic* fr. MF *angelique*, fr. LL *angelicus*, fr. Gk *angelikos*, fr. *angelos* angel + *-ikos* -ic; *angelical* fr. *angelic* + *-al*] **:** of, relating to, or proceeding from angels ⟨~ forms⟩ **:** resembling, characteristic of, or having the nature of an angel ⟨~ innocence⟩ ⟨~ beneficence⟩ **:** HEAVENLY, SAINTLY — **an·gel·i·cal·ly** \-ək(ə)lē, -ēk-, -li\ *adv*

an·gel·i·ca \an'jeləkə, aan-, -ēkə\ *n* [NL, fr. ML, angelica plant, fr. LL, fem. of *angelicus* angelic; fr. the supposed medicinal properties] **1** *cap* **:** a genus of herbs (family Umbelliferae) found in the temperate zone and New Zealand and having decompound leaves, mostly white flowers, and prominently dorsal-ribbed fruit **2** *also* **an·ge·lique** \¦anjə¦lēk, ¦aan-\ -s [*angelique* fr. F *angélique*] **:** any plant of the genus *Angelica; esp* **:** a biennial cultivated herb (*A. archangelica*) having rootstalks that are candied and roots and seeds that yield a flavoring oil — see ANGELICA OIL **3** -s *usu cap* [MexSp *angélica*, fr. fem. of *angélico* angelic, fr. LL *angelicus*] **:** a sweet straw-colored or amber-colored dessert wine produced in California **4** *or* **angelique** -s [*angelica* prob. fr. It, prob. fr. F *angélique*, fr. *angélique* angelic; *angelique* prob. fr. F *angélique*] **:** a lute with approximately 16 strings tuned scalewise — called also *angelot*

an·gel·ic acid \(')an¦jelik-\ *n* [NL *Angelica*] **:** an unsaturated crystalline acid $CH_3CH{=}C(CH_3)COOH$ obtained from angelica and some other plants; *cis*-α-methyl-crotonic acid — compare TIGLIC ACID

angelica lactone *n* **:** either of two lactones $C_5H_6O_2$ related to angelic acid

angelica oil *n* **:** either of two essential oils that have a musky odor and are obtained usu. from the roots but sometimes from the fruits of angelica and are used chiefly in making liqueurs

angelica tree *n* **:** HERCULES'-CLUB 3

an·gel·i·co \an'jelə,kō\ *n* -s [prob. alter. of *angelica*] **:** NONDO

an·gel·i·fy \an'jelə,fī\ *vt* -ED/-ING/-ES [¹*angel* + *-ify*] **:** to make into or like an angel **:** ANGELIZE

an·ge·lim \¦anjə¦lim\ *or* **an·ge·lin** \-in\ *n* -s [Pg *angelim*, fr. Tamil *anjili-maram, anjali-maram*] **:** any of several chiefly tropical American trees of the genus *Andira; esp* **:** CABBAGE BARK

angeling *pres part of* ANGEL

an·ge·lique \¦anjə¦lēk, ¦aan-\ *n* -s [F *angélique*, fr. MF *angélique* angelica (plant of the genus *Angelica*), fr. *angélique* angelic — more at ANGELIC] **1 a :** the wood of a So. American timber tree (*Dicorynia paraensis*) **b :** the tree that produces angelique **c :** ANGELICA 2 **2 :** a liqueur flavored with angelica oil and other flavoring agents (as coriander and oil of bitter almonds) **3 :** ANGELICA 4

an·gel·ism \'ānjə,lizəm\ *n* -s **:** the regarding of human affairs from an unrealistically sanguine point of view, as though a man were an angel

an·gel·ize \-,līz\ *vt* -ED/-ING/-s **:** to raise to the state of an angel **:** render angelic

angel light *n* **:** a small triangular light between subordinate arches of window tracery (as in English perpendicular style)

angel–noble *n* **:** ANGEL 7a

an·gel·ol·o·gy \,ānjə'läləjē\ *n* -ES [NL *angelologia*, fr. L *angelus* angel + NL *-o-* + *-logia* -logy — more at ANGEL] **:** the doctrine or theory of angels **:** beliefs concerning angels

an·ge·lón \¦anjə¦lōn\ *n* -s [AmerSp, fr. Sp, large angel, aug. of *ángel* angel, fr. LL *angelus* — more at ANGEL] **:** a plant of the genus *Angelonia*

an·ge·lo·nia \,anjə'lōnyə\ *n, cap* [NL, fr. AmerSp *angelón* + NL *-ia*] **:** a genus of tropical American herbs (family Scrophulariaceae) having long racemes of light purple flowers

an·ge·lot \'anjə,lät, ¦⸗⸗¦lō\ *n* -s [MF, fr. OF, little angel, dim. of *angele* angel — more at ANGEL] **1** [so called fr. the device on the obverse, showing the archangel Michael slaying a dragon] **:** an Anglo-Gallic gold coin issued by Henry VI of England **2 :** ANGELICA 4 **3 :** a small rich cheese made in Normandy

angel pie *n* **:** a dessert consisting of a baked shell of meringue filled with crushed fruit (as strawberries) and whipped cream

angel red *n* **:** COLCOTHAR 2

angels *pl of* ANGEL, *pres 3d sing of* ANGEL

angel's hair *n* **:** spun-glass strands used for Christmas-tree decoration

angel shark *n* [so called from its wing-shaped pectoral fins] **:** a shark of the family Squatinidae **:** MONKFISH 1

angel skin *n* [trans. of F *peau d'ange*] **:** PEAU D'ANGE

angel's kiss *n* **:** a cocktail made from crème de cacao and cream and occas. brandy and an additional liqueur and so poured into a glass that each ingredient forms a layer — compare POUSSE-CAFÉ 2

angel sleeve *n* **:** a very long wide sleeve usu. hanging loose from the shoulder often used on robes and gowns

angels on horseback : oysters wrapped in bacon and skewered, broiled, and served on toast

angel's seat *n, slang* **:** a raised observation seat in a railroad caboose

angel's–trumpet \'⸗⸗,⸗⸗\ *n, pl* **angel's–trumpets :** either of two So. American plants of the genus *Datura* (*D. suaveolens* and *D. arborea*) cultivated for their large and fragrant trumpet-shaped blossoms

angel's wing *or* **angel wing** *n* **:** a boring mollusk of the family Pholadidae **:** PIDDOCK

an·ge·lus \'anjələs, 'aan-\ *n* -ES *usu cap* [ML, fr. LL, angel; fr. the first word of the opening versicle — more at ANGEL] **1 :** a form of devotion that commemorates the Incarnation and is said in the morning, at noon, and at night by Roman Catholics usu. at the sounding of a bell **2 :** the bell announcing the time for the Angelus

angel–wing begonia *n* **:** any of several begonias having prominent basal leaf lobes that suggest the form of the upper part of the wing of an angel or bird

an·gen·e·sis \an'jenəsəs\ *n, pl* **angene·ses** \-ə,sēz\ [NL, fr. *ana-* + *genesis*] **:** regeneration esp. of tissues

¹**an·ger** \'aŋgə(r), 'aiŋ-\ *n* -s [ME, affliction, anger, fr. ON *angr* grief, sorrow; akin to OE *enge* narrow, OHG *engi*, ON *öngr*, Goth *aggwus*, L *angor* strangling, anguish, *angere* to strangle, distress, Gk *anchein* to strangle, Skt *aṁhas* anxiety] **1** *now dial Eng* **:** inflammation esp. of a wound or sore **2 a :** strong feeling of displeasure and usu. of antagonism ⟨an outburst of ~⟩ **3 :** a cause or manifestation of anger ⟨or if thy mistress some rich ~ shows —John Keats⟩ **4 :** something resembling the state, appearance, or behavior of an angry person ⟨the ~ of sea and sky⟩ ⟨the monstrous ~ of the guns —Wilfred Owen⟩

syn IRE, RAGE, FURY, INDIGNATION, WRATH: ANGER is the most general of these terms, merely indicating the emotional reaction of extreme displeasure and suggesting no definite degree of intensity ⟨boys and girls come to the hospitals full of fear and, sometimes, *anger* —J.N.Bell⟩ ⟨his *angers*, his personal spites reached metaphysical proportions —Lionel Abel⟩ IRE is literary, usu. suggesting a somewhat greater emotional turmoil than ANGER ⟨it turns the people's *ire* from local abuses —Stanley Ross⟩ ⟨undismayed by the dark flush of *ire* he kindled —George Meredith⟩ ⟨concealed his resentful *ire* —Jane Austen⟩ RAGE usu. adds to ANGER the idea of loss of control, of usu. strong outward display presumably reflecting an intense inner frustration, revengefulness, or temporary derangement ⟨his curses of *rage* and frustration tore the air and made the soldiers cringe —Allen Churchill⟩ ⟨hurled themselves at the spot, jaws snapping, trembling with violent *rage* —William Beebe⟩ FURY usu. indicates extreme overmastering rage; sometimes it applies to a violent and indignant anger kept barely under control ⟨the *fury* and devastation of World War II —*Lamp*⟩ ⟨phrases could move crowds to *fury* or pity —Arnold Bennett⟩ ⟨his anger deepened into *fury* —Agnes Repplier⟩ ⟨to watch in a cold *fury*⟩ INDIGNATION implies anger of no specified intensity or outward display but provoked by what one considers mean, shameful, unworthy, or outrageous ⟨the crime of aggression arouses their moral *indignation* —A.O. Wolfers⟩ ⟨the colonies were aflame with *indignation* —H.E. Scudder⟩ WRATH may imply either rage or indignation, usu. also implying a grievance and a desire to revenge or punish in return ⟨violent outbursts of *wrath* and summary chastisements do occur —Margaret Mead⟩ ⟨in *wrath* he had a widening glower that enveloped the offender — yet his eye seemed to stab — a flash shot from its center to transfix and pierce —G.D.Brown⟩ ⟨the *wrath* of God⟩

²**anger** \"\ *vb* **angered; angered; angering** \-g(ə)riŋ\ **angers** [ME *angren* to distress, anger, fr. ON *angra*, fr. *angr*] *vt* **1 :** to excite to anger **:** make angry ⟨her helplessness ~*ed* her —Robert Grant †1940⟩ **2** *chiefly dial* **:** to cause to smart **:** INFLAME ⟨the continued exertion ~*ed* his wound⟩ ~ *vi* **:** to become angry ⟨a man who ~*s* easily⟩

an·ger·ly *adv* [*'anger* + *-ly*] *archaic* **:** ANGRILY

an·gers \(')äⁿ¦zhā\ *adj, usu cap* [fr. *Angers*, France] **:** of or from the city of Angers, France **:** of the kind or style prevalent in Angers

-anges *pl of* -ANGE

¹**an·ge·vin** \'anjəvən, 'aan-\ *also* **an·ge·vine** \", -,vēn, -,vīn\ *adj, usu cap* [F, fr. OF, fr. ML *andegavinus*, fr. *Andegavia* Anjou, former province of France (fr. *Andegavum* Angers, former capital of Anjou) + L *-inus* -ine] **1 :** of, relating to, or characteristic of Anjou, France **2 :** of, relating to, or characteristic of the natives or inhabitants of Anjou **3 :** of, relating to, or characteristic of the Plantagenets **4 :** of or relating to the period of English history from the accession of Henry II in 1154 to the loss of Anjou in 1204 or to the division of the Plantagenets into the houses of Lancaster and York in 1399

²**angevin** \"\ *also* **angevine** \"\ *n* -s *cap* [F, fr. OF, fr. *angevin*, adj.] **1 :** a native or inhabitant of Anjou **2 :** any of the Plantagenet kings or their kinsmen or retainers

angi- *or* **angio-** *comb form* [NL, fr. Gk *angei-, angeio-* vessel, blood vessel, fr. *angeion*, dim. of *angos* vessel; perh. akin to L *angulus* angle — more at ANGLE] **1 a :** blood or lymph vessel ⟨*angi*oid⟩ ⟨*angio*lith⟩ ⟨*angi*osis⟩ **b :** angiomatous ⟨*angio*fibroma⟩ **:** angiomatous and ⟨*angio*cavernous⟩ **2 :** seed vessel ⟨*angio*carpous⟩

-angia *pl of* -ANGIUM

an·gi·co \an'jē(,)kü, -kō\ *n* -s [Pg] **:** any of various So. American trees of the family Leguminosae (esp. *Piptadenia rigida*) that yields a brown gum used in tanning

an·gi·i·tis \,anjē'īd·əs\ *n, pl* **angiit·i·des** \-ē'id·ə,dēz\ [NL, fr. *angi-* + *-itis*] **:** inflammation of a blood or lymph vessel or vessels

angild *n* -s [OE *āngilde, āngylde*, fr. *ān* one + *-gilde, -gylde* (akin to *gieldan* to pay for, reward, serve, punish) — more at ONE, YIELD] **:** a compensation in Anglo-Saxon times made in a single payment at a fixed valuation for a given injury to person or property

an·gi·na \an'jīnə, aan- *also* 'a(a)njənə\ *n* -s [L, quinsy, fr. L *angere* to strangle, distress, — more at ANGER] **:** a disease marked by spasmodic attacks of intense suffocative pain: as **a :** a severe inflammatory or ulcerated condition of the mouth or throat ⟨diphtheritic ~⟩ — compare LUDWIG'S ANGINA **b :** ANGINA PECTORIS — **an·gi·nal** \(')a(a)n¦jīnᵊl,'a(a)njənᵊl\ *adj*

angina pec·to·ris \-'pektərəs, *chiefly substand* -,pek'tōr-\ *n* [NL, lit., quinsy of the chest] **:** a disease characterized by paroxysmal attacks of substernal pain of short duration that is usu. associated with a sense of apprehension or fear of impending death, precipitated by effort or emotion, and relieved quickly by rest or administration of nitroglycerin — compare CORONARY INSUFFICIENCY, HEART FAILURE, MYOCARDIAL INFARCTION

an·gi·noid \'anjə,nȯid, an'jī-\ *adj* [*angina* + *-oid*] **:** resembling angina

an·gi·nose \'anjə,nōs, an'jī,-\ *or* **an·gi·nous** \(')an¦jīnəs, 'anjən-\ *adj* [*angina* + *-ose, -ous*] **:** relating to angina or angina pectoris

angio- *in pronunciations below*, ¦⸗⸗⸗ = ¦anjēō *or* ¦aan- *or* -ēə *or* -ē,ō\ — see ANGI-

an·gi·o·blast \'⸗⸗⸗,blast\ *n* -s [*angi-* + *-blast*] **:** one of the extraembryonic mesenchyme cells that differentiate into the endothelium of the embryonic blood vessels — **an·gi·o·blas·tic** \¦⸗⸗⸗¦tik\ *adj*

an·gi·o·car·di·o·gram \¦⸗⸗⸗-\ *n* -s [*angi-* + *cardiogram*] **:** a roentgenogram of the heart and its blood vessels after injection of a radiopaque substance

an·gi·o·car·di·o·graph·ic \¦⸗⸗⸗,⸗⸗⸗¦⸗⸗\ *adj* **:** of or by means of angiocardiography

an·gi·o·car·di·og·ra·phy \¦⸗⸗⸗-\ *n* -ES [*angi-* + *cardiography*] **:** the roentgenographic visualization of the heart and its blood vessels after injection of a radiopaque substance

an·gi·o·car·pous \¦⸗⸗⸗¦kärpəs\ *or* **an·gi·o·car·pic** \-pik\ *adj* [*angi-* + *-carpous, -carpic*] **1 :** having or being fruit enclosed within an external covering ⟨the acorn in its cupule is an ~ fruit⟩ — compare PYRENOCARPIC **2 :** having the hymenium enclosed or immersed in the thallus — used of some lichens and fungi; compare GYMNOCARPOUS, — **an·gi·o·car·py** \'⸗⸗⸗-,kärpē\ *n* -ES

an·gi·o·cho·li·tis \¦⸗⸗⸗-\ *n* -ES [NL, fr. *angi-* + *chol-* + *-itis*] **:** inflammation of the gall ducts **:** CHOLANGITIS

an·gi·o·cyst \'⸗⸗⸗,sist\ *n* -s [*angi-* + *cyst*] *anat* **:** a pouch of mesothelial tissue having blood-forming properties

an·gi·o·ede·ma \¦⸗⸗⸗-\ *n, pl* **angioedemas** *or* **angioede·ma·ta** [NL, fr. *angi-* + *edema*] **:** ANGIONEUROTIC EDEMA

an·gi·o·gen·e·sis \¦⸗⸗⸗-\ *n, pl* **angiogene·ses** [NL, fr. *angi-* + *genesis*] **:** the formation and differentiation of blood vessels; *esp* **:** the development of the vessels of the embryo from mesenchyme

an·gi·o·gen·ic \¦⸗⸗⸗¦jenik\ *adj* [*angi-* + *-genic*] **:** of or relating to the development of the embryonic circulatory system

an·gi·o·gram \'⸗⸗⸗,gram\ *n* -s [*angi-* + *-gram*] **:** a roentgenogram of the blood vessels after injection of a radiopaque substance

an·gi·og·ra·phy \,anjē'ägrəfē\ *n* -ES [*angi-* + *-graphy*] **:** the roentgenographic visualization of the blood vessels after injection of a radiopaque substance

an·gi·oid \'anjē,ȯid\ *adj* [*angi-* + *-oid*] **:** resembling a blood vessel or lymph vessel

an·gi·ol·o·gy \,anjē'äləjē\ *n* -ES [*angi-* + *-logy*] **:** a science dealing with the blood vessels and lymphatics

an·gi·o·ma \,anjē'ōmə\ *n, pl* **angiomas** *also* **angioma·ta** \-məd·ə\ [NL, fr. *angi-* + *-oma*] **:** a tumor composed chiefly of blood vessels or lymph vessels: as **a :** HEMANGIOMA **b :** LYMPHANGIOMA

an·gi·o·ma·to·sis \,anjē,ōmə'tōsəs\ *n, pl* **angiomato·ses** \-ō,sēz\ [NL, fr. *angiomat-*, *angioma* + *-osis*] **:** a condition characterized by the formation of multiple angiomas

an·gi·om·a·tous \¦anjē¦ämədəs, -ōm-\ *adj* [NL *angiomat-*, *angioma* + E *-ous*] **:** of, relating to, or having an angioma

an·gi·o·neu·rot·ic edema \¦⸗⸗(,)⸗¦⸗⸗-\ *n* [ISV *angi-* + *neurotic*] **:** a condition characterized by patches of circumscribed swelling of the skin, mucous membranes, and sometimes viscera and believed to be an expression of allergy

an·gi·op·ter·is \,anjē'äptərəs\ *n, cap* [NL, fr. *angi-* + *-pteris*] **:** a genus of tree ferns (family Marattiaceae) having sporangia closely arranged in two rows forming linear sori surrounded by a false indusium of fringed scales

an·gi·o·sco·to·ma \¦===-\ *n, pl* **angioscotomas** *also* **angio·scoto·ma·ta** [NL, fr. *angi-* + *scotoma*] **:** a blind spot or defect in the visual field produced by dilated retinal vessels that is esp. prevalent in persons long exposed to high altitudes

an·gi·o·sco·tom·e·try \¦===skō'tämə·trē\ *n* -ES [blend of NL *angioscotoma* and E *-metry*] **:** the charting of scotomas, esp. angioscotomas

an·gi·o·spasm \'===,spazəm\ *n* -S [*angi-* + *spasm*] **:** spasmodic contraction of the blood vessels with increase in blood pressure — **an·gi·o·spas·tic** \¦===¦spastik\ *adj*

an·gi·o·sperm \'===,spərm\ *n* -S [NL *Angiospermae*] **:** a plant of the class Angiospermae

an·gi·o·sper·mae \,===ˈspər,mē\ *n pl, cap* [NL, fr. *angi-* + *-spermae*] **:** a class of Pteropsida or in some classifications a subdivision of Spermatophyta comprising seed plants (as orchids or roses) that produce seeds enclosed in an ovary, including the vast majority of seed plants, and being divided into the subclasses Dicotyledoneae and Monocotyledoneae — compare FILICINEAE, GYMNOSPERMAE

an·gi·o·sper·mous \¦===¦=məs\ *or* **an·gi·o·sper·mal** \-məl\ *also* **an·gi·o·sper·ma·tous** \-mədəs\ *or* **an·gi·o·sper·mic** \-mik\ *adj* [*angi-* + *-spermous, -spermal, -spermatous, -spermic*] **:** of, relating to, or characteristic of the class Angiospermae; *often* **:** having ovules and seeds enclosed in an ovary — contrasted with *gymnospermous* — **an·gi·o·sper·my** \'===,=mē\ *n* -ES

an·gi·os·to·my \,anjēˈästəmē\ *n* -ES [*angi-* + *-stomy*] **:** the surgical establishment of an opening into a blood vessel esp. through a cannula

an·gi·o·tome \'===,tōm\ *n* -S [*angi-* + *-tome*] **:** a segment or unit of the vascular system in the embryo

an·gi·o·ton·ic \¦===¦tänik\ *adj* [*angi-* + *tonic*] **:** inducing or involving increased tonus in the wall of a blood vessel ⟨an ~ substance⟩ ⟨~ spasm⟩

an·gi·o·to·nin \,==='tōnən\ *n* -S [*angiotonic* + *-in*] **:** HYPERTENSIN

-an·gi·um \'anjēəm, 'aan-\ *n comb form, pl* **-an·gia** \-ēə\ [NL, fr. Gk *angeion* — more at ANGI-] **:** vessel **:** receptacle ⟨*gametangium*⟩ ⟨*gonangium*⟩

ang·ka \'aŋkə\ *n pl, usu cap* **:** a people in northern Assam, India

ang–khak \'aŋ,kak\ *n* -S [prob. fr. a Chin dial. phrase akin to Chin (Canton) *hung kuk* red rice, Chin (Peking) *hung² ku³*] **:** RED RICE 1

angklung *var of* ANKLONG

angl *abbr, often cap* **1** [L *Anglice*] in English **2** anglicized

¹an·glaise \(')äŋ¦glāz, (')aŋ,-,(')äⁿ¦-\ *n* -S [F, fr. fem. of *anglais* English, of Gmc origin; akin to OE *englisc* English — more at ENGLISH] **1 :** an old English country-dance **2 :** a lively musical dance form in duple time esp. as an optional member of the classical suite

²anglaise \"\ *adj* [F (*à la*) *anglaise* in the English manner; *anglaise*, fem. of *anglais* English] **1 :** boiled and served without sauce ⟨potatoes ~⟩ **2 :** BREADED ⟨cutlets ~⟩

¹an·gle \'aŋgəl, 'aiŋ-\ *n* -S *usu cap* [L *Angli*, pl., of Gmc origin; akin to OE *Engle*, pl., Angles] **:** a member of a Germanic people that entered and conquered England with the Saxons and Jutes in the 5th century A.D. and merged with them to form the Anglo-Saxon peoples

²angle \"\ *n* -S [ME *angel*, fr. OE *angel, ongul*, fr. *anga* hook; akin to OHG *angul* fishhook, *ango* hook, ON *öngull* fishhook, L *uncus* hook, Gk *onkos* barbed hook, *ankos* hollow, glen, Skt *aṅka* bend, hook] **1** *archaic* **:** FISHHOOK **2** *archaic* **:** fishing line, hook, and bait with or without rod

³angle \"\ *vb* **angled; angled; angling** \-g(ə)liŋ\ **angles** [ME *angelen*, fr. *angel*, n.] *vi* **1 :** to fish with a hook ⟨the fish one ~*s* for⟩ **2 :** to use artful bait or wily means **:** SCHEME ⟨~ for an invitation to the party⟩ ~ *vt* **:** FISH ⟨~ a stream⟩

⁴angle \"\ *n* -S [ME, fr. MF, fr. L *angulus*; akin to OE *anclēow* ankle, OHG *anchlāo, anchal, enchil*, ON *ökkla*, Gk *angos* pail, Skt *aṅga* limb, OE *angel, ongul* fishhook — more at ANGLE (fishhook)] **1 a** *archaic* **:** a corner or area near a corner **b** *archaic* **:** an out-of-the-way place ⟨into the utmost ~ of the world —Edmund Spenser⟩ **:** NOOK **2 a :** the figure formed by two lines diverging from the same point or by two surfaces diverging from the same line **b :** a representation of such a figure or space **3 :** one of the four astrological houses at the cardinal points of the compass **4 :** a projecting corner (as of a stone or building) **:** a pointed form or sharp fragment **5** *math* **:** a measure of the amount of rotation of either of two intersecting lines necessary to produce coincidence with the other, the rotation being in the plane of the lines and about the point of intersection; *also* **:** a measure based on this for indicating the divergence of two nonintersecting nonparallel lines, two intersecting planes, or two intersecting curves **6 a** (1) **:** the direction from which an object is viewed **:** POINT OF VIEW ⟨a camera ~⟩ **:** ASPECT, PHASE ⟨to discuss all ~*s* of a question⟩ (2) **:** the point of view or special interest or emphasis controlling a presentation (as of a story, article, or speech) or the phase of a presentation that is of interest to or bears upon a certain group or point of view **b** *slang* **:** SCHEME **:** a slick knowledge of method esp. in criminal activities **:** a method for illegal gain **7 :** a curving direction given a ball (as by a stroke or kick) ⟨put ~ on a tennis return⟩ **8 :** ANGLE IRON **syn** see PHASE

angles: *ABD* and *ABC* right angles; *FBD, F'BD, F"BD* acute angles; *EBD, E'BD, E"BD* obtuse angles; *CBD* straight angle; *GBD* reflex angle; *B* vertex

⁵angle \"\ *vb* **angled; angled; angling** \-g(ə)liŋ\ **angles** *vt* **1 a :** to turn, bend, move, or direct at an angle ⟨I *angled* a look behind me — *Think*⟩ **b :** to hit at an angle **:** strike or kick (a ball) toward the sidelines ⟨~ a tennis return⟩ **2 :** to adjust at an angle ⟨~ a camera⟩ **3 a :** to present the material of (as a news story, article, or speech) from a particular point of view or favorable to the interests of a particular group **b :** to warp (such a presentation) by emphasis or implication to favor a particular person, class, group, or race ~ *vi* **1 :** to change direction by making an angular turn or turns ⟨the road ~*s* up the hill⟩ **2 :** to go at an angle ⟨~ across the road⟩

angle bar *n* **1 :** ANGLE IRON **2 :** one of two bars used to splice the joint of two railroad rails

angle bead *n* **:** a corner bead set vertically at the meeting of two walls

angle beam *n* **:** a beam in which one part (as a flange) is at an angle with another

an·gle·ber·ry \'aŋgəl,berē\ *n* [prob. fr. (assumed) earlier E *angberry* — more at ANBURY] **:** a papilloma or warty growth of the skin or mucous membranes of cattle and sometimes horses often occurring in great numbers and thought to be caused by a filterable virus

angle brace *n* **1 :** a brace across two pieces that meet at an angle — called also *angle tie* **2 :** a boring brace for use in cramped places (as in a corner)

angle bracket *n* **1 :** a bracket in an angle or corner of a molded cornice **2 :** BRACKET 4b

angle brick *n* **:** a brick of oblique shape (as for use at a salient angle)

angle capital *n* **:** the capital of a corner column; *esp* **:** a capital modified from the ordinary form so as to face on both sides of the corner (as in the Ionic order)

angle chair *n* **:** a corner chair or desk chair

angle clip *n* **:** a short piece of angle iron for connecting structural parts (as plates) at angles

angled *adj* [⁴*angle* + *-ed*] **1 :** having an angle or angles — used of a geometric figure **:** having an angular outline ⟨an ~ sail⟩ **:** set or placed at angles rather than parallel **2 :** placed so that a part of the pool cushion at a pocket prevents a direct shot at an object ball ⟨the cue ball was ~⟩ **:** marked by such a situation **:** having to play with the cue ball so placed

angled draft *n* **:** a method of drawing cloth in which alternate twilling to left and right produces a herringbone

angle divider *n* **:** a square for bisecting or dividing angles

angledog \'==,=\ *n* [²*angle* + *dog*] *dial* **:** EARTHWORM

An·gle·doz·er \'aŋgəl,dōzə(r)\ *trademark* — used for a tractor-driven pusher and scraper with the blade at an angle for pushing material to one side or the other (as for clearing land or leveling runways)

angle float *n* **:** a plasterer's trowel having flat surfaces meeting at an angle used for finishing corners of plastered walls

angle gear *n* **:** a gear with teeth at an angle to its axis (as a bevel gear)

angle iron *n* **1 :** an iron or steel cleat or brace used to hold together two parts whose faces are at an angle **2** *also* **angle -s :** a piece of structural steel rolled with an L-shaped section

angle iron 1

angle meter *n* **:** an instrument for measuring angles; *esp* **:** CLINOMETER

angle of action : the angle of revolution of either of two wheels in gear during which any particular tooth continues in contact

angle of altitude : ANGLE OF ELEVATION 1

angle of approach : the angle turned through by either of a pair of wheels in gear from the first contact of a pair of teeth until the pitch points of these teeth fall together

angle of attack : the acute angle between the direction of the relative wind and a reference line (as the geometric chord) fixed in an airfoil

angle of bank : ANGLE OF ROLL

angle of climb : the angle between the horizontal and the flight path of a climbing airplane

angle of contact *physics* **:** the angle between the meniscus and the containing walls of a column of liquid measured from the vertical wall below the surface of the liquid to the position of the tangent to the meniscus at its point of contact with the wall

angle of declination 1 : the angle made by a descending line or plane with a horizontal plane **2 :** the angle between the direction indicated by a magnetic needle and the true meridian — called also *magnetic declination*

angle of departure : the vertical angle between the line of departure of a projectile and the line of site of the gun

angle of depression 1 : the angle that a descending line makes with a horizontal plane **2 :** the angle of elevation when the line of elevation of a gun falls below the horizontal

angle of elevation 1 : the angle that an ascending line makes with a horizontal plane **2 :** the vertical angle between the line of elevation and the line of site of a gun

angle of fall : the vertical angle between the horizontal and the tangent to the trajectory of a projectile at the point of fall —called also *striking angle*

angle of incidence 1 : ANGLE OF ATTACK **2 :** the angle that a line (as a ray of light) falling on a surface makes with a perpendicular to the surface at the point of incidence — see GLANCING ANGLE **3 :** the angle between the chord of an airplane wing section and the longitudinal axis of the airplane, being positive when the leading edge is higher than the trailing edge

angle of lag 1 : the angle through which the brushes of a commutator of a direct-current motor or generator must be shifted from the neutral plane on account of the armature reaction **2 :** the angle by which the current in an alternating-current circuit lags behind the electromotive force

angle of lead \-'lēd\ **:** the angle by which the current in an alternating-current circuit leads the electromotive force

angle of obliquity *or* **angle of pressure :** the angle that the line of pressure or of action of two gear teeth in contact makes with the tangent at the point of contact of the two pitch circles

angle of pitch : the angle between two planes one of which includes the lateral axis of an airplane and the direction of the relative wind and the other of which includes the lateral and the longitudinal axes that in normal flight is measured between the longitudinal axis and the direction of the relative wind and that is positive when the nose of the airplane rises

angle of position : ANGLE OF SITE

angle of recess : the angle turned through by either of a pair of wheels in gear from the coincidence of the pitch points of a pair of teeth until the last point of contact of the teeth

angle of reflection : the angle between a reflected ray and the normal drawn at the point of incidence to a reflecting surface — called also *specular angle*

angle of refraction : the angle between a refracted ray and the normal drawn at the point of incidence to the interface at which refraction occurs — called also *refraction angle*

angle of repose 1 *physics* **:** the angle that the plane of contact between two bodies makes with the horizontal when the upper body is just on the point of sliding **:** the angle whose tangent is the coefficient of friction between the two bodies **2** *or* **angle of rest :** the angle of maximum slope at which a heap of any loose solid material (as earth) will stand without sliding — compare ANGLE OF SLIDE

angle of roll : the angle through which an airplane must be rotated about its longitudinal axis to bring its lateral axis into a horizontal plane, being positive when the left wing is higher than the right — called also *angle of bank*

angle of site : the vertical angle between the line of site of a gun and the horizontal — called also *angle of position*

angle of slide : the angle of minimum slope usu. measured from the horizontal at which any loose solid material (as earth) will flow — compare ANGLE OF REPOSE

angle of the mandible *or* **angle of the jaw :** the angle formed by the junction of the ramus and the body of the human mandible

angle of thread : the angle between the sides of a screw thread measured in an axial plane

angle of torsion *or* **angle of twist :** the angle through which a radial section of a body (as a wire or a shaft) deflects from its normal position when the body is subjected to torque

angle of view : the angle in a lens between lines drawn from opposite edges of the image to the second nodal point of the lens

angle of yaw : the angle between the direction of the relative wind and the plane of symmetry of an airplane, being positive when the airplane turns to the right

angle of zero lift : ZERO-LIFT ANGLE

angle plate *n* **:** a plate having an L-shaped or angular section; *specif* **:** one of two such plates used to clamp and hold work in a shaper or other metalworking machine — compare ANGLE IRON

anglepod \'==,=\ *n* [⁴*angle* + *pod*] **:** any of several plants (genus *Gonolobus*) that have angled pods (as *G. gonocarpos*)

an·gler \'aŋglə(r), 'aiŋ-\ *n* -S [³*angle* + *-er*] **1 :** one that angles **2 a :** a European and American marine fish (*Lophius piscatorius*) of the order Pediculati that reaches a length of from three to five feet, has a large broad depressed head and large mouth, and lies partly buried on the bottom enticing other fishes within its reach by movements of a lure on its head and fleshy appendages around its mouth **b :** any of several closely related fishes (family Lophiidae)

angler (*Lophius piscatorius*)

angle rafter *n* **:** a rafter at the angle of a roof: as **a :** HIP RAFTER **b :** the principal rafter under the hip rafter

anglerfish \'==,=\ *n* **:** ANGLER 2

angle rib *n* **1 :** one of the great diagonal ribs that divide each rectangle of a Gothic vaulting and form the main part of the structure **2 :** a group of moldings ornamenting an angle in decorative work

angles *pl of* ANGLE, *pres 3d sing of* ANGLE

angle set *n* **1** *mining engin* **:** a timber set containing an angle brace **2** *mining engin* **:** one of a series of sets making angles with one another (as in a curving shaft or tunnel)

an·gle·sey \'aŋgəlsē, -si\ *adj, usu cap* [fr. *Anglesey*, island and county in Wales] **:** of or from the island or county of Anglesey, Wales **:** of the kind or style prevalent in Anglesey

angle shaft *n* **:** an enriched corner bead often having a capital or base or both

angle shear *n* **:** a machine for shearing or cutting angle irons

angle shot *n* **1 :** a picture taken with the camera pointed at an angle from the horizontal **2 :** a motion-picture shot duplicating or continuing the action of the previous shot but from a different position

an·gle·site \'aŋgəl,sīt, -glə,-\ *n* -S [F *anglésite*, fr. *Anglesey* island, Wales, its locality + F *-ite*] **:** a common secondary mineral consisting of lead sulfate $PbSO_4$ and formed by the oxidation of galena

anglesmith \'==,=\ *n* [⁴*angle* + *smith*] **1 :** one who bends and welds metal to form angular shapes (as angle irons or brackets) **2 :** a furnaceman who shapes steel structural members esp. for use in shipbuilding and repair — called also *slabman*

angle steel *n* **:** steel in bars rolled with an L section

angle tie *n* **1 :** ANGLE BRACE 1 **2 :** a tie to prevent displacement of building elements due to thrust

an·gle·ton grass \'aŋgəltən-, -tᵊn-\ *n* [prob. fr. *Angleton*, Texas, where it was introduced] **:** a grass (*Andropogon nodosus*) native to the Old World tropics and introduced in the West Indies having one or two racemes with the spikelets closely overlapping

an·gle·twitch \'aŋ(g)əl-,twich\ *also* **an·gle·touch** \-l,təch\ *n* -ES [ME *angeltwicche, angeltwacche*, fr. OE *angeltwæcce, angeltwicce*, fr. *angel* hook + *-twæcce, -twicce* (fr. *twiccian* to pluck, catch hold of) — more at ANGLE, TWITCH] *now dial Eng* **:** EARTHWORM

angle valve *n* **:** a valve with intake and exit ports at right angles

anglewing \'==,=\ *n* [⁴*angle* + *wing*] **:** one of numerous butterflies (including members of the genera *Polygonia, Nymphalis*, and *Anaea*) having the outer edge of the fore wings more or less notched or angular

anglewise \'==,=\ *adv* [⁴*angle* + *-wise*] **:** ANGULARLY

angleworm \'==,=\ *n* [²*angle* + *worm*] **:** EARTHWORM

¹an·gli·an \'aŋglēən, 'aiŋ-\ *adj, usu cap* [L *Angli* Angles + E *-an* — more at ANGLE] **1 :** of, relating to, or constituting the Angles or Anglian **2 :** East Anglian

²anglian \"\ *n* -S *usu cap* **1 :** ¹ANGLE **2 :** ²EAST ANGLIAN 1 **3 a :** the Old English dialects of Mercia and Northumbria **b :** ²EAST ANGLIAN 2

¹an·glic \-lik\ *adj, usu cap* [ML *Anglicus* English] **:** ANGLIAN

²anglic \"\ *n, usu cap* [ML *Anglicus*] **:** a proposed international language devised by R.E.Zachrisson †1937 Swedish philologist, and consisting of English written according to a system of simplified spelling without the introduction of any new letters

¹an·gli·can \'aŋglə̇kən, 'aiŋ-, -ēk-\ *adj, usu cap* [ML *Anglicanus*, fr. *Anglicus* English (fr. *Angli* English people, fr. L, Angles) + L *-anus* -an — more at ANGLE] **1 :** relating to or connected with the Church of England and churches in communion with it **2 :** of or relating to England or the English nation

²anglican \"\ *n* -S *usu cap* **:** one who acknowledges the faith and order common to the Anglican Communion

anglican chant *n, usu cap A* **:** a harmonized chant consisting of two strains of three and four measures respectively, the first measure of each containing a single reciting note and the remaining measures a cadence sung in strict rhythm

anglican communion *n, cap A&C* **:** a body of churches including the Church of England and those churches that hold essentially the same faith, order, and worship with it and are therefore in communion with each other (as the Church of Ireland, the Church in Wales, the Scottish Episcopal Church, the Protestant Episcopal Church in the U.S., the Anglican churches in the British dominions and colonies, and other kindred organizations)

an·gli·can·ism \-,nizəm\ *n* -S *cap* **1 :** the faith and order of the Anglican churches; *also* **:** adherence to the Anglican faith and order **2** *usu cap* **:** adherence or attachment to English attitudes and ways ⟨an extremely civilized literary and theatrical *Anglicanism* —John Gassner⟩

an·gli·ce \'aŋglə(,)sē, 'aiŋ-, -əsi\ *adv, usu cap* [ML, adv. of *Anglicus*] **:** in English; *esp* **:** in readily understood English ⟨the city of Livorno, *Anglice* Leghorn⟩

an·gli·cism \-,sizəm\ *n* -S *often cap* [ML *Anglicus* + E *-ism*] **1 a :** a characteristic feature of English occurring in another language **b :** a trend toward linguistic borrowing from English **2 :** the quality or qualities distinctive of the English **3 :** a partiality for English customs, manners, or ideas

an·gli·cist \-sə̇st\ *n* -S *usu cap* [ML *Anglicus* + E *-ist*] **:** a specialist in the English language or in English literature

an·gli·ci·za·tion \¦==sə̇'zāshən, -,sī'z-\ *n* -S *often cap* **:** the process or the result of anglicizing or being anglicized

an·gli·cize *or* **an·gli·cise** \-,sīz\ *vb* -ED/-ING/-S *often cap* [ML *Anglicus* + E *-ize, -ise*] *vt* **1 :** to make English in quality or characteristics **:** cause to become adapted in customs, manners, speech, or outlook to the culture of the English-speaking world and often esp. to the culture distinctive of England ⟨an *anglicized* Indian princess⟩ **2 :** to adapt (a foreign word or phrase) to English usage: as **a :** to alter to a characteristically English form, sound, or spelling (as *indexes* from Latin *indices*) **b :** to change to an English equivalent (as *John* for *Giovanni*) **c :** to borrow into English without alteration of form or spelling and with or without change in pronunciation (as *bona fide, soprano, kindergarten, matinee*) **3 :** to adapt to the characteristics of English meter or rhythm ~ *vi* **:** to take on English characteristics in conduct, speech, or outlook ⟨the immigrants gradually *anglicized*⟩

an·gli·fy \-,fī\ *vt* -ED/-ING/-ES *sometimes cap* [ML *Angli* English people (fr. L, Angles) + E *-fy* — more at ANGLE] **:** ANGLICIZE

an·gling \'aŋgliŋ, 'aiŋ-\ *n* -S [ME, fr. gerund of *angelen* to angle] **:** the act of one who angles; *esp* **:** the action or art of fishing with hook and line

an·glist \-glə̇st\ *n* -S *usu cap* [G, fr. ML *Angli* English people (fr. L, Angles) + G *-ist* — more at ANGLE] **:** ANGLICIST

an·glis·tics \aŋ'glistiks, aiŋ-\ *n pl but sing in constr, usu cap* [modif. of G *anglistik*, fr. *anglist* + *-ik* -ics] **:** the study of the English language or of literature composed in English

an·glo \'aŋ,glō, 'aiŋ-\ *n* -S *cap* [short for *Anglo-American*] *Southwest* **:** an Anglo-American as distinguished from a Spanish-American or a Mexican

an·glo- *in pronunciations below*, ¦== = ¦aŋ(,)glō *or* ¦aiŋ- *or* -ŋglə\ *comb form, usu cap* [NL, fr. ML *Angli* English people, fr. L, Angles — more at ANGLE] **1 :** English: **a :** of or belonging to England ⟨*Anglo*-Norman⟩ **b :** of English origin, descent, or culture ⟨*Anglo*-Indian⟩ ⟨*Anglo*-Irish⟩ **2 :** English and ⟨*Anglo*-Japanese⟩ ⟨*Anglo*-Russian⟩

anglo–american \¦==¦===\ *n, cap both As* [*Anglo-* + *American*] **1 :** a citizen of the U.S. of English origin or descent **2 :** a North American whose native language is English and whose culture is of English origin as distinguished from one whose language and culture are of non-English origin

anglo–arab \¦==ˈ==\ *n, usu cap both As* [*Anglo-* + *Arab* (horse)] **:** a horse produced by interbreeding Arab and Thoroughbred horses

anglo–burman \¦==¦==\ *n, cap A&B* [*Anglo-* + *Burman*] **1 :** a minority ethnic group in Burma deriving from intermarriage between British and Burmese **2 :** a member of the Anglo-Burman group

anglo–catholic \¦==¦=(=)=\ *n, usu cap A&C* [*Anglo-* + *Catholic*] **:** one who professes the tenets of Anglo-Catholicism **:** HIGH CHURCHMAN — compare LAUDIAN, TRACTARIAN

anglo–catholicism \¦==-\ *n, cap A&C* **:** the doctrines and practices of those in the Anglican Communion who maintain (1) that Catholicity is inherent in a church whose episcopate can trace its line of descent from the apostles and whose faith is agreed by all Catholics to be revealed truth and (2) that any church of the Anglican Communion is such a church, its method of church government and its doctrine remaining unchanged by the Reformation

anglo–french \¦==¦=\ *n, cap A&F* [*Anglo-* + *French*] **:** the French language used in medieval England: **a :** the French of Normandy used in England in the 11th and 12th centuries **b :** the French resulting from admixture of Norman and central French used from the 12th to the 15th centuries

an·glo·gae·an \¦==¦jēən\ *adj, usu cap* [NL *Anglogaea* Nearctica (fr. *Anglo-* + *-gaea*) + E *-an*] **:** NEARCTIC

anglo–gallic \¦==¦=\ *adj, usu cap A&G* [*Anglo-* + *Gallic*] **:** of or relating to one of the coins issued by English rulers from Henry II to Henry VIII in their territory in France

an·glo·hel·ve·ti·um \¦==,hel'vēshēəm\ *n* -S [NL, fr. *Anglo-* + *Helvetia* + *-ium*] **:** element 85 — a name superseded by *astatine*

¹anglo–indian \¦==¦-\ *adj, usu cap A&I* [*Anglo-* + *Indian* (of India)] **1 :** of, relating to, or characteristic of British India or the English in India **:** of or concerning the English and the

Indian peoples **2 :** of or belonging to the language of the English in India

²anglo-indian \"\ *n, cap A&I* **1 :** an Englishman living in India **2** *India* **:** a person of European (as British) and Indian ancestry — called also *Eurasian* **3 :** the terms adopted into English from the languages of India

anglo-irish \ˈ==ˈ-\ *n pl, cap A&I* [*Anglo-* + *Irish*] **1 :** persons of English origin or descent living in Ireland **2 :** persons of mixed English and Irish ancestry

anglo-israelism \ˈ==ˈ-\ *n, usu cap A&I* [*Anglo-* + *Israel* + E *-ism*] **:** the theory that the Anglo-Saxon peoples are descendants of the 10 lost tribes of Israel

anglo-israelite *n, usu cap A&I* **:** a believer in Anglo-Israelism

anglo-latin \ˈ==ˈ-\ *n, cap A&L* [*Anglo-* + *Latin*] **:** Medieval Latin as used in England

an·glo·ma·nia \ˌ==ˈmānēə, -nyə\ *n, often cap* [NL, fr. *Anglo-* + *mania*] **:** excessive fondness for what is English (as English customs and institutions) on the part of a foreigner

an·glo·ma·ni·ac \ˌ==ˈmānēˌak\ *n, usu cap* [*Anglo-* + *maniac*] **:** one affected with anglomania — **an·glo·ma·ni·a·cal** \ˌ==məˈnīəkəl\ *adj, usu cap*

anglo-norman \ˈ==ˈ==\ *n, cap A&N* [*Anglo-* + *Norman*] **1 :** one of the Normans who lived in England after the Conquest or any of their descendants **2 :** the form of Anglo-French used by Anglo-Normans

anglo-nubian \ˈ==ˈ===\ *n, usu cap A&N* [*Anglo-* + *Nubian* (goat)] **:** a British breed of goats developed by interbreeding native British goats with Nubians

an·glo·phile \ˈ==ˌfīl\ *also* **an·glo·phil** \-ˌfil\ *n* -s *often cap* [F *anglophile*, fr. *anglo-* Anglo- + *-phile* -phile, -phil] **:** one who esp. admires or is partial to England or English ways

an·glo·phil·ia \ˌ==ˈfilēə, -lyə\ *n* -s *often cap* [NL, fr. *Anglo-* + *-philia*] **:** particular unreasoned admiration of or partiality for England or English ways — **an·glo·phil·i·ac** \ˌ==ˈfilēˌak\ *or* **an·glo·phil·ic** \-lik\ *adj, often cap*

an·glo·phobe \ˈ==ˌfōb\ *n* -s *often cap* [prob. fr. F, fr. *anglo-* Anglo- + *-phobe*] **:** one who has anglophobia

an·glo·pho·bia \ˌ==ˈfōbēə\ *n* -s *often cap* [NL, fr. *Anglo-* + *-phobia*] **:** intense dislike or distrust of England, the English, or English ways — **an·glo·pho·bi·ac** \ˌ==ˈfōbēˌak\ *or* **an·glo·pho·bic** \ˈ==ˈfōbik *also* -äb-\ *adj, often cap*

anglos *pl of* ANGLO

an·glo-saxon \ˈ==ˈsaksən\ *n, cap A&S* [NL *Anglo-Saxones*, pl., alter. of ML *Angli Saxones*, fr. L *Angli* Angles + LL *Saxones* Saxons — more at ANGLE, SAXON] **1 a :** an Angle, Saxon, or Jute who came to England in the 5th century A.D. **b :** a descendant of one of these Anglo-Saxons **2 :** ENGLISHMAN; *broadly* **:** a person of English ancestry descended from the Anglo-Saxons **:** a white gentile whose native tongue is English **3 :** the language of the Anglo-Saxon people **:** OLD ENGLISH — see INDO-EUROPEAN LANGUAGES table **4 :** the Germanic element present in the English language since the emergence of the latter as a separate entity **5 a :** forthright direct plain English **b :** English employing words considered crude or vulgar ⟨the word-of-mouth version, which has come through generations of army men, is more bluntly *Anglo-Saxon* —Roger Butterfield⟩

anglo-saxon alphabet *n, usu cap 1st A&S* **:** the Latin alphabet as modified for writing Old English by the addition of the four characters æ or ę, edh, thorn, and wen — called also *Old English alphabet*

an·glo-sax·on·ism \ˈ==ˈ==ˌnizəm\ *n* -s *usu cap A&S* **1 :** a word or idiom that strongly suggests Anglo-Saxon origin **2 a :** the quality, qualities, traits, or outlook regarded as distinctive of the English or of the people of English descent **b :** the belief in the superiority of Anglo-Saxon characteristics or of the Anglo-Saxon people

an·glo-sax·on·ize \-ˌnīz\ *vt, sometimes cap A&S* **:** to inculcate with characteristics considered Anglo-Saxon or English

anglo-saxon word *n, usu cap A&S* **:** any of a group of monosyllabic English words whether or not of Anglo-Saxon origin that are considered vulgar and unacceptable in polite use — compare FOUR-LETTER WORD

anglo-vernacular \ˈ==ˈ===\ *adj, usu cap A&V* [*Anglo-* + *vernacular*] **:** using both English and a local vernacular — used esp. of schools in India, Burma, and Ceylon during the period of British rule

¹an·go·la \aŋˈgōlə, aiŋ-, an'-, aan'- *attrib* (ˈ)=ˈ==\ *n* -s *sometimes cap* [by alter.] **:** ANGORA

²angola *adj, usu cap* [fr. *Angola*, colony in southwestern Africa] **:** of or relating to Angola **:** of the kind or style prevalent in Angola

angola cloth *n, sometimes cap A* **1 :** a clothing fabric of plain or twill weave with cotton warp and wool weft **2 :** a cotton fabric with diaper pattern used for embroidery

angola grass *n, usu cap A* [fr. *Angola* (Port. West Africa), its place of origin] **:** PARA GRASS 1

an·go·lan \(ˈ)=ˈgōlən\ *n* -s *cap* [*Angola*, Africa + E *-an*] **:** a native or inhabitant of Angola — **angolan** *adj, usu cap*

angola pea *n, usu cap A* [fr. *Angola*, Africa] **:** PIGEON PEA

an·go·lar \aŋˈgōˌlär\ *n, pl* **angola·res** \ˌ==ˈlärēz\ [Pg, lit., of Angola, fr. *Angola* + Pg *-ar*] **1 :** the basic monetary unit of Angola established in 1928 and equal to the Portuguese escudo **2 :** a currency note representing one angolar

an·go·lese \ˌaŋgōˌlēz, ˌaiŋ-, -gə-, -ēs\ *n, pl* **angolese** *usu cap* [*Angola*, Africa + E *-ese*] **1 :** a member of any of the Bantu peoples of Angola **2 :** the Bantu language of the Angolese people

an·go·ni \aŋˈgōnē, an'-\ *n* -s *cap* [fr. *Angoni*land, plateau region in southwestern Nyasaland, Africa] **:** an animal of an eastern African native strain of zebu cattle

¹an·go·ra \aŋˈgōrə, aiŋ'-,an'-,aan'-, -ȯrə, *attrib also* ˈ=ˌ==\ *n* -s [prob. trans. of G *angorakaninchen* or F *lapin angora*, fr. *Angora* (Ankara), Turkey; prob. fr. the view that it originated in Asia Minor] **1** *also* **angora wool :** the hair of the Angora rabbit or the Angora goat **2 :** a yarn of Angora rabbit hair used esp. for knitting **3** *usu cap* **a :** ANGORA CAT **b :** ANGORA GOAT **c :** ANGORA RABBIT

²angora \"\ *adj* **:** of or relating to a mutant coat form in mammals characterized by great increase in length and silkiness of the hairs as compared with the wild type

angora cat *n, usu cap A* **1 :** a long-haired domestic cat with narrow pointed head and long slim body, tail, and limbs that prob. originated in the interior of Turkey and is nearly or wholly extinct as a pure breed in the U.S. — called also *coon cat, Maine cat* **2 :** a long-haired domestic cat

angora goat *n, usu cap A* **:** a breed or variety of the domestic goat reared for its long silky hair which is the true mohair of commerce and differs from the wool of the sheep in not felting

angora rabbit *n, usu cap A* **:** a long-haired rabbit usu. white with red eyes of a domestic breed raised for fine wool

an·gos·tu·ra bark \ˌaŋgəˌst(y)ùrə-, ˌaiŋ-, -ürə\ *also* **angostura** *n* -s [prob. trans. of AmerSp *corteza de Angostura*, lit., bark of Angostura, fr. *Angostura* (now Ciudad Bolívar), river port in Venezuela] **:** an aromatic bitter bark used as a tonic and antipyretic and obtained from either of two So. American trees (*Galipea officinalis* and *Cusparia trifoliata*) of the family Rutaceae, the latter yielding Brazilian angostura bark

an·gou·mois grain moth *also* **angoumois moth** \ˌäŋ-ˌgümˌwä-\ *n, often cap A* [fr. *Angoumois*, former province of France] **:** a small tineid moth (*Sitotroga cerealella*) of which the larva is a destructive pest of stored grain feeding in the interior of the kernels of various cereals

an·gre·cum \aŋˈgrēkəm\ *syn of* ANGRECUM

an·gre·cum \aŋˈgrēkəm\ *n, cap* [NL, modif. of Malay *anggĕrek* orchid] **:** a genus of epiphytic orchids found in tropical regions of the Old World with 2-ranked leaves and in several species grotesque showy flowers

an·gri·ly \ˈaŋgrəlē, ˈaiŋ-, -li\ *adv* [ME, fr. *angry* + *-ly*] **:** in an angry manner **:** with anger

an·gri·ness \-rēnəs, -rin-\ *n* -ES **:** the state of being angry

an·grite \ˈaŋˌgrīt\ *n* -s [*Angra* dos Reis, town near Rio de Janeiro, Brazil + E *-ite*] **:** a meteoritic stone consisting essentially of titanaugite and having no chondrules

an·gry \ˈaŋgrē, ˈaiŋ-, -ri, *chiefly substand* -ŋr-\ *adj, often* -ER/-EST [ME, fr. *anger* + *-y*] **1 :** feeling some degree of anger **:** showing vexation or hot resentment **:** WRATHFUL, IRATE ⟨~ with anyone who dislikes the Cockney manner —*Times Lit. Supp.*⟩ ⟨~ at the weather⟩ **2 a :** indicative of anger **:** proceeding from anger ⟨~ words⟩ **b :** seeming to show anger **:** threatening or seeming to threaten angrily ⟨an ~ sky⟩ ⟨a scorpion with wide ~ nippers —Robert Browning⟩ **3 :** inflamed and painful — used of a sore **4 a** *archaic* **:** habitually irascible and bad-tempered **b :** appearing or being naturally fierce or feral ⟨by ~ wolf —John Keats⟩ **5 :** having some characteristic associated with anger; *esp* **:** having a hue that suggests anger ⟨an ~ red⟩

syn MAD, IRATE, INDIGNANT, WRATHFUL, WROTH, ACRIMONIOUS: Although one may occasionally be inwardly and secretly ANGRY, the word commonly implies excited displeasure outwardly expressed ⟨she wanted somebody to be *angry* with, somebody to abuse —George Meredith⟩ Often but not always the word may imply a justifiable cause for displeasure ⟨he hardly ever gets *angry*, doesn't half stand up for his rights —Margaret Mead⟩ MAD is a close equivalent to ANGRY but lacks implications about expression ⟨Old Rough and Ready was getting *mad* . . . no official thanks for the victories had reached him —Bernard De Voto⟩ IRATE stresses vehement irascible expression of displeasure ⟨the men were getting more cautious and at the same time more *irate* and violent in their language —Anthony Trollope⟩ INDIGNANT always suggests some justification for wrath, some righteousness of anger ⟨he . . . grows very hot and *indignant* when he thinks of the disrespectful treatment he received —Rudyard Kipling⟩ ⟨the natives, *indignant* at the insult offered their laws . . ., made a dash at the rioters —Herman Melville⟩ WRATHFUL and the less common WROTH may express the vehemence of IRATE and the justification of INDIGNANT ⟨Mr. Seddon winced. Then he became *wrathful* in a dry legal fashion. "That", he said, "is a most improper question" —Agatha Christie⟩ ⟨eyes more wild than those of Moses when, at the sight of the golden calf and the dancing, his heart waxed *wroth* within him —L.P.Smith⟩ ACRIMONIOUS implies bitter feeling, rising temper, and caustic expression ⟨no modern subject, probably, has brought forth so much lyric liturgy and *acrimonious* debate —M.R.Cohen⟩ ANGRY and MAD are more common than the other words in reference to animals ⟨an *angry* hornet⟩ ⟨a *mad* bull⟩ and ANGRY and WRATHFUL are the most commonly used in the group in reference to raging or ominous natural phenomena ⟨*angry* storm clouds⟩ ⟨*wrathful* lightning⟩

angst \ˈäŋzt, ˈaŋ-, -ŋ(k)st\ *n, pl* **äng·ste** \ˈeŋztə, -ŋ(k)stə\ [Dan & G; Dan, fr. G, fr. OHG *angust*; akin to MLG *angest* dread, MD *anxt*, OFris *ångost* dread, OHG *engi* narrow — more at ANGER] **:** a feeling of anxiety **:** DREAD, ANGUISH

ang·ster \ˈäŋzte(r), -ŋ(k)st-\ *n* -s [G, fr. MHG, fr. ML *angustus* thin, fr. L, narrow — more at ANGUISH] **:** an old Swiss minor coin of copper coined in various cantons from the 15th to the 19th centuries

ang·strom \ˈaŋztrəm, ˈaiŋ-, -ŋst- *sometimes* ˈȯŋ-\ *or* **ang·strom unit** *n* -s [after Anders J. *Ångström* †1874 Swedish physicist] **:** either of two units of wavelength: **a :** one ten-billionth of a meter — called also *absolute angstrom* **b :** the wavelength of the red spectrum line of cadmium divided by 6438.4696 — called also *international angstrom*

an·gu·clast \ˈaŋgyüˌklast\ *n* -s [*angular* + *phenoclast*] **:** an angular phenoclast

an·gui·dae \ˈaŋgwəˌdē\ *n pl, cap* [NL, fr. *Anguis*, type genus + *-idae*] **:** a family of lizards some of which are limbless and all of which are entirely harmless and useful as destroyers of slugs, worms, and insects — compare BLINDWORM

an·gui·form \-ˌfȯrm\ *adj* [L *anguis* snake + E *-form*] *archaic* **:** having the form of a snake

an·guil·la \aŋˈgwilə\ *n, cap* [NL, fr. L, eel] **:** a genus (the type of the family Anguillidae) of fishes that includes the common eel and certain related forms and has the dorsal and anal fins continuous with the reduced caudal and pectoral fins

an·guil·lar·ia \ˌaŋgwəˈla(a)rēə\ *n, cap* [NL, fr. Luigi *Anguillara* †1570 Ital. botanist + NL *-ia*] **:** a small genus of herbs (family Melanthaceae) natives of Australia and Tasmania with sessile lilylike flowers

an·guil·li·form \aŋˈgwiləˌfȯrm\ *adj* [L *anguilla* eel + E *-iform*] *archaic* **:** having the form of an eel

an·guil·lu·la \aŋˈgwilyələ\ [NL, fr. L *anguilla* eel + NL *-ula*] *syn of* TURBATRIX

an·guil·lu·li·na \(ˌ)aŋˌgwilyəˈlīnə, -ēnə\ *n, cap* [NL, fr. *anguillula* (dim. of L *anguilla* eel) + NL *-ina*] *in some classifications* **:** a genus of widely distributed phasmid nematodes including free-living forms and a number of important plant pathogens and being approximately equal to *Tylenchus* and *Anguina* of other classifications

an·gui·mor·pha \ˌaŋgwəˈmȯrfə\ *n pl, cap* [NL, fr. *Anguis* + *-morpha*] **:** a section of the saurian division Autarchoglossa comprising the Anguidae and certain related families and characterized by simple clavicles, a smooth or papillate tongue, flounced hemipenes, and teeth that are usu. conical, pointed, or recurved — **an·gui·mor·phine** \ˌ==ˈ=ˌfīn, -ˌfən\ *adj*

an·gui·na \aŋˈgwīnə, an'-, -ēnə\ *n, cap* [NL, fr. L, fem. of *anguinus*] **:** a genus of plant-parasitic phasmid nematodes (family Tylenchidae) including several serious pests of cultivated crops and typically forming galls on leaves, stems, or roots — compare ANGUILLULINA; see TYLENCHUS

an·guine \ˈaŋˌgwīn\ *adj* [L *anguinus*, fr. *anguis* snake + *-inus* -ine — more at ANGUIS] *archaic* **:** of, relating to, or suggestive of a snake

an·guin·e·ous \(ˈ)aŋˈgwinēəs\ *adj* [L *anguineus*, fr. *anguin-*, *anguen* snake (fr. *anguis*) + *-eus* -eous] *archaic* **:** having the nature or appearance of a snake

an·guin·i·dae \aŋˈgwinəˌdē\ [NL, fr. *Anguin-*, *Anguis*, type genus + *-idae*] *syn of* ANGUIDAE

an·gui·ped \ˈaŋgwəˌped\ *adj* [L *anguiped-*, *anguipes*, fr. *anguis* + *ped-*, *pes* foot — more at FOOT] **:** having legs in the form of serpents — used esp. of a statue

an·guis \ˈaŋgwə̇s\ *n, cap* [NL, fr. L, snake; akin to OE & OHG *igil* hedgehog, OHG *unc* snake, L *anguilla* eel, Gk *enchelys* eel, *echidna* viper, *echinos* hedgehog, *ophis* snake, Skt *ahi*] **:** the type genus of Anguidae including only the limbless blindworm

¹an·guish \ˈaŋgwish, ˈaiŋ-, -ēsh *also* -əsh\ *n* -ES [ME *anguisshe*, fr. OF *angoisse* anguish, narrowness, restraint, fr. L *angustia* narrowness, difficulty, distress, fr. *angustus* narrow, difficult; akin to OE *enge* narrow — more at ANGER] **:** extreme pain either of body or mind **:** excruciating distress — usu. used in sing. ⟨the keenest of all ~, self-reproach —Jane Austen⟩ ⟨his whole frame quivering with ~ as kick followed kick in rapid succession —Charles Dickens⟩ **syn** see SORROW

²anguish \"\ *vb* -ED/-ING/-ES [ME *angwisshen*, fr. MF *angoissier*, fr. LL *angustiare* to distress, fr. L *angustia*] *vi* **:** to distress oneself **:** suffer intense pain or sorrow ⟨his heart ~*ed* within him —Edith Sitwell⟩ ~ *vt* **:** to cause to suffer anguish **:** distress severely ⟨a heart that had been ~*ed* with sorrow⟩

anguished *adj* [ME *angwisshed*, fr. past. part. of *angwisshen*] **:** produced, affected, or accompanied by anguish **:** TORMENTED ⟨an ~ conscience⟩ **:** AGONIZED ⟨an ~ shriek⟩

¹an·gu·lar \ˈaŋgyələ(r), ˈaiŋ-\ *adj* [MF or L; MF *angulaire*, fr. L *angularis*, fr. *angulus* angle, corner + *-aris* -ar — more at ANGLE] **1 :** having an angle or angles **:** forming an angle or corner **:** sharp-cornered ⟨an ~ brick structure —*Amer. Guide Series: Maine*⟩ **2 :** of or relating to the 1st, 4th, 7th, and 10th mundane houses of a horoscope **3 :** measured by an angle ⟨~ distance⟩ **4 a :** sharp and stiff in character or manner **:** lacking in smoothness ⟨a rough, ~, explosive poetry —*Saturday Rev.*⟩ **b :** having the bones prominent from lack of plumpness ⟨an ~ youth⟩ **5 :** relating to or having a chemical structure in which a ring or group is so joined as to form an angle and not a straight alignment ⟨an ~ methyl group⟩ **6** *anat* **:** relating to or situated near an angle ⟨the ~ head of the quadratus labii superioris⟩; *specif* **:** relating to or situated near the inner angle of the eye **syn** see LEAN

²angular \"\ *n* -s [NL *angulare*, fr. L, neut. of *angularis*, adj.] **:** a membrane bone in the lower posterior part of the lower jaw of most vertebrates except mammals

angular acceleration *n* **:** the time rate of change of angular velocity

angular aperture *n* **:** the angle subtended at the principal focus of an optical system by the diameter of its entrance pupil

angular artery *n* **:** the terminal part of the facial artery that passes up alongside the nose to the inner angle of the orbit

angular capital *n* **:** an Ionic capital with volutes on four faces, those of adjacent faces meeting and projecting diagonally under each corner of the abacus

angular convolution *or* **angular gyrus** *n* **:** one of the convolutions of the posterior part of the external surface of the parietal lobe of the cerebrum

angular cutter *n* **:** a tool-steel cutter for finishing surfaces at other than 90 degrees with its axis of rotation

angular displacement *n* **:** a definite amount of rotation (as of a disk) about a specified axis

an·gu·la·re \ˌaŋgyəˈlārē, -la(a)rē\ *n, pl* **angula·ria** \-ārēə, -a(a)rēə\ [NL, fr. L, neut. of *angularis* angular — more at ANGULAR] **:** ANGULAR

angular frequency *n* **:** frequency of a periodic process (as electric oscillation or sound vibration) expressed in radians per second, equivalent to frequency in cycles multiplied by 2π

angular impulse *n* **:** the product of a torque and its time of duration being equal to the change in angular momentum of a body free to rotate — compare IMPULSE 4a

an·gu·lar·i·ty \ˌaŋgyəˈlarəd·ē, ˌaiŋ-, -ətē, -i *also* -er-\ *n* -ES **1 :** the quality of being angular ⟨an almost impressionistic ~ —Robert Evett⟩ **2 a :** an ungainly appearance (as in dress or manner) **b :** lack of suaveness **:** CRANKINESS ⟨the ~ of his disposition⟩ **3 angularities** *pl* **:** angular outlines **:** sharp corners ⟨*angularities* of handwriting⟩

an·gu·lar·i·za·tion \ˌ==ˌlərəˈzāshən, -ˌrīˈz-\ *n* -s **:** the act, process, or result of angularizing

an·gu·lar·ize \ˈ===ˌrīz\ *vt* -ED/-ING/-S [ˈ*angular* + *-ize*] **:** to make angular; *esp* **:** to transform by changing curved lines into angular lines

angular leaf spot *also* **angular spot** *n* **:** a disease of plants in which the leaf spots have angular and usu. sharply limited outlines (as that of cotton caused by the bacterium *Xanthomonas malvacearum* and that of cucumber caused by the bacterium *Pseudomonas lachrymans*) — see BLACKFIRE

an·gu·lar·ly *adv* **:** in an angular manner

angular magnification *n* **:** the ratio of the angle subtended at the eye by the image formed by an optical instrument to that subtended at the eye by the object when not viewed through the instrument

angular milling *n* **:** the process of milling flat surfaces that are at an angle to the axis of the milling-machine spindle

angular momentum *n* **:** a vector quantity measuring the intensity of rotational motion and being equal in classical physics to the product of the angular velocity of a rotating body and its moment of inertia with respect to the rotation axis — called also *moment of momentum*

angular motion *n* **:** ROTATION 1a

angular position *n* **:** the orientation of a body or figure with respect to a specified reference position as expressed by the amount of rotation necessary to change from one orientation to the other about a specified axis

angular process *n* **:** any of the processes terminating the supraorbital arches of the frontal bone

angular speed *n* **:** the speed element of angular velocity

angular vein *n* **:** a vein that runs obliquely down at the side of the upper part of the nose and is continued across the cheek as the anterior facial vein

angular velocity *n* **:** the time rate of angular displacement usu. expressed in radians per second or in revolutions per second or per minute being a vector whose direction and sense are such that the motion appears clockwise to one looking in the direction of the vector

angular-wing katydid \ˈ===ˌwiŋd-\ *n* **:** a common large green long-horned grasshopper (*Microcentrum retinerve*) of the eastern U. S.

¹an·gu·late \ˈaŋgyələt, ˈaiŋ-, -ˌlāt *usu* -d·+V\ *adj* [L *angulatus*, fr. *angulus* angle, corner + *-atus* -ate] **:** formed with corners **:** ANGLED ⟨~ leaves⟩ — **an·gu·late·ly** *adv*

²an·gu·late \-ˌlāt *usu* -d·+V\ *vb* -ED/-ING/-S [ME *angulaten*, fr. L *angulatus*] *vt* **:** to make angulate ~ *vi* **:** to become angulate

an·gu·la·tion \ˌ==ˈlāshən\ *n* -s [ˈ*angulate* + *-ion*] **1 :** the action of making angulate **2 a :** an angular formation or shape **b** *med* **:** an abnormal bend or curve in an organ **3 :** the measurement of angles (as in surveying)

an·gu·la·tor \ˈ==ˌlād·ə(r)\ *n* -s **:** a mechanical device for converting angles measured in an oblique plane to their projections on a horizontal plane and used esp. in surveying

anguli *pl of* ANGULUS

anguli- *or* **angulo-** *comb form* [prob. fr. NL, fr. L *angulus* angle — more at ANGLE] **1 :** angle ⟨*angulo*meter⟩ **:** angular ⟨*anguli*nerved⟩ **2 :** of or belonging to the angular and ⟨*angulo*splenial⟩

an·gu·lif·er·ous \ˌaŋgyəˈlif(ə)rəs\ *adj* [*anguli-* + *-ferous*] *of a gastropod shell* **:** having the last whorl angular

an·gu·loa \ˌaŋgyəˈlōə, aŋˈgyüləwə\ *n, cap* [NL, after Francisco de *Angulo* 18th cent. Span. naturalist] **:** a small genus of So. American orchids with large plicate leaves cultivated for their showy fragrant flowers

¹an·gu·lo·sple·ni·al \ˌaŋgyə(ˌ)lōˈ-\ *adj* [*angulo-* + *splenial*] *anat* **:** of or relating to both the angular and the splenial

²angulosplenial \ˈ==(=)ˈ-\ *n* -s **:** the angulosplenial bone forming most of the inner and lower part of the mandible of amphibians

an·gu·lous \ˈaŋgyələs\ *also* **an·gu·lose** \-ˌlōs\ *adj* [F *anguleux*, fr. L *angulosus*, fr. *angulus* angle + *-osus* -ous, -ose] *archaic* **:** having angles or corners **:** ANGULAR

an·gu·lus \-ləs\ *n, pl* **angu·li** \-ˌlī, -ˌlē\ [L — more at ANGLE] *anat* **:** ANGLE; *also* **:** an angular part or relationship

¹an·gus \ˈaŋgəs, ˈaiŋ-\ *adj, usu cap* [fr. *Angus*, county in Scotland] **:** of or from the county of Angus, Scotland **:** of the kind or style prevalent in Angus

²angus \"\ *n, usu cap* [fr. *Angus*, county where the breed originated] **:** ABERDEEN ANGUS

angusti- *comb form* [prob. fr. L, fr. *angustus* — more at ANGUISH] **:** narrow ⟨*angusti*foliate⟩ ⟨*angusti*rostrate⟩

an·gus·ti·ros·trate \aŋˈgəstəˈ-\ *adj* [*angusti-* + *rostrate*] **:** having a narrow rostrum or snout

an·gus·ti·sel·late \ˈ=ˈ==ˈ-\ *adj* [*angusti-* + *sellate*] *paleontol* **:** having sutures in which there are a prominent ventral saddle, deep lateral lobes, and deep umbilical saddles — used of a stage in the development of the ammonoid shell

ang·wan·ti·bo \aŋˈ(g)wäntəˌbō\ *n* -s [Efik] **:** a small lemur (*Arctocebus calabarensis*) of western Africa having a rather long snout and a rudimentary tail

anh *abbr* anhydrous

an·ha·lo·ni·um alkaloid \ˌan(h)əˈlōnēəm-\ *n* [NL *Anhalonium*, genus of cacti, fr. Gk *an-* + *halōnion* small threshing floor (equated with NL *areola* areole, fr. L, small open space, dim. of *area* piece of level ground, threshing floor), dim. of *halōn* threshing floor; fr. the belief that the areoles were lacking — more at HALO] **:** any of a group of alkaloids (as hordenine, mescaline) that are found in mescal buttons and that are used as cerebral stimulants and motor depressants — called also *cactus alkaloid*

an·har·mon·ic \ˌan,=ˈ==\ *adj* [F *anharmonique*, fr. *an-* + *harmonique* harmonic, fr. L *harmonicus*] **:** not harmonic — **an·har·mo·nic·i·ty** \ˌan,härməˈnisəd·ē\ *n* -ES

an·he·do·nia \ˌanhēˈdōnēə\ *n* -s [NL, fr. *an-* + Gk *hēdonē* pleasure + NL *-ia* — more at HEDONIC] **1 :** insensitiveness to pleasure **2 :** incapacity for experiencing happiness — compare ANALGESIA — **an·he·don·ic** \ˈ==ˈdänik\ *adj*

an·he·dral \(ˈ)anˈhēdrəl\ *adj* [*an-* + *-hedral*] **:** ALLOTRIOMORPHIC

an·hi·dro·sis *or* **an·hy·dro·sis** \ˌanhīˈdrōsə̇s\ *also* **an·idro·sis** \ˌani'-\ *n, pl* **anhidro·ses** *or* **anhydro·ses** \-ōˌsēz\ [NL, fr. *an-* + *hidrosis*, *hydrosis*] **:** abnormal deficiency or absence of sweating

¹an·hi·drot·ic *or* **an·hy·drot·ic** *also* **an·idrot·ic** \ˈ==ˈdräd·ik\ *adj* [*an-* + *hidrotic*, *hydrotic*] **:** tending to check sweating

²anhidrotic *or* **anhydrotic** \"\ *also* **anidrotic** \"\ *n* -s **:** an anhidrotic agent

anhi·ma \anˈhīmə; əˈnēmə, aˈ-\ *n* [NL, fr. Pg, fr. Tupi] **1** -s **:** HORNED SCREAMER **2** *cap* **:** a genus of birds that includes only the horned screamer and is the type of the family Anhimidae

an·him·i·dae \anˈhiməˌdē\ *n pl, cap* [NL, fr. *Anhima*, type genus + *-idae*] **:** a family (coextensive with the suborder Anhimae of the order Anseriformes) of large stout-billed birds having spurred wings and more or less webbed feet and comprising the screamers of So. America

an·hin·ga \an'hiŋgə\ *n* [Pg, fr. Tupi] **1** -s **:** an American snakebird **2** *cap* [NL, fr. Pg] **:** a genus of aquatic birds related to the gannets and cormorants and consisting of the snakebirds

an·his·tous \(')an¦histəs\ *also* **an·his·tic** \-tik\ *adj* [*an-* + *hist-* + *-ous* or *-ic*] **:** not differentiated into tissues **:** NONCELLULAR ⟨~ matrix⟩ ⟨~ intercellular cement⟩

anhungered *adj* [ME *anhungred*, alter. of ME *ahungred* ahungered] **1** *obs* **:** HUNGRY **2** *archaic* **:** eagerly longing

anhungry *adj* [alter. of earlier *ahungry*] *obs* **:** HUNGRY

anhydr- *or* **anhydro-** *comb form* [modif. (influenced by *hydr-*, *hydro-*) of Gk *anydr-*, fr. *anydros* — more at ANHYDROUS] **1 a :** waterless ⟨*anhydremia*⟩ **b :** lacking fluid ⟨*anhydromyelia*⟩ **2 :** anhydride of ⟨*anhydroglucose*⟩

an·hy·drase \an'hī,drās\ *n* -s [*anhydr-* + *-ase*] **:** an enzyme (as carbonic anhydrase) promoting a specific dehydration reaction and the reverse hydration reaction

an·hy·drate \-,drāt, *usu* -ād·+V\ *vt* -ED/-ING/-S [*an-* + *hydrate*] **:** DEHYDRATE; *esp* **:** to dehydrate quickly in food processing — **an·hy·dra·tion** \,an,hī'drāshən\ *n* -s — **an·hy·dra·tor** \an'hī,drād·ə(r)\ *n* -s

an·hy·dre·mia *also* **an·hy·drae·mia** \,an,hī'drēmēə\ *n* -s [NL, fr. *anhydr-* + *-emia*] **:** an abnormal reduction of water in the blood — **an·hy·dre·mic** *also* **an·hy·drae·mic** \¦==¦drēmik\ *adj*

an·hy·dride \an'hī,drīd, -,drəd\ *n* -s [ISV *anhydr-* + *-ide*] **:** a compound derived from another compound (as an acid) by removal of the elements of water ⟨benzoic ~ $(C_6H_5CO)_2O$⟩

an·hy·drid·i·za·tion \(¦)an,hīdrədə'zāshən, -,dī'z-\ *or* **an·hy·dri·za·tion** \(,)an,hīdrə'z-\ *n* -s **:** the process of anhydridizing or the state of being anhydridized

an·hy·drid·ize \an'hīdrə,dīz\ *or* **an·hy·drize** \-,drīz\ *vt* -ED/-ING/-S **:** to convert into an anhydride

an·hy·drite \an'hī,drīt\ *n* -s [G *anhydrit*, fr. *anhydr-* + *-it* -ite] **:** a mineral consisting of an anhydrous calcium sulfate $CaSO_4$ occurring rarely in orthorhombic crystals usu. massive and white or slightly colored (hardness 3–3.5, sp. gr. 2.90 - 2.99) — compare GYPSUM

an·hy·dro \an'hī(,)drō\ *adj* [*anhydr-*] **:** of or relating to an anhydride ⟨~ sugars⟩ — compare DEHYDRO

anhydro base *n* **:** a dehydration product (as ammonia or an imine) of a base, usu. an oxygen-containing nitrogen base (as ammonium hydroxide or the color base of certain triphenylamine dyes)

an·hy·dro·bi·o·sis \(¦)an,hydrōbī'ōsəs\ *n, pl* **anhydrobio·ses** \-ō,sēz\ [NL, fr. *anhydr-* + *biosis*] **1** *of a usu aquatic organism* **:** life away from water **2 :** ANABIOSIS

an·hy·dro·hy·droxy·pro·ges·ter·one \an¦hīdrō,hī¦dräksēprō¦jestə,rōn\ *n* -s [*anhydr-* + *hydroxy-* + *progesterone*] **:** ETHISTERONE

an·hy·drous \(')an¦hīdrəs\ *adj* [modif. (influenced by *hydr-*, *hydro-*) of Gk *anydros* waterless, fr. *an-* + *-ydros* (fr. *hydōr* water) — more at WATER] **:** destitute of water — used of water of crystallization, dissolved or combined water, adsorbed water

anhydrous hydrofluoric acid *n* **:** HYDROGEN FLUORIDE

an·hys·ter·et·ic \¦an,histə¦red·ik, an¦h-\ *adj* [*an-* + *hysteretic*] **:** not subject to hysteresis

¹ani \ä'nē, ə'-\ *n* -s [Sp *ani* or Pg *ani*, fr. Tupi *ani*, *anú*] **:** any of several black cuckoos (genus *Crotophaga*) with arched laterally compressed bills found mostly in tropical America but occasionally (as the common ani *C. ani*) northward to the southern limits of the U.S.

²ani \'ā(,)nī\ *pl of* ANUS

ani·ba \ə'nībə, -ēbə\ *n, cap* [NL, prob. fr. Tupi *anhoaiba*, *anhuhyba*] **:** a genus of tropical American trees of the family Lauraceae with aromatic foliage, inconspicuous flowers, and succulent fruit, the seeds of some having tonic properties

an·i·can·o·don·ta \,anə,kanə'däntə\ [NL, fr. Gk *anikanos* insufficient + NL *-odonta*] *syn of* PILOSA

anic·ca \ə'nikə\ *n* -s [Pali, fr. Skt *anitya* not eternal, fr. *a-* ²a- + *nitya* eternal] *Buddhism* **:** evanescence or impermanence of existence

an·icon·ic \¦a,nī¦känik\ *adj* [*an-* + *iconic*] **1 :** symbolic or suggestive rather than literally representational **:** not made or designed as a likeness ⟨trees, boulders, and other ~ objects of primitive worship⟩ ⟨an ~ image⟩ **2 :** without idols or images **:** opposed to the use of idols or images ⟨an ~ religion⟩

an·icon·ism \(')a'nīkən,izəm\ *n* -s [*an-* + *iconism*] **1 :** worship of an aniconic object **2 :** opposition to the use of idols

an·ic·ter·ic \¦an(,)ik¦terik\ *adj* [ISV *an-* + *icteric*] **:** not accompanied or characterized by jaundice ⟨~ hepatitis⟩

an·i·cut *or* **an·ni·cut** \'anə,kət\ *n* -s [Tamil *aṇaikkaṭṭu*, fr. *aṇai* dam + *kaṭṭu* building, structure] **:** a dam made in a stream for maintaining and regulating irrigation

an·id·i·an \(')a¦nidēən\ *adj* [*an-* + Gk *eidos* form + E *-ian*] *of an embryo or fetus* **:** FORMLESS **:** lacking differentiation

anidrosis *var of* ANHIDROSIS

anidrotic *var of* ANHIDROTIC

an·i·el·li·dae \,anē'elə,dē\ *syn of* ANNIELLIDAE

an if *conj* [²*an*] *archaic* **:** provided that **:** IF ⟨these be fine things *an if* they be not sprites —Shak.⟩

¹anigh *prep* [¹*a-* + *nigh*] *archaic* **:** NIGH

²anigh *adv* -ER/-EST [¹*a-* + *nigh*] *archaic* **:** NIGH

anight *or* **anights** *adv* [ME, fr. OE *on niht*, fr. *on* + *niht* night — more at NIGHT] *archaic* **:** at night

an·il \'an³l\ *n* -s [ISV, fr. *aniline*] **:** a Schiff base derived from an aromatic amine; *esp* **:** one derived from aniline ⟨the ~ $C_6H_5CH{:}NC_6H_5$ of benzaldehyde⟩

ani·lao *or* **ani·lau** \ä'nē,lau̇\ *or* **ani·lo** \-(,)lō\ *n* -s [Tag] **1 :** a shrub (*Columbia serratifolia*) of the family Tiliaceae yielding a strong bast fiber that is found chiefly in the Philippines **2 :** any of several shrubs or trees of the genus *Grewia* yielding a cordage fiber

an·ile \'a,nīl, 'ā,-, -īəl\ *adj* [L *anilis*, fr. *anus* old woman + *-ilis* -ile; akin to OHG *ano* grandfather, male ancestor, Gk *annis* grandmother, Arm *han*, and perh. to L *senex* old man — more at SENIOR] **:** of, relating to, or suggesting a doddering old woman ⟨pathetic questions which showed an ~ loss of time sense —R.O Bowen⟩

anil·ic \ə'nilik, a'-\ *adj* [ISV *anil* + *-ic*] **:** of or relating to aniline or anil

anilic acid \ə'==-\ *or* **an·i·lid·ic acid** \¦an³l¦idik-\ *n* **:** a compound [as phthalanilic acid $C_6H_4(CONHC_6H_5)COOH$] that is both an anilide and an acid

anil·i·dae \ə'nilə,dē\ *syn of* ANILIIDAE

an·i·lide \'an³ləd, -,īd\ *n* -s [G *anilid*, fr. *anil* + *-id* -ide] **1 :** an amide (as acetanilide) in which hydrogen of the amido group is replaced by phenyl **:** an *N*-acyl derivative of aniline **2 :** ARYLIDE

an·i·li·id \,an³l'īəd\ *n* -s [NL *Aniliidae*] **:** a snake of the family Aniliidae

an·i·li·idae \-īə,dē\ *n pl, cap* [NL, fr. *Anilius*, type genus (irreg. fr. L *anulus* ring) + *-idae*] **:** a small family of tropical nonvenomous burrowing snakes with vestigial pelvis and vestigial hind legs

¹an·i·line \'an³lən *sometimes* -,īn *or* -,ēn\ *also* **an·i·lin** \-ən\ *n* -s [G *anilin*, fr. *anil* indigo, (fr. F, fr. Pg, fr. Ar *an-nīl* the indigo plant, fr. Skt *nīlī* indigo, fr. fem. of *nīla* dark blue) + *-in* -ine, -in] **:** an oily liquid poisonous amine $C_6H_5NH_2$ colorless when pure and obtainable by destructive distillation (as of indigo or coal) but now usu. made by the reduction of nitrobenzene or by the high-pressure reaction of chlorobenzene and ammonia and used chiefly in organic synthesis (as of dyes, pharmaceuticals, rubber chemicals, and explosives) and as a solvent; amino-benzene

²aniline \"\ *adj* **:** relating to aniline **:** made from or by the use of aniline or a chemically related compound

aniline black *n* **:** a black dye produced on fiber (as cotton) by the oxidation of aniline oil or aniline hydrochloride and noted for its fastness, intensity of color, and resistance to greening — see DYE table I (under *Oxidation Base 1* and *Pigment Black 1*)

aniline blue *n* **:** one of the soluble blue dyes used as a biological dye

aniline dye *n* **:** a dye made by the use of aniline **:** any of various chemically related dyes; *broadly* **:** any synthetic organic dye — compare COAL-TAR DYE

aniline-formaldehyde resin *n* **:** a synthetic usu. thermoplastic resin made from aniline and formaldehyde

aniline hydrochloride *n* **:** a white crystalline salt $C_6H_5NH_3Cl$ made from aniline and hydrochloric acid and used chiefly in the manufacture of dyes and in the production of aniline black

aniline ink *n* **:** a quick-drying printing ink usu. made with an alcohol as vehicle and with an organic or inorganic pigment

aniline oil *n* **:** ANILINE — used chiefly commercially; see DYE table I (under *Oxidation Base 1*)

aniline point *n* **:** the lowest temperature at which aniline and a solvent (as gasoline) are completely miscible and which serves as an indication of the type of hydrocarbons present in the solvent, the content of aromatics being higher according as the temperature is lower

aniline printing *also* **aniline process** *n* **:** a process in which nonabsorbent surfaces are printed with aniline inks

aniline salt *n* **:** ANILINE HYDROCHLORIDE — used chiefly commercially; see DYE table I (under *Oxidation Base 1*)

ani·lin·gus \,ānə'liŋgəs\ *or* **ani·linc·tus** \-ŋ(k)təs\ *n* -ES [NL, fr. *anus* + *-i-* + *-lingus*, *-linctus* (as in *cunnilingus*, *cunnilinctus*)] **:** erotic stimulation achieved by contact between mouth and anus

an·i·lin·ism \'an³lə,nizəm\ *n* -s [ISV *aniline* + *-ism*] **:** poisoning from fumes inhaled in the manufacture of aniline

an·i·li·no- \¦an³l¦ēnō, -nə\ *comb form* [ISV, fr. *aniline* + *-o-*] **:** containing the univalent radical $C_6H_5NH_2$— derived from aniline ⟨*anilino*phenol $C_6H_5NHC_6H_4OH$⟩

anil·i·ty \ə'niləd·ē, a'-\ *n* -ES [L *anilitas*, fr. *anilis* + *-tat-*, *-tas* -ty] **1 :** the state of being an old woman **2 :** an objectionable quality (as flightiness) felt to be typical of a doddering old woman ⟨the utter ~ of their political views⟩

anilo *var of* ANILAO

anils *pl of* ANIL

an·i·ma \'anəmə\ *n* -s [L — more at ANIMATE] **1 a :** SOUL, LIFE; *specif* **:** the passive or animal soul **b :** an individual's true inner self reflecting archetypal ideals of conduct — used esp. in contrast with *persona* in the analytic psychology of Carl Gustav Jung; compare ARCHETYPE **5** **2** [NL, fr. L, soul] *old pharmacy* **a :** the active ingredient of an animal or vegetable drug **b :** a dried plant juice or an aqueous extract

an·i·mad·ver·sion \,anə,mad'vərzhən, -,məd-, -ə̄|,-əi| *also* |sh-\ *n* -s [L *animadversion-*, *animadversio*, fr. *animadversus* (past part. of *animadvertere*) + *-ion-*, *-io* -ion — more at ANIMADVERT] **1 a :** criticism that is usu. adverse and prompted by some degree of hostility **:** CENSURE **:** a censorious remark or observation ⟨his ~ upon his old acquaintance and pupil —James Boswell⟩ ⟨the customary ~*s* of a reviewer —R.B. Gottfried⟩ **b :** an observation, remark, or commentary that is usu. based on careful analysis and impartial judgment ⟨illuminating and scholarly ~*s*⟩ **2** *archaic* **:** judicial cognizance and punishment of an offense

an·i·mad·vert \¦==(,)=¦vərt, -ət,-əit\ *vb* -ED/-ING/-S [L *animadvertere*, fr. *animus* mind, soul + *advertere* to advert — more at ANIMATE, ADVERT] *vt, archaic* **:** NOTICE, OBSERVE ~ *vi* **:** to make an animadversion ⟨~*ing* on a wide variety of things they disliked⟩ ⟨she ~*ed* upon her closest interests⟩

animae mundi *pl of* ANIMA MUNDI

¹an·i·mal \'anəməl\ *n* -s [L, fr. *animale*, neut. of *animalis* animate, fr. *anima* breath, soul, + *-alis* -al — more at ANIMATE] **1 :** an organism of the kingdom Animalia being characterized by a requirement for complex organic nutrients including proteins or their constituents which are usu. digested in an internal cavity before assimilation into the body proper and being distinguished from typical plants by lack of chlorophyll and inability to perform photosynthesis, by cells that lack cellulose walls, and usu. by greater mobility with some degree of voluntary locomotor ability, by greater irritability commonly mediated through a more or less centralized nervous system, and by the frequent presence of discrete complex sense organs **2 a :** one of the lower animals **:** a brute or beast as distinguished from man **:** any creature except a human being — compare DOMESTIC ANIMAL, FERAE NATURAE **b :** a mammal as distinguished from a bird, reptile, or other nonmammal **c** *North* **:** a male bovine **:** BULL **3 a :** a human being considered chiefly from the aspect of his animal nature and animal qualities ⟨a majestic ~ of a man —*Newsweek*⟩ **b :** a human being considered from a speculative or abstract viewpoint **:** PERSON, BEING, CREATURE ⟨women wonder so often about this strange creature, the male ~ —Theodor Reik⟩ **c :** THING ⟨the theater, obviously, is an entirely different ~ —Arthur Miller⟩ **4 :** animal nature **:** ANIMALITY ⟨unable to control the ~ in himself⟩

²animal \"\ *adj* **1 a :** of, relating to, resembling, or having the qualities of animals ⟨~ instincts⟩ ⟨~ behavior⟩; *esp* **:** more like a brute animal than a man ⟨the butler . . . betrayed a sullen and almost ~ affection for his master —G.K.Chesterton⟩ **b :** derived from animals as distinguished from vegetable or mineral sources ⟨furs and other ~ products⟩ **2 :** of or relating to the physical or sentient ⟨the savage, when he first began to lift his thoughts above the satisfaction of his merely ~ wants —J.G.Frazer⟩ — contrasted with *intellectual*, *rational*, *spiritual* **3 :** GROSS, CARNAL ⟨an ~ hunger for every pleasure⟩ **4 :** physically relaxing or soothing **:** pleasurable to the senses ⟨the ~ looseness of their summer home clothes —D.C.Peattie⟩ **5 :** of or relating to the animal pole of an egg or to that part of an egg from which ectoderm normally develops — compare VEGETAL **syn** see CARNAL

animal black *n* **:** a black pigment made by carbonizing animal matter: as **a :** BONE BLACK **b :** DROP BLACK **c :** IVORY BLACK

animal cellulose *n* **:** a substance like cellulose occurring in the test of certain tunicates

animal charcoal *n* **:** a charcoal of animal origin; *esp* **:** BONE BLACK

animal cracker *n* **:** a small semisweet animal-shaped cracker

an·i·mal·cu·lar \¦anə¦malkyələ(r)\ *also* **an·i·mal·cu·line** \-kyə,līn, -,lən\ *or* **an·i·mal·cu·lous** \-,ləs\ *adj* **:** of, relating to, or resembling animalcules

an·i·mal·cule \,anə'mal(,)kyül\ *or* **an·i·mal·cu·lum** \-kyələm\ *n, pl* **animalcules** \-kyülz\ *or* **animalcu·la** \-kyələ\ *also* **animalcu·lae** \-kyə,lē, -,lī\ [NL *animalculum*, dim. of L *animal*] **1** *archaic* **:** a tiny animal (as a fly) **2 a :** minute usu. microscopic organism — compare INFUSORIA

an·i·mal·cu·lism \-,kyə,lizəm\ *n* -s **1 :** a former theory in biology: various obscure physiological and pathological phenomena are caused by the activities of minute invisible animals **2 :** a former theory in biology: the spermatozoon contains the whole embryo in miniature — compare OVISM

an·i·mal·cu·list \-,ləst\ *n* -s **1 :** a specialist in animalcules **2 :** one that accepts animalculism

animal dance *n* **:** a stylized dance (as among American Indians) imitating or suggestive of the movements of an animal or bird (as a bear or owl) often marked by the use of masks

animal electricity *n* **:** electricity generated in the bodies of animals (as through friction); *specif* **:** electricity generated by specially adapted organs of some fishes (as the electric eel) and apparently used chiefly in attack or defense

animal faith *n* **:** instinctive belief without rational foundation — used esp. in the philosophy of George Santayana

animal flower *n* **:** an animal (as a hydroid) resembling a flower

animal glue *n* **:** an adhesive, sizing agent, and protective colloidal material that is obtained by hydrolysis of proteins of the skins, bones, connective tissues, and tendons of cattle, sheep, goats, horses, and other animals

animal heat *n* **:** heat produced in the body of a living animal by functional chemical and physical activities — called also *body heat;* compare TEMPERATURE 5b

animal husbandman *n* **1 :** a specialist in animal husbandry **2 :** one that keeps or tends livestock

animal husbandry *n* **:** a branch of agriculture concerned with the production and care of domestic animals; *specif* **:** scientific study of the problems of animal production (as breeding and feeding)

animal hypnosis *n* **:** CATAPLEXY

an·i·ma·lia \,anə'mālyə, -lēə\ *n pl, often cap* [NL, fr. L, pl. of *animal*] **:** that one of the basic groups of living things that comprises either all the animals or all the multicellular animals — compare ANIMAL KINGDOM, PLANTAE, PROTISTA

an·i·mal·ic \¦anə¦malik\ *also* **an·i·ma·li·an** \-'mālyən, -lēən\ *adj* **:** of or relating to animals or animalism

an·i·mal·ier \¦anəma¦li(ə)r\ *n* -s [F, fr. *animal* + *-ier* -er] **:** a sculptor or painter of animal subjects — compare ANIMALIST 2

an·i·mal·ism \'anəmə,lizəm\ *n* -s **1 a :** the aggregate of physical qualities felt to be typical of animals; *esp* **:** buoyant health and vitality and the uninhibited satisfaction of physical drives ⟨the joyous ~ of ancient Greece⟩ **b :** extreme preoccupation with the satisfaction of physical drives (as toward sex or food) sometimes accompanied by cruelty and brutality ⟨soldiers who passionately hated their enemies could revert to ~ —Webster Schott⟩ **2 :** a theory according to which human beings are basically brutes and little or nothing more ⟨a growing ~ that has accompanied the attempt to make social planning the be-all and end-all of human existence —R.M.Weaver⟩

an·i·mal·ist \-,ləst\ *n* -s **1 a :** one that follows animalism (sense 1b) as a mode of living **:** SENSUALIST **b :** one that accepts the theory of animalism **2 :** a painter, sculptor, or writer that deals with animal subjects — compare ANIMALIER

an·i·mal·is·tic \¦anəmə¦listik\ *adj* **1 :** of, relating to, or having the qualities of animals or animalism ⟨an ~ approach to life⟩ **2 :** resembling or suggestive of an animal ⟨an ~ door knocker⟩

an·i·mal·i·tar·i·an·ism \,anə,malə'terēə,nizəm\ *n* -s [¹*animal* + *-itarianism* (as in *humanitarianism*)] **:** the view that animals are more natural, happier, and admirable than human beings

an·i·mal·i·ty \,anə'maləd·ē, -ətē, -i\ *n* -ES [F *animalité*, fr. *animal* + *-ité* -ity] **1 :** animal healthiness, vitality, and absence of inhibitions **:** ANIMALISM ⟨the freedom of primitive sensuous ~ —John Dewey⟩ **2 a :** the state of being an animal **b :** animal nature esp. when not conferring of itself the faculty of reason ⟨that mental life which is characteristically human and above the level of sheer ~ —Susanne K. Langer⟩ **c :** a characteristic function or expression of animal nature ⟨the rude ~ of eating —R.L.Taylor⟩ **3 a :** animal life as distinguished from plant life ⟨the relationship of vegetable life and ~⟩ **b :** ANIMAL KINGDOM

an·i·mal·iv·o·ra \,anəmə'liv(ə)rə\ [NL, fr. L *animal* + NL *-i-* + *-vora*] *syn of* MICROCHIROPTERA

an·i·mal·i·vore \,anə'malə,vō(ə)r\ *n* -s [NL *Animalivora*] **:** MICROCHIROPTERAN — **an·i·mal·iv·o·rous** \¦anəmə¦liv(ə)rəs\ *adj*

an·i·mal·i·za·tion \,anəmələ'zāshən, -,lī'z-\ *n* -s **1 :** the act of animalizing or state of being animalized **2 :** regional distribution of animals by number and species **:** animal population

an·i·mal·ize \'anəmə,līz\ *vb* -ED/-ING/-S *vt* **1 a :** to represent in animal form ⟨the Egyptian god Sebek *animalized* as a crocodile⟩ **b** *fine art* **:** to endow (a human figure) with animal features **:** distort (human features) to make animallike **:** emphasize human features of animallike appearance ⟨a man's *animalized* head, adorned with ram's horns⟩ **2 :** to convert into animal matter ⟨*animalizing* food through digestion⟩ **3 a :** to reduce to the state of a lower animal **:** BRUTALIZE ⟨men that were *animalized* by war⟩ **b :** SENSUALIZE ⟨*animalized* by passion⟩ **4 :** to alter (vegetable fibers or synthetic fibers) by chemical treatment so as to cause to react like wool toward dyes **5 :** to cause (vegetal embryonic cells) to exhibit animal characteristics ~ *vi, of vegetal embryonic cells* **:** to exhibit animal characteristics

animal kingdom *n* **:** the one of the three basic groups of natural objects that comprises all living and extinct animals and includes about a million described species — compare MINERAL KINGDOM, PLANT KINGDOM

an·i·mal·like *adj* **:** having characteristics of an animal

an·i·mal·ly \-əlē, -li\ *adv* **:** in an animal manner

animal magnetism *n* **1 a :** a spiritlike force alleged by the Austrian physician Franz Anton Mesmer (1734–1815) to reside within himself and to be active in his use of therapeutical hypnosis — compare MESMERISM **b :** a spiritlike force held to reside in some individuals by the emanation of which a strong quasi-hypnotic influence can assertedly be exerted over others **2** *Christian Science* **:** ERROR, MORTAL MIND

animal mechanics *n* **:** the laws of equilibrium and motion in the animal body

animal mound *n* **:** EFFIGY MOUND

animal oil *n* **:** an oil obtained from animal substances; *specif* **:** BONE OIL 1

animal pole *n* **:** the point on the surface of an egg marking the center of the most active part of the protoplasm or the part containing least yolk, being in most animals whose embryology has been studied the point where the polar bodies are segmented off and where the protoplasm about it forms the ectoderm — opposed to *vegetal pole;* see BLASTULA illustration

animal protein factor *n* **:** vitamin B_{12} or a concentrate containing this vitamin and usu. antibiotics obtained esp. in the fermentation production of vitamin B_{12} and chlortetracycline and used as a supplement in some animal and poultry feeds

animal psychology *n* **:** the psychological behavior of animals other than man

animal rouge *n* **:** CARMINE 2

animals *pl of* ANIMAL

animal size *or* **animal sizing** *n* **1 :** an animal glue or gelatin used for surface-sizing the higher grades of paper **2 :** a solution or other preparation of animal size

animal-sized \'===¦=\ *adj* **:** sized with animal size

animal soul *n* **1 :** the soul that in the scholastic tradition is characteristic of an animal and has sensitive, appetitive, and locomotive faculties and controls a more developed form of vital activity than the lower vegetable soul but has no independent existence apart from the body and is distinguished thereby from the higher rational soul — compare RATIONAL SOUL, VEGETABLE SOUL **2** *theosophy* **:** the center of animal passions

animal spirits *n pl* [L *animalis* animate — more at ANIMAL] **1** *sometimes* **animal spirit** *obs* **:** the nervous energy that is the source of physical sensation and movement **2** [influenced in meaning by ¹*animal*] **:** vivacity arising from physical health and energy ⟨gay, full of contagious *animal spirits* —W.P.Eaton⟩

animal starch *n* **:** GLYCOGEN

animal step *n* **:** a dance step (as a fox trot, duck walk) named after and usu. imitative of a beast, bird, or fish

animal unit *n* **:** a unit expressing the feed requirements of different kinds of domestic animals on a common scale usu. based on the average or theoretical requirements of a mature cow ⟨100 hens equal one *animal unit*⟩

an·i·ma mun·di \,anəmə'mən,dī, -mün(,)dē\ *n, pl* **ani·mae mundi** \-,mē'mə-, -,mī'mü-\ [ML, vital force of the world] **:** a vital force or principle conceived of as permeating the world — compare ARCHEUS, WORLD SOUL

ani·man·do \,anə'män(,)dō, ,änə-\ *adj (or adv)* [It, animating, fr. L *animandum*, gerund of *animare*] **:** becoming animated — used as a direction in music

animas *pl of* ANIMA

¹an·i·mate \'anəmət, *sometimes* -,māt, *usu* -d·+V\ *adj* [ME *animat*, fr. L *animatus*, past part. of *animare* to quicken, enliven, endow with breath or soul, fr. *anima* breath, soul; akin to OE *ōthian*, *ēthian* to breathe, OFris *omma* breath, ON *önd*, gen. *andar* breath, life, soul, Goth *uzanan* to breathe one's last, expire, L *animus* soul, mind, Gk *anemos* breath, wind, Skt *aniti* he breathes] **1 :** possessing life **:** ALIVE, LIVING ⟨primitive worship of ~ and inanimate objects⟩ **2 a :** of, relating to, or associated with animal life as opposed to plant life ⟨the vast range of ~ and inanimate life⟩ **b :** marked by movement belonging to or suggesting the movement of animal life **:** MOVING **:** not static ⟨the swiftly flowing river was the only thing ~ in the valley⟩ **3 :** full of life **:** possessing to an intensive degree the qualities of a living being or suggesting such qualities **:** VIVACIOUS, ANIMATED, SPIRITED, LIVELY ⟨her happy laughter and the ~ sparkle of her eyes⟩ **4** *of a grammatical gender* **:** referring typically to living things or to things considered as living — opposed to *inanimate* — **an·i·mate·ly** *adv* — **an·i·mate·ness** *n* -ES

²an·i·mate \-,māt, *usu* -ād·+V\ *vt* -ED/-ING/-S **1 :** to give spirit and support to **:** stimulate to courage and perseverance **:** encourage or cheer up ⟨*animating* the tired men with a kind word⟩ **2 a :** to give life to **:** make alive **:** bring to life **:** fill with life ⟨the mysterious vital force that ~*s* the cells of the body⟩ **b :** to permeate deeply in such a way as to stimulate and enliven ⟨the forward-reaching spirit of inquiry which *animated* the study of logic —R.W.Southern⟩ **c :** to give vigor and vitality to **:** impart zest and color to **:** add sharply heightened interest and life to **:** brighten up ⟨an unusual gaiety . . . *animated* her conversation and actions —Osbert

Sitwell⟩ ⟨a smile *animated* his face⟩ **3 :** to move to action **:** MOTIVATE, PROMPT, INCITE **:** stir up ⟨all this apparatus of research *animated* the young historians —Van Wyck Brooks⟩ **4 :** to make, build, equip, or design in such a way that automatic, apparently spontaneous, and often lifelike movement is effected ⟨a miniature city of the future, completely *animated* —*Ford Times*⟩ ⟨*animated* puppets⟩ **5 a :** to produce in the form of an animated cartoon or of an animation ⟨three of the scenes in the musical will be *animated* by a New York studio⟩ **b :** to contribute to (the production of an animated cartoon or of an animation) by drawings or photographic work ⟨West Coast artists will ~ the last part of the film⟩ **syn** see QUICKEN

animated *adj* **1 a :** vibrantly alive ⟨she became intensely, rigidly ~ —Willa Cather⟩ **b :** full of the bustle and activity of life ⟨an ~ city street⟩ **c :** full of vigor and spirit **:** VIVACIOUS, LIVELY ⟨plunged into an ~ discussion —Dorothy Sayers⟩ **2 :** having the appearance of something alive **:** LIFELIKE ⟨an unusually ~ piece of sculpture⟩ **3 :** made in the form of an animated cartoon or of an animation ⟨the ~ sequences of the film are hilarious⟩ ⟨~ cutaways to show how the motors work⟩ **syn** see LIVELY

animated cartoon *n* **1** *also* **animated drawing a :** a series of drawings each of which shows a successive position of a figure or other object, the drawings being photographed on film or made directly on film so that projection of the film produces a picture in which the objects drawn seem to move in a lifelike and realistic manner **b :** a series of drawings similar to those of a film or tape animated cartoon but made on or transferred to a sequence of pages so that rapid flipping of the pages produces an illusion of movement in the objects drawn **2 :** ANIMATION 2a

an·i·mat·ed·ly \ˌanəˈmādədlē, -ātə-, -li\ *adv* **1 :** in a vivacious manner **:** with sparkling enthusiasm ⟨speaking ~ of vacation plans⟩ **2 :** with driving conviction often accompanied by a somewhat impatient vehemence **:** HEATEDLY ⟨the pros and cons were ~ argued⟩

animated oat *n* **:** an oat grass (*Avena sterilis*) marked by movements of the spikelets caused by twisting of the awns through changes in moisture

an·i·ma·tion \ˌanəˈmāshən\ *n* -s [L *animation-, animatio*, fr. *animatus* + *-ion-, -io* -ion] **1 a :** the act of animating or the state of being animate or animated ⟨cheerful words meant for the ~ of the discouraged⟩ **b :** the quality of being full of spirit and vigor **:** brightness of appearance or manner **:** VIVACIOUSNESS ⟨talking with great ~ —Dorothy Sayers⟩ **2 a :** a motion picture made by photographing successive positions or poses of puppets and other inanimate objects so that projection of the film produces a picture in which the puppets or other objects seem to move in a lifelike and realistic manner **b :** ANIMATED CARTOON 1 **c :** an inanimate object or group of objects designed for exhibit and illustration and usu. having movable and often automatically moving parts **3 :** production of an animated cartoon or animation

an·i·mat·ism \ˈanəməˌtizəm, -məd·ˌiz-\ *n* -s [[1]*animate* + *-ism*] **:** attribution of consciousness and personality but not of individual spirit to such natural phenomena as thunderstorms and earthquakes and to such objects as plants and stones — compare ANIMISM — **an·i·ma·tis·tic** \ˌ==məˈtistik, -məd·ˈis-\ *adj*

ani·ma·to \ˌanəˈmä(ˌ)tō, ˌän-, -äd·(ˌ)ō\ *adj (or adv)* [It, fr. L *animatus*, past part. of *animare* to animate — more at ANIMATE] **:** with animation — used as a direction in music

an·i·mat·o·graph \ˌanəˈmadəˌgraf\ *n* -s [[2]*animate* + *-ograph* (as in *cinematograph*)] **:** an early form of motion-picture projector

an·i·ma·tor *also* **an·i·ma·ter** \ˈanəˌmād·ə(r), -ātə-\ *n* -s **:** one that contributes to the production of an animated cartoon or animation (as by making drawings)

[1]**ani·mé** \əˈnēmē, ˌanəˈmā\ *or* **ane·mi** *or* **ani·mi** \əˈnēmē\ *n* -s [F *animé*, fr. Sp or Pg *anime*, fr. Tupi *ananim, oananim, oanani* resin] **:** any of various resins or oleoresins: as **a :** COPAL; *esp* **:** ZANZIBAR COPAL **b :** ELEMI

[2]**ani·mé** \ˌanəˈmā\ *adj (or adv)* [F, animated, past part. of *animer* to animate, fr. L *animare*] **:** ANIMATO — used as a direction in music

anim·i·ke·an \əˌniməˈkēən\ *or* **anim·i·ki** \əˈnimə(ˌ)kē\ *adj, usu cap* [Chippewa *animiki*] **:** of or relating to the series of Proterozoic rocks that underlies the Keweenawan

anim·i·kite \əˈniməˌkīt\ *n* -s [Chippewa *animiki* thunder (intended as trans. of *Thunder Bay*, inlet in northwestern Lake Superior, Ontario, Canada, near which it was discovered) + E *-ite*] **:** a mineral consisting of a silver antimonide occurring in white or gray granular masses

an·i·mism \ˈanəˌmizəm\ *n* -s [G *animismus*, fr. L *anima* soul + G *-ismus* -ism — more at ANIMATE] **1 :** a doctrine according to which the immaterial soul is the vital principle responsible for every organic development **2 :** attribution of conscious life and a discrete indwelling spirit to every material form of reality (as to such objects as plants and stones or to such natural phenomena as thunderstorms and earthquakes) often including belief in the continued existence of individual disembodied spirits capable of exercising a benignant or malignant influence — compare ANIMATISM

an·i·mist \-məst\ *n* -s *often attrib:* one who accepts the doctrine of animism — **an·i·mis·tic** \ˌ==ˈmistik\ *adj*

an·i·mos·i·ty \ˌanəˈmäsəd·ē, -ətē, -i\ *n* -ES [ME *animosite*, fr. MF or LL; MF *animosité*, fr. LL *animositat-, animositas*, fr. L *animosus* courageous, spirited (fr. *animus* soul, spirit + *-osus* -ose) + *-itat-, -itas* -ity — more at ANIMATE] **:** ill will or resentment tending toward hostile action **:** smoldering enmity **:** a feeling of antagonism ⟨growling, snarling ~ toward public officials —*New Republic*⟩ **syn** see ENMITY

ani·mo·so \ˌanəˈmō(ˌ)sō, ˌän-\ *adj (or adv)* [It, spirited, fr. L *animosus*] **:** ANIMATO — used as a direction in music

an·i·mus \ˈanəməs\ *n* -ES [L, mind, soul — more at ANIMATE] **1 a :** INTENTION, OBJECTIVE ⟨his ~ is not to overlook the progress made⟩ ⟨the ~ that led to the expansion of the machine was narrowly utilitarian —Lewis Mumford⟩ **b :** effort or tendency as directed toward a definite, often inevitable, but not always clearly or consciously recognized end ⟨the ~ of war is to enforce uniformity —Lewis Mumford⟩ ⟨youthful ~ toward happiness⟩ **c :** pervading and characteristic approach or treatment **:** dominant tone **:** ideological attitude **:** governing spirit ⟨other novelists of the same political ~ —*Partisan Rev.*⟩ ⟨the curious ~ of that philosophy⟩ **d :** breadth of vision esp. as a vitalizing and creative force **:** INSPIRATION ⟨too simple and too little charged with ~ —F.R.Leavis⟩ ⟨an important writer with a really interesting ~ —Donald Barr⟩ **2 :** life-giving spirit **:** animating principle of life; *specif* **:** the active or rational soul ⟨that spiritual ~ so universally needed —Mary B. Eddy⟩ **3 :** ill will, antagonism, or hostility usu. controlled but deep-seated and sometimes virulent **:** ANIMOSITY ⟨a large school of thought cherishes a curious ~ against what it calls intellectualism —W.R.Inge⟩ ⟨calmly and without ~⟩ ⟨an ~ against the plaintiff⟩ ⟨the antimodernistic ~ (whatever is, is wrong) —R.B.Heilman⟩ **syn** see ENMITY

an·ion \ˈaˌnīən *also* -ī,än\ *n* -s [Gk, neut. of *aniōn*, pres. part. of *anienai* to go up, fr. *ana-* + *ienai* to go — more at ISSUE] **1 :** a negatively charged ion (as a hydroxide, chloride, or acetate ion) — opposed to *cation* **2 a :** the ion in an electrolyzed solution that migrates to the anode and is there discharged and liberated or deposited **b :** a negative gaseous ion

anion-active *adj* **:** ANIONIC 2

anion exchange *n* **:** a chemical process in which anions are exchanged or removed: **a :** ion exchange in which one anion (as chloride or hydroxide) is substituted for one or more other anions (as sulfate) **b :** a process in which anions in the form of acids are adsorbed by a basic substance

anion exchanger *n* **:** an anion-exchange agent that can exchange its anion with the anion or anions of a solution passed through it or that can adsorb anions in the form of acids; *esp* **:** an insoluble basic synthetic organic resin usu. containing amine groups or quaternary ammonium groups

an·ion·ic \ˌaˌnīˈänik\ *adj* **1 :** relating to or consisting of anions **2 :** *of a chemical compound* **:** characterized by an active anion, esp. a surface-active anion (as a large hydrophobic organic acid group) ⟨~ emulsifying agent⟩ ⟨~ surface-active agent⟩

anionic detergent *n* **:** any of a class of synthetic detergents usu. consisting essentially of an alkali metal salt or an ammonium salt of a strong acid containing 12 to 24 carbon atoms together with an inorganic salt (as sodium sulfate) and, for heavy-duty laundering, a builder (as sodium tripolyphosphate): as **a :** an alkyl aryl sulfonate (as sodium dodecylbenzene-sulfonate $C_{12}H_{25}C_6H_4SO_3Na$) **b :** a salt (as sodium lauryl sulfate $C_{12}H_{25}SO_4Na$) of a sulfated alcohol

an·ion·oid \(ˈ)aˈnīəˌnȯid\ *adj* [*anion* + *-oid*] **:** NUCLEOPHILIC

an·ion·o·trop·ic \ˌaˌnīˌänəˈträpik\ *adj* **:** of, relating to, or marked by anionotropy

an·ion·ot·ro·py \ˌaˌnīəˈnä·trəpē\ *n* -ES [*anion* + *-o-* + *-tropy*] **:** tautomerism involving migration of an anion (as chloride, hydroxyl, or acetate), the best-known type being allylic rearrangement — distinguished from *cationotropy* and *prototropy*

an·irid·ia \ˌanīˈridēə\ *n* -s [NL, fr. *an-* + Gk *irid-, iris* iris + NL *-ia* — more at IRIS] **:** congenital absence or defect of the iris

anis *pl of* ANI

[1]**anis-** *or* **aniso-** *comb form* [NL, fr. Gk, fr. *anisos*, fr. *an-* + *isos* equal — more at IS-] **:** unequal ⟨*anisodont*⟩ ⟨*anisosthenic*⟩

[2]**an·is-** *or* **a·ni·so-** *comb form* [L *anisum* anise] **:** anise ⟨*anisic*⟩ **:** anisic acid ⟨*anisoyl*⟩

an·is·al·de·hyde \ˌanəˈsaldəˌhīd\ *n* -s [ISV [2]*anis-* + *aldehyde*] **:** a liquid aldehyde $CH_3OC_6H_4CHO$ obtained by mild oxidation of anethole, having a characteristic hawthorn odor, and used in making perfumes — called also *aubepine*

an·is·ate \ˈanəˌsāt, -sət\ *n* -s [ISV *anisic* + *-ate*] **:** a salt or ester of anisic acid

an·ise \ˈanəs\ *n, pl* **anises** *also* **anise** *often attrib* [ME *anis*, fr. OF, fr. L *anisum, anesum*, fr. Gk *anison, anēson*] **1 :** an herb (*Pimpinella anisum*) growing naturally in Egypt and cultivated in many lands for its carminative and aromatic seeds **2 :** the fruit or seeds of anise **:** ANISEED

anise alcohol *or* **anisic alcohol** *n* **:** ANISYL ALCOHOL

anise camphor *n* **:** ANETHOLE

an·i·seed *also* **an·ise·seed** \ˈanə(s)ˌsēd\ *n* -s [ME *anis seed*, fr. *anis* anise + *seed*] **:** the seed of anise often used as a flavoring in cordials and in cooking

aniseed star *n* **:** the fruit of the star anise

aniseed tree *n* **:** STAR ANISE

anise hyssop *n* [prob. so called fr. the aromatic nature of its seeds] **:** a No. American herb (*Agastache foeniculum*) with an odor like fennel

an·is·ei·ko·nia \ˌanˌīsīˈkōnēə\ *n* -s [NL, fr. [1]*anis-* + Gk *eikōn* image + NL *-ia* — more at ICON] **:** a defect of binocular vision in which the two retinal images of the same object are of unequal size — **an·is·ei·kon·ic** \-ˈkänik\ *adj*

anise oil *or* **aniseed oil** *n* **1 :** a colorless or pale yellow essential oil obtained from the dried fruits of anise and used as a flavoring agent and as a carminative **2 :** STAR ANISE OIL

anise plant *n* **:** an herb (*Seseli harveyanum*) that has an aroma like anise and that is found chiefly in Australia

aniseroot \ˈ==,=\ *n* -s [so called from the taste and odor of its root] **:** SWEET CHERVIL

an·is·ette \ˌanəˈset, -ˈzet\ *n* -s [F, fr. *anis* anise + *-ette* — more at ANISE] **:** a sweet usu. colorless liqueur with a flavor like licorice derived from aniseed and used as a cocktail ingredient and after-dinner drink

anis·ic acid \əˈnisik, (ˈ)aˈn- *also* -nī- *sometimes* -nē-\ *n* [ISV *anise* + *-ic*; orig. formed as F *anisique*] **:** a crystalline acid $CH_3OC_6H_4COOH$ obtained by oxidizing anethole or anisaldehyde — called also *para-anisic acid*

anisic aldehyde *n* **:** ANISALDEHYDE

anis·i·dine \əˈnisəˌdēn, -dən\ *n* -s [F, fr. *anis-* [2]*anis-* + *-ide* + *-ine*] **:** any of three isomeric bases $CH_3OC_6H_4NH_2$ that are amino derivatives of anisole and are used in the manufacture of guaiacol and of azo dyes

aniso- — see ANIS-

an·iso·car·pic \ˌaˌnīsəˈkärpik, aˌn-\ *or* **an·iso·car·pous** \-pəs\ *adj* [[1]*anis-* + *-carpic, -carpous*] *of flowers* **:** having fewer members in the whorl of carpels than in any of the other floral whorls — compare ISOCARPIC

an·iso·cer·cal \-ˈsarkəl\ *adj* [[1]*anis-* + *-cercal*] **:** not isocercal

an·iso·che·la \-ˈkēlə\ *n, pl* **anisochelas** \-ləz\ *or* **anisochelae** \-ˌlē\ [NL, fr. [1]*anis-* + *chela*] **:** a chelate sponge spicule having the ends dissimilar

an·iso·co·ria \-ˈkōrēə\ *n* -s [NL, fr. [1]*anis-* + Gk *korē* pupil of the eye + NL *-ia*] **:** inequality in the size of the pupils of the eyes

an·iso·cy·to·sis \-ˌsīˈtōsəs\ *n, pl* **anisocyto·ses** \-ōˌsēz\ [NL, fr. [1]*anis-* + *cyt-* + *-osis*] **:** variation in size of cells, esp. of the red blood cells (as in pernicious anemia) — **an·iso·cy·tot·ic** \-ˈtäd·ik\ *adj*

an·iso·dac·ty·lous \-ˈdaktələs\ *adj* [[1]*anis-* + *-dactylous*] **:** having unequal toes — used esp. of passerine and picarian birds having three toes turned forward and one backward

an·iso·ga·mete \-gəˈmēt, -ˈgaˌmēt\ *n* -s [[1]*anis-* + *gamete*] **:** HETEROGAMETE — **an·iso·ga·met·ic** \-gəˈmed·ik\ *adj*

an·isog·a·mous \ˌanˌīˈsägəməs\ *adj* [[1]*anis-* + *-gamous* or *-gamic*] *also* **an·iso·gam·ic** \ˌaˌnīsəˈgamik\ **1** *of sexual reproduction* **a :** characterized by fusion of unlike gametes or individuals usu. differing chiefly in size — used esp. of processes in lower organisms; see HETEROGAMOUS; compare OOGAMOUS **b :** HETEROGAMOUS a **2 :** having anisogamous reproduction — **an·isog·a·my** \ˌanˌīˈsägəmē\ *n* -ES

an·iso·ge·nous \ˌaˌnīˈsäjənəs\ *adj* **:** of, relating to, or marked by anisogeny

an·isog·e·ny \ˌaˌnīˈsäjənē\ *n* -ES [[1]*anis-* + *-geny*] **:** the property of exhibiting different inheritance in reciprocal crosses because of consistent differences in the male and female gametes of the parents

an·isog·na·thism \ˌaˌnīˈsägnəˌthizəm\ *n* -s [[1]*anis-* + *gnath-* + *-ism*] **:** the property of having the teeth in the two jaws unlike — **an·isog·na·thous** \ˌaˌnīˈsägnəthəs\ *adj*

an·is·ole \ˈanəˌsōl\ *n* -s [F *anisol*, fr. *anis-* [2]*anis-* + *-ol* -ole] **:** a colorless liquid ether $C_6H_5OCH_3$ of pleasant odor obtained by distilling anisic acid or by the action of dimethyl sulfate and alkali on phenol and used chiefly in perfumery; methyl phenyl ether

an·isom·e·les \ˌaˌnīˈsäməˌlēz\ *n, cap* [NL, fr. [1]*anis-* + *-meles* (fr. Gk *melē* cup); fr. the lack of uniformity in the anthers] **:** a small genus of herbs (family Labiatae) of tropical Asia and Australia with purplish cymose flowers

an·isom·er·ism \ˌaˌnīˈsäməˌrizəm\ *n* -s [*an-* + *isomere* + *-ism*] **:** the tendency of the primitive polyisomeres of an organism to become differentiated so that more highly evolved organisms do not consist of a linear series of similar and equivalent parts

an·iso·met·ric \ˌaˌnīsəˈme·trik, aˌn-\ *adj* [F *anisométrique*, fr. *an-* + *isométrique* isometric] **1 :** not isometric **:** having unsymmetrical parts — used of crystals with three unequal axes **2 :** of or relating to a rock of granular texture but with constituents of unequal size ⟨~ granite⟩ **3 :** not having equal or corresponding poetic meters

an·iso·me·tro·pia \-ˌməˈtrōpēə\ *n* -s [NL, fr. Gk *anisometros* of unequal measure + NL *-opia*] **:** unequal refractive power in the two eyes — **an·iso·me·trop·ic** \-ˈträpik\ *adj*

an·iso·my·ar·ia \-ˌmīˈa(a)rēə\ *n, pl, cap* [NL, fr. [1]*anis-* + *-myaria*] *in some classifications* **:** an order of Lamellibranchia comprising bivalve mollusks having the anterior adductor muscle highly developed and the posterior muscle only slightly developed — **an·iso·my·ar·i·an** \-ˈa(a)rēən\ *adj or n*

an·iso·my·o·di·an \-ˌmīˈōdēən\ *or* **an·iso·my·o·dous** \-ˈmīədəs\ *adj* [[1]*anis-* + Gk *myōdēs* muscular + E *-ian* or *-ous* — more at MYODES] **:** having the syringeal muscles inserted unequally either in the middle of the bronchial half rings or only upon the dorsal or ventral ends of the bronchial half rings — used of certain passerine birds

an·iso·mys \aˈnīsəˌmis\ *n, cap* [NL, fr. [1]*anis-* + *-mys*] **:** a genus of giant rats of New Guinea and Papua

an·iso·phyl·lous \ˌaˌnīsəˈfiləs, aˌn-\ *adj* [F *anisophylle*, fr. [1]*anis-* + *-phylle* -phyllous] **1 :** having leaves of two or more shapes and sizes ⟨some conifers and many aquatic plants are ~⟩ **2 :** having the leaves of a pair different in shape and size — compare ISOPHYLLOUS — **an·iso·phyl·ly** \(ˈ)aˈnīsəˌfilē\ *n* -ES

an·iso·ploid \(ˈ)aˈnīsəˌplȯid\ *adj* [[1]*anis-* + *-ploid*] **:** having a chromosome number (as triploid, pentaploid) that is an odd multiple of the basic number with consequent genetic incapability of sexual reproduction — **an·iso·ploi·dy** \(ˈ)aˈnīsəˌplȯidē\ *n* -ES

an·iso·pol·y·ploid \ˌaˌnīsəˈpäləˌplȯid, aˌn-\ *adj* [[1]*anis-* + *polyploid*] **:** ANISOPLOID — **an·iso·pol·y·ploi·dy** \-ˈpäləˌplȯidē\ *n* -ES

an·isop·tera \ˌaˌnīˈsäptərə\ *n pl, cap* [NL, fr. [1]*anis-* + *-ptera*] **:** a suborder of Odonata comprising the dragonflies that are larger stouter members of the order, hold the wings horizontally in repose, and have rectal gills during the naiad stage — compare ZYGOPTERA

an·iso·spore \(ˈ)aˈnīsəˌspō(ə)r\ *n* -s [[1]*anis-* + *spore*] **:** a sexual spore exhibiting sexual dimorphism esp. of size — opposed to *isospore*

an·iso·tre·mus \(ˌ)aˌnīsəˈtrēməs\ *n, cap* [NL, fr. [1]*anis-* + *-tremus* (fr. Gk *trēma* perforation, aperture)] **:** a genus of tropical American grunts (family Pomadasidae) including a number of food and game species (as the porkfish, the pompon, and the sargo)

an·iso·trop·ic \ˌaˌnīsəˈträpik, aˌn-\ *also* **an·isot·ro·pous** \ˌaˌnīˈsä·trəpəs\ *adj* [*an-* + *isotropic, isotropous*] **1** *physics* **:** exhibiting properties (as velocity of light transmission, conductivity of heat or electricity, compressibility) with different values when measured along axes in different directions **:** AEOLOTROPIC **:** not isotropic ⟨an ~ crystal⟩ **2** *bot* **:** assuming different positions in response to the action of external stimuli **3 :** having a predetermined axis or axes — used of the eggs of certain animals — **an·iso·trop·i·cal·ly** \(ˌ)aˌnīsəˈträpək(ə)lē, aˌn-\ *adv*

anisotropic liquid *n* **:** LIQUID CRYSTAL

an·isot·ro·py \ˌaˌnīˈsä·trəpē\ *or* **an·isot·ro·pism** \-ˌpizəm\ *n, pl* **anisotropies** *or* **anisotropisms** [*anisotropic* + *-y* or *-ism*] **:** the quality or property of being anisotropic

ani·sum \əˈnīsəm, -ēs-\ *n* -s [L *anisum, anesum* — more at ANISE] **:** ANISE

an·i·syl alcohol \ˈanəˌsil-\ *n* [ISV [2]*anis-* + *-yl*] **:** a colorless liquid alcohol $CH_3OC_6H_4CH_2OH$ having an odor like hawthorn and used in perfumery; *para*-methoxy-benzyl alcohol — called also *anise alcohol*

anith·er \əˈnithər\ *Scot var of* ANOTHER

ani·to \əˈnē(ˌ)tō\ *n* -s [Sp, fr. Tag] *Philippines* **:** a spirit esp. of an ancestor

an·jan \ˈanjən, -ˌjan\ *n* -s [native name in India] **1 :** a timber tree (*Hardwickia binata*) of India **2 :** the very hard dark red or purplish wood of the anjan tree

an·ka·ra \ˈaŋkərə, ˈaiŋ-, ˈäŋ-, ˈäŋ-\ *adj, usu cap* [fr. *Ankara*, Turkey] **:** of or from Ankara, the capital of Turkey **:** of the kind or style prevalent in Ankara

an·ka·ra·mite \ˌaŋkəˈräˌmīt\ *n* -s [F, fr. *Ankaramy*, Madagascar + F *-ite*] **:** a melanocratic basaltic rock with a feldspar content greater than picrite and less than basalt and differing from picrite in containing more augite than olivine

an·ka·ra·trite \-ˈä·ˌtrīt\ *n* -s [F *ankaratrite*, fr. *Ankaratra* mts., Madagascar, its locality + F *-ite*] **:** a melanocratic nephelite-basalt containing some feldspar, phenocrysts of olivine, microlites of titanaugite, and from 10 to 15 percent nephelite

an·ker \ˈäŋkər, ˈa-\ *n* -s [D, prob. fr. ML *ancheria, anceria*] **1 :** a unit of capacity: **a :** an old Dutch and German liquid measure used in various countries of Europe esp. for spirits and equal to about 9 to 10.5 U.S. gallons (30 to 40 liters) **b :** a U.S. unit equal to 10 gallons (37.85 liters) **c :** a unit of So. Africa equal to 7½ imperial gallons (34.10 liters) **2 :** a cask or keg having a capacity of one anker

an·ker·ite \ˈaŋkəˌrīt\ *n* -s [G *ankerit*, fr. M. J. *Anker* †1843 Austrian mineralogist + G *-it* -ite] **:** a variety of dolomite $Ca(Fe,Mg,Mn)(CO_3)_2$ containing much iron (sp. gr. 2.95–3.1)

ankh \ˈaŋk, ˈä-\ *n* -s [Egypt *ʿnḫ*] **:** a figure like a cross having a loop instead of an upper vertical arm used esp. in ancient Egypt as an attribute or sacred emblem symbolizing life—called also *ansate cross, crux ansata, handled cross, key of life*

ankh

an·king \ˈänˈkiŋ\ *adj, usu cap* [fr. *Anking*, China] **:** of or from the city of Anking, China **:** of the kind or style prevalent in Anking

[1]**an·kle** \ˈaŋkəl, ˈai-\ *n* -s [ME *ankel, anclowe*, fr. OE *anclēow*; akin to OHG *anchlāo, anchal, enchil* ankle, ON *ǫkkla*, L *angulus* angle, Gk *angos* pail, Skt *aṅga* limb — more at ANGLE] **1 a :** the joint between the foot and the leg corresponding to the wrist in the arm, the hock of a horse, and what is often called the knee of a bird and constituting in man a ginglymus joint between the tibia and fibula above and the talus below **b :** the joint between the cannon bone and pastern in certain hoofed quadrupeds (as horses) **:** FETLOCK JOINT **2 :** the region of this joint **:** TARSUS; *broadly* **:** this region together with the lower part of the leg below the calf

[2]**ankle** *vi* **ankled; ankled; ankling** \-k(ə)liŋ\ **ankles** *slang* **:** to move esp. by walking ⟨*ankling* down the street⟩

anklebone \ˈ==,=\ *n* [ME *anclebone*, fr. *ancle* ankle + *bone*] **:** TALUS

ankle boot *n* **1 :** a boot reaching only to the ankle **2 :** a protective covering for a horse's ankle

ankle-deep \ˈ==ˈ=\ *adj* **:** of depth sufficient to reach the ankles ⟨a street *ankle-deep* in mud⟩

ankle jerk *n* **:** a reflex downward movement of the foot due to a spasmodic contraction of the muscles of the calf caused by sudden extension of the leg or by striking the Achilles' tendon above the heel

ankle strap *n* **:** a single or multiple strap attached to a shoe to hold it on the foot or having a purely ornamental function and passing either above the instep near the arch or around the ankle

an·klet \ˈaŋklət, ˈai-\ *n* -s [*ankle* + *-let*] **1 a :** a bracelet or similar ornament worn around the ankle **b :** a brace that supports the ankle **c :** a fetter attached to the ankle **d :** ANKLE STRAP **2 a :** a short sock usu. extending only slightly above the ankle **b :** a knitted or woven band designed for protection from cold (as one attached to the bottom of a trouser leg or pajama leg) **3 :** a woman's or child's low shoe having one or more ankle straps

anklet 3

an·klong \ˈaŋˌklȯŋ\ *or* **an·klung** *or* **ang·klung** \-ˌkləŋ\ *n* -s [Malay *angkluŋ*] **:** a Malayan musical instrument made of suspended bamboo tubes

an·ko·le *also* **an·ko·li** \aŋˈkōlē\ *n, usu cap* [fr. *Ankole*, plateau region in Uganda, its native habitat] **:** an African breed of long-horned humpless cattle

an·kus \ˈaŋkəs, ˈəŋkəsh\ *also* **an·ku·sha** \ˈəŋkəshə\ *n, pl* **ankus** *also* **ankusha** *or* **ankuses** *also* **ankushas** [Hindi *aṅkus*, fr. Skt *aṅkuśa*; akin to Skt *aṅka* bend, hook — more at ANGLE (hook)] **:** an elephant goad used in India having a sharp spike and hook and resembling a short-handled boat hook

ankyl- *or* **ankylo-** *also* **anchyl-** *or* **anchylo-** *or* **ancyl-** *or* **ancylo-** *comb form* [NL, fr. Gk *ankyl-, ankylo-*, fr. *ankylos*; akin to Gk *ankos* glen — more at ANGLE] **1 :** crooked **:** curved ⟨*Ancylostoma*⟩ **2** [NL, fr. Gk *ankyl-, ankylo-*, fr. *ankylōsis*] **a :** stiff, immobile, constricted, or closed because of adhesion ⟨*ankyloglossia*⟩ ⟨*ankylurethria*⟩ **b :** ankylosis ⟨*ankylophobia*⟩

an·ky·lo·saur \ˈaŋkəlōˌsȯ(ə)r\ *n* -s [NL *Ankylosauria*, fr. *ankyl-* + *-sauria*] **:** any of a suborder (Ankylosauria) of heavily armored more or less dorsoventrally flattened Cretaceous dinosaurs somewhat resembling immense horned toads in shape

an·ky·lose *also* **an·chy·lose** \ˈaŋkəˌlōs, ˈai-, -kē,-, -ōz\ *or* **an·cy·lose** \"; ˈansə,-, ˈaa-\ *vb* -ED/-ING/-S [irreg. fr. NL *ankylosis, anchylosis, ancylosis*] *vt* **:** to unite or consolidate so as to make a more or less rigid and inflexible joint **:** cause to grow together into one **:** produce ankylosis in ⟨*ankylosed* bones⟩ ⟨a joint *ankylosed* by surgery⟩ ~ *vi* **:** to form a more or less rigid and inflexible joint **:** grow together into one **:** undergo ankylosis

an·ky·lo·sis *also* **an·chy·lo·sis** *or* **an·cy·lo·sis** \ˌ==ˈlōsəs\ *n, pl* **ankylo·ses** *also* **ancylo·ses** \-ōˌsēz\ [NL, fr. Gk *ankylōsis* stiffening, tongue-tie, adhesion of the eyelids, fr. *ankyloun* to crook, stiffen (fr. *ankylos* crooked) + *-ōsis* -osis — more at ANGLE] **1 :** stiffness or fixation of a joint by disease or surgery **:** formation of a stiff joint through obliteration of the joint space by fibrous or bony tissue **2 :** union of two or more separate bones or other hard parts to form a single bone or part without intervening soft tissues

an·ky·los·to·ma \,==ˈlästəmə\ *or* **an·ky·los·to·mum** \-məm\ [NL, fr. *ankyl-* + *-stoma, -stomum*] *syn of* ANCYLOSTOMA

ankylostome *var of* ANCYLOSTOME

ankylostomiasis *var of* ANCYLOSTOMIASIS

an·ky·lot·ic *also* **an·chy·lot·ic** *or* **an·cy·lot·ic** \ˈ==ˈlädik\ *adj* [fr. NL *ankylosis, ancylosis*, after such pairs as E *narcosis: narcotic*] **:** of, relating to, or marked by ankylosis **:** STIFFENED

an·ky·roid \aŋˈkī,rȯid, ˈaŋkə,-\ *also* **an·cy·roid** \anˈsī,-, ˈansə,-\ *adj* [Gk *ankyroeidēs* anchor-shaped, fr. *ankyra* anchor + *-oeidos* -oid — more at ANCHOR] *anat* **:** shaped like a hook

anl *abbr* **1** animal **2** anneal

an·lace \ˈanlәs, -,läs\ *n* -s [ME *anlas, anelas*, fr. OF *alenaz, alesnaz*, aug. of *alesne* awl, of Gmc origin; akin to OHG *alasna, alansa* awl, fr. *āla* — more at AWL] **:** a tapering medieval dagger

anlace

an·la·ge \ˈän,lägə, ˈän,lä-, *G* ˈän,lä=-\ *n, pl* **anla·gen** \-gən\ *also* **anlages** *sometimes cap* [G, fr. MHG *anlāge* request, ambush, fr. *ane* on, at (fr. OHG *ana*) + *lāge* act of laying, position, fr. OHG *lāga* laying; akin to OHG *ligen* to lie — more at ON, LIE] **:** the foundation or basis of a subsequent development **:** RUDIMENT; *specif* **:** the first accumulation of cells in an embryo recognizable as the commencement of a developing part or organ

an·laut \ˈän,laủt\ *n, pl* **anlau·te** \-aủd·ə,-aủtə\ *also* **anlauts** [G, fr. *an* on, at (fr. OHG *ana*) + *laut* sound, fr. OHG *lūt*; akin to OE *hlūd* loud — more at ON, LOUD] *phonetics* **:** initial sound or position of a word or syllable — compare AUSLAUT, INLAUT

ann \ˈan\ *or* **an·nat** \ˈa,nat, ˈanət\ *n* -s [Sc, fr. ML *annata* annates — more at ANNATES] *Scots law* **:** a half-year's stipend over and above what is owing for the incumbency due to a deceased minister's executors

ann *abbr* **1** annals **2** annealed **3** [L *anni*] years **4** annual **5** annuity

an·na *also* **ana** \ˈänə, ˈa-\ *n* -s [Hindi *ānā*] **1 a :** a former unit of value in Pakistan, India, and Burma equal to 1/16 rupee **b :** one sixteenth ⟨a 4-*anna* crop⟩ **2 :** a coin representing one anna unit

an·na·berg·ite \ˈanə,bərˌgīt\ *n* -s [*Annaberg*, Saxony, Germany, its locality + E *-ite*] **:** a mineral consisting of a hydrous nickel cobalt arsenate $(Ni,Co)_3(AsO_4)_2.8H_2O$ occurring in apple-green masses or capillary crystals and isomorphous with erythrite

annal *n* -s [back-formation fr. *annals*] *archaic* **:** ANNALS; *esp* **:** annals of a single year, locale, or people

an·nal·ist \ˈanᵊləst\ *n* -s [F *annaliste*, fr. MF, fr. *annales* annals (fr. L) + *-iste* -ist] **:** a writer of annals **:** HISTORIAN

an·nal·is·tic \,anᵊlˈistik, -ēk\ *adj* **:** of or relating to annals or an annalist ⟨a book with an ∼ approach⟩ — **an·nal·is·ti·cal·ly** \-ək(ə)lē,-li\ *adv*

an·nals \ˈanᵊlz\ *n pl* [L *annales*, fr. pl. of *annalis* yearly, fr. *annus* year + *-alis* -al — more at ANNUAL] **1 :** a record of events arranged in yearly sequence usu. without comment or interpretation by the compiler **2 :** historical records; *specif* **:** any of several histories of Roman times written by contemporary authors ⟨the ∼ of Tacitus⟩ **3** *sometimes sing in constr* **:** records of the activities of an organization, usu. published ⟨the ∼ of a welfare society⟩

¹an·nam·ese \,anəˈmēz, -ēs\ *or* **an·nam·ite** \ˈ==,mīt\ *adj, usu cap* [*Annam*, eastern section of Indochina + E *-ese* or *-ite*] **1 a :** of, relating to, or characteristic of Annam **b :** of, relating to, or characteristic of the Annamese people **2 :** of, relating to, or characteristic of the Annamese language

²annamese \"\ *n, pl* **annamese** *usu cap* **1 a :** a Mongolian people that occupies mainly Cochin China and the coast regions of Annam and Tonkin in eastern Indochina, being the dominant ethnic group among the Vietnamese **b** *or* **annamite** \"\ -s **:** a member of such people **2** *or* **annamite :** the language of the Annamese people **:** VIETNAMESE

an·nam–muong \(ˈ)aˈnamˈwȯŋ,əˈn-\ *n, usu cap A&M* [*Annamese* + *Muong*] **:** a language group of problematical status and relationship containing Annamese and Muong and perhaps related to Mon-Khmer or Thai

an·nam ulcer \(ˈ)aˈnam, əˈn-\ *n, usu cap A* [fr. *Annam*, Indochina] **:** TROPICAL ULCER 2

an·nap·o·lis \əˈnap(ə)ləs\ *adj, usu cap* [fr. *Annapolis*, Md.] **:** of or from Annapolis, the capital of Maryland **:** of the kind or style prevalent in Annapolis

an·na·pol·i·tan \,anəˈpälətᵊn\ *n* -s *cap* [*Annapolis*, Maryland + E *-itan* (as in *Neapolitan, metropolitan*)] **:** a native or resident of Annapolis, Md.

an·na's hummingbird \ˈanəz-\ *also* **anna hummingbird** *n, usu cap A* [after *Anna* *fl*1829 duchess of Rivoli] **:** a rather large hummingbird (*Calypte anna*) of western Mexico and California, the male being chiefly metallic bronze-green with rose-red forehead, crown, and throat and a dusky blackish tail, the female bronzy green above and dull gray below

annat *var of* ANN

an·nates \ˈa,nāts, ˈanəts\ *n pl* [ML *annata*, fr. L *annus* year — more at ANNUAL] **:** the first-fruits of an ecclesiastical benefice paid to the one presenting the benefice

an·nat·to *also* **ana·to** *or* **anat·to** \əˈnäd·(,)ō, əˈna,äˈnä, ˈd·ə, ˈ(,)tō,ˈ,tə\ *or* **an·nat·ta** \ˈd·ə,ˈ,tə\ *or* **ar·nat·ta** *or* **ar·nat·to** \ärˈn-,äˈn-\ *or* **ar·not·ta** *or* **ar·not·to** \-näˈ\ *n* -s [of Cariban origin; akin to Galibi *annoto* annatto tree] **1 a :** a red or yellowish red dyestuff containing bixin prepared from the pulp surrounding the seeds of the annatto tree and used esp. for coloring oils, butter, and cheese **b :** ANNATTO TREE **2 a :** a moderate yellowish pink that is yellower and less strong than coral pink and duller and slightly yellower than peach pink — called also *terra orellana* **b :** SALMON 4

annatto tree *n* **:** a tropical American tree (*Bixa orellana*) having cordate leaves and spinose capsules filled with seeds that yield annatto

anncr *abbr* announcer

¹an·neal \əˈnēl, -ēəl\ *vt* -ED/-ING/-S [ME *anelen*, fr. OE *onǣlan*, fr. *on* on + *ǣlan* to set on fire, burn, bake, fr. *āl* fire; akin to ON *eldr* fire, OE *ād* funeral pyre — more at EDIFY] **1 :** to heat (as glass) in order to fix laid-on colors **2 a :** to heat and then cool usu. for softening and rendering less brittle, gradual cooling being required for some materials (as steel and glass) but not for others (as copper and brass) — compare TEMPER **b :** to process (structural-clay products) by slow cooling after subjection to heat in order to prevent checking, cracking, and warping ⟨∼*ed* paving brick⟩ **3 :** STRENGTHEN, TOUGHEN ⟨a man rocklike in endurance, rocklike in insensibility, ∼*ed* by a simple, rigorous religion —Lionel Trilling⟩

²anneal \"\ *n* -s **:** the act, process, or result of annealing

an·neal·er \-lə(r)\ *n* -s **:** one that anneals

an·nec·tent *also* **an·nec·tant** \əˈnektənt, aˈ-\ *adj* [L *annectent-, annectens*, pres. part. of *annectere* to tie to, fr. *ad-* + *nectere* to tie, fasten together — more at ANNEX] *biol* **:** CONNECTING, LINKING — used esp. of species or groups having characters intermediate between those of two other species or groups

an·ne·la·ta \,anᵊlˈäd·ə, -ād·ə\ [NL, fr. F *annelès*, subdivision of invertebrates + NL *-ata*] *syn of* ANNELIDA

¹an·ne·lid \ˈanᵊləd\ *adj* [F *annélide*, adj. & n., fr. NL *Annelida*] **:** of or relating to the Annelida

²annelid \"\ *n* -s **:** an animal of the phylum Annelida

an·nel·i·da \əˈnelədə, aˈ-\ *n pl, cap* [NL, fr. F *annelés*, subdivision of invertebrates proposed 1801 by Lamarck, lit., ringed ones (fr. pl. of *annelé*, past part. of *anneler* to furnish or adorn with a ring or rings, fr. MF, fr. *annel-*, fr. OF, fr. *anel*, *annel* ring, fr. L *anellus* small ring, dim. of *anus* ring) + NL *-ida* — more at ANUS] **:** a phylum of typically elongated metameric animals having a voluminous true coelom, a closed vascular system usu. containing hemoglobin-bearing blood, a double ventral nervous system with anterior cerebral ganglion and esophageal ring, paired nephridia in one or many segments, and appendages that when present are not jointed as in arthropods — **an·nel·i·dan** \-dən, -dᵊn\ *adj or n*

an·nel·i·des \-,dēz\ *or* **an·nel·la·ta** \,anᵊlˈäd·ə, -ād·ə\ [NL, irreg. fr. F *annelés*] *syn of* ANNELIDA

an·ne·loid \ˈanᵊl,ȯid\ *n* -s [F *annelé* ringed + E *-oid*] **:** an animal resembling an annelid

an·ne·ro·dite \,anəˈrō,dīt\ *n* -s [Sw *ånnerödit*, fr. *Annerød*, town near Moss, Norway, its locality + *-it* -ite] **:** SAMARSKITE

¹an·nex \əˈneks, (ˈ)aˈn-\ *vt* -ED/-ING/-ES [ME *annexen*, fr. MF *annexer*, fr. OF, fr. *annexe* joined, fr. L *annexus*, past part. of *annectere, adnectere* to bind to, fr. *ad-* + *nectere* to tie, bind, alter. (prob. influenced by L *plectere* to plait) of a prehistoric form akin to L *nodus* knot — more at NET, PLY] **1 a :** to attach as a proper attribute or as a distinctive quality ⟨many privileges were ∼*ed* exclusively to royalty⟩ **b :** to attach as a necessary consequence ⟨happiness is not always ∼*ed* to wealth⟩ ⟨I would enjoy the pleasures of the table and of wine, but stop short of the pains inseparably ∼*ed* to an excess —Earl of Chesterfield⟩ **c :** to add or join as a condition ⟨only one requirement is ∼*ed* to this job⟩ **2 a** *archaic* **:** to add or join as an essential part **b** *archaic* **:** to add or join as a subordinate and accessory part ⟨this mansion, to which were ∼*ed* a tennis court, a bowling green, and a wilderness —T.B. Macaulay⟩ **3 a :** to add at the end of something written or spoken **:** SUBJOIN, APPEND ⟨a protocol ∼*ed* to the treaty—E.C. Helmreich⟩ ⟨a declaration with a promise ∼*ed*—W.F.Hambly⟩ **b :** to affix as an authoritative sanction ⟨∼*ing* his signature to the letter⟩ ⟨the president ∼*ed* his seal to the document⟩ **4 a :** to join in a closely united but subordinate capacity **:** take possession or control of **:** assume rights or jurisdiction over; *specif* **:** to incorporate (a country or other territory) within the sovereign domain of a state ⟨a move was made to ∼ Texas by a treaty —Dorothy B. Goebel⟩ **b :** to include (an area) within the limits of a governmental unit ⟨outlying districts were ∼*ed* by the city⟩ **5 a :** GET, OBTAIN ⟨we ∼*ed* a local guide —Thomas Barbour⟩ ⟨∼*ing* all the prizes in the dog show⟩ **b :** to appropriate esp. by highhanded or ethically questionable methods **:** get hold of **:** make off with; *often* **:** STEAL ⟨criminals trying to ∼ the miners' gold —Julian Dana⟩ ⟨she did not like to see him ∼*ed* by another woman —Joseph Conrad⟩

²annex \ˈa,neks, ˈani-,ˈanē-\ *n* -ES *often attrib* [MF *annexe*, fr. *annexe* joined] **:** something annexed or appended: as **a :** an added stipulation or statement; *esp* **:** an appendix of or codicil to a legislative document or international agreement ⟨the upper house approved two ∼*es* in the treaties —*Time*⟩ **b :** SUPPLEMENT; *esp* **:** a collection of supplementary matter ⟨this appendix is a worthwhile ∼ to the book⟩ ⟨anthropology was included as an ∼ to the regular curriculum⟩ **c :** a subsidiary supplementary structure either part of or separate from a main structure ⟨the new college wing was used as a science ∼⟩ **d :** a subsidiary district **:** SUBURB ⟨the big city and its ∼*es*⟩ **e** *Scots law* **:** FIXTURE, APPURTENANCE

an·nex·a *var of* ADNEXA

an·nex·a·tion \,a,nekˈsāshən, ,anə-, ,anē-\ *n* -s [*annex* + *-ation*] **1 :** the act of annexing or state of being annexed ⟨the possibility of cultural ∼⟩ **2 :** something that is annexed ⟨defended their ∼s with fire and sword —G.B.Shaw⟩ **3 :** the union of property with a freehold so as to become a fixture

an·nex·a·tion·al \ˈ=(,)=ˈ==shənᵊl\ *adj* **1 :** of or relating to annexation **2 :** favoring annexation

an·nex·a·tion·ism \,=(,)=ˈ==shə,nizəm\ *n* -s **:** the policy or advocacy of annexing territory

an·nex·a·tion·ist \-,nəst\ *n* -s **:** one who favors annexation

an·nexe \ˈa,neks, ˈani-\ *chiefly Brit var of* ²ANNEX

an·nex·ion \əˈnekshən, aˈ-\ *n* -s [LL *annexion-, annexio*, fr. L *annexus* + *-ion-, -io* -ion — more at ANNEX] **:** ANNEXATION

an·nex·ion·ist \-əst\ *n* -s **:** ANNEXATIONIST

an·nex·ive \əˈneksiv, (ˈ)aˈn-\ *adj* **:** COPULATIVE 1a, 1b

annexment *n* -s **1** *archaic* **:** ANNEXATION **2** *archaic* **:** ANNEX

an·nex·ure \əˈnekshə(r), (ˈ)aˈn-\ *n* -s **1** *chiefly Brit* **:** ANNEXATION **2** *chiefly Brit* **:** ANNEX

an·ni·cut *var of* ANICUT

an·ni·el·li·dae \,anēˈelə,dē\ *n pl, cap* [NL, fr. *Anniella*, type genus (irreg. fr. Sp *aniello, anillo* ring, fr. L *anellus* small ring) + *-idae* — more at ANNELIDA] **:** a family of degenerate wormlike California lizards apparently closely related to the Anguidae

an·nie oak·ley \ˈanēˈōklē, -li\ *n, pl* **annie oakleys** *usu cap A&O* [after *Annie Oakley* †1926 Am. markswoman; fr. the resemblance of a punched pass to a playing card with bullet holes through the spots] *slang* **:** a free ticket (as to a theater)

annie over *sometimes cap A, var of* ANTONY OVER

an·ni·hi·la·ble \əˈnīələbəl *sometimes* -īhə-\ *adj* [*annihilate* + *-able*] **:** capable of being annihilated

¹an·ni·hi·late \-lət, -,lāt\ *adj* [ME *adnichilat*, fr. LL *annihilatus*] *archaic* **:** ANNIHILATED

²an·ni·hi·late \-,lāt, *usu* -ād·+V\ *vt* -ED/-ING/-S [LL *annihilatus*, past part. of *annihilare*, fr. L *ad-* + *nihil* nothing — more at NIL] **1 a :** to cause to be of no effect **:** NULLIFY, ABROGATE ⟨a right to freedom that cannot be *annihilated*⟩ **b :** to destroy the substance or force of **:** totally weaken ⟨fear ∼*s* wit —Harvey Breit⟩ **2 :** to look upon as nothing **:** regard as of no consequence **:** make light of ⟨laughing at the past and *annihilating* its endeavors⟩ **3 a :** to do away with entirely so that nothing remains **:** reduce to nothing **:** cause to cease to exist **:** destroy totally **:** blot out entirely ⟨matter cannot be *annihilated*⟩ ⟨are we to suppose that I can ∼ so substantial an object simply by shutting my eyes —C.H. Whitely⟩ **b :** to strip of power and influence **:** check the activity of **:** neutralize the operations of ⟨*annihilating* the government's functions⟩ **c :** to destroy the interest and relevance of ⟨towering scenic backgrounds that *annihilated* the tiny figure on the stage⟩ ⟨a low building rightly placed will pull together surrounding high buildings instead of being *annihilated* by them —John Dewey⟩ **4 a :** to destroy a considerable part of **:** DECIMATE ⟨the army was *annihilated*⟩ ⟨little remained of the *annihilated* city⟩ **b :** to vanquish completely **:** CRUSH, ROUT ⟨the visiting football team was *annihilated*⟩ **syn** see ABOLISH

annihilating *adj* **:** CRUSHING, WITHERING ⟨a master of witty and ∼ rudeness —Edgar Johnson⟩ ⟨afire with ∼ invective —*Time*⟩

an·ni·hi·la·tion \=,==ˈlāshən\ *n* -s [LL *annihilation-, annihilatio*, fr. *annihilatus* + L *-ion-, -io* -ion] **1 :** the act of annihilating or state of being annihilated ⟨the ∼ of the individual is the worst perversity of man —W.L.Sullivan⟩ **2 :** cessation of being **:** NOTHINGNESS ⟨sentient beings are doomed to complete ∼ —C.R.Darwin⟩ **3 :** the process whereby an electron and a positron unite and consequently lose their identity as particles transforming themselves into short gamma rays — see ANNIHILATION RADIATION

an·ni·hi·la·tion·ism \-shə,nizəm\ *n* -s **:** the theological doctrine that the wicked will cease to exist after this life

an·ni·hi·la·tion·ist \-,nəst\ *n* -s **:** one who accepts annihilationism

annihilation radiation *n* **:** radiation produced by the mutually annihilating coalescence of an electron and a positron from which two radiation quanta travel in opposite directions with a wavelength corresponding to that of very short gamma rays, being approximately 0.024 angstrom

an·ni·hi·la·tive \əˈ==,lād·iv, -,ləd-\ *adj* **:** producing annihilation **:** DESTRUCTIVE ⟨an explosion that could be ∼ of nearly all life⟩

an·ni·hi·la·tor \-,lād·ə(r), -ātə-\ *n* -s **:** one that annihilates

an·ni·hi·la·to·ry \-,lə,tȯrē\ *adj* **:** ANNIHILATIVE

anni mirabiles *pl of* ANNUS MIRABILIS

an·ni·ver·sa·ry \,anəˈvərs(ə)rē, -vəs-,-vəis-, -ri\ *n* -ES *often attrib* [ME *anniversarie*, fr. ML *anniversaria, anniversarium*, fr. fem. & neut. of L *anniversarius*, fr. *annus* year + *versus* (past part. of *vertere* to turn) + *-arius* -ary — more at ANNUAL, WORTH] **1 a :** the annual recurrence of a date marking an event or occurrence of notable importance ⟨the ∼ of the Declaration of Independence⟩ ⟨the ∼ of the founding of a publishing house⟩ ⟨a wedding ∼⟩ **b :** the celebration or commemoration of an anniversary **2** *Roman Catholicism* **:** a mass said periodically for the soul of someone deceased

anniversary clock *n* **:** a clock with a slow torsion pendulum that enables it to run as long as 400 days on a single winding — called also *four-hundred-day clock*

anniversary day *n, usu cap A&D* **:** AUSTRALIA DAY

¹an·no dom·i·ni \ˈa(,)nōˈdämənē *also* ˈä- *or* -ōm- *or* -,nē *or* -,nī\ *adv, often cap A, usu cap D* [ML, in the year of the Lord (i.e., Jesus Christ)] — used to indicate that a time division falls within the Christian era, usu. being placed before the year ⟨*anno Domini* 1980⟩ and after other time divisions ⟨in the 8th century *anno Domini*⟩ ⟨within the 1st millennium *anno Domini*⟩; abbr. *A.D.* often printed in small capitals

²anno domini \"\ *n, usu cap A&D* **:** advancing years **:** old age ⟨*Anno Domini* softens even the cynics —*Atlantic*⟩

anno he·gi·rae \-,həˈjī(,)rē, -ˈhejə,rē\ *adv, often cap A&H* [NL, in the year of the Hegira] — used to indicate that a time division falls within the Muslim era; abbr. *A.H.* often printed in small capitals

annoint *var of* ANOINT

an·no lu·cis \-ˈlüsəs, -ük-\ *adv, often cap A&L* [NL, in the year of light; fr. the conception that God's word creating light in Gen 1:3 marks the beginning of creation] — used by many Freemasons with a year to indicate the number of years elapsed since 4000 B.C., 4000 being added to the usual computation of the year (A.D. 1980 is *Anno Lucis* 5980); abbr. *A.L.* often printed in small capitals

an·no·na \əˈnōnə\ *n, cap* [NL, fr. Sp *anona, anón* annona, fr. Taino *anon*] **:** a large genus of trees and shrubs (family Annonaceae) chiefly tropical American but widely cultivated having leathery leaves, solitary nodding flowers, and compound usu. edible fruit — see CUSTARD APPLE, SOURSOP, SWEETSOP

an·no·na·ce·ae \,anəˈnāsē,ē\ *n pl, cap* [NL, fr. *Annona*, type genus + *-aceae*] **:** a family of mostly tropical trees or shrubs (order Ranales) comprising the custard apples and related plants that have alternate leaves, flowers with three sepals and six petals, and fleshy fruits — **an·no·na·ceous** \ˈanəˈnāshəs\ *adj*

an·no·tate \ˈanə,tāt, -nō-, *usu* -ād·+V\ *vb* -ED/-ING/-S [L *annotatus*, past part. of *annotare*, fr. *ad-* + *notare* to mark — more at NOTE] *vi* **:** to make or furnish esp. critical or explanatory notes usu. on a literary work or subject ⟨he was always reading or *annotating*⟩ ∼ *vt* **:** to make or furnish esp. critical or explanatory notes on (a literary work or subject) ⟨she asked me to ∼ and introduce her book —W.B.Yeats⟩

an·no·ta·tion \,==ˈtāshən\ *n* -s [ME *annotacioun*, fr. L *annotation-, annotatio*, fr. *annotatus* + *-ion-, -io* -ion] **1 :** the act of annotating **2 a :** a note added by way of comment or explanation ⟨∼s on the text of an author⟩ **b :** an informational and descriptive note esp. about a book ⟨∼s on the newest acquisitions of the public library⟩ **3 :** a rescript in reply to a private citizen

an·no·ta·tor *also* **an·no·tat·er** \ˈ==,tād·ə(r), -ātə\ *n* -s [L *annotator*, fr. *annotatus* + *-or*] **:** one that makes annotations

an·no·ta·to·ry \ˈanə,tād·ərē, -,tə,tōrē; əˈnōd·ə,tōrē\ *adj* **:** of or belonging to an annotator or annotation

an·not·i·nous \əˈnätᵊnəs, aˈ-\ *adj* [L *annotinus*, fr. *annus* year — more at ANNUAL] *biol* **:** one year old

an·not·to \əˈnäd·(,)ō, äˈ-, -d·ə\ *n* -s [Galibi *annoto*] **:** ANNATTO

an·nounce \əˈnaủn(t)s\ *vb* -ED/-ING/-S [ME *announcen*, fr. MF *annoncer*, fr. L *annuntiare, adnuntiare*, fr. *ad-* + *nuntiare* to report, relate, fr. *nuntius* messenger] *vt* **1 a :** to give public notice of **:** make known officially or publicly **:** deliver news of **:** PROCLAIM ⟨the government *announced* a cut in taxes⟩ **b :** to state or declare often with some degree of self-importance or pomposity ⟨the child *announced* that the picnic had been fun⟩ **c :** to cause to cause (an individual) to be known in a specified role, capacity, or condition — usu. used with *as* ⟨was *announced* as a sponsor⟩ ⟨was *announced* as chief of cavalry —Eben Swift⟩ ⟨she could not live without *announcing* herself to him as his mother —Thomas Hardy⟩ **2 a :** to give notice of the arrival, presence, or readiness of ⟨∼ dinner⟩ **b :** to point to or indicate in advance **:** declare beforehand **:** FORETELL ⟨the invention of the printing press *announced* the diffusion of knowledge⟩ ⟨in 1926 Malraux was *announcing* the historical downfall of Europe —Ignazio Silone⟩ **3 :** to give evidence of esp. without oral communication ⟨his earlier work *announced* a lyric talent of the first order —Louise Bogan⟩ **:** indicate by action, appearance, or condition **:** make obvious by furnishing support for an inferrible conclusion ⟨loud shrieks *announced* his discovery —T.B.Costain⟩ **4 :** to serve as an announcer of ⟨he ∼s three programs a week⟩ ⟨he ∼s the biggest football games⟩ ∼ *vi* **1 :** to serve as an announcer ⟨he ∼s for a national network⟩ **2 a :** to declare one's candidacy — usu. used with *for* to specify the office sought ⟨12 days after he *announced* for governor —John Gunther⟩ **b :** to give one's support or allegiance — used with *for* to specify the recipient **syn** see DECLARE

an·nounce·ment \-mənt\ *n* -s **1 :** the act of announcing or of being announced ⟨during the long ∼ the crowd stirred restlessly⟩ **2 a :** public notification **:** official statement ⟨the governor will soon make a new ∼⟩ ⟨the college's ∼ of summer courses⟩ **b :** a usu. more or less formal declaration of an approaching or already realized event ⟨an ∼ of marriage⟩ **c :** a message delivered on radio or television **3 :** REMARK, OBSERVATION, STATEMENT ⟨every new ∼ of hers was greeted with shouts of laughter⟩ **4 :** a piece of formal stationery or a formal card designed for social or business purposes

an·nounc·er \-ə(r)\ *n* -s **1 :** one that introduces television or radio programs, often acts as master of ceremonies, makes commercial announcements, reads news summaries and sports reviews, gives station identification, and signals the control room for the switching of network broadcasts **2 :** one that comments on sports events (as baseball games) to television spectators or describes them to a radio audience

¹annoy *n* -s [ME *anoi*, fr. OF *anoi, enui*, fr. *anoier, enuier*] **1** *archaic* **:** a feeling of discomfort or vexation **:** ANNOYANCE **2** *obs* **:** something that is a source of annoyance or trouble

²an·noy \əˈnȯi\ *vb* -ED/-ING/-S [ME *anoien*, fr. OF *anoier, enuier*, fr. LL *inodiare* to make loathsome, fr. L *in odio* in hatred, odious, fr. *in* + *odio*, abl. of *odium* hatred — more at IN, ODIUM] *vt* **1 :** to irritate with a nettling or exasperating effect esp. by being a continuous or repeatedly renewed source of vexation **:** PROVOKE, VEX ⟨by living together they ∼*ed* the rest of the family even more than they irritated each other —William Thornton⟩ ⟨often puzzled and sometimes ∼*ed* by the ways of other peoples who are strange to us —W.A. Parker⟩ **2 a :** to harass esp. by quick and brief attacks ⟨dogs ∼*ing* a cornered bear⟩ ⟨infiltrating behind the lines so as to ∼ the enemy replacements⟩ **b** *obs* **:** to injure slightly **3** *obs* **:** to interfere with **:** affect detrimentally ∼ *vi* **:** to be a source of annoyance ⟨some personalities antagonize; others simply ∼⟩

syn VEX, IRK, BOTHER, WORRY: ANNOY suggests disturbed or irritated loss of composure, placidity, or patience through enduring affliction, molestation, slight, or discomfort ⟨Richard's absence *annoyed* him. The youth was vivacious, and his enthusiasm good fun —George Meredith⟩ ⟨*annoy* you with unnecessary details —P.B.Kyne⟩ ⟨Hopkinson *annoyed* the British in Philadelphia with a satirical ballad —*Amer. Guide Series: Pa.*⟩ VEX, somewhat stronger than ANNOY in implying a deep effect, applies to what provokes, disturbs, or perplexes ⟨the faulty translation that so *vexes* teachers —C.H. Grandgent⟩ ⟨you take delight in *vexing* me. You have no compassion on my poor nerves —Jane Austen⟩ ⟨Mr. Hudson, in his *La Plata*, has *vexed* himself with similar problems —Norman Douglas⟩ IRK now often applies to angering or provoking into a rejoinder; its older meaning of wearying and boring is becoming less common ⟨the supervision of the ubiquitous secret-service men *irked* his nerves —S.H.Adams⟩ ⟨the overiterated becomes the monotonous, and the monotonous *irks* and bores —J.L.Lowes⟩ BOTHER applies to whatever distracts, upsets, frets, or discomposes so that one cannot be placid or intent ⟨she is also a little *bothered*, I think, because the servant is going to leave —Arnold Bennett⟩ ⟨Jack and Ethel *bothered* him, they might think he'd quit on them —Oliver La Farge⟩ WORRY indicates suffering with fretting care or anxiety ⟨half sick and *worried* by debts⟩ ⟨one who has *worried* over governmental problems all of his mature life —Felix Frankfurter⟩ ⟨I'm to have my peace of mind destroyed — I'm to be *worried* into my grave —Douglas Jerrold⟩ **syn** see in addition WORRY

an·noy·ance \-ȯiən(t)s\ *n* -s [ME *anoiaunce*, fr. MF *anoiance, enuiance*, fr. OF, fr. *anoier, enuier* + *-ance*] **1 :** the act of annoying or of being annoyed ⟨her constant ~ of her grandmother⟩ **2 :** the state or feeling of being annoyed **:** VEXATION, IRRITATION ⟨he gave up the search and went on with rising ~ to find the address —Ethel Wilson⟩ **3 :** a source of vexation or irritation **:** bothersome disturbance **:** NUISANCE ⟨these attacks had proved to be an ~ rather than a menace —C.E.Black & E.C.Helmreich⟩ ⟨plaster cracks and other ~s —J.R.Dalzell⟩

annoying *adj* [ME *anoiing*, fr. pres. part. of *anoien* to annoy] **:** IRRITATING, VEXING — **an·noy·ing·ly** *adv*

¹an·nu·al \ˈanyə(wə)l\ *adj* [ME *annuel, annual*, fr. MF & LL; MF *annuel*, fr. LL *annualis*, blend of L *annuus* yearly (fr. *annus* year) and L *annalis* yearly (fr. *annus* year + *-alis* -al); akin to Goth *athnam* (dat. pl.) years, Skt *atati* he walks, goes] **1 a :** reckoned by the year ⟨~ value of coffee exports⟩ **b :** covering the period of a year **:** based on a year ⟨an ~ total⟩ ⟨~ statistics⟩ ⟨~ rainfall⟩ **2 :** occurring, appearing, made, done, or acted upon every year or once a year ⟨an ~ event⟩ ⟨an ~ magazine⟩ ⟨an ~ visit⟩ **3 :** completing the life cycle in one growing season **:** lasting one year or growing season ⟨an ~ plant⟩ — compare BIENNIAL, PERENNIAL — **an·nu·al·ly** \-lē, -i\ *adv*

²annual \"\ *n* -s **1 a :** a publication appearing yearly and often treating of matters of interest in a year just past ⟨editor of the high-school ~⟩; *specif* **:** a publication appearing as one of a series published to meet a yearly seasonal market ⟨a children's Christmas ~⟩ **b :** GIFTBOOK 2 **2 :** a yearly event; *specif* **:** an annual exhibition of paintings or sculpture **3 :** something that lasts one year or season; *specif* **:** a plant that completes its growth in one growing season

annual bluegrass *or* **annual meadowgrass** *n* **:** an annual European grass (*Poa annua*) of wide distribution introduced into No. America where it is often a weed esp. in lawns

annual epact *n* **:** EPACT 1a

annual improvement factor *n* **:** a provision in a labor contract calling for an annual increase in the hourly wage rates of the workers so as to provide a constantly rising standard of living

an·nu·al·ist \-əst\ *n* -s [²*annual* + *-ist*] **:** one who writes for an annual

an·nu·al·i·za·tion \ˌanyə(wə)ləˈzāshən, -ˌlīˈz-\ *n* -s **:** the act of annualizing or the state of being annualized

an·nu·al·ize \ˈanyə(wə)ˌlīz\ *vt* -ED/-ING/-S [¹*annual* + *-ize*] **:** to compute for periods of less than a year on a basis corresponding to that applicable to a full year ⟨*annualized* income⟩

annual leave *n* **:** free time granted annually to a jobholder

annual meeting *n* **:** a meeting (as of the stockholders of a business concern) held annually for reviewing developments of the year just past, electing new officers, and voting on major organizational policies

annual parallax *n* **:** HELIOCENTRIC PARALLAX

annual phlox *n* **:** any of various phloxes derived from an herb (*Phlox drummondii*) with erect stems usu. less than 18 inches high, leaves 1 to 3 inches long, the upper ones alternate, and flowers in close clusters — compare PERENNIAL PHLOX

annual rent *n* **1** *Scots law* **:** GROUND ANNUAL **2** *Scots law* **:** INTEREST

annual ring *n* **1** *of a woody plant* **:** the layer of wood produced by the growth of a single year and appearing in cross section as a ring or rings surrounding previously produced similar rings — called also *growth ring* **2 :** one of the markings or ridges on the scales of some fishes that correspond with a year's growth — called also *annulus*

transverse section of a twig of the tulip tree: *1* pith; *2* wood, showing three annual rings; *3* bark; *4* wood rays

annual sage *n* **1 :** CHIA 1 **2 :** THISTLE SAGE

annual variation *n* **:** the yearly change in a star's mean right ascension or declination produced by precession of the equinoxes and proper motion of the star

annual wage *n* **:** GUARANTEED ANNUAL WAGE

an·nu·ary \ˈanyəˌwerē\ *n* -ES [F *annuaire*, fr. LL *annuarius*, fr. L *annuus* yearly + *-arius* -ary — more at ANNUAL] **:** YEARBOOK, ANNUAL

an·nu·a·tion \ˌanyəˈwāshən\ *n* -s [L *annuus* yearly + E *-ation* — more at ANNUAL] **:** annual variation in the presence or absence or the abundance of particular members of a plant community usu. relatable to annual climatic variation — compare ASPECTION **2 :** ecological observations made over a period of years

an·nu·i·tant \əˈn(y)üəd·ənt, -ətənt *also* aˈ- *or* -ətˈnt\ *n* -s [*annuity* + *-ant*] **:** one that receives benefits or payments from an annuity or that is entitled to receive such benefits

an·nu·i·ty \-əd·ē, -ətē, -i\ *n* -ES *often attrib* [ME *annuite*, fr. MF *annuité*, fr. ML *annuitat-, annuitas*, fr. L *annuus* yearly + *-itat-, -itas* -ity — more at ANNUAL] **1 :** an amount payable yearly or at other regular intervals (as quarterly) for a certain or uncertain period (as for years, for life, or in perpetuity) **2 :** the grant of or the right to receive an annuity ⟨his will included *annuities* for several old servants⟩ **3 :** a contract or agreement under which one or more persons receive annuities in return for prior set payments made by themselves or another (as an employer) ⟨bought an ~ to take care of his parents⟩

annuity certain *n, pl* **annuities certain :** an annuity payable in any event for a term of years

annuity due *n, pl* **annuities due :** an annuity providing for the first payment at the beginning rather than at the end of the first period

an·nul \əˈnəl\ *vt* **annulled; annulled; annulling; annuls** [ME *annullen*, fr. MF *annuller*, fr. LL *annullare, adnullare* to destroy (trans. of Gk *exoudenein, exoudenoun*), fr. L *ad-* + LL *-nullare* (fr. L *nullus* none) — more at NULL] **1 a :** to cause to cease to exist **:** reduce to nothing **:** blot out **:** OBLITERATE ⟨*annulling* every memory⟩ **b :** to check effectively **:** make inoperative (as by an opposite influence or force) **:** NEUTRALIZE, CANCEL ⟨she stood very still, as if by her stillness to ~ the small leaden sound the key had made —Dorothy Baker⟩ **2 a :** to declare (a marriage) legally invalid ⟨he may then have the marriage *annulled* —S.G.Kling⟩ **b :** to make legally void **:** declare to be no longer of legal effect **:** ABOLISH **syn** see NULLIFY

an·nu·lar \ˈanyələ(r)\ *adj* [MF or L; MF *annulaire*, fr. L *annularis, anularis*, fr. *annulus, anulus* ring — more at ANNULUS] **1 a :** of or relating to a ring **:** forming a ring **:** shaped like a ring ⟨~ growths in the trunk of a tree⟩ **b** *chem* **:** CYCLIC **2 :** banded, marked, or thickened in circles ⟨an ~ cell of a plant⟩ — **an·nu·lar·ly** *adv*

annular auger *n* **:** a ring-shaped boring tool that cuts a circular channel leaving the center intact

annular budding *n* **:** budding in which a ring of bark is removed from the stock and replaced with one containing a bud of the desired species or variety

annular eclipse *n* **:** a solar eclipse in which a thin outer ring of the sun's disk is not covered by the apparently smaller dark disk of the moon

annular finger *n* **:** RING FINGER

annular gear *n* **:** INTERNAL GEAR

an·nu·lar·ia \ˌanyəˈla(a)rēə\ *n, cap* [NL, fr. L *annulus* + NL *-aria*] **:** a large genus of fossil pteridophytic plants of the order Equisetales having annuli formed by the basal sheaths of the leaf whorls

an·nu·lar·i·ty \-ˈlarəd·ē\ *n* -ES **:** annular state or form

annular ligament *n, anat* **:** a ringlike ligament or band of fibrous tissue encircling a part: **a :** any of the transverse bands holding in place the extensor and flexor tendons of the wrist and ankle **b :** a strong band of fibers surrounding the head of the radius and retaining it in the radial notch of the ulna — called also *orbicular ligament* **c :** any of certain strengthening bands of the tendon sheaths of the digits **d :** a ring attaching the base of the stapes to the fenestra vestibuli

annular solid *n, math* **:** a solid generated by a closed curve when rotated about a straight line lying in the plane of the curve and not intersecting the curve (as a torus)

annular vault *n* **:** a vault rising from two walls that are circular in plan (as above the walls of an ambulatory)

an·nu·lary \ˈanyəˌlerē\ *n* -ES [short for earlier *annulary finger*, fr. obs. E *annulary* of a ring (fr. L *annularius*) + *finger* — more at ANNULAR] **:** RING FINGER

¹an·nu·la·ta \ˌanyəˈläd·ə, -ˈād·ə\ [NL, fr. L, neut. pl. of *annulatus*] *syn of* ANNELIDA

²annulata \"\ *n pl, cap* [NL, fr. L] *in some classifications* **:** a major division of Invertebrata comprising bilaterally symmetrical animals with true metamerism and including the annelids, arthropods, and a few related forms

¹an·nu·late \ˈanyələt, -ˌlāt, *usu* -d·+V\ *or* **an·nu·lat·ed** \-ˌlād·əd\ *adj* [L *annulatus, anulatus*, fr. *annulus, anulus* ring + *-atus* -ate — more at ANNULUS] **1 :** having rings, ringlike structures, or ringlike characteristics **2 :** ANNULAR **3** [NL *Annulata*] **:** of or relating to the Annulata

²annulate \"\ *n* -s **:** an animal of the division Annulata

annulated column *or* **annulated shaft** *n* **:** a column made up of a cluster of shafts seemingly held together by an annular band at intervals but commonly worked on an interposed stone plate whose edge slightly projects and often found in clustered piers of Gothic churches

an·nu·la·tion \ˌanyəˈlāshən\ *n* -s **1 :** the formation of rings **2 :** a ringlike structure

an·nule \ˈa(ˌ)nyül\ *n* -s [L *annulus*] **:** ANNULUS; *specif* **:** a circular band formed by two transverse grooves in the cuticle of some nematodes with consequent apparent segmentation

an·nu·let \ˈanyələt, -ˌlet\ *n* -s [modif. (influenced by L *annulus, anulus* ring) of MF *annelet, anelet*, dim. of *anel*, fr. L *anellus* little ring, dim. of *annulus, anulus* ring — more at ANNULUS] **1 :** a little ring **2** *heraldry* **:** a ring-shaped charge that when borne as a cadency mark represents position as a 6th son or descendant of a 6th son **3** *archit* **:** a small molding or ridge forming a ring (as a list, fillet, or cincture); *esp* **:** one of the fillets used at the lower part of the Doric capital **4** *zool* **:** a narrow circle of some distinct color on a surface or around an organ

annulet 2

annuli *pl of* ANNULUS

an·nu·lism \-ˌlizəm\ *n* -s [*annulus* + *-ism*] **:** annulated state or structure

annulled *past of* ANNUL

an·nul·ler \əˈnələ(r)\ *n* -s **:** one that annuls

annulling *pres part of* ANNUL

an·nul·ment \əˈnəlmənt\ *n* -s **:** the act of annulling or of being annulled **:** NULLIFICATION; *specif* **:** a judicial pronouncement declaring the invalidity of a marriage — distinguished from *divorce* and *separation*

an·nu·lo·sa \ˌanyəˈlōsə, -ōzə\ *n pl, cap* [NL, fr. L *annulus* ring + *-osa* (neut. pl. of *-osus*) -ose] *in some classifications* **:** a subkingdom of animals including forms with articulate bodies and a double ventral chain of ganglia and comprising the annelid worms and the arthropods — **an·nu·losan** \-sən, -zən\ *n* -s — **an·nu·lose** \ˈanyəˌlōs\ *adj*

annuls *pres 3d sing of* ANNUL

an·nu·lus \ˈanyələs\ *n, pl* **annu·li** \-ˌlī\ *also* **annuluses** [L *annulus, anulus* ring, dim. of *anus* ring, circle, anus — more at ANUS] **1 :** a ringlike part, structure, or marking **2** *anat* **:** any of certain ringlike parts (as the abdominal ring) **3 :** ANNULET 3 **4 :** the plane space between two concentric circles one within the other **5 a** *of fungi* **:** a membranous or fleshy ring that surrounds the stipe of certain agarics after the expansion of the pileus **:** the remnant of the veil **b** *of a moss* **:** an elastic ring of cells between the operculum and the mouth of the capsule **c** *of a fern* **:** a line of cells partly or entirely surrounding the sporangium and each having inner tangential and radial walls thickened and outer wall thin and by its contraction bringing about rupture of the sporangium and assisting in spore discharge **d :** the fleshy rim of the corolla in some asclepiads (as of the genus *Stapelia*) **e :** the calyxlike whorl at the base of the strobilus of some horsetails (genus *Equisetum*) **6 a :** one of the ringlike but not truly segmented parts of the body of some annelids (as leeches) **b :** ANNUAL RING 2

an·nun·ci·ate \əˈnən(t)sēˌāt *also* aˈ-\ *vt* -ED/-ING/-S [L *annuntiatus, adnuntiatus*] **:** ANNOUNCE

an·nun·ci·a·tion \ə,ˌ==ˈāshən\ *n* -s [ME *annunciacioun*, fr. MF *anunciation, annonciation*, fr. LL *annuntiation-, annuntiatio*, fr. L *annuntiatus, adnuntiatus* (past part. of *annuntiare, adnuntiare* to announce) + *-ion-, -io* -ion — more at ANNOUNCE] **1 :** the act of announcing or of being announced **:** ANNOUNCEMENT ⟨~ of the good news⟩ **2** *also* **annunciation day** *usu cap A&D* **:** the 25th of March on which many Christian churches commemorate the announcement of the Incarnation related in Luke 1:28–35 — called also *Lady Day*

annunciation lily *n, usu cap A* [so called fr. its use by painters in pictures of the Annunciation] **1 :** MADONNA LILY **2 :** BERMUDA LILY

an·nun·ci·a·tor \ˈ==ˌād·ə(r), -ātə-\ *n* -s [LL, fr. L *annuntiatus* + *-or*] **1 :** one that annunciates **:** ANNOUNCER **2 :** a device for giving audible or visible directives or information: as **a :** an electrically controlled signaling apparatus for indicating which of the connecting lines is calling (as the rooms calling a hotel desk or the floors at which people are signaling for an elevator to stop) **b :** a device for transmitting speed orders to the engine room of a ship

an·nun·ci·a·to·ry \-əˌtōrē\ *adj* **:** serving to announce ⟨a condition ~ of what was to follow⟩

an·nus mi·ra·bi·lis \ˌanəsməˈräbələs, -rab-; ˈänəsməˈrä-\ *n, pl* **an·ni mirabi·les** \ˈaˌnīməˈräbəˌlēz, -rab-; ˈäˌnēməˈräbəˌlās\ *sometimes cap A&M* [L] **:** wonderful year — used of any esp. notable year ⟨1776 — an *annus mirabilis* in American history⟩

¹ano- *prefix* [NL, fr. Gk *anō* upward, above, fr. *ana* up, on — more at ON] **1 :** upward ⟨*anogenic*⟩ ⟨*anoopsia*⟩ **2 :** upper ⟨*anocarpous*⟩

²ano- *comb form* [NL, fr. L *anus*] **:** anus ⟨*anoscopy*⟩ **:** anal and ⟨*anococcygeal*⟩

anoa \əˈnōə\ *n* -s [native name in the Celebes] **:** a small wild ox of Celebes (*Anoa depressicornis*) related to the buffalo but having nearly straight horns

ano·bi·id \əˈnōbēəd\ *adj* [NL *Anobiidae*] **:** of or belonging to the Anobiidae

an·o·bi·i·dae \ˌanəˈbīəˌdē\ *n pl, cap* [NL, fr. *Anobium*, type genus + *-idae*] **:** a family of small hard-bodied beetles with 5-jointed tarsi and generally serrate clubbed antennae that feed on dry vegetable material and include destructive pests of stored foods and tobacco — see DRUGSTORE BEETLE

anobing *var of* ANUBING

ano·bi·um \əˈnōbēəm\ *n, cap* [NL, fr. ¹*ano-* + *-bium*] **:** a genus (the type of the family Anobiidae) of small beetles including a number of forms that bore in dry wood — compare FURNITURE BEETLE, POWDER-POST BEETLE

an·ode \ˈaˌnōd\ *n* -s [Gk *anodos* way up, rise, fr. *ana-* + *hodos* road; fr. the belief that the electric current passes from east to west — more at CEDE] **1 :** the electrode at which electrons leave a device to enter the external circuit — opposed to *cathode* **2 a :** the positive terminal of an electrolytic cell **b :** the negative terminal of a primary cell or of a storage battery that is delivering current **c :** the electron-collecting electrode of an electron tube **:** PLATE

anode current *n* **:** PLATE CURRENT

anode ray *n* **:** any of the streams of positively charged particles emitted by the metallic anode of a discharge tube or by impurities on the surface of the anode

an·od·ic \(ˈ)aˈnädik, -ōd-, əˈnä-\ *adj* [Gk *anodos* road up (fr. *ana-* + *hodos* road) + E *-ic*] **1 :** ASCENDING **2** *bot* **:** turned toward — used only of that half of a leaf which is turned toward the course of the genetic spiral; compare CATHODIC **3** [*anode* + *-ic*] **a :** of, at, or relating to an anode — opposed to *cathodic* **b :** *of a chemical element* **:** tending to form an anode in an electrochemical cell in relation to another element, often hydrogen ⟨zinc is ~ to copper⟩ **4 :** produced by or involving a process in which a metal is made to serve as the anode in an electrolytic cell (as for coating the metal with an oxide for protection) ⟨~ coating⟩ ⟨~ finish⟩ ⟨~ treatment⟩ — **an·od·i·cal·ly** \(ˈ)aˈnädək(ə)lē, -ōd-, əˈnä-\ *adv*

anodic coating *n* **:** the process of anodizing

an·od·ize *or* **an·od·ise** \ˈa(ˌ)nōˌdīz, ˈanə-\ *vt* -ED/-ING/-S [*anode* + *-ize*] **:** to subject (a metal) to electrolytic action by making (it) the anode of a cell before coating with a protective or decorative film

an·o·do·lu·mi·nes·cence \ˈanəˌdō-\ *n* -s [*anode* + *-o-* + *luminescence*] **:** luminescence excited by anode rays

¹an·o·don \ˈanəˌdän\ [NL, fr. Gk *anodōn* toothless, fr. *an-* + *odōn* tooth — more at TOOTH] *syn of* ANODONTA

²anodon \"\ *n* -s **:** a freshwater mussel of the genus *Anodonta*

an·o·don·ta \ˌanəˈdäntə\ *n, cap* [NL, fr. Gk *anodont-, anodōn* toothless] **:** a large genus of freshwater mussels (family Unionidae) having the hinge teeth rudimentary or wanting and the shell usu. thin and fragile

an·o·don·tia \ˌanōˈdänch(ē)ə\ *n* -s [NL, fr. *an-* + *-odontia*] **:** an esp. congenital absence of teeth

¹an·o·dyne \ˈanəˌdīn, -nō,-\ *adj* [L *anodynos*, fr. Gk *anōdynos*, fr. *an-* + *odynē* pain; akin to Arm *erkn* birth pains, Lith *ėdžiotis* to hurt, OE *etan* to eat — more at EAT] **1 :** serving to assuage pain **:** SOOTHING ⟨the ~ properties of certain drugs⟩ **2 :** serving or intended to soothe the mind or feelings **:** inducing forgetfulness, oblivion, or unconcern **:** RELAXING ⟨his pleasant voice and pious, ~ opinions making of his sentences so many gentle opiates —F.M.Ford⟩ ⟨all that doughy, woolly, ~ writing that exists merely to fill a gap of leisure —Aldous Huxley⟩ **3 :** marked by an absence of power of stimulation **:** BLAND ⟨~ translations from Homer and Sophocles in . . . sleepy prose —George Santayana⟩; *sometimes* **:** designedly weakened or softened (as by qualification or expurgation) ⟨read the ~ and doctored accounts of the transactions that had cost them their savings —*New Republic*⟩

²anodyne \"\ *n* -s [LL *anodynon*, fr. Gk *anōdynon*, fr. neut. of *anōdynos*] **1 :** a drug that allays pain (as an opiate or narcotic) **2 :** something that soothes, calms, or comforts ⟨the ~ of work⟩ ⟨old wounds heal; new friendships and associations come as ~s —Nevil Shute⟩ ⟨an escape, a distraction, an ~ —J.C.Powys⟩ — **an·o·dyn·ic** \ˌ==ˈdinik, -ēk\ *adj*

anodyne necklace *n* **1 :** a necklace usu. of henbane roots used in the 18th century esp. by teething children as a charm against illness **2 :** a hangman's noose

an·o·dyn·ia \ˌ==ˈdinēə, -dīn-\ *n* -s [NL, fr. Gk *anōdynia*, fr. *anōdynos* + *-ia*] **:** absence of pain

an·od·y·nous \aˈnäd°nəs; ˈanəˌdīnəs, -nō,-\ *adj* [L *anodynos*] **:** ANODYNE

an·o·e·sia \ˌanōˈēzh(ē)ə\ *n* -s [NL, fr. Gk *anoēsia* want of understanding, fr. *a-* ²*a-* + *noēsis*] **:** ANOIA

an·o·e·sis \ˌanōˈēsəs\ *n, pl* **anoe·ses** \-ˌsēz\ [²*a-* + *noesis*] **:** consciousness that is pure passive receptiveness without understanding or intellectual organization of the materials presented

anoestrous [*an-* + *oestrous*] *var of* ANESTROUS

anoestrus *or* **anoestrum** *var of* ANESTRUS

an·o·et·ic \ˌanōˈed·ik\ *adj* [²*a-* + *noetic*] **:** relating to or characterized by anoesis

ano·gra \əˈnōgrə\ *n cap* [NL anagram of *Onagra* (syn. of *Oenothera*) — more at ONAGRA] **:** a genus of herbs (family Onagraceae) found in the southern part of No. America and having alternate leaves and flowers with four notched petals

anoia \əˈnȯi(y)ə\ *n* -s [NL, fr. Gk *anoia* lack of understanding, fr. *a-* ²*a-* + *noos, nous* sense, mind, understanding + *-ia*] **:** mental deficiency; *esp* **:** IDIOCY

ano·ine \ˈanōˌīn, -ˌən\ *adj* [*anoa* + *-ine*] **:** of or relating to the anoa

anoint \əˈnȯint\ *vt* -ED/-ING/-S [ME *anointen, enointen*, fr. MF *enoint* (past part. of *enoindre*, fr. L *inunguere*), fr. L *inunctus*, past part. of *inunguere*, fr. *in* + *unguere, ungere* to smear, anoint — more at OINTMENT] **1 :** to rub over with oil or an oily substance ⟨~*ing* his boat —Herman Melville⟩ ⟨heron fat . . . was used by fishermen to ~ their lines —*Irish Digest*⟩ ⟨that road to ruin for which extravagant habits . . . were plentifully ~*ing* their wheels —George Eliot⟩ **:** RUB —used with *with* ⟨~*ing* one another with suntan oil⟩ ⟨drew the cork and ~*ed* his head with the lotion⟩ **2** *also* **an·noint** \"\ **a :** to apply oil to or pour oil upon as a sacred rite esp. for consecration ⟨they ~*ed* David king —2 Sam 2:4 (RSV)⟩ **b :** to choose by or as if by divine election **:** designate as if through the rite of anointment **:** CONSECRATE ⟨he has ~*ed* me to preach good news to the poor —Lk 4:18 (RSV)⟩ ⟨the elect and ~*ed* of God⟩ ⟨regarded by all as his ~*ed* successor⟩ **3** *chiefly dial* **:** BEAT, THRASH, CHASTISE

anoint·ment \-mənt\ *n* -s [ME, fr. *anointen* + *-ment*] **1 :** the action of anointing or state of being anointed **2** *archaic* **:** OINTMENT

ano·le \əˈnōlē\ *also* **ano·li** \"\ *n* -s [F *anolis*, fr. Island Carib *anoli*] **:** a lizard of the genus *Anolis*

ano·lis \əˈnōləs, ˈanə-\ *n, cap* [NL, fr. F *anolis*] **:** a genus of small American pleurodont lizards (family Iguanidae) comprising the New World chameleons that have the power of changing color like the true chameleons of the Old World

an·o·lyte \ˈanəˌlīt, -nō,-\ *n* -s [*anode* + *electrolyte*] **:** that portion of the electrolyte in the immediate vicinity of the anode in an electrolytic cell — opposed to *catholyte*

anom- *or* **anomo-** *comb form* [NL, fr. Gk *anom-* lawless, fr. *anomos*, fr. *a-* ²*a-* + *nomos* law, fr. *nemein* to distribute — more at NIMBLE] **:** unusual **:** abnormal **:** irregular ⟨*anomite*⟩ ⟨*anomocarpous*⟩

anomal- *or* **anomali-** *or* **anomalo-** *comb form* [L *anomal-*, fr. Gk, fr. *anōmalos* uneven, irregular — more at ANOMALOUS] **:** anomalous **:** irregular ⟨*anomali*florous⟩ ⟨*anomal*ism⟩ ⟨*anomalo*cephalus⟩

anom·a·la \əˈnäm(ə)lə\ *n, cap* [NL, fr. LL, fem. of *anomalus* anomalous] **:** a genus of beetles (family Scarabaeidae) having grubs that feed mainly on the roots of plants and including several pests of cultivated grasses — see ORIENTAL BEETLE

anomalies *pl of* ANOMALY

anom·a·li·ped \əˈnäməlǝˌped\ *or* **anom·a·li·pod** \-ˌpäd\ *adj* [F *anomalipède*, fr. *anomal-* + *-pède* -ped] **:** having more or less of the digits united ⟨the kingfisher and the kangaroo are ~⟩ **:** SYNDACTYLIC

anom·a·lism \əˈnäməˌlizəm\ *n* -s [*anomal-* + *-ism*] **1 :** the quality of being anomalous **2 :** ANOMALY

anom·a·list \-ləst\ *n* -s [perh. fr. G, fr. *anomal-* + *-ist*] **:** an adherent of the view held by certain Greek grammarians of the 2d century B.C. that in language the connection between the word and the idea is arbitrary and based on convention alone — opposed to *analogist*

anom·a·lis·tic \əˌnäməˈlistik, -ēk\ *also* **anom·a·lis·ti·cal** \ˌ=ˌ=ˈ=əkəl\ *adj* [*anomaly* + *-istic*] **1** *astron* **:** relating to the anomaly (sense 1a) **2** [*anomalist* + *-ic*] **:** of or relating to the anomalists **3 :** ANOMALOUS — **anom·a·lis·ti·cal·ly** \-ək(ə)lē, -li\ *adv*

anomalistic month *n* **:** the mean time of the moon's revolution from perigee to perigee again, being approximately 27.554550 days

anomalistic year *n* **:** the time of the earth's revolution from perihelion to perihelion again, being 365 days, 6 hours, 13 minutes, and 53.1 seconds

anom·a·lops \əˈnäməˌläps\ *n, cap* [NL, fr. *anomal-* + *-ops*] **:** a genus of fishes (order Berycomorphi) having a luminous organ beneath each eye filled with light-producing bacteria and known from warm seas of the southwestern Pacific and about Puerto Rico

anom·a·lop·ter·yx \əˌnäməˈläptəˌriks\ *n, cap* [NL, fr. *anomal-* + *-pteryx*] **:** a genus of moas of slender build and a height of three or four feet

anom·a·lo·scope \əˈnäməlǝˌskōp\ *n* -s [*anomal-* + *-scope*] **:** an optical device designed to test color vision by matching a yellow light which may be varied in intensity with a combination of red and green lights of constant intensity

anom·a·lous \əˈnäməlǝs\ *adj* [LL *anomalus*, fr. Gk *anōmalos*, lit., uneven, irregular, fr. *an-* + *homalos* even, level, fr. *homos* same, common — more at SAME] **1** *archaic* **:** UNCONFORMABLE, DISSIMILAR — used with *to* **2 :** deviating from a general rule, method, or analogy **:** ABNORMAL, IRREGULAR ⟨an ~ verb⟩ ⟨in nature, the ~ or lawless systems often are most interesting and instructive —Otto Glasser⟩ ⟨any hereditary peculiarity — as a supernumerary finger, or an ~ shape of feature —Nathaniel Hawthorne⟩ **3 :** not conformable to established or accepted conceptions of fitness or harmonious combination:

a : out of keeping with its recognized nature, characteristics, surroundings, or conditions of occurrence ⟨a person on a heath in raiment of modern cut and colors has more or less an ~ look —Thomas Hardy⟩ ⟨an ~ figure in the world of politics⟩ ⟨an ~ remark, coming from him⟩ **b :** exhibiting or containing incongruous or often contradictory elements ⟨the ~ position of the free Negro in the slave states —E.T.Price⟩ ⟨in the ~ position of being ranked second nationally . . . but first in the world —*New Yorker*⟩

anomalous dispersion *n* **:** dispersion of light in some refraction spectra in which the normal order of the separation of components is reversed in the vicinity of certain wavelengths

anomalous indorser *n* **:** a person other than the maker, payee, or holder of a negotiable bill or note who indorses it for some purpose other than to transfer it

anom·a·lous·ly *adv* **:** in an anomalous manner

anomalous plea *n, law* **:** a plea partly affirmative and partly negative, the one part being used to show that the other does not defeat the rights of the pleader

anomalous trichromatism *n* **:** a slight defect of color vision in which the proportions of the three primary colors required in color mixture deviate from the normal — compare COLOR 1

anom·a·lure \ə'nämə,lu̇(ə)r\ *n* -s [NL *Anomalurus*] **:** a member of the genus *Anomalurus* **:** SCALETAIL

anom·a·lu·rus \ə,nämə'lu̇rəs\ *n, cap* [NL, fr. *anomal-* + *-urus*] **:** a genus (the type of the family Anomaluridae) of sciuromorph rodents comprising the scaletails and resembling flying squirrels but having scaly tails used in climbing

anom·a·ly \ə'näməlē, -li\ *n* -ES [L *anomalia*, fr. Gk *anōmalia*, fr. *anōmalos* + *-ia*] **1 :** the state or fact of being out of place, out of true, or out of a normal or expected position **:** INEQUALITY, UNEVENNESS: as **a :** the angular distance of a planet from its perihelion as seen from the sun **b** (1) **:** the difference between the mean of any meteorological element or phase of that element over a given time at a particular place and the mean of the same element or phase over the same time for all other points on the same parallel of latitude (2) **:** the difference between the current value of a meteorological element and its long-term average **c :** a deviation of optical properties of a crystal from its apparent symmetry as expressed in its external form — usu. used in the phrase *optical anomaly* **2 :** deviation from the common rule **:** IRREGULARITY ⟨that supreme triumph of British ~, the unreformed House of Lords —R.W.Chapman⟩ **3 :** something anomalous **:** something irregular or abnormal: as **a :** a word form, set of inflectional forms, construction, or idiom analogous to few or no others (as the conjugation of the verb *to be* or *stood*, past tense of *stand*) **b** *biol* **:** a deviation in excess of normal variation from the form characteristic of a natural group **c** *geol* **:** a local departure from the general regional conditions (as of gravity, magnetism, radioactivity, or topography) **4 :** something out of keeping esp. with established or accepted notions of fitness or order ⟨her religion was no ~ but perfectly natural —George Santayana⟩

an·o·mer \'anəmər\ *n* -s [¹*ano-* + *-mer*] **:** a cyclic stereoisomer in the carbohydrate series with isomerism involving only the arrangement of atoms or groups at the aldehyde or ketone position (as in *alpha*-D-glucose and *beta*-D-glucose) — **an·o·mer·ic** \ˌanəˈmerik\ *adj*

ano·mia \ə'nōmēə\ *n, cap* [NL, fr. Gk *anomos* lawless + NL *-ia* — more at ANOM-] **:** a genus (the type of the family Anomiidae) of thin-shelled bivalve mollusks comprising the saddle oysters, having the right valve deeply notched for passage of the byssus, and forming with a few related forms a suborder of Filibranchia

anom·ic \ə'nämik, (ˌ)ā¦n-; -nō-\ *adj* [*anomie* + *-ic*] **:** relating to or characterized by anomie

anomic aphasia *n* **:** loss of the power to use or understand words denoting objects

an·o·mie \'anə,mē\ *also* **ano·mia** \ə'nōmēə, ā'n-, ˌanə'mēə\ *or* **an·o·my** \'anəmē, -mi\ *n* -s [*anomie, anomy* fr. F *anomie*, fr. Gk *anomia*, *anomiē* lawlessness; *anomia* fr. Gk — more at ANOMY] **:** a state of normlessness or lawlessness: **a :** a state of society in which normative standards of conduct and belief have weakened or disappeared **b :** a similar condition in an individual commonly characterized by personal disorientation, anxiety, and social isolation

an·o·mite \'anə,mīt\ *n* -s [ISV *anom-* + *-ite*; orig. formed as G *anomit*] **:** a variety of biotite differing optically from the ordinary kind

anomo- — see ANOM-

an·o·mo·coe·lous \ˌanə(ˌ)mō¦sēləs\ *adj* [*anom-* + *coelous*] **:** concave in front — used of a vertebra in which the anterior surface of the centrum is hollowed out while the posterior surface is flat or convex

¹an·o·mo·dont \'anə(ˌ)mō,dänt\ *adj* [NL *Anomodontia*] **:** of or belonging to Anomodontia

²anomodont \"\ *n* -s **:** an anomodont reptile

¹an·o·mo·don·tia \ˌanə(ˌ)mō'dänsh(ē)ə\ [NL, fr. *anom-* + *-odontia*] *syn of* PELYCOSAURIA

²anomodontia \"\ [NL, fr. *anom-* + *-odontia*] *syn of* DICYNODONTIA

¹an·o·moe·an \ˌanə'mēən\ *also* **an·o·moi·an** \-mȯiən\ *n* -s *usu cap* [LGk *Anomoios* (fr. Gk *anomoios*, adj., unlike, fr. *an-* + *homoios* similar, fr. *homos* same) + E *-an* — more at SAME] **:** a member of an extreme division of Arians of the 4th century A.D. who declared that since the Son of God is a created being he is unlike God in essence — called also EUNOMIAN

²anomoean \¦==¦==\ *adj, usu cap* **:** of, relating to, or belonging to the Anomoeans

an·o·mu·ra \ˌanə'm(y)u̇rə\ *also* **an·o·mou·ra** \-'mü-\ *n pl, cap* [NL, fr. *anom-* + *-ura*] **:** a tribe or other division of Reptantia including decapod crustaceans with the abdomen more or less reduced and usu. permanently flexed (as the hermit crabs), being in some classifications placed in Macrura or treated as a separate suborder intermediate between Macrura and Brachyura — **an·o·mu·ral** \¦==¦m(y)u̇rəl\ *adj* — **an·o·mu·ran** \-¦m(y)u̇rən\ *adj or n* — **an·o·mu·rous** \-¦m(y)u̇rəs\ *adj*

¹an·o·my \'anəmē, -mi\ *n* -ES [Gk *anomia*, *anomiē* lawlessness, fr. *anomos* + *-ia*, *-iē* -y] **1** *obs* **:** the state of being without law or order or esp. without natural law or uniformity **2 :** an act or phenomenon that can be ascribed to the operation of no known law **:** MIRACLE

²anomy *var of* ANOMIE

¹anon \ə'nän\ *adv* [ME *anon, onon*, fr. OE *on ān* in one, continually, immediately, fr. *on* in, on + *ān* one — more at ON, ONE] **1** *archaic* **:** at once **:** IMMEDIATELY, FORTHWITH ⟨he that heareth the word and ~ with joy receiveth it —Mt 13:20 (AV)⟩ — used esp. to express prompt response to a request or a summons **2 :** in a little while: **a :** SOON, PRESENTLY ⟨thou dost me yet but little hurt; thou wilt ~ —Shak.⟩ **b :** LATER ⟨but more of that ~⟩ **3 :** at another time **:** AGAIN, THEN ⟨on hill sometimes, ~ in shady vale —John Milton⟩ ⟨ever and ~⟩ ⟨now and ~⟩

²anon \"\ *interj, dial* — used to express failure to hear or understand something spoken or sometimes to express impatience or surprise

³anon \ä'nōn, ə'n-\ *n, pl* **ano·nes** \-(ˌ)nes, -äs\ [Sp *anón*, fr. Taino *anon*] **:** SWEETSOP 2

anon *abbr* anonymous

ano·na \ə'nōnə\ *syn of* ANNONA

ano·na·ce·ae \ˌanō'nāsē,ē\ *syn of* ANNONACEAE

ano·nang \ə'nō,näŋ\ *n* -s [Tag] **:** a Philippine tree (*Cordia myxa*) the inner bark of which furnishes a cordage fiber; *also* **:** the fiber itself

anon·cil·lo \ˌä(ˌ)nōn'sēl,yō\ *n* -s [AmerSp, dim. of Sp *anón*] **:** the fiber yielded by the bark of various Venezuelan trees of the genus *Annona*

an·o·nych·ia \ˌanə'nikēə\ *n* -s [NL, fr. *an-* + *-onychia*] *med* **:** congenital absence of the nails

an·o·nym *also* **an·o·nyme** \'anə,nim\ *n* -s [F *anonyme*, fr. *anonyme* anonymous, fr. LL *anonymus*] **1 a :** one that retains anonymity or is of unknown name ⟨the essential if vaguely defined role of the recording director seems to be played by complete ~s —R.D.Darrell⟩ ⟨the party is an omnipotent and all-present ~ —Sergey Levitsky⟩ **b :** an anonymous book **2 :** an idea that has no exact term to express it **3 :** PSEUDONYM

anon·y·ma \ə'nänəmə *also* a'-\ *n, pl* **anony·mae** \-,mē, -,mī\ *or* **anonymas** [NL fr. LL, fem. of *anonymus*] **:** the innominate artery

an·o·nym·i·ty \ˌanə'nimədē, -ətē, -i\ *n* -ES **1 :** the quality or state of being anonymous (as through absence or lack of identification, individuality, or personality) **:** ANONYMOUSNESS ⟨made it a rule not to debate important issues with men who . . . hide behind ~ —Norman Thomas⟩ ⟨the vast and kindly ~ of London life —James Hilton⟩ **2 :** someone or something that is anonymous ⟨*anonymities* made "immortal" by their chance mention in a diary or a letter —*New Republic*⟩

anon·y·mous \ə'nänəməs *also* (')a¦n-\ *adj* [LL *anonymus*, fr. Gk *anōnymos*, fr. *an-* + *onoma* name — more at NAME] **1 :** having or giving no name **:** of a name or with the name unknown or unrevealed **:** NAMELESS ⟨an ~ author⟩ ⟨giant corporations responsible to distant ~ owners⟩ ⟨the perfect type of the ~ assistant⟩ ⟨the ~ mass of mankind⟩ **2 a :** of unknown or unnamed source or origin (as authorship, donorship, workmanship) ⟨an ~ book⟩ ⟨~ furniture⟩ ⟨an ~ gift⟩ ⟨a bottle of imported but ~ claret⟩ **b** *of a coin or token* **:** bearing no indication (as name or insignia) of the issuer **3 :** not having or not imparting a sense of clearly marked individuality or personality **:** producing an effect of being without name or identity ⟨a sea of ~ faces⟩ ⟨a district of brown ~ houses —Sinclair Lewis⟩ ⟨its characters are both static and lifeless; they have names but they remain ~ —Bernard De Voto⟩ ⟨an ~ fear, the fear of forces rather than of men —Roger Burlingame⟩ **4 :** reported without the names of the persons involved — **anon·y·mous·ly** *adv* — **anon·y·mous·ness** *n* -ES

anon·y·mun·cule \ə,nänə'məŋ,kyül\ *n* -s [blend of *anonymous* and *homuncule* "homuncle", fr. L *homunculus*] **:** an insignificant anonymous writer

an·o·op·sia \ˌanō'äpsēə\ *or* **anop·sia** \ə'näp-\ *n* -s [NL, fr. ¹*ano-* + *-opsia*] *med* **:** upward strabismus

anoph·e·les \ə'näfə,lēz, -nō-\ *n, cap* [NL, fr. Gk *anōphelēs* useless, hurtful, fr. *an-* + *-ōphelēs* (fr. *ophelos* advantage, help) — more at OPHELIMITY] **:** a genus of mosquitoes that differ from most other mosquitoes in having the palpi slender and nearly as long as the beak, in holding the body and beak in a straight line pointed at the substratum when at rest, and in lacking a caudal breathing siphon in the larva and that includes all the mosquitoes capable of transmitting the malaria parasite to man — compare CULEX

¹anoph·e·line \ə'näfə,līn, -,lən\ *adj* [NL *Anopheles* + E *-ine*] **:** of, involving, or affecting mosquitoes of *Anopheles* or a closely related genus (as *Chagasia*) — compare CULICINE

²anopheline \"\ *n* -s **:** an anopheline mosquito

anoph·e·lism \-fə,lizəm\ *n* -s [NL *Anopheles* + E *-ism*] **:** infestation of a locality with anopheline mosquitoes

an·oph·thal·mia \ˌanəf'thalmēə\ *n* -s [NL, fr. *an-* + *-ophthalmia*] **:** congenital absence of the eyes

an·oph·thal·mos \-məs\ *n* -ES [NL, fr. MGk, without eyes] **1 :** ANOPHTHALMIA **2 :** an individual born without eyes

an·oph·thal·mus \"\ *n, cap* [NL, fr. MGk *anophthalmos* without eyes, fr. Gk *an-* an- + *ophthalmos* eye — more at OPHTHALMIA] **:** a genus of blind cave-inhabiting beetles (family Carabidae) of No. America

an·o·phyte \'anə,fīt\ *n* -s [¹*ano-* + *-phyte*] **:** BRYOPHYTE

an·o·pis·tho·graph·ic \ˌanə,pisthə¦==¦==\ *adj* [*an-* + *opisthographic*] **:** having writing or printing on one side only — **an·o·pis·tho·graph·i·cal·ly** \-ək(ə)lē\ *adv*

anopl- *or* **anoplo-** *comb form* [NL, fr. Gk *anoplos*, fr. *an-* + *-hoplos* (fr. *hoplon* tool, weapon) — more at HOPLITE] **:** unarmed — chiefly in names of zoological taxa ⟨*Anopl*anthus⟩ ⟨*anoplo*cephalic⟩

an·o·pla \'anəplə\ *n pl, cap* [NL, fr. Gk *anoplos*] **:** a class or other division of Nemertea comprising forms in which the mouth is posterior to the brain and the proboscis lacks stylets and including the orders Palaeonemertea and Heteronemertea

ano·pleu·ra \ˌanə'plu̇rə\ *syn of* ANOPLURA

an·op·lo·ceph·a·la \ˌanə(ˌ)plō'sefələ\ *n, cap* [NL, fr. *anopl-* + *-cephala* (fem. of *-cephalus*)] **:** a genus of taenioid tapeworms including certain parasites of horses that may be pathogenic when present in large numbers

an·op·lo·ce·phal·ic \¦==(ˌ)==sə¦falik\ *adj* [*anopl-* + *cephalic*] *zool* **:** lacking hooks on the scolex ⟨~ tapeworms⟩

an·op·lo·ceph·a·lid \¦==(ˌ)='sefələd\ *adj* [NL *Anoplocephalidae*] **:** of or belonging to the Anoplocephalidae

an·op·lo·ce·phal·i·dae \-sə'falə,dē\ *n pl, cap* [NL, fr. *Anoplocephala*, type genus + *-idae*] **:** a family of taenioid tapeworms with unarmed scolices that live as adults in the intestines of various herbivores and pass their larval stages in certain free-living mites

an·op·lo·nem·er·ti·ni \-,nemər'tī,nī\ [NL, fr. *anopl-* + *Nemertini*] *syn of* ANOPLA

an·op·lo·the·ri·um \-'thirēəm\ *n, cap* [NL, fr. *anopl-* + *-therium*] **:** a genus of hornless artiodactyl mammals with a long tail and weak canine teeth that is the type of a family (Anoplotheriidae) of the lower Oligocene of Europe

an·o·plu·ra \ˌanə'plu̇rə\ *n pl, cap* [NL, fr. *anopl-* + *-ura*] **:** an order of Insecta comprising the sucking lice and in some classifications the bird lice — compare MALLOPHAGA; see LOUSE 1a — **an·o·plu·ri·form** \¦==¦plu̇rə,fȯrm\ *adj*

anopsia *var of* ANOOPSIA

anor *abbr* another

an·o·rak \'anə,rak, 'änō,räk\ *n* -s [Greenland Esk *ánoráq*] **:** PARKA

an·or·chism \ə'nȯr,kizəm, a'n-\ *n* -s [NL *anorchus* + E *-ism*] **:** congenital absence of one or both testes

an·or·chous \-kəs\ *adj* [NL *anorchus*, fr. Gk *anorchos*, fr. *an-* + *orchis* testicle — more at ORCHIS] **:** having no testes

an·or·chus \"\ *n, pl* **anorchi** \-,kī\ [NL, fr. *anorchus*, adj.] **:** one without testes or whose testes have not descended

ano·rectal \ˌānō¦-\ *adj* [²*ano-* + *rectal*] **:** of, relating to, or involving both the anus and rectum ⟨~ surgery⟩

¹an·o·rec·tic \ˌanō¦rektik, -nə-\ *or* **an·o·ret·ic** \-¦red·ik\ *adj* [*anorectic* fr. Gk *anorektos* without appetite (fr. *an-* + *orektos* longed for, desired, stretched out, fr. *oregein*) + E *-ic*; *anoretic* alter. of *anorectic*] **1 :** lacking appetite ⟨an ~ patient⟩ **2 :** causing loss of appetite ⟨an ~ drug⟩

²anorectic \¦==¦rektik\ *or* **anoretic** *n* -s **:** an anorectic agent

an·o·rex·ia \-'reksēə\ *n* -s [NL, fr. Gk, fr. *an-* + *orexis* desire, appetite, fr. *oregein* to stretch out, reach after — more at RIGHT] **1 :** loss of appetite esp. when prolonged **2 :** ANOREXIA NERVOSA

anorexia ner·vo·sa \-(ˌ)nər'vōsə, -zə\ *n* [NL, nervous anorexia] **:** pathological loss of appetite from psychic causes typically accompanied by deficiency symptoms, emaciation, and wasting and atrophic changes

¹ano·rex·i·ant \ˌanō'reksēənt, -nə-\ *n* -s [NL *anorexia* + E *-ant*] **:** ANORECTIC

²anorexiant *adj* **:** ANORECTIC 2

ano·rex·i·gen·ic \¦==,reksə¦jenik\ *adj* [NL *anorexia* + E *-genic*] **:** causing loss of appetite ⟨an ~ drug⟩ **:** ANORECTIC 2

an·or·gan·ic \¦an+\ *adj* [*an-* + *organic*] **:** INORGANIC

anor·mal \(')ā¦==\ *adj* [F, fr. ML *anormalis*, fr. L *a-* ²*a-* + LL *normalis* according to rule — more at NORMAL] **:** not normal — used in distinction from the positive emphasis of *abnormal* — **anor·mal·i·ty** \¦ā(ˌ)=¦===\ *n* -ES

an·or·o·gen·ic \¦a,nȯ(ˌ)rō¦jenik\ *also* **an·or·o·ge·net·ic** \¦==(ˌ)=jə¦ned·ik\ *adj* [*an-* + *orogenic, orogenetic*] *geol* **:** free from mountain-making disturbance ⟨an ~ period⟩

an·or·thic \(')a¦nȯrthik, ə'n-\ *adj* [*an-* + *orth-* + *-ic*] *mineralogy* **:** having unequal oblique axes **:** TRICLINIC

an·or·thite \ə'nȯr,thīt\ *n* -s [F, fr. *an-* + Gk *orthos* straight + F *-ite*; fr. its oblique crystals — more at ORTH-] **:** a white, grayish, or reddish mineral consisting of feldspar of oblique triclinic crystallization, composed of calcium aluminum silicate $CaAl_2Si_2O_8$, and occurring in many igneous rocks (hardness 6–6.5, sp. gr. 2.74–2.76) — **an·or·thit·ic** \ˌa(ˌ)nȯr¦thid·ik\ *adj*

anorthite-basalt *n* **:** a rock consisting of a basic variety of basalt with anorthite instead of labradorite

an·or·thi·tite \ə'nȯrthə,tīt\ *n* -s [*anorthite* + *-ite*] **:** a leucocratic differentiation rock of the gabbro family consisting almost entirely of anorthite

an·or·tho·clase \ə'nȯrthə,klās, -āz\ *n* -s [ISV *an-* + *orthoclase*; orig. formed as G *anorthoklase*] **:** a feldspar of chiefly sodium potassium aluminum silicate that is closely related to orthoclase but triclinic

an·or·tho·pia \ˌa(ˌ)nȯr'thōpēə\ *n* -s [NL, fr. *an-* + *orth-* + *-opia*] **:** distorted vision in which straight lines appear bent or curved

an·or·those \ə'nȯr,thōs\ *n* -s [F, fr. *an-* + Gk *orthos* straight] **:** ANORTHOCLASE

an·or·tho·site \-,thə,sīt\ *n* -s [*anorthose* + *-ite*] **:** a granular plutonic igneous rock composed almost exclusively of a soda-lime feldspar (as labradorite) — **an·or·tho·sit·ic** \¦==¦sid·ik\ *adj*

ano·scope \'ānə,skōp\ *n* -s [²*ano-* + *-scope*] **:** an instrument for facilitating visual examination of the anal canal — **anos·co·py** \ā'näskəpē\ *n* -ES

ano·sia \ə'nōzh(ē)ə\ [NL, fr. Gk *anosos* harmless, healthy (fr. *a-* ²*a-* + *nosos* sickness) + NL *-ia*] *syn of* DANAUS

an·os·mat·ic \ˌa(ˌ)näz¦mad·ik, -ˌnəz¦-\ *adj* [*an-* + *osmatic*] **1 :** having the organs of smell rudimentary — used esp. of toothed cetaceans **2 :** lacking the sense of smell

an·os·mia \a'näzmēə, -äs-, a'n-\ *n* -s [NL, fr. *an-* + Gk *osmē* smell (fr. *ozein* to smell) + NL *-ia* — more at ODOR] **:** loss or impairment of the sense of smell — **an·os·mic** \ə'n-, (')a¦n-\ *adj*

an·os·phre·sia \ˌanəs'frēzh(ē)ə, -(ˌ)näs-\ *also* **an·os·phra·sia** \-'frā-\ *n* -s [NL, fr. *an-* + *-osphresia, -osphrasia*] **:** ANOSMIA

an·os·tra·ca \ə'nästrəkə\ *n pl, cap* [NL, fr. *an-* + *-ostraca*] **:** an order of small aquatic crustaceans (subclass Branchiopoda) lacking a carapace, having stalked eyes and 11 to 19 pairs of thoracic appendages, and including *Artemia* and similar freshwater forms — **an·os·tra·can** \-kən\ *adj or n*

¹an·oth·er \ə'nəthə(r), a'n-\ *adj* [ME, fr. *an* + *other*] **1 :** different or distinct from the one first named or considered ⟨the same scene viewed from ~ angle⟩: as **a :** altered or diametrically opposed ⟨it is ~ thing to ask us to affirm the reality of things we know to be illusions —G.F.Kennan⟩ **b :** changed in quality or behavior though the same in substance or identity ⟨a dog asleep was one thing, a dog very much awake and filled with active antagonism was ~ thing altogether —Jack McLaren⟩ ⟨since his illness he has been ~ man⟩ ⟨tomorrow is ~ day⟩ **c :** some other **:** LATER ⟨reserve this for ~ occasion⟩ ⟨~ time don't be so hasty⟩ **d :** FORMER, PAST ⟨the splendors of ~ age⟩ **2 a :** being one more in addition to one or a number of the same kind **:** ADDITIONAL ⟨have ~ slice of cake⟩ ⟨this wall needs ~ coat of paint⟩ ⟨it will take ~ two years to finish the building⟩ **b :** not different or not significantly differing from the first named or considered or from others — used often with *just* ⟨just ~ mishap in a long series of mishaps that day⟩ **c :** patterned after or equal to ⟨he fancies himself as ~ Napoleon⟩ **d :** NEW, FRESH ⟨bring me ~ cup, this one is chipped⟩

²another \"\ *pron* [ME, fr. *another*, adj.] **1 :** an additional one of the same kind **:** one more ⟨one copy to send out, ~ for the files⟩ — often used after *one* and in distinction to *the other* to indicate more than one other ⟨one carried a gun, ~ a knife⟩ **2 :** one other than oneself ⟨living subject to the will of ~⟩ **:** one that is different, separate, or in contrast to the first or present one ⟨peace is one thing but peace with dishonor is ~⟩ — often used reciprocally with *one* esp. of more than two ⟨and they said one to ~⟩; compare ONE ANOTHER **3 :** one of a set or group of unspecified or indefinite things ⟨in one way or ~⟩ ⟨for one reason or ~⟩

another-guess *adj* [earlier *anothergets, anothergates*, fr. ¹*another* + *gates*, gen. of *gate* (way)] *archaic* **:** of another sort ⟨I should behave to him in *another-guess* manner —Henry Fielding⟩

an·ou·ra \ə'nu̇rə, -nau̇-\ [NL, fr. *an-* + *-oura* (var. of *-ura*)] *syn of* SALIENTIA

anourous *var of* ANUROUS

an·o·üs \'anəwəs\ *n, cap* [NL, fr. Gk *anoos, anous* silly, fr. *a-* ²*a-* + *noos, nous* mind] **:** a genus of terns with a short tail and dark plumage found in warm countries — see NODDY 2a

an·o·vu·la·to·ry \(')a¦nōvyələ,tōrē, -näv-\ *adj* [*an-* + *ovulatory*] **:** without ovulation ⟨an ~ menstrual cycle⟩

an·ox·e·mia *also* **an·ox·ae·mia** \ˌa(ˌ)näk'sēmēə\ *n* -s [NL, fr. *an-* + *ox-* + *-emia, -aemia*] **:** a condition of subnormal oxygenation of the arterial blood — called also *anoxic anoxia* — **an·ox·e·mic** *also* **an·ox·ae·mic** \¦==(ˌ)=¦sēmik, -em-\ *adj*

an·ox·ia \a'näksēə, ə'n-\ *n* -s [NL, fr. *an-* + *ox-* + *-ia*] **:** hypoxia esp. of such severity or duration as to result in permanent damage to the affected individual or part

an·ox·ic \(')a¦näksik, ə'n-\ *adj* [NL *anoxia* + E *-ic*] **1 :** of, relating to, or marked by anoxia ⟨a severe ~ state⟩ **2** *of anoxia* **:** caused by inadequate oxygenation of the blood — see ANOXEMIA

an·ox·i·da·tive \(')a¦näksə,dād·iv, ə'n-\ *adj* [*an-* + *oxidative*] **:** not characterized by oxidation

an·ox·y·bi·o·sis \a,näksə,bī'ōsəs, ə'n-\ *n* [NL, fr. *an-* + *oxy-* (oxygen) + *-biosis*] **:** ANAEROBIOSIS

an·ox·y·bi·ot·ic \¦==,=¦äd·ik\ *adj* [*an-* + *oxy-* + *-biotic*] **:** of or relating to anoxybiosis

an·quera \an'kerə, aŋ-\ *n* -s [MexSp] *Southwest* **:** a tailpiece of leather for a stock saddle cut in the form of a crescent and attached to the base of the cantle from which it extends back to cover the rump and flanks of the horse

anr *abbr* another

-ans *pl of* -AN

ans *abbr* answer

ANS *abbr* autograph note signed

an·sa \'ansə\ *n, pl* **an·sae** \-,sē\ [NL, fr. L, handle; akin to MLG *öse* eye for a hook, loop, ON *æs* shoestring hole, Lith *qsà* pot handle, OPruss *ansis* kettle hook] **1 :** part of a celestial body having the appearance of a handle (as the projecting part of Saturn's rings) **2** *anat* **:** a loop or a structure resembling a loop

an·sar \'an,sär, ='=\ *n pl* [Ar *anṣār*, pl. of *nāṣir* helper] *often cap* **:** the citizens of Medina who received and supported Muhammad following the hegira

an·sar·ie \an'sa(a)rēə\ *or* **an·sar·i·yah** \-rē(y)ə\ *n, pl* **ansarie** *or* **ansaries** *or* **ansariyah** *usu cap* [Ar *an-Nuṣayrīyah* the Nusairis] **:** NUSAIRI

an·sate \'an,sāt, -ˌsət\ *or* **an·sat·ed** \-,sād·əd\ *adj* [L *ansatus*, fr. *ansa* + *-atus* -ate, -ated] **:** having a handle or handle-shaped part

ansate cross *n* **:** ANKH

an·sa·tion \an'sāshən\ *n* -s **:** the making or providing of handles

an·schau·ung \'än,shau̇əŋ, -au̇·(ˌ)u̇ŋ\ *n, pl* **an·schau·ung·en** \-ŋən\ *usu cap* [G, fr. MHG *aneschouwunge* contemplation, fr. *aneschouwen* to look at, contemplate (fr. OHG *anascouwōn*, fr *ana* on, at + *scouwōn* to look) + *-unge* (fr. OHG *-unga* -ing) — more at ON, SHOW] **1 :** INTUITION; *specif* **:** sense intuition **2 :** the element in knowledge that is directly given in sense awareness; *also* **:** sense perception or sense presentation **:** apprehension or immediate perception that involves fewest elements of rational thought

an·schluss \'än,shlu̇s\ *n* -ES *often cap* [G, lit., joining (after *anschliessen* to join), fr. *an* on, at (fr. OHG *ana*) + *schluss* closing, fr. MHG *sluz*; akin to OHG *sliozan* to close — more at ON, CLOSE] **:** UNION; *esp* **:** political or economic union of one government or territory with another ⟨some Austrians favored ~ with Germany⟩ ⟨the German-Austrian ~⟩ ⟨New Delhi then strongly protested against this forced ~ of Tibet —*New Republic*⟩ ⟨a campaign to effect an economic ~ of the notoriously jealous twin cities —*Newsweek*⟩

ansd *abbr* answered

anse de pa·nier \'äⁿsdə(ˌ)pàn'yā\ *n* [F, lit., basket handle] *archit* **:** a broadly elliptical or 3-centered curve

an·sel·mi·an \(')an¦selmēən\ *or* **an·sel·mic** \-mik\ *adj, usu cap* [St. *Anselm* of Canterbury †1109 Eng. scholastic philosopher + E *-ian* or *-ic*] **:** of or relating to the scholastic philosopher St. Anselm of Canterbury (1033–1109) ⟨the *Anselmian* logic⟩

an·ser \'an(t)sə(r), 'aan-\ *n, cap* [NL, fr. L, goose — more at GOOSE] **:** a genus of birds (family Anatidae) comprising the typical geese with large strongly serrated bills, rather simple plumage patterns, and comparatively short necks — compare BRANTA; see CHEN

an·ser·es \'==,rēz\ *n pl, cap* [NL, fr. L, pl. of *anser* goose] **:** a suborder of Anseriformes usu. being coextensive with the family Anatidae and including the ducks, geese, swans, and mergansers or in old classifications including most or all of the web-footed swimming birds and ranking as an order

an·ser·i·form \-,rə,fȯrm\ *adj* [NL *Anseriformes*] **:** of or belonging to the Anseriformes

an·ser·i·for·mes \\,===ˈfȯr,mēz\\ *n pl, cap* [NL, fr. *Anser* + *-iformes*] **:** an order of birds comprising the ducks, geese, swans, and mergansers and the screamers — see ANSERES

1an·ser·ine \\ˈ==,rīn, -,rən\\ *adj* [L *anserinus*, fr. *anser* goose + *-inus* -ine — more at GOOSE] **1 a :** of, relating to, or resembling a goose ⟨~ characteristics⟩ **b :** STUPID, SILLY ⟨ridiculous ~ behavior⟩ **2 :** of or belonging to the Anseres ⟨the ~ birds⟩

2an·ser·ine \\ˈ==,rēn, -,rən\\ *also* **an·ser·in** \\-,rən\\ *n* -s [ISV *anser-* (fr. L *anser* goose) + *-ine*] **:** a crystalline base $C_{10}H_{16}N_4O_3$ found in the muscles of birds; methyl-carnosine

anserine skin *n* **:** GOOSE FLESH

an·ser·ous \\ˈ==,rəs\\ *adj* [L *anser* goose + E *-ous*] **:** like a goose **:** STUPID, SILLY — compare 1ANSERINE

an·shan \\ˈän,shän\\ *adj, usu cap* [fr. *Anshan*, Manchuria] **:** of or from the city of Anshan, Manchuria **:** of the kind or style prevalent in Anshan

an·si·form \\ˈan(t)sə,fȯrm, ˈaan-\\ *adj* [L *ansa* handle + E *-iform* — more at ANSA] **:** having a shape like a loop

an·su \\ˈän,sü, -zü\\ *n* -s [Jap *anzu*, prob. fr. Chin *hsing*^{4} *tzu*^{3} apricot, fr. *hsing*^{4} apricot + *tzu*^{3}, diminutive suffix] **1 :** APRICOT 1 **2 :** an apricot (*Prunus armeniaca ansu*) that is native to Korea but is cultivated also in Japan

1an·swer \\ˈan(t)sə(r), ˈaan-,ˈain-,ˈán-\\ *n* -s [ME *answer, andswere*, fr. OE *andswaru* (akin to OFris *ondser*, OS *antswōr*, ON *andsvar*), fr. *and-* against + *-swaru* (fr. the root of OE *swerian* to swear) — more at ANTE-, SWEAR] **1 a :** something spoken or written in reply **:** a response to a question, call, summons, or appeal **:** a rejoinder to a remark, argument, or objection **:** a letter sent in return for one received **:** REPLY ⟨an honest ~ to a fair question⟩ ⟨a soft ~ turns away wrath —Prov 15:1 (RSV)⟩ ⟨I called him but he gave no ~ —Song of Sol 5:6 (RSV)⟩ ⟨sent him five letters without receiving a single ~⟩ **b :** a correct response to a question intended to test knowledge (as one asked as part of an examination or one implied in a topic assigned for discussion) ⟨knew the ~s to only 3 of the 10 questions⟩ **2 a :** a reply to a charge or accusation **:** DEFENSE ⟨at my first ~ no man stood with me —2 Tim 4:16 (AV)⟩ **b** *common law* **:** a counterstatement of facts in a course of pleadings; *esp* **:** the counterstatement made by the defendant in an equity case by way of reply to the charges made by the complainant in his bill — distinguished from *demurrer* **c** *modern statutory law* **:** the defendant's pleading made in either law or equity often including a demurrer or any other pleading whereby an issue is made or tendered by the defendant (as where a statute provides that judgment by default may be entered if no answer is filed) **d** *English law* **:** the plaintiff's reply to a defendant's plea setting up circumstances in defense **3 :** something done or given in response or in return for something else **:** a reply made through action ⟨its publication . . . comes as the ~ to an acute demand —*Survey Graphic*⟩ ⟨the Western ~ to this move was the use of planes to supply food⟩ ⟨his only ~ was to take his hat and walk out⟩; *also* **:** responsive action ⟨received a slap by way of ~⟩ ⟨men from the neighboring villages gathered in ~ to the warning⟩ ⟨in ~ to your request we are sending a catalog⟩ **4 :** a solution of a problem: **a :** a solution resulting from mathematical operation or other similar exercise of the reasoning power ⟨the ~ to a chess problem⟩ ⟨the ~ to a cryptogram⟩ **b :** a solution of any intricate problem **:** explanation of a perplexing or difficult situation offered or accepted as correct and as furnishing a guide to procedure ⟨the world situation is not one to which there is an easy ~ —Dean Acheson⟩ ⟨the search for an ~ to life⟩ **5** *of a fugue* **:** the imitation or exact transposition of the subject by a different voice usu. at the interval of a fifth above or a fourth below

2answer \\"\\ *vb* **answered; answered; answering** \\-s(ə)riŋ\\ **answers** [ME *answeren, andsweren*, fr. OE *andswarian, andswerian*, fr. *andswaru*, n.] *vi* **1 a :** to speak or write in reply to something said or written by another **:** REPLY, RESPOND, REJOIN ⟨too nervous to ~ effectively⟩ ⟨~*ed* well in all his examinations except one⟩ ⟨refused to ~ on grounds of possible self-incrimination⟩ ⟨should give the . . . organizations attacked by him a chance to ~ through public hearings —S.H.Slichter⟩ ⟨think carefully before ~*ing*⟩ **b :** to serve or file an answer (sense 2) **2 a :** to be or make oneself responsible or accountable **:** undertake responsibility **:** give assurance or guaranty — used with *for* ⟨stood ready to ~ for the conduct of his children⟩ ⟨unless immediate reforms are made, we cannot ~ for the consequences⟩ ⟨no one can ~ for the future⟩ **b :** to meet or suffer the consequences of responsibility **:** make amends **:** ATONE, PAY — used with *for* ⟨a crime for which he ~*ed* with his life⟩ ⟨someday you will ~ for this⟩ **3 :** to be in conformity or correspondence in size, shape, position, character, or quality **:** be similar or equivalent **:** CORRESPOND — usu. used with *to* ⟨as in water face ~*s* to face, so the mind of man reflects the man —Prov 27:19 (RSV)⟩ ⟨a result that did not ~ to expectations⟩ ⟨the boundless ocean of prairie vanishing into the far horizon, and above it the ~*ing* disk of sky —Meridel Le Sueur⟩ ⟨~*ed* perfectly to the description we had been given of it⟩ **4 :** to make a responsive sound (as of an echo) **5 :** to act in response to a request, a signal, a controlling action or instrument, or any action performed elsewhere or by another esp. in obedience or sympathy or suitably in return ⟨we rang several times but no one ~*ed*⟩ ⟨if you make the sign of the Man then she will ~ with the sign of the Fox —Lafcadio Hearn⟩ ⟨underground treasures . . . seldom ~ clearly when they are queried by the geologist's instruments —*Time*⟩ ⟨a flashing light ~*ed* on the leading destroyer —Wirt Williams⟩ **6 :** to serve the purpose **:** be adequate or sufficient **:** SERVE, DO ⟨in teaching the young to think hard, any subject will ~ —C.W.Eliot⟩ — often used with *for* ⟨a sofa that was quite often made to ~ for a bed⟩ **7 :** to repeat or imitate a musical theme stated by a preceding voice ⟨the second voice ~*s* in the dominant⟩ ~ *vt* **1 :** to speak or write in response to **:** reply to ⟨~ me when I speak to you⟩ ⟨you have not ~*ed* my question⟩ ⟨wrote him several letters which he did not ~⟩ ⟨a job which he secured by ~*ing* an advertisement⟩; *also* **:** to say or write by way of reply ⟨~*ed* that they would be happy to come⟩ ⟨~*ed* the first thing that came into his head⟩ **2 :** to reply to by way of rebuttal, justification, or satisfactory explanation **:** meet successfully in opposition ⟨an argument that is not easily ~*ed*⟩ ⟨the only faith that can immediately and finally ~ communism —Stephen Spender⟩ **3 :** to reply to (as a charge, accusation, or complaint) in defense **:** make a defense against ⟨was held in bail to ~ a charge of petty larceny⟩ **4 :** to act or be in correspondence to: **a :** to give back in kind or in retaliation **:** return esp. suitably or commensurately ⟨~*ing* blow with blow⟩ ⟨~*ed* the enemy's fire shell for shell⟩ **b :** to correspond or conform to **:** agree with **:** FIT, SUIT ⟨if thy appearance ~ loud report —John Milton⟩ ⟨a man exactly ~*ing* the description broadcast by the police⟩ ⟨all work must ~ the specifications laid down⟩ **c :** to correspond to in position ⟨the subtle antiphonal effects that come from curve ~*ing* curve, angle echoing angle —Hunter Mead⟩ ⟨parts that ~ each other on a blueprint⟩ **5 :** to fulfill, satisfy, or meet (as an obligation, requirement, expectation) ⟨studies day and night to ~ all the debt he owes unto you —Shak.⟩ **:** be sufficient for **:** SERVE ⟨a first-aid kit designed to ~ all common emergencies⟩ ⟨if peace did not serve his purposes, war might ~ them —Francis Hackett⟩ **6 :** to reply favorably to (as a petition) ⟨our prayers were ~*ed*⟩ **7** *obs* **:** to atone or make amends for **:** suffer the consequences of ⟨a grievous fault, and grievously hath Caesar ~*ed* it —Shak.⟩ **8 :** to act in or by way of response to ⟨a word of protest would be ~*ed* by a blow from a scimitar —C.S.Forester⟩ ⟨a call for 1000 bottles of blood was ~*ed* promptly —Irene Kuhn⟩ ⟨the ship was listing heavily and wouldn't ~ her rudder⟩ ⟨three fire companies ~*ed* the alarm⟩ ⟨the phone is ringing but nobody ~*s* it⟩ **9 :** to solve or offer a solution for ⟨can you ~ this riddle⟩ ⟨tried not only to ~ problems but to anticipate them⟩

syn RESPOND, REPLY, REJOIN, RETORT: ANSWER is the most general term of this group and is used without especial suggestion for any action of saying, writing, or doing something called for in return ⟨to *answer* a question⟩ ⟨to *answer* the telephone⟩ It may suggest full or ample return ⟨he could assert, produce arguments, opinions, and information but he couldn't meet or *answer* arguments —Rose Macaulay⟩ RESPOND may suggest a ready, willing, or immediate answering; it is used in connection with various stimuli, ANSWER being more limited ⟨*responding* to that appeal, many men and women went forth into the foreign field —Elmer Davis⟩ ⟨they were all quick to learn and *respond* to ethical values —Frances G. Patton⟩ ⟨*responding* to the threat of death with behavior that is a degradation of the human spirit —*Time*⟩ REPLY may focus attention on the act of answering in the same way, covering the same ground, giving an appropriate return ⟨to *reply* to a charge⟩ ⟨to *reply* to a salute⟩ ⟨"if anything starts, we are lost, sir", observed the first lieutenant again. "I'm perfectly aware of it", *replied* the captain, in a calm tone —Frederick Marryat⟩ ⟨three deep throaty blasts announce the approaching ship, to which the bridge *replies* with a like number of shrill signals —*Amer. Guide Series: Minn.*⟩ REJOIN means merely making an answer but may apply to a sharp or pointed reply to an ill-taken comment ⟨"he can't sleep comfortably on that ship", she said. "In his present state", *rejoined* Andrew, "he might not sleep comfortably anywhere" —L.C.Douglas⟩ RETORT applies to a retaliatory countering answer to some criticism, charge, rebuke, or argument ⟨the plundering soldier in Georgia who *retorted* to Sherman's sermon with "you can't expect all the cardinal virtues for thirteen dollars a month" —D.W. Brogan⟩ ⟨"you wouldn't let me send you a book or two just as a friendly memento?" she cried, incredulous. "I don't take anything from anybody", he *retorted* —S.H.Adams⟩ **syn** see in addition SATISFY

— **answer back :** to reply impertinently **:** RETORT — **answer to the name of :** to have as one's name

an·swer·a·bil·i·ty \\,=s(ə)rəˈbiləd·ē, -ətē, -i\\ *n* -ES **:** the quality or state of being answerable

an·swer·a·ble \\ˈ=s(ə)rəbəl\\ *adj* **1 :** liable to be called to account **:** ACCOUNTABLE, RESPONSIBLE ⟨was no one ~ for the grim despair of that half-starved wretch —Anthony Trollope⟩ ⟨a legislative body politically ~ to the people⟩ **2** *archaic* **:** able to serve a purpose or fill a need: **a :** SUITABLE, FITTING ⟨attended with an ~ train, in rich liveries —Anthony Wood⟩ **b :** EQUAL, EQUIVALENT, ADEQUATE ⟨had the valor of his soldiers been ~, he had reached that year . . . the utmost bounds of Britain —John Milton⟩ **3** *archaic* **:** in conformity **:** ACCORDANT, CORRESPONDING ⟨this revelation . . . was ~ to that of the apostle to the Thessalonians —John Milton⟩; *esp* **:** corresponding in quantity or degree ⟨render your future progress ~ to your past improvement —Joshua Reynolds⟩ **4 :** capable of being answered or refuted **:** admitting a satisfactory answer ⟨an ~ argument⟩ ⟨an interrogation confined to questions supposedly ~ in one word⟩ **syn** see RESPONSIBLE

answered *past of* ANSWER

an·swer·er \\ˈ=s(ə)rə(r)\\ *n* -s **:** one that answers **:** RESPONDENT

answering *pres part of* ANSWER

an·swer·ing·ly \\ˈ=s(ə)riŋlē, -li\\ *adv* [ME, fr. *answering* (pres. part. of *answeren*) + *-ly*] **1 :** in answer **2 :** CORRESPONDINGLY

answering pennant *n* **:** a red and white vertically striped pennant with the fly red used in the International Signal Code primarily for the reply "signal is received and understood"

an·swer·less \\ˈ=sə(r)lės\\ *adj* **:** without an answer: as **a :** giving no answer **:** UNANSWERING **b :** having received no answer **c :** impossible to be answered **:** UNANSWERABLE — **an·swer·less·ly** *adv*

answer print *n* **:** the first print of a motion-picture film in the form intended for release

answers *pl of* ANSWER, *pres 3d sing of* ANSWER

ant \\ˈant, ˈaa-,ˈai- *rarely* ˈá-\\ *n* -s *often attrib* [ME *ante, amete, emete*, fr. OE *ǣmette* (akin to OHG *āmeiza*), fr. *ǣ-* (fr. *of* from, off) + *-mette* cutter; akin to OHG *meizan* to cut — more at OF, MITE] **:** an insect of the family Formicidae (order Hymenoptera) all having a complex social organization, living in colonies with various castes performing special duties, usu. burrowing in the ground or in wood and making chambers and passages in which they store their food and raise their young, the adult males being winged and short-lived, the fertile females usu. temporarily winged, and the remainder of the colony made up of wingless sterile females called workers — compare CASTE, QUEEN; TERMITE, VELVET ANT — **ants in one's pants :** a usu. obvious and excessive eagerness for action **:** RESTLESSNESS, IMPATIENCE

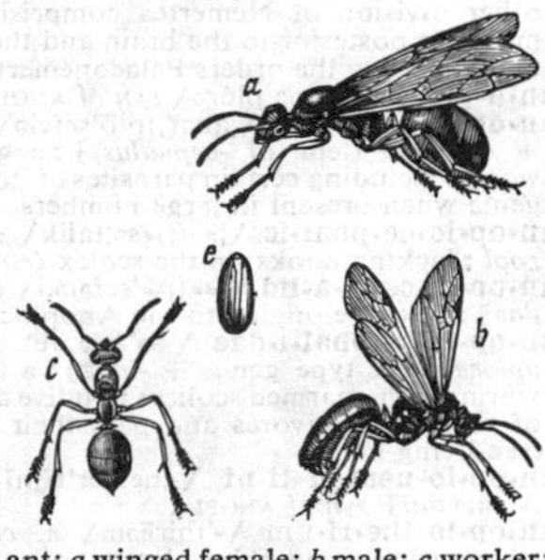

ant: *a* winged female; *b* male; *c* worker; *e* pupa

ant- — see 1ANTI-

1-ant \\ənt, ᵊnt\\ *n suffix* -s [ME, fr. OF, fr. *-ant*, pres. part. suffix, fr. L *-ant-, -ans*, pres. part. suffix of first conjugation, fr. *-a-* (vowel of first conjugation) + *-nt-, -ns*, pres. part. suffix; akin to OE *-nde*, pres. part. suffix, OHG *-nti*, ON *-ndi*, Goth *-nds*, Gk *-nt-, -n*, pres., fut., & aor. part. suffix, Skt *-nt*, pres., fut., & aor. act. part. suffix] **1 a :** one that performs (a specified action) **:** personal or impersonal agent ⟨assist*ant*⟩ ⟨claim*ant*⟩ ⟨cool*ant*⟩ ⟨deodor*ant*⟩ ⟨result*ant*⟩ **b :** thing that promotes (a specified action or process) ⟨expector*ant*⟩ **2 :** person or thing connected with ⟨annuit*ant*⟩ ⟨chemotherapeut*ant*⟩ **3 :** thing that is acted upon (in a specified manner) ⟨inhal*ant*⟩ ⟨ingest*ant*⟩ **4 :** thing that is used (for a specified purpose) ⟨antifogg*ant*⟩

2-ant \\"\\ *adj suffix* [ME, fr. OF, fr. *-ant*, pres. part. suffix] **1 :** performing (a specified action) or being (in a specified condition) ⟨denud*ant*⟩ ⟨propell*ant*⟩ ⟨somnambul*ant*⟩ **2 :** promoting (a specified action or process) ⟨expector*ant*⟩

ant *abbr* **1** antenna **2** anticipated **3** antiquarian; antiquity **4** antonym

1an't \\(ˌ)ant\\ [by contr.] **:** an it **:** if it — compare 2AN 2

2an't *var of* AIN'T

1an·ta \\ˈantə\\ *n, pl* **antas** \\-əz\\ *or* **an·tae** \\-,tē, -,tī\\ [L; akin to ON *önd* anteroom, Skt *ātā* doorframe, Arm dr-*and* doorjamb] **:** a pier produced by thickening a wall at its termination

2an·ta \\", ˈän-\\ *n* -s [Pg, tapir, elk, fr. Sp *anta* elk, modif. of Ar *lamṭ*] **:** TAPIR

3an·ta \\"\\ *n, pl* **anta** \\"\\ *or* **antas** \\-əz\\ *usu cap* [Pg, of AmerInd origin] **1 a :** a Tupian people dwelling west of the lower Tocantins river in northern Brazil — called also *Tapirana* **b :** a member of this people **2 :** the Tupian language of the Anta people

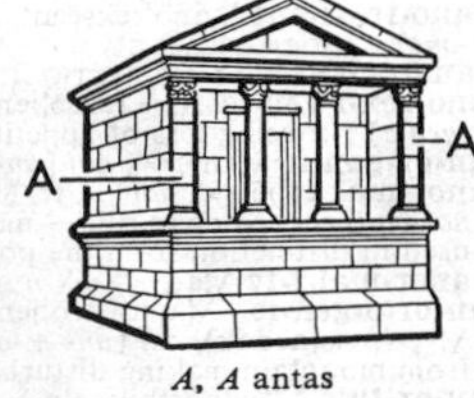

A, A antas

Ant·a·buse \\ˈantə,byüs\\ *trademark* — used for tetraethylthiuram disulfide

an·ta·cea \\anˈtāsēə\\ [NL] *syn of* CHONDRICHTHYES

1ant·ac·id \\(ˈ)ant·ˌ==, (ˈ)aan-, (ˈ)ain-\\ *also* **an·ti·ac·id** \\ˌ=,tī-ˌ==, -,tē-,-,tə-\\ *adj* [1*anti-* + *acid*] **:** counteractive of acidity

2antacid \\"\\ *also* **antiacid** \\"\\ *n* -s **:** an agent that counteracts or neutralizes acidity (as an alkali or absorbent)

antae *pl of* 1ANTA

an·tae·an \\(ˈ)an·ˌtēən\\ *adj, usu cap* [*Antaeus*, a mythical Libyan giant, son of Poseidon and Gaea (earth), who was long invincible because his strength was renewed by contact with the earth (fr. L, fr. Gk *Antaios*) + E *-an*] **:** possessed of superhuman strength with suggestions of earthiness ⟨an ~ figure⟩

an·tag·o·nism \\an·ˈtagə,nizəm, aan-\\ *n* -s [F *antagonisme*, fr. LGk *antagōnisma*, fr. Gk *antagōnizesthai* to contend with — more at ANTAGONIZE] **1 a :** actively expressed opposition, hostility, or antipathy ⟨~ between factions⟩ ⟨a yokel's ~ to city people⟩ **b :** opposition or contrariety of a conflicting activity, cause, or principle ⟨the ~ of democracy to dictatorship⟩ **:** contrariety of conflicting forces or tendencies ⟨alleged ~ between religion and science⟩ **2 :** opposition in physiological action: **a :** contrariety in the effect of contraction of muscles (as the extensors and flexors of a part) **b :** interaction of two or more substances such that the action of any one of them on living cells or tissues is modified (as by interference with the uptake or by an opposing physiological reaction) — opposed to *synergism* **3 :** the sum of the mutual interference between dissimilar organisms occupying or attempting to occupy the same ecological niche **syn** see ENMITY

an·tag·o·nist \\-,nəst\\ *n* -s [LL *antagonista*, fr. Gk *antagōnistēs*, fr. *antagōnizesthai*] **1 a :** one that contends with or opposes another (as in a fight, conflict, or other contest) **:** OPPONENT, ADVERSARY ⟨completely vanquishing his ~⟩ **b :** the principal opponent or foil of the main character in a drama or narrative ⟨the crook was the ~ to the detective hero⟩ — opposed to *protagonist* **2 :** an agent that acts in physiological opposition ⟨contact between a tooth and its ~ in the opposing jaw⟩: as **a :** a muscle that contracts with and limits the action of an agonist with which it is paired **b :** a drug that opposes the action on the organism of another drug by a physiological, chemical, or competitive mechanism

an·tag·o·nis·tic \\ˌ=,=əˌnistik, =ˌ=-, -ēk\\ *also* **an·tag·o·nis·ti·cal** \\-tėkəl, -ēk-\\ *adj* **1 :** characterized by or resulting from antagonism **:** marked by or arising from opposition, hostility, antipathy, or discord ⟨slaves ~ to their master⟩ ⟨~ criticisms⟩ **:** marked by counter tendencies **:** OPPOSING ⟨monopoly and free trade are ~⟩ **2** *of colors* **:** complementary or nearly so **syn** see ADVERSE

an·tag·o·nis·ti·cal·ly \\-ėk(ə)lē, -ēk-, -li\\ *adv* **:** in an antagonistic way **:** with antagonism

antagonistic cooperation *n* **:** the suppression of minor differences by two or more persons or groups to achieve a major common interest

antagonistic symbiosis *n* **:** PARASITISM 2

an·tag·o·nize *or* **an·tag·o·nise** \\an·ˈtagə,nīz, aan-\\ *vb* -ED/-ING/-S [Gk *antagōnizesthai*, fr. *anti-* 1anti- + *agōnizesthai* to struggle, fr. *agōn* contest — more at AGONY] *vt* **1 a** *archaic* **:** to contend with **:** OPPOSE ⟨stormed the castle and *antagonized* the enemy in pitched battle⟩ **b :** COUNTERACT ⟨the coldness of the air *antagonizing* the warmth of the metal⟩ **:** act in opposition to ⟨these effects are *antagonized* by atropine —Ernest Bueding & Harry Most⟩ **2 :** to make antagonistic **:** incur or provoke the hostility of ⟨~ his friends by open criticism of their actions⟩ ~ *vi* **:** to arouse antagonism against oneself ⟨a personality that ~*s* almost immediately⟩ **syn** see CONTEST

antaimerina *usu cap, var of* ANTIMERINA

ant·ambulacral \\ˌant·, ˌaant·+\\ *adj* [1*anti-* + *ambulacral*] **:** situated away from the ambulacral region

an·ta·nan·a·ri·vo \\ˌantə,nanəˌrē(,)vō\\ *adj, usu cap* [fr. *Antananarivo* (Tananarive), Madagascar] **:** TANANARIVE

ant·apex \\(ˈ)=·+\\ *n, pl* **antapexes** *or* **antapices** [1*anti-* + *apex*] **:** the point of the celestial sphere from which the solar system is moving — compare SOLAR APEX

an·ta·ra \\an·ˈtarə\\ *n* -s [AmerSp, fr. Quechua *antára*] **:** a Peruvian panpipe

ant·arc·ta·lian \\ˌant·,ärkˌtālyən, -lēən *also* -n·,tär-\\ *adj, usu cap* [NL *Antarctalia*, the antarctic marine realm (fr. L *antarcticus* antarctic + NL *-alia*) + E *-an*] **:** of, relating to, or being the marine biogeographic realm that comprises all regions south of a line at which mean temperatures approximate 44° F

ant·arctic \\(ˈ)ant·, (ˈ)aant· +ˌ- *also* -n·ˌtä- *or* -n·ˌtá-\\ *adj, often cap* [alter. (influenced by L *antarcticus*) of earlier *antartic*, fr. ME *antartik*, fr. ML *antarticus*, alter. of L *antarcticus*, fr. Gk *antarktikos*, fr. *anti-* 1anti- + *arktikos* arctic] **1 :** opposite to the north pole **:** relating to the south pole or to the region near it **2** *obs* **:** ANTIPODAL, OPPOSED, CONTRADICTORY

ant·arc·ti·ca \\(ˈ)ant·ˈärktėkə, -ˌärt-, -ˌákt-, -ˌát-, -ˌád-- *also* -n·ˌtä *or* -n·ˌtá-\\ *adj, usu cap* [fr. *Antarctica*, the continent, fr. fem. of L *antarcticus*] **:** of or relating to the continent of Antarctica **:** ANTARCTIC

antarctic beech *n* **:** any of various plants of the genus *Nothofagus*; *esp* **:** an evergreen tree (*N. antarctica*) common in rainy regions of extreme southern So. America

antarctic circle *n, often cap A&C* **:** the parallel of latitude that is approximately 66½° south of the equator and that circumscribes the southern frigid zone — see ZONE illustration

ant·arc·to·gae·an *or* **ant·arc·to·ge·an** \\(ˈ)ant·ˌärktəˌjēən *also* -n·ˌtär-\\ *adj, usu cap* [NL *Antarctogaea, Antarctogea*, a biogeographic realm (fr. L *antarcticus* + NL *-o-* + *-gaea, -gea*) + E *-an*] **:** of, relating to, or being a biogeographic realm that comprises New Zealand and the Antarctic continent and islands — compare NOTOGAEAN

antas *pl of* ANTA

ant bear *n* **1 :** a So. American mammal (*Myrmecophaga jubata*) of the order Edentata that is about four feet in length exclusive of the long tail, has long shaggy gray fur with a black breast band and white stripe on the shoulder, and is toothless but has a long slender tongue with which it licks up ants and powerful claws with which it tears up logs and anthills — called also *great anteater, tamanoir;* see ANTEATER **2 :** AARDVARK

ant·bird \\ˈ=,=\\ *n* **:** any of numerous birds believed to feed largely on ants; *esp* **:** a member of the family Formicariidae of the forest regions of tropical America that is small or medium sized, often black-and-white or brown, and of retiring habits — called also *ant thrush*

ant cattle *n pl* **:** plant lice or aphids tended by ants for the sake of their honeydew

ant cow *n* **:** an aphid from which ants obtain honeydew

1an·te \\ˈantē, ˈaan-\\ *adv or prep* [*ante-*] **:** BEFORE

2ante \\"\\ *n* -s **1 :** a poker stake usu. arbitrarily fixed and usu. put up before the deal to build the pot ⟨the dealer called for a dollar ~⟩ **2 :** an amount paid in advance esp. as a share in a joint financial venture **:** amount charged each entrant or participant **:** PRICE ⟨the ~ of these shareholders —*Atlantic*⟩ ⟨considerations that tend to raise the ~ —*Amer. Fabrics*⟩

3ante \\"\\ *vb* **anted; anted; anteing; antes** [2*ante*] *vt* **:** to put up (an ante) **:** PAY, PRODUCE ⟨~*ing* dollar bills for the next hand⟩ — often used with *up* ⟨they *anted* up $1,000,000 to build a pilot plant —*Newsweek*⟩ ⟨~ up ideas in a general conversation —George Biddle⟩ ~ *vi* **:** to pay up — usu. used with *up* ⟨~ up or move into the street —*Time*⟩

an·te- \\ˌantē, ˌaan-, -tə\\ *prefix* [ME, fr. L, fr. *ante* before, in front, in front of; akin to OE *and-, on-* against, OHG *ant-, int-*, ON *and-*, Goth *anda-, and-*, Gk *anti* before, against, Skt *anti* in the presence of, Hitt *hanti* in front — more at END] **1 a :** prior **:** precedent **:** earlier ⟨*ante*nati⟩ ⟨*ante*past⟩ ⟨*ante*type⟩ **b :** anterior ⟨*ante*room⟩ **:** forward ⟨*ante*flexion⟩ ⟨*ante*version⟩ **2 a :** prior to **:** earlier than ⟨*ante*classical⟩ ⟨*ante*natal⟩ ⟨*ante*partum⟩ **b :** in front of ⟨*ante*orbital⟩ ⟨*ante*temple⟩

anteater \\ˈ=,==\\ *n* **1 :** any of several mammals that feed largely or entirely on ants: **a :** any of certain edentates or related animals with the mouth modified for this purpose and having a long narrow snout, a long tongue with which they lick up the insects, and enormously developed salivary glands (as the ant bear, the tamandua, and the pangolins) **b :** ECHIDNA **c :** BANDED ANTEATER **d :** AARDVARK **2 :** ANTBIRD

an·te·bel·lum \\ˌantēˌbeləm, -tė-, ˌaan-\\ *adj* [L *ante bellum* before the war] **:** existing before the war ⟨the four ~ years from 1936 to 1939 —Otto Springer⟩ or esp. the Civil War (1861–65)

an·te·brach·i·al \\ˌantėˌ-, -tē-\\ *or* **an·ti·brach·i·al** \\"\\ *adj* [NL *antebrachium*, *antibrachium* + E *-al*] **:** relating to the antebrachium

an·te·bra·chi·um \\,==ˈ===\\ *or* **an·ti·bra·chi·um** \\"\\ *n, pl* **antebra·chia** *or* **antibrachia** [NL, fr. *ante-*, 2*anti-* + *brachium*] **:** the part of the arm or forelimb between the brachium and the carpus **:** FOREARM

an·te·cab·i·net \\ˈantė,-, -tē-\\ *n* [*ante-* + *cabinet*] **:** an antechamber to a private audience room

antecardium *var of* ANTICARDIUM

an·te·cede \\ˌantəˌsēd, ˌaan-\\ *vb* -ED/-ING/-S [L *antecedere*, fr. *ante-* + *cedere* to go, yield — more at CEDE] *vt* **:** to go before in time or place **:** PRECEDE ⟨thinkers who *anteceded* the rise of capitalism —Sidney Hook⟩ ~ *vi, obs* **:** to come before

an·te·ced·ence \\,==ˈsēdᵊn(t)s\\ *n* -s [L *antecedentia*] **1 :** PRIORITY, PRECEDENCE ⟨the ~ of certain institutions⟩ **2 :** a postulated sequence of erosional and orogenic events resulting in the development of an antecedent river or drainage system

an·te·ced·en·cy \-ᵊnsē, -si\ *n* -ES [L *antecedentia*, neut. pl. of *antecedent-, antecedens*, pres. part. of *antecedere* to go before — more at ANTECEDE] **1 :** the condition of being antecedent **:** PRIORITY **2 antecedencies** *pl* **:** antecedent events

¹an·te·ced·ent \,antə'sēdᵊnt, ,aan-\ *n* -S [ME, fr. ML & L; ML *antecedent-, antecedens* grammatical antecedent, logical antecedent, fr. L *antecedent-, antecedens* logical antecedent, lit., one that goes before, fr. neut. of *antecedent-, antecedens*, pres. part. of *antecedere*] **1 a :** a substantive word, phrase, or clause referred to by a pronoun, typically by a following pronoun (as *John* in "I saw John and spoke to him" or *that he is ill* in "I hear that he is ill and it worries me") **b :** any word or group of words replaced and referred to by a substitute (as *at the meeting* in "I looked for him at the meeting but he wasn't there") **2** *logic* **a** (1) **:** the conditional element in a proposition (as *if A* in the proposition "if A, then B") (2) **:** either premise in a categorical syllogism **b :** the condition upon which truth depends **3 :** the first term of a mathematical ratio (as *a* in the ratio *a* : *b*) **4 a :** an event, condition, situation, circumstance, or complex preceding and often influencing or conditioning an occurrence or issue — usu. used in pl. ⟨~s and consequences of the war⟩ **b antecedents** *pl* **:** the significant events, conditions, principles, traits, or activities of one's earlier life **5 a :** a predecessor in a series; *esp* **:** one that may serve as a model or stimulus for later developments in the series ⟨a stringed instrument believed to be an ~ of the banjo⟩ **b antecedents** *pl* **:** ANCESTORS, FOREFATHERS, PARENTS ⟨of English and Scotch-Irish ~s⟩ **6 a** *in canon and fugue* **:** the subject or opening theme restated by the consequent **b :** a proposing phrase or section of a musical passage as distinguished from the following responding phrase or section **syn** see CAUSE

²antecedent \¦==¦==\ *adj* [ME, fr. L *antecedent-, antecedens*, pres. part. of *antecedere*] **1 :** existing or occurring before in time or order often with consequential effects **:** PRIOR, ANTERIOR, PRECEDING ⟨a synthesis of much ~ thought —H.O. Taylor⟩ ⟨rights ~ to government —*Time*⟩ **2** *logic* **:** prior to investigation, further knowledge, or setting up of conditions **:** a priori **:** PRESUMPTIVE ⟨an ~ probability⟩ **3 :** established before the deformation of a surface and persisting after the deformation has taken place and in spite of it — used of drainage, a stream, or a valley; compare ²CONSEQUENT 5 — **an·te·ced·ent·ly** *adv*

an·te·ce·den·tal \¦==,sē¦dentᵊl\ *adj* **:** of or relating to an antecedent

an·te·ces·sor \'==,sesə(r), -ntē,-\ *n* -S [ME *antecessour*, fr. L *antecessor* — more at ANCESTOR] **1 :** one that goes before (as in office or the possession of property) **:** previous incumbent or owner **:** PREDECESSOR **2** *obs* **:** ANCESTOR, PROGENITOR

an·te·cham·ber \'antē,-, 'aan-, -tə-\ *n* [alter. (influenced by *ante-*) of earlier *antichamber*, fr. F *antichambre*, fr. MF (part trans. of It *anticamera*, fr. *anti-* — fr. L *ante-* ante- — + *camera* room), fr. It *anti-* + MF *chambre* room — more at CHAMBER] **:** a room or foyer placed before and leading into a chief apartment and serving as a waiting room

an·te·chap·el \'==,-\ *n* [*ante-* + *chapel*] **:** a vestibule or anteroom to a chapel

ant·echi·no·mys \,ant-ē'kīnə,mis\ *n, cap* [NL, fr. ¹*anti-* + *Echinomys*] **:** a genus of small insectivorous marsupials (family Dasyuridae) comprising the Australian jerboa pouched mice

ant·echi·nus \-'kīnəs\ *n, cap* [NL, fr. ¹*anti-* + L *echinus* hedgehog, sea urchin — more at ECHINUS] **:** a genus of Australian marsupial mice

an·te·choir \'antē,-, 'aan-, -tə-\ *n* [*ante-* + *choir*] **1 :** a space enclosed or reserved for the clergy and choristers at the entrance to a choir **2 :** the division of a divided choir that is farther away from the sanctuary

an·te·church \'==,=\ *n* [*ante-* + *church*] **:** a portico or narthex at the main entrance of a church

an·te·clyp·e·us \,==-'-\ *n, pl* **anteclyp·ei** [NL, fr. *ante-* + *clypeus*] **:** the lower or anterior portion of the clypeus of certain insects

an·te·col·ic \¦==¦==\ *adj* [*ante-* + *colic*] **:** situated in front of the colon

an·te·com·mun·ion \¦===¦==\ *n, usu cap A&C* [*ante-* + *communion*] **:** the part of the Anglican or Episcopal service of Holy Communion up to or including the prayer for the whole state of Christ's church that is used separately with a blessing when there is no Communion

an·te·con·se·quent \¦==¦===\ *adj* [*ante-* + *consequent*] **:** consequent in the earlier and antecedent in the later stages of erosional history ⟨an ~ river⟩

an·te·con·so·nan·tic \¦==¦==¦==\ *adj* [*ante-* + *consonantic*] **:** immediately preceding a consonant **:** PRECONSONANTAL

an·te·cor·nu \'==-,-\ *n* [NL, fr. *ante-* + *cornu*] **:** the anterior cornu of either lateral ventricle of the brain

an·te·cos·ta \'antə,-, -tē-\ *n, pl* **antecos·tae** *or* **antecostas** [NL, fr. *ante-* + *costa*] **:** the internal ridge that is externally manifested as a groove, that appears near the anterior margin of the typical dorsal or ventral plate of the primitive segment of an arthropod, and that provides attachment for the longitudinal muscles

an·te·cu·bi·tal \¦==¦-\ *adj* [*ante-* + *cubital*] **:** of or relating to the inner or front surface of the forearm

anted *past of* ANTE

¹an·te·date \'antə,dāt, 'aan-, -tē-\ *n* [earlier *antidate*, prob. fr. MF, fr. *anti-* ²*anti-* + *date*] **:** a prior date; *esp* **:** a date assigned to an event or affixed to a document that is earlier than the actual date of the event or document ⟨recognition of prior military service to establish the ~ of seniority in certain civilian categories⟩

²antedate \"\, ,==', *usu* -ad-+V\ *vt* [earlier *antidate*, prob. fr. MF *antidater*, fr. *antidate*, n.] **1 a :** to date (as a check or deed) as of a time prior to that of execution **b :** to assign (an event) to a date prior to that of actual occurrence ⟨archeological discoveries may show that the coming of man to this continent has not been *antedated*⟩ **2 a :** to transfer to an earlier date or period **b :** to cause to occur earlier than expected **:** ACCELERATE **3** *archaic* **:** ANTICIPATE **4 :** to precede in time **:** come before in date ⟨his death *antedated* his brother's⟩

¹an·te·di·lu·vi·an \,antēdə¦lüvēən ¦aan-, -tēd-, -,dī¦-, -vyən\ *also* **an·te·di·lu·vi·al** \-vēəl, -vyəl\ *adj* [*antediluvian* fr. *ante-* + L *diluvium* flood + E *-an; antediluvial* fr. *ante-* + *diluvial* — more at DELUGE] **1 :** of or relating to the period before the Flood described in the Bible ⟨~ man⟩ **2 :** ANTIQUATED **:** made, evolved, or developed a long time ago ⟨an ~ automobile⟩ **syn** see OLD

²antediluvian \"\ *n* -S **1 :** one that lived before the Flood described in the Bible **2 :** one that is very old or behind the times

an·te·don \an'tēdᵊn, -,dän\ *n, cap* [NL, perh. irreg. fr. Gk *Anthēdōn*, nymph associated with the ancient city Anthedon on the northern coast of Boeotia] **:** a large genus of recent and fossil comatulid crinoids having 10 or more arms

an·te·fix \'antə,fiks, -tē-\ *n* -ES [L *antefixum*, fr. neut. of *antefixus*, past part. of *antefigere* to fasten before, fr. *ante-* + *figere* to fasten — more at DIKE] **1** *classical archit* **:** an ornament at the eaves concealing the ends of the joint tiles of the roof **2** *classical archit* **:** an ornament of the cymatium of a classic cornice that is sometimes pierced for the escape of water — **an·te·fix·al** \¦==¦fiksəl\ *adj*

antefix 2

an·te·fixa \,=='fiksə\ *n pl* [L, pl. of *antefixum*] **:** ANTEFIXES

an·te·flex·ion \,=='-\ *n* [ISV *ante-* + *flexion*] **:** a displacement forward of an organ (as the uterus) so that its axis is bent upon itself

an·te·fur·ca \,=='-\ *n, pl* **antefurcae** [NL, fr. *ante-* + *furca*] **:** a forked chitinous process projecting into the thoracic cavity from the sternal wall of the anterior thoracic segment of certain insects — **an·te·fur·cal** \¦==¦-\ *adj*

ant egg *n* **:** one of the white egglike pupae or cocoons of ants that are often dried and sold for food for captive turtles, fish, and birds

an·te·hy·poph·y·sis \,antē,-, -tə-\ *n, pl* **antehypophyses** [NL, fr. *ante-* + *hypophysis*] **:** the anterior lobe of the pituitary gland

anteing *pres part of* ANTE

an·te·ju·ra·men·tum \,antē-, -tə-\ *n, pl* **antejuramenta** [ML, fr. L *ante-* + *juramentum* oath — more at JURAMENT] **:** the preliminary oath required of the accuser and accused in a trial by compurgation

an·te·la·bi·um \,=='-\ *n, pl* **antelabia** [NL, fr. *ante-* + L *labium* lip — more at LIP] **:** the exterior or protruding margin of a lip

an·te·lope \'antᵊl,ōp, 'aan-, -tə,lōp\ *n, pl* **antelope** *or* **antelopes** [ME, fabulous beast represented in heraldic devices, prob. fr. MF *antelop* savage animal with sawlike horns believed to live near the Euphrates, fr. ML *anthalopus*, fr. LGk *antholop-, antholops*] **1 a :** any of various Old World ruminant mammals of the family Bovidae that are esp. abundant in Africa, that differ from the true oxen by lighter racier build, horns directed upward and backward, and great variability in size, and that range from the ox-sized eland to forms scarcely larger than rabbits — see ADDAX, BLACK BUCK, DIK-DIK, GAZELLE **b :** any of various ruminant mammals chiefly of the family Bovidae that in appearance or behavior resemble true antelopes — compare PRONGHORN **2 :** leather made from the hide of an antelope **3 :** DUST 11

antelope brush *or* **antelope bitterbrush** *n* [so called fr. its use as browse] **:** BITTERBRUSH

antelope horn *n* **:** a spreading perennial (*Asclepidora decumbens*) of the family Asclepiadaceae resembling milkweed and having greenish white flowers and curved greenish pods — usu. used in pl.

antelope jack rabbit *n* **:** a very large pale jack rabbit (*Lepus alleni*) of the Arizona and western Mexican deserts having long ears and whitish sides suggesting the antelope's white rump when in motion

antelope squirrel *also* **antelope chipmunk** *n* **:** a small ground squirrel (*Citellus leucurus*) of the western U.S. having a white undersurface of the tail that when displayed over the back suggests the white rump of the American antelope; *also* **:** any of several similar and closely related rodents

an·te·lo·pi·an \¦==¦=pēən\ *or* **an·te·lo·pine** \-pən, -,pīn\ *adj* **:** resembling or relating to antelopes

an·te·lu·can \¦antə¦lükən\ *adj* [L *antelucanus*, fr. *ante-* + *luc-, lux* light + *-anus* -an — more at LIGHT] *archaic* **:** before dawn ⟨~ worship⟩

antemask *var of* ANTIMASQUE

an·te·me·rid·i·an \¦antēmə¦ridēən, -tə-\ *adj* [L *antemeridianus*, fr. *ante-* + *meridianus* of noon — more at MERIDIAN] **:** occurring before noon **:** of or relating to the forenoon ⟨~ chores⟩ ⟨at 9 o'clock ~⟩ — compare ANTE MERIDIEM

an·te me·rid·i·em \-¦ridēəm, -ē,em\ *adj* [L, before noon] **:** being before noon — abbr. *A.M.* or *a.m.*

an·te·mor·tem \-¦mȯrtəm\ *adj* [L] **:** before death ⟨~ diagnosis⟩

an·te·na·tal \¦antē¦-, -tə-\ *adj* [*ante-* + *natal*] **:** of or relating to an unborn child ⟨~ injury⟩ **:** occurring during pregnancy ⟨~ care⟩ — compare INTRANATAL, NEONATAL, POSTNATAL

an·te·na·tus \'=='nād-əs\ *n, pl* **antena·ti** \-ā,tī\ [ML, firstborn son, ancestor, predecessor, fr. L *ante-* + *natus*, past part. of *nasci* to be born — more at NATION] **:** a person born before a certain time or event esp. with reference to the existence of political rights (as a person born in an American colony before the Declaration of Independence) — usu. used in pl. ⟨eligibility of *antenati* to hold office⟩; opposed to *postnatus*

an·te·nave \'antē-, -tə-\ *n* [*ante-* + *nave*] **:** a church porch leading into the nave only or a part of a porch that leads directly into the nave

an·te–ni·cene \¦=='-\ *also* **an·te–ni·cae·an** \¦==¦=¦==\ *adj, usu cap N* [*ante-* + *Nicene, Nicaean*] **:** of or relating to the Christian church or era before the first council of Nicaea (A.D. 325)

an·ten·na \an-'tenə, aan-\ *n, pl* **anten·nae** \-(,)nē *also* -,nī\ *or* **antennas** [ML, fr. L *antemna, antenna* sail yard] **1 :** one of the paired movable sensory appendages of the preoral segments of the head of certain arthropods (two pairs being present in most crustaceans, one in insects and myriapods) consisting typically of basal scape, intermediate pedicel, and elongated multisegmented terminal flagellum, the last often much specialized and bearing numerous sensilla that function chiefly as touch and olfactory receptors — called also *feeler* **2 :** an organ on certain lower invertebrates (as rotifers) that is similar to the antenna of arthropods **3** *pl usu antennas* **:** a usu. metallic device (as a rod, wire, or arrangement of wires) for radiating or receiving radio waves

antennae of insects: *1* setaceous, *2* filiform, *3* moniliform, *4* serrate, *5* pectinate, *6* clavate, *7* capitate, *8* lamellate

antenna array *n* **:** a radio antenna consisting of numerous parallel wires arranged to transmit or receive substantially more in some directions than in others — called also *beam antenna*

antenna circuit *n* **:** the complete electric circuit of which the radio antenna is a part

antennae sword *n* **:** a sword of the late Bronze Age or early Iron Age whose hilt ends in a pair of ornaments suggesting antennae

antenna inductance *n* **1 :** the inductance of an antenna, its value varying at different frequencies as evidenced by the current distribution **2 :** the inductor or loading coil in an antenna circuit

an·ten·nal \(')an¦tenᵊl, (')aan-\ *adj* **:** of or relating to an antenna ⟨~ senses of insects⟩

antennal gland *n* **:** GREEN GLAND

an·ten·nar·ia \,an,te'na(a)rēə\ *n, cap* [NL, fr. ML *antenna* + NL *-aria*; fr. the resemblance of the pappus of the staminate flowers to the antennae of certain insects] **:** a genus of woolly or hoary herbs (family Compositae) that are natives mostly of temperate regions and have small whitish discoid flower heads and a pappus formed of club-shaped bristles — see CAT'S-FOOT

an·ten·na·ri·i·dae \an,tenə'rīə,dē\ *n pl, cap* [NL, fr. *Antennarius*, type genus (fr. ML *antenna* + L *-arius* -ary) + *-idae*; fr. the antennary process on the head] **:** a family of fishes (order Pediculati) that have an elongated somewhat compressed body, a short head deeper than broad, a large nearly vertical mouth with protrusible premaxillaries, rather large pectoral fins with elongated carpal bones forming a wrist, a first dorsal fin consisting of separate spines of which the first is usu. elongated and provided with a membranous flap that projects forward over the mouth and functions as a bait, that scramble about among seaweeds, and that include the frogfishes and sargassum fishes — compare ANGLER

an·ten·na·ry \(')an¦tenərē, -ri\ *adj* **:** of, relating to, or like an antenna **:** bearing antennae

antennary gland *n* **:** GREEN GLAND

antenna switch *n* **:** LIGHTNING SWITCH

an·ten·na·ta \,antə'nād-ə\ *n pl, cap* [NL, fr. ML *antenna* + NL *-ata*] *in some classifications* **:** a primary division of Arthropoda comprising the arthropods with antennae or less broadly the true insects and the myriapods

an·ten·nate \(')an¦tenət, -(,)nāt\ *adj* **:** having antennae

an·ten·ni·fer \an-'tenəfə(r)\ *n* -S [NL, fr. ML *antenna* + NL *-i-* + *-fer*] *zool* **:** the pivotal process that supports the base of an antenna — **an·ten·nif·er·ous** \¦an-,te¦nif(ə)rəs\ *adj*

an·ten·ni·form \an-'tenə,fȯrm\ *adj* **:** shaped like antenna

an·ten·nu·la \an-'tenyələ\ *n, pl* **antennu·lae** \-,lē, -ī\ [NL, dim. of ML *antenna*] **:** ANTENNULE

an·ten·nu·lar \(')an-¦tenyələ(r)\ *or* **an·ten·nu·lary** \-,lerē\ *adj* **:** of, relating to, or bearing antennules

an·ten·nule \an'te(,)nyül\ *n* -S [F, dim. of *antenne* antenna, fr. ML *antenna* — more at ANTENNA] **:** a small antenna or similar appendage; *specif* **:** one of the anterior pair of antennae of crustaceans

an·te·num·ber \'antē,-, -tə-\ *n* [*ante-* + *number*] **:** a number immediately preceding another

an·te·nup·tial \¦==¦-\ *adj* [*ante-* + *nuptial*] **:** preceding marriage ⟨an ~ contract⟩

an·te·o·per·cu·lum \,antēō'pərkyələm\ *also* **an·te·o·per·cle** \-'pərkəl\ *n, pl* **anteopercu·la** \-lə\ *or* **anteoperculums** *also* **anteopercles** [NL *anteoperculum*, fr. *ante-* + *operculum*] **:** PREOPERCLE

an·te·or·bit·al \¦==¦-\ *adj* [*ante-* + *orbital*] *anat* **:** situated in front of the eye or orbit

ante over *sometimes cap A, var of* ANTONY OVER

an·te·pag·ments \¦antē'pagmənts, -tə-\ *or* **an·te·pag·men·ta** \-,pag'mentə\ *n pl* [L *antepagmenta*, pl. of *antepagmentum*, fr. *ante-* + *pag-* (stem of *pangere* to make fast) + *-mentum* -ment — more at FANG] **:** trimmings added to a building esp. on the jambs of a door; *also* **:** a jamb so trimmed

an·te·pal·a·tal \¦==¦-\ *adj* [*ante-* + *palatal*] **:** articulated against the front half of the palate as a whole **:** articulated against the hard palate **:** PALATAL

an·te·par·tum \¦==¦pärd-əm\ *adj* [L *ante partum* before birth, fr. *ante* before + *partum*, acc. of *partus* birth, fr. *partus*, past part. of *parere* to bear offspring — more at ANTE-, PARE] **:** relating to the period before childbirth ⟨~ infection⟩

an·te·past \'antə,past, -tē-\ *n* -S [*ante-* + *-past* (as in *repast*)] *archaic* **:** FORETASTE; *specif* **:** a first course to whet the appetite

an·te·pen·di·um *also* **an·ti·pen·di·um** \,antə'pendēəm, ,antē-\ *n, pl* **antependiums** *or* **antepen·dia** *also* **antipendia** \-dēə\ [ML *antependium*, fr. (assumed) *antependēre* to hang in front, fr. L *ante-* + *pendēre* to hang — more at PENDANT] **:** a hanging for the front of an altar, pulpit, or lectern

an·te·pe·nult \'=='-\ *also* **an·te·pe·nul·ti·ma** \,==-'-\ *n* -S [LL *antepaenultima*, fem. of *antepaenultimus* preceding the next to last, fr. L *ante-* + *paenultimus* next to last — more at PENULTIMATE] **:** the third syllable of a word counting from the end **:** the syllable preceding the next-to-last syllable (as *cu* in *accumulate*)

¹an·te·pe·nul·ti·mate \¦===¦-\ *adj* [*ante* + *penultimate* (after LL *antepaenultimus*)] **1 :** of or relating to an antepenult **2 :** coming before the next to last in any series

²antepenultimate \"\ *n* -S **:** something that is antepenultimate; *specif* **:** an antepenultimate syllable

ant·ep·ir·rhe·ma \(,)ant-,epə'rēmə\ *n* [Gk *antepirrhēma*, fr. *anti-* ¹anti- + *epirrhēma* — more at EPIRRHEMA] **:** a continuation of an epirrhema following an antistrophe

anteport *n* [alter. (influenced by *ante-*) of earlier *antiport*, fr. It *antiporta*, fr. *anti-* ²anti- (fr. L) + *porta* gate, fr. L — more at PORT (gate)] *obs* **:** an outer port, gate, or door

an·te·po·si·tion \'antə,-, -tē-\ *n* [fr. L *anteponere* to place before, after such pairs as L *ponere* to place: E *position* — more at POSITION] **:** the placing of one word or word group before another or esp. before one which by usual usage would precede it (as in *fiddlers three*)

an·te·post \'antə,pōst\ *adj* [*ante-* + *post*] *Brit, of a horse-racing bet* **:** made before the racers' numbers are posted

an·te·predicament \¦==+\ *n* [*ante-* + *predicament*] **:** a prerequisite to a clear understanding of philosophical predicaments or categories (as the definition of equivocal, univocal, and denominative terms) — **an·te·predicamental** \"+\ *adj*

an·te rem \¦ant'ē¦rem, ¦än-\ *or* **ante res** \-¦rās\ *adv* [ML, lit., before the thing] **:** prior in reality or existence to particulars ⟨philosophical disputes over the proposition that universals exist *ante rem*⟩ — see AVICENNISM

an·te·rev·o·lu·tion·ary \¦antē,==¦==,==\ *adj* [*ante-* + *revolutionary*] **:** of or relating to the time before a revolution (as the American Revolution)

ant·er·gic \(')an¦tərjik\ *adj* [¹*anti-* + *-ergic* (as in *synergic*)] *of muscles* **:** ANTAGONISTIC — **ant·er·gism** \'antər,jizəm, an't-\ *n* -S

an·te·ri·ad \an'tirē,ad\ *adv* [*anterior* + *-ad*] **:** toward the anterior part of the body

an·te·ri·or \(')an¦tirē(r), -tēr-, (')aan-\ *adj* [L, comp. of *ante* before — more at ANTE-] **1 a :** situated toward the front **:** before in place — opposed to *posterior* **b :** relating to or situated near or toward the head or in headless animals the end most nearly corresponding **c** *bot* **:** ABAXIAL, INFERIOR **2 a :** before in time **:** ANTECEDENT **b :** logically prior or antecedent **3** *anat* **:** VENTRAL — used in ref. to man because of his upright position — **an·te·ri·or·ly** *adv*

anterior crural nerve *n* **:** FEMORAL NERVE

anterior horn *n* **1 :** either of the ventral gray columns of the spinal cord **2 :** the cornu of the lateral ventricle that curves outward and forward

anterior inferior spine *n* **:** the forward lower projection of the iliac crest

an·te·ri·or·i·ty \(,)an,tirē'ȯrəd-ē\ *n* -ES [prob. fr. F *antériorité*, fr. ML *anterioritat-, anterioritas*, fr. L *anterior* + *-itat-, -itas* -ity] **:** the quality or state of being anterior

anterior lingual gland *n* **:** any of the nonserous or mixed glands near the tip of the tongue secreting mucus

anterior nasal spine *n* **:** the nasal spine formed by the union of processes of the two premaxillaries and projecting upward between the anterior nares

anterior superior iliac spine *or* **anterior superior spine** *n* **:** the forward upper projection of the iliac crest

anterior tibial nerve *n* **:** PERONEAL NERVE

antero- *comb form* [NL, fr. L *anterior*] **:** anterior ⟨*anteroparietal*⟩ **:** anterior and ⟨*anterolateral*⟩ **:** from front to ⟨*anteroposterior*⟩

an·ter·o·grade \'antə(,)rō,-, -,rə-\ *adj* [*antero-* + *grade*] **:** effective for a period immediately following a shock or seizure; *sometimes* **:** effective for and in effect during the period from the seizure to the present — used esp. of amnesia

an·tero·lat·er·al \,==(,)=+\ *adj* [*antero-* + *lateral*] **:** situated or occurring in front and to the side

an·te·room \'antē,-, -tə-, 'aan-\ *n* [*ante-* + *room*] **1 :** a room placed before or forming an entrance to another and often used as a waiting room **2** *Brit* **:** a sitting room in an officers' mess

an·tero·pos·te·ri·or \,antə(,)rō-\ *adj* [*antero-* + *posterior*] **:** concerned with or extending along an axis or a direction from front to back or from anterior to posterior — **an·tero·pos·te·ri·or·ly** *adv*

¹an·tes \'an,tēz\ *n pl* [L] **:** ANTAE

²antes *pl of* ANTE, *pres 3d sing of* ANTE

an·te·script \'antē,skript\ *n* -S [*ante-* + *-script* (as in *postscript*)] **:** a passage (as a note affixed to a letter) written before or above — opposed to *postscript*

an·te·ster·num \,=='-\ *n, pl* **antesterna** [NL, fr. *ante-* + *sternum*] **:** the median underpart of an insect's prothorax

an·te·tem·ple \'==,-\ *n* [*ante-* + *temple*] **:** NARTHEX

an·te·type \'==,-\ *n* [*ante-* + *type*] **:** an earlier type

an·te·ver·sion \,=='-\ *n* -S [*ante-* + *version* (condition of the uterus)] **:** a condition of being anteverted — used esp. of the uterus

an·te·vert \'==,vərt, ,=='=\ *vt* -ED/-ING/-S [L *antevertere*, *anteverti* to come before, prevent, prefer, fr. *ante-* + *vertere* to turn — more at WORTH] **:** to displace (a body organ) so that the whole axis is directed farther forward than normal

an·te·vo·cal·ic \¦==(,)=¦=\ *adj* [*ante-* + *vocalic*] **:** immediately preceding a vowel **:** PREVOCALIC

¹anth- *or* **antho-** *comb form* [L *anth-*, fr. Gk *anth-, antho-*, fr. *anthos* — more at ANTHOLOGY] **1 :** flower ⟨*anthecology*⟩ ⟨*anthocyanin*⟩ **2 :** flowerlike ⟨*Anthozoa*⟩

²anth- — see ¹ANTI-

anth *abbr* anthology

ant heap *n* **:** ANTHILL

ant·he·li·on \(')ant¦hēlyən, (')an¦thē-, -lēən\ *n, pl* **anthe·lia** \-yə,-ēə\ *or* **anthelions** [Gk *anthēlion*, fr. neut. of *anthēlios*, alter. of *antēlios* opposite the sun, fr. *anti-* ¹anti- + *hēlios* sun — more at SOLAR] **:** the brightish white halolike spot appearing occas. on the parhelic circle opposite the sun — called also *antisun, countersun*

anthelix *var of* ANTIHELIX

¹anthel·min·tic \ˌant,helˈmintik, ˌan,thel-\ *also* **anthel·min·thic** \-nthik\ *adj* [¹*anti-* + Gk *helminth-, helmins* worm + E *-ic*] **:** expelling or destroying parasitic worms esp. of the intestine

²anthelmintic \"\ *also* **anthelminthic** \"\ *n* -s **:** an anthelmintic drug

¹an·them \ˈan(t)thəm, ˈaan-\ *n* -s [alter. of ME *antem, antefn,* fr. OE *antefn,* fr. LL *antiphona, antefana,* fr. LGk *antiphōna,* pl. of *antiphōnon,* fr. Gk, neut. of *antiphōnos* concordant, responsive, fr. *anti-* ¹anti- + *-phōnos* (fr. *phōnē* sound, voice) — more at BAN] **1 a :** a psalm or hymn sung antiphonally or responsively **b :** a sacred vocal composition with words usu. from the Scriptures that is usu. sung by a church choir **2 a :** a song or hymn of praise or gladness; *typically* **:** a patriotic song **b :** NATIONAL ANTHEM

²anthem \"\ *vt* -ED/-ING/-S **:** to praise with or as if with an anthem

-an·the·ma \ˌanˈthēmə\ *n comb form, pl* **-anthe·ma·ta** \-ēməd·ə, -em-\ *or* **-anthemas** \-ēməz\ [LL, fr. Gk *-anthēma;* akin to Gk *anthos* flower — more at ANTHOLOGY] **:** eruption **:** rash ⟨*enanthema*⟩

an·the·mi·on \anˈthēmēən, -ē,än\ *n, pl* **anthe·mia** \-ēə\ [Gk, lit., flower, dim. of *anthemon,* fr. *anthos* flower — more at ANTHOLOGY] **:** an ornament consisting of floral or foliated forms arranged in a radiating cluster but always flat (as in relief sculpture or in painting) — called also *honeysuckle ornament*

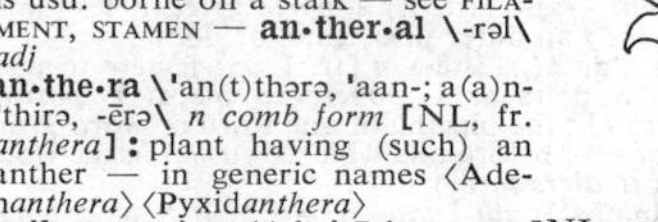
anthemion

an·the·mis \ˈan(t)thəməs\ *n* [NL, fr. L, chamomile, fr. Gk, fr. *anthos*] **1** *cap* **:** a large genus of Old World herbs (family Compositae) with pinnatifid leaves and daisylike heads in which the disk flowers are perfect and the ray flowers pistillate or neutral — see CHAMOMILE **2** -ES **:** the dried flower heads of a common chamomile (*Anthemis nobilis*) used as a bitter tonic and stomachic

-an·the·mum \ˈan(t)thəməm, ˈaan-\ *n comb form* [L, fr. Gk *anthemon* flower, fr. *anthos*] **:** plant having (such) a flower — in generic names ⟨Helianthemum⟩ ⟨Xeranthemum⟩

anthemwise \ˈ==,=\ *adv* [¹*anthem* + *-wise*] **:** ANTIPHONALLY

an·ther \ˈan(t)thə(r), ˈaan-\ *n* -s [NL *anthera,* fr. L, medicine made from flowers, fr. Gk *anthēra,* fr. fem. of *anthēros* flowery, fr. *anthos* flower — more at ANTHOLOGY] **:** the part of the stamen in seed plants that consists of microsporangia, develops and contains pollen, and though sometimes sessile is usu. borne on a stalk — see FILAMENT, STAMEN — **an·ther·al** \-rəl\ *adj*

anthers, *A*

-an·the·ra \ˈan(t)thərə, ˈaan-; a(a)nˈthirə, -ērə\ *n comb form* [NL, fr. *anthera*] **:** plant having (such) an anther — in generic names ⟨Adenanthera⟩ ⟨Pyxidanthera⟩

an·the·raea \ˌan(t)thəˈrēə\ *n, cap* [NL, prob. irreg. fr. Gk *anthēros* flowery] **:** a genus of large moths (family Saturniidae) including the American polyphemus moth and several Asiatic species with larvae that produce silk of high quality — see TUSSAH

anther cell *or* **anther sac** *n* **:** POLLEN SAC

an·ther·i·cum \anˈtherəkəm\ *n, cap* [NL, irreg. fr. Gk *antherikos* asphodel; akin to Gk *athēr* beard of grain — more at ATHEROMA] **:** a genus of mainly African plants (family Liliaceae) with rootstocks like tubers, narrow leaves, and racemes of small white flowers with a rotate perianth

an·ther·id·i·al \ˌan(t)thəˈridēəl\ *adj* [NL *antheridium* + E *-al*] **:** relating to or characterized by an antheridium

antheridial cell *n* **:** a cell that remains after one or more vegetative or prothallial cells are cut off from the microspore and that gives rise to tube and generative cells of the male gametophyte of gymnosperms

an·ther·id·i·o·phore \ˌan(t)thəˈridēə,fō(ə)r\ *n* -s [NL *antheridium* + E *-o-* + *-phore*] **:** a gametophore bearing antheridia only (as in certain mosses and liverworts)

an·ther·id·i·um \-ˈridēəm\ *n, pl* **antherid·ia** \-ēə\ [NL, fr. *anthera* anther + *-idium*] **1** *in cryptogamous plants* **:** the male reproductive organ within which the male sexual cells are organized — compare ANTHEROZOID, SPERM, SPERMATOZOID **2** *in seed plants* **:** a minute structure of only a few cells developed within the microspore or pollen grain

an·ther·less *adj* **:** lacking anthers

-an·ther·ous \ˌan(t)thərəs, ˈaan-\ *adj comb form* [prob. fr. NL *-antherus,* fr. *anthera* anther] **:** having (such) an anther or (such or so many) anthers ⟨decantherous⟩ ⟨phaenantherous⟩

an·ther·o·zo·id \ˌan(t)thərəˈzōəd\ *n* -s [*anther* + *-o-* + *-zoid*] *bot* **:** a motile male gamete **:** SPERMATOZOID — **an·ther·o·zo·i·dal** \-ōdᵊl\ *adj*

anther smut *n* **:** a smut fungus (*Ustilago violacea*) that attacks certain plants of the pink family and forms spores instead of pollen in the anthers

-an·thery \ˈan(t)thərē, ˈaan-,ˈain-, -ri\ *n comb form* -ES **:** possession of anthers, esp. as indicated ⟨phaenanthery⟩

-an·thes \ˈan,thēz, ˈaan-, ˈain-, -n(t),thēz\ *n comb form* [NL, fr. Gk *-anthēs* blooming, flowered, fr. *anthos* flower — more at ANTHOLOGY] **:** plant having (such) a flower — in generic names ⟨Achyranthes⟩ ⟨Polianthes⟩ ⟨Zephyranthes⟩

an·the·sis \anˈthēsəs\ *n, pl* **anthe·ses** \-ē,sēz\ [NL, fr. Gk *anthēsis* bloom, fr. *anthein* to flower (fr. *anthos* flower) + *-sis*] **:** the action or period of opening of a flower **:** full bloom

an·thid·i·um \anˈthidēəm\ *n* [NL, fr. ¹*anth-* + *-idium*] **1** *cap* **:** a genus of solitary bees that use resin as a cement in building their nests **2** *pl* **anthid·ia** \-ēə\ **:** a bee of the genus *Anthidium*

-anthies *pl of* -ANTHY

ant·hill \ˈ=,=\ *n* [ME *ante hil,* fr. *ante* ant + *hil* hill] **1 :** a mound thrown up by ants or by termites in digging their nest **2 :** a community congested with busy people unceasingly on the move ⟨the human ~ —H.G.Wells⟩

an·thine \ˈan,thīn, -,thən\ *adj* [NL *Anthus* + E *-ine*] **:** of or belonging to the genus *Anthus*

antho- — see ¹ANTH-

an·tho·car·pous \ˌan(t)thəˈkärpəs, -(,)thō-\ *adj* [¹*anth-* + *-carpous*] **1 :** having accessory parts ⟨~ fruits⟩ **2 :** composed chiefly of the enlarged and altered perianth or torus ⟨the ~ fruit of the wintergreen and the strawberry⟩

an·tho·cau·lus \ˌ==ˈkȯləs\ *n, pl* **anthocau·li** \-,lī\ [NL, fr. ¹*anth-* + Gk *kaulos* stem] **:** the stalklike basal portion of the zooid in certain solitary corals from which the oral portion is pinched off to form a new zooid

an·thoc·er·os \anˈthäsərəs\ *n, cap* [NL, fr. ¹*anth-* + *-ceros* (fr. Gk *keras* horn) — more at HORN] **:** a genus of liverworts (family Anthocerotaceae) having slender hornlike or awllike 2-valved capsules, the thallus more than one cell thick, and the involucre covering only the base of the sporangium

an·thoc·er·o·ta·ce·ae \an,thäs(ə)rōˈtāsē,ē, -,rə-\ *n pl, cap* [NL, fr. *Anthocerot-, Anthoceros,* type genus + *-aceae*] **:** a family of liverworts (order Anthocerotales) having the gametophyte without definite pores and with irregular or dichotomous lobing or branching

an·thoc·er·o·ta·les \-ˈtā(,)lēz\ *n pl, cap* [NL, fr. *Anthocerot-, Anthoceros* + *-ales*] **:** an order of liverworts (class Hepaticae) having a thalloid gametophyte, green cells with one or occas. two chloroplasts, and rhizoids smooth or punctate

an·thoc·er·ote \anˈthäsə,rōt\ *n* -s [NL *Anthocerotaceae* & *Anthocerotales* & *Anthocerotes*] **:** one of the Anthocerotaceae or of the Anthocerotales or Anthocerotes — **an·thoc·er·o·te·an** \=ˈ=;rōd·ēən\ *adj*

an·thoc·er·o·tes \=,==ˈrōd·(,)ēz\ *n pl, cap* [NL, fr. *Anthocerot-, Anthoceros*] *in some classifications* **:** a class of plants coextensive with the order Anthocerotales

an·tho·co·di·um \ˌan(t)thəˈkōdēəm, -(,)thō-\ *or* **an·tho·co·dia** \-dēə\ *n, pl* **anthoco·dia** \-dēə\ *or* **anthocodi·ae** \-dē,ē\ [NL, fr. ¹*anth-* + *-codium* (fr. Gk *kōdeia* head of a plant)] **:** the free oral end of an anthozoan polyp the basal portion of which is united with other zooids in a common mass

an·tho·cor·i·dae \-ˈkȯrə,dē\ *n pl* [NL, fr. *Anthocoris,* type genus (fr. ¹*anth-* + Gk *koris* bug) + *-idae*] **:** a family of small active bugs including a number predacious on other insects

an·tho·cy·an·i·din \-,sīˈanədən\ *n* -s [ISV ¹*anth-* + *cyanidin*] **:** a plant pigment (as cyanidin, delphinidin, or pelargonidin) formed by the hydrolysis of an anthocyanin and characterized by the same ring structure as the flavones and flavonols but having no ketone group

an·tho·cy·a·nin \-ˈsīənən\ *also* **an·tho·cy·an** \-ˈsīən\ *n* -s [*anthocyanin* fr. *anthocyan* + *-in; anthocyan* fr. ¹*anth-* + Gk *kyanos* dark blue] **:** any of a class of soluble glycoside pigments that are responsible for most of the blue to red colors in leaves, flowers, and other plant parts and differ from the plastid pigments in usu. being dissolved throughout the cell sap, that are reddish in an acid medium and violet or blue in an alkaline medium, and that yield anthocyanidins and sugars on hydrolysis

an·tho·cy·a·thus \-ˈsīəthəs\ *n, pl* **anthocya·thi** \-,thī\ [NL, fr. ¹*anth-* + *cyathus*] **:** the oral disk that is pinched off from the basal portion in some solitary corals (as members of the genus *Fungia*) and that enlarges to become a new zooid

an·tho·di·um \anˈthōdēəm\ *n, pl* **antho·dia** \-dēə\ [NL, fr. Gk *anthōdēs* flowerlike (fr. *anth-* ¹anth- + *-eidēs* -oid) + NL *-ium*] **1 :** the capitulum in plants of the family Compositae, the involucre simulating a calyx and the rays when present resembling petals **2 :** the involucre in the Compositae

an·tho·ecology \ˌan(t)(,)thō+\ *n* -ES [¹*anth-* + *ecology*] **:** the study of flowers as related to their environment

an·thog·ra·phy \anˈthägrəfē\ *n* -ES [¹*anth-* + *-graphy*] **:** the description of flowers

an·thoin·ite \anˈthȯi,nīt\ *n* -s [F, fr. Raymond *Anthoine,* 20th cent. Belgian mining engineer + F *-ite*] **:** a mineral $Al(WO_4)(OH).H_2O$ consisting of a hydrous basic aluminum tungstate

an·tho·log·i·cal \ˌan(t)thəˈläjəkəl, ˌaan-, -ēk-\ *adj* **:** resembling or having the characteristics of an anthology — **an·tho·log·i·cal·ly** \-jək(ə)lē, -ēk-, -li\ *adv*

an·thol·o·gist \anˈthäləjəst, aan-\ *n* -s **:** a maker of an anthology

an·thol·o·gize *or* **an·thol·o·gise** \-,jīz\ *vt* -ED/-ING/-S **1 :** to compile in an anthology **:** treat in an anthology ⟨~ American poetry⟩ **2 :** to publish (as a poem or piece of music) in an anthology ⟨the story has often been *anthologized*⟩

an·thol·o·gy \anˈthäləjē, aan-, -ji\ *n* -ES [NL *anthologia* collection of epigrams, fr. MGk, fr. Gk, flower-gathering, fr. *anthos* flower + *logia, logeia* collecting, fr. *legein* to collect, speak; akin to Skt *andha* herb, soma plant, and perh. to Alb *ëndë* blossom — more at LEGEND] **:** a usu. representative collection of selected literary pieces or passages ⟨an ~ of 19th century poetry⟩ or of selected pieces in any art form (as songs or recordings, paintings, or sculpture) ⟨a huge ~ of paintings, sculpture, and models for architecture⟩; *also* **:** something felt to resemble such a collection ⟨his performance was an ~ of hilarity⟩

an·thol·y·sis \anˈthäləsəs\ *n, pl* **antholy·ses** \-,sēz\ [NL, fr. ¹*anth-* + *-lysis*] **:** a metamorphosis of flower organs in which they become more or less foliaceous

an·tho·ly·za \ˌan(t)thəˈlīzə\ *n* [NL, irreg. fr. ¹*anth-* + Gk *lyssa* rage, rabies; fr. the gaping perianth, felt to resemble the open jaws of a rabid dog — more at LYSSA] **1** *cap* **:** a genus of southern African bulbous plants (family Iridaceae) with sword-shaped leaves and red and yellow flowers in 2-sided spikes **2** -s **:** a plant of the genus *Antholyza*

an·tho·me·du·sae \ˌan(,)thōˈ=(,)=, -(t),thə-\ *n pl, cap* [NL, fr. ¹*anth-* + *medusae* (pl. of *medusa*)] **:** a suborder of Hydroida that is sometimes regarded as a separate order of Hydrozoa and that includes hydrozoans, that has the hydranths and reproductive zooids unprotected by thecae, and that sometimes has medusae which bear the gonads in the manubrium and lack lithocysts — **an·tho·me·du·san** \ˌ=;=(,)==;==\ *adj or n*

¹an·tho·my·iid \ˌan(t)thəˈmīyəd\ *adj* [NL *Anthomyiidae*] **:** of or relating to the Anthomyiidae ⟨an ~ fly⟩

²anthomyiid \"\ *n* -s **:** one of the Anthomyiidae

an·tho·my·ii·dae \ˌ==ˈmīyə,dē\ *n pl, cap* [NL, fr. *Anthomyia,* type genus (fr. ¹*anth-* + *-myia*) + *-idae*] **:** a large family of two-winged flies closely related to the houseflies but usu. distinguished by a bristly abdomen and bristleless pleura and including a number of species of economic importance because of their plant-eating larvae (as the onion maggot, wheat bulb fly, and cabbage maggot)

an·thon·o·mus \anˈthänəməs\ *n, cap* [NL, fr. Gk *anthonomos* feeding on flowers, fr. ¹*anth-* + *-nomos* (fr. *nemein* to pasture) — more at NIMBLE] **:** a large genus of weevils (family Curculionidae) including a number of destructive pests of cultivated plants — see BOLL WEEVIL

anthony over *sometimes cap A, var of* ANTONY OVER

an·thoph·a·gous \(ˈ)anˈthäfəgəs\ *adj* [¹*anth-* + *-phagous*] **:** feeding on flowers ⟨~ larvae —*Biol. Abstracts*⟩

an·thoph·a·gy \-əjē\ *n* -ES [¹*anth-* + *-phagy*] **:** the practice of feeding on flowers

an·thoph·i·la \-ələ\ [NL, fr. ¹*anth-* + *-phila*] *syn of* APOIDEA

an·thoph·i·lous \anˈthäfələs\ *also* **an·tho·phil·i·an** \ˌan(t)thəˈfilēən, -(,)thō-\ *adj* [*anthophilous* ISV ¹*anth-* + *-philous; anthophilian* fr. ¹*anth-* + *-phil* + *-ian*] **1 :** feeding upon or living among flowers ⟨~ insects⟩ **2** [NL *Anthophila* + E *-ous* or *-ian*] **:** of or belonging to the Anthophila

an·thoph·o·ra \anˈthäfərə\ *n, cap* [NL, fr. ¹*anth-* + *-phora*] **:** a genus of solitary wood-boring bees (family Megachilidae)

an·tho·phore \ˈan(t)thə,fō(ə)r\ *n* -s [Gk *anthophoros* flower-bearing, fr. *anth-* ¹anth- + *-phoros* (fr. *pherein* to bear) — more at BEAR (carry)] **:** a stalklike extension of the receptacle on which the pistil and corolla are borne (as in the pinks) — compare GYNOPHORE, STIPE

an·thoph·o·rous \anˈthäfərəs\ *adj* [Gk *anthophoros*] **:** flower-bearing **:** FLORIFEROUS ⟨~ plants⟩

an·tho·phyl·lite \ˌan(,)thōˈfi,līt, -(t),thə-, -ˈthäfə-,\ *n* -s [G *anthophyllit,* fr. NL *anthophyllum* (fr. *anth-* ¹anth- + *-phyllum,* fr. Gk *phyllon* leaf) + G *-it* -ite] **:** an orthorhombic mineral $(Mg,Fe)_7Si_8O_{22}(OH)_2$ of the amphibole group that is often clove brown in color and lamellar or fibrous and is essentially a magnesium ferrous silicate — **an·tho·phyl·lit·ic** \ˌan(,)thōfəˈlidik, (t)thə-\ *adj*

section of pink showing anthophore, *a*

an·thoph·y·ta \anˈthäfəd·ə, ˌan(t)thəˈfīd·ə\ *n pl, cap* [NL, fr. ¹*anth-* + *-phyta*] *in some classifications* **:** a division including all the flowering plants

an·tho·sper·mum \ˌan(,)thōˈspərməm, -(t),thə-\ *n, cap* [NL, fr. ¹*anth-* + *-spermum*] **:** a genus of herbs and shrubs (family Rubiaceae) found in Africa and Madagascar and having small tubular flowers

-an·thous \ˈan(t)thəs, ˈaan-, ˈain-\ *adj comb form* [prob. fr. NL *-anthus,* fr. Gk *anthos* flower — more at ANTHOLOGY] **:** -flowered ⟨gymnanthous⟩ ⟨monanthous⟩ — **-an·thy** \ˌan(t)thē, ˌaan-, ˌain-, -thi\ *n comb form* -ES

an·tho·xan·thin \ˌan(t)thōˈzanthən, -(t),thə-\ *n* -s [¹*anth-* + Gk *xanthos* + E *-in*] **:** any of a group of ivory to yellow or orange crystalline pigments that are similar to anthocyanins in their solubility in plant cell sap but are derived in most cases from flavone or flavonol

an·tho·xan·thum \-thəm\ *n, cap* [NL, fr. *anth-* + *-xanthum* (fr. Gk *xanthos* yellow) — more at XANTHIC] **:** a genus of European grasses (family Poaceae) with contracted panicles, the spikelets consisting of one fertile floret and two sterile glumes below it — see SWEET VERNAL GRASS

an·tho·zoa \ˌan(,)thōˈzōə, -(+),thə-\ *n pl, cap* [NL, fr. ¹*anth-* + *-zoa*] **:** a class of marine coelenterates comprising the corals, sea anemones, and related forms all of which lack medusa generation and are distinguished by polyps with radial partitions or mesenteries projecting from the body wall into the gastrovascular cavity — see ALCYONARIA, ZOANTHARIA — **an·tho·zo·an** \ˌ=(,)=;zōən\ *adj or n* — **an·tho·zo·ic** \-;zōik\ *adj* — **an·tho·zo·on** \ˌ==ˈzō,än, -ən\ *n, pl* **anthozoa**

an·tho·zo·oid \-ˈzō,ȯid\ *n* -s [¹*anth-* + *zooid*] **:** an individual zooid of a compound anthozoan

anthr- *or* **anthra-** *comb form* [ISV *anthracene*] **:** anthracene nucleus ⟨*anthrol*⟩ ⟨*anthragallol*⟩

anthrac- *or* **anthraco-** *comb form* [L *anthrac-,* fr. Gk *anthrak-, anthrako-* charcoal, carbuncle, fr. *anthrak-, anthrax* — more at ANTHRAX] **1 :** coal **:** carbon ⟨*anthracosis*⟩ ⟨*anthracolithic*⟩ ⟨*Anthracosaurus*⟩ **2 :** carbuncle ⟨*anthracnose*⟩ **:** anthrax ⟨*anthracoid*⟩ ⟨*anthracocide*⟩

an·thra·cene \ˈan(t)thrə,sēn, ˈaan-\ *n* -s [ISV *anthrac-* + *-ene*] **:** a crystalline tricyclic hydrocarbon $C_6H_4(CH)_2C_6H_4$ that is white with violet fluorescence when pure and is obtained in the last stages of the distillation of coal tar and used esp. in coatings (as for absorbing ultraviolet light) and as a luminescent material (as in scintillation counters) — see ANTHRAQUINONE; compare STRUCTURAL FORMULA

anthracene

anthracene blue *n, often cap A&B* **:** any of various blue mordant or acid anthraquinone dyes — see DYE table I

anthracene brown *n* **:** ANTHRAGALLOL

anthracene dye *n* **:** any of several mordant azo dyes — see DYE table I

anthracene oil *n* **:** a heavy green oil that distills over from coal tar above 270° C and is the principal source of anthracene, phenanthrene, and carbazole

anthraces *pl of* ANTHRAX

an·thra·cif·er·ous \ˌan(t)thrəˈsif(ə)rəs, ˌaan-\ *adj* [*anthracite* + *-ferous*] **:** containing or yielding anthracite ⟨~ strata⟩

an·thra·cite \ˈan(t)thrə,sīt, ˈaan-\ *or* **anthracite coal** *n* -s [L *anthracites* a kind of bloodstone, fr. Gk *anthrakitēs,* fr. *anthrak-, anthrax* coal + *-itēs* -ite — more at ANTHRAX] **:** a hard compact natural coal of high luster differing from bituminous coal in containing only a small amount of volatile matter and burning with a nearly smokeless flame

ANTHRACITE COAL SIZES AS SORTED IN THE U.S.

Name of size	Will pass through	Will not pass through
Broken	4⅜ in. round mesh	3¼–3 in. round mesh
Egg	3¼–3 " " "	2 7/16 " " "
Stove	2 7/16 " " "	1⅝ " " "
Chestnut	1⅝ " " "	13/16 " " "
Pea	13/16 " " "	9/16 " " "
Buckwheat		
No. 1	9/16 " " "	5/16 " " "
" No. 2 (Rice)	5/16 " " "	3/16 " " "
" No. 3 (Barley)	3/16 " " "	3/32 " " "
" No. 4	3/32 " " "	3/64 " " "
" No. 5	3/64 " " "	

anthracite silt *n* **:** minute particles of anthracite too fine to be used in ordinary combustion

an·thra·cit·ic \ˌ==ˈsid·ik, -itik, -ēk\ *adj* **:** of, belonging to, or resembling anthracite

an·thra·cit·i·za·tion \ˌ==,sīd·əˈzāshən, -ītəˈ-\ *n* -s **:** the natural change of bituminous coal into anthracite by pressure or heat

an·thra·cit·ous \ˈan(t)thrə,sīd·əs, -ītəs, ˈaan-\ *adj* **:** containing anthracite

an·thrac·nose \anˈthrak,nōs\ *n* -s [F, fr. *anthrac-* + *-nose* (fr. Gk *nosos* disease)] **1 :** any of numerous plant diseases caused by imperfect fungi chiefly of the order Melanconiales, characterized by the formation of blisters, lesions like ulcers, or cankers often sunken and dark and with a brownish or purplish margin, and found destructive to important crop plants (as potatoes, melons, and cane fruits) **2 :** BITTER ROT

anthraco- — see ANTHRAC-

an·thrac·o·cide \(ˈ)anˈthrakə,sīd\ *adj* [*anthrac-* + *-cide*] **:** capable of destroying the bacteria of anthrax

an·thra·coid \ˈan(t)thrə,kȯid\ *adj* [ISV *anthrac-* + *-oid*] **1 :** resembling anthrax **2 :** resembling the carbuncle (sense 1) **3 :** resembling charcoal or carbon

an·thra·co·lith·ic \ˌ==kəˈlithik, -(,)kō-\ *adj* [ISV *anthrac-* + *-lithic*] **:** containing anthracite or graphite

an·thra·co·mar·ti \ˌ==(,)=ˈmärd,ī\ *n pl, cap* [NL, fr. *Anthracomartus,* type genus, irreg. fr. *anthrac-*] **:** an order of carboniferous arthropods related to the spiders — **an·thra·co·mar·tian** \ˌ==(,)=ˈmärshən\ *adj or n*

an·thra·co·saur \ˈ==(,)=,sȯ(ə)r\ *n* -s [NL *Anthracosaurus*] **:** a member of *Anthracosaurus* or a closely related genus of labyrinthodonts — **an·thra·co·sau·roid** \ˌ==(,)=ˈsȯ,rȯid\ *n* -s

an·thra·co·sau·rus \ˌ==(,)=ˈsȯrəs\ *n, cap* [NL, fr. *anthrac-* + *-saurus*] **:** a genus of labyrinthodonts from the coal measures of England perhaps in the direct ancestral line of the reptiles

an·thra·co·sil·i·co·sis \ˌ==(,)=,-\ *also* **an·thra·sil·i·co·sis** \ˌ==,-\ *n* \-,sēz\ [NL, fr. *anthrac-* + *silicosis*] **:** massive fibrosis of the lungs marked by shortness of breath from inhalation of carbon and quartz dusts — called also *miner's phthisis*

an·thra·co·sis \ˌan(t)thrəˈkōsəs\ *n, pl* **anthraco·ses** \-,sēz\ [NL, fr. *anthrac-* + *-osis*] **:** a benign deposition of coal dust within the lungs from inhalation of sooty air — compare ANTHRACOSILICOSIS — **an·thra·cot·ic** \ˌ==;käd·ik\ *adj*

an·thra·co·the·ri·um \ˌan(t)thrə(,)kōˈthirēəm, -kə-\ *n, cap* [NL, fr. *anthrac-* + *-therium*] **:** a genus of Tertiary artiodactyl mammals of Asia and Europe related to the pigs but sometimes as large as the rhinoceros

an·thra·fla·vic acid \ˌ==;flāvik-, -av-\ *n* [ISV *anthr-* + *flavic*] **:** a yellow crystalline compound $C_{14}H_6O_2(OH)_2$; 2,6-dihydroxy-anthraquinone

an·thra·fla·vin \ˈ==,flāvən, -av-\ *n* -s [ISV *anthr-* + *flavin*] **:** ANTHRAFLAVIC ACID

anthraflavone GC *n, usu cap* **:** a vat dye — see DYE table I (under *Vat Yellow 2*)

an·thra·gal·lol \-ˈga,lōl, -läl\ *n* -s [ISV *anthr-* + *gallic* + *-ol*] **:** an orange crystalline compound $C_{14}H_5O_2(OH)_3$ used as a brown mordant dye; 1,2,3-trihydroxy-anthraquinone — called also *alizarine brown, anthracene brown;* see DYE table I (under *Mordant Brown 42*)

anthra green B *n, usu cap A&G* **:** a vat dye — see DYE table I (under *Vat Green 9*)

an·thra·lin \ˈan(t)thrələn\ *n* -s [*anthr-* + *-al* + *-in*] **:** a yellowish brown crystalline triphenol $C_{14}H_7(OH)_3$ used in the treatment of skin diseases

an·thran·i·late \anˈthranə,lāt, -lət, ˈan(t)thrə-\ *n* -s [ISV *anthranilic* + *-ate*] **:** a salt or ester of anthranilic acid

an·thra·nil·ic acid \ˌan(t)thrəˈnilik-\ *n* [ISV *anthr-* + *anilic*] **:** a white to pale yellow crystalline acid $NH_2C_6H_4COOH$ orig. obtained by fusing indigo with alkali, now made chiefly from phthalimide, and used as an intermediate in the manufacture of dyes (as indigo), pharmaceuticals, and perfumes; *ortho*-aminobenzoic acid

an·thra·nol \ˈan(t)thrə,nōl, -äl-\ *n* -s [ISV *anthracene* + *-ol*] **:** an unstable brown-yellow alkali-soluble fluorescent solid phenol $C_{14}H_9OH$ formed from anthrone by alkaline treatment and changing to anthrone on standing — called also *9-anthrol*

an·thran·o·yl \anˈthranə,wil\ *n* -s [*anthranilic* + *-o-* + *-yl*] **:** the radical $NH_2C_6H_4CO$— of anthranilic acid; *ortho*-aminobenzoyl

an·thra·pur·pu·rin \ˌan(t)thrəˈpərp(y)ərən\ *n* -s [ISV *anthr-* + *purpurin*] **:** an orange crystalline compound $C_{14}H_5O_2(OH)_3$ found in commercial synthetic alizarin and also made separately; 1,2,7-trihydroxy-anthraquinone

an·thra·qui·none \-kwəˈnōn, -ˈkwi,nōn\ *n* -s [prob. fr. F, fr. *anthr-* + *quinone*] **:** a yellow crystalline diketone $C_6H_4(CO)_2C_6H_4$ obtained by oxidation of anthracene or by reaction of phthalic anhydride with benzene and used esp. in the manufacture of an important class of dyes

anthraquinone dye *n* **:** any of a large class of dyes (as mordant, acid, acetate, and vat dyes) derived from anthraquinone and noted for their fastness — see DYE table I

an·thra·qui·no·nyl \-,kwəˈnō,nil\ *n* -s [*anthraquinone* + *-yl*] **:** either of two univalent radicals $C_{14}H_7O_2$ derived from anthraquinone

an·thra·ru·fin \-ˈrüfən\ *n* -s [ISV *anthr-* + L *rufus* red + ISV *-in*] **:** a yellow crystalline compound $C_{14}H_6O_2(OH)_2$ used in dye manufacture; 1,5-dihydroxy-anthraquinone

anthrasilicosis *var of* ANTHRACOSILICOSIS

an·thrax \ˈan,thraks, ˈaan-\ *n, pl* **an·thra·ces** \-nthrə,sēz\ [ME *antrax* carbuncle, fr. L *anthrax,* fr. Gk, coal, charcoal, carbuncle; perh. akin to Arm *ant'el* glowing coal] **1** *archaic* **:** a carbuncle or malignant pustule **2 :** an infectious disease of warm-blooded animals (as cattle and sheep) caused by a spore-forming bacterium (*Bacillus anthracis*), transmissible from animals to man esp. by the handling of infected animal products (as hair), and characterized by external ulcerating nodules or by lesions in the lungs **3 :** the bacterium causing anthrax (sense 2)

an·thrax·o·lite \an'thraksə,līt\ *n* -s [Gk *anthrax* coal + E *-o-* + *-lite*] **:** a bituminous substance like coal that occurs in veins and masses in sedimentary rocks

an·thrax·y·lon \-sə,län\ *n* -s [NL, blend of Gk *anthrax* and *xylon* wood — more at XYL-] **:** the glossy jet-black constituent of banded bituminous coal including clarain and vitrain

-an·threne \'an,thrēn, 'aan-,'ain-\ *n comb form* -s [ISV *anthracene*] **:** substance related to anthracene ⟨phen*anthrene*⟩ ⟨chol*anthrene*⟩

an·thre·nus \an'thrēnəs\ *n, cap* [NL, irreg. fr. Gk *anthrēnē* hornet, wasp — more at ATHEROMA] **:** a genus of small beetles (family Dermestidae) having hairy larvae very destructive to woolen goods, fur, or other organic materials and including the carpet beetles and small gray and brown museum pests (*A. varius* and *A. musaeorum*) that destroy botanical and zoological specimens

an·thrib·i·dae \an'thribə,dē\ *n pl, cap* [NL, fr. *Anthribus*, type genus + *-idae*] **:** a small family of chiefly tropical short-snouted weevils mostly living and feeding on woody fungi or decaying wood

an·thris·cus \an'thriskəs\ *n, cap* [NL, fr. L, chervil, fr. Gk *anthriskos*; prob. akin to Gk *athēr* beard of grain — more at ATHEROMA] **:** a genus of Eurasian herbs (family Umbelliferae) with finely dissected leaves and short-beaked fruit

an·throne \'an,thrōn, ='=\ *n* -s [ISV *anthr-* + *-one*] **:** a pale yellow alkali-insoluble crystalline ketone $C_{14}H_{10}O$ formed by partial reduction of anthraquinone and used in sulfuric-acid solution as a colorimetric reagent for carbohydrates

anthrop- *or* **anthropo-** *comb form* [L *anthropo-*, fr. Gk *anthrōp-*, *anthrōpo-*, fr. *anthrōpos*, perh. irreg. fr. *andr-*, *anēr* man (male person) + *-ōpos* (fr. *ōps* face) — more at ANDR-, OPTIC] **:** human being ⟨*anthropoid*⟩ ⟨*anthropogenesis*⟩

an·thro·pe·ic \¦an(t)thrə¦pēik, ¦aan-\ *adj* [Gk *anthrōpikos* human, fr. *anthrōp-* anthrop- + *-ikos* -ic] **:** ANTHROPOGENIC

an·throp·ic \an'thräpik, -ēk, aan-\ *also* **an·throp·i·cal** \-əkəl\ *adj* [Gk *anthrōpikos*, fr. *anthrōpos* + *-ikos* -ic, -ical] **:** having to do with mankind or with the period of man's existence on earth ⟨~ gods⟩; *often* **:** ANTHROPOGENIC ⟨~ vegetation⟩

an·thro·pism \'=(t)thrə,pizəm, -(,)thrō-\ *n* -s [*anthrop-* + *-ism*] **:** ANTHROPOCENTRICISM

an·thro·po·cen·tric \¦an(t)thrə,pō¦sentrik, -ēk, -(,)thrō-, -,pə-, ¦aan-\ *adj* [*anthrop-* + *-centric*] **:** centering in man: **a :** considering man to be the central or most significant fact of the universe **b :** assuming man to be the measure of all things **c :** interpreting or regarding the world in terms of human values and experiences — **an·thro·po·cen·tric·al·ly** \-ək(ə)lē, -ēk-, -li\ *adv* — **an·thro·po·cen·tric·i·ty** \,=(,)=(,)='trisəd·ē; -ətē, -i\ *n* -ES

an·thro·po·cen·tri·cism \-'sentrə,sizəm\ *or* **an·thro·po·cen·trism** \-'sen,trizəm\ *n* -s **:** an anthropocentric theory or outlook

an·thro·po·chore \'=(,)=(,)=,kō(ə)r\ *n* -s [*anthrop-* + *-chore*] **:** a plant that is regularly distributed by man whether deliberately (as crop plants) or accidentally (as weeds) — **an·thro·po·cho·rous** \¦=(,)=(,)=¦kōrəs\ *adj*

an·thro·po·dermic \¦=(,)=(,)=¦==\ *adj* [*anthrop-* + *dermic*] **:** consisting of human skin

an·thro·po·gen·e·sis \-'===\ *n, pl* **anthropogene·ses** [NL, fr. *anthrop-* + L *genesis*] **:** the ontogenetic or phylogenetic origin and development of man — **an·thro·po·ge·net·ic** \¦=(,)=(,)==¦==\ *adj*

an·thro·po·gen·ic \¦=(,)=(,)=¦jenik, -ēk\ *adj* [*anthrop-* + *-genic*] **1 :** of or relating to anthropogenesis **2 :** involving the impact of man on nature **:** induced or altered by the presence and activities of man ⟨~ effects on vegetation⟩

an·thro·pog·e·ny \,=(,)='päjənē\ *n* -ES [*anthrop-* + *-geny*] **:** ANTHROPOGENESIS

an·thro·po·ge·og·ra·phy \¦an(t)thrə,pō-, -(,)thrō-, -,pə-, ¦aan-\ *n* -ES [ISV *anthrop-* + *geography*; orig. formed as G *anthropogeographie*] **:** the study of man's geographic distribution — compare ETHNOGEOGRAPHY

an·thro·po·gon·ic \¦=(,)=¦gänik\ *adj* **:** relating to anthropogony

an·thro·pog·o·ny \,=(,)='pägənē\ *n* -ES [*anthrop-* + *-gony*] **:** ANTHROPOGENESIS

an·thro·pog·ra·phy \-'pägrəfē\ *n* -ES [*anthrop-* + *-graphy*] **:** a branch of anthropology dealing with the distribution of the human race in its different divisions as distinguished by physical character, language, institutions, and customs — compare ANTHROPOLOGY, ETHNOGRAPHY

¹an·thro·poid \'an(t)thrə,pȯid, -thrō-, 'aan-; *sometimes* an-'thrō-\ *adj* [Gk *anthrōpoeidēs*, fr. *anthrōp-* anthrop- + *-eidos* -oid] **1 a :** resembling man — used esp. of the apes of the family Pongidae including the gibbons, chimpanzee, orangutan, and gorilla **b :** shaped like a man ⟨~ mummy cases⟩ **2** *anat* **:** like that of an ape ⟨an ~ pelvis⟩ **3 :** resembling or suggesting an ape in ugliness, brute strength, brutality, or lack of perception and appreciation ⟨~ mobsters⟩

²anthropoid \"\ *n* -s **1 :** a person resembling an ape either in stature and gait or in lack of knowledge, perception, and appreciation **2 :** an anthropoid ape

an·thro·poi·dal \¦=='pȯidᵊl\ *adj* **:** resembling or being an anthropoid

an·thro·poi·dea \,=='pȯidēə\ *n pl, cap* [NL, fr. *anthrop-* + *-oidea*] **1 :** the suborder of Primates including the monkeys, apes, and man, all being distinguished from the Lemuroidea by the larger cerebrum, more nearly enclosed orbit with the lachrymal gland opening within it, undivided uterus, and always pectoral mammae **2** *in some classifications* **:** HOMINOIDEA 1 — **an·thro·poi·de·an** \¦=¦=¦dēən\ *adj*

an·thro·pol·a·try \,=='pälə·trē, -tri\ *n* -ES [*anthrop-* + *-latry*] **:** the worship of a human **:** deification of a man

an·thro·po·lith \='thrōpə,lith, -'thrä-, '=(t)thrə-\ *or* **an·thro·po·lite** \-,līt\ *n* -s [ISV *anthrop-* + *-lith*, *-lite*] **:** a petrified human body or portion of it — **an·thro·po·lith·ic** \¦=thrəpə¦lithik\ *or* **an·thro·po·lit·ic** \-¦lid·ik\ *adj*

an·thro·po·log·i·cal \¦an(t)thrəpə¦läjəkəl, (,)thrō-, -,pō-, -ēk-, aan-\ *also* **an·thro·po·log·ic** \-jik, -ēk\ *adj* **:** of or relating to anthropology — **an·thro·po·log·i·cal·ly** \-ək(ə)lē, -li\ *adv*

an·thro·pol·o·gist \,=(,)='päləjəst, -lō-\ *n* -s **:** a specialist in anthropology

an·thro·pol·o·gy \-jē,-ji\ *n* -ES [NL *anthropologia*, fr. *anthrop-* + *-logia* -logy] **1 :** a study of man: as **a :** the study of body and mind and their interrelationships **b :** the study combining human anatomy and physiology **c :** ANTHROPOMETRY **d :** the study considering man's physical character, historical and present geographical distribution, racial classification, group relationships, and cultural history, the latter often limited to primitive stages **2 :** religious teaching about the origin, nature, and destiny of man from the perspective of his relation to God; *specif* **:** the branch of systematic theology dealing with anthropology

an·thro·po·man·cy \'=(,)=(,)=,mansē\ *n* -ES [*anthrop-* + *-mancy*] **:** divination from the entrails of a human being

an·thro·pom·e·ter \,=(,)='päməd·ə(r)\ *n* -s [ISV *anthrop-* + *-meter*] **:** an instrument used for making anthropometric measurements and consisting of four hollow graduated tubes that fit into one another to form a rigid rod

an·thro·po·met·ric \¦=(,)=(,)=¦me·trik, -ēk\ *also* **an·thro·po·met·ri·cal** \-rəkəl, -ēk-\ *adj* **:** involving or based on anthropometry ⟨~ examination⟩ — **an·thro·po·met·ri·cal·ly** \-rək(ə)lē, -li, -ēk-\ *adv*

an·thro·pom·e·trist \,=(,)='pämə·trəst\ *n* -s **:** a specialist in anthropometry

an·thro·pom·e·try \-mətrē\ *n* -ES [F *anthropométrie*, fr. *anthrop-* + *-métrie* -metry] **:** the science of measuring the human body and its parts and functional capacities esp. as an aid to the study of human evolution and variation

an·thro·po·morph \'an(t)thrəpə,mȯrf, -(,)thrō-, -(,)pō-, 'aan-\ *n* -s [LL *anthropomorphus* of human shape — more at ANTHROPOMORPHOUS] **1 :** a representation of the human figure — used esp. of conventionalized primitive art **2** [NL *Anthropomorpha*] **:** a member of the Anthropomorpha

an·thro·po·mor·pha \,=(,)=(,)='mȯrfə\ *n pl, cap* [NL, fr. Gk *anthrōpomorpha*, neut. pl. of *anthrōpomorphos* of human form] *in some former classifications* **:** a group of primates comprising the anthropoid apes and being equivalent to the family Pongidae; *broadly* **:** HOMINOIDEA 2

an·thro·po·morph·ic \¦=(,)=(,)=¦mȯrfik, -ēk\ *also* **an·thro·po·morph·i·cal** \-fəkəl, -ēk-\ *adj* [LL *anthropomorphus* + E *-ic*, *-ical*] **1 :** described or thought of as having human form or attributes **:** represented with human characteristics or under a human form **:** ascribing human characteristics to nonhuman things **:** crudely human or man-centered in character ⟨an ~ concept of God⟩ ⟨~ figurines⟩ ⟨crude ~ supernaturalism⟩ ⟨~ terms used in describing the activities of ants⟩ ⟨an ~ picture of the universe⟩ **2 :** derived from or having a human form ⟨an ~ monument⟩ ⟨geometric, zoomorphic, and ~ ornament⟩ — **an·thro·po·morph·i·cal·ly** \-fək(ə)lē, -li, -ēk-\ *adv*

an·thro·po·morph·i·dae \-fə,dē\ *n pl, cap* [NL, fr. *Anthropomorpha*, type genus (fr. LL, of human shape) + *-idae*] *syn of* PONGIDAE

an·thro·po·morph·ism \-,fizəm\ *n* -s [LL *anthropomorphus* + E *-ism*] **:** an interpretation of what is not human or personal in terms of human or personal characteristics **:** HUMANIZATION ⟨the language of ~ in saying that God sees, hears, knows, and loves⟩ **:** ANTHROPOCENTRICISM ⟨when a scientist speaks of force, he uses an ~ drawn from the act of will —W.L.Sullivan⟩ **:** PERSONIFICATION ⟨more of this ~: ". . . this was the mountain's first joyous cry as it awoke" —Joseph Braddock⟩

an·thro·po·morph·ist \-fəst\ *n* -s **:** a believer in anthropomorphism — **an·thro·po·mor·phis·tic** \¦=(,)=(,)=,=¦fistik, -ēk\ *adj*

an·thro·po·mor·phite \,=(,)=(,)='mȯr,fīt\ *n* -s [LL *anthropomorphita*, fr. LGk *anthrōpomorphitēs*, fr. *anthrōpomorphos* + *-itēs* -ite] **:** ANTHROPOMORPHIST

an·thro·po·mor·phi·za·tion \-,mȯrfə'zāshən\ *n* -s **:** the act or process of anthropomorphizing

an·thro·po·mor·phize *or* **an·thro·po·mor·phise** \-'mȯr,fīz\ *vb* -ED/-ING/-S [*anthropomorphous* + *-ize*, *-ise*] *vt* **:** to attribute a human form or personality to (as an animal or inanimate object) ⟨children ~ cats —Elmer Davis⟩ **~** *vi* **:** to attribute human form or personality to animals or things

an·thro·po·mor·phol·o·gy \-,mȯr'fäləjē, -ji\ *n* -ES [*anthropo-* + *morphology*] **:** the use of anthropomorphic language esp. in application to God or a god

an·thro·po·mor·pho·sis \-'mȯrfəsəs *sometimes* -,mȯr'fō-\ *n, pl* **anthropomorpho·ses** \-,sēz\ [*anthropomorphic* + *-osis* (as in *metamorphosis*)] **:** metamorphosis into human form

an·thro·po·mor·phous \¦=(,)=(,)=¦mȯrfəs\ *adj* [LL *anthropomorphus*, fr. Gk *anthrōpomorphos*, fr. *anthrōp-* + *-morphos* -morphous] **:** ANTHROPOMORPHIC — **an·thro·po·mor·phous·ly** *adv*

an·thro·pon·y·my \,an(t)thrə'pänəmē, -(,)thrō-, ,aan-\ *n* -ES [ISV *anthrop-* + *-onymy*] **:** a branch of onomastics that consists of the study of personal names

an·thro·po·path·ic \¦=(,)=¦pathik, -,pə¦p-, -ēk\ *adj* [*anthrop-* + *-pathic*] **:** ascribing human feelings to something that is not human ⟨~ writing⟩ — **an·thro·po·path·i·cal·ly** \-thək(ə)lē, -li, -ēk-\ *adv*

an·thro·pop·a·thism \,=(,)='päpə,thizəm\ *n* -s [*anthropopathy* + *-ism*] **:** the ascription of human feelings to something that is not human

an·thro·pop·a·thite \-'päpə,thīt\ *n* -s [*anthropopathy* + *-ite*] **:** one who ascribes human feelings to something not human

an·thro·pop·a·thy \-'päpəthē\ *n* -ES [LGk *anthrōpopatheia* humanity, possession of human feelings, fr. Gk *anthrōpopathēs* having human feelings (fr. *anthrōp-* anthrop- + *-pathēs* -path) + *-ia*] **:** ANTHROPOPATHISM

an·thro·poph·a·gite \-'päfə,jīt\ *n* -s [NL *anthropophagus* + E *-ite*] **:** CANNIBAL 1

an·thro·poph·a·gous \¦=¦päfəgəs\ *adj* [L *anthropophagus*] **:** feeding on human flesh **:** man-eating **:** CANNIBAL — **an·thro·poph·a·gous·ly** *adv*

an·thro·poph·a·gus \"\ *n, pl* **anthropopha·gi** \-ə,jī\ [L, adj. & n., fr. Gk *anthrōpophagos*, fr. *anthrōp-* anthrop- + *-phagos* -phagous] **:** MAN-EATER, CANNIBAL

an·thro·poph·a·gy \-'päfəjē\ *n* -ES [LL *anthropophagia*, fr. Gk *anthrōpophagia*, fr. *anthrōpophagos* + *-ia*] **:** the eating by man of human flesh **:** CANNIBALISM

an·thro·po·phil·ic \¦an(t)thrə,pō¦filik, -ēk, -(,)thrō-, -,pə-, ¦aan-\ *also* **an·thro·poph·i·lous** \¦=(,)=¦päfələs\ *adj* [*anthrop-* + *-philic*, *-philous*] **:** attracted to man esp. as a source of food ⟨~ mosquitoes⟩; *sometimes* **:** indicating relative attraction to man ⟨~ indices of certain forest insects⟩ — **an·thro·poph·i·lism** \-'päfə,lizəm\ *n* -s

an·thro·poph·u·ism \,=(,)='päfyü,izəm\ *n* -s [irreg. fr. *anthrop-* + Gk *phyē* growth, nature, character (fr. *phyein* to bring forth, arise) + E *-ism* — more at BE] **:** ascription of human nature to God or a god — **an·thro·poph·u·is·tic** \¦=(,)=,==¦istik\ *adj*

¹an·thro·po·pi·the·cus \,an(t)thrə,pōpə'thēkəs, ,aan-, -'pithikəs\ [NL, fr. *anthrop-* + *-pithecus*] *syn of* ⁷PAN

²anthropopithecus \"\ *n, pl* **anthropopithe·ci** \-,sī\ *sometimes cap* [NL, fr. *anthrop-* + *-pithecus*] **:** a hypothetical mammal or group of mammals intermediate in character between man and apes

an·thro·po·psy·chic \¦=(,)=¦=¦-\ *adj* [*anthrop-* + *psychic*] **:** relating to anthropopsychism — **an·thro·po·psy·chi·cal·ly** *adv*

an·thro·po·psy·chism \,=(,)=¦='-\ *n* -s [*anthrop-* + *psychism*] **:** ascription of a soul like that of man to nature or to something that governs natural processes

an·thro·po·scop·ic \¦=(,)=¦skäpik\ *adj* **:** involving or based on anthroposcopy ⟨~ method⟩ — **an·thro·po·scop·i·cal·ly** \-ək(ə)lē, -li\ *adv*

an·thro·pos·co·py \,=(,)='päskəpē\ *n* -ES [*anthrop-* + *-scopy*] **:** determination of human bodily characteristics by inspection as opposed to exact measurements — compare ANTHROPOMETRY

an·thro·po·so·ci·ol·o·gy \¦an(t)thrə,pō-, -thrō-, ¦aan-\ *n* -ES [*anthrop-* + *sociology*] **:** the sociological study of race by anthropological methods (as in the theories of Lapouge) as a means of establishing the social superiority of dolichocephalic peoples

an·thro·po·soph·i·cal \-¦säfəkəl\ *also* **an·thro·po·soph·ic** \-fik\ *adj* **:** relating to anthroposophy

an·thro·pos·o·phy \,=='päsəfē\ *n* -ES [*anthrop-* + *-sophy*] **1 a :** knowledge of the nature of man **b :** human wisdom **2 :** a spiritual and mystical doctrine that grew out of theosophy and derives mainly from the philosophy of Rudolf Steiner, Austrian social philosopher (1861–1925)

an·thro·po·the·ism \,an(t)thrə,pō'-, -thrō-, -,pə-, ,aan-\ *n* -s [*anthrop-* + *-theism*] **:** the doctrine that the gods originated as men or are essentially human in their nature

an·thro·po·tom·i·cal \¦=¦tämək əl\ *adj* **:** relating to anthropotomy

an·thro·pot·o·mist \,=(,)='päd·əməst\ *n* -s **:** a specialist in anthropotomy **:** ANATOMIST

an·thro·pot·o·my \-'päd·əmē\ *n* -ES [*anthrop-* + *anatomy*] **:** anatomy of the human body

-an·thro·pus \'an(t)thrəpəs, ,an'thrōpəs, -aan-,-ain-\ *n comb form* [NL, fr. Gk *anthrōpos* — more at ANTHROP-] **:** man — in generic names of primates ⟨Pithec*anthropus*⟩ ⟨Sin*anthropus*⟩

an·thryl \'an,thril, -ēl\ *n* -s [ISV *anthr-* + *-yl*] **:** any of three univalent radicals $C_{14}H_9$ derived from anthracene

an·thry·lene \'an(t)thrə,lēn\ *n* -s [*anthryl* + *-ene*] **:** any of several bivalent radicals $C_{14}H_8$ derived from anthracene

an·thu·ri·um \an'thyürēəm\ *n* [NL, fr. ¹*anth-* + *-urium* (fr. Gk *oura* tail); akin to Gk *orrhos* backside — more at ASS] **1** *cap* **:** a genus of tropical American plants (family Araceae) with large often highly colored leaves, a cylindrical spadix, and a colored spathe **2** -s **:** a plant of the genus *Anthurium*

an·thus \'an(t)thəs\ *n, cap* [NL, fr. L, a bird, prob. the yellow wagtail, fr. Gk *anthos*] **:** a genus of singing birds (family Motacillidae) comprising the typical pipits

-an·thus \'an(t)thəs, 'aan-,'ain-\ *n comb form* [NL, fr. Gk *anthos* flower — more at ANTHOLOGY] **:** organism having or resembling (such) a flower — in generic names in botany ⟨Cycl*anthus*⟩ ⟨Schiz*anthus*⟩ and zoology ⟨Oec*anthus*⟩

-anthy — see -ANTHOUS

an·thyl·lis \an'thiləs\ *n, cap* [NL, fr. L, a plant, fr. Gk] **:** a genus of Old World plants (family Leguminosae) with often yellowish red flowers and a pod enclosed in the calyx — see KIDNEY VETCH

¹an·ti \'an,tī, -,tē, 'aan-,'ain-\ *n* -s [¹*anti-*] **:** one who is opposed (as to a practice, law, policy, or movement) ⟨the division of the country into pros and ~s —*Atlantic*⟩

²anti \"\ *adj* [¹*anti-*] **1 :** opposed esp. to a proposal or policy ⟨the ~ group⟩ **2 :** TRANS — opposed to *syn*; compare ¹ANTI- 7

³anti \"\ *prep* [¹*anti-*] **:** in opposition or enmity to **:** AGAINST ⟨he has always been ~ sales tax⟩

⁴an·ti \'än(,)tē\ *n, pl* **anti** *or* **antis** *usu cap* [Sp, of AmerInd origin] **:** CAMPA

¹an·ti- *in pronunciations below*, ¦=(,)= = ¦an,tī *or* ¦an,tē *or* ¦antə (-tə *occurring chiefly before consonants*) *or* ¦aan- *or* ¦ain-\ *or* **ant-** *or* **anth-** *prefix* [*anti-* fr. ME, fr. OF & L; OF, fr. L, against, fr. Gk, fr. *anti*; *ant-* fr. ME, fr. L, against, fr. Gk, fr. *anti*; *anth-* fr. L, against, fr. Gk, fr. *anti* — more at ANTE-] **1 a :** one opposing the claims of **:** rival **:** spurious ⟨*anti*christ⟩ ⟨*anti*king⟩ ⟨*anti*pope⟩ **b :** of the same kind but situated opposite, exerting energy in the opposite direction, or pursuing an opposite policy ⟨*ant*apex⟩ ⟨*ant*arctic⟩ ⟨*anti*cline⟩ ⟨*anti*school⟩ ⟨*anti*volition⟩ **c :** one that is opposite in kind to ⟨*anti*climax⟩ ⟨*anti*hero⟩ ⟨*anti*religion⟩ — *anti-* before consonants other than *h* and sometimes *ant-* before vowels and *anth-* before *h* (which is not repeated), but more frequently *anti-* even before *h* or a vowel **2 a :** opposing or hostile to in opinion, sympathy, or practice ⟨*anti*capitalist⟩ ⟨*anti*democratic⟩ ⟨*anti*romantic⟩ ⟨*anti*slavery⟩ ⟨*anti*union⟩ **b :** opposing in effect or activity **:** inhibiting **:** preventing **:** counteracting ⟨*ant*acid⟩ ⟨*anth*elmintic⟩ ⟨*anti*aging⟩ ⟨*anti*-Comintern⟩ ⟨*anti*enzyme⟩ ⟨*anti*fat⟩ ⟨*anti*fogging⟩ ⟨*anti*-inflationary⟩ ⟨*anti*slip⟩ ⟨*anti*trust⟩ **3 :** not ⟨*anti*grammatical⟩ ⟨*anti*logical⟩ **4 :** serving to prevent, cure, or alleviate (a pathological condition) ⟨*anti*arthritic⟩ ⟨*anti*spasmodic⟩ **5 a :** combating or neutralizing another substance ⟨*anti*body⟩ ⟨*anti*serum⟩ **b :** substance that opposes or neutralizes (another substance); *esp* **:** substance that is an antibody to (a specified antigen) ⟨*anti*toxin⟩ **6 :** combating **:** destroying **:** defending against ⟨*anti*aircraft⟩ ⟨*anti*mine⟩ ⟨*anti*tank⟩ **7** *anti-* **:** TRANS- 3 — esp. in names of chemical structures in which the opposed atoms or groups are attached to carbon-to-nitrogen or nitrogen-to-nitrogen double bonds ⟨sodium *anti*-benzene-diazoate⟩; opposed to *syn-*; see BENZALDOXIME

²anti- *prefix* [MF & ML, fr. L *ante-*] **:** ANTE- — now little used because of possible confusion with ¹*anti-*

antiacid *var of* ANTACID

an·ti·air \¦=(,)= *at* ¹ANTI- + ¦=\ *adj* [by shortening] **:** ¹ANTIAIRCRAFT

an·ti·alien \¦=(,)=¦-\ *adj* [¹*anti-* + *alien*] **:** opposed or hostile to aliens

¹an·ti·air·craft \¦=(,)=¦-\ *adj* [¹*anti-* + *aircraft*] **:** designed for or concerned with defense against air attack ⟨~ battery⟩ ⟨~ shell⟩ ⟨~ training⟩

²antiaircraft \"\ *n* -s **1 :** an antiaircraft weapon or weapons **2 :** the organizations that serve antiaircraft weapons, lights, and pointing devices **3 :** the flight and burst of antiaircraft shells

an·ti·air·craft·er \¦=(,)=¦=,=ə(r)\ *n* -s **:** ANTIAIRCRAFTSMAN

an·ti·air·crafts·man \¦=(,)=¦=,smən\ *n* **:** a member of an antiaircraft unit

an·ti·al·co·hol·ism \¦=(,)=¦=-\ *n* -s [¹*anti-* + *alcohol* + *-ism*] **:** opposition to immoderate use of alcohol

an·ti·an·a·phy·lax·is \¦=(,)=,-\ *n, pl* **antianaphylax·es** [NL, fr. ¹*anti-* + NL *anaphylaxis*] **1 :** a condition in which an anaphylactic reaction is not obtained because of the presence of free antibodies in the blood **2 :** the state of desensitization to an antigen

an·ti·a·ne·mic \¦=(,)==¦=\ *adj* [¹*anti-* + *anemic*] **:** effective in or relating to the prevention or correction of anemia ⟨~ agent⟩ ⟨~ potency⟩

antianemic factor *or* **antianemic principle** *n* **:** a substance having antianemic activity; *esp* **:** VITAMIN B_{12}

an·ti·ar \'antē,är\ *n* -s [Jav *antjar* upas tree] **1 :** a poisonous gum resin from the upas tree **2 :** an arrow poison prepared from antiar

an·ti·arch \'antē,ärk\ *n* -s [NL *Antiarcha*] **:** one of the Antiarcha

an·ti·ar·cha \,=='ärkə\ *n pl, cap* [NL, fr. ¹*anti-* + *-archa* (fr. Gk *archos* anus); fr. the contrast in the location of the anus with that of the Urochorda] **:** a subclass or other division of Placodermi comprising small Devonian freshwater ostracoderms having complex bony armor on the anterior part of the body and a pair of pectoral appendages resembling paddles

an·ti·ar·chi \-'är,kī\ [NL, fr. ¹*anti-* + *-archi* (fr. Gk *archos*)] *syn of* ANTIARCHA

an·ti·a·rin \'antēərən\ *n* -s [ISV *antiar* + *-in*] **:** either of two crystalline glycosides $C_{29}H_{42}O_{11}$ that are obtained from antiar and are powerful cardiac poisons

an·ti·a·ris \,antē'a(a)rəs\ *n, cap* [NL, fr. Jav *antjar*] **:** a genus of East Indian trees (family Moraceae) with axillary clustered flowers and fleshy purple fruits — see UPAS

¹an·ti·bac·chic \¦=(,)= *at* ¹ANTI- + ¦==\ *adj* [LL *antibacchius* + E *-ic*] **:** relating to or composed of antibacchii

²antibacchic \"\ *n* -s **1 :** ANTIBACCHIUS **2 :** an antibacchic cadence

an·ti·bac·chi·us \¦=(,)=-\ *n, pl* **antibac·chii** [LL, fr. LGk *antibakcheios*, fr. Gk *anti-* ¹anti- + *bakcheios* bacchius — more at BACCHIUS] **:** a metrical foot of three syllables the first two having either primary or intermediate stress and the last being unstressed (as in accentual poetry) or the first two being long and the last short (as in classical prosody)

¹an·ti·bac·ter·i·al \¦=(,)=(')-\ *adj* [ISV ¹*anti-* + *bacterial*] **:** inimical to bacteria

²antibacterial \"\ *n* -s **:** an antibacterial agent

an·ti·bal·loon·er \¦=(,)=-\ *n* [¹*anti-* + *balloon* + *-er*] **:** SEPARATOR 3a(2)

an·ti·bi·ont \,=(,)= *at* ¹ANTI + 'bī,änt\ *n* -s [¹*anti-* + *symbiont*] **:** an organism participating in antibiosis

an·ti·bi·o·sis \,=(,)=,bī'ōsəs\ *n, pl* **antibio·ses** \-ō,sēz\ [NL, fr. ¹*anti-* + *-biosis*] **:** antagonistic association between organisms to the detriment of one of them or between one organism and a metabolic product of another (as that existing between certain bacteria and penicillin)

¹an·ti·bi·ot·ic \¦antē,bī¦äd·ik, -ätik, -ēk, -tə-, -,bē-, ¦aan-, ¦ain-; -,tī,bī-\ *adj* [prob. fr. NL *antibioticus*, fr. ¹*anti-* + Gk *biōtikos* of life — more at BIOTIC] **1 :** tending to prevent, inhibit, or destroy life **2 :** of or relating to antibiosis **3 :** of, with, or relating to an antibiotic — **an·ti·bi·ot·i·cal·ly** \-ək(ə)lē, -li\ *adv*

²antibiotic \"\ *n* -s **:** a substance produced by a microorganism (as a bacterium or a fungus) and in dilute solution having the capacity to inhibit the growth of or kill another microorganism (as a disease germ)

an·ti·blas·tic \¦=(,)= *at* ¹ANTI- + ¦blastik\ *adj* [¹*anti-* + *-blastic*] *biol* **:** antagonistic to growth; *esp* **:** of or relating to substances in the body of a host that interfere with normal metabolism of a parasite

an·ti·body \'antə,bädē, -ädi, -tē-, 'aan-, 'ain-\ *n* -ES [¹*anti-* + *body*; trans. of G *antikörper*] **:** any of various body globulins normally present or produced in response to infection or administration of suitable antigens or haptens that combine specifically with antigens (as bacteria, toxins, or foreign red blood cells) and neutralize toxins, agglutinate bacteria or cells, and precipitate soluble antigens — see AGGLUTININ, ANTITOXIN, PRECIPITIN

an·ti·bour·geois \¦=(,)=¦-\ *adj* [¹*anti-* + *bourgeois*] **:** opposed or hostile to people or things considered bourgeois

antibrachium *var of* ANTEBRACHIUM

an·ti·burgh·er \'an,tī, -,tē-, -tə-; *Scot* 'änti-\ *n* -s *usu cap* [¹*anti-* + *burgher*] **:** a member of the party of the Scottish Secession Church that held that its members could not conscientiously take the burgess oath — compare BURGHER 2

¹an·tic \'antik, 'aan-, -ēk\ *n* -s [It *antico* ancient thing or person, fr. *antico*, adj.] **1 :** an instance of grotesquely ludicrous or other unusual or unpredictable behavior **:** CAPER — usu. used in pl. ⟨the wondrous ~s of the financial community —C.J.Rolo⟩ ⟨blackbirds fill the air with their ~s —D.C.Peattie⟩ **2** *archaic* **a :** GROTESQUE **b :** a fantastic sculptured human figure or face; *esp* **:** one serving as an architectural support **3** *archaic* **:** one who performs a grotesque or ludicrous part (as in a play) **:** BUFFOON, MERRY-

ANDREW 4 *obs* : one of the people of ancient times : ANTIQUE 2a 5 *obs* : a grotesque pageant

²**antic** \"\ *also* **an·ti·cal** \-tə̇kəl, -ēk-\ *adj* [It *antico* ancient, fr. L *antiquus* — more at ANTIQUE] **1** *archaic* : having incongruous ornament of grotesque design : BIZARRE ⟨walls overlaid with ~ work⟩ **2 a** : characterized by ludicrous or clownish extravagance or absurdity ⟨the first specific instance of Hamlet's assumed ~ disposition —Harold Goddard⟩ **b** : fantastic in a light gay fashion : FROLICSOME ⟨music gives a humorous lift to the ~ words —Douglas Watt⟩ **syn** see FANTASTIC

³**antic** \"\ *vb* **anticked** *also* **antickt**; **anticked** *also* **antickt**; **antick·ing** \-tə̇kiŋ, -ēk-\ **antics** [¹*antic*] *vt*, *obs* : to make appear like a buffoon ~ *vi* : to perform antics ⟨minced, strode, and *anticked* in a parody of life and manners —Nora Waln⟩

antica *pl of* ANTICUM

an·ti·car·di·ac \¦antē¦kärdē,ak, -tə̇- *sometimes* -,tī-\ *adj* [NL *anticardium* + E *-ac* (as in *cardiac*)] : belonging or relating to the anticardium

an·ti·car·di·um \-'kärdēəm\ *or* **an·te·car·di·um** \¦antē, -tə̇-\ *n*, *pl* **anticar·dia** *or* **antecar·dia** \-dēə\ [NL, fr. ²*anti-* or *ante-* + *-cardium*] : the pit of the stomach : EPIGASTRIUM

an·ti·cat·a·lyst \¦=(,)= *at* ¹ANTI- + ¦=-\ *n* -s [¹*anti-* + *catalyst*] **1** : NEGATIVE CATALYST **2** : a catalytic poison

an·ti·cath·ode \¦=(,)='-\ *n* -s [ISV ¹*anti-* + *cathode*] : the target in an electron tube, esp. an X-ray tube

an·ti·cen·ter \¦=(,)='-\ *n* -s [¹*anti-* + *center*] : the direction in the sky opposite to that toward the center of the Milky Way galaxy

an·ti·chance \¦=(,)='-\ *n* -s [¹*anti-* + *chance*] : factors in evolution regarded as vitalistic and nonmaterialistic

an·ti·chlor \¦=(,)='klō(ə)r\ *n* -s [¹*anti-* + *chlorine*] : a substance used in removing the excess of chlorine or bleaching liquor left in paper pulp or textile fibers after bleaching

¹**an·ti·cho·lin·er·gic** \¦=(,)=,=-\ *adj* [¹*anti-* + *cholinergic*] : opposing or annulling the physiologic action of acetylcholine

²**anticholinergic** \"\ *n* -s : a substance having an anticholinergic action

an·ti·cho·lin·es·ter·ase \¦=(,)=,=-\ *n* -s [¹*anti-* + *cholinesterase*] : a substance that inhibits a cholinesterase by combination with it: as **a** : a drug (as physostigmine or neostigmine) useful as a cholinergic stimulant whose effect on a cholinesterase is reversible **b** : a nerve poison; *esp* : an organic phosphate derivative (as tetraethyl pyrophosphate or parathion) useful as an insecticide whose effect on a cholinesterase is irreversible or only partially reversible

an·ti·chre·sis \,antə̇'krēsə̇s\ *n*, *pl* **antichre·ses** \-ē,sēz\ [NL, fr. Gk, fr. *anti-* ¹anti- + *chrēsis* use, fr. *chrēsthai* to use, need — more at CHRESTOMATHY] : a mortgage contract by which the mortgagee takes possession of the mortgaged property and has its fruits or profits in lieu of interest — **an·ti·chret·ic** \-ed·ik, -ēd·ik\ *adj*

an·ti·christ \'=(,)= *at* ¹ANTI- + ,krīst\ *n* -s *often cap A*, *sometimes cap C with hyphen* [ME *anticrist*, *antecrist*, fr. OF & LL; OF *antecrist*, *anticrist*, fr. LL *Antichristus*, fr. Gk *Antichristos*, fr. ¹*anti-* + *Christos* Christ — more at CHRIST] : one who denies or opposes Christ

¹**an·ti·chris·tian** \¦=(,)=¦-\ *adj* [¹*anti-* + *Christian*] **1** : of or relating to an antichrist **2** : opposed to or rejecting Christ or Christianity — **an·ti·chris·tian·ism** \¦=(,)=¦-\ *n* -s

²**antichristian** \"\ *n* -s **1** *obs* : a follower of an antichrist **2** : one who is opposed to or rejects Christ or Christianity

antichristianity *n* -ES [¹*anti-* + *christianity*] *obs* : the system or rule of an antichrist

antichronism *n* -s [Gk *antichronismos* use of one tense for another, fr. *anti-* ¹anti- + *chronos* time + *-ismos* -ism] *obs* : ANACHRONISM

an·tich·thon \an'tik,thän, -,thōn, -thən\ *n*, *pl* **antichthones** \-,thə,nēz\ [LL, fr. Gk *antichthōn* counterearth, southern hemisphere, fr. *anti-* ¹anti- + *chthōn* earth — more at HUMBLE] **1** : COUNTEREARTH **2** [L *antichthones*, pl., fr. Gk, pl. of *antichthōn*] *obs* : an inhabitant of the antipodes — usu. used in pl.

¹**an·tic·i·pant** \an'tisəpənt, aan-\ *adj* [L *anticipant-*, *anticipans*, pres. part. of *anticipare*] : ANTICIPATING, EXPECTANT — usu. used with *of* ⟨~ of gaining support⟩

²**anticipant** \"\ *n* -s : one that anticipates ⟨he remains an ~ to the end —J.M.Grant⟩

an·tic·i·pate \an'tisə,pāt, aan-, *usu* -ād·+V\ *vb* -ED/-ING/-S [L *anticipatus*, past part. of *anticipare* to anticipate, fr. *anti-* ²ante- + *-cipare* (fr. *-cipere*, fr. *capere* to take) — more at HEAVE] *vt* **1** : to consider in advance : give advance thought, discussion, or treatment to ⟨the author had *anticipated* the question in a preceding chapter⟩ **2** : to cause to occur prematurely ⟨it is impossible for the bank to ~ payment —J.A. Todd⟩ : meet (an obligation) before a due date **3 a** : to deal with in advance : counter, guard against, or forestall by prior action ⟨*anticipating* the action of the enemy and taking due precautions⟩ **b** : to foresee and satisfy or fulfill beforehand ⟨*anticipating* the customers' demands⟩ **4** : to realize or actualize before an expected or plausible time ⟨*anticipating* the happiness of heaven⟩ **5** : to use or expend in advance of actual possession ⟨*anticipating* his salary and buying many clothes⟩ **6** : to act before (another) often with the intent or effect of checking or countering ⟨*anticipating* his opponent and protecting the threatened area⟩ **7** : look forward to as certain ⟨to ~ the stormy weather⟩ ~ *vi* **1** : to come before the expected time — usu. used of medical symptoms **2** : to speak or write in a way conditioned by knowledge or expectation of what will be treated later **syn** see FORESEE, PREVENT

an·tic·i·pa·tion \=,=='pāshən\ *n* -s [ME *anticipacioun*, fr. L *anticipation-*, *anticipatio*, fr. *anticipatus* + *-ion-*, *-io* -ion] **1** : the use or spending of money before it is due or available: as **a** : the taking or alienation (as by assignment) of the income of a trust estate before it is due **b** : a discount for advance payment of a bill for goods or services when no cash discount is specified in the terms of sale **2 a** : intuitive preconception : a priori knowledge : INTUITION **b** *obs* : formation of an opinion before all the facts are known : PREJUDICE, PREPOSSESSION **3** : a prior action that takes into account, deals with, or prevents the action of another **4 a** : occurrence before the normal or expected time **b** : assignment to or observance at a time earlier than the correct one; *specif* : regressive assimilation **c** : prior recognition, realization, invention, or accomplishment ⟨a species of early competitors or ~s of pocket watches —A.L.Kroeber⟩ **d** : the act of looking forward : EXPECTATION ⟨a mass meeting held in ~ of the visit —R.M.Lovett⟩; *specif* : pleasurable expectation ⟨look forward with ~ to his book —*Encounter*⟩ **5** : the entry of one or more tones of a succeeding chord or the entire chord as a rhythmic upbeat to the tone or tones anticipated **6** : a convention of bridge that a player making an opening suit-bid of one promises to rebid if his partner bids a different suit

an·tic·i·pa·tive \='==,pād·iv, -ātiv, -,pətiv, -ēv\ *adj* : given to anticipation : ANTICIPATING — **an·tic·i·pa·tive·ly** *adv*

an·tic·i·pa·tor \-,pād·ə(r), -ātə(r)\ *n* -s [L, fr. *anticipatus* + *-or*] : one that anticipates

an·tic·i·pa·to·ri·ly \¦='==_pə¦tōrəlē, -ōr-, -li\ *adv* : in an anticipatory manner

an·tic·i·pa·to·ry \='==pə,tōrē, -ōrē, -ri, *or chiefly Brit* -,pā·tə-\ *adj* **1** : characterized by anticipation ⟨could scarcely repress the ~ shiver —Mary Austin⟩ : ANTICIPATING ⟨an elder who has given a child a gift and waits, ~, for delighted thanks —J.H.Wheelwright⟩ **2** : standing as formal subject or object in place of a following word or word group esp. when it is the logical subject or object ⟨*it* in *it is customary to kiss the bride* and in *he found it necessary to tell us* or French *c'* in *c'est à vous que je parle* "it is to you that I am speaking" or German *es* in *es ist möglich, dass er kommen wird* "it is possible that he will come" are ~⟩

anticked *also* **antickt** *past of* ANTIC

anticking *pres part of* ANTIC

an·ti·clas·tic \¦=(,)= *at* ¹ANTI- + ¦klastik\ *adj* [¹*anti-* + Gk *klastos* (fr. *klan* to break) + E *-ic*] : having opposite curvatures at a given point; *specif* : curved convexly along a longitudinal plane section and concavely along the perpendicular section — used of a surface; opposed to *synclastic*

¹**an·ti·cler·i·cal** \¦=(,)=¦-\ *adj* [¹*anti-* + *clerical*] : opposed to clericalism or to the interference or influence of the clergy in secular affairs — **an·ti·cler·i·cal·ism** \¦=(,)=¦-\ *n* -s

²**anticlerical** \"\ *n* -s : a believer in anticlerical principles

an·ti·cli·mac·tic \¦=(,)=,=¦==\ *also* **an·ti·cli·mac·ti·cal** \-,=¦===\ *adj* [fr. *anticlimax*, after E *climax: climactic*, *climactical*] : relating to, attended by, or manifesting anticlimax — **an·ti·cli·mac·ti·cal·ly** \-,=¦=tə̇k(ə)lē, -li\ *adv*

an·ti·cli·max \¦=(,)=¦-\ *n* -ES [¹*anti-* + *climax*] **1** : the usu. sudden transition in writing or speaking from an idea of significance or dignity to an idea trivial or ludicrous by comparison esp. at the close of a series, sentence, or passage (as *a love of God, justice, and sports cars*); *also* : an instance of such transition **2 a** : an event or occurrence (as the last of a series) that is strikingly or ludicrously less important, significant, or dignified than what has preceded it **b** : a disappointment of expectation ⟨the ~ of his later years⟩

¹**an·ti·cli·nal** \¦=(,)=¦klīnᵊl\ *adj* [¹*anti-* + *clin-* (fr. Gk *klinein* to lean) + E *-al* — more at LEAN] : inclining in opposite directions: as **a** *geol* : having or relating to a fold in which the sides dip from a common line or crest — compare SYNCLINAL **b** *bot* : occurring at right angles to the surface or circumference of an organ — **an·ti·cli·nal·ly** \-īnᵊlē, -i\ *adv*

²**anticlinal** \"\ *n* -s : an anticlinal structure, fold, or axis

anticlinal theory *n* : a theory in geology: petroleum and natural gas migrate to the most elevated portions of permeable beds and so will usu. be found in anticlines

anticlinal valley *n* : a valley excavated by erosion along the axial portion of an anticlinal fold

anticlinal vertebra *n* : one of the dorsal vertebrae in many animals that has an upright spine toward which the spines of the neighboring vertebrae are inclined

an·ti·cline \'=(,)=,klīn\ *n* -s [back-formation fr. ¹*anticlinal*]

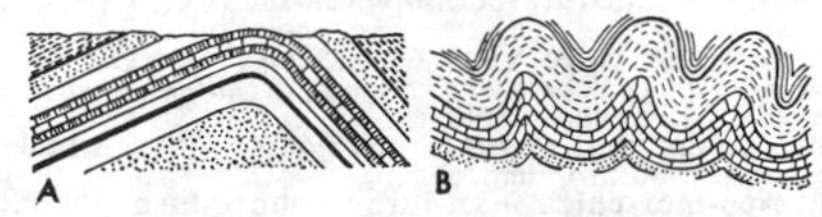

A, cross section of anticline 1; *B*, anticlinorium

1 : an upfold or arch of stratified rock in which the beds or layers bend downward in opposite directions from the crest or axis of the fold — compare SYNCLINE **2** *bot* : an anticlinal wall

an·ti·cli·no·ri·um \,=(,)=,klī'nōrēəm\ *n*, *pl* **anticlino·ria** \-rēə\ [NL, fr. ISV *anticline* + NL *-orium*] : a series of anticlines and synclines so grouped that taken together they have the general outline of an arch — opposed to *synclinorium*; see ANTICLINE illustration

an·ti·clock·wise \¦=(,)=¦-\ *adj* (*or adv*) [¹*anti-* + *clockwise*] : COUNTERCLOCKWISE

anticly *adv* [²*antic* + *-ly*] : in an antic manner

antic masque *n* [by alter.] *obs* : ANTIMASQUE

an·tic·ne·mi·on \,antik'nēmē,än, -,ōn, -ən\ *n* -s [Gk *antiknēmion*, fr. *anti-* ¹anti- + *knēmion* small leg, dim. of *knēmē* leg, shank — more at HAM] : the front of the leg

¹**an·ti·co·ag·u·lant** \¦=(,)= *at* ¹ANTI- + (,)=¦-\ *adj* [¹*anti-* + *coagulant*] : hindering coagulation esp. of blood

²**anticoagulant** \"\ *n* -s : a substance (as a drug) that hinders coagulation or clotting of blood

an·ti·co·ag·u·lin \¦=(,)=(,)='-\ *n* -s [¹*anti-* + *coagulate* + *-in*] : a substance present esp. in the saliva of blood-sucking insects that prevents or retards coagulation of vertebrate blood

an·ti·co·in·ci·dence \¦=(,)=(,)='-\ *n* -s [¹*anti-* + *coincidence*] : the indication of the passage of an ionizing particle through one counting tube only in a set, the circuit having been designed so that coincidences will not be registered

an·ti·co·mo·der·no \än¦tē(,)kōmə¦der(,)nō\ *adj* [It, artist that combines ancient and modern style, fr. *antico* ancient + *moderno* modern, fr. LL *modernus* — more at ANTIC, MODERN] : of or relating to modern imitations of antiques

an·ti·com·ple·men·ta·ry \¦=(,)= *at* ¹ANTI- + ,==¦-\ *adj* [¹*anti-* + *complementary*] *immunol* : having the power to remove or inactivate complement nonspecifically

an·ti·cor \'=(,),kō(ə)r\ *n* -s [NL, fr. ¹*anti-* + L *cor* heart — more at HEART] : an inflammatory swelling in the front of the chest of a horse caused by pressure or friction of the harness

an·ti·creep·er \'=(,)=,-\ *n* [¹*anti-* + *creeper*] : a device attached to a railroad rail to keep it from moving longitudinally

an·ti·cre·pus·cu·lar ray \¦=(,)==¦-\ *n* [¹*anti-* + *crepuscular*] : any of the extensions of the crepuscular rays that seem to converge to the antisolar point

an·ti·cro·tal·ic \¦=(,)=(')=¦-\ *adj* [¹*anti-* + *crotalic*] : effective against rattlesnake bites — used chiefly of antivenin serums

an·ti·cryp·tic \¦=(,)=¦-\ *adj* [¹*anti-* + *cryptic*] : of or relating to resemblance to surroundings that renders an animal less conspicuous to its prey — compare AGGRESSIVE 3a

antics *pl of* ANTIC, *pres 3d sing of* ANTIC

an·ti·cum \an'tīkəm\ *n*, *pl* **anti·ca** \-kə\ [*ante-* + *-icum* (as in *posticum*)] : a front porch — compare POSTICUM

an·ti·cus \an'tīkəs\ *adj* [L, fr. *ante* before + *-icus* -ic — more at ANTE-] : ANTERIOR

an·ti·cy·clo·gen·e·sis \¦=(,) *at* ¹ANTI- + ¦sīklō¦jenəsə̇s\ *n* [NL, fr. E *anticyclone* + L *genesis*] : the formation or development of an anticyclone

an·ti·cy·clol·y·sis \¦=(,)=,sī¦kläləsə̇s\ *n*, *pl* **anticycloly·ses** \-ə,sēz\ [NL, fr. E *anticyclone* + NL *-lysis*] : the destruction or weakening of an anticyclone

an·ti·cy·clone \'=(,)=,-\ *n* [¹*anti-* + *cyclone*] : a system of winds that rotates about a center of high atmospheric pressure clockwise in the northern hemisphere, counterclockwise in the southern, that usu. advances at 20 to 30 miles per hour, that often brings cool dry weather, and that usu. has a diameter of 1500 to 2500 miles — **an·ti·cy·clon·ic** \¦=(,)=,=¦-\ *adj*

an·ti·dac·tyl \'=(,)=,-\ *n* [LL *antidactylus*, fr. Gk *antidaktylos*, fr. *anti-* ¹anti- + *daktylos* dactyl — more at DACTYL] : reversed dactyl : ANAPEST

an·ti·de·riv·a·tive \¦=(,)=¦===\ *n* [¹*anti-* + *derivative*] : the inverse of a given mathematical function which can be obtained by differentiating the inverse ⟨$F(x)$ is the ~ of $f(x)$⟩

an·ti·det·o·nant \¦=(,)=¦detᵊnᵊnt\ *n* -s [¹*anti-* + *detonate* + *-ant*] : ANTIKNOCK

¹**an·ti·diph·the·rit·ic** \¦=(,)=,==¦-\ *adj* [ISV ¹*anti-* + *diphtheritic*] : preventing diphtheria esp. by immunization ⟨immunization with ~ toxoid⟩

²**antidiphtheritic** \"\ *n* -s : an agent that prevents or modifies the course of diphtheria ⟨antitoxin is an ~⟩

¹**an·ti·di·u·ret·ic** \¦=(,)=,==¦-\ *adj* [¹*anti-* + *diuretic*] *med* : tending to check or oppose excretion of urine

²**antidiuretic** \"\ *n* -s : an antidiuretic agent or substance ⟨some hormones are ~s⟩

an·ti·dor·cas \,antē'dȯrkəs, -,tī-\ *n*, *cap* [NL, fr. Gk *anti-* similar to, like (fr. *anti* against, instead of, equivalent to) + *dorkas* gazelle — more at ANTI-, DORCAS GAZELLE] : a genus of antelopes including only the springbok

an·ti·do·ron \-'dō,rän, -ōn, -rən\ *n*, *pl* **antido·ra** \-rə\ [LGk *antidōron* return gift, fr. Gk *anti-* ¹anti- + *dōron* gift, fr. *didonai* to give — more at DATE] : bread blessed but not consecrated and eaten in the Eucharist of the Eastern Church but instead distributed after the service as a sign of their participation in the blessing to worshipers who did not communicate : bread of fellowship — called also *eulogia*

an·ti·dot·al \¦antə̇¦dōd·ᵊl, -ōtᵊl, ¦aan-\ *adj* : consisting of, suited for, or acting as an antidote — **an·ti·dot·al·ly** \-ᵊlē, -ᵊli\ *adv*

antidotary *n* -ES [ML *antidotarius*, fr. L *antidotum*, *antidotus* + *-arius* -ary] *obs* : a book of antidotes

¹**an·ti·dote** \'antə̇,dōt, *usu* -ōd·+V\ *n* -s [ME *antidot*, *antidotum*, fr. L *antidotum*, *antidotus*, fr. Gk *antidoton*, *antidotos*, fr. neut. & fem. of (assumed) *antidotos*, verbal of *antididonai* to give in return, give as an antidote, fr. *anti-* ¹anti- + *didonai* to give — more at DATE (point of time)] **1** : a remedy to counteract the effects of poison ⟨an ~ for arsenic⟩ ⟨an ~ against several dangerous drugs⟩ **2** : something that relieves, prevents, or counteracts ⟨an ~ to complacency⟩ ⟨a soothing ~ for throats parched by a pungent Mexican repast —Green Peyton⟩

²**antidote** \"\ *vt* -ED/-ING/-S **1** : to counteract or neutralize by giving or taking an antidote ⟨*antidoted* the poison with quick medication⟩ **2** : to provide with an antidote ⟨kept whiskey to ~ himself against snake bite⟩

an·ti·drom·ic \¦antə̇¦drämik\ *or* **an·tid·ro·mal** \(')an¦tidrəməl\ *adj* [¹*anti-* + *drom-* + *-ic* or *-al*] : proceeding or conducting on a course opposite in direction to the usual — used esp. of a nerve impulse or fiber — **an·ti·drom·i·cal·ly** \¦antə̇¦drämə̇k(ə)lē\ *adv*

antient *archaic var of* ANCIENT

an·ti·en·zyme \¦=(,)= *at* ¹ANTI- + '=,=\ *n* [¹*anti-* + *enzyme*] : a substance that inhibits enzyme action; *esp* : an inhibitor (as antitrypsin) produced normally by animal and plant cells or following injection of an enzyme

an·ti·ep·i·cen·ter \¦=(,)=¦=-\ *n* -s [¹*anti-* + *epicenter*] : the point at which a straight line drawn through the epicenter of an earthquake and the earth's center would emerge on the opposite side of the globe

An·ti·fe·brin \¦=(,)=¦fēbrən, -fe-\ *trademark* — used for acetanilide

an·ti–fed·er·al·ist \¦=(,)=¦-\ *n* -s *usu cap F* [¹*anti-* + *Federalist*] : a member of the group that opposed the adoption of the U.S. Constitution

an·ti·fer·ro·mag·net \¦=(,)=,-\ *n* [¹*anti-* + *ferromagnet*] : a substance that exhibits antiferromagnetism

an·ti·fer·ro·mag·net·ic \¦=(,)=¦-\ *adj* [¹*anti-* + *ferromagnetic*] : of, relating to, or showing antiferromagnetism

an·ti·fer·ro·mag·net·ism \¦=(,)=,-\ *n* [¹*anti-* + *ferromagnetism*] : magnetic behavior characteristic of certain feebly magnetic substances (as manganese monoxide and chromium sesquioxide) thought to have two oppositely directed electron spins not quite neutralizing each other with the result that the magnetic susceptibility at first increases and then decreases as the substance is heated

an·ti·fi·bri·nol·y·sin \¦=(,) =,-\ *n* -s [¹*anti-* + *fibrinolysin*] : an antibody in the blood of persons convalescent from infection with hemolytic streptococci that specifically opposes fibrinolysins produced by these organisms and is used chiefly in certain diagnostic tests

an·ti·fi·bri·nol·y·sis \¦=(,)=,-\ *n*, *pl* **antifibrinoly·ses** [NL, fr. ¹*anti-* + *fibrinolysis*] : the action of an antifibrinolysin in opposing streptococcal fibrinolysis

an·ti·flash \¦=(,)=¦-\ *adj* [¹*anti-* + *flash*, n.] : capable of withstanding or minimizing the effects of flash or heat, esp. the intense heat encountered in fire fighting

an·ti·foam \'=(,)=,-\ *n* -s [¹*anti-* + *foam*] : a substance that reduces or prevents the formation of foam

an·ti·fog·gant \'=(,)=¦=ənt\ *n* -s [¹*anti-* + *fog* + *-ant*] : a reagent added to an emulsion, developer, or other photographic solution to reduce or prevent fog

an·ti·fog·mat·ic \¦=(,)=,=¦mad·ik\ *n* -s [¹*anti-* + *fog* + *-matic* (as in *rheumatic*)] : a drink of liquor taken to counteract the effect of fog or dampness

an·ti·for·eign·ism \¦=(,)=¦-\ *n* -s [¹*anti-* + *foreignism*] : aversion or opposition to foreigners

an·ti·foul·ing \¦=(,)=¦==\ *adj* [¹*anti-* + *fouling*] : intended to prevent fouling of underwater structures (as the bottoms of ships) ⟨~ paint⟩

an·ti·freeze \'=(,)=,-\ *n* -s [¹*anti-* + *freeze*, v.] : a substance (as alcohol) added to a liquid (as the coolant in an automobile, tractor, or airplane engine) to lower its freezing point

an·ti·fric·tion \¦=(,)=¦==\ *adj* [¹*anti-* + *friction*] : reducing friction; *specif* : having rolling contact instead of sliding contact ⟨~ ball bearing⟩

an·ti·gen \'antə̇jən, -,jen, -in\ *n* -s [ISV ¹*anti-* + *-gen*] **1** : a usu. protein or carbohydrate substance (as a toxin, enzyme, or any of certain constituents of blood corpuscles or of other cells), that when introduced into the body stimulates the production of an antibody **2** : a substance that reacts in complement fixation with an antibody to bind complement, the antigen and antibody usu. being specific — **an·ti·gen·ic** \¦=='jenik\ *adj* — **an·ti·gen·i·cal·ly** \-ə̇k(ə)lē\ *adv* — **an·ti·genicity** \-jə¦nisəd·ē\ *n* -ES

¹**an·ti·god·lin** \¦antə̇¦gädlə̇n, -gȯd,lēn\ *or* **an·ti·gog·lin** \-¦gäglə̇n\ *adj* [origin unknown] *chiefly Midland* : out of line : ASKEW

²**antigodlin** \"\ *or* **antigoglin** \"\ *adv*, *chiefly Midland* : at angles : CROSSWISE ⟨he went ~ across the field⟩

an·tig·o·non \an'tigə,nän\ *n*, *cap* [NL, fr. Gk *anti-* similar to, like (fr. *anti* against, instead of, equivalent to) + *-gonon*, fr. *polygonon* knotgrass (*Polygonum aviculare*) — more at ANTI-, POLYGONUM] : a genus of tropical American tendril-climbing herbs (family Polygonaceae) having petaloid flowers with brightly colored petaloid sepals — see CORALVINE

an·tig·o·rite \an'tigə,rīt\ *n* -s [G *antigorit*, fr. *Antigorio* valley, Piedmont, Italy, its locality + G *-it* -ite] : a brownish green lamellar variety of the mineral serpentine $Mg_3Si_2O_5(OH)_4$ — **an·tig·o·rit·ic** \(')=,==¦rid·ik\ *adj*

an·ti·grop·e·los \,antə̇'gräpələs, -,läs, -,lōs\ *n*, *pl* **antigropelos** \", -,lōz\ [perh. irreg. fr. Gk *anti-* ¹anti- + *hygros* wet + *pēlos* mud — more at HYGR-, SQUALOR] : waterproof leggings

an·ti–g suit \'=(,)= *at* ¹ANTI- + 'jē,-\ *n*, *usu cap G* [¹*anti-* + *G suit*] : G SUIT

¹**an·ti·guan** \(')an¦tēg(w)ən, -ig-\ *adj*, *usu cap* [*Antigua*, island in West Indies + E *-an*] **1** : of, relating to, or characteristic of the island of Antigua **2** : of, relating to, or characteristic of Antiguans

²**antiguan** \"\ *n* -s *cap* : a native or inhabitant of Antigua

an·ti·ha·la·tion \¦=(,)= *at* ¹ANTI- + ¦==\ *adj* [¹*anti-* + *halation*] : preventing halation

an·ti·ha·lo \'=(,)=,-\ *adj* [¹*anti-* + *halo*] : preventing halation ⟨film with ~ backing⟩

an·ti·he·lix \¦=(,)=¦-\ *also* **anthelix** \(')ant¦hē-, -¦thē-\ *n*, *pl* **antihelices** *or* **antihelixes** [¹*anti-* + *helix*] *anat* : the curved elevation of cartilage within or in front of the helix

an·ti·his·ta·mine \¦=(,)='-\ *or* **an·ti·his·ta·min·ic** \-,histə'minik, -ēk\ *n* -s [¹*anti-* + *histamine*] : any of various compounds used for treating certain allergic reactions and cold symptoms and presumably effective by inactivating histamine — **an·ti·his·ta·min·ic** \¦=(,)=,==¦==\ *adj*

an·ti·hor·mone \¦=(,)=¦-\ *n* -s [¹*anti-* + *hormone*] : a fraction of blood globulin that is capable of rendering ineffective a protein-containing heterologous hormone when the latter is administered over a period of time and that is now generally considered to be a true antibody formed in response to the presence of foreign protein

an·ti·ic·er \'=(,)=,-\ *n* -s [¹*anti-* + *ice* + *-er*] : a device serving to prevent ice formation esp. on an airplane (as a slinger ring, a windshield sprayer, a pump forcing alcohol and glycerin into the throat of a carburetor, or a thermal device supplying the leading edges of wings and tail with heated air

an·ti–in·tel·lec·tu·al·ism \¦=(,)=,-\ *n* -s [¹*anti-* + *intellectualism*] **1** : the philosophic attitude or doctrine that assigns intellect or reason to a subordinate place or denies the power of intellect to grasp the true nature of things — compare BERGSONISM **2** : hostility toward or suspicion of intellectuals : hostility toward inquiring, speculative, or academic habits of thought ⟨reflected trends toward *anti-intellectualism* by cutting the university's budget —Richard Schickel⟩

an·ti–in·tel·lec·tu·al·ist \¦=(,)=,-\ *n* -s : one given to anti-intellectualism

an·ti·jac·o·bin \¦=(,)=¦-\ *n*, *usu cap J* [¹*anti-* + *Jacobin*] : an opponent of the Jacobins — **an·ti·jac·o·bin·ism** \¦=(,)=¦-\ *n* -s *usu cap J*

an·ti·knock \'=(,)=,-\ *n* -s [¹*anti-* + *knock*] : a substance used as a fuel or fuel additive to prevent detonation in the combustion process of an internal-combustion engine

an·ti·lar·val \¦=(,)=¦-\ *adj* [¹*anti-* + *larval*] : directed against larvae — used of insect control measures designed to destroy larval insects, esp. disease-transmitting mosquitoes

an·ti–lea·guer \¦=(,)=,lēgə(r)\ *n*, *often cap L* [¹*anti-* + *League* (*of Nations*) + *-er*] : one opposed to the League of Nations or to the entrance of the U.S. into it

an·ti·le·gom·e·na \¦=(,)=lə¦gämənə\ *n pl*, *often cap* [Gk, fr. neut. pl. of *antilegomenos*, pres. part. pass. of *antilegein* to speak against, fr. *anti-* ¹anti- + *legein* to speak — more at LEGEND] : the books of the New Testament whose canonicity was for a time in dispute — compare HOMOLOGOUMENA

¹**an·til·le·an** \an¦tilēən, ¦aan-, (')=¦=lē=\ *adj*, *usu cap* [*Antilles*, islands in the West Indies + E *-an*] **1** : of, relating to, or characteristic of the Antilles **2** : of, relating to, or characteristic of Antilleans **3** : of, relating to, or being the biogeographic subregion of the Greater and Lesser Antilles

²**antillean** \"\ *n* -s *cap* : a native or inhabitant of the Antilles

an·ti·lo·bi·um \ˌ=(ˌ)=ˈlōbēəm\ *n, pl* **antilo·bia** \-bēə\ [NL, fr. Gk *antilobion*, fr. *anti-* ¹anti- + *lobion*, dim. of *lobos* lobe, pod — more at SLEEP] **:** TRAGUS

an·ti·lo·ca·pra \ˌantə(ˌ)lōˈkaprə\ *n, cap* [NL, fr. *antilo-* (fr. *Antilope*) + *Capra*] **:** a genus of ruminants (the type of the family Antilocapridae) consisting of the pronghorn — **an·ti·lo·cap·rid** \ˌ=(ˌ)=ˈkaprəd\ *adj or n*

an·ti·log·a·rithm \ˌ=(ˌ)=*at* ¹ANTI- +ˌ-\ *n* [*anti-* + *logarithm*] **:** the number corresponding to a logarithm ⟨in the common system, the ~ of 2 is 100, since the logarithm of 100 is 2⟩ —abbr. *antilog*

an·til·o·gism \anˈtiləˌjizəm\ *n* -s [LGk *antilogismos*, fr. Gk *anti-* ¹anti- + *logismos* calculating, reasoning, fr. *logizesthai* to calculate, fr. *logos* word, computation — more at LEGEND] **:** an inconsistent triad of propositions in logic of which two are premises of a valid syllogism while the third is the contradictory of its conclusion — **an·til·o·gis·tic** \(ˈ)=ˌ==ˈjistik\ *adj* — **an·til·o·gis·ti·cal·ly** \-tək(ə)lē\ *adv*

an·til·o·gous pole \(ˈ)anˈtiləgəs-\ *n* [Gk *antilogos* contradictory, fr. *anti-* ¹anti- + *logos* word — more at LEGEND] **:** the pole of a crystal that becomes negatively electrified when the crystal is heated

an·til·o·gy \anˈtiləjē\ *n* -ES [Gk *antilogia*, fr. *anti-* ¹anti- + *-logia* -logy] **:** a contradiction in terms or ideas

an·til·o·pe \anˈtiləˌpē\ *n, cap* [NL, prob. fr. obs. E *antilope*, fr. ME *antilope*, *antelope* fabulous beast represented in heraldic devices — more at ANTELOPE] **:** a genus of antelopes comprising the Indian black buck

an·ti·lu·et·ic \ˌ=(ˌ)= *at* ¹ANTI-+=ˈ==\ *n* -s [¹*anti-* + *luetic*] **:** ANTISYPHILITIC

an·ti·ly·sin \ˈ=(ˌ)=ˈ-\ *n* [¹*anti-* + *lysin*] **:** a substance antagonistic to a lysin and serving to protect the cells from the attacks of the lysin

an·ti·ly·sis \ˈ=(ˌ)=ˈ-\ *n, pl* **antily·ses** [NL, fr. ¹*anti-* + *-lysis*] **:** action of an antilysin — **an·ti·lyt·ic** \ˌ=(ˌ)=ˈ-\ *adj*

an·ti·ma·cas·sar \ˌantēməˈkasə(r), -tə-, ˌaan . . . ˈkaas-\ *n* -s [¹*anti-* + *Macassar (oil)*] **:** a cover to protect the back or arms of furniture from Macassar oil or other hair preparations **:** TIDY

an·ti·mag·ma·tist \ˌ=(ˌ)= *at* ¹ANTI- + ˈmagmətəst\ *n* -s [¹*anti-* + NL *magmat-*, *magma* + E *-ist*] **:** one that believes that granite and other similar igneous rocks are formed in situ by a process called granitization rather than intruded as magma

an·ti·mag·net·ic \ˌ=(ˌ)=ˌ=ˈ-\ *adj* [¹*anti-* + *magnetic*] *of a watch* **:** having a balance unit composed of alloys that will not remain magnetized thus reducing the extremes of error resulting from magnetism

¹**an·ti·ma·lar·i·al** \ˌ=(ˌ)==ˈ-\ *adj* [¹*anti-* + *malarial*] **:** serving to prevent, check, or cure malaria

²**antimalarial** \"\ *n* -s **:** an antimalarial drug

an·ti·ma·son \ˌ=(ˌ)=ˈ-\ *n, often cap A&M* [¹*anti* + *mason*] **:** one opposed to Freemasonry — used esp. of a member of an American political party — **an·ti·ma·son·ic** \-=ˈ==\ *adj, often cap A&M* — **an·ti·mason·ry** \-ˈ===\ *n, often cap A&M*

an·ti·masque *or* **an·ti·mask** *also* **an·te·mask** \ˈantē,-, -tə-\ *n* -s [²*anti-* or *ante-* + *masque, mask*] **:** an additional masque usu. preceding the main masque and introduced for comic or grotesque contrast

an·ti·mas·quer *or* **an·ti·mask·er** \ˈ==,-\ *n* -s **:** a performer in an antimasque

an·ti·mat·ter \ˈ=(ˌ)= *at* ¹ANTI- + ,==\ *n* -s [¹*anti-* + *matter*] **:** matter composed of the counterparts of ordinary matter, antiprotons instead of protons, positrons instead of electrons, and antineutrons instead of neutrons

an·ti·mech·a·nized \ˌ=(ˌ)=ˈ-\ *adj* [¹*anti-* + *mechanized*] **:** employed in defense against armored combat vehicles ⟨~ weapons⟩ ⟨~ firing⟩

an·ti·men·si·on \ˌantəˈmensēˌän, -tē-, -ōn, -ˌən\ *or* **an·ti·men·si·um** \-sēəm\ *or* **an·ti·mins** \-ˌminz\ *or* **an·ti·min·si·on** \-ˈminsēˌän, -ōn, -ˌən\ *n, pl* **antimensia** *or* **antimin·sia** \-sēə\ [ML *antimensium*, fr. MGk *antiminsion*, *antimēsion*, prob. fr. Gk *anti-* ¹anti- + L *mensa* table + Gk *-ion* -ium — more at MENSA] *Eastern Church* **:** a consecrated piece of silk or linen cloth containing relics consecrated by a bishop and kept on the altar

an·ti·mere \ˈ==ˌmi(ə)r\ *n* -s [¹*anti-* + *-mere*] **1** *zool* **:** one of opposite corresponding parts symmetrical with respect to a main axis (as the halves of bilaterally symmetrical animals) **:** one half of a metamere **2** *zool* **:** any of the segments essentially similar to an antimere into which a radially symmetrical animal can be divided — **an·ti·mer·ic** \ˌ==ˈmerik\ *adj*

an·ti·me·ri·na \ˌ==məˈrēnə\ *also* **an·tai·me·ri·na** \ˌanˌtī-\ *n, pl* **antimerina** *or* **antimerinas** *also* **antaimerina** *or* **antaimerinas** *usu cap* **:** HOVA

an·ti·mes·o·me·tri·al \ˌ=(ˌ)=ˈ-\ *adj* [¹*anti-* + *mesometrium* + *-al*] *anat* **:** of or relating to the front or ventral mesometrium

an·ti·me·tab·o·lite \ˌ=(ˌ)= *at* ¹ANTI- + =ˈ==\ *n* -s [¹*anti-* + *metabolite*] **:** a substance that inhibits the utilization of a metabolite (as by antagonistic action) — compare ANTIVITAMIN

an·ti·mi·cro·bi·al \ˌ=(ˌ)=ˌ=ˈ-\ *also* **an·ti·mi·cro·bic** \-ˌ=ˈ-\ *adj* [¹*anti-* + *microbial, microbic*] **:** inimical to microbes

an·ti·mis·sion \ˌ=(ˌ)ˈ-\ *adj* [¹*anti-* + *mission*] **:** opposed to foreign religious missions ⟨an ~ Baptist⟩

an·ti·mo·nate \ˈantəməˌnāt, -nət\ *also* **an·ti·mo·ni·ate** \ˌ=ˈmōnēˌāt, -ēət\ *n* -s [ISV *antimony* + *-ate*] **:** a salt [as potassium antimonate KSb(OH)$_6$] containing pentavalent antimony and oxygen in the anion

¹**an·ti·mo·ni·al** \ˌantəˈmōnēəl, -tē-, -nyəl, ˌaan-\ *adj* [*antimony* + *-al*] **:** of, relating to, or containing antimony

²**antimonial** \"\ *n* -s **:** an antimonial compound or preparation

antimonial lead *n* **:** lead containing antimony; *specif* **:** a hard alloy of lead containing 4 to 10 percent antimony used for the framework of storage-battery plates and tank linings — compare GRID METAL, HARD LEAD

antimonial powder *n* **:** a powder consisting of one part oxide of antimony and two parts phosphate of calcium that has been used as a diaphoretic, emetic, and cathartic — called also *James's powder*

an·ti·mon·ic \ˌ=ˈmänik, -ēk, -mō-\ *adj* [*antimony* + *-ic*] **:** of, relating to, or derived from antimony — used esp. of compounds in which antimony is pentavalent

an·ti·mo·nide \ˈ==məˌnīd -ˌnəd\ *n* -s [*antimony* + *-ide*] **:** a binary compound of antimony with a more positive element

an·ti·mo·nif·er·ous \ˌ===ˈnif(ə)rəs\ *adj* [ISV *antimony* + *-ferous*] **:** bearing antimony

an·ti·mo·ni·ous \ˌ==ˈmōnēəs\ *also* **an·ti·mo·nous** \ˈ==mənəs\ *adj* [*antimony* + *-ous*] **:** of, relating to, or derived from antimony — used esp. of compounds in which antimony is trivalent

antimonious oxide *n* **:** ANTIMONY TRIOXIDE

an·ti·mo·nite \ˈ==məˌnīt\ *n* -s [G *antimonit*, fr. *antimon* antimony + *-it* -ite] **:** STIBNITE

an·ti·mo·ni·um \ˌ==ˈmōnēəm\ *n, pl* **antimo·nia** \-nēə\ [ML] **:** ANTIMONY

an·ti·mo·ny \ˈantəˌmōnē, ˈaan-, -ni, *US also & Brit usu* -mən-\ *n* -ES [ME *antimonie*, fr. ML *antimonium*, perh. modif. of Ar *ithmid*, of Hamitic origin; akin to Egypt *sdm* antimony, Copt *stēm*] **1 :** STIBNITE **2 :** a trivalent and pentavalent metalloid element that is commonly metallic silvery white, crystalline, and brittle yet rather soft but is known also in black amorphous, unstable yellow, and explosive forms, that occurs in the free state but more often combined in minerals (as stibnite, kermesite, valentinite, and cervantite) and in ores of other metals (as lead), that is prepared chiefly from stibnite usu. by roasting and smelting, and that is used esp. as a constituent of alloys (as antimonial lead, type metals, and bearing metals) — symbol *Sb*; see ELEMENT table

antimony blende *n* **:** KERMESITE

antimony bloom *n* **:** VALENTINITE

antimony chloride *n* **:** either of two chlorides of antimony: **a :** the trichloride $SbCl_3$ obtained as a colorless hygroscopic caustic crystalline solid from antimony and chlorine and used chiefly in coloring metals (as iron, zinc), as a catalyst, and as a mordant — called also *butter of antimony* **b :** the pentachloride $SbCl_5$ obtained as a colorless to reddish yellow caustic oily liquid with an offensive odor and used chiefly as a chlorine carrier in organic synthesis and as a catalyst

antimony cinnabar *n* **:** ANTIMONY VERMILION

antimony crocus *n* **:** CROCUS OF ANTIMONY

antimony crude *n* **:** ANTIMONY SULFIDE

antimony glance *n* **:** STIBNITE

antimony hydride *n* **:** STIBINE

an·ti·mo·nyl \-məˌnil, -ēl\ *n* -s [ISV *antimony* + *-yl*] **:** a univalent radical SbO composed of antimony and oxygen held by some to exist in the molecules of tartar emetic and some basic salts of antimony

antimony ocher *n* **:** native antimony oxide; *esp* **:** CERVANTITE

antimony oxide *n* **:** an oxide of antimony; *esp* **:** ANTIMONY TRIOXIDE

antimony potassium tartrate *n* **:** TARTAR EMETIC

antimony regulus *n* **:** impure antimony made by smelting antimony ore

antimony salt *n* **:** a double salt of antimony fluoride (as with sodium fluoride or ammonium sulfate) used as a mordant — often used in pl.

antimony sulfide *n* **:** either of two sulfides of antimony: **a** *also* **antimony trisulfide :** the trisulfide Sb_2S_3 occurring native as stibnite, obtained synthetically as an orange-red precipitate, and used chiefly as a pigment (as in camouflage paints), in percussion primer compositions, and in fireworks — compare ANTIMONY VERMILION **b** *also* **antimony pentasulfide :** the pentasulfide Sb_2S_5 obtained as an orange-yellow precipitate and used chiefly as a pigment, in coloring and vulcanizing rubber, and in fireworks — called also *golden antimony sulfide*

antimony trioxide *n* **:** a white crystalline compound Sb_2O_3 or Sb_4O_6 occurring native as valentinite and senarmontite, formed when antimony burns, and used chiefly as a source of other antimony compounds and as a pigment esp. in fire-retardant paints — called also *antimonious oxide*

antimony vermilion *n* **:** a vermilion pigment made by treating a soluble antimony compound (as antimony trichloride) with a thiosulfate or hydrogen sulfide and consisting of antimony trisulfide or oxysulfide — called also *antimony cinnabar*

antimony white *n* **:** antimony trioxide used as a pigment

antimony yellow *n* **1 :** any of several yellow pigments containing antimony: as **a :** NAPLES YELLOW **b :** MÉRIMÉE'S YELLOW **2 a :** a moderate orange yellow that is paler than ocher yellow and yellower and less strong than deep chrome yellow — called also *sunray*

an·ti·morph \ˈ=(ˌ)= *at* ¹ANTI- + ˌmȯrf\ *n* -s [¹*anti-* + *-morph*] **:** a gene producing an effect opposite to that of the wild-type gene of the same locus — **an·ti·morph·ic** \ˌ=(ˌ)=ˈmȯrfik\ *adj*

an·ti·my·cin A \ˌ=(ˌ)=ˈmīsᵊnˈā\ *n* [¹*anti-* + *-mycin*] **:** a crystalline antibiotic $C_{28}H_{40}N_2O_9$ produced by an actinomycete (a species of *Streptomyces*) that is active against various fungi and insects

an·ti·neu·rit·ic \ˌ=(ˌ)==ˈ==\ *adj* [¹*anti-* + *neuritic*] **:** preventing or relieving neuritis ⟨an ~ vitamin⟩

an·ti·neu·tri·no \ˌ=(ˌ)=-\ *n* -s [¹*anti-* + *neutrino*] **:** an elementary particle which is identical to the neutrino in mass but opposite to it in electric and magnetic properties and whose encounter with a neutrino results in mutual annihilation

an·ti·neu·tron \ˌ=(ˌ)=ˈ-\ *n* -s [¹*anti-* + *neutron*] **:** an uncharged particle of mass equal to that of the neutron but having a magnetic moment in the opposite direction

ant·ing \ˈan(ˌ)tiŋ\ *n* -s [¹*ant* + *-ing*] *of certain birds* **:** the deliberate placing of living ants or other small invertebrates among the feathers

an·tin·i·al \(ˈ)anˈtinēəl\ *adj* **:** relating to the antinion

an·tin·i·on \anˈtinēən, -ēˌän\ *n* -s [¹*anti-* + Gk *inion* back of the head — more at INION] **:** the farthest projection of the forehead, opposite to the inion

an·ti·node \ˈantəˌnōd, -tē-\ *n* -s [ISV ¹*anti-* + *node*] **:** a region of maximum amplitude (as one of the vibrating segments of a musical string) situated between adjacent nodes in a field of wave interference — compare LOOP 4b, STANDING WAVE

an·ti·nome \-ˌnōm\ *n* -s [back-formation fr. *antinomy*] **:** a contradictory such as occurs in antinomy

¹**an·ti·no·mi·an** \ˌantəˈnōmēən, -tē-, -ˌtī-\ *adj* [ML *antinomus* (fr. L *anti-* ¹anti- + Gk *nomos* law) + E *-an* — more at NIMBLE] **:** relating to, proceeding from, or influenced by antinomianism

²**antinomian** \"\ *n* -s **:** an adherent of antinomianism

an·ti·no·mi·an·ism \ˌ=(ˌ)=ˈ==əˌnizəm\ *n* -s **:** the theological doctrine that by faith and God's gift of grace through the gospel a Christian is freed not only from the Old Testament law of Moses and all forms of legalism but also from all law including the generally accepted standards of morality prevailing in any given culture

an·ti·nom·ic \ˌ=(ˌ)=ˈnämik, -nō-\ *or* **an·ti·nom·i·cal** \-ˈnäməkəl\ *adj* **:** characterized by or involving antinomy — **an·ti·nom·i·cal·ly** \-mək(ə)lē, -li\ *adv*

an·tin·o·my \anˈtinəmē, -mi\ *n* -ES [L *antinomia*, fr. Gk, fr. *anti-* ¹anti- + *-nomia* (fr. *nomos* law) — more at NIMBLE] **1 :** opposition of one law or rule to another law or rule **:** contradiction within a law **2** *obs* **:** an opposing law or rule of any kind **:** a law that contradicts itself **3** [G *antinomie*, fr. L *antinomia*] **a :** a contradiction between two philosophical principles each of which is taken to be true or between inferences correctly drawn from such principles; *esp* **:** a conflict or opposition between the products of reason and of experience **b :** a statement embodying an antinomy **:** PARADOX **4 :** an apparent or real opposition, contradiction, conflict, or contrast

antinous release \anˈtanəs-\ *n* [perh. after *Antinous*, a Bithynian youth noted for his beauty, fr. L, fr. Gk *Antinoos*] **:** CABLE RELEASE

an·ti·nu·cle·on \ˌ=(ˌ)= *at* ¹ANTI- + ˈ-ˌ\ *n* -s [¹*anti-* + *nucleon*] **:** a particle of the same mass as a nucleon but differing from it in the sign of its electrical charge or the direction of its magnetic moment and capable of coalescing with the nucleon with the resultant annihilation of both

¹**an·ti·o·chene** \anˈtīəˌkēn, ˌantēˈäˌkēn\ *adj, usu cap* [LL *Antiochenus*, fr. *Antiochia* Antioch, ancient capital of Syria (now *Antakya*, Turkey) + L *-enus* -ene] **:** of or belonging to Antioch or to the theological doctrines associated with the Christian church at Syrian Antioch in the 4th and 5th centuries A.D. characterized by concern for the human and historical and by inductive and rationalistic method — compare ALEXANDRIAN SCHOOL 3

²**antiochene** \"\ *n* -s *usu cap* **:** a member of the church at Syrian Antioch or an adherent of its theological doctrines

¹**an·ti·och·i·an** \ˌantēˈäkēən, -ōk-\ *adj, usu cap* [*Antioch*us, name of thirteen kings of Syria who reigned from 280–64 B.C. + E *-ian*] **:** of or belonging to the Seleucidan kings of Syria who bore the name Antiochus

²**antiochian** \"\ *adj, usu cap* [*Antioch* + E *-ian*] **:** of, relating to, or characteristic of Antioch, esp. Syrian Antioch

³**antiochian** \"\ *n* -s *cap* **:** a native or inhabitant of Antioch, esp. Syrian Antioch

an·ti·o·dont \ˈantēəˌdänt, (ˈ)anˈtīə-\ *adj* [¹*anti-* + *-odont*] *zool* **:** relating to or being lophodont dentition in which the crests of opposing teeth meet

¹**an·ti·ox·i·dant** \ˈ=(ˌ)= *at* ¹ANTI- + ˈ-\ *n* -s [¹*anti-* + *oxidant*] **:** a substance that opposes oxidation or inhibits reactions promoted by oxygen or peroxides, many of these substances (as the tocopherols) being used as preservatives in various products (as in fats, oils, food products, and soaps for retarding the development of rancidity, in gasoline and other petroleum products for retarding gum formation and other undesirable changes, and in rubber for retarding aging)

²**antioxidant** \"\ *adj* **:** of or relating to an antioxidant

an·ti·ox·y·gen \ˌ=(ˌ)=ˈ-\ *n* -s [¹*anti-* + *oxygen*] **:** ANTIOXIDANT — **an·ti·ox·y·gen·ic** \ˌ=(ˌ)=ˌ==ˈ==\ *adj*

antipaedobaptism *often cap, var of* ANTIPEDOBAPTISM

an·ti·par·a·be·ma \ˌ=(ˌ)=ˌ-\ *n, pl* **antiparabema·ta** [¹*anti-* + *parabema*] **:** either of the two chapels opposite the parabemata in Byzantine architecture

an·ti·par·al·lel \ˌ=(ˌ)=ˈ-\ *adj* [¹*anti-* + *parallel*] *physics* **:** parallel but oppositely directed — used esp. of vectors

an·ti·pas·cha \ˌantēˈpaskə, -tə-\ *or* **an·ti·pasch** \-ˌpask\ *n* -s *usu cap* [MGk *antipascha*, fr. LGk, week immediately following Easter week, fr. Gk *anti-* ¹anti- + LGk *pascha* Easter — more at PASCH] *Eastern Church* **:** the first Sunday after Easter **:** LOW SUNDAY

an·ti·pas·to \ˌantēˈpastō, ˌän...ˈpä-, -tə-\ *n, pl* **antipas·ti** \-stē\ *or* **antipastos** [It, fr. *anti-* ²anti- (fr. L *ante-*) + *pasto* food, fr. L *pastus*, fr. *pastus*, past part. of *pascere* to feed — more at FOOD] **:** HORS D'OEUVRE

an·ti·pa·thar·ia \ˌantēpəˈtha(a)rēə, -tə-\ *n pl, cap* [NL, fr. *Antipathes* genus of antipatharian corals (fr. Gk *antipathes* black coral, lit., remedy for suffering, fr. neut. of *antipathēs* in exchange for suffering, of opposite feelings) + *-aria*] **:** an order or suborder of Anthozoa comprising the black or thorny corals, all having a usu. brown or black axial skeleton that is much branched and hornlike and polyps with few mesenteries or tentacles — **an·ti·pa·thar·i·an** \ˌ===ˈ==ən\ *adj or n*

an·ti·pa·thet·ic \ˌantəpəˈthed·ik, ˌaan-, -tēp-, -etik, -ēk, *also* anˌtip- *or* aan-\ *also* **an·ti·pa·thet·i·cal** \-ə̇kəl, -ēk-\ *adj* [L *antipathia* antipathy + E *-etic*, *-etical* (as in *pathetic*, *pathetical*)] **1 :** having a natural opposition or constitutional aversion ⟨~ variation of minerals in sedimentary rocks⟩ ⟨forces ~ to the spread of literacy—Helen Sullivan⟩ **2 a :** arousing antipathy ⟨mountains, which are most remote from the sea, are ~ to me—Havelock Ellis⟩ ⟨he really disliked Sir Theodosius, who was in every way ~ to him—Gabrielle Long⟩ **b :** instinctively averse — **an·ti·pa·thet·i·cal·ly** \-ə̇k(ə)lē, -ēk-, -li\ *adv*

an·ti·path·ic \ˌantəˈpathik\ *adj* [F *antipathique*, fr. *antipathie* antipathy + *-ique* -ic] **:** ANTIPATHETIC

an·ti·path·i·da \ˌantəˈpathədə\ [NL, fr. *Antipathes* genus of antipatharian corals + *-ida* — more at ANTIPATHARIA] *syn of* ANTIPATHARIA

an·tip·a·thist \anˈtipəthəst, aan-\ *n* -s **:** one who has an antipathy

antipathize *vi* -ED/-ING/-S *archaic* **:** to feel or show antipathy

an·tip·a·thy \anˈtipəthē, aan-, -thi\ *n* -ES [L *antipathia*, fr. Gk *antipatheia*, fr. *antipathēs* of opposite feelings (fr. *anti-* ¹anti- + *-pathēs* -path) + *-ia* -y] **1** *obs* **:** opposition in feeling **:** natural incompatibility **2 :** settled aversion or dislike **:** REPUGNANCE, DISTASTE ⟨some deep and secret ~ —Mary R. Rinehart⟩ ⟨*antipathies* against particular nations —George Washington⟩ ⟨Tolstoy's mounting ~ to the university —E.J. Simmons⟩ ⟨~ toward other persons or groups —E.A.Hoebel⟩ **3 :** an object of aversion ⟨evil is the greatest ~ of human nature —John Norris⟩ **syn** see ENMITY

an·ti·pa·tri·ot·ic \ˌ=(ˌ)= *at* ¹ANTI- + \ *adj* [¹*anti-* + *patriotic*] **:** tending to undermine patriotism ⟨~ propaganda⟩ ⟨~ activities⟩

an·ti·pe·dal \ˌ=(ˌ)= *at* ¹ANTI- + ˌpēdᵊl\ *adj* [¹*anti-* + *pedal*] **:** opposite to the foot — used of parts of the body of a mollusk

an·ti·pe·do·bap·tism *also* **an·ti·pae·do·bap·tism** \ˌ=(ˌ)=ˌpēdōˈbapˌtizəm\ *n* -s *often cap* [¹*anti-* + *pedobaptism, paedobaptism*] **:** the doctrine that infant baptism is scripturally unwarranted and inefficacious

an·ti·pe·do·bap·tist *or* **an·ti·pae·do·bap·tist** \ˌ=(ˌ)=ˌpēdōˈbaptəst\ *n* -s [¹*anti-* + *pedobaptist, paedobaptist*] **1** *usu cap* **:** one of a sect of Anabaptists opposed to infant baptism **2 :** an opponent of infant baptism

antipendium *var of* ANTEPENDIUM

¹**an·ti·pe·ri·od·ic** \ˌ=(ˌ)=-\ *adj* [ISV ¹*anti-* + *periodic*] **:** preventive of periodic returns of paroxysms or exacerbations of disease (as in intermittent fevers)

²**antiperiodic** \"\ *n* -s **:** an antiperiodic agent

an·ti·per·i·stal·sis \ˌ=(ˌ)=ˌ-\ *n* [NL, fr. ¹*anti-* + *peristalsis*] **:** reversed peristalsis

an·ti·per·i·stal·tic \ˌ=(ˌ)=ˌ==ˈ==\ *adj* [¹*anti-* + *peristaltic*] **1 :** opposed to or checking peristaltic motion **2 :** relating to antiperistalsis

an·ti·pe·ris·ta·sis \ˌ=(ˌ)=pəˈristəsə̇s\ *n, pl* **antiperista·ses** \-təˌsēz\ [Gk, fr. *anti-* ¹anti- + *peristasis* act of standing around, fr. *periistanai* to make stand around (fr. *peri-* + *histanai* to cause to stand) + *-sis* — more at STAND] *archaic* **:** resistance or reaction roused by opposition or by the action of an opposite principle or quality

an·ti·per·ni·cious anemia factor \ˌ=(ˌ)=-\ *n* [¹*anti-* + *pernicious*] **:** VITAMIN B_{12}

an·ti·per·son·nel \ˌ=(ˌ)=ˌ==ˈ=\ *adj* [¹*anti-* + *personnel*] **:** designed to destroy, maim, or obstruct military personnel ⟨~ bomb⟩ ⟨~ mine⟩ ⟨~ weapons⟩

an·ti·per·spi·rant \ˌ=(ˌ)=ˈpərspərənt, -ˈpə̄s- *sometimes* -ˌpə(r)ˈspīrənt\ *n* -s [¹*anti-* + *perspiration* + *-ant*] **:** a cosmetic preparation used to check excessive perspiration by astringent action when applied to the skin

an·ti·perth·ite \ˌ=(ˌ)=ˈpərˌthīt\ *n* -s [ISV ¹*anti-* + *perthite*] **:** a feldspar rock consisting of plagioclase containing lamellae of orthoclase — **an·ti·per·thit·ic** \ˌ=(ˌ)=ˌ=ˈthid·ik\ *adj*

an·ti·pet·al·ous \ˌ=(ˌ)=ˈ-\ *adj* [¹*anti-* + *petalous*] **:** having stamens opposite the petals

an·ti·phage \ˈ=(ˌ)=ˌfāj\ *adj* [¹*anti-* + *phage*] **:** inimical to phages

¹**an·ti·phlo·gis·tic** \ˌ=(ˌ)=-\ *adj* [¹*anti-* + *phlogistic*] **1 :** opposed to the doctrine of phlogiston **2 :** counteracting inflammation

²**antiphlogistic** \"\ *n* -s **:** an antiphlogistic agent

an·ti·phon \ˈantəfən, ˈaan-, -ˌfän\ *n* -s [LL *antiphona* — more at ANTHEM] **1 a :** a devotional verse sung responsively as a part of a liturgy by two choirs usu. by men's voices alternating with boys' or women's voices; *specif* **:** one of three of the chants of the mass: introit, offertory, and communion **b :** a liturgical verse or series of verses chanted responsively before the psalms or other hymns **2 :** RESPONSE, ANSWER ⟨deputies shrilled a dissenting ~ —*Time*⟩

¹**an·tiph·o·nal** \anˈtifənᵊl, aan-\ *n* -s **:** ANTIPHONARY

²**antiphonal** \(ˈ)=ˈ===\ *adj* **1 :** relating to or resembling an antiphon **2 :** answering or alternating (as in antiphony) — **an·tiph·o·nal·ly** \-ənᵊlē, -li\ *adv*

antiphonal organ *n* **:** an enclosed division of a pipe organ situated some distance from the main enclosure and permitting answering or antiphonal effects

¹**an·tiph·o·nary** \anˈtifəˌnerē, aan-, -ri\ *also* **antiphoner** *n, pl* **antiphonaries** *also* **antiphoners** [ME *antiphonary*, *antiphonarium*, fr. ML *antiphonarium*, fr. neut. of *antiphonarius*] **:** a book containing a collection of antiphons; *specif* **:** the book in which the choral parts of the breviary are contained

²**antiphonary** \(ˈ)"\ *adj* [ML *antiphonarius*, fr. LL *antiphona* antiphon + L *-arius* -ary — more at ANTHEM] **:** ANTIPHONAL

antiphone *archaic var of* ANTIPHON

an·tiph·o·net·ic \anˌtifəˈned·ik\ *adj* [*antiphon* + *-etic* (as in *phonetic*)] **:** RHYMING

an·ti·phon·ic \ˌantəˈfänik ˌaan-, -ēk\ *adj* [*antiphon* + *-ic*] **:** ANTIPHONAL — **an·ti·phon·i·cal·ly** \-ə̇k(ə)lē, -ēk-, -li\ *adv*

an·tiph·o·ny \anˈtifənē, aan-, -ni\ *n* -ES [Gk *antiphōnos* concordant, responsive + E *-y* — more at ANTHEM] **1 a :** musical response **b :** antiphonal chanting or singing; *broadly* **:** any alternation of voices **2 a :** an anthem, psalm, or musical composition sung alternately by divisions of a choir or congregation **b :** ANTIPHON 1 **3** *Greek music* **:** accompaniment or response in the octave **4 :** responsive movement between two dancers or groups of dancers

an·tiph·ra·sis \anˈtifrəsə̇s\ *n, pl* **antiphra·ses** \-əˌsēz\ [LL, fr. Gk, fr. *anti-* ¹anti- + *phrasis* diction — more at PHRASE] **:** the use of words in senses opposite to the generally accepted meanings or the use of a word in this way usu. for humorous or ironical purposes (as, a giant of three feet, four inches) — **an·ti·phras·tic** \ˌantəˈfrastik\ *adj* — **an·ti·phras·ti·cal·ly** \-tək(ə)lē, -li\ *adv*

an·ti·plas·tic \ˌ=(ˌ)= *at* ¹ANTI- + ˈ-\ *adj* [¹*anti-* + *plastic*] **:** preventing or checking the process of healing or granulation

an·ti·plum·ming \ˌ=(ˌ)=ˈ-\ *adj* [¹*anti-* + *plumming*] **:** preventing or reducing the tendency to undergo plumming ⟨an ~ agent in a photographic emulsion⟩

an·ti·pneu·mo·coc·cus \ˌ=(ˌ)=-\ *or* **an·ti·pneu·mo·coc·cic** \ˌ=(ˌ)=-\ *also* **an·ti·pneu·mo·coc·cal** \ˌ=(ˌ)=-\ *adj* [¹*anti-* + *pneumococcus, pneumococcic, pneumococcal*] **:** inimical to pneumococci

an·tip·o·dal \(ˈ)anˈtipədᵊl, (ˈ)aan-\ *also* **an·ti·pod·ic** \ˌ=təˈpädik, -ēk\ *adj* [*antipode* + *-al* or *-ic*] **1 :** of or relating to the antipodes; *specif* **:** situated at the opposite side of the earth ⟨~ latitudes⟩ ⟨~ to our region⟩ **2 :** diametrically opposite ⟨~ points on opposite sides of a sphere⟩ **3 :** OPPOSED **:** widely different ⟨nothing so ~ to his nature as this man's cold, unimaginative sagacity —Nathaniel Hawthorne⟩ ⟨have often marveled at the friendship of these two ~ men —W.H.Wright⟩ **syn** see OPPOSITE

²**an·tip·o·dal** \"\ *or* **antipodal cell** *n* -s **:** any of three cells in the female gametophyte of most angiosperms that are grouped at the end of the embryo sac farthest from the micropyle and

that usu. degenerate after fertilization but sometimes survive as part of the embryo

an·tip·o·dal·ly \(')=¦==dᵊlē, -li\ *adv* : in an antipodal position or manner

an·ti·pode \ˈantəˌpōd\ *n, pl* **an·tip·o·des** \anˈtipəˌdēz *sometimes* ˈantəˌpōdz *by those aware that there is a singular "antipode"*\ [back-formation fr. *antipodes*, pl., fr. ME, fr. L, fr. Gk, fr. pl. of *antipod-, antipous* with the feet opposite, fr. *anti-* ¹anti- + *pod-, pous* foot — more at FOOT] **1** *antipodes pl, archaic* **a** : persons dwelling at a directly opposite point on the globe of the earth **b** : those who are felt in some way to resemble such persons **2** *antipodes pl, sometimes cap* : the parts of the earth diametrically opposite — often used of Australia, New Zealand, and contiguous areas ⟨the churches of the ~s — *Christian Century*⟩; sometimes used in sing. ⟨the South Pole is the ~ of the North Pole —Irving Fisher & O.M.Miller⟩ **3** : the exact opposite or contrary ⟨virtue is the ~ of self-love —G.P.Fisher⟩ — often used in pl. ⟨the very ~s of scholarly humanism —A.L.Guérard⟩ **4** : a chemical compound having an exactly opposite configuration of its atoms in space — compare ENANTIOMORPH 2 **5** *antipodes pl* : antipodal points

¹an·tip·o·de·an \anˌtipəˈdēən, ¦an-ˌt-, aan-, ¦aan-\ *adj* [*antipode* + *-an*] **1** : ANTIPODAL **2** *sometimes cap, Brit* : AUSTRALIAN **syn** see OPPOSITE

²antipodean \"\ *n* -s **1** : one living at the antipodes **2** *sometimes cap, Brit* : AUSTRALIAN

an·ti·pole \ˈantəˌpōl, -tē-, ˈaan-\ *n* -s [¹*anti-* + *pole*] : the opposite pole

an·ti·po·lo \ˌäntēˈpōlō\ *n* -s [Tag] *Philippines* : BREADFRUIT 1

an·ti·pope \ˈantēˌpōp, -tə-, -tī-, ˈaan-\ *n* [alter. of earlier *antipape*, fr. MF, fr. ML *antipapa*, fr. *anti-* ¹anti- + *papa* pope] : one elected or claiming to be pope in opposition to the pope canonically chosen

an·ti·pros·tate \ˈantē,-, -tə-\ *n* -s [²*anti-* + *prostate*] : COWPER'S GLAND

an·ti·pro·throm·bic \¦=(ˌ)= *at* ¹ANTI- + ˌ=¦==\ *adj* : of or like that of an antiprothrombin

an·ti·pro·throm·bin \ˈ=(ˌ)=(ˌ)=¦==\ *n* -s [¹*anti-* + *prothrombin*] : a substance that interferes with the conversion of prothrombin to thrombin — compare ANTITHROMBIN, HEPARIN

an·ti·pro·ton \ˈ=(ˌ)=¦-\ *n* -s [¹*anti-* + *proton*] : a particle equal in mass but opposite in electrical charge to a proton

¹an·ti·pru·rit·ic \¦=(ˌ)==¦-\ *adj* [¹*anti-* + *pruritic*] : tending to check or alleviate itching

²antipruritic \"\ *n* -s : an antipruritic agent

an·ti·py·re·sis \ˌ=(ˌ)=ˌpīˈrēsəs\ *n* [NL, fr. E *antipyretic*, after such pairs as E *genetic*: L *genesis*] : treatment of fever by use of antipyretics

¹an·ti·py·ret·ic \ˌ=(ˌ)=ˌ-\ *n* -s [¹*anti-* + *pyretic*] : an antipyretic agent

²antipyretic \¦=(ˌ)=ˌ-\ *adj* : preventing, removing, or allaying fever

an·ti·py·rine \ˌ=(ˌ)=ˈpīˌrēn, -ˌrən\ *also* **an·ti·py·rin** \-ˌrən\ *n* -s [fr. G *antipyrin*, fr. *Antipyrin*, a trademark] : a white crystalline compound $C_{11}H_{12}N_2O$ derived from pyrazolone and formerly widely used as an antipyretic, analgesic, and antirheumatic but now largely replaced in oral use by less toxic substances (as aspirin)

¹an·ti·quar·i·an \ˌantəˈkwerēən, ˌaan-, -wa(a)r-, -wär-\ *n* -s [L *antiquarius* antiquary + E *-an*] **1** : ANTIQUARY **2** : a size of paper (as for drawing) 31 x 53 inches

²antiquarian \¦==¦===\ *adj* **1 a** : of or belonging to antiquaries, the study of antiquities, or old times **b** : connected with a dilettante interest in old things or former times **2** : dealing in old and rare books or in secondhand books ⟨~ booksellers⟩

an·ti·quar·i·an·ism \ˌ=='==əˌnizəm\ *n* -s : antiquarian interests or research : study or love of antiquities

¹an·ti·quary \ˈ==ˌkwerē, -ri\ *n* -ES [L *antiquarius* student of antiquities, fr. *antiquarius*, adj.] **1** *archaic* : an official custodian of antiquities **2** : one who studies the relics of antiquity : one who collects or studies antiquities

²antiquary \"\ *adj* [L *antiquarius*, fr. *antiquus* ancient — more at ANTIQUE] : belonging to or suggestive of antiquity

¹antiquate *adj* [LL *antiquatus*] *archaic* : ANTIQUATED

²an·ti·quate \ˈantəˌkwāt, -tē-, ˈaan-, *usu* -ād· + V\ *vt* -ED/-ING/-S [LL *antiquatus*, past part. of *antiquare* to make obsolete, fr. L *antiquus* old — more at ANTIQUE] **1 a** : to make old or obsolete ⟨new appliances ~ millions of old wiring systems — *Better Homes & Gardens*⟩ **b** : to make void or abolish as out of date ⟨the Copernican system . . . *antiquated* an astronomic theory —Jacob Taubes⟩ **2** : to make antique : ANTIQUE

an·ti·quat·ed \ˈ==ˌkwādəd, -ātəd\ *adj* **1** : fallen into disuse or lack of esteem because of age : OBSOLETE ⟨a calendar becomes ~ —A.L.Kroeber⟩ **2** : of long standing : DEEP-ROOTED, INVETERATE ⟨every royal master had whims of his own — ~ prejudices, family ties, fragments of knowledge —A.J.P. Taylor⟩ **3** : surviving from or imitating the past : OLD-FASHIONED ⟨~ legal ideas —Felix Frankfurter⟩ **4** : advanced in age : OLD **syn** see OLD

an·ti·qua·tion \ˌ=='kwāshən\ *n* -s [LL *antiquation-, antiquatio*, fr. L *antiquatus* + *-ion-, -io* -ion] : the act of making antiquated : the state of being antiquated

¹an·tique \(')anˈ¦tēk, (')aan-¦\ *adj* [MF, fr. L *antiquus, anticus*, fr. *ante* before — more at ANTE-] **1** : existing since ancient or former times : among the oldest of its class ⟨~ nations⟩ **2** : of or belonging to earlier periods : ANCIENT ⟨an ~ philosopher⟩ ⟨~ legends⟩ ⟨ruins of an ~ city⟩ **3** : exhibiting the style or fashion of ancient or former times : OLD-FASHIONED, ARCHAIC ⟨~ manners⟩ ⟨a mirror of ~ design⟩ **4** *of fabric* : having an indistinct design woven, printed, or watered in imitation of ancient silks **5 a** : embossed or impressed without ink, foil, or gold ⟨an ~ book cover⟩ : BLIND 6d **b** : having the appearance of age : suggesting the crafts of an older period ⟨~ decorations⟩ **syn** see OLD

²antique \"\ *n* -s **1 a** : a relic or object of ancient times or of an earlier period than the present **b** : a work of art, piece of furniture, or decorative object made at a much earlier period than the present and according to U.S. customs laws at least 100 years old **2 a** *obs* : a man of ancient times **b** : a person belonging to an older generation ⟨a handsome ~ —Wolcott Gibbs⟩ **3** : SYRUP 3 **4** : a paper having a rough finish and often relatively great bulk — compare EGGSHELL

³antique \"\ *vt* **an·tiqued**; **an·tiqued**; **an·tiqu·ing**; **antiques** **1** : to finish or refinish in antique style : give an appearance of age to **2** : to emboss or impress (lettering) without ink, foil, or gold ⟨a book with *antiqued* backbone⟩

antique brass *n* : a light to light grayish olive color

antique bronze *n* : a moderate yellowish brown that is redder and lighter than bronze, very slightly stronger than Bismarck brown, slightly yellower and very slightly stronger than cinnamon brown, and darker and very slightly yellower than maple sugar

antique brown *n* : a moderate brown that is yellower, lighter, and stronger than auburn, lighter, stronger, and slightly yellower than chestnut brown, and lighter, stronger, and slightly redder than coffee — called also *cigarette*

antique crown *n, heraldry* : a figure of a crown composed of a circular band with an indefinite number of pointed rays rising from it — called also *eastern crown*

antique crown

antique drab *n* : FOX 5

antique gold *n* **1** : a variable color averaging a dark yellow that is greener, lighter, and stronger than mustard (sense 3a) **2** : a strong yellowish brown that is redder, stronger, and slightly lighter than buckthorn brown and yellower and paler than orange rust

antique green *n* : a grayish to moderate green

an·tique·ly \(')=¦=lē, -li\ *adv* : in an antique manner

an·tique·ness *n* -ES : the quality or state of being antique

an·tiqu·er \=ˈtēkə(r)\ *n* -s [²*antique* + *-er*] **1** : a collector of antiques ⟨this is a book for ~s alone —*N.Y.Herald Tribune*⟩ **2** [³*antique* + *-er*] : one that antiques new furniture

antique red *n* : a dark reddish orange that is yellower and paler than average lacquer red and redder and paler than ocher red or burnt sienna — called also *canna, chaudron, Rembrandt's madder*

antique rose *n* : a grayish red that is yellower and darker than appleblossom and bluer and duller than bois de rose or Pompeian red

antiques and horribles *n pl* : fantastic impersonations forming part of a parade

an·tiqu·ing \=ˈtēkiŋ, -kēŋ\ *n* -s [²*antique* + *-ing*] : the collecting of antiques

an·tiq·ui·tar·i·an \(ˌ)anˌtikwəˈterēən\ *n* -s [*antiquity* + *-arian* (as in *humanitarian*)] : one who is attached to the opinions or practices of antiquity

an·tiq·ui·ty \anˈtikwədˌē, aan-, -ətē, -i\ *n* -ES [ME *antiquite*, fr. MF *antiquité*, fr. L *antiquitat-, antiquitas*, fr. *antiquus* ancient + *-itat-, -itas* -ity — more at ANTIQUE] **1** : ancient times : times long since past : former ages esp. when before the middle ages ⟨Greek ~⟩ ⟨Christian ~⟩ **2** : the quality of being ancient ⟨a castle of great ~⟩ **3 antiquities** *pl* **a** : relics or monuments of ancient times (as coins, statues, or buildings) **b** : matters relating to the life or culture of ancient times ⟨the study of Germanic *antiquities*⟩ **4** : the people of ancient times ⟨the records left by ~⟩ **5** *obs* **a** : old age **b** : an old man ⟨you are a shrewd ~, neighbor —Ben Jonson⟩

an·ti·rab·ic \¦=(ˌ)= *at* ¹ANTI- + ¦==\ *adj* [¹*anti-* + *rabic*] : tending to prevent or control rabies

an·ti·rac·er \ˈ=(ˌ)=ˌ-\ *n* [¹*anti-* + *racer*] : a device to prevent the racing of a ship's propeller

¹an·ti·ra·chit·ic \¦=(ˌ)==¦-\ *adj* [¹*anti-* + *rachitic*] : opposing or preventing the development of rickets ⟨an ~ vitamin⟩

²antirachitic \"\ *n* -s : an antirachitic agent

an·ti·re·flec·tion film \¦=(ˌ)==¦-\ *or* **antireflection coating** *n* [¹*anti-* + *reflection*] : a transparent film applied to an optical surface (as glass) of such thickness and refractive index as to reduce the intensity of reflected light almost to zero

an·ti·re·li·gious \¦=(ˌ)==¦-\ *adj* [¹*anti-* + *religious*] : opposing or hostile to religion or to the power and influence of organized religion

an·ti·re·mon·strant \ˌ=(ˌ)==-\ *n, usu cap* [¹*anti-* + *Remonstrant*] : one of the Dutch Calvinistic party that opposed the Remonstrants or Arminians

an·ti·rent \ˈ=(ˌ)=ˌ-\ *adj, usu cap* [¹*anti-* + *rent*] : of or relating to a political party (1839–47) in the state of New York that supported those tenants resisting collection of rents by patroons — **an·ti·rent·er** \¦=(ˌ)=¦-\ *n* -s *usu cap*

an·ti·res·o·nance \¦=(ˌ)=¦-\ *n* -s [¹*anti-* + *resonance*] : the state of adjustment of the components of an alternating current or acoustic network that produces for a given frequency minimum amplitude and intensity of current or acoustic flux — **an·ti·res·o·nant** \¦=(ˌ)=¦-\ *adj*

an·ti·re·tic·u·lar cytotoxic serum \¦=(ˌ)==¦-\ *n* [ISV ¹*anti-* + *reticular*] : a serum prepared from blood of horses inoculated with cells of normal human spleen and bone marrow and claimed to have restorative and regenerative effects on certain reticular tissues in humans

¹an·ti·rheu·mat·ic \¦=(ˌ)==¦-\ *adj* [¹*anti-* + *rheumatic*] : alleviating or preventing rheumatism

²antirheumatic *n* : an antirheumatic agent

an·tir·rhi·num \ˌantəˈrīnəm, -tē-\ *n* [NL, fr. L, snapdragon, fr. Gk *antirrhinon*, fr. *anti-* similar to, like (fr. *anti* against, instead of, equivalent to) + *-rrhinon* (fr. *rhin-, rhis* nose, snout); fr. the resemblance of the flower to a calf's snout] **1** *cap* : a genus of herbs (family Scrophulariaceae) of the northern hemisphere with brightly colored irregular flowers distinguished from those of *Linaria* by the absence of a spur — see SNAPDRAGON **2** -s : any plant of the genus *Antirrhinum*

antis *pl of* ANTI

anti-sabbatarian *n* [¹*anti-* + *sabbatarian*] : one who denies any obligation for observing the Sabbath day

antiscion *n, pl* **antiscia** [Gk *antiskion*, fr. *anti-* ¹anti- + *-skion* (fr. *skia* shadow) — more at SCENE] *archaic* : either of any two signs of the zodiac equally distant from Cancer and Capricorn on opposite sides

¹an·ti·scor·bu·tic \¦=(ˌ)= *at* ¹ANTI- + ˌ=¦==\ *adj* [¹*anti-* + *scorbutic*] : counteracting scurvy ⟨the ~ vitamin is vitamin C⟩

²antiscorbutic \"\ *n* -s : a remedy for scurvy

an·ti·se·le·ne \ˌ=(ˌ)=səˈlēnē\ *n* -s [NL, fr. *anti-* ¹anti- + Gk *selēnē* moon — more at SELEN-] : a white luminous spot like a halo occurring rarely at the same elevation as the moon and in the opposite azimuth

an·ti-sem·ite \ˌ=(ˌ)=¦-\ *n, usu cap S* [¹*anti-* + *Semite*] : one who is hostile to Jews or who practices anti-Semitism

an·ti-se·mit·ic \¦=(ˌ)==¦==\ *adj, often cap S* [¹*anti-* + *Semitic*] : relating to or characterized by anti-Semitism

an·ti-sem·i·tism \ˌ=(ˌ)=¦-\ *n, usu cap S* **1** : hostility toward Jews as a religious or racial minority group often accompanied by social, economic, and political discrimination — compare RACISM **2** : opposition to Zionism : sympathy with opponents of the state of Israel

an·ti·sep·sis \ˌantəˈsepsəs, ˌaan-\ *n, pl* **an·ti·sep·ses** \-pˌsēz\ [NL, fr. E *antiseptic*, after such pairs as E *septic*: NL *sepsis*] : the process of inhibiting the growth and multiplication of microorganisms : the prevention or treatment of sepsis by antiseptic means — compare ASEPSIS, DISINFECTION, STERILIZATION

¹an·ti·sep·tic \¦==¦septik, -ēk\ *adj* [¹*anti-* + Gk *sēptikos* putrefying — more at SEPTIC] **1 a** : opposing sepsis, putrefaction, or decay : having the properties of an antiseptic : preventing or arresting the growth or action of microorganisms esp. on or in living tissue — compare DISINFECTANT **b** : acting like an antiseptic : CLEANSING, PURIFYING ⟨the ~ effect of sturdy criticism —*New Republic*⟩; *also* : BRACING ⟨smelling the crisp ~ air —Berton Roueché⟩ **c** : giving protection from what is contaminating ⟨new settlements a safe number of ~ miles from Johannesburg's whites —*Time*⟩ **2** : relating to or characterized by the use of antiseptics ⟨~ treatment⟩ — compare ASEPTIC **3 a** : free from living microorganisms : characterized by scrupulous cleanliness, sterilization, exclusion of bacteria : ASEPTIC ⟨a technician in an ~ white jacket —*Monsanto Mag.*⟩ **b** (1) : suggestive of a hospital or operating room (as in cleanliness or orderliness) ⟨abstract art's ~ charm —Lewis Mumford⟩ ⟨the ~ world of interstellar mathematics —*Time*⟩ (2) : excessively neat, well-ordered, or severe ⟨the room itself was bare, almost ~ —Nicholas Blake⟩ (3) : lacking warmth or vitality ⟨a conception that was much too meek and ~ —Joseph Katz⟩ (4) : DULL, VAPID, UNIMAGINATIVE ⟨main building of ~ institutional Georgian —Nathaniel Burt⟩ **c** : free or protected from what is contaminating ⟨lyrics that were ~ as Sunday school —*Saturday Rev.*⟩ ⟨two romances of a lively but ~ nature —Wolcott Gibbs⟩ **d** : marked by objectivity or detachment; *esp* : coldly impersonal ⟨gave the score an ~ reading —Horst Koegler⟩ — **an·ti·sep·ti·cal·ly** \-tək(ə)lē, -ēk-, -li\ *adv*

²antiseptic \"\ *n* -s : a substance that opposes sepsis, putrefaction, or decay : one that prevents or arrests the growth or action of microorganisms either by inhibiting their activity or by destroying them — used esp. of agents applied to living tissue; compare DISINFECTANT, GERMICIDE

an·ti·sep·ti·cize \ˌ=='=təˌsīz\ *vt* -ED/-ING/-S : to make antiseptic

an·ti·se·rum \ˈ=(ˌ)= *at* ¹ANTI-+ˌ==\ *n* [ISV ¹*anti-* + *serum*] : a serum containing antibodies that is obtained from the blood of an animal subjected to repeated sublethal doses of a microorganism or a specific toxin and that is used in treatment of the disease caused by the respective microorganism or toxin (as diphtheria or tetanus) — compare ANTITOXIN

an·ti·si \ˈäntēˌsē\ *also* **an·ti·si·ans** \ˌ=='sēənz\ *n pl, usu cap* [modif. of Sp *antis*, of AmerInd origin] : the Indian peoples of the eastern slopes of the Andes

an·ti·si·der·ic \¦=(ˌ)=*at* ¹ANTI- + səˈderik\ *n* -s [¹*anti-* + Gk *sidēros* iron + E *-ic*] : a pharmaceutical agent that counteracts the physiological action of iron

an·ti·si·phon \ˌ=(ˌ)='-\ *adj* [¹*anti-* + *siphon*] : designed to prevent the emptying of a sanitary trap because of difference of pressure

an·ti·si·phon·al \¦=(ˌ)=¦-\ *adj* [¹*anti-* + *siphonal*] : opposite the siphuncle or siphon — used esp. of an unpaired lobe of the suture on the dorsal side of a cephalopod

an·ti·skid plate \¦=(ˌ)=¦-\ *n* [¹*anti-* + *skid*] : a piece of sheet iron roughed on both sides by punching holes through it alternately on each side, and placed between piled boxes or other objects to prevent sliding (as in a freight car)

an·ti·skin·ning \¦=(ˌ)=¦-\ *adj* [¹*anti-* + *skinning*, gerund of *skin*] : serving to prevent the formation of skin (as on paint)

an·ti·slav·ery *n, often attrib* [¹*anti-* + *slavery*] : opposition to slavery

an·ti·so·cial \¦=(ˌ)=¦-\ *adj* [¹*anti-* + *social*] **1 a** : tending to interrupt or destroy social intercourse **b** : hostile to the well-being of society **c** : characterized by markedly deviating behavior ⟨~ actions⟩ ⟨crime is ~⟩ ⟨~ persons⟩ **2** : averse to the society of others or to social intercourse : MISANTHROPIC ⟨stand-offish and ~ —Hamilton Basso⟩ — **an·ti·so·ci·al·i·ty** \ˌ=(ˌ)=ˌ-\ *n* -ES — **an·ti·so·cial·ly** \¦=(ˌ)=¦-\ *adv*

an·ti·so·lar \¦=(ˌ)=¦-\ *adj* [¹*anti-* + *solar*] : directly opposite the sun on the celestial sphere

an·ti·spa·dix \¦=(ˌ)=¦-\ *n* [¹*anti-* + *spadix*] : the four modified tentacles opposite the spadix in mollusks of the genus *Nautilus*

¹an·ti·spas·mod·ic \ˌ=(ˌ)=ˌ-\ *n* -s [¹*anti-* + *spasmodic*] : an antispasmodic agent

²antispasmodic \¦=(ˌ)=ˌ-\ *adj* : tending or having the power to prevent or relieve spasms or convulsions : SPASMOLYTIC

an·ti·spast \ˈantēˌspast, -tə-\ *n* -s [LL *antispastus*, fr. Gk *antispastos* drawn in the contrary direction, fr. *antispan* to draw in the contrary direction, fr. *anti-* ¹anti- + *span* to draw — more at SPAN] : a metrical foot or system of four syllables in which an iambic cadence is followed by a trochaic

an·ti·spas·tic \¦==¦spastik\ *adj* [LL *antispasticus*, fr. Gk *antispastikos*, fr. *antispastos* + *-ikos* -ic] : relating to, consisting of, or containing antispasts

an·ti·squa·ma \ˌ=='-\ *or* **an·ti·squame** \ˌ=='-\ *n, pl* **antisqua·mae** *or* **antisquames** [NL *antisquama*, fr. ¹*anti-* + *squama*] : a scalelike lobe between the base of the wing and the squama of various two-winged flies

an·tis·tes \anˈtisˌtēz\ *n, pl* **antis·ti·tes** \-təˌtēz\ [LL, priest, bishop, fr. L, overseer, high priest, fr. *ante-* + *-stes* (fr. *stare* to stand) — more at STAND] **1** : a presiding officer in the church : PRESBYTER **2** : a Moravian bishop

an·ti·stokes line \¦=(ˌ)= *at* ¹ANTI- + ˈstōks-\ *n, usu cap S* [¹*anti-* + *Stokes' (law)* + *line*] : a spectrum line of radiation not conforming to Stokes' law (sense 1)

an·ti·strep·tol·y·sin \ˌ=(ˌ)=ˌ-\ *n* -s [¹*anti-* + *streptolysin*] : an antibody against a streptolysin produced by the body of an individual injected with a streptolysin-forming streptococcus

an·tis·tro·phe \anˈtistrə(ˌ)fē, -ˌfi\ *n* -s [LL, fr. Gk *antistrophē*, fr. Gk *anti-* ¹anti- + *strophē* turning, movement of the chorus in Greek drama — more at STROPHE] **1** *in the Greek choral dance* **a** : the returning of the chorus exactly answering to a previous strophe **b** : the part of a choral song corresponding to this returning **2** *archaic* : an inverse relation or correspondence — **an·ti·stroph·ic** \ˌantəˈsträfik *also* -ōf-\ *adj* — **an·ti·stroph·i·cal·ly** \-fək(ə)lē\ *adv*

an·ti·sub·ma·rine \¦=(ˌ)= *at* ¹ANTI- + \ *adj* [¹*anti-* + *submarine*] : designed or waged to destroy submarines ⟨~ warfare⟩

an·ti·sun \ˈ=(ˌ)= *at* ¹ANTI- + ˌ=\ *n* [¹*anti-* + *sun*] : ANTHELION

an·ti·sym·met·ric \¦=(ˌ)==¦-\ *adj* [¹*anti-* + *symmetric*] *of a square matrix or a tensor* : having the sign of every element or component changed by the interchange of any two indices of that element or component

an·ti·sym·pa·tho·mi·met·ic \¦=(ˌ)==(ˌ)=(ˌ)=¦-\ *adj* [¹*anti-* + *sympathomimetic*] : SYMPATHOLYTIC

¹an·ti·syph·i·lit·ic \¦=(ˌ)=ˌ==¦-\ *adj* [¹*anti-* + *syphilitic*] : effective against syphilis ⟨~ treatment⟩

²antisyphilitic \"\ *n* -s : an agent effective against syphilis

an·ti·tank \¦=(ˌ)=¦=\ *adj* [¹*anti-* + *tank*] : designed to destroy or check tanks ⟨an ~ gun⟩

an·ti·the·nar \ˌantəˈthēnər, -tē-, -ˌnär, (')an¦tithə-\ *adj* [ISV ¹*anti-* + Gk *thenar* palm of the hand; akin to OHG *tenar* palm of the hand — more at DEN] **1** : situated opposite to the palm or sole **2** : HYPOTHENAR

an·tith·e·sis \anˈtithəsəs, aan-\ *n, pl* **antithe·ses** \-əˌsēz\ [LL, fr. Gk, lit., opposition, fr. *antithe-* (stem of *antitithenai* to set against, oppose, fr. *anti-* ¹anti- + *tithenai* to set) + *-sis* — more at DO] **1 a** : the rhetorical opposing or contrasting of ideas by means of grammatically parallel arrangements of words, clauses, or sentences (as *action*, not *words* or they *promised freedom* and *provided slavery*); *broadly* : a balanced contrast formed by a pair or several pairs of objects or concepts, each member in a pair being the opposite of the other in essence or in particulars ⟨the ~ of prose and verse⟩ **b** (1) : the second of the two opposing constituents of an antithesis ⟨~ opposed to thesis⟩ (2) : an object or concept that counteracts or contradicts another ⟨that mystic faith in unseen powers which is the ~ of materialism —Rose Macaulay⟩ : the direct opposite : CONTRARY ⟨his temperament is the very ~ of mine⟩ **2 a** : a philosophical proposition opposed to a given thesis: **a** *Kantianism* : the negative member of one of the antinomies of reason **b** *Hegelianism* : the negative moment in the movement of thought that denies the thesis and is in turn transcended in the synthesis **syn** see COMPARISON

antithet *n* -s [L, fr. Gk, fr. neut. of *antithetos*, fr. *antitithenai*] *archaic* : ANTITHESIS 1

an·ti·thet·i·cal \¦antə¦thedəkəl, ¦aan-, -etək-, -ēk-\ *or* **an·ti·thet·ic** \-ik, -ēk\ *adj* [LL *antitheticus*, fr. LGk *antithetikos*, fr. Gk *antithetos* placed in opposition (fr. *antitithenai*) + *-ikos* -ical, -ic] **1** : constituting or resembling antithesis : containing or marked by antithesis ⟨~ symbolism of ice and flame—Leslie Rees⟩ **2** : marked by direct opposition : exactly opposite : COUNTER, OPPOSING ⟨respective ways of life which looked to wholly *antithetic* ends —H.J.Laski⟩ **syn** see OPPOSITE

an·ti·thet·i·cal·ly \-ək(ə)lē, -ēk-, -li\ *adv* : with antithesis in an antithetical manner

antithetic theory *n* : a theory in botany: the sporophyte and gametophyte are basically distinct with the gametophyte representing the primitive ancestral phase and the sporophyte being a new structure resulting from increasingly retarded zygotic reduction — compare HOMOLOGOUS THEORY

an·ti·throm·bic \¦=(ˌ)= *at* ¹ANTI- + ¦thrämbik\ *adj* : of or like that of an antithrombin

an·ti·throm·bin \¦=(ˌ)=¦-\ *n* [ISV ¹*anti-* + *thrombin*] : a substance in blood that inactivates thrombin and prevents conversion of fibrinogen to fibrin — compare HEPARIN

an·ti·thy·roid \¦=(ˌ)=¦-\ *adj* [¹*anti-* + *thyroid*] : tending or having power to counteract thyroid overactivity ⟨~ drugs⟩

an·ti·torque rotor \¦=(ˌ)=¦-\ *n* [¹*anti-* + *torque*] : a small rotor mounted on the tail of a helicopter that balances the torque reaction of the main lifting rotor and thus permits the craft to maintain a desired heading

an·ti·tox·ic \¦=(ˌ)=¦-\ *adj* [¹*anti-* + *toxic*] **1** : counteracting toxins ⟨~ versus antibacterial immunity⟩ **2** : being or containing antitoxins ⟨~ serum⟩

an·ti·tox·in \ˌ=tēˈtäksən, -tə'-\ *n* [ISV ¹*anti-* + *toxin*] : an antibody that is capable of neutralizing the specific toxin (as a specific causative agent of disease) that stimulated its production in the body and is produced in animals for medical purposes by injection of a toxin or toxoid with the resulting serum being used to counteract the toxin in other individuals; *also* : a serum containing antitoxins — compare ANTIVENIN

an·ti·trades \ˈ=(ˌ)=ˌ=\ *n pl* [¹*anti-* + *trades* (trade winds)] : the prevailing westerly winds of middle latitudes : the westerly winds above the trade winds

an·ti·trag·i·cus \ˌantēˈtrajəkəs, -ntə-\ *n, pl* **antitragi·ci** \-jəˌsī\ [NL, fr. *antitragus* + L *-icus* -ic] : a small muscle arising from the outer part of the antitragus and inserted into the antihelix

an·ti·tra·gus \¦==¦trāgəs\ *n, pl* **antitra·gi** \-āˌjī, -əˌgī\ [NL, fr. Gk *antitragos*, fr. *anti-* ¹anti- + *tragos* he-goat, part of the inner ear] : a prominence on the lower posterior portion of the concha of the external ear opposite the tragus

an·ti·tro·chan·ter \-trōˈkantər\ *n* [¹*anti-* + *trochanter*] : an articular surface on the ilium of birds against which the great trochanter of the femur plays

an·ti·trope \ˈantēˌtrōp, -tə-\ *n* -s [¹*anti-* + *-trope*] *zool* : an antitropic part or appendage — opposed to *syntrope*

an·ti·trop·ic \¦==¦träpik\ *adj* [¹*anti-* + *-tropic*] **1** : SINISTRORSE **2** : repeated and reversed symmetrically ⟨the corresponding limbs on the right and left sides of a vertebrate are ~⟩ — opposed to *syntropic*

an·tit·ro·py \anˈti·trəpē\ *n* -ES [¹*anti-* + *-tropy*] : the condition or quality of being antitropic

an·ti·trust \¦=(ˌ)= *at* ¹ANTI- + ¦=\ *adj* [¹*anti-* + *trust*] : of or relating to opposition to trusts or combinations; *specif* : consisting of federal and state laws and their enforcement for the protection of trade and commerce from unlawful restraints and monopolies or unfair business practices

an·ti·tryp·sin \ˈ=(ˌ)=ˌtripsən\ *n* -s [ISV ¹*anti-* + *trypsin*;

orig. formed in G] **:** a substance (as one obtained from pancreatic extracts or from soybeans) that inhibits the action of trypsin — **an·ti·tryp·tic** \¦=(,)=¦triptik\ *adj*
an·ti·tus·sive \¦=(,)=¦-\ *adj* [¹*anti-* + *tussive*] **:** tending or having the power to control or prevent cough
an·ti·twi·light \'antē,-, -tə-\ *or* **antitwilight arch** *n* [¹*anti-* + *twilight*] **:** the pink or purplish glow in the eastern sky after sunset
an·ti·type \'antə,tīp, -tē- *also* -(,)tī-, 'aan-\ *n* [LL *antitypus* (fr. LGk *antitypos*) or NL *antitypum*, fr. LGk *antitypon*; both fr. Gk, masc. & neut. of *antitypos* repelled by a hard body, corresponding to a die, fr. *antitypoun* to strike against, fr. *anti-* ¹anti- + *typoun* to stamp, fr. *typos* blow, mark of a blow, mold — more at TYPE] **1 a :** something that corresponds to or is foreshadowed in a type **b :** an opposite type **2 :** ANTITROPE
an·ti·typ·i·cal \¦=(,)=¦tipəkəl, -ēk-\ *or* **an·ti·typ·ic** \-¦tipik, -ēk\ *adj* **1 :** of or relating to an antitype **2 :** ANTITROPIC 2 — **an·ti·typ·i·cal·ly** \-ək(ə)lē, -li, -ēk-\ *adv*
an·ti·ty·py \an'tid·əpē, -pi, -titə-\ *n* -ES [Gk *antitypia*, fr. *antitypos* + *-ia*] **:** resistance offered esp. by matter to penetrative force, alteration, or change
an·ti·ven·in \¦=(,)= *at* ¹ANTI- + ¦venən, ¦vē-\ *also* **an·ti·venene** \-və¦nēn, -¦ve,nēn, -¦vē,-\ *n* -S [ISV ¹*anti-* + *venin*, *venene*] **:** an antitoxin to a venom; *also* **:** an antiserum containing such an antitoxin
an·ti·viral \¦=(,)=¦-\ *adj* [¹*anti-* + *viral*] **:** acting to make a virus ineffective
an·ti·vi·rot·ic \¦=(,)=,vī¦räd·ik, -ätik, -ēk\ *n* -S [¹*anti-* + *virus* + *-otic*] **:** an antibiotic effective against viruses
an·ti·vi·ta·min \¦=(,)=,-\ *n* [¹*anti-* + *vitamin*] **:** a substance that renders a vitamin ineffective either by converting it into a compound of different structure or by making it unavailable through combination with it — compare ANTIMETABOLITE
an·ti·viv·i·sec·tion·ist \,=(,)=,-\ *n* -S [¹*anti-* + *vivisection* + *-ist*] **:** a person opposed to animal experimentation
an·ti·xe·roph·thal·mic vitamin \¦=(,)=,ziräf¦thalmik-\ *n* [¹*anti-* + *xerophthalmia* + *-ic*] **:** VITAMIN A
an·ti·zi·on·ism \,=(,)=¦-\ *n* -S *usu cap Z* [¹*anti-* + *Zionism*] **:** opposition to the establishment or support of the state of Israel
an·ti·zo·ea \,antē,zō'ēə, -tə-\ *n*, *pl* **antizoe·ae** \-'ē,ē, -'ē,ī\ [NL, fr. ²*anti-* + *zoea*] **:** an early stomatopod larva
ant·ler \'antlə(r), 'aan-\ *n* -S [ME *aunteler*, fr. MF *antoillier*, fr. (assumed) VL *anteoculare*, fr. neut. of *anteocularis* located before the eye, fr. L *ante-* + *oculus* eye + *-aris* -ar — more at EYE] **:** a horn of an animal of the deer family being typically present only in the male and differing from the horns of other ruminants in being a solid generally branched bony outgrowth that is shed and renewed annually; *sometimes* **:** a branch of an antler — see BEAM; compare VELVET

antler: *a* brow antler, *b* bay antler, *c* royal antler, *d* surroyal antler

ant·lered crab \-lə(d)-\ *n* **:** an Australian deepwater crab (*Latreillopsis petterdi*) with a tuberculated carapace and an antler-shaped spine over each eye
ant·ler·ite \lə,rīt\ *n* -S [*Antler* Mine, Arizona, its locality + E *-ite*] **:** a mineral $Cu_3SO_4(OH)_4$ consisting of a basic copper sulfate, occurring in green crystals, and interlaced aggregates of needlelike crystals
antler lichen *n* **:** a fruticose antler-shaped lichen (*Evernia cladonia*)
antler moth *n* **:** a brownish white-marked European moth (*Charaeas graminis*) whose larva devastates grasslands
antler sponge *n* **:** any of several branching erect calcareous sponges suggesting an antler in form
ant lion *n* **:** an insect of *Myrmeleon* or related genera (order Neuroptera), most having a larva that digs a small conical pit in sandy soil in the bottom of which it lies buried with its long jaws protruding to catch any insects (as ants) which fall into the pit
antney over *sometimes cap A*, *var of* ANTONY OVER
an·toe·ci \an·'tē,sī\ *also* **an·toe·cians** \-,shənz\ *n pl* [*antoec* fr. LL, fr. Gk *antoikoi*, fr. *anti-* ¹anti- + *oikos* house; *antoecians* fr. LL *antoeci* + E *-an* + *-s* — more at VICINITY] **:** those who live under the same meridian but on opposite parallels of latitude equidistant north and south of the equator
an·to·nine \'antə,nīn\ *also* **an·to·nin·i·an** \¦antə¦ninēən, -ninyən\ *adj*, *usu cap* [*Antonine* fr. L *Antoninus* Pius † A.D. 161 and Marcus Aurelius *Antoninus* † A.D. 180 Roman emperors; *Antoninian* fr. L *Antoninus* + E *-ian*] **:** characteristic of the Roman emperors Antoninus Pius and Marcus Aurelius Antoninus or their rule
an·to·nin·i·a·nus \,antə,ninē'ānəs\ *n*, *pl* **antoninia·ni** \-'ā,nī\ [LL, lit., of Antoninus, fr. Marcus Aurelius *Antoninus* Caracalla † A.D. 217 Roman emperor who introduced it + L *-ianus* -ian] **:** an ancient Roman coin orig. worth two denarii
an·ton·o·ma·sia \(,)an,tänə'māzh(ē)ə\ *n* -S [L, fr. Gk, fr. *antonomazein* to name instead (fr. *anti-* instead, against + *onomazein* to name, fr. *onoma* name) + *-ia* — more at ANTI-, NAME] **1 :** the substitution of another designation for a common, obvious, or normal one: as **a :** the use of an official title or an epithet in place of a proper name (as *his honor* for *Judge Doe*) or ordinary appellative (as *chief executive* for *the president*) **b :** the use of a proper name to designate a member of a class (as a *Solomon* for *a wise ruler*); *also* **:** the making of a common noun or verb from a proper name (as *pasteurize* from *Pasteur*) **2 :** the giving of a proper name (as to a character in fiction) that names or suggests a leading quality (as Squire *Allworthy*, Doctor *Sawbones*)
an·to·nym \'antə,nim, 'aan-, -tᵊn,im\ *n* -S [¹*anti-* + *-onym*] **:** a word of opposite meaning ⟨the usual ~ of *good* is *bad*⟩ — opposed to *synonym* — **an·ton·y·my** \an·'tänəmē, aan-, -mi\ *n* -ES
an·ton·y·mous \(')=¦tänəməs\ *adj* **:** being an antonym **:** indicating an opposite significance **:** OPPOSING, CONTRADICTING
syn see OPPOSITE
an·to·ny over \'ant(ᵊ)nē·, 'aan-,'ain-\ *or* **an·dy over** \'andē-, 'aan-\ *or* **an·nie over** \'anē-, -ni\ *also* **an·te over** \'antē-, 'aan-,'ain-, -ti\ *or* **an·tho·ny over** *like* ANTONY OVER; *or*, *sometimes*, -thən-\ *or* **ant·ney over** *or* **an·ty over** *n* -S *sometimes cap A* [origin unknown] **:** a game played by two teams (as of schoolboys) in which a ball is tossed back and forth over any small building or bounced against its side
ant·or·bi·tal \¦ant·¦=-\ *adj* [¹*anti-* + *orbital*] **:** situated in front of the orbit
ant plant *n* **:** MYRMECOPHYTE
antr- *or* **antro-** *comb form* [NL, fr. LL *antrum* cavity in the body — more at ANTRUM] **1 :** antrum ⟨*antritis*⟩ **2 :** antral and ⟨*antronasal*⟩
antra *pl of* ANTRUM
an·tral \'antrəl, 'aan-, 'ain-\ *adj* **:** of or relating to an antrum
an·tre \'antə(r)\ *n* -S [F, fr. L *antrum* — more at ANTRUM] **:** CAVE 1
an·trim \'an·trəm\ *adj*, *usu cap* [fr. *Antrim*, county of Ireland] **:** of or from County Antrim, Northern Ireland **:** of the kind or style prevalent in Antrim
an·trin \'äntrən\ *adj* [fr. past part. of Sc *anter* to adventure, to chance on, fr. ME *auntren*, *aventuren* — more at ADVENTURE] *Scot* **:** RARE, OCCASIONAL ⟨he comes around at ~ times⟩
an·trorse \'an·,trȯrs, =¦=\ *adj* [NL *antrorsus*, irreg. fr. *antero-* + *-orsus* (as in *dextrorsus* toward the right) — more at DEXTRORSE] **:** directed forward or upward — compare RETRORSE — **an·trorse·ly** *adv*
an·tros·to·mus \an·'trästəməs\ *n*, *cap* [NL, fr. *antro-* (fr. L *antrum* cave) + *-stomus*] *in some classifications* **:** a genus of birds including the whippoorwill and chuck-will's-widow
an·tros·to·my \-təmē\ *n* -ES [*antr-* + *-stomy*] **:** the operation of opening an antrum (as for drainage); *also* **:** the opening made in such an operation
an·trot·o·my \an·'träd·əmē\ *n* -ES [ISV *antr-* + *-tomy*] **:** ANTROSTOMY
an·trum \'an·trəm\ *n*, *pl* **an·tra** \-rə\ [LL, cavity in the body, fr. L, cave, fr. Gk *antron*; perh. akin to Gk *anemos* wind — more at ANIMATE] **:** the cavity of a hollow organ or a sinus ⟨the ~ of the Graafian follicle⟩
antrum of high·more \-'hī,mō(ə)r\ *usu cap H* [after Nathaniel *Highmore* †1685 Eng. physician who first described it] **:** MAXILLARY SINUS
an·trus·tion \an'trəschən\ *n* -S [ML *antrustion-*, *antrustio*, of Gmc origin; akin to OHG *ant-*, *int-* against and OHG *trōst* help, comfort — more at ANTE-, TRUST] **:** a follower usu. in the bodyguard of Frankish princes of the 5th to 7th centuries
An·try·cide \'antrə,sīd\ *trademark* — used for a white crystalline compound derived from quinoline and used in the control of trypanosomiasis in cattle
ants *pl of* ANT
ant·shrike \'ant,shrīk\ *n* [*ant*bird + *shrike*] **:** any of numerous tropical American antbirds (family Formicariidae) resembling shrikes
ant's-wood *n*, *pl* **ant's-woods :** SAFFRON PLUM; *broadly* **:** BUCKTHORN 2
antsy \'an(t)sē, 'aan-, 'ain-\ *adj*, *usu* -ER/-EST [*ants* (pl. of ¹*ant*) + *-y*] *slang* **:** EAGER, IMPATIENT, RESTLESS; *sometimes* **:** CONCUPISCENT
ant thrush *n* **1 :** ANTBIRD **2 :** PITTA 2
ant tree *n* **:** any of several So. American trees of the genus *Triplaris* having hollow stems inhabited by venomous ants which repel intruders
ANTU \'an,tü\ *abbr or n* -S *sometimes not cap* [*a*lpha-*n*aphthyl*t*hio*u*rea] **:** a chemical $C_{10}H_7NHCSNH_2$ produced as a gray powder for use as a rat poison; alpha-naphthylthiourea
an·tung \'än·,tu̇ŋ, -,du̇ŋ\ *adj*, *usu cap* [fr. *Antung*, Manchuria] **:** of or from the city of Antung, Manchuria **:** of the kind or style prevalent in Antung
ant·werp \'ant·,wərp, 'aan-, 'ain-, -,wəp, -,wə(r)p\ *adj*, *usu cap* [fr. *Antwerp*, Belgium] **:** of or from the city of Antwerp, Belgium **:** of the kind or style prevalent in Antwerp
antwerp *or* **antwerp pigeon** *n* -S *usu cap A* [fr. *Antwerp*, Belgium] **:** one of a Belgian variety of homing pigeons
antwerp blue *n*, *usu cap A* **1 :** any of various iron-blue pigments (as one containing alumina or a zinc compound) **2 :** a moderate blue that is greener and duller than average copen and greener and deeper than azurite blue, Dresden blue, or pompadour — called also *Harlem blue*, *mineral blue*
antwerp brown *n*, *often cap A* **:** CONGO 4
antwerp red *n*, *often cap A* **:** ²BOLE 3
antwren \'=,=\ *n* [*ant* + *wren*] **:** any of various small antbirds having short tails like wrens
anty over *sometimes cap A*, *var of* ANTONY OVER
anu \'ä,nü, -,nyü, 'a-\ *also* **an·yu** \-,nyü\ *n* -S [AmerSp *añú*, fr. Quechua *áñu*] **1 :** a So. American herb (*Tropaeolum tuberosum*) cultivated for its edible tubers **2 :** the tuber produced by the anu
anu·bing \'änü,biŋ, ,==¦=\ *also* **anu·bin** \-,bēn\ *or* **ano·bing** \-nō,biŋ\ *n* -S [Tag *anubing*] **1 :** any of several trees of the genus *Artocarpus* **2 :** the wood of the anubing
anu·bis baboon \ə'n(y)übəs-\ *n* [after *Anubis*, a jackal god in ancient Egyptian religion the pictorial representation of which the animal was thought to resemble, fr. L, fr. Gk *Anoubis*, fr. Egypt *Ȧnpu*, *Ȧnp*] **:** a rather rare Sudanese baboon (*Papio doguera*)
anucleate *also* **anucleated** \(')ā+\ *adj* [²*a-* + *nucleate*, *nucleated*] **:** lacking a nucleus
a number 1 \'ā¦=¦=¦wən\ *adj*, *cap A* **:** A1 (sense 2)
an·under \ə'nən(d)ə(r)\ *prep* [ME, fr. *an*, *on* on + *under*] *chiefly dial* **:** UNDER
an·u·ra \ə'n(y)u̇rə, a'-\ [NL, fr. *an-* + *-ura*] *syn of* SALIENTIA
an·u·ran \-'n(y)u̇rən\ *adj or n* [NL *Anura* + E *-an*] **:** SALIENTIAN
an·u·re·sis \,anyə'rēsəs, -nə'-\ *n*, *pl* **anure·ses** \-ē,sēz\ [NL, fr. *an-* + *uresis*] **:** retention of urine in the urinary bladder **:** failure or inability to void urine — compare ANURIA — **an·u·ret·ic** \¦==¦red·ik\ *adj*
an·u·ria \ə'n(y)u̇rēə, a'-\ *n* -S [NL, fr. *an-* + *-uria*] **:** absence or defective excretion of urine — compare ANURESIS — **an·u·ric** \-u̇rik\ *adj*
an·u·rous \ə'n(y)u̇rəs, a'-\ *or* **an·our·ous** \-'nu̇rəs\ *adj* [*an-* + *-urous*, *-ourous*] *zool* **:** having no tail ⟨~ toads⟩ ⟨~ frogs⟩
an·u·ry \'anyərē, -ri\ *n* -ES [*an-* + Gk *oura* tail + E *-y*] *zool* **:** absence of a tail ⟨the inheritance of ~ in mice⟩
anus \'ānəs\ *n*, *pl* **anuses** *also* **ani** \'ā(,)nī\ [L, ring, anus; akin to OIr *áinne* and perh. to Arm *anur* necklace, ring] **:** the posterior opening of the alimentary canal
an·us·va·ra \,anəs'värə, ,än-\ *n* -S [Skt *anusvāra*] **1 :** a Sanskrit postvocalic nasal sound or group of sounds occurring in the interior of a morpheme only before *ś*, *ṣ*, *s*, or *h* and at the end of a morpheme only before an initial consonant of a following morpheme **2 :** a sign used in writing Sanskrit to represent the anusvara sound or sounds and in some manuscripts and editions certain other postvocalic nasal sounds — see ALPHABET table
¹**an·vil** \'anvəl, 'aan- *sometimes* -(,)vil\ *n* -S [alter. of ME *anfilt*, *anfelt*, fr. OE *anfealt*, *anfilt* (akin to OHG *anafalz*, G dial. *änefilt*, MD *anvilt*), fr. *an* on + *-fealt*, *-filt* (akin to Sw dial. *filta* to beat) — more at ON, FELT] **1 a :** a heavy usu. steel-faced iron block on which metal is shaped (as by hand hammering or forging) **b :** a machine part that serves a similar purpose — compare SNARLING IRON **2 :** something that resembles an anvil in shape or use ⟨bold imagination, able thought, and discussion . . . are the ~ of public policy —A.E.Stevenson b.1900⟩: as **a :** INCUS **b :** the metal structure of a cartridge against which the percussion composition is exploded by the blow of the firing pin upon the head of the primer **c :** the lower contact of a telegraphic key **d :** the fixed jaw in a measuring instrument (as a micrometer caliper) **e :** a musical percussion instrument consisting of a steel bar that when struck with a hammer sounds like an anvil — **on the anvil** *adv* (*or adj*) **:** under discussion or in preparation

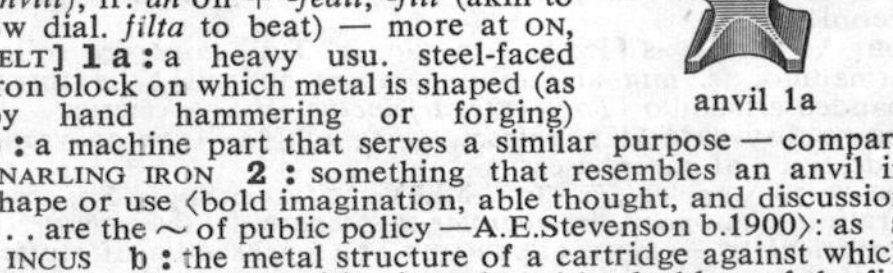
anvil 1a

²**anvil** \"\ *vt* **anvilled; anvilled; anvilling; anvils** *obs* **:** to shape on an anvil **:** hammer out
anvil bat *n* **:** EPAULET BAT
anvil block *n* **:** the anvil for a power hammer
anvil chisel *n* **:** HARDIE
anvil cloud *n* **:** the anvil-shaped top of a cumulonimbus
anx·i·ety \aŋ'zīəd·ē, aiŋ-, -ətē, -i\ *n* -ES [L *anxietas*, fr. *anxius* + *-tas* -ty] **1 a** (1) **:** a state of being anxious or of experiencing a strong or dominating blend of uncertainty, agitation or dread, and brooding fear about some contingency **:** UNEASINESS ⟨your ~ about the child's health . . . is . . . unfounded —Agnes Repplier⟩ (2) **:** the cause for such a state ⟨there was no escaping his *anxieties*, and plagued as he was by them, he sought solitude —Jean Stafford⟩ **b :** a strong concern about some imminent development or a strong desire, mixed with doubt and fear, for some event or issue ⟨~ to succeed had dragged her out of her capable and mechanical indifference —Arnold Bennett⟩ **2 a :** an abnormal and overwhelming sense of apprehension and of fear often marked by such physical symptoms as tension, tremor, sweating, palpitation, and increased pulse rate **b** (1) **:** an unpleasant feeling of helplessness and isolation sometimes accompanied by physiological manifestations of fear, consciously accounted for by the anticipation of pain, death, or some unknown catastrophe but without sufficient objective justification, and explained on the basis of repressed libidinal expression resulting from parental apprehension and rejection (2) **:** a condition experimentally produced in laboratory animals and manifested by the physiological changes that in man accompany fear **3** *existentialism* **:** a state of mind that is deeply troubled or distressed; *esp* **:** one that results from apparently being confronted with nothingness (as in a situation involving the need or the responsibility to make valuations and decisions and to take actions without the guidance of tradition or society) **syn** see CARE
anxiety attack *n* **:** an acute psychobiologic reaction manifested by anxiety or panic and by the physiologic changes characteristically accompanying fear
anxiety equivalent *n* **:** a spontaneous attack in which an intense somatic symptom (as palpitation of the heart) replaces fear
anxiety hysteria *n* **:** a psychoneurotic disorder with features of both conversion reaction and anxiety neurosis
anxiety neurosis *or* **anxiety reaction** *or* **anxiety state** *n* **:** a psychoneurotic disorder characterized by diffuse anxiety often accompanied by somatic manifestations of fear
anx·ious \'aŋ(k)shəs, 'aiŋ-\ *adj* [L *anxius*, fr. *angere* to strangle, distress — more at ANGER] **1 :** characterized by extreme uneasiness of mind about some contingency **:** experiencing a sense of brooding fear **:** APPREHENSIVE, WORRIED ⟨wounded by the disapproval of . . . her friends and ~ for the future —R.M.Lovett⟩ ⟨a timid young woman, not used to cities, ~ about small things —Leslie Rees⟩ **2 :** characterized by, resulting from, or causing anxiety **:** WORRYING ⟨two ~ days followed while the ship was being loaded —T.B. Costain⟩ ⟨bid my ~ fears subside —William Williams⟩ **3 :** characterized by strong earnest desire **:** ardently wishing ⟨a kindhearted landlord ever ~ to ameliorate the condition of the poor —Anthony Trollope⟩ **syn** see AFRAID, EAGER
anxious bench *or* **anxious seat** *n* **1 :** a seat near the pulpit reserved at some revival meetings for persons esp. concerned about their spiritual condition — called also *mourners' bench* **2 :** a state of worry or anxiety caused by uncertainty ⟨everybody was kept on the *anxious seat* by this system of perpetual probation —Alva Johnston⟩
anx·ious·ly *adv* **:** in an anxious manner
anx·ious·ness *n* -ES **:** the state of being anxious
¹**any** \¦enē, -ni *sometimes* ,ən- *or*, *after* t *or* d, ᵊn-\ *adj* [ME *any*, *eny*, fr. OE *ǣnig* (akin to OFris *ēnig*, OHG *einag*, ON *einigr* anyone, no one), fr. *ān* one + *-ig* -y — more at ONE] **1 :** one indifferently out of more than two **:** one or some indiscriminately of whatever kind: **a :** one or another **:** this, that, or the other — used as a function word esp. in interrogative and conditional expressions to indicate one that is not a particular or definite individual of the given category but whichever one chance may select ⟨did you experience ~ trouble⟩ ⟨if ~ defect appears⟩ ⟨ask ~ man you meet⟩ **b :** one, no matter what one **:** EVERY — used as a function word esp. in assertions and denials to indicate one that is selected without restriction or limitation of choice ⟨~ child would know that⟩ ⟨forbidden to enter ~ house⟩ **c :** one or some of whatever kind or sort; *esp* **:** one or some however imperfect — used as a function word to indicate one that is selected with indifference to quality ⟨~ plan is better than no plan⟩ **2 :** one, some, or all indiscriminately of whatever quantity: **a :** one or more **:** not none — used as a function word to indicate a positive but undetermined number or amount ⟨I can't find ~ stamps⟩ ⟨have you ~ money⟩ **b :** ALL — used as a function word to indicate the maximum or whole of a number or quantity ⟨give me ~ letters you find⟩ ⟨he needs ~ help he can get⟩ **c :** a or some no matter how great or small — used as a function word to indicate what is considered despite its quantity or extent ⟨determined to win at ~ cost⟩ ⟨it is good of you to pay ~ attention to him⟩ **3 a :** great, unmeasured, or unlimited in amount, quantity, number, time, or extent **:** up to whatever measure may be needed or desired ⟨the falls can produce ~ quantity of water power⟩ ⟨could have seen him ~ time last week⟩ **b :** appreciably or at all large, prolonged, or extended in amount, quantity, time, or extent — used with a preceding negative ⟨could not endure it ~ length of time⟩ ⟨could not walk ~ distance without falling⟩
²**any** \"\ *pron*, *pl* **any** [ME *any*, *eny* fr. OE *ǣnig*, fr. *ǣnig*, adj.] **1 :** one or more indiscriminately from all those of a kind: **a :** any person or persons **:** ANYBODY ⟨asked if there were ~ present who had remembered⟩ ⟨~ of them could answer the question⟩ **b :** any thing or things **:** any part, quantity, or number ⟨promised not to lose ~ of the books⟩ ⟨a scene as effective as ~ in modern drama⟩ ⟨no money and no prospect of ~⟩ **2** *now dial Eng* **:** one of two **:** EITHER
³**any** \"\ *adv* [ME *any*, *eny*, fr. *any*, *eny*, adj.] **:** to any extent **:** in any degree **:** at all ⟨he won't be ~ happier there⟩ ⟨he could not walk ~ farther⟩ ⟨you certainly aren't helping me ~⟩
an·yath·i·an \(')an¦yathēən\ *adj*, *usu cap* [Burmese *ān-ya=thā* native of upper Burma + E *-ian*] **:** of or belonging to a lower Paleolithic culture of Burma and Thailand characterized by distinctive chopping tools
¹**any·body** \'enē,bädē, -(,)bədē, -ni...di\ *pron* [¹*any* + *body*] **:** a person out of an indefinite number **:** any person **:** ANYONE ⟨is ~ home⟩ ⟨had forgotten to ask ~ to come⟩
²**anybody** \"\ *n* **:** a person of some importance ⟨everybody who was ~ was at all was at the dance⟩
anyhow \'==,=\ *adv* **1 a :** in any manner whatever **:** ANYWISE ⟨wheat may be sown almost ~ —Adrian Bell⟩ **b :** without order or arrangement **:** HAPHAZARDLY ⟨untidy scrambles of bed linen . . . flung ~ over balustrades —Richard Llewellyn⟩ **2 :** in any case **:** at any rate **:** in any event ⟨and ~ it was very much better for the generals to go on with the military operations —Sir Winston Churchill⟩
anymore \¦==¦=\ *adv* [³*any* + *more*] **:** at the present time **:** NOWADAYS, CURRENTLY, NOW — used only in a negative context ⟨I am not lucky ~ —Ernest Hemingway⟩ or a statement with negative implication ⟨he rarely comes here ~⟩ except in dial. ⟨used to be I had to . . . carry my own whiskey out of the Hollow, but ~ I'm such a good customer they tote it up here . . . for me —Charley Robertson⟩ ⟨every time I even smile at a man ~ the papers have me practically married to him —Betty Grable⟩
any·one \'==(,)wən\ *pron* [ME *any on*, *eny on*, fr. *any*, *eny* + *on* one] **:** any person indiscriminately **:** ANYBODY ⟨~ on the lookout for good prose —J.W.Beach⟩ ⟨did ~ care for her opinion —Hugh Walpole⟩
anyplace \'==,=\ *adv* [¹*any* + *place*] **:** in any place **:** ANYWHERE ⟨wouldn't let you work ~ else —Edmund Wilson⟩
any-quantity rate *n* **:** a freight rate with the charge per unit the same regardless of the quantity offered for shipment — abbr. *AQ*
anys·ti·dae \ə'nistə,dē\ *n pl*, *cap* [NL, fr. *Anystis*, type genus + *-idae*] **:** a family of predatory mites having no median groove in the cephalothorax and the last joint of the first pair of legs not swollen though usu. long
¹**any·thing** \'enē,thiŋ, -ni,-, *often* -,thin *or* -,thēŋ *when another word follows without pause*\ *pron* [ME *anything*, *enything* fr. OE *ǣnig thing*, fr. *ǣnig* any + *thing*] **:** any thing whatever **:** something or other **:** AUGHT ⟨does not include ~ he does not need —E.R.Bentley⟩ ⟨don't bother to do ~ about it —W.J. Reilly⟩
²**anything** \"\ *adv* [ME, fr. OE *ǣngi thinga* to any extent, inst. of *ǣnig thing* anything] **:** in any measure **:** to any extent **:** at all ⟨if the remaining books . . . are ~ up to the standard of those already published —*Times Lit. Supp.*⟩
³**anything** \"\ *n* [¹*anything*] **:** thing of whatever kind **:** thing of any sort ⟨my horse, my ox, my ass, my ~ —Shak.⟩
any·thing·ar·i·an \,==(,)=¦ereən\ *n* -S [¹*anything* + *-arian* (as in *unitarian*)] **:** one that holds no particular creed or dogma
anything but *adv* **:** not at all **:** by no means **:** in no respect ⟨it was *anything but* clear . . . what the political democracy . . . would be like —John Strachey⟩
anything like *adv* **:** in any way **:** to any extent **:** at all ⟨give *anything like* an adequate image of the phonetic facts —R.M.S. Heffner⟩
anytime \'==,=\ *adv* [¹*any* + *time*] **:** at any time whatever **:** under any circumstances ⟨can get a job anywhere ~ —Jack Kerouac⟩
anyu *var of* ANU
anyway *adv* [¹*any* + *way*] **1 :** in any way whatever **:** ANYWISE ⟨told him to do the job ~ he wanted⟩ **2 :** at all events **:** in any case **:** ANYHOW ⟨~ he would not forget⟩
anyways \'==,=\ *adv* [¹*any* + *-ways*] **1 a** *archaic* **:** in any manner or respect **:** ANYWISE **b** *dial* **:** to any degree at all ⟨it didn't look ~ good for him⟩ **2** *chiefly dial* **:** in any case
anywhen \'==¦=\ *adv* [¹*any* + *when*] *chiefly dial* **:** at any time ⟨will vote ~ and anywhere —William Faulkner⟩
¹**anywhere** \'==,(h)we(ə)r, -eə, -,(h)wə(r)\ *adv* [ME *anywhere*, *enywhere*, fr. *any*, *eny* + *where*] **1 :** at, in, or to any place or point ⟨could sail ~ along the coast⟩ **2 :** at all **:** to any extent ⟨do not rank ~ near the other species —J.B.Robson⟩ **3 —** used as a function word to indicate limits of variation ⟨~ from 10 to 30 minutes⟩ ⟨~ from 40 to 60 students⟩
²**anywhere** \"\ *n* [ME, fr. *anywhere*, adv.] **:** any place ⟨will flock to the cities, to the new world, to ~ where it can have a full life —*Irish Statesman*⟩ ⟨welcomes visitors from ~⟩
any·wheres \-rz, -əz, -,(h)wərz, -wə̄z\ *adv* [*anywhere* + *-s*] *chiefly dial* **:** ANYWHERE

any which way *adv* : in any way or direction at all : HAPHAZARDLY ⟨the . . . fence lay *any which way* between the bare black yard and the broken sidewalk —Marcia Davenport⟩
anywhither \ˈ==ˌ==\ *adv* [³*any* + *whither*] *archaic* : in any direction whatever ⟨rivers ran ~ —J.B.Cabell⟩
any·wise \ˈ==ˌwīz\ *adv* [ME *anywise, enywise*, fr. OE (*on*) *ǣnige wīsan* in any way, fr. *ǣnige* (acc. fem. of *ǣnig*) + *wīsan*, acc. of *wise* wise, way — more at WISE] : in any way or manner whatever : at all ⟨nor was it ~ important⟩
an·zac \ˈanˌzak, ˈaan-\ *n* -S *cap* [Australian and New Zealand Army Corps] : an Australian or New Zealander ⟨the burly *Anzac* saw his chance and merely kept the ball in play —J.R. Tunis⟩; *specif* : a soldier from Australia or New Zealand
anzac day *n, usu cap A&D* : April 25 observed as a legal holiday in Australia and New Zealand in celebration of the anniversary of the landing of Australian and New Zealand forces at Gallipoli in 1915
an·zan·ite \ˈanzəˌnīt\ *n* -S *usu cap* [*Anzan* (*Anshan*), region of ancient Persia + E *-ite*] : ELAMITE
AO *abbr, often not cap* **1** account of **2** among others **3** and others
AOL *abbr* absent over leave
aonach *var of* AENACH
A1 \ˈāˈwən\ *adj* [¹*a*] **1** : having the highest possible classification — used as a symbol by Lloyd's Register of Shipping to designate the characteristics of a ship **2** : of the highest quality : FIRST-CLASS, FIRST-RATE, SUPERIOR ⟨can *A1* man of music as well as an *A1* man of the orchestra —Virgil Thomson⟩
ao·ni·an \(ˈ)āˈōnēən, -nyən\ *adj, usu cap* [*Aonia*, district of ancient Greece (fr. L, fr. Gk) + E *-an*] : of or relating to Aonia or to the Muses ⟨to waste and spoil the sweet *Aonian* fields —Christopher Marlowe⟩
ao·nid·i·el·la \ˌāəˌnidēˈelə\ *n, cap* [NL] : a genus of widely distributed chiefly tropical armored scales including several pests of cultivated plants (as the red scale of citrus)
aor \ˈaü(ə)r\ *n* -S *usu cap* : one of a group of related peoples inhabiting the Naga hills in eastern Assam
ao·rist \ˈāərəst, ˈa(a)r-\ *n* -S [LL & Gk; LL *aoristos*, fr. Gk, fr. *aoristos* undefined, fr. *a-* ²*a-* + *horistos* definable, fr. *horizein* to define — more at HORIZON] : a set or one of a set of inflectional forms of a verb typically denoting simple occurrence of an action without reference to its completeness or incompleteness, duration, or repetition and typically without reference to its position in time but sometimes (as in the indicative mood in Greek and Sanskrit) with reference to past time — used first in Greek grammar and later in the grammar of Sanskrit and various other languages
ao·ris·tic \ˌāəˈristik, (ˈ)a(a)ˈr-\ *adj* [MGk *aoristikos*, fr. *aoristos* + *-ikos* -ic] **1** : of or belonging to the aorist : like the aorist **2** : INDEFINITE, INDETERMINATE — **ao·ris·ti·cal·ly** \-tək(ə)lē\ *adv*
aort- *or* **aorto-** *comb form* [NL, fr. *aorta*] : aorta ⟨*aortitis*⟩ ⟨*aortolith*⟩
aor·ta \āˈȯrd·ə, -ȯ(ə)|, |tə\ *n, pl* **aortas** \-əz\ *or* **aor·tae** \|ˌtē\ [NL, fr. Gk *aortē*, fr. *aeirein*, *airein* to lift, heave; perh. akin to Alb *vjer* I hang up] **1** : the chief arterial trunk of the vertebrate body that carries blood from the heart to be distributed to all parts of the body reached by the systemic circulation, being divided in lower vertebrates and embryos of higher forms into an ascending portion arising from the ventricle of the heart and a descending or dorsal portion continuous with the former through the aortic arches but in birds and mammals arising from the left ventricle and continuing over the root of the lung through the single remaining aortic arch then passing posteriorly beside the spinal column to bifurcate into the common iliac arteries after having given off various branches to the head, forelimbs, and trunk **2** : a large dorsal blood vessel in various invertebrates; *esp* : the anterior prolongation of the heart of an insect or other arthropod

diagram of the heart showing *a* aorta, *l* left ventricle, *r* right ventricle

aor·tic \(ˈ)āˈȯrd·ik, -ȯ(ə)|, |tik, -ēk\ *or* **aor·tal** \|d·ᵊl, |tᵊl\ *adj* [*aort-* + *-ic* or *-al*] : of or relating to the aorta
aortic arch *n* : one of the branches that arise from the ascending aorta in pairs in fishes and the embryos of higher vertebrates and pass to the gill clefts of either side and thence round the esophagus to fuse into the dorsal aorta and that are reduced in adult higher forms, one pair persisting in most amphibians and reptiles and a single arch, forming the base of the aortic trunk, in warm-blooded vertebrates, in birds the right and in mammals the left
aortic insufficiency *or* **aortic incompetence** *n* : leakage of blood from the aorta back into the left ventricle during diastole because of failure of an aortic valve to close properly
aortic murmur *n* : a heart murmur originating at the aortic valve
aortic stenosis *n* : a condition usu. the result of disease in which the aorta, esp. its orifice, is abnormally narrow
aortic valve *n* : the semilunar valve separating the aorta from the left ventricle
aor·ti·tis \ˌāˌȯ(r)ˈtīd·əs\ *n* -ES [NL, fr. *aort-* + *-itis*] : inflammation of the aorta
aorto- — see AORT-
aor·to·graphic \(ˌ)āˌȯ(r)d·əˈgrafik, -ȯ(ə)d-, -ēk\ *adj* [*aortography* + *-ic*] : of or by means of aortography (~ examination)
aor·tog·ra·phy \ˌāˌȯ(r)ˈtägrəfē\ *n* -ES [ISV *aort-* + *-graphy*] : arteriography of the aorta
ao·tes \āˈōd·ēz, -ōˌtēz\ *n, cap* [NL, prob. irreg. fr. Gk *aōtos* without ears, fr. *a-* ²*a-* + *ōt-*, *ous* ear — more at EAR] : a genus of tropical American nocturnal monkeys (family Cebidae) having long nonprehensile tails, projecting lower incisors, and very large eyes and comprising the douroucoulis
ao·tus \āˈōd·əs\ [NL, fr. Gk *aōtos*] *syn of* AOTES
aou·dad *also* **au·dad** \ˈaüˌdad\ *n* -S [F *aoudad*, fr. Berber *audad*] : a wild sheep (*Ammotragus lervia*) of No. Africa thought to be the chamois of the Old Testament — called also *arui, maned sheep*
¹**aoul** \ˈaü(ə)l\ *n* -S *cap* [Nepali *aul* marsh, fever] : a member of any of several small peoples living in the malarial terai districts of Nepal
²**aoul** \"\ *n* -S [native name in Ethiopia] : an Abyssinian gazelle (*Gazella soemmerringii soemmerringii*)
a ou·trance \ˌäˌüˈträⁿs\ *also* **à l'ou·trance** \ˌäˌlü-\ *adv* [F] : to the utmost : to the death : UNSPARINGLY ⟨planned in secrecy and waged *à outrance* —E.M. Earle⟩

aoudad (*Ammotragus lervia*)

ao·ya·ma's fluid \aüˈyäməz-\ *n, usu cap A* [after Fumio *Aoyama*, 20th cent. Jap. anatomist] : a solution of cadmium chloride and neutral formalin used for fixing tissues prior to osmic acid impregnation of the Golgi apparatus
¹**ap-** — see AD-
²**ap-** — see APO-
ap *abbr* **1** apostle **2** apothecaries' **3** [L *apud*] according to or in the works of
AP *abbr* **1** above proof **2** account paid **3** accounts payable **4** additional premium **5** advanced post **6** advice of payment **7** airplane **8** airplane pilot **9** antipersonnel **10** armor-piercing **11** as purchased **12** assessment paid **13** assumed position **14** authority to pay **15** authority to purchase **16** author's proof
apa \əˈpä\ *n* -S [Pg, fr. Tupi, fr. Galibi] : WALLABA
apa·bhram·sa \ˌäpəˈbrəmshə\ *n* -S *usu cap* [Skt *apabhraṁśa*, lit., fall] : a stage of an Indic language characterized by linguistic changes not found in a more conservative stage that serves as a standard of correctness: **a** : non-Sanskrit linguistic forms in Indic speech prior to approximately the 3d century A.D. **b** : an Indic language spoken in approximately the 3d to the 5th centuries A.D. and differing from the literary Prakrit **c** : an Indic language that was used as a vehicle for poetry from approximately the 6th to the 12th centuries and that shows linguistic changes not found in Prakrit
apace \əˈpās\ *adv* [ME *apas, apace* step by step, slowly, rapidly, prob. fr. MF *à pas*, fr. *à* to, at, on (fr. L *ad*) + *pas* step — more at AT, PACE] : at a quick pace : SPEEDILY, SWIFTLY, FAST ⟨the concentration of corporate wealth has proceeded ~ —G.B.Hurff⟩
apache *in senses 1 & 2 & prob 4* əˈpachē *or* -chi *sometimes* -pä- *or* -pȧ-; *in sense 3* əˈpash *or* -paa- *or* -pai- *or* -pä- *or* -pȧ-\ *n, pl* **apache** *or* **apaches** [Sp, prob. fr. Zuñi *Ápachu*, lit., enemy] **1** *usu cap* **a** : an Athapaskan people of Arizona, New Mexico, Texas, and northern Mexico **b** : a member of such people **2** *usu cap* : any of the Athapaskan languages of the Apache people **3** [F, fr. *Apache* Apache Indian, prob. fr. E] *a sometimes cap* : a member of a gang of criminals esp. in Paris noted for their crimes of violence **b** : RUFFIAN **4** : SIENNA BROWN
apach·e·an \-chēən\ *adj, usu cap* : of or relating to the Apache people or their languages
apache dance \-sh|d-\ *n* **1 a** : a violent duet dance of the Parisian underworld **b** : a subdued version of such a dance in vaudeville, burlesque, and revues **2** : a ballroom dance with close contact, jerks, and spins
apache devil dance \-chē'd-\ *n, usu cap A* : a dance of the Apache Indian gahe in which the performer crouches with arms in angular position and the knees turned outward and jumps in even rhythm with both feet at the same time or at intervals with one leg extended and a jumping movement on the other foot
apache pine \-chē-\ *n, usu cap A* : a 3-leaved pine (*Pinus latifolia*) of Arizona and New Mexico resembling the ponderosa pine but having very long leaves when young
apache plume \-chē-\ *n, usu cap A* : an evergreen shrub (*Fallugia paradoxa*) of the family Rosaceae of the southwestern U. S. and Mexico having showy plumed fruits
apach·ite \əˈpaˌchīt\ *n* -S [G *apachit*, fr. *Apache* mts., Texas, its locality + G *-it* -ite] : a phonolitic rock containing abundant amphibole and aenigmatite associated with the pyroxene and microperthite as the feldspar
apa·da·na \ˌäpəˈdänə, ˌäp-\ *n* -S [OPer *apadāna* palace, fr. *apa-* away + *dāna* container, receptacle, fr. *dā* to put, make, create; akin to Av & Skt *apa* away and to Av *dadāiti* he puts, gives, Skt *dadhāti* — more at OF, DO] : the great hall in ancient Persian palaces
ap·a·go·ge \ˈapəˌgōjē *sometimes* -gäjē *or* ˌ==ˈ==\ *n* -S [Gk *apagōgē*, lit., act of leading away, fr. *apo-* + *agōgē* leading, carrying away, fr. *agein* to lead, drive, act, do — more at AGENT] **1** : ABDUCTION 3 **2** : argument by the reductio ad absurdum
ap·a·gog·ic \ˌapəˈgäjik\ *or* **ap·a·gog·i·cal** \-jəkəl\ *adj* : of, relating to, or involving an apagoge; *esp* : proceeding by the method of disproving the proposition that contradicts the one to be established — **ap·a·gog·i·cal·ly** \-jək(ə)lē\ *adv*
apagogic reduction *n* : INDIRECT REDUCTION
apaid *adj* [ME *apayed, apaid*, fr. past part. of *apayen, apaien* to satisfy, please, requite — more at APPAY] *archaic* : SATISFIED, PLEASED, REWARDED
ap·a·lach·ee *also* **apa·lach·i** \ˌapəˈlachē\ *n, pl* **apalachee** *or* **apalachees** *also* **apalachi** *or* **apalachis** *usu cap* [prob. fr. Choctaw *apelachi* helper, ally] **1 a** : a Muskogean people of northwestern Florida **b** : a member of such people **2** : the language of the Apalachee people
ap·a·lach·i·co·la \ˌapəˌlachəˈkōlə\ *n, pl* **apalachicola** *or* **apalachicolas** *usu cap* [Hitchiti *Apolachicoli* or Muskogee *Apalachicolo*, lit., people of the other side] **1** : a Muskogean people of Georgia, Alabama, and Florida **2** : a member of the Apalachicola people — compare CREEK
apa·lai \ˈäpəˈlī\ *n, pl* **apalai** *or* **apalais** *usu cap* [Pg, of AmerInd origin] **1 a** : a Cariban people of the north bank of the mouth of the Amazon **b** : a member of such people **2** : the language of the Apalai people
apanage *var of* APPANAGE
ap·an·drous \(ˈ)aˈpandrəs\ *adj* [*apo-* + *-androus*] *bot* : having functionless male organs (~ fungi) — **ap·an·dry** \ˈaˌpandrē\ *n* -ES
apan·te·les \əˈpantᵊlˌēz\ *n, cap* [NL, fr. ²*a-* + Gk *pantelēs* altogether complete, fr. *pan-* + *-telēs* (fr. *telos* end, completion); fr. the lack of a caudal appendage — more at WHEEL] : a genus of small wasps (family Braconidae) parasitic as larvae on caterpillars and used in the biological control of certain destructive caterpillars
ap·an·te·sis \ˌapənˈtēsəs\ *n, cap* [NL, perh. fr. Gk *apantēsis* encounter, fr. *apantan* to meet, fr. *apo-* + *antan* to meet face to face, fr. *anta* face to face; akin to Gk *anti* against — more at ANTE-] : a genus of tiger moths frequently having the fore wings velvety black with branching light colored stripes and the hind wings red, pink, or yellow with black spots
apan·to \əˈpanˌtō\ *n, pl* **apanto** *or* **apantos** *usu cap* [Pg, of AmerInd origin] **1 a** : a Tupian people of northern Brazil **b** : a member of such people **2** : the language of the Apanto people
apar \əˈpär\ *n* -S [Pg or AmerSp, fr. Tupi *tatuapára* rolled armadillo, fr. *tatu* armadillo + *iapára* to roll] : the three-banded armadillo (*Tolypeutes tricinctus*) of So. America
apa·raph·y·sate \ˌāpəˈrafəsət, -ˌsāt\ *adj* [²*a-* + *paraphysate*] : destitute of paraphyses
apa·re·jo \ˌapəˈrā(ˌ)ō, ˌäp-, -āˌhō\ *n* -S [AmerSp, fr. Sp, preparation, equipment, fr. *aparejar* to prepare, fr. (assumed) VL *apparīculare* — more at APPAREL] : a packsaddle of stuffed leather or canvas
¹**apart** \əˈpärt, -pȧt, *usu* -d· + V\ *adv* [ME, fr. MF *a part*, lit., at the side, to the side, fr. (assumed) VL *ad partem*, fr. L *ad* at, to + LL *partem*, accus. of *pars* side, fr. L, part — more at AT, PART] **1** : to or at one side : at a little distance ⟨the kitchen stood ~ from the house⟩ **2** : separately in space or time : away from one another ⟨towns five miles ~⟩ ⟨children born two years ~⟩ **3** : as a separate or distinct object of thought : INDEPENDENTLY, INDIVIDUALLY ⟨viewed ~, his arguments were unsound⟩ **4** : excluded from consideration : ASIDE ⟨these things ~, I have been working steadily —H.J.Laski⟩ **5** : in or into two or more parts : to pieces : ASUNDER ⟨was showing signs of coming ~ at the seams —Milton Hindus⟩ **6** : aside from common use : above the general level ⟨the elite were definitely set ~ from the mass —A.N.Christensen⟩
²**apart** \"\ *adj* **1 a** : having particular characteristics not shared with any others ⟨scientists felt they were a group ~, entitled to special privilege—Vannevar Bush⟩ **b** : being out of the way : remote, secluded ⟨had been preserved because they inhabited a place ~ —W.H.Hudson †1922⟩ **2** : holding different opinions : in disagreement : DIVERGENT ⟨the allies are still ~ —*Time*⟩
apart from *prep* : other than : BESIDES ⟨*apart from* his legal avocations his only interest was music —H.W.H.Knott⟩
apart·heid \əˈpärˌtˌāt, -pȧˌt|, |īt, -ärt,h|, -ȧt,h|\ *n* -S [Afrik, lit., separateness, fr. D, fr. *apart* separate (fr. F *à part*) + *-heid* -hood — more at APART] : racial segregation; *specif* : a policy of segregation and political and economic discrimination against non-European groups in the Republic of So. Africa
apart·ment \əˈpärtmənt, -pȧt-\ *n* -S *often attrib* [F *appartement*, fr. It *appartamento* (trans. of Sp *apartamiento*, lit., separation), fr. *appartare* to put aside, separate (fr. *a parte* aside, separately, lit., at the side, to the side, fr. assumed VL *ad partem*) + *-mento* -ment (fr. L *-mentum*)] **1** : a room or a set of rooms used as a dwelling and located in a private house, a hotel, or a building containing only such rooms or suites with necessary passages and hallways : FLAT **2** *obs* **a** : a separate or special abode : a dwelling place ⟨came down from my ~ in the tree —Daniel Defoe⟩ **b** : COMPARTMENT **3** : any room in a building ⟨the dining room at the hall was not a cheerful ~ —Osbert Lancaster⟩ **4** : a building made up of individual dwelling units ⟨these new ~s have intensified the parking problem⟩ — **a·part·men·tal** \əˌpärtˈmentᵊl, ˌaˌp-, -pȧt-\ *adj*
apartment building *or* **apartment house** *n* : a building containing a number of separate residential units and usu. having conveniences (as heat and elevators) in common
apartment hotel *n* : an apartment house containing suites equipped for housekeeping purposes and in addition furnished rooms and dining service for transient and permanent guests
apart·ness \əˈpärtnəs, -pȧt-\ *n* -ES [²*apart* + *-ness*] : the quality or state of being apart : ALOOFNESS, ISOLATION ⟨our own . . . grandiose ~ and air of exclusive ease . . . threatened to defeat us —W.H.Hale⟩
apas *pl of* APA
apast \əˈp-\ *adv or prep* [¹*a-* + *past*] *chiefly Midland* : PAST
ap·as·tron \(ˈ)aˈpastrən, -ˌsträn\ *n, pl* **apas·tra** \-strə\ [NL, fr. *apo-* + Gk *astron* star — more at STAR] : the point in the orbit of one star of a binary where it is farthest from the other — compare PERIASTRON
apa ta·ni \ˌäpəˈtänē\ *n, pl* **apa tani** *or* **apa tanis** *usu cap A&T* **1** : an Assamese people of the eastern outer Himalaya mountain region **2** : a member of the Apa Tani people
ap·a·tet·ic \ˌapəˈted·ik\ *adj* [Gk *apatētikos* fallacious, fr. *apatan* to deceive, cheat, fr. *apatē* deceit — more at APATITE] *zool* : imitative in color or form
ap·a·theia \ˌapəˈthēə\ *or* **apath·ia** \əˈpathēə\ *n* -S [Gk — more at APATHY] : freedom or release from emotion or excitement
ap·a·thet·ic \ˌapəˈthed·ik, -etik, -ēk\ *adj* [*apathy* + *-etic* (as in *pathetic*)] **1** : having or showing little or no feeling or emotion : SPIRITLESS, IMPASSIVE ⟨rare women who . . . become active instead of ~ as they grow older —Ellen Glasgow⟩ **2** : having or showing little or no interest or concern : INDIFFERENT ⟨not that the people were ~ . . . for they were . . . curious about everything —L.C.Stevens⟩ **syn** see IMPASSIVE
ap·a·thet·i·cal·ly \-ək(ə)lē, -ēk-, -li\ *adv* : in an apathetic manner
apath·o·gen·ic \ˌāˌpathəˈjenik, āˈp-\ *adj* [²*a-* + *pathogenic*] : not capable of causing disease : NONPATHOGENIC
ap·a·thy \ˈapəthē, -thi\ *n* -ES [Gk *apatheia, apathia*, fr. *apathēs* without feeling (fr. *a-* ²*a-* + *pathos* feeling, suffering) + *-ia* -y — more at PATHOS] **1** : release or freedom from passion, excitement, or emotion ⟨this attitude of calm is the Epicurean counterpart of the Stoic ~ —Frank Thilly⟩ **2 a** : absence or lack of feeling or emotion : UNFEELINGNESS, IMPASSIVENESS ⟨the dull ~ of despair —Oscar Wilde⟩ **b** : absence or lack of interest or concern : LISTLESSNESS, INDIFFERENCE ⟨an alarming degree of ~ among the party's rank and file —G.C.Wright⟩
ap·a·tite \ˈapəˌtīt\ *n* -S [G *apatit*, fr. Gk *apatē* deceit (perh. fr. *apo-* + *patos* path) + G *-it* -ite; fr. its being taken for other minerals — more at FIND] : any of a group of calcium phosphate minerals containing other elements or radicals (as fluorine, chlorine, hydroxyl, or carbonate), having the approximate general formula $Ca_5(F,Cl,OH,\frac{1}{2}CO_3)(PO_4)_3$, and occurring variously as hexagonal crystals, as granular masses, or in fine-grained often impure masses as the chief constituent of phosphate rock and of most or all bones and teeth; *specif* : FLUORAPATITE — see CARBONATE-APATITE, CHLORAPATITE, HYDROXYLAPATITE
ap·a·tor·nis \ˌapəˈtȯrnəs\ *n, cap* [NL, fr. Gk *apatē* + NL *-ornis*] : a genus of toothed birds from the Cretaceous of Kansas related to *Ichthyornis*
ap·a·to·sau·rus \ˌapətōˈsȯrəs\ *n, cap* [NL, fr. *apato-* (fr. Gk *apatē*) + *-saurus*] : a genus of American Jurassic herbivorous dinosaurs (order Sauropoda) that reached a length of over 65 feet and a height of 12 feet and are thought to have attained a weight of up to 30 tons
apaumé *var of* APPAUMÉ
apa·yao \ˌäpəˈyaü\ *n, pl* **apayao** *or* **apayaos** *usu cap* [Sp, fr. native name in northern Luzon] **1 a** : a predominantly pagan people of northern Luzon, Philippines **b** : a member of such people **2** : the Austronesian language of the Apayao people
APC *abbr* **1** aspirin, phenacetin, caffeine **2** autographed presentation copy
¹**ape** \ˈāp\ *n* -S [ME, fr. OE *apa*; akin to OS *apo*, OHG *affo*, ON *api*] **1 a** : MONKEY — used esp. of the larger tailless Old World forms **b** : a member of the family Pongidae **2** : one that imitates or copies : MIMIC ⟨be his duplicate but not his ~ —Earl of Chesterfield⟩ ⟨the ~s of fashion —Malcolm Cowley⟩ **3** *obs* : DUPE, FOOL **4** : one that is felt to resemble an ape esp. in appearance and manners : a large uncouth person ⟨didn't know who the big ~ was —Edwin Corle⟩
²**ape** *vt* -ED/-ING/-S : to follow as a pattern or example : IMITATE, COPY, MIMIC ⟨had *aped* the styles of various authors — Van Wyck Brooks⟩ **syn** see COPY
³**ape** \ˈä(ˌ)pā\ *n* -S [Hawaiian *'ape*] **1** : any of several herbaceous aroids (as *Alocasia macrorrhiza* and some members of the genus *Xanthosoma*) having large heart-shaped blades rising on long petioles from short trunks and being cultivated as ornamentals esp. in Hawaii **2** : APE-APE
apeak \əˈpēk\ *adv (or adj)* [alter. (influenced by *peak*) of earlier *apike*, prob. fr. F *à pic* vertically] : in a vertical position : held vertically ⟨the oars were all ~ —W.J.Dakin⟩
ape-ape \ˌäpēˈäpē\ *n* -S [Hawaiian *'ape'ape*] : a rhizomatous perennial herb (*Gunnera petaloidea*) of Hawaiian uplands having a branched inflorescence and bluntly heart-shaped leaves several feet in diameter that rise from a short fleshy crown
ape fissure *n* : SULCUS LUNATUS
ape hand *n* : a wasting deformity of the hand seen in muscular dystrophy
apei·ron \əˈpīˌrän, -pā-\ *n, pl* **apei·ra** \-rə, -ˌrä\ [Gk, fr. neut. of *apeiros* endless, infinite, fr. *a-* ²*a-* + *-peiron* (fr. *peirat-*, *peirar* end, conclusion); akin to *peri* around — more at FAR] : the unlimited, indeterminate, and indefinite ground, origin, or primal principle of all matter postulated esp. by Anaximander
ape·let \ˈāplət\ *or* **ape·ling** \ˈāpliŋ, -lēŋ\ *n* -S : a little ape
ape-man \ˈ=ˌ=\ *n, pl* **ape-men** : a primate (as a member of the genera *Pithecanthropus, Australopithecus*, and *Sinanthropus*) intermediate in character between true man (*Homo sapiens*) and the higher apes
ap·en·nine \ˈapəˌnīn\ *adj, usu cap* [L *Appenninus, Apenninus*, a chain of mountains in Italy] : of or relating to the Apennines
¹**ap·er** \ˈāpə(r)\ *n* -S [²*ape* + *-er*] : one that apes ⟨~s of the nobility⟩
²**aper** \ˈäpə(r), ˈā-\ *n* -S [L; akin to OE *eofor* wild boar, OS *ebur*, OHG *ebur*, ON *jöfurr* prince, chieftain, Umbrian *apruf*, *abrof* wild boar (acc. pl.), OSlav *vepri*, Lith *vepris*] : the European wild boar
aper·çu \ˌäpə(r)ˈsü, *F* äpersü̅\ *n* -S [F, fr. *aperçu*, past part. of *apercevoir* to perceive, fr. OF, fr. *a-* (fr. L *ad-*) + *perceivre* to perceive, fr. L *percipere* — more at PERCEIVE] **1** : a brief glimpse or immediate impression; *esp* : an intuitive insight ⟨the many brilliant ~s that illustrate and illuminate the main theme —D.W.Brogan⟩ **2** : a brief survey or sketch : OUTLINE ⟨if reduced to . . . two pages it would be the profoundest ~ of the universe that I ever have read —O.W.Holmes †1935⟩ **syn** see COMPENDIUM
ape·rea \ˌäpeˈrēə\ *or* **pe·rea** \ˌperēˈä\ *n* -S [Sp & Pg *apereá*, *aperea*, fr. Tupi *apereá*] : a wild cavy (*Cavia porcellus*) possibly ancestral to the domesticated guinea pig
¹**ape·ri·ent** \əˈpirēənt\ *adj* [L *aperient-, aperiens*, pres. part. of *aperire* to uncover, open — more at APERTURE] : gently moving the bowels : LAXATIVE
²**aperient** \"\ *n* -S : an aperient agent
aperies *pl of* APERY
ape·ri·od·ic \ˌāˌpirēˈädik, āˈp-\ *adj* [²*a-* + *periodic*] **1** : of irregular occurrence : not periodic ⟨~ floods⟩ **2** : not having periodic vibrations : nonoscillatory and hence capable of moving steadily to a position of equilibrium **3** *cryptology* : not repeating or not repeating with a short or easily discoverable period ⟨an ~ key⟩ — **ape·ri·od·i·cal·ly** \-dək(ə)lē\ *adv* — **ape·ri·o·dic·i·ty** \ˌāˌpirēəˈdisəd·ē\ *n* -ES
aper·i·tif \ˌäˌperəˈtēf, -rēˈ-; äˈ==ˌ=, əˈ-\ *n* -S [F *apéritif* aperitif, aperient, fr. MF *aperitif*, adj., aperient, fr. ML *aperitivus*, irreg. fr. L *aperire* to open + *-ivus* -ive — more at APERTURE] **1** : APPETIZER; *esp* : an alcoholic drink (as a cocktail or glass of appetizer wine) often taken before a meal **2** *also* **aperitif wine** : an appetizer wine that is chiefly of French or Italian origin, flavored with herbs and other substances, and used as an appetizer or cocktail ingredient
¹**aper·i·tive** \əˈperəd·iv\ *adj* [ML *aperitivus*] **1** : APERIENT **2** [F *apéritif* aperient, stimulating the appetite, fr. MF *aperitif* aperient] : stimulating the appetite
²**aperitive** \"\ *n* -S **1** : APERIENT **2** [F *apéritif*] : APERITIF
apert *adj* [ME, fr. OF, fr. L *apertus*, fr. past part. of *aperire* to open] **1** *archaic* : OPEN, MANIFEST, EVIDENT **2** *obs* : BOLD, STRAIGHTFORWARD, OUTSPOKEN — **apertly** *adv, archaic*
apertion *n* -S [L *apertion-*, *apertio*, fr. *apertus* (past part. of

aperire to open) + *-ion-, -io* -ion — more at APERTURE] **1** *obs* **:** the act of opening **2** *obs* **:** an opening or aperture

ap·er·tom·e·ter \ˌapə(r)ˈtäməd·ə(r)\ *n* -s [*aperture* + *-o-* + *-meter*] **:** an instrument for measuring the numerical aperture of objectives (as those of a microscope)

ap·er·tur·al \ˈapə(r),chu̇rəl\ *adj* **:** of, relating to, or like an aperture

apertural canal *n* **:** the basal extension of the aperture affording lodgment for the siphon in univalve shells

ap·er·ture *R* ˈapə(r),chu̇(ə)r, -ˌchər; *–R* -pə,chu̇ə, -pəchə\ *n* -s [ME, fr. L *apertura*, fr. *apertus* open (fr. past part. of *aperire* to open, uncover, prob. fr. *ap-* — akin to L *ab* from — + — assumed — *verire* to cover) + *-ura* -ure — more at OF, WEIR] **1** *obs* **:** the act or process of opening **2 :** an opening or open space (as between parts or sections of solid matter) **:** HOLE, GAP, CLEFT, CHASM, SLIT ⟨the only light . . . came through the narrow ~ between the stone lips —Willa Cather⟩ **3 a :** an opening that restricts a beam of radiation or a stream of particles; *specif* **:** the opening in a photographic lens that admits the light passing through, the size often being controlled by an iris diaphragm **b :** the diameter of the entrance pupil of an optical system **4 :** the opening of a univalve shell

ap·er·tured \-,chu̇(ə)rd, -u̇əd, -ˌchə(r)d\ *adj* **:** having an aperture

aperture plate *n* **:** a smooth plate that establishes the film plane in a motion-picture camera or projector and that has a rectangular opening defining the margins of the picture area as recorded or projected

aperture ratio *n* **:** RELATIVE APERTURE

aperture vignette *n* **:** MASK 2d (1)

ap·ery \ˈāpərē, -ri\ *n* -ES [¹*ape* + *-ery*] **:** the act or practice of aping **:** MIMICRY

apes *pl of* APE, *pres 3d sing of* APE

apes–earring \ˈ≈ˈ≈(,)≈\ *n* **:** MANILA TAMARIND

apet·a·lae \(ˈ)āˈped·ᵊl,ē\ *n pl, cap* [NL, fr. ²*a-* + *-petalae*] *in some classifications* **:** a group of the Archichlamydeae comprising plants whose flowers have no petals — compare CHORIPETALAE

apet·al·ous \(ˈ)āˌped·ᵊləs\ *adj* [²*a-* + *-petalous*] **1 :** of, relating to, or characteristic of the Apetalae; *often, of flowers* **:** having no petals **2 :** not petaloid; *specif* **:** lacking the petallike expansion of the ambulacra ⟨~ sea urchins⟩ — **apet·aly** \(ˈ)≈ˈ≈lē\ *n* -ES

à pe·tits fers \ˌäp(ə),tēˈfe(ə)r, ˌap-\ *adj* [F, lit., with small tools] **:** made up of small decorative elements ⟨a book binding with a design *à petits fers*⟩

¹**apex** \ˈāˌpeks\ *n, pl* **apexes** \-ksəz\ *or* **api·ces** \ˈāpə,sēz *also* ˈap-\ [L, summit, small rod at top of flamen's cap; prob. akin to L *aptus* fastened, attached — more at APT] **1 a :** the highest or uppermost point **:** SUMMIT, TOP, PEAK ⟨the ~ of the mountain⟩: as (1) **:** the vertex of an angle, a cone, or a pyramid (2) **:** the point of the heavens toward which a celestial body is moving at a given time ⟨solar ~⟩ **b :** the pointed end **:** TIP ⟨the ~ of the tongue⟩ **2 :** the highest or culminating point **:** CLIMAX, ACME, CULMINATION ⟨the ~ of his career⟩ ⟨the ~ of an era⟩ **3 :** the end, edge, or crest of a vein of mineral nearest the surface **4** *in palmistry* **:** a triangle formed by capillary lines on the pads of the fingers and the mounts **5 a :** the narrow somewhat conical upper part of a lung extending into the root **b :** the lower pointed end of the heart situated in man opposite the space between the cartilages of the fifth and sixth ribs on the left side **c :** the extremity of the root of a tooth

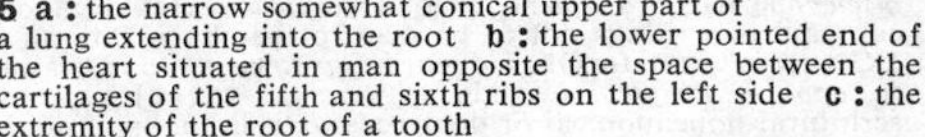

a apex (1b) of a leaf

²**apex** \"\ *vi* -ED/-ING/-ES *of a vein of mineral* **:** to form an apex **:** present an upper edge

apex beat *n* **:** the pulsation made by the apex of the left ventricle of the heart heard or felt at the fifth left intercostal space

apexed \ˈāˌpekst\ *adj* **:** having an apex

apex stone *n* **:** the top stone in a gable end — called also *saddle stone*

APF *abbr* animal protein factor

aph- — see APO-

aphaer·e·sis *or* **apher·e·sis** \əˈferəsəs, a'-, -fir-\ *n, pl* **aphaere·ses** *or* **aphere·ses** \-ə,sēz\ [LL, fr. Gk *aphairesis*, lit., taking off, fr. *aphairein* to take away (fr. *apo-* + *hairein* to take) + *-sis* — more at HERESY] **1 :** the loss of one or more sounds or letters at the beginning of a word (as in *round* for *around*, *coon* for *raccoon*, baby talk *'top* for *stop*) — compare APHESIS 1, APOCOPE, SYNCOPE 2a **2 :** the omission of one or more syllables at the beginning of a member or verse — used esp. in ref. to Greek and Latin prosody; compare PROSTHESIS

aph·ae·ret·ic *or* **aph·er·et·ic** \ˌafəˈred·ik\ *adj* [Gk *aphairetikos* fit for taking away, fr. *aphairein*] **:** of or relating to aphaeresis **:** formed by aphaeresis **:** consisting of aphaeresis

apha·gia \əˈfāj(ē)ə, a'-\ *n* -s [NL, fr. ²*a-* + *-phagia*] **1 :** loss of the ability to swallow **2 :** an inability to feed — used of the state of certain insect imagos (as mayflies) in which the adult is dependent on reserves stored during larval life and takes no food

apha·kia \əˈfākēə, a'-\ *also* **apha·cia** \-ash(ē)ə\ *n* -s [NL, fr. ²*a-* + Gk *phakos* lentil + NL *-ia* — more at BEAN] **:** absence of the crystalline lens of the eye; *also* **:** the anomalous state of refraction resulting therefrom — **apha·kic** \-ākik\ *adj or n*

aphan- *or* **aphano-** *comb form* [F *aphan-*, fr. Gk *aphanēs*, fr. *a-* ²*a-* + *-phanēs* (fr. *phainesthai* to appear) — more at PHENOMENON] **:** invisible **:** obscure ⟨*aphanite*⟩ ⟨*Aphanomyces*⟩

aph·a·nap·ter·yx \ˌafəˈnaptə(,)riks\ *n, cap* [NL, fr. *aphan-* + *Apteryx*] **:** a genus comprising a large long-billed flightless rail of Mauritius that has been exterminated by man

aph·a·nip·tera \ˌafəˈniptərə\ [NL, fr. *aphan-* + *-i-* + *-ptera*] *syn of* SIPHONAPTERA

aph·a·ni·sia \ˌafəˈnizh(ē)ə, -nēzh-\ *n* -s [NL, fr. Gk *aphanisis* disappearance + NL *-ia*] **:** early normal development of a vestigial organ followed by regression — compare RUDIMENTATION

aph·a·nite \ˈafə,nīt, *usu* -d·+V\ *n* -s [F, fr. *aphan-* + *-ite*] **:** a dark rock of such close texture that its separate grains are invisible to the naked eye — **aph·a·nit·ic** \ˌafəˈnid·ik\ *adj* — **aph·a·nit·ism** \ˈafə,nīd·,izəm; əˈfanə,tiz-, a'-\ *n* -s

aph·a·no·my·ces \ˌafənōˈmī,sēz\ *n, cap* [NL, fr. *aphan-* + *-myces*] **:** a genus of fungi (order Saprolegniales) characterized by slender zoosporangia with but one row of zoospores and occurring as parasites in algae and roots of higher plants

aphan·o·phyre \əˈfanə,fī(ə)r, a'-\ *n* -s [*aphan-* + *-phyre*] **:** a porphyry with aphanitic groundmass

aph·a·no·zy·gous \ˌāfəˈnōˈzīgəs\ *adj* [*aphan-* + *-zygous*] **:** CRYPTOZYGOUS

apha·ryn·gent \ˌāfəˈrinjənt\ *adj* [²*a-* + *pharyng-* + *-ent*] **:** lacking a pharynx

apha·sia \əˈfāzh(ē)ə\ *n* -s [NL, fr. Gk, fr. *a-* ²*a-* + *-phasia*] **:** the loss or impairment of the power to use words as symbols of ideas that results from a brain lesion — see AUDITORY APHASIA, MOTOR APHASIA

¹**apha·sic** \-āzik\ *adj* [NL *aphasia* + E *-ic*] **:** of, relating to, or affected by aphasia

²**aphasic** \"\ *n* -s **:** an aphasic person **:** one suffering from aphasia

aphas·mid·ia \ˌāˌfazˈmidēə\ *n pl, cap* [NL, fr. ²*a-* + *Phasmidia*] *in many classifications* **:** a subclass of Nematoda comprising worms in which phasmids are lacking or greatly reduced, deirids are absent, and amphids are usu. modified while sensory organs are often setose — compare PHASMIDIA

aph·e·lan·dra \ˌafəˈlandrə\ *n, cap* [NL, fr. Gk *aphelēs* simple, lit., smooth + NL *-andra*; fr. the one-celled anthers] **:** a genus of tropical American plants (family Acanthaceae) having quadrangular spikes of red 2-lipped flowers

aph·e·len·chi·dae \ˌafəˈleŋkə,dē\ *n pl, cap* [NL, fr. *Aphelenchus*, type genus + *-idae*] **:** a family of soil-dwelling and plant-parasitic nematodes (superfamily Rhabditoidea) sometimes regarded as constituting a distinct superfamily nearly related to Tylenchoidea — see APHELENCHOIDES

aph·e·len·choi·des \ˌafə,leŋˈkȯi(,)dēz\ *n, cap* [NL, fr. *Aphelenchus* + *-oides*] **:** a large cosmopolitan genus of nematodes (family Aphelenchidae) including free-living forms, insect parasites, and a number of serious plant pathogens that attack the leaves and buds of various cultivated plants

aph·e·len·chus \ˌafəˈleŋkəs\ *n, cap* [NL, fr. Gk *aphelēs* simple, lit., smooth + *enchos* spear; fr. the absence of basal knobs on the stylet] **:** a genus of rhabditoid nematode worms that is the type of the family Aphelenchidae and that includes several important plant pathogens

aph·e·li·nid \ˌafəˈlīnəd, -ēn-,-in-\ *n* -s [NL *Aphelinidae*] **:** an insect of the family Aphelinidae

aph·e·lin·i·dae \ˌafəˈlinə,dē\ *n pl, cap* [NL, fr. *Aphelinus*, type genus + *-idae*] **:** a family of small narrow-winged hymenopterous flies closely related to the chalcid flies and parasitic as larvae on plant lice and scales

aph·e·li·nus \ˌafəˈlīnəs, -ēn-\ *n, cap* [NL, fr. Gk *aphelēs* smooth (fr. *a-* ²*a-* + *-phelēs*, fr. *phelleus* stony ground) + L *-inus* -ine; prob. akin to L *follis* bellows — more at BLOW] **:** a genus of hymenopterous flies that is the type of the family Aphelinidae and that includes a species (*A. mali*) important in the biological control of the woolly apple aphid

aph·e·lion \(ˈ)aˈfēlyən, (ˈ)afˈhē-, (ˈ)apˈhē-, -lēən\ *n, pl* **aphe·lia** \-yə,-ēə\ [NL, alter. (influenced by Gk words in *-ion*, dim. suffix) of *aphelium*, fr. *apo-* + *-helium* (fr. Gk *hēlios* sun) — more at SOLAR] **:** the point of a planet's or comet's orbit most distant from the sun — opposed to *perihelion*

diagram of earth's orbit (actually an ellipse): position of the earth in July, A; in January, P; sun, S; minor axis, aa; major axis, AP; aphelion distance, AS; perihelion distance, PS

aph·e·li·o·trop·ic \ˌafˌhēlēəˈträpik, ˌaˌfē-, ˌapˌhē-\ *adj* [*apo-* + *heliotropic*] **:** characterized by apheliotropism — **aph·e·li·o·trop·i·cal·ly** \-pək(ə)lē\ *adv*

aph·e·li·ot·ro·pism \ˌ≈ˌ≈≈ˈä·trə,pizəm\ *n* -s [*apo-* + *heliotropism*] **:** negative heliotropism (as in certain roots that turn away from the sun)

aph·e·lops \ˈafə,läps\ *n, cap* [NL, fr. Gk *aphelēs* smooth + *ōps* face; fr. the absence of a horn — more at OPTIC] **:** a genus of fossil rhinoceroses of very robust build and with very short legs found in the Miocene and Pliocene of America

aphe·mia \əˈfēmēə\ *n* -s [NL, fr. ²*a-* + *-phemia*] **:** MOTOR APHASIA — **aphe·mic** \-mik\ *adj*

apheresis *var of* APHAERESIS

aph·e·sis \ˈafəsəs\ *n, pl* **aphe·ses** \-ə,sēz\ [NL, fr. Gk, release, dismissal, fr. *aphienai* to let go, dismiss (fr. *apo-* + *hienai* to let go, send, throw, hurl, cast) — more at JET] **1 :** aphaeresis consisting of the loss of a short unaccented vowel at the beginning of a word (as in *lone* for *alone*) **2 :** APHAERESIS 1

aph·e·ta \ˈafəd·ə\ *n* -s [NL, fr. Gk *aphetēs* heavenly body determining the vital quadrant, fr. *aphienai* to send forth, fr. *apo-* + *hienai* to send — more at JET (to spout)] *in astrology* **:** the ruler or giver of life in a nativity

aphet·ic \əˈfed·ik, (ˈ)aˌf-\ *adj* [Gk *aphetos* let loose (fr. *aphienai*) + E *-ic*] **:** produced by aphesis or aphaeresis ⟨the ~ form *dobe* for *adobe*⟩ — **aphet·i·cal·ly** \-d·ək(ə)lē\ *adv*

aph·e·tize \ˈafə,tīz\ *vt* -ED/-ING/-S [*aphetic* + *-ize*] **:** to shorten by aphesis ⟨*esquire* was *aphetized* to *squire*⟩ **:** produce by aphesis ⟨the *aphetized* form *down*, from *adown*⟩

aph·e·to·hy·oi·dea \ˌafə,tōˌhīˈȯidēə\ [NL, fr. Gk *aphetos* let loose, free + NL *-hyoidea* (fr. Gk *hyoeidēs* shaped like an upsilon, fr. *hy*, *y* upsilon + *-oeidēs* -oid)] *syn of* PLACODERMI

aph·e·to·hy·oi·de·an \-ēən\ *n* -s [NL *Aphetohyoidea* + E *-an*] **:** PLACODERM

aphi·cid·al \ˌāfəˈsīdᵊl *also* ˌaf-\ *adj* [*aphid* + *-cidal*] **:** toxic to or used for killing aphids

aphi·cide \ˈ≈fə,sīd\ *n* -s [*aphid* + *-cide*] **:** a substance used to kill aphids

aphid \ˈāfəd *also* ˈaf-\ *n* -s [NL *Aphid-, Aphis*] **:** any of numerous small sluggish homopterous insects (superfamily Aphidoidea) that suck the juices of plants thereby causing wilting, distorted growth, or gall formation, serve as vectors of certain important virus diseases of plants, and excrete as a by≈product of their metabolism a sweet liquid very attractive to ants — see PHYLLOXERA, PLANT LOUSE, WOOLLY APPLE APHID; compare APHIDIDAE, APHIS

aphi·dae \ˈ≈fə,dē\ *syn of* APHIDIDAE

aphides *pl of* APHIS

aphid·i·dae \əˈfidə,dē, āˈ-,aˈ-\ *n pl, cap* [NL, fr. *Aphid-, Aphis*, type genus + *-idae*] **:** a large family of Homoptera comprising small soft-bodied plant lice that are usu. somewhat pear≈shaped with wings if present held vertically over the back when at rest, well-developed antennae, and a pair of prominent wax-secreting cornicles on the posterior part of the abdomen from which the covering of white waxy filaments typical of many species is produced and that have a complex life cycle in which resistant fertilized eggs produced in the fall hatch out parthenogenetic females in the spring that give birth to repeated generations of winged or wingless parthenogenetic females on the same or other kinds of host plants, finally producing a generation of winged males and winged or wingless females that mate and produce the fertilized eggs

aphid·iv·o·rous \ˌāfəˈdivərəs *also* ˌaf-\ *adj* [*aphid* + *-i-* + *-vorous*] **:** APHIDOPHAGOUS

aphid lion *n* **:** APHIS LION

aphi·doi·dea \ˌāfəˈdȯidēə *also* ˌaf-\ *n pl, cap* [NL, fr. *Aphid-, Aphis* + *-oidea*] **:** a superfamily of Homoptera comprising the aphids and now usu. divided into a number of families (as Aphididae, Eriosomatidae, and Phylloxeridae)

aphid·ol·o·gist \-ˈdäləjəst\ *n* -s [*aphid* + *-ologist* (as in *biologist*)] **:** one specializing in the study of aphids

aphid·oph·a·gous \ˌāfəˈdäfəgəs *also* ˌaf-\ *adj* [*aphid* + *-o-* + *-phagous*] **:** feeding on aphids ⟨~ syrphus fly larvae⟩

aphid·oph·i·lous \-ˈdäfələs\ *adj* [*aphid* + *-o-* + *-philous*] **:** of or relating to certain ants that nurture aphids in return for the honeydew they obtain from them

aphi·doz·er \ˈ≈≈,dōzə(r)\ *n* -s [blend of *aphid* and *hopper-dozer*] **:** a device consisting of a hopper and revolving brushes used to brush off and collect aphids from cultivated crops

aphis \ˈāfəs *also* ˈaf-\ *n* [NL, perh. irreg. fr. Gk *apheidēs* unsparing, lavish, fr. *a-* ²*a-* + *-pheidēs* (fr. *pheidesthai* to spare); prob. akin to L *findere* to split — more at BITE] **1** *cap* **:** the type genus of Aphididae comprising many aphids injurious to fruit trees and vegetables **2** *pl* **aphi·des** \-fə,dēz\ **a :** an insect of the genus *Aphis* **b :** APHID

aphis lion *n* **:** a larval lacewing that is usu. vigorously predaceous on aphids; *also* **:** any of certain other insect larvae (as of the ladybird and syrphus fly) that feed on aphids

aphle·bia \(ˈ)aˈflēbēə, -leb-\ *n* -s [NL, fr. Gk *aphlebos* without veins, fr. *a-* ²*a-* + *phleb-, phleps* vein — more at PHLEB-] **:** one of the imperfect pinnae found in certain fossil ferns of the Carboniferous age

aph·o·dal \ˈafədᵊl\ *adj* [NL *aphodus* + E *-al*] **:** of or relating to an aphodus **:** having aphodi

apho·di·us \əˈfōdēəs\ *n, cap* [NL, fr. Gk *aphodos* excrement, fr. *apo-* + *hodos* way, road — more at CEDE] **:** a large genus of small somewhat elongated dung beetles commonly placed in the family Scarabaeidae — see PASTURE COCKCHAFER

aph·o·dus \ˈafədəs\ *n, pl* **apho·di** \-,dī, -,dē\ [NL, fr. Gk *aphodos* going away, fr. *apo-* + *hodos* way — more at CEDE] **:** a short canal in rhagon sponges leading from a flagellated chamber to an excurrent canal

apho·nia \(ˈ)āˈfōnēə, əˈ-\ *n* -s [NL, fr. Gk *aphōnia*, fr. *aphōnos* voiceless, (fr. *a-* ²*a-* + *phōnē* sound, voice) + *-ia*] — more at BAN] **:** loss of voice and of all but whispered speech as a result of hysteria, disease, or overuse of the vocal cords

aphon·ic \(ˈ)āˈfänik\ *adj* [²*a-* + *phonic*] **1 a :** having no sound or pronunciation **:** SILENT, NOISELESS **b** *phonetics* **:** VOICELESS **2 :** of, relating to, or characterized by aphonia

aph·o·rism \ˈafə,rizəm\ *n* -s [MF *aphorisme*, fr. LL *aphorismus*, fr. Gk *aphorismos* definition, short, pithy sentence, fr. *aphorizein* to mark off by boundaries, set aside, cast out, define (fr. *apo-* + *horizein* to separate, part) + *-ismos* -ism — more at HORIZON] **1 :** a concise statement of a principle **2 :** a terse and often ingenious formulation of a truth or sentiment usu. in a single sentence **:** ADAGE, MAXIM ⟨one must reverse the ~ "the style is the man" —Emily Genauer⟩

aph·o·ris·mat·ic \ˌafə,rizˈmad·ik\ *adj* **:** APHORISTIC

aph·o·ris·mic \ˌafəˈrizmik\ *adj* **:** APHORISTIC

apho·ris·mos \ˌäfərēzˈmȯs\ *n, pl* **aphoris·moi** \-ˈmē\ [LGk (influenced in meaning by *aphorizein* to excommunicate, fr. Gk, to cast out), fr. Gk, definition, short, pithy sentence] *Eastern Church* **:** temporary excommunication

aph·o·rist \ˈafərəst\ *n* -s **:** one who formulates or repeats aphorisms

aph·o·ris·tic \ˌafəˈristik\ *adj* [Gk *aphoristikos* delimiting, aphoristic, fr. (assumed) *aphoristos* (verbal of *aphorizein*) + *-ikos* -ic] **1 :** of, resembling, or characterized by aphorisms **:** TERSE, PITHY ⟨the suggestive virtues of the ~ style —Douglas Bush⟩ **2 :** given to the use of aphorisms ⟨do not be brilliant and ~ —J.B.Cabell⟩ — **aph·o·ris·ti·cal·ly** \-tək(ə)lē\ *adv*

aph·o·rize \ˈafə,rīz\ *vi* -ED/-ING/-S [fr. *aphorism*, after such pairs as E *baptism: baptize*] **:** to write or speak in or as if in aphorisms **:** express terse general opinions

aphos·pho·ro·sis \ˌāˌfäsfəˈrōsəs\ *n, pl* **aphosphoro·ses** \-ō,sēz\ [NL, fr. ²*a-* + *phosphor-* + *-osis*] **:** a deficiency disease esp. of domestic cattle caused by inadequate intake of dietary phosphorus and marked by inappetence, unthriftiness, lameness, and scouring and in affected animals commonly by depraved appetite and the avid devouring of bones and other materials containing phosphates — compare LAMSIEKTE, PICA

aphos·pho·rot·ic \ˌ≈ˌ≈≈ˈräd·ik, ≈ˌ≈≈ˌ≈-\ *adj* [²*a-* + *phosphor-* + *-otic*] **:** characterized or accompanied by aphosphorosis

apho·tic \(ˈ)āˈfōd·ik\ *adj* [²*a-* + *photic*] **:** without light ⟨~ depths⟩

aphotic region *n* **:** the lightless biogeographic region of deep water where organisms directly dependent on photosynthesis cannot exist

apho·to·tax·is \ˌāˌfōd·əˈtaksəs, (ˈ)āˈ≈≈ˌ≈≈\ *n, pl* **aphototax·es** \-k,sēz\ [NL, fr. ²*a-* + *phototaxis*] **:** absence of phototaxis

apho·to·trop·ic \ˌāˌfōd·əˈträpik, āˌf-\ *adj* [²*a-* + *phototropic*] **:** turning away from the source of light ⟨~ roots⟩ — **apho·tot·ro·pism** \ˌāfōˈtä·trə,pizəm\ *n* -s

aphr- *or* **aphro-** *comb form* [G *aphr-*, fr. Gk *aphr-, aphro-*, fr. *aphros*; perh. akin to L *imber* rain — more at IMBRICATE] **:** foam ⟨*aphrite*⟩ ⟨*aphrometer*⟩

aphra·sia \əˈfrāzh(ē)ə, a'-\ *n* -s [NL, fr. ²*a-* + *-phrasia*] **1 :** an inability to utter words in intelligible order **2 :** pathological refusal to speak — **aphra·sic** \-āzik\ *adj*

aph·rite \ˈa,frīt\ *n* -s [G *aphrit*, fr. *aphr-* foam + G *-it* -ite] **:** a foliated or chalky variety of calcite that is pearly in luster

aph·ro·di·sia \ˌafrəˈdizh(ē)ə\ *n* -s [NL, irreg. fr. Gk, pl., sexual pleasures, fr. neut. pl. of *aphrodisios* of Aphrodite, of sexual love, fr. *Aphroditē*] **:** sexual desire esp. when violent

¹**aph·ro·dis·i·ac** \ˌ≈≈ˈdizē,ak\ *or* **aph·ro·di·si·a·cal** \-,diˈsīəkəl, -ˈzī-\ *adj* [Gk *aphrodisiakos* sexual, fr. *aphrodisia*] **:** provocative of or exciting sexual desire ⟨the labored unreserve of ~ novels —C.E.Montague⟩ ⟨hatches *aphrodisiacal* schemes . . . when confronted with temptations of the flesh —*Time*⟩

²**aphrodisiac** \"\ *n* -s **:** an aphrodisiac agent ⟨odors and . . . other chemical stimuli which are ~*s* —A.C.Kinsey⟩ ⟨the reputation of cantharides as an ~ —C.H.Thienes⟩

aph·ro·di·te \ˌafrōˈdīd·ē, -rəˈ-, -ītē, -i\ *n* [NL, after *Aphrodite*, Greek goddess of love, fr. Gk *Aphroditē*] **1** *cap* **:** a genus (the type of the family Aphroditidae) of large marine polychaetous annelids covered with long lustrous golden hairlike setae — compare SEA MOUSE **2** -s *sometimes cap* [NL (specific epithet of *Argynnis aphrodite*), after *Aphrodite*, goddess] **:** a brown black-spotted butterfly (*Speyeria aphrodite*) of the U.S. with silver spots on the underside **3** -s *often cap* [after *Aphrodite*, goddess] **:** a light bluish green that is greener and deeper than average aqua green (sense 1) or robin's-egg blue (sense 2) and greener and darker than average turquoise green

aph·ro·lite \ˈafrō,līt\ *n* -s [alter. of earlier *aphrolith*, fr. *aphr-* + *-lith*] **:** AA

aph·ro·sid·er·ite \ˌafrōˈsidə,rīt\ *n* -s [G *aphrosiderit*, fr. *aphr-* + *siderit* siderite] **:** a mineral consisting of a hydrous silicate of the chlorite group

aph·tha \ˈafthə, ˈapthə\ *also* **ap·tha** \ˈap-\ *n, pl* **aph·thae** \-,thē\ [NL, back-formation fr. LL *aphthae*, pl., fr. Gk *aphthai*, pl. of *aphtha*, perh. fr. *haptein* to fasten, seize, set on fire — more at HAPTO-] **1 :** a speck, flake, or blister on the mucous membranes (as in the mouth or gastrointestinal tract or on the lips) characteristic of some diseases (as thrush) **2 :** one of the vesicles filled with clear serous fluid that occur in the mouth, on the udder, and in the spaces between the digits of cloven-footed animals in certain diseases — usu. used in pl. **3 :** a disease characterized by aphthae (as foot-and≈mouth disease) — **aph·thic** \-,thik\ *adj*

aph·thar·to·do·ce·tae \afˌthärd·ōdōˈsēd·ē, apˌth-, -sē(,)tē\ *n pl, usu cap* [NL, pl., fr. LGk *aphthartodokētai*, pl. of *aphthartodokētēs*, fr. Gk *aphthartos* incorruptible (fr. *a-* ²*a-* + *phthartos* destructible, fr. *phtheirein* to corrupt, defile) + *-dokētēs* (fr. *dokein* to think) — more at PHTHIRIASIS, DECENT] **:** a 6th century Monophysitic sect that taught that from the moment of the union with the divine nature the body of Christ was incorruptible — compare PHTHARTOLATRAE

aph·thar·to·do·ce·tism \-ˈsēd·,izəm, -ē,tiz-\ *n* -s *usu cap* **:** the doctrines of the Aphthartodocetae

aph·thar·to·do·ce·tist \-ˈsēd·əst\ *n* -s *usu cap* **:** a member of the Aphthartodocetae

aph·thit·a·lite \afˈthid·ᵊl,īt, apˈth-\ *n* -s [Gk *aphthitos* indestructible (fr. *a-* ²*a-* + — assumed — *phthitos*, verbal of *phthiein* to waste away) + *hal-, hals* salt + E *-ite* — more at PHTHISIS, SALT] **:** a mineral $(K,Na)_3Na(SO_4)_2$ consisting of potassium sodium sulfate occurring massive or in white rhombohedral crystals

aph·thoid \ˈaf,thȯid, ˈap,-\ *adj* [NL *aptha* + E *-oid*] **:** having the characteristics of aphthae; *specif* **:** resembling thrush

aph·tho·sis \afˈthōsəs\ *n, pl* **aphtho·ses** \-ō,sēz\ [NL, fr. *aphtha* + *-osis*] **:** a condition characterized by the formation of aphthae

aph·thous \ˈafthəs, ˈapth-\ *adj* [NL *aphtha* + ISV *-ous*] **:** of, relating to, or characterized by aphthae

aphthous fever *n* **:** FOOT-AND-MOUTH DISEASE

aph·y·dro·trop·ic \ˌafˌhīˌ≈≈, ˌaˌfī-, ˌapˌhī-, ≈ˌ≈≈ˌ≈≈\ *also* **ap·o·hy·dro·trop·ic** \ˌapōˌhī≈ˌ≈≈\ *adj* [*apo-* + *hydrotropic*] **:** turning away from or shunning moisture ⟨an ~ plant⟩ — **aph·y·drot·ro·pism** \ˌafˌhīˈdrä·trə,pizəm, ˌaˌfī-, ˌapˌhī-\ *n* -s

aphyl·lous \(ˈ)āˈfiləs\ *adj* [Gk *aphyllos*, fr. *a-* ²*a-* + *phyllon* leaf — more at BLADE] **:** destitute of foliage leaves — **aphyl·ly** \ˈā,filē\ *n* -ES

aphyr·ic \(ˈ)āˈfirik, -fīr-\ *adj* [ISV ²*a-* + *-phyric*; orig formed as G *aphyrisch*] **:** not porphyritic

aphy·tal zone \(ˈ)āˈfid·ᵊl-\ *n* [²*a-* + Gk *phyton* plant + E *-al*] **:** APHOTIC REGION; *esp* **:** the plantless depths of a lake floor

api- *comb form* [L, fr. *apis*] **:** bee ⟨*apiculture*⟩ ⟨*apiphobia*⟩

api·a·ca \ˌapēəˈkä, ˌäp-\ *n, pl* **apiaca** *or* **apiacas** *usu cap* [Pg *apiacá*, of AmerInd origin] **1 a :** a Cariban people living near the mouth of the Tocantins river, Brazil **b :** a member of such people **2 a :** a Tupi-Guaranian people living on the Tapajoz river, Mato Grosso, Brazil **b :** a member of such people **3 :** the language of the Tupi-Guaranian Apiaca people

api·a·ce·ae \ˌāpēˈāsē,ē, ˌap-\ [NL, fr. *Apium*, type genus + *-aceae*] *syn of* UMBELLIFERAE

api·a·ceous \ˌāpēˈāshəs, ˌap-\ *adj* [NL *Apiaceae* + E *-ous*] **:** UMBELLIFEROUS

a pia·ce·re \ˌäpyäˈchāre, -erē\ *adv* [It] **:** at pleasure **:** ad libitum — used in ref. to a musical performance

api·an \ˈāpēən\ *adj* [L *apianus*, fr. *apis* + *-anus* -an] **:** of or relating to bees

api·ar·i·an \ˌāpēˈerēən, -ˈa(a)r-,-ˈär-\ *adj* **:** of or relating to beekeeping or bees

api·a·rist \ˈāpēərəst\ *n* -s **:** BEEKEEPER

api·ary \ˈāpē,erē, -ri\ *n* -ES [L *apiarium*, fr. *apis* bee + *-arium* -ary] **:** a place where bees are kept; *esp* **:** a collection of hives or colonies of bees kept for their honey

apic- *or* **apici-** *or* **apico-** *comb form* [prob. fr. NL, fr. L *apic-*, *apex*] **1 :** apex **:** tip esp. of an organ ⟨*apicad*⟩ ⟨*apicifixed*⟩ ⟨*apicoectomy*⟩ **2 :** apical and ⟨*apicodental* consonant⟩

ap·i·cad \ˈapə,kad, ˈāp-\ *adv* [*apic-* + *-ad*] **:** toward the apex

¹**ap·i·cal** \ˈapəkəl, ˈāp-, -ēk-\ *adj* [prob. fr. NL *apicalis*, fr. *apic-* + L *-alis* -al] **1 :** at or belonging to an apex, tip, or summit **2** *phonetics* **:** of, relating to, or formed with the participation of the tip of the tongue — **ap·i·cal·ly** \-k(ə)lē, -li\ *adv*

²**apical** \"\ *n* -s **:** an apical speech sound

apical cap *n* **:** one of a series of bands resembling collars formed at the ends of the cells of green algae of the genus *Oedogonium* as a result of cell divisions

apical cell *n* **:** the single cell that terminates the vegetative axis in many cryptogamous plants **:** the initial point of longitudinal growth

apical dominance *n* **:** inhibition of the growth of lateral buds by the terminal bud of a shoot that is believed to be effected principally or at least in part by auxins produced by the terminal bud

apical meristem *n* **:** a meristem located at the apex of a root or shoot and responsible for increase in length of the organ — compare INTERCALARY MERISTEM, LATERAL MERISTEM

apical plate *n* **:** a group of specialized cells of nervous and sensory function at the anterior end of the trochophore larva of certain invertebrates

apices *pl of* APEX

api·cian \ə'pishən\ *adj, usu cap* [L *apicianus*, fr. Marcus Gavius *Apicius fl* A.D. 14–37 Roman epicure + L *-anus* -an] **:** befitting Apicius; *specif* **:** EPICUREAN

ap·i·ci·fixed \'apəsə,fikst\ *adj* [*apic-* + *fixed*] **:** attached by the apex

apick·a·back \ə'-\ *archaic var of* PIGGYBACK

ap·i·co·bas·al \ˌapə(ˌ)kō¦-, ¦āp-\ *adj* [*apic-* + *basal*] **:** of or relating to apex and base ⟨an ~ axis⟩

apic·u·late \ə'pikyələt, ā'-, -ˌlāt, *usu* -d·+V\ *also* **apic·u·lat·ed** \-ˌlād·əd\ *adj* [NL *apiculus* + E *-ate*, *-ated*] **:** ending abruptly in a small distinct point ⟨an ~ leaf⟩

apic·u·la·tion \ˌ=ˌ=='lāshən\ *n* -s **:** APICULUS

api·cul·tur·al \ˌ¦āpə¦-\ *adj* **:** of, relating to, or affecting apiculture

api·cul·ture \'āpə,-\ *n* -s [prob. fr. F, fr. *api-* + *culture*] **:** beekeeping esp. when pursued on a large scale

api·cul·tur·ist \ˌ¦āpə¦-\ *n* -s **:** one who specializes in the breeding and culture of bees **:** BEEKEEPER

apic·u·lus \ə'pikyələs, ā'-\ *n, pl* **apicu·li** \-ˌlī, -ˌlē\ [NL, dim. of L *apic-, apex* summit] **:** a small acute point or tip

ap·i·dae \'apəˌdē\ *n pl, cap* [NL, fr. *Apis*, type genus + *-idae*] **:** a family of social bees having the glossa and basal joints of the labial palpi elongate and including the common honeybees and the stingless bees, in some classifications also the bumblebees and some solitary bees, and formerly all the bees

apiece \ə'pēs\ *adv* [ME *a pece*, fr. ²*a* (for each) + *pece* piece — more at PIECE] **:** for each person or thing **:** for each one **:** EACH, INDIVIDUALLY, SEVERALLY ⟨available at a dollar ~⟩ ⟨took an hour ~ to work the problems⟩

apieces *adv* [¹*a-* + *pieces*] *archaic* **:** in or to pieces

api·gen·in \ˌāpə'jenən, ˌap-\ *n* -s [ISV *apiin* + *-gen* + *-in*] **:** a yellowish crystalline compound $C_{15}H_{10}O_5$ occurring usu. as glycosides (as apiin) in various plants; 4′,5,7-trihydroxy= flavone

api·in \'āpēən, 'ap-\ *n* -s [ISV *api-* (fr. L *apium* parsley, celery) + *-in* — more at APIUM] **:** a crystalline glycoside $C_{26}H_{28}O_{14}$ obtained from parsley

api·ko·res *or* **api·ko·ros** \ˌäpē'kōrəs\ *n, pl* **apikor·sim** \-rsəm\ [Yiddish & Heb; Yiddish *apikurus*, fr. Heb *apīqōrōs*, fr. Gk *Epikouros* Epicurus — more at EPICURE] **:** a Jew who is lax in observing Jewish law or who does not believe in Judaism; *also* **:** SKEPTIC, ATHEIST

api·na·yé \ˌäpē(ˌ)nä'yā\ *n, pl* **apinayé** *usu cap* [Pg, of Amer-Ind origin] **1 a :** a Gesan people of north central Brazil **b :** a member of such people **2 :** the language of the Apinayé people

aping *pres part of* APE

apio \'äpē,ō\ *n* -s [AmerSp, fr. Sp, celery, fr. L *apium* — more at APIUM] **:** ARRACACHA

api·ole \'āpē,ōl, 'ap-\ *also* **api·ol** \-,ōl, -,ȯl\ *n* -s [ISV *api-* (fr. L *apium* parsley, celery) + *-ole*, *-ol* — more at APIUM] **1 a :** a colorless crystalline diether $C_{12}H_{14}O_4$ of the aromatic series found esp. in the plant and fruit of parsley — called also *parsley camphor* **b :** an isomeric liquid ether from certain dill oils — called also *dill apiole* **2 :** an oleoresin from parsley fruit used as an emmenagogue and antiperiodic

api·ol·o·gy \ˌāpē'äləjē\ *n* -ES [*api-* + *-logy*] **:** the scientific study of honeybees

api·on \'āpē,än\ *n, cap* [NL, fr. Gk, pear; fr. the shape of the beak — more at PEAR] **:** a large cosmopolitan genus of small long-beaked weevils including a number of serious pests of cultivated plants

api·os \'āpē,äs\ *n, cap* [NL, fr. Gk, pear tree; fr. the shape of the tubers — more at PEAR] **:** a widely distributed genus of trailing or climbing herbs (family Leguminosae) having tuberous roots, compound leaves, small racemose flowers, and linear pods — see GROUNDNUT

api·ose \'āpē,ōs, 'ap-\ *n* -s [*apiin* + *-ose*] **:** a branched-chain pentose $(HOCH_2)_2C(OH)CHOHCHO$ obtained as a syrup by hydrolyzing apiin

api·o·so·ma \ˌāpēō'sōmə, ˌap-\ [NL] *syn of* BABESIA

apis \'āpəs\ *n, cap* [NL, fr. L, bee] **:** the type genus of Apidae including brownish social bees lacking spurs but having scopae on the hind tibiae and including the common honeybee

ap·ish \'āpish, -ēsh\ *adj* **:** like an ape: as **a :** given to servile imitation **b :** extremely silly or affected ⟨the ~ gallantry of a fantastic boy —Sir Walter Scott⟩ — **ap·ish·ly** *adv*

apish·a·more \ə'pishəˌmō(ə)r\ *n* -s [modif. of Ojibwa *apishamon* something to lie down on] **:** a saddle blanket usu. of buffalo hide

apis·to·gram·ma \ə,pistə'gramə\ *n, cap* [NL, perh. fr. Gk *apistos* untrustworthy (fr. *a-* ²*a-* + *pistos* trustworthy) + *gramma* letter] **:** a genus of small cichlid fishes including a species (*A. agassizi*) commonly kept in the tropical aquarium

api·tong \'äpē,tȯŋ\ *n* -s [Tag] **1 :** any of several trees of the genus *Dipterocarpus*; *esp* **:** an important Philippine timber tree (*D. grandiflorus*) yielding a resin used as an illuminant or varnish or for calking boats **2 :** the reddish brown wood of an apitong tree

api·um \'āpēəm, 'ap-\ *n, cap* [NL, fr. L, parsley, celery; perh. akin to Skt *ap-* water — more at ABKAR] **:** a genus of Eurasian herbs of the carrot family having pinnate leaves and white or yellowish flowers in compound umbels — see CELERY

apiv·o·rous \(ˈ)ā¦pivərəs\ *adj* [prob. fr. F *apivore*, fr. *api-* + *-vore* -vorous] **:** bee-eating ⟨~ birds⟩

ap·john·ite \'ap,jä,nīt\ *n* -s [G *apjohnit*, fr. James *Apjohn* †1886 Ir. chemist who first examined it + G *-it* -ite] **:** a mineral $MnSO_4.Al_2(SO_4)_3.22H_2O$ consisting of manganese aluminum sulfate containing water and occurring in crusts or fibrous masses

apl- — see HAPL-

apla·cen·tal \¦ā=¦==\ *adj* [²*a-* + *placental*] **:** having or developing no placenta

apla·coph·o·ra \ˌā,pla'käfərə, ˌaplə'-\ *n pl, cap* [NL, fr. ²*a-* + *plac-* + *-phora*] **:** an order of Amphineura comprising wormlike mollusks in which the body is without calcareous plates but the mantle bears numerous calcified spicules over its entire surface — **apla·coph·o·ran** \¦=(ˌ)=¦==rən\ *adj or n* — **apla·coph·o·rous** \-rəs\ *adj*

ap·la·nat \'aplə,nat, *usu* -ad·+V\ *n* -s [G, back-formation fr. *aplanatisch*, fr. E *aplanatic*] **:** an aplanatic lens

ap·la·nat·ic \ˌaplə¦nad·ik\ *adj* [irreg. fr. Gk *aplanētos* that cannot go astray (fr. *a-* ²*a-* + *planētos* wandering) + E *-ic* — more at PLANET] **:** free from or corrected for spherical aberration ⟨an ~ lens⟩ — **ap·la·nat·i·cal·ly** \-d·ək(ə)lē\ *adv*

aplan·a·tism \ā'planə,tizəm, ə'-; 'aplə,nad·,izəm\ *n* -s **:** freedom from spherical aberration

aplan·e·tism \ā'planə,tizəm, ə'-\ *n* -s [Gk *aplanētos* that cannot go astray + E *-ism*] **:** the state of producing nonmotile asexual spores

aplano- *comb form* [prob. fr. NL, fr. Gk *aplanēs* not wandering, fixed, fr. *a-* ²*a-* + *-planēs* wandering, fr. *planasthai* to wander — more at PLANET] **:** nonmotile ⟨*Aplano*bacter⟩ ⟨*aplano*spore⟩

aplan·o·bac·ter \(ˈ)ā¦planə,baktə(r)\ [NL, fr. *aplano-* + *-bacter*] *syn of* ¹BACILLUS

aplan·o·ga·mete \(ˈ)ā¦planəgə,mēt, ˌā,planəgə'm-, ¦ā,planə'ga,m-\ *n* -s [*aplano-* + *gamete*] **:** a nonmotile gamete (as in certain lower algae) — compare PLANOGAMETE

apla·nog·a·mous \ˌā,pla¦nägəməs, ¦aplə'-\ *adj* [*aplano-* + *-gamous*] **:** having nonmotile gametes — **apla·nog·a·my** \-'nägəmē\ *n* -ES

aplan·o·spore \(ˈ)ā¦planə,spō(ə)r\ *n* -s [*aplano-* + *spore*] **1 :** a nonmotile asexual spore formed by rejuvenescence in certain algae and distinguished from an akinete by developing a new cell wall distinct from that of the parent cell — compare HYPNOSPORE, ZOOSPORE **2 :** a nonmotile asexual spore produced within the sporangium in certain fungi (as Mucoraceae)

apla·sia \(ˈ)ā'plāzh(ē)ə, ə'p-, (ˈ)a'p-\ *n* -s [NL, fr. ²*a-* + *-plasia*] **:** the incomplete or faulty development of an organ or part

aplas·tic \(ˈ)ā¦-\ *adj* [²*a-* + *plastic*] **1 a :** not plastic **:** not easily molded **b :** not exhibiting growth or change in structure **2 :** of, relating to, or exhibiting aplasia

aplastic anemia *n* **:** anemia characterized by defective function of the blood-forming organs (as the bone marrow) and believed to be caused by toxic agents

¹**aplen·ty** \ə'-\ *adj* [¹*a-* + *plenty*] **:** in plenty or abundance **:** enough and to spare **:** ABUNDANT ⟨money ~ for all our needs⟩ — used postpositively or predicatively

²**aplenty** \"\ *adv* [¹*a-* + *plenty*] **1 :** in abundance **:** PLENTIFULLY ⟨germs are present ~ in addition to the venom —W.L. Gresham⟩ **2 :** VERY, EXTREMELY ⟨scared ~ —Booth Tarkington⟩

³**aplenty** \"\ *n* [¹*aplenty*] **:** ABUNDANCE, PLENTY ⟨wished now to get ~ while they were getting —*Nation*⟩

ap·lite \'a,plīt\ *also* **hap·lite** \'ha-\ *n* -s [ISV *hapl-* + *-ite*; prob. orig. formed as G *aplit*] **:** a fine-grained light-colored differentiation rock; *specif* **:** a differentiate of granite consisting almost entirely of quartz and feldspar and generally occurring in dikes — **ap·lit·ic** \(ˈ)a¦plid·ik\ *adj*

aplo- — see HAPL-

ap·lo·chei·lus \ˌaplō'kīləs\ *n, cap* [NL, fr. *hapl-* + Gk *cheilos* lip — more at GILL] **:** a genus of tropical killifishes including the panchaxes

ap·lo·di·no·tus \ˌa(ˌ)plōdə'nōd·əs\ *n, cap* [NL, fr. *hapl-* + Gk *dinōtos* round] **:** a genus of freshwater fishes (family Scaenidae) including the freshwater drum or sheepshead (*A. grunniens*) widely distributed in larger rivers and lakes of No. America

ap·lo·don·tia \ˌaplō'dänch(ē)ə\ *n, cap* [NL, fr. *hapl-* + *-odontia*] **:** a genus (the type of the family Aplodontiidae) of rodents comprising the mountain beavers — **ap·lo·don·ti·id** \¦aplō¦dänchēəd\ *adj or n*

ap·lo·don·toi·dea \ˌaplō,dän'tȯidēə\ *n pl, cap* [NL, fr. *Aplodontia* + *-oidea*] **:** a superfamily of primitive rodents represented among modern forms by the mountain beaver

ap·lo·gran·ite \¦aplō¦granət\ *n* -s [*hapl-* + *granite*] **:** a rock of granitic texture consisting of alkali-feldspar and quartz with some biotite

aplomb \ə'pläm, -əm *also* -ōm *or* -ōm; *F* äplō^n\ *n* -s [F, lit., perpendicularity, fr. MF, fr. *a plomb* perpendicularly, lit., according to the plummet, fr. *a* to, at, according to (fr. L *ad* to, at) + *plomb* lead, plummet — more at AT, PLUMB] **1 :** complete confidence or assurance in oneself **:** SELF-POSSESSION, POISE ⟨summed up the situation with his usual ~ —John Marks⟩ ⟨few of them, however, possess the ~ to order a martini before lunch —Edward Newhouse⟩ **2 :** the perpendicular position **:** PERPENDICULARITY **3** *of a ballet dancer* **:** the perfect equilibrium required to maintain stability in a pose or movement

ap·lome \'a,plōm\ *n* -s [F, fr. *hapl-* + *-ome*] **:** a dark brown or green variety of andradite containing manganese — compare GARNET

ap·lo·pap·pus \ˌaplō'papəs\ *syn of* HAPLOPAPPUS

ap·lo·per·i·stom·a·tous \¦aplō,perə'stäməd·əs, -ōm-\ *adj* [*hapl-* + NL *peristomat-*, *peristoma* + E *-ous*] *of a moss* **:** having in the peristome a single row of teeth or none

aplus·tre \ə'plästrē\ *n, pl* **aplus·tria** \-rēə\ *or* **aplus·tra** \-rə\ [L, prob. fr. an Etruscan word borrowed fr. Gk *aphlaston*] **:** the curved ornamented stern of an ancient Greek or Roman ship

aply·sia \ə'plizh(ē)ə\ [NL, fr. Gk, a kind of sponge, fr. *aplytos* unwashed (fr. *a-* ²*a-* + *plytos* washed) + *-ia*; akin to *plynein* to wash, *plein* to sail, float, swim — more at FLOW] *syn of* TETHYS

ap·ly·si·i·dae \ˌaplə'sīə,dē\ [NL, fr. *Aplysia*, type genus + *-idae*] *syn of* TETHYIDAE

ap·nea *or* **ap·noea** \'apnēə, ap'n-\ *n* -s [NL, fr. ²*a-* + *-pnea*, *-pnoea*] **1 :** transient cessation of respiration whether normal (as in hibernating animals) or abnormal (as that caused by certain drugs) **2 :** ASPHYXIA — **ap·ne·ic** *or* **ap·noe·ic** \(ˈ)ap¦nēik\ *adj*

apneu·mo·na \(ˈ)ā'n(y)ümənə, ap'n-\ *or* **apneu·mo·nes** \-məˌnēz\ *n pl, cap* [NL, fr. ²*a-* + *-pneumona*, *-pneumones* (fr. Gk *pneumon-*, *pneumōn* lung) — more at PNEUMONIA] **:** a formerly recognized division of Holothurioidea comprising forms lacking an internal respiratory apparatus — compare PNEUMONOPHORA — **apneu·mo·nous** \(ˈ)ā¦n-,(ˈ)ap¦n-\ *adj*

apneu·mo·no·mor·phae \=,==nō'mȯr,fē\ *n pl, cap* [NL, fr. *Apneumona* + *-o-* + *-morphae*] *in some classifications* **:** a suborder of Arachnida comprising the arachnomorph spiders that lack book lungs

ap·neu·sis \ap'n(y)üsəs\ *n, pl* **apneu·ses** \-ü,sēz\ [NL, fr. ²*a-* + Gk *pneusis* breathing, fr. *pnein* to breathe — more at SNEEZE] **:** sustained tonic contraction of the respiratory muscles resulting in the prolonged inspiration characteristic of many lower vertebrates

ap·neus·tic \(ˈ)=¦=,stik\ *adj* [²*a-* + Gk *pneustikos* of or for breathing, fr. (assumed) Gk *pneustos* (verbal of *pnein* to breathe) + Gk *-ikos* -ic] **1** *of an insect larva* **:** having all the spiracles absent or closed **2 :** exhibiting apneusis

apo- *or* **ap-** *or* **aph-** *prefix* [*apo-* fr. ME, fr. MF & L; MF, fr. L, fr. Gk, fr. *apo*; *ap-* fr. Gk, fr. *apo*; *aph-* fr. LL, fr. Gk, fr. *apo* — more at OF] **1 :** away from **:** off ⟨*apo*stron⟩ ⟨*aph*elion⟩ **2 :** detached **:** separate ⟨*apo*carpous⟩ **3 :** formed from **:** related to — in names of chemical compounds ⟨*apo*codeine⟩; *apo-* before consonants other than *h* and sometimes *ap-* before vowels and *aph-* before *h* (which is not repeated) but frequently *apo-* even before *h* or a vowel

apo *abbr* apogee

APO *abbr* army post office

apo·at·ro·pine \ˌapō'a·\ *n* [ISV *apo-* + *atropine*] **:** a bitter crystalline poisonous alkaloid $C_{17}H_{21}NO_2$ occurring naturally in belladonna root or prepared synthetically by the action of nitric acid on atropine and having no mydriatic effect

apoc·a·lypse \ə'päkə,lips\ *n* -s [ME *apocalipse* Revelation of St. John (book of the New Testament), revelation, vision, fr. LL *apocalypsis*, fr. Gk *apokalypsis*, lit., uncovering, revelation, fr. *apokalyptein* to uncover, reveal (fr. *apo-* + *kalyptein* to cover, conceal) + *-sis* — more at HELL] **1 :** a writing professing to reveal the future; *esp* **:** such a pseudonymous writing in Jewish or early Christian circles between about 200 B.C. and A.D. 150 predicting the ultimate future shape of eschatological events by means of a symbolism understandable to the faithful but hidden from others **2 :** something viewed as a revelation **:** DISCLOSURE

¹**apoc·a·lyp·tic** \ə¦päkə¦liptik *also* ¦a,päkə- *sometimes* ¦apəkə-\ *also* **apoc·a·lyp·ti·cal** \-təkəl, -ēk-\ *adj* [LGk *apokalyptikos*, fr. Gk *apokalyptein* + *-ikos* -ic, -ical] **1 a :** of or relating to an apocalypse **b :** resembling or having the characteristics of an apocalypse **2 a :** forecasting or predicting the ultimate destiny of the world in the shape of future events **b :** PROPHETIC, REVELATORY **3 :** foreboding imminent disaster or final doom **4 :** wildly unrestrained **:** GRANDIOSE **5 :** ultimately decisive — **apoc·a·lyp·ti·cal·ly** \-tək(ə)lē, -ēk-, -li\ *adv*

²**apocalyptic** \"\ *n* -s **:** literature resembling or having characteristics of an apocalypse

apoc·a·lyp·ti·cism \ə,päkə'liptə,sizəm *also* ,a,päk- *sometimes* ,apək-\ *or* **apoc·a·lyp·tism** \ə¦päkə¦lip,tiz-, ,a,päkə'l-, ,apəkə'l-\ *n* -s **:** apocalyptic expectation; *esp* **:** a doctrine distinguished by the expectation of an imminent end of the present temporal world, the final destruction of the unrighteous in a purging holocaust engulfing the earth, and the resurrection of the righteous to a purified world of bliss

apoc·a·lyp·tist \ə¦päkə¦liptəst, ,a,päkə'l-, ,apəkə'l-\ *n* -s **:** the writer of an apocalypse

ap·o·car·pous \¦apə¦kärpəs\ *adj* [*apo-* + *-carpous*] **:** having the carpels of the gynoecium separate ⟨the buttercup is ~⟩ — opposed to *syncarpous*

ap·o·car·py \'apə,kärpē\ *n* -ES [*apocarpous* + *-y*] **:** the state of being apocarpous

ap·o·ca·tas·ta·sis *or* **ap·o·ka·tas·ta·sis** \¦apəkə'tastəsəs\ *n, pl* **apocatasta·ses** *or* **apokatasta·ses** \-ə,sēz\ [NL, fr. LL, fr. Gk *apokatastasis*, lit. restitution, recovery, fr. *apo-* + *katastasis* restoration, condition — more at CATASTASIS] **:** RESTITUTION, RESTORATION; *esp* **:** the doctrine of the final restoration of all sinful beings to God and to the state of blessedness — compare UNIVERSALISM — **ap·o·cat·a·stat·ic** \¦apə,kad·ə¦stad·ik\ *adj*

ap·o·cen·ter \'apə,-\ *n* -s [*apo-* + *center*, *centre*] **:** the point of an orbit farthest from the center of attraction

ap·o·cen·tric \¦==¦-\ *adj* [*apo-* + *centric*] *biol* **:** deviating from the archetype — opposed to *archecentric* — **ap·o·cen·tric·i·ty** \ˌapə,sen'trisəd·ē, -,sən-\ *n* -ES

ap·o·cha \'apəkə\ *n, pl* **apo·chae** \-,kī, -,kē\ [LL, fr. Gk *apochē* receipt] *Roman & civil law* **:** a written receipt for the payment of money

apocha tri·um an·no·rum \-¦trēəmə'nōrəm, -¦trīə-\ *n, pl* **apochae trium annorum** [NL, lit., three year receipt] *Scots law* **:** a written receipt for a debt due (as rent or interest) for three consecutive separate yearly or periodical payments from which the payment of the preceding installments is presumed

ap·o·chro·mat \¦apəkrō¦mat, ,apə'krō,m-, *usu* -ad·+V\ *n* -s [G, back-formation fr. *apochromatisch* apochromatic] **:** an apochromatic lens

ap·o·chro·mat·ic \¦apəkrō¦mad·ik\ *adj* [ISV *apo-* + *chromatic*] **:** free from chromatic and spherical aberration — used of a lens in which rays of three or more colors are brought to the same focus, the degree of achromatism thus obtained being more nearly complete than where two rays only are thus focused

apoc·o·pate \ə'päkə,pāt, *usu* -ād·+V\ *vt* -ED/-ING/-s [*apocope* + *-ate*] **:** to shorten by apocope — **apoc·o·pa·tion** \ə,päkə'pāshən\ *n* -s

apoc·o·pe \ə'päkə(,)pē\ *n* -s [LL, fr. Gk *apokopē*, lit., cutting off, fr. *apokoptein* to cut off, fr. *apo-* + *koptein* to strike, cut off — more at CAPON] **:** the loss of one or more sounds or letters at the end of a word (as in *sing* from Old English *singan*, *my* from Old English *mīn*, or *tho* for *though*) — compare APHAERESIS, SYNCOPE

ap·o·crine \'apəkrən; -,krin, -īn,-ēn\ *adj* [ISV *apo-* + *-crine* (fr. Gk *krinein* to separate)] **:** producing a secretion that involves breaking off of the part of the cytoplasm of the secreting cells above the nucleus **:** produced by an apocrine gland — compare ECCRINE, MEROCRINE

apocrine gland *n* **:** any of the large sweat glands that produce both a fluid and an apocrine secretion, are restricted in man to hairy regions of the body, and are lined by a single layer of tall columnar cells with acidophile cytoplasm — compare ECCRINE GLAND

ap·o·cri·si·ar·i·us \ˌapə,kriz(h)ē'a(a)rēəs\ *also* **ap·o·cri·si·ary** \-'kriz(h)ē,erē, -zhərē\ *n, pl* **apocrisiar·ii** \-a(a)rē,ī, -rē,ē\ *or* **apocrisiar·ies** [LL *apocrisiarius*, *apocrisarius*, fr. LGk *apokrisis* message (fr. Gk, answer, fr. *apokrinesthai* to answer — fr. *apokrinein* to separate, choose, fr. *apo-* + *krinein* to separate, distinguish, decide — + *-sis*) + L *-arius* -ary — more at RIDDLE (sieve)] **:** a plenipotentiary delegate formerly representing a power and residing at a foreign capital; *esp* **:** a papal nuncio serving at the imperial court in Constantinople during the early centuries of the medieval era

apoc·ri·ta \ə'päkrəd·ə\ [NL, fr. Gk *apokrita*, neut. pl. of *apokritos* separated, fr. *apokrinein* to separate] *syn of* CLISTOGASTRA

ap·o·cryph \'apə,krif\ *n* -s [ME *apocrife*, fr. MF, fr. ML *apocrypha*] **:** an apocryphal writing

apoc·ry·pha \ə'päkrəfə\ *n pl but sometimes sing in constr, often cap* [ML, fr. LL, neut. pl. of *apocryphus* secret, uncanonical (said of writings not to be read to the congregation), fr. LGk *apokryphos*, fr. Gk, hidden, fr. *apokryptein* to hide away, fr. *apo-* + *kryptein* to hide — more at CRYPT] **1 :** quasi-scriptural noncanonical or deuterocanonical books of doubtful authorship and authority ⟨the Old Testament *Apocrypha*⟩ ⟨in these ~ we find Confucius being regarded as a superhuman being —Yu-lan Feng⟩ **2 :** writings or statements of doubtful or spurious authorship ⟨his early rise is shrouded in ~ —E.S.Turner⟩

apoc·ry·phal \-fəl\ *adj* **1** *often cap* **:** similar to the Apocrypha **2 :** not canonical **:** of doubtful authenticity **:** FICTITIOUS, SPURIOUS, UNTRUSTWORTHY ⟨noting which works are regarded as authentic and which ~ —L.J.Thro⟩ ⟨a story, possibly ~ but completely credible —Robert Campbell⟩ **3** *archaic* **:** COUNTERFEIT, IMITATIVE, SHAM **syn** see FICTITIOUS

apoc·ry·phal·ly \-fəlē, -li\ *adv* **:** in an apocryphal manner **:** without authenticity

apoc·ry·phon \-,fän\ *sing of* APOCRYPHA

ap·o·cy·a·nine \¦apə¦-\ *n* -s [ISV *apo-* + *cyanine*] **:** any of a class of cyanine dyes in whose structure the two heterocyclic rings are directly attached to each other by a double bond

apoc·y·na·ce·ae \ə,päsə'nāsē,ē, ,apəsə'-, -ə,sī'-\ *n pl, cap* [NL, fr. *Apocynum*, type genus + *-aceae*] **:** a family of chiefly tropical herbs, shrubs, or trees (order Gentianales) having a milky juice, simple entire leaves, often showy flowers, and a fruit consisting of two follicles or drupes — compare DOGBANE, OLEANDER, PERIWINKLE — **apoc·y·na·ceous** \=¦==¦nāshəs, ¦==(,)=¦-\ *adj*

apoc·y·nin \ə'päsənən\ *n* -s [ISV *apocyn-* (fr. NL *Apocynum*) + *-in*] **:** ACETOVANILLONE

apoc·y·num \-sənəm\ *n, cap* [NL, fr. L, dogbane, fr. Gk *apokynon*, fr. *apo-* + *-kynon* (fr. *kyn-*, *kyōn* dog) — more at HOUND] **:** a genus of chiefly American perennial herbs (family Apocynaceae) with opposite leaves and small white or pink flowers in corymbose cymes — see INDIAN HEMP 1

ap·o·cyte \'apə,sīt\ *n* -s [ISV *apo-* + *-cyte*] **:** a multinucleate cell

ap·o·da \'apədə\ *n pl, cap* [NL, fr. Gk, neut. pl. of *apod-*, *apous* footless] **:** any of several different groups of animals that have been so named from their lacking limbs or feet: as **a :** an order of slender wormlike holothurians that lack tube feet and radial ambulacral vessels — compare HOLOTHURIOIDEA **b :** a group of fishes without pelvic fins **c :** CAECILIANS **d :** an order or suborder of parasitic segmented cirripedes **e :** worms without appendages (as the leeches)

¹**ap·o·dal** \'apəd^əl\ *also* **ap·o·dan** \-dən, -d^ən\ *or* **ap·o·dous** \-dəs\ *adj* [Gk *apod-*, *apous* + E *-al* or *-an* or *-ous*] **1 :** having no feet **:** FOOTLESS **2 :** lacking appendages ⟨eels and some insect larvae are ~⟩ **3** [NL *Apodes* & *Apoda* + E *-al* or *-an* or *-ous*] **:** of or relating to the Apoda or Apodes

²**apodal** \"\ *also* **apodan** \"\ *n* -s **:** an apodal animal

apodeictic *var of* APODICTIC

apo·deip·non \ä'pōdēp,nōn\ *n, pl* **apodeip·na** \-,nä\ *often cap* [MGk, fr. Gk *apo-* + *deipnon* meal] **:** the last part of the divine office in the Eastern Church — compare COMPLINE

apod·e·mal \ə'pädəməl, ¦apə¦dēm-\ *adj* **:** of, relating to, or functioning as an apodeme

ap·o·deme \'apə,dēm\ *also* **apod·e·ma** \ə'pädəmə\ *n, pl* **apodemes** \-ēmz\ *also* **apodemas** \-məz\ *or* **apodem·a·ta** \ˌapə'demədə\ [NL *apodema*, fr. *apo-* + *-dema* (fr. Gk *demas* body, build); akin to Gk *demein* to build — more at TIMBER] **:** one of the internal ridges or ingrowths from the exoskeleton of most arthropods that support the internal organs, provide points of attachment for the muscles, and constitute the endoskeleton of the animal

ap·o·de·mus \ˌapə'dēməs\ *n, cap* [NL, fr. Gk *apodēmos* abroad, fr. *apodēmein* to go abroad, be abroad, fr. *apo-* + *dēmos* country, people — more at DEMOCRACY] **:** a genus consisting of the Old World field mice

¹**ap·o·des** \'apə,dēz\ *n pl, cap* [NL, fr. Gk, masc. & fem. pl. of *apod-*, *apous* footless] **1 :** a group of soft-finned, elongated, and probably degenerate fishes consisting of the eels, often including the morays and in old classifications also many others having no pelvic fins, and being now commonly treated as an order but sometimes as including several orders or, formerly, made a division of the Physostomi **2 :** any of several groups of animals lacking appendages; *specif* **:** APODA a, c

²**apodes** *pl of* APUS

ap·o·di \'apə,dī, -,dē\ *n pl, cap* [NL, fr. Gk *apodoi*, pl. of *apous* footless, fr. *a-* ²*a-* + *-pous* (fr. *pous* foot) — more at FOOT] **:** a suborder of Apodiformes that comprises the swifts

apo·dia \ā'pōdēə, a'-,ə'-\ *n* -s [NL, fr. Gk, fr. *apod-*, *apous* + *-ia*] **:** APODA a

ap·o·dic·tic \¦apə¦diktik\ *also* **ap·o·dic·ti·cal** \-təkəl\ *also* **ap·o·deic·tic** \-'dīktik\ *adj* [L *apodicticus*, fr. Gk *apodeiktikos*, fr. *apodeiktos*, verbal of *apodeiknynai* to demonstrate (fr. *apo-* + *deiknynai* to show) + *-ikos* -ic, -ical — more at TOKEN] **1 :** expressing necessary truth **:** absolutely certain ⟨categories of human action . . . are ~ and absolute and do not admit of any gradation —Alfred Sherrard⟩ **2 :** capable of clear and certain demonstration ⟨an ~ theory⟩ — **ap·o·dic·ti·cal·ly** \-tәk(ә)lē\ *adv*

[1]**apod·i·dae** \ә'pädә,dē\ [NL, fr. *Apod-*, *Apus* (syn. of *Triops*), type genus + *-idae* — more at APUS] *syn of* TRIOPIDAE

[2]**apodidae** \"\ *n pl, cap* [NL, fr. *Apod-*, *Apus*, type genus + *-idae* — more at APUS] **:** a widely distributed family of birds (order Apodiformes) comprising the swifts and having flat skulls and all toes pointing forward but being swallowlike in appearance and behavior

apod·i·form \ә'pädә,fȯrm\ *adj* [NL *Apodiformes*] **:** of or relating to the Apodiformes

apod·i·for·mes \ә,pädә'fȯr,mēz\ *n pl, cap* [NL, fr. *Apod-*, *Apus* + *-iformes*] **:** an order of birds with long narrow wings and weak feet that comprises the swifts and the humming birds

apod·o·sis \ә'pädәsәs\ *n, pl* **apodo·ses** \-ә,sēz\ [NL, fr. Gk, restitution, definition, apodosis, fr. *apodidonai* to restore, define, make an apodosis (fr. *apo-* + *didonai* to give) + *-sis* — more at DATE (point of time)] **1 :** CONCLUSION 7 — contrasted with *protasis* **2 :** the last day of a festival period in the Eastern Church comparable to the last day of an octave in the Western Church except in the variable duration of the period

ap·o·dy·te·ri·um \,apә,dī'tirēәm\ *n, pl* **apodyte·ria** \-rēә\ [L, fr. Gk *apodytērion*, fr. *apodyein* to strip off, fr. *apo-* + *dyein* to dive in, put on (clothes) — more at ADYTUM] **:** a dressing room in an ancient Greek or Roman bath or palaestra

ap·o·en·zyme \¦apō¦-\ *n* -s [ISV *apo-* + *enzyme*] **:** any protein that forms an active enzyme system by combination with a coenzyme and that determines the specificity of this system for any one substrate

ap·o·fer·ri·tin \¦apә¦-\ *n* -s [ISV *apo-* + *ferritin*] **:** a colorless crystalline protein capable of storing iron in the cells of the body — compare FERRITIN

ap·o·gae·ic \¦apә¦jēik\ *or* **ap·o·ga·ic** \-¦gāik\ *adj* [NL *apogaeum* & Gk *apogaion* apogee + E *-ic*] **:** APOGEAN

ap·o·ga·lac·te·um \,apәgә'laktēәm, -kshēәm; -,ga,lak'tē-\ *n* -s [NL, fr. *apo-* + *-galacteum* (fr. Gk *galakt-*, *gala* milk) — more at GALAXY] **:** the point of the hypothetical orbit of the sun or another star at which it is most remote from the galactic nucleus

ap·o·gam·ic \¦apә¦gamik\ *or* **ap·o·ga·met·ic** \-gә¦med·ik\ *or* **apog·a·mous** \ә'pägәmәs, a'-\ *adj* **:** of or relating to apogamy — **ap·o·gam·i·cal·ly** \¦apә¦gamәk(ә)lē\ *adv* — **apog·a·mous·ly** \ә'pägәmәslē, a'-\ *adv*

apog·a·my \ә'pägәmē, (')a¦p-\ *n* -ES [ISV *apo-* + *-gamy*] **1** *biol* **:** interbreeding within a segregated group not having any common differentiating character — compare HOMOGAMY **2** *bot* **:** development of the sporophyte from the gametophyte without fertilization — used esp. of a form of apomixis in seed plants wherein an embryo arises from a cell or cells other than the egg and without fertilization

ap·o·ge·an \¦apә¦jēәn\ *also* **ap·o·ge·al** \-ēәl\ *or* **ap·o·ge·ic** \-ēik\ *adj* **:** of or connected with the apogee ⟨~ tides that occur when the moon is at the apogee of its orbit⟩

ap·o·gee \'apә(,)jē, -әji\ *n* -s [It & Gk & F & NL; It *apogeo* & F *apogée* & NL *apogaeum*, fr. Gk *apogeion*, *apogaion*, fr. neut. of *apogeios*, *apogaios* far from the earth, fr. *apo-* + *-geios*, *-gaios* (fr. *gē* earth)] **1 :** the point in the orbit of a satellite of the earth (as the moon or an artificial body) at the greatest distance from the center of the earth **2 :** the farthest or highest point **:** APEX ⟨the ~ of Renaissance art —*Time*⟩

apog·e·nous \ә'päjәnәs, (')a¦p-\ *adj* [*apo-* + *-genous*] **:** relating to or causing apogeny

apog·e·ny \ә'päjәnē, a'-\ *n* -ES [*apo-* + *-geny*] *bot* **:** loss of the reproductive function

ap·o·ge·o·trop·ic \¦apә¦==¦==\ *adj* [*apo-* + *geotropic*] **:** bending up or away from the ground ⟨the short ~ roots of the mangrove⟩ — **ap·o·ge·o·trop·i·cal·ly** \¦==,==¦=pәk(ә)lē\ *adv*

ap·o·ge·ot·ro·pism \¦apә=¦====\ *n* -s [*apo-* + *geotropism*] *bot* **:** the state of being apogeotropic **:** negative geotropism

apo·gon \ә'pō,gän, ā'-\ *n, cap* [NL, fr. MGk *apōgōn* beardless, fr. Gk *a-* [2]a- + *pōgōn* beard — more at -POGON] **:** a genus of large-headed marine percoid fishes having the body oblong and compressed and comprising the cardinal fishes — see APOGONIDAE

apo·gon·id \ә'pōgәnәd, ā'-; ,apә'gän-\ *n* -s [NL *Apogonidae*] **:** a fish of the genus *Apogon* or family Apogonidae

ap·o·gon·i·dae \,apә'gänә,dē\ *n pl, cap* [NL, fr. *Apogon*, type genus + *-idae*] *in many classifications* **:** a family (type genus *Apogon*) of bright-colored tropical marine percoid fishes many of which incubate the eggs in the mouth

apogon iris *n, usu cap A* **:** BEARDLESS IRIS

ap·o·graph \'apә,graf\ *n, pl* **apog·ra·pha** \ә'pägrәfә, a'-\ [L *apographon*, fr. Gk, fr. neut. of *apographos* copied, fr. *apo-* + *-graphos* -graph] **:** COPY, TRANSCRIPT — **apog·ra·phal** \ә'pägrәfәl, (')a¦p-\ *adj*

ap·o·hy·al \¦apә¦hīәl\ *n* -s [*apo-* + *hyoidal*] **:** CERATOBRANCHIAL

apohydrotropic *var of* APHYDROTROPIC

ap·oid \'a,pȯid, 'ā,-\ *adj* [NL *Apoidea*] **:** of or relating to the Apoidea **:** resembling one of the Apoidea or some part of one of these insects ⟨~ mouth parts⟩

apoi·de·a \ә'pȯidēә, ā'p-,a'p-\ *n pl, cap* [NL, fr. *Apis* + *-oidea*] **:** a superfamily of Hymenoptera comprising the true bees — compare APIDAE, SPHECOIDEA

apoise \ә'-\ *adj* [[1]*a-* + *poise* (v.)] **:** in readiness **:** POISED ⟨bridesmaids were ~ to resume their places —Edith Wharton⟩

ap·o·jove \'apә,jōv\ *n* -s [NL *apojovium*, fr. *apo-* + *-jovium* (fr. *Jovis* Jupiter) — more at JOVE] **:** the point farthest from the planet Jupiter in the orbit of each of its satellites

apokatastasis *var of* APOCATASTASIS

apo koi·nou \,ä(,)pō,kȯi'nü, ä,p-\ *n, pl* **apo koinous** \-nüz\ [Gk, lit., in common] **:** the occurrence of one and the same word or word group, not repeated, in two constructions (as *three crows* in "there were three crows sat on a tree")

apo·lar \(')ā¦-\ *adj* [[2]*a-* + *polar*] **:** having no poles — used esp. of nerve cells formerly believed to lack processes

ap·o·laus·tic \¦apә¦lȯstik\ *adj* [Gk *apolaustikos*, fr. *apolaustos* enjoyed, enjoyable (fr. *apolauein* to enjoy, benefit from, fr. *apo-* + *-lauein*, akin to *leia* booty, prey) + *-ikos* -ic — more at LUCRE] **:** devoted to enjoyment ⟨a learned, ~ buffoon who loved good food —James Stern⟩

ap·o·le·gam·ic \¦apәlә¦gamik\ *adj* [Gk *apolegein* to pick out (fr. *apo-* + *legein* to gather) + E *-gamic* — more at LEGEND] *biol* **:** relating to selection — used specif. of mating based on sexual selection

apo·lis·ta \,äpә'lēstә\ *n, pl* **apolista** *or* **apolistas** *usu cap* [Sp, of AmerInd origin] **1 a :** a people of the Apolo river valley, Bolivia **b :** a member of such people **2 :** the language of the Apolista people

apo·lit·i·cal \¦ā=¦===\ *adj* [[2]*a-* + *political*] **1 :** having an aversion for or no interest or involvement in political affairs **2 :** without political significance

[1]**apol·li·nar·i·an** \ә¦pälә¦na(a)rēәn\ *adj, usu cap* [L *Apollinaris* (fr. *Apollin-*, *Apollo* + L *-aris* -ary) + E *-an*] **:** relating to or in honor of Apollo

[2]**apollinarian** \"\ *adj, usu cap* [LL *Apollinarianus*, fr. LGk *Apollinarianos*, fr. *Apollinaris* of Laodicea †*ab* A.D. 390 Syrian teacher & theologian + Gk *-anos* -an] **:** relating to Apollinaris of Laodicea or to the doctrine held by Apollinarians

[3]**apollinarian** \"\ *n* -s *usu cap* **:** an adherent of the Christological doctrine that asserted that in Jesus Christ a perfect divine nature in the form of the divine Logos assumed an imperfect human body with the Logos taking the controlling place ordinarily held by the mind

apol·line \ә'pälәn, -,līn\ *adj, usu cap* [L *Apollineus*, fr. *Apollin-*, *Apollo* + *-eus* -eous] **:** of or relating to Apollo or his worship ⟨~ serenity⟩ ⟨~ choruses⟩

ap·ol·lin·i·an \¦apә¦linēәn *also* ¦a,pä¦-\ *adj, usu cap* [L *Apollineus* of Apollo + E *-ian*] **:** [1]APOLLONIAN

apol·lo \ә'pä(,)lō\ *n* -s *usu cap* [after *Apollo*, Graeco-Roman god of manly beauty, of poetry and music, and of the wisdom of oracles, fr. L, fr. Gk *Apollōn*] **1 :** a man of graceful beauty esp. when young **2** *or* **apollo butterfly** [*apollo*, NL, specific epithet of *Parnassius apollo*, after *Apollo*, the god] **:** a European alpine butterfly (*Parnassius apollo*), largely white with eyelike markings; *also* **:** a related but darker butterfly (*P. mnemosyne*)

[1]**ap·ol·lo·ni·an** \¦apә¦lōnēәn, -nyәn *also* ¦a,pä¦-\ *also* **ap·ol·lon·ic** \-¦länik\ *or* **apol·lo·nis·tic** \ә¦pälō¦nistik\ *adj, usu cap* [Gk *Apollōn* + E *-ian* or *-ic* or *-istic*] **1 :** of, relating to, or resembling the god Apollo **2** [trans. of G *apollonisch*] **:** harmonious, measured, ordered, or balanced in character **:** of a rational or nomothetic nature fundamentally temperate, restrained, or meditative — contrasted with *dionysian*

[2]**apollonian** \"\ *adj, usu cap* [*Apollonius* of Perga, 3d cent. B.C. Greek mathematician & *Apollonius* of Tyana, 1st cent. A.D. Greek philosopher + E *-an*] **:** of or named after Apollonius, esp. Apollonius of Perga or Apollonius of Tyana

[3]**apollonian** *n* -s *usu cap* **:** one that has a well-developed Mount of Apollo and a long and large finger of Apollo and that is usu. held by palmists to be characterized by health, versatility, and an attractive personality

apollonian problem *n, usu cap A* [[2]*Apollonian*, after *Apollonius* of Perga] **:** the problem in geometry of the construction of a circle touching three given circles

apol·lyon \ә'pälyәn, -lēәn\ *n* -s *usu cap* [after *Apollyon*, "the angel of the bottomless pit" (Rev 9:11)] **:** DEVIL 1

apol·o·gete \ә'pälә,jēt\ *n* -s [back-formation fr. *apologetic*] **:** one skilled in apologetics **:** APOLOGIST

[1]**apol·o·get·ic** \ә¦pälә¦jed·ik, -etik, -ēk\ *adj* [prob. back-formation fr. *apologetical*, fr. LL *apologeticus* formal apology or justification + E *-al*] **1 :** defending by discourse ⟨modern tolerance often listens benevolently to many ~ pleas —G.G. Coulton⟩ **:** said, written, or done in defense or by way of apology ⟨her little ~ titter —Audrey Barker⟩ **2 :** regretfully excusing or acknowledging ⟨an ~ essay⟩ — **apol·o·get·i·cal·ly** \-әk(ә)lē, -ēk-, -li\ *adv*

[2]**apologetic** \"\ *n* -s [LL *apologeticus*, fr. *apologeticus* suitable for defense, fr. Gk *apologētikos*, fr. *apologeisthai* to speak in defense, defend oneself verbally, fr. *apo-* + *-logeisthai* (fr. *logos* speech) — more at LEGEND] **1 :** a formal apology or justification ⟨a type of ~ for natural laissez-faire and the pursuit of narrow individual self-interest —P.H.Douglas⟩ **2 :** APOLOGETICS; *esp* **:** the systematic defense and exposition of the Christian faith addressed primarily to non-Christians

apol·o·get·i·cal \-әkәl\ *archaic var of* APOLOGETIC

apol·o·get·ics \-iks\ *n pl but usu sing in constr* **1 :** systematic argumentative tactics or discourse in defense (as of a doctrine, a historical character, or particular actions) **2 :** that branch of theology devoted to the defense of a religious faith and addressed primarily to criticism originating from outside the religious faith; *esp* **:** such defense of the Christian faith

ap·o·lo·gia \,apә'lōj(ē)ә, ә,pōlә'jēә\ *n, pl* **apologias** \-әz\ *also* **apologi·ae** \,apә'lōjē,ē, ә,pōlә'jē,ā\ [LL — more at APOLOGY] **1 :** an apology or a defense ⟨the present volume is no ~, on the contrary, it is the pugnacious self-vindication of an . . . able man —*Times Lit. Supp.*⟩ **2 :** justification of the acts of a person's life ⟨*En Miroir* turns out to be an ~, suffering from all the faults of self-justification —*Times Lit. Supp.*⟩ **syn** see APOLOGY

apol·o·gist \ә'pälәjәst *sometimes* ,apә'lōj-\ *n* -s [F *apologiste*, fr. *apologie* apology + *-iste* -ist] **1 :** one who makes an apology or defense **:** one who speaks or writes in defense of a faith, a cause, or an institution; *esp* **:** one who makes a systematic defense of Christianity **2** *usu cap* **:** one of a number of 2d century church fathers who wrote treatises in defense of the Christian faith

apol·o·gize *also* **apol·o·gise** \ә'pälә,jīz\ *vi* -ED/-ING/-S [[1]*apology* + *-ize*] **1 :** to offer a defense or excuse **2 :** to acknowledge a fault or offense with expression of regret by way of amends ⟨when he gives an assignment to a reporter it seems he is doing all but ~ for troubling him —Stanley Walker⟩ ⟨the least you can do is ~⟩ — **apol·o·giz·er** \-zә(r)\ *n* -s

ap·o·logue \'apә,lȯg *also* -äg\ *n* -s [alter. of earlier *apology*, modif. (influenced by *apology*) of F *apologue*, fr. L *apologus*, fr. Gk *apologos*, fr. *apo-* + *logos* word — more at LEGEND] **:** an allegorical narrative (as a beast fable) usu. intended to convey a moral ⟨Aesop was the master of the ~⟩ **syn** see ALLEGORY

apol·o·gy \ә'pälәjē\ *n* -ES [MF or LL; MF *apologie*, fr. LL *apologia*, fr. Gk, fr. *apo-* + *-logia* (fr. *logos* speech) — more at LEGEND] **1 :** something said or written in defense or justification of what appears to others to be wrong or of what may be liable to disapprobation ⟨an ~ for a country's foreign policy⟩ **2 :** an attempt to justify or excuse ⟨a convenient ~ for their ruthlessness in Darwinian philosophy —J.D. Hicks⟩ **3 :** an acknowledgment intended as an atonement for some improper or injurious remark or act **:** an admission to another of a wrong or discourtesy done him accompanied by an expression of regret ⟨an ~ to a hostess for being late⟩ **4 :** something that serves as an excuse for the absence of something **:** a poor specimen or substitute **:** MAKESHIFT ⟨devising *apologies* for window curtains —Charles Dickens⟩ **syn** APOLOGIA, EXCUSE, PLEA, PRETEXT, ALIBI: APOLOGY in today's English usu. indicates either a frank regretful admission that one has been wrong or a defense involving mitigating or extenuating circumstances ⟨an *apology* for the offense⟩ ⟨traffic congestion was their *apology* for being so late⟩ Sometimes, like the word APOLOGIA, it is used without suggestions of guilt or error simply to indicate an explanation for a course or belief ⟨Justin Martyr, a native of Samaria, who wrote one of the more famous of the *apologies* for Christianity, and who won his sobriquet by his death for the faith —K.S.Latourette⟩ ⟨the preface to Mirsky's book on Lenin contains his *apologia* for his shift of allegiance to the Soviet power —Edmund Wilson⟩ EXCUSE indicates an explanation offered to escape censure or blame ⟨it matters not that some uncontrollable impulse, the product of mental disease, may have driven the defendant to the commission of the murderous act. The law knows nothing of such *excuses* —B.N.Cardozo⟩ PLEA usu. involves an appeal for understanding, sympathy, or clemency ⟨old Hepzibah's scowl could no longer vindicate itself entirely on the *plea* of nearsightedness —Nathaniel Hawthorne⟩ PRETEXT suggests a subterfuge, an offer of an untrue reason or motive ⟨he made my health a *pretext* for taking all the heavy chores, long after I was as well as he was —Willa Cather⟩ ⟨the hypocrisy that covers gainful exploitation by the *pretext* of a civilizing mission, concerned with the elevation of the native population —J.A.Hobson⟩ ALIBI, legally a plea that one was elsewhere than at the place at which a crime was committed, may be applied to a mitigating or placating explanation ⟨the *alibis* of many churches for their failure to provide qualified chaplains —Scott Hershey & Harry Tennant⟩ ⟨federal taxes are already being used as an *alibi* for cuts in local school budgets —H.M.Groves⟩

apo·lou·sis *or* **apo·lu·sis** \ä'pȯlü,sēs, ,apә'lüsәs\ *n* [MGk *apolousis*, fr. Gk, act of washing off, fr. *apolouein* to wash off, fr. *apo-* + *louein* to wash — more at LYE] **:** the ceremony in the Eastern Church of washing away the baptismal chrism performed by a priest on the eighth day after baptism

[1]**apo·ly·sis** \ä'pȯlē,sēs\ *n* [LGk, fr. Gk, loosening, dismissal, fr. *apolyein* to loose from, release, dismiss (fr. *apo-* + *lyein* to loosen, free, destroy) + *-sis* — more at LOSE] **:** the prayer of dismissal used at the conclusion of a service in the Eastern Church

[2]**apol·y·sis** \ә'pälәsәs\ *n, pl* **apoly·ses** \-ә,sēz\ [NL, fr. *apo-* + *-lysis*] **:** the shedding of ripe proglottids during life (as in most tapeworms) — compare ANAPOLYSIS

apo·ly·ti·kion \,ä,pȯlē'tē,kyȯn\ *n, pl* **apolyti·kia** \-yä\ [MGk, alter. of *apolytikon*, fr. neut. of *apolytikos* absolving, dismissing, fr. Gk *apolytos* freed, dismissed (fr. *apolyein* to dismiss) + *-ikos* -ic] **:** the concluding hymn sung in the Eastern Church at the end of offices (as matins and vespers) and varying from day to day according to the calendar

ap·o·mei·o·sis \¦apә,mī¦ōsәs\ *n, pl* **apomeio·ses** \-ō,sēz\ [NL, fr. *apo-* + *meiosis*] **:** imperfect or suppressed meiosis, a characteristic of the life cycle of many higher polyploids

ap·o·mei·ot·ic \-ī¦äd·ik\ *adj* [fr. NL *apomeiosis*, after such pairs as NL *hypnosis*: E *hypnotic*] **:** relating to or marked by apomeiosis **:** formed without meiosis

ap·o·mict \'apә,mikt\ *n* -s [prob. back-formation fr. ISV *apomictic*, fr. *apo-* + Gk *miktos* mixed] *biol* **:** an individual or species produced by or reproducing by apomixis — **ap·o·mic·tic** \¦apә¦miktik\ *or* **ap·o·mic·ti·cal** \-tәkәl\ *adj* — **ap·o·mic·ti·cal·ly** \-tәk(ә)lē\ *adv*

ap·o·mix·is \,apә'miksәs\ *n, pl* **apomix·es** \-k,sēz\ [NL, fr. *apo-* + *-mixis*] **1** *biol* **:** reproduction involving the specialized generative tissues but not dependent upon fertilization (as apogamy or parthenogenesis) **2** *biol* **:** APOMIXY

ap·o·mixy \'apә,miksē\ *n* -ES [*apo-* + *-mixy* (as in *panmixy*)] **:** the total absence or great limitation of interbreeding restricting the possibility of genetic exchange — opposed to *panmixia*

ap·o·mor·phine \¦apә¦-\ *n* [ISV *apo-* + *morphine*] **:** an artificial crystalline alkaloid $C_{17}H_{17}NO_2$ obtained from morphine by dehydration and having a powerful emetic action when injected hypodermically usu. in the form of its hydrochloride

ap·o·neu·ro·sis \,apәnә'rōsәs, -n(y)ü'-\ *n, pl* **aponeuro·ses** \-ō,sēz\ [NL, fr. Gk *aponeurōsis*, fr. *aponeurousthai* to pass into a tendon (fr. *apo-* + *neuron* sinew, nerve) + *-sis* — more at NERVE] **:** any of the thicker and denser of the deep fasciae that cover, invest, and form the terminations and attachments of certain muscles and differ from tendons in being flat and thin

ap·o·neu·rot·ic \¦===¦räd·ik\ *adj* [fr. NL *aponeurosis*, after NL *neurosis*: E *neurotic*] **:** of or relating to an aponeurosis

ap·o·no·ge·ton \,apә(,)nō'jē,tän\ *n* [NL, fr. *apono-* (prob. fr. L *Aponus*, hot mineral spring near Padua in northeastern Italy) + Gk *geitōn* neighbor] **1** *cap* **:** a genus (coextensive with the family Aponogetonaceae) of 25 species of Old World aquatic herbs (order Naiadales) with oblong often skeletonized leaves and small spicate flowers — see LATTICE PLANT **2** -s **:** a plant of the genus *Aponogeton* — **ap·o·no·ge·to·na·ceous** \¦apә(,)nō,jēd·ә-'nāshәs\ *adj*

apoop \ә'püp\ *adv* (*or adj*) [[1]*a-* + *poop*] **:** ASTERN

ap·o·pemp·tic \¦apә¦pem(p)tik\ *adj* [LGk *apopemptikos*, fr. Gk *apopemptos* dimissed (fr. *apopempein* to send off, dismiss, fr. *apo-* + *pempein* to send) + *-ikos* -ic — more at POMP] *archaic* **:** sung or addressed to one departing **:** VALEDICTORY ⟨~ hymns⟩

ap·o·pet·al·ous \¦apә¦-\ *adj* [*apo-* + *-petalous*] *bot* **:** POLYPETALOUS

ap·o·phan·tic \,apә'fantik\ *n* -s [Gk *apophantikos*, adj., categorical, declaratory, fr. *apophantos* declared (fr. *apophainein* to declare, display, fr. *apo-* + *phainein* to show) + *-ikos* -ic — more at FANCY] *logic* **:** the doctrine of predicative judgment

ap·o·phon·ic \¦apә¦fanik\ *adj* **:** of or relating to ablaut **:** cognate in a manner explainable in terms of apophony

apoph·o·ny \ә'päfәnē, a'-\ *n* -ES [*apo-* + *-phony*; trans. of G *ablaut*] **:** ABLAUT

ap·o·pho·rom·e·ter \,apәfә'rämәd·ә(r)\ *n* -s [Gk *apophora* act of carrying away, absorption (fr. *apopherein* to carry away, fr. *apo-* + *pherein* to carry) + E *-o-* + *-meter* — more at BEAR] **:** an apparatus for identifying minerals by sublimation

apophthegm *var of* APOTHEGM

apoph·y·ge \ә'päfә(,)jē\ *n* -s [Gk *apophygē*, lit., escape, fr. *apo-* + *phygē* flight, fr. *pheugein* to flee — more at BOW (to bend)] **:** the small hollow curvature given to the top (as in a Doric column) or bottom (as in an Ionic or Corinthian column) of the shaft of a column where it expands to meet the edge of the fillet — compare CONGÉ 4, SCAPE

ap·o·phyl·lite \,apә'fi,līt, ә'päfә,l-\ *n* -s [F, fr. *apo-* + *phyllite*] **:** a mineral $KCa_4Si_8O_{20}(F,OH).8H_2O$ composed of a hydrous potassium calcium silicate related to the zeolites and usu. occurring in transparent square prisms or white or grayish masses (hardness 4.5-5, sp. gr., 2.3-2.4)

ap·o·phyl·lous \¦apә¦filәs\ *adj* [*apo-* + *-phyllous*] *bot* **:** having the parts distinct — used of a whorl of the perianth

apoph·y·sal \ә'päfәsәl\ *adj* [NL *apophysis* + E *-al*] *geol* **:** of or relating to an apophysis

apoph·y·sate \-sәt,-,sāt\ *adj* [ISV *apophys-* (fr. NL *apophysis*) + *-ate*] *bot* **:** having an apophysis

apoph·y·se·al \ә¦päfә¦sēәl, -¦zē- *also* ¦apә¦fizē-\ *also* **ap·o·phys·i·al** \¦apә¦fizēәl\ *or* **apoph·y·sary** \ә'päfә,serē\ *adj* [*apophyseal* alter. of *apophysial*; *apophysial* fr. *apophysis* + *-al*; *apophysary* fr. *apophysis* + *-ary*] **:** of or relating to an apophysis

apoph·y·sis \ә'päfәsәs\ *n, pl* **apophy·ses** \-ә,sēz\ [NL, fr. Gk, offshoot, process of a bone, fr. *apo-* + *-physis* (fr. *phyein*, *phyesthai* to grow, produce) — more at BE] **1 :** a process of a bone (as a vertebra) **2 :** a swelling of the seta at the base of the capsule of certain mosses often provided with many stomata and functioning as the chief assimilative part of the sporogonium **3 :** a swelling on the cone scale of certain conifers **4** *of certain fungi* **:** a swollen part of the filament or a swelling of the stalk (as in certain members of the genus *Geaster*) **5 :** an expansion or swelling of the hypha (as that below the sporangium in *Mucor*) **6 :** an offshoot from an intrusive body of igneous rock **7 :** a process of the exoskeleton of an insect (as an apodeme or an external spur)

ap·o·plec·tic \¦apә¦plektik, -ēk\ *also* **ap·o·plec·ti·cal** \-tәkәl, -ēk-\ *adj* [*apoplectic* fr. F or LL; F *apoplectique*, fr. LL *apoplecticus*, fr. Gk *apoplēktikos*, fr. *apoplēssein* to cripple by a stroke; *apoplectical* prob. fr. LL *apoplecticus* + E *-al* — more at APOPLEXY] **:** of, relating to, or causing apoplexy ⟨~ stroke⟩ **:** affected with, inclined to, or symptomatic of apoplexy ⟨an ~ person⟩ — **ap·o·plec·ti·cal·ly** \-tәk(ә)lē, -ēk-, -li\ *adv*

ap·o·plec·ti·form \¦==¦=tә,fȯrm\ *also* **ap·o·plec·toid** \,=='= ,tȯid\ *adj* [*apoplectic* + *-iform* or *-oid*] **:** resembling apoplexy

apoplectiform septicemia *n* **:** a highly infectious disease of gallinaceous birds caused by a bacterium (*Streptococcus gallinarum*) and characterized by depression, listlessness, and a staggering gait usu. followed by prostration and death

[1]**apoplex** *n* -ES [LL *apoplexis*] *obs* **:** APOPLEXY

[2]**ap·o·plex** \'apә,pleks\ *vt* -ED/-ING/-ES *archaic* **:** to strike with apoplexy

ap·o·plexy \'apә,pleksē, -si\ *n* -ES [ME *apoplexie*, fr. MF & LL; MF *apoplexie*, fr. LL *apoplexia*, *apoplexis*, fr. Gk *apoplēxia*, *apoplēxis*, fr. *apoplēssein* to cripple by a stroke, fr. *apo-* + *plēssein* to strike — more at PLAINT] **1 a :** a sudden loss of consciousness followed by paralysis caused by hemorrhage into the brain from rupture of an artery or by sudden anemia of a part of the brain from obstruction of its artery either by a blood clot or by the lodgment of an embolus — called also *stroke*; compare CEREBRAL HEMORRHAGE, CEREBRAL THROMBOSIS **b :** gross hemorrhage into a cavity or into the substance of an organ ⟨abdominal ~⟩ ⟨adrenal ~⟩ **2** [so called fr. the rapid drying of the vine] *bot* **:** BLACK MEASLES

ap·o·pyle \'apә,pīl\ *n* -s [*apo-* + Gk *pylē* gate — more at PYLON] *zool* **:** one of the openings by which the water passes out of a radial canal or flagellated chamber of a sponge

apor·al \(')ā¦pōrәl, (')a¦-\ *adj* [irreg. fr. [1]*ab-* + *poral*] **:** located farther from a pore than another structure ⟨on the ~ side of the ovary⟩

ap·o·ret·ic \¦apә¦red·ik\ *also* **ap·o·re·mat·ic** \-rә¦mad·ik\ *adj* [Gk *aporētikos*, *aporēmatikos*, fr. *aporein* to doubt] **:** SKEPTICAL

ap·o·rhy·o·lite \¦apә¦rīә,līt\ *n* -s [*apo-* + *rhyolite*] **:** a rock consisting of a felsite whose structure shows it to have been orig. vitreous like some rhyolites

apo·ria \ә'pōrēә, -ȯr-\ *n, pl* **aporias** \-ēәz\ *or* **apori·ae** \-ē,ē\ [NL, fr. LL, doubt, perplexity, fr. Gk, difficulty, perplexity, fr. *aporos* impassable, difficult (fr. *a-* [2]a- + *poros* passage, path) + *-ia* — more at FARE] **1 :** a problem or difficulty arising from an awareness of opposing or incompatible views on the same theoretic matter; *esp* **:** one giving rise to philosophically systematic doubt **2 :** a passage in speech or writing incorporating or presenting a difficulty or doubt

ap·o·rid·ea \,apә'ridēә\ *n pl, cap* [NL, fr. Gk *aporos* + NL *-idea*] *in some classifications* **:** an order of Cestoda including a single genus (*Nematoparataenia*) of unsegmented tapeworms parasitic in swans

apo·ro·sa \,āpә'rōsә, ,ap-, -ōzә\ *n pl, cap* [NL, fr. [2]*a-* + *Porosa* (syn. of *Perforata*), fr. ML, neut. pl. of *porosus* porous — more at POROUS] **:** a division of corals (order Madreporaria) having the corallum solid — opposed to *Perforata* — **apo·rose** \(')ā¦pōr,ōs, 'apә,rōs\ *adj*

ap·or·phine \'a,pȯr,fēn, 'apәr,-; (')a'pȯr,-\ *n* -s [ISV *apo-* + *morphine*] **:** a synthetic alkaloid $C_{17}H_{17}N$ regarded as the parent from which morphine, bulbocapnine, and related alkaloids are derived

ap·or·rha·is \,apә'rāәs\ *n, cap* [NL, fr. Gk, a shellfish (perh. a species of *Aporrhais*)] **:** a genus of small solid long-spired marine snails related to *Strombus* but having the foot broad and flat — **ap·or·rha·oid** \-ā,ȯid\ *adj*

aporrhoea *n* -s [NL, fr. *apo-* + *-rrhoea*] *obs* **:** EFFLUVIUM, EMANATION

aport \ə'-\ *adv* (*or adj*) [¹*a-* + *port* (left side)] **:** on or toward the left side of a ship — used esp. of the helm

apos *abbr* apostrophe

ap·o·se·mat·ic \ˌapəsə¦mad·ik\ *adj* [*apo-* + *sematic*] *zool* **:** CONSPICUOUS, WARNING — used of colors or structures indicative of special means of defense against enemies (as in the skunk and certain actinians and insects) — **ap·o·se·mat·i·cal·ly** \-d·ək(ə)lē\ *adv*

ap·o·seme \ˈapəˌsēm\ *n* -s [*apo-* + *-seme*] *zool* **:** a group distinguished by possession of similar aposematic coloration

ap·o·sep·al·ous \¦apə¦-\ *adj* [*apo-* + *-sepalous*] *bot* **:** POLYSEPALOUS

ap·o·si·o·pe·sis \ˌapəˌsīə'pēsəs\ *n, pl* **aposiope·ses** \-ēˌsēz\ [LL, fr. Gk *aposiōpēsis*, fr. *aposiōpan* to be quite silent, fr. *apo-* + *siōpan* to be silent, fr. *siōpē* silence] **:** the leaving of a thought explicitly incomplete in writing or speaking often by a sudden breaking off and shifting of grammatical construction for rhetorical purposes (as *his behavior was — but I blush to mention that*) or by the use of *etc.* — **ap·o·si·o·pet·ic** \¦apəˌsīə¦ped·ik\ *adj*

ap·o·so·ro \ˌapə'sōr(ˌ)ō\ *n* -s [prob. native name in Africa] **:** POTTO

ap·o·spor·ic \¦apə¦spōrik\ *or* **ap·o·spor·ous** \¦apə¦spōrəs; ə'päspər-, a'-\ *adj* **:** of or relating to apospory

ap·o·spor·i·cal·ly \¦apə¦spōrək(ə)lē\ *adv* **:** in an aposporic manner

ap·o·spo·rog·o·ny \¦apə¦=¦==\ *n* -ES [*apo-* + *sporogony*] *biol* **:** suppression of sporogony

ap·o·spory \ˈapəˌspōrē; ə'päspərē, a'-\ *n* -ES [*apo-* + *-spory*] **:** production of gametophytes directly from somatic cells of the sporophytes without spore formation (as in certain ferns and mosses)

apos·ta·cize *or* **apos·ta·size** \ə'pästəˌsīz *also* -ōs-\ *vi* -ED/-ING/-S **:** APOSTATIZE

apos·ta·cy \-sē\ *archaic var of* APOSTASY

apos·ta·sy \ə'pästəsē, -si *also* -ōs-\ *n* -ES [ME *apostasie*, fr. LL *apostasia*, fr. Gk, lit., revolt, defection, fr. *aphistanai* to remove, cause to revolt, fr. *apo-* + *histanai* to cause to stand — more at STAND] **1 :** the renunciation of a religious faith **2 :** an abandonment of what one has voluntarily professed **:** a total desertion or departure (as from one's principles or party) ⟨*apostasies* of disciples who refused to accept Freud's theories —*Time*⟩

¹**apos·tate** \ə'päˌstāt, -ˌstət *also* -ōˌs-; *usu* -d·+V\ *n* -s [ME, fr. MF & LL; MF *apostate*, fr. LL *apostata*, fr. Gk *apostatēs*, lit., deserter, rebel, fr. *aphistanai*] **1 :** one who has renounced or forsaken his religious faith or given up his moral allegiance ⟨a Church decree . . . excommunicated as ∼*s* all . . . "who profess . . . the materialistic and anti-Christian doctrine" —H.L.Matthews⟩ **2 :** one who has given up the principles or party to which he adhered **:** RENEGADE ⟨that incomparable ∼ from intelligence, George Moore —H.J.Laski⟩

²**apostate** \"\ *adj* [ME, fr. *apostate*, n.] **1 :** relating to or characterized by apostasy ⟨the child of an ∼ . . . Catholic —*Time*⟩ **:** faithless to moral allegiance **:** RENEGADE ⟨so spoke the ∼ angel —John Milton⟩ **2 :** abandoning or involving the abandonment of any form of allegiance ⟨an ∼ and unnatural connection with any foreign power —George Washington⟩

ap·o·stat·ic \¦apə¦stad·ik\ *or* **ap·o·stat·i·cal** \-d·əkəl\ *adj* **:** APOSTATE — **ap·o·stat·i·cal·ly** \-d·ək(ə)lē\ *adv*

apos·ta·tize \ə'pästəˌtīz *also* -ōs-\ *vi* -ED/-ING/-S [MF or LL; MF *apostatiser*, fr. LL *apostatizare*, fr. L *apostata* + *-izare* -ize] **:** to commit apostasy **:** to renounce one's faith, party, or principles ⟨the church had *apostatized* and gone against the commandment —Edson Jessop⟩

ap·o·stax·is \ˌapə'staksəs\ *n, pl* **apostax·es** \-kˌsēz\ [NL, fr. Gk *apostaxis* drippings, fr. *apostazein* to drip off, fr. *apo-* + *stazein* to drip — more at STAGNATE] *bot* **:** an abnormal exudation

ap·o·steme *n* -s [ME, fr. MF, fr. L *apostema*, fr. Gk *apostēma* abscess, distance, fr. *aphistanai* to remove — more at APOSTASY] *obs* **:** a swelling filled with purulent matter **:** ABSCESS

a pos·te·ri·o·ri \ˈä,pä,stirē'ōr,ī, -'ō.rī; ¦ä,pä,sterē'ōr(ˌ)ē, ¦ā,-, -'ō(ˌ)rē, -ī\ *adj* [L, lit., from the latter] **1 :** of or relating to the kind of reasoning that derives propositions from the observation of facts or that by generalizations from facts arrives at principles ⟨*a posteriori* demonstration⟩ — contrasted with *a priori* **2 :** of or relating to what cannot be known except from experience **:** proved by induction from facts obtained by observation or experiment ⟨*a posteriori* truth⟩

apos·til *or* **apos·tille** \ə'pästəl\ *n* -s [MF *apostille*, fr. *apostiller* to annotate, fr. *a-* (fr. L *ad-*) + *postiller* to annotate — more at POSTIL] *archaic* **:** a marginal note **:** ANNOTATION

apos·tle \ə'päsəl *also* -ōs-\ *n* -s [ME *apostle*, *apostel*, fr. OF & OE; OF *apostle* & OE *apostol*, fr. LL *apostolus*, fr. Gk *apostolos*, lit., messenger, fr. *apostellein* to send away, fr. *apo-* + *stellein* to send — more at STALL] **1 a :** one who is sent forth **:** MESSENGER; *specif* **:** one of the 12 disciples of Christ **b :** one of certain early Christian missionaries (as Paul and Barnabas) or in Eastern orthodoxy one of the 70 disciples of Jesus **2 a :** the first or the first prominent Christian missionary in any part of the world **:** one who has extraordinary success as a missionary or reformer ⟨St. Boniface, ∼ to Germany⟩ **b :** one who initiates a great moral reform or first advocates any important belief or system **3 :** the highest ecclesiastical official in some church organizations (as in the Church of God in Christ and in the New Apostolic Church of No. America) **4 apostles** *pl, civil & admiralty law* **:** a brief letter dimissory sent by a court appealed from to the superior court, stating the case **:** papers sent up on appeal, equivalent to the record in a case at law **5 :** one of a council or quorum of 12 men in the Mormon Church acting principally as administrators **6 apostles** *pl* **:** bollards and bitts in a sailing ship

apostle bird *n, Austral* **:** a bird that goes about in small flocks: **a :** BABBLER; *esp* **:** GRAY-CROWNED BABBLER **b :** a loud-voiced gray crowlike bird (*Struthidea cinerea*) with brown wings and black legs and bill

apos·tle·hood \-ˌhu̇d\ *n* [ME *apostlehed*, *apostlehod*, fr. OE *apostolhād*, fr. *apostol* + *-hād* -hood] **:** the office or status of an apostle

apostle jug *n* **:** a jug with raised figures of apostles on it

apostle plant *or* **apostle flower** *n* **:** an irislike plant (*Neomarica gracilis*) of the family Iridaceae having flat leaflike stems, ribbonlike leaves, and flowers with the outer perianth members white with basal brown and yellow marking or blotching and inner members blue and strongly reflexed

apos·tle·ship \-ˌship\ *n* **:** the status, rank, or office of an apostle

apostle spoon *n* **:** a silver spoon with the handle terminating in the figure of an apostle formerly often presented by sponsors at baptism to the godchild

apos·to·late \ə'pästəˌlāt, -lət *also* -ōs-; *usu* -d·+V\ *n* -s [LL *apostolatus*, fr. *apostolus* + L *-atus* -ate] **1 :** the office or mission of an apostle **:** APOSTLESHIP ⟨fulfillment of an ∼ to the world⟩ **2 :** an association of persons dedicated to the propagation of a religious faith or doctrine

apos·to·li \-ˌlī, -ˌlē\ *n pl* [L, pl. of *apostolus*, fr. Gk *apostolos* messenger — more at APOSTLE] *civil law* **:** letters dimissory from an inferior court to a superior court

¹**ap·os·tol·ic** \¦apə¦stälik, -ēk *sometimes* ə¦pä¦- *or* ə¦pō¦-\ *also* **ap·os·tol·i·cal** \-ləkəl, -ēk-\ *adj* [*apostolic* fr. ME *apostolik*, fr. LL *apostolicus*, fr. Gk *apostolikos*, fr. *apostolos* apostle + *-ikos* -ic; *apostolical* fr. ME, fr. *apostolik* + *-al*] **1 :** of, relating to, or resembling an apostle or the apostles, their times, or their spirit ⟨∼ fervor⟩ **2 a :** according to the doctrine of the apostles **:** taught by or in the tradition of the apostles **b :** genuine and authoritative ⟨∼ faith⟩ **3** *Roman Catholicism* **:** PAPAL ⟨∼ indulgences⟩ **4** *usu cap* **:** of or relating to one of various Christian religious bodies usu. with the term *Apostolic* included in the official name that seek to bring doctrine and practice into close accord with that of the first Christian apostles and usu. distinguished from other organized forms of Christianity by their emphasis on evangelistic methods, the doctrines of entire sanctification and the direct operation of the Holy Spirit, a fundamentalistic theology, and such practices as foot washing, the gift of tongues, divine healing, and spirit baptism — **ap·os·tol·i·cal·ly** \-lək(ə)lē, -ēk-, -li\ *adv*

²**apostolic** \"\ *n* -s *cap* **:** a member of an Apostolic church

apostolic church *n* **1** *usu cap A&C* **:** the Christian church as founded by the apostles **2 :** a church founded by an apostle

apostolic delegate *n* **:** an ecclesiastical diplomatic representing a church in a country that has no formal diplomatic relations with the church's headquarters

apostolic father *n, usu cap A&F* **:** one of the authors of a collection of 2d century A.D. writings of religious significance

ap·os·tol·i·ci \ˌapə'stäləˌsī\ *n pl, usu cap* [LL, fr. pl. of *apostolicus* apostolic] **:** members of various ascetic sects of the 3d and 4th centuries A.D. in Phrygia, Cilicia, and Pamphylia who sought apostolic purity of life by renouncing marriage and private property — called also *Apotactici*, *Apotactites*

apos·to·lic·i·ty \əˌpästə'lisəd·ē, -ətē, -i *also* əˌpōs- *sometimes* ˌapəs-\ *n* -ES **:** the quality or character of being apostolic

apostolic see *n* **1 :** a see established by an apostle (as Jerusalem, Antioch, or Rome) **2** *usu cap A, Roman Catholicism* **:** the Roman see

apostolic succession *n* **:** the succession or descent believed to be uninterrupted from the apostles and perpetuated by successive ordinations of bishops, held (as by Roman Catholics, Anglicans, and Eastern Orthodox) to be necessary for valid administration of the sacraments and the transmission of orders

apostolize *vb* -ED/-ING/-S [LL *apostolus* + E *-ize*] *vt, obs* **:** PROCLAIM ∼ *vi, obs* **:** to act as an apostle

apos·to·los \ə'pästəˌläs, -ōstəˌlōs\ *n, pl* **aposto·loi** \-ˌlȯi, -ˌlē\ *cap* [LGk, fr. Gk, apostle] *Eastern Church* **:** EPISTLE 1a

¹**apos·tro·phe** \ə'pästrə(ˌ)fē *also* -ōs-\ *n* -s [L, fr. Gk *apostrophē*, lit., turning away, fr. *apo-* + *strophē* turning — more at STROPHE] **1 :** the addressing of a person usu. not present or of a thing usu. personified for rhetorical purposes ⟨an ∼ to Shakespeare⟩ **2 :** the arrangement of chloroplasts along the lateral walls of leaf cells — called *positive* when caused by intense light and *negative* when by prolonged darkness

²**apostrophe** \"\ *n* -s [MF & LL; MF *apostrophe*, fr. LL *apostrophus*, fr. Gk *apostrophos*, fr. *apostrophos* turned away, fr. *apostrephein* to turn away, fr. *apo-* + *strephein* to turn — more at STROPHE] **:** the mark ' or ' used to indicate omission of one or more letters or figures (as in *can't* for *cannot*, *judg'd* for *judged*, *wish'd* for *wished*, *mascara'd* for *mascaraed*, *'76* for *1776*), to mark the possessive case of English nouns and of certain English pronouns (as in *Bill's*, *Moses'*, *women's*, *boys'*, *anyone's*) or the plural of letters (as in *two a's*) or of figures (as in *three 7's*) and sometimes of words that are not normally nouns (as in *no if's or but's*), to set off an inflectional or derivational suffix from a word that is pronounced by uttering the name of each of its letters (as in *their IQ's*, *he OK's it*, *GOP'er*), or to constitute a terminal quotation mark

¹**ap·os·troph·ic** \¦apə¦sträfik *also* ¦aˌpä¦- *or* ¦aˌpō¦- *or* -ōfik\ *adj* [¹*apostrophe* + *-ic*] **:** of or characteristic of apostrophe ⟨a passage of ∼ grandeur⟩ ⟨an ∼ manner of writing⟩; *also* **:** given to the use of apostrophe ⟨an ∼ writer⟩

²**apostrophic** \"\ *adj* [²*apostrophe* + *-ic*] **:** associated with or including the mark called an apostrophe ⟨the ∼ possessive ending⟩ **:** being an apostrophe

¹**apos·tro·phize** \ə'pästrəˌfīz *also* -ōs-\ *vb* -ED/-ING/-S [¹*apostrophe* + *-ize*] *vt* **:** to address by or in apostrophe ⟨∼ the spirit of freedom⟩ ∼ *vi* **:** to express an apostrophe

²**apostrophize** \"\ *vt* -ED/-ING/-S [²*apostrophe* + *-ize*] **:** to shorten by omitting a letter **:** mark with an apostrophe

apos·tro·phus \-fəs\ *n, pl* **apostro·phi** \-ˌfī\ [LL — more at APOSTROPHE] **1 :** ²APOSTROPHE **2 :** the symbol Ↄ of the ancient Roman numeral system used for indicating the number 500 — see NUMBER table

ap·o·tac·ti·ci \ˌapə'taktəˌsī\ *n pl, cap* [LL or ML, pl. of *Apotacticus*, fr. LGk *Apotaktikos*, lit., renouncer, fr. *apotaktikos* disposed to renounce, fr. Gk *apotassein* to set apart, fr. *apo-* + *tassein* to put in order, arrange — more at TACTICS] **:** APOSTOLICI

ap·o·tac·tites \-kˌtīts\ *n pl, cap* [ML *Apotactitae*, fr. LGk *Apotaktitai*, fr. Gk *apotaktos* set apart (fr. *apotassein* to set apart, fr. *apo-* + *tassein* to arrange, put in a certain order) + *-itai* (pl. of *-ites* -ite) — more at TACTICS] **:** APOSTOLICI

apotelesm *n* -s [LL *apotelesma* effect, effect of the stars on human destiny, fr. Gk, fr. *apotelein* to complete, fr. *apo-* + *telein* to complete, fr. *telos* goal — more at WHEEL] *archaic* **:** the casting of a horoscope

apotelesmatic *adj* [Gk *apotelesmatikos*, productive, astrologically influential, fr. *apotelesmat-*, *apotelesma* + *-ikos* -ic] *archaic* **:** of or relating to the casting of horoscopes

apothecaries' measure *or* **apothecary measure** *n* **:** the series of liquid units of capacity (gallon, pint, fluid ounce, fluid dram, minim) that are used by pharmacists

apothecaries' weight *or* **apothecary weight** *n* **:** the series of units of weight, including the pound of 12 ounces, the dram of 60 grains, and the scruple, used chiefly by pharmacists in compounding medical prescriptions — see MEASURE table

apoth·e·cary \ə'päthəˌkerē, -ri\ *n* -ES [ME *apotecarie*, fr. ML *apothecarius*, fr. LL, shopkeeper, warehouseman, fr. L *apotheca* warehouse (fr. Gk *apothēkē*, fr. *apotithenai* to put away, fr. *apo-* + *tithenai* to put, place) + *-arius* -ary — more at DO] **1 :** one who prepares and sells drugs or compounds for medicinal purposes **:** DRUGGIST, PHARMACIST **2 :** PHARMACY

apothecary jar *n* **:** a usu. wide-mouthed covered and ornamented jar (as for drugs, herbs, or bathroom and kitchen supplies)

apothecary jars

ap·o·the·cial \ˌapə¦thēsh(ē)əl, -ēsēəl\ *adj* [NL *apothecium* + E *-al*] **:** of or relating to an apothecium

ap·o·the·ci·um \-ēs(h)ēəm\ *n, pl* **apothecia** \-s(h)ēə\ [NL, fr. L *apotheca* storehouse + NL *-ium*] **:** a spore-bearing structure in many lichens and ascomycetous fungi consisting of a disklike, saucer-shaped, or cuplike body bearing asci in an extended layer (the hymenium) on the exposed flat or concave surface

ap·o·thegm *or* **ap·o·phthegm** \ˈapəˌthem\ *n* -s [Gk *apophthegma*, fr. *apo-* + *phthegma* voice, saying, word, fr. *phthengesthai* to speak out] **:** a short, pointed, and instructive saying **:** a short usu. pointedly concise formulation of a truth or precept **:** a terse aphorism

ap·o·theg·mat·ic \¦apəˌtheg¦mad·ik\ *or* **ap·o·theg·mat·i·cal** \-d·əkəl\ *also* **ap·o·phtheg·mat·ic** *or* **ap·o·phtheg·mat·i·cal** \¦apəˌth-\ *adj* [Gk *apophthegmatikos*, fr. *apophthegmat-*, *apophthegma* + *-ikos* -ic] **:** relating to or characteristic of apothegms **:** given to apothegms **:** characterized by apothegms — **ap·o·theg·mat·i·cal·ly** \-d·ək(ə)lē\ *adv*

ap·o·them \ˈapəˌthem\ *n* -s [ISV *apo-* + *-them* (fr. *thema* that which is laid down, proposition) — more at THEME] **:** the perpendicular from the center to one of the sides of a regular polygon

A
B C D

regular polygon showing A center; BD side; C midpoint of BD; AC apothem

apoth·e·ose \ə'pätheˌōz, -ōs\ *vt* -ED/-ING/-S [back-formation fr. *apotheosis*] *archaic* **:** APOTHEOSIZE

apoth·e·o·sis \əˌpäthē'ōsəs, ˌapə'thēəs- *also* (ˌ)aˌpäthē'ōs- *sometimes* ˌapəthē'ōs-\ *n, pl* **apotheo·ses** \-ˌsēz\ [LL, fr. Gk *apotheōsis*, fr. *apotheoun* to deify (fr. *apo-* + *theos* god) + *-sis* — more at THEISM] **1 :** the elevation of a human to the rank of a god **:** the raising of a person or thing to divine status **:** DEIFICATION **2 :** the culmination or highest development of a thing **:** the ultimate, quintessential, or final form ⟨she is the ∼ of womanhood⟩ ⟨the ∼ of brute force and vulgarity⟩ **3 a :** the exaltation of a person or a thing to a final state of triumph or glory **b :** the ascension of a person or a thing from earthly existence to heavenly glory

ap·o·the·o·size \ˌapə'thēəˌsīz, ə'päthēə-\ *vt* -ED/-ING/-S **:** raise to an apotheosis **:** DEIFY, GLORIFY

apot·o·me \ə'päd·ə(ˌ)mē\ *n* -s [Gk *apotomē*, lit., cutting off, fr. *apotemnein* to cut off, fr. *apo-* + *temnein* to cut — more at CONTEMN] *in Greek music* **:** the interval of a semitone in the Pythagorean scale that is slightly greater than half a whole tone and is equal to the difference between the tetrachord and two whole tones

ap·o·tra·che·al \¦apə¦-\ *adj* [*apo-* + *tracheal*] **:** not associated or contiguous with vessels or vascular tracheids ⟨∼ parenchyma⟩ — compare METATRACHEAL, PARATRACHEAL, VASICENTRIC

ap·o·tro·pa·ic \¦apətrə¦pāik\ *adj* [Gk *apotropaios* (fr. *apotrepein* to turn away, fr. *apo-* + *trepein* to turn) + E *-ic* — more at TROPE] **:** designed to avert or turn aside evil ⟨an ∼ ritual —J.H.Moulton⟩

ap·o·tro·pa·ism \ˌ=¦==¦=ˌizəm\ *n* -s **:** the performance of magic ritual or incantatory formulas in order to avert evil

ap·o·type \ˈapəˌtīp\ *n* -s [*apo-* + *type*] **:** HYPOTYPE

ap·o·typ·ic \¦apə¦tipik\ *adj, biol* **:** varying or departing from a type

a power supply \ˈā-\ *n, usu cap A* [¹A] **:** a battery or transformer supplying electric power to heat the cathode in an electron tube — compare B POWER SUPPLY, C POWER SUPPLY; A BATTERY

ap·o·zem \ˈapəˌzem\ *also* **apoz·e·ma** \ə'päzəmə\ *n* -s [*apozem* prob. fr. F *apozème*, fr. L *apozema*, fr. Gk, fr. *apozein* to boil till the scum is thrown off, fr. *apo-* + *zein* to boil; *apozema* fr. L — more at YEAST] *pharmacy* **:** DECOCTION — **ap·o·zem·i·cal** \¦apə¦zeməkəl\ *adj*

apo·zy·mase \¦apə¦-\ *n* [*apo-* + *zymase*] **:** the protein portion of a zymase

app *abbr* **1** apparatus **2** apparent **3** appeal; appellate **4** appended; appendix **5** applied **6** appointed **7** apprentice

¹**ap·pa·la·chian** \¦apə¦lāchən, *chiefly southeastern U.S.* -achən, -āshən, *also* -chēən *sometimes* -āshēən\ *adj, usu cap* [prob. irreg. fr. *Apalachee* + E *-an*] **1 :** of or relating to a system of mountains in the eastern U.S. or to the region where they are found **2 :** of or relating to the mountain-making movements in No. America in or near the Pennsylvanian period — see GEOLOGIC TIME table

²**appalachian** \"\ *n* -s *usu cap* **:** APALACHEE

appalachian tea *n, usu cap A* **1 :** the leaves of either of two shrubs (*Ilex glabra* and *I. vomitoria*) of the eastern U.S. locally used as a tea **2 :** any plant that yields Appalachian tea **3 :** WITHE ROD

ap·pall *also* **ap·pal** \ə'pȯl\ *vb* **appalled; appalled; appalling; appalls** *also* **appals** [ME *appallen*, *apallen*, fr. MF *appalir*, *apalir* to grow pale, make pale, fr. OF, fr. *a-* (fr. L *ad-*) + *palir* to grow pale, fr. L *pallescere*, incho. of *pallēre* to be pale — more at FALLOW] *vi, obs* **:** to become pale, faint, or weak **:** FAIL ⟨therewith her wrathful courage gan ∼ —Edmund Spenser⟩ ∼ *vt* **:** to overcome with consternation or horror **:** fill with fear, astonishment, or amazement **:** DISMAY, SHOCK ⟨∼*ed* at the deadly nature of the duel —R.W.Thorp⟩ **syn** see DISMAY

appalling *adj* **:** tending to appall **:** capable of appalling **:** inspiring dismay **:** SHOCKING ⟨an ∼ accident⟩ — often used to show intense displeasure ⟨eating the most ∼ food — stew, mostly, made of old mutton or goat —Oliver La Farge⟩ **syn** see FEARFUL

appallingly *adv* **:** in an appalling manner

ap·pa·loo·sa \ˌapə'lüsə, ˌäp-\ *n* -s *usu cap* [prob. after the *Palouse* Indians] **:** one of a breed of rugged saddle horses developed in western No. America from stock of Spanish origin and distinguished by a mottled skin, vertically striped hoofs, and a patch of white hair over the rump and loins that is blotched or dotted with darker color

¹**ap·pa·nage** *also* **ap·a·nage** \ˈapənij\ *n* -s [F *apanage*, fr. OF, fr. *apaner* to make suitable provision for a younger son or a daughter (fr. OProv *apanar* to feed, support, fr. *a-* — fr. L *ad-* — + *-panar*, fr. *pan* bread, fr. L *panis*) + *-age* — more at FOOD] **1 a :** a grant (as of lands, offices, state revenues, or money) made by a sovereign or a legislative body for the support of dependent members of the royal family or of the ruler's principal liege men **b :** a property or a privilege appropriated to or by a person as his share or perquisite ⟨religious supremacy became a kind of ∼ to the civil sovereignty —H.H.Milman⟩ **2 :** a customary or rightful endowment or adjunct ⟨beauty which is the natural ∼ of happiness —C.K.D.Patmore⟩ **3 a :** a territory or province held in possession as an appanage **:** PRINCIPALITY **b :** a territory subject to outside rule **:** DEPENDENCY **syn** see RIGHT

²**appanage** *also* **apanage** *vt* -ED/-ING/-S **:** to provide or endow with an appanage

ap·pa·rat \ˈapəˌrat, ˈäpəˌrät, ˌ==ˈ=\ *n* -s [Russ, lit., apparatus, prob. fr. G, fr. L *apparatus*] **1 :** the political machine of the Communist party ⟨no other book throws so much light on the inside story of Joseph Stalin's ∼ . . . , secret police, and rise to absolute power —B.D.Wolfe⟩ **2 :** APPARATUS 3 ⟨control the . . . power ∼ of the . . . larger cities —M.J.Arlen⟩

ap·pa·ra·tchik \ˌäpə'rächik\ *n, pl* **apparatchiks** \-iks\ *or* **apparatchi·ki** \-rächəkē\ [Russ, fr. *apparat* + *-chik* (agent suffix)] **1 a :** a Communist secret agent ⟨after her return to Germany bean work as an ∼ —J.H.Lichtblau⟩ **b :** a member of a Communist apparat **2 :** an official blindly devoted to his superiors or organization ⟨the Establishment man par excellence, the perfect ∼ —Frank Getlein⟩

ap·pa·ra·tus \ˌapə'rad·əs, -ād, ¦təs *sometimes* -ál\ *n, pl* **apparatuses** *or* **apparatus** [L, preparation, equipment, fr. *apparatus*, past part. of *apparare* to prepare, fr. *ad-* + *parare* to make ready — more at PARE] **1** *obs* **:** a preparation for action **2 a :** a collection or set of materials, instruments, appliances, or machinery designed for a particular use ⟨the ∼ of art —Arnold Bennett⟩: as (1) **:** scholarly resources used in the critical study of documents and texts (2) **:** FIRE APPARATUS (3) **:** gymnastic equipment (as parallel bars) ⟨worked out on the ∼ for an hour⟩ **b :** any compound instrument or appliance designed for a specific mechanical or chemical action or operation **:** MACHINERY, MECHANISM **c :** a system or group of physical organs that unite in a common function ⟨the respiratory ∼⟩ **3 :** the complex of instrumentalities and processes by means of which an organization functions or a systematized activity is carried out: **a :** the machinery of government **b :** the organization of a political party or of an underground movement **syn** see EQUIPMENT, MACHINE

apparatus crit·i·cus \¦==¦==ˈkrid·ikəs, -it|, |ēk-\ *n* [NL, critical apparatus] **:** supplementary data (as variant readings) provided as part of an edition of a text as a basis for critical study

¹**ap·par·el** \ə'parəl *also* -er-\ *vt* **appareled** *or* **apparelled; appareled** *or* **apparelled; appareling** *or* **apparelling; apparels** [ME *appareillen*, fr. OF *apareillier* to prepare, fr. (assumed) VL *appariculare*, irreg. fr. L *apparare*] **1** *obs* **:** to make or get ready **:** prepare or prepare for **2 :** DRESS, CLOTHE **:** ATTIRE ⟨∼*ed* like circuit riders in Missouri —Frederick O'Brien⟩ **3** *archaic* **:** to furnish (as a ship) with apparatus **:** fit out **:** EQUIP ⟨how are such ships . . . rigged and ∼*ed* —Alan Moore⟩ **4 :** to clothe with ornaments **:** cover with something ornamental **:** ADORN, DECK, EMBELLISH ⟨the work is magnificently printed and tastefully ∼*ed* —E.E.Noth⟩

²**apparel** \"\ *n* -s [ME *appareil*, fr. OF *apareil* preparation, provision, furniture, fr. *apareillier*] **1 a** *obs* **:** material designed for a particular use **:** APPARATUS **b :** the equipment of a ship (as masts, sails, rigging, and anchors) **2 a :** a person's clothing **:** DRESS, ATTIRE, RAIMENT ⟨his daily ∼ was rough and shabby —Willa Cather⟩ **b :** something that clothes or adorns as if with garments ⟨the gay ∼ of spring⟩ **3** *archaic* **:** outward appearance **:** ASPECT, GUISE ⟨so correct that she had puzzled the acutest hinters without the ∼ of being circumspect —Lord Byron⟩ **4 :** an oblong piece of embroidery on certain ecclesiastical vestments (as on an alb or amice)

ap·par·en·cy \ə'parənsē, -si *also* -aar- *or* -er-\ *n* -ES [L *apparentia*, fr. *apparent-*, *apparens* + *-ia* -y] **1** *obs* **:** APPEARANCE, SEMBLANCE **2 :** the quality or state of being apparent **3 :** the position of being heir apparent ⟨the bare right of ∼ carried certain privileges with it —John Erskine †1951⟩

¹**ap·par·ent** \-rənt\ *adj* [ME *apparaunt*, *apparent*, fr. OF *aparant*, *aparent*, pres. part. of *aparoir* to appear), fr. L *apparent-*, *apparens*, pres. part. of *apparēre* to appear — more at APPEAR] **1 :** capable of easy perception: as **a :** readily perceptible to the senses, esp. sight **:** open to ready observation or full view **:** unobstructed and unconcealed ⟨an ∼ change⟩ ⟨the flaw in the metal was ∼⟩ ⟨deposits of transported material left by the retreating ice are perhaps the most widely ∼ results of the glaciation —*Amer. Guide Series: N. H.*⟩ **b :** capable of being readily perceived by the sensibilities or understanding as certainly existent or present ⟨a face in which a strange strife . . . was ∼ —Thomas Hardy⟩ ⟨"you see — my wife — " he let it go at that because it was ∼ that they understood —John Steinbeck⟩ **2 :** readily manifest to senses or mind as real or true and supported by credible evidence of genuine existence but possibly distinct from or contrary to reality or truth ⟨the states are very jealous of any even ∼ encroachment by the

federal government —Stephen Duggan⟩ ⟨to this end his ~ digressions eventually return —H.O.Taylor⟩ — distinguished from *actual* **3** *obs* **:** LIKELY, PROBABLE ⟨as well the fear of harm as harm ~ . . . ought to be prevented —Shak.⟩ **4 :** entitled (as by right of birth) to inherit (as property) or succeed (as to a throne) in the ordinary course of events — see HEIR APPARENT; compare PRESUMPTIVE

syn SEEMING, OSTENSIBLE, ILLUSORY: APPARENT may imply only distinctness from reality or truth ⟨most children have periods of *apparent* stagnation . . . but probably throughout these periods there is progress in ways that are not easily perceptible —Bertrand Russell⟩ It may also describe a semblance contrary to truth and actuality, a likeness dissipated by close scrutiny or consideration of all facts ⟨the high mineral content is the reason why irrigation often produces bumper crops from *apparent* deserts —Stuart Chase⟩ It usu. does not suggest a reprehensible intent to deceive ⟨the long corridor . . . carpeted with a narrow bordered carpet whose parallel lines increased its *apparent* length —Arnold Bennett⟩ SEEMING stresses a close resemblance to reality detected only by correcting faulty observation or analysis ⟨John had doubtless no wish to be entangled in a long quarrel . . . and the Archbishop's mediation allowed him to withdraw with *seeming* dignity —J.R.Green⟩ It is not derogatory in suggesting deception ⟨the whole of Burns' song has an air of straight dealing . . . but these *seeming* simplicities are craftily charged —C.E.Montague⟩ OSTENSIBLE applies to what is explicitly declared or avowed or to what one would naturally and logically assume from what appears ⟨it is by no means true that every law is void which may seem . . . unsuited to its *ostensible* end —O.W.Holmes †1935⟩ It often applies to differences between such declarations or appearances and a true or actual end, aim, purpose, or character ⟨natives . . . whose *ostensible* business was the repair of broken necklaces . . . but whose real end seemed to be to raise money for angry Maharanees —Rudyard Kipling⟩ It often applies to conscious deception ⟨the first time that he had been *ostensibly* frank as to his purpose while really concealing it —Thomas Hardy⟩ ILLUSORY definitely states that the described impressions of truth or actuality are illusions based on deceptive semblances, formed through faulty observation or analysis, or warped by emotional forces ⟨the multiplication of wants, real or *illusory* —Lewis Mumford⟩ ⟨we need a deeper reality to take the place of these early beliefs which the growth of intelligence necessarily shows to be *illusory* —Havelock Ellis⟩ ⟨but hopes may be *illusory* or ill-founded — they may even attach to what is demonstrably impossible —M.R.Cohen⟩ **syn** see in addition EVIDENT

²apparent \"\ *n* -s [by shortening] *obs* **:** HEIR APPARENT

³ap·par·ent \ə'pa(a)rənt, a'-, -per- *sometimes* -pär-\ *vt* -ED/-ING/-S [*ad-* + L *parent-, parens* parent, relative — more at PARENT] **:** to bring into close relationship **:** connect (as by way of descent or derivation) ⟨Islam, the universal church through which . . . Syriac society came . . . to be ~*ed* to the Iranic and Arabic societies —A.J.Toynbee⟩

ap·par·en·ta·tion \=,=ən'tāshən, ,a,p-\ *n* -s **:** the process of apparenting **:** AFFILIATION

apparent authority *n* **:** the authority that an agent appears to have by reason of his actual agency or by such acts or conduct of the principal as estop the latter from denying the authority

apparent candle power *n* **:** the candle power of an extended source of light that is equal to the candle power of a point source of light which if located at the extended source would produce an equivalent illumination at the distance specified

apparent danger *n* **:** danger that appears from overt actual demonstration (as by conduct and acts indicative of a design to take life or inflict great personal injury) to make homicide appear necessary to self-preservation

apparent easement *or* **apparent servitude** *n* **:** an easement that involves (as in its nature or as a means of its enjoyment) some permanent visible sign of its existence (as the bed of a stream, an overhanging roof, or a water pipe)

ap·pa·rente·ment \àpärä^n^tmä^n^\ *n* -s [F, lit., alliance by marriage, fr. *apparenter* to ally by marriage (fr. OF *aparenter* to take or treat as a relative, fr. *a-* — fr. L *ad-* — + *parent* relative, parent) + *-ment* — more at PARENT] **:** an alliance of French political parties formed during an election

apparent expansion *n* **:** the thermal expansion of a liquid as measured in a graduated container without allowance for the expansion of the container

apparent horizon *n* **:** the somewhat irregular boundary between the sky and the land or water surface of the earth as viewed from any given point — called also *visible horizon*

ap·par·ent·ly \ə'par(ə)ntlē, -lı *also* -aar- *or* -er-\ *adv* [¹*apparent* + *-ly*] **:** in an apparent manner **:** SEEMINGLY, EVIDENTLY

apparent magnitude *n* **:** the observed or apparent brightness of a celestial body expressed on the magnitude scale and varying in accordance with the spectral sensitivity of the means of observing (as the eye, a photographic material, or an instrument)

apparent motion *or* **apparent movement** *n* **:** an optical illusion in which stationary objects viewed in quick succession or in relation to moving objects appear to be in motion

apparent noon *n* **:** the instant of transit of the sun's center over the meridian at any particular place — compare APPARENT TIME

apparent photosynthesis *n* **:** the rate of photosynthesis less the rate of respiration

apparent power *n* **:** the product of the effective electromotive force and the effective current in an alternating-current circuit

apparent time *or* **apparent solar time** *n* **:** the time of day at any particular place indicated by the hour angle of the apparent or true sun or by a simple sundial and differing from mean time by the equation of time

apparent variable *n* **:** BOUND VARIABLE — opposed to *real variable*

apparent volume *n* **:** the result obtained by subtracting from the volume of a binary solution the volume of the pure solvent entering into it at the same temperature, being in general somewhat less than the volume of the pure solute

apparent weight *n* **:** the weight of a body as affected by the buoyancy of a fluid (as air) in which it is immersed, being the true weight minus the weight of the displaced fluid — compare ARCHIMEDES' PRINCIPLE

apparent wind *n* **:** the wind as observed aboard a moving vessel, being the vectorial combination of the true wind and the wind due to the ship's motion

ap·pa·ri·tion \,apə'rishən\ *n* -s [ME *appariciouin*, fr. LL *apparition-, apparitio* appearance, epiphany (trans. of Gk *epiphaneia*), fr. L *apparitus* (past part. of *apparēre* to appear) + *-ion-, -io* -ion — more at APPEAR] **1 a :** someone or something unusual or unexpected that appears **:** PHENOMENON ⟨Shakespeare is an ~ as genius forever is —W.L.Sullivan⟩ **b :** a supernatural appearance **:** GHOST, PHANTOM, SPECTER ⟨was never allowed to hear of a goblin or ~ or scarcely to be told of bad men —Charles Lamb⟩ **2 a :** the act of becoming visible **:** APPEARANCE ⟨I was recalled to the present by the ~ of my adversary riding his pony toward me —R.H.Davis⟩ **b (1) :** the first appearance of a planet, comet, star, or other luminary after being invisible or obscured **(2) :** the period during which such a body is visible **3** *obs* **:** SEMBLANCE, ASPECT **4** *usu cap, obs* **:** EPIPHANY

ap·pa·ri·tion·al \,apə'rishən³l, -shnəl\ *adj* **:** of, relating to, or being a phantom **:** SPECTRAL

ap·par·i·tor \ə'parəd·ə(r)\ *n* -s [L, fr. *apparitus* (past part. of *apparēre* to appear) + *-or* — more at APPEAR] **1 :** one that attends or serves an officer or authority: **a :** an officer who executed the orders of a Roman magistrate **b :** an officer who executed the orders and decrees of an ecclesiastical court esp. by serving summonses **c :** an officer formerly present to execute the order of the magistrate or judge of a civil court **2** *obs* **:** one that acts as a forerunner **:** HERALD

ap·pas·si·o·na·ta·men·te \ə'pàsēə,nàd·ə'mentē, -as-, -syə,-, ə,pasha,n-\ *adv* [It, fr. *appassionato*] **:** with passion — used as a direction in music

¹ap·pas·si·o·na·to \¦=(=)=¦näd·(,)ō\ *or* **ap·pas·si·o·na·ta** \-äd·ə\ *adj* [It *appassionato* (masc.) & *appassionata* (fem.), past part. of *appassionare* to impassion, fr. *ap-* (fr. L *ad-*) + *passionare* to impassion, fr. *passione* passion, fr. LL *passion-, passio* — more at PASSION] **:** deeply emotional **:** IMPASSIONED — used as a direction in music

²appassionato \"\ *n* -s [It, fr. *appassionato*, past part.] **:** a musical movement or piece marked *appassionato*

ap·pau·mé *or* **ap·pau·mée** *also* **apau·mé** \¦a(,)pō¦mā\ *adj* [F *appaumé*, fr. *ap-* (fr. L, fr. *ad-*) + *-paumé* (fr. *paume* palm of the hand) — more at PALM] *heraldry* **:** opened out so as to show the palm of the hand

appay *vt* [ME *apaien*, fr. OF *apaier*, fr. *a-* (fr. L *ad-*) + *paier* to pacify, fr. L *pacare* — more at PAY] **1** *obs* **:** SATISFY, CONTENT **2** *obs* **:** REPAY, REQUITE

appd *abbr* approved

appeach *vb* -ED/-ING/-ES [ME *apechen*, fr. (assumed) AF *apecher, anpecher*, fr. LL *impedicare* to entangle — more at IMPEACH] *vt* **1** *obs* **:** to bring a charge against **:** ACCUSE **2** *obs* **:** to cast aspersions on ~ *vi, obs* **:** to bring accusation

¹ap·peal \ə'pēl, -ēəl\ *n* -s [ME *appel, apel*, fr. OF *apel*, fr. *apeler*] **1 a :** a legal proceeding by which a case is brought from a lower to a higher court for rehearing — compare WRIT OF ERROR **b :** a request for such an appeal **c :** the right to such an appeal **d :** a case so appealed **2 :** a formal accusation of a felony or heinous crime made against a person by another who demands punishment for the private injury rather than for the public offense **3** *obs* **:** a challenge to defend oneself (as by a duel) against a charge **4 :** an application or reference (as to a recognized authority) for corroboration, vindication, or decision ⟨an ~ to his superiors⟩ ⟨an ~ to the umpire⟩ ⟨an ~ to reason⟩ **5 :** an earnest plea or request (as for help or support) **:** ENTREATY ⟨~*s* for current support from alumni —T.L.Hungate⟩ **6 :** the power or property of arousing a sympathetic response **:** ATTRACTION ⟨the great ~ of a freighter crossing is . . . its . . . informality —Richard Joseph⟩ **syn** see PRAYER

²appeal \"\ *vb* -ED/-ING/-S [ME *appelen, apelen* to appeal, accuse, fr. MF *apeler*, fr. L *appellare* to address, entreat, appeal to, accuse, summon, call by name, fr. *appellere* to drive to, fr. *ad-* + *pellere* to drive, strike — more at PULSE] *vt* **1 :** to charge with a crime **:** ACCUSE; *specif* **:** to institute a private criminal prosecution against for a felony or heinous crime **2 :** to take proceedings for the removal of (a case) from a lower to a higher court for rehearing **3** *archaic* **:** CHALLENGE ⟨man to man I will ~ the Norman to the lists —Sir Walter Scott⟩ **4** *obs* **:** to call to witness **:** INVOKE ~ *vi* **1 :** to apply for the removal of a case from a lower to a higher court for rehearing **2 :** to call upon or refer to another as a recognized authority for corroboration, vindication, or decision ⟨to what sources of information do I ~ —B.N.Cardozo⟩ ⟨Burke's teaching . . . ~*ed* from the spoken to the unspoken rules of freedom —Michael Polanyi⟩ **3 :** to plead seriously **:** make an earnest request ⟨both contestants ~*ed* for the ballots of the . . . electors —M.M.Quaife⟩ ⟨~*ed* to the president for aid⟩ **4 :** to have a particular interest or attraction **:** arouse a sympathetic response ⟨the idea of a European federation has ~*ed* to many statesmen —Vera M. Dean⟩ ⟨educational questions . . . ~ to their sense of duty —J.B.Conant⟩

ap·peal·a·bil·i·ty \ə,pēlə'biləd·ē\ *n* -ES **:** the quality or state of being appealable ⟨on the question of ~ the court relied entirely on United States v. Snyder —*Harvard Law Rev.*⟩

ap·peal·a·ble \ə'pēləbəl\ *adj* **:** capable of being appealed esp. to a higher tribunal ⟨decisions . . . ~ to the head of the agency —*New Republic*⟩

ap·peal·er \-ēlə(r)\ *n* -s **:** APPELLANT

ap·peal·ing \-ēliŋ, -lēŋ\ *adj* **1 :** having appeal **:** ATTRACTIVE, PLEASING ⟨he added an ~ and memorable figure to popular American mythology —Vincent Starrett⟩ **2 :** PLEADING, IMPLORING ⟨the ~ and frightened look worn by a domestic dog when injured—James Stevenson-Hamilton⟩ — **ap·peal·ing·ly** *adv* — **ap·peal·ing·ness** *n* -ES

appeals *pl of* APPEAL, *pres 3d sing of* APPEAL

appeal to the country : a British general election after a government measure has been defeated and parliament dissolved

ap·pear \ə'pi(ə)r, -iə\ *vi* -ED/-ING/-S [ME *apperen, aperen*, fr. OF *aparoir* (3d pers. pl. pres. indic. *aperent*), fr. L *apparēre*, fr. *ad-* + *parēre* to come forth, be visible; akin to Gk *peparein* to display] **1 a :** to come into view (as from a distance or a place of concealment) **:** become visible ⟨sandbars which ~ in the river bed at low water —P.E.James⟩ **b :** to be in sight **:** be visible ⟨a faint but courteous smile occasionally ~*ed* upon the veteran's lips —E.H.Collis⟩ **2 :** to come formally before an authoritative body ⟨I ~*ed* before the committee in executive session —R.M.Lovett⟩; *specif* **:** to present oneself formally as plaintiff, defendant, or counsel ⟨was instructed to ~ in court the next morning⟩ **3 :** to be taken as **:** LOOK, SEEM ⟨a spirit of tolerance which allows the expression of all opinions, however heretical they may ~ —J.B.Conant⟩ **4 a :** to be clear to the mind **:** be obvious or evident ⟨it perpetually ~*s* throughout history that one man achieves and is the true creator of a capital event —Hilaire Belloc⟩ **b :** to reveal itself to an observer or reader **:** be manifest ⟨his range of interest ~*s* also in his books —Allan Westcott⟩ **5 :** to come before the public or into public view ⟨thank the delegates for the great honor they have done me in inviting me to ~ before them —D.D. Eisenhower⟩: **a :** to come before the public as an actor ⟨he first ~*ed* on Broadway last year⟩ **b :** to come before the public as an author ⟨he ~*ed* in print for the first time⟩ **c :** to come out in published form ⟨his papers ~*ed* in various scientific journals⟩ **:** be out ⟨a new recording of the symphony ~*ed* last week⟩ **6 :** to come into existence ⟨primitives may very well ~ at any stage of a country's development —Bernard Smith⟩ **:** become created, developed, discovered, founded, or invented ⟨the sources whence civilization flowed westward centuries before Greece and Rome ~ —Edward Clodd⟩

ap·pear·ance \ə'pirən(t)s\ *n* -s [ME *apparaunce*, alter. (influenced by *apperen* to appear) of *apparaunce, apparence*, fr. MF *aparance, apparence*, fr. LL *apparentia*, fr. L *apparent-, apparens* (pres. part. of *apparēre* to appear) + *-ia* -y] **1 :** the act, action, or process of appearing: as **a :** the act or action of coming into view or being visible ⟨the sudden ~ of enemy troops⟩ ⟨the unexpected ~ of smoke on the horizon⟩ **b :** the act or action of coming before the public or into public view ⟨his last ~ on the London stage⟩ ⟨financially secure since the ~ of his last novel⟩ **c :** the action or process of coming into existence (as by development, discovery, or invention) ⟨within a few years after the ~ of the . . . canal boat —*Amer. Guide Series: N.Y.*⟩ **d :** the act or action of coming formally before an authoritative body ⟨his ~ before the board⟩ **e (1) :** the coming into court of either of the parties to a suit **(2) :** the coming into court of a party summoned in an action or his attorney **(3) :** the act or proceeding by which a party proceeded against places himself before the court and submits to its jurisdiction (as by making the proper entry in the court records and remaining within reach of its process) **2 a :** the state or form in which one appears **:** ASPECT, LOOK, MIEN ⟨his whole ~ was markedly different from that of the guests usually to be seen —Archibald Marshall⟩ **b (1) :** an outward state of appearing as opposed to an actual state **:** external show or pretense **:** SEMBLANCE ⟨traders, though hostile to the settlement, had to preserve an ~ of neutrality —B.K.Sandwell⟩ **(2) appearances** *pl* **:** outward show intended esp. to conceal a real or fancied disgrace or to avoid a social lapse ⟨they spent their lives trying to keep up ~*s* and to make his salary do more than it could —Willa Cather⟩ **c appearances** *pl* **:** outward indications, circumstances, or events ⟨to all ~*s* he was guilty⟩ **d (1) :** a sense impression of a thing as distinguished from its true nature or real existence ⟨the blue of distant hills is only an ~⟩ **(2) :** a sensation of an object as produced or modified by the character of the sense organs or by particular circumstances ⟨the different ~*s* of a penny viewed from different angles⟩ **e :** the phenomenal as opposed to the real: **(1) :** something given in sensation or impression as contrasted with something subject to rational verification **(2) :** the sum total of human or finite experience as contrasted with the reality of the absolute ⟨that philosophic legerdemain which, with only experience for its datum, would condemn this experience to the status of ~ and disclose a reality more edifying —C.I.Lewis⟩ **3 a :** something that appears: **(1) :** PHENOMENON ⟨a great observer of natural ~*s* —William Cowper⟩ **(2)** *archaic* **:** APPARITION ⟨this of that ~ passed for as real a thing as the blazing star itself —Daniel Defoe⟩ **b :** an instance of appearing **:** OCCURRENCE ⟨the first ~ of that word in English⟩ **4** *obs* **:** a gathering or company **:** ATTENDANCE ⟨an innumerable ~ of gallants —John Evelyn⟩

syn APPEARANCE, LOOK, ASPECT, SEMBLANCE can mean, in common, the outward show or image presented by a person or thing. APPEARANCE usu. suggests no more than the meaning common to the group ⟨the *appearance* of the house has been unfortunately altered by the addition of an upper gallery —*Amer. Guide Series: La.*⟩ ⟨his long, flowing beard, whitening with the years, gave to his countenance a patriarchal *appearance* —H.A.Bridgman⟩ but can suggest a dissembling or pretense ⟨giving highway robbery the *appearance* of legality —H.W.Carter⟩ ⟨going into debt to keep up an *appearance* of prosperity⟩ LOOK usu. carries the meaning common to the group but often (generally in the plural) suggests a more objective condition than APPEARANCE, stressing the concrete details of outward appearance ⟨he's wearing a queer kind of knickerbocker suit. He hasn't the *look* of a journalist —John Buchan⟩ ⟨did not care for the *looks* of Labrador —Russell Lord⟩ ⟨nor has she lost her dark, good *looks* —*Irish Digest*⟩ ASPECT is like LOOK in stressing the features, usu. suggesting a characteristic or habitual appearance, esp. facial expression, but most commonly is applied to nonconcrete things ⟨his voice and *aspect* were quite friendly —George Meredith⟩ ⟨this was the dreariest evening *aspect* of the sea he had ever seen —Joseph Conrad⟩ ⟨such is the lot of the man who writes upon the subject of the day; the *aspect* of affairs changes in an hour or two —William Cowper⟩ ⟨"Democracy," he says, "has different *aspects* in different lands" —C.L.Sulzberger⟩ SEMBLANCE can signify an outward seeming, an approximation, without suggesting falseness or hypocrisy, but generally implies a difference between outward appearance and inner reality ⟨it is the *semblance* which interests the painter, not the actual object —*Times Lit. Supp.*⟩ ⟨this mission has recently been restored to some *semblance* of its former grandeur —*Amer. Guide Series: Texas*⟩ ⟨giving defeat the *semblance* of victory —H.A.Overstreet⟩ ⟨a regime with efficient instruments of terror must cloak its power so as to give it a *semblance* of legitimacy —Julian Towster⟩

appeared *past of* APPEAR

appearing *pres part of* APPEAR

ap·pear·ing·ly *adv, now dial* **:** APPARENTLY

appears *pres 3d sing of* APPEAR

ap·peas·a·ble \ə'pēzəbəl\ *adj* **:** capable of being appeased **:** PLACABLE

ap·pease \ə'pēz\ *vt* -ED/-ING/-S [ME *appesen, apesen*, fr. OF *apaisier*, fr. *a-* (fr. L *ad-*) + *-paisier* (fr. *pais* peace) — more at PEACE] **1 :** to bring to a state of peace or quiet **:** CALM, SETTLE ⟨instead of *appeasing* the quarrel the government's action intensified it —J.H.Plumb⟩ **2 :** to cause to subside **:** ALLAY, ASSUAGE ⟨the man had *appeased* his great hunger —Elizabeth M.Roberts⟩ ⟨the same kind of supposition which had *appeased* Mrs. Bennet's curiosity —Jane Austen⟩ **3 a :** to bring to a state of ease or content **:** CONCILIATE, SATISFY ⟨when he has once tasted the blood of popular applause, he is a tiger, nevermore to be *appeased* —C.H.Grandgent⟩ **b :** to conciliate or buy off (a potential aggressor) by political or economic concessions usu. at the sacrifice of principles ⟨the attempt to ~ the Nazis at Munich⟩ **syn** see PACIFY

ap·pease·ment \-smənt\ *n* -s [ME *appesement*, fr. MF *apaisement*, fr. OF, fr. *apaisier* + *-ment*] **1 a :** the act or action of appeasing **:** PACIFICATION ⟨one tribe may go in for the ~ of local ghosts —W.D.Howells⟩ **:** CONCILIATION ⟨that we should accept wrong and call it right . . . would be ~ at its most cowardly —A.L.Guérard⟩ **b :** the state of being appeased **:** SATISFACTION ⟨an experience from which he derived little ~⟩ **2 :** a policy of appeasing a potential aggressor ⟨some defensible reasons for the ~ which London and Paris practiced in the thirties —D.F.Fleming⟩

ap·peas·er \-zə(r)\ *n* -s **:** one that appeases

¹ap·pel·lant \ə'pelənt\ *adj* [ME, fr. MF *apelant* (pres. part. of *apeler* to appeal), fr. L *appellant-, appellans*, pres. part. of *appellare* to appeal to — more at APPEAL] **:** relating to an appeal **:** APPEALING, APPELLATE ⟨~ jurisdiction⟩

²appellant \"\ *n* -s **1 a :** one that accuses another of treason or felony **b** *obs* **:** one that challenges another to combat esp. to prove treason or felony **2 :** one that appeals; *specif* **:** one that appeals from a judicial decision or decree — opposed to *appellee*

ap·pel·late \ə'pelət, *outside the legal profession sometimes* 'apə,lāt *or* 'apələt; *usu* -d·+V\ *adj* [L *appellatus*, past. part. of *appellare* to appeal to, call by name — more at APPEAL] **:** of, relating to, or taking cognizance of appeals; *specif* **:** having the power to review and affirm, reverse, or modify the judgment or decision of another tribunal ⟨an ~ court⟩

ap·pel·la·tion \,apə'lāshən\ *n* -s [ME *appellacioun*, fr. L *appellation-, appellatio*, fr. *appellatus* + *-ion-, -io* -ion] **1** *obs* **:** the act of appealing esp. to a higher court or authority **2** *archaic* **:** the act of calling by a name **3 :** a name or title by which a person, thing, or clan is called and known **:** DESIGNATION ⟨he had received the added ~ of Jerry —Charles Dickens⟩ ⟨none of us was well acquainted with the road; indeed, I could see nothing which was fairly entitled to that ~ —George Borrow⟩

¹ap·pel·la·tive \ə'peləd·iv, -ətiv\ *adj* [ME, fr. LL *appellativus*, fr. L *appellatus* + *-ivus* -ive] **1 :** designating a being or thing of which more than one specimen exists **:** being a common noun **:** dealing with common nouns **2 :** of, relating to, or inclined to the giving of names ⟨the ~ faculty of children⟩ — **ap·pel·la·tive·ly** *adv*

²appellative \"\ *n* -s **1 :** COMMON NOUN **2 :** APPELLATION 3

ap·pel·lee \¦apə¦lē\ *n* -s [MF *appelé, apelé*, fr. past part. of *appeler, apeler* to appeal — more at APPEAL] **:** one against whom an appeal is taken **:** the respondent to an appeal — opposed to *appellant*

ap·pel·lor \¦apə¦lò(ə)r, ə'pelər\ *n* -s [ME *appellour, apellour*, fr. AF *apelour*, fr. L *appellator* appellant, fr. *appellatus* (past part. of *appellare* to address, appeal to) + *-or* — more at APPEAL] **:** APPELLANT 1a

ap·pend \ə'pend *also* a'-\ *vt* -ED/-ING/-S [F *appendre*, fr. LL *appendere*, fr. L, to weigh, fr. *ad-* + *pendere* to weigh — more at PENDANT] **1 :** to hang or suspend (as by a string) **:** ATTACH ⟨a seal ~*ed* to a document⟩ **2 :** to add as something secondary or subordinate ⟨the final summary of his views which he enjoyed ~*ing* to his long-winded discourses —I.V.Morris⟩; *specif* **:** to add as a supplement or appendix ⟨notes ~*ed* to a chapter⟩

append- *or* **appendo-** *or* **appendic-** *or* **appendico-** *comb form* [NL, fr. *appendic-, appendix*, fr. L, appendage, supplement] **:** vermiform appendix ⟨*append*ectomy⟩ ⟨*appendic*itis⟩ ⟨*appendico*stomy⟩ ⟨*appendo*tome⟩

ap·pend·age \ə'pendij, -dēj *also* a'-\ *n* -s **1 :** something accompanying or appended to another thing and usu. subordinate or not essential to it **:** ADJUNCT, APPURTENANCE ⟨most factories are an accumulation of ~*s* — something tacked on here, something tacked on there —G.S.Perry⟩ ⟨music . . . had been treated for the most part as a kind of decorative ~ to life —H.A.Overstreet⟩ ⟨the vermiform appendix is a small tubular ~ of the cecum⟩ **2 :** a person accompanying or in constant attendance on another usu. as a subordinate **:** HANGER-ON ⟨occupation forces and their civilian ~*s* constantly traveling about on cut-rate military tickets —*N.Y.Times*⟩ **3 :** LIMB 2a; *broadly* **:** any peripheral extension of an animal body esp. when functioning as a limb (as a seta or cirrus)

ap·pend·aged \-jd\ *adj* **:** having an appendage

ap·pend·ance \-dən(t)s\ *or* **ap·pend·an·cy** \-dənsē, -si\ *n, pl* **appendances** *or* **appendancies** [MF *apendance*, fr. OF, fr. *apendre* to be attached, depend, belong, append (fr. LL *appendere* to suspend) + *-ance*] **:** the quality or state of being appendant

¹ap·pend·ant \-dənt\ *adj* [ME *appendaunt, apendaunt*, fr. MF *apendant*, fr. OF, pres. part. of *apendre*] **1 :** associated as an attendant circumstance or consequence ⟨as they have transmitted the benefit to us, it is but reasonable we should suffer the ~ calamity —Jeremy Taylor⟩ **2 :** annexed or belonging as a right — used in English law of certain ancient immemorial rights in land (as an advowson or common) that are annexed to the land of the persons claiming them **3 :** attached as an appendage **:** ANNEXED ⟨the governor of a colony has jurisdiction within the ~ protectorate —Martin Wight⟩ ⟨a seal ~ to a document⟩

²appendant \"\ *n* -s **1 :** an appendant inheritance or right **2 :** APPENDAGE

ap·pen·dec·to·my \ˌapənˈdektəmē, -mi, ˌaˌpen-\ *n* -ES [*append-* + *-ectomy*] : surgical removal of the vermiform appendix
appended *past of* APPEND
ap·pen·di·ceal \ˌapənˈdishəl, ˈaˌpen-; əˌpendəˈsēəl, ˈaˌp-\ *also* **ap·pen·di·cal** \əˈpendəkəl, (ˈ)aˈp-, -dēk-\ *or* **ap·pen·di·cial** \ˌapənˈdishəl, ˈaˌpen-\ *adj* [*appendic-* + *-eal, -al, -ial*] : of, relating to, or involving the vermiform appendix
ap·pen·di·cec·to·my \əˌpendəˈsektəmi, (ˌ)aˌp-\ *n* -ES [ISV *appendic-* + *-ectomy*] *Brit* : APPENDECTOMY
appendices *pl of* APPENDIX
ap·pen·di·ci·tis \əˌpendəˈsīd·əs\ *n* -ES [NL, fr. *appendic-* + *-itis*] : inflammation of the vermiform appendix characterized by usu. right-sided abdominal pain and sometimes by nausea and vomiting
ap·pen·di·cle \əˈpendəkəl\ *n* -S [F or L; F *appendicule*, fr. L *appendicula*, fr. *appendic-, appendix* + *-ula*] : a small appendage
appendico- — see APPEND-
ap·pen·dic·u·lar \ˌapənˈdikyələ(r), ˈaˌpen-\ *adj* [L *appendicula* + E *-ar*] : of or relating to an appendage: **a** : of or relating to a limb or limbs ⟨the ~ skeleton⟩ **b** : APPENDICEAL ⟨~ inflammation⟩
¹ap·pen·dic·u·lar·ia \ˌ=(ˌ)=ˌ==ˈla(a)rēə\ *n, cap* [NL, fr. L *appendicula* appendicle + NL *-aria*] : a genus of small free-swimming pelagic tunicates shaped somewhat like a tadpole and remarkable for resemblances to the larvae of other tunicates
²appendicularia \"\ *or* **ap·pen·dic·u·lar·i·ae** \-rēˌē\ [NL, fr. L *appendicula* + NL *-aria, -ariae*] *syn of* LARVACEA
¹ap·pen·dic·u·lar·i·an \ˌ=(ˌ)=ˌ==ˈēən\ *adj* [NL ²*Appendicularia* + E *-an*] : of or relating to the Larvacea
²appendicularian \"\ *n* -S : a tunicate of the order Larvacea
ap·pen·dic·u·la·ta \ˌ=(ˌ)=ˌ==ˈläd·ə, -ād·ə\ *n pl, cap* [NL, fr. L *appendicula* + NL *-ata*] *in some classifications* : a group that together with the Chaetopoda and Rotifera is nearly equivalent to the Arthropoda
ap·pen·dic·u·late \ˌ=(ˌ)=ˈ==ˌlət, -ˌlāt, *usu* -d·+V\ *also* **ap·pen·dic·u·lat·ed** \-ˌlād·əd\ *adj* [L *appendicula* + E *-ate, -ated* — more at APPENDICLE] : having appendages ⟨~ corolla⟩ : forming an appendage
appending *pres part of* APPEND
¹ap·pen·dix \əˈpendiks, -ēks\ *n, pl* **appendixes** \-ksəz\ *or* **appendi·ces** \-də(ˌ)sēz\ [L *appendic-, appendix*, fr. *appendere* to attach — more at APPEND (attach)] **1** : APPENDAGE ⟨the principle of official management was invented . . . as a natural ~ to political dictatorship —N.S.Timasheff⟩ **2** : matter added to a book but not essential to its completeness (as a bibliography or a series of tables usu. following the text) **3** : a supplementary part or process attached to another part; *specif* : VERMIFORM APPENDIX **4** : the tube that is located at the bottom of a balloon and used in inflation and deflation
²appendix \"\ *vt* -ED/-ING/-ES : to add as an appendix : APPEND ⟨~*ed*, indexed, and footnoted the book in bang-up scholarly fashion —*New Yorker*⟩
appendix dig·i·ti·for·mis \-ˌdijəd·əˈfȯrməs\ *n* [NL, finger-shaped appendix] : the finger-shaped anal gland in elasmobranchs
appendo- — see APPEND-
appends *pres 3d sing of* APPEND
ap·pen·zell \ˈapənˌzel, ˈäpəntˌsel\ *n* -S *sometimes cap* [fr. *Appenzell*, canton and commune in Switzerland, where it is made] : a fine hand or machine embroidery of Swiss origin usu. worked in pale blue thread on white cloth
ap·per·ceive \ˌapə(r)ˈsēv\ *vt* -ED/-ING/-S [ME *apperceiven, aperceiven*, fr. OF *aperceivre*, fr. *a-* (fr. L *ad-*) + *perceivre* to perceive — more at PERCEIVE] **1** *obs* : PERCEIVE, OBSERVE **2** *philos* : to possess apperception of **3** *psychol* : to understand (as a new percept) in terms of previous experience — compare APPERCEPTIVE MASS
ap·per·cep·tion \ˌapə(r)ˈsepshən\ *n* -S [F *aperception*, fr. *apercevoir* to apperceive, perceive (after F *percevoir: perception*), fr. OF, to perceive, fr. *a-* (fr. L *ad-*) + *percevoir* to perceive, fr. L *percipere* — more at PERCEIVE] **1** *philos* **a** *in Leibnitz* : a mental act in which the mind becomes aware or has knowledge of itself as it perceives **b** *in Kant* (1) : consciousness of oneself as a changing phenomenon with a variable content — called also *empirical apperception* (2) : consciousness of the persisting identity of oneself, irrespective of changing representations, as a necessary prerequisite to any experience — called also *pure apperception, transcendental apperception* **2** : mental perception : RECOGNITION **3** *psychol* **a** : the process of understanding (as of a new percept) in terms of one's previous experience — compare APPERCEPTIVE MASS, ASSIMILATION 5 **b** : the perception of meaning
ap·per·cep·tion·ism \ˌ==ˈ==ˌnizəm\ *n* -S : the theory that mental development is determined chiefly by apperception rather than by association — opposed to *associationism*
ap·per·cep·tion·ist \-ˌnəst\ *n* -S : one who believes in apperceptionism — **ap·per·cep·tion·is·tic** \ˌ==ˌ==ˈnistik\ *adj*
ap·per·cep·tive \ˌ==ˈ=tiv\ *adj* [*apperception* + *-ive*] : relating to, involved in, or produced by apperception : capable of apperceiving — **ap·per·cep·tive·ly** *adv*
apperceptive mass *n, psychol* : the whole of a person's previous experience that is used in understanding a new percept or idea — called also *apperceiving mass, apperception mass*
¹ap·per·cip·i·ent \ˌapə(r)ˈsipēənt\ *adj* [fr. *apperception*, after E *perception: percipient*] : possessing apperception : APPERCEPTIVE
²appercipient \"\ *n* -S : one who apperceives
apperil *n* -S [*ad-* + *peril*] *obs* : PERIL
ap·per·son·ate \aˈpərsᵊnˌāt, əˈ-\ *vt* -ED/-ING/-S [back-formation fr. *appersonation*] : to subject to appersonation
ap·per·son·a·tion \(ˌ)aˌpərsᵊnˈāshən, əˌp-\ *n* -S [*ad-* + *personation*; part trans. of G *appersonierung*] : the incorporation of characteristics of external objects or persons through a process of ego extension
ap·per·tain \ˌapə(r)ˈtān\ *vi* -ED/-ING/-S [ME *apperteinen, apertenen, apertenen*, fr. MF *apartenir*, fr. (assumed) VL *appartenēre*, alter. (influenced by L *part-, pars* part) of LL *appertinēre*, fr. L *ad-* + *pertinēre* to reach to, belong — more at PERTAIN] : to belong either as something appropriate or as a part, possession, right, or attribute : PERTAIN ⟨he will grow into an adult with the privileges and obligations ~*ing* thereto —Richard Joseph⟩ ⟨islands which have been determined by the President to ~ to the U. S. —E.D.Dickinson⟩
appertinent *adj* [ME *apertinent* — more at APPURTENANT] *archaic* : APPURTENANT 2
ap·pe·stat \ˈapəˌstat\ *n* -S [*appetite* + *-stat*] : a neural center in the hypothalamus believed to regulate appetite
ap·pe·ten·cy \ˈapəd·ənsē, ǀtən-, -si *also* ǀtᵊn-\ *or* **ap·pe·tence** \-n(t)s\ *n, pl* **appetencies** *or* **appetences** [L *appetentia*, fr. *appetent-, appetens* + *-ia*] **1** : a strong ingrained desire : APPETITE, CRAVING ⟨the object of life is to satisfy as many *appetencies* as possible —Granville Hicks⟩ **2** : a natural affinity of a substance or inanimate object for another ⟨the ~ of substance for oxygen⟩ **3** : an instinctive inclination or propensity in animals to perform certain actions **syn** see DESIRE
ap·pe·tent \-nt\ *adj* [ME, fr. L *appetent-, appetens*, pres. part. of *appetere*] : marked by eager desire : LONGING ⟨the crash and scramble of that big rich ~ Western city —Willa Cather⟩
ap·pet·i·bil·i·ty \(ˌ)aˌped·əˈbiləd·ē, əˌp-; ˌapəd·ə-\ *n* -ES : the quality or state of being appetible ⟨beauty is the ~ of truth —*Liturgical Arts*⟩
ap·pet·i·ble \aˈped·əbəl, əˈ-; ˈapəd·əbəl\ *adj* [L *appetibilis*, fr. *appetere* to strive after, long for + *-ibilis* -ible — more at APPETITE] : worthy of desire : DESIRABLE
ap·pe·tite \ˈapəˌtīt, *usu* -īd·+V\ *n* -S [ME *appetit, apetit*, fr. MF *apetit*, fr. L *appetitus*, fr. *appetitus*, past part. of *appetere* to strive after, long for, fr. *ad-* + *petere* to go to, head for — more at FEATHER] **1** : a natural desire : one of the instinctive desires necessary to keep up organic life; *esp* : the immediate desire to eat when food is present **2 a** : an inherent or habitual desire or propensity for gratification or satisfaction ⟨an ~ for life, a robust reaching out to life —V.S.Pritchett⟩ ⟨an insatiable ~⟩ ⟨~ for the acquisition of more territory —A.J.Toynbee⟩ **b** : TASTE, LIKING, PREFERENCE ⟨a faculty for idleness implies a catholic ~ —R.L.Stevenson⟩ ⟨the cultural ~s of the time —J.D.Hart⟩ **c** *obs* : APPETENCY 2 **3** *archaic* : an object of desire ⟨power being the natural ~ of princes —Jonathan Swift⟩ **syn** see DESIRE
ap·pe·ti·tion \ˌapəˈtishən\ *n* -S [L *appetition-, appetitio*, fr. *appetitus* + *-ion-, -io* -ion] : a longing for or seeking after something : DESIRE ⟨something which creates an informed ~ for the good —R.M.Weaver⟩
ap·pe·ti·tious \ˌapəˈtishəs\ *adj, archaic* : suited to appetite ⟨thick slabs of ~ meat —William Sansom⟩
ap·pet·i·tive \(ˈ)aˈped·əd·iv, əˈp-\ *adj* [MF *appetitif*, fr. ML *appetitivus*, fr. L *appetitus* appetite + *-ivus* -ive] : belonging or relating to appetite ⟨~ needs⟩ ⟨~ behavior⟩
ap·pe·tit·ost \ˈäpəˌtēd-ˌüst\ *n* -S [Dan, fr. *appetit* appetite (fr. G, fr. MHG, fr. MF *apetit*) + *ost* cheese; akin to OSwed *öster* cheese, ON *ostr* — more at JUICE] : a soft Danish cheese made from sour buttermilk
ap·pe·tiz·er *also* **ap·pe·tis·er** \ˈapəˌtīzə(r)\ *n* -S **1** : a food or drink that stimulates the appetite and is usu. served before a meal (as a canapé, hors d'oeuvre, aperitif, or cocktail) **2** : something that stimulates a desire for more ⟨the street events are but an ~ to the carnival —Louise Gerdts⟩ ⟨a mere ~ for the more formidable pleasure of reading the whole —*New Yorker*⟩ ⟨the preliminaries were an effective ~ for the main bout⟩
appetizer wine *n* : an extra-dry to semisweet fortified wine (as sherry or vermouth) usu. served before a meal or used as a cocktail ingredient
ap·pe·tiz·ing *also* **ap·pe·tis·ing** \-īziŋ, -zēŋ\ *adj* : appealing to the appetite esp. in appearance ⟨~ fruit⟩ ⟨an ~ newcomer from Hollywood —Wolcott Gibbs⟩ ⟨an expert at preparing ~ dishes⟩ **syn** see PALATABLE
ap·pe·tiz·ing·ly *adv* : in an appetizing manner
ap·pin·ite \ˈapəˌnīt\ *n* -S [*Appin*, Loch Linnhe, Scotland, its locality + E *-ite*] : any of a group of melanocratic hornblende-rich syenite, monzonite, or diorite rocks
appl *abbr* **1** appeal **2** applied; applicable
ap·pla·nate \ˈapləˌnāt, (ˈ)aˈplāˌn-\ *adj* [ML *applanatus*, past part. of *applanare* to flatten, fr. L *ad-* + LL *planare* to flatten, fr. L *planus* even — more at FIELD] : flattened or horizontally expanded ⟨the ~ thallus of certain liverworts and lichens⟩
ap·plaud \əˈplȯd\ *vb* -ED/-ING/-S [MF or L; MF *applaudir*, fr. L *applaudere*, fr. *ad-* + *plaudere* to beat, clap, applaud] *vi* : to express approval esp. by clapping the hands repeatedly and usu. loudly ⟨the audience ~*ed* vigorously⟩ ~ *vt* **1** : to express approval of : PRAISE, COMMEND ⟨the only foreign policy which a democratic public opinion can ~ —A.J.P.Taylor⟩ **2** : to show approval of esp. by clapping the hands ⟨everywhere on the streets there were Romans who ~*ed* the passing troops —Eric Linklater⟩ ⟨spectators ~*ing* his performance⟩
ap·plaud·a·ble \-dəbəl\ *adj* : worthy of being applauded — **ap·plaud·a·bly** \-dəblē, -li\ *adv*
ap·plaud·ing·ly *adv* : in an applauding manner
ap·plause \əˈplȯz\ *n* -S [ML *applausus*, fr. L, clashing noise, fr. *applausus*, past part. of *applaudere*] : approval publicly expressed (as by clapping hands) : marked commendation ⟨long and vociferous ~ —A.R.Williams⟩ ⟨the kind of ~ every really creative writer wants —Robert Tallant⟩
ap·plaus·ive \əˈplȯziv, aˈ-, -ȯs-\ *adj* [ML *applausivus*, fr. *applausus* + L *-ivus* -ive] **1** *obs* : APPLAUDABLE **2** *archaic* : expressing approval or applause — **ap·plaus·ive·ly** *adv*
ap·ple \ˈapəl\ *n* -S *often attrib* [ME *appel*, fr. OE *æppel*; akin to OHG *apful, afful*, ON *apall, epli*, Crimean Goth *apel*, OIr *ubull*, OSlav *ablŭko, jablŭko*] **1 a** : the pome fruit of any tree of the genus *Malus* being important economically esp. in No. America, Europe, and Australasia and markedly variable but usu. round in shape and red, yellow, or greenish in color ⟨~ dumpling⟩ **b** : any fruit or other vegetable production that resembles the apple ⟨balsam ~⟩ ⟨oak ~⟩ ⟨thorn ~⟩ **2 a** : a tree of the genus *Malus* : APPLE TREE **b** : the wood of the apple tree **3** : something that resembles an apple esp. in shape (as a baseball) or color ⟨~ cheeks⟩ **4** : APPLE OF ONE'S EYE **5** *Austral* : any of several trees: as **a** : a eucalypt (*Eucalyptus stuartiana*) with pendulous branches and soft whitish bark **b** : any tree of a genus of the myrtle family having opposite leaves and flowers in corymbose panicles
apple anthracnose *n* : a disease of the apple, pear, and quince in the Pacific coast region of northwestern America caused by a fungus (*Neofabraea malicorticis*) producing limb cankers and esp. after storage a rot of the fruit — called also *black spot*
apple aphid *n* : an aphid that infests the apple; *specif* : a bright-green aphid (*Aphis pomi*) that feeds on and causes curling of apple leaves — called also *green apple aphid;* see ROSY APPLE APHID, WOOLLY APPLE APHID
apple banana *n* [so called fr. its applelike flavor] : a banana (*Musa sapientum cubensis*) having fruit much smaller than that of the common banana and with a very thin skin
apple bee *n* : a bee at which apples are prepared for drying
ap·ple·ber·ry \ˈ==- — *see* BERRY\ *n* **1** : an Australian woody vine (*Billardiera scandens*) with showy flowers **2** : the pleasant subacid fruit of the appleberry
apple blight *n* **1** : any of various plant lice attacking the apple; *esp* : WOOLLY APPLE APHID **2** : FIRE BLIGHT
appleblossom \ˈ==ˌ==\ *or* **appleblossom pink** *n* : a grayish red that is bluer, less strong, and slightly lighter than bois de rose, bluer and slightly less strong than Pompeian red, and bluer, lighter, and stronger than livid brown
apple blossom weevil *n* : a European weevil (*Anthonomus pomorum*) that is related to the American boll weevil and that feeds as an adult on the leaves of apple and lays its eggs in the young flower buds where the developing larva feeds and causes the bud to turn brown and fail to open
apple blotch *n* : BLOTCH 2a
apple box *n, Austral* : any of several trees of the genus *Eucalyptus* with gray bark (as *E. bicolor* and *E. baueriana*)
apple brandy *n* : brandy that is distilled from fermented apple juice
apple bucculatrix *n* : a small tineid moth (*Bucculatrix pomifoliella*) having a yellowish green brown-headed larva that feeds upon apple leaves
apple butter *n* : a spread made of apples stewed down with sugar and spices usu. in cider
apple canker *n* : any of several diseases of the apple tree that produce cankers (as bark canker, bitter rot, black rot, blister canker, European canker, fire blight, or perennial canker)
applecart \ˈ==ˌ=\ *n* [*apple* + *cart*] : a plan, scheme, system, undertaking, or situation that is or may be overturned or disrupted often unexpectedly — used esp. with *upset* ⟨upset the whole Darwinian ~ —Julian Huxley⟩ ⟨we might make a wrong move and upset somebody's ~ —*Survey Graphic*⟩
apple cheese *n* : the cake of apple pomace from a cider press
apple curculio *n* : a small weevil (*Tachypterellus quadrigibbus*) the larva of which feeds about the core in the fruits of apple and pear
apple essence *n* : apple oil (sense 2) esp. when in alcohol solution
apple family *n* : MALACEAE
apple flea weevil *n* : a minute dull-black weevil (*Rhynchaenus pallicornis*) that feeds as an adult on the undersurface of apple and cherry leaves, the larvae burrowing and feeding within the leaves
apple fly *n* : FRUIT FLY
apple geranium *n* : NUTMEG GERANIUM
apple grain aphid *n* : a yellowish green aphid (*Rhopalosiphum fitchii*) with dark bands on the abdomen that produces its fertilized eggs on apple and related trees and feeds on their leaves in early spring but passes most of the growing season on various small grains and grasses
apple green *n* **1** : a moderate yellow green that is greener, lighter, and stronger than average moss green or mosstone and lighter and stronger than average pea green or spinach green **2** : a light yellowish green that is greener and deeper than ocean green, pistachio, or crayon green
apple grunt *n, chiefly New Eng* : a dessert made with apples and pie crust; *esp* : a deep-dish apple pie
apple gum *n* : an Australian timber tree (*Eucalyptus stuartiana*) resembling the apple tree
apple haw *n* : MAYHAW
apple head *n* : a domed or rounded skull typical of certain toy dogs — **ap·ple-head·ed** \ˈ==ˌ==\ *adj*
apple honey *n* : a clarified condensation of apple syrup used as a sweetening agent in the food industry
ap·ple·jack \-ˌjak\ *n* [*apple* + *jack* (man)] **1** : APPLE BRANDY **2** : an alcoholic beverage consisting of the central unfrozen portion of a container (as a keg) of frozen hard cider; *also* : HARD CIDER
applejohn *n, often cap* [*apple* + *John*, the name; prob. fr. St. John's Day, when it was said to get ripe] *archaic* : a variety of apple the flavor of which is said to be improved by drying
apple knocker *n* **1** *slang* : an apple picker : fruit picker **2** *slang* : HICK, RUBE **3** *slang* : one beginning a new job : BEGINNER, GREENHORN
apple leafhopper *n* : a small greenish leafhopper (*Empoasca maligna*) that injures the foliage of apple trees and many other plants; *also* : a related Australian insect (*Typhlocyba frogatti*)
apple leaf skeletonizer *n* : a small dark-brownish moth (*Psorosina hammondi*) having a brownish green caterpillar that feeds on the interveinal tissue of apple leaves
apple-leaf trumpet miner *n* : a leaf-mining caterpillar (*Tischeria malifoliella*) that injures the leaves of apple trees by excavating trumpet-shaped burrows
apple maggot *n* : the larva of a dark brown and yellowish trypetid fly (*Rhagoletis pomonella*) with dark-marked wings that burrows in and feeds on apples or sometimes other fruits and is a vector of a bacterial rot of this fruit — called also *railroad worm*
apple mealybug *n* : a mealybug (*Phenacoccus aceris*) common on apple trees in parts of Canada
apple mildew *n* **1** : a disease of the apple caused by a powdery mildew (*Podosphaera leucotricha*) **2** : the fungus that causes apple mildew
apple mint *n* : a European mint (*Mentha rotundifolia*) naturalized in the U.S.
apple moss *n* : a moss of the genus *Bartramia* having spherical capsules
apple moth *n* : a moth whose larva feeds on apple trees or fruits; *specif* : a pale brownish moth (*Tortrix postvittana*) of which the larvae feed on the leaves and fruit of apples and many other cultivated plants in Australia, New Zealand, and various Pacific islands
applenut \ˈ==ˌ=\ *n* : the apple-shaped nut of an ivory palm (*Coelococcus amicarum*) — called also *ivory nut*
apple of discord [trans. of LL *malum Discordiae*; fr. the golden apple inscribed "for the fairest" which was thrown into an assembly of the gods by the goddess Discord (L *Discordia*, Gk *Eris*) and claimed by Hera, Athena, and Aphrodite] : a subject of contention and envy ⟨the chief *apple of discord* was western lands —T.A.Bailey⟩
apple of one's eye [obs. *apple of the eye* pupil of the eye] : something highly cherished ⟨his daughter is the *apple of his eye*⟩
apple of pe·ru \-pəˈrü, -pēˈ-\ *usu cap P* [fr. *Peru*, country in So. America] **1** : a coarse herb (*Nicandra physalodes*) bearing pale blue flowers and a bladderlike fruit enclosing a dry berry **2** : JIMSONWEED
apple of sod·om \-ˈsädəm\ *usu cap S* [fr. *Sodom*, biblical city destroyed by God (Gen 10)] **1 a** : a fruit described by ancient writers as externally of fair appearance but dissolving into smoke and ashes when plucked — called also *Dead Sea apple* **b** : an empty mockery ⟨had seen the fruits of victory turn into *apples of Sodom* —R.M.Lovett⟩ **2 a** : the small yellow tomato-like fruit of a prickly shrub (*Solanum sodomeum*) **b** : a spiny herb (*Solanum carolinense*) that bears yellow and orange berries
apple oil *n* **1** : the essential oil of apples **2** : an artificially prepared oil (as amyl isovalerate) used to imitate the odor or flavor of apples
apple pandowdy *n* : PANDOWDY
apple paring *n* : APPLE BEE
apple-pie \ˈ=ˈ=\ *adj* : PERFECT, EXCELLENT, FIRST-RATE — used esp. in the phrase *apple-pie order*
apple-pie bed *n* : a bed in which as a joke the sheets are doubled like the cover of an apple turnover to prevent anyone from stretching at full length between them
apple-pol·ish \ˈ==ˌ==\ *vi* : to attempt to ingratiate oneself : TOADY ⟨this called for some extra *apple-polishing* by employees —M.S.Davis⟩ ~ *vt* : to curry favor with (as by flattery or services) ⟨he hopes to pass the course by *apple-polishing* the instructor⟩ — **apple-polisher** \ˈ==ˌ===\ *n*
apple pox *n* : BLISTER CANKER
apple red *n* : a vivid red that is yellower and slightly lighter and stronger than carmine, duller and slightly bluer than Castilian red, yellower and paler than madder crimson, bluer and duller than pimento, and bluer and slightly deeper than scarlet
apple red bug *n* : a small plump reddish bug (*Lygidea mendax*) that feeds on young apple foliage and developing fruits causing russeting, dwarfing, and catfacing of the mature apples
apple rose *n* : a rose (*Rosa pomifera*) of central Europe often cultivated for its showy scarlet fruits that are about an inch in diameter
apple rust *n* **1** : any of several diseases caused by fungi of the genus *Gymnosporangium*; *esp* : a destructive fungous disease esp. of the apple but also attacking pears and quinces that is caused by a rust (*G. juniperi-virginianae*) having its pycnial and aecial stages on the leaves and fruit of the apple and the telial stage on species of *Juniperus*, esp. a common red cedar (*J. virginiana*) **2** : the fungus causing apple rust — called also *cedar apple rust, cedar rust;* compare CEDAR APPLE
apples *pl of* APPLE
applesauce \ˈ==ˌ=\ *n* **1** : a relish or dessert made of apples sweetened and stewed to a pulp **2** *slang* : an insincere expression of opinion : an assertion that is patently absurd and usu. phrased in exaggerated terms : BUNK, BALONEY ⟨I know ~ when I hear it —Ring Lardner⟩
apple sawfly *n* : a sawfly (*Hoplocampa testudinea*) native to Europe but now established in the eastern U.S. that lays its eggs singly in the calyx or receptacle of the apple flower, the larva feeding in the core of the developing fruit
apple scab *n* : a widespread destructive disease caused by a fungus (*Venturia inaequalis*) producing dark or sooty blotches on the leaves and blackish scurfy or scablike lesions on the fruit and sometimes on the young twigs
apple scald *n* : a brown discoloration of apples in storage
apple scale *n* : any scale infesting the apple tree; *esp* : OYSTER-SHELL SCALE
apple-seed chalcid *n* : a chalcid fly (*Torymus varians*) whose larva feeds on the seed of the apple
apple shell *n* : the apple snail or its shell
apple skin worm *n* : a larval moth (*Argyrotaenia franciscana*) that is related to the red-banded leaf roller and that feeds on the surface of the developing fruits of apple and a number of other cultivated fruits
apple snail *n* : any of a number of large rounded smooth-shelled freshwater snails of the family Pilidae — see PILA
apple-squire *n, obs* : a kept gallant : PIMP
apple sucker *n* : a small jumping plant louse (*Psylla mali* or *Psyllia mali*) the larva of which feeds in and injures developing apple blossoms in Europe and eastern No. America
ap·ple·ton layer \ˈapəltən-, -tᵊn-\ *n, usu cap A* [after Sir Edward *Appleton* †1965 Eng. physicist] : F LAYER
apple tree *n* **1** : any tree that bears apples **2** *Austral* : APPLE GUM **3** : an Australian tree (*Angophora subvelutina*) that yields kino
apple tree borer *n* : a beetle having larvae that bore in apple trees: **a** : FLATHEADED APPLE TREE BORER **b** : a large beetle (*Saperda candida*) brown striped with white above and dull white beneath that is esp. destructive to apple and other fruit trees — called also *roundheaded apple tree borer*
apple tree canker *n* : APPLE CANKER
apple twig borer *n* : a small brown cylindrical beetle (*Amphicerus bicaudatus*) that bores into the twigs of esp. fruit trees
apple weevil *n* : any of several weevils that feed chiefly on apple, the adults on the foliage, the larvae in the fruit
applewife \ˈ==ˌ=\ *n, pl* **applewives** : a woman who sells apples
applewood \ˈ==ˌ=\ *n* : the wood of an apple tree esp. of the genus *Malus*
apple worm *n* : an insect larva that burrows in the interior of apples; *esp* : the larva of the codling moth
ap·pli·a·ble \əˈplīəbəl\ *adj* [ME, fr. *applien* to apply + *-able* — more at APPLY] **1** *obs* : COMPLIANT **2** : APPLICABLE — **ap·pli·a·bly** \-əblē\ *adv*
ap·pli·ance \əˈplīən(t)s\ *n* -S [*apply* + *-ance*] **1** : the act of applying or using : APPLICATION ⟨when schoolboys were punished by ~ of the birch⟩ **2** : something applied to a pur-

pose or use: as **a** *archaic* **:** DEVICE, MEASURE, STRATAGEM **b :** a piece of equipment for adapting a tool or machine to a special purpose **:** ACCESSORY, FIXTURE, ATTACHMENT **c :** a tool, instrument, or device specially designed for a particular use **:** APPARATUS ⟨fire-fighting ~*s*⟩ **d :** a household or office utensil, apparatus, instrument, or machine that utilizes a power supply, esp. electric current (as a vacuum cleaner, a refrigerator, a toaster, an air conditioner) **3** *obs* **:** obedient service **:** COMPLIANCE **syn** see IMPLEMENT, MACHINE

ap·pli·ca·bil·i·ty \ˌaplәkә'bilәd·ē, -lēk-, -әtē, -i *sometimes* әˌplik- *or* aˌplik-\ *n* -ES **:** the quality or state of being applicable

ap·pli·ca·ble \'aplәkәbәl, 'aplēk-,'aˌplik- *sometimes* ә'plik- *or* a'plik-\ *adj* [F, fr. *appliquer* to apply (fr. L *applicare* to attach to, devote to) + *-able*] **1 :** capable of being applied **:** having relevance ⟨a basic technique of musical rendition that is ~ to any piece —Virgil Thomson⟩ **2 :** fit, suitable, or right to be applied **:** APPROPRIATE ⟨prosecuted in any ~ court —*U.S. Code*⟩ **syn** see RELEVANT

ap·pli·ca·ble·ness *n* -ES **:** APPLICABILITY

applicable surfaces *n pl, math* **:** two surfaces that may be deformed one into the other without stretching or tearing

ap·pli·ca·bly \-blē,-bli\ *adj* **:** in an applicable manner

ap·pli·cant \'aplәkәnt, -lēk-\ *n* -S [L *applicant-, applicans,* pres. part. of *applicare*] **:** one who applies for something **:** one who makes a usu. formal request esp. for something of benefit to himself ⟨an ~ for a job⟩ ⟨an ~ for a scholarship⟩

applicate *adj* [L *applicatus,* past part. of *applicare*] *archaic* **:** put to use **:** APPLIED ⟨those ~ sciences that extend the power of man over the elements —Isaac Taylor †1865⟩

ap·pli·ca·tion \ˌaplә'kāshәn\ *n* -S [ME *applicacioun,* fr. ML *application-, applicatio,* fr. L, inclination, fr. *applicatus* (past part. of *applicare* to attach) + *-ion-, -io* -ion — more at APPLY] **1 :** the act of applying: **a :** the bringing to bear (as of one general statement upon another) by way of elucidation ⟨the ~ of a theory to a case⟩ **b :** employment as a means **:** specific use ⟨the ~ of certain new techniques⟩ **c :** the act of laying on or of bringing into contact ⟨the ~ of a dressing to the wound⟩ **d :** the act of fixing one's mind closely or attentively **:** assiduous attention ⟨learn by intense ~⟩ **2** *in astrology* **:** approach (as of one planet to another) **3 :** APPEAL, REQUEST, PETITION ⟨an ~ for a position⟩ ⟨an ~ to an underwriter for insurance⟩ **4 :** something applied or used in applying: as **a** (1) **:** the part of a discourse in which principles stated previously are applied to practical uses (2) **:** the moral lesson or inference to be derived from a moral tale; *esp* **:** the explicit formulation of this often given at the end of the tale **b :** something applied to the body locally as a remedial device (as a tourniquet, ointment, or poultice) **5 :** capacity of being practically applied or used **:** RELEVANCY ⟨words of varied ~⟩ **6 :** the denotation of a term in logic

¹ap·pli·ca·tive \'aplәˌkād·iv, -ˌkәd·-; ә'plikәd·-, a'-\ *adj* [obs. E *applicate* + E *-ive*] **1 :** APPLICABLE **2 :** put to use **:** APPLIED — **ap·pli·ca·tive·ly** *adv*

²applicative \"\ *n* -S **:** QUANTIFIER

ap·pli·ca·tor \'aplәˌkād·ә(r), -ātә-\ *n* -S [obs. E *applicate* to apply (fr. L *applicatus*) + E *-or*] **1 :** a device (as a cotton-tipped rod, a pad, or a nozzle) for applying substances (as medicine, cosmetics, polish, or chemical foam) **2 :** one that applies substances ⟨urges that ~*s* avoid using sprays during windy weather —*Country Gentleman*⟩

ap·pli·ca·to·ry \'aplәkәˌtōrē, ә'plik-\ *adj* [obs. E *applicate* + E *-ory*] **:** capable of being applied

ap·plied \ә'plīd\ *adj* **1 :** put to practical use **:** engaged in for a utilitarian or contributory purpose **:** concerned with concrete problems or data rather than with fundamental principles ⟨~ mathematics⟩ ⟨~ psychology⟩ ⟨technical problems in medicine, engineering, economics, and other ~ disciplines —Sidney Hook⟩ — contrasted with *pure;* compare ABSTRACT, THEORETICAL **2** *of art* **:** employed in the decoration, design, or execution of useful objects **3 :** APPLIQUÉD

applied music *n* **:** vocal or instrumental musical performance subject to instruction in college or school as contrasted with musical theory and literature — called also *practical music*

applied ornament *n* **:** appliquéd ornament **:** APPLIQUÉ

ap·pli·er \ә'plī(ә)r, -īә\ *n* -S **:** one that applies

¹ap·pli·qué \ˌaplә¦kā\ *n* -S *often attrib* [F *appliqué* (past part. of *appliquer* to put on), fr. L *applicatus,* past part. of *applicare* to attach — more at APPLY] **:** a cutout decoration of a material laid on and fastened to a larger piece of the same or different material: **a :** a design composed of various fabric shapes stitched, embroidered, or sometimes pasted onto a surface (as of a quilt, skirt, or tablecloth) **b :** a lace motif made separately and attached to a ground of net or lace **c :** a shaped piece of wood or metal attached as a decoration to furniture **d :** something usu. of metal applied decoratively (as a wall sconce)

²appliqué \"\ *vt* **appliquéd; appliquéd; appliquéing** \-kāiŋ\ **appliqués :** to apply (as a decoration or ornament) **:** OVERLAY — used esp. of fabrics ⟨of finest percale with *appliquéd* designs —*New Yorker*⟩

ap·pli·quer \ˌaplә¦kā(r)\ *n* -S **:** one that appliqués; *esp* **:** a worker who stitches monograms or ornamental patches to knitted garments

appln *abbr* application

ap·plo·sion \ә'plōzhәn, (')a¦p-\ *n* -S [*ad-* + *-plosion* (as in *explosion, implosion*)] *phonetics* **:** interruption and compression of the breath in the production of a stop

ap·plot \ә'plät, a'-\ *vt* -ED/-ING/-S [*ad-* + *plot*] *archaic* **:** to divide into parts **:** APPORTION — **ap·plot·ment** \-mәnt\ *n* -S *archaic*

ap·ply \ә'plī\ *vb* -ED/-ING/-ES [ME *applien, aplien,* fr. MF *aplier,* fr. L *applicare* to apply, attach, devote, fr. *ad-* + *plicare* to fold, twist together — more at PLY] *vt* **1 a :** to make use of as suitable, fitting, or relevant ⟨~ the rule to each situation⟩ ⟨~ an epithet to a person⟩ ⟨~ a word to a new idea⟩ **b :** to put to use esp. for some practical purpose ⟨~ knowledge⟩ **:** to use for a particular purpose or in a particular case ⟨~ money to the payment of a debt⟩ **c :** to bring into action ⟨he *applied* his brakes quickly⟩ **d :** to put into effect **:** IMPOSE ⟨~ an embargo⟩ **e** (1) **:** to place in contact ⟨~ an antiseptic to a cut⟩ **:** lay or spread on **:** OVERLAY ⟨sand the wood before ~*ing* the varnish⟩ (2) **:** SUPERPOSE ⟨~ one triangle upon another⟩ **2 :** to devote or employ diligently or with close attention ⟨~ oneself to a task⟩ ⟨~ your wits to this problem⟩ **3** *obs* **:** PRACTICE **:** carry on **:** PLY ~ *vi* **1 a :** to be in contact **:** ADHERE, FIT ⟨nails ~ in prebored holes⟩ **b :** to have a valid connection, agreement, or analogy **:** have a bearing **:** be pertinent ⟨the argument *applies* to the case⟩ **2 a** *obs* **:** to be adapted **:** SUIT **b :** to devote oneself **:** attend closely ⟨the more you ~ the quicker you will learn⟩ **3 :** to make an appeal or a request esp. formally and often in writing and usu. for something of benefit to oneself ⟨~ to an employer for a job⟩ ⟨~ to a bank for a loan⟩ **syn** see DIRECT, USE

appmt *abbr* appointment

ap·pog·gia·tu·ra \әˌpäjә'türә, -tü-\ *n* -S [It, lit., support, fr. *appoggiare* to lean, rest, fr. (assumed) VL *appodiare,* fr. L *ad-* + (assumed) VL *-podiare* (fr. L *podium* balcony) — more at PEW] **:** an accessory embellishing note or tone preceding an essential melodic note or tone and usu. written as a note of smaller size — see LONG APPOGGIATURA, SHORT APPOGGIATURA

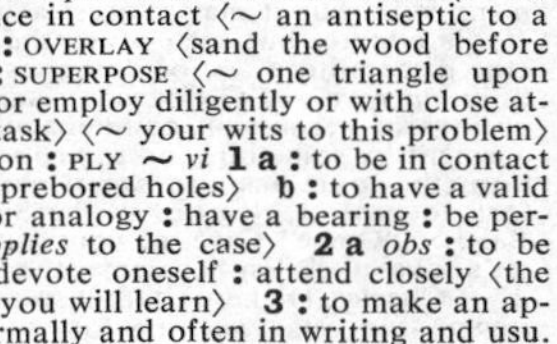

long written played
short written played
double written played

appoggiatura

ap·point \ә'pȯint\ *vb* -ED/-ING/-S [ME *appointen, apointen,* fr. MF *apointier* to arrange, settle, equip, fr. OF, fr. *a-* (fr. L *ad-*) + *-pointier* (fr. *point*) — more at POINT] *vt* **1 a** (1) **:** to fix by a decree, order, command, resolve, decision, or mutual agreement **:** ORDAIN, PRESCRIBE (2) **:** to establish with power or firmness **:** mark out **b** (1) **:** to designate (the person) in whom shall be vested an estate subject to a power of appointment (2) **:** to direct or determine the disposition of (an estate) by designating the person or persons in whom it shall vest by virtue of a power of appointment **c :** to assign, designate, or set apart by authority ⟨~ each man to his position⟩: (1) *archaic* **:** DESTINE, ASSIGN, DEVOTE ⟨sheep ~*ed* to be slain⟩ (2) **:** DESIGNATE ⟨~ an officer⟩⟨~an official⟩ **:** place in an office or post ⟨~ a superintendent⟩ ⟨~ a committee⟩ **d** (1) *archaic* **:** to arrange for a meeting with (a person) (2) *archaic* **:** to fix the time and place of ⟨~ the meeting, even at his father's house —Shak.⟩ (3) **:** to fix (the time) for an event ⟨in our places at the ~*ed* hour⟩ **2 :** to provide with necessary equipment **:** FURNISH, EQUIP **:** fit out ⟨beautifully ~*ed* public rooms —*N.Y. Times Mag.*⟩ ~ *vi* **1** *obs* **:** SETTLE, ARRANGE **2** *obs* **:** ORDAIN, DETERMINE **3** *archaic* **:** to make an engagement **:** arrange a meeting with a person **syn** see DESIGNATE, FURNISH

ap·poin·tee \әˌpȯin·'tē *also* ˌaˌp- *sometimes* aˌpȯint·'ē *or* ә'=(ˌ)=\ *n* -S [*appoint* + *-ee*] **1 :** one that is appointed (as to an office) **2 :** one to whom an estate is appointed

ap·point·ive \ә'pȯintiv, -ēv *also* -әv\ *adj* **1 :** of or relating to the act or power of appointing ⟨the president's ~ powers⟩ **2 :** subject to appointment ⟨an ~ office⟩

ap·point·ment \ә'pȯintmәnt\ *n* -S [ME *appointement, apointement,* fr. MF *apointement,* fr. *apointier* to arrange + *-ment* — more at APPOINT] **1 :** act of appointing: **a** *obs* **:** the act of coming to terms of capitulation **b :** designation by virtue of a vested power of a person to enjoy an estate or other specific property subject to that power **c :** designation of a person to hold a nonelective office or perform a function ⟨exercise the right of ~⟩ **2 a** *obs* **:** terms made with an opponent (as for surrender) **:** CAPITULATION, AGREEMENT **b** *archaic* **:** ORDINANCE, DISPENSATION ⟨the merciful ~ of Providence⟩ **c** (1) **:** OFFICE, POSITION ⟨he received the ~ of ambassador⟩ (2) *archaic* **:** a monetary allowance esp. to a public officer **:** PERQUISITE — usu. used in pl. **3 :** an arrangement for a meeting **:** ENGAGEMENT ⟨an ~ for an interview⟩ ⟨broke his ~ with the dentist⟩ **4 :** equipment or furnishings esp. for a hotel or a ship **:** ACCOUTERMENTS — usu. used in pl. ⟨~*s* for a soldier or a horse⟩ ⟨famous for the luxury and comfort of its ~*s*⟩ ⟨the coat of arms appeared on the ~*s* of the knight and his mount⟩ **syn** see ENGAGEMENT

ap·poin·tor \әˌpȯin·'tȯ(ә)r *also* ˌaˌp- *or* ә'pȯintәr *sometimes* әˌpȯint·'ȯ(ә)r *or* ә'pȯin·ˌtȯ- *or* ә'pȯint·ˌȯ-\ *n* -S **:** one that appoints an estate under a power of appointment

appoints *pres 3d sing of* APPOINT

¹ap·port \ә'pō(ә)rt, a'-, -ȯ(ә)rt\ *n* -S [ME *aport, apport,* alter. (influenced by ME *aport, apport* offering, contribution, fr. MF *aport,* fr. OF, fr. *aporter* to bring, fr. L *apportare*) of *port* — more at PORT] **1** *obs* **:** BEARING, PORT **2** [F, lit., action of bringing, thing brought, fr. *apporter* to bring, fr. L *apportare*] **:** motion or production of an object by a spiritualist medium without apparent physical agency; *also* **:** the object so produced

²apport \"\ *vt* -ED/-ING/-S [prob. fr. F *apporter,* lit., to bring, fr. L *apportare,* fr. *ad-* + *portare* to carry — more at PORT] **:** to produce (a material object) at a spiritualist séance without any apparent physical means

ap·por·tion \ә'pōrshәn, -orsh-,-ōәsh-,-ȯ(ә)sh- *also* a'-\ *vt* **apportioned; apportioned; apportioning** \-sh(ә)niŋ\ **apportions** [MF *apportionner,* fr. *a-* (fr. L *ad-*) + *portionner* to portion — more at PORTION] **:** to divide and assign in proportion **:** divide and distribute proportionately **:** make an apportionment of **:** portion out **:** ALLOT ⟨~ time among various employments⟩; *specif* **:** to assign (a capitation or other direct federal tax) among the states in proportion to population as provided in the U.S. Constitution

syn PORTION, PARCEL, RATION, PRORATE: APPORTION applies to distribution on an equitable, or suitable basis ⟨representatives shall be *apportioned* among the several states according to their respective numbers, counting the whole number of persons in each —*U. S. Constitution*⟩ ⟨he will be a brave man who will *apportion* responsibility for Britain's attitude between parties and classes —Roy Lewis & Angus Maude⟩ ⟨nature seems to have *apportioned* the voices of many of her creatures with sensitive regard for their environment —William Beebe⟩ PORTION may apply to distribution of more or less equal shares ⟨firing 270 rounds *portioned* equally among pistols of three calibers —*Time*⟩ PARCEL, usu. used with *out,* may indicate division into many small pieces, lots, or units for subsequent delivery, claim, or execution ⟨being compelled to *parcel* out its inadequate combat resources sparingly between the many vulnerable points —Herbert Feis⟩ ⟨Mother would *parcel* out her year: three months with Herbert and Mabel, three with Carrie and Roland —Victoria Sackville-West⟩ RATION may apply to division by authority, presumably equitably, on some such basis as need ⟨where capital is short, it must be *rationed* intelligently, in the same way as gasoline and sugar were *rationed* in wartime —A.B.Lans⟩ ⟨he *rationed* his time, told visitors he could give them three minutes —*Time*⟩ PRORATE suggests equitable proportional distribution according to authority or common agreement ⟨the entire field was to be put in truck crops, and the yield *prorated* to the workers —Russell Lord⟩ **syn** see in addition ALLOT

apportionate *vt* -ED/-ING/-S [ML *apportionatus,* past part. of *apportionare,* fr. MF *apportionner*] *obs* **:** APPORTION

ap·por·tion·ment \-shәnmәnt\ *n* -S [prob. fr. MF *apportionnement,* fr. *apportionner* + *-ment*] **1 :** the act or result of apportioning ⟨the ~ of lands among settlers⟩ **2 :** the division of rights or liabilities among several persons entitled or liable to them in accordance with their respective interests (as where a contractor is given part payment in return for part performance or where rents are divided according to some scale of interest) **3 :** the apportioning of representatives or taxes to the several states according to U. S. law

apportionment clause *n* **:** a clause in an insurance policy that prescribes the method of determining the insurer's portion of liability for loss where property is covered by other insurance

ap·pose \a'pōz\ *vt* -ED/-ING/-S [MF *aposer,* fr. OF, fr. *a-* (fr. L *ad-*) + *poser* to put, place — more at POSE] **1** *archaic* **:** to place opposite or before **:** apply (one thing) to another ⟨~ a seal to a document⟩ **2 :** to place in juxtaposition or proximity ⟨chromosomes . . . with their transverse bands exactly *apposed* —*Discovery*⟩

ap·po·site \'apәzәt *sometimes* ә'päz- *or* a'päz-\ *adj* [L *appositus,* fr. past part. of *apponere* to place near, apply to, fr. *ad-* + *ponere* to put — more at POSITION] **:** highly pertinent or appropriate **:** RELEVANT, APT ⟨examples more or less ~ to one subject —Edward Clodd⟩ ⟨~ illustrations may be found in recent statutes —B.N.Cardozo⟩ ⟨her use of anecdote is ~ —Carl Van Vechten⟩ **syn** see RELEVANT

ap·po·site·ly *adv* **:** in an apposite manner **:** RELEVANTLY

ap·po·site·ness *n* -ES **:** the quality or state of being apposite **:** APTNESS

ap·po·si·tion \ˌapә'zishәn\ *n* -S [ME *apposicioun,* fr. ML *apposition-, appositio,* fr. LL, act of setting before, fr. L *appositus* (past part. of *apponere*) + *-ion-, -io* -ion] **1 a :** a grammatical construction that consists of two nouns or noun equivalents referring to the same person or thing, standing in the same syntactical relation to the rest of the sentence without being joined to each other by a coordinating conjunction, and typically adjacent to each other (as *the poet* and *Burns* in "a biography of the poet Burns", *my sister* and *Jane* in "this is my sister Jane", *John* and *a bashful child* in "John, a bashful child, was afraid of strangers", or *the fact* and *that he is rich* in "the fact that he is rich is obvious") **b :** the relation of one of such a pair of nouns or noun equivalents to the other, esp. of the second to the first **2** [F fr. LL *apposition-, appositio*] **a** *archaic* **:** the application of one thing to another (as a seal to a document) **b :** the placing of things in juxtaposition or proximity; *specif* **:** deposition of successive layers upon those already present (as in cell walls) — compare INTUSSUSCEPTION **3 :** the state of being in juxtaposition or proximity (as in the drawing together of cut edges of tissue in healing)

ap·po·si·tion·al \¦==¦=shәn°l, -shnәl\ *adj* **:** relating to or being in apposition — **ap·po·si·tion·al·ly** \-shәn°lē,-shnәlē, -li\ *adv*

apposition beach *n* **:** one of a series of beaches successively formed on the seaward side of an older beach

apposition eye *n* **:** a compound eye that is characteristic of diurnal insects and in which entering light reaches the retina of each ommatidium as a single spot and the image is a composite of all the spots — compare SUPERPOSITION EYE

¹ap·pos·i·tive \ә'päzәd·iv, -әtiv *also* a'-\ *adj* [*apposition* + *-ive*] **1 :** standing in grammatical apposition ⟨an ~ noun⟩ **:** being a grammatical apposition ⟨an ~ construction⟩ **2** *of an adjective or adjective equivalent* **:** standing in a relation to its noun like that of the second noun or noun equivalent to the first in an apposition (as *shy* and *embarrassed* in "the child, shy and embarrassed, said nothing") — compare ADHERENT 4, ATTRIBUTIVE 1a, ¹PREDICATE 2 — **appositively** *adv*

²appositive \"\ *n* -S **:** an appositive noun, noun equivalent, adjective, or adjective equivalent

appr *abbr* apprentice

ap·prais·al \ә'prāzәl, a'-\ *also* **ap·praise·ment** \-zmәnt\ *n* -S [*appraise* + *-al* or *-ment*] **1 :** an act of estimating or evaluating (as quality, status, or character) esp. by one fitted to judge ⟨a more realistic ~ of the difficulties inherent in the undertaking —J.B.Conant⟩ ⟨a swift ~ by shrewd eyes —George Whiting⟩; *also* **:** the stated result of such an act ⟨an overgenerous ~ of his worth⟩ ⟨a detailed ~ of a program⟩ **2 :** a valuation of property by the estimate of an authorized person; *specif* **:** the valuation of imported goods according to methods set forth in the tariff laws of a country

appraisal clause *n* **:** the provision in fire and certain other insurance policies for a procedure to be followed in determining the amount of loss when the insurer and insured cannot agree

ap·praise \ә'prāz, a'-\ *vt* -ED/-ING/-S [ME *appreisen,* modif. (influenced by *preisen* to set a value on) of MF *aprisier* — more at APPRIZE] **1 :** to set a value on (as goods, lands, or the estate of a deceased person) **:** estimate the amount of (as a loss by fire) **2 :** to judge and analyze the worth, significance or status of; *esp* **:** to give a definitive expert judgment of the merit, rank, or importance of ⟨~ recent American poetry⟩ ⟨~ a political trend⟩ ⟨~ the cost of an objective in terms of human life —O.N.Bradley⟩ **syn** see ESTIMATE

ap·prais·er \-zә(r)\ *n* -S **1 :** one that appraises (as real estate for determining tax rates or sales prices, imported articles for the assessing of tariff duties, damaged goods for salvage, or the property of bankrupt businesses for auction-sale value of assets) **2 :** one that estimates status, excellence, or potentiality; *specif* **:** one that as a guide to the establishment of new businesses or advertising contracts studies a neighborhood to appraise its buying power, class of goods used, or services desired **3 :** one that determines the authenticity of works of art by means of X ray and other scientific methods of examination

appraiser's store *n* **:** a storeroom or building where goods are held by U.S. customs officials for appraisal

ap·prais·ing·ly *adv* **:** in an appraising manner ⟨looked about him ~ —Erle Stanley Gardner⟩

ap·prais·ive \-āziv\ *adj* **:** forming an appraisal ⟨both aesthetic and ethical discourse . . . are treated as primarily ~ in their mode of signifying —P.B.Rice⟩ **:** APPRAISING ⟨so many harshly ~ eyes fixed upon her —I.S.Cobb⟩

apprecate *vt* -ED/-ING/-S [L *apprecatus,* past part. of *apprecari,* fr. *ad-* + *precari* to pray — more at PRAY] *obs* **:** to pray for — **apprecation** *n* -S *obs* — **apprecatory** *adj, obs*

ap·pre·cia·ble \ә'prēshәbәl *sometimes* -rishә- *or* -rēshēә-\ *adj* [F *appréciable,* fr. MF *appreciable,* fr. *apprecier, aprecier* to appraise (fr. LL *appretiare*) + *-able*] **:** capable of being perceived and recognized or of being weighed and appraised ⟨seldom capable of any ~ color change —W.H.Dowdeswell⟩ ⟨voters were unable to exert any ~ influence upon the selection of the candidates put forward by their party —F.A.Ogg & P.O.Ray⟩ **syn** see PERCEPTIBLE

ap·pre·cia·bly \-әblē, -li\ *adv* **:** to an appreciable extent or degree **:** NOTICEABLY

ap·pre·ci·ate \ә'prēshēˌāt *sometimes* -rishē- *rarely* -rēsē-, *usu* -ād·+V\ *vb* -ED/-ING/-S [ML & LL; ML *appreciatus* (past part. of *appretiare* to value, esteem), fr. LL, past part. of *appretiare* to appraise, put a price on, fr. L *ad-* + *pretium* price, value — more at PRICE] *vt* **1 a** (1) **:** to evaluate highly or approve warmly often with expressions or tokens of liking ⟨to be loved, to be *appreciated,* to be admired and highly valued —Theodor Reik⟩ (2) **:** to judge or evaluate the worth, merit, quality, or significance of **:** comprehend with knowledge, judgment, and discrimination ⟨incapable of *appreciating* the difference between right and wrong —B.N.Cardozo⟩ ⟨*appreciated* that a new era was beginning —David Fairchild⟩ ⟨my power of *appreciating* your many charms and my desire that you should become my wife —Samuel Butler †1902⟩ **b :** to judge with heightened perception or understanding: (1) **:** to be critically and emotionally aware of delicate subtle aesthetic or artistic values ⟨he could not ~ artistic quality⟩ (2) **:** to be fully sensible of often through or as if through personal experience ⟨must be experienced to be *appreciated* —Rudyard Kipling⟩ **c :** to esteem highly and express thanks or gratitude for ⟨I ~ your kindness but I should be much happier alone —Louis Bromfield⟩ **2 :** to raise the value of **:** increase the market price of ⟨from 1820 onwards gold was mainly *appreciated* —J.A.Todd⟩ — opposed to *depreciate* ~ *vi* **:** to rise in value or quantity ⟨apples *appreciated* 2 to 5 cents per box —*Wall Street Jour.*⟩ ⟨the calving and lambing season is good and numbers greatly ~ —James Stevenson-Hamilton⟩

syn VALUE, PRIZE, TREASURE, CHERISH: APPRECIATE connotes recognition of worth or merit through wise judgment, analytical perception, and keen insight ⟨the author *appreciates* the historical development of the Roman law and the character of its various sources —H.O.Taylor⟩ ⟨he liked to be near people and have his talent as a whittler *appreciated* —Sherwood Anderson⟩ It is rarely used without these notions, although in less precise use it may carry added notions of warm hearty approval or full or delicate enjoyment ⟨attach herself to someone who knew how to *appreciate* the fullness of her ardor —Morley Callaghan⟩ ⟨youth *appreciates* that sort of recognition which is the subtlest form of flattery age can offer —Joseph Conrad⟩ In this series VALUE is less rich in suggestion than the others. It may suggest judgment blending the analytic and the subjective ⟨she only *valued* rest to herself when it came in the midst of other people's labor —Thomas Hardy⟩ ⟨suddenly Gard was smitten by the tragedy of plain women; to be *valued,* but not loved —Mary Austin⟩ PRIZE stresses high evaluation, often subjective; it may suggest a sense of pride in acquisition or possession and reluctance to lose or be deprived of the thing in question ⟨his grandfather's two *prized* standing cups —T.B.Costain⟩ ⟨we had *prized* our solitude when we had to fight for it —Virginia D. Dawson & Betty D. Wilson⟩ ⟨what is freedom and why is it *prized?* —John Dewey⟩ TREASURE, used with things considered or felt to be of extreme value, stresses notions of storing or of jealous guarding against loss or theft, notions of cleaving to and preserving ⟨that the volumes I write will be *treasured* up with the utmost care for ages —William Cowper⟩ ⟨ecstatic moments for him, to be *treasured* and conned over —T.B.Costain⟩ ⟨if . . . I have your friendship, I shall *treasure* it —Edna S. V. Millay⟩ CHERISH, rich in affective suggestion, adds the idea of deep-seated, perhaps tacit affection or intimate fond reflection on ⟨he *cherished* a painfully nostalgic memory of his childhood sweetheart —Saxe Commins⟩ ⟨troubled by the conflict of many ideas in his fruitful mind, and ardently *cherishing* those he thought true and good —Carl Van Doren⟩ ⟨*cherish* their allegiance to Christ in solitude and silence —Katharine F. Gerould⟩ **syn** see in addition UNDERSTAND

appreciated surplus *n* **:** a surplus due to increase in the book value of the capital assets of a corporation

ap·pre·ci·a·tion \әˌprēshē'āshәn *also* -rēsē'- *sometimes* -rishē- — -ēsē- *is more freq in "appreciation" than in "appreciate", as a result of sh- dissimilation*\ *n* -S [F & LL; F *appréciation,* fr. MF *appreciation,* prob. fr. *apprecier* + *-ation;* LL *appretiation-, appretiatio* valuation, fr. *appretiatus* + L *-ion-, -io* -ion — more at APPRECIABLE] **1 a :** recognition through the senses esp. with delicacy of perception ⟨an ~ of fine shades of meaning⟩; *specif* **:** sensitive awareness of worth or esp. aesthetic value ⟨his fine ~ of painting⟩ **b :** ESTIMATION, JUDGMENT ⟨~ of quality or character⟩; *specif* **:** a written or spoken critical estimate esp. when favorable ⟨write a brief ~ of a book⟩ **c :** expression of gratification and approval, of gratitude, or of aesthetic satisfaction ⟨in ~ of your work⟩ ⟨we offer this small token by way of ~⟩ **d :** recognition of aesthetic values that is cultivated in students esp. through courses emphasizing enjoyment and discrimination rather than historical background or scholarly method **2 :** increase in exchangeable value (as of money, goods, or property) — opposed to *depreciation*

ap·pre·cia·tive \ə'prēshə|d·iv, |tiv *sometimes* -rishə| *or* -rēshē,ā| *or* -rēshēə|\ *also* **ap·pre·cia·to·ry** \ə'prēshə,tōrē, -tȯ-, -ri *sometimes* -rishə,- *or* -rēshēə,-\ *adj* **:** having or showing appreciation ⟨an ~ audience⟩ ⟨~ of a beautiful landscape⟩ — **ap·pre·cia·tive·ly** *adv* — **ap·pre·cia·tive·ness** *n* -ES

ap·pre·ci·a·tor \ə'prēshē,ād·ə(r), -ātə- *sometimes* -rishē- *rarely* -rēsē-\ *n* -S **:** one that appreciates ⟨the artist and his ~*s* —Hunter Mead⟩

ap·pre·hend \ˌaprə̇ˈhend, -rēˌ-\ *vb* -ED/-ING/-S [ME *apprehenden*, fr. L *apprehendere* to grasp mentally, seize, fr. *ad-* + *prehendere* to seize — more at PREHENSILE] *vt* **1 a** *obs* **:** to come to know **:** LEARN **b :** to lay hold of with the understanding **:** recognize the existence or meaning of **c** *obs* **:** to sense emotionally **:** APPRECIATE **d :** to anticipate esp. with anxiety, dread, or fear **e :** to become aware of through the senses ⟨~ the flame of a candle⟩ **f :** to view or consider as being of a certain description ⟨~ eternal truths⟩ **2 a** *obs* **:** to take possession of **:** take hold of **b :** to take (a person) in legal process **:** ARREST, SEIZE ⟨~ a thief⟩ ~ *vi* **:** to receive knowledge or grasp notions **syn** see FORESEE

ap·pre·hen·si·bil·i·ty \ˌ==ˌhen(t)sə'biləd·ē\ *n* -ES **:** the quality or state of being apprehensible

ap·pre·hen·si·ble \ˌ==ˌhen(t)səbəl\ *adj* [LL *apprehensibilis*, fr. L *apprehensus* (past part. of *apprehendere*) + *-ibilis* -ible] **:** capable of being apprehended or conceived — **ap·pre·hen·si·bly** \-blē, -i\ *adv*

ap·pre·hen·sion \ˌ=='henchən\ *n* -S [ME *apprehensioun*, fr. LL *apprehension-*, *apprehensio*, fr. L *apprehensus* (past part. of *apprehendere*) + *-ion-*, *-io* -ion] **1 a** *obs* **:** the act of learning **b :** the faculty of grasping with the intellect **:** UNDERSTANDING ⟨a man of dull ~⟩ **c :** the act of grasping with the intellect **:** INTELLECTION, PERCEPTION **d** (1) **:** the result of apprehending mentally **:** OPINION, CONCEPTION ⟨according to popular ~⟩ (2) **:** NOTION, SENTIMENT, IDEA ⟨to mistrust one's own ~*s*⟩ **e** *philos* **:** the act of mentally grasping or of bringing before the mind; *specif* **:** a perception that is comparatively simple, direct, and immediate and has as its object something considered to be directly and nondiscursively understandable; *broadly* **:** an intellectual awareness **:** a relatively simple or unreflective idea, opinion, or belief **f** *in traditional logic* **:** that one of the three operations of thought by which one grasps what is expressed by a term or name — contrasted with *judgment* and *reasoning* **g** *psychol* **:** the observing of an object as a whole without distinguishing its parts **2 :** the taking by legal, esp. criminal, process **:** ARREST ⟨~ of a felon⟩ **3 :** anticipation esp. of unfavorable things **:** suspicion or fear esp. of future evil

syn FOREBODING, MISGIVING, PRESENTIMENT: APPREHENSION may refer to a fear, sometimes vague, that obsesses and keeps one anxious about the future ⟨peasants who have survived a famine will be perpetually haunted by memory and *apprehension* —Bertrand Russell⟩ ⟨daily *apprehension* lest the wholesome sons and daughters whom they commit to a college return to them as brazen fools without culture —W.L.Sullivan⟩ FOREBODING applies to oppressive anticipatory fear, often ill-grounded, ill-defined, or superstitious ⟨my wife was curiously silent throughout the drive and seemed oppressed with *forebodings* of evil —H.G.Wells⟩ ⟨there was a sadness and constraint about all persons that day, which filled Mr. Esmond with gloomy *forebodings* —W.M.Thackeray⟩ MISGIVING applies to sudden uneasy fear and worried doubt rather than due anxiety or dread ⟨a *misgiving* arose within him that such dread experiences would revive the old danger —Charles Dickens⟩ ⟨his self-confidence had given place to a *misgiving* that he had been making a fool of himself —G.B.Shaw⟩ PRESENTIMENT indicates a shadowy, almost mystical, intuitive perception of some coming event, often unpleasant and fearful ⟨this unfortunate accident has upset me. I have a horrible *presentiment* that something of the kind may happen to me —Oscar Wilde⟩

ap·pre·hen·sive \ˌ==ˌhen(t)siv, -ēv *also* -əv\ *adj* [ME, fr. ML *apprehensivus*, fr. L *apprehensus* + *-ivus* -ive] **1** *archaic* **:** serving for apprehension **2 :** capable of apprehending or quick to do so **:** APT, DISCERNING ⟨a kind and ~ friend —Nathaniel Hawthorne⟩ **3 :** having apprehension **:** KNOWING, CONSCIOUS, COGNIZANT ⟨~ of one's youthful folly⟩ **4 :** anticipative of something unfavorable **:** fearful of what may be coming **:** in dread of possible evil or harm ⟨~ of danger⟩ ⟨~ for one's life⟩ **5 :** relating to the faculty of apprehension ⟨judgment is implied in every ~ act —William Hamilton †1856⟩ — **ap·pre·hen·sive·ly** *adv* — **ap·pre·hen·sive·ness** *n* -ES

[1]**ap·pren·tice** \ə'prentə̇s\ *n* -S *often attrib* [ME *apprentis*, *aprentis*, fr. MF *aprentis*, fr. OF, fr. *aprendre* to learn, fr. L *apprendere* to grasp mentally, seize, contr. of *apprehendere* — more at APPREHEND] **1 a :** one who is bound by indentures or by legal agreement to serve another person for a certain time with a view to learning an art or trade in consideration of instruction therein and formerly usu. of maintenance by the master **b :** one who is learning by practical experience under skilled workers a trade, art, or calling usu. for a prescribed period of time and at a prescribed rate of pay ⟨~ bricklayer⟩ ⟨actor's ~⟩ ⟨~ teacher⟩ **2 a** *English law, archaic* **:** a barrister-at-law of less than 16 years' standing and ranking below a serjeant-at-law **b :** an enlisted man in the U.S. Navy who has completed recruit training at a training center ashore but who has not been promoted to seaman or airman **c :** a jockey who has yet to win 40 races or has ridden less than a year **d :** the lowest rank in the exploring program of the Boy Scouts of America **3 :** one not well versed in a subject **:** an inexperienced person **:** TYRO, NOVICE ⟨an ~ in suffering and humiliation —Saul Bellow⟩ **syn** see NOVICE

[2]**apprentice** \"\ *vt* -ED/-ING/-S **:** to bind by contract or indenture; *also* **:** to set at work as an apprentice ⟨at the age of sixteen he was *apprenticed* to a blacksmith —H.U.Faulkner⟩

apprenticeage *n* -S [MF *aprentissage*, fr. *aprentis* apprentice + *-age*] *obs* **:** APPRENTICESHIP

apprenticehood *n* -S [ME *apprentishod*, *aprentishod*, fr. *apprentis*, *aprentis* apprentice + *-hod* -hood] *obs* **:** APPRENTICESHIP

ap·pren·tice·ship \-tə̇(sh),ship *also* -tə̇s,sh-\ *n* -S **1 :** service or status as an apprentice or novice ⟨begin one's ~⟩ ⟨his early intellectual ~ —Paul Willen⟩ **2 :** the time during which an apprentice or novice serves ⟨the customary three years of ~ —*Current Biog.*⟩ ⟨a writer with a long ~ in reporting the inner and outer lives of the maladjusted —R.N.Denney⟩

ap·pressed \ə'prest, (')aˌp-\ *or* **ad·pressed** \(')adˌp-\ *adj* [L *appressus*, *adpressus* (past part. of *apprimere*, *adprimere*, fr. *ad-* + *primere* to press) + E *-ed* — more at PRESS] **:** pressed close to or lying flat against something ⟨closely ~ to the lower surface of the much larger dorsal lobe —D.H.Campbell⟩ ⟨igneous rocks . . . folded and closely ~ by this force —L.V.Pirsson⟩

ap·pres·sion \a'preshən\ *n* -S **:** the state of being appressed

ap·pres·so·ri·al \ˌaprəˌsōrēəl\ *adj* [NL *appressorium* + E *-al*] **:** belonging or relating to an appressorium

ap·pres·so·ri·um \ˌapre'sōrēəm\ *n, pl* **appresso·ria** \-rēə\ [NL, fr. L *appressus* + NL *-orium*] **:** the flattened, thickened, or tuftlike tip of a hyphal branch by which certain parasitic fungi are attached to their hosts, giving rise to either haustoria or infection hyphae

ap·prise *also* **ap·prize** \ə'prīz, a'-\ *vt* -ED/-ING/-S [F *appris* (fem. *apprise*), past part. of *apprendre* to learn, teach, inform, fr. OF *aprendre* to learn, teach — more at APPRENTICE] **1 :** to give oral or written notice to (a person) **:** INFORM ⟨Mrs. Berry came in to ~ Lucy that she was wanted —George Meredith⟩ ⟨Emily was fairly *apprised* of the situation —Mary Austin⟩ **2 :** to give notice of (a thing) **syn** see INFORM

ap·priz·al *also* **ap·pris·al** \-zəl\ *n* -S **:** APPRAISAL

ap·prize *also* **ap·prise** \-īz\ *vt* -ED/-ING/-S [ME *apprisen*, *aprisen*, fr. MF *aprisier*, fr. OF, fr. *a-* (fr. L *ad-*) + *prisier* to value, appraise — more at PRIZE] **1** *obs* **:** to put a value upon **:** APPRAISE **2 :** to value or appreciate ⟨learn to ~ knowledge for the sake of knowledge —*U.S. Daily*⟩ **3** *Scots law, obs* **:** to make a judicial sale of (a heritable estate) for the benefit of a creditor — compare ADJUDGE 5

ap·prize·ment *also* **ap·prise·ment** \-mənt\ *n* -S [ME *apprisement*, fr. MF *aprisement*, fr. *aprisier* + *-ment*] *archaic* **:** APPRAISAL

ap·priz·er \-zə(r)\ *n* -S **1** *archaic* **:** APPRAISER **2** *Scots law* **:** a creditor who had an apprizing made

appro *abbr* **1** approbation **2** approval

[1]**ap·proach** \ə'prōch\ *vb* -ED/-ING/-ES [ME *approchen*, *aprochen*, fr. OF *aprochier*, fr. LL *appropiare*, fr. L *ad-* + LL *-propiare* (fr. L *prope* near); akin to L *pro* before, for — more at FOR] *vt* **1 a :** to come or go near or nearer to in place or time **:** draw nearer to ⟨we ~*ed* the city⟩ ⟨~ the hour of departure with dread⟩ **b :** to come or go near or nearer to in character or quality ⟨~ manhood⟩ ⟨a performance that ~*es* perfection⟩ or quantity ⟨an error that ~*es* zero as a limit⟩ **2 :** to bring near or nearer ⟨he ~*ed* the drill to the work⟩ **3 :** to address tentatively or make an overture to esp. in order to create a desired point of view or result: **a :** to take preliminary steps toward accomplishment or full knowledge or experience of ⟨~ a task⟩ ⟨~ a problem⟩ ⟨~ an author's works⟩ **b :** to begin discussion of ⟨having discussed crime, they ~*ed* its elimination⟩ **c** (1) **:** to make advances to **:** SOLICIT (as a prospective purchaser or contributor) (2) **:** to attempt to bribe or influence ⟨~ a member of the legislature⟩ ~ *vi* **1 a :** to come or go near or nearer in place or time **:** to draw nearer ⟨the sound ~*ed* more rapidly⟩ ⟨as daylight ~*es*⟩ **b :** to come or go near or nearer in character or quality ⟨~ to or recede from a line⟩ **2 :** to make a golfing approach ⟨he spoils his game by ~*ing* badly⟩ **syn** see MATCH

[2]**approach** \"\ *n* -ES [ME *approche*, fr. *approchen*, v.] **1 a :** a drawing near in space or time ⟨the rapid ~ of a tornado⟩ ⟨the ~ of summer⟩ **b :** a coming or being near in quality or character ⟨the ~ of dictatorship was foreshadowed by certain events⟩ ⟨in this fine work he made his closest ~ to true greatness⟩ **2 a** *obs* **:** ability to approach **:** opportunity of approaching **b :** a way of gaining access (as to the understanding of a subject) ⟨this book provides a good ~ to nuclear physics⟩ **3 a approaches** *pl, obs* **:** advances or maneuvers toward one **b** (1) **:** the taking of tentative or introductory steps for a particular purpose (as full accomplishment, discussion, acquaintance, or solicitation) ⟨his method of ~ to the subject repels most readers⟩ ⟨new lines of ~⟩ (2) **:** a particular manner of taking such steps ⟨her ~ was obviously friendly⟩ **4 a** (1) **:** a way, passage, or avenue by which a place or a building can be approached ⟨the ~ to the park⟩ (2) **approaches** *pl* **:** the means of approaching an area ⟨air ~*es* between the continental U.S. and outlying bases⟩ **b approaches** *pl* **:** means of approach (as zigzag trenches) prepared by besiegers in advancing toward fortifications **c :** an embankment, trestle, or other construction that provides access at either end of a bridge or tunnel **d :** a portion of railroad track along which a train passes before entering an area controlled by a signal **5** *also* **approaching :** APPROACH GRAFT **6 a :** a golfing stroke from the fairway for the green **b** (1) **:** the steps and motion of a bowler before he delivers the ball (2) **:** the part of the alley in front of the foul line from which a bowler delivers the ball **7 :** descent of an airplane toward a landing strip

ap·proach·a·bil·i·ty \ə,prōchə'biləd·ē\ *n* -ES **:** the quality or state of being approachable

ap·proach·a·ble \-əbəl\ *adj* **:** capable of being approached ⟨a squalid place ~ from a complicated branch of the Niger —H.H.Johnston⟩ ⟨the tales ... seem more ~ than his more difficult novels —F.B.Millett⟩; *specif* **:** easy to meet, converse with, or do business with ⟨a friendly ~ person —C.H. Voss⟩

approach bid *n* **:** a bid in auction bridge or contract bridge in a particular suit on a hand that would justify either a suit bid or a no-trump bid

approach–forcing system \='=,==-\ *n* **:** CULBERTSON SYSTEM

approach graft *n* **:** a plant graft made by joining stock and scion laterally at an intermediate point but leaving both rooted and uncut until firm union is established when the stock is cut above and the scion below the union

approach light *n* **:** one of a group of usu. green lights placed outside a landing area and arranged to indicate to the pilot of an approaching airplane the direction and termination of a runway or landing strip

ap·proach·ment \-mənt\ *n* -S [MF *aprochement*, fr. *aprochier* to approach + *-ment* — more at APPROACH] **:** [2]APPROACH 1a

approach signal *n* **:** DISTANT SIGNAL

approach trench *n* **:** a trench providing protected passage between the front and rear elements of a defensive position

ap·pro·bate \'aprə,bāt\ *vt* -ED/-ING/-S [ME *approbaten*, fr. L *approbatus*, past part. of *approbare* — more at APPROVE (sanction)] **1 :** to express approval of formally or legally **:** sanction officially ⟨a certificate *approbating* the hotel⟩: **a :** to certify (a person) as officially licensed to preach ⟨an *approbated* minister⟩ **b** *Scots law* **:** to accept as legal or valid (as part of a deed) — used esp. in the phrase *approbate and reprobate* ⟨a deed cannot be both *approbated* and reprobated⟩ **2 :** to have a favorable opinion of **:** approve of ⟨everyone ~*s* him⟩

ap·pro·ba·tion \,aprə'bāshən\ *n* -S [ME *approbacioun*, fr. MF *approbation*, fr. L *approbation-*, *approbatio*, fr. *approbatus* (past part. of *approbare* to approve, prove) + *-ion-*, *-io* -ion — more at APPROVE] **1** *obs* **:** PROOF, ATTESTATION, CONFIRMATION **2 a :** act of approving formally or authoritatively **:** SANCTION ⟨without the previous ~ of any public officer —T.B.Macaulay⟩; *specif* **:** official certification that a person is authorized to perform the functions of an ecclesiastic **b :** an assenting to anything usu. with some degree of pleasure or satisfaction **:** COMMENDATION ⟨one of his early books . . . received the ~ of scholars —*Current Biog.*⟩ ⟨deportment that wins ~ —George Meredith⟩ ⟨the pleasure of social ~ —Bertrand Russell⟩ **3** *obs* **:** PROBATION, NOVITIATE, TRIAL

ap·pro·ba·tive \'aprə,bād·iv, -ˌbəd·-; ə'prōbəd·-, ə'präb-\ *adj* [F *approbatif*, fr. ML *approbativus* proving, fr. LL, giving a reason, fr. L *approbatus* + *-ivus* -ive] **:** FAVORABLE ⟨once criticism of the plan took a favorable turn, it remained ~⟩

ap·pro·ba·to·ry \'aprəbə,tōrē, ə'prōb-,ə'präb-\ *adj* [*approbate* + *-ory*] **:** expressing approbation **:** COMMENDATORY

ap·proof \a'prüf, ə'-\ *n* -S [fr. [1]*approve*, after E *prove*: *proof*] **1** *archaic* **:** TRIAL, PROOF, TEST **2** *archaic* **:** APPROVAL

ap·pro·pin·quate \,aprə'piŋ·,kwāt\ *vi* -ED/-ING/-S [L *appropinquatus*, past part. of *appropinquare* to approach, fr. *ad-* + *propinquare* to approach, fr. *propinquus* near — more at PROPINQUITY] *archaic* **:** APPROACH — **ap·pro·pin·qua·tion** \,aprə,piŋ·'kwāshən\ *n* -S

ap·pro·pin·qui·ty \,aprə'piŋkwəd·ē\ *n* -ES [*ad-* + *propinquity*] **:** NEARNESS, PROPINQUITY

ap·pro·pri·a·ble \ə'prōprēəbəl, *chiefly substand* (*by r-dissimilation*) ə'pōprē-\ *adj* [*appropriate* + *-able*] **:** capable of being appropriated

[1]**ap·pro·pri·ate** \-ē,āt, *usu* -ād·+V\ *vt* -ED/-ING/-S [ME *appropriaten*, fr. LL *appropriatus*, past part. of *appropriare*, fr. L *ad-* + *propriare* to appropriate, fr. *proprius* own — more at PROPER] **1 :** to annex (a benefice) to a spiritual corporation to its perpetual use — distinguished from *impropriate* **2** *archaic* **:** to assign or attribute as specially belonging **3 a :** to make peculiarly the possession of someone ⟨~ goods to the lord⟩ ⟨~ the money to himself⟩ **b :** to claim or use as if by an exclusive or preeminent right ⟨let no man ~ a common benefit⟩ **4** *archaic* **:** to make suitable **:** SUIT ⟨terms so exquisitely *appropriated* to the character he draws —E.V.Lucas⟩ **5 :** to set apart for or assign to a particular purpose or use in exclusion of all others ⟨~ money for the navy⟩ ⟨~ the building for storage⟩ **6 :** to take without permission **:** PILFER, PURLOIN ⟨he *appropriated* my notebook —R.M.Lovett⟩

syn PREEMPT, USURP, ARROGATE, CONFISCATE: these verbs all mean to seize or take over more or less dictatorially. In the order APPROPRIATE, PREEMPT, USURP, ARROGATE, CONFISCATE they may be said to form an ascending scale of highhandedness. APPROPRIATE has the common meaning of to set aside for a special purpose ⟨it would not be easy to induce the town to *appropriate* money for improvements —*Amer. Guide Series: Maine*⟩ but it signifies more generally to take over or acquire without authority or with questionable authority, usu. also implying a conversion to one's own use of the thing taken over ⟨to the natives, it is sacrilegious . . . for the white men to *appropriate* the sacred watering places —Rex Ingamells⟩ ⟨the winners *appropriated* all of the best jobs —Charlton Laird⟩ PREEMPT adds to APPROPRIATE the idea of beforehandedness and suggests a stronger action, as a seizure, esp. of something desired by others ⟨*preempt* a lion's share of the profits⟩ ⟨the Hindu Maharajah . . . *preempted* the country's entire public motor transport —Faubion Bowers⟩ ⟨tall, modern apartments *preempt* Washington Square West —*Amer. Guide Series: N. Y. City*⟩ USURP stresses more the idea of the unlawfulness or unwarranted nature of the action and more frequently has as its object rather powers, rights, or offices taken by strong-arm methods than tangible goods seized by force ⟨new rulers have to prove that they have not *usurped* their title, but possess some higher right to govern than the mere fact of having grabbed power —Aldous Huxley⟩ ⟨the executive officer of the *Caine* who *usurps* command from Captain Queeg in the midst of the typhoon —H.W.Baldwin⟩ ⟨legislative assemblies have *usurped* the powers which rightfully belong to the executive branch —H.J.Morgenthau⟩ ⟨the persistence with which certain birds *usurped* and clung to favorite perches —William Beebe⟩ ARROGATE stresses an extreme highhandedness, as of presumption or insolence, and usu. has as its object a right, power, or function ⟨a ruthlessness that *arrogates* to them sole control of local political life —T.H.White⟩ ⟨not only did he reconstitute himself the final court of appeals, but he gradually *arrogated* to himself the function of all the courts —G.W.Johnson⟩ ⟨the artist's productivity pretends to be creation, that is, it *arrogates* to man what is the privilege of God —Hannah Arendt⟩ ⟨the clique which had *arrogated* to itself the function of dictating to Ireland in all things literary —M.P.Linehan⟩ CONFISCATE stresses stongly the idea of unwarranted seizure itself, suggesting often rather a display of power or control than any conversion of the thing seized to one's own purpose ⟨they *confiscated* Tory property worth a million dollars —*Amer. Guide Series: N. C.*⟩ ⟨eight were banished from the United States and their property *confiscated* —H.S.Canby⟩ ⟨pots and pans *confiscated* from the kitchen —R.M.Lovett⟩

[2]**ap·pro·pri·ate** \-ēə̇t *sometimes* -ē,āt; *usu* -d·+V\ *adj* [ME *appropriat*, fr. LL *appropriatus*] **1 :** specially suitable **:** FIT, PROPER ⟨sit down anywhere and the ~ waiter comes up —P.E. Deutschman⟩ ⟨gift packages are likewise ~ for the girls you regularly remember —*Phoenix Flame*⟩ ⟨by any means ~ to our use —George Meredith⟩ **2 :** belonging peculiarly **:** SPECIAL ⟨an ~ symbol of that swanky and luxurious town —Virgil Thomson⟩ ⟨the pupil lacks the qualities ~ to the master's style —David Sylvester⟩ **3** *obs* **:** attached as an accessory possession **syn** see FIT

ap·pro·pri·ate·ly *adv* **:** in an appropriate manner

ap·pro·pri·ate·ness *n* -ES **:** the quality or state of being appropriate

ap·pro·pri·a·tion \=,=='āshən\ *n* -S [ME *appropriacioun*, fr. MF or LL; MF *appropriation*, fr. LL *appropriation-*, *appropriatio*, fr. *appropriatus* + L *-ion-*, *-io* -ion] **1 a :** the act of appropriating to oneself or another person or to a particular use ⟨he was punished for his ~ of their belongings⟩ **b :** something that has been appropriated; *specif* **:** a sum of money set aside or allotted by official or formal action for a specific use (as from public revenue by a legislative body that stipulates the amount, manner, and purpose of items of expenditure) ⟨~ bill⟩ ⟨an annual ~ for flood control⟩ **2** [ML, fr. LL] *ecclesiastical law* **:** transference of a benefice with its spiritual or temporal interests to a spiritual corporation, provision for the service of the church being made in return; *also* **:** the benefice so transferred **3** *obs* **:** a special attribute or application **4 :** a taking over of a reaction pattern or activity by members of one species (as of birds) or group from those of another group with which the former is associated **:** imitative behavior

ap·pro·pri·a·tive \='==,ā|d·iv, -ˌə|, |tiv\ *adj* **:** relating to appropriation **:** APPROPRIATING

ap·pro·pri·a·tor \-,ād·ə(r), -,ātə-\ *n* -S **1 :** one that appropriates **2** *ecclesiastical law* **:** a religious corporation that owns an appropriated benefice

ap·prov·a·bil·i·ty \ə,prüvə'biləd·ē *also* a,-\ *n* -ES **:** the quality or state of being approvable

ap·prov·a·ble \='=vəbəl\ *adj* [ME, fr. *approven* + *-able*] **:** capable of being approved — **ap·prov·a·bly** \-əblē\ *adv*

ap·prov·al \-vəl\ *n* -S **1 :** the act of approving **:** APPROBATION, SANCTION ⟨a procedure likely to meet with the ~ of the circumspect —S.H.Adams⟩ **2 :** certification as to acceptability (as of a request for capital expenditure) ⟨these ~*s* are usually indicated on the invoice before the voucher is prepared —H.S.Noble⟩ — **on approval** *adv* (*or adj*) **:** subject to a prospective purchaser's decision to accept or refuse ⟨goods sent out *on approval*⟩

approval book *n* **:** a set of small approval sheets in book form

approval sheet *n* **:** a sheet of paper on which postage stamps are mounted for sending on approval to purchasers

ap·prov·ance \-vən(t)s\ *n* -S [[1]*approve* + *-ance*] *archaic* **:** APPROVAL

[1]**ap·prove** \ə'prüv *also* a'-\ *vb* -ED/-ING/-S [ME *approven*, *aproven*, fr. OF *aprover*, fr. L *approbare* to approve, prove, fr. *ad-* + *probare* to approve, prove — more at PROVE] *vt* **1 a** *obs* **:** to demonstrate the truth or correctness of **:** establish as fact or as being sound **b** *archaic* **:** CORROBORATE, AUTHENTICATE **c** *obs* **:** CONVICT ⟨*approved* in this offense —Shak.⟩ **2** *obs* **a :** TEST, TRY **b :** EXPERIENCE **3** *archaic* **a :** to make or show to be worthy of approbation or acceptance — used reflexively with *to* ⟨the first care and concern must be to ~ himself to God —John Rogers⟩ **b :** to offer proof of by active demonstration **:** manifest or display actually or practically **:** EXHIBIT ⟨his behavior under fire *approved* him a man of courage⟩ **4 :** to judge and find commendable or acceptable **:** think well of **:** have or express a favorable opinion or judgment of ⟨a friend, whom he liked, but whose conduct he could not ~ —Osbert Sitwell⟩ ⟨Jane secretly *approved* his discernment —Rose Macaulay⟩ **5 a :** to express often formally agreement with and support of or commendation of as meeting a standard ⟨the governor *approved* the project⟩ ⟨one of the first hospitals in the state to be *approved* by the organization⟩ **b :** to vote into effect **:** pass formally ⟨the legislature *approved* the bill⟩ ~ *vi* **:** to have or express a favorable opinion **:** judge favorably — usu. used with *of* ⟨she wants to teach him not to fight; she doesn't ~ of fighting —Margaret Mead⟩

syn SANCTION, ENDORSE, ACCREDIT, CERTIFY: APPROVE applies to a feeling or expression of commendation or of agreement with, but it may suggest a judicious attitude involved ⟨fools admire, but men of wits *approve* —Joseph Furphey⟩ ⟨the discomfiture . . . of doing, as he must, what he did not fully *approve* —J.G.Cozzens⟩ SANCTION adds to APPROVE notions of permission, countenancing, authorization, encouragement by something or someone in an authoritative position ⟨the court has also *sanctioned* recently some federal efforts to protect Negroes in the South from violence —Alan Barth⟩ ⟨"Come! Give me your authority . . . For his daughter's sake . . ." "In her name, then, let it be done; I *sanction* it" —Charles Dickens⟩ ENDORSE or INDORSE (see note at ENDORSE) suggests vouching for, supporting, or explicitly expressing approval of and is often used in reference to things needing promotion or publicity ⟨the Kentucky Republicans *endorsed* him for the presidential nomination —E.M.Coulter⟩ ⟨the view that increasing money wages is the only road to permanent prosperity has in recent years been *endorsed* by many business leaders —*Fortune*⟩ ACCREDIT is likely to indicate an approved status confirmed by some authoritative force or conformity to a standard officially vouched for ⟨few of us think of turning to the dictionary before writing a sentence to see if all the words we propose to use are properly *accredited* in the language —M.M.Mathews⟩ ⟨institutions not *accredited* by a regional association —*Bull. of Bates College*⟩ CERTIFY is often a close synonym for ACCREDIT; it may stress a formal act of writing or attesting to conformity with a standard or to being as represented ⟨labels by which brain merit is advertised and *certified* — medals, honors, degrees —Virginia Woolf⟩ ⟨the nearly two billion that these utilities have had *certified* for rapid tax write-off —*New Republic*⟩

[2]**approve** \"\ *vt* -ED/-ING/-S [ME *approven*, *aproven*, *approuen*, *aprouen*, fr. MF *aprouer* to cause to profit, fr. OF, fr. *a-* (fr. L *ad-*) + *-prouer* (fr. *prou* profit, advantage) — more at PROW] **:** to enclose or appropriate (wasteland or common land) for one's own benefit (as permitted esp. to the lord of a manor in English law before the Enclosure acts)

approved school *n, Brit* **:** a school for juvenile delinquents

[1]**ap·prove·ment** \-vmənt\ *n* -S [ME *approvement*, *approuement*, fr. MF *approuement*, *aprouement*, fr. OF, fr. *aprouer* + *-ment*] *English law* **:** the act of approving lands

[2]**approvement** \"\ *n* -S [[1]*approve* + *-ment*] **1** *obs* **:** APPROBA-

TION, APPROVAL **2** *Old English law* **:** the act of one that when appealed of a felony confessed his guilt and appealed another as an accomplice of the same crime to obtain his own pardon

¹ap·prov·er \-və(r)\ *n* -s [AF *aprouour*, fr. MF *aprouer* to cause to profit + *-our* -or — more at APPROVE] *English law*, *obs* **:** BAILIFF, STEWARD, AGENT

²approver \"\ *n* -s [¹*approve* + *-er*] *Old English law* **:** one that makes an approvement

approves *pres 3d sing of* APPROVE

ap·prov·ing·ly *adv* **:** in an approving manner

ap·prox·i·mal \ə'präksəməl, (')a¦p-\ *adj* [*ad-* + L *proximus* nearest, next + E *-al*] **:** CONTIGUOUS ⟨~ surfaces of teeth⟩

¹ap·prox·i·mate \ə'präksəmət, *usu* -əd·+V\ *adj* [LL *approximatus*, past part. of *approximare* to come near, fr. L *ad-* + *proximare* to come near — more at PROXIMATE] **1 :** nearly resembling ⟨doing such ~ justice as we could —W.A.White⟩ **2 :** near to correctness or accuracy **:** nearly exact ⟨a sketch map with ~ topography —C.B.Hitchcock⟩ ⟨an ~ idea of the agricultural area —J.M.Mogey⟩ ⟨at the ~ center of the state⟩ **3 :** located very close together ⟨leaves that are ovate and ~⟩

²ap·prox·i·mate \-,māt, *usu* -ād·+V\ *vb* -ED/ -ING/ -S *vt* **1 a :** to bring near or close to **:** cause to approach **:** make approximate ⟨the closer the performing conditions for Sebastian Bach's concerted music are *approximated* to those of early eighteenth century provincial Germany —Virgil Thomson⟩ **b** *med* **:** to bring together (cut edges of tissue) **2 :** to come near to **:** APPROACH ⟨the candidate's memory should closely ~ a hypothetical norm —H.G.Armstrong⟩ ⟨nothing *approximating* a history of American letters was printed —H.M.Jones⟩ **3 :** to set by hasty and crude calculation **:** ESTIMATE ⟨maybe the map is just *approximated* when it comes to precise distances —A.R.Marcus⟩ ~ *vi* **:** to come close ⟨to make the effects of poetry ~ to those of music —Edmund Wilson⟩

ap·prox·i·mate·ly \-,mətlē, -li\ *adv* **:** reasonably close to **:** NEARLY, ALMOST, ABOUT

ap·prox·i·ma·tion \ə,präksə'māshən\ *n* -s **1 :** the action of coming or bringing near or close together ⟨effectively prevents ~ of viable parietal and visceral tissues —*Surgical Forum*⟩ **2 :** the state of being near ⟨an ~ to the truth⟩ **:** an approach esp. to a correct estimate, calculation, or conception or to a given quantity or quality ⟨to deal with crude ~*s* and somewhat meaningless generalities —W.A.Noyes⟩ **3** *math* **a :** a continual approach to a correct result ⟨solve an equation by successive ~*s*⟩ **b :** a value that is nearly but not exactly correct

ap·prox·i·ma·tive \ə'==,mād·iv, -,məd-\ *adj* **:** APPROACHING, APPROXIMATE — **ap·prox·i·ma·tive·ly** *adv*

appt *abbr* appoint; appointment

apptd *abbr* appointed

ap·pulse \ə'pəls, a'p-, 'a,p- *also* -lts\ *n* -s [L *appulsus* driving forward, approach, fr. *appulsus*, past part. of *appellere* to drive toward, strike against, fr. *ad-* + *pellere* to drive, beat, push — more at FELT] **1 :** a driving or running toward (as a place) **:** act of striking against (as a point) ⟨the days have passed when national differences could be settled by the ~ of small professional armies —R.S.Ellery⟩ **2 :** the apparent very near approach of one celestial body to another **:** a coming into conjunction — see LUNAR APPULSE

ap·pur·te·nance \ə'pərt(ᵊ)nən(t)s, -pət-,-pəit-\ *n* -s [ME *appurtenaunce*, *apurtenaunce*, fr. AF *apurtenance*, alter. (prob. influenced by OF *pour*, *pur* for) of OF *apartenance*, fr. *apartenir* to belong + *-ance* — more at APPERTAIN, PURCHASE] **1 :** an incidental property right or privilege (as to a right of way, a barn, or an orchard) belonging to a principal right and passing in possession with it **2 :** a subordinate part, adjunct, or accessory ⟨an ~ to his own vast vanity —Donn Byrne⟩ — usu. used in pl. ⟨the swashbuckling ~*s* of the historical novel⟩ **3 appurtenances** *pl* **:** accessory objects used in any function **:** APPARATUS, GEAR ⟨from cameras and lenses to all the ~*s* of the darkroom —J.T.Soby⟩ ⟨all the ~*s* of their daily existence —Marcia Davenport⟩

¹ap·pur·te·nant \-ənt\ *adj* [ME *appurtenaunt*, *apurtenaunt*, alter. (prob. influenced by ME *appurtenaunce*) of *appertenant*, *apertenant*, *apertinent*, fr. MF *apertenant*, *apartenant*, fr. OF, pres. part. of *apartenir*] **1 a :** annexed or belonging legally to some more important thing ⟨a right-of-way ~ to land or buildings⟩ **b :** incident to and passing in possession with real estate — used of certain profits or easements; compare APPENDANT 2 **2 :** BELONGING, APPROPRIATE, ACCESSORY ⟨all other necessary ~ equipment —*Military Engineer*⟩ ⟨compressor station facilities ~ to this line —*Annual Report of Cities Service Co.*⟩

²appurtenant \"\ *n* -s **:** APPURTENANCE

appx *abbr* appendix

aprac·tic \(')ā¦praktik\ *or* **aprax·ic** \-aksik\ *adj* [*apractic* fr. Gk *apraktos* not taking part in action, fr. *a-* ²a- + *-praktos* (fr. *prattein*, *prassein* to do, carry out); *apraxic* fr. NL *apraxia* + E *-ic*] **:** of, relating to, or marked by apraxia

aprax·ia \ā'praksēə\ *n* -s [NL, fr. Gk, inaction, fr. *a-* ²a- + *praxis* action (fr. *prattein*, *prassein* to do, carry out + *-sis*) + *-ia* — more at PRACTICAL] **:** loss or impairment of ability to execute movements (as in manipulating objects) without muscular paralysis

après \ä'prā\ *adv* [F, fr. LL *ad pressum* near, fr. L *ad* to, at + *pressum*, accus. neut. of *pressus*, past part. of *premere* to press — more at AT, PRESS] **:** AFTER, AFTERWARD — used specif. in the game of rouge et noir to announce a refait

aprick·le \ə'-\ *adj* [¹*a-* + *prickle* (*v.*)] **:** PRICKLY

apricock *archaic var of* APRICOT

apri·cot \'aprə,kät, āp-, *usu* kād·+V; 'ap- *is more freq than* 'āp- *in N*, 'āp- *is much more freq than* 'ap- *in S*\ *n* -s [alter. (prob. nfluenced by L *apricum* sunny place and MF *abricot* apricot) of earlier *abrecock*, prob. fr. obs. Catal *abercoc*, fr. Ar *al-birqūq* the apricot, fr. *al-* the + *birqūq* apricot, prob. fr. Gk *praikokion*, fr. L *praecocia* (in *persica praecocia*, lit., early ripening peaches), neut. pl. of *praecox* early ripening — more at PRECOCIOUS] **1 a :** the oval orange-colored fruit of a temperate-zone tree (*Prunus armeniaca*) resembling both peach and plum in flavor **b :** any tree that bears apricots **2 :** a variable color averaging a moderate orange that is yellower, less strong, and slightly lighter than honeydew, yellower and paler than Persian orange, and paler and slightly yellower than other brown

apricot-kernel oil *n* **:** either of two oils obtained from apricot kernels and very similar in properties and uses to the true almond oils: **a :** a colorless or straw-colored nondrying fatty oil obtained by expression — called also *persic oil* **b :** a colorless to yellow aromatic toxic essential oil obtained by steam distillation — called also *bitter almond oil*

apricot palm *n* **:** a small Brazilian palm (*Cocos eriospatha*) that bears apricot-flavored fruit and is cultivated in California

apricot plum *n* **1 :** a Chinese tree (*Prunus simonii*) yielding an inferior fruit but used in hybridizing **2 :** the slightly astringent fruit of the apricot plum

apricot vine *n* **:** MAYPOP 1

apricot yellow *n* **:** a light to moderate yellow that is redder than amber yellow, snapdragon, or primrose yellow (sense 2)

april \'āprəl *sometimes* -(,)pril\ *n* -s *usu cap, often attrib* [ME *April*, *Averil*, *Aperil*, fr. OF & L; OF *avrill*, fr. L *Aprilis*, prob. of Etruscan origin; akin to Etruscan *apru* April, perh. fr. Gk *Aphrō*, short for *Aphroditē* Greek goddess of love, perh. orig. a goddess of the underworld] **1 :** the fourth month of the Gregorian calendar — abbr. *Apr.*; see MONTH table **2 :** the season of spring ⟨something fresh and full of hope, an *April* of the spirit —Alzada Comstock⟩

april fool *n*, *usu cap A* **1 :** the butt or victim of a joke or trick played on April Fools' Day; *also* **:** such a joke or trick **2 :** PASQUEFLOWER

april fools' day *n*, *usu cap A&F&D* **:** April 1st, when practical jokes are played on the unwary — called also *All Fools' Day*

april·i·an \(')ā¦prilēən\ *adj*, *usu cap* [*April* + *-ian*] **:** of, relating to, or like April

¹a pri·o·ri \¦äprē¦ōrē, ¦ä-, ¦a-, ¦ā-, -ōr-, -ri; ¦āprī¦ōr,ī, -ō,rī, -ōrē, -ōr,ē, -ri\ *adv* [L, lit., from the former] **1 :** by reasoning from definitions formed or principles assumed **:** DEDUCTIVELY **2 :** without examination or analysis **:** PRESUMPTIVELY **3 :** independently of experience **:** INTUITIVELY

²a priori \"\ *adj* **1 a :** marked by reasoning or by deducing consequences from definitions formed or principles assumed **:** DEDUCTIVE ⟨an *a priori* argument⟩ ⟨an *a priori* order of propositions⟩ **b** (1) **:** of or relating to something that can be known by reason alone ⟨*a priori* geometrical propositions⟩ (2) **:** of or relating to reasoning from mere examination of ideas alone **:** marked by being knowable by reasoning from what is considered self-evident and therefore without appeal to the particular facts of experience **c :** of or relating to something that is presupposed by experience in general **:** considered as antecedently necessary in order that experience in general should be intelligible — used in Kantianism **d :** true or false by definition or convention alone **:** ANALYTIC ⟨*a priori* statements⟩ **e :** arbitrarily or conventionally postulated for formalization or axiomatization — contrasted with *a posteriori* **2 :** without examination or analysis **:** PRESUMPTIVE ⟨*a priori* acceptance of the greatness of a book —Norman Cousins⟩

³a priori \"\ *n*, *pl* **a prioris :** something that is a priori; *esp* **:** an a priori conception or proposition ⟨the *a priori* coextensive with the formal —W.S.Sellars⟩

apri·o·rism \,==(,)='ōr,izəm, -'ō,ri-\ *n* -s [prob. trans. of D *apriorisme*] **1 :** belief in a priori principles or reasoning; *specif* **:** the doctrine that knowledge rests upon principles that are self-evident to reason or are presupposed by experience in general **2 a :** an a priori principle **:** ASSUMPTION **b :** an example of a priori reasoning **c :** a statement that makes evident a belief in a priori principles

apri·o·rist \-'ōrəst, -'ōr-\ *n* -s **:** one who believes in a priori principles or seeks to establish his position by a priori reasoning

apri·o·ris·tic \¦=,prē,ōr¦istik, -,prī,-, -,ō¦ris-; ¦=,prī,ə¦ri-\ *adj* **:** based upon a priori principles **:** A PRIORI ⟨~ positivism⟩ — **apri·o·ris·ti·cal·ly** \-tək(ə)lē\ *adv*

apri·or·i·ty \,=,prē'ōrəd·ē, ¦=,prī'-, -'ärə-\ *n* -ES **1 :** the quality or state of being a priori **2 :** the character in a proposition of following from principles that are a priori

apris·mo \ä'prēz(,)mō\ *n* -s *usu cap* [AmerSp, fr. *Apra*, Peruvian political party (fr. *Alianza Popular Revolucionaria Americana* American Popular Revolutionary Alliance) + Sp *-ismo* -ism] **:** the political philosophy and policies advocated by Apristas

apris·ta \ä'prēstə\ *n* -s *usu cap* [AmerSp, fr. *Apra* + Sp *-ista* -ist] **:** a member or adherent of any of various Latin-American socialist parties advocating division of landed estates, domestic social reform, and cooperation among Latin-American countries

aproc·ta \(')ā¦präktə\ [NL, fr. ²*a-* + *-procta*] *syn of* TURBELLARIA

aproc·tous \(')ā¦präktəs\ *adj* [²*a-* + *-proctous*] **:** without an anal orifice

¹apron \'āprən, *less often in stand than in substand speech* -pə(r)n\ *n* -s *often attrib* [ME, alter. (resulting from incorrect division of *a napron*) of *napron*, fr. MF *naperon*, dim. of *nape* cloth, tablecloth, modif. of L *mappa* napkin — more at MAP] **1 a :** an article made of cloth, plastic, leather, or other material, usu worn on the front of the body and tied around the waist with strings, and used to protect the clothing, to cover the body, or to adorn a costume **b :** a part of certain official costumes ⟨the ~ and gaiters of a bishop —Donn Byrne⟩ **2 :** a horizontal or vertical cover appended to a structure for protection and often serving also as a brace or decoration: as **a :** an extension of a building material (as trim or flashing) along another surface for the purpose of decorating, hiding unfinished surfaces, or protecting against impact or the elements; *specif* **:** the lower member under the sill of the interior casing of a window **b** (1) **:** a downward extension of the frame of a piece of furniture (as immediately below a table top or chair seat) (2) **:** an upward or downward vertical extension of a sink or lavatory **c** (1) **:** a strip of planking along the side of a boat (2) **:** a reinforcing piece of timber behind the stempost of a boat **d :** a swinging part of a gun shield **e** (1) **:** a piece of waterproof cloth or other material spread out (as before the seat of a vehicle) as a protection from rain or mud (2) **:** a horizontal or vertical metal shield extending across the front of an automobile below the radiator **f :** a covering or casing (as of sheet metal) for protecting parts of machinery **g :** a strip of leather forming part of the upper of an oxford shoe and extending from the shank over the waist and instep **h :** a canvas jacket fitted over the back of a hen turkey to prevent injury during mating **3 a :** a device or mechanism serving to move or guide material into or retain it in a desired position: as (1) **:** an endless belt for carrying material of any kind — called also *traveling apron* (2) **:** a receptacle for conveying material (as rock) by a cableway and trolley (3) **:** a revolving canvas for conveying cut grain (as wheat) to the binding mechanism of a harvester **:** a platform or elevator canvas (4) **:** a flap on which paper pulp is led from the strainer **b** (1) **:** a moving lattice for feeding loose fibers to a machine (as in a cotton picker) (2) **:** a leather or composition belt operating in conjunction with other devices to draft, rub, or condense roving in preparatory and spinning processes (3) **:** a means (as a fabric) for attaching warp threads to the cloth roller in weaving **c** (1) **:** a flat plate or lip serving as a chute or deflector in mining engineering (2) **:** a copper plate coated with amalgam used outside a stamp battery in gold mining — called also *apron plate* (3) **:** the canvas-covered frame used in a gold miner's cradle to deflect material washed and to catch the fine gold **d** (1) **:** the vertical front plate of a lathe carriage that bears the mechanism by which the carriage is moved (2) **:** the piece to which the cutting tool of a planer is clamped — called also *tool apron* **e** (1) **:** a metal strip used in turpentining to support the cup and to guide the crude turpentine into it (2) **:** a piece of leather or board for conducting loose material (as grain) past an opening (as in a separator) **f :** a broad shallow vat used for evaporating **g :** a strip of often embossed plastic material used to separate the turns of a film rolled up for development in a tank **4 :** an anatomical structure that resembles an apron: as **a :** HOTTENTOT APRON **b** (1) **:** the diaphragm or midriff of an animal (2) **:** a thick transverse fold of skin on the fore part of the breast or lower part of the neck of a ram (3) **:** the fat skin covering the belly of a goose or duck (4) **:** the infolded abdomen of a crab (5) **:** a frill of esp. long hair on the lower throat and chest of a long-haired dog **5 :** an extensive usu. unconsolidated alluvial, glaciofluvial, eolian, or marine deposit spread outward from an identifiable source **:** a piedmont alluvial plain **:** ALLUVIAL FAN **:** OUTWASH PLAIN **6 a :** the part of the stage in front of the proscenium arch and the curtain **:** FORESTAGE ⟨stepped to the ~ of the stage and took the bow —Bennett Cerf⟩ **b :** the part of the boxing-ring floor that extends beyond the ropes **c :** the part of a golf course immediately surrounding a green **7 a :** a flat steel plate between a railroad locomotive and tender used as a standing place by the fireman **b** (1) **:** the area along the waterfront edge of a pier or wharf used for the direct transfer of cargo between ship's hold and railroad cars (2) **:** a bridge structure supporting railroad tracks that connects a car ferry with the tracks extending to land **8 a :** a shield (as of concrete, planking, or brushwood) along the bank of a river, along a sea wall, or below a dam **b** (1) **:** a cover (as of concrete or metal) that protects an inclined surface of a fortification (2) **:** a strip of barbed-wire entanglements **c** (1) **:** the extensive paved part of an airport located immediately adjacent to the terminal area or hangars and used for loading, unloading, and parking aircraft (2) **:** an extensive usu. hard-surfaced area; *esp* **:** such an area used for stopping or parking automobiles **9 :** a sheet attached to or a space on an invoice for notations or facts relative to payment

²apron \"\ *vt* -ED/-ING/-S **:** to put an apron on **:** cover with or as if with an apron

apron conveyor *n* **:** a chain conveyor having plates attached to the chain for carrying material — compare APRON 3a(1)

apron feeder *n* **:** an apron conveyor so operated as to control the rate of delivery of material to be processed by a machine

apron lining *n* **:** the casing of the apron piece that forms part of the finish of a staircase

apron man *n*, *obs* **:** a man who wears an apron **:** WORKMAN, TRADESMAN

apron piece *n* **:** a beam supporting a landing or a series of winders in a staircase

apron stage *n* **:** the flat wide part of the Elizabethan stage projecting into the audience and used as the main acting area

apron string *n* **:** the string of an apron — usu. used in pl. as a symbol of complete dependence on or domineering control by a wife or mother ⟨succeeds . . . in tying him to her *apron strings* forever —J.H.Lawson⟩

apron wall *n* **:** SPANDREL 3

¹ap·ro·pos \,aprə¦pō\ *adv* [F *à propos*, lit., to the purpose] **1 :** at an opportune time **:** SEASONABLY, FITLY ⟨your letter comes ~ as usual —O.W.Holmes †1935⟩ **2 :** by the way **:** INCIDENTALLY ⟨~, are there any cases of women being held captive by the sirens —Norman Douglas⟩

²apropos \"\ *adj* **:** to the point **:** APPROPRIATE, PERTINENT, RELEVANT ⟨have some ~ comments —Dorothy Barclay⟩ **syn** see RELEVANT

³apropos \"\ *prep* **:** with respect to **:** CONCERNING, REGARDING ⟨~ the return of young Americans to lyricism —Peter Viereck⟩ — often used with *of* ⟨his remark to Emerson ~ of diplomas —H.S.Canby⟩

apros·cop·i·nous \¦ā,prä¦skäpənəs\ *adj* [²*a-* + *proscopinous*] **:** lacking the supraorbital ridge — **apros·cop·i·ny** \-'skäpənē\ *n* -ES

apros·ex·ia \¦ā,prä'seksēə\ *n* -s [NL, fr. Gk, want of attention, fr. *a-* ²a- + *-prosexia* (fr. *prosechein* to turn something, as one's mind or attention, to, fr. *pros* toward + *echein* to hold — more at SCHEME] **:** abnormal inability to sustain attention

aprot·er·o·dont \(')ā¦prädərə,dänt, ¦āprō¦terə,-\ *adj* [²*a-* + *proter-* + *-odont*] **:** having the intermaxillaries toothless

apro·tic \(')ā¦prōd·ik\ *adj* [²*a-* + *proton* + *-ic*] **:** incapable of acting as a proton acceptor or proton donor or as an acid or a base ⟨~ solvent⟩

aprowl \ə'-\ *adj* [¹*a-* + *prowl*, v.] **:** in a state of activity or motion **:** on the prowl ⟨battleships and cruisers were ~ —J.A.Michener⟩

apse \'aps\ *n* -s [ML & L; ML *apsis*, *absis* apse of a church, fr. L, vault, arch, orbit of a heavenly body — more at APSIS] **1 :** a projecting part of a building (as a church) usu. semicircular in plan and vaulted; *specif* **:** the bishop's seat or throne in ancient churches usu. in the apse at the eastern end of the choir — see BASILICA illustration **2** [NL, fr. L] **:** APSIS 2

apse aisle *n* **:** an aisle or ambulatory continuing a choir aisle around an apse or chevet

ap·si·dal \'apsədᵊl\ *adj* [L *apsid-*, *apsis* + E *-al*] **1 :** of or relating to the apsides of an orbit ⟨~ motion⟩ **2** [ML *apsid-*, *apsis* + E *-al*] **:** of or relating to the apse of a church — **ap·si·dal·ly** \-dəlē *also* -dᵊlē\ *adv*

apsides *pl of* APSIS

ap·sid·i·ole \ap'sidē,ōl\ *also* **ab·sid·i·ole** \ab's-\ *n* -s [F *absidiole*, fr. *abside* apse (fr. ML *absid-*, *absis*) + *-i-* + *-ole* — more at APSE] **:** a small apse; *specif* **:** one of the smaller or secondary apses in a church having several apses

ap·sis \'apsəs\ *n*, *pl* **apsi·des** \-psə,dēz, ap'sī(,)dēz\ [L *apsis*, *absis*, fr. Gk *apsid-*, *apsis*, *hapsid-*, *hapsis* loop, wheel, arch, orbit, fr. *haptein* to fasten; perh. akin to Gk *oipheín* to copulate with, Skt *yabhati* he copulates with] **1** *obs* **:** CIRCUMFERENCE, ORBIT **2** [NL, fr. L] **:** the point in an orbit at which the distance of the body from the center of attraction is either greatest or least (as the apogee or perigee of the moon or the aphelion or perihelion of a planet) **3** [ML, fr. L] **:** APSE 1

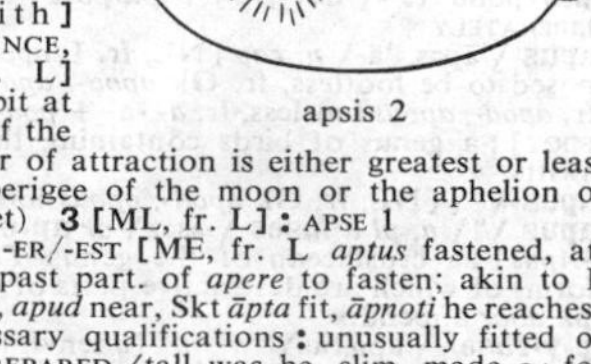

apsis 2

¹apt \'apt\ *adj*, *usu* -ER/-EST [ME, fr. L *aptus* fastened, attached, suitable, fr. past part. of *apere* to fasten; akin to L *apisci* to reach, attain, *apud* near, Skt *āpta* fit, *āpnoti* he reaches] **1 :** having the necessary qualifications **:** unusually fitted or qualified **:** READY, PREPARED ⟨tall was he, slim, made ~ for feats of war —William Morris⟩ **2 a :** having an habitual tendency or inclination **:** LIKELY ⟨the fish is ~ to be lighter in shallower water —Francesca R. La Monte⟩ **b :** ordinarily disposed **:** GIVEN, INCLINED, PRONE ⟨are ~ to believe what we like to believe —John Mason Brown⟩ **3 :** suited to its purpose **:** FITTING, SUITABLE ⟨picking out every term or figure ~ for literary use —C.E.Montague⟩; *specif* **:** to the point **:** APPOSITE, APPROPRIATE, PAT ⟨words were ~ and well chosen —Osbert Sitwell⟩ ⟨~ quotations from classical Arabic travelers —W.L.Wright⟩ **4 :** keenly intelligent **:** mentally alert **:** QUICK-WITTED, QUICK ⟨an ~ student⟩ ⟨an ~ wit —Samuel Johnson⟩ ⟨the boy was observant and ~ to learn —J.G. Cozzens⟩ **syn** see FIT, QUICK

²apt *vt* -ED/ -ING/ -S [L *aptare*, fr. *aptus*] *obs* **:** to make fit or suitable **:** DISPOSE

apt *abbr* apartment

ap·tal \'ap,tal\ *n* -s *usu cap* **:** a member of a Gypsy people of northern Syria

ap·te·no·dy·tes \,aptə,tēnə'dīd·ēz, -ī,tēz\ *n*, *cap* [NL, fr. *apteno-* (fr. Gk *aptēn* wingless, fr. *a-* ²a- + *-ptēn*, fr. *ptēnos* winged) + *-dytes*; akin to Gk *petesthai* to fly — more at FEATHER] **:** a genus of large penguins including the king penguin and emperor penguin

¹ap·tera \'aptərə\ *n pl*, *cap* [NL, fr. Gk, neut. pl. of *apteros*] **1** *in former classifications* **:** an order comprising various wingless arthropods (as spiders, centipedes, and certain insects) **2** *in some modern classifications* **a :** an order of insects coextensive with Entotrophi **b :** an order of insects coextensive with Apterygota — **ap·ter·an** \-rən\ *adj or n*

²aptera \"\ *n*, *pl* **apter·ae** \-ə,rē\ [NL, fr. Gk *apterē*, fem. of *apteros*] **:** a wingless parthenogenetic female aphid that lives on the definitive host plants producing other generations of like aphids and later a generation of alates

ap·ter·al \'aptərəl\ *adj* [Gk *apteros* + E *-al*] **1 :** APTEROUS, WINGLESS **2 :** marked by columniation consisting of a portico at one or both ends but no lateral columns — see COLUMNIATION illustration

ap·te·ri·al \(')ap¦tirēəl\ *adj* [NL *apterium* + E *-al*] **:** of or relating to an apterium

ap·te·ri·um \ap'tirēəm\ *n*, *pl* **apte·ria** \-ēə\ [NL, fr. *a-* ²a- + *pter-* + *-ium*] **:** one of the bare spaces between the feathered areas on the body of a bird

ap·ter·ous \'aptərəs\ *adj* [Gk *apteros*, fr. *a-* ²a- + *-pteros* (fr. *pteron* wing) — more at FEATHER] **1 :** lacking wings ⟨an ~ insect⟩ **2 :** lacking winglike expansions ⟨~ petioles⟩ ⟨an ~ seed⟩

ap·tery \-rē\ *n* -ES [²*a-* + *pter-* + *-y*] *zool* **:** the state of being wingless

ap·ter·y·ges \ap'terə,jēz\ [NL, fr. pl. of *Apteryg-*, *Apteryx*] *syn of* APTERYGIFORMES

ap·ter·yg·ial \¦aptə¦rij(ē)əl\ *adj* [²*a-* + Gk *pterygion* fin, lit., little wing + E *-al* — more at PTERYGIUM] **:** without paired fins or limbs (as of the cyclostomes)

ap·ter·yg·i·for·mes \,aptə,rijə'fōr,mēz\ *n pl*, *cap* [NL, fr. *Apteryg-*, *Apteryx* + *-iformes*] **:** an order of flightless ground birds (superorder Palaeognathae) having vestigial wings, long bills, and small eyes and being coextensive with a family (Apterygidae) that includes the New Zealand kiwis and extinct related birds of Australia and New Zealand — see APTERYX

ap·ter·yg·o·ge·nea \ap,terə(,)gō'jēnēə\ [NL, fr. *a-* ²a- + *pteryg-* + *-genea* (fr. Gk *genos* race, kin) — more at KIN] *syn of* APTERYGOTA

ap·ter·y·go·ta \(,)ap,terə'gōd·ə, ¦a,te-\ *n pl*, *cap* [NL, fr. ²*a-* + *Pterygota*] **:** a subclass of Insecta comprising primitive insects that are presumed never to have developed wings and have no conspicuous metamorphosis — compare PTERYGOTA

ap·ter·y·gote \(')ap¦terə,gōt, (')ā¦te-\ *or* **ap·ter·y·go·tous** \¦ap,terə¦gōd·əs, ¦ā,te\ *adj* [*apterygote* fr. NL *Apterygota*; *apterygotous*, fr. NL *Apterygota* + E *-ous*] **:** of or relating to the subclass Apterygota

ap·ter·y·la \(')ap¦terələ, (')ā¦te-\ *n*, *pl* **aptery·lae** \-,lē, -,lī\ [NL, fr. ²*a-* + *pteryla*] **:** one of the spaces between the feather tracts of birds

ap·ter·yx \'aptə(,)riks\ *n* [NL, fr. ²*a-* + *-pteryx*] **1** *cap* **:** a genus (the type of the family Apterygidae) of flightless birds comprising the kiwis and including all surviving members of the order Apterygiformes **2** -ES **:** KIWI

aptest *superlative of* APT

aptha *var of* APHTHA

apt·i·an \'aptēən, -psh(ē)ən\ *adj, usu cap* [F *aptien,* fr. *Apt,* commune near Avignon, France + F *-ien* -ian] **:** of or relating to a subdivision of the European Lower Cretaceous — see GEOLOGIC TIME table

ap·ti·ana \,aptē'anə, -'ä-,-'ā- *also* -'ā-\ *n, cap* [NL, fr. ISV *Aptian*] **:** a genus of fossil plants of the Lower Cretaceous of England said to represent one of the earliest known ancestors of existing angiosperms

apting *pres part of* APT

ap·ti·tude \'aptə,tüd, -ptə-,tyüd\ *n* -s [ME, fr. ML *aptitudo,* fr. LL, fitness, fr. L *aptus* fit + *-i-* + *-tudo* -tude — more at APT] **1 :** a tendency, capacity, or inclination to learn or understand **:** mental alertness **:** QUICK-WITTEDNESS, APTNESS ⟨boys of real ability with an ~ for classics —A.C.Benson⟩ **2 a :** a natural inclination or acquired disposition ⟨beavers have an ~ for building dams⟩ **b :** a natural or acquired capacity or ability endowed . . . with a stubborn ~ for facing facts —Ellen Glasgow⟩ **3 :** a general fitness or suitableness **:** APPROPRIATENESS ⟨that sociable and helpful ~ which God implanted between man and woman —John Milton⟩ **4** *obs* **:** ATTITUDE 1 **5 :** any constellation of measurable characteristics known to predispose to the learning of certain skills **syn** see GIFT

aptitude test *n* **:** a standardized test designed to predict an individual's ability to learn certain skills — compare INTELLIGENCE TEST

ap·ti·tu·di·nal \¦==¦=dᵊnəl\ *adj* [ML *aptitudin-, aptitudo* + E *-al*] **:** of or relating to aptitude — **ap·ti·tu·di·nal·ly** \-əlē, -li\ *adv*

apt·ly \'aptlē, -li, *rap.* -pl-\ *adv* **1 :** in an apt manner **:** APPROPRIATELY, FITTINGLY, READILY **2** *archaic* **:** with exact adjustment or correspondence

apt·ness \'ap(t)nəs\ *n* -ES **:** the quality or state of being apt: **a :** FITNESS, SUITABLENESS ⟨the universal ~ of a religious system —A.W.Kinglake⟩ **b :** habitual tendency or inclination **:** LIKELIHOOD ⟨the ~ of iron to rust⟩ **:** PROPENSITY, PRONENESS ⟨the ~ of men to sin⟩ **c :** APPROPRIATENESS, APPOSITENESS ⟨this last metaphor has a peculiar ~ —F.R.Leavis⟩ **d :** mental alertness **:** QUICK-WITTEDNESS, APTITUDE ⟨his ~ in illustration was as charming as it was effective —Broadus Mitchell⟩

apts *pres 3d sing of* APT

apty·a·lism \(')ā'tīə,lizəm\ *also* **apty·a·lia** \,ā,tī'ālyə, -lēə\ *n* -s [*aptyalism,* fr. ²*a-* + *ptyalism; aptyalia,* NL, fr. ²*a-* + *ptyal-* + *-ia*] **:** absence of or deficiency in secretion of saliva

ap·ty·chus \'aptəkəs\ *n, pl* **ap·ty·chi** \-,kī\ [NL, fr. ²*a-* + Gk *ptychē* fold — more at PTYCH-] **:** a shelly plate usu. of two pieces found in ammonites and regarded as an operculum

¹**apu·lian** \ə'pyülēən, -lyən\ *adj, usu cap* [*Apulia* (It *Puglia*), compartimento of southeastern Italy + E *-an*] **:** of or relating to Apulia or the Apulians

²**apulian** \"\ *n* -s *cap* **:** a native or inhabitant of Apulia

apulian pottery *n, usu cap A* **:** a kind of ancient pottery found in Apulia; *esp* **:** a species of vase or stamnos having red designs on a lustrous black surface

a pun·ta d'ar·co \ä¦püntə'där(,)kō\ *adv* [It] **:** with or at the point of the bow — used as a direction for players of stringed instruments

apur·pose \ə'-\ *adv* [¹*a-* + *purpose*] *dial* **:** on purpose **:** DELIBERATELY

¹**apus** \'āpəs, 'ä-\ *n, cap* [NL, fr. L *apod-, apus* swallow supposed to be footless, fr. Gk *apod-, apous* sand-martin, swift, fr. *apod-, apous* footless, fr. *a-* ²*a-* + *pod-, pous* foot — more at FOOT] **:** a genus of birds containing the typical Old World swifts

²**apus** \"\ [NL, fr. Gk *apod-, apous* footless] *syn of* TRIOPS

³**apus** \"\ *n, pl* **apuses** \-əsəz\ *or* **ap·o·des** \'apə,dēz\ [NL ²*Apus*] **:** a crustacean of the genus *Triops* certain tropical forms of which are destructive pests of young rice

apx *abbr* appendix

ap·y·rase \'apə,rās\ *n* -s [adenyl*pyro*phosphat*ase*] **:** any enzyme that hydrolyzes adenosine triphosphate with the liberation of phosphate — compare ADENOSINE TRIPHOSPHATASE

apy·rene \(')ā¦pī,rēn\ *adj* [ISV ²*a-* + *-pyrene* (fr. Gk *pyrēn* stone of a fruit) — more at FURZE] **:** lacking a nucleus ⟨~ spermatozoa⟩

apy·ret·ic \¦ā,pī¦red·ik, ¦apə¦r-\ *adj* [²*a-* + *pyretic*] **:** without fever **:** AFEBRILE

apy·rex·ia \¦ā,pī'reksēə, ,apə'r-\ *also* **apy·rexy** \(')ā'pī,reksē, 'apə,r-\ *n, pl* **apyrexias** *also* **apyrexies** [NL *apyrexia,* fr. Gk, fr. *a-* ²*a-* + *-pyrexia* (fr. *pyressein* to be feverish, fr. *pyr* fire) — more at FIRE] **:** absence or intermission of fever — **apy·rex·i·al** \¦ā,pī¦reksēəl, ¦apə¦r-\ *adj*

apy·rous \(')ā¦pīrəs\ *adj* [Gk *apyros* without fire, fr. *a-* ²*a-* + *pyr* fire] **:** NONCOMBUSTIBLE

aq *abbr* aqua; aqueous

AQ *abbr* accomplishment quotient; achievement quotient

aq bull *abbr* [L *aqua bulliens*] boiling water

aq dest *abbr* [NL *aqua destillata*] distilled water

aq ferv *abbr* [L *aqua fervens*] warm water

aq font *abbr* [L *aqua fontana*] spring water

aq·ua \'akwə, 'äkwə, 'ȧ- *sometimes* -(,)kwä; *sometimes* 'ākwə\ *n, pl* **aq·uae** \'a(,)kwē, 'a,kwī; 'ä,kwī, 'ȧ-\ *or* **aquas** [L — more at ISLAND] **1** *pl* **aquae :** WATER **: a** (1) *in old chem* **:** LIQUID (2) **:** a solution esp. in water **b :** an indefinite usu. infinitely large amount of water — used in abbreviated form in chemical formulas ⟨$CaCl_2$ *.aq*⟩ **2** *pl* **aquas :** a variable color averaging a light greenish blue that is greener and paler than average robin's-egg blue (sense 1), paler and slightly bluer than average turquoise (sense 2a), paler and very slightly bluer than average turquoise blue, and greener and slightly deeper than average aqua blue

aqua- — see AQUI-

aqua am·mo·nia \-ə'mōnēə, -nyə\ *or* **aqua am·mo·ni·ae** \-nē,ē\ *n, pl* **aquae ammo·ni·ae** \-nē,ē\ [NL] **:** AMMONIA WATER; *esp* **:** a solution of ammonia containing 10 percent of ammonia by weight

aqua ar·o·mat·i·ca \-,arə'mad·əkə\ *n, pl* **aquae ar·o·mat·i·cae** \-ad·ə,sē\ [NL] **:** AROMATIC WATER

aq·ua·belle \'akwə,bel, 'ä-\ *n* -s [prob. fr. *aquacade* + *belle*] **:** an attractive young woman in a bathing suit

aqua blue *n* **:** a variable color averaging a light greenish blue that is greener and paler than average robin's-egg blue (sense 1), bluer and slightly paler than average aqua, and bluer and paler than average turquoise blue

aq·ua·cade \'akwə,kād, 'äk-\ *n* -s [after *Aquacade,* a water entertainment spectacle at the Cleveland, O. Great Lakes Exposition of 1937 and the New York World's Fair of 1939-40] **:** a water spectacle that consists usu. of exhibitions of swimming and diving with musical accompaniment

aqua cam·pho·rae \-'kam(p)fə,rē\ *n, pl* **aquae camphorae** [NL, water of camphor] **:** CAMPHOR WATER

aq·ua·cul·tur·al *also* **aq·ui·cul·tur·al** \¦akwə¦-\ *adj* **:** of, relating to, or involving aquaculture

aq·ua·cul·ture \'==,-\ *or* **aq·ui·cul·ture** \"\ *n* -s [*aqua-* or *aqui-* + *culture* (as in *agriculture*)] **1 a :** the art of cultivating the natural produce of water **b :** the raising or fattening of fish in enclosed ponds **2 :** HYDROPONICS

Aq·ua·dag \'akwə,dag\ *trademark* — used for a substance that consists of a colloidal suspension of fine particles of graphite in water and is used esp. as a lubricant

aqua des·til·la·ta \-,destə'läd·ə\ *n, pl* **aquae destilla·tae** \-ä,tē\ [NL] **:** DISTILLED WATER

aq·uae·duc·tus \,akwə'dəktəs, -wē'-\ *n, pl* **aquaeduc·ti** \-,tī,-,tē\ [L, lit., conveying of water, aqueduct — more at AQUEDUCT] **:** the right in law to lead or conduct water over the land of another

aquae·haus·tus \-'hȯstəs, -haùs-\ *n, pl* **aquaehaus·ti** \-ō,stī, -aù,stē\ [L *aquae haustus* drawing of water, fr. *aquae* (gen. of *aqua* water) + *haustus* act of drawing, fr. *haustus,* past part. of *haurire* to draw — more at ISLAND, EXHAUST] **:** the right in law to draw water from a well, spring, or stream on another's land

aquae im·mit·ten·dae \-,imə'ten,dē, -,dī — *see* AQUA\ *n pl but sing in constr* [L, waters to be thrown out] **:** the right in law to throw water from one's windows on a neighbor's buildings or soil

aquafer *var of* AQUIFER

aq·ua·flo·ri·um \,akwə'flōrēəm, ,äk-, -ȯr-\ *n* -s [NL, fr. L *aqua* water + *flor-, flos* flower + NL *-ium* — more at ISLAND, BLOSSOM] **:** an inverted glass bowl resting on a base and containing a flower or flowers submerged in water

aq·ua·for·tis \-'fȯrd·əs\ *n* -ES [NL *aqua fortis,* lit., strong water, fr. L *aqua* water + *fortis* strong — more at FORT] **1 :** NITRIC ACID **2 :** etching in which nitric acid is used as a mordant

aq·ua·for·tist \-rd·əst\ *n* -s [prob. fr. F *aquafortiste,* irreg. fr. NL *aqua fortis* + F *-iste* -ist] **:** one who uses aquafortis in etching

aqua gray *n* **:** a variable color averaging a pale blue that is greener and paler than average powder blue, Sistine, or average cadet gray

aqua green *n* **1 :** a variable color averaging a light bluish green that is bluer, lighter, and stronger than robin's-egg blue (sense 2), greener, lighter, and stronger than Eton blue, and slightly paler and very slightly greener than turquoise (sense 2 b) **2 :** a light yellowish green that is greener, stronger, and slightly lighter than pistachio, yellower and paler than apple green (sense 2), greener and deeper than ocean green, and deeper than crayon green

aqua green tint *n* **:** a variable color averaging a very pale green that is paler and slightly bluer than tourmaline and bluer and duller than emerald tint or celadon tint

aquake \ə'-\ *adj* [¹*a-* + *quake* (v.)] **:** QUAKING

aq·ua·lung·er \-,ləŋə(r)\ *n* -s [fr. *Aqualung,* a trademark] **:** an underwater swimmer who uses a breathing device (as a cylinder of compressed air and a watertight face mask)

aq·ua·ma·ni·le \,akwəmə'nī(,)lē, ,äkwəmə'nēlē\ *n, pl* **aqua·mani·les** \-ī(,)lēz, -ēlēz, -lās\ *or* **aquamanil·ia** \-'nilēə\ [LL, alter. of L *aquae manale,* fr. *aquae* (gen. of *aqua* water) + *manale* ewer, fr. neut. of *manalis* flowing, fr. *manare* to flow + *-alis* -al — more at EMANATE] **:** a water vessel or ewer; *specif* **:** a basin used by the priest for washing his hands during the celebration of Mass

aq·ua·ma·rine \,akwəmə'rēn *also* ,äk- *or* ,ȧk-; *attrib* ¦==¦=\ *n* -s *often attrib* [NL *aqua marina,* fr. L, sea water, fr. *aqua* water + *marina,* fem. of *marinus* of the sea — more at MARINE] **1 :** a transparent variety of beryl that is blue, blue-green, or green in color **2 :** a pale blue to light greenish blue

aquamarine chrysolite *n* **:** a beryl of a greenish yellow color

aquamarine topaz *n* **:** a topaz shading to green

aquameter *var of* AQUOMETER

aquam·e·try \ə'kwämə·trē\ *n* -ES [*aqua* + *-metry*] **:** determination of amount of water esp. by means of the Karl Fischer reagent

aqua mi·ra·bi·lis \-mə'räbələs, -rab-\ *n, pl* **aquae mirabi·les** \-ābə,lēz, -lās; -abə,lēz\ [NL, wonderful water] **:** a distilled cordial of old pharmacy made of spirits, sage, betony, balm, and other aromatic ingredients

¹**aq·ua·plane** \'akwə,plān *also* 'äk- *or* 'ȧk-\ *n* [L *aqua* water + E *plane* (surface) — more at ISLAND] **:** a board on which a person stands and which when towed behind a speedboat planes on the surface of the water

²**aquaplane** \"\ *vi* -ED/-ING/-S **:** to ride on an aquaplane

aq·ua·plan·er \-,plānə(r)\ *n* -s **:** one that aquaplanes

aqua pu·ra \-'pyürə, 'pürə\ *n, pl* **aquae pu·rae** \-ē'pyü(,)rē, -ī'pü,rī — *see* AQUA\ [L] **:** pure water

aquardiente *var of* AGUARDIENTE

aqua re·gia \-'rēj(ē)ə\ *n, pl* **aquae regi·ae** \-jē,ē\ [NL, lit., royal water; fr. its ability to dissolve gold] **:** a very corrosive fuming yellow liquid made by mixing nitric and hydrochloric acids usu. in the proportion of one volume of nitric to three or four of hydrochloric and used in dissolving metals (as gold or platinum) and in etching — called also *nitrohydrochloric acid*

aq·ua·relle \¦akwə¦rel, ¦äk- \ *n* -s [F, fr. obs. It *acquarella* (now *acquerello*), fr. *acqua* water, fr. L *aqua*] **1 a :** drawing or painting in watercolor, esp. transparent watercolor — compare GOUACHE **b :** a watercolor drawing or painting esp. when executed in transparent colors **2 :** a picture produced by printing from a key plate and then with brushes applying watercolors through stencils placed over the print — **aq·ua·rel·list** \,==¦reləst\ *n* -s

aquar·i·an \ə'kwa(a)rēən, -wer-, -wär-\ *n* -s *usu cap* [LL *Aquarius* (fr. L *aqua* + *-arius* -ary) + E *-an*] **:** a member of any of certain sects in the early church (as the Encratites) that used water instead of wine in the Eucharist

aquar·ii \-rē,ī, -rē,ē\ *n pl, usu cap* [LL, pl. of *Aquarius*] **:** AQUARIANS

aquar·ist \-rəst\ *n* -s [*aquarium* + *-ist*] **:** one who keeps an aquarium

aquar·i·um \-rēəm\ *n, pl* **aquariums** \-ēəmz\ *or* **aquar·ia** \-ēə\ [L, watering place for cattle, fr. neut. of *aquarius* of water, fr. *aqua* + *-arius* -ary — more at ISLAND] **1 :** a glass bowl or globe, a tank usu. having glass sides, or an artificial pond in which living aquatic animals or plants are kept **2 :** a place or establishment in which aquatic collections are kept and exhibited

aquarium

aquar·i·us \-rēəs\ *n, pl* **aquar·ii** \-ē,ī, -ē,ē\ *or* **aquariuses** *usu cap* [ME, fr. L (trans. of Gk *Hydrochoos*), lit., water carrier, fr. *aqua* + *-arius* -ary] **:** the 11th sign of the zodiac — see SIGN table; ZODIAC illustration

aquas *pl of* AQUA

Aq·ua·stat \'akwə,stat *also* 'äk-\ *trademark* — used for an automatic device for regulating the temperature of water heated by a boiler or furnace

aqua system *n* **:** a system for storing fuel oil or gasoline in tanks having the lower part filled with water upon which the lighter oil rests, water being pumped in from below to maintain the pressure as oil is withdrawn

aquate \ə'kwāt\ *vt* -ED/-ING/-S [back-formation fr. *aquation*] **:** to subject to aquation **:** combine with water (as in the formation of coordination complexes, esp. ions) — compare HYDRATE

aq·ua·terrarium \¦akwə, ¦äk-+\ *n* [*aqua* + *terrarium*] **:** a box or aquarium adapted for water and a sloping bank of earth and rocks in which to culture snails and other amphibious animals

¹**aquat·ic** \ə'kwä¦d·ik, -wa¦, ¦tik, -ēk\ *adj* [MF *aquatique,* fr. L *aquaticus,* fr. *aqua* water] **:** of or relating to water **:** WATER**: a** (1) **:** living wholly or chiefly in or on water ⟨porpoises and seals are ~ animals⟩ (2) **:** growing in or on water ⟨~ plants⟩ (3) **:** living near or frequenting water ⟨gulls and herons are ~ birds⟩ **b :** engaged in or performed in or on water ⟨~ sports⟩ — **aquat·i·cal·ly** \-ək(ə)lē, -ēk-, -li\ *adv*

²**aquatic** \"\ *n* -s **1 :** an aquatic animal or plant **2 :** one given to bathing or swimming or to taking part in aquatic sports **3 aquat·ics** \-ks\ *pl but sometimes sing in constr* **:** water sports

aquatic plant *n* **:** a plant that grows in water (as the water lily, floating heart, or lattice plant) whether rooted in the mud (as a lotus) or floating without anchorage (as the water hyacinth)

¹**aq·ua·tile** \'akwə,tīl\ *adj* [L *aquatilis,* fr. *aqua*] **:** AQUATIC

²**aquatile** *n* -s *obs* **:** an aquatic animal or plant

¹**aq·ua·tint** \'akwə,tint, 'äk-\ *n* -s [It *acqua tinta* dyed water] **1 :** a process of etching in which the plate is grained by an application of powdered rosin and subjected to a series of bitings between some of which certain areas are stopped out, the resulting print resembling a watercolor made with flat washes of different strengths **2 :** an engraving produced by the aquatint process

²**aquatint** \"\ *vt* -ED/-ING/-S **:** to etch by aquatint

aq·ua·tin·ta \¦==¦tintə\ *adj* [It *acqua tinta* dyed water] **:** in aquatint ⟨~ engravings⟩

aqua·tion \ə'kwāshən\ *n* -s [L *aquation-, aquatio* act of fetching water, fr. *aquatus* (past part. of *aquari* to bring or fetch water, fr. *aqua* water) + *-ion-, -io* -ion] **:** the replacement by water molecules of a coordinated atom or group in a coordination complex

aq·ua·ti·za·tion \,akwəd·ə'zāshən, -wə,tī'z-\ *n* -s [*aquate* + *-ization*] **:** AQUATION

aq·ua·tone \'akwə,tōn, 'äk-\ *n* -s [*aqua* + *tone*] **1 :** an offset printing method utilizing a gelatin-coated zinc plate hardened and sensitized to print type, line illustrations, and fine-screen halftones **2 :** a print produced by aquatone

à qua·tre mains \äkatrəmaⁿ\ *adj* [F, lit., for four hands] **:** to be played as a duet at one keyboard — used as a direction in music

aq·ua·vit *also* **ak·va·vit** \'äkwə,vēt, 'ak-; 'äk(,)vä-, 'ȧk(,)vä-; *also* -,vit *or* ,==¦vēt\ *n* -s [Sw, Dan & Norw *akvavit,* fr. ML *aqua vitae*] **:** a colorless or slightly yellow alcoholic liquor produced in the Scandinavian countries by redistilling neutral spirits from grain, potatoes, or esp. wood waste, flavored with caraway seeds, and often taken neat as an aperitif

aqua vi·tae \-'vīd·ē, -ī,tē\ *n* [ME *aqua vite,* fr. ML *aqua vitae,* lit., water of life; prob. fr. the use of brandy as a medicine] **1 :** ALCOHOL; *esp* **:** alcohol obtained by distilling vinous liquids **2 :** a strong liquor (as brandy or whiskey)

aq·ue·duct \'akwə,dəkt\ *n* -s [L *aquaeductus,* fr. *aquae* (gen. of *aqua* water) + *ductus* leading, conducting — more at ISLAND, DUCT] **1 a :** a conduit or artificial channel for conveying water; *esp* **:** one for carrying a large quantity of water which flows by gravitation **b** *or* **aqueduct bridge :** a structure for conveying a canal over a river or hollow **2 :** a canal or passage in a part or organ

aqueduct of fal·lo·pi·us \-fə'lōpēəs\ *usu cap F* [trans. of NL *aquaeductus Fallopii,* after Gabriel *Fallopius* — more at FALLOPIAN TUBE] **:** FACIAL CANAL

aqueduct of syl·vi·us \-'silvēəs\ *usu cap S* [trans. of NL *aquaeductus Sylvii,* after *Sylvius* (Jacques Dubois) †1555 Fr. anatomist] **:** a channel connecting the third and fourth ventricles of the brain

aque·ous \'ākwēəs, 'ak-\ *adj* [ML *aqueus,* fr. L *aqua* + *-eus* -eous] **1 a :** of, relating to, or having the characteristics of water **:** WATERY ⟨the ~ vapor of the air —John Tyndall⟩ **b :** made from, with, or by means of water ⟨~ solutions⟩ **c :** produced by the action of water ⟨~ deposits⟩ **2 :** of or relating to the aqueous humor — **aque·ous·ly** *adv*

aqueous ammonia *n* **:** AMMONIA WATER

aqueous extract *n* **:** an extract prepared by evaporating a watery solution of the soluble principles of a vegetable drug (as licorice) to a semisolid or solid consistency

aqueous humor *n* **:** a limpid fluid occupying the space between the crystalline lens and the cornea of the eye

aqueous meteor *n* **:** a meteor consisting of rain, hail, snow, or dew

aqueous rock *n* **:** a sedimentary rock deposited by or in water — compare EOLIAN

aqui- *also* **aqua-** *comb form* [L *aqui-,* fr. *aqua* — more at ISLAND] **:** water ⟨*aqui*culture⟩ ⟨*aqui*ferous⟩ ⟨*aqua*cade⟩

aq·ui·clude \'akwə,klüd, 'äk-\ *n* -s [*aqui-* + L *cludere, claudere* to close, shut up, block up — more at CLOSE] **:** a geologic formation or stratum that confines water in an adjacent aquifer

aquicultural, aquiculture *var of* AQUACULTURAL, AQUACULTURE

aq·ui·fer *also* **aq·ua·fer** \'akwəfə(r)\ *n* -s [NL, fr. L *aqui-* or *aqua* + *-fer*] **:** a water-bearing bed or stratum of permeable rock, sand, or gravel capable of yielding considerable quantities of water to wells or springs — **aquif·er·ous**\ə'kwifərəs*adj*

aquifer spring *n* **:** a spring whose water rises from an aquifer

aq·ui·fo·li·a·ce·ae \,akwə,fōlē'āsē,ē\ *n pl, cap* [NL, fr. *Aquifolium,* type genus (fr. L, holly tree, fr. *aqui-* — fr. *acer* sharp — + *folium* leaf) + *-aceae* — more at EDGE, BLADE] **:** a family of widely distributed shrubs and trees (order Sapindales) having alternate simple often evergreen leaves, small dioecious flowers usu. in axillary clusters, and berrylike drupes — see ILEX — **aq·ui·fo·li·a·ceous** \¦==,==¦āshəs\ *adj*

aq·ui·fuge \'==,fyüj\ *n* -s [prob. fr. *aqui-* + *-fuge* (as in *refuge*)] **:** AQUICLUDE

aq·ui·la \'akwələ\ *n, cap* [NL, fr. L, eagle] **:** a cosmopolitan genus of eagles (as the golden eagle) including a number of typical forms with the legs feathered to the toes

aq·ui·la·ria \,akwə'la(a)rēə\ *n, cap* [NL (prob. approximate trans. of F *bois d'aigle* agalloch), fr. L *aquila* + NL *-aria* — more at EAGLEWOOD] **:** a genus of Asiatic trees (family Thymelaeaceae) having lanceolate leaves and nearly sessile umbels of flowers — see AGALLOCH

aq·ui·lege \'==,lēj\ *n* -s [NL *aquilegia*] **:** COLUMBINE 1

aq·ui·le·gia \,==¦lēj(ē)ə\ *n* [NL, fr. *aquilegia, aquileia* columbine] **1** *cap* **:** a genus of herbs (family Ranunculaceae) having irregular showy spurred flowers — see COLUMBINE **2** -s **:** COLUMBINE 1

aquil·i·an \ə'kwilēən\ *adj, usu cap* [L *Aquilianus,* fr. C. *Aquilius* Gallus 1st cent. B.C. Roman jurist + L *-anus* -an] **:** arising from or governed by a statute of the Roman republic with respect to wrongful damage to property — used of a fault or liability in civil and Roman law

aquilian stipulation *n, usu cap A* **:** a stipulation in civil and Roman law whereby an obligation can be reduced to a stipulation and then discharged by an acceptilation

aq·ui·line \'akwə,līn, -lən\ *adj* [L *aquilinus,* fr. *aquila* eagle + *-inus* -ine — more at EAGLE] **1 :** of, belonging to, or like an eagle **2 :** curving or hooked like an eagle's beak **:** PROMINENT ⟨an ~ nose⟩ ⟨the ~ profile of a Roman senator —Ellen Glasgow⟩ — **aq·ui·lin·i·ty** \,==¦linəd·ē, -ətē, -i\ *n* -ES

aqui·li·no \,äkwə'lēnō\ *n* -s [It, fr. *aquila* eagle, fr. L] **:** any of several silver coins having the device of an eagle and issued by various Italian states; *esp* **:** the one first issued by Padua in the 13th century

aqui·nist \ə'kwīnəst\ *n* -s *usu cap* [Thomas *Aquinas* †1274, It. scholastic philosopher + E *-ist*] **:** a follower of or specialist in the study of St. Thomas Aquinas **:** THOMIST

¹**aq·ui·ta·ni·an** \¦akwə¦tānēən, -nyən\ *adj, usu cap* [*Aquitania,* Roman division of southwestern Gaul + E *-ian*] **1 :** of or relating to Aquitania **2 :** of or relating to a subdivision of the European Oligocene

²**aquitanian** \"\ *n* -s *cap* **1 :** a native or inhabitant of Aquitania **2 :** the Aquitanian geologic stage

aquiv·er \ə'-\ *adj* [¹*a-* + *quiver,* v.] **:** QUIVERING, TREMBLING

aq·uo \'a(,)kwō, 'ä-\ *adj* [*aquo-*] **:** of or relating to compounds derived from water ⟨lithium hydroxide LiOH is an ~ base⟩ — compare AMMONO

aquo- *comb form* [ISV, fr. L *aqua* water + ISV *-o-*] **1 :** containing a molecule of water as part of a coordination complex ⟨hex*aquo*cobalt (III) chloride $[Co(H_2O)_6]Cl_3$⟩ **2 :** derived from water — in names of chemical compounds ⟨*aquo*carbonic acid $OC(OH)_2$⟩; compare AMMONO- 2

aquo ion *n* **1 :** a complex ion containing one or more water molecules **2 :** an ion formed by aquation

aq·uo·me·ter *also* **aq·ua·me·ter** \'akwə,med·ə(r), ə'kwämed·-\ *n* [*aquometer* fr. L *aqua* water + E *-o-* + *-meter; aquameter* fr. *aqua-* + *-meter*] **:** PULSOMETER

aquos·i·ty \ə'kwäsəd·ē, ā'-\ *n* -ES [LL *aquositas,* fr. L *aquosus* aqueous (fr. *aqua* + *-osus* -ose) + *-itas* -ity] **:** the quality or state of being moist or wet **:** WATERINESS

aq·uo·ti·za·tion \,akwəd·ə'zāshən, -wə,tī'z-\ *n* -s **:** AQUATION

aq·uo·tize \'akwə,tīz\ *vi* -ED/-ING/-S [*aquo-* + connective *-t-* + *-ize*] **:** to undergo aquotization

ar \'är, 'ä\ *n* -s [ME] **:** the letter *r*

-ar \ə(r) *sometimes* ,är *or* ,ä\ *adj suffix* [ME *-ar, -er,* fr. OF & L; OF *-er,* fr. L *-aris,* alter. (after bases containing *l*) of *-alis* -al] **:** of or belonging to ⟨linear⟩ ⟨molecular⟩ ⟨nuclear⟩ ⟨polar⟩ **:** being ⟨spectacular⟩ ⟨triangular⟩ **:** resembling ⟨annular⟩ ⟨oracular⟩ — chiefly in words containing *l* and often accompanied by change of final postconsonantal *-le* of the base word to *-ul-* ⟨angular⟩ ⟨muscular⟩ ⟨titular⟩

ar *abbr* **1** area **2** argent; argentum **3** aromatic **4** arrival; arrive

AR *abbr* **1** account receivable **2** acknowledgment of receipt **3** all rail **4** all risks **5** analyzed reagent **6** [L *anno regni*] in the year of the reign **7** annual return **8** army regulation **9** autonomous republic

Ar *symbol* **1** argon **2** aryl

¹**ara** \'a(a)rə, 'ārə\ *n, cap* [NL, prob. modif. of Tupi *arara* macaw] **:** a genus of macaws containing the blue-and-yellow macaw and the military macaw

²**ara** \"\ *n* -s [origin unknown] **:** TEXTILE SCREW PINE

¹**ar·ab** \'arəb *also* 'er-; *usual or frequent in sense 2, chiefly old-fash in other senses* 'ā,rab *or* 'ā,raa(ə)b\ *n* -s [ME, fr. L *Arabus, Arabs,* fr. Gk *Arab-, Araps,* fr. Ar *'Arab*] **1** *cap* **a :** a member of the Semitic people of the Arabian peninsula, orig. of the Bedouin tribes in the north of the peninsula and east of Palestine **:** ²ARABIAN 1 **b :** a member of any Arabic-speaking people **c :** a tent-dwelling nomadic Arab as distinguished from the oasis or town dweller **2** *sometimes cap* **a :** STREET ARAB **b** *dial* **:** a street peddler or house-to-house peddler of fruits and vegetables **3** *usu cap* **:** a horse of the stock used

by the natives of Arabia, adjacent regions of Asia, and parts of northern Africa; *specif* **:** a horse of a breed noted for its graceful build, speed, intelligence, and spirit and often used as sires to improve or modify other stocks — compare THOROUGHBRED 1 **4** *also* **arab brown** *often cap A* **:** a strong brown that is yellower, less strong, and slightly lighter than average russet and yellower and paler than average copper brown — called also *rugby tan*

²arab \"\ *adj, usu cap* **:** of, relating to, or characteristic of the Arabs **:** ARABIAN

arab- *or* **arabo-** *comb form* [ISV, fr. *arabinose*] **1 :** related to arabinose ⟨*arabo*ascorbic acid⟩ **2** *arabo-, usu ital* **:** having the stereochemical arrangement of atoms or groups found in arabinose ⟨D-*arabo*-3-hexulose⟩

¹ara·ba \ə'räbə\ *also* **aro·ba** \"\ *or* **ar·ba** \'ärbə\ *n* -s [Russ & Turk; Russ *arba*, fr. Turk *araba*] **:** a carriage (as a cab or coach) used in Turkey and neighboring countries

²ar·a·ba \'arəbə\ *n* -s [Pg, prob. fr. Tupi] **:** a So. American howler monkey (*Alouatta straminea*)

ar·a·ban \'arə,ban\ *n* -s [*arab-* + *-an*] **:** a pentosan yielding arabinose on hydrolysis

ar·a·bel·la \,arə'belə\ *n, cap* [NL] **:** a common genus of slender cylindrical polychaete worms

¹ar·a·besque \¦arə¦besk *also* ¦er-\ *adj* [F, fr. It *arabesco*, fr. *arabesco* Arabic, made or done in the Arabic fashion, fr. *Arabo* Arab (fr. L *Arabus*) + *-esco* -esque — more at ARAB] **:** relating to or exhibiting the style of ornament called arabesque ⟨~ frescoes⟩

²arabesque \"\ *n* -s **1 a :** an ornament or a style of ornamentation found in painting, low-relief carving, mosaic, and textile design that employs flower, foliage, or fruit and sometimes animal and figural outlines or forms so as to produce an intricate pattern of interlaced lines sometimes geometric and angular in character (as in Islamic art) and sometimes curviform and flowing (as in Renaissance decoration) **b :** a linear design motif of the kind occurring in arabesque ornament **2 :** musical embellishment; *specif* **:** a passage of music suggestive of an arabesque **3 :** a posture (as in ballet dancing) in which the body is bent forward from the hip on one leg with the corresponding arm extended forward and the other arm and leg backward in a line parallel to the floor

arabesque 1

³arabesque \"\ *vt* -ED/-ING/-S [²*arabesque*] **:** to ornament with or in the style of arabesques

arabesque spin *n* **:** a forward or backward skating spiral done in arabesque position

¹ara·bi·an \ə'rābēən *also* -byən\ *adj, usu cap* [*Arabia*, peninsula in southwestern Asia + E *-an*] **:** of, relating to, or characteristic of Arabia or Arabians ⟨*Arabian* nomads⟩

²arabian \"\ *n* -s *cap* **1 :** a native or inhabitant of Arabia **2 :** ARAB 3

arabian baboon *n, usu cap A* **:** SACRED BABOON

arabian brown *n, often cap A* **:** a moderate to strong brown that is redder and slightly darker than oak and darker than Vassar tan

arabian camel *n, usu cap A* **:** the one-humped camel (*Camelus dromedarius*) of western Asia and northern Africa — called also *dromedary*

arabian coffee *n, usu cap A* **:** a large evergreen shrub or small tree (*Coffea arabica*) native to tropical Africa but widely cultivated in a number of horticultural varieties in tropical and subtropical regions for its seeds which form most of the coffee of commerce

arabian gum *n, usu cap A* **:** KORDOFAN GUM

arabian horse *n, usu cap A* **:** ARAB 3

arabian hyrax *n, usu cap A* **:** SYRIAN HYRAX

arabian jasmine *or* **arabian jessamine** *n, usu cap A* **:** an East Indian vine (*Jasminum sambac*) cultivated for its profuse fragrant white flowers

arabian red *n, often cap A* **:** INDIA RED

arabian senna *n, usu cap A* **:** an Arabian form of senna derived from a shrub (*Cassia acutifolia*)

arabian tea *n, usu cap A* **:** KAT

¹ar·a·bic \'arəbik *also* 'er-\ *adj, usu cap* [ME *arabik*, fr. MF *arabic*, fr. L *Arabicus*, fr. *Arabus* Arab + *-icus* -ic — more at ARAB] **1 :** of, relating to, or characteristic of Arabia **2 :** of, relating to, or characteristic of the Arabs **3 :** of, relating to, characteristic of, or constituting the language Arabic **4 :** of, relating to, constituting, or written in the Arabic alphabet **5 :** expressed in or utilizing arabic numerals ⟨21 is an *Arabic* number⟩ ⟨*Arabic* notation⟩

²arabic \"\ *n* -s *cap* [ME *arabik*, fr. MF *arabic*, fr. *arabic*, adj.] **:** a Semitic language orig. of the Arabs of the Hejaz and Nejd that is now the prevailing speech of Arabia, Jordan, Lebanon, Syria, Iraq, Egypt, and parts of northern Africa and that has numerous dialects but in the written form usu. conforms to the classical standards of the Koran — see AFRO-ASIATIC LANGUAGES table

arab·i·ca coffee *also* **arabica** \ə'rabəkə\ *n, often cap A* [NL *arabica* (specific epithet of *Coffea arabica*), fr. L, fem. of *Arabicus*] **:** coffee (sense 2) produced from Arabian coffee — compare MOCHA

arabic alphabet *n, usu cap 1st A* **:** the alphabet of 28 letters derived from the Aramaic which is used for writing Arabic and also with adaptations for numerous other languages of Asia, Africa, and Europe of peoples professing the Muslim religion — see ALPHABET table

arabic architecture *n, usu cap 1st A* **:** the Saracenic architecture of the Arab dominions established in Syria and Egypt during the 1st century after the hegira (A.D. 622–722)

arab·i·cism \ə'rabə,sizəm\ *n* -s *usu cap* [*arabic* + *-ism*] **:** ARABISM 1

arab·i·cize \-,sīz\ *vt* -ED/-ING/-S *often cap* [*arabic* + *-ize*] **1 :** to adapt (a language or elements of language) to the phonetic or structural pattern of Arabic **2 :** ARABIZE 1

arabic numeral *or* **arabic figure** *n, often cap A* **:** one of the number symbols 0, 1, 2, 3, 4, 5, 6, 7, 8, 9 conventionally so written for enumeration and for arithmetical computation — called also *Hindu numeral*; see NUMBER table

ar·a·bi·dopsis \,arəbə'däpsəs\ *n, cap* [NL, fr. *Arabid-*, *Arabis* + *-opsis*] **:** a small genus of annual or biennial herbs (family Brassicaceae) of north temperate regions with basal rosettes of petioled leaves, cauline leaves short-petioled or clasping, and flowers white, purplish, or sometimes yellow petals — see MOUSE-EAR CRESS

ar·a·bil·i·ty \,arə'biləd·ē, -ətē, -i *also* ,er-\ *n* -ES **:** the state of being arable

arab·i·nose \ə'rabə,nōs, 'arəb-\ *n* -s [ISV *arabin*, the solid principle in gum arabic (fr. — *gum — arabic* + *-in*) + *-ose*] **:** a crystalline aldose sugar $C_5H_{10}O_5$ of the pentose class obtained in the dextrorotatory L-form esp. from cherry-tree gum or mesquite gum or prepared synthetically in the levorotatory D-form from D-glucose — **arab·i·nos·ic** \ə¦rabə¦nōsik, ¦arəb-\ *adj*

ar·a·bin·o·side \,arə'binə,sīd, ə'rabənō-\ *n* -s [*arabinose* + *-ide*] **:** a glycoside that yields arabinose on hydrolysis

ar·a·bis \'arəbəs\ *n, cap* [NL, fr. Gk *arabid-, arabis*, a brassicaceous plant, prob. fr. *Arab-, Araps* Arab; fr. its ability to grow in rocky or sandy soil] **:** a large genus of herbs (family Cruciferae) with white or purple flowers and flat siliques with nerved valves — see SICKLEPOD, TOWER MUSTARD

ar·ab·ism \'arə,bizəm\ *n* -s *usu cap* [²*arab* + *-ism*] **1 :** a characteristic feature of Arabic occurring in another language **2 :** devotion to Arab interests, customs, culture, ideas, or ideals

ar·ab·ist \-bəst\ *n* -s *usu cap* [²*arab* + *-ist*] **:** a specialist in the Arabic language or in the culture of the Arabic-speaking peoples

arab·i·tol \ə'rabə,tōl, -ōl\ *n* -s [*arab-* + *-itol*] **:** a sweet crystalline pentahydroxy alcohol $C_5H_7(OH)_5$ obtained by the reduction of arabinose

ar·ab·i·za·tion \,arəbə'zāshən\ *n* -s *usu cap* **:** the act or process of arabizing or of being arabized

ar·ab·ize \'arə,bīz\ *vt* -ED/-ING/ -S *often cap* [²*arab* + *-ize*] **1 a :** to cause to acquire Arab customs, manners, speech, or outlook **b :** to modify (a racial or national stock) by an admixture of Arab blood **2 :** ARABICIZE 1

¹ar·a·ble \'arəbəl *also* 'er-\ *adj* [MF or L; MF *arable*, fr. L *arabilis*, fr. *arare* to plow + *-abilis* -able — more at EAR] **1 a :** capable of being plowed **:** fit for tillage and crop production ⟨~ land⟩ **b** *Brit* **:** engaged in or involving the production of cultivated crops ⟨~ farmer⟩ ⟨~ farming⟩ **c** *Brit, of crops* **:** requiring cultivation; *esp* **:** seeded and grown annually rather than from the regrowth of an established sod ⟨small grains or other ~ crops⟩ **2** *Brit, of livestock* **:** fed on cultivated crops (as roots) ⟨the ~ ewe going back on to the rough grazing —S.J.Watson⟩

²arable \"\ *n* -s **1 :** land that is tilled or tillable **2** *Brit* **:** TILLAGE

arabo- — see ARAB-

ar·a·bo·galactan \¦arə,bō+\ *n* -s [*arab-* + *galactan*] **:** a gummy substance that is found esp. in the wood of the western larch and that yields arabinose and galactose on hydrolysis

ar·a·bon·ic acid \¦arə¦bänik-\ *n* [ISV *arab-* + *-onic*] **:** a crystalline acid $HOCH_2(CHOH)_3COOH$ obtained by oxidation of arabinose, dextrose, or levulose and used in synthesizing riboflavin

ar·a·ça \¦arə¦sä\ *n* -s [Pg *araçá*, fr. Tupi] **:** a Brazilian timber tree (*Terminalia januarensis*) suggesting birch in its working properties

ar·a·can·ga \,arə'kaŋgə\ *n* -s [Pg, fr. Tupi *araracanga*] **:** SCARLET MACAW

ar·a·ca·ri \,ärə'särē\ *n* -s [Pg *araçari*, fr. Tupi] **:** any of several brilliantly colored tropical American toucans

ara·ce·ae \ə'rāsē,ē\ *n pl, cap* [NL, fr. *Arum*, type genus + *-aceae* — more at ARUM] **:** a family of plants (order Arales) chiefly of tropical distribution distinguished by having the flowers on a fleshy spadix subtended by a leafy spathe — **ara·ceous** \-shəs\ *adj*

arach *abbr* ARACHNOLOGY

ar·a·chide \'arə,kīd, -,kəd\ *n* -s [F, fr. NL *Arachid-, Arachis*] **:** PEANUT 1

ar·a·chid·ic acid \,arə'kidik-\ *also* **arach·ic acid** \ə'rakik-\ *n* [ISV *arachid-* or *arach-* (fr. NL *Arachid-, Arachis*) + *-ic*] **:** a white crystalline saturated fatty acid $CH_3(CH_2)_{18}COOH$ found in the form of esters esp. in vegetable fats and oils (as peanut oil) — called also *eicosanoic acid*

ar·a·chi·don·ic acid \,arəkə'dänik-\ *n* [ISV *arachidic* + *-onic*] **:** a liquid unsaturated acid $C_{19}H_{31}COOH$ occurring in most animal fats (as in the phosphatides of beef adrenal glands and the lipids of the liver) and considered essential in animal nutrition

ar·a·chin \'arəkən\ *n* -s [ISV *arachic* + *-in*] **:** a globulin constituting the chief protein of the peanut

ar·a·chis \-kəs\ *n* [NL, perh. modif. of Gk *arakis* chickling vetch, dim. of *arakos* chickling vetch; perh. akin to L *arinca*, a cereal grain] **1** *cap* **:** a small genus of mostly Brazilian herbs (family Leguminosae) with yellow flowers and pods that ripen underground — see PEANUT **2** -ES **:** a plant of the genus *Arachis*

arachis oil *n* **:** PEANUT OIL

arachn- *or* **arachno-** *comb form* [NL & Gk; NL, fr. Gk, fr. *arachnē*; perh. akin to L *aranea* spider, Gk *arkys* net] **1 :** spider ⟨*arachno*logy⟩ **2 :** arachnoid membrane ⟨*arachn*itis⟩

ar·ach·nac·tis \,a,rak'naktəs\ *n, pl* **arach·nac·ti·nes** \ə,rak,nak'tī(,)nēz\ [NL, fr. *arachn-* + Gk *aktis* ray — more at ACTIN-] **:** a free-swimming larva of certain actinians

arach·ne·an \ə'raknēən, ¦a,rak¦nēən\ *adj* [*arachn-* + *-ean*] **:** having the lightness or fineness of texture of a spider's web **:** GOSSAMER

arach·ni·cide \ə'raknə,sīd\ *n* -s [*arachnid* + *-cide*] **:** a substance that kills arachnids (as mites)

arach·nid \ə'raknəd\ *n* -s [NL *Arachnida*] **:** one of the Arachnida

arach·ni·da \-nədə\ *n pl, cap* [NL, fr. *arachn-* + *-ida*] **1 :** a large class of arthropods including scorpions, spiders, mites, and related forms all lacking wings and free first antennae and having highly modified prehensile second antennae and most being also air-breathing by means of tracheae or book lungs and having head and thorax fused to form a cephalothorax that bears six pairs of appendages consisting of four pairs of walking legs, a pair of pedipalpi variously specialized in different groups, and a pair of buccal chelicerae often provided with poison glands **2** *in former classifications* **:** a more extensive group including the Arachnida together with the king crabs, tongue worms, sea spiders, water bears, and sometimes the extinct eurypterids

arach·nid·ism \-nə,dizəm\ *n* -s [*arachnid* + *-ism*] **:** poisoning caused by the bite or sting of an arachnid (as a spider, tick, or scorpion); *esp* **:** a syndrome marked by extreme pain and muscular rigidity due to the bite of a black widow spider

ar·ach·nid·i·um \,a,rak'nidēəm\ *n, pl* **arachnid·ia** \-ēə\ [NL, fr. *Arachnida* + *-ium*] **:** the apparatus by which a spider's web is produced consisting of the silk glands and their ducts and the spinnerets

arach·nid·ol·o·gy \ə,raknə'däləjē\ *n* -ES [*arachnid* + *-ology*] **:** ARACHNOLOGY

ar·ach·ni·tis \,a,rak'nīd·əs\ *n* -ES [NL, fr. *arachn-* + *-itis*] **:** ARACHNOIDITIS

arach·no·dac·ty·ly \ə,raknō'daktəlē\ *n* -ES [*arachn-* + *-dactyly* (fr. NL *-dactylia*)] **:** a hereditary abnormality characterized by excessive length of the long bones (as of the fingers and toes) and usu. associated with other abnormalities

¹arach·noid \ə'rak,nȯid\ *n* -s [NL *arachnoides*, fr. Gk *arachnoeidēs* cobweblike, fr. *arachn-* + *-eidēs* -oid] **:** a thin membrane of the brain and spinal cord that lies between the dura mater and the pia mater

²arachnoid \"\ *adj* **:** of or relating to the arachnoid ⟨the ~ membrane⟩

³arachnoid \"\ *adj* [*arachn-* + *-oid*] **:** of, relating to, or characterizing the Arachnida **:** like arachnids

⁴arachnoid \"\ *n* -s **:** ARACHNID; *broadly* **:** any of various invertebrate animals that resemble or are related to arachnids

⁵arachnoid \"\ *adj* [Gk *arachnoeidēs*] **:** resembling a spider's web; *specif* **:** covered with or composed of soft loose hairs or fibers — used esp. of plants ⟨an ~ leaf⟩

ar·ach·noi·dal \¦a,rak¦nȯidᵊl\ *also* **ar·ach·noi·de·an** \-dēən\ *adj* **:** ²ARACHNOID

¹ar·ach·noi·dea \,a,rak'nȯidēə\ [NL, fr. Gk *arachnoeidēs*] *syn of* ARACHNIDA

²arachnoidea \"\ *n* -s [NL, alter. of *arachnoides* — more at ARACHNOID] **:** ¹ARACHNOID

arachnoid granulation *n* **:** PACCHIONIAN BODY

arach·noid·ism \ə'rak,nȯi,dizəm\ *n* -s [⁴*arachnoid* + *-ism*] **:** ARACHNIDISM

arach·noid·i·tis \ə,rak,nȯi'dīd·əs\ *n* -ES [NL, fr. *arachnoides* or *arachnoidea* + *-itis*] **:** inflammation of the arachnoid membrane

ar·ach·nol·o·gist \,a,rak'näləjəst\ *n* -s **:** a specialist in arachnology

ar·ach·nol·o·gy \-jē\ *n* -ES [ISV *arachn-* + *-logy*] **:** the branch of zoology that deals with spiders and other arachnids

arach·no·ly·sin \ə,raknō'līsᵊn\ *n* -s [ISV *arachn-* + *-lysin*] **:** a hemolysin secreted by certain spiders

arach·no·morph \ə'raknō,mȯrf\ *adj* [NL *Arachnomorphae*] **:** of or relating to the Arachnomorphae

arach·no·mor·phae \⸗,⸗⸗'mȯr,fē\ *n pl, cap* [NL, fr. *arachn-* + *-morphae*] *in some classifications* **:** a suborder of Araneida including the great majority of spiders and distinguished by having the poison fangs moving in and out and the venom glands extending beyond the base of the fangs

ar·ach·noph·a·gous \,a,rak'näfəgəs\ *adj* [*arachn-* + *-phagous*] **:** feeding on spiders

ar·ach·no·pia \-'nōpēə\ *n* -s [NL, fr. *arachn-* + *pia* (membrane)] **:** PIA-ARACHNOID

ar·a·did \'arədəd, -,did\ *n* -s [NL *Aradidae*] **:** one of the Aradidae

arad·i·dae \ə'radə,dē\ *n pl, cap* [NL, fr. *Aradus*, type genus (perh. fr. Gk *arados* disturbance) + *-idae*] **:** a family of small flat narrow-headed bugs usu. living under bark and including a So. American species capable of inflicting severe bites

arae·o·style \ə'rēə,stīl\ *or* **are·o·style** \", 'arēō-\ *n* -s [earlier *areostylos*, fr. L *araeostylos*, adj., having such an intercolumniation, fr. Gk *araiostylos*, fr. *araios* thin, weak, intermittent + *stylos* pillar — more at STEER] **:** an intercolumniation of usu. four or more diameters — see INTERCOLUMNIATION illustration

araeo·systyle \ə¦rēō+\ *or* **areo·systle** \", ¦arē(,)ō+\ *n* -s [F *aréosystyle*, fr. Gk *araios* + F *systyle*, fr. L *systylos* — more at SYSTYLE] **:** an intercolumniation that is alternately a systyle and an araeostyle

ar·a·go·ne·sa \,arəgō'nāsə, -āzə\ *n* -s *often cap* [Sp (*jota*) *aragonesa* Aragonese jota; *aragonesa*, fem. of *aragonés*] **:** a Spanish couple folk dance from Aragon — called also *jota aragonesa*

¹ar·a·go·nese \¦arəgə¦nēz, -ēs\ *adj, usu cap* [Sp *aragonés*, fr. *Aragón*, region and ancient kingdom in northeastern Spain + Sp *-és* -ese (fr. L *-ensis*)] **:** of or relating to the Aragon region and former kingdom of northeastern Spain or to its inhabitants

²aragonese \"\ *n, pl* **aragonese** *cap* **1 :** a native or inhabitant of Aragon **2 :** the dialect of Spanish spoken in Aragon

arag·o·nite \ə'ragə,nīt, 'arəgə,nīt\ *n* -s [G *aragonit*, fr. *Aragon*, its locality + G *-it* -ite] **:** a mineral consisting like calcite of calcium carbonate $CaCO_3$ but differing from calcite esp. in its orthorhombic crystallization, greater density, and less distinct cleavage and occurring most commonly in beds of gypsum and of iron ore (hardness 3.5–4, sp. gr. 2.93–2.95)

ar·a·gon spar \'arə,gän-, -,gən-\ *n, usu cap A & sometimes cap S* **:** ARAGONITE

ara·gua·nay *also* **ara·gua·ne** *or* **ara·gua·ney** \,ärəgwä'nā\ *n* -s [AmerSp *araguaney*] **:** any of several trees of the genus *Tecoma*

ara·gua·to \,ärə'gwä,d·ō\ *n* -ES [modif. of F *araguate*, of Cariban origin — more at ALOUATTE] **:** URSINE HOWLER

arahat *or* **arahant** *often cap, var of* ARHAT

¹arain \'ārən\ *n* -s [ME *arain, irain, aran*, fr. MF & L; MF *araigne, iraigne*, fr. L *aranea* — more at ARACHN-] *now dial* **:** SPIDER

²arain \ə'rīn\ *n* -s *usu cap* **1 :** a Muslim people of the Punjab region in India **2 :** a member of the Arain people

araire \ə're(ə)r\ *n* -s [F, fr. Prov, fr. L *aratrum*, fr. *arare* to plow — more at EAR] **:** a primitive plow used in southern Europe

araise *vt* -ED/-ING/-S [ME *araisen, areisen*, fr. *a-* (perfective prefix) + *raisen, reisen* to raise — more at ABEAR, RAISE] *obs* **:** to raise esp. from the dead

arak *var of* ARRACK

ar·a·ka·nese \¦arəkə¦nēz, -ēs\ *n, pl* **arakanese** *usu cap* [*Arakan*, division of Lower Burma + E *-ese*] **1 a :** a Burmese people of the western Arakan coastlands of Burma who have been strongly influenced by contact with Muslim culture in India **b :** a member of such people **2 :** the language of the Arakanese

ara·ka·wa·ite \,ärə'käwə,īt\ *n* -s [*Arakawa* mine, Akita prefecture, Japan, its locality + E *-ite*] **:** VESZELYITE

arake \ə'rāk\ *adj* [¹*a-* + *rake*] **:** inclined from the perpendicular **:** RAKED

ara·les \ə'rā,lēz\ *n pl, cap* [NL, fr. *Arum* genus of araceous plants + *-ales* — more at ARUM] **:** an order of monocotyledonous woody or herbaceous plants that are usu. sympodial with cyclic flowers on a spadix — see ARACEAE, LEMNACEAE

ara·lia \ə'rālēə, -lyə\ *n* [NL] **1** *cap* **:** a large genus (the type of the family Araliaceae) of widely distributed often aromatic herbs, shrubs, and trees with compound leaves and umbellate flowers — see HERCULES'-CLUB, SPIKENARD **2 2** -s **:** a plant of the genus *Aralia* **3 :** the dried rhizome and roots of a plant (*Aralia racemosa*) used as a diaphoretic and aromatic

ara·li·a·ce·ae \ə,rālē'āsē,ē\ *n pl, cap* [NL, fr. *Aralia*, type genus + *-aceae*] **:** a widely distributed family of plants (order Umbellales) with flowers typically pentamerous and umbellate and fruit a drupe or berry — compare GINSENG, HEDERA

ara·li·a·ceous \ə¦rālē¦āshəs\ *adj* [NL *Araliaceae* + E *-ous*] **:** of or belonging to the Araliaceae

ara·li·ad \ə'rālē,ad\ *n* -s [NL *Aralia* + E *-ad*] **:** an araliaceous plant

ar·al·i·phat·ic \¦a,ralə¦fad·ik\ *adj* [*aryl* + *aliphatic*] **:** of or relating to an essentially aliphatic compound containing one or more aryl groups ⟨~ amines⟩

ar·al·koxy \¦arəl¦käksē\ *adj* [*aralkoxy-*, fr. *aralkyl* + *oxy-*] **:** of, relating to, or containing a univalent radical composed of an aralkyl group united with one atom of oxygen

ar·al·kyl \a'ral,kil\ *n* -s [ISV *aryl* + *alkyl*] **:** an aryl-substituted alkyl radical ⟨benzyl is the best-known ~⟩

ar·al·kyl·ate \a'ralkə,lāt, -lət, *usu* -d·+V\ *vt* -ED/-ING/-S **:** to introduce aralkyl into (a compound)

¹ar·a·mae·an *also* **ar·a·me·an** \¦arə¦mēən\ *adj, usu cap* [L *Aramaeus* (fr. Gk *Aramaios*, fr. Heb *'Ărām* Aram, ancient name for Syria) + E *-an*] **1 :** of, relating to, or characteristic of ancient Aram or the Aramaeans **2 :** ARAMAIC

²aramaean *also* **aramean** \"\ *n, pl* **aramaeans** *or* **arameans** *usu cap* **1 :** a member of a Semitic people that settled in the second millennium B.C. in Syria and Upper Mesopotamia, where they established a number of city-states and came to be engaged extensively in overland trade **2 :** ARAMAIC

¹ar·a·ma·ic \¦arə¦māik\ *adj, usu cap* [Gk *Aramaios* + E *-ic*] **:** of, relating to, characteristic of, or composed in Aramaic

²aramaic \"\ *n* -s *cap* **:** a Semitic language of which documents are known from as early as the 9th century B.C., orig. the speech of the Aramaeans but later used extensively in southwest Asia as a commercial lingua franca and governmental language and adopted as their customary speech by various non-Aramaean peoples including the Jews among whom it replaced Hebrew after the Babylonian exile, developing into an eastern and a western type, each having various dialects some of which are often regarded as separate languages, but ultimately being largely displaced by Arabic as a consequence of the Muslim conquests, only neo-Syriac of the eastern group and Modern Western Aramaic of the western group being still spoken

aramaic alphabet *n, usu cap 1st A* **1 :** an extinct North Semitic alphabet dating from the 9th century B.C. which was for several centuries the commercial alphabet of southwest Asia and was the parent of the Syriac, Arabic, and numerous other alphabets **2 :** the square Hebrew alphabet as distinguished from the early Hebrew alphabet

ar·a·ma·ism \,arə'mā,izəm, 'arə(,)mā-\ *also* **ar·a·ma·i·cism** \,arə'māə,sizəm\ *n* -s *usu cap* [¹*aramaic* + *-ism*] **:** a characteristic feature of Aramaic occurring in another language

ar·a·ma·ize \-,īz\ *vt* -ED /-ING/ -S *often cap* [¹*aramaic* + *-ize*] **1 :** to tincture with Aramaisms ⟨*aramaized* Greek⟩ **2 :** to cause to become Aramaean in culture or Aramaic in language ⟨Syria . . . became thoroughly *Aramaized* —David Diringer⟩

ar·a·may·o·ite \,arə'mīə,wīt\ *n* -s [F. A. *Aramayo*, 20th cent. mine director in Bolivia + E *-ite*] **:** a black metallic mineral consisting of silver antimony bismuth sulfide $Ag(Sb,Bi)S_2$ related in crystal structure to galena

ar·a·mi·na \,arə'mēnə\ *n* -s [Pg, dim. of *arame* wire, fr. LL *aeramen* copper, fr. L *aes* copper, ore — more at ORE] **:** the fiber of the Caesar weed — called also *Congo jute*

ara·ña \ə'ränyə\ *n* -s [AmerSp, fr. Sp, spider, fr. L *aranea* — more at ARACHN-] **:** a Mexican 2-wheeled horse-drawn cab

araña del mar \-,del'mär\ *n* [Sp, lit., spider of the sea] **:** ARROW CRAB

aranda *or* **arunta** *usu cap, var of* ARUNTA

ara·nea \ə'rānēə\ *n, cap* [NL, fr. L, spider — more at ARACHN-] **:** a genus of orb-weaving spiders (family Argiopidae) including the common garden spiders

ara·ne·ae \-nē,ē\ [NL, fr. pl. of *Aranea*] *syn of* ARANEIDA

araneae ther·a·pho·sae \-,therə'fō,sē\ *n pl, cap A* [NL, theraphose *Araneae*] *in some classifications* **:** a division of spiders that comprises those with vertically articulated chelicerae and is equivalent to the Liphistiomorphae plus the Mygalomorphae

araneae ve·rae \-'vi,rē\ *n pl, cap A* [NL, lit., true spiders] *in some classifications* **:** a division of spiders that comprises those with laterally articulated chelicerae and is equivalent to the Apneumonomorphae, Dipneumonomorphae, and Hypochilomorphae

ara·ne·id \ə'rānēəd, ,arə'n-, -,id\ *n* -s [NL *Araneida*] **:** SPIDER 1

ar·a·ne·i·da \,arə'nēədə\ *n pl, cap* [NL, fr. *Aranea* + *-ida*] **:** the order of Arachnida consisting of the spiders, all having the body divided into a cephalothorax and a short usu. unsegmented abdomen, the chelicerae modified into poison fangs, leglike pedipalpi, simple eyes, a web-spinning apparatus at the end of the abdomen, and respiratory lung sacs or tracheae in the abdomen — **ar·a·ne·i·dal** \ˌ=ˌ=ˈ=ədᵊl\ *adj* — **ar·a·ne·i·dan** \-ədᵊn\ *adj or n*

ar·a·ne·i·form \ˌ=ˌ=ˈ=əˌfȯrm\ *adj* [L *aranea* + E *-iform*] **:** like a spider

ar·a·ne·i·for·mes \ˌ=ˌ=ˌ=ˈfȯrˌmēz\ *also* **araneifor·mia** \-ˌmēə\ *n pl, cap* [*Araneiformes* fr. NL, fr. L *aranea* spider + NL *-iformes*; *Araneiformia* fr. NL, prob. alter. of *Araneiformes*] *in old classifications* **:** PYCNOGONIDA

ara·ne·i·na \əˌrāˌnēˈīnə\ *or* **ara·ne·oi·dea** \-ˈȯidēə\ [NL, fr. *Aranea* + *-ina* or *-oidea*] *syn of* ARANEIDA

ara·ne·ol·o·gist \-ˈäləjəst\ *n* -s **:** a specialist in the study of spiders

ara·ne·ol·o·gy \-jē, -i\ *n* -ES [F *aranéologie*, fr. L *aranea* + F *-o-* + *-logie* -logy] **:** the branch of zoology that deals with spiders

ara·ne·o·morph \əˈrānēəˌmȯrf\ *adj* [NL *Araneomorphae*] **:** ARACHNOMORPH

ara·ne·o·mor·phae \ˌ=ˌ=ˌ=ˈmȯrˌfē\ [NL, fr. *araneo-* (fr. *Aranea*) + *-morphae*] *syn of* ARACHNOMORPHAE

ara·ne·ous \əˈrānēəs\ *also* **ara·ne·ose** \-ˌōs\ *adj* [*araneous* prob. modif. (influenced by L *araneus* of a spider, fr. *aranea* spider) of L *araneosus*, fr. *aranea* spider + *-osus* -ose; *araneose* fr. L *araneosus*] **:** ²ARACHNOID

ara·ne·us \-əs\ [NL, fr. L, of a spider, fr. *aranea* spider] *syn of* ARANEA

aran·ga \əˈräŋgə\ *n* -s [Tag] **1** *Philippines* **:** a tree of the genus *Homalium* (esp. *H. luzoniense*) **2** *Philippines* **:** the hard reddish wood of aranga

aran·ya·ka \äˈrənyəkə\ *n* -s *usu cap* [Skt *āraṇyaka*, lit., forest treatise] **:** one of a group of sacred Hindu writings composed between the Brahmanas and the Upanishads and used in Vedic ritual

ara·ona \ˌarəˈōnə\ *or* **ara·una** \ˌarəˈünə\ *n, pl* **araona** *or* **araonas** *or* **arauna** *or* **araunas** *usu cap* [Sp *araona* & Pg *araúna*, of AmerInd origin] **1 a :** a Tacanan people of northwest Bolivia and adjacent parts of Brazil **b :** a member of such people **2 :** the language of the Araona people

arap·a·hite \əˈrapəˌhīt\ *n* -s [*Arapaho* + E *-ite*; fr. its discovery on land owned by Arapahos] **:** a basic basalt rock containing bytownite, augite, over 50 percent of magnetite, and abundant apatite

arap·a·ho *or* **arap·a·hoe** \əˈrapəˌhō\ *n, pl* **arapaho** *or* **arapahos** *or* **arapahoe** *or* **arapahoes** *usu cap* [perh. fr. Crow *aa·raxpé-ahu*, lit., tattoo, fr. *aa-* with + *raxpé* skin + *-ahu* lots, many] **1 a :** an Algonquian people ranging over the plains region from southern Saskatchewan and Manitoba to New Mexico and Texas **b :** a member of such people **2 :** the Algonquian language of the Arapaho people

ar·a·pai·ma \ˌarəˈpīmə\ *n* [NL, fr. Pg & Sp, pirarucu, of Tupian origin; akin to Mura *uarapâinu*] **1** *cap* **:** a genus of Osteoglossidae comprising the pirarucu **2** -s [Pg & Sp] **:** PIRARUCU

ar·a·pesh \ˈarəˌpesh\ *n, pl* **arapesh** *or* **arapeshes** *usu cap* **1 :** a Papuan people inhabiting the Sepik district, Territory of New Guinea **2 :** a member of the Arapesh people

ar·a·pho·ros·tic \ˌarəfəˈrästik\ *or* **ar·a·phos·tic** \ˌ=ˈ=ˈfästik\ *adj* [irreg., fr. Gk *arrhaphos* (fr. *a-* ²*a-* + *-rhaphos*, fr. *rhaptein* to sew) + E *-ic* — more at RHAPSODY] **:** lacking seams **:** UNSEWED ⟨an ~ shoe⟩

ar·a·pon·ga \ˌarəˈpäŋgə\ *n* -s [Pg] **:** BELLBIRD a

ara·ri·ba \ˌarərēˈbä\ *n* -s [Pg *araribá*, fr. Tupi] **1 :** any of several trees of the genus *Centrolobium* (family Leguminosae); *esp* **:** a Brazilian tree (*C. robustum*) — called also *zebrawood* **2 :** any of several trees of the genus *Sickingia* usu. with heavy dark red wood **3 :** the wood of an arariba tree

ara·ro·ba \ˌarəˈrōbə\ *n* -s [Pg, of Tupian origin; akin to Tupi *araribá*] **1 :** GOA POWDER **2 :** ARARIBA

arastra *var of* ARRASTRA

ar·a·tin·ga \ˌarəˈtiŋgə\ *n* [NL, fr. Pg] **1** *cap* **:** a genus of rather large chiefly green parrakeets of tropical America **2** -s **:** a parrakeet of the genus *Aratinga* **:** CONURE

arau \äˈrau̇\ *n, pl* **arau** *or* **araus** *usu cap* **1 :** a Papuan people of western New Guinea **2 :** a member of the Arau people

arauá \ˌarəˈwä\ *n, pl* **arauá** *or* **arauás** *usu cap* [Sp *araua, arauá, aragua*, of AmerInd origin] **1 a :** a group of Indian peoples of western Brazil **b :** a member of one of these peoples **2 :** the language of the Arauá people considered by some Americanists to constitute an independent language family and by others to be a branch of Arawakan

arau·ca·na \əˌrau̇ˈkänə\ *n* -s *usu cap* [AmerSp, fr. fem. of *araucano* of Arauco, fr. *Arauco*, district in Chile + Sp *-ano* -an] **:** a chicken of a So. American breed distinguished by lack of tail feathers, by bushy tufts of feathers on each side of the head, and by the production of blue eggs

¹**arau·ca·nian** \əˌrau̇ˈkānēən, -kā-, -nyən; ˌaˌrȯˈkān-\ *also* **arau·can** \əˈrau̇kən\ *or* **arau·ca·no** \əˌrau̇ˈkä(ˌ)nō\ *n, pl* **araucanians** *also* **araucan** *or* **araucans** *or* **araucano** *or* **araucanos** *usu cap* [Sp *araucano*, fr. *Arauco*, locality (now a province) in Chile (fr. Araucan *ragh, raq, rau* clay + *ko, co* water) + *-ano* -an] **1 :** a member of a group of Indian peoples of south central Chile and adjacent regions of Argentina **2 :** the language of the Araucanian people, constituting an independent language family

²**araucanian** \"\ *adj, usu cap* **:** of or relating to Araucanian or Araucanians

ar·au·car·ia \ˌaˌrȯˈka(a)rēə\ *n* [NL, fr. *Arauco*, locality in Chile + NL *-aria*] **1** *cap* **:** a small genus of tall So. American or Australian trees (family Pinaceae) with branches usu. in whorls, stiff broad scalelike leaves, large cones, and edible seeds — see MONKEY PUZZLE, NORFOLK ISLAND PINE **2** -s **:** a plant of the genus *Araucaria* — **ar·au·car·i·an** \-ēən\ *adj*

ar·au·car·i·a·ce·ae \-ˌka(a)rēˈāsēˌē\ *n pl, cap* [NL, fr. *Araucaria*, type genus + *-aceae*] *in some classifications* **:** a family of plants comprising *Araucaria* and *Agathis* and often included in the Pinaceae

ar·au·car·i·ox·y·lon \-ˌka(a)rēˈäksəˌlän, -ˌlən\ *n* [NL, fr. *Araucaria* + *-o-* + *-xylon*] **1** *cap* **:** a genus of widely distributed fossil conifers of late Paleozoic to late Mesozoic time having a wood structure resembling that of modern araucarias **2 :** any of several fossil woods having a structure like that of modern araucarias

arau·jia \əˈrōjēə, -rau̇j-\ *n, cap* [NL, fr. Antônio de *Araujo* de Azevedo †1817 Port. statesman + NL *-ia*] **:** a small genus of So. American vines (family Asclepiadaceae) sometimes cultivated in greenhouses for their white or pink flowers

arauna *var of* ARAONA

ar·a·wa \ˈärəwə\ *n, pl* **arawa** *or* **arawas** *cap* [Maori] **:** a Maori people of New Zealand

ar·a·wak *also* **ar·ra·wak** \ˈarəˌwäk, -ˌwak\ *n, pl* **arawak** *or* **arawaks** *usu cap* **1 a :** an Indian people or peoples of the Arawakan group formerly occupying most of the Greater Antilles but now scattered in small numbers along the coast of Guyana **b :** a member of such people **2 :** the language of the Arawak people **3 :** ARAWAKAN

¹**ar·a·wak·an** \ˌ=ˈ=kən\ *adj, usu cap* **:** of or belonging to Arawakan or the Arawakan peoples

²**arawakan** \"\ *n, pl* **arawakan** *or* **arawakans** *usu cap* **1 a :** a group of Indian peoples of Bolivia, Brazil, Colombia, Guiana, Paraguay, Peru, Venezuela, and, formerly, the West Indies whose languages constitute a large language family **b :** a member of such peoples **2 :** the language family of the Arawakan peoples

arba *var of* ARABA

ar·ba·cia \ärˈbāsēə\ *n* [NL, fr. *Arbaces* †*ab*848 B.C. king of Media + NL *-ia*] **1** *cap* **:** a genus of sea urchins (order Centrechinoida) having the ambulacral plates with three pairs of pores, the periproct covered by four triangular plates, the test rather low and stout, and the spines short with those near the mouth having enameled flattened tips **2** -s **:** a sea urchin of the genus *Arbacia*

ar·ba kan·foth *or* **arba kan·fot** \ˌärbəˈkänfəs, -ˌfōs, -ˌfōt\ *n* [Heb *arba' kanphōth* four corners] **:** a rectangular strip of cloth that has fringes fastened to its four corners and has an opening for the head and is worn under the ordinary clothes by orthodox male Jews — compare TALLITH

ar·ba·lest \ˈärbələst, -ˌlest\ *also* **ar·ba·list** \-ˌləst, -ˌlist\ *n* -s [ME *arbelast, arblast*, fr. OE *arblast*, fr. OF *arbaleste*, fr. LL *arcoballista, arcuballista*, fr. L *arcu-* (fr. *arcus* bow) + *ballista* — more at ARROW, BALLISTA] **:** CROSSBOW; *esp* **:** one used as a military weapon in medieval and early modern times often having a steel bow and sometimes used to throw balls or stones as well as quarrels

ar·ba·lest·er \ˈ=ˌ=ˌlestə(r)\ *also* **ar·ba·les·tri·er** \ˌ=ˌ=ˈlestrēə(r)\ *or* **ar·ba·list·er** \ˈ=ˌ=ˌlistə(r)\ *n* -s [ME *arbalaster, arblaster*, fr. OF *arbalestier*, fr. LL *arcuballistarius*, fr. *arcuballista* + L *-arius* -ary] **:** a user of an arbalest **:** CROSSBOWMAN

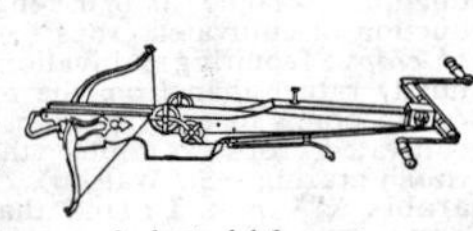
arbalest, 14th century

ar·bi·ter \ˈärbəd·ər, ˈäbəd·ə, ǀtə(r) *sometimes* ÷ -ˌbī\ *n* -s [ME *arbitre, arbitour*, fr. MF *arbitre*, fr. L *arbiter* (akin to Umbrian *ařputrati* according to judgment), perh. fr. *ad-* + *-biter* (fr. *baetere* to go)] **1 :** a person having the authority to decide a matter in dispute **:** JUDGE; *esp* **:** one chosen by parties or appointed in their behalf by a court to determine a controversy between them ⟨whenever a political body controls arbitration machinery, appoints ~*s*, and enforces rulings —*Christian Science Monitor*⟩ **2 :** a person or agency having absolute power of judging, determining, or ruling or one whose decisions are accepted as final ⟨she . . . became the supreme ~ of skating fashions —Maribel Y. Vinson⟩ ⟨the market, overseas and at home, will be the final ~ —*Economist*⟩

arbiter ele·gan·ti·ae \-ˌeləˈganshēˌē\ *or* **arbiter eleganti·a·rum** \-ˌganshēˈä(a)rəm\ *n* [L, judge of elegance] **:** a person who prescribes, rules on, or is a recognized authority on matters of social behavior and taste

ar·bith *or* **ar·bit** \ärˈbēt, ˈ=ˌ=; ˈärvəs\ *n* -s [Heb *'arbīth*] **:** MAARIB

ar·bi·tra·ble \ˈärbəˌtrəbəl, (ˈ)ärǀbi·tr-\ *adj* [L *arbitrari* to judge + E *-able* — more at ARBITRATE] **:** subject to decision by arbitration **:** referable to an arbitrator or arbiter ⟨the issues were not ~ according to the contract⟩

¹**ar·bi·trage** *in sense 2* ˈärbəˌträzh *or* ˌ=ˌ=ˈ=; *in sense 1 possibly* ˈärbəˌtrij\ *n* -s [ME, fr. MF, fr. OF, fr. *arbitrer* to render judgment (fr. L *arbitrari*) + *-age*] **1** *archaic* **:** judgment by an arbiter **:** authoritative determination **:** ARBITRATION **2 :** simultaneous purchase and sale of the same or equivalent security, commodity contract, insurance, or foreign exchange on the same or different markets in order to profit from price discrepancies — compare ARBITRATION OF EXCHANGE

²**ar·bi·trage** \-ˌäzh\ *vi* -ED/-ING/-S **:** to practice arbitrage ⟨~ in stock rights⟩

ar·bi·trag·er \-äzhər\ *also* **ar·bi·tra·geur** \ˌ=ˌ=-(ˌ)träˈzhər\ *n* -s [F *arbitrageur*, fr. *arbitrage* + *-eur* -or] **:** one that practices arbitrage

ar·bi·tra·gist \ˌ=ˌ=ˈträzhəst\ *n* -s [F *arbitragiste*, fr. *arbitrage* + *-iste* -ist] **:** ARBITRAGER

ar·bi·tral \ˈärbəˌtrəl, ˈäb-\ *adj* [ME, fr. MF, fr. LL *arbitralis*, fr. L *arbitr-, arbiter* + *-alis* -al — more at ARBITER] **:** of or concerning arbiters or arbitration ⟨the ~ adjustment of controversial legal questions —S.F.Bemis⟩

ar·bit·ra·ment *also* **ar·bit·re·ment** \ärˈbi·trəmənt, äˈb-\ *n* -s [ME, fr. MF *arbitrement*, fr. *arbitrer* to render judgment (fr. L *arbitrari*) + *-ment* — more at ARBITRATE] **1** *archaic* **:** the right or power of deciding, directing, or controlling ⟨thou seest thy life . . . at my ~ —Christopher Marlowe⟩ **2 :** the act of deciding as an arbiter **:** authoritative decision **:** ARBITRATION ⟨submit a case to the ~ of the judges⟩ **3 :** the judgment given by an arbitrator **:** DECISION

ar·bi·trar·i·ly \ˌärbəˈtrerəlē, ˌäb-, -li\ *adv* **:** in an arbitrary manner **:** at will ⟨the genus will here be rather ~ described as though it were one man —W.S.White⟩ ⟨inflexible rules, ~ ordained—Havelock Ellis⟩ ⟨~set the lunch hour at one o'clock⟩

ar·bi·trar·i·ness *n* -ES **:** the quality or state of being arbitrary

arbitrarious *adj* [L *arbitrarius*] *obs* **:** ARBITRARY — **ar·bi·trar·i·ous·ly** *adv, obs*

¹**ar·bi·trary** \ˈärbəˌtrerē, ˈäb-, -ri\ *adj* [ME, fr. MF or L; MF *arbitraire*, fr. L *arbitrarius*, fr. *arbitr-, arbiter* judge + *-arius* -ary — more at ARBITER] **1 :** depending on choice or discretion; *specif* **:** determinable by decision of a judge or tribunal rather than defined by statute ⟨an ~ decision⟩ ⟨~ punishment⟩ **2 a** (1) **:** arising from unrestrained exercise of the will, caprice, or personal preference **:** given to expressing opinions that arise thus (2) **:** selected at random or as a typical example ⟨such ~ items as clothing, room furnishings, travel — *Official Register of Harvard Univ.*⟩ **b :** based on random or convenient selection or choice rather than on reason or nature ⟨an ~ symbol⟩ ⟨~ division of historical studies into watertight compartments —A.J.Toynbee⟩ **c** *Brit, of a printing character* **:** not usu. found in the ordinary type font **3 a :** given to willful irrational choices and demands **:** IMPERIOUS ⟨a man of iron will and ~ decision⟩ **b :** characterized by absolute power or authority **:** DESPOTIC, TYRANNICAL ⟨~ rule⟩ ⟨an ~ governor⟩ **syn** see ABSOLUTE

²**arbitrary** \"\ *n* -ES **1 :** something that is arbitrary ⟨the . . . conception of cosmic rule, into which an element of the ~ had found its way —S.F.Mason⟩ **2 a :** a fixed sum allowed a carrier in making or dividing a through rate **b :** an amount added to or deducted from a basic transportation rate, fare, or charge (as an increment for abnormal services or features); *also* **:** a payment to employees for work other than regular duties

arbitrary constant *n, math* **:** a symbol to which various values may be assigned but which remains unaffected by the changes in the values of the variables of the equation

arbitrary function *n* **:** a symbol that may be considered to represent any one function of a set of functions

ar·bi·trate \-ˌtrāt, *usu* -ād·+V\ *vb* -ED/-ING/-S [L *arbitratus*, past part. of *arbitrari* to render judgment, consider as, fr. *arbitr-, arbiter* judge — more at ARBITER] *vi* **:** to act as arbitrator or judge ⟨~ upon several reports⟩ ⟨~ between parties to a suit⟩ ~ *vt* **1 :** to act as arbiter upon (a disputed question) ⟨political leaders deem themselves competent to ~ scientific disputes —Martin Gardner⟩ ⟨the commission *arbitrated* boundaries between the countries⟩ **2 :** to submit or refer for decision (as a quarrel) to an arbiter ⟨she was invariably right when we *arbitrated* our dispute —Ernest Beaglehole⟩ **3** *archaic* **:** to make authoritative decisions concerning **:** DECIDE, DETERMINE ⟨decides that which long process could not ~ —Shak.⟩

ar·bi·tra·tion \ˌ=ˌ=ˈtrāshən\ *n* -s [ME *arbitracioun*, fr. MF *arbitration*, fr. L *arbitration-, arbitratio*, fr. *arbitratus* + *-ion-, -io* -ion] **:** the act of arbitrating; *esp* **:** the hearing and determination of a case between parties in controversy by a person or persons chosen by the parties or appointed under statutory authority instead of by a judicial tribunal provided by law ⟨~ of a dispute between management and labor⟩

ar·bi·tra·tion·al \ˌ=ˌ=ǀshənᵊl, -shnəl\ *adj* **:** relating to or resulting from arbitration ⟨an ~ settlement⟩

ar·bi·tra·tion·ist \ˌ=ˌ=ˈsh(ə)nəst\ *n* -s **:** a person in favor of arbitration

arbitration of exchange : simultaneous purchase and sale of foreign exchanges in two or more markets to profit from discrepancies in quotations — compare ARBITRAGE

ar·bi·tra·tive \ˈ=ˌ=ˌtrād·iv\ *adj* **:** of or relating to arbitration **:** having the authority to arbitrate ⟨an ~ board⟩ **:** done by arbitration

ar·bi·tra·tor \-ˌtrād·ə(r), -ātə-\ *n* -s [ME *arbitratour*, fr. MF, fr. LL *arbitrator*, fr. L *arbitratus* (past part. of *arbitrari* to render judgment) + *-or* — more at ARBITRATE] **1 :** a person or one of two or more persons chosen to settle by arbitration the differences between two parties in controversy **:** CONCILIATOR — distinguished from *mediator* **2 :** one with absolute power of deciding **:** ARBITER ⟨made himself the ~ of his own destiny —Geoffrey Clive⟩

arbitrement *var of* ARBITRAMENT

arbitrer *n* -s [ME *arbitrour*, fr. OF *arbitreor*, fr. LL *arbitrator*] *obs* **:** ARBITRATOR

ar·bi·tress \ˈärbə·trəs, ˈäb-\ *n* -ES [ME *arbitres*, fr. MF *arbitresse*, fem. of *arbitre* judge — more at ARBITER] **:** a female arbiter

arblast *archaic var of* ARBALEST

ar·bo·lo·co \ˌärbəˈlō(ˌ)kō\ *n* -ES [AmerSp, fr. Sp *árbol* tree (fr. L *arbor*) + *loco* mad — more at ARBOR, LOCO] **:** a Colombian tree (*Montanoa lehmannii*) of the family Compositae whose wood is used esp. for making billiard cues

¹**ar·bor** \ˈärbər, ˈäbə\ *n* -s *see -or in Explan Notes* [ME *erber, herber* plot of grass, herb garden, shady bower, fr. OF *erbier, herbier* plot of grass, fr. *herbe* herb, grass — more at HERB] **1 :** a bower formed of vines or branches or of latticework covered with climbing shrubs or vines **:** a shaded retreat **2** *obs* **:** a shaded or covered walk

arbor 1

²**ar·bor** \"\ *n* [L, tree, beam; perh. akin to L *arduus* steep, high — more at ARDUOUS] **1** -s **:** a principal supporting rod or bar: as **a :** a spindle or axle of a wheel (as in a clock or watch) **b :** a metal shaft or axis on which a revolving cutting tool (as a circular saw) is mounted; *sometimes* **:** a spindle or bar on a cutting machine that holds the work to be cut — compare MANDREL **c :** the central bar or support of a mold core **2** *pl* **ar·bo·res** \ˈärbəˌrēz, ˈäb-\ **:** a tree as distinguished from a shrub

ar·bo·ra·ceous \ˌärbəˈrāshəs, ˌäb-\ *or* **ar·bo·ral** \ˈ=b(ə)rəl\ *adj* [²*arbor* (tree) + *-aceous* or *-al*] **:** ARBOREAL

ar·bo·rary \ˈ=bəˌrerē\ *adj* [L *arborarius*, fr. *arbor* tree + *-arius* -ary] **:** ARBOREAL

arbor day *n, usu cap A&D* **:** a day in April or May designated in most states as a tree-planting day

ar·bo·re·al \(ˈ)ärǀbōrēəl, (ˈ)äǀb-, -ȯr-\ *also* **ar·bo·re·an** \-ēən\ *adj* [L *arboreus* + E *-al* or *-an*] **1 :** of or relating to a tree **:** resembling a tree **2 :** inhabiting or frequenting trees ⟨~ animals⟩ — **ar·bo·re·al·ly** \-ēəlē, -li\ *adv*

ar·bored \ˈärbərd, ˈäbəd\ *adj* [¹*arbor* + *-ed*] **:** furnished with an arbor **:** lined with trees **:** having trees **:** EMBOWERED ⟨an ~ walk⟩

ar·bo·re·ous \(ˈ)ärǀbōrēəs, (ˈ)äǀb-, -ȯr-\ *adj* [L *arboreus* of a tree, fr. *arbor* + *-eus* -eous] **1 :** abounding in trees **:** WOODED ⟨an ~ landscape⟩ **2 :** having the form, duration of life, or structure of a tree in distinction from an herb or shrub **3 :** ARBOREAL 2

ar·bor·er \ˈärbərər, ˈäbərə\ *n* -s [²*arbor* + *-er*] **:** a jewelry worker who shapes rings on an arbor

ar·bo·res·cence \ˌ=ˌ=ˈresᵊn(t)s\ *n* -s **:** the state of being arborescent **:** treelike form or appearance (as in minerals)

ar·bo·res·cent \ˌ=ˌ=ǀsᵊnt\ *adj* [L *arborescent-, arborescens*, pres. part. of *arborescere* to become a tree, fr. *arbor*] **1 :** resembling a tree in growth, structure, or appearance; *esp* **:** branching like a tree **2 :** having crystallizations disposed like the branches and twigs of a tree ⟨~ frost-growths —F.C. Phillips⟩ — **ar·bo·res·cent·ly** *adv*

arborescent appendage *n* **:** any branched accessory vascular structure in the gill chamber of certain fishes that leave the water (as the climbing perch) by which they are enabled to breathe air

ar·bo·resque \ˌ=ˌ=ˈresk\ *adj* [²*arbor* (tree) + E *-esque*] **:** like a tree

ar·bo·ret \ˌ=ˌ=ˈret\ *n* -s [L *arbor* tree + E *-et*] **:** a small tree **:** SHRUB

ar·bo·re·tum \ˌärbəˈrēd·əm, ˌäb-, -ētˌ\ *n, pl* **arboretums** \ǀəmz\ *also* **arbore·ta** \ǀə\ [NL, fr. L, a place grown with trees, fr. *arbor* + *-etum*] **:** a place where trees, shrubs, and herbaceous plants are cultivated for scientific and educational purposes **:** a botanic garden of trees

ar·bor·i·cal \(ˈ)ärǀbȯrəkəl\ *adj* [²*arbor* (tree) + *-ical*] **:** ARBOREAL 1

ar·bor·i·cole \ˌ=ˈ=rəˌkōl\ *also* **ar·bo·ric·o·lous** \ˌärbəˈrikələs\ *adj* [F, fr. L *arbor* tree + F *-i-* + *-cole* -colous] **:** inhabiting trees ⟨certain mollusks are ~⟩

ar·bo·ri·cul·tur·al \ˌärbərə-ˌ ärǀbȯrə-ˌ\ *adj* **:** of or relating to arboriculture

ar·bo·ri·cul·ture \ˈärbərə-, ärˈbȯrə-\ *n* -s [²*arbor* (tree) + *-iculture* (as in *agriculture*)] **:** the cultivation of trees and shrubs esp. for ornamental purposes — compare SILVICULTURE — **ar·bo·ri·cul·tur·ist** \ˌ=ˌ=ˈ=-, =ˌ=-\ *n* -s

ar·bo·ri·form \ˈärbərəˌfȯrm, ärˈbȯrə-\ *adj* [²*arbor* (tree) + *-iform*] **:** resembling a tree in shape or appearance

ar·bo·rist \ˈärbərəst\ *n* -s [L *arbor* tree + E *-ist*] **:** a specialist in planting and transplanting, pruning, and diagnosing the ailments of trees and in tree surgery and tree maintenance

ar·bo·ri·za·tion \ˌ=ˌ=rəˈzāshən, -ˌrīˈz-\ *n* -s **1 :** formation of or into a figure or arrangement resembling a tree or shrub **:** RAMIFICATION ⟨the extent of the ~ of axons and dendrites⟩ **2 :** a treelike figure or arrangement of branching parts: as **a :** an outline or impression of a tree or plant in fossils **b :** DENDRITE 1 **c :** a treelike process of a nerve cell ⟨the terminal ~ of an axon⟩

ar·bo·rize \ˈärbəˌrīz\ *vb* -ED/-ING/-S [F *arboriser*, fr. L *arbor* tree + F *-iser* -ize] *vt* **:** to give a treelike appearance to ~ *vi* **:** to assume a treelike appearance ⟨the nerve fibers *arborized*⟩

ar·bo·rous \-rəs\ *adj* [L *arbor* tree + E *-ous*] **:** of, relating to, or formed by trees ⟨an ~ roof⟩

arbor por·phyr·i·ana \-(ˌ)pȯrˌfirēˈanə\ *n, sometimes cap A & usu cap P* [prob. fr. ML — more at TREE OF PORPHYRY] **:** TREE OF PORPHYRY

arbor press *n* [²*arbor*] **1 :** MANDREL PRESS **2 :** a light press commonly operated by a hand lever

ar·bor·vi·tae \ˌärbərˈvīd·ē, ˌäbəˈv-, -ītǀ, ǀi\ *n* -s [NL *arbor vitae*, lit., tree of life] **1 :** a tree or shrub of the genus *Thuja* or the closely related *Thujopsis* — see AMERICAN ARBORVITAE, ORIENTAL ARBORVITAE; TREE illustration **2 :** any of several plants of the genus *Libocedrus* **3** *usu* **arbor vitae :** a treelike structure or arrangement (as of nervous tissue in the cerebellum)

arborvitae leaf miner *n* **:** the larva of a small moth (*Argyresthia thuiella*) that mines in the leaves of the arborvitae

arborway \ˈ=ˌ=ˌ=\ *n* [¹*arbor* + *way*] **:** an arbored passage or walk

arbour *chiefly Brit var of* ARBOR

arbtrn *abbr* arbitration

ar·bus·cle \ˈärˌbəsəl\ *or* **ar·bus·cu·la** \ärˈbəskyələ\ *n* -s [L *arbuscula*, dim. of *arbor* tree] **:** a dwarf tree or treelike shrub

ar·bus·cu·lar \(ˈ)ärǀbəskyələr\ *adj* **:** of or relating to an arbuscule

ar·bus·cule \ˈ=ˈ=(ˌ)kyül\ *n* -s [L *arbuscula*] **1 :** a tuft of hairs or cilia **2 :** a branched treelike organ; *specif* **:** one of the treelike haustorial organs in certain mycorhizal fungi

ar·bus·tum \ärˈbəstəm\ *n, pl* **arbus·ta** \-tə\ [L, fr. *arbor* tree] **:** a plantation of shrubs or small trees **:** COPSE, ORCHARD

arbute *n* -s [L *arbutus*] *archaic* **:** a tree of the genus *Arbutus* — **arbutean** *adj, archaic*

ar·bu·tin \ärˈbyütᵊn, ˈärbyətᵊn\ *n* -s [ISV *arbut-* (fr. NL *arbutus*) + *-in*] **:** a crystalline glucoside $C_{12}H_{16}O_7$ found in the leaves of the bearberry and in other plants and sometimes used as a urinary antiseptic

ar·bu·tus \ärˈbyüd·əs, äˈb-, -ütəs\ *n* [NL, fr. L, strawberry tree] **1** *cap* **:** a genus of evergreen shrubs or trees (family Ericaceae) of southern Europe and western No. America with white or pink flowers and many-seeded scarlet berries — see STRAWBERRY TREE **2** -ES **:** a tree of the genus *Arbutus* **3** -ES **:** a trailing plant (*Epigaea repens*) of eastern No. America with oblong hairy leaves and fragrant pink or white spring-blooming flowers with a 5-parted salver-shaped corolla — called also *ground laurel, mayflower, trailing arbutus* **4** -ES **:** a deep pink to purplish pink that is paler than France rose

arbutus pink *n* **:** a moderate pink that is bluer and paler than blossom pink, bluer, lighter, and stronger than chalk pink, and bluer and stronger than hydrangea pink

¹**arc** \ˈärk, ˈäk\ *n* -s [ME *ark*, fr. MF *arc*, fr. L *arcus* bow, arc — more at ARROW] **1 :** the apparent path described above and below the horizon by the sun or other celestial body **2 :** something that is arched or curved **:** an arched or curved shape or figure ⟨with eyebrows raised in a quizzical ~⟩ ⟨he bent the twig into an ~⟩: as **a** *obs* **:** ARCH ⟨triumphal ~*s* —John Milton⟩ **b :** a geologic or topographic feature repeated along a curving line on the earth's surface ⟨island ~*s* . . . so well developed in the western Pacific —F.P.Shepard⟩ ⟨volcanic ~*s*⟩ **c** (1) **:** a sustained brilliantly luminous glow sometimes having the appearance of a curved line of flame that is formed under certain conditions when a break is made in an electric circuit

arcs 3

(2) **:** a spotlight or lamp that uses an electric arc as the light source **d :** one of the curved stripes that close the open angle at the bottom or top of certain chevrons on military uniforms **e :** the quarter circle enclosing the service box on a squash rackets court **3 :** a continuous portion of a curved line or path (as part of a circle or an ellipse) **4 :** angular measure — used chiefly in the phrase *of arc* ⟨11 minutes 3 seconds of ~⟩

²arc \"\ *vi* **arced** \-kt\ **arced** \"\ **arcing** \-kiŋ\ **arcs** **1 :** to form an electric arc **2 :** to follow or describe a curving course resembling the form of an arc ⟨waterfalls ~ outward into . . . white plumes —C.H.Baker⟩ ⟨the meandering Kum river, ~*ing* around Taejon —*Newsweek*⟩

ar·ca \'ärkə\ *n* [NL, fr. L, chest, box — more at ARK] **1** *pl* **ar·cae** \-ˌkī, -ˌsē\ [L] **:** a chest or strong box used in ancient times as a receptacle for money or valuables and also by primitive Christians for reserving the consecrated bread of the Eucharist **2** *cap* **:** a genus (the type of the family Arcidae) of bivalve mollusks having small ark shells and blood clams

ar·ca·cea \är'kāshēə\ *n pl, cap* [NL, fr. *Arca* + *-acea*] **:** a suborder of the order Filibranchia including the ark shells and related forms

ar·cade \(')är¦kād, (')ä¦k-\ *n* -s [F, fr. (assumed) It dial. (northern) *arcada*, fr. It *arco* arch, bow, arc (fr. L *arcus*) + *-ada* -ade (fr. LL *-ata*) — more at ARROW] **1 a** *obs* **:** an arched or vaulted place **:** an arched opening with its structural parts **b :** a long arched building or gallery **2 a :** an arched or curved passageway or avenue **b :** a covered passageway along which rows of shops are located **3 :** a series of arches with the columns or piers that support them, the spandrels above, and other necessary appurtenances, sometimes open and serving as an entrance or to give light, sometimes closed at the back and forming a decorative feature **4** *anat* **a :** a structure comprising a series of arches **b :** DENTAL ARCH

arcade 3

ar·cad·ed \-ādəd\ *adj* **:** having arcades **:** lined with arcades ⟨~ streets⟩ **:** formed in, furnished, or decorated with arches or arcades ⟨a chair with an ~ back design⟩ ⟨an ~ courtyard⟩

ar·ca·dia \är'kādēə, ä'k-\ *also* **ar·ca·dy** \'ärkədē, 'äk-, -di\ *n, pl* **arcadias** *also* **arcadies** *often cap* [fr. *Arcadia*, pastoral region of ancient Greece regarded as a rural paradise, fr. L, fr. Gk *Arkadia*] **:** a usu. idealized region or scene of simple pleasure, rustic innocence, and uninterrupted quiet ⟨Jefferson . . . with his dream of . . . an 18th century rural ~ —W.H. Hale⟩

¹ar·ca·di·an \är'kādēən, ä'k-\ *n* -s [*Arcadia* + E *-an*] **1** *often cap* **:** a person who lives a life of simple pleasure, rustic innocence, and untroubled quiet **2** *cap* **:** a native or inhabitant of Arcadia, a region of ancient Greece **3** *cap* **:** a dialect of ancient Greek used in Arcadia

²arcadian \(')=¦===\ *adj, sometimes cap* **1 :** of, belonging to, or characteristic of the idealized representations of pastoral life in literature **2 :** idyllically pastoral; *esp* **:** idyllically innocent, simple, or untroubled ⟨in retrospect the past sometimes seems ~⟩ **3 a** *usu cap* **:** of or relating to Arcadia or to the Arcadians **b :** of or relating to Arcadian

ar·ca·di·an·ism \=¦==ə,nizəm\ *n* -s *often cap* **1 :** adoption or affectation of conduct or dress imitative of or suggestive of that depicted in arcadian literature **2 :** the use of arcadian literary conventions in writing

ar·cad·ing \=¦kādiŋ, -dēŋ\ *n* -s **:** the series of arches or arcades used in the construction or decoration of a building or other object ⟨the ~ of the walls is in two stories —Ian Finlay⟩

arcana *pl of* ARCANUM

ar·cane \(')är¦kān\ *adj* [L *arcanus* — more at ARCANUM] **:** being or resembling an arcanum **:** SECRET, MYSTERIOUS ⟨what is ~ to them is lucid to Dr. Leavis —*Times Lit. Supp.*⟩ — **ar·cane·ly** *adv*

ar·ca·nist \är'kānəst\ *n* -s [*arcanum* + *-ist*] **:** a workman having knowledge of a secret process of manufacture (as of the manufacture of porcelain)

ar·ca·nite \-ˌnīt, 'ärkə,-\ *n* -s [G *arkanit*, fr. NL *arcanum* (*duplicatum*), lit., double arcanum + G *-it* -ite] **:** POTASSIUM SULFATE

ar·ca·num \är'kānəm *sometimes* -an- *or* -än-\ *n, pl* **arca·na** \-nə\ [L, fr. neut. of *arcanus* closed, secret, fr. *arca* chest — more at ARK] **1 :** a secret or mysterious knowledge or information known only to the initiate ⟨an ~ of prosodic theory which is the province of specialists —P.F.Baum⟩ ⟨certain *arcana* . . . which you must with the utmost care conceal, and never seem to know —Earl of Chesterfield⟩ **2** [NL, fr. L] **:** an extract of the vital nature of something **:** a powerful natural agent **:** ELIXIR ⟨the search of the alchemists for the grand ~⟩

arcanum ar·ca·no·rum \-nə,märkə'nōrəm\ *n* [NL] **:** the mystery of mysteries; *specif* **:** the one ultimate secret supposed to lie behind all astrology, alchemy, and magic

ar·ca·to \är'käd·(ˌ)ō\ *adj (or adv)* [It, fr. *arco* bow (fr. L *arcus* bow, arc) + *-ato* (fr. L *-atus* -ate) — more at ARROW] **:** COLL'ARCO — usu. used as a direction in music

ar·ca·ture \'ärkə,chü(ə)r, -ˌchər\ *n* -s [F, prob. irreg. fr. *arcade* + *-ure*] **1 :** a small arcade (as in a balustrade) **2 :** a blind arcade; *esp* **:** one that is decorative rather than structural

arcature 2

arc–back \'=,=\ *n* **:** failure of a gas-filled or mercury= vapor rectifier to suppress the current during the inverse-voltage half of a cycle due to overheating of the anode or to other causes

arc–bou·tant \ärbütäⁿ\ *n, pl* **arcs–boutants** \-äⁿ(z)\ [F, fr. MF *arc boutant*, lit., thrusting arch, fr. *arc* arch, bow, arc (fr. L *arcus*) + *boutant*, pres. part. of *bouter* to thrust — more at ARROW, BUTT] **:** FLYING BUTTRESS

arc chute *n* **:** a set of insulating barriers on a circuit breaker arranged to confine the arc and prevent it from causing damage

arc cosecant *n* **:** the inverse function to the cosecant ⟨if *y* is the cosecant of *θ*, then *θ* is the *arc cosecant of y*⟩ — called also *inverse cosecant*

arc cosine *n* **:** the inverse function to the cosine ⟨if *y* is the cosine of *θ*, then *θ* is the *arc cosine of y*⟩ — called also *inverse cosine*

arc cotangent *n* **:** the inverse function to the cotangent ⟨if *y* is the cotangent of *θ*, then *θ* is the *arc cotangent of y*⟩ — called also *inverse cotangent*

arc de tri·omphe \ˌärkdə(ˌ)trē'ōⁿf\ *n, pl* **arcs de triomphe** \-k(s)d-\ [F] **:** TRIUMPHAL ARCH

arced *past of* ARC

ar·cel·la \är'selə\ *n* [NL, fr. L *arca* box, chest + NL *-ella*] **1** *cap* **:** the type genus of Arcellidae comprising protozoans resembling amoebas and provided with a chitinous shell suggesting an umbrella **2** -s **:** a protozoan of the genus *Arcella*

ar·cel·li·dae \-ə,dē\ *n pl, cap* [NL, fr. *Arcella*, type genus + *-idae*] **:** a cosmopolitan family of soil and freshwater protozoans related to the amoebas but commonly enclosed in a test — see ARCELLA

ar·ceu·tho·bi·um \ˌärsyə'thōbēəm, ˌär,sü'-\ *n, cap* [NL, fr. Gk *arkeuthos* juniper + NL *-bium*; fr. its parasitism on conifers; perh. akin to Gk *arkys* net — more at ARACHN-] **:** a genus of chiefly American plants (family Loranthaceae) parasitic on various conifers and having 4-angled branches, scalelike leaves, dioecious flowers, and fleshy stalked berries — see AMERICAN MISTLETOE

arc furnace *n* **:** an electric furnace in which the heat is provided by an arc formed between two electrodes — compare INDUCTION FURNACE

¹arch \'ärch, 'äch\ *n* -ES [ME *arche*, fr. OF, fr. (assumed) VL

arches: *1* round (*ext* extrados, *int* intrados, *imp* impost, *k* keystone, *sp* springer, *v* voussoir); *2* horseshoe; *3* lancet; *4* ogee; *5* trefoil; *6* basket-handle; *7* Tudor

arca, fr. L *arcus* arch, bow, arc — more at ARROW] **1** *archaic* **:** a part of a curve **:** ARC **2 :** a typically curved structural member spanning an opening and serving as a support (as for the wall or other weight above the opening) by resolving vertical pressure into horizontal thrust, sometimes consisting of a framed structure similar in construction to a truss, sometimes made up of wedge-shaped solids with their joints at right angles to the curve **3 :** a structure or other object having the form of an arch or resembling an arch in form or function: as **a :** either of two vaulted portions of the bony structure of the foot that impart elasticity to and cushion the foot against shock (as in walking, running, leaping): (1) **:** a longitudinal arch supported posteriorly by the basal tuberosity of the calcaneus and anteriorly by the heads of the metatarsal bones (2) **:** a transverse arch consisting of the metatarsals and 1st row of tarsals and resulting from elevation of the central anterior portion of the median longitudinal arch **b :** one of the fire chambers of a brick kiln; *also* **:** the fire chamber in certain kinds of furnaces and ovens **c :** the arched top of a furnace or gas retort **d :** a round transverse bar shaped like an inverted U whose ends form the wheel axles of a row-crop cultivator, the arch providing clearance for the plants as they are cultivated **e :** a fingerprint in which all the ridges run from side to side and make no backward turn — compare LOOP, WHORL **f :** a natural bridge resulting from erosion **g** *geol* **:** an upward flexure of sedimentary rocks ⟨the Cincinnati ~⟩ **:** a broad anticline **h :** an arch formed in dancing by raised and joined hands, kerchiefs, or swords by a couple, a pair, or a row of couples for the passage of a soloist or the remaining couples in line **i :** the lengthwise frame piece of a loom beneath which the warp travels and the cloth is woven **j :** the semicircular side plates of a carding machine **k :** a derricklike device consisting of a metal frame and fairlead mounted on the rear of a tractor or on separate wheels or tracks and used for lifting log ends clear of the ground so as to facilitate their skidding — compare SULKY **4 a :** a curvature having or approximating the form of an arch ⟨a slight ~ to her eyebrows⟩ ⟨an ~ in the cat's back⟩ **b :** the perpendicular distance from the master leaf of a leaf spring to a line drawn through the centers of the spring eyes **5 :** a place covered by an arch **:** ARCHWAY

²arch \"\ *vb* -ED/-ING/-ES [ME *archen*, fr. *arche*, n.] *vt* **1 :** to cover or provide with an arch or arches **:** span with an arch ⟨a bridge ~*es* the stream⟩ ⟨the high blue heaven that ~*es* our continent —D.C.Peattie⟩ **2 :** to form or bend into the shape of an arch **:** CURVE ⟨~ her eyebrows⟩ ⟨~ the ball a trifle higher —W.L.Hughes⟩ ~ *vi* **1 :** to form into an arch **:** take the shape of an arch ⟨trees ~ above the promenade —*Amer. Guide Series: Maine*⟩ **2 :** to follow or take an arch-shaped path or course ⟨the ball ~*ed* toward the basket⟩ ⟨the meteor ~*ed* across the sky⟩ **3** *dancing* **a :** to form an arch by joining hands with the dance partner or neighbor **b :** to place the toe of the free foot against the arch of the supporting foot

³arch \"\ *adj* [¹*arch-*] **1 :** most important or outstanding **:** PRINCIPAL, CHIEF — used attributively usu. with a hyphen ⟨an *arch*-villain⟩ ⟨the life of Thoreau as an ~ Yankee —H.S. Canby⟩ **2** [¹*arch-*; fr. its use as an intensifying prefix in such compounds as *archrogue, archwag*, whereby some of the semantic range of *rogue* and *wag* was extended to the prefix] **a :** characterized by clever or sly alertness ⟨that ~ eye of yours! it sees through everything —Jane Austen⟩ **b :** playfully saucy **:** ROGUISH ⟨an ~ look⟩ **:** having an exaggerated often forced or artificial playfulness ⟨simpering expressions and ~ posturing —Osbert Lancaster⟩

⁴arch *n* -ES *obs* **:** one that is preeminent **:** CHIEF

¹arch– \¦ärch, ¦äch, *but* ¦ärk *or* ¦äk *in "archangel" and derivatives*\ *prefix* [ME *arche-, arch-*, fr. OE & OF; OE *arce-, erce-*, fr. LL *arch-* & L *archi-*, fr. Gk *arch-, archi-*; OF *arch-, arche-*, fr. LL *arch-* & L *archi-* — more at ARCHI-] **1 :** chief **:** principal ⟨*arch*angel⟩ ⟨*arch*bishop⟩ ⟨*arch*diocese⟩ ⟨*arch*duke⟩ ⟨*arch*pillar⟩ **2 :** preeminent **:** extreme **:** most fully embodying the qualities of his or its kind ⟨*arch*antiquary⟩ ⟨*arch*capitalist⟩ ⟨*arch*fool⟩ ⟨*arch*infamy⟩ ⟨*arch*philosopher⟩ ⟨*arch*puritan⟩ ⟨*arch*rogue⟩ **3 :** first in time ⟨*arch*father⟩ **:** primitive ⟨*arch*form⟩

²arch– — see ARCHI-

¹–arch \ˌärk, ˌäk, *alternatively* -ə(r)k *in a few common words (as "monarch") in which the preceding syllable has stress*\ *n comb form* -s [ME *-arke, -arche*, fr. OF & LL & L; OF *-arche*, fr. LL *-archa*, fr. L *-arches, -archus*, fr. Gk *-archēs, archos* — more at ARCHI-] **:** ruler **:** leader ⟨*matri*arch⟩ ⟨*nom*arch⟩

²–arch \ˌärk, ˌäk\ *adj comb form* [prob. fr. G, fr. Gk *archē* beginning — more at ARCHI-] **:** having (such) a point or (so many) points of origin ⟨*end*arch⟩ ⟨*pent*arch⟩

arch *abbr* **1** archaic **2** *often cap* archbishop **3** archery **4** archipelago **5** architecture **6** archive

archabbey \'=¦==\ *n* [¹*arch-* + *abbey*] **:** a chief Benedictine abbey

archabbot \'=¦==\ *n* [¹*arch-* + *abbot*] **:** the superior of an archabbey

archae– *or* **archaeo–** *also* **archeo–** *in pronunciations below*, ¦==(ˌ)= = ¦ärkē(ˌ)ō *or* ¦äk- *or* -ēə, =¦== = är¦kēō *or* ä¦k- *or* -ēə\ *comb form* [Gk *archaio-*, fr. *archaios* ancient, fr. *archē* beginning — more at ARCHI-] **1 :** antiquity ⟨*archaeo*graphy⟩ **2 :** ancient **:** primitive ⟨*archae*craniate⟩ ⟨*archaeo*lithic⟩ ⟨*archeo*zoic⟩

archaean *usu cap, var of* ARCHEAN

ar·chae·cra·ni·ate \¦ärkē¦-\ *adj* [*archae-* + *craniate*] **:** of, relating to, or having a primitive type of skull (as that of Amphibia) — opposed to *syncraniate*

archaei *pl of* ARCHAEUS

ar·chaeo·calamites \¦==(ˌ)= *or* =¦== *at* ARCHAE- +\ *n, cap* [NL, fr. *archae-* + *Calamites*] **:** a genus of fossil plants related to *Calamites*, found in the oldest Carboniferous strata, and having large repeatedly dichotomous leaves and a strobilus like an equisetum

ar·chaeo·cete \'=== *or* =¦== *at* ARCHAE- + ˌsēt\ *adj or n* [NL *Archaeoceti*] **:** ZEUGLODON

ar·chaeo·ce·ti \ˌ=== *or* =ˌ== *at* ARCHAE- + 'sēˌtī\ [NL, fr. *archae-* + *ceti*, pl. of L *cetus* whale — more at CETE] *syn of* ZEUGLODONTIA

ar·chaeo·cy·a·tha \ˌ=== *or* =ˌ== *at* ARCHAE- + 'sīəthə\ *n pl, cap* [NL, fr. *Archaeocyathus*] *in some classifications* **:** a phylum of extinct animals of uncertain systematic relations represented by fossils of the genus *Archaeocyathus*

ar·chaeo·cy·a·thus \-thəs\ *n, cap* [NL, fr. *archae-* + L *cyathus* cup — more at CYATHUS] **:** a genus of Cambrian fossils with characteristics of both sponges and corals that is included among the pleosponges or placed in Archaeocyatha

ar·chaeo·cyte *also* **ar·che·o·cyte** \'=== *or* =¦== *at* ARCHAE- + ˌsīt\ *n* -s [*archae-* + *-cyte*] **:** an indifferent commonly amoeboid interstitial cell; *specif* **:** any of certain amoebocytes of sponges that have large nuclei and blunt pseudopods, are believed to be persistent undifferentiated embryonic cells, and develop into the sex cells

ar·chaeo·gastropod \¦==(ˌ)= *or* =ˌ== *at* ARCHAE- +\ *n* -s [NL *Archaeogastropoda*] **:** one of the Aspidobranchia

ar·chaeo·gastropoda \¦==(ˌ)= *or* =ˌ== *at* ARCHAE- +\ [NL, fr. *archae-* + *Gastropoda*] *syn of* ASPIDOBRANCHIA

ar·chaeo·geology \"\ *n* -ES [*archae-* + *geology*] **:** the geology of the most ancient periods

ar·chaeo·hippus \¦==(ˌ)= *or* =ˌ== *at* ARCHAE- + 'hipəs\ *n, cap* [NL, fr. *archae-* + *-hippus*] **:** a genus of small No. American Miocene horses ancestral to modern horses

ar·chae·ol·a·try \ˌärkē'äl-ə-trē\ *n* -ES [*archae-* + *-latry*] **:** the worship of archaism

ar·chae·o·log·i·cal *or* **ar·che·o·log·i·cal** \¦ärkēə¦läjəkəl, ¦äk-, -jēk-\ *also* **ar·chae·o·log·ic** *or* **ar·che·o·log·ic** \-jik, -ēk\ *adj* **:** of, belonging to, or relating to archaeology; *also* **:** dealing with or devoted to archaeology

ar·chae·o·log·i·cal·ly *or* **ar·che·o·log·i·cal·ly** \-ək(ə)lē, -ēk-, -li\ *adv* **:** in or according to archaeology **:** from an archaeological standpoint ⟨an ~ rich country⟩

ar·chae·ol·o·gist *or* **ar·che·ol·o·gist** \ˌ=='äləjəst\ *n* -s **:** a specialist in archaeology

ar·chae·ol·o·gy *or* **ar·che·ol·o·gy** \-jē, -i\ *n* -ES [LL *archaeologia* antiquarian lore, fr. Gk *archaiologia*, fr. *archaio-* archae- + *-logia* -logy] **1** *archaic* **:** ancient history **2** [F *archéologie*, fr. LL *archaeologia*] **:** the scientific study of extinct peoples or of past phases of the culture of historic peoples through skeletal remains, fossils, and objects of human workmanship (as implements, artifacts, monuments, or inscriptions) found in the earth **3 :** remains of the culture of a people **:** ANTIQUITIES ⟨the ~ of the Incas⟩ ⟨the museum displayed Aztec ~⟩

ar·chaeo·pithecus \¦==(ˌ)= *or* =¦== *at* ARCHAE- + \ *n, cap* [NL, fr. *archae-* + *-pithecus*] **:** a genus of extinct So. American Eocene mammals once supposed to be ancestral to Pithecanthropus but now recognized as notoungulates

ar·chae·op·ter·is \ˌärkē'äptərəs\ *n, cap* [NL, fr. *archae-* + *-pteris*] **:** a genus of fossil plants esp. characteristic of the Devonian that were formerly regarded as ferns but are now generally included in the order Cycadofilicales

ar·chae·op·ter·yg·i·for·mes \ˌärkē¦äptə,rijə'fȯr,mēz\ *n pl, cap* [NL, fr. *Archaeopteryg-*, *Archaeopteryx* + *-iformes*] **:** an order of extinct toothed birds including the genera *Archaeopteryx* and *Archaeornis*

ar·chae·op·ter·yx \ˌärkē¦äptə(ˌ)riks\ *n* [NL, fr. *archae-* + *-pteryx*] **1** *cap* **:** a genus of primitive reptilelike birds (subclass Archaeornithes) known from only a few specimens from the Upper Jurassic of Europe and having a long slender tail with feathers along each side **2** -ES **:** a bird or fossil of the genus *Archaeopteryx* or of the subclass Archaeornithes

ar·chae·or·nis \ˌärkē'ȯrnəs\ *n* [NL, fr. *archae-* + *-ornis*] **1** *cap* **:** a genus of Upper Jurassic birds (subclass Archaeornithes) having a long feathered tail, showing reptilian characteristics in the absence of a bill, presence of teeth in the jaws, and on the wings three free digits with claws **2** -ES **:** a bird or fossil of the genus *Archaeornis*

ar·chae·or·ni·thes \-'ȯrnə,thēz, -ˌȯr'nī(ˌ)thēz\ *n pl, cap* [NL, fr. *archae-* + *-ornithes*] **:** a subclass of Aves comprising the earliest and most primitive of fossil birds, retaining distinctive reptilian characters, and including the two genera *Archaeornis* and *Archaeopteryx*

archaeozoic *usu cap, var of* ARCHEOZOIC

archaeus *var of* ARCHEUS

archai *pl of* ARCHE

ar·cha·ic \(')är¦kāik, (')ä¦k-\ *adj* [F or Gk; F *archaïque*, fr. Gk *archaïkos* old-fashioned, fr. *archaios* ancient + *-ikos* -ic — more at ARCHAE-] **1 :** relating to, belonging to, or having the characteristics of an earlier and often more primitive time **:** OLD-FASHIONED, ANTIQUATED ⟨many procedures of the law have long seemed ~ to laymen —W.O.Douglas⟩ **2 a :** having the characteristics of the language of the past and surviving in the present chiefly in legal language (as *malice aforethought*), in biblical or ecclesiastical language (as *thou art, brethren, saith*), or in the language of poetry, imaginative prose, and esp. historical fiction (as *belike, methinks, in sooth*)

☞ In this dict. the label *archaic* is affixed to words and senses relatively common in earlier times but infrequently used in present-day English

b : current without restriction in the present stage of a language but surviving from an earlier stage or from a parent language ⟨verbs like *sing-sang-sung* which form their past and past participle by vowel change are an ~ feature of English⟩ **c** *of a writer or literary work* **:** characterized by the intentional use of old-fashioned language **3 :** of or belonging to an early or formative stage or period in the development of an artistic style, esp. a period immediately preceding one of fully realized expression ⟨the ~ Greek art of the 6th century B.C.⟩ **4 :** surviving essentially unchanged from an earlier period ⟨~ usages govern his conduct toward all the crucial issues of life —Norman Lewis⟩; *specif* **:** typical of a previously dominant evolutionary stage ⟨sphenodon is an ~ reptile⟩ **5 :** having the characteristics of primitive man and his animal forebears esp. as represented in the unconscious and appearing in behavior as manifestations of the unconscious **6** *usu cap* **:** of or belonging to a prehistoric period to which has been assigned the earliest known culture or cultures of a particular area **syn** see OLD

ar·cha·i·cal·ly \-āək(ə)lē, -li\ *adv* **:** in an archaic manner or form **:** with archaic characteristics

ar·cha·i·cism \=¦=ə,sizəm\ *n* -s **:** ARCHAISM

archaic smile *n* **:** a facial expression determined by prominent cheekbones and upturned mouth corners and resembling a smile — used esp. in ref. to archaic Greek sculpture

ar·cha·ism \'ärkē,izəm, 'äk-, -kā-\ *n* -s [NL *archaismus*, fr. Gk *archaïsmos* use of obsolete expressions, fr. *archaios* ancient + *-ismos* -ism — more at ARCHAE-] **1 :** the use of obsolete or old-fashioned diction, idiom, or style in writing or speaking or of the style of an earlier period in painting or other arts; *also* **:** old-fashionedness in diction and style ⟨by 1377 the idiom of 1311 was . . . an ~ already withering into anachronism —*Bull. of Inst. of Historical Research*⟩ **2 :** an instance of archaic usage **:** an archaic word, idiom, or style occurring in such usage ⟨the ~ *thou art*⟩ **3 :** something archaic: as **a** *biol* **:** a survivor from a past period distinguished by retained characteristics out of keeping with its present surroundings **b :** an outmoded or inefficient custom, method, or way of thinking that survives from a past era ⟨we must discard the ~*s* that retard our culture⟩ **c :** the preference for standards, customs, or behavior characteristic of a past era ⟨~ — the referring of everything to the infallible authority of antiquity —*Times Lit. Supp.*⟩

ar·cha·ist \-əst\ *n* -s [*archaism* + *-ist*] **:** ANTIQUARY; *also* **:** one who archaizes

ar·cha·is·tic \¦=kē¦istik, -(ˌ)kā-, -tēk\ *adj* **1 :** imitative of archaic style, form, manner ⟨~ writing⟩ ⟨~ pottery⟩ **:** using or affecting archaisms ⟨an ~ writer⟩ ⟨~ behavior⟩ **2 :** ARCHAIC ⟨an ~ word⟩ ⟨an ~ fear of foreigners⟩ **:** characterized by archaism ⟨an ~ taste in manners and speech⟩ **3 :** tending to preserve or return to the methods, customs, art, or culture of the past ⟨~ or culturally reactionary tendencies⟩ — **ar·cha·is·ti·cal·ly** \-tək(ə)lē, -ēk-, -li\ *adv*

ar·cha·ize \'=ˌkēˌīz, -ˌkā-\ *vb* -ED/-ING/-S [Gk *archaïzein*, fr. *archaios* + *-izein* -ize] *vt* **:** to make appear archaic or antique ⟨~ the styles⟩ ~ *vi* **:** to use archaisms ⟨conscious *archaizing* of the language by the translator⟩

ar·chal·lax·is \ˌärkə'laksəs\ *n, pl* **archallax·es** \-kˌsēz\ [NL, fr. *archi-* + Gk *allaxis* exchange, barter, fr. *allassein* to exchange, fr. *allos* other — more at ELSE] *biol* **:** the early deviation from an ancestral development pattern eliminating recapitulation

¹arch·angel \'ärk-, 'äk-+-, ; (')=-+'-\ *n* -s [ME, fr. OF or LL; OF *archangele*, fr. LL *archangelus*, fr. Gk *archangelos*, fr. Gk *arch-* ¹arch- + *angelos* angel — more at ANGEL] **1 :** an angel of high rank **2 :** a being in the heavenly hierarchy ranking above an angel — see CELESTIAL HIERARCHY **3 a :** ANGELICA 2 **b :** any of several plants of the mint family: as (1) **:** BLACK HOREHOUND (2) **:** RED ARCHANGEL (3) **:** WHITE DEAD NETTLE

²archangel \'=,==\ *or* **ar·khan·gelsk** \är'kan,gelsk\ *adj, usu cap* [fr. *Archangel* or *Arkhangelsk*, U.S.S.R.] **:** of or from the city of Archangel, U.S.S.R. **:** of the kind or style prevalent in Archangel

arch·angelic \¦ärk-, ¦äk- + ,=¦=\ *or* **arch·angelical** \+,= ¦===\ *adj* [LL *archangelicus*, fr. LGk *archangelikos*, fr. Gk *archangelos* + *-ikos* -ic] **:** of or relating to archangels **:** being or resembling an archangel ⟨a face with a look of ~ power⟩

arch·an·gel·i·ca \¦ärk·ˌan'jeləkə\ [NL, fr. *archi-* + *Angelica*] *syn of* ANGELICA

arch·an·thro·pi·nae \¦ärk·ˌanthrō'pī(ˌ)nē\ *n pl, cap* [NL, fr. *archi-* + *anthrop-* + *-inae*] **:** an anthropological subdivision of

Hominidae regarded as comparable to a subfamily and including *Pithecanthropus* and related forms distinguished by extreme development of the occipital torus — compare NEOANTHROPINAE, PALEOANTHROPINAE
arch·an·thro·pine \ärk'anthrə,pīn\ *n* -s *usu cap* [NL *Archanthropinae*] **:** a member of the Archanthropinae
ar·cha·rios \är'käryōs\ *n* -ES [LGk, fr. Gk *archē* beginning + *-arios* (fr. L *-arius* -ary) — more at ARCHI-] **:** a novice in a monastic community of the Eastern Orthodox Church
archband \ˈ=,=\ *n* -s [¹*arch* + *band*] **:** a strip of masonry connected with an arch surface: as **a :** ARCHIVOLT **b :** the part of an arch or rib visible below the vaulting surface
arch bar *n* **:** a bar of arched shape: as **a :** a curved bar in a window sash **b :** an iron bar arching over an ashpit
arch·bishop \(ˈ)ärch,(ˈ)ȧch+ˌ-\ *n* [ME *erchebishop, archebishop*, fr. OE *ærcebiscop, arcebiscop*, fr. LL *archiepiscopus*, fr. LGk *archiepiskopos*, fr. Gk *archi-* + *episkopos* bishop — more at BISHOP] **:** a chief bishop **:** a prelate at the head of an ecclesiastical province or one of equivalent honorary rank with duties and dignities variously comprised in the titles of exarch, patriarch, metropolitan, or primate
arch·bishopric \(ˈ)=+ˈ-\ *n* -s [ME *archebischopric*, fr. OE *arcebiscoprice*, fr. *arcebiscop* + *-rice* -ric] **1 :** the jurisdiction or office of an archbishop **2 :** the see or province over which an archbishop exercises authority
archbp *abbr, often cap* archbishop
arch brace *n* **:** a curved brace in a wooden truss
arch brick *n* **1 :** a wedge-shaped brick used in the building of an arch — compare COMPASS BRICK **2 :** brick that has been overburned through being placed in contact with the fire in the arch of a kiln **:** CLINKER BRICK; *also* **:** one such brick
arch bridge *n* **:** a bridge in which the main supporting elements are arches
arch buttress *n* **:** FLYING BUTTRESS
arch center *n* **:** a temporary structure supporting a concrete or masonry arch during construction
arch·confraternity \ˈärch+\ *n* -ES [¹*arch-* + *confraternity*; trans. of It *arciconfraternità*] *Roman Catholicism* **:** a confraternity canonically empowered to affiliate with and confer its privileges and indulgences on other confraternities with similar purposes
archd *abbr, often cap* **1** archdeacon **2** archduke
arch dam *n* **:** a dam built in a gorge in the form of a horizontal arch having the convex side upstream and abutting against the side walls
arch·deacon \(ˈ)ärch,(ˈ)ȧch+ˌ-\ *n* [ME *erchedeken, archedeken*, fr. OE *ærcediacon, arcediacon*, fr. LL *archidiaconus*, fr. LGk *archidiakonos*, fr. Gk *archi-* + *diakonos* deacon — more at DEACON] **1 :** a chief deacon **:** an ecclesiastical dignitary next in rank below a bishop or in most Eastern Orthodox churches below an archpriest **2 :** a priest in the Episcopal Church who supervises an archdeaconry or who superintends the missionary work of a district
arch·deaconate \(ˈ)=+ˈ-\ *n* -s **:** the position of archdeacon
arch·deaconry \(ˈ)=+ˈ-\ *n* -ES **:** the office, tenure, or state of an archdeacon **:** the district or residence of an archdeacon
arch·dean \ˈärch-,ˈȧch+ˌ-\ *n* [ME *archdene*, fr. ¹*arch-* + *dene* dean] **:** a chief dean **:** one who supervises other deans
arch·diocesan \ˌärch,ˌȧch+,=ˈ===\ *adj* **:** of or relating to an archdiocese
arch·diocese \(ˈ)=+\ *n* [¹*arch-* + *diocese*] **:** the diocese of an archbishop
arch·ducal \(ˈ)=+ˈ==\ *adj* [earlier *archiducal*, fr. F, fr. *archiduc* archduke + *-al*] **:** of, belonging to, or befitting an archduke or archduchy
arch·duchess \ˈ=+ˈ==\ *n* [F *archiduchesse*, fem. of *archiduc* archduke, fr. MF *archeduc*] **1 :** the wife or widow of an archduke **2 :** a woman who holds an archducal title in her own right; *specif* **:** a princess of the imperial family of Austria
arch·duchy \ˈ=+ˈ==\ *n* -ES [F *archeduché* (now *archiduché*), fr. MF, fr. *arche-* ¹arch- + *duché* duchy — more at DUCHY] **:** the territory of an archduke or archduchess
arch·duke \ˈ=+ˌ-\ *n* [MF *archeduc*, fr. *arche-* ¹arch- + *duc* duke — more at DUKE] **:** a sovereign prince; *specif* **:** a prince of the imperial family of Austria
arch·dukedom \ˈ=+ˌ-\ *n* -s **:** ARCHDUCHY
ar·che \ˈär,kē; ärˈkā, -ˈkē\ *n, pl* **ar·chai** \-kī\ [Gk *archē*, lit., beginning — more at ARCHI-] **:** something that was in the beginning **:** a first principle: **a** *in early Greek philosophy* **:** a substance or primal element **b** *in Aristotle* **:** an actuating principle (as a cause)
arche- *prefix* [L, fr. Gk, fr. *archein* to begin — more at ARCHI-] **:** primitive **:** original ⟨*arche*centric⟩ ⟨*arche*spore⟩
¹**ar·che·an** *or* **ar·chae·an** \(ˈ)ärˈkēən, ˈär̦k-\ *adj, usu cap* [Gk *archaios* ancient + E *-an* — more at ARCHAE-] **:** of, belonging to, or contemporary with the oldest known group of rocks, usu. with the earlier portion of the Precambrian; *sometimes* **:** PRECAMBRIAN — see GEOLOGIC TIME table
²**archean** *or* **archaean** \"\ *n* -s *usu cap* **:** the Archean era or system of rocks
archean protaxis *n, usu cap A* **:** the area or mass of Archean rocks in any continent that throughout post-Archeozoic time remained a land area
ar·che·bi·o·sis \ˌärkə,bīˈōsəs\ *n* [NL, fr. *arche-* + *-biosis*] **:** abiogenesis esp. as relating to the initial formation of living matter on earth
ar·che·centric \ˌ==+ˈ-\ *adj* [*arche-* + *centric*] **:** of, relating to, or designating an archetype (sense 3a) — opposed to *apocentric*
arched \ˈärcht, ˈȧcht\ *adj* **:** made with or formed in an arch or arches ⟨an ~ beam⟩ **:** covered with an arch ⟨an ~ door⟩
ar·che·dic·ty·on \ˌärkəˈdiktē,än\ *n* -s [NL, fr. *arche-* + Gk *diktyon* net, fr. *dikein* to throw] **:** a fine veinlike network on the wings of primitive insects esp. of some extinct groups
arched squall *n* **:** a violent thunder squall advancing broadside, its front seeming to form an arch
ar·che·gone \ˈärkə,gōn\ *n* -s [F, fr. NL *archegonium*] **:** ARCHEGONIUM
archegonia *pl of* ARCHEGONIUM
ar·che·go·ni·al \ˌärkəˈgōnēəl\ *adj* [NL *archegonium* + E *-al*] **:** of or relating to an archegonium **:** ARCHEGONIATE
archegonial chamber *n* **:** a cavity above the archegonium in the female gametophyte of some gymnosperms (as ginkgo and the cycads)
ar·che·go·ni·a·ta \ˌärkə,gōnēˈädə, -ˈād-ə\ [NL, fr. *archegonium* + *-ata*] *syn of* ARCHEGONIATAE
ar·che·go·ni·a·tae \-nēˈā,tē, -ˈä,-\ *n pl, cap* [NL, fr. *archegonium* + *-atae* (fr. fem. pl. of L *-atus* -ate)] *in some classifications* **:** a primary division of the plant kingdom coextensive with the subkingdom Embryophyta and containing all the plants that produce archegonia (as the mosses, ferns, horsetails, and club mosses)
¹**ar·che·go·ni·ate** \ˌ==ˈgōnēət, -ē,āt\ *adj* [NL *archegonium* + E *-ate*] **:** bearing archegonia
²**archegoniate** \"\ *n* -s **1 :** a plant bearing archegonia **2** [NL *Archegoniatae*] **:** a plant belonging to the division Archegoniatae
ar·che·go·ni·o·phore \ˌ==ˈgōnēə,fō(ə)r\ *n* -s [NL *archegonium* + E *-o-* + *-phore*] **:** the stalk or other outgrowth of a prothallium upon which archegonia are borne (as in liverworts of the genus *Marchantia*) — compare CARPOCEPHALUM
ar·che·go·ni·um \ˌärkəˈgōnēəm\ *n, pl* **archego·nia** \-nēə\ [NL, fr. Gk *archegonos* original, primal (fr. *arche-* + *-gonos*, akin to *gignesthai* to be born) + NL *-ium* — more at KIN] **:** the flask-shaped female sex organ in mosses and ferns and some gymnosperms
ar·che·go·sau·rus \ˌär,kēgōˈsȯrəs\ *n, cap* [NL, fr. Gk *archēgos* primary, originating (fr. *archē* beginning + *-ēgos*, akin to Gk *agein* to lead, drive) + NL *-saurus* — more at ARCHI-, AGENT] **:** a genus of extinct long-snouted aquatic labyrinthodont amphibians from the Lower Permian of Europe
ar·chel·o·gy \ärˈkeləjē\ *n* -ES [NL *archelogia*, fr. Gk *archē* beginning, element + L *-logia* -logy] **:** the science of first principles
ar·che·lon \ˈärkə,län\ *n, cap* [NL, prob. irreg. fr. *archi-* + Gk *chelōnē* tortoise; akin to Gk *chelys* tortoise — more at CHELYS] **:** a genus of very large extinct marine turtles from the Cretaceous of So. Dakota having a well-developed plastron but poorly developed carapace
¹**arch·en·ceph·a·la** \ˌärk-,enˈsefələ\ *n pl, cap* [NL, fr. *archi-* + *encephala* (pl. of *encephalon*) — more at ENCEPHALON] **:** man regarded as constituting a separate subclass of Mammalia — not now used as an acceptable taxonomic concept
²**archencephala** *pl of* ARCHENCEPHALON
arch·en·ce·phal·ic \ˌärk,ensəˈfalik\ *adj* [NL *archencephalon* + E *-ic*] **:** of or relating to the archencephalon
arch·encephalon \ˌärk+,-\ *n, pl* **archencephala** [NL, fr. *archi-* + *encephalon*] **:** the primitive forebrain of the early embryo
arch·enemy \ˈärˈchen-\ *n* -ES [¹*arch-* + *enemy*] **:** a principal enemy **:** a great enemy
arch·en·ter·ic \ˌärk-,enˈterik, ˌärkən-\ *adj* [NL *archenteron* + E *-ic*] **:** of or relating to the archenteron
archenteric pouch *n* **:** one of the paired pouches budded off the dorsolateral aspect of the archenteron of amphioxus and some other chordates giving rise to the anterior somites and coelomic mesoderm
arch·en·ter·on \(ˈ)ärk-ˈentə,rän\ *n, pl* **archen·tera** \-tərə\ [NL, fr. *archi-* + Gk *enteron* intestine] **:** the cavity formed by the invagination or ingrowth of cells of the gastrula stage of the embryo (as that of the frog)
archeo- — see ARCHAE-
archeocyte *var of* ARCHAEOCYTE
archeology *var of* ARCHAEOLOGY
¹**ar·cheo·zo·ic** *also* **ar·chaeo·zo·ic** \ˌärkēəˈzōik *sometimes* ˌär̦k-\ *adj, usu cap* [*archae-* + *-zoic*] **:** of, belonging to, or relating to the earliest era of geological history, the era of the Archean rocks — see GEOLOGIC TIME table
²**archeozoic** *also* **archaeozoic** \"\ *n* -s *usu cap* **:** the Archeozoic era or system of rocks
archepiscopal *var of* ARCHIEPISCOPAL
arch·er \ˈärchər, ˈȧchə\ *n* -s [ME, fr. OF *archier, archer*, fr. LL *arcarius*, alter. of *arcuarius*, fr. *arcuarius* of a bow, fr. L *arcus* bow + *-arius* -ary — more at ARROW] **1 :** one skilled in the use of the bow and arrow **:** BOWMAN **2 :** ARCHERFISH **3 :** a shoe worker who operates a machine for shaping the arch or shank of outsoles and insoles
archerfish \ˈ==,=\ *n* **:** a small fish (*Toxotes jaculator*) of the East Indies that ejects drops of water from its mouth at insects resting on objects over the water causing them to fall so that it can capture them; *also* **:** any of several other closely related fishes of similar habits

archerfish (*Toxotes jaculator*)

arch·ery \ˈärch(ə)rē, ˈȧch-, -ri\ *n* -ES [ME *archerie*, fr. MF, fr. OF, fr. *archier*, *archer* + *-ie* -y] **1 :** the use of bow and arrows (as in battle or as a sport) **:** the art, practice, or skill of shooting with bow and arrow ⟨he excels in ~⟩ **2 :** an archer's weapons (as bows and arrows) ⟨the troops were supplied with new ~⟩ **3 :** a body of archers (as a company or corps) ⟨the order was given for the ~ to advance⟩
arches *pl of* ARCH, *pres 3d sing of* ARCH
ar·che·spore \ˈärkə,spō(ə)r\ *or* **ar·che·spo·ri·um** \ˌ==ˈspōrēəm\ *n, pl* **arche·spores** \-rz\ *or* **archespo·ria** \-ōrēə\ [NL *archesporium*, fr. *arche-* + *-sporium*] **:** the cell or group of cells from which spore mother cells develop (as those from which the microspores develop in the pollen sac or the megaspore in the ovule) — **ar·che·spo·ri·al** \ˌ==ˈspōrēəl\ *adj*
ar·che·tis·ta \ˌärkəˈtistə\ *n pl, cap* [NL] **:** a hypothetical assemblage of primitive organisms comprising viruses, bacteriophages, and supposed free-living related viroids
ar·che·typ·al \ˌärkəˈtīpəl, ˌäk-\ *or* **ar·che·typ·i·cal** \-ˈtipəkəl, -ēk-\ *adj* **:** of, relating to, or representing an archetype or archetypes ⟨~ patterns and images⟩ **:** constituting a model either actual or ideal ⟨~ figures and characters⟩ — **ar·che·typ·al·ly** \-īpəlē, -li\ *or* **ar·che·typ·i·cal·ly** \-ipək(ə)lē, -ēk-, -li\ *adv*
ar·che·type \ˈärkə,tīp, ˈäk-\ *n* -s [L *archetypum*, fr. Gk *archetypon*, fr. neut. of *archetypos* molded first as a model, exemplary, fr. *arche-* + *typos* impression of a seal, mold, replica — more at TYPE] **1 :** the original model, form, or pattern from which something is made or from which something develops ⟨in . . . oral ballads, variation has gone so far that it is impossible to reconstruct the exact words of the ~ —M.J.C.Hodgart⟩ ⟨the House of Commons, the ~ of all the representative assemblies which now meet —T.B.Macaulay⟩ **2 a** *in Platonism* **:** one of the ideas of which existent things are imitations — compare IDEA 1 **b** *in scholastic philosophy* **:** the idea in the divine intellect that determines the form of a created thing **c** *in Locke* **:** one of the external realities with which our ideas and impressions to some extent correspond **3 a :** a primitive generalized plan of structure deduced from the characters of the members of a natural group of animals or plants and assumed to be the type from which they have been modified **b :** the original ancestor of a group of animals or plants **4 :** a manuscript usu. no longer extant from which others were copied **5** *in the psychology of C.G.Jung* **:** an inherited idea or mode of thought derived from the experiences of the race and present in the unconscious of the individual **6 a :** a perfectly typical example **:** a perfect example of a particular type ⟨the ~ of his profession — stocky, thick-chested, bull-necked —*New Yorker*⟩ **:** the most extreme example ⟨the ~ of the stuffy aesthetic reactionary —*N.Y. Herald Tribune*⟩ **b :** an abstract or ideal conception of a type ⟨the various . . . ideals or ~s; the gentleman, the scholar . . . the go-getter . . . the captain of industry —Walter Moberly⟩
ar·che·us *also* **ar·chae·us** \ärˈkēəs\ *n, pl* **ar·chei** *also* **ar·chaei** \-ē,ī\ [NL, fr. Gk *archos* ruler — more at ARCHI-] **:** the vital principle that according to Paracelsians directs and maintains the growth and continuation of living beings
archfiend \ˈärchˈfēnd, ˈȧch-\ *n* -s [¹*arch-* + *fiend*] **:** a chief fiend; *esp* **:** SATAN
arch-gravity dam *n* [¹*arch*] **:** an arch dam having also sufficient mass and breadth of base to provide gravity stability
archi- *or* **arch-** *prefix* [MF & It & L; MF *archi-* & It *arci-*, fr. L *archi-*, fr. Gk *arch-, archi-*; akin to Gk *archein* to begin, *archē* beginning, *archos* ruler] **1 :** chief **:** principal ⟨*archi*episcopal⟩ — *archi-* before consonants, *arch-* or more frequently *archi-* before vowels **2 :** primitive **:** original **:** primary ⟨*arch*enteron⟩ ⟨*archi*blast⟩ ⟨*archi*carp⟩ ⟨*archi*continent⟩ ⟨*archi*pterygium⟩
ar·chi·acanthocephala \ˌärkē+\ *n pl, cap* [NL, fr. *archi-* + *Acanthocephala*] **:** an order of Acanthocephala comprising parasites of terrestrial vertebrates having the proboscis hooks arranged in concentric circles and lacking trunk spines
ar·chi·annelida \ˌ==+\ *n pl, cap* [NL, fr. *archi-* + *Annelida*] **:** a group, usu. a class, of small primitive or secondarily simplified annelid worms lacking external segmentation and resembling polychaete larvae — compare POLYGORDIUS
ar·chi·a·ter \ˈärkē,ād·ər, -ˌ==ˈ==\ *n* -s [LL *archiater, archiatrus*, fr. Gk *archiatros*, fr. *archi-* + *iatros* physician — more at IATRO-] **:** a chief physician orig. of the court of a Hellenistic king or a Roman emperor
ar·chi·benthic *also* **ar·chi·benthal** \ˌärkē+ˌ-\ *adj* [*archi-* + *benthic, benthal*] **:** of, relating to, or being the upper part of the benthic region that includes the continental shelf and extends from the sublittoral to the abyssal
ar·chi·benthos \ˌärkē+\ *n* [NL, fr. *archi-* + *benthos*] **:** MESOBENTHOS
ar·chi·blast \ˈärkə,blast\ *n* -s [*archi-* + *-blast*] **1 :** the active protoplasmic components of the egg in contrast to the stored yolk and other reserves **2 :** EPIBLAST
ar·chi·blas·tic \ˌ==ˈblastik\ *adj* **:** of, relating to, or derived from the archiblast
ar·chi·blastula \ˌärkē+ˌ-\ *n* -s [NL, fr. *archi-* + *blastula*] **:** COELOBLASTULA
ar·chi·carp \ˈärkē,kärp\ *n* -s [*archi-* + *-carp*] **:** the female reproductive organ in ascomycetous fungi; *specif* **:** one consisting of a carpogonium and a trichogyne
ar·chi·cephalic \ˌärkē+=ˈ==\ *adj* [NL *archicephalon* + E *-ic*] **:** of or relating to the archicephalon
ar·chi·ceph·a·lon \ˌ==ˈsefə,län\ *n* [NL, fr. *archi-* + *cephalon*] **:** the primitive head region in insects consisting of the preoral segments and probably equivalent to the prostomium of annelid worms
ar·chi·cerebellum \ˌärkē+\ *n* [NL, fr. *archi-* + *cerebellum*] **:** the part of the cerebellum related to labyrinthine sense and comprising the flocculus, nodulus, and part of the vermis — compare NEOCEREBELLUM, PALEOCEREBELLUM
ar·chi·cerebrum \ˌärkē+\ *n* [NL, fr. *archi-* + *cerebrum*] **:** the supra-esophageal ganglia of invertebrates
ar·chi·chla·myd·e·ae \ˌärkēklə'midē,ē\ *n pl, cap* [NL, fr. *archi-* + *-chlamydeae* (fr. Gk *chlamyd-, chlamys* cloak, mantle)] **:** a group of Dicotyledoneae comprising plants in which the petals of the flowers are separate or absent — compare METACHLAMYDEAE; see APETALAE, CHORIPETALAE — **ar·chi·chla·myd·e·ous** \ˌ===ˈ=ēəs\ *adj*
ar·chi·cleistogamous \ˌärkē+,=ˈ===\ *adj* **:** of or relating to archicleistogamy
ar·chi·cleistogamy \ˌärkē+,=ˈ===\ *n* -ES [*archi-* + *cleistogamy*] **:** permanent cleistogamy
ar·chi·coele *also* **ar·chi·coel** \ˈärkē,sēl\ *n* -s [*archi-* + *-coele, -coel*] **:** the segmentation cavity in some forms persisting as a body cavity between the ectoderm and endoderm
ar·chi·continent \ˌärkē+ˌ-\ *n* [*archi-* + *continent*] **:** a continental nucleus that has persisted throughout the recorded portion of geologic time
ar·chi·diaconal \ˌärkē+,=ˈ===\ *adj* [LL *archidiaconus* archdeacon + E *-al* — more at ARCHDEACON] **:** of or relating to an archdeacon or his office ⟨~ visitation⟩
ar·chi·diaconate \ˌärkē+\ *n* -s [ML *archidiaconatus*, fr. LL *archidiaconus* + L *-atus* -ate] **:** the office or order of an archdeacon
ar·chi·did·as·ca·li·an \ˌärkē,didəˈskālēən, -lyən\ *or* **ar·chi·di·das·ca·line** \-ˌdəˈdaskələn, -ˌdī'd-, -ˌlīn\ *adj* **:** of or relating to an archididascalos
ar·chi·di·das·ca·los \ˌ==dəˈdaskə,läs, -ˌdīˈd-, -ˌləs\ *or* **ar·chi·di·das·ca·lus** \-ˌləs\ *n, pl* **archididasca·li** \-ˌlī\ [LGk *archididaskalos*, fr. Gk *archi-* + *didaskalos* teacher, fr. *didaskein* to teach — more at DOCILE] **:** a chief teacher (as a headmaster in a school)
ar·chid·i·um \ärˈkidēəm\ *n, cap* [NL] **:** a genus of acrocarpous mosses related to *Dicranum* but having sessile capsules and sometimes made type of a separate family
ar·chie \ˈärchē\ *n* -s *often cap* [prob. fr. *Archie*, nickname for *Archibald*] *slang* **:** ANTIAIRCRAFT
ar·chi·episcopacy \ˌärkē, ˌäkē+\ *n* [LL *archiepiscopus* archbishop + E *-acy* — more at ARCHBISHOP] **1 :** the form of episcopacy in which the chief power is in the hands of archbishops **2 :** ARCHIEPISCOPATE
ar·chi·episcopal \+=ˈ===\ *also* **arch·episcopal** \ˌärk, ˌäk+=ˈ===\ *adj* [ML *archiepiscopalis*, fr. LL *archiepiscopus* + L *-alis* -al] **:** of or relating to an archbishop ⟨an ~ see⟩ — **ar·chi·episcopally** *adv*
archiepiscopal cross *n* **:** PATRIARCHAL CROSS
archiepiscopal staff *n* **:** CROSS-STAFF 1a
ar·chi·episcopate \ˌärkē, ˌäkē+\ *n* [ML *archiepiscopatus*, fr. LL *archiepiscopus* + L *-atus* -ate] **:** the office, tenure, or state of an archbishop **:** ARCHBISHOPRIC

archiepiscopal cross

-archies *pl of* -ARCHY
ar·chi·gas·ter \ˈärkē,gastə(r), ˌ==ˈ=\ *n* -s [*archi-* + *gaster*] **:** ARCHENTERON
ar·chi·gastrula \ˌärkē+ˌ-\ *n* [NL, fr. *archi-* + *gastrula*] **:** a gastrula formed by simple invagination
ar·chi·gen·e·sis \ˌärkē+\ *n* [NL, fr. *archi-* + *genesis*] **:** ARCHEBIOSIS
ar·chi·ge·tes \ˌärkəˈjēd·ēz, ärˈkijə,tēz\ *n, cap* [NL] **:** a genus of pseudophyllidean tapeworms living as neotenic larvae in the coelom of aquatic oligochaete worms, some being reported to develop into typical caryophyllid worms when the host is ingested by a suitable fish — compare CARYOPHYLLAEIDAE
ar·chil \ˈärchəl\ *also* **or·chil** \ˈȯr-\ *or* **ar·chil·la** \ärˈchilə\ *n* -s [ME *orchell*, prob. fr. OIt *oricello*] **1 :** a violet dye obtained as a pasty mass from certain lichens of the genera *Roccella* and *Lecanora* by fermentation with alkali (as ammonia) — compare CUDBEAR, LITMUS **2 :** a plant that yields archil **3 :** any of the colors imparted by the dye archil varying from moderate red to dark purplish red according as the dye bath is acid or alkaline — called also *corcir*
¹**ar·chi·lo·chi·an** \ˌärkəˈlōkēən\ *adj, usu cap* [*Archilochus*, 7th cent. B.C. Greek poet (fr. L, fr. Gk *Archilochos*) + E *-ian*] **1 a :** of or relating to Archilochus **b :** TRENCHANT, SARCASTIC, BITTER **2 :** marked by use of Archilochians or of Archilochian strophes
²**archilochian** \"\ *n* -s *usu cap* **:** a verse form ascribed to Archilochus: as **a :** a line composed of a dactylic tetrapody followed by a trochaic tripody — called also *greater Archilochian* **b :** a dactylic tripody catalectic — sometimes called also *lesser Archilochian* **c :** a dactylic tetrapody with spondee or trochee as the fourth foot **d :** a dicolon composed of a complete prosodiac followed by an ithyphallic
archilochian strophe *n* **1 :** a dactylic hexameter followed by a lesser Archilochian **2 :** a dactylic hexameter followed by an iambelegus **3 :** an iambic trimeter followed by an elegiambus **4 :** a greater Archilochian followed by an iambic trimeter catalectic
archilowe *n* -s [origin unknown] *Scot* **:** the return that one who has been treated in an inn makes to the company
ar·chi·mage \ˈärkə,māj\ *n* -s [NL *archimagus*, fr. LGk *archimagos*, fr. Gk *archi-* + *magos* magus, wizard — more at MAGIC] **:** a great magician, wizard, or enchanter
ar·chi·man·drite \ˌärkəˈman,drīt\ *n* -s [LL *archimandrites, archimandrita*, fr. LGk *archimandritēs*, fr. Gk *archi-* + LGk *mandra* monastery, fr. Gk, fold, pen] **1** *Eastern Church* **:** the superior or abbot of a larger monastery — compare HEGUMEN **2** *Eastern Church* **:** an honorary title bestowed by a patriarch, catholicos, or bishop (as upon heads of a number of monasteries or prominent hieromonks)
ar·chi·me·de·an \ˌärkəˈmēdēən, ˌäk-ˌmə'd-\ *adj, usu cap* [*Archimedes* (fr. Gk *Archimēdēs*) †212 B.C. Greek mathematician & inventor + E *-an*] **:** of, relating to, or invented by Archimedes **:** constructed on the principle of an invention by Archimedes ⟨~ drill⟩ ⟨~ lever⟩
archimedean solid *n, usu cap A* **:** one of 13 possible solids each of which has plane faces that are all regular polygons though not all of the polygons are of the same species and each of which has all its polyhedral angles equal
archimedean spiral *n, usu cap A* **:** a plane curve generated by a point moving away from or toward a fixed point at a constant rate while the radius vector from the fixed point rotates at a constant rate
ar·chi·me·des \ˌärkəˈmē(ˌ)dēz\ *n* [NL, fr. *Archimedes* †212 B.C.; fr. the screwlike axis] **1** *cap* **:** a genus of extinct colonial bryozoans having a spiral screwlike axis and being typical of Mississippian formations but known also from Pennsylvanian and Permian rocks **2** *pl* **archimedes :** any bryozoan or fossil of the genus *Archimedes*

archimedes: *a* zoarium, *b* axis

ar·chi·me·des' principle \-dēz'p-\ *n, usu cap A & sometimes cap P* **:** a law of fluid mechanics: a body while wholly or partly immersed in a fluid apparently loses weight by an amount equal to that of the fluid displaced
archimedes' problem *n, usu cap A* **:** the mathematical problem of bisecting the volume of a hemisphere by means of a plane parallel to the base insoluble by Euclidean methods
archimedes' screw *n, usu cap A* **:** a device consisting of a tube bent spirally around an axis or of a broad-threaded screw incased by a hollow open cylinder and used to raise water by rotating the apparatus when partly immersed in a slantwise direction

archimedes' screw

ar·chi·mime \ˈärkə,mīm\ *n* -s [L *archimimus*, fr. Gk *archimimos*, fr. *archi-* + *mimos* mime — more at MIME] **:** the chief performer in the Roman mime
ar·chi·my·ce·tes \ˌärkə,mīˈsēd·ēz\ *n pl, cap* [NL, fr. *archi-* + *-mycetes*] **1** *in some classifications* **:** a subclass or order of

Phycomycetes coextensive with Chytridiales **2** *in some classifications* **:** a class of primitive fungi comprising the Chytridiales and certain related forms

archin *or* **archine** *var of* ARSHIN

ar·chi·nephridium \ˌärkē+\ *n* [NL, fr. *archi-* + *nephridium*] **:** the primitive nephridium found paired in each segment of certain annelid larvae

arch·ing \ˈärchiŋ, ˈäch-, -ēŋ\ *n* -s [fr. gerund of ²*arch*] **:** the arched part of a structure **:** a system of arches

ar·chi·oligochaeta \ˌärkē+\ *n pl, cap* [NL, fr. *archi-* + *Oligochaeta*] *in some classifications* **:** a division of Oligochaeta comprising relatively small aquatic worms of few segments that reproduce vegetatively by fission as well as by sexual means (as members of the genera *Aeolosoma, Nais,* and *Dero*) — compare LIMICOLAE, MICRODRILI — **ar·chi·oligo·chaete** \+ˈ-\ *adj or n*

ar·chi·pallial \ˌärkē+\ *adj* [NL *archipallium* + E *-al*] **:** of or relating to the archipallium

ar·chi·pallium \+\ *n* -s [NL, fr. *archi-* + *pallium*] **:** the olfactory part of the pallium comprising the hippocampus and part of the hippocampal gyrus and evolved earlier than the neopallium

ar·chi·pe·lag·ic \ˌärkəpəˈlajik, -rchə-\ *also* **ar·chi·pe·la·gian** \-ˈlāj(ē)ən\ *adj* [*archipelago* + *-ic* or *-ian*] **:** of, relating to, or located in an archipelago ⟨an ~ war —*New Republic*⟩

ar·chi·pel·a·go \ˌärkəˈpeləˌgō, ˌärchə-, ˌäk-, ˌäch-; *the Italian source word "Arcipelago" (see etymology) is pronounced* ˌärch-\ *n, pl* **archipelagoes** *or* **archipelagos** [*Archipelago* Aegean sea, fr. It *Arcipelago*] **1 :** a sea or other expanse of water having many scattered islands **2 :** a group or cluster of islands

ar·chi·phoneme \ˈärkē, -kə+ˌ-\ *n* -s [ISV *archi-* + *phoneme*] **:** a class of phonemes consisting usu. of a pair sharing all distinctive features except one (as *d* and *t* share all distinctive features except that *d* is voiced and *t* is voiceless); *esp* **:** a structurally descriptive category in which a sound may be placed when it occurs in a position where it may belong to any of two or more phonemes because of neutralization or suspension of the usual contrast between them (as German *t* in final position where it may correspond either to medial *t* or to medial *d*)

ar·chi·plasm \ˈärkəˌplazəm\ *n* -s [G *archiplasma*, fr. *archi-* + *-plasma* -plasm] **1 :** a hypothetical primitive undifferentiated protoplasm **2 :** ARCHOPLASM — **ar·chi·plas·mic** \ˌ==ˈplazmik\ *adj*

archipresbyter *var of* ARCHPRESBYTER

archipresbyterate *var of* ARCHPRESBYTERATE

ar·chips \ˈärˌkips\ *n, cap* [NL, fr. *archi-* + Gk *ips* woodworm] **:** a large genus of tortricid moths including a number with larvae that are serious pests of economically important plants, feeding on and webbing the leaves and causing defoliation — compare UGLY-NEST CATERPILLAR

ar·chip·te·ryg·i·al \ˌärˌkiptəˈrij(ē)əl, ˌäˌk-\ *adj* [NL *archipterygium* + E *-al*] **:** of or relating to archipterygium

ar·chip·te·ryg·i·um \(ˌ)==ˌ==ˈjēəm\ *n* [NL, fr. *archi-* + Gk *pterygion* little wing, fin — more at PTERYGIUM] **:** a primitive form of fin having a long segmented axis (as that of *Neoceratodus*)

ar·chi·sper·mae \ˌärkəˈspərˌmē\ *n pl, cap* [NL, fr. *archi-* + *-spermae;* fr. their presumed antiquity] *in some classifications* **:** a class equivalent to Gymnospermae

ar·chis·tia \ärˈkistēə\ *n pl, cap* [NL, fr. *archi-* + *-istia* (as in *Cladistia*)] **:** an order of primitive Paleozoic ganoid fishes of moderate size superficially resembling modern herrings but having heterocercal tails, the maxilla expanded over the cheek, and a true clavicle in the pectoral girdle

ar·chi·stome \ˈärkəˌstōm\ *n* -s [*archi-* + *-stome*] **:** BLASTOPORE

¹**ar·chi·tect** \ˈärkəˌtekt, ˈäk-\ *n* -s [MF *architecte*, fr. L *architectus, architecton*, fr. Gk *architektōn* chief artificer, master builder, fr. *archi-* + *tektōn* workman, carpenter — more at TECHNICAL] **1 :** a person skilled in the art of building **:** a professional student of architecture or one who makes it his occupation to form plans and designs of and to draw up specifications for an building and to superintend their execution — compare LANDSCAPE ARCHITECT, MARINE ARCHITECT **2 :** one that plans and achieves esp. an objective that is felt to be the product of painstaking construction ⟨the . . . ~s of Portugal's . . . empire in the Far East —S.E.Morison⟩ ⟨the great ~ of the military victory —*Time*⟩

²**architect** \"\ *vt* -ED/-ING/-S **:** to plan and contrive as an architect ⟨the book is not well ~*ed* —*Times Lit. Supp.*⟩

ar·chi·tec·ton·ic \ˌärkəˌtekˈtänik, ˌäk-\ *adj* [L *architectonicus* of architecture, fr. Gk *architektonikos* of a master builder, fr. *architektōn-, architektōn* + *-ikos* -ic] **1 :** of, related to, or in accordance with the technical principles of architecture **:** ARCHITECTURAL ⟨~ feature⟩ ⟨~ purposes⟩ **2 a :** having the organized structural and rational qualities of architecture ⟨severe and ~ landscape —Osbert Sitwell⟩ ⟨make his book a series of essays rather than an ~ whole —D.W.Petegorsky⟩ **b :** giving, creating, or tending to give the quality of structural unity or order ⟨creative energy . . . is . . . ~, and it imposes upon the lyric impulse an ordered sequence and an organic unity —J.L.Lowes⟩

ar·chi·tec·ton·i·ca \ˌ==ˌ==ˈnəkə\ *n, cap* [NL, fr. L, fem. of *architectonicus*] **:** a genus of tropical marine snails having a depressed conical shell the umbilicus of which is wide so that the upper whorls can be seen in it

ar·chi·tec·ton·i·cal·ly \ˌ==ˌ==ˈnək(ə)lē\ *adv* **:** with respect to or in terms of architectonics

ar·chi·tec·ton·ics \ˌ==ˌ==ˈniks\ *n pl but sing in constr, also* **ar·chi·tec·ton·ic** \-ik\ **1 :** the science of architecture **2** *philos* **a :** the doctrine of pure method or of the abstract systematization of knowledge **b :** the abstract scheme or plan or the purely formal elucidation of something **3 a :** the structural design that imposes order, balance, and unity upon a work or an entity **:** the element of form that relates the parts to each other and to the whole ⟨good novels . . . have rhythm, ~, focus —*New Republic*⟩ ⟨drawing is the ~, . . . the living skeleton of painting —George Biddle⟩ **b :** system of structure **:** plan of order ⟨Dante's . . . ~ of the relationships of authority and obedience —Israel Knox⟩

architector *n* -s [MF *architecteur*, fr. L *architectus, architecton* + MF *-eur* -or — more at ARCHITECT] *obs* **:** ARCHITECT

architects' scale *n* **:** a scale or rule usu. of triangular section made of boxwood and having a variety of graduations on its edges, one edge usu. being graduated in inches and sixteenths of an inch, the other edges graduated in twelfths and fractions thereof for lengths of 3 inches, 1½ inches, and 1 inch so that dimensions of reduced-scale drawings may be measured directly in feet and inches

ar·chi·tec·tur·al \ˌärkəˈtekchərəl, ˌäk-, -ksh(ə)rəl\ *adj* **1 :** of, resembling, or relating to architecture **:** characteristic of architecture **:** conforming to the rules of architecture ⟨~ effects⟩ ⟨~ quality⟩ **2 :** used for construction and esp. for ornamentation in architecture ⟨~ bronze⟩ ⟨~ glass⟩ **3 :** having features, ornaments, or motifs characteristic of some type or style of architecture ⟨~ canopy⟩ — **ar·chi·tec·tur·al·ly** \-kchərəlē, -ksh(ə)rəlē, -li\ *adv*

architectural concrete *n* **:** concrete used for the exterior or interior ornamentation or finish of a building or structure, often being cast integral with the reinforced concrete frame

architectural engineering *n* **:** the art and science of engineering and construction as practiced in regard to buildings as distinguished from architecture as an art of design

architectural furniture *n* **:** furniture designed to match or to accord with the architectural features of the rooms for which it is intended

architectural projected window *n* **:** a better grade of projected window for use in buildings where the architectural effect is important

ar·chi·tec·ture \ˈärkəˌtekchər, ˈäkəˌtekchə, -ksh-\ *n* -s [MF, fr. L *architectura*, fr. *architectus* architect + *-ura* -ure — more at ARCHITECT] **1 :** the art or science of building; *specif* **:** the art or practice of designing and building structures, esp. habitable structures, in accordance with principles determined by aesthetic and practical or material considerations **2 :** formation or construction whether the result of conscious act or of growth or of random disposition of the parts ⟨~ and function of the cerebral cortex⟩ ⟨the fountains blow their ~ of slender pillars —Aldous Huxley⟩ ⟨the careful ~ of *Tom Jones* in the innumerable subplots which give the book the proportions of life, the personal story of Jones taking its place in the general orchestration —Graham Greene⟩ **3 :** the exercise or an instance of the exercise of the art or science of architecture ⟨building must go beyond mere building for shelter to become ~ —T.E.Sanford⟩ **:** architectural product **:** architectural work ⟨the mansions which comprise the entire ~ of the Square —Blake Ehrlich⟩ **4 :** a method or style of building characterized by certain peculiarities of structure or ornamentation ⟨many other ~s besides Gothic —John Ruskin⟩

ar·chi·teu·this \ˌärkəˈt(y)üthəs\ *n, cap* [NL, fr. *archi-* + *Teuthis*] **:** a genus of gigantic squids containing the largest mollusks known, some being 40 feet long inclusive of the long arms

ar·chit·o·my \ärˈkidəmē\ *n* -ES [*archi-* + *-tomy*] **:** reproduction by fission followed by bodily reorganization (as in certain annelids) — compare PARATOMY

ar·chi·trave \ˈärkəˌtrāv, ˈäˌk-\ *n* -s [MF, fr. OIt, fr. *archi-* (fr. L *archi-*) + *trave* beam, fr. L *trabs* — more at THORP] **1 :** the lowest division of an entablature resting (as in classical architecture) immediately on the capital of the column — see ENTABLATURE illustration **2 :** the molded band, group of moldings, or other architectural member around a door or other opening esp. if rectangular in form

ar·chi·traved \-vd\ *adj* **:** furnished with an architrave

ar·chi·val \(ˈ)ärˈkīvəl, (ˈ)äˈk-; ˈ=ˌkəvəl\ *adj* [¹*archive* + *-al*] **:** of, relating to, contained in, or constituting archives or records

ar·chi·va·lia \ˌärkəˈvālēə, -lyə\ *n pl* [NL, fr. L *archivum* + NL *-alia*] **:** material preserved in or suitable for preservation in archives **:** ARCHIVE 2

¹**ar·chive** \ˈärˌkīv, ˈäˌk-\ *n* -s [F & L; obs. F *archive* (now *archives*, pl.), fr. L *archivum, archium*, fr. Gk *archeion* government house, *archeia* (pl. of *archeion*) archives, fr. *archē* beginning, first place, government — more at ARCHI-] **1 a :** a place in which public or institutional records (as minutes, correspondence, reports, accounts) are systematically preserved — usu. used in pl. **b :** a repository for any documents or other materials esp. of historical value (as diaries, photographs, private correspondence) ⟨the Trotsky ~s at Harvard⟩ — usu. used in pl. **c :** any repository or collection esp. of information ⟨the ~s of memory⟩ **2 :** public or institutional records, historic documents, and other materials that have been preserved — usu. used in pl.

²**archive** \"\ *vt* -ED/-ING/-S **:** to file or collect (as records or documents) in an archive or other repository ⟨methods for *archiving* languages of the world —*Linguistic Institute*⟩

ar·chi·vism \ˈärkəˌvizəm\ *n* -s **:** the process of archiving

ar·chi·vist \ˈärkəvəst, -ˌkīv-, ˈä(ˌ)k-\ *n* -s [prob. fr. F *archiviste*, fr. *archives* + *-iste* -ist] **:** one who is in charge of archives **:** one responsible for the collection, cataloging, and preservation of archives

ar·chi·vis·tic \ˌärkəˈvistik, ˌäk-, -tēk\ *adj* **:** of or relating to archives

ar·chi·volt \ˈärkəˌvōlt, ˈäk-\ *n* -s [It *archivolto*, fr. ML *archivoltum*, prob. modif. (influenced by ML *archi-* bow, fr. L *arqui-, arci-*, fr. *arcus*) of OF *arvolt, arcvolt* arch, arcade, fr. *arc* arch (fr. L *arcus*) + *volt* curved, fr. (assumed) VL *volvitus*, past part. of L *volvere* to roll — more at ARROW, VOLUBLE] **1 :** the architectural member or members forming the inner surface of an arch **2 a :** the usu. ornamental band or molding surrounding an arch and corresponding to the architrave of a rectangular opening **b :** the molding or other ornaments on the wall face of the voussoirs

archivolt 2a

ar·chi·zo·ic \ˌ==ˈzōik\ *adj* [*archi-* + *-zoic*] **:** of or relating to the earliest forms of life

archlike \ˈ=ˌ=\ *adj* **:** resembling an arch

arch·lute \ˈärchˌlüt\ *n* [F or It; F *archiluth*, fr. It *arciliuto, arcileuto*, fr. *arci-* archi- + *liuto, leuto* lute, fr. Ar *al-ʿūd* the lute, the wood] **:** a large lute **:** CHITARRONE, THEORBO

arch·ly \ˈärchlē, ˈäch-, -li\ *adv* [³*arch* + *-ly*] **:** in an arch manner **:** with playful slyness or roguishness

arch·ness \-nəs\ *n* -ES [³*arch* + *-ness*] **:** the quality of being arch **:** playful slyness or roguishness

arch of corti *usu cap C* [after Alfonso *Corti* †1876 Ital. anatomist] *anat* **:** any of the series of arches composing the tunnel of Corti — compare ORGAN OF CORTI

arch of the fauces : PILLAR OF THE FAUCES

ar·chol·o·gy \ärˈkäləjē\ *n* -ES [*archi* + *-ology*] **:** the doctrine of origins

ar·chon \ˈärˌkän, -kən\ *n* -s [L, fr. Gk *archōn*, fr. pres. part. of *archein* to rule, begin — more at ARCHI-] **1 :** a chief magistrate in ancient Athens; *esp* **:** one of nine chief magistrates in Athens after 683 B.C. with executive, judicial, religious, military, legislative, and administrative functions **2 :** a magistrate of any of the Jewish communities of the Diaspora in the Greco-Roman period **3 :** a ruler, high official, presiding officer, or leader ⟨George Ripley, ~ of the Farm, built Brook Farm in the image of his belief —Tom Brooks⟩ **4** [MGk, fr. Gk] *Eastern Church* **a :** an ecclesiastical official who directs special services of a cathedral **b :** an ecclesiastic who administers various business matters of the churches of a patriarchate

ar·chon·tate \ˈ=ˌkənˌtāt\ *n* -s [F *archontat*, fr. *archonte* archon (fr. L *archont-, archōn*) + *-at* -ate] **:** an archon's term of office

ar·chon·tia \ärˈkänch(ē)ə\ *n pl, cap* [NL, fr. Gk *archont-, archōn*, pres. part. of *archein*] **:** ARCHENCEPHALA

ar·cho·plasm \ˈärkəˌplazəm\ *also* **ar·cho·plas·ma** \ˌ==ˈplazmə\ *n* -s [NL *archoplasma*, fr. *archo-* (fr. Gk *archōn* ruler) + *-plasma* — more at ARCHON] **:** supposedly specialized protoplasm formerly held to constitute the achromatic figure but now usu. regarded as an optical artifact indicative of changes in colloidal state occurring during mitosis — opposed to *trophoplasm* — **ar·cho·plas·mic** \ˌ==ˈplazmik\ *adj*

arch order *n* **:** the system in classical architecture of framing arches with columns and entablatures — called also *Roman order*

ar·cho·sau·ria \ˌärkəˈsȯrēə\ *n pl, cap* [NL, fr. *archo-* (fr. Gk *archōn*) + *-sauria*] **:** a large subclass of Reptilia comprising the dinosaurs, pterosaurs, and crocodilians all distinguished by possessing temporal openings separated from each other by a postorbitosquamosal arch — **ar·cho·sau·ri·an** \ˌ==ˈrēən\ *adj or n*

arch-poet \ˈärch, ˈäch +ˌ-\ *n* [¹*arch-* + *poet*] **:** a chief poet ⟨*arch-poet* in the king's court⟩

arch-presbyter \(ˈ)ärch +ˈ-\ *or* **ar·chi·presbyter** \ˌärkē +ˈ-\ *n* [LL *archipresbyter* — more at ARCHPRIEST] **:** ARCHPRIEST

arch·presbyterate \ˌärch+\ *or* **ar·chi·presbyterate** \ˌärkē +\ *n* [ML *archipresbyteratus*, fr. LL *archipresbyter* + L *-atus* -ate] **1 :** a district or part of a medieval diocese under an archpriest **2 :** a rural deanery

arch press *n* **:** a punch press having an arch-shaped frame giving greater width at the bolster plate and permitting operations on wider work at the expense of strength and rigidity in the frame

arch·priest \ˈärchˈprēst, ˈäch-\ *n* [ME *archeprest*, fr. MF *archeprestre*, fr. LL *archipresbyter*, fr. L *archi-* + LL *presbyter* priest — more at PRIEST] **1 :** a chief priest **:** a priest who formerly acted as the chief assistant or as the vicar of a bishop in a cathedral particularly in liturgical functions — later called *dean* **2 :** a priest who formerly supervised the clergy of a town other than an episcopal city and the surrounding rural area — later called *rural dean* **3** *Eastern Church* **:** the highest title of honor given a member of the secular clergy

arch ring *n* **:** the curved member which is the main supporting element in an arched structure

-archs *pl of* -ARCH

arch·see \ˈärchˌsē\ *n* [¹*arch-* + *see*] **:** an archbishop's see

arch spring *n* **:** the upward curve in the shank of a shoe or last measured from a straight line drawn from the ball to the heel

arch stone *also* **arch solid** *n* **:** VOUSSOIR

arch support *n* **:** a corrective device worn in the shoe and so molded as to provide support for the natural arch of the foot

archt *abbr* architect

arch·type \ˈärchˌtīp\ *n* [alter. of *archetype*] **:** ARCHETYPE 6

archway \ˈ=ˌ=\ *n* **:** a way or passage under an arch; *also* **:** an arch over a passage

-ar·chy \ˌärkē, ˌäkē, -ki, *alternatively* -ə(r)kē *or* -ki *in a few common words (as "monarchy") in which the preceding syllable has stress*\ *n comb form* -ES [ME *-archie*, fr. MF, fr. L *-archia*, fr. Gk, fr. *-archēs* ¹-arch + *-ia* -y] **:** rule **:** government ⟨*dyarchy*⟩ ⟨squire*archy*⟩

ar·ci·dae \ˈärsəˌdē\ *n pl, cap* [NL, fr. *Arca*, type genus + *-idae*] **:** a large family of chiefly tropical lamellibranch mollusks (order Filibranchia) with ribbed equivalve shell having a strong toothed hinge — see ARK SHELL

ar·cif·era \ärˈsif(ə)rə\ *n pl, cap* [NL, fr. L *arci-* (fr. *arcus* bow) + NL *-fera* (neut. pl. of *-fer* -ferous) — more at ARROW] **:** a division of the amphibian suborder Linguata including most of the frogs of the world and characterized by having the epicoracoids of the two sides overlapping each other — **ar·cif·er·al** \(ˈ)=ˈ=(=)rəl\ *or* **ar·cif·er·ous** \-rəs\ *adj*

ar·ci·fin·i·ous \ˌärsəˈfinēəs\ *adj* [L *arcifinius*, prob. fr. *arcēre* to hold off, enclose + *-i-* + *finis* boundary — more at ARK, FINAL] **1** *law* **:** having a natural boundary ⟨an ~ estate bounded by a river⟩ **2** *of a nation* **:** having a frontier forming a natural defense

ar·ci·form \ˈärsəˌfȯrm\ *adj* [L *arci-* (fr. *arcus* bow) + E *-form*] **:** having the form of an arch **:** CURVED

arcing *pres part of* ARC

arcing contact *n* **1 :** one of the readily replaceable parts (as of a circuit breaker) on which the arc, because of the opening of an electric circuit, is drawn after the main contacts have opened **2 :** BREAK JAW

arc lamp *n* **:** an electric lamp that produces light by means of an arc made when a current passes between two incandescent carbon or metal electrodes, the gas about the electrodes being at atmospheric pressure — see ENCLOSED ARC LAMP

arc light *n* **:** ARC LAMP; *also* **:** the light from an arc lamp

ar·co \ˈär(ˌ)kō\ *adv (or adj)* [It, bow, fr. L *arcus* — more at ARROW] **:** with the bow — usu. used as a direction in music for players of stringed instruments; compare PIZZICATO

ar·co·cen·trum \ˌärkōˈsen·trəm\ *n* [NL, fr. *arco-* (fr. L *arcus* bow) + *centrum*] **:** a centrum of a vertebra formed of basal parts or segments of the neural and hemal arches more or less modified and fused together — compare CHORDACENTRUM

arc of action : the arc made up in gearing of the arcs of approach and recess

arc of approach : the part of the arc of contact of toothed gearing along which the flank of the driving wheel touches the face of the driven wheel

arc of contact : the portion of a circular surface that is in contact with another surface (as that between a belt and a pulley); *specif* **:** the arc on a toothed gear between the point where the teeth first make contact with another gear wheel and the point where that contact ends

arc of lo·witz \-ˈlōˌvits\ *usu cap L* [after J. T. *Lowitz fl* 1794 Russ. astronomer] **:** a rare halo extending obliquely downward and inward from a 22 degree parhelion

arc of meridian 1 : a portion of a great circle of a sphere — used esp. with reference to the earth or the celestial sphere **2 :** a portion of a meridian curve

arc of recess *or* **arc of recession :** the part of the arc of contact in toothed gearing in which the face of the driving wheel touches the flank of the driven wheel

¹**ar·co sal·tan·do** \ˌär(ˌ)kō,sälˈtän(ˌ)dō\ *n* [It, jumping bow] **:** a rapid staccato in which the bow rebounds from the string at each tone

²**arco saltando** \"\ *adv (or adj)* **:** with arco saltando **:** SALTATO, SAUTILLÉ, SPICCATO

arcose *var of* ARKOSE

ar·co·so·li·um \ˌärkəˈsōlēəm\ *n, pl* **arcoso·lia** \-lēə\ [NL, fr. *arco-* (fr. L *arcus* bow) + L *solium* seat, sarcophagus, fr. *sedēre* to sit — more at ARROW, SIT] **:** an arched cell in a Roman catacomb; *esp* **:** one designed to receive a sarcophagus

arc-over \ˈ=ˌ==\ *n* -s **:** an undesired arc following the opening of a switch or a breakdown of insulation

arcs *pl of* ARC, *pres 3d sing of* ARC

arc secant *n* **:** the inverse function to the secant ⟨if *y* is the secant of θ, then θ is the *arc secant of y*⟩ — called also *inverse secant*

arc sine *n* **:** the inverse function to the sine ⟨if y is the sine of θ, then θ is the *arc sine of* y⟩ — called also *inverse sine*

arc spectrum *n* **:** the spectrum of a substance that is vaporized by introducing it into an electric arc — compare SPARK SPECTRUM

arct- *or* **arcto-** *comb form* [L *arct-*, fr. Gk *arkt-, arkto-*, fr. *arktos* bear, Ursa Major, north — more at ARCTIC] **1 :** north **:** arctic ⟨*Arct*alia⟩ ⟨*Arcto*gaea⟩ **2 :** bear ⟨*Arct*oidea⟩ ⟨*Arcto*staphylus⟩

arc·ta·lian \(ˈ)ärkˈtālyən, -lēən\ *adj, usu cap* [NL *Arctalia* northern biogeographic realm (fr. *arct-* + *-alia*) + E *-an*] **:** of, relating to, or being the biogeographic realm that comprises all northern seas and extends southward as far as floating ice occurs

arct-american \ˌärkt+\ *adj, usu cap* [*arct-* + *American*] **:** NEARCTIC

arc tangent *n* **:** the inverse function to the tangent ⟨if y is the tangent of θ, then θ is the *arc tangent of* y⟩ — called also *inverse tangent*

¹**arc·tic** \ˈärktik, ˈärd·ik, ˈärtik, ˈäkt-, ˈäd-, ˈät-, -ēk — *the pronunciation without the first* k *is the original one in English (see etymology) and has centuries of oral tradition behind it*\ *adj* [alter. (influenced by L *arcticus*) of earlier *artic*, fr. ME *artik*, fr. ML *articus*, alter. of L *arcticus*, fr. Gk *arktikos*, fr. *arktos* bear, Ursa Major, north + *-ikos* -ic; akin to MIr *art* bear, L *ursus*, Skt *ṛkṣa*] **1** *sometimes cap* **:** of, in, characteristic of, or used in the region around the north pole to approximately 65° N ⟨~ nights⟩ ⟨~ waters⟩ ⟨~ clothing⟩ **2 a :** bitter cold **:** FRIGID ⟨~ temperatures⟩ **b :** cold in temper or mood ⟨an ~ smile⟩ **3** *usu cap* **:** of or belonging to an early Stone Age culture of northwestern Europe or to a culture based on the hunting of sea mammals on the islands of Bering strait **4** *usu cap* **:** of, relating to, or being a biogeographic realm or zone that comprises the tundra and treeless grounds lying north of timberline in the northern hemisphere or this together with more southerly areas that are above timberline — compare ALPINE, BOREAL — **arc·ti·cal·ly** \-t|ək(ə)lē, -d·|, |ēk-, li\ *adv*

²**arctic** \"\ *n* -s **:** a fabric-lined rubber overshoe reaching to the ankle or above and having a fastening device (as a buckle or zipper)

arctic air *n* **:** an air mass characterized by cold dry air from the arctic region — compare POLAR AIR

arctic-alpine \ˌ==ˌ=(ˌ)=\ *adj, usu cap both A's* **:** NEARCTIC

arctic birch *n* **:** a low shrub (*Betula nana*) having small roundish leaves and found in northern boreal regions

arctic bluebell *n* **:** an arctic or alpine harebell (*Campanula uniflora*) with a solitary blue flower and narrow leaves

arctic

arctic chamomile *n* **:** a white-flowered herb (*Matricaria ambigua*) with dissected foliage found in northern Canada and Alaska

arctic char *n* **:** a char (*Salvelinus alpinus*) known from lakes and streams of arctic No. America but probably circumpolar in distribution — called also *arctic trout*

arctic circle *n, often cap A&C* **:** the parallel of latitude that is approximately 66½° north of the equator and that circumscribes the northern frigid zone — see ZONE illustration

arctic dog disease *n, usu cap A* **:** a destructive disease of dogs in northwestern No. America related to or possibly identical with rabies

arctic fox *n, often cap A* **:** a small fox (*Alopex lagopus*) of the arctic regions of both hemispheres having valuable fur that is blue-gray or brownish in summer and white in winter — see BLUE FOX

arctic front *n* **:** the boundary between an arctic and a polar air mass

arctic grass *n* **:** RESCUE GRASS

arctic grayling *n, often cap A* **:** a grayling (*Thymallus signifer*)

ARCHITECTURE

Historic Styles	Types and Examples	Characteristic Features
EGYPTIAN		Mass, solidity, colossal size; source of the columnar orders and of lotiform ornament
Old Kingdom: B.C. 2980–2475	*Pyramids* at Giza	Simplicity of geometrical form; highly finished stonework
Middle Kingdom: B.C. 2160–1788	*Tombs* at Beni Hasan	Hewn in cliffs; open porticoes with columns, some of proto-Doric type
Empire: B.C. 1580–1090	*Temple* at Der-el-Bahri	Terraced courts with colonnades; ascent by ramp
	Great temples, Karnak (Thebes)	Pylons, peristylar forecourts, hypostyle hall, and sanctuary; clerestory lighting; obelisks; colossi
	Temple at Elephantine	Exterior peristyle
Ptolemaic and Roman: B.C. 324–A.D. 330	*Temples* at Edfu and Philae	Rich elaboration and variety of detail; screen walls; Hathor-headed capitals
MESOPOTAMIAN		Massive brick construction with arches; terraced roofs; colored tile ornament; ziggurats
Old Babylonian Kingdom: B.C. 2100–1750	*Houses* and *temples* at Babylon	Square open court, arched doorways, battlemented walls
Assyrian Empire: B.C. 885–607	*Palaces* at Khorsabad and Nineveh	Complex plan with interior courts; fortified walls with flanking towers, barbicans, etc.; doorways flanked with winged bulls; continuous friezes of sculpture
New Babylonian Kingdom: B.C. 612–538	*Temples* and *palaces* at Babylon	Great ziggurat, or "Tower of Babel"; vaulted substructure of "Hanging Gardens"
PERSIAN		Derivative forms from Egypt, Assyria, and Greece; native columnar forms with bull capitals
B.C. 550–330	*Palaces* and *tombs* at Persepolis	Propylaea and throne rooms, or apadanas, with slender columns
GREEK		Simplicity, symmetry; column and lintel construction in masonry
Minoan: B.C. 3000–1400	*Palaces* at Knossos	Complex plan with terraced roofs, courts and light wells, stories and staircases
Mycenaean: B.C. 1500–1100	*Palaces* at Mycenae and Tiryns	Megaron with gabled roof and vestibule in antis; propylaea
	Beehive tombs at Mycenae	Circular chamber with pointed corbel vault
Archaic: B.C. 776–480	*Doric temples* at Selinus and Akragas	Long narrow cella with exterior peristyle and gable roof; stout columns
Transitional: B.C. 480–460	*Temple* of Zeus at Olympia	Broader cella divided by longitudinal colonnades; sculptured pediments
Periclean: B.C. 460–400	*Temples,* Theseum, Parthenon, Erechtheum, Wingless Victory, at Athens	Subtle design and execution in marble; sculptured pediments and continuous friezes; delicate optical refinements; entasis and inclinations; Ionic order (of Asian origin) attains its established form
Fourth Century: B.C. 400–330	*Mausoleum* at Halicarnassus	High basement supporting peristyle crowned by pyramid; many friezes
	Tholos at Epidaurus	Circular cella with outer and inner peristyles, latter of the Corinthian order
Hellenistic: B.C. 330–146	*Altar* at Pergamum	Vast flight of steps leading to Ionic colonnade above basement with colossal sculptured frieze
	Pharos at Alexandria	Lighthouse tower of diminishing stages, square, octagonal, and circular
Greco-Roman: B.C. 146–A.D. 330	*Temple* of Olympian Zeus at Athens	Colossal columns of the Corinthian order
ROMAN		Greek orders with arched construction; civil buildings for varied uses
Etruscan: B.C. 500–300	*Tombs; temples; sewers,* Cloaca Maxima; *Gateway* at Perugia	Molded arch ring in stone, ample abutment
Republican: B.C. 300–50	*Basilicas, bridges, aqueducts, theaters; temples,* "Fortuna Virilis"	Cella with engaged columns at sides and rear
Imperial: B.C. 50–A.D. 330	*Fora; thermae,* Diocletian; *basilicas,* Constantine; *commemorative arches* and *columns; palaces* and villas; *amphitheaters,* Colosseum	Axial planning with vaulted interiors in groupings over extended areas; massive concrete cores with incrustation of marble
MEDIEVAL	The basilican *church*	Arched construction functionally used; freedom of craftsmanship
Early Christian: 325–525	*Basilicas,* Santa Maria Maggiore, St. Paul beyond the Walls, Rome; *baptisteries*	T plan; light walls and wooden truss roofs; mosaic decoration
Byzantine: in Eastern Europe, 525–1453	*Domed churches,* St. Sophia, Constantinople; St. Mark's, Venice	Domed basilica, or Greek-cross plan, the dome placed over a square by means of pendentives; construction without centering; incised carving; mosaics
Romanesque: in Western Europe, about 775–1200	*Churches,* esp. *monastic; castles*	Vaulted basilica; massive stone construction; round arched openings
Italian:	Sant' Ambrogio, Milan	Ribbed groined vaults with compound piers; arcaded and corbeled cornices
	Cathedral, baptistery, and Leaning Tower at Pisa	Wooden-roofed basilica; exterior arcading in multiplied stories; optical refinements
French:	*Abbeys* of Cluny, Clairvaux, and Citeaux; Saint-Martin, Tours; Saint-Sernin, Toulouse	Experiments in vaulting, culminating in Île de France with Gothic system; Latin-cross plan; chevet with apse aisle and radiating chapels; west front with twin towers
English ("Norman"):	Durham Cathedral	Roofs mostly wooden, permitting high clerestory
German ("Rhenish"):	*Cathedrals* of Worms, Mainz, and Speyer	Double-ended church with two transepts and many turrets; triconch plans
Spanish:	Santiago de Compostela	Profusion of sculptured decoration
Gothic: 1160–1530	*Cathedrals; castles,* Coucy, Pierrefonds; *colleges,* Christ Church, Oxford; *town* and *guild halls,* Cloth Hall, Louvain	Ribbed vaulting, pointed arches, vertical lines; concentrated and balanced thrusts, making possible substitution for walls of large windows with tracery and stained glass; effects of complexity and mystery; scientific fortification
French: 12th Century:	Notre-Dame, Paris	Solution of structural problems; sexpartite vaults; relative solidity
13th Century:	Amiens; Reims; Sainte-Chapelle, Paris	Greater slenderness and height; quadripartite vaults; rose windows; vertical effect
14th Century:	Transept of Notre-Dame; Saint-Ouen, Rouen	Extremely thin geometrical lines
"Flamboyant": 1450–1530	Saint-Maclou, Rouen; N spire of Chartres	Flowing or flaming lines in tracery; profuse decoration
English:	Fountains Abbey, Ripon	Lancet-shaped windows without mullions; naves of great length
Early English "Lancet": 1180–1250	Salisbury Cathedral	Square east end
"Decorated" or "Geometric": 1250–1380	Lichfield Cathedral, "Angel Choir" of Lincoln	Multiple ribs and liernes; tracery at first geometric, then flowing or curvilinear; rich floral decoration
"Perpendicular": 1380–1530	King's College Chapel; St. George's, Windsor; Henry VII Chapel, Westminster	Fan vaulting with tracery and pendants; four-centered arches; perpendicular mullions with horizontal transoms
German:	Strasbourg and Ulm cathedrals	Nave and aisles sometimes of equal height; vault ribs fancifully curved
Italian:	*Cathedrals* of Florence, Siena, Orvieto	Relatively large wall surfaces with smaller windows; surface decoration of marble, mosaic, and painting
RENAISSANCE	*Palaces, villas, churches*	Revival and adaptation of classic orders and Roman types
Italian: Early Renaissance: 1420–1500	Church of San Lorenzo, Pazzi Chapel, Riccardi Palace, Florence; Loggia, Verona	Reversion to basilican type with columns and wooden roof; dome over square, polygonal, and Greek-cross plans; delicate arabesque ornament
"High Renaissance": 1500–1540	Sant' Andrea, Mantua; Cancelleria Palace, St. Peter's, Vatican, Rome; Library of St. Mark's, Venice	Facades with superposed orders; classic proportions and detail with little decorative carving; repetition of uniform self-sufficient elements; calm serenity of horizontal lines and harmonious proportions
Spanish: 1480–1570	Town Hall, Seville; Palace of Charles V, Granada	Plateresque ornament, Mudejar style with Moorish elements
French: 1495–1590	*Châteaux,* Blois, Chambord; Court of the Louvre, Paris	Classic ornaments on northern body; steep roofs, dormers, high chimneys; pavilions
English: 1520–1625	*Country houses,* Longleat, Kirby	E and H plans; hall with tall mullioned windows, plaster ceilings, oak wainscot
German: 1520–1600	*Castles,* Heidelberg; *town halls,* Cologne	Fanciful arabesque decoration on northern body; stepped gables and dormers
ACADEMIC and BAROQUE 1540–1780	*Royal palaces, churches*	Strict classic proportions of the orders; plastic freedom of composition in mass and space
Italian:	Colonnades of St. Peter's; Sant' Agnese, Rome; Santa Maria della Salute, Venice; *villas*	Dynamic opposition of unbalanced masses and lines; rustic columns, broken pediments; union of building and environment; terraced gardens
French:	Palace of Versailles; Colonnade of the Louvre	Stately formal exteriors with rich interior decoration culminating in rocaille ornament; plan with cour d'honneur
Spanish:	Escorial; Town Hall of Salamanca	Somber walls with concentrated adornment of entrance; churrigueresque ornament
English:	Banqueting House, Whitehall; St. Paul's Cathedral; *country houses*	Sober monumental treatment on Palladian models; adoption of Roman elements; garden temples of classic design
German:	Zwinger, Dresden	Lavish use of baroque forms
MODERN		Influence of historical and natural science, pure and applied
Classic Revival: 1760–1830	*Churches,* Madeleine, Paris; *government buildings; monuments*	Literal imitation of classic buildings, first Roman, then Greek; supremacy of abstract form over practical convenience
Gothic Revival: 1750–1870	*Churches; college buildings;* Houses of Parliament, London	Imitation of medieval forms; revival of handicraft
Eclecticism: 1820–1900	*Theaters* and *opera houses,* Opera, Paris; *government buildings; libraries*	Free choice between the historic styles according to supposed appropriateness to use or to national and local traditions
Functionalism: 1860–	*Railroad stations, factories, office buildings, exposition buildings;* Reliance Building, Chicago	Expression of use and material; exploitation of new materials (as iron and steel, glass, concrete)
International: 1920–	*Public buildings; residences; commercial structures;* Salvation Army building, Paris	Expression of contemporary techniques and design philosophies liberated from the limitations of historic or local influence

that is widely distributed in northern No. America and represented more southerly by two varieties, the Montana grayling and the Michigan grayling

arctic hare *n, usu cap A* : POLAR HARE

arctic hysteria *n* : a form of individual and mass hysteria that is peculiar to Arctic peoples and is characterized by compulsive mimicry

arc·ti·cize \-tə,sīz, -d-ə,-\ *vt* -ED/-ING/-S : to acclimate to or make suitable for arctic conditions

arctic moss *n, often cap A* : REINDEER MOSS

arctic owl *n, often cap A* : SNOWY OWL

arctic penguin *n, often cap A* : GREAT AUK

arctic poppy *n* : ICELAND POPPY

arctic seal *n, often cap A* : rabbit fur processed to simulate seal

arctic sea smoke *also* **arctic smoke** *or* **arctic mist** *n* : a fog that forms in arctic regions when very cold air flows over warmer waters

arctic skua *n, often cap A* : PARASITIC JAEGER

arctic tern *n, sometimes cap A* : a tern (*Sterna paradisaea*) resembling the common tern but breeding in the northern circumpolar regions and migrating to southern Africa and So. America

arctic timothy *n, sometimes cap A* : a grass (*Alopecurus alpinus*) used by the Eskimos for padding, insulation, and in a variety of other ways

arc·tic·tis \ärk'tiktəs\ *n, cap* [NL, fr. *arct-* + Gk *iktis* yellow-breasted marten] : the genus of aeluroid mammals (family Viverridae) consisting of the binturong

arctic trout *n* : ARCTIC CHARR

arctic willow *n, sometimes cap A* : a low shrub (*Salix arctica*) with pale foliage and stalked catkins found in arctic America and Asia

arctic wolf *n, often cap A* : a wolf of the arctic regions having white fur and a black-tipped tail and being perhaps a variety (*Canis lupus tundrarum*) of the timber wolf

arc·ti·id \'ärktēəd, -kshē-\ *adj* [NL *Arctiidae*] : of or relating to the Arctiidae

arc·ti·i·dae \ärk'tīə,dē\ *n pl, cap* [NL, fr. *Arctia*, type genus (fr. Gk *arktos* bear + NL *-ia*) + *-idae*; fr. the furry appearance — more at ARCTIC] : a large and variously delimited family of moths typically having stout bodies and broad wings often conspicuously striped or spotted, the larvae being usu. hairy caterpillars — see TIGER MOTH, WOOLLY BEAR

arc·tis·ca \ärk'tiskə\ [NL, fr. Gk *arktos* bear] *syn of* TARDIGRADA

arc·ti·um \'ärkshēəm, -ktēəm\ *n, cap* [NL, fr. Gk *arktion*, a plant, prob. fr. *arktos* bear] : a genus of Old World coarse biennial herbs (family Compositae) distinguished by the bristly receptacle of the flower heads and by the hooked involucral bracts — see BURDOCK

arcto- — see ARCT-

arc·to·ceph·a·lus \,ärk(,)tō'sefələs\ *n, cap* [NL, fr. *arct-* + *-cephalus*] : the genus containing the fur seals of the southern hemisphere

arc·to·cy·on·i·dae \;≈(,)≈,sī'änə,dē\ *n pl, cap* [NL, fr. *Arctocyon*, type genus (fr. *arct-* + Gk *kyōn* dog) + *-idae*] : a family of primitive generalized early Tertiary mammals that may belong to the direct ancestral line of the Carnivora

arc·to·gae·an *or* **arc·to·ge·an** \;ärktə;jēən\ *also* **arc·to·gae·al** *or* **arc·to·ge·al** \-ēəl\ *adj, usu cap* [NL *Arctogaea*, *Arctogea*, a biogeographic realm (fr. *arct-* + *-gaea*, *-gea*) + E *-an*] : of, relating to, or being a biogeographic realm that comprises the Holarctic, Ethiopian, and Oriental regions

[1]**arc·toid** \'ärk,tȯid\ *adj* [NL *Arctoidea*] : of, relating to, or like the Arctoidea : URSINE

[2]**arctoid** \"\ *n* -S : an animal of the superfamily Arctoidea

arc·toi·dea \ärk'tȯidēə\ *n pl, cap* [NL, fr. *arct-* + *-oidea*] : a superfamily of Carnivora comprising bears, raccoons, weasels, and related forms and now but not formerly including the dogs — **arc·toi·de·an** \(')≈;≈dēən\ *adj*

arc·to·mys \'ärktə,mis\ [NL, fr. *arct-* + *-mys*] *syn of* MARMOTA

arc·to·nyx \-,niks\ *n, cap* [NL, fr. *arct-* + Gk *onyx* talon, claw — more at NAIL] : the genus that consists of the hog-nosed badgers

arc·to·staph·y·los \,ärk(,)tō'stafələs, -,läs\ *n* [NL, irreg. fr. *arct-* + Gk *staphylē* bunch of grapes — more at STAPHYLE] **1** *cap* : a genus of chiefly No. American woody plants (family Ericaceae) with alternate evergreen leaves, nodding flowers, and drupaceous fruits **2** -ES : a plant of the genus *Arctostaphylos* — see BEARBERRY

arc·to·tis \ärk'tōd·əs\ *n, cap* [NL, irreg. fr. *arct-* + Gk *ōt-*, *ous* ear; fr. the earlike pappus scales — more at EAR] : a genus of African herbs (family Compositae) having white woolly foliage and long-stalked flower heads — see AFRICAN DAISY 2

arc triangulation *n* : a triangulation that follows approximately the arc of a great circle on the earth's surface in order to tie in two distant control points — compare AREA TRIANGULATION, CONTROL 3c

ar·cu·al \'ärkyəwəl\ *adj* [L *arcus* bow, arc + E *-al* — more at ARROW] : of or relating to an arc

ar·cu·a·le \,ärkyə'wā(,)lē\ *n, pl* **arcua·lia** \-lēə\ [NL, fr. L *arcus* bow + *-ale* (neut. of *-alis* -al)] : any of the primitive cartilages or structural elements of which a typical vertebra is formed, there being four pairs, two dorsal and two ventral, usu. combined with various dorsal and ventral accessory elements

ar·cu·ate \'ärkyəwət, -,wāt\ *adj* [L *arcuatus*, past part. of *arcuare* to bend like a bow, fr. *arcus* bow] : bent or curved in the form of a bow ⟨~ veins in a leaf⟩ — **ar·cu·ate·ly** *adv*

ar·cu·at·ed \-,wād·əd\ *adj* [L *arcuatus* + E *-ed*] **1** : ARCUATE **2** *archit* : having arches

ar·cu·a·tion \,≈≈'wāshən\ *n* -S [L *arcuation-*, *arcuatio* arch, fr. *arcuatus* + *-ion-*, *-io* -ion] **1** : an arching or curving : INCURVATION ⟨the ~ of the face of a cliff⟩ **2** *archit* : the employment of arches; *also* : a system of arches

arcubalist *n* -S [LL *arcoballista*, *arcuballista* — more at ARBALEST] *obs* : ARBALEST

arcubalister *n* -S [LL *arcoballista*, *arcuballista* + E *-er*] *obs* : ARBALESTER

ar·cus \'ärkəs\ *n* -ES [NL, fr. L, bow, arch, arc — more at ARROW] **1** : a whitish ring-shaped or bow-shaped deposit sometimes seen in the cornea **2** : an arch-shaped cloud that sometimes accompanies a cumulonimbus

arc weld *n* : a weld made by arc welding

arc-weld \'≈;≈\ *vt* : to join by means of a form of fusion welding in which the heat for fusion is supplied by an electric arc formed between a metal or carbon electrode and the part being welded or between two separate electrodes or between the two separate pieces being welded — **arc welding** *n*

-ard \ə(r)d *or, in a few loan words from French (as "communard")*, ;ärd *or* ;äd\ *also* **-art** \ə(r)t\ *n suffix* -S [ME, fr. OF, of Gmc origin; akin to OHG *-hart* (in personal names such as *Gērhart* Gerard); akin to OE *heard* hard — more at HARD] : one that is characterized by performing some action, possessing some quality, or being associated with some thing esp. conspicuously or excessively ⟨bragg*art*⟩ ⟨drunk*ard*⟩ ⟨dull*ard*⟩ ⟨poll*ard*⟩ ⟨slugg*ard*⟩ ⟨stink*ard*⟩ ⟨wiz*ard*⟩ : a large one of its kind ⟨stagg*ard*⟩

ar·da \'är(,)dä\ *n* -S *usu cap* [Sp, of AmerInd origin] : an extinct language family of southeastern Colombia

ar·dea \'ärdēə\ *n, cap* [NL, fr. L, heron; akin to ON *arta* garganey, Gk *erōdios* heron] : the type genus of Ardeidae including a number of large strong-flying New and Old World herons

ar·de·ae \'ärdē,ē\ *n pl, cap* [NL, fr. L, pl. of *ardea* heron] : the suborder of Ciconiiformes comprising the herons

ar·de·al·ite \,ärdē'ä,līt\ *n* -S [G *ardealit*, fr. *Ardeal* Transylvania, region of Romania + G *-it* -ite] : a mineral $Ca_2H(PO_4)(SO_4).4H_2O$ consisting of a hydrous acid calcium phosphate-sulfate

ar·deb \'är,deb\ *also* **ar·dab** \-,dab\ *n* -S [colloq. Ar *ardabb* (class. Ar *irdabb*), fr. Gk *artabē*] : any of a number of Egyptian units of capacity; *esp* : the customs unit equal to 5.44 imperial or 5.619 U.S. bushels

ar·de·id \'ärdēəd\ *adj* [NL *Ardeidae*] : of or belonging to the Ardeidae

ar·de·i·dae \är'dēə,dē\ *n pl, cap* [NL, fr. *Ardea*, type genus + *-idae*] : a family of long-legged and long-necked migratory wading birds (order Ciconiiformes) comprising the herons and bitterns

ar·del·la \är'delə\ *n, pl* **ardel·lae** \-'del,ē\ [NL, perh. fr. Gk *arda* dirt (perh. fr. *ardein* to water) + NL *-ella*; akin to Skt *vari* water] : any of the small dust-resembling apothecia of certain lichens

ar·den·cy \'ärdᵊnsē, 'äd-, -si\ *n* -ES : the quality or state of being ardent : ARDOR, WARMTH ⟨the spirituality of Channing was enriched in Parker by the ~ of his loving nature —V.L. Parrington⟩

ar·dennes \(')är¦den(z)\ *n, pl* **ardennes** *usu cap* [fr. the *Ardennes* region in France and Belgium, where it originated] : a strong rugged medium-sized horse of draft type esp. popular in Sweden and Russia

ar·den·nite \är'de,nīt\ *n* -S [G *ardennit*, fr. *Ardennes* region, Belgium, its locality + G *-it* -ite] : a mineral $Mn_5Al_5(VO_4)(SiO_4)_5(OH)_2.2H_2O$ consisting of a hydrous silicate vanadate and arsenate of manganese and aluminum

[1]**ar·dent** \'ärdᵊnt, 'äd-\ *adj* [ME *ardaunt*, *ardent*, fr. MF *ardant*, *ardent*, fr. L *ardent-*, *ardens*, pres. part. of *ardēre* to burn — more at ARDOR] **1 a** : characterized by warmth or heat of emotion, feeling, or sentiment : WARM, PASSIONATE ⟨a faint influence of his ~ spirit reached the West—R.W.Southern⟩ ⟨has left me a less ~ lover than I should perhaps otherwise have been —Samuel Butler †1902⟩ **b** : characterized by intensity : very strong or great : EXTREME ⟨gave constant proofs of his ~ longing for an education —R.B.Merriman⟩ ⟨glanced with ~ loathing at Mrs. Follansbee —Jean Stafford⟩ **c** (1) : extremely enthusiastic : EAGER, ZEALOUS ⟨an ~ naturalist⟩ (2) : extremely loyal : DEVOTED, FAITHFUL ⟨an ~ supporter of Gladstone —H.D.Jordan⟩ **2** : burning or causing a sensation of burning : FIERY, HOT ⟨an ~ fever⟩ ⟨the ~ sun⟩ **3** : INFLAMMABLE, COMBUSTIBLE — now used only in the phrase *ardent spirits* **4** : having the appearance of fire : GLOWING, SHINING ⟨from rank to rank she darts her ~ eyes —Alexander Pope⟩ **syn** see IMPASSIONED

[2]**ardent** \"\ *n* -S : ARDENT SPIRITS — used with *the* ⟨a man extremely fond of the ~⟩

ar·dent·ly *adv* [ME *ardauntly*, *ardently*, fr. *ardaunt*, *ardent* + *-ly*] : in an ardent manner

ar·dent·ness *n* -ES : the quality or state of being ardent

ardent spirits *n pl* : strong alcoholic liquors (as brandy, rum, whiskey) obtained by distillation : spirituous liquors

arder *n* -S [prob. fr. ON *arthr* plow; akin to *erja* to plow — more at EAR (to plow)] **1** *obs* : plowing or fallowing **2** *obs* : land left fallow

ar·dha·ma·ga·dhi \,ärdə'mägədē\ *n* -S *usu cap* : a Prakrit language of north India used in a large part of the Jain canon

ar·dis·ia \är'dizh(ē)ə\ *n* [NL, fr. Gk *ardis* point of an arrow + NL *-ia*; fr. the shape of the lobes of the corolla; perh. akin to OIr *aird* point, height] **1** *cap* : a genus of tropical evergreen shrubs and trees (family Myrsinaceae) having panicled flowers and drupaceous fruits **2** -S : a plant of the genus *Ardisia*

ar·doise \är'dwäz\ *n* [F, lit., slate] : a grayish purple that is stronger than telegraph blue, bluer and deeper than mauve gray, and bluer and paler than average rose mauve

ar·dor *or* **ar·dour** \'ärdər, 'ädə(r)\ *n* -S [ME *ardour*, fr. MF & L; MF *ardour*, fr. L *ardor*, fr. *ardēre* to burn; akin to OHG *essa* forge, ON *arinn* hearth, L *ārēre* to be dry, *aridus* dry, Gk *azein* to parch, Skt *āsa* ashes, dust] **1 a** : warmth or heat of emotion, feeling, or sentiment ⟨enough ~ in his tone to melt a heart of ice —Joseph Conrad⟩ : SPIRIT ⟨impressed the House as much by candor as by ~ —S.E.Morison⟩ : PASSION ⟨gave him love potions and herb teas to increase his ~ —Willa Cather⟩ **b** : extreme vigor, force, or energy : INTENSITY ⟨its ~ was the greater for being so long delayed —V.L.Parrington⟩ **c** (1) : intense enthusiasm or eagerness : FERVOR, ZEAL ⟨his ~ cooled off in the course of the war —Edmund Wilson⟩ ⟨desired it with an ~ that far exceeded moderation —Mary W. Shelley⟩ (2) : deep-seated devotion : FIDELITY, LOYALTY ⟨loving this country with that extra ~ of the immigrant —John Mason Brown⟩ **2** : strong or burning heat : FIRE, FLAME ⟨the ~ of the noonday sun⟩ **3** : an instance or an expression of an ardent emotion ⟨the stress of unbridled ~s —H.M.Parshley⟩ **syn** see PASSION

ar·dor uri·nae \'är,dȯryu̇'rī,nē, -,nī, -,dər-, -yə-\ *n* [NL, lit., heat of urine] : a scalding sensation during urination

ard·ri *also* **ard·righ** \ȯr'drē, är'-, '≈,≈\ *n* -S [IrGael *ārdrī*, fr. *ārd* high, noble (fr. OIr *ard*) + *rī* king, fr. OIr — more at ROYAL, RICH] : the high king in ancient Ireland — compare [9]RIG

-ards *pl of* -ARD

ar·du·i·nite \,ärdə'wē,nīt, är'düə,n-\ *n* -S [Giovanni *Arduino* †1795 Ital. geologist + E *-ite*] : MORDENITE

ar·du·ous \'är|jəwəs, 'ä|, *Brit usu & US sometimes* |dyəw-\ *adj* [L *arduus* high, steep, difficult; akin to ON *ōrthigr*, *ōrthugr* high, steep, bold, OIr *ard* high, tall, Toch A *orto* up, Av *ərədva* high] **1 a** : hard to accomplish or achieve : DIFFICULT, ONEROUS ⟨building a college curriculum . . . is a long, ~, and difficult task —J.P.Leonard⟩ **b** : marked by great labor or effort : STRENUOUS, EXACTING ⟨determined to save him from a life of ~ toil —A.C.Cole⟩ **2** : hard to climb : STEEP, LOFTY ⟨those ~ paths they trod —Alexander Pope⟩ **3** : hard to endure : full of difficulties and hardships : TRYING ⟨your willingness after these six ~ days to remain here —F.D.Roosevelt⟩ **syn** see HARD

ar·du·ous·ly *adv* : in an arduous manner

ar·du·ous·ness *n* -ES : the quality or state of being arduous

[1]**are** [ME *are*, *arne*, fr. OE *aron*, *earun*; akin to ON *eru* (they) are, *erum* (we) are, OE *is* — more at IS] *pres 2d sing or pres pl of* BE

[2]**are** \'a(a)(ə)r, 'e(ə)r, 'är\ *n* -S [F, fr. L *area*] : a metric unit of area equal to the area of a square 10 meters long on each side : 100 square meters — see METRIC SYSTEM table

ar·ea \'arēə, 'er-,'aar-,'är-\ *n* -S [L, piece of level ground, threshing floor, fr. *ārēre* to be dry; fr. its use as a place to dry grain, or fr. the vegetation's having been burned off — more at ARDOR] **1 a** : a level or relatively level piece of unoccupied or unused ground : a clear or open space of land ⟨plants his crops on any ~ he can find —P.E.James⟩ **b** : a definitely bounded piece of ground set aside for a specific use or purpose ⟨the state has provided several picnic ~s along the new highway⟩ ⟨a free parking ~ in the center of town⟩ **2** : the superficial contents of any figure : superficial extent : the surface included within any set of lines; *specif* : the number of squares, each with a side one unit long, that exactly cover a surface (as in certain rectangles) when it can be covered in such a manner or a number that is equally acceptable as a measure of the surface (as in spheres or circles) when it cannot be covered in this manner **3 a** : the enclosed space or site on which a building stands **b** : AREAWAY ⟨went down the steps into the ~ of a house —James Joyce⟩ **4 a** : a clear or open space within a building ⟨the communion table should be removed from the middle of the ~ —David Hume †1776⟩ **b** : a definitely bounded part or section of a building set aside for a specific use or purpose ⟨the house has a large kitchen ~⟩ **5** : any particular extent of space or surface: as **a** : a part of the surface of the human body ⟨if the ethyl fluid should come in contact with the skin, wash the ~ immediately —H.G.Armstrong⟩ **b** : an expanse or tract of the earth's surface ⟨a large ~ outside the marshes is submerged —Wilfred Thesiger⟩ **c** : a section, district, or zone of a town or city ⟨the shopping ~⟩ ⟨the residential ~⟩ **d** : a region or territory including and surrounding a city, consisting of a large part of a state or country or several states or countries, or embracing an entire continent or parts of more than one continent ⟨the Chicago ~⟩ ⟨the West Virginia mining ~⟩ ⟨the Caribbean ~⟩ ⟨Europe . . . was considered the chief danger ~ —A.O.Wolfers⟩ **e** : the territory assigned to a military unit ⟨the battalion's new ~ was on the fringe of the town —Bill Davidson⟩ **f** : CULTURE AREA **6 a** : the range or extent covered by or included in some thing or concept : the sphere or scope of operation or action : FIELD ⟨the whole ~ of foreign policy⟩ ⟨the novel has steadily widened the ~s of experience it will deal with —Bernard De Voto⟩ **b** : a system or sphere of intellectual activity or study; *specif* : a major section of a curriculum ⟨courses in the ~ of the humanities⟩ **7** : a part of the cerebral cortex regarded as having a particular function — see ASSOCIATION AREA, MOTOR AREA, SENSORY AREA **syn** see SIZE

COMMON AREA FORMULAS

FIGURE	FORMULA	MEANING OF LETTERS
rectangle	A=ab	a=base; b=height
square	$A=a^2$	a=a side
triangle	$A=\frac{ab}{2}$	a=base; b=height
trapezoid	$A=\frac{h(a+b)}{2}$	h=height; a=the longer parallel side; b=the shorter side
parallelogram	A=ab	a=base; b=height
regular pentagon	$A=1.720a^2$	a=a side
regular hexagon	$A=2.598a^2$	a=a side
regular octagon	$A=4.828a^2$	a=a side
circle	$A=\pi r^2$	r=radius; π=3.1416

area am·ni·ot·i·ca \-,amnē'äd·əkə, -ēkə\ *n* [NL, amniotic area] : the transparent part of the mammalian blastodisc corresponding approximately to the area pellucida

area bombing *n* : air bombardment in which all attacking aircraft release their bombs in a fairly large target area instead of attempting to hit one specific target — called also *carpet bombing, pattern bombing, saturation bombing*; compare PRECISION BOMBING

aread *or* **areed** \ə'rēd\ *vt* **ared** \ə'red\ **ared**; **areading** *or* **areeding**; **areads** *or* **areeds** [ME *areden*, fr. OE *ārǣdan*, fr. *ā-* (perfective prefix) + *rǣdan* to advise, explain, read — more at ABEAR, READ] **1** *obs* : to make known : DECLARE, TELL **2** *archaic* : to explain the meaning of : INTERPRET ⟨rightly he *ared* the maid's intent —Robert Southey⟩ **3** *obs* : to give counsel to : ADVISE **4** *archaic* : ADJUDGE, DECREE ⟨did plain *areed* that unto him the horse belonged —Edmund Spenser⟩

ar·e·al \-ēəl\ *adj* [*area* + *-al*] : of, relating to, or involving an area; *specif* : of or belonging to the school of areal linguistics : interpreted in the manner of the school of areal linguistics

areal linguistics *also* **area linguistics** *n* : a school of historical and comparative linguistics that denies the existence of phonetic laws without exceptions, questions the value of attempts to trace individual languages back to a common ancestral language, and chiefly emphasizes the study of the transmission through space of linguistic innovations which is considered as taking place quite readily even between languages that are not of common origin — called also *neolinguistics*

ar·e·al·ly \-ēəlē, -li\ *adv* : in or according to area

area of langerhans *usu cap L* : ISLET OF LANGERHANS

area opa·ca \-ō'pākə\ *n* [NL, opaque area] : the peripheral opaque area surrounding the area pellucida of vertebrate embryos with discoidal cleavage

area pel·lu·ci·da \-pə'lüsədə\ *n* [NL, pellucid area] : the pellucid central area immediately surrounding the embryo in vertebrates with discoidal cleavage

area pla·cen·ta·lis \-,plasən'tāləs\ *n* [NL, placental area] : the part of the trophoblast in early placental vertebrate embryos that lies in immediate contact with the uterine mucosa

[1]**arear** *vt* -ED/-ING/-S [ME *arearen*, *areren*, fr. OE *ārǣran* (akin to Goth *urraisjan*), fr. *ā-* (perfective prefix) + *rǣran* to rear, raise — more at ABEAR, REAR] *obs* : to raise up: as **a** : to set up : ERECT **b** : to raise in rank or status

[2]**arear** \ə'-\ *adv* [*'a-* + *rear* (n.)] : in or to the rear ⟨went ~ for rest and rehabilitation⟩

area research *n* : interdisciplinary research (as in the social sciences) in a distinct geographic, sociocultural, or political area aimed at a scientific understanding of the area as an entity and at relating it to other areas

areas *pl of* AREA

area study *n* : a study of a political or geographical area including its history, geography, language, and general culture

area target *n* : a target most profitably attacked by area bombing or for which the tactical or strategic situation demands area bombing

area triangulation *n* : triangulation extending in various directions from a control point and covering the region surrounding it — compare ARC TRIANGULATION, CONTROL 3c

area vas·cu·lo·sa \-,vaskyə'lōsə\ *n* [NL, vascular area] : the inner portion of the area opaca in which blood and blood-vessel formation is initiated

area vector *n* : the vector of a plane surface whose magnitude is the area of the figure and whose direction is that of a perpendicular to the plane of the figure

area vit·el·li·na \-,vid·ə'līnə, -,vī-\ *n* [NL, vitelline area] : the outer nonvascular portion of the area opaca

area wall *n* : a retaining wall surrounding an areaway

ar·ea·way \'≈≈≈,≈\ *n* : an open subsurface space adjacent to a building for affording access to or for lighting or ventilating a basement

are·ca \ə'rēkə, 'arəkə\ *n* [NL, fr. Pg *areca* betel palm, fr. Malayalam *aṭekka*, *aṭakka*] **1** *cap* : a small but important genus of pinnate-leaved palms of tropical Asia and the Malay archipelago characterized by the thick-rinded fruits — see BETEL PALM **2** -S : a palm of the genus *Areca* or of any of several genera related to *Areca* (as *Chrysalidocarpus lutescens*)

ar·e·ca·ce·ae \,arə'kāsē,ē\ *n pl, cap* [NL, fr. *Areca*, type genus + *-aceae*] *in some classifications* : a family of palms that is coextensive with Palmae or restricted to forms closely related to the areca palm

areca nut *n* : BETEL NUT

areca palm *n* : a palm of the genus *Areca*

are·co·line \ə'rēkə,lēn, -lən\ *n* -S [ISV *arec-* (fr. NL *Areca*) + *-ol* + *-ine*] : a colorless oily toxic alkaloid $C_8H_{13}NO_2$ that is a derivative of nicotinic acid and constitutes the active principle of betel nuts

are·cu·na *or* **are·ku·na** \,ärə'künə\ *n, pl* **arecuna** *or* **arecunas** *or* **arekuna** *or* **arekunas** *usu cap* [Sp, of AmerInd origin] **1 a** : a Cariban people dwelling on the headwaters of the Caroni river in southeastern Venezuela **b** : a member of such people **2** : the language of the Arecuna people

ared *past of* AREAD

areed *var of* AREAD

a·re·flex·ia \,ārə'fleksēə\ *n* -S [NL, fr. [2]*a-* + ISV *reflex* + NL *-ia*] : absence of reflexes — **a·re·flex·ic** \;≈≈;≈ik\ *adj*

aregenerative \;ā + ≈;≈≈(,)≈≈\ *adj* [[2]*a-* + *regenerative*] : not regenerating after disease or injury

arei·to \ə'rā,tō\ *n* -S [Sp, fr. Taino *areyto* historical poem, song, dance] : a ceremonial dance among the Indians of Spanish America; *also* : the songs and masks associated with the dance

a-religious \;ā + ≈;≈≈\ *adj* [[2]*a-* + *religious*] : noncommittal or professedly neutral concerning religious matters

are·na \ə'rēnə\ *n* -S [L *harena*, *arena* sand, sandy place, arena] **1** : the area in the central part of a Roman amphitheater where gladiatorial combats and other spectacles took place **2 a** : a central area or open space within an enclosure used for public entertainment ⟨the circus elephants were led into the ~⟩ ⟨the livestock ~ had once been a small auto race track⟩ ⟨the side ~ seats in Madison Square Garden were full⟩ **b** : a building containing an arena used esp. for indoor sports ⟨the wrestling ~ burned to the ground⟩ **3 a** : a sphere or field of interest, activity, or controversy : SCENE ⟨left in undisputed control of the political ~ —H.S.Commager⟩

arenaceo- *comb form* [perh. fr. F *arénacé-*, fr. L *arenaceus*] : arenaceous and ⟨*arenaceo*-argillaceous⟩

ar·e·na·ceous \,arə¦nāshəs\ *adj* [L *harenaceus*, *arenaceus*, fr. *harena*, *arena* + *-aceus* -aceous] **1** : resembling, made of, or containing sand or sandy particles : SANDY ⟨~ limestone⟩ ⟨the ~ elytra of a beetle⟩ **2** : growing in sandy places

ar·e·nar·ia \,≈≈'na(a)rēə\ *n, cap* [NL, fr. LL *harenaria*, *arenaria*, fem. of *harenarius*, *arenarius* of sand] : a genus of widely distributed chiefly low-tufted herbs with sessile leaves (family Caryophyllaceae) — see THYME-LEAVED SANDWORT

ar·e·nar·i·ous \;≈≈;≈ēəs\ *adj* [LL *harenarius*, *arenarius*, fr. L *harena*, *arena* + *-arius* -ary] : ARENACEOUS

arena theater *n* **1** : a theater having the acting area in the center of the auditorium with the audience seated on all sides of the stage — called also *theater-in-the-round* **2** : the style or method of staging plays in an arena theater

aren·dal·ite \ə'rendᵊl,īt\ *n* -S [G *arendalit*, fr. *Arendal*, Norway, its locality + G *-it* -ite] : a variety of epidote

ar·ene \'a,rēn, ='=\ *n* -s [aromatic + *-ene*] **:** an aromatic hydrocarbon (as benzene, toluene, naphthalene)

aren·ga \ə'reŋgə, -engə\ *n, cap* [NL, fr. Jav *arèn*] **:** a genus of tropical Asiatic and Malaysian palms having pendent branching spadices and large berrylike fruits — see GOMUTI

ar·e·nic·o·la \,arə'nikələ\ *n, cap* [NL, fr. L *hareni-, areni-* (fr. *harena, arena* sand) + *-cola* inhabitant — more at -COLOUS] **:** a genus of stout-bodied burrowing polychaete worms comprising the lugworms — **ar·e·nic·o·lid** \-ələd\ *adj or n*

ar·e·nic·o·lite \-ə,līt\ *n* -s [NL *Arenicola* + E *-ite*] **:** a marking found on certain stratified rocks generally regarded as the trail of a mollusk or crustacean though formerly supposed to represent arenicolous worm burrows or trails

ar·e·nic·o·lous \¦==¦=ələs\ *adj* [L *arena, harena* sand + E *-i-* + *-colous*] **:** inhabiting or burrowing in sand **:** growing in sand soil

are·nig \'a'rānig\ *adj, usu cap* [fr. *Arenig* mountains, Wales] **:** of or relating to a subdivision of the European Ordovician — see GEOLOGIC TIME table

ar·e·nite \'arə,nīt, ə'rē,-\ *n* -s [L *arena, harena* sand + E *-ite*] **:** medium-grained detrital rock (as sandstone, graywacke, arkose, and orthoquartzite) — **ar·e·nit·ic** \¦arə¦nid·ik\ *adj*

aren't \="*are not*", (¦)ärnt, (¦)ȧnt *also* (*esp when emphatic or sentence-final*) ¦ärənt *or* ¦ärənt; = "*am not*" (*most often in the speech of r-droppers*), (¦)ȧnt, (¦)ärnt\ [by contr.] **1 :** are not ⟨they *aren't* going⟩ **2 :** am not — used in questions ⟨the thing is, Sidney, *aren't* I ever to know you?—Elizabeth Bowen⟩

areo- *comb form* [Gk *Arēs* Ares (god of war), Mars (planet)] **:** the planet Mars ⟨*areo*centric longitude⟩ **:** of or belonging to the planet Mars ⟨*areo*graphy⟩

¹ar·e·og·ra·phy \,a(a)rē'ägrəfē\ *n* -ES [*areo-* + *-graphy*] **:** description of the surface of the planet Mars

²areography \"\ *n* -ES [*area* + *-o-* + *-graphy*] **:** descriptive biogeography

are·o·la \ə'rēələ\ *n, pl* **areolae** \-ə,lē, -lī\ *or* **areolas** [NL, fr. L, small open space, dim. of *area* piece of level ground — more at AREA] **:** a small area: as **a :** an interstice or small space (as between the veins of leaves, between the cracks of the surface in certain crustaceous lichens, between the fibers composing organs or vessels that interlace, or between the nervures of an insect's wing) **b :** the colored ring around the nipple or around a vesicle or pustule **c :** the portion of the iris that borders the pupil of the eye

are·o·lar \-ələ(r)\ *adj* **1 :** of, relating to, or like an areola **:** filled with interstices **2 :** of, relating to, or consisting of areolar tissue

areolar tissue *n* **:** fibrous connective tissue having the fibers loosely arranged in a net or meshwork

are·o·late \-ələt, -,lāt\ *also* **are·o·lat·ed** \-ə,lād·əd\ *adj* [NL *areola* + E *-ate, -ated*] **:** divided into or marked by areolae

areolate mildew *n* **:** a leaf spot of cotton caused by an imperfect fungus (*Ramularia areola*)

are·o·la·tion \ə,rēə'lāshən, ,a(a)rē-\ *n* -s **1 :** division into areolae **2 :** an areola or space marked by areolae

ar·e·ole \'a(a)rē,ōl\ *n* -s [F *aréole*, fr. L *areola*] **1 :** AREOLA **2 a :** one of the thinner areas arranged in characteristic pattern in the siliceous deposit on the wall of diatoms — compare PUNCTA **b :** a small pit or cavity (as that from which the spines arise in cacti)

are·o·let \ə'rēələt, 'a(a)rēə,let\ *n* -s [blend of NL *areola* and E *-let*] **:** a small areola

ar·e·ol·o·gy \,arē'äləjē, -ji\ *n* -ES [*areo-* + *-logy*] **:** the scientific study of the planet Mars

ar·e·om·e·ter \,arē'ämədə(r)\ *n* -s [prob. fr. F *aréomètre*, fr. Gk *araios* thin + F *-mètre* -meter] **:** HYDROMETER — **ar·e·o·met·ric** \¦==ə¦me·trik\ *or* **ar·e·o·met·ri·cal** \-trəkəl\ *adj* — **ar·e·o·met·ri·cal·ly** \-ək(ə)lē\ *adv*

ar·e·op·a·gite \,arē'äpə,jīt, -,gīt\ *n* -s *usu cap* [L *Areopagites*, fr. Gk *Areopagitēs*, fr. *Areiopagos* + *-itēs* -ite] **:** a member of the tribunal of the Areopagus

ar·e·op·a·git·ic \¦==,==¦jid·ik\ *adj, usu cap* [LL *Areopagiticus*, fr. Gk *Areopagitikos*, fr. *Areopagitēs* + *-ikos* -ic] **:** of or relating to the Areopagus

ar·e·op·a·gus \,arē'äpəgəs\ *n* -ES *usu cap* [L, fr. Gk *Areiopagos*, alter. of *Areios pagos*, lit., hill of Ares (a hill in Athens where the supreme tribunal met), fr. *Areios* of Ares (fr. *Arēs* Ares, Greek god of war) + *pagos* rocky hill, frost — more at PAGOSCOPE] **1 :** the supreme tribunal of Athens **2 :** any tribunal or group of persons whose judgments are decisive or authoritative

areostyle *var of* ARAEOSTYLE

areosystyle *var of* ARAEOSYSTYLE

are·re \ə'rerē\ *n* -s [native name in Africa] **:** OBECHE

ares *pl of* ARE

ar·e·ta·ics \,arə'tāiks\ *n pl but sing in constr* [irreg. fr. Gk *aretē* + E *-ics*] **:** science of virtue — contrasted with *eudaemonics*

ar·e·tal·o·gy \,arə'taləjē\ *n* -ES [Gk *aretalogia*, fr. *aretē* virtue + *-logia* -logy] **:** a narrative of the miraculous deeds of a god or hero

¹arête \ə'rāt, a'-\ *n* -s [F, ridge, fishbone, beard of grain, fr. LL *arista* fishbone, fr. L, beard of grain] **:** a sharp-crested ridge in rugged mountains commonly present in those (as the Alps) that have been sculptured by glaciers

²ar·e·te \,arə'tā, -tē\ *n* -s [Gk *aretē*, fr. *areskein* to appease, please, satisfy; akin to *ararískein* to fit — more at ARM] **:** the sum of good qualities that make character **:** EXCELLENCE, VALOR, VIRTUE, MANLINESS

ar·e·thu·sa \,arə'th(y)üzə, -sə\ *n* [NL, fr. L *Arethusa*, fountain nymph of Elis transported to Sicily to escape from the pursuit of the river god Alpheus, fr. Gk *Arethousa*] **1** *cap* **:** a genus of bog orchids having small bulbs with a single linear leaf and a solitary purple-fringed flower that appears in late spring **2** -s **:** a plant of the genus *Arethusa*

ar·e·tin·i·an \¦==¦tinēən, -tē-\ *adj, usu cap* [It *aretino* of Guido d'Arezzo †*ab* 1050 Ital. monk and musician, lit., of Arezzo, city in Tuscany, Italy, where he lived (fr. L *Arretinus*, fr. *Arretium* Arezzo + *-inus* -ine) + E *-ian*] **:** GUIDONIAN

arf·ved·son·ite \'ärvədsə,nīt\ *n* -s [J.A.*Arfvedson* †1841 Swedish chemist + E *-ite*] **:** a sodium, silicate, of sodium, calcium, and iron, approximately $Na_{2-3}(Fe,Mg,Al)_5Si_8O_{22}(OH)_2$, of the amphibole group occurring in black monoclinic strongly pleochroic prisms in certain igneous rocks

arg *abbr* **1** argent; argentum **2** argument

¹ar·gal \'ärgəl\ *adv* [alter. of *ergo*] **:** THEREFORE — used chiefly to imply that the reasoning is specious or absurd

²argal *var of* ARGOL

ar·ga·li \'ärgəlē, -li\ *n, pl* **argali** *or* **argalis** [Mongolian] **1 :** a large wild sheep (*Ovis ammon*) having immense horns, widely distributed in mountainous central and eastern Asia, and being probably not on the direct ancestral line of domesticated sheep though some authorities regard certain of its races as an ancestor of the fat-tailed sheep **2 :** any of several large wild sheep (as the bighorn or the aoudad) **3 :** HAIR BROWN

argali (*Ovis ammon*)

ar·gand burner \'är,gan(d)-, -än(d)-, -gən(d)-\ *n, usu cap A* [after Aimé *Argand* †1803 Swiss physicist and inventor] **:** a burner for an Argand lamp or a gas burner applying the principle of that lamp

argand diagram *n, usu cap A* [after Jean Robert *Argand* †1825 Fr. mathematician] **:** a conventional diagram or graph in which the complex number $x + iy$ is represented by the point whose rectangular coordinates are x and y

argand lamp *n, usu cap A* [after Aimé *Argand*] **:** a lamp with a tubular wick that admits a current of air inside as well as outside of the flame

ar·gan oil \'ärgən-, -,gan-\ *n* **:** a fatty oil obtained from the seeds of the argan tree and used in cooking

ar·gan·ti·dae \är'gantə,dē\ [NL, fr. *Argant-, Argas*, type genus + *-idae*] *syn of* ARGASIDAE

ar·gan tree *n* [Ar *arjān*] **:** a tall Moroccan tree (*Argania sideroxylon*) of the family Sapotaceae bearing fruits like olives that are used as a cattle food and seeds that yield argan oil

ar·gas \'ärgəs, -,gas\ *n, cap* [NL, perh. irreg. fr. Gk *argos* idle, fr. *a-* ²a- + *-ergos* (fr. *ergon* work) — more at WORK] **:** a genus (the type of the family Argasidae) of ticks including the cosmopolitan chicken tick (*A. persicus*), a serious enemy of poultry in warmer countries

ar·ga·sid \'=gasəd\ *adj* [NL *Argasidae*] **:** of or relating to the Argasidae

ar·gas·i·dae \är'gasə,dē\ *n pl, cap* [NL, fr. *Argas*, type genus + *-idae*] **:** a family of ticks that includes a number of medically and economically important ticks all of which lack a scutum and exhibit no marked sexual dimorphism — see ARGAS, ORNITHODOROS

¹ar·ge·an \(')är'jēən\ *adj, usu cap* [*Argo*, ship in which the Argonauts sailed, constellation in the southern hemisphere (fr. Gk *Argō*) + E *-ean*] **:** relating to the ship or the constellation Argo

²argean \"\ *adj, usu cap* [*Argeia* or *Argos*, district of ancient Greece (fr. Gk) + E *-an, -ean*] **:** of or relating to the district of Argeia or Argos or its inhabitants

ar·gel \'ärgəl, -,gel\ *n* -s [EgyptAr *ḥargel*] **:** either of two related African plants (*Solenostemma argel* and *Asclepias fruticosus*) whose leaves have been used to adulterate senna

ar·ge·lan·der's method \'ärgə,landərz-, -län-\ *n, cap A* [after F.W.A. *Argelander* †1875 Ger. astronomer] **:** a method of visual photometry that determines the magnitude of a star or the extent of changes in brightness of a variable star by comparisons with a sequence of neighboring stars of slightly different magnitudes

ar·gem·o·ne \är'jemənē; 'ärjə,mōnē, ,=='==\ *n* [NL, fr. L, wind rose (*Papaver argemone*), fr. Gk *argemōnē*] **1** *cap* **:** a genus of American herbs (family Papaveraceae) having yellow sap, prickly leaves, and showy white or yellow flowers — see PRICKLY POPPY **2** -s **:** a plant of the genus *Argemone*

argemone oil *n* **:** a semidrying fatty oil obtained from the prickly poppy

¹ar·gent \'ärjənt, 'äj-\ *n* -s [ME, fr. MF & L; MF *argent*, fr. L *argentum*; akin to OIr *arggat* silver, L *arguere* to make clear, Gk *argyros* silver, *argos* white, Skt *rajata* silver, whitish] **1** *archaic* **a :** the metal silver **b :** WHITENESS ⟨the polished ~ of her breast —Alfred Tennyson⟩ **2** *obs* **:** silver coin **:** MONEY **3 :** a metal tincture used in heraldry and conventionally supposed to be represented by silver but in practice represented by either silver or white **4 :** SILVER 6b

²argent \"\ *adj* **1 :** made of or resembling silver **:** SILVERY **2 :** shining like silver **:** silvery white ⟨the prophet was already erect with ~ garments and uplifted hands —G.K.Chesterton⟩ **3 :** of the heraldic metal argent — abbr. *arg.*

argent- *or* **argenti-** *or* **argento-** *comb form* [MF *argent-*, fr. L, fr. *argentum*] **:** silver ⟨*argent*amide⟩ ⟨*argenti*nitrate⟩ ⟨*argento*metry⟩

argenta dei *pl of* ARGENTUM DEI

ar·gen·taf·fin \är'jentəfən\ *or* **ar·gen·taf·fine** \", -ə,fēn\ *adj* [prob. back-formation fr. *argentaffinity*, fr. *argent-* + *affinity*] **1 a :** depositing reduced silver from ammoniated silver hydroxide solutions — used of certain cell granules containing phenols or polyamines **b :** of, relating to, or being a cell type of the gastrointestinal tract that is postulated to have a role in the production of intrinsic factor **2 :** ARGENTOPHIL — **ar·gen·taf·fin·i·ty** \=,=ə'finəd·ē\ *n*

ar·gen·taf·fi·no·ma \,ärjentəfə'nōmə, ,är,jən,tafə'-\ *n* -s [NL, fr. E *argentaffin* + NL *-oma*] **:** CARCINOID

ar·gen·tal mercury \(')är'jentᵊl-\ *n* [part trans. of F *mercure argental; argental*, fr. *argent* silver + *-al* — more at ARGENT] **:** a native silver amalgam

ar·gen·tan \'ärjən,tan\ *n* -s *usu cap* [fr. *Argentan*, commune in France where it is made] **:** a needlepoint lace of the Alençon type with bold designs

ar·gen·tate \'ärjən,tāt\ *adj* [L *argentatus* silver-plated, fr. *argentum* silver + *-atus* -ate — more at ARGENT] **:** SILVERY

ar·gen·te·ous \(')är¦jentēəs, (')ȧ¦j-\ *adj* [L *argenteus*, fr. *argentum* + *-eus* -eous] **:** SILVERY

ar·gen·te·um \-tēəm\ *n* -s [NL, fr. L, neut. of *argenteus*] **:** a layer of connective tissue containing microscopic crystals of guanine that forms a reflecting surface in the skin of many fishes and is the source of pearl essence

ar·gen·tian \(')är¦jenchən\ *adj* [*argent-* + *-ian*] **:** containing silver ⟨~ galena⟩

ar·gen·tic \(')är¦jentik, -ēk, (')ȧ¦j-\ *adj* [*argent-* + *-ic*] **:** of, relating to, or containing silver — used esp. of compounds in which this element is bivalent; compare ARGENTOUS

ar·gen·tif·er·ous \¦=,jən¦tif(ə)rəs\ *adj* **:** producing or containing silver

¹ar·gen·ti·na \,ärjən¦tēnə, ¦äj-\ *adj, usu cap* [fr. *Argentina*, country in So. America] **:** of or from Argentina **:** of the kind or style prevalent in Argentina **:** ARGENTINE

²argentina \", -īnə\ *n, cap* [NL, fr. *argent-* + *-ina* (fr. L, fem. of *-inus* -ine)] **:** the type genus of the family Argentinidae

³argentina \"\ *n* -s *often cap* [prob. fr. *Argentina*, country in So. America] **:** ART BROWN

¹ar·gen·tine \'=,=,tīn *also* -,tən *or* -,tēn\ *adj* [ME, fr. MF *argentin*, fr. OF, fr. *argent* silver + *-in* -ine — more at ARGENT] **:** relating to, containing, or resembling silver **:** SILVERY

²argentine \"\ *n* -s **1 :** SILVER; *also* **:** any of various materials resembling it (as plate metal) **2 :** any of various small silvery-scaled marine fishes: as **a :** PEARLSIDES **b :** any of various fishes of the genera *Argentina* or *Myctophum* **3 :** a pearly variety of calcite with undulating lamellae

³argentine \-,tēn, -īn\ *adj, usu cap* [Sp *argentino*, adj. & n., fr. *Argentina*, country in So. America] **:** of or relating to Argentina

⁴argentine \"\ *n* -s [Sp *argentino*] **1** *cap* **:** a native or inhabitant of Argentina **2 :** a ballroom dance similar to the tango but distinguished by low dips, scissors, and twisting steps on the toes

¹ar·gen·tin·e·an *or* **ar·gen·tin·i·an** \¦ärjən¦tinēən, ¦äj-, -¦tē-, -nyən\ *adj, usu cap* [*Argentina* + E *-ean* or *-ian*] **:** ³ARGENTINE

²argentinean *or* **argentinian** \"\ *n* -s *cap* **:** ⁴ARGENTINE 1

argentine ant *n, usu cap 1st A* [³*Argentine*] **:** a small brown ant (*Iridomyrmex humilis*) introduced from So. America into the southern and western U.S., southern Africa, and other warm regions where it has become a household and orchard pest

ar·gen·tin·i·dae \,ärjən'tinə,dē\ *n pl, cap* [NL, fr. *Argentina*, type genus + *-idae*] **:** a family of small silvery marine fishes related to the salmons and trouts and including the capelins and a few other fishes and formerly the true smelts

ar·gen·ti·no \-'tē(,)nō\ *n* -s [Sp — more at ARGENTINE] **1** *cap* **:** ⁴ARGENTINE 1 **2 :** a gold coin of Argentina worth five pesos and issued between 1880 and 1914

ar·gen·tite \'ärjən,tīt\ *n* -s [G *argentit*, fr. *argent-* + *-it* -ite] **:** a sectile mineral Ag_2S consisting of native silver sulfide, having a metallic luster and dark lead-gray color, occurring in isometric crystals and in masses and coatings, and constituting a valuable ore of silver (hardness 2–2.5, sp. gr. 7.20–7.36)

argento- — see ARGENT-

ar·gen·to·cyanide \är,jentō+\ *n* [*argent-* + *cyanide*] **:** any of a series of complex salts (as sodium argentocyanide $Na[Ag(CN)_2]$ formed in the cyanide process for silver) made by the union of silver cyanide with another cyanide

ar·gen·to·jarosite \=,==+\ *n* [*argent-* + *jarosite*] **:** a mineral $AgFe_3(SO_4)_2(OH)_6$ consisting of basic silver ferric sulfate resembling jarosite but with silver replacing potassium

ar·gen·tom·e·ter \,ärjən'tämədə(r)\ *n* -s [*argent-* + *-meter*] **:** an instrument for measuring the amount of silver salt in a solution (as by finding the specific gravity or by photoelectric means)

ar·gen·to·met·ric \(')är¦jentə¦me·trik\ *adj* [*argent-* + *-metric*] **:** relating to or making use of argentometry — **ar·gen·to·met·ri·cal·ly** \-trək(ə)lē\ *adv*

ar·gen·tom·e·try \,ärjən'tämə·trē\ *n* -ES [*argent-* + *-metry*] **:** chemical analysis involving the use of silver compounds; *esp* **:** a volumetric method employing a silver salt solution

ar·gen·ton \är'jentᵊn\ *n* -s [modif. of L *argentum* silver — more at ARGENT] **:** an alloy of nickel, copper, and zinc first used for coins by the Swiss in 1850

ar·gen·to·phil \(')är¦jentə,fil\ *or* **ar·gen·to·phile** \-,fīl\ *or* **ar·gen·to·phil·ic** \¦=¦==¦filik\ *adj* [*argent-* + *-phil, -phile, -philic*] **:** having an affinity for silver — used of certain cells, structures, or tissues that selectively reduce silver salts to metallic silver

ar·gen·to·pro·te·i·num \är¦jentō,prōtē'īnəm\ *n* -s [NL, fr. *argent-* + ISV *protein*] **:** SILVER PROTEIN

ar·gen·tose \'ärjən,tōs, är'jen-\ *n* -s [*argent-* + *-ose*] **:** a compound of silver and a nucleoprotein used like silver nitrate as an astringent antiseptic

argen·tous \(')är¦jentəs\ *adj* [*argent-* + *-ous*] **:** of, relating to, or containing silver — used esp. of compounds in which this element is univalent; compare ARGENTIC

ar·gen·tum \är'jentəm\ *n* -s [L — more at ARGENT] **:** SILVER — symbol *Ag*

ar·gen·tum dei \-'dē,ī, -'dā,ē\ *n, pl* **argen·ta dei** \-tə-\ *usu cap D* [ML, lit., God's silver] **:** GOD'S PENNY

argh \'ärf, 'ärk\ *adj* [ME, cowardly, lazy, slow, wretched, fr. OE *earg*; akin to OFris *erg* evil, bad, OHG *arg, arag* cowardly, worthless, stingy, ON *argr* evil, homosexual, effeminate, Av *ərəgant-* evil, repulsive, Lith *aržùs* sensual, lustful] *dial Eng* **:** TIMID, COWARDLY

ar·ghan \'ärgən\ *n* -s [origin unknown] **:** PITA 1c

ar·ghool *also* **ar·ghoul** \är'gül\ *n* -s [Ar *arghūl*] **:** an Egyptian musical reed instrument

ar·gi·dae \'ärjə,dē\ *n pl, cap* [NL, fr. *Arge*, type genus (perh. fr. Gk *argēs* bright) + *-idae*; akin to Gk *argos* white — more at ARGENT] **:** a family of sawflies having 3-jointed antennae

ar·gil \'ärjəl\ *n* -s [ME *argil, argilla*, fr. L *argilla*, fr. Gk *argillos*; akin to Gk *argos* white] **1 :** CLAY; *esp* **:** POTTER'S CLAY **2 :** ALUMINA

argill- *or* **argilli-** *or* **argillo-** *comb form* [ME *argill-*, fr. L, fr. *argilla*] **1 :** clay ⟨*argilli*ferous⟩ ⟨*argill*oid⟩ **2 :** argillaceous and ⟨*argillo*arenaceous⟩

argillaceo- *comb form* [*argillaceous*] **:** argillaceous and ⟨*argillaceo*calcareous⟩

ar·gil·la·ceous \¦ärjə¦lāshəs\ *adj* [L *argillaceus*, fr. *argilla* + *-aceus* -aceous] **:** of, relating to, or containing clay or clay minerals **:** CLAYEY ⟨~ rocks⟩

ar·gil·lic \(')är¦jilik\ *adj* [*argill-* + *-ic*] **:** of or relating to clay or clay minerals **:** ARGILLACEOUS ⟨~ alteration⟩

ar·gil·lif·er·ous \¦ärjə¦lif(ə)rəs\ *adj* [*argill-* + *-ferous*] **:** producing or abounding in clay

ar·gil·lite \'ärjə,līt\ *n* -s [*argill-* + *-ite*] **:** a compact argillaceous rock differing from shale in being cemented by silica and from slate in having no slaty cleavage — **ar·gil·lit·ic** \¦==¦lid·ik\ *adj*

ar·gil·loid \'==,lȯid\ *adj* [ISV *argill-* + *-oid*] **:** like clay

ar·gil·lous \(')är¦jiləs\ *adj* [ME *argillose, argillous*, fr. L *argillosus*, fr. *argilla* + *-osus* -ose] **:** ARGILLACEOUS

ar·gi·nase \'ärjə,nās\ *n* -s [ISV *arginine* + *-ase*] **:** a crystalline enzyme obtained esp. from liver that converts naturally occurring arginine into ornithine and urea

ar·gi·nine \-,nēn, -,nən\ *n* -s [ISV *argin-* (perh. fr. Gk *arginoeis* bright, white) + *-ine*; orig. formed as G *arginin*] **:** a crystalline basic amino acid $C_6H_{13}N_4COOH$ that is essential in the nutrition of rats, is derived from guanidine, is obtained esp. from certain vegetable tissues and from the decomposition of protamines and proteins, and is also made synthetically — see ORNITHINE

ar·gi·ope \är'jīə(,)pē\ *n, cap* [NL, fr. Gk *Argiopē*, nymph who was mother of the mythical bard Thamyris] **:** a small genus (the type of the family Argiopidae) of orb-weaving spiders including the common black and gold garden spider (*A. aurantia*)

ar·gi·op·i·dae \,är,jī'äpə,dē, -jē-\ *n pl, cap* [NL, fr. *Argiope*, type genus + *-idae*] **:** a cosmopolitan family of orb-weaving spiders with eight similar eyes, legs hairy or spiny, and no stridulating organs and including many well-known large or brightly colored garden spiders

¹ar·give \'är,jīv, -gīv\ *adj, usu cap* [L *Argivus*, adj. & n., fr. (assumed) Gk *Argeiwos* (whence Gk *Argeios*) lit., of Argos, fr. *Argos* city-state of ancient Greece + (assumed) Gk *-eiwos* (whence Gk *-eios* -ive)] **:** of or relating to the Greeks or Greece, esp. the Achaean city of Argos or the surrounding territory of Argolis

²argive \"\ *n* -s *cap* [L *Argivus*] **:** GREEK; *esp* **:** a Greek of Argos

ar·gle \'ärgəl\ *dial var of* ARGUE

ar·gle-bar·gle \'ärgəl'bärgəl\ *n* -s [redupl. of *argle*] *chiefly Scot* **:** ARGY-BARGY

ar·gob·ba \är'gäbə\ *n* -s *usu cap* **:** a Semitic language closely related to Amharic and spoken in east-central Ethiopia

¹ar·gol *or* **ar·gal** \'ärgəl\ *n* -s [ME *argoile*, prob. fr. AF *argoil*] **:** a grayish or reddish crystalline crust deposited in wine casks during aging

²argol \"\ *n* -s [Mongolian] **:** dry dung (as of camels or cattle) used as fuel esp. in Central Asia

ar·gon \'är,gän, 'äg-\ *n* -s [Gk, neut. of *argos* idle, lazy, fr. *a-* ²a- + *ergon* work — more at WORK] **:** a colorless odorless inert gaseous element that occurs in the air to the extent of 0.94 percent by volume and in volcanic gases, is obtained by separation from liquid air, and is used chiefly as a protecting atmosphere during fabrication and arc welding of metals and as a filler for electric incandescent and fluorescent bulbs, for gas-filled electron tubes, and for Geiger-Müller counters — symbol *A* or *Ar*; see ELEMENT table

ar·go·naut \'ärgə,nȯt, 'äg-\ *n* -s [L *Argonauta, Argonautes*, fr. Gk *Argonautēs*, fr. *Argō*, ship in which the Argonauts sailed + Gk *nautēs* sailor — more at NAUTICAL] **1 a** *usu cap* **:** one of the legendary heroes who sailed with Jason on the ship Argo in quest of the Golden Fleece **b :** *often cap* **:** an adventurer or traveler engaged in a particular quest; *specif* **:** one of those who went to California in 1849 in search of gold **2 :** PAPER NAUTILUS

ar·go·nau·ta \,=='nȯd·ə\ *n, cap* [NL, fr. L, *Argonaut*] **:** a genus of cephalopods (order Dibranchia) including a single recent form, the paper nautilus (*A. argos*), related to the octopus and like it having eight arms two of which in the female are expanded at the tips to clasp the thin fragile unchambered shell — compare NAUTILUS

ar·go·nau·tic \¦==¦nȯd·ik\ *adj, usu cap* [L *Argonauticus*, fr. Gk *Argonautikos*, fr. *Argonautēs* + *-ikos* -ic] **:** of or relating to the Argonauts

ar·go·nau·ti·dae \,=='nȯd·ə,dē\ *n pl, cap* [NL, fr. *Argonauta*, type genus + *-idae*] **:** a family of cephalopods now represented solely by the genus *Argonauta*

ar·go·sy \'ärgəsē, 'äg-, -si\ *n* -ES [alter. of earlier *ragusye*, fr. It *ragusea* Ragusan vessel, fr. *Ragusa*, port of Dalmatia (now Dubrovnik, Yugoslavia)] **1 :** a large ship; *esp* **:** a richly laden merchant ship ⟨three of your *argosies* are . . . come to harbor —Shak.⟩ **2 :** a fleet of ships or of anything likened to ships ⟨white clouds sailed in splendid *argosies* across the sea of the sky —B.A.Williams⟩ **3 :** a rich store or supply **:** STOREHOUSE ⟨an ~ of railway folklore for all time —F.P.Donovan⟩

ar·got \'ärgət, 'äg-, -(,)gō *sometimes* -,gät; *usu* -əd· *or* -äd· + V\ *n* -s [F] **1 :** a special vocabulary and idiom used by a particular underworld group esp. as a means of private communication ⟨the ~ of pickpockets⟩ **2 :** the special vocabulary and idiom (as slang) of a particular social group or class ⟨the ~ of sport⟩ ⟨the ~ of teen-agers⟩ **3 :** SLANG 2 — used esp. of French **syn** see DIALECT

ar·gu·a·ble \'ärgyəwəbəl, 'äg-\ *adj* **:** capable of being argued **:** open to argument, dispute, or question ⟨~ matters of policy still undecided⟩

ar·gu·a·bly \-blē, -i\ *adv* **:** as may be shown by argument

ar·gue \'är(,)gyü, 'äg-, -gyə, *often* -gyəw+V\ *vb* **argued; argued; arguing; argues** [ME *arguen*, fr. MF *arguer* to accuse, reason & L *arguere* to accuse, assert, make clear; MF *arguer*, fr. L *argutare* to prate, fr. *argutus*, past part. of *arguere* — more at ARGENT] *vi* **1 :** to give or provide reasons for or against a matter under discussion or in dispute **:** make statements or present facts in support of or in opposition to a proposal or opinion ⟨three considerations . . . ~ against increasing the fee —T.L.Hungate⟩ ⟨am not *arguing* for an emotional art —H.S.Langfeld⟩ ⟨by *arguing* thus he showed that he had missed my meaning completely⟩ **2 :** to contend or disagree in words **:** DISPUTE, DEBATE ⟨you can always come and ~ with me about it —C.B.Flood⟩ ⟨they have been *arguing* for the past hour⟩ ~ *vt* **1** *obs* **:** to bring evidence against **:** accuse or convict **2 :** to give evidence of **:** suggest strongly **:** imply clearly **:** INDICATE, SHOW ⟨the presence of a large population in a restricted area generally ~s long occupancy —Edward Sapir⟩ **3 :** to give reasons for or against **:** consider the pros and cons of **:** DISCUSS ⟨cadets should be allowed to ~ any question that troubles the world —J.M.Burns⟩ **4** : to prove or try to prove by giving reasons : MAINTAIN, CONTEND ⟨*argued* that this would jeopardize the Monroe Doctrine —Vera M. Dean⟩ **5** *obs* : to give as a reason : ADDUCE **6** : to persuade by giving reasons : INDUCE ⟨~*s* an elderly rabbi . . . into holding services frequently —*Saturday Rev.*⟩ **syn** see DISCUSS, INDICATE

argue away *vt* : to get rid of by argument or by giving reasons ⟨*argue away* the fact that he had not kept his promises⟩

ar·gu·en·do \ˌärgyəˈwen(ˌ)dō\ *adv* [L, abl. of *arguendum*, gerund of *arguere*] : in the course of the argument

ar·gu·er \ˈärgyəwər, ˈȧgyəwə(r)\ *n* -s [ME, fr. *arguen* + *-er*] : one that argues

ar·gu·fi·er \-yəˌfī(ə)r, -īə\ *n* -s : one that argufies

ar·gu·fy \-ˌfī\ *vb* -ED/-ING/-ES [*argue* + *-fy*] *vt* **1** : to persuade by argument : prevail on ⟨~ a judge —Adria Langley⟩ **2** : DISPUTE, DEBATE ⟨ready to ~ the point⟩ ~ *vi* **1** : to argue obstinately : WRANGLE ⟨like lawyers in a murder case they stoutly ~ —Carl Sandburg⟩ **2** *archaic* : to be of consequence : be of use : MATTER

ar·gu·lus \ˈärgyələs\ *n* [NL, fr. *Argus*, mythological being + NL *-ulus* — more at ARGUS] **1** *cap* : a common genus of fish lice including forms highly destructive to goldfish and related forms **2** *pl* **ar·gu·li** \-ˌlī\ : a fish louse of the genus *Argulus* : CARP LOUSE

ar·gu·ment \ˈärgyəmənt, ˈȧg-\ *n* -s [ME, fr. MF, fr. L *argumentum*, fr. *arguere* to make clear + *-mentum* -ment] **1** *obs* : an outward sign : EVIDENCE, INDICATION ⟨it is no addition to her wit nor no great ~ of her folly —Shak.⟩ **2 a** : a reason given for or against a matter under discussion : a statement made or a fact presented in support of or in opposition to a proposal or opinion ⟨paper was a party organ providing usable facts and ~*s* in terse paragraphs —Helen C.Boatfield⟩; *specif* : the middle term of a syllogism **b** : a form of rhetorical expression intended to convince or persuade ⟨the textbook contained good examples of exposition and ~⟩ **3 a** : the act or process of arguing, reasoning, or discussing : ARGUMENTATION, DISPUTATION ⟨reiteration is not ~ —C.M.Fuess⟩ **b** : a coherent series of reasons, statements, or facts intended to support or establish a point of view : a discussion often involving a controversial topic ⟨the plaintiff has made his closing ~ —W.E. Sedgwick⟩ ⟨keep to the single thread of my ~ —E.R.Bentley⟩ **c** : an instance of arguing : a difference of opinion : DISAGREEMENT, DISPUTE, QUARREL ⟨the ~ . . . will not be settled by any showdown —*Saturday Rev.*⟩ **4** : an abstract or summary esp. of a poem, play, or part of a literary work ⟨a later editor added the ~ to the poem⟩ **5** : the subject matter, plot, or central idea esp. of a novel, poem, or speech ⟨the ~ of the book is as simple as you could wish for —Robert Parris⟩ **6** *math* **a** : one of the independent variables upon whose value that of a function depends **b** : the angle that fixes the direction of a complex number — compare ARGAND DIAGRAM **syn** see REASON

ar·gu·men·tal \ˌ⸗⸗ˈmentᵊl\ *adj* [LL *argumentalis*, fr. L *argumentum* + *-alis* -al] : ARGUMENTATIVE

ar·gu·men·ta·tion \ˌ⸗⸗mənˈtāshən, -ˌmen-\ *n* -s [ME *argumentacioun*, fr. L *argumentation-*, *argumentatio*, fr. *argumentatus* (past part. of *argumentari* to bring forward proof, fr. *argumentum*) + *-ion-*, *-io* -ion] **1 a** : the act of forming reasons, making inductions, drawing conclusions, and applying them to the case in discussion : the operation of inferring propositions not known or admitted as true from facts or principles known, admitted, or proved to be true **b** : a process of reasoning : the result of an argument : a series of arguments : a reasoning process ⟨ingenious ~*s*⟩ **2 a** : discussion esp. of a controversial topic : DEBATE **b** : ARGUMENT 2b

ar·gu·men·ta·tive \ˌ⸗⸗ˈmentəd·iv, -ətiv\ *or* **ar·gu·men·tive** \-ntiv\ *adj* **1** : consisting of or characterized by argument : containing a process of reasoning : CONTROVERSIAL ⟨an ~ discourse⟩ **2** : PRESUMPTIVE, INDICATIVE, SUGGESTIVE ⟨his silence is ~ of guilt⟩ **3** : given to or fond of argument : CONTENTIOUS, DISPUTATIOUS ⟨~ to the point of being cantankerous —J.S.Clarke⟩ — **ar·gu·men·ta·tive·ly** *adv*

ar·gu·men·ta·tor \ˈ⸗⸗mənˌtād·ə(r), -ˌmen-\ *n* -s [LL, fr. L *argumentatus* + *-or*] : one who engages in argument : CONTROVERSIALIST

argument from design : an argument for the existence of God based on the hypothesis of an ultimate design, intention, or purpose in the universe

ar·gu·men·tize *vi* -ED/-ING/-S *obs* : ARGUE

ar·gu·men·tum \ˌ⸗⸗ˈmentəm\ *n, pl* **argumen·ta** \-tə\ [L — more at ARGUMENT] : an argument, proof, or appeal to reason — used as the first term in many technical phrases designating forms both of sound and of fallacious reasoning ⟨~ ad hominem⟩ ⟨~ ad captandum⟩; compare AD CAPTANDUM, AD HOMINEM

¹**ar·gus** \ˈärgəs, ˈȧg-\ *n* -ES [after *Argus*, mythological being with many eyes some of which were always open, known as a zealous watchman, fr. L, fr. Gk *Argos*] **1** *usu cap* : a very watchful person : a vigilant guardian **2** *or* **argus pheasant** [NL, fr. L; fr. the many eyelike spots, likened to the eyes of Argus] : any of several large brilliantly patterned East Indian pheasants chiefly of the genus *Argusianus* that are closely related to the peacocks **3** : any of several butterflies esp. of the family Satyridae with numerous circular eyespots on the wings

²**argus** \"\ [NL, after *Argus*, mythological being] *syn of* ARGAS

³**argus** \"\ [NL, after *Argus*, mythological being] *syn of* ARGUSIANUS

argus brown *n* [¹*argus* (pheasant)] : a moderate brown that is yellower, stronger, and slightly darker than bay, redder, stronger, and slightly lighter than coffee, and deeper and slightly redder than chestnut brown — called also *cochin*, *Mars brown*, *moccasin*

argus–eyed \ˈ⸗⸗ˈ⸗\ *adj, often cap A* [¹*argus*] : vigilantly observant : SHARP-SIGHTED

argusfish \ˈ⸗⸗ˌ⸗\ *n* [after *Argus*, mythological being; fr. its eyelike spots] : a small spotted scaly-finned fish (*Ephippus argus*) from brackish waters of India

ar·gu·si·a·nus \ˌär,gyüzēˈānəs, -üsē-\ *n, cap* [NL, irreg. fr. ³*Argus* + L *-ianus* -ian] : a genus of East Indian pheasants (family Phasianidae) including the typical argus pheasants

argus shell *n* [after *Argus*, mythological being; fr. its spots] : a tropical marine gastropod shell (*Cypraea argus*) having ocellate spots

argus tortoise beetle *n* [after *Argus*, mythological being; fr. its spots] : a reddish tortoise beetle (*Chelymorpha cassidea*) spotted with black

ar·gute \(ˈ)ärˈgyüt\ *adj* [L *argutus*, fr. past part. of *arguere* to make clear — more at ARGUE] **1** : characterized by shrewdness, acuteness, or sagacity ⟨an ~ critic⟩ **2** : SHRILL ⟨a rich but too ~ guitar —W.S.Landor⟩ **3** : sharply serrate — **ar·gute·ly** *adv* — **ar·gute·ness** *n* -ES

¹**ar·gy–bar·gy** \ˈärgēˈbärgē\ *vi* -ED/-ING/-ES [redupl. of Sc & E dial. *argy*, alter. of *argue*] *chiefly dial* : to engage in argument : WRANGLE, HAGGLE

²**argy–bargy** \"\ *n* -ES **1** *chiefly dial* : ARGUMENT, DISPUTE **2** *chiefly dial* : a lively discussion

ar·gyle *also* **ar·gyll** \ärˈgīl, ˈä,g-, ⸗ˈ⸗\ *n* -s [after *Argyle*, *Argyll*, branch of the Scottish clan of Campbell, from whose tartan the design was adapted] **1** *often cap A* : any of various geometric knitting patterns that are balanced patterns of varicolored diamond figures in solid and outline shapes on a single background color **b** : a sock knit in such a pattern **2** [prob. after a duke of *Argyle*] : a serving vessel for gravy or sauce having either an outer compartment for holding hot water or an inner one for a heated iron to keep the contents warm

argyle 1a

argyle purple *n, often cap A* : a pale to grayish reddish purple that is stronger than crocus (sense 3a)

ar·gyll–rob·ert·son pupil \ärˌgīlˈräbərtsən-\ *n, usu cap A&R* [after D. *Argyll-Robertson* †1909 Scot. physician] : a pupil that fails to react to light but still reacts in accommodation to distance and that is characteristic of neurosyphilis

ar·gyll·shire \ärˈgīl,shi(ə)r, -,shə(r)\ *or* **ar·gyll** \ˈ⸗,⸗, ⸗ˈ⸗\ *adj, usu cap* [fr. *Argyllshire* or *Argyll*, county in western Scotland] : of or from Argyllshire : of the kind or style prevalent in Argyllshire

ar·gyn·nis \ärˈjinə̇s\ *n, cap* [NL, prob. fr. Gk *Argynnis*, epithet of Aphrodite as worshiped in the Boeotian town Argynnos] : a genus of nymphalid butterflies mostly fulvous above with small black spots or markings and with silvery spots on the underside of the hind wings — see FRITILLARY

argyr- *or* **argyro-** *comb form* [NL, fr. Gk, fr. *argyros* — more at ARGENT] : silver ⟨*argyr*ite⟩ ⟨*argyro*cephalous⟩

ar·gyr·ia \ärˈjirēə\ *n* -s [NL, fr. *argyr-* + *-ia*] : permanent dark discoloration of the skin due to absorption following overuse of medicinal silver preparations

ar·gyr·ic \(ˈ)ärˈjirik\ *adj* [Gk *argyrikos* of silver, fr. *argyros* + *-ikos* -ic] : ARGENTIC

ar·gyr·o·dite \⸗ˈjirə,dīt\ *n* -s [ISV *argyrod-* (fr. Gk *argyrōdēs* rich in silver, fr. *argyros* silver + *-ōdēs* -ode) + *-ite*; orig. formed as G *argyrodit*] : a steel-gray mineral Ag_8GeS_6 consisting of silver, germanium, and sulfur

ar·gy·ro·pel·e·cus \ˌärjə(ˌ)rōˈpeləkəs\ *n, cap* [NL, fr. *argyr-* + Gk *pelekys* ax; fr. the shape — more at PELICAN] : a genus of small deep-sea fishes (order Stomiatoidea) having short deep bodies with a silvery sheen and luminous spots

ar·gyr·o·phil \ˈärjə(ˌ)rō,fil, -,rə-\ *or* **ar·gyr·o·phile** \-,fīl\ *also* **ar·gyr·o·phil·ic** \ˌ⸗⸗(ˌ)⸗ˈfilik\ *or* **ar·gyr·oph·i·lous** \ˌ⸗⸗ˈräfələs\ *adj* [*argyr-* + *-phil*, *-phile*, *-philic*, *-philous*] : ARGENTOPHIL — **ar·gyr·o·phil·ia** \ˌ⸗⸗(ˌ)rōˈfilēə, -,rə-\ *n* -s

ar·gy·ro·sis \ˌärjəˈrōsə̇s\ *n, pl* **argyro·ses** \-ˈrō,sēz\ [NL, fr. *argyr-* + *-osis*] : ARGYRIA

ar·gyr·o·tae·nia \ˌ⸗⸗(ˌ)rōˈtēnēə, -,rə-\ *n, cap* [NL, fr. *argyr-* + *taenia*] : a genus of tortricid moths including a number having larvae that are serious leaf-rolling pests of economic plants — compare ORANGE TORTRIX, RED-BANDED LEAF ROLLER

ar·har \ˈärˌhär\ *n* -s [Hindi *arhar*, *arhar*, perh. fr. Skt *āḍhakī* (*Cajanus indicus*)] : PIGEON PEA

ar·hat \ˈär(ˌ)hət\ *also* **ar·a·hat** \ˈarə(ˌ)hət\ *or* **ar·a·hant** \-,hant\ *n* -s *often cap* [Skt *arhat*, lit., deserving respect, fr. *arhati* he deserves; akin to Gk *alphein* to gain, Av *arəzhaiti* it is worth, Lith *algà* wage, salary] : a Buddhist monk who has attained Nirvana

ar·hat·ship \ˈ⸗(ˌ)⸗,ship\ *n* -s *sometimes cap* : the state of being an arhat ⟨trying to attain ~⟩

ar·hua·co \ärˈwä(ˌ)kō\ *or* **aro·a·co** \ˌärōˈä-\ *or* **aru·ac** \ˈärüˌäk\ *n, pl* **arhuaco** *or* **arhuacos** *or* **aroaco** *or* **aroacos** *or* **aruac** *or* **aruacs** *usu cap* [Sp, of AmerInd origin] **1** : a Chibchan people of northern Colombia **2** : a member of the Arhuaco people

arhyn·chob·del·li·da \ˌā,riŋ,käbˈdeləda\ *n pl, cap* [NL, fr. ²*a-* + *rhynch-* + *-bdellida* (fr. *-bdella* + *-ida*)] *in some classifications* : an order or other division of leeches comprising the Gnathobdellida and Pharyngobdellida

arhythmia *var of* ARRHYTHMIA

arhythmicity \ˌā+ˌ⸗ˈ⸗⸗⸗\ *n* -ES [²*a-* + *rhythm* + *-icity*] *ecol* : a condition characterized by the absence of some rhythm of behavior or physiology that might be expected to be present

¹**aria** \ˈärēə, ˈär- *also* ˈar- *or* ˈer- *or* ˈār-\ *n* -s *pl* **ari·as** \-ēəz *also* **arie** \-ē,ā\ [It, lit., atmospheric air, fr. L *aera* (accus. of *aer*), fr. Gk *aera*, accus. of *aēr* — more at AIR] : AIR, MELODY, TUNE; *specif* : an accompanied, extended, and usu. elaborate melody sung by a single voice (as in an opera or oratorio) — compare RECITATIVE

²**aria** \əˈrēə\ *n* -s [NL, fr. Gk, a kind of tree] : WHITEBEAM

-aria *pl of* -ARIUM

²**-ar·ia** \ˈa(a)rēə, ˈer-, ˈār-\ *n suffix* [NL, fr. L, fem. sing. & neut. pl. of *-arius* -ary] : one or ones like or connected with — esp. in biological taxonomic names ⟨Campanul*aria*⟩ ⟨Madrepor*aria*⟩ ⟨Utricul*aria*⟩

aria da ca·po \ˈärēədəˈkä(ˌ)pō\ *n, pl* **arias da capo** \-ēəzd-\ *also* **arie da capo** \-ē,äd-\ [It, air from the beginning] : an aria in 3-part musical form comprising a theme, a secondary contrasting part, and a repetition of the first part

aria d'i·mi·ta·zi·o·ne \-,dēmə,tätsēˈō,nā\ *n, pl* **arias d'imitazione** \-ēəz,d-\ *also* **arie d'imitazione** \-ē,ä,d-\ [It, air of imitation] : an aria in which the voice or accompaniment imitates sounds of nature or is otherwise descriptive

¹**ar·i·an** \ˈa(a)rēən, ˈer-, ˈār-\ *n* -s *usu cap* [LL *Arianus*, adj. & n., fr. *Arius* †A.D.336 Alexandrian Greek theologian + L *-anus* -an] : one adhering to or supporting Arianism

²**arian** \"\ *adj, usu cap* [LL *Arianus*] : of or relating to Arius, the Arians, or Arianism

³**arian** *usu cap, var of* ARYAN

-ar·i·an \ˈ⸗⸗⸗\ *n suffix* -s [L *-arius* -ary + E ¹*-an*] **1** : believer ⟨necessit*arian*⟩ : advocate ⟨latitudin*arian*⟩ **2** : producer ⟨platitudin*arian*⟩ ⟨tract*arian*⟩

ar·i·an·ism \ˈ⸗⸗ə,nizəm\ *n* -s *usu cap* [²*arian* + *-ism*] **1** : a theological movement initiated by Arius in opposition to Sabellianism that won strong support during the 4th century A.D. chiefly in the Eastern churches but that was condemned in general councils at Nicaea (A.D.325) and Constantinople (A.D.381), the doctrine being marked by the following principles: (1) God is absolutely alone, unknowable, and separate from every created being; (2) the Christ, the Logos or Son of God, preexistent but not eternally real, is a created being and so not God in the fullest sense, though as maker of all other creatures he may be regarded and worshiped as a secondary divinity; (3) in the incarnation the Logos assumed a body but not a human soul, and so Jesus Christ was neither truly God nor truly man — compare ANOMOEAN, HOMOEAN **2 a** : Arian doctrine **b** : adherence to or advocacy of Arian doctrine

ar·i·an·is·tic \ˌ⸗⸗⸗ˈnistik\ *or* **ar·i·an·is·ti·cal** \-tə̇kəl\ *adj, usu cap* [ML *Arianista* (fr. LL *Arianus* + L *-ista* -ist) + E *-ic*, *-ical*] : of, relating to, or characterized by Arianism

aria par·lan·te \-,pärˈlän,tā\ *n, pl* **arias parlante** \-ēz,p-\ *also* **arie parlan·ti** \-ē,ä,pärˈlän(ˌ)tē\ [It, speaking air] : an aria characterized by a declamatory melodic style

ari·bo·fla·vin·o·sis \ˌā,rībə,flāvəˈnōsə̇s *also* -rib- *or* -lav-\ *n, pl* **ariboflavino·ses** \-ō,sēz\ [NL, fr. ²*a-* + ISV *riboflavin* + NL *-osis*] **1** : a deficiency disease due to inadequate intake of riboflavin that is marked by cheilosis, scaling around the nose, and sensitivity to light **2** : CURLED-TOE PARALYSIS

aricara *usu cap, var of* ARIKARA

aricuri *var of* OURICURY

ar·id \ˈarə̇d *also* ˈer-\ *adj, sometimes* -ER/-EST [F or L; F *aride*, fr. L *aridus* — more at ARDOR] **1** : without moisture : excessively dry : parched and barren; *specif* : having insufficient rainfall to support agriculture, usu. less than 10 to 15 inches annually ⟨~ miles of brushland —Green Peyton⟩ **2** : devoid of interest and life : dry and monotonous : JEJUNE ⟨the dullest and most ~ documents —J.L.Lowes⟩ **syn** see DRY

arid cycle *n* : the cycle of erosion in an arid region as contrasted with that in a humid region

arid·i·ty \əˈridəd·ē, aˈ-,e-, -ətē, -i\ *n* -ES [L *ariditas*, fr. *aridus* + *-itas* -ity] **1** : the quality or state of being arid : DRYNESS ⟨the ~ of desert sands⟩ **2** : unavailability of water present in a habitat to organisms occupying that habitat whether caused by inability of the organisms to remove the water or to the ability of the soil to withhold it

ar·id·ly *adv* : in an arid manner : DRILY, MONOTONOUSLY

ar·id·ness *n* -ES : ARIDITY

ar·i·e·gite \ˌarēˈā,zhīt\ *n* -s [F *ariégite*, fr. Dept. Ariège, France, its locality + F *-ite*] : a rock consisting of granular pyroxenite with dark green spinel and pyrope and sometimes biotite or hornblende

¹**ar·i·el** \ˈa(a)rēəl, ˈer-, ˈār-\ *n* -s [prob. fr. *Ariel*, an airy spirit in Shakespeare's *Tempest*] : an Australian flying phalanger of the genus *Petaurus*

²**ariel** \"\ *or* **ariel gazelle** *n* -s [Ar *aryal*, var of *ayyil* stag] : a gazelle (*Gazella arabica*) of Arabia and adjacent regions

aries \ˈe(ə)rˌēz, ˈa(a)r-, ˈär-, -rē,ēz\ *n, usu cap* [L, lit., ram; akin to Umbrian *erietu*, acc., ram, Gk *eriphos* kid, OIr *heirp* doe, female goat, *erb* cow, Arm *or-oj* lamb] : the 1st sign of the zodiac — see SIGN table; ZODIAC illustration

-aries *pl of* -ARY

ar·i·et·ta \ˌarēˈed·ə, ˌär- *also* **ar·i·ette** \ˌ⸗⸗ˈet\ *n* -s [*arietta* fr. It, dim. of *aria*; *ariette* fr. F, fr. It *arietta*] : a short aria

aright \əˈ-\ *adv* [ME, fr. OE *ariht*, fr. ¹*a-* + *riht* right (n.) — more at RIGHT] : RIGHTLY, CORRECTLY ⟨if I remember ~⟩

ari·id \əˈrīəd\ *adj* [NL *Ariidae*] : belonging to the Ariidae

ar·i·i·dae \əˈrīə,dē\ *n pl, cap* [NL, fr. *Arius*, type genus (prob. fr. Gk *areios* warlike, devoted to Ares, fr. *Arēs* Ares, god of war) + *-idae*] : a family of marine fishes (order Ostariophysi) comprising the sea catfishes and usu. having a bony buckler from the skull to the dorsal spine — compare CRUCIFIX FISH

arik·a·ra *also* **aric·a·ra** \əˈrikərə\ *n, pl* **arikara** *or* **arikaras** *also* **aricara** *or* **aricaras** *usu cap* [Skidi Pawnee *Arikara*, lit., horns, fr. pl. of *ariki* horn; fr. their hair style with hornlike bones inserted] **1 a** : a Caddo people west of the Missouri river in the Dakotas **b** : a member of such people **2** : the language of the Arikara people

ariki *or* **arii** *var of* ALII

ar·il \ˈarəl\ *n* -s [prob. fr. NL *arillus*, fr. ML, raisin, grape seed] : an exterior covering or appendage of certain seeds that develops after fertilization as an outgrowth from the funiculus and envelops the seed — see ARILLODE

ar·il·late \ˈarəlāt, -ə,lāt\ *or* **ar·il·lat·ed** \-ə,lād·əd\ *or* **ar·iled** *or* **ar·illed** \ˈarəld\ *adj* [*aril* + *-ate*, *-ated* or *-ed*] : having an aril

ar·il·lode \ˈarə,lōd\ *or* **ar·il·lo·di·um** \ˌarəˈlōdēəm\ *n* -s [*arillode* fr. *aril* + *-ode*; *arillodium* fr. NL, fr. *arillus* + *-odium* (fr. *-odes* -ode — fr. Gk *-ōdēs* — + *-ium*)] : a false aril : an aril originating from tissue in the region of the micropyle instead of from the funicle or chalaza of the ovule

ar·il·loid \ˈarə,lȯid\ *adj* [*aril* + *-oid*] : resembling an aril

aril·lus \əˈriləs\ *n, pl* **aril·li** \-ˌri,lī, -i(ˌ)lē\ *or* **arilluses** [NL — more at ARIL] : ARIL

ar·i·masp \ˈarə,masp\ *or* **ar·i·mas·pi·an** \ˌ⸗⸗ˈmaspēən\ *n, pl* **arimasps** *or* **arimaspians** *also* **arimas·pi** \ˌ⸗⸗ˈma,spī, -(ˌ)spē\ *often cap* [*Arimasp* fr. L *Arimaspus*, fr. Gk *Arimaspos*; *Arimaspian* fr. L *Arimaspus* + E *-ian*] : one of a mythical race of one-eyed men of Scythia represented in ancient art as in constant strife with griffins for gold guarded by the griffins — **arimaspian** \ˌ⸗⸗ˈmaspēən\ *adj, often cap*

ar·i·o·car·pus \ˌarē(ˌ)ōˈkärpəs, -rēəˈk-\ *n, cap* [NL, fr. *ario-* (fr. *Aria* section of *Sorbus* once considered a separate genus of Malaceae, fr. Gk *aria* holm oak) + *-carpus*] : a genus of spineless cacti found in Texas and adjacent Mexico consisting of spirally arranged triangular horny tubercles

ari·on \əˈrīən\ *n, cap* [NL, fr. *Arion*, 7th cent. B.C. semilegendary Greek poet, fr. L, fr. Gk *Ariōn*] : a genus of slugs including a common European black slug (*A. ater*)

ari·ose \ˈärē,ōs, ˈar-\ *adj* [It *arioso*, f . *aria* + *-oso* -ose (fr. L *-osus*)] : characterized by melody — distinguished from *recitative*

¹**ari·o·so** \ˌärēˈō(ˌ)sō, ˌar-, -(ˌ)zō\ *adj* [It] : resembling an aria: as **a** *of a vocal passage* : involving a mixture of free recitative and metrical song **b** *of an instrumental passage* : resembling an accompanied recitative or aria

²**arioso** \"\ *adv* : in arioso style — used as a direction in music

³**arioso** \"\ *n, pl* **ariosos** *also* **ario·si** \-(ˌ)sē\ : an arioso composition or passage

ari·ot \əˈ-\ *adj* [¹*a-* + *riot*, v.] : running riot ⟨vines ~ everywhere⟩

arip·ple \əˈ-\ *adj* [¹*a-* + *ripple*, v.] : RIPPLING ⟨the lake was quiet, its waters ~⟩

aris *var of* ARRIS

ar·i·sae·ma \ˌarə̇ˈsēmə\ *n, cap* [NL, fr. L *aris* arum (fr. Gk) + Gk *haima* blood; fr. the red-spotted leaves of some species; akin to Gk *aron* arum — more at ARUM, HEM-] : a genus of herbs (family Araceae) of temperate and subtropical regions having flowers without perianth that are borne at the base of the spadix which is prolonged into a fleshy tip — see GREEN DRAGON, JACK-IN-THE-PULPIT

arisaid *n* -s [Sc, fr. earlier *arisad*, *arrisat*] : a full robe or skirt of tartan gathered and girdled at the waist

ari·sa·ka *or* **arisaka rifle** \ˌarə̇ˈsäkə, ˌär-\ *n* -s *usu cap A* [after Col. Nariaka *Arisaka* †1915 Jap. army officer & superintendent of Tokyo arsenal] : any of a series of bolt-action rifles of about .30 caliber that were standard issue to Japanese forces from about 1905 until 1945

¹**arise** \əˈrīz\ *vi* **arose** \-rōz\ **arisen** \-rizᵊn\ **arising**; **arises** [ME *arisen*, fr. OE *ārīsan* (akin to OS *arīsan*, OHG *irrīsan*, Goth *urreisan*), fr. *ā-* (perfective prefix) + *rīsan* to rise — more at ABEAR, RISE] **1 a** : to rise from a fallen position ⟨he *arose* slowly, brushing the dust of the street from his clothes⟩ **b** : to get up from a lying, sitting, or kneeling position ⟨when they finally stood up to look at the finished table, Millie *arose* too —J.M.MacDonald⟩ **c** : to shake off a state of inactivity : pursue a less tranquil way of living or course of procedure; *esp* : to rise belligerently, hostilely, or in rebellion ⟨~ from your torpor and taste life⟩ ⟨every group or institution ~*s* in defense of an ideal —*Encounter*⟩ ⟨no rival native house *arose* to dispute the throne —Kemp Malone⟩ **2 a** : to rise from sleep or rest ⟨*arising* early in the morning⟩ **b** : to return from death to life ⟨they firmly believed that the dead ~⟩ **3** : to become violently active (as of the sea, the wind, or a deep emotion) **4 a** : to originate from a specified source ⟨a historical precedent for it *arising* out of the period of English rule —G.G. Weigend⟩ **b** : to come into being ⟨no poets, no historians had *arisen* —Van Wyck Brooks⟩ ⟨local cultures *arose* which were distinguished for fine pottery —Angélica Mendoza⟩ **c** : to become operative esp. in such a way as to attract attention ⟨a group of enthusiastic naturalists had *arisen* —H.A. Pilsbry⟩ **5 a** : to appear above the horizon (as of the sun) **b** : to move upward physically : MOUNT, ASCEND ⟨a heavy mist *arose* and hung over the city⟩ **6** *of circumstances and occurrences* **a** : to come about : come up : take place ⟨a situation almost unique in the world has *arisen* —L.D.Stamp⟩ **b** : to become apparent in such a way as to demand attention ⟨various claims in the economic sphere which *arose* at the end of World War II —G.W.Hoffman⟩ ⟨important problems which ~ when two different groups having diverse languages and cultures meet —T.A.Sebeok⟩ **7** : to become audible : become heard ⟨a storm of protest immediately *arose* —*Current Biog.*⟩ **8** *obs* : to attain a higher rank : come into greater eminence **syn** see RISE, SPRING

²**arise** *n* -s *obs* : RISING ⟨his morning's next ~ — Christopher Marlowe⟩

aris·ings \əˈrīziŋz, -zēŋz\ *n pl* : surplus products or salvageable leftover materials (as in manufacturing)

aris·ta \əˈristə\ *n, pl* **aris·tae** \-(ˌ)stē, -,stī\ *or* **aristas** [NL, fr. L, beard of grain] : the bristlelike structure near or at the tip of the antenna of many two-winged flies

aristapedia *var of* ARISTOPEDIA

ar·is·tarch \ˈarə̇,stärk\ *n* -s *sometimes cap* [after *Aristarchus* †*ab* 145B.C. Greek grammarian and critic] : a severe critic

aris·tate \əˈri,stāt, -,stət\ *adj* [L *aristatus* having beards of grain, fr. *arista* + *-atus* -ate] *biol* : having a slender sharp or spinelike tip : having an arista

aris·ti·da \əˈristədə\ *n, cap* [NL, irreg. fr. L *arista* beard of grain] : a genus of grasses with one-flowered spikelets and a hard sharp-pointed lemma terminating in three awns — see DOGTOWN GRASS

aris·to \əˈri(ˌ)stō, F ȧrestō\ *n* -s [F, short for *aristocrate*] *chiefly Brit* : ARISTOCRAT

aris·to- *in pronunciations below*, ⸗ˈ⸗(ˌ)⸗=⸗ˈri(ˌ)stō *or* -stə *sometimes* ˌa\ *comb form* [MF & LL; MF, fr. LL, fr. Gk, fr. *aristos*; akin to Gk *ararískein* to fit — more at ARM] **1** : best ⟨*aristo*genesis⟩ **2** : aristocracy and ⟨*aristo*democracy⟩ : aristocratic and ⟨*aristo*democratic⟩

ar·is·toc·ra·cy \ˌarə̇ˈstäkrəsē, -si *also* ˌer-\ *n* -ES [MF & LL; MF *aristocratie*, fr. LL *aristocratia*, fr. Gk *aristokratia*, fr. *aristo-* + *-kratia* -cracy] **1** : government by the best individuals or by a relatively small privileged class **2 a** : a form of government in which the power is vested in a minority consisting of those felt to be best qualified to rule **b** : a state having such a government **3** : a governing body made up of those felt to be outstanding citizens, esp. nobles or others of high rank : an upper class usu. made up of an hereditary nobility : a patrician order **4** : the aggregate of those felt to be superior (as in rank, wealth, or intellect)

aris·to·crat \əˈristə,krat *sometimes* aˈ- *or* eˈ-, *Brit usu & US sometimes* ˈaris-; *usu* -ad-+V\ *n* -s [F *aristocrate*, back-formation fr. *aristocratie* & *aristocratique*] **1** : a high-ranking or otherwise superior individual : a member of an aristocracy; *esp* : NOBLE **2** : one who has the bearing and viewpoint typical of a ruling, privileged, or otherwise superior class; *sometimes* : one who favors aristocracy

aris·to·crat·ic \əˌristəˈkrad·ik, -atik, -ēk *sometimes* a- *or* e-, *Brit usu & US sometimes* ˌa(ˌ)ris- *or* ˌarəs-\ *also* **aris·to·crat·i·cal** \-ə̇kəl, -ēk-\ *adj* [*aristocratic* fr. MF *aristocratique*, fr. ML *aristocraticus*, fr. Gk *aristokratikos*, fr. *aristo-* + *-kratikos* -cratic; *aristocratical* fr. MF *aristocratique* + E *-al*] **1** : belonging to, having the qualities of, or favoring aristocracy ⟨an ~ government⟩ **2 :** socially exclusive ⟨an ~ neighborhood⟩; *sometimes* **:** SNOBBISH ⟨an essentially ~ movement — superior, sniffish, and antidemocratic —H.L.Mencken⟩ — **aris·to·crat·i·cal·ly** \-ək(ə)lē, -ēk-, -li\ *adv*

ar·is·toc·ra·tism \,arə'stäkrə,tizəm, ə'ristə,krad·,iz-\ *n* -s [*aristocrat* + *-ism*] **:** the principles or practices of aristocracy

aristo·genesis \ₑ₌(,)₌ *at* ARISTO- + \ *n, pl* **aristogeneses** [*aristo-* + *genesis*] **:** a theory now not widely accepted in biology: evolution is the product of a continuous orderly creative faculty innate in living matter and manifested in response to external stimuli at such a rate that perfection of an adaptation anticipates the need of that adaptation — **aristo·genetic** \(')₌;₌(,)₌₌;-\ *adj* — **aris·to·gen·ic** \(')₌;₌(,)₌;jenik, -ēk\ *adj*

ar·is·toi \'arə,stȯi\ *n pl* [Gk, fr. pl. of *aristos* best, noblest — more at ARISTO-] **1 :** ARISTOCRATS ⟨every country has its bourgeois and its ~⟩ **2** *usu sing in constr* **:** aristocratic class

aris·to·lo·chia \₌,₌(,)₌ *at* ARISTO- + 'lōkēə\ *n, cap* [NL, fr. L, birthwort, fr. Gk *aristolocheia*, fr. *aristo-* + *locheia* childbirth; akin to *lechos* bed — more at LIE] **:** a large genus (the type of the family Aristolochiaceae) of mostly tropical herbs or woody vines with pungent aromatic rootstocks and very irregular flowers — see BIRTHWORT, DUTCHMAN'S-PIPE, PELICAN FLOWER

aris·to·lo·chi·a·ce·ae \₌,₌(,)₌,lōkē'āsē,ē\ *n pl, cap* [NL, fr. *Aristolochia*, type genus + *-aceae*] **:** a family of erect or climbing herbs or shrubs (order Aristolochiales) having alternate petioled leaves and apetalous flowers with a petaloid calyx and stamens adnate to the style — see ARISTOLOCHIA —**aris·to·lo·chi·a·ceous** \(')₌;₌(,)₌;₌₌;āshəs\ *adj*

aris·to·lo·chi·a·les \₌,₌(,)₌;₌₌'ā,lēz\ *n pl, cap* [NL, fr. *Aristolochia* + *-ales*] **:** an order of metachlamydeous dicotyledonous plants embracing the families Aristolochiaceae, Rafflesiaceae, and Hydnoraceae and distinguished by the tubular petaloid perianth, inferior ovary, and numerous stamens free from the perianth

aris·to·pe·dia \ə,ristə'pēdēə\ *also* **aris·ta·pe·dia** *n* -s [NL, fr. *aristo-* (fr. *arista*), *arista* + *ped-* + *-ia*] *of insects* **:** the replacement of an antennal arista by a more or less perfect leg, a not uncommon developmental aberration in drosophilas

¹**ar·is·to·phan·ic** \;arəstə;fanik, ¦a,ris-\ *adj, usu cap* [LL *Aristophanicus*, fr. *Aristophanes* (Gk *Aristophanēs*) †ab 380 B.C. Athenian comic dramatist + L *-icus* -ic] **:** of, relating to, or characteristic of Aristophanes or his dramas

²**aristophanic** \"\ *n* -s **:** PHERECRATIC

aristos *pl of* ARISTO

¹**ar·is·to·te·lian** *also* **ar·is·to·te·lean** \;arəstə;tēlyən, ¦a,ris-, -lēən *also* ¦er- *or* ə;ris- *or* a;ris-\ *or* **ar·is·to·tel·ic** \-;telik\ *adj, usu cap* [L *Aristoteles* Aristotle †322 B.C. Greek philosopher (fr. Gk *Aristotelēs*) + E *-ian*, *-ean*, *-ic*] **:** of or relating to Aristotle or his philosophy

²**aristotelian** \"\ *n* -s *usu cap* **:** a follower of Aristotle or adherent of Aristotelianism

ar·is·to·te·lian·ism \-,nizəm\ *also* **ar·is·tot·e·lism** \'arə-,städ·ᵊl,izəm, -ät·ᵊl- *also* 'er- *or* ,₌₌'₌₌,₌₌\ *n* -s *usu cap* **1 :** the philosophy of Aristotle that elaborates the fundamental principles of formal logic esp. through the doctrine of the syllogism and holds that all reality is of particular things each of which is the union of matter and a form which is characteristic of its kind except that God is pure actuality, being the unmoved mover and unchanging cause of all change, and except that prime matter is pure potentiality — compare CATEGORY, CATHARSIS, CAUSE, FORM, MATTER, PREDICABLE **2 :** a philosophy incorporating essential features of that of Aristotle with usu. the inclusion of factors stemming from later ideological traditions ⟨a mystical *Aristotelianism* also got into parts of the Jewish Cabala —S.P.Lamprecht⟩

aristotelian logic *n, usu cap A* **:** the logic of Aristotle: **a :** the total organon of Aristotle including his theories of the predicables and categories, of definition and syllogistic **b :** the traditional formal logic inaugurated by Aristotle — compare TRADITIONAL LOGIC

ar·is·to·tle's dictum \'arə,städ·ᵊlz-, -ät·ᵊlz- *also* 'er-\ *n, usu cap A* **:** DICTUM DE OMNI ET NULLO

aristotle's lantern *n, usu cap A* [*lantern*, trans. of Gk *lamptēr*; fr. a passage in Aristotle where the shape of a sea urchin is said to resemble the frame of a lantern] **:** the protrusible 5-sided masticatory apparatus of a sea urchin, each side being made up of a tooth with its supporting ossicles and the muscles that activate it

ari·ta ware *or* **arita porcelain** \ə'rēd·ə,-, ä'r-\ *n, usu cap A* [fr. *Arita*, Japan] **:** Japanese porcelain produced in and about Arita on Kyushu Island and including blue-and-white and enamel-decorated ware (as Imari and Kakiemon wares)

ar·ith·log paper \'arəth,lȯg-, -äg-\ *n* [*arithmetic* + *logarithm*] **:** semilogarithmic coordinate paper

¹**arith·me·tic** \ə'rithmə,tik\ *n* -s [alter. (influenced by Gk *arithmētikē*) of earlier *arithmetrik*, fr. ME, alter. (influenced by L *arithmetica* or Gk *arithmētikē*) of *arsmetrike*, modif. (influenced by L *ars* art & L *metricus* of measurement) of OF *arismetique*, fr. L & Gk; L *arithmetica*, fr. Gk *arithmētikē*, fr. fem. of *arithmētikos* arithmetical, fr. *arithmein* to count, fr. *arithmos* number — more at ARITHMO-, ART, METRIC] **1 a :** the branch of mathematics that treats of the properties and relationships of real numbers and of computations with them involving chiefly addition, subtraction, multiplication, and division **b :** a textbook or treatise on the principles of arithmetic **2 :** application of arithmetic **:** COMPUTATION, CALCULATION, RECKONING ⟨your ~ is pretty bad⟩ ⟨he jogged himself into an ~ of the number of nips of liquor he had taken —George Meredith⟩

²**ar·ith·met·ic** \¦a(,)rith¦med·ik, -rəth-, -etik, -ēk *also* ¦e-\ *or* **ar·ith·met·i·cal** \-ēkəl, -ēk-\ *adj* **1 :** of or relating to arithmetic **:** in agreement with the rules or methods of arithmetic **2 :** proceeding by an arithmetic progression; *esp* **:** having equal spacing between divisions corresponding to successive positive or negative integers ⟨~ scale⟩ — **ar·ith·met·i·cal·ly** \-ək(ə)lē, -li\ *adv*

arithmetical discount *n* **:** the interest discounted in advance on a note and computed on the principal of the note ⟨the *arithmetical discount* on a $1000 note for one year at 5% is $47.62⟩ — called also *true discount*; compare BANK DISCOUNT

arithmetical sum *n* **:** the sum of two or more positive quantities ⟨the *arithmetical sum* of 2, 8, and 1 is 11⟩ — compare ALGEBRAIC SUM

arithmetic graph *or* **arithmetic chart** *n* **:** a graph on which both coordinates are plotted on arithmetic scales

arith·me·ti·cian \ə,rithmə'tishən *sometimes* ,a,ri- *or* ,e,ri-\ *n* -s [MF *arithmeticien*, fr. *arithmetique* arithmetic (alter. — influenced by L *arithmetica* or Gk *arithmētikē* — of *arismetique*) + *-ien* -ian] **:** one skilled in arithmetic

arithmetic mean *n* **:** a quantity formed by adding quantities together in any order and dividing by their number ⟨the *arithmetic mean* of 6, 4, and 5 is 5⟩

arithmetic progression *n* **:** a sequence of numbers (as 3, 5, 7, 9 etc.) in which the difference between any number of the sequence and the number immediately preceding it is always the same

arith·me·ti·za·tion \ə,rithməd·ə'zāshən, -ə,tī'z-; ,a(,)rith-,med·ə'z-\ *n* -s **:** the treatment of various branches of higher mathematics by methods involving only the fundamental concepts and operations of arithmetic

arithmo- *comb form* [prob. fr. NL, fr. LGk, fr. Gk *arithmos*; akin to Gk *arariskein* to fit — more at ARM] **:** number ⟨*arithmograph*⟩ ⟨*arithmomania*⟩

ar·ith·moc·ra·cy \,a(,)rith'mäkrəsē\ *n* -ES [*arithmo-* + *-cracy*] **:** rule of the majority

ar·ith·mom·e·ter \-'mäməd·ə(r)\ *n* -s [F *arithmomètre*, fr. *arithmo-* + *-mètre* -meter] **:** an early type of adding machine

-ar·i·um \'a(ə)r-,'ār-, 'erēəm\ *n suffix, pl* **-ariums** *or* **-aria** [L, fr. neut. of *-arius* -ary] **:** thing or place belonging to or connected with ⟨*aquarium*⟩ ⟨*planetarium*⟩

ar·i·vai·pa \,arə'vīpə\ *n, pl* **arivaipa** *or* **arivaipas** *usu cap* [perh. fr. Pima *aarivapa*, lit., girls] **:** SAN CARLOS

ar·i·zo·na \,arə¦zōnə *also* ¦er-\ *adj, usu cap* [fr. *Arizona*, state in the southwestern U. S., fr. AmerSp, prob. fr. Papago *arizonac*, lit., few springs, small springs] **:** of or from the state of Arizona **:** of the kind or style prevalent in Arizona **:** ARIZONAN

arizona ash *n, usu cap 1st A* **:** an ash (*Fraxinus velutina*) of the southern U. S. and Mexico having leaves with 3 to 5 leaflets and fruit less than an inch long

arizona cardinal *n, usu cap A* **:** a rather large pale cardinal bird (*Richmondena cardinalis superba*) that ranges from Arizona to Mexico

arizona crested flycatcher *n, usu cap A* **:** a rather large crested flycatcher (*Myiarchus tyrannulus magister*) of the southern Arizona desert

arizona cypress *n, usu cap A* **:** a timber tree (*Cupressus arizonica*) with bluish silvery foliage found chiefly in Arizona

arizona gourd *n, usu cap A* **:** CALABAZILLA

arizona hooded oriole *n, usu cap A* **:** a hooded oriole (*Icterus cucullatus nelsoni*) that breeds in the extreme southwestern U.S. and winters in Mexico

arizona jay *n, usu cap A* **:** a blue and gray crestless jay (*Aphelocoma ultramarina arizonae*) of Arizona and New Mexico

arizona longleaf pine *n, usu cap A* **:** APACHE PINE

¹**ar·i·zo·nan** \,₌₌'zōnən\ *also* **ar·i·zo·ni·an** \-nēən, -nyən\ *n* -s *cap* [*Arizona* + E *-an*, *-ian*] **:** a native or resident of the state of Arizona

²**arizonan** \¦₌₌¦₌₌\ *also* **arizonian** \¦₌₌¦₌(₌)₌\ *adj, usu cap* **:** of, relating to, or characteristic of Arizona or Arizonans

arizona pine *n, usu cap A* **:** a timber tree (*Pinus arizonica*) of Arizona and adjacent regions with leaves clustered in groups of three, four, or five and tufted at the ends of branches

arizona ruby *n, usu cap A* **:** a ruby-colored pyrope garnet of igneous origin from the southwestern U. S.

arizona sycamore *n, usu cap A* **:** a medium-sized tree (*Platanus wrightii*) of Arizona and adjacent regions with deeply lobed leaves and collective fruits in groups of from three to five

arizona walnut *n, usu cap A* **:** a short stout tree (*Juglans major*) with a thin-shelled edible nut found in the southwestern U. S. and adjacent Mexico

arizona white oak *n, usu cap A* **:** an oak (*Quercus arizonica*) of Arizona and Mexico with entire oblong to obovate leaves and a hemispherical cup around the acorn

ar·i·zo·nite \,arə'zō,nīt\ *n* -s [*Arizona*, its locality + E *-ite*] **:** a mineral $Fe_2Ti_3O_9$ consisting of ferric titanium oxide found in irregular metallic steel-gray masses

ar·jun *also* **ar·jan** \'ärjən\ *n* -s [Hindi *arjun*, fr. Skt *arjuna*, lit., white; akin to L *argentum* — more at ARGENT] **:** either of two trees of the genus *Terminalia* (*T. arjuna* and *T. glabra*) found in tropical Asia and characterized by astringent bark that is used in tanning — called also *kumbuk*

ark \'ärk, 'ȧk\ *n* -s [ME, fr. OE *arc, earc*; akin to OHG *arahha* ark, ON *örk*, Goth *arka*, all fr. a prehistoric Gmc word borrowed fr. L *arca*; akin to L *arcēre* to hold off, enclose, Gk *arkein* to ward off, defend, Lith *rãktas* key, Hitt *ḫark-* to have, hold and perh. to ME *rail*, OHG *rigil*; basic meaning: protecting, locking in] **1** *now chiefly dial* **a :** a chest, coffer, covered basket, or other closed receptacle **b :** BIN, HUTCH **c** *Brit* **:** a small movable poultry house having the shape of an inverted V **2 a :** a boat or ship felt to resemble in some way that in which according to Gen 6 Noah and his family together with pairs of animals were preserved from the Deluge **b :** a large flatboat formerly used on American rivers to carry produce and stock to market — called also *broadhorn* **c :** a wanigan on a log raft **d :** something that affords protection and safety ⟨many look to the U. S. as an ~ of refuge⟩ **3 :** an ornamental somewhat elevated closet or recess traditionally built into or placed against the wall of a synagogue on the side nearest Jerusalem and serving as a repository for the scrolls of the Torah used in public worship **4 :** a storage vat for potter's clay slip **5 :** ARK SHELL

ar·kan·san \är'kanzən, ȧ'k₌, -kaan- *sometimes* -n(t)sən\ *also* **ar·kan·si·an** \-zēən, -(t)sēən\ *n* -s *cap* [²*Arkansas* + E *-an*, *-ian*] **:** a native or resident of the state of Arkansas

²**arkansan** \(')₌¦₌₌\ *also* **arkansi·an** \(')₌¦₌₌₌\ *adj, usu cap* **1 :** of, relating to, or characteristic of the state of Arkansas **2 :** of, relating to, or characteristic of Arkansans

¹**ar·kan·sas** \'ärkən,sȯ, 'ȧk-, *rap. also* -kᵊŋ,-\ *n, pl* **arkansas** \-ȯ(z)\ *usu cap* [F (recorded in the 17th cent. also as *Acansa*, *Acansas*), of AmerInd origin] **:** QUAPAW

²**arkansas** \"\ *adj, usu cap* [fr. *Arkansas*, state in the south central U. S., fr. ¹*arkansas*] **:** of or from the state of Arkansas **:** of the kind or style prevalent in Arkansas

arkansas goldfinch *n, usu cap A* **:** a small goldfinch (*Spinus psaltria psaltria*) of southwestern No. America from Colorado and New Mexico south into Mexico, the adult males being black-backed, the females somewhat greenish

arkansas kingbird *n, usu cap A* **:** a kingbird (*Tyrannus verticalis*) appearing widely in the western U. S. and having the head and back pale gray, the underparts yellowish, and the tail black narrowly bordered with white — called also *western kingbird*

arkansas soft pine *n, usu cap A* **:** the lumber of any of several soft pines: as **a :** LOBLOLLY PINE 1 **b :** SHORTLEAF PINE 1

arkansas stone *n, usu cap A* **1 :** a superior variety of novaculite found in the Ouachita mountains in Arkansas **2 :** a whetstone made of Arkansas stone

arkansas toothpick *n, usu cap A* **1 :** BOWIE KNIFE **2 :** a long pointed often double-edged sheath knife used esp. as a weapon

ar·kan·saw·yer \'ärkən,sȯyər, 'ȧk . . . yə(r), ,₌₌'₌₌\ *n* -s *usu cap* [*Arkansaw* (older spelling of *Arkansas*) + *-yer* (as in *sawyer*)] **:** ARKANSAN — used as a nickname

ar·kar \'är,kär\ *n, pl* **arkars** *also* **arkar** [origin unknown] **:** ARGALI

arkhangelsk *usu cap, var of* ARCHANGEL

ar·kie \'ärkē, 'ȧkē, -ki\ *n* -s *usu cap* [*Arkansas* + *-ie*] **:** an itinerant agricultural worker; *esp* **:** such a worker from Arkansas — compare OKIE

¹**ar·kite** \'är,kīt\ *n* -s *usu cap* [Heb 'Arqī + E *-ite*] **1 :** a member of an ancient Canaanite people **2 :** a member of the Arkite people

²**arkite** \"\ *n* -s [*Arkansas*, its locality + E *-ite*] **:** a porphyritic leucite rock consisting of pseudoleucite, orthoclase, nepheline, diopside, aegirite, and garnet

ark of the law *n, often cap A&L* **:** ARK 3

ar·kose *also* **ar·cose** \'är,kōs *also* -ōz\ *n* -s [F *arkose*] **:** a sandstone derived from the rapid disintegration of granite or gneiss and characterized by feldspar fragments

ar·ko·sic \(')är¦kōsik *also* -ōz-\ *adj* **:** of or relating to arkose

ark shell *n* [so called fr. the boat-shaped interior of the shell] **:** a marine bivalve mollusk of the family Arcidae

ar·leng \'är,leŋ\ *n, pl* **arleng** *or* **arlengs** *usu cap* **:** MIKIR

arles \'är(ə)lz\ *n pl* [ME *erles*, modif. of OF *erres* (pl.) — more at EARNEST] *chiefly Scot* **:** EARNEST MONEY

¹**arm** \'ärm, 'ȧm\ *n* -s [ME, fr. OE *arm, earm*; akin to OHG *aram* arm, ON *armr*, Goth *arms*, L *armus* shoulder, Gk *harmos* joint, Skt *īrma* arm, L *arma* tools, weapons, *art-, ars* skill, Gk *arariskein* to fit; basic meaning: joining, fitting] **1 a** (1) **:** a human upper limb (2) **:** the part of an arm between the shoulder and the wrist; *sometimes* **:** the part of an arm above the elbow **b :** the corresponding part of any other vertebrate **c :** HUMERUS ⟨a broken ~⟩ **2 a :** a limb or a locomotive or prehensile organ of an invertebrate animal: as (1) **:** a ray of a starfish or brittle star (2) **:** a brachium of a brachiopod or crinoid **b :** either of the two portions of a chromosome that lie lateral to the centromere **3 a :** an inlet of water from the sea or from some other body of water **:** an often long and relatively narrow bay in the shoreline of a body of water **b :** a tributary or branch of a river or stream **4 a :** a narrow extension of a larger area, mass or group ⟨Baja California, the long, narrow ~ of western Mexico —Marion Wilhelm⟩ ⟨the spiral ~s of the Milky Way —George Gamow⟩ ⟨an ~ of the population⟩ **b :** a ridge or elevation extending from a mountain **:** SPUR ⟨two enormous parallel ~s with a high plateau between —Forrest Morgan⟩ **c :** an extension of a building or of a group of buildings **:** WING ⟨a cruciform church with three equilateral ~s⟩ **5 a :** POWER, MIGHT ⟨the ~ of the law⟩ **b :** STRENGTH, SUPPORT ⟨the governor relied on diplomacy and his own capable ~⟩ **6 a :** BRANCH ⟨the sheltering ~s of the great birches and maples —John Burroughs⟩ **b :** a lateral shoot (as of the grape, hop, or other plants); *specif* **:** a main division of the trunk of a grapevine **7 :** a support for the elbow and forearm ⟨his elbow resting on the left ~ of the chair⟩ **8 :** a projecting part of a machine or mechanical appliance that often moves up and down or rotates ⟨the ~s of a windmill⟩ ⟨a long derrick ~ —E.S.Gardner⟩ **9 a :** a lateral and usu. horizontally extended attachment or device ⟨a metal ~ to support a wall rack⟩ **b :** one of two or more lateral and usu. horizontally extended parts ⟨the ~s of a candelabrum⟩ ⟨the ~s of a pair of eyeglasses⟩ **c** (1) **:** the end of a yard (as of a ship) (2) **:** the part of an anchor from the crown to the fluke — see ANCHOR illustration **10 :** SLEEVE ⟨both ~s of the shirt were torn⟩ **11** *baseball* **:** ability to throw or pitch ⟨to lose one's ~⟩ **12 :** an extension, division, or supplement of a specified group or activity esp. when viewed as accomplishing a functional and operative aim of the group or activity ⟨the logistical ~ of the air force⟩ ⟨because it is an ~ of merchandising, the sales finance company is under a special incentive to promote consumer goodwill —C.W.Phelps⟩ ⟨making literature serve utilitarian and ulterior ends as an ~ of propaganda —C.I.Glicksberg⟩ **13 :** TONE ARM ⟨use of a properly adjusted professional-type pickup ~ with diamond styli —R.D.Darrell⟩ **14 :** a shoulder cut of meat containing a small round bone and cross sections of three to five ribs — see BEEF illustration **syn** see POWER — **arm in arm :** with arms linked together ⟨they walked down the street *arm in arm*⟩ — **in arms :** extremely young and unable to walk independently **:** requiring to be carried ⟨still a babe *in arms*⟩ — **in the arms of morpheus** *usu cap M* **:** ASLEEP

²**arm** \"\ *vb* -ED/-ING/-S *vt* **1** *obs* **:** EMBRACE **2 :** to take or hold by the arm (as in guiding) ⟨~*ing* her friend along through the town⟩ ~ *vi* **:** to develop lateral shoots or branches (as of the hop or pole bean)

³**arm** \"\ *vb* -ED/-ING/-S [ME *armen*, fr. OF *armer*, fr. L *armare*, fr. *arma* (pl.) tools, weapons] *vt* **1 :** to furnish or equip with weapons ⟨~*ing* the soldiers for battle⟩ **2 :** to furnish or equip with something that adds strength, force, security, or efficiency ⟨an animal ~*ed* with a protective shell⟩ ⟨~*ed* with a good meal⟩ ⟨the divers were ~*ed* with cameras and collecting gear —T.A.Manar⟩ **3 :** to prepare for struggle or resistance by some means other than physical **:** fortify morally ⟨~*ed* only with knowledge —J.F.Golay⟩ **4 :** to equip, fit out, or ready for action or operation: as **a :** to free the plunger of (a percussion fuze) from the wire, pin, or other safety device so as to allow the plunger to be driven against the cap **b :** to apply grease or tallow to the socket at the end of (a sounding lead) so as to bring up a specimen of the sea bottom ⟨~ your lead with soap and sound all around the boat —H.A.Calahan⟩ **c :** to make an adjustment in (a bomb, torpedo, or grenade) so that all safety devices are released and the mechanism is in such condition that it will function under predetermined conditions (as impact, pressure, proximity, preset time) ~ *vi* **:** to prepare oneself (as with weapons) for struggle or resistance ⟨~*ing* for the fight⟩ **syn** see FURNISH

⁴**arm** \"\ *n* -s [back-formation fr. *arms*, pl., fr. ME *armes*, fr. OF, fr. L *arma*] **1 a :** a means of offense or defense **:** WEAPON ⟨air power today is the dominant ~ in war —Donald Armstrong⟩ ⟨he had been found to be in possession of a prohibited ~ —F.M.Ford⟩; *esp* **:** FIREARM ⟨an ~s manufacturer⟩ — often used in pl. ⟨taking up ~s to defend themselves⟩ **b :** a combat branch (as of an army) ⟨the coast artillery is an important ~ of the military⟩ **c :** an organized branch of national defense (as the navy) **2 arms** *pl* **a :** the hereditary ensigns armorial of a family consisting of figures and colors borne (as on shields or banners) as marks of dignity and distinction **b :** heraldic devices adopted by governments as a symbol of authority or official dignity and used esp. on seals and documents **c :** heraldic devices granted to or adopted by towns, corporations, and others as a badge or trademark **3 arms** *pl, archaic* **:** defensive covering **:** ARMOR ⟨clothed in brilliantly polished ~s⟩ **4 arms** *pl* **:** active hostilities **:** WARFARE ⟨the call to ~s⟩ **5 arms** *pl* **:** military service **:** a military career ⟨choosing ~s as his profession⟩ **syn** see WEAPON — **in arms :** ARMED **:** in a state of hostility — **under arms 1 :** in battle order **2 :** enrolled for military service — **up in arms :** aroused and ready to undertake hostilities

arm *abbr* **1** armature **2** armament

ar·ma·da \är'mädə, ȧ'mä- *also* -ādə *sometimes* -adə\ *n* -s [Sp, fr. ML *armata* army, fleet, fr. L, fem. of *armatus*, past part. of *armare*] **1 a :** a fleet of warships **b :** a large number of ships **:** FLEET **c :** a large force, body, or number of things, esp. moving things (as vehicles) ⟨an ~ of planes⟩ ⟨an ~ of buses⟩ **2 :** an arrangement of two tiers of fixed guns simultaneously fired and used in Mexico for the mass shooting of duck

ar·ma·dil·li·di·i·dae \,ärmə,dilə'dīə,dē\ *n pl, cap* [NL, fr. *Armadillidium*, type genus (fr. ²*Armadillo* + *-idium*) + *-idae*; fr. the habit of rolling the body up into a ball when touched] **:** a cosmopolitan family (type genus *Armadillidium*) of terrestrial isopods having arched bodies that can be rolled into a ball and including all the pill bugs

¹**ar·ma·dil·lo** \,ärmə'di(,)lō, ,ȧm-, -dilə *sometimes* -dē(,)(y)ō\ *n, pl* **armadillos** *also* **armadilloes** [Sp, dim. of *armado* armed one (past part. of *armar* to arm), fr. L *armatus*] **:** any of several burrowing chiefly nocturnal mammals (family Dasypodidae) having body and head encased in an armor of small bony plates in which many of them can curl up into a ball presenting the armor on all sides when attacked, being widely distributed in warmer parts of the Americas and in some areas esteemed as food — see PEBA, PELUDO

armadillo (*Dasypus sexcinctus*)

²**armadillo** \"\ [NL, fr. Sp] *syn of* ARMADILLIDIUM; see ARMADILLIDIIDAE

armado *obs var of* ARMADA

ar·ma·ged·don \,ärmə'gedᵊn, ,ȧm-\ *n* -s *usu cap* [LL *Armagedon*, scene of a battle between good and evil to take place on Judgment Day according to Rev 16:14–16, fr. Gk *Armageddōn*, *Harmagedōn*] **1 a :** final and conclusive conflict between the forces of good and evil **:** an apocalyptic battle **b :** the site or time of Armageddon **2 :** a widespread annihilating war **:** a vast conflict that is marked by great slaughter and widespread destruction and that is usu. so decisive as to make further or renewed conflict impossible

ar·magh \(')är¦mä\ *adj, usu cap* [fr. *Armagh*, county in Ireland] **1 :** of or from the urban district of Armagh, Ireland **:** of the kind or style prevalent in Armagh **2 :** of or from County Armagh **:** of the kind or style prevalent in County Armagh

ar·ma·gnac \¦ärmən¦yak\ *n* -s *often cap* [F, fr. *Armagnac*, region in southwest France] **:** a brown dry brandy from the department of Gers in southern France distilled from grape wine and aged in oak barrels

ar·ma·ment \'ärməmənt, 'ȧm-\ *n* -s *often attrib* [modif. (influenced by L *armamenta* utensils) of F *armement*, partly fr. L *armer* to arm + *-ment*, partly fr. LL *armamentum* arms, fr. L, utensil, fr. *arma* weapons, tools + *-mentum* -ment — more at ARM] **1 :** an army, air, or naval force **:** a combat or defense unit **:** a military detachment ⟨the last ~ sent by the Roman emperor crossed the sea⟩ **2** *often pl* **a :** the aggregate of a nation's military strength **:** military, air, and naval personnel, their weapons and equipment, and full manpower of a nation when organized for war or defense together with essential industry, raw materials, and stockpiles of manufactured goods ⟨a small nation that is determined to have adequate ~s⟩ **b :** arms and accessory equipment of a combat or defense unit ⟨planes with the newest ~⟩ **c :** means of protection or defense **:** ARMOR ⟨a rosebush well protected by thorns, its natural ~⟩ **3 :** the process of readying or equipping for war (as through building up an arms supply) ⟨the country's ~ will take years⟩

ar·ma·men·tar·i·um \,ärməmən'terēəm, -₌mən-\ *n, pl* **armamentar·ia** \-ēə\ *also* **armamentariums** [L, armory, arsenal, fr. *armamentum* + *-arium* -ary] **1 :** the total store of available resources: **a :** the equipment (as drugs or instruments) and methods used in an activity or profession, esp. in medicine ⟨new medicines that are a welcome addition to the ~ of the medical profession⟩ ⟨the whole ~ of science is being marshaled to increase our understanding of life —J.R.Killian⟩ **b :** factual, experimental, and speculative data ⟨adding to the ~ of knowledge⟩ **2 :** array (as of materials) : COLLECTION ⟨an immense ~ of new antibiotics —*Newsweek*⟩ **3** : essential components : APPARATUS ⟨the ~ used in producing intelligible speech⟩

ar·man·gite \är'man,gīt, -aŋ,-; 'ärmən,gīt\ *n* -s [*arsenite* of *manganese* + *-ite*] : a mineral $Mn_3(AsO_3)_2$ consisting of a manganese arsenite occurring in black rhombohedral crystals

ar·mar·i·um \är'ma(a)rēəm\ *n, pl* **armar·ia** \-ēə\ *or* **ar·mariums** [L — more at AMBRY] : AMBRY

ar·ma·ta \är'mäd·ə, -ād·ə\ [NL, fr. L, neut. pl. of *armatus*] *syn of* ECHIUROIDEA

ar·ma·ture \'ärmə,chu̇(ə)r, -,chər, -,tu̇(ə)r, -,tyu̇(ə)r; 'àmə-,chu̇ə, -,chə, -,tu̇ə, -,tyu̇ə\ *n* -s [L *armatura*, fr. *armatus* (past part. of *armare* to arm) + *-ura* -ure — more at ARM] **1** : ARMOR **2** : iron bars or framing employed for the consolidation of a building (as in sustaining slender columns, holding up canopies, stiffening glass windows) **3** : an organ or structure having a protective function ⟨the ~ of armadillos⟩; *sometimes* : an organ or structure used for attack ⟨a small animal having sharp teeth for its ~⟩ **4** : any of various spinous or sclerotized processes on insects; *esp* : the corneous parts of the genitalia **5** [NL *armatura*, fr. L] **a** : a piece of soft iron or steel that connects the poles of a magnet or of adjacent magnets to preserve the intensity of magnetization, produce signals (as in the telegraph), or do mechanical work by its motions to and from the magnet **b** : the part of a dynamoelectric machine carrying the conductors whose relative movement through the magnetic field between the pole pieces causes an electric current to be induced in the conductors (as in the dynamo) or which by having a current passed through them are caused by electromagnetic induction to move through this field (as in the motor) **c** : the movable part of an electromagnetic device (as a relay, buzzer, loudspeaker, or pickup) **6** : a skeleton or framework used by a sculptor to support a figure being modeled in a plastic material

armature reaction *n* : a magnetomotive force set up by the current induced in the armature of a dynamo that results in altering as to both magnitude and direction the flux due to the field magnet

armband \'=,=\ *n* -s [¹*arm* + *band*] : a band of cloth or other material usu. worn round the upper part of a sleeve esp. in mourning or for identification

arm bar *n* : ¹BAR 11

arm board *n* [so called fr. its being strapped to the worker's arm] : a graining board used in leatherworking and made from the outer bark of the cork oak

¹**armchair** \'=,=\ *n* [¹*arm* + *chair*] : a chair with armrests

²**armchair** \'=,=\ *adj* **1** : characterized by comfort, ease, and lazy inactivity ⟨an atmosphere of relaxation, almost of ~ leisure —M.A.C.Gorham⟩ **2** : remote from the necessity of dealing directly with the solution of problems : given to a purely speculative approach to the demands of reality : theoretical rather than practical : lacking firsthand knowledge and experience ⟨an ~ strategist⟩ ⟨~ authorities, whose concern is with contemplation, not action —F.C.Neff⟩ ⟨from ~ speculation to empirical investigation —P.H.Odegard⟩ **3** : sharing vicariously in another's experiences (as through reading) ⟨an ~ traveler⟩

armd *abbr* armored

arme blanche \'ärm'blänsh, *F* ärməbläⁿsh\ *n, pl* **armes blanches** \-m(z)'b-, *F* ärməbläⁿsh\ [F, lit., white weapon] : a cutting or thrusting weapon (as a sword or lance) as distinguished from a firearm

armed \'ärmd, 'àmd\ *adj* [ME, fr. past part. of *armen* to arm] **1 a** : furnished with weapons of offense or defense : FORTIFIED, EQUIPPED ⟨~ forces⟩ **b** : furnished with something that provides security, strength, or efficacy ⟨~ with letters of recommendation⟩ **c** : furnished with organs or structures esp. adapted to defense or attack ⟨the mandibles of the ~ soldier ants⟩ ⟨rosebushes and other ~ shrubs⟩ **2** *heraldry* **a** : BLAZONED **b** : represented with horns, beak, or talons or having them of a specified tincture — used of beasts and birds of prey ⟨an eagle gules, ~ or⟩ **3** : marked by the maintenance of armed forces in readiness for possible conflict ⟨~ peace⟩ ⟨an ~ truce⟩

armed forces *n pl* : the combined military, naval, and air forces of a nation or a group of nations

armed guard *n* : a naval detachment aboard a merchant ship in wartime

armed neutrality *n* : the position taken by a neutral country during war in which it is prepared to maintain its neutral rights against the belligerents by force if necessary

armed reconnaissance *n* **1** : reconnaissance by aircraft to locate and attack targets of opportunity in a general area rather than to attack predesignated targets **2** : air reconnaissance to locate and gather intelligence on targets in areas where lack of air superiority makes it necessary for the aircraft to fight its way in and out again

armed tapeworm *n* : a tapeworm with a spiny rostellum (as the pork tapeworm)

¹**ar·me·nian** \(')är¦mēnēən, -ä¦m-, -nyən\ *adj, usu cap* [*Armenia* (fr. L, fr. Gk) ancient country in western Asia, now divided among U.S.S.R., Turkey, & Iran + E *-an*] : of or relating to Armenia, Armenians, or the language of Armenians

²**armenian** \"\ *n* -s *cap* **1** : a member of a people dwelling chiefly in Armenia but also dispersed throughout the Middle East and emigrated to the New World **2** : the Indo-European language of the Armenians — see INDO-EUROPEAN LANGUAGES table **3** *usu cap* : a member of the Armenian Church which was established about A.D. 302 by St. Gregory the Illuminator as the earliest national Christian church and which professes a modified Monophysitism but otherwise agrees doctrinally with the Eastern Orthodox Church

armenian alphabet *n, usu cap 1st A* : the alphabet of 38 letters in which Armenian is written and of which the invention is ascribed to the bishop Mesrob in the early 5th century A.D.

armenian blue *n, often cap A* [prob. fr. *Armenian* (*stone*), n.] : ULTRAMARINE

armenian bole *n, often cap A* **1** : a soft clayey bright red earth found chiefly in Armenia and Tuscany and used esp. as a coloring material **2** : ²BOLE 3

armenian catholic *n, usu cap A&C* : an Eastern-rite Armenian united with the Roman Catholic Church — see UNIATE

armenian red *n, often cap A* : a strong brown that is yellower and stronger than average russet, stronger and slightly yellower and lighter than average copper brown, and yellower and deeper than rust

armenian stone *n, often cap A* [*Armenian stone*, n., "lapis lazuli", source of blue pigment] : AZURITE BLUE

ar·men·ic \(')=¦menik\ *adj, cap* [*Armenia* + *-ic*] : of or relating to the Armenian language or tongues of the same stock

ar·me·nite \är'mē,nīt, 'ärmə,n-\ *n* -s [F *arménite*, fr. *Arménie* Armenia + *-ite*] : a mineral $BaCa_2Al_6Si_8O_{28}.2H_2O$ consisting of a hydrous calcium barium aluminosilicate

ar·me·noid \är'mē,nȯid, 'ärmə,n-\ *n* -s *usu cap* [²*Armenian* + *-oid*] : one having the physical characters of the eastern branch of the Alpine subrace chiefly characterized by dark skin, prominent nose, and broad short skull often flat in the back with a sloping forehead

ar·me·no-turk·ish \är'mē(,)nō'-\ *n, cap A&T* [*Armeno-* (fr. ¹*Armenian*) + *Turkish*] : Turkish as used by Armenians in Turkey with an admixture of Armenian words

ar·me·ria \är'mirēə\ *n, cap* [NL] : a genus of evergreen tufted herbs or subshrubs (family Plumbaginaceae) formerly included in *Limonium* but distinguished by narrow often linear leaves and flowers in dense globular heads — see THRIFT

ar·me·ri·a·ce·ae \(,)är,mirē'āsē,ē\ [NL, fr. *Armeria*, type genus + *-aceae*] *syn of* PLUMBAGINACEAE

armes blanches *pl of* ARME BLANCHE

armes par·lantes \ärmə̇pärläⁿt\ *n pl* [F, lit., speaking arms] *heraldry* : punning arms : canting arms

ar·met \'ärmə̇t\ *n* -s [MF, modif. (influenced by *arme* arm, weapon) of OSp *almete*, fr. OF *helmet* — more at HELMET] : a late and perfected medieval helmet of many light parts closing neatly round the head by means of hinges following the contour of chin and neck

arm·ful \'ärm,fu̇l, 'àm-\ *n, pl* **armfuls** \-lz\ *or* **arms·ful** \-mz,fu̇l\ : as much as the arm can hold ⟨a huge ~ of red roses —L.C.Douglas⟩

arm garter *n* : GARTER 1c

armguard \'=,=\ *n* [¹*arm* + *guard*] : a covering to protect the arm; *specif* : ¹BRACER

armhole \'=,=\ *n* [ME, fr. ¹*arm* + *hole*] **1** *obs* : ARMPIT **2** : an opening for the arm in the body of a garment **3** : ARMSCYE

armies *pl of* ARMY

ar·mi·ger \'ärmə̇jər\ *n, pl* **armigers** \-rz\ *also* **armig·eri** \är'mijə,rī\ [ML, squire, fr. L, armor-bearer, fr. *armiger* armor-bearing, fr. *arma* weapons, armor + *-i-* + *-ger* -gerous — more at ARM] **1** : ARMOR-BEARER, SQUIRE ⟨~ of a knight⟩ **2** : one entitled to armorial bearings — **ar·mig·er·al** \(')är¦mijərəl\ *adj*

ar·mig·er·ous \(')är¦mijərəs\ *adj* [L *armiger* armor-bearing + E *-ous*] : bearing heraldic arms ⟨the ~ part of the population —Thomas De Quincey⟩

ar·mil *or* **ar·mill** \'ärməl, -(,)mil\ *n* -s [ME *armille* bracelet, fr. MF, fr. L *armilla*] **1** : ARMILLA 1, 3 **2** [earlier *armilla*, fr. ML, fr. L] : an ancient astronomical instrument for determining equinoxes and solstices by the shadows cast by the sun

ar·mil·la \är'milə\ *n, pl* **armil·lae** \-i(,)lē, -,lī\ *or* **armillas** [L, bracelet, iron ring, fr. *armus* shoulder, arm — more at ARM] **1** : BRACELET; *esp* : a gold coronation bracelet **2** [NL, fr. L] : the annular ligament of the wrist **3** : a stole similar to the ecclesiastical stole and used in the British coronation ceremony

ar·mil·lar·ia \,ärmə'la(a)rēə\ *n, cap* [NL, fr. L *armilla* + NL *-aria*; fr. the ring-shaped veil] : a genus of edible agarics having white spores, an annulus, decurrent gills, and blue juice — see HONEY MUSHROOM, SHOESTRING FUNGUS

ar·mil·lary sphere \'ärmə,lerē, är'milərē\ *n* [MF *armillaire*, fr. ML *armilla* + MF *-aire* -ary] : an ancient astronomical instrument composed of an assemblage of rings, designed to represent the positions of important circles of the celestial sphere, and turning on its polar axis within a meridian and horizon

armillary sphere

arming \'ärmiŋ, 'àm-\ *n* -s [ME, fr. gerund of *armen* to arm] : something that arms or that is used to arm; *specif* : tallow or grease used in arming a sounding lead

arming press *n* : a press for stamping a design on a book cover

¹**ar·min·ian** \(')är¦minēən, -nyən\ *adj, usu cap* [Jacobus *Arminius* (Jacob Harmensen or Hermansz) †1609 Dutch Protestant theologian + E *-ian*] : of or relating to the theologian Arminius, his followers, or their doctrines — see ARMINIANISM

²**arminian** \"\ *n* -s *usu cap* : a follower of Arminius : a believer in Arminianism

arminian baptist *n, usu cap A&B* **1** : GENERAL BAPTIST **2** : a Baptist holding Arminian doctrinal principles

ar·min·ian·ism \-,nizəm\ *n* -s *usu cap* : the doctrines or teachings of Arminius who opposed the absolute predestination taught by Calvin and maintained the real possibility of salvation for all — compare CALVINISM

ar·mip·o·tent \(')är¦mipəd·ənt\ *adj* [ME, fr. L *armipotent-*, *armipotens*, fr. *arma* arms + *potent-*, *potens* powerful — more at ARM, POTENT] *archaic* : powerful in arms : mighty in battle

ar·mi·stice \'ärmə̇stə̇s, 'àm-, *rapid* -mstə̇s; är'mis- *and* à'mis-, *often heard immediately after the 1918 armistice, is now chiefly substand*\ *n* -s [F or NL; F *armistice*, fr. NL *armistitium*, fr. L *armi-* (fr. *arma* weapons) + *-stitium* (as in *solstitium* solstice) — more at ARM] : temporary suspension of hostilities as agreed upon by those engaged in the hostilities : a truce either localized or general

armistice day *n, usu cap A&D* : November 11, observed as a legal holiday in the U.S. and Canada in commemoration of the end of hostilities in 1918 and 1945 — used before the official adoption of *Veterans Day* in 1954; called also *Remembrance Day*

ar·mi·tas \är'mēd·əz\ *n pl* [MexSp, pl. of *armita*, dim. of Sp *arma* weapon, fr. L, weapons — more at ARM] : ankle-length divided leather aprons tying around waist and knees formerly worn by cowboys

arm·less \'ärmlə̇s, 'àm-\ *adj* : lacking arms

arm·let \'ärmlə̇t, 'àm-\ *n* -s [¹*arm* + *-let*] **1** : a band of cloth, metal, or other material worn around the upper arm for ornament, identification, or protection **2** : a small arm (as of the sea)

armload \'=,=\ *n* : as much as an arm can carry ⟨~s of firewood⟩

armlock \'=,=\ *n* [¹*arm* + *lock*] : HAMMERLOCK

ar·moire \'ärmwär, 'àmə(r\ *n* -s [MF, alter. of OF *armaire*, fr. L *armarium* — more at AMBRY] : a usu. large and ornate cupboard, wardrobe, or clothespress

armonica *n* -s [It, fem. of *armonico* harmonious, fr. L *harmonicus* musical — more at HARMONIC] : GLASS HARMONICA

¹**ar·mor** \'ärmər, 'àmə(r\ *n* -s *see -or in Explan Notes* [ME *armour*, alter. of *armure*, fr. OF, fr. L *armatura* — more at ARMATURE] **1** : defensive covering for the body: **a** : the usu. metal defensive covering worn in combat in the medieval period ⟨suits of ~⟩ — see MAIL 1 **b** : the defensive covering (as that made of resin-treated glass-fiber cloth) used esp. in modern warfare ⟨troops with body ~ and helmets⟩ **c** : the watertight pressure-resistant gear of a diver (as in deep-sea diving) **2** : a quality or circumstance that affords protection ⟨the ~ of courage⟩ ⟨the ~ of prosperity⟩ **3** : steel or iron plating designed to resist gunfire and used esp. to protect ships, tanks, and aircraft **4** : a more or less hard and rigid protective covering of an animal or plant; *esp* : the vegetable tissue enveloping the ligneous interior of certain fossil tree trunks — see BENNETTITALES **5 a** : a protective sheathing on wire, cordage, or hose **b** : a metal sheath commonly of woven wire or spiraled tape covering the insulation of an electrical conducting cable and serving both as a mechanical protection and as a shield against electrostatic or electromagnetic induction **6** : armored forces and vehicles (as mechanized artillery and tanks) ⟨night attacks with ~ —V.G. Gilbert⟩

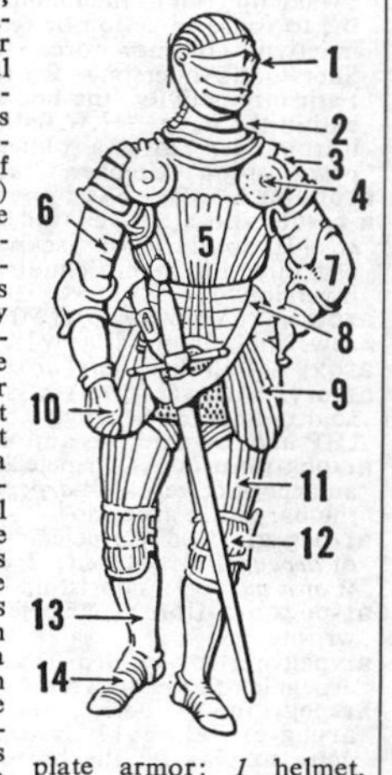

plate armor: *1* helmet, *2* gorget, *3* épaulière, *4* pallette, *5* breastplate, *6* brassard, *7* cubitiere, *8* skirt of tasses, *9* tuille, *10* gauntlet, *11* cuisse, *12* knee piece, *13* jambeau, *14* solleret

²**armor** \"\ *vt* **armored; armored; armoring** \-m(ə)riŋ\ **armors** : to equip with armor ⟨four divisions were being ~*ed*⟩

armor-bearer \'==,==\ *n* : one that bears armor; *specif* : SQUIRE

¹**armor-clad** \'==¦=\ *adj* [¹*armor* + *clad*] : sheathed in or protected by armor

²**armor-clad** \'==,=\ *n* -s : a ship (as a warship) protected by armor

armored *adj* **1** : equipped with armor ⟨an ~ ship⟩ ⟨~ concrete⟩ **2** : marked by the use of armor ⟨an ~ attack⟩ **3** : of or relating to an armored force ⟨an ~ training center⟩

armored cable *n* : an electrical conducting cable with a wrapping of metal (as tape or wire) — compare ¹ARMOR 5b

armored car *n* **1** : an armored wheeled vehicle (as an automobile) often mounting machine guns and light cannon — compare TANK **2** : a railroad car protected by armor

armored catfish *n* : any of certain So. American catfishes chiefly of the family Loricariidae having the body covered by rough and often interlocking bony plates

armored scale *n* : any of numerous scales constituting the family Diaspididae and having a firm covering of wax best developed in the female that is secreted from special glands — compare SOFT SCALE

ar·mor·er \'ärmərər, 'àmərə\ *n* -s [ME *armourer*, alter. (influenced by ME *armour* armor) of *armurer*, fr. MF *armurier*, fr. OF, fr. *armure* armor — more at ARMOR] **1** : one that makes armor or arms ⟨a sword made by a British ~⟩ **2** : an attendant to assist in the donning of a suit of armor ⟨the knight's young ~⟩ **3** : one that repairs, assembles, and tests firearms: as **a** : an enlisted man having charge of the repair and maintenance of the small arms of his unit **b** : a member of a ground crew charged with repair and service of aircraft armament including bombs and machine guns

¹**ar·mo·ri·al** \(')är¦mōrēəl, -ä¦m-, -ȯr-\ *adj* [²*armory* + *-al*] : belonging to or bearing heraldic arms — **ar·mo·ri·al·ly** \-ēəlē, -li\ *adv*

²**armorial** \"\ *n* -s **1** : a book of heraldic arms **2** : ⁴ARM 2a

armorial bearing *n* : ⁴ARM 2a — usu. used in pl.

¹**ar·mor·i·can** \(')är¦mȯrə̇kən, -mär-\ *also* **ar·mor·ic** \-rik\ *adj, usu cap* [*armorican* fr. L *Armorica*e (pl.) Armorica, region comprising the coast of Gaul between the Seine and Loire rivers + E *-an*; *armoric* prob. fr. L *armoricus* (akin to *Armoricae*, n. pl.)] **1 a** : of or relating to the region in northwest France between the Seine and Loire rivers; *esp* : of or relating to Brittany **b** : of or relating to the people of that region **c** : of or relating to the language of the Armorican people **2** : HERCYNIAN

²**armorican** \"\ *also* **armoric** \"\ *n* -s *cap* **1** : a native or inhabitant of Armorica (now Brittany) : BRETON **2** : the language of the Armoricans

ar·mo·ried \'ärm(ə)rēd\ *adj* [²*armory* + *-ed*] : decked with armorial bearings

ar·mor·ist \'ärmərə̇st\ *n* -s : one skilled in the study of coat armor or heraldry

armor-piercing \'==,==\ *adj* : capable of or used for piercing armor — used esp. of rifle bullets, artillery projectiles, and antitank grenades

armor-plated \'==¦==\ *adj* : covered with or protected by plating of armor ⟨the barge had *armor-plated* sides⟩

armors *pl of* ARMOR, *pres 3d sing of* ARMOR

¹**ar·mo·ry** \'ärm(ə)rē, 'àm-, -ri\ *n* -ES [ME *armourie*, alter. (influenced by ME *armour* armor) of *armurie*, fr. *armure* armor + *-ie* -y — more at ARMOR] **1 a** *archaic* : ARMOR : defensive and offensive arms **b** *archaic* : protective trappings : defensive gear **c** : ensemble of arms for defense or attack : array of weapons ⟨an important weapon in the antiaircraft ~⟩ **d** : the storehouse of resources : repository of usable material : collection of available data ⟨within the ~ of the artist⟩ ⟨a whole ~ of intellectual tools —Sidney Hook⟩ ⟨his ~ of mythological lore —Dudley Fitts⟩ **2** : a place where arms and military equipment are deposited, often being a large building including also a drill hall and offices **3** : a usu. government-owned building or site where arms (as rifles, pistols, bayonets, and swords) are manufactured

²**armory** \"\ *n* -ES [MF *armoierie*, fr. OF, fr. *armoier* to blazon (fr. *armes* arms, coat of arms) + *-erie* -ery — more at ARM] **1** : the art of blazoning arms : HERALDRY **2** : ⁴ARM 2a **3 a** : a branch of heraldry that treats of coat armor **b** : the use and display of coat armor **c** : a book of coats of arms arranged in the order of the bearers' names — compare ORDINARY

ar·mour \'àmə(r\ *chiefly Brit var of* ARMOR

ar·mo·zeen *or* **ar·mo·zine** \¦ärmə¦zēn\ *n* -s [prob. fr. It *ermesino*, fr. *Harmozia* (now *Hormuz*, *Ormuz*), ancient town on coast of Persia] : a heavy generally black taffeta-weave silk used for clerical robes and mourning

armpit \'=,=\ *n* [ME, fr. ¹*arm* + *pit*] : the hollow beneath the junction of the arm and shoulder : AXILLA

armrack \'=,=\ *n* [⁴*arm* + *rack*] : a frame for holding pistols or other small arms

armrest \'=,=\ *n* : a support for the arm (as on a chair)

arms *pl of* ARM, *pres 3d sing of* ARM

arm·scye \'ärm,sī, -,zī\ *also* **arms·eye** \-,zī\ *n* -s [*armscye* fr. ¹*arm* + E dial. *scye*, *sey* armhole; *armseye* prob. by folk etymology fr. *armscye*] : ARMHOLE; *specif, in tailoring and dressmaking* : the shape or outline of the armhole

armsful *pl of* ARMFUL

arm's length *n* : a distance preventing or excluding personal contact, familiarity, or intimacy ⟨pompous and ornate and keeps us stiffly at *arm's length* —Virginia Woolf⟩; *specif* : the condition or fact that the parties to a transaction or negotiation are independent and that one does not dominate the other ⟨sale at *arm's length*⟩ ⟨*arm's-length* bargaining⟩

arms of adoption *heraldry* : arms taken by a stranger in blood in compliance with the will of a testator

arms of affection *heraldry* : arms assumed out of gratitude to a benefactor and borne quartered with one's paternal arms

arms of alliance **1** *heraldry* : arms taken up by the issue of heiresses to show their maternal descent **2** *heraldry* : arms acquired by marriage

arms of augmentation *heraldry* : armorial bearings additional to those already possessed and conferred by special grant for distinguished services to the state

arms of community *heraldry* : arms of corporate and other bodies (as bishops' sees, abbeys, universities, and towns)

arms of dominion *also* **arms of sovereignty** *heraldry* : national arms borne by a sovereign

arms of office *heraldry* : arms borne by virtue of tenancy of an office or dignity ⟨a bishop's *arms of office*⟩

arms of pretension *heraldry* : arms of a sovereignty or other rank that are assumed to denote a claim to a realm or rank by one not in possession of it (as the fleurs-de-lis of France borne on the shield of England from 1340 to 1801)

arms of succession *heraldry* : arms denoting inheritance

arm spread *n* : SPAN 1b

arm stake *n* : ¹STAKE 9

armt *abbr* armament

ar·mure \'är,myu̇(ə)r, -,myər\ *n* -s [F, lit., armor — more at ARMOR] : a pebbly-surfaced fabric made from various fibers or combinations of fibers and used for clothing and interior decoration, the usual armure pattern being an allover one of small conventional motifs floated on a twilled or rep ground

ar·my \'ärmē, 'àm-, -mi\ *n* -ES [ME *armee*, fr. MF *armée*, fr. ML *armata* army, fleet — more at ARMADA] **1 a** : a large organized body of men armed and trained for war and destined chiefly for land service **b** : a unit organized to be capable of independent action and consisting conventionally of a headquarters, two or more corps, and auxiliary troops **c** *often cap* : the complete military organization of a nation for land warfare ⟨the ~ of the U.S.⟩ **2** : a great number : vast multitude : ARRAY ⟨an ~ of skilled technicians would be necessary⟩ **3** : a body of persons organized for the advancement of a cause ⟨an ~ of dedicated doctors⟩ ⟨the Salvation *Army*⟩

army ant *n* [so called fr. its moving in large groups] : any of a number of nomadic social ants constituting a subfamily (Dorylinae) of the Formicidae, ranging and foraging freely, and establishing temporary bivouacs rather than permanent nests — compare DRIVER ANT, LEGIONARY ANT

army aviation *n* : aircraft with necessary personnel and equipment organized as a part of the army rather than the air force

army brat *n, often cap A, slang* : the son or daughter of a regular-army officer or enlisted man

army brown *n* : a light brown that is darker and slightly yellower than blush and redder and darker than cork — called also *rosario*

army corps *n* : CORPS 1b

army cutworm *n* [so called fr. its moving in large groups] : a cutworm (*Chorizagrotis auxiliaris*) destructive mainly to forage crops and small grains

army group *n* : a primarily tactical organization that consists of two or more armies (sense 1b)

army of occupation : an army sent to hold and exercise a military government in the territory of the enemy after his subjugation in war usu. to ensure compliance with peace terms

armyworm \'==,=\ *n* **1** : any of a number of larval noctuid moths that often travel in great multitudes from field to field destroying grass, grain, and other crops; *esp* : the common armyworm (*Pseudaletia unipuncta*) of the northern U.S. — see BEET ARMYWORM, FALL ARMYWORM **2** : one of the larvae of certain small two-winged flies (genus *Sciara*) that march in large companies in regular order

arn \'ärn\ *n* -s [earlier *alryne*, *alrone*, fr. ME *alloren*, *allerne* of alder, fr. OE *ælren*, fr. *alor*, *aler* alder + *-en* — more at ALDER] *Scot* : the alder tree

ar·na \'är,nä\ *n* -s [Hindi *arnā*; akin to Skt *araṇya* forest, fr. *araṇa* foreign, distant; akin to Av *auruna-* wild and perh. to L *alius* other — more at ELSE] : a wild water buffalo

arnatta *or* **arnatto** *var of* ANNATTO
ar·naut \'är,naüt, ⸗'⸗\ *n* -s *usu cap* [Turk *arnavut* Albanian, perh. fr. MGk *Arbanitēs*, alter. of *Albanitēs*, fr. *Albania* (fr. ML) + Gk *-itēs* -ite] **:** an inhabitant of Albania and neighboring mountainous regions; *esp* **:** an Albanian serving in the Turkish army
ar·ne·bia \är'nēbēə, ,ärnə'bēə\ *n, cap* [NL, fr. Ar *arnabīyah*] **:** a genus of Asiatic and northern African herbs (family Boraginaceae) having alternate leaves and yellow or violet flowers that change color in age — see PROPHET FLOWER
ar·nee \'är,nē\ *n* -s [Hindi *arnī*, fem. of *arnā* — more at ARNA] **:** ARNA; *esp* **:** the female arna
ar·neth index \'är,net·'-, -ed·'-\ *n, cap A* [after Joseph *Arneth* †1955 Ger. physician] **:** an age classification of blood granulocytes, specif. neutrophils, based on the number of lobes of the nucleus, increasing lobulation being regarded as a criterion of increasing age — compare SCHILLING INDEX, SHIFT TO THE LEFT, SHIFT TO THE RIGHT
arn·hem \'ärnəm, -n,hem\ *adj, usu cap* [fr. *Arnhem*, Netherlands] **:** of or from Arnhem, Netherlands **:** of the kind or style prevalent in Arnhem
ar·ni·ca \'ärnikə, -nē-, *dial* -nəkē\ *n* [NL] **1 a** *cap* **:** a large genus of herbs (family Compositae) of the northern hemisphere having opposite leaves and flower heads that are discoid or have bright yellow rays — see LEOPARD'S BANE 2 **b** -s **:** a plant of the genus *Arnica* **2** -s **a :** the dried flower head of an herb (*Arnica montana*) and other plants of the genus *Arnica* used for stimulant and local irritant effect esp. in the form of the tincture as an embrocation for bruises, sprains, and swellings **b :** the tincture made from arnica
arnica bud *n* [*arnica*, fr. the appearance of its leaves] **:** FALL DANDELION
ar·nim·ite \'ärnə,mīt\ *n* -s [G *arnimit*, fr. von *Arnim*, name of the German family owning a mine near Planitz, Germany, its locality + G *-it* -ite] **:** a mineral $Cu_5(SO_4)_2(OH)_6.3H_2O$ consisting of a basic copper carbonate
ar·nold·ist \'ärnᵊldəst\ *n* -s *cap* [*Arnold* of Brescia (Arnaldo da Brescia) †1155 Ital. political reformer + E *-ist*] **:** one of the followers of Arnold of Brescia, who preached against clerical riches and corruption and instigated the Romans to rebel against the temporal power of the pope
ar·nold's ganglion \'ärnᵊl(d)z-\ *n, usu cap A* [after Friedrich *Arnold* †1890 Ger. anatomist] **:** OTIC GANGLION
ar·nold sterilizer \-nᵊl(d)'st-\ *n, usu cap A* [after Julius *Arnold* †1915 Ger. pathologist] **:** a sterilizer used for fractional sterilization at 212°F by the free circulation of steam at atmospheric pressure
arnotta *or* **arnotto** *var of* ANNATTO
aroaco *cap, var of* ARHUACO
aroar \ə'-\ *adj* [¹*a-* + *roar*, v.] **:** ROARING
aroba *var of* ARABA
aro·ei·ra \,arə'wārə\ *n* -s [Pg] **:** any of several So. American resin-yielding timber trees of the genera *Schinus* and *Astronium* of the family Anacardiaceae
¹ar·oid \'a(ə),rȯid\ *or* **aroi·de·ous** \(')⸗;⸗dēəs, ə'rȯid-\ *adj* [*aroid* fr. NL *Arum* + E *-oid*; *aroideous* fr. ²*aroid* + *-eous*] **:** belonging to the family Araceae **:** ARACEOUS
²aroid \"\ *n* -s **:** a plant of the family Araceae
aroint \ə'rȯint\ *vb* [origin unknown] *v imper* **:** BEGONE — used with reflexive *thee* ⟨~ thee, witch —Shak.⟩ ~ *vt* -ED/-ING/-S **:** to drive away by or as if by an exclamation or curse ⟨the . . . church duly ~*ed* witches —D.C.Peattie⟩
aro·li·um \ə'rōlēəm\ *n, pl* **aro·lia** \-ēə\ [NL, fr. ML, roll of cloth] **:** a padlike lobe projecting between the tarsal claws of many insects
arol·la \ə'rälə, -ōlə,-ȯlə\ *or* **arolla pine** *n* -s [F dial. (Valais canton, Switzerland) *arolla*, prob. of non-IE origin; akin to G dial. (Switzerland) *arve* Swiss pine] **:** SWISS PINE
¹aro·ma \ə'rōmə\ *n* -s [alter. (influenced by L *aroma*) of earlier *aromat*, fr. ME, fr. OF, fr. L *aromat-, aroma*, fr. Gk *arōmat-, arōma*] **1** *obs* **:** SPICE — usu. used in pl. **2 a** (1) **:** a distinctive pleasing odor **:** FRAGRANCE ⟨the ~ of fresh coffee⟩ ⟨the ~ of a wood fire⟩ (2) **:** the fragrance of a wine derived from the particular variety of grape used **:** BOUQUET **b :** any smell or odor ⟨the gruesomely strong ~ of the old dog —Christopher Morley⟩ **3 :** a distinctive pervasive quality, characteristic, or atmosphere **:** FLAVOR ⟨ancient capitals around which hang an ~ and mystery —Lin Yutang⟩ ⟨the ~ and fragrance of new thought were perceptible —Nathaniel Hawthorne⟩
syn see SMELL
²aro·ma \"\ *or* **aro·mo** \-(,)mō\ *n* -s [AmerSp, fr. Sp *aroma* flower of the huisache, lit., fragrant plant product, fr. L, spice] **:** any of several spiny shrubs and trees (as the huisache)
aro·ma·den·drene \ə,rōmə'den,drēn\ *n* -s [ISV ¹*aroma* + *dendr-* + *-ene*] **:** a sesquiterpenoid hydrocarbon $C_{15}H_{24}$ occurring as a major constituent of oils from several eucalyptus trees
aro·mal \ə'rōməl\ *adj* [¹*aroma* + *-al*] **:** AROMATIC
¹ar·o·mat·ic \,arə¦mad·ik, -atik, -ēk *also* ¦er-\ *adj* [ME *aromatyk*, fr. MF *aromatique*, fr. LL *aromaticus*, fr. Gk *arōmatikos*, fr. *arōmat-, arōma* + *-ikos* -ic] **1 :** of, relating to, or having aroma: **a :** having a distinctive pleasing odor **:** sweet⸗smelling **:** FRAGRANT ⟨the ~ breath of spruce and pine —Willa Cather⟩ ⟨an ~ blend of domestic and imported tobaccos⟩ **b :** having a strong smell or odor ⟨steerage accommodations . . . were at best congested and strikingly ~ —Robert Rice⟩ **c :** having a distinctive pervasive quality or atmosphere ⟨all the places with ~ names —John Woodburn⟩ **2 a :** of, relating to, or characterized by the presence of at least one benzene ring — used of a large class of monocyclic, bicyclic, and polycyclic hydrocarbons and their derivatives (as benzene, toluene, naphthalene, phenol, aniline, salicylic acid); distinguished from *alicyclic, aliphatic, heterocyclic;* see CARBOCYCLIC; compare BENZENOID **b :** similar in chemical properties to the benzene ring or to compounds containing it — used esp. in relation to some unsaturated heterocyclic compounds (as thiophene and pyridine) — **ar·o·mat·i·cal·ly** \-ək(ə)lē, -ēk-, -lī\ *adv* — **ar·o·mat·ic·ness** \-iknəs, -ēk-\ *n* -ES
²aromatic \"\ *n* -s **1 :** a plant, drug, or medicine characterized by a fragrant smell and usu. by a warm pungent taste (as ginger, cinnamon, and spices) **2 :** an organic compound of the aromatic class
aromatical [¹*aromatic* + *-al*] *archaic var of* AROMATIC
aromatic bitters *n* **:** bitters that contain aromatic oils but little tannin
ar·o·ma·tic·i·ty \,arəmə'tisəd·ē, ,ərōm-\ *n* -ES **1 :** aromatic quality **2 :** the quality of being or resembling a member of the aromatic class of chemical compounds
aromatic spirit of ammonia : a solution of ammonia and ammonium carbonate in alcohol and distilled water perfumed with the oils of lemon, lavender, and nutmeg and used as a stimulant, carminative, and antacid
aromatic sulfuric acid *n* **:** a mixture of sulfuric acid, tincture of ginger, oil or spirit of cinnamon, and alcohol formerly used as a tonic and astringent
aromatic vinegar *n* **:** a solution of acetic acid highly flavored with fragrant substances and used as smelling salts
aromatic water *n* **:** a saturated aqueous solution of a volatile oil or other volatile substance prepared either by distillation or by dissolving the substance
aromatic wintergreen *n* **:** WINTERGREEN 2a
aro·ma·ti·tes \ə,rōmə'tīd·ēz\ *n, pl* **aromati·tae** \-ī,tē\ [L, fr. Gk *arōmatitēs*, fr. *arōmatitēs* aromatic, fr. *arōmat-, arōma* + *-itēs* -ite — more at AROMA] **:** a precious stone of ancient Arabia and Egypt
aro·ma·ti·za·tion \ə,rōmad·ə'zāshən, -mədə-, -mə,tī'z-\ *n* -s **1 :** the act or process of making aromatic or the quality or state of being aromatic **2 a :** chemical conversion into one or more aromatic compounds **b** *in petroleum refining* **:** conversion of aliphatic or alicyclic hydrocarbons into aromatic hydrocarbons by cyclization or dehydrogenation or both (as heptane into toluene or cyclohexane into benzene) — see HYDROFORMING
aro·ma·tize \ə'rōmə,tīz\ *vt* -ED/-ING/-S [MF *aromatiser*, fr. LL *aromatizare*, fr. Gk *arōmatizein*, fr. *arōmat-, arōma* + *-izein* -ize] **1 :** to make aromatic (as with herbs) **:** give a fragrant scent to **:** FLAVOR **2 :** to subject to chemical aromatization
aromo *var of* AROMA
ar·o·mor·pho·sis \,arə'mȯrfəsəs *sometimes* -,mȯr'fō-\ *n, pl* **aromorpho·ses** \-,sēz\ [NL, fr. *aro-* (fr. Gk *ara, ar* there and then, straightway; also, interrogative and connective particle) + *morphosis;* akin to Lith *ir̃* and, also, *ar̃*, interrogative particle] **:** biological evolution marked by general increase in degree of organization without sharp specialization — compare ALLOMORPHOSIS
aro·nia \ə'rōnēə\ *n, cap* [NL, fr. Gk *arōnia* medlar tree] **:** a small genus of shrubs (family Rosaceae) comprising the chokeberries and having white or pink flowers in terminal compound cymes
aroon \ə'rün\ *n* -s [IrGael *a rūn* oh darling, fr. *a* oh + *rūn* darling, lit., secret, fr. OIr — more at RUNE] *Irish* **:** DARLING
aroosha *var of* ARUSHA
aro·ras \ə'rōrəz\ *n pl, usu cap* [native name in India] **:** a prosperous mercantile caste of Hindus of the Punjab region of the Indian subcontinent
arose *past of* ARISE
¹around \ə'raůnd\ *adv* [ME, prob. fr. ¹*a-* + *round*, n.] **1 a :** in a circle or in circumference **:** ROUND ⟨the wheel kept going ~⟩ ⟨the track is a mile ~⟩ **b :** in a course making a circle or part of a circle ⟨waltz your partner ~ again⟩ ⟨the wind has gone ~ to the south⟩ **c :** by a circuitous route **:** in a roundabout way ⟨the road goes ~ by the lake⟩ **2 a :** on every side **:** in all or various directions from a fixed point ⟨the water of this well is famous for miles ~⟩ **b :** in close from all sides so as to surround, confine, or envelop **:** close about ⟨the old house is hemmed ~ by new apartments⟩ ⟨people crowded ~ to look at the wreck⟩ **c :** in or near one's present situation ⟨you have time to stay ~ a while⟩ **3 a :** here and there at random **:** at, in, or to various places **:** from one place to another **:** all about ⟨for a year he traveled ~ from state to state⟩ ⟨the news soon got ~⟩ **b :** to a particular place either specified or understood ⟨invited him to come ~ for supper⟩ **c :** into a situation permitting doing or attending — used with *to* ⟨it was a long time before he got ~ to reading the book⟩ ⟨we'll get ~ to the work in the morning⟩ **4 a :** in rotation or succession **:** in turn ⟨another winter has come ~⟩ ⟨he passed the candy ~ to his guests⟩ **b :** from beginning to end **:** THROUGH ⟨the region has a mild climate the year ~⟩ **c :** in order ⟨the other way ~⟩ **d :** to a customary condition (as of health or consciousness) **:** to an improved state ⟨medicines that will bring the invalids ~⟩ **5 :** somewhere close by **:** in the vicinity or neighborhood **:** NEARBY ⟨all he could do was stand ~ and wait⟩ **6 a :** in the reverse or opposite direction **:** to the rear ⟨suddenly he turned ~⟩ **b :** from one opinion, belief, or point of view to another **:** to an altogether different position or attitude ⟨the public's reaction soon brought the legislators ~⟩ **7 :** in the neighborhood of **:** APPROXIMATELY, ABOUT ⟨the book runs to ~ 500 pages⟩ ⟨he comes at ~ the same time every day⟩ —**been around :** undergone many varied experiences **:** become worldly-wise or sophisticated ⟨what most of them need is just a little advice from somebody who's *been around* —W.L. Gresham⟩
²around \"\ *prep* [ME, fr. *around*, adv.] **1 a :** along the outer edge or boundary of **:** on all sides of ⟨a neat yard with a fence ~ it⟩ **:** so as to encircle or enclose **:** ABOUT ⟨threw her arm ~ his neck⟩ ⟨several people seated ~ the table⟩ **b :** so as to make the circuit of ⟨~ the world in 80 days⟩ or partial circuit of ⟨a voyage ~ Cape Horn⟩ **:** so as to follow the curving course of ⟨coming ~ the bend of the river⟩ **c :** so as to avoid or get past ⟨leaping over fences and dodging ~ boulders⟩ **2 a :** in the neighborhood of **:** NEAR ⟨the fields ~ the village⟩ **:** in the same region with ⟨the country ~ the source of the Nile⟩ **b :** close to ⟨only the men ~ the president knew of his illness⟩ **3 a :** in all directions outward from ⟨stood looking ~ him⟩ **b :** so as to have a center or basis in ⟨primitive societies which are organized ~ kinship ties —Weston La Barre⟩ **4 a :** here and there at random in or throughout **:** ABOUT, OVER ⟨constantly traveling ~ the country⟩ **b :** from one part to another of ⟨wandering restlessly ~ the house⟩
³around \"\ *adj* [¹*around*] **1 :** going or moving about **:** ASTIR ⟨he has been up and ~ for two days⟩ **2 :** in existence **:** ALIVE, LIVING, PRESENT ⟨one of the most alertly intelligent of the artists ~ today —R.M.Coates⟩ ⟨the troubles arising out of lack of money have been ~ for a long time —Murray Illson⟩
around-the-clock \⸗¦⸗¦⸗⸗\ *adj* **:** being in effect, continuing, or lasting 24 hours a day **:** UNCEASING, CONSTANT ⟨an *around⸗the-clock* operation⟩
aroura *or* **arura** \ə'rürə\ *n, pl* **arourae** *or* **arurae** \-,rē\ [Gk *aroura*, lit., tilled or arable land, fr. *aroun* to plow — more at EAR (to plow)] **:** an ancient Egyptian unit of land measure equal to 0.677 acres (27.4 ares)
arous·al \ə'raůzəl\ *n* -s **:** the act of arousing **:** the state of being aroused
arouse \ə'raůz\ *vb* -ED/-ING/-S [*a-* (perfective prefix) + *rouse* — more at ABEAR] *vt* **1 a :** to awake from or as if from sleep **:** wake up ⟨ran to the flaming house and *aroused* the old man⟩ **b :** to rouse to action or readiness for action from a state of inactivity ⟨the new force stirred and *aroused* the people —Sherwood Anderson⟩ **2 :** to give rise to **:** EXCITE, STIMULATE **:** stir into activity ⟨the book and the play . . . *aroused* debate within the navy —H.W.Baldwin⟩ ~ *vi* **:** to awake from or as if from sleep **:** STIR ⟨a soldier would ~ and turn his body to a new position —Stephen Crane⟩ **syn** see STIR
arous·er \-zə(r)\ *n* -s **:** one that arouses
a ro·ve·scio \,ärō've(,)shō, -eshē,ō\ *also* **al rovescio** \,äl·r-\ *adv* [It, upside down, backwards] **:** in contrary motion — used as a direction in music indicating imitation by reversion or by inversion
arow \ə'rō\ *adv (or adj)* [ME *arewe, arowe*, fr. ¹*a-* + *rewe, rowe* row, line — more at ROW] **:** in a row, line, or rank
aroxy \(')a¦räksē\ *adj* [*aroxy-*, fr. *aryl* + *oxy-*] **:** ARYLOXY
ar·o·yl \'arəwəl, -,wēl\ *n* -s [*aromatic* + *-yl*] **:** an aromatic acid radical (as benzoyl)
ARP *abbr* air raid precautions
ar·peg·gian·do \(,)är,pejē'än(,)dō, ¦ärpe¦jä-\ *adv* [It, playing an arpeggio, verbal of *arpeggiare* to play an arpeggio, play on the harp] **:** in arpeggio
ar·peg·gi·at·ed \är'pejē,ād·əd\ *adj* [It *arpeggiato* (past part. of *arpeggiare*) + E *-ed*] **1** *of a chord* **:** played as an arpeggio **2** *of a passage* **:** consisting of or played as arpeggios
ar·peg·gi·a·tion \(,)är,pejē'āshən\ *n* -s **:** arpeggio playing or writing
ar·peg·gia·to \(,)är,pejē'äd·(,)ō, ¦ärpe¦jä-\ *adj* [It] **:** in arpeggios **:** ARPEGGIATED
ar·peg·gio \är'pejē,ō, -e(,)jō\ *n, pl* **arpeggios** \-ōz\ *or* **arpeg·gi** \-e(,)jē\ [It, fr. *arpeggiare* to play on the harp, fr. *arpa* harp, of Gmc origin; akin to OHG *harpha* harp — more at HARP] **1 :** production of the tones of a chord in succession and not simultaneously **2 :** a chord played in arpeggio

arpeggio 2

ar·peg·gioed \-ōd\ *adj* **:** ARPEGGIATED
ar·peg·gio·ne \(,)är,pejē'ōnē, ,ärpe'jō-\ *n* -s [G, fr. It *arpeggio*] **:** a cellolike bowed instrument of the early 19th century having frets and drone strings
ar·pent \'ärpənt, -,pänt\ *also* **ar·pen** \-,pən, -,päⁿ\ *n* -s [MF *arpent*, fr. (assumed) VL *arependis*, prob. alter. of L *arepennis*, fr. Gaulish; akin to MIr *airchenn*, a measure of land area; both fr. a prehistoric Celtic compound whose first and second constituents respectively are akin to Gaulish *are* by, in front of (akin to OHG *furi* for, in front of) and to OIr *cenn* head, end, W *pen* — more at FOR] **1 :** any of various old French units of land area; *esp* **:** a unit still used in certain French sections of Canada and the U. S. equal to about 0.85 acre **2 :** a unit of length equal to one side of a square constituting one arpent
arquebus *var of* HARQUEBUS
ar·que·rite \är'ke,rīt\ *n* -s [F *arquérite*, fr. *Arqueros*, Chile, its locality + F *-ite*] **:** a mineral consisting of a soft malleable variety of amalgam
arr \'er, 'ar\ *n* -s [ME *erre, arre*, of Scand origin; akin to ON *ørr, örr* scar, OSw *ær, ar*, Dan *ar, arr;* akin to MLG *are* scar, G dial. *arbe*, Skt *aru* wound and perh. to ON *rögg* long hair, long wool — more at RUG] *now dial Brit* **:** ²SCAR
arr *abbr* **1** arranged; arrangement **2** arrival; arrive
ARR *abbr* [L *anno regni regis* or *reginae*] in the year of the king's or queen's reign
ar·ra·ca·cha \,arə'kachə, ,ärə'kä-, '⸗⸗,⸗⸗\ *also* **ar·ra·cach** \,⸗⸗'kach, '⸗⸗,⸗\ *n, pl* **arracachas** *also* **arracaches** [Sp *arracacha, aracacha*, fr. Quechua *rakkácha*] **:** a tropical American perennial herb (*Arracacia xanthorrhiza* or *A. esculenta*) that is related to the carrot and is cultivated in the uplands of northern and western So. America for its edible root — called also *apio, Peruvian carrot*
ar·ra·ca·cia \,arə'kāsh(ē)ə\ *n, cap* [NL, fr. Sp *arracacha*] **:** a genus of chiefly Mexican herbs (family Umbelliferae) having compound leaves, white flowers in umbels without an involucre, and a distinct stylopodium — see ARRACACHA
ar·rack *also* **ar·ak** *or* **ar·rak** \'arək, 'a,rak\ *n* -s [Ar *'araq* sweet juice, liquor] **:** an alcoholic beverage from the Far East or Near East; *esp* **:** a liquor of high alcoholic content resembling rum in taste and distilled in the Far East from the fermented juice of the coconut palm or from a fermented mash of rice and molasses
arrack punsch *or* **arrack punch** *n* [Sw *arrakpunsch*, fr. *arrak* arrack (fr. E *arrack*) + *punsch* punch, fr. E *punch* — more at PUNCH] **:** SWEDISH PUNSCH
ar·rah \'arə\ *interj* [IrGael *ara*] *Irish* — used to express surprise or excitement
¹ar·raign \ə'rān *also* a'-\ *vt* -ED/-ING/-S [ME *arreinen*, fr. MF *araisnier* to speak to, arraign, fr. OF, fr. *a-* (fr. L *ad-*) + *raisnier* to speak, fr. (assumed) VL *rationare*, fr. L *ration-, ratio* reason, reasoning — more at REASON] **1 :** to call (a prisoner) to the bar of a court to answer to the charge of an indictment **:** ACCUSE, CHARGE **2 :** to accuse of wrong, inadequacy, or imperfection **:** find fault with **:** DENOUNCE ⟨St. Peter Damiani . . . ~*s* the monks for teaching grammar rather than things spiritual —H.O.Taylor⟩ **syn** see ACCUSE
²arraign \"\ *vt* -ED/-ING/-S [AF *arrainer*, alter. of *arramer*, irreg. fr. ML *adhramire, arramire* to promise to perform a juridical act, to arraign, fr. L *ad-* + ML *-hramire*, of Gmc origin; akin to OE *hremman* to hinder, ON *hremma* to clutch, Goth *hramjan* to crucify; akin to Russ *kromy* (pl.) loom] **:** to appeal to **:** DEMAND
ar·raign·er \-nə(r)\ *n* -s **:** one that arraigns
ar·raign·ment \-nmənt\ *n* -s [ME *arreinement*, fr. MF *araisnement* action of speaking to, fr. OF, fr. *araisnier* + *-ment*] **:** the act of arraigning or the state of being arraigned **:** ACCUSATION, DENUNCIATION ⟨the wholesale ~ of existing educational standards —F.N.Robinson⟩
ar·rame \ə'rām\ *vt* -ED/-ING/-S [ML *arramire* to arraign (as in *arramire assisam* to hold an assize) — more at ARRAIGN] *law* **:** COMMENCE ⟨~ the assize⟩
arrand *var of* ARAIN
ar·range \ə'rānj *also* a'-\ *vb* -ED/-ING/-S [ME *arangen, arengen*, fr. MF *arangier, arengier*, fr. OF, fr. *a-* (fr. L *ad-*) + *rengier* to set in a row — more at RANGE] *vt* **1 :** to put in correct, convenient, or desired order **:** adjust properly **:** DISPOSE, PLACE ⟨the girl carefully *arranged* her hair⟩ ⟨minerals *arranged* according to the Dana classification⟩ **2 :** to put in order beforehand **:** make preparations for **:** PLAN ⟨would be grateful to them for *arranging* her few remaining years —Victoria Sackville-West⟩ **3 :** to effect usu. by consulting **:** come to an agreement or understanding about **:** SETTLE ⟨decided as a matter of wisdom to ~ a truce —C.B.Hitchcock⟩ ⟨the date of the marriage was finally *arranged*⟩ **4 a :** to adapt (a musical composition) by rescoring to voices or instruments other than those for which orig. written **b :** ORCHESTRATE ⟨~ a folk melody⟩ ~ *vi* **1 :** to come to an agreement, understanding, or settlement ⟨*arranged* with the travel agent for a June passage⟩ **2 :** to make preparations **:** PLAN ⟨the band *arranged* for a series of concerts⟩ **syn** see ORDER
ar·range·ment \-jmənt\ *n* -s [F, fr. MF *arengement*, fr. *arengier* + *-ment*] **1 a :** the act or action of arranging or putting in correct, convenient, or desired order ⟨there was time only for the quickest ~ of mind —Jane Austen⟩ **b :** the quality or state of being arranged or put in order **2 :** the style, manner, or way in which things are arranged **:** ORDER, SYSTEM ⟨was shocked at the helter-skelter ~ of the papers —Jean Stafford⟩ **3 :** a preliminary step or measure **:** PREPARATION, PLAN — usu. used in pl. ⟨when the emigration to America was decided upon, he was one of four to complete the ~*s* —R.G.Usher⟩ **4 a :** a structure or combination of things arranged in a particular way or for a specific purpose **:** COMBINATION ⟨this does not prevent his paintings from being handsome aesthetic ~*s* —*Encounter*⟩ ⟨the church was decorated with ~*s* of roses and snapdragons⟩ **b :** CONTRIVANCE, AFFAIR, THING ⟨the machine was powered by a man who pumped a bicycle ~⟩ **5 a :** adaptation by rescoring of a musical composition to voices or instruments for which it was not orig. written **b :** a piece so adapted ⟨an orchestral ~ of a song⟩ **6 a :** a settlement or adjustment esp. of a dispute or claim ⟨I'm in a very delicate position but I'll fall in with any ~ Thespis may propose —W.S.Gilbert⟩ **b** (1) **:** a mutual agreement or understanding (as between persons or nations) ⟨nothing . . . precludes the existence of regional ~*s* or agencies —Vera M. Dean⟩ (2) **:** an agreement between a debtor and his creditors modifying his obligations to them **7 :** PERMUTATION 3
ar·rang·er \-jə(r)\ *n* -s **1 :** one that arranges **2 :** one that transcribes music for voices or instruments for which it was not orig. written or adapts it to a style suitable to a particular group of performers — called also *adapter*
ar·rant \'arənt *also* 'er-\ *adj* [alter. of *errant*] **1 :** wandering or roving about **:** ITINERANT, VAGRANT ⟨an ~ thief⟩ **2 a :** OUT-AND-OUT, THOROUGHGOING, CONFIRMED, EXTREME ⟨~ individualists pursuing separate courses —C.M.Smith⟩ ⟨his own perilous air of ~ omniscience —C.E.Montague⟩ **b :** notoriously or outstandingly bad **:** SHAMELESS ⟨is an ~ coward and shows the white feather at the slightest display of pluck in his antagonist —John Burroughs⟩ — **ar·rant·ly** *adv*
¹ar·ras \'arəs *also* 'er- *sometimes* -,ras *or* -aa(ə)s\ *n, pl* **arras** [ME, fr. *Arras*, city in northern France] **1 a :** a high-warp tapestry of 14th and 15th century Flemish origin having rich pictorial designs and being used for wall hangings and curtains **b :** any tapestry of similar design **2 :** a wall hanging or hanging screen of tapestry ⟨behind the ~ I'll convey myself —Shak.⟩
²ar·ras \'ä,räs\ *n pl* [Sp, fr. LL *arrae*, fr. L, pl. of *arra* earnest — more at EARNEST] *Spanish law* **:** a gift made by a husband to his wife upon marriage
ar·ra·sene \,arə'sēn, '⸗⸗,⸗\ *n* -s [¹*arras* + *-ene* (as in *damascene*)] **:** a silk or wool embroidery cord resembling chenille
ar·ras·tra \ə'rästrə\ *or* **ar·ras·tre** \-,strā\ *or* **aras·tra** \ə'rästrə\ *n* -s [modif. of MexSp *arrastre*, fr. Sp, haulage, dragging, fr. *arrastrar* to drag, fr. *a-* (fr. L *ad-*) + *rastrar* to drag, fr. *rastro* rake, harrow, fr. L *rastrum* rake — more at RASTER] **:** a rude drag-stone mill for pulverizing ores (as those containing free gold)
ar·ras·tre \ə'rä,strā\ *n* -s [PhilSp, fr. Sp, haulage, dragging] **1** *Philippines* **:** the operation of receiving, conveying, and loading or unloading merchandise on piers or wharves **2** [Sp, lit., dragging] **:** the act or process of dragging a dead bull from the ring after a bullfight
ar·rau \ä'raů, ə'raů, ə'räü\ *n* -s [AmerSp & Pg, fr. Maipure *arráu*] **:** a large turtle (*Podocnemis expansa*) of the group Pleurodira found in the Amazon river and valued for its edible eggs and as a source of oil
arrawak *usu cap, var of* ARAWAK
¹ar·ray \ə'rā, a'-\ *vt* -ED/-ING/-S [ME *arayen, arrayen*, fr. OF *areer, arayer*, fr. (assumed) VL *arredare* to arrange, fr. L *ad-* + (assumed) VL *redare* to provide, of Gmc origin; akin to Goth *garaiths* arranged — more at READY] **1 a :** to set or place in order **:** draw up **:** MARSHAL ⟨time to ~ his men at the town-ward wall —A.C.Whitehead⟩ ⟨served only to ~ public sentiment . . . against the owners —W.J.Ghent⟩ **b :** to set or set forth in order (as a jury) for the trial of a cause **:** call (as a jury) man by man **2 :** to clothe or dress esp. in splendid or impressive attire **:** dress up **:** deck out **:** ADORN ⟨did she not ~ herself in what seemed unbelievably beautiful clothes —Sherwood Anderson⟩
²array \"\ *n* -s [ME *aray, array*, fr. OF *arrai, arroi, aroi* order, arrangement, dress, fr. *areer, arayer*] **1 a :** a regular and imposing grouping or arrangement **:** ORDER ⟨tending to place the great geographical interests in hostile ~ —U.B.Phillips⟩ **b :** military order ⟨with horse and chariots ranked in loose ~ —John Milton⟩ **c** (1) **:** an orderly listing of jurors impaneled (2) **:** JURY **d :** a group of individuals or kinds of individuals that has a definite modal point forming a center of variation ⟨an interesting ~ of halophiles⟩ **2 a :** CLOTHING, ATTIRE

⟨clad in white ~⟩ **b :** rich or beautiful apparel **:** FINERY ⟨my silks and fine ~ —William Blake⟩ **3 a :** the summoning of a military force **b :** a body of soldiers **:** MILITIA ⟨the rule was established that foreign wars should be conducted by the feudal ~ —Edward Jenks⟩ **4 a :** an imposing group of company or persons **:** large number ⟨such an ~ of attorneys —Sinclair Lewis⟩ **b :** an impressive list, series, or group of things **:** SUPPLY, DISPLAY ⟨it revives the past as no ~ of facts can do —H.C.Perkins⟩ ⟨this rather bewildering ~ of records and playing equipment —Herbert Kupferberg⟩ **5 a :** a number of mathematical elements arranged in rows and columns ⟨a square determinant ~⟩ ⟨a rectangular ~⟩ **b :** a series of statistical observations or data arranged in classes in order of magnitude **:** a statistical distribution **6 :** ANTENNA ARRAY **syn** see DISPLAY

ar·ray·al \-āəl\ *n* -s **1 :** the act or process of arraying **2 :** something that is arrayed

ar·ra·yán \ˌärəˈyän, ˈ==ˌ=\ *n* -s [MexSp, fr. Sp, myrtle, fr. Ar *ar-raiḥān*, any fragrant plant] **1 :** any of several Mexican trees or shrubs of the genera *Psidium, Myrtus, Gaultheria, Pernettya,* and *Rapanea* **2** [AmerSp, fr. Sp] *in the West Indies* **a :** WAX MYRTLE **b :** any of several plants of the genus *Ardisia* **3** [AmerSp, fr. Sp] **a :** an ornamental shrub (*Eugenia apiculata*) of Chile **b :** a shrub (*Eugenia arayan*) of Colombia and Ecuador

ar·ray·er \əˈrāə(r), aˈ-\ *n* -s **:** one that arrays

ar·ray·ment \-āmənt\ *n* -s [ME *arayment, arrayment,* fr. MF *araiement, areement,* fr. OF, fr. *areer, arayer* + *-ment*] **1 :** the act of arraying or the quality or state of being arrayed ⟨then in ~ close . . . rush to war —William Morris⟩ **2 :** CLOTHING, DRESS ⟨titled ladies in fine ~⟩

ar·rear \əˈri(ə)r, -iə *also* aˈ-\ *n* -s [obs. *arrear,* adv., behindhand, fr. ME *arrere* behind, backward, fr. MF, fr. OF *ariere, arriere, arrere,* fr. (assumed) VL *ad retro* backward, fr. L *ad* to + *retro* backward, behind — more at AT, RETRO-] **1 :** the state of being behind in the discharge of duties, obligations, or responsibilities — usu. used in pl. ⟨he is in ~s with his payments⟩ **2** *archaic* **:** the rear part (as of a procession) **3** *usu pl* **a :** an obligation that has not been met on time or duty that is unfinished ⟨set about the ~s of work that had piled up —Nevil Shute⟩ **b :** an unpaid and overdue debt; *esp* **:** a remainder or balance due ⟨after securing to the present incumbents all ~s in salary —C.G.Bowers⟩ **4** *archaic* **:** something that is held back or in reserve **syn** see DEBT

ar·rear·age \-rij, -ēj\ *n* -s [ME *arrerage,* fr. MF, fr. OF, fr. *arrere* + *-age*] **1 :** the condition of being in arrears **2 :** something that is in arrears; *esp* **:** something that remains unpaid and overdue after previous payment of a part — often used in pl. ⟨a formal demand for the payment of ~s —Washington Irving⟩ **3** *archaic* **:** something that is held back or in reserve **syn** see DEBT

ar·rect \(ˈ)əˌrekt\ *adj* [L *arrectus,* past part. of *arrigere* to raise up, fr. *ad-* + *-rigere* (fr. *regere* to direct, guide) — more at RIGHT] **1 :** rigidly erect **:** lifted up **:** RAISED ⟨a rabbit with ears ~⟩ **2 :** ATTENTIVE, ALERT ⟨God speaks . . . to the vigilant and ~ —George Smalridge⟩

ar·rec·tor \əˈrektə(r)\ *n, pl* **arrecto·res** \ˌaˌrekˈtōr(ˌ)ēz\ *or* **arrectors** [NL, fr. L *arrectus* + *-or*] **:** ERECTOR a

arrenotokous *var of* ARRHENOTOKOUS

ar·rent \aˈrent, əˈ-\ *vt* -ED/-ING/-S [ME *arenten,* fr. MF *arenter,* fr. OF, fr. *a-* (fr. L *ad-*) + *-renter* (fr. *rente* income from a property) — more at RENT] **:** to let or farm out at a rent; *specif* **:** to permit the enclosure of (forest lands) with a low hedge and a ditch under a yearly rent — **ar·ren·ta·tion** \ˌaˌrenˈtāshən\ *n* -s

¹ar·rest \əˈrest *also* aˈ-\ *vt* -ED/-ING/-S [ME *aresten,* fr. MF *arester,* fr. (assumed) VL *arrestare,* fr. L *ad-* + *restare* to stay back, remain — more at REST] **1 a :** to bring to a stop or halt the motion, course, or progress of **:** halt or prevent the development of ⟨the girl was caught in a pine tree which ~*ed* her fall —Willa Cather⟩ ⟨the physician cannot ~ the coming on of age —J.A.Froude⟩ **b :** to check, hinder, or slow down the course or progress of **:** moderate the force of ⟨various expedients to ~ fierce willful human nature in its outward course —J.H.Newman⟩ **c :** to bring to a standstill or state of inactivity ⟨~*ed* tuberculosis⟩ ⟨~*ed* labor⟩ **2 :** to catch or take hold of **:** SEIZE, CAPTURE; *specif* **:** to take or keep in custody by authority of law ⟨they ~*ed* him for speeding⟩ **3 a :** to catch and hold (as the senses or intellectual faculties) ⟨the racial difference that at once ~s attention is skin color —Ruth Benedict⟩ **b :** to seize or hold in focus the attention, thought, or consideration of ⟨an easy beauty of style which ~s even the least prepared reader —T.S. Eliot⟩

syn CHECK, INTERRUPT **:** ARREST indicates a stopping or holding fixed in the midst of motion, progress, development, or course with suddenness and with such power, force, or decisiveness that some sort of release is needed for resumed advance or motion ⟨he had gone from task to task until this last attack of blackwater fever had *arrested* his activities —H.G.Wells⟩ ⟨thought was *arrested* by utter bewilderment —George Eliot⟩ CHECK may suggest a quite sudden stopping, perhaps with force, with no implication at all about possible resumption of advance or activity in question ⟨Lucian . . . seemed about to speak but *checked* himself —G.B.Shaw⟩ ⟨while making a tour of his northern provinces he was *checked* by the information that the Penobscot Indians . . . were about to go on the warpath —*Encycl. Americana*⟩ INTERRUPT indicates some sort of breaking in and stopping smooth continuation of action under way; it stresses the fact of breaking in and is usu. used in situations in which a resumption of activity by the performer, doer, or speaker is possible ⟨he entered the Lawrence Scientific School . . . where his studies in chemistry and natural history were *interrupted* by the Civil War —F.H.Garrison⟩ ⟨Emily could never have suspected that she had *interrupted* Mrs. Hetherington on the point of establishing an emotional mastery over the situation —Mary Austin⟩

²ar·rest \"\ *n* -s [ME *arest, areste,* fr. MF, fr. OF, fr. *arester*] **1 a :** the act of stopping or restraining (as from further motion) **:** CHECK, STAY, STOPPAGE ⟨in my attempt to explain the ~ of the scientific spirit among the Greeks —Benjamin Farrington⟩ **b :** the condition of being stopped ⟨since the heart was in complete ~, massage was immediately started⟩ **2 a :** the act of seizing or taking hold of **:** SEIZURE ⟨the first ~s of sleep —Charles Lamb⟩ **b (1) :** the taking or detaining of a person in custody by authority of law **(2) :** legal restraint of the person **:** CUSTODY, IMPRISONMENT **(3) :** seizure or detention of chattels under process of law, esp. of vessels in admiralty cases or of movable obligations in a proceeding in Scots law analogous to garnishment **3** *obs* **:** A JUDGMENT, DECREE, SENTENCE **:** ARRET **4 :** a device for arresting motion (as one for checking the swinging of the beam or pans of a balance) — **under arrest :** in legal custody **:** ARRESTED

ar·res·ta·tion \ˌaˌreˈstāshən\ *n* -s [F, fr. MF *arestation,* fr. *arester* + *-ation*] **:** ARREST: **a :** STOPPING ⟨the sudden ~ of life under the magic spell —E.V.Lucas⟩ **b :** apprehension by legal authority ⟨the ~ of the criminal⟩

arrested *adj* **:** showing cessation of growth or activity ⟨~ tuberculous activity⟩ ⟨~ development⟩

ar·rest·ee \ˌaˌreˈstē, əˌreˈstē, aˈ-\ *n* -s [¹*arrest* + *-ee*] **1** *Scots law* **:** the person who holds property attached by arrestment **2 :** one who is under arrest ⟨follow the ~s to city hall and the magistrate's court —Saul Bellow⟩

ar·rest·er *or* **ar·res·tor** \əˈrestə(r), aˈ-\ *n* -s [ME *arester,* fr. *aresten* + *-er*] **:** one that arrests: as **a :** one that arrests by legal authority **b :** LIGHTNING ARRESTER **c :** SPARK ARRESTER

arrester hook *n* **:** a retractable hook on the underside of the tail of a carrier-based airplane extended in landing to engage an arresting-gear cable on the deck of the carrier

arresting *adj* **:** catching or holding the attention, thought, or feelings **:** GRIPPING, STRIKING, INTERESTING ⟨a cryptic and ~ personality that compels attention —Geoffrey Bruun⟩ ⟨an ~ and sensitively written contribution to the still slim literature of undersea warfare —Walter Millis⟩ **syn** see NOTICEABLE

arresting gear *n* **:** a series of rather widely spaced parallel wire cables held taut by strong springs and extending across the flight deck of an aircraft carrier, one such cable by being caught by the arrester hook of an airplane in the process of landing halting the forward motion of the plane within a limited space

ar·rest·ing·ly *adv* **:** in an arresting manner

ar·res·tive \əˈrestiv, aˈ-, -ēv\ *adj* **:** tending to arrest or catch the attention or interest **:** STRIKING

ar·rest·ment \-s(t)mənt\ *n* -s [ME *arestment,* fr. MF *arestement,* fr. OF, fr. *arester* + *-ment*] **1 a :** the arrest of a person or the seizure of his personal property to secure his presence at a trial or the satisfaction of any judgment against him **b** *Scots law* **:** a process secured by a second creditor whereby a debtor is prohibited from making payment or delivery of movable property to one of his creditors until that creditor's debt to the second creditor is settled or secured — compare EQUITABLE ATTACHMENT, GARNISHMENT, TRUSTEE PROCESS **c** *Scots law* **:** a process whereby the movable property of one domiciled outside of Scotland is seized in order to give jurisdiction against him — called also *arrestment jurisdictionis fundae causa* **2 a :** the action of stopping or checking **b :** a stoppage or check

arrest of judgment : the staying or stopping of a judgment after verdict for legal cause

arrests *pres 3d sing of* ARREST, *pl of* ARREST

ar·ret \aˈre, -rā\ *n* -s [F *arrêt* decision of a court, act of stopping, fr. MF *arest* — more at ARREST] **:** a judgment, decision, or decree of a court or sovereign

ar·re·tine \ˈarəˌtīn, -ēn\ *adj, usu cap* [L *Arretinus,* fr. *Arretium* (now *Arezzo*), ancient city of Italy + L *-inus* -ine] **:** of or relating to the ancient Arretium

arretine ware *n, usu cap A* **:** red terracotta ware usu. decorated in relief made at Arretium and elsewhere in Italy from about 100 B.C. to about A.D. 100 — called also *Samian ware, terra sigillata*

arrgt *abbr* arrangement

ar·rha \ˈarə\ *n, pl* **arrhae** \-(ˌ)rē\ [L *arra, arrha* — more at EARNEST] **:** EARNEST MONEY — **ar·rhal** \ˈarəl\ *adj*

ar·rhe·nath·er·um \ˌarəˈnathərəm\ *n, cap* [NL, fr. Gk *arrhen-, arrhēn* male + *ather-, athēr* awn; fr. the awned staminate lemma; akin to Skt *arṣati* it flows, *ṛṣabha* bull, L *ros* dew — more at RORIC] **:** a genus of Eurasiatic grasses that have 2-flowered spikelets, the first floret staminate and awned from the back and are naturalized in cooler parts of No. America — see TALL OAT GRASS

ar·rhe·nite \ˈarəˌnīt\ *n* -s [Sw or G *arrhenit,* fr. Col. Carl A. *Arrhenius,* 19th cent. Swedish army officer + Sw or G *-it* -ite] **:** an altered variety of fergusonite

ar·rhe·no·blas·to·ma \ˌarəˌnōˌblaˈstōmə, əˌrē,-\ *n, pl* **arrhenoblastomas** *also* **arrhenoblasto·ma·ta** \-məd·ə\ [NL, fr. Gk *arrhen-, arrhēn* male + NL *-o-* + *blastoma*] **:** a sometimes malignant tumor of the ovary that by the secretion of male hormone induces development of secondary male characteristics

ar·rhe·no·kar·y·ot·ic \ˌarəˌnōˌkarēˈäd·ik, əˌrē,-\ *adj* [Gk *arrhen-, arrhēn* male + E *-o-* + *kary-* + *-otic*] **:** of or relating to a blastomere possessing only chromosomes of paternal origin

ar·rhe·not·o·kous *also* **ar·re·not·o·kous** \ˌarəˈnäd·əkəs\ *adj* [Gk *arrhenotokos* bearing male children] **:** of, relating to, or involving arrhenotoky

ar·rhe·not·o·ky *also* **ar·re·not·o·ky** \ˌ==ˈnäd·əkē\ *n* -ES [LGk *arrhenotokia* act of bearing male children, fr. Gk *arrhenotokos* bearing male children (fr. *arrhenotokein* to bear male children, fr. *arrhen-, arrhēn* male + *tokein* to bear) + *-ia* -y] **:** parthenogenesis in which only male offspring are produced — compare THELYTOKY

ar·rho·stia \əˈrōstēə\ *n* -s [NL, fr. Gk *arrhōstia* sickness, weakness, fr. *arrhōstos* sickly, weak (fr. *a-* ²a- + *-rhōstos,* fr. *rhōsis* strength) + *-ia* -y] **:** an evolutionary product or trend that appears to be more or less pathological (as the immense size attained by certain dinosaurs) — **ar·rhos·tic** \əˈrästik\ *adj*

ar·rhyth·mia *also* **ar·ryth·mia** \āˈrithmēə, aˈr- *also* -th-\ *n* -s [NL, fr. Gk, lack of rhythm, fr. *arrhythmos* unrhythmical (fr. *a-* ²a- + *rhythmos* rhythm) + *-ia* — more at RHYTHM] **:** an alteration in the rhythm of the heartbeat either in time or force that is of functional or organic origin — compare BRADYCARDIA, TACHYCARDIA; FIBRILLATION

ar·rhyth·mic \(ˈ)=ˈ=mik\ *or* **ar·rhyth·mi·cal** \-məkəl\ *adj* [Gk *arrhythmos* + E *-ic, -ical*] **:** lacking rhythm or regularity — **ar·rhyth·mi·cal·ly** \-mək(ə)lē\ *adv*

ar·ric·cio \əˈrē(ˌ)chō\ *n* -s [It, fr. *arricciare* to bristle up, curl, groove (a plastered wall), fr. *a-* (fr. L *ad-*) + *riccio* hedgehog, curl, fr. L *ericius* hedgehog — more at URCHIN] **:** the rough first coat of plaster in fresco painting — compare INTONACO

ar·ride \əˈrīd, aˈ-\ *vt* -ED/-ING/-S [L *arridēre,* fr. *ad-* + *ridēre* to laugh — more at RIDICULOUS] **1** *obs* **:** to smile or laugh at **2 :** PLEASE, GRATIFY, DELIGHT ⟨I . . . was greatly *arrided* . . . by what I saw —William Hardman⟩ **syn** see PLEASE

ar·ridge \ˈarij\ *n* -s [alter. (influenced by *ridge*) of *arris*] *dial Brit* **:** ARRIS

ar·rie \ˈarē\ *n* -s [prob. native name in the Aleutians] **:** MURRE

ar·rière–ban \ˈarēˌerˈbän\ *n* -s [F, fr. OF *arriereban,* alter. (influenced by *ariere, arriere* behind) of *herban* proclamation to serve in the army, of Gmc origin; akin to OHG *heri* army and to OHG *ban* proclamation — more at HARRY, BAN] **1 :** a proclamation of a king (as of France) calling to arms his immediate feudatories and their vassals **2 :** the body of vassals summoned to military service

ar·ri·ere fee *or* **arriere fief** \ˈarēˌer-\ *n* [MF *arriere fie, arriere fief,* fr. OF *arierefief,* fr. *ariere, arriere* behind + *fief* fee — more at ARREAR, FEE] **:** a fee or fief dependent on a fee **:** a fee held of a feudatory **:** SUBFIEF

arrière–pen·sée \-ˌpäⁿˈsā\ *n* -s [F, fr. MF *arriere pensee,* fr. *arriere* behind + *pensee* thought, fr. fem. of *pensé,* past par of *penser* to think — more at PENSIVE] **:** an undisclosed thought or intention **:** mental reservation

arrière–vous·sure \-ˌvüˈsü(ə)r\ *n* -s [F, lit., rear arching, fr. *arrière* rear, behind + *voussure* arching, bend of an arch, fr. (assumed) VL *volsura,* fr. *volsus* (past part. of L *volvere* to roll) + L *-ura* -ure — more at VOLUBLE] **1 :** an inner or rear arch in a thick wall that carries the inner part of that wall; *esp* **:** such an arch over a door or window frame **2 :** a relieving arch behind the face of a wall

ar·rie·ro \ˌarēˈe(ˌ)rō\ *n* -s [Sp, fr. *arre* get up!, giddap!] **:** MULETEER

ar·rie·ros \-ōz, -ōs\ *n pl* [MexSp (*baile de los*) *arrieros* the muleteers' dance] **:** Mexican men's fiesta dances that follow two local patterns, one portraying a muleteers' camp and the other including votive flagellation and hymns — compare PENITENTE

ar·ris *also* **ar·is** \ˈarəs *also* ˈer-\ *n, pl* **arris** *or* **arrises** *also* **aris** *or* **arises** [prob. modif. of MF *areste* arris, fishbone, beard of grain, fr. LL *arista* fishbone, fr. L, beard of grain] **:** the sharp edge or salient angle formed by the meeting of two surfaces whether plane or curved — used esp. of the edges in moldings and of the raised edges separating the flutings in a Doric column

arris fillet *n* **:** a triangular piece of wood used to raise the slates of a roof against a chimney or wall to shed the rain

arris gutter *n* **:** a V-shaped gutter at the eaves of a building

ar·rish \ˈarish\ *n* -ES [alter. of *eddish*] **1** *dial Eng* **:** the stubble of wheat or grass **2** *dial Eng* **:** STUBBLE FIELD

arris rail *n* **:** a rail (as of wood) of triangular section

ar·ris·ways \ˈarəsˌwāz\ *also* **ar·ris·wise** \-wīz\ *adv* **:** with the angle or edge presented

ar·riv·al \əˈrīvəl\ *n* -s [ME *arrivaille,* fr. MF, fr. *ariver*] **1 :** the act of arriving: as **a :** the act of reaching a destination or of coming to the end of a journey ⟨bad weather delayed our ~⟩ **b :** the act of making an appearance or of coming upon the scene ⟨his ~ brought complete silence to the room⟩ **c :** the attainment or reaching of an end, a state of mind, or a position esp. by conscious effort ⟨his ~ at this conclusion was the result of much thought⟩ **d :** the attainment of or coming to a stage of development esp. by the passage of time ⟨on his ~ at thirty he began to work harder⟩ **2 :** one that is arriving or has arrived ⟨the beach was crowded with recent ~s⟩

arrival draft *n* **:** a draft drawn in foreign trade payable upon receipt of the goods by the buyer

ar·riv·ance \-vən(t)s\ *n* -s [¹*arrive* + *-ance* (as in *entrance*)] *now dial* **:** ARRIVAL

¹ar·rive \əˈrīv\ *vb* -ED/-ING/-S [ME *ariven,* fr. OF *ariver,* fr. (assumed) VL *arripare* to land, come to shore, fr. L *ad-* + (assumed) VL *-ripare* (fr. L *ripa* bank, shore) — more at RIVE] *vi* **1 a :** to reach a destination **:** come to the end of a journey ⟨they *arrived* by plane at midnight⟩ **b :** to make an appearance **:** come upon the scene ⟨the crowd became silent when the officers *arrived*⟩ **2 a :** to gain or achieve an end esp. by conscious effort **:** attain or reach a state of mind or a position — used with *at* ⟨many attempts to ~ at an understanding —C.L.Jones⟩ **b :** to reach or come to a stage of development esp. by the passage of time **:** ATTAIN — used with *at* ⟨moved out to the suburb last year when their eldest child was *arriving* at school age —F.L.Allen⟩ **3 a** *archaic* **:** to come to pass **:** HAPPEN, OCCUR ⟨any such event may ~ to a woman —Henry Fielding⟩ **b :** to be near or at hand in time **:** COME ⟨the time to go finally *arrived*⟩ **4 :** to achieve success or gain recognition **:** be successful ⟨believed that a man who has not arrived by forty will never ~ —Catherine D. Bowen⟩ ~ *vt* **1** *obs* **:** to cause to arrive **:** BRING, CONVEY ⟨and made the sea-trod ship ~ them near —George Chapman⟩ **2** *archaic* **:** to come to **:** REACH ⟨ere he ~ the happy isle —John Milton⟩

²ar·ri·vé \ˌa(ˌ)rēˈvā\ *n* -s [F, fr. past part. of *arriver* to arrive, fr. OF *ariver*] **:** one who has arrived; *specif* **:** one who has risen rapidly to success, power, or fame ⟨the upstart or ~ who has made his fortune in trade —*Fortnightly Rev.*⟩

ar·riv·er \əˈrīvə(r)\ *n* -s **:** one that arrives

ar·ri·vism \ˌa(ˌ)rēˈvēzəm, -viz-\ *n* -s [F *arrivisme,* fr. *arriviste* + *-isme* -ism] **:** the practice or conduct of an arriviste ⟨middle-class ~⟩

ar·ri·viste *also* **ar·ri·vist** \ˌa(ˌ)rēˈvēst, -vist\ *n* -s [F *arriviste,* fr. *arriver* + *-iste* -ist] **:** one who employs any means however questionable or unscrupulous to achieve success **:** an aggressive pushing person **:** PARVENU, UPSTART ⟨an impoverished family of high breeding and training sneers self-consolingly at vulgar ~s —John Hersey⟩

ar·ro·ba \əˈrōbə\ *n* -s [Sp & Pg, fr. Ar *ar-rub'* the quarter (of the weight *al-qinṭār*)] **:** a unit of weight: **a :** an old Spanish unit equal to about 25 pounds now used locally in certain Spanish-American countries **b :** an old Portuguese unit equal to about 32 pounds now used locally in Brazil

ar·ro·gance \ˈarəgən(t)s *also* ˈer- *sometimes* -rē- *or* -ri-\ *n* -s [ME *arrogaunce,* fr. MF *arrogance,* fr. L *arrogantia,* fr. *arrogant-, arrogans* + *-ia* -y] **:** a genuine or assumed feeling of superiority that shows itself in an overbearing manner or attitude or in excessive claims of position, dignity, or power or that unduly exalts one's own worth or importance **:** overbearing pride ⟨all his words and actions had an irritating ~; he was always right —O.E.Rölvaag⟩

ar·ro·gan·cy \-gənsē, -si\ *n* -ES [L *arrogantia* — more at ARROGANCE] **:** the quality or state of being arrogant

ar·ro·gant \-gənt\ *adj* [ME, fr. L *arrogant-, arrogans,* pres. part. of *arrogare*] **1 :** having a feeling of superiority that shows or is inclined to show itself in an overbearing attitude or in claiming more consideration than is due to one's position, dignity, or power **:** exaggerating or disposed to exaggerate one's own worth or importance **:** overbearingly haughty ⟨he was ~, overbearing, conceited, and passionate — without any rank which could excuse pride —Anthony Trollope⟩ **2 :** proceeding from or characterized by arrogance ⟨his administration had been ~ and despotic —Willa Cather⟩ **syn** see PROUD

ar·ro·gant·ly *adv* **:** in an arrogant manner

ar·ro·gant·ness *n* -ES **:** ARROGANCE

ar·ro·gate \-rəˌgāt, *usu* -ād·+V\ *vt* -ED/-ING/-S [L *arrogatus,* past part. of *arrogare* to appropriate to oneself, fr. *ad-* + *rogare* to ask — more at RIGHT] **1 a :** to claim or seize as one's right (something one is not entitled to) **:** APPROPRIATE ⟨the sweeping powers the federal government would ~ . . . over a domain that had always hitherto been under the states —T.H.White⟩ **b :** to make undue claims to the possession of **:** maintain without reason that one has **:** ASSUME ⟨the unwarranted importance *arrogated* to themselves by public men —Kenneth Roberts⟩ **2 :** to lay claim to on behalf of another **:** ASCRIBE, ATTRIBUTE ⟨a proposal which would have *arrogated* to the four general staff sections all the functions of a headquarters⟩ **3 :** to adopt (as a person sui juris and independent) in the form and under the special circumstances permitted under the Roman law — see ARROGATION; compare POTESTAS **syn** see APPROPRIATE

ar·ro·ga·tion \ˌ==ˈgāshən\ *n* -s [L *arrogation-, arrogatio,* fr. *arrogatus* + *-ion-, -io* -ion] **1 :** the act of arrogating or the state of being arrogated ⟨an ~ by Congress of a role that belongs to the courts —*New Republic*⟩ **2** *Roman law* **:** the adoption of a person sui juris and independent, the person adopted losing his independence and together with his children and his property becoming subject to the paternal power of the adopting father

ar·ro·ja·dite \ˌarəˈjäˌdīt\ *n* -s [Pg *arrojadita,* fr. Miguel *Arrojado* Lisbôa 20th cent. Brazilian geologist + Pg *-ita* -ite] **:** a mineral $Na_2(Fe,Mn)_5(PO_4)_4$ consisting of a phosphate of sodium, iron, and manganese occurring in Brazil as dark green monoclinic masses

ar·ron·di \ˌa,rōⁿˈdē\ *adj* [F, past part. of *arrondir*] **:** CURVED, ROUNDED ⟨~ arm posture or leg movement in ballet dancing⟩

ar·ron·disse·ment \əˈrändəsmənt, ˌaranˈdēsmənt, ˌa'rändē-ˌsmäⁿ, *F* ärōⁿdēsmäⁿ\ *n, pl* **arrondissements** \-ənts, -äⁿz, *F* -äⁿ\ [F, fr. MF, action of making round, fr. *arrondiss-* (stem of *arrondir* to make round, fr. OF *arondir, areondir,* fr. *a-* — fr. L *ad-* — + *-rondir, -reondir,* fr. *reont, roont* round) + connective *-e-* + MF *-ment* — more at ROUND] **1 :** the largest administrative subdivision of a French department **2 :** a ward or administrative district of some large cities of France ⟨Paris is subdivided into 20 ~s⟩

¹ar·row \ˈa(ˌ)rō, ˈarə *also* ˈe-; *often* -ˌrəw+V\ *n* -s *often attrib* [ME *arewe, arwe,* fr. OE *arewe, earh*; akin to ON *ǫr* arrow, Goth *arhwazna,* L *arcus* bow, arc] **1 :** a missile weapon shot from a bow and usu. consisting of a straight slender shaft that has a point or sharp head of stone or metal, feathers or vanes fastened near the butt, and a nock to be fitted to a bowstring **2 :** something felt to resemble an arrow esp. in shape: as **a :** a mark (as on a map or signboard) to indicate direction **b :** the inflorescence of the sugarcane or the shoot that develops into the inflorescence **c :** a surveyor's marking pin used to mark the ground at each chain's length — called also *chain pin*

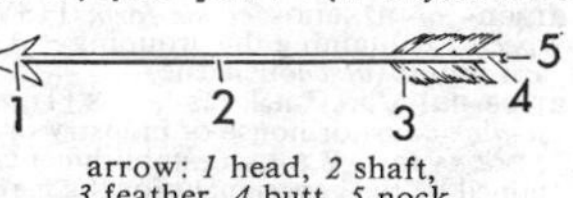

arrow: *1* head, *2* shaft, *3* feather, *4* butt, *5* nock

²arrow \"\ *vi* -ED/-ING/-S **1 :** to move fast and straight like an arrow in flight **:** DART ⟨the wild geese could not ~ through the storm —S.V.Benét⟩ **2** *of sugarcane* **:** to develop arrows **:** FLOWER

³arrow \ˈarə\ *adj* [by folk etymology fr. *e'er a*] *dial Eng* **:** ever a

arrow arum *n* **:** a plant of the genus *Peltandra* (as *P. virginica*)

arrow–back chair *n* **:** a chair having a back with vertical balusters that are broadened and flattened near one end

arrow crab *n* **:** a brilliantly colored crab (*Stenorhynchus seticornis*) that is widely distributed in the southern Atlantic

ar·rowed \ˈa(ˌ)rōd, ˈe-, -ˌrəd\ *adj* **:** shaped like or furnished with an arrow

arrow grass *n* [so called fr. the shape of the burst capsules] **1 :** a plant of the genus *Triglochin*; *esp* **:** an herb (*T. maritima*) that sometimes poisons livestock **2 :** any of several grasses of the genus *Aristida* (as *A. purpurascens*) **3 :** PORCUPINE GRASS 1

arrow–grass family *n* **:** SCHEUCHZERIACEAE

arrow·head \ˈ=(ˌ)=+ˌ=\ *n* [ME *arewe hed,* fr. *arewe* arrow + *hed* head] **1 :** the striking end of an arrow usu. separate from the shaft, shaped like a thin wedge, and having a barb or barbs **2 :** something resembling an arrowhead: as **a :** a stroke or mark (as on a drawing) to limit a dimension line or indicate a note **b :** the dart of an egg-and-dart molding **c :** a triangular decoration or reinforcement consisting of intercrossed satin stitches used on tailored garments **3 :** a plant of the genus *Sagittaria*

arrowhead 2c

arrow horn *n* **:** a wedge usu. of horn or fiber set in the butt of an arrow shaft and containing a nock
arrow·leaf \ˈ=(,)=+,=\ *n* **:** ARROWHEAD 3
arrow·plate \ˈ"+,=\ *n* **:** an inlaid strip (as of ivory) set in a bow where the arrow crosses it when shot or released and designed to prevent wear
arrow·point \ˈ"+,=\ *n* **:** a stone arrowhead
arrow rest *n* **:** a shoulder of horn or metal used on some bows to support the arrow
arrow·root \ˈ=(,)=+,=\ *n* [prob. so called fr. its use by American Indians to heal wounds from poisoned arrows] **1 a :** a tropical American plant of the genus *Maranta* (as the widely cultivated *M. arundinacea*) **b :** a plant or root yielding arrowroot starch **2 a :** a nutritive starch obtained from the rootstock of the arrowroot (*M. arundinacea*) that is used esp. in foods prepared for children and invalids **b :** any of various starches used as substitutes for arrowroot and obtained from other plants of the genus *Maranta* or from plants of other genera (as *Zamia, Curcuma, Tacca, Canna,* and *Musa*) — see PORTLAND ARROWROOT
arrowroot family *n* **:** MARANTACEAE
arrow·stone \ˈ=(,)=+,=\ *n* **:** BELEMNITE
arrow straightener *n* **:** an instrument used by the Eskimo consisting of a piece of bone, horn, ivory, or wood having at one end a hole through which a heated shaft (as of an arrow) is drawn for straightening — compare BATON 5
arrow–toothed halibut \ˈ=(,)=,tütht- *sometimes* -ütthd-\ *or* **arrowtooth halibut** *or* **arrowtooth sole** *n* **:** a flatfish (*Atheresthes stomias*) of the northern Pacific coasts of America
arrow·weed \ˈ=(,)=+,=\ *n* **:** ARROWWOOD 1b
arrow·wood \ˈ"+,=\ *n* **1 :** any of several shrubs having tough pliant shoots formerly used to make arrows: as **a :** any of various plants of the genus *Viburnum* (as *V. dentatum*) **b :** a low composite shrub (*Pluchea sericea*) of the southwestern U.S. and Mexico **c :** OCEAN SPRAY **d :** ALDER BUCKTHORN **2 :** BURROBRUSH
arrow·worm \ˈ"+,=\ *n* **:** a worm of the class Chaetognatha — see SAGITTA

arrowworm: *1* spines, *2* mouth, *3* jaws, *4* alimentary canal, *5* ventral ganglion, *6* ovary, *7* oviduct, *8* anus, *9* vas deferens, *10* seminal vesicle, *11* fins, *12* testis

ar·rowy \ˈarəwē, ˈer-, -wi\ *adj* **1 :** consisting of or full of arrows **2 :** like an arrow or arrows (as in appearance, motion, or effect) **:** SWIFT, DARTING, PIERCING ⟨that frail ~ figure was invariably clothed in black —Norman Douglas⟩ ⟨fish darting in an ~ rush⟩ ⟨deflates tower and university with one ~ pun —Florence B.Lennon⟩
ar·royo \əˈrȯi(,)yə, -rō(,)yō, -rȯi(,)(y)ō\ *also* **ar·roya** \-rȯi-(y)ə\ *n* -s [Sp *arroyo*, prob. of non-IE origin; akin to the source of L *arrugia* gallery in a mine] **1 :** BROOK, CREEK, STREAM **:** WATERCOURSE ⟨around all of these lakes are extensive flood lands, and stemming from each are brooks or ~s which drain into other lakes —A.R.Holmberg⟩ **2 :** a water-carved gully or channel **:** DRY WASH, RAVINE ⟨he rode out of a deep ~ between bare mountainsides —S.H.Adams⟩
arroyo grape *n* **:** CHICKEN GRAPE
arroyo willow *n* **:** a shrubby willow (*Salix lasiolepis*) of the western U.S.
arroz \äˈrōth, -ōs\ *n* [Sp, fr. Ar *ar-ruzz* the rice] **:** RICE
arroz con po·llo \-ōth(,)kōnˈpōl(,)yō, -ō(s)(,)kōnˈpō(,)yō\ *n* [Sp, lit., rice with chicken] **:** rice and chicken cooked together and seasoned usu. with saffron, garlic, and other condiments
arrs *pl of* ARR
arrythmia *var of* ARRHYTHMIA
ars *pl of* AR
ars- *comb form* [ISV, fr. ¹*arsenic*] **:** arsenic ⟨*arsine*⟩ ⟨*arsphenamine*⟩
ars *abbr* arsenal
¹**ar·sac·id** \ärˈsasəd, ˈärsəs-\ *n, pl* **arsacids** \-dz\ *or* **arsacidae** \ärˈsasə,dē\ *or* **arsac·ides** \ärˈsasədz; ˈärsəsədz, -,sīdz\ *usu cap* [L *Arsacides*, fr. *Arsaces* I *fl ab* 250 B.C. king of Parthia, founder of the dynasty (fr. Gk *Arsakēs*) + L *-ides* (patronymic suffix) — more at -IDAE] **:** a member of a dynasty of Parthian rulers established in revolt against the Seleucids about 250 B.C. and overthrown by the Persian Sassanids A.D. 226
²**arsacid** \(ˈ)ärˈsasəd, ˈärsəs-\ *adj, usu cap* **:** of or relating to the empire of the Arsacids
ars·anil·ic acid \ˌärsəˈnilik-\ *n* [*ars-* + *aniline* + *-ic*] **:** any of three poisonous crystalline isomeric acids $NH_2C_6H_4AsO(OH)_2$; amino-benzene-arsonic acid; *esp* **:** the para isomer analogous to sulfanilic acid used in making organic arsenical drugs
ars an·ti·qua \ˈär,sanˈtēkwə, -r,za-\ *n* [ML, old art] **:** the style of musical composition before about 1300 and esp. of the 13th century — contrasted with *ars nova*
ars ar·ti·um \ˈärˈsärd-ēəm, ˈärs-ˈär-, (ˈ)ärˈzärshēəm\ *n* [ML, lit., art of arts] **:** LOGIC 1
¹**arse** *var of* ASS
²**arse** \ˈärs, ˈäs\ *n* -s [¹*arse*] **:** the bottom end of a wooden pulley block in which is the score for the rope strap
ar·se·dine \ˈärsə,dēn, -dīn\ *n* -s [ME *assady, assadyn, assaden*] **:** an alloy of copper and zinc made into very thin sheets like gold leaf and used in decoration
ar·sem furnace \ˈärsəm,-\ *n, usu cap A* [after William C. *Arsem b*1880, Am. chemical engineer] **:** an electric furnace usu. of the vacuum type heated by electrical resistance
arsen- *or* **arseno-** *comb form* [ISV, fr. *arsenic*] **:** arsenic; *specif* **:** containing the grouping —As=As— analogous to the azo group ⟨*arsenobenzene*⟩
ar·se·nal \ˈärs(ᵊ)nəl, ˈäs-\ *n* -s [It *arsenale*, modif. of Ar *dār ṣinā'ah* court or house of industry or manufacture] **1** *archaic* **:** DOCKYARD **2 a :** an establishment often operated and maintained by the government for the manufacture, repair, storage, or issue of arms and other military equipment **b :** a storehouse or source of supply for arms, ammunition, or other military equipment ⟨we must be the great ~ of democracy —F.D. Roosevelt⟩ **c :** a stock or collection of weapons ⟨Wild Bill added one item to his usual ~ of two revolvers and bowie knife —S.H.Holbrook⟩ **3 :** STORE, STOREHOUSE **:** SUPPLY, REPERTORY ⟨this was the ~ of learning from which he drew —Van Wyck Brooks⟩ ⟨will have occasion to use her full ~ of charm, clear thinking, and equanimity —Robert Rice⟩
ar·se·nate \ˈärs(ᵊ)nət, ˈäs-, -sᵊn,āt, *usu* -d·+V\ *n* -s [earlier *arseniate*, prob. fr. F *arséniate*, fr. *arsenic* + *-ate*] **:** a salt or ester of an arsenic acid
ar·se·nian \ärˈsēnēən, -nyən\ *adj* **:** containing arsenic
¹**ar·se·nic** \ˈärs(ᵊ)nik, ˈäs-, -ēk — see ²ARSENIC\ *n* -s [ME *arsenic, arsenicum*, fr. MF & L; MF *arsenic*, fr. L *arsenicum*, fr. Gk *arsenikon, arrhenikon* yellow orpiment, by folk etymology (influence of Gk *arsenikos, arrhenikos* male, virile, fr. *arsen-, arrhen-, arsēn, arrhēn* male + *-ikos* -ic) fr. Syr *zarnīg*, of Iranian origin; akin to Av *zaranya* gold, OPer *daraniya*; akin to Skt *hiraṇya* gold, *hari* yellowish — more at ARRHENATHERUM, YELLOW] **1 :** a trivalent and pentavalent metalloid element commonly metallic steel-gray, crystalline, and brittle but known also in other forms (as black amorphous and yellow crystalline forms), that occurs in the free state (as in tarnished granular or kidney-shaped masses having a sp. gr. of 5.73) and also combined in minerals (as arsenopyrite, orpiment, realgar, arsenolite) and in ores of other metals (as copper, gold) from which it is usu. separated as a by-product in the form of arsenic trioxide, and that is used in small amounts in alloys (as an alloy with lead for shot) and in the form of its compounds chiefly as poisons (as insecticides), in pharmaceutical preparations, and in glass — symbol *As;* see ELEMENT table **2 :** ARSENIC TRIOXIDE — used chiefly commercially
²**ar·sen·ic** \(ˈ)ärˈsenik, (ˈ)äˈs-, -ēk; *in names of compounds below beginning with "arsenic", the usu pronunc in "arsenic acid" is that found here, the usu pronunc in other cases is that found at* ¹ARSENIC\ *adj* **:** of, relating to, or containing arsenic — used esp. of compounds in which this element is pentavalent
arsenic acid *n* **1 :** any of three acids derived from arsenic pentoxide analogous to the phosphoric acids; *esp* **:** the ortho acid obtained as the white crystalline hemihydrate $H_3AsO_4.½H_2O$ **2 :** ARSENIC PENTOXIDE — not used scientifically
¹**ar·sen·i·cal** \(ˈ)ärˈsenəkəl, (ˈ)äˈ-, -ēk-\ *adj* [¹*arsenic* + *-al*] **:** of, relating to, or containing arsenic ⟨~ vapor⟩ ⟨~ wallpapers⟩
²**arsenical** \"\ *n* -s **:** a compound or preparation containing arsenic
arsenical antimony *n* **:** ALLEMONTITE
ar·sen·i·cal·ism \=ˈ===,lizəm\ *n* -s **:** chronic arsenic poisoning
arsenical pyrites *n* **:** ARSENOPYRITE
arsenic antidote *n* **:** a preparation of ferric hydroxide and magnesia that envelops or occludes arsenic thus rendering it inert
ar·sen·i·cate \ärˈsenə,kāt\ *vt* -ED/-ING/-S **:** to combine, treat, or impregnate with arsenic
arsenic bloom *n* **:** ARSENOLITE
arsenic disulfide *or* **arsenic monosulfide** *n* **:** an orange, red, or black compound As_4S_4, As_2S_2, or AsS occurring native as realgar, also prepared artificially, and used esp. in fireworks and formerly as a pigment
arsenic oxide *n* **:** an oxide of arsenic: as **a :** ARSENIC TRIOXIDE **b :** ARSENIC PENTOXIDE
arsenic pentoxide *n* **:** a white amorphous deliquescent compound As_2O_5 or As_4O_{10} usu. made by oxidizing arsenic trioxide and used in making arsenates
arsenic trichloride *n* **:** a colorless oily liquid $AsCl_3$ obtained by burning arsenic in chlorine and used in making organic arsenicals and in ceramics
arsenic trioxide *n* **:** a white or transparent glassy extremely poisonous compound As_2O_3 or As_4O_6 that occurs naturally as arsenolite and claudetite, that is obtained usu. from the flue dusts from smelters roasting arsenic-containing ores, and that is used esp. as a decolorizing agent chiefly in making insecticides, weed killers, pigments, and glass — called also *arsenious oxide, white arsenic*
arsenic trisulfide *n* **:** a yellow compound As_2S_3 or As_4S_6 occurring native as orpiment, also prepared artificially, and used in fireworks and as a pigment — called also *king's yellow*
ar·se·nide \ˈärsᵊn,īd\ *n* -s [F, fr. *arsen-* + *-ide*] **:** a binary compound of arsenic with a more positive element
ar·se·nif·er·ous \ˌärsᵊnˈif(ə)rəs\ *adj* [*arsen-* + *-i-* + *-ferous*] **:** yielding arsenic
ar·se·ni·llo \ˌärsᵊnˈē(,)(y)ō\ *n* -s [AmerSp] **:** powdered or granulated atacamite
ar·se·ni·o·ple·ite \ärˈsēnē(,)ōˈplē,īt\ *n* -s [ISV *arsenio-* (fr. *arsenic*) + Gk *pleiōn* more + ISV *-ite;* orig. formed as G *arseniopleit*] **:** a mineral consisting of a basic arsenate of manganese, calcium, iron, and other metals occurring in brownish red cleavable masses
ar·se·ni·o·sid·er·ite \-ˈsidə,rīt\ *n* -s [F *arsénio-sidérite*, fr. *arsénio-* + *sidérite* siderite, fr. G *siderit*] **:** a mineral $Ca_3Fe_4(AsO_4)_4(OH)_{4}.4H_2O$ consisting of a basic iron calcium arsenate occurring as yellowish brown concretions
ar·se·ni·ous \(ˈ)ärˈsēnēəs, (ˈ)äˈs- *also* -nyəs\ *also* **ar·se·nous** \ˈ=s(ᵊ)nəs\ *adj* [F *arsénieux*, fr. *arsenic* + *-eux* -ous] **:** of, relating to, or containing arsenic — used esp. of compounds in which this element is trivalent
arsenious acid *n* **1 :** an acid (as ortho-arsenious acid H_3AsO_3) derived from arsenic trioxide known only in solution and esp. in the form of salts (as sodium arsenite) **2 :** ARSENIC TRIOXIDE
arsenious anhydride *or* **arsenious oxide** *n* **:** ARSENIC TRIOXIDE
ar·se·nite \ˈärsə,nīt\ *n* -s [F *arsénite*, fr. *arsén-* arsen- + *-ite*] **:** a salt or ester of an arsenious acid
ar·se·ni·um \ärˈsēnēəm\ *n* -s [NL, fr. *arsen-* + *-ium*] **:** ARSENIC
ar·sen·iu·ret·ted *or* **ar·sen·iu·ret·ed** \ärˈsenyə,red·əd, -sēn-\ *adj* [*arseniuret*, old name for *arsenide* (fr. F *arséniure*, fr. *arsenic* + *-ure* -uret) + *-ed*] **:** combined with arsenic
arseniuretted hydrogen *n* **:** ARSINE 1
arseno- — see ARSEN-
ar·se·no·ben·zene \ˌärs(ᵊ)nō, ärˌsenō+\ *n* [*arsen-* + *benzene*] **:** a pale yellow crystalline compound C_6H_5As: AsC_6H_5, derivatives of which are used in medicine — see ARSPHENAMINE
ar·se·no·bis·mite \"+\ *n* -s [*arsen-* + *bismite*] **:** a mineral consisting of a hydrous bismuth arsenate occurring in yellowish green aggregates
ar·se·no·cla·site \"+ˈklā,sīt, -,zīt\ *n* -s [ISV *arsen-* + Gk *klasis* breaking, fracture + ISV *-ite;* orig. formed as Sw or G *arsenoklasit*] **:** a mineral $Mn_5AsO_4(OH)_4$ consisting of a basic manganese arsenate
ar·sen·o·lite \ärˈsenᵊl,īt\ *n* -s [*arsen-* + *-lite*] **:** a mineral As_2O_3 consisting of a native arsenic trioxide usu. occurring as a white bloom or crust — compare CLAUDETITE
ar·se·no·py·rite \ˌärs(ᵊ)nō, ärˌsenō+\ *n* -s [*arsen-* + *pyrite*] **:** a mineral FeAsS consisting of a hard tin-white or grayish iron sulfarsenide occurring in prismatic orthorhombic crystals or in masses or grains, found chiefly in crystalline rocks, and constituting the principal ore of arsenic (hardness 5.5–6, sp. gr. 5.9–6.2) — called also *arsenical pyrites, mispickel*
ar·se·no·so \ˌärsᵊnˈō(,)sō\ *adj* [*arsenoso-*] **:** relating to or containing the radical —AsO
arsenoso- \"\ *comb form* [ISV, fr. *arsen-* + *-oso-* (as in *ferroso-*)] **:** containing the univalent radical —AsO composed of arsenic and oxygen ⟨*arsenoso*phenol⟩
ar·se·no·therapy \ˌärs(ᵊ)nō, ärˌsenō+\ *n* -ES [ISV *arsen-* + *therapy*] **:** treatment of disease with any form of arsenic
ar·se·nous *var of* ARSENIOUS
ar·sen·oxide \ˌärsᵊn+\ *n* [ISV *arsen-* + *oxide*] **:** an organic arsenoso compound RAsO; *specif* **:** oxophenarsine hydrochloride — used chiefly in pharmaceutical names
arses *pl of* ARSIS *or of* ARSE
arse·smart \ˈ=,= — see ASS\ *n* -s [*arse* + *smart*, v.] *dial* **:** a plant of the genus *Polygonum*; *esp* **:** SMARTWEED
ar·shin *or* **ar·shine** *or* **ar·chine** \ärˈshēn\ *n* -s [Russ, of Turkic origin; akin to Turk *arşın*, Kazan Tatar *aršyn*, Jagatai *aršun*] **:** a Russian unit of length equal to 28 inches
ar·sine \ärˈsēn, ˈär,s-\ *n* -s [ISV *ars-* + *-ine*] **1 :** a colorless extremely poisonous gas AsH_3 having an odor like garlic, burning with a bluish flame, and made by reaction of an arsenide (as zinc arsenide) with an acid and in other ways — see MARSH TEST **2 :** any of a class of very poisonous organic compounds derived from arsine that are analogous to the amines and phosphines — compare DIPHENYLCHLOROARSINE, LEWISITE
ar·sin·ic acid \(ˈ)ärˈsinik-\ *n* [ISV *arsine* + *-ic*] **1 :** any of a series of organic acids (as cacodylic acid) having the general formula RR'AsOOH and obtainable by oxidizing disubstituted organic arsines [as dimethyl-arsine $(CH_3)_2AsH$] **2 :** ARSONIC ACID 1
arsino- *comb form* [ISV, fr. *arsine* + *-o-*] **:** arsine **:** containing the univalent radical AsH_2
ar·si·noi·the·ri·um \ˌärsə,nȯiˈthirēəm\ *n, cap* [NL, irreg. fr. *Arsinoë* II †271B.C. queen of Egypt + NL *-therium*] **:** a genus of extinct mammals (order Embrithopoda) of the Oligocene of Egypt having limbs resembling those of the elephant and a pair of large horns
ar·sis \ˈärsəs, ˈäs-\ *n, pl* **ar·ses** \-,sēz\ [LL & Gk; LL, accented syllable of a metrical foot, fr. Gk, unaccented syllable of a metrical foot, lifting of the foot in beating time, irreg. fr. *aeirein* to lift + *-sis* — more at AORTA] **1 a :** the lighter or shorter part of a poetic foot esp. in quantitative verse **b :** the accented or longer part of a poetic foot esp. in accentual verse **2 :** the weak or unaccented part of a musical measure **:** UPBEAT — compare THESIS
ar·sle \ˈärsəl\ *vi* -ED/-ING/-S [¹*arse* + *-le*] *dial* **:** to move backward
ars mag·na \ˈärs·ˈmägnə, ˈärz-, -ag-\ *n, usu cap A&M* [ML, lit., great art] **:** a logistic system designed to function as a universal science that would be basic to all others; *specif* **:** the combinative method orig. designed by Raymond Lully
ars no·va \-ˈnōvə\ *n* [ML, new art] **:** the style of musical composition of the late middle ages and esp. of the 14th century — contrasted with *ars antiqua*
ar·so·ite \ˈär(,)sō,īt\ *n* -s [G *arsoit*, fr. *Arso*, town on the island of Ischia, Italy + G *-it* -ite] **:** a dark gray porous rock consisting of trachyandesite containing phenocrysts of andesine, sanidine, diopside, and a little olivine in a trachytic groundmass of sanidine, a little oligoclase, much diopside, and magnetite
arson- *or* **arsono-** *comb form* [ISV, fr. *arsonic*] **:** containing the radical —AsO(OH)₂ characteristic of the arsonic acids ⟨*arsonate*⟩ ⟨*arsono*acetic acid⟩
ar·son \ˈärsᵊn, ˈäs-\ *n* -s [obs. F, fr. OF, fr. *ars*, past part. of *ardre* to burn, fr. L *ardēre* — more at ARDOR] **:** the willful and malicious burning of or attempt to burn any building, structure, or property of another (as a house, a church, or a boat) or of one's own usu. with criminal or fraudulent intent
¹**ar·so·nate** \ˈärsᵊn,āt, -ət\ *n* -s [*arsonic* + *-ate*] **:** a salt or ester of an arsonic acid
²**arsonate** \-,āt\ *vt* -ED/-ING/-S [*arson-* + *-ate*] **:** to introduce the arsono group into **:** convert into an arsonic acid or derivative—**ar·so·na·tion** \ˌ==ˈāshən\ *n* -s
ar·son·ic acid \(ˈ)ärˈsänik-, -sō-\ *n* [ISV *arsonium* + *-ic*] **1 :** any of a series of organic acids (as the arsanilic acids) having the general formula $RAsO(OH)_2$ and obtainable by oxidizing monosubstituted organic arsines (as phenyl-arsine $C_6H_5AsH_2$) **2 :** ARSINIC ACID 1
ar·son·ist \ˈärs(ᵊ)nəst, ˈäs-\ *n* -s **:** one who commits arson **:** INCENDIARY, FIREBUG
ar·so·ni·um \ärˈsōnēəm\ *n* -s [*ars-* + *ammonium*] **:** a univalent radical AsH_4 containing arsenic analogous to ammonium and known in the form of organic derivatives (as tetramethyl-arsonium iodide $As(CH_3)_4I$) — compare QUATERNARY AMMONIUM COMPOUND
ar·so·no \ärˈsō(,)nō\ *adj* [*arsono-*] **:** containing the radical —$AsO(OH)_2$ — compare ARSON-
ars·phen·a·mine \ärsˈfenə,mēn, -,mən\ *n* -s [ISV *ars-* + *phenamine*] **:** a light-yellow toxic hygroscopic powder $C_{12}H_{12}As_2N_2O_2.2HCl.2H_2O$ derived from arsenobenzene that was formerly used in the treatment of spirochetal diseases (as syphilis, relapsing fever) — see NEOARSPHENAMINE
ars po·et·i·ca \ˈärs(,)pōˈed·əkə, ˈärz-, -etə-, -ēkə\ *n, pl* **ars poeticas** [L *Ars Poetica* The Art of Poetry, poetic epistle by Horace †8 B.C. Roman poet] **:** a treatise on the art of literary and esp. poetic composition
¹**ar·sy–var·sy** \ˌärsēˈvärsē\ *or* **ar·sy–ver·sy** \-ˈvar-\ *adv* [redupl. (prob. influenced by L *versus*) of *arsy*, fr. ¹*arse* + *-y*] **:** backside forward **:** head over heels **:** TOPSY-TURVY ⟨knocked him *arsy-varsy*⟩
²**arsy–varsy** *or* **arsy–versy** \ˌ==ˈ==\ *adj* **:** upside down **:** TOPSY-TURVY
¹**art** [ME *art, ert*, fr. OE *eart*; akin to ON *est, ert*, (thou) art, Goth *is*, L *es*, Gk *essi*, Skt *asi*, OE *is* is — more at IS] *archaic pres 2d sing of* BE
²**art** \ˈärt, ˈät, *usu* -d·+V\ *n* -s *often attrib* [ME, fr. OF, fr. L *art-, ars* — more at ARM] **1 a :** the power of performing certain actions esp. as acquired by experience, study, or observation **:** SKILL, DEXTERITY ⟨there's an ~ to tightrope walking⟩ **b** (1) **:** skill in the adaptation of things in the natural world to the uses of human life **:** human contrivance or ingenuity ⟨are these chipped stones the product of ~⟩ (2) *obs* **:** technical skill often as though aided by magic **2 :** a branch of learning: **a :** one of the humanities traditionally including history, philosophy, literature, languages, and the fine arts ⟨the College of *Arts* and Sciences⟩ **b arts** *pl* **:** the liberal arts ⟨bachelor of *arts*⟩ **c** *archaic* **:** LEARNING, SCHOLARSHIP **3 a :** an occupation or business requiring knowledge or skill **:** CRAFT **b :** an organization of men practicing a craft or trade ⟨the ~ of Wool, that is, . . . the corporation of the dealers in wool —C.E.Norton⟩ **c :** the general principles of any branch of learning or of any developed craft **:** a system of rules or of organized modes of operation serving to facilitate the performance of certain actions ⟨the ~ of building⟩ ⟨the ~ of engraving⟩ ⟨the ~ of navigation⟩ **d :** systematic application of knowledge or skill in effecting a desired result **4 a :** application of skill and taste to production according to aesthetic principles **:** the conscious use of skill, taste, and creative imagination in the practical definition or production of beauty **b :** the product of skill and taste applied according to aesthetic principles **:** expression of beauty **:** works of art ⟨an ~ gallery⟩ **5 a** *archaic* **:** a skillful plan or device ⟨employed every ~ to soothe the discontented —T.B.Macaulay⟩ **b :** CUNNING, ARTIFICE ⟨I swear I use no ~ at all —Shak.⟩ ⟨she owes her wavy hair to ~ rather than to nature⟩ **c :** artificial and studied behavior ⟨~s that allure, the magic nod and wink —Robert Browning⟩ **6 a :** the craft of the artist; *specif* **:** the technical devices used by a painter regarded esp. as a subject of study **b :** a method or device that produces an artistic effect or is used for decorative purposes ⟨~ needlework⟩ **7 a :** FINE ARTS **b :** one of the fine arts **c :** a plastic art **d :** a graphic art **e :** PAINTING **8 :** decorative or illustrative elements in printed matter as distinguished from the text or other parts printed from standard alphabetic types; *esp* **:** the illustrative material of a newspaper or periodical

syn SKILL, CUNNING, ARTIFICE, CRAFT, ART can mean, in common, the faculty, usu. expert, of performing or executing what is planned or devised. SKILL stresses technical knowledge, proficiency, or expertness ⟨a first-rate specimen of the composer's art, the interpreter's *skill* and the engineer's craft —Herbert Weinstock⟩ ⟨dentistry as a *skill* alone is limited at present largely to repair and restoration —J.B. Conant⟩ ⟨varying *skill* and thoroughness in the detection of crime —Havelock Ellis⟩ ⟨a *skilled* toolmaker⟩ CUNNING may emphasize special, often tricky, inventive or creative power ⟨the *cunning* and consummate artistry by which he has achieved certain effects —J.D.Adams⟩ ⟨his unerring eye and his incomparable *cunning* of hand . . . a most able painter —Laurence Binyon⟩ ⟨a scout whose *cunning* exceeded that of the Indian —*Amer. Guide Series: Ariz.*⟩ ARTIFICE can stress skill or intelligence in contriving or devising, but usu. stresses at the same time a certain lack of true creative power, a certain artificiality ⟨what amazing *artifice* is found under that apparently straightforward tale —A.T.Quiller-Couch⟩ ⟨no matter what skill is displayed toward objectifying fiction, the omniscience of the author is naturally assumed . . . but such is *artifice* that it attempts to conceal this basic convention —Robert Humphrey⟩ ⟨he heightened the *artifice* of this style — its inversions, its verbal encrustation, its complexity of syntax, yet combined it with the natural speech rhythms and homely idioms —C.D.Lewis⟩ CRAFT can suggest ingenuity and subtlety in workmanship or trickery or guile; applied to a skilled pursuit or vocation, it may suggest a lower type of skill or inventive power joined with mastery of materials and technique but lacking true creative force or quality ⟨professional writers who take their *craft* seriously —M.D.Geismar⟩ ⟨small teams of dressmakers, each of them a mistress of her *craft* —*Choice of Careers: Dressmaking*⟩ ⟨no great artist but a master of his *craft*⟩ ART is the most variable of these words in meaning, often interchangeable with, often contrasting with, the others: its significant weight can fall upon recondite, inventive, or creative power ⟨the rare *art* of the alchemist or witch doctor⟩ It can, like SKILL, suggest proficiency or expertness ⟨the shoemaker's *art*⟩ ⟨*arts* such as medicine, husbandry —Benjamin Farrington⟩ or, like CRAFT, or, rarely, like ARTIFICE, can point to skill, ingenuity, and inventiveness in contriving even though the act or result lacks any true creative force or quality ⟨handmade tools, utensils, and furniture of the premachine age, . . . are interesting as *art* because of skillful handling of materials —*Amer. Guide Series: Mich.*⟩ ⟨practicing their *arts* as masons, brickmakers, carpenters, leather dressers —*Amer. Guide Series: Md.*⟩ ⟨to gain an end by one *art* or another⟩ But more frequently and in its most distinct sense ART contrasts with SKILL, ARTIFICE, and CRAFT in putting stress upon something more, in implying a personal, unanalyzable creative force that transmits and raises the art or product beyond a skill, artifice, or craft though it may involve the essential elements of all of these ⟨to turn from the mere skill of figurine making to the *art* of sculpture⟩ ⟨most of the symbolic details are examples of artifice rather than of *art* —R.M. Kain⟩ ⟨so much English acting which is very fine . . . is so satisfactory as craft and so limited as *art* —H.E.Clurman⟩
³**art** \"\ *adj* **1 :** composed or created with conscious artistry — opposed to *folk* ⟨an ~ ballad⟩ ⟨an ~ song⟩ **2 :** designed for decorative purposes or to produce an artistic effect ⟨~ pottery⟩
-art — see -ARD
art *abbr* **1** article **2** artificial **3** artillery **4** artist
artal *or* **artel** [Ar *arṭāl*, pl. of *raṭl* rotl] *pl of* ROTL — sometimes used as sing.

1art and part \,ärtᵊn'pärt\ *n* [ME; *art,* prob. fr. OF *hart* segment (in the expression *ne hart ne part* nothing at all), branch, willow withe, noose, of Gmc origin; perh. akin to OE *heordan* hurds — more at HURDS] *Scots law* : indirect participation in a crime by instigating, counseling, or assisting the actual perpetrator

2art and part *adv, Scots law* : by being an accessory before the fact or an accomplice in a crime ⟨pronounced guilty *art and part*⟩

art brown *n* : a dark brown that is darker than leafmold — called also *Argentina, mirador*

art director *n* **1** : one who directs the artistic features of a theatrical production (as scenic, costume, and lighting effects) **2** *also* **art editor** : one who executes, supervises, or coordinates designs, illustrations, and layouts to be used in printed matter

artefact *or* **artefac** *var of* ARTIFACT

1artel *var of* ARTAL

2ar·tel \är'tel(ʸ)\ *n* -s [Russ *artel'*, fr. It *artieri*, pl. of *artiere* artisan, fr. *arte* art, fr. L *art-, ars* — more at ARM] : the traditional Russian association of laborers for collective work : a cooperative craft society

ar·te·mia \är'tēmēə\ *n* [NL, irreg. fr. *Artemis*, Greek goddess of forests and hills (fr. L, fr. Gk) + NL *-ia*] **1** *cap* : a genus of crustaceans (order Anostraca) found in salt lakes and the brines of saltworks **2** -s : any crustacean of the genus *Artemia* : BRINE SHRIMP

ar·te·mis·ia \,ärd·ə'mizh(ē)ə, -rtə'-, -izēə, -is-\ *n* [NL *Artemisia*, fr. L *artemisia* mugwort, fr. Gk, prob. irreg. fr. *Artemid-, Artemis* + *-ia*] **1** *cap* : a genus of shrubs and herbs (family Compositae) widely distributed in temperate and cool regions and having strongly scented foliage and small rayless flower heads **2** -s : any plant of the genus *Artemisia*, abundant in the western U.S.

artemisia green *n* : a greenish gray that is slightly yellower and stronger than cabbage green

ar·te·mon \'ärd·ə,män\ *n, pl* **artem·o·nes** \är'temə,nēz\ [LL, foresail, fr. Gk *artemōn*] **1** : a mast in ancient sailing ships forward of the foremast and raking forward **2** : the sail set on an artemon

ar·ten·kreis \'ärtᵊn,krīs\ *n, pl* **artenkrei·se** \-īzə\ *or* **artenkreis·es** \-īsəz\ *usu cap* [G, lit., cycle of species, fr. *arten* (pl. of *art* species, kind, type, nature, fr. MHG) + *kreis* cycle, circle, fr. OHG *kreiz*; akin to MLG *kreit, krēt* circle, enclosed dueling space, OHG *krizzōn* to scratch in (as letters), *krazzōn* to scratch — more at ARTICLE, SCRATCH] : a group of species that replace one another in geographic sequence, presumably trace ultimately to a common ancestral form, and are equivalent as a group to a subgenus

ar·ter \'ärd·ər, 'ād·ə(r)\ *dial var of* AFTER

ar·te·re·nol \,ärd·ə'rē,nōl, -rtə'-, -ōl\ *n* -s [fr. *Arterenol*, a trademark] : NOREPINEPHRINE

arteri- *or* **arterio-** *comb form* [MF, fr. LL, fr. Gk *artēri-, artērio-*, fr. *artēria* — more at ARTERY] **1** : artery ⟨*arteri*ectasia⟩ ⟨*arterio*logy⟩ **2** : arterial and ⟨*arterio*venous⟩

ar·te·ria \är'tirēə\ *n, pl* **arteri·ae** \-ē,ē\ [L — more at ARTERY] : ARTERY

1ar·te·ri·al \(')är¦tirēəl, (')ä¦-, -tēr-\ *adj* [MF *arterial, arteriel*, fr. (assumed) ML *arterialis*, fr. L *arteria* + *-alis* -al] **1 a** : of or relating to an artery or arteries ⟨the ~ system⟩ **b** : relating to the bright red blood present in most arteries and a few veins that has been oxygenated and arterialized during passage through lungs or gills — compare PULMONARY VEIN, VENOUS **2** : of, relating to, or constituting through-traffic facilities ⟨newly widened ~ avenues —Duncan Aikman⟩ ⟨its tributaries form the ~ system of the continent —W.W.Huggett⟩ — **ar·te·ri·al·ly** \-rēəlē, -li\ *adv*

2arterial \"\ *n* -s : a through street or arterial highway

arterial bulb *n* : BULBUS ARTERIOSUS

arterial gland *n* : any of certain small masses of vascular and chromaffin tissue found in several parts of the body (as the carotid and coccygeal glands)

ar·te·ri·al·i·za·tion \är,tirēələ'zāshən, -,lī'-\ *n* -s : the process of arterializing

ar·te·ri·al·ize \är'tirēə,līz\ *vt* -ED/-ING/-S : to transform (venous blood) into arterial blood by exposure to oxygen in lungs or other respiratory organs, oxygen being taken up and carbon dioxide given off : make blood arterial

ar·te·ri·o·gram \är'tirēə,gram, -rēō,-\ *n* -s [ISV *arteri-* + *-gram*] : a roentgenogram of an artery made by arteriography

ar·te·ri·o·graph·ic \=¦===¦grafik\ *adj* [ISV *arteriography* + *-ic*] : of, by, or relating to arteriography ⟨~ and histological studies have shown that circulation in bone follows particular rules —M.J.Dallemagne⟩

ar·te·ri·og·ra·phy \är,tirē'ägrəfē\ *n* -ES [ISV *arteri-* + *-graphy*] : the roentgenographic visualization of an artery after injection of a radiopaque substance

ar·te·ri·o·lar \är,tirē¦ōlər, -lär, -lər\ *adj* : of, relating to, or involving an arteriole ⟨associated with arterial and ~ disease —*Jour. Amer. Med. Assoc.*⟩

ar·te·ri·ole \är'tirē,ōl\ *n* -s [F or NL; F *artériole*, prob. fr. NL *arteriola*, fr. L *arteria* artery + *-ola* -ole] : one of the small terminal twigs of an artery that joins the artery to its capillary bed

ar·te·ri·o·lop·a·thy \är,tirēə'läpəthē, -rē(,)ō'-\ *n* -ES [*arteriole* + *-o-* + *-pathy*] : disease of the arterioles

ar·te·ri·o·lo·sclerosis \=,==¦ōlō, =¦==,ə,lō + =¦=\ *n, pl* **arteriolosclero·ses** [NL, fr. *arteriola* + *-o-* + *sclerosis*] : thickening of the intima of arterioles by hyaline and fatty deposits resulting in reduction of the lumen with obstruction to blood flow, seen chiefly in the kidneys (as in hypertension) but occurring also in other tissues and organs

ar·te·ri·o·sclerosis \=,==(,)ō, -,ə+\ *n, pl* **arterioscleroses** [NL, fr. *arteri-* + *sclerosis*] : a chronic disease of the arteries characterized by abnormal thickening and hardening of the vessel walls resulting in loss of elasticity — compare ATHEROSCLEROSIS

1ar·te·ri·o·scle·rot·ic \=¦==(,)ə¦sklə¦räd·ik\ *adj* [fr. NL *arteriosclerosis*, after such pairs as NL *hypnosis*: E *hypnotic*] : of, relating to, or affected by arteriosclerosis

2arteriosclerotic \"\ *n* -s : an arteriosclerotic individual

ar·te·ri·ot·o·my \är,tirē'äd·əmē\ *n* -ES [LL *arteriotomia*, fr. Gk *artēriotomia*, fr. *artēri-* arteri- + *-tomia* -tomy] : the surgical incision of an artery

ar·te·ri·ous \(')är¦tirēəs\ *adj* [*arteri-* + *-ous*] *archaic* : ARTERIAL

ar·te·ri·o·venous \är¦tirē(,)ō, -rē,ə+¦==\ *adj* [ISV *arteri-* + *venous*] : of, relating to, or connecting the arteries and veins ⟨an ~ fistula⟩

ar·te·ri·tis \,ärd·ə'rīd·əs, ,ärtə-, -ītəs\ *n* -ES [NL, irreg. fr. *arteri-* + *-itis*] : inflammation of an artery

ar·tery \'ärd·ərē, 'ā¦, ¦tə-, -ri *sometimes* ¦trē or -i\ *n* -ES [ME *arterie*, fr. L *arteria* windpipe, artery, fr. Gk *artēria*; akin to Gk *aortē* aorta — more at AORTA] **1 a** : one of the tubular branching vessels that carry blood from the heart to the various parts and organs of the body and have thicker more muscular and elastic walls than veins, the outer coating being in smaller arteries increasingly reduced until the ultimate capillaries connecting them with the veins possess only the innermost endothelial layer, blood in the arteries being under pressure and flowing in waves due to beats of the heart — compare ADVENTITIA, INTIMA, MEDIA; PULMONARY ARTERY, SYSTEMIC; CIRCULATION **b** : an often contractile vessel distributing blood to the tissues of an invertebrate animal **2** *obs* : TRACHEA 1 **3 a** : the main waterway of a river system ⟨he had stood at the confluence of the Monongahela and the Alleghany and seen the great ~ of the Ohio flow out of them —Roger Burlingame⟩ **b** : a channel of transportation or communication; *esp* : the principal channel in a branching system ⟨~ of trade⟩ ⟨through many *arteries* — publications, radio and television programs, movies, lectures —J.H.Baker⟩ **c** : a principal street or road ⟨they issue from a side road into a main ~ —Green Peyton⟩ **syn** see WAY

ar·te·sian \(')är¦tēzhən, (')ä¦-\ *adj* [F *artésien*, lit., of Artois, fr. OF, fr. *Arteis* Artois, region of northern France + OF *-ien* -ian; fr. the wells of this type bored in Artois in the 18th century] : involving, relating to, or supplied by the upward movement of water under hydrostatic pressure in rocks or unconsolidated material beneath the earth's surface ⟨~ spring⟩ ⟨~ water⟩ ⟨~ pressure⟩ — distinguished from *subartesian*

artesian well *n* **1** : a usu. deep and narrow well made by boring until water is reached that will flow upward through artesian pressures **2** : any deep-bored well

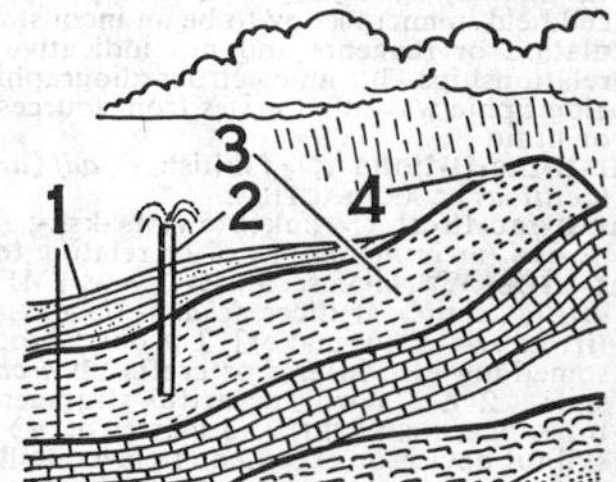

section of an artesian well: *1* impervious layers, *2* well, *3* inclined water-bearing strata, *4* catchment area

art film *n* **1** : a motion picture produced as an artistic or experimental venture **2** : a film documentary depicting works of art or artists at work

art form *n* **1 a** : a recognized form in which artistic expression is cast (as a sonnet or a symphony) **b** : a recognized medium of artistic expression (as writing or painting) **2** : an unconventional form or medium in which expression regarded as artistic may be cast ⟨fireworks are an *art form* of the Mexican provinces⟩ ⟨baseball is a popular American *art form*⟩ **3 a** : a production that is regarded as a work of art **b** : a production outside the realm of painting and sculpture in which are discerned elements in some way comparable with those involved in artistic creation ⟨a snuffbox valued as an *art form* by connoisseurs⟩

art·ful \'ärtfəl, 'āt-\ *adj* [2*art* + *-ful*] **1 a** : performed with, characterized by, or exhibiting art or skill ⟨so ~ is the choice of detail that the reader is given the illusion of having lived through every painful minute of the lengthy trial —Howard Haycraft⟩ **b** : produced by art : ARTIFICIAL ⟨the wording a shade too clever, the vowel-patterns too ~ —*Times Lit. Supp.*⟩ **c** (1) : ingeniously designed ⟨~ vases and pitchers—*N.Y.Times*⟩ (2) : craftily deceptive ⟨she hit upon an ~ conjecture —George Meredith⟩ **2 a** : using art or skill : DEXTEROUS, SKILLFUL ⟨something more than the mere ~ prose stylist he is so often considered —David Daiches⟩ **b** : adroit in taking advantage usu. unfairly : CRAFTY, DECEITFUL ⟨many an ~ shipmaster who thought the barristers were fools . . . has seen his nautical evidence torn to shreds by a lawyer who had never been to sea —*N.Y.Herald Tribune*⟩ **syn** see SLY

art·ful·ly \-fəlē, -li\ *adv* : in an artful manner : with art, dexterity, or craft

art·ful·ness \-fəlnəs\ *n* -ES : the quality or state of being artful

art glass *n* : articles of glass designed primarily for decorative purposes; *esp* : novelty glassware

art gray *n* : a purplish gray that is bluer and lighter than crane, bluer and less strong than dove gray, and bluer than cinder gray — called also *Quaker, sea mist*

art green *n* : a moderate yellow green to olive green that is greener and less strong than woodbine green

art–historical \¦==¦===\ *adj* : of or relating to the history of art ⟨the current direction of *art-historical* research⟩

art house *n* : ART THEATER

arthr- *or* **arthro-** *comb form* [L *arthr-*, fr. Gk *arthr-, arthro-*, fr. *arthron*; akin to Gk *arariskein* to fit — more at ARM] : joint ⟨*arthr*algia⟩ ⟨*arthro*pathy⟩

arthra *pl of* ARTHRON

ar·thral \'ärthrəl\ *adj* [*arthr-* + *-al*] : of or relating to a joint

ar·thral·gia \är'thralj(ē)ə\ *n* -s [NL, fr. *arthr-* + *-algia*] : neuralgic pain in one or more joints esp. accompanying systemic infections (as scarlet fever)

1ar·thrit·ic \(')är¦thrid·ik, (')ä¦-, -itik, -ēk\ *also* **ar·thrit·i·cal** \-ðkəl, -ēk-\ *adj* [*arthritic* alter. (influenced by L *arthriticus*) of earlier *artetic, arthetic*, fr. ME *artetyk, arthretik*, fr. MF *artetique*, modif. of L *arthriticus*, fr. Gk *arthritikos*, fr. *arthritis* + *-ikos* -ic; *arthritical* alter. (influenced by L *arthriticus*) of earlier *artetical*, fr. *artetic* + *-al*] **1** : of, relating to, or affected with arthritis **2** : creaky esp. with age ⟨enough singable songs have been produced to take the place of the present ~ repertory —*New Yorker*⟩ — **ar·thrit·i·cal·ly** \-ðk(ə)lē, -ēk-, -li\ *adv*

2arthritic \"\ *n* -s : a person affected with arthritis

ar·thri·tis \är'thrīdəs, ä'-, -ītəs\ *n, pl* **ar·thrit·i·des** \-'thridə,dēz, -itə-\ [L, fr. Gk, fr. *arthron* joint + *-itis*] : inflammation of one or more joints due to infectious, metabolic, or constitutional causes — compare DEGENERATIVE ARTHRITIS, GOUT, RHEUMATOID ARTHRITIS

arthritis de·for·mans \-dē'fór,manz\ *n* [NL, deforming arthritis] : a chronic arthritis marked by deformation of affected joints

arthro- *in pronunciations below,* ¦=(,)== ¦är(,)thrō *or* ¦ä(,)thr- *or* -,thrə\ — see ARTHR-

ar·thro·bac·ter \'=(,)=,baktə(r)\ *n, cap* [NL, fr. *arthr-* + *-bacter*] : a genus of soil bacteria comprising cellulolytic forms that resemble and are often considered to be members of *Corynebacterium*

ar·thro·branch \'=(,)=,braŋk\ *also* **ar·thro·bran·chia** \,=(,)=¦=kēə\ *n, pl* **arthrobranchs** *also* **arthrobranchi·ae** \-kē,ē\ [NL *arthrobranchia*, fr. *arthr-* + *-branchia*] : a gill attached to the articular membrane between the body and the basal joint of a leg of a crustacean

ar·thro·derm \'=(,)=,dərm\ *n* -s [*arthr-* + *-derm*] : the external covering of an arthropod

ar·thro·dese \'==,dēz, ,==¦=\ *vt* -ED/-ING/-S [back-formation fr. *arthrodesis*] : IMMOBILIZE ⟨a hip *arthrodesed* by polio⟩

ar·throd·e·sis \är'thrädəsəs\ *n, pl* **arthrode·ses** \-ə,sēz\ [NL, fr. *arthr-* + *-desis*] : the surgical operation of immobilizing a joint by removing the cartilaginous surfaces so that the bones grow solidly together : artificial ankylosis

ar·thro·dia \är'thrōdēə\ *n, pl* **arthrodi·ae** \-dē,ē\ [NL, fr. Gk *arthrōdia*, fr. *arthrōdēs* articulated (fr. *arthron* joint + *-ōdēs* -ode) + *-ia*] : a gliding joint : a diarthrosis in which the articular surfaces glide upon each other without axial motion — **ar·thro·di·al** \(')=¦=dēəl\ *adj* — **ar·throd·ic** \-¦thrädik\ *adj*

ar·thro·di·ra \,== *at* ARTHRO- + 'dīrə\ *n pl, cap* [NL, fr. *arthr-* + *-dira* (fr. Gk *deirē* neck); akin to Latvian *grīva* mouth of a river, OSlav *griva* mane, Skt *grīva* neck, L *vorare* to devour — more at VORACIOUS] : a group of Devonian fishes forming a subclass of Placodermi or esp. formerly an order of Ostracodermi or a separate class and having the forepart of the body protected by bony plates and with an imperfectly ossified internal skeleton — see COCCOSTEIDAE, DINICHTHYS — **ar·thro·di·ran** \¦==¦dīrən\ *adj or n* — **ar·thro·dire** \'==,dī(ə)r\ *n* -s — **ar·thro·di·rous** \-¦dīrəs\ *adj*

ar·thro·gastra \,==+'gastrə\ *n pl, cap* [NL, fr. *arthr-* + *-gastra* (fr. Gk *gastr-, gastēr* stomach) — more at GASTRIC] *in some classifications* : a primary division of the Arachnida comprising those which have the abdomen segmented (as the scorpions) — **ar·thro·gas·tran** \¦==¦gastrən\ *adj or n*

ar·throg·e·nous \(')är¦thräjənəs\ *adj* [*arthrospore* + *-genous*] : developing vegetative resting cells (as arthrospores) that function as spores ⟨~ algae⟩ ⟨~ fungi⟩

ar·thro·gram \'== *at* ARTHRO- + ,gram\ *n* -s [ISV *arthr-* + *-gram*] : a roentgenogram of a joint made by arthrography

ar·throg·ra·phy \är'thrägrəfē\ *n* -ES [ISV *arthr-* + *-graphy*] : the roentgenographic visualization of a joint after the injection of an opaque substance

ar·thro·lite \'== *at* ARTHRO- + ,līt\ *n* -s [*arthr-* + *-lite*] : a cylindrical concretion with transverse joints occas. found in clays or shales

ar·thro·mere \'==,mi(ə)r\ *n* -s [*arthr-* + *-mere*] : one of the body segments of jointed animals — **ar·thro·mer·ic** \¦==¦merik\ *adj*

ar·thron \'är,thrän\ *n, pl* **ar·thra** \-,thrə\ [NL, fr. Gk] : ARTICULATION, JOINT

ar·throp·a·thy \är'thräpəthē\ *n* -ES [ISV *arthr-* + *-pathy*] : a disease of a joint

ar·thro·plas·ty \'== *at* ARTHRO- + ,plastē\ *n* -ES [ISV *arthr-* + *-plasty*] : plastic surgery of a joint : the operative formation or restoration of a joint

ar·thro·ple·o·na \,==+'plēənə\ *n pl, cap* [NL, fr. *arthr-* + *-pleona* (fr. Gk *plein* to swim, float) — more at FLOW] : a suborder of Collembola including most of the springtails and characterized by an elongate body and distinct abdominal segmentation — compare SYMPHYPLEONA

ar·thro·pleure \'==,plú(ə)r\ *also* **ar·thro·pleu·ra** \,==plúrə\ *n, pl* **arthropleures** \'==,plú(ə)rz\ *also* **arthropleu·rae** \,=='plú,rē\ [NL *arthropleura*, fr. *arthr-* + *pleura*] : the lateral or limb-bearing portion of an arthromere

1ar·thro·pod \'==,päd\ *adj* [NL *Arthropoda*] : of or belonging to the Arthropoda

2arthropod \"\ *n* -s : one of the Arthropoda

ar·throp·o·da \är'thräpədə\ *n pl, cap* [NL, fr. *arthr-* + *-poda*] : a phylum consisting of articulate invertebrate animals with jointed limbs, the body divided into metameric segments, the brain dorsal to the alimentary canal and connected with a ventral chain of ganglia, and the body generally covered with a chitinous shell that is molted at intervals and including the crustaceans, insects, and spiders and related forms as well as several less prominent groups (as the millepedes and onychophores), often the trilobites, and sometimes the tongue worms, sea spiders, and water bears — **ar·throp·o·dal** \(')=¦=pədᵊl\ *adj* — **ar·throp·o·dan** \-dən\ *adj* — **ar·throp·o·dous** \-dəs\ *adj*

ar·thro·po·ma·ta \,== *at* ARTHRO- + 'pōməd·ə, -äm-, -ətə\ [NL, fr. *arthr-* + *-pomata* (fr. Gk *pōmat-, pōma* lid) — more at POMACENTRIDAE] *syn of* ARTICULATA 2

ar·thro·pom·a·tous \¦==¦pämədəs, -ōm-, -ətəs\ *adj* [NL *Arthropomata* + E *-ous*] : of or relating to the Arthropomata

ar·throp·ter·ous \(')är¦thräptərəs\ *adj* [ISV *arthr-* + *-pterous*] : having jointed fin rays ⟨most fishes are ~⟩

ar·thro·sis \är'thrōsəs\ *n, pl* **arthro·ses** \-ō,sēz\ [NL, fr. Gk *arthrōsis*, fr. *arthroun* to articulate (fr. *arthron* joint) + *-ōsis* -osis] : an articulation or suture uniting two bones

ar·thro·spore \'== *at* ARTHRO- + ,spō(ə)r\ *n* -s [*arthr-* + *spore*] **1 a** : a thick-walled vegetative resting cell formed by segmentation of the filament in certain blue-green algae esp. of the genus *Nostoc* **b** : an oidium in fungi **2** : a refractile body other than an endospore encountered in bacterial cultures and variously regarded as degenerate cells, as resistant vegetative forms, or as forms associated with a sexual cycle — **ar·thro·spor·ic** \¦==¦spórik\ *adj* — **ar·thro·spor·ous** \-¦spórəs, (')=¦thräspərəs\ *adj*

ar·thro·stome \'==,stōm\ *n* -s [*arthr-* + *-stome*] : a mouth with complex jointed mouthparts that are modified segmental appendages — used typically of the Arthropoda

ar·thros·tra·ca \är'thrästrəkə\ *n pl, cap* [NL, fr. *arthr-* + *-ostraca*] *in some classifications* : a division of Crustacea comprising the orders Amphipoda, Isopoda, and usu. Tanaidacea in which both thorax and abdomen are segmented and there are seven pairs of thoracic appendages

ar·throus \'ärthrəs\ *adj* [*arthr-* + *-ous*] : ARTHRAL, JOINTED

ar·thro·zoa \,==¦zōə\ *n pl, cap* [NL, fr. *arthr-* + *-zoa*] : a primary division of Invertebrata in which the Arthropoda and certain worms were formerly grouped — **ar·thro·zo·an** \¦==¦zōən\ *adj or n* — **ar·thro·zo·ic** \-¦zōik\ *adj*

ar·thu·ri·an \(')är¦thúrēən, (')ä¦-, -ür-\ *adj, usu cap* [fr. *Arthur*, semilegendary 6th cent. king of the Britons + E *-ian*] : of, relating to, or characteristic of the legends or romances built around King Arthur and his knights ⟨the ~ legend⟩

ar·thu·ri·ana \(,)==,=='anə, -'ä-, -'a-, -'ā- *also* -'ā-\ *n pl, usu cap* [NL, fr. *Arthur* + *-i-* + *-ana*] : writings and other materials concerning the Arthurian story

ar·thus phenomenon \'ärthəs-, *F* ärtüs-\ *n, usu cap A* [prob. trans. of F *phénomène d'Arthus*, after Nicholas M. Arthus †1945 Fr. bacteriologist] : a reaction following injection of an antigen into an animal in which hypersensitivity has been previously established involving infiltrations, edema, sterile abscesses, and in severe cases gangrene

ar·ti·ad \'ärd·ē,ad, -rshē,-\ *n* -s [Gk *artios* even + E *-ad*] **1 a** *obs* : an element or radical of even valence **b** : an element of even atomic number — contrasted with *perissad* **2** : one of the Artiodactyla

artic *obs var of* ARCTIC

ar·ti·choke \'är¦d·ə,chōk, 'ā¦, ¦tə-\ *n* -s [It dial. (Lombardy) *articiocco*, fr. Ar *al-khurshūf* the artichoke] **1** : a tall herb (*Cynara scolymus*) that resembles a thistle and has coarse pinnately incised leaves **2** : the flower head of the artichoke having large oval involucral bracts with fleshy bases that with the receptacle are cooked as a vegetable — called also *globe artichoke* **3** : JERUSALEM ARTICHOKE

artichoke flower head

artichoke green *n* : a grayish yellow green that is yellower and paler than palmetto or average sage green and yellower and lighter than mermaid or celadon

artichoke thistle *n* : CARDOON

1ar·ti·cle \'ärd·əkəl, 'ā¦, ¦tə-, -ēk-\ *n* -s [ME, fr. OF, fr. L *articulus* division, part, joint, dim. of *artus* joint; akin to OE *eard* condition, fate, MHG *art* innate character, nature, ON *einarthr* firm, single, L *art-, ars* skill, Gk *artyein* to arrange, prepare, Skt *ṛta* fit, right — more at ARM] **1 a** : a distinguishable and usu. separately marked section (as of a creed, statute, indictment, treaty, legacy, or other writing consisting of two or more such sections) ⟨an ~ of the constitution⟩ **b** : a distinct and separate point, count, charge, or clause ⟨an explanation of the statute in six ~s⟩ **c** : a condition or stipulation esp. in a contract or a creed — often used in pl. ⟨sign ship's ~s⟩ ⟨~s of indenture⟩ ⟨~s of faith⟩ **d** : a paragraph, section, or other distinct part of a document ⟨mentioned in the next ~⟩ **e** : a generally short nonfictional prose composition usu. forming an independent portion of a publication (as a newspaper, magazine, or encyclopedia) ⟨write an ~ for a magazine⟩ ⟨have you seen the ~ in the morning newspaper⟩ **2** *archaic* : a particular juncture, point of time, or moment — used esp. in the phrase *article of death* **3 a** : a particular item of business : MATTER ⟨a very great revolution that has happened in this ~ of good breeding —Joseph Addison⟩ **b** : a distinct detail or particular (as of an action or proceeding) ⟨each ~ of human duty —William Paley⟩ **4** : any of a usu. small set of words or affixes used with substantives (as nouns) to limit, individualize, or give definiteness or indefiniteness to their application (as *a, an, the*) — traditionally considered an adjective; compare 1DEFINITE 3a, 1INDEFINITE **5** : a material thing : ITEM, OBJECT ⟨~s of diet⟩ ⟨scarce ~s command high prices⟩ **6 a** : a thing of a particular class or kind as distinct from a thing of another class or kind ⟨this disclaimer to any resemblance between a real cowhand and the Hollywood ~ —M.C.Boatright⟩ **b** : one who is adept or practiced ⟨as a professional gambler was about the slickest ~ in his line —H.E.Fosdick⟩ **c** : PERSON ⟨the second clerk . . . was a fairly smooth ~ —Frederick Way⟩ **7 a** *obs* : a joint of the body **b** : an articulated segment of an appendage in arthropods

2article \"\ *vb* **articled; articled; articling** \-k(ə)liŋ\ **articles** [ME *articlen*, fr. *article*, n.] *vt* **1** *archaic* **a** : to set forth in distinct particulars : SPECIFY **b** : to set forth or charge someone with (offenses) **2 a** *obs* : to stipulate esp. in a treaty **b** : to bind by articles (as of apprenticeship) ⟨*articled* at seventeen to a well-known London architect —J.D.Beresford⟩ ~ *vi* **1** *archaic* : to bring a particularized charge or accusation **2** *archaic* : to make an arrangement or agreement : STIPULATE

articled *adj* : bound by articles of apprenticeship : APPRENTICED

articles of association **1** : a written agreement embodying the purposes or other terms and conditions of the association of a number of persons for the prosecution of a joint enterprise; *specif* : a written agreement duly executed and filed so as to have the force of a charter under general incorporation laws **2** : a written agreement that in England under the Companies Act may accompany the memorandum of association of a company with a liability limited by shares, that must accompany that of a company with a liability limited by guarantee or unlimited, and that prescribes the regulations for the government of the company

ar·tic·u·la·ble \är'tikyələbəl, ä'-\ *adj* [*articulate* + *-able*] : capable of being articulated

ar·tic·u·la·cy \-ləsē\ *n* -ES [1*articulate* + *-cy*] : the quality or state of being articulate

ar·tic·u·la·men·tum \är,tikyələ'mentəm\ *n, pl* **articula·men·ta** \-tə\ [NL, fr. L, articulation of the limbs, joint, fr.

articulare to divide into joints + *-mentum* -ment — more at ARTICULATE] **:** the inner layer of a plate of a chiton projecting anteriorly and articulating with the plate in front — compare TEGUMENTUM

¹ar·tic·u·lar \är'tikyələr, ä'tikyələ(r)\ *adj* [ME *articuler*, fr. L *articularis*, fr. *articulus* joint + *-aris* -ar, -ary — more at ARTICLE] **1** *also* **ar·tic·u·lary** \-,lerē\ **:** of or relating to a joint or joints ⟨~ disease⟩ ⟨an ~ condyle⟩ **2** [LL *articularis*, fr. L] **:** being an article **:** accompanied by an article ⟨the ~ infinitive in Greek⟩ **:** characteristic of an article ⟨~ use of a former demonstrative adjective⟩

²articular \"\ *also* **articulary** \"\ *or* **ar·tic·u·lare** \=,== 'lärē, -la(ə)rē\ *n, pl* **articulars** \-ə(r)z\ *also* **articularies** \-erēz\ *or* **articula·ria** \-ärēə,-a(ə)rēə\ [NL *articulare*, fr. L, neut. of *articularis*] **:** a bone in the base of the lower jaw of most vertebrates except mammals by which the jaw usu. articulates with the quadrate bone — compare MECKEL'S CARTILAGE

articular cartilage *n* **:** cartilage that covers the articular surfaces of bones

articular disk *n* **:** a cartilage interposed between two articular surfaces and partially or completely separating the joint cavity into two compartments

articular lamella *n* **:** the layer of compact bone to which the articular cartilage is attached

articularly *adv, obs* **:** in separate items

articular membrane *n* **:** a region of flexible unsclerotized cuticle between areas of sclerotization in the exoskeleton of an arthropod that functions as a joint permitting movement of the body or its parts

ar·tic·u·la·ta \är,tikyə'läd·ə, -ād·ə\ *n pl, cap* [NL, fr. neut. pl. of *articulatus* jointed, fr. L, uttered distinctly, past part. of *articulare*] **1 :** one of the four subkingdoms in the classification of Cuvier comprising invertebrates having the body composed of a series of ringlike segments (as arthromeres, somites, or metameres) **2 :** a class or other division of Brachiopoda comprising forms with the valves hinged and usu. bearing teeth — compare INARTICULATA

¹ar·tic·u·late \är'tikyələt, ä'- *sometimes* -,lāt; *usu* -d·+V\ *adj* [NL *articulatus*, fr. L, past part. of *articulare* to divide into joints, utter distinctly, fr. *articulus* division, part, joint] **1** *obs* **:** expressed in separate items or particulars **2 a :** segmented into syllables or esp. into words meaningfully arranged **:** constituting intelligible speech ⟨an ~ cry⟩ **b :** possessing the faculty or power of speech **c :** expressing oneself readily **:** not reserved **:** not reticent ⟨too ~ to be trusted with a secret⟩ **:** expressed readily ⟨gratitude is one of the least ~ of the emotions —*Survey Graphic*⟩ **d :** expressing oneself clearly and effectively enough to gain attention; *also* **:** expressed in such a manner ⟨the primitive poet . . . was used by the community to make its spiritual needs ~ —C.D.Lewis⟩ **3 a :** jointed or consisting of segments united by joints **:** JOINTED ⟨~ animals⟩ ⟨~ plants⟩ **b :** distinctly marked off **:** formulated in clearly distinguished parts **:** DISTINCT ⟨an ~ period of history⟩ ⟨the way in which an ~ system blinds the thinker —Irwin Edman⟩ **syn** see VOCAL

²articulate \-,lāt, *usu* -ād·+V\ *vb* -ED/-ING/-S *vt* **1** *obs* **:** to draw up or write in separate articles **:** SPECIFY, PARTICULARIZE **2 a** (1) **:** to make (the breath stream) articulate ⟨speech is *articulated* air⟩ (2) **:** to pronounce distinctly (a syllable, word, or speech sound) **b :** to give clear and effective utterance to ⟨~ the dumb, deep want of the people —Thomas Carlyle⟩ **3 a** (1) **:** to unite by means of a joint **:** put together with joints or at the joints ⟨*articulated* mastodon remains —*Jour. of Geol.*⟩ (2) **:** to join together permanently or semipermanently by means of a pivot connection for operating separate forms, frames, or segments as a unit ⟨*articulated* locomotive⟩ ⟨*articulated* railroad car⟩ **b :** to form or fit into a systematically related whole **:** interrelate systematically **:** coordinate coherently ⟨the high schools have been *articulated* with the state university⟩ ⟨the problem is to ~ the ideas —E.D. Canham⟩ **4 :** to arrange (artificial teeth) on an articulator ~ *vi* **1** *obs* **:** to make or come to terms **2 a :** to utter articulate sounds or utter intelligible speech **:** speak distinctly ⟨too frightened to ~⟩ **b :** to manipulate the vocal organs so as to produce a speech sound **3 a :** to become jointed **:** become united or connected by means of a joint ⟨bones that ~ with each other⟩ **b :** to be united or connected in a systematic interrelation ⟨at the beginning of the 19th century there were a number of school units in existence, none of which *articulated* with the others —J.D.Russell & C.H.Judd⟩

³articulate \-,lət, -,lāt, *usu* -d·+V\ *n* -S [NL *Articulata*] **:** one of the Articulata

articulated train *n* **:** a railroad train whose cars are permanently or semipermanently joined together for operation as a unit as distinguished from one whose cars may be readily uncoupled and operated in other trains

ar·tic·u·late·ly \-,lətlē, -li\ *adv* **:** in an articulate manner

ar·tic·u·late·ness *n* -ES **:** the quality or state of being articulate

ar·tic·u·la·tion \(,)är,tikyə'lāshən, (,)ä,t-\ *n* -S [F, fr. MF, fr. L *articulatus* + F *-ion*] **1 a :** the action or manner of jointing or interrelating ⟨a sketch showing the ~ of the limbs⟩ ⟨try to show them the inner structure, the ~ of the parts —M.J.Adler⟩ **b :** the state of being jointed or systematically interrelated into a whole ⟨~ of the detail with the central thought —Gilbert Highet⟩ ⟨the potency of movies depends upon the quality of their dramatic ~ —Bosley Crowther⟩; *specif* **:** interrelation of different levels of education (as elementary education, secondary education, higher education) for ensuring continuous advancement in learning **c :** the clarification of an architectural design by emphasizing certain parts of the structure (as stairs, corridors, or floors) **2 a** (1) **:** a joint or juncture between bones or cartilages in the skeleton of a vertebrate, being immovable when the bones are directly united, slightly movable when they are united by an intervening substance, or more or less freely movable when the articular surfaces are covered with smooth cartilage and surrounded by a fibrous capsule lined with synovial membrane — see AMPHIARTHROSIS, DIARTHROSIS, SYNARTHROSIS (2) **:** a movable joint between rigid parts of any animal (as between the segments of an insect appendage) **b** (1) **:** a joint or connection between two parts capable of spontaneous separation (as the base of a leafstalk or of the peduncle of a flower) (2) **:** a node or thickened portion of a stem or the interval between two such points **3 a** (1) **:** the act or manner of articulating (2) **:** an articulated utterance or sound; *specif* **:** CONSONANT **b :** a measure of the extent to which a transmission system is capable of reproducing the original speech **c :** the manner of sounding or uttering the separate notes or phrases that make up a melodic line in music **4 a** (1) **:** the act of properly arranging artificial teeth (2) **:** an arrangement of artificial teeth **b :** OCCLUSION 2a

articulation index *n* **:** an indication based on a test consisting of the utterance of nonsense words or syllables of the percentage of speech sounds that would be heard correctly without contextual help

ar·tic·u·la·tion·ist \-nəst\ *n* -S **:** one who uses or favors the oral method of teaching the deaf

ar·tic·u·la·tive \=ˈ==,ləd·iv, -,lāl, |tiv, -ēv\ *adj* **:** of or relating to articulation

ar·tic·u·la·tor \-,lād·ə(r), -ātə-\ *n* -S **1 :** one that speaks distinctly **2 :** a movable vocal organ (as the tongue) — compare POINT OF ARTICULATION **3 :** an apparatus used in dentistry for obtaining correct articulation in artificial teeth

ar·tic·u·la·to·ri·ly \=ˈ==lə,tōrəlē, -ōr-, -li\ *adv* **:** in an articulatory manner

ar·tic·u·la·to·ry \=ˈ==lə,tōrē, -ōr-, -ri\ *adj* **:** of or relating to articulation

ar·tic·u·lite \är'tikyə,līt\ *n* -S [L *articulus* joint + E *-ite* — more at ARTICLE] **:** ITACOLUMITE

ar·tic·u·lus \-ləs\ *n, pl* **articu·li** \-,lī\ [NL, fr. L, joint — more at ARTICLE] **:** the hinge including the hinge plate, teeth, and ligament in bivalve mollusks

artier *comparative of* ARTY

artiest *superlative of* ARTY

ar·ti·fact *or* **ar·te·fact** \'ärd·ə,fakt, 'ä|, |tə-, -ē,f-\ *also* **ar·te·fac** \-ak\ *n* -S [*artifact* alter. (prob. influenced by *artifice*) of *artefact*, fr. L *arte* by skill (abl. of *art-, ars* skill) + *factum* something done, fr. neut. of *factus*, past part. of *facere* to do, make; *artefac* alter. of *artefact* — more at ARM, DO] **1 :** a usu. simple object (as a tool or ornament) showing human workmanship or modification as distinguished from a natural object **2 a :** a product of artificial character due to extraneous (as human) agency; *specif* **:** an appearance in a fixed tissue or cell held in microscopy to be an inconstant product of manipulation or reagents and not indicative of actual structural relationships **b :** an electrocardiographic and electroencephalographic wave that arises from sources other than the heart or brain

ar·ti·fac·ti·tious \ˈ==,fak¦tishəs\ *adj* [*artifact* + *-itious* (as in *factitious*)] **:** ARTIFACTUAL

ar·ti·fac·tu·al \ˈ==¦fakch(əw)əl, -ksh-; -kshwəl\ *adj* [*artifact* + *-ual* (as in *factual*)] **:** of or relating to an artifact

ar·ti·fice \'ärd·əfəs, 'ä|, |tə-\ *n* -S [MF, fr. L *artificium*, fr. *artific-, artifex* artificer, fr. *arti-* (fr. *art-, ars* skill) + *-fic-, -fex* (fr. *facere* to do, make)] **1 a** *obs* **:** production or making of something esp. in arts or crafts **b** *archaic* **:** artistic skill or style **2 a :** a wily or artful stratagem **:** TRICK, TRICKERY **b :** GUILE, INSINCERITY ⟨a master of ~⟩ **3 :** an ingenious or skillful device or expedient **:** clever skill **:** INGENUITY, INVENTIVENESS ⟨the sum total of all this ~, melodrama, and incredible behavior is a warm, witty, profoundly tragic portrait —*Time*⟩ **syn** see ART, TRICK

ar·ti·ficed \-fəst\ *adj* **:** fashioned with artifice ⟨a plot too ingeniously ~ to be the inevitable outcome of the characters' motivation —Frederic Morton⟩

ar·tif·i·cer \är'tifəsər, ä'tifəsə(r) *sometimes* 'ärd·əf- *or* 'ä| *or* |təf-\ *n* -S [ME *artificier, artificer*, fr. (assumed) AF *artificier*, fr. MF *artifice* + *-ier* -er] **1 a :** a skilled or artistic worker **:** a mechanic or craftsman whose handicraft requires skill or knowledge of a special kind (as a silversmith) **b :** an enlisted man or noncommissioned officer in the army or navy with specialized technical duties **:** ARMORER ⟨Royal Navy engine= room ~⟩ ⟨U.S. Army small arms ~⟩ **2 :** one that makes or contrives **:** DEVISER, INVENTOR, FRAMER ⟨the grand ~ of the national life —L.P.Curtis⟩ **3** *obs* **:** a cunning or artful fellow ⟨these base and illiterate ~*s* —Robert Burton⟩

¹ar·ti·fi·cial \ˌär|də¦fishəl, ¦ä|, |tə-\ *adj* [ME, fr. MF or L; MF *artificial, artificiel*, fr. L *artificialis* according to the rules of art, fr. *artificium* artifice + *-alis* -al] **1 :** contrived through human art or effort and not by natural causes detached from human agency **:** relating to human direction or effect in contrast to nature: **a :** formed or established by man's efforts, not by nature ⟨the people do not resort to ~ irrigation —J.G. Frazer⟩ **b :** produced or effected by man's skill to imitate nature **:** SIMULATED ⟨whether Milly's bloom was natural, as it appeared, or ~, as Victoria suspected —Ellen Glasgow⟩ ⟨the use of live bait versus ~ flies in angling⟩ ⟨an ~ limb replacing the amputated leg⟩ **:** made esp. by chemical process to resemble a raw material or something derived from it **:** SYNTHETIC ⟨~ silk⟩ ⟨~ cotton⟩ ⟨~ diamonds⟩ **c :** of, relating to, or produced by artificial insemination ⟨~ daughters of all breeds of cattle⟩ ⟨first ~ breeding association formed in U.S. —*New England Homestead*⟩ **2 a :** characteristic of human social, economic, or legal organization or structure and devoid of or contrary to actual existence in nature as detached from man **b :** taking form from an exceptional legalistic, economic, or social situation **:** palpably unnatural **:** FABRICATED ⟨the empire must be felt not as an ~ novelty but as the natural extension of the republican tradition —John Buchan⟩ ⟨most of the inequalities in the existing world are ~ —Bertrand Russell⟩ **3** *obs* **a :** displaying skill **:** SKILLFUL **b :** ARTFUL, CUNNING, CRAFTY **c :** of or according to fine or practical art **4 a :** not genuinely and spontaneously felt or experienced **:** seemingly not genuine **:** achieved through effort, not naturally **:** FEIGNED, ASSUMED, SPURIOUS ⟨the common tone was ~, was unreal —C.E.Norton⟩ ⟨none of that ~ shamefacedness which her husband mistook for delicacy —W.M.Thackeray⟩ **b :** AFFECTED, SHALLOW, CONVENTIONALIZED, STILTED **:** not natural, spontaneous, or free ⟨so affected, so fussy, so ~ —Kenneth Roberts⟩ ⟨to disregard the ~ rules of somewhat emptied rhetoric —H.O. Taylor⟩ **c :** IMITATION, SHAM ⟨a training army which has not been equipped with guns and artillery and tanks uses ~ guns and masquerading trucks —John Steinbeck⟩ **5 :** of or relating to a bid or bidding system in contract bridge intended to inform one's partner as to the nature of the hand held but not necessarily to show strength in the suit named or willingness to undertake the contract named

syn SYNTHETIC, FACTITIOUS: ARTIFICIAL and SYNTHETIC are often interchangeable when applied to fabrication ⟨rayon is called *artificial* silk and is spoken of as a *synthetic* fabric⟩ ARTIFICIAL contrasts with *natural* ⟨*artificial* and natural silks⟩ ⟨*artificial* and natural heat⟩ ⟨the miner must work by *artificial* light even though the sun be shining outside: still further down in the seams, he must work by *artificial* ventilation, too —Lewis Mumford⟩ SYNTHETIC is likely to connote chemical combination or similar processes ⟨*synthetic* flavors or dyes⟩ ⟨synthesis always means synthesis. *Synthetic* camphor and *synthetic* quinine mean just that —H.L.Fisher⟩ ARTIFICIAL may apply to anything existing in human but not in natural affairs ⟨a corporation is an *artificial* being, invisible, intangible and existing only in contemplation of law —John Marshall⟩ ⟨now magicians or medicine men appear to constitute the oldest *artificial* or professional class in the evolution of society —J.G.Frazer⟩ ARTIFICIAL, FACTITIOUS, and SYNTHETIC may all describe the forced, constrained, simulated, fabricated, or unnatural in matters social or personal; they all indicate a lack of the natural or spontaneous ⟨the strained *artificial* romanticism of Kotzebue's lugubrious dramas —J.W.Krutch⟩ ⟨at her best she is *artificial* . . . one can always feel the heavily conscious performer —G.J.Nathan⟩ ⟨in the degree in which decorative effect is achieved in isolation, it becomes empty embellishment, *factitious* ornamentation — like sugar figures on a cake —John Dewey⟩ ⟨emotional depths which till now had seemed to him unreal, theatrical, *factitious* —B.A.Williams⟩ ⟨an esoteric jargon which did not even have the authentic ring of American slang. It was purely *synthetic* —Stanley Walker⟩ ⟨the usually *synthetic* obscenities of the popular joke, the remote glamor of the embraces of moving-picture stars —Lewis Mumford⟩ FACTITIOUS is less common than ARTIFICIAL; SYNTHETIC is more recent in this use and more likely to suggest technological fabrication.

²artificial \"\ *n* -S **1 :** an imitation of a natural object ⟨there are many live-bait fishermen but the advocates of ~*s* are agreed on one thing —Eddie Finlay⟩; *specif* **:** an artificial flower **2 artificials** *pl, chiefly Brit* **:** artificial manure **:** chemical fertilizer ⟨this crop grows easily on poor soil and although it responds to lime it does not like ~*s* —*Farming*⟩

artificial accession *n* **:** INDUSTRIAL ACCESSION

artificial asphalt *n* **:** the solid residuum from the refining of certain kinds of petroleum

artificial bitter almond oil *n* **:** BENZALDEHYDE

artificial fever *n* **:** FEVER THERAPY

artificial harmonic *n* **:** a harmonic produced on a stopped string on a stringed instrument — compare NATURAL HARMONIC

artificial heart *n* **:** MECHANICAL HEART

artificial horizon *n* **1 :** HORIZON 1b (4) **2 :** an aeronautical instrument based upon a gyroscope and designed to furnish a surface constantly perpendicular to the vertical and therefore parallel to the horizon

artificial insemination *n* **:** introduction of semen into the uterus or oviduct by other than natural means either in order to increase the probability of conception or to extend the usefulness of a valued and prepotent male

ar·ti·fi·ci·al·i·ty \,==,fishē'aləd·ē, -ətē, -i *sometimes* -(,)fi-'shal-\ *n* -ES **:** the quality or state of being artificial **:** the appearance of being artificial **:** something that is artificial

ar·ti·fi·cial·ize \,=='fishə,līz\ *vt* -ED/-ING/-S **:** to make artificial ⟨~ sport for profit —A.S.Leopold⟩ ⟨a singularly *artificialized* life —*Harper's*⟩

artificial key *n* **:** a key used to determine the name of a plant or animal and based on convenient differential morphological characters that do not necessarily indicate natural relationships

artificial kidney *n* **:** an apparatus designed to do the work of the kidney in instances of temporary stoppage of kidney function

artificial language *n* **:** a language devised by an individual or a small group of individuals and proposed for an international language or for some more specific purpose (as aptitude testing) but not functioning as the native speech of its users — compare NATURAL LANGUAGE

ar·ti·fi·cial·ly \¦==¦=shəlē, -li, *rap.* -shl-\ *adv* **:** in an artificial manner

ar·ti·fi·cial·ness *n* -ES **:** ARTIFICIALITY

artificial nucleation *n* **:** a process in which a cloud of liquid-water droplets at below-freezing temperature is converted to an ice crystal-cloud by artificial means

artificial person *n* **:** JURISTIC PERSON

artificial radioactivity *n* **:** radioactivity produced in a substance by bombardment with high-speed particles (as protons or neutrons) — called also *induced radioactivity*

artificial respiration *n* **:** the restoration or initiation by manual or mechanical means of breathing that has failed or that has never begun consisting essentially of forcing air into and out of the lungs to establish the rhythm of inspiration and expiration — compare ELECTROPHRENIC RESPIRATION, IRON LUNG, RESPIRATOR

artificial selection *n* **:** the process of modifying organisms by selection in breeding controlled by man

artificial system *n* **:** a system of classification based on characters that do not indicate natural relationship; *specif* **:** LINNAEAN CLASSIFICATION

artificial ultramarine *n* **:** FRENCH BLUE

artificial vagina *n* **:** a device for collecting semen for artificial insemination

artificious *adj* [prob. fr. MF *artificieux*, fr. L *artificiosus*, fr. *artificium* artifice + *-osus* -ose, -ous — more at ARTIFICE] *obs* **:** displaying skill or artifice — **artificiously** *adv*

ar·til·ler·ist \är'til(ə)rəst, ä'-\ *n* -S **:** one skilled in artillery **:** GUNNER, ARTILLERYMAN

ar·til·lery \är'til(ə)rē, ä'-, -ri, *attrib* (')=¦=(=)=\ *n* -ES *often attrib* [ME *artilrie, artillerie*, fr. MF *artillerie*, fr. OF, fr. *artillier* to furnish with implements esp. for warfare (prob. fr. *art* skill) + *-erie* -ery — more at ART] **1 a** *archaic* **:** munitions of war **:** implements for offensive and defensive warfare **b :** weapons (as bows, slings, arbalests, and catapults) for discharging missiles **c :** crew-served carriage-mounted firearms used in modern warfare that are of caliber greater than that of small arms **:** ordnance (as guns or howitzers) with its equipment **:** CANNON **d** *slang* **:** personal weapons **:** SMALL ARMS **2 a** (1) **:** the missiles discharged by the weapons of war, esp. from modern ordnance (2) **:** the massed fire of artillery weapons **b :** means of arguing or persuading ⟨his own high-powered conversational ~ —*Newsweek*⟩ **3** *obs* **:** the practice of archery **4 :** the branch or analogous organization of an army that is armed with artillery and whose primary missions are furnishing close-fire support to forward combat units, supplying counterbattery fire and fire directed against the enemy's rear areas, and using antiaircraft weapons against enemy planes **5 :** CARTHAMUS RED

ar·til·lery·man \='=(=)=mən\ *n, pl* **artillerymen :** a soldier who belongs to the artillery **:** a person who manages or serves a piece of artillery

artillery plant *n* **:** a tropical American herb (*Pilea microphylla*) that discharges its pollen explosively

artillery wheel *n* **:** a heavily built dished wheel with a long axle box used on gun carriages and usu. having 14 spokes and 7 fellies

art·i·ly \'ärd·ᵊlē, 'äd·|, -t|, |əlē, -li\ *adv* [*arty* + *-ly*] **:** in an arty manner

art·i·ness \ēnəs, |in-\ *n* -ES **:** the quality or state of being arty ⟨substitute ~ for taste⟩

ar·ti·nite \är'tē,nīt, 'ärtᵊn,īt\ *n* -S [It *artinite*, fr. Ettore *Artini* †1928 Ital. mineralogist + It *-ite*] **:** a hydrous magnesium carbonate $Mg_2(CO_3)(OH)_2.3H_2O$ occurring in white orthorhombic crystals and fibrous aggregates

¹ar·ti·o·dac·tyl \¦ärd·ē·ō¦daktᵊl, -rshē-\ *or* **ar·ti·o·dac·tyle** \", -,tīl\ *adj* [NL *Artiodactyla*] **:** of, relating to, or belonging to the Artiodactyla **:** even-toed

²artiodactyl \"\ *or* **artiodactyle** \"\ *n* -S **:** one of the Artiodactyla

ar·ti·o·dac·ty·la \,===ˈdaktələ\ *n pl, cap* [NL, fr. neut. pl. of *artiodactylus* having an even number of toes, fr. Gk *artios* complete, even, even-numbered + *daktylos* finger, toe; akin to L *artus* joint — more at ARTICLE, DACTYL] **:** an order of ungulate mammals including the ox, sheep, goat, antelope, deer, giraffe, camel, hippopotamus, pig, and related forms all having the functional toes of the hind feet and forefeet even in number and the 3d digit of each foot symmetrical with and paired with the 4th digit — compare PERISSODACTYLA

ar·ti·o·dac·ty·lous \¦===¦daktələs\ *adj* [NL *Artiodactyla* + E *-ous*] **:** ARTIODACTYL

ar·ti·san *also* **ar·ti·zan** \'är|d·əzən, 'ä|, |tə-, -əsən *sometimes* -,zan *or* -aa(ə)n, *Brit usu* ¦äti¦zan\ *n* -S [MF, fr. OIt *artigiano*, fr. *arte* art, fr. L *art-, ars* skill — more at ARM] **1** *obs* **:** one who practices an art **:** ARTIST **2 :** one trained to manual dexterity or skill in a trade **:** HANDICRAFTSMAN **3 :** the second rank earned by members of a Horizon Club, senior program of the Camp Fire Girls — compare JOURNEYMAN

ar·ti·san·al \'==zənᵊl, -sən-\ *adj* [F, fr. *artisan* + *-al*] **:** of or relating to artisans

ar·ti·san·ship \-,zən,ship, -sən-, -¦zan, -aan-\ *or* **ar·ti·san·ry** \'==,zənrē, -sən-, -ri\ *n, pl* **artisanships** *or* **artisanries :** the work or workmanship of an artisan

art·ist \'ärd·əst, 'ä|, |tə-\ *n* -S [MF *artiste* artist, artisan, learned man, fr. ML *artista* student or master of the liberal arts, fr. L *art-, ars* art, skill + *-ista* -ist] **1 a :** one who professes and practices an art in which conception and execution are governed by imagination and taste **b :** a person skilled in one of the fine arts; *esp* **:** PAINTER **2a :** a performer of music in public (as a singer, pianist, or conductor) **b :** a theatrical performer ⟨a dramatic ~⟩; *broadly* **:** a usu. adept or skillful public performer or entertainer ⟨a trapeze ~⟩ **:** ARTISTE **3 a** *obs* **:** one skilled or versed in learned arts — used esp. of philosophers, savants, physicians or surgeons, astrologers, or alchemists **b** *archaic* **:** one skilled in some technical or mechanical art or trade (as a cobbler, miner, surveyor, or seaman) **:** ARTISAN **4 :** one who is adept esp. at deception, fraud, artifice, or stratagem **:** one who is expert esp. at something dubious or reprehensible ⟨an ~ with loaded dice⟩ ⟨a short-weight ~ in the coal business⟩ **5 :** one whose vocation involves drawing, painting, designing, or layout work ⟨landscape ~⟩ **syn** see EXPERT

ar·tiste \är'tēst, ä'-\ *n* -S [F, artist, skilled performer or workman] **1 :** a skilled adept performer, often a woman; *specif* **:** a musical or theatrical entertainer **2 :** a skillful and pleasing worker (as a cook or milliner) **syn** see EXPERT

ar·tis·tic \(')är¦tistik, (')ä¦-, -ēk\ *also* **ar·tis·ti·cal** \-əkəl, -ēk-\ *adj* **1 :** relating to, suitable for, or characteristic of art or artists ⟨certain subjects are considered ~ subjects —Bernard Smith⟩ **2 :** characterized by taste, discrimination, and judgment or by art and skill ⟨you may have an ~ interior or you may have a museum —Herbert Spencer⟩ **3 a :** produced by human art ⟨for Plato ~ production is but an imitation of an imitation —A.E.Vassilion⟩ **b :** appropriate for or relevant to a fine-arts presentation ⟨~ subjects⟩ **:** associated with the arts **:** compatible with an artist's attitudes or intentions **:** not material, objective, or moralistic ⟨the difference between mechanical or purely objective construction and ~ production —John Dewey⟩ **c :** suggestive often speciously of art or artists **:** seemingly frequented by artists **:** BOHEMIAN ⟨the people who came to this Soho restaurant because it was notoriously so ~ —Aldous Huxley⟩

syn AESTHETIC: ARTISTIC may stress the viewpoint or suggest the aspirations of the artist as the producer of beautiful things, and AESTHETIC the appreciative attitude of one who views with enjoyment the resulting product or situation ⟨we have no word in the English language that unambiguously includes what is signified by the two words *artistic* and *aesthetic*. Since *artistic* refers primarily to the act of production and *aesthetic* to that of perception and enjoyment, the absence of a term designating the two processes taken together is unfortunate —John Dewey⟩ ⟨the intensity of the *artistic* process, the pressure . . . under which the fusion takes place —T.S.Eliot⟩ ⟨the artist's work in life is full of struggle and toil; it is only the spectator of morals who can assume the calm *aesthetic* attitude —Havelock Ellis⟩ Sometimes this distinction is not followed ⟨an *artistic* satisfaction in the contemplation of evil —W.S. Maugham⟩ ⟨that loveliness which is the creation of the *aesthetic* human spirit —John Galsworthy⟩

ar·tis·ti·cal·ly \-ək(ə)lē, -ēk-, -li\ *adv* **:** in an artistic manner

artist lithography *n* : AUTOLITHOGRAPHY
art·ist·ry \ˈärd·əstrē, ˈȧ|, |tə-, -ri\ *n* -ES **1** : artistic quality of effect or workmanship ⟨the ~ of this first chapter —G.H. Genzmer⟩ **2** : artistic ability ⟨to be on the winning side in every argument requires an ~ not always fully appreciated —Julian Dana⟩
artist's proof *n* : one of the first and therefore best proofs printed from an engraved plate
art·less \ˈärtləs, ˈȧt-\ *adj* **1 a** : lacking art, skill, or knowledge : IGNORANT, UNSKILLFUL ⟨to be ~ is to be dehumanized —E.A. Hoebel⟩ **b** : devoid of artistic quality or taste : UNCULTURED ⟨the land vaguely realizing westward but still unstoried, ~ —Robert Frost⟩ **2** : free from the artificial : easy, natural, and not contrived ⟨its atmosphere of something we call an ~ charm pervades through the narrative —H.V.Gregory⟩ **3** : made or contrived without skill or art : CRUDE, INARTISTIC ⟨marred by an ~ summerhouse in the garden⟩ **4** : marked by freedom from calculated craft, guile, and duplicity and by sincerity, simplicity, and genuineness ⟨open, candid, ~, guileless, with affections strong, but simple, forming no pretensions, and knowing no disguise —Jane Austen⟩ **syn** see NATURAL
art·less·ly *adv* : in an artless manner : without art, skill, or guile : UNAFFECTEDLY
art·less·ness *n* -ES : the quality or state of being artless
art marble *n* : a cast stone made of crushed marble with the exposed surface highly polished to resemble natural marble
art music *n* : music composed by the trained musician as contrasted with folk music and often with popular music
art nou·veau \ˌär,nüˈvō\ *n, often cap A&N* [F, lit., new art] : a late 19th century and early 20th century decorative style characterized by organic foliate forms, sinuous lines, and nongeometric curves
arto- *comb form* [L, fr. Gk, fr. *artos*; perh. akin to Gk *arariskein* to fit — more at ARM] : bread ⟨*Arto*carpus⟩
art object *n* [by trans.] : OBJET D'ART
ar·to·car·pus \ˌärd·əˈkärpəs\ *n* [NL, fr. *arto-* + *-carpus*] **1** *cap* : a large genus of tall evergreen milky-juiced trees (family Moraceae) orig. Asiatic but now grown throughout the tropics having large alternate entire or lobed leaves and flowers in catkinlike clusters with the pistillate ones in crowded heads that produce a multiple fleshy fruit **2** -ES : a plant of the genus *Artocarpus* : BREADFRUIT, JACKFRUIT
art of self-defense 1 : BOXING **2** : FENCING
ar·to·gra·vure \ˌärd·əgrəˈvyu̇(ə)r\ *n* -S [²*art* + *-o-* + *gravure*] : the process of preparing silk-screen stencils photographically by sensitizing the silk and printing the image on it
ar·to·pho·ri·on \-ˈfōrē,än\ *n, pl* **artopho·ria** \-rēə\ [MGk, fr. Gk, bread basket, fr. *arto-* + *-phorion* (akin to *pherein* to carry) — more at BEAR] : a container for the reserved sacrament in the Eastern Church
ar·to·type \ˈärd·ə,tīp\ *n* -S [²*art* + *-o-* + *type*] : COLLOTYPE
ar·to·ty·rite \ˌärd·əˈtī,rīt\ *n* -S *usu cap* [LL *Artotyrita*, fr. LGk *Artotyritēs*, fr. Gk *artotyros* bread and cheese (fr. *arto-* + *tyros* cheese) + *-itēs* -ite — more at TYR-] : one of a Montanist sect that according to its opponents used bread and cheese in the celebration of the Lord's Supper
art paper *n* **1** *Brit* : coated paper **2** : heavy colored paper used esp. by students for art or craft projects — compare CONSTRUCTION PAPER
arts *pl of* ART
-arts *pl of* -ART
arts and crafts *n pl* : the arts of decorative design and handicraft (as bookbinding, weaving, and needlework) that are concerned with objects of use
arts college *n* : a college in which the liberal arts are the only or the principal studies
artsman *n, pl* **artsmen** *obs* : a man skilled in an art
arts master *n, obs* : a teacher or master of art or of an art
art song *n* : a song that is lyric in character with melody and accompaniment usu. through-composed by a trained musician — see LIED; compare FOLK SONG
art square *n* : a patterned rectangle of carpet woven in one piece for a rug
art theater *n* : a theater that specializes in the presentation of artistic dramatic productions and esp. foreign films
art union *n* : any of several 19th century American associations for promoting the arts esp. through the distribution of paintings and prints by lottery
artware \ˈ⸗,⸗\ *n* : merchandise (as knickknacks) that is aesthetic as well as utilitarian
artwork \ˈ⸗,⸗\ *n* **1 a** : the making of decorative or artistic objects by hand **b** : the decoration of artistic objects so made **2** : artistic work produced in quantity; *specif* : 19th century factory-made objects **3** : ART 8
arty \ˈär|d·ē, ˈȧ|, |tē, -i\ *adj* -ER/-EST **1** : imitative often unsuccessfully of art : having some of the showier characteristics of art ⟨no ~ or pretentious line ever got into his daily cartoon —James Thurber⟩ **2** : aspiring often unsuccessfully to be artistic : showing dilettante interests : marked by concern with accidental rather than essential characteristics of art ⟨his ~ but beautiful wife —V.P.Hass⟩
arty *abbr* artillery
arty-crafty \ˌ⸗⸗ˈ⸗⸗\ *also* **arty-and-crafty** \ˌ⸗⸗⸗ˈ⸗⸗\ *or* **artsy-craftsy** \ˌärtsēˈkraf(t)sē\ *adj* [irreg. fr. *arts and crafts*] **1 a** : simultaneously arty and somewhat useless, novel, and often expensive and uncomfortable ⟨*arty-crafty* lawn furniture⟩ **b** : marked by pretension esp. to artlessness or simplicity ⟨*arty-crafty* street terminology that garden suburbs have lately made their own —*Architectural Rev.*⟩ **2** : ARTY 2 ⟨a free-thinking, *arty-crafty* little sculptress —Eleazar Lipsky⟩
arua \ˈärəˌwä\ *n, pl* **arua** *or* **aruas** *usu cap* [Pg *aruá*, of Amer Ind origin] **1 a** : an Arawakan people of French Guiana and Brazil **b** : a member of such people **2** : the language of the Arua people
aruac *usu cap, var of* ARHUACO
arui \ˈärüˌē\ *n* -S [native name in eastern Africa] : AOUDAD
aru·ke \ˈärüˌkā\ *n* -S [Maori *aruhe*] *New Zeal* : the starchy rhizome of the brake (*Pteridium aquilinum*)
ar·um \ˈa(a)rəm, ˈer-, ˈär-\ *n* [NL, fr. L, arum, fr. Gk *aron*; perh. akin to L *arundo* reed] **1** *cap* : a genus (the type of the family Araceae) of herbs of Europe and Asia with usu. heart-shaped leaves and a large spathe with edges involute at the base **2** -S : any of several plants of the family Araceae, esp. of the genus *Arum* — see CUCKOOPINT **3** -S : a sagolike starch obtained from cuckoopint root : PORTLAND ARROWROOT
arum family *n* : ARACEAE
arum lily *n* : CALLA LILY
arun·cus \əˈrəŋkəs\ *n, cap* [NL, fr. L, beard of a goat, fr. (assumed) Gk (Dor) *aryngos*; akin to Gk (Attic) *ēryngos*] : a small genus of herbs (family Rosaceae) found in No. America and Japan and having compound leaves and a showy branched cluster of white flowers — see GOATSBEARD
arun·del \əˈrənd°l\ *adj, usu cap* [fr. Anne Arundel county, Md.] : of or relating to a subdivision of the Lower Cretaceous
arun·di·na·ceous \əˌrəndəˈnāshəs\ *adj* [L *arundinaceus*, *harundinaceus* reedlike, fr. *arundin-*, *arundo*, *harundin-*, *harundo* reed + *-aceus* -aceous] : of or relating to a reed : resembling reed or cane
arun·di·nar·ia \əˌrəndəˈna(a)rēə\ *n, cap* [NL, fr. L *arundin-*, *arundo*, *harundin-*, *harundo* reed + NL *-aria*] : a genus of large woody bamboo grasses that are natives of Asia and America and have terete culms, persistent leaf sheaths with stiff scabrous bristles, and flower spikelets arranged in racemes or panicles — compare CANEBRAKE, GIANT CANE, SMALL CANE
arun·do \əˈrən(ˌ)dō\ *n, cap* [NL, fr. L *arundo*, *harundo* reed] : a small genus of coarse tall grasses found in most warm countries and having conspicuous 2-ranked long leaves and an erect panicle up to 2 feet or more in length — see GIANT REED
arun·ta \əˈrəntə\ *or* **aran·da** \-andə, -än-\ *or* **aran·ta** \-antə, -än-\ *n, pl* **arunta** *or* **aruntas** *or* **aranda** *or* **arandas** *or* **aranta** *or* **arantas** *usu cap* **1 a** : an aboriginal people in central Australia **b** : a member of such people **2** : the language of the Arunta people
arura *var of* AROURA
aru·sa \əˈrüsə\ *n* -S [modif. of Hindi *arus*, perh. fr. Skt *aṭaruṣa*] **1** : a small shrub (*Adhatoda vasica*) found in India **2** : a yellow dye derived from arusa leaves
aru·sha *also* **aroo·sha** \əˈrüshə\ *n* -S [perh. fr. Skt *aruṣa* red] : an Indian shrub (*Callicarpa cana*) yielding a flaxlike fiber

aruspex *var of* HARUSPEX
arv *abbr* arrive
¹**ar·val** *also* **ar·vel** \ˈärvəl\ *n* -S [ME *arvell*, of Scand origin; akin to ON *erfiöl* funeral feast, fr. *erfi* inheritance, funeral feast + *öl* ale, drinking bout, banquet; akin to ON *arfi* inheritance — more at ORPHAN, ALE] *dial Brit* : a funeral feast
²**arval** \ˈ"\ *adj, usu cap* [L *arvalis*, lit., of cultivated field, fr. *arvum* cultivated field + *-alis* -al] : relating to a body of ancient Roman priests who presided over an annual fertility festival in May
ar·ver·ni \ärˈvər,nī\ *n pl, usu cap* [L] : a powerful and civilized people of southern Gaul that were conquered by Caesar in his Gallic wars
¹**ar·vic·o·la** \-ˈvikələ\ *n, cap* [NL, fr. LL *arvi-* (fr. L *arvum* cultivated field, fr. neut. of *arvus* arable) + L *-cola* inhabitant; akin to L *arare* to plow — more at EAR, -COLOUS] : a genus of rodents consisting of the water voles
²**arvicola** \ˈ"\ [NL, fr. LL *arvi-* + L *-cola*] *syn of* MICROTUS
ar·vi·cole \ˈärvə,kōl\ *n* -S [NL *Arvicola*] : a member of the genus *Arvicola*
ar·vi·cul·ture \-,kəlchər *also* ,⸗⸗ˈ⸗⸗\ *n* -S [prob. fr. F, fr. LL *arvi-* + F *culture*] : the cultivation of field crops : the science and art of growing field crops
ARW *abbr* air raid warden
ary \ˈarē, ˈer-, ˈaar-, -ri *S also* ˈar *or* ˈaə\ *adj* [alter. of *e'er a*, fr. *e'er* + ²*a*] *dial* : ANY, A ⟨was there ~ thing I could do —Marjorie K. Rawlings⟩
¹**-ary** *US*: ,erē, ,eri, *infrequently* ərē *or* r-, *S also* ,är-, *when an unstressed syllable precedes;* ər- *also* r-, *in a few words* ,er- *S also* ,är-, *when a stressed syllable precedes. Brit: whatever the preceding stress, usu* əri, *alternatively often* ri *when a vowel or semivowel does not immediately precede*\ *n suffix* -ES [ME *-arie*, fr. OF & L; OF *-arie*, *-aire*, fr. L *-arius*, *-aria*, *-arium*, fr. *-arius*, adj. suffix] : one that belongs to or is connected with: **a** : thing belonging to or connected with; *esp* : place of ⟨avi*ary*⟩ ⟨besti*ary*⟩ ⟨herb*ary*⟩ ⟨semin*ary*⟩ ⟨termit*ary*⟩ **b** : person belonging to, connected with, or engaged in ⟨function*ary*⟩ ⟨sedition*ary*⟩
²**-ary** \ˈ"\ *adj suffix* [ME *-arie*, fr. MF & L; MF *-aire*, fr. L *-arius*] : of or belonging to or connected with ⟨budget*ary*⟩ ⟨discretion*ary*⟩ ⟨parliament*ary*⟩ ⟨unit*ary*⟩
ar·ya *like next without* n\ *n, pl* **aryas** *also* **arya** *usu cap* [Skt *ārya*] : ARYAN
¹**ar·yan** *also* **ar·ian** \ˈa(a)rēən, ˈer-, ˈär- *sometimes* ˈärēən *or* ˈäryən *or* ˈārē- *or* ˈāy-\ *adj, usu cap* [Skt *ārya*, adj. & n., noble, Aryan, member of the upper castes, prob. fr. *ari* stranger, enemy; akin to Av *airyō* Aryan, OPer *ariya*, and prob. to L *alius* other — more at ELSE] **1** : of or relating to the Indo-European family of languages or to their hypothetical prototype **2** : of or relating to speakers of Indo-European languages **3 a** : of or relating to a hypothetical ethnic type illustrated by or descended from early speakers of Indo-European languages **b** : NORDIC **4** : of or relating to the Indo-Iranians or their speech
²**aryan** *also* **arian** \ˈ"\ *n* -S *usu cap* [Skt *ārya*] **1** : a member of the Indo-European-speaking people one branch of which early occupied the Iranian plateau while another branch entered India and conquered and amalgamated with the earlier non-Indo-European inhabitants : INDO-IRANIAN **2 a** : member of the people that spoke the language from which the Indo-European languages are derived **b** : an individual of any of those peoples who have spoken these languages since prehistoric times : INDO-EUROPEAN **c** : NORDIC **d** : GENTILE **3** : a member of the Indo-European-speaking modern peoples of India as opposed to the Dravidian-speaking ones
ar·yan·ism \-,nizəm\ *n* -S *usu cap* **1** : the doctrine popularized by Nazism that the so-called Aryan peoples possess superior capacities for government, social organization, and civilization **2** : the belief in the doctrine of Aryanism and acceptance of its social and ethical implications often accompanied by suppression of the so-called non-Aryan peoples (as the Jews) — compare NORDICISM
ar·yan·ist \-nəst\ *n* -S *usu cap* : one who makes a special study of the facts bearing on the Aryan race as a homogeneous group; *specif* : one who argues the existence of the Aryan race or credits the hypothetical Aryans with racially superior capacities or traits
ar·yan·i·za·tion \ˌ⸗(⸗)⸗nəˈzāshən, -,nīˈz-\ *n* -S *usu cap* : the act or process of aryanizing
ar·yan·ize \ˈ⸗(⸗)⸗,nīz\ *vt* -ED/-ING/-S *often cap* **1** : to make Aryan in speech characteristics or culture **2** : to clear of non-Aryan (as Semitic) personnel, control, or influence
ar·y·bal·los *or* **ar·y·bal·lus** \ˌarəˈbaləs\ *n* -ES [Gk *aryballos* bag, purse, aryballos, perh. fr. *ary-* (fr. *aryein* to draw — water) + *-ballos* (fr. *ballein* to throw) — more at DEVIL] : a flask or bottle that has a short neck, single handle, small orifice with a flaring lip, and globular body often elaborately decorated and that is used for holding oils or ointments — compare ALABASTRUM

aryballos

ar·y·epiglottic \ˌarē + ˌ⸗⸗ˈ⸗⸗\ *adj* [Gk *ary-* (fr. *aryein* to draw — water) + E *epiglottic*] : ARYTENOEPIGLOTTIC
ar·yl \ˈarəl\ *n* -S [ISV *aromatic* + *-yl*; prob. orig. formed in G] **1** : a univalent aromatic radical (as phenyl or tolyl) derived from an arene by removal of one hydrogen atom from a carbon atom of the nucleus — compare ARALKYL **2** : a compound of one or more aryl radicals with a metal ⟨sodium ~s⟩
ar·yl·amine \ˌarəl + \ *n* -S [ISV *aryl* + *amine*] : an amine (as aniline) containing aryl attached to amino nitrogen
ar·yl·a·mi·no \ˌ⸗⸗ˈmē(,)nō, -ˈamə,nō\ *adj* [ISV *arylamino-*, fr. *arylamine*] : of, relating to, or containing an arylamine
ar·yl·ate \ˈarə,lāt\ *vt* -ED/-ING/-S [ISV *aryl* + *-ate*] : to introduce one or more aryl groups into (a compound)
ar·yl·a·tion \ˌ⸗⸗ˈlāshən\ *n* -S : the act or process of arylating
ar·yl·ene \ˈarə,lēn\ *n* -S [ISV *aryl-* + *-ene*] : a bivalent radical (as phenylene) derived from an aromatic hydrocarbon by removal of a hydrogen atom from each of two carbon atoms of the nucleus
ar·yl·ide \-,līd\ *n* -S [*aryl* + *amide*] : a usu. acid amide (as an anilide) in which hydrogen of the amido group is replaced by aryl (as phenyl)
ar·yl·oxy \-,läksē\ *adj* [*aryloxy-*, fr. *aryl* + *oxy-*] : of, relating to, or containing a univalent radical ArO (as phenoxy) composed of an aryl radical united with oxygen
¹**ar·yo-dravidian** \ˌa(a)rē,ō, ˌer-, ˌär- *sometimes* ˈärē,ō *or* ˈär(,)yō *or* ˈārē,ō *or* ˈā(,)yō+\ *adj, usu cap A&D* [*Aryo-* (fr. ¹*Aryan*) + *Dravidian*] : of, relating to, or characteristic of the Indian people having a mixture of Aryan and Dravidian blood that constitute the chief population of northern India between the Punjab and Bengal and of the southern half of Ceylon
²**aryo-dravidian** \ˈ"\ *n* -S *cap A&D* : one of the Aryo-Dravidian people
aryo-indian \ˈ"+\ *n, cap A&I* : a person of a native race in India having an Aryan element in his ancestry
ar·y·te·no·epiglottic \ˌarə,tē(,)nō, əˌrit°n,ō+\ *or* **ar·y·te·no·epiglottidean** \ˈ"+\ *adj* [*aryteno-* (fr. NL *arytenoides*) + *epiglottic* or *epiglottidean*] : relating to or linking the arytenoid cartilage and the epiglottis ⟨~ folds⟩
¹**ar·y·te·noid** \ˌarəˈtē,nȯid, əˈrit°n,ȯid\ *also* **ar·y·te·noi·dal** \ˌarə(,)tēˈnȯid°l, əˌrit°nˈȯi-\ *adj* [*arytaenoid* fr. NL *arytaenoides*, fr. Gk *arytainoeidēs*, lit., ladle-shaped, fr. *arytaina* ladle (fr. *aryein* to draw —water—, prob. fr. a prehistoric Gk compound whose first and second constituents are akin respectively to Skt *vār* water and to L *haurire* to draw) + *-oeidēs* -oid; *arytenoidal* fr. ²*arytenoid* + *-al* — more at URINE, EXHAUST] **1** : relating to or being either of two small cartilages to which the vocal cords are attached and which are situated at the upper back part of the larynx **2** : relating to or being either of a pair of small muscles or an unpaired muscle of the larynx
²**arytenoid** \ˈ"\ *n* -S [NL *arytaenoides*, fr. Gk *arytainoeidēs*, adj.] : an arytenoid cartilage or muscle
arz·ru·nite \ˈärzˈrü,nīt, ˈärts-\ *n* -S [G *arzrunit*, fr. Andreas *Arzruni* †1898 Ger. mineralogist who first recognized it + G *-it*] : a mineral consisting of a basic copper sulfate with copper chloride occurring as bluish green incrustations

¹**as** \əz, (ˈ)az\ *adv* [ME *as, alse, also*, adv. & conj., fr. OE *alswā, ealswā, ælswā* just as, likewise — more at ALSO] **1** : to the same degree or amount : to such an extent : EQUALLY — used to modify an adjective or an adverb ⟨I haven't found any new poems ~ good as my old favorites —Randall Jarrell⟩ ⟨neither of them wrote ~ well after the experience as before it —Van Wyck Brooks⟩ ⟨nowhere else in the world is there a people ~ intelligent or ~ perceptive of humor —F.P.Adams⟩ **2** : for instance : by way of example : THUS — usu. used to introduce illustrative details ⟨high-pitched sounds come to suggest spatial height, ~ in bird songs —Thomas Munro⟩
²**as** \ˈ"\ *conj* [ME *as, alse, alswa*] **1** : to which (degree or amount) : in which (degree or extent) : in or to the same degree in which — usu. used as a correlative after an adjective or adverb modified by adverbial *as* or *so* and often followed by a noun or pronoun representing an incomplete clause whose verb would be the same as that of the main clause ⟨the position of this science is as honorable ~ it is secure —L.A.White⟩ ⟨no general presentation . . . can interest the children as much ~ the learning of the foreign language —Ruth Mays⟩ ⟨his dull red hair was snow-powdered nearly as white ~ that of a British grenadier⟩ **2** : in the same way or manner that : in the form or condition in which ⟨his hair is brown ~ are his eyes⟩ ⟨studied the simile ~ Horner used it⟩ — sometimes followed by a noun or pronoun representing an incomplete clause whose verb would be the same as that of the main clause ⟨during his stay on the island he lived ~ an islander⟩ **3** : according to what : in accordance with that which or the way in which ⟨~ he said, the stream was full of trout⟩ ⟨his criticisms, ~ I remember, were coldly received⟩ ⟨he is really quite good ~ boys go⟩ **4** : as if ⟨were saying farewell to each other ~ to their childhood —Edith Sitwell⟩ ⟨this mechanical thought is crushing ~ with an iron roller all that is organic —W.B.Yeats⟩ **5** : during or at the same time that : WHILE, WHEN ⟨promptly opened fire again ~ he turned away —C.S.Forester⟩ ⟨~ he paced back and forth the idea occurred to him⟩ ⟨you will see the tower ~ you cross the bridge⟩ **6** : notwithstanding the degree to which : THOUGH ⟨some see in him, Gael ~ he was, the earliest Protestant —Gilbert Highet⟩ **7** : in a manner or degree befitting or having equal certainty with the fact, belief, or hope that ⟨this swears he, ~ he is a prince, is just and ~ I am a gentleman, I credit him —Shak.⟩ ⟨~ I live, I cannot believe it⟩ **8** : for the reason that : BECAUSE, SINCE ⟨remained in great loneliness and considerable privation ~ he had no income —W.L.Sullivan⟩ **9** *dial* : THAN — used in comparisons ⟨he better not be later ~ midnight —T.B.Costain⟩ **10 a** : that the result is : THAT — used with preceding *so* or *such* ⟨so clearly guilty ~ to leave no doubt of his conviction⟩ ⟨and such a son ~ all men hailed me happy —John Milton⟩ **b** : THAT — used to introduce a noun clause and now dial. except in certain negative expressions with *know, say*, or *see* that have wide usage in informal speech ⟨he said ~ he would come⟩ ⟨I don't know ~ it makes any difference⟩ **c** *dial* : in so far as : THAT — used to introduce an adverbial clause ⟨he hasn't come out again ~ I've seen⟩ — **as is** \(ˈ)aˈziz, əˈz-\ : in its present condition : without any repairs, improvements, or alterations being made ⟨the car was priced at $1000 *as is*⟩ — **as it were** : as if it were so : in a manner of speaking ⟨her triumph, *as it were*, did not last long⟩ — **as new** : practically new : in the best secondhand condition ⟨the clothes offered for sale were all prewar and all *as new*⟩ — **as you were** — a military command used (1) to cancel another command that has not yet been executed or (2) to direct troops to return to the position occupied before the last command
³**as** \ˈ"\ *pron* **1 a** : THAT, WHO, WHICH — used to introduce an adjectival clause and having *same* or *such* as antecedent ⟨their children should grow up in the same intellectual culture ~ they have enjoyed —G.B.Jeffery⟩ ⟨tears such ~ angels weep burst forth —John Milton⟩ **b** *now dial* : THAT, WHO, WHICH — used to introduce an adjectival clause and having a noun or pronoun as antecedent ⟨a lot of things happened . . . ~ never ought to —Richard Llewellyn⟩ ⟨was going to tell the gospel to them ~ had ears —R.P.Warren⟩ **2** : a fact that : THAT ⟨he is a foreigner, ~ is evident from his accent⟩ ⟨I have used thee, filth ~ thou art, with humane care —Shak.⟩
⁴**as** \ˈ"\ *prep* [¹*as*] **1** : after the manner of : the same as : LIKE ⟨had seen strong men become ~ weaklings when they were faced with . . . being shipwrecked —H.A.Chippendale⟩ ⟨his face was ~ a mask of gauze through which nothing was quite clearly visible —Max Beerbohm⟩ **2 a** : in the character, role, function, capacity, condition, or sense of ⟨more interested in . . . attitudes ~ attitudes than he is in their definition and embodiment in aesthetic forms —Mark Schorer⟩ ⟨eager for power ~ power⟩ ⟨his appearance ~ Hamlet⟩ ⟨his appointment ~ instructor⟩ **b** : in a way or of a nature constituting ⟨he comes home at six ~ a rule⟩ ⟨~ a result of the trip he was exhausted⟩ **c** : for consideration or considered in a specified form or relation — usu. used before prepositions and participles (as *against, between, distinguished*, and *opposed*) ⟨his argument ~ against yours⟩ ⟨my opinion ~ distinguished from theirs⟩
⁵**as** \ˈas\ *n, pl* **as·ses** \ˈa(,)sēz, -səz\ [L — more at ACE] **1** : LIBRA 2 **2 a (1)** : a bronze coin of the ancient Roman republic varying in weight from 1 as, or 12 ounces, to ½ ounce **(2)** : one of several similar coins issued by some of the Roman emperors **b** : a unit of value equivalent to an as coin
⁶**as** *sing of* AESIR
⁷**as** \ˈäs\ *also* **as nas** \-näs\ *n* [Per] : a Persian card game similar to poker and by some thought to be its progenitor

Roman as, showing head of Janus

¹**as-** — see AD-
²**as-** *also* **asym-** *comb form, usu ital* [ISV *asymmetric*] : asymmetric — in names of organic compounds ⟨*as*-dichloro-ethylene⟩
-as *pl of* -A
AS *abbr* **1** account sales **2** after sight **3** air service **4** air speed **5** alongside **6** [ML *anno salutis*] in the year of redemption **7** antisubmarine **8** applied science **9** apprentice seaman **10** at sight
As *symbol* arsenic
a's *or* **as** *pl of* A
asa·do \əˈsä(,)dō\ *n* -S [AmerSp, fr. Sp, roast meat, fr. *asado* (past part. of *asar* to roast), fr. L *assatus*, past part. of *assare* to roast, fr. *assus* roasted; akin to L *ardēre* to burn — more at ARDOR] : BARBECUE
asa dul·cis \ˌasəˈdəlsəs, ˌäs-\ *n* [NL, lit., sweet gum] : BENZOIN 1
as·a·fet·i·da *or* **as·a·foet·i·da** *or* **as·sa·fet·i·da** *or* **as·sa·foet·i·da** \ˌasəˈfid·ədē, -fed·ə-, -fetə-, asˈf-, aas-,ais-; -fed·ədə, -fetədə\ *also* **as·fet·i·da** \asˈf-,aasˈf-,aisˈf-\ *n* -S [ME *asafetida*, fr. ML *asafoetida*, fr. *asa* gum (of Iranian origin; akin to Per *azā* mastic) + L *foetida*, fem. of *foetidus* fetid] : the fetid gum resin of various Persian and East Indian plants of the genus *Ferula* (esp. *F. assafoetida*, *F. foetida*, or *F. narthex*) occurring in the form of tears and dark-colored masses, having a strong odor and taste, and formerly used in medicine as an antispasmodic
asa·hi·ka·wa \ˌäsəhēˈkäwə\ *adj, usu cap* [fr. *Asahikawa*, city on Hokkaido island, Japan] : of or from Asahikawa, Japan : of the kind or style prevalent in Asahikawa
¹**asak** *var of* ASOKA
²**as·ak** \ˈasək\ *n* -S [Hindi *asok* — more at ASOKA] : MAST TREE
¹**asa·na** \ˈäsənə\ *n* -S [Skt *āsana*, fr. *āste* he sits; akin to Gk *hēsthai* to sit, Av *āstē* he sits, Hitt *es-* to sit] : manner of sitting (as in the practice of yoga) : POSTURE
²**asa·na** \ˌäsəˈnä\ *n* -S [PhilSp *asana*, fr. Tag *asanā*] : NARRA
asante *usu cap, var of* ASHANTI
asaph·ic \(ˈ)āˈsafik\ *adj, usu cap* [*Asaph*, 10th cent. B.C. Levite and musician mentioned in 1 Chron 16:5, 25:1–2 + E *-ic*] : of or relating to Asaph, chief musician of the sanctuary in the time of David, or to the hereditary musical guild founded by him ⟨*Asaphic* psalms⟩
asaph·ite \ˈāsa,fīt\ *n* -S *usu cap* [*Asaph* + E *-ite*] : a descendant of the Levite Asaph

as·a·phus \'asəfəs\ *n, cap* [NL, irreg. fr. Gk *asaphēs* indistinct, dim, fr. *a-* ²a- + *saphēs* distinct, clear] **:** a genus of trilobites occurring abundantly in the Ordovician of northern Europe and having subequal cephala and pygidia

as·a·ra·bac·ca \,asərə'bakə\ *n* -s [alter. of earlier *asarabacara*, prob. fr. Sp *asarabácara*, irreg. fr. *ásaro* asarabacca (fr. L *asarum* hazelwort) + *bácara* clary (*Salvia sclarea*), fr. L *baccaris*, a plant with an aromatic root, fr. Gk *bakkaris*] **:** a plant of the genus *Asarum*

asa·rah b'te·bet \ä¦sō,rōbə'tā(,)ves\ *n* -s *usu cap A&T* [Heb *'ăsārāh bĕṭēbhēth*] **:** a Jewish fast day observed on the 10th day of Tebet to mark the beginning of the siege of Jerusalem by Nebuchadnezzar in 586 B.C.

asarh \'ä,sär\ *n* -s *usu cap* [Skt *Āṣāḍha*] **:** a month of the Hindu year — see MONTH table

as·a·ron \'asə,rän\ *also* **as·a·rone** \-,rōn\ *n* -s [ISV *asar-* (fr. NL *Asarum*) + *-on, -one*] **:** a crystalline phenolic ether $C_{12}H_{16}O_3$ found in the oils of a number of plants esp. of the genus *Asarum* — called also *asarum camphor*

as·a·ro·tum \,asə'rōd·əm\ *n, pl* **asaro·ta** \-ōd·ə\ [L, fr. Gk *asarōton*, neut. of *asarōtos* paved in mosaic resembling an unswept floor, lit., unswept, fr. *a-* ²a- + *sarōtos*, verbal of *saroun* to sweep, fr. *saron* broom; prob. akin to L *turba* disturbance, tumult — more at TURBID] **:** ancient Roman painted pavement

as·a·rum \'asərəm\ *n* [NL, fr. L, hazelwort, fr. Gk *asaron*] **1** *cap* **:** a genus of acaulescent herbs (family Aristolochiaceae) native to north-temperate regions and having pungent aromatic roots and dull-colored flowers — see WILD GINGER **2** -s **:** the dried rhizome and roots of wild ginger used as an aromatic bitters and flavoring agent

asarum camphor *n* **:** ASARON

as·best \'as,best, ≈'≈ *also* (')az-\ *n* -s *archaic* **:** ASBESTOS

as·bes·tic \(')as¦bestik, -z¦b-\ *n* -s **:** a fibrous sand formed by mixing second-grade asbestos and serpentine and used when crushed and mixed with lime to form a fireproof wall plaster

as·bes·ti·form \as'bestə,fȯrm, az-\ *adj* [¹*asbestos* + *-iform*] **:** having the form or appearance of asbestos

as·bes·tine \(')≈¦≈stən, ≈'≈,stēn\ *or* **as·bes·tous** \(')≈¦≈stəs\ *or* **as·bes·tic** \(')≈¦≈stik\ *adj* [*asbestos* + *-ine* or *-ous* or *-ic*] **:** of, relating to, or having the characteristics of asbestos **:** INCOMBUSTIBLE

Asbestine \≈'≈,stēn, -,stən\ *trademark* — used for a finely fibrous variety of talc used esp. as a filler for rubber and paper and as an extender and white pigment in paints

as·bes·toid \≈'≈,stȯid\ *or* **as·bes·toi·dal** \¦≈¦≈¦stȯidᵊl\ *adj* [¹*asbestos* + *-oid, -oidal*] **:** resembling asbestos

¹**as·bes·tos** *also* **as·bes·tus** \as'bestəs *also* az'- *or* əs'- *or* əz'-\ *n* -ES [ME *asbestus* mineral supposed to be inextinguishable when set on fire, alter. (influenced by L & Gk *asbestos*) of *albeston*, prob. fr. MF, alter. (prob. influenced by L *albus* white) of *abeston*, fr. ML *asbeston*, alter. of L *asbestos*, fr. Gk, unslaked lime, fr. *asbestos* inextinguishable, unextinguished, fr. *a-* ²a- + (assumed) *sbestos*, verbal of *sbennynai* to quench, extinguish; akin to Lith *gesti* to be extinguished, Skt *jasate* he is exhausted and perh. to OHG *quist* annihilation, Goth *qistjan* to destroy, Toch B *käs-* to pass out of existence] **1 :** a mineral (as chrysotile, tremolite, or actinolite) that readily separates into long flexible fibers suitable for uses where incombustible, nonconducting, or chemically resistant material is required **2 a :** a mineral fiber usu. long, smooth, and white **b** *or* **asbestos yarn :** a yarn usu. made of asbestos or of asbestos and other fibers **3** *or* **asbestos curtain :** a fireproof curtain made of asbestos or other material and used in a theater to close the proscenium opening in case of fire

²**asbestos** \"\ *adj* **:** made of, containing, or resembling asbestos

asbestos cement *n* **:** a hardened mixture of asbestos fibers, portland cement, and water used in relatively thin slabs for shingles, wallboard, and siding

as·bes·to·sis \,as,be'stōsəs, ,az-\ *n, pl* **asbesto·ses** \-ō,sēz\ [NL, fr. L *asbestos* + NL *-osis*] **:** a form of pneumoconiosis caused by the inhalation of fine particles of asbestos

as·bo·lite \'azbə,līt, 'as-\ *also* **as·bo·lan** \-,lan\ *or* **as·bo·lane** \-,lān\ *n* -s [*asbolite*, modif. (influenced by *-ite*) of G *asbolan*, fr. Gk *asbolos* soot + G *-an* -an, -ane; *asbolan*, *asbolane* fr. G *asbolan*; perh. akin to Goth *azgo* ash — more at ASH] **:** an earthy mineral aggregate containing manganese and cobalt oxides

asc- *or* **asci-** *or* **asco-** *comb form* [NL, fr. *ascus*] **:** bladder **:** ascus ⟨*asc*ula⟩ ⟨*asci*gerous⟩ ⟨*asco*spore⟩

as·ca·la·bo·ta \,askələ'bōd·ə\ *n, pl, cap* [NL, fr. *Ascalabotes*, type genus, fr. Gk *askalabōtēs* spotted lizard] *zool* **:** a division of Lacertilia comprising the Gekkones, Iguania, and Rhiptoglossa

as·ca·laph·i·dae \,askə'lafə,dē\ *n pl, cap* [NL, fr. *Ascalaphus*, type genus (fr. Gk *askalaphos*, a kind of owl) + *-idae*] **:** a family of rather large nocturnal insects (order Neuroptera) superficially resembling dragonflies but having long club-tipped antennae

as·caph·i·dae \ə'skafə,dē\ *n pl, cap* [NL, fr. *Ascaphus*, type genus + *-idae*] *in some classifications* **:** a family of western No. American toads — see ASCAPHUS

as·ca·phus \'askəfəs\ *n, cap* [NL, fr. Gk *askaphos* not dug about, fr. *a-* ²a- + *-skaphos* (fr. *skaptein* to dig); akin to L *capo* capon — more at CAPON] **:** a genus of western No. American toads including only the bell toad which is distinguished by a taillike copulatory organ in the male cloaca and which is sometimes isolated in a separate family (Ascaphidae) but usu. included in the Liopelmidae

ascared \ə'-\ *adj* [*a-* (as in *afraid*) + *scared*] *chiefly dial* **:** AFRAID

as·ca·ri·a·sis \,askə'rīəsəs\ *n, pl* **ascaria·ses** \-ə,sēz\ [NL, fr. *Ascaris* + *-iasis*] **:** infestation with or disease caused by ascarids; *specif* **:** infestation of the human intestine by the large roundworm (*Ascaris lumbricoides*) usu. accompanied by colicky pains and diarrhea

as·car·i·cid·al \ə,skarə¦sīdᵊl\ *adj* **:** capable of destroying ascarids

as·car·i·cide \ə'skarə,sīd\ *n* -s [F, fr. *ascaride* ascarid + *-cide*] **:** an agent destructive of ascarids

as·ca·rid \'askərəd, -,rid\ *n, pl* **as·ca·rids** \-dz\ *also* **as·car·i·des** \ə'skarə,dēz\ [LL *ascarid-*, *ascaris* intestinal worm — more at ASCARIS] **:** a roundworm of the family Ascaridae

as·car·i·dae \ə'skarə,dē\ *n pl, cap* [NL, fr. *Ascarid-*, *Ascaris* type genus + *-idae*] **:** a large family of nematode worms (superfamily Ascaridoidea) usu. parasitic in the intestines of vertebrates, of large size, and having three well-developed lips and a simple cylindrical esophagus — see ASCARIDIA, ASCARIS

as·car·i·da·ta \ə,skarə'dād·ə, -ād·ə\ [NL, fr. *Ascarid-*, *Ascaris* + *-ata*] *syn of* ASCARIDINA

ascarides *pl of* ASCARID *or of* ASCARIS

as·ca·rid·ia \,askə'ridēə\ *n, cap* [NL, fr. LL *ascarid-*, *ascaris* intestinal worm + NL *-ia*] **:** a genus of nematode worms (family Ascaridae) including an important intestinal parasite (*A. galli*) of chickens and other domestic fowls and being distinguished from other ascarids by the presence of a preanal sucker — **as·ca·rid·i·al** \¦≈≈¦≈dēəl\ *adj*

as·car·i·di·a·sis \ə,skarə'dīəsəs\ *also* **as·ca·rid·i·o·sis** \,askə,ridē'ōsəs\ *n, pl* **ascaridia·ses** \-ə,sēz\ *also* **ascaridio·ses** \-ō,sēz\ [NL, fr. *Ascarid-*, *Ascaris* + *-iasis* or *-iosis* (fr. *-i-* + *-osis*)] **:** ASCARIASIS

as·car·i·di·na \ə,skarə'dīnə\ *n pl, cap* [NL, fr. *Ascarid-*, *Ascaris* + *-ina*] **:** a suborder of Rhabditida comprising comparatively large nematode worms without a stylet and parasitic in arthropods, mollusks, and vertebrates including man — compare ASCARIDATA

as·car·i·doi·dea \-dȯidēə\ *n pl, cap* [NL, fr. *Ascarid-*, *Ascaris* + *-oidea*] **:** a superfamily of Ascaridina comprising polymyarian nematodes (as *Ascaris* and *Heterakis*) with cervical papillae and the esophagus highly muscular

as·car·i·dole \ə'skarə,dōl\ *also* **as·car·i·dol** \-,dōl, -ōl\ *n* -s [ISV *ascarid* + *-ole*, *-ol*] **:** a liquid terpenoid peroxide $C_{10}H_{16}O_2$ constituting the active anthelmintic and toxic principle of chenopodium oil, made by addition of oxygen to alpha-terpinene, and used as a catalyst in promoting polymerization reactions

as·ca·ris \'askərəs\ *n* [NL, fr. LL *ascaris* intestinal worm, fr. Gk *askaris*; akin to Gk *skairein* to gambol — more at CARDINAL] **1** *cap* **:** the type genus of Ascaridae comprising nematode worms having a 3-lipped mouth, including the common roundworm (*A. lumbricoides*) parasitic in the human intestines and like an earthworm in size and superficial appearance, and including also many other species that infest animals **2** *pl* **ascar·i·des** \ə'skarə,dēz\ **:** ASCARID

as·ca·roid \'askə,rȯid\ *adj* [NL *Ascaroidea*] **:** of or belonging to the Ascaridoidea

as·ca·roi·dea \,askə'rȯidēə\ [NL, fr. *Ascaris* + *-oidea*] *syn of* ASCARIDOIDEA

as·ca·rops \'askə,räps\ *n, cap* [NL, fr. LL *ascaris* intestinal worm + NL *-ops*] **:** a genus of nematode worms (family Spiruridae) that includes a common reddish stomach worm (*A. strongylina*) of wild and domestic swine and is sometimes made type of a separate family

as·cend \ə'send *also* a'-\ *vb* -ED/-ING/-S [ME *ascenden*, fr. L *ascendere*, *adscendere*, fr. *ad-* + *-scendere* (fr. *scandere* to climb) — more at SCAN] *vi* **1 a :** to move upward **:** go up sometimes by stages with gradual motion **:** become raised ⟨~*ed* to Mistover by a circuitous and easy incline —Thomas Hardy⟩ ⟨~ to the roof of her dwelling house —Lafcadio Hearn⟩ **b :** to appear above the horizon and approach the zenith ⟨higher yet that star ~*s* —John Bowring⟩ **c :** to attain height through growth or construction **:** rise up **:** TOWER ⟨the city ~*ed* . . . taking the firmness of its foundation for granted —Frederic Beck⟩ ⟨the redwood trees ~ over the others⟩ **d :** to slope upward **:** lie along a rising slope ⟨the paths ~ through pine woods to the mountain lake⟩ **2 a :** to go up or upward from a lower level or degree **:** RISE ⟨when man ceases to wander he will cease to ~ in the scale of being —A.N.Whitehead⟩ ⟨doomed always to ~ to power under the worst possible objective conditions —Arthur Koestler⟩ **b :** to go back in time or in order of genealogical succession ⟨female kin in the ~*ing* generations are excluded —Mary Tew⟩ **c** *of a sound* **:** to rise in pitch ~ *vt* **1 :** to go or move up, upon, along, to the top of, or over **:** CLIMB, MOUNT ⟨began to ~ the vale towards Mistover —Thomas Hardy⟩ ⟨~*ed* the river farther than any white man had been before —L.H.Bolander⟩ **2 :** to come to hold or occupy **:** succeed to ⟨~*ed* the throne on the death of his father⟩

syn MOUNT, CLIMB, SCALE: ASCEND, a general term, lacks vivid connotation; it suggests merely upward movement, often with gradual or steady motion ⟨to *ascend* a mountain⟩ ⟨an *ascending* elevator⟩ MOUNT, in its transitive uses particularly, implies getting up on something raised, something above the ground ⟨to *mount* a horse⟩ ⟨the speaker *mounting* the platform⟩ ⟨the condemned king *mounting* the scaffold⟩ Intransitively, MOUNT is a close synonym for ASCEND ⟨as he proceeded south, his crossness seemed to *mount* with the temperature —Osbert Sitwell⟩ CLIMB may suggest sustained effort to reach a height or to go over something; it is esp. likely to be used in situations involving clambering or scrambling ⟨*climbing* out of the gulch⟩ ⟨*climbing* up the rigging⟩ ⟨*climbing* into the window⟩ SCALE is likely to add to CLIMB notions of dexterity and adroitness, as of an alpinist, athlete, or esp. trained ladderman ⟨*scaling* the highest peaks⟩ ⟨the baron's men *scaling* the ramparts⟩ ⟨a fireman *scaling* the wall⟩ **syn** see in addition RISE

as·cend·ance *also* **as·cend·ence** \ə'sendən(t)s *also* a'-\ *n* -s **:** ASCENDANCY, LEADERSHIP, DOMINATION

as·cend·an·cy *or* **as·cend·en·cy** \-dənsē, -si\ *n* -ES **:** the quality or state of being in the ascendant **:** controlling influence **:** governing power **:** DOMINATION ⟨dominant castes seek to retain their ~ —Bertrand Russell⟩ ⟨the growing ~ of brains and skills over capital power —Bud Wilson⟩ ⟨would not patiently submit to the ~ of France —T. B. Macaulay⟩

¹**as·cend·ant** *also* **as·cend·ent** \-dənt\ *n* -s [ME *ascendent*, fr. ML *ascendent-*, *ascendens*, fr. L, pres. part. of *ascendere* to ascend] **1 :** the point of the ecliptic or degree of the zodiac that rises above the eastern horizon at any moment (as that of one's birth) **2 :** the quality, state, or position of being supreme, dominant, or in power **:** the point of highest development or influence **:** PREEMINENCE, SUPERIORITY ⟨men who want the president to fight for this program now appear to be in the ~ —E.K.Lindley⟩ ⟨conservatism was in the ~ —C.L. Jones⟩ **3 :** a lineal or collateral relative in the ascending line **:** one that precedes in genealogical succession **:** ANCESTOR ⟨nearly the whole of a man's heredity must be supplied by his immediate ~*s* —Havelock Ellis⟩

²**ascendant** *also* **ascendent** \"\ *adj* [ME *ascendent*, fr. L *ascendent-*, *ascendens*] **1 a :** moving or tending upward **:** RISING ⟨rooted and ~ strength like that of foliage —John Ruskin⟩ **b :** directed upward ⟨an ~ stem⟩ ⟨an ~ leaf⟩ ⟨an ~ inflorescence⟩ **2 a :** in a supreme, dominant, or powerful position **:** SUPERIOR, PREEMINENT, CONTROLLING ⟨the proletariat, the ~ class —Granville Hicks⟩ **b :** inclined to dominate **:** DOMINANT ⟨the chief difference between the ~ and nonascendant child was in the amount of self-confidence —K.C.Garrison⟩

as·cend·er \-də(r)\ *n* -s **:** one that ascends: as **a :** the part of a lowercase letter that exceeds x height (as in "b" or "t") **b :** an ascending letter or character ⟨Aldus used only one size of capitals but they did not reach the height of the lowercase ~*s* —J.C.Oswald⟩

as·cend·ing \(')a¦sendiŋ, ə's-\ *adj* **1 :** that ascends **:** mounting up or sloping upward **:** RISING **2 :** rising upward usu. from a more or less prostrate base or point of attachment ⟨the ~ stems of chickweed⟩ — **as·cend·ing·ly** *adv*

ascending aorta *n* **:** the part of the aorta from its origin to the beginning of the arch

ascending diphthong *n* **:** RISING DIPHTHONG

ascending frontal convolution *n* **:** a frontal convolution lying immediately behind the precentral sulcus

ascending node *n, astron* **:** the node passed as the body goes north

ascending rhythm *n* **:** RISING RHYTHM

ascending series *n* **1 :** a mathematical series arranged according to the ascending powers of a quantity **2 :** a mathematical series in which each term is greater than the preceding

ascends *pres 3d sing of* ASCEND

as·cen·sion \ə'senchən *also* a'-\ *n* -s [ME *ascencioun*, fr. MF & L; MF *ascension* ascension of Jesus into heaven, fr. LL *ascension-*, *ascensio*, fr. L, ascent, fr. *ascensus* (past part. of *ascendere* to ascend) + *-ion-*, *-io* -ion] **1 :** the act or process of ascending ⟨balloon ~⟩ ⟨thin ~*s* of smoke from the breached roof —Ambrose Bierce⟩ **2 a** *often cap* **:** the ascending of Jesus to heaven on the 40th day after his resurrection **b** *usu cap* **:** ASCENSION DAY **3** *archaic* **:** DISTILLATION, EVAPORATION

as·cen·sion·al \-chənᵊl,-chnəl\ *adj* **:** of or relating to ascension or ascent **:** tending upward

ascension day *n, usu cap A&D* **:** the Thursday 40 days after Easter on which is commemorated Christ's ascension after his resurrection — called also *Holy Thursday*

as·cen·sion·ist \-ch(ə)nəst\ *n* -s **1 :** one that makes ascensions or ascents ⟨a balloon ~⟩ **2** *often cap* **:** one of a group of 19th century Christians that prepared for the coming of Christ, the end of the world, and the ascension of the faithful; *specif* **:** MILLERITE

ascensiontide \≈'≈≈,≈\ *n, usu cap* [*ascension* + *tide*] **:** the period of 10 days from Ascension Day to Whitsunday

as·cen·sive \(')a¦sen(t)siv, ə's-\ *adj* [*ascension* + *-ive*] **1 :** rising or tending to rise **:** ASCENDING **2 :** INTENSIVE 2 b

as·cen·sor \ə'sen(t)sə(r), a'-\ *n, pl* **ascenso·res** \,a,sen'sōr(,)ēz\ [Sp, fr. L, one that ascends, fr. *ascensus* (past part. of *ascendere* to ascend) + *-or* — more at ASCEND] **:** a nearly vertical funicular railway used on very steep ascents

as·cent \ə'sent *also* a'-\ *n* -s [fr. *ascend*, after E *descend*: *descent*] **1 a :** the act of ascending or rising **:** a moving or mounting upward ⟨the ~ of vapors from the earth⟩ **b :** a going, traveling, or climbing up (as to the top of a hill or the source of a river) ⟨their ~ of the mountain⟩ ⟨his ~ of the river in a canoe⟩ **c :** the way or means of ascending **:** an upward slope or rising grade **:** ACCLIVITY ⟨the ~ by which he goes up on to the roof of the house to get in at the window of his workshop —R.F.Kilvert⟩ **d :** the degree of elevation or upward slope **:** INCLINATION, GRADIENT ⟨the road has an ~ of six degrees⟩ **2 :** a rising or ascending from a lower level or degree **:** advancement esp. in social status, intellectual achievement, or reputation **:** PROGRESS ⟨the ~ from the working class to the middle class —Liam O'Flaherty⟩ ⟨the long ages of struggle and ~ —B.N.Cardozo⟩ **3 :** a going back in time or upward in order of genealogical succession ⟨any person in the line of ~ from the claimant to the common ancestor —Morris Ploscowe⟩

as·cer·tain \,asə(r)¦tān, ,aas-\ *vt* -ED/-ING/-S [ME *acertainen*, fr. MF *acertainer*, *acertener*, fr. OF *acertener*, fr. *a-* (fr. L *ad-*) + *-certener* (fr. *certain*) — more at CERTAIN] **1 a** *obs* **:** to make (a person) certain, sure, or confident **:** ASSURE ⟨but how shall I be ~*ed* that I also shall be entertained —John Bunyan⟩ **b** *archaic* **:** to make (a thing) certain **:** establish as a certainty **:** determine with certainty ⟨but who shall exactly ~ to us what superstition is —George Horne †1792⟩ **c** *obs* **:** to make certain the possession of **:** SECURE ⟨no diligence can ~ success —Samuel Johnson⟩ **d** *obs* **:** to bring or deliver (a person) certainly **:** DESTINE ⟨would ~ us into a possession of all the promises —Jeremy Taylor⟩ **e** *archaic* **:** to make (a thing) certain, exact, or precise **:** SETTLE, FIX ⟨some effectual method for correcting, enlarging, and ~*ing* our language —Jonathan Swift⟩ **2 :** to find out or learn for a certainty (as by examination or investigation) **:** make sure of **:** DISCOVER ⟨a sensitive instrument for ~*ing* the people's ideas and wishes —A.R.Williams⟩ ⟨had ~*ed* . . . that his son-in-law was among the living prisoners —Charles Dickens⟩ **syn** see DISCOVER

as·cer·tain·a·ble \-nəbəl\ *adj* **:** capable of being ascertained ⟨~ facts⟩ — **as·cer·tain·a·bly** \-blē, -li\ *adv*

as·cer·tain·ment \,≈≈'≈mənt\ *n* -s **:** the act of ascertaining: **a** *archaic* **:** a reducing to certainty **:** exact determination ⟨that a period might be put and some ~ made and a time fixed —Oliver Cromwell⟩ **b :** a finding out (as by investigation) **:** DISCOVERY ⟨his work . . . was the ~ of historical truth —Arnold Bennett⟩

as·ce·sis \ə'sēsəs, a'-\ *or* **as·ke·sis** \-'skēsəs\ *n, pl* **asce·ses** *or* **aske·ses** \-ē,sēz\ [LL or Gk; LL, fr. Gk *askēsis*, lit., exercise, fr. *askein* to work, exercise + *-ēsis* -esis] **:** rigorous training, self-discipline, or self-restraint **:** ASCETICISM

¹**as·cet·ic** \ə'sed·ik, a'-, -etik\ *also* **as·cet·i·cal** \-ə̇kəl, -ēk-\ *adj* [Gk *askētikos*, lit., laborious, fr. *askētēs* one that exercises, hermit (fr. *askein* to work, exercise) + *-ikos* -ic, -ical] **1 :** extremely strict in religious exercises **:** religiously austere ⟨the monastic profession was then a little more than a vow of celibacy and his devotion took no ~ turn —J.R.Green⟩ **2 :** refraining from self-indulgence **:** SELF-DENYING, SELF-DISCIPLINED, AUSTERE ⟨the severely ~ life and cold personality of the celebrated scholar —Dorothy C. Fisher⟩ **syn** see SEVERE

²**ascetic** \"\ *n* -s **1 a :** one who devotes himself to a life of solitude and contemplation and practices such methods of self-discipline as celibacy, fasting, and self-mortification ⟨the desert was often the abode of the ~*s*⟩ **b :** one who is rigorously strict in religious exercises ⟨his predecessor, Ignatius, a zealous and devout ~ . . . allowed himself to be used by the extremists —R.M.French⟩ **2 :** one who leads a life of self-denial, rigorous self-discipline, or austerity ⟨he is no ~ — he loves food and drink and friendly talk —Katherine Simonds⟩

as·cet·i·cal·ly \-ə̇k(ə)lē, -ēk-, -li\ *adv* **:** in an ascetic manner

ascetical theology *n* **:** the branch of Roman Catholic theology that deals with the practice of virtue and the means of attaining holiness and perfection

as·cet·i·cism \-ə,sizəm\ *n* -s **1 a :** the condition, practice, or mode of life of an ascetic **:** rigorous abstention from self-indulgence ⟨his direction toward a life of ~ and contemplation was already clear —W.P.Clancy⟩ **b :** a disciplinary course of conduct in which certain actions (as contemplation and fasting) are performed for their intellectual, moral, or religious effect ⟨for the Catholic ~ of poverty the Protestant substituted the ~ of work —Stringfellow Barr⟩ **2 :** the doctrine that through the renunciation of the desires of the flesh and of pleasure in worldly things and through self-mortification or self-denial one can subdue his appetites and discipline himself so as to reach a high spiritual or intellectual state ⟨the Greek ideal was far removed from ~ —G.L.Dickinson⟩

aschaf·fite \ə'sha,fīt\ *n* -s [G *aschaffit*, fr. *Aschaffenburg*, Bavaria, Germany, its locality + G *-it* -ite] **:** a lamprophyric dike rock that is related to the quartz-diorites and contains phenocrysts of quartz, plagioclase, and biotite

as·cham \'askəm\ *n* -s [after Roger *Ascham* †1568 Eng. scholar, author of a treatise on archery] **:** a tall narrow locker or box in which bows and arrows are kept

asc·hel·min·thes \,ask,hel'min,thēz, ,a,skel-\ *n pl, cap* [NL, fr. *asc-* + *Helminthes*] *in some classifications* **:** a phylum of pseudocoelomate animals including the Rotifera, Gastrotricha, Kinorhyncha, Nematoda, Nematomorpha, and sometimes the Acanthocephala all of which are sometimes regarded as independent phyla — compare ENTOPROCTA

asch·er·so·nia \,ashə(r)'sōnyə\ *n, cap* [NL, fr. Paul F. A. *Ascherson* †1913 Ger. botanist + NL *-ia*] **:** a genus of imperfect fungi (family Phyllostictaceae) parasitic on whiteflies and soft scales and characterized by development of characteristic often highly colored stromata in which conidia and occas. later ascospores of the perfect stage are produced

asch·heim-zon·dek test \'ä,shīm'zän¦dik-, 'äsh,hīm-, -m'ts¦, ¦ōn- -,dek-\ *n, usu cap A&Z* [after Selmar *Aschheim* *b*1878 and Bernhard *Zondek* *b*1891 Ger. gynecologists] **:** a test used (1) to determine human pregnancy in its early stages on the basis of the effect of a subcutaneous injection of the patient's urine on the ovaries of an immature female mouse or (2) to diagnose the presence in a man or woman of a tumor containing embryonic elements (as choriocarcinoma)

aschistic \(')ā+¦≈≈\ *adj* [²*a-* + *schistic*] *of rock* **:** not differentiated — opposed to *diaschistic*

aschi·za \ə'skīzə\ *n pl, cap* [NL, fr. ²*a-* + Gk *schiza* splinter] **:** a group of cyclorrhaphous Diptera comprising two-winged flies (as syrphus flies) that lack a lunule and do not suck blood

aschoff body *or* **aschoff nodule** \'ä,shȯf-\ *n, usu cap A* [after Ludwig *Aschoff* †1942 Ger. pathologist] **:** one of the tiny lumps consisting of swollen collagen, cells, and fibrils found in the heart muscle and typical of rheumatic heart disease; *also* **:** one of the similar but larger lumps found under the skin esp. in rheumatic fever or polyarthritis

asci *pl of* **ascus**

asci- — see ASC-

as·ci·an \'ash(ē)ən\ *n* -s [L *ascius* (fr. Gk *askios*, fr. *a-* ²a- + *skia* shadow) + E *-an* — more at SCENE] **:** one that has no shadow; *specif* **:** an inhabitant of the torrid zone where the sun is vertical at noon for a few days every year

ascidi- *or* **ascidio-** *comb form* [NL, fr. ²*Ascidia* & *ascidium*] **:** ascidian ⟨*ascidio*zooid⟩ **:** ascidium ⟨*ascidi*ferous⟩

¹**as·cid·ia** \ə'sidēə, a'-\ *n, cap* [NL, fr. Gk *askidion* little wineskin + NL *-ia* — more at ASCIDIUM] **:** a genus of simple ascidians now restricted to a few typical species or replaced by *Phallusia* but formerly including all the simple Ascidiacea

²**ascidia** \"\ [NL, fr. Gk *askidia*, pl. of *askidion*] *syn of* UROCHORDA

as·cid·i·a·cea \≈,≈≈'āshēə\ *n pl, cap* [NL, fr. ¹*Ascidia* + *-acea*] **:** an order of tunicates comprising simple ascidians, compound ascidians that reproduce by budding and remain connected together embedded in a common test, and certain atypical pelagic compound ascidians (as of the genus *Pyrosoma*)

as·cid·i·ae \≈'≈dē,ē\ [NL, fr. pl. of ¹*Ascidia*] *syn of* ASCIDIACEA

as·cid·i·an \-ēən\ *n* -s [NL ²*Ascidia* + E *-an*] **:** a simple or compound tunicate of the order Ascidiacea suggesting as a larva a minute active tadpole with an elongated tail that contains a distinct notochord and dorsal nerve chord showing obvious relationship to the vertebrates but as an adult lacking the tail and being reduced to a sessile saclike form with an anterior branchial opening through which water passes to a branchial sac having perforated walls which strain microscopic food into the digestive tract before the water emerges by way of an atrium and dorsal atrial opening; *broadly* **:** TUNICATE

as·cid·i·ar·i·um \≈,≈dē'a(a)rēəm\ *n, pl* **ascidiar·ia** \-ēə\ [NL, fr. *ascidi-* + *-arium*] **:** an entire compound ascidian

¹**as·cid·i·ate** \≈'≈dēət, -ē,āt\ *adj* [*ascidi-* + *-ate*] **:** resembling an ascidium

²**ascidiate** \"\ *adj* [NL *ascidium* + E *-ate*] **:** having ascidia

as·ci·dic·o·lous \¦asə¦dikələs\ *adj* [*ascidi-* + *-colous*] **:** commensal with or parasitic in an ascidian

as·cid·i·form \ə'sidə,fȯrm, a'-\ *adj* [ISV *ascidi-* + *-form*] **1 :** shaped like a pitcher ⟨an ~ leaf⟩ **2 :** shaped like an ascidian or an ascidium

as·cid·i·oi·da \ə,sidē'ȯidə, a,-\ *or* **as·cid·i·oi·dea** \-dēə\ [NL, fr. *ascidi-* + *-oida*, *-oidea*] *syn of* ASCIDIACEA

as·cid·i·ol·o·gy \-ˈäləjē\ *n* -ES [*ascidi-* + *-logy*] **:** a branch of zoology that deals with the Ascidiacea or broadly the Urochorda

as·cid·i·o·zoa \-dēəˈzōə\ [NL, fr. *ascidi-* + *-zoa*] *syn of* UROCHORDA

as·cid·i·o·zo·oid \ˌ≈ˌ≈≈ˈzōˌöid\ *n* -S [*ascidi-* + *zooid*] **:** one of the individual zooids of a compound ascidian

as·cid·i·um \əˈsidēəm, aˈ-\ *n, pl* **ascid·ia** \-ēə\ [NL, fr. Gk *askidion* little wineskin, fr. *askos* wineskin + *-idion* -idium] **:** a pitcher-shaped or flask-shaped organ or appendage of a plant (as the leaf of the pitcher plant)

as·cig·er·ous \əˈsijərəs\ *also* **as·cif·er·ous** \əˈsifər-\ *a* [*asc-* + *-gerous* or *-ferous*] **:** bearing or associated with asci ⟨an ~ fruit⟩

as·ci·tes \əˈsīd·ēz, aˈ-\ *n, pl* **ascites** [ME *aschytes*, fr. LL *ascites*, fr. Gk *askitēs*, fr. *askos* wineskin, bladder, belly — more at ASCUS] **:** the abnormal accumulation of serous fluid in the abdominal cavity — called also *hydroperitoneum;* compare EDEMA — **as·cit·ic** \-ˈsid·ik\ *adj*

as·ci·ti·tious \ˌasəˈtishəs\ *var of* ADSCITITIOUS

¹as·cle·pi·ad \əˈsklēpēˌad, aˈ-, -ēˌad\ *n* -S *usu cap* [Gk *asklēpiadeios*, fr. *asklēpiadeios* asclepiadean, fr. *Asklēpiadēs* Asclepiades, 3d cent. B.C. Greek poet] **:** a Greek lyric verse that extends a glyconic base by repetition of the choriambic cadence (1) once before the final iambus (as ‒‒‒◡◡‒‒◡◡‒◡‒) or (2) twice (as ‒‒‒◡◡‒‒◡◡‒‒◡◡‒◡‒) — called also respectively (1) *lesser asclepiad, minor asclepiad;* (2) *greater asclepiad, major asclepiad*

²asclepiad \"\ *n* -S [NL *Asclepiad-, Asclepias*] **:** a plant of the family Asclepiadaceae

as·cle·pi·a·da·ce·ae \ˌ≈ˌ≈≈ˈdāsēˌē\ *n pl, cap* [NL, fr. *Asclepiad-, Asclepias*, type genus + *-aceae*] **:** a widely distributed family of herbs or shrubs (order Gentianales) mostly with milky juice and with umbellate flowers that have a prominent corona between corolla and stamens — see MILKWEED — **as·cle·pi·a·da·ceous** \ˌ≈ˌ≈≈ˌ≈ˈshəs\ *adj*

¹as·cle·pi·a·de·an \ˌ≈ˌ≈≈ˈdēən\ *or* **as·cle·pi·ad·ic** \-ˈadik\ *adj, usu cap* [LL *asclepiadeus, asclepiadius* asclepiadean (fr. Gk *asklēpiadeios*) + E *-an* or *-ic*] **1 :** relating to the Greek poet Asclepiades of Samos **2 :** relating to, containing, or consisting of asclepiads

²asclepiadean \"\ *or* **asclepiadic** \"\ *n* -S *usu cap* **1 :** ASCLEPIAD **2 :** a distich or strophe constructed with asclepiads

as·cle·pi·as \əˈsklēpēəs, aˈ-\ *n* [NL, fr. L, swallowwort (*Cynanchum vincetoxicum*), fr. Gk *asklēpias*, fr. *Asklēpios*, physician-hero of Greek myth sometimes worshiped as god of healing] **1** *cap* **:** a genus (the type of the family Asclepiadaceae) of perennial herbs found chiefly in No. America with flowers having a corona of five concave hoods each of which bears a slender horn — see BUTTERFLY WEED, MILKWEED **2** -ES **:** a plant of the genus *Asclepias* **3** -ES **a :** the dried root of the butterfly weed formerly used as a diaphoretic and expectorant — called also *pleurisy root* **b :** the root of the swamp milkweed used similarly

as·cle·pi·o·do·ra \ˌ≈ˌ≈≈ˈdōrə\ *n, cap* [prob. irreg. fr. *Asclepias*] **:** a genus of American plants (family Asclepiadaceae) with alternate leaves and a crest on each hood of the corona

asco- — see ASC-

as·co·carp \ˈaskəˌkärp\ *n* -S [*asc-* + *-carp*] **:** the mature fruiting body of an ascomycetous fungus; *broadly* **:** such a body including the enclosed asci, spores, and paraphyses — see ASCOMA; compare APOTHECIUM, PERITHECIUM — **as·co·car·pous** \ˌ≈≈ˈkärpəs\ *adj*

as·coch·y·ta \aˈskäkəd·ə\ *n, cap* [NL, fr. *asc-* + *-chyta* (prob. fr. Gk. *chytos* poured, verbal of *chein* to pour) — more at FOUND] **:** a form genus of imperfect fungi (order Sphaeropsidales) with hyaline 2-celled pycnospores formed in pycnidia located in discolored spots in leaves, stems, or fruits

as·cog·e·nous \aˈskäjənəs\ *adj* [*asc-* + *-genous*] **:** of, relating to, or producing asci

as·co·go·ni·al \ˌaskəˈgōnēəl\ *adj* [NL *ascogonium* + E *-al*] **:** of or relating to an ascogonium

as·co·go·ni·um \ˌ≈≈ˈgōnēəm\ *also* **as·co·gone** \ˈ≈≈ˌgōn\ *n, pl* **ascogo·nia** \-ˈgōnēə\ *also* **ascogones** [NL *ascogonium*, fr. *asc-* + *gonium*] **:** the female sexual organ in many ascomycetous fungi consisting of a single cell or a group of cells — compare ARCHICARP

as·co·li·chen \ˌaskōˈlīkən\ *n* -S [NL *Ascolichenes*] **:** a lichen of the group Ascolichenes — compare BASIDIOLICHEN

as·co·li·che·nes \ˌ≈≈ˌlīˈkē(ˌ)nēz\ *n pl, cap* [NL, fr. *asc-* + *Lichenes*] **:** a group of lichens comprising all those in which the fungous component is an ascomycete — compare BASIDIOLICHENES, DISCOLICHEN, PYRENOLICHEN

as·co·ma \aˈskōmə\ *n, pl* **ascoma·ta** \-məd·ə\ [NL, fr. Gk *askōma* leather lining protecting the aperture for the oar, fr. *askos* wineskin — more at ASCUS] **:** an ascocarp having the hymenium on a broadly expanded or disklike receptacle esp. characteristic of the order Helvellales; *specif* **:** the simple type of fruiting body made up of an undifferentiated mass of tissue on or in which the asci are borne

as·co·my·cete \ˌaskōˈmīˌsēt, -ˌmīˈsēt\ *n* -S [NL *Ascomycetes*] **:** a fungus of the class Ascomycetes

as·co·my·ce·tes \-ˌmīˈsēd·ēz\ *n pl, cap* [NL, fr. *asc-* + *-mycetes*] **:** a large class of higher fungi distinguished by having septate hyphae and spores formed in asci and comprising the two subclasses Hemiascomycetes and Euascomycetes and in some classifications also the subclass Protoascomycetes and many orders, mainly in the Euascomycetes — **as·co·my·ce·tous** \ˌ≈≈ˌ≈ˈsēd·əs\ *adj*

¹as·con \ˈaˌskän\ *n* -S [NL, fr. Gk *askos* wineskin] **:** a sponge or sponge larva having incurrent canals that lead directly to the paragaster — compare LEUCON, SYCON — **as·co·noid** \ˈaskəˌnȯid\ *adj or n*

²ascon \äskōⁿ\ *n* -S [origin unknown] **:** a Haitian voodoo fetish made of a gourd entwined with snake vertebrae and beads and shaken to summon the gods

¹as·co·nes \aˈskō(ˌ)nēz\ [NL, fr. pl. of ¹*ascon*] *syn of* ASCONOSA

²ascones \"\ *n pl* [NL, pl. of ¹*ascon*] **1 :** the ascon sponges **2** *cap* **:** a suborder of Homocoela

as·co·no·sa \ˌaskəˈnōsə\ *n pl, cap* [NL, fr. ¹*ascon* + *-osa* (neut. pl. of L *-osus* -ose)] **:** an order of Calcispongiae comprising simple asconoid sponges and others derived from this type — compare LEUCETTA

diagram of canal system of an ascon type of sponge: *1* gastral layer, *2* dermal layer, *3* osculum, *4* gastral cavity

a–scope \ˈāˌskōp\ *n, usu cap A* [¹*A* + *-scope*] **:** a radarscope on which signals appear as displacements of the trace and indicate only range of the target — compare B-SCOPE

as·co·phore \ˈaskəˌfō(ə)r\ *n* -S [prob. fr. F, fr. *asc-* + *-phore*] **1 :** an ascus-bearing hypha **2 :** ASCOCARP

as·coph·o·rous \(ˈ)aˈskäfərəs\ *adj* **:** ASCOGENOUS

as·co·phyl·lum \ˌaskəˈfiləm\ *n, cap* [NL, fr. *asc-* + *-phyllum*] **:** a genus of brown algae (family Fucaceae) distinguished by clavate, compressed, or somewhat inflated branchlets scattered along the axis and constituting with *Fucus* the bladder-bearing rockweeds of the northern Atlantic coast of which some species are used in the kelp industry

ascor·bate \əˈskȯrbāt\ *n* -S [*ascorbic* + *-ate*] **:** a salt of ascorbic acid

ascor·bic acid \əˈskȯrbik-\ *n* [²*a-* + NL *scorbutus* scurvy + E *-ic* — more at SCORBUTIC] **1 :** a crystalline water-soluble vitamin $C_6H_8O_6$ that occurs esp. in fruits (as citrus fruits, tomatoes), vegetables (as leafy vegetables, new potatoes), and fresh tea leaves, that is usu. obtained commercially from sorbitol by a series of synthetic steps, that is a strong reducing agent and is reversibly oxidized to dehydroascorbic acid, and that is used chiefly in the prevention and cure of scurvy and in antioxidants for food; an enolic lactone of a 2- or 3-keto aldonic acid related to xylose — called also L-*ascorbic acid, vitamin C,* L-*xylo-ascorbic acid* **2 :** any of several enolic lactones of keto aldonic acids that are stereoisomers of ascorbic acid

as·co·spore \ˈaskəˌspō(ə)r\ *n* -S [prob. fr. F *ascospore*, fr. *asc-* + *spore*] **:** one of the spores contained in an ascus and upon germination usu. producing mycelium upon which sexual organs are developed — **as·co·spor·ic** \ˌ≈≈ˈspȯrik\ *adj* — **as·co·spor·ous** \ˌaskəˈspōrəs, (ˈ)aˈskäspər-\ *adj*

as·cot \ˈaskət, ˈaas-, -ˌskät\ *n* -S *often attrib* [fr. *Ascot* Heath, fashionable racetrack near Ascot, village in Berkshire, England; fr. the neckwear worn by men of fashion there] **1 :** a broad necktie whose usu. square ends are tied in a knot, crossed diagonally, and then pinned **2 :** a broad neck scarf that is looped under the chin and sometimes secured by a pin

ascot 2

as·co·tho·rac·i·ca \ˌaskōthəˈrasəkə\ *n pl, cap* [NL, fr. *asc-* + *Thoracica*] **:** a minor order or suborder of small hermaphrodite barnacles that live enveloped in a soft mantle and partly buried in other animals (as black corals)

ascot tan *n, often cap A* **:** COCONUT 4

as·crib·a·ble \əˈskrībəbəl *also* aˈ-\ *adj* **:** capable of being ascribed **:** ATTRIBUTABLE ⟨punctuation errors ~ to careless proofreading⟩

as·cribe \əˈskrīb *also* aˈ-\ *vt* -ED/-ING/-S [ME *ascriben*, alter. (influenced by L *ascribere*) of *ascriven*, fr. MF *ascrivre*, fr. L *ascribere, adscribere* to ascribe, add to, fr. *ad-* + *scribere* to write — more at SCRIBE] **1 :** to refer esp. to a supposed cause, source, or author **:** ASSIGN, ATTRIBUTE ⟨it is conventional to ~ this mastery to the development of scientific method —P.W.Bridgman⟩ ⟨in so far as we can ~ those changes to individuals —Christopher Hollis⟩ **2** *obs* **:** to add in writing **:** SUBSCRIBE **3** *obs* **:** INSCRIBE, DEDICATE

syn ATTRIBUTE, ASSIGN, REFER, CREDIT, ACCREDIT, IMPUTE, CHARGE: ASCRIBE may suggest tentative, conjectural, inferential, or accustomed indication of cause or characteristic ⟨they have *ascribed* their victories — in superstitious terms — to the operations of fortune —A.J.Toynbee⟩ ⟨disinclined to *ascribe* to her more than an indiscreet friendship with Wildeve —Thomas Hardy⟩ ATTRIBUTE may imply less of the tentative than ASCRIBE; in its suggestion it falls between ASCRIBE and ASSIGN ⟨this knowledge was partly communicated by visions and revelations, to which St. Paul *attributed* some importance —W.R.Inge⟩ ⟨the French had then given up their conventional trick of *attributing* Eleanor's acts to her want of morals —Henry Adams⟩ ASSIGN may suggest the certainty and definiteness of cause, characterization, or placement that comes with deliberate consideration ⟨more than one rejoinder declared that the importance I here *assigned* to criticism was excessive —Matthew Arnold⟩ ⟨they bore a strong likeness to the poems of Henry Vaughan the Silurist, and he concluded that they must be *assigned* to Vaughan —A.T.Quiller-Couch⟩ REFER, now less frequent in this sense, suggests explaining or characterizing by adducing an ultimate cause of major significance or by subsuming in a comprehensive group ⟨I am convinced that at least one half of their bad manners may be *referred* to their education —A.T.Quiller-Couch⟩ CREDIT and ACCREDIT usu. suggest favorable ascription bringing credit, although they may be used in unfavorable situations ⟨I am sure both parties *credited* them with too much idealism and too little plain horse sense —Rose Macaulay⟩ ⟨literary style . . . is *credited* with being a mysterious preservative for subject matter which no longer interests —T.S.Eliot⟩ ⟨several Bangor houses have been *accredited* to Bulfinch —*Amer. Guide Series: Maine*⟩ IMPUTE is likely to be used with discreditable ascription ranging from accusation to implication ⟨you *imputed* mean motives to them for giving such advice and cowardice to me for listening to them —Oscar Wilde⟩ ⟨no one should . . . find it necessary to *impute* to the critic . . . a puritanic way —F.R. Leavis⟩ Unlike IMPUTE, CHARGE always suggests unfavorable ascription, usu. in direct accusation ⟨the tyrannies . . . *charged* upon the New England oligarchy —V.L.Parrington⟩ ⟨crimes as base as any *charged* on me —William Cowper⟩

as·crip·tion \əˈskripshən *also* aˈ-\ *n* -S [LL *ascription-, ascriptio*, fr. L, written addition, fr. *ascriptus* (past part. of *ascribere* to ascribe, add in writing) + *-ion-, -io* -ion] **1 :** the act of ascribing ⟨the common ~ of special religiousness to the middle ages —G.C.Sellery⟩ **2 :** a statement or declaration that ascribes ⟨"most gracious" as an ~ applied to the king first appears in the litany in 1559 —F.H.A.Micklewright⟩; *specif* **:** a form of prayer ascribing praise to God spoken by a minister usu. after the sermon **3 :** the quality or state of being adscript

ascrip·tive \əˈskriptiv *also* aˈ-\ *adj* [L *ascriptivus, adscriptivus*, fr. *ascriptus, adscriptus* + *-ivus* -ive] **:** relating to or involving ascription; *specif* **:** entailing elements that attribute or impute rather than factually describe ⟨some ethical statements have a noncognitive function in the sense of being emotive or ~⟩

as·cu·la \ˈaskyələ\ *n, pl* **ascu·lae** \-ˌlē, -ˌlī\ [NL, fr. *asc-* + *-ula*] **:** OLYNTHUS

as·cus \ˈaskəs\ *n, pl* **as·ci** \ˈaˌsī, ˈaˌskē\ [NL, fr. Gk *askos* wineskin, bladder, belly; prob. akin to Skt *atka* garment] **:** the membranous oval or tubular spore sac in fungi of the class Ascomycetes that is produced either directly from the fertilized ascogonium or from ascogenous hyphae produced therefrom and that bears within it, following nuclear fusion, ascospores, typically eight in number — compare APOTHECIUM, ASCOCARP, PERITHECIUM

ascy·phous \(ˈ)āˌsīfəs\ *adj* [²*a-* + NL *scyphus*] **:** having no scyphi

as·cy·rum \əˈsīrəm, ˈasərəm\ *n, cap* [NL, fr. Gk *askyron* St.-John's-wort] **:** a genus of American subshrubs (family Hypericaceae) having short leafy branches, yellow flowers, and one-celled capsular fruit — see SAINT-PETER'S-WORT

as·dic \ˈazˌdik\ *n* -S [*A*nti-*S*ubmarine *D*etection *I*nvestigation *C*ommittee] **:** SONAR

-ase \ˌās\ *n suffix* -S [F, fr. *diastase*] **:** enzyme **:** destroying substance ⟨aureomycin*ase*⟩ ⟨prote*ase*⟩ ⟨ure*ase*⟩

a-sea \əˈ-\ *adv* [¹*a-* + *sea*] **:** at sea **:** SEAWARD

aseel *or* **asil** \əˈsē(ə)l\ *n* -S *often cap* [prob. native name in India] **:** MALAY 3

aseethe \əˈ-\ *adj* [¹*a-* + *seethe*, v.] **:** SEETHING

aseismatic \ˌā+\ *adj* [²*a-* + Gk *seismat-, seisma* shaking + E *-ic* — more at SEISMATICAL] **:** withstanding or mitigating the effects of earthquake shocks

aseismic \(ˈ)ā+\ *adj* [ISV ²*a-* + *seismic*] **1 :** not subject to earthquakes ⟨an ~ region⟩ **2 :** resisting the destructive forces of earthquakes — **aseismicity** \ˌā+ˌ-\ *n* -ES

as·e·i·ty \aˈsēəd·ē, əˈ-\ *also* **ase·i·tas** \-ēəˌtas\ *n, pl* **asei·ties** \-əd·ēz\ *also* **aseita·tes** \ˌ(ˌ)≈ˌ≈ˈtād·ēz\ [ML *aseitas*, fr. L *a se* from oneself (fr. *a, ab* from + *se* oneself) + *-itas* -ity — more at OF, SUICIDE] **:** the quality or state of being self-derived or self-originated; *specif* **:** the absolute self-sufficiency, independence, and autonomy of God

asel·late \(ˈ)āˈselət, (ˈ)āˈseˌlāt\ *adj* [²*a-* + L *sella* saddle + E *-ate* — more at SETTLE] *paleontol* **:** without saddles — used specif. of the simplest known ammonoid suture

asel·li·dae \əˈseləˌdē\ *n pl, cap* [NL, fr. *Asellus*, type genus + *-idae*] **:** a family of chiefly freshwater isopod crustaceans having terminal biramous uropods and a single shieldlike plate covering the abdomen

asel·lus \əˈseləs\ *n* [NL, fr. L, small ass, dim. of *asinus* ass — more at ASS] **1** *cap* **:** the type genus of Asellidae **2** *pl* **asel·li** \-ˌlī, -ˌlē\ **:** an isopod of the genus *Asellus* or of the family Asellidae

asepsis \(ˈ)ā+\ *n, pl* **asepses** [NL, fr. ²*a-* + *sepsis*] **1 :** the quality or state of being aseptic — compare ANTISEPSIS **2 :** the methods of making or keeping aseptic

aseptate \(ˈ)ā+\ *adj* [²*a-* + *septate*] **:** not septate

aseptic \(ˈ)ā+\ *adj* [ISV ²*a-* + *septic*] **1 :** preventing or not involving infection ⟨an ~ wound⟩; *specif* **:** free or freed from pathogenic microorganisms by special methods ⟨~ surgery⟩ ⟨instruments sterilized by heat are ~⟩ — compare ANTISEPTIC **2 a :** lacking vitality, emotion, or warmth ⟨the bureaucrat's world is prim and proper and ~ —R.M.Weaver⟩ **b :** DETACHED, OBJECTIVE ⟨the more ~ idealism of the social philosopher —H.L.Smith⟩ **c :** CLEANSING, PURIFYING ⟨~ laughter to cut through . . . fears —*Saturday Night*⟩ — **aseptically** *adv*

asexual \(ˈ)ā+\ *adj* [²*a-* + *sexual*] **:** not sexual: **a :** having no sex or functional sexual organs **b :** produced without sexual action or differentiation ⟨an ~ spore⟩ **c :** not relating to sex — **asexually** \(ˈ)ā+\ *adv*

asexual generation *n* **:** the generation that reproduces only by asexual processes — used of plants or animals exhibiting alternation of generations; compare ASEXUAL REPRODUCTION

asexuality \ˌā+\ *n* -ES [ISV *asexual* + *-ity*] **:** absence of sex

asexualization \ˌā+\ *n* -S [²*a-* + *sexualization*] **:** the act or process of rendering incapable of reproduction **:** STERILIZATION, CASTRATION

asexual reproduction *n* **:** a process of reproduction (as cell division, spore formation, fission, or budding) that does not involve or directly follow the union of individuals or germ cells of two different sexes — compare ALTERNATION OF GENERATIONS

asexual spore *n* **:** a spore produced by cell division or encystment and capable of developing without conjugation into a new individual (as the spores developed by a sporophyte)

as far as *conj* **:** to the degree or extent that ⟨*as far as* I know, he can come⟩

asfetida *var of* ASAFETIDA

as for \ˈazfə(r), ˌazfə(r)\ *prep* **:** with reference to **:** CONCERNING ⟨*as for* me, give me liberty —Patrick Henry⟩

asgd *abbr* assigned

¹ash \ˈash, ˈaa(ə)sh, ˈaish\ *n* -ES [ME *asshe*, fr. OE *æsc;* akin to OHG *ask* ash, ON *askr*, L *ornus* wild mountain ash, Gk *oxyē* beech, Lith *uosis* ash] **1 :** a tree of the genus *Fraxinus* — see TREE illustration **2 :** the wood of ash which is tough and elastic and is used esp. to make tool handles, skis, and bats **3 :** any of numerous Australian trees of various genera (as *Acronychia, Alphitonia, Cupania, Elaeocarpus, Eucalyptus, Flindersia, Litsea, Malaisia, Panax,* and *Schizomeria*) having tough strong wood — see BLACK ASH, BLUE ASH, MOUNTAIN ASH **4** [OE *æsc*, name of the corresponding runic letter] **:** the ligature æ used in Old English to represent a low front vowel

²ash \"\ *adj* **1 :** of or relating to the ash **2 :** made of ash wood

³ash \"\ *n* -ES *often attrib* [ME *asshe*, fr. OE *asce, æsce;* akin to OHG *asca* ash, ON *aska*, Goth *azgo*, L *arēre* to be dry — more at ARDOR] **1 a :** the earthy or mineral residue that remains after combustible substances (as coal) have been thoroughly burned — usu. used in pl. ⟨carried the ~*es* from the cellar to the alley⟩ **b :** the solid residue of nonvolatile oxides or salts of metals (as sodium, calcium, magnesium, iron) or of nonmetallic atoms (as silica) or of pure metal (as platinum) left when combustible substances (as plants, foods) have been thoroughly oxidized (as by nitric acid or some other wet oxidizing agent) and frequently used in quantitative analysis as a measure of the mineral-matter content of the original material **c :** fine particles of mineral matter ejected from a volcanic vent during an explosive eruption ⟨lava may be blown out as fragments by explosions of steam, to fall as dust, ~, and cinders —L.V.Pirsson⟩ **d :** SODA ASH — used chiefly commercially **2 ashes** *pl* **:** the ruins or remains of anything that has been destroyed esp. by fire **:** the last traces ⟨a new city was built on the ~*es* of the old⟩ **3 ashes** *pl* **a :** whatever remains after the cremation or disintegration of the human body ⟨having collected from the funeral pile the ~*es* of her lover —Lafcadio Hearn⟩ **b :** man or his body as mortal or subject to decay ⟨we are ~*es* and dust —Alfred Tennyson⟩ **4 ashes** *pl* **:** something that symbolizes grief, repentance, or humiliation ⟨there was room for an innocent mistake but he cast ~*es* on his head that it should have happened to Mr. Tibbets —John Buchan⟩ **5 a ashes** *pl* **:** deathlike pallor ⟨the lip of ~*es* and the cheek of flame —Lord Byron⟩ **b ashes** *pl but sing in constr* **:** a light brownish gray that is paler than slate gray and redder and darker than silver gray **c :** ASH GRAY **6 ashes** *pl* **:** the mythical symbol of supremacy contested for in Australia-versus-England cricket test matches ⟨England . . . retains the ~*es* —*Australian Weekly Rev.*⟩

⁴ash \"\ *vt* -ED/-ING/-ES **1 :** to sprinkle with ashes ⟨the corn was ~*ed* to keep away weevils⟩ **2 :** to convert into ash **:** burn to ashes ⟨the bones were ~*ed* in a furnace⟩ **3 :** to buff or scour with a wet paste of pumice or other abrasive

ashake \əˈ-\ *adj* [¹*a-* + *shake*, v.] **:** SHAKING ⟨their long manes ~ —W.B.Yeats⟩

ashamed \əˈshāmd\ *adj* [ME, fr. OE *āscamod*, past part. of *āscamian* to shame, fr. *ā-* (perfective prefix) + *scamian* to shame — more at ABEAR, SHAME] **1 a :** feeling shame **:** humiliated or disconcerted by feelings of guilt, disgrace, or impropriety about something discreditable or indecorous ⟨rather ~ that on my first appearance I had stayed so late —Scott Fitzgerald⟩ — usu. used predicatively **b :** ill at ease or subdued by feelings of inferiority or unworthiness ⟨they can't afford the stalls and are ~ to be seen in the gallery —G.B. Shaw⟩ **2 :** restrained by anticipation of feelings of shame **:** reluctant or unwilling to undertake an action likely to involve shame ⟨he looked at his own shabby person and was ~ to enter —Sherwood Anderson⟩ **3** *chiefly Midland* **:** TIMID, BASHFUL

syn MORTIFIED, CHAGRINED: MORTIFIED and CHAGRINED also apply to feelings and situations involving embarrassment and humiliation. ASHAMED stresses regretful feelings of guilt, discredit, or disgrace at one's own or another's shameful or discreditable actions, behavior, or condition ⟨you were *ashamed* because you had gone against the community judgment —Mary Austin⟩ ⟨the hunter, who is *ashamed* if he does not hit his quarry in the appointed, difficult, and honorable spot —Margaret Mead⟩ ⟨Catherine, recollecting herself, grew *ashamed* of her eagerness —Jane Austen⟩ ⟨I have been *ashamed* of your moroseness there! Your manners have been of that silent and sullen and hangdog kind —Charles Dickens⟩ MORTIFIED suggests sorry or resentful hurt pride at being put into a false and embarrassing but not necessarily shameful position ⟨*mortified* at finding the house shut —Harriet Martineau⟩ CHAGRINED stresses the feeling of vexation at a rebuff or disappointment ⟨"you've done your best, Blundell, but I think we had better hand the thing over . . . to Scotland Yard. . ." Mr. Blundell looked *chagrined* —Dorothy Sayers⟩ ⟨Tony, somewhat *chagrined* at his mistake, said he should like to see the other pictures —Archibald Marshall⟩

ashamed·ly \-mədlē, -lī\ *adv* **:** in an embarrassed manner

ashamed·ness \-mədnəs, -m(d)n-\ *n* -ES **:** the quality or state of being ashamed

ashan·go \əˈshaŋ(ˌ)gō\ *n, pl* **ashango** *or* **ashangos** *usu cap* **1 :** a pygmy people of central Africa **2 :** a member of the Ashango people

ashan·ti \əˈshantē, -aan-,-ain-,-än-,-ån-; aˈshan-, -aan-,-ain-; äˈshän-, -ån-; äˈshän-\ *also* **asan·te** \-ˈsantē, -saan-,-sain-,-sän-, -sån-\ *n, pl* **ashanti** *or* **ashantis** *also* **asante** *or* **asantes** *usu cap* [Ashanti *Asanteˀ*] **1 :** a West African people that are divided into various tribes organized as a kingdom in Ghana and that are skilled in cotton weaving, goldbeating and gold casting, and agriculture **2 :** a dialect of Akan spoken by the Ashanti people

ashanti pepper *n, usu cap A* **:** AFRICAN CUBEB

ash·a·rite *or* **ash·a·rite** \ˈashəˌrīt\ *n* -S *usu cap* [Ali al-*Ash'ari* †935 Muslim theologian + E *-ite*] **:** an adherent of the doctrine of al-Ash'ari, who reconciled a dialectic method with orthodox beliefs to form a scholasticism of primary importance in Islam

a sharp \ˈā+ˈ-\ *n, usu cap A* **1 :** the keynote of A-sharp minor **2 :** the tone a half step above A

a–sharp minor \ˈ≈ˌ≈ˈ≈-\ *n, usu cap A* **:** the minor musical key having a signature of seven sharps

ash–blonde \ˈ≈ˈ≈\ *adj* [³*ash*] *of hair* **:** light in color without reddish tint or tinge **:** pale blonde

ash borer *n* [¹*ash*] **:** any of various insect larvae that bore in the wood of ash trees; *esp* **:** a larval clearwing (*Podosesia syringae fraxini*) of eastern and central No. America

ashcake \ˈ≈ˌ≈\ *n* [³*ash* + *cake*] *South & Midland* **:** a cake of corn meal baked in hot ashes

ash can *n* [³*ash*] **1 :** a metal receptacle for refuse (as ashes) — see CAN illustration **2** *slang* **:** DEPTH CHARGE

ashcan \ˈ≈ˌ≈\ *adj, often cap* **:** relating to the street life of a city, esp. to its unidealized or seamy aspects; *specif* **:** depicting or working to depict genre scenes of city life realistically — used esp. of an early 20th century school of American artists

ash cone *n* [³*ash*] **:** a conical accumulation of volcanic ash around a vent

ash dump *n* [³*ash*] **:** an opening in the bottom of a fireplace or furnace leading to an ashpit below

¹ash·en \ˈashən, ˈaa-,ˈai-\ *adj* [ME *asshen*, fr. *asshe* ash (tree) + *-en*] **:** ²ASH

²ashen \"\ *adj* [ME *asshen*, fr. *asshe* ash (residue of combustion) + *-en*] **1 :** consisting of or resembling ashes **2 a :** of the color of ashes **b :** of the color of ash gray **3 :** deadly pale **:** BLANCHED, PALLID ⟨his face was ~ with rage and apprehension —P.B.Kyne⟩

ashe·rah \ə'shirə\ *n, pl* **ashe·rim** \-rəm\ *or* **asherahs** *usu cap* [Heb *ăshērāh*] **:** a sacred wooden post, pole, or pillar that stood near the altar in various Canaanite high places and that symbolized the goddess Asherah

ash·er·ite \'ashə,rīt\ *n* -s *usu cap* [*Asher*, Jacob's 8th son (Gen 30:12-13) + E *-ite*] **:** a member of the Hebrew tribe of Asher **:** a descendant of Asher

ash·ery \'ashərē, 'aa-, 'ai- -ri\ *n* -ES [³*ash* + *-ery*] **:** a place where potash is made

ashes *pl of* ASH, *pres 3d sing of* ASH

ashes of rose *or* **ashes of roses** **1 :** a variable color averaging a light grayish red that is yellower and very slightly darker than livid violet — called also *rose gray* **2** *of textiles* **:** a grayish purplish red that is redder and slightly darker than tourmaline pink

ash·et \'ashət\ *n* -s [F *assiette* — more at ASSIETTE] *chiefly Scot* **:** PLATTER

ashfall \'=,=\ *n* [³*ash* + *fall*] **:** a deposit of volcanic ash — called also *ash shower*

ash field *n* [³*ash*] **:** a thick widespread deposit of volcanic ash — called also *ash plain*

ash furnace *n* [³*ash*] **:** a furnace or oven for fritting materials for glassmaking — called also *ash oven*

ash gray *n* [³*ash*] **:** a light greenish gray that is yellower, lighter, and stronger than French gray and yellower than lichen green

ashier *comparative of* ASHY

ashiest *superlative of* ASHY

ashim·mer \ə'-\ *adj* [¹*a-* + *shimmer*, v.] **:** SHIMMERING

ashine \ə'-\ *adj* [¹*a-* + *shine*, v.] **:** SHINING

ashing *pres part of* ASH

aship·board \ə'-\ *adv* [¹*a-* + *shipboard*] **:** on shipboard

ashiv·er \ə'-\ *adj* [¹*a-* + *shiver*, v.] **:** SHIVERING

ash·ke·na·zi \,ashkə'nazē, ,äshkə'nä-, -zi\ *n, pl* **ashkena·zim** \-(,)zim\ *also* **ashkenazi** *usu cap* [Heb *Ashkĕnāzī*] **:** a member of one of the two great divisions of Jews comprising the eastern European Yiddish-speaking Jews — compare SEPHARDI

ash·ke·naz·ic \¦=='zik\ *or* **ash·ke·na·zi** \-zē, -zi\ *adj, usu cap* **:** of, belonging to, or characteristic of the Ashkenazim — compare SEPHARDIC

ashkh·a·bad \'ashkə,bad\ *adj, usu cap* [fr. *Ashkhabad*, city in southern U.S.S.R.] **:** of or from Ashkhabad, Turkmen S.S.R., U.S.S.R. **:** of the kind or style prevalent in Ashkhabad

ash·ko·ko \ash'kō(,)kō, 'ashkə,kō\ *n* -s [Amharic *askoko*] **:** ²HYRAX

¹ash·lar *also* **ash·ler** \'ashlə(r), 'aa-,'ai-\ *n* -s *often attrib* [ME *asheler*, fr. MF *aisselier* crossbeam, fr. OF, fr. *ais* board, plank, fr. L *axis*, by folk etymology (influence of L *axis* axle) fr. *assis* — more at ACE, AXIS] **1 a :** hewn or squared stone **:** masonry of such stone **b :** a thin squared and dressed stone for facing a wall of rubble or brick **2 :** one of the short upright studs between the floor beams and the rafters of a garret cutting off the sharp side angles

²ashlar \"\ *vt* -ED/-ING/-S **:** to cover with ashlar

ashlar brick *n* **:** a brick with the faces rough-hackled to resemble stone

ashlar facing *n* **:** sawed or dressed squared stones used in facing masonry walls

ashlaring *n* -s **1 :** ASHLAR MASONRY **2 :** ASHLAR 2

ashlar line *n* **:** the outer line of an exterior wall above any projecting base

ashlar masonry *n* **:** masonry made of sawed, dressed, tooled, or quarry-faced stone with proper bond

ash–leaved maple \'=,=-\ *n* [¹*ash*] **:** BOX ELDER

ash·lu·slay \,ashlü'slī\ *n, pl* **ashluslay** *usu cap* **1 a :** a Matacan people of southwestern Paraguay **b :** a member of such people **2 :** the language of the Ashluslay people

ash·man \'=,=\ *n, pl* **ashmen** [³*ash*] **:** a worker who removes ashes — called also *cinderman*

ash·o·chi·mi \,ashə'chēmē\ *n, pl* **ashochimi** *or* **ashochimis** *usu cap* **:** WAPPO

ashore \ə'-\ *adv (or adj)* [¹*a-* + *shore*] **:** on or to the shore **:** on or to land ⟨the troops came ~ at midnight⟩ ⟨the captain was ~ for two hours⟩

ash oven *n* [³*ash*] **:** ASH FURNACE

as how *conj* **1** *dial* **:** ³THAT ⟨seeing *as how* the captain had been hauling him over the coals —Frederick Marryat⟩ **2** *dial* **:** IF, WHETHER ⟨I don't know *as how* this will be any better⟩

ashpan \'=,=\ *n* [³*ash* + *pan*] **:** a pan under a grate for collecting and removing ashes

ashpit \'=,=\ *n* [³*ash* + *pit*] **:** a pit for ashes esp. under a grate

ash plain *n* [³*ash*] **:** ASH FIELD

ashplant \'=,=\ *n* [¹*ash* + *plant*] **1 :** an ash sapling **2 :** a walking stick; *esp* **:** one made from an ash sapling

ashraf \ä'shräf\ *n pl, often cap* [Ar *ashrāf*, pl. of *sharīf* noble] **:** descendants of the prophet Muhammad regarded as of noble lineage and preeminence in Islam — compare SAYYID, SHARIF

ashram \'äshrəm\ *n* -s [Skt *āśrama*, fr. *ā* towards, near to + *śrama* fatigue, exertion, religious exercise; akin to Skt *śrāmyati*, *klāmyati*, *klāmati* he gets tired, OIr *clam* leprous, W *claf* ill, Bret *klañv*, *klañ*, Corn *clāf* ill, leprous — more at ACHARYA] **1** *India* **:** HERMITAGE **2** *India* **:** a religious retreat for a colony of disciples

ashra·ma *also* **asra·ma** \'äshrəmə\ *n* -s [Skt *āśrama*] **1** *India* **:** ASHRAM **2 :** any one of the four stages of the Brahmanic scheme of life — compare BRAHMACHARYA, GRIHASTHA, SANNYASI, VANAPRASTHA

ashra·mite \'äshrə,mīt\ *n* -s **:** a member of an ashram

ashre \ä'shrā\ *n, pl* **ashre** [Heb *ashrē* happy, the first word of the first two verses (Psalms 84:4 & 144:15) of the recital] **:** a recital in the daily liturgy of the Jews of the two verses from Psalms 84 and 144 followed by the recitation of Psalm 145

ash rock *n* [³*ash*] **:** rock consisting of volcanic ash

ash rose *n* [³*ash*] **:** a variable color averaging a grayish red that is bluer and paler than bois de rose, bluer and less strong than appleblossom or Pompeian red, and bluer, lighter, and stronger than livid brown

ash rust *n* [¹*ash*] **:** a rust disease of ash trees caused by a fungus (*Puccinia peridermiospora*)

ash sawfly *n* **:** any of various sawflies (esp. *Tomostethus multicinctus* and *Tethida cordigera*) having larvae that feed on and defoliate ash trees

ash shower *or* **ash spread** *n* **:** ASHFALL

ashstone \'=,=\ *n* [³*ash* + *stone*] **:** a rock composed of particles of volcanic ash less than 0.06 millimeter in greatest dimension

ash–throated flycatcher \'=,==-\ *n* [³*ash*] **:** a common flycatcher (*Myiarchus cinerascens*) of the western U.S. and northern Mexico that resembles the crested flycatcher but has the throat and chest ashy to white and the outer web of the outer tail feather white

ashtray \'=,=\ *n* [³*ash* + *tray*] **:** a receptacle for tobacco ashes and for cigar and cigarette butts

¹ashu·ra \ə'shúrə\ *n* -s *often cap* [Ar *'ashūrā*, fr. *'asharah* ten] **:** a Muslim voluntary fast day observed on the 10th day of Muharram and esp. sacred to Shiites

²ashura \"\ *n, usu cap* [Jap] **:** a Japanese breed of medium-sized game fowls

ash wednesday *n, usu cap A & W* [ME *Asshe Wednesday*, fr. *asshe* ash + *Wednesday*] **:** the first day of Lent in Western Christendom

ashy \'ashē, 'aa-,'ai-, -i\ *adj* -ER/-EST [ME *asshy*, fr. *asshe* ash (residue of combustion) + *-y*] **1 :** composed of, covered with, or resembling ashes ⟨the carpet would be dim with a gray ~ dust from the tobacco —Elizabeth M. Roberts⟩ ⟨all these things ~ to his taste —J.L.Liebman⟩ **2 :** like ashes in color **:** deadly pale **:** ASHEN ⟨some return of color to the ~ cheeks —Bram Stoker⟩ **3** *chiefly Midland* **:** ANGRY, ENRAGED

ASI *abbr* air-speed indicator

asia \'āzhə *also* -shə *sometimes* -zhēə\ *adj, usu cap* [fr. *Asia*, largest continent in the world] **:** of or from the continent of Asia **:** of the kind or style prevalent in Asia **:** ASIAN

asia·go \,äsē'ä(,)gō, ä'syä-\ *n* -s [fr. *Asiago*, commune in province of Vicenza, Italy, where it originated] **:** a sweet-curd semicooked Italian cheese with pungent aroma

¹asian \'āzhən *also* -shən *sometimes* -zhēən *or* -shēən *or (esp Brit)* -syən *or* -siən\ *adj, usu cap* [L *asianus*, adj. & n., fr. Gk *asianos*, fr. *Asia* + *-anos* -an] **1 :** of, relating to, or characteristic of the continent of Asia **2 :** of, relating to, or characteristic of the people of Asia

²asian \"\ *n* -s *cap* [L *asianus*] **:** a native or inhabitant of Asia

asi·an·ic \¦āzhē¦anik *also* -shē-\ *adj, usu cap* [*Asian* + *-ic*] **1 :** ASIAN **2 :** of, belonging to, or constituting a group of non-Indo-European languages not admitted by many linguists to be demonstrably or even plausibly of common origin, spoken in Asia Minor or in southwestern Asia and southern Europe before the coming of the Indo-Europeans, and perhaps including Lycian, Lydian, Etruscan, and the languages ancestral to Basque and some Caucasian languages

asian influenza *n, usu cap A* **:** influenza caused by a mutant strain of the influenza virus

asi·arch \'āzhē,ärk *also* -shē-\ *n* -s *usu cap* [LL *Asiarcha*, fr. Gk *Asiarchēs*, fr. *Asia* Asia, Roman province in western Asia Minor + *-archēs* -arch] **:** one of a group of civil and priestly officials in the Roman province of Asia who presided over the public games and religious rites

¹asi·at·ic \¦āzhē¦ad·ik, -atik, -ēk *also* ¦āzē-*or* ¦āshē- *sometimes* ¦äsē-\ *adj, usu cap* [L *Asiaticus*, adj. & n., fr. Gk *Asiatikos*, fr. *Asia*] **1 :** ASIAN — now often taken to be offensive **2 :** tending to excessive ornamentation or emotionalism in literary or oratorical style **:** FLORID

²asiatic \"\ *n* -s *cap* [L *Asiaticus*] **1 :** ASIAN — now often taken to be offensive **2** *Africa* **:** one of Indian descent

asiatic beetle *n, usu cap A* **:** ORIENTAL BEETLE

asiatic bronze *n, often cap A* **:** BRONZE BROWN

asiatic cholera *n, usu cap A* **:** an acute infectious epidemic and endemic disease of man esp. in Asia involving the small intestine, characterized by severe effortless diarrhea with rice-water stools, vomiting, and muscle cramps, marked by toxemia, dehydration, and collapse, caused by a bacterium (*Vibrio comma*), and spread by contaminated food and water

asiatic class *n, usu cap A* **:** a group of breeds of domestic fowls supposed to have originated in eastern Asia and containing the Brahmas, Cochins, and Langshans, all consisting of large heavy birds that have feathered legs and red ear lobes and lay brown-shelled eggs — compare MEDITERRANEAN CLASS

asiatic cockroach *n, usu cap A* **:** ORIENTAL COCKROACH

asiatic elephant *n, usu cap A* **:** a forest-dwelling elephant (*Elephas maximus*) with relatively small ears that occurs in southeastern Asia from India to Ceylon and Borneo — compare AFRICAN ELEPHANT

asiatic garden beetle *n, usu cap A* **:** a small brown beetle (*Maladera castanea*) resembling the related Oriental beetle in appearance and habits and like the latter introduced into eastern No. America from Asia

asi·at·i·cism \,==='ə,sizəm\ *n, usu cap* **:** a literary, oratorical, or architectural style characterized by excessive ornamentation or emotionalism **:** FLORIDITY

asi·at·i·cize \-ə,sīz\ *also* **asi·a·tize** \'===ə,tīz; ,=='ad·,īz -'a,tīz\ *vt* -ED/-ING/-S *often cap* **:** to make Asian or partially Asian in customs or ideas

asiatic sweetleaf *n, usu cap A* **:** an eastern Asian shrub (*Symplocos paniculata*) cultivated for its fragrant white flowers and bright blue fruits

asiatic white pine *n, usu cap A* **:** HIMALAYAN PINE

¹aside \ə'-\ *adv* [ME, fr. ¹*a-* + *side*] **1 a :** to or toward one side ⟨draw ~ the curtains⟩ **b :** SIDEWISE, ASLANT, OBLIQUELY ⟨practiced to lisp and hang the head ~ —Alexander Pope⟩ **2** *now dial* **:** by the side **:** ALONGSIDE — usu. used with following *of* ⟨he sat down ~ of me⟩ **3 a :** out of the way **:** away from a group **:** in or into privacy **:** APART ⟨had been taken ~ by his father —Rex Ingamells⟩ **b :** away from oneself ⟨he threw his coat ~⟩ **c :** away from one's thought or use **:** out of consideration ⟨all such protests were brushed ~ as purely superficial —Osbert Lancaster⟩ **d** *archaic* **:** away from the correct or right way **:** ASTRAY ⟨they are all gone ~ —Ps 14:3 (AV)⟩ **4 :** set to one side ⟨matters which, exceptional cases ~, no investor can settle with the foreign government —M.A.Heilperin⟩ **5** on each side **:** to a side ⟨a football match in the High Street with 50 or 60 ~ —G.G.Carter⟩

²aside \"\ *prep* **1** *obs* **:** BEYOND, PAST ⟨the kind prince . . . hath rushed ~ the law —Shak.⟩ **2** *dial* **:** BESIDE, NEAR ⟨was always at the wheel with the little boy ~ him —Karlton Kelm⟩

³aside \"\ *n* -s **1 a :** words spoken aside or in a low tone so as to be inaudible to some person or persons present ⟨after a few parting ~s to Mrs. Wales she led Cecily into the house —Hamilton Basso⟩ **b** (1) **:** words spoken by a character in a play that are heard by the audience but are supposedly not heard by other characters on stage (2) **:** a stage convention using such words **2 :** a departure from the subject or principal theme (as of an essay or lecture) **:** DIGRESSION, PARENTHESIS ⟨the author frequently stops the narrative for caustic ~s and remarks on a wide variety of subjects —R.A.Cordell⟩

aside from *prep* **1 :** in addition to **:** BESIDES ⟨*aside from* being a plane stop, [it] is the most important station for the river steamers —Tom Marvel⟩ **2 :** except for **:** apart from ⟨they were farmers almost to a man, *aside from* a few mechanics —Van Wyck Brooks⟩

asid·en \ə'sīd³n\ *adv* [prob. fr. ME *asidenhand* aside, aslant, fr. *aside* + *hand*] *now dial Eng* **:** SIDEWISE, AWRY

asien·to *or* **as·sien·to** \,asē'en(,)tō, ,äs-\ *n* -s [Sp *asiento* seat, meeting place of a tribunal, treaty, contract, fr. *asentar* to seat, make an agreement, fr. *a-* (fr. L *ad-*) + *sentar* to seat] **:** a contract or convention between Spain and another power or company or individual for furnishing Negro slaves for the Spanish dominions in America

¹as if *conj* **:** as it would be if ⟨it was *as if* he had lost his last friend⟩ **:** as one would do if ⟨he ran *as if* ghosts were chasing him⟩ **:** THAT ⟨it seemed *as if* the day would never end⟩

²as if *n* **:** ALS OB

asigmatic \¦ā+¦=¦==\ *adj* [²*a-* + *sigmatic*] *of a tense* **:** formed without the addition of *s* to the root — opposed to *sigmatic*

asil *often cap, var of* ASEEL

¹asi·lid \ə'sīləd, -il-\ *adj* [NL *Asilidae*] **:** of or relating to the Asilidae

²asilid \"\ *n* -s **:** one of the Asilidae **:** ROBBER FLY

asil·i·dae \ə'silə,dē\ *n pl, cap* [NL, fr. *Asilus*, type genus + *-idae*] **:** a family of rather large usu. slender two-winged flies with strong legs and wings and the proboscis a hardened beak used for sucking the body fluids of other insects which they capture on the wing — compare ROBBER FLY

asi·lus \ə'sīləs\ *n, cap* [NL, fr. L, gadfly] **:** the type genus of Asilidae

asim·i·na \ə'simənə\ *n, cap* [NL, fr. AmerF *assimine* papaw, modif. of Illinois *rassimina*, fr. *rassi* divided lengthwise into equal parts + *mina* seeds] **:** a small genus of eastern No. American shrubs and small trees (family Annonaceae) having aromatic alternate leaves and flowers with 3 to 15 stamens and carpels — see PAPAW

asim·mer \ə'-\ *adj* [¹*a-* + *simmer*, v.] **:** SIMMERING ⟨the stuff and nonsense long ~ in their noddles —Robert Browning⟩

asin \'äsən\ *n* -s *usu cap* [Skt *Āśvina*] **:** a month of the Hindu year — see MONTH table

asinego *n* -ES [alter. of earlier *asinico*, modif. (influenced by L *asinus*) of Sp *asnico*, dim. of *asno* ass, fr. L *asinus*] **1** *obs* **:** a little ass **2** *obs* **:** FOOL

as·i·nine \'asᵊn,īn, 'aas- *sometimes* 'az-\ *adj* [L *asininus*, fr. *asinus* ass + *-inus* -ine — more at ASS] **1 :** of, relating to, or resembling an ass or asses ⟨this interesting animal is definitely horselike although it has ~ characteristics as well —R.S. Summerhays⟩ **2 :** UNINTELLIGENT, STUPID, SILLY, OBSTINATE ⟨a man so ~ that he looks for gratitude in this world —H.L. Mencken⟩ ⟨a polite smile at what he thought an ~ joke —Dashiell Hammett⟩ **syn** see SIMPLE

as·i·nin·i·ty \,==='inəd·ē, -ətē, -i\ *n* -ES **1 :** the quality or state of being asinine ⟨capable of an ~ that can snatch defeat from the very jaws of victory —G.W.Johnson⟩ **2 :** something that is asinine ⟨that sickening list of asininities —Max Ascoli⟩

¹asiphonate \(')ā+¦-\ *adj* [²*a-* + *siphonate*] **:** having no siphon ⟨an ~ oyster⟩

²asiphonate \"\ *n* -s **:** an asiphonate mollusk

¹ask \'ask, 'aa(ə)-,'ai-,'á-, *chiefly substand* -st\ *vb* **asked** \-s(k)t, *before a word (esp consonant-initial) following without pause, often* -sk\ **asked** \"\ **asking** \-skiŋ, *chiefly substand* -stiŋ *or* -stən\ **asks** \-sks, *chiefly substand* -s(t)s\ [ME *asken*, *axen*, fr. OE *āscian*, *ācsian* to ask, demand; akin to OFris *āskia* to demand, OS *ēscon*, OHG *eiscōn* to ask, L *aeruscare* to beg, Gk *himeros* longing, Skt *icchati* he seeks, desires] *vt* **1 a :** to call upon for an answer or informative response **:** put a question to **:** inquire of ⟨he ~*ed* him about his trip⟩ **b :** to seek to be informed about **:** put a question about **:** inquire concerning ⟨the two or three people of whom I ~*ed* his whereabouts —Scott Fitzgerald⟩ **c :** to speak or utter (a question or a request for information) ⟨he never ~*s* foolish questions⟩ **2 a :** to make a request of **:** BEG, PETITION ⟨they ~*ed* him to be quiet⟩ **b :** to make a request for **:** seek by words to obtain ⟨she ~*ed* help from her teacher⟩ ⟨he ~*ed* advice of several friends⟩ **3 :** to call for **:** NEED, REQUIRE ⟨it ~*s* some strenuous agility to keep them both in the mind together —Donald Davie⟩ **4** *archaic* **:** to make known publicly **:** PUBLISH ⟨the day when I shall ~ the banns —Shak.⟩ **5 :** to set as a price **:** DEMAND, EXPECT ⟨the dealer ~*ed* $2000 for the car⟩ **6 :** to extend an invitation to **:** INVITE ⟨we ~*ed* him to come to lunch⟩ ~ *vi* **1 :** to seek information **:** make inquiries **:** INQUIRE ⟨he ~*ed* about your job⟩ ⟨he ~*ed* for the owner⟩ ⟨he ~*ed* after the old man's health⟩ **2 :** to make a request **:** SEEK, PETITION ⟨they ~*ed* for food and lodging⟩ **3 :** to seek or invite punishment or retaliation ⟨if you do that you're just ~*ing* for trouble⟩ — often used with following phrase *for it* ⟨the Nazis and the Fascists have ~*ed* for it and they are going to get it —F.D.Roosevelt⟩

syn INQUIRE, QUERY, QUESTION, INTERROGATE, EXAMINE, QUIZ, CATECHIZE: ASK is a general and colorless term suggesting mainly the placing of a single question in order to gain information. It may verge onto connoting seeking or requesting ⟨where lies the land to which your ship must go . . . yet still I *ask*, what haven is her mark? —William Wordsworth⟩ ⟨an increasing number were *asking* many things from philosophy —H.O.Taylor⟩ INQUIRE in this sense is likely to indicate an honest request for information, a question asked solely to lead to enlightening the questioner on the matter ostensibly under primary consideration ⟨my literary conscience . . . *inquires* if ideas were really free at Oxford —Ellen Glasgow⟩ QUERY indicates asking for an answer which clarifies, substantiates, removes doubt from the questioner's mind ⟨the anthropologist, on the other hand, might *query* the statement —J.F.Embree⟩ QUESTION heightens the implication that the questioner finds an assertion or notion doubtful, unconvincing, and perhaps incorrect ⟨*Newsweek's* incoming mail sacks bulge. Some letters *query*, others *question* facts —*Newsweek*⟩ ⟨even today *questioning* a statement made by a person is often taken by him as a reflection upon his integrity, and is resented —John Dewey⟩ To QUESTION a person is to keep asking him searching questions ⟨*question* the committee about the deficit⟩ INTERROGATE may suggest systematic and thorough questions; it implies, however, a simple search for facts and indicates nothing about the attitude of the questioner ⟨he had landed on the Arno and *interrogated* the natives with the help of an interpreter —John Dos Passos⟩ EXAMINE, in reference to things, is a synonym for *inspect* rather than for QUESTION; in reference to persons, it may suggest either detailed questions intended to discover the correctness of a person's conduct or beliefs or the scope of his knowledge or abilities, the examiner often having knowledge of the correct or preferred answers ⟨where he had himself *examined* for three days by the learned and wise king of Naples —R.A.Hall b.1911⟩ QUIZ suggests the asking of a series of questions by one knowing the answers in order to test another's knowledge; it may suggest a lighter, more casual, less significant procedure than EXAMINE ⟨*quizzed* by feature writers in magazines —G.A. Miller⟩ CATECHIZE, which often pertains to matters religious, may suggest systematic, rapid questioning, often calling for answers by rote, to verify accuracy, correctness, or orthodoxy of another's notions, and to trip him up if possible ⟨the awkward situation in which you found yourself on receiving a visit from an authoress whose works though presented to you . . . you had never read. . . . I hope she *catechized* you well —William Cowper⟩

syn ASK, REQUEST, SOLICIT mean, in a common application, to try to obtain by making one's wants known. ASK implies little more than the statement of the desire ⟨*ask* the cooperation of all concerned⟩ ⟨what more can be *asked* of books than that they provoke laughter, more reading, discussion, a pilgrimage —D.S.Davis⟩ REQUEST implies more formality, greater display of courtesy, and anticipation of affirmative response ⟨*request* the cooperation of neighboring towns in the control of Dutch elm disease⟩ ⟨*request* a meeting to discuss common problems and the possibility of mutual help⟩ ⟨*requesting* that Italy be given the trusteeship of that territory —*Collier's Yr. Bk.*⟩ ⟨16 nations *requesting* aid under the European Recovery Program —*Current Biog.*⟩ SOLICIT, in modern use and in this connection, commonly means no more than calling attention to one's wants or desires ⟨*solicit* trade or patronage by advertisement⟩ ⟨*solicit* funds for flood relief⟩ ⟨our interest is *solicited* by the characters themselves rather than by anything that they do —A.J.Ayer⟩

²ask \'ask\ *n* -s [ME *aske*, *ascre*, fr. OE *āthexe* (akin to OHG *egidehsa*, OS *egithassa*, MD *haghedisse*), fr. *ā-* (perh. akin to Gk *ophis* snake) + *-thexe* (perh. akin to MHG *dehse* spindle) — more at ANGUIS] *dial Brit* **:** WATER NEWT

¹askance \ə'skan(t)s, -aa(ə)n-,-ain- *also* -än-\ *adv* [origin unknown] **1 :** with a side glance **:** SIDEWAYS, OBLIQUELY ⟨did not now turn quite all the way back but looked at me ~ with her bright steady eyes —Edmund Wilson⟩ **2 :** with disapproval or distrust **:** SUSPICIOUSLY, ⟨one trained in . . . the basic sciences may look ~ at this process —D.H.K. Lee⟩

²askance \"\ *adj* **:** turned askance **:** SIDEWAYS ⟨her eyes with their misted ~ look —Elizabeth Bowen⟩

¹askant \-ant, -aa(ə)nt,-aint\ *adv* [prob. alter. (influenced by *aslant*) of ¹*askance*] **:** ASKANCE ⟨and I saw ~ the armies —Walt Whitman⟩

²askant \"\ *adj* [alter. of ²*askance*] **:** ASKANCE ⟨oil lamps often with wick ~ in the socket —George Meredith⟩

as·kar \'askə(r)\ *n, pl* **askar** [Ar *'askar* soldier] **:** a native infantryman in the army of Morocco or any other Arabic-speaking country

as·ka·rel \'askə¦rel\ *n* -s [origin unknown] **:** a synthetic electrically insulating liquid that is nonflammable

as·ka·ri \'askərē; ə'skärē, a's-\ *n, pl* **askaris** [Ar *'askarī*] **1 :** a native soldier esp. of eastern Africa in the service of a European power **2 :** a native policeman, guard, or watchman esp. of eastern Africa

asked *past of* ASK

askeletal \(')ā+¦-\ *adj* [²*a-* + *skeletal*] **:** without a skeleton — used esp. of sponges

¹ask·er \'askə(r), 'aa-,ai-,á-\ *n* -s [ME, fr. *asken* + *-er*] **:** one that asks: **a :** one that asks questions **:** INQUIRER **b :** one that asks favors, gifts, or alms **:** SUPPLIANT, BEGGAR

²as·ker \'askə(r)\ *n* -s [ME *ascre* — more at ASK (n.)] *dial Eng* **:** WATER NEWT

askesis *var of* ASCESIS

¹askew \ə'skyü\ *adv* [prob. fr. ¹*a-* + *skew*] **1 :** out of line **:** to one side **:** AWRY, OBLIQUELY ⟨something has gone seriously ~ with the show —Angelica Gibbs⟩ ⟨the gate hung ~ —Agatha Christie⟩ **2 :** with contempt or disdain **:** SCORNFULLY ⟨looked somewhat ~ at his tipsy, giggling wife⟩

²askew \"\ *adj* **:** made or standing out of line **:** set or turned to one side **:** AWRY, SKEW ⟨leaning against an ~ lamppost to light a cigarette —R.P.Warren⟩

asking *pres part of* ASK

asking bid *n* **:** an artificial bid in contract bridge that asks for certain information from the bidder's partner

ask·ing·ly *adv* **:** in an entreating or inquiring manner

asking price *n* **:** the price at which something is offered for sale

asklent \ə'sklent\ *dial Scot var of* ASLANT

asks *pres 3d sing of* ASK, *pl of* ASK

aslake \ə'slāk\ *vt* -ED/-ING/-S [ME *aslaken*, fr. OE *āslacian* to become or make slack, diminish, loosen, fr. *ā-* (perfective prefix) + *slacian* to slacken — more at ABEAR, SLAKE] *archaic* **:** to cause to abate or diminish ⟨waits for the prey . . . its hunger to ~ —Robert Southey⟩

¹aslant \ə'slant, -aa(ə)nt,-aint,-ánt\ *adv* [ME *aslante*, *aslonte*, *aslunte*, prob. fr. ¹*a-* + the root of ME *slente* slope — more at SLANT (n.)] **:** in a slanting or sloping direction **:** toward one side **:** OBLIQUELY ⟨the sun shone ~ across his face —Elizabeth M. Roberts⟩

²aslant \"\ *prep* **:** over or across in a slanting direction **:** ATHWART ⟨there is a willow grows ~ a brook —Shak.⟩

³aslant \"\ *adj* : SLANTING, OBLIQUE ⟨with head ~⟩

¹asleep \ə'slēp\ *adj* [ME *aslepe*, adj. & adv., fr. ¹*a-* + *slepe* sleep] **1** : being in a state of sleep : SLEEPING ⟨he has been ~ since noon⟩ **2** : being in the sleep of death : DEAD ⟨we would not have you ignorant . . . concerning those who are ~ —1 Thess 4:13 (RSV)⟩ **3** : lacking sensation or feeling : NUMB ⟨my arm is ~⟩ **4** : being in a state of mental or physical inactivity, sluggishness, or indifference : not alert : INACTIVE, DORMANT ⟨a weak, timid, lethargic government usually ~ —Sir Winston Churchill⟩ ⟨the sea ~ and at peace —Thomas Wood †1950⟩ **5** *of a sail* : MOTIONLESS, UNRUFFLED — **asleep at the switch** : not alert to a duty or opportunity

²asleep \"\ *adv* [ME *aslepe*] **1** : into a state of sleep ⟨he fell ~ at noon⟩ **2** : into the sleep of death : DEAD ⟨God will bring with him those who have fallen ~ —1 Thess 4:14 (RSV)⟩ **3** : into a state of inactivity, sluggishness, or indifference ⟨the falling ~ of the critical faculty —R.W. Southern⟩

as long as *conj* **1** : during the time that : WHILE ⟨enjoyed success *as long as* she lived⟩ **2** : provided that ⟨they can go where they please *as long as* they return on time⟩ **3** : inasmuch as : SINCE ⟨*as long as* you are going, I'll go too⟩

¹aslope \ə'slōp\ *adj* [ME, adj. & adv.] : SLOPING, SLANTING

²aslope \"\ *adv* [ME] : in a sloping or slanting direction : SLOPINGLY ⟨he was leaning ~ against the building⟩

asm *abbr* assembly

as·ma·ra \azmärə, as'-, -marə\ *adj, usu cap* [fr. *Asmara*, Eritrea] : of or from Asmara, the capital of Eritrea : of the kind or style prevalent in Asmara

asmoke \ə'-\ *adj* [¹*a-* + *smoke*, v.] : SMOKING

asmonaean *or* **asmonean** *usu cap, var of* HASMONAEAN

asmt *abbr* assortment

as much *pron* : nearly the same

as much as *adv* : in effect : ALMOST ⟨he *as much as* admitted the whole story⟩

as nas *var of* ⁷AS

asocial \(')ā+¦-\ *adj* [²*a-* + *social*] **1** : inconsiderate of or hostile to the needs, desires, or customs of others : SELFISH ⟨a defensory wall of ~ behavior —F.H.Allport⟩ **2** : withdrawn from society and from normal social intercourse : unable or unwilling to conform to social demands — sometimes distinguished from *antisocial* ⟨a vast difference between an acceptable social attitude and an ~ or reclusive attitude —A.T.Weaver⟩ — **asocialism** \(')ā+\ *n* -s — **asociality** \¦ā+\ *n* -ES

as of \¦azə(v)\ *prep* : at or on (a specific time or date) ⟨the rule takes effect *as of* July 1⟩

aso·ka \ə's(h)ōkə\ *also* **as·ak** *or* **as·ok** \'asək\ *n* -s [Hindi *asok*, fr. Skt *aśoka*] : a showy tree (*Saraca indica*) of the family Leguminosae of tropical Asia that is cultivated for its orange scarlet flowers and is used to decorate temples

aso·kan column \ə's(h)ōkən-\ *n, usu cap A* [*Asoka* the Great †232 B.C. king of Magadha, ancient kingdom of India, at whose behest they were erected + E *-an*] : a stone column found in India and usu. of considerable height on which Buddhist inscriptions were cut — compare ²LAT

aso·ma·tog·no·sia \¦ā,sōmə,täg'nōzh(ē)ə\ *n* [NL, fr. ²*a-* + *somat-* + *-gnosia*] : ignorance of paralysis as a result of brain damage

asomatophyte \¦ā+\ *n* -s [²*a-* + *somat-* + *-phyte*] : a plant in which body and reproductive cells are not distinct and which lacking permanent tissue loses none of its capacity to grow and multiply — compare SOMATOPHYTE

aso·ma·tous \(')ā¦sōmədəs\ *adj* [LL *asomatus*, fr. Gk *asōmatos*, fr. *a-* ²*a-* + *-sōmatos* (fr. *sōmat-, sōma* body) — more at -SOMA] : INCORPOREAL, IMMATERIAL

asonant \(')ā+¦-\ *adj* [²*a-* + *sonant*] : not sonant

as·or \'a,sȯ(ə)r\ *n* -s [Heb *'āśōr*, fr. *'āśār* ten] : an ancient Hebrew zitherlike instrument having 10 strings and played with a plectrum

¹asp \'asp, 'aa(ə)-, 'ai- *also* 'ȧ-\ *n* -s [ME *aspe* — more at ASPEN] : ASPEN

²asp \"\ *n* -s [ME *aspis*, fr. L, fr. Gk] : a small venomous snake of Egypt variously identified as the horned viper or a small African cobra (*Naja haje*) — see URAEUS

as·pal·a·thus \a'spaləthəs\ *n* [L, fr. Gk *aspalathos*] **1** -ES : a biblical shrub yielding a fragrant oil and generally believed to be a member of the genus *Alhagi* or of the genus *Convolvulus* **2** [NL, fr. L] *cap* : a genus of southern African shrubs (family Fabaceae) with heathlike often tufted leaves and yellow or rarely purple flowers

aspar \ə'spär\ *adv* [¹*a-* + *spar*] *chiefly Scot* : wide apart

as·pa·rag·i·nase \,aspə'rajə,nās, -āz\ *n* -s [*asparagine* + *-ase*] : an enzyme obtained esp. from liver extracts that hydrolyzes asparagine to aspartic acid and ammonia

as·par·a·gine \ə'sparə,jēn, -jən\ *n* -s [F, fr. L *asparagus* + F *-ine*] : a white crystalline amino acid $H_2NOCCH_2CH(NH_2)COOH$ found in most plants (as asparagus and leguminous plants) and used in culture media for some bacteria (as lactobacilli and tubercle bacilli); α-amino-succinamic acid

as·pa·rag·i·nyl \,aspə'rajənəl, -,nēl\ *n* [*asparagine* + *-yl*] : the univalent acyl radical $H_2NCOCH_2CH(NH_2)CO$— of asparagine

as·par·a·gus \ə'sparəgəs *also* -er-\ *n* [in sense 1, fr. NL, fr. L, asparagus (plant), fr. Gk *asparagos, aspharagos;* in other senses, fr. L, asparagus (plant); akin to Gk *spargan* to swell — more at SPARK] **1** *cap* : a genus of Old World perennial herbs (family Liliaceae) having erect much-branched stems, minute scalelike leaves, and linear cladophylls often mistaken for leaves **2** -ES **a** : any plant of the genus *Asparagus; esp* : a plant (*A. officinalis*) widely cultivated for its tender edible young shoots **b** : the root of cultivated asparagus formerly used as a diuretic

asparagus bean *n* : a So. American bean (*Vigna sesquipedalis*) having very long succulent pods

asparagus bed *n* : a military obstacle consisting of series of steel, wood, or concrete uprights planted in the ground

asparagus beetle *n* : a small dark-colored but brightly marked beetle (*Crioceris asparagi*) of which both the adult and larva feed on asparagus; *also* : SPOTTED ASPARAGUS BEETLE

asparagus broccoli *n* : CALABRESE

asparagus fern *n* : a feathery cultivated asparagus (*A. plumosus*) resembling a fern

asparagus lettuce *n* : a variety (*Lactuca sativa angustana*) of the common lettuce grown for its thick edible stem

asparagus pea *n* : GOA BEAN

asparagus stone *n* : a variety of apatite occurring in yellow-green crystals

as·par·tase \ə'spär,tās, -āz\ *n* -s [*aspartic* + *-ase*] : an enzyme that occurs in various bacteria, yeasts, and higher plants and that catalyzes the conversion reaction of aspartic acid to fumaric acid by the removal of ammonia and also the reverse reaction of the addition of ammonia to fumaric acid

as·par·tate \-,tāt\ *n* -s [ISV *aspartic* + *-ate*] : a salt or ester of aspartic acid

as·par·tic acid \-,tik-\ *n* [ISV *aspar-* (fr. L *asparagus*) + connective *-t-* + *-ic*] : a crystalline amino dicarboxylic acid $HOOCCH_2CH(NH_2)COOH$ that is found esp. in many plants (as young sugar cane) and is obtained by hydrolysis of asparagine and proteins, that takes part in transamination reactions in the living organism, and that is used in bacteriological culture media; amino-succinic acid

as·par·to·yl \-tə,wil\ *also* **as·par·tyl** \-rd-ᵊl, -r,tēl\ *n* -s [*aspartic* + *-oyl, -yl*] : the bivalent radical $—OCCH_2CH(NH_2)CO—$ of aspartic acid; amino-succinyl

¹as·pect \'a,spekt, 'aa- *sometimes* -,spēkt *or* -,spikt\ *n* -s [ME, fr. L *aspectus*, fr. *aspectus*, past part. of *aspicere, adspicere* to look at, fr. *ad-* + *-spicere* (fr. *specere* to look) — more at SPY] **1 a** (1) : the position of planets or stars with respect to one another held by astrologers to exert an influence upon human affairs : the joint look of planets or stars upon each other or upon the earth ⟨the shepherd's issue at whose birth heaven did afford a gracious ~ —Christopher Marlowe⟩ (2) : the effect of this position ⟨astrologers call the evil influences of the stars evil ~*s* —Francis Bacon⟩ **b** *archaic* : the direction in which influence is brought to bear **c** (1) : a position facing or fronting a particular direction : a position in relation to the points of the compass : EXPOSURE ⟨the house has a southern ~⟩ (2) : a view of a plane from a given direction : the manner of presentation of a plane to a fluid (as the air) through which it is moving or to a current (3) : orientation of a slope in respect to the compass : exposure to sunlight ⟨lands are planted with vines where soil and ~ permit⟩ **d** : the part of an object in a particular position ⟨a sandbag placed over the dorsal ~*s* of the feet will prevent them from slipping —*Med. Radiography & Photography*⟩ **2 a** (1) *obs* : CONSIDERATION, RESPECT (2) : appearance to the eye or mind ⟨the ~ of affairs —T.B.Macaulay⟩ (3) : a particular status or phase in which anything appears or may be regarded ⟨a question having many ~*s*⟩ ⟨in other ~*s* of our living conditions —W.C.Allee⟩ **b** (1) : a particular appearance of the face : COUNTENANCE, MIEN, AIR ⟨serious in ~ —John Dryden⟩ (2) : the apparent position of a body in the solar system with reference to the sun including conjunction, quadrature, and opposition (3) : the appearance of a fixed railroad signal as viewed from the direction of an approaching train or the appearance of a cab signal as viewed by an observer in the cab **c** : the distinctive seasonal appearance of a plant community ⟨spring ~⟩ — see ASPECTION **3** *archaic* **a** : act of looking or gazing : GAZE ⟨his ~ was bent on the ground —Sir Walter Scott⟩ **b** : GLANCE, LOOK **4** [trans. of Russ *vid*] **a** : a set of inflectional forms of a verb that indicate the nature of the action or the manner in which the action is regarded esp. with reference to its beginning, duration, completion, or repetition and without reference to its position in time — used first of the Slavic languages, later of many others; compare COMPLETIVE, IMPERFECTIVE, INCHOATIVE, ITERATIVE, PERFECTIVE **b** : the nature of the action of a verb or the manner in which that action is regarded esp. with reference to its beginning, duration, completion, or repetition and without reference to its position in time, whether indicated by a set of inflectional forms (as in sense 4a), by the meaning of the verb itself (as in *find*, expressing momentary or completed action, by contrast with *seek*, expressing continuing action), by an adverbial modifier (as in *sit down*, meaning "get into a sitting position", by contrast with *sit there till the doctor is ready*, where *sit* means "remain in a sitting position"), by such devices as the so-called progressive tenses in English (as *was eating*, which expresses continuing action, by contrast with *left*, which expresses momentary or completed action, in "he left while I was eating"), or by some other means **5** *in the Midwestern system for American archaeology* : a unit of classification constituting a group of foci that have an approximate majority of determinant types in common — see PHASE; compare COMPONENT, PATTERN **syn** see APPEARANCE, PHASE

²as·pect \", a'spekt\ *vt* -ED/-ING/-S [L *aspectare*, fr. *aspectus*, past part. of *aspicere*] **1** *astrol, of a planet or constellation* : to look upon (a person, house, or another planet) in a particular aspect ⟨when badly ~*ed* the subjects of Scorpio are, however, most destructive —W.T.&Kate Pavitt⟩ **2** *obs* : to look at : BEHOLD

as·pect·a·ble \a'spektəbəl, 'a,spek-\ *adj* [L *aspectabilis*, fr. *aspectare* to look at + *-abilis* -able] *archaic* : capable of being seen : VISIBLE

as·pec·tion \a'spekshən\ *n* -s [L *aspection-, aspectio*, fr. L *aspectus* (past part. of *aspicere*) + *-ion-, -io* -ion] **1** *archaic* : VIEWING **2** : seasonal variation in the appearance or makeup of a plant community usu. relatable to seasonal climatic variation — compare ANNUATION

aspect ratio *n* **1** : the ratio of span to mean chord of an airfoil **2** : the ratio of the width of a television image to its height **3** : the ratio of the longer to the shorter dimension of the cross section of an air duct opening in an air-conditioning system

as·pec·tu·al \a'spekchə(wə)l, 'a,s-\ *adj* [L *aspectus* aspect + E *-al*] : of or belonging to an aspect (as the aspect of a verb)

¹as·pen \'aspən, 'aas-,'ais- *also* 'ȧs- *or* -pin\ *adj* [ME, fr. *aspe*, n. + *-en*] **1 a** : of, relating to, or resembling the aspen **b** : made of the wood of the aspen **2** : quivering like the leaves of the aspen : TREMULOUS, QUAKING

²aspen \"\ *n* -s [alter. (influenced by ¹*aspen*) of ME *aspe*, fr. OE *æspe, æpse;* akin to OHG *aspa* aspen, ON *ösp*, Latvian *apsa*, Russ *osina*] : any of several poplars (esp. *Populus tremula* of Europe and *P. tremuloides* and *P. grandidentata* of No. America) the leaves of which flutter in the lightest wind on account of their flattened petioles

aspen poplar *n* : WHITE POPLAR 1b

aspen tortrix *n* : a tortricid moth (*Archips conflictana*) having a larva that feeds on and may seriously defoliate various species of aspen esp. in parts of Canada

¹asper *adj* [ME *aspre, asper*, fr. MF & L; MF *aspre*, fr. L *asper*, lit., rough] *obs* : HARSH, BITTER, STERN

²as·per \'aspə(r)\ *n* -s [ME, fr. MF *aspre* or It *aspro*, fr. MGk *aspron*, fr. neut. of *aspros* white, fr. L *asper* rough, newly minted] **1** : any one of several small silver coins circulating in the eastern Mediterranean area from the 12th to the 17th centuries: **a** : a coin issued by the Comneni of Trebizond **b** : a coin issued by the Knights of Rhodes equivalent to the denier of western Europe **c** : a Turkish coin first issued in the 14th century **2** : a Turkish unit of value that continued in use after the disappearance of the Turkish asper at one time equivalent to the 120th part of a piaster

¹as·per·ate \'aspərət\ *adj* [L *asperatus*, past part. of *asperare* to make rough, fr. *asper* rough] *archaic* : somewhat rough or harsh to the touch : ASPEROUS

²as·per·ate \-,rāt\ *vt* -ED/-ING/-S [L *asperatus*] *archaic* : to make rough or harsh

as·perge \ə'spərj, a'-\ *vt* -ED/-ING/-S [MF *asperger*, fr. L *aspergere* — more at ASPERSE] : to sprinkle esp. with holy water

as·per·ges \-(,)jēz\ *n, sometimes cap* [L, thou wilt sprinkle, 2d pers. sing. fut. indic. of *aspergere*] : the ceremony of sprinkling altar, clergy, and people with holy water

as·per·gil·la·ce·ae \,aspərjə'lāsē,ē\ *n pl, cap* [NL, fr. *Aspergillus*, type genus + *-aceae*] : a family of fungi (order Eurotiales) including the common molds of the genera *Aspergillus* and *Penicillium* and the fungus *Thielavia basicola* which is the cause of root rot or black root rot of numerous hosts

as·per·gil·la·les \-ā(,)lēz\ *n* [NL, fr. *Aspergillus* + *-ales*] *syn of* EUROTIALES

as·per·gil·li·form \¦aspər¦jilə,fȯrm\ *adj* [ISV *aspergill-* (fr. NL *aspergillus*) + *-iform*] : like a brush; *specif* : resembling the sporophore of *Aspergillus* ⟨an ~ stigma⟩

as·per·gil·lin \-lən\ *n* -s [ISV *aspergill-* (fr. NL *Aspergillus*) + *-in*] **1** : an amorphous black pigment found in the spores of various fungi of the genus *Aspergillus* **2** : an antibacterial substance obtained from cultures of two molds (*Aspergillus flavus* and *A. fumigatus*) reported to possess activity against both gram-positive and gram-negative bacteria

as·per·gil·lo·sis \,aspərjə'lōsəs\ *n, pl* **aspergillo·ses** \-ō,sēz\ [NL, fr. *Aspergillus* + *-osis*] : infection with or disease caused by molds of the genus *Aspergillus*: **a** : a severe respiratory disease of birds caused by a mold (*A. fumigatus* or rarely *A. niger*) and marked by unthriftiness, emaciation, and pulmonary calcification resembling that of tuberculosis or in young chickens and turkeys taking the form of an acute rapidly fatal pneumonia — called also *brooder pneumonia* **b** : a disease of man usu. occurring in agricultural workers, hair or fur cleaners and others exposed to inhalation of spores (esp. *A. fumigatus*) and characterized by formation of lumps in the skin, ears, sinuses, and respiratory organs

as·per·gil·lum \,aspə(r)'jiləm\ *or* **as·per·gil** *or* **as·per·gill** \'aspə(r),jil\ *n, pl* **aspergil·la** \-'jilə\ *or* **aspergil·lums** \-'jiləmz\ *or* **aspergils** *or* **aspergills** \-,jilz\ [NL *aspergillum*, fr. L *aspergere* to sprinkle] : a short-handled brush or a perforated globe holding a sponge used for sprinkling holy water

aspergillum

as·per·gil·lus \,aspə(r)'jiləs\ *n* [NL, alter. of *aspergillum*] **1** *pl* **aspergil·li** \-,lī\ : ASPERGILLUM **2** *cap* : a genus (the type of the family Aspergillaceae) of fungi including besides common molds species pathogenic to plants and animals and characterized by spores borne in chains on numerous simple or branched usu. bottle-shaped sterigmata that radiate from the upper part or the whole of the swollen tip of the conidiophore — see ASPERGILLOSIS

as·per·i·fo·li·ate \¦aspərə¦fōlēət, -ē,āt\ *or* **as·per·i·fo·li·ous** \-ēəs\ *adj* [*asperifoliate* fr. NL *asperifolius* + E *-ate; asperifolious* fr. NL *asperifolius*, fr. L *asper* rough + *-i-* + *-folius* (fr. *folium* leaf) — more at BLADE] : rough-leaved

as·per·i·ty \a'sperəd-ē, ə'-, -ətē, -i\ *n* -ES [alter. (influenced by MF *asperité* — fr. L *asperitat-, asperitas*, fr. *asper* rough + *-itat-, -itas* -ity — or by L *asperitas*) of ME *asprete*, fr. OF *aspreté*, fr. *aspre* rough (fr. L *asper*) + *-té* -ty] **1** : a characteristic making for hardship : RIGOR, SEVERITY ⟨the path of beauty is not soft and smooth, but full of harshness and ~ —Havelock Ellis⟩ **2 a** (1) : roughness of surface (as of a leaf) : UNEVENNESS (2) **asperities** *pl* : rough places : EXCRESCENCES ⟨ultramicroscopic *asperities* . . . upon the solid surface —J.W.McBain⟩ **b** *obs* : roughness to the taste : SOURNESS, TARTNESS **c** : roughness or harshness of sound : RAUCOUSNESS ⟨the elderly ladies in his audience had been shocked by the *asperities* of the new style in music —Aaron Copland⟩ **3** : a characteristic making for bitterness : roughness of manner or of temper ⟨he repented of his ~, however, when he saw Shiloh droop his head and wither visibly into sadness —Elinor Wylie⟩ ⟨it caused him a passing ~ to observe her lay places for three —A.J.Cronin⟩ : SEVERITY ⟨the portrait . . . on the wall, whose painted eyes, it seemed, were now inhumanly surveying them . . . with some little ~ —Walter de la Mare⟩ : TARTNESS ⟨a little ~ was in her voice —George Meredith⟩

aspermatism \(')ā+\ *n* -s [ISV ²*a-* + *spermatism*] : ASPERMIA

asper·mia \ā'spərmēə\ *n* -s [NL, fr. ²*a-* + *-spermia*] : inability to produce or ejaculate semen — compare AZOOSPERMIA — **asper·mic** \(')ā¦spərmik\ *adj*

as·per·ous \'asp(ə)rəs\ *adj* [L *asper* rough + E *-ous*] : ROUGH, SCABROUS — **as·per·ous·ly** *adv*

aspers *pl of* ASPER

as·perse \ə'spərs, a'-, -əs, -əis\ *vt* -ED/-ING/-S [L *aspersus*, past part. of *aspergere, adspergere* to sprinkle, fr. *ad-* + *-spergere* (fr. *spargere* to strew, scatter) — more at SPARK] **1 a** *archaic* (1) : to besprinkle (a person or thing) with a liquid or with dust (2) : to sprinkle (as water or dust) upon anybody or anything **b** (1) : to baptize by sprinkling ⟨use of sprinkling and *aspersing* was made in old times but only exceptionally and in the case of dying and dangerously sick persons —C.N.Callinicos⟩ (2) : to sprinkle with holy water **2** : to attack with foul reports or false and injurious charges : utter damaging charges or implications against in order to hurt the reputation of ⟨~ a man's character⟩ **syn** see MALIGN

as·pers·er \-sə(r)\ *n* -s : one that asperses

as·per·sion \ə'spərzhən, -ə̄zh-, -əizh- *also* a's-, *Brit usu & US also* -shən\ *n* -s [L *aspersion-, aspersio*, fr. *aspersus* + *-ion-, -io* -ion] **1 a** : a sprinkling with water esp. in religious ceremonies (as some forms of baptism) ⟨~*s* of holy water —F.B.Artz⟩ **b** *archaic* : SHOWER, SPRAY **2 a** : the act of calumniating : DEFAMATION ⟨groundless ~ of his wife's fidelity⟩ **b** : a calumnious or defamatory expression or reflection ⟨some of his more detailed ~*s* seem trigger-happy —P.H.Nowell-Smith⟩ ⟨greets you by casting ~*s* on your honesty —E.W.Lumsden⟩

as·per·so·ri·um \,aspər'sōrēəm, -sȯrē-\ *n, pl* **asperso·ria** \-ēə\ *or* **aspersoriums** [ML, fr. L *aspersus* + *-orium*] **1** : a stoup, basin, or other vessel for holy water **2** : ASPERGILLUM

as·per·so·ry \a'spərsərē, ə'-\ *n* -ES [ML *aspersorium*] : ASPERGILLUM

as·per·u·la \a'sper(y)ələ, ə'-\ *n, cap* [NL, fr. fem. of *asperulus*] : a genus of Old World herbs (family Rubiaceae) with small flowers and whorled leaves — see WOODRUFF

as·per·u·late \-,lāt,-lət\ *adj* [NL *asperulus* + E *-ate*] *bot* : delicately roughened

as·per·u·lous \-ləs\ *adj* [NL *asperulus*, fr. L *asper* rough + *-ulus*] *bot* : slightly rough

¹as·phalt \'a,sfȯlt, 'aa-, *Brit usu & US sometimes* -falt, *sporadic & old-fash* -felt\ *or* **as·phal·tum** \=ˈ=təm\ *also* **as·phalte** *like* ASPHALT\ *n* -s *often attrib* [alter. (prob. influenced by LL *asphaltus*, fr. Gk *asphaltos*) of earlier *aspaltum*, alter. (prob. influenced by assumed ML *aspaltum*, alter. of LL *aspaltus*) of ME *aspaltoun, aspalt*, fr. (assumed) ML *aspaltum* & LL *aspaltus*, fr. Gk *asphaltos, asphalton*, perh. fr. *a-* ²*a-* + *-sphaltos, -sphalton* (akin to Gk *sphallein* to cause to fall); fr. its possible use as a binding agent in stone walls — more at SPELL] **1** : a brown to black bituminous substance found native around the Dead sea, in Trinidad, and elsewhere and also obtained as a residue from certain petroleums consisting chiefly of a mixture of hydrocarbons, varying from hard and brittle to plastic in form, melting on heating, being insoluble in water but soluble in gasoline, and used esp. for paving and roofing, in paints and varnishes, and because light renders certain grades insoluble in oil of turpentine for photomechanical work **2 a** : a composition of ground asphalt rock and bitumen, of bitumen, lime, and gravel, or even of coal tar, lime, and sand used for forming pavements and as a waterproof cement (as for bridges and roofs) **b** : a surface (as a path or roadway) paved with asphalt **3 a** : SMOKE BROWN **b** *asphaltum* : CONGO 4

²asphalt \"\ *vt* -ED/-ING/-S **1** : to cover or pave with asphalt or a mixture containing asphalt ⟨the road itself was magnificently ~*ed* from side to side —Max Beerbohm⟩ **2** : to impregnate (as paper) with asphalt ⟨~*ed* bags, placed between the outer case and the packaged food —*Science News Letter*⟩

asphalt-base \'=,=¦=\ *adj* : containing relatively large amounts of asphalt-forming substances : yielding asphaltic residues on refining — used esp. of crude petroleum; compare NAPHTHENE-BASE, PARAFFIN-BASE

asphalt cement *n* : a refined asphalt free from water and coarse foreign material and containing less than one percent of ash

as·phal·tene \=ˈ=,tēn\ *n* -s [F *asphaltène*, fr. *asphalte* asphalt + *-ène* -ene] : any of the components of a bitumen (as asphalt) that are soluble in carbon disulfide but not in paraffin naphtha and that are held to constitute the solid dispersed particles of the bitumen and to consist chiefly of high-molecular-weight hydrocarbons — compare CARBENE

as·phal·tic \(')=¦=,tik, -ēk\ *adj* : of or containing asphalt

asphaltic felt *n* : a roofing and waterproofing material consisting of saturated asbestos or rag felt cemented together with asphalt or tar pitch

as·phal·tite \=ˈ=,tīt, '=,=,=\ *n* -s [Gk *asphaltitēs*, fr. *asphaltos* + *-itēs* -ite] : a native asphalt occurring in vein deposits below the surface of the ground

asphalt lamination *n* : lamination (as of kraft papers) in which asphalt is used as the adhesive

asphalt macadam *n* : a pavement similar to tarmacadam but having asphaltic binder in place of tar

asphalt mastic *n* : a mixture of asphalt and other material (as sand, crushed rock, or asbestos) used like cement

asphalt paper *n* : paper that is impregnated, coated, or laminated with asphalt

asphalt process *n* : BITUMEN PROCESS

asphalt rock *n* : rock (as sandstone or limestone) impregnated naturally with asphalt

asphaltum *var of* ASPHALT

asphaltus *n* [LL — more at ASPHALT] *obs* : ASPHALT

aspheric \(')ā+¦-\ *or* **aspherical** \(')ā+¦-\ *adj* [²*a-* + *spheric, spherical*] **1** : departing slightly from the spherical form — used of an optical surface **2** : free from spherical aberration

as·pho·del \'asfə,del, 'aas-\ *n, pl* **asphodel** *also* **asphodels** [L *asphodelus*, fr. Gk *asphodelos*] : any of various Old World usu. perennial herbs of the family Liliaceae and chiefly of the genera *Asphodelus* and *Asphodeline* that bear their flowers in long erect racemes — see FALSE ASPHODEL

asphodel green *n* : a moderate yellow green that is greener and paler than average moss green, yellower and less strong than average pea green, and yellower and paler than spinach green

as·pho·del·i·ne \,asfə'delə,nē\ *n, cap* [NL, fr. Gk *asphodelinē*, fem. of *asphodelinos* of asphodel, fr. *asphodelos*] : a genus of asphodels native to the Mediterranean region that have usu. yellow or white flowers in long bracted racemes

as·phod·e·lus \a'sfädᵊləs\ *n, cap* [NL, fr. L] : a genus of asphodels native to southern Asia and the Mediterranean region that have white, pink, or yellow flowers and clustered fleshy roots

as·phyx·ia \a'sfiksēə, ə's-, -kshə\ *n* -s [NL, fr. Gk, stopping of the pulse, fr. *a-* ²*a-* + *-sphyxia* (fr. *sphyzein* to throb)] : local or systemic deficiency of oxygen and excess of carbon dioxide in living tissues usu. as a result of interruption of respiration; *broadly* : ANOXIA — compare SUFFOCATION

as·phyx·i·al \-ksēəl\ *adj* [NL *asphyxia* + E *-al*] : marked by or relating to asphyxia

as·phyx·i·ant \-ksēənt\ *n* -s [*asphyxiate* + *-ant*] : an agent (as a gas) capable of causing asphyxia

as·phyx·i·ate \-ē,āt, *usu* -ād.+V\ *vb* -ED/-ING/-S [NL *asphyxia* + E *-ate*] *vt* **:** to cause asphyxia in **:** kill, suspend animation in, or make unconscious through want of adequate oxygen, presence of noxious agents, or other obstruction to normal breathing ⟨*asphyxiated* by carbon monoxide in the garage⟩ ~ *vi* **:** to suffer asphyxia **:** die, be overcome, or faint typically because of noxious gas or want of adequate oxygen ⟨the rescue squad almost *asphyxiated*⟩ **syn** see SUFFOCATE

as·phyx·i·a·tion \(,)a,sfiksē'āshən, ə,s-\ *n* -S **1 :** act of causing asphyxia **:** a state of asphyxia **:** SUFFOCATION **2 :** a physiological disorder of plants caused by shortage of air and characterized by failure of seeds to germinate or by yellowing or blighting of established plants

as·phyx·i·a·tor \a'sfiksē,ād·ə(r), ə's-\ *n* -S **:** one that asphyxiates: as **a :** an asphyxiating agent **b :** a device for killing animals by asphyxiation

as·phyxy \a'sfiksē, ə's-, 'a,s-\ *n* -ES [F *asphyxie*, fr. NL *asphyxia*] **:** ASPHYXIA

¹as·pic \'aspik, 'aas-,'ais-, -ēk\ *n* -S [MF, fr. OF, alter. of *aspe*, fr. L *aspis* — more at ASP] *obs* **:** the venomous asp

²aspic \"\ *n* -S [F, fr. MF, modif. of OProv *espic* head (of grain), spike, fr. L *spica* — more at SPIKE] **:** a European lavender (*Lavandula spica*) that produces a volatile oil — compare SPIKE LAVENDER

³aspic \"\ *n* -S [F, lit., asp] **:** a savory jelly made from fish or meat stock thickened with gelatin and seasoned and used cold to garnish meat or fish or to make a mold of meat, fish, or vegetables

aspiculate \(')ā+ⱼ-\ *or* **aspiculous** \(')ā+ⱼ-\ *adj* [²*a-* + *spiculate, spiculous*] **:** without spicules ⟨~ sponges⟩

aspid- *or* **aspido-** *comb form* [NL, fr. Gk, fr. *aspid-, aspis*; perh. akin to Gk *aspidēs* vast, broad, L *spatium* space — more at SPEED] **:** shield ⟨*aspidate*⟩ ⟨*Aspidosperma*⟩

as·pid·i·nol \a'spid°n,ȯl, -ōl\ *n* -S [ISV *aspidin* $C_{25}H_{32}O_8$ (fr. *aspid-* — fr. NL *Aspidium* — + *-in*; orig. formed in G) + *-ol*; orig. formed in G] **:** a yellow crystalline compound $C_{12}H_{16}O_4$ found in the rhizome of the male fern

as·pid·i·o·tus \(,)a,spidē'ōd·əs\ *n, cap* [NL, modif. of Gk *aspidiōtēs* one bearing a shield, fr. *aspid-, aspis* shield] **:** a genus of armored scales including the San Jose scale and several others that are very destructive to orchard trees

as·pi·dis·tra \,aspə'distrə, ,aas-\ *n* [NL, irreg. fr. Gk *aspid-, aspis* shield] **1** *cap* **:** a genus of Asiatic herbs (family Liliaceae) with large handsome basal leaves and tetramerous flowers borne close to the ground — see CAST-IRON PLANT **2** -S **:** any plant of the genus *Aspidistra*

¹as·pid·i·um \a'spidēəm\ [NL, fr. Gk *aspidion* small shield, dim. of *aspid-, aspis*] *syn of* DRYOPTERIS

²aspidium \"\ *n* [NL, fr. Gk *aspidion*] **1** *cap, in some classifications* **:** a genus of ferns including those otherwise divided among the genera *Dryopteris, Polystichum,* and *Tectaria* **2** *pl* **aspidia** \-ēə\ **:** any fern belonging to the genus *Dryopteris, Polystichum,* or *Tectaria* **3** *pl* **aspidia :** a drug consisting of the rhizome and stipes esp. of the male fern used as the oleoresinous extract for the expulsion of tapeworms

as·pi·do·both·ria \,aspə,dō'bäthrēə\ *or* **aspidoboth·rii** \-rē,ī\ [NL, fr. *aspid-* + *-bothria, -bothrii* (fr. *bothrium*)] *syn of* ASPIDOGASTREA

as·pi·do·bran·chia \-'braŋkēə\ *n pl, cap* [NL, fr. *aspid-* + *-branchia*] **:** an order of Streptoneura comprising marine gastropods having the nervous system only slightly concentrated, usu. exhibiting clear traces of ancestral bilateral symmetry, with two kidneys and two auricles, and including the limpets and other primitive forms — **as·pi·do·bran·chi·ate** \-'braŋkēət, -ē,āt\ *adj or n*

as·pi·do·ceph·a·li \-'sefə,lī\ [NL, fr. *aspid-* + *-cephali*] *syn of* CEPHALASPIDA

as·pi·do·chi·ro·ta \-,kī'rōd·ə\ *n pl, cap* [NL, fr. *aspid-* + Gk *-cheirōta* (neut. pl. of *-cheirōtos*, fr. *cheir* hand) — more at CHIR-] **:** an order of chiefly tropical holothurians having tube feet and having the branches of the tentacles confined to the tip where they form a more or less circular shield-shaped terminal disk

as·pi·do·co·tyl·ea \-kə'tilēə, -,käd·°l'ēə\ [NL, fr. *aspid-* + *-cotylea* (fr. Gk *kotylē* anything hollow)] *syn of* ASPIDOGASTREA

as·pi·do·gas·trea \-'gastrēə\ *n pl, cap* [NL, fr. *aspid-* + *-gastrea* (fr. Gk *gastr-, gastēr* stomach) — more at GASTRIC] **:** a small subclass of Trematoda comprising flukes with large complex ventral sucking disks that are intermediate in some respects between monogenetic and digenetic trematodes and are internal or external parasites of aquatic animals, sometimes having alternation of hosts though completely lacking sexual reproduction — **as·pi·do·gas·trid** \-'gastrəd\ *adj or n*

as·pi·do·sper·ma \-'spərmə\ *n* [NL, fr. *aspid-* + *-sperma*] **1** *cap* **:** a genus of tropical American trees or rarely shrubs (family Apocynaceae) having alternate leaves, small flowers, follicular fruits, and peltate compressed seeds with a flat papery wing — see PADDLEWOOD, QUEBRACHO **2** -S **:** the dried bark of the white quebracho used as a respiratory sedative in dyspnea and in asthma

as·pi·do·sper·mine \-'spər,mēn, -,mən\ *n* -S [ISV *aspidosperm-* (fr. NL *Aspidosperma*) + *-ine*] **:** a bitter crystalline alkaloid $C_{22}H_{30}N_2O_2$ obtained from quebracho bark, its sulfate having been used formerly as a respiratory stimulant and antispasmodic and as an antipyretic in typhoid fever

aspinose \(')ā+\ *adj* [²*a-* + *-spinose*] *zool* **:** without a spine

¹as·pi·rant \'asp(ə)rənt, 'aas- *also* ə'spīr-\ *n* -S [L *aspirant-, aspirans*, pres. part. of *aspirare* to aspire] **:** one who aspires **:** one who is ambitious of advancement or attainment ⟨any ~, whoever he may be, can try his hand at writing —James Britton⟩ ⟨~s to medicine and philosophy —Benjamin Farrington⟩

²aspirant \"\ *adj* [L *aspirant-, aspirans*] **:** ASPIRING ⟨good American historical writing is the work of professors and of ~ professors —*Times Lit. Supp.*⟩

as·pi·ra·ta \,aspə'rād·ə, -ād·ə\ *n, pl* **aspira·tae** \-ä,tē, -ä,tī, -ā,tē\ [NL, fr. L, fem. of past part. of *aspirare* to aspirate] **:** ROUGH STOP

¹as·pi·rate \'asp(ə)rət, 'aas-, *usu* -əd.+V\ *adj* [L *aspiratus*, past part. of *aspirare*, lit., to breathe upon — more at ASPIRE] **1 :** ASPIRATED **2 :** silent but not preceded by liaison or elision — used of *h* in modern French

²as·pi·rate \-pə,rāt, *usu* -ād.+V\ *vt* -ED/-ING/-S [L *aspiratus*] **1 a :** to pronounce or to mark so as to be pronounced (a vowel or word) with an *h*-sound as the initial element (as in ancient Greek) **b :** to pronounce (a stop consonant) with an immediately following *h*-sound in a syllable in which the *h* is not usu. represented (as in English) **2 a :** to draw by suction ⟨a new charge is simultaneously being *aspirated* by the lower cylinder by way of inlet ports —G.G.Smith⟩ **b :** to remove (material) by aspiration ⟨the portal vein is exposed and blood is *aspirated* with a 50-ml. syringe —*Biol. Abstracts*⟩ ⟨mucus *aspirated* from the bronchus by bronchoscopy⟩ **c :** INHALE ⟨~ food particles⟩

³as·pi·rate \-p(ə)rət, *usu* -əd.+V\ *n* -S ['*aspirate*] **1 :** \h\ as an independent sound or a character representing it (as the letter *h* or the rough breathing symbol in Greek) — compare BREATHING 2 **2 :** a consonant having as its final element aspiration in the same syllable; *broadly* **:** a combination of letters of which the last is *h* or the sound of such a combination **3 :** material removed by aspiration ⟨parasites may be more readily found in ~s from the sputum —K.F.Maxcy⟩

aspirating stroke *n* **:** SUCTION STROKE

as·pi·ra·tion \,aspə'rāshən, ,aas- *sometimes* -(,)spī- *or* -,spē-\ *n* -S [ME *aspiracioun*, fr. L *aspiration-, aspiratio* breathing, blowing, aspiration, fr. *aspiratus* + *-ion-, -io* -ion] **1 a :** the act of aspirating **:** addition of an aspirate sound **:** pronunciation of an aspirate **b :** an aspirated sound (as \h\) **:** a breathed sound in Greek **2 a :** act of breathing, esp. breathing in, sometimes audibly **b** (1) **:** the withdrawal esp. by means of suction of fluids or friable tissue from the body (2) **:** the operation of making such a withdrawal — compare ASPIRATOR 2 **3** [ML *aspiration-, aspiratio* aspiration, desire, fr. L] **a :** a strong desire for realization (as of ambitions, ideals, or accomplishment) ⟨the ~ of America is still upward, toward a better job —Bernard De Voto⟩ ⟨the religious ~ which raised the first Gothic cathedrals —O. Elfrida Saunders⟩ ⟨the only independent institution of learning of any size with liberal ~s is the university —Green Peyton⟩ **b :** an end or goal aspired to **:** a condition strongly desired ⟨the democratic ideal . . . was the common ~ of men —W.A.White⟩ ⟨flying is her ~ and her passion —E.A.Weeks⟩

as·pi·ra·tion·al \¦ₑₑ(,)ₑ¦ₑshən°l, -shnəl\ *adj* **:** of or relating to aspiration ⟨an adequate moral and ~ life —K.L.Patton⟩

aspiration biopsy *n* **:** biopsy by means of aspiration

aspiration pneumonia *n* **:** pneumonia resulting from inhalation of foreign bodies (as food particles)

as·pi·ra·tor \'aspə,rād·ə(r), 'aas-, -ātə-\ *n* -S [G, fr. L *aspiratus* + *-or*] **1 :** an apparatus for moving gases, liquids, or granular substances by suction ⟨grain ~s probe the holds of a . . . merchantman with long tentaclelike tubes and discharge her cargo into canalboats —D.S.Boyer⟩ **2 a :** an instrument for collecting material by suction; *specif* **:** a hollow needle or cannula connected with a reservoir in which a partial vacuum can be created and used for the removal of foreign bodies, or the collection of secretions or tissue from the body esp. for diagnostic purposes **b :** any of various devices for producing suction; *esp* **:** a device in which a fluid at high velocity passes an orifice thus creating a partial vacuum behind the orifice **3 :** RESPIRATOR

aspire \ə'spī(ə)r, -īə *also* a'-\ *vb* -ED/-ING/-S [ME *aspiren*, fr. MF or L; MF *aspirer*, fr. L *aspirare, adspirare*, lit., to breathe upon, fr. *ad-* + *spirare* to breathe — more at SPIRIT] *vi* **1 :** to be ambitious **:** YEARN, LONG **:** seek to attain or accomplish something, esp. something high or great — used often with *to* or *after* ⟨souls will still live and will ~ —W.L.Sullivan⟩ ⟨Romans who *aspired* to philosophy —Benjamin Farrington⟩ ⟨self-realization to which they *aspired* —G.L.Dickinson⟩ ⟨the perfect lyrist should ~, if not to epics, at least to odes —Herbert Read⟩ ⟨dictatorships that ~ to control the economy —Peter Wiles⟩ **2 :** RISE, ASCEND, TOWER, SOAR ⟨a tall thin flame that *aspired* —J.B.Cabell⟩ ⟨here still an aged elm ~s —Philip Freneau⟩ ~ *vt* **1** *obs* **:** to mount to **:** ATTAIN ⟨our souls ~ celestial thrones —Christopher Marlowe⟩ **2** *archaic* **:** to long for

aspi·ré *or* **aspi·rée** \,aspə'rā, -pē-\ *adj* [F, lit., aspirated, fr. masc. & fem. respectively of pres. part. of *aspirer* to aspirate, breathe] *of h in French* **:** initial in the orthography of a word before which elision and liaison do not occur — compare MUET

aspir·er \ə'spīrə(r) *also* a'-\ *n* -S **:** one that aspires

as·pi·rin \'asp(ə)rən, 'aas- *also* -pərn\ *n, pl* **aspirin** *or* **aspirins** [ISV, *acetyl* + *spir-* (fr. *spiraeic acid*, old name for salicylic acid (fr. ISV *spirae-* — fr. NL *Spiraea* — + *-ic* + *acid*; orig. formed as G *spirsäure*) + *-in*; orig. formed in G] **1 :** a white crystalline compound $CH_3COOC_6H_4COOH$ of salicylic acid used esp. in tablet form as an antipyretic and analgesic like the salicylates but producing fewer undesirable effects — called also *acetylsalicylic acid* **2 :** a tablet of aspirin

as·pis \'aspəs, 'aas-\ *n, cap* [NL, fr. L, asp, viper, fr. Gk] **:** a genus of vipers including the horned viper and related hornless forms

-aspis \"\ *n comb form* [NL, fr. Gk *aspis* shield — more at ASPID-] **:** one having (such) a shield — in generic names in zoology and paleontology ⟨Cephal*aspis*⟩ ⟨Odont*aspis*⟩

asp·ish \'aspish, 'aas-,'ais-, -ēsh\ *adj* [²*asp* + *-ish*] **:** like that of an asp ⟨~ venom⟩ — **asp·ish·ly** *adv*

asplanchnic \(')ā+ⱼ-\ *adj* [Gk *asplanchnos* without bowels (fr. *a-* ²*a-* + *-splanchnos*, fr. *splanchnon* entrail) + E *-ic* — more at SPLANCHNO-] **:** having no alimentary canal

as·ple·ni·oid \a'splēnē,ȯid\ *adj* [ISV *aspleni-* (fr. NL *Asplenium*) + *-oid*] **:** of or resembling ferns of the genus *Asplenium*

as·ple·ni·um \-ēəm\ *n, cap* [NL, alter. of L *asplenum* spleenwort, fr. Gk *asplēnon*, irreg. fr. *splēn* spleen — more at SPLEEN] **:** a widely distributed genus of ferns (family Polypodiaceae) having linear or oblong sori borne obliquely on the upper side of a veinlet and comprising the spleenworts — see EBONY SPLEENWORT, WALL RUE

asporogenous \¦ā+ₑ¦ₑₑₑ\ *or* **asporogenic** \¦ā+ₑₑ¦ₑₑ\ *adj* [ISV ²*a-* + *sporogenous, sporogenic*] **:** not spore-bearing **:** not producing spores — used esp. of yeasts

asporous \(')ā+ⱼ-\ *adj* [ISV ²*a-* + *-sporous*] **:** without true spores

as·por·ta·tion \,aspə(r)'tāshən\ *n* -S [ME *asportacioun*, fr. L *asportation-, asportatio*, fr. *asportatus* (past part. of *asportare* to carry off, fr. *as-* — fr. *abs, ab* away — + *portare* to carry) + *-ion-, -io* -ion — more at OF, PORT] **:** a carrying away; *specif* **:** felonious removal of goods

asporulate \(')ā+ⱼ-\ *adj* [²*a-* + *sporulate*, v., taken as an adj.] **:** not sporulating

asprawl \ə'-\ *adv (or adj)* ['*a-* + *sprawl*, v.] **:** in or into a sprawling position ⟨landed ~ on the floor⟩ ⟨with legs ~⟩

aspre *var of* ¹ASPER

aspread \ə'-\ *adj* ['*a-* + *spread*, v.] **:** spread out **:** SPREADING

aspre·do \a'sprē(,)dō\ *n, cap* [NL, fr. L, roughness, fr. *asper* rough] **:** a genus of So. American catfishes the females of which carry their eggs attached to the skin of the lower surface of the body until hatched

asps *pl of* ASP

asquat \ə'-\ *adj* ['*a-* + *squat*, v.] **:** SQUATTING

asquint \ə'-\ *adv (or adj)* [ME] **:** with the eye directed to one side, obliquely, or squintingly as if with distorted vision or as if to peer or glance furtively or slyly ⟨when he . . . speaks falsely, the eye is muddy and sometimes ~ —R.W.Emerson⟩

asquirm \ə'-\ *adj* ['*a-* + *squirm*, v.] **:** SQUIRMING

asram \'äs(h)rəm\ *n* -S [Skt *āśrama* — more at ASHRAM] **:** ASHRAM

asrama *var of* ASHRAMA

as regards *or* **as respects** *prep* **:** in regard to **:** with respect to **:** CONCERNING ⟨*as regards* his suggestions I was noncommittal⟩

¹ass \'as, 'aa(ə)s,'ais *also* 'äs *in NE & Brit esp (in Brit at least) in sense 2*\ *n* -ES [ME *asse*, fr. OE *assa*, perh. fr. OIr *asan*, fr. L *asinus*, prob. fr. a language of Asia Minor; akin to the source of Gk *onos* ass] **1 :** any of several mammals of the genus *Equus* that are smaller than the horse, with a shorter mane and shorter hair on the tail, with long ears, and without callosities on the inner surface of the hind limbs, that are hardy and gregarious sure-footed natives of Asia and No. Africa, and of which one species (*E. asinus*) is the domestic ass, a rugged, patient, but somewhat stubborn beast of burden, made a popular symbol of obstinacy and stupidity — see KIANG, MULE **2 :** one that is utterly silly **:** a simple-minded fool often marked by stubbornness or stolidity ⟨when they make ~es of themselves they do it in the grand style —Leonard Bacon⟩

wild ass

²ass \"\ *vi* -ED/-ING/-ES **:** to act like an ass **:** play the ass ⟨~*ing* along . . . as though we were still back in the nineteen-twenties —Margery Allingham⟩

³ass \'as\ *Scot var of* ¹ASH

⁴ass *or* **arse** \ *in the U S* 'as, 'aa(ə)s, 'ais *also* 'äs, *and sometimes* 'ärs *euphemistically by speakers who have preconsonantal r and who are aware that there is a spelling "arse"*; 'äs *in standard Brit and* 'ä(r)s *or* 'ārs *or* 'ers *in Brit and Scot dialect; in the US the pronunc* 'äs *occurs chiefly in NE and is there prob more often associated with the spelling "ass" than with "arse"*\ *n* -ES [ME *ars, ers*, fr. OE *ærs, ears*; akin to OHG & ON *ars* buttocks, Gk *orrhos*, Arm *or*, Hitt *arraš*, OIr *err* tail] **1 a :** BUTTOCKS, RUMP — often considered vulgar **b :** ANUS — often considered vulgar **2** *dial Brit* **:** the lower or rear end of anything **:** BOTTOM **3 :** SEXUAL INTERCOURSE — usu. considered vulgar

ass *abbr* **1** assembly **2** assistant **3** association

as·sa·cu \¦asə¦kü\ *n* -S [Pg *assacú*, fr. Tupi] **:** SANDBOX TREE

assafetida *or* **assafoetida** *var of* ASAFETIDA

assagai *var of* ASSEGAI

¹as·sai \ä'sī, -sä·ē\ *adv* [It, fr. (assumed) VL *ad satis* enough — more at ASSET] **:** VERY — used with tempo direction in music ⟨allegro ~⟩

²as·sai *also* **as·sa·hy** \¦äsä¦ē\ *n, pl* **assa·is** *or* **assa·hies** [Pg *assaí*, fr. Tupi] **1** *or* **assai palm :** a slender pinnate-leaved palm (*Euterpe edulis*) of Brazil and British Guiana having dark purple fleshy fibrous edible fruit **2 a :** a nutritious Brazilian drink made by infusion from the fruit of the assai palm with the addition of cassava **b :** a flavor (as for desserts or ice cream) made from the assai fruit

¹as·sail \ə'sāl *also* a'-\ *vt* -ED/-ING/-S [ME *assailen*, fr. OF *assaillir*, fr. (assumed) VL *assalire*, alter. (influenced by *salire*) of L *assilire, adsilire* to leap upon, fr. *ad-* + *salire* to leap — more at SALLY] **1 :** to attack with violence or vehemence **:** ASSAULT ⟨~ a man with blows⟩ ⟨~ a city⟩ ⟨the noise ~*ed* his ears⟩ **2 :** to attack forcefully or violently by nonphysical means (as with words) ⟨the adherents of the new learning were ~*ed* with every sort of ridicule —G.G.Coulton⟩ **:** beset strongly with or as if with intent to overcome ⟨~*ed* by a cloud of disturbing thoughts —T.B.Costain⟩ **3** *archaic* **:** WOO ⟨~ her with tenderness⟩ **4 :** to encounter or confront (as an obstacle) in order to prevail over ⟨~ the slope below the cliff⟩ **5 :** to make an impact upon ⟨the faint smell of copper ~*ed* my nostrils —Amy Lowell⟩ **syn** see ATTACK

²assail \"\ *n* -S [ME, fr. *assailen*] *archaic* **:** ATTACK

as·sail·a·ble \-ləbəl\ *adj* **:** capable of being assailed

as·sail·ant \-ənt\ *n* -S [MF *assaillant*, fr. *assaillant*, pres. part. of *assaillir*] **1 :** one who assails or attacks ⟨met by ~s and in the scuffle one worker was killed —*Current Biog.*⟩ **2 :** an aggressive opponent in controversy ⟨an ~ of the religious belief of the day —Leslie Stephen⟩

²assailant \"\ *adj* [MF *assaillant*, pres. part. of *assaillir*, fr. OF *assaillir*] *archaic* **:** ASSAILING

as·sail·ment \-mənt\ *n* -S **:** act of assailing **:** ATTACK, ASSAULT

assai palm *n* [²*assai* + *palm*] **:** ²ASSAI 1

as·sam \ə'sam, a'-, -saa(ə)m, 'a,sa-\ *also* **assam tea** *n* -S *usu cap A* [fr. *Assam*, state of northeastern India] **:** tea from Assam

¹as·sam·ese \,asə'mēz, -ēs\ *n, pl* **assamese** *cap* [*Assam* + *-ese*] **1 :** a native or inhabitant of Assam, India **2 :** the language of Assam the alphabet of which is the same as that of Bengali with one additional letter for the sound of *w*

²assamese \¦ₑₑ¦ₑ\ *adj, usu cap* **1 a :** of, relating to, or characteristic of Assam **b :** of, relating to, or characteristic of the natives or inhabitants of Assam **2 :** of, relating to, or characteristic of the Assamese language

assam rubber *n, usu cap A* **:** a rubber obtained from a rubber tree (*Ficus elastica*) **:** RAMBONG RUBBER

as·sa·pan \'asə,pan\ *also* **as·sa·pan·ic** \,ₑₑ'ₑnik\ *n* -S [of Virginian origin; akin to Sac & Fox *äsepäna* raccoon, Ojibwa *assänogo* gray squirrel] **:** the American flying squirrel

¹as·sart \ə'särt\ *also* **es·sart** \ė'-\ *vt* -ED/-ING/-S [MF *essarter*, fr. OF, fr. *essart*] *English law* **:** to grub up trees and bushes to make land arable

²assart \"\ *also* **essart** \"\ *n* -S [MF *essart*, fr. OF, fr. LL *exartum*, fr. (assumed) VL *exsartum*, neut. of *exsartus*, past part. of *exsarire* to weed out, fr. L *ex* out + *sarire* to hoe, weed; akin to OHG *sarf* sharp, L *sarpere* to prune, Gk *harpagē* hook, rake, Skt *sṛṇī* sickle — more at EX-] **1** *English law* **:** act of grubbing up trees or bushes usu. in converting forest land into arable land **2** *English law* **:** a piece of land cleared

¹as·sas·sin \ə'sas°n, -saas- *sometimes* -sin\ *n* -S [ML *assassinus*, fr. Ar *ḥashshāshīn*, pl. of *ḥashshāsh* one who smokes or chews hashish, hashish addict, fr. *ḥashīsh* hemp, hashish] **1** *usu cap* **:** one of a secret order of Muslims that at the time of the Crusades terrorized Christians and other enemies by secret murder committed under the influence of hashish **2 :** MURDERER; *esp* **:** one that murders either for hire or from fanatic adherence to a cause

²assassin *vt* -ED/-ING/-S *obs* **:** ASSASSINATE

¹assassinate *n* -S [MF *assassinat*, fr. ML *assassinatus*, fr. *assassinatus*, past part. of *assassinare*] **1** *obs* **:** ASSASSINATION **2** *obs* **:** ASSASSIN

²as·sas·si·nate \ə'sas°n,āt, -saas-, *usu* -ād.+V\ *vt* -ED/-ING/-S [ML *assassinatus*, past part. of *assassinare*, fr. *assassinus*] **1 :** to murder (a usu. prominent person) violently **2** *obs* **:** to assail with murderous intent **3 :** to injure, wound, or destroy usu. unexpectedly and treacherously ⟨he was *assassinating* a man's character —*Atlantic*⟩ **syn** see KILL

as·sas·si·na·tion \ₑ,ₑₑ'āshən\ *n* -S **1 :** act of assassinating **:** killing by violence **2 :** destruction esp. of reputation

assassin bug *n* **:** a predaceous bug of the family Reduviidae living mostly on other insects though a few attack mammals and even man **:** CONENOSE

assassin fly *n* **:** ROBBER FLY

as·sa·tion \a'sāshən\ *n* -S [F, fr. MF, fr. L *assatus* (past part. of *assare* to roast, fr. *assus* roasted, fr. *ardēre* to burn) + MF *-ion* — more at ARDOR] *archaic* **:** the act of baking or roasting

¹as·sault \ə'sȯlt\ *n* -S [ME *assaut*, fr. OF *asaut, assaut*, fr. (assumed) VL *assaltus*, fr. *assaltus*, past part. of *assalire* to assail — more at ASSAIL] **1 :** a violent attack with physical means (as blows or weapons): as **a :** a military charge or onslaught esp. against a walled or defended position **b :** the phase of an attack in which the attacker moves forward and by means of close combat seeks to eliminate enemy resistance and establish control of the objective **c :** a part of an offensive action in which close firing develops or may be expected to develop ⟨an ~ on beaches⟩ ⟨~ troops⟩ ⟨~ guns⟩ **2 :** a violent attack with nonphysical weapons (as words, arguments, or appeals) ⟨an ~ upon science —W.L.Sullivan⟩ ⟨an ~ on his character⟩ **3 a :** an apparently violent attempt or a willful offer with force or violence to do hurt to another without the actual doing of the hurt threatened (as by lifting the fist or a cane in a threatening manner) — compare ASSAULT AND BATTERY, BATTERY 2b **b :** RAPE **:** indecent attack or overture forcibly effected **4 :** a bout with foils, broadswords, or similar weapons

²assault \"\ *vb* -ED/-ING/-S [ME *assauten*, fr. MF *assauter*, fr. (assumed) VL *assaltare*, fr. *assaltus*] *vt* **1 a :** to make an assault upon **:** rush violently and hostilely against **:** attack with strong violent onslaught ⟨the soldiers were ~*ing* the castle⟩ **b :** to attack (a person) typically with brutal violence ⟨a policeman ~*ed* by the mob⟩ **c :** to commit rape upon **:** subject to indecent attack **2** *obs* **:** TEMPT **3 :** to attack violently by nonphysical means (as words, arguments, or unfriendly measures) **:** ASSAIL ⟨~ the Constitution —J.B.Oakes⟩ **4 :** to strike against violently ⟨we ~ our eyes with colors unknown in the natural world —T.F.Hamlin⟩ **:** impinge upon ⟨an ounce of fact is ~*ed* by a ton of footnotes —L.Ruth Middlebrook⟩ ~ *vi* **:** to make an assault ⟨within 50 yards of their objective, they ~*ed* —Mack Morriss⟩ **syn** see ATTACK

as·sault·a·ble \-ləbəl\ *adj* **:** exposed to assault

assault and battery *n* **:** assault (sense 3a) combined with the actual doing of an injury — compare BATTERY 2b

assault-at-arms \ₑ¦ₑₑ'ₑ\ *n, pl* **assaults-at-arms** *Brit* **:** a public team contest in which individual boxers, wrestlers, and fencers of various weights and classes are matched

assault boat *n* **:** a small portable boat used in an amphibious military attack or in land warfare for crossing rivers or lakes

assault fire *n* **:** fire delivered by infantry in the assault esp. with rifles fired from the hip or rapidly from the shoulder

as·sault·ive \ə'sȯltiv\ *adj* **:** inclined toward or disposed to committing assault ⟨viciously ~ even to the point of homicide —Richard Warden⟩ — **as·sault·ive·ness** *n* -ES

¹as·say \'a,sā, a'sā\ *n* -S [ME, fr. ONF *assai*, alter. (influenced by *a* to, fr. L *ad*) of OF *essai* — more at AT, ESSAY] **1 a** *archaic* (1) **:** trial in order to test **:** TESTING (2) **:** EXPERIMENT (3) **:** TRIAL, AFFLICTION **b :** examination and determination as to characteristics (as weight, measure, or quality) ⟨an ~ merely of the technical operations of the poem —*Amer. Scholar*⟩ ⟨~ of the historical role of the individual —Jerome Nathanson⟩ ⟨microbiological ~ methods —*U. S. Dept. Agric. Report on Experiment Stations*⟩ ⟨under the ~ conditions employed —*Biol. Abstracts*⟩: (1) **:** a chemical test to determine the presence or absence or more often the quantity of one or more components of a material (as an ore, alloy, drug, antibiotic, or dietary substance) (2) *archaic* **:** a testing by taste **:** TASTING (3) *obs* **:** the usu. complimentary or courteous act of tasting food or drink before offering it to a person (4) *obs* **:** testing as to compliance with a standard (as of weights, measures, or foodstuffs) **c :** tested purity, value, or character ⟨of high poetic ~ —Roland Gelatt⟩ **d** (1) **:** a substance to be tested or being tested ⟨the blowpipe test was made on the ~⟩ (2) **:** the reported result of such testing **:** measurable quantity ⟨the town always had a fairly high ~ of Nazis —Paul Moor⟩ **2 a** *archaic* **:** ASSAULT, ATTACK

⟨the men . . . strove vainly at the first ~ by dint of climbing on other men's shoulders to storm the platform —*Century Mag.*⟩ **b** *obs* **:** initial or tentative effort **3 a** *archaic* **:** an effort to accomplish **:** ENDEAVOR, ATTEMPT ⟨two brief ~*s* at teaching —*Americana Annual*⟩ — now rarely used in this sense; compare ESSAY **b** *archaic* **:** best effort or maximum exertion — **at all assays 1** *obs* **:** at or for any emergency **2** *obs* **:** in any case **:** ALWAYS

²as·say \a'sā *also* 'a,sā *sometimes* ə'sā\ *vb* -ED/-ING/-S [ME *assayen*, fr. ONF *assayer*, fr. *assai*] *vt* **1 :** TRY, ATTEMPT, ESSAY ⟨here we have two authors ~*ing* that task once more —Oscar Lewis⟩ ⟨has ~*ed* to penetrate a field that by its very nature requires consummate skill —J.W.Chase⟩ **2** *obs* **:** to learn from experience **3** *obs* **a :** to taste (food or drink) before serving (as to a person of rank) **b :** to practice experimentally **c :** to subject to the trial of afflictions or temptations **4 a :** to analyze (an impure substance or mixture) for one or more valuable components — used esp. of determinations in mining, metallurgy, pharmacy, food chemistry **b :** to analyze and judge the significance, worth, or status of ⟨~ a play⟩ ⟨~ an event⟩ ⟨~ the various intellectual changes which the great reformers within and without the Catholic Church accomplished —J.H.Randall⟩ **~** *vi* **:** to show or prove to be of a particular nature by means of an assay ⟨the ore ~*s* high in silver⟩ **syn** see ESTIMATE

as·say·a·ble \(')a¦sāəbəl\ *adj* **:** capable of being assayed

assay bar *n* **:** a bar of pure or nearly pure gold or silver manufactured by the government as a standard

as·say·er \a'sāə(r), 'a,s-, ə's-\ *n* -S [ME, fr. *assayen* + *-er*] **:** one that assays; *specif* **:** a chemist who assays the value and amount of metals in ores and alloys

assay office *n* **:** a government or commercial office and laboratory in which assays are made (as of precious metals)

assay ton *n* **:** a unit of weight of ore taken for assay equal to 29166⅔ milligrams, the number of milligrams of precious metal in this amount of ore being equal to the number of troy ounces per 2000-pound ton

¹ass-backward \'¦=¦==\ *adj* [*ass* + *backward*] **:** ludicrously disordered **:** showing an arrangement grotesquely counter to the usual or workable ⟨incompetents doing their work in an *ass-backward* way⟩

²ass-backward *or* **ass-backwards** \'=¦==\ *adv* **:** in an ass-backward way ⟨an inexperienced assistant filing everything *ass-backward*⟩

assce *abbr* assurance

assd *abbr* **1** assessed **2** assigned **3** assured

asse \'as\ *n* -S [prob. native name in southern Africa] **:** a fox of southern Africa (*Vulpes chama*)

¹as·se·gai *or* **as·sa·gai** \'asə,gī, ,==¦=\ *n* -S [prob. fr. MF *azagaie*, fr. OSp *azagaya* the assegai, fr. Ar *az-zaghāya* the assegai, fr. Ar *al-* the + *zaghāya*, fr. Berber] **1 :** a slender hardwood spear or light javelin usu. tipped with iron and used by tribes in southern Africa **2 :** a southern African tree (*Curtisia faginea*) of the dogwood family, whose wood may be used in making assegais

assegai

²assegai *or* **assagai** \"\ *vt* -ED/-ING/-S **:** to pierce with an assegai

asselar man \'asə,lär-\ *n*, *usu cap A* [fr. *Asselar*, Fr. garrison near Tombouctou, Fr. West Africa, near where it was found] **:** a post-Paleolithic negroid type of man known from a single tall dolichocephalic skeleton from the southern Sahara having points of resemblance to both Boskop and Grimaldi man

as·self \a'self\ *vt* -ED/-ING/-S [*ad-* + *self*] *archaic* **:** to take to oneself **:** APPROPRIATE

as·sem·blage \ə'semblij, -ēj\ *n* -S [F, fr. MF, fr. *assembler* + *-age*] **1 a :** a collection of individuals or of particular things **:** AGGREGATION ⟨a strange ~ of human beings —Bertrand Russell⟩ ⟨the ~ of forms of mosquitoes formerly included in the species —G.S.Carter⟩ ⟨a slow but general southward migration of the various plant ~*s* —C.O.Dunbar⟩ **b :** a group of organisms or fossils sharing a common situation (as a microhabitat) essentially by chance **2 a :** the act of assembling ⟨building became the ~ of accurately measured elements —Lewis Mumford⟩ **:** ASSEMBLY **b :** the state of being assembled ⟨a motion-picture theater or other place of public ~⟩ **3 :** AGGREGATE 5 **4 :** the cost of bringing two or more parcels of land under a single ownership **:** PLOTTAGE ⟨the entire Dodge ~ designated by (B) on the map is $1,140,000 for land and $1,270,000 for land and buildings —*N. Y. Herald Tribune*⟩ **5 :** the total of related culture traits and artifacts associated with any one archaeological manifestation

as·sem·blance \-blən(t)s, a's-\ *n* -S [MF, fr. *a-* (fr. L *ad-*) + *semblance* — more at SEMBLANCE] *archaic* **:** SEMBLANCE, APPEARANCE

¹as·sem·ble \ə'sembəl\ *vb* **assembled**; **assembled**; **assembling** \-b(ə)liŋ\ **assembles** [ME *assemblen*, fr. OF *assembler*, fr. (assumed) VL *assimulare*, fr. L *ad-* + (assumed) VL *-similare* (fr. L *simul* together, at the same time) — more at SAME] *vt* **1 :** to bring or summon together into a group, crowd, company, assembly, or unit ⟨even after a new crew had, at great pains, been *assembled* —V.G.Heiser⟩ ⟨hold all planes until a striking force could be *assembled* —H.L. Merillat⟩ **2 :** to bring together: as **a :** to put or join together usu. in an orderly way with logical selection or sequence ⟨~ statistics⟩ ⟨evaluating the data *assembled*⟩ ⟨he *assembled* a large library⟩ **b :** to fit together various parts of so as to make into an operative whole ⟨~ a radio set⟩ ⟨airplanes being *assembled*⟩ **~** *vi* **:** to come or meet together in a group, company, assembly, or unit often purposively, sometimes formally ⟨the right of the people peaceably to ~ —*U. S. Constitution*⟩ ⟨help drill Federal volunteers then *assembling* about Washington —Robert Bruce⟩ ⟨~ at one of the taverns for convivial purposes —*Amer. Guide Series: N. H.*⟩ **syn** see GATHER

²as·sem·blé \äsäⁿblā\ *n* -S [F, fr. *assemblé*, past part. of *assembler*] **:** a figure of two successive movements in ballet dancing in the first of which one leg is extended outward in any direction from the hip while the other leaps from the floor and in the second both feet come to rest crossed and with toes turned outward in fifth position

as·sem·bler \ə'sembl(ə)r\ *n* -S **1 :** one that assembles: as **a :** a worker who assembles component parts of an item of manufacture **b :** a middleman who buys mainly farm products from small and scattered producers and prepares them for shipment in economical quantities to the city markets **2** *obs* **:** one of an assembly

assembling *n* -S **:** the act or action of those that assemble: as **a :** the gathering of the males of certain moths over considerable distances in response to odors produced by sexually receptive females **b :** the concentrating of goods or the achieving of control of goods to facilitate sales or purchases

as·sem·bly \ə'semblē, -li\ *n* -ES *often attrib* [ME *assemblee*, fr. MF, fr. OF, fem. of *assemblé*, past part. of *assembler*] **1 :** a company of persons collected together in one place usu. for some common purpose (as deliberation and legislation, worship, or entertainment): **a** *usu cap* **:** a legislative body; *specif* **:** the lower house of a legislature ⟨the *Assembly* of New York State⟩ ⟨the National *Assembly* of France⟩ — compare GENERAL ASSEMBLY, HOUSE OF ASSEMBLY, LEGISLATIVE ASSEMBLY **b** *usu cap* **:** the highest judiciary or governing board in any of various religious denominations ⟨the General *Assembly* of the Presbyterian Church⟩ **c :** a formal social gathering (as a subscription ball) **d :** a local congregation or religious association similar to a church **e :** a scheduled meeting of the whole student body and usu. the faculty of a school or college either for purposes of administrative routine or for educational or recreational programs **2 :** the act of coming together **:** the state of being assembled ⟨prohibits unlawful ~⟩ **3 :** ASSEMBLAGE 1b **4 a :** a signal given by drum, bugle, trumpet, or all field music for troops to assemble or fall in **b :** the collection of the elements of a military command into a given locality **5 a :** the act or process of building up a complete unit (as a motor vehicle) using parts already in themselves finished manufactured products ⟨to work on the ~ line⟩ **b :** a collection of parts so assembled as to form a complete machine, structure, or unit of a machine ⟨a hub ~⟩ ⟨a dome ~⟩ **6 :** a hall or room in which an assembly is held

assembly district *n* **:** an election district in some states of the U. S. (as New York) that returns a member to the state legislature

assembly line *n* **1 :** an arrangement of machines, equipment, and workers so that work passes from operation to operation in direct line until the product is assembled **2 :** a process for turning out a finished product in an efficient impartial often cursory manner ⟨war criminals . . . rolling off the Allied amnesty *assembly line* —*Nation*⟩

as·sem·bly·man \-mən\ *n*, *pl* **assemblymen 1 :** a member of an assembly, esp. of a legislative assembly **2 :** one that assembles components usu. in a manufacturing process to produce finished goods **:** ASSEMBLER

assembly mark *or* **assembling mark** *n* **:** one of a number of marks placed on the parts of a machine or structure to define the position or order in which the parts are to be assembled

¹as·sent \ə'sent *also* a'-\ *vi* -ED/-ING/-S [ME *assenten*, fr. OF *assenter*, fr. L *assentari*, fr. *assentire*, *adsentire*, fr. *ad-* + *sentire* to feel, think — more at SENSE] **1 :** to give or express one's concurrence, acquiescence, or compliance **:** CONSENT ⟨he at once ~*ed* to my wishes —W.F.DeMorgan⟩ **2 :** to admit as true **:** express one's agreement or concession ⟨we see and immediately ~ to the beauty of an object —Joseph Addison⟩

syn CONSENT, ACCEDE, ACQUIESCE, AGREE, SUBSCRIBE: ASSENT indicates a concurring, either a positive agreeing or more passive conceding, without expressed doubts or objections ⟨I fully *assent* to the proposition that here as elsewhere the distinctions of the law are distinctions of degree —O.W. Holmes †1935⟩ ("Yes, of course", said the lady, vaguely, evidently *assenting* to the doctor's remark rather than expressing a conviction of her own —G.B.Shaw⟩ CONSENT indicates a complying, granting, or yielding, willing or reluctant, to request or demand ⟨whatever you ask of me I will *consent* to —George Meredith⟩ ⟨at first Mary would not wed the white man, but in the end *consented* to do so in order to help forward conversions among her people to the Christian faith —I.B. Richman⟩ ACCEDE may heighten suggestions of conceding or yielding to something proposed, with or without pressure or importunity ⟨he suggested that they go to his room and talk it over. She *acceded* without demur —S.H.Adams⟩ ⟨Mr. Bennet could have no hesitation in *acceding* to the proposal before him —Jane Austen⟩ ACQUIESCE stresses the fact of compliance without effective opposition or resistance ⟨it seemed mad and stupid to Ripton's sense of reason, but he was a bondsman and bound to *acquiesce* —George Meredith⟩ ⟨he was obliged to *acquiesce* in the repression of his individuality —Van Wyck Brooks⟩ AGREE may suggest an according or concurring, often one arrived at after settling differences and points at issue ⟨it might make a bad impression. Myles had to *agree* with that, if reluctantly —J.F.Powers⟩ ⟨whatever answers the philosophers of history might eventually *agree* on —C.E. Black & E.C.Helmreich⟩ ⟨the United States has tacitly *agreed* to Russia's occupation of the Kurile islands —Vera M. Dean⟩ SUBSCRIBE may indicate a ready willingness not only to concur in but to endorse and maintain ⟨those scientists who *subscribe* to the current program in its entirety, who would follow blindly, who could produce a synthetic enthusiasm even if they retained doubts —Vannevar Bush⟩ ⟨Russia declared war on Japan and *subscribed* to the terms presented to Tokyo by its three great allies —Vera M. Dean⟩

²assent \"\ *n* -S [ME, fr. OF, fr. *assenter*] **1 a** *archaic* **:** ACQUIESCENCE, COMPLIANCE, CONSENT **b** *obs* **:** common accord **:** general approval **c :** concurrence with approval **:** SANCTION ⟨~ to ratification would be by simple majority —F.A.Ogg & P.O.Ray⟩ — compare ROYAL ASSENT **2 :** the accepting as true or certain of something (as a doctrine or conclusion) proposed for belief ⟨rational ~ may arrive late, intellectual conviction may come slowly —T.S.Eliot⟩ **3 :** agreement with a statement or proposal esp. in a matter of minor importance or one detached from personal concern **:** mere acquiescence ⟨give a nod of ~⟩ — distinguished from *consent*

as·sen·ta·tion \,asᵊn'tāshən, ,a,sen't-\ *n* -S [L *assentation-*, *assentatio*, fr. *assentatus* (past part. of *assentari*) + *-ion-*, *-io* -ion] **:** ready assent esp. when insincere or obsequious ⟨a tame and banal ~ —George Saintsbury⟩

assented *or* **assenting** *adj*, *of securities* **:** subject to deposit under an agreement by which the owners assent to some proposed change affecting or affected by amount, nature, or status of the securities

as·sent·ing·ly *adv* **:** in an assenting manner **:** so as to give or express assent

as·sen·tor \ə'sentə(r), a'-\ *n* -S *English law* **:** one of the voters in addition to the proposer and seconder required to endorse the nomination of a candidate for election (as to Parliament)

as·sert \ə'sərt, -ət,-əit *also* a'-; *usu* -d·+V\ *vt* -ED/-ING/-S [L *assertus*, *adsertus*, past part. of *asserere*, *adserere* to assert, lay claim to, liberate, fr. *ad-* + *serere* to join — more at SERIES] **1 :** to state or affirm positively, assuredly, plainly, or strongly ⟨I am far from ~*ing* it was the actual way —Havelock Ellis⟩ **2 a :** to demonstrate the existence of (an attribute) **:** SIGNIFY ⟨~ his manhood —James Joyce⟩ **b :** to demand and compel recognition of ⟨he was never able to ~ himself sufficiently⟩ **c :** to postulate or to affirm the existence of ⟨by again ~*ing* God as an active force in history —*Time*⟩ **3** *archaic* **a :** to lay claim to as a possession or attribute **b :** to take a stand with or for **:** CHAMPION, DEFEND ⟨I will ~ it from the scandal —Jeremy Taylor⟩

syn DECLARE, PROFESS, AFFIRM, AVER, PROTEST, AVOUCH, AVOW, PREDICATE, WARRANT: ASSERT puts stress on the fact of positive statement; it may imply noteworthy assuredness or force on the speaker's part or lack of proof for the statement ⟨we dissect and study and describe a language in modern times on the basis of a structural analysis, and then *assert* what its usage is —Joshua Whatmough⟩ ⟨as early as 1808 Jefferson's cabinet *asserted* that the United States had a common interest with the revolutionists in excluding European influence —A.P.Whitaker⟩ ⟨hill-dwellers, whose language, it is *asserted*, resembles Elizabethan English —*Amer. Guide Series: Ark.*⟩ DECLARE is sometimes used in reference to explicit, open, public statement, perhaps formal ⟨almost without exception, the New Jersey press daily *declares* its independence from its metropolitan rivals —*Amer. Guide Series: N. J.*⟩ ⟨the law in many states *declared* mixed marriages illegal —Oscar Handlin⟩ PROFESS may refer to open declaration, perhaps repeated, esp. of one's own inclinations or capacities, sometimes hypocritical ⟨if judicial critics do not learn modesty from the past they *profess* to esteem, it is not from lack of material —John Dewey⟩ ⟨an orthodox Communist leader who *professed* to speak for the submerged masses —Allan Murray⟩ ⟨enjoyment in occasionally *professing* opinions which in fact are not your own —Jane Austen⟩ AFFIRM may suggest delivery of a statement with an earnest appearance of truth and conviction, sometimes a factitious appearance ⟨*affirmed* that he took no part in this black deed —W.H.Hudson †1922⟩ ⟨it will be *affirmed* that much learning deadens or perverts poetic sensibility —T.S.Eliot⟩ ⟨politicians more often *affirm* their desire for retirement than show that they really mean it —*Times Lit. Supp.*⟩ AVER may suggest confidence and genuine belief in the truth of a statement that might be questioned ⟨Sedgwick *averred* that he had wasted two years' work through adhering to Werner's notions —S.F.Mason⟩ ⟨*averring* that leniency would be a mistake in the case of the confirmed young criminal —*Current Biog.*⟩ PROTEST may indicate forceful declaration in the face of doubt or contradiction ⟨Streicher *protesting* he'd never hurt a soul —*Current Biog.*⟩ ⟨we tend to suspect that a man who *protests* that his aim is the production of beauty and goodness is something of a charlatan —T.D.Weldon⟩ AVOUCH, less used than others in this group, may apply to statements substantiated by certain personal knowledge or by irrefutable authority ⟨as anyone who is familiar with Communist tactics can *avouch* —W.R.Kintner⟩ AVOW stresses open, frank declaration, with full personal acknowledgment and responsibility ⟨communists, fascists, and other *avowed* enemies of parliamentarism —F.Ogg & H.Zink⟩ ("as to the great service," said Carton, "I am bound to *avow* to you, when you speak of it in that way, that it was mere professional claptrap" —Charles Dickens⟩ PREDICATE in this sense may indicate an affirming of something as a quality, attribute, or concomitant ⟨to *predicate* of diabolic agencies, which are gifted with angelic intellects, the highly ridiculous activities which are so characteristic of poltergeist visitations —J.McCarthy⟩ ⟨logic works by *predicating* of the single instance what is true of all its kind —William James⟩ WARRANT may apply to assured statement made without brooking contradiction, with or as if with one's personal guarantee ⟨I'll *warrant* he's as good a gentleman as any —John Buchan⟩ **syn** see in addition MAINTAIN

as·sert·a·tive \-d·əd·iv, -tətiv\ *adj* [by alter.] **:** ASSERTIVE

as·sert·ed·ly *adv* **:** by positive and usu. unsubstantiated assertion **:** ALLEGEDLY ⟨a lens . . . for goggles which would ~ protect the eyes from atomic glare —*Newsweek*⟩

as·sert·i·ble \-d·əbəl, -təb-\ *adj* **:** capable of being asserted or affirmed **:** NONCONTRADICTORY

as·ser·tion \ə'sərshən, -əsh-,-əish- *also* a'-\ *n* -S [ME *assercioun*, fr. MF or LL; MF *assertion*, fr. LL *assertion-*, *assertio*, fr. L, formal declaration of free or servile status, fr. *assertus* + *-ion-*, *-io* -ion] **:** the act of asserting or something that is asserted: as **a** *archaic* **:** a defense from attack ⟨the ~ of a friend's character⟩ **b :** insistent and positive affirming, maintaining, or defending (as of a right or attribute) ⟨an ~ of ownership⟩ **c :** a declaration that something is the case (as that a proposition is true or that a formula is a theorem in an axiomatized system)

as·ser·tion·al \-shənᵊl, -shnəl\ *adj* **:** of or relating to assertion

assertion of the consequent : AFFIRMATION OF THE CONSEQUENT

as·ser·tive \ə'sərd·iv, -ət-,-əit-, -ēv *also* a'-\ *adj* [*assertion* + *-ive*] **1 :** resembling, suited to, or characterized by assertion **2 :** disposed to make assertions **:** characterized by self-confidence, determination, and boldness in asserting opinions or in otherwise making one's presence or influence felt **syn** see AGGRESSIVE

as·ser·tive·ly *adv* **:** in an assertive manner **:** with assertion

as·ser·tive·ness *n* -ES **:** the quality or state of being assertive

as·ser·tor \-d·ə(r), -tə(r)\ *n* -S **:** one that asserts something

as·ser·to·ri·al \¦asə(r)¦tōrēəl, -ȯr-\ *adj* **:** ASSERTORIC — **as·ser·to·ri·al·ly** \-ēəlē\ *adv*

as·ser·to·ric \-¦tȯrik, -ōr-,-är-\ *adj* **:** of or relating to assertion — **as·ser·tor·i·cal·ly** \-ək(ə)lē\ *adv*

as·ser·to·ry \ə'sərd·ərē *also* a'-\ *adj* **:** ASSERTORIC, ASSERTIVE

as·ser·tum \ə'sərd·əm *also* a'-\ *n*, *pl* **asser·ta** \-d·ə\ [NL, fr. LL, assertion, fr. L, neut. of *assertus*] **:** something that is asserted

asses *pl of* AS *or of* ASS

asses' bridge *n* [trans. of NL *pons asinorum*; prob. fr. the similarity of the geometrical construction demonstrating it to the trusses of a bridge and fr. its being considered a difficulty for poor students of geometry] **:** the fifth proposition of the first book of Euclid: the angles at the base of an isosceles triangle are equal to one another ⟨a schoolboy, stammering out his *asses' bridge* —Frederic Harrison⟩

as·sess \ə'ses, (')a¦ses\ *vt* -ED/-ING/-ES [ME *assessen*, prob. fr. ML *assessus*, past part. of *assidēre*, fr. L, to sit beside, assist in the office of judge — more at ASSIZE] **1 :** to determine the rate or amount of (as a tax, charge, or fine) ⟨~ damages after an accident⟩ **2 a :** to determine the amount of and impose (as a tax, charge, or fine) according to an established rate or apportionment ⟨the tax to be ~*ed* upon all retail sales⟩ **b :** to subject to a tax, charge, or levy so determined ⟨each member will be ~*ed* $25⟩ **3 :** to make an official valuation or estimate of (property) esp. for the purposes of taxation **4 :** to analyze critically and judge definitively the nature, significance, status, or merit of **:** determine the importance, size, or value of ⟨~ men as leaders⟩ ⟨properly ~*ing* the financial needs of individual students —J.B.Conant⟩ **syn** see ESTIMATE

as·sess·a·ble \=¦=əbəl\ *adj* **:** capable of being assessed

as·sess·ee \,a,se¦sē, ə,se'sē; ə'se,sē, a'-\ *n* -S **:** one upon whom a payment is assessed

as·ses·sion \ə'seshən, a'-\ *n* -S [L *assession-*, *assessio*, fr. *assessus* (past part. of *assidēre* to sit beside) + *-ion-*, *-io* -ion] **1** *archaic* **:** SESSION **2** [prob. fr. *assess* + *-ion*] **:** the assessing or renting of a lord's demesnes in the duchy of Cornwall — **as·ses·sion·a·ble** \-sh(ə)nəbəl\ *adj* — **as·ses·sion·al** \-shənᵊl,-shnəl\ *adj*

as·sess·ment \ə'sesmənt *also* a'-\ *n* -S **1 a :** a valuation of property usu. for the purpose of taxation **b :** a valuation and an adjudging of the sum to be levied on property **2 :** the act of assessing **:** the act of apportioning or determining an amount to be paid ⟨an ~ of damages⟩ **3 :** an appraisal or evaluation (as of merit) ⟨a critical ~ of the composer's work⟩ **4 a :** a specific charge or tax determined upon by assessing **:** amount assessed **b :** the entire plan or scheme fixed upon for charging or taxing **5 a** (1) **:** an apportionment of an amount subscribed for stock into successive installments (2) **:** one of these installments **b :** a demand by a company for payment of the remainder or part of the remainder of the price of stock not yet fully paid for — called also *call* **c** (1) **:** a demand made under various statutory provisions upon holders of stock in a bank for proportional contribution to make good capital losses (2) **:** a similar demand on holders of other kinds of stock **d :** a levy variable in amount collected by insurance companies from certificate or policy holders in order to meet their obligations **e :** a levy made by an American political party on appointive officers for campaign expenses **f :** a levy made on members of an organization (as a club or union) for a special purpose not covered by dues

assessment company *n* **:** a company that issues assessment insurance

assessment insurance *n* **:** insurance providing for the payment of claims in whole or in part from the proceeds of assessments levied upon the members of an association for that purpose

assessment work *n* **:** the annual work upon an unpatented mining claim on the public domain necessary under the U. S. law for the maintenance of the possessory title thereto

as·ses·sor \ə'sesə(r) *also* a'-\ *n* -S [ME *assessour*, fr. MF or L; MF *assesseur*, fr. L *assessor* assistant, judge's assistant, fr. *assessus* (past part. of *assidēre* to sit beside, assist in the office of judge) + *-or*] **1 :** one appointed or elected to assist a judge or magistrate; *esp* **:** one with special knowledge of the subject to be decided ⟨legal ~*s*⟩ ⟨nautical ~*s*⟩ **2** [ML, fr. L] **:** one that assesses; *specif* **:** one that is authorized to assess property for taxation **3** *archaic* **:** one that sits by another as next in dignity or as an assistant and adviser **:** an associate in office **4** *Brit* **:** INSURANCE ADJUSTER

as·ses·so·ri·al \ə,se'sōrēəl, ¦a,se¦s-, ¦asə¦s-, -ȯr-\ *adj* **:** of or relating to an assessor or a court of assessors

as·ses·sor·ship \ə'sesə(r),ship *also* a'-\ *n* -S **:** the position of assessor

as·set \'a,set, 'aa,- *sometimes* ˌsət; *usu* -d·+V\ *n* -S [back-formation fr. *assets*, sing., sufficient property to pay debts and legacies, fr. AF *asetz*, fr. OF *asez*, *assez* enough, fr. (assumed) VL *ad satis*, fr. L *ad* to + *satis* enough — more at AT, SAD] **1 assets** *pl* **a** (1) **:** the property of a deceased person that in the hands of his heir or executor is sufficient to pay his debts and legacies (2) **:** the property of a deceased person subject by law to the payment of his debts and legacies **b :** the entire property of all sorts of an insolvent or bankrupt or of a person, association, corporation, or estate applicable or subject to the payment of his or its debts **2 :** a quality, condition, or entity that serves as an advantage, support, resource, or source of strength ⟨wit, a good deal of shrewd classical allusion, and a Voltairean satire are the book's ~*s* —Edmund Fuller⟩ ⟨a college degree is considered a valuable ~ for the beginner —A.W.McCain⟩ ⟨his was a most useful ~ when it came to practical affairs —J.D.Beresford⟩ **3 a :** an item of value owned **b assets** *pl* **:** the series of items on a balance sheet representing the book values at a given date of resources, rights, or items of property owned grouped under appropriate headings according to their nature — see CAPITAL ASSETS, CASH ASSETS, CURRENT ASSETS, FIXED ASSETS, NET ASSETS; ²INTANGIBLE, ²TANGIBLE

asset currency *n* **:** currency secured exclusively by the general assets of the issuing bank as distinguished from that secured by special deposits (as of government bonds or commercial paper)

assets by descent *or* **assets per descent :** assets descending to the heir and rendering him liable to their extent for specialty debts of his ancestor — used in the older law of the administration of estates

assets en·tre main \ˌän·trə'mān\ [AF *asetz entre maines*] : ASSETS IN HAND

assets in hand [trans. of AF *asetz entre maines*] : assets going directly to the executor or other trustee to satisfy the claims against him as such — used in the older law of the administration of estates; called also *assets entre main*

as·sev·er \ə'sevə(r), a'-\ *vt* **assevered; assevered; assevering** \-v(ə)riŋ\ **assevers** [L *asseverare*] *archaic* : ASSEVERATE

as·sev·er·ate \ə'sevə,rāt, a'-, *usu* -ād·+V\ *vt* -ED/-ING/-S [L *asseveratus, adseveratus*, past part. of *asseverare, adseverare*, fr. *ad-* + *-severare* (fr. *severus* serious, severe) — more at SEVERE] : to affirm or aver positively or earnestly ⟨admit or ~ the necessity and inevitability of almost everything that follows —S.C.Pepper⟩ **syn** see SWEAR

as·sev·er·a·tion \ə,sevə'rāshən\ *n* -S [L *asseveration-, asseveratio*, fr. *asseveratus* + *-ion-, -io* -ion] : the act of asseverating : positive or emphatic affirmation or assertion : solemn declaration ⟨a simple factual account of the author's ~s —Muna Lee⟩

as·sev·er·a·tive \ə'sevə,rād·iv, a'-, -,rəd·iv\ *adj* : characterized by asseveration : ASSEVERATING

asshead \'=,=\ *n* [¹*ass* + *head*] : BLOCKHEAD, ASS

as·si \'asē\ *n* -S [Creek *ássi*, short for *ássi-lupútski* small leaves] : YAUPON

as·sib·i·late \ə'sibə,lāt, a'-, *usu* -ād·+V\ *vb* -ED/-ING/-S [*ad-* + *sibilate*] *vt* **1** : to introduce a sibilant sound after or less often before ⟨z was an *assibilated* d in primitive Greek — either \dz\ or \zd\⟩ **2** : to convert to or replace by a sibilant sound or a sound of which a sibilant is one constituent (as when the pronunciation \'indyən\ for *Indian* becomes \'injən\; \j\ = \d\ + \zh\) ~ *vi* : to change by introducing a sibilant sound ⟨(noninitial) Indo-European *ti* (unless preceded by *s*) ~s (through palatalization) to *si* —G.U.Bonfante⟩

as·sib·i·la·tion \=,=='lāshən\ *n* -S : the development of a sound into a sibilant or into an affricate whose second element is a sibilant

as·si·de·an *or* **as·si·dae·an** \ˌasə'dēən\ *or* **has·i·de·an** *or* **has·i·dae·an** *also* **has·si·de·an** *or* **has·si·dae·an** \ˌhas-\ *n* -S *usu cap* [Gk *Asidaioi*, pl. (fr. Heb *ḥăsīdhīm* pious ones) + E *-an* — more at HASID] : HASID 1

as·si·du·i·ty \ˌasə'd(y)üəd·ē, ˌaas-, -ətē, -i\ *n* -ES [L *assiduitas*, fr. *assiduus* assiduous + *-itas* -ity] **1** : the quality or state of being assiduous : constant or close application or attention esp. to some business or enterprise : DILIGENCE **2** *obs* : frequent repetition **3** : solicitous or obsequious attention to a person : persistent personal attention — often used in pl. ⟨vanquish her coldness . . . by my *assiduities* —Tobias Smollett⟩

as·sid·u·ous \ə'sijəwəs, a'-\ *adj* [L *assiduus*, fr. *assidēre* to sit beside, take care of — more at ASSIZE] **1** : marked or characterized by constant unremitting attention or by persistent energetic application ⟨an ~ servant⟩ ⟨~ labor⟩ **2** : SOLICITOUS, OBSEQUIOUS **syn** see BUSY

as·sid·u·ous·ly *adv* : in an assiduous manner : with assiduity ⟨tried ~ to make the sale⟩

as·sid·u·ous·ness *n* -ES : ASSIDUITY

assiege *vt* -ED/-ING/-S [ME *asegen, assegen*, fr. MF *assegier*, fr. OF, prob. fr. *a-* (fr. L *ad-*) + *sege* seat, siege — more at SIEGE] *obs* : BESIEGE — **assiegement** *n* -S *archaic*

assiento *var of* ASIENTO

as·si·ette \"\ *n* -S [F, fr. MF, seating of guests at table, course (of a meal), fr. OF, assessment (of a tax), fr. (assumed) VL *assedita* action of seating or placing, fr. fem. of *asseditus*, past part. of *assedēre* to seat, place — more at ASSIZE] **1 a** : PLATE 3c **b** : hors d'oeuvres or cold cuts served on one plate **2** : a mixture of bole, bloodstone, and galena used as a gilding surface (as by bookbinders)

¹as·sign \ə'sīn *also* a'-\ *vt* -ED/-ING/-S [ME *assignen*, fr. OF *assigner*, fr. L *assignare, adsignare*, fr. *ad-* + *signare* to mark, mark out, designate — more at SIGN] **1** : to transfer to another in writing (one's title to or interest in property, esp. intangible property) ⟨~ a bond by an endorsement⟩; *specif* : to transfer (property) to another in trust or for the benefit of creditors ⟨the bankrupt must also ~ all of his patents to the receiver⟩ **2 a** : to appoint (one) to a post or duty ⟨was ~*ed* to the laboratory and school —*Current Biog.*⟩ ⟨though ~*ed* only menial tasks —B.L.Robinson⟩; *specif* : to order (an individual or unit) to serve more or less permanently as an organic member of a particular military organization — distinguished from *attach* **b** : PRESCRIBE ⟨carbines are ~*ed* for guard duty⟩ ⟨the teacher ~*ed* the next 20 pages of the text⟩ **3** : SPECIFY, SELECT, DESIGNATE : fix authoritatively or exactly ⟨~ a limit⟩ ⟨~ counsel⟩ ⟨~ a day for trial⟩ **4 a** : to give, adduce, or allege by way of explanation or cause esp. after deliberation ⟨financial difficulties . . . were ~*ed* as the probable cause of his suicide —G.S.Bryan⟩ **b** : to think of after deliberation as characterizing or being possessed as indicated : ALLOT, ENDOW ⟨by ~*ing* to a nation energy and honesty as its chief spiritual characteristics —Matthew Arnold⟩ **c** : to regard as done by or during : reckon as composed, made, or executed as indicated ⟨the temple of Baal Lebanon, which is ~*ed* to the eleventh century B.C. —Edward Clodd⟩ **5** *archaic* : to point out : SHOW ⟨the dwarf the way to her ~*ed* —Edmund Spenser⟩ **syn** see ALLOT, ASCRIBE, PRESCRIBE

²assign \"\ *n* -S [ME *assigne*, fr. MF *assigné* — more at ASSIGNEE] **1** : ASSIGNEE **2** *obs* : ASSIGNEE a

as·sign·a·bil·i·ty \=,=ə'biləd·ē, -ətē, -i\ *n* -ES : the quality of being assignable

as·sign·a·ble \='=əbəl\ *adj* : capable of being assigned ⟨definite, ~ reasons —William James⟩ ⟨the bill of exchange is par excellence an ~ debt —W.M.Dacey⟩ — **as·sign·a·bly** \-əblē, -li\ *adv*

as·sig·nat \'asig,nat, F åsēnʸå\ *n* -S [F, fr. L *assignatus*, past part. of *assignare* to assign] : one of the bills issued as currency by the Revolutionary government of France (1790-95) and based on the security of the lands that had been appropriated by the state

as·sig·na·tion \ˌasig'nāshən, ˌaseg-\ *n* -S [ME *assignacion*, fr. MF, fr. L *assignation-, assignatio*, fr. *assignatus* + *-ion-, -io* -ion] **1** *obs* : authoritative order **2 a** *obs* : assignment of funds : ALLOWANCE **b** : something assigned (as a sum of money) **c** *obs* : a piece of paper currency **3 a** : a making over by transfer of title : ASSIGNMENT **b** : an assigning by allotment : APPORTIONMENT **4** : an appointment of time and place for a meeting esp. for illicit sexual relations ⟨known places of ~ —E.A.Armstrong⟩ ⟨returned from an ~ with his mistress —W.B.Yeats⟩ **5** : ATTRIBUTION, ASCRIPTION ⟨the ~ to Mark Twain of "everybody talks about the weather, but nobody does anything about it" —*Saturday Rev.*⟩ **syn** see ENGAGEMENT

assigned risk *n* : a risk that qualified underwriters of workmen's compensation or automobile liability insurance would reject under applicable standards but accept so as to permit compliance with state law, the insurance being handled through a pool of insurers and assigned to companies in turn

as·sign·ee \ə,sī'nē, ¦a,sī¦nē; ə'sī(,)nē, a'sī(,)nē, -ˌni; *Brit usu* ¦asə¦nē\ *n* -S [ME *assigne*, fr. MF *assigné*, past part. of *assigner* to assign — more at ASSIGN] : one to whom an assignment is made: as **a** : one appointed to act for another: AGENT, REPRESENTATIVE **b** : one to whom a right or property is legally transferred — **as·sign·ee·ship** \-,ship\ *n* -S

as·sign·er \ə'sīnə(r) *also* a'-\ *n* -S : one that assigns or makes an assignment

as·sign·ment \-nmənt\ *n* -S [ME *assignement*, fr. MF, fr. OF, fr. *assigner* to assign + *-ment*] **1** : the act of assigning: as **a** : ALLOTMENT ⟨the ~ of land to veterans⟩ **b** : a pointing out or specifying ⟨~ of error in proceedings for review⟩ **c** : ALLEGEMENT, STATEMENT ⟨the ~ of these reasons⟩ **d** : ATTRIBUTION ⟨his ~ of different functions to different parts⟩ **2 a** : a position, post, or office to which one is assigned : APPOINTMENT ⟨his ~ as vice-consul in Liverpool⟩ ⟨his ~ as minister of two rural churches⟩ **b** : a specified amount of work or a definite task or mission assigned by authority or undertaken as though so assigned ⟨an ~ of 10 arithmetic problems⟩ ⟨the reporter's ~ was to interview the congressman⟩ **3 a** : the transfer to another of one's legal interest or right; *esp* : the transfer of property to be held in trust or to be used for the benefit of creditors **b** : the document by which such an interest or right is transferred **syn** see TASK

as·sign·or \ə'sīnər, a'-, -,nȯ(ə)r; ə,sī'nȯ(ə)r, ¦a,sī¦nȯ(ə)r; *Brit usu* ¦asə¦nȯ(ə)r\ *n* -S : one that makes an assignment; *esp* : one that transfers to another a legal interest or right

assigt *abbr* assignment

as·sim·i·la·bil·i·ty \ə,simələ'biləd·ē, -ətē, -i\ *n* -ES : the quality or state of being assimilable ⟨the ~ of new immigrants⟩

as·sim·i·la·ble \ə'====bəl\ *adj* : capable of being assimilated

¹as·sim·i·late \ə'simə,lāt, *usu* -ād·+V\ *vb* -ED/-ING/-S [ML *assimilatus*, past part. of *assimilare*, fr. L *assimulare, assimilare, adsimulare, adsimilare* to make similar, compare, fr. *ad-* + *simulare, similare* to make similar, simulate — more at SIMULATE] *vt* **1 a** : to appropriate and transform or incorporate into the substance of the assimilator : take in and appropriate as nourishment : absorb into the system ⟨the body ~s digested food into its protoplasm⟩ **b** : to take in and absorb as one's own: receive into the mind and consider and thoroughly comprehend ⟨the wide range of influences . . . which he *assimilated* in his years of apprenticeship —Herbert Read⟩ ⟨an amazing amount of scientific information which he had *assimilated* —V.G.Heiser⟩ **2 a** : to make similar or alike : cause to resemble — usu. used with *to* or *with* ⟨~ our law in this respect to the law of Scotland —John Bright⟩ ⟨stains, and vegetation, which ~ the architecture with the work of nature —John Ruskin⟩ **b** : to alter by the process of assimilation ⟨the prefix *im-* is an *assimilated* form of *in-*⟩ **c** : to absorb into the cultural tradition of a population or group ⟨the community *assimilated* persons of many nationalities⟩ **3** : to represent as similar or alike : COMPARE, LIKEN ⟨*assimilated* the career of a conqueror to that of a simple robber —W.E.H.Lecky⟩ — usu. used with following *to* or *with* **4** *archaic* : to bring into conformity : ADAPT ~ *vi* **1 a** : to become of the same substance : become absorbed or incorporated into the system ⟨some foods ~ more readily than others⟩ **b** : to become absorbed ⟨cannot ~ with the Church of England —J.H. Newman⟩ **2 a** : to be or become similar or alike : RESEMBLE — usu. used with following *to* or *with* ⟨~s with the character of English scenery⟩ **b** : to become altered by the process of assimilation ⟨the sound *m* often ~s before a following *n*⟩ **c** : to become culturally assimilated : undergo cultural assimilation **3** *archaic* : to become adapted : CONFORM

²as·sim·i·late \-,lət, -,lāt, *usu* -d·+V\ *n* -S : something that is assimilated

as·sim·i·la·tion \=,=='lāshən\ *n* -S [prob. fr. ML *assimilation-, assimilatio* physiological assimilation, fr. L *assimulatio, assimilatio* similarity, fr. *assimulatus, assimilatus* (past part. of *assimulare, assimilare* to make similar) + *-ion-, -io* -ion] **1 a** : the act or process of assimilating ⟨this creative ~ of what is handed down constitutes the great conservative force in poetry —J.L.Lowes⟩ **b** : the quality or state of being assimilated ⟨some writings had to be translated many times before reaching their final ~ —G.A.L.Sarton⟩ **2 a** : the conversion or incorporation of nutritive material into the fluid or solid substance of the body and being the last stage or series of stages in the process of nutrition following after digestion and absorption or occurring with the latter **b** : the incorporation of foreign blastematous material into the organized pattern of an embryo or blastema (as in certain experimental transfers of tissue) **c** (1) : the incorporation of food materials into the protoplasm : photosynthesis together with root absorption (2) : PHOTOSYNTHESIS — used esp. in England **3** : the process in which the chemical composition of molten magmas is changed by the fusion of the country rock with which they come in contact **4** : partial or total adaptation of the position or type of articulation of a particular sound (as a consonant) to that of an adjacent or neighboring sound — compare UMLAUT ⟨in the word *cupboard* the \p\ sound of the word *cup* has undergone complete ~⟩ ⟨in *conduct* the \m\ of the prefix *com-* shows ~⟩ **5** : the process of receiving new facts or responding to new situations in conformity with what is already available to consciousness — compare APPERCEPTION **6** : sociocultural fusion wherein individuals and groups of differing ethnic heritage acquire the basic habits, attitudes, and mode of life of an embracing national culture — distinguished from *acculturation*

as·sim·i·la·tion·ist \-əst\ *n* -S : one that believes in or advocates a policy of assimilation of differing racial or cultural groups, sometimes specif. of the Jews

as·sim·i·la·tive \='==,lād·iv, -,ləd·-\ *adj* [ML *assimilativus*, lit., making similar, fr. L *assimulatus, assimilatus* + *-ivus* -ive] : tending to, characterized by, or causing assimilation : ASSIMILATING ⟨an ~ pattern⟩ ⟨an ~ process⟩

as·sim·i·la·tor \-,lād·ə(r)\ *n* -S : one that assimilates

as·sim·i·la·to·ry \-,lə,tōrē, -,ȯr-\ *adj* : ASSIMILATIVE

as·sim·i·nea \ə,simə'nēə\ *n, cap* [NL] : a genus (the type of the widely distributed family Assimineidae) of small conical operculate pulmonate snails (order Pectinibranchia) of brackish water including a species (*A. lutea*) sometimes serving as an intermediate host of the lung fluke

as·sin·i·boin *also* **as·sin·i·boine** \ə'sinə,bȯin\ *n, pl* **assiniboin** *or* **assiniboins** *also* **assiniboine** *or* **assiniboines** *usu cap* [Ojibwa *ūsini-ūpwäwᵃ*, lit., one who cooks by use of stones, fr. *ūsini* stone + *ūpwäwᵃ* he cooks by roasting] **1 a** : a Siouan people of the area between the upper Missouri and middle Saskatchewan rivers **b** : a member of such people **2** : a dialect of Dakota spoken by the Assiniboin people

¹as·sis \a'sē\ *adj* [F, past part. of *asseoir* to seat — more at ASSIZE] : sitting down — used of animals in heraldry

²assis *pl of* ASSI

as·sise \a'sēz\ *n* -S [F, fr. *assise*, fem. of *assis*] : a succession of two or more paleontologic zones bearing typical fossils of the same species or genera

as·si·si \ə'sē(,)sē, ə'sēzē *also* ə'sisē *or* ə'sizē\ *n* -S [fr. *Assisi*, commune, Perugia province, Italy, where it was originally made] : an embroidery with unworked designs outlined by a solid background of cross-stitch

¹as·sist \ə'sist\ *vb* -ED/-ING/-S [MF or L: MF *assister* to help, be present, fr. L *assistere, adsistere* to help, stand by, fr. *ad-* + *sistere* to cause to stand, stand; akin to L *stare* to stand — more at STAND] *vi* **1** : to give support or aid : HELP ⟨refused to ~ in the campaign⟩ ⟨waited to see if he could ~ in any way⟩ **2** : to be present as a spectator ⟨unwilling to ~ at an interview between Amy and Amy's mistress —Arnold Bennett⟩ **3 a** *in euchre* : to order the dealer when he is the partner to take up the turned trump **b** *in bridge* : RAISE ~ *vt* **1 a** : to give support or aid to esp. in some undertaking or effort : AID ⟨diligently endeavored to ~ his search for a mate —George Meredith⟩ ⟨~*ed* the boy with his lessons⟩ **b** : to perform some service for : HELP ⟨a good and faithful helpmate ~*ed* me much by attending the shop —Benjamin Franklin⟩ ⟨~*ed* the old man up the stairs⟩ **2** *obs* : to take one's place with : JOIN, ATTEND **syn** see HELP

²assist \"\ *sometimes* 'a,s- *in sense 2*\ *n* -S **1** : an act of assistance : AID ⟨without any ~ from her brother . . . she has written . . . a breezy novel —Bernard Kalb⟩ **2 a** : the act of a player who by handling the ball (as in baseball) or passing the puck (as in hockey) enables a teammate to make a put-out or score a goal **b** : the official credit given a player for making such a play **3** : an act or circumstance that helps to bring about a decisive result ⟨the winning candidate got an ~ from his opponent's inept tactics⟩

as·sist·ance \ə'sistən(t)s\ *n* -S [ME *assistence* (fr. ML *assistentia*, fr. L *assistent-, assistens* + *-ia* -y) & *assistance*, fr. MF, fr. *assister* + *-ance*] **1 a** : the act or action of assisting : AID, HELP ⟨might from time to time require the ~ of a mild digestive —Dorothy Sayers⟩ **b** : the help supplied or given : SUPPORT ⟨economic ~ to several countries⟩; *specif* : aid (often financial) to the needy ⟨a program of public ~⟩ **2** *archaic* **a** : PRESENCE, ATTENDANCE **b** : AUDIENCE

¹as·sist·ant \-tənt\ *adj* [ME *assistant* (fr. MF, pres. part. of *assister*) & *assistent*, fr. L *assistent-, assistens*, pres. part. of *assistere*] **1** : giving aid or support : HELPFUL, AUXILIARY ⟨the guilty trade and the innocent manufacture were mutually ~ in more ways than one —G.M.Trevelyan⟩ **2** : acting as a subordinate to another : having a subordinate position or rank ⟨an ~ editor⟩ ⟨an ~ minister⟩

²assistant \"\ *n* -S [alter. (influenced by MF *assistant*) of ME *assistent*, fr. L *assistent-, assistens*] **1** *archaic* : one who is present : SPECTATOR **2 a** : one who assists : HELPER ⟨my close associate and invaluable ~ throughout the struggle⟩ **b** : one who acts as a subordinate to another or as an official in a subordinate capacity ⟨accepted a post as resident ~ in a large hospital⟩ ⟨was elected ~ and was for three years the only other officer —R.G.Usher⟩ **c** : a member usu. of the lowest rank of a college or university faculty whose duties may include grading papers, supervising laboratories, or teaching classes ⟨was appointed ~ in English⟩ **3** : a means of help : AUXILIARY ⟨rhyme is an ~ to memory⟩ **4** : a substance that aids in the processing of textile fibers; *esp* : a substance (as sodium sulfate) added to a dyebath for helping fix the dye or mordant to the yarn or fabric, for promoting level dyeing, or for promoting exhaustion of the dyebath

assistant professor *n* : a member of a college or university faculty who ranks immediately above an instructor and immediately below an associate professor

as·sist·ant·ship \-,ship\ *n* : the position of assistant at a college or university often given to a graduate student working for an advanced degree ⟨an ~ in chemistry⟩

as·sist·er \ə'sistə(r)\ *n* -S **1** *archaic* : one that is present **2** : one that assists

as·sist·ive \-tiv\ *adj* : giving aid : HELPFUL

¹as·size \ə'sīz *also* a'-\ *n* -S [ME *assise*, fr. OF, session, settlement, assessment, fr. fem. of *assis*, past part. of *asseoir* to seat, place, fr. (assumed) VL *assedēre*, alter. (influenced by L *sedēre*) of L *assidēre, adsidēre* to sit beside, assist in the office of judge, fr. *ad-* + *sedēre* to sit — more at SIT] **1** : an instruction, decree, or enactment made or issued at a legislative sitting or assembly : EDICT, ORDINANCE ⟨the *Assize* of Clarendon⟩ ⟨the *Assize* of Arms⟩ **2 a** : a statute or ordinance regulating weights and measures or the weight, measure, proportions of ingredients, or price of articles sold in the market ⟨the *Assize* of Weights and Measures⟩ **b** : the regulation of the price of bread or ale by the price of grain **3** : a fixed or customary standard (as of quantity, quality, or price) **4 a** : a trial or hearing in the nature of an inquest or recognition before sworn jurymen or assessors : judicial inquest **b** : an action to be decided by such a hearing, the writ for instituting it, or the verdict or finding rendered by the jury **5 a** : the periodical sessions of the judges of the superior courts in every county of England for the purpose of administering justice in the trial and determination of civil and criminal cases — usu. used in pl. **b** : the time or place of holding such a court, the court itself, or a session of it — usu. used in pl. **c** *Scot* (1) : a jury trial (2) : JURY, PANEL **6** : a cylinder-shaped block of stone forming part of a column or of a layer of stone in a building

²assize *vt* -ED/-ING/-S [ME *assisen*, fr *assise*, n.] *obs* : to regulate or fix (as a price) according to an ordinance or standard

as·siz·er \-zə(r)\ *n* -S [ME *assisour*, fr. AF, fr. OF *assise* + *-our* -or] **1** : a member of an assize : JURYMAN **2** : an officer appointed to execute the provisions of various assizes (sense 2a)

assmt *abbr* assessment

assn *abbr* association

as·so·cia·bil·i·ty \ə,sōsh(ē)ə'biləd·ē, -ōsēə-, -lətē, -i *also* a,s-\ *n* -ES : the quality or state of being associable

as·so·cia·ble \ə'=(=)=,bəl\ *adj* [ISV ¹*associate* + *-able*] : capable of being associated, joined, or connected in thought ⟨a word . . . easily ~ with collective nouns —Yakov Malkiel⟩

¹as·so·ci·ate \ə'sōs(h)ē,āt, *usu* -ād·+V\ *vb* -ED/-ING/-S [ME *associat* (3d pers. sing. past indic.), fr. L *associatus*, past part. of *associare*] *vt* **1 a** : to join often in a loose relationship as a partner, fellow worker, colleague, friend, companion, or ally ⟨was *associated* with him in a large law firm⟩ ⟨were closely *associated* with each other during the war⟩ **b** : to elect as an associate ⟨was *associated* to the Royal Academy —Robert Southey⟩ **2** *obs* : to keep company with : ATTEND ⟨friends should ~ friends in grief and woe —Shak.⟩ **3** : to join (things) together or connect (one thing) with another : COMBINE ⟨particles of gold *associated* with heavy minerals⟩ **4** : to join or connect in any of various intangible or unspecified ways (as in general mental, legendary, or historical relationship, in unspecified causal relationship, or in unspecified professional or scholarly relationship) ⟨surrealism has been *associated* with psychological and intellectual atmosphere common to periods of war —Bernard Smith⟩ ⟨she wished to ~ him with her unusual mood —J.C.Powys⟩ **5** : to submit to public identification (as with a principle or sentiment) ⟨the House will ~ itself with these expressions —Sir Winston Churchill⟩ ⟨I should wholeheartedly ~ myself with the general libertarian views —Felix Frankfurter⟩ **6** *chem* : to join in loose combinations — see ASSOCIATION 7 ~ *vi* **1** : to come together as partners, fellow workers, colleagues, friends, companions, or allies ⟨my father's conviction that they were too lowly to ~ with me —G.B.Shaw⟩ **2** : to combine or join with another or others as component parts : UNITE ⟨protons and neutrons with their encircling electrons ~ together to form atoms —G.W.Gray⟩ **3** : to engage in free association ⟨the patient *associated* freely about his childhood⟩ — see FREE ASSOCIATION **syn** see JOIN

²as·so·ciate \-s(h)ēət, -shət, -shē,āt, -sē,āt, *usu* -d·+V\ *adj* [ME *associat*, fr. L *associatus, adsociatus*, past part. of *associare, adsociare* to join, unite, fr. *ad-* + *sociare* to join, share, fr. *socius* companion — more at SOCIAL] **1** : closely connected, joined, or united with another (as in interest, function, activity, or office) : sharing in responsibility or authority ⟨descent through darkness . . . to my ~ powers —John Milton⟩ ⟨an ~ judge⟩ **2** : closely related esp. in the mind : ALLIED, ACCOMPANYING ⟨they want some ~ sounds to make them harmonious —Samuel Johnson⟩ **3** : admitted to some but not to all rights and privileges : having a secondary or subordinate status ⟨admitted to ~ membership in the society⟩

³associate \"\ *n* -S **1** : one associated with another: **a** : one who shares with another an enterprise, business, or action : a fellow worker : PARTNER ⟨the chemist and his ~s finally completed their experiment⟩ **b** : one who shares with another an office or position of authority : COLLEAGUE ⟨they were ~s on the bench for 20 years⟩ **c** : one who is frequently in company with another : COMPANION, COMRADE ⟨his most intimate ~ during his college years⟩ **2** : something that is closely connected with or that usu. accompanies another : ACCOMPANIMENT, CONCOMITANT; *esp* : a word or concept linked to another by association ⟨no sooner at any time comes into the understanding but its ~ appears with it —John Locke⟩ **3 a** : an officer of the superior common-law courts in England **b** : a member of a learned society or academy ranking below a fellow ⟨an ~ of the Royal Academy⟩ **c** : a research worker or teacher affiliated with a college, university, or some other professional organization or institution and ranking below a professor or full member ⟨research ~ in anthropology⟩ ⟨~ in German⟩ ⟨~ in medicine⟩ **4** *often cap* **a** : a degree conferred by a junior college upon its graduates ⟨~ in arts⟩ **b** : a degree or title granted by some colleges and universities to students who finish a course that is complete in itself but shorter than that leading to a bachelor's degree

associated state *n, often cap A&S* [trans. of F *état associé*] : a semi-independent state within the French Union bound to France by special treaties ⟨most of the *associated states* were once protectorates⟩

associate professor *n* : a faculty member in a college or university who ranks immediately below a professor and above an assistant professor

as·so·ci·a·tion \ə,sōsē'āshən, -ōshē- — -ōsh- *is somewhat less freq in this than in the other associ- words, by reason of* sh- *dissimilation*\ *n* -S [MF or ML; MF *association*, fr. ML *association-, associatio*, fr. L *associatus* (past part. of *associare* to join, unite) + *-ion-, -io* -ion — more at ASSOCIATE] **1 a** : the act or action of associating ⟨there is no such thing as criminal guilt by ~ in Anglo-American law —Sidney Hook⟩ ⟨the house dog's intimate ~ with people —J.W.Cross⟩ **b** : the quality or state of being associated : COMPANIONSHIP, PARTNERSHIP, CONNECTION, COMBINATION ⟨my four years of close ~ with Alec —Sidney Lovett⟩ ⟨the cerebrospinal fluid, due to its intimate ~ with the central nervous system —H.G.Armstrong⟩ ⟨flint implements in ~ with the remains of the extinct prehistoric cave bear —R.W.Murray⟩ **2** *archaic* : a written pledge to carry out an undertaking ⟨the six men had forged the ~⟩ **3** : an organization of persons having a common interest : SOCIETY, LEAGUE, UNION ⟨the Modern Language *Association* of America⟩: as **a** (1) : a voluntary union of neighboring self-governing local churches of the same denomination ⟨~ of the Baptists⟩ (2) : a stated meeting of the clergymen and other appointed delegates of such churches b : a body of persons organized for the prosecution of some purpose, having no charter from the state, but having the general form and mode of procedure of a corporation — distinguished from *corporation* **4 :** a feeling, thought, or recollection linked in the mind or associated in the memory with a thing or person : CONNOTATION, OVERTONE ⟨words stir our feelings . . . through their enveloping atmosphere of ~s —J.L.Lowes⟩ ⟨each new hearing yields some new richness in tonal ~ —Richard Eberhart⟩ **5 a :** the mental connection or bond existing between any sensations, perceptions, ideas, or feelings that to a subject or observer have a relational significance with one another ⟨the laws of ~⟩ **b :** the process of forming mental connections or bonds between sensations, perceptions, ideas, or feelings — compare LEARNING 1a(2) **c :** FREE ASSOCIATION **6** [short for *association football*] *Brit* : SOCCER **7** *chem* : aggregation to form (as with hydrogen bonds) loosely bound complexes **8 a :** a major unit often taken to be the fundamental unit in ecological community organization that is characterized by essential uniformity in physiognomy, composition, and structure and has usu. two or more dominant species of a particular life form or habit **b :** such a unit when considered a major subdivision of a formation or biome **c :** a group of organisms usu. of similar life form associated in a given environment and distinguishable as a group from neighboring groups of like nature **9** *sociol* **:** a formal or secondary social group that has been expressly organized to satisfy the specific intents and purposes of its members **10 :** a group of defined and named soils usu. having different characteristics and regularly associated in a geographic pattern

as·so·ci·a·tion·al \¦=¦==¦=shən³l, -shnəl\ *adj* **:** of or relating to association, associationism, or an association

as·so·ci·a·tion·al·ism \=,==¦=shən³l,izəm, -shnə,li-\ *n* -S : ASSOCIATIONISM

as·so·ci·a·tion·al·ist \-¸əst\ *n* -S : an adherent of associationalism

association area *n* **:** an area of the cerebral cortex considered to function in linking and coordinating the projection areas

association book *n* **:** a copy of a book prized for its association with some prominent person

association center *n* **:** a nervous center of an invertebrate concerned with the coordination and distribution of stimuli from sensory receptors

association fibers *n pl* **:** nerve fibers connecting different parts of the brain; *specif* **:** fibers connecting different areas within the cortex of each cerebral hemisphere

association football *n* **:** SOCCER

as·so·ci·a·tion·ism \=,==¦āshə,nizəm\ *n* -S [prob. fr. F *associationisme*, fr. *association* + *-isme* -ism] **:** a school of psychology that holds that the content of consciousness can be explained by the association and reassociation of irreducible sensory and perceptual elements — opposed to *apperceptionism*; compare MENTAL CHEMISTRY

¹as·so·ci·a·tion·ist \-sh(ə)nəst\ *n* -S [prob. fr. F *associationiste*, fr. *association* + *-iste* -ist] **:** an adherent of associationism

²associationist \=¦=¦=(=)=\ *also* **as·so·ci·a·tion·is·tic** \=¦==¦=shə¦nistik\ *adj* **:** of or relating to associationists or associationism

association psychology *or* **association theory** *n* : ASSOCIATIONISM

association test *n* : WORD ASSOCIATION TEST

as·so·ci·a·tive \ə'sōs(h)ē,ād·iv, -ōshəd·iv,-ōs(h)ēəd·iv\ *adj* **1 :** tending to, inducing, or characterized by association esp. of ideas or images ⟨an ~ symbol⟩ **2 a :** dependent on or characterized by association ⟨an ~ reaction⟩ **b :** acquired by a process of learning ⟨an ~ reflex⟩ **3 :** of, relating to, or being a mathematical operation that combines elements such that when the order of elements is preserved the result is independent of the grouping ⟨addition is ~ since $(a + b) + c = a + (b + c)$⟩ — **as·so·ci·a·tive·ly** *adv* — **as·so·ci·a·tiv·i·ty** \ə,sōs(h)ēə'tivəd·ē\ *n* -ES

associative anamnesis *n* **:** the taking of a psychiatric history by the method of free association

associative law *n* **:** a law indicating immateriality in the grouping of variables; *specif* **:** any law of the form $(\phi R\chi)R\psi = \phi R(\chi R\psi)$ where ϕ, χ, ψ are variables and R a dyadic operator [as $(a+b)+c=a+(b+c)$ in arithmetic or $(pvq)vr.\equiv.pv(qvr)$ in the propositional calculus] — called also *principle of association*

associative learning *n* **:** the learning process whereby discrete ideas and percepts become linked with one another

as·so·ci·a·tor \ə'sōs(h)ē,ād·ə(r), -,ātə-\ *n* -S : ASSOCIATE, CONFEDERATE

as·so·cia·to·ry \ə'sōs(h)ēə,tōrē, -ōshə,-\ *adj* : ASSOCIATIVE

as·so·ci·es \ə'sōsē,ēz\ *n, pl* **associes** [NL, prob. irreg. fr. L *associare*] **:** an impermanent nonclimax biotic community similar in scope to an association

as·soil \ə'sȯi(ə)l, a'-\ *vt* -ED/-ING/-S [ME *assoilen*, fr. OF *assoldre, assoudre* (1st pers. sing. pres. indic. *assoil*), fr. L *absolvere* — more at ABSOLVE] **1 a** *archaic* **:** to absolve or set free from sin : PARDON, FORGIVE ⟨the work of our brother in Christ and St. Francis . . . whom God ~ —Mary Austin⟩ **b** *obs* **:** to absolve or set free from an ecclesiastical punishment **c** *archaic* **:** to set free : RELEASE, DELIVER ⟨till from her bands the spright ~*ed* is —Edmund Spenser⟩ **2** *obs* **:** to clear up (a doubt or problem) : RESOLVE, SOLVE **3** *archaic* **:** to acquit of a criminal charge : CLEAR ⟨thou art ~*ed* of man-slaying —Gilbert Murray⟩ **4** *archaic* **:** to atone for : EXPIATE ⟨let each act ~ a fault —Edwin Arnold⟩

as·soil·ment \-mənt\ *n* -S *archaic* : ABSOLUTION ⟨a station of purification and ~ —Thomas De Quincey⟩

as·soil·zie \ə'sȯil(y)ē\ *vt* -ED/-ING/-S [ME (Scots dial.) *assoilyen, assolyen*, fr. MF *assoudre* (1st pers. sing. pres. indic. *assoil*, 3d pers. sing. pres. subj. *assoille*)] *Scot* : ASSOIL; *specif* **:** to acquit by sentence of court

as·so·nance \'as³nən(t)s, 'aas-\ *n* -S [F, fr. L *assonare* + F *-ance*] **1 :** resemblance of sound in words or syllables ⟨notice the ~ in *ring* and *hild* —George Saintsbury⟩ **2 a :** relatively close juxtaposition of similar sounds esp. of vowels **b :** repetition of vowels without repetition of consonants (as in *cálamo* and *plátano*) used as an alternative to rhyme in verse — called also *vowel rhyme* **3 :** incomplete correspondence : RESEMBLANCE ⟨~ between facts seemingly remote —J.R. Lowell⟩ — compare CONSONANCE

¹as·so·nant \-ənt\ *adj* [F or L; F *assonant*, fr. L *assonant-, assonans, adsonant-, adsonans*, pres. part. of *assonare, adsonare* to answer with the same sound, fr. *ad-* + *sonare* to sound — more at SOUND] **:** of, relating to, or marked by assonance ⟨an ~ pun⟩

²assonant \"\ *n* -S **:** a word or syllable that is assonant with another word or syllable

as·so·nan·tal \¦==¦antəl\ *also* **as·so·nan·tic** \-tik\ *adj* : ASSONANT

as·so·nate \'==,āt\ *vi* -ED/-ING/-S [L *assonatus, assonitus*, past part. of *assonare*] **:** to correspond in sound esp. by assonance ⟨syllables that ~⟩

as·so·nia \ə'sōnēə\ [NL, fr. I. J. de *Asso* y del Río †1814 Span. naturalist + NL connective *-n-* + *-ia*] *syn of* DOMBEYA

as soon as *conj* **:** immediately at or just after the time that ⟨*as soon as* he came, the meeting began⟩

as·sort \ə'sȯ(ə)rt, -ȯ(ə)t, *usu* -d·+V\ *vb* -ED/-ING/-S [MF *assortir*, fr. *a-* (fr. L *ad-*) + *-sortir* (fr. *sorte* sort, kind) — more at SORT] *vt* **1 :** to separate and distribute into groups of a like kind, quality, or purpose : CLASSIFY, SORT ⟨her mind was busily ~*ing* and grouping the faces before her —Ellen Glasgow⟩ **2 :** to supply with a suitable assortment or variety (as of goods) ⟨helped to balance and ~ that month's listings —*Atlantic Bull.*⟩ **3 :** to place in the same group with others : associate in a class : CLASS ⟨~ this fiction with the short stories and novelettes⟩ ~ *vi* **1 :** to fall into a class or place : agree in sort or kind : become adapted or suited : MATCH, HARMONIZE ⟨the donkey trail ~*ed* oddly with the house —D.C.Peattie⟩ **2 :** to keep company : ASSOCIATE, CONSORT ⟨I could abide to ~ with fisher-swains —Charles Lamb⟩

as·sort·a·tive \ə'sȯ(r)d·əd·iv, ¦tətiv\ *also* **as·sort·ive** \ə'sȯr|d·iv, -ȯ(ə)|, |tiv, -ēv\ *adj* **1 :** ASSORTING **2 :** of or relating to selection on the basis of likeness — **as·sor·ta·tive·ly** *adv*

assortative mating *n* **:** nonrandom mating: as **a :** mating between the more similar individuals of a population esp. when regarded as a factor in evolutionary differentiation within a population **b :** selective mating between individuals whose choice of marriage partners is determined by similarity of social environment — see HOMOGAMY

as·sort·ed \ə'sȯr|d·əd, -ȯ(ə)|, |təd\ *adj* **1 a :** consisting of selected kinds or sorts ⟨a box of ~ chocolates⟩ **b :** consisting of various kinds or sorts : MISCELLANEOUS, HETEROGENEOUS ⟨the hotel was full of ~ British and American accents —Arnold Bennett⟩ **2 :** MATCHED, SUITED, FITTED ⟨the doctor and his wife . . . had been a curiously ~ pair —Alan Hynd⟩

as·sort·er \-d·ə(r),-tə(r)\ *n* -S **:** one that assorts; *specif* **:** a garment worker who matches pieces or bundles garments

as·sort·ment \ə'sȯrtmənt, -ȯ(ə)t-\ *n* -S **1 a :** the act of assorting : arrangement into kinds and sorts ⟨Harnwell's household goods got mingled in the roadway with those appertaining to the Fishers and their ~ . . . was a task —Arthur Morrison⟩ **b :** the quality or state of being assorted : VARIETY ⟨the absence of quantity and ~ in his wares —W.D.Howells⟩ **2 :** an assorted group or collection: as **a :** a selected group or collection consisting of one sort **b :** a collection containing a variety of sorts adapted to various wants, demands, or purposes ⟨an ~ of tools⟩ **c :** a miscellaneous group or collection consisting of various sorts ⟨canoes . . . loaded with an ~ of yabbering, singing natives, whining dogs, cooked reptiles and fish —Francis Birtles⟩ **3 :** the separation and segregation of homologous genes at meiosis — compare MENDEL'S LAW

ass's-ear \'==,=\ *n, pl* **ass's-ears :** a slender tropical abalone (*Haliotis asinina*) common in the Pacific islands and northern Australia

asst *abbr* assistant

asstd *abbr* **1** assented **2** associated **3** assorted

as·suage \ə'swāj\ *also* -āzh *or* -äzh\ *vb* -ED/-ING/-S [ME *aswagen*, fr. OF *assouagier*, fr. (assumed) VL *assuaviare, adsuaviare*, fr. L *ad-* + (assumed) VL *-suaviare* (fr. L *suavis* sweet) — more at SWEET] *vt* **1 :** to reduce the intensity of : make less severe or violent : ALLAY, MITIGATE, EASE ⟨stroking her right wrist with her left hand as though to ~ the ache —Jean Stafford⟩ ⟨forgetting her own sorrow in her effort to ~ his —B.A. Williams⟩ **2 :** to reduce to a state of peace, calm, or quiet : MOLLIFY, PACIFY ⟨she found herself . . . pleasantly *assuaged* by the sense of anonymity which enveloped her —Helen Howe⟩ **3 :** to put an end to by satisfying : APPEASE, QUENCH ⟨surrounded with more than enough to ~ its hunger —F.G. Kay⟩ **4** *obs* **:** to reduce esp. in size : DIMINISH ~ *vi*, *archaic* **:** to grow less : ABATE, SUBSIDE ⟨God made a wind to pass over the earth and the waters *assuaged* —Gen 8: 1 (AV)⟩ **syn** see RELIEVE

as·suage·ment \-mənt\ *n* -S **1 a :** the act of assuaging : ALLEVIATION, RELIEF ⟨the ~ of their hunger by a few more mouthfuls than usual —Glenway Wescott⟩ **b :** the quality or state of being assuaged ⟨the founts whereat my soul . . . may cool ~ find —Selwyn Image⟩ **2 :** something that assuages : ALLEVIATIVE ⟨his social . . . inadequacies led him to the ~s of anti-Semitism and a superpatriotism —*Time*⟩

as·sua·sive \ə, a+\ *adj* [*ad-* + *suasive*] **:** having a pleasantly soothing quality or effect : CALMING ⟨he feels the earth under him germinating in the spring night, the sweet ~ air —Norman Mailer⟩

assubjugate *vt* -ED/-ING/-S [*ad-* + *subjugate*] *archaic* **:** to reduce to subjugation

assuefaction *n* -S [F, fr. OF, fr. L *assuefactus* (past part. of *assuefacere* to accustom, fr. *assuetus* + *facere* to make, do) + OF *-ion* — more at DO] *obs* : HABITUATION, USE

as·sue·tude \'aswē,tüd, -ē-,tyüd\ *n* -S [L *assuetudo*, fr. *assuetus*, past part. of *assuescere* to be accustomed, fr. *ad-* + *suescere* to become accustomed; akin to L *suus* one's own — more at SUICIDE] : ACCUSTOMEDNESS, HABIT

as·sum·a·ble \ə'süməbəl\ *adj* **:** capable of being assumed

as·sum·a·bly \-blē, -li\ *adv* **:** as may be assumed : PRESUMABLY

as·sume \ə'süm\ *vb* -ED/-ING/-S [ME *assumen*, fr. L *assumere, adsumere*, fr. *ad-* + *sumere* to take, fr. *sub* under + *emere* to buy, obtain — more at SUB-, REDEEM] *vt* **1 :** to take up or into : RECEIVE, ACCEPT: **a :** to receive into heaven ⟨in what wise the Mother of God had been *assumed* into her place in Heaven —William James⟩ **b :** to take into partnership, employment, or use : receive as an associate ⟨revealed religion ~s them into her service —R.C.Trench⟩ **2 :** to take to or upon oneself : UNDERTAKE: **a :** to invest oneself with (a form, attribute, or aspect) ⟨anxious in this lecture not to ~ the role of a Christian apologist —W.R.Inge⟩ ⟨visits of inspection often ~ a dramatic character —C.L.Jones⟩ **b :** to put on (an article of clothing) : DON ⟨had *assumed* her bonnet and shawl —Arnold Bennett⟩ **c :** to invest oneself formally with (an office or its symbols) : enter upon the duties of ⟨at the age of 40 he *assumed* the presidency of the college⟩ **d :** to take upon oneself (to do or perform) : UNDERTAKE — used chiefly in law and with following infinitive ⟨did ~ to carry his horse . . . over the water of Humber sound —William Fulbecke⟩ **3 :** to take as one's right or possession : ARROGATE, SEIZE, USURP ⟨the king *assumed* to himself the right of filling up the chief municipal offices —T.B.Macaulay⟩ **4 :** to take in appearance only : pretend to have or be : FEIGN ⟨she felt, without knowing why, that the gaiety was *assumed* —Ellen Glasgow⟩ **5 :** to take for granted : accept arbitrarily or tentatively : SUPPOSE ⟨we simply *assumed* that we were going to be married —R.P.Warren⟩ **6 :** to take as an assumption or premise in logic **7 :** to take over as one's own (the debts of another) : make oneself formally liable for ⟨the public debt which the incorporators *assumed* —W.P.Webb⟩ ~ *vi* **:** to claim more than is due : be pretentious ⟨in the absence of proof history has no right to ~ —Hilaire Belloc⟩

syn AFFECT, PRETEND, SIMULATE, FEIGN, COUNTERFEIT, SHAM: ASSUME may apply to putting on a false or deceptive appearance through either pardonable or blameworthy motives ⟨by *assuming* an air of cheerfulness we become cheerful in reality —William Cowper⟩ ⟨an elderly "buck" with an air of *assumed* juvenility —W.S.Gilbert⟩ ⟨the defense counsel *assumes* great friendliness and the inexperienced witness assumes that this friendliness may be genuine —Paul Wilson⟩ ⟨*assume* a meek look⟩ AFFECT indicates making a false show of possessing, using, feeling, or preferring ⟨Gayerson, a Bengal Civilian, who *affected* the customs—as he had the heart—of youth —Rudyard Kipling⟩ ⟨Elizabeth could but just *affect* concern in missing him; she really rejoiced at it —Jane Austen⟩ ⟨a tramp cyclist, *affecting* turtleneck sweaters and gray flannel bags —P.G.Wodehouse⟩ PRETEND may suggest sustained profession of or adherence to what is false ⟨I shall find myself *pretending* that I am so full of resources that I do not require any outside help to enjoy a holiday in a lovely place —O.S.J.Gogarty⟩ ⟨absurd to *pretend* that the young men of Europe ever wanted to hunt each other into holes in the ground and throw bombs into the holes to disembowel one another —G.B.Shaw⟩ ⟨they had high critical standards; even their clowns had to be learned or to *pretend* learning —Gilbert Highet⟩ SIMULATE indicates factitiously appearing or imitating for a purpose ⟨Tibetan women do not like to appear sunburnt, even powdering their faces to *simulate* a fair complexion —Heinrich Harrer⟩ ⟨since few cannon were available, trees hewn to *simulate* formidable artillery pieces were dragged into position all along the ramparts —*Amer. Guide Series: La.*⟩ ⟨casting myself face downwards on the earth, . . . *simulating* death —W.H.Hudson †1922⟩ FEIGN, often interchangeable with SIMULATE, may suggest calculated intent and artful execution ⟨a clever young man who had evaded conscription by *feigning* epilepsy —Eric Linklater⟩ ⟨Bouquet, *feigning* retreat, drew the Indians forward to receive a flanking fire from companies ambushed for the purpose —S.J.Buck⟩ COUNTERFEIT may imply imitation that copies very closely ⟨*counterfeit* coins⟩ ⟨many noblemen gave the actor-manager access to their collections of armor and weapons in order that his accouterment should exactly *counterfeit* that of a Norman baron —G.B. Shaw⟩ SHAM may apply to deception so obvious that it deceives only the gullible ⟨when the curtain falls there are more actors *shamming* dead upon the stage than actors upright —H.A.L.Craig⟩ **syn** see in addition PRESUPPOSE

as·sumed \-ümd\ *adj* **1 :** taken as one's right or possession : APPROPRIATED, USURPED ⟨hearing evi ence in an ~ capacity⟩ **2 a :** MAKE-BELIEVE, PRETENDED, FEIGNED ⟨an ~ cheerfulness⟩ **b :** FICTITIOUS, FALSE ⟨an ~ name⟩ **3 :** taken for granted : SUPPOSED ⟨the ~ reason for his absence⟩ — **as·sum·ed·ly** \-mədlē, -li\ *adv*

assumed bond *n* **:** a bond issued by one corporation and assumed by another

assumed position *n* **:** the position at which a craft is assumed to be located for the determination of a line of position

as·sum·er \-mə(r)\ *n* -S **:** one that assumes

assuming *adj* **:** taking too much upon oneself : PRETENTIOUS, PRESUMPTUOUS ⟨upon a subject like this . . . it would be altogether too ~ for a single individual to decide —Herman Melville⟩ — **as·sum·ing·ly** *adv*

as·sump·sit \ə'səm(p)sət, a'-\ *n* -S [NL, he undertook, 3d pers. sing. perf. indic. act. of *assumere* to undertake, fr. L, to take up — more at ASSUME] **1 a :** a form of common-law action on the case not now used in which the plaintiff alleged a breach of agreement by the defendant from which the plaintiff had suffered legal damage **b :** an action on contract to recover damages for a breach or nonperformance of a contract or promise express or implied, oral or in writing, and formerly not under seal — see NON ASSUMPSIT **2 :** a promise or contract not under seal on which an action of assumpsit may be brought

assumpt *vt* -ED/-ING/-S [L *assumptus*, past part. of *assumere*] *obs* : ASSUME

as·sump·tion \ə'səm(p)shən\ *n* -S [ME, fr. LL *assumption-, assumptio*, fr. L, reception, taking up, adoption, fr. *assumptus* (past part. of *assumere* to take up) + *-ion-, -io* -ion] **1** *usu cap* **a :** the bodily taking up of a person into heaven ⟨the dogma of the *Assumption* of the Virgin Mary⟩ **b :** the church feast commemorating the Assumption of the Virgin Mary that is observed on August 15 — compare FALLING ASLEEP **2** *archaic* **:** the taking into association or union : ADOPTION, INCORPORATION **3 a :** the act of taking to or upon oneself an attribute, form, duty, or office ⟨his meek ~ of innocence⟩ ⟨a delay in the ~ of his new position⟩ **b :** the act of laying claim to or taking possession of : APPROPRIATION, USURPATION ⟨the Nazi ~ of power in 1934⟩ **4 :** unwarranted pretentiousness : ARROGANCE ⟨his usual air of haughty ~ —Sir Walter Scott⟩ **5 a :** the act of taking for granted or supposing that a thing is true ⟨the structural characteristics of the order and the fallacies in ~ —R.E.Montgomery⟩ **b :** something that is taken for granted : SUPPOSITION ⟨it was, like all societies, built on certain ~s —M.C.Hollis⟩ **6 :** the taking over of debts or obligations by another; *specif* **:** the adoption by the federal government of the states' debts incurred during the American Revolution **7 a :** the proposition, axiom, postulate, or notion assumed **b :** the minor or second premise in a categorical syllogism

as·sump·tion·ist \-shənəst\ *n* -S **1 :** one who favored the taking over by the federal government of the states' debts incurred during the American Revolution **2** *usu cap* : AUGUSTINIAN OF THE ASSUMPTION

assumption of risk : a rule of common law that an employee entering upon employment assumes risks of injury incident to such employment

as·sump·tious \ə'səm(p)shəs\ *adj* [*assumption* + *-ous*] : ASSUMING

as·sump·tive \-(p)tiv\ *adj* [prob. fr. (assumed) NL *assumptivus*, fr. L *assumptus*, past part. of *assumere* + *-ivus* -ive] : ASSUMED, ASSUMING: as **a :** taken as one's own ⟨upstarts with their ~ arms⟩ **b :** taken for granted or inclined to take for granted ⟨~ beliefs⟩ ⟨the ~ habits of her mind⟩ **c :** making undue claims ⟨an ~ person⟩

as·sur·ance \ə'shürən(t)s, a'-\ *n* -S [ME *assuraunce*, fr. MF *assurance*, fr. OF *aseürance*, fr. *aseürer* + *-ance*] **1 a :** the act of assuring : PLEDGE, GUARANTEE ⟨can tell you . . . with my most solemn ~ that it's true —Richard Joseph⟩ **b** *archaic* **:** a guarantee or pledge of peace and safety — usu. used in pl. ⟨angry that ~s had been given the enemy⟩ **2 :** something that inspires or tends to inspire confidence ⟨~s of support came pouring in daily —T.B.Macaulay⟩ **3 a :** the quality or state of being sure or certain : freedom from doubt : CERTAINTY ⟨said with as much ~ as is ever brought to human affairs —*Time*⟩ **b :** assuredness of divine grace or of forgiveness and salvation : consciousness of personal fellowship with God ⟨blessed ~, Jesus is mine —Fanny J.Crosby⟩ **4 :** the quality or state of being sure or safe : SECURITY, SAFETY ⟨the king's ascent to the crown and ~ therein —Thomas Keightley⟩ **5 :** the act of conveying or the instrument or other legal evidence of the conveyance of real property — called also *common assurance* **6** *now chiefly Brit* : INSURANCE **7 :** confidence of manner : freedom from timidity : SELF-CONFIDENCE, SELF-RELIANCE ⟨to face a good orchestra with inward and outward authority and ~ —J.N.Burk⟩ **8 :** excessive or presumptuous boldness : IMPUDENCE, AUDACITY ⟨no experience so far served to reveal the whole offensiveness of the man's ~ —Mary Austin⟩

as·sure \ə'shü(ə)r, a'-, -üə\ *vt* -ED/-ING/-S [ME *assuren*, fr. MF *assurer*, fr. OF *aseürer*, fr. ML *assecurare*, fr. L *ad-* + ML *-securare* (fr. L *securus* secure) — more at SECURE] **1 :** to make safe (as from risks or against overthrow) : INSURE, SECURE ⟨an international organization capable of *assuring* the security of all nations —Vera M. Dean⟩ **2 :** to give confidence to : REASSURE, ENCOURAGE, STRENGTHEN ⟨a pure man forgives or pleads for mercy or ~s the penitent —F.W.Robertson⟩ **3 :** to make sure or certain : put beyond all doubt : CONVINCE ⟨glancing backward . . . to ~ himself that neither of his late antagonists was returning —C.G.D.Roberts⟩ **4 :** to inform positively : tell earnestly : declare confidently to ⟨Constance *assured* her that the doctor would have nothing new to advise —Arnold Bennett⟩ ⟨I can ~ you of his reliability⟩ **5** *obs* **a :** to give a pledge or guarantee of : PROMISE ⟨*assuring* the king perpetual love —John Smith †1631⟩ **b :** to state with assurance ⟨about which neither . . . could ~ anything —Isaac Barrow⟩ **c :** to make sure the possession of : secure the title of ⟨and with my proper blood ~ any soul to be great Lucifer's —Christopher Marlowe⟩ **6 :** to make certain the coming or attainment of : ENSURE ⟨spent the better part of a year in painstaking research to ~ accuracy —A.W.Barkley⟩ **syn** see ENSURE

¹as·sured \-ü(ə)rd, -üəd\ *adj* [ME, fr. past part. of *assuren*] **1 a :** characterized by certainty or security : SURE ⟨deluded into believing that we can ever have completely ~ lives —C.C. Furnas⟩ **b :** beyond doubt or question : UNQUESTIONABLE, CERTAIN ⟨beliefs that were ~ became doubtful —C.W. de Kiewiet⟩ **c :** GUARANTEED, INSURED ⟨a tiny but ~ income for the rest of his life —Elinor Wylie⟩ **2** *obs* : ENGAGED, PLEDGED; *specif* : BETROTHED **3 a :** characterized by self-assurance : CONFIDENT, SELF-POSSESSED ⟨most ~ of all in appearance was the commissary of prisoners —Kenneth Roberts⟩ ⟨an art so ~ as to appear casual —Margery Bailey⟩ **b :** characterized by undue or excessive self-confidence : SELF-SATISFIED ⟨with an air of ~ ignorance —Isaac Watts⟩ **4 :** satisfied as to the certainty or truth of a matter : CONVINCED ⟨so ~ was Augustus of the merits of his plan —John Buchan⟩ **syn** see CONFIDENT

²assured \"\ *n, pl* **assured** *or* **assureds 1 :** the person in whose favor an insurance policy stands **2 :** the person who is insured

as·sur·ed·ly \-ürədlē, -li\ *adv* **1 :** without a doubt : CERTAINLY, SURELY **2 :** with assurance : CONFIDENTLY

as·sur·ed·ness *n* -ES **:** the quality or state of being assured

as·sur·er *or* **as·sur·or** \-ürə(r)\ *n* -S **:** one that assures; *specif* **:** one that gives or underwrites an insurance policy

as·sur·gen·cy \ə'sərjənsē\ *n* -ES [*assurgent* + *-cy*] **:** the tendency to rise

as·sur·gent \-jənt\ *adj* [L *assurgent-, assurgens, adsurgent-, adsurgens*, pres. part. of *assurgere, adsurgere* to rise, fr. *ad-* + *surgere* to rise — more at SURGE] : ASCENDING, RISING: as **a** *heraldry* **:** rising from the sea ⟨a sea horse ~⟩ **b :** ASCENDANT 1b

assuring *adj* **:** that assures or tends to assure : giving confidence — **as·sur·ing·ly** *adv*

asswage *obs var of* ASSUAGE

assy *abbr* assembly

¹as·syr·i·an \ə'sirēən *also* a'-\ *adj, usu cap* [*Assyria*, ancient empire of western Asia + E *-an*] **1 a :** of, relating to, or characteristic of Assyria, an ancient empire of western Asia **b :** of, relating to, or characteristic of Assyrians **2 :** of, relating to, or characteristic of the Assyrian language

[2]**assyrian** \"\ n -s cap **1 a :** a member of an ancient Semitic race forming the Assyrian nation and characterized physically by a muscular frame, brachycephaly, a tawny complexion, and a prominent hooked nose **b :** a Babylonian Semite **2 :** the Semitic language of the Assyrians, a dialect of Akkadian — see AFRO-ASIATIC LANGUAGES table **3 :** a member of a brunette Caucasian ethnic group in Asia Minor and Iraq whose language is neo-Syriac — compare CHALDEAN

assyrian plum n, usu cap A **:** SEBESTEN

as·syr·i·ol·o·gist \ˌ==ˈäləjəst\ n -s usu cap **:** a specialist in Assyriology

as·syr·i·ol·o·gy \-jē, -i\ n -ES usu cap [Assyria + E -o- + -logy] **:** the science or study of the history, language, and antiquities of ancient Assyria and Babylonia

[1]**as·syro–babylonian** \əˈsi(ˌ)rō, aˈs-+ˌ==ˈ=(=)=\ adj, usu cap A&B [Assyro- (fr. Assyria) + Babylonian] **:** of, relating to, or characteristic of Assyria and Babylonia or their common culture

[2]**assyro–babylonian** n, usu cap A&B **:** AKKADIAN 3a

assythment n -s [Sc assythe to compensate, satisfy (fr. ME assithen, assethen, fr. assith, asseth, n., satisfaction, reparation, fr. MF asseit, back-formation fr. assez enough) + E -ment — more at ASSET] Scot law **:** indemnification for injury; specif **:** the satisfaction formerly demandable by the family of a person slain but now superseded by damages recoverable by an action — compare MANBOTE

[1]**ast** \ˈast, aa(ə)-,ai-,á-\ dial var of ASK

[2]**ast** \"\ **:** ASKED — used esp. in written dialogue to represent a supposed dialect or substandard speech

-ast \ˌast, ˌaa(ə)-, ˌəst\ n suffix -s [ME -aste, fr. L -astes, fr. Gk -astēs (akin to -istēs -ist)] **:** one connected with ⟨ecdysiast⟩ ⟨hypochondriast⟩

AST abbr Atlantic standard time

as·ta·cid·ea \ˌastəˈsidēə\ [NL, fr. Astacus + -idea] syn of ASTACURA

as·ta·cin \ˈastəsən\ also **as·ta·cene** \-ˌsēn\ n -s [ISV astac- (fr. NL Astacus) + -in or -ene] **:** a red carotenoid ketone pigment $C_{40}H_{48}O_4$ found esp. in crustaceans (as in boiled lobster shell) and obtained by oxidation of astaxanthin

as·ta·cu·ra \ˌastəˈkyu̇rə\ n pl, cap [NL, fr. Astacus + -ura] zool **:** a tribe of Reptantia that includes the freshwater crayfishes and the true lobsters both formerly placed in the suborder Macrura — **as·ta·cu·ran** \ˌ==ˈ=rən\ adj or n

as·ta·cus \ˈastəkəs\ n, cap [NL, fr. L, crab, fr. Gk astakos, ostakos lobster, crayfish; akin to Gk osteon bone — more at OSSEOUS] **:** a genus (the type of the family Astacidae) of crustaceans containing the freshwater crayfishes of Europe and related species of western No. America

a–stage resin \ˈā,-\ n, usu cap A [[1]a] **:** RESOLE

a star \ˈā-\ n, usu cap A [[1]a] **:** a star of spectral type A — see SPECTRAL TYPE table

astar·board \əˈ-\ adv [[1]a- + starboard] **:** over toward or on the starboard side of a ship — usu. used of the helm ⟨put the helm hard ~⟩

astare \əˈ-\ adj [[1]a- + stare, v.] **:** STARING ⟨the round face . . . high-collared and ~ —Maurice Hewlett⟩ ⟨with eyes ~⟩

astart \əˈ-\ adv [[1]a- + start (to move convulsively)] **:** with a start **:** SUDDENLY

as·tar·te \əˈstärd·ē, aˈ-\ n [NL, fr. L Astarte, principal goddess of Tyre and Sidon (often identified with Aphrodite by the Greeks), fr. Gk Astartē, of Sem origin; akin to Heb ʿAshtōreth, Phoenician and Canaanite goddess] **1** cap **:** a genus (the type of the family Astartidae) comprising marine bivalve mollusks (order Eulamellibranchia) with thick equivalved shells often concentrically ridged and with well-developed hinge teeth **2** -s **:** any member of the genus Astarte

asta·sia \əˈstāzh(ē)ə\ n -s [NL, fr. Gk, unsteadiness, fr. astatos unsteady (fr. a- [2]a- + statos standing, fr. histanai to cause to stand) + -ia — more at STAND] med **:** muscular incoordination in standing — compare ABASIA

asta·sia–abasia \"+\ n -s [NL, fr. astasia + abasia] med **:** inability to stand and walk resulting from muscular incoordination

astatic \(ˈ)ā+ˈ-\ adj [[2]a- + static] **1 :** not static **:** not stable or steady **2** physics **:** having little or no tendency to take a fixed or definite position or direction — **astatically** adv — **astat·i·cism** \(ˈ)āˈstad·əˌsizəm\ n -s

astatic galvanometer n **:** a galvanometer having two needles with opposite polarities that reduce the effect of the earth's magnetism

astatic pair n **:** two small coplanar magnets of equal moment rigidly attached at right angles to a stiff wire with their moments oppositely directed and forming a system that experiences no directive influence when suspended in a uniform magnetic field

as·ta·tine \ˈastəˌtēn, -ˌtən\ n -s [Gk astatos unsteady, unstable + E -ine] **:** a radioactive element belonging to the halogens discovered by bombarding bismuth with helium nuclei and also formed by radioactive decay — symbol At; see ELEMENT table

as·ta·tize \-ˌtīz\ vt -ED/-ING/-S [astatic + -ize] **:** to render astatic

as·ta·xanthin \ˌastə+\ n -s [NL Astacus + E xanthin] **:** a violet crystalline carotenoid pigment $C_{40}H_{52}O_4$ found combined (as with proteins) esp. in the shells of crustaceans and the feathers of birds

astay \əˈstā\ adj [[1]a- + stay (rope)] of an anchor being hove in **:** having its cable parallel to one of the ship's stays

ast·bury \ˈas(t)b(ə)rē, -ri\ or **ast·bury·ware** \ˈ=(=)=ˌ=\ n -s usu cap [after John Astbury †1743 Eng. potter] **:** 18th century English pottery including red stoneware with sprigged or molded ornamentation and mottled lead-glazed earthenware figures

asteep \əˈ-\ adj [[1]a- + steep, v.] **:** undergoing steeping

asteer \əˈstēr\ Scot var of ASTIR

aste·lic \(ˈ)āˈstēlik\ adj [[2]a- + -stelic] **:** lacking a stele or having the cylindrical arrangement of the vascular bundles discontinuous or disrupted — **aste·ly** \ˈāˌstēlē\ n -ES

as·ter \ˈastə(r), ˈaas-\ n [in senses 1 and 2, fr. NL, fr. L, aster, fr. Gk aster-, astēr star, aster; in sense 3, fr. NL, fr. LL, star, fr. Gk aster-, astēr; in sense 4, fr. MGk aster-, astēr, fr. Gk, star — more at STAR] **1** cap **:** a large genus of chiefly fall-blooming leafy-stemmed herbaceous plants (family Compositae) native of temperate regions and having discoid and usu. daisylike radiate heads, a multiseriate involucre, and a pappus of a single series of capillary bristles — see MICHAELMAS DAISY **2** -s **a :** any plant of the genus Aster or its immediate related forms **b :** any of a number of plants derived from the China aster **3** -s biol **:** a system of gelated cytoplasmic rays (aster rays) typically arranged radially about a centrosome at either end of the mitotic spindle and sometimes persisting between mitoses — called also cytaster **4** Eastern Church **:** ASTERISK 2

aster- or **astero-** comb form [Gk, fr. aster-, astēr] **:** star ⟨Asterolepis⟩

[1]**-as·ter** \ˌastə(r), ˌaas-\ n suffix -s [ME, fr. L, suffix denoting partial resemblance] **:** one that is inferior, worthless, or not genuine ⟨criticaster⟩ ⟨poetaster⟩

[2]**-aster** \ˌ==\ n comb form -s [NL, fr. Gk astēr] **:** star — in structural and generic names in biology ⟨diaster⟩ ⟨Geaster⟩

as·ter·a·ce·ae \ˌastəˈrāsēˌē\ [NL, fr. Aster, type genus + -aceae] syn of COMPOSITAE

as·ter·a·ceous \ˌ==ˈrāshəs\ adj [NL Asteraceae + E -ous] **:** COMPOSITE b

as·ter·a·les \ˌ==ˈrā(ˌ)lēz\ n pl, cap [NL, fr. Aster + -ales] in some classifications **:** an order of flowering plants coextensive with the superfamily Compositae and now usu. included in Campanulales

aster cloth n **:** a fine-mesh cotton fabric used to shade growing plants and to exclude insects — compare TOBACCO CLOTH

as·ter·el·la \ˌastəˈrelə\ [NL, fr. L aster star + NL -ella] syn of REBOULIA

astereognosis \(ˈ)ā+\ n, pl **astereognoses** [NL, fr. a- [2]a- + stereognosis] med **:** loss of the ability to recognize the shapes of objects by handling them

aster family n **:** COMPOSITAE

[1]**as·te·ria** \aˈstirēə\ n -s [L, a precious stone, perh. the star sapphire, fr. Gk, fem. of asterios starry, fr. aster-, astēr star] **:** a gem stone cut so as to show asterism

[2]**asteria** pl of ASTERION

as·te·ri·al \(ˈ)aˈstirēəl\ adj [L aster or Gk aster-, astēr star + E -ial] **:** of or relating to stars **:** like a star

as·te·ri·as \aˈstirēəs\ n, cap [NL, fr. Gk, starred, fr. aster-, astēr] **:** a genus of echinoderms formerly comprising nearly all starfishes and ophiurans but now restricted to certain typical starfishes including the common littoral forms of Europe and eastern No. America

as·te·ri·at·ed \=ˈ==ˌād·əd\ adj [Gk asterios starry, of a star + E -ate + -ed — more at ASTERIA] **:** exhibiting asterism

as·ter·i·i·dae \ˌastəˈrīəˌdē\ n pl, cap [NL, fr. Asterias, type genus + -idae] **:** a large and important family of starfishes including the common species of No. America and Europe and having Asterias as its type and best-known genus

as·ter·in·i·dae \-ˈrinəˌdē\ n pl, cap [NL, fr. Asterina, type genus (fr. Gk aster-, astēr star, starfish + NL -ina) + -idae] **:** a widely distributed family of usu. pentagonal quite flat starfishes

[1]**as·te·ri·oid** \aˈstirēˌȯid\ adj [NL Asterioidea] **:** ASTEROID 2

[2]**asterioid** \"\ n -s **:** ASTEROID 2

as·te·ri·oi·dea \=ˌ==ˈȯidēə\ [NL Asterias + -oidea] syn of ASTEROIDEA

as·te·ri·on \aˈstirēˌän, -ˌən\ n, pl **aste·ria** \-ēə\ [NL, fr. Gk, neut. of asterios starry] **:** the point behind the ear where the parietal, temporal, and occipital bones meet — see CRANIOMETRY illustration — **as·te·ri·on·ic** \(ˈ)=ˌ==ˈänik\ adj

as·te·ri·o·nel·la \=ˌ==əˈnelə\ n [NL, fr. Gk asterion (neut. of asterios starry) + NL -ella] **1** cap **:** a small genus of narrowly linear diatoms (family Fragilariaceae) arranged in stellate free-floating colonies and often causing geraniumlike or fishy odors in public water supplies **2** -s **:** a diatom of the genus Asterionella

[1]**as·ter·isk** \ˈastəˌrisk, ˈaas-\ n -s [LL asteriscus, fr. Gk asteriskos, lit., little star, dim. of aster-, astēr star] **1 :** the character * used in printing as the first in series of the reference marks, to indicate the omission of letters or words, in linguistic works to mark hypothetical forms belonging to a reconstructed ancestral language, and in various arbitrary uses — called also star **2** also **as·te·ris·kos** \ˌästəˈrēˌskȯs\ -ES Eastern Church **:** a star-shaped liturgical utensil used to cover the eucharistic elements lying in a paten and to guard them from contact with the first veil

[2]**asterisk** \"\ vt -ED/-ING/-S **:** to mark with an asterisk **:** STAR

as·ter·ism \-ˌrizəm\ n -s [Gk asterismos, fr. asterizein to arrange in constellations, fr. aster-, astēr star + -izein -ize] **1 a :** CONSTELLATION **b :** a small group of stars **2 :** the optical phenomenon of a star-shaped figure exhibited by some crystals by reflected light (as in a star sapphire) or by transmitted light (as in some mica) **3 :** three asterisks arranged in the form of an inverted or upright pyramid (as ⁂ or ⁂) esp. in order to direct attention to a following passage

as·ter·is·mal \ˌ==ˈrizməl\ adj **:** of or relating to asterisms or constellations

aster leafhopper n **:** SIX-SPOTTED LEAFHOPPER

[1]**astern** \əˈ-\ adv [[1]a- + stern (n.)] **1 :** behind a ship or aircraft **:** in the rear ⟨we were sailing due east and the setting sun was now directly ~⟩ ⟨~, the sea gulls wheeled and dipped⟩ **2 :** at or toward the stern of a ship or aircraft ⟨it ended ~ in a clumsy-looking bulge that was closed by a pair of huge clamshell doors —W.F.Jenkins⟩ ⟨he paused ~, gazing over the rail at the wake of the ship⟩ **3 :** stern foremost **:** to the rear **:** BACKWARD ⟨rang full ~ on the telegraph⟩ ⟨maneuvers that involve going ~ should never be taken until the dinghy line is shortened —W.P.Moore⟩

[2]**astern** \"\ adj **1 :** placed or situated astern **2 :** directing astern **:** signaling motion astern

asternal \(ˈ)ā+ˈ-\ adj [[2]a- + sternal] anat **:** not sternal: **a :** unattached to the sternum ⟨the floating ribs are ~⟩ **b :** having no sternum

astero- — see ASTER-

as·tero·calamites \ˌastə(ˌ)rō+\ [NL, fr. aster- + Calamites] syn of ARCHAEOCALAMITES

[1]**as·tero·coc·cus** \ˌastərōˈkäkəs\ [NL, fr. aster- + -coccus] syn of MYCOPLASMA

[2]**asterococcus** \"\ n, pl **asterococ·ci** \-äˌkī, -äkē, -äkˌsī, -äksē\ [NL, fr. aster- + -coccus] **1 :** an organism of the genus Mycoplasma **2 :** a disk-shaped developmental form of an asterococcus

[1]**as·ter·oid** \ˈastəˌrȯid, ˈaas-\ n -s [Gk asteroeidēs starlike] **1 :** a celestial body resembling a star in appearance; specif **:** one of thousands of small planets most of which have orbits between those of Mars and Jupiter, approximating on the average the orbit at 2.8 astronomical units assigned by Bode's law, and ranging in size from a fraction of a mile in largest dimension to nearly 500 miles in diameter — called also minor planet, planetoid **2** [NL Asteroidea] **:** one of the Asteroidea **:** STARFISH

[2]**asteroid** \"\ adj [ISV, fr. Gk asteroeidēs starlike, fr. aster-, astēr star + -oeidēs -oid] **1 :** like a star **2** [NL Asteroidea] **:** of or resembling a starfish **3** [NL Aster + E -oid] **:** resembling or belonging to the genus Aster

as·ter·oi·dal \ˌ==ˈrȯidᵊl\ adj **:** of or belonging to an asteroid or the asteroids

as·ter·oi·dea \ˌ==ˈrȯidēə\ n pl, cap [NL, fr. Asterias + -oidea] **:** the class of echinoderms comprising the starfishes, all being unattached, having (1) a star-shaped or pentagonal body, the rays or arms (usu. 5 in number) hollow and containing prolongations of the coelom and alimentary and other viscera, (2) a skeleton of calcareous plates and ossicles somewhat loosely united, often allowing the arms great freedom of movement, and (3) a mouth on the lower surface without jaws or teeth, an aboral madreporic plate, and the anus often wanting or functionless (undigested matter being thrown out at the mouth), and moving by means of the arms or of long spines on the sides of the arms or by rows of tube feet that occur in a furrow on the lower surface of each arm — **as·ter·oi·de·an** \ˌ==ˈ==dēən\ adj or n

as·tero·lecanium \ˌastə(ˌ)rō+\ n, cap [NL, fr. aster- + Lecanium] **:** a large genus of chiefly tropical scales including some that are pests of oaks and ornamental plantings in California — compare PIT SCALE

as·ter·ol·e·pis \ˌastəˈräləpəs\ n, cap [NL, fr. aster- + -lepis] **:** a genus of Middle Devonian ostracoderms (subclass Antiarcha) with greatly developed pectoral spines

as·tero·phyl·li·tes \ˌastə(ˌ)rōfəˈlīd·ēz\ n, cap [NL, fr. aster- + Gk phyllon leaf + NL -ites -ite — more at BLADE] **:** a form genus of fossil plants abundantly represented in the coal measures, having a starlike disposition of the leaves, and considered now to be branches of Calamites

as·tero·spon·dy·li \-ˈspändəˌlī\ n pl, cap [NL, fr. aster- + -spondyli] in some classifications **:** an order of Elasmobranchii comprising forms having asterospondylic vertebrae and including most of the recent sharks and dogfishes

as·tero·spon·dyl·ic \ˌ==(ˌ)=ˌspänˈdilik\ or **as·tero·spon·dy·lous** \-ˈspändələs\ adj [aster- + spondylic, spondylous] **1 :** having the vertebral centra strengthened by longitudinal calcified plates radiating outward from a central cylinder surrounding the notochord — compare CYCLOSPONDYLIC **2** [NL Asterospondyli + E -ic or -ous] **:** of or relating to the Asterospondyli

as·tero·the·ca \ˌ==(ˌ)=ˈthēkə\ n, cap [NL, fr. aster- + -theca] **:** a form genus of Paleozoic fossil ferns based on the sporangia which are grouped in a circular sorus

as·ter·oxy·la·ce·ae \ˌastəˌräksəˈlāsēˌē\ n pl, cap [NL, fr. Asteroxylon, type genus (fr. aster- + -xylon) + -aceae] **:** a family of Paleozoic plants (order Psilophytales) having a xylem that is star-shaped in cross section

as·ter·oxy·lon \-ˈräksəˌlän\ n, cap [NL, fr. aster- + -xylon] **:** a genus of Paleozoic plants (family Asteroxylaceae) having a single star-shaped vascular strand in the shoot

as·tero·zoa \ˌastərəˈzōə\ n pl, cap [NL, fr. aster- + -zoa] in some classifications **:** a subphylum of echinoderms comprising the starfishes (Asteroidea) and brittle stars (Ophiuroidea)

aster purple n **:** a deep purplish red that is bluer and deeper than American beauty, redder and duller than magenta (sense 2a), and bluer and less strong than hollyhock

aster ray n **:** one of the rays making up an aster (sense 3)

asters pl of ASTER

-asters pl of -ASTER

aster yellows n pl **:** a widespread virus disease of the aster and many other plants characterized by yellowing and dwarfing and a greenish tinge to the flower heads and transmitted by leafhoppers

asthen- or **astheno-** comb form [Gk, fr. asthenēs weak, fr. a- [2]a- + -sthenēs (fr. sthenos strength); perh. akin to Skt saghnoti he takes upon himself, is a match for] **:** weak ⟨asthenopia⟩ **:** weakness ⟨asthenology⟩

as·the·nia \asˈthēnēə, əs- also ˌasthəˈnēə\ n -s [NL, fr. Gk astheneia, fr. asthenēs + -ia] **:** lack or loss of strength **:** DEBILITY **:** deficient vitality

as·then·ic \(ˈ)asˈthenik, əsˈth-\ adj [fr. Gk asthenikos, fr. astheneia + -ikos -ic] **1 :** belonging to or characterized by asthenia **:** WEAK, DEBILITATED **2 :** characterized by slender build and slight muscular development **:** ECTOMORPHIC — compare ATHLETIC, PYKNIC

as·the·no·bi·o·sis \ˈasthə(ˌ)nōˌbīˈōsəs\ n, pl **asthenobio·ses** \-ōˌsēz\ [NL, fr. asthen- + -biosis] **:** a state of reduced activity that precedes pupation in the larvae of certain insects

as·then·o·lith \asˈthenəˌlith, əs-\ n -s [asthen- + -lith] **:** the material in the asthenosphere

as·the·no·pia \ˌasthəˈnōpēə\ n -s [NL, fr. asthen- + -opia] **:** weakness or rapid fatigue of the eyes often accompanied by pain and headache — **as·the·nop·ic** \ˌ==ˈnäpik, -ōp-\ adj

as·theno·sphere \asˈthenəˌsfi(ə)r, əsˈth-\ n -s [asthen- + -sphere] **:** a hypothetical earth-circling shell or zone which lies from 30 to 75 miles below the earth's surface and within which the material not necessarily molten is believed to yield more readily to persistent stresses than the rigid crust above or the solid nucleus below — called also tectosphere, zone of mobility, zone of weakness; compare SIMA, ZONE OF FLOW

asth·ma \ˈazmə, Brit usu & US rarely ˈasmə\ n -s [alter. (influenced by Gk asthma) of earlier asma, fr. ME, fr. ML, modif. of Gk asthma; perh. akin to Gk aēnai to blow — more at WIND] **:** labored breathing either continuous or paroxysmal accompanied by wheezing, a sense of constriction in the chest, and often by attacks of coughing or gasping caused by conditions that interfere with the normal inflow and outflow of air in the lungs (as swelling of the mucous membrane of the bronchi or constriction of the bronchial or bronchiolar walls with resultant narrowing of the lumen) — see BRONCHIAL ASTHMA; compare CARDIAC ASTHMA

asthma herb n **:** a tropical weed (Euphorbia hirta) reputed in Australia to be effective in the treatment of asthma

asthma paper n **:** paper impregnated with saltpeter whose fumes when burned are sometimes inhaled as an alleviative for asthma

[1]**asth·mat·ic** \(ˈ)azˈmad·ik, -atik, -ēk\ also **asth·mat·i·cal** \-əkəl, -ēk-\ adj [L asthmaticus, fr. Gk asthmatikos, fr. asthmat-, asthma + -ikos -ic] **1 :** caused by or affected with asthma ⟨an ~ cough⟩ ⟨an ~ patient⟩ **:** relating to asthma **2 :** suggesting the breathing of an asthmatic person **:** WHEEZY ⟨traveling in ancient and ~ cars⟩ **:** PANTING, SHORT-BREATHED ⟨the coarse tone and ~ phrasing of Bach's oboe —Ralph Vaughan Williams⟩ — **asth·mat·i·cal·ly** \-ək(ə)lē, -ēk-, -li\ adv

[2]**asthmatic** \"\ n -s **:** an asthmatic person

asthmatic cigarette n **:** a medicated cigarette smoked for the relief of spasmodic asthma

asth·ma·toid \ˈazməˌtȯid\ adj [ISV asthmat- (fr. Gk asthmat-, arthma) + -oid] **:** resembling asthma ⟨an ~ wheeze⟩

asthma weed n **:** INDIAN TOBACCO

asth·mo·gen·ic \ˌazməˈjenik\ adj [ISV asthmo- (fr. asthma) + -genic] **:** causing asthmatic attacks

asthore \əsˈthȯr\ n -s [IrGael a stōr oh treasure, fr. a oh + stōr treasure] Irish **:** TREASURE — a term of endearment

as though conj **:** as if ⟨the Charter makes "aggression" synonymous with "wrongdoing" but drops the matter there, as though everyone understood the nature of sin —E.B.White⟩

as·ti·chous \ˈastəkəs\ adj [[2]a- + -stichous] bot **:** not arranged in rows

as·tig·mat \ˈastigˌmat, əˈstig-\ n -s [short for astigmatic] **:** an astigmatic person

as·tig·mat·ic \ˌastigˈmad·ik, -tēg-, -atik, -ēk\ also **as·tig·mat·i·cal** \-əkəl, -ēk-\ adj [[2]a- + Gk stigmat-, stigma spot, mark + E -ic, -ical] **1 :** affected with or relating to astigmatism ⟨~ eyes⟩ **:** correcting astigmatism ⟨~ lenses⟩ **2 :** having or showing an inability or unwillingness to observe, discriminate, or evaluate closely or in accordance with fact ⟨~, flabby, and bemused writing about the Civil War —Bernard De Voto⟩ ⟨an ~ fanaticism, a disregard for the facts —N.Y. Herald Tribune⟩ — **as·tig·mat·i·cal·ly** \-ək(ə)lē, -ēk-, -li\ adv

astig·ma·tism \əˈstigməˌtizəm, aˈ-\ n -s [astigmatic + -ism] **1** physics **:** a defect of an optical system (as a lens or mirror) in consequence of which rays from a single point of an object fail to meet in a single focal point thus causing the image of a point to be drawn out into a line and the images of lines having a certain direction to be less distinct than those of lines transverse to that direction **2 :** a defect of vision due to astigmatism of the refractive system of the eye commonly caused by irregular conformation of the cornea **3 :** distorted mental perception suggestive of the blurred vision of a person affected with astigmatism of the eyes **:** want of true discernment or appreciation esp. when resulting from prejudice or deliberate obtuseness ⟨foreign travelers . . . whose subjective observations were highly colored by their own mental ~, provincialism, and an absurd moral rectitude —E.J.Simmons⟩ ⟨swayed . . . by his ~ and his hates —H.L.Ickes⟩

astig·ma·tiz·er \-ˌtīzə(r)\ n -s **:** a device used for drawing out a point of light into a line (as in a range finder)

astig·mia \-mēə\ n -s [NL, fr. [2]a- + Gk stigma spot, mark + NL -ia — more at STIGMA] **:** ASTIGMATISM

as·tig·mom·e·ter \ˌa(ˌ)stigˈmämad·ə(r), ˌastēg-\ or **astig·ma·tom·e·ter** \əˌstigməˈtämad·ə(r), aˌs-\ n -s [ISV astigmo-, astigmato- (fr. astigmatism) + -meter; orig. formed as F astigmomètre] **:** an apparatus for measuring the degree of astigmatism — **as·tig·mom·e·try** \ˌaˌstigˈmämətrē, -i\ n -ES

astil·be \əˈstil(ˌ)bē\ n [NL, fr. [2]a- + Gk stilbē, fem. of stilbos glistening — more at STILBUM] **1** cap **:** a genus of chiefly Asiatic perennials (family Saxifragaceae) with ample ternately compound leaves and large terminal panicles composed of spikes and small white flowers — see FALSE GOATSBEARD **2** -s **:** any plant of the genus Astilbe ⟨the feathery charm of the ~s⟩

[1]**astipulate** vb -ED/-ING/-S [L astipulatus, past part. of astipulari, fr. ad- + stipulari to stipulate — more at STIPULATE] vi, obs **:** AGREE, ASSENT ~ vt, obs **:** to agree to — **astipulation** n -s

[2]**astipulate** \(ˈ)ā+ˈ-\ adj [[2]a- + stipulate] bot **:** EXSTIPULATE

astir \əˈstər, +V -ər-; əˈstə, +V -ər- also -ōr\ adj [prob. alter. of Sc asteer, fr. [1]a- + steer, var. of stir] **1 :** STIRRING **:** in a state of activity or motion ⟨a fresh and more vigorous spirit was plainly ~ —Van Wyck Brooks⟩ ⟨hundreds of men moved restlessly, so that the whole hill was ~ —Kenneth Roberts⟩ — often used with with ⟨streams ~ with trout⟩ ⟨the ship was ~ with agitated passengers —Ngaio Marsh⟩ **2 :** out of bed **:** UP

as·tite \əˈstīt\ adv [ME, fr. as + tite] dial Brit **:** as soon **:** RATHER

as to prep [ME, fr. as + to] **:** with reference to **:** in regard to **:** as regards: **a :** ABOUT, CONCERNING, RESPECTING ⟨a matter as to which opinions might differ⟩ ⟨stopped short of their objective as to production⟩ ⟨felt somewhat at a loss as to how to begin —Life⟩ ⟨as to my own views, they will be mentioned later⟩ ⟨uncertain as to what to do next⟩ **b :** according to **:** BY ⟨classified and graded as to size and color⟩

as·to·gen·ic \ˌastəˈjenik\ adj **:** relating to or marked by astogeny

as·tog·e·ny \aˈstäjənē\ n -ES [prob. fr. Gk astos inhabitant of a city (fr. asty city) + E -geny] **:** a more or less marked change in size or form shown by all the zooids in colonial animals (as graptolites) as the colony grows older

astomatal \(ˈ)ā+ˈ-\ adj [[2]a- + stomatal] **:** without stomata — used of green plants or their parts ⟨an ~ leaf⟩

astomatous \(ˈ)ā+ˈ-\ adj [[2]a- + stomatous] **:** having no mouth; esp **:** lacking a cytostome ⟨~ ciliates⟩

as·to·mous \ˈastəməs\ adj [[2]a- + -stomous] **1 :** ASTOMATAL **2 :** having a capsule that bursts irregularly and is not dehiscent by an operculum — used of certain mosses

as·ton dark space \ˈastən-\ n, usu cap A [after Francis W. Aston †1945 Eng. chemist and physicist] **:** a nonluminous layer between the cathode surface and the cathode glow in a vacuum tube

astonied *past of* ASTONY

as·ton·ish \ə'stänish, -ēsh, *esp in pres part* -əsh\ *vt* -ED/-ING/-ES [prob. fr. *astony* + *-ish* (as in *abolish*)] **1** *obs* **:** to render senseless (as by a blow) **:** STUN, PARALYZE, DEADEN ⟨enough, Captain; you have ~*ed* him —Shak.⟩ **2** *obs* **:** to stupefy the mind of **:** BEWILDER, DAZE, CONFUSE ⟨had his wits ~*ed* with sorrow —Philip Sidney⟩ ⟨blind, ~*ed*, and struck with superstition as with a planet —John Milton⟩ **3** *obs* **:** to strike with sudden fear or dismay ⟨that with the very shaking of their chains they may ~ these fell-lurking curs —Shak.⟩ **4 :** to strike with a sudden sense of surprise or wonder esp. through something unexpected or difficult to accept as true or reasonable **:** surprise greatly **:** AMAZE ⟨was ~*ed* to find a thick forest where in 1915 I had mowed thick grass with a scythe —S.H. Holbrook⟩ ⟨~*ed* by the vastness and majesty of the cathedral⟩ ⟨a gross desire to ~ his friends with his sudden wealth⟩ ⟨the customs of non-European groups were treated as curios with which to ~ the uninformed —Ralph Linton⟩ **syn** see SURPRISE

astonishable *adj, obs* **:** ASTONISHING

as·ton·ished·ly \-shtlē\ *adv* **:** in an astonished manner **:** with astonishment

astonishing *adj* **:** causing or tending to cause astonishment esp. by surpassing expectation or ready belief **:** SURPRISING, AMAZING ⟨the longbow and the arrow which whizzed from it with ~ power —Hardiman Scott⟩ ⟨an ~ success story⟩ ⟨an ~ eye for seeing sermons in stones —C.D.Lewis⟩ — **as·ton·ish·ing·ly** *adv* — **as·ton·ish·ing·ness** *n* -ES

as·ton·ish·ment \ə'stänishmənt, -ēsh-\ *n* -S **1 :** the state of being astonished or of one who is astonished: as **a** *obs* **:** PARALYSIS, NUMBNESS **b** *obs* **:** STUPOR, BEWILDERMENT **c** *archaic* **:** DISMAY, CONSTERNATION ⟨~ though not in itself fear is nevertheless a good stage towards it —T.L.Peacock⟩ **d :** great surprise or wonder **:** AMAZEMENT ⟨saw ~ giving place to horror on the faces of the people —H.G.Wells⟩ ⟨children watching with ~ and delight⟩ ⟨in his first ~ he had stopped dead short —Joseph Conrad⟩ ⟨sincere women sometimes express their ~ over the exaggerated sense of romance . . . which many men show —Theodor Reik⟩ **2 :** one that astonishes; *esp* **:** a cause of amazement or wonder ⟨a never-ending ~ to his parents⟩ ⟨my first meeting with Oscar Wilde was an ~ —W.B.Yeats⟩ ⟨the book races on from one ~ to the next —Dan Wickenden⟩

as·tony \ə'stänē\ *vt* -ED/-ING/-S [ME *astonien*, alter. of *astonen*, modif. of OF *estoner*, fr. (assumed) VL *extonare*, fr. L *ex-* + *tonare* to thunder — more at THUNDER] **1** *obs* **:** STUN, PARALYZE **2** *archaic* **:** DAZE, DISMAY, AMAZE ⟨then Daniel was *astonied* for one hour —Dan 4:19 (AV)⟩ ⟨I rent my garment and my mantle . . . and sat down *astonied* —Ezra 9:3 (AV)⟩ ⟨and I *astonied* fell and could not pray —Elizabeth B. Browning⟩

astoop \ə'-\ *adj* [*¹a-* + *stoop* (act of stooping)] **:** in an inclined position **:** TILTED, STOOPING

¹as·to·ri·an \a'stōrēən, ə'-, -ōr-\ *n* -S *usu cap* [*Astoria*, former trading post in Oregon (now site of Astoria, Oregon) founded 1811 by John J. Astor †1848 Am. merchant + E *-an*] **:** a fur trader of the Astoria trading post

²astorian \"\ *adj, usu cap* **:** relating to the Astoria trading post or to its activities

¹as·tound \ə'staủnd\ *adj* [ME *astouned, astoned*, fr. past part. of *astounen, astonen* to stun, astound — more at ASTONY] *archaic* **:** ASTOUNDED ⟨dizzy and ~, as sudden ruin yawned around —Sir Walter Scott⟩

²astound \"\ *vb* -ED/-ING/-S [partly fr. ¹*astound*, partly backformation fr. *astounded*, fr. ME, alter. of *astouned*] **1** *obs* **:** STUN, STUPEFY **2 :** to stun with bewildered or incredulous wonder **:** overwhelm with astonishment or amazement ⟨Constance was ~*ed* at her sister's self-control, which entirely passed her comprehension —Arnold Bennett⟩ ⟨it was naval disasters or failures that ~*ed* and angered the man in the street —D.W.Brogan⟩ **syn** see SURPRISE

astounding *adj* **:** calculated to astound **:** causing or capable of causing wonder and surprise in high degree **:** AMAZING ⟨the look of a man who has come up against ~ things but always with the determination not to be astounded —Mary Austin⟩ ⟨a fascinating account of an ~ epoch⟩ ⟨an ~ recovery⟩ — **astound·ing·ly** *adv*

as·tound·ment \-n(d)mənt\ *n* -S *archaic* **1 :** the state of being astounded **:** AMAZEMENT, ASTONISHMENT

astr- *or* **astro-** *comb form* [ME *astro-*, fr. OF, fr. L *astr-, astro-*, fr. Gk, fr. *astron* star — more at STAR] **1 :** star ⟨*astr*oid⟩ ⟨*astro*meter⟩ **:** the heavens ⟨*astro*graphy⟩ ⟨*astro*nautics⟩ **:** astronomical ⟨*astro*physics⟩ **2 :** astrological ⟨*astro*diagnosis⟩ **:** astrological and ⟨*astro*medical⟩ **3 :** aster in cells ⟨*astro*sphere⟩

astrachan *often cap, var of* ASTRAKHAN

¹astrad·dle \ə'-\ *adv* [*¹a-* + *straddle* (v.)] **:** ASTRIDE ⟨sit ~ on the horse⟩ **:** on or above and extending onto both sides ⟨the battle was fought ~ of the road⟩

²astraddle \"\ *prep* **:** with one leg on each side of **:** ASTRIDE ⟨seated ~ a horse⟩ ⟨with one foot in either hemisphere, ~ longitude 0 —C.S.Forester⟩

¹as·trae·an \a'strēən\ *adj* [NL *Astraea*, genus of corals (fr. Gk *astraios* starry, fr. *astr-, astēr* star) + E *-an* — more at STAR] **:** of or relating to the star corals

²astraean \"\ *n* -S **:** STAR CORAL

as·traeo·spon·gia \a¦strē(,)ō'spənjēə, -pän-\ *n, cap* [NL, fr. *astraeo-* (fr. Gk *astraios* starry, fr. *aster-, astēr* star) + *-spongia* — more at STAR] **:** a genus of saucer-shaped Silurian fossil sponges having 6-rayed stellate spicules and important as Paleozoic index fossils

as·tra·gal \'astrəgəl\ *n* -S [L *astragalus*, fr. Gk *astragalos* vertebra, anklebone, molding, milk vetch; prob. akin to Gk *osteon* bone — more at OSSEOUS] **1 :** a small convex molding of rounded surface generally from half to three quarters of a circle: as **a :** a projecting strip on the edge of folding doors **b :** BAR 1d(3) — compare BEAD 5 **2 :** a molding encircling a cannon near the muzzle **3** [prob. fr. NL *astragalus*, fr. Gk *astragalos*] **:** TALUS

astragal- *or* **astragalo-** *comb form* [Gk, fr. *astragalos*] **1 :** dice ⟨*astragalo*mancy⟩ **2** [NL *astragalus*, fr. Gk *astragalos*] **:** a the bone astragalus ⟨*astragal*ectomy⟩ **b :** astragalar and ⟨*astragalo*calcaneal⟩

as·trag·a·lar \ə'stragələ(r), a'-\ *adj* **:** of or relating to the astragalus

as·trag·a·lo·man·cy \-lō,man(t)sē\ *n* -ES [*astragal-* + *-mancy*] **:** divination by means of small bones or dice

as·trag·a·lus \-ləs\ *n* [prob. NL, fr. Gk *astragalos*] **1** *pl* **astraga·li** \-,lī, -,lē\ **:** one of the proximal bones of the tarsus of the higher vertebrates supposed to represent the united tibiale and intermedium of many lower vertebrates — usu. called in man *talus* or *anklebone;* see TALUS **2** *cap* [NL, fr. L, milk vetch, fr. Gk *astragalos*] **:** a large genus of herbs and shrubs (family Leguminosae) characterized by the narrow standard of the corolla, the blunt keel, and the fleshy or papery uninflated pod — see LOCOWEED, MILK VETCH, TRAGACANTH **3** *pl* **astragali** *or* **astragaluses** [L, fr. Gk *astragalos*] **:** ASTRAGAL 1

astrain \ə'-\ *adj* [*¹a-* + *strain* (v.)] **:** STRAINING ⟨with all his senses ~, afraid to move a step —Arnold Bennett⟩

as·tra·kan·ite *or* **as·tra·khan·ite** \'astrəkə,nīt\ *n* -S [G *astrakanit*, irreg. fr. *Astrakhan*, region in U.S.S.R., its locality + G *-it* -ite] **:** a variety of the mineral bloedite

¹as·tra·khan \'astrəkən, 'aas-, -kan, -,kaa(ə)n\ *adj, usu cap* [fr. *Astrakhan*, U.S.S.R.] **:** of or from the city or region of Astrakhan, U.S.S.R. **:** of the kind or style prevalent in Astrakhan

²astrakhan \"\ *also* **as·tra·chan** \"\ *n* -S *often cap* **1 :** the fur or skin of a karakul lamb of Russian breeding — now seldom used because of confusion resulting from varied and conflicting application within the fur trade **2 :** a lustrous cloth of wool or of cotton and wool made with a curled and looped pile often cut to imitate astrakhan fur

¹as·tral \'astrəl, 'aas-\ *adj* [LL *astralis*, fr. L *astrum* star (fr. Gk *astron*) + *-alis* -al — more at STAR] **1 a :** of or relating to the stars ⟨~ myths⟩ ⟨~ imagery⟩ **:** coming or thought of as coming from the stars ⟨~ beams⟩ ⟨~ influences⟩ **b :** consisting of stars **:** like stars ⟨~ showers⟩ **:** STARRY ⟨an ~ gleam⟩ **2** *biol* **:** of or relating to an aster ⟨~ rays⟩ **3** *theosophy* **:** consisting of, belonging to, or being a supersensible substance supposed to be next above the tangible world in refinement **4 :** suggestive of the remoteness of the stars (as from common concerns or values): as **a :** VISIONARY, UNWORLDLY ⟨an ~ and most impractical thinker⟩ **b :** EXALTED ⟨the most ~ circles of society⟩ — **as·tral·ly** \-əlē, -li\ *adv*

²astral \"\ *n* -S **1 :** ASTRAL LAMP **2** *theosophy* **:** an astral body or spirit

astral body *n, theosophy* **:** a subtle counterpart of the physical human body accompanying but not usu. separated from it in life and surviving its death — compare KAMARUPA

astral crown *n* **1 :** CELESTIAL CROWN **2 :** a figure of a coronet having along the rim 8 low points from every other one of which arises a 6-pointed star between 2 wings — used in heraldry esp. to symbolize association with aviation

astral lamp *n* **:** an Argand lamp so constructed that no interruption of the light upon the table is made by the flattened ring-shaped reservoir containing the oil

astral spirit *n* **1 :** one of various celestial intelligences (as the souls of dead men, demons, or spirits originating in fire) formerly thought to live in and control the movements of stars and planets **2** *theosophy* **:** a spirit composed of astral substance

astrand \ə'-\ *adj* [*¹a-* + *strand* (v.)] **:** STRANDED

as·tran·tia \ə'stranch(ē)ə, -ntēə\ *n, cap* [NL] **:** a small genus of Eurasian herbs (family Umbelliferae) having aromatic roots, palmate leaves, and showy flowers in starlike bracted umbels — see MASTERWORT b

as·tra·po·there \'astrəpō,thi(ə)r\ *n* -S [NL *Astrapotheria*] **:** an animal or fossil of the Astrapotheria

as·tra·po·the·ria \,ˌˌ'thirēə\ *n pl, cap* [NL, fr. Gk *astrapo-* (fr. *astrapē* lightning) + NL *-theria;* akin to Gk *aster-, astēr* star — more at STAR] **:** an order of extinct So. American ungulates that may have diverged from primitive notoungulates in the Paleocene, flourished in the Oligocene and Miocene, and were distinguished by large size with marked disproportion between the powerful forequarters and feebly developed hindquarters, cowlike incisors accompanied by immense persistently growing canines and huge molars, and probably an elephantine proboscis

astray \ə'strā\ *adv* (*or adj*) [ME *astray, astrayey*, fr. MF *estraié* wandering, masterless, fr. *estraier* to roam about without a master — more at STRAY] **1 :** out of the right way **:** off the right path or route ⟨mark the trail so travelers will not go ~⟩ **:** away from native or familiar surroundings **:** lost or wandering ⟨some circus juggernaut ~ from winter quarters —A.T.Lougee⟩ **2 :** into a wrong or mistaken way of thinking or acting **:** in or into error **:** WRONG ⟨the desire to escape from subjectivity . . . has led some modern philosophers ~ —Bertrand Russell⟩ ⟨his calculations were ~⟩ **:** away from a proper or desirable course or development ⟨originality gone ~, seduced . . . by the mania for novelty —J.L.Lowes⟩ **3 :** wandering in mind or fancy **:** lost in thought ⟨her thoughts had been entirely ~ during . . . family devotions —W.M.Thackeray⟩

astray freight *n* **:** freight marked for destination but separated from the waybill

astre *n* -S [ME *aster, ayster*, fr. MF *astre, aistre* hearth, fr. ML *astracus, ostracus* pavement of potsherds, pavement, fr. Gk *ostrakon* pot, potsherd, hard shell — more at OYSTER] **:** HEARTH, HOME — compare ASTRER

¹astream \ə'-\ *adj* [*¹a-* + *stream*, v.] **:** STREAMING ⟨glorious the northern lights ~ —Christopher Smart⟩

²astream \"\ *adv* [*¹a-* + *stream*, n.] **:** in line with the stream ⟨swinging ~ of the tide⟩

astrer *or* **astrier** *n* -S [*astrer* fr. *astre* + *-er; astrier*, alter. of *astrer*] *old English law* **:** one belonging to the hearth or home — used of various persons having certain rights or disabilities by reason of their residence or holding of tenements

ast·rex \'a,streks\ *n* -ES *usu cap* [blend of *Astrakhan* and *rex*] **:** a rex rabbit of a variety characterized by curled or wavy fur that suggests broadtail

as·trict \ə'strikt\ *vt* -ED/-ING/-S [L *astrictus*, past part. of *astringere* to bind fast] **1 :** to bind up **:** CONFINE, CONSTRICT; *sometimes* **:** CONSTIPATE **2 :** to bind by a moral or legal obligation **:** CONSTRAIN, RESTRICT, LIMIT ⟨trade unions were illegal and peasants were ~*ed* to the soil⟩

as·tric·tion \ə'strikshən\ *n* -S [ML *astriction-, astrictio* restriction, obligation, fr. L, astringency, fr. *astrictus* (past part. of *astringere*) + *-ion-, -io* -ion] **1 :** the act of binding or the state of being bound **:** CONSTRICTION, RESTRICTION **2** *obs* **:** ASTRINGENCY

as·tric·tive \ə'striktiv\ *adj or n* **:** ASTRINGENT — **as·tric·tive·ly** *adv*

¹astride \ə'-\ *adv* [*¹a-* + *stride* (n.)] **1 :** with one leg on each side ⟨women seldom rode ~⟩ **2 :** with the legs stretched wide apart ⟨standing ~ with arms folded⟩

²astride \"\ *prep* **1 :** on or above and with one leg on each side of **:** BESTRIDING ⟨~ a horse⟩ **:** STRADDLING ⟨her little baby ~ her hips —William Beebe⟩ **2 :** placed or lying on both sides of ⟨established frontier provinces along or ~ the river —W.G.East⟩ ⟨an enemy roadblock ~ his regiment's supply route —*N. Y. Times*⟩ **3 :** extending or stretching over or across (as from one limit to another) **:** SPANNING, BRIDGING ⟨no single individual stands more firmly ~ the history of England from 1906 onwards —*Times Lit. Supp.*⟩ ⟨stands ~ two worlds — our own and the utterly alien world of the Greenland Eskimos —Jeannette Mirsky⟩

as·trild \'a,strild\ *n* -S [Afrik] **:** a southern African waxbill (*Estrilda astrild*) often kept as a cage bird

as·tringe \ə'strinj\ *vt* -ED/-ING/-S [L *astringere, adstringere* to bind fast, fr. *ad-* + *stringere* to bind tight — more at STRAIN] **:** to bind together **:** cause (tissue) to draw together **:** CONSTRICT, COMPRESS

as·trin·gence \ə'strinjən(t)s\ *n* -S **:** ASTRINGENCY ⟨the first tartness of fall, the ~ of winter —Marc Brandel⟩

as·trin·gen·cy \-jənsē, -si\ *n* -ES **:** the quality or state of being astringent ⟨pungency is a sensation of the gums . . . a roughness or ~ in the mouth —W.H.Ukers⟩ ⟨the soldier's traditional bluntness, and also an ~ of phrases —*Saturday Rev.*⟩

¹as·trin·gent \-jənt\ *adj* [prob. fr. MF, fr. L *astringent-, astringens*, pres. part. of *astringere*] **1 :** having the property of drawing together the soft organic tissues **:** CONTRACTING, CONSTRICTING ⟨~ cosmetic lotions⟩ ⟨the air was so ~ with pine scent that it tightened the nostrils —Grace Campbell⟩: **a :** tending to shrink mucous membranes or raw or exposed tissues **:** checking discharge (as of serum or mucus) **:** STYPTIC **b :** tending to pucker the tissues of the mouth ⟨~ fruits and wines⟩ ⟨green persimmons are strongly ~⟩ ⟨he remembered the musty ~ taste of his own cup of tea —Elinor Wylie⟩ **2 :** suggestive of an astringent effect upon tissue **:** free of slackness or expansiveness **:** SEVERE, AUSTERE ⟨his own writing has an ~ quality which often matches the sharp, clear outlines of the Greek landscape —*Spectator*⟩ **:** SHARP, TONIC ⟨there was something ~ and bracing about that man's mind —William McFee⟩ **:** STERN, STRICT ⟨made enemies by his ~ honesty —*Time*⟩ — **as·trin·gent·ly** *adv*

²astringent \"\ *n* -S **:** an astringent agent or substance: as **a :** a medicine for checking the discharge of mucus or serum by causing shrinkage of tissue **b :** a liquid cosmetic for cleansing the skin and contracting the pores

astringent bitters *n pl* **:** bitters containing tannin but little aromatic oil

astringent clay *n* **:** a clay containing an astringent salt (as alum)

astringent root *n* **:** SPOTTED CRANESBILL

as·tro- *in pronunciations below*, ¦ˌ(,)ˌ = ¦a(,)strō *or* ¦aa- *or* -,strə\ — see ASTR-

as·tro·blast \'ˌˌ,blast\ *n* -S [*astr-* + *-blast*] *anat* **:** a primordial astrocyte — **as·tro·blas·tic** \¦ˌˌ¦blastik\ *adj*

as·tro·car·y·um \,ˌˌ'ka(a)rēəm\ *n, cap* [NL, fr. *astr-* + *-caryum* (fr. Gk *karyon* nut); prob. fr. the radiating arrangement of the pores on the kernel of the fruit — more at CAREEN] **:** a genus of very spiny pinnate-leaved tropical American palms (family Palmae), some with edible fruit, others grown for ornament

as·tro·chronological \¦ˌ(,)ˌ+\ *adj* [*astr-* + *chronological*] **:** relating to the chronology of heavenly bodies

as·tro·compass \'ˌˌ+,-\ *n* -S [*astr-* + *compass*] **:** a device that by mechanically solving the astronomical triangle reveals the bearing of any recognized celestial body to a navigator and is used esp. near the earth's magnetic pole where magnetic compasses are not reliable

as·tro·cyte \'astrə,sīt\ *n* -S [ISV *astr-* + *-cyte*] *anat* **:** a star-shaped cell: as **a :** any comparatively large much-branched neuroglial cell **:** MOSSY CELL, SPIDER CELL **b :** OSTEOBLAST

as·tro·cy·to·ma \,ˌˌsī'tōmə\ *n, pl* **astrocytomas** \-məz\ *or* **astrocyto·ma·ta** \-məd·ə\ [NL, fr. ISV *astrocyte* + NL *-oma*] **:** a nerve-tissue tumor composed of astrocytes

as·tro·diagnosis \¦ˌˌ+\ *n* [*astr-* + *diagnosis*] **:** diagnosis by means of horoscopy and palmistry

as·tro·dome \'astrə,dōm\ *n* -S [ISV *astr-* + *dome*] **:** a transparent dome-shaped projection in the upper surface of an aircraft from within which the navigator makes celestial observations

as·tro·gate \-,gāt\ *vb* -ED/-ING/-S [*astr-* + *-gate* (as in *navigate*)] *vt* **:** to guide (as a spaceship or rocket) in interplanetary flight ~ *vi* **:** to navigate in space

as·tro·ga·tion \,ˌˌ'gāshən\ *n* -S [*astr-* + *-gation* (as in *navigation*)] **:** the science or art of navigating a spaceship **:** space navigation

as·tro·ga·tor \'ˌˌ,gād·ə(r)\ *n* -S [*astr-* + *-gator* (as in *navigator*)] **1 :** one that is qualified in the science or skilled in the art of astrogation **2 :** the pilot of a spaceship

as·trog·lia \a'sträglēə, ,astrə'glīə\ *n* -S [NL, fr. *astro-* (as in ISV *astrocyte*) + *-glia* (as in *neuroglia*)] **:** neuroglia tissue composed of astrocytes

as·trog·no·sy \a'strägnəsē\ *n* -ES [*astr-* + *-gnosy*] **:** a branch of astronomy having to do with the fixed stars

as·tro·gon·ic \¦ˌˌ *at* ASTRO- + ¦gänik\ *adj* **:** of or relating to astrogony

as·trog·o·ny \a'strägənē\ *n* -ES [*astr-* + *-gony*] **:** stellar cosmogony

as·tro·graph \'astrō,graf\ *n* -S [ISV *astr-* + *-graph*] **1 :** a photographic telescope designed for use in mapping the heavens **2 :** a now little used navigational instrument for projecting star-altitude curves from film directly onto a Mercator chart of proper scale

as·tro·graph·ic \¦ˌˌ¦grafik\ *adj* **:** relating to or used in astrography ⟨~ camera⟩

as·trog·ra·phy \a'strägrəfē\ *n* -ES [*astr-* + *-graphy*] **:** description or mapping of the heavens

¹as·troid \'a,strȯid\ *adj* [Gk *astroeidēs* starlike, fr. *astr-* + *-oeidēs* -oid] **:** shaped like a star

²astroid \"\ *n* -S [*astr-* + *-oid*] **:** a hypocycloid of four cusps, the radius of the rolling circle being one fourth that of the fixed circle

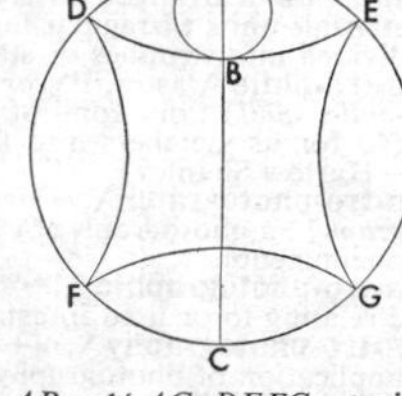

AB = ¼ *AC; DEFG* astroid

astroite *n* -S [L *astroites* asteriated gem, fr. (assumed) Gk *astroitēs*, fr. Gk *astron* star + *-itēs* -ite — more at STAR] *obs* **:** a radiated or star-shaped mineral or fossil

as·tro·labe \'astrə,lāb, 'aas-, *sometimes* -lab *or* -laa(ə)b\ *n* -S [ME *astrolabe, astrilabie*, fr. MF & ML; MF *astrolabe*, fr. ML *astrolabium*, fr. LGk *astrolábion*, dim. of Gk *astrolabos*, fr. *astr-* + *-labos* (fr. *lambanein* to take) — more at LEMMA] **1 :** a compact instrument for observing the positions of the celestial bodies, among the ancients often having been essentially the armillary sphere, in the 18th century a graduated circle for taking altitudes at sea, and now having been superseded by the sextant — see PRISMATIC ASTROLABE **2 :** a stereographic projection of the sphere on the plane of a great circle (as the equator or meridian) **:** PLANISPHERE

as·tro·lab·i·cal \¦ˌˌ¦labəkəl, -āb-\ *adj* **:** of or relating to an astrolabe

as·trol·a·ter \ə'strälad·ə(r)\ *n* -S [fr. *astrolatry*, after E *idolatry: idolater*] **:** one that practices astrolatry

as·trol·a·try \-ə·trē, -i\ *n* -ES [*astr-* + *-latry*] **:** worship of the heavenly bodies

as·tro·lithology \¦astrō+\ *n* -ES [*astr-* + *lithology*] **:** the science dealing with meteoritic stones

as·tol·o·ger \ə'strälaja(r)\ *n* -S [ME, astronomer, prob. modif. (influenced by *-er*) of MF *astrologien*] **1** *obs* **:** one that studies the stars **:** ASTRONOMER **2 :** one that practices astrology

¹as·tro·lo·gian \,astrə'lōj(ē)ən\ *n* -S [ME *astrologien*, fr. MF, fr. *astrologie* astrology] **:** ASTROLOGER

²astrologian *adj, obs* **:** ASTROLOGICAL

as·tro·log·i·cal \¦ˌˌ¦läjəkəl, -ēk-\ *also* **as·tro·log·ic** \-jik, -ēk\ *adj* [*astrological* fr. LL *astrologicus* of astrology (fr. Gk *astrologikos* of astronomy, fr. *astrologos* astronomer + *-ikos* -ic) + E *-al; astrologic* fr. LL *astrologicus*] **:** of or belonging to astrology **:** professing astrology — **as·tro·log·i·cal·ly** \-jək-(ə)lē, -ēk-, -li\ *adv*

as·trol·o·gist \ə'strälajəst\ *n* -S **:** ASTROLOGER

as·trol·o·gis·tic \¦ˌ¦ˌjistik\ *adj* **:** using astrology

as·trol·o·gize \ˌ'ˌˌ,jīz\ *vb* -ED/-ING/-S *vt* **:** to apply astrology to ~ *vi* **:** to study or practice astrology

as·trol·o·gous \-ləgəs\ *adj* [*astrology* + *-ous*] **:** ASTROLOGICAL

as·trol·o·gy \ə'strälajē, -ji\ *n* -ES [ME *astrologie* astronomy, applied astronomy, fr. MF, fr. L *astrologia* astronomy, fr. Gk, fr. *astrologos* astronomer (fr. *astr-* + *logos* speech, discourse) + *-ia* -y — more at LEGEND] **1 :** divination that treats of the supposed influences of the stars upon human affairs and of foretelling terrestrial events by their positions and aspects — see JUDICIAL ASTROLOGY, NATURAL ASTROLOGY; compare HOROSCOPE **2** *obs* **:** ASTRONOMY

as·tro·meteorological \¦astrō+\ *adj* **:** relating to astrometeorology

as·tro·meteorologist \"+\ *n* -S **:** a specialist in astrometeorology

as·tro·meteorology \"+\ *n* -ES [*astr-* + *meteorology*] **:** investigation of the supposed relation between the celestial bodies and the weather

as·tro·met·ric \¦astrō¦me·trik\ *or* **as·tro·met·ri·cal** \-rəkəl\ *adj* **:** of or relating to astrometry

as·trom·e·try \ə'strämə·trē\ *n* -ES [*astr-* + *-metry*] **:** a branch of astronomy that deals with measurements of the celestial bodies, esp. those made to determine their positions and movements

as·tro·naut \'astrə,nȯt, -ät\ *n* -S [*astr-* + *-naut* (as in *aeronaut*)] **1 :** a traveler in interplanetary space **2 :** a student, devotee, or advocate of astronautics

as·tro·nau·ti·cal \¦ˌˌ¦nȯd·əkəl, -nä-\ *adj* [*astr-* + *-nautical* (as in *aeronautical*)] **:** of or belonging to astronautics or to astronauts — **as·tro·nau·ti·cal·ly** \-d·ək(ə)lē\ *adv*

as·tro·nau·tics \¦ˌˌ'ˌd·iks\ *n pl but usu sing in constr* [ISV *astr-* + *-nautics* (as in *aeronautics*)] **1 :** the science that treats of the construction and operation of vehicles designed to travel in interplanetary or interstellar space **2 :** ASTROGATION

as·tro·navigation \¦astrō+\ *n* [*astr-* + *navigation*] **:** CELESTIAL NAVIGATION

as·tron·o·mer \ə'stränəmə(r)\ *n* -S [ME, alter. of *astronomien*, fr. MF, fr. LL *astronomus* (fr. Gk *astronomos*) + MF *-ien* -ian] **1** *obs* **:** ASTROLOGER **2 :** one skilled in astronomy **:** one having a knowledge of the laws and phenomena of the celestial bodies **:** one that makes observations of celestial phenomena

astronomer royal *n, pl* **astronomers royal** *usu cap A&R* **:** the director of one of the royal observatories of Great Britain

astronomer's staff *n* **:** ALMUCANTAR STAFF

as·tro·nom·i·cal \-mәkəl, -ēk-\ *or* **as·tro·nom·ic** \¦astrə¦nämik, ¦aas-, -mēk\ *adj* [*astronomical* fr. L *astronomicus* + E *-al; astronomic* fr. L *astronomicus*, fr. Gk *astronomikos*, fr. *astronomos* astronomer + *-ikos* -ic] **1 :** of or belonging to astronomy **2 :** suggestive of astronomy or of the magnitude of the forces and phenomena treated or of the quantities used by the astronomer ⟨the change must come, if come it did, with ~ slowness, like the cooling of the sun —W.B.Yeats⟩; *esp* **:** enormously or inconceivably large or great in extent or degree ⟨300¹⁶⁰⁰, a truly ~ number —G.A.Miller⟩ ⟨voted ~ sums for rearmament⟩ ⟨inflation on an ~ scale —Bruce Bliven b. 1889⟩

astronomical clock *n* **1 :** a high-precision clock (as a

Riefler clock or a quartz-crystal clock) used in an astronomical observatory to time the movements of celestial bodies or assist in locating them or to serve as the basis of standard time **2 :** a clock with mechanism and dials for indicating various astronomical phenomena (as phases of the moon, movements of the planets)

astronomical coordinate *n* **:** CELESTIAL COORDINATE

astronomical geography *n* **:** the part of mathematical geography that treats of the earth in its relation to the other celestial bodies

astronomical latitude *n* **:** the angle between the plane of the earth's equator and the plumb line (direction of gravity) at a given point on the earth's surface — compare TERRESTRIAL LATITUDE

as·tro·nom·i·cal·ly \-mək(ə)lē, -ēk-, -li\ *adv* **1 :** in accordance with the methods or principles of astronomy **2 :** in or to a degree suggestive of the quantities and measurements used in astronomy ⟨an ~ costly system of government⟩ ⟨prices in this field have risen ~⟩ **:** in or to an astronomical degree

astronomical telescope *n* **:** a telescope that is designed for observing celestial bodies and that requires no image-erecting system — compare TERRESTRIAL TELESCOPE

astronomical time *n* **:** time reckoned in mean solar time units continuously through the 24 hours beginning either at noon or since 1925 at midnight of each civil day — compare GREENWICH TIME

astronomical triangle *n* **:** a triangle on the celestial sphere whose vertices are the pole, the zenith, and the observed body

astronomical twilight *n* **:** the period after sunset or before sunrise ending or beginning when the sun is about 18 degrees below the horizon

astronomical unit *n* **:** a unit of length used in astronomy equal to the mean radius of the earth's orbit or about 93 million miles

as·tron·o·mize \ə'strānə,mīz\ *vi* -ED/-ING/-S [*astronomy* + *-ize*] **1 :** to study or practice astronomy **2 :** to discourse on astronomy **:** talk astronomically

as·tron·o·my \-mē, -i\ *n* -ES [ME *astronomie*, fr. OF, fr. L *astronomia*, fr. Gk, fr. *astronomos* astronomer (fr. *astr-* + *nomos* law) + *-ia* -y — more at NIMBLE] **1 :** the science that treats of the celestial bodies, of their positions, magnitudes, motions, distances, constitution, physical condition, mutual relations, history, and destiny — formerly used as synonymous with *astrology* **2 :** a treatise on this science

as·tro·pec·ten \,astrō'pektən\ *n, cap* [NL, fr. *astr-* + L *pecten* comb — more at PECTINATE] **:** a large genus of chiefly tropical starfishes of shallow water that are markedly stellate in form with the disk and arms flat, the largest species being a foot or more across

astrophic \(')ā+\ *adj* [[2]*a-* + *strophic*] **1** *of stanzas or stanzaic structure* **:** arranged in series without regular repetition of stanzaic units **:** irregular in arrangement **2 :** not arranged or divided into strophes or stanzas **:** not stanzaic

as·tro·phile \'astrə,fīl\ *or* **as·tro·phil** \-,fil\ *n* -S [*astr-* + *-phile*, *-phil*] **:** one fond of star lore **:** an amateur astronomer ⟨go for its members into the ranks of the amateurs and ~*s* —Harlow Shapley⟩

as·tro·photograph \,== *at* ASTRO-+\ *n* [ISV *astr-* + *photograph*] **:** a photograph of a celestial body or any astronomical phenomenon

as·tro·photographic \¦==+\ *adj* [ISV *astr-* + *photographic*] **:** relating to or used in astrophotography ⟨~ telescope⟩

as·tro·photography \,==+\ *n* [ISV *astr-* + *photography*] **:** the application of photography to astronomical investigations

as·tro·phyl·lite \,astrə'fi,līt\ *n* -S [ISV *astr-* + Gk *phyllon* leaf + ISV *-ite;* orig. formed as G *astrophyllit* — more at BLADE] **:** a mineral $(K,Na)_2(Fe,Mn)TiSi_4O_{14}(OH)_2$ consisting of a basic silicate of potassium or sodium, iron or manganese, and titanium

as·tro·physical \¦== *at* ASTRO-+¦-\ *adj* [*astr-* + *physical*] **:** of or relating to astrophysics

as·tro·physicist \,==+\ *n* **:** a specialist in astrophysics

as·tro·physics \"+\ *n pl but usu sing in constr* [ISV *astr-* + *physics;* orig. formed as G *astrophysik*] **:** a branch of astronomy dealing principally with the physical and chemical natures of the heavenly bodies and their origin and evolution

as·troph·y·ton \a'strāfə,tän\ *n, cap* [NL, fr. *astr-* + Gk *phyton* plant — more at PHYT-] **:** a genus of ophiuroids having complexly branching arms and including many of the basket stars

as·tro·sclereid \,== *at* ASTRO-+\ *n* -S [*astr-* + *sclereid*] **:** a sclereid having its cell wall drawn out into lobes or arms to form a more or less stellate body (as those in the leaves and stems of certain xerophytes)

as·trose \'a,strōs\ *adj* [*astr-* + *-ose*] *of a sponge spicule* **:** STELLATE

as·tro·sphere \'== *at* ASTRO-+,-\ *n* -S [ISV *astr-* + *-sphere*] **1 :** the central mass of the aster exclusive of the rays **:** CENTROSPHERE **2 :** the entire aster exclusive of the centrosome — compare ASTER 3

as·tro·stereogram \¦==+\ *n* -S [*astr-* + *stereogram*] **:** a pair of stereoscopic photographs of a celestial body

astrut \ə'strət\ *adj* [ME *astrout*, *astrut*, fr. [1]*a-* + *strout*, *strut* strut — more at STRUT] **:** puffed up (as with conceit)

-asts *pl of* -AST

as·tu·cious \ə'st(y)üshəs, a'-\ *adj* [F *astucieux*, fr. MF, fr. *astuce* astuteness (fr. L *astutia*, fr. *astutus* astute + *-ia* -y) + *-ieux* -ious] **:** ASTUTE — **as·tu·cious·ly** *adv*

as·tu·ci·ty \-üsəd·ē\ *n* -ES [fr. *astucious*, after such pairs as E *ferocious: ferocity*] **:** the quality of being astute **:** ASTUTENESS ⟨they had been fools (to put it mildly), while the M'gai had been devils of ~ and treachery —John Masefield⟩

as·tur \'astə(r)\ *n* [NL, fr. *astur*, a hawk (prob. a 16th cent. insertion in the MS of a LL writer), prob. fr. Romansh, hawk, fr. L *accipiter* — more at ACCIPITER] **1** *cap* **:** a genus consisting of the goshawks and sometimes considered a subgenus of *Accipiter* **2** -S **:** GOSHAWK

[1]**as·tu·ri·an** \a'st(y)ürēən, ə'-\ *adj, usu cap* [Sp *asturiano*, adj. & n., fr. *Asturias*, region in northwestern Spain + Sp *-ano* -an (fr. L *-anus*)] **1 :** of, relating to, or characteristic of Asturias, now the province of Oviedo, in Spain **2 :** belonging to a late Mesolithic culture of northern Spain characterized by picks chipped from cobblestones and by subsistence on shellfish

[2]**asturian** \"\ *n* -S *cap* [Sp *asturiano*] **:** a native or inhabitant of Asturias

as·tute \ə'st(y)üt, a'-, *attrib sometimes* 'a,s-; *usu* -üd·+V\ *adj* [L *astutus*, fr. *astus* craft, cunning] **1 :** having or displaying shrewd discernment and sagacity ⟨an ~ and trustworthy observer of the political scene⟩ ⟨one of the most ~ field workers in American anthropology⟩ ⟨an ~ study of a complex subject⟩ **2 :** CRAFTY, CUNNING, WILY ⟨sold . . . on the basis of clever packaging and ~ advertising —Lewis Mumford⟩ **syn** see SHREWD

as·tute·ly *adv* **:** in an astute manner **:** SHREWDLY, CLEVERLY

as·tute·ness *n* -ES **:** the quality or state of being astute

as·ty·a·nax \ə'stīə,naks, a'-\ *n, cap* [NL, fr. *Astyanax*, young son of Hector and Andromache of Troy, fr. L, fr. Gk] **:** a genus of small brightly colored So. and Central American fishes (order Ostariophysi) including a silvery black-spotted species (*A. bimaculatus*) with orange-red fins and tail that is popular in the tropical aquarium

asty·lar \(')ā¦stīlə(r)\ *adj* [[2]*a-* + Gk *stylos* pillar + E *-ar*] *archit* **:** without columns or pilasters

asty·lo·spon·gia \¦ā,stīlə'spənjēə, -pän-\ *n, cap* [NL, fr. *astyl-*, *astylo-* (fr. [2]*a-* + *styl-*) + *-spongia*] **:** a genus of small pear-shaped siliceous fossil sponges including important index fossils occurring in Middle Silurian strata

asud·den \ə'-\ *adv* [[1]*a-* + *sudden*] **:** SUDDENLY

asun·ci·ón *or* **asun·ci·on** \ə¦sün(t)sē¦ōn, ä¦s-, -sün-,-sən-, -ē¦än, -ē¦ōn\ *adj, usu cap* [fr. *Asunción*, capital of Paraguay] **:** of or from Asunción, the capital of Paraguay **:** of the kind or style prevalent in Asunción

asun·der \ə'səndə(r)\ *adv* (*or adj*) [ME *asonder*, *asunder*, fr. OE *onsundran*, *onsundrum*, fr. *on* + *sundran*, *sundrum* apart, fr. *sunder*, *sundor* apart, separate — more at SUNDER] **1 :** into parts **:** into different pieces ⟨the American constitutional fabric would be torn ~ —H.S.Commager⟩ **2 :** apart from each other in position ⟨as wide ~ as pole and pole —J.A. Froude⟩ **3 :** distinct from each other in kind, quality, or nature ⟨I do not know their faces ~ —Thomas Gray⟩ ⟨their philosophies are poles ~⟩

asu·ra \'əsərə, (,)ə'sürə\ *n* -S *usu cap* [Skt — more at AESIR] **1 :** one of a class of beneficent celestial spirits of early Vedic and Zoroastrian mythology higher than men but lower than gods **2 :** one of a class of demons or titans in later Hinduism and Buddhism, the enemies of the gods

asu·ri \-(,)rē\ *n, usu cap* **:** a dialect of the Munda group of languages in central India

asu·ri·ní \¦äsərə¦nē\ *n, pl* **asuriní** *or* **asurinís** *usu cap* [Pg, of AmerInd origin] **1 a :** a Tupi-Guaranian people of the southern part of the state of Mato Grosso, Brazil **b :** a member of such people **2 :** the language of the Asuriní people

aswang \ä'swäŋ\ *also* **asu·wang** \,äsə'w-\ *or* **asuang** \ä'swäŋ\ *n* -S [Tag *asuwáng*, *aswáng*] *Philippines* **:** WITCH **:** evil spirit

aswarm \ə'-\ *adj* [[1]*a-* + *swarm*, v.] **:** SWARMING ⟨boulevards and cafés ~ with people⟩

asway \ə'-\ *adj* [[1]*a-* + *sway*, v.] **:** SWAYING ⟨buzz of bees in blooms ~ —G.F.Savage-Armstrong⟩

asweat \ə'-\ *adj* [[1]*a-* + *sweat*, v.] **:** SWEATING, SWEATY ⟨all the stone vault ~ with steam —Robinson Jeffers⟩

aswell \ə'-\ *adj* [[1]*a-* + *swell*, v.] **:** SWELLING ⟨with sails ~⟩

as well *adv* **:** in addition **:** BESIDES, ALSO, TOO ⟨there were other features *as well*⟩

as well as *prep* **:** in addition to **:** BESIDES ⟨a real scholar *as well as* . . . a composer of the highest integrity —Norman Demuth⟩

aswim \ə'-\ *adj* [[1]*a-* + *swim*, v.] **:** SWIMMING

aswing \ə'-\ *adj* [[1]*a-* + *swing*, v.] **:** SWINGING

aswirl \ə'-\ *adj* [[1]*a-* + *swirl*, v.] **:** SWIRLING

aswoon \ə'swün\ *adj* [ME *aswoue*, *aswoune*, *aswone*, fr. OE *geswōgen*] **:** SWOONING

as yet *adv* **:** up to the present time **:** so far ⟨he has not *as yet* arrived⟩

asyl·la·bia \,āsə'lābēə\ *n* -S [NL, fr. [2]*a-* + L *syllaba* syllable + NL *-ia* — more at SYLLABLE] **:** aphasia in which the patient can recognize letters but cannot form their sounds into syllables

asyllabic \¦ā+=¦==\ *also* **asyl·lab·i·cal** \¦ā+=¦===\ *adj* [[2]*a-* + *syllabic*, *syllabical*] **:** not syllabic

asy·lum \ə'sīləm\ *n, pl* **asy·lums** \-ləmz\ [ME *asilum*, fr. L *asylum*, fr. Gk *asylon*, neut. of *asylos* exempt from spoliation, inviolable, fr. *a-* [2]a- + *sylon* right of seizure] **1 a :** a place of refuge and protection (as a temple, altar, or statue of a god or in later times a Christian church) where criminals and debtors found shelter and from which they could not be forcibly taken without sacrilege **:** SANCTUARY **b** *international law* **:** a place exempted by custom or convention from the territorial jurisdiction of a state within which it is so that refugees may not be followed to or taken from it except by the consent of the state enjoying the immunity **2 :** a place of retreat and security **:** SHELTER ⟨the land of the free and the ~ of the downtrodden —G.W.Pierson⟩ ⟨the ideal world . . . is an ~ in which he takes refuge from the troubles of existence —John Dewey⟩ **3 a :** the protection or inviolability afforded by an asylum **:** REFUGE ⟨the right to seek and to enjoy in other countries ~ from persecution —*U.N. Declaration of Human Rights*⟩ ⟨fled to England, where he requested and has received political ~ —*Encounter*⟩ ⟨he can, if he wishes, seek ~ from present tumults in a past period of history —Reinhold Niebuhr⟩ **b :** the act or the custom of affording shelter or protection to one under or in danger of persecution ⟨the controversial custom of ~ —*Time*⟩ ⟨for the United States diplomatic ~ is not a principle of international law —Alona Evans⟩ **4 :** an institution for the protection or relief of some class of destitute, afflicted, or otherwise unfortunate persons ⟨an orphan ~⟩ ⟨an ~ for the deaf and dumb⟩; *esp* **:** an institution for the care of the insane

asym- — see AS-

asym·bo·lia \,ā,sim'bōlēə\ *n* -S [NL, fr. [2]*a-* + L *symbolus*, *symbolum* symbol + NL *-ia* — more at SYMBOL] **:** loss of power to understand previously familiar symbols and signs usu. in consequence of brain lesion

asymbolic \¦ā+,=¦==\ *also* **asymbolical** \¦ā+,=¦===\ *adj* [[2]*a-* + *symbolic*] **:** not symbolic

asymmetric \¦ā, ¦a+=¦==\ *or* **asymmetrical** \"+=¦===\ *adj* [*asymmetry* + *-ic*, *-ical*] **:** not symmetrical ⟨an ~ face⟩ ⟨~ growth or development⟩ ⟨a strikingly ~ architectural design⟩: **a** *bot* (1) **:** not isobilateral (2) **:** ZYGOMORPHIC ⟨an ~ flower⟩ ⟨an ~ corolla⟩ **b :** relating to derivatives in which groups are substituted unsymmetrically in the molecule ⟨~ dichloroethylene $CH_2{=}CCl_2$⟩ ⟨~ or 1,2,4-trinitro-benzene⟩ **c :** relating to or characterized by asymmetry in spatial arrangement or in the placement of parts or components **d :** of, belonging to, or designating the crystallographic system having no plane of symmetry or the group of this system having no plane, axis, or center of symmetry **e :** so constituted as never to hold when related arguments are interchanged (as in the relation *x* is the father of *y*) — **asymmetrically** *adv*

asymmetric carbon atom *n* **:** a carbon atom in union with four atoms or groups no two of which are alike, compounds containing such a carbon atom being capable of existing in two optically active forms which are distinguished by being respectively levorotatory and dextrorotatory and also in some cases by having enantiomorphous crystal forms

asymmetric carbon atom: the two tetrahedrons illustrate the two ways in which four different atoms or groups, *a*, *b*, *c*, *d*, may be arranged in mirror-image relationship about a carbon atom assumed to be at the center of each tetrahedron

asymmetric synthesis *n, chem* **:** a process that directly produces an optically active compound (as one containing an asymmetric carbon atom) from symmetrically constituted molecules without requiring resolution of a racemic mixture

asym·me·tron \ā'simə·,trän\ *n, cap* [NL, fr. Gk, neut. of *asymmetros*] **:** a genus of lancelets (family Epigonichthyidae) differing from *Branchiostoma* in having asymmetrical metapleura and but one series of gonads, the right — compare AMPHIOXUS

asymmetry \(')ā, (')a+\ *n* -ES [Gk *asymmetria* incommensurability, lack of proportion, fr. *asymmetros* incommensurable, ill-proportioned (fr. *a-* [2]a- + *symmetros* commensurate, suitable, symmetrical) + *-ia* -y — more at SYMMETRY] **1** *math* **a** *obs* **:** INCOMMENSURABILITY **b :** SKEWNESS **2 :** lack or absence of symmetry ⟨the ideal of nonmetrical rhythm, like that of atonality, is ~ —Virgil Thomson⟩ ⟨the *Art Nouveau's* wriggling *asymmetries* —T.H.Robsjohn-Gibbings⟩: as **a :** lack of proportion between the parts of a thing; *esp* **:** want of bilateral symmetry ⟨~ in the development of the two sides of the brain⟩ **b :** lack of coordination of two parts acting in connection with one another ⟨~ of convergence of the eyes⟩ **3 :** want of symmetry in spatial arrangement of atoms and groups in a molecule (as similar to two nonsuperimposable mirror images) which may result from the presence of an asymmetric atom (as carbon, nitrogen, or sulfur) or if none is present in molecules with rigid structures (as in certain allenes, spirans, or cycloparaffin) or in molecules with restricted rotation about single bonds (as in certain biphenyls) — called also *molecular asymmetry;* see OPTICAL ISOMERISM

asymptomatic \(')ā+\ *adj* [[2]*a-* + *symptomatic*] **:** SYMPTOMLESS **:** presenting no subjective evidence of disease — **asymptomatically** *adv*

as·ymp·tote \'asəm(p),tōt, *usu* -ōd·+-V\ *n* -S [prob. fr. (assumed) NL *asymptotus*, fr. Gk *asymptōtos*, fr. *asymptōtos* not meeting, fr. *a-* [2]a- + *symptōtos*, verbal of *sympiptein* to meet, fall together — more at SYMPTOM] *math* **:** a straight line associated with a curve such that as a point P moves out along an infinite branch of the curve the distance from the point P to the line approaches zero and the slope of the curve at P approaches the slope of the line ⟨not all curves have ~*s*⟩ ⟨the hyperbola has two ~*s* while the parabola has none⟩

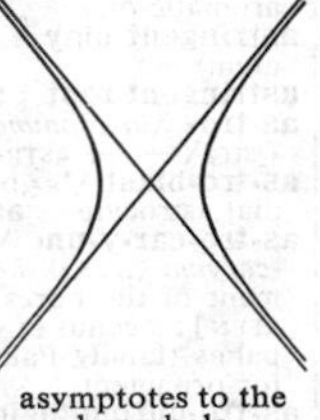

asymptotes to the hyperbola

as·ymp·tot·ic \¦==¦täd·ik\ *also* **as·ymp·tot·i·cal** \-d·əkəl\ *adj* **:** of, relating to, or of the nature of an asymptote — **as·ymp·tot·i·cal·ly** \-d·ək(ə)lē\ *adv*

asymptotic curve *or* **asymptotic line** *n* **:** a curve on a surface whose osculating plane at each point coincides with the tangent plane to the surface at that point

asymptotic developable *n* **:** the developable surface generated by the tangent planes of a ruled surface whose rulings are supposed not to be minimal lines

asymptotic formula *n* **:** a formula that approaches perfect accuracy as the independent variable increases indefinitely

asynapsis \,ā+\ *n, pl* **asynapses** [NL, fr. [2]*a-* + *synapsis*] **:** failure of synapsis or pairing of homologous chromosomes in meiosis — compare DESYNAPSIS, SYNAPSIS — **asynaptic** \¦ā+=¦==\ *adj* — **asynaptically** *adv*

asynartetic \(')ā+\ *adj* [*asynartete* asynartetic verse (fr. Gk *asynartētos* asynartetic, fr. *a-* [2]a- + — assumed — *synartētos*, verbal of Gk *synartan* to join together, fr. *syn-* + *artan* to fasten, hang) + *-ic;* perh. akin to Gk *aeirein* to lift — more at AORTA] *of a line of verse* **:** containing disparate or unconnected rhythmic units: as **a :** with unhomogeneous rhythms in the two members distinguished by the caesura **b :** with diaeresis, hiatus, or syllaba anceps at the caesura so that a quasi independence of the two members is effected

asynchronism \(')ā+\ *or* **asynchrony** \(')ā+\ *n, pl* **asynchronisms** *or* **asynchronies** [[2]*a-* + *synchronism*, *synchrony*] **:** the quality or state of being asynchronous **:** absence or lack of concurrence in time

asynchronistic \(')ā+\ *adj* [[2]*a-* + *synchronistic*] **:** ASYNCHRONOUS

asynchronous \(')ā+¦-\ *adj* [[2]*a-* + *synchronous*] **:** not simultaneous **:** not concurrent in time — opposed to *synchronous* — **asynchronously** *adv*

asyndesis \(')ā+\ *n, pl* **asyndeses** [NL, fr. [2]*a-* + *syndesis*] **:** ASYNAPSIS

[1]**asyn·det·ic** \¦asᵊn¦ded·ik, ¦ās-, -(,)sin-\ *adj* [ISV *asyndeton* + *-ic*] **:** characterized by asyndeton ⟨the ~ and not altogether logical sequence of thought —Norah K. Chadwick⟩ — **asyn·det·i·cal·ly** \-ək(ə)lē\ *adv*

[2]**asyndetic** \"\ *adj* [NL *asyndesis* + E *-etic*] **:** ASYNAPTIC ⟨~ hybrids . . . where the satellite chromosomes do not conjugate —*Biol. Abstracts*⟩ — **asyn·det·i·cal·ly** \-ək(ə)lē\ *adv*

asyn·de·ton \ə'sində-,tän, -,tən\ *n, pl* **asynde·tons** \-nz\ *or* **asynde·ta** \,dətə\ [LL, fr. Gk, fr. neut. of *asyndetos* unconnected, fr. *a-* [2]a- + *syndetos* bound together, verbal of *syndein* to bind together, fr. *syn-* + *dein* to bind — more at DIADEM] **:** omission of the conjunctions that ordinarily join coordinate words or clauses (as in *I came, I saw, I conquered*)

asy·ner·gia \,āsi'nərj(ē)ə\ *also* **asyn·er·gy** \ā'sinərjē\ *n, pl* **asynergias** *also* **asynergies** [NL *asynergia*, fr. [2]*a-* + *synergia* synergy] *med* **:** lack of coordination (as of muscles) ⟨~ results in jerkiness, overaction and imperfect muscle control —C.H.Best & N.B.Taylor⟩ — **asy·ner·gic** \¦āsi¦nərjik\ *adj*

asyn·tac·tic \¦ā+(,)=¦==\ *also* **asyntactical** \¦ā+(,)=¦===\ *adj* [Gk *asyntaktikos*, fr. *a-* [2]a- + *syntaktikos* syntactic, syntactical — more at SYNTACTIC] **:** not syntactic ⟨an ~ narrative⟩ ⟨an ~ compound such as *star-spangled*, with a structure differing from that of the phrase *spangled with stars*⟩

asystole \(')ā+\ *n* -S [[2]*a-* + *systole*] *physiol* **:** a condition of weakening or cessation of systole — **asystolic** \¦ā+\ *adj* — **asys·to·lism** \(')ā'sistə,lizəm\ *n* -S

[1]**at** \ət, (')at, *usu* -d·+V\ *prep* [ME, fr. OE *æt;* akin to OHG *az* at, to, ON & Goth *at*, L *ad*, OIr *ad-*] **1** — used as a function word to indicate presence in, on, or near: as (1) presence or occurrence in a particular place ⟨lying ~ the bottom of the sea⟩ ⟨staying ~ a hotel⟩ ⟨road ~ the edge of the woods⟩ ⟨enter ~ the south gate⟩ ⟨walk ~ my side⟩; used dial. with a point of the compass to designate an area of the country ⟨transportation to cities ~ the South⟩; (2) attendance as a spectator ⟨~ the wedding⟩ or attendance as a participant or as one connected with an activity ⟨been ~ college since September⟩; (3) location of a feeling, quality, or condition ⟨sick ~ heart⟩ ⟨out ~ the elbows⟩ **2 a** — used as a function word to indicate that which is the goal of an action or that toward which an action or motion is directed ⟨aimed the arrow ~ the target⟩ ⟨snatched ~ the purse but missed⟩ ⟨laughed ~ him⟩ ⟨hinted ~ the answer⟩ ⟨angry ~ his brother⟩ **b** (1) **:** in personal contact with **:** into the presence of ⟨hard to get ~ the president⟩ (2) **:** in active or aggressive pursuit of or contact with ⟨creditors are ~ him again⟩ **3** — used as a function word to indicate that with which one is occupied or employed ⟨a student ~ work on his experiment⟩ ⟨the pilot ~ the controls⟩ ⟨an expert ~ chess⟩ **4** — used as a function word to indicate situation in an active or passive state or condition ⟨two nations ~ war⟩ ⟨negotiations ~ a standstill⟩ ⟨a criminal ~ liberty⟩ ⟨the people ~ rest⟩ **5** — used as a function word to indicate means, agency, cause, source, or manner ⟨sell the goods ~ auction⟩ ⟨laughed ~ his joke⟩ ⟨angry ~ his reply⟩ ⟨the child jumped ~ his command⟩ ⟨suffered ~ his hands⟩ ⟨act ~ your own discretion⟩ **6** — used as a function word to indicate (1) rate, degree, or position in a scale or series ⟨proceed ~ 20 miles an hour⟩ ⟨the temperature ~ 90⟩ ⟨a bargain ~ five dollars⟩ ⟨a crowd estimated ~ 10,000⟩ or (2) relative order or value ⟨the news came ~ first as a terrific shock⟩ ⟨the performance was ~ its best mediocre⟩ **7** — used as a function word to indicate age or position in time ⟨retire ~ 65⟩ ⟨ready for college ~ 18⟩ ⟨awoke ~ midnight⟩ ⟨president of the company ~ his death⟩ ⟨was serving on four committees ~ this time⟩ **8** — used substand. as an intensive with *where* ⟨don't know where they are ~⟩ — **at after** *now dial Eng* **:** AFTER, AFTERWARD — **at and from** *insurance* **:** covering a ship at the port of departure as well as on the voyage — **at it :** busily engaged in some particular activity (as work, play, or fighting) ⟨he was up and *at it* before breakfast⟩ ⟨the neighbors are *at it* again⟩ — **at law :** under or within the provisions of the law **:** as required by law **:** according to law practice ⟨enforceable *at law*⟩ ⟨*at* common *law*⟩ — see ATTORNEY-AT-LAW — **at that 1 :** without further effort, argument, or consideration **:** as matters now stand ⟨we'll let it go *at that*⟩ **2 :** over and above what is expected or bargained for **:** BESIDES ⟨an interesting experience but a painful one *at that*⟩ **3 :** even so **:** notwithstanding that ⟨*at that*, you can still make a good profit⟩

[2]**at** \ət, *usu* əd·+V\ *conj* [ME, alter. of *that*] *now dial* **:** THAT

[3]**at** \(')at, *usu* (')ad·+V\ *pron* [ME, alter. of *that*] *now dial* **:** THAT

[4]**at** *var of* ATT

[5]**at** \'ät, 'at\ *n, pl* **at** [Siamese] **:** a subsidiary unit of value of Laos from 1955 equal to $1/100$ kip

at- — see AD-

at *abbr* **1** airtight **2** atmosphere; atmospheric **3** atomic **4** attorney

AT *abbr* **1** American terms **2** ampere-turn **3** antitank **4** assay ton

At *symbol* astatine

[1]**ata** *var of* [1]ATTA

[2]**ata** \'äd·ə, -d·,ä\ *n, pl* **ata** *or* **atas** *usu cap* **1 a :** a predominantly pagan people near Mount Apo in central Mindanao, Philippines **b :** a member of such people **2 :** an Austronesian language of the Ata people

-a·ta \'ä|d·ə, 'ā|, 'å|, |tə — *in the pronunc of words containing this suffix, usu only the first two variants are shown*\ *n pl suffix* [NL, fr. L, neut. pl. of *-atus* -ate] **:** ones characterized by having (such a feature) — in names of zoological groups ⟨Coelenter*ata*⟩ ⟨Vertebr*ata*⟩ ⟨Chord*ata*⟩ ⟨Branchi*ata*⟩

at·a·bal \'ad·ə,bal, -äl, ,=='=\ *n* -S [Sp, fr. Ar *aṭ-ṭabl* the drum] **1 :** an Arabian kettledrum **2 :** a small So. American drum

ata·beg \'ad·ə,beg, 'äd·ə-, ,=='=\ *or* **ata·bek** \-,bek\ *n* -S [Russ, of Turkic origin; akin to Jagatai *atabäg*, Turk *atabey*, fr. *ata* father + *bäg*, *bey* prince — more at BEY] **1 :** a Seljuk provincial governor **2 :** any of various Turkish high officials (as a vizier or prime minister)

at about *adv* **:** nearly at **:** ABOUT ⟨who were arriving *at about* the same time —Thomas Pyles⟩ ⟨paid *at about* that rate —Anthony Trollope⟩ ⟨*at about* the western border —Bernard De Voto⟩ ⟨*at about* five o'clock —Florette Henri⟩

At·a·brine \'ad·əbrən, 'atə-, -,brēn *also* -īn\ *trademark* — used for quinacrine

ata·ca·me·ñan \¦ad·əkə¦mānyən, ¦äd·ə-\ *adj, usu cap* **1 :** relating or belonging to the Atacameño people **2 :** of or relating to the language of the Atacameño people

ata·ca·me·ño \\,⸗⸗⸗'mān(,)yō\\ *or* **at·a·ca·ma** \\,⸗⸗'kämə\\ *n, pl* **atacameño** *or* **atacameños** *or* **atacama** *or* **atacamas** *usu cap* [Sp, fr. the *Atacama* desert, northern Chile, their locality] **1 a :** a So. American Indian people of the Atacama desert in northern Chile **b :** a member of such people **2 :** the language formerly spoken by the Atacameño people

at·a·cam·ite \\,ad·ə'ka,mīt, ə'takə,m-\\ *n* -s [F, fr. *Atacama* desert, its locality + F *-ite*] **:** a mineral $Cu_2Cl(OH)_3$ consisting of a basic copper chloride that is transparent or translucent and of various shades of green and occurs usu. in prismatic orthorhombic crystals but also in crystalline aggregates or in massive form (hardness 3–3.5, sp. gr. 3.75–3.77)

atac·tic \\(')ā¦taktik, -ēk\\ *adj* [Gk *ataktos* not ordered (fr. *a-* [2]a- + *taktos* ordered, fr. *tassein* to arrange, put in order) + E *-ic* — more at TACTICS] **1 :** lacking regularity or coordination; *specif* **:** ATAXIC **2 :** having no syntactic connection

atac·ti·form \\(')ā¦taktə,fȯrm\\ *adj* [*atact-* (fr. NL *ataxia*) + *-iform*] **:** resembling ataxia

ataghan *var of* YATAGHAN

ata·jo \\ə'tä(,)hō, -ta-, -tā-\\ *n* -s [Sp, fr. *atajar* to intercept, cut off, take a short cut, fr. *a-* (fr. L *ad-*) + *tajar* to divide, slice, fr. (assumed) VL *taliare* — more at TAILOR] **1** *chiefly Southwest* **:** a drove of mules or horses **2** *chiefly Southwest* **:** an expedient of any kind **:** SHORT CUT

ata·ka·pa *or* **at·ta·ca·pa** \\ə'takəpə, -äk-, -,pä,-,pȯ\\ *n, pl* **atakapa** *or* **atakapas** *or* **attacapa** *or* **attacapas** *usu cap* [F *Atac-Apa*, fr. Choctaw *hatak-apa* cannibal, fr. *hatak* man + *apa* eats] **1 a :** an Indian people of the Gulf coast of Louisiana and Texas **b :** a member of such people **2 :** the language of the Atakapa people

ata·ka·pan *or* **at·ta·ca·pan** \\-,pən,-,pän,-,pȯn\\ *n, pl* **atakapan** *or* **atakapans** *or* **attacapan** *or* **attacapans** *usu cap* **:** a language family of the Gulf phylum in Louisiana and Texas comprising the Atakapa language

ata·la·lá \\,ad·ələ'lä\\ *n, pl* **atalalá** *or* **atalalás** *usu cap* [Sp, of AmerInd origin] **1 :** a people of the Vilela group **2 :** a member of the Vilela people

ata·lán \\,ad·ᵊl'än\\ *n, pl* **atalán** *or* **ataláns** *usu cap* [Sp *atalán*, of AmerInd origin] **:** a language family of Ecuador

at all \\əd·'ȯl, ə'tȯl, ad·'ȯl\\ *adv (or adj)* **:** in any way or respect **:** to even the least extent or degree **:** under any circumstances — used chiefly for emphasis esp. in negative, conditional, or interrogative sentences or phrases ⟨he has no ambition *at all*⟩ ⟨not *at all* likely⟩ ⟨wherever an *at all* Catholic culture exists —R.G.Davis⟩

at·a·man \\,ad·ə'man\\ *n* -s [Russ, fr. ORuss *vatamanŭ*] **:** HETMAN

at·a·mas·co lily \\¦ad·ə¦ma(,)skō-\\ *also* **atamasco** *n* [Virginia *attamusco*, lit., it is red] **:** a plant of the genus *Zephyranthes* (esp. *Z. atamasco* and *Z. longifolia*)

at·ap *or* **at·tap** \\'a,tap\\ *n* -s [Malay *atap* roof, thatch] **1 :** NIPA PALM **2 :** the leaves of the nipa palm used esp. for thatching in Malayan countries **3 :** a thatched roof often made with the leaves of the nipa palm

atar *var of* ATTAR

[1]at·a·rac·tic \\¦ad·ə¦raktik\\ *adj* [Gk *ataraktos* + E *-ic*] **1** *or* **at·a·rax·ic** \\-raksik\\ **:** tending to tranquilize — used of drugs for the treatment of anxiety and tension states or mental diseases **2 :** of or relating to mental tranquillity ⟨~ effect⟩

[2]ataractic \\"\\ *or* **ataraxic** \\"\\ *n* -s [*ataractic* fr. [1]*ataractic*; *ataraxic* fr. *ataraxy* + *-ic*] **:** an ataractic drug

at·a·raxy \\'ad·ə,raksē\\ *also* **at·a·rax·ia** \\,⸗⸗'raksēə\\ *n, pl* **ataraxies** *also* **ataraxias** [MF & Gk; MF *ataraxie*, fr. Gk *ataraxia*, fr. *ataraktos* undisturbed (fr. *a-* [2]a- + *taraktos*, verbal of *tarattein*, *tarassein* to disturb, stir) + *-ia* -y — more at DREG] **:** calmness untroubled by mental or emotional disquiet **:** intellectual detachment **:** IMPERTURBABILITY

ataroi *usu cap, var of* ATORAI

atas *pl of* ATA

ataunt \\ə'tȯnt, -änt\\ *or* **ataun·to** \\-(,)tō\\ *adj* [*ataunt* fr. ME, as much as possible, fr. MF *autant* as much, as much as possible, fr. OF *altant*, *autant* as much, fr. *al*, *el* other, other thing (fr. assumed VL *ale*, alter. of L *aliud*, neut. of *alius* other) + *tant* so much, fr. L *tantum*, neut. of *tantus* so great; *ataunto*, alter. of *ataunt* — more at ELSE, TANTAMOUNT] **1 :** fully rigged; *esp* **:** with all light upper spars hoisted and rigged **2 :** completely in order **:** SHIPSHAPE

at·a·vic \\'ad·ə(,)vik, 'atə-; ə'tav-, (')a¦t-\\ *adj* [prob. fr. F *atavique*, fr. L *atavus* ancestor + F *-ique* -ic] **:** ATAVISTIC

at·a·vism \\'ad·ə,vizəm, 'atə,-\\ *n* -s [F *atavisme*, fr. L *atavus* ancestor, grandfather's or grandmother's great-grandfather (perh. fr. *atta* daddy + *avus* grandfather) + F *-isme* -ism] **1 :** recurrence in an organism or in any of its parts of a form typical of ancestors more remote than the parents usu. due to recombination of ancestral genes **2 :** an individual or character manifesting atavism **:** THROWBACK, REVERSION ⟨he was a magnificent ~, a man so purely primitive —Jack London⟩

at·a·vist \\-,vəst\\ *n* -s [*atavism* + *-ist*] **:** one that is marked by atavism

at·a·vis·tic \\¦⸗⸗¦vistik, -ēk\\ *adj* **:** of, relating to, tending to, or marked by atavism ⟨from some ~ inheritance of the cave dweller he always disliked people on first acquaintance —W.S. Maugham⟩ ⟨called his work uncultured and ~⟩ — **at·a·vis·ti·cal·ly** \\-tək(ə)lē, -ēk-, -li\\ *adv*

at·a·vus \\'ad·əvəs\\ *n, pl* **ata·vi** \\-,vī, -,vē\\ [L] **:** an ancestor or ancestral type from which a character is assumed to be inherited

atax·aphasia \\ə,taks +\\ *or* **ataxi·aphasia** \\ə,taksē +\\ *n* -s [NL, fr. *ataxia* + *aphasia*] **:** aphasia marked by inability to order words into sentences

atax·ia \\ə'taksēə, (')ā-\\ *also* **ataxy** \\ə'taksē, 'a,t-\\ *n, pl* **ataxias** *also* **ataxies** [Gk *ataxia*, fr. *ataktos* disorderly (fr. *a-* [2]a- + *taktos* ordered, verbal of *tattein*, *tassein* to put in order) + *-ia* -y — more at TACTICS] **1 :** lack of order **:** CONFUSION ⟨their political ~ . . . kept them unaware of themselves and unaware of each other —Waldo Frank⟩ **2** [NL, fr. Gk] **:** an inability to coordinate voluntary muscular movements that is symptomatic of any of several disorders of the nervous system; *specif* **:** such an abnormality in sheep associated with inadequate intake of copper and common in parts of Australia

atax·ia·gram \\ə'taksēə,gram\\ *n* -s [NL *ataxia* + E *-gram*] **:** a record obtained with an ataxiameter

atax·i·am·e·ter \\ə,taksē'aməd·ə(r)\\ *or* **atax·ia·graph** \\⸗'⸗⸗ə,graf\\ *n* -s [NL *ataxia* + E *-meter* or *-graph*] **:** an instrument for measuring involuntary tremor and unsteadiness (as the swaying of the whole body in the erect posture)

atax·ic \\ə'taksik\\ *adj* **1 :** marked or caused by ataxia **2 :** of or relating to unstratified ore deposits — opposed to *eutaxic*

atax·ite \\ə'tak,sīt, ā'-\\ *n* -s [ISV *atax-* (fr. Gk *ataxia* disorder) + *-ite;* orig. formed as G *ataxit* — more at ATAXIA] **1 :** a taxitic rock whose components have no definite arrangement, simulating a breccia **2 :** an iron meteorite lacking the structure of either hexahedrites or octahedrites — **atax·it·ic** \\¦ā,tak¦sid·ik\\ *adj*

ataxonomic \\(')ā + ¦⸗⸗¦⸗⸗\\ *adj* [[2]*a-* + *taxonomic*] **:** not concerned with classification or systematic botany and zoology — compare TAXONOMY

atayal *usu cap, var of* TAYAL

atbash *var of* ATHBASH

at bat \\⸗'⸗\\ *n, pl* **at bats** **1 :** a turn at attempting to hit a ball thrown by a baseball or softball pitcher **2 :** an official time at the plate charged to the batter except when he walks, sacrifices, is hit by a pitched ball, or is interfered with by the catcher ⟨the shortstop made three hits in five *at bats*⟩

atdt *abbr* attendant

[1]ate *past of* EAT

[2]ate \\'äd·ē, 'ā-; 'ä,tā, 'ā,tē\\ *n* -s [Gk *atē;* prob. akin to Latvian *vâts* wound] **:** blind impulse, reckless ambition, or excessive folly that drives men to ruin

[1]-ate \\ət, ,āt, *usu* -d·+V\\ *n suffix* -s [ME *-at*, fr. OF, fr. L *-atus* (nom. sing. masc.), *-atum* (nom. sing. neut.), fr. *-atus*, past part. ending of 1st conj. verbs] **1 :** one acted upon (in a specified way) ⟨advoc*ate*⟩ ⟨leg*ate*⟩ ⟨centrifug*ate*⟩ ⟨duplic*ate*⟩ ⟨mand*ate*⟩ ⟨vulcaniz*ate*⟩ **2** [NL *-atum*, fr. L, neut. of *-atus*] **:** chemical compound or complex anion derived from a (specified) compound or element ⟨alcohol*ate*⟩ ⟨ferr*ate*⟩; *esp* **:** salt or ester of an acid with a name ending in *-ic* and not beginning with *hydro-* ⟨acet*ate*⟩ ⟨carbon*ate*⟩ — compare STOCK SYSTEM

[2]-ate \\"\\ *n suffix* -s [ME *-at*, fr. OF, fr. L *-atus*, fr. *-atus*, past part. ending of 1st conj. verbs] **:** office **:** function **:** rank **:** state **:** group of persons holding a (specified) office or rank, having a (specified) function, or being in a (specified) state ⟨episcop*ate*⟩ ⟨pontific*ate*⟩ ⟨professor*ate*⟩ ⟨rabbin*ate*⟩

[3]-ate \\"\\ *adj suffix* [ME *-at*, fr. L *-atus*, past part. ending of 1st conj. verbs, fr. *-a-* (thematic vowel of 1st conj.) + *-tus*, past part. ending — more at -ED] **1 :** acted upon (in a specified way) **:** brought into or being in a (specified) state ⟨consumm*ate*⟩ ⟨degener*ate*⟩ ⟨inanim*ate*⟩ ⟨Italian*ate*⟩ ⟨temper*ate*⟩ **2 :** characterized by having ⟨branchi*ate*⟩ ⟨chord*ate*⟩ ⟨foli*ate*⟩

[4]-ate \\¦āt, *usu* ¦ād·+V\\ *vb suffix* -ED/-ING/-S [ME *-aten*, fr. L *-atus*, past part. ending of 1st conj. verbs] **:** to act (in a specified way) ⟨negoti*ate*⟩ ⟨pontific*ate*⟩ **:** act upon (in a specified way) ⟨assassin*ate*⟩ ⟨vener*ate*⟩ **:** cause to be modified or affected by ⟨camphor*ate*⟩ ⟨hyphen*ate*⟩ ⟨pollin*ate*⟩ **:** cause to become ⟨activ*ate*⟩ ⟨domestic*ate*⟩ ⟨fraction*ate*⟩ **:** furnish with ⟨capacit*ate*⟩ ⟨substanti*ate*⟩

A·te·brin \\'ad·əbrən, 'atə-, *also* -,brēn\\ *trademark* — used for quinacrine

atef \\'ä,tef\\ *n* -s [alternate transliteration of Egypt *ꜣtf*] **:** a tall crown with a long feather on each side shown in the art of ancient Upper Egypt as worn by Osiris

atel- *or* **atelo-** *comb form* [NL, fr. Gk *atel-* imperfect, incomplete, fr. *atelēs*, fr. *a-* [2]a- + *-telēs* (fr. *telos* end) — more at WHEEL] **:** defective ⟨*atel*ectasis⟩ ⟨*atelo*myelia⟩

at·el·ec·ta·sis \\,ad·ᵊl'ektəsəs\\ *n, pl* **atelecta·ses** \\-ə,sēz\\ [NL, fr. *atel-* + Gk *ektasis* extension — more at ECTASIS] **:** collapse of the expanded lung; *also* **:** defective expansion of the pulmonary alveoli at birth — **at·e·lec·tat·ic** \\¦⸗⸗,lek¦tad·ik\\ *adj*

at·e·les \\'ad·ᵊl,ēz\\ *n, cap* [NL, fr. Gk *atelēs;* fr. the absence or rudimentary development of the thumb] **:** a genus comprising the spider monkeys

at·e·les·tite \\,ad·ᵊl'e,stīt\\ *n* -s [G *atelestit*, fr. Gk *atelestos* unaccomplished (fr. *a-* [2]a- + *telestos* accomplished, fr. *telein* to accomplish, fr. *telos* end) + G *-it* -ite] **:** a mineral consisting of basic bismuth arsenate occurring in minute yellow crystals (sp. gr. 6.82)

atel·ic \\(')ā¦telik\\ *adj* [[2]*a-* + *telic*] **:** IMPERFECTIVE 2 — contrasted with *telic*

ate·lier \\¦ad·ᵊl¦yā, ¦atᵊl- *also* a'tel,yā *or* ə't-\\ *n* -s [F, fr. MF *astelier* woodpile, construction yard, workshop, fr. *astele* splinter, chip of wood, fr. LL *astella* splinter, alter. (influenced by L *-ella*) of L *astula*, alter. of *assula*, dim. of *assis* board — more at ACE] **1 a :** an artist's studio or workroom **b :** a studio in which students of art or architecture receive instruction **2 :** WORKSHOP: **a :** an artist's studio or workshop in which several assistants or apprentices contribute toward the execution of a work bearing a master's signature ⟨Rubens's ~⟩ **b :** a workshop in which several people are employed at artisans' tasks ⟨had spent their apprenticeships in the metal, jewelry, and glass ~*s* —Sherrill Whiton⟩ **3 :** a business establishment devoted to the design and execution of women's fine clothing ⟨a showing of summer models at a Paris ~⟩

atel·i·o·sis \\ə,telē'ōsəs, -tē-\\ *also* **atel·ei·o·sis** \\", -lī-\\ *n, pl* **atelio·ses** *also* **ateleio·ses** \\-'ō,sēz\\ [NL, fr. Gk *ateleia* incompleteness (fr. *atelēs* incomplete) + NL *-osis*] **:** incomplete development **:** INFANTILISM; *esp* **:** dwarfism associated with anterior pituitary deficiencies and marked by essentially normal intelligence and proportions though often retarded sexual development — compare ACHONDROPLASIA — **atel·i·ot·ic** \\ə¦telē¦äd·ik, -tēl-\\ *also* **atel·ei·ot·ic** \\", -lī-\\ *adj*

atel·lan \\ə'telən\\ *also* **atel·lane** \\", -,lān\\ *adj, usu cap* [L *Atellanus* of Atella, fr. *Atella*, ancient Oscan town in southern Italy where the Roman farce originated + L *-anus* -an] **:** of, relating to, or having the characteristics of a Roman genre of farce developed from impromptu rustic plays of country life and adopted for interludes and afterpieces during the Republic and up to the time of Tiberius

atelomitic \\¦ā + ¦⸗⸗¦⸗⸗\\ *adj* [[2]*a-* + *telomitic*] **:** NONTERMINAL ⟨the ~ centromeres and spindle attachment of certain chromosomes⟩

ate·moya \\,äd·ə'mȯiə, ,a-, -tə-\\ *n* -s [*ates* + cheri*moya*] **:** a white-pulped tropical fruit produced by crossing the sweetsop and the cherimoya

a tempo \\ä +\\ *adv (or adj)* [It] **:** in time — used as a direction in music to return to the original rate of speed of a piece after any change in the tempo

atentaculata \\¦ā +\\ [NL, fr. [2]*a-* + *Tentaculata*] *syn of* NUDA

a ter·go \\ä'ter(,)gō\\ *adv* [L] **:** from behind ⟨assisted him out *a tergo* with his own footwear —H.W.Thompson⟩

ate·ri·an \\ə'tirēən\\ *adj, usu cap* [F *atérien*, fr. Bir el-*Ater* (Constantine), Algeria + F *-ien* -ian] **:** of or belonging to a derived Mousterian culture of northern Africa which has in addition to the usual European Mousterian traits tanged and winged arrow points and leaf-shaped spearheads and which may be said to carry on the Mousterian tradition into upper Paleolithic times

à terre \\ä'te(ə)r, *F* àter\\ *adv (or adj)* [F] *ballet* **:** on the ground **:** PAR TERRE

[1]ates *pl of* ATE

[2]ates \\'ä,tes\\ *n, pl* **ates** [Tag] **:** SWEETSOP

-ates *pl of* -ATE, *present 3d sing of* -ATE

[1]ates·tine \\ə'testən, -,tīn\\ *adj, usu cap* [L *atestinus*, fr. *Ateste*, city in northeastern Italy + L *-inus* -ine] **:** of or belonging to the early Roman Iron Age culture of Ateste related to the Villanova culture but later influenced by the Etruscans

[2]atestine \\"\\ *n* -s *usu cap* **:** one of the people of Ateste (modern Este, Italy) esp. of the period 800-400 B.C.

at·fa·la·ti \\at'fäləd·ē\\ *n, pl* **atfalati** *or* **atfalatis** *usu cap* [perh. fr. Kalapooia *Tfalati*, fr. Shahaptian *Twalatin*, lit., river people, fr. *wala* river + *tin* people] **1 :** a people of the northern dialectic branch of the Kalapooian language family **2 :** a member of the Atfalati people

ath *abbr* athletic

athabascan *or* **athabaskan** *usu cap, var of* ATHAPASKAN

athal·a·mous \\(')ā'thaləməs\\ *adj* [[2]*a-* + L *thalam*us marriage bed, bedroom (fr. Gk *thalamos* bedroom, room) + E *-ous;* akin to Gk *tholos* rotunda — more at DALE] **1 :** lacking a torus or receptacle ⟨~ flowers⟩ **2 :** without apothecia, beds, or shields for spores ⟨~ lichens⟩

[1]ath·a·na·sian \\¦athə¦nāzhən, -nāsh-\\ *adj, usu cap* [*Athanasius* the Great †373 Greek church father & patriarch of Alexandria + E *-an*] **:** of or relating to Athanasius, who advocated the homoousian doctrine against Arianism

[2]athanasian \\"\\ *n* -s *usu cap* **:** an adherent of Athanasius or of his teachings

ath·a·na·sian·ism \\,⸗⸗'⸗⸗,nizəm\\ *n* -s *usu cap* **:** the theological doctrine of Athanasius; *esp* **:** the doctrine that the Son is of the same substance with the Father — opposed to *Arianism*

ath·a·nor \\'athə,nȯ(ə)r\\ *n* -s [ME, fr. (assumed) ML, fr. Ar *at-tannūr* the oven, fr. Aram *tannūr* oven] **:** a self-feeding digesting furnace that maintained a uniform and durable heat and was used by alchemists

ath·a·pas·kan *or* **ath·a·pas·can** \\¦athə¦paskən\\ *or* **ath·a·bas·can** *or* **ath·a·bas·kan** \\- ¦ba-\\ *n* -s *usu cap* [*Athapaska*, *Athapasca*, *Athabasca*, *Athabaska* an Athapaskan people (fr. Cree *Athap-askaw*, lit., grass or reeds here and there) + E *-an*] **1 :** a language stock of the Na-dene phylum in No. America consisting of the three groups Apachean, Pacific Athapaskan, and Déné or Northern Athapaskan **2 a :** a people speaking an Athapaskan language **b :** a member of any such people

athar *var of* ATTAR

ath·bash \\ät'bäsh, äth-, '⸗,⸗\\ *also* **at·bash** \\ät-, '⸗,⸗\\ *n* -ES [Heb *athbash*, a word formed from the first, last, second, and next-to-last letters of the Hebrew alphabet] **:** a cipher used in Jewish mystical and allegorical writing in which each letter of a word is replaced by that letter which stands as many places from the end of the Hebrew alphabet as the letter replaced stands from the beginning — compare ALBAM

athe·cae \\ə'thē(,)sē\\ *n pl, cap* [NL, fr. fem. pl. of (assumed) NL *athecus* having no cover, fr. NL [2]*a-* + (assumed) NL *-thecus* (fr. L *theca* cover, sheath) — more at TICK] **:** a division usu. made a suborder of Testudinata comprising turtles with the carapace separate from the internal skeleton and usu. with greatly reduced ossification and represented among recent forms by the marine leatherback — **athe·can** \\-ēkən\\ *adj or n*

ath·e·ca·ta \\,athə'käd·ə, -ād·ə\\ [NL, fr. [2]*a-* + *thec-* + *-ata*] *syn of* ANTHOMEDUSAE

athe·cate \\(')ā¦-; *in sense 2 also* 'athə,kāt, -,kət\\ *adj* **1** [[2]*a-* + *thecate*] **:** lacking a theca **2** [NL *Athecata*] **:** of or belonging to the gymnoblastic hydroids

ath·e·coi·dea \\,athə'kȯidēə\\ [NL, fr. [2]*a-* + *thec-* + *-oidea*] *syn of* ATHECAE

athe·ism \\'āthē,izəm\\ *n* -s [MF *athéisme*, fr. *athée* atheist (fr. Gk *atheos* godless, not believing in the existence of gods, fr. *a-* [2]a- + *theos* god) + *-isme* -ism — more at THE-] **1 a :** disbelief in the existence of God or any other deity **b :** the doctrine that there is neither God nor any other deity — compare AGNOSTICISM **2 :** godlessness esp. in conduct **:** UNGODLINESS, WICKEDNESS

[1]athe·ist \\-,əst\\ *n* -s [MF *athéiste*, fr. *athée* + *-iste* -ist] **:** one who subscribes to, advocates, or practices atheism **syn** see AGNOSTIC

[2]atheist \\"\\ *adj* **:** ATHEISTIC ⟨~ radicalism⟩

athe·is·tic \\¦āthē¦istik, -ēk\\ *also* **athe·is·ti·cal** \\-təkəl, -ēk-\\ *adj* **:** relating to, characterized by, or given to atheism **:** GODLESS, IMPIOUS, IRREVERENT — **athe·is·ti·cal·ly** \\-tək(ə)lē, -ēk-, -li\\ *adv* — **athe·is·tic·ness** *n* -ES

athe·ize \\'āthē,īz\\ *vt* -ED/-ING/-S [*athe*istic + *-ize*] **:** to make atheistic

ath·e·ling *also* **aeth·e·ling** \\'athəliŋ, -th-\\ *or* **eth·e·ling** \\'e-\\ *n* -s *often cap* [ME, fr. OE *ætheling* (akin to OHG *adalung* nobleman, OS *ethiling*, ON *öthlingr*), fr. *æthelu* nobility, family, nature + *-ling;* akin to OHG *adal* family, noble family, nobility, OS *athal*, ON *athal* nature, disposition, offspring, OE *ōthel* property, inheritance, OHG *uodal*, ON *ōthal*] **:** an Anglo-Saxon prince or nobleman; *esp* **:** the heir apparent or a prince of the royal family

athel tree \\'athəl-\\ *also* **athel tamarisk** *or* **athel** *n* -s [Ar *athlah*] **:** a small drought-resistant evergreen tree (*Tamarix aphylla*) native to southern and western Asia but now widely planted as an ornamental or shelter-belt tree in warm dry regions (as of the southwestern U. S. and Australia); *broadly* **:** any of several other trees or shrubs of the genus *Tamarix*

athematic \\¦ā + ⸗¦⸗⸗\\ *adj* [[2]*a-* + *thematic*] **1** *of a verb or class of verbs* **:** having no thematic vowel ⟨Sanskrit *as-ti* "he is", Greek *es-ti*, Latin *es-t* are ~ verbs⟩ **2** *music* **:** not based on the repetition or elaboration of themes ⟨an ~ style⟩

ath·e·nae·um *or* **ath·e·ne·um** \\,athə'nēəm\\ *n* -s [L *Athenaeum*, a school in ancient Rome for the study of the arts, fr. Gk *Athēnaion*, a temple of Athena in Athens where poets read their works, fr. *Athēna*, *Athēnē*, major Greek deity, goddess of war, fertility, arts, and wisdom] **1 :** a literary or scientific association or club **2 :** a building or a room in which books, periodicals, and newspapers are kept for use **:** READING ROOM, LIBRARY

[1]athe·ni·an \\ə'thēnēən, -nyən\\ *adj, usu cap* [L *Atheniensis*, adj. & n., fr. *Athenae* Athens (fr. Gk *Athēnai*) + L *-iensis* -ian] **:** of, relating to, or having the characteristics of Athens or its ancient civilization

[2]athenian \\"\\ *n* -s *cap* [L *Atheniensis*] **:** a native or inhabitant of Athens, esp. Athens, Greece

[1]ath·ens \\'athənz\\ *n* -ES *cap* [fr. *Athens*, city-state and cultural center of ancient Greece, fr. L *Athenae*, fr. Gk *Athēnai*] **:** a city regarded as a center of culture and intellectual achievement ⟨Boston has often been called the *Athens* of America⟩

[2]athens *adj, usu cap* [fr. *Athens*, Greece] **:** of or from Athens, the capital of Greece **:** of the kind or style prevalent in Athens **:** ATHENIAN

atheology \\¦ā+\\ *n* -ES [[2]*a-* + *theology*] **:** opposition to theology

athe·ous \\'āthēəs\\ *adj* [Gk *atheos* without god, fr. *a-* [2]a- + *theos* god — more at THEISM] **1** *obs* **:** ATHEISTIC **2 :** neither accepting nor denying the existence of God

ath·e·ric·era \\,athə'risərə\\ *n pl, cap* [NL, fr. Gk *athēr* barb, awn + NL *-cera*] *in some classifications* **:** a group of two-winged flies part of the suborder Cyclorrhapha and having three basal joints to the antennae and a bristle arising from the base of the third — **ath·e·ric·er·an** \\¦⸗⸗¦⸗⸗rən\\ *adj or n* — **ath·e·ric·er·ous** \\-rəs\\ *adj*

ath·er·i·na \\,athə'rīnə\\ *n* [NL, fr. Gk *atherinē* smelt] **1** *cap* **:** the type genus of Atherinidae **2** -s **:** a fish of the genus *Atherina*

ath·er·ine \\'⸗⸗,rīn, -,rən\\ *n* -s [NL *Atherina*] **:** any of numerous small fishes of the family Atherinidae; *esp* **:** a European food fish (*Atherina presbyter*)

ath·er·in·id \\,athə'rinəd, -rī-\\ *n* -s [NL *Atherinidae*] **:** a fish of the family Atherinidae **:** SILVERSIDES 1

ath·er·in·i·dae \\,⸗⸗'rinə,dē\\ *n pl, cap* [NL, fr. *Atherina*, type genus + *-idae*] **:** a family of small spiny-finned fishes of both salt and fresh water, all having a silvery band along the sides sometimes underlaid by black pigment — see SILVERSIDES

athe·ri·o·gae·an *or* **athe·ri·o·ge·an** \\ə¦thirēō¦jēən\\ *adj, usu cap* [NL *Atheriogaea*, *Atheriogea* Antarctogaea (fr. [2]*a-* + Gk *thērion* wild animal, animal — dim. of *thēr* beast of prey, wild animal — + NL *-gaea*, *-gea*) + E *-an* — more at FIERCE] **:** ANTARCTOGAEAN

ather·mal·ize \\¦a¦thərmə,līz, -thō-\\ *vt* -ED/-ING/-S [[2]*a-* + *thermal* + *-ize*] **:** to render (as an optical system) independent of temperature or of thermal effects

ather·man·cy \\¦⸗¦⸗mənsē\\ *n* -ES [[2]*a-* + *-thermancy* (as in *diathermancy*)] **:** inability to transmit infrared radiation — compare DIATHERMANCY

ather·ma·nous \\¦⸗¦⸗mənəs\\ *adj* [[2]*a-* + *-thermanous* (as in *diathermanous*)] **:** not transmitting infrared radiation — compare DIATHERMANOUS

athermic \\¦ā+¦⸗⸗\\ *adj* [[2]*a-* + *thermic*] **:** HEATLESS ⟨an ~ motor⟩

athero- *comb form* [NL, fr. *atheroma*] **:** atheroma ⟨*athero*genesis⟩

ath·er·o·ma \\,athə'rōmə\\ *n, pl* **atheromas** *also* **atheroma·ta** \\-'rōməd·ə\\ [NL, fr. L, a tumor containing gruellike matter, fr. Gk *athērōma*, fr. *athērē*, *athēra* gruel, fr. *ather-*, *athēr* beard of grain, point of a lance, barb; akin to Gk *antherix* beard of grain, stalk, *anthereōn* chin, *anthryskion* chervil, *anthrēnē* hornet, wasp] **:** a disease characterized by fatty degeneration of the inner coat of the arteries

ath·er·o·ma·to·sis \\,⸗⸗,⸗mə'tōsəs\\ *n, pl* **atheromato·ses** \\-ō,sēz\\ [NL, fr. *atheromat-*, *atheroma* + *-osis*] **:** a disease characterized by more or less generalized atheromatous degeneration of the arteries

ath·er·om·a·tous \\¦⸗⸗¦rämәd·əs, -ōm-\\ *also* **ath·er·o·mat·ic** \\-(,)rō¦mad·ik\\ *adj* [NL *atheromat-*, *atheroma* + E *-ous* or *-ic*] **:** of, relating to, or having the characteristics of atheroma

ath·er·o·sclerosis \\,athə(,)rō+\\ *n, pl* **atheroscleroses** [NL, fr. *athero-* + *sclerosis*] **:** a degenerative disease of the arteries that is a stage of arteriosclerosis and is characterized by the deposition of fatty substances in and the fibrous thickening of the intima, resulting in the narrowing of the vessel passages and ultimately hardening and loss of elasticity — **ath·er·o·sclerotic** \\¦⸗⸗(,)⸗ + ⸗¦⸗⸗\\ *adj*

ath·e·ru·rus \\,athə'ru̇rəs\\ *n, cap* [NL, fr. Gk *athēr* barb, awn + NL *-urus*] **:** a genus of long-bodied Old World porcupines having the tail scaly except at its spiny tip and comprising the brush-tailed porcupines

ath·e·te·sis \\,athə'tēsəs\\ *n, pl* **athete·ses** \\-ē,sēz\\ [Gk *athetēsis* art of setting aside, abolition, annulling, fr. *athetos* + *-ēsis* -esis] **:** the rejecting or marking of a passage (as in a poem) as spurious

ath·e·tize \\'⸗⸗,tīz\\ *vt* -ED/-ING/-S [Gk *athetein* (fr. *athetos* set aside, not fixed, fr. *a-* [2]a- + *thetos* placed, fr. *tithenai* to place) + E *-ize* — more at DO] **:** to reject or mark (a passage) as spurious ⟨the *athetized* lines of the Iliad⟩

[1]ath·e·toid \\'athə,tȯid\\ *adj* [ISV *athet-* (fr. NL *athetosis*) + *-oid*] **:** exhibiting or characteristic of athetosis ⟨~ children⟩ ⟨~ movements⟩

[2]athetoid \\"\\ *n* -s **:** an athetoid individual

ath·e·to·sis \\,athə'tōsəs\\ *n, pl* **atheto·ses** \\-ō,sēz\\ [NL, fr. Gk *athetos* + NL *-osis*] **:** a nervous disorder seen chiefly in children that is marked by continual slow movements esp. of the extremities and is usu. due to a brain lesion

ath·e·tot·ic \\¦⸗⸗¦täd·ik\\ *or* **ath·e·to·sic** \\-¦tōsik\\ *adj* [*athetotic* fr. NL *athetosis*, after such pairs as NL *hypnosis:* E *hypnotic; athetosic* fr. NL *athetosis* + E *-ic*] **:** relating to athetosis **:** ATHETOID

athing \əˈth(ˌ)iŋ, ˈä-\ *n* -s [7*a* + *thing*] *Scot* : EVERYTHING
athi·o·rho·da·ce·ae \a͟thˌthīəˌrōˈdāsēˌē\ *n pl, cap* [NL, fr. 2*a-* + *thi-* + *rhod-* + *-aceae*] : a family of small motile sulfur bacteria having polar flagella and red to brown coloration due to various combinations of bacteriochlorophyll and carotenoid pigments
athirst \əˈthərst, -ə̄st,-əist\ *adj* [ME *athirst, athurst,* fr. OE *ofthyrst, ofthyrsted,* past part. of *ofthyrstan* to suffer from thirst, fr. *of-* overcoming, destroying (fr. *of* off, from) + *thyrstan* to thirst — more at OF, THIRST] : THIRSTY: **a** : suffering from or experiencing thirst ⟨and when thou art ~ go unto the vessels and drink —Ruth 2:9 (AV)⟩ **b** : having a strong desire or yearning : EAGER, LONGING ⟨these that gather in mid-Manhattan . . . ~ for merriment —R.L.Shayon⟩ **syn** see EAGER
ath·lete \ˈath,lēt, *chiefly substand* -thə,l-; *usu* -ēd·+V\ *n* -s [ME, fr. L *athleta,* fr. Gk *athlētēs, aethlētēs,* fr. *athlein, aethlein* to contend for a prize, fr. *athlos, aethlos* contest, or *athlon, aethlon* prize, contest; perh. akin to L *vad-, vas* bail, security — more at WED] **1** : one who competed for a prize in the public games of ancient Greece and Rome **2 a** : one who is trained to compete either professionally or as an amateur in exercises, sports, or games requiring physical strength, agility, or stamina **b** : one who has a natural aptitude for or is reasonably skilled in physical exercises, sports, or games **3** : one who takes part in or is capable of taking part in exercises or activities requiring mental agility, endurance, or strength ⟨nor does the world cheer the natural ~s of the mind —J.M.Barzun⟩
athlete's foot *n* : ringworm of the feet characterized by softening and cracking of the skin between the toes, accompanied by painful itching, and caused by infection with any of several fungi and occasionally by unrelated organisms
athlete's heart *n* : a supposed hypertrophic dilated heart attributed to the effects of repeated overexertion (as on the part of professional athletes) — not used technically
ath·let·ic \(ˈ)athˈled·ik, -etik, -ēk, *chiefly substand* ˌathəˈl-\ *adj* [L *athleticus,* fr. Gk *athlētikos,* fr. *athlētēs* + *-ikos* -ic] **1** : of or relating to athletes or athletics ⟨the college ~ association⟩ **2** : having the characteristics of or befitting an athlete : STRONG, MUSCULAR, ROBUST, VIGOROUS, AGILE, ACTIVE ⟨an ~ build⟩ ⟨a powerful and ~ mind⟩ **3** : characterized by heavy frame, large chest, and powerful muscular development : MESOMORPHIC — compare ASTHENIC, PYKNIC **4** : designed or suitable for use or wear by athletes ⟨a new ~ dormitory⟩ ⟨~ shorts⟩ — **ath·let·i·cal·ly** \-ək(ə)lē, -ēk-, -li\ *adv*
ath·let·i·cism \athˈled·ə,sizəm, -letə-\ *n* -s **1 a** : an intense interest in athletics ⟨you carry your disdain of ~ too far —Christopher Isherwood⟩ **b** : an ardent participation in athletics **c** : a zealous encouragement of athletics **2** : intense energy or activity : STRENUOSITY ⟨an objective and healthy, almost happy ~ about his later works such as the *Third Symphony* —Aaron Copland⟩
ath·let·ics \athˈled·iks, -etiks, -ēks\ *n pl* **1** *sometimes sing in constr* **a** : the physical exercises, sports, or games engaged in by athletes ⟨intercollegiate ~⟩ **b** *Brit* : track-and-field sports **2** *usu sing in constr* **a** : the practice of athletic activities **b** : the principles of athletic activities and training
ath·o·dyd \ˈathəˌdid\ *n* -s [*aero-* + *thermodynamic* + *duct*] : a jet engine consisting essentially of a continuous duct or tube of varying diameter which admits air at the forward end, adds heat to it by the combustion of fuel, and discharges it from the after end
athole brose *or* **atholl brose** \ˈathəlˈbrōz\ *n, usu cap A* [fr. *Athole, Atholl,* district in Scotland] *Scot* : whiskey mixed with honey or meal
at home \ətˈhōm, *Brit sometimes* əˈtōm\ *n* : a reception given at one's home ⟨if you are serving tea and chocolate and a variety of food . . . call it an *at home* —Emily Post⟩
at-home·ness \ˈ"+nəs\ *n* -ES : the quality or state of being at home ⟨his complete *at-homeness* in Chopin's music —Virgil Thomson⟩
1**atho·nite** \ˈathəˌnīt\ *adj, usu cap* [L *Athon-, Athos* Athos, mountain in northeastern Greece (fr. Gk *Athōs* — acc. sometimes *Athōn*) + E *-ite*] : of or relating to Mount Athos, an important monastic center of the Eastern Orthodox Church
2**athonite** \"\ *n* -s *usu cap* : a monk of Mount Athos, Greece
athort \əˈthȯrt\ *Scot var of* ATHWART
athrep·sia \əˈthrepsēə, āˈ-\ *n* -s [NL, fr. 2*a-* + Gk *threpsis* nourishing + NL *-ia*] : MARASMUS — **athrep·tic** \əˈthreptik, (ˈ)āˈ-\ *adj*
athrill \əˈ-\ *adj* [1*a-* + *thrill* (v.)] : in a state of thrill : EXCITED ⟨his whole being was ~ with excitement —O.E.Rölvaag⟩
athrob \əˈ-\ *adj* [1*a-* + *throb* (v.)] : THROBBING
ath·ro·cyte \ˈathrəˌsīt\ *n* -s [ISV *athro-* (fr. Gk *athroos* collected) + *-cyte*] : a cell (as a Kupffer cell) having the property of picking up extraneous material and storing it in granular form in its cytoplasm — compare PHAGOCYTE — **ath·ro·cy·to·sis** \ˌ==ˌsīˈtōsəs\ *n, pl* **athrocytoses**
ath·ro·gen·ic \ˌathrəˈjenik\ *adj* [F *athrogénique,* fr. Gk *athroos, hathroos* together, collected + F *-génique* -genic; akin to Skt *sādhati* he comes to his goal, Av *āsna* successful, Gk *ithys* straight] : of or relating to clastic rocks of igneous origin
1**athwart** \əˈ-\ *adv* [ME, adv. & prep., fr. 1*a-* + *thwart*] **1 a** : from side to side : across esp. in an oblique direction : TRANSVERSELY ⟨the line of probable advance runs ~ to the high chains of mountains —W.V.Pratt⟩ **b** : at right angles to the center line (of a ship) **2** : in opposition to the right or expected course : CROSSWISE, AWRY ⟨and quite ~ goes all decorum —Shak.⟩
2**athwart** \"\ *prep* [ME] **1 a** : from side to side of : transversely over : ACROSS ⟨a row of steppingstones set ~ the creek —Eden Phillpotts⟩ **b** : from side to side of the length, direction, or course of (a ship) : ACROSS ⟨a fleet standing ~ our course⟩ **2** : in opposition to : contrary to ⟨a procedure directly ~ the New England prejudices —R.G.Cole⟩
athwart·hawse \" + ˌ-\ *adv (or adj)* : across the cable or stem (of another ship) — used with following *of*
athwart·ship \"+ˌ-\ *adj* : across the ship from side to side ⟨this vessel has two watertight ~ bulkheads in the middle portion —E.L.Attwood⟩ — opposed to *fore-and-aft*
athwart·ships \-ˌships\ *adv* [*athwart* + *ship* + *-s*] : across the ship from side to side ⟨the boilers were installed ~⟩
athwart·wise \-t·ˌwīz\ *adv (or adj)* : CROSSWISE
athy·re·o·sis \ˌāˌthīrēˈōsəs\ *n, pl* **athyreo·ses** \-ōˌsēz\ [NL, fr. 2*a-* + *thyreo-* + *-osis*] : an abnormal condition caused by absence or functional deficiency of the thyroid gland — **athy·re·ot·ic** \ˌ;==ˈäd·ik\ *adj*
ath·y·ris \ˈathərəs\ *n, cap* [NL, fr. 2*a-* + Gk *thyris* valve, opening] : a genus of smooth biconvex extinct brachiopods having the plates of the brachidium prolonged into spirally rolled laterally directed processes
athyr·i·um \əˈthirēəm\ *n, cap* [NL, irreg. fr. Gk *athoros* without sperm (fr. *a-* 2*a-* + *thoros* semen) + NL *-ium;* akin to MIr *dairim* I leap upon, Skt *dhārā* stream] : a genus of ferns (family Polypodiaceae) differing from *Asplenium* (in which it is often included) in having curved or lunate sori — compare LADY FERN
1**athyroid** \ˈathəˌrȯid\ *adj* [NL *Athyris* + E *-oid*] : belonging to or characteristic of the genus *Athyris*
2**athyroid** \"\ *n* -s : a brachiopod of the genus *Athyris* — see BRACHIOPOD illustration
ati \ˈäd·ē\ *n, pl* **ati** *or* **atis** *usu cap* [Hiligaynon] **1** : a predominantly pagan Negritoid people on Panay, Philippines **2** : a member of the Ati people
at·i·ko·ka·nia \ˌad·ə(ˌ)kōˈkānēə, -nyə\ *n, cap* [NL, fr. *Atikokan* river, Ontario, Canada + NL *-ia*] : a genus of Precambrian fossils possibly of siliceous sponges and if actually such the only fossil animal known from this early period
atilt \əˈ-\ *adj (or adv)* [1*a-* + *tilt,* v.] **1** : in a tilting position ⟨huge trees dangerously ~ were still falling —G.S.Perry⟩ **2** : with lance in hand (as in a tourney) ⟨run ~ at men —Samuel Butler †1680⟩
-ating *pres part of* -ATE
atin·gle \əˈ-\ *adj* [1*a-* + *tingle,* v.] : TINGLING
-a·tion \ˈāshən\ *n suffix* -s [ME *-acioun,* fr. OF *-ation,* fr. L *-ation-, -atio,* fr. *-atus* -ate + *-ion-, -io* -ion] : action or process ⟨computa*tion*⟩ ⟨flirta*tion*⟩ ⟨visita*tion*⟩ : something connected with an action or process ⟨civiliza*tion*⟩ ⟨discolora*tion*⟩
a·tip·toe \əˈ-\ *adv (or adj)* [1*a-* + *tiptoe*] **1** : on the tip of one's toes ⟨stood ~ by the terrace wall watching the barges —Anne Green⟩ **2** : in a state of expectancy : alert and expectant ⟨it was disquieting news and the ordnance . . . is ~ —*Nation*⟩
1**atis** \əˈtēs\ *n* -ES [Hindi *atīs*] **1** : a monkshood (*Aconitum heterophyllum*) found in the Himalayas **2** : any of several trees of the genus *Annona; esp* : SWEETSOP
2**atis** *pl of* ATI
ati·u·an \ˌädˈēˈüən\ *adj, usu cap* [*Atiu,* one of the Cook islands in the So. Pacific + E *-an*] : of or concerning the island of Atiu
-a·tive *When the preceding syllable has a stress (as in "purgative") əd·iv or ətiv or, sometimes in some words (as "rotative") answering to paroxytone disyllabic verbs in "-ate", ˌād·iv or ˌātiv or -ēv also -əv; when the preceding syllable is noninitial and unstressed (as in "legislative" or "nominative") ˌā- or ˌə-; in some words (as "elative") answering to oxytone verbs in "-ate",* ˈā-\ *adj suffix* [ME, fr. MF *-atif,* fr. L *-ativus,* fr. *-atus* -ate + *-ivus* -ive] : of, relating to, or connected with ⟨authorit*ative*⟩ ⟨consult*ative*⟩ ⟨norm*ative*⟩ ⟨quantit*ative*⟩ : tending to ⟨fix*ative*⟩ ⟨form*ative*⟩ ⟨lax*ative*⟩ ⟨talk*ative*⟩
atjeh·nese \ˌachəˈnēz, ˌä-, -ēs\ *n, pl* **atjehnese** *usu cap* [*Atjeh,* part of Sumatra + E *-nese* (as in *Japanese*)] **1** : a Muslim Indonesian people of northern Sumatra **2** : a member of the Atjehnese people
at·ka mackerel *also* **atka fish** \ˈatkə-, ˈät-\ *n, usu cap A* [fr. *Atka* Island, Alaska, its locality] : a valuable marine food fish (*Pleurogrammus monopterygius*) of the family Hexagrammidae of Alaska and adjacent regions
atlant- *or* **atlanto-** *comb form* [NL *atlant-, atlas*] **1** : atlas (sense 3) ⟨*atlant*ad⟩ **2** : atlantal and ⟨*atlanto*axial⟩ ⟨*atlanto*-odontoid⟩
1**at·lan·ta** \ətˈlantə, at-\ *n, cap* [NL, prob. irreg. fr. L (*mare*) *Atlanticum* Atlantic ocean, fr. *Atlanticum,* neut. of *Atlanticus* Atlantic] : a cosmopolitan genus (the type of the small family Atlantidae) comprising small transparent heteropod mollusks with a sharply keeled spiral shell
2**at·lan·ta** \ətˈlantə, -aan-\ *adj, usu cap* [fr. *Atlanta,* Ga.] : of or from Atlanta, the capital of Georgia ⟨an *Atlanta* businessman⟩ : of the kind or style prevalent in Atlanta
at·lan·tad \-ˌtad\ *adv* [NL *atlant-, atlas* + E *-ad*] *anat* : toward the atlas
at·lan·tal \ətˈlantᵊl, (ˈ)atˈ-\ *adj* [NL *atlant-, atlas* + E *-al*] **1** *anat* : of or relating to the atlas **2** *anat* : ANTERIOR, CEPHALIC
1**at·lan·tan** \ətˈlantᵊn, -ntən\ *or* **at·lan·ti·an** \-ntēən\ *adj, usu cap* [*Atlanta,* Georgia + E *-an, -ian*] **1** : of, relating to, or characteristic of Atlanta, the capital of Georgia **2** : of, relating to, or characteristic of the people of Atlanta
2**atlantan** \"\ *or* **atlantian** \"\ *n* -s *cap* : a native or resident of Atlanta
1**at·lan·te·an** \ˌatˌlanˈtēən, -ˌlən-; ətˈlant-, (ˈ)atˈlant-\ *adj, usu cap* [L *Atlanteus* (fr. *Atlant-, Atlas*) + E *-an*] : of, relating to, or resembling Atlas : STRONG ⟨my *Atlantean* shoulders are bent beneath the load of the firmament —L.P.Smith⟩
2**atlantean** \"\ *adj, usu cap* [*Atlantis,* legendary sunken continent in the Atlantic ocean, mentioned by Pliny and Plato (fr. L, fr. Gk, prob. fr. *Atlantis* Atlantic ocean) + E *-ean*] : of or relating to Atlantis or its hypothetical culture
atlantes *pl of* ATLAS
at·lan·tic \ətˈlantik, -aan-, -ēk\ *adj* [L *Atlanticus,* fr. Gk *Atlantikos,* fr. *Atlantis* Atlantic ocean (fr. *Atlant-, Atlas,* the Titan or the Atlas mountains in southern Mauretania, named after him) + *-ikos* -ic] **1** *usu cap* **a** : of, relating to, or found in, on, or near the Atlantic ocean ⟨the author's picture is fundamentally valid for our *Atlantic* civilization as a whole —H.M.Parshley⟩ **b** : of, relating to, or found on or near the east coast of the U.S. ⟨the chief *Atlantic* ports⟩ ⟨the middle-*Atlantic* states⟩ **2** [NL *atlant-, atlas* + E *-ic*] *anat* : of or relating to the atlas
atlantic bonito *n, usu cap A* : an oily-fleshed bonito (*Sarda sarda*) of the western Atlantic that is marked with oblique dark stripes, is highly regarded as a sport fish, but is little used for food — compare CHILE BONITO, PACIFIC BONITO
atlantic brant *n, usu cap A* : AMERICAN BRANT
atlantic croaker *n, usu cap A* : a small but important food fish (*Micropogon undulatus*) of the Gulf coast and the Atlantic coast south of Cape Cod
atlantic flyway *n, usu cap A* : the easternmost of the American flyways extending northward between the Atlantic ocean and the Appalachians and dividing northerly into a western branch through West Virginia and Pennsylvania, a central up the Hudson river to Canada, and a northeasterly across New England
atlantic halibut *n, usu cap A* : the halibut (*Hippoglossus hippoglossus*) of the No. Atlantic
atlantic kittiwake *n, usu cap A* : a kittiwake (*Rissa tridactyla*) of the No. Atlantic coasts largely pure white with pale gray mantling and black wing tips and feet — compare PACIFIC KITTIWAKE
atlantic puffin *n, usu cap A* : a puffin (*Fratercula arctica*) of the No. Atlantic largely white below but with the upper parts blackish
atlantic sailfish *n, usu cap A* : a sailfish (*Istiophorus americanus*) common in the warmer parts of the Atlantic and the Gulf of Mexico that is highly esteemed as a sport fish and whose smoked flesh is considered a delicacy
atlantic salmon *n, usu cap A* : SALMON 1a
atlantic time *or* **atlantic standard time** *n, cap A* : the time of the 4th time zone west of Greenwich that is based on the 60th meridian, is used in Nova Scotia, New Brunswick, Prince Edward Island, eastern Quebec, Puerto Rico, and the Virgin islands, and is one hour faster than eastern time
at·lan·tite \ətˈlanˌtīt\ *n* -s [ISV *Atlantic* + *-ite;* orig. formed as G *atlantit;* fr. its occurrence in the Atlantic petrographic province] : a melanocratic nephelite-basalt rock consisting of plagioclase, augite, and olivine phenocrysts in a groundmass predominantly nephelite
atlanto- — see ATLANT-
at·lan·to·sau·rus \ətˌlantəˈsȯrəs\ [NL, fr. L *Atlant-, Atlas* (fr. Gk) + NL *-o-* + *-saurus*] *syn of* CAMARASAURUS
1**at·las** \ˈatləs\ *n* -ES *see sense 4* [after *Atlas,* a Titan of Greek mythology often represented as bearing the heavens on his shoulders, fr. L *Atlant-, Atlas,* fr. Gk] **1** *usu cap* : one who bears a heavy burden : chief supporter : MAINSTAY **2** [fr. NL *Atlas,* title of a cartographical work (published in 1595) by Gerhardus Mercator (Gerhard Kremer) †1594 Flemish geographer; prob. fr. the fact that the title pages of cartographical works of this period often had a representation of Atlas bearing the heavens] **a** : a bound collection of maps ⟨a glance at the ~ showed that the city is near the coast⟩ **b** : a bound collection of tables, charts, or plates illustrating any subject ⟨an ~ of peripheral nerve injuries⟩ ⟨a chromosome ~⟩ ⟨an ~ of climatic charts⟩ **3** [NL, fr. Gk, after *Atlas,* the Titan] : the first cervical vertebra articulating immediately with the skull and thus sustaining the globe of the head **4** *pl usu* **at·lan·tes** \ətˈlan(ˌ)tēz, at-, -aan-\ [Gk, after *Atlas,* the Titan] : a figure or half figure of a man used as a column to support an entablature — called also *telamon;* compare CARYATID

atlas 4: one of the atlantes from Theater of Bacchus, Athens

2**atlas** \"\ *n* -ES [Ar *aṭlas*] : a rich satin made in the Far East
atlas beetle *n, usu cap A* : a very large shining mahogany-colored grotesquely horned beetle (*Chalcosoma atlas*) of the Old World tropics
atlas cedar *n, usu cap A* : an Algerian evergreen tree (*Cedrus atlantica*) much planted for ornament esp. in some of its horticultural bluish-foliaged forms
atlas moth *n, usu cap A* **1** : a giant silk moth (*Attacus atlas*) widespread and often abundant in Asia that is cultured for silk in some places **2** : any of several giant silk moths of the East Indies and southern Asia
at·latl \ˈatˌlatᵊl, ätˌlä-\ *n* -s [of Uto-Aztecan origin; akin to Nahuatl *atlatl* spear thrower] : THROWING-STICK; *specif* : the spear thrower of ancient Mexico
at·le *or* **at·lee** \ˈatlē\ *n* -s [Ar *athlah* tamarisk] : ATHEL TREE
atlo- *comb form* [*atlas*] : atlantal and ⟨*atlo*axoid⟩
at·loid \ˈatˌlȯid\ *or* **at·loi·de·an** \ətˈlȯidēən, (ˈ)atˈ-\ *adj* [F *atloïde,* fr. NL *atlas* + F *-oïde* -oid] : ATLANTAL
atloido- *comb form* [F *atloïdo-,* fr. *atloïde*] : atlantal and ⟨*atloido*axoid⟩
atm- *or* **atmo-** *comb form* [NL *atmo-* vapor, fr. Gk *atm-, atmo-,* fr. *atmos;* akin to Gk *aēnai* to blow — more at WIND] : vapor ⟨*atm*iatry⟩ : air ⟨*atmo*genic⟩
atm *abbr* atmosphere
at·man \ˈätmən\ *n* -s *often cap* [Skt *ātman* breath, self, soul, Universal Self, Supreme Spirit; akin to OHG *ātum* breath] *Hinduism* : the innermost essence of each individual; *often* : the supreme universal self
atmid- *or* **atmido-** *comb form* [ISV, fr. Gk, fr. *atmid-, atmis,* fr. *atmos*] : steam ⟨*atmid*albumin⟩ ⟨*atmido*meter⟩
at·mo·clas·tic \ˌatməˈklastik\ *adj* [*atm-* + *clastic*] : disintegrated by atmospheric action and consolidated or cemented without transportation — used of rock
at·mo·gen·ic \-ˈjenik\ *adj* [*atm-* + *-genic*] : of atmospheric origin by condensation, wind action, or deposition from volcanic vapors ⟨~ glacial ice⟩—used chiefly of rocks and minerals
at·mol·y·sis \ətˈmäləsəs, at-\ *n, pl* **atmoly·ses** \-əˌsēz\ [NL, fr. *atm-* + *-lysis*] : the act or process of separating mingled gases of unequal diffusibility by transmission through porous substances
at·mom·e·ter \-ˈmäməd·ə(r), -ətə-\ *n* -s [*atm-* + *-meter*] : an instrument for measuring the evaporating capacity of the air
at·mo·phile \ˈatməˌfīl\ *or* **at·mo·phil** \-ˌfil\ *adj* [*atm-* + *-phile, -phil*] : found in, attracted to, or having a tendency to occur in the atmosphere — used esp. of chemical elements or compounds
1**at·mo·sphere** \ˈatməˌsfi(ə)r, -iə\ *n* -s [NL *atmosphaera,* fr. Gk *atm-* + L *sphaera* sphere — more at SPHERE] **1 a** : a gaseous mass enveloping a heavenly body (as a planet or satellite) ⟨the ~ of Mars⟩ **b** : the whole mass of air surrounding the earth **c** : a gaseous envelope or medium ⟨an inert ~⟩ **2** : a supposed medium around various bodies : any surrounding envelope ⟨the ~ of electrons⟩ **3** : the air of a given place or locality esp. as affected by a particular characteristic (as heat, moisture, wholesomeness, or unwholesomeness) ⟨the close ~ of the schoolroom⟩ ⟨the fetid swamp ~⟩ ⟨a refreshing mountain ~⟩ **4 a** : a conditioning surrounding influence : mental or moral environment : physical milieu viewed as having a mental or moral influence ⟨an ~ of war, of blood, of excitement —Stuart Cloete⟩ ⟨the Sunday-school ~ of conventional religiosity —Havelock Ellis⟩ **b** : the typical environment of a given locality or period, class of people, or way of life : characteristic background or setting ⟨the ~ of a New England college town —C.G.Poore⟩ **5** : a unit of pressure equal to 101,325 newtons per square meter and very nearly equal to the pressure exerted by a vertical column of mercury 760 millimeters high at a temperature of 0°C under standard gravity **6 a** : the pervasive strongly dominant mood of a creative work (as a painting, symphony, or poem) evoked by and dependent on the successful suggestion, delineation, and heightening of elements vital to the desired effect ⟨the brooding ~ of *Macbeth*⟩ **b** : overall aesthetic effect of a creative work (as of art) that succeeds in producing a sense of intimate contact with and sharing in its physical or psychic environment ⟨a novel rich in ~⟩ **c** : color, interest, and appeal : FASCINATION : individual or exotic tone or effect ⟨a tiny inn that was full of ~⟩ **d** : intriguing effect esp. when arising from exotic, bizarre, or other beguilingly unusual qualities ⟨the languorous, bewitching ~ of a pagan island⟩ **7** : a brownish pink that is slightly redder and duller than nude — called also *mauve blush* **8** : an effect of slight haziness or mistiness (as that caused by particles of dust or moisture suspended in the air and leading to the diffusion of light rays); *specif* : such an effect in a painting
2**atmosphere** \"\ *vb* -ED/ -ING/ -S *vt* : to provide with atmosphere or an atmosphere ⟨the play needs to be *atmosphered*⟩ ~ *vi* : to be accessible to the atmosphere : VENT ⟨a water tank with a single pipe for *atmosphering*⟩
at·mo·spher·ic \ˌ==ˈsfirik, -er-, -ēk\ *also* **at·mo·spher·i·cal** \-rəkəl, -ēk-\ *adj* **1 a** : of or relating to the atmosphere ⟨favorable ~ conditions⟩ **b** : like the atmosphere : AIRY ⟨fine lace with an ~ lightness⟩ **c** : occurring in or actuated by the atmosphere ⟨~ disturbances⟩ ⟨~ moisture⟩ **2** : having, marked by, or contributing atmosphere or an atmosphere ⟨an engaging ~ book⟩ ⟨tales handled in a poetic ~ way⟩ ⟨~ music⟩ **3** : having an effect of haziness ⟨~ subdued colors⟩ — **at·mo·spher·i·cal·ly** \-rək(ə)lē, -ēk-, -li\ *adv*
atmospheric absorption *n* : absorption of radio waves by the atmosphere
atmospheric electricity *n* : electricity involved in such natural phenomena as lightning, St. Elmo's fire, or the aurora borealis
atmospheric perspective *n* : AERIAL PERSPECTIVE
atmospheric pressure *n* : the pressure exerted in every direction at any given point by the weight of the atmosphere
at·mo·spher·ics \ˌatməˈsfiriks, -er-, -ēks\ *n pl* **1 a** : disturbances produced in radio receiving apparatus by atmospheric electrical phenomena (as electrical storms) : STATIC **b** : atmospheric electrical phenomena **2** : ATMOSPHERE 6 ⟨midnight, rain-swept, graveyard ~ —W.T.Scott⟩
atmospheric tide *n* : one of the tidal movements of the atmosphere resembling those of the ocean but produced mainly by diurnal temperature changes
ato \ˈäd·ō\ *n, pl* **atos** *or* **ato** [Bontok] : a political division of a Bontok village
ato·cha \əˈtōchə, āˈ-\ *n* -s [Sp] : ESPARTO 1
ato·kan \əˈtōkən\ *adj, usu cap* [*Atoka* county, Okla. + E *-an*] : of or relating to a subdivision of the Pennsylvanian geologic period — see GEOLOGIC TIME table
atoke \ˈaˌtōk, ˈā-\ *n* -s [Gk *atokos* without offspring, fr. *a-* 2*a-* + *tokos* childbirth, offspring; akin to Gk *teknon* child — more at THANE] : the anterior sexless part of certain polychaete worms from which grows the sexual portion — compare EPITOKE — **at·o·kous** *also* **at·o·cous** \ˈad·əkəs\ *or* **at·o·kal** \-kəl\ *adj*
ato·le \əˈtō(ˌ)lā\ *n* -s [Sp, fr. Nahuatl *atolli*] : corn meal that is cooked and eaten as mush or that is drunk as a thin gruel
at·oll \ˈaˌtȯl, -äl, -ōl *also* ˈā- *sometimes* aˈt- *or* əˈt-\ *n* -s [native name in the Maldive islands] : a coral reef appearing above the sea as a low ring-shaped coral island or as a chain of closely spaced coral islets enclosing or nearly enclosing a shallow lagoon that may vary in diameter from less than a mile to 80 or more miles
at·om \ˈad·əm, ˈatəm\ *n* -s *often attrib* [ME *atome,* fr. L *atomus,* fr. Gk *atomos,* fr. *atomos* indivisible, fr. *a-* 2*a-* + *tomos,* verbal of *temnein* to cut — more at TOME] **1** *philos* **a** : one of the minute, indivisible, discrete, and concrete particles of which according to ancient materialism the universe is composed; *often* : a similar particle considered as being of the stuff of which the mind is composed **b** : one of the various final irreducible or basic units or constituents of which according to different theories the universe is ultimately constructed (as minute things or processes in physicalistic theories and presentations or sense qualia in phenomenalistic theories); *often* : a logical construct that is formed from such basic units **c** : a particular or an element that is considered to be ultimate or unanalyzable for the purposes of a given system **2 a** : a tiny particle : MOTE, BIT ⟨~s of dust dancing in the sunlight⟩ ⟨the glass bowl was smashed to ~s⟩ **b** : the smallest possible part : minute fragment : tiny portion or quantity ⟨not an ~ of water to drink⟩ ⟨without an ~ of common sense⟩ **c** : a very small creature or object : MITE ⟨brilliant hummingbirds, flashing ~s of color⟩ **d** : a small individual unit usu. viewed as a relatively independent member of a group ⟨every man is a social ~⟩ **3 a** *according to the atomic theory* : the smallest particle of an element that can exist either alone or in combination with similar particles of the same or of a different element : the smallest particle of an element that enters into the composition of molecules — see ATOMIC THEORY 2 **b** : a group of such particles constituting the smallest quantity of a radical ⟨an ~ of ammonium⟩ **c** : MOLECULE — used esp. in earlier literature **d** : a quantity proportional to the atomic weight : the atomic weight in grams : GRAM ATOM **4** : the atom

considered as a source of vast potential destructive or constructive energy ⟨attempts to use the ~ in peacetime projects⟩; *esp* **:** the atom as the core nucleus of the fission bomb ⟨trying to defend our cities against the ~⟩

at·om·ate \-,māt, -mət\ *adj, bot* **:** sprinkled with small particles

atom beam *or* **atomic beam** *n* **:** a beam of molecular rays composed of the monatomic molecules of a vaporized metal

atom bomb *or* **atomic bomb** *n* **1 :** a bomb whose violent explosive power is due to the sudden release of atomic energy resulting from the splitting of nuclei of a heavy chemical element (as plutonium or uranium) by neutrons in a very rapid chain reaction — called also *fission bomb;* contrasted with *fusion bomb* **2 :** any bomb whose explosive power is due to the release of atomic energy

atom–bomb \'=‚=\ *vt* **:** to bomb with an atom bomb ~ *vi* **:** to drop an atom bomb

atomic \ə'tämik, -ēk *also* a'-\ *also* **atomical** \-məkəl, -ēk-\ *adj* **1 :** of, relating to, or concerned with atoms **2 :** marked by acceptance of the theory of atomism **3 :** MINUTE **:** divided into minute particles **4 :** being ultimate, logically simple, unanalyzable, or noncompound either actually or taken as such within a given universe of discourse ⟨"this is red" may be considered an ~ proposition⟩; *specif* **:** without sentential connectives and variables — compare MONADIC 5 *of a chemical element* **:** in the state of separate atoms **:** not combined with itself or with other elements ⟨~ hydrogen⟩ **6 :** of, relating to, or utilizing changes in the nucleus of an atom: **a :** utilizing atomic energy ⟨~ power⟩ ⟨~ weapons⟩ **b :** utilizing or resulting from an atom bomb ⟨~ armaments⟩ ⟨~ warfare⟩ ⟨an ~ explosion⟩ — **atom·i·cal·ly** \-mək(ə)lē, -ēk-, -li\ *adv*

atomic clock *n* **:** a precision clock that depends for its operation on an electrical oscillator (as a quartz crystal) regulated by the natural vibration frequencies of an atomic system (as a beam of cesium atoms or of ammonia molecules)

atomic cocktail *n* **:** a radioactive substance (as sodium iodide) administered orally in water to patients with cancer

atomic constant *n* **:** any one of certain fundamental constants (as the electronic charge *e*, the electronic mass *m*, and the Planck constant *h*) relating to all atoms

atomic energy *n* **:** energy that can be liberated by changes in the nucleus of an atom (as by fission of a heavy nucleus or fusion of light nuclei into heavier ones with accompanying loss of mass)

atomic furnace *n* **:** REACTOR

atomic heat *n* **:** the thermal capacity per gram atom of any element, being the specific heat in calories per degree per gram multiplied by the atomic weight — compare DULONG AND PETIT'S LAW, MOLECULAR HEAT

atomic hydrogen welding *n* **:** arc welding that utilizes an alternating-current arc between two metal electrodes to dissociate hydrogen from a surrounding stream so that when the hydrogen atoms recombine into molecules at the surface of the part being welded they supply to the surface for fusion the heat that was absorbed in the arc during dissociation

at·o·mic·i·ty \‚ad·ə'misəd·ē, ‚atə-, -ətē, -i\ *n* -ES [ISV *atomic* + *-ity*] **1 a :** VALENCE **b :** the number of atoms in the molecule of an element **c :** the number of replaceable atoms or groups in the molecule of a compound **2 :** the state of consisting of atoms **3** *philos* **:** the nature, character, or property of being atomic

atomic mass *n* **:** the mass of any species of atom usu. expressed in atomic mass units

atomic mass unit *n* **:** a unit of mass for expressing masses of atoms, molecules, or nuclear particles equal to $\frac{1}{12}$ of the atomic mass of the most abundant carbon isotope, $_6C^{12}$, which is about 1.66043×10^{-27} kilogram or in terms of equivalent energy to about 9.31478×10^8 electron volts — called also *mass unit*

atomic number *n* **:** a number characteristic of an element and taken to represent the positive charge on the nucleus of an atom of the element, being equal to the number of protons in the nucleus and in a neutral atom to the number of electrons outside the nucleus, an atomic number as determined experimentally by X-ray spectra being assigned to each element and determining its place in the periodic table and its properties except those depending on atomic weight — symbol *Z;* abbr. *at. no.;* see ELEMENT table; ISOTOPE, PERIODIC TABLE

atomic pile *n* **:** REACTOR

atom·ics \ə'tämiks, -ēks *also* a'-\ *n pl but sing in constr* **:** the science of atoms esp. as applied in the development and utilization of atomic energy for bombs or power

atomic spectrum *n* **:** a spectrum of radiation due to electron transitions within atoms and consisting mainly of series of spectrum lines characteristic of the element

atomic theory *n* **1 :** ATOMISM 1 **2** *also* **atomic hypothesis :** a theory of the nature of matter: all material substances are composed of minute particles or atoms of a comparatively small number of kinds, all the atoms of the same kind being uniform in size, weight, and other properties **3 :** any of several theories of the structure of the atom, most modern ones, based on experimentation and theoretical considerations, holding that the atom is composed essentially of a small positively charged comparatively heavy nucleus surrounded by a comparatively large arrangement of electrons — compare THOMSON'S HYPOTHESIS, RUTHERFORD ATOM, LEWIS-LANGMUIR THEORY, BOHR THEORY, SCHRÖDINGER ATOM

atomic volume *n* **:** the quotient obtained by dividing the atomic weight of an element by its specific gravity

atomic weight *n* **:** the average relative weight of an element as it occurs in nature referred to some element taken as a standard, hydrogen sometimes being assigned an atomic weight of 1 but oxygen with an atomic weight of 16 or carbon with an atomic weight of 12 usu. being taken as a basis — abbr. *at. wt.;* see ELEMENT table, PERIODIC TABLE; compare ATOMIC MASS, ISOTOPE

at·om·ism \'ad·ə‚mizəm, 'atə-\ *n* -S **1 :** a doctrine according to which either the physical universe or the physical and mental universe is composed of simple, indivisible, and minute particles or atoms: as **a :** the theory formulated in pre-Socratic times by Leucippus and Democritus who taught that all phenomena are to be explained by the incessant movement of atoms differing only in shape, order, and position **b :** one of the various modern philosophical theories treating atoms as composed either of sense elements or as matter of which the mind is made up — compare NEUTRAL MONISM, PANPSYCHISM, PHENOMENALISM **2 a :** ATOMIC THEORY 3 **b :** ATOMICITY **3 :** the psychological doctrine that perceptions, thoughts, and all mental processes are built up by the combination of simple elements **4 a :** division of society into individual units or groups ⟨the caste ~ of India⟩ **b :** a theory or doctrine holding that the individual is the only objective unit of analysis **c :** a tendency toward individualism; *esp* **:** mutually opposed or antagonistic action of the members of a group or society

at·om·ist \-məst\ *n* -S **:** an adherent of atomism

at·om·is·tic \‚ad·ə'mistik, ‚atə-, -ēk\ *also* **at·om·is·ti·cal** \-tәkəl, -ēk-\ *adj* **1 :** of or relating to atoms **2 a :** relating to, based on, or characterized by atomism **b :** viewing the content of consciousness or the succession of ideas or mental experiences as the primary concern of psychology (as among structuralists and existentialists) rather than the integrated conscious self (as among holists and personalists) **3 :** characterized by a structure made up of sharply distinct and independent individuals or units ⟨an ~ society⟩ ⟨an ~ economy⟩ **:** tending toward atomism or individualism ⟨~ social structure⟩ — **at·om·is·ti·cal·ly** \-tək(ə)lē, -ēk-, -li\ *adv*

at·om·is·tics \‚=='mistiks, -ēks\ *n pl but sing in constr* **:** a branch of science dealing with the atom **:** the art of applied use of atomic energy

at·om·i·za·tion \‚ad·əmə'zāshən, ‚atəm-, -‚mī'z-\ *n* -S **:** the act or process of atomizing

at·om·ize \'==‚mīz\ *vt* -ED/-ING/-S *see -ize in Explan Notes* **1 :** to reduce to minute particles ⟨the TNT *atomized* the bridge⟩ **2 :** to convert (a liquid or solid) to a fine spray, minute particles, or light dust ⟨*atomized* fuel oil⟩ ⟨*atomized* soft coal⟩ ⟨an *atomized* medicated powder⟩ **3 a :** to divide in atomistic multiplicity ⟨alone in an unsympathetic *atomized* society⟩ **b :** to view or treat as made up of discrete or atomistic units rather than as an organismic whole ⟨*atomizing* human behavior⟩ **4 :** to subject (a place) to an atomic attack **:** devastate by atomic bombing **5 :** to individualize or cause to lose social cohesion ⟨contacts with Europeans have *atomized* some native cultures⟩

at·om·iz·er \-zə(r)\ *n* -S **1 :** one that atomizes **2 :** an instrument for atomizing; *esp* **:** an instrument that atomizes a perfume or disinfectant

atomizer

atoms *pl of* ATOM

atom smasher *n* **:** ACCELERATOR 1g

¹**at·o·my** \'ad·əmē, 'atə-, -mi\ *n* -ES [irreg. fr. L *atomi,* pl. (taken as sing.) of *atomus* atom — more at ATOM] **1 :** a tiny particle **:** MOTE, ATOM ⟨specks of dust, swirling *atomies*⟩ **2 :** a tiny and often contemptible creature or object ⟨the army was still so far distant that it seemed a mere swarm of *atomies*⟩

²**atomy** \"\ *n* -ES [for *anatomy* (*an-* being taken as the indefinite article)] **1 :** a body used in anatomy; *often* **:** SKELETON **2 :** an extremely gaunt emaciated body **:** a living skeleton ⟨hunger made them waste away to *atomies*⟩

aton·a·ble *also* **atone·a·ble** \ə'tōnəbəl\ *adj* **:** able to be atoned for

aton·al \(')ā¦tōnᵊl, (')a¦- *also* ə'-\ *adj* [²*a-* + *tonal*] **:** characterized by avoidance of traditional tonality — **aton·al·ly** \-ᵊlē, -i\ *adv*

aton·al·ism \(')=¦=ᵊl‚izəm\ *n* -S **1 :** the avoidance of traditional tonality as a principle of musical composition **2 :** musical composition in atonal style **3 :** the theory of atonal composition

aton·al·ist \-ᵊləst\ *n* -S **:** one who advocates or practices atonalism — **aton·al·is·tic** \(')ā¦tōnᵊl¦istik, (')a¦-, -ēk\ *adj*

ato·nal·i·ty \¦ātō'naləd·ē, ¦a-, -tə'n-, -lətē, -i\ *n* -ES **:** a style of composition in which the musical material is organized without reference to key or tonal center and in which the tones of the chromatic scale are used impartially

at once *adv* [ME *at ones,* fr. *at* + *ones* once] **1 a :** at the same time **:** SIMULTANEOUSLY ⟨the two events happened *at once*⟩ **b :** IMMEDIATELY ⟨don't delay; do your work *at once*⟩ **2 :** in one and the same way, manner, degree, or condition ⟨a plan that is *at once* stupid and dangerous⟩

at one *adv* [ME *at on,* fr. *at* + *on* one] **1 a :** in a state of unity of feeling **:** in harmony **:** in a closely united friendly relationship ⟨the poet felt *at one* with nature⟩ **b** *archaic* **:** into peaceful agreement **:** into harmony — used esp. with *bring, make,* or *set* ⟨he showed himself unto them as they strove, and would have set them *at one* again, saying, Sirs, ye are brethren — Acts 7:26 (AV)⟩ **2 :** of an identical or sympathetic frame of mind **:** of the same opinion **:** in a state of agreement ⟨on these points we are *at one*⟩ **3** *obs* **:** TOGETHER

atone \ə'tōn\ *vb* -ED/-ING/-S [ME *atonen,* fr. *at on*] *vt* **1** *archaic* **:** to bring from a state of enmity or opposition to a state of friendliness, toleration, or harmony **:** RECONCILE **2 a** *archaic* **:** to make reparation to **:** PROPITIATE, CONCILIATE ⟨with prayers and vows the dryads I ~ —John Dryden⟩ **b :** to make reparation or supply satisfaction for **:** EXPIATE — used in the passive voice with *for* ⟨the crime must be *atoned* for⟩; passive use without *for* and active use are archaic ~ *vi* **1** *obs* **:** to enjoy a peaceful harmonious relationship **:** AGREE **2 :** to make amends — used with *for* ⟨colorful description ~*s* for the story's lack of cohesion⟩

atone·ment \-mənt\ *n* -S **1** *obs* **:** restoration of friendly relations **:** RECONCILIATION **2** *sometimes cap* **:** a theological doctrine concerning the reconciliation of God and man esp. as effected by the saving and redeeming work of Jesus Christ **3 :** reparation esp. for an offense or injury **4** *Christian Science* **:** the exemplifying of man's oneness with God

¹**aton·ic** \(')ā¦tänik, (')a¦-, ə'-, -ēk\ *adj* [prob. fr. F *atonique,* fr. Gk *atonos* + F *-ique* -ic (fr. L *-icus*)] **1 :** characterized by atony ⟨an ~ bladder⟩ **2 :** uttered without accent (sense 2) ⟨an ~ word⟩ ⟨an ~ syllable⟩

²**atonic** \"\ *n* -S **:** a word or syllable uttered without accent or written without an accent mark

ato·nic·i·ty \¦atə'nisəd·ē, ¦at-, -tō-, -ətē, -i\ *n* -ES **:** lack of normal tension or tonus ⟨intestinal ~ as a cause of constipation⟩

at·o·ny \'atᵊnē, -ni\ *also* **ato·nia** \ə'tōnēə, ā'-\ *n, pl* **atonies** *also* **atonias** [LL *atonia,* fr. Gk, fr. *atonos* slack, without tone (fr. *a-* ²*a-* + *tonos* tone) + *-ia* -y — more at TONE] **1 :** lack of tonus or vital energy **:** weakness esp. of a contractile organ **2** *phonetics* **:** lack of stress or accent

¹**atop** \ə'-\ *also* **atop of** *prep* [¹*a-* + *top*] **:** on top of ⟨standing ~ the tall building⟩ ⟨a tile cottage *atop of* the hill⟩

²**atop** \"\ *adv* **:** to or at the top

³**atop** \"\ *adj* **:** on or at the top — used postpositively ⟨tall trees with clusters of coconuts ~⟩

ato·pen \'ad·əpən, -‚pen\ *n* -S [*atopic allergen*] **:** an agent inducing atopic allergy

atop·ic \(')ā¦täpik, (')a¦-, ə'-, -ēk\ *adj* [in sense 1, fr. ²*a-* + Gk *topos* place + E *-ic;* in sense 2, fr. *atopy* + *-ic* — more at TOPIC] **1** *of an organ of the body* **:** not in the usual place **2 :** relating to or characterized by atopy ⟨~ dermatitis⟩

at·o·pite \'ad·ə‚pīt\ *n* -S [ISV *atop-* (fr. Gk *atopos* out of the way, unusual, fr. *a-* ²*a-* + *topos* place) + *-ite;* prob. orig. formed as Sw *atopit*] **:** a yellow or brown variety of romeite

atopognosis \¦ā+\ *n* [NL, fr. ²*a-* + *topognosis*] **:** absence or loss of the power of topognosia

at·o·py \'ad·əpē, -pi\ *n* -ES [Gk *atopia* unusualness, fr. *atopos* out of the way, unusual + *-ia* -y] **1 :** a probably hereditary allergy characterized by symptoms (as hay fever, asthma, or hives) produced upon exposure to the exciting antigen without inoculation **2 :** hypersensitivity in which reagin is formed in place of the usual precipitins or agglutinins

-a·tor \¦ād·ə(r), ¦ātə(r) *sometimes* ¦ā‚tó(ə)r *or* -‚tó(ə)\ *n suffix* -S [ME *-atour,* fr. OF & L; OF *-atour, -ator,* fr. L *-ator,* fr. *-atus* -ate + *-or*] **:** one that does ⟨calorizator⟩ ⟨totalizator⟩

ato·rai \¦äd·ə¦rī\ *also* **ata·roi** \¦äd·ə¦rȯi\ *n, pl* **atorai** *or* **atorais** *also* **ataroi** *or* **atarois** *usu cap* [Sp & Pg, of AmerInd origin] **1 a :** an Arawakan people of the headwaters of the Essequibo river in British Guiana **b :** a member of such people **2 :** the language of the Atorai people

-a·to·ry \ə‚tōrē, -tȯr-, -ri; *esp Brit* ətəri *or* ətri *or sometimes when an unstressed syllable precedes* ¦ātəri *or* ¦ā·tri\ *adj suffix* [ME, fr. L *-atorius,* fr. *-atus* -ate + *-orius* -ory] **:** of, belonging to, or connected with ⟨perspir*atory*⟩ **:** serving or tending to ⟨amend*atory*⟩

atos *pl of* ATO

atour \ə'tór\ *adv or prep* [ME (northern dial.), fr. ¹*at* + (northern dial.) *our,* alter. of *over*] *Scot* **:** OVER

atox·yl \ə'täksəl, ā'-, -ēl\ *n* -S [ISV ²*a-* + *toxic* + *-yl;* orig. formed in G] **:** a white crystalline compound $C_6H_7AsNNaO_3.4H_2O$ formerly used in the treatment of syphilis and sleeping sickness, its use frequently causing blindness **:** the monosodium salt of *para*-arsanilic acid

ATP *abbr* adenosine triphosphate

at·ra·bi·lar·i·ous \‚a·trəbə¦la(a)rēəs\ *adj* [NL *atrabilarius,* fr. L *atra bilis* black bile (fr. *atra* — fem. of *ater* black — + *bilis* bile) + *-arius* -ary — more at BILE] *archaic* **:** ATRABILIOUS

at·ra·bil·i·ar \-¦bilēə(r), -lyə(r)\ *adj* [NL *atrabiliarius*] **:** ATRABILIOUS

at·ra·bil·i·ous \-¦bilyəs, -lēəs\ *adj* [L *atra bilis* + E *-ous*] **1 :** given to or marked by melancholy **:** GLOOMY ⟨an ~ outlook on life⟩ **2 :** ILL-NATURED, PEEVISH ⟨an ~ scowl⟩

atracheate \(')ā+¦-\ *adj* [²*a-* + *tracheate*] **:** without tracheae

at·rac·tas·pis \‚a·trak'taspəs\ *n, cap* [NL, fr. Gk *atraktos* spindle, arrow + L *aspis* asp — more at TORTURE, ASP] **:** a genus of slender African burrowing oviparous vipers having large head shields like harmless snakes of the region but provided with long poison fangs

atrag·e·ne \ə'trajə‚nē\ *n* [NL, modif. of Gk *athragenē* traveler's-joy] **1** *cap* **:** a small genus of perennial vines (family Ranunculaceae) with small spatulate petals **2** -S **:** a plant of the genus *Atragene*

at·ra·ment \'a·trəmənt\ *n* -S [ME, fr. L *atramentum,* fr. (assumed) L *atrare* to make black (fr. L *atr-, ater* black) + L *-mentum* -ment — more at ATROCIOUS] **1** *obs* **:** INK ⟨writing with ~⟩ **2 :** a very dark substance — usu. used of liquids ⟨a puff of ~ emitted by the octopus⟩

at·ra·men·tous \‚==¦mentəs\ *adj* **:** black as ink **:** INKY

atraumatic \¦ā+‚=¦==\ *adj* [²*a-* + *traumatic*] *med* **:** specially designed or planned to minimize injurious effects ⟨~ suture⟩

atraumatically \¦ā+‚=¦==(ə)=\ *adv* **:** in a way that is marked by the use of atraumatic methods or instruments ⟨surgery performed as ~ as possible⟩

¹**atrem·a·ta** \ə'treməd·ə, -trē-, ā'-\ *n pl, cap* [NL, fr. ²*a-* + *-tremata*] **:** an order of inarticulate Brachiopoda having the peduncle emerging freely from between the valves

²**atremata** \"\ [NL, fr. ²*a-* + *-tremata*] *syn of* LARVACEA

atrem·ate \ə'tremət\ *n* -S [NL ¹*Atremata*] **:** a brachiopod of the order Atremata

atrem·a·tous \ə'tremədəs, (')ā·¦-\ *adj* [NL ¹*Atremata* + E *-ous*] **:** of or belonging to the Atremata

atrem·ble \ə't-\ *adj* [¹*a-* + *tremble* (v.)] **:** TREMBLING, QUIVERING — usu. used postpositively or predicatively ⟨~ like an aspen leaf —Seyril Schochen⟩

atre·sia \ə'trēzh(ē)ə\ *n* -S [NL, fr. ²*a-* + *-tresia*] **1** *med* **:** absence or closure of a natural passage of the body **:** IMPERFORATION ⟨~ of the small intestine⟩ **2** *med* **:** involution of a part (as of an ovarian follicle not destined to produce a functional ovum)

atre·sic \-zik,-sik\ *adj* [NL *atresia* + E *-ic*] **:** ATRETIC

atretic \-'tred·ik\ *adj* [NL *atresia* + E *-etic*] **:** of, relating to, or marked by atresia

atri- *or* **atrio-** *comb form* [NL *atrium,* fr. L] **1 :** atrium (sense 3, 4) ⟨*atrial*⟩ ⟨*atrio*pore⟩ **2 :** atrial and ⟨*atrio*coelomic⟩ ⟨*atrio*ventricular⟩

atria *pl of* ATRIUM

atri·al \'ā·trēəl\ *adj* [*atrium* + *-al*] **:** of or relating to an atrium — often used in combination ⟨sino*atrial*⟩

atrich·ia \ā'trikēə, ə'-\ *n* -S [NL, fr. ²*a-* + *-trichia*] **:** congenital or acquired baldness **:** ALOPECIA

atrich·ic \-kik\ *adj* [Gk *atrichos* + E *-ic*] **:** HAIRLESS

atrichosis \‚ā·trə'kōsəs\ *n, pl* **atrichoses** \-ō‚sēz\ [NL, fr. Gk *atrichos* hairless + NL *-osis*] **:** ATRICHIA

at·ri·chous \'a·trəkəs, (')ā¦trik-\ *adj* [Gk *atrichos* hairless, fr. *a-* ²*a-* + *trich-, thrix* hair — more at TRICH-] **:** having no flagellum

atrio \'ä·trē‚ō\ *n* -S [It, fr. L *atrium*] **:** the valley between two cones of a volcano

atri·o·pore \'ā·trēə‚pō(ə)r\ *n* -S [*atri-* + *-pore*] *zool* **:** the opening of an atrium **:** an atrial pore (as in amphioxus)

atri·o·ventricular \¦ā·trē(‚)ō+‚=¦===\ *adj* [*atri-* + *ventricular*] **1 :** of, relating to, or between an atrium and ventricle ⟨an ~ valve⟩ **2 :** of, involving, or being the atrioventricular node

atrioventricular bundle *n* **:** a slender bundle of modified cardiac muscle that passes from the atrioventricular node in the right atrium to the right and left ventricles by way of the septum and that conducts the wave of excitation from the right atrium to the ventricles, thus maintaining the normal sequence of the heartbeat — see PURKINJE'S NETWORK

atrioventricular node *n* **:** a small mass of tissue lying in the wall of the right auricle adjacent to the septum between the auricles, being structurally and functionally related to the sinoatrial node, passing impulses received from the latter by way of the atrioventricular bundles, and in certain pathological states replacing the sinoatrial node as pacemaker of the heart

atrip \ə'trip\ *adj* [¹*a-* + *trip* (v.)] **1 :** hove just clear of the ground — used of an anchor **2 :** sheeted home, hoisted taut up, and ready for trimming — used of sails **3 :** hoisted up and ready to be swayed across — used of light yards **4 :** with the fid out and ready for lowering — used of upper masts

at·ri·plex \'a·trə‚pleks\ *n, cap* [NL, fr. L, orache — more at ORACHE] **:** a widely distributed genus of herbs or subshrubs (family Chenopodiaceae) with small diclinous flowers and utricular fruit enclosed in two bracts — see ORACHE

atri·um \'ā·trēəm *also esp in senses 1 & 2* 'ä·-\ *n, pl* **atria** \-ēə\ [L] **1 :** the central hall of a Roman house **2 a :** the open court leading to a basilica or dwelling having a covered way on three or (as in a cloister) on all four sides **b :** a square hall from which other rooms open and which is used as a sitting room in a modern house **3** [NL, fr. L] **:** an anatomical cavity or chamber: as **a :** the chamber or one of the two chambers of the heart by which the blood is received from the veins and forced into the ventricle or ventricles and which in man consists of a main cavity and an auricular appendage **b :** the main part of the tympanic cavity **4** [NL, fr. L] **:** an anatomical entrance or passage: **a :** an external chamber in tunicates and lancelets that receives water from the gills **b :** a vestibule in various insects from which one or more tracheae extend into the body

atro- *comb form* [L *atr-, ater* black + E *-o-*] **:** black and ⟨*atro*castaneous⟩

at·ro·cha \'a·trəkə\ *n* -S [NL, fr. ²*a-* + *-trocha* (fr. Gk *trochos* wheel) — more at -TROCH] **:** a chaetopod larva lacking the preoral circle of cilia and having most of the body uniformly ciliated — **at·ro·chal** \-kəl\ *adj*

atro·cious \ə'trōshəs\ *adj* [L *atroc-, atrox* gloomy, cruel, atrocious (fr. *atr-, ater* black + *-oc-, -ox* looking, appearing — akin to L *oculus* eye) + E *-ious;* akin to Arm *airem* I set on fire, Av *ātar-* fire, and perh. to W *odyn* kiln — more at EYE] **1 :** marked by or given to extreme wickedness ⟨leading an ~ life⟩ ⟨an ~ criminal⟩ **2 a :** marked by or given to extreme brutality or cruelty **:** grossly inhumane ⟨his ~ treatment in prison —Hugh Byas⟩ ⟨an ~ dictatorship⟩ **b :** OUTRAGEOUS **:** violating the bounds of common decency **:** UNCIVILIZED, BARBARIC ⟨the ~ exploitation of human beings in mines and mills —M.R.Cohen⟩ **3 a :** extremely painful **:** marked by intense distress **:** GRIEVOUS ⟨he had known long and ~ sufferings from wounds in the war —Rebecca West⟩ **b :** marked by extreme violence **:** savagely fierce **:** MURDEROUS ⟨~ assault and battery⟩ **4 :** of such a kind as to fill with fright or dismay **:** APPALLING, TERRIBLE ⟨the ~ truth blazed in the night like lightning —Elinor Wylie⟩ ⟨an ~ accident⟩ **5 a :** utterly revolting **:** ABOMINABLE ⟨~ weather⟩ ⟨~ working conditions⟩ **b :** markedly inferior in quality ⟨an ~ speller⟩ ⟨~ manners⟩

syn see OUTRAGEOUS

atro·cious·ly *adv* **:** in an atrocious manner

atro·cious·ness *n* -ES **:** ATROCITY

atroc·i·ty \ə'träsəd·ē, -ətē, -i, *rap. also* -stē, -i\ *n* -ES [MF *atrocité,* fr. L *atrocitat-, atrocitas,* fr. *atroc-, atrox* + *-itat-, -itas* -ity] **1 a :** the quality or state of being atrocious ⟨the tyrant's ~ in dealing with the prisoners⟩ **b :** something that is atrocious: as (1) **:** an execrable situation or circumstance ⟨having to put up with the *atrocities* of living in a narrow-minded society⟩ (2) **:** a gross departure from social correctness or good taste ⟨drunken guests committing one ~ after another⟩ ⟨a hat that was an utter ~⟩ **2 :** a savagely brutal or cruel deed; *esp* **:** an act violating the code of humane restrictions morally imposed on belligerents ⟨accused of war *atrocities*⟩

à trois \ä·'trwä, *F* àtrwà\ *adj* [F] **:** designed for or shared among three individuals — usu. used postpositively ⟨a pleasant little dinner *à trois*⟩ ⟨a discussion *à trois*⟩

at·ro·pa \'a·trəpə\ *n, cap* [NL, fr. Gk *Atropos,* that one of the three mythological Fates who severs the thread of life] **:** a genus of Eurasian and African herbs (family Solanaceae) with leaves entire, calyx, and corolla, the fruit being a berry subtended by the enlarged calyx lobes — see BELLADONNA 1

at·ro·pa·ceous \‚a·trə¦pāshəs\ *adj* [NL *Atropa* + E *-aceous*] **:** of or relating to the genus *Atropa*

atro·phia \ə'trōfēə\ *n* -S [LL] **:** ATROPHY

atroph·ic \(')ā'träfik, ə't-, -trä-, -ēk\ *adj* **:** relating to or characterized by atrophy

atrophic arthritis *n* **:** RHEUMATOID ARTHRITIS

atrophied *adj* **:** affected with atrophy **:** SHRUNKEN, WASTED, EMACIATED

¹**at·ro·phy** \'a·trəfē, -fi\ *n* -ES [LL *atrophia,* fr. Gk *atrophia,* fr. *atrophos* ill fed (fr. *a-* ²*a-* + *trophos* feeder, fr. *trephein* to nourish, curdle) + *-ia* -y; akin to Gk *thremma* nursling, *trophis* fat, *thrombos* clot, curd, and perh. to Skt *drapsa* drop] **1 :** decrease in size of a part or tissue after full development has been attained **:** a wasting away of tissue (as from disuse, old age, injury, or disease) ⟨senile ~⟩ ⟨muscular ~⟩ **2 :** a stoppage of development of a part or organ incidental to the normal development or life of an animal or plant often followed by diminution in size or of complete disappearance of the part or organ **3 :** a wasting away or progressive decline **:** DEGENERATION ⟨the ~ of freedom⟩ ⟨the ~ of an empire⟩

²**at·ro·phy** \-fē, -fi, -‚fī\ *vb* -ED/-ING/-ES *vi* **:** to undergo atrophy ⟨the inactive muscles *atrophied*⟩ ~ *vt* **:** to cause to undergo atrophy ⟨disuse *atrophied* the arm⟩

atro·pia \ə'trōpēə\ *n* -s [NL, fr. *Atropa* + *-ia*] : ATROPINE

atrop·i·dae \ə'träpə,dē\ *n pl, cap* [NL, fr. *Atropos*, type genus (fr. Gk *Atropos*) + *-idae*; fr. the belief that the ticking sound made by some species of book lice forebodes a death] : a widely distributed family of wingless insects (order Corrodentia) that include most book lice and that feed on organic debris and often damage various stored products (as processed foods, book bindings, and herbarium specimens)

at·ro·pine \'a·trə,pēn, -,pən\ *n* -s [G *atropin*, fr. NL *Atropa* (genus name of *Atropa belladonna*) + G *-in* -ine] : a racemic mixture of hyoscyamine extracted from the belladonna and other plants of the family Solanaceae and used esp. in the form of its sulfate to relieve spasms, to diminish secretions, to relieve pain, and to dilate the pupil of the eye; racemic hyoscyamine

at·ro·pin·ize \-pə,nīz\ *vt* -ED/-ING/-S : to bring under the influence of atropine

at·ro·pous \'a·trəpəs\ *adj* [Gk *atropos* not to be turned, fr. *a-* ²a + *-tropos* -trope] *bot* : not inverted : ORTHOTROPOUS

at·ro·scine \-,sēn,-sən\ *n* -s [ISV *atro-* (fr. NL *Atropa*) + *hyoscine*] : racemic scopolamine

atry \ə'trī\ *adj* [¹*a-* + *try* ("to lie to")] : kept bow on to the sea by a balance of sails

atry·pa \ə'trīpə\ *n, cap* [NL, fr. ²*a-* + Gk *trypa* hole — more at TRYPA] : a genus of extinct Silurian and Devonian plicate-shelled or costate-shelled brachiopods having the plates of the brachidium produced into spirally rolled processes with the apices usu. directed toward the plane of symmetry of the valve

¹atry·poid \-,pȯid\ *adj* [NL *Atrypa* + E *-oid*] : belonging to or characteristic of the genus *Atrypa*

²atrypoid \"\ *n* -s : a brachiopod of the genus *Atrypa* — see BRACHIOPOD illustration

ats *pl of* ⁴AT

ats *abbr* at the suit of

atsara *var of* ACHARA

at·si·na \at'sēnə\ *n, pl* **atsina** *or* **atsinas** *usu cap* [Blackfoot, lit., good people] **1 a** : an Indian people in Montana and southern Saskatchewan that are part of the Arapaho **b** : a member of such people **2** : a dialect of Arapaho

at·su·ge·wi \,atsü'gāwē\ *n, pl* **atsugewi** *or* **atsugewis** *usu cap* [Atsugewi] **1 a** : an Indian people of the Pit river valley in northern California **b** : a member of such people **2** : a Shastan language of the Atsugewi people

att *also* **at** \'ät\ *n* -s [Siamese] **1** : an old subsidiary coin of Siam worth 1/64 of a tical issued before 1868 in pewter and after that up to 1906 in copper **2** : a unit of value corresponding to the att ⟨2-*att* postage stamp⟩ ⟨½-*att* coin⟩

att *abbr* **1** attaché **2** attached **3** attention **4** *often cap* attorney

¹at·ta \'ä,tä\ *n* -s [Hindi *āṭā*] *India* : unsorted wheat flour or meal

²at·ta \'ad·ə\ *n, cap* [NL] : a New World genus of typical leaf-cutting chiefly tropical ants often very destructive to crops

at·ta·boy \'ad·ə,bȯi, 'atə-, ,==ˈ=\ *interj* [alter. of *that's the boy*] — used to express encouragement, approval, or admiration

attacapa *usu cap, var of* ATAKAPA

at·tac·ca \ə'täkə, -akə\ *v imper* [It, lit., attack, imper. sing. of *attaccare* to attack — more at ATTACK] : attack at once — used as a direction in music at the end of a movement to begin the next without pause

at·tac·co \ə'tä(,)kō, -ta-\ *n* -s [It, lit., attachment, connection, fr. *attaccare* to attach, attack] : a motive or short phrase in music presented in contrapuntal imitation and introduced in the course of a composition as development or as the feature of a fugue exposition

at·tach \ə'tach\ *vb* -ED/-ING/-ES [ME *attachen*, fr. MF *attacher*, fr. OF *atachier*, alter. (influenced by *a* to, fr. L *ad*) of *estachier*, fr. *estache* stake, of Gmc origin; akin to OE *staca* stake — more at AT, STAKE] *vt* **1** : to take by legal authority: **a** : to arrest by writ and bring before a court (as to answer for a debt or a contempt) — now applied chiefly to a taking of the person by a civil process **b** : to seize or take (property) by virtue of a writ or precept to hold the same to satisfy a judgment that may be rendered in the suit — compare ATTACHMENT 1 **2** *obs* **a** : INDICT, ACCUSE ⟨of capital treason I ~ you both —Shak.⟩ **b** : to lay hold of : SEIZE ⟨him to ~ and down to hell to throw —Edmund Spenser⟩ **3 a** : to bring (oneself) into an association ⟨consider to what branch of the law to ~ himself⟩ **b** : to fasten (itself) firmly ⟨a figure of universal fame, of a kind that scarcely ~*es* itself to anyone in this age —Osbert Sitwell⟩ **c** : to order (an individual or unit in the military) to serve more or less temporarily with another organization **d** : to place (an individual or unit in the military) under the control of another organization for specific purposes (as for rations, quarters, or training) — distinguished from *assign* **4** : to bind by personal ties (as of affection or sympathy) : win to affection or devotion — used with *to* ⟨she undertakes to ~ him to her by strong ties: a child, or marriage —H.M.Parshley⟩ **5** : make fast or join (as by string or glue) : BIND, FASTEN, TIE ⟨~ price tags on each article⟩ **6** : to connect by attribution : ASCRIBE — used with *to* ⟨the fetish worshiper ~*es* magical potency to stones —M.R.Cohen⟩ **7** : to associate as a property or adjunct ⟨to this treasure a curse is ~*ed* —Bayard Taylor⟩ ~ *vi* **1** : to fix or fasten itself : ADHERE ⟨the suspicion that he is guilty ~*es* upon his strange actions⟩ ⟨all the advantages that ~ to the office⟩ **2** : to come into legal operation : VEST ⟨an ancient law ~*ed* in this case⟩ **syn** see FASTEN

at·tach·a·ble \-əbəl\ *adj* **1** : liable to arrest or legal seizure ⟨goods that are ~ for debt⟩ **2 a** : capable of being fastened or added to something ⟨a handle ~ by two bolts⟩ **b** : capable of being attributed as an adjunct ⟨complete cooperativeness was not ~ to his actions⟩

at·ta·ché \,ad·ə'shā, ,atə'shā, ,a,ta'shā *also* ə,ta'shā *sometimes* ad·ə,a'shā, *Brit usu & US sometimes* ə'ta(,)shā *or* a't-\ *n* -s [F, past part. of *attacher* to attach] : one attached to another person or to a group: *specif* : an expert (as in science or aviation) on duty with the diplomatic representative of his country at a foreign capital ⟨a military ~⟩ — see COMMERCIAL ATTACHÉ

at·ta·ché case \ə'tashē-, -aash-, -aish-, -(,)shā, *less often one of the other pronunciations at* ATTACHÉ, *sometimes* ə'tachə-\ *n* **1** : a traveling case like a suitcase but smaller **2** : BRIEFCASE

attaché case

attached *adj* **1** : permanently fixed when adult ⟨an ~ barnacle⟩ ⟨an ~ oyster⟩ **2** *archit* : ENGAGED

at·tach·ment \ə'tachmənt\ *n* -s [ME *attachement*, fr. MF, fr. OF *atachement*, fr. *atachier* to attach + *-ment* — more at ATTACH] **1 a** : a seizure or taking into custody (of persons or property) by virtue of a legal process **b** : the writ or precept commanding such seizure — compare GARNISHMENT **2 a** : the state of being attached (as by affection, sympathy, or self-interest) : FIDELITY ⟨~ to a friend⟩ ⟨~ to a cause⟩ **b** : a feeling (as affection) that binds a person : REGARD ⟨sense a growing ~ for a person⟩ **3** : a device that is attached (as to a machine) esp. for doing special work ⟨~s for a vacuum cleaner⟩ **4** : the physical connection by which one thing is attached to another : FASTENING ⟨cut the ~s of a muscle to a bone⟩ **5** : an attaching by physical connection ⟨the ~ of a recording device to a telephone⟩

syn AFFECTION, LOVE: ATTACHMENT implies strong liking, devotion, or loyalty ⟨the *attachment* which they all so obviously felt for him —W.S.Maugham⟩ ⟨are not to lose their *attachment* to the land —*Farmer's Weekly (So. Africa)*⟩ ⟨strong party *attachments*⟩ ⟨an *attachment* to a lost cause⟩ AFFECTION, usu. having as its object a sentient thing, implies warmth and tenderness of sentiment, usu. settled and regulated ⟨a vast amount of quiet, restrained *affection*, of mutual confidence and respect, even of tenderness —Arnold Bennett⟩ ⟨*affection* for a dog⟩ ⟨widespread American *affection* for France and respect for her very special culture —E.B.George⟩ ⟨heightened *affection* for the memory of the dead —W.D.Howells⟩ LOVE implies a feeling stronger and more intense than AFFECTION, often connoting passion ⟨a *love* of parent for child⟩ ⟨a *love* of man for woman⟩ ⟨a *love* of God⟩ ⟨a *love* of painting⟩

attachment disk *n* : the holdfast of an alga

attachment plug *n* : a plug consisting usu. of a screw-shell body and cap and connecting a flexible conductor to a lamp holder or receptacle

¹at·tack \ə'tak, *chiefly substand* -kt\ *vb* **attacked** \-kt, *chiefly substand* -ktəd\ **attacked**; **attacking**; **attacks** [MF *attaquer*, fr. OIt *attaccare* to attach, attack, alter. (influenced by *a* to, fr. L *ad*) of (assumed) OIt *estaccare* to attach, fr. (assumed) OIt *stacca* stake, of Gmc origin; akin to OE *staca* stake — more at AT, STAKE] *vt* **1 a** : to set upon or work against forcefully ⟨~ a man without warning⟩ ⟨if we study any modern river we note how determinedly it ~*s* its banks —W.E.Swinton⟩ : assail esp. with force and weapons ⟨~ the enemy positions⟩ : ASSAULT **b** : to set upon forcibly with sexual intent : subject to indecent assault : RAPE, RAVISH **2** : to threaten (a piece in chess) with immediate capture ⟨the rook is ~*ing* the queen⟩ **3** : to assail with unfriendly or bitter words : begin a controversy with : attempt to overthrow or bring into disrepute (as by criticism or satire) **4** : to begin to affect : seize upon ⟨the kidneys are ~*ed* by an embryonic tumor —H.R.Litchfield & L.H.Dembo⟩ ⟨~*ed* by a fever⟩ **5 a** : to begin to injure, damage, or eat ⟨worms ~*ed* the cabbage plants⟩ **b** : to act upon destructively : DECOMPOSE ⟨the acid ~*s* the metal cup⟩ **6** : to set to work upon (as a problem or an investigation) esp. vigorously : TACKLE ⟨a plan which ~*s* the four basic problems —*Collier's Yr. Bk.*⟩ ~ *vi* : to make an attack ⟨waiting for the enemy to ~⟩ ⟨they ~*ed* furiously in an effort to score the tying goal⟩

syn ATTACK, ASSAIL, ASSAULT, BOMBARD, STORM mean to make a more or less violent onslaught upon, literally or figuratively. ATTACK means to move against with more or less violent intent, implying aggression in any sense and the initiative in the onset ⟨the infantry and air force *attacked* the town in coordinated waves⟩ ⟨he and other union leaders were physically *attacked* —*Current Biog.*⟩ ⟨erosion *attacked* the range and began its relentless work of reducing the land to sea level once more —*Amer. Guide Series: N.Y.*⟩ ASSAIL suggests repeated blows in an attack, as with or as if with shells or sword thrusts ⟨the expedition . . . *assailed* by a fleet of fifty-four war canoes —Tom Marvel⟩ ⟨the rain *assailed* him and thorns tore him —H.G.Wells⟩ ⟨*assailed* by doubts⟩ ASSAULT stresses attack at close quarters, the use of brute strength, suddenness, and violence ⟨pilots hammered a rail marshaling yard, bombing twenty boxcars, while other aircraft *assaulted* supply buildings —*N.Y.Times*⟩ ⟨adult ears are not to be *assaulted* by the sudden screams of childish exuberance —Richard Joseph⟩ BOMBARD means to assail with bombs, suggesting by extension an unremitting importuning or pestering with a series of similar things ⟨naval artillery *bombarded* the shore fortifications⟩ ⟨magazine editors are *bombarded* with manuscripts —L.D.Rubin⟩ ⟨he and his office associates were *bombarded* with requests for box seats —*New Yorker*⟩ STORM stresses a violence, rush, and effectiveness of assault that usu. and summarily clears all opposition out of the way ⟨the waves of light tanks *stormed* the infantry positions —S.L.A.Marshall⟩ ⟨a group of soldiers in the International Brigade *stormed* the jail —*Current Biog.*⟩

²attack \"\ *n* -s **1** : the act of falling on with force or violence : ONSET, ASSAULT, OFFENSE ⟨retreat before the infantry ~⟩ — opposed to *defense* **2 a** : an offensive or antagonistic movement or action of any kind ⟨television was used in many parts of the country as an instrument of ~, rather than of argument —Gilbert Seldes⟩ ⟨the team launched an ~ that carried deep into enemy territory⟩ **b** : RAPE, INDECENT ASSAULT **3 a** : an assault with unfriendly or bitter words ⟨her vocal ~*s* are less savage than they once were —*Newsweek*⟩ **b** : the beginning of corrosive, decomposing, or destructive action by a chemical agent **4 a** : the setting to work upon some undertaking : beginning or method of procedure ⟨the solution in each problem calls for a different ~⟩ **b** : an often extraordinary Salvationist effort to make converts **5** : the act or manner of beginning a musical tone or phrase: as **a** : unanimity of entrance of several performers ⟨a ragged ~⟩ **b** : suddenness or gradualness of beginning a tone **c** : the initial precision of pitch and quality esp. in singing **6** : the initiation or onset of the articulation of a speech sound **7 a** : an offensive or scoring action ⟨won the game with a 16-hit ~⟩ **b** : offensive players or the positions taken up by them **c** : a series of aggressive moves in chess usu. for positional advantage; *also* : a threat to capture an opponent's man **d** : cricket bowling esp. as contrasted with batting; *also* : the bowlers of a cricket team **e** : an effort to hit in fencing — used also as a word of command **f** : any of three lacrosse positions or players between out home and center — called respectively in their order from the opponents' goal *first attack, second attack, third attack* **8** : the setting in or the duration of a depressive or destructive process: as **a** : an access of disease : fit of sickness ⟨an ~ of bronchitis⟩ **b** : a period of being strongly affected by some particular desire or mood ⟨an ~ of melancholy⟩

³attack \"\ *adj* [²*attack*] : designed, planned, or employed for initiating, supporting, or carrying out a military attack ⟨an ~ formation⟩ ⟨an ~ bomber⟩

at·tack·a·ble \-əbəl\ *adj* : that can be attacked esp. with some prospect of success

attack cargo ship *n* : a naval ship with specially trained boat crews for landing material in an amphibious assault

attack plane *n* : a military airplane designed and armed for attacking the enemy's ground forces

attack transport *n* : a naval ship with specially trained boat crews for landing troops in an amphibious assault

at·ta·cus \'ad·əkəs\ *n* [LL, fr. Gk *attakos*] **1** -ES : an edible insect mentioned in Lev 11:22(DV) — called *bald locust* in the Authorized and Revised Standard versions **2** *cap* [NL, fr. LL] : a widely distributed genus of large chiefly tropical moths (family Saturniidae) that include the Asiatic Atlas moth

at·tain \ə'tān\ *vb* -ED/-ING/-S [ME *atteynen, ateignen*, fr. OF *ataign-*, stem of *ataindre*, fr. (assumed) VL *attangere*, alter. (influenced by L *tangere*) of L *attingere*, fr. *ad-* + *tangere* to touch, reach — more at TANGENT] *vt* **1** : REACH, GAIN, ACHIEVE, ACCOMPLISH ⟨difficult to ~ a realistic effect⟩ ⟨~ repose⟩ ⟨~ his goal⟩ **2** *obs* : to get at the knowledge of : ASCERTAIN **3** : to come into possession of : OBTAIN ⟨~ a kingdom⟩ ⟨~ preferment⟩ **4** *obs* : get at : OVERTAKE, CATCH **5** : to reach or come to by progression or motion : arrive at ⟨~ the top of the hill⟩ ⟨~ a ripe old age⟩ ~ *vi* : to come or arrive by motion, growth, or effort toward a place, object, or state : REACH ⟨to his stature we . . . may in time ~ —C.W.Eliot⟩ — usu. used with *to* or *unto* ⟨this plant ~*s* to a height of 10 feet⟩ **syn** see REACH

at·tain·a·bil·i·ty \ə,tānə'biləd·ē, -ətē, -i\ *n* -ES : the quality or state of being attainable

at·tain·a·ble \ə'tānəbəl\ *adj* : capable of being attained

at·tain·a·ble·ness *n* -ES : ATTAINABILITY

at·tain·der \ə'tāndə(r)\ *n* -s [ME *attaynder*, fr. MF *ataindre* to accuse, convict, attain] **1** : the act of attainting or state of being attainted : extinction of the civil rights and capacities of a person consequent upon sentence of death or outlawry ⟨an act of ~⟩ ⟨no ~ of treason shall work corruption of blood or forfeiture except during the life of the person attainted —*U.S. Constitution*⟩ **2** *obs* **a** : dishonoring accusation : SENTENCE **b** : the stain of dishonor

at·tain·ment \ə'tānmənt\ *n* -s **1** : the act of attaining : the condition of being attained ⟨the ~ of her life ambition⟩ ⟨notions difficult of ~⟩ **2** : something that is attained or attained to (as a mental acquirement or social accomplishment) ⟨famous for his scientific ~*s*⟩

¹at·taint \ə'tānt, a'-\ *vt* **attainted**; **attainted** *or archaic* **attaint**; **attainting**; **attaints** [ME *attaynten*, fr. MF *ataint*, past part. of *ataindre*] **1** *obs* : to prove guilty **2** *obs* : to find guilty : CONVICT — used esp. of a jury on trial for giving a false verdict **3** : to subject (a person) to the legal condition formerly resulting from a sentence of death or outlawry for treason or felony : affect by attainder **4 a** : to affect or infect esp. with disease **b** : to taint esp. with corruption or poison **5** *archaic* : to charge with a crime or a dishonorable act : ACCUSE **6** *archaic* : SULLY **syn** see CONTAMINATE

²attaint \"\ *n* -s [MF *atainte*, fr. fem. of *ataint*] **1 a** : a legal proceeding or process formerly instituted by writ after judgment to inquire and try by a grand jury whether a trial jury has given a false verdict **b** : the convicting of the jury so tried **c** : ATTAINDER **2** *obs* : TOUCH — used specif. in tilting **3** *obs* : a stain esp. upon honor or purity : DISGRACE

at·taint·ment \-mənt\ *n* -s : ATTAINDER

attainture *n* -s **1** *obs* : ATTAINDER **2** *obs* : an imputation of disgrace : STAIN

at·ta·lea \ə'tālēə\ *n, cap* [NL, after *Attalus* I †197 B.C. king of Pergamum] : a genus of tropical American pinnate-leaved palms with ringed stems and immense leaves — see COQUILLA NUT, PIASSAVA

at·ta·lid \'ad·ᵊləd, -,id\ *n, pl* **attalids** \-dz\ *or* **attal·i·dae** \ə'talə,dē, a'-\ *cap* [*Attal*us I †197 B.C. king of Pergamum, victor in a decisive battle with the Gauls of Asia Minor and first of his line to bear the title of king + E *-id*] : a member of a Hellenistic dynasty that ruled Pergamum from about 283 to 133 B.C.

attap *var of* ATAP

at·ta·pul·gite \,ad·ə'pəl,jīt\ *n* -s [*Attapulgus*, Ga. + E *-ite*] : a fibrous clay mineral typically $(OH_2)_4Mg_5Si_8O_{20}(OH)_2 \cdot 4H_2O$

at·tar *also* **at·ar** \'ad·ə(r), 'atə-, 'a,tär, 'a,tȧ(r *also* 'ä|d·ə(r) *or* 'ä| *or* |tə-\ *or* **ath·ar** \'athə(r), -,thär, -,thȧ(r\ *or* **ot·tar** \'äd·ə(r), 'ätə-, 'ä,tär, 'ä,tȧ(r\ *or* **ot·to** \'äd·(,)ō, 'ä(,)tō\ *n* -s [Per *'aṭir* perfumed, fr. *'iṭr* perfume, fr. Ar] : a perfume obtained from flowers; *specif* : ATTAR OF ROSES

attar of roses : a fragrant essential oil obtained by distillation from petals esp. of damask rose and with geraniol and citronellol as its principal odorous constituents : ROSE OIL

attas *pl of* ATTA

attask *vt* -ED/-ING/-S [¹*a-* + *task*] *obs* : to take to task : BLAME

at·tem·per \ə'tempə(r), a'-\ *vt* -ED/-ING/-S [ME *attempren*, fr. MF *atemprer*, fr. L *attemperare* to adjust, accommodate, fr. *ad-* + *temperare* to temper — more at TEMPER] **1** *obs* : REGULATE, CONTROL, ORDER **2** *archaic* **a** : SOFTEN, MITIGATE **b** : SOOTHE, APPEASE **3 a** *archaic* : to reduce, modify, or moderate by mixture **b** : to modify the temperature of : make (as air) warmer or colder **4** *archaic* : to make suitable : ACCOMMODATE, ADAPT **5** *archaic* : to bring into harmony : ATTUNE **syn** see MODERATE

at·tem·per·a·ment \-p(ə)rəmənt\ *n* -s [fr. *attemper*, after E *temper: temperament*] *archaic* : a mixing in proper proportion

at·tem·per·ate \-pə,rāt, *usu* -ād·+V\ *vt* -ED/-ING/-S [L *attemperatus*, past part. of *attemperare*] : ATTEMPER 3b — **at·tem·per·a·tion** \=,==ˈrāshən\ *n* -s

at·tem·per·a·tor \-ād·ə(r), -ātə-\ *n* -s : a coil of pipe through which hot or cold water may be run for regulating temperature

¹at·tempt \ə'tem(p)t *also* a'-\ *vb* -ED/-ING/-S [L *attemptare*, fr. *ad-* + *temptare* to touch, try — more at TEMPT] *vt* **1** : to make an effort to do, accomplish, solve, or effect ⟨~ to swim⟩ ⟨~ a problem⟩ — often used in venturous or experimental situations sometimes with implications of failure ⟨I doubted at first whether I should ~ the creation of a being like myself —Mary W.Shelley⟩ **2 a** *archaic* : to try to win over by temptations : TEMPT **b** : to try to seduce or ravish **3** *obs* **a** : to try to get or win (as by tempting) **b** : to try to persuade : seek to influence (as by entreaty or reasoning) **4** *archaic* : to try to subdue, overcome, or take by force : ATTACK, ASSAIL ~ *vi, obs* : to make an attempt — used with *on* or *upon* **syn** see TRY

²attempt \"\ *n* -s **1** : the act of attempting : ESSAY, TRIAL, ENDEAVOR, UNDERTAKING; *esp* : an unsuccessful effort **2** : an effort to achieve something by force: as **a** : ATTACK ⟨the enemy's ~ against our lines⟩ **b** : an assault esp. upon a person's life or a woman's honor **3** *obs* : the thing attempted : AIM

at·tempt·a·ble \-əbəl\ *adj* : capable of being attempted

at·tend \ə'tend *also* a'-\ *vb* -ED/-ING/-S [ME *attenden*, fr. OF *atendre*, fr. L *attendere* to stretch, apply the mind to, fr. *ad-* + *tendere* to stretch — more at THIN] *vt* **1** : to direct the attention to : fix the mind upon : give heed to : listen to ⟨~ the warning of the soothsayer⟩ ⟨~ my words⟩ **2** : to look after : take charge of : watch over the working of ⟨the prisoners were ~*ed* by guards⟩ **3** *archaic* **a** : to wait for ⟨three days I promised to ~ my doom —John Dryden⟩ **b** : to be in store for ⟨the state that ~*s* all men after this —John Locke⟩ **4** : to go or stay with as a companion, nurse, or servant : visit professionally as a physician : accompany in order to do service : ESCORT : wait on ⟨fawning ministers who ~ the king⟩ **5** *obs* : to follow up : CONJOIN, ASSOCIATE **6** : to be present with : ACCOMPANY : be united or consequent to ⟨the immense amount of work that has ~*ed* the creation of these lists —C.C.Fries & A.A.Traver⟩ ⟨what cares must then ~ the toiling swain —John Dryden⟩ **7** : to be present at : go to ⟨~ a meeting⟩ ⟨~ college⟩ ~ *vi* **1** : to direct one's energies : apply oneself ⟨~ to your work⟩ ⟨~ strictly to business⟩ **2** : to apply the mind or pay attention with a view to perceiving, understanding, or complying : pay regard : HEED, LISTEN — usu. followed by *to* ⟨one is lucky to meet six or seven people who know how to ~; the rest have fidgety ears —J.M.Barzun⟩ ⟨~ to the voice of my supplications —Ps 86: 6(AV)⟩ **3** : to be present or near at hand in pursuance of duty ⟨the good lord was dismissed, and has not ~*ed* in the drawing room since —Mary W. Montagu⟩ : be ready for service : wait or be in waiting — often used with *on* or *upon* ⟨ministers who ~ upon the king⟩ **4** *obs* : WAIT, STAY, DELAY — often used with *for* **5** : to direct one's care : SEE — used with *to* ⟨producers should ~ to the following important aspects of marketing —*Farmer's Weekly (So. Africa)*⟩

at·tend·ance \ə'tendən(t)s\ *n* -s [ME *attendaunce*, fr. MF *atendance*, fr. OF, fr. *atendre* to attend + *-ance*] **1** : the act or fact of attending: as **a** : the act or state of being in waiting : service esp. at court or at a hospital ⟨a physician in ~⟩ **b** : a being present : PRESENCE ⟨~ at a play⟩ **2** : the persons attending: **a** *obs* : a body of attendants : RETINUE ⟨the king, with his ~ of court officials⟩ **b** : the persons or number of persons present (as at a public performance or a session of school) ⟨the broadcasting of plays . . . does not seem to diminish the ~*s* at original performances —Joseph Trenaman⟩

attendance area *n* : the territory served by a given public school

attendance officer *n* : one employed by a public-school system to investigate the continued absences of pupils — called also *truant officer*

attendancy *n* -ES *obs* : ATTENDANCE

¹at·tend·ant \ə'tendənt\ *adj* [ME, fr. MF *atendant*, pres. part. of *atendre*] **1** : accompanying, waiting upon, or following in order to perform service ⟨the defensive responsibilities of the fleet's ~ aircraft —S.L.A.Marshall⟩ — often used with *on* or *upon* ⟨Cherub and Seraph . . . ~ on their Lord —John Milton⟩ **2** *law* : owing duty or service : DEPENDING — used with *on* or *to* ⟨the widow ~ to the heir⟩ **3** : accompanying, connected with, or immediately following as consequential : CONSEQUENT ⟨a community fight against . . . the ~ theft problems so often found where drug traffic is heavy —John Egerton⟩ ⟨the relentless rains and their ~ evils —J.W.Berry⟩ — often used with *on* or *upon* ⟨the disadvantages ~ upon being jealous —F.R.Leavis⟩

²attendant \"\ *n* -s **1** *law* : one owing duty or service to or depending on another **2** : one who attends or accompanies another in order to render a service (as a companion, servant, keeper, or agent) ⟨the bride's ~*s* at the wedding⟩ ⟨ward ~*s* in a hospital⟩; *esp* : an employee who waits on customers ⟨a gasoline-station ~⟩ **3** : something that accompanies as a circumstance : ACCOMPANIMENT, CONCOMITANT ⟨the love of luxury and its literary and artistic ~*s* —*Encyc. Americana*⟩ **4** : one who is present on a given occasion or at a given place ⟨~*s* at the festival⟩

attendant term *n* : a mortgage or long lease kept in force in form to protect the title of the owner of an English estate

attended *past of* ATTEND

at·tend·ee \ə,ten'dē, ,a,t-; ə'ten,dē\ *n* -s : ATTENDANT 4

¹attending *pres part of* ATTEND

²attending *adj* : serving as a physician on the staff of a teaching hospital ⟨~ surgeon⟩ ⟨a large ~ staff⟩

attends *pres 3d sing of* ATTEND

at·ten·si·ty \a'ten(t)səd·ē, ə'-\ *n* -ES [*attributive* + *-tensity* (as in *protensity*)] : sensory clearness (as in differentiating between a sensation that is in the focus of attention and one that is not)

at·ten·tat \(,)a,tän'tä, (,)a,tänⁿt-, -'tä\ *n, pl* **attentats** \-äz,-äz\ [F] : an attempt to commit a crime of violence — usu. used of an unsuccessful attempt at a political crime

attentate *n* -s [F *attentat*, fr. MF *attentat, attemptat*, fr. *attenter, attempter* to attempt (fr. L *attentare, attemptare*) + *-at* -ate — more at ATTEMPT, -ATE (office)] *obs* : any step wrongly innovated or attempted in a suit by an inferior judge pending an appeal or after inhibition

at·ten·tion \ə'tenchən *also* a'-; *as a command in sense 5* (ə)¦ten'shən *or* (a)¦-, *with prolongation of* -ten-\ *n* -s [ME *attencioun*, fr. L *attention-, attentio*, fr. *attentus* (past part. of *attendere* to attend) + *-ion-* -*io* -ion — more at ATTEND] **1** : the act or state of attending : the application of the mind to any object of sense or thought ⟨the magnitude of his literary output . . . engaged his undivided ~ —H.W.H.Knott⟩ : CONSIDERATION, NOTICE ⟨gain worldwide ~ for a contribution to science⟩ : mental power of attending ⟨call ~ to an error⟩ ⟨fix ~ on a moving light⟩ **2** : consideration with a view to action : observant care ⟨call this to the manager's ~⟩ **3** : an act of civility or courtesy : care for the wishes, comfort, or pleasure of others : ATTENTIVENESS ⟨she loved her children, but did not . . . spoil them . . . with injudicious ~s —Rose Macaulay⟩; *specif* : interest and concern expressed in courtship ⟨she would now marry Voldi whose constant ~s . . . were unmistakable —L.C.Douglas⟩ **4 a** : an organismic condition of selective awareness or perceptual receptivity; *specif* : the complex of neuromuscular adjustments that permit maximum excitability or responsiveness to a given class of stimuli **b** : the process of focusing consciousness to produce greater vividness and clarity of certain of its contents relative to others **5** : a position assumed by a soldier with heels together at a 45 degree angle, body erect, arms and hands hanging naturally at the sides and eyes to the front — often used as a command

attention 5

at·ten·tion·al \ə'tenchən°l, -chnəl *also* a'-\ *adj* : of or relating to attention ⟨~ factors in reaction time —*Psychological Abstracts*⟩

attention line *n* : a line usu. placed above the salutation in a business letter directing the letter to a specific individual, office, or department esp. when the name of the person to whom the letter should go is unknown

attention span *n* : the length of time during which an individual is able to concentrate

at·ten·tive \ə'tentiv, -ēv *also* a'- *or* -əv\ *adj* [ME *attentif*, fr. MF *atentif*, fr. *atente* expectation (fr. OF, fr. fem. of assumed *atent*, past part. of OF *atendre* to attend, direct the attention to) + *-if* -ive — more at ATTEND] **1** : regarding with care or attention : HEEDFUL, OBSERVANT, INTENT ⟨certain of an ~ ear and reasonable counsel —W.S.Maugham⟩ **2** : heedful of the comfort of others : COURTEOUS, POLITE ⟨his behavior to us . . . was more than civil; it was really ~ —Jane Austen⟩ **3** : paying attentions (as in courting) — **at·ten·tive·ly** \-əvlē, -li\ *adv*

at·ten·tive·ness *n* -ES : the quality or state of being attentive

¹at·ten·u·ate \ə'tenyə,wāt *also* a'-; *usu* -ād·+V\ *vb* -ED/ -ING/ -S [L *attenuatus*, past part. of *attenuare* to make thin, fr. *ad-* + *tenuare* to make thin, fr. *tenuis* thin — more at THIN] *vt* **1** : to make thin or slender (as by mechanical or chemical action) ⟨glass . . . may be *attenuated* into the finest of fibers —M.F.Brooke⟩ **2** : to lessen the amount, force, or value of : make less complex : WEAKEN ⟨he refuses to ~ human life —Hardin Craig⟩ ⟨a cloudburst will ~ UHF signals —*RCA Review*⟩ **3** : to reduce the severity of (a disease) or the virulence or vitality of (a pathogenic agent) **4** *archaic* : to break into finer parts (as the humors of the body) **5** : to make thin in consistency : render less viscid or dense : RAREFY ⟨~ oil by heating it⟩ ~ *vi* : to become thin, fine, or less : LESSEN ⟨the vividness of a memory ~s with time⟩ **syn** see THIN

²at·ten·u·ate \-yəwət, -,wāt, *usu* -d·+V\ *adj* [L *attenuatus*] **1** : attenuated esp. in thickness, density, or force : SLENDER, THIN ⟨the ~ limbs of a starving person⟩ **2** *bot* : tapering gradually often into a long slender point ⟨narrow ~ leaves⟩ **3** : thin in consistency : RAREFIED, FINE, REFINED ⟨an ~ kind of beauty⟩

at·ten·u·a·tion \ə,‚‚'wāshən\ *n* -s [L *attenuation-, attenuatio*, fr. *attenuatus* + *-ion-*, *-io* -ion] **1** : the act or process of attenuating ⟨the treble can stand a little ~ —P.H.Lang⟩ : the state of being attenuated ⟨the city of Duluth shows an . . . ~ between Lake Superior and the uplands —C.L.White & G.T.Renner⟩: as **a** : diminution of thickness : THINNING, EMACIATION ⟨the patient shows the ~ characteristic of that disease⟩ **b** : diminution of density ⟨~ of a country's population⟩ **c** : diminution of force or intensity : WEAKENING ⟨~ of the volume of sound⟩ **2** : a decrease in the pathogenicity or vitality of a microorganism or in the severity of a disease **3** : the diminution of density of wort resulting from its fermentation **4** : the decrease in amplitude of a wave or current with increasing distance from the source of transmission

attenuation constant *n* : DECAY CONSTANT

attenuation factor *n* : TRANSMISSION 1a

at·ten·u·a·tor \ə'‚‚,wād·ə(r), -ātə-\ *n* -s : a device for reducing the amplitude of an alternating-current wave without introducing appreciable distortion

at·ter \'ad·ər\ *n* -s [ME, fr. OE *ātor;* akin to OHG *eitar* poison, OS *ettar*, ON *eitr*, OHG *eiz* pustule, boil, Gk *oidos* swelling, tumor, OSlav *jadŭ* poison, and perh. to Skt *indrastronga*, and perh. to OE *āte* oat] *chiefly Scot* : corrupt matter from a sore

at·ter·cop \'ad·ər,käp\ *dial Eng var of* ETTERCAP

at·ter·mine \ə'tərmən, a'-\ *vt* -ED/-ING/-S [ME *atermynen*, fr. MF *aterminer*, fr. LL *atterminare*, fr. L *ad-* + *terminare* to limit — more at TERMINATE] : to fix the term or limit of; *esp* : to put off payment of (a debt) until an appointed date — **at·ter·mine·ment** \-mənmənt\ *n* -s

atterrate *vt* -ED/-ING/-S [It *atterrato*, past part. of *atterrare*, fr. *a-* (fr. L *ad-*) + *terra* earth, fr. L — more at TERRACE] *obs* : to fill up with alluvium or other earth — **atterration** *n* -s *obs*

¹at·test \ə'test, a'-\ *vb* -ED/-ING/-S [MF *attester*, fr. L *attestari*, fr. *ad-* + *testari* to be a witness — more at TESTAMENT] *vt* **1 a** : to bear witness to : affirm to be true or genuine : CERTIFY; *specif* : to witness and authenticate by signing as a witness **b** : to authenticate officially (as the truth of a writing) **c** *Brit* : to authenticate officially the freedom of (livestock) from a specified disease ⟨an ~ed herd⟩ **2** : to establish or verify the usage of ⟨*railroad* is ~ed earlier than *railway* — by one year —R.A.Hall b.1911⟩ **3** : to be or stand as proof of : MANIFEST ⟨the ruins of Palmyra ~ its ancient magnificence⟩ **4** *obs* : to call to witness : INVOKE **5** : to put on oath or solemn declaration **6** : to enroll for military service ⟨the day on which the recruits were ~ed⟩ ~ *vi* **1** : to bear witness : TESTIFY — often used with *to* ⟨~ to the truth of the statement⟩ **2** : to enroll oneself for service in the armed forces ⟨the day on which the recruits ~ed⟩ **syn** see INDICATE

²attest *n* -s *obs* : TESTIMONY, WITNESS

at·test·a·ble \-əbəl\ *adj* : capable of being attested

at·test·ant \-stənt\ *n* -s [L *attestant-, attestans*, pres. part. of *attestari* to bear witness] : one who attests

at·tes·ta·tion \,a,te'stāshən, ,ad·ə's-, ,atə's-, ,ə,te's-\ *n* -s [MF, fr. LL *attestation-, attestatio*, fr. L *attestatus* (past part. of *attestari*) + *-ion-*, *-io* -ion] **1** : the act of attesting **2** : the proof or evidence by which something is attested ⟨the . . . volumes . . . stand, like a solid ~ of the victory —Edmund Wilson⟩ **3** : the formal authentication of an act or instrument by a subscribing witness or an official **4** *Brit* : the giving of an oath (as the oath of allegiance to an army recruit)

at·tes·ta·tive \ə'testəd·iv, a'-\ *adj* [*attestation* + *-ive*] : of or relating to attestation

at·tes·ta·tor \ə'te,stād·ə(r), a'-, 'ad·ə,s-\ *n* -s [L *attestatus* + E *-or*] : one that attests

at·test·er \ə'testə(r), a'- *or* **at·tes·tor** \" *also* -,stȯr *or* -,stō(ə)r\ *n* -s : one that attests

at·tes·tive \-,stiv\ *adj* : ATTESTING

¹at·tic \'ad·ik, 'atik, -ēk\ *adj, usu cap* [L *Atticus*, adj. & n., fr Gk *Attikos*, fr. *Attikē* (Attica), region of ancient Greece] **1** : ATHENIAN **2** : marked by simplicity, purity, and refinement ⟨*Attic* taste⟩ ⟨an *Attic* style⟩

²attic \"\ *n* -s *cap* [L *Atticus*] **1** : GREEK; *specif* : ATHENIAN **2** : a dialect of ancient Greek that was originally used in Attica and became the literary language of the entire Greek-speaking world

³attic \"\ *n* -s [F *attique*, fr. *attique* Attic, of Attica, fr. L *Atticus;* fr. the use of pilasters in the Attic style] **1 a** : a low story or wall above the main order or orders of a façade in the classical styles **b** : a room or rooms behind an attic **c** : the part of a building immediately below the roof and wholly or partly within the roof framing : a garret or storage space under the roof **2** : the small upper space of the tympanic cavity

attic base *n, usu cap A* : a molded base consisting of an upper and lower torus separated by a scotia and two narrow fillets and assumed to be the typical form of base for the Ionic and Corinthian orders

at·ti·cism \'ad·ə,sizəm, 'atə-\ *n* -s *often cap* [L *Atticismus*, fr. Gk *Attikismos*, fr. *Attikos* + *-ismos* -ism] **1** : a favoring of or attachment to the Athenians **2** : a characteristic feature of Attic Greek occurring in another language or dialect **3** : a concisely witty or well-turned phrase or sentence **4 a** : a style like that of Attic writers or orators **b** : adherence to or practice of Attic manner or style

at·ti·cist \-,səst\ *n* -s *usu cap* [Gk *Attikistēs*, fr. *Attikos* + *-istēs* -ist] : one who affects Atticisms

at·ti·cize \-,sīz\ *vb* -ED/-ING/-S *often cap* [¹*Attic* + *-ize*, after Gk *attikizein*, fr. *Attikos* + *-izein* -ize] *vt* : to make conformable to Athenian or Greek language or customs ~ *vi* **1** : to favor or side with the Athenians **2** : to speak or write in Attic

at·ti·co·mastoid \¦ad·ə(,)kō+¦-\ *adj* [³*attic* + *-o-* + *mastoid*] *anat* : of or relating to the attic and the mastoid

attic order *n* [³*attic*] : an order (as of pilasters) adorning the front of an attic

attic salt *or* **attic wit** *n, often cap A* [¹*Attic*] : poignant delicate wit

attic story *n* [³*attic*] : the space enclosed by the attic : the top story of a house

at·tid \'ad·əd\ *adj or n* [NL *Attidae*] : SALTICID

At·ti·dae \'ad·ə,dē\ [NL, fr. *Attus*, type genus (prob. fr. L *atta* one that walks on tiptoes) + *-idae*] *syn of* SALTICIDAE

at·tine \'a,tīn\ *adj* [NL *Atta* + E *-ine*] : of or relating to the genus *Atta* or to the ants constituting this genus

attinge *vt* **attinged**; **attinged**; **attinging**; **attinges** [L *attingere*, fr. *ad-* + *-tingere* (fr. *tangere* to touch) — more at TANGENT] **1** *obs* : TOUCH : come in contact with **2** *obs* : INFLUENCE, AFFECT

at·tin·gent \ə'tinjənt, a'-\ *adj* [L *attingent-, attingens*, pres. part. of *attingere*] *archaic* : in contact : TOUCHING

¹at·tire \ə'tī(ə)r, a'-, -īə\ *vt* -ED/-ING/-S [ME *attiren*, fr. OF *atirier*, fr. *a-* (fr. L *ad-*) + *-tirier* (fr. *tire* order, rank, of Gmc origin; akin to OE *tīr* glory, OHG *ziarī* adorned, ON *tīrr* glory); akin to Lith *dyrėti* to gaze, Toch A *tiri* manner, L *deus* god — more at DEITY] **1** : to put garments on : DRESS, ARRAY ⟨a shabby look, common to all thus *attired*⟩ ⟨*attired* himself in a gray business suit⟩ **2** : to clothe in fancy or rich garments : ADORN ⟨*attired* in the huge black cloak and the large black hat which he always affected —Osbert Sitwell⟩

²attire \"\ *n* -s [ME, fr. *attiren* to attire] **1** : DRESS, CLOTHING, CLOTHES ⟨the usual ~ of a gentleman —W.M.Thackeray⟩ ⟨his unfashionable ~ and clumsy manners —A.C.Cole⟩; *esp* : splendid or decorative clothing ⟨the king in his royal ~⟩ **2** : the antlers or antlers and scalp of a stag or buck **3** *obs* : DRESS, GARMENT, HEADDRESS, ORNAMENT — usu. used in pl. **4** : something felt to dress or adorn ⟨the sparkling ~ of trees after a snowstorm⟩

at·tired \-ī(ə)rd, -īəd\ *adj* [ME, past part. of *attiren* to attire] : emblazoned with antlers ⟨a stag argent ~ sable⟩

at·tire·ment \-ī(ə)rmənt, -īəm-\ *n* -s : ATTIRE

at·ti·tude \'ad·ə,tüd, 'atə-, -ə,tyüd *also* -d·ē- *or* -tē-\ *n* -s [F, fr. It *attitudine* (influenced in meaning by It *atto* act, action, fr. L *actus* act), fr. *attitudine* aptitude, natural tendency, fr. LL *aptitudin-, aptitudo* fitness — more at APTITUDE, ACT] **1 a** : the arrangement of the parts of a sculptured or painted figure **b** : the posture of a figure in a sculpture or a painting **2 a** : a position or bearing as indicating action, feeling, or mood ⟨a firm ~⟩ **b** : the feeling or mood itself ⟨one's ~ regarding vivisection⟩ **3 a** : the posture or position of a person, an animal, or an inanimate object or the manner in which the parts of the body are disposed ⟨toys lying in tumbled ~s on the nursery floor⟩ **b** : a position assumed to serve a purpose ⟨strike a threatening ~⟩ **4 a** : behavior representative of feeling or conviction **b** : a disposition that is primarily grounded in affect and emotion and is expressive of opinions rather than belief **c** : an organismic state of readiness to act that is often accompanied by considerable affect and that may be activated by an appropriate stimulus into significant or meaningful behavior **d** : a persistent disposition to act either positively or negatively toward a person, group, object, situation, or value **5** *geol* : the position of a bed, fault plane, or other planar body or surface with respect to a horizontal plane **6 a** : any posture held momentarily in dancing **b** : a variation of the arabesque used in ballet with the lifted leg bent sharply at the knee, the body held upright, the corresponding arm usu. raised forward, and the opposite arm extended to the side **7** : the position or orientation of an aircraft in the air as seen by an observer stationary on the earth determined and expressed mathematically by the inclination of the axes of the aircraft to three fixed axes on the earth that form a frame of reference

attitude gyro *n* : an instrument that indicates continuously the attitude of an airplane in flight in relation to a horizontal plane

attitude of flight : inclination of the three principal axes of an airplane in flight to the relative wind

attitude scale *n* : a measure of the relative quantity of an attitude possessed by an individual as contrasted with a reference group

at·ti·tu·di·nal \¦‚‚¦‚d°nəl\ *adj* [*attitude* + *-inal* (as in *aptitudinal*)] : relating to, based on, or expressive of personal attitudes or feelings ⟨moving one's attitudes toward the ~ standards set by others —M.J.Rosenberg⟩

at·ti·tu·di·nar·i·an \,‚‚,‚‚'erēən\ *n* -s [*attitude* + *-inarian* (as in *valetudinarian*)] : one who attitudinizes : POSTURER — **at·ti·tu·di·nar·i·an·ism** \-rēə,nizəm\ *n* -s

at·ti·tu·di·nize \,‚‚'‚d°n,īz\ *vi* -ED/-ING/-S *see -ize in Explan Notes* [*attitude* + *-in-* (fr. L, suffixal element of oblique cases of nouns ending in *-udo*) + *-ize*] : to assume or practice attitudes : strike an attitude : pose for effect ⟨below the conventional *attitudinizing* a man lies hid —H.S.Bennett⟩

at·ti·wan·da·ronk \,ad·ə'wändə,räŋk\ *n -s usu cap* : an Indian of the Neutral people

attn *abbr* attention

at·torn \ə'tərn\ *vb* -ED/-ING/-S [ME *attournen*, fr. MF *atorner* to direct, dispose, attorn, fr. OF, fr. *a* to (fr. L *ad*) + *torner* to turn — more at AT, TURN] *vi* **1** *feudal law* : to turn or transfer homage and service from one lord to another : render homage and service to a lord **2** *modern law* : to agree to become tenant to one as owner or landlord of an estate previously held of another : recognize one expressly or by implication as landlord or the person in whose behalf one holds something — see ATTORNMENT 2 ~ *vt* : TRANSFER

at·tor·ney \ə'tərnē, -tən-, -təin-, -ni\ *n* -s [ME *attourney*, fr. MF *atorné*, past part. of *atorner*] : one who is legally appointed by another to transact business for him; *specif* : a legal agent qualified to act for suitors and defendants in legal proceedings — **at·tor·ney·ship** \‚'‚‚,ship\ *n* -s

attorney–at–law \‚¦‚‚‚'‚\ *n, pl* **attorneys–at–law** : a practitioner in a court of law who is legally qualified to prosecute and defend actions in such court on the retainer of clients — compare ADVOCATE, BARRISTER, LAWYER, PROCTOR, SOLICITOR

attorney general *n, pl* **attorneys general** *or* **attorney generals** : the chief law officer of a state who is empowered to act in all litigation in which the government is a party and to advise the chief executive whenever required — **attorney generalship** *n*

attorney–in–fact \‚¦‚‚‚'‚\ *n, pl* **attorneys–in–fact** **1** : a person appointed by another by a letter or power of attorney to transact any business for him out of court — compare ATTORNEY-AT-LAW **2** : an agent employed in any business or to do any act in pais for another

at·torn·ment \ə'tərnmənt\ *n* -s [MF *atornement*, fr. OF, fr. *atorner* + *-ment*] **1** : the act of a feudatory, vassal, or tenant by which he consents upon the alienation of an estate to receive a new lord or superior and transfers to him his homage and service : the agreement or acknowledgment by a tenant that he holds his tenement of a new person as landlord **2** : the acknowledgment by a bailee that he holds a property on behalf of a new party

at·tour \ə'tōr\ *var of* ATOUR

at·tract \ə'trakt\ *vb* -ED/-ING/-S [ME *attracten*, fr. L *attractus*, past part. of *attrahere*, fr. *ad-* + *trahere* to draw — more at DRAW] *vt* **1** *obs* : to draw or draw in esp. by suction or pulling : INHALE **2** : to cause to approach or adhere: as **a** : to draw to or toward oneself ⟨a magnet ~s iron⟩ **b** : to call forth or compel (as interest in or appreciation of) ⟨often ~s admiring glances⟩ ⟨her agitation at a steeplechase . . . ~s her husband's notice —Matthew Arnold⟩ **c** : to invite or draw by exposure or openness or by some natural appeal ⟨a swarm in the tree for weeks, ~ed by some secretion —Richard Jefferies⟩ ⟨~ bitter criticism⟩ **d** : to draw or entice to one by an aesthetic or emotional appeal ⟨clad in a pale buff frock . . she ~ed every eye —John Galsworthy⟩ **e** : to interest and lead to consideration, participation, or attendance ⟨the talent which the organization ~ed⟩ ~ *vi* : to exercise or exhibit attraction ⟨her voice has the power to ~⟩ ⟨opposites ~⟩

syn ALLURE, CAPTIVATE, FASCINATE, BEWITCH, CHARM, ENCHANT, TAKE: of these words ATTRACT is at once the widest in its use and the least rich in connotation. It stresses the fact of one thing's being able to draw another to it in some way or other ⟨tempting summer, when song and shade and colour *attract* every one to the field —Richard Jefferies⟩ ⟨to Papa, who had begun to be *attracted* rather against his will —Virginia Woolf⟩ ⟨men could be *attracted* into these by higher pay or shorter hours —Bertrand Russell⟩ ALLURE may add the notion of the enticement of something good or enjoyable being offered or withheld ⟨new class of technicians, *allured* by their wide opportunities of service —Bernard Pares⟩ ⟨the beauty that *allured* men for pleasure had failed to hold them —Ellen Glasgow⟩ CAPTIVATE, like the succeeding words in this list, suggests an appeal irresistible and blocking rational consideration which might diminish its force. CAPTIVATE is less strong than the following words since it may be used for fleeting or short-lived impressions produced by an individual trait ⟨a serene expression upon her face which *captivated* almost all who saw her —Samuel Butler †1902⟩ ⟨the Republican State Convention . . . *captivated* by his address as temporary chairman, nominated him for governor —A.C.Flick⟩ FASCINATE, in older usage and sometimes in today's, implies a spell which irresistibly transfixes the victim ⟨the younger and weaker man was *fascinated* and helpless before the creeping approach of so monstrous a wrath —G.D.Brown⟩ It often indicates a compelling attraction or interest or enthusiasm ⟨James . . . carried the exploration of the technics of his craft into depths and recesses almost as *fascinating* as Leonardo da Vinci's abstruse, inspired-looking speculations about his —C.E.Montague⟩ BEWITCH suggests domination and absorption of interest or liking precluding any check and possibly against the subject's will ⟨if you suffer yourself to think how pretty they are, you are *bewitched* and vanquished —Lafcadio Hearn⟩ ⟨these small splinters of perfection in the art of letters would still *bewitch* us if they had no context at all —C.E.Montague⟩ CHARM suggests domination as by magic; it indicates pleasure on the subject's part and may be used with reference to sensuous or social traits that appeal ⟨she gave some attention to her flowers, but it was perfunctorily bestowed, for they no longer *charmed* her —Thomas Hardy⟩ ⟨a grace about him which *charmed*, and a hint of latent power which impressed —John Buchan⟩ ENCHANT is possibly the strongest word in the list; it may suggest a more complex appeal, its irresistibility, utter absence of thoughtful reservation, and sheer delight on the part of the subject ⟨a mature person . . . cannot be utterly *enchanted* by what he feels to be trivial or false —George Santayana⟩ ⟨man's power to *enchant* himself with his own dreams —Irving Babbitt⟩ TAKE, usu. used in the passive, is somewhat informal and has suggestions ranging from those of ATTRACT to those of CAPTIVATE ⟨he stared at her . . . the more he stared, the more *taken* was he —Rudyard Kipling⟩

at·tract·a·ble \-əbəl\ *adj* : capable of being attracted

at·tract·ance \-ən(t)s\ *also* **at·tract·an·cy** \-ənsē, -si\ *n, pl* **attractances** *also* **attractancies** : the tendency (as of an insecticide) to attract positively

at·tract·ant \-ənt\ *n* -s : something that attracts; *specif* : a substance used to attract insects or other animals

at·tract·ing·ly *adv* : in an attracting manner

at·trac·tion \ə'trakshən\ *n* -s [MF & ML; MF, attraction, contraction, fr. ML *attraction-, attractio* attraction, fr. L, contraction, fr. *attractus* (past part. of *attrahere* to attract, contract) + *-ion-*, *-io* -ion] **1 a** : a characteristic that elicits interest or admiration : an attracting quality — usu. used in pl. ⟨relationships between individual members are based primarily on spontaneous mutual ~s —*Jour. of Communication*⟩ **b** : personal magnetic charm ⟨unable to resist her mysterious ~s⟩ **2** : a force acting between oppositely electrified bodies or oppositely magnetized bodies that tends to draw them together and resist their separation **3 a** : the action or power of drawing forth a response (as interest or affection) : attractive quality ⟨the career of the father came to have an ~ for the son⟩ **b (1)** : something that draws people by appealing to their desires and tastes **(2)** : a person, thing, or performance that attracts crowds ⟨another $100 dinner, with the presidential candidate as the main ~⟩ **4** : grammatical agreement between two words usu. near each other that are not syntactically connected in a way that makes it normal for them to agree (as between *books* and *were* in "neither of the books were sold")

at·trac·tion·al·ly \-shən°lē, -shnəlē\ *adv* [*attraction* + *-al* + ²*-ly*] : by means of attraction

attraction cone *n* : ENTRANCE CONE

attraction sphere *n* : the central mass of the aster in mitotic cell division : CENTROSPHERE

¹at·trac·tive \ə'traktiv, -ēv *also* -əv\ *adj* [ME, fr. MF & LL; MF *attractif*, fr. LL *attractivus*, fr. L *attractus* + *-ivus* -ive] **1 a** : able to cause (a person or animal) to approach by influencing the will or appealing to the senses ⟨a sanctuary ~ to birds⟩ **b** : able to draw to itself objects not attached to it ⟨~ powers of a magnet⟩ **2** : having qualities that arouse interest, pleasure, or affection in the observer : PLEASING ⟨an ~ personality⟩ ⟨goods ~ in price or quality⟩ — used esp. of pleasing in appearance — **at·tract·ive·ly** \-təvlē, -li\ *adv* — **at·tract·ive·ness** \-tivnəs, -tēv- *also* -təv-\ *n* -ES

²attractive \"\ *n* -s [ME] *archaic* : ATTRACTION

attractive nuisance *n* : something (as a turntable or scaffold) unsafe and unprotected and often under construction that tempts children to risk injury by playing with, in, or on it

at·trac·tor \-ktə(r) *also* -,tȯ(ə)r *or* -ō(ə)\ *also* **at·tract·er** \-ktə(r)\ *n* -s : one that attracts

attracts *pres 3d sing of* ATTRACT

at·tra·hent \'a·trəhənt\ *n* -s [L *attrahent-, attrahens*, pres. part. of *attrahere* to attract — more at ATTRACT] : ATTRACTANT

at·trib·ut·a·ble \ə'tribyəd·əbəl, -yətə-\ *adj* : capable of being attributed

at·trib·u·tal \-yəd·°l\ *adj* : DESCRIPTIVE

¹at·tri·bute \'a·trə,byüt, *usu* -üd·+V\ *n* -s [ME, fr. L *attributus*, past part. of *attribuere* to attribute, fr. *ad-* + *tribuere* to bestow — more at TRIBUTE] **1** : a quality, character, or characteristic ascribed usu. commonly: **a** : a characteristic either essential and intrinsic or accidental and concomitant ⟨to endow her with all the ~s of a mythological paragon upon Olympus —Elinor Wylie⟩ **b** : a quality intrinsic, inherent, naturally belonging to a thing or person ⟨not in spiritual nor even in moral ~s —G.L.Dickinson⟩ **2** : an object closely associated with and thought of as belonging to a specific person, thing, or office ⟨a scepter is the ~ of power⟩ ⟨all his ~s are here — ring, cigarette case, tiepin, cane —Osbert Sitwell⟩; *esp* : such an accessory object used for identification or association in painting or sculpture (as a club for Hercules) **3 a** *logic* : any quality or characteristic that may be predicated of some subject — compare PREDICATE **b** *philos* **:** a necessary or essential quality or characteristic of substance — compare CARTESIANISM, SPINOZISM **4 a :** a word ascribing a quality; *esp* **:** ADJECTIVE, ADJECTIVE EQUIVALENT **b :** that one of the two immediate constituents of an endocentric compound or construction that does not have the same grammatical function as the whole (as *this* in *this paper, completely* in *completely new, black* in *blackbird*) — opposed to *head* **5 :** any one of the ways (as intensity, duration, or quality) in which one sensation, image, or feeling can differ from another **syn** see QUALITY, SYMBOL

²at·trib·ute \ə'tribyət *also* -i(,)byüt, *chiefly substand* -,bət; *usu* -d·+V\ *vt* **attributed** \-yəd·əd,-yətəd\ **attributed** \"\ **attributing** \-yəd·iŋ,-yətiŋ\ **attributes** \-yəts *also* -yüts\ [L *attributus*] **1** *archaic* **:** to bestow as a right **2 :** to explain as caused or brought about by **:** regard as occurring in consequence of or on account of ⟨the collapse of the movement can be *attributed* to lack of morale⟩ **3 :** to regard as possessed, owned, originated, characterized, or described as indicated: as **a :** to reckon as a quality, characteristic, or trait possessed sometimes fitly or properly ⟨Delia reproached herself for *attributing* feelings of jealousy to her cousin —Edith Wharton⟩ **b :** to reckon as executed, made, originated, or achieved as indicated ⟨*attributed* the invention to a Russian⟩ **c :** CLASSIFY, DESIGNATE, DATE ⟨a manuscript *attributed* to the 10th century⟩ **syn** see ASCRIBE

at·tri·bu·tion \,a·trə'byüshən\ *n* -s [ME, fr. MF, fr. L *attribution-, attributio* assignment of a debt of money, fr. *attributus* (past part. of *attribuere* to attribute, assign) + *-ion-, -io* -ion] **1 :** the action of bestowing or assigning ⟨~ of a gift⟩ **2 :** the process of ascribing to someone or something ⟨the ~ of guilt to the accused⟩ **3 :** the ascribing of a work to an author, date, or place; *esp* **:** the ascribing of a work of art to a particular artist **4 :** the fact of being an attribute **:** the logical relation of an attribute to its subject

¹at·trib·u·tive \ə'tribyəd·iv, -yətiv\ *adj* [F *attributif*, fr. MF, fr. *attribution*, after such pairs as MF *distribution: distributif* distributive] **1 :** ATTRIBUTING **:** relating to or of the nature of an attribute **:** expressing or assigning an attribute: as **a** *of an adjective or adjective equivalent* **:** joined directly to a modified noun without a copulative verb and in English usu. preceding the noun (as of *red* in *red hair, city* in *city streets, militant* in *the church militant*) but in some other languages (as French) typically following it (as *moderne* in *un roman moderne* "a modern novel") — compare ADHERENT 4, APPOSITIVE 2, PREDICATE 2 **b :** of or belonging to an attributive adjective or adjective equivalent ⟨~ position⟩ ⟨~ function⟩ **:** including an attributive adjective or adjective equivalent ⟨an ~ collocation⟩ **2 :** ADJECTIVAL — used of a term ⟨*redness* is abstract but *red* is ~⟩ **3 :** of an attributed or assigned nature or origin — used of the authorship of a work of art — **at·trib·u·tive·ly** \-əvlē, -li\ *adv*

²attributive \"\ *n* -s **:** an attributive word; *esp* **:** ADJECTIVE, ADJECTIVE EQUIVALENT

attrist *vt* -ED/ING/-S [F *attrister*, fr. MF, fr. *a-* (fr. L *ad-*) + *-trister* (fr. *triste* sad, fr. L *tristis*) — more at TRISTE] *obs* **:** SADDEN

at·tri·tal \ə'trīd·ᵊl, a'-, -ītᵊl\ *adj* [L *attritus* + E *-al*] **:** of or relating to matter that has been worn by attrition ⟨~ coal⟩

at·trite \ə'trīt, a'-\ *adj* [L *attritus*, past part. of *atterere* to rub against, rub away, fr. *ad-* + *terere* to rub — more at THROW] **:** having attrition

at·trit·ed \ə'trīd·əd\ *adj* **:** worn by attrition

at·tri·tion \ə'trishən *also* a'-\ *n* -s [L *attrition-, attritio*, fr. *attritus* + *-ion-, -io* -ion] **1** [ME *attricioun*, fr. (assumed) ML *attrition-, attritio*, fr. L] **:** sorrow for one's own sins that arises from a motive considered lower than that of the love of God (as a fear of punishment or a sense of shame) **:** imperfect contrition — used in Roman Catholic theology **2 :** the act of rubbing together or wearing down **:** the condition of being worn down or ground down by friction ⟨withstand moisture, pressure, and ~ —*Farmer's Weekly (So. Africa)*⟩ ⟨tweeds that drag out into woolly knots and strings wherever there is ~ —H.G.Wells⟩ **3 :** the act of weakening to the point of exhaustion by constant harassment, use, or abuse ⟨the slow ~ of the soul by the conduct of life —Thornton Wilder⟩ **:** a breaking down or wearing down from repeated attacks or constant diminution ⟨war of ~⟩ ⟨the rate of ~ in some industries⟩ **:** gradual loss of strength from attrition **4 :** the wear of rock particles while being moved about by wind, stream currents, waves, or glaciers; *also* **:** the removal of ice from a glacier by melting or evaporation **5 :** the absence of a consonant sound (as of a sound no longer pronounced) **6 :** the portion of a maturing debt issue not turned in for exchange into new securities in a refunding **syn** see PENITENCE

at·tri·tion·al \-shənᵊl,-shnəl\ *adj* **:** relating to or caused by attrition

attrition mill *n* **:** a machine in which materials (as grain or spices) are pulverized between two toothed metal disks rotating in opposite directions

at·tri·tive \ə'trīd·iv, a'-\ *adj* [*attrition* + *-ive*] **:** causing attrition

at·tri·tus \ə'trīd·əs, a'-, -ītəs\ *n* -ES [NL, fr. L, act of rubbing against, rubbing away, fr. *attritus* past part. of *atterere* to rub against, rub away — more at ATTRITE] **:** matter pulverized or finely divided by attrition; *specif* **:** one of the constituents of durain consisting of a macerated plant debris including leaves, bark, cuticle, spore and pollen extines, resins, and mineral matter

atts *pl of* ATT

at·tune \ə'tün, ə'tyün *also* a-\ *vt* -ED/-ING/-S [*ad-* + *tune*] **1 :** to bring into harmony or accord, esp. musical harmony **:** make melodious **2 :** to put in tune **:** TUNE ⟨*attuned* the violin⟩

at·tune·ment \-mənt\ *n* -s **:** the act of attuning **:** the state of being attuned ⟨a delicate ~ to the written word —*Atlantic*⟩

atty *abbr* attorney

atua \ə'tüə\ *or* **akua** \-'küə\ *n, pl* **atua** *or* **atuas** *or* **akua** *or* **akuas** [Tahitian, Maori, or Samoan *atua*, Hawaiian *akua*] **:** a Polynesian supernatural being or spirit

atu·a·mi \,äd·ə'wämē\ *n, pl* **atuami** *or* **atuamis** *usu cap* **1 :** a Palaihnihan Indian people of Shastan stock **2 :** a member of the Atuami people

atule *var of* AKULE

atun \ä'tün\ *n* -s [Sp *atún*, fr. Ar *at-tūn, at-tunn* the tunny, fr. L *thunnus* — more at TUNNY] **:** TUNA

atwain \ə'twān\ *adv* [ME *atweyne*, fr. ¹*a-* + *tweyne* twain] *archaic* **:** in twain **:** in two parts **:** ASUNDER

atweel \ə'twēl\ *adv* [alter. of Sc (*I*) *wat weel* I well know] *Scot* **:** SURELY, TRULY

atween \ə'twēn\ *prep or adv* [ME *atwene*, fr. ¹*a-* + *-twene* (as in *betwene*)] *now dial* **:** BETWEEN

atwist \ə+\ *adv* [¹*a-* + *twist*, v.] **:** in a twisted manner **:** TWISTED

atwitter \ə+\ *adj* [¹*a-* + *twitter*, v.] **:** nervously concerned ⟨~ . . . thinking of her among all those Indians —Kenneth Roberts⟩ **:** EXCITED, TWITTERING ⟨Hollywood gossips ~ with speculation —*Time*⟩

atwixt \ə'twikst\ *prep* [ME, fr. ¹*a-* + *-twixt* (as in *betwixt*)] *dial* **:** BETWIXT, BETWEEN

atwo \ə'tü\ *adv* [ME *atwo, ato*, fr. OE *on twā, on tū*, fr. *on* + *twā, tū* two — more at TWO] *dial Brit* **:** in two **:** into two parts

a2–horizon \ā'tü+\ *n, usu cap A* [¹*A*] **:** the often whitish gray or ash-gray portion of the A-horizon below the dark layer at the immediate surface

at·wood's machine \'at-,wůdz-\ *n, usu cap A* [after George *Atwood* †1807 Eng. mathematician, its inventor] **:** an apparatus for demonstrating the laws of accelerated motion by means of a light nearly frictionless pulley wheel over which passes a thread having at its ends fairly heavy masses whose slight difference in weight is the cause of the acceleration

a–type star \'ā,=-\ *n, usu cap A* [¹*A*] **:** A STAR

atyp·ia \(')ā'tipēə\ *n* -s [NL, fr. ²*a-* + L *typus* type + NL *-ia* — more at TYPE] **:** ATYPISM

atypical \(')ā+¦==\ *adj* [²*a-* + *typical*] **:** not typical **:** unlike the type **:** IRREGULAR ⟨this sample is ~⟩ **:** ABNORMAL ⟨~ behavior . . . not the accepted type of response that we expect from children —G.E.Gardner⟩ — **atypically** *adv*

atyp·ism \(')ā'tī,pizəm\ *n* -s [²*a-* + *type* + *-ism*] **:** the condition of being uncharacteristic or lacking uniformity ⟨nuclear ~ of cells characterizes certain precancerous conditions⟩

AU *abbr* **1** *often not cap* [L *ad usum*] according to custom **2** angstrom unit **3** astronomical unit

Au [L *aurum*] *symbol* gold

a'u \'ä,ü\ *n* -s [Hawaiian] *Hawaii* **:** any of certain scombroid fishes: **a :** a member of the family Istiophoridae (as a sailfish or marlin) **b :** SWORDFISH 1a

au·bade \ō'bäd, -ad\ *n* -s [F, fr. MF, fr. (assumed) OProv *aubada*, fr. OProv *auba, alba* dawn — more at ALBA] **1 :** a song or poem greeting the dawn **:** a walking or rising song — called also *matin song* **2 a :** a morning love song **b :** a song or poem of lovers parting at daybreak **3 :** morning music — compare SERENADE, NOCTURNE

au·bain \ō'ban\ *n* -s [F, fr. OF *aubain, albain*, prob. fr. (assumed) OFrk *aliban* one belonging to another jurisdiction, fr. (assumed) OFrk *ali-* (akin to Goth *aljis* other) + OFrk *ban* jurisdiction — more at ELSE, BAN] **:** a resident alien subject to the droit d'aubaine

aubaine \"\ *n* [by shortening] **:** DROIT D'AUBAINE

aube \'ōb\ *n* -s [ME, fr. MF, fr. ML *alba* — more at ALB] **1** *archaic* **:** ALB 1 **2 :** ¹ALBA 1

au·be·pine \'ōbə,pēn, -bā-, -,pən, ōbā'pēn\ *n* -s [F *aubépine*, fr. OF *aubespin*, fr. (assumed) VL *albispina*, fr. (assumed) L *alba spina* (attested as *spina alba*), fr. L *alba* white (fem. of *albus*) + *spina* thorn — more at ELF, SPINE] **:** ANISALDEHYDE

au·berge \ō'berzh\ *n* -s [F, of Gmc origin; akin to OHG *heriberga* army encampment — more at HARBOR] **:** INN

au·ber·gine \'ōbər,zhēn, 'ō,ber-, -,jēn, ,=(,)='=\ *n* -s [F, fr. Catal *alberginia*, fr. Ar *al-bādhinjān* the eggplant — more at BRINJAL] **:** EGGPLANT

aubergine purple *n* **:** BISHOP'S PURPLE 1

au·brie·tia \ō'brēsh(ē)ə, ó'-\ *n* [NL, fr. Claude *Aubriet* †1742 Fr. painter of flowers and animals + NL *-ia*] **1** *cap* **:** a genus of Mediterranean herbs (family Cruciferae) often growing in dense mats and cultivated in rock gardens, and having showy purplish flowers **2** *also* **aubretia** -s **:** a plant of the genus *Aubrietia*

au·brite \'ó,brīt\ *n* -s [*Aubres*, commune near Nyons, Dept. Drôme, France, where a meteorite containing it fell in 1836 + E *-ite*] **:** an achondrite containing enstatite

¹au·burn \'óbə(r)n\ *adj* [ME *aborne* blond, fr. MF *auborne*, fr. OF *auborne, alborne*, fr. ML *alburnus* whitish, fr. L *albus* white — more at ELF] **1 :** of the color auburn **2 :** having reddish brown hair

²auburn \"\ *n* -s **:** a moderate brown that is yellower and duller than toast brown, lighter and slightly yellower than tobacco, paler and slightly yellower than bay, redder and slightly lighter and stronger than chestnut brown, and redder, lighter, and slightly stronger than coffee — called also *cashew lake, gorevan, tulipwood, Zuñi brown*

¹au·bus·son \'ōbə,sō", ,==¦=\ *n* -s *usu cap* [fr. *Aubusson*, France, where it was made] **1 :** a tapestry woven orig. in the 16th century, noted for its figure and scenic designs, and used for wall hangings and upholstery **2 :** a fine usu. wool or silk rug with ornate floral, scroll, and medallion designs woven without pile to resemble the tapestry Aubusson; *also* **:** any rug with similar designs usu. in pastel colors

²aubusson \"\ *n* -s **:** a dark red that is less strong and slightly yellower and darker than cranberry and bluer and paler than average garnet or average wine

AUC *abbr* **1** [L *ab urbe condita*] from the founding of the city **2** [L *anno urbis conditae*] in the year from the founding of the city

au·ca \'aůkə, -,kä *also* 'ókə\ *n* -s [Sp., fr. Araucanian, lit., enemy, fr. Quechua *áukka* enemy, rebel] **1** *sometimes cap* **:** a primitive Indian of western or southern So. America **2** *usu cap* **:** ARAUCANIAN

au·can \'aůkən, 'ók-\ *also* **au·ca·ni·an** \(')=¦kānēən, -nyən\ *n* -s *usu cap* [*Aucan* fr. Sp *aucano*, fr. *auca* + *-ano* -an; *Aucanian* fr. Sp *aucano* + E *-ian*] **:** ARAUCANIAN

au·can·er *or* **au·kan·er** \'ókanər\ *n* -s *usu cap* **:** one of the Bush Negroes dwelling on the upper Cormotibo river in Dutch Guiana

au·che·nia \ó'kēnēə\ [NL, fr. Gk *auchēn* neck + NL *-ia*] *syn of* ²LAMA 1

aucht \'äkt, 'ó-\ *var of* AUGHT

auchten *pres part of* AUGHT

auchts *pres 3d sing of* AUGHT

auck·land \'óklənd\ *adj, usu cap* [fr. *Auckland*, New Zealand] **:** of or from the city or provincial district of Auckland, New Zealand **:** of the kind or style prevalent in Auckland

au cou·rant \,ō,kü'räⁿ\ *adj* [F, lit., in the current] **1 a :** marked by keen awareness of latest developments and trends **:** fully informed ⟨people who consider themselves to be *au courant* and indisputably advanced — J.T.Farrell⟩ ⟨he seemed to be *au courant* of everything —Arnold Bennett⟩ **b :** UP-TO-DATE, ABREAST ⟨keeping its public *au courant* with recent significant work —Dwight Macdonald⟩ ⟨the book stays *au courant* by constant revision⟩ **2 :** fully familiar (as with a given object of knowledge or experience) **:** ACQUAINTED, CONVERSANT ⟨very *au courant* with the little things that gave life its color and texture —Margaret Evans⟩ **3 :** not lacking knowledge **:** COGNIZANT ⟨she was *au courant* of what had happened⟩

¹auc·tion \'ókshən\ *n* -s [L *auction-, auctio*, lit., increase, fr. *auctus* (past part. of *augēre* to increase) + *-ion-, -io* -ion — more at EKE] **1 :** a public sale of property to the highest bidder (as by successive increased bids) ⟨going to an ~ of household goods⟩ ⟨two cows bought at the ~⟩ — sometimes used with *at* ⟨sell at ~⟩ **2** *in card games* **a :** the act or process of bidding (as in auction bridge) **b :** the final declaration **:** CONTRACT **c :** any game (as auction pinochle) marked by bidding with the exception of contract bridge; *esp* **:** AUCTION BRIDGE ⟨playing a game of ~⟩ **3 :** an organization of wholesale dealers who make offers in a year-round competitive selling system marked by leisurely bidding ⟨some poultrymen sell eggs through an egg ~⟩

²auction \"\ *vt* **auctioned; auctioned; auctioning** \-sh(ə)niŋ\ **auctions :** to sell at auction — often used with *off* ⟨all the books were ~ed off⟩

auction bridge *n* **:** a bridge game differing from contract bridge in that tricks made in excess of the contract are scored toward game

¹auc·tion·eer \¦ókshə¦ni(ə)r, -iə\ *n* -s [¹*auction* + *-eer*] **:** one who conducts the sale of goods at public auction usu. as an agent on commission

²auctioneer \"\ *vt* -ED/-ING/-S **:** AUCTION

auction forty-fives *n pl but sing or pl in constr, also* **auction forty-five :** a card game that is a variant of spoil five and forty-five

auction market *n* **:** a trading center operating without set prices, terms and transactions being arranged between sellers offering lowest prices and buyers offering highest

auction pinochle *n* **1 :** a pinochle game usu. for four players, sometimes for three or five, only three being active on each deal, active players being dealt 15 cards each and bidding for the privilege of using the 3-card widow, melding, designating the trump, and leading to the first trick **2 :** any pinochle game in which the players bid for the privilege of designating the trump

auction pitch *n* **:** an all-fours game in which the players bid for the privilege of leading a card of the suit that is to be the trump — called also *setback*

auction pool *n* **:** a betting pool in which selections (as of starters in a horse race) are sold at auction, the auctioneer usu. retaining a percentage of the pool

auc·tor \'ók,tó(ə)r, 'aůk-\ *n, pl* **auctors** \-rz\ *also* **aucto·res** \=¦tō,rēz\ [L, author — more at AUTHOR] **:** the author or source (as a vendor or assignor) of a right or title **:** PRINCIPAL

auc·to·ri·al \(')ók¦tōrēəl, (')aůk-\ *adj* [L *auctor* + E *-ial*] **:** of, coming from, or typical of an author **:** AUTHORIAL ⟨~ flights of imagination⟩ ⟨~ comment⟩

au·cu·ba \'ókyəbə\ *n* [NL, fr. Jap *aokoba* aucuba, fr. *ao* green + *ki, ko* tree + *ba* leaf] **1** *cap* **:** a genus of shrubs (family Cornaceae) native to eastern Asia and having persistent often mottled foliage, small purple flowers in terminal panicles, and red berries **2** -s **:** a plant of the genus *Aucuba*

aucuba green *n* **:** a light olive that is greener and stronger than citrine, deeper and slightly greener than grape green, and greener and very slightly lighter than old moss green — called also *oak green, sea moss*

aucuba mosaic *n* **:** a mosaic of the potato and other plants of the family Solanaceae, the leaves of affected plants resembling the normal leaves of the Japanese laurel (*Aucuba japonica*)

aud *abbr* **1** audible **2** audit; auditor

au·da·ce \aů'dä,chā, -,chē\ *adj* [It, fr. L *audac-, audax*] **:** BOLD, SPIRITED — used as a direction in music

¹au·da·cious \(')ó¦dāshəs\ *adj* [MF *audacieux*, fr. *audace* audacity, fr. L *audacia*, fr. *audac-, audax* bold (fr. *audēre* to dare) + *-ia* -y; akin to L *avidus* greedy — more at AVID] **1 a :** marked by spirited fearless daring **:** intrepidly adventurous ⟨~ visions of the total conquest of space⟩ **b :** recklessly venturesome **:** presumptuously bold **:** RASH ⟨an ~ disregard for physical limitations⟩ **2 a :** manifesting defiance of or contempt for the restrictions of law, religion, social codes, or tradition **:** arrogantly rebellious **:** INSOLENT ⟨~ individualists in love with absolute freedom⟩ **b :** marked by originality and verve **:** untrammeled by formalistic restraint **:** free of cautionary inhibitions ⟨making life an ~ experiment⟩ **syn** see BRAVE

²audacious \", (')aů(t)¦d-\ *adv, dial Eng* **:** EXTREMELY, VERY ⟨~ cold weather⟩

au·da·cious·ly \(')ó¦d-\ *adv* [¹*audacious* + *-ly*] **:** in an audacious manner

au·da·cious·ness \ó'd-\ *n* -s **:** AUDACITY

au·dac·i·ty \ó'dasəd·ē, -aas-, -ətē, -i *sometimes* ə'-\ *n* -ES [ME *audacite*, fr. L *audac-, audax* + ME *-ite* -ity] **1 :** the quality or state of being audacious **:** daring boldness with assurance, presumption, or open disdain of restraint ⟨an innovating ~ for the form is unrelated to any traditional model —J.E. Gloag⟩ **2 :** an instance of audacity **:** an audacious act — usu. used in pl. ⟨my mind kindled at the thought of these *audacities* —L.P.Smith⟩ **syn** see TEMERITY

audad *var of* AOUDAD

au·dae·an \ó'dēən\ *or* **au·di·an** \'ódē-\ *n* -s *usu cap* [*Audaeus* or *Audius*, 4th cent. A.D. Mesopotamian religious reformer + E *-an*] **:** a member of an anthropomorphistic Christian sect founded by Audius in Asia in the 4th century A.D.

au·di·ber·tia \,ódə'bersh(ē)ə, ,ó-\ *n, cap* [NL, fr. Urbain *Audibert* †1846 Fr. botanist + NL *-ia*] **:** a genus of low shrubs (family Labiatae) of the western U.S. and adjacent Mexico with often hoary or canescent foliage and small spicate flowers — see BLACK SAGE 5

au·di·bil·i·ty \,ódə'biləd·ē, -ətē, -i\ *n* -ES **:** the quality or state of being audible; *specif* **:** the degree of intensity of a received radio signal estimated as the ratio of the current in the telephone receiver to that producing a signal that is sufficiently audible to permit the differentiation of telegraphic dot and dash elements of letters

audibility meter *n* **:** an instrument for measuring the intensity of radio signals that consists essentially of a variable resistor and a telephone receiver

au·di blade \'ō,dē-\ *n, usu cap A* [origin unknown] **:** an implement found in early Aurignacian cultural levels that is a development of a Mousterian flake tool

au·di·ble \'ódəbəl\ *adj* [LL *audibilis*, fr. L *audire* to hear + *-ibilis* -ible; akin to Gk *aiein* to hear, *aisthanesthai* to perceive, Skt *āvis* evidently, Av *āviš*, OSlav *avě, javě* evident] **:** capable of being heard **:** actually heard ⟨he spoke in an ~ whisper⟩ — **au·di·ble·ness** *n* -ES

audible control *n* **:** remote supervisory radio control that uses audible signals in conveying information or instructions

au·di·bly \-blē, -i\ *adv* **:** in such a way as to be audible ⟨expressed their disapproval ~⟩

au·di·ence \'ódēən(t)s, 'äd-, *Brit often & US sometimes* -dyən-\ *n* -s *often attrib* [ME, fr. MF, fr. L *audientia*, fr. *audient-, audiens* (pres. part. of *audire* to hear) + *-ia* -y] **1 a :** the act of hearing; *esp* **:** attention to that which is heard, usu. to words ⟨give me ~ and heed what I say⟩ **b** *archaic* **:** the state of hearing **:** the condition of being within hearing distance **:** HEARING ⟨he said this in the ~ of all⟩ **2 a :** formal hearing **:** formal interview (as with a sovereign or the head of a government) — often used with *with*, sometimes with *of* ⟨an ~ with the king⟩ ⟨they were received in the royal ~ chamber⟩ **b :** an opportunity of being heard ⟨he would succeed if he were once given an ~⟩ **3 a :** a group or assembly of listeners ⟨the lecturer spoke to a large ~⟩ ⟨the pianist had a very appreciative ~⟩ ⟨a nationwide radio ~⟩ **b :** a group or assembly of spectators ⟨a varied ~ attended the science exhibit⟩ ⟨a tremendous ~ of sports enthusiasts⟩ **c :** those attending a stage or film production or viewing a televised program ⟨the play met with favorable ~ reaction⟩ **d :** the public reached by books, newspapers, magazines, or other similar media ⟨influencing an ~ of millions through his books⟩ **4 :** those interested in, responsive to, or otherwise supporting an individual (as a writer), an ideology (as liberalism), an art form (as poetry), or other object of public interest **:** FOLLOWING ⟨developing an enthusiastic ~ for the free expression of ideas⟩

audience court *n* **:** the court held by an archbishop

audience flow *n* **:** the flux in audience size from one television or radio program to the next

au·di·en·cia \,aůdē'en(t)sēə, -nch(ē)ə\ *n* -s [Sp, lit., hearing, fr. L *audientia*] **1 a :** a tribunal in which the sovereign of Spain gave his personal attention to matters of justice **b :** an ecclesiastical or secular court representing the king of Spain **2 :** a high court of justice in a Spanish colony frequently exercising military power as well as judicial and political functions **3 :** a provincial or territorial high court in modern Spain **4 :** the jurisdiction of an audiencia

au·di·ent \'ódēənt, 'äd-, -dyənt\ *n* -s [L *audient-, audiens*] **1 :** HEARER **2** *in the early Christian Church:* **a :** one permitted to attend services in the narthex but dismissed after the sermon **b :** a catechumen in the early stages of instruction for admission to the church but not yet an applicant for baptism

¹au·dile \'ó,dīl\ *n* -s [L *audire* to hear + E *-ile* — more at AUDIBLE] **:** one whose mental imagery is auditory rather than visual or motor — compare MOTILE, VISUALIZER

²audile \"\ *adj* [L *audire* + E *-ile*] **1 a :** AUDITORY **b :** of or relating to an audile **2 :** relating to or transmitted by the cochlear nerves and auditory tracts

aud·ing \'ódiŋ\ *n* -s [L *audire* + E *-ing*] **:** the process of hearing, listening to, recognizing, and interpreting spoken language

¹au·di·o \'ódē,ō\ *adj* [*audio-*] **1 :** of or relating to acoustic, mechanical, or electrical frequencies in the range of audible sound ⟨~ signal⟩ ⟨~ amplifier⟩ ⟨~ transformer⟩ **2 a :** of, relating to, or dealing with sound ⟨~ waves⟩ ⟨~ research⟩ ⟨a new ~ book⟩ **b :** relating to or used in the reproduction of sound (as in high-fidelity equipment) ⟨an ~ set⟩ **c :** relating to or used in the transmission or reception of sound (as in radio or television) ⟨~ components of a television set⟩ — compare VIDEO **3 a :** marked by special interest in and usu. a technical knowledge of the mechanics of sound, esp. its transmission, reception, and reproduction ⟨~ experts⟩ ⟨~ enthusiasts⟩ **b :** specializing in the manufacture, distribution, sale, or promotion of audio equipment ⟨an ~ supply house⟩ ⟨an ~ fair⟩ **4 :** of or relating to high fidelity ⟨a disc that pleases any ~ connoisseur⟩ ⟨a tape meeting exacting ~ standards⟩

²audio \"\ *n* -s **1 :** the transmission, reception, or reproduction of sound esp. in high fidelity **2 a :** the section of television equipment used to supply sound **:** electronic equipment primarily designed to handle signals of an audible frequency **b :** the part of an electric or acoustic signal that falls in the audible frequency spectrum

audio- *comb form* [L *audire* to hear + E *-o-*] **1 :** hearing ⟨*audiology*⟩ ⟨*audiometer*⟩ **2 :** sound **:** frequencies in the range of audible sound ⟨*audiogenic*⟩ **3 :** auditory and ⟨*audiovisual*⟩

audio frequency *n* **:** the frequency of any normally audible sound wave; *also* **:** any frequency in the range approximately between 15 and 20,000 cycles per second

au·di·o·gen·ic \¦ódē(,)ō¦jenik, -dēə¦-\ *adj* [*audio-* + *-genic*] **:** produced by frequencies corresponding to sound waves — used esp. of epileptoid responses ⟨~ seizures⟩

au·di·o·gram \'==(,)=,gram\ *n* -s [*audio-* + *-gram*] **:** a graphic representation of the relation of vibrational frequency and the auditory minimal threshold

au·di·ol·o·gist \,=='äləjəst\ *n* -s **:** a specialist in audiology

au·di·ol·o·gy \-'äləjē\ *n* -ES [*audio-* + *-logy*] **:** the branch of science dealing with hearing; *specif* **:** therapy of individuals having impaired hearing — distinguished from *otology*

au·di·om·e·ter \-'ämǝd·ǝ(r)\ *n* -s [*audio-* + *-meter*] **:** an instrument used in measuring the acuity of hearing in the individual ear for sounds of various frequencies esp. with a view to detecting departures from normal hearing

au·di·o·metric \ˌȯdē(ˌ)ō, -dēə + ¦==\ *adj* [*audio-* + *metric*] **:** of or relating to audiometry **:** marked by the use of audiometry

au·di·o·metrically \"+¦==(=)=\ *adv* **:** through the use of audiometry **:** in a manner marked by audiometric theory or methods ⟨testing prospective air pilots ~⟩

au·di·om·e·trist \ˌȯdēˈämətrəst\ *n* -s **:** a specialist in audiometry

au·di·om·e·try \-ˈämətrē\ *n* -ES [*audio-* + *-metry*] **:** the testing and measurement of hearing acuity for variations in sound intensity and pitch and for tonal purity

Au·di·on \ˈȯdēən, -ˌän\ *trademark* — used for a 3-electrode tube

au·di·o·phile \ˈȯdēōˌfīl, -ēə-\ *n* -s [*audio-* + *-phile*] **:** an audio enthusiast

au·di·o·spectrograph \ˌȯdē(ˌ)ō +\ *n* -s [*audio-* + *spectrograph*] **:** an instrument that measures sound and records the measurement on a record sheet

audio spectrometer *n* **:** an instrument that records the relative intensities in a complex sound over a succession of equal frequency ranges

au·dio·visual \ˌȯdē(ˌ)ō + ¦-\ *adj* [*audio-* + *visual*] **1 :** of or relating to both hearing and sight **2 :** designed to aid in learning and teaching by making use of both hearing and sight ⟨an ~ education program⟩ ⟨an extensive ~ department of films and recordings⟩

au·di·phone \ˈȯdəˌfōn\ *n* -s [*audi-* (fr. L *audire* to hear) + *-phone*] **:** an instrument consisting of a diaphragm or plate that is placed against the teeth and conveys sound vibrations to the inner ear enabling persons with certain types of deafness to hear more or less distinctly

[1]**au·dit** \ˈȯdət, *usu* -dəd·+V\ *n* -s [ME, fr. L *auditus* hearing, fr. *auditus*, past part. of *audire* to hear — more at AUDIBLE] **1 a :** a formal or official examination and verification of books of account (as for reporting on the financial condition of a business at a given date or on the results of its operations for a given period) **b :** a methodical examination and review of a situation or condition (as within a business enterprise) concluding with a detailed report of findings **:** a rendering and settling of accounts **2 :** the final report following a formal examination of books of account **:** an account as adjusted by auditors **:** final statement of account **3** *archaic* **:** a judicial examination (as in a court) **4 :** AUDIT ALE **5 :** a check of publishers' records to verify claims as to the extent of a publication's circulation

[2]**audit** \"\ *vb* -ED/-ING/-S *vt* **1 :** to examine and verify (as the books of account of a company or a treasurer's accounts) **2 :** to attend (a course esp. in a college or university) without working for or expecting to receive formal credit ~ *vi* **:** to make an audit **syn** see SCRUTINIZE

audit- *or* **audito-** *comb form* [ME *audit-*, fr. MF & L; MF *audit-*, fr. L, fr. *auditus*, past part. of *audire* to hear] **1 :** hearing **:** sound ⟨*auditize*⟩ **2 :** auditory and ⟨*auditopsychic*⟩ ⟨*auditosensory*⟩

audit ale *n* [so called fr. its original use on the day of audit] **:** a strong ale brewed at some English universities, esp. at Cambridge and Oxford

au·di·ta que·re·la \au̇ˈdēd·əkwəˈrālə\ *n* [L, the complaint having been heard] **:** a largely disused or abolished common-law writ lying for a party against whom judgment is recovered but to whom facts constituting a good basis for discharge have subsequently accrued or become possible that could not have been availed of to prevent such judgment

auditing *n* -s [fr. gerund of [2]*audit*] **:** a branch of accounting that deals with the examination and verification of accounts or books of account and with making the final reports

[1]**au·di·tion** \ȯˈdishən\ *n* -s [MF or L; MF, fr. L *audition-*, *auditio*, fr. *auditus* + *-ion-*, *-io* -ion] **1 :** the power or sense of hearing **:** ability to hear **2 :** the act of hearing **3 :** the act of listening to intently **:** a critical hearing ⟨an ~ of new recordings⟩ **4 :** a trial performance to appraise an entertainer's merits

[2]**audition** \"\ *vb* **auditioned**; **auditioned**; **auditioning** \-sh(ə)niŋ\ **auditions** *vt* **:** to try out in an audition ⟨the producer ~*ed* the choreography group⟩ ~ *vi* **:** to give a trial performance ⟨she ~*ed* for the leading role⟩

au·di·tive \ˈȯdəd·iv, -ətiv\ *adj* [F *auditif*, fr. MF, fr. *audition*, after such pairs as MF *attraction*: *attractif* attractive] **:** AUDITORY

au·di·tor \ˈȯdəd·ə(r), -ətə(r)\ *n* -s [ME *auditour*, fr. MF & ML; MF *auditeur* hearer, judge's assistant & ML *auditor* one that audits accounts, fr. L *auditor* hearer, fr. *auditus* + *-or*] **1 :** one that hears or listens; *specif* **:** one that is part of an audience ⟨~s and viewers of radio and television programs⟩ **2 a :** one that audits **b :** one authorized to examine and verify accounts **c :** one skilled in the technique of auditing **3 :** DISCIPLE, CATECHUMEN ⟨the elect were a class above the ~s or novices —G.P.Fisher⟩ **4 :** one that hears judicially: as **a :** the presiding official of a court of inquiry in criminal cases in some European countries **b :** a judicial assessor to courts-martial in some countries **c :** one of the lowest rank of special members of the French Council of State **d :** a referee appointed by a court in a civil action in some jurisdictions; *esp* **:** one designated to take an account and report to the court **5 :** one that audits a course of study esp. in a college or university

auditor-general *n*, *pl* **auditors-general :** a chief auditorial officer

au·di·to·ri·al \ˌȯdəˈtōrēəl\ *adj* **:** of or relating to an audit or an auditor of accounts

au·di·to·ri·um \ˌȯdəˈtōrēəm, -ȯr-\ *n*, *pl* **auditoriums** \-ēəmz\ *also* **audito·ria** \-ēə\ [L, fr. *auditus* (past part. of *audire* to hear) + *-orium*] **1 :** the part of a usu. public building (as a theater) assigned to the audience **:** a place of assemblage of spectators and listeners **2 :** a room, hall, or entire building specially designed for stage and film presentations, concerts, recitals, lectures, and audio-visual features and activities ⟨a magnificent civic ~⟩ ⟨a school ~⟩

[1]**au·di·to·ry** \ˈȯdəˌtōrē, -ȯr-, -ri\ *n* -ES [ME *auditorie*, fr. L *auditorium* auditorium] **1** *archaic* **:** an assemblage of listeners and spectators **:** AUDIENCE **2** *archaic* **:** AUDITORIUM

[2]**auditory** \"\ *adj* [LL *auditorius*, fr. L *auditus* + *-orius* -ory] **1 :** of or relating to hearing **2 :** attained, produced, or experienced through hearing ⟨~ images⟩ ⟨the enjoyment of ~ rhythm⟩ **3 :** marked by great or sometimes extreme susceptibility to impressions and reactions produced by acoustic stimuli **:** AUDILE ⟨an ~ type of individual⟩

auditory aphasia *n* **:** inability to understand spoken words

auditory area *or* **auditory center** *n* **:** a sensory area in the temporal cortex associated with the organ of hearing

auditory capsule *also* **auditory vesicle** *n* **:** OTIC VESICLE

auditory cell *n* **:** a hair cell of the organ of Corti

auditory ganglion *n* **:** ACOUSTIC TUBERCLE

auditory meatus *or* **auditory canal** *n* **:** either of two passages of the ear — in human anatomy sometimes called *acoustic meatus*; compare EXTERNAL AUDITORY MEATUS, INTERNAL AUDITORY MEATUS; see EAR illustration

auditory nerve *also* **auditory** *n* **:** either of the 8th pair of cranial nerves being a sensory nerve composed of two parts: (1) a part arising in the spiral ganglion of the cochlea and serving to conduct sensory stimuli from the organ of hearing to the brain and (2) a part arising from the vestibular ganglion of the internal auditory meatus and serving to conduct stimuli having to do with the maintenance of bodily equilibrium, the two entering the brain together through the lateral wall of the medulla — called also respectively (1) *cochlear nerve*, (2) *vestibular nerve*; see EAR illustration

auditory pit *n* **:** the indentation of thickened surface ectoderm to form the embryonic ear

auditory placode *n* **:** either of the anterior lateral areas of ectoderm that invaginate and sink beneath the body surface to form the internal ear structures of vertebrate embryos

auditory point *n* **:** the lowest part of the notch between the incurved rim of the outer ear and the tragus

auditory tube *n* **:** EUSTACHIAN TUBE

au·di·tress \ˈȯdətrəs\ *n* -ES [*auditor* + *-ess*] **:** a female auditor

audits *pl of* AUDIT, *pres 3d sing of* AUDIT

au·di·vise \ˈȯdəˌvīz\ *vb* -ED/-ING/-S [back-formation fr. *audivision*] **:** to transmit or receive by audivision

au·di·vi·sion \ˈȯdəˌvizhən *sometimes* ˌ==ˈ==\ *n* -s [*audi-* (fr. L *audire* to hear) + *vision* — more at AUDIBLE] **:** the transmission or reception of a succession of images with accompanying sounds over wire or wireless circuits by electrical means

au·du·bon's caracara \ˈȯdəbənz-, -ˌbänz *sometimes* ˈȯdyə- *or* ˈōjə-\ *n*, *usu cap A* [after J. J. *Audubon* †1851 Am. ornithologist] **:** a No. American caracara (*Polyborus cheriway audubonii*) that is widespread from the southern U. S. through Mexico to Central America and is rusty black above with a bright bare face, a small black crest, and the breast and tail white marked with black

audubon's shearwater *n*, *usu cap A* **:** a small dark-footed shearwater (*Puffinus lherminieri* or *Procellaria lherminieri*) chiefly of the West Indies and the Florida coast

audubon warbler *also* **audubon's warbler** *n*, *usu cap A* **:** a common warbler (*Dendroica auduboni*) of western No. America resembling the myrtle warbler but more extensively yellow on the breast

aue *or* **au·we** \au̇ˈwā\ *interj* [Maori, Hawaiian, Tahitian, Marquesan, & Samoan *auē*, *auwē*] — used in Polynesia to express an emotional reaction (as sorrow, surprise, or affection)

auer·bach's plexus \ˈau̇(ə)rˌbäks-\ *n*, *usu cap A* [G *Auerbachscher plexus*, after Leopold *Auerbach* †1897 Ger. anatomist] **:** a network of nerve fibers and ganglia between the longitudinal and circular muscular layers of the intestine — called also *myenteric plexus*

au·e·tö \ˌau̇əˈtō\ *n*, *pl* **auetö** *or* **auetös** *usu cap* [G *Auetö*, of AmerInd origin] **1 a :** a Tupian people of the upper Xingú river basin in the state of Mato Grosso, Brazil **b :** a member of such people **2 :** the language of the Auetö people

auf *or* **awf** \ˈȯf\ *n* -s [prob. fr. ON *alfr* elf — more at ELF] **1** *now dial Eng* **:** CHANGELING **2** *now dial Eng* **:** SIMPLETON

au fait \ōˈfā\ *adj* [F, lit., to the point] **1 :** fully competent **:** up to the mark **:** CAPABLE ⟨he is remarkably *au fait* in business⟩ ⟨quite *au fait* at playing tennis⟩ **2 :** FAMILIAR **:** fully informed **:** in touch **:** au courant ⟨they are always *au fait* on the latest events⟩ ⟨putting her *au fait* with what had happened⟩ **3 :** socially correct **:** PROPER **:** in good form ⟨a somewhat unusual piece of interior decoration, but really quite *au fait*⟩

au·fait \"\ *n* -s [prob. alter. (influenced by [1]*au fait*) of *parfait*] **:** brick ice cream in layers with frozen candied fruit between the layers

auf·ga·be \ˈau̇fˌgäbə\ *n*, *pl* **aufga·ben** \-bən\ *usu cap* [G (influenced in meaning by *aufgeben* to assign), fr. MHG *ūfgābe* act of handing over, fr. *ūf* up, on (fr. OHG) + *gābe* gift; akin to OHG *geban* to give — more at UP, GIVE] **:** a task esp. when assigned experimentally or as a test (as in psychology) **:** EXERCISE

auf·klä·rung \ˈau̇fˌklārəŋ, -ler-, -laar-, -(ˌ)ru̇ŋ\ *n* -s *usu cap* [G, fr. *aufklären* to enlighten, clear up (fr. *auf* up — fr. OHG *ūf* — + *klären* to clear, explain, fr. MHG *klæren*, fr. *klār* clear, fr. MD *claer*, fr. L *clarus*) + *-ung* -ing (fr. OHG *-unga*) — more at UP, CLEAR] **:** ENLIGHTENMENT 2

au fond \ōˈfōⁿ\ *adv* [F, lit., at the bottom] **:** at bottom **:** FUNDAMENTALLY, ESSENTIALLY

auf·takt \ˈau̇fˌtäkt\ *n* -s [G, fr. *auf* up + *takt*] **:** UPBEAT

auf·tak·tig·keit \ˈau̇fˌtäktikˌkīt\ *n* -s [G, fr. *auftakt*] **:** a principle in music: all musical phrases begin on an upbeat

auf wie·der·sehen \au̇fˈvēdərˌzā(ə)n\ *interj*, *usu cap W* [G, trans. of F *au revoir*] **:** GOOD-BYE

aug *abbr* augmentative; augmented

au·ga·nite \ˈȯgəˌnīt\ *n* -s [*augite* + *andesite*] **:** an olivine-free basaltic rock whose essential minerals are calcic plagioclase and augite

[1]**auge** *n* -s [MF, fr. Ar *awj* top, summit] **1** *obs* **:** APSIS 1 **2** *obs* **:** APOGEE

[2]**au·ge** \ˈau̇gə\ *n*, *pl* **au·gen** \-gən\ [G, lit., eye, fr. OHG *ouga* — more at EYE] **:** an elliptical or lens-shaped aggregate produced by the squeezing of the constituents of certain metamorphic rocks into an eyelike form

au·ge·an \(ˈ)ȯˈjēən\ *adj*, *usu cap* [*Augeas* legendary king of Elis whose immense stable, left unclean for 30 years, was cleaned by Hercules (fr. L, fr. Gk *Augeias*) + E *-an*] **:** extremely difficult and usu. very distasteful ⟨an *Augean* task⟩

augean stable *n*, *usu cap A* **:** a condition or place marked by a staggering accumulation of corruption and filth ⟨every government ought to attend to cleaning its own *Augean stables*⟩

au·ge·lite \ˈȯjəˌlīt, -gə-\ *n* -s [ISV *auge-* (fr. Gk *augē* brightness) + *-lite*; prob. orig. formed as G *augelith*; akin to Alb *agój* to dawn, OSlav *jugŭ* south; basic meaning: brightness] **:** a mineral $Al_2(OH)_3PO_4$ consisting of a colorless or white basic aluminum phosphate (sp. gr. 2.7)

au·gend \ˈȯˌjend\ *n* -s [L *augendum*, neut. of *augendus*, gerundive of *augēre* to increase — more at EKE] **:** the quantity to which an addend is added

au·gen·phi·lo·lo·gie \ˈau̇gənˌfēlōlōˈgē, -ˌfēˌlōl-\ *n* -s [G, lit., philology of the eyes, fr. *augen* (pl. of *auge* eye) + *philologie* philology] **:** linguistics that misrepresents the realities of speech because of overemphasis on writing

[1]**au·ger** \ˈȯgə(r)\ *n* -s [ME, alter. (resulting from incorrect division of *a nauger*) of *nauger*, *navegar*, fr. OE *nafogār* (akin to OHG *nabugēr*, OS *nabugēr*, ON *nafarr*), fr. *nafu* nave (of a wheel) + *gār* spear — more at NAVE, GORE] **1 :** a tool for boring holes in wood consisting of a shank with a crosswise handle for turning and having spiral channels that end in two spurs for marking the outline of the hole, a central tapered feed screw, and a pair of cutting lips **2 :** any of various augerlike tools designed for boring into soil and used esp. for such purposes as prospecting, drilling for oil or water, and digging postholes **3 :** a large spiral bit used to mix a material and force it through a die (as in a brickmaking machine or a meat grinder) **4 :** the rotating helical member of a screw conveyor

screw auger

[2]**auger** \"\ *vt* -ED/-ING/-S **:** to move by use of an auger ⟨chopped and ~*ed* into silos —Ross Wurm⟩

auger beetle *n* **:** any of a number of elongated cylindrical beetles (family Bostrychidae) having the head protected by the heavy often spiny prothorax and boring in and feeding on wood

auger bit *n* **:** a wood-boring bit shaped like an auger but without a handle, one end of which usu. has a square tang to fit the chuck of a brace

auger conveyor *n* **:** CONVEYER 2a(8)

au·ger effect \(ˈ)ōˌzhā-\ *n*, *usu cap A* [after Pierre V. *Auger* *b*1899 Fr. physicist] **:** a process in which an atom singly ionized by emitting one electron with energy in the X-ray range instead of emitting the usual X-ray photon on recovery undergoes a transition in which a second electron is emitted

auger electron *n*, *usu cap A* [after P. V. *Auger*] **:** one of the electrons ejected from an atom as a result of the internal conversion of its own X rays in the Auger effect

auger shell \ˈȯgə(r)-\ *n* **:** a gastropod mollusk of the family Terebridae with an elongated spiral shell; *also* **:** the shell itself

auger shower \(ˈ)ōˌzhā-\ *n*, *usu cap A* [after P. V. *Auger*] **:** an extensive air shower

auger stem \ˈȯgə(r)-\ *n* **:** a long round bar of iron to which the bit and the rope socket or jars may be attached for oil-well drilling

[1]**aught** \ˈȯt, ˈät\ *n* -s [ME *aught*, *aughte* property, possession, fr. OE *ǣht*; akin to OHG *ēht* property, ON *ātt*, *ætt* family, race, generation, Goth *aihts* property, possession, OE *āgan* to own — more at OWN] **1** *Scot* **:** OWNERSHIP, POSSESSION ⟨I am as weel worth looking at as ony book in your ~ —Sir Walter Scott⟩ **2** *Scot* **:** PROPERTY

[2]**aught** *also* **ought** \ˈȯt, ˈät\ *pron* [ME *aught*, *awiht*, fr. OE *āwiht*, *ōwiht* (akin to OHG *eowiht*), fr. *ā*, *ō* ever + *wiht* creature, thing — more at AYE, WIGHT] **1** *archaic* **:** any least part **:** anything whatsoever ⟨go, my son, and see if ~ be wanting —Joseph Addison⟩ **2 :** ALL ⟨for ~ he knew to the contrary, it might have been some quack —G.W. Johnson⟩

[3]**aught** \"\ *adv* [ME, fr. [2]*aught*] *archaic* **:** at all **:** in any degree **:** to any extent ⟨he doesn't care ~ for that⟩

[4]**aught** *or* **aucht** \ˈäkt, ˈȯ-\ *vt past* **aught** *or* **aucht** \"\ *pres part* **aught·ing** \-tən, -tiŋ\ *or* **aucht·en** \-tən\ *pres 3d sing* **aughts** *or* **aught** *or* **auchts** *or* **aucht** [ME *aghten*, *aughten*, *oughten* to be obliged to, to owe — more at OUGHT] **1** *Scot* **:** OWN **2** *Scot* **:** OWE

[5]**aught** \ˈäkt, ˈȯ-\ *adj* [ME *aghte*, *aughte*, *oughte* possessed, owned, owed, past & past part. of *aghen*, *aughen*, *awen* to possess, own, owe — more at OWE] *Scot* **:** possessed of

[6]**aught** \ˈäkt\ *adj* [ME *aghte*, *aughte*, var. of *eighte* — more at EIGHT] **1** *Scot* **:** EIGHT **2** *Scot* **:** EIGHTH

[7]**aught** \ˈȯt, ˈät\ *n* -s [alter. (resulting from incorrect division of *a naught*) of *naught*] **1 :** ZERO, CIPHER **2** *archaic* **:** NONENTITY, NOTHING

aught·lins \ˈäktlənz\ *var of* OUGHTLINS

au·gite \ˈȯˌjīt, -gīt\ *n* -s [L *augites*, a precious stone, fr. Gk *augitēs*, fr. Gk *augē* brightness + *-itēs* -ite — more at AUGELITE] **1 :** a mineral principally $(Ca,Na)(Mg,Fe,Al)(Si,Al)_2O_6$ consisting of an aluminous usu. black or dark green variety of pyroxene occurring in igneous rocks such as basalt **2 :** PYROXENE

au·git·ic \(ˈ)ȯˈjid·ik\ *adj* **:** of or relating to augite

au·gi·tite \ˈȯjəd·ˌīt, -gə-, -əˌtīt\ *n* -s [ISV *augite* + *-ite*; prob. orig. formed as G *augitit*] **:** an extrusive porphyritic rock consisting essentially of augite with small amounts of amphibole magnetite or ilmenite and apatite in a glassy groundmass

au·git·o·phyre \ȯˈjid·əˌfī(ə)r\ *n* -s [ISV *augite* + *-o-* + *-phyre*] **:** a porphyritic rock with augite phenocrysts in a groundmass of potash feldspar

[1]**aug·ment** \ȯgˈment, ˈ=ˌ=\ *vb* -ED/-ING/-S [ME *augmenten*, fr. MF *augmenter*, fr. LL *augmentare*, fr. *augmentum* increase, fr. L *augēre* to increase + *-mentum* -ment — more at EKE] *vi* **:** to become augmented **:** INCREASE ⟨as the morning advances, the din of labor ~*s* —Washington Irving⟩ ~ *vt* **1 :** to enlarge or increase esp. in size, amount, or degree **:** make bigger **:** SWELL ⟨the army was ~*ed* by reinforcements⟩ ⟨rain ~*ed* the stream⟩ **2 :** to make an augmentation to (a coat of arms) **3 :** to add an augment to **4 a :** to increase by a half step (a perfect or a major interval in music) **b :** to double the note values in the development of (a theme in music) **syn** see INCREASE

[2]**aug·ment** \ˈȯgˌment, *Brit usu* -ˌmənt\ *n* -s [ME, fr. MF, fr. LL *augmentum*] **:** a prefixed vowel (as epsilon in Greek, usu. short *a-* in Sanskrit) or a lengthening or diphthongization of the initial vowel in certain verb forms to indicate past time (as in Skt *asicat* "he poured" from *sic* "to pour", Gk *egrapse* "he wrote" from *graphein* "to write", Gk *ērche* "he began" from *archein* "to begin")

aug·men·ta·tion \ˌȯgmənˈtāshən, -ˌmen-\ *n* -s [ME *augmentacioun*, fr. MF *augmentation*, fr. LL *augmentation-*, *augmentatio*, fr. *augmentatus* (past part. of *augmentare*) + L *-ion-*, *-io* -ion] **1 a :** the act, action, or process of augmenting **b :** the process of becoming augmented **:** GROWTH, INCREASE **2 :** the state of being augmented ⟨a general ~ of wealth and leisure⟩ **3 :** something that augments **:** ADDITION ⟨a fleet of new jets was a notable ~ for the air force⟩ **4 :** the device of modifying a musical subject or theme by repetition in tones of usu. twice the original length (as in polyphonic music) **5** *Scots law* **:** increase of stipend obtained by a parish minister **6 :** an additional charge to a coat of arms given as an honor

[1]**aug·men·ta·tive** \(ˈ)ȯgˈmentəd·iv, -ətiv\ *adj* [MF or ML; MF *augmentatif*, fr. ML *augmentativus*, fr. LL *augmentatus* + L *-ivus* -ive] **1 :** having the quality or power of augmenting **2 :** indicating large size and sometimes awkwardness or unattractiveness — used of affixes and of words formed with them (as Italian *casone* "big house", from *casa* "house", and Italian *-one* in words like *casone*); contrasted with *diminutive*

[2]**augmentative** \"\ *n* -s **:** an augmentative word or affix

augmented *adj* **:** INCREASED, ENLARGED; *sometimes* **:** ENHANCED ⟨~ renown⟩ — **aug·ment·ed·ly** *adv*

augmented interval *n* **:** an interval in music greater by one half step than a major or perfect interval or greater by two half steps than a minor interval

augmented pedal *n* **:** the pedal division in an organ in which borrowing and unification are used

augmented triad *n* **:** a triad having a major third and an augmented fifth — see TRIAD illustration

aug·men·tor *also* **aug·ment·er** \ȯgˈmentə(r), ˈȯgˌm-\ *n* -s **:** one that augments; *specif* **:** a tube enclosing the exhaust jet of a jet engine to give more thrust — called also *thrust augmentor*

au gra·tin \ōˈgrätᵊn, ȯ-, -rat-\ *adj* [F, lit., with the burnt particles left on the bottom of the pan] **:** browned under a flame or in a hot oven; *specif* **:** covered with bread crumbs, butter, and cheese and then browned ⟨potatoes *au gratin*⟩

augs·burg \ˈau̇gzˌbu̇rg, ˈau̇ks-, -rk; ˈȯgzˌbərg\ *adj*, *usu cap* [fr. *Augsburg*, Germany] **:** of or from the city of Augsburg, Germany **:** of the kind or style prevalent in Augsburg

[1]**au·gur** \ˈȯgə(r) *also* ˈȯgyə(r)\ *n* -s [L, prob. fr. *augēre* to increase — more at EKE] **1 :** a member of the highest class of official diviners of ancient Rome **2 :** one reputed to foretell events by omens **:** SOOTHSAYER, PROPHET

[2]**augur** \"\ *vb* -ED/-ING/-S [L *augurari*, *augurare*, fr. *augur*, n.] *vt* **1 :** to predict or foretell esp. from signs or omens ⟨an unloved brother, of whom worse things had been ~*ed* —George Eliot⟩ — often used with *well* or *ill* ⟨he ~*ed* well for his plan⟩ **2 :** to give promise of **:** give indirect evidence of **:** PORTEND, PRESAGE, BETOKEN ⟨their enthusiasm ~*s* continued success⟩ ⟨ominous delays that ~ the failure of the venture⟩ ~ *vi* **:** to predict the future (as from signs or omens) **:** make an augury ⟨she starts ~*ing* on the least pretext⟩ **syn** see FORETELL

au·gu·ral \ˈȯg(y)ərəl\ *adj* [L *auguralis*, fr. *augur* + *-alis* -al] **1 :** of or relating to an augur or augury **2 :** signifying the future **:** ominous, portentous, or auspicious

augurate *vb* -ED/-ING/-S [L, *auguratus*, past part. of *augurare*, *augurari* to augur] *vt*, *obs* **:** to infer from signs or omens ~ *vi*, *obs* **:** to make an augury

au·gur·er \ˈȯgərə(r) *also* ˈȯgyə-\ *n* -s [[2]*augur* + *-er*] **1** *obs* **:** AUGUR 1 **2 :** AUGUR 2

au·gu·ry \ˈȯgyərē, -ri *also* ˈȯgə-\ *n* -ES [ME *augurie*, fr. MF, fr. L *augurium*, fr. *augur*] **1 a :** divination by the interpretation of omens or portents (as inspection of the flight of birds or the entrails of sacrificed animals) or of chance phenomena (as the fall of lots) — see AUSPICE 1; compare SORTILEGE **b :** the rite or ceremony of divination followed by an augur **2 :** a sign or omen taken as an indication of the future **:** PORTENT ⟨like an ~, the night was coming closer —Norman Mailer⟩ **3 :** an indication of the future or of future events ⟨an exciting ~ of things to come —Bennett Cerf⟩

[1]**au·gust** \ˈȯgəst\ *n* -s *usu cap* [ME, fr. OE, fr L *Augustus*, after *Augustus* Caesar †A.D. 14 1st Roman emperor] **:** the 8th month of the year in the Gregorian calendar — abbr. *Aug.*; see MONTH table

[2]**au·gust** \(ˈ)ȯˈgəst *sometimes* əˈg- *or* ˈȯˌg-\ *adj*, *sometimes* -ER/-EST [L *augustus*, fr. *augēre* to increase — more at EKE] **:** of majestic dignity or grandeur **:** marked by stateliness or magnificence **syn** see GRAND

au·gus·ta \ȯˈgəstə, əˈ-\ *adj*, *usu cap* [fr. *Augusta*, Maine] **:** of the kind or style prevalent in Augusta

au·gus·tal \ȯˈgəstᵊl, əˈ-\ *or* **au·gus·ta·le** \ˌau̇gəˈstälē\ *or* **au·gus·ta·lis** \ˌau̇gəˈstäləs\ *n*, *pl* **augustals** \-tᵊlz\ *or* **augusta·les** \ˌau̇gəˈstälēz, ˌȯgəˈstā(ˌ)lēz\ [It & ML; It *augustale*, fr. ML *augustalis*, fr. *Augustalis* of Frederick II †1250 Holy Roman Emperor, bearing, like all Roman emperors, the surname *Augustus*, fr. L, of Caesar Augustus, fr. Caesar *Augustus* + L *-alis* -al] **:** a medieval Italian gold coin struck in the 13th century by Frederick II, patterned after the Roman aureus, and having on the obverse the emperor's bust draped in Roman garb

[1]**au·gus·tan** \(ˈ)ȯˈgəstən, əˈ-\ *adj*, *usu cap* [ML *Augustanus*, fr. L *Augusta* (Vindelicorum), Roman colony in Germany (now *Augsburg*) + L *-anus* -an] **:** of or relating to the town of Augsburg, Germany

[2]**augustan** \"\ *adj*, *usu cap* [L *Augustanus*, fr. *Augustus* + *-anus* -an] **1 :** of, relating to, or characteristic of Augustus Caesar or his age **2 :** of, relating to, or characteristic of any age felt to resemble that of Augustus Caesar (as the neoclassic period in England or esp. the reign of Queen Anne) — compare CLASSICAL 2

[3]**augustan** \"\ *n* -s *usu cap* **1 :** an English Augustan writer ⟨Alexander Pope and Joseph Addison were *Augustans*⟩ **2 :** a person of the Augustan period in England; *esp* **:** one sharing the neoclassic belief of the period ⟨an *Augustan* in spirit⟩

au·gus·tana lutheran \ˌȯgəˌstanə-\ *n*, *usu cap A&L* [NL *Augustana* (in *Confessio Augustana* Augsburg Confession, famous Lutheran document of 1530), fr. ML, fem. of *Augustanus* of Augsburg] **:** a member of the Augustana Evangelical

Lutheran Church organized chiefly by Swedish immigrants in the midwestern U. S. in 1860

au·guste \'aùgəst\ *n* -s *often cap* [F, prob. fr. G *august*, fr. the name *August*] : a circus clown who appears in white makeup and follows a chiefly slapstick routine

augusti *pl of* AUGUSTUS

¹au·gus·tin·ian \¦ȯgə¦stinēən, -tēn-, -nyən\ *adj, usu cap* [St. *Augustine* (Aurelius Augustinus) †430 Numidian church father and philosopher, bishop of Hippo (ancient city near what is now Bône, Algeria) + E *-ian*] **1** : of or relating to St. Augustine or his doctrines (as the tenets of absolute predestination and the immediate efficacy of grace) **2** : of or relating to any of several orders deriving their name from St. Augustine

²augustinian \"\ *n* -s *usu cap* **1** : a follower of St. Augustine; *specif* : one who accepts the views of Augustine on predestination and grace **2** : a member of an Augustinian order

augustinian hermit *n, usu cap A & sometimes cap H* : HERMIT OF ST. AUGUSTINE

au·gus·tin·ian·ism \-,nizəm\ *also* **au·gus·tin·ism** \ȯ'gəstə,ni-, ə'-; 'ȯgə,stē,ni-\ *n* -s *cap* : the philosophical or theological doctrine of or body of Christian teaching traceable to St. Augustine embodying a distinctive synthetic reconciliation of the doctrines of the fall, predestination, irresistible grace, and free will

augustinian of the assumption *usu cap both As* : a member of a religious congregation founded by D'Alzon in 1844 at Nîmes — called also *Assumptionist*

au·gus·tin process \'aùgə,stēn-\ *n, usu cap A* [trans. of G *Augustinverfahren*, fr. the name *Augustin*] : a process for extracting silver by converting it into chloride by roasting, leaching with salt solution, and precipitating by metallic copper

august lily *n, usu cap A* [¹*August*] : PLANTAIN LILY

au·gust·ly \(')ȯ¦gəstlē, -li *sometimes* ə'g- *or* 'ȯ,g-\ *adv* : in an august manner

august meteor *n, usu cap A* [¹*August*] : one of the Perseids

au·gust·ness *n* -ES : the quality or state of being august

au·gus·tus \ȯ'gəstəs, ə'-\ *n, pl* **augus·ti** \-,stī, aù'gù,stē\ *usu cap* [L, fr. *augustus* exalted, sacred — more at AUGUST] **1 a** : imperial majesty — a title conferred upon Gaius Julius Caesar Octavianus in 27 B.C. and assumed by subsequent Roman emperors **b** : one of the Roman emperors with the title *Augustus* **2** : one of the rulers of the Eastern and Western Roman empires (as Diocletian, A.D. 286)

au·jesz·ky's disease \'aù,yeskēz-\ *n, usu cap A* [after Aladar *Aujeszky* †1933 Hungarian pathologist] : PSEUDORABIES

au jus \ō'zhüs, ō'jüs, *F* ōzhü\ *adj* [F, lit., with juice] : served in the meat juice obtained from roasting ⟨roast beef *au jus*⟩

¹auk \'ȯk\ *n* -s [Norw. or Icel. *alk, alka*, fr. ON *ālka*; akin to L *olor* swan, MIr *ela*, and perh. to Gk *elea* a marsh bird] : any of several black and white short-necked diving seabirds of the family Alcidae that breed in colder parts of the northern hemisphere, laying their eggs in the open on ledges of cliffs or sometimes in burrows — see GREAT AUK, RAZORBILL

²auk \'ȯk, 'aùk\ *n, pl* **auk** *or* **auks** *usu cap* **1** : a Tlingit people on Stephens Passage and Douglas and Admiralty islands, Alaska **2** : a member of the Auk people

aukaner *usu cap, var of* AUCANER

auk·let \'ȯklət\ *n* -s [¹*auk* + *-let*] : any of several small auks of the No. Pacific coasts — see CASSIN'S AUKLET

aul \'aù(ə)l\ *n* -s [Russ, fr. Kazan Tatar & Kirghiz] **1** : a Caucasian mountain or desert settlement (as a village) **2** : a Central Asiatic tent made of felt or skins fastened over a circular wooden framework

razor-billed auk

aul- *or* **aulo-** *comb form* [NL, fr. Gk, fr. *aulos* — more at ALVEOLUS] : flute : pipe ⟨*Aulacanthus*⟩ ⟨*Aulostomus*⟩ ⟨*aulophyte*⟩

¹au·la \'aùlə, 'ȯlə\ *n, pl* **aulas** \-əz\ *or* **au·lae** \'aù,lī, 'ȯ,lē\ [G, fr. L, court, hall, fr. Gk *aulē*; prob. akin to Gk *iauein* to rest, sleep, Arm *aganim* I spend the night, and perh. to OE *wērig* weary — more at WEARY] **1** : a hall or large room; *specif* : the assembly hall in a German school or university **2** [NL, fr. L] : the anterior part of the third ventricle of the brain leading to the lateral ventricles

²au·la \'aùlə\ *n* -s [Marathi *āvḷā*, fr. Skt *āmalaka*] : EMBLIC

au·la·com·ni·um \,ȯlə'kämnēəm\ *n, cap* [NL, fr. Gk *aulak-, aulax* furrow + NL *-o-* + *Mnium*] : a small genus (the type of the family Aulacomniaceae) of tufted mosses closely related to the genus *Mnium* with each leaf cell having a conical central papilla and the capsules being striate and with double peristomes

¹au·lar·i·an \(')ȯ¦la(a)rēən\ *adj, sometimes cap* [ML *aularius* (fr. L *aula* hall) + E *-an*] : of or belonging to a hall; *specif* : belonging to an English university hall

²aularian \"\ *n* -s : a member of an English university hall

auld \'ȯl(d), 'äl(d)\ *adj* -ER/-EST [ME (northern dial.), alter. of ME *ald old* — more at OLD] *chiefly Scot* : OLD

auld-far·ant *or* **auld-far·ran** \(')ₑ¦farən, -ənt,-ənd\ *adj* [Sc *auld* + *farrant, farran*] *chiefly Scot* : wise beyond one's years : SAGACIOUS, CUNNING

auld kirk \'ₑ¦kirk\ *n* [fr. *Auld Kirk*, lit., old church, the established Church of Scotland; prob. fr. the more lenient attitude toward strong drink of Auld Kirkers compared with dissenters] *Scot* : WHISKEY

auld kirk·er \ₑ,kirkər\ *n, usu cap A&K* [*Auld Kirk* + E *-er*] : a member of the established church of Scotland

auld lang syne \¦ōl,laŋ'zīn, ¦ōl,laŋ-, ¦ōl,daŋ-, -aiŋ- *also* ¦ōl,dla- *or* ¦ōl- *or* ¦äl- *or* ¦äl- *or* -'sīn\ *n* [Sc, old long ago] : the good old times ⟨let's drink to *auld lang syne*⟩

auld licht \'ȯl,(d)likt, 'äl-\ *n, usu cap A&L* [Sc, lit., old light] : a member of one of those parties in the Scottish Secession churches, both Burgher and Antiburgher, that continued to hold to the principle of the connection between church and state in opposition to the voluntarism of the New Lichts

auld wife *n* **1** *Scot* : OLD WIFE **2** *Scot* : a fussy nervous person

au·lic \'ȯlik, 'aùl-\ *adj* [F *aulique*, fr. L *aulicus*, fr. Gk *aulikos*, fr.Gk *aulē* + *-ikos* -ic] **1** : of or relating to a court : COURTLY ⟨ecclesiastical wealth and ~ dignities —W.S.Landor⟩ **2** [NL *aula* + E *-ic*] *anat* : of or relating to the aula

aulo- — see AUL-

au·lo·phyte \'ȯlə,fīt\ *n* -s [*aul-* + *-phyte*] : a plant that lives within the cavity of another plant but that is neither a symbiont nor a parasite

au·los \'ȯ,läs\ *n, pl* **au·loi** \-,lȯi\ [Gk — more at ALVEOLUS] : a Greek woodwind musical instrument that is commonly called a flute but is in fact a reed instrument similar to an oboe

au·lo·sto·mat·i·dae \,ȯləstə'mad·ə,dē\ [NL, fr. *Aulostomat-, Aulostoma*, type genus (fr. *aul-* + *-stomat-, -stoma*) + *-idae*] *syn of* AULOSTOMIDAE

au·los·to·mi \ȯ'lästə,mī, ə-, -,mē\ *n pl, cap* [NL, fr. *aul-* + *-stomi*] *in some classifications* : an order comprising the cornetfishes, bellows fishes, and shrimpfishes all having a tubelike snout with small terminal mouth

au·lo·stom·i·dae \,ȯlə'stämə,dē\ *n pl, cap* [NL *Aulostomus*, type genus + *-idae*] : a family (order Solenichthyes or Aulostomi) of elongated compressed small-scaled fishes of warm seas having a group of separate dorsal spines and a single barbel under the chin — see AULOSTOMUS

au·los·to·mus \ȯ'lästəməs, ə-\ *n, cap* [NL, fr. *aul-* + *-stomus*] : a genus of tropical marine fishes comprising the flutemouths and constituting the monotypic family Aulostomidae

auls *pl of* AUL

au·lu \'aù(,)lü, 'äü,-\ *n* -s [Hawaiian] **1** : a Hawaiian tree (*Sideroxylon sandwicense*) the milky juice of which is used as birdlime **2** : a Hawaiian tree (*Sapindus oahuensis*) the fruit of which yields a native soap

¹aum \'ōm\ *n* -s [D *aam*, fr. MD *āme*; akin to OE *ōme, ōma*, a liquid measure, MHG *ōme*, Icel *āma*; all fr. a prehistoric NGmc-WGmc word borrowed fr. L *ama* pail, fr. Gk *amē*; akin to L *sentina* bilge water, Lith *semti* to draw (water)] : an old Dutch and German unit of liquid capacity (as for wine) varying from 36 to 42 gallons

²aum *var of* OM

au·ma·ga \aù'mäŋə\ *n* -s [Samoan *'aumāga*] : the village organization of untitled men in Samoa

aumakua \,aùmə'küə\ *n, pl* **aumakua** [Hawaiian *'aumakua*] : a Hawaiian personal and family god

aumbry *var of* AMBRY

au·mil \'ȯməl, -,mil\ *n* -s [Hindi *'āmil*, lit., worker, agent, fr. Ar] : a revenue collector under a local government in India

au·mil·dar \¦ȯməl¦där\ *n* -s [Hindi *'amaldār*, fr. Ar *'amal* work + Per *-dār* (agent suffix)] *India* : AGENT, FACTOR, MANAGER; *specif* : a revenue collector

au·mous \'äməs, 'ō-\ *n, pl* **aumous** [ME (northern dial.) *almouse, almus, awmus* — more at ALMOUS] *chiefly Scot* : ALMS

aum·rie *or* **aum·ry** \'ämri, 'ō-\ *var of* AMBRY 1b

AUN *abbr, often not cap* [L *absque ulla nota*] free from marking

au na·tu·rel \,ō,nad·ə'rel, ō'nachərəl, ō'nad·ərəl\ *adj* [F] **1 a** : in natural style or condition ⟨a remarkably *au naturel* attitude⟩ **b** : NUDE ⟨we went swimming *au naturel*⟩ **2 a** : cooked without dressing : cooked plainly ⟨oysters *au naturel*⟩ **b** : UNCOOKED

aun·cel \'ȯnsəl, 'ä-\ *n* -s [ME, fr. AF *auncelle*, perh. alter. (resulting from incorrect division into definite article *l'* + noun) of (assumed) OF *lancelle*, fr. OIt *lancella* small balance, fr. *lance* balance (fr. L *lanc-, lanx* plate, scalepan) + *-ella* (fr. L) — more at BALANCE] : a medieval English balance for weighing or a weight used in medieval England

aune \'ōn\ *n* -s [F, fr. OF *aulne* — more at ALNAGE] : any of various old French units of length for cloth corresponding to the English ell: as **a** : a Paris unit equal to 46.79 inches **b** : a unit used in Belgium and Switzerland and equal to 47.24 inches

aun·je·titz \'aùnyə,tits\ *adj, usu cap* [fr. *Aunjetitz*, village near Prague, Czechoslovakia] : of or belonging to an early Bronze Age culture of central Europe

aunt \'ant, 'aa(ə)-,'ai-,'á-,'ä-\ *n* -s [ME *aunte*, fr. OF *ante*, fr. L *amita* father's sister — more at AMATEUR] **1 a** : the sister of one's father or mother **b** : the wife of one's uncle — often used as a term of endearment for any woman (as an older one) who is regarded with benevolent affection **2** *obs* : an old crone or bawd

aunt·ie *or* **aunty** \-tē,-ti\ *n, pl* **aunties** : AUNT — often used as a term of endearment

aunt jer·i·cho \-'jerə,kō, -rē,-\ *n, pl* **aunt jerichos** *usu cap A&J* [by folk etymology fr. NL *Angelica*] : a plant of the genus *Angelica*

auntly \'ₑlē, -li\ *adj, sometimes* -ER/-EST : of, relating to, or suggesting an aunt ⟨telephones her . . . nearly every day with ~ advice —*Newsweek*⟩

aunt sally \-'salē, -li\ *n, pl* **aunt sallies** *also* **aunt sallys** *usu cap A&S* **1** *Brit* : a representation (as an effigy or puppet figure) of a woman usu. with a pipe in her mouth **2** *Brit* : a sport consisting in trying to break the pipe of an Aunt Sally or to knock the figure down by throwing sticks or balls

aunt·sary \-'serē\ *n* -ES [perh. alter. of *Aunt Sarah*] *Canad* : a catamaran turned up at both ends

au pair \(')ō¦pa(a)(ə)r, -pe(ə)r\ *adj* [F, lit., on equal terms] : consisting of an arrangement whereby one thing is exchanged for another of a similar nature ⟨an *au pair* tutoring post that enables one to learn a foreign language in return for English lessons⟩

au pied de la let·tre \ō¦pyādəlä'letr(ᵊ), -et(rə)\ *adv* [F, lit., to the foot of the letter] : LITERALLY ⟨don't take everything I say *au pied de la lettre*⟩

aur *abbr* aurum

aur- *or* **auri-** *comb form* [L, fr. *auris* — more at EAR] **1** : ear ⟨*aural*⟩ ⟨*auriscope*⟩ **2** : aural and ⟨*aurinasal*⟩

au·ra \'ȯrə\ *n, pl* **auras** \-əz\ *or* **au·rae** \-,rē\ [ME, fr. L, breeze, air, fr. Gk; akin to OE *weder* weather — more at WEATHER] **1 a** : a distinctive and often subtle sensory stimulus (as an aroma) ⟨an ~ of rosebuds filled the room⟩ **b** : a distinctive highly individualized atmosphere surrounding or attributed to a given source ⟨the warm earthy ~ of an old country inn, breathing friendliness and cheer⟩ **c** : distinctive appearance or impression : ASPECT ⟨everything they did had a smug ~ of respectability⟩ **2 a** : a luminous radiation : enveloping glow : NIMBUS ⟨she sparkled with vitality and seemed always to move in an ~ of brightness⟩ **b** : ASTRAL BODY **3** : a subjective sensation (as of voices, colored lights, or crawling and numbness) experienced before an attack of epilepsy, migraine, or certain other nervous disorders **4** *geol* : a zone of metamorphism surrounding an intrusive igneous body

au·ral \'ȯrəl *also* 'är-\ *adj* [L *auris* ear + E *-al* — more at EAR] **1** : of or relating to the ear ⟨an animal with a remarkably sensitive ~ apparatus⟩ **2** : of or relating to the sense of hearing ⟨a new musical with plenty of visual and ~ appeal⟩ — **au·ral·ly** *adv*

aural harmonic *n* : an overtone that is heard by the normal ear when a pure tone of suitable frequency and intensity is sounded and that is presumably due to the nonlinear response of the ear mechanism — compare COMBINATION TONE, DIFFERENCE TONE, SUMMATION TONE

au·ra·mine \'ȯrə,mēn, -,mən, ₌ₑ'mēn\ *also* **au·ra·min** \'ₑₑmən\ *n* -s [ISV *aur-* (fr. L *aurum* gold) + *amine*; orig. formed as G *auramin* — more at ORIOLE] : a bright yellow ketonimine dye $C_{17}H_{22}ClN_3$ of poor lightfastness and stability derived from diphenylmethane and used chiefly in coloring paper, in making pigments, in signal smokes, and as a fluorescent biological stain — called in full *auramine O*; see DYE table 1 (under *Basic yellow 2* and *Solvent yellow 34*)

au·ran·tia \ȯ'ranch(ē)ə\ *n* -s [NL, fr. L *aurant-, aurans* (pres. part. of *aurare* to gild, fr. *aurum* gold) + NL *-ia* — more at ORIOLE] : a poisonous red-brown crystalline alcohol-soluble dye $C_{12}H_8N_8O_{12}$ used in biological staining, in desensitizing photographic plates, and in colored photographic filters; the ammonium salt of hexanitrodiphenylamine

au·ran·ti·a·ce·ae \ə,rantē'āsē,ē\ [NL, fr. *Aurantium*, type genus (fr. L *aurant-, aurans*, pres. part. of *aurare* to gild + NL *-ium*) + *-aceae*] *syn of* RUTACEAE

au·ran·ti·a·ceous \ₑ¦ₑₑ¦āshəs\ *adj* [in sense 1, fr. NL *aurantium* (specific epithet of *Citrus aurantium*) + E *-aceous*; in sense 2, fr. NL *Aurantiaceae* + E *-ous*] **1** : relating to or resembling the sour orange **2** : of or relating to the family Rutaceae

aurar *pl of* EYRIR

au·rate \'ȯrāt, -,rāt\ *n* -s [*auric* + *-ate*] : a salt of auric acid

au·re·ate \'ȯrēət *also* -ē,āt; *usu* -d·+V\ *adj* [ME *aureat*, fr. ML *aureatus* decorated with gold, prob. blend of L *auratus* decorated with gold, gilded, golden (fr. *aurum* gold + *-atus* -ate) and L *aureus* golden (fr. *aurum* gold) — more at ORIOLE] **1 a** : golden in color ⟨her long ~ hair⟩ **b** : marked by a golden brilliance : RESPLENDENT ⟨the sea lay shimmering in ~ splendor⟩ **2** : marked by a style that is affected, grandiloquent, and heavily ornamental, that uses rhetorical flourishes excessively, and that often employs interlarded foreign words and phrases ⟨an early Renaissance poet using ~ language⟩

aurei *pl of* AUREUS

au·re·i·ty \ȯ'rēəd·ē\ *n* -ES [L *aureus* golden + E *-ity*] : the distinctive properties of gold

¹au·re·lia \ȯ'rēlyə, -lēə\ *n* -s [It & NL; NL, fr. It, fr. L *aurum* gold] : a chrysalis esp. of a lepidopterous insect

²aurelia \"\ *n* [NL, prob. fr. L *aurum*] **1** *cap* : a genus of large jellyfishes often studied as typical of the class Scyphozoa **2** -s : a jellyfish of *Aurelia* or of related genera

¹au·re·lian \(')ȯ¦rēlyən, -lēən\ *adj* [NL ¹*aurelia* + E *-an*] **1** : golden in color **2** : of or relating to an aurelia

²aurelian \"\ *n* -s [NL ¹*aurelia* + E *-an*] : a collector and breeder of moths and butterflies

³aurelian \"\ *adj* [NL ²*Aurelia* + E *-an*] : of or relating to *Aurelia* or related genera

au·rel·lia \ȯ'relyə, -elēə\ *syn of* AURELIA 2a

au·rene \'ȯrēn\ *n* -s [fr. *Aurene*, a trademark] : an early 20th century American iridescent glassware

¹au·re·ole \'ȯrē,ōl\ *or* **au·re·o·la** \ȯ'rēələ, ə'-\ *n, pl* **aureoles** \-ōlz\ *or* **aureolas** \-ələz\ *or* **aureo·lae** \-'rēə(,)lē\ [ME & ML; ME *aureole, auriole*, fr. OF *auriole*, fr. ML *aureola*, fr. L, fem. of *aureolus* golden, fr. *aureus* golden] **1** *Roman Catholicism* : a special heavenly reward marked by a special degree of glory and given to those (as martyrs) who have practiced heroic virtue **2** *fine art* : an indication of radiant light around the head (as a nimbus) or body (as a vesica piscis) of a sacred personage **3** : a quality, condition, or circumstance that surrounds and glorifies a given object : RADIANCE ⟨the sweet ~ of youth⟩ **4 a** : the luminous area surrounding the sun or other bright light when seen through thin cloud, fog, or mist : CORONA, GLORY **b** : the inner portion of a corona : the whole of an incompletely developed corona **5** *geol* : a more or less ring-shaped contact zone surrounding a comparatively small igneous intrusion

²aureole \"\ *vt* -ED/-ING/-S : to surround with an aureole ⟨her head was *aureoled* with soft moonlight⟩

au·re·o·lin \ȯ'rēələn, ə-\ *n* -s [ISV *aureol-* (fr. L *aureolus* golden) + *-in*; prob. orig. formed in G] : COBALT YELLOW

au·re·o·lus trout \ȯ'rēələs-, ə-\ *n* [NL *aureolus* (specific epithet of the Sunapee trout *Salvelinus aureolus*), fr. L, golden] : SUNAPEE TROUT

Au·re·o·my·cin \,ȯrē(,)ō'mīsᵊn, -ēə'm-\ *trademark* — used for chlortetracycline

au·re·ous \'ȯrēəs\ *adj* [L *aureus*] : golden in color

au·re·us \'ȯrēəs\ *n, pl* **au·rei** \-rē,ī\ [L, lit., golden] : a gold coin of ancient Rome varying in weight from ¹⁄₃₀ libra to ¹⁄₇₀ libra

au re·voir \,ōrəv'wär, ,ȯr-, -wå, *F* ōr(ə)vwåär *or* ōrwåär *or* ȯr- *or* ȯvwå(är)\ *n* [F, lit., to the seeing again] : GOOD-BYE — often used interjectionally

¹auri- *comb form* [ME, fr. L, fr. *aurum* — more at ORIOLE] **1** : gold ⟨*auriferous*⟩ **2** : of, relating to, or containing trivalent gold : auric ⟨*auri*-iodide⟩ ⟨*auri*cyanide⟩

²auri- — see AUR-

au·ric \'ȯrik\ *adj* [L *aurum* gold + E *-ic*] : of, relating to, or like gold : derived from gold — used esp. of compounds in which this element is trivalent ⟨~ oxide Au_2O_3⟩

auric acid *n* : a weak acid $HAuO_2$ said to be obtained as a brown powder practically insoluble in water

au·ri·chal·cite \,ȯrə'kal,sīt\ *n* -s [G *aurichalzit*, fr. L *aurichalcum* yellow copper ore (alter. — influenced by *aurum* gold — of *orichalcum*) + G *-it* -ite — more at ORICHALC] : a mineral $(Zn,Cu)_5(OH)_6(CO_3)_2$ consisting of a basic copper zinc carbonate found in pale green or pale blue crystalline incrustations

au·ri·chloride \,ₑₑ+\ *n* -s [¹*auri-* + *chloride*] : CHLOROAURATE

au·ri·cle \'ȯrəkəl, -rēk-\ *n* -s [L *auricula*, dim. of *auris* ear — more at EAR] **1 a** : the pinna of the ear **b** [so called fr. a resemblance to the external ear of some quadrupeds] : an atrium of the heart **c** : AURICULAR APPENDAGE **2** : an angular or earlike lobe or process: as **a** : one of the plates of the jaw to which the jaw muscles are attached in certain sea urchins with jaws **b** : one of a pair of ciliated pitlike organs eversible for swimming in certain rotifers **c** : either of the wings at the hinged border of the shell in certain bivalve mollusks (as the scallop) **3** : an ear-shaped appendage (as that at the base of the leaf blade of many grasses) — **au·ri·cled** \-ld\ *adj*

¹au·ric·u·la \ȯ'rikyələ, ə-\ *n, pl* **auriculas** \-ləz\ *also* **auricu·lae** \-,lē,-lī\ [NL, fr. L, external ear] **1** : a yellow-flowered primrose (*Primula auricula*) native to the Alps and commonly cultivated — called also *bear's-ear* **2** : AURICLE; *esp* : the auricular appendix of the heart

²auricula \"\ [NL, fr. L] *syn of* ELLOBIUM

auricula purple *n* : a dark reddish purple that is redder and less strong than patriarch or amaranth and redder, stronger, and slightly lighter than raisin purple

¹au·ric·u·lar \(')ȯ¦rikyələ(r)\ *adj* [LL *auricularis*, fr. L *auricula* + *-aris* -ar] **1** : of, relating to, or using the ear or the sense of hearing **2** : told in the ear : told privately ⟨~ confession⟩ **3** : understood or recognized by the ear : known by the sense of hearing ⟨my apprehension of words is ~; I must hear what I read —George Santayana⟩ ⟨~ proof⟩ **4** : of, like, or relating to an auricle or auricula

²auricular \"\ *n* -s : one of the loose-webbed feathers overlying the opening of the ear of birds — usu. used in pl.

auricular appendage *or* **auricular appendix** *n* : an anterior ear-shaped pouch in each atrium of the human heart

au·ric·u·lare \ȯ,rikyə'la(a)rē, -lärē\ *n, pl* **auricular·ia** \-a(a)rēə,-lärēə\ [NL, fr. LL, neut. of *auricularis*] : SUPRA-AURICULAR POINT

auricular fibrillation *n* : very rapid uncoordinated contractions of the auricles of the heart resulting in a lack of synchronism between heartbeat and pulse beat

auricular finger *n* [so called fr. the fact that it can be introduced into the ear passage] : LITTLE FINGER

auricular flutter *n* : an irregularity of the heartbeat in which the contractions of the auricle exceed in number those of the ventricle — compare AURICULAR FIBRILLATION

auricular height *n* **1** *anthrop* : cranial height as measured from the auditory point to the vertex **2** *anthrop* : the vertical section of the triangle formed by the distance between the poria and that from each porion to the bregma

¹au·ric·u·lar·ia \ȯ,rikyə'la(a)rēə\ *n, cap* [NL, fr. L *auricula* + NL *-aria*] : the type genus of Auriculariaceae — see JEW'S-EAR

²auricularia \"\ *n, pl* **auricularias** \-əz\ *also* **auriculari·ae** \-rē,ē,-rē,ī\ [NL, fr. *auricula* + *-aria*] : a free-swimming holothurian larva of which the body has short blunt lobes

au·ric·u·lar·i·a·ce·ae \ₑ,ₑₑ,ₑrē'āsē,ē\ *n pl, cap* [NL, fr. *Auricularia*, type genus + *-aceae*] : a family of basidiomycetous fungi (order Tremellales) with transversely septate basidia and gelatinous sporophores

au·ric·u·lar·i·a·les \ₑ,ₑₑ,ₑrē'ā,lēz\ *n pl, cap* [NL, fr. ¹*Auricularia* + *-ales*] *in some classifications* : an order of basidiomycetous fungi coextensive with the family Auriculariaceae

au·ric·u·lar·ian \ȯ¦rikyə¦la(a)rēən, -ler-\ *adj* [NL ²*auricularia* + E *-an*] : of or relating to an auricularia

au·ric·u·la·ris \ₑ,ₑₑ'la(a)rəs, -lär-\ *n, pl* **auricula·res** \-,rēz\ [NL, fr. LL, of the ear] : any of three muscles attached to the cartilage of the external ear, one anterior, one superior, and one posterior in position — called also *auricular muscle*

auricular point *n, anthrop* : the center of the external auditory meatus — see CRANIOMETRY illustration

auricular witness *n* : one who witnesses to what he has heard

au·ric·u·late \(')ȯ¦rikyələt, -,lāt\ *also* **au·ric·u·lat·ed** \-,lād·əd\ *adj* [fr. (assumed) NL *auriculatus*, fr. LL, having ears, fr. L *auricula* + *-atus* -ate, -ated] : having ears or earlike appendages : having auricles : EARED ⟨an ~ leaf⟩

au·ri·cu·li·dae \,ȯrə'kyülə,dē\ [NL, fr. ²*Auricula*, type genus + *-idae*] *syn of* ELLOBIIDAE

auriculo- *comb form* [prob. fr. NL, fr. *auricula* auricle of the heart, fr. L, external ear — more at AURICLE] **1** : of or belonging to an auricle of the heart and ⟨*auriculo*ventricular⟩ **2** : aural and ⟨*auriculo*parietal⟩ ⟨*auriculo*temporal⟩

au·ric·u·lo-infraorbital plane \ȯ¦rikyə,lō, -¦lə +\ *n* : the plane that passes through the auricular points and the lowest points of the orbits — see CRANIOMETRY illustration

auriculo-parietal angle \" + ₑ¦ₑₑₑ-\ *n* [*auriculo-* + *parietal*] : PARIETAL ANGLE

auriculo-temporal nerve \" + ¦ₑₑₑ-\ *n* [*auriculo-* + *temporal* (of the temple)] : the branch of the mandibular nerve that supplies sensory fibers to the skin of the external ear and temporal region and autonomic fibers from the otic ganglion to the parotid gland

auriculo-ventricular \" + (,)ₑ¦ₑₑₑ\ *adj* [*auriculo-* + *ventricular*] : ATRIOVENTRICULAR

auriculoventricular valve *n* : a valve between an auricle and ventricle of the heart: **a** : MITRAL VALVE **b** : TRICUSPID VALVE

au·ri·cyanic acid \¦ȯrē, -,rī + (,)ₑ¦ₑₑ-\ *n* [¹*auri-* + *cyanic*] : CYANOAURIC ACID

au·rif·er·ous \(')ȯ¦rifərəs\ *adj* [L *aurifer*, fr. *auri-* ¹auri- + *-fer* -ferous] : gold-bearing — used of gravels and rocks ⟨~ quartz veins⟩

au·rif·ic \(')ȯ¦rifik\ *adj* [¹*auri-* + *-fic*] : producing gold

au·ri·fi·ca·tion \,ȯrəfə'kāshən\ *n* -s [¹*auri-* + *-fication*] : the act of working with or in gold

au·ri·form \'ȯrə,fȯrm\ *adj* [*aur-* + *-form*] : shaped like the human ear — used esp. of mollusk shells

au·ri·fy \'ȯrə,fī\ *vb* -ED/-ING/-ES [¹*auri-* + *-fy*] : to turn into gold

au·ri·gna·cian \¦ȯrən¦yāshən\ *adj, usu cap* [F *aurignacien*, fr. *Aurignac*, commune in Haute-Garonne dept., France, near which there are caves with paleolithic remains + F *-ien* -ian] : of or belonging to the epoch of the Upper Paleolithic period following the Mousterian and preceding the Solutrean that was characterized by stone artifacts some of Mousterian type but smaller and more finely made, figures and other artifacts of bone, and paintings and engravings on walls and bone

aurignacian man *n, usu cap A* **1** *or* **aurignacian race :** man (*Homo sapiens*) of the Aurignacian period: as **a :** COMBE-CAPELLE MAN **b :** CRO-MAGNON **2 :** an individual belonging to Aurignacian man

au·rin \'ȯrən\ *n* -S [prob. fr. G *aurin*, fr. *auri-* ¹auri- + *-in*] **:** a poisonous red dye $C_{19}H_{14}O_3$ derived from triphenylmethane often obtained commercially in impure yellowish brown lumps and used chiefly as a dye intermediate — called also *pararosolic acid, rosolic acid*

au·ri·nasal \,ȯrə + \ *adj* [*aur-* + *nasal*] **:** of or relating to the ear and nose

au·ri·phryg·i·ate \,ȯrə-'frijēət, -jē,āt\ *adj* [modif. (influenced by L *Phrygius* Phrygian) of ML *aurifrigiatus*, fr. *aurifrigium* orphrey + L *-atus* -ate — more at ORPHREY] **:** adorned with orphrey

au·ri·scope \'ȯrə,skōp\ *n* -S [*aur-* + *-scope*] **:** OTOSCOPE

auro- *comb form* [ISV, fr. L *aurum* — more at ORIOLE] **1 a :** gold ⟨*aurophobia*⟩ **b :** gold and ⟨*auro*-plumbiferous⟩ **2 :** of, relating to, or containing univalent gold **:** aurous ⟨*auro*-bromide⟩ ⟨*auro*thiosulfate⟩

au·rochs \'au̇,räks, 'ȯ,r-\ *also* **au·roch** \-äk\ *n, pl* **aurochs** *also* **aurochses** [G (now usu. *auerochs*), fr. OHG *ūrohso*, fr. *ūro* aurochs + *ohso* head of cattle, ox; akin to OE *ūr* aurochs, ON *ūrr*, Goth *uraz*, a runic name, and prob. to ON *ūr* drizzle — more at URINE, OX] **1 :** URUS **2 :** WISENT

au·ro·cyanide \,ȯrō, -rə + \ *n* -S [ISV *auro-* + *cyanide*] **:** a complex salt (as sodium aurocyanide $Na[Au(CN)_2]$ formed in the cyanide process for gold) made by the union of aurous cyanide with another cyanide

au·ro·ra \ə'rōrə, ȯ'-, -rȯrə\ *n, pl* **auroras** *see senses 1 & 2* [L — more at EAST] **1** *or pl* **auro·rae** \-(,)rē\ **:** the rising light of the morning **:** the dawn of day **:** the redness of the sky just before the sun rises **2** *or pl* **aurorae :** a luminous phenomenon that consists of streamers or arches of light appearing in the upper atmosphere of a planet's polar regions and is caused by the emission of light from atoms excited by electrons accelerated along the planet's magnetic field lines **3** *or* **aurora orange :** a moderate reddish orange that is redder and paler than flamingo, crab apple, or burnt ocher — called also *orange aurora*

aurora aus·tra·lis \-(,)ȯ'strāləs\ *n, pl* **aurorae austra·les** \-(,)lēz\ [NL, lit., southern aurora] **:** an aurora that occurs in earth's southern hemisphere — called also *southern lights*

aurora bo·re·al·is \-,bōrē'aləs, -,bȯr- *also* -ē'āl-\ *n, pl* **aurorae boreal·es** \-(,)lēz\ [NL, lit., northern aurora] **:** an aurora that occurs in earth's northern hemisphere — called also *northern lights*

aurora glory *n* **:** the corona of the aurora borealis

au·ro·ral \ə'rōrəl, ȯ'-, -rȯr-\ *adj* **:** of, relating to, or resembling the dawn or the aurora borealis **:** ROSY, RADIANT ⟨a dim ~ glow⟩ ⟨a gorgeous ~ sunrise⟩

auroral line *n* **:** a prominent green line in the spectrum of the aurora borealis and aurora australis apparently due to the presence of oxygen in the upper atmosphere

aurora po·lar·is \-pə'larəs, -pō-\ *n, pl* **aurorae polar·es** \-(,)rēz\ [NL, lit., polar aurora] **:** a high-latitude aurora borealis or aurora australis

aurora yellow *n* **:** CADMIUM YELLOW

¹au·rore \ə'rō(ə)r, ȯ'-, -rȯ(ə)r\ *n* -S [F, lit., dawn, fr. L *aurora*] **:** HYDRANGEA PINK

²aurore \"\ *adj* [F, fr. *aurore*, n.] **:** marked by or relating to a yellow or pink tint given a white sauce by the addition of egg yolks, tomato puree, or lobster coral

au·ro·re·an \-rōrēən, -rȯr-\ *adj* [*aurora* + *-ean*] **:** AURORAL

au·ro·thioglucose \,ȯrō, -rə + \ *n* -S [*auro-* + *thi-* + *glucose*] **:** an organic compound of gold $C_6H_{11}AuO_5S$ injected intramuscularly in the treatment of active rheumatoid arthritis and nondisseminated lupus erythematosus

auro·thiosulfate \" + \ *n* -S [*auro-* + *thiosulfate*] **:** a complex salt containing gold in the anion $[Au(S_2O_3)_2]^{3-}$ and formed by the reaction of gold salts with thiosulfates

au·rous \'ȯrəs\ *adj* [prob. fr. F *aureux*, fr. LL *aurosus* goldlike, fr. L *aurum* gold + *-osus* -ous] **:** of, relating to, or containing gold — used esp. of compounds in which this element is univalent

au·rox \'au̇,räks, 'ȯ,r-\ *n, pl* **aurox** \"\ *or* **auroxes** \-ksəz\ *also* **aurox·en** \-ksən\ [part. trans. of G *aurochs* — more at AUROCHS] **:** AUROCHS

au·ru·lent \'ȯr(y)ələnt\ *adj* [LL *aurulentus*, fr. L *aurum* gold + *-ulentus* -ulent — more at ORIOLE] **:** golden in color

¹au·rum \'ȯrəm, 'au̇r-\ *n* -S [L — more at ORIOLE] **1 :** GOLD — symbol *Au* **2 :** the color gold

²au·rum \'au̇rəm\ *n* -S [fr. *Aurum*, a trademark] **:** a golden-colored Italian liqueur

au·rum po·ta·bi·le \,au̇rəmpə'täbəlē, ¦ȯr . . . tab-\ *n* [NL, lit., drinkable gold] **:** a formerly used cordial or medicine consisting of some volatile oil in which minute particles of gold were suspended

¹aus \'au̇s\ *n, pl* **aus** *usu cap* [Ar *Aws*] **:** one of an Arab people at Medina in the time of Muhammad

²aus *n, pl* **aus** \"\ [Hindi *āūs*] **:** short-stemmed rice grown in the dry season in India

aus·cul·tate \'ȯskəl,tāt\ *vt* -ED/ -ING/ -S [back-formation fr. *auscultation*] **:** to examine by auscultation

aus·cul·ta·tion \,ȯskəl'tāshən\ *n* -S [L *auscultation-*, *auscultatio*, fr. *auscultatus* (past part. of *auscultare* to listen, fr. *aus-* — akin to L *auris* ear — + *-cultare*, prob. akin to L *cluēre* to be named, be called) + *-ion-*, *-io* -ion — more at EAR, LOUD] **:** the act of listening to sounds arising within organs (as the lungs or heart) as an aid to diagnosis and treatment, the examination being made either by use of the stethoscope or by direct application of the ear to the body

aus·cul·ta·to·ry \ȯ'skəltə,tōrē\ *adj* [L *auscultatus* + E *-ory*] **:** of or relating to auscultation

au·shar \'au̇(,)shär\ *n, pl* **aushar** *or* **aushars** *usu cap* **:** AISSOR

aus·land·er \'au̇,slendə(r), -lan-; 'ȯ,slan-\ *n* -S [G *ausländer*, fr. MHG *ūzlender*, fr. *ūz* out (fr. OHG) + *-lender* (fr. *lend*— mutated stem of *lant* land, province, fr. OHG *land* — + *-er*) — more at OUT, LAND] **:** OUTSIDER, FOREIGNER

aus·laut \'au̇,slau̇t, *usu* -d·+V\ *n, pl* **auslau·te** \-lau̇d·ə\ *or* **auslauts** [G, fr. *aus* out (fr. OHG *ūz*) + *laut* sound, fr. MHG *lūt*; akin to OE *hlūd* loud — more at OUT, LOUD] **:** final sound in a word or syllable **:** end position of a sound in a word or syllable — compare ANLAUT, INLAUT

au·so·nian \(')ȯ¦sōnyən, -nyən\ *adj, usu cap* [L *Ausonia* southern Italy, Italy + E *-an*] **:** ITALIAN — used in poetry

aus·pex \'ȯ,speks, 'au̇,-\ *n, pl* **auspi·ces** \-,spə,sēz\ [L] **:** AUGUR

aus·pi·cate \'ȯspə,kāt\ *vt* -ED/-ING/-S [L *auspicatus*, past part. of *auspicari* to take auspices, fr. *auspic-*, *auspex*] **1** *archaic* **:** to indicate in advance as though by an omen **:** PORTEND, AUGUR **2 :** to initiate or enter upon esp. under circumstances or with a procedure (as drinking a toast) calculated to ensure prosperity and good luck ⟨*auspicating* the trip with a cocktail⟩

aus·pice \'ȯspəs\ *n, pl* **auspic·es** \-əsəz *also* -ə,sēz\ [L *auspicium*, fr. *auspic-*, *auspex* bird seer, augur, fr. *au-* (fr. *avis* bird) + *-spic-*, *-spex* (fr. *spicere*, *specere* to look) — more at AVIARY, SPY] **1 :** observation (as in augury) esp. of the flight and feeding of birds intended to discover a sign of the future; *also* **:** an omen based on such observation **2 a :** any sign or portent apparently indicative of the future **:** prophetic token ⟨under these unpromising ~s the parting took place —Jane Austen⟩; *esp* **:** a sign taken as being a favorable indication of the future ⟨he took her gentle words as an ~ of happiness⟩ **b :** the interplay of events and circumstances esp. when favorable — usu. used in pl. ⟨with the right ~s, they will succeed⟩ **3 auspices** *pl* **:** patronage and kindly guidance **:** PROTECTION ⟨under the ~s of the United Nations⟩

auspices *pl of* AUSPEX *or of* AUSPICE

aus·pi·cious \(')ȯ¦spishəs\ *also* **aus·pi·cial** \-shəl\ *adj* [L *auspicium* + E *-ous* or *-al*] **1 :** affording an esp. favorable auspice **:** favoring or conducive to success **:** PROPITIOUS ⟨an ~ beginning⟩ **2 :** attended by good auspices **:** FORTUNATE, PROSPEROUS **3** *archaic* **:** kindly disposed **syn** see FAVORABLE

aus·pi·cious·ly *adv* **:** in an auspicious manner

aus·pi·cious·ness \¦==¦==\ *n* -ES **:** the quality or state of being auspicious

aus·sa·ge test \'au̇s,zägə-\ *n* [G *aussage* deposition, declaration, fr. *aussagen* to depose, declare, fr. MHG *ūzsagen*, fr. *ūz* out (fr. OHG) + *sagen* to say, fr. OHG *sagēn* — more at OUT, SAY] *psychol* **:** a test of reliability of testimony in which the subject is required to describe a situation or event familiar to the examiner

aus·sie \'ȯsē, 'ä-, -si\ *n* -S *cap, often attrib* [by shortening & alter.] **:** AUSTRALIAN

aus·tausch \'au̇s,tau̇sh\ *n, pl* **austau·sche** \-shə\ [G, lit., exchange, fr. *austauschen* to exchange, fr. *aus* out (fr. OHG *ūz*) + *tauschen* to exchange, barter, fr. MHG *tūschen*, *tiuschen* to barter, deceive, mock, fr. MLG *tūschen*, lit., to tell a lie] **1 :** an effect of turbulent motion in the atmosphere that is manifested by an exchange of air and water vapor molecules, together with their momentum and heat energy, from one horizontal layer to another **2 :** the viscosity coefficient for horizontal flow in the atmosphere where it is affected by turbulence

aus·tem·per \ȯs-'tempə(r)\ *vt* -ED/-ING/-S [*austenite* + *temper*] **:** to quench (steel) from above the transformation temperature in a bath between 350° and 600° F and hold it there until transformation of austenite stops, for rendering it hard and tough

aus·ten·ite \'ȯstə,nīt\ *n* -S [F, fr. Sir William C. Roberts-*Austen* †1902 Eng. metallurgist + F *-ite*] **:** a solid solution in gamma iron of carbon and sometimes other solutes that is characterized by face-centered cubic crystal structure (as in austenitic alloy steel)

aus·ten·it·ic \¦==¦nid·ik\ *adj* **:** composed principally of austenite ⟨~ stainless steel⟩

aus·ten·it·ize \'ȯstənə,tīz\ *or* **aus·ten·ize** \-tə,nīz\ *vt* -ED/-ING/-S **:** to produce austenite of (a ferrous alloy) by heating above the transformation temperature

aus·tere \(')ȯ¦sti(ə)r, -iə\ *adj, sometimes* -ER/-EST [ME, fr. MF, fr. L *austerus*, fr. Gk *austēros*; akin to Gk *hauein* to parch, dry — more at SERE] **1 a :** stern and cold in appearance or manner ⟨~ Puritans⟩ **b :** marked by gravity and seriousness **:** UNSMILING ⟨the most ~ of critics —Virginia Woolf⟩ **2 :** rigidly self-disciplined and morally strict **:** ASCETIC ⟨an ~ old hermit⟩ **3 :** astringent to the taste and marked by sourness or bitterness ⟨a dry white wine with enough body so as never to seem ~⟩ **4 :** plainly simple and unadorned **:** UNEMBELLISHED ⟨an ~ office⟩ ⟨an ~ style of writing⟩ **5 :** giving little or no scope for pleasure or indulgence ⟨an ~ meal⟩ ⟨~ diets⟩ ⟨an ~ budget⟩ **syn** see SEVERE

aus·tere·ly *adv* **:** in an austere manner

aus·tere·ness *n* -ES **:** AUSTERITY

aus·ter·i·ty \ȯ'sterəd·ē, -ətē, -i\ *n* -ES [ME *austerite*, fr. MF *austerité*, fr. L *austeritat-*, *austeritas*, fr. *austerus* + *-itat-*, *-itas* -ity] **1 :** the quality or state of being austere **:** SEVERITY, STERNNESS, RIGOR **2 a :** an austere act, manner, or attitude **b :** an ascetic practice ⟨early Christian *austerities*⟩ **3 :** lack of luxuries **:** enforced or extreme economy esp. on a national scale ⟨live on an ~ diet⟩

austerity program *n* **:** a program of economic controls aimed at reducing current consumption so as to improve the national economy esp. by increased exports

¹aus·tin \'ȯstən, 'äs-\ *adj, usu cap* [ME *Austyn*, modif. of LL *Augustinus* Augustine †430 early Christian church father, bishop of Hippo in northern Africa] *chiefly Brit* **:** ¹AUGUSTINIAN

²austin \"\ *adj, usu cap* [fr. *Austin*, Texas] **:** of or from Austin, the capital of Texas **:** of the kind or style prevalent in Austin

aus·tin·i·an \(')ȯ¦stinēən, (')ä¦-\ *adj, usu cap* [John *Austin* †1859 Eng. jurist + E *-ian*] **:** of or relating to the theories of law and jurisprudence of Austin

aus·tin·ite \'ȯstə,nīt, 'äs-\ *n* -S [*Austin* F. Rogers †1957 Am. mineralogist + E *-ite*] **:** a mineral $CaZn(AsO_4)(OH)$ consisting of a basic calcium zinc arsenate (hardness 4.5, sp. gr. 4.13)

¹austr- *or* **austro-** *comb form, usu cap* [ME *austr-*, fr. L, south, fr. *austr-*, *auster* south wind, south; akin to L *aurora* dawn — more at EAST] **1 :** south **:** southern ⟨*Austro*asiatic⟩ ⟨*Austro*riparian⟩ **2 :** Australian and ⟨*Austro*-Malayan⟩

²austr- *or* **austro-** *comb form, usu cap* [prob. fr. NL, fr. *Austria*] **1 :** Austrian and ⟨*Austro*-Hungarian⟩ **2 :** Austria ⟨*Austr*ium⟩ ⟨*Austro*phobia⟩

¹aus·tral \'ȯstrəl\ *adj* [ME, fr. L *australis*, fr. *austr-*, *auster* + *-alis* -al] **1 :** SOUTHERN ⟨sailing the ~ seas⟩ **2** *usu cap* **:** of, relating to, or being a biogeographic zone extending across No. America between the transition and tropical zones **3** *usu cap* **:** AUSTRALIAN

²austral \"\ *n* -S *usu cap* **:** the language of the Austral islands

¹aus·tra·la·sian \¦ȯstrə¦lāzhən, -āsh-\ *adj, usu cap* [*Australasia* islands of the central and southern Pacific (fr. F *Australasie*) + E *-an*] **1 :** of or relating to the lands of the central and southern Pacific ocean (as Polynesia) **2 :** AUSTRALIAN — used in biogeographic description

²australasian \"\ *n* -S *cap* **:** a native or inhabitant of Australasian lands

austral english *n, cap A&E* **:** the language of most inhabitants of Australia and New Zealand — used esp. with the implication that it is a variety of English distinct from that used in Great Britain yet not so divergent as to be a separate language; compare AMERICAN ENGLISH, AUSTRALIAN ENGLISH, BRITISH ENGLISH

aus·tra·lia \ȯ'strālyə, ä's-, *US also &* *Australian appar usu* ə's-; *sometimes* -lēə\ *adj, usu cap* [fr. *Australia*, island continent of the southern Pacific] **:** of or from the continent or the commonwealth of Australia **:** of the kind or style prevalent in Australia **:** AUSTRALIAN

australia day *n, usu cap A&D* **:** a national holiday in Australia that commemorates the landing of the British under Arthur Phillip at Sydney Cove in 1788 and is observed on Jan. 26 when that date is a Monday, otherwise on the following Monday — called also *Anniversary Day*

¹aus·tra·lian \-lyən *sometimes* -lēən\ *n* -S *cap* [*Australia* + E *-an*] **1 :** an aborigine of Australia whose physical characters include dolichocephaly, dark brown skin, black often wavy hair, heavy beard, prominent brow ridges and marked prognathism, and medium stature **2 :** a native or inhabitant of the Australian commonwealth **3 :** AUSTRALIAN ENGLISH **4 :** the speech of the aboriginal inhabitants of Australia

²australian \"\ *adj, usu cap* **1 :** of or relating to the continent or commonwealth of Australia, its inhabitants, or the languages spoken there **2 a :** of, relating to, or being a biogeographic region that comprises Australia and the islands north of it from Celebes eastward, Tasmania, New Zealand, and Polynesia **b :** of, relating to, or being the subregion of the Australian region that comprises Australia and Tasmania — compare AUSTROGAEAN **3 :** native to Australia — often used to indicate organisms with but superficial resemblance to those designated by the substantive

australian anteater *n, usu cap 1st A* **:** ECHIDNA

australian badger *n, usu cap A* **:** WOMBAT

australian ballot *n, usu cap A* **:** an official ballot printed at public expense on which the names of all the nominated candidates appear and which is distributed only at the polling place and marked in secret — see INDIANA BALLOT, MASSACHUSETTS BALLOT

australian banyan *n, usu cap A* **:** MORETON BAY FIG

australian baobab *n, usu cap A* **:** CREAM-OF-TARTAR TREE

australian bean tree *n, usu cap A* **1 :** a tall tree (*Castanospermum australe*) with pealike flowers and long pods **2 :** a tall spreading tree (*Bauhinia hookeri*) with broad flat pods

australian bear *n, usu cap A* **:** KOALA

australian beech *n, usu cap A* **:** a gum tree (*Eucalyptus polyanthemos*) with small flowers in many-flowered panicles

australian beech cherry *n, usu cap A* **:** a shrub or small tree (*Trochocarpa laurina*) with globular fruits

australian blackwood *n, usu cap A* **:** LIGHTWOOD 2a

australian bluebell *or* **australian bluebell creeper** *n, usu cap A* **:** a slender evergreen vine (*Sollya fusiformis*) with nodding blue flowers

australian bluegrass *n, usu cap A* **:** an Australian pasture grass (*Andropogon sericeus*) introduced into the West Indies

australian brake *n, usu cap A* **:** a bright green Australian fern (*Pteris tremula*) cultivated for its ornamental fronds

australian cat *n, usu cap A* **:** a variety of the Siamese cat developed in Australia

australian cattle dog *n, usu cap A* **:** a large-sized dog of a breed developed by crossing the dingo with the smooth-coated blue merle Scotch collie and having the face and ears black or red and the body dark blue evenly speckled with a lighter blue — called also *Australian heeler, blue heeler, merle*

australian cherry *n, usu cap A* **:** NATIVE CHERRY

australian cockroach *n, usu cap A* **:** a cockroach (*Periplaneta australasiae*) now widely distributed in warm countries

australian cranberry *n, usu cap A* **1 :** the edible berry of an Australian shrub (*Lissanthe sapida*) resembling the European cranberry **2 :** any plant that bears the Australian cranberry **3 :** a prostrate shrub (*Astroloma humifusum*) having cranberrylike leaves and nearly globular edible fruit

australian crawl *n, usu cap A* **:** a crawl stroke in swimming; *specif* **:** a 2-beat crawl

australian currant *n, usu cap A* **:** a shrub or small tree (*Leucopogon richei*) having oblong leaves, terminal spikes of small tubular flowers, and edible white fruits

australian desert kumquat *n, usu cap A* **:** DESERT LEMON

australian english *n, cap A&E* **:** the language of most inhabitants of Australia — used esp. with the implication that it is a variety of English distinct from that used in Great Britain yet not so divergent as to be a separate language; compare AMERICAN ENGLISH, AUSTRAL ENGLISH, BRITISH ENGLISH

australian football *n, usu cap A* **:** AUSTRALIAN RULES FOOTBALL

australian glasswort *n, usu cap A* **:** a leafless herb (*Salicornia australis*) with fleshy scaly branches

australian gourd *n, usu cap A* **:** STAR CUCUMBER — used of the plant when adventive in Australia

australian grass tree *n, usu cap A* **1 :** GRASS TREE 1 **2 :** a plant (*Kingia australis*) of western Australia that is variously assigned to Juncaceae or Liliaceae and has an erect black woody trunk crowned with long slender silvery leaves **3 :** a stout shrub (*Richea dracophylla*) with narrow leaves crowded at the ends of the branches and with dense terminal clusters of white or pink flowers

australian gum *n, usu cap A* **:** gum arabic from certain Australian wattles or acacias

australian heath *n, usu cap A* **:** any heathlike plant of the family Epacridaceae

australian heeler *n, usu cap A* **:** AUSTRALIAN CATTLE DOG

australian honeysuckle *n, usu cap A* **:** any of several plants of the genus *Banksia*; *esp* **:** a shrub or bushy tree (*B. integrifolia*) with silky foliage and cylindrical flower spikes

australian ironbark *n, usu cap A* **:** any of several trees of the genus *Eucalyptus*

aus·tra·lian·ism \-,nizəm\ *n* -S *usu cap* **1 :** a characteristic feature of Australian English esp. as contrasted with British English **2 :** patriotic or partisan feeling for Australia

aus·tra·lian·ize \-,nīz\ *vt* -ED/-ING/-S *often cap* **1 :** to cause to acquire traits distinctive of Australians **2 :** to cause to become devoted to Australia **3 :** to naturalize as an Australian

australian laurel *n, usu cap A* **1 :** NATIVE LAUREL 1 **2 :** AUSTRALIAN WALNUT

australian lilac *n, usu cap A* **:** AUSTRALIAN SARSAPARILLA

australian magpie *n, usu cap A* **:** PIPING CROW

australian mahogany *n, usu cap A* **1 :** JARRAH 1 **2 :** AUSTRALIAN ROSEWOOD 2

australian millet *n, usu cap A* **:** an Australian grass (*Panicum divaricatissimum*) with edible seeds

australian nettle tree *n, usu cap A* **:** any of several tall Australian trees of the genus *Laportea*

australian nut *n, usu cap A* **:** MACADAMIA 2

australian oak *n, usu cap A* **:** any of several Australian trees: as **a :** SILK OAK **b :** either of two mountain ashes (*Eucalyptus regnans* and *E. delagatensis*) having rather hard heavy durable pinkish or light brown wood that works and polishes well

australian oat *n, usu cap A* **:** RESCUE GRASS

australian opossum *n, usu cap A* **:** OPOSSUM 2

australian pea *n, usu cap A* **:** an evergreen partly woody vine (*Dolichos lignosus*) having 3-foliolate leaves, rose-purple or white flowers, and black seeds in a flat pod

australian pine *n, usu cap A* **1 :** any of several trees of the genus *Casuarina* **:** BEEFWOOD **2 :** a dark yellowish green that is yellower and paler than holly green (sense 1), lighter and stronger than deep chrome green, and yellower, lighter, and stronger than average hunter green

australian piripiri *n, usu cap A* **:** a silky herb (*Acaena ovina*) with flowers in an interrupted spike and prickly fruits

australian pitcher plant *n, usu cap A* **:** a scapose herb (*Cephalotus follicularis*) with leaves in a basal cluster and white flowers in a spike

australian plague locust *n, usu cap A* **:** a very destructive large migratory grasshopper (*Chortoicetes terminifera*) of the southern parts of Australia; *also* **:** a smaller form (*Austroicetes cruciata*) of similar habits

australian poker *n, usu cap A* **:** a British draw poker with blind opening

australian red snail *or* **australian snail** *n, usu cap A* **:** a brilliant red Australian pulmonate snail (*Lenameria dispar*) with red blood often kept as a scavenger in freshwater aquaria

australian rosewood *n, usu cap A* **1 :** BASTARD ROSEWOOD 2 **2 :** a tall tree (*Dysoxylum fraserianum*) of New South Wales having flowers with a united calyx

australian rules football *n, usu cap A&R* **:** a football game played on a field having 4 goalposts at each end between teams of 18 players of whom 3 play no fixed position, the players advancing the ball by kicking, underhand passing, and, provided it is bounced every 10 yards, running

australian salmon *n, usu cap A* **:** a common percoid fish (*Arripis trutta*) that occurs in schools along the coasts of New South Wales, Tasmania, and New Zealand and is fished with beach seines for food and bait

australian saltbush *n, usu cap A* **:** any of several Australian shrubs of the family Chenopodiaceae (as of the genus *Atriplex*) cultivated in the western U.S. as forage plants

australian sarsaparilla *n, usu cap A* **:** an Australian shrub (*Hardenbergia monophylla*) used as a substitute for sarsaparilla and often cultivated for ornament

australian sassafras *n, usu cap A* **1 :** a tall tree (*Doryphora sassafras*) of the family Monimiaceae with aromatic bark and leaves **2 :** a tree (*Atherosperma moschata*) of the family Monimiaceae with dark gray wood

australian sea holly *n, usu cap A* **:** a prostrate prickly herb (*Eryngium vesiculosum*) with a bracted flower cluster

australian shamrock *n, usu cap A* **:** MENINDIE CLOVER

australian sugar tree *n, usu cap A* [so called fr. its sweetish resin] **:** SUGAR TREE

australian swamp oak *n, usu cap A* **:** a small beefwood (*Casuarina glauca*) sometimes cultivated for ornament

australian tamarind *n, usu cap A* **:** a low tree (*Diploglottis cunninghamii*) yielding subacid fruits

australian teak *n, usu cap A* **:** any of several trees having teaklike timber: as **a :** a small tree (*Endiandra glauca*) of the family Lauraceae **b :** FLINDOSA

australian terrier *n, usu cap A* **:** a small rather short-legged wirehaired terrier of an Australian breed usu. grayish or bluish in color and with tan legs

australian turpentine tree *n, usu cap A* **1 :** BRUSH BOX **2 :** a medium-sized or large tree (*Syncarpia laurifolia*) of the family Myrtaceae with fibrous bark, opposite ovate thick leaves, and white flowers in dense round heads

australian walnut *n, usu cap A* **:** a timber tree (*Endiandra palmerstonii*) with brown to black and variegated wood

australian water lily *n, usu cap A* **:** an immense water lily (*Nymphaea gigantea*) with round leaves 18 inches wide and blue or purple-pink flowers nearly as large

australian water rat *n, usu cap A* **:** BEAVER RAT

australian willow *n, usu cap A* **:** WILGA

australian x-disease *also* **australian x encephalitis** *n, usu cap A&X* **:** X-DISEASE

aus·tra·lic \ȯ'stralik, ä's-,ə's-\ *adj, usu cap* [*Australia* + E *-ic*] **:** of or belonging to aboriginal Australians

aus·tra·lite \'ȯstrə,līt\ *n* -S [*Australia*, its locality + E *-ite*] **:** a natural meteoritic glass found in Australia

aus·tra·lo·an·thro·pus \ȯ,strālō'an(t)thrəpəs, ä,-, -,an-'thrōpəs\ *n, cap* [NL, fr. Australia + NL *-o-* + *-anthropus*] *in some classifications* **:** a subgenus of *Homo* comprising the Australian aborigines and their extinct related forms, the Solo and Wadjak men

¹aus·tra·loid \'ȯstrə,lȯid, 'äs-\ *also* **aus·tra·li·oid** \(')=

¦strālē,ȯid\ *adj, usu cap* [*Australia* + E *-oid*] **:** relating or belonging to an ethnic group including the Australian aborigines, the autochthonous Dravidians of southern India, and other peoples of southern Asia and Pacific islands sometimes including the Ainu

²australoid \"\ *n* -s *usu cap* **:** a person having the physical characteristics common to aboriginal Australians

aus·tra·lo·pith·e·ci·dae \ȯ,strā(,)lōpə'thēsə,dē, ä,-\ *n pl, cap* [NL, fr. *Australopithecus*, type genus + *-idae*] **:** the Australopithecinae regarded as a family of Hominoidea distinct from the Pongidae

aus·tra·lo·pith·e·ci·nae \-,pithə'sī(,)nē\ *n pl, cap* [NL, fr. *Australopithecus*, type genus + *-inae*] **:** a subfamily of Pongidae including extinct apes with near-human dentition and constituting *Australopithecus* and according to some authorities other genera all from southern Africa

¹aus·tra·lo·pith·e·cine \⸗¦⸗⸗¦pithə,sīn, -,sən\ *adj* [NL *Australopithecinae*] **:** of or belonging to Australopithecinae or the australopithecines

²aus·tra·lo·pith·e·cine \"\ *also* **aus·tra·lo·pith·e·cid** \-pə'thēsəd, -'pithə,sid\ *or* **aus·tra·lo·pith** \⸗'⸗⸗,pith\ *n* -s [*australopithecine* fr. NL *Australopithecinae; australopithecid* fr. NL *Australopithecidae; australopith* fr. NL *Australopithecinae* or *Australopithecidae*] **:** an individual or fossil of the subfamily Australopithecinae

aus·tra·lo·pith·e·cus \⸗,⸗(,)⸗pə'thēkəs, -'pithikəs\ *n, cap* [NL, fr. L *australis* southern + NL *-o-* + *-pithecus* — more at AUSTRAL] **:** a genus of extinct generalized anthropoid apes (family Pongidae) known chiefly from skulls from the middle Pleistocene or possibly Upper Pliocene deposits of southern Africa which are all essentially apelike though showing advances towards the hominid condition in cranial capacity, in the form of the dental arch, and in dentition and that is usu. regarded as too recent to have been ancestral to man — see AUSTRALOPITHECINAE

aus·tral·or·bis \,ȯstrə'lȯrbəs, ¦äs-\ *n, cap* [NL, fr. L *australis* southern + *orbis* ring, circle] **:** a genus of New World pulmonate snails (family Planorbidae) including important So. and Central American intermediate hosts of the schistosome (*Schistosoma mansoni*)

aus·tral·orp \'⸗⸗,lȯrp\ *n* -s *usu cap* [*Austral*ian + *Orp*ington] **:** a utility type of black Orpington fowl developed in Australia and now a widely distributed and valued egg-producing breed, a white sport being less common

¹aus·tra·sian \(')ȯ¦strāzhən, -āsh-\ *adj, usu cap* [*Austrasia, Ostrasia*, eastern division of the Frankish dominions (fr. ML) + E *-an*] **1 :** of, relating to, or characteristic of Austrasia, the eastern part of the kingdom of the Franks **2 :** of, relating to, or characteristic of Austrasians

²austrasian \"\ *n* -s *cap* **:** a native or inhabitant of Austrasia

aus·tria \'ȯstrēə, 'äs-\ *adj, usu cap* [fr. *Austria*, country in central Europe] **:** of or from Austria **:** of the kind or style prevalent in Austria **:** AUSTRIAN

¹aus·tri·an \-ēən\ *adj, usu cap* [*Austria* + E *-an*] **1 a :** of, relating to, or characteristic of Austria **b :** of, relating to, or characteristic of the Austrians **2 :** of or relating to the Austrian school of economic theory

²austrian \"\ *n* -s **1** *cap* **a :** a native or inhabitant of Austria **b :** a native or inhabitant of Austria-Hungary **2** *usu cap* **:** a member of the Austrian school of economic theory

austrian brier *n, usu cap A* **:** a yellow rose (*Rosa foetida*) with an unpleasant odor

austrian copper *n, usu cap A* **:** a variety (*Rosa foetida bicolor*) of the Austrian brier rose with copper-colored petals

austrian fieldcress *or* **austrian cress** *n, usu cap A* **:** a perennial cress (*Rorippa austriaca*) with auricled stem leaves and fruiting pedicels three to four times the length of the ellipsoid fruit pods

austrian oak *n, usu cap A* **:** ENGLISH OAK

austrian pine *n, usu cap A* **:** a tall pine (*Pinus nigra*) of central Europe widely cultivated for ornament and having needles two in a cluster and grayish twigs

austrian school *n, usu cap A & sometimes cap S* **:** the proponents of and adherents to the economic theories developed by Karl Menger (1840-1921), Friedrich von Wieser (1851-1926), and Eugen Böhm-Bawerk (1851-1914) of Vienna, Austria, who originated a subjective theory of value that utilizes the doctrine of marginal utility rather than the Ricardian labor theory of value and who formulated a productivity theory of interest and capital that emphasizes the importance of the time element in production — compare MARGINAL UTILITY

austrian winter pea *n, usu cap A* **:** FIELD PEA

¹aus·tric \'ȯstrik, 'äs-\ *adj, usu cap* [*Austria* + E *-ic*] **:** AUSTRIAN

²austric \"\ *adj, usu cap* [¹*austr-* + *-ic*] **:** of, relating to, or belonging to the related Austronesian and Austroasiatic families of languages considered as subfamilies of a vast family of languages extending from northern India across the islands of the Pacific

aus·trin·ger \'ästrinjər, 'ȯ-\ *n* -s [alter. of *ostreger* — more at OSTREGER] **:** one that keeps goshawks

¹austro- — see ¹AUSTR-

²austro- — see ²AUSTR-

aus·tro·asiatic \¦ȯ(,)strō, ¦ä-+,⸗⸗¦⸗⸗\ *adj, usu cap* [¹*austr-* + *Asiatic*] **:** of, relating to, or belonging to a family of languages once widespread over northeastern India and Indo-China and comprising (1) the older now almost extinct Malacca group in the Malay peninsula, including Semang, Sakai; (2) Khasi, including Nicobarese, Palaung, Wa, Khasi; (3) Mon-Khmer, including Mon, Khmer, Jakun; and (4) Munda, including Santali, Ho, Mundari, Korwa, Asuri, Korku, Kharia, Juang, Savara, Gadaba — see ²AUSTRIC

austro-columbian \"+\ *adj, usu cap A&C* [NL *Austro⸗Columbia*, the neotropical region (fr. ¹*austr-* + *Columbia* America) + E *-an*] **:** NEOTROPICAL

aus·tro·gae·an *or* **aus·tro·ge·an** \¦ȯstrō¦jēən, ¦äs-\ *adj, usu cap* [NL *Austrogaea, Austrogea*, a biogeographic region (fr. ¹*austr-* + *-gaea, -gea*) + E *-an*] **:** of, relating to, or being a biogeographic region that comprises the Australian region except Polynesia

¹aus·tro-hungarian \¦ȯ(,)strō, ¦ä- +,⸗¦⸗⸗⸗\ *adj, usu cap A&H* [²*Austr-* + *Hungarian*] **:** of or relating to the former dual monarchy of Austria-Hungary

²austro-hungarian \"\ *n, cap A&H* **:** a native or inhabitant of Austria-Hungary

austro-malayan \"+⸗¦⸗⸗, ¦⸗,⸗⸗\ *adj, usu cap A&M* [¹*austr-* + *Malayan*] **:** PAPUAN

¹aus·tro·ne·sian \¦ȯstrō¦nēzhən, ¦äs-, -ēsh-\ *adj, usu cap* [ISV, fr. NL *Austronesia*, islands of the southern Pacific + ISV *-an;* orig. formed as G *austronesisch*] **:** belonging or relating to a family of agglutinative languages spoken in the area extending from Madagascar in the west through the Malay peninsula and archipelago to Hawaii and Easter Island in the east and including practically all the native languages of the Pacific islands with exception of the Australian, Papuan, and Negrito languages — compare AUSTRIC 2, INDONESIAN

²austronesian \"\ *n* -s *usu cap* **:** the Austronesian language family

aus·tro·riparian \¦ȯstrō, ¦äs+(,)⸗¦⸗⸗⸗\ *adj, usu cap* [¹*austr-* + *riparian*] **:** of, relating to, or being the humid division of the Lower Austral life zone including the lower Mississippi valley and the greater part of the So. Atlantic and Gulf states from Virginia to eastern Texas

au·su \aü'sü\ *n* -s [Sp *ausú*] **:** any of several West Indian trees of the myrtle family; *esp* **:** BAYBERRY 1

au·su·bo \aü'sü(,)bō\ *n* -s [Sp] **1 a :** MASTIC TREE **b :** BUSTIC **2 :** the dark heavy strong and valuable wood of an ausubo

aut- *or* **auto-** *comb form* [Gk, fr. *autos;* perh. akin to L *aut* or — more at EKE] **1 a :** self **:** same one ⟨*autecology*⟩ ⟨*autism*⟩ ⟨*autobiography*⟩ ⟨*autogenetic*⟩ ⟨*autokinetic*⟩ ⟨*autolysis*⟩ **b** *usu auto-* **:** having similar genomes ⟨*autohexaploid*⟩ ⟨*autopolyploid*⟩ — opposed to *all-* **2 :** automatic **:** self-acting **:** self⸗regulating ⟨*autoalarm*⟩ ⟨*autofeed*⟩ ⟨*autowind*⟩ **3** *auto-* **a :** of, by, affecting, or for the same individual ⟨*autohemagglutination*⟩ ⟨*autovaccine*⟩ **b :** self-caused **:** self-induced **:** occurring within one's own body sometimes pathologically ⟨*autointoxication*⟩ **c :** acting as an antibody on or produced as an antibody for a person's or animal's own antigens ⟨*autoagglutinin*⟩ ⟨*autohemolysin*⟩

au·ta·coid \'ȯd·ə,kȯid\ *n* -s [*aut-* + Gk *akos* remedy + E *-oid;* akin to OIr *hīcc* healing, payment, W *iach* healthy, Corn *yogh*] **:** a specific organic substance formed by the cells of one part and transported in the body fluid or the sap of an organism and producing a specific effect on the activity of the cells of another part **:** an internal secretion (as a hormone or chalone) — **au·ta·coid·al** \¦⸗⸗¦kȯid°l\ *adj*

aut·allotriomorphic \'aůd·+⸗¦⸗⸗⸗¦⸗⸗\ *adj* [*aut-* + *allotriomorphic*, fr. Gk *allotrios* strange (fr. *allos* other) + E *-morphic* — more at ELSE] **:** of, relating to, or like an aplitic texture of rock in which all of the constituents have crystallized simultaneously and mutually interfered

au·tarch \'ȯ,tärk\ *n* -s [Gk *autarchos*, fr. *autarchos* autocratic, fr. *aut-* self, independent, independently + *archos* ruler — more at ARCHI-] **:** AUTOCRAT, DESPOT

au·tar·chic \(')ȯ¦tärkik\ *or* **au·tar·chi·cal** \-rkəkəl\ *adj* **1 a :** of, relating to, or marked by autarchy ⟨an ~ government⟩ **b :** AUTARKIC **2 :** unaffected by adjacent genes — used of genes in mosaic tissues; compare HYPARCHIC **syn** see FREE

au·tar·chi·cal·ly \-rkək(ə)lē\ *adv* **:** in an autarchic manner

au·tar·chist \'⸗,⸗kəst\ *n* -s [by alter.] **:** AUTARKIST

au·tar·cho·glos·sa \ȯ,tärkō'gläsə, -ȯsə\ *n pl, cap* [NL, fr. Gk *autarchos* autocratic (fr. *aut-* + *-archos* -arch) + NL *-glossa*] **:** a division comprising all lizards except the Ascalabota

¹au·tar·chy \'ȯ,tärkē, -tȧk-, -ki *sometimes* 'ȯd·ə(r)k- *or* 'ȯtə-\ *n* -ES [Gk *autarchia*, fr. *autarchos* self-ruling + *-ia* -y] **:** absolute sovereignty **:** absolute or autocratic rule

²autarchy \"\ *n* -ES [by alter.] **:** AUTARKY

au·tar·kic \(')ȯ¦tärkik\ *or* **au·tar·ki·cal** \-rkəkəl\ *adj* **:** of, relating to, or marked by autarky **syn** see FREE

au·tar·ki·cal·ly \-rkək(ə)lē\ *adv* **:** in an autarkic manner

¹au·tar·kist \'⸗,⸗kəst\ *adj* **1 :** favoring autarky **2 :** AUTARKIC

²autarkist \"\ *n* -s **:** an advocate of autarky

au·tar·ky \'ȯ,tärkē, -tȧk-, -ki *sometimes* 'ȯd·ə(r)k- *or* 'ȯtə-\ *n* -ES [modif. of G *autarkie*, fr. Gk *autarkeia* personal self⸗sufficiency, fr. *autarkēs* self-sufficient + *-ia* -y] **1 :** SELF⸗SUFFICIENCY, INDEPENDENCE; *specif* **:** national economic self⸗sufficiency and independence ⟨under a system of ~, trade between countries dwindled to almost nothing⟩ **2 :** a policy of establishing a national economy that is completely self-sufficient and independent of imports from other countries **3 :** an economically independent and self-sufficient region or nation

au·te \'aůd·ē\ *n* -s [Tahitian & Samoan *'aute*, or Maori *aute*] *in Tahiti & New Zealand* **:** PAPER MULBERRY

autecious *var of* AUTOECIOUS

aut·ecologic *or* **aut·ecological** \¦aůd·+\ *adj* **:** of, relating to, or involving autecology — **autecologically** *adv*

aut·ecology \,aůd·+\ *n* -ES [ISV *aut-* + *ecology;* orig. formed as G *autökologie*] **:** a branch of ecology dealing with the interrelations between individual organisms or individual kinds of organisms (as species) and their environment — compare SYNECOLOGY

auth *abbr* **1** authentic **2** author **3** authority; authorized

au·then·tic \ə'thentik, ȯ'-, -tēk\ *adj* [alter. (influenced by Gk *authentikos*) of earlier *autentyke*, fr. ME *autentik*, fr. MF *autentique*, fr. LL *authenticus*, fr. Gk *authentikos*, fr. *authentēs* murderer, master, doer (fr. *aut-* + *-hentēs* one that accomplishes) + *-ikos* -ic; akin to Gk *anyein, anein* to accomplish, *entea* (pl.) armor, Skt *sanoti* he gains] **1** *obs* **:** possessing authority that is not usu. open to challenge **:** AUTHORITATIVE **2 :** worthy of acceptance or belief by reason of conformity to fact and reality **:** not contradicted by evidence **:** TRUSTWORTHY, CREDIBLE, CONVINCING ⟨an ~ book on medieval customs⟩ ⟨an ~ portrayal⟩ **3 a :** vested with due formalities and legally attested **:** legally valid ⟨an ~ act⟩ **b** *obs* **:** properly qualified **:** AUTHORIZED **4 a :** not imaginary or specious **:** REAL, GENUINE ⟨~ joy over her return⟩ **b :** not copied **:** ORIGINAL ⟨an ~ manuscript⟩ ⟨an ~ Chippendale chair⟩ **5** *of a church mode* **:** ranging upwards from the keynote — distinguished from *plagal* **6 :** of an origin that cannot be questioned **:** indisputably proceeding from a given source that is avowed or implied **:** not spurious ⟨an ~ historical reference⟩ **7 a :** marked by conformity to widespread or long-continued tradition ⟨an ~ English custom⟩ **b :** marked by close conformity to an original **:** accurately and satisfyingly reproducing essential features ⟨an ~ portrait⟩ **8** *biol* **:** VALID

syn GENUINE, VERITABLE, BONA FIDE: AUTHENTIC stresses fidelity to actuality and fact, compatibility with a certain source or origin, accordance with usage or tradition, or complete sincerity without feigning or hypocrisy ⟨he told his grandfather that he had been in combat with a giant, and frightened his poor mother . . . with long, and by no means *authentic*, accounts of the battle —W.M.Thackeray⟩ ⟨an esoteric jargon which does not even have the *authentic* ring of American slang —Stanley Walker⟩ ⟨only the *authentic* Christian tradition has the answer to our present problems —*Times Lit. Supp.*⟩ ⟨an *authentic* passion for concrete detail, in the mind of the author himself —C.E.Montague⟩ GENUINE may stress definite origin from a certain source ⟨whose letter — *genuine* or counterfeited — had been so instrumental in hastening this outbreak —J.L.Motley⟩ GENUINE chiefly emphasizes a real actual character as contrasted with a fraudulent, deceptive appearance ⟨whether it is a *genuine* insight into the workings of his own mind or only a false explanation of them —C.D. Lewis⟩ ⟨sham motor bus companies which if *genuine* would have been very sensible and publicly useful investments — G.B.Shaw⟩ ⟨palming off paper imitations of all kinds of valuables on the simple-minded ghosts and gods, who take them in all good faith for the *genuine* articles —J.G.Frazer⟩ GENUINE may also describe emotions or mental states really experienced and not feigned ⟨that was no conventional expected shock that she had received. It was *genuine* unforeseen shock —Arnold Bennett⟩ In "a genuine authentic Gilbert Stuart portrait of Washington", GENUINE emphasizes certainty of ascription to Stuart and AUTHENTIC emphasizes the close similarity between portrait and subject. VERITABLE indicates a true existence or actual identity ⟨the ruffians were so utterly appalled, not only by the false powers of magic, but by *veritable* powers of majesty and eloquence —Charles Kingsley⟩ It may indicate a very close similarity and stress the suitability of a metaphor ⟨an old gray-haired lady, a *veritable* saint who had not been soured by her many deeds of charity —P.E.More⟩ BONA FIDE, often commercial or legal in suggestion, stresses good faith and lack of intent to deceive or the avoidance of equivocal casuistry ⟨*bona fide* residents who . . . maintained homes in no other places —*Harper's*⟩

authentical *archaic var of* AUTHENTIC

au·then·ti·cal·ly \-tə̇k(ə)lē, -ēk-, -li\ *adv* **:** REALLY, GENUINELY, VALIDLY **:** with authority

au·then·ti·cate \-tə,kāt, *usu* -ād·+V\ *vt* -ED/-ING/-s [ML *authenticatus*, past part. of *authenticare*, fr. LL *authenticus* authentic] **:** to make authentic: **a :** to make authoritative **:** give authority to ⟨a book that is *authenticated* by the renown of those who contributed to it⟩ **b :** to make valid and effective by the proof, attestation, or formalities required by law ⟨an *authenticated* grant of land⟩ **c :** to make credible **:** make evident the reasonableness or logical necessity of accepting (a theory, assertion, or reputed fact) ⟨*authenticating* her testimony by her obvious sincerity⟩ ⟨the date can be *authenticated* by documentary proof⟩ **d :** to establish convincingly as accurate, true, real, or genuine ⟨well-*authenticated* information⟩ ⟨an *authenticated* diamond⟩ **e :** to establish a conclusive basis for accepting as truly of an averred character, function, or position ⟨a diplomat *authenticating* himself and the object of his mission⟩ **f :** to verify the origin of **:** prove the authorship of ⟨a priceless and *authenticated* painting of Rembrandt⟩ **syn** see CONFIRM

au·then·ti·ca·tion \ə,thentə'kāshən, (,)ȯ,th-\ *n* -s **1 :** the action or process of authenticating **2 :** the state of being authenticated

au·then·ti·ca·tor \ə'thentə,kād·ə(r), ȯ'th-, -ātə-\ *n* -s **:** one that authenticates

authentic cadence *n* **:** a cadence consisting of the resolution of the dominant or the dominant seventh chord to the tonic

au·then·tic·i·ty \,ȯ,then·'tisəd·ē, -ətē, -i *also* ,ȯthən-\ *n* -ES **:** the quality of being authentic **:** the quality of being authoritative, valid, true, real, or genuine ⟨a good adventure story with the added merit of complete ~ —Margaret B. Hexter⟩

au·thi·gen·e·sis \,ȯthə'jenəsəs\ *n, pl* **authigene·ses** \-ə,sēz\ [NL, fr. Gk *authi* + NL *genesis*] **:** the process by which minerals form in a sedimentary rock after its deposition

au·thi·gen·ic \¦ȯthə¦jenik\ *or* **au·thig·e·nous** \(')ȯ¦thijənəs\ *adj* [G *authigen* authigenic (fr. Gk *authigenēs* born in that place, native, fr. *authi* there + *-genēs* born) + E *-ic* or *-ous;* akin to Gk *au* again — more at EKE, -GEN] **:** formed where found — used of mineral particles of rocks formed by crystallization in the place they occupy; opposed to *allothogenic*

¹au·thor \'ȯthə(r)\ *n* -s [alter. of ME *autour, auctour*, fr. OF *autor, auctor*, fr. L *auctor*, fr. *auctus* (past part. of *augēre* to increase) + *-or* — more at EKE] **1 :** one that fathers **:** PROCREATOR, PARENT, ANCESTOR ⟨the ~ of his being was a shiftless, drunken, ill-tempered hack musician —H.W.Van Loon⟩ **2 a :** one that is the source of some form of intellectual or creative work ⟨the ~ of the theory of relativity⟩ ⟨the ~ of a beautifully designed mural⟩; *esp* **:** one that writes or otherwise composes a book, article, poem, play, or other work which involves literary composition and is intended for publication ⟨favorite American ~s⟩ ⟨~ of a textbook⟩ ⟨the ~s of a tariff law⟩ — compare COMPILER, EDITOR, TRANSLATOR **b :** one that compiles material (as for publication) in such a way that the finished compilation can be regarded as a relatively original work ⟨~ of an anthology of French poetry⟩ **c :** one (as an author's agent) having the right to make author's alterations **d :** a printer's customer **e :** a corporate author **3 a :** one that originates, makes, or gives existence **:** SOURCE, CREATOR; *esp, cap* **:** GOD ⟨Eternal King . . . *Author* of all being —John Milton⟩ **b :** one that brings about or is the efficient cause of an action, event, circumstance, or condition ⟨the ~ of a plan for social improvement⟩ ⟨an ~ of world tension⟩ **c :** one that prompts to an action **:** INSTIGATOR ⟨~ of a mutiny⟩ **4** *obs* **:** one that is pointed out or appealed to as the source of an opinion **:** INFORMANT **5 authors** *pl but sing in constr, often cap* **:** a game played with special cards divided into sets or books, each set relating to a different author; *also* **:** this game played with standard playing cards **6 :** one that originally names and describes a particular taxon

²author \"\ *vt* **authored; authored; authoring** \-th(ə)riŋ\ **authors 1 :** to be the author of; *esp* **:** WRITE ⟨he ~*ed* a series of best sellers⟩ **2 :** MAKE, ORIGINATE, CREATE ⟨~*ing* a radically new fashion trend⟩

author catalog *n* **:** an alphabetical catalog in which titles are listed usu. under the names of authors only but sometimes also under the names of editors and compilers — compare DICTIONARY CATALOG

authorcraft \'⸗⸗,⸗\ *n* **:** skill in or practice of authorship ⟨a man remarkable for his ~⟩

author entry *n* **:** a catalog entry of a writing under its author's name usu. with the surname placed first

au·thor·ess \'ȯthərəs *also* -thr-\ *n* -ES **:** a female author — now usu. replaced by *author*

au·tho·ri·al \(')ȯ¦thōrēəl, -ȯr-\ *adj* **:** AUCTORIAL

authorise *Brit var of* AUTHORIZE

¹au·thor·i·tar·i·an \ȯ,thärə'terēən, ə,th-, -,thȯr-, -'ta(a)r-, -'tär- *sometimes* ¦ȯthərə¦t-\ *adj* [*authority* + *-arian* (as in *humanitarian*)] **1 :** of, relating to, or favoring a principle of often blind submission to authority as opposed to individual freedom of thought and action ⟨a strict ~ hierarchy in which every man has his place, every class a defined function, a set of commands issuing from above, a group of subordinates below to be ordered ruthlessly about —Roy Lewis & Angus Maude⟩ **2 :** of, relating to, or favoring a political system that concentrates power in the hands of a leader or a small autocratic elite not constitutionally responsible to the body of the people — opposed to *democratic* ⟨an ~ regime⟩

²authoritarian \"\ *n* -s **:** one who advocates, supports, or furthers authoritarian principles and practices ⟨uncompromising ~s, contemptuous of the individual —B.R.Redman⟩

au·thor·i·tar·i·an·ism \-,nizəm\ *n* -s **:** an authoritarian system **:** authoritarian principles

au·thor·i·ta·tive \ə'thärə,tā|d·iv, -thȯr-, -,tə|, |tiv, -ēv *also* ȯ'th-\ *adj* [*authority* + *-ative*] **1 a :** of the nature of authority **:** marked by, possessing, or proceeding from authority **:** OFFICIAL ⟨an ~ decision⟩ **b :** exercising or assuming authority **:** having an air of authority; *sometimes* **:** demanding submission and conformity **:** PEREMPTORY, DICTATORIAL ⟨an ~ young officer⟩ **2 :** possessing recognized or evident authority that elicits acquiescence and acceptance **:** having qualities that mark as definitive **:** CONCLUSIVE, CONVINCING ⟨~ literature on the functioning of the human mind —Elspeth Mosscrop⟩ ⟨an ~ interpretation of the great composer⟩ ⟨a more sober and ~ view of the situation —D.W.Maurer & V.H.Vogel⟩ — **au·thor·i·ta·tive·ly** *adv* **au·thor·i·ta·tive·ness** *n* -ES

au·thor·i·ty \ə'thärəd·ē, -thȯr-, -ətē, -i *also* ȯ'th-\ *n* -ES [ME *auctorite, autorite*, fr. OF *autorité, auctorité*, fr. L *auctoritat-, auctoritas*, fr. *auctor* originator, author + *-itat-, -itas* -ity] **1 a :** a citation (as from a book) used in defense or support of one's actions, opinions, or beliefs; *also* **:** the source from which such a citation is drawn ⟨they used a brief passage from the book as their ~⟩ ⟨he quoted extensively from the Bible, his sole ~⟩ **b :** a conclusive statement or aggregate of statements (as an official decision of a court) **:** decisive declaration taken as a precedent; *also* **:** TESTIMONY ⟨they viewed the court's decision as an unquestionable ~ for their action⟩ ⟨heard on the best ~⟩ **c :** an individual (as a specialist in a given field) who is the source of conclusive statements or testimony **:** one who is cited or appealed to as an expert whose opinion deserves acceptance ⟨there was a long and fierce dispute between scholars who held that Cicero was an unchallengeable ~ —Gilbert Highet⟩ ⟨one should always be prepared to quote *authorities* in support of one's theories —Aldous Huxley⟩ **2 a :** power to require and receive submission **:** the right to expect obedience **:** superiority derived from a status that carries with it the right to command and give final decisions **:** DOMINION, JURISDICTION ⟨the ~ of parents over their children⟩ ⟨the ~ of the president⟩ ⟨the ~ of a judge⟩ **b :** delegated power over others **:** AUTHORIZATION ⟨he acted with the full ~ of the government⟩ **c :** freedom granted by one in authority **:** RIGHT ⟨do you have the ~ to leave when you want to⟩ **3 a :** power to influence thought and opinion **:** intellectual influence ⟨Voltaire had his enemies, but his ~ could not be denied⟩ **b :** power to influence the outward behavior of others **:** practical personal influence ⟨the ~ of fashion⟩ **4 a :** persons in command; *specif* **:** GOVERNMENT — now usu. used in pl. in the concrete ⟨the local *authorities* of each state⟩ and sing. in the abstract ⟨the public ~ is responsible for our protection⟩ **b :** a public administrative agency or corporation having quasi-governmental powers and authorized to administer a revenue-producing public enterprise ⟨the port ~⟩ ⟨the valley ~⟩ **5 :** justifying grounds **:** BASIS, WARRANT ⟨on what ~ can you act as you do⟩ **6 :** convincing force **:** WEIGHT ⟨his sincerity added much more ~ to the story⟩ **7 :** a combination of unstrained definitive masterfulness, clear-sighted ingenuity and skill, and economical attainment of an objective (as in a piece of writing or in a musical performance) ⟨a recording that is unequaled for its finesse and ~⟩ **8 :** AUTHOR 6 **syn** see INFLUENCE, POWER

authority to pay : LETTER OF CREDIT

authority to purchase : an instrument similar to a letter of credit under which drafts are drawn by the seller or exporter directly upon the buyer or importer rather than on a bank

au·tho·ri·za·tion \,ȯthərə'zāshən, -,rī'z-\ *n* -s **1 :** the act of authorizing **:** the state of being authorized **:** SANCTION, WARRANT **2 :** a grant of authority to the executive branch of a government to spend money for specified purposes or to contract for spending in the future

au·tho·rize \'ȯthə,rīz\ *vt* -ED/-ING/-s *see -ize in Explan Notes* [alter. of ME *autorisen*, fr. MF *autoriser*, fr. ML *auctorizare*, fr. L *auctor* + LL *-izare* -ize] **1 a :** to endorse, empower, justify, or permit by or as if by some recognized or proper authority (as custom, evidence, personal right, or regulating power) ⟨~ a new version⟩ **:** SANCTION ⟨idiom *authorized* by use⟩ ⟨he was not *authorized* to use my name⟩ ⟨I would on no account ~ in my girls the smallest degree of arrogance —Jane Austen⟩ **b** *archaic* **:** to furnish grounds for **:** JUSTIFY **2** *obs* **:** to vouch for **:** confirm the truth or reality of by alleging one's own or another's authority **3** *obs* **:** to give legality or effective force to (a power, instrument, order) **4 a :** to endow with authority or effective legal power, warrant, or right **:** appoint, empower, or warrant regularly, legally, or officially ⟨Congress has *authorized* the President to suspend the operation of a Statute —O.W.Holmes †1935⟩ ⟨before Ferdinand

and Isabella *authorized* the first voyage —*Times Lit. Supp.*⟩ **b :** to grant or allot by proper authority ⟨a million dollars *authorized* for the new bridge⟩

syn ACCREDIT, COMMISSION, LICENSE: AUTHORIZE indicates endowing formally with a power or right to act, usu. with discretionary privileges ⟨a whipping post was erected and the keeper *authorized* to punish the convicts —Marjorie Freer⟩ Sometimes it applies to the sanction of any force viewed as authoritative ⟨an informality *authorized* by custom⟩ ⟨an agent *authorized* by the heirs⟩ ⟨a rite *authorized* by a church council⟩ ACCREDIT may imply endowing or giving formal credentials or proof of authorization to ⟨all ambassadors, ministers, and consuls *accredited* to foreign states —F.A.Ogg & Harold Zink⟩ ⟨the Association of American Railroads has had a competent mechanical engineer duly *accredited* to the Atomic Energy Commission —W.T.Faricy⟩ COMMISSION may imply the conferring, usu. formal, of rank, office, or status, or specific instructions about duties and missions ⟨Delaware, in *commissioning* its delegates, restrained them from assenting to any change in the "rule of suffrage" —E.K.Alden⟩ ⟨I *commissioned* a mutual friend . . . to break the matter to this gentleman as delicately as possible —W.M.Thackeray⟩ LICENSE may indicate issuance of a formal legal document setting forth a particular permission or right ⟨*licensed* to dispense narcotics⟩ ⟨he was *licensed* as a pilot⟩ In other senses LICENSE may suggest a certain sanction in proceeding with what might be questioned or questionable ⟨through the character of Huck, that disreputable, illiterate little boy . . . he [Mark Twain] was *licensed* to let himself go —Van Wyck Brooks⟩

authorized *or* **authorised** *adj* [alter. of ME *autorised*, fr. past part. of *autorisen*] **1** *archaic* **:** having authority **:** marked by authority **:** recognized as having authority **2 :** endowed with authority ⟨an ~ representative⟩ **3 :** sanctioned by authority **:** APPROVED ⟨an ~ biography⟩ ⟨an ~ translation⟩

authorized capital *n* **:** the amount of capital stock that a corporation is authorized to issue under the terms of its charter

au·tho·riz·er \-zə(r)\ *n* -S **1 :** one that authorizes **2 :** a clerk who verifies the credit standing of customers and approves or disapproves charges against their accounts

au·thor·less \ˈȯthə(r)ləs\ *adj* **:** having no author; *also* **:** having an unknown author **:** ANONYMOUS

author number *also* **author mark** *n* **:** a character or characters representing an author's surname in a call number — see CUTTER NUMBER

authors *pl of* AUTHOR, *pres 3d sing of* AUTHOR

author's alteration *n* **:** a change or correction not of a printer's error ordered in a printer's proof by and customarily chargeable to an author — abbr. *AA*

author's correction *n* **:** AUTHOR'S ALTERATION — abbr. *AC*

author's edition *n* **:** an edition of a book for which the printing and publishing costs are borne by the author

au·thor·ship \ˈȯthə(r),ship\ *n* -S **1 a :** the profession of writing (as books, stories, or articles) **b :** the function or dignity of an author **2 a :** the origin of a literary production ⟨the disputed ~ of the miracle plays⟩ **b :** the state or act of creating or causing **:** INSTIGATION ⟨the ~ of a crime⟩

au·tism \ˈȯ,tizəm, ˈȯd-,iz-\ *n* -S [NL *autismus*, fr. L *aut-* + *-ismus* -ism] **:** absorption in self-centered subjective mental activity (as daydreams, fantasies, delusions, and hallucinations) esp. when accompanied by marked withdrawal from reality

au·tis·tic \(ˈ)ȯ¦tistik\ *adj* **:** of, relating to, or marked by autism — **au·tis·ti·cal·ly** \-k(ə)lē\ *adv*

¹au·to \ˈau̇(ˌ)d-(ˌ)ō, ˈȯ|, |(ˌ)tō, *Pg* ˈau̇(ˌ)tü\ *n* -S [Sp & Pg, fr. L *actus* act (of a play), act (in general) — more at ACT] **1 a :** short medieval play on a sacred or biblical subject (as a miracle or morality play) flourishing up to the middle of the 18th century and esp. popular among the Spanish and Portuguese **2 :** AUTO-DA-FÉ

²au·to \ˈȯd-(ˌ)ō, ˈȯ,tō\ *n* -S [by shortening] **:** AUTOMOBILE

³auto \ˈ"\ *vi* -ED/-ING/-S **:** to drive an automobile or ride in one **:** MOTOR

⁴auto \ˈ"\ *adj or n* [by shortening] **:** AUTOMATIC

¹auto- *in pronunciations below*, ¦=(ˌ)= = ¦ȯd-(ˌ)ō *or* ¦ȯ(ˌ)tō *also before consonants* -ə\ — see AUT-

²auto- \ˈ"\ *comb form* [¹*automobile*] **:** self-propelling **:** automotive ⟨*autocab*⟩ ⟨*autocar*⟩

au·to·ag·glu·ti·na·tion \¦=(ˌ)= *at* ¹AUTO- +\ *n* -S [*aut-* + *agglutination*] **:** agglutination of an individual's red blood cells by cold agglutinins in his own serum usu. at lower than body temperature — called also *cold agglutination*

au·to·ag·glu·ti·nin \ˈ" +\ *n* -S [*aut-* + *agglutinin*] **:** an antibody that agglutinates the red blood cells of the individual that produces it — compare COLD AGGLUTININ

au·to·alarm \ˈ=(ˌ)= + =,=\ *n* -S [*aut-* + *alarm*] **:** a radio receiving device used on ships that rings an alarm bell when a distress signal is received

au·to·an·ti·body \ˈ" +\ *n* -ES [*aut-* + *antibody*] **:** an antibody against one of the constituents of the tissues of the individual that produces it — compare AUTOAGGLUTININ

au·to·as·phyx·i·a·tion \¦=(ˌ)= +\ *n* -S [*aut-* + *asphyxiation*] **:** asphyxiation of an organism by the products of its own metabolism

au·to·bahn \ˈau̇d-ō,bän, ˈȯd-ō-\ *n, pl* **autobahns** \-nz\ *also* **au·to·bah·nen** \-nən\ *sometimes cap* [G (prob. trans. of It *autostrada*), fr. *auto-* ²auto- + *bahn* track, road, fr. MHG *ban, bane*; akin to G dial. (Westphalia) *baanen* to hammer out, OHG *bano* death, destruction — more at BANE] **:** a road in Germany with double traffic lanes in each direction separated by a parkway

au·to·ba·sid·ii \¦=(ˌ)= *at* ¹AUTO + bəˈsidē,ī\ *n pl, cap* [NL, fr. *aut-* + *basidii* (fr. *basidium*)] *in some classifications* **:** EUBASIDII

au·to·ba·sid·i·o·my·ce·tes \ˈ" +\ [NL, fr. *aut-* + *Basidiomycetes*] *syn of* AUTOBASIDII

au·to·ba·sid·i·um \ˈ"+\ *n, pl* **autobasidia** [NL, fr. *aut-* + *basidium*] **:** an undivided basidium typical of the higher basidiomycetes — compare HEMIBASIDIUM, PROMYCELIUM

au·to·bi·og·ra·pher \,ȯd-|ə,bīˈägrəfə(r), ,ȯt|, |ō- *also* -,bē-\ *n* -S [*aut-* + *biographer*] **:** one who writes his own biography

au·to·bi·o·graph·i·cal \¦==,bīə¦grafəkəl, -raif-, -fēk- *sometimes* -,bēə-\ *or* **au·to·bi·o·graph·ic** \-fik, -fēk\ *adj* **1 :** in the style of, suggestive of, or relating to an autobiography ⟨a book based on personal incidents without being ~⟩ **:** of the nature of an autobiography ⟨an ~ film⟩ **2 :** of or relating to an autobiographer **:** marked by qualities associated with an autobiographer ⟨the ~ impulse is normal in old age —Van Wyck Brooks⟩ — **au·to·bi·o·graph·i·cal·ly** \-fək(ə)lē, -ēk-, -li\ *adv*

au·to·bi·og·ra·phist \,==,bīˈägrəfəst *also* -,bē-\ *n* -S **:** AUTOBIOGRAPHER

au·to·bi·og·ra·phy \-fē, -fi\ *n* -ES [*aut-* + *biography*] **:** the biography of oneself narrated by oneself

au·to·boat \ˈ== *at* ¹AUTO- + ,=\ *n* -S [²*auto-* + *boat*] **:** MOTORBOAT

au·to·bo·lide \ˈ" + =,=\ *n* -S [F, fr. *auto-* ²auto- + *bolide*] **:** an automobile designed to be projected through the air from a specially constructed track

au·to·bus \ˈ" + ,=\ *n* [²*auto-* + *bus*] **:** OMNIBUS 1

au·to·cade \¦== + ¦kād\ *n* -S [²*auto* + *-cade* (as in *motorcade*)] **:** MOTORCADE

au·to·camp \ˈ== + ,=\ *n* [²*auto* + *camp*] **:** a camping ground often provided with cabins or tents and designed for the accommodation of automobile tourists

au·to·car \ˈ" + ,=\ *n* [²*auto-* + *car*] **:** AUTOMOBILE — now usu. shortened to *auto* or *car*

au·to·carp \ˈ== + ,kärp\ *n* -S [*aut-* + *-carp*] **1 :** a fruit resulting from self-fertilization **2 :** a fruit consisting of the ripened pericarp without adnate parts

au·to·car·pous \¦== + ¦kärpəs\ *or* **au·to·car·pi·an** \-¦kärpēən\ *or* **au·to·car·pic** \-¦kärpik\ *adj* [*autocarpous, autocarpic* fr. *aut-* + *-carpous, -carpic*; *autocarpian* fr. *aut-* + *carp-* + *-an*] **:** consisting of the ripened pericarp with no adnate parts

au·to·car·py \ˈ== + ,kärpē\ *n* -ES [*aut-* + *-carpy*] **:** the producing of fruit by self-fertilization

au·to·ca·tal·y·sis \¦=(ˌ)= +\ *n, pl* **autocatalyses** [NL, fr. *aut-* + *catalysis*] **:** SELF-CATALYSIS **:** catalysis of a reaction by one of its own products (as the reduction of silver oxide by the silver formed by reduction of a small portion of it or the activation of an enzyme precursor by the enzyme itself)

au·to·cat·a·lyt·ic \ˈ" + ,==¦==\ *adj* [fr. NL *autocatalysis*, after NL *catalysis*: E *catalytic*] **:** relating to or proceeding by autocatalysis — **au·to·cat·a·lyt·i·cal·ly** \ˈ" + ,==¦==(ə)=\ *adv*

au·to·ceph·a·lic·i·ty \ˈ" + ,sefəˈlisəd-ē\ *or* **au·to·ceph·a·lism** \-ˈsefə,lizəm\ *n, pl* **autocephalicities** *or* **autocephalisms** [*autocephalicity* fr. *autocephalous* + *-ic* + *-ity*; *autocephalism* fr. *autocephalous* + *-ism*] **:** AUTOCEPHALY

au·to·ceph·a·lous \¦== + ¦sefələs\ *adj* [LGk *autokephalos*, fr. Gk *aut-* + *-kephalos* (fr. *kephalē* head) — more at CEPHALIC] *Eastern Orthodox Church* **:** INDEPENDENT, SELF-GOVERNING **:** not under the jurisdiction of another — used of a church that appoints its own chief bishop without outside sanction and enters into direct relations with other churches but is in communion with the ecumenical patriarch of Constantinople and thus with all other Orthodox churches

au·to·ceph·a·ly \ˈ== + ,sefəlē\ *n* -ES [LL *autocephalia*, fr. LGk *autokephalos* + L *-ia* -y] **:** the state of being autocephalous

au·to·chore \ˈȯd-ə,kō(ə)r\ *n* -S [*aut-* + *-chore*] **:** a plant that is the major agent in the distribution of its own seeds or spores (as by special ejecting organs) — **au·to·cho·rous** \¦ȯd-ə-¦kōrəs\ *adj*

¹au·to·chrome \ˈ== + ,krōm\ *n* -S [ISV *aut-* + *-chrome*; orig. formed in F] **:** a plate for additive color photography that uses a layer of minute grains of starch dyed red, green, and blue coated with a panchromatic emulsion

²autochrome \ˈ"\ *adj* **:** METACHROME

au·toch·thon \ȯˈtäkthən, -,thän\ *n, pl* **autochthons** \-nz\ *or* **autochtho·nes** \-,thə,nēz\ [modif. (influenced by Gk *autochthōn*) of L *autocthon*, fr. Gk *autochthon-, autochthōn*, fr. *aut-* + *chthon-, chthōn* earth — more at HUMBLE] **1 a :** one supposed to have risen or sprung from the ground of the region he inhabits **b :** one of the original inhabitants of a region **:** ABORIGINE **2 :** something that is autochthonous; *esp* **:** an indigenous plant or animal **3** *or* **au·toch·thone** \-,thōn\ **:** rock essentially in its place of origin in contrast to the adjacent rock of an allochthon

au·toch·tho·nism \-,thə,nizəm\ *n* -S **1 :** origin from the soil **2 :** the state of being aboriginal **:** the state of being native to a region

au·toch·tho·nous \(ˈ)ȯ¦täkthənəs\ *also* **au·toch·tho·nal** \-nᵊl\ *or* **au·toch·thon·ic** \¦ȯ,täk¦thänik\ *adj* **1 :** INDIGENOUS, NATIVE, ABORIGINAL — used esp. of floras and faunas **2 a :** formed or occurring in the place where found **:** AUTHIGENIC ⟨~ rock⟩ ⟨~ minerals⟩ **b :** indigenous to a region ⟨~ fossils⟩ **:** ENDEMIC ⟨~ malaria⟩ **:** not imported **:** NATIVE ⟨~ culture⟩ ⟨~ literature⟩ **3** *geol* **:** not displaced by overthrusting ⟨an ~ zone⟩ **4 :** originating in that part of the body where found — used chiefly of pathological conditions **syn** see NATIVE

autochthonous idea *n* **:** an abnormally dominating idea seeming to a psychiatric patient to have been thrust upon him and not to have developed out of his content of consciousness — compare FIXED IDEA

au·toch·tho·nous·ly \(ˈ)ȯ¦täkthənəslē\ *adv* **:** in an autochthonous manner

au·toch·tho·ny \ȯˈtäkthənē\ *n* -ES **:** autochthonous condition

autocinesis *var of* AUTOKINESIS

au·to·clas·tic \¦== *at* ¹AUTO- + ¦==\ *adj* [*aut-* + *clastic*] **:** broken in place — used of rocks having a broken or brecciated structure due to crushing in contrast to those of brecciated materials brought from a distance

¹au·to·clave \ˈ== + ,klāv\ *n* -S [F, fr. *aut-* (fr. Gk) + L *clavis* key — more at CLAVICLE] **:** an airtight chamber that can be filled with steam under pressure or surrounded by another chamber for the steam and that is used for sterilizing, cooking, or other purposes requiring moist or dry temperatures above 212° F without boiling — compare PRESSURE COOKER

²autoclave \ˈ"\ *vt* -ED/-ING/-S **:** to subject to the action of an autoclave

autoclave cipher *n* [*aut-* + *-clave* (fr. L *clavis* key) — more at CLAVICLE] **:** AUTOKEY CIPHER

au·to·col·li·ma·tion \¦== +\ *n* -S [*aut-* + *collimation*] **:** the process of collimating an instrument (as a telescope) having objective and cross hairs by directing it toward a plane mirror and adjusting the lens and cross hairs so that the latter coincide with their own reflected image

au·to·col·li·ma·tor \ˈ" +\ *n* -S [*aut-* + *collimator*] **:** a telescope with eyepiece adapted to the method of autocollimation either to collimate the instrument itself or to ensure that its axis is perpendicular to a reflecting surface

au·to·col·o·ny \ˈ" +\ *n* -ES [*aut-* + *colony*] *bot* **:** a daughter colony formed within one of the cells of a colony and duplicating in miniature the parent colony

au·to·cop·u·la·tion \ˈ" +\ *n* [*aut-* + *copulation*] **:** self-copulation that infrequently occurs in some hermaphroditic worms

au·to·cosm \ˈȯd-ō,käzəm\ *n* -S [*auto-* + *-cosm*] **:** a self-created microcosm **:** a private world

au·to·cos·mic \¦==¦käzmik\ *adj* [*aut-* + *cosmic*] **:** of or relating to an autocosm **:** highly personalistic **:** AUTISTIC

auto court *n* [²*auto*] **:** MOTEL

au·toc·ra·cy \ȯˈtäkrəsē, -si\ *n* -ES [prob. fr. *autocrat*, after such pairs as E *aristocrat*: *aristocracy*] **1 :** a form of government in which one person possesses unlimited power — compare ABSOLUTISM **2 :** the unlimited authority or rule of an autocrat **3 :** a community or state governed by autocracy **:** an autocratic community or state

au·to·crat \ˈȯd-|ə,krat, ˈȯt|, |ō-, *usu* -ad- + V\ *n* -S [F *autocrate*, fr. Gk *autokratēs* ruling by oneself, absolute, fr. *aut-* + *-kratēs* (fr. *kratos* strength, power) — more at HARD] **1 a :** a monarch ruling with unlimited authority **b :** a governor with absolute power **2 :** one who rules with undisputed sway in any relationship ⟨he was the ~ of his household⟩

au·to·crat·ic \,ȯd-ə¦krad-ik, ¦ȯt|, |ō-, -atik, -ēk\ *also* **au·to·crat·i·cal** \-ə̇kəl, -ēk-\ *adj* **1 :** of the nature of or relating to an autocrat **:** having unlimited and sole control **:** favoring autocracy **:** DESPOTIC ⟨an ~ ruler⟩ ⟨those who have long been in the habit of exercising power become ~ and quarrelsome —Bertrand Russell⟩ **2 :** of the nature of or relating to an autocracy **:** having the characteristics of an autocracy **:** marked by the exercising or favoring of absolute and sole control ⟨an ~ government⟩ ⟨history of ~ political rule and economic backwardness —Vera M. Dean⟩ **syn** see ABSOLUTE

au·to·crat·i·cal·ly \-ə̇k(ə)lē, -ēk-, -li\ *adv* **:** in an autocratic manner

au·toc·ra·tor \ȯˈtäkrəd-ə(r)\ *n* -S [Russ & LL; Russ *avtokrator* & LL *autocrator*, fr. Gk *autokratōr* absolute ruler, absolute, fr. *aut-* + *-kratōr* (fr. *kratein* to rule, fr. *kratos* power)] **:** AUTOCRAT

au·to·crit·i·cal \¦== *at* ¹AUTO- + ¦===\ *adj* [*aut-* + *critical*] **:** of or relating to autocriticism **:** disposed to or marked by the exercise of autocriticism ⟨the ~ habit of mind indispensable to a genuine philosopher —David Gascoyne⟩

au·to·crit·i·cism \ˈ" +\ *n* -S [*aut-* + *criticism*] **:** criticism of oneself **:** searching self-examination

au·to·cy·tol·y·sis \ˈ" +\ *n, pl* **autocytolyses** [NL, fr. *aut-* + *cyt-* + *-lysis*] **:** autolysis of cells

au·to–da–fé \¦au̇|d-ədəˈfā, ¦ȯ|, |d-(ˌ)ōd-,|təd-,|(ˌ)tōd-\ *n, pl* **autos-da-fé** \-əzd-, -ōzd-\ [Pg *auto da fé*, lit., act of the faith] **:** the ceremony accompanying the pronouncement of judgment by the Inquisition and followed by the execution of sentence by the secular authorities; *esp* **:** the burning of a person condemned as a heretic or of writings condemned as heretical

auto de fé \ˈ"\ *n, pl* **autos de fé** [Sp, fr. Pg *auto da fé*] **:** AUTO-DA-FÉ

au·to·di·dact \,ȯd-ōˈdī,dakt, -,dīˈd-, -,dəˈd-\ *n* -S [Gk *autodidaktos* self-taught, fr. *aut-* + *didaktos* taught, fr. *didaskein* to teach] **:** one who is self-taught

au·to·di·dac·tic \,==,dīˈdaktik, -,dəˈd-\ *adj* **:** of or relating to an autodidact **:** having the characteristics of an autodidact

au·to·di·ges·tion \¦=(ˌ)= *at* ¹AUTO- +\ *n* -S [*aut-* + *digestion*] **:** AUTOLYSIS

au·to·dyne \ˈ==+,=\ *n* -S [ISV *aut-* + *dyne*] **:** a special heterodyne in which the auxiliary current is generated in the device used for rectification

¹au·toe·cious *also* **au·te·cious** \(ˈ)ȯ¦tēshəs, (ˈ)ȯd-¦ē-\ *adj* [*aut-* + *-oecious, -ecious* (fr. Gk *oikia* house + E *-ous*) — more at VICINITY] **:** passing through all the stages in its life history on the same host or on closely related hosts ⟨certain parasitic fungi such as rusts are ~⟩ — compare HETEROECIOUS — **au·toe·cious·ly** *also* **au·te·cious·ly** *adv* — **au·toe·cism** *also* **au·te·cism** \ȯˈtē,sizəm, ȯd-ˈē,-\ *n* -S

²autoecious *var of* AUTOICOUS

autoed *past of* AUTO

au·to·erot·ic \¦=(ˌ)= *at* ¹AUTO- + =¦==\ *adj* [*aut-* + *erotic*] **:** of, relating to, or marked by autoerotism — **au·to·erot·i·cal·ly** \ˈ"+=¦==(ə)=\ *adv*

au·to·erot·ism \¦==+\ *also* **au·to·erot·i·cism** \ˈ"+\ *n* -S [*aut-* + *erotism, eroticism*] **1 :** sexual gratification obtained through one's own organism without the participation or stimulus of another individual — contrasted with *alloerotism* **2 :** sexual feeling or desire arising endogenously without known external stimulation

au·to·ette \¦ȯd-ə¦wet\ *n* -S [²*auto-* + *-ette*] **:** a 3-wheeled motorcycle provided usu. with a box or trunk for packages and used for light deliveries (as by parcel-post carriers)

au·to·fo·cal \¦== *at* ¹AUTO- + ¦==\ *adj* [*aut-* + *focal*] **:** being a photographic enlarger that is automatically kept in focus as the enlarger head is moved up or down to secure the desired degree of enlargement

au·to·fret·tage \ˈ== + ,==\ *n* -S [prob. fr. F, fr. *aut-* + *frettage*] **:** the application of such interior pressure to the bore of a heavy ordnance gun as will deform the inner layers of steel beyond the elastic limit that would be reached by the explosion of any charge to be used subsequently in the gun

au·tog·a·mous \(ˈ)ȯ¦tägəməs, ə¦-\ *also* **au·to·gam·ic** \¦ȯd-ō-¦gamik\ *adj* **:** of, relating to, or reproducing by autogamy

au·tog·a·my \ȯˈtägəmē, əˈ-\ *n* -ES [ISV *aut-* + *-gamy*] **:** SELF-FERTILIZATION: as **a :** pollination of a flower by its own pollen **b :** conjugation of two sister cells or sister nuclei of protozoans or fungi

au·to·gen·e·sis \¦== *at* ¹AUTO-+\ *n, pl* **autogeneses** [NL, fr. L *aut-* + *genesis*] **1 :** ABIOGENESIS **2 :** a concept that evolution is directed by innate orienting factors independent of the interaction of organism and environment

au·to·ge·net·ic \¦=(ˌ)=+=¦==\ *adj* [ISV, fr. NL *autogenesis*, after such pairs as E *antithesis: antithetic*] **1 :** SELF-GENERATED **2 :** of or relating to autogenesis **3** *geol* **:** determined by or developed under strictly local conditions **4** *of plankton* **:** originating where found — opposed to *allogenetic* — **au·to·ge·net·i·cal·ly** \ˈ"+=¦==(ə)=\ *adv*

autogenetic drainage *n* **:** drainage by streams whose courses have been determined solely by the conditions of the land surface over which they flow — compare EPIGENETIC DRAINAGE

au·to·gen·ic \¦ȯd-ə¦jenik\ *adj* [*aut-* + *-genic*] **:** involving or resulting from biotic reaction — used chiefly in the phrase *autogenic succession*

au·to·gen·i·tal \ˈ"+¦===\ *adj* [*aut-* + *genital*] **:** of or relating to one's own genital organs

au·to·gen·o·type \ˈ"+\ *n* -S [*aut-* + *genotype*] **:** a genotype specif. established in the original publication of a genus

au·tog·e·nous \(ˈ)ȯ¦täjənəs, ə¦-\ *also* **au·to·gen·ic** \¦ȯd-ō-¦jenik\ *adj* [Gk *autogenēs* self-produced (fr. *aut-* + *-genēs* -gen) + E *-ous* or *-ic*] **1 :** SELF-GENERATED **:** produced independently of external influence or aid **:** ENDOGENOUS **2** *anat* **:** ossifying from an independent center **3** *med* **:** of origin within or from oneself ⟨~ skin graft⟩ **4 :** AUTOGENETIC 3 **5 :** achieved without external aid — used esp. of a union of parts or surfaces without use of adhesives or solder ⟨~ welding⟩ ⟨~ healing of a crack in asphalt paving⟩ ⟨~ tin-plating on sheet iron⟩ **6** *biol* **a :** originating within the same individual **b :** caused by factors within the individual **:** not directly due to environmental influences ⟨an ~ variation⟩ — **au·tog·e·nous·ly** \(ˈ)ȯ¦täjənəslē, ə¦-\ *adv*

autogenous graft *n* **:** AUTOGRAFT

autogenous vaccine *n* **:** a vaccine prepared from cultures obtained from a specific lesion of the patient himself and used to immunize him against further spread and progress of the same organism

au·tog·e·ny \ȯˈtäjənē\ *n* -ES [alter. of earlier *autogony*, fr. G *autogonie*, fr. *aut-* + *-gonie* -gony] **:** SELF-GENERATION

au·to·geo·syn·cli·nal \¦== *at* ¹AUTO- + \ *adj* **:** of, relating to, or marked by the presence of an autogeosyncline

au·to·geo·syn·cline \ˈ"+\ *n* -S [*aut-* + *geosyncline*] *geol* **:** an isolated basin which is relatively remote from uplifted source areas and in which fine clastic sediments, carbonate rocks, and evaporites are usu. deposited

au·to·gi·ro *also* **au·to·gy·ro** \,ȯd-|ōˈjī(ˌ)rō, ,ȯt|, |əˈ-, ˈ==,=(ˌ)=\ *n* -S [fr. *Autogiro*, a trademark] **:** a rotating-wing aircraft that achieves slow flight and vertical takeoff by the use of a freely rotating rotor replacing or supplementing the wings but is driven forward by a conventional propeller — compare HELICOPTER

au·tog·no·sis \,ȯd-əgˈnōsə̇s\ *n, pl* **autogno·ses** \-ō,sēz\ [NL, fr. *aut-* + *-gnosis*] **:** SELF-KNOWLEDGE; *esp* **:** an understanding of one's own psychodynamics

au·tog·nos·tic \¦==¦nästik\ *adj* [fr. NL *autognosis*, after NL *-gnosis*: E *Gnostic*] **:** of, relating to, or characterized by autognosis

¹au·to·graft \ˈ== *at* ¹AUTO- + ,=\ *n* -S [*aut-* + *graft*] **:** a tissue or organ that is transplanted from one part to another part of the same body

²autograft \ˈ"\ *vt* **:** to transplant as an autograft ⟨~*ing* skin⟩

¹au·to·graph \ˈȯd-ə,graf, ˈȯtə-, -raa(ə)f,-raif,-räf\ *n* -S [LL *autographum*, fr. L, neut. of *autographus* written with one's own hand, fr. Gk *autographos*, fr. *aut-* + *-graphos* -graph] **1 :** something that is written with one's own hand **:** **a :** an original handwritten manuscript (as of an author's or composer's work) ⟨valuable old ~*s* of Dickens⟩ **b :** a person's handwritten signature ⟨a book with the author's ~⟩ ⟨teenagers clamoring for the ~*s* of their favorite stars⟩ **2 :** an autographic recorder **3 :** a print made by autography **4** *photog* **:** a representation or trace of an object produced with the object close to the emulsion or (as in the case of ions or elementary particles) with the object passing through the emulsion, the image being formed by mechanical, electrical, chemical, or radiation effects of the object itself and usu. being made visible by development — compare AUTORADIOGRAPH

²autograph \ˈ"\ *adj* **:** in the writer's own handwriting **:** not copied nor duplicated **:** ORIGINAL ⟨an ~ letter⟩ ⟨an ~ will⟩

³autograph \ˈ"\ *vt* -ED/-ING/-S **1 :** to write with one's own hand **2 :** to write one's autograph or signature in or on

au·tog·ra·pher \ȯˈtägrəfə(r)\ *n* -S **:** one who copies the clef signs, key, title, instructions, and lyrics from original music manuscript to serve as a pattern for engravers

au·to·graph·ic \,ȯd-əˈgrafik, ,ȯtə-, -fēk\ *also* **au·to·graph·i·cal** \-fəkəl, -ēk-\ *adj* **1 :** of or relating to an autograph **:** of the nature of an autograph **:** written in the author's own handwriting ⟨an unquestionably ~ document⟩ **2 :** using or made by autography **3 a** *of an instrument* **:** SELF-RECORDING **b** *of a record* **:** recorded by a self-recording instrument — **au·to·graph·i·cal·ly** \-fək(ə)lē, -ēk-, -li\ *adv*

au·tog·ra·phy \ȯˈtägrəfē\ *n* -ES [*aut-* + *-graphy*] **1 a :** the action of writing with one's own hand **:** one's own handwriting **:** AUTOGRAPH **b :** a collection of autographs **2 :** any process in which original copy is made on or transferred direct to the printing surface

Au·to·harp \ˈȯd-ō,härp\ *trademark* — used for a musical instrument which is somewhat like a zither and on which simple harmony is obtained by button-controlled dampers operating in sets that when depressed leave free the strings of the desired chord

au·to·hem·or·rhage \¦== *at* ¹AUTO- +\ *n* -S [*aut-* + *hemorrhage*] **:** the voluntary exudation or ejection by certain insects of blood which is nauseous or poisonous and hence protective against enemies

au·to·he·mo·ther·a·py \ˈ"+\ *n* -ES [ISV *aut-* + *hemotherapy*; orig. formed as F *autohémothérapie*] **:** treatment of disease with the patient's own blood either modified (as by irradiation) or introduced outside the blood stream (as by intramuscular injection)

au·toi·cous \(ˈ)ȯ¦tȯikəs, (ˈ)ȯd-¦ȯi-\ *also* **autoecious** *adj* [*aut-* + *-oicous, -oecious* (fr. Gk *oikos* dwelling + E *-ous*) — more at VICINITY] **:** having male and female organs on the same plant but on separate branches ⟨certain mosses are ~⟩ — compare DIOICOUS, PAROICOUS, SYNOICOUS

au·to·ig·ni·tion \¦=(ˌ)= *at* ¹AUTO- +\ *n* -S [*aut-* + *ignition*] **1 :** self-ignition in an internal-combustion engine cylinder either as a result of the heat of the compression alone or from this in combination with glowing carbon — compare PREIGNITION **2** : SPONTANEOUS COMBUSTION

au·to·immunization \"+\ *n* -s [ISV *aut-* + *immunization*] : production by an individual of antibodies against constituents of his own tissues that is a possible cause of a number of serious and apparently incurable diseases

au·to·infection \"+\ *n* -s [ISV *aut-* + *infection*] : reinfection (as through self-contamination) with larvae produced by parasitic worms already in the body — compare HYPERINFECTION

autoing *pres part of* AUTO

au·to·inoculability \"+\ *n* -ES : the condition of being autoinoculable

au·to·inoculable \"+ˌ‧ˈ‧‧‧‧\ *adj* [*aut-* + *inoculable*] : capable of being transmitted by inoculation from one part of the body to another ⟨certain kinds of warts are ~⟩

au·to·inoculation \"+\ *n* -s [ISV *aut-* + *inoculation*] **1** : inoculation of an individual with vaccine prepared from material from his own body **2** : spread of infection from one part to other parts of the same body

au·to·intoxicated \"+ˌ‧ˈ‧‧‧‧\ *adj* [*aut-* + *intoxicated*] : affected by autointoxication

au·to·intoxication \"+\ *n* -s [ISV *aut-* + *intoxication*; originally formed in F] **1** : a state of being poisoned by absorption of toxic substances produced within the body either by body cells or by microorganisms **2** : the act of arousing oneself psychologically to a state resembling drunkenness

au·to·ist \ˈȯd·əwəst, ˈȯd·ˌō‧\ *n* -s [²*auto* + *-ist*] : AUTOMOBILIST, MOTORIST

au·to·key cipher \ˈ‧‧ *at* ¹AUTO-+ˌ‧-\ *n* [*aut-* + *key*] : a cipher in which each letter serves as key for the next letter or for one at a constant interval

au·to·kinesis \ˌ‧(ˌ)‧+\ *also* **autocinesis** \"+\ *n, pl* **autokineses** *also* **autocineses** [NL, fr. *aut-* + *kinesis*] : spontaneous movement; *esp* : apparent spontaneous movement of an actually stationary object

au·to·kinetic \"+ˌ‧ˈ‧‧\ *adj* [*aut-* + *kinetic*] : of, relating to, or marked by autokinesis

autokinetic system *n* : a system of fire-alarm telegraphy so arranged that when one alarm is being transmitted no other alarm will be transmitted until after the first alarm has been disposed of

auto lift *n* [²*auto*] : a hydraulic machine by which automobiles are hoisted above the floor to give access to the underparts

au·to·lith \ˈ‧‧+ˌlith\ *n* -s [*aut-* + *-lith*] : a fragment of a previously crystallized portion of rock enclosed in material from the same magma which solidified later

¹**au·to·lithograph** \ˌ‧‧+\ *n* -s [*aut-* + *lithograph*] : a print made by autolithography

²**autolithograph** \"\ *vt* : to make (a print) by autolithography

au·to·lithographic \ˌ‧‧+\ *adj* : relating to or produced by autolithography

au·to·lithography \ˌ‧(ˌ)‧+\ *n* [ISV *aut-* + *lithography*] : lithography in which an artist makes his original drawing direct on the printing surface — called also *artist lithography*

au·to·loader \ˈ‧‧+ˌ‧‧\ *n* -s [*aut-* + *loader*] : an autoloading firearm

au·to·loading \ˌ‧‧+ˈ‧‧\ *adj* [*aut-* + *loading*] : SEMIAUTOMATIC — used of firearms

au·tol·o·gous \(ˈ)ȯˈtäləgəs\ *adj* [*aut-* + *-ologous* (as in *homologous*)] : derived from the same individual ⟨an ~ graft is taken from one part of the body and transplanted into another⟩ — compare HOMOLOGOUS

au·to·luminescence \ˌ‧‧ *at* ¹AUTO-+\ *n* -s [*aut-* + *luminescence*] : luminescence of a substance (as a radioactive material) due to energy originating within itself

au·to·luminescent \"+\ *adj* [*aut-* + *luminescent*] : of, relating to, or marked by autoluminescence

au·tol·y·sate \ȯˈtäləˌsāt, -ˌsət\ *n* -s [ISV *autolys-* (fr. NL *autolysis*) + *-ate*] : a product of autolysis

au·tol·y·sin \ȯˈtäləsən, ˌȯd·əˈlīs-\ *n* -s [ISV *autolys-* (fr. NL *autolysis*) + *-in*] : any substance that produces autolysis (as certain proteolytic enzymes)

au·tol·y·sis \ȯˈtäləsəs\ *n* [NL, fr. *aut-* + *-lysis*] : self-digestion (as in fruit after picking, meat, or a diseased part of the body or one in which circulation has stopped) occurring in plant and animal tissues particularly after they have ceased to be a normal part of the organism to which they belong

au·to·lyt·ic \ˌȯd·ᵊlˌid·ik\ *adj* [fr. NL *autolysis*, after such pairs as ML *analysis*: E *analytic*] : of or relating to autolysis

au·tol·y·tus \ȯˈtäləd·əs\ *n, cap* [NL, fr. *aut-* + Gk *lytos* capable of being unfastened or dissolved, verbal of *lyein* to unfasten, dissolve, break up into parts — more at LOSE] : a genus of marine annelids (family Syllidae) that reproduce asexually by producing numerous new segments at a point near the posterior end, each of which develops into a new individual but remains attached for a time, a long chain of worms being thus formed

au·tol·y·zate \ȯˈtäləˌzāt, -ˌzət\ *n* -s [*autolyze* + *-ate*] : AUTOLYSATE

au·to·lyze \ˈȯd·ᵊlˌīz\ *vb* -ED/-ING/-S [fr. NL *autolysis*, after such pairs as ML *analysis*: E *analyze*] *vi* : to undergo autolysis ~ *vt* : to subject to autolysis

au·to·mak·er \ˈ‧‧ˌ‧‧\ *n* : a manufacturer of automobiles

au·to·mak·ing \ˈ‧‧ˌ‧‧\ *n* : the manufacturing of automobiles

au·to·manual \ˌ‧‧ *at* ¹AUTO- + ˈ‧‧‧\ *adj* [*aut-* + *manual*] : of or relating to a railroad signal system in which the signals are operated manually but return to the danger position automatically after a train passes

Au·to·mat \ˈȯd·əˌmat, ˈȯtə-\ *service mark* — used for a cafeteria in which food is obtained esp. from coin-operated compartments

automat- *or* **automato-** *comb form* [Gk, self-acting, fr. *automatos* — more at AUTOMATON] : self-acting : self-regulating : automatic ⟨*automat*in⟩ ⟨*automato*graph⟩

automata *pl of* AUTOMATON

au·to·mate \ˈȯd·əˌmāt, ˈȯtə-, *usu* -mād·+V\ *vt* -ED/-ING/-S [back-formation fr. *automation*] : to operate by automation : mechanize through automation : convert to largely automatic operation : make automatic : AUTOMATIZE ⟨*automated* business equipment⟩ ⟨*automating* a factory⟩

¹**au·to·mat·ic** \ˌȯd·əˈmad·ik, ˌȯtə-, -atik, -ēk\ *also* **au·to·mat·i·cal** \-ə̇kəl, -ēk-\ *adj* [Gk *automatos* self-acting + E *-ic*, *-ical* — more at AUTOMATON] **1 a** : involuntary either wholly or to a major extent so that any activity of the will is largely negligible : of a reflex nature : without volition ⟨the ~ blinking of the eyelids⟩ **b** : like or suggestive of an automaton : MECHANICAL ⟨the ~ smile of a tired store clerk⟩ **c** : performed without conscious awareness ⟨an unthinking ~ response⟩ **2** *archaic* : able to move and act in total independence of any outside cause : having the power of motion and action entirely within self **3** : having a self-acting or self-regulating mechanism that performs a required act at a predetermined point in an operation ⟨~ feed of a lathe⟩ ⟨~ record changer⟩ **4** : marked by spontaneous or apparently spontaneous action : marked by action that is unpremeditated and that arises as a really or apparently necessary reaction to or consequence of a given set of circumstances ⟨the ~ enthusiasm of the crowd over the returning heroes⟩ ⟨~ branding of the suspect as a traitor⟩ **5** *of a firearm* : marked by the use of either gas pressure or force of recoil and mechanical spring action for ejecting the empty cartridge case after the first shot, loading the next cartridge from the magazine, firing, ejecting the spent case, and repeating the above cycle as long as the pressure on the trigger is maintained and there is ammunition in the magazine or other loading device ⟨~ weapons⟩ — compare SEMIAUTOMATIC **syn** see SPONTANEOUS

²**automatic** \"\ *n* -s : a machine or apparatus that operates automatically; *esp* : an automatic or autoloading firearm

au·to·mat·i·cal·ly \-ə̇k(ə)lē, -ēk-, -li\ *adv* : in an automatic manner : without thought or conscious intention

automatic block signal *n* : a railroad signal at the entrance of a block actuated automatically by and governing the movement of trains entering and using the block

automatic coverage *n* : insurance that provides automatic adjustment of amount to correspond with fluctuating property values

automatic currency *n* : an elastic currency that adapts itself to business needs with little government intervention — contrasted with *managed currency*

automatic drill *n* : a straight brace for bits the shank of which consists of a screw of very coarse pitch sliding within a correspondingly threaded tube having a handle at the end, the tool being actuated by pushing the handle

automatic drive *n* : AUTOMATIC TRANSMISSION

au·to·ma·tic·i·ty \ˌȯd·ˌəmə'tisəd·ē, ˌȯt|, |ȯm-, -ətē, -i\ *n* -ES : the quality or state of being automatic ⟨the increasing ~ in industry⟩ ⟨the ~ of an habitual gesture⟩

automatic jointer *n* : a jointer that automatically assumes the proper position to turn under trash just before the plow turns over the furrow

automatic line finder *n* : a lever on a typewriter that when depressed disengages the line-spacing ratchet to allow writing between lines and when lifted returns the ratchet to place at the original line spacing

automatic machine *n* : a machine or machine tool (as a spinning machine or lathe) that after once being set operates automatically except for applying the power, lubricating, supplying material, and shutting off the power

automatic pilot *n* : a device for automatically steering ships and aircraft and automatically stabilizing aircraft

automatic pistol *n* : a pistol capable of automatic or semiautomatic fire

automatic premium loan *n* : an insurance policy loan made automatically to cover a premium due and unpaid at the end of the grace period

automatic progression *n* : the granting of advances in wages or salary on a scale between minimum and maximum strictly on a periodic basis

automatic reel *n* : a fly-fishing reel that retrieves line by a spring device

automatic reinstatement *n* : the reinstatement of the face value of an insurance policy after a loss has been incurred and paid for

automatic rifle *n* : a rifle capable commonly of either semiautomatic or full automatic fire and designed to be fired without a mount — compare MACHINE GUN

automatics *pl of* AUTOMATIC

automatic selling *n* : selling by vending machines or by self-service

automatic sequence *n* : the arrangement of a recording on successive sides of two or more phonograph discs so that the continuity of the recording is preserved when the discs are played on a record changer

automatic switch *n* : an electrical switch (as on a telephone) that is controlled from a central point

automatic transmission *n* : a usu. hydraulic or pneumatic mechanism whereby a motor vehicle automatically shifts gear according to actual car speed — called also *automatic drive*

automatic writing *n* : writing performed without conscious intention and sometimes without awareness as if of telepathic or spiritualistic origin

automating *pres part of* AUTOMATE

au·to·ma·tion \ˌȯd·əˈmāshən, ˌȯtə-\ *n* -s [*automat-* + *-ion*] **1** : the technique of making an apparatus (as a calculating machine), a process (as of manufacturing), or a system (as of bookkeeping) operate automatically **2** : the state of being operated automatically **3** : automatically controlled operation of an apparatus, process, or system by mechanical or electronic devices that take the place of human organs of observation, effort, and decision

au·tom·a·tism \ȯˈtäməˌtizəm *also* əˈt-\ *n* -s [F *automatisme*, fr. *automate* automaton + *-isme* -ism] **1 a** : the quality or state of being automatic **b** : an automatic action; *esp* : any action performed without the doer's intention or awareness **2** : a theory that views the body analogically as a machine and the mind or consciousness as a noncontrolling adjunct of the body **3** : the power or fact of moving without conscious control either without dependence on external stimulation (as in the beating of the heart) or more or less directly under the influence of external stimuli (as in the dilating or contracting of the pupil of the eye) **4** : suspension of the conscious mind to release subconscious images — used of technique in surrealist painting

au·tom·a·tist \-məd·ə̇st, -mətə̇-\ *n* -s **1** : one who accepts the theory of automatism **2 a** : one that performs automatic acts; *esp* : one that does automatic writing **b** : MEDIUM 7

au·tom·a·ti·za·tion \ȯˌtäməd·ə̇ˈzāshən, -məˌtīˈz- *also* əˌt-\ *n* -s : the action or process of automatizing : the state of being automatized : AUTOMATION

au·tom·a·tize \ȯˈtäməˌtīz *also* əˈt-\ *vt* -ED/-ING/-S *see -ize in Explan Notes* [*automaton* + *-ize*] **1** : to make an automaton of **2** [*automat-* + *-ize*] : to make automatic : reduce (as an habitual action) to an automatic condition ⟨*automatized* responses⟩ **3** : AUTOMATE

automato- — see AUTOMAT-

au·to·mat·o·graph \ˌȯd·əˈmad·əˌgraf\ *n* -s [*automat-* + *-graph*] : AUTOSCOPE

au·tom·a·ton \ȯˈtämətən, -əd·ən, -ətᵊn *also* əˈtäm- *or* -məˌtän\ *n, pl* **automatons** \-nz\ *also* **automa·ta** \-mətə, -əd·ə *sometimes* -əˌtä *or* -əˌtȧ\ [L, fr. Gk, neut. of *automatos* self-acting, fr. *aut-* + *-matos* (akin to Skt *mata* thought) — more at MIND] **1** *archaic* : something that has within itself the principle of its movements **2 a** : a mechanism that is relatively self-moving **b** : a contrivance or figure that appears to imitate the motions of men or animals : ROBOT ⟨tiny wooden soldiers that could be wound with a key and that would then march stiffly along — wonderful little ~s⟩ **3** : a machine or a controlling mechanism designed to follow automatically a predetermined sequence of operations or respond to encoded instructions and correct errors or deviations occurring during operation **4** : a creature whose actions are fixed, routine, and mechanical with little or no indication of active intelligence ⟨dull unthinking human ~s⟩

au·tom·a·tous \-məd·əs\ *adj* [L *automatus*, fr. Gk *automatos*] : of, like, or suggestive of an automaton : AUTOMATIC, MECHANICAL ⟨the relentless ~ march of an army⟩

au·to·mechanism \ˈ‧‧ *at* ¹AUTO- +\ *n* -s [*aut-* + *mechanism*] : a machine or other device that works automatically or under servo control

au·to·metamorphic \ˌ‧‧ +\ *adj* [*aut-* + *metamorphic*] : of or relating to autometamorphism

au·to·metamorphism \" +\ *n* [*aut-* + *metamorphism*] : alteration of igneous rocks by their own residual solutions without introduction of extraneous matter

au·to·metasomatic \" +\ *adj* [*aut-* + *metasomatic*] : AUTOMETAMORPHIC

au·to·metasomatism \" +\ *n* [*aut-* + *metasomatism*] : AUTOMETAMORPHISM

au·to·mix·is \" + ˈmiksə̇s\ *n, pl* **automix·es** \-kˌsēz\ [NL, fr. *aut-* + *-mixis*] : parthenogenesis in which the chromosomes of a haploid gamete divide without nuclear division resulting in formation of a diploid restitution nucleus — called also *automictic parthenogenesis*; compare AUTOGAMY

au·tomne·sia \ˌȯd·əmˈnēzh(ē)ə, ˌȯd·ōˈn-\ *n* -s [NL, fr. *auto-* + *-mnesia*] : memory of earlier experience without any apparent associative condition

¹**automobile** *like next*\ *adj* [F, fr. *aut-* + *mobile*] : AUTOMOTIVE

²**au·to·mo·bile** \ˌȯd·əmōˈbēl, ˌȯtəm-, ˈ‧‧‧ˌ‧ *also* ˌ‧‧ˈmō,bēl *or* ˌ‧‧ məˌbēl *sometimes* ˌ‧‧ˈbil *or* ˌ‧‧ˈmōbəl *or* ˌ‧‧ˈmō,bil\ *n* -s [F, fr. *automobile*, adj.] : a usu. 4-wheeled automotive vehicle designed for passenger transportation on streets and roadways and commonly propelled by an internal-combustion engine using a volatile fuel (as gasoline) — called also *car* or esp. Brit. *motorcar*

³**automobile** \"\ *vi* -ED/-ING/-S : to ride in or drive an automobile

automobile insurance *n* : insurance against loss arising from destruction of or damage to an insured motor vehicle; *also* : AUTOMOBILE LIABILITY INSURANCE

automobile liability insurance *n* : insurance against loss from or legal liability for damages arising out of ownership, maintenance, or operation of a motor vehicle

automobile sled *n* : AUTOSLED

automobile-weed \-ˌwēd\ *n* : a low European herb (*Tribulus terrestris*) having sharp stout spines on the fruits and occurring as a roadside weed in America

au·to·mo·bil·i·ana \ˌ‧‧‧bēlē, -ˌbilē + \ *n pl* [*automobile* + *-i-* + *-ana*] : a collection of automobiles or of items relating to automobiles esp. of the early kinds

au·to·mo·bil·ism \-ˌlizəm\ *n* -s : the use of automobiles : MOTORING

au·to·mo·bil·ist \-ˌlə̇st\ *n* -s : one who uses an automobile : MOTORIST

au·to·mo·bil·i·ty \ˌ‧‧mōˈbiləd·ē, -məb\ *n* -ES [²*automobile* + *-ity*] : use of automobiles : condition or capability of transportation by automobile

au·tom·o·lite \ȯˈtäməˌlīt\ *n* -s [Sw *automolit*, fr. Gk *automolos* deserter (fr. *aut-* + *-molos*, fr. *molein* to come, go, fr. aorist inf. of *blōskein*) + Sw *-it* -ite; akin to MIr *mell* hill, Slovenian *moliti* to stretch out, Alb *mal* mountain and perh. to Skt *mani* pearl; basic meaning: coming forth, going up] : a variety of gahnite

au·to·mor·phic \ˌȯd·əˈmȯrfik\ *adj* [*aut-* + *-morphic*] **1** : patterned after self ⟨an ~ concept⟩ **2** [ISV *aut-* + *-morphic*; orig. formed as G *automorph*] : IDIOMORPHIC

automorphic-granular \"+ˈ‧-\ *adj, of a rock* : characterized by a texture whose constituents are all automorphic — called also *idiomorphic-granular*

au·to·mo·tive \ˌȯd·əˈmōd·iv, ˌȯtəˈmōtiv, -ēv *also* -əv\ *adj* [*aut-* + *motive*] **1** : containing within itself the means of propulsion : SELF-PROPELLING **2** : of, relating to, or concerned with vehicles or machines that propel themselves (as automobiles, trucks, airplanes, motorboats) ⟨~ principles⟩

au·to·narcosis \ˌ‧(ˌ)‧ *at* ¹AUTO- +\ *n* [NL, fr. *aut-* + *narcosis*] : narcotization of members of a colony of insects by a chemical substance released by one or more of them

¹**au·to·nom·ic** \ˌȯd·əˈnämik\ *also* **au·to·nom·i·cal** \-mə̇kəl\ *adj* [*autonomy* + *-ic*, *-ical*] **1** *archaic* : AUTONOMOUS **2 a** : acting independently of volition ⟨~ reflexes⟩ **b** : of, relating to, affecting, or controlled by the autonomic nervous system **3** *bot* : due to internal causes or influences : SPONTANEOUS ⟨~ movements⟩ — compare PARATONIC **4** *of a drug* : having an effect upon a tissue supplied by the autonomic nervous system — **au·to·nom·i·cal·ly** \ˌ‧‧ˈmə̇k(ə)lē\ *adv*

²**autonomic** \"\ *n* -s **1** : AUTONOMIC NERVOUS SYSTEM **2** : one of the parts (as a nerve or ganglion) of the autonomic nervous system

autonomic nervous system *n* **1** : a part of the vertebrate nervous system that innervates smooth and cardiac muscle and glandular tissues, governs actions that are more or less automatic (as secretion, vasoconstriction, or peristalsis), and consists of the sympathetic nervous system and the parasympathetic nervous system **2** : PARASYMPATHETIC NERVOUS SYSTEM

autonomic system *n* : AUTONOMIC NERVOUS SYSTEM

au·ton·o·mism \ȯˈtänəˌmizəm, əˈ-\ *n* -s [*autonomous* + *-ism*] : the principle or system of independent self-government

au·ton·o·mist \-ˌməst\ *n* -s : one who advocates autonomy

au·ton·o·mous \ȯˈtänəməs, əˈ-\ *adj* [Gk *autonomos* living under one's own laws, independent, fr. *aut-* + *nomos* law — more at NIMBLE] **1** : of, relating to, or marked by autonomy **2 a** : having the right or power of self-government : possessing a certain degree of political autonomy ⟨~ states⟩ **b** : undertaken or carried on without outside control : SELF-CONTAINED ⟨an ~ school system⟩ **c** : possessing individual autonomy : morally self-legislating ⟨an ~ will⟩ : self-directed in personality ⟨he is no mere conformist — he's ~⟩ **3** *biol* **a** : existing or capable of existing independently ⟨an ~ zooid⟩ : being a perfect whole : not forming a part (as does an embryo or seed) in the developmental sequence of an organism **b** : responding, reacting, or developing independently of the whole ⟨a tumor is an ~ growth⟩ **4** : AUTONOMIC 3 **5** : under control of the autonomic nervous system : AUTOMATIC **6** : issued by a political entity having the right of independent coinage ⟨ancient ~ coins minted by a subject city in the Roman Empire⟩ **7** : semi-independent and partially self-governing — used of some Eastern Orthodox churches **syn** see FREE

autonomous investment *n* : that portion of total investment not directly attributable to short-term changes in total output but correlated with the long-term growth of the economy — distinguished from *induced investment*

au·ton·o·mous·ly *adv* : in an autonomous manner : INDEPENDENTLY

au·ton·o·my \-mē, -mi\ *n* -ES [Gk *autonomia*, fr. *autonomos* + *-ia* -y] **1** : the quality or state of being independent, free, and self-directing : individual or group freedom ⟨the ~ of every individual should be respected⟩ **2 a** : the degree of self-determination or political control possessed by a minority group, territorial division, or political unit in its relations to the state or political community of which it forms a part and extending from local self-government to full independence (as in the dominions of the British Commonwealth) **b** : an autonomous body or community **3** : the sovereignty of reason in the sphere of morals : possession of moral freedom or self-determination : power of the individual to be self-legislating in the realm of morals — opposed to *heteronomy* **4** *biol* : independence from the organism as a whole in the capacity of a part for growth, reactivity, or responsiveness

au·ton·y·mous \(ˈ)ȯˈtänəməs\ *adj* [*aut-* + *-onymous* (as in *anonymous*)] : naming or designating itself — used of symbols and expressions

auto-oxidation *var of* AUTOXIDATION

au·top·a·thy \ȯˈtäpəthē\ *n* -ES [Gk *autopatheia*, fr. *aut-* + *-patheia* -pathy] : IDIOPATHY

au·to·pelagic \ˌ‧‧ *at* ¹AUTO- +\ *adj* [*aut-* + *pelagic*] *of plankton* : strictly pelagic — compare SPANIPELAGIC

au·toph·a·gous \(ˈ)ȯˈtäfəgəs\ *adj* [Gk *autophagos*, fr. *aut-* + *-phagos* -phagous] : SELF-DEVOURING

au·to·pho·bia \ˌȯd·əˈfōbēə\ *n* [NL, fr. *aut-* + *-phobia*] : morbid fear of solitude

au·to·phone \ˈ‧‧ *at* ¹AUTO- + ˌ‧\ *n* -s [Gk *autophōnos* self-sounding, fr. *aut-* + *-phōnos* (fr. *phōnē* sound) — more at PHONE] : IDIOPHONE — **autophonic** *adj*

au·to·phyte \" + ˌfīt\ *n* -s [*aut-* + *-phyte*] : a plant capable of synthesizing its own food from simple inorganic substances — compare HETEROPHYTE, PARASITE, SAPROPHYTE — **au·to·phyt·ic** \ˌ‧‧ˈfid·ik\ *adj* — **au·to·phyt·i·cal·ly** \-d·ə̇k(ə)lē\ *adv*

au·to·phytograph \ˌ‧‧ +\ *n* -s [*aut-* + *phytograph*] : the outline or imprint produced upon a rock by the chemical action of a plant or plant fragment

au·to·phytography \" +\ *n* -ES [*aut-* + *phytography*] : the process by which an autophytograph is produced

au·to·pilot \ˈ‧‧ + ˌ‧‧\ *n* -s [*automatic pilot*] : AUTOMATIC PILOT

au·to·pistol \" + ˌ‧‧\ *n* -s [*automatic pistol*] : AUTOMATIC PISTOL

au·to·plastic \ˌ‧‧ + ˈ‧‧\ *adj* **1** : of, relating to, or characterized by autoplasty ⟨~ transplant⟩ **2** : relating to or characterized by adaptation of oneself to one's environment ⟨~ evolution⟩ — contrasted with *alloplastic* — **au·to·plastically** \" + ˈ‧(‧)‧\ *adv*

autoplastic graft *n* : AUTOGRAFT

au·to·plasticity \ˌ‧(ˌ)‧ +\ *or* **au·to·plas·ty** \ˈ‧‧ + ˌplastē\ *n* -ES [*aut-* + *plasticity* or *-plasty*] : the capacity or tendency for intrapsychic molding of the mechanism for dealing with the external world — contrasted with *alloplasticity*

au·to·plas·ty \ˈ‧‧ + ˌplastē\ *n* -ES [prob. fr. F *autoplastie*, fr. *aut-* + *-plastie* -plasty] : the repairing of lesions with tissue from the same body — compare GRAFT 2b

Au·to·plate \ˈ‧‧ + ˌ‧\ *trademark* — used for a machine that casts, shaves, and cools curved stereotype plates

au·to·ploid \ˈ‧‧ + ˌplȯid\ *n* -s [by contr.] : AUTOPOLYPLOID

au·to·ploidy \ˈ‧‧ + ˌplȯidē\ *n* -ES [by contr.] : AUTOPOLYPLOIDY

au·to·pneumatolytic \ˌ‧(ˌ)‧ +\ *adj* [*aut-* + *pneumatolytic*] : AUTOMETAMORPHIC

¹**au·to·polyploid** \" +\ *n* -s [*aut-* + *polyploid*] : an individual or strain exhibiting autopolyploidy

²**au·to·polyploid** \ˌ‧‧ + ˌ‧‧ˌ‧\ *also* **au·to·polyploidic** \" +\ *adj* : exhibiting autopolyploidy : being an autopolyploid

au·to·polyploidy \" +\ *n* -ES [*aut-* + *polyploidy*] : the state of having more than two genomes, all being alike and derived from a single ancestral species — compare ALLOPOLYPLOIDY

au·to·pore \ˈ‧‧ + ˌ\ *n* -s [*aut-* + *-pore*] : ZOOECIUM

au·to·potamic \ˌ‧‧ *at* ¹AUTO- +\ *adj* [*aut-* + *potamic*] *of algae* : adapted to life in flowing streams — compare EUPOTAMIC, TYCHOPOTAMIC

au·top·sist \-sə̇st — *see* ¹AUTOPSY\ *n* -s [*autopsy* + *-ist*] **:** one who performs an autopsy

¹au·top·sy \'ȯ,täpsē, 'ȯdəp-, 'ȯtəp-, -si *sometimes* ȯ'täp- *or* ə'täp-\ *n* -ES [Gk *autopsia* seeing with one's own eyes, fr. *aut-* + *-opsia* (fr. *opsis* sight) — more at OPTIC] **1 :** POSTMORTEM EXAMINATION, NECROPSY; *also* **:** permission to make such an examination ⟨~ was refused⟩ **2 :** a critical analysis either hostile or dispassionate of a past event or a completed creative process ⟨history is at best ~ —F.L.Wright⟩

²autopsy \"\ *vt* -ED/-ING/-ES **:** to perform a postmortem examination upon

au·to·psychic \¦==+¦==\ *at* ¹AUTO- + ¦==\ *adj* [*aut-* + *psychic*] **:** of or relating to one's own mind — contrasted with *allopsychic*

au·top·tic \(')ȯ¦täptik\ *adj* [Gk *autoptikos* of an eyewitness, fr. *aut-* + *optikos* of sight — more at OPTIC] **:** based on one's own observation ⟨an ~ report on the Far East⟩

au·to·radiograph \¦== *at* ¹AUTO- +\ *or* **au·to·radiogram** \" +\ *n* [ISV *aut-* + *radiograph* or *radiogram*] **:** an image produced on a photographic film or plate by the radiations from a radioactive substance in an object which is in close contact with the emulsion — called also *radioautograph* — **au·to·radiographic** \" +\ *adj*

au·to·radiography \" +\ *n* [*aut-* + *radiography*] **:** the process of making autoradiographs

au·to·rail \'== +,=\ *or* **au·to·railer** \" + ,==\ *n* -s [²*auto-* + *rail* or *railer*] **:** a self-propelled vehicle equipped with both flange wheels and pneumatic tires and thus adaptable to either railway or highway operation

au·to–rifle \'ȯd-ō,==\ *n* [*automatic rifle*] **:** AUTOMATIC RIFLE

au·to roller \'ȯd-ō,-\ *n* [*automatic*] **:** a worker who feeds and operates an automatic machine for cutting wrapper leaves and rolling cigars

au·to·rotation \¦=(,)= *at* ¹AUTO- +\ *n* -s [ISV *aut-* + *rotation*] **:** the turning of the rotor of an autogiro or a helicopter with resulting lift caused solely by the aerodynamic forces induced by motion of the rotor along its flight path — **au·to·rota·tional** \" +\ *adj*

autos *pl of* AUTO, *pres 3d sing of* AUTO

au·to·sau·ri \" + ¦sȯ,rī, -(,)rē\ *or* **au·to·sau·ri·a** \-¦sȯrēə\ [NL, fr. *aut-* + *-sauri* (pl. of *-saurus*) or *-sauria*] *syn of* LACERTILIA

au·to·sche·di·asm \,== + 'skēdē,azəm\ *n* -s [Gk *autoschediasma*, fr. *autoschediazein* to extemporize, fr. *aut-* + *schediazein* to improvise, do something offhand, fr. *schedios* casual; akin to Gk *schein*, *echein* to have, hold — more at SCHEME] **:** something that is done offhand **:** IMPROVISATION

au·to·sche·di·as·tic \¦== + ¦skēdē¦astik\ *adj* [Gk *autoschediastikos*, fr. *autoschediastos* extemporary (fr. *autoschediazein*) + *-ikos* -ic] **:** EXTEMPORARY, OFFHAND

au·to·scope \'== + ,skōp\ *n* -s [ISV *aut-* + *-scope*; prob. orig. formed as G *autoskop*] **:** a device for recording or magnifying small involuntary movements of the body

au·to·scopic \¦== + ¦==\ *adj* **:** of, relating to, or marked by autoscopy

au·tos·co·py \ȯ'täskəpē\ *n* -ES [ISV *aut-* + *-scopy*; prob. orig. formed as G *autoskopie*] **:** visual hallucination of one's body image

autos–da–fé *pl of* AUTO-DA-FÉ

autos de fé *pl of* AUTO DE FÉ

au·to·sensitization \¦=(,)= *at* ¹AUTO- + \ *n* -s [*aut-* + *sensitization*] **:** AUTOIMMUNIZATION

au·to·serum \'== + ,==\ *n* -s [ISV *aut-* + *serum*] **:** a serum obtained from a patient for use in treating that patient

au·to·sexing \" + ,==\ *adj* [*aut-* + *sexing*, pres. part. of *sex*] **:** showing characters that are differential for sex at birth or hatching — used esp. of domestic fowls crossbred for characteristic color or pattern differences in the two sexes

au·to·site \" + ,sīt\ *n* -s [F, fr. *aut-* + *-site* (as in *parasite*)] **:** that part of a double fetal monster that nourishes both itself and the parasitic twin

au·to·sit·ic \¦== + ¦sid·ik\ *adj* **:** of the nature of an autosite

au·to·skeleton \'== + ,===\ *n* -s [*aut-* + *skeleton*] **:** an internal skeleton; *specif* **:** the endoskeleton of sponges consisting of spicules or spongin fibers secreted by the cells — opposed to *pseudoskeleton*

au·to·sled \" + ,=\ *n* -s [²*auto-* + *sled*] **1 :** a vehicle with four retractable runners and wheels that is driven by propeller blades and is capable of traveling on bare roads, packed snow, or ice **2 :** a vehicle like an autosled but that has only the front wheels retractable and that is driven by the rear wheels

au·to·som·al \¦== + ¦sōməl\ *adj* **:** of, belonging to, located on, or transmitted by an autosome — used chiefly of genes

au·to·some \'== + ,sōm\ *n* -s [*aut-* + *-some*] **:** a chromosome other than a sex chromosome — called also *euchromosome*; compare ALLOSOME

au·to·spore \" + ,=\ *n* -s [*aut-* + *-spore*] **:** one of the daughter cells formed by the internal division of a single cell esp. in such unicellular algae as members of the order Chroococcales and duplicating in miniature the parent cell

au·to·spor·ic \¦== + ¦spōrik\ *adj* **:** of, relating to, or characterized by autospores

au·to·stability \" + \ *n* -ES [*aut-* + *stability*] **:** the ability (as of an airplane) to keep in steady poise either by virtue of its inherent shape and proportions or by a self-operative controlling mechanism

au·to·sty·lic \¦== + ¦stīlik\ *adj* [*aut-* + *-stylic*] **:** having the jaws connected directly with the cranium (as chimaeras, lungfishes, amphibians, and higher vertebrates) instead of indirectly by the hyoid arch — sometimes distinguished from *holostylic* to denote lack of fusion of the pterygoquadrate with the cranium; compare AMPHISTYLIC, HYOSTYLIC

au·to·sty·lism \" + ¦stī,lizəm\ *or* **au·to·sty·ly** \'== + ,stīlē\ *n*, *pl* **autostylisms** *or* **autostylies** [*autostylic* + *-ism* or *-y*] **:** condition of being autostylic

au·to·suggestibility \¦=(,)= + \ *n* -ES **:** the quality or state of being autosuggestible

au·to·suggestible \" + =¦===\ *adj* [*autosuggestion* + *-ible*] **:** subject to autosuggestion

au·to·suggestion \" + \ *n* -s [ISV *aut-* + *suggestion*; orig. formed in G] **:** an influencing of one's own attitudes, behavior, or physical condition by mental processes other than conscious thought **:** SELF-HYPNOSIS

au·to·suggestive \" + =¦==\ *adj* [*autosuggestion* + *-ive*] **:** of, relating to, or marked by autosuggestion

au·to·synapsis \" + \ *n* [NL, fr. *aut-* + *synapsis*] **:** AUTOSYNDESIS

au·to·syndesis \" + \ *n* [NL, fr. *aut-* + *syndesis*] **:** pairing at meiosis of homologous chromosomes from the similar sets of an allopolyploid individual

au·to·syndetic \" + =¦==\ *adj* [*aut-* + *syndetic*] **:** of, relating to, or marked by autosyndesis — **au·to·syndetically** \" + =¦==(ə)lē\ *adv*

au·to·tel·ic \¦==+¦telik\ *adj* [Gk *autotelēs* complete in itself (fr. *aut-* + *telos* end) + E *-ic*] **:** having an end or purpose in and not apart from itself ⟨poetry is . . . , like mathematics, an ~ activity —Louis MacNeice⟩ — contrasted with *heterotelic*

au·to·tel·ism \,== + 'te,lizəm, -'tē,l- *also* ȯ'tätᵊl,iz-\ *n* -s **:** the belief that a work of art, esp. a work of literature, is an end in itself or provides its own justification

au·to·tetraploid \¦==+\ *n* -s [*aut-* + *tetraploid*] **:** an individual or strain exhibiting autotetraploidy

au·to·tetraploidy \" + \ *n* -ES [*aut-* + *tetraploidy*] **:** the state of having four genomes due to doubling of the ancestral chromosome complement — compare C-MITOSIS

au·to·the·ism \'=(,)= + (,)thē,izəm, -'th-\ *n* -s [LGk *autotheos* very God (fr. Gk *aut-* + *theos* god) + E *-ism* — more at THEISM] **1 :** the doctrine of the self-existence of God; *esp* **:** the doctrine that Christ is the self-existent God himself **2 :** deification of oneself **:** SELF-WORSHIP

au·to·the·ist \'=(,)= + ,thēə̇st, ,thē,ist\ *n* -s **:** one who believes in or practices autotheism

au·to·theistic \¦=(,)= + =¦==\ *adj* **:** of, relating to, or marked by autotheism

au·to·therapy \¦==+¦==\ *n* -ES [*aut-* + *therapy*] **:** medication of oneself or treatment of one's own disease without medical supervision or prescription

au·to·tomic \" + ¦tämik\ *or* **au·tot·o·mous** \ȯ'tädəməs\ *adj* [*aut-* + Gk *tomos* cutting + E *-ic* or *-ous*] **:** of, relating to, or characterized by autotomy

au·tot·o·mize \ȯ'täd·ə,mīz\ *vb* -ED/-ING/-S *vt* **:** to effect autotomy of ~ *vi* **:** to undergo autotomy

autotomizer muscle *n* **:** a muscle that contracts in such a way as to cause autotomy (as in the limbs of a crayfish)

au·tot·o·my \ȯ'täd·əmē\ *n* -ES [ISV *aut-* + *-tomy*] **:** reflex separation of a part or limb from the body **:** division of the whole into two or more pieces (as in crustaceans, echinoderms, or worms)

au·to·toxemia *also* **au·to·toxaemia** \¦=(,)= *at* ¹AUTO- + =¦===\ *n* -s [NL, fr. *aut-* + *toxemia*, *toxaemia*] **:** AUTOINTOXICATION

au·to·toxin \" + ¦==\ *n* -s [ISV *aut-* + *toxin*] **:** any toxin produced within the body

au·to·transformer \" + =¦==\ *n* -s [*aut-* + *transformer*] **:** a transformer in which the primary and secondary coils have part or all of their turns in common

au·to·transplant \" + =¦=, ,=\ *vt* [*aut-* + *transplant*] **:** AUTOGRAFT

au·to·transplantation \" + ¦==¦==\ *n* -s **:** the action of autotransplanting or the condition of being autotransplanted

¹au·to·triploid \¦== + ¦=,=\ *adj* [*aut-* + *triploid*] **:** having a triploid set of chromosomes made up of like genomes — **au·to·triploidy** \+¦=,==\ *n* -ES

²autotriploid \"\ *n* -s **:** an autotriploid individual

au·to·tron·ic \¦==+¦tränik\ *adj* [fr. *Autotronic*, a trademark] **:** capable of automatically regulating the operation of banks of elevators in office buildings

au·to·troph \'== + ,träf, -ȯf\ *also* **au·to·trophe** \-,trōf\ *n* -s [G, fr. *autotroph*, adj., autotrophic] **:** an autotrophic organism **:** AUTOPHYTE — **au·tot·ro·phy** \ȯ'tä·trəfē\ *n* -ES

autotroph hypothesis *n* **:** a hypothesis in biology: the most primitive first life was autotrophic — compare HETEROTROPH HYPOTHESIS

au·to·troph·ic \¦== + ¦träfik, -trō-\ *adj* [ISV *aut-* + *-trophic*; prob. orig. formed as G *autotroph*] **1 :** capable of self-nourishment; *specif* **:** capable of using carbon dioxide or carbonates as a sole source of carbon and a simple inorganic nitrogen compound for metabolic synthesis — used of green plants and certain chemoautotrophic bacteria and protozoans; opposed to *heterotrophic*; see PHOTOAUTOTROPHIC **2 :** not requiring a specified exogenous factor for normal metabolism — usu. used in combination ⟨strictly auxo*autotrophic*⟩ — **au·to·troph·i·cal·ly** \¦==¦=fə̇k(ə)lē\ *adv*

au·to·truck \'== + ,=\ *n* -s [²*auto-* + *truck*] **:** a motor-driven truck

¹au·to·type \" + ,=\ *n* -s [*aut-* + *type*] **1 :** FACSIMILE **2 a :** CARBON PROCESS **b :** a picture made by the carbon process **3 a :** HYPOTYPE **b :** AUTOGENOTYPE

²autotype \"\ *vt* -ED/-ING/-S **:** to make or copy by autotypy

au·to·typ·ic \¦== + ¦==\ *adj* **1 :** reproduced by the carbon process **2 :** of, relating to, or of the nature of an autotype

au·to·typy \'== + ,tīpē; ȯ'täd·əpē\ *n* -ES **:** process of making autotypes (sense 2)

au·to·vaccine \'== +\ *n* -s [*autogenous vaccine*] **:** AUTOGENOUS VACCINE

auto wrench *also* **automobile wrench** *n* **:** a lightweight all-metal monkey wrench

au·tox·i·da·tion \ȯ,täksə̇'dāshən, ȯd·,äk-\ *also* **au·to–oxidation** \¦== *at* ¹AUTO- + ==¦==\ *n* [ISV *aut-* + *oxidation*] **:** oxidation by direct combination with oxygen (as in air) at ordinary temperatures ⟨the rancidity of fats and oils is caused by ~⟩

au·tox·i·da·tive \ȯ¦täksə̇¦dād·iv, ȯd·¦äk-\ *adj* **:** of, relating to, or caused by autoxidation

au·tox·i·diz·a·ble \=¦==¦dīzəbəl\ *adj* **:** capable of undergoing autoxidation

au·tox·i·dize \='==,dīz\ *also* **au·to–oxidize** \¦== *at* ¹AUTO- + ¦==,=\ *vi* [*aut-* + *oxidize*] **:** to undergo autoxidation

au·to·zooid \¦== *at* ¹AUTO- + ¦=,=\ *n* -s [*aut-* + *zooid*] **:** a fully formed alcyonarian zooid as distinguished from a siphonozooid

au·tre·fois ac·quit \¦ō·trəf,wä(,)a'kē\ *n* [AF, formerly acquitted] **:** a defendant's plea alleging previous trial and acquittal of the same offense

autrefois con·vict \-,kən'vikt\ *n* [AF, formerly convicted] **:** a defendant's plea alleging previous trial and conviction for the same offense

au·tumn \'ȯd·əm, 'ä|, |təm\ *n* -s *often attrib* [ME *autumpne*, fr. L *autumnus*] **1 a :** the season between summer and winter reckoned astronomically as extending from the September equinox to the December solstice **b :** the season comprising the months of September, October, and November — called also *fall* **c** *Brit* **:** the season comprising the months of August, September, and October **d :** the season reckoned astronomically in the southern hemisphere as extending from the March equinox to the June solstice **2 :** time of full maturity or incipient decline **:** latter portion **:** third stage ⟨the ~ of life⟩ **3 :** a moderate olive brown that is darker and very slightly greener than the typical or average olive brown

autumn adonis *n*, *usu cap 2d A* **:** PHEASANT'S-EYE 1

au·tum·nal \(')ȯ¦təmnəl *sometimes* 'ȯd·əm- *or* 'ä| *or* |tə-\ *adj* [L *autumnalis*, fr. *autumnus* + *-alis* -al] **1 :** of, belonging to, or peculiar to autumn ⟨mild, ~ sunshine —Nathaniel Hawthorne⟩ **2 :** produced or gathered in autumn **:** maturing in autumn ⟨~ fruits⟩ **3 :** characterized by qualities associated with or suggested by autumn ⟨a serene ~ mood⟩ — **au·tum·nal·ly** *adv*

autumnal tea *n* **:** a black tea grown during the autumn in certain Indian tea districts (as Assam, Darjeeling, Duars)

autumn blond *n* **:** FAWN 3

autumn brown *n* **:** a grayish to moderate brown that is yellower and darker than dark beaver

autumn crocus *n* **:** MEADOW SAFFRON

autumn elaeagnus *n*, *pl* **autumn elaeagnuses :** an Asiatic shrub (*Elaeagnus umbellata*) often escaped from cultivation esp. in the eastern U.S. with flowers in umbels and with the corolla tube much longer than the lobes

autumn glory *n* **:** a dark red to reddish orange that is slightly yellower and stronger than Moroccan

autumn green *n* **:** SPINACH GREEN

autumn leaf *n* [after F *feuille-morte*, lit., dead leaf] **:** FEUILLE MORTE

autumn mange *n* **:** a skin disease of domestic animals that is caused by the bites of chiggers, is characterized by papules and severe itching, and is most common in late summer and autumn

autumn oak *n* **:** LIVER 5

autumn snowflake *n* **:** a bulbous herb (*Leucojum autumnale*) with filiform leaves and the fall-blooming white flowers tinged with red — see SNOWFLAKE

autumn squill *n* **:** a hardy European bulbous garden plant (*Scilla autumnalis*) with persistent leaves that are produced after the naked raceme of pink flowers

autumn willow *n* **:** a bog shrub (*Salix serissima*) of northern No. America with shining dark-green leaves and fruits that persist until autumn

au·tun·ite \'ōtə,nīt\ *n* -s [*Autun*, dist. Saône-et-Loire, France, its locality + E *-ite*] **:** a radioactive lemon-yellow mineral composed of uranyl calcium phosphate $Ca(UO_2)_2(PO_4)_2.10\text{–}12H_2O$ occurring in tabular crystals with basal cleavage and in micalike scales (sp. gr. 3.05–3.19)

au·ver·gnat \¦ō,vern¦yä\ *n* -s *cap* [F, fr. *Auvergne*, region of south central France] **:** a native or inhabitant of Auvergne, France

au·wai \'aů,wī\ *n* -s [Hawaiian *'auwai*] *Hawaii* **:** a watercourse or channel esp. for irrigation

au·we \'aů(,)wā\ *var of* AUE

aux *abbr* auxiliary

auxano- *comb form* [ISV, fr. Gk *auxanein* to increase; akin to Gk *auxein* to increase — more at EKE] **:** growth ⟨*auxano*gram⟩ ⟨*auxano*logy⟩

aux·an·o·gram \ȯg'zanə,gram, ȯk'sa-\ *n* -s [*auxano-* + *-gram*] **:** a plate culture (as of bacteria) in which variable conditions are provided for growth that is used as a means of determining the effects of a particular condition or agent on the growth of a test organism

aux·an·o·graph·ic \¦=¦=¦grafik\ *adj* **:** of, belonging to, or by means of auxanography — **aux·an·o·graph·i·cal·ly** \-fə̇k(ə)lē\ *adv*

aux·a·nog·ra·phy \,ȯgzə'nägrəfē, ,ȯksə'-\ *n* -ES [*auxano-* + *-graphy*] **:** the study of growth-promoting or growth-inhibiting agents by means of auxanograms

aux·a·nom·e·ter \,==¦nämәd·ə(r)\ *n* -s [ISV *auxano-* + *-meter*] **:** an instrument for determining and measuring the rate of growth in plants consisting essentially of a lever with a long and a short arm which is attached to the plant

-auxe \'ȯk(,)sē\ *n comb form*, *pl* **-auxae** [NL, fr. Gk *auxē* growth; akin to Gk *auxein* to increase — more at EKE] **:** enlargement **:** hypertrophy ⟨enter*auxe*⟩

aux·e·sis \ȯg'zēsə̇s, ȯk'se-\ *n*, *pl* **aux·e·ses** \-ē,sēz\ [NL, fr. Gk *auxēsis* increase, fr. *auxanein*, *auxein* to increase + *-ēsis* -esis — more at EKE] **1 :** GROWTH; *specif* **:** increase of cell size without cell division — compare MERISIS **2 :** the process by which certain diatoms that have become small through repeated asexual divisions are restored to normal size, the protoplasts escaping from the cell wall and increasing to normal size or fusing to form auxospores or zygospores that then increase to normal size before new cell walls form

aux·et·ic \(')ȯg¦zed·ik, (')ȯk¦se-\ *adj* [Gk *auxētikos* growing, promoting growth, fr. *auxētos* increased, capable of being increased (fr. *auxanein*, *auxein* to increase) + *-ikos* -ic] **1 :** characterized by auxesis **2 :** inducing auxesis — **aux·et·i·cal·ly** \-d·ək(ə)lē\ *adv*

aux·il·i·an \ȯg'zilyən\ *n* -s [*auxiliary* + *-ian*] **:** a member of a hospital auxiliary group

auxiliar *adj or n* [L *auxiliaris*, fr. *auxilium* + *-aris* -ar] *archaic* **:** AUXILIARY

¹aux·il·ia·ry \(')ȯg¦zilyərē, əg'z-, ÷ -l(ə)r-, -ri *sometimes* -k¦s- *or* -k's- *or* -lē,er-\ *adj* [L *auxiliarius*, fr. *auxilium* help (akin to L *augēre* to increase) + *-arius* -ary — more at EKE] **1 a :** offering or providing help, assistance, or support esp. by interaction ⟨neither philosophy nor science has ever been more closely ~ to literature than at the moment —Wylie Sypher⟩ **b :** functioning in a subsidiary capacity ⟨an ~ branch of the state university⟩ **2** *of a verb* **:** accompanying a nonfinite verb form that expresses the main verbal meaning of its clause, expressing typically such things as person, number, mood, and tense, and finite in form unless accompanied by another auxiliary verb, in which case only one is finite (as *be*, *have*, *do*, *will*, *can*, in such expressions as "we were standing there", "I move the nominations be closed", "he has been informed", "where do they live?", "he will write", "I can swim", German *haben*, *sein*, *werden*, *dürfen*, or French *avoir*, *être*, *pouvoir*, *devoir*, in similar expressions) **3 :** augmenting or available to augment a basic power, potential, or ability: as **a :** SUPPLEMENTARY ⟨with ~ instruments the new telescope has more power⟩ **b :** RESERVE ⟨the ~ police were called to the disaster area⟩ ⟨~ power plant⟩ **4** *of a boat* **:** equipped with an inboard engine to supplement the motive power of sails ⟨an ~ sloop⟩

²auxiliary \"\ *n* -ES **1 :** one that helps **:** one that functions or serves in a supplementary often subordinate position **2 a :** an allied or foreign armed force in the service of a nation at war — usu. used in pl. **b :** a member of such a force **3** *or* **auxiliary bishop :** a titular bishop in the Roman Catholic Church who assists the ordinary of a diocese **4 a :** an auxiliary engine (as on a sailboat) **b :** an auxiliary boat (as a tanker, tender, or supply ship) — see NAVAL AUXILIARY **c :** a sailboat with an auxiliary engine **5 :** a member of an auxiliary group (as of police or firemen) **6 :** ASSISTANT 3 **7 :** an auxiliary verb **8 :** AUXILIARY INFLECTION **9 a :** an organization that is adjunct to one having a restricted membership; *esp* **:** an organization for wives and women relatives of such members ⟨the American Legion *Auxiliary*⟩ ⟨Women's *Auxiliary* of the State Medical Society⟩ **b :** an organization often of women that assists esp. by donations or volunteer services the work of a church, hospital, or charitable institution ⟨the Lutheran Home *Auxiliary*⟩

auxiliary cell *n* **:** a specialized cell in certain red algae often some distance from the carpogonium into which the diploid zygote nucleus migrates after fertilization sometimes by special threads called ooblasts and from which the carpospores eventually develop

auxiliary circle *n* **:** a circle described on the major or minor axis of an ellipse as diameter

auxiliary equation *n* **:** an equation obtained from the standard form of a linear differential equation by replacing the right member by zero

auxiliary goods *n pl* **:** PRODUCER GOODS

auxiliary inflection *n*, *paleontol* **:** any lateral lobe or saddle of the ammonoid suture added later than the first two or three pairs

auxiliary language *n* **:** a language (as Esperanto or pidgin English) used for communication between persons that do not understand each other's native language — compare INTERLANGUAGE

auxiliary rafter *n* **:** a rafter used to strengthen the principal rafter in a truss

auxiliary switch *n* **:** an electrical switch actuated by a main device (as a circuit breaker) for signaling or interlocking

auxiliary target *n* **:** a point of known location used as an adjusting point for subsequent fire on other targets

auxiliary tone *or* **auxiliary note** *n* **:** an unaccented nonharmonic tone approached from above or below by stepwise motion and returning to the original tone

aux·il·i·um \ȯg'zilēəm\ *n* -s [L] **:** an aid or tribute — compare AID 4

aux·i·mone \'ȯksə,mōn\ *n* -s [Gk *auximos* promoting growth + *-one* (as in hormone)] **:** any of certain substances considered necessary, though only in small quantities, for the vigorous growth of plants and occurring esp. in sphagnum peat decomposed by nitrogen bacteria — compare VITAMIN

aux·in \'ȯksə̇n\ *n* -s [ISV *aux-* (fr. Gk *auxein* to increase) + *-in* — more at EKE] **:** any organic substance (as indoleacetic acid) characterized by its ability in low concentrations to promote growth of plant shoots along the longitudinal axis (as in the Avena test) and to produce various other effects (as root formation and bud inhibition) — compare PLANT HORMONE — **aux·in·ic** \(')ȯk¦sinik\ *or* **aux·in·i·cal** \-nə̇kəl\ *adj* — **aux·in·i·cal·ly** \-ək(ə)lē\ *adv*

aux·i·thal \'ȯksə̇,thal\ *n* -s [*auxi-* (fr. Gk *auxein* to increase) + *-thal* (fr. *thiamine* + *-al*)] **:** AUXIN

auxo- *comb form* [ISV, fr. Gk, fr. *auxein* to increase — more at EKE] **1 :** growth ⟨*auxo*body⟩ ⟨*auxo*substance⟩ **:** increase ⟨*auxo*graph⟩ **2 :** accelerating **:** stimulating ⟨*auxo*chrome⟩

aux·o·autotrophic \¦ȯk(,)sō¦==¦==\ *adj* [*auxo-* + *autotrophic*] *biol* **:** requiring no exogenous growth factors

aux·o·chrome \'ȯksə,krōm\ *n* -s [ISV *auxo-* + *-chrome*] **:** a salt-forming group (as hydroxyl or amino) that when introduced into a chromogen produces a dye — see CHROMOPHORE — **aux·o·chrom·ic** \¦==¦krōmik\ *adj*

aux·o·cyte \'ȯksə,sīt\ *n* -s [*auxo-* + *-cyte*] *biol* **:** a gamete-forming cell (as an oocyte) or a sporocyte during its growth period

aux·o·drome \-,drōm\ *n* -s [*auxo-* + *drome*] **:** a plotted curve indicating the relative development of a child at any given age

aux·o·graph \'ȯksə,graf\ *n* -s [*auxo-* + *-graph*] **:** an instrument for the automatic recording of variations in volume of any body and orig. used to measure the swelling and shrinking of parts of plants — **aux·o·graph·ic** \¦==¦grafik\ *adj*

aux·o·heterotrophic \¦ȯk(,)sō+¦===¦=\ *adj* [*auxo-* + *heterotrophic*] *biol* **:** requiring exogenous growth factors or stimulants

aux·o·spore \'ȯksə,spō(ə)r\ *n* -s [ISV *auxo-* + *-spore*; prob. orig. formed in G] **:** a reproductive cell in diatoms usu. resulting from the union of two smaller cells or their contents and associated with rejuvenescence in cells that have become progressively smaller because of repeated divisions

aux·o·tonic \¦ȯksə¦tänik\ *adj* [ISV *auxo-* + *tonic*] *plant physiol* **:** determined or induced by growth rather than by external stimulus — opposed to *allassotonic*

av *usu cap*, *var of* AB

av *abbr* **1** avenue **2** average **3** aviation **4** avoirdupois

AV *abbr* **1** ad valorem **2** [L *annos vixit*] he lived (a given number of) years **3** audio-visual **4** average variability

ava *or* **ava'** \ə'vä, -vȯ\ *adv* [Sc *av* (alter. of E *of*) + ²*a*] **1** *Scot* **:** of all ⟨this pleased them warst ~ —Robert Burns⟩ **2** *Scot* **:** at all ⟨not like a gentleman ~⟩

'ava \'(ʔ)ävə\ *n* -s [Tahitian or Samoan *'ava*] *Central Polynesia* **:** KAVA

av·a·da·vat \'avədə,vat\ *also* **am·a·da·vat** \'amə-\ *n* -s [irreg. fr. *Ahmadabad*, city in India from which it was imported to Europe] **:** a very small weaverbird (*Estrilda aman-*

dava) native to southeast Asia but often kept as a cage bird, having the breeding male scarlet, darker above, and with white dots on wings and sides and the female and eclipse male olive brown above and grayish buff below — called also *strawberry finch*

ava·hi \ə'vä,hē\ *n* -s [native name in Madagascar] : WOOLLY LEMUR

1**avail** \ə'vāl, *esp bef pause or cons* -āəl\ *vb* -ED/-ING/-S [ME *availen*, prob. fr. *a-* (as in *abaten* to abate) + *vailen* to avail — more at VAIL] *vi* **1** : to function effectively or advantageously in the accomplishment of an objective : be useful or beneficial for a specific purpose ⟨apparatus and pretension ~ nothing⟩ ⟨heroism could not ~ against the enemy fire⟩ ⟨the wall could not ~ to protect the town against cannon⟩ **2** : to be of profit or value : serve to clarify or improve a situation ⟨no comparison would ~, he was one of a kind⟩ ⟨the forces of which judges avowedly ~ to shape the form and content of their judgments —B.N.Cardozo⟩ ~ *vt* **1** : to be of service or advantage to : BENEFIT, PROFIT **2** *archaic* : to give (someone) a specific advantage or benefit — used with *of* ⟨~ Mr. Barclay of that fund —Thomas Jefferson⟩ **3 a** : to take advantage : make use — used with *of* ⟨far from resenting such tutelage I am only too glad to ~ myself of it —G.B.Shaw⟩ **b** : to use or apply to good advantage **syn** see USE

2**avail** \"\ *n* -s [ME, fr. *availen*, v.] **1** *obs* : PROFIT, BENEFIT, VALUE ⟨the ~ of a deathbed repentance —Jeremy Taylor⟩ **2** : effective advantage toward attainment of a goal or purpose : USE — used chiefly after *of* or *to* and now usu. in negative contexts ⟨his effort was of no ~⟩ **3 avails** *pl, archaic* : profits or proceeds esp. from a business or from the sale of property ⟨I made it clear that none of my ~*s* were going to be dissipated —S.H.Adams⟩ **syn** see USE

avail·a·bil·i·ty \ə,vālə'biləd·ē, -ətē, -i\ *n* -ES **1** : the quality or state of being available; *specif* : the calculated promise of a political candidate's success based chiefly on his personal popularity and appeal irrespective of ability or special fitness ⟨the emphasis has not been upon greatness in the candidate but upon ~ —D.D.McKean⟩ — compare AVAILABLE 5a **2** : an available person or thing ⟨trying to furnish a house from local *availabilities*⟩

avail·a·ble \ə'vāləbəl\ *adj* [ME, fr. *availen* + *-able*] **1 a** *obs* : capable of availing : having sufficient power or force to achieve an end **b** *archaic* : having a beneficial effect **2** : VALID — used of a legal plea or charge ⟨all charges must be good and ~⟩ or of a taxonomic designation not currently preferred but properly published and not invalidated by other usages **3** : such as may be availed of : capable of use for the accomplishment of a purpose : immediately utilizable ⟨the first thing to concentrate on was the sinking of the German navy on any ~ pretext —G.B.Shaw⟩ **4** : that is accessible or may be obtained : personally obtainable (as for employment) ⟨physicist, industrial and academic experience, wants position, ~ late summer⟩ : at disposal esp. for sale or utilization ⟨~ in many colors and sizes⟩ ⟨latest readily ~ information⟩ **5 a** : having the requisite political associations and circumstantial qualifications for winning election to office — compare AVAILABILITY 1 **b** : willing to accept nomination for or election to an office ⟨he announced that he was ~ for the nomination⟩ **6 a** : present in such chemical or physical form esp. in the soil as to be capable of being utilized by a plant or animal ⟨~ nitrogen⟩ ⟨~ phosphorus⟩ ⟨~ water⟩ **b** : *of a chemical element or compound* : in a reactive form ⟨~ alkali⟩ — **avail·a·ble·ness** *n* -ES — **avail·a·bly** *adv*

available assets *n pl* : assets available for use as collateral

available chlorine *n* : the amount of free chlorine that a substance (as bleaching powder) yields when treated with an acid in the presence of a chloride (as sodium chloride or calcium chloride), one atom of chlorine in a hypochlorite being thus computed as equivalent to a molecule of elemental chlorine

available energy *n, physics* : that part of the energy of bodies or systems which exists under such conditions that work may be theoretically derived from it — compare DEGRADATION OF ENERGY, ENTROPY, UNAVAILABLE ENERGY

aval \a'val\ *n* -s [F] *civil law* : a written engagement by one not a drawer, acceptor, or indorser of a note or bill of exchange that it will be paid at maturity

1**av·a·lanche** \'avə,lanch, -aa(ə)n-,-ain-\ *n* -s *often attrib* [F, fr. F dial. (northwestern Alps) *avalantse*, alter. (influenced by F *avaler* to lower, go downstream) of F dial. (northwestern Alps) *lavantse*, prob. of non-IE origin; akin to the source of OProv *lavanca* avalanche, It *valanga*] **1** : a large mass of snow, ice, earth, rock, or other material in swift motion down a mountainside or over a precipice **2** : any sudden great or overwhelming rush or flood ⟨an ~ of water smashing on the decks —*Harper's*⟩ **3** : an electric breakdown which occurs under an applied electric field and in which an electron released from an atom acquires enough energy from the electric field to cause the release of two or more electrons from an atom with which it collides thus initiating an electronic chain reaction — called also *electron avalanche*, *Townsend avalanche*

2**avalanche** \"\ *vb* -ED/-ING/-S *vi* : to rush or slide in or in the manner of an avalanche ⟨a pile of junk ~*s* out of the hall closet when you open the door⟩ ~ *vt* : to present or supply at one time with a superabundance of anything : OVERWHELM, FLOOD ⟨the office was *avalanched* with applications⟩

avalanche conduction *n* : conduction of the nervous impulse from one neuron through several others so as to converge on one point where the intensity of the discharge is increased by summation

avalanche lily *n* : a perennial herb (*Erythronium montanum*) having large white orange-marked flowers and commonly found near the snow line in the northwestern U. S.

avale *vb* -ED/-ING/-S [ME *avalen*, fr. MF *avaler*, fr. OF, fr. *aval* downward, fr. *a* to (fr. L *ad*) + *val* valley — more at AT, VALE] *vt* **1** *obs* : LOWER : let fall **2** *obs* : to bring low : ABASE ~ *vi* **1** *obs* : DESCEND, DISMOUNT **2** *obs* : to sink down : flow down

avalvular \(')ā+¦-\ *adj* [2*a-* + *valvular*] **1** *anat* : lacking valves **2** *anat* : not affecting valves

avant-corps \(¦)ä,vänt'kō(ə)r, -ȯ(ə)r\ *n* [F, fr. *avant* forward + *corps* body, fr. L *corpus* — more at AVAUNT, MIDRIFF] : a part which projects out from the main mass of a building (as a pavilion in front of the façade)

avant-courier \(¦)ä,vänt+'-\ *n* -s [F *avant-courrier*, fr. *avant* + *courrier* courier — more at COURIER] **1 avant-couriers** *pl, archaic* : the scouts or advance guard of an army **2** : one that goes or comes before another — called also *herald*

avant-garde \(¦)ä,vän(t)'gärd, ¦a,v-, ə,v-, (¦)å,v-, -vän 'g-, -vȯn(t)'g-,-vȯn 'g-, -gȧd\ *n* -s *often attrib* [F, vanguard] **1** : those who create, produce, or apply new, original, or experimental ideas, designs, and techniques in any field, esp. in the arts — used usu. with *the* **2** : a group (as of writers or artists) that is unorthodox and untraditional in its approach; *sometimes* : such a group that is extremist, bizarre, or arty and affected **3** : advocates and admirers of the avant-garde

avant-gard·ism \-,dizəm\ *n* -s : predilection for or practice of intellectual or artistic experimentalism : participation in activity or effort associated with the avant-garde

avant-gard·ist \-,dəst\ *also* **avant-gar·diste** \-,gär'dēst, -,gȧ'd-\ *n* -s : a member of the avant-garde

avanturine *var of* AVENTURINE

avanyo *or* **avanyu** *var of* AWANYU

avar \'ä,vär\ *n* -s *usu cap* **1** : a member of a people of Eastern origin now belonging to the Lezghian division of the peoples of the Caucasus prominent from the 6th to the 9th centuries at first in Dacia and later in Pannonia **2** *or* **avar·ish** \ä'värish\ : the No. Caucasic language of the Avars

ava·ram bark \'ävərəm,-\ *also* **avaram** *n* -s [Malayalam *āvīram*] : a tanbark from a bush or tree (*Cassia auriculata*) of India

avar·i·an \ä'värēən\ *or* **avar·ic** \-rik\ *adj, usu cap* : of or relating to the Avars

av·a·rice \'avərəs, *rap.* -vr-\ *n* -s [ME, fr. OF, fr. L *avaritia*, fr. *avarus* avaricious, fr. *avēre* to covet, long for — more at AVID] : excessive or insatiable desire for wealth or gain : GREEDINESS, CUPIDITY ⟨they scrimped and stinted and starved themselves . . . out of ~ and the will-to-power —Lewis Mumford⟩ **syn** see CUPIDITY

av·a·ri·cious \¦avə¦rishəs\ *adj* [MF *avaricieux*, fr. OF, fr. *avarice*] : actuated by avarice : inordinately desirous of accumulating wealth, often in niggardly ways and merely in order to hoard it ⟨[they] were furtively ~; they couldn't help being stingy, since parsimony ran in their blood, but they were not frank about it —Victoria Sackville-West⟩ **syn** see COVETOUS

av·a·ri·cious·ly *adv* : in an avaricious manner

av·a·ri·cious·ness *n* -ES : AVARICE

avarish *usu cap, var of* AVAR

'avas *pl of* 'AVA

avascular \(')ā+¦-\ *adj* [2*a-* + *vascular*] : having few or no blood vessels ⟨the lens is a very ~ structure⟩ : lacking vascular tissue ⟨~ plants⟩ — **avascularity** *n* -ES

avast \ə'vast, -aa(ə)st,-aist,-ȧst\ *v imper* [perh. fr. D *houd vast* hold fast, stop, fr. *houd* (imp. of *houden* to hold, stop, fr. MD) + *vast* fast, fr. MD; akin to OHG *haltan* to hold and to OE *fæst* fast — more at HOLD, FAST] — a nautical command to stop or cease ⟨~ heaving⟩ ⟨~ lowering⟩

av·a·tar \'avə,tär, -tȧ(r, ,==':\ *n* -s [Skt *avatāra* descent, fr. *avatarati* he descends, fr. *ava* off, down + *tarati* he passes across or over (akin to L *trans* across, over) — more at TRANS-] **1** *or* **ava·ta·ra** \(,)əvə'tärə, -ȧrə\ : the descent and incarnation of a deity in earthly form — chiefly associated in Hinduism with the incarnations of Vishnu **2 a** : an incarnation or embodiment in human form — usu. used hyperbolically in comparisons ⟨here, one almost fancies, is an Eastern ~ of Mark Twain, telling fresh tales of Huckleberry Finn —*Times Lit. Supp.*⟩ **b** : a remarkably complete manifestation or embodiment usu. in a person, of a concept, philosophy, or tradition ⟨[he] is not merely a conservative, but the very archetype, the ~ of conservatism, since to him conservatism is a condition of existence —*N. Y. Herald Tribune*⟩ **3** : a variant phase or version of a continuing basic entity sometimes implying no more than a change in name ⟨the privileges of the proprietary, whose current ~ was called the Company of the Indies —Bernard De Voto⟩

1**avaunt** \ə'vȯnt, -änt,-ȧnt\ *vb* -ED/-ING/-S [ME *avaunten*, fr. MF *avanter*, fr. *a-* (fr. L *ad-*) + *vanter* to boast — more at VAUNT] *obs* : BOAST, VAUNT

2**avaunt** \"\ *adv* [ME, fr. MF *avant*, fr. L *abante* forward, before, fr. *ab* from, away + *ante* before — more at OF, ANTE-] *archaic* : HENCE 1 ⟨walks thrice round them, bidding malicious spirits ~ —J.G.Frazer⟩ ⟨~ thou very idiot —T.B.Costain⟩

3**avaunt** \"\ *n* -s *obs* : an order to be gone ⟨the devil tempted him but he gave him the ~ —William Barlow⟩

AVC *abbr* automatic volume control

avdp *abbr* avoirdupois

ave \'ä(,)vā, 'ȧ-, -,vē,-vi\ *n* -s [ME, fr. L *ave, have* hail, prob. fr. Punic *ḥwy* live!] **1** : a salutation of greeting or of leave-taking : HAIL, FAREWELL — often used interjectionally **2** [short for *Ave Maria*] **a** *often cap* : AVE MARIA 1 ⟨saying *Aves* and Paternosters⟩ **b** *obs* : AVE MARIA 3

ave *abbr* avenue

AVE *abbr* automatic volume expansion

avel·lan \ə'velən, 'avəl-\ *or* **avel·lane** \-,lān\ *adj* [L *abellana*, *avellana* hazel nut, filbert, fr. fem. of *Abellanus*, *Avellanus* of Abella, fr. *Abella*, *Avella*, ancient town in Italy] **1** : relating to the filbert or hazel **2** *of a cross* : having each of the four arms shaped like a conventional filbert — see CROSS illustration

ave·lla·ne·da \¦ävəzhə¦nāthə, ¦ävələ¦nādə\ *adj, usu cap* [fr. *Avellaneda*, Argentina] : of or from Avellaneda, Argentina : of the kind or style prevalent in Avellaneda

av·el·la·neous \¦avə¦lānēəs, -nyəs\ *adj* [L *abellana*, *avellana* + E *-eous*] : HAZEL

avel·la·no \,ävə'länō, ,a-, -vəl'yä-\ *n* -s [Sp, fr. *avellana* hazelnut, filbert, fr. L *abellana*, *avellana*] : a Chilean tree (*Gevuina avellana*) of the family Proteaceae with tough wood, evergreen foliage, and white flowers succeeded by red fruit containing oily edible seeds

ave ma·ria \¦=(,)= *as at* AVE + mə'rēə, -mä-,-mȧ-\ *also* **ave mary** \-'merē, -mār-,-ma(a)r-, -ri\ *n usu cap A&M* [ME *ave Maria*, fr. ML, hail, Mary!] **1** : a salutation to the Virgin Mary combined as now used in the Roman Catholic Church with a prayer to her as mother of God **2** : a particular time (as in Italy at the ringing of the bells about half an hour after sunset and also at early dawn) when the people repeat the Ave Maria **3** : one of the small beads of a rosary by which Ave Marias are counted

ave·na \ə'vēnə\ *n, cap* [NL, fr. L, oats; akin to Lith *aviža* oats, Russ *oves*] : a genus of widely distributed grasses (family Gramineae) having a loosely paniculate inflorescence, lemmas 2-toothed and usu. awned near the apex, and deeply furrowed grains enclosed in the glumes and sometimes adherent to them — see OAT

avena test *n, usu cap A* [NL *Avena*] : a test of the growth-promoting or sometimes inhibiting value of a substance as judged by the reaction of a growing oat (genus *Avena*) coleoptile to which the substance is applied — see AUXIN

avenge \ə'venj\ *vb* -ED/-ING/-S [ME *avengen*, prob. fr. *a-* (as in *abaten* to abate) + *vengen* to avenge, fr. OF *vengier* — more at VENGEANCE] *vt* **1** : to take vengeance for or on behalf of (oneself or another) ⟨~, O Lord, thy slaughtered saints —John Milton⟩ ⟨he *avenged* himself on his brother's killer⟩ **2** : to exact satisfaction for (a wrong) by punishing the injurer ⟨though he always *avenged* an injury, he never bore malice for one —Charles Kingsley⟩ ~ *vi* : to take vengeance

syn AVENGE and REVENGE agree in meaning to punish a person who has wronged one or someone close to one. They are often used interchangeably but AVENGE more often suggests punishing a person when one is vindicating someone else than oneself or is serving the ends of justice, the suggestion of justice achieved being strong in any application of the word ⟨after all, if other people's children do not like him, he can always *avenge* himself by disliking them twice as much —Robert Lynd⟩ ⟨it was a son who would some day *avenge* his father —Charles Dickens⟩ ⟨his wife . . . entered the gubernatorial campaign to *avenge* her husband —*Amer. Guide Series: Texas*⟩ REVENGE more often applies to vindicating oneself and usu. suggests an evening up of scores or a personal satisfaction more than an achievement of justice, often connoting malice, spite, or vindictive retaliation ⟨the novelist obsessed with the errors of his past . . . is irresistibly drawn to *revenge* himself on his past by rewriting it —C.J.Rolo⟩ ⟨the hope of *revenging* himself on me was a strong inducement —Jane Austen⟩

avenge·ment \-mənt\ *n* -s [ME, fr. *avengen* + *-ment*] : act of taking vengeance

aveng·er \-njə(r)\ *n* -s : one that avenges

aveng·ing *adj* : that takes vengeance or treats revengefully — **aveng·ing·ly** *adv*

ave·nin \ə'vēnən, 'avən-\ *or* **ave·nine** \-,nēn\ *n* -s [ISV *aven-* (fr. L *avena* oats) + *-in*, *-ine*] : the glutelin of oats

av·ens \'avənz\ *n, pl* **avens** [ME *avence*, fr. OF] : a plant of the genus *Geum* — compare HERB BENNET, WATER AVENS

av·en·tail \'avən,tāl\ *n* -s [ME *aventaile*, prob. fr. (assumed) AF *aventaille*, alter. (resulting from incorrect division of *la ventaille* the aventail) of OF *ventaille* — more at VENTAIL] : VENTAIL

aventure *archaic var of* ADVENTURE

1**aven·tu·rine** \ə'venchə,rēn, -,rən\ *also* **avan·tu·rine** \ə'vän-\ *n* -s [F *aventurine*, fr. *aventure* chance; fr. its chance discovery — more at ADVENTURE] **1** : glass containing opaque sparkling particles of foreign material, usu. (1) copper or (2) chromic oxide — called also respectively (1) *gold aventurine* or (2) *chrome aventurine*, *green aventurine* **2** : a translucent quartz spangled throughout with scales of mica or other mineral

2**aventurine** \"\ *also* **avanturine** \"\ *adj* : having the brilliant spangled appearance of aventurine

av·e·nue \'avə,n(y)ü *also* 'aav-, *rapid sometimes* -v(,)nü *or* -vənyə\ *n* -s [MF, fr. fem. of *avenu*, past part. of *avenir* to come to, fr. L *advenire* — more at ADVENE] **1** : an opening or passageway permitting actual approach or entry to a place — often followed by a prepositional phrase indicating a specific purpose ⟨the river is a great ~ of commerce⟩ ⟨a new ~ to India⟩ **2** : a way or means by which an esp. intangible end may be pursued, approached, or accomplished ⟨an ~ of research⟩ ⟨new ~*s* to fame⟩ **3 a** *chiefly Brit* : the principal walk or driveway to a house situated off the main road **b** : a broad passageway bordered on either side by trees ⟨an ~ of poplars⟩ **4** : a city street esp. when broad and attractive

1**aver** \'āvər\ *now chiefly Scot var of* AIVER

2**aver** \ə'vər, +V -ər·; -vā, +V -ər· *also* -ār\ *vt* **averred**; **averred; averring; avers** [ME *averren*, fr. MF *averer*, fr. ML *adverare* to confirm as authentic, fr. L *ad-* + ML *-verare* (fr. L *verus* true) — more at VERY] **1** *obs* : to acknowledge (a statement) as true **2** *archaic* : to acknowledge the existence of : admit as valid or real **3 a** : AVOUCH, VERIFY **b** : ASSERT, CLAIM, DECLARE **4** : to affirm or declare in a positive confident manner : insist emphatically ⟨he had proudly *averred* that he needed no help⟩ **syn** see ASSERT

1**av·er·age** \'av(ə)rij, -rēj\ *n* -s [modif. (influenced by E *-age*) of MF *avarie* damage to ship or cargo, port dues, fr. OIt *avaria* damage to ship or cargo, fr. Ar *'awārīyah* damaged merchandise, fr. *'awār* defect, damage, fr. *'ār* to harm] **1** *obs* : a tariff on goods transported by ship **2 a** *obs* : a charge payable by the owner or consignor in addition to the regular charge for freight of goods shipped **b** : sundry petty charges regularly and necessarily defrayed by the master (as port charges, pilotage) formerly borne partly by the ship and partly by the cargo but now usu. included in the freight **3** *marine insurance* **a** : a less than total loss sustained by a ship or cargo **b** : a charge arising from damage caused by sea perils customarily distributed equitably and proportionately among all chargeable with it **c** : an incidence of such loss or charge **4** : ARITHMETIC MEAN **5** : an estimate or approximate representation of an arithmetic mean ⟨students are expected to maintain a B ~ or better⟩ **6** : something felt as representing an arithmetic average and hence typical of a group, class, or series ⟨the simple act of ringing doorbells while seeking votes introduced him to the ~ —John Mason Brown⟩ **7** : a ratio expressing the average performance esp. of an athletic team or an athlete computed according to the number of opportunities for successful performance ⟨in a batting slump his ~ dropped from .303 to .261⟩ ⟨the team ~ so far this season⟩ **8** : the average price of a group of securities or stocks (as industrials or railroads) used as a measure of changes in price levels — usu. used in pl. ⟨the current position of leading ~*s*⟩

syn AVERAGE, MEAN, MEDIAN, NORM, PAR can mean in common a number, quantity, or condition that represents a middle point between extremes. AVERAGE is chiefly an arithmetical term to indicate the figure arrived at by finding the sum of a given number of unequal figures and dividing by the number of figures ⟨the *average* of 10, 12, 14, 16, 18, and 20 is 15, that is, 90 divided by 6⟩ and is usu. computed as a means of getting a fair general estimate of something comprising a series of unequal but like things (as grades in school courses, depths of snowfall in successive years, weekly sales over a period of weeks). In certain applications, as in sports or gambling, an AVERAGE is usu. the proportion, expressed in a percentage, of successful performances (as hits achieved in a single baseball season by a ballplayer) to opportunities for or attempts at successful performance (as the total number of times a ballplayer goes to bat in a single baseball season); in other applications, as in statistical analysis, it may be, for example, the proportion, expressed in a percentage, of deaths in a given period for every 1000 citizens over 50 years old or automobile accidents in a given area over a given time for every 100 drivers. It may extend to designate a person who stands at a roughly estimated middle level in a scale presumably determining the intellectual or cultural capacity or quality of a group, esp. a society ⟨Dartmouth's Shattuck Observatory has been measuring snowfall since 1867, and the *average* at Hanover is six feet —R.S.Monahan⟩ ⟨only those renters are admitted whose incomes fall within certain fixed limits — limits which are, however, higher than the *average* of the people who formerly lived in the area —*Amer. Guide Series: Minn.*⟩ ⟨it is enough if we are of the same moral and mental stature as the "main" or "mean" part of men — that is to say as the *average* —Samuel Butler †1902⟩ ⟨the cleverest boys go to the École Normale Supérieure and do not mix any longer with the *average* —Bertrand Russell⟩ MEAN indicates a point midway between extremes, in an older sense signifying a point midway between any two extremes (as of condition, quality, or intensity) but today being confined chiefly to mathematics or statistics in which it may signify either an arithmetical or geometric midpoint, that is, a figure midway between two others (as a lowest and a highest figure in a series of temperature readings) or a figure arrived at by finding the square root of the product of two numbers or quantities ⟨a golden *mean* between extravagance and miserliness⟩ ⟨10 is the arithmetical *mean* of 4 and 16⟩ ⟨8 is the geometric *mean* of 4 and 16, that is, the square root of 64⟩ MEDIAN indicates a midpoint in position but is used chiefly in statistics to indicate the point below which there are as many instances as there are above ⟨a *median* of public opinion⟩ ⟨the average pay of five men earning respectively 10, 14, 20, 26, and 40 dollars a day is $22 but the *median* is only $20 since there are two men earning below and two above this⟩ NORM designates the sometimes computed sometimes estimated average performance or achievement or, often, average minimum performance or achievement, of a group, class, or category, set up as the standard for members ⟨demands made upon children of a certain age should be adjusted to the *norm* for children of that age group⟩ ⟨construction workers . . . protesting the imposition of a 10 percent increase in the working *norm* —*Newsweek*⟩ ⟨those which fall below the required level of academic decency are encouraged to bring their curricula and degrees up to the *norm* —W.L.Sperry⟩ PAR in this connection more frequently refers to the average performance or condition of an individual or established for an individual, analogous to a norm for a group, though sometimes and esp. in British use PAR may refer to an average in amount (as of barometric pressure) ⟨*par* for a fast typist in English: 120 words⟩ ⟨40 pounds a day is considered *par* for a Holstein —*New Yorker*⟩ ⟨while 200 pounds or slightly thereunder is *par* for him, he has a tendency toward fatness —E.J.Kahn⟩

— **on an average** *or* **on the average** : taking the mean of unequal numbers or quantities : taking the typical example of the group under consideration ⟨these are, *on the average*, a better class of article⟩

2**average** \"\ *adj* **1** : equaling an arithmetic mean ⟨an ~ annual rainfall of 20 inches⟩ **2 a** : approximating or resembling an arithmetic mean specif. in being about midway between extremes : not out of the ordinary for members of the group under consideration ⟨served with ~ merit under Grant —H.E.Nettles⟩ ⟨a man of ~ height⟩ : TYPICAL, COMMON, ORDINARY ⟨not an ~ wind but a decidedly abnormal one⟩ ⟨typical of the middle class at its most ~ —*N.Y.Herald Tribune*⟩ **b** *of a color* : medial in value ⟨slightly redder than ~ mustard tan⟩ **3** *maritime law* : assessed according to the laws of average

3**average** \"\ *vb* -ED/-ING/-S *vi* **1 a** : to be, on an average ⟨in these waters the fish ~ larger⟩ : amount to or come to, on an average ⟨losses will ~ 5000 dollars a year⟩ ⟨these poles ~ 10 feet in length⟩ — sometimes used with *out* ⟨the gain *averaged* out to 20 percent⟩ **b** *of a color* : to have a medial value of a specified color **2** : to buy or sell additional shares or commodities when the price falls or rises so as to obtain a more favorable average price — often used with *up* or *to* ~ *vt* **1** : to do, get, make, spend, have, on the average or as an average sum or quantity ⟨~*s* 20 inches a year rainfall⟩ ⟨~ two days a week on the golf course⟩ ⟨a writer who ~*s* three stories a month⟩ **2** : to find the arithmetic mean of (a series of unequal quantities) : obtain an average of ⟨~ the hourly temperature readings⟩ **3 a** : to bring toward the average : reduce or level out to an average ⟨the *averaging* of tendencies, a movement toward a mean —John Dewey⟩ — sometimes used with *out* **b** : to divide among a number according to a given proportion ⟨~ a loss⟩

average agreement *n* : an arrangement by which penalties for failure to meet a requirement in certain instances (as in demurrage) may be offset by more than meeting it in others

average bond *n, marine insurance* : a bond required to procure delivery of goods and given by a consignee to the master of a ship for prompt payment of any chargeable general average when its amount is ascertained

average clause *n* **1** : a clause in an insurance policy that restricts the amount payable to a sum not to exceed the value of the property destroyed and that bears the same proportion to the loss as the face of the policy does to the value of the property insured — compare COINSURANCE **2** : a clause in a marine insurance policy that exempts the insurer from particular average and in respect of some things from all average

average due date *n* : a computed date on which with fairness to debtor and creditor one settlement in full may be made for all variously dated items in an account

average life *n, of a radioactive substance* : the average of the times required for the disintegration of all the atoms, being 1.443 times the half-life

av·er·age·ly *adv* : to a degree representative of some understood average or norm : MODERATELY, FAIRLY ⟨he was an ~ good barber — as good as could be expected —Robert Lynd⟩ ⟨a more than ~ happy marriage —Edward Sapir⟩

av·er·age·ness \-nəs\ *n* -ES : the quality or state of being average — often used to imply mediocrity or ordinariness

average out *vi* : to close out a stock or commodity transaction without loss or at a profit by averaging

average tare *n* : tare estimated from the weight of a number of packages selected from a large number of similar ones

aver·ment \ə'vərmənt, -vəm-\ *n* -S [ME *averrement*, fr. MF *averement*, fr. *averer* to verify + *-ment* — more at AVER] **1** *obs* : the establishment of a fact by evidence **2** *law* : a positive statement of facts : an allegation made with an offer to justify or prove what is alleged : VERIFICATION ⟨the ~ alleged negligence on the part of the defendant⟩ **3 a** : the act of making an averment **b** : a positive assertion : AFFIRMATION

aver·nal \ə'vərnᵊl\ *or* **aver·ni·an** \-nēən, -nyən\ *adj, sometimes cap* [*avernal* fr. L *Avernalis* of Avernus, fr. *Avernus*, lake near Pozzuoli, Italy (now *Lago Averno*), reputed because of its depth and stench to lead to the underworld, underworld + L *-alis* -al; *avernian* fr. *Avernus* + E *-ian*] : INFERNAL

averred *past of* AVER

av·er·rhoa \,avə'rōə, ə'verəwə\ *n, cap* [NL, fr. *Averroës, Averrhoës* †1198 Spanish-Arabian philosopher] : a genus of East Indian trees (family Oxalidaceae) with pinnate leaves — see BILIMBI, CARAMBOLA

averring *pres part of* AVER

aver·ro·ism \ə'verə,wizəm, a'v- *also* ,avə'rō,iz-\ *n* -S *usu cap* [*Averroës* + E *-ism*] **1** : the doctrines of Averroës whose teachings were mainly written in the form of Neoplatonically influenced commentaries on Aristotle and differed from Avicennism in affirming that the whole world is created all at once by God directly, eternally, and continuously and that individual souls are not immortal except insofar as they participate in a universal intellect **2** : any of numerous and widely diverse doctrines of Jewish and Christian teachers in the 13th and later centuries regarded by themselves or by their critics as followers of Averroes and repeatedly condemned esp. because of their real or supposed denial of human freedom and personal immortality

aver·ro·ist \-rawəst,-rōəst\ *n* -S *usu cap* : an adherent to the doctrines of Averroism

aver·ro·is·tic \ə¦verə¦wistik, a¦v- *also* ,avərō¦is-\ *adj, usu cap* : of, relating to, or characteristic of Averroism

averruncate *vt* -ED/-ING/-S [E *averruncate* (partly influenced in meaning by L *eruncare* to weed out), fr. L *averruncatus*, past part. of *averruncare* to avert, fr. *a*, *ab* from, away + *verruncare* to turn; perh. akin to L *verrere* to sweep — more at OF, WAR] **1** *obs* : to ward off or avert (as an evil) **2** *obs* : to weed out : UPROOT : cut away (as weeds) : REMOVE — **averruncation** *n* -S

avers *pres 3d sing of* AVER

aversation *n* -S [L *aversation-, aversatio*, fr. *aversatus* (past part. of *aversari* to turn away, fr. *aversus*) + *-ion-, -io* -ion] **1** *obs* : an act of turning away : ESTRANGEMENT **2** *archaic* : AVERSION

¹averse \ə'vərs, -vōs,-vəis\ *adj* [L *aversus*, past part. of *avertere* to avert] **1** : having an active feeling of repugnance, dislike, or distaste for something and tending to avoid, spurn, or evade it as a result — used postpositively and predicatively, followed by *to* or chiefly Brit. *from* ⟨what cat's ~ to fish —Thomas Gray⟩ ⟨I am inveterately ~ from any sort of fuss —Max Beerbohm⟩ ⟨he is not ~ to a glass of wine or two with his friends —Green Peyton⟩ **2** *archaic* : turned backward or away **3** *archaic* **a** : ADVERSE **b** : OPPOSITE **4** *bot* : turned away from the stem or axis — opposed to *adverse* **syn** see DISINCLINED

²averse *vb* -ED/-ING/-S *obs* : to turn away

averse·ly \ə'vərslē, -vōs-,-vəis-, -li\ *adv* : in an averse manner, direction, or position

averse·ness *n* -ES : AVERSION

aver·sion \ə'vərzhən, -vōzh-,-vəizh- *also* a'v-; *Brit usu & US also* -shən\ *n* -S [L *aversion-, aversio*, fr. *aversus* + *-ion-, -io* -ion] **1** *obs* : the physical or mental act of averting **2** [LL *aversion-, aversio*, fr. L] **a** : a feeling of revulsion and repugnance towards something usu. coupled with an intense desire to avoid or turn from it ⟨what had been terror and dislike before, was now absolute ~ —Jane Austen⟩ **b** : a firmly settled and vehement dislike : ANTIPATHY — used usu. with *to, for*, or *from* ⟨an ~ to crowds and crowd behavior —H.G.Wells⟩ ⟨he had the most unconquerable ~ for Tristram —Laurence Sterne⟩ ⟨a corpulency of the body, accentuated by an unhappy ~ from exercise —Ernest Barker⟩ **3** : a person or thing that is the object of aversion ⟨Mrs. Susan Crosstitch, whom you know to be my utter ~ —Henry Fielding⟩ ⟨a writer whose pet ~ was the use of clichés⟩ **4** : antagonism (sense 3) between colonies of microorganisms **syn** see DISLIKE

aver·sive \-siv,-ziv\ *adj* [L *aversus* + E *-ive*] **1** : showing aversion : characterized by aversion **2** : tending to avert : for the purpose of averting ⟨~ magic to drive off evil⟩

avert \ə'vərt, -vōt,-vəit *also* a'v-; *usu* -d·+V\ *vb* -ED/-ING/-S [ME *averten*, fr. MF *avertir*, fr. L *avertere*, fr. *a*, *ab* from, away + *vertere* to turn — more at OF, WORTH] *vt* **1** : to turn away or aside (one's face, eyes, thoughts) esp. in order to escape something dangerous, unpleasant, or disconcerting ⟨some mortar and dust came dropping down, which he ~*ed* his face to avoid —Charles Dickens⟩ ⟨he . . . ~*s* his attention from an uncomfortable topic as soon as possible —Walter Moberly⟩ **2** *archaic* : to cause to turn, change, or deviate : ESTRANGE, ALIENATE ⟨so many discordant and contrary opinions . . . ~ them from the church —Francis Bacon⟩ **3** : to anticipate and ward off : prevent the occurrence or unfortunate, dangerous, and dire effects of ⟨war was ~*ed* by a timely peace mission⟩ ⟨many highway accidents can be ~*ed* by courtesy⟩ ~ *vi, archaic* : to turn away — usu. used with *from* **syn** see PREVENT, TURN

averted *adj* : turned away esp. with the intention of avoiding ⟨she closed it, with ~ eyes, and pushed it away —Jane Austen⟩

Av·er·tin \ə'vərtən, ə'vərtᵊn\ *trademark* — used for tribromoethanol

¹aves *pl of* AVE

²aves \'ā(,)vēz\ *n pl, cap* [NL, fr. L, pl. of *avis* bird — more at AVIARY] : a class of Vertebrata derived from Reptilia and including all fossil and recent birds

¹aves·tan \ə'vestən\ *adj, usu cap* [*Avesta*, sacred books of the ancient Zoroastrian religion (fr. MPer *Avastāk*) + E *-an*] : of or relating to the Avesta or to Avestan

²avestan \"\ *or* **aves·tic** \-tik\ *n, cap* [*Avesta* + E *-an* or *-ic*] : one of the two ancient languages comprising Old Iranian and that in which the sacred books of the Zoroastrian religion were written — compare OLD PERSIAN

avg *abbr* average

av·gas \'av + ,-\ *n* [aviation *gas*oline] : gasoline produced for aircraft engines

avian \'āvēən\ *also* **avine** \-,vīn,-,vən\ *adj* [L *avis* bird + E *-ian* or *-ine*] **1** : of, relating to, or characteristic of birds ⟨~ families⟩ ⟨~ studies⟩ **2** : derived from a bird ⟨~ tubercle bacilli in a goat⟩

avian diphtheria *n* : FOWL POX b

avian encephalomyelitis *n* : an acute usu. fatal virus infection of young chickens characterized by ataxic gait and weakening of the legs and by tremor esp. of the head and neck

avi·an·ize \'āvēə,nīz\ *vt* -ED/-ING/-S : to modify (microorganisms) by repeated culture in the developing chick embryo; *specif* : to attenuate (a virus in the preparation of vaccines) by such means

avian leukosis complex *or* **avian lymphomatosis** *n* : the leukoses of fowls

avian monocytosis *n* : BLUE COMB

avian osteopetrosis *n* : OSTEOPETROSIS 2

avian pneumoencephalitis *n* : NEWCASTLE DISEASE

avian tuberculosis *n* : bird tuberculosis usu. caused by a bacterium (*Mycobacterium avium*); *also* : infection of mammals (as swine) by this species of *Mycobacterium*

avi·a·rist \'āvēərəst, -ē,er-\ *n* -S : one who keeps an aviary

avi·ary \'āvē,erē, *esp Brit* -vyər-\ *n* -ES [L *aviarium*, fr. *avis* bird + *-arium*; akin to Gk *aetos* eagle, Skt *vi* bird] : a house, enclosure, or large cage for confining live birds ⟨a glass-domed ~ . . . houses more than 500 birds —*Amer. Guide Series: Mich.*⟩

avi·ate \'āvē,āt, 'av-\ *vi* -ED/-ING/-S [back-formation fr. *aviation & aviator*] : to navigate the air (as by operating an aircraft) : FLY

avi·a·tion \,āvē'āshən, ,av- — *the variant with* a *in 1st syll seems to be more frequent for "aviation" than for "aviator"*\ *n* -S *often attrib* [F, fr. *avi-* (fr. L *avis*) + *-ation*] **1** : the operation of heavier-than-air aircraft **2** : military aircraft ⟨carrier-based ~⟩ ⟨his ~ had sunk or damaged 52 Japanese vessels —*Newsweek*⟩ **3** : aircraft manufacture, development, and design esp. of a particular group or nation ⟨advances in American ~⟩

aviation badge *n* : WINGS

aviation cadet *n* : a person in training to become an air-force officer with an aeronautical rating — abbr. *AC*

aviation engineer *n* : one who constructs runways or other field installations required for air operations

aviation insurance *n* : insurance against claims and losses arising from the ownership, maintenance, or use of aircraft, hangars, or airports including damage to aircraft, personal injury, and property damage

aviation medicine *n* : a branch of medicine including aeromedicine and space medicine and dealing with the study, prevention, alleviation, and cure of diseases and ailments connected with aviation

avi·a·tor \'āvē,ād·ə(r), 'av-, -,ātə- — *see* AVIATION\ *n* -S [F *aviateur*, fr. *avi-* (fr. L *avis*) + *-ateur* (as in *amateur*)] **1** *obs* : FLYING MACHINE **2** : the operator or pilot of an airplane

avi·a·to·ri·al \¦==,ə¦tōrēəl\ *adj* : of or relating to aviation or an aviator

aviator's ear *n* : AERO-OTITIS MEDIA

avi·a·trix \,==¦ā·triks, -ēks\ *also* **avi·a·tress** \'==,ā·trəs\ *n, pl* **aviatrixes** \-ksəz\ *or* **aviatri·ces** \,==¦ā·trə,sēz\ *also* **aviatresses** \'==,ā·trəsəz\ : a woman aviator

av·i·cen·nia \,avə'senēə\ *n, cap* [NL, fr. *Avicenna* †1037 Arab physician and philosopher + NL *-ia*] : a small genus of tropical shrubs or trees (family Verbenaceae) having opposite evergreen leaves and terminal clusters of small flowers with five sepals, four petals, and a capsular fruit — see AVICENNIACEAE, BLACK MANGROVE, WHITE MANGROVE

av·i·cen·ni·a·ce·ae \,==,==¦āsē,ē\ *n pl, cap* [NL, fr. *Avicennia*, type genus + *-aceae*] *in some classifications* : a family coextensive with the genus *Avicennia*

av·i·cen·nism \,avə'se,nizəm\ *n* -S *usu cap* [*Avicenna* + E *-ism*] : the doctrines of the philosopher Avicenna who taught a theory of emanation and a doctrine widely accepted in the middle ages that universals exist in rebus as the general characters of particulars but ante res only in the mind of God and post res only as abstractions in the human mind

avi·cide \'āvə,sīd, 'av-\ *n* -S [L *avis* bird + E *-cide* — more at AVIARY] : the killing of birds

avic·o·lous \ā'vikələs, ə'v-\ *adj* [L *avis* + E *-colous*] : living on birds ⟨~ bird lice⟩

avic·u·lar·ia \ə,vikyə'la(a)rēə\ *n, cap* [NL, fr. L *avicula* small bird (dim. of *avis* bird) + NL *-aria*] : a genus of large tropical spiders containing a number of typical bird spiders

avic·u·lar·i·an \¦==¦==rēən\ *adj* [NL *avicularium* + E *-an*] : of or relating to an avicularium or avicularia

avic·u·la·ri·idae \ə,vikyələ'rīə,dē\ [NL, fr. *Avicularia*, type genus + *-idae*] *syn of* THERAPHOSIDAE

avic·u·lar·i·um \ə,vikyə'la(a)rēəm\ *n, pl* **avicular·ia** \-ēə\ [NL, fr. L *avicula* + *-arium* -ary] : a small prehensile process resembling a bird's head with a movable mandible found on many bryozoans

av·i·cu·li·dae \,avə'kyülə,dē\ [NL, fr. *Avicula* (syn. of *Pteria*), type genus (fr. L *avicula* small bird) + *-idae*; fr. the winglike expansions of the hinge of some species] *syn of* PTERIIDAE

av·i·cul·tur·al \¦āvə¦kəlch(ə)rəl, ¦av-\ *adj* : of, relating, or devoted to the interests of aviculture ⟨an ~ society⟩

avi·cul·ture \'āvə,kəlchə(r), 'av-\ *n* -S [L *avis* bird + E *culture*] : the rearing and care of birds, esp. of wild birds in captivity — **avi·cul·tur·ist** \¦==¦==ch(ə)rəst\ *n* -S

av·id \'avəd *sometimes* 'āv-\ *adj* [F or L; F *avide*, fr. L *avidus*, fr. *avēre* to long for; akin to Goth *awiliuþ* thanks, Gk *enēēs* gentle, Skt *avati* he favors] **1** : craving eagerly : desirous to the point of greed ⟨his ~ fondness for the limelight —*Time*⟩ — often used with *for*, sometimes with *of* ⟨convivial, bawdy, robustly ~ for pleasure —Scott Fitzgerald⟩ ⟨a powerful will . . . ~ of glory —H.A.Overstreet⟩ **2** : characterized by enthusiasm, ardor, and vigorous pursuit ⟨an ~ reader⟩ ⟨an ~ gardener⟩ **syn** see EAGER

av·i·din \'avədən\ *n* -S [*avid* + *-in*; fr. its having an avidity for biotin] : a protein found in white of egg that combines with biotin, rendering it inactive and leading to egg-white injury

avid·i·ty \ə'vidəd·ē, -dətē, -i *also* a'v- *or* ā'v-\ *n* -ES [ME *avidite*, fr. MF or L; MF *avidité*, fr. L *aviditat-, aviditas*, fr. *avidus* + *-itat-, -itas* -ity] **1** : the quality or state of being avid : great or extreme eagerness or enthusiasm ⟨he seized his opportunity with ~⟩ ⟨all the ~ of a love-hungered soul —Joseph Furphy⟩ **2** : an intense desire for gain or profit : AVARICE **3** *chem* **a** : the strength of an acid or base dependent on its degree of dissociation **b** : AFFINITY 2b **4** : a characteristic of antibodies (as antitoxins) that tends to enhance their rate of combination or firmness of combination with antigen

av·id·ly \'avədlē, -li *sometimes* 'āv-\ *adv* : in an avid manner

avi·dya \(,)ə'vid(,)yä\ *also* **avij·ja** \-i(,)jä\ *n* -S [Skt *avidyā*, lit., ignorance, fr. *a-* ²a- + *vidyā* knowledge — more at WIT] *Hinduism & Buddhism* : IGNORANCE; *specif* : blindness to ultimate truth

avi·fau·na \¦āvə¦fònə, ¦av-\ *n* -S [NL, fr. L *avis* bird + NL *fauna*] : the birds or the kinds of birds of a region, period, or environment — **avi·fau·nal** \¦==¦==nᵊl\ *adj* — **avi·fau·nal·ly** \-nᵊlē\ *adv* — **avi·fau·nis·tic** \¦==¦==¦nistik\ *adj*

av·i·ga·tion \,avə'gāshən, ,āv-\ *n* -S [L *avis* bird + E *-gation* (as in *navigation*) — more at AVIARY] : navigation of aircraft

avi·gnon berry *or* **avignon grain** \ä'vinyən-\ *n, usu cap A* [fr. *Avignon*, France] : any of several buckthorn berries from France — called also *French berry*; compare PERSIAN BERRY

avi·gnon·ese \¦ä¦vinyə¦nēz, -ēs\ *adj, usu cap* [*Avignon* + E *-ese*] : of or belonging to Avignon or to the residence there of the popes during the period 1309–1377

avile *vt* -ED/-ING/-S [ME *avilen*, fr. OF *avilier*, fr. *a* to (fr. L *ad*) + *-viler* (fr. *vil* vile) — more at AT, VILE] *obs* : ABASE, DEBASE, VILIFY

a vin·cu·lo ma·tri·mo·nii \ä¦viŋkü(,)lō ,mä·trē'mōnē,ē, ā¦v . . . kyə . . . ,ma . . . nē,ī\ *also* **a vinculo** *adj* [NL, lit., from the bond of marriage] *of a divorce* : ABSOLUTE ⟨granted a decree *a vinculo*⟩

avine *var of* AVIAN

avion \ävyōⁿ\ *n* -S [F, fr. L *avis* bird — more at AVIARY] : AIRPLANE

avi·on·ic \¦āvē¦änik, ¦av-, -ēk\ *adj* [back-formation fr. *avionics*] : of, for, or relating to the field of avionics

avi·on·ics \,==¦==niks\ *n pl* [*avi*ation electr*onics*] : the development and production of electrical and electronic devices for use in aviation, esp. of electronic control systems for aircraft and airborne weapons; *also* : the devices and systems so developed ⟨~ design and procurement⟩

avirulence \(')ā+\ *n* -S [²a- + *virulence*] : lack of virulence

avirulent \(')ā+\ *adj* [ISV ²a- + *virulent*] : not virulent — compare NONPATHOGENIC

avi·ta·min·o·sis \¦ā,vīd·əmə'nōsəs\ *n, pl* **avitamino·ses** \-ō,sēz\ [NL, fr. ²a- + ISV *vitamin* + NL *-osis*] : a disease in man and animals resulting from a deficiency of one or more vitamins — often used in combination to identify the vitamin involved ⟨~ A⟩ — **avi·ta·mi·not·ic** \-¦näd·ik\ *adj*

avizandum \,avi'zandəm\ *n* -S [ML, neut. of *avizandus*, gerundive of *avizare, avisare, advisare* to consider, fr. MF *aviser* — more at ADVISE] *Scots law* : private consideration

avn *abbr* aviation

avo \'ä(,)vü\ *n* -S [Pg] **1** : a unit of value in Macao equal to ¹⁄₁₀₀ pataca — see MONEY table **2** : a former unit of value in Timor

avo·ca·do \,avə'käd(,)dō, -'kä-, (*esp when "pear" follows*) -,də, *also* ,äv- *or* ,āv-\ *also* **avocado pear** *n, pl* **avocados** *also* **avocadoes** [modif. of Sp *aguacate*, fr. Nahuatl *ahuacatl*, short for *ahuacacuahuitl*, lit., testicle tree, fr. *ahuacatl* testicle + *cuahuitl* tree; fr. its use as an aphrodisiac] **1** : the pulpy green or purple somewhat pear-shaped edible fruit of various tropical American trees of the genus *Persea*, esp. of cultivated varieties originating in the West Indies, Guatemala, and Mexico — called also *alligator pear* **2** : a tree bearing avocados

av·o·ca·tion \,avə'kāshən\ *n* -S [L *avocation-, avocatio*, fr. *avocatus* (past part. of *avocare* to call away, fr. *a*, *ab* from, away + *vocare* to call, fr. *voc-, vox* voice) + *-ion-, -io* -ion — more at OF, VOICE] **1** *archaic* : a calling away : DIVERSION, DISTRACTION ⟨try, by every method of ~ and amusement, whether you cannot get the better of that dejection —Thomas Gray⟩ **2** : a subordinate occupation pursued in addition to one's regular work esp. for enjoyment : HOBBY ⟨a lawyer by profession but painting has been his ~ for years⟩ — opposed to *vocation* **3** : regular or customary work or employment : VOCATION — **av·o·ca·tion·al** \¦==¦==shənᵊl, -shnəl\ *adj*

av·o·cet \'avə,set\ *n* -S [F & It; F *avocette*, fr. It *avocetta*, *avosetta*] : any of several rather large long-legged shore birds (genus *Recurvirostra*) having webbed feet and a slender upwardly curved bill — compare STILT

European avocet

av·o·di·re \¦avədə¦rā\ *n* -S [F *avodiré*] **1** : the smooth-textured decorative whitish to pale yellow wood of a large tropical West African tree (*Turraeanthus africana*) of the mahogany family used for cabinetmaking **2** : the tree that produces avodire

avo·ga·drite \,avə'gä,drīt, ,äv-\ *n* -S [It *avogadrite*, fr. Count Amedeo *Avogadro* †1856 Ital. chemist and physicist + It *-ite*] : a potassium and cesium fluoborate $(K,Cs)BF_4$ occurring in small crystals on Vesuvian lava

avo·ga·dro number *or* **avogadro constant** \¦==¦=(,)drō-\ *n, usu cap A* [after Count *Avogadro*] : the number of atoms in a gram atom or of molecules in a gram molecule of any substance (as for oxygen the number of atoms in 16 grams), its value being 6.023×10^{23} — compare AVOGADRO'S LAW

avogadro's law *or* **avogadro's hypothesis** *n, usu cap A* : a law in chemistry: equal volumes of all gases at the same temperature and pressure contain equal numbers of molecules — compare GAY-LUSSAC'S LAW 1

avo·gram \'avə,gram\ *n* -S [*Avogadro* + *gram*] : a unit of mass and weight equal to one gram divided by the Avogadro number

avoid \ə'vȯid\ *vb* -ED/-ING/-S [ME *avoiden*, fr. OF *esvuidier*, fr. *es-* (fr. L *ex* out) + *vuidier* to empty — more at EX-, VOID] *vt* **1** *obs* **a** : VOID **b** : EXPEL **2** *archaic* : to depart or withdraw from : LEAVE **3** *law* : to make void : ANNUL, VACATE, DEFEAT, EVADE, INVALIDATE ⟨~ a plea⟩ **4 a** : to keep away from : stay clear of ⟨she was a professional do-gooder . . . and Horace Mann ~*ed* her —H.S.Commager⟩ **b** : to prevent the occurrence or effectiveness of ⟨be careful to ~ cracking the glass⟩ : SIDESTEP : BYPASS ⟨he is also a Puritan who does not smoke and drinks only to ~ an issue —*Amer. Fabrics*⟩ : refrain from ⟨they should ~ bringing out sensational books even if they promise to sell well —Lister Hill⟩ ~ *vi, obs* : RETREAT, WITHDRAW — usu. followed by a preposition ⟨David ~*ed* out of his presence —1 Sam 18:11 (AV)⟩ **syn** see ESCAPE

avoid·a·ble \-dəbəl\ *adj* : that can be avoided — **avoid·a·bly** \-blē, -li\ *adv*

avoid·ance \-dᵊn(t)s\ *n* -S [ME *avoidaunce*, fr. *avoiden* to avoid + *-aunce* -ance] **1** *obs* **a** : an action of emptying, vacating, or clearing away **b** : OUTLET **2** : VACANCY — used esp. of an office or benefice ⟨the next ~ of an abbacy⟩ **3** : the act of annulling or making void : ANNULMENT ⟨~ of a contract⟩ **4** : an act or practice of avoiding something undesirable or unwelcome ⟨~ of danger⟩ ⟨the use of merger agreements . . . as a means of tax ~ —*Va. Law Rev.*⟩ **5** : abstention from various types of social contact with persons of specified relationships, esp. with those of the opposite sex that are related by marriage (as a parent-in-law), a custom overtly signifying respect and difference in status and amounting to a taboo among some primitive peoples — compare JOKING RELATIONSHIP **6** : the introduction of new material in pleading in order to avoid the effect of known and admitted facts presented in an adversary's former pleading ⟨a plea in ~⟩

avoiding reaction *n* : a reaction away from a stimulus : a negative tropism or taxis

¹av·oir·du·pois \,avə(r)də'pȯiz, '==,=\ *n* [alter. (influenced by F *du* of the) of earlier *averdepois*, *avoir de pois*, fr. ME *avoir de pois, aver de peis* goods sold by weight, fr. OF, lit., goods of weight, fr. *aver* property, goods + *de* of (fr. L *de* from) + *pois, peis* weight — more at AIVER, DE-, POISE] **1** : AVOIRDUPOIS WEIGHT **2** : WEIGHT, HEAVINESS; *specif* : pėrsonal weight : FATNESS, FAT ⟨the best advertisements for ~ since Santa Claus —Coulton Waugh⟩

²avoirdupois \"\ *adj* : expressed in avoirdupois weight ⟨~ units⟩ ⟨ounce ~⟩ — abbr. *av, avdp, avoir*

avoirdupois pound *n* : POUND 1b

avoirdupois weight *n* : the series of units of weight based on the pound of 16 ounces and the ounce of 16 drams — see MEASURE table

avond·bloem \'ävən,blüm\ *n* -S [obs. Afrik (now *aandblom*), fr. *avond* evening (fr. MD *āvont, āvent*) + *bloem* flower, fr. MD *bloeme*; akin to OHG *āband* evening and to OHG *bluoma* flower — more at EVEN, BLOOM] : a southern African irislike bulbous plant (*Hesperantha falcata*) having claret-red flowers

avos *pl of* AVO

¹avouch \ə'vaůch\ *vb* -ED/-ING/-ES [ME *avouchen*, fr. MF *avochier* to summon, call to one's aid, fr. L *advocare* — more at ADVOCATE] *vt* **1** *obs* **a** : to appeal to or cite as an authority for a statement **2** : to declare as a matter of fact or as a thing that can be proved : AFFIRM ⟨~ the contrary⟩ ⟨unless Mr. Smith ~*es* and proves that she changed the spelling —Isabel Paterson⟩ **3** : to maintain as just or true : vouch for : GUARANTEE ⟨~*ed* it for the law of God —John Milton⟩ **4** : to acknowledge esp. as one's own : ACCEPT, CONFESS ⟨thou hast ~*ed* the Lord . . . to be thy God —Deut 26:17 (AV)⟩ : take responsibility for ⟨~ those unjust actions⟩ ~ *vi, archaic* : to give guarantee or assurance : VOUCH ⟨I cannot ~ for her reputation —Daniel Defoe⟩ **syn** see ASSERT

²avouch \"\ *n* -ES : the act of avouching

avouch·ment \-mənt\ *n* -S : the act of avouching : AFFIRMATION, ASSURANCE

avour·neen \ə'vůr,nēn\ *n* -S [IrGael *a mhuirnīn* oh, darling!, fr. *a* oh + *muirnīn* darling, fr. MIr *mūirnīn*, dim. of *mūirn* affection, joy] *Irish* : DARLING, SWEETHEART

¹avow \ə'vaů\ *vt* -ED/-ING/-S [ME *avowen*, fr. OF *avouer*, fr. L *advocare* to summon, call to one's aid] **1** *obs* : to acknowledge (a person) as one's own : acknowledge with approval (an agent's actions) **2 a** : to assert or declare as a fact : CLAIM ⟨the modest procedure is not to ~ loudly . . . our love of truth —G.W.Sherburn⟩ ⟨I can . . . ~ him to be the best family a boy ever had —W.J.Locke⟩ **b** : to acknowledge and assert (an act, a purpose) with frankness and determination : declare openly, bluntly, and without shame ⟨the frankness to ~ poverty —G.B.Shaw⟩ **3** *law* : to acknowledge and justify (an act done); *specif* : to make an avowry of **syn** see ACKNOWLEDGE, ASSERT

²avow \"\ *n* -S [ME, fr. *avowen* to avow, to bind by a vow, fr. MF *avouer*, fr. *a-* (fr. L *ad-*) + *vouer* to vow — more at VOW] *archaic* : a solemn promise : VOW

avow·al \ə'vaů(ə)l\ *n* -S [*avow* + *-al*] : an open declaration or frank acknowledgment ⟨an ~ of principle⟩

avow·ant \-aůənt\ *n* -S [MF *avouant*, pres. part. of *avouer* to avow] : the defendant in replevin who avows the distress of the goods and justifies the taking

avowed \-aůd\ *adj* [ME, fr. past part. of *avowen* to avow, to declare openly] : openly acknowledged or declared : ADMITTED ⟨as an ~ Jeffersonian he has been . . . a guardian of constitutional checks and guarantees —*Current Biog.*⟩ ⟨~ aims⟩ : SWORN ⟨an ~ enemy⟩ — **avow·ed·ly** \-au̇ədlē, -li\ *adv*

avow·ry \-au̇(ə)rē, -ri\ *n* -ES [ME *avowrie*, fr. MF *avouerie* protection, patronage, fr. OF, fr. *avouer* to avow + -*erie* -ery] **1 a** *obs* : ADVOCACY, PATRONAGE, PROTECTION **b** : ADVOCATE, PATRON; *esp* : PATRON SAINT **2** : the act of one who avows something; *esp* : the act of the distrainer of goods who in an action of replevin avows and justifies the taking in his own right — compare COGNIZANCE 5

avoy·el \ə'vȯiəl, a'- *also* ȧvwȧ(y)el\ *n, pl* **avoyel** *or* **avoyels** *usu cap* [F, of AmerInd origin] **1** : a Natchesan people of central Louisiana **2** : a member of the Avoyel people

avulse \ə'vəls\ *vt* -ED/-ING/-S [L *avulsus*, past part. of *avellere* to tear off] : to pull off or tear away; *specif* : to separate by avulsion ⟨an *avulsed* ligament⟩

avul·sion \-lshən\ *n* -S [L *avulsion-, avulsio*, fr. *avulsus* (past part. of *avellere* to tear off, fr. *a, ab* from, away + *vellere* to pluck, pull) + -*ion-*, -*io* -ion — more at OF, VULNERABLE] : a forcible separation or detachment: as **a** *med* : a tearing away of a structure or part accidentally or surgically ⟨surgical ~ of a part of the phrenic nerve to rest a diseased lung⟩ **b** : a sudden cutting off of land by flood, currents, or change in course of a body of water; *esp* : one that separates a portion from one person's property and joins it to that of another

avun·cu·lar \ə'vəŋkyələ(r)\ *adj* [L *avunculus* maternal uncle (dim. of *avus* grandfather) + E -*ar* — more at UNCLE] **1** : of, being, or relating to an uncle, specif. a maternal uncle **2** : acting or speaking with the familiarity, kindness, or indulgence of an uncle; *sometimes* : unduly benevolent and condescending ⟨then one evening he decided to join in. He was robust, ~, patronizing —Elizabeth Taylor⟩ — **avun·cu·lar·i·ty** \ə,==ˈlarəd·ē\ *n* -ES

avun·cu·late \=ˈ==,lət, -,lāt\ *n* -S [L *avunculus* + E -*ate*] **1** : a special relationship obtaining among some tribal peoples between a nephew and his maternal uncle **2** : authority of a man over his sister's family affairs but esp. over her children and the rights and responsibilities associated therewith — compare AMITATE

avun·cu·lo·cal \ə'vəŋkyə'lōkəl\ *adj* [L *avunculus* + E *local*] **1** : located at or centered around the residence of the husband's maternal uncle **2** : belonging to a maternal uncle — compare MATRILOCAL, PATRILOCAL, NEOLOCAL

aw \'ȯ, 'ä\ *interj* — used to express mild remonstrance, incredulity, or disgust

AW *abbr* **1** above water **2** actual weight **3** aircraft warning **4** all water **5** all widths **6** articles of war **7** automatic weapon

1awa \ə'wȧ, -wȯ\ *adv* [by alter.] *Scot* : AWAY

2awa \'ä(,)vä, -wä\ *n* -S [Hawaiian] : MILKFISH

3awa \'(ʔ)ävə\ *n* -S [Hawaiian *'awa*] : KAVA

awa·bi \ə'wäbē\ *n, pl* **awabi** [Jap] : an abalone (*Haliotis gigantea*)

awa·dhi \'äwə(,)dē\ *n* -S *usu cap* [Hindi *Avadhī*] : a literary dialect of Eastern Hindi

1await \ə'wāt, *usu* -ād+V\ *vb* -ED/-ING/-S [ME *awaiten*, fr. ONF *awaitier*, fr. *a-* (fr. L *ad-*) + *waitier* to watch — more at WAIT] *vt* **1** *obs* : to watch for esp. with hostile intent : lie in wait for ⟨your ill-meaning politician lords . . . appointed to ~ me thirty spies —John Milton⟩ **2** : to wait for : stay for ⟨you must ~ the sequel —Walter de la Mare⟩ ⟨had decided to ~ me in the mountains —D.L.Busk⟩ **3** : to be in store for : be ready or in waiting for ⟨a lavish Sunday dinner ~*ing* them —Ellen Glasgow⟩ ~ *vi* **1** *obs* : to wait on someone : ATTEND ⟨on whom three hundred gold-capped youths ~ —Alexander Pope⟩ **2** : to stay or be in waiting : WAIT ⟨the people ~*ed* outside the building⟩ **3** : to be in store ⟨marched . . . north to civilization where fame and fortune ~*ed* —Tom Marvel⟩ **syn** see EXPECT

2await *n* -S [ME, fr. ONF, fr. *awaitier*] *obs* : a lying in wait or watching for with hostile intent : AMBUSH

1awake \ə'wāk\ *vb* **awoke** \-wōk\ *also* **awaked** \-wākt\ **awaked** \"\ *also* **awoke** \-wōk\ *or* **awok·en** \-wōkən\ **awaking; awakes** [ME *awaken* (fr. OE *awacan*, fr. *1a-* + *wacan* to awake, arise, be born) & *awakien*, fr. OE *awacian*, fr. *1a-* + *wacian* to be awake, watch — more at WAKE] *vi* **1** : to emerge from sleep : regain consciousness after natural sleep : cease sleeping, dozing, or dreaming ⟨the elderly bellboy *awoke* from his dreams —Sinclair Lewis⟩ **2 a** : to emerge from a sleeplike state (as from inaction, indifference, or death) : bestir oneself ⟨cast off your bonds, ~, arise —William Wordsworth⟩ **b** : to become active again : be resurgent **3** : to become conscious or aware — usu. used with following *to* ⟨unless the bar ~*s* to its opportunity and power —B.N.Cardozo⟩ ⟨they *awoke* to their danger⟩ ~ *vt* **1** : to arouse from sleep : bring back to consciousness after sleep ⟨the sound of heavy footsteps in the driveway *awoke* the watchdogs⟩ **2 a** : to arouse from a sleeplike state (as from inaction, indifference, or death) ⟨I was soon *awaked* from this disagreeable reverie —Oliver Goldsmith⟩ **b** : to incite to activity : make active : stir up ⟨certain of them *awoke* in me feelings of fear —Osbert Lancaster⟩

2awake \"\ *adj* [ME *awake, awaken*, past part. of *awaken*] **1** : not asleep, dormant, or notably lethargic ⟨the boys sat in their chairs half asleep but Mack was ~ —John Steinbeck⟩ **2 a** : in a state of vigilance, arousal, or activity ⟨all the nationalistic elements now ~ on the African continent —J.M.Houston⟩ **b** : fully conscious or appreciative : AWARE — usu. used with following *to* ⟨was ~ to the dangers and disgrace of the existing maladministration —J.A.Froude⟩ **c** : brought back to consciousness : REACTIVATED, REANIMATED ⟨old memories suddenly ~ again⟩ **syn** see AWARE

awak·en \ə'wākən\ *vb* **awakened; awakened; awakening** \-k(ə)niŋ\ **awakens** [ME *awakenen*, fr. OE *awæcnian, onwæcnian*, fr. *1a-, on* + *wæcnian, wæcnan* to awake — more at WAKEN] *vi* : AWAKE ⟨the youth ~*ed* slowly —Stephen Crane⟩ ⟨England . . . had ~*ed* from its age-old isolation —Van Wyck Brooks⟩ ⟨old infirmities ~ under our skins —V.S.Pritchett⟩ ⟨we have ~*ed* to this fact —G.W.Chapman⟩ ~ *vt* : AWAKE ⟨wondering what had ~*ed* her —Ann Petry⟩ ⟨a rare gift of ~*ing* the keen interest of his students —H.K.Barrows⟩ ⟨did more than any other to ~ the churches of this faith to the value of their heritage —C.A.Dinsmore⟩ **syn** see STIR

awak·en·er \-k(ə)nə(r)\ *n* -S : one that awakens

1awakening *n* -S **1** : a rousing from sleep **2 a** : a rousing from inactivity, sloth, or indifference ⟨ancient and somnolent institutions were once again spared an ~ —E.B.George⟩ ⟨the most significant fact in the world today is the ~ that is going on in the East —Wendell Willkie⟩ **b** : a revival of interest in religion ⟨the later ~*s* in Protestantism gave rise to novel movements in education and thought —K.S.Latourette⟩ **3** : a coming into consciousness or awareness : REALIZATION, RECOGNITION — usu. used with following *to* ⟨a gradual ~ to the facts of the country's military position⟩

2awakening *adj* : AWAKING — **awak·en·ing·ly** *adv*

awak·en·ment \-kənmənt\ *n* -S : AWAKENING

awan \ə'wän\ *n* -S *usu cap* [native name in India] : a member of a people of the northwestern Indian subcontinent, mainly along the Indus

awant·ing \ə+\ *adj* [*1a-* + *wanting*] : WANTING ⟨jesters and jugglers were not ~ —Sir Walter Scott⟩

awanyu \ə'wän(,)yü\ *also* **awanyo** \-vän(,)yō\ *or* **avanyu** \-(,)yü\ *n* -S [Tewa] : a sacred plumed serpent in the mythology and art of the Tewa Indians

1award \ə'wȯ(ə)rd, -ō(ə)d\ *vt* -ED/-ING/-S [ME *awarden*, fr. ONF *eswarder*, fr. *es-* (fr. L *ex* out) + *warder* to observe, keep, guard; akin to OF *guarder, garder* to observe, keep, guard — more at EX-, GUARD] **1** *obs* : to determine after careful consideration : JUDGE, DECIDE ⟨shall then the testament ~ the right —John Dryden⟩ **2** : to give by judicial decree : assign after careful judgment : ADJUDGE ⟨the arbitrators ~*ed* heavy damages⟩ **3** : to confer or bestow upon : GRANT, GIVE ⟨the university ~*ed* him an honorary degree⟩ **syn** see GRANT

2award \"\ *n* -S [ME, fr. ONF *eswart*, fr. *eswarder*] **1 a** : a judgment, sentence, or final decision; *esp* : the decision of arbitrators in a case submitted to them ⟨following the arbitration ~ . . . he was retained as counsel by . . . the more important claimants —H.W.H.Knott⟩ **b** : the document containing the decision of arbitrators **2 a** : something that is conferred or bestowed upon a person : GRANT ⟨candidates for the ~*s* in chemistry⟩ **b** : an emblem or medal symbolizing such an award ⟨the ~ is a blue-and-gold pin with an appropriate inscription⟩

3award *vt* -ED/-ING/-S [*a-* (perfective prefix) + *ward* — more at ABEAR] *obs* : to ward off

award clerk *n* : PROCUREMENT CLERK

award·ee \ə,=ˈdē, =ˈ=,dē\ *n* -S : one that receives an award

award·er \ə'=də(r)\ *n* -S : one that awards

aware \ə'wa(a)(ə)r, -we(ə)r,-wa(a)ə,-weə\ *adj* [ME *iwar*, fr. OE *gewær*, fr. *ge-* (collective prefix) + *wær* wary — more at CO-, WARY] **1** *archaic* : on guard : WATCHFUL, VIGILANT ⟨are you all ~ of . . . talebearing and evil-speaking —John Wesley⟩ **2 a** : marked by realization, perception, or knowledge : CONSCIOUS, SENSIBLE, COGNIZANT ⟨he was never fully ~ of the extent of his failures —O.S.Nock⟩ ⟨Adams was ~ that the arrival of the tea ships might be used to precipitate a crisis —C.L.Becker⟩ **b** : showing heightened perception and ready comprehension and appreciation : INFORMED, KNOWING, ALERT ⟨the most intellectually ambitious and the most technically ~ of the novelists under thirty —W.S.Graham⟩

syn COGNIZANT, CONSCIOUS, SENSIBLE, ALIVE, AWAKE: AWARE may indicate either general information, wide knowledge, interpretative power, or vigilant perception ⟨few, so far as I am *aware*, now claim the free speech to call a knave a knave —T.S.Eliot⟩ ⟨more widely *aware* of the phenomena of biological chemistry —Sinclair Lewis⟩ ⟨Americans are becoming *aware* that American destiny can be pursued only in a world framework —Max Lerner⟩ COGNIZANT may imply the gradual impingement of knowledge or perception on one's consciousness or may connote special efforts to know ⟨Soapy's mind became *cognizant* of the fact —O.Henry⟩ ⟨through the servants, or from some other means, he had made himself *cognizant* of the projected elopement —Anthony Trollope⟩ It may imply arch knowingness ⟨"ah!" went the other eyeing Ripton in lordly *cognizant* style —George Meredith⟩ CONSCIOUS may indicate impingement on one's mind so that one recognizes the fact or existence of something ⟨dimly *conscious* that Hallward was speaking to him but not catching the meaning of the words —Oscar Wilde⟩ It may also indicate an extreme and dominating realization, even a preoccupation ⟨what makes a writer most acutely *conscious* of his place in time —T.S.Eliot⟩ SENSIBLE may apply to situations in which a thing is intuitively sensed and also to those in which it is rationally perceived, known, and admitted ⟨for my part, though deeply *sensible* of its influence, I cannot seize it —Nathaniel Hawthorne⟩ ⟨I am *sensible* that I write you short letters but I write you all I know —Horace Walpole⟩ It is often used to indicate awareness and acknowledgment of gratitude, pleasure, resentment, or pain ⟨I am *sensible* I may be indebted to you, sir —Charles Dickens⟩ ALIVE may suggest vivid awareness, certain keen perception ⟨Cromwell . . . was keenly *alive* to all that concerned England's honor and strength —A.T.Mahan⟩ ⟨these two had a certain cool judgment, and they were fully *alive* to the danger of thwarting Barbara —John Galsworthy⟩ AWAKE may suggest alert perception ⟨a large number of her [Britain's] leaders seem *awake* to the saving qualities of compromise —Leland Stowe⟩

aware·ness \-nəs\ *n* -ES : the quality or state of being aware ⟨the crash of music broke into his ~ —Hamilton Basso⟩ ⟨their intelligence, social consciousness, and political ~ are of the highest degree —T.H.Fielding⟩

awa·ru·ite \,äwä'rü,īt\ *n* -S [*Awarua*, South Island, New Zealand, its locality + E -*ite*] : a mineral consisting of a rare natural alloy of nickel and iron

awas *pl of* AWA

awash \ə+\ *adv* (*or adj*) [*1a-* + *wash*, v.] **1 a** : alternately covered and exposed by the waves or tide : washed by the sea ⟨two whales spouting close to the factory and lying carelessly ~ —R.B.Robertson⟩ ⟨a group of great islands almost ~ with the sea —C.O.Dunbar⟩ **b** : washing about : AFLOAT ⟨everything movable on deck was ~⟩ **c** : covered with water : FLOODED ⟨the street was ~ after the sudden storm⟩ **2** : marked by an abundance : FULL, OVERFLOWING ⟨the resulting music is ~ with decayed Viennese romanticism —Herbert Weinstock⟩ ⟨here is the household ~ with children —Brendan Gill⟩

awave \ə+\ *adj* [*1a-* + *wave*, v.] : moving in or as if in waves : WAVING

1away \ə'wā\ *adv* [ME *away, on way*, fr. OE *aweg, onweg*, fr. *1a-, on* + *weg* way — more at WAY] **1** : on the way : ONWARD, ALONG ⟨come ~ death —Shak.⟩ **2** : from this or that place : HENCE, THENCE ⟨the lone and level sands stretch far ~ —P.B.Shelley⟩ ⟨go ~⟩ — sometimes used to indicate motion from a place with no expressed verb of motion or no expressed verb at all ⟨we must ~⟩ ⟨whither ~⟩ **3 a** : from contact or close association : ASIDE ⟨she folded her work and laid it ~ —H.W.Longfellow⟩ **b** : at a little distance : OFF ⟨he was a good boxer inside as well as ~ —A.J.Liebling⟩ **c** : in another direction; *esp* : in the opposite direction ⟨we've turned . . . hard ~ in a tight circle to port to get out of this area —Richard Dimbleby⟩ **4** : from a condition of being : out of existence : to an end : to nothing ⟨tried to explain ~ the affair of the letter —H.E.Scudder⟩ ⟨a progressive twitching of the muscles with increasing weakness and wasting ~ —Morris Fishbein⟩ **5** : from one's possession or use ⟨it is given ~ to a friend by the householder —J.G.Frazer⟩ **6 a** : onward in time : UNINTERRUPTEDLY, CONSTANTLY, ON ⟨a distinct compartment in one's mind that works ~ no matter what is going on —O.W. Holmes †1935⟩ **b** : without hesitation or delay : FORTHWITH, IMMEDIATELY ⟨the troops were ordered to fire ~⟩ **7** : to a considerable degree : by a long distance or interval : FAR ⟨he is far and ~ the best player on the team⟩ ⟨the trouble began ~ back in 1910⟩

2away \"\ *adj* **1 a** : absent from a place : GONE ⟨he is ~ from home⟩ **b** : started on the way : OFF ⟨he was ~ at a gallop —Winston Churchill⟩ **2** : distant in space or time : ⟨a lake 10 miles ~⟩ ⟨the opening of the season is only a week ~⟩ **3** *chiefly Scot* : gone out of or as if out of existence : dead, mad, or in a faint ⟨she was ~ in her head —Mary Deasy⟩ **4 a** : played on an opponent's home grounds ⟨league headquarters arranges the schedule of home and ~ games⟩ **b** *of a golf ball* : lying farthest from the cup and to be played first **c** *baseball* : OUT ⟨the home run came with two ~ in the 9th inning⟩

away-going crop \=ˈ=,==-\ *n* : a crop that a tenant is under certain conditions entitled to remove after the end of his tenancy : EMBLEMENT

away·ness \ə'wānəs\ *n* -ES : the quality or state of being out of the way : REMOTENESS ⟨it was the ~ of it that first attracted me to the place —Aldous Huxley⟩

1awe \'ȯ\ *n* -S [ME *awe, age, aghe*, fr. ON *agi*; akin to OE *ege* awe, fear, terror — more at AIL] **1** *obs* : intense fear : DREAD, TERROR ⟨waits for death with dread and trembling ~ —Edmund Spenser⟩ **2** *archaic* : the power to inspire fear or reverence ⟨you see, my lord, what an ~ you have upon me —John Dryden⟩ **3** : fear mixed with dread, veneration, reverence, or wonder: as **a** : profound and reverent fear inspired by deity ⟨~ of the judgments of God —Daniel Defoe⟩ **b** : abashed reverence and fear inspired by authority or power ⟨nothing but an extreme ~ of your authority has hitherto prevented me from forcing my impertinent attentions upon you —Dorothy Sayers⟩ **c** : veneration and latent fear inspired by something sacred, mysterious, or morally impressive ⟨jaguars were regarded with religious ~ and were the object of a cult —Alfred Métraux⟩ **d** : reverent wonder with a touch of fear inspired by the grand or sublime esp. in nature or art ⟨the bird was so beautiful that the vision of it . . . seemed to bring with it an overpowering sense of ~ —J.C.Powys⟩

2awe \"\ *vt* **awed; awed; awing** \'ȯ(·)iŋ\ **awes** [ME *awen*, fr. *awe*, n.] **1** : to inspire with awe : FRIGHTEN, TERRIFY ⟨the exalted nature of the personage to whom she was being taken *awed* her —P.I.Wellman⟩ ⟨nature among the mountains is too fierce, too strong for man . . . and she ~*s* him —Charles Kingsley⟩ **2** : to influence, control, or check by inspiring with awe ⟨her pained reserve had no power to ~ them into decency —Joseph Conrad⟩

3awe \'ȯ, 'ä\ *n* -S [MF *auve, aube*, perh. fr. L *alapa* box on the ear; perh. akin to ON *lōfi* palm of the hand — more at GLOVE] **1** : one of the boards or buckets against which the water acts in an undershot mill wheel **2** : one of the sails of a windmill

awearied \ə+\ *adj* [*1a-* + *wearied*] : WEARIED

aweary \ə+\ *adj* [*1a-* + *weary*] : WEARY, TIRED

aweather \ə+\ *adv* [*1a-* + *weather*] : on or toward the weather or windward side — opposed to *alee*

awed \'ȯd\ *adj* : feeling or showing awe — **awed·ly** \'ȯ(ə)dlē, -li\ *adv* — **awed·ness** \'ȯ(ə)dnəs\ *n* -ES

awee \ə'wē\ *adv* [*2a* + *wee*] *chiefly Scot* : a little while

aweel \ə'wēl, -wel\ *interj* [ah + Sc *weel*] *Scot* : well then

aweigh \ə'wā\ *adj* [*1a-* + *weigh* (to heave up)] *of an anchor* : just clear of the ground and hanging perpendicularly : ATRIP

awei·ko·ma \,äwä'kōmə\ *n, pl* **aweikoma** *or* **aweikomas** *usu cap* : CAINGANG

awe-inspiring \'=,==,==\ *adj* : that arouses awe ⟨*awe-inspiring* bravery⟩ ⟨an *awe-inspiring* cathedral⟩

awe·less *or* **aw·less** \'ȯləs\ *adj* [ME *aweless, awlesse, ageless*, fr. *awe, age* + *-lesse* -less] **1** : lacking awe: **a** : FEARLESS **b** : IRREVERENT **2** *obs* : inspiring no awe

awe·some \'ȯsəm\ *adj* **1** : expressive of awe : deeply reverent ⟨has paid ~ tribute to British soldiery —I.L.Salomon⟩ **2** : causing awe : AWE-INSPIRING, DREADFUL, AWFUL ⟨one of the most ~ jungles in the world —John Hersey⟩ — **awe·some·ly** *adv* — **awe·some·ness** *n* -ES

awestricken \'=,==\ *adj* : AWESTRUCK ⟨in grim despair and ~ wonder —O.E.Rölvaag⟩

awe-strike \'=,=\ *vt, archaic* : to strike with awe

awestruck \'=,=\ *adj* : filled with awe ⟨his eyes had an ~ expression —Stephen Crane⟩

aweto \ä'wed·(,)ō, ä'fe-\ *n* -S [Maori] : a composite structure that occurs in New Zealand, that when dried and burned yields a useful black pigment, and that is made up of the mummified body of a caterpillar killed by the attack of a parasitic ascomycetous fungus (*Cordyceps robustus*) together with the elongated fruiting body of the fungus which projects from the neck of the mummy — called also *vegetable caterpillar*

awf *var of* AUF

1aw·ful \'ȯfəl\ *adj, sometimes* **awfuller**; *sometimes* **awfullest** [ME *awful, aweful, ageful*, fr. *awe, age* + *-ful*] **1** : inspiring awe: as **a** : causing dread or terror : APPALLING ⟨I am in fear — in ~ fear — and there is no escape for me —Bram Stoker⟩ **b** : commanding reverential fear or profound respect ⟨they may hold converse with some saint, their ~, kindly friend —Nathaniel Hawthorne⟩ **c** : solemnly impressive ⟨Westminster Hall . . . had an ~ majesty, so vast, so high, and so silent —E.W.Weeks⟩ **2** : filled with awe: as **a** *obs* : terror-stricken ⟨great potentates do kneel with ~ fear —Christopher Marlowe⟩ **b** : deeply respectful ⟨towards the East our ~ greetings are wafted —John Keble⟩ **3** : extremely unpleasant, disagreeable, or objectionable — often a generalized expression of disapproval ⟨she has an ~ voice⟩ ⟨an ~ person⟩ ⟨~ manners⟩ ⟨an ~ hat⟩ **4** : very great — used as an intensive ⟨does an ~ lot of talking⟩ ⟨took an ~ chance⟩ **syn** see FEARFUL

2awful \"\ *adv* : AWFULLY, VERY, EXTREMELY ⟨my papa always said you were an ~ smart boy —Willa Cather⟩ — not often in formal use

aw·ful·ly *in senses 3 & 4* 'ȯflē *or* -li *also* -fəl-, *in senses 1 & 2* 'ȯfəl-l\ *adv* [ME, fr. *awful* + *-ly*] **1** : in a manner that inspires awe ⟨the drawing room in which New York's most chosen company was somewhat ~ assembled —Edith Wharton⟩ **2** *archaic* : with a feeling of awe ⟨and timorous passed and ~ withdrew —Alexander Pope⟩ **3** : in an unpleasant, disagreeable, or objectionable manner — often a generalized expression of disapproval ⟨he of the red nightcap now commenced snoring ~ —George Borrow⟩ **4** : EXCEEDINGLY, EXTREMELY, VERY — an intensive ⟨an ~ hard rain⟩ ⟨thanks ~⟩

aw·ful·ness \-fəlnəs\ *n* -ES : the quality or state of being awful

AWG *abbr* American wire gauge

awheel \ə+\ *adv* (*or adj*) [*1a-* (as in *afoot*) + *wheel*] : riding (as on a bicycle or in an automobile) ⟨a concourse of citizens ~ and afoot —Winston Churchill⟩ ⟨the lure of a spring holiday ~ —Bert Pierce⟩

awhile \ə+\ *adv* [ME *awhile, on while*, fr. *1a-, on* + *while*] : for a time ⟨the father of these girls . . . had settled ~ in Virginia —Dixon Wecter⟩ : for a brief period — often used for *a while* as the object of a preposition ⟨for ~ there is silence —Lord Dunsany⟩

awhirl \ə+\ *adj* [*1a-* + *whirl*, v.] : in a whirl : WHIRLING ⟨his head ~ with fantastic schemes⟩

awin \'ȯən\ [ME (northern dial.) *awen* to possess, own, owe — more at OWE] *Scot var of* 1OWN

1aw·ing \'ȯ(·)iŋ\ *pres part of* AWE

2awing \ə'wiŋ\ *adv* (*or adj*) [*1a-* + *wing*] : on the wing : FLYING

awi·shi·ra \,äwə'shērə\ *n, pl* **awishira** *or* **awishiras** *usu cap* [Sp *avixira*, of AmerInd origin] **1 a** : an Indian people of northeastern Peru **b** : a member of such people **2** : the language of the Awishira people

1awk *adj* [ME *awke*] **1** *obs* : turned or done the wrong way **2** *obs* : PERVERSE **3** *obs* : AWKWARD, CLUMSY

2awk *or* **awkly** *adv, obs* : in the wrong way

awk·ward \'ȯkwə(r)d\ *adj* -ER/-EST [ME *awkeward* in the wrong direction, upside down, fr. *awke* turned the wrong way, left-handed (fr. ON *öfugr* turned the wrong way) + *-ward*; akin to OHG *abuh* turned the wrong way, bad, evil, OS *abuh*, L *opacus* shady, obscure, OSlav *opaky* turned backward, Arm *haka-* toward] **1** *obs* **a** : PERVERSE, FROWARD ⟨an ~ pride in my nature —Henry Fielding⟩ **b** : ADVERSE, UNFAVORABLE ⟨with ~ winds and with sore tempests driven —Christopher Marlowe⟩ **2 a** : lacking dexterity or skill esp. in the use of the hands or of instruments : CLUMSY ⟨she was too ~ with a needle to make her own clothes⟩ **b** : showing the result of inexpert handling or faulty craftsmanship : ILL-MADE ⟨the form of writing used . . . was extremely crude and was confined chiefly to expressing thoughts by means of ~ pictures —R.W.Murray⟩ **3 a** : lacking ease, grace, or deftness of movement : not graceful ⟨she had large feet and her walk was ~ and ungainly⟩ **b** : appearing ill-proportioned, outsize, or poorly fitted together : UNGAINLY ⟨how long, tall, quick, strong, or ~ in looks he was —Carl Sandburg⟩ **4** : lacking ease, grace, or effectiveness of expression : CUMBERSOME ⟨an ~ piece of writing⟩ ⟨a title which is extremely ~ in English —R.A.Hall b.1911⟩ **5 a** : lacking social grace and assurance : feeling or showing embarrassment : ill at ease ⟨he hesitated, ~ and bashful, shifted his weight from one leg to the other —Jack London⟩ **b** : causing embarrassment : INCONVENIENT, DIFFICULT ⟨sometimes his quick brain runs him into ~ situations —John Ennis⟩ ⟨spared her from explanations and professions which it was exceedingly ~ to give —Jane Austen⟩ **6** : inexpertly designed, placed, or organized : poorly adapted for use or handling ⟨attempts to combine . . . a single picture out of these ~ and contradictory tests —Havelock Ellis⟩ ⟨the dykes and drains make these roads so very ~ —Dorothy Sayers⟩ **7** : requiring caution : somewhat dangerous ⟨the guide let himself down an ~ cliff⟩

syn CLUMSY, INEPT, MALADROIT, GAUCHE, UNGAINLY, LUMBERING, GAWKY: AWKWARD, CLUMSY, INEPT, MALADROIT, and GAUCHE denote lack of grace, ease, skill, or fitness in appearance or movement, action or speech, use or function; UNGAINLY, LUMBERING, and GAWKY denote a similar lack, usu. due to cumbersome build or ill-proportioned structure. AWKWARD may apply to a person who is lacking in muscular coordination or is deficient in poise ⟨you're as *awkward*, McGovery, as a bull calf —Anthony Trollope⟩ It often implies shyness and self-consciousness ⟨I, sitting in silence, felt *awkward*; but I was too shy to break into any of the groups that seemed absorbed in their own affairs —W.S.Maugham⟩ It may apply to an object that is not easily handled or dexterously managed ⟨*awkward* round boats⟩ to a situation or action likely to cause embarrassment or discomfiture ⟨an easy and welcome solution to an otherwise *awkward* problem —W.L. Sperry⟩ or to modes of expression that are cumbersome or confused ⟨an *awkward* sentence⟩ CLUMSY may denote a person or an animal that is blundering or lacking in skill or grace and often describes one who is grotesque and clattering from awkwardness, esp. as an inherent tendency ⟨a *clumsy* bear⟩ ⟨a *clumsy* and timid horseman —W.M.Thackeray⟩ It may also denote a person or object that is heavy or unwieldy ⟨the *clumsy* machinery of the plot —T.S.Eliot⟩ ⟨a *clumsy* horse⟩ INEPT, which applies to both persons and their actions or products, is the strongest word of those here compared, for it suggests total failure ⟨an *inept* mechanic⟩ ⟨an *inept* administrator⟩

⟨an *inept* translation⟩ and carries a suggestion of futility or absurdity ⟨by what *inept* logic must we bow to our creation if it be a machine and spurn it as "unreal" if it happens to be a painting or a poem? —Lewis Mumford⟩ MALADROIT may describe remarks or actions that are out of place, ill-timed, or tasteless and that cause embarrassment or resentment, or persons responsible for them ⟨Lloyd George, though a brilliant statesman, was often a *maladroit* politician —Malcolm Thomson⟩ GAUCHE also describes a person or something he says or does and often refers to a general tendency to be ill at ease from shyness, inexperience, or lack of breeding, and to increase one's discomfiture by inappropriate acts or remarks ⟨these *gauche* characters just don't know the rules of the game —John Farrelly⟩ ⟨that shy, rather *gauche* fellow, slinking nervously about the corridors —H.J.Laski⟩ UNGAINLY indicates marked physical gracelessness often due to excessive size ⟨she had long *ungainly* limbs and was very awkward in the use of them —Anthony Trollope⟩ LUMBERING describes one that is large and ponderous, formidable when at rest and moving, if at all, with real or apparent difficulty ⟨so that his slow *lumbering* plane would not be left behind by the faster bombers —H.L.Merillat⟩ GAWKY suggests graceless proportions and the self-consciousness often attendant on such an appearance ⟨one of these abrupt, rather *gawky* women, all hands and feet —Valentine Williams⟩

awkward age *n* **:** the age of early adolescence usu. characterized by awkwardness and shyness

awk·ward·ly *adv* **:** in an awkward manner: **a :** CLUMSILY **b :** EMBARRASSINGLY

awk·ward·ness \-nəs\ *n* -ES **1 :** the quality or state of being awkward: **a :** lack of dexterity or skill **:** CLUMSINESS ⟨a puppy's ~⟩ **b :** lack of ease or grace **:** INELEGANCE ⟨the ~ of his prose style⟩ **c :** lack of composure **:** EMBARRASSMENT ⟨the silence conveyed to neither any sense of ~ —Thomas Hardy⟩ **2 :** something that is awkward ⟨conscious of these minor ~*es* and disfigurements —Geoffrey Gorer⟩

awkward squad *n* **:** a group of inept recruits undergoing special drill

awl \'ȯl\ *n* -S [ME *al*, fr. OE *æl;* akin to OHG *āla* awl, ON *alr*, (assumed) Goth *ela* (whence Lith *yla*), Skt *ārā*] **:** a pointed instrument for marking surfaces or piercing small holes (as in leather or wood), the blade being differently shaped and pointed for different uses

1 awl, *2* sewing awl

AWL *abbr* absent with leave

awless *var of* AWELESS

awl-shaped \'ˌˌ\ *adj* **:** shaped like an awl; *specif* **:** linear and tapering to a fine point ⟨an *awl-shaped* onion leaf⟩

awl·wort \'ȯl,wərt, -ȯrt\ *n* -S [*awl* + *wort*] **:** a small aquatic plant (*Subularia aquatica*) of the family Cruciferae with tufted awl-shaped leaves and minute white flowers

aw·mous \'ȧməs, 'ȯm-\ *n, pl* **awmous** [ME (northern dial.) *almouse, almus, awmus* — more at ALMOUS] *Scot* **:** ALMS

¹awn \'ȯn\ *n* -S [ME *awne*, fr. OE *agen* ear of grain, of Scand origin; akin to ON *ōgn* chaff; akin to OE *egenu* chaff, Goth *ahana*, L *agna* ear of grain, Gk *akōn* javelin, Skt *aśani* arrowhead, missile, OE *ecg* edge, sword — more at EDGE] **1 a :** one of the slender bristles that terminate the glumes or bracts of the spikelet in barley, oats, some varieties of wheat, and other grasses **b :** a small pointed process (as that which terminates the anthers in members of the genus *Vaccinium*) **2 :** one of the barbed processes on the hemipenis of a reptile

²awn \"\ *vt* -ED/-ING/-S **:** to remove the awns from

³awn \'ȯn\ [ME (northern dial.) *awen* to possess, own, owe — more at OWE] *chiefly Scot var of* OWN

⁴awn \'ȯn\ *vt* -ED/-ING/-S [back-formation fr. *awning*] **:** to cover with or as if with an awning ⟨this green pavilion ~*ing* the moles —Daniel Sargent⟩

awned \'ȯnd\ *adj* [¹*awn* + *-ed*] **:** furnished with an awn **:** BEARDED

awned wheatgrass *n* **:** BEARDED WHEATGRASS

awn·er \'ȯnə(r)\ *n* -S **:** a machine for removing awns from grain

awn grass *n* **:** a tufted grass (*Chrysopogon aciculatus*) of tropical Asia and Pacific Islands with sharp-pointed seeds that penetrate clothing and sheep's wool

aw·ning \'ȯniŋ, 'ȧn-, -nēŋ\ *n* -S [origin unknown] **1 :** a usu. canvas rooflike cover extended over or before any place as a shelter from the sun, rain, or wind (as over the deck of a ship or slanting outward before a window) **2 :** a shelter resembling an awning

awning cloth *or* **awning stripe** *n* **:** cloth suitable for awnings; *specif* **:** a heavy cotton duck or canvas with printed, painted, or woven stripes of bright colors

awning deck *n* **:** a light deck extending over the main deck from stem to stern — called also *hurricane deck*

aw·ninged \-ŋd\ *adj* **:** covered with an awning

awning window *n* **:** a window consisting of several top-hinged sections arranged in a vertical series, operated by one or more control devices that swing the bottom edges of the sections outward, and designed esp. to admit air while excluding rain

awning window

awn·less \'ȯnləs\ *adj* **:** without awns

awnless bromegrass *n* **:** a drought-resistant perennial bromegrass (*Bromus inermis*) with awns lacking or very short that spreads by creeping rhizomes, is native to Europe, and is cultivated for forage and hay

awn·let \'ȯnlət\ *n* -S [*awn* + *-let*] **:** a small awn

awny \'ȯnē, -i\ *adj* [¹*awn* + *-y*] **:** having awns **:** BEARDED

awoke *past of* AWAKE

awoken *past part of* AWAKE

¹awol \'ā,wȯl, ˌā,dəbəl(ˌ)yü,ō'el — *the first is prob more freq for the form "awol", the second for the form "AWOL"*\ *abbr or adj (or adv), often cap A & W & O & L* [*a*bsent *w*ithout *l*eave] **:** absent without leave ⟨an ~ private returning to barracks —Nelson Algren⟩ ⟨had gone *AWOL* from the British hospitals to get back into the fight —H.H.Martin⟩

²awol \"\ *n* -S *often cap A & W & O & L* **:** one who is absent without leave ⟨most of these *AWOLs* are soldiers on their first furlough —*Infantry Jour.*⟩

awork \ə+\ *adv (or adj)* [ME, fr. ¹*a-* + *work*, n.] **:** at work **:** in an active state

awry \ə'rī\ *adv (or adj)* [ME *on wry*, fr. *on* + *wry*] **1 :** turned or twisted toward one side **:** OBLIQUELY, OBLIQUE **:** not straight **:** ASKEW ⟨a dissipated-looking youth with a gorgeous red necktie all ~ —G.K.Chesterton⟩ **2 :** out of the right, expected, or hoped-for course **:** wide of the mark **:** WRONG, AMISS ⟨after three years of schooling in New York something went ~ in his education —S.H.Adams⟩

ax- *or* **axo-** *comb form* [ISV, fr. Gk *axōn* axle, axis — more at AXIS] **1 :** axis ⟨*axophyte*⟩ **2 :** axis cylinder ⟨*axite*⟩ ⟨*axodendrite*⟩

¹ax *or* **axe** \'aks\ *n, pl* **axes** [ME, fr. OE *æx, æces, acus:* akin to OHG *acchus, acchus*, ON *ōx*, Goth *aqizi*, L *ascia*, Gk *axinē*, and perh. to OE *ecg* edge, sword — more at EDGE] **1 a :** a cutting tool or implement that consists of a relatively heavy edged head fixed to a handle, the edge or edges being parallel to the handle so as to be suited for striking, and that is used esp. for felling trees, chopping and splitting wood, and hewing timber **2 :** a hammer with a sharp edge for dressing or spalling stone **:** AXHAMMER **3 :** removal from office or release from employment **:** DISMISSAL, DISCHARGE — usu. used with *the* ⟨one of the leading candidates for the ~ when and if the expected purge comes —John Dean⟩ ⟨boys who had got the ~ —John McNulty⟩ — **ax to grind :** a selfish end to gain **:** an ulterior purpose to further

axes: *1* common ax; *2* double-bitted ax; *3* broad-ax; *4* section of 3; *5* fireman's ax

²ax \"\ *or* **axe** *vt* **axed; axed; axing; axes 1 a :** to shape, dress, or trim with an ax ⟨~ stone⟩ ⟨~ bricks⟩ **b :** to chop, cut, split, or sever with an ax ⟨~ branches from a tree⟩ **2 :** to relieve of office or employment **:** DISMISS, DISCHARGE ⟨columnists and correspondents were ~*ed* —*Time*⟩ **3 :** to put an end to, curtail, or impair ⟨congressmen who want to ~ the subsidy program —J.C.Cort⟩

³ax \'aks\ *vb* -ED/-ING/-ES [ME *axen* — more at ASK] *dial* **:** ASK

ax *abbr* **1** axiom **2** axis

axbreaker *or* **axebreaker** \'ˌˌˌ\ *n* -S **1 :** an Australian tree (*Notelaea longifolia*) with very hard wood **2 :** QUEBRACHO 1b

¹axe *var of* AX

²axe \'aks\ *n* -S [MF, fr. L *axis* — more at AXIS] *archaic* **:** AXIS

ax·el \'aksəl\ *n* -S *sometimes cap* [after *Axel* Paulsen *fl ab* 1890, its inventor] *figure skating* **:** a jump from the outer forward edge of one skate with 1½ turns taken in the air and a return to the outer backward edge of the other skate

axeman *var of* AXMAN

axen·ic \(')ā¦zenik, -zēn-\ *adj* [²*a-* + *xen-* + *-ic*] **:** STERILE — used esp. of animals isolated from all other living things ⟨~ worms⟩ or of their environment ⟨~ conditions⟩

axes *pl of* AXIS *or of* AX, *pres 3d sing of* AX

axes of coordinates \'ak,sēz-\ **1 :** two intersecting straight lines used as reference lines in plane Cartesian geometry **2 :** the three straight lines having a common point that are the intersections of the three coordinate planes of reference in three-dimensional Cartesian geometry

ax-grinder *or* **axe-grinder** \'ˌˌˌ\ *n* **:** one that has an ax to grind

ax-grinding *or* **axe-grinding** \'ˌˌˌ\ *n* **:** working for an ulterior purpose or toward a selfish end ⟨fulfills the . . . aims of its author with a minimum of *ax-grinding* —A.C.Danto⟩

axhammer \'ˌˌˌ\ *n* **:** an ax having two cutting edges or one cutting edge and one hammer face and used for dressing or spalling the rougher kinds of stone

axhead \'ˌˌ\ *n* **:** the head of an ax

axi- *comb form* [L, axle, axis, fr. *axis* — more at AXIS] **1 :** axis ⟨*axiform*⟩ **2 :** axis cylinder ⟨*axilemma*⟩

ax·i·al \'aksēəl\ *or* **ax·al** \-ksəl\ *adj* [*axi-, ax-* + *-al*] **1 a :** of or relating to an axis **b :** having the characteristics of or resembling an axis **2 a :** around an axis **:** in the direction of the axis **:** on or along the axis **b :** extending in a direction essentially parallel to the main axis of a cyclohexane or similar cyclic structure or characterized by bonds extending in this manner — distinguished from *equatorial* ⟨~ bonds⟩ ⟨~ hydrogen atoms⟩ — **ax·i·al·ly** \-ēəlē, -li\ *adv*

axial angle *n* **1 :** the angle between the two optic axes of a biaxial mineral **2 :** the angle between an axis of a plant and one of its appendages (as between a stem and a branch) — compare ABAXIAL, ADAXIAL

axial elements *n* **:** the angles between the crystallographic axes and the ratios of the unit-cell dimensions parallel to the axes of a crystal

axial feather *n* **:** a small feather between the primary and secondary wing feathers of some birds

axial filament *n* **:** a central often contractile filament of a flagellum **:** AXONEME

axial-flow \'ˌˌˌ¦ˌ\ *adj* **:** having the fluid or gas flowing parallel to the axis ⟨*axial-flow* turbine⟩ ⟨*axial-flow* pump⟩ — compare RADIAL-FLOW

axial gradient *n* **:** GRADIENT 4

ax·i·al·i·ty \,aksē'aləd·ē\ *n* -ES **:** the quality or state of being axial

axial pencil *n* **:** a system of planes intersecting on a straight line

axial plane *n* **:** the imaginary plane bisecting the angle between the limbs of an anticline or syncline

axial skeleton *n* **:** the skeleton of the trunk and head — compare APPENDICULAR

ax·i·ate \'aksēˌāt, -ē,āt\ *adj* [*axi-* + *-ate*] **:** AXIAL

axiate gradient *n* **:** GRADIENT 4

ax·i·a·tion \,aksē'āshən\ *n* -S [*axi-* + *-ation*] **:** the development of polarity in an embryo or its parts

ax·if·era \ak'sifərə\ [NL, fr. *axi-* + *-fera* (neut. pl. of *-fer*)] *syn of* GORGONACEA

ax·il \'aksəl, -(ˌ)sil\ *n* -S [NL *axilla*, fr. L, armpit — more at AXIS] **:** the distal usu. upper angle or point of divergence between a branch or leaf and the axis from which it arises

ax·ile \'ak,sīl\ *adj* [*ax-* + *-ile*] **:** belonging to or situated in the axis ⟨~ placentation⟩

ax·il·la \ak'silə\ *n, pl* **axil·lae** \-i(ˌ)lē, -i,lī\ *or* **axillas** [L] **1 :** the cavity beneath the junction of the arm or anterior appendage and shoulder or pectoral girdle containing the axillary artery and vein, a part of the brachial nerve plexus, many lymph nodes, and fat and areolar tissue **:** ARMPIT **2 :** SHOULDER

ax·il·lant \'aksələnt, (')ak¦silənt\ *adj* [ISV *axil* + *-ant*] **:** forming, subtending, or growing in an axil

ax·il·lar \ak'silə(r), 'aksəl-\ *n* -S [*axilla* + *-ar*] **:** an axillary part (as a vein, nerve, or feather)

¹ax·il·lary \'aksə,lerē, -ri *also (esp in sense 1)* (')ak¦silər-\ *also* **ax·il·lar** *usu* (')ak¦silə(r) *in sense 1 and* 'aksəl- *in sense 2*\ *adj* [prob. fr. F *axillaire*, fr. MF, fr. L *axilla* + MF *-aire* -ary] **1 :** of, near, or relating to the axilla ⟨an ~ nerve⟩ ⟨an ~ feather⟩ ⟨an ~ plate⟩ **2** [*axil* + *-ary, -ar*] **:** situated in, growing from, or relating to an axil ⟨~ buds⟩

²axillary \"\ *n* -ES **:** AXILLAR: as **a :** one of a group of feathers arising from the axilla and closing the space between flight feathers and body when a bird is flying **b :** one of the small lateral sclerites of the thorax with which the wing of an insect articulates and flexes

axillary artery *n* **:** the part of the main artery of the arm that lies in the axilla and that is continuous with the subclavian above and the brachial below

axillary fossa *n* **:** AXILLA 1

axillary gland *n* **:** any of the lymph nodes of the axilla

axillary nerve *n* **:** a large nerve arising from the posterior cord of the brachial plexus and supplying the deltoid and teres minor muscles and the skin of the shoulder

axillary scale *n* **:** ACCESSORY SCALE

axillary vein *n* **:** the large vein passing through the axilla continuous with the basilic below and the subclavian above

ax·ine \'ak,sīn\ *adj* [NL ²*Axis* + E *-ine*] **:** relating to or resembling the axis deer

axing *pres part of* AXE *or of* AX

ax·i·nite \'aksə,nīt\ *n* -S [F, fr. Gk *axinē* axhead, ax + F *-ite;* fr. its ax-shaped crystals] **:** a mineral $Ca_2(MnFe)Al_2BSi_4O_{15}OH$, consisting of borosilicate of aluminum and calcium with varying amounts of iron and manganese commonly in brown glassy sharp-edged triclinic crystals (hardness 6.5–7, sp. gr. 3.27–3.29)

ax·in·o·man·cy \'aksənə,mansē, ak'sin-\ *n* -ES [L *axinomantia*, fr. (assumed) Gk *axinomanteia*, fr. Gk *axino-* (fr. *axinē* axhead, ax) + *manteia* divination — more at AX, -MANCY] **:** divination by means of the movements of an ax placed on a post

ax·i·o·lite \'aksēə,līt\ *n* -S [ISV *axi-* + *-o-* + *-lite;* orig. formed as G *axiolit*] **:** a spherulitic aggregate rock with grouping about a line or axis — **ax·i·o·lit·ic** \¦ˌˌ¦lid·ik\ *adj*

ax·i·o·log·i·cal \¦ˌˌ¦läjəkəl\ *adj* **1 :** of or relating to axiology ⟨~ investigations⟩ **2 a :** based on or involving intrinsic or fundamental values ⟨an ~ absolutism⟩ ⟨the ~ crisis⟩ **b :** making moral obligations dependent on values ⟨~ ethical theories⟩ — contrasted with *deontological* — **ax·i·o·log·i·cal·ly** \-jək(ə)lē\ *adv*

ax·i·ol·o·gist \,aksē'äləjəst\ *n* -S **1 :** a student of or specialist in axiology **2 :** a philosopher advocating an axiological theory of ethics — contrasted with *deontologist*

ax·i·ol·o·gy \-'äləjē\ *n* -ES [ISV *axio-* (fr. Gk *axios* worth, worthy) + *-logy*] **:** the theory or study of values, primarily of intrinsic values (as those in ethics, aesthetics, and religion) but also of instrumental values (as those in economics) particularly with reference to the manner in which they can be known or experienced, their nature and kinds, and their ontological status

ax·i·om \'aksēəm\ *n* -S [L *axioma*, fr. Gk *axiōma*, fr. *axioun* to think worthy, think fit, fr. *axios* worth, worthy, fit; akin to Gk *agein* to lead, drive, weigh as much as — more at AGENT] **1 a :** a proposition, principle, rule, or maxim that has found general acceptance or is thought worthy thereof whether by virtue of a claim to intrinsic merit ⟨the ~*s* of wisdom⟩ or on the basis of an appeal to self-evidence ⟨the ~*s* of euclidean geometry⟩ **b** (1) *Baconianism* **:** an empirical rule or generalization based on experience (2) *Kantianism* **:** an immediately certain synthetic a priori proposition **2 :** a self-consistent statement about the primitive terms or undefinable objects that form the basis for discourse **:** POSTULATE ⟨the statement that there is one and only one straight line passing through two given points is an ~⟩ **syn** see PRINCIPLE

ax·i·o·ma·ta me·dia \,aksē'ōməd·ə'mēdēə, -sē'äm-\ *n pl* [NL, middle principles] **:** the general principles that are above simple empirical laws yet inferior to the highest generalizations or to those that are taken to be fundamental **:** middle principles

ax·i·o·mat·ic \¦aksēə¦mad·ik, -matik, -ēk\ *also* **ax·i·o·mat·i·cal** \-ə̇kəl, -ēk-\ *adj* [MGk *axiōmatikos*, fr. Gk, dignified, honorable, fr. *axiōmat-, axiōma* honor, axiom + *-ikos* -ic] **:** of or relating to an axiom or axioms: as **a :** taken for granted **:** SELF-EVIDENT ⟨an ~ truth⟩ **b :** APHORISTIC ⟨~ wisdom⟩ **c :** POSTULATIONAL, HYPOTHETICO-DEDUCTIVE — **ax·i·o·mat·i·cal·ly** \-ə̇k(ə)lē, -ēk-, -li\ *adv*

ax·i·o·mat·i·cist \-d·əsəst, -təsə̇-\ *n* -S **:** a student of or a specialist in axiomatics

ax·i·o·mat·ics \-d·iks, -tiks, -ēks\ *n pl but sing in constr* **1 :** a set of axioms **:** an axiomatized system **2 :** the study or a theory of axioms or axiom systems

ax·i·om·a·ti·za·tion \,aksē,ämədˌə̇'zāshən, -mə,tī'z-\ *n* -S **:** the act or process of axiomatizing — compare FORMALIZATION

ax·i·om·a·tize \,aksē'ämə,tīz\ *vt* -ED/-ING/-S [*axiomatic* + *-ize*] **1 :** to make axiomatic **2 :** to reduce to axioms or an axiom system

axiom of parallels : PARALLEL POSTULATE

axiom system *n* **:** a set of axioms together with formal rules for derivation of theorems — compare TRANSFORMATION RULE

¹ax·is \'aksə̇s\ *n, pl* **ax·es** \-k,sēz\ [L, axis, axle; akin to OE *eax* axis, axle, OHG *ahsa*, ON *öxull* axle, L *ala* wing, *axilla* armpit, Gk *axōn* axle, axis, Skt *akṣa* axle, axis, L *agere* to drive — more at AGENT] **1 a :** a straight line about which a body or a 3-dimensional figure rotates or may be supposed to rotate ⟨the earth's ~⟩ **b :** a straight line with respect to which a body, figure, or system of points is either radially or bilaterally symmetrical ⟨the ~ of a cone⟩ **c :** a straight line about which a line, curve, or plane figure is conceived to revolve in generating a solid of revolution ⟨the ~ of a hyperboloid⟩ **d :** one of the reference lines of a coordinate system ⟨the X ~ of a rectangular coordinate system⟩ **2** *archaic* **:** the axle of a wheel **3 a** (1) **:** the second vertebra of the neck of the higher vertebrates that is prolonged anteriorly within the foramen of the first vertebra and united with the odontoid process which serves as a pivot for the atlas and head to turn upon — called also *epistropheus* (2) **:** the first vertebra of amphibians **b :** any of various central, fundamental, or axial parts ⟨the cerebrospinal ~⟩ ⟨the skeletal ~⟩ **c :** AXILLA **4 :** the median lobe of a trilobite **5 :** the stem of a plant **:** the longitudinal support on which organs are arranged often including also the root, esp. a taproot **:** the hypothetical central line of any body or organ ⟨the ~ of a stem, petiole, or inflorescence⟩ **6 :** one of several imaginary lines assumed in describing the positions of the planes by which a crystal is bounded, the positions of atoms in the structure of the crystal, and the directions associated with vectorial and tensorial physical properties **7 :** a main line of direction, motion, growth, or extension ⟨the ~ of a city⟩ **8 a :** a line following the crest of a ridge or mountain range or the bottom of a depression in the earth's surface: as (1) **:** the crest line of an anticline ⟨anticlinal ~⟩ (2) **:** the trough line of a syncline ⟨synclinal ~⟩ **b :** the average direction of current at flood or ebb tide ⟨flood ~⟩ ⟨ebb ~⟩ **9 a** *in painting and sculpture* **:** an implied line through a composition to which elements in the composition are referred ⟨fruit and flowers arranged about a diagonal ~⟩ **b :** a line actually drawn and used as the basis of measurements in an architectural or other working drawing **10 :** any of three fixed lines of reference in an aircraft, usu. centroidal and mutually perpendicular, (1) one being the principal longitudinal line in the plane of symmetry, (2) one being perpendicular to this in the plane of symmetry, (3) one being perpendicular to the other two — called also respectively (1) *longitudinal axis*, (2) *normal axis*, (3) *lateral axis* **11** *dancing* **a :** the part of the body around which movements center and revolve **b :** the person, object, or imaginary line around which the dancers and dance patterns evolve or revolve **12 a :** an agreement entered into by two or more powers to demonstrate their solidarity of interest and to insure a common front and mutual support in foreign policies ⟨the Nazi-Fascist ~⟩ **b :** the countries adhering to such an agreement ⟨in the hope that either China or the London-Washington *Axis* . . . would listen —*Time*⟩ **13 :** any agreement of two or more in a common objective **:** PARTNERSHIP, ALLIANCE ⟨this unhealthy ~ . . . made it so difficult to bring any real democratic reform to the graft-ridden docks —Budd Schulberg⟩

²axis \"\ *n* [NL, fr. L, a wild animal of India] **1** *also* **axis deer** -ES **:** a deer (*Axis axis*) of India and other parts of southern Asia having rusine antlers and white-spotted body **2** *cap* **:** a genus of Cervidae containing the axis and hog deer

axis cylinder *n* **1 :** the central portion of a nerve fiber visibly divided into central and peripheral zones **2 :** the essential protoplasmic core of a medullated nerve fiber **:** AXON

axis cylinder process *n* **:** AXON

ax·ised \'aksə̇st\ *adj* **:** having an axis

axis of abscissas *in plane Cartesian coordinates* **:** the axis parallel to which abscissas are measured

axis of a curve : a straight line that bisects at right angles a system of parallel chords and divides the curve into two symmetrical portions (as in the parabola which has one such axis, the ellipse which has two, or the circle which has an infinite number)

axis of a lens : the common axis of symmetry of all the lens surfaces — compare OPTICAL AXIS

axis of an airfoil : a line perpendicular to an airfoil section

axis of ordinates *in plane Cartesian coordinates* **:** the axis parallel to which ordinates are measured

axis of rotation : the straight line through all fixed points of a rotating rigid body around which all other points of the body move in circles

axis of symmetry : the line about which a geometrical figure or drawing is symmetric

ax·i·symmetric \¦aksə +\ *also* **ax·i·symmetrical** \" +\ *adj* [*axi-* + *symmetric, symmetrical*] **:** symmetric in respect to an axis

ax·ite \'ak,sīt\ *n* -S [*ax-* + *-ite*] **1 :** AXON **2 :** any of the terminal branches of an axon

ax·le \'aksəl\ *n* -S [ME *axel-* (as in *axeltre* axletree) — more at AXLETREE] **1** *archaic* **:** AXIS ⟨the ~ of the earth⟩ **2 a :** the pin, bar, or shaft on which or with which a wheel or pair of wheels revolves — see DEAD AXLE, FLOATING AXLE, LIVE AXLE **b** (1) **:** the spindle of an axletree (2) **:** AXLETREE

axle bar *n* **:** an iron bar serving as an axletree

axle box *n* **1 :** a bushing in the hub of a wheel through which the axle passes **2** *Brit* **:** JOURNAL BOX

ax·led \'aksəld\ *adj* **:** having an axle

axle load *n* **:** the load of a vehicle applied through the wheels at both ends of an axle and equaling twice the wheel load

ax·le·tree \'aksəl,trē, -ltri\ *n* -S [ME *axeltre*, fr. ON *öxultrē*, fr. *öxull* axle + *trē* beam, tree — more at AXIS, TREE] **1 :** a fixed bar or beam having bearings at its ends upon which the wheels (as of a carriage, cart, or wagon) revolve **2** *obs* **:** AXIS

ax·man *or* **axe·man** \'aksmən, -,man, -maa(ə)n\ *n, pl* **axmen** *or* **axemen :** one that wields an ax; *specif* **:** a worker who uses an ax to chop trees and logs for firewood or to clear away trees and brush

ax·master *or* **axe·master** \'aks +,-\ *n* -S **1 :** BLACK IRONWOOD **1 2 :** QUEBRACHO 1

ax·min·ster \'ak,sminztə(r), -n(t)st-\ *n* -S *usu cap, often attrib* [fr. *Axminster*, England, its place of manufacture] **:** a machine-woven carpet having pile tufts of many types and colors inserted mechanically to form a variety of textures and patterns

axo- — see AX-

ax·o·den·drite \ˌaksə'denˌdrīt\ *n* -s [*ax-* + *dendrite*] **:** a nonmedullated process branching laterally from a nerve-cell axon

ax·og·a·my \ak'sägəmē\ *n* -ES [*ax-* + *-gamy*] **:** the condition of bearing sexual organs on a leafy stem

ax·oid \'akˌsȯid\ *or* **ax·oi·de·an** \(')ak¦sȯidēən\ *adj* [ISV *ax-* + *-oid*] **:** of or relating to the axis vertebra

ax·o·lotl \'aksəˌläd·ᵊl, -ät·ᵊl\ *n* -s [Nahuatl, lit., water doll, toy, fr. *atl* water + *xolotl* doll, toy, mythological personality] **:** any of several larval salamanders of the genus *Ambystoma* (as *A. tigrinum*) found in the mountain lakes of Mexico and the western U.S. ordinarily living and breeding in the larval condition but being capable when the pond it inhabits dries up of gradually losing the gills and fins while beginning to breathe air at the surface and of eventually emerging as an adult salamander — compare NEOTENY; see SIREDON

ax·om·e·ter \ak'sämad·ə(r)\ *n* -s [ISV *ax-* + *-meter*] **:** an instrument used to locate the position of optical axes; *esp* **:** one used to adjust a pair of spectacles properly with respect to the axes of the eyes

ax·on \'akˌsän\ *also* **ax·one** \'akˌsōn\ *n* -s [NL *axon*, fr. Gk *axōn* axis, vertebra] **:** a nerve-cell process that is typically single and long, that terminates in short branches relatively far from the cell body, and that as a rule except in certain sensory neurones conducts impulses away from the cell body — called also *axis cylinder process, axite, neuraxis, neurite*

ax·o·nal \'aksənᵊl\ *or* **ax·on·ic** \(')ak¦sänik\ *adj* [NL *axon* + E *-al* or *-ic*] **:** of or relating to an axon

ax·o·neme \'aksəˌnēm\ *n* -s [*ax-* + *-neme*] **:** a central fibril or bundle of fibrils in a flagellum

axon hillock *n* **:** the prominence on a nerve-cell body from which an axon arises

ax·o·nia \ak'sōnēə\ *n pl, usu cap* [NL, fr. Gk *axōn* axis + NL *-ia*] **:** organisms having a distinct axis or axes — opposed to *Anaxonia*

axono- *comb form* [ISV, fr. Gk *axon-, axōn* axle, axis — more at AXIS] **:** axis ⟨*axono*metry⟩ ⟨*Axono*phora⟩

ax·o·nol·i·pa \aksə'näləpə\ *n pl, cap* [NL, fr. *axono-* + *-lipa* (irreg. fr. Gk *leipein* to leave, be lacking) — more at LOAN] **:** a suborder of Graptoloidea including all nondendroid forms lacking an axial support — **ax·o·nol·i·pous** \¦==¦='əpəs\ *adj*

ax·o·no·met·ric projection \¦aksə(ˌ)nō¦metrik-\ *n* [*axono-* + *-metric*] **:** the representation on a single plane (as a drawing surface) of a three-dimensional object placed at an angle to the plane of projection

ax·o·noph·o·ra \ˌaksə'näf(ə)rə\ *n pl, cap* [NL, fr. *axono-* + *-phora*] **:** a suborder of Graptoloidea in which the colony has a virgula — **ax·on·o·phore** \ak'sänəˌfō(ə)r\ *adj* — **ax·o·noph·o·rous** \¦aksə¦näf(ə)rəs\ *adj*

ax·on·o·pus \ak'sänəpəs\ *n, cap* [NL, fr. *axono-* + *-pus*] **:** a genus of American grasses with oblong one-flowered spikelets in one-sided spikelike racemes — see CARPET GRASS

ax·o·nost \'aksəˌnäst\ *n* -s [NL *axon* + E *-ost*] **:** any of the interspinal bones supporting the dorsal and anal fins of a fish

axo·plasm \-ˌplazəm\ *n* -s [ISV *ax-* + *-plasm*] **:** the protoplasm of an axon usu. visibly distinct from that of a nerve-cell body or a dendrite

axo·plas·mic \ˌaksə'plazmək, -ksō-\ *adj* [*axoplasm* + *-ic*] **:** relating to or taking place in or along axoplasm ⟨~ transport in nerves⟩

axo·po·di·um \ˌaksə'pōdēəm\ *also* **axo·pod** \'aksəˌpäd\ *n, pl* **axopo·dia** \-'pōdēə\ *also* **axopods** [NL *axopodium*, fr. *ax-* + *-podium*] **:** a semipermanent pseudopodium that consists of an axial rod surrounded by an ectoplasmic sheath and that is typically present in Radiolaria and Heliozoa

axo·style \'aksə + ˌ-\ *n* -s [*ax-* + *-style*] **:** an axial rod present in many parasitic flagellates that is variously regarded as locomotor or supporting in function

ax·seed \'akˌsēd\ *n* **:** a European vetchlike herb (*Coronilla varia*) naturalized in the eastern U.S. and having umbels of pink-and-white flowers and sharp-angled pods — called also *crown vetch*

¹**ax·um·ite** *or* **ak·sum·ite** \'aksəˌmīt\ *adj, usu cap* [*Axum, Aksum*, ancient city of Ethiopia + E *-ite*] **:** of or relating to the ancient city or empire of Aksum

²**axumite** *or* **aksumite** \"\ *n* -s *usu cap* **1 :** one of the Axumite people **2 :** the language of the Axumite people

ax·unge \'akˌsənj\ *n* -s [MF & LL; MF *axunge*, fr. LL *axungia*, fr. L, axle grease, fr. *axis* axle + *-ungia* (fr. *ungere, unguere* to grease, anoint) — more at AXIS, OINTMENT] **:** fat or grease usu. of pigs or of geese; *esp* **:** lard prepared for medicinal use

¹**ay** *var of* AYE

²**ay** \'ī *sometimes* 'ā\ *interj* [ME *aymi* ay me] — usu. used with following *me* to express sorrow or regret ⟨~ me! I fondly dream —John Milton⟩

aya·ca·hui·te \ˌīyəkə'wēd·ā\ *or* **ayacahuite pine** *n* -s [Sp, fr. Nahuatl *ayacahuitl*, fr. *ayatl*, a kind of cloth + *cuahuitl* tree] **1 :** a large Mexican pine tree (*Pinus ayacahuite*) with long needles and extremely large yellowish red cones **2 :** the wood of ayacahuite

ayah \'īə, 'äyə\ *n* -s [Hindi *āyā, āya* (also in other languages of India), fr. Pg *aia* governess, nursemaid, chambermaid, fr. L *avia* grandmother] *India* **:** a native nurse or maid

aya·huas·co \ˌīə'wä(ˌ)skō, -ˌskə\ *n* -s [AmerSp *ayahuasca*, fr. Quechua *ayawáskha*] **:** a So. American vine (*Banisteria caapi*) of the family Malpighiaceae having roots that yield a drink which produces a delirious psychosis that alternates with prolonged hallucinations and dreams

aya·pa·na \ˌīyə'pänə\ *n* -s [Sp & Pg; Sp *ayapaná*, fr. Pg *aiapana, aiapina*, fr. Tupi *ayapana*] **:** a low spreading herbaceous Brazilian shrub (*Eupatorium aya-pana*) whose long narrow leaves are used to make a mildly stimulating decoction resembling tea

¹**aye** *also* **ay** \'ā, *in Brit dial* " *or* 'əi *or* 'ai\ *adv* [ME *aye, ai, agg*, fr. ON *ei*; akin to OE *ā*, *ō* always, OHG *eo, io*, Goth *aiws* time, eternity, L *aevum* age, lifetime, Gk *aiōn* age, eon, Skt *āyus* life] **:** for all time or for an indefinite time **:** FOREVER, EVER, ALWAYS, CONTINUALLY ⟨love that will ~ endure —W.S.Gilbert⟩ ⟨I ~ thought the quotations from him . . . most appetizing —John Buchan⟩

²**aye** *also* **ay** \'ī\ *adv* [earlier *I*, perh. fr. ME *yie*, alter. of *ye, ya* yes — more at YEA] **:** YES, CERTAINLY ⟨~, I mind him well —John Buchan⟩ — used as an affirmative response esp. in viva-voce voting, nautical language, and dialect speech; used reduplicatively in nautical language in response to an order or command ⟨*aye, aye*, sir means "I understand, sir, and I will do it"⟩

³**aye** *also* **ay** \'ī\ *n, pl* **ayes 1 :** an affirmative vote ⟨cast an ~ for all administration measures⟩ **2 :** one who votes affirmatively ⟨the ~s have it⟩

aye–aye \'īˌī\ *n* -s [F, fr. Malagasy *aiay*, of imit. origin] **:** a nocturnal lemur (*Daubentonia madagascariensis*) found in Madagascar that has incisor teeth like those of a rodent and long fingers with sharp nails

ayer·za's disease \ə'yerzəz-\ *n, usu cap A* [after Abel *Ayerza* †1918 Argentine physician] **:** a complex of symptoms marked esp. by cyanosis, dyspnea, polycythemia, and sclerosis of the pulmonary artery

ay·in *or* **'ay·in** *or* **ain** \'īən\ *n* -s [Heb *'ayin*] **1 :** the 16th letter of the Hebrew alphabet — symbol ע; see ALPHABET table **2 :** the letter of the Phoenician or of any of various other Semitic alphabets corresponding to Hebrew ayin

ayles·bury \'ālzbərē, -brē, -i\ *n* -s *usu cap* [fr. *Aylesbury*, England] **:** a breed of large white ducks somewhat similar to the Pekins

ayl·lu \'ī(ˌ)lü\ *n* -s [Quechua *áyllu*] **1 :** a sib or clan that constituted the basic socioeconomic unit of Inca society **2 :** a present-day Peruvian highland community of extended families that owns some land in common and that serves as an administrative unit

ay·ma·ra *also* **ai·ma·ra** \¦īmə¦rä\ *n, pl* **aymara** *or* **aymaras** *also* **aimara** *or* **aimaras** *usu cap* [Sp *aymará, aimará*, of AmerInd origin] **1 a :** an Indian people of Bolivia and Peru **b :** a member of such people **2 a :** the language of the Aymara people **b :** a language family of the Kechumaran stock comprising Aymara and formerly held to be an independent stock

aymara deformation *n, usu cap A* **:** a conoidal or oxycephalic head produced by binding the head of an infant with bands or with frontal pads and a band

ay·ma·ran \¦īmə¦rän\ *n* -s *usu cap* **:** AYMARA 2b

'ayn *or* **'ain** *or* **ain** \'īn, 'ān\ *n* -s [Ar *'ayn*] **:** the 18th letter of the Arabic alphabet — see ALPHABET table

ayont \ə'yänt\ *prep* [¹*a-* + *yont*] *dial* **:** BEYOND

ayous \ā'yüs\ *n* -ES [F, of African origin; akin to Yoruba *a²wu¹sa³* (*Monodora brevipes*)] **:** OBECHE

ayr *see* ¹AYRSHIRE\ *adj, usu cap* [fr. *Ayr*, burgh in Scotland] **1 :** of or from the burgh of Ayr, Scotland **:** of the kind or style prevalent in Ayr **2 :** AYRSHIRE

ayre *var of* AIR

¹**ayr·shire** \'a(a)(ə)rˌshi(ə)r, 'e(ə)r-; 'a(a)əˌshiə(r, 'eə,-; *also* -ˌshə(r); *sometimes by r-dissimilation* 'aˌshi(ə)r *or* 'aa,- *or* 'ai,-\ *or* **ayr** \'a(a)(ə)r, 'e(ə)r, 'a(a)ə\ *adj, usu cap* [fr. *Ayrshire* or *Ayr*, county in Scotland] **:** of or from the county of Ayr, Scotland **:** of the kind or style prevalent in the county of Ayr

²**ayrshire** \"\ *n* -s *usu cap* **:** an animal of a breed of hardy dairy cattle that originated in Ayr, that vary in color from white to red or brown, and that are esp. adapted to market milk production

ayrshire rose *n, usu cap A* **:** any of certain formerly popular double often scentless garden roses derived from the species rose (*Rosa arvensis*)

ayr stone \'a(a)(ə)r-, 'e(ə)r-\ *n, usu cap A* [fr. *Ayr*, Scotland] **:** a stone used as a whetstone and for surfacing and polishing

ayr·ton shunt \'a(a)(ə)rtᵊn-, 'e(ə)r-\ *n, usu cap A* [after William E. *Ayrton* †1908 Eng. electrical engineer and inventor] **:** a shunt used to increase the range of a galvanometer — called also *universal shunt*

ay·thya \ī'thīə\ *n, cap* [NL, fr. Gk *aithyia*, a kind of diving bird] **:** a genus of diving ducks including the canvasback, redhead, pochard, and related forms

ayu \'ä(ˌ)yü, 'ī(ˌ)(y)ü\ *also* **ai** \'ī\ *n* -s [Jap *ayu, ai*] **:** a small salmonlike anadromous fish (*Plecoglossus altivelis*) of Japan that is highly esteemed as a food fish — called also *sweetfish*

ayun·ta·mien·to \ī,yün(ˌ)tämē'entō\ *n* -s [Sp, fr. OSp, fr. *ayuntar* to join, unite (fr. *a* to — fr. L *ad* — + *yuntar, juntar* to join, fr. L *junctus*, past part. of *jungere* to join) + *-miento* -ment (fr. L *-mentum*) — more at AT, YOKE] **1 :** the municipal council or governing body of a town or city in Spain or the former Spanish colonies **2 :** a town hall in Spain or the former Spanish colonies

ayur·ve·da \'äyərˌvādə\ *n* -s *usu cap* [Skt *āyurveda*, fr. *āyur* life, vital power + *veda* knowledge] **:** the traditional Hindu system of medicine based largely on homeopathy and naturopathy — **ayur·ve·dic** \-dik\ *adj, usu cap*

ay·yub·id \ī'yübəd\ *also* **ay·yub·ite** \-üˌbīt\ *n* -s *usu cap* [*Ayyub* ibn-Shadhi †1173 Kurd general, father of the founder of the dynasty + E *-id* (patronymic suffix) or *-ite*] **:** a member of a Muslim dynasty founded in 1171 the separate branches of which flourished in Egypt, Syria, Palestine, Mesopotamia, and southern Arabia until the middle of the 13th century

az- *or* **azo-** *comb form* [ISV, fr. *azote*] **1 :** containing nitrogen ⟨*az*olitmin⟩ **2** *azo-* **:** containing the bivalent group —N=N— composed of doubly bonded nitrogen atoms united usu. on both sides to carbon ⟨*azo*methane $CH_3N{=}NCH_3$⟩ — compare DIAZ- 1

az *abbr* **1** azimuth **2** azure **3** *often cap A* nitrogen

aza- *or* **az-** *comb form* [ISV, fr. *az-* + *-a-*] **:** containing nitrogen in place of carbon, usu. the group —NH— for the group —CH_2— or a single nitrogen atom =N— for the group =CH— ⟨*aza*cyanine⟩ ⟨*aza*phenanthrene⟩ — compare OXA-, THIA-

aza·cyanine \ˌazə + \ *or* **azacyanine dye** *n* [*aza-* + *cyanine*] **:** any of a class of dyes differing from the cyanines in that the chain joining the heterocyclic rings contains one or more nitrogen atoms

azad·i·rach·ta \əˌzadə'raktə\ *n* -s [NL, fr. Per *āzād dirakht*, lit., free or noble tree] **:** MARGOSA

aza·fran \ˌäsə'frän, '==ˌ=\ *n* -s [Sp *azafrán*, fr. Ar *al-za'farān* the saffron] **:** SAFFRON

aza·lea \ə'zālyə *also* -lēə\ *n* [NL, fr. Gk, fem. of *azaleos* dry; fr. the supposition that it grows well in dry ground; akin to Czech *ozd* malt kiln, Gk *azein* to parch — more at ARDOR] **1** *cap, in some classifications* **:** a genus of shrubs or trees with deciduous leaves and funnel-shaped flowers now usu. considered a subgenus of *Rhododendron* **2** -s **:** any plant of the genus or subgenus *Azalea* **3** -s **:** a grayish red that is bluer than bois de rose, bluer, stronger, and slightly darker than Pompeian red, and stronger than appleblossom

aza·lea·mum \-(ˌ)məm\ *n* -s [*azalea* + chrysanthe*mum*] **:** any of various profusely flowering dwarf chrysanthemums

azan·de \ə'zandē\ *n, pl* **azande** *or* **azandes** *usu cap* **:** ZANDE

aza·ra's dog \ə'zärəz-\ *or* **azara's fox** *n, usu cap A* [trans. of NL *Canis Azarae*, after Félix de *Azara* †1821 Sp. soldier and naturalist] **:** a foxlike mammal (*Dusicyon gymnocercus* or *D. azarae*) of eastern and southern So. America

az·a·role \'azəˌrōl\ *n* -s [F *azerole*, fr. Sp *acerola*, fr. Ar *az-zu'rūr* the azarole] **1 :** the fruit of a shrub (*Crataegus azarolus*) of southern Europe **2 :** the shrub that bears azaroles

azed·a·rach \ə'zedəˌrak\ *n* -s [F *azédarac*, fr. Per *āzād dirakht*, lit., free or noble tree] **1 :** CHINABERRY 2 **2 :** the bark of the roots of the azedarach, formerly used as an emetic and anthelmintic

az·e·la·ic acid \¦azə¦lāik-\ *n* [*az-* + Gk *elaion* olive oil + E *-ic* — more at OIL] **:** a crystalline dicarboxylic acid $HOOC(CH_2)_7COOH$ made usu. by the oxidation of oleic acid or the acids from castor oil (as with nitric acid or ozone) and used in the form of derivatives esp. in lubricants and as plasticizers

az·e·late \'azᵊlˌāt, -ət\ *n* -s [ISV *azelaic* + *-ate*] **:** a salt or ester of azelaic acid

aze·o·trope \ā'zēəˌtrōp\ *n* -s [ISV ²*a-* + *zeo-* (fr. Gk *zein* to boil) + *-trope* — more at YEAST] **:** a liquid mixture that is characterized by a constant minimum or maximum boiling point which is lower or higher than that of any of the components and that distills without change in composition

aze·o·trop·ic \¦āˌzēə¦träpik\ *adj* [ISV *azeotrope* + *-ic*] **1 :** being an azeotrope **:** relating to or having the characteristics of an azeotrope **2 :** involving an azeotrope or components that can form an azeotrope ⟨~ separation⟩

azeotropic distillation *n* **:** distillation involving the presence of a compound that forms an azeotrope with at least one of the components of a liquid mixture which can thereby be more readily separated because of the resulting increase in the difference between the volatilities of the components of the mixture

aze·ot·ro·pism \ˌāzē'ä·trəˌpizəm\ *n* -s [ISV *azeotrope* + *-ism*] **:** AZEOTROPY

aze·ot·ro·py \ˌāzē'ä·trəpē\ *n* -ES [ISV *azeotrope* + *-y*] **:** the phenomenon of being an azeotrope

azer·bai·ja·ni \ˌazə(r)ˌbī'jänē, ˌäz-\ *also* **azer·bai·ja·nese** \-¦bījə¦nēz, -ēs\ *or* **azer·bai·ja·ni·an** \-ˌbī'jänēən\ *n, pl* **azerbaijani** *or* **azerbaijanis** *also* **azerbaijanese** *or* **azerbaijanians** *usu cap* [fr. *Azerbaijan*, region of southwestern Asia comprised of Azerbaijan, province of Iran, and Azerbaidzhan, republic of the U.S.S.R.] **1 :** a member of a Turkic-speaking people of the Azerbaidzhan Soviet Socialist Republic or the province of Azerbaijan in northwestern Iran **2 :** the Turkic language of the Azerbaijani

az·ha·roth \ˌäz(·h)ə'rōt, az-, -ōth,-ōs *also* ä'zō(ˌ)rōs\ *or* **az·ha·rot** \-ə'rōt,-ə'rōs\ *n pl, often cap* [Heb *azhārōth* warnings, exhortations] **:** Jewish liturgical poems containing exhortations to obedience to the religious commandments in the Torah

az·ide \'aˌzīd, 'ā-, -ˌzəd\ *n* -s [ISV *az-* + *-ide*] **:** a compound containing the azido group combined with an element or radical **:** HYDRAZOATE ⟨potassium ~ KN_3⟩ ⟨acid ~s⟩

az·i·do \'azə(ˌ)dō\ *adj* [*azido-*] **:** relating to or containing the group N_3

azido- \"\ *comb form* [ISV, fr. *azide* + *-o-*] **:** containing the univalent group N_3 derived from hydrazoic acid ⟨*azido*acetic acid⟩

azil·ian \ə'zēlyən, -zil-, -lēən\ *adj, usu cap* [Le Mas d' *Azil*, dept. Ariège, France, its type station + E *-ian*] **:** of or belonging to an early Mesolithic culture found primarily in France and characterized by stone and bone implements of degenerate Magdalenian type and esp. by pebbles painted with lines, dots, and geometric figures

az·i·muth \'azəməth\ *n* -s [ME *azimut, azimuth*, fr. (assumed) ML, fr. Ar *as-sumūt* the azimuth, pl. of *as-samt* the way, direction] **1 a :** an arc of the horizon measured between a fixed point (as true north) and the vertical circle passing through the center of an object, usu. in astronomy and navigation being measured clockwise from the north point through 360 degrees and in surveying clockwise from the south point ⟨the ~ of a star⟩ **b :** horizontal direction expressed as the angular distance between the direction of a fixed point (as the observer's heading) and the direction of the object **:** BEARING 7c **2 a :** the angle that the plane of polarization of polarized light makes with a specified reference plane **b :** a vectorial angle (as that defining the position of a particle in an orbit or of a point in an image field as measured around the instrumental axis) **3 :** a line or course **:** DIRECTION ⟨the ~ we must take to confirm the victories already won —F.R.Fogle⟩

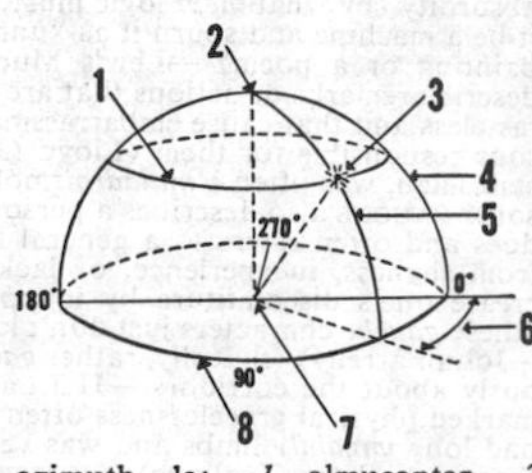

azimuth 1a: *1* almucantar, *2* zenith, *3* star, *4* meridian passing through north, *5* arc of vertical circle, *6* azimuth, *7* observer, *8* horizon

az·i·muth·al \ˌazə¦məthəl, -myüth-\ *adj* **:** of or relating to azimuth **:** in azimuth — **az·i·muth·al·ly** \-əlē\ *adv*

azimuthal equidistant projection *n* **:** a map projection of the surface of the earth so centered at any given point that a straight line radiating from the center to any other point represents the shortest distance and can be measured to scale

azimuthal equidistant projection centered on Washington, D.C.: *1* London, *2* Algiers, *3* Moscow, *4* Buenos Aires, *5* Tokyo, *6* Auckland

azimuthal quantum number *n* **:** an integer associated with the angular momentum of an atomic electron in any one of its possible stationary states, each state corresponding to a different integer — compare PRINCIPAL QUANTUM NUMBER, RADIAL QUANTUM NUMBER

azimuth circle *n* **1 :** one of the great circles of the celestial sphere intersecting each other in the zenith and nadir — called also *vertical circle;* compare MERIDIAN 2 **2 :** a horizontal graduated circle for indicating azimuth (as one having sight vanes and screens and attached to a compass to show magnetic azimuths or one having a telescope for accurate measurement of differences of azimuth)

azimuth compass *n* **:** a compass resembling the mariner's compass and having vertical sights used for taking the magnetic azimuth of a celestial body

azimuth dial *n* **:** a horizontal sundial whose gnomon is at right angles to the plane of the horizon

az·ine \'aˌzēn, 'ā-, -ˌzən\ *n* -s [ISV *az-* + *-ine*] **1 a :** any of a large class of organic compounds that is characterized by a 6-membered ring containing two or more atoms of nitrogen or at least one atom of nitrogen and one other hetero atom (as oxygen or sulfur) and that is subdivided according to the kind and number of hetero atoms (as diazines, triazines, oxazines, thiazines); *esp* **:** a paradiazine or analogous oxazine or thiazine **b :** AZINE DYE **2 :** a compound of the general formula $RCH{=}NN{=}CHR$ or $R_2C{=}NN{=}CR_2$ formed by the action of hydrazine on aldehydes or ketones

azine dye *also* **azine** *n* -s **:** any of a class of acid quinonoid-type dyes containing a paradiazine ring fused to one or more aromatic rings and used esp. in dyeing wool, silk, paper, and leather and in coloring fats, oils, lacquers, and plastics; *also* **:** an oxazine or thiazine dye

az·lactone \az + \ *n* -s [*az-* + *lactone*] **:** a lactone of an unsaturated nitrogenous hydroxy acid (as the enol form $C_6H_5C(OH){=}NCH_2COOH$ of hippuric acid), some lactones being useful in the synthesis of alpha-amino acids

az·lon \'azˌlän\ *n* -s [*az-* + *-lon* (as in *nylon*)] **:** any of various textile fibers made from protein sources (as zein and casein)

azo \'a(ˌ)zō\ *adj* [*az-*] **:** relating to or containing the group —N=N— united at both ends to carbon usu. in two univalent organic radicals, esp. aryl radicals with the formation of solid compounds varying in color from yellow to red to violet and blue — see COUPLE *vi* 2b, DISAZO, TRISAZO; compare DIAZO

azo- — see AZ-

az·o·benzene \ˌazō, ˌā- + \ *n* -s [ISV *az-* + *benzene*] **:** an orange-red crystalline compound $C_6H_5N{=}NC_6H_5$ obtained by reducing nitrobenzene and used as an insecticide esp. for spider mites in greenhouses

azo dye *n* **:** any of a very large class of dyes characterized by the presence of one or more azo groups, made by coupling an aromatic diazonium compound with a coupling component (as a phenol, an aromatic amine, or a pyrazolone), and noted for their versatility, being applied by various processes in dyeing or coloring a wide range of materials (as textile fibers, leather, plastics, foods, drugs, and cosmetics) and being used in making pigments and diazotypes — see DYE table I

az·o·fi·ca·tion \ˌazōfə'kāshən, ˌāz-\ *n* -s [*az-* + *-fication*] **:** nonsymbiotic fixation of atmospheric nitrogen in soil by bacteria

¹**azo·ic** \(')ā¦zōik, ə'z-\ *adj* [²*a-* + *-zoic*] **:** without life; *specif* **:** of or relating to the part of geologic time that antedates life — compare ARCHEAN

²**azo·ic** \(')a¦zōik *also* (')ā¦-, ə¦-\ *adj* [ISV *az-* + *-ic*; prob. orig. formed as F *azoique*] **:** AZO — now usu. restricted to insoluble dyes formed on the fiber

azoic dye *also* **azoic** *n* -s **:** any of a group of water-insoluble azo dyes formed by coupling of the components on the fiber — called also *ice color, ingrain dye;* see DYE table I

az·o·im·ide \ˌazō'iˌmīd, ˌāz-, -məd\ *also* **az·o·im·id** \-'iməd\ *n* -s [ISV *az-* + *imide;* orig. formed as G *azoimid*] **:** HYDRAZOIC ACID

az·ole \'aˌzōl, 'ā-\ *n* -s [ISV *az-* + *-ole*] **1 :** any of a large class of organic compounds that is characterized by a 5-membered ring containing two or more hetero atoms at least one of which is nitrogen and that is subdivided analogously to the azines (as diazoles, triazoles, thiazoles) **2 :** PYRROLE

az·o·lit·min \ˌazō'litmən, ˌā-\ *n* -s [ISV *az-* + *litmus* + *-in*] **:** a dark red nitrogenous coloring matter obtained from litmus and used as an acid-base indicator

azol·la \ə'zälə\ *n, cap* [NL] **:** a genus of minute water ferns (family Salviniaceae) having a sporophyte consisting of pinnately branching stems with small distichous 2-lobed leaves

az·o·methine \ˌazō, ˌā +\ *n* -s [*az-* + *methine*] **1 :** METHYLENIMINE **2** *or* **azomethine compound :** any of a class of compounds regarded as derivatives of methylenimine and characterized by the grouping −CH=N− or >C=N− **:** SCHIFF BASE — used esp. of dyes important in color photography

azon \'āˌzōn, -än\ *or* **azon bomb** *n* -s *often cap A* [*az*imuth *only*] **:** an aerial bomb that can be guided to the left or right by radio control — compare RAZON

azon·al \(ˈ)ā+\ *adj* [[2]*a-* + *zonal*] **:** not arranged in zones ⟨~ heating⟩

azonal soil *n* **1 :** a major soil group often classified as a category of the highest rank and embracing soils that lack well-developed horizons because of immaturity or other factors that have prevented their development — compare INTRAZONAL SOIL, ZONAL SOIL **2 :** any soil belonging to the azonal soil group (as the rocky soils on steep slopes)

azo·osper·mia \āˌzōə'spərmēə, əˌz-\ *n* -s [NL, fr. Gk *azōos* lifeless (fr. *a-* [2]a- + *-zōos*, fr. *zōē* life) + NL *-spermia* — more at QUICK] **:** absence of spermatozoa from the seminal fluid — compare ASPERMIA — **azo·osper·mic** \-mik, -ēk\ *adj*

azo·protein \ˈa(ˌ)zō+\ *n* -s [*az-* + *protein*] **:** any of various compounds made by coupling a protein (as serum albumin) with a diazotized amine (as histamine or sulfanilamide), and sometimes used as synthetic antigens

[1]**azor·e·an** \(ˈ)āˈzōrēən, -ȯr- *also* ə'z-\ *adj, usu cap* [*Azores*, islands in the No. Atlantic + E *-an*] **1 :** of, relating to, or characteristic of the Azores **2 :** of, relating to, or characteristic of Azoreans

[2]**azorean** \"\ *n* -s *cap* **:** a native or inhabitant of the Azores

azo ru·bine \ˌazō'rüˌbēn, ˌāz-, -ˌbən\ *n, usu cap A&R* [*az-* + L *rub*eus red + E *-ine* — more at RUBY] **:** a mordant acid azo dye that dyes wool bluish red — called also *carmoisin;* see DYE table I (under *Acid Red 14*)

az·o·sulfamide *also* **az·o·sulphamide** \ˌazō, ˌā- +\ *n* -s [*az-* + *sulfamide*] **:** a dark red crystalline azo compound $C_{18}H_{14}N_4Na_2O_{10}S_3$ of the sulfa class having antibacterial effect similar to that of sulfanilamide

azote \'aˌzōt, ə'z-\ *n* -s [F, fr. *a-* [2]a- (fr. Gk) + *-zote* (irreg. fr. Gk *zōē* life); fr. the observation that it cannot take the place of air in supporting life — more at QUICK] **:** NITROGEN

azo·tea \ˌazō'tāə\ *n* -s [Sp, fr. Ar *as-suṭayḥ* the azotea] **:** a flat roof or platform on the top of a house or other building

az·o·te·mia *also* **az·o·tae·mia** \ˌazə'tēmēə\ *n* -s [NL, fr. ISV *azote* + NL *-emia, -aemia*] **:** an excess of nitrogenous bodies in the blood as a result of kidney insufficiency associated with kidney disease or secondary to disease in other organs — compare AZOTURIA — **az·o·tem·ic** \ˈ==ˈtemik, -tē-\ *adj*

az·oth \'aˌzȯth, -ōth, -äth\ *n* -s [Ar *az-zā'ūq* the mercury] **1 :** mercury regarded by alchemists as the first principle of metals **2 :** the universal remedy of Paracelsus

azot·ic \(ˈ)aˈzäd·ik, ə'z-\ *adj* [F *azotique*, fr. *azote* + *-ique* -ic] **:** NITROGENOUS, NITRIC ⟨~ gas⟩ ⟨~ acid⟩

azo·to·bac·ter \a'zōd·əˌbaktə(r), ə'z-\ *n* [NL, fr. ISV *azote* + NL *-o-* + *-bacter*] **1** *cap* **:** a genus of large flagellated gram-negative rod-shaped or spherical nonsymbiotic bacteria (order Eubacteriales) occurring in soil and sewage that fix atmospheric nitrogen in the presence of carbohydrates and derive growth energy from oxidation of carbohydrates **2** -s *sometimes cap* **:** a bacterium of the genus *Azotobacter*

az·o·tom·e·ter \ˌazə'tämәd·ə(r)\ *n* -s [ISV *azote* + *-o-* + *-meter;* orig. formed in G] **:** NITROMETER

azot·uria \ˌazə'tu̇rēə, -ə·'tyu̇-\ *n* -s [NL, fr. ISV *azote* + NL *-uria*] **:** an excess of urea or other nitrogenous substances in the urine; *specif* **:** an acute disease of horses marked by passage of dark urine rich in nitrogenous compounds, stiffening and muscular paralysis, profuse sweating, and collapse that occurs in animals brought back to work after being heavily fed and inadequately exercised for several days — compare AZOTEMIA

az·oxy \(ˈ)a'zäksē, (ˈ)ā-\ *adj* [*azoxy-*] **:** relating to or containing the group −N(O)=N−

azoxy- *comb form* [ISV, fr. *az-* + *oxy-*] **:** containing the bivalent group −N(O)=N− composed of two nitrogen atoms and one oxygen atom united usu. on both sides to carbon ⟨*azoxy*naphthalene $C_{10}H_7N(O)=NC_{10}H_7$⟩

az·oxy·benzene \ˌa(ˌ)zäksē, ˌā- +\ *n* -s [ISV *azoxy-* + *benzene*] **:** a yellow crystalline compound $C_6H_5N(O)=NC_6H_5$ formed by reduction of nitrobenzene and yielding azobenzene on further reduction

azo yellow *n* **:** an acid dye — see DYE table I (under *Acid Yellow 63*)

az·ra·el \'azrāˌel\ *n* -s *usu cap* [Ar *'Azrā'īl*, fr. Heb *'Ăzar'ēl*, lit., God has helped] **:** the angel of death in Jewish and Islamic thought who watches over the dying and separates the soul from the body

az·tec \'azˌtek *sometimes* 'aˌstek\ *n* -s [Sp *azteca*, fr. Nahuatl, pl. of *aztecatl*, fr. *Aztlan*, *Aztatlan*, their legendary place of origin, lit., near the cranes (fr. *azta* — pl. of *aztatl* crane — + *tlan* near) + *-tecatl* (suffix denoting origin)] **1** *usu cap* **a :** a Nahuatl people that founded the Mexican empire conquered by Cortes in 1519 **b** (1) **:** a member of such people (2) **:** a member of any Nahuatl people or of any people under Aztec influence **2** *usu cap* **a :** the language of the Aztec people **b :** NAHUATL **3** *often cap* **:** a moderate to strong yellowish brown that is lighter and slightly redder than tobacco brown and slightly redder and darker than clay — called also *Indian tan*

az·te·ca \az'tākə, a'stā-\ *n, pl* **azteca** *or* **aztecas** *usu cap* [Sp] **:** AZTEC 1

az·tec·an \'azˌtekən *sometimes* 'aˌste-\ *adj, usu cap* **:** of or relating to the Aztec people or their language

aztec lily *n, usu cap A* **:** JACOBEAN LILY

aztec marigold *n, usu cap A* **:** AFRICAN MARIGOLD

aztec maroon *n, often cap A* **:** a grayish purplish red that is redder and deeper than average rose plum and redder and duller than tourmaline pink or daphne pink

azu·lene \'azhəˌlēn\ *n* -s [ISV *azul-* (fr. Sp *azul* blue, fr. OSp *azur, azul*) + *-ene* — more at AZURE] **1 a :** a liquid hydrocarbon $C_{15}H_{18}$ of intense blue color found in some essential oils (as oil of cubebs) and in lignite tar **b :** any of various blue to violet or green hydrocarbons closely related chemically to this hydrocarbon and occurring naturally in essential oils or formed from various colorless naturally occurring sesquiterpenes **2 :** a synthetic blue crystalline unsaturated bicyclic hydrocarbon $C_{10}H_8$ that resembles the isomeric naphthalene in some properties but is more active chemically and that is the parent compound of the azulenes; cyclo-penta-cyclo-heptene

azu·lite \-ˌlīt\ *n* -s [Sp *azul* blue + E *-ite*] **:** a mineral consisting of translucent pale blue smithsonite often found in Arizona and Greece in masses weighing over 20 pounds

[1]**azure** \'azhə(r), 'aizh-, *rare in stand speech in US at least* 'āzh-\ *n* -s [ME *asur*, fr. OF *azur*, prob. fr. OSp *azur, azul*, alter. of Ar *lāzaward, lāzuward* lapis lazuli, blue, fr. Per *lāzhuward*] **1** *archaic* **:** LAPIS LAZULI **2 :** the heraldic color blue **3 a :** the blue color of the clear sky **b :** any blue somewhat resembling that of the sky **4 :** the unclouded sky ⟨above, the crystal ~, perfect, pale —F.T.Palgrave⟩

[2]**azure** \"\ *adj* [ME *asur*, fr. *asur*, n.] **1 :** of the heraldic color blue **2 :** resembling the color of the unclouded sky **3 :** resembling the unclouded sky **:** CLOUDLESS, CLEAR **4 :** composed of horizontal parallel lines (as a tooled or stamped design on a book cover)

[3]**azure** \"\ *vt* -ED/-ING/-S **:** to make blue in color ⟨morning up the eastern stair marches, *azuring* the air —A.E.Housman⟩

azu·rean \ˈazhəˈrēən; ə'zhu̇r-, a'-\ *adj* [*azure* + *-ean* (as in *cerulean*)] **:** [2]AZURE 2

azure blue *n* **1 :** [1]AZURE 3 **2 :** any of several blue pigments: as **a :** COBALT BLUE 1a **b :** SMALT 1 **3** *often cap A & B* **:** any of several dyes — see DYE table I (under *Acid Blue*)

azured *adj* **:** [2]AZURE 2

azure stone *n* **1 :** LAPIS LAZULI **2 :** LAZULITE

azur·ite \'azhəˌrīt\ *n* -s [F, fr. *azur* azure + *-ite*] **1 :** a mineral $Cu_3(OH)_2(CO_3)_2$ consisting of blue basic carbonate of copper, occurring in monoclinic crystals, massive, and in earthy form, being an ore of copper, and formerly used as a pigment (hardness 3.5–4, sp. gr. 3.77–3.83) — compare MALACHITE **2 :** a semiprecious stone derived from azurite when compact

azurite blue *n* **:** a moderate blue that is greener and duller than Dresden blue or average copen, greener and paler than smalt or bluebird, and greener and slightly duller than pompadour — called also *air blue*, *Armenian stone*, *bice blue*, *blue ashes*, *blue bice*, *blue verditer*, *cendre*, *ceramic*, *chessylite blue*, *copper blue*, *Hungarian blue*, *Lambert's blue*, *lime blue*, *mineral blue*, *mountain blue*, *stone blue*, *verditer blue*

az·ur·malachite \ˌazhər +\ *n* -s [*azur*ite + *malachite*] **:** azurite mixed with malachite, usu. occurring massive and concentrically banded, and used as ornamental stone

azury \'azhərē\ *adj* [[2]*azure* + *-y*] **:** azure or tinted with azure

azygo- *comb form* [ISV, fr. Gk *azygos*] **:** azygous ⟨*azygo*spore⟩

azygomatous \ˈā +\ *adj* [[2]*a-* + *zygomatous*] **:** without zygomatic arches

azy·go·spore \ā'zīgōˌspō(ə)r, ə'z-\ *n* -s [*azygo-* + *spore*] **:** a reproductive body found in certain fungi (class Phycomycetes) and in some algae that resembles a zygospore but is formed without gametic fusion

azygote \ā, ə +\ *n* -s [[2]*a-* + *zygote*] **:** an individual produced by haploid parthenogenesis

[1]**az·y·gous** *or* **az·y·gos** \'azəgəs\ *adj* [NL *azygos*, fr. Gk, fr. *a-* [2]a- + *-zygos* (fr. *zygon* yoke) — more at YOKE] **:** not one of a pair **:** ODD, SINGLE ⟨the ~ muscle of the uvula⟩

[2]**azygous** *or* **azygos** \"\ *n* -ES **:** an azygous part

azygous vein *n* **:** any of a system of three veins which drain the thoracic wall and much of the abdominal wall and which form a collateral circulation when either the inferior or superior vena cava is obstructed; *esp* **:** a vein that receives blood from the right half of the thoracic and abdominal walls, ascends along the right side of the vertebral column, and empties into the superior vena cava — see HEMIAZYGOUS VEIN

azyme \'aˌzīm\ *also* **azym** \-zəm\ *n* -s [LL *azyma*, fr. L, neut. pl. of *azymus* unleavened, fr. Gk *azymos*, fr. *a-* [2]a- + *-zymos* (fr. *zymē* leaven); prob. akin to L *jus* broth — more at JUICE] **:** unleavened bread: **a :** such bread eaten by the Jews at the Passover **b :** such bread consecrated by Christians of the Western church in celebrating the Eucharist

az·zaz·a·me \ə'zazəmē\ *or* **az·zaz·i·mah** \-mə\ *n* -s *usu cap* [Ar *'Azāzamiyah*, colloq. Ar *'Az(z)āzme*] **1 :** an Arab people living chiefly in the Sinai peninsula but found scattered throughout the Arab world **2 :** a member of the Azzazame people

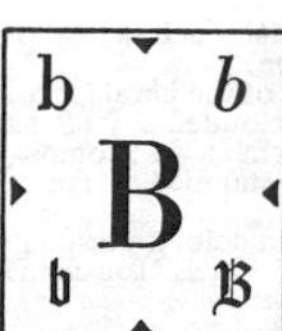

¹b \'bē\ *n, pl* **b's** *or* **bs** \'bēz\ *often cap, often attrib* **1 a :** the second letter of the English alphabet **b :** an instance of this letter printed, written, or otherwise represented **c :** a speech counterpart of orthographic *b* (as *b* in *bib, baby, dabbed,* or German *bühne*) **2 a :** the keynote of B major or B minor **b :** the tone B **3 :** a printer's type, a stamp, or some other instrument for reproducing the letter *b* **4 :** someone or something arbitrarily or conveniently designated *b* esp. as the second in order or class ⟨A deeded land to *B*⟩ **5 a :** a grade assigned by a teacher or examiner rating a student's work as good, better than average, but short of excellent ⟨the typical student begins at D, moves up steadily, and is doing C or *B* work at the finish —Philip Marsh⟩ **b :** one graded or rated with a B ⟨a *B* student⟩ **c :** a motion picture produced on a small budget and usu. shown as a supplement to the main feature of a program **6 :** something having the shape of the capital letter B

²b *abbr, often cap* **1** bachelor **2** bacillus **3** back **4** bag **5** baht **6** balboa **7** bale **8** ball **9** ban **10** [ML *bancus*] bench **11** band **12** bar **13** barge **14** baron **15** base **16** bass **17** basso **18** bat **19** bath **20** battery **21** battle **22** Baumé **23** bay **24** bearing **25** [L *beata* (fem.) & *beatus* (masc.) — more at BEATIFY] blessed **26** before **27** bel **28** Bible **29** bid **30** bishop **31** bitch **32** black **33** blend **34** blue **35** boatswain **36** bogach **37** boils at **38** bolivar **39** boliviano **40** bomber **41** bond **42** book **43** born **44** bottom **45** bowled **46** brass **47** breadth **48** breezing **49** brick **50** brightness **51** British **52** British thermal unit **53** broadcast **54** broken **55** brotherhood **56** bulb **57** bulletin **58** bye

³b *symbol, cap* **1** boron **2** magnetic induction

ba \'bä\ *n* -s [alternate transliteration of Egypt *b*ꜣ] **:** the living, immortal, eternal, and ultimately divine soul in Egyptian religious belief represented as a bird with a human head and believed to leave the body at death and return eventually to revivify the body if it is preserved

BA \(')bē¦ā\ *abbr or n* -s Bachelor of Arts

Ba *symbol* barium

¹baa *or* **ba** \'ba, 'baa, 'bä, 'bȧ\ *n* -s [imit.] **:** the bleat of a sheep

²baa *or* **ba** \"\ *vi* -ED/-ING/-S **:** to cry baa **:** BLEAT ⟨the black goats and the dirty, gray-white sheep began slowly to amble down the slope, *~ing* —Nora B. Kubie⟩

baal \'bā(ə)l\ *n, pl* **baa·lim** \'bā(ə)ləm, 'bāə,lim\ *or* **baals** \-(ə)lz\ [Heb *ba'al* lord, name of a divinity] **1** *often cap* **:** any of a multitude of Canaanite and Phoenician chief deities worshiped individually rather than collectively at localized sanctuaries and commonly distinguished by name according to area or function (as Baal-peor, Baal of Peor) **2 :** a false god **:** IDOL

baal–ha–bos *var of* BALABOS

baal·ism \'bā(ə),lizəm\ *n* -s *often cap* **1 :** the worship of Baal **2 :** IDOLATRY

baal·ist·ic \¦bāə¦listik, (')bā¦l-\ *adj, often cap* **:** of or relating to baalism

baal·ite \'bā(ə),līt\ *n* -s *often cap* **:** an adherent of or believer in baalism

baal·ize \'bā(ə),līz\ *vt* -ED/-ING/-S **:** to convert to or influence toward the worship of Baal or to some other form of idolatry

baal ko·re \bäl'kō(,)rā\ *n* [Heb *ba'al qōrē'*, lit., reading master] **:** the person (as the cantor) who reads the weekly excerpt from the Torah during synagogue services

baal·shem *also* **bal·shem** \bäl'shām\ *n, often cap* [Heb *ba'al shēm* one who possesses or works through the (divine) name] **:** one believed among Jews (as earlier Polish Jews) to work wonders by the use of the name of God

baas \'bäs, 'bȧs\ *n* -ES [Afrik, fr. MD *baes* — more at BOSS] *Africa* **:** MASTER, BOSS — often used as a form of address

¹ba·ba *or* **baba au rhum** \'bä,bä'ō'rəm, *F* bȧbȧōrôm\ *n, pl* **babas** *or* **babas au rhum** \-äzō-,-äzō-\ [*baba* fr. F, fr. Pol, lit., old woman; *baba au rhum* fr. F, baba with rum — more at BABUSHKA] **:** a rich yeast-leavened usu. fruited cake soaked in a rum and sugar syrup before serving

²ba·ba \'bä,bä\ *n* -s [Malay, colonial-born] *in the southern part of the Malay peninsula* **:** a Chinese or sometimes a European or Eurasian male born in Malacca, Penang, or the crown colony of Singapore

³baba \"\ *n* -s [Hindi *bābā* father, prob. fr. Ar; fr. the use in India of parent terms when addressing children] *India* **:** BABY, CHILD

ba·ba·coo·te \,bäbə'küd·ē\ *also* **ba·ba·ko·to** \-kōd·(,)ō\ *n* -s [Malagasy *babakoto*] **:** a large Madagascan short-tailed lemur (*Indri indri*)

ba·ba·la \'bäbə,lä, -,lə\ *n* -s [Afrik] **:** PEARL MILLET

babasco *var of* BARBASCO

ba·bas·su \¦bäbə¦sü\ *n* -s [Pg *babaçú*] **:** a tall pinnate-leaved palm (*Orbignya speciosa* or *O. martiana*) of northeastern Brazil with hard-shelled nuts yielding a valuable oil

babassu oil \"-\ *also* **ba·ba·çu oil** \"\ *n* **:** a fatty oil obtained from kernels of babassu nuts that is similar in properties and uses to coconut oil

ba·bay·lan *or* **ba·bai·lan** \,bäbī'län\ *or* **ba·bal·yan** \-bəl'yän\ *or* **ba·ba·li·an** \-bəlē'än\ *n, pl* **ba·bay·la·nes** \-ä,nās\ [of Philippine origin; akin to Tagbanuwa *babalyan*, fr. *balyan* mediumship, esoteric religious skill] *in central and southern Philippines* **:** a pagan priest, priestess, or medium

¹bab·bitt *also* **bab·bit** \'babət, *usu* -əd·+V\ *n* -s *sometimes cap* [*babbitt* (*metal*)] **1 :** BABBITT METAL **2 :** a babbitt-metal lining for a bearing

²babbitt \"\ *also* **babbit** *adj, sometimes cap* **:** made of or relating to babbitt metal

³babbitt \"\ *vt* -ED/-ING/-S **:** to line or furnish with babbitt metal

⁴babbitt \"\ *also* **babbit** *n* -s *usu cap* [after George F. *Babbitt*, stereotype Am. businessman portrayed in the novel *Babbitt* (1922) by Sinclair Lewis †1951 Am. novelist] **:** a person (as a business or professional man) who conforms unthinkingly and complacently to prevailing middle-class standards of respectability, who makes a cult of material success, and who is contemptuous of or incapable of appreciating artistic or intellectual values ⟨he was repelled by the prosperous and patronizing *Babbitts*⟩ — **bab·bitt·i·cal** \(')ba¦bid·əkəl\ *adj, usu cap* — **bab·bitty** \'babəd·ē\ *adj, usu cap*

bab·bitt·er \-əd·ə(r)\ *n* -s [³*babbitt* + -*er*] **:** a worker who applies babbitt metal to bearings or other surfaces

babbitting jig *n* [fr. pres. part. of ³*babbitt*] **:** a molding box in which bearings or bearing brasses are placed while being babbitted

bab·bitt·ism \-əd·,izəm\ *n* -s *often cap* [George F. *Babbitt* + E -*ism*] **:** BABBITTRY

babbitt metal *also* **babbit metal** *n, sometimes cap B* [after Isaac *Babbitt* †1862 Am. inventor] **:** either of two alloys used for lining bearings: **a :** a tin-base alloy; *esp* **:** one containing 2 to 8 percent copper and 5 to 15 percent antimony **b :** a lead-base alloy containing 1 to 10 percent tin and 10 to 15 percent antimony with or without some arsenic

bab·bitt·ry *also* **bab·bit·ry** \-ətrē\ *n* -ES *often cap* [George F. *Babbitt* + E -*ry*] **:** the attitudes, beliefs, and conduct characteristic of Babbitts ⟨the obvious ~ and middle-class convention are always being challenged on some level by the individual —Elizabeth Janeway⟩

bab·bla·tive \'babləd·iv\ *adj* [¹*babble* + -*ative* (as in *talkative*)] **:** GARRULOUS

¹bab·ble \'babəl\ *vb* **babbled; babbled; babbling** \-b(ə)liŋ\ **babbles** [ME *babelen;* prob. of imit. origin like ME *babe*, babe baby, LG *babbeln* to babble, ON *babba*, L *babulus* babbler, Gk *barbaros* foreign, LGk *babazein* to speak inarticulately, Skt *balbalā* stammering sound, *barbara* stammering] *vi* **1 a :** to utter meaningless sounds as though talking ⟨a baby *babbling* in his crib⟩ **b :** to talk foolishly **:** PRATTLE ⟨~ about his responsibilities⟩ **c :** to talk excessively **:** CHATTER ⟨*babbling* about their plans for the coming holidays —Mabel C. Widdemer⟩ **2 a :** to make sounds as though babbling ⟨the *babbling* of a mountain stream⟩ ⟨birds *babbling* in the hedge⟩ **b** *of a hound* **:** to bay before picking up the scent ~ *vt* **1 :** to utter in an incoherent, inane, or meaninglessly repetitious manner ⟨why did the red-haired man ~ those excuses —Max Beerbohm⟩ **2 :** to reveal (as a secret) by talking too freely or thoughtlessly ⟨before we could stop him he had *babbled* our plans to the group⟩

²babble \"\ *n* -s [ME *bable*, fr. *babelen*] **1 :** foolish or idle talk **:** CHATTER, NONSENSE ⟨making ~ at an afternoon tea⟩ **2 :** continuous meaningless vocal sounds ⟨the ~ of a baby in the next room⟩ **:** a murmur or a continuity of confused sounds ⟨the ~ of four or more voices going on at once —G.A.Miller⟩ ⟨the ~ of birds⟩; *specif* **:** the unwanted disturbing sounds in a telephone circuit resulting from cross-talk interference from a large number of other active circuits

bab·ble·ment \-bəlmənt\ *n* -s **:** ²BABBLE

bab·bler \'bab(ə)lə(r)\ *n* -s **:** one that babbles; *specif* **:** any of numerous birds esp. of the family Timaliidae having loud chattering notes

babbling *n* -s [ME *babeling*, fr. gerund of *babelen*] **:** idle talk or chatter **:** BABBLE ⟨her early love letters are almost childish ~*s* —*Britain Today*⟩

babbling·ly *adv* **:** in a babbling manner

babbling thrush *n* **:** any of several thrushlike babblers

bab·bly \'bab(ə)lē\ *adj* **:** CHATTERING, GARRULOUS

bab·by \'babē\ *dial var of* BABY

bab·cock test \'bab,käk-\ *n, usu cap B* [after Stephen M. *Babcock* †1931 Am. agricultural chemist] **:** a test for determining the butter value of milk and milk products by treating with acid and whirling by means of a centrifugal apparatus in a bottle with a long graduated neck, the fat being brought to the top and its amount being read off directly

babe \'bāb\ *n* -s [ME — more at BABBLE] **1 a :** INFANT, BABY ⟨a ~ in arms⟩ ⟨the book is not milk for ~*s* —Thomas Pyles⟩ **b** *slang* **:** GIRL, WOMAN ⟨the blond ~ who helps the gangster —P.T.Hartung⟩ **2** *obs* **:** DOLL **3 :** an innocent, inexperienced, or ignorant person ⟨in the matter of handling money, he was just a ~⟩ — **babe in the woods :** an innocent trusting guileless person esp. in circumstances calling for sophistication or cunning ⟨made him an easy victim for the blandishments of tougher-minded men among whom he literally was a *babe in the woods* —A.L.Sachar⟩

ba·bel \'bābəl, 'ba-\ *n* -s *often cap* [fr. the Tower of *Babel*, biblical structure (Gen 11:4–9) that was erected for the purpose of reaching heaven and incurred the wrath of God, who as punishment made the builders' speech mutually unintelligible, fr. Assyr-Bab *bāb-ilu* gate of god] **1 a :** a confusion or medley of sounds, voices, languages, or ideas ⟨such a ~! Everyone talking at once and nobody listening to anyone —Hugh Walpole⟩ ⟨a ~ of birds fills the nearby woods —Joseph Chiari⟩ ⟨a ~ of controversy —Gene Baro⟩ **b :** a place or scene of noise or confusion, esp. of mingled and confused noises ⟨all races and nationalities meet and talk in the streets to make the town a ~⟩ **2 a :** a lofty or towering structure **b :** an excessively grandiose or visionary scheme or project ⟨the ~ of their ambitions must totter to the ground⟩ **syn** see DIN

ba·bel·ism \-,lizəm\ *n* -s *sometimes cap* **:** a confusion of sound or sense

ba·bel·i·za·tion \-,lə'zāshən, -,lī'z-\ *n* -s *often cap* **:** the state of being babelized or the process of babelizing ⟨the ~ of city speech⟩ ⟨an approach to the problem of our ~ . . . let every man everywhere become at least bilingual —*N.Y.Times*⟩

ba·bel·ize \'==,līz\ *vt* -ED/-ING/-S *often cap* [*babel* + -*ize*] **:** to confuse esp. through the mingling of markedly different languages and cultures **:** CONFOUND ⟨the mounting needs of intercourse between *Babelized* peoples —A.D.Sheffield⟩

ba·bes–ernst body *or* **babes–ernst granule** \'bä,be¦shərn(t)st-\ *n, usu cap 1st B&E* [after Victor *Babeș* †1926 Romanian bacteriologist and H.C.*Ernst* †1922 Am. bacteriologist] **:** a metachromatic granule in protoplasm

ba·be·sia \bə'bēzh(ē)ə\ *n* [NL, fr. Victor *Babeș* + NL -*ia*] **1** *cap* **:** the type genus of Babesiidae **2 -s a :** a protozoan of the genus *Babesia* **b :** PIROPLASM — **ba·be·sial** \-zh(ē)əl\ *adj*

bab·e·si·a·sis \,babə'zīəsəs, -ē'z-\ *n, pl* **babesia·ses** \-ə,sēz\ [NL, fr. *Babesia* + -*iasis*] **:** infection with or disease caused by protozoans of the genus *Babesia* or the family Babesiidae **:** PIROPLASMOSIS

ba·be·si·el·la \bə,bēzē'elə\ *n, cap* [NL, fr. *Babesia* + -*ella*] *in some classifications* **:** a genus of very small bacterialike piroplasms that are usu. included in *Babesia*

ba·be·si·el·lo·sis \-zēə'lōsəs\ *n, pl* **babesiello·ses** \-'lō,sēz\ [NL, fr. *Babesiella* + -*osis*] **:** babesiasis caused by members of the genus *Babesiella*

ba·be·si·i·dae \,babə'zīə,dē, -zē-\ *n pl, cap* [NL, fr. *Babesia*, type genus + -*idae*] **:** a family of Haemosporidia comprising minute parasites of the red blood cells of mammals that are transmitted from host to host by the bite of a tick intermediate host and cause certain destructive diseases of domestic animals — see BABESIA, PIROPLASM, THEILERIA

ba·be·si·o·sis \bə,bēzē'ōsəs\ *n, pl* **babesio·ses** \-'ō,sēz\ [NL, fr. *Babesia* + -*osis*] **:** BABESIASIS

ba·bhan \'bäbən\ *n* -s *cap* [Bihari *bābhan*, fr. Skt *brāhmaṇa* Brahman — more at BRAHMAN] **:** a Hindu of a high caste of the Aryo-Dravidian ethnic type that dwells mainly in Bihar

babi \'bä(,)bē\ *n* -s *usu cap* [after *Bab*, title of its founder — more at BABISM] **1 :** a sect professing Babism **2 :** an adherent of Babism

bab·i·a·na \,babē'anə, -'ä-,-'á- *also* -'ā-\ *n* [NL, fr. D *babianer*, fr. obs. D *babiaen* baboon (now *baviaan*), fr. MF *babouin* baboon; fr. the fact that its stems are eaten by baboons — more at BABOON] **1** *cap* **:** a genus of bulbous herbs (family Iridaceae) having showy red or yellow spicate flowers **2 -s :** a plant of the genus *Babiana*

ba·biche \bə'bēsh\ *n* -s [CanF, of Algonquian origin; akin to Micmac *ababich* cord, Ojibwa *assabābish* thread] **:** thread or thong of sinew, gut, or rawhide

babied *past of* BABY

babier *comparative of* BABY

babies *pl of* BABY, *pres 3d sing of* BABY

babies'–feet \'==,=\ *n pl but sing or pl in constr* [so called fr. its dainty pink blossoms] **:** GAYWINGS

babies'–slippers \'==,==\ *n pl but sing or pl in constr* [so called fr. the shape of the pods] **:** BIRD'S-FOOT TREFOIL 1a

babiest *superlative of* BABY

babies'–toes \'==,=\ *n pl but sing or pl in constr* **:** BABIES'-FEET

ba·bine \bə'bēn\ *n, pl* **babine** *or* **babines** *usu cap* [F, lit., thick-lipped person, thick lip — more at BABOON] **1 :** an Athapaskan people closely related to or a subdivision of the Carriers and living in central British Columbia **2 :** a member of the Babine people

bab·ing·ton·ite \'babiŋtə,nīt\ *n* -s [William *Babington* †1833 Eng. mineralogist + E -*ite*] **:** a greenish black mineral $Ca_2(Fe,Mn)Si_5O_{14}OH$ consisting of a silicate of iron and calcium occurring in triclinic crystals (hardness 5.5–6)

ba·bin·ski reflex *or* **babinski sign** \bə'binskē-\ *also* **babinski's reflex** *or* **babinski's sign** *n, usu cap B* [after J.F.F. *Babinski* †1932 Fr. neurologist] **:** a reflex movement in which when the sole is tickled the great toe turns upward instead of downward indicating an organic lesion in the brain or spinal cord

babion *n* -s [F, prob. alter. of *babouin* — more at BABOON] *obs* **:** BABOON

bab·i·ru·sa *or* **bab·i·rous·sa** *or* **bab·i·rus·sa** \,babə'rüsə, ,bä-\ *n* -s [Malay *bābīrūsa*, fr. *bābī* hog + *rūsa* deer] **:** a large hoglike sometimes domesticated quadruped (*Babirussa babyrussa*) of the East Indies whose upper canine teeth in the male are large and recurved, coming out through the lips

babish *adj* [¹*baby* + -*ish*] *obs* **:** like a baby **:** BABYISH

bab·ism \'bä,bizəm\ *n* -s *usu cap* [*Bab*, title of Ali Mohammed of Shiraz †1850 Persian religious leader, its founder + E -*ism*] **:** the doctrine and practice of a 19th century Iranian sect that affirmed the progressiveness of revelation, held that no revelation was final, and forbade concubinage and polygamy, mendicancy, the use of intoxicating liquors and drugs, and dealing in slaves

bab·ist \-bəst\ *n* -s *usu cap* **:** an adherent of Babism

ba·boen \'bä,bün\ *n* -s [D, short for *baboen hoedoe*, prob. native name in Surinam] **:** a tropical American timber tree (*Myristica surinamensis*) with reddish wood

ba·boon \(')ba¦bün, *Brit usu & US sometimes* bə'b-\ *n* -s [ME *babewin*, *baboin*, fr. MF *babouin*, fr. *baboue* grimace; akin to MF *babine* thick lip, *babiller* to babble, prob. of imit. origin like ME *babelen* to babble — more at BABBLE] **1** *obs* **:** a grotesque figure in architectural or decorative work **2 a :** any of various large African and Asiatic cercopithecoid primates constituting the genus *Papio* and related genera and having doglike muzzles, large canine teeth, cheek pouches, usu. a short tail, and naked callosities on the buttocks— see CHACMA, ⁶DRILL, MANDRILL **b :** an uncouth, coarse, or ugly person; *esp* **:** one that combines the qualities of great physical strength, low intelligence, and brutish appearance

baboon (*Papio leucophaeus*)

ba·boon·ery \==ˈnərē\ *n* -ES [ME *babwinrie*, fr. *babewin* + -*rie* -ry] **:** conduct, activity, or attitudes that are brutish, degrading, or grotesquely humorous ⟨never . . . in the history of architecture has taste . . . descended to similar ~ —*Architect & Building News*⟩

ba·bouche \bə'büsh, bä-\ *n* -s [F, fr. Ar *bābūj*, *bābūsh*, fr. Per *pāpūsh*] **:** a chiefly oriental slipper made without heel or quarters

babouche

ba·bou·vism \bə'bü,vizəm, bä-\ *n* -s *usu cap* [F *babouvisme*, fr. François Émile *Babeuf* or *Babœuf* †1797 Fr. revolutionary + F -*isme* -ism] **:** a social and political doctrine or movement advocating a program of egalitarianism and communism esp. as formulated by Babeuf

ba·bou·vist \-,vəst\ *n* -s *usu cap* [F *babouviste*, fr. F.E. *Babeuf* + F -*iste* -ist] **:** an advocate of Babouvism

bab·ra·cot \'babrə,kät\ *n* -s [prob. native name in So. America] **:** a 3-legged or 4-legged wooden grating used by So. American Indians for the drying and smoking of meat and other foods

bab·root \'bab+,-\ *n* [origin unknown] **:** SAMPSON SNAKEROOT

ba·bu *also* **ba·boo** \'bä(,)bü\ *n* -s [Hindi *bābū*, *bābu*, lit., father] **1 :** a Hindu gentleman — a form of address corresponding to *Mr.* or *Esquire* **2 a :** an Indian clerk who writes English **b :** an Indian having some education in English — often used disparagingly

bab·u·i·na \,babə'wēnə\ *n* -s [NL, fr. F *babouin* baboon — more at BABOON] **:** a female baboon

ba·bul *or* **ba·bool** \bə'bül\ *or* **ba·blah** \-'blä\ *n* -s [Per *babūl*; akin to Skt *babbula*, *babbūla* (*Acacia arabica*)] **1 a :** an acacia tree (*Acacia arabica*) that is probably native to the Sudan but is widespread in northern Africa and across Asia through much of India and that is a source of gum arabic and of tannins and in part of its range of fodder and timber — compare AMRAD GUM **b :** the hard tough durable reddish woods of babul which is used esp. in India for agricultural implements, general construction, and carving **2** *usu* **bablah :** the pods and sometimes the bark of the babul that are rich in tannin and used in tanning and dyeing; *also* **:** the pods of any of several acacias that are similarly used

ba·bush·ka \'bäbəshkə, -,kä, *in sense 2 usu* bə'bu̇shkə *or* bä-, *sometimes* -'bü-\ *n* -s [Russ, grandmother, dim. of *baba* old woman; akin to Pol *baba* grandmother, old woman, Lith *bóba* old woman, Latvian *bāba*] **1 :** GRANDMOTHER, GRANNY **2 a :** a usu. triangular or triangularly folded kerchief worn over the head and usu. tied under the chin **b :** a head covering resembling a babushka

¹ba·by \'bābē, -bi\ *n* -ES [ME *babie* — more at BABBLE] **1 a** (1) **:** an extremely young child; *esp* **:** one that is still in arms **:** INFANT (2) **:** the young of an animal ⟨of the nation's 640 full species of breeding birds, 170 raise their *babies* . . . along the Mexican border —W.F.Heald⟩ ⟨a ~ lamb⟩ **b :** the youngest member of a group, esp. of a family ⟨the ~ of the family⟩ ⟨the ~ member of the Eisenhower subcabinet —Drew Pearson⟩ **c** *slang* **:** something that is one's personal responsibility, achievement, or interest ⟨though other . . . detectives have helped out, the case is really the bomb squad's ~ —Joseph Carter⟩ **2 a** *obs* **:** DOLL **b** *archaic* **:** a diminutive reflection of oneself in the pupil of another's eye — used chiefly in the phrase *to look babies in (another's) eyes* **3 :** one that is like a baby in character or conduct; *esp* **:** one that is petulant, dependent on another, or unable to endure even mild pain or deprivation **4** *slang* **a :** GIRL, WOMAN — often used in address **b :** BOY, MAN — often used in address **5** *slang* **:** PERSON, THING ⟨this chap . . . is a tough ~ —D.G. Gerahty⟩ ⟨the young airman had sent a picture of the plane . . . with the notation, "This is the ~ I'm going to fly" —*Springfield (Mass.) Daily News*⟩

babushka 2a

²baby \"\ *adj* -ER/-EST **1 :** of or relating to a baby **2 :** much smaller in size than is usual for a particular class of things **:** SMALL, DIMINUTIVE ⟨the Depot Commander had set forth in the *babiest* of baby cars —*Blackwood's*⟩ ⟨a ~ extension ladder —*Training Manual for Auxiliary Firemen*⟩ ⟨~ pine trees⟩

³baby \"\ *vt* -ED/-ING/-ES **1 a :** to tend solicitously **:** make much of **:** gratify the whims of **:** HUMOR ⟨*babied* her strapping big son till he was thoroughly spoiled⟩ ⟨~ a sick husband⟩ **b :** to operate, handle, or treat with special or fond care ⟨~ the engine of a racing car⟩ ⟨windows, behind any one of which a German sniper might be hiding, *~ing* his rifle —Irwin Shaw⟩ **2 :** to hit (a ball) with a gentle stroke of the bat or racket (as in badminton) **syn** see INDULGE

baby beef *n* **1 :** a fat young beef steer or heifer ready for market (as a yearling) **2 :** meat from a baby beef

baby blue *n* **1 :** a very pale blue that is greener, lighter, and stronger than pastel blue (sense 2) and stronger and slightly greener and darker than cloud blue **2 :** a pale blue that is greener and paler than average powder blue, Sistine, or average cadet gray

baby blue–eyes \,==ˈ=,=\ *n pl but sing or pl in constr* [so called fr. the eyelike spots] **:** a delicate California herb (*Nemophila menziesii*) having blue flowers marked with dark spots

baby bond *n* **:** a bond having a face value of $10, $25, $50, or $100 as distinguished from one of $500 or $1000 — called also *small bond*

baby carriage *or* **baby buggy** *n* **:** a 4-wheeled push carriage usu. with a folding top for a baby

baby carrier *or* **baby flattop** *n* **:** ESCORT CARRIER

baby coach *n, chiefly North Midland* **:** BABY CARRIAGE

baby eyes *n pl but sing or pl in constr* **:** a variety (*Nemophila menziesii intermedia*) of baby blue-eyes with white or pale blue flowers

baby face *n* **:** a usu. rounded face that gives the impression of extreme youth and innocence — **baby–faced** \'==¦=\ *adj*

baby farm *n* **:** a place where nursing and care of babies is provided for a fee — usu. used derogatorily — **baby farming** *n*

baby grand *n* **:** a small grand piano five to six feet in length

ba·by·hood \'==,hu̇d\ *n* -s **:** INFANCY

ba·by·ish \'bābēish\ *adj* **:** resembling a baby **:** CHILDISH, INFANTILE ⟨a rounded face that gave her a peculiarly ~ appearance⟩ ⟨~ tears and petulance⟩ — **ba·by·ish·ly** *adv*

bab·y·lon \'babələn *also* -ə,län *sometimes* -i,län *or* -ē,län\ *n* -s *usu cap* [fr. *Babylon*, ancient city of Babylonia noted for its luxurious living, fr. ME *Babilon*, *Babiloine*, fr. L *Babylon*, fr. Gk *Babylōn*, fr. Heb *Bābhel*] **:** a large city regarded as luxurious, wicked, or given to the gratification of the senses

¹bab·y·lo·nian \,babə'lōnyən, -nēən\ *n* -s *usu cap* [*Babylonia*, ancient country of southwestern Asia + E -*an*] **1 :** a native or resident of ancient Babylonia or of its capital city, Babylon **2 :** the form of the Akkadian language that was used in ancient Babylonia and was also employed widely as a diplomatic language

²babylonian \¦==¦=(=)=\ *adj, usu cap* [*Babylon* or *Babylonia* + E -*an*] **1 :** of, relating to, or characteristic of Babylonia, an ancient country of southern Mesopotamia, or its capital city, Babylon **2 :** of, relating to, or characteristic of the people of

Babylonia or Babylon **3 :** affording abundant or excessive gratification to the senses **:** LUXURIOUS, SUMPTUOUS, LAVISH **4 :** of, relating to, or characteristic of the Babylonian language **5** *obs* **:** ROMAN CATHOLIC

babylonian–assyrian *n, usu cap B&A* **:** ²AKKADIAN 3a

bab·y·lon·ic \ˌbabəˈlänik\ *adj, usu cap* [*Babylonia* or *Babylon* + E *-ic*] **1 :** ²BABYLONIAN 1 **2 :** ²BABYLONIAN 3

bab·y·lon·ish \ˈbabəˌlänish, ¦babə¦lōnish, ˈbabələnish\ *adj, usu cap* [*Babylonia* or *Babylon* + E *-ish*] **1 :** ²BABYLONIAN 1 — usu. used in the phrase *Babylonish captivity* **2 :** ²BABYLONIAN 3

baby louis heel *n, usu cap L* **:** a low Louis heel

baby–minder \ˈ==,==\ *n, Brit* **:** BABY-SITTER

baby orchid *n* **:** a Guatemalan epiphytic orchid (*Odontoglossum grande*) that is often cultivated in the greenhouse for its large typically orange-yellow flowers which have a wavy-edged creamy lip and are blotched and barred with darker color and usu. chestnut brown

baby–pig disease *n* **:** an acute hypoglycemia of newborn pigs accompanied by weakness, loss of appetite, and diarrhea, and usu. fatal if untreated

baby pink *n* **:** a variable color averaging a light yellowish pink that is redder and deeper than average shell pink (sense 1) or petal pink and redder and stronger than opera pink

baby primrose *n* **1 :** a Chinese primrose (*Primula forbesii*) having numerous small pale lilac flowers **2 :** FAIRY PRIMROSE

baby rambler *n* **:** POLYANTHA

ba·by's breath *or* **ba·bies' breath** *n* [so called fr. its light fragrance and dainty blossoms] **1 :** a plant of the genus *Gypsophila:* as **a :** a tall much-branched perennial herb (*G. paniculata*) having clusters of small fragrant white or pink flowers **b :** an annual herb (*G. elegans*) with larger white or rosy flowers **2 :** any of several plants having delicately scented flowers: as **a :** GRAPE HYACINTH **b :** a bedstraw (*Galium sylvaticum*) with thin lanceolate leaves and white flowers

baby–sit \ˈ==,=\ *vi* **:** to act or become employed as a baby-sitter ⟨ask her to *baby-sit* during church service⟩ ⟨I had to *baby-sit* with my grandchildren —Robert Frost⟩

baby–sitter \ˈ==,==\ *n* **:** a person engaged usu. for pay and for relatively short periods of time to take care of a child or children while the parents are away from the home

baby spot *n* **:** a small usu. hooded spotlight used to concentrate light on an object or area (as on a stage) from a short distance

baby's tears *also* **baby tears** *n pl but sing or pl in constr* **:** a prostrate or creeping sparsely hairy Corsican herb (*Helxine soleirolii*) of the family Urticaceae often grown esp. as a house plant for its mosslike small round short-stalked leaves

baby talk *n* **1 a :** the syntactically imperfect speech or phonetically modified forms used by small children learning to talk **b :** the consciously imperfect or mutilated speech or prattle often used by adults in speaking to small children **2 :** a deliberately oversimplified, ingenuous, or naïve talk or explanation ⟨indulge in intellectual *baby talk* —S.L.Payne⟩

baby tooth *n* **:** MILK TOOTH

baby walker *n* **:** WALKER

bac *abbr* [ML *baccalaureus*] bachelor

ba·ca·ba \bəˈkäbə\ *or* **bacaba palm** *n* -s [Pg *bacaba* fruit of the bacaba palm, fr. Tupi] **:** a palm of the genus *Oenocarpus* (esp. *O. bacaba* and *O. distichus*) the drupelike fruits of which yield oil used in soap manufacture

ba·ca·lao \ˌbäkəˈlau̇, ˌba-\ *n* -s [Sp] **1 :** CODFISH **2 :** any of various locally important marine food fishes

ba·ca·uan \bəˈkäwən\ *also* **ba·cao** \bəˈkau̇\ *n* -s [Tag *bakawan, bakaw*] *Philippines* **:** any of various Asiatic mangroves (as those of the genera *Rhizophora* and *Bruguiera*)

bac·ba·ki·ri *or* **back·bac·ki·ri** \ˌbakbəˈkirē\ *n* -s [imit.] **:** BOKMAKIERIE

¹**bac·ca** \ˈbakə\ *n, pl* **bac·cae** \-aˌkē, -aˌkī, -akˌsē, -akˌsī\ [L *baca, bacca* — more at BAY] **:** BERRY 1c

²**bac·ca** \ˈbakə\ *n* -s [by shortening & alter.] *slang* **:** TOBACCO

¹**bac·ca·lau·re·ate** \ˌbakəˈlȯrēət, -lär-\ *n* -s [ML *baccalaureatus*, fr. *baccalaureus* advanced student, bachelor (alter. — influenced by L *bacca* berry & *laureus* laurel — of *baccalarius* dependent farmer, tenant, young clerk, advanced student) + L *-atus* -ate — more at BACHELOR] **1 :** the degree of bachelor conferred by universities and colleges **2 a :** a religious or semireligious service held at many educational institutions the Sunday before commencement **b :** the sermon or address delivered at this service

²**baccalaureate** \"\ *adj* **:** of or relating to the degree of bachelor or to the ceremonies attending the conferral of that degree ⟨a ~ degree is required for many jobs⟩ ⟨the ~ service⟩ ⟨a ~ address⟩

bac·ca·rat *also* **bac·ca·ra** \ˈbäkəˌrä, ˌ==ˈ= *also* -ak-\ *n* -s [F *baccara*] **1 :** a card game played in European casinos identical with chemin de fer except that in baccarat the dealer gives hands to each of two opponents and to himself **2 :** a hand counting zero in this game or in chemin de fer

bac·ca·rat glass \"-\ *n, usu cap B* [fr. *Baccarat*, a trademark] **:** fine blown, molded, and cut glass made at Baccarat, France, from 1765 to the present time

bac·cate \ˈbakˌāt\ *adj* [L *baca, bacca* berry + E *-ate*] **1 :** pulpy throughout like a berry **2 :** bearing berries

bac·chae \ˈbakˌē, -kˌī\ *n pl, cap* [L, fr. Gk *Bakchai*, pl. of *Bakchē* maenad] **:** MAENADS

¹**bac·cha·nal** \ˈbakənᵊl\ *adj* [L *bacchanalis* of Bacchus, irreg. fr. *Bacchus*, a name of Dionysus, god of fruits including esp. the grape (fr. Gk *Bakchos*, prob. of non-IE origin) + *-alis* -al — more at BAY] **:** BACCHANALIAN

²**bac·cha·nal** \ˈbäkəˌnäl, ¦bakə¦nal, ¦bak-; ¦bakə¦nal\ *n* -s **1 :** a devotee of Bacchus; *esp* **:** one who celebrates the bacchanalian rites **:** REVELER, CAROUSER **2 a :** drunken revelry or carousal **:** excessive indulgence **:** BACCHANALIA **b :** a bacchanalian song or dance

bac·cha·nale \"\ *n* -s [F, back-formation fr. *bacchanales* bacchanalia, fr. L *bacchanalia*] **:** a ballet whose dances are marked by voluptuousness or pagan abandon

bac·cha·na·lia \ˌbakəˈnālyə, -lēə\ *n, pl* **bacchanalia** *or* **bacchanalias** [L, fr. neut. pl. of *bacchanalis*] **:** a bacchanalian celebration **:** a drunken feast **:** ORGY

¹**bac·cha·na·lian** \¦bakə¦nālyən, -lēən\ *adj* **:** of, relating to, or suggesting the ancient Roman religious rites marked by orgiastic revelry and drunkenness that were held in honor of Bacchus, the god of wine

²**bacchanalian** \"\ *n* -s **:** a bacchanalian reveler **:** ²BACCHANAL 1

¹**bac·chant** \bəˈkant, ba-, -aa(ə)nt; bəˈkä-, ba-, -ˈkȧ-, ˈbäˌkä-, bäˈkȧ-; ˈbakənt\ *n, pl* **bacchants** \-n(t)s\ *or* **bac·chantes** *as at* BACCHANTE\ [L *bacchant-, bacchans*, pres. part. of *bacchari* to celebrate the festival of Bacchus, fr. *Bacchus*] **:** BACCHANALIAN

²**bacchant** \"\ *adj* **:** of or belonging to a bacchant

bac·chante \bəˈkant(ē), ba-, -aa(ə)nt(ē); bəˈkä-, ba-, -ˈkȧ-, bäˈkä-,bäˈkȧ-\ *n* -s [F, fr. L *bacchant-, bacchans*, pres. part.] **:** a priestess or female follower of Bacchus **:** MAENAD

bac·chan·tic \-ntik, -ēk\ *adj* **:** of, relating to, or like a bacchant

bac·cha·ris \ˈbakərəs\ *n, cap* [NL, fr. L *baccar, bacchar*, a plant having a fragrant root, fr. Gk *bakcharis* sowbread] **:** a genus of smooth and resinous or glutinous shrubs (family Compositae) having whitish or yellow flower heads in pyramidal panicles

bac·cha·roid \-ˌrȯid\ *adj* [NL *Baccharis* + E *-oid*] **:** belonging to or resembling the genus *Baccharis*

bac·chi·ac \bəˈkīək, ba-; ˈbakēˌak\ *adj* [Gk *bakcheiakos*, fr. *bakcheios* bacchius] **:** composed of or relating to bacchii

¹**bac·chic** \ˈbakik, -ēk\ *adj* [L *Bacchicus*, fr. Gk *Bakchikos*, fr. *Bakchos* Bacchus + *-ikos* -ic] **:** BACCHANALIAN

²**bacchic** \"\ *adj* [L *bacchius* + E *-ic*] **:** relating to or composed of bacchii

³**bacchic** \"\ *n* -s **:** a bacchius or bacchic cadence

bac·chi·us \bəˈkīəs, ba-\ *n, pl* **bac·chii** \-ˌīˌī\ [L, fr. Gk *Bakcheios*, fr. *Bakcheios*, adj., of Bacchus, fr. *Bakchos* Bacchus] **1** *in accentual prosody* **:** a metrical foot of three syllables, the first unstressed, the other two having either primary or intermediate stress **2** *in classical prosody* **:** a foot of three syllables, the first short, the other two long

bac·cif·er·ous \(ˈ)bakˈsif(ə)rəs\ *adj* [L *bacifer, baccifer* bearing berries (fr. *baca, bacca* berry + *-fer* -ferous) + E *-ous*] **:** bearing berries

baccubert *usu cap, var of* BACUBERT

bac·cy \ˈbakē\ *n* -ES [by shortening & alter.] *slang* **:** TOBACCO

¹**bach** \ˈbach\ *n* -ES [by shortening] *slang* **:** BACHELOR

²**bach** *also* **batch** \"\ *vi* -ED/-ING/-ES *slang* **:** to live as a bachelor; *esp* **:** to keep house in the absence of a wife — often used with *it* ⟨while their wives were away the two men ~*ed* it in a cabin by a lake and fished⟩

³**bach** \"\ *n* -ES [prob. fr. ¹*bach*] *NewZeal* **:** a small house or weekend cottage

bache \ˈbach\ *n* -s [ME, fr. OE *bæce, bece* — more at BECK] *dial Eng* **:** the valley of a small stream — now used chiefly in place names

bach·e·lor \ˈbach(ə)lə(r)\ *n* -s [ME *bacheler*, fr. OF, young man, squire, fr. ML *baccalarius* dependent farmer, tenant, young clerk, advanced student, of Celt origin; akin to IrGael *bachlach* peasant, shepherd, fr. OIr *bachall* staff, fr. L *baculus, baculum* — more at BACTERIUM] **1 a :** a usu. young knight who was entitled to display his own pennon but who followed the banner of another **:** KNIGHT BACHELOR **b :** an apprentice or novice knight **2 :** a person who has received what is usu. the first or lowest degree conferred by a college or university or by some professional schools ⟨~ of letters⟩ ⟨~ of divinity⟩ ⟨~ of laws⟩ **3 a :** an unmarried person of marriageable age; *esp* **:** a man of marriageable age ⟨remained a ~ for seven years after his first wife's death⟩ ⟨a ~ girl⟩ **b :** a male animal; *specif* **:** a young male fur seal when without a mate during breeding time **4 :** WHITE CRAPPIE — **bach·e·lor·dom** \-dəm\ *n* -s — **bach·e·lor·hood** \-ˌhu̇d\ *n* -s

bachelor dinner *n* **:** a party attended only by men and given by or for a man just prior to his wedding

bach·e·lor·ism \-ləˌrizəm\ *n* -s **1 :** the state of being a bachelor **2 :** a peculiarity of a bachelor

bach·e·lor·ly \-lə(r)lē\ *adj* **:** of or like a bachelor

bachelor of arts *usu cap B&A* **1 :** the recipient of a bachelor's degree which usu. signifies that the recipient has passed a certain number of courses in the humanities — abbr. *B.A., A.B.* ⟨became a *Bachelor of Arts* after only three years of university attendance⟩ ⟨requires a year of Latin of the *Bachelors of Arts*⟩ **2 :** the degree making one a Bachelor of Arts — abbr. *B.A., A.B.* ⟨require a *Bachelor of Arts* of all high-school teachers⟩ ⟨get an *A.B.* in classics⟩ ⟨get a *B.A.* in history⟩

bachelor of science *usu cap B&S* **1 :** the recipient of a bachelor's degree which usu. signifies that the recipient has done the greater part of his course work in the sciences with some specialization in a particular science **2 :** the degree making one a Bachelor of Science — abbr. *B.S., B.Sc., S.B.* ⟨the degree of *Bachelor of Science* in agronomy⟩ ⟨a *B.S.* in chemical engineering⟩ ⟨a *B.Sc.* in architecture⟩

bachelor's–breeches \ˈ=(=)=¦==\ *n pl but sing or pl in constr* **:** DUTCHMAN'S-BREECHES

bachelor's button \ˈ=(=)=¦==\ *also* **bachelor button** \ˈ=(=)=-,==\ *n, pl* **bachelor's buttons** *also* **bachelor buttons** **1 :** any of numerous plants with flowers or flower heads that suggest buttons: as **a :** DAISY 1a **b :** ORANGE MILKWORT **c :** BLUE-EYED GRASS **d :** GLOBE AMARANTH **e :** BLUEBOTTLE 1a **2** *usu* **bachelor button :** a deep pink that is bluer than average coral (sense 3b) and bluer and duller than fiesta or begonia

bachelor's button 1e

bachelor's chest *n* **:** a low chest of drawers with a pull-out slide for writing

bachelor's hall *n* **:** the residence of a bachelor or of a man whose wife is absent — usu. used in the phrase *to keep bachelor's hall*

bach·e·lor·ship \-lə(r)ˌship\ *n* -s **:** the state of being unmarried

bachman sparrow \ˈbäkmənz-\ *also* **bach·man sparrow** \-ən-\ *n, usu cap B* [after John *Bachman* †1874 Am. Lutheran clergyman and naturalist] **:** a sparrow (*Aimophila aestivalis bachmani*) of the central and southern U.S. that is reddish brown above and white below with the breast and sides washed with warm light brown

bach trumpet \ˈbäk, ˈbȧ-, -k\ *n, usu cap B* [after Johann S. *Bach* †1750 Ger. composer and organist] **:** a trumpet of high pitch designed esp. for performing J.S.Bach's original trumpet parts

bachur *var of* BAHUR

bacill– *or* **bacilli–** *or* **bacillo–** *comb form* [NL *bacillus*] **:** bacillus ⟨*bacillosis*⟩ ⟨*bacilliculture*⟩ ⟨*bacillogenic*⟩

bac·il·la·ce·ae \ˌbasəˈlāsēˌē\ *n pl, cap* [NL, fr. *Bacillus*, type genus + *-aceae*] **:** a family comprising typically rod-shaped usu. gram-positive bacteria (order Eubacteriales) that produce endospores and including the genera *Bacillus* and *Clostridium*

bac·il·la·ri·a·ce·ae \ˌbasəˌlerēˈāsēˌē\ *n pl, cap* [NL, fr. *Bacillaria*, type genus, fr. NL *bacillus* small rod + NL *-aria*) + *-aceae* — more at BACILLUS] *in some esp former classifications* **:** a family equivalent to Bacillariophyceae — **bac·il·la·ri·a·ceous** \¦==¦==¦āshəs\ *adj*

bac·il·la·ri·a·les \ˌbasəˌlerēˈā(ˌ)lēz\ *n pl, cap* [NL, fr. *Bacillaria* + *-ales*] *in some esp former classifications* **:** an order equivalent to Bacillariophyceae

bac·il·la·ri·e·ae \-ˈēˌē\ *n pl, cap* [NL fr. *Bacillaria* + *-eae*] *in some classifications* **:** a group of algae comprising the diatoms and usu. regarded as a distinct class but sometimes esp. formerly treated as a subclass and included in the Zygophyceae

bac·il·lar·i·o·phy·ce·ae \-əˈfīsēˌē, -əˈfis-\ *n pl, cap* [NL, fr. *Bacillaria* + *-o-* + *-phyceae*] **:** a class of yellow-green algae (division Chrysophyta) comprising the diatoms

bac·il·la·ri·oph·y·ta \-ˈäfəd·ə\ *n pl, cap* [NL, fr. *Bacillaria* + *-o-* + *-phyta*] *in some classifications* **:** a division of plants coextensive with the class Bacillariophyceae

bac·il·lary \ˈbasəˌlerē, -ri *also* bəˈsilər-\ *or* **ba·cil·lar** \bəˈsilə(r), ˈbasəl-\ *adj* [ISV *bacill-* + *-ary, -ar*] **1 :** shaped like a rod **:** consisting of small rods or rodlike bodies **2 :** belonging to, resembling, produced by, or containing bacilli

bacillary dysentery *n* **:** SHIGELLOSIS

bacillary white diarrhea *n* **:** pullorum disease of the young bird

bac·il·le·mia \ˌbasəˈlēmēə\ *n* -s [NL, fr. *bacill-* + *-emia*] **:** BACTEREMIA

bacilli *pl of* BACILLUS

ba·cil·li·form \bəˈsiləˌfȯrm, -fō(ə)m\ *adj* [NL *bacilliformis*, fr. *bacill-* + L *-formis* -form] **:** shaped like a rod **:** BACILLARY

ba·cil·lite \bəˈsiˌlīt\ *n* -s [L *bacillum* + E *-ite*] **:** a rodlike crystallite formed by a number of parallel longulites

bac·il·lo·sis \ˌbasəˈlōsəs\ *n, pl* **bacillo·ses** \-ōˌsēz\ [NL, fr. *bacill-* + *-osis*] **:** a state of infection with bacilli

bac·il·lu·ria \ˌbasəˈlu̇rēə, -səlˈyu̇-\ *n* -s [NL, fr. *bacill-* + *-uria*] **:** the passage of bacilli with the urine — **bac·il·lu·ric** \¦==¦rik\ *adj*

¹**ba·cil·lus** \bəˈsiləs\ *n* [NL, fr. ML *bacillus* small staff, alter. of L *baculum* — more at BACTERIUM] **1** *cap* **:** a large genus (the type of the family Bacillaceae) of aerobic rod-shaped bacteria producing endospores that do not thicken the rod, often forming long chains and rhizoid colonies, and as now restricted including (1) many saprophytes of soil, water, and comparable habitats that are important in the natural decay of organic matter and (2) a number of parasites (as *B. anthracis* the cause of anthrax, *B. larvae* of American foulbrood, and *B. popilliae* causing milky disease in the Japanese beetle) — compare CLOSTRIDIUM **2** *pl* **bacil·li** \-ˌlī, -lē\ **a :** any member of the genus *Bacillus; broadly* **:** any straight rod-shaped bacterium — distinguished from *coccus* and *spirillum* **b :** BACTERIUM; *esp* **:** a disease-producing bacterium **syn** see MICROORGANISM

²**bacillus** \"\ *n, cap* [NL, fr. ML, small staff] **:** a genus of long slender wingless Old World stick insects commonly made the type of a widely distributed family

bacillus cal·mette–gué·rin \-ˌkalˈmet(ˌ)gāˈraⁿ, -ran\ *n, usu cap C&G* [trans. of F *bacille Calmette-Guérin*, after Albert L.C.*Calmette* †1933 and Camille *Guérin* *b*1872 Fr. bacteriologists] **:** an attenuated strain of tubercle bacillus developed by repeated culture on a medium containing bile and used in preparation of tuberculosis vaccines — compare BCG VACCINE

ba·ci·roa \ˌbasəˈrōə\ *n, pl* **baciroa** *or* **baciroas** *usu cap* [Sp, of AmerInd origin] **1 :** a Taracahitian people in the state of Sonora, Mexico **2 :** a member of the Baciroa people

bac·i·tra·cin \ˌbasəˈtrāsᵊn\ *n* -s [NL *Bacillus* (genus name of *Bacillus subtilis*, the species producing the toxin) + Margaret *Tracy* *b ab*1936 Am. child in whose tissue it was found + E *-in*] **:** a water-soluble toxic polypeptide antibiotic or mixture of antibiotics isolated as a whitish powder from one strain of the hay bacillus, effective esp. against streptococci, staphylococci, pneumococci, and other gram-positive organisms, and administered chiefly topically

¹**back** \ˈbak\ *n* -s [ME *bak, back*, fr. OE *bæc*; akin to OHG *bah* back, ON *bak*, OHG *bahho* side of bacon] **1 a** (1) **:** the rear part of the human body extending from the neck to the end of the spine, esp. the portion from shoulder to waist ⟨turned his ~ to the fire⟩ ⟨trudging down the road with a load on his ~⟩ (2) **:** the whole body considered as the wearer of clothing ⟨food for his belly and a fine blue uniform for his ~⟩ (3) **:** capacity esp. for labor, effort, or endurance ⟨imposing crushing burdens on the ~*s* of the working class⟩ ⟨know where you desire to go in life and put your ~ into getting there —*Architect & Building News*⟩ **b :** the corresponding part of the body of vertebrates other than man **:** DORSUM ⟨ride on a horse's ~⟩ ⟨a bird with reddish coloring on ~ and wings⟩ ⟨an odd marking along the ~ of a snake⟩ **c :** the backbone or the muscles and ligaments of this part of the body ⟨break your ~⟩ ⟨strain her ~⟩ **d :** a surface analogous to this portion of a vertebrate ⟨riding the ~*s* of waves⟩ **e :** the portion of a tanned leather hide resulting from cutting longitudinally down the backbone of the hide and trimming off the head and belly **f :** BACKBONE 3 **g** *in leapfrog* **:** the position of the player who is to be jumped over ⟨make a ~⟩; *also* **:** the player who is jumped over **2 a** (1) **:** the side or surface of something that is opposite to the side that is regarded as its front or face ⟨the ~ of the head⟩ or that is opposite to the more important, functional, or useful side ⟨scribbling his verses on the ~*s* of old letters⟩ ⟨the dingy ~ of the hotel contrasting with its brilliant facade⟩ (2) **:** the side that is opposite to the side approached or seen ⟨the ~ of the mountain⟩ ⟨the ~ of the door⟩ (3) **:** the side or part of any object or space that is most remote from the observer or from its front or forward part ⟨the chorus was massed at the ~ of the stage⟩ ⟨moved to the ~ of the room⟩ ⟨a journey into the thinly settled ~ of the province⟩ **b** (1) **:** the upper, outer, or convex side or part of something as opposed to the inner, lower, or concave side or part ⟨rest a hand on the ~ of a handrail⟩ ⟨the ~ of an arch⟩ ⟨~ of a hoop⟩ (2) **:** the upper surface of a beam (3) **:** the side of a piece of printer's type opposite the belly — see TYPE illustration (4) **:** the roof, arch, or top surface of mine workings (5) **:** the mass of ore existing above a mine working — sometimes used in pl. (6) **:** a plane of cleavage in a coal seam **c :** the side or edge of something opposite to a side or edge designed for grasping, cutting, or striking ⟨the ~ of a knife⟩ ⟨the ~ of a saw⟩ ⟨the ~ of an ax⟩ **d :** the portion of a chair that supports the back of a sitter **e :** BACKING **f** (1) **:** the last few pages of a book (2) **:** the inside margin of a printed page **g :** the reverse of a currency note **h :** BACKYARD ⟨leave a bicycle in the ~⟩ **i :** the main or longest leaf of a leaf spring **j :** the upper part or convex portion of a saw tooth **3** *of a bird dog* **:** the action of backing **4 :** the part of the upper surface of the tongue behind the front and lying opposite the soft palate when the tongue is at rest **5 a :** a primarily defensive player (as in soccer or polo) with a position nearest his own goal — compare FORWARD **b :** a rugby player who is not a forward; *esp* **:** FULLBACK **c :** a primarily offensive player in football whose position is behind that of his linemen ⟨starred as a triple-threat ~⟩ — see FULLBACK, HALFBACK, QUARTERBACK — **at one's back :** close behind in support or pursuit ⟨in the battle the infantry stayed right *at our backs*⟩ — **behind one's back :** when one is not present **:** without one's knowledge **:** in secret ⟨make vicious remarks about you *behind your back*⟩ — **in back of** *prep* **:** BEHIND ⟨the tiny parlor *in back of* the store —John McNulty⟩ ⟨always been strongly *in back of* the venture —Thomas Wood b. 1910⟩ — **the back of beyond :** a place far out of the way **:** a remote region — **the back of one's hand :** a show of one's contempt — **the back of one's mind :** the remote or hidden part of one's thoughts ⟨the stranger's name hovered in *the back of his mind*⟩; *also* **:** the store of thoughts or memories that can be drawn upon on the appropriate occasion ⟨to keep someone's good advice in *the back of your mind* as a constant goad to activity⟩ — **with one's back to the wall :** at bay **:** in a position from which there is no retreat **:** CORNERED

²**back** \"\ *adv* [ME *bak*, fr. *bak*, n.] **1 a :** to or toward the rear **:** to or toward a place away from any place regarded as the front, center, or forward position ⟨move ~ from the front lines⟩ ⟨move ~ in a bus⟩ ⟨ask the crowd to move ~ from the scene of an accident⟩ **b :** at the rear or a position behind **:** at a place considered away from the front, center, or forward position ⟨a chapter beginning several pages ~⟩ ⟨left his friends two miles ~⟩ **c :** in or into the past ⟨to look ~ on his youth⟩ ⟨an event ~ in the last century⟩ **:** AGO ⟨several years ~⟩ ⟨met him in the street two days ~⟩ **d :** at an angle off the vertical ⟨banks slant evenly ~ from the highway⟩; *esp* **:** in a reclining position ⟨lying ~ in the boat —Frank Gallagher⟩ ⟨lie ~ on a couch⟩ **e** (1) **:** in a condition of check or restraint ⟨would have leaped if his friends had not held him ~⟩ ⟨poverty may hold a talented man ~⟩ ⟨hold ~ a laugh⟩ (2) **:** in a delayed or retarded condition **:** in a condition less advanced or advantageous than before — often used with *set* ⟨landslides set the construction job ~ many days⟩ ⟨unfortunate speculations set the firm ~⟩ **f :** in one's keeping or possession — usu. used of something that should be given up, yielded, or declared freely ⟨hold ~ part of the money⟩ ⟨keep ~ the truth⟩ **g :** in arrears ⟨he was ~ in payment of rent⟩ **h :** BACKSTAGE 1 **2 a :** to, toward, or in a place from which a person or thing came or was taken ⟨go ~ home⟩ ⟨put a book ~⟩ **b :** to or toward a former condition **:** to or toward a former or original state (as of activity, consciousness, or productivity) ⟨go ~ to private life⟩ ⟨go ~ to barbarism⟩ ⟨needed two transfusions to bring him ~ —Bill Alcine⟩ ⟨good farming practices were needed to bring the fields ~⟩ **c** (1) **:** in repayment or return (as of a loan or favor) ⟨gave ~ the borrowed money⟩ (2) **:** in retaliation ⟨hit him right ~⟩ (3) **:** in reply usu. in the manner of a retort ⟨repressed a strong impulse to talk ~⟩ or a retraction ⟨refused to take ~ his charges⟩ or a withdrawal ⟨drew ~ from his earlier promise⟩ **3 :** OVER ⟨read your shorthand notes ~⟩

³**back** \"\ *adj* [ME *bak*, fr. *bak*, n.] **1 a :** being at the back or in the rear ⟨the ~ door⟩ ⟨the ~ porch⟩ ⟨a ~ alley⟩ **b :** distant from a center of population or habitation or off the main routes of travel ⟨~ settlements⟩ ⟨the near woodlands and ~ pastures afford good hunting —*Amer. Guide Series: Tenn.*⟩ ⟨a ~ river port⟩ ⟨~ roads and picturesque lanes⟩ **c** *comparative sometimes* **backer :** articulated at or toward the back of the oral passage ⟨the vowels \ü\ and \ä\ and \g\ in *go* are ~ sounds⟩ **2 a :** OVERDUE **:** in arrears ⟨pay ~ rent due for several months⟩ **b :** due for services performed prior to the latest pay period ⟨a retroactive increase results in ~ wages for workers⟩ **3 a :** moving or operating backward ⟨~ action with oars that drives a boat sternward⟩ **b :** moved or moving in a return direction ⟨pick up ~ cargo⟩ ⟨~ freight⟩ ⟨a ~ current⟩ **c :** constituting the second 9 holes of an 18-hole golf course ⟨play the ~ nine in record time⟩ **4** *of a publication* **:** not current ⟨a ~ number of a magazine⟩ ⟨a ~ issue⟩

⁴**back** \"\ *vb* -ED/-ING/-S [¹*back*] *vt* **1 a :** to support or help by physical, moral, or financial assistance **:** UPHOLD **:** strengthen or encourage by aid or influence — often used with *up* ⟨~ a candidate for office⟩ ⟨~ up his son⟩; *specif* **:** to move into a position behind (a teammate) in order to assist in a play (as in stopping an offensive play in football or by retrieving a missed ball in baseball or cricket) **b :** to increase the persuasive or logical force of **:** SUBSTANTIATE — often used with *up* ⟨~ up an argument with forceful illustrations⟩ **c :** to bet on the success of ⟨~ a racehorse⟩ **d :** COUNTERSIGN, ENDORSE ⟨the warrant . . . had to be ~*ed* or countersigned by a magistrate of the county to which the offender had fled —Edward Jenks & D.J.L.Davies⟩ ⟨~ a check⟩; *also* **:** to assume financial responsibility for **:** provide financial security for ⟨~ an enterprise⟩ ⟨~ a currency⟩ **e :** to supply the first stage of exhaustion in a pumping operation in connection with (another pump) ⟨a mechanical rotary pump ~*ing* an oil diffusion pump⟩ **2 :** to get upon the back of **:** MOUNT ⟨~ a

horse); *esp* **:** to break (a horse) to the saddle **3 a :** to drive, force, or cause to move back, retreat, recede, or go in reverse — often used with *up* ⟨~ a car into a garage⟩ ⟨~ a car up⟩ ⟨~ a propeller at full speed⟩ **b :** to articulate (a sound) with the tongue further back **4 a :** to make or form a back for **:** furnish with a back **:** put a back to — often used with *up*, sometimes with *off* ⟨a row of hills ~*s* the town⟩ ⟨~ a skirt with stiff material⟩ ⟨~ up a bookcase with cardboard⟩ ⟨~ off a wall with bricks⟩ **b :** to be at the back of — often used with *up* ⟨a barn ~*ing* the house⟩ ⟨a row of garages ~ the building up⟩ **c** (1) **:** to print the second side of (a sheet with one printed side) **:** PERFECT, REITERATE; *esp* **:** to so print in close register — often used with *up* (2) **:** to fill (an electrotype shell) with molten metal to form a printing plate — often used with *up* (3) **:** to reinforce (a stereotype matrix) to enable to withstand molten-metal pressure in molding **d :** to widen the backbone of (an unbound book) by spreading the backs of the sections gradually from the center of the back thereby forming longitudinal ridges at each side in order to strengthen (the book) and facilitate attachment of the cover **e :** to provide (a film or plate) with a photographic backing **5** *dial* **:** to write an address on (an envelope) **6** *of a bird dog* **:** to assume pointing stance behind (another dog that has pointed a covey of birds) **7 :** to fasten a weight (as a second anchor) to the rear of (an anchor) to increase holding power **8 :** to brace (a sail) so that the wind presses upon the forward side thus checking headway or driving the bow over onto a new course ~ *vi* **1 :** to move backward ⟨~ up three paces⟩ ⟨~*ed* off in preparation for his leap⟩ ⟨~*ed* away from the door⟩ **2** *of a bird dog* **:** to stop and point behind another pointing dog **3** *of the wind* **:** to shift in a counterclockwise direction — opposed to *veer* **4 :** to have the back in the direction of and often close to something — used with *on, onto,* or *against* ⟨seaside resorts . . . seem to ~ onto the sea, instead of facing it —Stephen Potter⟩ ⟨house ~*s* onto a wall⟩ **syn** see RECEDE — **back and fill 1 :** to alternately back the sails and fill the sails of a ship so as to keep it clear of the shore and obstructions while the current of a river or channel carries it down **2 :** to take opposite positions alternately **:** alternately favor and disfavor **:** SHILLY-SHALLY ⟨he *backed and filled* and finally came to no decision at all⟩ **3 :** to maneuver esp. backward and forward ⟨turn the wheel to *back and fill* the car around⟩ ⟨the boar *backed and filled* as the dogs circulated and took nips —*Newsweek*⟩

⁵back \"\ *n* -s [D *bak*, fr. MD *bac*, fr. OF, fr. (assumed) VL *bacca* water vessel — more at BASIN] **:** a large shallow vat **:** a cistern, tub, or trough used (as by brewers, dyers, or gluemakers) esp. for mixing or cooling wort or holding water or hot glue

back *abbr* backwardation

backache \ˈ=,=\ *n* **:** a pain in the lower back ⟨complains of ~*s*⟩

backache brake *or* **backache fern** \ˈ=,=-\ *n* **:** LADY FERN

backaching \ˈ=,==\ *adj* **:** demanding much physical exertion ⟨a ~ job⟩

back action *n* **:** action reversing the usual or direct action

back-alley *adj* **:** having a mean, furtive, or squalid character or air ⟨*back-alley* gossip⟩

back along *adv, dial* **:** some time back **:** in the past **:** some time ago ⟨a good old-timer dating *back along* —Robert Frost⟩

back and forth *adv* **:** backwards and forwards **:** to and fro ⟨a loose window shutter swinging *back and forth*⟩ ⟨to rock *back and forth* on his heels⟩

back answer *n* [³*back*] **:** a disrespectful retort ⟨hero-worshiping girl, absolutely dependent and submissive, with never a *back answer* —Richard Mallett⟩

back away *vi* **:** to withdraw or retreat gradually (as from a principle or a theoretical position) ⟨*back* slowly *away* from their insistence on repeal —Benjamin Rathbun⟩

backbackiri *var of* BACBAKIRI

back bacon *n* **:** CANADIAN BACON

backband \ˈ=,=\ *n* **1 :** a band passing over a horse's neck and holding up the shafts of a vehicle **2 :** the outside molding of the trim around an opening (as a door or window)

backbar \ˈ=ˈ=\ *n* **1 :** a horizontal bar in the chimney of an open fireplace on which to hang a vessel over the fire **2 :** the shelf or counter space along the wall or backing of a bar area

back beam *n* **:** the cylinder of wood on a loom on which the warp is wound before the weaving process

back bench *n* **:** a bench in the British House of Commons or House of Lords occupied by backbenchers ⟨he would leave the shadow cabinet and return to the freedom of the *back benches* —Denis Healey⟩ — compare FRONT BENCH

backbencher \ˈ=ˈ=\ *n* -s **:** a rank-and-file member of a legislature; *esp* **:** such a member of the British House of Commons or House of Lords ⟨is cordially disliked by the ~*s* in Commons and some of the party intellectuals —M.H.Rubin⟩

backbend \ˈ=,=\ *n* **:** a tumbling stunt in which from a standing position with the knees straight the body is arched backwards until the hands touch the floor over the head

back·ber·end *or* **back·ber·and** \ˈbak,berənd\ *or* **back·bear·ing** \ˈ=,==\ *adj* [ME *bakberende*, fr. *bak* back + *berende*, pres. part. of *beren* to bear — more at BACK, BEAR] *law* **:** having in one's possession — used of a person carrying away stolen property

¹back·bite \ˈbak,bīt, *usu* -īd· +V\ *vb* [ME *bakbiten*, fr. *bak* back + *biten* to bite — more at BITE] *vt* **:** to say mean or spiteful things about (one absent) **:** SLANDER ⟨if a reader does not like what you have written, he ~*s* you to the editor, but if he is particularly pleased, he writes to you personally —Corra Harris⟩ ⟨had all *backbitten* and double-crossed each other while pretending to work together —Sir Winston Churchill⟩ ~ *vi* **:** to backbite a person

²backbite \"\ *n* **:** the act or an instance of backbiting ⟨manipulating a hundred and one strands of gossip and ~ —Eugene Walter⟩

back·bit·er \-īd·ə(r), -ītə-\ *n* -s [ME *bacbiter*, fr. *bakbiten* v.] **:** one that backbites

backbiting *n* -s [ME *bakbiting*, fr. *bak* back + *biting*] **:** the action of one who backbites or an instance of such action ⟨bickering and ~ —Margaret Stewart⟩ **syn** see DETRACTION

backblast \ˈ=,=\ *n* **:** the rush of powder gases from the open or vented breech of a recoilless weapon

backblock \ˈ=,=\ *n, Austral* **:** remote or sparsely settled country esp. far from a river or seacoast — usu. used in pl. ⟨he lived in the ~*s* of Queensland⟩ ⟨the difficulties of a ~*s* sheep farmer⟩

backboard \ˈ=,=\ *n* **:** a board or other construction placed at or fastened to the back of some object (as a picture) or serving as the back (as of a wagon); *specif* **:** a rounded or rectangular board that is behind the basket on a basketball court and that serves to keep missed shots from going out of bounds and as a surface from which the ball can be made to rebound into the basket

back bond *n* [³*back*] *Scots law* **:** an instrument by which one apparently taking as absolute owner under another instrument acknowledges that he is only a trustee or mortgagee

backbone \ˈ=ˈ=\ *n* [ME *bakbon*, fr. *bak* back + *bon* bone] **1 :** SPINE, SPINAL COLUMN, VERTEBRAL COLUMN **2 a** (1) **:** the chief mountain ridge, range, or system of a country or region ⟨the broad uplands of the Pennines form . . . the ~ of England —L.D.Stamp⟩ ⟨down the small pod-shaped peninsula . . . runs a ~ of high mountains —J.B.P.Robinson⟩ (2) **:** the foundation or most substantial or sturdiest part of any material object ⟨a heavy length of wood . . . which forms the ~ of the boat —*Manual of Seamanship*⟩ ⟨saw the girders, the gaunt steel ~ of the building, rising in the air⟩ **b** (1) **:** the mainstay, principal support, or most substantial element or part of something ⟨the clothiers have been described as the ~ of the middle class —Roy Lewis & Angus Maude⟩ ⟨those branches of general medicine which form the ~ of aviation medicine —H.G. Armstrong⟩ ⟨corn is the ~ of our agriculture —P.C.Mangelsdorf⟩ (2) **:** firm and resolute character **:** strength of will ⟨she is dealing with a man who has ~ —Margaret Deland⟩ ⟨displayed ~ by his frank admission of guilt⟩ **3 :** the edge of a book along which the sections are secured together in binding **:** the part that shows as the book ordinarily stands on a shelf and that is often lettered with the title and the author's and publisher's names — called also *back, backstrip, shelfback, spine* **4 :** a rope attached fore and aft along the center of a ship's awning to support and strengthen it **5 :** a main railroad-yard track from which other tracks branch **syn** see FORTITUDE — **to the backbone** *adv* **:** THOROUGHLY, COMPLETELY ⟨O'Connor was Irish *to the backbone* —*Irish Digest*⟩

backboned \ˈ=ˈ=\ *adj* **:** having a backbone **:** VERTEBRATE

back·bone·less \ˈ=ˈ=ləs\ *adj* **1 :** without backbone or a backbone **2 :** SPINELESS, PLIANT ⟨a ~ submission to ill-treatment⟩ — **back·bone·less·ness** \(ˈ)=ˈ==nəs\ *n* -ES

backbreak \ˈ=,=\ *n* -s **:** backbreaking labor ⟨a countryman tired of the ~ of a tenant farm —Hamilton Basso⟩

backbreaker \ˈ=,==\ *n* -s **1 :** a backbreaking task **2 :** a refinery worker who breaks crust formed on the surface of the electrolytic bath in aluminum-reduction pots to free anode for lowering or raising during tapping

backbreaking \ˈ=,==\ *adj* [*back* + *breaking*] **:** greatly taxing one's strength or endurance ⟨~ labor⟩ ⟨a ~ effort⟩

back bulb *n* **:** a pseudobulb on certain types of orchid plants that remains on the plant after the terminal growth has been removed and is used in the propagation of certain orchids

back-calving \ˈ=,==\ *adj, Scot* **:** calving during the last part of the year

backcast \ˈ=,=\ *n* -s [³*back* + *cast*] *dial Brit* **:** a relapse esp. during convalescence **:** REVERSAL

back center *n* **:** the center in the tailstock of a lathe

backchain \ˈ=,=\ *n* **:** a chain attached to each side of a rudder and to a point under the counter to support the rudder in backing

backchat \ˈ=,=\ *n* [³*back* + *chat*] **:** gossipy or bantering conversation **:** SMALL TALK ⟨~ that hardly went beyond tennis and dancing and cricket —Frank Sargeson⟩ **:** REPARTEE ⟨good humored ~ between audience and speaker —Alan Edwards⟩

back-check \ˈ=,=\ *vb* [²*back*] *vt* **:** to check over (as a computation) ~ *vi* **:** to skate back towards one's own goal covering the rushes of opposing players in a hockey game

back choir *n* **:** RETROCHOIR

back cloth *n* **1 :** a piece of canvas secured to the after part of a topsail yard to stow the bunt of the topsail in **2** *or* **back gray :** an unfinished cloth used in cylinder printing of fabrics to absorb excess dye **3** *chiefly Brit* **:** BACKDROP

back comb *n* **:** an ornamental comb with a wide top and a few long teeth worn high at the back of the head

back·coun·try \ˈ=ˈ==\ *n* **1 :** a rural and relatively thinly settled and undeveloped area to the rear of a more densely peopled and developed region containing the main centers of population ⟨the antagonism between Tidewater and ~ in colonial Virginia⟩ **:** farming area ⟨trucks daily bring in produce from the ~⟩ **2 :** the country to the rear of a settled district **:** a frontier area **:** BORDERLAND ⟨the first white men to set foot in that vast ~⟩

back comb

backcourt \ˈ=,=\ *n* **1 :** the part of a tennis court between the service line and the base line **2 :** the space near or nearest the back boundary lines or back wall or walls of the playing area in net and wall games; *esp* **:** a basketball team's defensive half of the court

¹backcross \ˈ=,=\ *vt* [²*back* + *cross*] **:** to cross (a first-generation hybrid) with one parent or with an individual of the same genetic composition as the parent

²backcross \"\ *n* -ES **:** an instance of backcrossing; *also* **:** an individual produced by backcrossing

³backcross \"\ *adj* [²*backcross*] **:** of, relating to, or produced by a backcross or by backcrossing

backdate \ˈ=ˈ=\ *vt* [²*back* + *date*] **:** PREDATE ⟨indicted for *backdating* tax returns to save interest and penalty payments —*Time*⟩

back dive *n* [³*back*] **1 :** a dive from a position facing the diving board — see CUTAWAY; compare BACKWARD DIVE **2 :** a category in competitive diving that includes those dives in which the body rotates backward from a backward standing takeoff — compare FRONT DIVE, REVERSE DIVE, TWIST DIVE

back door *n* **1 a :** a door in the back or to the rear of something, esp. a habitation **b :** an entrance or approach (as to a country) regarded as at the back and usu. distant or geographically opposite the main route of approach ⟨but the richest area of all the peninsula was found . . . at the *back door* of Nome —*Encyc. Americana*⟩ ⟨the *back door* of Egypt —Hassoldt Davis⟩ **2 :** an indirect, surreptitious, underhanded, or illegal means or way ⟨the West entered America's popular literature through the *back door* of humor —J.D. Hart⟩ ⟨depends more and more on western *back doors* for essential war supplies —*Amerasia*⟩ ⟨a junk shop with a *back-door* trade in hides from illegally killed cattle —H.L.Davis⟩

backdoor trots *n pl but sing or pl in constr, dial* **:** DIARRHEA

back down *vi* **:** to retreat or withdraw from a previous commitment, position, or claim ⟨wished he had not undertaken the errand, but he was afraid to *back down* —Harold Sinclair⟩

backdown \ˈ=,=\ *n* -s [*back down*] **:** the action or an instance of backing down on a stand or position ⟨a ~ on the explosive German question —*Newsweek*⟩

back draft *n* **:** an explosion of the gaseous products of incomplete combustion in admixture with air sometimes occurring during a fire (as in a building or mine) — called also *smoke explosion*

backdrop \ˈ=,=\ *n* -s **1 a :** a cloth usu. painted or decorated in some way and hung across the rear of a stage or stage setting to mask the backstage area or to serve as scenic background **b :** a background used by a photographer consisting of a drapery or painted canvas stretched on a frame or hung from a support **2 :** BACKGROUND; *esp* **:** a background against which something is observed or stands out ⟨Indochina is the ~ for this tensely written story —*N.Y. Times*⟩

back drop *n* **:** a fundamental trampoline stunt in which from a bounce the performer lands on his back on the bed with head forward, hands in front of the body, and the legs at a 45 degree angle, then rebounds to an erect standing position

backed \ˈbakt\ *adj* [ME, having a back, fr. ¹*back* + *-ed*] **1** *of an archer's bow* **:** made of two or more strips glued together, one piece forming the back and another the belly — contrasted with *self* **2** *of cloth* **:** woven with a second set of threads in the warp or weft for additional weight or reversibility — see DOUBLE CLOTH **3** *of photographic film or plate* **:** coated on the side opposite the emulsion with a substance to absorb light and hence reduce halation

backed-blade \ˈ=ˈ=\ *n* **:** a prehistoric flint knife having one edge blunted

backed-off \ˈ=ˈ=\ *adj* **:** having metal removed from the back to provide clearance — used esp. of a milling cutter

back electromotive force *n* **:** COUNTER ELECTROMOTIVE FORCE

back·en \ˈbakən\ *vt* -ED/-ING/-S [³*back* + *-en*] *now dial* **:** to retard the progress of **:** DELAY ⟨cold weather will ~ the corn⟩

back end *n* **1 :** the rear end **2** *dial Brit* **:** the latter part of the year **:** the autumn and early winter

¹back·er \ˈbakə(r)\ *comparative of* BACK

²backer \"\ *n* -s **1 :** one that supports **2 :** a worker who works with backs or backing: as **a :** a slaughterhouse worker who removes the back, shoulders, and base of the tail of a hide from a carcass **b :** a worker who reinforces parts of shoes (as vamps, uppers, or straps) by pasting in pieces of lining material **c :** a worker who forms the ridges to which covers are hinged at the back of rounded book bodies **3 :** material used for backing; *specif* **:** a piece of canvas, flannel, or other material used to reinforce parts of linings or uppers of shoes **4 :** a strap usu. of sennit secured to a ship's yard and carrying a thimble through which an earing runs

³backer \"\ *n* -s [by shortening & alter.] *dial* **:** TOBACCO

backer-up \ˈ==ˈ=\ *n, pl* **backers-up :** one that backs up: as **a :** SPONSOR **b :** a linebacker in football **c :** a worker who mounts calendars between metal strips and staples calendar pads to metal

back·et \ˈbakət\ *n* -s [F *baquet*, dim. of *bac* tub — more at BACK] *Scot* **:** a shallow wooden box used esp. to carry fuel or ashes

backfall \ˈ=,=\ *n* [³*back* + *fall*] **1** *obs* **:** a descending appoggiatura in music **2 :** the sloping surface in a beater or washing engine down which paper pulp passes on leaving the knives

back-fanged \ˈ=ˈ=\ *adj, of a snake* **:** having grooved venom-conducting teeth located posteriorly in the roof of the mouth — compare FRONT-FANGED, OPISTHOGLYPHA

back-feed *vt* **:** to put (as a paper) into a typewriter by inserting it bottom-first behind the top of a paper already in the machine and rolling the platen backward

back-fence \ˈ=ˈ=\ *adj* [*back fence*] **:** having an intimate informal but often malicious or slanderous character — used chiefly of conversation ⟨cheery *back-fence* chats⟩ ⟨vicious *back-fence* gossip⟩

back·field \ˈ=,=\ *n* **:** the football players whose positions are behind the line of scrimmage; *also* **:** the positions themselves

back file *n* [³*back*] **:** a file of back numbers (as of a newspaper or documentary matter to be saved for use in the future

¹backfill \ˈ=,=\ *vt* [²*back* + *fill*] **:** to replace earth in (as a trench or the open space around a foundation wall); *also* **:** to refill (as an excavation) with any material

²backfill \"\ *n* -s **1 :** the refilling of a trench or other excavation or of the space around a foundation **2 :** the material used in backfilling

backfilled \ˈ=,=\ *adj* [¹*back* + *filled*] *of an esp cotton fabric* **:** stiffened by applying size or finish to the back only

back·fill·er \ˈ=,==\ *n* -s [¹*backfill* + *-er*] **1 :** a machine for backfilling **2 :** a worker who moves backfilling material

back fillet *n* **:** the edge or fillet by which a slightly projecting part (as a quoin or architrave) returns to the face of the wall — **back-filleted** \ˈ=ˈ==\ *adj*

back·fill·ing \ˈ=,==\ *n* -s [³*back* + *filling*] **:** ²BACKFILL

¹backfire \ˈ=,=\ *n* [³*back* + *fire*] **1 a :** a fire started counter to an advancing forest or prairie fire to check the latter by clearing an area **b :** a vigorous countermovement or activity ⟨delegates come under the influence of a strong ~ of opinion from the country —Allen Johnson⟩ **2 a :** an improperly timed explosion of fuel mixture in the cylinder of an internal-combustion engine; *esp* **:** one occurring when either the exhaust or intake valve is open and resulting in a loud detonation **b :** combustion in a fuel-supply line (as of a welding torch)

²backfire \"\ *vi* **1 a :** to make a backfire **b :** to make a sound like that of a backfire ⟨a big coffee urn *backfiring* with alarming pops and bangs —Frederick Way⟩ **2 :** to have or experience a backfire or backfires — used of an internal-combustion engine or a firearm **3 :** to light so that the flame proceeds from the internal gas jet instead of from the external jet of mixed gas and air — used of a Bunsen or similar air-fed burner **4 :** to have the reverse of the desired effect by causing loss or injury to the user or doer **:** BOOMERANG ⟨when the opposition publicized the lady candidate's photograph in a bathing suit, the strategy *backfired* —Emily T. Douglas⟩ **:** fail to have the desired effect **:** MISCARRY ⟨some of the marriages have been happy, some have badly *backfired* —Frank Gibney⟩ — **backfiring** *n* -s

back·fisch \ˈbäk,fish\ *n, pl* **back·fische** \-shə\ [G, lit., fish for baking or frying, fr. *backen* to bake, fry (fr. OHG *backan*) + *fisch* fish, fr. OHG *fisc* — more at BAKE, FISH] **:** an adolescent immature girl ⟨his family . . . two grown-up gawky sons, and a ~ daughter —A.L.Mikhelson⟩

backflap \ˈ=,=\ *n* **:** a flap that folds back or hangs down in back; *specif* **:** the part of a book jacket that folds over and onto the inside of the back cover

¹backflash \ˈ=,=\ *n* -ES [³*back* + *flash*] **1 :** FLASHBACK **2 :** the act or an instance of backflashing **3 :** a groove formed around the outer portion of the flash to receive the metal squeezed through the flash in sinking an upper die — called also *gutter*

²backflash \"\ *vi* **1 :** to flash back (as of a gas) and burn at a point where combustion is not intended **2** *of a literary or dramatic work* **:** to introduce a flashback into the narrative ⟨the script ~*es* to a day in his life 10 years before⟩

¹backflip \ˈ=,=\ *n* [³*back* + *flip*] **1 :** a backward somersault **2 :** a complete reversal of position or belief **:** VOLTE-FACE

²backflip \"\ *vi* **:** to do a backflip ⟨~ off a diving board⟩

backflow \ˈ=,=\ *n* [³*back* + *flow*] **1 :** a flowing back or returning toward a source **2 :** the entrance of water or other liquid from any but the regular source of a potable water supply system — compare CROSS-CONNECTION

back focus *n* **:** the distance from the rear glass surface of a photographic lens to the focal plane when the lens is focused on a very distant object

back-formation \ˈ=ˌ=ˈ==\ *n* **1 :** a word formed by subtraction of a real or supposed affix (as a suffix) from an already existing longer word (as *buttle* from *butler*, the final *-er* being taken as the suffix found in such words as *maker* or *player*, or as *pea* from *pease*, the final *-se* \z\ being taken as a plural ending) **2 :** the formation of a back-formation

back-friend \ˈ=,=\ *n* [perh. fr. ³*back* + *friend*] *archaic* **:** a seeming friend who is secretly an enemy

back-front \ˈ=,=\ *n* **:** the rear facade of a building

backfurrow \ˈ=,==\ *vb* [²*back* + *furrow*] **:** to plow by throwing or turning the soil from the first two furrows together, leaving clear furrows on the sides

backgame \ˈ=,=\ *n* **:** a strategy in backgammon that aims at hindering the opponent's progress instead of advancing one's own men

¹back·gam·mon \ˈbak,gamən, ==ˈ= *sometimes* ˈbagəmən *or* baˈgam- *or* bəˈgam-\ *n* -s [perh. fr. ³*back* + *gammon*, alter. of ME *gamen* game, sport — more at GAME] **1 :** a game played with dice and counters on a board divided into two tables each marked with 12 points in which each player tries to move his own counters from point to point and off the board trying at the same time to block or capture those of his opponent — called also *tables* **2 :** the winning of a backgammon game before the loser has borne off any men and while one or more men remain on the winner's inner table or on the bar, the winner receiving triple score

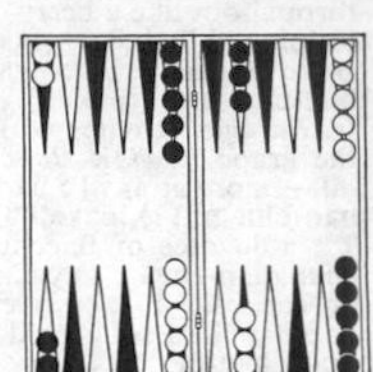
backgammon board with pieces arranged as at beginning of game

²backgammon \"\ *vt* -ED/-ING/-S **:** to beat (an opponent) in backgammon by scoring a backgammon

back gear *or* **back gearing** *n* **:** the gearing at the headstock of a lathe for reducing the speed of the spindle from that of the driving pulley — **back-geared** \ˈ=ˈ=\ *adj*

back gray *n* **:** BACK CLOTH 2

¹background \ˈ=,=\ *n, often attrib* **1 a :** the ground, space, or its contents being or represented as being at the rear or behind the principal object or objects observed: as (1) **:** the rear part of a stage or its contents (as painted scenery) ⟨as the curtain rises, a rustic festival is in progress in the ~⟩ (2) **:** the space or ground and its contents shown in a pictorial representation as being at the rear of the principal figure or figures ⟨stands in a graceful pose against a ~ of peaceful stream and rolling hills⟩ **b :** the surface upon or against which the principal figures or parts of a two-dimensional representation or pattern are seen ⟨a study of white flowers against a solid black ~⟩ **2 :** a position away from that which holds the center of attention **:** an obscure, less prominent, or not readily noticed position or status ⟨the parents stayed in the ~ during the children's party⟩ ⟨pushed into the ~ by the brilliance and glamor of his rival⟩ **3 a** (1) **:** the natural, physical, or material conditions that form the setting within which something is viewed or experienced ⟨attractive private dwellings, all set in a ~ of tropical luxuriance —Tom Marvel⟩ ⟨a hum of distant street noises made a gentle ~ to the strident tootings of the big . . . American cars —Mollie Panter-Downes⟩ (2) **:** an harmonic or rhythmic accompaniment to a melodic line played or sung ⟨a violin duet with a bare viola and cello harmonic ~ —Ralph Hill⟩ **b** (1) **:** the conditions, circumstances, ideas, or events that stand in an antecedent, causal, or intimate relation to any phenomenon or development **:** SETTING, MILIEU ⟨made an exhaustive study of the ~ of the Crimean War⟩ ⟨the social and economic ~ of the Renaissance⟩ ⟨police probed into the ~ of the murder⟩ (2) **:** factual and circumstantial information that is essential to full understanding of a particular problem or situation ⟨take along a good standard book on British history to give you some ~ on what you'll be seeing —Richard Joseph⟩ **c** (1) **:** the environmental conditions or circumstances esp. of childhood and youth that form or contribute to the formation of an individual's character, personality, and cultural makeup ⟨Lincoln's pioneer ~⟩ ⟨a family ~ of wealth, leisure, and cultivated tastes⟩ ⟨a German ~ on his mother's side⟩ (2) **:** the area or areas of past experience or concentration (as in training or employment) ⟨a ~ in sales promotion⟩ ⟨a ~ in medieval history⟩ ⟨a ~ of gold mining and prospecting for oil⟩ ⟨has unusual ~*s* of study and experience in international affairs —F.L.Mott⟩ (3) **:** an individual's life history or past career ⟨investigated the ~ of the suspect⟩ ⟨a ~ of success in all his varied enterprises⟩ **4 a :** intrusive often constant sound that confuses, distorts, or interferes with received or recorded electronic signals (as in radio reception or recording); *also* **:** adventitious flicks interfering with electronic instrument readings **b :** the more or less steady level of radiation or sound above which the effect (as radioactivity) being measured by an apparatus (as a Geiger counter) is detected

²**background** \"\ *vt* [¹*background*] **1 :** to form a background to ⟨elms that have ~*ed* memorable scenes in our history —Frank Thone⟩ **2 :** to provide with a background ⟨a richly ~*ed* study of a silent movie star —Hollis Alpert⟩

background music *also* **background** *n* **:** music performed esp. by unseen performers as an accompaniment to some activity essentially unrelated to it (as dining, shopping, or factory work); *specif* **:** music specially composed or arranged to accompany the dialogue or action (but not dancing or singing) of a motion picture or radio or television drama

background projection *n* **:** the projection of still or motion pictures onto a translucent screen that is then photographed from the opposite side and used as the background for live action sequences of a photoplay — called also *back projection, process projection*

¹**backhand** \ˈ=,= *sometimes* ˈ=ˈ=\ *n* [³*back* + *hand*] **1 a :** a stroke with the back of the hand turned in the direction of the movement ⟨a sharp ~ across the cheek⟩ **b :** a stroke (as in tennis) made from his left by a right-handed player or from his right by a left-handed player — opposed to *forehand* ⟨a good ~ in squash⟩ ⟨a good-~ game⟩ **2 :** handwriting whose up-and-down strokes slant at a downward angle from left to right ⟨to write a bold ~⟩ ⟨~ writing⟩

backhand 1b

²**backhand** \"\ *or* **back·hand·ed** *also* **back·hand·ed·ly** *adv* **1 :** using a backhand ⟨deliver a slap ~⟩ ⟨hit the tennis ball ~ on a tricky bounce⟩ **2** *of a catch in baseball* **:** with the glove hand across the body to the right in right-handed throwers or to the left in left-handed ones ⟨catch a long fly ~ on the run⟩

³**backhand** \"\ *vt* **:** to do or hit with the back of the hand or a backhand ⟨I ~*ed* the coffee right into the lap of the lippy guy —R.V.Williams⟩ ⟨he ~*ed* the man with a sharp slap across the cheek⟩ ⟨~ a tricky bounce on a tennis court⟩

back·hand·ed \ˈ=ˈ==\ *adj* **1 :** using or consisting of backhand or a backhand ⟨~ writing⟩ ⟨a ~ slap in the face⟩ ⟨a ~ shot in tennis⟩ **2 :** HESITANT, DIFFIDENT ⟨not at all ~ in asking for second helpings⟩ **3 :** indirect, roundabout, or devious ⟨a ~, dishonest way of achieving his end⟩ — often used of an outcome opposed to the real or seeming intent of an act or statement ⟨attacks from that source amounted to a ~ compliment to the man's integrity⟩ ⟨the ~ censorship of providing information "channels" . . . actually aimed at hiding facts —Dale Kramer⟩ — compare LEFT-HANDED 3 **4** *of written letters of the alphabet* **:** inclining from upper left to lower right

backhanded rope *or* **backhand rope** *n* **:** LEFT-HANDED ROPE

back·hand·er \ˈ=,== *also* ˈ=ˈ==\ *n* -s [¹*backhand* + *-er*] **:** a backhanded blow, stroke, or catch

backhaul \ˈ=,=\ *n* [³*back* + *haul*] **:** the return movement of a transportation vehicle from the direction of its principal haul esp. transporting a shipment back over part or all of the route

back·heel \ˈ=,=\ *n* [³*back* + *heel*] **:** a method of tripping a wrestling opponent by getting a foot behind his heel and pushing him backward; *also* **:** a throw made in this way

backhoe \ˈ=,=\ *n* [³*back* + *hoe*] **:** an excavating machine in which the bucket is rigidly attached to a hinged stick on the boom and is drawn toward the machine in operation — compare DRAGLINE

backhouse \ˈ=,=\ *n* **:** PRIVY 2

back in *vi* **1** *in poker* **:** to bet after having passed at the first opportunity **2** *in bridge* **:** to overcall or double or to reopen the bidding after having passed in the first round

¹**backing** *pres part of* BACK

²**backing** *n* -s **1 :** something forming or used to form a back: as **a :** unsquared stone or rubble, brick, hollow tile, or concrete block used at the back of a wall in masonry or such supporting masonry itself **b :** a piece of cloth or other material serving as a foundation or used for stiffening ⟨a leather ~ on a cloth belt⟩ **c :** a thick layer of wood behind the armor of a warship **d :** the silvering on the back of a mirror **e :** a piece of scenery placed behind an opening (as a door or arch) in a stage setting to prevent the audience from seeing what lies behind it **f :** the metal portion of a dental crown, bridge, or similar structure to which a porcelain or plastic tooth facing is attached **g :** a light-absorbing coating either on the back of a photographic plate or film or between the emulsion and the base reducing interreflections between the surfaces and hence reducing halation **2 backings** *pl, Scot* **:** refuse of wool, flax, or cloth **3 a :** SUPPORT, AID ⟨his campaign had the solid ~ of the party leadership⟩; **:** the persons or elements providing support or aid ⟨his ~ includes all the substantial elements in the community⟩ **b :** endorsement esp. of a warrant by a magistrate **4 :** a secondary line attached to a casting line and wound onto the fishing reel spool before it

backing hammer *n* **:** a hammer with a broad claw at one end of the head and a flat head at the other end used in shaping the backbones of books

backing light *or* **backing lamp** *n* **:** BACKUP LIGHT

backing pump *n* **:** FOREPUMP

backing ring *n* **:** a metal ring used inside a butt-welded joint to reinforce the joint and to prevent weld metal from entering the pipe at the joint

backing strip *n* **:** long lighting units used for stage illumination (as behind doors, windows, or portholes)

backing yarn *n* **:** the yarn that holds the tufts and forms the skeleton of a pile fabric

backjoint \ˈ=,=\ *n* **:** a rabbet or chase in masonry left to receive a permanent slab or other filling

backkick \ˈ=,=\ *n* **:** KICKBACK

backland \ˈ=,=\ *n* -s **1 :** BACKCOUNTRY, HINTERLAND — often used in pl. ⟨the remote ~*s* of the country⟩ **2 :** the part of a river floodplain separated from the river by a natural levee

¹**backlash** \ˈ=,=\ *n* [³*back* + *lash*] **1 a :** a sudden often violent backward movement or recoil **b :** the clearance, slack, or play between adjacent movable parts (as in a train of cars or series of gears) or the jar or reaction often caused by such clearance when the parts are suddenly put in action or are in irregular action **c :** an action or reaction in a reverse direction suggesting such a backward movement or recoil **2 :** a snarl in that part of a fishing line which is wound on the spool of the reel caused by overrunning of the spool **3 :** a rearward movement of the trigger of a firearm past the position where hammer or firing pin is released **4 :** the small reverse phase of an imperfectly rectified alternating current resulting from positive ions produced in the gas of the rectifier tube by the impact of thermoelectrons

²**backlash** \"\ *vi* **:** to make or execute a backlash

back·less \ˈbakləs\ *adj* **:** not having a back

¹**backlight** \ˈ=,=\ *n* [³*back* + *light*] **:** illumination falling upon an object from behind esp. throwing it into relief ⟨a feather floating white in the dazzling ~ of the sun —Ralph Ellison⟩

²**backlight** \"\ *vt* **:** to illuminate with a backlight or backlighting ⟨the sun dropped lower, ~*ing* the peaks —Douglass Wallop⟩ ⟨a ~*ed* camera shot⟩

backlighting *n* -s **:** controlled lighting of an object from the rear or from the side away from the camera for special photographic effects

backlining \ˈ=,==\ *n* -s [¹*back* + *lining*] **:** the material fastened to the backbone of a book or to the inside of the cover in the backbone area to provide strength and rigidity

back·lins \ˈbaklənz\ *adv* [ME (northern dial.) *bakling*, fr. *bak* back + *-ling*] *dial Brit* **:** BACKWARD

backlist \ˈ=,=\ *n* **:** the books kept in print as distinguished from books newly published

back load *n* **:** a load or burden carried or suitable to be carried on the back ⟨a ~ of firewood⟩

¹**backlog** \ˈ=,=\ *n* [³*back* + *log*] **1 :** a large log of wood forming the back of a campfire or hearthfire **2 :** a reserve that promises continuing work and profit ⟨a vast ~ of orders may soon make possible the greatest peacetime industrial activity that we have ever seen —H.S.Truman⟩ **3 :** an increasing accumulation of tasks unperformed or materials not processed ⟨eliminate the ~ of uncataloged books⟩ ⟨judges met . . . to discuss how to clear the ~ of 15,000 cases —*N.Y. Times*⟩

²**backlog** \"\ *vb* **:** to accumulate as a backlog

back loop jump *n* **:** a jump in figure skating executed from an outside backward loop and consisting of a full revolution of the body in the air landing on the same outside backward edge

back·lot·ter \ˈ=,lädər\ *or* **back·yard·er** \-ˌyärdər\ *n* [*back lot* or *back yard* + *-er*] **1 :** one who raises poultry or rabbits on a small lot, usu. a back lot **2 :** a breeder on a small scale

back marker *n, Brit* **:** one starting a handicapped race, game, or match with a high adverse handicap

back matter *n* **:** matter following the main text of a book — compare FRONT MATTER

back·most \ˈbak,mōst *esp Brit also* -məst\ *superlative of* BACK

back mutation *n* **:** atavistic biological mutation **:** mutation of a previously mutated gene to its former condition

back number *n* **1 :** an issue (as of a magazine) preceding the current one **2 :** something that is out of date ⟨the building has become a *back number* in construction and design —Lee Graham⟩

back of *prep* **1 :** BEHIND ⟨a hall *back of* the main staircase —*New Yorker*⟩ **2 :** beyond in past time **:** BEFORE ⟨the history of the islands goes far *back of* this —Nathaniel Burt⟩ ⟨two centuries *back of* the oldest complete Greek texts —I.M. Price⟩ **3 :** in a hidden causal or background relation to ⟨soon learned that the hardest kind of work was *back of* every success —Edward Bok⟩ ⟨wondered what was *back of* his strange remark⟩ **4 :** in support of ⟨*back of* the legislation stood those likely to gain by its passage⟩

back off *vt* **1 :** to reverse the direction of rotation of (a spindle) for a few turns in mule spinning so that the yarn between the nose of the cop and the point of the spindle may be uncoiled **2 a :** to remove metal from the back of (a cutting tool) to provide clearance from the work (as in cutting a screw thread) **b :** to remove (as part of a well casing) by unscrewing **3 :** to cut away or relieve on the back ⟨*back off* a cutter or drill to make a clearance⟩ **~** *vi* **:** to back down or back out

back office *n* **:** the inner private office or area of a business or institution

back order *n* **1 :** an unfulfilled order held for future completion or delivery **2 :** a new order made up of previously unavailable items of an old order

¹**back out** *vi* [⁴*back* + *out*] **:** to withdraw esp. from an agreement, commitment, or contest — often used with *of* ⟨*back out* of a fight⟩ ⟨agreed to come, then *backed out*⟩ ⟨*backed out* of their treaty obligations⟩

²**back out** *n* **:** the act or an instance of backing out of something ⟨a fight from which there was no chance of a *back out*⟩

¹**backpack** \ˈ=,=\ *n* [¹*back* + *pack*] **1 :** a load carried on the back (as by knapsack) **2 :** a piece of equipment (as a fire extinguisher) designed for operation while being carried on the back

²**backpack** \"\ *vt* **:** to carry (food or equipment) on the back esp. in camping ⟨each wooden roof beam . . . had to be ~*ed* from the plain below up the steep trail —*Holiday*⟩ ⟨summer hikers who are ~*ing* all their equipment —K.A.Henderson⟩ **~** *vi* **:** to carry one's food or equipment on the back esp. in camping ⟨crampons would have been useful, but when ~*ing*, we hadn't considered their extra weight worth taking —*Appalachia*⟩

back–page \ˈ=ˈ=\ *adj* [*back page*] **:** of or relating to the back pages of a newspaper **:** of small news value — opposed to *front-page*

back–paint \ˈ=,=\ *vt* **:** to paint the back or concealed portion of (as wood trim)

back–palm \ˈ=,=\ *vt* **:** to conceal (as cards or coins) on the side of the hand away from the audience in sleight of hand

back parlor *n* **:** a private usu. second parlor in the back or the main living area of a house or inn

back–patting *n* -s **:** the act or an instance of complimenting or congratulating (as for merit or achievement) ⟨the time for *back-patting* is not yet —*Manufacturing Confectioner*⟩

backpedal \ˈ=,==\ *vi* [²*back* + *pedal*] **1 :** to press backward on the pedals of a bicycle to check the forward motion **2 a :** to retreat or back away esp. in boxing ⟨hamper . . . troops trying to ~ northward —*Newsweek*⟩ ⟨he sent several jolting hooks to the heart, forcing the defending champion to ~ —Nat Fleischer⟩ **b :** to back down from or reverse a previous opinion or stand ⟨a politician *backpedaling* on an earlier promise⟩

backpiece \ˈ=,=\ *n* **:** a piece at the back or serving as a back; *esp* **:** a piece of armor designed to protect the back

back pitch *n* **:** the center-to-center distance between two parallel rows of rivets in riveted joints

backplaster \ˈ=,==\ *vt* **:** to apply plaster on the back of (lathing) or mortar on the back of (a masonry wall) — **backplastering** *n* -s

back·plate \ˈ=,=\ *n* **:** a metal piece in back or forming a back esp. of a suit of armor

back play *n, cricket* **:** batting in which the batsman steps back toward his wicket and plays the ball well behind the popping crease — contrasted with *forward play*

back pressure *n* **1 :** residual pressure on the exhaust side of a steam-engine piston against which the steam on the intake side must work **2 :** opposition to flow of a liquid or gas due to friction, inertia, gravity, or other cause

back pressure–arm lift method *n* **:** artificial respiration in which the operator kneels at the head of the victim, compresses the chest manually, then pulls up the elbows thereby expanding the lungs and repeats this sequence in a regular rhythm as long as considered necessary

back projection *n* **:** BACKGROUND PROJECTION

back–putty \ˈ=,==\ *vt* **:** to force putty into any space in a window sash that may be left between the edges of the rabbet and the glass

back–rake \ˈ=,=\ *vt* [²*back*] **:** ²RAKE 4

back–reef \ˈ=ˈ=\ *adj* [*back reef*] **:** consisting of or belonging to a restricted lagoon behind barrier reefs ⟨a *back-reef* area⟩ ⟨*back-reef* geologic formations⟩

backrest *n* **:** a rest at the back: as **a :** a follow rest in a lathe **b** *Brit* **:** WHIP ROLL **c :** a grinding-machine rest that is fastened to the machine table to support the work

back room *n* **1 :** a room situated in the rear; *esp* **:** one accessible only to special or private groups ⟨in the *back room* of every tavern, clubs held meetings several times a week —Bernard Faÿ⟩ **2 :** the meeting place of a leadership or directing group (as of a political party) that wields its influence and authority in an informal, inconspicuous, and often indirect way reaching decisions through negotiation among its members and sometimes making use of dubious or underhanded methods ⟨the man in the *back room*, avoiding direct contacts, weaving a web of intrigue and influence —M.W. Straight⟩ ⟨delegates . . . were merely marking time until the real decisions were made in the *back rooms* —*Time*⟩

backroom boy \ˈ=,=-\ *n, slang chiefly Brit* **:** a person engaged in scientific esp. secret research; *also* **:** an expert adviser or aide **:** BRAIN TRUSTER

backrope \ˈ=,=\ *n* **1 :** a rope or chain extending aft on each side of a sailing ship from the lower end of the dolphin striker to the bows — see SHIP illustration **2 :** CAT BACK

back rubber *n* [¹*back*] **:** a device that automatically applies insecticide to cattle as they rub against it

back run *n* [³*back*] **:** the period in an industrial process in which the flow of materials (as of steam and gas in water-gas manufacture) is reversed

backs *pl of* BACK, *pres 3d sing of* BACK

back sail *n* **:** a sail upon which the wind pressure is on the forward side

backs and cutters *n pl* **:** any two main series of fractures that produce jointed rock structure by crossing each other at steep angles — used in quarrying

backsaw \ˈ=,=\ *n* [so called fr. the stiffened back] **:** a short fine-toothed saw stiffened by a metal rib along its back edge

backsaw

backsawn \ˈ=,=\ *adj* [²*back* + *sawn*] **:** sawed at right angles to the medullary rays ⟨~ wood⟩

backscatter \ˈ=,==\ *or* **backscattering** \ˈ=,===\ *n* [²*back* + *scatter* or *scattering*] **:** the scattering of radiation (as X rays) in a direction approximately opposite to that of the incident radiation and due to reflection from particles of the medium traversed; *also* **:** the radiation so reversed in direction

backscattered *adj* **:** produced by backscatter

back score *n* **1 :** a line in curling drawn tangent to the parish and parallel with and midway between the sweeping score and the foot score — see CURLING illustration **2 :** a record in bridge of the number of points each player has won or lost in the course of the game

back scratcher *n* **:** a device shaped like a hand, mounted at the end of a stick, and used to scratch one's own back

back scratching *n* **:** the reciprocal exchange of favors, services, or assistance tending to the private advantage or interest of the parties to the exchange ⟨promotion becomes no longer a matter of merit but of log-rolling, *back scratching*, and of obsequious toadying —F.D.Roosevelt⟩ ⟨*back-scratching* alliances with . . . lobbies —*Progressive Labor World*⟩

backseat \ˈ=ˈ=\ *n* **:** a secondary, inferior, or inconspicuous position or status in relation to the position or status of something else — usu. used in the phrase *take a backseat* ⟨the poems were first-rate, but the comments didn't have to take a ~ —Harvey Breit⟩ ⟨foreign requirements for new freight cars will have to take a ~ to domestic needs —*Jour. of Commerce*⟩

backseat driver \ˈ=,=-\ *n* **1 :** a person who directs or attempts to direct the actions of the driver of a car from the backseat (as by unsolicited advice or warnings) **2 :** any person esp. in a subordinate position who intervenes or tries to intervene in the direction or conduct of affairs that are not his proper concern or responsibility — **backseat driving** *n*

¹**backset** \ˈ=,=\ *n* -s [³*back* + *set*] **1 :** SETBACK ⟨a ~ in his own personal finances —F.W.Crofts⟩ ⟨get out of bed too soon after an illness and suffer a ~⟩ **2 :** an eddy or countercurrent of water **3 :** the distance from the face of a lock to the center of the keyhole

²**backset** \"\ *vt* [²*back* + *set*] *West* **:** to plow again in the fall (prairie land broken up in the spring)

back–set bed \ˈ=,=-\ *n* **:** a stratum deposited on the rear slope of a glacial apron or sand plain as the ice retreats and consequently dipping toward the retreating ice

backsetting *n* [fr. gerund of ²*backset*] *West* **:** newly broken prairie land after the second plowing of broken sod

backsey \ˈbakˈsī\ *n* -s [³*back* + *sey*] *Scot* **:** a cut of meat usu. including all or most of the loin

back shaft *n* **1 :** a countershaft driven by a back gear **2 :** any shaft placed at the back of a machine

back·sheesh *or* **back·shish** \ˈbak,shēsh, =ˈ=\ *var of* BAKSHEESH

backshift \ˈ=,=\ *n* **:** the second shift of workers for the day in a mine

back shop *n* **1 :** a usu. private shop or area to the rear of the main shop or establishment; *specif* **:** the printing room of a newspaper or periodical **2 :** a locomotive repair shop

backshore \ˈ=,=\ *n* **:** the part of the seashore between the foreshore and the coastline covered by water only during storms of exceptional severity

back shutter *n* **:** the backflap of a shutter

backside \ˈ=ˈ=\ *n* [ME *bakside*, fr. *bak* back + *side*] **1** *now dial Brit* **a :** the backyard of a house **b :** BARNYARD, FARMYARD **2 :** BUTTOCKS — often used in pl. **3 :** BACKSTRETCH

backsight \ˈ=,=\ *n* **1** *surveying* **:** a reading of the leveling rod in its unchanged position when the leveling instrument has been taken to a new position **2** *surveying* **:** a sight directed backward to a previous station

back sinew *n* **:** the large flexor tendon at the back of the cannon bones of quadrupeds — called also *back tendon*

back slang *n* **:** a secret language in which each word is pronounced exactly or approximately as if spelled backwards (as *nam* for *man; nird* for *drink*) ⟨Cockney *back slang*⟩

¹**backslap** \ˈ=,=\ *n* [¹*back* + *slap*] **1 :** a slap on the back esp. as an indication of good-fellowship ⟨the symbols . . . of quick liking and respect — the handshake, the ~ —James Thurber⟩ **2 :** a slap or blow caused by a sudden backward motion

²**backslap** \"\ *vt* **:** to slap on the back familiarly or approvingly; *also* **:** to make an excessive or effusive display of approval of ⟨many of the critics . . . tend to browbeat some authors as they can be guaranteed to ~ others —Vera Brittain⟩ **~** *vi* **:** to engage in backslapping **:** make a pronounced or excessive display of cheerfulness, cordiality, or good-fellowship ⟨would have puffed up and blustered and laughed and *backslapped* —T.W.Duncan⟩ — **back·slap·per** \-pə(r)\ *n*

¹**backslapping** *adj* **1 :** characterized by a tendency to backslap ⟨a jovial, hearty, ~ type⟩ **2 :** having an excessively hearty or boisterous character ⟨the ~ jocosity that passes for humor here —Sinclair Lewis⟩

²**backslapping** *n* -s **:** the effusive display of approval, cordiality, or good-fellowship ⟨there has been much satisfied ~ over the presentation —Bosley Crowther⟩ ⟨a field where social drinking and hearty ~ had heretofore been prerequisites for success —Ralph de Toledano⟩

¹**backslide** \ˈ=,= *also* (ˈ)=ˈ=\ *vi* **backslid; backslid** *or* **backslidden; backsliding; backslides** [²*back* + *slide*] **:** to fall away or relapse from a previously adopted faith, position, or line of conduct ⟨when an earnest Christian encounters one who has *backslidden* —A.J.Russell⟩ ⟨had *backslid* so far as to bargain with the infidel —*Time*⟩ **:** revert to an earlier and worse condition **:** RETROGRESS, DECLINE ⟨a world that . . . had certainly *backslidden* in the ways of culture —V.L.Parrington⟩

²**backslide** \ˈ=,=\ *n* **:** the act or an instance of backsliding ⟨a moral ~ —*New Republic*⟩

backslider \ˈ=,==\ *n* **:** one that backslides ⟨nor will a ~ be able to plead his former righteousness —W.L.Wardle⟩

backspace \ˈ=,=\ *vi* [²*back* + *space*] **:** to move the carriage of a typewriter back one space with each depression of a key

back·spac·er \-sə(r)\ *n* **:** the typewriter key used for backspacing — called also *backspace key*

backspang \ˈ=,=\ *n* -s [³*back* + *spang*] *chiefly Scot* **:** a trick or loophole that enables one to retreat from a bargain

backspin \ˈ=,=\ *n* **:** a backward rotary motion imparted esp. to a ball (as a billiard or golf ball) that causes the ball on touching the ground or some other surface to recoil, bounce backward, stop dead, or roll forward only a short distance

backsplash \ˈ=,=\ *or* **backsplasher** \-shə(r)\ *n* [³*back* + *splash* or *splasher*] **:** a plate or panel erected at the back of a fixture (as an electric range) usu. supporting control devices

backsplice \ˈ=,=\ *n* [³*back* + *splice*] **:** a finish for the end of a rope that consists of a crown knot with the strands tucked over and under in the standing part

¹**backspread** \ˈ=,=\ *vi* [²*back* + *spread*] **1** *in stock speculation* **:** to close the transactions previously made in a spreading operation **2** *in stock speculation* **:** to transfer a hedge from one market to another

²**backspread** \"\ *n* **:** an arbitrage operation like a spread but performed when the difference in price between the two markets is less than the normal one

backspring \ˈ=,=\ *n* [³*back* + *spring*] **:** a spring hawser led at a forward angle to the wharf from the stern or midships

backstab \ˈ=,=\ *vt* [¹*back* + *stab*] **:** to attack (a person) behind his back (as by making unfounded accusations) ⟨unscrupulous politicos ~*ing* opponents⟩

backstaff \ˈ=,=\ *n* [¹*back* + *staff;* fr. the position of the observer, who has his back to the sun when using it] **:** an instrument similar to a cross-staff but fitted with a reflector and formerly used for taking the altitudes of heavenly bodies

[1]**backstage** \'⸗'⸗\ *adv* [[2]*back* (used prepositionally by analogy with *upstage, downstage*) + *stage*] **1 :** in or to a backstage area ⟨changes of costume to be made ~ —Winifred Bambrick⟩ ⟨rushed ~ after the performance⟩ **2 :** in a backstage setting **:** SECRETLY, PRIVATELY ⟨officers of the convention were chosen ~⟩ ⟨working ~ to gain support for his plan⟩

[2]**backstage** \'⸗'⸗\ *adj* **1 :** of, relating to, or occurring or carried on in a backstage ⟨~ voices and sounds to give the impression of a mob⟩ ⟨a ~ worker shifting scenery⟩ ⟨her ~ impersonations of the company's principal dancers —*Current Biog.*⟩ **2 :** of or relating to the private lives of actors, actresses, or theater people ⟨a ~ love affair⟩ or purporting to depict the private lives of theater people ⟨a ~ musical⟩ **3 :** of or relating to the hidden, inner, or behind-the-scenes workings or operations (as of an organization or institution) ⟨a key ~ figure in the new regime —*Newsweek*⟩ **:** concealed from public view ⟨~ deals and promises⟩

[3]**backstage** \'⸗'⸗\ *n* [[3]*back* + *stage*] **:** the whole or any part of the area of a stage that is behind the proscenium; *specif* **:** the dressing rooms of a theater

back·stairs *also* **back·stair** \'⸗¦⸗\ *adj* [*back stairs*, n.] **1 :** characterized by a quality and air of secrecy and intrigue ⟨~ deals⟩ ⟨~ gossip⟩ **:** FURTIVE, DEVIOUS ⟨his low ~ cunning —A.L. Guérard⟩ **2 :** having a sordid or scandalous character ⟨~ intimacies —A.L.Kroeber⟩ ⟨cheap ~ fiction —E.A.Weeks⟩

[1]**backstamp** \'⸗'⸗\ *vt* [[1]*back* + *stamp*] **:** to stamp on the back; *specif* **:** to stamp (a piece of mail) with the date of receipt and the name of the receiving post office along the transportation route

[2]**backstamp** \"\ *n* **:** a stamp (as a date stamp or postmark) on the back of a piece of mail

backstand \'⸗'⸗\ *n* **:** a device for regulating machinery belt tension

[1]**backstay** \'⸗'⸗\ *n* [[3]*back* + *stay*] **1 a :** a stay extending from the mastheads to the side of a ship and slanting a little aft — see SHIP illustration **b :** a supporting cable (as on a derrick) that prevents a falling forward of a more or less vertical part **2 :** any of various strengthening or supporting devices at the back or rear: as **a :** a rope or strap to prevent excessive forward motion (as of the carriage in a hand printing press) **b :** a spring used to keep the cutting edges of purchase shears in contact **c :** a bar topped with a glass rod running across a loom below the lowest motion of the warp yarns **d :** a rod extending from either end of the rear axle of a carriage to the reach **e :** a strip of leather covering and strengthening the back seam of a shoe

[2]**backstay** \"\ *vt* **:** to rig with backstays

backstay stool *n* **:** STOOL 6a

back·stein \'bäk,s(h)tīn\ *also* **back·stei·ner** \-nə(r)\ *n* -s *usu cap* [G *backsteinkäse*, lit., brick cheese, fr. *backstein* brick (fr. *backen* to bake — fr. OHG *backan* — + *stein* stone, fr. OHG) + *käse* cheese; akin to OHG *bahhan* to bake — more at BAKE, STONE] **:** a German cheese resembling limburger that is produced in brick shape

backstick \'⸗'⸗\ *n* **:** a large stick placed on or used as a backlog

[1]**backstitch** \'⸗'⸗\ *n* [[3]*back* + *stitch*] **:** a hand stitch resembling machine stitching that is made by inserting the needle a stitch length to the right and bringing it up an equal distance to the left

[2]**backstitch** \"\ *vb* **:** to sew with backstitches

back·stone \'bak,stōn, -stən\ *dial Eng var of* BAKESTONE

back stool *n* **:** a stool with a back added for extra comfort **:** an early form of side chair

[1]**back·stop** \'bak,stäp\ *n* [[3]*back* + *stop*] **:** something serving as a stop behind something else: as **a :** a screen or fence (as that behind home plate in baseball or that behind the base line of a tennis court) intended to stop balls leaving the field of play **b :** a player (as the catcher in baseball or the wicketkeeper in cricket) whose position is behind the batter **c :** a stop (as a pawl) that prevents a backward movement (as of a wheel, elevator, or conveyor) beyond a certain point **d :** a dirt mound or other obstruction to catch the bullets going through or beyond the target in a rifle or pistol range

[2]**backstop** \"\ *vt* **1 :** to serve as a backstop to ⟨barberry hedge . . . did its poor best to ~ errant baseballs —Philip Brady⟩ **2 :** to provide with backing or support **:** BOLSTER ⟨a lawyer, who ~s the president on problems involving national security —*Newsweek*⟩ ⟨no reserves except a British tank division which *backstopped* the line wherever it weakened —*Time*⟩

back straddle vault *n* **:** a gymnastics straddle vault in which the performer passes the left leg over the right side of the buck or horse and the right leg over the left side and clears the apparatus backward to land in a position the reverse of the starting position

back·strap \'⸗,⸗\ *n* **1 :** a pull strap attached to the top of the backstay of a shoe or boot **2 :** BACKBONE 3

back–strapped \'⸗,⸗\ *adj* [[2]*back*] *of a sailing ship* **:** forced by adverse winds or currents to leeward of a point to be weathered

back stream *n* **:** EDDY

back street *n* **:** a street away or far from the main thoroughfares

backstretch \'⸗¦⸗\ *n* **:** the far straightaway opposite the homestretch on an oval racecourse

back·strip \'⸗,⸗\ *n* [[1]*back* + *strip*] **:** BACKBONE 3

backstroke \'⸗,⸗\ *n* **1 :** a swimming stroke executed on the back and resembling an inverted crawl or inverted butterfly breaststroke but with more knee flexion and usu. six inverted crawl leg beats to an arm cycle **2 :** the bell ringer's pull on the rope that starts the bell down from its poised mouth-up position in full ringing — compare HANDSTROKE 2

backswamp \'⸗,⸗\ *n* **:** a swamp in a backland ⟨a ~ area⟩

back swath *n* **:** the swath that is next to the first one cut, that is usu. cut in the opposite direction, and that the tractor or horses have traveled over in cutting the first swath

back·swept \'⸗¦⸗\ *adj* [[2]*back* + *swept*] **:** swept, brushed, slanted, or slanting backward ⟨his gray ~ hair⟩ ⟨a full ~ skirt⟩; *specif* **:** characterized by or possessing sweepback ⟨a ~ airplane wing⟩

back swimmer *n* [[1]*back*] **:** an insect of the family Notonectidae characterized by swimming with the ventral surface uppermost

backswing \'⸗,⸗\ *n* [[3]*back* + *swing*] **:** the movement of a club, racket, or bat backward to the position from which the downward or forward stroke is made

backsword \'⸗,⸗\ *n* [[1]*back* + *sword*] **1 :** a sword with only one sharp edge **2 :** SINGLESTICK **3 :** *or* **back·sword·man** \-mən\ *pl* **backswordmen :** a fencer with the backsword

back·sword·ing \-diŋ\ *or* **backsword** *n* -s **:** fencing with a backsword or singlestick

back talk *n* [[3]*back* + *talk* (after *talk back*, v.)] **:** an impudent, insolent, or argumentative reply esp. from a subordinate ⟨would take no *back talk* from his children⟩

back–tan \'⸗,⸗\ *vt* [[2]*back*] **:** to treat (dyed material) with tannin in order to fix the dye — **back–tanning** \'⸗,⸗⸗\ *n* -s

back taper *n* **:** a slight relief on a tap or drill causing it to have a larger diameter at the point than at the shank

back·tend·er \'⸗,⸗⸗\ *n* **:** a worker who tends the discharge end of an industrial machine: as **a :** one who tends the drier, calender, and slitting and rewinding sections of a paper machine **b :** a textile worker who rolls or folds cloth

back tendon *n* **:** BACK SINEW

back·ten·ter \'⸗,tentə(r)\ *Brit var of* BACKTENDER a

back–titrate \(')⸗¦⸗,⸗\ *vt, chem* **:** to titrate back to the end point after it has been passed — **back–titration** \'⸗,⸗¦⸗⸗\ *n*

back to back *adj* **1 :** facing in opposite directions and often touching ⟨standing in a row *back to back*⟩ ⟨train seats *back to back*⟩ **2 :** dealt one in the hole and one face up — used of a pair in stud poker ⟨aces *back to back*⟩ **3 :** one after the other **:** CONSECUTIVE ⟨two home runs *back to back* in the third inning⟩ ⟨*back to back* telecasts⟩ **4** *of a letter of credit* **:** granted by a bank to an exporter to finance purchase of goods already covered by a letter of credit in his favor taken out by the importer

back–to–work \'⸗⸗'⸗\ *adj* **:** urging or directing the return of strikers to their jobs ⟨a *back-to-work* movement⟩ ⟨a *back-to-work* injunction⟩

back track *n* [[3]*back* + *track*] **1 :** a return track or course **:** a track leading back to one's starting point; *also* **:** a retracing of one's steps ⟨took the *back track* through the woods⟩ ⟨beat a *back track* through the woods⟩ **2 :** a retreat from or reversal of a position or stand once taken ⟨after his assurance that he would help out, we did not expect so quick a *back track*⟩

backtrack \'⸗,⸗\ *vi* **1 :** to take or follow a back track **:** retrace one's steps ⟨when the trail became impassable, we ~*ed* to camp⟩ **2 :** to modify, retreat from, or reverse a position or stand once taken ⟨first thumping the table and laying down the law, then ~*ing* when the reaction sets in —*New Republic*⟩ ~ *vt* **:** to follow in the tracks of ⟨~*ed* many a Methodist circuit rider while educating himself in the mill towns of the Deep South —R.P.Ramsey⟩

back trail *n* **:** BACK TRACK

backtrail \'⸗,⸗\ *vb* [*back trail*] **:** BACKTRACK

back turn *n, music* **:** an inverted turn

back up *vi* **1** *of water checked by an obstruction* **:** to rise and flow backward or overflow adjacent areas ⟨clogged pipes caused drain water to *back up* into the house⟩ ⟨a dammed stream that *backs up* and floods a meadow⟩ **2** *of nonliquid objects* **:** to accumulate through lack of an outlet in undesirable or unmanageable excess or in a congested state ⟨supplies are ample, if not already *backing up* in the hands of the producers —*Biddle Survey*⟩ ⟨cars *back up* for blocks on either side of the Main Street traffic light —Louise Levitas⟩ **3** *cricket* **a** *of a batsman* **:** to move forward of one's crease in readiness to run **b** *of a nonstriker* **:** to so move as the ball is delivered ~ *vt* **:** to hold back (as a river) usu. causing an accumulation ⟨this dam . . . *backs up* billions of gallons of water to prevent floods —N.M.Clark⟩

backup \'⸗,⸗\ *n* -s [*back up*] **1 :** BACKING ⟨supported by military strength in being and strength in potential timely ~ —M.B.Ridgway⟩ ⟨a stiff ~ to the sheet so that it would not bend⟩ **2 :** an accumulation esp. as a result of the stoppage of a flow ⟨a ~ of sewage⟩ ⟨a ~ of cars before the intersection⟩ **:** RESERVE ⟨a ~ of material for emergency use⟩ **3 :** a backward movement **:** a retreat from a position ⟨asked Congress for a ~ on its policy and a repeal of the law⟩ **4 :** a ball that curves or fades to the right in bowling **5 :** a masonry backing to a wall **6 :** the presswork on the second side of a printed sheet

backup light *n* **:** a light mounted at the rear of a motor vehicle and so connected that it shines only when the vehicle is in reverse gear illuminating the road behind

backup relay *n* **:** a secondary relay to protect a power system against faults in the event of failure of the primary relay to function as desired

backup signal *n* **:** DWARF SIGNAL

backveld \'⸗,⸗\ *n* [[3]*back* + *veld*; prob. part trans. of Afrik *agterveld*] *Africa* **:** BACKCOUNTRY

back vent *n* **:** a ventilating pipe attached to a waste pipe on the sewer side of its trap to prevent siphonage — **back venting** *n*

[1]**back·ward** \'bakwə(r)d\ *or* **back·wards** \-dz\ *adv* [ME *bakward, bakwardes*, fr. *bak* back + *-ward, -wardes*] **1 a :** toward the back or rear ⟨throw the arms out and ~⟩ **b :** with the back in advance or foremost ⟨pull a chair ~ away from a table⟩ ⟨drive ~ up a driveway⟩ **2 a :** in the direction from which one came **:** in a reverse or contrary direction or way ⟨read ~⟩ ⟨do things ~⟩ ⟨turn a handle ~⟩ ⟨the tide ebbs ~ toward the sea —John DeMeyer⟩ **b :** toward the past ⟨lovers of romance who look fondly ~⟩ **c :** in a regressive direction ⟨under his administration the community was not only at a standstill but going ~⟩ **:** toward an earlier and worse state ⟨moving ~ culturally and morally⟩

[2]**backward** \"\ *adj* [ME *bakward*, fr. *bakward*, adv.] **1 a :** directed or turned backward ⟨a ~ glance⟩ ⟨a ~ movement of the train⟩ ⟨a ~ jerk of the arm —Wirt Williams⟩ ⟨a ~ slant to his handwriting⟩ **b :** done or executed backward ⟨a ~ twist of a handle⟩ **2** *archaic* **:** situated or placed toward or in the back or rear **3 :** RELUCTANT, DIFFIDENT, SHY ⟨a man hardly ~ in asserting himself⟩ ⟨a ~ suitor⟩ ⟨I have been ~ to begin my canvass —Edmund Burke⟩ **4 a :** slow to learn or dull of comprehension **:** mentally retarded ⟨a ~ child⟩ **b :** holding to outworn or traditional ideas, views, or principles **:** REACTIONARY, UNPROGRESSIVE ⟨a ~ person, imbued with strong and irrational prejudices⟩ **c :** in a relatively underdeveloped state esp. economically and socially ⟨technological assistance to the ~ areas of the world⟩ ⟨a ~ agrarian country⟩ ⟨desires to elevate the more ~ portions of the human family —Philip Mason⟩ **5 :** unsupported by a fellow pawn in chess and not readily movable to a position to be so supported — **back·ward·ly** *adv*

[3]**backward** \"\ *n* -s **:** the part behind or past ⟨the dark ~ . . . of time —Shak.⟩

back ward *n* **:** a ward where mentally ill patients whose prognosis is poor are housed and where patients typically receive only custodial care

back·ward·a·tion \,bakwə(r)'dāshən\ *n* -s [[1]*backward* + *-ation*] **1 :** the seller's postponement of delivery of stock or shares on the London Stock Exchange with the consent of the buyer upon payment of a premium to the latter **2 :** the premium paid in backwardation — compare CONTANGO

backward dive *n* **:** a dive in fancy diving from a position facing the board and keeping the back toward the water throughout — compare CUTAWAY

back·ward·ness \'bakwə(r)dnəs\ *n* -ES **:** the quality or state of being backward

backward pass *n* **:** a pass in football thrown at right angles to the direction of play or obliquely to the rear

[1]**backwash** \'⸗,⸗\ *n* [[3]*back* + *wash*] **1 a :** the motion of water or waves washed or thrown back (as by the propeller or oars of a boat) **b :** a backward flow or movement (as of air or matter) produced by and incidental or residual to some action or process ⟨the turbojet generates a ~ of such high velocity that the conventional wooden fences blow away —*Boeing Mag.*⟩ **2 :** a condition, movement, or event that is a reaction to or an extension, consequence, or by-product of some other event or development **:** SEQUEL, AFTERMATH, REPERCUSSION ⟨the ~ of English deism reached the shores of New England —V.L.Parrington⟩ ⟨Australians should have no fear of their ability to weather the ~ of an American recession —*Sydney (Australia) Bulletin*⟩ ⟨economic and social problems . . . are by no means the mere ~ of war and German occupation —Robert Strausz-Hupé⟩ **3 :** BACKWATER 4 ⟨an unspoiled rural paradise — called by some a ~ of eighteenth century manners and customs —*Amer. Guide Series: Del.*⟩

[2]**backwash** \"\ *vt* **1 :** to affect with backwash ⟨a steamer ~*ing* our small craft⟩ **2 :** to scour and dry (wool) in sliver form before or after combing **3 :** to clean (a water filter) by reversing the flow — **back·wash·er** \-shə(r)\ *n*

[1]**backwater** \'⸗,⸗⸗\ *n* [ME *bakwater*, fr. *bak* back + *water*] **1 a :** water turned back in its course (as in a sewer or river channel) by an obstruction, an opposing current, or the flow of the tide **b :** a body or accumulation of water resulting from this esp. when overflowing lowlands or forming a body fed by a side channel from the main current or sea **2 :** BACKWASH 1 **3 :** WHITE WATER 2 **4 :** an isolated, secluded, or backward place, section, or condition ⟨one of the cultural ~*s* of civilization⟩ ⟨the quiet ~ of a classroom —Anna M.Wells⟩ ⟨a rural New England ~ —R.F.Nichols⟩ **5 :** a large grayish or mottled Indo-Pacific ray (*Gymnura japonica*) esteemed for food

[2]**backwater** \"\ *vi* [[4]*back* + *water*, n.] **1 :** to reverse the usual forward rowing or paddling stroke usu. to check the forward motion of a boat or canoe or propel it backward **2 :** to retreat from a stand taken ⟨~ publicly on several issues⟩

backwearing \'⸗,⸗⸗\ *n* [[3]*back* + *wearing*] **:** erosion that causes an escarpment or mountain slope to retreat without changing its declivity

[1]**backwind** \'⸗,⸗\ *n* [[3]*back* + *wind*] **:** a wind blowing onto the wrong side of a sail; *esp* **:** one directed upon a mainsail by a wrongly trimmed jib

[2]**backwind** \"\ *vt* **1 :** to direct a backwind upon ⟨a jib thus bellied is most apt to ~ the mainsail⟩ **2 :** to sail to windward of (another sailing ship) so as to blanket or interfere with the wind ⟨~ his opponent in a yacht race⟩

backwoods \'⸗¦⸗\ *n pl but sing or pl in constr, often attrib* **1 :** the wooded or outlying and only partly cleared areas on the frontier or in the backcountry ⟨the farmers who lived in the ~ and wrestled to clear the land —*Amer Guide Series: Ind.*⟩ **2 :** a rural area that is provincial or backward in culture or remote from the main centers of civilization ⟨a ~ newspaper⟩ ⟨the idiom of the East Texas ~ —G.S.Perry⟩

back·woods·er \-zə(r)\ *n* -s [*backwoods* + *-er*] **:** *chiefly Midland* **:** HICK, RUSTIC, BACKWOODSMAN

back·woods·man \'⸗¦⸗mən, '⸗⸗mən\ *n, pl* **backwoodsmen** [*backwoods* + *man*] **1 :** one who lives in the backwoods **2** *Brit* **:** a member of the British House of Lords who takes little active part in the business of the house and rarely attends its meetings

back·woodsy \'⸗¦⸗ē, ⸗'⸗ē\ *adj* [*backwoods* + *-y*] **:** marked by plain, rustic, or uncouth speech, manners, or conduct ⟨five or six preachers . . . rough-cut and ~ —H.L.Davis⟩

back·wort \'bak,wərt, -wȯrt\ *n* -s [[1]*back* + *wort*] **:** COMFREY 1

backy \'bakē\ *n* -ES [by shortening & alter.] *dial* **:** TOBACCO

backyard \'⸗'⸗ *attrib* '⸗,⸗\ *n, often attrib* **1 a :** an area often enclosed by a fence in the rear of a house or other habitation ⟨admired a lilac in his ~ —Nell G.Ahern⟩ ⟨a ~ shed⟩ **b :** an area or lot behind the main tent of a circus where property tents and dressing tents are located ⟨in the ~ . . . the equestrian director was given a dressing wagon —Hartzell Spence⟩ **2 :** an area that is close, easily accessible, and in a peculiarly intimate relation to a person, group, or another area ⟨right here in our own ~ we have some of the finest designers in the world —*New Englander*⟩ ⟨Latin America was the air ~ of the U.S. —A.P. de Seversky⟩

backyarder *var of* BACKLOTTER

ba·co·lod \bə'kō,lōd\ *adj, usu cap* [fr. *Bacolod*, Philippines] **:** of or from the city of Bacolod, Philippines **:** of the kind or style prevalent in Bacolod

ba·con \'bākən *sometimes* -k[ə]ŋ\ *n* -s [ME *bacon, bacoun*, fr. MF *bacon*, of Gmc origin; akin to OHG *bahho* side of bacon — more at BACK] **1 :** a side of a pig after removal of spareribs and after being cured dry or in pickle and smoked **2** *obs slang* **:** HICK, RUSTIC **3** *South & Midland* **:** brine-cured bacon **:** SALT PORK — called also *white bacon*

bacon beetle *n* **:** LARDER BEETLE

bacon biliteral cipher \"-\ *n, cap 1st B* [after Francis *Bacon*, who proposed it] **:** a cipher that hides a message in a cover text by representing the letters of the plaintext by different combinations of two letter forms (as italic and roman) in each sequence of five letters of the cover text (as when "Springfield, Mass" hides the word CAB by the code *xxxxx*=A, xxxx*x*=B, xxx*xx*=C)

ba·con·er \'bākənə(r)\ *n* -s *Brit* **:** BACON HOG

bacon hog *also* **bacon pig** *n* **:** a hog raised for bacon or of a type fit to be made into bacon and other cured products **:** a meat-type hog

[1]**ba·co·nian** \(')bā¦kōnēən *also* bə'k- *or* -nyən\ *also* **ba·con·ic** \-känik\ *adj, usu cap* [Francis *Bacon* †1626 Eng. philosopher & author + E *-ian* or *-ic*] **1 a :** of or relating to Francis Bacon or his doctrines, esp. his belief in the inductive origin of valid ideas, the testing of ideas by controlled and scientific methods, and human progress and improvement by the control of nature through scientific knowledge ⟨their *Baconian* fear of speculative hypotheses —Sidney Ratner⟩ ⟨the *Baconian* principle of scientific investigation —C.W.Shumaker⟩ ⟨the *Baconian* theory of the experiential origin of all ideas to counter . . . intuitionism and absolutism —Willis Moore⟩ **b** *of a logical method* **:** consisting of the process of attaining general statements on the basis of observations, comparisons, and experiments through intermediate generalizations and with regard for negative as well as positive instances — compare INDUCTION **2 :** of or relating to the Baconians who believe that Francis Bacon was the author of the dramatic works usu. attributed to Shakespeare

[2]**baconian** \"\ *n* -s *usu cap* **:** one who supports or believes in Baconian doctrines

baconian induction *n, usu cap B* **:** the inductive method developed by Francis Bacon that consists in inferring that what has been observed or established in respect to a part, individual, or species may on the ground of analogy be affirmed or received of the whole to which it belongs — compare INDUCTION

ba·co·nian·ism \⸗'⸗(⸗)⸗,nizəm\ *n* -s *usu cap* **:** Baconian philosophy or scientific method

ba·con·ism \'bākə,nizəm\ *n, usu cap* [Francis *Bacon* + E *-ism*] **:** BACONIANISM

bacon square *n* **:** the jowl of a pig trimmed square, cured, and smoked

bacon type *n* **:** a type of hog adapted to producing the largest possible proportion of high-grade bacon

ba·con·weed \'⸗⸗,⸗\ *n* **:** LAMB'S-QUARTERS 1

ba·co·pa \bə'kōpə\ *n, cap* [NL, prob. fr. a native name in the Guianas] **:** a genus of chiefly tropical herbs (family Scrophulariaceae) with opposite leaves and small solitary flowers — see WATER HYSSOP

bac·so·ni·an \(')bak¦sōnēən\ *adj, usu cap* [*Bac-son*, locality in Tonkin, northern Vietnam, where the remains were found + E *-ian*] **:** of or relating to a Neolithic culture of southeast Asia characterized by unpainted pottery and polished stone implements

bact *abbr* **1** bacteriological; bacteriology **2** bacterium

-bac·ter \,baktə(r)\ *n comb form* [NL, fr. *bacterium*] **:** bacterial organism — in generic names ⟨*Aerobacter*⟩ ⟨*Nitrobacter*⟩

bac·te·re·mia \,baktə'rēmēə\ *or* **bac·te·ri·e·mia** *also* **bac·te·ri·ae·mia** \(,)bak,tirē'ēmēə\ *n* -s [NL, alter. of *bacteriemia, bacteriaemia; bacteriemia, bacteriaemia*, NL, fr. *bacteri-* + *-emia, -aemia*] **:** the usu. transient presence of bacteria or other microorganisms in the blood — compare SEPTICEMIA

bac·te·re·mic \¦baktə¦rēmik\ *adj* [NL *bacteremia* + E *-ic*] **:** being, relating to, or having bacteremia

bacteri- *or* **bacterio-** *comb form* [*bacterium*] **:** bacteria **:** bacterial ⟨*bacteri*form⟩ ⟨*bacterio*blast⟩ ⟨*bacterio*lysis⟩

bacteria *pl of* BACTERIUM

bac·te·ri·a·ce·ae \(,)bak,tirē'āsē,ē\ *n pl, cap* [NL, fr. *Bacterium*, type genus + *-aceae*] **1** *in some classifications* **:** a large family of rod-shaped usu. gram-negative bacteria (order Eubacteriales) that produce no spores and have a complex metabolism utilizing amino acids and generally carbohydrates **2** *in former classifications* **:** a family comprising all simple cylindrical bacteria lacking a sheath and including Bacteriaceae, *Bacillus*, and a number of other groups — **bac·te·ri·a·ceous** \(')⸗¦⸗⸗¦āshəs\ *adj*

bac·te·ri·a·cide \bak'tirēə,sīd\ *n* -s [by alter.] **:** BACTERICIDE

bac·te·ri·al \(')bak¦tirēəl, -tēr-\ *adj* [ISV *bacteri-* + *-al*] **:** belonging to, consisting of, resulting from, or caused by bacteria ⟨~ ooze⟩ ⟨~ decomposition⟩ ⟨~ wilt⟩ — **bac·te·ri·al·ly** \-rēəlē, -li\ *adv*

bacterial blight *n* **:** a blight of plants caused by bacteria: as **a :** HALO BLIGHT **b :** ANGULAR LEAF SPOT **c :** CELERY BLIGHT

bacterial canker *n* **:** any of various plant diseases caused by bacteria and characterized by the formation of cankers: as **a :** a disease of stone fruits (as plums and cherries) caused by bacteria of the genus *Pseudomonas* and marked by cankers on affected branches with copious exudation of gum and often severe dieback of affected areas **b :** TOMATO CANKER

bacterial nodule *n* **:** NODULE 2b(3)

bacterial speck *n* **:** a bacterial plant disease characterized by the production of small lesions — compare SPECK 3b

bacterial spot *n* **:** a bacterial plant disease characterized by spotting of the affected parts

bacterial vaccine *n* **:** BACTERIN

bacterial virus *n* **:** BACTERIOPHAGE

bacterial warfare *n* **:** BIOLOGICAL WARFARE

bac·te·ri·cid·al \(')bak¦tirə¦sīdᵊl\ *adj* **:** of or relating to a bactericide **:** destroying bacteria — **bac·te·ri·cid·al·ly** \-ᵊlē\ *adv*

bac·te·ri·cide \bak'tirə,sīd\ *n* -s [ISV *bacteri-* + *-cide*] **:** something that destroys bacteria

bac·te·ri·cid·in \bak¦tirə¦sīdᵊn\ *or* **bac·te·ri·o·cid·in** \bak,tirēə'sī-\ *n* -s [*bactericide* + *-in*] **:** an antibody that kills microorganisms against which it is active

bac·ter·id \'baktərəd\ *n* -s [*bacteri-* + *-id*] **:** a skin eruption associated with bacterial infection — compare ID

bacteriemia *also* **bacteriaemia** *var of* BACTEREMIA

bac·ter·in \'baktərən\ *n* -s [*bacteri-* + *-in*] **:** a suspension of killed or attenuated bacteria injected into a living body to stimulate the development of immunity to the same kind of bacteria

bacterio- — see BACTERI-

bac·te·rio·chlorophyll \bak¦tirē+\ *n* -s [*bacteri-* + *chlorophyll*] **:** a pyrrole derivative in photosynthetic bacteria related to but not identical with the chlorophyll of higher plants

bac·te·rio·cid·al \(ˈ)bak¦tirēə¦sīdᵊl\ *adj* [*bacteri-* + *-cidal*] : BACTERICIDAL

bac·te·rio·cyte \bakˈtirēə,sīt, -ˈtē-\ *n* -S [ISV *bacteri-* + *-cyte*] : a modified fat cell occurring in the fat body of certain insects and containing groups of bacterium-shaped rods that are believed to be symbiotic bacteria — compare MYCETOCYTE

bac·te·rio·fre·nic \bak¦tirēə¦frēnik\ *adj* [*bacteri-* + L *frenare* to curb, bridle (fr. *frenum* bridle) + E *-ic* — more at FRENUM] : checking the development of bacteria

bac·te·rio·gen·ic \-əˈjenik, -ēk\ *also* **bac·te·ri·og·e·nous** \-ˈäjənəs\ *adj* [*bacteri-* + *-genic, -genous*] : caused by bacteria

bacterioid *also* **bacterioidal** *var of* BACTEROID

bac·te·rio·log·ic \(ˈ)bak¦tirēə¦läjik, -tēr-, -jēk\ *or* **bac·te·rio·log·i·cal** \-jəkəl, -ēk-\ *adj* : of or belonging to bacteriology — **bac·te·rio·log·i·cal·ly** \-jək(ə)lē, -ēk-, -li\ *adv*

bacteriological warfare *n* : BIOLOGICAL WARFARE

bac·te·ri·ol·o·gist \(,)=,==ˈäləjəst\ *n* -S : one who specializes in the study of bacteria

bac·te·ri·ol·o·gy \(,)bak,tirēˈäləjē, -tēr-, -ji\ *n* -ES [ISV *bacteri-* + *-logy*] **1** : a science that deals with the study of bacteria and with their relations to medicine, industry, and agriculture **2** : bacterial life and phenomena ⟨the ~ of a water supply⟩ ⟨the ~ of a disease⟩

bac·te·rio·ly·sin \bak,tirēəˈlīsᵊn\ *n* -S [ISV *bacteri-* + *lysin*] **1** : an antibody that acting together with its complement causes the dissolution of the microorganism against which it is directed **2** : an antibody that kills the microorganism against which it is active with or without lysis : BACTERICIDIN

bac·te·ri·ol·y·sis \(,)=,==ˈäləsəs\ *n, pl* **bacterioly·ses** \-ə,sēz\ [NL, fr. *bacteri-* + *-lysis*] : the destruction or dissolution of bacterial cells (as by antibodies)

bac·te·rio·lyt·ic \bak¦tirēə¦lid·ik\ *adj* [fr. NL *bacteriolysis*, after such pairs as E *analysis: analytic*] : of, belonging to, or producing bacteriolysis

bac·te·rio·phage \bakˈtirēə,fāj\ *n* -S [ISV *bacteri-* + *-phage*; orig. formed in F] : any of various specific bacteriolytic viruses or bacteria-destroying agents that are normally present in sewage, in the intestinal tracts of man and animals esp. when recovering from a bacterial infection, and in blood, pus, urine, or other body products and that are of uncertain nature though possessing definite organization and certain other attributes of living matter — **bac·te·rio·phag·ic** \=¦===¦fajik\ *or* **bac·te·ri·oph·a·gous** \=,=¦äfəgəs\ *adj* — **bac·te·ri·oph·a·gy** \(,)=,==ˈäfəjē\ *n* -ES

bac·te·rio·purpurin \bak¦tirē(,)ō+\ *n* [*bacteri-* + *purpurin*] : a red coloring matter present in some bacteria that has the power of reducing highly oxidized compounds by absorption of certain rays of light; *broadly* : any of several bacterial photosynthetic pigments

bac·te·rio·scop·ic \bak¦tirēə¦skäpik\ *adj* : of, belonging to, or involving bacterioscopy

bac·te·ri·os·co·py \=,==ˈäskəpē\ *n* -ES [*bacteri-* + *-scopy*] : microscopic examination or investigation of bacteria

bac·te·rio·sis \(,)=,=ˈōsəs\ *n, pl* **bacterio·ses** \-ō,sēz\ [NL, fr. *bacteri-* + *-osis*] : any bacterial disease of plants

bac·te·ri·osta·sis \bak,tirēōˈstāsəs, -rēˈästəsəs, -rēōˈstasəs\ *n, pl* **bacteriosta·ses** \-,sēz\ [NL, fr. *bacteri-* + *-stasis*] : inhibition of the growth of bacteria without destruction — **bac·te·rio·stat·ic** \=¦==ō¦stad·ik\ *adj* — **bac·te·rio·stat·i·cal·ly** \-d·ək(ə)lē\ *adv*

bac·te·rio·stat \bakˈtirēə,stat\ *also* **bac·te·rio·stat·ic** \=,===ˈstad·ik\ *n* -S [*bacteriostatic*, adj.] : an agent that causes bacteriostasis

bac·te·rio·tome \bakˈtirēə,tōm\ *n* -S [*bacteri-* + *-tome*] : a mycetome containing bacteria

bac·te·rio·tox·in \=¦===¦täksən\ *n* [ISV *bacteri-* + *toxin*] : a specific substance that destroys or inhibits bacteria growth

bac·te·rio·trop·ic \=¦===¦träpik\ *adj* [ISV *bacteri-* + *-tropic*] : directed toward bacteria or affecting them in a specific way

bac·te·ri·ot·ro·pin \(,)=,==ˈä·trəpən\ *n* -S [ISV *bacteri-* + *-trope* + *-in*; orig. formed in G] : any of certain constituents (probably antibodies) of serum that unite with bacteria and make them more susceptible to phagocytosis

bac·te·rit·ic \¦baktə¦rid·ik\ *adj* [*bacteri-* + *-itic*] : showing the presence of or caused by bacteria

bac·te·ri·um \bakˈtirēəm, -tēr-\ *n* [NL, fr. Gk *baktērion* small staff, dim. of *baktēria* staff; akin to L *baculum* staff, Gk *baktron* stick] **1** *cap, in some classifications* : a more or less inclusive genus comprising straight rod-shaped bacteria with no flagella and (in modern usage) no spores and including a variable assemblage of species most of which are more commonly placed in other genera — compare ACETOBACTER, AEROBACTER, ALCALIGENES **2** *pl* **bacte·ria** \-rēə\ : any of a large group of microscopic plants constituting the class Schizomycetes, having round, rodlike, spiral, or filamentous single-celled or noncellular bodies that are often aggregated into colonies, are enclosed by a cell wall or membrane, usu. lack fully differentiated nuclei, and are often motile by means of flagella, reproducing by fission, by the formation of asexual resting spores or, in some higher forms, by conidia or by imperfectly understood sexual processes, living in soil, water, organic matter or the live bodies of plants and animals, and being autotrophic, saprophytic, or parasitic in nutrition and important to man because of their chemical effects (as in nitrogen fixation, putrefaction, and various fermentations) and as pathogens **syn** see MICROORGANISM

bacteria

bac·te·ri·uria \(,)=,==ˈyürēə\ *n* -S [NL, fr. *bacteri-* + *-uria*] : BACILLURIA

bac·te·ri·za·tion \,baktərəˈzāshən\ *n* -S : the act of bacterizing : the state of being bacterized

bac·te·rize \ˈbaktə,rīz\ *vt* -ED/-ING/-S [*bacteri-* + *-ize*] : to subject to or modify by bacterial action ⟨*bacterized* peat⟩

[1]**bac·te·roid** \ˈbaktə,rȯid\ *or* **bac·te·roi·dal** \¦==¦rȯidᵊl\ *also* **bac·te·ri·oid** \bakˈtirē,ȯid\ *or* **bac·te·ri·oi·dal** \(ˈ)bak¦tirē¦ȯidᵊl\ *adj* [ISV *bacter-, bacteri-* (fr. NL *bacterium*) + *-oid, -oidal*] : resembling bacteria

[2]**bacteroid** \"\ *n* -S **1** : an enlarged branched bacterium (as the rhizobia found in the tubercles of leguminous plants) **2** : a symbiotic bacterium or an inclusion like a bacterium in the bacteriocytes of the fat body of certain insects

bac·te·roi·da·ce·ae \,baktə,rȯiˈdāsē,ē\ *n pl, cap* [NL, fr. *Bacteroides*, type genus + *-aceae*] : a family of extremely varied gram-negative bacteria (order Eubacteriales) that usu. live in the alimentary canal or on mucous surfaces of warm-blooded animals and are sometimes associated with acute infective processes — see BACTEROIDES

bacteroidal cell *n* : a peritoneal or coelomic cell in certain invertebrates that is packed with rodlike inclusions thought by some to be bacterial symbionts and by others excretory products

bac·te·roi·des \,baktəˈrȯi(,)dēz\ *n* [NL, fr. *bacterium* + *-oides*] **1** *cap* : a genus (the type of the family Bacteroidaceae) of gram-negative anaerobic bacteria having rounded ends, producing no endospores and no pigment, and living usu. in the normal intestinal tract **2** *pl* **bacteroides** : a bacterium of *Bacteroides* or a closely related genus

[1]**bac·tri·an** \ˈbaktrēən\ *n* -S *usu cap* [L *Bactrianus*, adj. & n, fr. Gk *Baktrianos*, fr. *Baktria* Bactria, ancient country of southwestern Asia + Gk *-anos* -an] **1** : one of an ancient Iranian people located between the Hindu Kush and the Oxus **2** : the language of the Bactrians

[2]**bactrian** \"\ *adj, usu cap* [L *Bactrianus*] : of or relating to Bactria, a satrapy of ancient Persia

bactrian camel *also* **bactrian** *n, usu cap B* : the 2-humped camel

bac·tris \ˈbaktrəs\ *n, cap* [NL, modif. of Gk *baktron* stick, staff — more at BACTERIUM] : a large genus of tropical American pinnate-leaved usu. spiny palms (family Palmae) with small fruit consisting of a fibrous pulp enclosing a hard, mostly oily, and sometimes edible nut

bac·tri·tes \bakˈtrīd·ēz\ *n, cap* [NL, fr. Gk *baktron* stick, staff + L *-ites* -ite] : a genus of Devonian ammonoids with straight tapering shells and simple sutures — **bac·tri·toid** \ˈbaktrə,tȯid\ *adj*

bac·trit·i·cone \bakˈtrid·ə,kōn\ *n* -S [NL *Bactrites* + E *-i-* + *cone*] : a straight ammonoid with simple sutures corresponding to the orthoceracone among the nautiloids

ba·cu·bert *also* **bac·cu·bert** \ˈba(,)kyü¦be(ə)r\ *n*, -S *usu cap* [F] : a semiceremonial sword dance of Dauphiné and Piedmont, France

bacula *pl of* BACULUM

baculi *pl of* BACULUS

bac·u·li·form \ˈbakyələ,fȯrm; baˈkyül-, bə-\ *adj* [L *baculum* + E *-iform*] : shaped like a rod ⟨~ chromosomes⟩

bac·u·lite \ˈbakyə,līt\ *n* -S [NL *Baculites*] : an ammonoid of the genus *Baculites*

bac·u·li·tes \,bakyəˈlīd·ēz\ *n, cap* [NL, fr. L *baculum* + *-ites* -ite] : a genus of extinct Cretaceous ammonoids having the shell straight like a tapering rod — **baculitic** \¦==¦lid·ik\ *adj* — **baculoid** \ˈ==,lȯid\ *n* -S

bac·u·lit·i·cone \-ˈlid·ə,kōn\ *n* -S [*baculite* + *-i-* + *cone*] : any ammonoid (as a baculite) with a straight shell

bac·u·lum \ˈbakyələm\ *n, pl* **baculums** \-ləmz\ *or* **bacu·la** \-lə\ [NL, fr. L, staff, stick — more at BACTERIUM] : a slender bone reinforcing the penis in many mammals

bac·u·lus \-ləs\ *n, pl* **bacu·li** \-,lī, -,lē\ [LL; akin to L *baculum* staff] : a staff esp. one that is symbolic of authority (as the pastoral staff of a bishop)

ba·cu·ry *also* **ba·cu·ri** *or* **ba·ku·ri** \¦bäk(y)ə¦rē, ¦bak-\ *n, pl* **bacuries** *also* **bacuris** *or* **bakuris** [Pg *bacuri*, fr. Tupi] : a tropical So. American timber tree (*Platonia insignis*) valued for its yellowish brown wood and for its pleasantly perfumed edible fruits which yield an oil used in soapmaking

[1]**bad** *archaic past of* BID *or of* BIDE

[2]**bad** \ˈbad, -aa(ə)d,-aid\ *adj* **worse** \ˈwərs, -ōs,-əis\ *also sometimes* **badder** *also substand* **wors·er** \-sə(r)\ **worst** \ˈwərst, -ōst, -əist\ *also sometimes* **baddest** [ME *badde*; prob. akin to OE *bǣddel* hermaphrodite, *bǣdan* to defile] **1 a** : failing to come up to or achieve a certain standard : failing to display or attain the worth, quality, shape, or appearance proper or appropriate to its type or species : POOR, WORTHLESS, BLEMISHED ⟨a ~ car⟩ ⟨a ~ complexion⟩ ⟨a ~ book⟩ ⟨a ~ repair job⟩ **b** : unfavorable or derogatory in significance or tendency ⟨made a ~ impression on the examiners⟩ ⟨had ~ reports about his conduct⟩ ⟨youthful escapades gave him a ~ name⟩ : marked by unfavorable or unfortunate events, trends, or occurrences ⟨a ~ year for Rome —Robert Graves⟩ : contrary to expectations or hopes : INAUSPICIOUS ⟨the messenger brought ~ news⟩ ⟨regard the present as a ~ time to buy durable consumer goods —S.H.Slichter⟩ **c** : DECAYED, ROTTEN, SPOILED ⟨meat has gone ~⟩ **d** : DILAPIDATED, RUNDOWN ⟨a farmhouse in a ~ state⟩ **2 a** : having an evil, depraved, or vicious character or tendency ⟨a thoroughly ~ man, without a trace of feeling or conscience⟩ ⟨a ~ book, sowing harmful deluding ideas⟩ : IMMORAL ⟨gossip had it that she was a ~ girl⟩ **b** : MISCHIEVOUS, INTRACTABLE, DISOBEDIENT ⟨a ~ child⟩ **3 a** : inadequate or unsuited to its purpose : UNSATISFACTORY ⟨a ~ plan⟩ ⟨a ~ light to read by⟩ **b** : unsuccessful or unprofitable esp. on account of a lack (as of good judgment or skill) ⟨a ~ buy⟩ ⟨a ~ investment⟩ ⟨a ~ shot⟩ : displaying or revealing poor judgment or lack of skill ⟨a wild golf shot caused by ~ timing on the down stroke⟩ **4 a** (1) : offensive or painful to one's senses : DISAGREEABLE, DISPLEASING, UNPLEASANT ⟨a ~ smell⟩ ⟨a ~ taste⟩ (2) : causing or attended by sensations of discomfort or unease ⟨spent a few ~ minutes waiting for the jury's decision⟩ **b** *of language* : IMPROPER, BLASPHEMOUS ⟨scolded the boy for using ~ language⟩ **5 a** : inimical to welfare : INJURIOUS, DELETERIOUS, HARMFUL ⟨too close reading is often ~ for the eyes⟩ ⟨a climate ~ for the health⟩ **b** : severe or distressing esp. more so than is usual or customary ⟨a ~ cold⟩ ⟨a ~ shock⟩ **c** : DISASTROUS, CALAMITOUS ⟨a ~ train wreck⟩ ⟨a ~ forest fire⟩ **d** : causing or offering difficulty ⟨as languages go, I'd say Japanese isn't ~ —Bernard Bloch⟩ ⟨we went up the Elena Glacier . . . and found it as ~ as we had feared —D.L.Busk⟩ **6** : INCORRECT, FAULTY, SUBSTANDARD ⟨~ grammar⟩ ⟨conduct in the *worst* taste⟩ **7 a** : in pain or discomfort : ILL, SICK ⟨~ with fever⟩ ⟨the cold made him feel generally ~⟩ **b** : DISEASED, UNHEALTHY, DEFICIENT ⟨~ teeth⟩ ⟨a ~ constitution⟩ **8 a** : SORROWFUL, DOWNCAST, DEJECTED ⟨feel ~ at the death of a friend⟩ **b** : SORRY, REGRETFUL, REMORSEFUL ⟨feel ~ about slighting a friend⟩ **c** *of a person's character or disposition* : IRRITABLE, CROSS, SURLY ⟨everybody was in a ~ humor except the chief —Dashiell Hammett⟩ **9 a** : not legally good : INVALID, VOID ⟨a ~ claim⟩ **b** *of a debt* : not collectible **c** *of a check* : issued without sufficient funds in the bank to cover **d** *in games* : FOUL : not counted or counted against a player according to the rules ⟨a ~ tennis shot falling several feet outside the base line⟩

syn ILL, EVIL, WICKED, NAUGHTY: BAD, a very general term, applies to anything or anyone reprehensible, for whatever reason and to whatever degree ⟨Svengali walking up and down the earth seeking whom he might cheat, betray, exploit, borrow money from, make brutal fun of, bully if he dared, cringe to if he must — man, woman, child, or dog — was about as *bad* as they make 'em —George du Maurier⟩ ⟨that *bad* man in one of his raving outbursts threatened us with a terrifying increase in the numbers and activities of his U-boats . . . —Sir Winston Churchill⟩ ⟨she often stole little foods from the table and . . . ate them at odd hours of the night, with the pleased expression of a *bad* child —Sinclair Lewis⟩ ILL may imply vice or malevolence ⟨it was *ill* counsel had misled the girl —Alfred Tennyson⟩ ⟨the far results of an *ill* deed involve the innocent with the guilty —H.O.Taylor⟩ EVIL often adds the sinister to the reprehensible ⟨who attended him as his shadow and his *evil* genius — a confidential colleague who betrayed his confidence, mocked his projects, derided his authority —J.L.Motley⟩ ⟨the *evil* counselors who . . . abused his youth —J.R.Green⟩ ⟨an *evil* and treacherous folk, and they lied and murdered for gold —William Morris⟩ WICKED usually implies severe moral reprehensibility ⟨the *wicked* sorcerers who have done people to death by their charms —J.G.Frazer⟩ It may also suggest malevolence or malice ⟨this injury . . . has rankled in his *wicked*, scheming brain, and all his life he has longed for vengeance —A. Conan Doyle⟩ NAUGHTY generally applies to trivial misbehavior of children ⟨Charles never was a *naughty* boy. He never robbed birds' nests, or smoked behind the barn, or played marbles on Sunday —Margaret Deland⟩ Sometimes it suggests reprehensibility in a light and playful way ⟨can't I be a *naughty* little thing? —J.M.Cain⟩ ⟨the still popular, and still *naughty*, and perpetually profane Decameron —Gilbert Highet⟩

— **in a bad way** : having serious difficulty ⟨public schools are at the present time *in a bad way* —M.B.Smith⟩ ⟨the stricken man was in *such a bad way* he was immediately hospitalized⟩ — **too bad** : REGRETTABLE ⟨it is *too bad* that rewards often do not come to deserving men⟩

[3]**bad** \"\ *n* -S [ME *badde*, fr. *badde*, adj.] **1 a** : something that is bad ⟨the ~ or good I say of myself I say of them —Walt Whitman⟩ **b** : the bad part or portion of something ⟨the good in him was at constant variance with the ~⟩ **2** : an evil, unhappy, or degenerate state ⟨from ~ to worse⟩ ⟨he went to the ~ early in life⟩ — **in bad** *adv* : in or into disfavor ⟨lose a job by getting *in bad* with the boss⟩

[4]**bad** \"\ *adv* **worse** \"\ **worst** \"\ [[2]*bad*] **1** : BADLY ⟨want something ~ enough to fight for it⟩ ⟨the man was not doing so ~ despite handicaps⟩ ⟨the Americans didn't know how ~ off they were until daylight —E.J.Kahn⟩ **2** *substand* : SEVERELY, SERIOUSLY ⟨in the fight he was roughed up ~ and ended in the hospital⟩ ⟨mess up a plan real ~⟩ ⟨being ~ sick —James Jones⟩ ⟨put his fist through a window and cut it up ~⟩

bad actor *n* : an unruly, turbulent, or contentious individual : TROUBLEMAKER ⟨Nick's horse was a notorious *bad actor*, a kicker —D.M.Mankiewicz⟩ ⟨the boy became a *bad actor* early and ended in reform school⟩

ba·da·ga \bəˈdägə\ *n, pl* **badaga** *or* **badagas** *usu cap* [Kanarese *badaga*, lit., northman] **1 a** : a Dravidian agricultural people of southern India **b** : a member of such people **2** : the dialect of Kanarese that is the language of the Badaga people

ba·dak \ˈbä,däk\ *n* -S [native name in Java] : JAVAN RHINOCEROS

ba·dan \bəˈdän, -an\ *n* -S [Russ] : a Siberian plant of the genus *Saxifraga* (*S. crassifolia*) with roots that are used as a tanning material

[1]**ba·da·ri·an** \bəˈdärēən\ *adj, usu cap* [*Badari*, village in Upper Egypt, where the discoveries were made + E *-an*] : of or belonging to an Egyptian predynastic neolithic culture dated about 5000 B.C. and characterized by fine handmade pottery (as black beakers with incised designs in white), flint tools, and polished stone axes

[2]**badarian** \"\ *n* -S *usu cap* : one of the ancient Egyptian people who produced the Badarian culture

badawi *often cap, var of* BEDAWI

bad blood *n* : RESENTMENT : ill feeling : BITTERNESS ⟨*bad blood* existing between Beaver Island Mormons and mainland fishermen —*Amer. Guide Series: Mich.*⟩

bad books *n pl* : DISFAVOR ⟨got into the president's *bad books*⟩

bad boy *n* : one who shocks or scandalizes by flouting or defying the moral or artistic conventions of a period ⟨the *bad boy* of English dramatic criticism —Leo Lerman⟩

bad·chan *or* **bad·han** *or* **bad·chen** \ˈbätkən, -ädk-\ *n, pl* **bad·cha·nim** *or* **bad·ha·nim** \=ˈkōnəm, -ənem *also* -kän-\ *or* **badchens** [Heb *badhān*] : a professional jester and topical minstrel esp. at Jewish wedding celebrations

bad conduct discharge *n* : a discharge from one of the armed services given at the recommendation of a court-martial after conviction for an offense less serious than one leading to a dishonorable discharge

badde·ley·ite \ˈbad(ᵊ)lē,īt\ *n* -S [Joseph *Baddeley*, 19th cent. Englishman who brought the first specimens from Ceylon + E *-ite*] : a mineral ZrO_2 consisting of zirconium oxide occurring in colorless, yellow, brown, or black tabular crystals

bad delivery *n* : a tender of securities on a stock exchange that are not in proper transferable or negotiable form or not in compliance with the terms of a contract or the rules of an exchange

badder *comparative of* BAD

bad·der·locks \ˈbadə(r),läks\ *n pl but sing in constr* [origin unknown] : a large brownish black seaweed (*Alaria esculenta*) often eaten as a vegetable in Europe — called also *henware, murlin*

baddest *superlative of* BAD

bad·die *or* **bad·dy** \ˈbadē, ˈbaa-, ˈbai-, -di\ *n, pl* **baddies** [[2]*bad* + *-ie, -y*] *slang* : a hoodlum or other malefactor; *esp* : a movie, radio, or TV villain or bad woman ⟨gathered together all the ace *baddies* of the West into one high-pressure action picture —*Argus*⟩

bad·dish \-dish,-dēsh\ *adj* : somewhat bad : INFERIOR ⟨a mediocre to ~ book⟩

bad doer *n* : a domestic animal that with normal care fails to develop or produce normally

bade *past of* BID *or of* BIDE

bad egg *n, slang* : a worthless, untrustworthy person : MALEFACTOR, CROOK, TROUBLEMAKER

bad·e·nite \ˈbadᵊn,īt, bəˈden,-\ *n* -S [prob. fr. F, fr. *Badeni*, near Botosani, Romania + F *-ite*] : a mineral consisting of cobalt, nickel, and iron bismuth-arsenide and occurring in metallic steel-gray masses

ba·de·ous *also* **ba·di·us** \ˈbādēəs\ *adj* [L *badius* brown, chestnut-colored — more at BAY] : of a bay color

[1]**badge** \ˈbaj, -aa(ə)j\ *n* -S [ME *bagge, bage*, prob. fr. AF *bageys*] **1** : a distinctive or distinguishing mark, token, device, or sign esp. of membership in a society or group and usu. worn on the person ⟨a knight in armor wearing his lady's scarf as a ~⟩ ⟨a policeman's ~⟩ ⟨no ~ of authority such as a cap or uniform to distinguish them⟩ ⟨the yacht club ~ on the flag flying from the mainmast⟩ **2** : something so characteristic as to suggest or serve as a badge ⟨the black coat and green eyeshade that were the recognized ~ of his calling —Oscar Lewis⟩ ⟨higher education, or what passes for that, is neither a birthright nor a necessary ~ of respectability —Douglas Bush⟩ ⟨the contemporary ~s of boyhood — visor cap, short-pants suit, and black cotton stockings —Jack Alexander⟩ **3** : an emblem awarded for a particular accomplishment (as proficiency in marksmanship) ⟨a scout's merit ~⟩ ⟨combat infantryman's ~⟩ **syn** see SIGN

[2]**badge** \"\ *vt* -ED/-ING/-S [ME *baggen*, fr. *bagge*, n.] : to mark or distinguish with a badge

badge of ul·ster \-jəˈvəlztə(r), -lst-\ *usu cap B&U, heraldry* : RED HAND

[1]**badg·er** \ˈbajə(r)\ *n* -S [ME *bagger*] **1** : a dealer licensed in former times to buy grain in one place and sell it in another **2** *now dial Eng* : an itinerant dealer in commodities used for food : HAWKER, HUCKSTER

[2]**badger** \"\ *n* -S [prob. fr. [1]*badge* + *-er*; fr. the white mark on its forehead] **1 a** (1) : any of certain strong sturdily built burrowing mammals constituting two genera (*Meles* and *Taxidea*) of the family Mustelidae and being widely distributed in the northern hemisphere, represented in western No. America by a mammal (*T. taxus*) and in Europe and northern Asia by another (*M. meles*) (2) : the pelt or fur of one of these animals **b** : a related animal (as the teledu or ratel) **2** *Austral* **a** : WOMBAT **b** : BANDICOOT **3** *usu cap* : WISCONSINITE — used as a nickname **4** *or* **badgerweed** \ˈ==,=\ : AMERICAN PASQUEFLOWER **5** : a bundle of sacks tied to the end of a rope and pulled through a line of drain tile as it is laid to clear away loose material

[3]**badger** \"\ *vt* **badgered; badgered; badgering** \-j(ə)riŋ\ **badgers** : to harass, pester, or bedevil persistently esp. in a manner likely or designed to confuse, annoy, or wear down ⟨~ed the witness out of her wits⟩ ⟨the mill foreman . . . taunted the workers . . ., ~ed them, and told them that they dared not quit —Sinclair Lewis⟩ **syn** see BAIT

badger baiting *or* **badger drawing** *n* : the former sport of setting dogs to pull a badger from an artificially made hole or from a barrel or box

badger bird *n* : MARBLED GODWIT

badger dog *n* [trans. of G *dachshund*] : DACHSHUND

badger game *n* [[3]*badger*] : an extortion racket in which a man is lured by a woman into a compromising position and is then confronted with and blackmailed by the woman's accomplice posing as her husband or brother

badg·er·ing·ly *adv* : in a badgering manner

badger skunk *n* : HOG-NOSED SKUNK

badhan *var of* BADCHAN

bad hat *n, slang Brit* : a disreputable dissolute person : BAD EGG ⟨the man is a *bad hat*, a swindler or worse —Joyce Cary⟩

ba·di·an \ˈbädēən, ˈbad-\ *n* -S [F *badiane*, fr. Per *bādiān* anise] : the carminative fruit of the Chinese anise resembling true anise in flavor

[1]**ba·di·geon** \bəˈdijən\ *n* -S [F] : a cement or paste (as of plaster and powdered freestone) used to fill holes or cover defects in wood or stone

[2]**badigeon** \"\ *vt* -ED/-ING/-S : to cover with badigeon

bad·i·nage \,badᵊnˈäzh, -ázh, ˈ==,=\ *n* -S [F, fr. *badiner* to joke (fr. MF, fr. *badin* joker, fool, fr. OProv. fr. *badar* to gape, fr. (assumed) VL *batare*) + MF *-age*] : light and playful repartee or wit : BANTER ⟨will read the deepest and eternal truths into your most topical ~ —Stella Campbell⟩ ⟨risen from the level of ~ to that of real grandiloquence —Frederic Prokosch⟩

ba·dis \ˈbādəs\ *n, cap* [NL] : a genus of small freshwater fishes (family Nandidae) including an Indian species (*B. badis*) that is yellowish brown with iridescent blue markings and a transparent tail and that is favored in tropical aquariums

badius *var of* BADEOUS

badjoo *or* **badju** *var of* BAJU

badland \ˈ=,=\ *n* -S *often attrib* : a region characterized by the intricate and sharp erosional sculpture of generally weak rocks usu. forming nearly horizontal beds, generally developing in decomposed granite, loess, or other soft material, lacking or having only scanty vegetation, and consisting of steep, furrowed, or fantastically formed hills, labyrinthine drainage, and normally dry watercourses or arroyos ⟨the ~s of So. Dakota⟩ ⟨~ topography⟩

bad lot *n, slang* : a worthless, unreliable, immoral, or dishonest person : CROOK, TROUBLEMAKER ⟨decoyed by a thoroughly *bad lot* of a friend into helping him in a burglary —M.R.Ridley⟩

[1]**bad·ly** \ˈbadlē, -aad-,-aid-, -li\ *adv* [ME *baddely*, fr. *badde* bad + *-ly*] **1** : in a bad manner: as **a** : POORLY, FAULTILY, DEFECTIVELY ⟨the car ran ~⟩ ⟨a picture ~ executed⟩ **b** : UNFAVORABLY ⟨the enterprise turned out ~ for the investors⟩ **c** : WRONGLY, EVILLY ⟨to steal is to act ~⟩ **d** : DISOBEDIENTLY, NAUGHTILY ⟨the child acted ~ in company⟩ **e** : INADEQUATELY, INCOMPLETELY, INEFFECTIVELY ⟨a picnic ~ planned⟩ ⟨provide ~ for emergencies⟩ **2 a** : very much : to a great or intense degree ⟨want something ~⟩ ⟨~ in need of help⟩ ⟨the cables of the Delei bridge had sagged ~ —Francis Kingdon-Ward⟩ ⟨the victim was not so ~ off⟩ ⟨the situation was ~ un-

balanced —*Collier's Yr. Bk.*⟩ **b :** STRONGLY, COMPELLINGLY ⟨want something ~ enough to work hard for it⟩ **c :** SEVERELY ⟨so ~ frozen that . . . several fingers had to be amputated —*Amer. Guide Series: Minn.*⟩

2**badly** \"\ *adj* **1** *chiefly dial Brit* **:** SICK, UNWELL ⟨he has been ~ for a long time⟩ **2 :** BAD 8a, b ⟨feel ~ about a spiteful remark⟩ ⟨feel ~ about another's misfortune⟩

badly off *adv (or adj)* **1 :** in an unsatisfactory condition esp. in respect to money ⟨thanks to a private income, he's not *badly off*⟩ **2 :** suffering from a deficiency or shortage ⟨the company is *badly off* for experienced engineers⟩

badman \'ˌ=ˌ=\ *n, pl* **badmen :** OUTLAW, DESPERADO ⟨Jesse James, Missouri ~ —*Amer. Guide Series: Minn.*⟩ ⟨the classic western with its quick-drawing, dead-shot *badmen* and good men —*Time*⟩ ⟨a bunch of *badmen* who have kidnapped a blind girl —John McCarten⟩

bad·mash \'bədˌmäsh\ *var of* BUDMASH

bad·min·ton \'badˌmintᵊn, -tən\ *n* -s [fr. *Badminton,* resi-

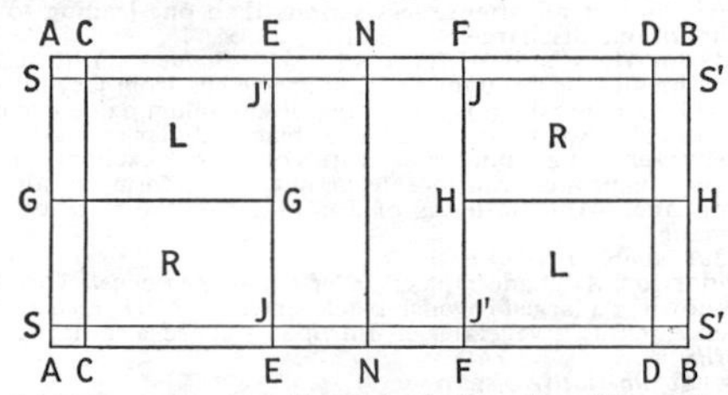

badminton court: *AA, BB* back boundary lines; *AB* doubles side boundary line; *SS'* singles side boundary line; *CC, DD* long-service lines (doubles only; the back boundary lines are long-service lines in singles); *EE, FF* short-service lines; *GG, HH* center lines; *R* right doubles service court; *L* left doubles service court; *GSJ'G, HS'J'H* left singles service courts; *GSJG, HS'JH* right singles service courts

dence of the duke of Beaufort, Gloucestershire, where it was first played in England] **:** a court game played by two or four persons with light long-handled rackets and a shuttlecock volleyed over a net suspended across the middle of the court surface — see RACKET illustration

bad·ness *n* -ES **:** the quality or state of being bad

bad·rans \'badrənz, -athr-\ *var of* BAUDRONS

bads *pl of* BAD

bad time *n* **:** the period of time that is not considered part of a serviceman's military service (as when he is AWOL or in prison for a military offense) and that must be made up before his release from duty

baeck·e·ol \'bākēˌōl, -ōl\ *n* -s [NL *Baeckea* (genus name of *Baeckea crenulata,* a species of myrtle that produces it) + E *-ol*] **:** a pale yellow crystalline phenolic ketone $C_{13}H_{18}O_4$ found in oils from various plants of various species of the myrtle family (esp. *Baeckea crenulata*)

baed *past of* BA

bae·de·ker \'bādəkə(r), -dēk-\ *n* -s *usu cap* [after Karl *Baedeker* †1859 Ger. publisher of guidebooks] **1 :** any one of a series of guidebooks devoted chiefly to European countries and cities ⟨seeing Paris with a *Baedeker*⟩ **2 :** GUIDEBOOK, HANDBOOK ⟨a *Baedeker* of contemporary arts⟩

bael *var of* BEL

baer·ia \'ba(a)rēə\ *n, cap* [NL, fr. Karl E. von *Baer* †1876 Estonian naturalist + NL *-ia*] **:** a genus of annual herbs (family Compositae) having opposite hairy leaves and showy yellow flowers — see GOLD FIELDS

baer·mann apparatus \'ba(ə)rmən-\ *n, usu cap B* [fr. the name *Baermann*] **:** an apparatus consisting essentially of a funnel containing muslin filters for straining out larvae or worms from fecal or other specimens

baermann technique *also* **baermann method** *n, usu cap B* **:** isolation of nematode or other minute worms or larvae by means of the Baermann apparatus

bae·tyl \'bēdᵊl\ *or* **bae·tu·lus** \'bēchələs\ *or* **bae·ty·lus** \'bēdᵊləs\ *n, pl* **baetyls** \-ᵊlz\ *or* **baetu·li** \-chəˌlī\ *or* **baety·li** \-dᵊˌlī\ [L *baetulus,* fr. Gk *baitylos,* a sacred meteorite] **:** a roughly shaped stone (as a meteorite) held sacred or worshiped as of divine origin — **bae·tyl·ic** \(')bē¦tilik\ *adj*

bae·yer strain theory \'bā(y)ə(r)-\ *n, usu cap B* [after Adolf von *Baeyer* †1917 Ger. chemist] **:** a theory in chemistry: the four valences of carbon are normally directed symmetrically in space making angles of 109° 28′ with one another and deflection of these directions produces strain in the molecule (as in the formation of rings)

ba·fa·ro \bə'fä(ˌ)rō\ *n* -s [Afrik, prob. fr. a native name in southern Africa] *Africa* **:** a stonebass (*Polyprion americanus*)

1**baff** \'baf, -aa(ə)f, -aif, -äf\ *n* -s [prob. of imit. origin] **1** *Scot* **:** BLOW, STROKE, THUD ⟨she struck him on the face with a resounding ~⟩ **2 :** a golf stroke in which the sole of the club hits the ground and drives the ball aloft

2**baff** \"\ *vt* -ED/-ING/-S **:** STRIKE; *specif* **:** to make a stroke with a golf club so that the sole of the club strikes the ground and lofts (the ball)

baffing spoon *n* [fr. pres. part. of 2*baff*] **:** BAFFY

1**baf·fle** \'bafəl\ *vt* **baffled; baffled; baffling** \-f(ə)liŋ\ **baffles** [prob. alter. of ME (Scots dial.) *bawchillen, bachlen* to denounce or discredit publicly] **1** *obs* **a :** to subject to a disgraceful punishment or to infamy **b :** to subject to any disgrace or contumely **c :** CHEAT, TRICK **d :** to reduce to ineffectiveness **2 :** to defeat or check (as understanding, plans, efforts, actions) by confusing or puzzling **:** DISCONCERT, PERPLEX, FRUSTRATE ⟨with postwar verse, the . . . untutored reader is apt to admit himself quite *baffled* —C.D.Lewis⟩ ⟨the swiftness of his marches *baffled* alike flight and resistance —J.A.Froude⟩ **3 :** to check or break the force of **:** deflect or stop the flow of ⟨guard plates to ~ the steam⟩ **:** interfere with the free or straight motion of **:** disperse the effective force of ⟨the yawl was *baffled* by the changing winds⟩ **4 :** to equip with a baffle **5 :** to prevent (two or more sets of sound waves) from interfering with each other (as by introducing a partition between the front and back of a loudspeaker) **syn** see FRUSTRATE

2**baffle** \"\ *n* -s **1 :** BAFFLEMENT, CONFUSION, UNCERTAINTY **2 :** something for deflecting, checking, or otherwise regulating flow: as **a :** a plate or wall for deflecting gases or other fluids (as in a steam-boiler flue, a reverberatory furnace, or a gasoline-engine muffler) **b :** a plate or grating in a channel or a pipe conveying fluid to check eddy currents and thus cause a uniform flow **c :** a device or structure (as a vane or partition) for preventing the passage of, deflecting, or regulating the intensity of light **d :** a device or structure for deadening, preventing the transmission of, or deflecting sound **3 :** a partition or cabinet used with the diaphragm of a loudspeaker to impede the exchange of sound waves between front and back

baffle gate *n* **:** a gate that permits passage in one direction only

baf·fle·ment \-fəlmənt\ *n* -s **1 :** the action of baffling **:** the fact of being baffled ⟨their best efforts met with persistent ~⟩ **2 :** the state of being baffled **:** PERPLEXITY, CONFUSION ⟨she couldn't understand the meaning of all this and he gloated over her ~ —Adria Langley⟩

baffle painting *n* **:** camouflage of a ship to give it a deceptive appearance as to size, form, course, and speed

baffle plate *n* **:** a plate used as a baffle (sense 2)

baf·fler \'baf(ə)lə(r)\ *n* -s **1 :** one that baffles **2 :** BAFFLE 2

baffling *adj* **:** causing bafflement **:** PERPLEXING, CONFUSING ⟨a ~ problem⟩ ⟨a detective's most ~ case⟩ — **baf·fling·ly** *adv* — **baf·fling·ness** *n* -ES

baffling wind *n* **:** a light wind that frequently shifts from one point to another

baffy \'bafē, -aaf-, -aif-, -äf-, -fi\ *n* -ES [2*baff* + *-y*] **:** a short wooden golf club with a deeply lofted face

baft *adv* [ME *bafte, baften,* fr. OE *bæftan, beæftan* behind fr. *be-* + *æftan* from behind — more at AFT] *archaic* **:** ABAFT ASTERN

1**bag** \'bag, -aa(ə)g, -aig\ *n* -s [ME *bagge,* fr. ON *baggi*] **1 :** a container made of paper, cloth, mesh, metal foil, plastic, or other flexible material and usu. closed on all sides except for an opening that may be closed (as by folding, pasting, tying, or sewing), being of sizes ranging from small to very large and being specially designed and treated for properly holding, storing, carrying, shipping, or distributing any material or product — compare POUCH, SACK **2 :** a bag for a particular purpose: as **a :** a bag to hold money **:** PURSE; *esp* **:** a woman's pocketbook **:** HANDBAG **b :** a bag for carrying game **:** GAME BAG ⟨several squirrels and a rabbit in his ~⟩ **c :** a silk pouch used to hold up the back hair (as of a powdered wig) **d :** MAILBAG **e :** TRAVELING BAG, VALISE, SUITCASE **3 :** something felt to resemble a bag (as in form or capaciousness): as **a :** a pouched or pendulous bodily part or organ: (1) **:** a sac or space containing a secretion or other fluid ⟨the poison ~ of a snake⟩ ⟨the honey ~ of a bee⟩ (2) **:** UDDER (3) *dial Brit* **:** BELLY (4) **:** a pendulous outpouching of flabby skin ⟨an aging face with ~*s* below the eyes⟩ (5) *slang* **:** SCROTUM **b :** a puffed out sag or bulge (as of cloth) suggestive of a bag ⟨~*s* at the knees of trousers⟩ ⟨the ~ in the sail of a ship⟩ **c bags** *pl, chiefly Brit* **:** SLACKS ⟨dressed with casual undergraduate elegance in sports coat, silk pullover, and flannel ~*s* —Christopher Isherwood⟩ **d :** a square white canvas container filled with sawdust that is fastened to the ground to mark the position of first, second, or third base in baseball **e :** PUNCHING BAG **f :** SLEEPING BAG **g :** any of the small upright chimneys inside a ceramic kiln through which the flames pass into the body of the structure **h :** a cavity filled with water or gas in a mine **4 :** something that is bagged: as **a :** the amount contained in a bag esp. when fixed (as by law) for a particular commodity and used as a unit of weight ⟨25 ~*s* to the ton⟩; *broadly* **:** a bag and its contents ⟨don't forget to get a ~ of potatoes⟩ **b :** a quantity of game taken during a particular hunt or during a particular period usu. by one person ⟨the ~ included an elephant, and a magnificent male tiger⟩; *often* **:** the amount of game permitted (as by law) to be taken by one hunter ⟨he got his ~ early and was home before lunch⟩ **c :** something likened to the bag taken by a hunter or fisherman esp. in being won, captured, seized, or otherwise taken by personal effort **:** TROPHY, SPOILS ⟨the flier finished the day with a ~ of four enemy planes⟩; *sometimes* **:** a group of persons or things **:** COLLECTION, ASSORTMENT ⟨a mixed ~ of bystanders —Ken Purdy⟩ ⟨a large ~ of special techniques —Greer Williams⟩ **5** *slang* **a :** PROSTITUTE **b :** WOMAN; *esp* **:** a slovenly unattractive woman — used chiefly in the phrase *old bag;* usu. used disparagingly — **in the bag 1 :** marked by evidence and surrounding circumstances that make the attainment of a given objective a virtual certainty **:** practically unquestionable **:** as good as already gained, acquired, or won **:** ASSURED, CERTAIN ⟨his nomination was *in the bag*⟩ — not often in formal use **2** *slang* **:** DRUNK ⟨was half *in the bag* and staggering slightly⟩

bag 2a

2**bag** \"\ *vb* **bagged; bagged; bagging; bags** [ME *baggen,* fr. *bagge,* n.] *vi* **1 a :** to swell out **:** BULGE ⟨the entire side of the tent *bagged* outward under the force of the gale⟩ **b :** to hang loosely (as of clothing) like a bag ⟨her dress *bagged* shapelessly about her⟩ **2** *of a milch animal* **:** to develop the udder — usu. used with *up* ⟨this heifer is *bagging up* well⟩ ~ *vt* **1 :** to cause to bulge or swell out ⟨the rush of air at once *bagged* and filled out the parachute⟩ **2 a :** to put into a bag ⟨*bagging* and shipping the sugar⟩ — often used with *up* ⟨don't sweep until you have *bagged up* the beans⟩ **b :** to cover (as plants) with bags so as to exclude insects or foreign pollen ⟨long rows of carefully *bagged* zinnias⟩ **3 a :** to take (animals) as game **:** to kill or capture (game) ⟨he *bagged* a fine 10-point buck⟩ **b :** to get possession of esp. by strategy or stealth **:** GAIN, ACQUIRE ⟨his shrewd business speculation helped him to ~ a fabulous fortune⟩; *also* **:** make off with **:** STEAL ⟨two little boys were caught *bagging* apples⟩ **c :** to win a victory over **:** get the mastery of **:** CAPTURE, SEIZE ⟨the police *bagged* the entire dope ring⟩; *also* **:** to shoot down **:** DESTROY ⟨his first day he *bagged* three enemy planes⟩ **syn** see CATCH

3**bag** \"\ *vt* **bagged; bagged; bagging; bags** [origin unknown] **:** to cut (as grain) with a heavy sickle and gather the cut produce into bundles

bag *abbr* baggage

ba·gac \bə'gak\ *n* -s [native name in the Philippines] **:** APITONG

bag and baggage *adv* **:** with all one's belongings **:** COMPLETELY ⟨he got rid of all the visitors, *bag and baggage*⟩

ba·ga·ni \bə'gänē\ *n* -s *often cap* **:** MAGANI

ba·gasse *also* **be·gass** *or* **be·gasse** \bə'gas, -aa(ə)s, -ais, -äs\ *n, pl* **bagasses** *also* **begasses** [F *bagasse,* fr. Sp *bagazo,* fr. *baga* seed pod of flax, fr. L *baca, bacca* berry] **:** the crushed juiceless remains of sugar cane as it comes from the mill often used as fuel in the mill and sometimes commercially as a source of cellulose (as for papermaking) or as an ingredient in animal feeds; *sometimes* **:** similar plant residue remaining after extraction of a juice (as from sugar beets or grapes), an oil (as from olives), or a fiber (as from sisal)

bagasse disease *n* **:** an industrial disease characterized by cough, difficult breathing, chills, fever, and prolonged weakness and caused by the inhalation of the dust of bagasse

bag·as·so·sis \ˌbagə'sōsəs\ *n, pl* **bagasso·ses** \-ōˌsēz\ [NL, fr. F *bagasse* + NL *-osis*] **:** BAGASSE DISEASE

bagataway *var of* BAGGATAWAY

ba·ga·telle \¦bagə¦tel\ *n* -s [F, fr. It *bagattella,* prob. fr. L *baca, bacca* berry] **1 :** a thing of little or no importance or value **:** a mere nothing **:** TRIFLE ⟨to him money was a ~⟩ **2 :** a game played with a cue and usu. nine balls on an oblong table having cups or both cups and arches at one end **3 :** a short piece of music or verse in a light style; *esp* **:** a short light piece for the piano

bagdad *usu cap, var of* BAGHDAD

bagdad boil [after *Baghdad, Bagdad,* Iraq] *n, usu cap 1st B* **:** ORIENTAL SORE

bag·di \'bägdē\ *n* -s *cap* [Bengali] **:** a member of a numerous caste of field laborers of Bengal

ba·gel \'bāgəl\ *n* -s [Yiddish *beygel,* fr. (assumed) MHG *böugel* (whence G dial. *beugel, bäugl*), dim. of MHG *boug-, bouc* ring, bracelet, fr. OHG *boug;* akin to OE *bēag, bēah* ring, bracelet — more at BEE] **:** a hard roll shaped like a doughnut that is made of raised dough and cooked by simmering in water and then baked to give it a glazed browned exterior over a firm white interior

bag filter *n* **:** a filter made of a cloth bag ordinarily about 30 feet long for recovery of metal oxides and other solid particles suspended in a gas (as from smelting or other furnaces)

bag fox *n* **:** a fox taken to a covert in a bag to be released before hounds

bag·ful \'bagˌfu̇l, -aag-, -aig-\ *n, pl* **bagfuls** *also* **bagsful** \-gˌfu̇lz, -gzˌfu̇l\ [ME *baggeful,* fr. *bagge* bag + *-ful*] **:** the quantity held by a bag; *esp* **:** an indeterminate but usu. rather large quantity ⟨investors will come flocking in with ~*s* of money —Tom Fitzsimmons⟩

1**bag·gage** \'bagij, -aig-, -gēj\ *n* -s [ME *bagage,* fr. MF, fr. *bague* bundle (perh. fr. ON *baggi* bag) + *-age*] **1 :** a group of traveling bags, trunks, or both esp. when packed and in transit **:** personal belongings of travelers either carried by hand or checked with a carrier **:** LUGGAGE ⟨the ~ was brought from the attic for packing⟩ ⟨since there were only a couple of small pieces, the traveler carried his own ~⟩ **2 :** equipment that is transported or that can be transported ⟨the ~ of an army⟩ **:** FURNISHINGS, APPARATUS ⟨the ~ of a science laboratory⟩ **3 a :** a combination of extraneous, superfluous, or intrusive things and circumstances that may impede free activity, progress, or the attainment of a specific goal ⟨smooth speech and writing depend very much upon freedom from purist grammar and from other linguistic ~⟩ **b :** theories, notions, or practices viewed as outmoded or as otherwise obstructing with and retarding desirable development ⟨cultural ~ which the Puritans brought from England to America in the seventeenth century —I.V.Brown⟩ ⟨mental ~ from bygone days —D.G. Haring⟩ **4** [prob. by folk etymology fr. MF *bagasse,* fr. OProv *bagassa*] **a :** a worthless or vile woman ⟨and it's wicked of me. You must think me a shameless ~ —Max Peacock⟩ ⟨a disreputable old ~, dealing in grass skirts and shrunken human heads —Wolcott Gibbs⟩; *esp* **:** a woman of loose morals **:** PROSTITUTE **b :** a young woman or girl; *esp* **:** a girl or young woman who is the object of affection, playfulness, usu. gentle criticism, or a somewhat patronizing attitude ⟨a toothsome blond ~ —*New Yorker*⟩ ⟨she's a pretty little ~ —Walter O'Meara⟩

2**baggage** \"\ *adj, obs* **:** WORTHLESS, TRASHY, RUBBISHY ⟨a ~ scoundrel⟩

baggage car *n* **:** a railroad car for passengers' baggage

bag·gage·man \-ˌman, -aa(ə)n *also* -ˌmən\ *n, pl* **baggagemen** **1 :** a railroad employee who is in charge of the checked baggage of passengers during the run of a train and unloads it at the proper destination **2 :** a porter in a hotel who carries heavy luggage, arranges for receipt and shipment of baggage, sets up sample rooms, and supplies travel information **3 :** an employee at a bus terminal who takes care of the checking, loading, or release of travelers' baggage

baggagemaster \'ˌ=ˌ=ˌ=\ *n* **1 :** a railroad employee in charge of a baggage car or baggage train **2 :** an employee on a ship who is responsible for the stowing, care, and removal of baggage **3 :** a bus company employee who traces and settles claims for baggage and other articles lost or damaged in shipment

baggage rack *n* **:** a shelf in a railroad passenger car or a bus for the accommodation of hand baggage and parcels

baggage-smasher \'ˌ=ˌ=ˌ=\ *n, slang* **:** a person (as a baggageman) who handles the baggage of others esp. in a baggage car or steamship

baggage train *n* **:** a train of vehicles carrying baggage

bag·ga·la \'bəgəˌlä, -ˌlə\ *n* -s [Marathi *baglā, bagalā,* prob. fr. Pg *baixel,* fr. Catal *vaixell,* fr. L *vascellum* small vase — more at VESSEL] **:** a 2-masted trading vessel used in the Indian ocean

bag·gat·a·way *also* **ba·gat·a·way** \bə'gadəˌwā\ *n* -s [of Algonquian origin] **:** a Canadian Indian game from which lacrosse developed

bagged \'bagd, -aa(ə)gd, -aigd\ *adj* **1 :** hanging in bags **:** hanging loosely ⟨~ cheeks⟩ ⟨~ ropes⟩ **2 :** having a bag or bags ⟨she gave him an ugly look with her ~, spectacled eyes —Marcia Davenport⟩ **3** *slang* **:** DRUNK ⟨was so ~ he could hardly stand up⟩

bag·ger \-gə(r)\ *n* -s [2*bag* + *-er*] **:** one that bags: as **a :** one that fills bags with such goods as food, tobacco, and cement **b :** one that places stockings in bags to prepare them for dyeing — called also *batcher*

bag·gi·ly \-gəlē, -li\ *adv* **:** in a loose baggy way ⟨his clothes hung about him ~⟩

bag·gi·ness \-gēnəs, -gin-\ *n* -ES [*baggy* + *-ness*] **:** the quality or state of being baggy

1**bag·ging** \-giŋ, -gēŋ\ *n* -s [1*bag* + *-ing*] **1** *dial Eng* **:** food eaten between meals; *esp* **:** a midafternoon lunch **2 :** material for bags; *usu* **:** a coarse fabric (as burlap or gunny)

2**bagging** \"\ *n* -s [fr. gerund of 2*bag*] **:** filtration through a bag (as of sperm oil)

bag·git \'bagət\ *n* -s [Sc *baggit* pregnant, fr. ME *bagged,* fr. past part. of *baggen* to bag, swell — more at BAG] *Brit* **:** a female salmon just after spawning

bag·gy \'bagē, -aag-, -aig-, -gi\ *adj, usu* -ER/-EST **:** loose, puffed out, or hanging like a bag ⟨~ trousers⟩ ⟨~ cheeks⟩ ⟨round ~ shoulders —Thomas Wolfe⟩ ⟨~ generalities and shabby prejudices —H.J.Muller⟩

baggy crop *n* **:** PENDULOUS CROP

bag·gy·wrin·kle *also* **bagy·wrin·kle** \-ˌriŋkəl\ *n* -s **:** protective gear made from frayed out rope and used on ship rigging to prevent chafing

bag handle *vt* **:** to mar (as coins) by handling or storing in a bag or other container that allows the rubbing together of the contents ⟨gold coins that show evidence of having been *bag handled*⟩

bagh·dad *or* **bag·dad** \'bagˌdad, 'bagˌdaa(ə)d, 'baigˌdad\ *adj, usu cap* [fr. *Baghdad* or *Bagdad,* Iraq] **:** of or from Baghdad, the capital of Iraq **:** of the kind or style prevalent in Baghdad

bagh·dadi \(')=¦=dē, -di\ *n* -s *cap* [fr. *Baghdad,* Iraq] **:** a native or inhabitant of Baghdad, Iraq

baghouse \'=ˌ=\ *n* **1 :** a building in which bag filters are used for filtering gas **2 :** BAG FILTER

ba·gio \ˌbäge'ō, bäg'yō\ *var of* BAGUIO

ba·gir·mi \bə'girmē\ *n, pl* **bagirmi** *or* **bagirmis** *usu cap* **1 a :** a Muslim people of a mixed Negroid stock living southeast of Lake Chad in the central Sudan **b :** a member of such people **2 :** a Central Sudanic language of the Bagirmi people

bagleaves \'=ˌ=\ *n pl but sing or pl in constr* **:** ORPINE

bag limit *n* **:** the maximum number of fish or game animals permitted by law to be taken by one person in a given period

bag·man \'bagmən, -aag-, -aig-\ *n, pl* **bagmen** **1** *chiefly Brit* **:** TRAVELING SALESMAN ⟨*bagmen,* who did not in those days aspire to the title of commercial travelers —Hugh McCausland⟩ **2** *slang* **:** BAG FOX **3** *Austral* **:** TRAMP 1a, 1b **4 :** a person who collects or distributes money usu. illicitly on behalf of another (as in making payoffs or collecting bribes)

bag molding *n* **:** a technique or process in which plastic or plywood-plastic combinations are molded to curved forms by use of a rigid die within a flexible cover through which fluid pressure (as of steam, air, or vacuum) may act on the material to be molded

bag·net \'bagˌnet, 'bäg-, -ˌnət\ *dial var of* BAYONET

bag net *n* **:** a bag-shaped net for catching fish

ba·gnio \'ban(ˌ)yō, 'bän-\ *n* -s [It *bagno,* fr. L *balneum,* fr. Gk *balaneion;* akin to Gk *balaneus* bather, *blyein, blyzein* to gush forth, Skt *galati* it drips — more at DEVIL] **1** *obs* **:** an establishment providing Turkish baths **2** *obs* **:** PRISON **3 :** house of prostitution **:** BROTHEL

ba·go \'bä(ˌ)gō\ *n* -s [Tag, Cebuan, & Bikol] **:** an evergreen Asiatic shrub (*Gnetum gnemon*) having edible young leaves and seeds

ba·go·bo \bə'gō(ˌ)bō\ *n, pl* **bagobo** *or* **bagobos** *usu cap* **1 a :** a predominantly pagan people inhabiting southern Mindanao, Philippines **b :** a member of such people **2 :** the Austronesian language of the Bagobo people

bag of bones : an extremely thin individual

bag of tricks : a supply of expedients or devices **:** stock of resources ⟨in their attempts to be original they have pretty well exhausted their *bag of tricks*⟩

bag of waters : the double-walled fluid-filled sac that encloses and protects the fetus in the mother's womb and breaks releasing its fluid during the birth process

bag of wind : WINDBAG 2

bag·o·net \'bag(ə)ˌnet, -ˌnət\ *dial var of* BAYONET

ba·go·ong \bä'gōˌōŋ\ *n* -s [Tag] *Philippines* **:** a paste or sauce of small fish and prawns which have been salted and fermented that is much used as seasoning

bagpipe \'=ˌ=\ *n* [ME *baggepipe,* fr. *bagge* bag + *pipe*] **:** a musical instrument consisting of a double-reed melody pipe and one or more single-reed drone pipes that are sounded by air from a flexible bag which is in turn kept inflated either by a mouth tube or by an elbow-worked bellows — often used in pl.; compare MUSETTE; see CHANTER

bag·pip·er \-ˌīpə(r)\ *n* [ME *baggepiper,* fr. *baggepipe* + *-er*] **:** a player on a bagpipe **:** PIPER

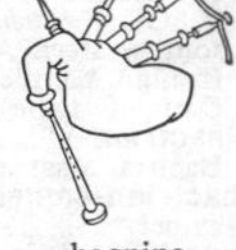
bagpipe

bagpod \'=ˌ=\ *n* **:** an annual herb (*Glottidium vesicarium*) of the pea family having pinnate leaves with numerous leaflets, flowers in axillary clusters, and elliptic pods that taper at both ends — called also *bladderpod*

bag pudding *n* **:** a dessert pudding boiled or steamed in a bag

ba·gre \'bä(ˌ)grā, 'ba-, -ˌgrē, -ˌgrə\ *n* [Sp & Pg, fr. Ar *bāghir, baghār,* prob. fr. L *pagrus,* a bream — more at PARGO] **1** -s **:** any of various catfishes esp. of Spanish-American waters **2** *cap* **:** the genus (family Ariidae) to which the gaff-topsail catfish belongs

bagreef \'=ˌ=\ *n* [2*bag* + *reef;* fr. its use in preventing a large sail from bagging] **1 :** the lower reef of fore-and-aft sails **2 :** a single reef in a square topsail

bags *pl of* BAG, *pres 3d sing of* BAG

bag table n : a small light worktable with one or two drawers the lower of which forms a frame from which is suspended a bag for needlework

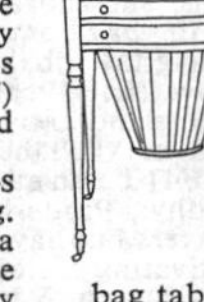
bag table

bag·ti·kan \bäg'tēkən\ n -s [native name in the Philippines] : the reddish gray heavy wood of either of two trees of the genus *Parashorea* (*P. malaanon* and *P. warburgii*) of the family Dipterocarpaceae — called also *Philippine mahogany*

ba·guette also **ba·guet** \ba'get, bai-\ n -s [F *baguette*, lit., rod, fr. It *bacchetta*, irreg. fr. L *baculum* — more at BACTERIUM] **1 a :** a small molding like but smaller than the astragal : BEAD **b :** a molding formerly placed along the angle between two planes of a hip roof **2 :** a table-cut gem having the shape of a long, narrow, and sometimes tapered rectangle; *also* : the shape itself **3 :** a very small narrow rectangular watch movement used esp. for bracelet and ring watches; *sometimes* : a wristwatch of which the movement is a baguette **4 a :** DRUMSTICK 1 **b :** the wooden part of a violin bow **c :** BATON 4

ba·guio \,bägē'ō, bäg'yō\ n -s [Sp, fr. Tag *bagyó*] *Philippines* : TROPICAL CYCLONE

bag-wall \'=,=\ n : a low wall inside a furnace or kiln against and over which the flame plays

bagwig \'=,=\ n : an 18th century wig with the back hair enclosed in a small silk bag

bagworm \'=,=\ n : a moth larva of the family Psychidae constructing and living in a silk case which is usu. covered with bits of plant debris; *esp* : an often destructive pest (*Thyridopteryx ephemeraeformis*) of trees and shrubs in the eastern U.S. — compare CASEWORM

bag·wyn \'bagwən\ n -s [origin unknown] : a fabulous beast like an antelope but having a goat's horns and a horse's tail

bagywrinkle var of BAGGYWRINKLE

bah \'bä, 'ba, 'bȧ, 'baa\ *interj* — used to express disdain or contempt

ba·ha·dur \bə'hȯdə(r), -'hä-,-'hȧ-\ n -s [Hindi *bahādur* hero, champion, fr. Per] *India* : a distinguished person — used as a title of respect

ba·hai \bä'hä·ē, bə-, -R sometimes -ä'rē\ or **ba·ha·ist** \-ä(,)ist, -ärəst\ n -s *usu cap* [Per *bahā'ī*, lit., of glory, fr. *bahā* glory, splendor, fr. Ar *bahā'*] : an adherent of Bahaism

ba·ha·ism \-ä,izəm, -ä,ri-\ n -s *usu cap* : the doctrine and practice of a sect founded in Iran in the 19th century that emphasizes the spiritual unity of mankind, advocates peace and universal education, and affirms the equality of men and women

ba·ha·ma \bə'hämə, -hā- (*pronunc in Bahamas*); -hā-\ *adj, usu cap* [fr. *Bahama* islands] : of or from the Bahama islands : of the kind or style prevalent in the Bahama islands

bahama duck also **bahama pintail** n, *usu cap B* [fr. the *Bahama* islands in the Atlantic southeast of Florida] : a pin-tailed duck (*Anas bahamensis*) with a white face and throat, red base to the bill, and pale buff tail that is widely distributed in the Caribbean islands and through much of So. America — called also *white-cheeked pintail*

bahama grass n, *usu cap B* : BERMUDA GRASS

bahama sisal n, *usu cap B* : SISAL 1a

1ba·ha·mi·an \bə'hāmēən, -hä-,-hā-—ä *is used in this word by many Bahamians but apparently not in* "bahama(s)"\ *adj, usu cap* [*Bahama* islands + E *-ian*] **1 :** of, relating to, or characteristic of the Bahama islands **2 :** of, relating to, or characteristic of Bahamians

2bahamian \"\ n -s *cap* : a native or inhabitant of the Bahama islands

ba·hau \bə'hau̇\ n, pl **bahau** or **bahaus** *usu cap* **1 :** a Dayak people of northern Borneo — see KAYAN, KENYA **2 :** a member of the Bahau people

ba·he·ra \'bəhə,rä\ n -s [Hindi *baherā*] : an important East Indian tree (*Terminalia bellerica*) yielding an oil from its seed kernels, a dye and tanning extract from its fruits, and a gum from its bark — compare MYROBALAN

1ba·hia \bə'hēə\ n -s *usu cap* [fr. *Bahia* (now Baía), state in Brazil] : Brazilian piassava

2bahia \"\ *adj, usu cap* [fr. *Bahia*, old name for Salvador, Brazil] : 2SALVADOR

ba·hía blan·ca or **ba·hia blan·ca** \bə¦hēə¦bläŋkə\ *adj, usu cap both Bs* [fr. *Bahía Blanca*, Argentina] : of or from the city of Bahía Blanca, Argentina : of the kind or style prevalent in Bahía Blanca

bahia grass n, *usu cap B* [fr. *Bahia*, state of Brazil] : a perennial tropical American grass (*Paspalum notatum*) used in the Gulf states as a pasture grass esp. in arid regions

bahia powder n, *usu cap B* [fr. *Bahia*, Brazil] : GOA POWDER

ba·his·ti \bə'hēstē\ var of BHEESTY

baho var of PAHO

bahr \'bär, 'bȧ(r\ n -s [Ar *baḥr*] : a body of water (as a lake, river, or sea)

bah·rain or **bah·rein** \bä¦rān\ *adj, usu cap* [fr. *Bahrain*, country in the Persian Gulf] : of or from Bahrain : of the kind or style prevalent in Bahrain

1bah·raini also **bah·reini** \bä'rānē\ n, pl **bahraini** or **bahrainis** also **bahreini** or **bahreinis** *cap* [modif. of Ar *baḥrānīy*, fr. *Baḥrayn* Bahrain] : a native or inhabitant of Bahrain

2bahraini also **bahreini** *adj, usu cap* : of or relating to Bahrain or its inhabitants

baht or **bat** \'bät\ n, pl **bahts** also **baht** or **bat** also **bats** [Thai *bāt*] **1 :** TICAL 1 **2 :** the basic monetary unit of Thailand; *also* : a coin or note representing one baht — see MONEY table

bahu \'bä(,)hü, 'bä·(,)ü, 'bau̇\ n -s [Jav] : BOUW

ba·hur or **ba·chur** also **bo·chur** \'bȯkər\ or **bo·cher** \'bəkər\ n, pl **ba·hu·rim** or **ba·chu·rim** also **bo·chu·rim** \'bȯkürəm, 'bəkər-, -rēm\ or **bo·che·rim** \'bəkər-\ [Heb *bāḥūr* youth] *in Jewish use* : a young unmarried man : YOUTH; *specif* : a student in a Talmudic academy — called also *yeshiva bocher*

ba·hut \'bä,hüt, bə'hüt, -üt, F bȧüē\ n -s [F] **1 :** a chest or cabinet; *esp* : one having a rounded top and used as furniture **2 a :** a low wall raised above the main cornice of a building and carrying the roof — compare ATTIC **b :** a parapet wall solid and generally not decorative; *often* : the rounded top course of masonry of such a wall

ba·hu·vri·hi \,bä(,)hüv'rēhē\ n -s [Skt *bahuvrīhi*, lit., having much rice (a compound of this type), fr. *bahu* much + *vrīhi* rice — more at PACHY-, RICE] : a class of compound words whose meanings follow the formula "(one) having a *B* that is *A*" where *A* stands for the first constituent of the compound and *B* for the second; *also* : a compound word belonging to this class (as *graybeard, blockhead, barefoot*) — see 1POSSESSIVE 1b

ba·ian·ism \'bāyə,nizəm\ also **ba·jan·ism** \", 'bajə-\ n -s *usu cap* [F *baïanisme*, fr. *Baius* (Michel de Bay) †1589 Belgian theologian + F *-isme* -ism] : the doctrine of Baius according to which divine grace is neither gratuitous nor truly necessary, man's nature and actions are essentially evil through original sin, man's will is not really free, and the sacraments have a highly limited purpose and efficacy

baib grass \'bīb-\ n [prob. native name in India] : BHABAR 1

baidar var of BIDAR

baidarka var of BIDARKA

bai·dya \'bīdyə\ n -s *cap* [Skt *vaidya* lit., possessing knowledge, fr. *vidyā* knowledge — more at WIT] : a member of a high caste of eastern Bengal traditionally made up of physicians

bai·era \'bīərə\ n, *cap* [NL, after J.J. *Baier* †1735 Ger. naturalist] : a genus of fossil gymnosperms (family Ginkgoaceae) that are known from the Trias to the Lower Cretaceous and are considered by some paleobotanists to be ancestors of the fossil and surviving ginkgoes

bai·ga \'bīgə\ n, pl **baiga** or **baigas** *usu cap* **1 :** an aboriginal hill people living in the Central Provinces of India **2 :** a member of the Baiga people

bai·gi·net \'bāg(ə),net, -nət\ *Scot var of* BAYONET

bai·gnoire \bān'wär, '=,=\ n -s [F, lit., bathtub, fr. *baigner* to bathe, fr. LL *balneare*, fr. L *balneum* bath — more at BAGNIO] : a theater box having low partitions that is in the lowest tier

bai·kal·ite \bī'kä,līt, 'bīkə,l-\ n -s [G *baikalit*, fr. Lake *Baikal*, Siberia + G *-it* -ite] : a dark green variety of hedenbergite

bai·ker·in·ite \'bīkərə,nīt\ n -s [G *baikerinit*, blend of *baikerit* and *-in*] : a tarry hydrocarbon constituting about one third of baikerite

bai·ker·ite \'bīkə,rīt\ n -s [G *baikerit*, irreg. fr. Lake *Baikal* + G *-it* -ite] : a mineral wax apparently a mixture of ozokerite with other tarry, waxy, and resinous hydrocarbons

1bail \'bāl, *esp bef pause or cons* -āəl\ n -s [ME *bail, baille*, fr. MF *bail*, fr. *baillier* to give, deliver, fr. L *bajulare* to bear a burden, keep in custody, fr. *bajulus* porter, load carrier] **1** *obs* : CUSTODY, JURISDICTION **2 a** *obs* : the custody of a prisoner or one under arrest by one who procures the release of the prisoner or arrested individual by giving surety for his due appearance **b :** the security or obligation given for the due appearance of a prisoner in order to obtain his release from imprisonment ⟨the man is out on ~⟩ **c :** the temporary delivery or release of a prisoner upon security for his due appearance **d :** one that agrees to assume legal liability for a money forfeit or damages if a prisoner released on bail fails to make his due appearance in court — compare MAINPRISE **e :** the process by which a person is released from custody

2bail \"\ *vt* -ED/-ING/-S **1 :** to deliver (personal property) to another under an agreement express or implied that some special purpose be accomplished by the bailee with respect to the property and that at some time the property be returned to the bailor ⟨she ~*ed* the cloth to the tailor to be made into a dress⟩ **2 :** to set free, deliver from arrest, or deliver out of custody on an undertaking of another to be responsible for the due appearance of the one so released ⟨the magistrate ~*ed* the prisoner⟩ **3 :** to procure the release of by giving bail — often used with *out* ⟨his lawyer ~*ed* him out⟩ **4 :** to set free from an unpleasant or difficult situation : come to the help of usu. through financial aid — used with *out*

3bail \"\ n -s [ME *bail, baile*, fr. OF, fortification, stake, perh. fr. L *bajulus* porter, load carrier] **1 :** an outer wall of a feudal castle; *also* : the space enclosed by such a wall : COURT **2 :** either of two crosspieces placed end to end on top of the stumps in cricket **3** *chiefly Brit* **a :** a bar, pole, or partition of suspended boards separating animals (as in an open stable or on shipboard) **b :** a frame for confining the head of a cow : STANCHION **c :** a movable open shed often on wheels that is used for milking and supplying concentrates to milch cows : MILKING PARLOR

4bail \"\ *vt* -ED/-ING/-S **1** *archaic* : CONFINE ⟨a lofty spirit ~*ed* by human limitation⟩ **2** *Brit* : to make fast with or in a bail — used with *up* ⟨~ a cow up for milking⟩ **3** *Austral* : to force to a halt : ACCOST, CHECK : detain esp. for purposes of robbery — used with *up* ⟨they were ~*ed up* by a gang of bushrangers —Bill Beatty⟩

5bail \"\ n -s [ME *baile, baille*, fr. MF *baille*, fr. (assumed) VL *bajula*, alter of L *bajulus*] : a bucket, dipper, or other container used to remove water that has entered a boat

6bail also **bale** \"\ *vb* -ED/-ING/-S *vt* : to dip up and throw; *esp* : to clear (water) from a boat by dipping and throwing over the side — usu. used with *out* ⟨they spent half an hour ~*ing* out the rowboat⟩ ~ *vi* **1 :** to dip up and throw out water from a boat ⟨they ~*ed* for hours but the water slowly deepened⟩ **2 a :** to parachute from an aircraft — used with *out* **b :** to escape from a predicament or avoid responsibility — used with *out*

7bail also **bale** \"\ n -s [ME *beil, baile*, prob. of Scand origin; akin to ON *beygja* to bend — more at BOW] **1 a :** a supporting half hoop or horseshoe-shaped strip (as for the cover of a delivery wagon or the canopy of a small boat) **b :** an iron yoke on a life car to suspend it from the hawser **c :** a yoke to the trunnions of a cannon to raise it from the carriage **d :** pivoted arched steel bow on a road scraper to which the motive power is attached **e :** either of the two metal clamps that hold a tympan sheet in place in a platen printing press **f :** a hinged bar for holding the paper against the platen of a typewriter **g** *angling* : an attachment of certain spinning reels that picks up the line for rewinding on the spool **2 :** the usual arched handle of a kettle, pail, or similar vessel

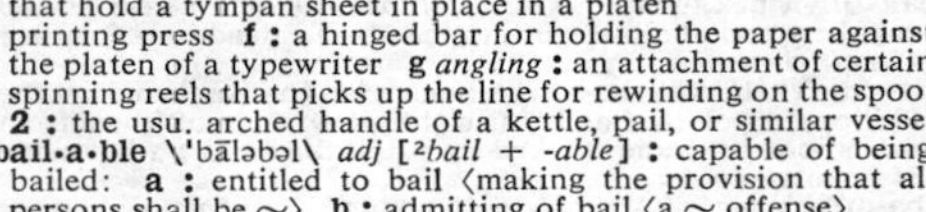
1, 1 bail 2

bail·a·ble \'bāləbəl\ *adj* [2*bail* + *-able*] : capable of being bailed: **a :** entitled to bail ⟨making the provision that all persons shall be ~⟩ **b :** admitting of bail ⟨a ~ offense⟩

bail above \'=='=\ n : bail given by a defendant after his appearance in court as a guarantee that he will satisfy the judgment of the court in damages, debt, or costs or failing to do so surrender himself in person to the court — called also *bail to the action, special bail*

bail below \'=='=\ n **1 :** bail given by two sureties to the sheriff for the due appearance of the defendant **2 :** a mere form with imaginary persons as sureties used as a method of entering the appearance of the defendant in civil actions — called also *common bail*

bail bond n [1*bail*] : a bond by which bail is given

bai·le \'bī,lā\ n -s [Sp, fr. *bailar* to dance, fr. OSp, modif. of OProv *balar*, fr. LL *ballare* — more at BALL] *Southwest* : DANCE : a social gathering for dancing; *specif* : one at which Spanish or Mexican folk dances are performed

bailed past of BAIL

bail·ee \(')bā¦lē\ n -s [2*bail* + *-ee*] : the person to whom goods are committed in trust and who has a temporary possession and a qualified property in them for the purposes of the trust : one that receives goods under a contract of bailment

1bail·er \'bālə(r)\ var of BAILOR

2bailer \"\ n -s [7*bail* + *-er*] : a worker who attaches handles to pails or buckets

3bailer \"\ n -s [3*bail* + *-er*] : a cricket ball bowled so that it hits and removes one or both bails

4bailer \"\ n -s [6*bail* + *-er*] : one that bails (as water); *esp* : a device used for bailing

bailer shell also **bailer** n -s [4*bailer*; fr. its capacity to hold water] : MELON SHELL

bai·ley \'bālē, -li\ n -s [ME *bailli*, fr. OF *balie*, var. of *baile* — more at BAIL (outer wall)] **1 :** the outer wall of a medieval castle or any of the several walls surrounding the keep **2 :** the space immediately within the external wall of a castle or fortress or between any two outer walls

bailey bridge \"-\ n, *usu cap 1st B* [After Sir Donald C. *Bailey* b1901 Eng. engineer who designed it] : a bridge designed for rapid construction from interchangeable latticed panels of high-tensile steel that are coupled with alloy steel pins set into ready-made holes to form girders and laid double or triple or superposed to suit the span and load

bai·lie \'bālē, -li\ n -s [ME] **1** *dial* : BAILIFF **2 a :** a onetime chief magistrate of a Scottish barony with duties similar to those of a sheriff **b :** a municipal magistrate in Scotland corresponding to the English alderman

bai·li·ery also **bai·li·ary** \'bālē,erē, -ri\ n -ES [ME *baillierie* fr. *baillie* + *-erie* -ery] : the jurisdicton of a bailie

bai·liff \'bāləf\ n -s [ME *baillif, bailiff, bailie*, fr. OF *baillif, baillu, baillu*, fr. *bail* jurisdiction — more at BAIL] **1 :** one deputed to exercise public administrative authority locally; *specif, chiefly Brit* : a sheriff's deputy — used formerly as a title of nearly any officer (as a mayor, sheriff, or chief officer of a hundred) in England nominated by the king; now used (1) as a title of the chief magistrate of some British towns and of a keeper of some royal castles and (2) as the English equivalent of the title of certain magistrates (as the Scottish bailie or the German landvogt) in countries other than England **2 :** one having the custody and management of property for another: as **a** *Brit* : the agent of a lord (as for the collection of rents) **b** *chiefly Brit* : one that manages an estate or farm for another **3 :** a court officer who seats witnesses and spectators, announces the entrance of the judge, and keeps order in the court — **bai·liff·ship** \-,ship\ n -s

bai·liff·ry \-rē\ n -ES : the office or jurisdiction of a bailiff : BAILIWICK

bailing pres part of BAIL

bai·li·wick \'bālē,wik, -lə-\ n -s [ME *baillifwik, bailliwik*, fr. *baillif, bailie* bailiff + *wik* wick] **1** *law* : office or jurisdiction esp. of a bailiff : range of authority **2 a :** the special province or domain in which one has superior aptitude, knowledge, or experience or in which one has a particular right to enjoy free activity, exercise authority, and command attention and respect ⟨a scientist intruding in a clergyman's ~⟩ **b :** field of activity : sphere of operations ⟨highly successful in the political ~⟩ **3 :** surrounding territory : VICINITY, NEIGHBORHOOD ⟨the coastal areas in Florida's ~⟩ **syn** see FIELD

bail·li \bȧyē\ n -s [F, fr. OF *baillif* — more at BAILIFF] : a medieval officer representing the king or seignior and having wide judicial, financial, and military powers

bail·liage \'bä'yäzh\ n -s [ME, fr. MF, fr. *baillir* to administer (fr. *bail* jurisdiction) + *-age* — more at BAIL] : a bailli's bailiwick

bail·ment \'bā(ə)lmənt\ n -s [MF *baillement*, fr. *baillier* to deliver + *-ment* — more at BAIL] **1 :** the act of bailing a prisoner or a person accused **2 :** a delivery of personal property by a bailor to a bailee for specific purposes under an express or implied agreement of the parties that when those purposes are accomplished the property will be returned to the bailor, kept until he reclaims it, or disposed of according to the agreement — compare MANDATE, PLEDGE

bailment for hire : a bailment for the mutual benefit of the bailor and bailee for compensation (as where one hires the use of another's property or agrees to keep it safely or to transport it or where one bestows care, labor, or attention upon it) — compare PLEDGE

bail·or \(')bā¦lȯ(ə)r, -ȯ(ə); 'bālə(r)\ or **bail·er** \'bālə(r)\ n -s [2*bail* + *-or*] : one that delivers goods or money to another in trust

bailout \'=,=\ n -s [6*bail* + *out*, v.] : an emergency departure and parachute descent from an aircraft aloft

bailpiece \'=,=\ n [1*bail* + *piece*] **1 :** a certificate formerly issued to the surety attesting his act of offering bail **2 :** a warrant issued to the surety upon which he may arrest the person bailed by him

bails *pl of* BAIL, *pres 3d sing of* BAIL

bails·man \'bā(ə)lzmən\ n, pl **bailsmen** [fr. poss. of 1*bail* + *man*] : one who gives bail for another : SURETY

bail to the action [1*bail*] : BAIL ABOVE

bai·ly *dial var of* BAILIE

bai·ly's beads \'bālēz-, -liz-\ n pl, *usu cap 1st B* [after Francis *Baily* †1844 Eng. astronomer who described them] : the row of brilliant points of sunlight shining through valleys on the edge of the moon that are seen for a few seconds just before and after the central phase in an eclipse of the sun

1bain \'bān\ *adj, usu* -ER/-EST [ME, fr. ON *beinn* straight, ready, hospitable] **1** *now dial Eng* **a :** WILLING, READY **b :** LITHE, SUPPLE **2** *dial Eng* : DIRECT, NEAR, SHORT ⟨the ~*est* way⟩

2bain \"\ n -s [ME, fr. MF, fr. L *balneum* — more at BAGNIO] *obs* : BATH

bain·bridge reflex \'bān(,)brij-\ n, *usu cap B* [after Francis A. *Bainbridge* †1921 Eng. physiologist] : a reflex mechanism adjusting the rate of the heartbeat to the bodily need and consisting of response by local stretch receptors of the great veins and auricles to increase in venous pressure with consequent acceleration of the heartbeat

baing *pres part of* BA

bai·ning \'bīniŋ\ n, pl **baining** or **bainings** *usu cap* **1 a :** a Papuan people of New Britain **b :** a member of such people **2 :** the language of the Baining people

bain·ite \'bā,nīt\ n -s [Edgar C. *Bain* b1891 Am. physicist and metallurgist + E *-ite*] : a transformation product in solid steel developed from austenite at temperatures intermediate between those where pearlite and martensite form

bain-ma·rie \,baⁿmə'rē, bā'merē\ n, pl **bains-marie** \,baⁿm-, bā'm-\ [F, fr. MF, lit., bath (of) Mary, after *Mary* or *Miriam*, Moses' sister (Exod 15:20), to whom is ascribed a treatise on alchemy] **1 :** WATER BATH **2 :** STEAM TABLE

bai·noa \bī'nōə\ n, pl **bainoa** or **bainoas** *usu cap* [Sp, of AmerInd origin] **1 :** an Arawakan people of Haiti and southwestern Santo Domingo **2 :** a member of the Bainoa people

ba·ioc·co or **ba·joc·co** \bə'yȯ(,)kō\ or **ba·ioc** \bə'yȯk\ n, pl **baioc·chi** \-ȯkē\ or **baioccos** \-ȯ(,)kōz\ or **bajoc·chi** \-ȯkē\ or **bajoccos** \-ȯ(,)kōz\ or **baiocs** \-ȯks\ [It *baiocco*, prob. fr. ML *Baiocas* Bayeux, city in Normandy, France (appearing in inscriptions on certain Merovingian coins)] **1 :** a minor billon or copper coin of the former Papal States equal to 1/100 scudo **2 :** a unit of value equivalent to one baiocco coin ⟨coins worth 2 and 5 *baiocchi*⟩ ⟨postage stamps worth 6 and 8 *baiocchi* were issued⟩

baira var of BEIRA

bai·ram \(')bī¦räm\ n -s *usu cap* [Turk *bayram*] : either or both of two Muslim festivals held after Ramadan

baird's sandpiper \'ba(a)(ə)rdz-, 'be(ə)r-\ n, *usu cap B* [after Spencer F. *Baird* †1888 Am. zoologist] : a small migratory sandpiper (*Erolia bairdii*) chiefly of western No. America that breeds in the arctic tundras and winters in So. America and is mottled buff and gray with a dark rump and a short slender bill

bairn \'ba(a)(ə)rn,'be(ə)rn,'bārn\ n -s [ME *bern, barn*, fr. OE *bearn* & ON *barn*; akin to OS, OHG & Goth *barn* child, OE *beran* to bear — more at BEAR] *chiefly Scot* : CHILD

bairn·ie \-nē\ n -s *chiefly Scot* : a small child

bairn·ish \-nish\ *adj, chiefly Scot* : CHILDISH

bairn·ly \-nlē\ *adj* -ER/-EST *Scot* : CHILDISH

bairn's part n : LEGITIM

bairn·time \-n-,tīm\ also **bairn·team** \-ēm\ n -s [ME *bernteam, barnteam, barntime*, fr. OE *bearntēam*, fr. *bearn* child + *tēam* family, brood, team — more at BAIRN, TEAM] *Scot* : BROOD, OFFSPRING

bai·ru \'bī(,)rü\ n, pl **bairu** or **bairus** *usu cap* : a member of the peasant segment of the population of the kingdom of Ankole in Uganda — compare HERA, RUNDI

bai·sakh \'bī,säk\ n -s *usu cap* [Skt *Vaiśākha*] : a month of the Hindu year — see MONTH table

baise-mains \,bāz(ə)'maⁿ, ,bez-\ n pl [F, fr. *baiser* to kiss (fr. OF *baisier*, fr. L *basiare*) + *mains*, pl. of *main* hand, fr. L *manus*] : RESPECTS, COMPLIMENTS ⟨greeted the owners with curtsies and *baise-mains* — Natacha Stewart⟩

baist \'bāst\ *Brit var of* BASTE

1bait \'bāt\ *vb* -ED/-ING/-S [ME *baiten*, fr. ON *beita*; akin to OE *bǣtan* to bait, worry, OHG *beizen*; causative fr. the root of E *bite* — more at BITE] *vt* **1 a :** to attack in speech or writing (as by derision or insult) usu. with malice : harass (an individual or group) in such a way as to wound the feelings or injure the reputation : PERSECUTE : gall or exasperate by repeated wanton attacks ⟨~*ing* minority groups in a cheap display of prejudice⟩ **b :** to nag at : goad in a carping way : HOUND ⟨his wife constantly ~*ed* him for not having more money⟩ **c :** to ruffle or rouse usu. in a playful good-natured way : TEASE ⟨she kept ~*ing* him about her other love affairs⟩ **2 a :** to harass (as a chained animal) by setting on dogs to worry and bite usu. as a sport ⟨the hunters captured a large bear and ~*ed* him⟩ **b :** to attack by biting and tearing : WORRY ⟨the dogs yapped with excitement as they ~*ed* the badger⟩ **3 a :** to furnish (as a hook or trap) with bait ⟨they sat along the riverbank, carefully ~*ing* the fish lines⟩ **b :** to place poisoned bait on or around (as a field or building) in order to kill pests ⟨he ~*ed* the crop for wireworms⟩; *also* : to provide or distribute bait for the consumption of (a pest) ⟨~ the rats for several days before putting out the poison⟩ **c :** to impale (bait) on or as if on a hook ⟨a ~*ed* earthworm⟩ **d :** to entice by or as if by bait ⟨~*ing* him by promises of a good job⟩ : lure esp. by trickery, duplicity, or strategy ⟨some planes were ~*ed* off course by false radio signals⟩ **4** *now dial* : to give a portion of food and drink to (an animal) esp. upon the road : FEED ⟨the travelers paused to ~ their horses⟩ **5 :** to feed (a furnace) with fuel ~ *vi* **1** *archaic* **a :** to stop for food and drink (as when traveling) **b :** to make a brief halt **2** *archaic* : FEED ⟨the horses ~*ed* at the edge of the road⟩

syn RIDE, BADGER, HOUND, HECTOR, HECKLE, CHIVY: all these words indicate persistent harassing or annoying and are frequently interchangeable. BAIT may still be used in reference to wanton, malicious worrying or tormenting of a chained or tethered animal ⟨*baiting* the prisoner, terrorizing him —Liam O'Flaherty⟩ Common in politics today, it suggests any malicious or scornful attack, ridicule, calumny, esp. one goading a weak or defenseless opponent ⟨*baiting* these hapless citizens who had the gall to have Japanese parents —G.S. Schuyler⟩ RIDE in this sense suggests harassing by stringent unfair criticism, derision, or onerous imposition of tasks and charges ⟨the foreman *rides* him. They transfer him from one job to another —Lawrence Lader⟩ BADGER suggests bedeviling persistently with tactics calculated to confuse, madden, or enervate completely ⟨the mill foreman so taunted the workers, so *badgered* them —Sinclair Lewis⟩ ⟨she can't sit and think quietly anywhere else without being *badgered* —Nevil Shute⟩ HOUND implies persistent dogged pursuit and harassing ⟨how Grandfather was *hounded* out of his congregation because he couldn't hold her to their standards of behavior for a minister's wife —Mary Austin⟩ HECTOR suggests any sustained domineering esp. by bullying or scolding ⟨he will speak in a loud voice, and will *hector*, because he wishes to prove that he is "somebody" —F.A.Swinnerton⟩ HECKLE is esp. likely to suggest harassing of a speaker or spokesman by disconcerting tactics, although it may be used for other situations in which one is harried ⟨*heckling* the candidate with constant questions and interruptions⟩ CHIVY is now applicable to any situation involving persistent petty harassing and vexation ⟨having seen two successive wives of the delicate poet *chivied* and worried into their graves —Joseph Conrad⟩

²**bait** \"\ *n* -s [ME, fr. ON *beit* pasturage & *beita* food, bait; akin to OHG *beiza* corrosion, maceration, MLG *bēte*, ON *bīta* to bite — more at BITE] **1 a :** a lure (as a piece of meat) used to attract fish or other animals (as to a hook or trap) so that they can be caught **b :** the specific lure (as worms or an animal decoy) used in catching fish or other animals **c :** a poisonous material distributed where it will be eaten by pests (as rats or insects) **2 :** an attraction meant to win to or make compliant with an ulterior and often not immediately evident objective (as an objective that would otherwise be rejected or viewed with apathy); *also* **:** an enticement that is marked by trickery or duplicity ⟨asking harder work and holding up before them the ~ of higher commissions⟩ **3** *now dial* **a :** FOOD; *esp* **:** a light lunch or snack **b :** refreshment taken during a pause in a journey or during work **4** *obs* **:** a stopping (as for refreshment) in the course of traveling or other activity **5** *slang Brit* **:** a fit of temper **:** RAGE ⟨he'd be in an awful ~ if he knew⟩ **6** *chiefly South* **:** an indefinite but adequate amount **:** PLENTY ⟨a big ~ of pie⟩ ⟨a good ~ of firewood⟩ **7 a :** a preheated iron used for attaching one end of a gather of molten glass that is to be drawn into a cylindrical shape **b :** a device that is lowered into molten glass to start a drawing operation esp. of a sheet

³**bait** \"\ *dial Brit var of* ³BEET

⁴**bait** \"\ *archaic var of* BATE

bait bug *n* **:** a small crustacean of the genus *Emerita* found burrowing in sandy beaches and used for fish bait

bait casting *n* **:** the single-handed rod casting of a relatively heavy and usu. artificial bait which carries out with it the light and soft line from a free-spool reel

baited *past of* BAIT

baitfish \'ˌ=,=\ *n* **:** a fish suitable for or used for bait

baith \'bāth\ *adj or pron or conj* [ME (northern dial.) *bathe, baithe*, fr. ON *bāthir* — more at BOTH] *Scot* **:** BOTH

baiting *pres part of* BAIT

baits *pres 3d sing of* BAIT, *pl of* BAIT

bait set *n* **:** a baited trap — compare BLIND SET, WATER SET

bai·tsi \'bītsē\ *n, pl* **baitsi** *or* **baitsis** *usu cap* **1 a :** a Papuan people on Bougainville Island **b :** a member of such people **2 :** the language of the Baitsi people

bait·tle \'bāt³l\ *adj* [prob. of Scand origin; akin to ON *beiti* pasturage] *Scot* **:** RICH, NOURISHING — used of pasture

bai-u \(')bī¦ü\ *adj* [Jap, rain of the rainy season, fr. *bai* plum + *u* rain] **:** relating to the spring or early summer rainy season in China and Japan

bai·za \'bīzə\ *n* -s [colloq. Ar, fr. Hindi *paisā*] **1 :** a monetary unit of Oman equivalent to ¹⁄₁₀₀₀ rial — see MONEY table **2 :** a coin representing one baiza

baize \'bāz\ *n* -s *often attrib* [MF *baies*, pl. (taken as sing.) of *baie* baize, fr. fem. of *bai* bay-colored — more at BAY] **1 :** a coarsely woven woolen or cotton fabric napped to imitate felt and dyed in solid colors **2 :** a baize drapery, table cover, or lining for furniture

ba·ja·da *also* **ba·ha·da** \bə'hädə\ *n* -s [Sp *bajada* slope, descent, fr. fem. of *bajado*, past part. of *bajar* to descend, fr. (assumed) VL *bassiare*, fr. LL *bassus* fat, short, low] **1** *Southwest* **:** a steep curved descending road or trail **2 :** a broad alluvial slope extending from the base of a mountain range out into a basin and formed by coalescence of separate alluvial fans

ba·jan \'bājən\ *var of* BEJAN

bajanism *usu cap, var of* BAIANISM

ba·jau \bə'jaů\ *n, pl* **bajau** *or* **bajaus** *usu cap* **1 :** a Malay people inhabiting coastal regions of Borneo and the southern Philippines — called also *orang laut* **2 :** a member of the Bajau people — called also *sea gypsy*

bajocco *var of* BAIOCCO

ba·jo·na·do \ˌbäkə'nä(ˌ)dō\ *n* -s [Sp] **:** JOLTHEAD PORGY

ba·jou·ri \bə'jůrē\ *n, pl* **bajouri** *or* **bajouris** *usu cap* **1 :** a Pathan people in the Afghan-Pakistan frontier region **2 :** a member of the Bajouri people

baj·ra \'bäjrə, -(ˌ)rä\ *or* **baj·ri** *or* **baj·ree** \-(ˌ)rē\ *n* -s [Hindi *bājrā, bājrī*] *India* **:** PEARL MILLET 1

ba·ju *also* **badjoo** *or* **badju** \'bä(ˌ)jü\ *n* -s [Malay] **:** a Malay short jacket

ba·ka bomb *also* **baka** \'bäkə\ *n* -s [Jap *baka*, lit., fool, fr. *ba* horse + *ka* deer] **:** a Japanese rocket-propelled bomb-carrying airplane guided by a suicide pilot and used in World War II

ba·kau·an \bə'häwən\ *var of* BACAUAN

¹**bake** \'bāk\ *vb* **baked; baked** \-kt\ *or archaic* **bak·en** \-kən\ **baking; bakes** [ME *baken*, fr. OE *bacan*; akin to OHG *bahhan* to warm, *bahhan* to bake, ON *baka*, Gk *phōgein* to roast] *vt* **1 :** to prepare (as food) by a dry heat either in an oven or on heated metal or stone or under coals **2 :** to dry or harden by subjecting to heat ⟨the ground was *baked* by the hot sun⟩ ⟨*baked* bricks⟩ **3** *obs* **a :** to make into a hard or solid mass **b :** to harden by cold ~ *vi* **1 :** to prepare food by baking it **2 :** to undergo the process of baking ⟨the potatoes were *baking* in the oven⟩ **3 :** to be subjected to intense heat ⟨the rocks ~ in the desert sun⟩ ⟨a sizable audience, *baking* in a blaze of newsreel and television lights —Truman Capote⟩ **syn** see DRY

²**bake** \"\ *n* -s **1 :** the action or process of baking **:** subjection to or preparation by baking ⟨for best results a slow ~ at a moderate temperature is essential⟩ **2** *Scot* **:** a hard biscuit **3 a :** a meal or individual dish consisting largely of baked food ⟨a delicious vegetable ~⟩ **b :** a social gathering at which a baked specialty is served as the main dish; *esp* **:** CLAMBAKE **4 :** a batch of baked goods **:** production or total output of baked goods ⟨turning out a huge daily ~ of fresh bread⟩

bakeboard \'=,=\ *n, chiefly Brit* **:** a board on which dough is kneaded or rolled

baked alaska *n, often cap B & usu cap A* **:** a dessert consisting of cake topped with ice cream covered with meringue which then is quickly browned in an oven

baked-ap·ple \(')=ˌ==\ *or* **baked-apple berry** *also* **bakeapple** \'=,==\ *or* **bake-apple berry** *n* [so called fr. its wrinkly appearance] **:** CLOUDBERRY 2

baked beans *n pl* **:** beans softened by soaking and boiling and then baked usu. with salt pork and seasoning — see BOSTON BAKED BEANS

bakehead \'=,=\ *n, slang* **:** a locomotive fireman

bakehouse \'=,=\ *n* [ME *bakhous*, fr. *baken* to bake + *hous* house] **:** BAKERY

Bake·lite \'bākə,līt, -āk-,l-\ *trademark* — used for any of various synthetic resins and plastics

bakemeat *or* **baked meat** *n* [ME *bakemete*, fr. *baken* to bake + *mete* food — more at BAKE, MEAT] *obs* **:** cooked usu. baked food; *specif* **:** a meat pie

baken *archaic past part of* BAKE

Bake-Off \'=,=\ *service mark* — used for a public contest for amateur cooks in which contestants must prepare and bake their entries within a stated time

bakeout \'=,=\ *n* -s **:** protracted heating for the purpose of removing adsorbed substances (as moisture or gas)

¹**bak·er** \'bākə(r)\ *n* -s [ME, fr. OE *bæcere*, fr. *bacan* to bake + *-ere* -er — more at BAKE] **1 :** one that bakes: as **a :** one that specializes in the making of breads, cakes, cookies, and pastries **b :** an operator of equipment for the flaking, toasting, and cooling of cereals **c :** BURNER 1a(1) **2 a :** a utensil used for baking **b :** a food (as a meat, fruit, or vegetable) that is suitable for baking ⟨Idaho potatoes are esteemed as good ~s⟩ **3** *or* **baker bird** [so called fr. its ovenlike nest] **:** a So. American ovenbird (*Furnarius rufus*)

²**baker** \"\ *usu cap* — a communications code word for the letter *b*

ba·ker·ite \'bākə,rīt\ *n* -s [R.C.*Baker*, 20th cent. Englishman, its discoverer + E *-ite*] **:** a variety of the mineral datolite occurring in white fine-grained masses resembling marble, containing boron in place of some of the silicon, and having the probable formula $CaB_4(BO_4)(SiO_4)_3(OH)_3.H_2O$ (hardness 4.5)

baker's cheese *also* **bakers' cheese** *n* **:** soft uncooked cottage cheese

baker's dozen *n* **1 :** THIRTEEN ⟨a *baker's dozen* of eggs⟩ **2 :** a small unspecified number ⟨very few persons were there, and only a *baker's dozen* showed any real interest⟩

baker's itch *n* **:** GROCER'S ITCH

bakers' yeast *n* **:** a yeast (commonly *Saccharomyces cerevisiae*) used or suitable for use as leaven; *esp* **:** any yeast strain yielding maximum growth rather than high alcohol production — compare BREWERS' YEAST

bak·ery \'bāk(ə)rē, -ri\ *n* -ES [¹*bake* + *-ery*] **1** *archaic* **:** the work of a baker **2 :** a place in which baked products (as bread, cakes, cookies) are made **3 :** an establishment (as a retail shop) that sells baked products chiefly or exclusively

bakes *pres 3d sing of* BAKE, *pl of* BAKE

bakeshop \'=,=\ *n* **:** BAKERY

bake·stone \'bāk,stōn, -,stən\ *n* **:** a flat piece of stone or iron formerly used for baking (as of scones, cakes, or tarts)

bakeware \'=,=\ *n* **:** heat-resistant dishes (as of pottery) used for baking and serving food ⟨a set of ~⟩ ⟨this ~ is both durable and attractive⟩

bakh·tia·ri \ˌbäktē'ärē, bäk'tyä-\ *n, pl* **bakhtiari** *or* **bakhtiaris** *usu cap* [Per *Bakhtyārī*, perh. fr. *bakhtyār* fortunate, rich, fr. *bakht* fortune, prosperity] **1 :** a nomadic people ranging between Isfahan and Kermanshah, Iran **2 :** a member of the Bakhtiari people

ba·kie \'bāki\ *n* -s [prob. fr. ScGael *bacaid*, perh. fr. F *baquet* — more at BACKET] *Scot* **:** a square wooden vessel; *esp* **:** one for carrying ashes or fodder

¹**baking** *n* -s [ME, fr. gerund of *baken*] **1 :** the action or process of baking **2 :** a quantity baked at or within a given time **:** BATCH ⟨served . . . wild turkey and deer and a week's ~ of mince and apple pies —Marjory S. Douglas⟩

²**baking** *adj* **1 :** designed for or used in baking ⟨a ~ utensil⟩ ⟨an essential ~ ingredient⟩ **2 :** marked by intense dry heat **:** SCORCHING ⟨the arid ~ sands of the desert⟩ — **baking·ly** *adv*

baking powder *n* **:** a powder used as a leavening agent in making baked goods (as quick breads or cake) and consisting essentially of a carbonate (as baking soda), an acid substance (as cream of tartar), and starch or flour so that when the mixture is moistened the carbonate and acid react, liberating carbon dioxide which raises the dough

baking soda *n* **:** SODIUM BICARBONATE

ba·kla·va *also* **ba·kla·wa** \'bäklə,vä, ˌ==ˌ=\ *n* -s [Turk *baklava*] **:** a dessert of wafer-thin sheets of pastry put together with nuts and honey or a sugar syrup and cut usu. in diamond-shaped pieces for serving

bak·shaish \(')bäk¦shīsh\ *n* -ES *usu cap* [fr. *Bakhshis*, village in northwestern Iran] **:** a semiantique or antique Persian carpet with usu. angular designs

bak·sheesh *also* **bak·shish** *or* **bakh·sheesh** *or* **bakh·shish** \'bak,shēsh, =ˈ=\ *n, pl* **baksheesh** [Per *bakhshīsh*, fr. *bakhshīdan* to give, fr. MPer; akin to Av *baxshaiti* he has or gives a share, Gk *phagein* to eat, Toch A *pāk* part, OSlav *bogatŭ* rich, *bogŭ* god, Skt *bhakṣati* he enjoys, consumes, *bhajati* he allots, and perh. to OHG *backe, bahho* cheek; basic meaning: allot] *esp in northern Africa & southwestern Asia* **:** a gift of money (as for a favor or as a reward) **:** TIP ⟨knowing our porters could go no farther in their light clothes, we gave them their wages, plus liberal ~, and sent them back —Edmund Hillary⟩; *also* **:** ALMS ⟨assailed by hordes of homeless street waifs and their age-old wail of "~" —C.G.Pepper⟩

bak·tun \'bäk,tün\ *n* -s [Maya, fr. *bak* 400 + *tun* year of 360 days] **:** a period of 400 tuns in the Maya calendar — compare KATUN, PICTUN

¹**ba·ku** \'bä(ˌ)kü\ *n* -s *sometimes cap* [native name in the Philippines] **1 :** a fine lightweight straw made of fibers from the talipot palm and marked by a dull finish **2 :** a hat made of baku straw

²**baku** \"\ *n* -s [of African origin; akin to Twi *abako* mahogany tree, *bakua* stalk of a plantain or banana tree] **1 :** either of two tropical African timber trees (*Mimusops heckelii* and *M. djave*) **2 :** the hard heavy wood of the baku trees

³**ba·ku** \(')bä¦kü *also* (')ba-\ *adj, usu cap* [fr. *Baku*, U.S.S.R.] **:** of or from the city of Baku, Azerbaidzhan S.S.R., U.S.S.R. **:** of the kind or style prevalent in Baku

⁴**baku** \"\ *n* -s *usu cap* **:** a fine western Caucasian rug with angular designs

ba·ku·la \'bəkələ\ *n* -s [Skt, perh. of Dravidian origin; akin to Kanarese *pagaḍe*] **:** a tropical Asiatic tree (*Mimusops elengi*) with fragrant white flowers

ba·ku·nin·ism \bə'kün(y)ə,nizəm\ *n* -s *usu cap* [Mikhail A. *Bakunin* †1876 Russian anarchist and writer + E *-ism*] **:** a doctrine of revolutionary anarchism; *also* **:** its militant tenets

ba·ku·nin·ist \-ün(y)ənəst\ *also* **ba·ku·nist** \-ün(y)əst\ *n* -s *usu cap* [M.A.*Bakunin* + E *-ist*] **:** an advocate of Bakuninism

ba·ku·pa·ri \ˌbä(ˌ)küpə'rē\ *n* -s [modif. of Pg *bacopari*, fr. Tupi] **:** a Brazilian tree (*Rheedia brasiliensis*) of the family Guttiferae with an edible fruit having snow-white slightly acid pulp

bakuri *var of* BACURY

¹**bal** \'bal\ *n* -s [Corn] *chiefly in Cornwall* **:** MINE

²**bal** \"\ *n* -s [by shortening] **:** BALMACAAN

³**bal** \"\ *n* -s [by shortening] **:** BALMORAL 1

bal *abbr* balance

BAL \"\ *abbr or n* -s [*British Anti-Lewisite*] **:** DIMERCAPROL

bala \'balə\ *adj, usu cap* [*Bala*, town in north Wales] **:** of or relating to a subdivision of the European Ordovician

ba·laam \'bāləm\ *n* -s [after *Balaam*, biblical prophet rebuked by his ass (Num 22–24); prob. fr. newspaper fillers being regarded as asinine] **1** *slang* **:** FILLER 1d(1) **2** *slang* **:** worthless or rejected newspaper or magazine copy ⟨could not prevent the publication of a certain amount of ~ —J.B.Hubbell⟩

bal·a·bos *or* **bal·ebos** \ˌbälə'bós\ *or* **baal-ha-bos** \ˌbäl(h)ä'-\ *n, pl* **bal·a·ba·tim** *or* **baal-ha-ba·tim** \-'bätəm, -,tēm\ [Yiddish *balebos*, fr. Heb *ba'al habbayith*, lit., lord of the house] **:** a Jewish master of the house **:** a Jewish house owner or host

ba·la·bos·ta *or* **ba·le·bos·ta** \ˌbälə'bóstə\ *or* **baal-ha-bos·ta** \ˌbäl(h)ä-\ *n* -s [Yiddish *baleboste*, fr. *balebos*] **:** a Jewish mistress of the house; *esp* **:** an efficient or competent Jewish housewife or hostess

bal·a·cla·va \ˌbalə'klävə, -avə, *attrib* ¦=ˈ=¦==\ *or* **balaclava helmet** *n* -s [fr. *Balaclava* (now usu. *Balaklava*), village in the Crimea, U.S.S.R., where a battle of the Crimean War was fought on Oct. 25, 1854] **:** a hoodlike knitted cap covering the head, neck, and part of the shoulders and worn esp. by soldiers and mountaineers

bal·a·dine \ˌbalə'dēn\ *n* -s [MF *baladin*, fr. OProv, fr. *balar* to dance — more at BALLAD] *archaic* **:** a professional dancer esp. in a troupe of street entertainers

ba·lae·na \bə'lēnə\ *n, cap* [NL, fr. L, whale, modif. of Gk *phalaina, phallaina*; akin to Gk *phallos* penis — more at BLOW] **:** the genus consisting of the Greenland whale — compare RIGHT WHALE

ba·lae·ni·cip·i·tes \bə,lēnə'sipə,tēz\ *n pl, cap* [NL, fr. *Balaenicip-, Balaeniceps*, genus of Ciconiiformes (fr. L *balaena* whale + NL *-cip-, -ceps*, fr. L *caput* head) + *-ites* -ite — more at HEAD] **:** a suborder of Ciconiiformes constituted by the shoebill

ba·lae·nid \bə'lēnəd\ *n* -s [NL *Balaenidae*] **:** a whale of the family Balaenidae

ba·lae·ni·dae \bə'lēnə,dē\ *n pl, cap* [NL, fr. *Balaena*, type genus + *-idae*] **:** a family of whales comprising the right whales and extinct related forms

ba·lae·noid \-,nóid\ *n* -s [NL *Balaenoidea*] **:** WHALEBONE WHALE — **bal·ae·noi·de·an** \¦balə¦nóidēən\ *adj or n*

bal·ae·noi·dea \ˌbalə'nóidēə\ [NL, fr. *Balaena* + *-oidea*] *syn of* MYSTICETI

bal·ae·nop·tera \-'näptərə\ *n pl, cap* [NL, fr. *balaeno-* (fr. L *balaena* whale) + *-ptera*] **:** a genus (the type of the family Balaenopteridae) of whalebone whales that comprises the rorquals

bal·ae·nop·ter·i·dae \-(ˌ)näp'terə,dē\ *n pl, cap* [NL, fr. *Balaenoptera*, type genus + *-idae*] **:** a family of whalebone whales that comprise the rorquals and humpbacks and are distinguished from the right whales by the dorsal fin, gular folds, and short whalebone

balafo *var of* BALAPHON

ba·la·ghat \¦bälə¦gôt, -ät\ *n* -s [prob. fr. Hindi, fr. Per *bālā* above (fr. MPer) + Hindi *ghāṭ* pass — more at GHAT] *India* **:** tableland above mountain passes

ba·la·hi \bə'lähē\ *n, pl* **balahi** *or* **balahis** *usu cap* [Hindi *balāhī*] **1 :** an ethnic group among the untouchables inhabiting Madhya Pradesh state, India, who once were spinners and weavers but have become predominantly farm laborers for the cultivating castes **2 :** a member of the Balahi

bal·a·lai·ka \ˌbalə'līkə\ *n* -s [Russ *balalaika, balabaika*; akin to Ukrainian *balabajka* balalaika; perh. akin to Russ *balabolit'* to chatter, Czech *blaboliti* to murmur] **:** an instrument of the guitar kind used esp. in the U.S.S.R. and having a triangular wooden body and from two to four strings

balalaika

ba·lam \'bäləm\ *n* -s [Maya] **:** a supernatural being in Mayan religion that guards cornfields and villages ⟨the Mayas of Central America speak of *Balam* as a god of agriculture, describing him as an old fellow with a long head. He walks in the air and whistles as he goes — a much-dreaded nocturnal being —W.D.Wallis⟩

balan- *or* **balano-** *comb form* [NL, fr. Gk *balan-, balano-* acorn, fr. *balanos* acorn, glans penis — more at GLAND] **1 :** glans penis ⟨*balanitis*⟩ ⟨*balanoblennorrhea*⟩ **2 :** acorn ⟨*Balanops*⟩

¹**bal·ance** \'balən(t)s\ *n* -s [ME, fr. OF, modif. of (assumed) VL *bilancia*, fr. LL *bilanc-, bilanx* having two scalepans, fr. L *bi-* + *lanc-, lanx* plate, scalepan; akin to Gk *lekos* dish, Lith *uolektis* ell, OE *eln* ell — more at ELL] **1 a :** a device or apparatus designed esp. to measure the weight of an object: as (1) **:** a beam or lever supported by a fulcrum at the midpoint to form two equal arms, having a pan or tray suspended from each arm, one to hold an object of known weight and the other to hold an object to be weighed, and registering the weight of this object by the deflection of a pointer fastened to the beam and provided with a scale before which it swings (2) **:** a similar device but with unequal arms, the body to be weighed being suspended from the shorter arm while a sliding counterpoise is moved along the graduated scale that forms the other arm to produce equilibrium and indicate the body's weight (3) **:** a device using the elasticity of a spiral spring to measure weight (as of a body suspended from a spring) or force (as of a pull exerted upon the spring) by means of the extension produced in the coil to which is attached a pointer moving along a graduated scale — called also *spring balance* (4) **:** a measuring apparatus in which opposing phenomena (as forces or resistances) neutralize each other — compare NULL METHOD **b** *obs* **:** the tray or dish of a balance **:** SCALE ⟨a pair of ~s⟩ **2 a :** a means that judges or decides ⟨a nomination arrived at in the ~ of a free election⟩ — often used in pl. ⟨the peoples of Africa place insistently on the world's agenda matters of still greater weight in the ~s of human affairs —Alan Paton & H.R.Isaacs⟩ **b** *archaic* **:** the power to make authoritative judgments **3 :** an element, influence, or part that serves as a counterbalance or counterpart esp. to secure harmony, proportion, or symmetry **:** COUNTERPOISE ⟨the minstrel show . . . was soon introduced as a ~ to many heavy dramatic bills —*Amer. Guide Series: La.*⟩ **4 :** a vibrating wheel operating in conjunction with a hairspring to regulate the movement of a timepiece **5 a :** stability (as of an upright body) produced by even distribution of weight on each side of the vertical axis ⟨lose his ~ and fall⟩ **b :** equipoise produced between two contrasting or opposing elements whereby one neutralizes, makes up for, or offsets the other ⟨the benign ~ in him between science and humanism —Lucien Price⟩ ⟨the ~ we strike between security and freedom —Earl Warren⟩ **c :** equality between the totals of the two sides of an account **d :** the quality or state of having weight (as of a pulley or shaft) so distributed that (1) there will be no vibration when running or that (2) the body (as a shaft or a pulley mounted on a balanced shaft) will stand in any position in which it may be placed on a pair of knife-ways — called also respectively (1) *dynamic balance* or *running balance*, (2) *standing balance* or *static balance* **6 a** (1) **:** an aesthetically pleasing integration of elements (as in a work of art) achieved usu. by giving each element only its due prominence or significance and often by allowing one element to stand in contrast to, oppose, or otherwise be matched by another element **:** PROPORTION, HARMONY (2) **:** the juxtaposition in writing of two or more syntactically parallel constructions (as phrases or clauses) containing similar, contrasting, or opposing ideas (as "to err is human; to forgive, divine") **b :** the distribution of weight (as in an implement, device, or moving part of a mechanism) that promotes ease of handling or smoothness of performance **7 a :** physical equilibrium (as of an athlete) maintained before or returned to after a motion or series of motions that upsets the normal weight distribution of the body ⟨a gymnast with a fine sense of ~⟩ ⟨a fighter kept off ~ for a whole round⟩ **b** (1) **:** a controlled state in dancing of maintaining an erect posture (2) **:** a rocking shift from foot to foot esp. in ballroom dancing **8 a :** the weight that one side, faction, or element has in excess of another or others ⟨the ~ of the evidence lay on the side of the defendant⟩ **b :** something that is left over **:** REMAINDER ⟨answers will be given in the ~ of this chapter —R.W.Murray⟩ **c :** an excess or an amount in excess on either side of an account; *esp* **:** an amount in excess on the credit side of an account ⟨to have a comfortable ~ in the bank⟩ **9 a :** control of emotional bias and maintenance of the power of sober judgment esp. under stress **:** SANITY, COMMON SENSE **b :** normal psychological composure **:** EQUANIMITY ⟨I doubt that Thoreau would be thrown off ~ by the fantastic sights and sounds of the 20th century —E.B.White⟩ **10 a :** the relation in physiology between the intake of a particular nutrient and its excretion — used with *positive* when the nutrient is in excess of the bodily metabolic requirement ⟨a positive nitrogen ~⟩ and with *negative* when dietary inadequacy and withdrawal of bodily reserves is present ⟨a negative calcium ~⟩ **b :** the maintenance (as in laboratory cultures and natural habitats) of a population in about the same condition and level ⟨a ~ of biological life or of organic groups had been set up through the ages —*Science*⟩ **11 :** the point in the length of an object at which the moment of force on one side of the point equals that on the other ⟨a rifle with the ~ just two inches in front of the trigger guard⟩

balance 1a(1)

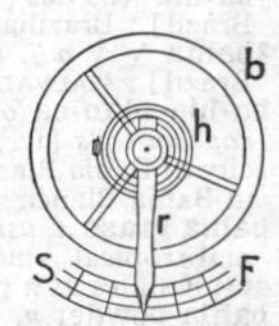

balance 4 : *S* slow, *F* fast, *r* regulating lever, *h* hairspring, *b* balance

syn BALANCE, EQUILIBRIUM, EQUIPOISE, POISE, and TENSION can denote, in common, the stability or efficiency resulting from the equalization or exact adjustment of opposing forces. BALANCE suggests a steadiness that results when all parts are properly adjusted to each other, when no one part or constituting force outweighs or is out of proportion to another ⟨to keep her *balance* on an icy street⟩ ⟨to keep his emotional *balance* under stress⟩ ⟨the *balance* between civilian and military needs —*Collier's Yr. Bk.*⟩ ⟨establish an acceptable *balance* between satisfactions and frustrations —Abram Kardiner⟩ ⟨the inevitable outgrowth of the *balance* of character, theme, atmosphere, and structure —F.O.Baker⟩ EQUILIBRIUM, often interchangeable with BALANCE ⟨to keep her physical and emotional *equilibrium* under stress⟩, is more often restricted to a mechanically produced or producible property deriving from a thing's construction, support, or relation to external forces, often suggesting a tendency to return to an original position after disturbance ⟨a ship's *equilibrium*⟩ ⟨an *equilibrium* of opposing human impulses —Sinclair Lewis⟩ ⟨establishing an *equilibrium* between the Western forces and a possible aggressor —*Current History*⟩ ⟨a fundamental lack of *equilibrium* between different aspects of the constitutional distribution of power —R.M.Dawson⟩ EQUIPOISE suggests perfection of balance or stability of equilibrium ⟨to maintain . . . *equipoise* among contending interests —L.H.Butterfield⟩ ⟨the structure remains upright, a marvel of *equipoise* —Norman Douglas⟩ ⟨the *equipoise* of intellectual and pietistic interests in him —H.O.Taylor⟩ POISE denotes an equality of opposing or different things or forces, often designating the state or appearance of perfect balance or serenity, esp. of mind ⟨the condition of a *poise* between widely divergent impulses and emotions that produces a strange serenity —F.R.Leavis⟩ ⟨the main characteristic of their blond gray-eyed colleague is quiet *poise* that stands her in good stead in the exciting, high-pressure work —*Newsweek*⟩ TENSION, rare in this connection, implies strain, either a pull from both ends or an outward pressure in every direction, of such equality that there results a tautness without undue strain at any point; applied to a mental condition it implies an inner balanced vital opposition of moral or intellectual forces, powers, or qualities ⟨indolent as he was on all occasions which required *tension* of the mind, he was active and persevering in bodily exercise —T.B. Macaulay⟩ ⟨the whole *tension* of Gide's work is characterized in those sentences: the incessant dialectic of a man who knows no peace but the precarious equilibrium of opposites —*Times Lit. Supp.*⟩ ⟨in letting the whole physical system lose tone, for lack of the *tension* which gaiety imparts —W.C.Brownell⟩ — **in the balance** *or* **in balance** : in an uncertain critical position : with the fate or outcome about to be determined one way or the other ⟨some human being's right to life hangs *in the balance* —Lucius Garvin⟩ ⟨his . . . authority and his manly strength hesitating and hanging *in the balance* —Glenway Wescott⟩ — **on balance** *also* **in balance** : all things considered : in a final analysis ⟨economic aid has, *on balance*, been justified —H.C.Wolfe⟩ ⟨a . . . noble experiment which, *on balance*, has already proved itself an inexpensive insurance policy against social collapse —C.R.Decker⟩

[2]**balance** \"\ *vb* -ED/-ING/-s [prob. fr. [1]*balance*] *vt* **1 a (1) :** to compute the difference if any between the debits and credits of (an account) : arrange or prove (as an account or a book of accounts) so that the sum of the debits equals the sum of the credits ⟨~ the books of a company⟩ **(2) :** to pay the amount due on : SETTLE ⟨send a check to ~ her account⟩ **(3) :** to equalize the total debits and credits of (an account) **b :** to complete (an equation in chemistry) so that the same number of atoms of each kind appears on each side **2 a :** to set off : COUNTERBALANCE, COUNTERPOISE ⟨the pressures of business, labor, and farmers . . . manage to check and ~ each other —Max Ascoli⟩ ⟨~ one consideration against another⟩ ⟨a large expenditure *balanced* only by his large income⟩ — often used with *up* or *out* ⟨~ up the frustrations of their lives by . . . escapist types of recreation —Ernest & Pearl Beaglehole⟩ **b :** to equal or equalize in weight, number, form, or proportion : arrange in balance ⟨duties and pleasures *balanced* each other in his well-planned life⟩ **3 a :** to weigh (two things) in or as if in a balance : compare the relative weight, force, importance, or value of ⟨~ the profit and loss to see what had been gained⟩ **b :** to deliberate upon esp. by weighing opposing considerations : PONDER ⟨*balancing* the issues for hours on end with no decision ever reached⟩ **4 a :** to bring to a state or position of equipoise ⟨~ scales by adjusting the opposing weights⟩ **b :** to poise or arrange in or as if in balance ⟨a hat *balanced* precariously on his head⟩ ⟨~ a stick on his finger⟩ ⟨*balanced* a set of equations⟩ **c :** to adjust or apportion (as by even or due distribution of elements) to achieve proportion, harmony, or symmetry ⟨regulate your activities and ~ your diet⟩ ⟨~ the national economy⟩; *specif* : to bring (a body, as a flywheel) into balance by removing portions where the weight is excessive or by adding weight to lighter sections — see [1]BALANCE 5d ~ *vi* **1 a :** to become balanced or established in balance esp. in a position difficult to maintain ⟨~ on one hand on a diving board⟩ ⟨sit *balancing* on a porch rail⟩ ⟨an intellect that ~s between foolishness and genius⟩ **b :** to stay poised in dancing in an upright position that requires unusual control **2 :** to be an equal counterpoise ⟨his periods of frenzy *balanced* with periods of cool meticulous deliberation⟩ **3 :** FLUCTUATE, WAVER, HESITATE ⟨~ and temporize on all matters that demand action⟩ ⟨feel something like contempt for the mind that ~s and waits —P.E.More⟩ **4 a :** to move with a swaying or swinging motion; *esp* : to shift the weight lightly back and forth from foot to foot in dancing bending the body to the side on which the weight is placed **b :** to move in dancing toward a person or couple usu. with four steps and then back **5 :** to bid in contract bridge on the assumption that one's partner must have a strong hand because the opponents have bid weakly **syn** see STABILIZE

[3]**ba·lan·cé** \bə'länˈ¦sā, 'ba,länˈ¦sā\ *adj* [F, past part. of *balancer* to balance, fr. *balance*, n.] **:** changing the weight in ballet lightly from foot to foot with knee flexion accompanied by closing in of the free foot and by body sway

balance beam *n* **1 :** a beam used as a counterpoise (as to a drawbridge) **2 :** a thin rail used for feats of balancing in gymnastics

balance cock *or* **balance bridge** *n* **:** the bridge that carries the top pivot of the balance staff in a watch

balance coil *n* **:** an iron-cored solenoid with a tap at the center or neutral point used to provide a neutral terminal in a three-wire system

balance crane *n* **:** a crane in which there is a counterbalancing weight opposite the load

balanced *adj* **1 a :** being in a state of balance : PROPORTIONATE, SYMMETRICAL, HARMONIOUS ⟨one of the notable early builders of the closed and ~ couplet —Douglas Bush⟩ ⟨the properly ~ classical symphonic orchestra —Ralph Hill⟩ ⟨a more sober and perhaps more ~ assessment of modern intellectual and cultural history —F.L.Baumer⟩ ⟨a ~ blend of Virginia and Oriental tobaccos —*Punch*⟩ ⟨prided herself on possessing a well-*balanced* mind —Dorothy Sayers⟩ ⟨the educated man shows a ~ development of all his powers —*Report: (Canadian) Royal Commission on Nat'l Development*⟩ **b :** having the physiologically active elements mutually counteracting ⟨a ~ solution⟩ **c :** possessing in proper proportions the living and nonliving elements necessary for the existence and continuation of an effective food chain ⟨a ~ pond⟩ ⟨a ~ aquarium⟩ **d** *of a diet or ration* **:** furnishing all needed nutrients in just the quantity, form, and proportion needed to support healthy growth and productivity ⟨a ~ chicken mash is essential for the first four to six weeks —*Farmer's Weekly (So. Africa)*⟩ ⟨low-cost ~ luncheons —*Current Biog.*⟩ **e** *of fishing tackle* **:** having rod, reel, line, and lure properly matched to provide maximum angling efficiency **f :** having players equally distributed on each side of the center — used of an offensive line or backfield formation in football; compare UNBALANCED **g** *of cards* **:** evenly distributed among the four suits **h** *of a budget* **:** having expenditures no greater than income ⟨insisted on a ~ budget and refused to permit government subsidies —*Collier's Yr. Bk.*⟩ **i** *of an electrical transmission line* **:** having equal impedance in each separate line and equal impedance from each line to ground **2 a** *of a fabric* **:** having the same type and number of yarns in weft and warp **b** *of twisted plied yarns* **:** that do not curl or kink

balanced anesthesia *n* **:** anesthesia produced by smaller doses of two or more agents considered safer than the usual large dose of a single agent

balanced fund *n* **:** a security portfolio comprising both bonds and stocks

balanced lethal *n* **:** a true-breeding heterozygous organism maintained in a stable state through the existence of different lethals on each of a pair of homologous chromosomes and resulting in loss of all homozygotes

balanced population *n* **:** a natural population in a particular land area or body of water that maintains itself year after year with little fluctuation in numbers of individuals in spite of regulated fishing or hunting

balanced rock *n* **:** an angular, subangular, or rounded rock of considerable size that rests more or less precariously on its base and is the result of weathering and erosion in situ — compare PERCHED BOULDER

balanced rudder *or* **balance rudder** *n* **:** a rudder hung with part of its area forward of the vertical axis to counterbalance the force of the water on the part abaft of the axis

balanced step *n* **:** any of a series of winders so arranged that their small ends are only a little narrower than the fliers

balanced ticket *n* **:** a political party ticket with a list of candidates designed to appeal to the major racial, national, and religious groups of the electorate

balance fish *n* **:** HAMMERHEAD 3a

balance frame *n* **:** the frame of a walking wheel cultivator having axles offset to the front to enable the weight of the machine to overcome the tendency of the tongue to fly upward when the gangs are hung up

balance gate *n* **:** a gate (as a floodgate) hung in the middle on a horizontal axis to facilitate turning

bal·an·celle \¦balən¦sel\ *n* -s [F, fr. It dial. (Genoa) *balanzella*] **:** a Mediterranean coasting and fishing boat with a single lateen sail

balance lugsail *n* **:** a lugsail not lowered in tacking and having the foot laced to a boom extending forward of the mast or with the tack fitted to travel on a horse set in the deck forward of the mast — see LUGSAIL illustration

balance of mind : emotional equilibrium : SANITY ⟨had taken her life when her *balance of mind* was disturbed⟩

balance of nature : a state of equilibrium in nature due to the constant interaction of the whole biotic and environmental complex, interference with this equilibrium (as by human intervention) being often extremely destructive — compare EROSION

balance of payments *also* **balance of international payments :** a summary of the international transactions of a country or region over a period of time including commodity and service transactions, capital transactions, and gold movements

balance of power : an equilibrium or adjustment of power (as between potentially opposing sovereign states) such that no one state is willing or able to upset the equilibrium by waging war or interfering with the independence of other states

balance of trade : the difference in value over a period of time between imports and exports of commodities or formerly of commodities and such transactions as services and remittances

balance piston *n* **:** a small piston moving in a steam cylinder and attached directly to a vertically reciprocating piece so as partly to balance its dead weight

bal·anc·er \'balən(t)sə(r)\ *n* -s **:** one that balances: as **a (1) :** [3]HALTER **(2) :** a rodlike lateral protuberance of the head in certain larval salamanders **b (1) :** an electronic appliance (as a balancing condenser) used with a direction finder to improve the sharpness of the direction indication **(2) :** BALANCER SET

balance reef *n* **1 :** the last reef used in a fore-and-aft sail and taken diagonally from the throat to the close-reef cringle of the leech **2 :** the ordinary last reef or close reef used to steady a ship

balancer set *n* **1 :** two or more similar direct-current machines directly coupled together and connected in series across the outer conductors of a multiple-wire system of distribution for the purpose of maintaining the potentials of the intermediate wires of the system, which are connected to the junction points between the machines — called also *compensator, equalizer set* **2 :** reactors or transformers with their wires so interconnected as to equalize the voltages between the wires of a multiple-wire alternating-current system — called also *static balancer*

balance rudder *var of* BALANCED RUDDER

balances *pl of* BALANCE, *pres 3d sing of* BALANCE

balance screw *n* **:** one of the screws set into the rim of a watch balance or chronometer balance and used for regulating the poise of the balance and thereby the timekeeping rate — compare MEANTIME SCREW

balance sheet *n* **1 :** a statement of the financial condition (as of a corporation) at a given date showing the equality of total assets to total liabilities plus net worth or of total liabilities to total assets plus deficit **2 :** an accounting showing the relationship of counterpoised things (as profit and loss, achievement and lag, or activity and rest) ⟨a *balance sheet* of military government, showing its difficulties and achievements —Sigmund Neumann⟩ ⟨set up a *balance sheet* on each possible solution, stating your evidence for and against that course of action —W.J.Reilly⟩

balance spring *n* **:** HAIRSPRING

balance staff *n* **:** the pivoted arbor of a balance wheel

balance wheel *n* **1 a :** a wheel that regulates or stabilizes the motion of a mechanism (as a sewing machine or timepiece) — compare [1]BALANCE 4 **b :** FLYWHEEL **2 :** something suggesting a balance wheel in acting as a regulating and stabilizing force ⟨George Washington . . . was the *balance wheel* of the convention —*World Today*⟩ ⟨a sense of humor that acts as a *balance wheel* in a man's life⟩

balancing *pres part of* BALANCE

balancing band *n* **:** a band fitted with a link or ring on each side of the shank at the balancing point of the ship's anchor — called also *gravity band*

balancing condenser *n* **:** a variable condenser used in an auxiliary way with a direction finder to make the indications of the instrument more precise — called also *compensating condenser*

balancing ring *n* **:** a ring attached to the balancing band of an anchor

ba·lan·gay \¦balan¦gī\ *also* **ba·ran·gay** \¦barən-\ *n* -s [*balangay* fr. Tag; *barangay* fr. Ilako or Bisayan] **:** a large swift canoe or boat of the Philippines

ba·lan·ic \bə'lanik\ *adj* [*balan-* + *-ic*] **:** of or relating to the glans of the penis or of the clitoris

[1]**bal·a·nid** \'balənəd\ *adj* [NL *Balanidae*] **:** of or relating to the genus *Balanus*

[2]**balanid** \"\ *n* -s **:** a barnacle of the genus *Balanus*

ba·lan·i·dae \bə'lanə,dē\ *n pl, cap* [NL, fr. *Balanus*, type genus + *-idae*] **:** a family of highly evolved sessile barnacles comprising the acorn barnacles

bal·a·nite \'balə,nīt\ *n* -s [*balan-* + *-ite*] **:** a fossil balanoid shell

bal·a·ni·tes \,balə'nīd·ēz\ *n, cap* [NL, fr. Gk *balanitēs* acorn-shaped, fr. *balan-* + *-itēs* -ite] **:** a small genus of Old World tropical trees of the family Zygophyllaceae distinguished by the one-seeded drupe

bal·a·ni·tis \-īd·əs\ *n* -ES [NL, fr. *balan-* + *-itis*] **:** inflammation of the glans penis

balano- — see BALAN-

bal·a·no·glos·sid \,balə(,)nō'gläsəd\ *n* -s [NL *Balanoglossida*] **:** ENTEROPNEUST

bal·a·no·glos·si·da \-sədə\ [NL, fr. *Balanoglossus* + *-ida*] *syn of* ENTEROPNEUSTA

bal·a·no·glos·sus \-səs\ *n, cap* [NL, fr. *balan-* + *-glossus* (fr. Gk *glōssa* tongue) — more at GLOSS] **:** a genus of marine burrowing wormlike animals that because of certain vertebrate-like characters are now usu. classed as chordates and made with certain closely related forms (as *Dolichoglossus*) to constitute an order (Enteropneusta) of the Hemichorda

[1]**bal·a·noid** \'balə,nȯid\ *adj* [Gk *balanoeidēs* like an acorn, fr. *balan-* + *-eidēs* -oid] **:** of or relating to the acorn barnacles

[2]**balanoid** \"\ *n* -s **:** ACORN BARNACLE

bal·a·noph·o·ra \,balə'näfərə\ *n, cap* [NL, fr. *balan-* + *-phora*] **:** a genus (typifying the family Balanophoraceae) of Asiatic parasitic plants having pistillate flowers without perianth and with one pistil

bal·a·noph·o·ra·ce·ae \,balə,näfə'rāsē,ē\ *n pl, cap* [NL, fr. *Balanophora*, type genus + *-aceae*] **:** a family of yellow or red tropical root parasitic dicotyledonous plants related to and sometimes included among the Santalales — **bal·a·noph·o·ra·ceous** \¦==¦==¦=shəs\ *adj*

ba·lan·o·phore \bə'lanə,fō(ə)r, 'balənə,f-\ *adj* [NL *Balanophora*] **:** of or relating to the Balanophoraceae

bal·a·no·pos·thi·tis \¦balə(,)nō(,)päs'thīd·əs\ *n* -ES [NL, fr. *balan-* + *posthitis*] **:** inflammation of the glans penis and of the prepuce

bal·a·nops \'balə,näps\ *n, cap* [NL, fr. *balan-* + *-ops*] **:** a small genus (constituting the family Balanopsidaceae and order Balanopsidales) of tall little-known Australian dicotyledonous trees having large simple leaves, flowers in catkins, and a nutlike fruit enclosed in an involucre

ba·lante \bə'länt\ *also* **ba·lan·ta** \-ləntə\ *n, pl* **balante** *or* **balantes** *also* **balanta** *or* **balantas** *usu cap* [*Balante* fr. F; *Balanta* fr. Pg] **1 a :** a Sudanese Negro people of French Senegal and Angola **b :** a member of such people **2 :** the West-Atlantic language of the Balante people

bal·an·tid·i·al \¦balən¦tidēəl\ *or* **bal·an·tid·ic** \-dik\ *adj* [NL *Balantidium* + E *-al* or *-ic*] **:** of, relating to, or caused by protozoans of the genus *Balantidium*

bal·an·ti·di·a·sis \,balənt·ə'dīəsəs, bə,lan-\ *also* **bal·an·tid·i·o·sis** \,balən,tidē'ōsəs\ *n, pl* **balantidia·ses** *also* **balantidio·ses** \-sēz\ [NL, fr. *Balantidium* + *-asis* or *-osis*] **:** infection with or disease caused by protozoans of the genus *Balantidium*

bal·an·tid·i·um \,balən-'tidēəm\ *n* [NL, fr. Gk *balantidion* little bag, dim. of *balantion* bag, pouch, purse] **1** *cap* **:** a genus of large parasitic ciliate protozoans (order Heterotricha) having the peristome beginning near the anterior tip of the body and containing a species (*Balantidium coli*) that infests the intestines of swine and other mammals and may cause a chronic ulcerative dysentery in man **2** *pl* **balantid·ia** \-ēə\ **:** a protozoan of the genus *Balantidium*

bal·a·nus \'balənəs\ *n, cap* [NL, fr. L, acorn, fr. Gk *balanos* — more at GLAND] **:** a very large genus (the type of the family Balanidae) of barnacles comprising the sessile acorn barnacles and including littoral and deepwater forms some of which cause destructive fouling of ships and of underwater cables

ba·lao \bə'laù\ *n* -s [Sp] **:** HALFBEAK

bal·a·phon \'balə,fōn, -än\ *also* **balafo** \-,fō\ *n* -s [F & Bambara; F *balafon*, fr. Bambara *balafo* to play the xylophone, fr. *bala* xylophone] **:** a West African xylophone with gourd resonators

bal·as \'baləs\ *or* **balas ruby** *n* -ES [ME *baleis, balis, balas*, fr. MF *balais*, fr. Ar *balakhsh*, fr. *Badhakhshān, Balakhshān*, ancient region of Afghanistan] **:** a ruby spinel of a pale rose-red or orange

ba·la·ta \bə'läd·ə\ *n* -s [Sp, of Cariban origin; akin to Galibi *balata*] **1 :** a hard substance produced by drying the milky juice of a bully tree (*Manilkara bidentata*) and that possess properties similar to those of gutta percha and is used chiefly in the manufacture of belting and golf balls — called also *gutta balata* **2 :** any of certain tropical American trees of the genus *Manilkara* that yield balata; *esp* **:** a bully tree (*M. bidentata*)

ba·la·tong \'bälə,tôŋ\ *n* -s [Tag] *Philippines* **:** MUNG BEAN

ba·latte \bə'lat\ *n* -s [origin unknown] **:** a cut slab of soft white limestone providing good reflective insulation owing to its natural white color

ba·laus·tre \bə'laù,strā\ *n* -s [AmerSp, fr. Sp *balaustre, balaústre* baluster, fr. It *balaustro* — more at BALUSTER] **1 :** either of two So. American timber trees (*Centrolobium robustum* or *C. paraense*) with yellowish brown to purplish or rose-colored glossy wood **2 :** the wood of the balaustre

ba·la·wa \bə'läwə\ *n, pl* **balawa** *or* **balawas** *usu cap* **:** a division of the Andamanese

bal·boa \bal'bōə\ *n* -s [Sp, after Vasco Núñez de *Balboa* †1517 Span. explorer] **1 :** the basic monetary unit of Panama — see MONEY table **2 :** a silver coin representing one balboa

bal·brig·gan \bal'brigən\ *n* -s [fr. *Balbriggan*, seaport town in Ireland where it was orig. manufactured] **1 :** a plain-stitch knitted often tubular usu. cotton fabric used esp. for underwear, hosiery, or sweaters **2 :** clothing (as pajamas) made of balbriggan — usu. used in pl.

bal·che *also* **bal·ché** \(')bäl¦chā\ *n* -s [AmerSp *balché*, fr. Maya] **:** a fermented drink prepared by the natives of Yucatan from the bark of a tree of the genus *Lonchocarpus* and honey

bal·co·net *or* **bal·co·nette** \¦balkə¦net\ *n* -s [*balcony* + *-et*, *-ette*] **:** a railing or balustrade on the outside of a window and in the form of a balcony

bal·co·nied \'balkənēd, -id\ *adj* **:** having balconies ⟨a ~ façade⟩ ⟨a spacious, turreted, ~ structure of dark, weather-beaten shingles —E.A.Weeks⟩

bal·co·ny \'balkənē, 'baùk-, -ni\ *n* -ES [It *balcone*, fr. OIt, scaffold, of Gmc origin; akin to OHG *balko, balcho* beam — more at BALK] **1 a :** a usu. unroofed platform projecting from the wall of a building, enclosed by a parapet or railing, and usu. resting on brackets or consoles **b :** an interior projecting gallery in a public building (as a theater); *specif* **:** such a gallery immediately above the main floor **2 :** an elevated usu. railed platform similar to or suggesting a balcony (as on the side of a large cylinder printing press)

balcony 1a

syn GALLERY, LOGGIA, VERANDA, PIAZZA, PORCH, PORTICO, STOOP: these words often show considerable variation in use, esp. regional; the following comments bear on only those applications that appear to meet with approval in historical and architectural use. BALCONY in this comparison is applicable to any unroofed structure resting on brackets or corbels enclosed by balustrade or railing and extending along a side of a building. GALLERY applies to a long narrow structure roofed over and often enclosed. LOGGIA may apply to a balcony or gallery that is architecturally well integrated in a building's design. VERANDA applies to a roofed structure or area facilitating out-of-door activities. PIAZZA, orig. indicating an open square in a town, is interchangeable with, and may be a rather modish synonym for, VERANDA. PORCH orig. indicated a covered entrance affording protection but now is applicable to all but the largest verandas. PORTICO is likely to suggest a roofed gallery or gallerylike structure fronting a more or less large or imposing building. STOOP is applicable in regional speech to any relatively unpretentious construction outside an entrance, esp. to a small porch or to a flight of steps with a landing before a door

[1]**bald** \'bȯld\ *adj* -ER/-EST [ME *ballede*; akin to OE *bǣl* fire, pyre, OHG *belihha* coot, ON *bāl* pyre, Dan *bældet* bald, Goth *bala* white-faced horse, L *fulica* coot, Gk *phalios* having a white spot, Skt *bhāla* forehead, luster] **1 a :** lacking all or a significant portion of the natural or usual covering of hair on the head or sometimes on other parts of the body ⟨his big head was ~ except for a wisp or two of brown hair —G.K.Chesterton⟩ ⟨comb the hair from the sides of the head across the top to disguise the fact that he is ~⟩ ⟨looking as ~ and hairless in a bathing suit as a plucked chicken⟩ ⟨a bearded or ~ face⟩ **b :** lacking some natural or expected covering (as of foliage, feathers, trees, soil, or nap) ⟨the trees were brown and ~ as in winter —George Borrow⟩ ⟨~, featureless, fire-blackened mountains —John Muir⟩ ⟨the banks rise suddenly, sometimes covered with timber and sometimes ~ —Anthony Trollope⟩ ⟨the ~ seat of his trousers⟩ **c** *of wheat* **:** lacking a beard **d :** not having a flange — used of a mechanical part **2** *archaic* **:** lacking merit, import, or effect : WORTHLESS, PALTRY **3 a :** lacking amplification, adornment, or decoration : SPARSE, PLAIN, MEAGER ⟨offered not a shred of evidence — nothing but ~ assertion —C.H.Grandgent⟩ ⟨a ~ statement of the facts⟩ ⟨only the ~ outlines of his legal career —George Bellairs⟩ ⟨the more poetic the theme, the ~*er*, at least the briefer, its expression —W.C.Brownell⟩ **b :** UNDISGUISED, PATENT, PALPABLE, OUTRIGHT ⟨~ egotism —J.R.Lowell⟩ ⟨a ~ lie⟩ ⟨the ~, inaccurate . . . realism of the present theater —J.P.Marquand⟩ ⟨the present outcome is a ~ political compromise —*New Republic*⟩ **4** *of a horse* **:** having the face including the skin about the eyes and nostrils white **syn** see BARE

[2]**bald** \"\ *n* -s *chiefly Midland* **:** an often grassy mountain summit or other elevated area naturally bare of forest ⟨the grass-covered ~s of the Blue Ridge in North Carolina —*Fortune*⟩

[3]**bald** \"\ *vi* -ED/-ING/-s **:** to become bald ⟨was starting to ~ noticeably⟩ ⟨a young man as diplomats go, still under fifty, ~*ing* rapidly —J.P.O'Donnell⟩

bal·da·chin \'bȯldəkən, 'bal-\ *or* **bal·da·chi·no** *or* **bal·dac·chi·no** \,baldə'kē(,)nō\ *or* **bal·da·quin** \'bȯldəkən, 'bal-\ *n* -s [*baldachin, baldachino, baldacchino* fr. It *baldacchino*, fr. OIt, fr. *Baldacco* Bagdad, city in Iraq + OIt *-ino* (fr. L *-inus* -ine); *baldaquin* fr. MF *baldequin, baudequin*, fr. OF, fr. OIt *baldacchino*] **1** : an embroidered fabric of silk and gold esp. for church vestments, ceremonial robes, and decorations **2** : a cloth canopy fixed or carried over an important person or a sacred object often as a mark of honor **3** : an ornamental canopylike structure that projects from a wall, is suspended from above, or is supported by columns and that is used esp. over an altar or a seat of honor — compare CIBORIUM

baldachin 3

bald brant *n* : BLUE GOOSE

bald coot *n* **1** : the Old World coot **2** : FLORIDA GALLINULE **3** : COOT 4

baldcrown \'ₛ,ₛ\ *n* : BALDPATE 2

bald cypress *n* [so called fr. the fact that it is deciduous] **1** : either of two large swamp trees (*Taxodium distichum* and *T. ascendens*) of the southern states — see POND CYPRESS **2** : the hard red wood of bald cypress much used for shingles

bald eagle *also* **bald-headed eagle** *n* : the common eagle (*Haliaeetus leucocephalus*) of No. America that is wholly brown when young but in full adult plumage has white head and neck feathers and a white tail — see AMERICAN EAGLE

balder *comparative of* BALD

¹**bal·der·dash** \'bȯldə(r),dash, -aa(ə)sh,-aish\ *n* -ES [origin unknown] **1** *obs* : an odd and usu. objectionable mixture of drinks (as beer and milk or beer and wine) **2** : NONSENSE, TRASH ⟨writers of this kind of sophomoric ~ —F.L.Mott⟩ ⟨poetry, some of it excellent, much of it ~ —J.D.Adams⟩

²**balderdash** \"\ *vt* -ED/-ING/-ES *archaic* : to make balderdash of ⟨wine ~*ed* with milk⟩ ⟨poetry . . . ~*ed* with false sentiment —Washington Irving⟩

baldest *superlative of* BALD

bald face *n* **1** : a bald-faced horse : a bald horse **2** *archaic* : raw or inferior whiskey

bald-faced \'ₛ;ₛ\ *adj* **1** : having a white face or a white mark on the face — usu. used of an animal (as a horse, cow, or stag) **2** : BAREFACED ⟨a plain, *bald-faced* case of highhanded graft —F.B.Gipson⟩ ⟨a *bald-faced* lie⟩ — compare BALD

bald-faced hornet *n* : WHITE-FACED HORNET

bald-faced widgeon *n* : BALDPATE 2

baldhead \'ₛ,ₛ\ *n* **1** : a bald-headed person **2 a** : BALDPATE 2 **b** : a breed or color variety of domestic pigeon **3** : an abnormality of seedlings esp. common among beans characterized by deformity, decay, or death of the growing point and the appearance of a bare stump above the cotyledons resulting from damage to the seed by mechanical, biological, or other factors; *also* : the stump itself

¹**bald-headed** \'ₛ;ₛₛ\ *adj* **1** : BALD **2** *of a schooner* : without topmasts

²**bald-headed** \'ₛ;ₛₛ\ *adv* [¹*bald-headed*] : in a rush without care or caution : PRECIPITATELY ⟨she came out *bald-headed* and accused me of having stolen the case —Valentine Williams⟩ ⟨the planes went *bald-headed* for the enemy squadron⟩

bal·die \'bȯldē\ *n* -s [prob. short for Giuseppe *Garibaldi* †1882 Ital. patriot] : a small double-ended fishing boat used on the east coast of Scotland

bald·ing \'bȯldiŋ, -ēŋ\ *adj* : getting bald ⟨a short stout ~ man —W.G.Smith⟩ ⟨a ~ head thinly sprinkled with grey hairs —Mervyn Wall⟩

bald·ish \'bȯldish, -ēsh\ *adj* : somewhat bald ⟨sixty years old now . . . gnarled and ~ —Stanley Walker⟩

bald locust *n* : ATTACUS 1

bald·ly \'bȯl(d)lē, -li\ *adv* : in a bald manner ⟨to put the case ~ without vain recrimination —Edith Wharton⟩ ⟨this evidence, which is only ~ summarized —Edward Clodd⟩ ⟨the appeal is simply and ~ to morbid curiosity —F.L.Mott⟩

baldmoney \"\ *n, pl* **baldmoneys** [by folk etymology fr. ME *baldemoine, baldemonie*] **1** : any of several gentians (esp. *Gentiana amarella*) **2** : SPICKNEL

bald·ness *n* -ES : the state of being bald

¹**baldpate** \'ₛ,ₛ\ *or* **bald-pated** \'ₛ;ₛₛ\ *adj* [¹*bald* + *-pate* or *-pated*] : BALD-HEADED

²**baldpate** \"\ *n* **1** : BALDHEAD 1 **2** : a white-crowned widgeon (*Mareca americana* or *Anas americana*) with a short narrow bill that breeds in northwestern No. America and winters along both coasts of the U.S. and in Mexico

baldrib \'ₛ,ₛ\ *n, dial Eng* : a lean piece of pork cut from nearer the rump than the sparerib

bal·dric *also* **bal·drick** \'bȯldrik, -ēk\ *n* -s [ME *baudry, baudrik*, prob. modif. of OF *baudré*] **1** : an often richly ornamented belt worn over one shoulder, across the breast, and under the opposite arm to support a sword or bugle **2** : a belt resembling a baldric worn about the waist

baldric 1

bald rush *n* : an American sedge of the genus *Psilocarya*

balds *pres 3d sing of* BALD, *pl of* BALD

bald tire *n* : a flangeless steel tire shrunk or bolted to a locomotive drive wheel —called also *blind tire, flangeless tire, plain tire*

bald·win hoe \'bȯldwən-\ *n, usu cap B* [prob. after Henry I. *Baldwin* b1896 Am. research forester] : a heavy hoe with a long narrow blade used in planting small forest trees

baldwin spot *n, usu cap B* [fr. *Baldwin*, a variety of winter apple, after Col. Loammi *Baldwin* †1807 Am. civil engineer & soldier who developed it] : BITTER PIT

baldy \'bȯldē, -i\ *n* -ES **1** *slang* : one that is bald **2** : a white-headed pigeon (*Columba norfolciensis*) of Australia that feeds on fruits and seeds

¹**bale** \'bāl, *esp bef pause or cons* -āəl\ *n* -s [ME, fr. OE *bealu, balu*; akin to OHG *balo* evil, ON *böl*, Goth *balwawesei* malice, OCorn *bal* plague, OBulg *bolŭ* sick man] **1** : great evil : a malign pernicious influence : HARM, DISASTER ⟨gave him a final look, in which Reith read nothing but ~ —D.C. Peattie⟩ ⟨the day would come when the thunderous shout "Nika!" would mean ~ and woe to her —P.I.Wellman⟩ **2** : pain or mental suffering : TORMENT, WOE, SORROW ⟨bring us ~ and bitter sorrowings, instead of comfort, which we should embrace —Edmund Spenser⟩

²**bale** \"\ *n* -s [ME, fr. OE *bǣl* fire, pyre; akin to ON *bál* flame, pyre — more at BALD] *archaic* : a great fire; *esp* : a signal fire

³**bale** \"\ *n* -s [ME, fr. OF, of Gmc origin; akin to OHG *balla* ball — more at BALL] **1 a** : a large bundle of goods for storage or transportation; *specif* : a large closely pressed package of merchandise bound with cord, wire, or hoops and usu. protected by a wrapping (as of burlap) ⟨a ~ of paper⟩ ⟨a ~ of hay⟩ **b** : the amount contained in a bale esp. when fixed for a certain commodity and sometimes used as a unit of measure (as in the U. S. 500 pounds of cotton) **2** *archaic* : a set usu. of three — used of dice

⁴**bale** \"\ *vt* -ED/-ING/-S [³*bale*] : to make up into a bale ⟨loose pulp is *baled* in units measuring about 18x23x43 inches —H.R.Mauersberger⟩ ⟨spend an afternoon *baling* hay⟩

⁵**bale** *var of* BAIL

bale·age \'bālij, -ēj\ *n* -s [³*bale* + *-age*] : the total number of bales (as of cotton produced)

bal·e·ar·ic \¦balē¦arik, -ēk, *also* -¦er- *sometimes* bə'lir-\ *adj, usu cap* [L *Baliaricus, Balearicus* of the Balearic islands, fr. Gk *Baliarikos*, fr. *Baliareis* Balearic islands + *-ikos* -ic] : of or relating to a group of islands in the Mediterranean sea off the coast of Spain including esp. Majorca, Minorca, and Iviza

bal·e·ar·i·ca \,balē'arəkə\ *n, cap* [NL, fr. L, fem. of *Balearicus*] : the genus comprising the crowned cranes

balearic crane *n, usu cap B* : a crowned crane (*Balearica pavonina*) of Africa

balebos *var of* BALABOS

baleboste *var of* BALABOSTA

bale breaker *n* [³*bale*] : a breaker for baled material (as cotton)

bale cubic *n* [³*bale*] : the space available for cargo in a ship's hold that is measured in cubic feet to the inside of the cargo battens and to the underside of the beams

ba·leen \bə'lēn\ *n* -s [ME *baleine* whale, baleen, fr. OF, fr. L *balaena* whale — more at BALAENA] : a horny substance growing in the mouth of whales of the suborder Mysticeti that is esp. developed in the right whale and grows in dependent plates from 2 to 12 feet long attached in 2 ranks along the upper jaw forming a fringelike sieve to collect and retain food — called also *whalebone*

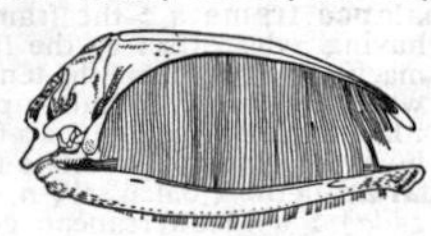
skull of right whale showing plates of baleen

baleen whale *n* : WHALEBONE WHALE

bale·fire \'bā(ə)l,fī(ə)r\ *n* [ME, fr. OE *bǣlfȳr* funeral fire, fr. *bǣl* pyre + *fȳr* fire — more at BALE, FIRE] : a large outdoor fire: **a** : a funeral pyre **b** : a signal fire : BEACON **c** : BONFIRE 2

bale·ful \'bālfəl\ *adj* [ME, fr. OE *bealuful, baluful*, fr. *bealu, balu* bale + *-ful* — more at BALE] **1** : marked by a deadly, malign, or pernicious influence or effect : MALEFICENT ⟨the ~ arts of sorcerers —J.G.Frazer⟩ ⟨their pale and ghastly features, more ghastly in that ~ and malignant light —T.L. Peacock⟩ ⟨the grating supervision of one particularly ~ sergeant —Byron Bentley⟩ **2** : foreboding evil : OMINOUS ⟨the . . . company, despite the ~ economic outlook, decided to seek national distribution of its products —D.C.Morrill⟩ ⟨a man full of gloom and ~ predictions⟩ — **bale·ful·ly** \-fəlē, -li\ *adv* — **bale·ful·ness** *n* -ES

bale·less \'bā(ə)lləs\ *adj* : being without a bale

bal·er \'bālə(r)\ *n* -s [⁴*bale* + *-er*] : one that bales (as a machine that bales hay, straw, cotton, and similar products or a person who operates such a machine)

baler bag *or* **baler sack** *n* : a large sack of cloth or multi-ply paper designed to hold a number of smaller filled bags or boxes under little or no compression

bale rope *n* [³*bale*] : a heavy unpolished twine esp. for bales

bales *pl of* BALE, *pres 3d sing of* BALE

bale sling *n* [³*bale*] : a length of rope with its ends spliced together that is used as a loading sling by being passed under an object (as a bale or barrel) so that its two loops meet on top with one being drawn under the other and placed over the hook of a hoisting block

ba·les·tra \bə'lestrə\ *n* -s [It, lit., crossbow, fr. L *ballista* — more at BALLISTA] : a jump forward in fencing followed by a lunge

ba·le·te *also* **ba·li·ti** \bə'lēd·ē\ *n* -s [Tag *baliti*] : any of several Philippine figs with aerial roots (as *Ficus indica* and *F. palawanensis*) used for rope making

balewort \'ₛ,ₛ\ *n* -s [¹*bale* + *wort*] : OPIUM POPPY

bal·four pine \'bal,fȯr-, -ūr-,-ōr-\ *n, usu cap B* [after John H. *Balfour* †1884 Scottish botanist] : FOXTAIL PINE

balge yellow *pronunc unknown*\ *n* [origin unknown] : SUNFLOWER YELLOW

ba·li aga \,bälē'ägə\ *n, pl* **bali aga** *or* **bali agas** *usu cap B&A* **1** : a people inhabiting the interior of the island of Bali, Indonesia **2** : a member of the Bali Aga

ba·li·an \'bälēən\ *n, pl* **balian** *or* **balians** [Malay *bĕlian* medium, shaman] : a Malaysian medium who employs trances in practicing the art of a medicine man

ba·li·ba·go \,bälē'bä(,)gō\ *n* -s [Tag & Bisayan] *Philippines* : MAJAGUA a

ba·li·bun·tal *or* **ba·li·bun·tl** \,balē'bənt°l, -lə'-\ *n* -s [*bali-* (fr. *Balinog*, town on Luzon, Philippines) + Tag *buntál* talipot-palm fiber, hat made of talipot-palm fiber] **1** : a fine lightweight straw of glossy smooth buntal **2** : a hat made of balibuntal

ba·li·ja \bə'lējə\ *n* -s *usu cap* : a member of a numerous caste of traders of Madras and Madhya Pradesh states, India

ba·lim·bing \bə'lim(,)biŋ\ *n* -s [Tag] *Philippines* : CARAMBOLA

¹**ba·li·nese** \¦bälə¦nēz, ¦ba-, -lē-, -nēs\ *n, pl* **balinese** *usu cap* [D *Balinees*, adj. & n., fr. *Bali*, island of Indonesia + connective *-n-* + D *-ees* -ese] **1 a** : a people of chiefly Hinduₛ Javanese extraction prob. with Papuan and Polynesian admixture inhabiting the island of Bali **b** : a member of such people **2** : the Malayo-Javanese language of the Balinese people

²**balinese** \"\ *adj, usu cap* [D *Balinees*] : of or relating to the island of Bali or its inhabitants or their language or culture

baling *pres part of* BALE

bal·in·ger \'balənjə(r)\ *n* -s [ME *balynger*, fr. MF *balengier, baleinier* whale ship, fr. *baleine* whale — more at BALEEN] : a small British seagoing ship of the 15th to 17th centuries

baling hook *n* [fr. pres. part. of ⁴*bale*] : a longshoreman's implement consisting of a metal hook with short shank and wooden handle at right angles to the shank

ba·lin·ta·wak \bə¦lintə¦wäk\ *n* -s [Tag] : a native dress of Filipino women consisting of dress and skirt woven of local fibers with a kerchief and apron to match

ba·li·saur \'bälə,sȯ(ə)r\ *n* -s [Hindi *bālū* sand (fr. Skt *vālukā*, prob. fr. *valate* he turns) + *sūar* pig, fr. Skt *sūkara* — more at VOLUBLE, SOW] : HOG-NOSED BADGER

ba·li·sier \bə'lēzē,ā\ *n* -s [F] *in the West Indies* : WILD PLANTAIN

balista *var of* BALLISTA

ba·lis·tes \bə'li(,)stēz\ *n, cap* [NL, fr. L *balista, ballista*; fr. the way in which the first spine snaps down when pressure is applied on the second spine — more at BALLISTA] : the type genus of Balistidae

¹**ba·lis·tid** \-stə̇d\ *adj* [NL *Balistidae*] : of or relating to the family Balistidae

²**balistid** \"\ *n* -s : a fish of the family Balistidae

ba·lis·ti·dae \-stə,dē\ *n pl, cap* [NL, fr. *Balistes*, type genus + *-idae*] : a family of long-snouted small-eyed marine fishes having a deep compressed body and rough spinose scales, comprising the triggerfishes and sometimes the filefishes, and with a few related forms constituting a suborder of Plectognathi

bal·is·toi·dea \,balə'stȯidēə\ *n pl, cap* [NL, fr. *Balistes* + *-oidea*] : a suborder of marine plectognath fishes including the filefishes, triggerfishes, and related chiefly tropical forms

bal·is·trar·ia \,balə'stra(a)rēə\ *n, pl* **balistrari·ae** \-rē,ē\ [NL, fr. LL, fem. of *balistrarius, ballistrarius* of slinging, fr. L *balista, ballista* sling — more at BALLISTA] : a narrow often cruciform opening in a wall (as of a tower or fortress) for discharging arrows (as from a crossbow)

ba·li·tao \¦bälə¦tau̇\ *n* -s [native name in the Philippines] : a Philippine peasant dance in mazurka rhythm and semiₛ European style depicting work movements

baliti *var of* BALETE

¹**balk** *or* **baulk** \'bȯk *sometimes* -ȯlk\ *n* -s [ME *balke*, fr. OE *balca* ridge; akin to OHG *balko* beam, ON *bjálki*, L *fulcire* to prop, Gk *phalanx* log, line of battle, Skt *bhurij* arm] **1 a** : a ridge of land left unplowed between furrows or formerly between the acres or fields in common lands **b** : a piece missed in plowing (as by carelessness) **2** : a rough-squared length of timber : BEAM, RAFTER, TIE BEAM **3** *dial Eng* **a** : the beam of a balance **b** : the often unfloored loft above the tie beams of a house — usu. used in pl. **4** *obs* : OMISSION **5** : HINDRANCE, DISAPPOINTMENT, CHECK, DEFEAT **6 a** : the space behind the balkline on a billiard table **b** : any of the eight outside divisions of a billiard table made by the four balklines **7** : headrope connecting fishing nets **8 a** : a failure of a competitor after making his approach to the starting line to follow through with his jump, vault, or dive **b** : an illegal motion by the pitcher in baseball toward the plate or toward a base when there are men on base esp. without delivering the ball, the baserunners automatically advancing a base **c** *in racket games* : interference with an opponent's stroke **9** : one of the stringers placed from boat to boat on which the flooring is placed in a floating bridge **10** : an abrupt thinning out of a coal seam

²**balk** *or* **baulk** \"\ *vb* -ED/-ING/-S [ME *balken* to make balks in plowing, to pass over, fr. *balke*, n.] *vt* **1** *archaic* : to pass over : let pass by : OVERLOOK, IGNORE, AVOID ⟨and such an age as ours ~*s* no expense —William Cowper⟩ **2** : to defeat, check, or stop by or as if by an obstacle, block, or barrier : block from things wished, contemplated, or planned causing ensuing disappointment and vexation : block or halt occurrence, indication, performance, or execution of ⟨the French ambassadors had neither been ~*ed* nor been frightened —Francis Hackett⟩ ⟨snarled in a knot of words which ~*s* the understanding —Edmund Wilson⟩ **3** *cribbage* : to give (the dealer's crib) cards that are unlikely to make fifteens or sequences ~ *vi* **1 a** : to stop short and refuse to go ⟨they ~*ed* like seasoned steers at a loading-chute gate —Lewis Nordyke⟩ : cease or decline progress, action, or development suddenly, arbitrarily, or unexpectedly ⟨many of the more interesting bacteria distinctly prefer to grow at this higher temperature and . . . are apt to ~ if not provided with their favorite heat —Justina Hill⟩ **b** : to refuse abruptly or decisively (as for reasons of taste, propriety, or temperament) : RECOIL — used with *at* ⟨his aggressive nature ~*ed* at the association —*Amer. Guide Series: Oregon*⟩ ⟨I ~*ed* at snails but Bill got them down without a quiver —W.A.White⟩ **c** : to commit a balk in sports **2** : to engage in foolish or trivial argument : QUIBBLE **syn** see DEMUR, FRUSTRATE

bal·kan \'bȯlkən *sometimes* 'bal-\ *also* **bal·kan·ic** \(')ₛ¦kanik\ *adj, usu cap* [fr. the *Balkan* peninsula in southeastern Europe] : of or relating to the Balkan peninsula, the Balkan mountain range, or the people of Balkan states

balkan frame *n, usu cap B* [fr. the *Balkan* countries, where it was first used] : a frame employed in the treatment of fractured bones of the leg or arm that provides overhead weights and pulleys for suspension, traction, and continuous extension of the splinted fractured limb

balkan grippe *n, usu cap B* : Q FEVER

bal·kan·ism \-,nizəm\ *n* -s *usu cap* **1** : the quality or state of being balkanized ⟨a country fated to endure a century of ~⟩ **2** : BALKANIZATION

bal·kan·ite \-,nīt\ *n* -s *cap* : a native or inhabitant of the Balkan states

bal·kan·i·za·tion \,ₛₛnə'zāshən, -,nī'z-\ *n* -s *often cap* : the process of balkanizing : the state of being balkanized ⟨regretted the ~ of South Africa and were anxious for some form of federation —Leo Marquard⟩ ⟨perpetuate the ~ of the Christian Commonwealth by validating the concept of separate sovereignties —E.A.Walsh⟩

bal·kan·ize \'ₛₛ,nīz\ *vt* -ED/-ING/-S *often cap* [*Balkan* peninsula + E *-ize*; fr. the way in which this territory has been broken up into many small states] : to break up (as a region) into smaller ineffectual and frequently conflicting units ⟨opposes the partition of Germany, and holds that the economic consequences of *Balkanizing* the country would be serious —*Times Lit. Supp.*⟩

balkan pine *n, usu cap B* : an ornamental pine (*Pinus peuce*) of the Balkan mountains of dense pyramidal habit and having needles in fascicles of five

bal·kar \'bäl,kär\ *n* -s *cap* [Russ, of Turkic origin; akin to Karachai *balqar*, Balkar *bolqar*, OTurk *bulgar* mixed breed] **1** : one of a mixed Mongoloid people of the Caucasus in the Kabardino-Balkarian Republic, U.S.S.R. **2** : the Turkic language of the Balkar people

balk·i·ly \'bȯkəlē, -li *sometimes* 'bȯlk-\ *adv* [*balky* + *-ly*] : in a balky manner ⟨the horse crossed the river ~ and only with severe coercion from the whip⟩

balk·i·ness \-kēnəs, -ki-\ *n* -ES : the quality or state of being balky

balk·ing·ly *adv* : in a balking manner

balkline \'ₛ,ₛ\ *n* **1** : a line across a billiard table near one end behind which the cue balls are placed in lagging for lead and making opening shots (as in English billiards, pool, or bagatelle) **2 a** : one of four lines drawn parallel to and 14 or 18 inches from the cushions of a billiard table dividing it into nine compartments **b** : a carom billiards game that sets restrictions (as in scoring) determined by these lines; *specif* : the billiard game in which it is ruled that if the two object balls rest in one of the eight compartments formed by the cushions and these lines at least one of the balls must be driven out at the second shot or sometimes at each shot

balks *pl of* BALK, *pres 3d sing of* BALK

balky \'bȯkē, -i *sometimes* 'bȯlk-\ *adj* -ER/-EST [¹*balk* + *-y*] : balking or likely to balk : refusing or apt to refuse to proceed in an indicated or expected direction or to act according to direction or suggestion ⟨will appeal directly to the voters for support if Congress gets ~ —*Look*⟩ ⟨order ~ witnesses to appear⟩ ⟨a ~ horse⟩ ⟨acting just like a ~ mule⟩ **syn** see CONTRARY

¹**ball** \'bȯl\ *n* -s [ME *bal*, fr. ON *böllr*; akin to OE *bealluc* testis, OHG *balla* ball, OE *bula* bull — more at BULL] **1** : a round or roundish body or mass: as **a** : a spherical or ovoid body of any kind for throwing, hitting, or kicking in games or sports ⟨the baseball player knocked the ~ down the third-base line⟩ ⟨kick the ~ over the goalposts⟩ **b** : a celestial body : EARTH, GLOBE **c** : any of various spherical, rounded, or conical missiles or projectiles (as for a catapult, cannon, or firearm); *also* : projectiles used in firearms : BULLETS ⟨powder and ~⟩ **d** : a roundish protuberant part of the body: as (1) : the rounded eminence by which the base of the thumb is continuous with the palm of the hand (2) : the rounded broad part of the sole of the human foot between toes and arch and on which the main weight of the body first rests in normal walking; *also* : the corresponding part of a shoe or of a last (3) : the padded rounded underside of a human finger or toe near the tip **e** : EYEBALL **f** : a ball-shaped dabber made usu. of pelt stuffed with wool and fastened to a handle and formerly used by printers for inking a form **g** : a mandrel upon which steel piping is welded by concave rolls **h** : BALL BEARING **i** : TESTIS — usu. considered vulgar **j** : a spherical architectural ornament often hollow and of considerable size crowning a cupola or dome **k** : a small globose fruit or seed pod : SEED BALL **l** : the compact mass of earth and roots often tightly bound (as with burlap) and moved with a transplanted tree, shrub, or herbaceous plant **m** : a solidified mass of iron in the manufacture of wrought iron intimately mixed with siliceous slag and being the result of puddling or of pouring molten refined iron into slag **n** : a large pill (as one used in veterinary medicine) : BOLUS **o** (1) : a ball-shaped mass (as of candy, pastry, vegetable, minced fish, or meat) (2) : a small roundish mass ranging in consistency from soft to hard and formed when sugar is boiled to a certain temperature and then quickly chilled **2** : a game in which a ball is thrown, kicked, or struck; *esp* : BASEBALL ⟨play ~ for two hours⟩ **3 a** : the delivery of the ball (as in baseball) ⟨a fast ~⟩ ⟨a curve ~⟩ **b** : a pitched baseball not struck at by the batter that fails to pass through the strike zone ⟨a count of three ~*s* and two strikes⟩ **c** *cricket* : a fair delivery of the ball by bowling — opposed to *no ball*; compare WIDE **4** *slang* : FELLOW, CHARACTER ⟨this narrator . . . is an odd ~ indeed —Hollis Alpert⟩ **5 balls** *pl* [fr. pl. of *ball* (testis)] : NONSENSE — often used interjectionally to express disapproval or annoyance; often considered vulgar **6** : main authority over or direction of an enterprise or activity : RESPONSIBILITY ⟨to take the ~ away from the incompetent director and give it to a new man⟩ — **get the ball rolling** *or* **start the ball rolling** : to initiate an activity usu. to be engaged in by two or more people hesitant to begin ⟨the teacher *started the ball rolling* by posing a large and general question on which all were sure to have an opinion⟩ — **keep the ball rolling** : to give continued impetus or momentum to an activity already in progress ⟨when the conversation began to lag, the host always *kept the ball rolling* by introducing a new topic of common interest without seeming to have done it purposely⟩ — **on the ball** *adv (or adj)* **1** *slang* : knowledgeable and competent : purposively active : ALERT ⟨she was no chicken perhaps, but she was *on the ball* —Theodora Keogh⟩ ⟨when the men know some of the lesson, the instructor really

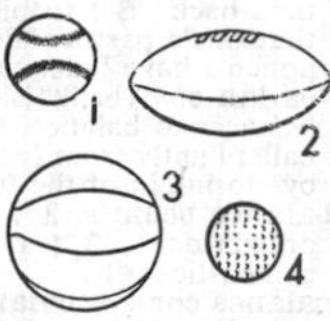
ball 1a: *1* baseball, *2* football, *3* basketball, *4* golf ball

has to stay *on the ball* —*Infantry Jour.*⟩ **2** *slang* **:** of ability **:** of competence ⟨to have a lot *on the ball*⟩ ⟨the average man of 40 had appreciably more *on the ball* than the person of 30 —J.E.Gibson⟩

²ball \"\ *vb* -ED/-ING/-S *vt* **1 :** to form into a ball: as **a :** to squeeze into a more or less compact mass ⟨~*ing* each sheet of paper into a wad before throwing it away⟩ — often used with *up* **b :** to wind up (as string) upon itself **c :** to form (as molten iron) into balls in the manufacture of wrought iron **d :** to cluster densely about (the queen bee) — used of bees **2 :** to clog (the hoof of an animal) with balls ⟨the pony's hoofs got badly ~*ed* in the mud⟩ **3 :** to compact a ball of earth about (a tree, shrub, or herbaceous plant or its roots) for storing or transporting **4 :** to give a medicinal ball to (as a horse) ~ *vi* **:** to form, gather, collect, or pack into a ball or balls ⟨the stallion's right forefoot ~*ed* with snow and sand —W.V.T.Clark⟩ ⟨the boiled sugar ~*ed* when dropped into cold water⟩ ⟨smaller shotgun pellets liable to ~ in the barrel⟩ — often used with *up* ⟨danger of the stuff ~*ing* up, i. e. the fibers clot up into small inseparable balls of fiber —F.H.Norris⟩ — **ball the jack** *slang* **:** to go fast **:** HURRY ⟨a hot rodder *balling the jack* up highway 102⟩

³ball \"\ *n* -S [F *bal*, fr. OF, fr. *baller* to dance, fr. LL *ballare*, fr. Gk *ballizein;* akin to Skt *balbaliti* he whirls] **1 :** a large formal gathering for social dancing **2 :** a good time **:** PICNIC ⟨a fairly monstrous cowboy actor in from the Coast for a ~ —Gilbert Millstein⟩ ⟨it's a ~ for a while, but it's no life to lead —David Hulburd⟩

bal·la·bi·le \bä'läbə,lā\ *n* -S [It, fr. *ballare* to dance (fr. LL) + *-abile* -able — more at BALL] **:** a dance in classic ballet performed by the corps de ballet by itself or with the principal dancers

¹bal·lad \'baləd\ *n* -S [ME *balade*, fr. MF, fr. OProv *balada* dancing song, dance, fr. *balar* to dance, fr. LL *ballare* — more at BALL] **1 :** a song sung while dancing or to accompany a dance **2 :** a part-song often in stanzas with a refrain **:** a light madrigal **3 a :** a narrative composition in verse of strongly marked rhythm suited to simple singing or dancing; *specif* **:** a composition handed down by oral transmission from medieval and early modern times and having narrative combined with lyrical and sometimes dramatic elements — see BALLAD METER, BALLAD STANZA **b :** an art song imitating such a composition **c :** BROADSIDE BALLAD **4 :** BALLADE **5 :** a popular song; *esp* **:** a dance song of romantic or sentimental character and slow tempo

²ballad \"\ *vt* -ED/-ING/-S [ME *baladen*, fr. *balade*, n.] *obs* **:** to tell or sing of in ballads

bal·lade \bə'läd, ba-, -ȧd,-ad; bá'lȧd, bä'läd\ *n* -S [ME *balade*] **1 :** a medieval French verse form or the English verse form derived from it having usu. three stanzas of 7, 8, or 10 lines, maintaining the same three or four rhymes throughout, and concluding with an envoi of half the stanzaic length usu. in the form of an apostrophe addressed to an individual, the last line of each stanza and of the envoi being an identical refrain **2 a :** an elaborate musical setting of a ballad with or without text **b :** a musical composition usu. for piano suggesting the theme or spirit of an epic ballad

bal·lad·eer *also* **bal·lad·ier** \,balə'di(ə)r, -iə\ *n* -S [¹*ballad* + *-eer*, *-ier*] **:** a singer of ballads ⟨guitar-strumming ~*s*⟩

ballade royal \-'-'rȯiəl; bȧlȧdrwäyȧl\ *n, pl* **ballade royals** \-əlz,-ȧl\ [ME *balade royal*, fr. MF, royal ballade] **:** a ballade having its stanzas usu. in rhyme royal

ballad horn *n* **:** a circular althorn

bal·lad·ic \bə'ladik, (')ba¦l-\ *adj* **:** of or relating to a ballad

bal·lad·ist \-dəst\ *n* -S **:** one who writes or sings ballads

ballad meter *n* **:** the meter common in English ballads consisting chiefly of iambic lines of 7 accents each arranged in rhymed pairs and usu. printed as the 4-line ballad stanza

balladmonger \'==,==\ *n* **1 :** a seller or composer of ballads **2 :** a poor or inferior poet

balladmongering \'==,=(=)=\ *n* **1 :** the selling or composing of ballads **2 :** the composing of popular verse having little or no artistic value

ballad opera *n* **:** a theatrical entertainment consisting of folk melodies and popular airs with new texts interspersed with spoken dialogue

bal·lad·ry \'baladrē, -ri\ *n* -ES **1 :** the art or practice of ballad singing **2 :** BALLADS ⟨the ~ of Scotland⟩

ballad stanza *n* **:** a verse stanza common in English ballads that consists of 2 lines in ballad meter usu. printed as a 4-line stanza with lines 1 and 3 of 4 accents each unrhymed and with lines 2 and 4 of 3 accents each rhymed

bal·la·hoo *or* **bal·la·hou** \¦balə¦hü\ *n* -S [Sp *balahú*] **1 :** a schooner of Bermuda and the West Indies having its foremast raking forward and mainmast aft **2 :** a lubberly untrim ship

ball alley *n* [¹*ball*] **:** ¹ALLEY 2a

bal·lam \bə'läm\ *n* -S [Malayalam *vaḷḷam*] **:** a canoe of the Malabar coast

bal·lan *or* **ballan wrasse** *also* **bal·len wrasse** \'balən-\ *n* -S [origin unknown] **:** a European wrasse (*Labrus bergylta*)

ball and chain *n, pl* **balls and chains** [so called fr. the ball and chain stereotypically attached to prisoners' legs to prevent escape] **1 :** something that severely restricts one's activity usu. oppressively ⟨marriage, intended to enslave woman, was also a *ball and chain* for man —H.M.Parshley⟩ ⟨his aristocratic birth proved a *ball and chain* throughout his life⟩ **2** *slang* **:** WIFE ⟨this is a book for females, but if any male can get the *ball and chain* to read it, maybe the skillets won't fly so fast —Burton Rascoe⟩

ball-and-claw foot *n* **:** CLAW-AND-BALL FOOT

ball-and-socket joint *n* **:** a joint in which a ball moves within a socket so as to admit of rotary motion in every direction within certain limits (as the hip joint) — called also *ball joint*

ball-and-socket joint (with part of socket cut away)

bal·lant \'balənt\ *n* -S [by alter.] *chiefly Scot* **:** BALLAD

bal·las \'baləs\ *n, pl* **ballas** [prob. fr. Pg *balas*, pl. of *bala*, lit., ball, bullet, fr. It *palla*, of Gmc origin; akin to OHG *balla* ball — more at BALL] **:** a nearly spherical aggregate of diamond grains having a radial or granular structure and used as an industrial diamond because of a toughness that is due to the lack of throughgoing cleavage planes

¹bal·last \'baləst\ *n* -S [prob. fr. LG, of Scand origin; akin to Dan & Sw *barlast*, lit., mere load, fr. *bar* bare (fr. ODan & OSw) + *last* load, fr. MLG; akin to ON *berr* bare and to OHG *hlast* load — more at BARE, LAST] **1 :** a relatively heavy substance used to maintain a ship at its proper draft or trim or to improve its stability (as rock stowed in holds or water in tanks) **2 :** something that gives stability or weight esp. in character, conduct, ideas, or morals ⟨it is profitable for cultures to carry a considerable degree of ~ in the shape of consistency and continuity —A.L.Kroeber⟩ **3 :** something heavy (as sand or water) put into the car of a balloon to be thrown out if necessary to reduce the load **4 a :** gravel or broken stone laid in a roadbed esp. of a railroad to provide a firm surface for the track, to hold the track in line, and to facilitate drainage **b :** the larger solids (as broken stone or gravel) used in making concrete — compare ³AGGREGATE 3b **5 :** a resistance used to stabilize the current in a circuit (as of an arc lamp, a mercury-vapor lamp, or a fluorescent lamp) **6 :** ROUGHAGE — **in ballast** *of a ship* **:** with only ballast as a load

²ballast \"\ *vt* -ED/-ING/-S **1 :** to steady or equip with ballast ⟨~ a canoe with large rocks⟩ **2** *archaic* **:** weight down **:** BURDEN, LOAD **3 a :** to steady or stabilize in mind, morals, or conduct ⟨a little security to ~ your life⟩ **b :** to act as a counterpoise to ⟨some common sense to ~ the general flightiness of the group⟩ **4 :** to fill in (as a railroad bed) with ballast

syn see STABILIZE

bal·last·age \-ij\ *n* -S [¹*ballast* + *-age*] **:** a toll paid for the privilege of taking up ballast in a port or harbor

ballast car *n* **:** a freight car (as for carrying ballast) that may be unloaded from the side or bottom

ballast engine *n* **:** a steam engine used in excavating and for digging and raising stones and gravel for ballast

ballast fin *n* **:** a fin-shaped metal extension of the keel of a yacht that acts as ballast **:** FIN KEEL

ballasting *n* -S [¹*ballast* + *-ing*] **:** material used for ballast

ballast line *n* **:** the water line of a ship in ballast

ballast master *n* **:** a harbor official who sees that ships take on and discharge ballast according to regulations

ballast port *n* **:** a large port in the side of a ship for taking in or discharging ballast

ballast pump *n* **:** a pump for discharging water ballast

ballast tank *n* **:** a tank in the hold of a ship that can be pumped full of or free from water ballast

bal·lat \'balət\ *archaic var of* BALLAD

bal·la·ta \bə'läd·ə\ *n, pl* **bal·la·te** \-ä,tā\ [It, fr. OIt, fr. OProv *balada* — more at BALLAD] **:** a medieval Italian song accompanied by or alternated with dancing and having stanzas and refrain alternating

ball-bank indicator *n* **:** a bank indicator consisting of a slightly curved tube in which a ball remains centered while the airplane is flying straight and level or while the airplane is making a properly banked turn

ball bat *n* **:** a baseball bat

ball bearing *n* **1 a :** a bearing in which the journal turns upon loose hardened steel balls that roll easily in a race and thus convert sliding friction into rolling friction **b :** any of the balls in such a bearing **2 :** a bearing in which the disk of a watt-hour meter is mounted on a vertical shaft that rotates with minimized friction because of rolling action on a single steel ball between cupped jewels

ball boy *n* [¹*ball*] **:** a tennis court attendant who retrieves balls for the players

ball breaker *n* **:** SKULL CRACKER

ball cactus *n* **:** a low tuberculated cactus (*Neobessya missouriensis*) having short spines and predominantly yellow flowers and resembling a ball

ballcarrier \'=,==\ *n* **:** the football player carrying the ball in an offensive play

ball cartridge *n* **:** a general-purpose cartridge having a ball, a primer, and a full charge of powder

ball change *n* **:** a quick change of weight from the ball of one foot to the other in ballroom and tap dancing

ball-check valve *n* **:** a ball valve in which the ball is pushed against or away from its seat by fluid pressure opposed to the action of a spring

ball clay *n* [fr. its formation into balls for transport from the mines] **:** a very plastic high-firing clay that fires white to light buff and is used esp. to give plasticity to clayware bodies containing short clays

ball clover *n* **:** any of certain clovers with globular flower heads (as cluster clover)

ball club *n* **1 :** a club or professional organization whose main purpose is the support and building up of a baseball team **2 :** a team of ballplayers; *esp* **:** a baseball team

ball cock *n* **:** a float valve with a spherical float — called also *ball valve*

ball dahlia *n* **:** any of a class of dahlias having globular flower heads usu. more than three inches in diameter — compare POMPON 2c

balldress \'=,=\ *n* [³*ball* + *dress*] **1** *Brit* **:** a suit or dress worn on official or formal occasions **2** *Brit* **:** formal attire

balled *past of* BALL

ballen wrasse *var of* BALLAN

ball·er \'bȯlə(r)\ *n* -S **1 :** one that makes something into balls: as **a :** a warper who balls the warp **b :** *or* **baller-out** \¦==¦=\ **:** BATTER 2a (1) **2 :** a laundry worker who irons parts of garments that cannot be ironed on a flat press or with a hand iron by moving them back and forth over heated metal forms — called also *puffer*

bal·le·ri·na \,balə'rēnə\ *n* -S [It, fr. *ballare* to dance, fr. LL — more at BALL] **1 a :** a female ballet dancer **:** DANSEUSE **b :** PRIMA BALLERINA **2 :** a lightweight flexible slipper with a very low heel for street and evening wear by women — compare BALLET SLIPPER

¹bal·let \'balət\ *n* -S [alter. of ¹*ballad*] **1** *dial* **:** BALLAD 3 **2** *also* **bal·lett** \"\ **:** BALLAD 2

²bal·let \'ba,lā, ba'lā *sometimes* bə'lā *or* 'ba,la *or* 'balē *or* 'bali\ *n* -S [F, fr. It *balletto*, dim. of *ballo* dance, fr. *ballare* to dance, fr. LL — more at BALL] **1 :** artistic dancing in which conventionalized poses and steps are combined with light and flowing figures and movements (as leaps and turns) ⟨a lesson in ~ usu. includes exercises in balancing⟩ **2 a :** a theatrical art form by which ballet dancing together with music, scenery, costume, and sometimes pantomime or speech conveys a story, theme, or atmosphere to the audience **b :** a theatrical performance of the ballet art form ⟨attend the ~⟩ **c :** a musical score for such a performance **d :** the script for a ballet performance ⟨the microfilm copy of a ~⟩ **e :** a performance resembling a ballet (as by a troupe of ice skaters or trapeze artists) **3 :** a company of persons who perform ballets ⟨the New York City *Ballet*⟩ **4 :** BALLET SLIPPER

ballet blanc \¦=(,)='blän, =¦='=\ *n, pl* **ballets blancs** \-āz'blän, -ēz'-,-iz'-; -ā'blän(z), -ē'-,-i'-\ [F, lit., white ballet] **:** a ballet in which the ballerinas wear white skirts

ballet bouffe \-'büf\ *n, pl* **ballets bouffes** \-āz'büf, -ēz'-,-iz'-; -ā'büf(s), -ē'-,-i'-\ [F] **:** a comic ballet usu. with stock characters

bal·let d'ac·tion \bȧlādȧksyōn\ *n, pl* **ballets d'action** \"\ [F] **:** a ballet with a plot

ballet girl *pronunc at* ²BALLET +,-\ *n* **:** a female ballet dancer

bal·let·ic \(')ba¦led·ik\ *adj* [²*ballet* + *-ic*] **:** of, typical of, relating to, resembling, or suitable for ballet — **bal·let·i·cal·ly** \-d·ək(ə)lē\ *adv*

ballet leg *n* **:** a synchronized group-swimming stunt in which from a starting back floating position with legs extended one knee is drawn to the chest, the leg is then extended vertically, the knee then bent, and the leg then returned to the starting position

ballet master *n* [²*ballet*] **:** a man who directs, trains, and sometimes acts as choreographer for a ballet company

ballet mistress *n* [²*ballet*] **:** a woman who directs, trains, and sometimes acts as choreographer for a ballet company

bal·let·o·mane \ba'led·ə,mān, bə-\ *n* -S [*ballet* + *-o-* + *-mane* (fr. *mania*)] **:** one who takes extraordinary delight in ballets

bal·leto·mania \=¦==+\ *n* [²*ballet* + *-o-* + *mania*] **:** extraordinary enthusiasm for ballets

ballet slipper *or* **ballet shoe** *n* [²*ballet*] **1 :** a slipper without a heel made usu. of kid or fabric, often reinforced in the toe, and worn by ballet dancers **2 :** a woman's shoe for street or evening wear resembling a ballet slipper

ball fern *n* **:** a feathery fern (*Davallia bullata*) of tropical Asia and Malaya cultivated chiefly in fern balls that its creeping rhizomes help to form

ball-flower \'=,=\ *n* **:** an ornament characteristic of 13th century English Gothic architecture consisting of a ball placed in the hollow of a circular flower and usu. inserted in a hollow molding

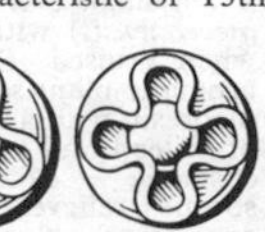

ball-flowers

ball foot *n* **:** a large turned foot often found on 17th-century case furniture — see BUN FOOT, MELON FOOT, TURNIP FOOT; FOOT illustration

ball fringe *n* **:** a decorative fringe (as for upholstery, curtains, or clothing) made with covered balls or yarn balls hanging at even intervals along one edge

ball game *n* **:** a game played with a ball; *esp* **:** a baseball game

ball governor *n* [¹*ball*] **:** a governor that operates by the centrifugal force of revolving balls

ball handler *n* **:** one who controls the ball in a ball game (as basketball or football) — **ball handling** *n*

ball hawk *n* **1 :** one skillful in taking the ball away from opponents (as in basketball or football) **2 :** a fielder in baseball skilled in catching fly balls — **ball hawking** *n*

ballhooter \'=,==\ *n* **:** a logger who rolls logs down slopes too steep for teams — called also *brutter*

ballibuntl *var of* BALIBUNTAL

ballies *pl of* BALLY

¹bal·ling \'bōliŋ, 'bäl-, -lēŋ\ *adj, usu cap* [*Balling* (*scale*)] **1 :** according to a Balling scale ⟨a sugar solution of 19° *Balling*⟩ **2 :** calibrated in accordance with a Balling scale ⟨a *Balling* hydrometer⟩

²balling \"\ *n* -S *usu cap* **:** concentration in percent by weight of a soluble solid (as sugar) according to a Balling scale ⟨the *Balling* of a syrup⟩

ball·ing furnace \'bȯl-\ *n* **:** PUDDLING FURNACE

ball·ing iron *or* **balling gun** \"\ *n* **:** a long metal instrument with a cup-shaped depression at one end for placing solid medicine in the form of a ball or cylinder in the posterior part of the mouth of a horse or ox so that it will have to be swallowed whole

bal·ling scale \'bȯl-,'bäl-\ *n, usu cap B* [after Karl J. N. *Balling* †1868 Ger. chemist] **:** a hydrometer scale that registers the percentage by weight of soluble solids in a solution (as sugar in grape juice or wine), one degree on the scale being equal to one percent

bal·lism \'ba,lizəm\ *or* **bal·lis·mus** \ba'lizməs\ *n, pl* **ballisms** *or* **ballismuses** [NL *ballismus*, fr. Gk *ballismos* dance, act of jumping about, fr. *ballizein* to dance, jump about, fr. *ballein* to throw] **:** the abnormal swinging jerking movements sometimes seen in chorea

bal·lis·ta \bə'listə *also* ba-\ *also* **ba·lis·ta** \"\ *n, pl* **ballis·tae** \-,tē, -,tī\ *also* **ballistas** \-,təz\ *or* **balis·tae** \-,tē, -,tī\ *or* **bali·stas** \-,təz\ [L, fr. (assumed) Gk *ballistas* or *ballistēs*, fr. *ballein* to throw — more at DEVIL] **:** an ancient military engine often in the form of a crossbow for hurling large missiles

bal·lis·ter \'baləstə(r)\ *n* -S [by alter.] **:** BALUSTER

bal·lis·tic \bə'listik, -ēk *also* ba-\ *adj* [L *ballista* + E *-ic*] **1 :** of or belonging to the hurling of missiles ⟨the ~ power of a crossbow⟩ **2 :** of or relating to ballistics or to a body in motion when the characteristics of such motion are determined by the laws of ballistics **3 :** belonging to or actuated by a sudden impulse (as that due to an electric discharge) — **bal·lis·ti·cal·ly** \-tək(ə)lē, -tēk-, -li\ *adv*

ballistic cap *n* **:** a hollow metal cap placed over an armor-piercing cap to continue the ogival curve of the head of the projectile and reduce the resistance to the air

ballistic coefficient *n* **:** a constant in ballistics that represents the efficiency of a projectile in overcoming air resistance

ballistic galvanometer *n* **:** a moving-coil galvanometer that indicates the presence of an electric charge by the single impulse imparted to the coil by a sudden brief current, the quantity of electricity that passes being proportionate to the first deflection of the coil

bal·lis·ti·cian \,balə'stishən\ *n* -S [fr. *ballistics*, after such pairs as E *statistics: statistician*] **:** an authority on or one versed in ballistics; *esp* **:** a member of a police force who studies the evidence and determines the facts relating to the use of firearms in criminal cases

ballistic missile *n* **:** a guided missile designed to fly roughly in the high-arch trajectory of a true ballistic object, self-powered for most of its ascent and guided in the ascending part of its flight but becoming a free-falling object in descent

ballistic pendulum *n* **:** a pendulum with a bifilarly suspended bob that retains objects striking it and registers the amplitude of the swing caused by the impact, the velocity of the object (as a rifle bullet) penetrating the bob being computed by application of the principles of conservation of momentum and energy — compare GUN PENDULUM

bal·lis·tics \bə'listiks, -ēks *also* ba-\ *n pl* **1 a** *usu sing in constr* **:** the science of the motion of powder-propelled projectiles in flight — compare EXTERIOR BALLISTICS, INTERIOR BALLISTICS **b** *sometimes sing in constr* **:** the characteristics of flight of a projectile **c** *sometimes sing in constr* **:** the firing characteristics of a firearm or cartridge **2** *usu sing in constr* **:** the cardiac movements involved in the forcing of blood into the arteries and the bodily recoil movements that maintain adjustment within the body

bal·lis·tite \'balə,stīt\ *n* -S [fr. *Ballistite*, a trademark] **:** a smokeless powder consisting essentially of soluble cellulose nitrates and nitroglycerin approximately in equal parts

bal·lis·to·cardiogram \bə¦li(,)stō, ba-+\ *n* -S [*ballistic* + *-o-* + *cardiogram*] **:** the record made by a ballistocardiograph

bal·lis·to·cardiograph \"+\ *n* -S [*ballistic* + *-o-* + *cardiograph*] **:** a device for measuring the amount of blood passing through the heart in a specified time by recording the recoil movements of the body that result from contraction of heart muscle in ejecting blood from the ventricles — **bal·lis·to·cardiographic** \"+\ *adj* — **bal·lis·to·cardiography** \"+\ *n*

bal·lis·to·spore \bə'listə,spō(ə)r\ *n* -S [L *ballista* + E *-o-* + *-spore* — more at BALLISTA] **:** one of the spores borne on sterigmata of certain fungi and forcibly discharged at maturity

bal·li·um \'balēəm\ *n* -S [ML, fr. ME *baile* — more at BAIL (outer wall)] **:** BAILEY

ball·iz·ing \'bȯ,līziŋ\ *n* -S [fr. gerund of *ballize*, fr. ¹*ball* + *-ize*] **:** the process of sizing and surface-finishing a hole by pressing a hardened steel ball through it

ball joint *n* **:** BALL-AND-SOCKET JOINT

ball jointing *n* **:** concentric joints in homogeneous rock

ball lightning *n* **:** an extremely rare form of lightning consisting of highly luminous balls that move with moderate speed and usu. disappear without an explosion

ball mill *n* **:** a pulverizing machine consisting of a hollow drum that contains material to be pulverized along with pebbles or heavy steel balls and sometimes also water or some other liquid and that is revolved or agitated so that the pebbles or balls crush the material as they roll about

ball-mill *vt* **:** to pulverize in a ball mill

ball moss *n* **:** an epiphytic plant (*Tillandsia recurvata*) of the southern U. S. that often grows in compact masses

ball mustard *n* **:** a yellow-flowered European plant (*Neslia paniculata*) of the family Cruciferae having globose seed pods and being adventive in eastern No. America

ball nettle *n* **:** HORSE NETTLE

ball nut *n* **:** a nut having ball bearings that run (as in a ball race) between its threads and those of the screw it engages

bal·lock \'bälik, -ēk,-ək\ *n* -S [ME *ballok*, fr. OE *beallucs* — more at BALL] **:** TESTIS — usu. considered vulgar

ball of fire **:** a person of unusual energy, vitality, or drive esp. manifest in speed of accomplishment ⟨no mental *ball of fire*, but a few things quickly become clear to her —*Time*⟩

bal·lo·gan \'bäl(ə)gən\ *n* -S [ScGael *bolgan*, dim. of *bolg* bag, swelling, pimple; akin to OE *belg* bag, skin — more at BELLY] **:** NIPPLEWORT

bal·lon *also* **ba·lon** \ba'lōn\ *n* -S [F *ballon*, lit., balloon] **:** the lightness of movement that allows a ballet dancer to appear to remain in the air unusually long during a jump **:** BUOYANCY

bal·lon d'es·sai \bȧlōndāsā\ *n, pl* **ballons d'essai** \"\ [F] **:** TRIAL BALLOON

bal·lo·net *or* **bal·lon·net** \¦balə¦nā\ *n* -S [F *ballonnet*, dim. of *ballon*] **:** a gas-tight compartment of variable volume within the interior of a balloon or airship used for controlling its ascent or descent and for maintaining pressure on the outer envelope so as to prevent deformation and kept inflated under the control of valves by a blower or by the action of wind caught in an air scoop

bal·lon·né \¦balə¦nā\ *n* -S [F, fr. *ballon*] **:** a wide circular jump in ballet with a battement

¹bal·loon \bə'lün\ *n* -S [It dial. *ballone* (It *pallone*), aug. of It dial. *balla*, of Gmc origin; akin to OHG *balla* ball — more at BALL] **1 a** (1) **:** a large inflated leather ball used in a now obsolete sport that involved striking and kicking the ball back and forth (2) **:** the game formerly played with such a ball **b** (1) **:** a bag of silk or other tough light material shaped usu. like a sphere, made nonporous, and filled with heated air or a gas lighter than air **:** an aerostat without a propelling system — see FREE BALLOON, KITE BALLOON, PILOT BALLOON, SOUNDING BALLOON (2) **:** a small-necked inflatable bag of thin usu. gaily colored rubber used as a toy ⟨held a bright red ~⟩ **2 :** something resembling a balloon in contour, buoyancy, inflation, or insubstantiality: as **a** *obs* **:** a fireworks shell **b :** BALL 1j **c :** a spherical glass vessel usu. with a short neck (as a receiver) or with a stopcock

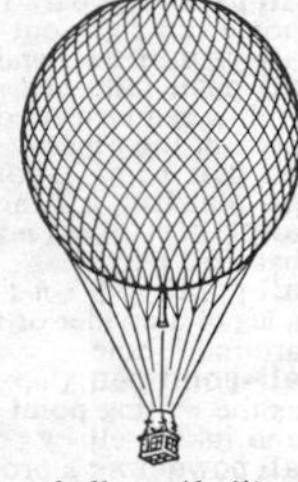

balloon 1b (1)

for use in weighing gases **d** : an area (as of a cartoon) in which presumed spoken words are printed or thoughts represented typically having a rounded outline and being connected with the speaker's or thinker's mouth by a single line **e** : BALLOON TIRE **f** (1) : the ball-shaped mass of yarn strands produced in the mechanical spinning, twisting, or winding of thread as the strands pass between a guide and the revolving spool on which they are wound (2) : a revolving cylindrical reel used in woolen warp drying **g** *or* **balloon glass** : SNIFTER **3 a** : outward appearance : SHOW, DISPLAY ⟨punctured their ~ of confidence —Speed Lamkin⟩ **b** : a poorly substantiated or shallow attitude, belief, or assumption ⟨dogmatists who take delight in shooting ~*s* and asking a man for proofs —Van Wyck Brooks⟩

²balloon \"\ *vb* -ED/-ING/-S *vt* **1** : to cause to assume a smooth rounded form by or as if by inflation : DISTEND ⟨a sudden breeze ~*ing* the spinnaker⟩ ⟨he ~*ed* his cheeks in imitation of a fat lady⟩ **2** : to increase or augment usu. beyond what is average, normal, or expected ⟨a lusty increase in European consumption helped ~ prices —*Wall Street Jour.*⟩ ~ *vi* **1 a** : to ascend or travel in a balloon ⟨in 1935 he had ~*ed* to a world's altitude record —*Time*⟩ **b** : to rise abruptly and become fully airborne in an airplane after the initial landing impact **c** *of a young spider* : to travel through the air supported by a strand of silk that catches the wind **2 a** : to swell out into a smoothly rounded surface : belly out ⟨the curtains ~*ing* in the morning breeze⟩ **b** : to issue or burst forth in or as if in rounded distended form ⟨the fat mushroom of smoke that ~*ed* out of the mouth of the English chase guns —Frank Yerby⟩ ⟨magniloquent phrases ~ from his lips —Neville Cardus⟩ **3** : to increase rapidly ⟨clerical costs ~*ed* . . . in every department of business —*Newsweek*⟩ : grow suddenly and beyond average proportion or normal expectation ⟨the church's enrollment has ~*ed* 130% —*Time*⟩ — sometimes used with *out* or *up* ⟨houses in fashionable architectural styles ~*ed* up and expired in endless succession —T.H.Robsjohn-Gibbings⟩ ⟨the young republic ~*ed* out to its present proportions in a few decades⟩

³balloon \"\ *adj* **1** : of, relating to, resembling, or suggesting a balloon esp. in contour or silhouette ⟨a ~ sleeve⟩ ⟨a ~ figure⟩ ⟨a ~ sail⟩ **2** *of cargo* : consisting of light bulky goods **3** : having a final installment that is much larger than preceding ones in a term or installment loan ⟨a ~ note⟩ ⟨a ~ payment mortgage⟩

balloon back *n* : a chair back of rounded outline

balloon barrage *n* : a screen of balloons moored to the ground as a barrage against enemy airplanes

balloonberry \ˈ=ˌ==\ *n* : STRAWBERRY RASPBERRY

balloon cloth *or* **balloon fabric** *n* : a fine strong cloth of plain weave made usu. of cotton and used primarily with special finishes for balloons and airplanes

bal·loon·er \bəˈlünə(r)\ *n* -S : BALLOON SAIL

balloon feather *n* : an arrow vane with convex outline

balloonfish \ˈ=ˌ=\ *n* [so called fr. its ability to distend its body] : GLOBEFISH

balloonflower \ˈ=ˌ=\ *n* : an Asiatic plant (*Platycodon grandiflorum*) with showy corollas like balloons — called also *bellflower, Chinese bellflower*

balloon fly *n* : a small fly (family Empididae) in whose courtship ritual the male presents the female with food supported by a silken balloon

balloon foresail *or* **balloon jib** *n* : a large sail set usu. between the fore-topmast head and the end of the bowsprit or jib boom with the clew led abaft the foremast — compare BALLOON SAIL

balloon frame *also* **balloon framing** *n* **1** : a frame for a building constructed of small members nailed together instead of heavy timbers joined by mortises and tenons — compare BRACED FRAME **2** : construction utilizing the balloon frame

ballooning *pres part of* BALLOON

bal·loon·ist \bəˈlünəst\ *n* -S : one that ascends in a balloon (as for exhibition purposes)

balloons *pl of* BALLOON, *pres 3d sing of* BALLOON

balloon sail *n* : a large light sail (as a spinnaker) set in addition to or in place of an ordinary light sail esp. by yachts in moderate weather

balloon tire *n* : a pneumatic tire with a light flexible carcass and large cross section designed to provide cushioning through a large volume of air at low pressure

balloon trawl *n* : a trawl designed to skim over rather than thoroughly drag the bottom

balloon vine *n* : a cultivated vine (*Cardiospermum halicacabum*) introduced into northern No. America from tropical America and bearing numerous large ornamental bladdery pods

¹bal·lot \ˈbalət, *usu* -əd·+V\ *n* -S [It *ballotta*, fr. It dial., dim. of *balla* ball — more at BALLOON] **1 a** : a small ball dropped into a box or urn in secret voting **b** : a ticket or sheet of paper (as one printed with the candidates' names or the proposition to be voted on) used to cast a secret vote (as during public elections) — see AUSTRALIAN BALLOT **2 a** : the action or system of secret voting by the use of ballots or by any device for casting or recording votes (as a voting machine) **b** : the right to vote in such a way **c** : ¹VOTE 1a **3** : the whole number of votes cast at an election **4** : the drawing of lots

²ballot \"\ *vb* -ED/-ING/-S [It *ballottare*, fr. *ballotta*] *vi* : to vote or decide by ballot ⟨~ for a candidate⟩ ⟨~ against a referendum⟩ ⟨the ~*ing* continued until eight in the evening⟩ ~ *vt* **1** : to obtain a vote from (a body of voters) ⟨~ the men on the proposal⟩ **2** : to select by ballot or by the drawing of lots ⟨~ all able-bodied men for service in the army⟩

bal·lo·ta \bəˈlōd·ə\ *n*, *cap* [NL, alter. of L *ballote* black horehound, fr. Gk *ballōtē*] : a genus of plants (family Labiatae) having small bracteate flowers in axillary clusters — see BLACK HOREHOUND

bal·lo·tade \ˌbaləˈtād, -ād\ *n* -S [F *ballottade*, fr. *ballotter* to toss (fr. *ballotte* small ball, fr. It dial. *ballotta*) + *-ade* — more at BALLOT] : a forward leap performed by a horse trained in manège in which fore and hind legs are gathered under the body and the hind hoofs are turned outward so that the shoes are visible

bal·lo·tage \ˌbaləˈtäzh\ *n* -S [F *ballottage*, fr. *ballotter* to subject to a second ballot, lit., shake, toss + *-age*] : a second ballot taken to decide between the two or three highest candidates when no candidate receives a majority of the votes on the first ballot

ballot box *n* **1** : a box for receiving ballots **2** : the system or practice of secret voting : ¹BALLOT 2

bal·lot·ta·ble \bəˈläd·əbəl, ba-\ *adj* [*ballottement* + *-able*] : identifiable by ballottement

bal·lot·té \ˌbaləˈtā\ *adj* [F, fr. past part. of *ballotter*] *of a leap* : made in ballet with a rocking motion and with the free leg cut out to the side

bal·lotte·ment \bəˈlätmənt, ba-, F bȧlȯtmäⁿ\ *n* -S [F, lit., act of tossing, shaking, fr. *ballotter* + *-ment*] *med* : a method of determining the presence or absence of a floating object by using the sense of touch: as **a** : the act of pushing up the uterus with a finger inserted below in order to detect pregnancy by feeling the return impact when a fetus displaced in the amniotic fluid sinks back **b** : a similar procedure for diagnosing floating kidney

ballow *n* -S [origin unknown] *obs* : CUDGEL, STICK

ball park *n* : a park in which ball games are played ⟨knocked a home run right out of the *ball park*⟩

ball peen *n* : a hemispherical peen

ball peen hammer *n* : a machinist's hammer having a head with a cylindrical convex-faced surface at one end and a ball peen at the other

ball pen *n* : BALL-POINT PEN

ball planting *n* : the transplanting of balled plants

ballplayer \ˈ=ˌ==\ *n* : one that plays ball; *specif* : a professional baseball player

ball point \ˈ=ˌ=\ *n* : a device like a ball for forming a seat for a leg of a divider or the head of a trammel in describing curves around a hole

ball-point pen \ˈ=ˌ=-\ *also* **ball-point** \ˈ=ˌ=\ *n* : a pen having as the writing point a small steel ball that rotates in its socket and inks itself by contact with an inner magazine of ink

ball powder *n* : a progressive-burning spherical-grained smokeless gunpowder

ball python *n* **1** : a small burrowing Central African snake (*Calabaria reinhardti*) that twists itself into a tight ball when alarmed **2** : a small West African python (*Python regius*) — called also *royal python*

ball race *n* : one of the races in a ball bearing

ball rest *n* : a lathe rest having a circular traverse and a radial feed for turning spherical objects

ballroom \ˈ=ˌ=\ *n* : a large room (as in a hotel) set aside or suitable for dances

ballroom dance *also* **ballroom** *n* : a social dance adapted to the modern ballroom and including couple dances in embrace position (as the fox trot, tango, two-step, waltz), face-to-face jazz dances (as the charleston), and certain folk dances (as the czardas, mazurka, polka, schottische) done usu. for recreation and sometimes for exhibition

balls *pl of* BALL, *pres 3d sing of* BALL

ball sage *n* : BLACK SAGE 3

ball screw *n* : a screw attachable to a ramrod used to extract lead bullets from muzzle-loading guns

ball signal *n* : an object like a ball hoisted manually to the top of a track-side pole in early railroading to indicate that the way was clear for an approaching train — compare HIGHBALL

ball smut *n* : ²BUNT

ball snake *n* : RUBBER BOA

ballstock \ˈ=ˌ=\ *n* [¹*ball* + *stock*] : the handle on a printer's ink ball

ball turret *n* : a usu. retractable gun turret used on large combat aircraft and capable of being rotated so that a gunner may obtain a full circle of fire

¹bal·lup \ˈbaləp\ *n* -S [alter. of earlier *baglap*, fr. ¹*bag* + *lap* (flap of cloth)] *now dial* : a flap resembling a codpiece on the front of the trousers

²ball·up \ˈbȯˌləp\ *n* -S [*ball up*] *slang* : a balled up state of affairs : CONFUSION

ball up *vt* : to make a mess of : CONFUSE, MUDDLE ⟨a mind that could *ball* anything *up*⟩ ⟨my educational routine was so hopelessly *balled up* that my mother made only one more effort to reform me —Elsa Maxwell⟩ ⟨got his signals crossed and hopelessly *balled up* the program⟩ ~ *vi* : to get balled up : become badly muddled or confused ⟨so tired he *balled up* on even simple problems⟩

ball valve *n* **1** : a valve in which a ball fits into a spherical seat and regulates the aperture by its rise and fall due to fluid pressure, to a spring, or to its own weight **2** : BALL COCK

¹bal·ly \ˈbalī\ *adv (or adj)* [euphemism for ³*bloody*] *slang Brit* — used as a mild imprecation and intensifier ⟨he was ~ well sure he was right⟩ ⟨ask the whole ~ lot to . . . dinner —John Buchan⟩

²bal·ly \ˈbalē, -li\ *n* -ES [by shortening] : ¹BALLYHOO 1

³bally \"\ *vt* -ED/-ING/-ES [by shortening] : ²BALLYHOO 1 ⟨a sideshow barker noisily ~*ing* a group of loiterers⟩

bal·ly gum \ˈbälē-\ *n* [by alter.] : BOLLY GUM

bal·ly·hack \ˈbalēˌhak\ *n* [origin unknown] *slang* : HELL, HADES, PERDITION — used especially in the expression *go to ballyhack*

¹bal·ly·hoo \ˈbalēˌhü, -li-\ *n* -S [origin unknown] **1** : an attention-getting demonstration or talk (as by a barker) to arouse interest in an entertainment ⟨a stunt of sticking a trick knife through one arm to attract a crowd and then starting his ~ —F.B.Gipson⟩ **2 a** : publicity characterized by exaggeration, gross flamboyant display, or excessive sensationalism ⟨a good deal of ~ for safer driving⟩ ⟨burlesque . . . election campaign tactics and advertising ~ —W.R.Frye⟩ **b** : empty or false talk : NONSENSE ⟨every face powder must claim a "scientific" uniqueness, and by this ~ millions are impressed —Ruth Benedict⟩ ⟨this claim cannot be dismissed as mere . . . ~ —L.G.Pine⟩ **syn** see PUBLICITY

²ballyhoo \" *sometimes* ˌ==ˈ=\ *vt* **ballyhooed; ballyhooed; ballyhooing; ballyhoos 1** : to direct ballyhoo at ⟨~ the crowd with songs and speeches⟩ ⟨~ the public with false advertising⟩ **2** : to drum up interest in by means of ballyhoo : PUBLICIZE ⟨gladiatorial meets were ~*ed* on the walls of ancient Rome —*Dun's Rev.*⟩ ⟨new cars carry on their bodies a shield or some such insigne ~*ing* the dealer from whom they were bought —*New Yorker*⟩

³bal·ly·hoo *also* **bal·ly·hu** \ˈbalēˌhü, -li-\ *n* -S [by folk etymology fr. AmerSp *balajú*] : HALFBEAK; *esp* : either of two common tropical American halfbeaks (*Hemiramphus brasiliensis* and *Hyporamphus unifasciatus*) much used for bait

bally platform *n* : a platform at a carnival or sideshow on which a barker stands

ballyrag *var of* BULLYRAG

¹balm \ˈbä|m, ˈbȧ| *also* |lm; *sporadic & archaic* ˈbam\ *n* -S [ME *baume, basme*, fr. OF *basme*, fr. L *balsamum* balsam, fr. Gk *balsamon*, prob. of Sem origin; akin to Heb *bāsām* spice, balsam] **1** : any of several balsamic resins; *esp* : the resinous and aromatic exudation from trees of the genus *Commiphora* **2** : an aromatic preparation: as **a** : a healing ointment ⟨his hands were covered with blisters . . . doctored with some smelly iodine ~ —Vicki Baum⟩ **b** *obs* : an oil or ointment for anointing **3** : any of various aromatic plants: as **a** : a plant of the genus *Melissa*; *esp* : LEMON BALM **b** : a plant of the genus *Monarda*; *esp* : OSWEGO TEA **4** : a spicy odor : an agreeably pungent or aromatic redolence ⟨the white lilies in the garden, the herb bed near the bees — everything sent out fragrance and ~ into the soft air —Agnes S. Turnbull⟩ **5** : a soothing restorative agency : something that brings comfort and relieves pain ⟨bound up her wound . . . with the ~ of understanding —Josephine Pinckney⟩ ⟨friendship is . . . the finest ~ for the pangs of disappointed love —Jane Austen⟩ **6** : a sticky resinous substance used by honey bees to varnish the inside of certain cells in the hive before eggs are laid in them — compare PROPOLIS

²balm \"\ *vt* -ED/-ING/-S [ME *baumen*, fr. *baume*, n.] **1** *obs* : to anoint esp. with balm **2** : SOOTHE, ALLEVIATE ⟨~ one's injured feelings⟩

bal·ma·caan \ˌbalməˈkan, -aa(ə)n *sometimes* -än *or* -ȧn\ *n* -S [fr. *Balmacaan*, estate near Inverness, Scot.] : a loose boxy overcoat made orig. of rough woolens and with raglan sleeves, a short turnover collar, and a closing that may be buttoned to the throat ⟨a ~ collar⟩ — called also *bal*

bal mas·qué \bȧlmȧskā\ *n*, *pl* **bals masqués** \"\ [F] : a masked ball

balm cricket *n* [by folk etymology fr. *baum-cricket*, part trans. of G *baumgrille*, fr. *baum* tree (fr. OHG *boum*) + *grille* cricket — more at BEAM] : CICADA

balm·i·ly *pronunc at* ¹BALM + əlē, -li\ *adv* : in a balmy manner

balm·i·ness *pronunc at* ¹BALM + -ēnəs, -in-\ *n* -ES [*balmy* + *-ness*] : the quality or state of being balmy ⟨the ~ of the warm summer air⟩

balm of gil·ead \-ˈgilēəd, -lyəd, -lē,ad\ *usu cap G* [fr. *Gilead*, region of ancient Palestine known for its "balm" (Jer 8:22)] **1** : a small evergreen African and Asian tree (*Commiphora meccanensis*) with leaves that yield a strong aromatic odor when bruised **2** *also* **balm in gilead a** : any of several aromatic plant secretions; *esp* : a fragrant yellow or greenish oleoresin with a somewhat bitter taste obtained from the balm of Gilead and valued esp. in biblical times as an unguent and cosmetic — called also *Mecca balsam* **b** : an agency that soothes, relieves, or heals **3** : a fragrant herb (*Dracocephalum canariense*) **4** : BALSAM FIR 1 **5** : either of two poplars: **a** : a hybrid northern tree (*Populus gileadensis*) used in cultivation and differing from the balsam poplar in having broadly cordate leaves that are pubescent esp. on the under side **b** : BALSAM POPLAR

bal·mo·ny \ˈba(l)mənē\ *n* -ES [origin unknown] : a turtlehead (*Chelone glabra*)

bal·mor·al \balˈmȯrəl, -mär-\ *n* -S [fr. *Balmoral* Castle, Aberdeen, Scot.] **1** : a boot or shoe that is laced in front; *esp* : an oxford shoe with quarters meeting and centered over a separate tongue — called also *bal* **2** *usu cap* : a round flat cap with a top projecting all around, somewhat resembling a tam-o'-shanter, and worn esp. in Scotland

balmy *pronunc at* ¹BALM +ē, i\ *adj* -ER/-EST [¹*balm* + *-y*] **1 a** : having the soothing, healing, or aromatic qualities of balm or suggesting those attributed to balm ⟨the first ~ presage of this repose —Laurence Sterne⟩ ⟨~ flowery vegetation —John Muir †1914⟩ ⟨a ~ medicinal syrup⟩ **b** : MILD ⟨the ~ breeze of morning —T.L.Peacock⟩ ⟨a pleasant ~ climate⟩ **2** [alter. of BARMY] : FOOLISH, SILLY, INSANE ⟨with weather so cold, one would be ~ to think of going swimming⟩ ⟨the country has gone slightly ~ —G.A.Parks⟩ **syn** see SOFT

balne- *or* **balneo-** *comb form* [L *balne-*, fr. *balneum* bath — more at BAGNIO] : bath : bathing ⟨*balneal*⟩ ⟨*balneotherapy*⟩

bal·ne·al \ˈbalnēəl\ *or* **bal·ne·ary** \-ē,erē\ *adj* [L *balneum* bath + E *-al, -ary*] : of or relating to a bath, bathing, or a bathroom ⟨the *balneal* reek of grim-tiled lavatories —William Sansom⟩ ⟨not . . . the slightest sign of the presence of *balneary* appurtenances in bedrooms; not even of ewers, lavers, and basins, nor of pails and tubs —E.V.Mitchell⟩

bal·ne·a·tion \ˌbalnēˈāshən\ *n* -S [LL *balneatus* (past part. of *balneare* to bathe, fr. L *balneum* bath) + E *-ion*] : the act or action of bathing

bal·neo·log·ic \ˌbalnēəˈläjik\ *or* **bal·neo·log·i·cal** \-jəkəl\ *adj* : of or relating to balneology

bal·ne·ol·o·gist \ˌbalnēˈäləjəst\ *n* -S : an expert in balneology

bal·ne·ol·o·gy \-jē\ *n* -ES [ISV *balne-* + *-logy*] : the science of the therapeutic application of baths esp. with natural mineral waters

bal·neo-therapy *also* **bal·neo·therapeutics** \ˌbalnēō +\ *n* [ISV *balne-* + *-therapy, -therapeutics*] : the treatment of disease by baths

balochi *or* **baloch** *usu cap, var of* BALUCHI

ba·lo·ghia \bəˈlōgēə\ *n*, *cap* [NL, fr. Joseph *Balogh*, 19th cent Hung. botanist + NL *-ia*] : a small genus of Australasian trees and shrubs (family Euphorbiaceae) with opposite-stalked leaves and small dioecious flowers — see BLOODWOOD a(2)

balon *var of* BALLON

¹ba·lo·ney \bəˈlōnē, -ni\ *var of* BOLOGNA

²baloney \"\ *n* -S [alter. of ²*bologna*] *slang* : pretentious nonsense : something false or insincere : BUNKUM — often a generalized expression of disagreement ⟨everything he says is just plain ~⟩ ⟨forget this ~ about temperament and concentrate more on the game —Jack Crawford⟩

bal·op \ˈbaˌläp\ *n* -S [short for *balopticon*] **1** : a balopticon for projecting images into a television transmitting apparatus **2** : the slide or card bearing the picture or other visual material for projection by the balop; *also* : the visual material for projection

bal·op·ti·con \baˈläptəˌkän, bə-\ *n* -S [fr. *Balopticon*, a trademark] : a projector that utilizes reflected light for projecting the images of opaque objects

ba·low \baˈlō\ *or* **ba·loo** \-ˈlü\ *n* -S *now chiefly Scot* : LULLABY

bals *pl of* BAL

bal·sa \ˈbȯlsə *also* -äl-\ *n* -S [Sp] **1 a** : a tree (*Ochroma lagopus*) of Central America, the West Indies, and northern So. America with wood that is lighter than cork but strong and used esp. for floats **b** : the wood of this tree **2** : a Central American, So. American, or Philippine raft made of bundles of grass or reeds lashed together **3** : a life raft made of two cylinders of metal or wood joined by a framework and often used for landing through surf

bal·sam \ˈbȯlsəm\ *n* -S *often attrib* [L *balsamum* — more at BALM] **1 a** : an aromatic substance flowing spontaneously or by incision from a plant and not necessarily remaining liquid **b** (1) : any of various oleoresins (as copaiba and Canada balsam) (2) : any of several resinous substances (as balm of Gilead and benzoin) that contain benzoic or cinnamic acid in addition to resin and usu. essential oil — called also *true balsam* **c** : any of various pharmaceutical preparations containing resinous substances and having a balsamic odor **2** : any of several balsam-yielding trees: as **a** : BALSAM FIR **b** : BALSAM POPLAR **c** : the tree that produces balsam of Tolu **3** : something that heals or soothes ⟨music was ~ to the senses⟩ ⟨the ~ of flattery⟩ **4** : a plant of the genus *Impatiens*; *esp* : GARDEN BALSAM **5** : CYPRESS SPURGE **6** : BALSAMWEED 1

balsam apple *n* **1** : either of two small East Indian ornamental vines of the gourd family (*Momordica balsamina* and *M. charantia*) with red or orange oblong warty fruits extensively naturalized in the West Indies and used sometimes for poultices and for liniments **2** : the fruit of the balsam apple plant

balsam bog *n* **1** : a plant (*Azorella glebaria*) of the Falkland islands and Patagonia that belongs to the carrot family, forms dense woody hillocks often several feet in height, and yields a gum used as a folk remedy **2** : a usu. sphagnous bog in northeastern America containing the balsam fir

balsam bottle *n* : a bottle fitted with a dropper and glass cap to prevent evaporation and exclude dust and used for storing Canada balsam

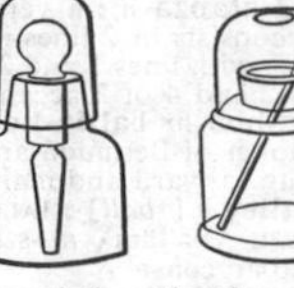
balsam bottles

balsam copaiba *n* : COPAIBA

balsam fig *n* : PITCH APPLE

balsam fir *n* **1** : a medium-sized fir (*Abies balsamea*) that is widely distributed in northeastern No. America, has a rather smooth gray or brown bark with many resin-filled blisters, flat dark green needles with rounded tips, upright purplish cones, and soft weak wood resembling but inferior as lumber to that of the eastern spruce, is the source of Canada balsam, and is much used for pulpwood and for Christmas trees — called also *balm of Gilead*; see TREE illustration **2** : any of certain southern and western firs of the genus *Abies*: as **a** : FRASER FIR **b** : WHITE FIR 1a(1)

balsam-fir sawfly *n* : a greenish sawfly (*Neodiprion abietis*) that is widespread in the northern U.S. and Canada and has larvae which feed on and defoliate various spruces and the balsam fir

balsam herb *n* : COSTMARY

balsam hickory *n* : a No. American tree (*Carya ovalis*) having a small sweet nut and aromatic hard tough wood

bal·sam·ic \(ˈ)bȯlˈsamik\ *adj* **1** : of, relating to, yielding, or containing balsam ⟨a ~ wood⟩ ⟨leaves which exude a ~ fragrance —David Fairchild⟩ **2** : having the qualities of balsam : SOOTHING, HEALING, RESTORATIVE, BALMY ⟨a ~ medicinal preparation⟩

bal·sam·if·er·ous \ˌbȯlsəˈmif(ə)rəs\ *adj* [*balsam* + *-i-* + *-ferous*] : producing balsam

bal·sa·mi·na·ce·ae \ˌbȯlsəməˈnāsēˌē, -ˌsam-\ *n pl*, *cap* [NL, fr. *Balsamina*, type genus (fr. Gk *balsaminē*) + *-aceae*] : a family of plants (order Geraniales) distinguished from members of the Geraniaceae by the irregular flowers — see IMPATIENS — **bal·sa·mi·na·ceous** \ˌ(ˌ)==ˈ=ˈnāshəs\ *adj*

bal·sa·mine \ˈbȯlsəˌmēn\ *or* **bal·sam·i·na** \bȯlˈsamənə\ *n* -S [F *balsamine*, fr. Gk *balsaminē*, fr. *balsamon* balsam — more at BALM] : GARDEN BALSAM

bal·sa·mo \ˈbȯlsəˌmō\ *n* -S [AmerSp *bálsamo*, fr. Sp, balsam, fr. L *balsamum* — more at BALM] : BALSAM OF TOLU

balsam of copaiba : COPAIBA

balsam-of-copaiba tree *n* : a tree yielding true copaiba

balsam of fir : CANADA BALSAM

balsam of pe·ru \-pəˈrü, -pē-\ *usu cap P* : a dark brown syrupy balsam obtained from a tropical American tree (*Myroxylon pereirae*) growing esp. in El Salvador and used chiefly in perfumery and in medicine (as in dressing wounds and in certain skin diseases)

balsam of to·lu \-təˈlü, -tō-\ *usu cap T* [fr. Santiago de *Tolú*, Colombia] : a brown or yellowish brown plastic solid balsam obtained from a tropical American tree (*Myroxylon balsamum* or *M. toluiferum*) and used as a stimulating expectorant and a flavoring for cough syrups and in perfumes

bal·sa·mor·rhi·za \ˌbȯlsəməˈrīzə\ *n*, *cap* [NL, fr. Gk *balsamon* balsam + NL *-rhiza*] : a small genus of coarse western American perennial herbs (family Compositae) with large roots containing an aromatic balsam, velvety basal leaves, and large heads of yellow flowers — see BALSAMROOT

balsam pear *n* : a balsam apple (*Momordica charantia*)

balsam poplar *n* : a No. American poplar (*Populus balsamifera* syn. *P. tacamahaca*) that is often cultivated as a shade tree and has buds thickly coated with an aromatic resin — called also *balm of Gilead, tacamahac*

balsamroot \ˈ=ˌ==\ *n* : a plant of the genus *Balsamorrhiza*

balsams *pl of* BALSAM

balsam tree *n* : a tree that yields balsam: as **a** : BALSAM FIR **b** : MASTIC TREE **c** : BALSAM POPLAR **d** : a large tropical tree (*Myroxylon balsamum*) with small pinnate dark green leaves that yields balsam of Tolu

balsam-tree family *n* : GUTTIFERAE

balsam twig aphid *n* **:** a common aphid (*Mindarus abietinus*) of the northern U.S. and Canada feeding chiefly on spruces and balsam fir and often producing much honeydew

balsamum *n, pl* **balsami** [ME, fr. L — more at BALM] *obs* **:** BALSAM

balsamweed \'==,=\ *n* **1 :** either of two fragrant American everlastings (*Gnaphalium macounii* and *G. obtusifolium*) **2 :** JEWELWEED

balsam willow *n* **:** a low shrub or small tree (*Salix pyrifolia*) of northern No. America often occurring up to the tree line and having leaves prominently reticulate when mature and balsamic when crushed

balsam woolly aphid *n* **:** an aphid (*Adelges piceae*) native to northern Europe and widespread in No. America that severely damages fir (as balsam fir) causing swollen twigs and abnormal growth and covering the stems with a dirty white flocculent encrustation

bal·samy \'bȯlsəmē, -mi\ *adj* **:** like balsam (as in fragrance)

balshem *var of* BAALSHEM

balt \'bȯlt\ *n* -s *usu cap* [LL *Balti, Balthi, Balthae*, pl., fr. a Gothic word akin to *balthei* boldness — more at BOLD] **1 a :** one of the Lithuanians or Letts identified with the Aestii of Tacitus **b :** a native or inhabitant of the Baltic states of Lithuania, Latvia, and Estonia **2 :** a German born or resident in one of the Baltic states; *esp* **:** a member or descendant of the former German-speaking landed aristocracy of the Baltic states **3** *Austral* **:** a recently arrived immigrant from Central Europe

balter *vi* -ED/-ING/-S [ME *balteren*] *archaic* **:** to dance or tread clumsily

bal·te·us \'baltēəs, 'bȯl-\ *n, pl* **bal·tei** \-ē,ī\ [L] **1 a :** an ancient Roman belt or baldric **b :** one of the passages between the tiers of seats in an auditorium of ancient Rome **2** *also* **bal·the·us** \-lthēəs\ **:** a belt worn by an ecclesiastic; *specif* **:** SUBCINCTORIUM

bal·thaz·ar \bal'thazə(r), bȯl-\ *n* -s *usu cap* [after *Balthazar* (Belshazzar), 6th cent. B.C. king of Babylon mentioned in the Bible (Dan 5)] **1 :** an oversize wine bottle holding about 16 quarts ⟨a ~ of champagne⟩

bal·ti \'bəltē\ *n, pl* **balti** *or* **baltis** *usu cap* **1 a :** a muslimized Tibetan people in northern Kashmir having some physical resemblances to the Indo-Aryan Dards, having a castelike system of social hierarchy, and possibly being descendants of the Scythian Sacae **b :** a member of such people **2 :** a Tibeto-Himalayan language of the Balti people

¹bal·tic \'bȯltik, -ēk\ *adj, usu cap* [ML *balticus*, fr. LL *Balti*, pl., Balts + L *-icus* -ic] **1 a :** of or relating to the sea enclosed by Sweden, Denmark, Germany, Poland, the Baltic States, and Finland **b :** situated on the Baltic sea **c :** of or relating to the Baltic states of Lithuania, Latvia, and Estonia ⟨two *Baltic* ministers in Washington⟩ **2 :** of or relating to a branch of the Indo-European languages containing Latvian, Lithuanian, and Old Prussian

²baltic \"\ *n* -s **1** *cap* **:** the Baltic languages **2** *often cap* **:** MYRTLE 3b

baltic ivy *n, usu cap B* **:** a small-leaved hardy form (*Hedera helix baltica*) of English ivy

baltic pine *n, usu cap B* **:** SCOTCH PINE

baltic rush *n, usu cap B* **:** a small tufted rush (*Juncus balticus*) of cool regions that grows from extensively creeping and forking rootstocks and has usu. loosely forking flower clusters

¹bal·ti·more \'bȯltə,mō(ə)r, -mȯ(ə)r, -mōə, -mȯ(ə),-,mə(r) *sometimes* -ltēm- *or, locally & in rapid speech*, -ləm-\ *adj, usu cap* [fr. *Baltimore*, Maryland] **:** of or from the city of Baltimore, Md. ⟨*Baltimore* crowds⟩ **:** of the kind or style prevalent in Baltimore

²baltimore \"\ *n* -s *usu cap* [after Lord *Baltimore* (George Calvert) †1632 Eng. proprietor and colonizer of Maryland] **:** an eastern No. American nymphalid butterfly (*Euphydryas phaëton*) that is black above with orange-red, yellow, and white spots, has a larva which is social in nests when young, hibernates before maturity, and feeds on turtlehead and related plants

bal·ti·mor·e·an \,bȯltə'mōrēən, -ȯr-\ *n* -s *cap* [*Baltimore*, Maryland + E *-an*] **:** a native or resident of Baltimore, Md.

baltimore clipper *n, usu cap B* [fr. *Baltimore*, Maryland] **:** a fast sharp-hulled ship of usu. less than 200 tons built chiefly between 1830 and 1850 on Chesapeake Bay and usu. having sharply raked masts and a brig or schooner rig

baltimore oriole *or* **baltimore bird** *n, usu cap B* [after Lord *Baltimore*] **:** a common American oriole (*Icterus galbula*) that builds a finely woven pendent nest of various fibers and grasses and that in the female has prevailingly brown and greenish yellow plumage and in the male has a black head, upper back, and tail base, black and white wings, and a yellow-orange outer part of the outer tail feathers and has the remaining plumage a brilliant orange

bal·to-slavic \;bȯl,tō+\ *n, cap B&S* [*Balto-* (fr. *Baltic*) + *Slavic*] **:** a subfamily of Indo-European languages consisting of the Baltic and the Slavic branches

balts *pl of* BALT

ba·lu·chi \bə'lüchē\ *or* **ba·luch** \-ch\ *also* **ba·lo·chi** \-lōchē\ *or* **ba·loch** \-ōch\ *or* **be·lu·chi** \bə'lüchē\ *n, pl* **baluchi** *or* **baluchis** *or* **baluch** *or* **baluches** *usu cap* [Per *Balūch*, *Balūchī*] **1 a :** an Indo-Iranian people blended from a mixture of the Veddoid type isolated in the Hadhramaut and of the Irano-Afghan type and located in Baluchistan in the southwestern part of Pakistan **b :** a member of such people **2 :** the Iranian language of the Baluchi people

ba·lu·chi·stan *or* **be·lu·chi·stan** \bə;lüchə;stan, -ȧn\ *n* -s *usu cap* [fr. *Baluchistan*, country of western Asia, fr. Per *Balūchistān*] **:** a rug in somber colors (as mulberry and deep blue) woven by nomad tribes in Baluchistan and esp. Seistan

ba·lu·chi·there \bə'lüchə,thi(ə)r\ *n* -s [NL *Baluchitherium*] **:** BALUCHITHERIUM 2

ba·lu·chi·the·ri·um \bə,lüchə'thirēəm\ *n* [NL, fr. *Baluchistan* (country) + NL *-therium*] **1** *cap* **:** a genus of very large Oligocene mammals related to the rhinoceros the remains of which are found in central Asia **2** *pl* **baluchithe·ria** \-ēə\ **:** an animal or fossil of the genus *Baluchitherium*

ba·lu·ga \;bälə;gä\ *n, pl* **baluga** *or* **balugas** *usu cap* [Tag *balugá*] **:** a person of mixed Negrito and non-Negrito Philippine ancestry in central Luzon

bal·un \'ba,lən\ *n* -s [*balanced* + *un*balanced] **:** a radio device for converting from a balanced to an unbalanced line and usu. used at high radio frequencies

bal·us·ter \'baləstə(r)\ *n* -s [F *balustre*, fr. It *balaustro*, fr. *balaustra* flower of the wild pomegranate, modif. of L *balaustium*, fr. Gk *balaustion*; fr. the similarity of form] **1 :** a short support like a column often with a circular section and a molded vaselike outline; *esp* **:** one of a series (as in a balustrade or stair rail) **2 :** a vertical member (as the leg of a table, a round in the back of a chair, the stem of a glass, the shaft of a candlestick) having a vaselike or turned outline

balusters 1

¹bal·us·trade \'balə,strād, ,==;=\ *n* -s [F, fr. It *balaustrata*, fr. *balaustro* baluster] **1 a :** a row of balusters topped by a rail to serve as an open parapet (as along the edge of a balcony, terrace, bridge, staircase, or the eaves of a building) **b :** a stair rail; *esp* **:** a wide rail having massive supports **2 :** a low parapet or barrier

²balustrade \"\ *vt* -ED/-ING/-S **:** to furnish with a balustrade

bal·us·trad·ing \-diŋ\ *n* -s **:** the architectural members that constitute a balustrade

ba·lut \bä'lüt, bə-\ *n* -s [Tag *balót, balút*] **:** a food in the Philippines consisting of duck eggs incubated almost to the point of hatching and then boiled

bal·zacian \(')bal;zāshən; (')bȯl;zakēən, (')bal;zak-\ *adj, usu cap* [Honoré de *Balzac* †1850 French novelist + E *-ian*] **1 :** of, relating to, or befitting Balzac or his voluminous writings **2** *of a literary work* **:** large and comprehensive or minute and faithful in presentation of the realistic details of contemporary life or of lives of odd and undistinguished types

¹bam \'bam\ *vt* **bammed; bammed; bamming; bams** [perh. short for *bamboozle*] *archaic* **:** FOOL, HOAX ⟨now you're *bamming* me — don't attempt to put such stories off on your old granny —Frederick Marryat⟩

²bam \"\ *n* -s [imit.] **:** a dull resounding noise (as one made by a flat surface of a bulky object striking against another flat surface) ⟨the crates fell with ~s and crashes⟩

³bam \"\ *vi* **bammed; bammed; bamming; bams :** to make or emit a bam **:** strike making the noise of a bam ⟨the planes *bammed* against the deck of the carrier⟩

ba·mah \'bä,mä, =';=\ *n, pl* **ba·moth** \-mōth, -ōt,-ōs\ [Heb *bāmāh*] **:** a high place; *esp* **:** one that serves as a sanctuary (as one orig. devoted to a non-Israelite religion that later served as a place where Yahweh was worshiped)

ba·ma·ko \'bämə,kō, bä'ma(,)kō\ *adj, usu cap* [fr. *Bamako*, Mali, West Africa] **:** of or relating to Bamako, capital of Mali, West Africa **:** of the kind or style prevalent in Bamako

bam·ba \'bämbə\ *n* -s *often cap* [AmerSp] **:** a foot-tapping couple dance deriving from one of the huapangos of the Mexican Pacific-coast Negro-Indian population and danced in ballrooms of the U.S. — called also *la bamba*

bam·ba·ra \bäm'bärə\ *n, pl* **bambara** *or* **bambaras** *usu cap* **1 a :** a Negroid people of the upper Niger noted for their delicate mask carving **b :** a member of the Bambara people **2 :** a Mande language of the Bambara people widely used as a trade language in French Sudan — compare MANDINGO

bam·bar·ra groundnut *also* **bambarra nut** \"-\ *n, usu cap B* **:** a tropical leguminous African creeping herb (*Voandzeia subterranea*) that ripens its edible fruits underground

bam·bi·no \bam'bē(,)nō, bäm-\ *n, pl* **bambinos** \-(,)nōz\ *or* **bambi·ni** \-,nē\ [It, dim. of *bambo* child, simpleton] **1 :** CHILD, BABY **2** *pl usu* **bambini :** a representation of the infant Christ

bam·boche \bäm'bōsh\ *n* -s [AmerF (Haiti), fr. F, spree, back-formation fr. *bambochade* spree, rustic genre painting often depicting drinking scenes, fr. It *bambocciata* rustic genre painting, fr. It *Bamboccio* (lit., the simpleton, fr. *bambo* child, simpleton), nickname of Pieter van Laar (or Laer) †1642 Dutch painter] **:** a social get-together in Haiti characterized by noisy singing and dancing

¹bam·boo \(')bam;bü, -aam-\ *n* -s [Malay *bambu*, fr. Kannada *or* Tulu] **1 :** a woody or arborescent grass of *Bambusa, Arundinaria, Dendrocalamus*, and related genera (tribe Bambuseae) widely distributed chiefly in the tropics and subtropics of both hemispheres; *esp* **:** a large woody plant (*B. arundinacea*) having hollow stems that attain a diameter of five or six inches and are so hard and durable as to be used for furniture, cooking utensils, and structural framing, the smaller stalks being also used (as for walking sticks and flutes) and the young shoots utilized as food **2 a :** a variable color averaging a grayish yellow that is greener, lighter, and stronger than chamois, lighter and stronger than old ivory, and redder, lighter, and stronger than crash **b :** a light to moderate yellowish brown that is yellower than lion

A portion of bamboo stem; *B* longitudinal section of *A*

²bamboo \"\ *adj* **1 :** of, relating to, or made of bamboo ⟨a ~ hut⟩ **2 :** belonging or peculiar to or suggestive of a native population esp. of a tropical Pacific area ⟨a ~ train⟩ ⟨a ~ prison⟩; *specif* **:** having dropped Western habits and affiliations — used of an American or European ⟨Mac stayed because he was ~, but you couldn't use that word to his face —R.O.Bowen⟩

bamboo borer *n* **:** BAMBOO POWDER-POST BEETLE

bamboo brier *n* **:** BULLBRIER

bamboo cocktail *n* **:** a cocktail consisting of dry sherry, French vermouth, and usu. a dash of bitters

bamboo curtain *n, often cap B&C* **:** a political, military, and ideological barrier in the Orient (as that isolating territory controlled by Communist China) — compare IRON CURTAIN

bamboo dance *n* **:** a popular dance in India and the Philippines that involves skillful hopping over and between bamboo poles as they are manipulated by two or four men

bamboo fern *n* **:** a fast-growing sturdy Japanese fern (*Coniogramme japonica*) having mostly once-pinnate fronds and grown esp. under glass and for ornament

bamboo fish *n* **:** a southern African fish (*Sarpa salpa*) of the family Sparidae often used as bait

bamboo grass *n* **1 :** BAMBOO **2 :** a grass resembling the bamboo (*Bambusa arundinacea*) in structure or appearance **3 :** a cane grass (*Glyceria ramigera*)

bamboo oyster *n* **:** a small oyster of the Chinese coast cultivated on bamboo stakes thrust into the mud

bamboo palm *n* **1 :** ¹BAMBOO **2 :** any of several palms of the genus *Raphia* (esp. *R. vinifera*)

bamboo partridge *n* **:** any of certain east Asian partridges (genus *Bambusicola*) having a spurred tarsus, 14 tail feathers, and the first primary shorter than the tenth

bamboo pipe *n* **:** a simple easily made whistle flute

bamboo powder-post beetle *n* **:** an auger beetle (*Dinoderus minutus*) that is blackish with yellow markings on the elytra, green on the thorax, and red on the antenna bases and that bores in bamboo and in the southern U.S. attacks stored grain

bamboo rat *n* **1 :** any of several burrowing ratlike rodents of the genus *Rhizomys* found in the Orient **2 :** CANE RAT 1

bamboo reed *n* **:** GIANT REED 1

bamboo seaweed *n* **:** a brown seaweed (*Ecklonia buccinalis*) common on the coasts of southern Africa and resembling the bladder kelps of the No. Pacific ocean

bamboo shoot *n* **:** one of the young expanding buds from the rhizome of bamboo cut as soon as it appears aboveground and used as a vegetable esp. by Chinese and Japanese

bamboo sugar *n* **:** TABASHEER

bamboo telegraph *or* **bamboo wireless** *n* **:** the Oceanian native grapevine telegraph

bamboo vine *n* **:** a bull brier (*Smilax bona-nox*) having 4-angled stems with stellate scurfy bases

bamboo ware *n* [so called fr. its color] **:** a ware resembling but darker than caneware introduced by Josiah Wedgwood in 1770

bamboo worm *n* [so called fr. the resemblance of the segmentally striped body to a jointed bamboo stalk] **:** a common slender cylindrical reddish polychaete worm (*Clymenella torquata*) dwelling in tubes in the littoral zone along the New England coast

bam·boo·zle \bam'büzəl, baam-\ *vt* **bamboozled; bamboozled; bamboozling** \-z(ə)liŋ\ **bamboozles** [origin unknown] **:** to conceal one's true motives from esp. by elaborately feigning good intentions so as to gain an end or achieve an advantage **:** MISLEAD, HOODWINK — often used with *into* ⟨campaigns to ~ workers into turning out more work for less pay —*Progressive Labor World*⟩ ⟨she'd *bamboozled* Grandfather into marrying her —Ngaio Marsh⟩ **syn** see DUPE

bam·boo·zle·ment \-zəlmənt\ *n* -s **:** the quality or state of being bamboozled

bam·bou·la \bam'bülə, bäm-\ *n* -s [F, fr. Bantu] **1 :** a primitive drum used by Negroes of western Africa and the West Indies esp. in voodoo ceremonies and incantations **2 :** the dance performed to the beating of the bamboula

bam·bu·co \bam'bü(,)kō\ *n* -s [AmerSp] **:** a Colombian dance song with alternating six-eight and three-quarter meter

bam·buk butter \'bam,bük-\ *n, often cap 1st B* [fr. *Bambuk*, region in western Africa] **:** SHEA BUTTER

bam·bu·sa \bam'byüsə\ *n, cap* [NL, fr. D *bamboes* bamboo, modif. of Malay *bambu*] **:** a genus (tribe Bambuseae) comprising typical bamboos that are woody or arborescent grasses native to the warmer parts of Asia, Africa, and So. America sometimes attaining a height of 120 feet, growing in clumps, and having spikelets bearing several flowers

bam·bu·se·ae \-sē,ē\ *n pl, cap* [NL, fr. *Bambusa* + *-eae* (fem. pl. of *-eus*)] **:** a tribe of the family Gramineae comprising the bamboos and being characterized by perennial usu. rhizomatous rootstocks that send up numerous culms which typically form clumps but are sometimes solitary or climbing

ba·mia \'bämyə\ *n* -s [Turk *bamya*] **:** OKRA

bammed *past of* BAM

bamming *pres part of* BAM

bamoth *pl of* BAMAH

bams *pl of* BAM, *pres 3d sing of* BAM

¹ban \'ban, -aa(ə)n\ *vb* **banned; banned; banning; bans** [ME *bannen* to curse, summon, fr. OE *bannan* to summon; akin to OHG *bannan* to command, ON *banna* to prohibit, L *fari* to speak, Gk *phanai* to say, *phōnē* sound, voice, Skt *bhanati* he speaks] *vt* **1** *archaic* **:** CURSE ⟨he blessed his friend and *banned* his foe⟩ **2 :** to prohibit esp. by legal means or social pressure the performance, activities, dissemination, or use of ⟨~ a political party⟩ ⟨~ a book⟩ ⟨good manners ~ slovenly dress in restaurants⟩ ⟨a bill to ~ birth-control literature⟩ ~ *vi* **:** to utter maledictions ⟨the serious world will scold and ~ —J.R.Drake⟩ **syn** see FORBID

²ban \"\ *n* -s [ME, partly fr. *bannen*, v. & partly fr. OF *ban* summoning of the king's vassals for military service, of Gmc origin; akin to OHG *ban* command, prohibition, jurisdiction, *bannan* to command, ON *bann* prohibition] **1 :** the summoning in feudal times of the king's vassals for military service; *also* **:** the body of feudal vassals so summoned — compare ARRIÈRE-BAN **2 a** *obs* **:** a public proclamation or edict **:** summons by public proclamation **b** *archaic* **:** BANNS 1 **3 :** a solemn curse formally made by ecclesiastical authority **:** ANATHEMA ⟨a person under the pope's ~⟩ ⟨a city placed under ~ of pope and church⟩ **4 a :** a curse that calls down evil or harm upon a person or thing **:** an incantatory malediction ⟨a father's ~ upon his wayward son⟩ **b** *archaic* **:** a maledictory oath **:** a profane exclamation ⟨blasphemous ~s and shouts⟩ **5 :** legal prohibition **:** official interdict ⟨the Senate committee also voted to continue the ~ on price support of potatoes —*Wall Street Jour.*⟩ ⟨lift the ~ on the sale of a product⟩ ⟨the delegates voted against the ~ of Communists from the teaching profession —*Key Reporter*⟩ **6 :** censure or condemnation esp. through public opinion, social pressure, or moral or ethical considerations **:** severe disapproval ⟨a ~ on the use of atomic weapons⟩ ⟨a ~ on high-pressure salesmanship⟩ ⟨he became a lawyer; but the profession was under ~ with the upper classes —*Encyc. Americana*⟩

³ban \'bän\ *n* -s [Serbo-Croatian *bān* lord, ruler; akin to ORuss *bojanŭ* rhapsodist, of Turkic origin; akin to Turk *bay* rich man] **:** a provincial governor of former times in Hungary, Croatia, or Slavonia with military powers in time of war

⁴ban \'bän\ *n, pl* **ba·ni** \'bä(,)nē\ [Romanian] **1 :** a Romanian unit of value equal to ¹⁄₁₀₀ leu — see MONEY table **2 :** a coin representing one ban

ba·na·ba \;bänə;bä\ *n* -s [Tag & Bisayan] **1 :** an Asiatic timber tree (*Lagerstroemia speciosa*) with large red or rose-purple flowers **2 :** the tough durable reddish wood of the banaba much used for ship planking

ba·nak \'bä,näk\ *n* -s [prob. native name in Honduras] **:** any of several Central American timber trees of the genus *Virola* (esp. *V. merendonia*) extensively shipped from British Honduras

¹ba·nal \'bānᵊl; bə'nal, -äl,-ål *also* ba-\ *adj* [F, fr. MF, of compulsory feudal service, possessed in common, commonplace, fr. *ban* summoning of the king's vassals + *-al* — more at BAN] **1 :** wanting originality, freshness, or novelty **:** failing to stimulate, appeal, or arrest attention **:** TRITE, WORN-OUT, COMMONPLACE ⟨the poor working girl of the ~ songs —J.T. Farrell⟩ ⟨little books on great subjects are generally intolerably ~ —*Times Lit. Supp.*⟩ ⟨the food there was ~ —Jean Stafford⟩ ⟨the new Custom House, a towering structure, sound in plan but ~ in decoration —Lewis Mumford⟩ **2** *med* **:** COMMON, ORDINARY ⟨~ inflammation⟩ **syn** see INSIPID

²ban·al \'bänᵊl\ *adj* [³*ban* + *-al*] **:** of or relating to a ban or banat

ba·nal·i·ty \bā'naləd·ē, bə-, -ətē, -i *also* ba-\ *n* -ES [F *banalité*, fr. *banal* + *-ité* -ity] **1 a :** the quality or state of being banal ⟨their love affairs had a tedious ~ —W.S.Maugham⟩ **b :** something banal **:** COMMONPLACE ⟨the *banalities* of our rhymed radio commercials —C.M.Fuess⟩ **2 :** a lord's right in old French law to require his vassals to use his wine press, oven, or mill

ba·nal·ly \'bānᵊlē; bə'nallē, -ällē,-ållē *also* ba-; -i\ *adv* **:** in a banal manner

ba·na·na \bə'nanə, *chiefly Brit* -'nå-\ *n* -s *often attrib* [Sp or Pg; Sp, fr. Pg, of African origin; akin to Wolof *banäna*, Mandingo *banäna*, *banända*, *barända* plantain] **1 a :** the elongated often curved and usu. tapering fruit of the banana plant having soft pulpy flesh and a rind that is usu. yellow or orange-colored when ripe and dark brown to black at full maturity — see DWARF BANANA, PLANTAIN **b :** any of several treelike perennial herbs of the genus *Musa* (esp. *M. paradisiaca sapientum*) that are native to tropical Asia but are cultivated or naturalized throughout the tropics, that have a soft herbaceous stalk, very large simple leaves, flowers enveloped in colored bracts and collected into a large pendent bunch each flower of which produces a single usu. seedless fruit, and that usu. reproduce only vegetatively by means of suckers formed at the base of the plant **2 :** a grayish yellow that is paler and slightly greener than chamois, redder, lighter, and stronger than crash, and lighter, stronger, and very slightly redder than old ivory — called also *sunbeam*

banana 1a

banana bird *n* **1 :** BANANA QUIT **2 :** any of several Australian birds

banana boa *n* **:** a boa frequenting bananas; *specif* **:** a moderate-sized snake (*Boa imperator*) often imported with bunches of bananas

banana family *n* **:** MUSACEAE

banana fish *n* **:** BONEFISH 1

banana freckle *n* **:** a disease of the fruit and leaves of the banana caused by an imperfect fungus (*Macrophoma musae*) producing brown or black spots

banana melon *or* **banana muskmelon** *n* **:** a long slender muskmelon with salmon-colored flesh and a shallow-ribbed rind that is not netted

banana oil *n* **1 a** (1) **:** ISOAMYL ACETATE (2) **:** AMYL ACETATE **a b :** a lacquer containing amyl acetate; *often* **:** a solution of cellulose nitrate usu. in amyl acetate **2** *slang* **:** HOKUM, BLARNEY ⟨the pure *banana oil* of the propagandist —Hesketh Pearson⟩

banana-plant \=';==,=\ *n* **:** an aquatic perennial herb (*Nymphoides aquatica*) with cordate leaves and tubers in clusters like bananas

banana plug *n* **:** a single-conductor electrical plug with a banana-shaped tip of spring metal

banana quit *n* **:** any of several typical honeycreepers (genus *Coereba*)

banana republic *n* [so called fr. the fact that some small tropical countries are economically dependent on their fruit exporting trade] **:** a small country usu. in the tropics that is economically dependent on foreign capital and dominated by it

banana root borer *also* **banana root weevil** *n* **:** a stout orange or reddish black-marked weevil (*Cosmopolites sordidus*) whose larvae bore in banana plant roots

banana shrub *n* **:** a Chinese evergreen shrub (*Michelia fuscata*) with flowers having a fragrance like banana

banana spider *n* **1 :** a large tropical crab spider (*Heteropoda venatoria*) often introduced into temperate regions with bunches of bananas **2 :** TARANTULA

banana split *n* **:** a dessert consisting of a banana sliced in half lengthwise, topped with one or more balls of ice cream, and usu. garnished with whipped cream and nuts

banana squash *n* **:** a winter squash having elongated fruits that taper at both ends

banana water lily *n* **:** a yellow-flowered water lily (*Nymphaea mexicana*) having seeds that serve as feed for wild fowl esp. from Florida to Mexico

banana wilt *n* **:** PANAMA DISEASE

ba·na·ras \bə'närəs\ *or* **be·na·res** \", -rēz\ *adj, usu cap* [fr. *Banaras* or *Benares*, India] **:** of or from the city of Banaras, India **:** of the kind or style prevalent in Banaras

ba·na·ro \'bänə,rō\ *n, pl* **banaro** *or* **banaros** *usu cap* **1 :** a Papuan people of the Sepik district, Territory of New Guinea **2 :** a member of the Banaro people

ban·at *also* **ban·ate** *or* **ban·nat** \'bänət\ *n* -s [Serbo-Croatian *bānat*, fr. *bān* lord, ruler — more at BAN] **:** a province under the jurisdiction of a ban

ba·nau·sic \bə'nȯsik, -ȯzik\ *adj* [Gk *banausikos* of artisans, fr. *banausos* artisan + *-ikos* -ic] **1 a :** governed by or suggestive of utilitarian purposes **:** PRACTICAL ⟨my approach to this literature was . . . ~. I wanted advice, instruction, not aids to reflection —John Buchan⟩ **b :** common in taste, thought, or intention **:** dull and menial ⟨this sort of ~ performance is not mitigated by the striking of a few brave attitudes —John Wain⟩ **2 :** MONEYMAKING, BREADWINNING **:** VOCATIONAL ⟨a class freed from ~ pursuits and enjoying its leisure⟩ **:** commercially minded **:** MATERIALISTIC ⟨a ~ civilization⟩

Ban·bury \'ban,berē-, -,bəre\ *trademark* — used for any of various mechanical mixers for processing rubber, plastic, and other compositions

banbury tart *n, usu cap B* [fr. *Banbury*, England] **:** an often triangular tart with a fruit filling esp. of raisins

banc \'baŋk, -ai-\ *n* -s [ME *banck*, fr. OF *banc* — more at BANK] **:** the bench on which the judges of a court sit — **in banc** *also* **in ban·co** \-'bæŋ(,)kō, -aiŋ-\ **:** in full court **:** with full judicial authority ⟨sittings *in banc*⟩ — used of a court held by such a number of judges as constitute a quorum; compare NISI PRIUS

ban·ca *also* **bang·ka** *or* **ban·ka** \'bäŋkə\ *n* -s [PhilSp & Tag; PhilSp *banca*, fr. Tag *bangkâ*] **:** a small boat found in Pacific waters esp. around the Philippines; *usu* **:** a dugout canoe often provided with outriggers and a roof of bamboo

ban·cal \bäŋ-'käl\ *n* -s [Sp, fr. Bisayan *bañkal*] *Philippines* **:** a large tree (*Nauclea orientalis*) of the family Rubiaceae that has rather soft straight-grained yellow to orange wood which is used locally for cabinetwork and construction

ban·cha \'bän(,)chä\ *also* **bancha tea** *n* -s [Jap *bancha*, fr. *ban* number + *cha* tea] **:** a coarse Japanese tea that is usu. not exported

¹ban·co \'baŋ(,)kō, -aiŋ-\ *adj* [It, money of account, bank, bench, var. of *banca* bank, bench — more at BANK] *of a coin, note, unit of value* **:** issued or used by a bank at the time of a depreciated government currency ⟨a 19th century Swedish skilling ~⟩

²banco \"\ *n* -s [F, fr. It, total sum offered by the banker in a gambling game, fr. *banco* bank, bench] **:** an announcement by a bettor in certain gambling games (as baccarat or chemin-de-fer) signifying that he elects to accept alone the entire sum offered by the banker to meet the bets of all bettors, his bet taking precedence over any lower bet previously offered — often used interjectionally

³banco \"\ *n* -s [Sp, sandbar, bench, of Gmc origin; akin to OHG *bank* bench — more at BENCH] **:** a portion of the floodplain or channel of a river cut off and left dry by the shifting of its course

ban·croft·i·an filariasis \'ban,krȯftēən-, *also* -aŋ,k- *or* ≠'≠≠≠-\ *or* **ban·croft's filariasis** \'≠,krȯf(t)s-\ *n, usu cap B* [Joseph *Bancroft* †1894 Eng. physician + E *-ian*] **:** filariasis caused by a slender white filaria (*Wuchereria bancrofti*) that is transmitted in larval form by mosquitoes, lives in lymph vessels and lymphoid tissues periodically shedding larvae into the peripheral blood stream, and often causes elephantiasis by blocking the lymphatic drainage of a part

bancroft's law *n, usu cap B* [after Dr. Edith S. W. *Bancroft* *b*1893 Am. botanist] **:** a statement in ecology: a community or an organism tends to attain a state of dynamic equilibrium with its environment

¹band \'band, -aa(ə)-\ *n* -s [ME *band, bond*, fr. ON *band*; akin to OE *bend* fetter, OHG *bant*, Goth *bandi*, Skt *bandha* fetter, OE *bindan* to bind — more at BIND] **1 :** something that confines or constricts while allowing or imparting a limited or necessary degree of movement: **a** (1) *archaic* **:** something used to make fast the body or limbs (as a fetter, manacle, shackle) (2) *obs* **:** a leading string **:** TETHER **b** *obs* **:** a hinge of a gate or door; *esp* **:** STRAP HINGE **2 :** something that binds or restrains by legal, moral, or spiritual authority: as **a :** a restraining obligation or tie affecting one's relations to another, to others, or to a tradition, concept, or condition ⟨two New Jersey sculptors of the same period who helped break the ~*s* of neoclassic traditions —*Amer. Guide Series: N.J.*⟩ **b** *archaic* (1) **:** a formal promise or guarantee **:** BOND (2) **:** a pledge given **:** SECURITY, SURETY **3** [partly fr. ME *bande* strip, fr. MF *bande, bende*] **:** a strip serving to join, hold together, or integrate two or more things: as **a :** a string or tie (as of hay, straw, rushes) used to bind stalks into a sheaf or bundle **b :** BELT 2 **c :** the endless loop of cotton cord on a spinning frame or twister that is used as a belt to drive individual spindles — called also *spinning band* **d :** a cord or strip which crosses the backbone of a book and to which the sections are sewn **e :** a window came **f :** a metallic hoop or sleeve used to hold the barrel and stock of a gun together — called also *barrel band* **g :** a printed strip used as a label ⟨a large collection of cigar ~*s*⟩ **4** [ME *bande* strip, fr. MF *bande, bende*, fr. (assumed) VL *binda*, of Gmc origin; akin to OHG *binta* fillet; akin to OHG *bintan* to bind — more at BIND] **:** a thin flat encircling strip, strap, or flat belt of material serving chiefly to bind or contain something: as **a :** a close-fitting strip that confines material at the waist, neck, or cuff of clothing; *specif* **:** HATBAND **b** (1) *obs* **:** a strip of cloth for swathing the body **:** BANDAGE (2) **:** a strip of cloth used to protect a newborn baby's navel — called also *bellyband* **c :** a ring or endless strip of elastic (as for holding or compressing wrapping or keeping small objects together) **d :** a strengthening piece of canvas sewed across a sail (as at the eyelet holes used in reefing) **e :** a container without a bottom and usu. of wood-veneer or treated paper in which plants are grown individually prior to transplanting or benching — called also *plant band* **5** [ME *bande* strip, fr. MF *bande, bende*] **:** an elongated surface or section with parallel or roughly parallel sides: as **a :** a strip separated by some characteristic color or texture or considered apart from what is adjacent ⟨a yellow ~ of light upon the street pours from an open door —Amy Lowell⟩: as (1) **:** a stripe, streak, or other elongated mark on an animal; *esp* **:** one transverse to the long axis of the body ⟨the ~ is an important show feature on a Hampshire hog⟩ (2) **:** a line or streak of differentiated cells; *often* **:** GERM BAND (3) **:** one of the alternating dark and light segments of skeletal muscle fibers (4) **:** STAB CELL (5) **:** a strip of abnormal tissue either congenital or acquired; *esp* **:** a strip of connective tissue that causes obstruction of the bowel (6) **:** a thin seam of ore or other mineral stratified between other kinds of rock **b** (1) **:** a transverse ridge raised by a cord or strip on the backbone of a book and often continued onto the front and back covers — see RAISED BAND (2) **:** a false ridge raised on the binding of a book for decoration or to protect lettering — compare HUB 4 **c :** a long narrow feature or surface running along, across, or around something ⟨along the coast . . . lies a ~ of sand dunes —Samuel Van Valkenburg & Ellsworth Huntington⟩ **d :** a more or less well-defined range of wavelengths, frequencies, or energies of optical, electric, or acoustic radiation ⟨~ spectrum⟩ ⟨radio-frequency ~⟩ **6** [ME *bande* strip, fr. MF *bande, bende*] **:** a narrow circular, curved, or straight strip serving chiefly as decoration: as **a :** a narrow strip of material (as cloth) applied as binding, trimming, or finish to an article of dress **b** (1) **bands** *pl* **:** a pair of strips hanging at the front of the neck as part of a clerical, legal, or academic dress — compare GENEVA BANDS (2) **:** FALL 1d (2) **c :** any of several flat lines stamped or tooled on a book cover in gold or color or blind to simulate bands — compare FILLET 5b **d :** a flat usu. horizontal member (as a continuous tablet, a stripe, or a series of ornaments as of carved foliage, of color, or of brickwork) dividing or ornamenting a wall or part (as the molding or suite of moldings which encircles the pillars and small shafts in Gothic architecture or one of the sections of the banded column used in French Renaissance) **e :** a ring without raised portions ⟨a wedding ~⟩ **7** [ME *bande* strip, fr. MF *bande, bende*] **:** ¹BAND SHELL **8 :** a strip of the grooves of a phonograph record on which a single piece or a section of a long piece is recorded

²band \"\ *vb* -ED/-ING/-S *vt* **1 :** to affix a band to: as **a :** to bind together or tie up with a band ⟨~ asparagus⟩ ⟨automatically ~*ed* and delivered in 5 packs of 50 cards each —*Theory & Practice of Presswork*⟩ **b :** to encircle (a tree trunk) with a band of cloth, paper, or sticky substance as protection against injurious insects **c :** to mark (a bird) with a band for identification **2 a :** to finish with a band ⟨the jacket was ~*ed* with black⟩ ⟨the interior walls, ~*ed* in light and dark gray stone —*Amer. Guide Series: Minn.*⟩ **b :** to create or form a band on ⟨wide gray eyes ~*ed* her face with intensity and intellect —Elizabeth Pollet⟩ **3 a :** to attach (oneself) to a group ⟨the royalists ~*ed* themselves against the popular movement⟩ **b :** to gather together or summon esp. for some purpose ⟨he ~*ed* all his resources together against the coming struggle⟩ **c :** to unite in a troop, company, or confederacy ⟨farmers had long been ~*ed* against certain government controls⟩ **4 :** to distribute (as grass seed, legume seed, or fertilizer) in strips under the soil surface rather than broadcast ~ *vi* **:** to confederate esp. for some common purpose **:** UNITE ⟨all the first-rate critics are, in some measure, ~*ed* in one army —C.E. Montague⟩ — often used with *together* ⟨housewives ~ together and serve chicken and turkey —*Amer. Guide Series: Texas*⟩

³band \"\ *n* -s [MF *bande* troop, prob. fr. OProv *banda*, of Gmc origin; akin to Goth *bandwa, bandwo* sign; fr. the use of a standard by a troop of soldiers — more at BANNER] **:** a group of persons, animals, or things: as **a :** a body of armed men **:** GANG ⟨a guerrilla ~⟩ ⟨a ~ of Indians⟩ ⟨a ~ of outlaws⟩ ⟨a ~ of men who wrecked the tobacco crop of those of their neighbors who refused to join a would-be monopolistic association —E.R.Bentley⟩ **b :** a body of persons often brought together by a common purpose or bound together by a common fate or lot ⟨a ~ of refugees⟩ ⟨a ~ of patriotic ladies who made clothing for the soldiers —*Encyc. Americana*⟩ ⟨the small and select ~ of Europeans who have made the overland journey from China to India —*Geog. Jour.*⟩; *specif* **:** a relatively self-sufficient tribal subgroup that is mainly united for social and economic reasons **c :** a group of animals sharing often more or less permanently a common existence either in nature or under domestication: as (1) **:** a herd or flock usu. of domestic mammals ⟨a ~ of well-fattened cattle⟩; *esp* **:** a large flock of range sheep tended by one herder (2) **:** a flock of birds ⟨a ~ of jays⟩ (3) **:** a swarm of insects; *specif* **:** a circumscribed aggregation of migratory grasshoppers functioning as a unit — used often of the immature hoppers as distinguished from swarms of flying adults **d :** a group of musicians organized for playing together **:** ORCHESTRA: as (1) **:** a group composed chiefly of percussion and wind instruments ⟨military ~⟩ or of percussion and brass wind instruments only ⟨brass ~⟩ (2) **:** any group capable of playing while marching (3) **:** a group composed chiefly of one kind of instrument ⟨a harmonica ~⟩ ⟨a pipe ~⟩ (4) **:** a dance orchestra of any composition (5) **:** one of the groups of related instruments in an orchestra **e :** AGGREGATE, COLLECTION, NUMBER ⟨a ~ of ideas⟩ ⟨the small numerable ~ of runaway planets —A.N.Whitehead⟩

⁴band \"\ *vt* -ED/-ING/-S [prob. fr. MF *bander*, lit., to be tight — more at BANDY] **:** BANDY

ban·da \'bandə\ *n* -s [native name in Africa] **:** a thatched house of central Africa

¹ban·dage \'bandij, -aan-, -dēj\ *n* -s [ME, fr. *bande* strip + *-age* — more at BAND] **1 :** a narrow length of fabric used to cover a wound, hold a dressing in place, immobilize an injured part, or apply pressure **2 :** a flexible strip used like a bandage (as one bound over or around something to cover, strengthen, or compress it); *specif* **:** a strip of coarse-mesh fabric (as cheesecloth) used in cheesemaking to line the hoop before the curd is put in for pressing

bandages: *1* spiral bandage of finger, *2* gauntlet bandage, *3* spiral reverse bandage of forearm, *4* figure-of-eight bandage of knee and spiral reverse below knee

²bandage \"\ *esp in pres part* -dəj\ *vb* -ED/-ING/-S *vt* **:** to bind, dress, or cover with a bandage ⟨~ a wound⟩ ⟨~ a sprained ankle⟩ ⟨*bandaging* and whitewashing the apple trees —Miles Franklin⟩ ~ *vi* **:** to apply a bandage ⟨were taught how to ~⟩

ban·dag·er \-jə(r)\ *n* -s **:** one that bandages

Band–Aid \'ban,dād, -aan-\ *trademark* — used for a small adhesive strip with a gauze pad for covering minor wounds

ban·da·ite \'bandə,īt, -n,dīt\ *n* -s [*Bandai*, volcano on Honshu Island, Japan + E *-ite*] **:** a siliceous often quartz-bearing basalt of andesitic texture with labradorite as its feldspar

ban·da·ka *also* **ban·dak·ka** \'bandəkə\ *or* **ban·di·kai** \-də-,kī\ *n* -s [Kanarese *bende-kāyi* or Telugu *benda-kāya*] **:** OKRA

ban·da·lore \'bandə,lō(ə)r\ *n* -s [origin unknown] **:** a toy with an automatically winding cord by which it is brought back to the hand when thrown — called also *quiz*

ban·dan·na *also* **ban·dana** \ban'danə, baan-, *Brit also* -dà-; *attrib* (')≠'≠≠\ *n* -s [Hindi *bādhnū*, a variegated-color dyeing process involving tying the cloth in knots, cloth so dyed, fr. *bādhnā* to tie, fr. Skt *badhnāti* he ties — more at BIND] **1 :** a large cotton or silk handkerchief that usu. has a solid background of red or blue with simple figures or geometrical forms in white or yellow and is printed by tie-and-dye **2 :** any of various large plain or printed handkerchiefs or kerchiefs often made to imitate the tied-and-dyed ones

ban·dan·naed \-nəd\ *adj* **:** covered with a bandanna

ban·dar *also* **bhun·der** *or* **bun·der** \'bəndə(r)\ *n* -s [Hindi *bādar, bãdar* monkey, fr. Skt *vānara*, fr. *vanar-, vana* forest; akin to Av *vana* forest] **:** RHESUS

ban·dar–log \'bəndə(r),lóg, -läg\ *n, pl* **bandar–log** *or* **bandar–logs** [Hindi *bãdar* monkey + *log* people; fr. the portrayal of the monkey race as chatterers and poseurs in the jungle stories of Rudyard Kipling †1936 Eng. writer — more at LOG] **:** a vacuous chattering person ⟨he's evidently picked up some congenial *bandar-logs* —Booth Tarkington⟩

¹band·box \'ban(d),bäks, -aan-\ *n* [¹*band* + *box*] **1 :** a usu. cylindrical box of pasteboard or thin wood for holding light articles of attire (as ruffs, collars, hats) **2 :** a structure (as a baseball park) resembling a bandbox esp. in having relatively small interior dimensions — **band·box·i·cal** \(')≠¦≠ə̇kəl\ *adj* — **band·boxy** \'≠,≠ē\ *adj*

²bandbox \"\ *adj* **1 :** of flimsy unsubstantial nature or construction ⟨a fragile ~ reputation⟩ **2 :** exquisitely neat, clean, or ordered **:** being as though fresh-taken from a bandbox ⟨the quiet ~ scenery of cultivated England —Leslie Stephen⟩

band brake *n* **:** a friction brake used esp. in vehicles, cranes, and hoists that consists of a flexible band around a revolving drum and is operated by tightening the band

band cell *n* **:** STAB CELL

band clutch *n* **:** a clutch in which a friction band resembling a brake band tightens around a shaft or drum

band conveyor *n* **:** CONVEYER 2a (1)

band course *n* **:** BELT COURSE

band creaser *n* **:** a tool used in bookbinding to crease lines on either side of bands

ban·deau \'ban,dō, -aan-, ≠'≠\ *n, pl* **ban·deaux** \-ōz\ [F, dim. of *bande* strip — more at BAND] **1 a :** a fillet or a wide band (as for the hair) **b :** a bandlike hat for women **2 :** BRASSIERE; *esp* **:** a lightweight narrow one for a young figure

banded *adj* **1 a :** having a band or bands; *esp* **:** marked with or showing bands or stripes ⟨a ~ collar⟩ ⟨a ~ rock⟩ **b** *heraldry* **:** having a band of a specified color **2** *of an architectural feature* **:** having the regular profile interrupted by blocks or projections crossing it at right angles ⟨a ~ architrave⟩ ⟨a series of ~ piers⟩

banded anteater *n* **:** a marsupial anteater of the genus *Myrmecobius* of Australia — called also *numbat*

banded drum *n* **1 :** the black drum when immature **2** *or* **banded croaker :** a sciaenid fish (*Larimus fasciatus*) of the So. Atlantic and the Gulf coast of the U.S.

banded duiker *n* **:** a small forest antelope (*Cephalophus doriae*) of Liberia with dark cross stripes on a fulvous ground

banded krait *or* **banded adder** *n* **:** a sluggish krait (*Bungarus fasciatus*) banded with black and yellow or buff

banded leaf monkey *n* **:** a Malayan langur of the genus *Presbytis*

banded mackerel *n* **:** BANDED RUDDERFISH

banded olive snake *n* **:** a small harmless snake (*Natrix olivaceus*) of tropical and southern Africa

banded palm civet *n* **:** any of several East Indian civets that constitute the genus *Hemigalus* and usu. have a light coat with dark transverse stripes

banded pickerel *n* **:** CHAIN PICKEREL

banded purple *n* **:** a nymphalid butterfly (*Limenitis arthemis*) of northeastern No. America with blue-black wings crossed by a broad white band — called also *white admiral*

banded rattlesnake *n* **:** TIMBER RATTLESNAKE

banded rudderfish *n* **:** a common amberfish (*Seriola zonata*) of the western Atlantic — called also *banded mackerel*

banded spindle *n* **:** ¹BAND SHELL

banded stilt *n* **:** a web-footed Australian stilt (*Cladorhynchus leucocephalum*) with reddish brown pectoral markings

banded structure *n* **:** a geological structure characterized by an arrangement of different minerals in layers that appear as bands in cross section (as in a fissure vein) or of different colors or textures in layers in a rock consisting of one mineral (as in onyx marble)

banded sunfish *n* **:** BLACK-BANDED SUNFISH

banded veins *n pl* **:** mineral veins that when seen in cross section present a banded structure

banded water snake *n* **:** a common No. American water snake (*Natrix sipedon*) represented in the U.S. by several widely distributed subspecies

banded whelk *n* **:** ¹BAND SHELL

ban·de·let \,bandə¦let, 'bandlət\ *also* **ban·de·lette** \,bandə-¦let\ *or* **band·let** \'bandlət\ *n* -s [F *bandelette*, dim. of *bande* strip — more at BAND] *archit* **:** a little band or flat molding about a column

bandelier *var of* BANDOLIER

ban·deng \'ban,deŋ\ *n* -s [native name in Indonesia] **:** the milkfish (*Chanos chanos*) used for mosquito control and cultivated in ponds in Indonesia

band·er \'bandə(r), -aan-\ *n* -s **:** one that bands: as **a :** a sewing-machine operator who attaches neckbands, waistbands, and trimming bands to garments **b :** a worker who wraps labels around items (as shoelaces or cigars) or who bands together a specified number of articles (as envelopes, hose, or knitted garments)

ban·de·ri·lla \,bandə'rē(y)ə, ,bän-, -ēlyə\ *n* -s [Sp, dim. of *bandera* banner, of Gmc origin; akin to Goth *bandwa* sign — more at BANNER] **:** a decorated barbed dart that the banderillero thrusts into the neck or shoulder of the bull in a bullfight

ban·de·ril·le·ro \,bandərē(l)'ye(,)rō, ,bän-\ *n* -s [Sp, fr. *banderilla*] **:** one who thrusts in the banderillas in bullfighting

ban·de·role *or* **ban·de·rol** \'bandə,rōl\ *or* **ban·drol** \-,drōl\ *n* -s [F *banderole*, fr. It *banderuola*, dim. of *bandiera* banner, of Gmc origin; akin to Goth *bandwa* sign — more at BANNER] **1 :** a long narrow forked flag or streamer **2 :** a ribbonlike scroll bearing an inscription or a device; *specif* **:** a sculptured band often bearing an inscription and used as architectural decoration esp. in the Renaissance period **3 :** a flag about one yard square formerly displayed at funerals of great men

ban·der·snatch \'bandə(r),snach\ *n* -ES [fr. *Bandersnatch*, a fabulous animal in *Through the Looking Glass* (1872) by Lewis Carroll (Charles L. Dodgson) †1898 Eng. mathematician & writer] **:** a wildly grotesque or bizarre individual ⟨like teaching metaphysics to a ~ —F.B.Ebersole⟩

band file *n* **:** a machine tool resembling a band saw but with a cutting edge in the form of a file

bandfish \'≠,≠\ *n* **:** RIBBONFISH 1b

band form *n* **:** STAB CELL

ban·di·coot \'bandē,küt\ *n* -s [Telugu *pandikokku*, fr. *pandi* pig + *kokku* bandicoot] **1** *or* **bandicoot rat :** any of several very large rats of *Nesokia* and related genera of India and Ceylon that do much injury to rice fields and gardens **2 :** any of certain small active insectivorous and herbivorous marsupial mammals constituting the family Peramelidae and found in Australia, Tasmania, and New Guinea — see RABBIT BANDICOOT

Australian bandicoot

ban·di·do \ban'dē(,)dō\ *n* -s [Sp, fr. It *bandito* — more at BANDIT] *Southwest* **:** an outlaw esp. of Mexican extraction or origin

ban·die \'bandē\ *n* -s [prob. alter. of *banstickle*] *chiefly Scot* **:** STICKLEBACK

bandied *past of* BANDY

bandies *pres 3d sing of* BANDY, *pl of* BANDY

bandikai *var of* BANDAKA

bandileer *var of* BANDOLIER

banding *n* -s [fr. gerund of ²*band*] **1 :** a uniting or confederating ⟨a ~ of man and man⟩ **2 a :** narrow fabric (as tape, braid, or ribbon) that is used for bands **b :** a series or configuration of bands ⟨the ~ on a sectionalized mineral⟩ ⟨veneer ~ on furniture⟩

ban·dit \'bandə̇t, -aan-, *usu* -ə̇d-+V\ *n, pl* **bandits** \-ə̇ts\ *also* **bandit·ti** \≠'did·|ē, -it|, |i\ *see sense 1* [It *bandito*, fr. past part. of *bandire* to banish, of Gmc origin; akin to OHG *ban* command, prohibition, prob. influenced in form by a Gmc word akin to Goth *bandwa* sign — more at BAN, BANNER] **1** *pl often* banditti **:** one who is outlawed **:** BRIGAND — often used of a member of one of the marauding bands in the mountainous districts of the Mediterranean lands **2** *pl bandits* **:** one who steals, profiteers, or kills esp. in a shameless, inglorious, or pitiless manner **:** GANGSTER ⟨~ killings⟩ ⟨a theater held up by masked ~*s*⟩ ⟨the war against the Communist ~*s* —Amry Vandenbosch⟩ **3** *pl bandits, slang* **:** one who takes unfair advantage over others usu. to procure inordinate payment or profit ⟨the taxi ~*s* who tie up traffic —Bennett Cerf⟩ **4** *pl bandits* **:** an enemy plane — used in the armed forces in the identification and recognition of aircraft ⟨a ~ approaching at 15,000 feet⟩

ban·dit·ry \'bandə̇trē, -aan-, -ri\ *n* -ES **:** the practice of marauding esp. in semiorganized groups ⟨juvenile ~⟩ ⟨civil wars and ~ are still common in Tibet —Christopher Rand⟩

band·ke·ram·ik \,bäntkä¦rämik, *Ger* -rääm-\ *n* -s *usu cap* [G, fr. *band* band (fr. OHG *bant*) + *keramik* ceramics, fr. F *céramique* — more at BAND, CERAMICS] **:** a European Neolithic pottery with banded decoration

band knife *n* **:** a knife having the form of an endless belt running over a set of pulleys and used for splitting hides into two or more thicknesses and for cutting many thicknesses of cloth

B and L *abbr* building and loan

bandleader \'≠,≠≠\ *n* [³*band* + *leader*] **:** the director of a band (as a dance band)

band·less \'bandlə̇s, 'baan-\ *adj* **:** being without a band

bandlet *var of* BANDELET

bandman *var of* BANDSMAN

band·mas·ter \'≠,≠≠\ *n* [³*band* + *master*] **:** a conductor of a military or concert band

band mill *n* [*band (saw)*] **:** a sawmill whose headsaw is a band saw

band neutrophil *n* **:** STAB CELL

band nippers *n pl but sometimes sing in constr* **:** metal pliers designed for shaping the bands on the backbone of a book

ban·do·bust \'bəndə,bəst\ *var of* BUNDOBUST

bandoeng *var of* BANDUNG

ban·dog \'ban, -aan +\ *n* -s [ME *bandogge, band-dogge*, fr. *band* + *dogge* dog] **:** a dog (as a mastiff or bloodhound) formerly kept tied or chained as a watchdog or because ferocious

bandoleer fruit *see* BANDOLIER\ *n* **:** the fleshy berrylike fruit of an East Indian vine (*Zanonia indica*)

ban·do·le·ris·mo \,bandə(,)le'riz(,)mō, ,bän-\ *n* -ES [Sp, fr. *bandolero* + *-ismo* -ism] *Philippines* **:** HIGHWAY ROBBERY

ban·do·lier *or* **ban·do·leer** *also* **ban·de·lier** *or* **ban·di·leer** \,bandə¦li(ə)r, -aan-, -liə\ *n* -s [MF *bandouliere*, fr. OSp *bandolera*, fr. *bandolero* highwayman, partisan, fr. Catal *bandoler*, fr. *bàndol* band, fr. Sp *bando*, of Gmc origin; akin to

Goth *bandwo, bandwa* sign — more at BANNER] **:** a belt worn over the shoulder and across the breast often for the suspending of some article or as a part of an official or ceremonial dress: **a** *obs* **:** one used to carry a wallet **b :** one from which the small tubular cases containing charges for a musket were suspended **c** (1) **:** one having a series of loops for individual cartridges (2) **:** one having a series of pouches, each holding one or more cartridge clips, and now used chiefly for carrying ammunition supplementary to that in the cartridge belt

ban·do·ni·on *or* **ban·do·ne·on** \ban'dōnē,än\ *n* -s [*bandonion* fr. G, fr. Heinrich *Band*, 19th cent. German musician, its inventor + G *-on-* (as in *harmonika* harmonica, accordion, fr. E *harmonica*) + *-ion* (as in *akkordion* accordion); *bandoneon*, fr. Sp *bandoneón*, fr. G *bandonion* — more at HARMONICA, ACCORDION] **:** an accordion popular in So. America having buttons for both treble and bass notes with each bass button representing or sounding a single note not a chord

ban·dore \'ban,dō(ə)r\ *or* **ban·do·ra** \ban'dōrə\ *n* -s [Sp *bandurria* or Pg *bandurra*, fr. LL *pandura, pandurium* — three-stringed lute, fr. Gk *pandoura*] **:** a bass stringed instrument that resembles a guitar with scalloped sides and that was popular in the Renaissance — called also *pandora*

band-pass filter \'=,=-\ *n* **:** FILTER 3a

bandrol *var of* BANDEROLE

bands *pl of* BAND, *pres 3d sing of* BAND

B and S *abbr* brandy and soda

band saw *n* **:** a saw in the form of an endless steel belt running over pulleys; *also* **:** a power sawing machine using this device — compare SCROLL SAW

[1]**band shell** *n* [[1]*band*] **:** any of numerous large marine snails that have thick-walled spiral shells with an expanded body whorl, constitute *Fasciolaria* and related genera, and are common in warm shallow seas — called also *banded spindle, banded whelk*

[2]**band shell** *n* [[3]*band*] **:** a bandstand having at the rear a sounding board shaped like a huge concave seashell

bands·man \'ban(d)zmən, 'baan-\ *also* **band·man** \-n(d)mən, -,man, -,maa(ə)n\ *n, pl* **bandsmen** *also* **bandmen :** a member of a band esp. of musicians

band spectrum *n* **:** an optical spectrum consisting of groups of narrowly spaced lines — used of a molecular spectrum

bandstand \'=,=\ *n* [[3]*band* + *stand*] **1 :** a stand in which a band may play an outdoor concert; *usu* **:** a roofed platform open on all sides — see BAND SHELL **2 :** a raised platform (as in a hall or restaurant) on which a band or orchestra performs

band·stra·tion \(')ban(d)z¦trāshən, -n(d)¦st-\ *n* -s [[3]*band* + *orchestration*] **:** the scoring of music for a band

bandstring \'=,=\ *n* [[1]*band* (collar) + *string*] **:** one of a pair of strings for fastening a 16th century ruff or a 17th century collar

band-tailed \'=¦=\ *adj* **:** marked by a band or bands upon the tail

band-tailed pigeon *also* **band-tail pigeon** \'=,=-\ *or* **bandtail** \'=,=\ *n* **:** a wild pigeon (*Columba fasciata*) of western No. America that is often confused with the now extinct passenger pigeon but is distinguished by a rounded tail with a black transverse band

band tool *n* **:** a machine tool having an endless belt (often of metal) that contains cutting elements (as for sawing, shaping, or finishing materials)

ban·dung *or* **ban·doeng** \'bän,dün, 'ban,dün, 'ban,dəŋ *sometimes* 'bän,dəŋ\ *adj, usu cap* [fr. *Bandung* or *Bandoeng*, Indonesia] **:** of or from the city of Bandung, Indonesia **:** of the kind or style prevalent in Bandung

ban·du·ra \ban'dùrə\ *n* -s [Russ, fr. Pol, fr. It *pandura, pandora*, fr. LL *pandura, pandurium* three-stringed lute — more at BANDORE] **:** a Russian stringed instrument of the lute class — **ban·du·rist** \-rəst\ *n* -s

ban·dur·ria \ban'dùryə\ *n* -s [Sp — more at BANDORE] **:** a Spanish stringed instrument of the lute family

b and w *abbr, often cap B & W* **1** black and white **2** bread and water

bandwagon \'=,=\ *n* [[3]*band* + *wagon*] **1 :** a usu. ornate and high wagon for a band of musicians esp. in a circus parade **2 a :** a party, faction, or other element that attracts adherents by its timeliness, showmanship, vigor, or novelty ⟨the Prohibition ~ rolled victoriously through several states⟩; *specif* **:** such a party, faction, or other element held together by or capable of attracting new members through opportunity for personal gain ⟨the ~ mentality⟩ **b :** a social, cultural, or racial movement that amasses power by or as if by sheer size, momentum, or internal unity ⟨fascists certain they were on history's ~⟩ ⟨the reform ~ that swept across the country⟩ **c :** a current or fashionable taste or trend ⟨the sports car ~⟩ ⟨to beat the Mozart ~ as early as 1903 with a penetrating study of the classical concerto —Joseph Kerman⟩

band wheel *n* **1 :** BELT PULLEY **2 :** a wheel on which a band saw runs

bandwidth \'=¦=\ *n* **:** the range within a band of wavelengths, frequencies, or energies; *specif* **:** the number of cycles per second expressing the difference between the limiting frequencies of a band ⟨a television channel with a ~ of 6 megacycles⟩

bandworm \'=,=\ *n* **:** TAPEWORM

[1]**ban·dy** \'bandē, -aan-, -di\ *vb* -ED/-ING/-ES [prob. fr. MF *bander* to be tight, to bandy at tennis, fr. *bande* strip — more at BAND] *vt* **1 :** to bat (as a tennis ball) to and fro **2** *obs* **:** to toss aside (as rumors) **:** drive or throw away **:** REJECT ⟨a ~ suitor⟩ **3 a :** to toss from side to side or from one to another in a rough or inappropriate manner ⟨a firearm is no toy to be *bandied* about⟩ **:** treat carelessly or highhandedly ⟨so that's the way he *bandies* me about, I'll teach him —Anne Green⟩ **b :** EXCHANGE ⟨~ blows⟩ ⟨~ compliments⟩; *esp* **:** to exchange (words) petulantly, heatedly, or argumentatively ⟨the senator never deigned to ~ words with members of the opposition⟩ **c :** to discuss lightly or banteringly esp. among a number of people ⟨the ~*ing* of statistics⟩ **:** use (as in writing or conversation) in a glib, facile, or offhand manner — often used with *about* ⟨I beg the privilege of ~*ing* generalizations and theories —E.R.Bentley⟩ **4** *archaic* **:** to band together **:** UNITE ~ *vi* **1** *obs* **:** CONTEND, STRIVE — usu. used with *with* **2** *archaic* **:** UNITE

[2]**bandy** \"\ *n* -ES [perh. fr. MF *bandé*, past part. of *bander*] **1** *obs* **:** an old game played with a ball and racket; *also* **:** a stroke or return in this game **2 :** a game similar to and reputedly the prototype of hockey; *also* **:** the bent club with which the ball is struck in this game

[3]**bandy** \"\ *adj* [prob. fr. [2]*bandy* (hockey stick)] **1** *of legs* **:** BOWED **2 :** BOWLEGGED ⟨a case of china . . . stood beyond the ~ table —Dylan Thomas⟩

[4]**bandy** \", 'bə-\ *n* -ES [Kanarese-Telugu *baṇḍi*] **:** a carriage or cart used in India; *esp* **:** one drawn by bullocks

ban·dy-ban·dy \'bandē,bandē\ *n* [native name in Australia] **:** a common poisonous ringed snake (*Furina annulata*) of Australia with a mouth so small as to be incapable of biting a man

bandy-leg \'==,=\ *n* [[3]*bandy*] **1 :** BOWLEG **2 :** a cabriole furniture leg

ban·dy-legged \¦==¦leg(ə)d\ *adj* **:** BOW-LEGGED

ban·dy·lite \'bandē,līt\ *n* -s [after Mark C. *Bandy*, 20th cent. mining engineer who collected it + E *-lite*] **:** a mineral $Cu_2B_2O_4Cl_2.4H_2O$ consisting of a rare hydrous borate and chloride found near Calama, Chile

ban·dy·man \'bandēmən, 'bə-\ *n, pl* **bandymen** [[4]*bandy* + *man*] *India* **:** a driver of a bandy

[1]**bane** \'bān\ *n* -s [ME, fr. OE *bana*; akin to OE *benn* wound, OHG *bano* death, destruction, ON *ben* wound, *bani* slayer, Goth *banja* wound, Av *banta* ill] **1 a** *obs* **:** one that causes death **:** MURDERER, SLAYER **b :** POISON ⟨was there ~ in that tea you did tell Tivvy to give Mother —Mary Webb⟩ — see HENBANE, RATSBANE **c** (1) **:** DEATH, DESTRUCTION ⟨drink will be the ~ of him⟩ ⟨money, thou ~ of bliss, and source of woe —George Herbert⟩ ⟨the cup of deception spiced and tempered to their ~ —John Milton⟩ (2) **:** HARM, WOE ⟨from deepest ~ will he bring her back to highest blessing —George Meredith⟩ **2 a :** any pernicious or fatal element, feature, or flaw **:** CURSE ⟨the aristocratic tradition embedded in British higher education is its ~ —Bertrand Russell⟩ ⟨used cars have been called the ~ of the automobile industry —C.W.Phelps⟩ ⟨this rage for novelty is the ~ of literature —T.L.Peacock⟩ **b :** a person who makes another completely miserable ⟨the ~ of my existence⟩ **:** one that perversely or persistently spoils or thwarts ⟨the pitcher was the ~ of right-handed batters⟩ **syn** see POISON

[2]**bane** \"\ *vb* -ED/-ING/-S *vt, obs* **:** to kill esp. with poison ~ *vi, archaic* **:** to do injury **:** HARM

[3]**bane** \"\ *n* -s [ME (northern dial.) *ban*, fr. OE *bān* — more at BONE] *chiefly Scot* **:** BONE

baneberry \'=,==\ *n* [*bane* (poison) + *berry*] **1 :** the acrid poisonous berry of any plant of the genus *Actaea* **2 :** a plant of the genus *Actaea*

bane·ful \'bānfəl\ *adj* [[1]*bane* + *-ful*] **1** *archaic* **:** having poisonous qualities **:** NOXIOUS **2 :** creating destruction, woe, or ruin **:** RUINOUS, HARMFUL ⟨~ effects⟩ ⟨constantly influencing our foreign policy in a ~ way —S.F.Bemis⟩ **3 :** perversely productive of discomfort or misery ⟨then came an east wind, ~ to me at all times —William Cowper⟩ ⟨her love for him is a possessive and ~ love —J.D.Scott b.1915⟩ ⟨students undergoing three hours of ~ examinations⟩ **4 :** darkly or grimly threatening or foreboding **:** OMINOUS ⟨picturing their country in more lurid and ~ lights —Robert Brennan⟩ ⟨the story, which has been acquiring a ~ intensity —Malcolm Cowley⟩ **syn** see PERNICIOUS

bane·ful·ly \-fəlē, -li\ *adv* **:** in a baneful manner **:** with a baneful effect

banes *obs var of* BANNS

banewort \'=,=\ *n* [[1]*bane* + *wort*] **1 :** BELLADONNA 1 **2** *Brit* **:** LESSER SPEARWORT

banff·shire \'bam(p)f,shi(ə)r, -,shər\ *or* **banff** \-f\ *adj, usu cap* [fr. *Banffshire* or *Banff*, Scotland] **:** of or from the county of Banff, Scotland **:** of the kind or style prevalent in Banff

[1]**bang** \'baŋ, -aiŋ\ *vb* -ED/-ING/-S [prob. of Scand origin; akin to Icel *banga* to hammer, OSw *banga*; prob. of imit. origin like ON *bang* hammering, MHG *bungen* to drum] *vt* **1** *archaic* **:** to beat soundly (as with a cudgel) **:** THRASH **2 :** to strike against **:** BUMP ⟨fall and ~ one's knee⟩ **3 :** to knock (an object) a distance with noisy vigor ⟨~*ed* a homer over the center-field bleachers⟩ **4 a :** to thrust, put, push, or force vigorously often with a sharp noise ⟨~ a book down⟩ ⟨~ a receiver up⟩ ⟨the driver ~*ed* in the clutch —G.A.Wagner⟩ **b :** to copulate with — usu. considered vulgar **5 :** to produce a resounding report or series of reports by striking ⟨~ a drum⟩ ⟨don't ~ the door⟩ ⟨~ a gavel⟩ **6 a :** to treat roughly or carelessly ⟨packages badly ~*ed* around by the post office⟩ **:** mistreat so as to leave dents, bruises, or other signs of damage ⟨~ furniture⟩ **b :** to cause extensive damage to **:** RUIN — used with *up* ⟨~*ed* up his car⟩ **7** *chiefly dial* **:** BEAT, SURPASS, OUTDO ⟨don't it just ~ anything you ever heard of —Mark Twain⟩ ~ *vi* **1 a :** to strike with a sharp noise ⟨the falling chair ~*ed* against the wall⟩ ⟨the door ~*ed* shut⟩ **b :** to strike repeatedly ⟨buckles of his helmet straps ~*ing* against his cheeks —K.M. Dodson⟩ **:** beat or thump with a resounding series of blows ⟨~ on a door⟩ **2 :** to produce a sharp often metallic explosive or percussive noise or series of such noises ⟨drums thumped, crackers ~*ed*, horns screamed —John Blofeld⟩ ⟨a brass band ~*ing* away on the village green⟩ **3 a :** to move or proceed rapidly or noisily **:** DASH, RUSH ⟨we grab our coats and ~ down the stairs⟩ ⟨a train ~*ing* along down the valley⟩ **b :** to go from one thing to another **:** frequent a place without definite or sustained purpose — used with *about* or *around* ⟨in 1923, when I was ~*ing* around Madison Avenue —William Benton⟩ **4 :** to shoot esp. in a sporadic or desultory manner — usu. used with *away* ⟨the town got out its shotguns . . . and ~*ed* away at the flock going over —Paul Annixter⟩

[2]**bang** \"\ *n* -s [prob. of Scand origin, akin to ON *bang* hammering] **1 :** a resounding blow **:** THUMP, WHACK ⟨gave the ball a terrific ~⟩ ⟨a ~ on the head⟩ **2 a :** a sudden loud noise ⟨closed the door with a ~⟩ ⟨the ~ of a rifle⟩ — often used interjectionally ⟨saw flashes and heard an automatic go ~ ~ —Erle Stanley Gardner⟩ **b :** earsplitting noise often of a metallic quality ⟨the deafening clang and ~ of a . . . boiler factory —*Lamp*⟩ ⟨they played with a virile blare and ~ —S.H. Adams⟩ **3 :** sudden emotional pleasure **:** THRILL ⟨the kind that will try anything once — for the ~ of it —J.P.Marquand⟩ — often used with *get* or *give* ⟨I get a ~ out of all this —W.H. Whyte⟩ ⟨Jean looked very beautiful and it gave him a ~ to be with her —Frederic Wakeman⟩ **4 a :** a sudden or abrupt burst of showiness, brilliancy, or éclat ⟨you've got to have a press campaign. Not a big one, necessarily, after the first big ~ —Dorothy Sayers⟩ **b :** sudden effectiveness or success ⟨went over with a ~⟩ **5 a :** emotional or physical vitality ⟨no ~ left in him⟩ **b :** a quick burst of energy or activity ⟨start off with a ~⟩ **:** sudden fervor ⟨fell for her with a ~⟩

[3]**bang** \"\ *vt* -ED/-ING/-S **1 :** to cut (the hair) in a bang **2 :** to cut (the hair of an animal) like a bang ⟨~ a horse's tail⟩

[4]**bang** \"\ *adv* **:** RIGHT, DIRECTLY, EXACTLY ⟨~ on time⟩ ⟨married ~ in the middle of the war⟩ ⟨ran ~ up against more trouble⟩ ⟨open spaces . . . ~ on top of old colliery workings —Sam Pollock⟩

[5]**bang** \"\ *n* -s [prob. back-formation fr. *bangtail* short tail — more at BANGTAIL] **:** the front hair or a section of it cut short and worn straight or curled over the forehead — usu. used in pl.

A bang

[6]**bang** \"\ *n* -s [origin unknown] **1 :** a common sardine (*Sardinella anchovia*) of the western Atlantic esp. abundant in the Caribbean area **2 :** ALEWIFE

[7]**bang** \"\ *var of* BHANG

[8]**bang** \"\ *n* -s *usu cap* [Skt *Vaṅga* Bengal] **1 :** an ancient people of Bengal, India, differing racially and culturally from the Aryans whose literature refers to them disdainfully **2 :** a member of the Bang people

ban·ga \'bäŋ'ä\ *n* -s [Tag] **:** a large spherical baked-clay water jar of the Philippines

bang·al·ay \baŋ'alē\ *n* -s [native name in Australia] **:** BASTARD MAHOGANY 1a(1)

ban·ga·lore \'baŋgə,lō(ə)r\ *adj, usu cap* [fr. *Bangalore*, India] **:** of or from the city of Bangalore, India **:** of the kind or style prevalent in Bangalore

bangalore torpedo \"\ *also* **bangalore** \'==,=, ,==='\ *n* -s [fr. *Bangalore*, city in India] **:** a metal tube containing explosives and a firing mechanism often designed so that it can be joined to other such tubes and used to cut wire entanglements and detonate buried mines by being exploded flat on the ground

ban·ga·low palm *also* **bangalow** \'baŋgə,lō\ *n* -s [native name in Australia] **:** either of two Australian palms (*Auchontophoenix alexandrae* and *A. cunninghamii*) cultivated for their tall erect form and pinnate foliage and having a terminal bud that is sometimes used as food

ban·gash \'ban,gash\ *n, pl* **bangash** *or* **bangashes** *usu cap* **1 :** a Pathan people in the Punjab **2 :** a member of the Bangash people

bang away *vi* **1 :** to work with determined effort ⟨students *banging away* on their homework⟩ **2 :** to attack esp. in an indirect, persistent, hounding way — used with *at* ⟨police are going to keep *banging away* at you —Erle Stanley Gardner⟩

bang-bang \'=,=\ *n* **:** SHOOTING; *broadly* **:** violent action ⟨plenty of *bang-bang* in that movie⟩

bangboard \'=,=\ *n* [[1]*bang* + *board*] **1 :** an extra sidepiece mounted above the far sideboard of a wagon from which the ears of corn tossed by a husker rebound into the wagon **2 :** a tennis practice board usu. of plywood with a line marked at the height of a net

bange \'banj\ *vi* **banged; banged; bangeing; banges** [origin unknown] *NewEng* **:** to lounge about **:** LOAF

ban·ghy \'baŋgē\ *n* -ES [Hindi *bahaṅgī*] *India* **:** a shoulder yoke for carrying loads; *also* **:** the yoke with its pair of suspended boxes or baskets

bang·i·a·ce·ae \,baŋē'āsē,ē\ *n pl, cap* [NL, fr. *Bangia*, type genus (fr. Hoffman *Bang*, 19th cent. Dan. botanist + NL *-ia*) + *-aceae*] **:** a family of chiefly marine red algae (order Bangiales) having a simple unbranched mostly thin or membranaceous thallus with a single stellate axile chromatophore in each cell and no pits in the cell walls — **bang·i·a·ceous** \¦==¦=shəs\ *adj*

bang·i·a·les \,baŋē'ā(,)lēz\ *n pl, cap* [NL, fr. *Bangia* + *-ales*] **:** an order of red algae usu. considered coextensive with the subclass Bangioideae

bang·ing \'baŋiŋ, ŋēŋ\ *adj* [fr. pres. part. of [1]*bang*] **:** HUGE, WHOPPING ⟨a ~ lie⟩

bang·i·oi·de·ae \,baŋē'ōidē,ē\ *n pl, cap* [NL, fr. *Bangia* genus of algae + *-oideae* — more at BANGIACEAE] **:** a subclass of Rhodophyceae comprising red algae that usu. lack a growing point, undergo diffuse growth, and have a filamentous or foliose and often unbranched thallus — compare FLORIDEAE

bangka *var of* BANCA

bang·kal \bäŋ·'käl\ *n* -s [Bisayan *baṅkal*] **:** BANCAL

[1]**bang·kok** \'baŋ·,käk, -aiŋ·-, =¦=\ *adj, usu cap* [fr. *Bangkok*, Thailand] **:** of or from Bangkok, the capital of Thailand **:** of the kind or style prevalent in Bangkok

[2]**bangkok** \"\ *n* -s **1 :** a fine buntal **2 :** a hat made of bangkok

[1]**bang·le** \'baŋəl\ *vt* -ED/-ING/-S [origin unknown] *now dial Eng* **:** to fritter away **:** WASTE ⟨~ away a fortune⟩

[2]**ban·gle** \'baŋgəl, -aiŋ-\ *n* -s [Hindi *baṅgrī, baṅgrī, baṅglī*] **1 :** a stiff usu. ornamental bracelet or anklet slipped or clasped on **2 :** something that hangs loosely; *esp* **:** an ornamental disk (as on a bracelet, necklace, tambourine)

ban·go \'baŋ(,)gō\ *or* **bango reed** *n* -s [native name in East Africa] **:** an East African grass (*Phragmites mauritianus*) used in thatching buildings

bang off *vi, of a loom* **:** to stop normal operation due to the failure of the shuttle to enter the box

ban·gón \baŋ'gōn\ *n, pl* **bangón** *or* **bangóns** *usu cap* [Tag] **1 :** a pagan people inhabiting central Mindoro, Philippines **2 :** a member of the Bangón people

ban·gor ladder *also* **bangor** \'baŋ,gò(ə)r, -aiŋ-, -,gò(ə),-,gə(r)\ *n, usu cap B* [fr. *Bangor*, Maine, where it was invented] **:** a long extension ladder controlled by means of poles and used in fire fighting

bang·os \'bäŋōs\ *n, pl* **bangos** [Tag] *Philippines* **:** MILKFISH

bang out *vt* **:** to produce in a hurried manner ⟨a typist *banging out* copy⟩ ⟨authors continually are being importuned to *bang out* a brief article, speech, or foreword —Bennett Cerf⟩

bangs *pres 3d sing of* BANG, *pl of* BANG

bang's disease *also* **bang's** \'baŋz-, -aiŋz-\ *n, usu cap B* [after Bernhard L.F. *Bang* †1932 Dan. veterinarian] **:** BRUCELLOSIS; *specif* **:** contagious abortion of cattle

bangsring *var of* BANXRING

bang·ster \'baŋztər, -ŋ(k)st-\ *n* -s [[1]*bang* + *-ster*] **1** *Scot* **:** BULLY, ROUGHNECK **2** *Scot* **:** WINNER, VICTOR

bangtail \'=,=\ *n* [fr. *bangtail* short tail, prob. fr. [1]*bang* + *tail*] **1 a :** RACEHORSE **b :** a wild horse; *esp* **:** one with a short stubby tail **2** *Austral* **:** any bovine that has had its tail banged to indicate that it has been counted during a muster and to prevent the possibility of recounting it

bangtail muster *n* [*bangtail* short tail; fr. the practice of cutting the tuft at the end of the tail straight across as the animal is counted] *Austral* **:** a roundup of cattle for counting them

ban·gui \'bäŋ(,)gē\ *adj, usu cap* [fr. *Bangui*, Central African Republic] **:** of or from Bangui, capital of the Central African Republic **:** of the kind or style prevalent in Bangui

[1]**bang-up** \'=,=\ *adj* [[1]*bang*] **:** FIRST-RATE, EXCELLENT ⟨a *bang-up* job⟩

[2]**bang-up** \"\ *n* -s [origin unknown] **:** a heavy overcoat

ban·gy \'baŋgē\ *var of* BANGHY

bani *pl of* BAN

bania *or* **banian** *var of* BANYAN

ba·nig \bä'nēg\ *n* -s [Tag *banig*] *Philippines* **:** PETATE

baning *pres part of* BANE

ban·ish \'banish, -ēsh, *esp in pres part* -əsh\ *vt* -ED/-ING/-ES [ME *banishen*, fr. *baniss-*, stem of MF *banir*, of Gmc origin; akin to OHG *ban* command, prohibition — more at BAN] **1 a :** to require (a person) by authority to leave esp. his own country or the country in which he is staying ⟨political foes ~*ed* by the dictator⟩ **b :** to forbid (a person) to frequent a certain area, group, or class ⟨~ from court⟩ ⟨~ newsmen from the captured city⟩ **c :** to send (a person) away often in a summary manner **:** DISMISS ⟨stood confronting her visitor as though to ~ her from the house —Robert Grant †1940⟩ **2 a :** to remove esp. from a significant or dominant position **:** DEPOSE ⟨genetic theories . . . are to be ~*ed* from Russian laboratories —*Collier's Yr. Bk.*⟩ ⟨the . . . towboat is fighting the railroad that ~*ed* the packet boat —Murray Schumach⟩ **b :** to do away with or cast out esp. in a retributive, truculent, or vindictive manner ⟨the club signified its displeasure by ~*ing* his portrait from the library — *Amer. Guide Series: N.Y. City*⟩ ⟨the gray squirrels will entirely ~ the old red ones —Lord Dunsany⟩ **3 :** to clear away **:** DISSIPATE, DISPEL ⟨a smudge to ~ mosquitoes —B.A.Williams⟩ ⟨literacy . . . will ~ the desperation on which communism feeds —Jerome Ellison⟩ ⟨anesthesia has done much to ~ the fear of operations⟩

syn BANISH, EXILE, EXPATRIATE, OSTRACIZE, DEPORT, TRANSPORT, and EXTRADITE mean, in common, to remove by force or authority from a country, state, or sovereignty. To BANISH is usu. to compel, usu. by public edict or sentence, to leave and stay out of a country or section, although not necessarily one's own ⟨the Reverend John Wheelwright, who had been *banished* from the Massachusetts Bay Colony —*Amer. Guide Series: N.H.*⟩ ⟨the Newtonian scheme of the universe does not *banish* God from the universe —*Times Lit. Supp.*⟩ ⟨Plato wished to *banish* poetry utterly from the Republic because it could be intoxicating to its victims —Max Lerner & Edwin Mims⟩ To EXILE is usu. to banish a person from his own country or section or oneself voluntarily from one's own country ⟨*exiled* to Siberia for political offenses⟩ ⟨many American writers *exiled* themselves in Paris⟩ ⟨the fallen champion chose to *exile* himself to his southern ranch —*Time*⟩ To EXPATRIATE implies not only exile but often a loss of citizenship in one's country, often voluntarily imposed by naturalization in another country ⟨a man all too willing to be *expatriated*⟩ ⟨*expatriate* oneself to England for emotional reasons for a number of years⟩ To OSTRACIZE is to exclude by common consent from recognition or acceptance by society ⟨a person *ostracized* for religious reasons⟩ ⟨the dangers inherent in *ostracizing* from public service men of eminence —Kimmis Hendrick⟩ ⟨after the Normans conquered England in 1066, Anglo-Saxon was *ostracized* from the schools⟩ To DEPORT is to banish (a person) from a country of which he is not a citizen, often to the country from which he came ⟨aiding the Chinese government to *deport* to their homeland the remnants of Japanese forces —*Current Biog.*⟩ ⟨an alien *deported* because of illegal entry into the country⟩ To TRANSPORT, in this sense, is to banish a person convicted of crime to a penal colony or a place regarded as like one ⟨English convicts *transported* to Australia⟩ To EXTRADITE is to deliver over (a person, usu. an alleged criminal) to authorities of another jurisdiction ⟨a criminal *extradited* by Texas at the request of Massachusetts for a confessed murder in Massachusetts⟩

ban·ish·ment \-mənt\ *n* -s **1 a :** legal expulsion from a country ⟨in 1940 his sentence was changed to ~ —*Current Biog.*⟩ **b :** exclusion or dismissal, self-imposed or prescribed by some authority, esp. from a particular area, group, or class ⟨his ~ from amateur sports⟩ ⟨~ from good society⟩ **2 :** a casting off **:** DISCARDING ⟨the ~ of the textbook from the classroom —Theodore Collier⟩

ban·is·ter *also* **ban·nis·ter** \'banəstə(r)\ *n* -s [alter. of *baluster*] **1 :** a slender vertical post sometimes having a turned or molded outline; *specif* **:** one of the upright supports of a handrail alongside a staircase — compare BALUSTER **2** *often pl but sing or pl in constr* **a :** a handrail (as of a staircase) and its supporting posts **b :** the handrail esp. of a staircase ⟨Alice went downstairs, walking with one hand on the ~*s* —Audrey Barker⟩ **3 :** one of several upright members, typically split turnings, that support the crest rail of a chair back

ba·ni·va *also* **ba·ni·wa** \bə'nēvə\ *n, pl* **baniva** *or* **banivas** *usu cap* [Sp *baniva*, of AmerInd origin] **1 a :** an Arawakan people of the upper Orinoco and Río Negro, Venezuela and Colombia **b :** a member of such people **2 :** the language of the Baniva people

baniya *var of* BANYAN

ban·jo \'ban(,)jō, -aan-, *in S often* -jə\ *n, pl* **banjos** *also* **banjoes** [prob. of African origin; akin to Kimbundu *mbanza*, a similar stringed instrument] **1 a :** a musical instrument of the guitar class with a long narrow fretted neck and small drumlike body and usu. five strings plucked or strummed

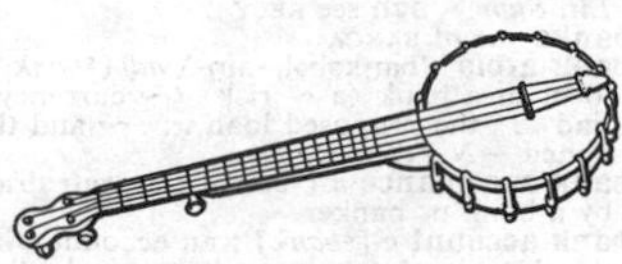

banjo 1b

with the fingers **b :** a banjo with a larger body and four wire strings played usu. with a pick — called also *tenor banjo* **2 :** BANJO SIGNAL **3 :** something bearing some resemblance to a banjo in shape: as **a :** a miner's shovel **b :** a working device for the placer mining of tin **c :** a transmission housing of a certain design

banjo clock *n* **:** a shelf or wall pendulum clock whose shape suggests a banjo; *esp* **:** such a clock designed by Simon Willard of Roxbury, Mass. and patented by him in 1802

a banjo clock

banjo hit *n* **:** BLOOPER 3b

ban·jo·ist \-,jōəst, -,jəwə-\ *n* -s **:** a banjo player

ban·jo·rine \,banjə¦rēn\ *n* -s [*banjo* + *-rine* (as in *tambourine*)] **:** a banjo with a short neck, tuned a fourth higher than the common banjo

banjo signal *n* **:** a former railroad-signal apparatus having a circular box with a glass window in which a red disk appeared as the danger signal

ban·jo–uku·le·le \¦==(,)= +\ *also* **ban·jo–uke** \"+\ *n* **:** a ukulele with a drumlike body

[1]**bank** \'baŋk, -aiŋk\ *n* -s [ME *banke*, prob. of Scand origin; akin to ON *bakki* ridge, bank; akin to OE *benc* bench — more at BENCH] **1 :** a mound, pile, or ridge raised by natural processes or artificial means above the surrounding level: **a** *now dial Eng* **:** ELEVATION, HILL **b** *obs* **:** EARTHWORK **c :** something piled or accumulated in the form of a mound and often having a broad or long base and flat top ⟨a ~ of snow⟩; *specif* **:** a piled-up mass of cloud, fog, or mist often extending upward from the horizon **d :** an underwater elevation of mud, gravel, or sand; *specif* **:** an undersea elevation rising esp. from the continental shelf and usu. with a broad flat top ⟨the cod ~s off Norway —Irwin Shaw⟩ — compare REEF, SEAMOUNT, SHOAL **2 a :** the margin of a watercourse **:** the rising ground bordering a lake, river, or sea or forming the edge of a cut or other hollow **b** *obs* **:** SEACOAST **3 a :** a steep acclivity (as the side of a hill, pile, or mound) **:** GRADE, SLOPE **b :** the lateral inward tilt of a vehicle or other moving object when taking a curve ⟨the bomber crossed the target area in a sharp ~⟩ **:** the lateral inward tip of a surface (as a road or track) along a curve ⟨the engineers hadn't given the road enough ~⟩ **4 :** a protective or cushioning rim or piece: as **a** (1) **:** the slightly elevated ground surrounding a bowling green on the outer side of the ditch (2) **:** CUSHION 3e **b :** a ramp of earth (as that leading to the upper story of some bank barns) **c :** BANKING PIN **5 a** *Brit* **:** the place in a bog where peat is dug **b** (1) **:** the face of coal being worked (2) **:** a deposit of ore or coal worked by excavations above water level (3) **:** the ground at the top of a shaft ⟨the cost of an ore on the ~⟩

[2]**bank** \"\ *vb* -ED/-ING/-S *vt* **1 :** to raise a bank about **:** enclose, protect, or fortify with a bank **:** EMBANK: as **a :** to cover (as a fire) with fresh fuel or other material, usu. adjusting the draft to slow the rate of burning and maintain fire for a prolonged period — often used with *up* **b :** to heap earth along the row of (a growing crop, as of celery) to protect or blanch **:** HILL, EARTH **c :** to build (a railway curve) with the outer rail elevated above the inner rail or to build (a curve in a road or track) with the roadbed or track inclined laterally upward from the inside edge to the outside edge so as to prevent a fast-moving vehicle or runner from being carried off the track or toppled over by centrifugal force in rounding the curve ⟨it is necessary to ~ the curves very steeply for bobsled racing⟩ **2** *obs* **:** to pass by the banks of **:** SKIRT **3 :** to heap (as sand) or pile (as logs) in a bank ⟨lumberjacks . . . ~*ed* the cut timber on rollways to await the spring drives —*Amer. Guide Series: Mich.*⟩ — often used with *up* ⟨there is ~*ed* up a great mass of purchasing power —Clement Atlee⟩ **4 a :** to drive (the cue ball in billiards) into a cushion before striking an object ball **b** (1) **:** to drive (an object ball in pool) into a cushion in an attempt to pocket or to place advantageously on the rebound (2) **:** to drive (a cue ball in pool) into a cushion to hit an object ball on the rebound or to play a safe shot **5 :** to form or group in a tier ⟨~ electric lights⟩ ~ *vi* **1 :** to rise in or form a bank **:** lie in banks (as of clouds) — often used with *up* ⟨in the rainy season the clouds would ~ up about midday, and showers fall with true tropical violence —William Beebe⟩ **2 :** to swing so far as to strike against a banking pin — used of the lever of a lever escapement in a watch or clock **3 :** to fish on the banks of Newfoundland **4 a** (1) **:** to incline an airplane laterally (2) *of an airplane* **:** to incline laterally ⟨torpedo planes . . . darting in to attack, then ~*ing* off —K.M.Dodson⟩ **b :** to execute a movement like that of an airplane banking ⟨comets . . . appear without warning, race in through the planets, ~ sharply around the sun, then head out toward the stars —A.C. Clarke⟩ — used esp. of birds in flight and fishes swimming

[3]**bank** \"\ *n* -s [ME *banck*, fr. OF *banc*, of Gmc origin; akin to OHG *bank* bench — more at BENCH] **1 a** *obs* **:** the bench or seat on which the judges of a court of law sit **b :** a bench upon which the rowers of a galley sit **2 :** a group or series of objects arranged near together in a row or a tier: as **a :** a tier of oars esp. of an ancient galley **b :** a tier of keys belonging to a keyboard **c :** a set of two or more elevators ⟨eighteen passenger elevators, in three ~s of six —*New Yorker*⟩ **3 a** *archaic* **:** a table for holding unprinted and printed sheets **b :** a slant-topped stand or sometimes a flat-topped table on which type matter in galleys is corrected and prepared for makeup **4 :** one of the horizontal divisions of a headline; *esp* **:** a secondary or lower division — compare [1]DECK 6 **5 :** the backboard to which a basketball hoop is attached — **in bank** *adv, law* **:** in full court — compare BANC

[4]**bank** \"\ *n* -s [ME, fr. MF or OIt; MF *banque*, fr. OIt *banca*, lit., bench, of Gmc origin; akin to OHG *bank* bench] **1 a** (1) *obs* **:** the table, counter, or place of business of a money-changer (2) **:** an establishment for the custody, loan, exchange, or issue of money, for the extension of credit, and for facilitating the transmission of funds by drafts or bills of exchange; *also* **:** an institution incorporated for performing one or more of such functions **b :** GAMBLING HOUSE **2 a :** the stockholders or directors of a bank acting in their corporate capacity **b :** a person or persons conducting a gambling house or game; *specif* **:** DEALER **3 :** a supply of something useful or valuable held in reserve: as **a** (1) *obs* **:** a sum of money (2) **:** the sum of money in certain gambling games (as chemin de fer) that is deposited or stated by the dealer as a fund from which to pay his losses **b** (1) **:** the whole supply of chips available for purchase and use by players in a game played with chips (as poker) (2) **:** a fund of pieces belonging to a game (as dominoes) from which the players are allowed to draw **c :** an excess of logs cut or skidded during a given period and held as a reserve to make up deficiencies in daily quotas **4 :** a place where something useful or valuable is held available: as **a :** LANDING 2b **b :** a small container for holding coins to be accumulated as savings or for a special purpose — see PIGGY BANK **c :** a depot for the collection and storage of a biological product of human origin for medical use ⟨a semen ~⟩ ⟨a nerve ~⟩ ⟨bone ~⟩ — **in the bank** *adv (or adj), Brit* **:** in debt

[5]**bank** \"\ *vb* -ED/-ING/-S *vi* **1 a :** to keep a bank **b :** to carry out the business of banking **2 a :** to deposit money in a bank ⟨a trip into town to shop and ~⟩ **b :** to have an account with a bank or banker ⟨the company ~s at the First National⟩ ~ *vt* **1 :** to deposit in a bank ⟨~ your salary⟩ **2 :** to deposit (as blood, plasma, bone) for storage in a bank (sense 4c) ⟨whole blood . . . could be ~*ed* indefinitely —*Time*⟩ **3 :** to act as banker for (as a gambling game) **4 :** FINANCE ⟨members who help ~ political campaigns —*New Republic*⟩ — **bank on** *or* **bank upon :** to expect with confidence or assurance **:** depend upon **:** rely on ⟨*bank on* a person's help⟩ ⟨Hitler . . . *banked on* the moral collapse of the Western Powers —*Times Lit. Supp.*⟩ **syn** see RELY

banka *var of* BANCA

bank·a·ble \'baŋkəbəl, -aiŋ-\ *adj* [[5]*bank* + *-able*] **:** acceptable to or at a bank ⟨a ~ risk⟩ ⟨~ currency⟩ ⟨the bank did not find . . . the proposed loan . . . ~ and the project was abandoned —*N.Y.Times*⟩

bank acceptance *n* [[4]*bank*] **:** a draft drawn on and accepted by a bank or banker

bank account *n* [[4]*bank*] **:** an account with a bank created by the deposit of money or its equivalent and subject to withdrawal of money (as by check or passbook) ⟨thought it wise to put his savings in a *bank account*⟩

bank and turn indicator *n* [[1]*bank*] **:** TURN AND BANK INDICATOR

bank annuities *n pl* [[4]*bank*] **:** CONSOLS

bank balance *n* [[4]*bank*] **1 :** the amount credited to a depositor of a bank as of a particular time **2 :** a balance against or in favor of a bank at a financial clearinghouse ⟨an increasingly substantial *bank balance*⟩

bank barn *n* [[1]*bank*] **:** a two-story barn, typical of northern and central parts of No. America, built into a slope of earth that provides an outside entrance into the second story on one side, the lower story being enterable from the other side

bank beaver *n* [[1]*bank*] **1 :** OTTER **2 :** a beaver that inhabits burrows in stream banks instead of making a house and dam

bank bill *n* [[4]*bank*] **1 :** an obsolete Bank of England note — called also *sealed bank bill* **2 :** BANK NOTE 1

bankbook \'=,=\ *n* [[4]*bank* + *book*] **:** the depositor's book in which a bank enters his deposits and withdrawals — called also *passbook*

bank call *n* [[4]*bank*] **:** a periodic demand made usu. quarterly by the Comptroller of Currency of the U.S. upon national banks and by the heads of the banking departments of the several states upon state banks and trust companies for sworn detailed statements showing the condition of the banks as of a definite date

bank check *n* [[4]*bank*] **:** an order by a depositor on a commercial bank to pay a specified sum on demand to a designated payee or, when the check is endorsed by the payee, to others

bank commissioner *n* [[4]*bank*] **:** an appointed official in charge of supervising banks; *esp* **:** a state superintendent of banks

bank craps *n* [[4]*bank*] **:** the game of craps played in gambling houses where every bet made against the house is under special rules established by the house

bank debit *n* [[4]*bank*] **:** the charge against a bank-deposit account resulting from the drawing of checks or from cash withdrawals

bank deposit *n* [[4]*bank*] **:** any funds credited to a depositor's account by a bank

bank deposit insurance *n* **:** the insurance of deposit accounts up to $10,000 (formerly up to $5000) in banks in the U.S. that belong to the Federal Deposit Insurance Corporation

bank discount *n* [[4]*bank*] **:** the interest discounted in advance on a note and computed on the face value of the note ⟨the *bank discount* on $1000 for one year at 5% is $50⟩ — compare ARITHMETICAL DISCOUNT

bank draft *n* [[4]*bank*] **:** a demand draft drawn by one bank upon funds to its account in another bank

banked *adj* [fr. past part. of [2]*bank*] **1 :** arranged in tiers ⟨~ microphones⟩ ⟨~ windows⟩ **2 :** laterally tipped or made while laterally tipped esp. inward along or while taking a curve ⟨a ~ railroad track⟩ ⟨the ~ glide of an airplane⟩ **3 a :** piled up into or as if into a bank ⟨~ earth⟩ ⟨~ clouds⟩ **b :** protected by a bank ⟨~ cellar windows⟩ ⟨guns ~ in concrete⟩

bank engine *n* [[1]*bank* (slope)] *Brit* **:** a helper locomotive used to assist heavy trains over steep grades — called also *banker*

[1]**ban·ker** \'baŋkə(r), -aiŋ-\ *n* -s [ME, fr. OF *banquier*, fr. *banc* bench — more at BANK] *archaic* **:** a covering (as of tapestry) for a bench or chair

[2]**bank·er** \"\ *n* -s [MF *banquier*, fr. *banque* bench, table, bank + *-ier* -er — more at BANK] **1 :** one who engages in the business of commercial or investment banking **2 a :** the player who keeps, sells, and redeems the supply of chips used in a game — compare [4]BANK 3b(1) **b :** the person who agrees to cover the bets of all players up to a certain limit established as the bank **c :** a dealer (as in blackjack) or a gambling house or its representative against whom all bets must be placed **d :** BANKER AND BROKER

[3]**bank·er** \"\ *n* -s [[1]*bank* + *-er*] **1 :** a man or a vessel employed in the cod fishery on the banks of Newfoundland **2** *Austral* **:** a river running full to the top of its banks

[4]**bank·er** \"\ *n* -s [[3]*bank* + *-er*] **:** a bench of stone or wood or a support on which a sculptor, mason, or bricklayer shapes or gauges his material

[5]**bank·er** \"\ *n* -s [[1]*bank* + *-er*] **:** BANK ENGINE

banker and broker *n* [[2]*banker*] **:** any of various card games in which two or more opposing players lift off a packet from the deck and show the card at the bottom of the packet, the highest-ranking card so shown determining the winner

banker–mark \'==,=\ *n* [[4]*banker*] **:** a mark cut by the stonecutter on dressed stones in medieval times to identify the person preparing the stone — called also *mason's mark*

banker mason *n* [[4]*banker*] **:** a workman who does by hand the final preparation work on stone-masonry blocks

banker's acceptance *n* [[2]*banker*] **:** BANK ACCEPTANCE

banker's bank *n* [[2]*banker*] **:** a bank that deals only with other banks; *specif* **:** a central bank (as a U.S. Federal Reserve bank or the Bank of England)

banker's bill *n* [[2]*banker*] **:** a bill of exchange drawn by a bank on a foreign bank

bankers' blanket bond *n* [[2]*banker*] **:** insurance sold to financial institutions covering theft by employees and losses due to burglary, robbery, or forgery — compare FIDELITY BOND

banker's check *n* [[2]*banker*] **:** TRAVELER'S CHECK

banker's draft *n* [[2]*banker*] **:** a check or bill drawn by one bank against balances deposited with another

ban·ket \(')baŋ¦ket\ *n* -s [Afrik, lit., a kind of confectionery, banquet, fr. MD, banquet, fr. MF *banquet* — more at BANQUET] **:** the auriferous conglomerate rock of the Transvaal

bank examiner *n* [[4]*bank*] **:** a federal or state official empowered to examine the records and affairs of a bank

bank fish *n* [[1]*bank*; so called fr. its being caught on the banks of Newfoundland] **:** COD

bank–full \'=¦=\ *adj* [[1]*bank* + *full*] **:** full to the top of the banks ⟨a *bank-full* river⟩

bank gravel *n* [[1]*bank*] **:** gravel or sand as found in natural deposits

bank guarantee *n* [[4]*bank*] **:** a statement issued by an importer's bank guaranteeing the payment of drafts to the exporter

bank guaranty *n* [[4]*bank*] **:** insurance to protect depositors in a bank against loss in case of failure — see DEPOSITORY BOND

bank head *n* [[1]*bank* + *head*] **:** the mouth and immediate environs of a coalmine

bank holiday *n* [[4]*bank*] **1** *Brit* **:** a holiday on which banks are closed by law **:** LEGAL HOLIDAY **2 :** a period when banks in general are closed often by government fiat (as for the stabilization of currency or for the reform of banking practices)

ban·kia \'baŋkēə\ *n, cap* [NL, fr. Sir Joseph *Banks* †1820 Eng. naturalist + NL *-ia*] **:** a genus of boring mollusks (family Teredinidae) including the giant northwest shipworm (*B. setacea*) of the Pacific coast of No. America

bank indicator *also* **banking indicator** *n* [[1]*bank*] **:** RELATIVE INCLINOMETER

[1]**banking** *n* -s [fr. gerund of [5]*bank*] **:** the business of a bank, orig. restricted to money changing and now devoted to taking money on deposit subject to check or draft, loaning money and credit (as by discounting notes and bills), issuing drafts, and any other associated form of general dealing in money or credit

[2]**banking** *n* -s [fr. gerund of [2]*bank*] **1 a :** the construction of embankments **b :** [1]BANK 2a **:** EMBANKMENT **2 :** fishing on the banks of Newfoundland

banking doctrine *also* **banking principle** *n* **:** the principle that bank notes represent a form of banker's credit and should not be subject to special regulation and that freedom from regulation is essential to an elastic currency the fluctuation of which will be regulated by business conditions — compare CURRENCY DOCTRINE

banking game *n* **:** a gambling game in which bets must be laid against a gambling house, banker, or dealer

banking pin *n* [fr. pres. part. of [2]*bank*] **1 :** either of two upright pins limiting the angular motion of the pallet fork in a timepiece having a lever escapement **2 :** a pin emerging horizontally from the rim of a balance in a cylinder escapement or verge escapement to limit the arc of the balance **3 :** REGULATOR PIN

banking screw *n* [fr. pres. part. of [2]*bank*] **:** an adjustable screw in a chronometer escapement for regulating the depth of escape-tooth locking

bank kiln *n* [[1]*bank*] **:** an Oriental kiln (as in China) built on a slope of a hill to obtain draft

bank letter *n* [[4]*bank*] **:** a periodical reviewing economic and financial developments that is issued by a bank

bank line *n* [[1]*bank*] **:** a fishing line attached to the shore and not tended by a fisherman **:** SETLINE

bank loan *n* [[4]*bank*] **:** a loan by a bank to be repaid at a fixed future date with interest — compare DISCOUNT

bank·man \'baŋkmən, -aiŋ-\ *n, pl* **bankmen** [[1]*bank* + *man*] **:** a compositor or apprentice who works at a stand on which type matter in galleys is corrected and prepared for makeup

bank martin *n* [[1]*bank*] **:** BANK SWALLOW

bank money *n* [[4]*bank*] **:** the equivalent of money as a medium of exchange constituted by checks, drafts, or bank credits other than bank notes — compare CURRENCY

bank night *n* [[4]*bank*] **:** a copyright form of lottery conducted by proprietors of motion-picture theaters with a drawing of prizes for distribution among patrons who have registered and are present at an appointed evening performance

bank note *n* [[4]*bank*] **1 :** a promissory note issued by a bank payable to bearer on demand but without interest and circulating as money — compare NATIONAL BANK NOTE **2 :** a strong durable pliable bond paper made of cotton and linen rags and used in paper money

bank of deposit [[4]*bank*] **:** a bank that receives money for safe-keeping

bank of issue *also* **bank of circulation** [[4]*bank*] **:** a bank authorized by law to issue bank notes (as the Bank of England or the U.S. Federal Reserve banks)

bank paper *n* [[4]*bank*] **1 a :** circulating bank notes **b :** bankable commercial paper (as drafts or bills accepted by a bank or notes good enough to be discounted at a bank) **2 :** a thin strong paper similar to but lighter than bond paper and commonly used for business letterheads

bank pole *n* [[1]*bank*] **:** a fishing pole secured to the shore and not tended by a fisherman

bank rate *n* [[4]*bank*] **:** the discount rate fixed by a central bank (as by the Bank of England) — compare DISCOUNT RATE

[1]**bankroll** \'=,=\ *n* [[4]*bank* + *roll*] **:** supply of money **:** FUNDS ⟨rising taxes had made a great dent in the family ~⟩

[2]**bankroll** \"\ *vt* **:** to supply the capital for or pay the cost of (a business or project) ⟨the project was ~*ed* by the government⟩

bank·roll·er \"ə(r)\ *n* [*bankroll* + *-er*] **:** one that bankrolls ⟨was ~ for a television show⟩

bank run *n* [[1]*bank*] **:** BANK GRAVEL

[1]**bank·rupt** \'baŋk·,rəpt, -aiŋ-, -ŋ krəpt\ *n* -s [modif. (influenced by L *ruptus*) of MF & OIt; MF *banqueroute*, fr. OIt *bancarotta*, fr. *banca* bank + *rotta* broken, fr. L *rupta*, fem. of *ruptus*, past part. of *rumpere* to break — more at BANK, REAVE] **1** *obs* **:** BANKRUPTCY **2 a** *obs* **:** a person who to avoid payment of his debts secretes himself, flees the country, or defrauds or simply avoids his creditors and is in consequence legally a criminal **b :** any person who has done any of the acts that the law provides shall entitle his creditors to have his estate administered for their benefit (as by the making of a general assignment) **c :** a person who has on the petition of his creditors or on his own petition been judicially declared subject to having his estate administered under the bankrupt laws for the benefit of his creditors **d :** a person who becomes insolvent — not used technically **3 :** one who is destitute of or completely lacking in a particular thing ⟨a moral ~⟩ ⟨a ~ in all that is intellectually valuable⟩

[2]**bankrupt** \"\ *vt* -ED/-ING/-S **1 a :** to bring about the legal bankruptcy of ⟨high taxes and poor sales ~*ed* the company⟩ **b :** DEPLETE, IMPOVERISH ⟨war had ~*ed* the nation's natural resources and manpower⟩ **2 a :** to render destitute of **:** DEPRIVE ⟨a nervous breakdown ~*ed* him of courage to face society⟩ **b :** to spoil completely **:** RUIN ⟨his revision made the novel more accurate historically but ~*ed* it as a work of art⟩ **syn** see DEPLETE

[3]**bankrupt** \"\ *adj* **1 a :** in a state of financial ruin ⟨the nation's finances are ~⟩ **:** IMPOVERISHED ⟨~ peasantry⟩; *specif* **:** declared legally insolvent and with assets taken over by judicial process in order that they may be distributed among creditors ⟨a ~ corporation⟩ ⟨the original owner of the company went ~⟩ **b :** having to do with bankrupts or bankruptcy ⟨~ laws⟩ **2 a :** BROKEN, RUINED ⟨a ~ professional career⟩ **:** come to an end **:** FINISHED ⟨~ politicians⟩ **b :** DEPLETED, STERILE, EXHAUSTED ⟨the conviction . . . that the world was morally and religiously ~ —G.G.Coulton⟩ ⟨a ~ old culture⟩ **c :** DESTITUTE, DEPRIVED — used with *of* or *in* ⟨~ of all merciful feelings⟩ ⟨~ in resources⟩

bank·rupt·cy \-p(t)sē, -si\ *n* -ES [[3]*bankrupt* + *-cy*] **1 :** the quality or state of being bankrupt ⟨the company went into ~⟩ **2 a :** utter failure ⟨the ~ of Hitler's soaring ambitions —G.P. Gooch⟩ **:** RUIN ⟨our policy . . . in ~, the nation in mortal peril —C.B.Marshall⟩ **b :** DEPLETION, EXHAUSTION ⟨physical ~⟩ ⟨quitting is a tacit admission of moral ~ —W.R.Miller⟩ **c :** STERILITY, BARRENNESS ⟨the ~ of his propaganda⟩

bankrupt worm *n* [so called fr. its injurious effect on sheep and cattle] **:** a roundworm of the genus *Trichostrongylus*

banks *pl of* BANK, *pres 3d sing of* BANK

banks·hall \'baŋks,hȯl\ *n* -s [by folk etymology fr. Malay *bangsal* shed] **1** *India* **:** WAREHOUSE **2** *India* **:** the office of a harbor master or port officer

bank shot *n* [[1]*bank*] **1 :** a shot in billiards and pool in which a player banks the cue ball or the object ball **2 :** a shot in basketball played to rebound from the backboard into the basket

banks·ia \'baŋksēə\ *n* [NL, fr. Sir Joseph *Banks* †1820 Eng. naturalist + NL *-ia*] **1** *cap* **:** an important genus of Australian evergreen trees or shrubs (family Proteaceae) with alternate coriaceous leaves, apetalous yellowish flowers often in showy heads, and large woody follicles containing winged seeds — see AUSTRALIAN HONEYSUCKLE **2 -s :** a plant of the genus *Banksia*

banks·ian pine \-ēən-\ *also* **banks' pine** \-ŋks(əz)-\ *or* **banks' air pine** *n, usu cap B* [after Sir Joseph *Banks*] **:** JACK PINE 1

banksia rose *also* **banksian rose** *n, sometimes cap B* **:** a Chinese evergreen climbing rose (*Rosa banksiae*) having yellow or white single flowers and being cultivated in several horticultural varieties in mild climates

bankside \'=,=\ *n* [[1]*bank* + *side*] **:** the slope of a bank esp. of a stream

bank·sku·ta \'baŋk,skūd·ə\ *also* **bank·skoi·te** \-kȯid·ə\ *n* -s [*bankskuta* fr. Sw, fr. *bank* + *skuta* sloop, smack; *bankskoite* fr. Norw *bankskøite*, fr. *bank* + *skøite* sloop, smack] **:** a usu. ketch-rigged Scandinavian fishing craft designed for use in the North Sea bank fisheries and averaging from 30 to 70 tons burden

banks·man \'baŋksmən\ *n, pl* **banksmen** [[1]*bank* + *-s* + *man*] **:** an overseer at the bank of a mine drift

banksring *var of* BANXRING

bank statement *n* [[4]*bank*] **1 :** a statement showing the condition of a bank or banks **2 :** a statement by a bank of a customer's account

bank stock *n* [[4]*bank*] **:** the capital stock of any banking company

bank superintendent *n* [[4]*bank*] **:** BANK COMMISSIONER

bank swallow *n* [[1]*bank*] **:** a small swallow (*Riparia riparia*) of the northern hemisphere that nests in a hole it makes in a bank — called also *bank martin*

bank vole *n* [[1]*bank*] **:** the common red-backed mouse (*Clethrionomys glareolus*) of Europe

bank winding *n* [[1]*bank*] **:** a type of winding of coils which is used esp. in radios and in which the turns are staggered so as to reduce the capacity of the whole coil

bank–wound \'=,=\ *adj* [[1]*bank*] **:** of or having to do with bank winding

ban·lieue *also* **ban·lieu** \bäⁿlyœ\ *n, pl* **banlieues** *also* **banlieux** \"\ [F *banlieue*, fr. OF, fr. *ban* summoning of the king's vassals, tribute, ban + *lieue* league, fr. LL *leuca* — more at BAN, LEAGUE] **:** the outlying residential area of a city **:** ENVIRONS — often used in pl. ⟨trainload after trainload of young men and women from the ~ was disgorged into the capital —Max Beerbohm⟩ ⟨from the location of all these puppet theaters in the ~s of town it is evident that they were the resorts . . . of common people —Paul McPharlin⟩

bannack *var of* BANNOCK

bannat *var of* BANAT

banned *past of* BAN

¹**ban·ner** \'banə(r)\ *n* -s [ME *baner, banere,* fr. OF *banere, baniere,* fr. *ban-* (modif. — influenced by OF *ban* proclamation, summons — of an assumed word in some Gmc language akin to Goth *bandwa, bandwo* sign) + *-ere, -iere* (fr. L *-aria* -ary); akin to ON *benda* to give a sign and prob. to Gk *phainein* to show — more at FANCY, BAN] **1 a :** a piece of cloth attached by one edge to a staff and used by a monarch, feudal lord, knight, or other commander as his standard which served as a rallying point for his men in battle **b :** FLAG 1 — used esp. in literary context or for emotional effect **c :** a quadrangular piece of cloth bearing armorial ensigns (as of an individual) **d** (1) **:** an ensign displaying some distinctive or symbolic device, motto, or legend; *esp* **:** one used as the emblem of a guild, fraternity, club, or other organization or presented as an award of honor or distinction (2) **:** such an ensign extended on a crosspiece, in a frame, or between poles **2 :** STANDARD 16a **3 a :** any of the primary divisions of the Manchu army, each having its distinctive banner **b :** a military subdivision of Mongolian tribes **4 :** a headline in large type running across an entire newspaper page usu. the first page **5 :** the actuated part of a disk or wigwag signal on a railroad **6 :** a strip of cloth on which a sign is painted ⟨welcoming ~s stretched across the street⟩ ⟨political ~s⟩ ⟨sideshow ~s — the pictorials that describe the freaks and the wonders on the midways —Emmett Kelly⟩ **syn** see FLAG

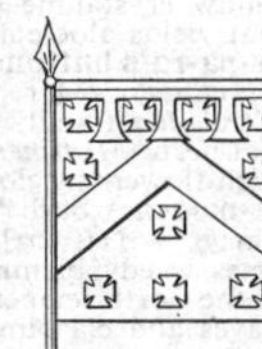
banner 1a

²**banner** \"\ *vt* -ED/-ING/-S **1 :** to furnish with a banner **2 :** to give extreme prominence to; *esp* **:** to print (a news story) under a banner usu. on the front page

³**banner** \"\ *adj* **:** distinguished from all others esp. in excellence **:** OUTSTANDING ⟨a ~ year for business⟩ ⟨a ~ student⟩ ⟨a bureau that has done ~ work in drawing up scientific recipes —*Consumers' Guide*⟩

banner cloud *n* **:** a cloud touching and extending out from the lee side of a mountain peak

bannered *adj* **1 :** bearing or furnished with a banner **:** hung with banners **2 :** blazoned or borne on a banner

¹**ban·ner·et** \'banərət, ˌ==ˈret\ *n* -s *often cap* [ME *baneret,* fr. OF *baneret, banerez,* fr. *banere* banner — more at BANNER] **1 :** a knight who was entitled to lead his vassals into the field under his own banner and who therefore ranked above a knight bachelor **:** KNIGHT BANNERET **2 :** a civil officer in some of the Swiss cantons and Italian republics

²**ban·ner·et** *also* **ban·ner·ette** \ˌbanəˈret\ *n* -s [ME *banerett,* fr. MF *banerete,* dim. of *banere*] **:** a small banner

banner head *or* **banner headline** *n* **:** BANNER 4

ban·ner·less \'banərləs, *-R* -nəl- *or* -nᵊl-\ *adj* **:** lacking a banner

¹**bannerline** \'==ˌ=\ *n* [¹*banner* + *line*] **:** ¹BANNER 4

²**bannerline** \"\ *vt* **:** ²BANNER 2

ban·ner·man \'banə(r)mən\ *n, pl* **bannermen 1 :** STANDARD-BEARER **2 :** a Manchu belonging to a banner

banner man \-ˌman\ *n* **:** one who posts bills advertising coming amusements

ban·ne·rol *also* **ban·ner roll** \'banəˌrōl\ *n* -s [*bannerol* fr. MF, var. of *banderole; banner roll* by folk etymology fr. *bannerol* — more at BANDEROLE] **:** BANDEROLE; *esp* **:** a banner displayed at a funeral and set over the tomb

banner plant *n* **:** any of several plants constituting the genus *Anthurium* and having a bright-colored reflexed bannerlike spathe

banner pompano *n* [so called fr. its long dorsal and anal fins] **:** LONGFIN POMPANO

banner screen *n* **:** a fire screen consisting of an upright pole usu. mounted on a tripod and carrying a rectangular frame covered with tapestry or needlework

bannerstone \'==ˌ=\ *n* **:** a perforated stone reported only from archaic sites in midwestern and eastern No. America and having usu. two symmetrical wings that was apparently used primarily as a weight attached to a throwing stick but doubtless had considerable ceremonial significance, having been often buried with the dead — compare ATLATL

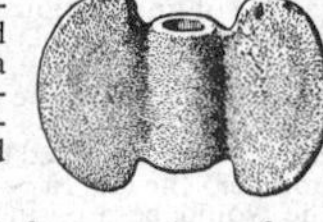
bannerstone from Rhea county, Tenn.

banning *pres part of* BAN

bannister *var of* BANISTER

ban·nis·ter harness \'banəstə(r)-\ *n, usu cap B* [prob. fr. the name *Bannister*] **:** a harness used for weaving wide patterns in fine reeds from a small jacquard loom

¹**ban·nock** \'banək, -nik\ *n* -s [ME *bannok,* prob. fr. ScGael *bannach, bonnach*] **1 :** an often unleavened bread of oat or barley flour baked in flattish loaves that is common in the British isles esp. in the north **2** *NewEng* **:** CORNBREAD; *esp* **:** a thin cake baked on a griddle

²**bannock** \"\ *also* **ban·nack** \"\ *n, pl* **bannock** *or* **bannocks** *also* **bannack** *or* **bannacks** *usu cap* [Bannock *Banákwŭt*] **1 a :** a Shoshonean people of southern Utah and neighboring states **b :** a member of such people **2 :** the language of the Bannock people

banns \'banz, -aa(ə)-\ *n pl* [pl. of *bann,* alter. (influenced by ²*ban*) of earlier *bane,* fr. ME, var. of ²*ban* (proclamation)] **1 :** notice of a proposed marriage proclaimed in a church or other place prescribed by law in order that any person may object if he knows any impediment to the marriage **2** *obs* **:** the proclamation or prologue of a play

ban·nut \'banət\ *n* -s [ME *bannenote*] *dial Eng* **:** ENGLISH WALNUT

ba·no·vi·na \'bänəˌvēnə\ *n, pl* **banovi·ne** \-ˌnā\ [Serbo-Croatian *bānovina,* fr. *bān* lord, ruler] **:** a former administrative subdivision of Yugoslavia

¹**ban·quet** \'baŋkwət, 'bank-,'baank- *sometimes* -nˌkwet *or* -ŋ-ˌkwet; *usu* -d+V\ *n* -s [MF, fr. OIt *banchetto* judge's bench, banquet, dim. of *banco* bench — more at BANCO] **1 a :** an elaborate and often ceremonious meal attended by numerous people and often honoring a person or marking some incident (as an anniversary or reunion) **b** *obs* **:** a drinking feast **2** *obs* **a :** DESSERT **b :** a repast between meals

²**banquet** \"\ *vb* -ED/-ING/-S [MF *banqueter,* fr. *banquet*] *vt* **:** to treat with a banquet **:** FEAST ⟨~*ed* the visiting notables⟩ ~ *vi* **:** to partake of a banquet **:** enjoy good food and drink ⟨didn't just eat; we ~*ed*⟩

ban·que·teer \ˌbaŋkwəˈti(ə)r, -a(a)nk-\ *n* -s **:** BANQUETER 2

ban·quet·er *pronunc at* ¹BANQUET + ə(r)\ *n* -s **1** *obs* **:** a host at a banquet **2 :** a guest at a banquet **:** a person prone to participate in banquets

ban·quette \(ˈ)baŋ·ˈket, -aiŋ·-, -anˈk-,-aanˈk-, *in sense 2b often* 'baŋkət *or* -aiŋ-\ *n* -s [F, fr. Prov *banqueta,* dim. of *banc* bench, of Gmc origin; akin to OHG *bank* bench — more at BENCH] **1 a :** a raised way or foot bank along the inside of a parapet or trench on which soldiers and guns are posted to fire upon the enemy — see BASTION illustration **b** *South* **:** a raised footway beside a thoroughfare **:** SIDEWALK **2 a :** a benchlike upholstered seat **b :** a narrow window seat **c :** a sofa having one roll-over arm **d :** a built-in upholstered bench along a wall or partition (as in a restaurant) **e :** a raised shelf (as at the back of a buffet) **3 :** an elevated platform or bench along the wall in a cliff dwelling or a kiva **4 :** an embankment constructed at the toe of the land side of a levee to protect the levee from sloughing off when saturated with water

banquette slope *n* **:** the slope of earth connecting the banquette tread of a fortification with the terreplein or parade

banquette tread *n* **:** the standing surface of a banquette (sense 1a) — called also *firing tread*

bans *pl of* BAN, *pres 3d sing of* BAN

ban·sal·a·guin \(ˌ)bänˌsäləˈgēn\ *also* **ban·sal·a·gue** *or* **ban·sal·a·gui** \bänˈsäləgē\ *or* **ban·sal·a·que** \-əkē\ *n* -s [Tag & Bisayan *bansalagin*] **1 :** a large tree (*Mimusops parvifolia*) of the Philippines and southwest Pacific area that produces an edible fruit and a very dense fine-grained wood that is reddish or reddish white in color **2 :** the wood of the bansalaguin

ban·shee *also* **ban·shie** \'ban(ˌ)shē\ *n* -s [ScGael *bean-sìth,* fr. or akin to OIr *ben síde* woman of fairyland, fr. *ben* woman + *síde,* gen. of *síd* fairy abode; akin to Gk *gynē* woman — more at QUEAN, SIDHE] **:** a female spirit in Gaelic folklore that warns a family of the approaching death of a member by her appearance or esp. by wailing unseen under the windows of the house a night or two before the time of the death she foretells

ban·stick·le \'banzˌtikəl, -nˌst-\ *n* -s [ME *banstickel,* prob. fr. *ban-* (fr. OE *bān* bone) + *stickel* sting, fr. OE *sticel* — more at BONE, STICKLE] **:** THREE-SPINED STICKLEBACK

bant \'bant\ *vi* -ED/-ING/-S [short for *bantingize* to reduce by bantingism, fr. *banting* + *-ize*] **:** to practice banting **:** DIET

¹**ban·tam** \'bantəm, -aan-\ *n* -s [fr. *Bantam,* former residency in Java] **1** *usu cap* **a :** a very small domestic fowl having feathered legs and feet and believed to have come from Java **b :** any of numerous small chiefly ornamental domestic fowls that are often miniatures of members of the standard breeds ⟨a Cochin ~⟩ ⟨a Brahma ~⟩ **2 :** a person of diminutive stature and often combative disposition **3 :** BANTAMWEIGHT **4 :** JEEP

²**bantam** \"\ *adj* **1 a :** SMALL ⟨~ sized⟩ **b :** easily handled **:** small and manageable ⟨a ~ edition of Shakespeare's complete works⟩ ⟨~ English cars⟩ **2 :** SAUCY **:** pertly combative ⟨her valiant ~ spirit —H.G.Wells⟩ **3 :** of the junior age-group ⟨a ~ baseball team⟩

ban·tam·ize \-ˌmīz\ *vt* -ED/-ING/-S *see -ize in Explan Notes* **:** to cause (a breed of fowls) to become bantam or to produce a bantam strain

bantamweight \'==ˌ=\ *n* **:** a boxer of the class whose maximum weight is 118 pounds — compare FEATHERWEIGHT

ban·tay \bänˈtī\ *n* -s [Tag *bantáy*] *Philippines* **:** a guard or sentinel

ban·ta·yan \bänˈtäˌyän\ *n* -s [Tag, fr. *bantáy*] *Philippines* **:** LOOKOUT, SIGNAL TOWER

ban·teng \'bänˌteŋ\ *also* **ban·tin** \-ntᵊn, -n(ˌ)tin\ *or* **bant·ing** \-nˌtiŋ\ *n* -s [Malay *banteng, banting*] **:** a wild ox (*Bibos banting,* syn. *sondaicus*) of the Malay peninsula and archipelago sometimes used for draft

¹**ban·ter** \'bantə(r), -aan-\ *vb* **bantered**; **bantered**; **bantering** \-ntəriŋ *also* -nˌtriŋ\ **banters** [origin unknown] *vt* **1 :** to speak to or address in a witty and teasing manner ⟨the students enjoyed their teacher's ~*ing* them about mistakes⟩ **:** act playfully and teasingly with ⟨~ the ladies⟩ **2** *archaic* **:** to delude or trick esp. by way of jest **3** *obs* **:** RIDICULE **4** *chiefly South & Midland* **:** DARE, CHALLENGE ⟨I'll ~ you to a game of checkers⟩ ⟨he ~*ed* him for a fight⟩ **5 :** *chiefly South & Midland* **:** to coax into action by argument or haggling **:** WHEEDLE ⟨he'd like to ~ you for a horse swap⟩ ~ *vi* **:** to tease good-naturedly **:** speak or act playfully or wittily ⟨he ~*ed* and romped with his grandchildren —*Time*⟩

²**banter** \"\ *n* -s **1 a** *obs* **:** absurd or nonsensical language used as ridicule **b :** good-natured and usu. witty and playful teasing ⟨the sprightly ~ of a tea party⟩ **:** animated joking back and forth ⟨~ between husband and wife⟩ **:** PLAYFULNESS ⟨the tragic mood predominates but a considerable infusion of delightful ~ relieves it —Arthur Berger⟩ **2** *archaic* **:** an instance of good-natured teasing

ban·ter·ing·ly *adv* **:** in a bantering manner

Ban·thine \'banˌthēn\ *trademark* — used for methantheline

¹**ban·ting** \'bantiŋ\ *also* **ban·ting·ism** \-ˌizəm\ *n* -s *often cap* [after William *Banting* †1878 Eng. undertaker and writer] **:** a method of dieting for obesity by avoiding sweets and carbohydrates

²**ban·ting** \", 'bän-\ *n* -s [Malay] **:** a sailing dugout of Johore, Malaya

ban·ti's disease *or* **banti's syndrome** \'bäntēz-\ *n, usu cap B* [after Guido *Banti* †1925 Ital. physician] **:** a disorder characterized by congestion and great enlargement of the spleen usu. accompanied by anemia, leukopenia, and cirrhosis of the liver

bant·ling \'bantliŋ\ *n* -s [perh. modif. of G *bänkling* bastard, fr. *bank* bench (fr. OHG) + *-ling* — more at BENCH] **:** a very young child **:** INFANT ⟨a woman with a ~ in her arms⟩ ⟨the record of the ~ American language remains incomplete —H.M.Reynolds⟩

ban·toid \'banˌtȯid\ *adj, usu cap* [*Bantu* + *-oid*] **1 :** of, relating to, or characteristic of the Bantu people **2 :** of, relating to, or characteristic of the Bantu language

ban·tu \'banˌtü, -aan- *also* -än- *or* -ȧn-\ *n, pl* **bantu** *or* **bantus** *usu cap* **1 a :** a family of Negroid peoples (as the Ngoni, Ganda, Kikuyu, Lunda, Zulu, Swahili, and peoples whose names begin with *Aba-, Ama-, Ma-, Wa-,* and other variants of the Bantu plural personal prefix *Aba-*) who occupy equatorial and southern Africa and who apart from language do not show a great degree of racial or cultural uniformity — used chiefly in linguistic classification; see KAFFIR **b :** a member of such people **2 a** *in former classifications* **:** an independent family of African languages **b :** a group of African languages within the Central branch of the Niger-Congo family, comprising over 300 languages, spoken generally south of a line from Cameroons to Kenya, and being generally very similar in structure, characteristically having a highly developed system of noun classes marked by prefixes and determining a system of concord, each dependent word having a prefix of the same class as the noun

ban·tu·ist \-üəst\ *n* -s *usu cap* **:** a specialist in the Bantu languages or the Bantu-speaking peoples

bantu ka·vi·ron·do \-ˌkävəˈrän(ˌ)dō\ *n, usu cap B&K* **:** a group consisting of two distinct but neighboring and related Bantu-speaking peoples, the Logoli and Vugusa of eastern Africa

ban·ty \'bantē, -aan-, -ain-, -ti\ *n or adj* [by alter.] **:** BANTAM

ba·nus \'bänəs\ *n* -ES [ML, fr. Serbo-Croatian *bān* lord, ruler — more at BAN] **:** ³BAN

ba·nu·yo \bəˈnü(ˌ)yō\ *n* -s [Tag] **1 :** a Philippine timber tree (*Wallaceodendron celebicum*) of the family Leguminosae **2 :** the fine hard wood of the banuyo, similar to acle, of pale golden-brown or dark coffee color, much used in cabinetwork

banx·ring \'baŋksˌriŋ\ *or* **bangs·ring** \-aŋz.r-\ *or* **banks·ring** \-aŋks.r-\ *n* -s [Jav *bangsring*] **:** TREE SHREW

ban·yan *or* **ban·ian** \'banyən *sometimes* -nˌyan *or* -nēən *or* -nēˌan *or* 'bənyən\ *n* -s [Hindi *baniyā,* fr. Skt *vāṇija* merchant, fr. *vaṇij* merchant] **1** *or* **ba·nia** *or* **ba·niya** \-nyə,-nēə,-nē,(y)ä\ **a :** one of a caste of Hindu merchants and traders **b :** a loose shirt, gown, or jacket that is worn in India **2** [fr. a banyan pagoda erected under a tree of the species grown near Bandar Abbas, southern Iran] *also* **ban·yan tree :** an East Indian tree (*Ficus bengalensis*) the branches of which send out numerous trunks that grow down to the soil and form props so that a single tree thus covers a very large area

banyan 2

banyan day *n* [so called fr. the banyans' abstinence fr. flesh] **1 :** a day on which no meat is served to the crew of a ship **2** *Austral* **:** a day on which the food is of inferior quality (as on the last day of a weekly ration)

ban·zai \(ˈ)bänˈzī, -ȧn-\ *n* -s [Jap, hurrah, fr. *ban* ten thousand + *sai* year] **:** a Japanese cheer **:** a cry of enthusiasm or triumph — usu. used interjectionally

ban·zai attack *or* **banzai charge** \'bänˌzī, -an-,-aan-,-ȧn-\ *n* **:** a reckless desperate mass attack originated by Japanese soldiers and accompanied by yells of "banzai" and insulting taunts

bao·bab \'bau̇ˌbab, 'bāə,-\ *n* -s [prob. native name in Africa] **:** a tree (*Adansonia digitata*) esp. of Africa, India, and Australia having a trunk that often grows to a diameter of 30 feet, a gourdlike fruit that yields a pleasantly acid edible pulp which also furnishes a beverage, leaves and bark formerly used medicinally, and bark that is used in papermaking and that is also made into cloth and ropes by the natives — see MONKEY BREAD

bap \'bap\ *n* -s [origin unknown] *chiefly Scot* **:** a small loaf or roll of bread

bap *or* **bapt** *abbr* baptized

baph·ia \'bafēə\ *n, cap* [NL, fr. Gk *baphē* dye (fr. *baptein* to dip, dye) + NL *-ia* — more at BAPTIZE] **:** a small genus of trees and shrubs (family Leguminosae) native to tropical Africa and Madagascar having unifoliolate leaves and bracteolate flowers with a sheathing calyx and 10 free stamens — see CAMWOOD

baph·o·met·ic \ˌbafəˈmed·ik\ *adj, usu cap* [*Baphomet,* idol the Templars were accused of worshiping (fr. F, alter. of *Mahomet* Muhammad †632 Arabian prophet, fr. Ar *Muḥammad*) + E *-ic*] **:** of or relating to the idol Baphomet

bap·tise *chiefly Brit var of* BAPTIZE

bap·ti·sia \bapˈtizh(ē)ə, -ēzh-\ *n, cap* [NL, fr. Gk *baptisis* baptism (fr. *baptein* to dip) + NL *-ia* — more at BAPTIZE] **:** a genus of No. American herbs (family Leguminosae) with showy yellow, blue, or white pealike flowers and an inflated pod — see WILD INDIGO

bap·tism \'bapˌtizəm, ÷'babˌt-\ *n* -s [ME *bapteme, baptisme,* fr. OF & LL; OF *baptesme,* fr. LL *baptisma,* fr. Gk, fr. *baptizein* to baptize — more at BAPTIZE] **1 a :** the ceremony of proclaiming one a Christian or of admitting one into membership in a Christian church with the use of water by immersion, pouring, or sprinkling and with the recital of a form of words (as "I baptize thee in the name of the Father and of the Son and of the Holy Ghost") **b :** the Christian sacrament (as in the Roman Catholic and many Protestant churches) of purification from sin and of spiritual rebirth as a Christian that is administered before any other sacrament (often in infancy) **c :** a rite resembling Christian baptism usu. in using water for ritual purification **d :** an experience of spiritual purification and renewal **e** *Christian Science* **:** purification by or submergence in Spirit **2 :** an act, experience, or ordeal by which one is purified, sanctified, initiated, or named ⟨the ~ of the gutter —W.B.Yeats⟩ ⟨giving bomber crews their ~ in mock atomic warfare —*N.Y.Times*⟩ ⟨the official ~ of a new battleship⟩

bap·tis·mal \(ˈ)=ˈtizməl\ *adj* [ML *baptismalis,* fr. LL *baptisma* + L *-alis* -al] **:** of or relating to baptism ⟨~ certificates⟩ ⟨~ vows⟩ ⟨the first ~ shock . . . had worn off —Evelyn Barkins⟩ — **bap·tis·mal·ly** \-məlē, -li\ *adv*

baptismal name *n* **:** CHRISTIAN NAME; *esp* **:** one given at baptism

baptismal regeneration *n* **:** the theological doctrine that regeneration is effected in and through Christian baptism

baptism for the dead : the baptism of a living person as proxy for one who has died unbaptized (as practiced in modern times by Mormons)

baptism of fire [trans. of LGk *baptisma pyros*] **1 :** a spiritual baptism by the gift of the Holy Spirit — often used in allusion to Acts 2:3–4; Mt 3:11 (RSV) **2 :** an introductory or initial experience that is a severe ordeal; *specif* **:** a soldier's first exposure to enemy fire

¹**bap·tist** \'baptəst, ÷'babtə-, ÷'babdə-\ *n* -s [ME *baptiste,* fr. OF, fr. LL *baptista,* fr. Gk *baptistēs,* fr. *baptizein* to baptize — more at BAPTIZE] **1 :** one that baptizes **2** *cap* **:** a member or adherent of a denomination of Trinitarian Protestant Christians that are congregational in polity and for the most part doctrinally Calvinistic and maintain that baptism should be administered by immersion to believers only

²**baptist** \"\ *adj, usu cap* **:** of or relating to Baptists or their doctrines and practices

bap·tis·tery \'baptəstrē, -ri, ÷'babtə-, ÷'babdə- *also* -stər- *sometimes* bapˈtis-tər- *or* ÷ babˈt-\ *or* **bap·tis·try** \'==-trē, -ri\ *n* -ES [ME *baptisterie,* fr. MF, fr. LL *baptisterium,* fr. LGk *baptistērion,* fr. Gk, swimming tank, fr. *baptizein* to dip, baptize — more at BAPTIZE] **1 :** a usu. round or polygonal building used in early times for baptismal services **2 a :** a part of a church containing a font and used for baptismal services **b :** a large tank used in modern Baptist and other churches for immersion

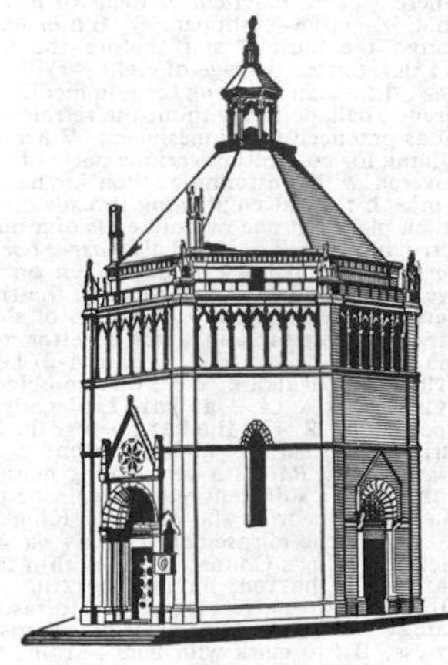
baptistery 1

bap·tis·tic \(ˈ)bapˈtistik, ÷-abˈt-\ *adj, usu cap* **:** of or relating to Baptists; *esp* **:** in accord with Baptist doctrines and practices

bap·tize \bapˈtīz, ÷babˈt-, 'ˌ=\ *vb* -ED/-ING/-S *see -ize in Explan Notes* [ME *baptizen,* fr. OF *baptiser,* fr. LL *baptizare,* fr. Gk *baptizein* to dip, baptize, fr. *baptein* to dip; akin to ON *kafa* to dive, swim under water, *kvefja* to quench] *vt* **1 a :** to dip or immerse in water or to pour or sprinkle water on as a rite of spiritual or moral purification or of initiation into a religious society **:** administer baptism to ⟨~ a child in the Episcopal Church⟩ **b :** to make a member of (a particular sect) by baptism ⟨in San Antonio, he was *baptized* a Catholic —Green Peyton⟩ **2 a :** to initiate or launch ⟨both developments were *baptized* under last season's conditions of scanty snow —*N.Y.Times*⟩ **b :** to purify or cleanse spiritually esp. by a purging experience or ordeal ⟨*baptized* with pain and rapture, tears and fire —Sidney Lanier⟩ **3 :** to give a name to (as at baptism) **:** CHRISTEN ⟨I know you're not always called the name you're *baptized* by —Agatha Christie⟩ ⟨he was *baptized* Samuel⟩ ~ *vi* **:** to administer baptism

bap·tiz·er \-zə(r)\ *n* -s [ME, fr. *baptizen* to immerse + *-er*] **:** one that baptizes **:** BAPTIST

bap·tor·nis \bapˈtȯrnəs\ *n, cap* [NL, fr. Gk *baptein* to dip + *-ornis*] **:** a genus of swimming birds from the Cretaceous of Kansas that is imperfectly known but prob. related to *Hesperornis*

ba·pu \'bəˌpü, 'bä-\ *n* -s [Hindi, fr. Skt *papu* protector] *India* **:** FATHER

¹**bar** \'bär, 'bȧ(r\ *n* -s *often attrib* [ME *barre,* fr. OF] **1 a** (1) **:** a straight piece of wood or metal that is longer than it is wide, is used to fasten (as a door), and that can be unlatched or unfastened (2) **:** a similar piece of wood or metal so fixed or placed as to obstruct passage through any opening or over any way and often forming a part of a continuous barrier (as of a fence or grating) ⟨heavy ~s across prison windows⟩ **b :** a rodlike piece of iron or steel often pointed at one or both ends or terminating at one end in a cutting edge and used as a digging, breaking, or prying tool **c :** a solid piece or block of some material usu. rectangular and considerably longer than it is wide ⟨a ~ of gold⟩ **d :** a piece (as of wood or metal) longer than it is wide and usu. having considerable rigidity that is used as a lever, handle, support, or division maker: as (1) **:** a part of a machine usu. designed to activate a certain mechanism or to hold replaceable parts (as cutting teeth or needles)

bars 6a, *B;* double bar, *D*

(2) **:** a handrail along the walls of a dance studio used as an aid to maintain balance during ballet exercises (3) **:** a slender strip of wood that divides and supports the glass in a window **:** SASH — called also *sash bar* **e** (1) **:** the part of the wall of a horse's hoof that is bent inward toward the frog at the heel on each side and that extends toward the center of the sole (2) **:** the sidepiece joining the pommel and cantle of a saddle (3) **:** the mouthpiece of a bridle when solid **2 :** BARRIER, IMPEDIMENT **:** something that obstructs, hinders, or prevents passage, progress, or action: as **a :** the gate or the gatehouse of a castle or fortified town ⟨the four principal entrances along the main highroads were defended by the four ~*s* —Edwin Benson⟩ **b :** the complete and permanent destruction of an action or claim in law ⟨matter in ~⟩ ⟨defense in ~⟩; *also* **:** a plea or objection that effects such destruction **c** (1) **:** any intangible or nonphysical impediment or obstacle ⟨agreed that long sentences are a ~ to easy reading —F.L.Mott⟩ ⟨one of the biggest ~*s* standing in the way of developing a vaccine —*Monsanto Mag.*⟩ (2) **bars** *pl* **:** standards of inclusion or admission **:** restrictions or precautions against inclusion or admission of undesirable or supposedly inferior elements ⟨let down the ~*s* against this microbial enemy —Justina Hill⟩ ⟨the club will not let down its ~*s*⟩ **d :** a submerged or partly submerged bank of sand, gravel, or other material along a shore or in a river often obstructing navigation esp. at the mouth of the river or approaching a harbor — compare BANK 1d, BARRIER 2b (1), HOOK, REEF, SPIT, TOMBOLO **3 a** (1) **:** the railing in a courtroom that encloses the place about the judge where prisoners are stationed for arraignment, trial, or sentence or where the business of the court is transacted in civil cases ⟨summoned the prisoner to the ~⟩ (2) **:** COURT, TRIBUNAL ⟨see that justice is done at the ~⟩ (3) **:** a particular system of courts ⟨the New York bench and ~ acquitted themselves wisely . . . in defense of liberty and law —Telford Taylor⟩ ⟨practice at the Massachusetts ~⟩ (4) **:** any authority or tribunal that renders judgment or makes a final evaluation ⟨he must summon to the ~ of a nobler philosophy the current standards of value and conduct —V.L.Parrington⟩ ⟨be judged at the ~ of public opinion⟩ **b** (1) **:** the barrier or partition in the English Inns of Court that formerly separated the seats of the benchers or readers from the body of the hall occupied by the students who in time were called to take their place within the barrier to enter into the debates of the house — called also *utter bar* (2) **:** the whole body of barristers or lawyers qualified to practice in any jurisdiction ⟨be admitted to the ~⟩ ⟨a ~ association⟩ (3) **:** the profession of barrister or lawyer ⟨heighten respect for members of the ~ and judiciary —W.L.Hoyt⟩ **c :** a railing in a room, office, or hall of assembly designed to reserve a space for those having special privileges ⟨the ~ of the House of Commons⟩ **4 :** a straight stripe, band, or line much longer than it is wide: as **a :** one of two or more horizontal stripes on a heraldic shield — see FESS **b :** a transverse ridge on the roof of a horse's mouth — usu. used in pl. **c :** the space in front of the molar teeth of a horse in which the bit is placed **d :** a metal or embroidered strip worn on a uniform to indicate rank or service in the armed forces ⟨a second lieutenant's ~⟩ ⟨overseas ~*s*⟩ or as an award for merit or achievement ⟨awarded ~*s* to volunteer Red Cross workers⟩ or to signify that the holder of a medal or similar distinction has again merited its award ⟨a Distinguished Flying Cross with ~⟩ **e :** RIBBON 1c **f :** a mark or stripe crossing at right angles to the length of a feather **g :** the space between the inner and outer table on a backgammon board **h** *geol* **:** VEIN, DIKE **i :** a mark long in proportion to its width, used in print or writing (as the superscript mark in ā or the subscript mark in t̲h̲ or the mark |) **5 a :** a counter at which food or esp. alcoholic beverages are served ⟨had a cocktail at the ~⟩ ⟨snack ~⟩ ⟨milk ~⟩ **b :** a room or public establishment containing such a counter **:** BARROOM **c :** a piece of furniture on wheels to be moved about having a counter on top and storage space for liquor and equipment below **d :** a counter or section of a store where a particular item or items of merchandise are featured ⟨hat ~⟩ ⟨gift ~⟩ ⟨slipper ~⟩ **6 a** *or* **bar line :** a vertical line across the musical staff before the initial measure accent **b :** MEASURE ⟨a passage of eight ~*s*⟩ ⟨two ~*s*' rest⟩ **c :** BASS BAR **d :** a stanzaic song form in medieval music related to the French ballade but without the refrain; *specif* **:** this form (a a b) as practiced by minnesingers **7 a :** a lace and embroidery joining for connecting various parts of the pattern that is usu. covered with buttonhole stitch for needlepoint lace and cutwork **b :** the strengthening threads covered with buttonhole stitch placed at one or both ends of a buttonhole **8 :** banded ferruginous rock — called also *jasper bar* **9 :** a recorded time of performance in horse racing taken on an occasion or at an event not conducted according to the rules of racing that debars a horse from entry in a class of slower record **10 :** an area of a crap table in which a bettor may place a bet against the caster, one cast (1-1, 6-6, or 1-2) being barred **11** *or* **bar arm :** HAMMERLOCK; *esp* **:** one combined with another hold **syn** see OBSTACLE — **at bar 1 :** legally before the court **:** in open court **2** *or* **at the bar :** before the full court ⟨trial *at bar*⟩ ⟨trial *at the bar*⟩ — **go to the bar :** to become a barrister ⟨*went to the Bar* as a very young man —W.S.Gilbert⟩ — **in bar of :** as a sufficient reason against **:** PREVENTING — **within the bar :** in or to the office of King's or Queen's Counsel — used in the phrase *called within the bar;* in allusion to the fact that King's Counsel plead within the bar of the court

²bar \ "\ *vt* **barred; barred; barring; bars** [ME *barren,* fr. OF *barrer,* fr. *barre* bar] **1 a :** to fasten with a bar ⟨~ the gate⟩ ⟨~ a door⟩ **b :** to place bars across to prevent ingress or egress **2 :** to mark with bars **:** STRIPE ⟨a feather *barred* with brown⟩ **3 a :** to confine or shut in by or as if by bars ⟨~ a prisoner in his cell⟩ **b :** not to take into consideration **:** set aside ⟨the picnic will be on Saturday, *barring* the possibility of rain⟩ ⟨if man does not want to change his culture, then, *barring* outside compulsions, it will not be changed —W.D.Wallis⟩ **c :** to shut or keep out **:** EXCLUDE — often used with *from* ⟨*barred* enlisted men from the club⟩ ⟨*barred* aliens from sensitive positions⟩; *also, archaic* **:** to exclude from ⟨I will ~ no honest man my house —*Shak.*⟩ **4 a :** to interpose or serve as a sufficient and permanent legal objection to (as an action) or to the claim of (as a person) **b :** PREVENT, HINDER ⟨nothing *barred* them from meeting together⟩ **c :** FORBID, PROHIBIT ⟨a convention *barring* the use of poison gas in war⟩ **d :** to obstruct, block up, or shut off (as an entrance or road) by or as if by a barrier ⟨~ a residential street to heavy traffic⟩ **e :** OBSTRUCT, PREVENT ⟨rushed fresh reserves to the front to ~ the enemy's advance⟩ **5 :** to reinforce (as a buttonhole) with a bar **6 :** to move or turn (as a flywheel or a locomotive driving wheel) by a bar used as a lever **7 :** to divide (a music staff) into measures with bar lines **8** *in veterinary practice* **:** to dissect free and ligate (a vein in a horse's leg) above and below the site of a projected operative procedure **syn** see HINDER

³bar \ "\ *prep* **:** EXCEPT, SAVE, EXCLUDING ⟨all was over ~ the formal recording of the votes —*Sydney (Australia) Bull.*⟩ ⟨language can describe anything ~ the ineffable —Edna Daitz⟩

⁴bar \ "\ *n* -s [F, fr. OF, fr. MD *baers;* akin to OE *bærs* bass — more at BASS] **:** ²MAIGRE

⁵bar \ "\ *n* -s [LaF *boire* mosquito net] **:** MOSQUITO NET ⟨see that you drive all the mosquitoes out of their ~ —Mark Twain⟩

⁶bar *n* -s [ScGael *bàir* game, goal] **1** *Scot* **:** PRACTICAL JOKE **2** *Scot* **:** an amusing situation

⁷bar \ "\ *n* -s [G, fr. Gk *baros* weight — more at GRIEVE] **1 a :** a unit of pressure equal to one million dynes per square centimeter or about 0.98697 standard atmosphere **2 :** the absolute cgs unit of pressure equal to one dyne per square centimeter — called also *barye*

BAR \ˌbēˌāˈär, -āˈä(r\ *abbr or n* -s Browning automatic rifle ⟨an infantry squad leader . . . carries a *BAR* —Donald Howard⟩

bar *abbr* **1** bark; barque **2** barometer; barometric **3** barrel

bar- *or* **baro-** *comb form* [Gk *baros* — more at GRIEVE] **:** weight **:** pressure ⟨*bar*agnosis⟩ ⟨*baro*graph⟩

ba·ra \ˈbə(ˌ)rä\ *var of* BURRA

ba·ra·ba·ra \ˌbärəˈbärə\ *or* **ba·ra·bo·ra** \ˌ==ˈbō=\ *n* -s [Russ dial. *barabora*] **:** a sod or turf hut of northern Siberia or of Alaska; *esp* **:** a hut of the Aleutian islanders built partly or wholly underground

bar·a·boo \ˈbarəˌbü, ˌ==ˈ=\ *n* -s [fr. *Baraboo* mts., Wis.] **:** a disinterred monadnock

bar·ag·no·sis \ˌbaˌragˈnōsəs, baˈragˌnō-\ *n, pl* **baragno·ses** \-ōˌsēz\ [NL, fr. *bar-* + ²*a-* + *-gnosis*] **:** loss of barognosis

ba·ra·gouin \ˌbarəˌgwaⁿ\ *n* -s [F] **:** outlandish unintelligible speech **:** JARGON

ba·rai·ta *or* **ba·rai·tha** \bəˈrītə\ *n, pl* **baraitas** *or* **baraithas** *also* **ba·rai·toth** \ˌbärīˈtōt, -tōth,-tōs\ *or* **ba·rai·tot** \-ˈtōt, -ˈtōs\ *or* **barai·thoth** \-t,-th,-s\ *or* **barai·thot** \-t,-s\ *usu cap* [Aram *barrāythā* extraneous matter] **:** a traditional Jewish interpretation or statement of biblical law dating from the tannaitic period but not included in the Mishnah

ba·ra·ji·llo \ˌbarəˈhē(ˌ)(y)ō\ *n* -s [AmerSp, perh. fr. Sp *barajar* to entangle] **:** a Central American perennial herb (*Desmodium rensoni*) used as forage

ba·ra·ka \bəˈräkə\ *n* -s [Ar *barakah*] **:** a blessing that is regarded in various Eastern religions as an indwelling spiritual force and divine gift inhering in saints, charismatic leaders, and natural objects

bar·a·min \ˈbarəmən\ *n* -s [Heb *bara* created + *min* kind] *among some antievolutionists* **:** a created plant or animal as distinguished from one that has developed through the process of evolution

bar-and-dot \ˌ==ˈ=\ *adj* [¹*bar*] **:** of or relating to a system of writing numbers used by the Maya and some other ancient peoples of Middle America in which a bar stood for five and a dot for one (as in the following examples)

•	••	—	•̲	•••• (bar)	=	••• ≡
1	2	5	6	9	10	18

baranduki *var of* BARONDUKI

¹ba·ran·gay \ˌbaranˈgī\ *n* -s [Iloko *baranggáy* hamlet, community] **:** a unit of administration in primitive Philippine society consisting of from 50 to 100 families under a headman

²barangay *var of* BALANGAY

ba·rani \bəˈranē, -ränē\ *or* **ba·roni** \-ränē\ *n* -s [prob. fr. the name *Barani*] **:** a trampoline and tumbling stunt in which the performer does a front somersault with a half twist

bá·rá·ny chair \bəˈränē-, *Hung* ˈbäˌrānʸ-\ *n, usu cap B* [after Robert *Bárány* †1936 Austrian physician] **:** a chair for testing the effects of circular motion esp. on airplane pilots

ba·rar·ite \bəˈrärˌrīt\ *n* -s *cap* [*Barari,* Bengal, India + E *-ite*] **:** a mineral $(NH_4)_2SiF_6$ consisting of ammonium fluosilicate occurring in hexagonal crystals and in crusts on the rocks about Vesuvius

bar arm *n* [¹*bar*] **:** ¹BAR 11

ba·ra·singh \ˈbärəˌsiŋ\ *or* **ba·ra·sin·gha** \ˌbärəˈsiŋgə\ *n* -s *sometimes cap* [Hindi *bārahsīṅghā,* lit., having twelve tines, fr. *bārah* twelve + *sīg* horn (fr. Skt *śṛṅga*) — more at HORN] **:** SWAMP DEER

¹ba·rat \bəˈrät\ *n* -s [native name in Indonesia] **:** a violent squall from the northwest that occurs in Menando Bay on the coast of Celebes Island and is prevalent from December to February

²barat *var of* BERAT

bar·a·thea \ˌbarəˈthēə\ *n* -s [fr. *Barathea,* a trademark] **:** a closely woven clothing fabric that has a broken twill weave which produces a pebbly-surface effect and is made of silk, rayon, cotton, wool, or combinations of these yarns

bar·a·thrum \ˈbarəthrəm\ *n, pl* **bara·thra** \-rə\ [L & Gk; L *barathrum,* fr. Gk *barathron;* akin to Gk *bibrōskein* to devour — more at VORACIOUS] **:** a bottomless pit or abyss **:** HELL

ba·ratte \bəˈrat\ *n* -s [F, churn, fr. MF, fr. *baratter* to shake, fr. *baratte, barate* agitation, confusion] **:** a churn in which alkali cellulose is converted into cellulose xanthate in the manufacture of viscose

¹barb \ˈbärb, ˈbȧb\ *n* -s [ME *barbe* barb, beard, fr. MF, fr. L *barba* — more at BEARD] **1 a :** a sharp projection extending backwards (as from the point of an arrow, spear, or fishhook) preventing easy extraction from a wound; *also* **:** any sharp projection with its point similarly oblique or crosswise to something else **b :** the point of a weapon or missile **c :** a biting or pointedly critical remark or comment ⟨~*s* of ridicule⟩ ⟨attacks the . . . government and its leaders with personal ~*s* of astonishing virulence —Faubion Bowers⟩ **:** painful impact or effect ⟨the first violators felt the ~ of Mulrain's enforcement tactics —G.S.Perry⟩ **2 :** a part of a medieval linen or cotton headdress that is usu. starched and sometimes pleated, that passes over or under the chin and covers the neck and sometimes the shoulders, and that is now worn only by nuns of certain orders **3 :** a fleshy projection under the snout or around the mouth in fishes like sturgeons or cod; *esp* **:** BARBEL **4 :** one of the little projections of the mucous membrane that mark the opening of the submaxillary glands under the tongue in horses and cattle; *esp* **:** such a projection when inflamed and swollen — usu. used in pl. **5** *heraldry* **:** one of the projecting leaves of the calyx of a rose **6 :** one of the side branches of the shaft of a bird's feather **7 :** one of the minute branches on fur fiber **8** *bot* **:** a hair or bristle ending in a hook, often a double one

barb 1a

²barb \ "\ *vb* -ED/-ING/-S [ME & MF; ME *barben* to clip wool, fr. MF *barber* to shave, clip, fr. *barbe* beard, barb] *vt* **1 a** *obs* **:** to shave or trim the beard of **b :** CLIP, MOW **2** [¹*barb*] **:** to furnish (as an arrow or fishhook) with a barb ⟨~ arrows with points of fish bone⟩ ~ *vi, obs* **:** to shave or trim the beard

³barb \ "\ *n* -s [by alter.] *obs* **:** ²BARD 1

⁴barb \ "\ *n* -s [F *barbe,* fr. It *barbero,* fr. *barbero* of Barbary, fr. *Barberia* Barbary, coastal region of northern Africa] **1 a :** a horse of the stock native to Barbary **b** *usu cap* **:** a horse of a breed related to the Arabs that is noted for speed and endurance and was introduced into Spain by the Moors **2 :** a pigeon of a domestic breed related to the carriers that has a short broad beak, much bare skin about the eyes, and the skin about the nostrils swollen **3 :** a black kelpie

⁵barb \ "\ *n* -s [prob. fr. ¹*barb*] **1 :** any of several whitings of the eastern and southeastern coasts of the U.S. **2 :** any of several brightly colored tropical fishes (genus *Barbus*) kept in aquariums

⁶barb \ "\ *n* -s [by shortening] *slang* **:** BARBARIAN 2

bar·ba am·a·ril·la \ˌbärbəˌaməˈrilə, -rē(y)ə\ *n, pl* **barba amarillas** [AmerSp, lit., yellow beard] **:** FER-DE-LANCE

bar·ba·coa \ˌbärbəˈkōə\ *n, pl* **barbacoa** *or* **barbacoas** *usu cap* [Sp, of AmerInd origin] **1 a :** a Chibchan people of northern Ecuador and southern Colombia **b :** a member of such people **2 :** a language of the Barbacoa people — **bar·ba·co·an** \ˌ==ˈ==ən\ *adj, usu cap*

¹bar·ba·di·an \(ˈ)bärˈbādēən\ *adj, usu cap* [*Barbados,* island in the West Indies + E *-ian*] **1 :** of, relating to, or characteristic of Barbados, West Indies **2 :** of, relating to, or characteristic of Barbadians

²barbadian \ "\ *n* -s *cap* **:** a native or resident of Barbados

bar·ba·dos \(ˈ)bärˈbādəs, -(ˌ)ōs,-(ˌ)ōz\ *adj, usu cap* [fr. *Barbados,* West Indies] **:** of or from the island of Barbados, West Indies **:** of the kind or style prevalent in Barbados

bar·ba·dos aloe *n, usu cap B* **:** a stemless aloe (*Aloe vera*) with grayish green spiny-margined leaves and spikes of yellow flowers that is native to northern Africa but naturalized throughout the tropics and widely grown as a greenhouse ornamental

barbados cherry *n, usu cap B* **1 :** any of several West Indian shrubs of the genera *Malpighia* and *Bunchosia* (esp. *M. urens*) **2 :** the slightly acid berry of the Barbados cherry somewhat resembling cherries in flavor **3 :** SURINAM CHERRY 2

barbados-cherry family *n, usu cap B* **:** MALPIGHIACEAE

barbados earth *n, usu cap B* **:** an earthy marl of Miocene age occurring in Barbados and noted for its richness in radiolarians

barbados flower fence *n, usu cap B* **:** any of several tropical shrubs or small trees used for hedges: as **a :** PRIDE OF BARBADOS **b :** BRASILETTO **c :** JERUSALEM THORN 2

barbados gooseberry *n, usu cap B* **1 :** a West Indian cactus (*Peireskia aculeata*) **2 :** the smooth edible fruit of the Barbados gooseberry

barbados lily *n, usu cap B* **:** a bulbous tropical American herb (*Hippeastrum puniceum*) related to the amaryllis

barbados pride *n, usu cap B* **1 :** PRIDE OF BARBADOS **2 :** RED SANDALWOOD 2

barbados tar *n, usu cap B* **:** a thick black petroleum from Barbados

barb·al·o·in \bärˈbaləwən\ *n* -s [*Barbados aloe* + *-in*] **:** a yellow crystalline compound $C_{20}H_{18}O_9$ isolated from aloin that yields aloe-emodin and D-arabinose on hydrolysis

bar·ba·ra's buttons \ˈbärb(ə)rəz-\ *n pl but sing or pl in constr, usu cap 1st B* [fr. the name *Barbara*] **:** a plant of the genus *Marshallia* (family Compositae); *esp* **:** a low-growing perennial herb (*M. trinervia*) sometimes cultivated and having purplish flowers in globose heads

bar·ba·rea \ˌbärbəˈrēə\ *n, cap* [NL, fr. St. *Barbara,* 3d cent. martyr + NL *-ea*] **:** a small genus of yellow-flowered sometimes weedy biennial or perennial herbs (family Cruciferae) of the north temperate zone having lyrate or pinnatifid lower leaves and clasping stem leaves and basal rosettes of leaves that overwinter — see WINTER CRESS

¹bar·ba·resque \ˌbärbəˈresk\ *adj* [F, fr. It *barbaresco,* fr. *Barbaria, Barberia* Barbary, coastal region of northern Africa + It *-esco* -esque] **1** *usu cap* **:** of, relating to, or characteristic of Barbary **2 :** barbaric in style ⟨~ architecture⟩

²barbaresque \ "\ *n* -s *cap* **:** one of the natives of Barbary formerly noted for their piratical activity ⟨seventy thousand peasants huddled together because it had not been safe to remain out for fear of the ~*s* —Bernhard Berenson⟩

¹bar·bar·i·an \(ˈ)bärˈberēən, (ˈ)bȧˈ-, -ˈba(ə)r-, -ˈbär-\ *adj* [L *barbarus* + E *-ian* — more at BARBAROUS] **1 :** of or relating to a land, culture, or people alien and usu. believed to be inferior to one's own ⟨~ tribes massing on the borders of the Roman Empire⟩ ⟨the Chinese emperor received with civility a mission from the ~ West⟩ **2 :** lacking refinement, gentleness, learning, or artistic or literary culture **:** marked by a tendency toward brutality, violence, or lawlessness but sometimes displaying a rough vigor or vitality ⟨introduced me to his loud, boisterous, ~ mother⟩ ⟨a ~ race which possesses neither virtue nor humanity —R.L.Bruckberger⟩ **3 :** of or relating to a people or group in a stage of cultural development about midway between savagery and full civilization; *also* **:** of or relating to such a stage

syn BARBARIC, BARBAROUS, SAVAGE: BARBARIAN frequently applies to a state about midway between full civilization and tribal savagery ⟨some *barbarian* peoples have brought their mores into true adjustment to their life conditions and have gone on for centuries without change —W.G.Sumner⟩ BARBARIC and BARBAROUS may also be used to express this notion ⟨they had passed the *barbaric* stage when they invaded Chaldea. They knew the use of metals; they were skillful architects and . . . good engineers —Edward Clodd⟩ ⟨Caesar's short sketch of the Germans gives the impression of *barbarous* peoples . . . they had not yet reached the agricultural stage, but were devoted to war and hunting —H.O.Taylor⟩ SAVAGE implies even less advancement ⟨for *savage* or semicivilized men . . . authority is needed to restrain them from injuring themselves —C.W.Eliot⟩ BARBAROUS and SAVAGE are somewhat more common than BARBARIC and BARBARIAN to indicate uncivilized cruelty, but all may be used ⟨he required as a condition of peace that they should sacrifice their children to Baal no longer. But the *barbarous* custom was too inveterate —J.G.Frazer⟩ ⟨the King's greed passed into *savage* menace. He would hang all, he swore — man, woman, the very child at the breast —J.R.Green⟩ ⟨they had further traits and customs which are *barbaric* rather than specifically Teutonic: cruelty and faithlessness toward enemies, feuds, wergeld —H.O.Taylor⟩ ⟨for him those chambers held *barbarian* hordes, hyena foeman, and hot-blooded lords —John Keats⟩ BARBARIC and BARBAROUS are more common in relation to taste and refinement. BARBARIC connotes a wild, profuse lack of restraint ⟨this audacious and *barbaric* profusion of words — chosen always for their color and their vividly expressive quality —Arthur Symons⟩ ⟨the march became rather splendid and *barbaric*. First rode Feisal in white, then Sharraf at his right in red headcloth and henna-dyed tunic and cloak, myself on his left in white and scarlet, behind us three banners of faded crimson silk with gilt spikes —T.E.Lawrence⟩ BARBAROUS implies an utter lack of cultivated taste and refinement ⟨a race of unconscious spiritual helots. We shall become utterly *barbarous* and desolate —Ludwig Lewisohn⟩ ⟨but this deeply *barbarous* book may, in its very vulgarity of expression, be in advance of its time —Dorothy Thompson⟩

²barbarian \ "\ *n* -s **1 :** one that is barbarian ⟨a cultural conceit which divided the world into Greeks and ~*s* —Frederick Bodmer⟩ ⟨he is . . . a ~ in the arts of the table —Sinclair Lewis⟩ ⟨he would be a ~ indeed who failed to appreciate exquisite flowers, rare lace, . . . and feminine charm —H.M.Parshley⟩ **2** *slang* **:** an undergraduate not a member of a fraternity or sorority

bar·bar·i·an·ism \ˌ=ˈ===ˌnizəm\ *n* -s **:** BARBARISM, BARBARITY

bar·bar·ic \(ˈ)bärˈbarik, (ˈ)bȧˈ-, -rēk *also* -ˈber-\ *adj* [L *barbaricus* foreign, barbaric, fr. Gk *barbarikos,* fr. *barbaros* foreign + *-ikos* -ic — more at BARBAROUS] **1 :** of, relating to, or characteristic of barbarians ⟨we wage bloodier and more bestial wars than our ~ ancestors —Edward Glover⟩ ⟨full of the virility of ~ health and vigor —William Baucke⟩ ⟨men may be considered to have risen into the ~ state when they take to agriculture —E.B.Tylor⟩ **2** *of artistic style or expression* **:** marked by a lack of restraint or by unchecked exuberance ⟨the ~ use of color or ornament⟩ **:** having a bizarre, primitive, or unsophisticated quality ⟨the ~ splendor of the carving —*Notes and Queries*⟩ ⟨the ~ richness of color of Stravinsky's *Rite of Spring*⟩ ⟨I sound my ~ yawp —Walt Whitman⟩ ⟨wild ~ music —Sir Walter Scott⟩ ⟨the tangled, loose ~ magnificence of the Elizabethan drama —*Think*⟩ **syn** see BARBARIAN

bar·bar·i·cal·ly \-ək(ə)lē, -ēk-, -li\ *adv* **:** in a barbaric manner

bar·bar·i·ous \(ˈ)=ˈberēəs, -ˈba(ə)r-,-ˈbär-\ *adj* [by alter.] **:** BARBAROUS

bar·ba·rism \ˈbärbəˌrizəm, ˈbȧb-\ *n* -s [MF *barbarisme,* fr. L *barbarismus,* fr. Gk *barbarismos,* fr. *barbaros* foreign + *-ismos* -ism — more at BARBAROUS] **1 a :** a word or expression which in form or use offends against contemporary standards of acceptability in a language esp. in the derivative construction of words **b :** any idea, act, or performance that runs counter to prevailing standards of good taste or of what is intellectually or artistically sound or correct ⟨the ~ seen on some of the Assyrian sculpture, where inscriptions were scrawled right across the work without regard to design —Edward Clodd⟩ ⟨the idea of . . . a unit of international exchange based upon an unchanging value in terms of gold is an economic ~ —E.H.Collins⟩ **2 a :** a barbarian or barbarous social or intellectual condition ⟨that peculiar taint of ~ which makes men prefer occasional disobedience to systematic liberty —H.T.Buckle⟩ **:** BACKWARDNESS ⟨drew the country out of its economic ~ and illiteracy⟩ **b** (1) **:** the practice or display of barbarian acts, attitudes, or ideas esp. of barbarous cruelty or brutality ⟨the reversion to ~ in political trials and punishments —Alfred Cobban⟩ ⟨the ~ with which the revolt was suppressed⟩ (2) **:** a particular trait or characteristic of this condition ⟨I had been taught that war was an outmoded ~ —A.W.Turnbull⟩ **c** *among some anthropologists* **:** a stage of cultural development between savagery and civilization characterized by a primitive agricultural and pastoral economy but lacking a written language

bar·bar·i·ty \bärˈbarəd·ē, bäˈb-, -ətē, -i *also* -ˈber-\ *n* -ES [L *barbarus* + E *-ity*] **1 :** BARBARISM ⟨liberties . . . which were now threatened by the rising tide of ~ —Walter Lippmann⟩ ⟨many American writers fled to exile . . . in disgust at the ~ of their homeland —Horace Sutton⟩ ⟨a ~ which deserves the ridicule which we bestow upon the rites of savages —Virginia Woolf⟩ **2 a :** barbarous cruelty **:** INHUMANITY ⟨to mitigate the ~ of the criminal law —W.R.Inge⟩ **b :** an act or instance of barbarous cruelty **:** ATROCITY ⟨there were few inhuman *barbarities* aside from the custom of scalping —*Amer. Guide Series: Maine*⟩

bar·ba·ri·za·tion \ˌbärbərəˈzāshən, ˌbȧb-, -ˌrīˈz-\ *n* -s **1 :** the act of making barbarous **:** the action of becoming barbarous **2 :** the state of being barbarized

bar·ba·rize \ˈ==ˌrīz\ *vb* -ED/-ING/-S [partly fr. Gk *barbarizein* to act or speak like a barbarian, fr. *barbaros* + *-izein* -ize; partly fr. E *barbarous* + *-ize*] *vi* **1 :** to use barbarisms in speech or writing **2 :** to become barbarous ⟨Christianity began rapidly to ~ —H.H.Milman⟩ ~ *vt* **:** to make barbarian or barbarous ⟨the Greek world had been cut off and the Roman world barbarized —Gilbert Highet⟩ ⟨an aristocratic and ruling class may just as well ~ culture as revive it —William Barrett⟩

⟨with the end of the Roman schools the Latin used was terribly *barbarized* —F.B.Artz⟩

bar·ba·rous \ˈbärb(ə)rəs, ˈbȧb-\ *adj* [L *barbarus*, fr. Gk *barbaros* foreign, rude, ignorant; perh. akin to Skt *barbara* stammering, non-Aryan — more at BABBLE] **1 :** characterized by the use of barbarisms in speech or writing ⟨~ language⟩ **:** constituting a barbarism in speech or writing ⟨a ~ phrase⟩ **2 a :** BARBARIAN, UNCIVILIZED ⟨so ~ are some of these jungle lands that when . . . mapping planes dipped low, savage Indians launched futile spears . . . at them —*Nat'l Geographic*⟩ **b :** lacking culture or refinement **:** PHILISTINE ⟨a large enough advance to permit him to escape . . . from this ~ country to lodgings in Paris or Rome —Harrison Smith⟩ **c :** contrary to good or fashionable standards (as of taste or deportment) ⟨the ~ taste of our time and country, which had loaded . . . the furniture with bric-a-brac —Ambrose Bierce⟩ ⟨wolfing my dinner in order to arrive at the opera house at the ~ hour of seven-fifteen —Winthrop Sargeant⟩ **d :** BARBARIC, INHUMANE ⟨the crimes in this country are more ~ —W.C.Reckless⟩ **syn** see BARBARIAN, FIERCE

barbarously *adv* **:** in a barbarous manner

bar·ba·rous·ness \-nəs\ *n* -ES **:** BARBARISM, BARBARITY ⟨the provincialism and crudity, if not outright ~, of . . . society —R.T.LaPiere⟩

bar·ba·ry ape \ˈbärb(ə)rē-, ˈbȧb-, -ri-\ *n, usu cap B* [fr. *Barbary*, coastal region in northern Africa] **:** a tailless monkey (*Macaca sylvana*) of No. Africa and the Rock of Gibraltar that is the only monkey now native to Europe and is often trained by showmen

barbary coast *n, usu cap B & often cap C* [fr. the *Barbary Coast*, former notorious vice-ridden section of San Francisco, after the *Barbary coast* of northern Africa, former pirate center] **:** a district or section of a city noted as a center of gambling, prostitution, and riotous night life ⟨a *Barbary Coast* in the Colorado desert —Frank Waters⟩

barbary fig *n, usu cap B* **:** a common prickly pear (*Opuntia vulgaris*) of the eastern U.S. introduced into No. Africa

barbary horse *n, usu cap B* **:** ⁴BARB 1

barbary lion *n, usu cap B* **:** the No. African lion

barbary mastic *n, usu cap B* **:** a mastic obtained from a plant (*Pistacia atlantica*) of the Mediterranean region; *also* **:** the plant itself

barbary sheep *n, usu cap B* **:** AOUDAD

bar·bas \ˈbärbəs, -bəz\ *n, pl* **barbas** \-bəz,-bəs\ [Pg, lit., beards, pl. of *barba* beard, fr. L — more at BEARD] **:** a tropical American timber tree (*Vitex longeracemosa*) with yellowish brown lustrous wood — called also *jocote de mico*

bar·bas·co \bärˈba(ˌ)skō, -rˈbä-\ *also* **ba·bas·co** \bäˈb-,bəˈb-\ *n* -S [AmerSp *barbasco*, perh. alter. of Sp *verbasco*, *varbasco* mullein, fr. L *verbascum*] **1 :** WILD CINNAMON 1 **2 :** JOEWOOD **3 a :** any of various plants used by the Indians of northern So. America in making fish poison; *esp* **:** ³CUBE 1 **b :** the poison (as rotenone) contained in these plants

bar bass *n* [¹*bar*; fr. its resting on gravel bed bars] **:** CHANNEL BASS

bar·ba·stel *or* **bar·ba·stelle** \ˌbärbəˈstel\ *n* -S [F *barbastelle*, fr. It *barbastello*, fr. It dial. (Ferrara) *barbastel*, *barbastrel*, fr. L *vespertilio* bat — more at VESPERTILIO] **:** a long-eared European bat (*Barbastellus barbastellus*)

bar·bate \ˈbärˌbāt\ *adj* [L *barbatus*, fr. *barba* beard + *-atus* -ate — more at BEARD] **1 :** BEARDED **2** *bot* **:** bearing long stiff hairs

bar·ba·ti·mao \ˌbärbətēˈmaůⁿ\ *n* -S [Pg *barbatimão*, fr. Tupi *barbatimão*] **:** a Brazilian tree (*Stryphnodendron barbatimao*) of the family Mimosaceae that yields tanning material

barb bolt *n* [¹*barb*] **:** RAG BOLT

barbe \ˈbärb, ˈbȧb\ *n* -S [ME, fr. MF, lit., beard — more at BARB] **1 :** ¹BARB 2 **2 :** a short scarf or lappet of lace formerly worn at the throat or on the head

bar·beau \bärˈbō, ˌ==ˈ=\ *n* -S [F, fr. *barbe* beard] **:** CORNFLOWER 1b

¹**bar·be·cue** *also* **bar·be·que** \ˈbärbəˌkyü, ˈbȧb-, -bēˌk-\ *n* -S *often attrib* [AmerSp *barbacoa*, prob. fr. Taino] **1 a :** a metal rack on which meat and fish are roasted **b :** an often portable fireplace with such a rack **2 a :** a hog, steer, or other large animal roasted or broiled, whole or split, over an open fire or barbecue pit **b :** a social gathering of many people esp. in the open air at which whole or sides of large animals (as beef) are roasted over a barbecue pit **c :** pieces of meat, chicken, or fish broiled over or in front of a source of cooking heat outdoors or indoors **d :** meat or chicken cooked in a barbecue sauce **3 :** a place where barbecued meat is sold

barbecue 1b

²**barbecue** \"\ *vt* -ED/-ING/-S **1 :** to dry or cure (as meat) by exposure to heat **2 :** to roast or broil (as beef or fish) on a rack over hot coals or on a revolving spit before or over a source of cooking heat **3 :** to cook (as beef or fish) in a highly seasoned vinegar sauce

barbecue pit *n* **:** a trench in which wood is burned to make a bed of hot coals over which meat is barbecued

bar·be·cu·er \-üə(r)\ *n* -S **:** one that barbecues

barbecue sauce *n* **:** a highly seasoned sauce of vinegar, condiments, and spices that may be used in cooking, basting, or serving meat or fish

¹**barbed** \ˈbärbd, ˈbȧbd\ *adj* [³*barb* + *-ed*] **:** equipped with barbs ⟨under his feet he treads the armed Saracens and ~ steeds —Richard Carew⟩

²**barbed** \"\ *adj* [obs. E *barb* beard (fr. ME) + *-ed* — more at BARB] **1 a :** emblazoned with a beard ⟨an antelope argent ~ or⟩ **b :** emblazoned with wattles ⟨a cock vert ~ gules⟩ **c :** emblazoned with sepals showing between petals ⟨a rose gules ~ vert⟩ **d :** emblazoned with a pointed head ⟨an arrow argent ~ azure⟩ **2** [fr. past part. of ²*barb*] **a** *of a stream* **:** joined by tributaries at an acute angle pointed upstream ⟨a ~ tributary⟩ **b :** consisting of streams of this nature ⟨~ drainage⟩

barbed wire \ˈbä(r)bˈ(d)wī(ə)r; ˈbȧbˈ(d)wīə, ˈbäb-; *attrib* ˈ=ˌ=\ *n* [fr. past part. of ²*barb*] **:** a wire or a strand of twisted wires armed with barbs or sharp points

barbed wire

bar·bei·ro \bärˈbā(ˌ)rü, -rō\ *n* -S [Pg, lit., barber, fr. *barba* beard, fr. L; fr. its blood-sucking apparatus — more at BEARD] **:** a large black red-spotted cone-nose bug (*Triatoma*, or *Conorhinus*, *megistus*) of the American tropics that transmits the trypanosome causing Chagas' disease

¹**bar·bel** \ˈbärbəl, ˈbȧb-\ *n* -S [ME, fr. MF, fr. (assumed) VL *barbellus*, dim. of L *barbus* barbel — more at BARBUS] **1 :** a large European freshwater fish (*Barbus fluviatilis*) with four barbels on its upper jaw **2 :** any of various species of the genus *Barbus*

²**barbel** \"\ *n* -S [obs. F (now *barbeau*), fr. MF, dim. of *barbe* barb, beard, fr. L *barba* — more at BEARD] **1 :** a slender tactile process on the lips of certain fishes (as catfishes and cyprinoids) **2 barbels** *pl* **:** ¹BARB 4 — used esp. when the processes are inflamed and turgid **3 :** a fleshy process on the chin or neck of some turtles

bar·bell \ˈbärˌbel, ˈbȧb-\ *n* [¹*bar* + *bell*] **:** a bar with adjustable weighted disks attached to each end used for exercise and in weight lifting

bar·bel·late \ˈbärbəˌlāt, (ˈ)bärˈbelət\ *adj* [NL *barbella* short stiff hair (dim. of L *barbula*, dim. of *barba* beard + E *-ate* — more at BEARD] *biol* **:** having short stiff hooked bristles or hairs

bar·bel·lu·la \bärˈbelyələ\ *n, pl* **barbellu·lae** \-ˌlē\ [NL, dim. of *barbella* short stiff hair, dim. of L *barbula* little beard — more at BARBULA] *biol* **:** a very small barb or bristle — **barbel·lu·late** \(ˈ)=ˈ==lət, -ˌlāt\ *adj*

barbeque *var of* BARBECUE

¹**bar·ber** \ˈbärbər, ˈbȧbə(r\ *n* -S [ME *barbour*, *barber*, fr. MF *barbeor*, fr. *barbe*, fr. L *barba* beard + *-eor* -or — more at BEARD] **1 :** one whose business is cutting and dressing hair, shaving and trimming beards, and performing related services (as giving facials or scalp treatments or formerly performing dentistry and surgery) **2 a :** a Tasmanian fish (*Caesioperca rasor*) of the family Serranidae **b :** an African catfish (*Clarias capensis*) **3 :** FROST SMOKE

²**barber** \"\ *vb* **barbered**; **barbered**; **barbering** \-b(ə)riŋ\ **barbers** *vt* **1 :** to render the services of a barber to; *esp* **:** to cut, trim, dress, or groom the hair or beard of ⟨~*ed* him and bathed him and sent him to a tailor —T.W.Duncan⟩ **2 :** to cut or trim closely (as a lawn) ⟨green acres of ~*ed* landscape —*Time*⟩ ~ *vi* **:** to perform usu. professionally the actions or services of a barber ⟨he'd been ~*ing* . . . for well over twenty years —G.S.Perry⟩

barber chair *n* **1 :** a specially constructed chair used in barbershops and usu. having a footrest, a backrest that may be lowered to reclining position, and a hydraulic mechanism for adjusting the height of the chair **2 :** a stump on which a slab is left standing when a tree is felled

barberfish \ˈ==ˌ=\ *n* **:** any of several bright red fishes of the genus *Anthias* (family Berycidae); *esp* **:** a fish (*A. anthias*) of Madeira and the Mediterranean

barbermonger \ˈ==ˌ==\ *n* [¹*barber* + *monger*] *obs* **:** FOP

bar·bero \bärˈbe(ˌ)rō\ *n* -S [AmerSp, fr. Sp, barber, fr. *barba* beard, fr. L — more at BEARD] **:** SURGEONFISH

barber pole *or* **barber's pole** *n* **:** a usu. rotating pole with diagonal stripes of red and white or of red, white, and blue used as a sign for a barbershop

bar·ber·ry \ˈbärˌberē, ˈbȧˌ-, -ˌb(ə)rē, -ri\ *also* **ber·ber·ry** *or* **ber·bery** \ˈbərˌ-, ˈbəˌ-\ *n* [by folk etymology (influence of ¹*berry*) fr. ME *barbere*, fr. MF *barbarin*, *berberis*, *berbere*, fr. Ar *barbārīs*] **1 :** any shrub of the genus *Berberis* — see AMERICAN BARBERRY, COMMON BARBERRY, JAPANESE BARBERRY **2 :** the dried rhizome and roots of various shrubs of the genus *Mahonia* used as a bitter tonic

barberry family *n* **:** BERBERIDACEAE

barberry rust *n* **:** the wheat stem rust in its aecial stage on barberry, formerly thought to be a distinct species (*Aecidium berberidis*)

¹**bar·ber·shop** \ˈ==ˌ=\ *n* **:** a barber's place of business

²**barbershop** \"\ *adj* [fr. *barbershop (quartet)*, male quartet traditionally associated with old-style barbershops] **1** *of singing* **:** in the style of impromptu unaccompanied vocal harmonizing of popular songs esp. by a male quartet or any informal singing group **2 a** *of harmony* **:** marked by avoidance of spread chords and by the favoring of chromatically altered tones — compare CLOSE HARMONY **b :** of, relating to, or marked by such harmony ⟨a ~ quartet⟩ ⟨a ~ chord⟩

³**barbershop** \"\ *n* **:** barbershop singing **:** barbershop harmony ⟨singing ~ for an hour after supper⟩

barber's itch *n* **:** ringworm of parts of the face and neck caused by any of several parasitic fungi

barber's pole worm *n* **:** a stomach worm (*Haemonchus contorbus*)

bar·ber·ton daisy \ˈbärbərtᵊn-, -tən-, ˈbȧbət-, *prob also* ˈbärbət- *by r-dissimilation*\ *n, usu cap B* [fr. *Barberton*, town in eastern Transvaal, Union of South Africa] **:** TRANSVAAL DAISY

bar·ber·ton·ite \-tᵊnˌīt, -təˌnīt\ *n* -S [*Barberton* + E *-ite*] **:** a mineral $Mg_6Cr_2(OH)_{16}(CO_3){\cdot}4H_2O$ consisting of a hydrous basic carbonate of magnesium and chromium

bar·bery \ˈbärbərē\ *n* -ES [MF *barberie*, fr. *barbier* barber (fr. *barbe* beard, fr. L *barba*) + *-ie* -y — more at BEARD] **:** the craft of a barber ⟨a fashionable dentist . . . who seems to have graduated from ~ to dentistry —Harvey Graham⟩

barbes *pl of* BARBE

bar·bet \ˈbärbət\ *n* -S [prob. fr. ¹*barb* + *-et*] **1 :** any of numerous loud-voiced tropical birds constituting a family (Capitonidae) of the Piciformes being closely related to the honey guides but having a large stout bill bearing bristles and usu. swollen at the base — see COPPERSMITH **2 :** PUFFBIRD

barbet

bar·bette \(ˈ)bärˈbet\ *n* -S [F, dim. of *barbe* nun's barb — more at BARB] **1 :** a nun's barb; *often* **:** one consisting only of a band passing under the chin and pinned on top of the head **2** [so called fr. the resemblance of the earthwork encircling the cannon to a nun's barb] **:** a mound of earth or an often specially protected platform on which guns are mounted to fire over a parapet **3 :** a cylinder of armor on a warship that gives protection to the rotating part of the turret below the gunhouse — **in barbette** *of a gun* **:** in such a position as to fire over a parapet rather than through embrasures

barbette carriage *n* **:** a gun carriage that elevates the gun sufficiently for it to be in barbette

barbette gun *n* **:** a gun mounted in barbette

bar·bi·can \ˈbärbəkən\ *n* -S [ME, fr. OF *barbacane*, fr. ML *barbacana*] **:** an outer defensive work of a city or castle; *esp* **:** a tower at a gate or bridge

bar·bi·cel \ˈbärbəˌsel\ *n* -S [NL *barbicella*, dim. of L *barba* beard — more at BEARD] **:** one of the small processes on a barbule of the distal side of a barb of a feather that bear the hooks which hold the web of the feather together

bar·bier·ite \bärˈbiˌrīt\ *n* -S [Philippe *Barbier* fl1908 French chemist + E *-ite*] **:** a hypothetical monoclinic soda feldspar $NaAlSi_3O_8$ believed to be isomorphous with orthoclase

barb·ing \ˈbärbiŋ, ˈbȧb-, -bēŋ\ *n* -S [fr. gerund of ²*barb*] **:** oblique cutting to form sharp points when forming barbed wire

bar bit *n* [¹*bar*] **:** a bit for horses of which the mouthpiece is a solid bar of metal sometimes covered (as with rubber) and having no lever action — see BIT illustration

bar·bi·tal \ˈbärbəˌtȯl, ˈbȧb- *sometimes* -bəd·ᵊl *or* -bətᵊl *or* bəˌtal\ *n* -S [*barbit*uric + *-al* (as in *Veronal*)] **:** a white crystalline habit-forming hypnotic $C_8H_{12}N_2O_3$ often administered in the form of its soluble sodium salt; diethyl-barbituric acid

bar·bi·ton \ˈ==ˌtän\ *n, pl* **barbitons** *or* **barbita** [L *barbitos*, *barbiton*, fr. Gk] **1** *also* **barbitos :** an ancient Greek musical instrument resembling a lyre **2** *obs* **:** LUTE, VIOL

bar·bi·tone \ˈ==ˌtōn\ *n* -S *sometimes cap* [*barbit*uric + *-one*] *Brit* **:** BARBITAL

bar·bi·tu·rate \bärˈbichərət, bȧˈb-, -ˌrāt *sometimes* -chrət; *also* ˌbärbəˈtu̇ˌrāt *or* ˌbȧb- *or* -əˈtyü- *or* -(y)ü- *sometimes* -əˈchü- *or* -əˈchü- *or* ˈ==ˌ=ˌ=; *substand* =ˈbichəwət *or* -chəˌwāt; *usu* -əd· *or* -äd· + V\ *n* -S [*barbituric* + *-ate*] **1 :** a salt or ester of barbituric acid **2 :** any of a large group of slightly bitter crystalline acids (as barbital, phenobarbital) or their salts derived from barbituric acid that are used as sedatives, hypnotics, and antispasmodics

bar·bi·tu·ric acid \ˌbärbəˈtu̇rik-, ˌbȧb-, -əˈtyü-, -t(y)ü-, -rēk-\ *n* [part trans. of G *barbitursäure*, irreg. fr. the name *Barbara* + G *-ur-* (fr. ISV *uric*) + *säure* acid] **:** a crystalline acid $CH_2(CONH)_2CO$ that is a derivative of pyrimidine and is usu. obtained from malonic acid and urea; malonylurea; *also* **:** any of the acids derived from this acid, many of them being used as hypnotics

bar·bi·zon \ˈbärbəˌzän\ *adj, usu cap* [fr. *Barbizon*, village near Fontainebleau Forest, France] **:** depicting landscape and rural genre subjects from direct observation of nature and with much attention to the expression of light and atmosphere — used esp. of a middle 19th century school of French painting

bar·ble \ˈbärbəl\ *n* -S [by alter.] **:** ¹BARB 4

barb·less \ˈbärbləs, ˈbȧb-\ *adj* **:** being without a barb ⟨considered it unsporting to use anything other than a ~ hook⟩

barb·let \ˈbärblət\ *n* -S [irreg. fr. ²*barbel* + *-let*] **:** a small barbel

bar·bo·la work \bärˈbōlə, bȧˈb-\ *also* **barbola** *n* -S [origin unknown] **:** the decoration of small articles (as of wood or glass) with colored models of flowers, fruit, or other ornamental objects made from a plastic paste

bar·bo·ne \bärˈbōnē\ *also* **barbone disease** *n* -S [It, lit., long beard, aug. of *barba* beard, fr. L — more at BEARD] **:** pasteurellosis of the domestic buffalo

bar·bo·tine \ˌbärbəˈtēn\ *n* -S [F, fr. *barboter* to splash about + *-ine*] **1 :** ⁷SLIP 1a **2** *or* **barbotine ware :** early European ware decorated with raised slip designs

bar·botte \(ˈ)bärˈbät\ *also* **bar·booth** \-ˈbüt(h)\ *or* **bar·bu·di** \bärˈbüdē\ *n* -S [CanF & Turk; CanF *barbotte*, fr. Turk *barbut*] **:** a dice game in which a throw of 3-3, 5-5, 6-6, or 6-5 wins, a throw of 1-1, 1-2, 2-2, or 4-4 loses, and other throws do not count

barboy \ˈ=ˌ=\ *n* [¹*bar* (counter) + *boy*] **:** a bartender's helper who keeps the bar supplied (as with glasses and ice) and performs related duties (as peeling fruit and carrying off waste)

barbs *pl of* BARB, *pres 3d sing of* BARB

bar·bu·do \bärˈbü(ˌ)dō\ *n* -S [AmerSp, fr. Sp, adj., bearded, fr. *barba* beard, fr. L; fr. the barbels — more at BEARD] **1 :** any of several threadfins used as food; *esp* **:** a common species (*Polynemus virginicus*) of the Caribbean and adjacent areas **2 :** any of several berycoid fishes (genus *Polymixia*) widely distributed in the deeper waters of the Atlantic and Pacific oceans

bar·bu·la \ˈbärbyələ\ *n, cap* [NL, fr. L *barbula* little beard, dim. of *barba* beard — more at BEARD] **:** a large genus of slender tufted mosses (family Pottiaceae) with 16 mostly long spirally twisted peristome teeth

bar·bu·la·tion \ˌbärbyəˈlāshən\ *n* -S [*barbule* + *-ation*] **:** the occurrence of barbules — used of feathers

bar·bule \ˈbär(ˌ)byül\ *n* -S [L *barbula* little beard] **:** a minute barb or beard: **a :** ²BARBEL 1 **b :** one of the processes along either side of a barb of a feather, those on the upper side resembling slender scroll-like plates and terminating in a thickened flange with which the hooks of the barbicels that terminate the barbules of the lower margin of an adjacent barb mesh

bar·buled \-ld\ *adj* **:** having barbules

bar burner *n* [¹*bar*] **:** one who secures samples of steel bars from each heat and prepares them for carbon analysis

bar·bus \ˈbärbəs\ *n, cap* [NL, fr. L, barbel] **:** a very large genus of chiefly small often brilliantly colored Old World fishes related to the carps and including a number that are popular in the tropical aquarium

barb·wire \ˈbä(r)bˈwī(ə)r; ˈbȧbˈwīə, ˈbäb-; *attrib* ˈ=ˌ=\ *n* [¹*barb* + *wire*] **:** BARBED WIRE

bar car *n* [¹*bar*] **:** a parlor car or lounge car with facilities for preparing and serving beverages or other refreshments

bar·ca·role *or* **bar·ca·rolle** \ˈbärkəˌrōl, ˈbȧk-\ *n* -S [F *barcarolle*, fr. It *barcarola*, fr. *barcarolo* gondolier, fr. *barca* bark, barge, fr. LL — more at BARK] **1 :** a boat song esp. as sung by Venetian gondoliers and typically characterized by the alternation of a strong and a weak beat in ⁶⁄₈ time and suggesting a rowing rhythm **2 :** an art song or other piece of music imitating a barcarole

¹**bar·ce·lo·na** \ˌbärsəˈlōnə, ˈbȧs-\ *adj, usu cap* [fr. *Barcelona*, Spain] **:** of or from the city of Barcelona, Spain **:** of the kind or style prevalent in Barcelona

²**barcelona** \"\ *n* -S **:** a handkerchief or scarf of twilled silk

barcelona nut *n, usu cap B* **:** a Spanish variety of hazelnut kiln-dried before exportation to preserve its flavor

bar·ce·lo·nese \ˌ==(ˌ)lōˈnēz, -ēs\ *n, pl* **barcelonese** *usu cap* [*Barcelona*, city & province of Spain + E *-ese*] **:** a native or resident of Barcelona, esp. Barcelona, Spain

bar·chan *or* **bar·chane** *or* **bar·khan** \(ˈ)bärˈkän, -ˈk-\ *n* -S [Russ *barkhan*, fr. Kirghiz] **:** a moving sand dune shaped like a crescent and found in several very dry regions of the world

bar chart *n* [¹*bar*] **:** a graphic representation for comparing numbers by means of rectangles of uniform widths but of lengths proportional to the numbers being represented — called also *bar graph*

bar clamp *n* [¹*bar*] **:** a frame consisting of a long bar with two adjustable clamping jaws that is used usu. in woodwork or cabinetmaking for holding large work

bar·coo rot \(ˈ)bärˈkü-\ *n, often cap B* [fr. *Barcoo*, district of Australia, where the disease was common] **:** DESERT SORE

barcoo spew *or* **barcoo vomit** *n, often cap B* **:** a sickness occurring in Australia that is characterized by painless attacks of vomiting

bar creaser *n* [¹*bar*] **:** an operator of a machine for creasing paper-box blanks along lines where they are to be folded

¹**bard** \ˈbärd, ˈbȧd\ *n* -S [ME, fr. ScGael & MIr; akin to W *bardd* poet and prob. to Skt *gṛṇāti* he praises — more at GRACE] **1 a :** a tribal poet-singer (as among the ancient Celts) gifted in composing and reciting verses usu. to harp accompaniment in honor of the chief or successive chiefs and their deeds and as a record in verse of tribal history, tradition, genealogy, or religious law **b :** any similar poet-singer of the period before the use of writing; *esp* **:** a composer, singer, or declaimer of epic or heroic verse **2** *obs* **:** one of a class of wandering musicians or minstrels in early Scotland often treated as vagabonds in Scottish law and opinion **3 a :** POET; *esp* **:** a poet who writes impassioned, lyrical, or epic verse ⟨the ~ walks in advance, leader of leaders —Walt Whitman⟩ **b :** a writer of insipid or mediocre verse **:** VERSIFIER ⟨newspaper ~*s*⟩

²**bard** *or* **barde** \"\ *n* -S [MF *barde*, fr. OSp *barda* horse armor, fr. Ar *barda'ah*] **1 a :** a piece of spiked or bossed armor for a horse's neck, breast, or flank — usu. used in pl. **b :** an ornamental imitation of such armor made of velvet or other rich cloth and often used in tournaments — usu. used in pl. **2 bards** *pl* **:** plate armor formerly worn by a man-at-arms **3 :** a slice of bacon used to cover meat or game for cooking

³**bard** \"\ *vt* -ED/-ING/-S [MF *barder*, fr. *barde*] **1 :** to equip or accouter with bards **2 :** to cover (meat or game) with slices of bacon for cooking

bar·dane \(ˈ)bärˈdän\ *n* -S [F] **:** BURDOCK

bar·dash \(ˈ)bärˈdash\ *n* -ES [MF *bardache*, fr. OIt dial. *bardascia* youth, homosexual, fr. Ar *bardaj* slave, fr. Per *bardah*] **:** a homosexual male **:** CATAMITE

bar·dé \(ˈ)bärˈdā *F* bȧrdā\ *adj* [F, past part. of *barder* to bard (cover with bacon)] **:** covered with salt pork or slices of bacon before cooking

bar·dee *also* **bar·dy** \ˈbärdē\ *n, pl* **bardees** *also* **bardies** [prob. a native name in Australia] **:** a large Australian roundheaded borer that is the larva of a beetle (*Bardistus cibarius*) and is esteemed as food by the aborigines

bard·ic \ˈbärdik, ˈbȧd-, -ēk\ *adj* [¹*bard* + *-ic*] **:** being, belonging, or relating to a bard or his poetry ⟨a ~ poet⟩ ⟨a ~ lay⟩

bard·ie \ˈbärdi\ *n* -S [¹*bard* + *-ie*] *Scot* **:** a minor poet

bar·di·glio \bärˈdēl(ˌ)yō\ *n* -S [It, fr. It dial. *bardiglio* grayish (It *pardiglio*) fr. Sp *pardillo* grayish, brown, fr. *pardo* gray, brown, prob. fr. L *pardus* panther; fr. the color of the panther — more at PARD] **:** an Italian marble commonly having a dark gray or bluish ground traversed by veins and occurring in its principal varieties in the neighborhood of Carrara and in Corsica

bard·ing \ˈbärdiŋ\ *n* -S [fr. gerund of ³*bard*] **:** the armorial or armorlike ornamental trappings of a horse — usu. used in pl.

bar ditch \ˈbärˌ-\ *n* [alter. of *borrow*] *chiefly West* **:** BORROW DITCH

bard·let \ˈbärdlət\ *or* **bard·ling** \-liŋ\ *n* -S **:** POETASTER

bar·do \ˈbär(ˌ)dō\ *n* -S *often cap* [Tibetan, lit., between two] *Lamaism* **:** the intermediate or astral state of the soul after death and before rebirth

bard·ol·a·ter \bärˈdäləd·ər\ *also* **bard·ol·a·trist** \-lə·trəst\ *n* -S *sometimes cap* [*Bard* (*of Avon*), nickname of William Shakespeare †1616 Eng. poet & playwright + *idolater*] **:** one who idolizes Shakespeare ⟨an ardent ~⟩

bard·ol·a·try \-ə·trē\ *n* -ES *sometimes cap* **:** the worship of Shakespeare

bard·ship \ˈbärdˌship\ *n* [¹*bard* + *-ship*] **:** the office of or condition of a bard

bardy \ˈbärdi\ *adj* -ER/-EST [prob. fr. ¹*bard* (minstrel) + *-y*] *Scot* **:** BOLD, FORWARD, INSOLENT

¹**bare** \ˈba(a)(ə)r, ˈbe(ə)r,ˈba(a)ə, ˈbeə\ *adj* -ER/-EST [ME, fr. OE *bær*; akin to OHG *bar* naked, ON *berr*, Lith *basas* barefoot, Arm *bok*] **1 a :** lacking its natural covering (as of hair, flesh, bark, or foliage) ⟨a stroke that left the bone ~⟩ ⟨a ~ hillside⟩ ⟨trees standing gaunt and ~⟩ ⟨a ~ scalp⟩ **b (1) :** lacking clothing **:** UNCOVERED ⟨expose a ~ back to the sun⟩ ⟨walk in ~ feet⟩ **(2)** *obs* **:** BAREHEADED **c (1) :** lacking its customary or appropriate covering (as of paint or carpets) ⟨~ aluminum gutters⟩ ⟨a ~ floor⟩ **(2) :** lacking armor or weapons **:** UNARMED — usu. used in the phrase *bare hands* or the word *bare-handed* ⟨fought and killed him with ~ hands⟩ **(3)** *of cloth* **:** THREADBARE **(4)** *of a sword* **:** UNSHEATHED ⟨and ~ was the Niblung sword —William Morris⟩ **(5)** *of a ship's mast* **:** having no sails set ⟨rode out the storm with ~ poles⟩ **d** *obs* **:** laid waste or desolate **2 :** exposed or open to view or

comprehension — often used in the phrase *lay bare* ⟨lays ~ with admirable simplicity the essentials of the problem⟩ ⟨laid ~ the innermost secrets of the society⟩ **3 a :** lacking the usual or appropriate furnishings, equipment, or contents **:** EMPTY **:** unfurnished or scantily supplied ⟨tenant farmers who live in ~ shacks —*Amer. Guide Series: Texas*⟩ ⟨a ~ room, dusty and cold⟩ **b :** DESTITUTE, NEEDY, LACKING — usu. used with *of* ⟨a house ~ of all comforts save the devotion of the parents⟩ ⟨deny the right to livelihood of individuals ~ of all legal protection —Robert Lekachman⟩ **4 a :** having nothing left over or added ⟨a ~ living⟩ ⟨the ~ dinner of potatoes —Lewis Mumford⟩ **:** MINIMUM ⟨the ~ necessities of life⟩ **:** MERE ⟨the father drowned . . . when Nathan was a ~ two years old —Mary S. Watts⟩ ⟨rage . . . at the ~ idea that the tenant of a furnished house should interfere with the owner's timber —F.M.Ford⟩ **b :** having no more or little more than essentials **:** devoid of amplification or of adornment, refinement, or polish **:** severely plain **:** AUSTERE ⟨state the ~ truth⟩ ⟨the ~ folk tale, a simple narration of some happening or action —R.A.Hall b. 1911⟩ ⟨a ~ outline of a novelette⟩ **c :** SCANTY, MEAGER ⟨only a ~ portion of the available gold was being secured —Irving Stone⟩ **5** *obs* **:** WORTHLESS, PALTRY, INADEQUATE **6** *bridge* **:** unaccompanied by others of the same suit ⟨a ~ king⟩ ⟨hold the ace ~⟩

syn BARE, NAKED, NUDE, BALD, BARREN all indicate lack of some usual covering, shrouding, or overlaying. In reference to bodily matters, BARE usu. describes bodily parts, indicates simply an unclothed or uncovered condition, and lacks especial connotation ⟨maidens whose *bare* feet make no sound —Lafcadio Hearn⟩ ⟨legs *bare* or swathed from the knee to the ankle —Edna S. V. Millay⟩ NAKED usu. indicates complete lack of clothing; it may suggest a primitive or natural condition, rare and complete beauty, pitiful destitution, or wanton and shameless exhibitionism ⟨a boy and an old man — both islanders, the former nearly *naked* and the latter dressed in an old naval frock coat —Herman Melville⟩ ⟨a radiant spirit arose all beautiful in *naked* purity —P.B.Shelley⟩ ⟨hunt for food and be a *naked* man —S.T.Coleridge⟩ ⟨down with Reticence, down with Reverence — forward — *naked* — let them stare —Alfred Tennyson⟩ Especial connotations are lacking for NUDE, a synonym more sophisticated and less common before the 20th century, except that it is frequently used in relation to artistic productions ⟨standing before a picture of *nude* beauty —P.E.More⟩ In reference to bodily matters BALD also lacks especial connotation. In other contexts BARE stresses a lack of some covering, furniture, addition, or amplification usu. expected ⟨the house seemed *bare* and cold, a bareness scarcely modified by the few old pieces of furniture —Mary Austin⟩ ⟨scorched and blackened by the long summer, the country was as *bare* as a conquered province after the march of an invader —Ellen Glasgow⟩ ⟨the *bare* statement that "art is useless" is so vague as to be really meaningless, if not inaccurate and misleading —Havelock Ellis⟩ NAKED strongly suggests exposure or revelation ⟨it is not asked that poetry should offer *naked* argument and skeleton plans —C.D. Lewis⟩ ⟨numberless *naked*, detached coral formations are seen, just emerging, as it were, from the ocean —Herman Melville⟩ BALD indicates absence of natural covering, particularly on the top of something ⟨Texas, spanning a widely divergent region between the lush green coastal prairies and a semiarid trans-Pecos expanse of *bald* hills —*Amer. Guide Series: Tex.*⟩ It may also imply severe curt plainness and lack of adornment ⟨he invented no fancy phrases to decorate a *bald* fact —Agnes Repplier⟩ ⟨lend verisimilitude to an otherwise *bald* and unconvincing narrative —W.S.Gilbert⟩ BARREN stresses lack of natural covering ⟨the country was *barren* and rocks stuck up through the clay. There was no grass —Ernest Hemingway⟩ Otherwise it suggests impoverishment or fruitlessness ⟨my life is a *barren* and lonely one, and so full of work that I have not had much time for friendships —Bram Stoker⟩

²bare \"\ *vt* -ED/-ING/-S [ME *baren*, fr. OE *barian;* causative fr. the root of E ¹*bare*] **:** to make or lay bare **:** UNCOVER, REVEAL ⟨~ his back to the sun⟩ ⟨~ her teeth in a smile⟩ ⟨~*s* the remote origins of bolshevism —S.T.Possony⟩ ⟨demanding that men ~ their private opinion or else go to jail —Herbert Agar⟩ **syn** see STRIP

³bare \"\ *adv* [ME, fr. *bare*, adj.] *obs* **:** BARELY

⁴bare \"\ *archaic past of* BEAR

⁵ba·ré \bəˈrā, ˈbä(ˌ)rā\ *n, pl* **baré** *or* **barés** *usu cap* [Sp & Pg, of AmerInd origin] **1 a :** an Arawakan people on the Rio Negro and Rio Cassiquiare in northern Brazil and Venezuela **b :** a member of such people **2 :** the language of the Baré people

bare–assed \ˈ⸗ˌ⸗\ *adv* (*or adj*) **:** in the nude **:** UNCLOTHED — sometimes considered vulgar ⟨a boy swimming *bare-assed*⟩ ⟨a small *bare-assed* boy running along the beach⟩

bareback *or* **barebacked** \ˈ⸗ˌ⸗\ *adv* (*or adj*) **:** on the bare back of a horse without using a saddle ⟨a young boy riding ~⟩ ⟨learned ~ riding among the Indians⟩

bareback rider *n* **:** an entertainer (as in a circus) who performs acrobatic feats or feats of balance bareback while the horse is trotting or cantering

bareboat \ˈ⸗ˌ⸗\ *adj, of a charter* **:** placing on the charterer of a vessel once it has been outfitted and equipped by the owner full responsibility for operating and manning it and paying operation, repair, and insurance costs as if it were his own

bare bones *n pl* **:** the barest essentials, facts, or elements (as of a situation) ⟨the afternoon paper had reported the *bare bones* of the case —Thomas Thursday⟩ ⟨he finally stripped his proposition to its *bare bones* —A.H.Vandenberg †1951⟩

ba·re'e \bəˈrā,ā\ *n* -S **:** an Austronesian language of central Celebes

bare–eyed cockatoo \ˈ⸗ˌ⸗-\ *n* **:** a widely distributed small corella (*Kakatoe sanguinea*) with patches of bare bluish gray skin about the eyes

bareface \ˈ⸗ˌ⸗\ *adj, of a fabric* **:** having a clear finish and no nap

barefaced \ˈ⸗ˌ⸗\ *adj* **1 :** having the face uncovered: **a :** having no beard or whiskers **:** BEARDLESS **b :** wearing no mask **2 a :** UNCONCEALED, OPEN, OBVIOUS ⟨a ~ mockery of the new . . . trading class —Sam Pollock⟩ ⟨out of this ~ and unashamed formula evolves one of the most entertaining . . . tales of the lightly fantastic —John Nerber⟩ **b :** lacking scruples **:** SHAMELESS, BRAZEN ⟨a policy of ~ imperialism —W.K. Ferguson⟩ ⟨cheat each other in ways that were often ~ and sometimes violent —Havelock Ellis⟩ ⟨a ~ lie⟩ **c :** BLUNT, STRAIGHTFORWARD ⟨never slandered personalities, but he was . . . ~ about facts as he saw them —Peggy Bennett⟩ **syn** see SHAMELESS

bare·fac·ed·ly \(ˈ)⸗ˈfāsədlē, -stlē, -li\ *adv* **:** in a barefaced manner

barefaced tenon *n* **:** a tenon having a shoulder on one side only

bare fallow *n* **:** land remaining uncropped for a season and kept free from vegetation by cultivation

barefisted \ˈ⸗ˈ⸗⸗\ *adv* (*or adj*) **:** BAREKNUCKLE ⟨fight ~⟩ ⟨a ~ exchange of blows⟩

bare·fit \ˈbär(ˌ)fit, -er-,-ār-\ *adj* [by alter.] *Scot* **:** BAREFOOT

barefoot \ˈ⸗ˌ⸗\ *or* **barefooted** \ˈ⸗ˈ⸗⸗\ *adv* (*or adj*) [ME *barefot*, fr. OE *bærfōt* (akin to MHG *barvuoz*, OFris *berfōt*, ON *berfœttr*), fr. *bær* bare + *fōt* foot — more at BARE, FOOT] **1 a :** with the feet bare **:** without shoes or stockings ⟨a ~ boy⟩ ⟨go ~ in the summertime⟩ **b** *of a horse* **:** UNSHOD **2 :** wearing only sandals on the feet — used esp. of certain religious communities **3 :** set up and fastened without a mortise and tenon (as a post or stud in a balloon frame) **4** *of an oil well* **:** drilled without a casing

B
B
B barefaced tenon

barefoot auger *n* **:** SHIP AUGER

ba·rege \bəˈrezh\ *n* -S [F *barège*, fr. *Barèges*, a town in the Pyrenees, France] **:** a sheer fabric of open weave for women's clothing usu. made of wool in combination with silk or cotton

bare–handed \ˈ⸗ˈ⸗⸗\ *adv* (*or adj*) **1 :** without covering on the hands **:** UNGLOVED ⟨box *bare-handed*⟩ **2 :** without tools, implements, or weapons ⟨fight an animal *bare-handed*⟩ ⟨efforts to survive *bare-handed* in a hostile world —Lewis Mumford⟩

bareheaded \ˈ⸗ˈ⸗⸗\ *also* **barehead** \ˈ⸗ˌ⸗\ *adv* (*or adj*) [ME *barehed*, fr. *bare* + *hed* head] **:** without a hat or other covering for the head ⟨standing ~ in the rain —*New Republic*⟩ ⟨go ~ in the hot sun⟩ ⟨a ~ boy who had lost his cap⟩ — **bare·head·ed·ness** *n* -ES

ba·reil·ly \bəˈrālē\ *adj, usu cap* [fr. *Bareilly*, India] **:** of or from the city of Bareilly, India **:** of the kind or style prevalent in Bareilly

¹bareknuckle *or* **bareknuckled** \ˈ⸗ˈ⸗⸗\ *adj* [¹*bare* + *knuckle* or *knuckled*] **1 :** not using boxing gloves — used of fighting or a fighter ⟨champion ~ prizefighter of England —Dennis Craig⟩ **2 :** having an aggressive fierce unrelenting character ⟨led a *bareknuckled* fight against waste of public funds —J.R. Aswell & E.J.Michelson⟩

²bareknuckle *or* **bareknuckled** \ˈ⸗ˈ⸗⸗\ *adv* **:** in a bareknuckle way ⟨the early days of pugilism in which men fought ~⟩ ⟨fighting ~ in congress for his beliefs⟩

barely *adv* [ME, fr. ¹*bare* + *-ly*] **1 :** by the narrowest margin ⟨~ escaped injury⟩ **:** lacking any excess **:** with nothing to spare **:** SCARCELY, HARDLY ⟨~ enough food to sustain life⟩ **2 :** SCANTILY, MEAGERLY, PLAINLY ⟨a ~ furnished room⟩

ba·ren \(ˈ)bäˈren\ *n* -S [prob. fr. Jap] **:** a pad of twisted cord covered with paper, cloth, and bamboo leaf with which a printmaker transmits pressure typically by rubbing to paper laid on an inked woodcut

bare·ness *n* -ES [¹*bare* + *-ness*] **:** the quality or state of being bare ⟨a room furnished with a simplicity bordering on ~⟩ ⟨a story with a marked ~ of outline⟩

bare·sark \ˈ⸗ˌsärk\ *n* -S [intended as trans. of ON *berserkr* — more at BERSERK] **:** BERSERKER

ba·res·ma \ˈbarəsmə, -əzmə\ *n* -S [Av *barəsman-*] **:** BARSOM

bare trust *n* **:** PASSIVE TRUST

ba·ret·ta \bəˈred·ə\ *n* -S [modif. of MexSp *barreta*, fr. Sp *barreta*, *barrete* cap, biretta, fr. Catal *barret*, fr. Prov *berret* — more at BERET] **:** a rutaceous evergreen shrub (*Helietta parvifolia*) of Texas with opposite trifoliolate leaves and purple flowers

barff \ˈbärf\ *vt* -ED/-ING/-S [after F.S.*Barff* — more at BOWER-BARFF PROCESS] **:** to protect (iron or steel) with a coating of iron oxide Fe_3O_4 by the Bower-Barff process

barfish \ˈ⸗ˌ⸗\ *n* [¹*bar;* fr. the stripes on the back] **1 :** WHITE BASS 1 **2 :** YELLOW BASS

barfly \ˈ⸗ˌ⸗\ *n* -ES [¹*bar* (counter) + *fly*] **:** a drinker who frequents bars

¹bar·gain \ˈbärgən, ˈbȧg-\ *n* -S *often attrib* [ME *bargayn*, fr. MF *bargaigne*, fr. OF, fr. *bargaignier*] **1** *obs* **:** discussion of terms of agreement **:** HAGGLING **2 a :** an agreement between parties settling what each gives or receives in a transaction between them or what course of action or policy each pursues in respect to the other ⟨struck a ~ to sell only to each other⟩ ⟨the two armed camps made a ~ to cease fire⟩ **b** *dial Eng* **:** a piece of contract work at an agreed rate esp. in mining and quarrying **3 a :** a thing acquired by or as if by bargaining ⟨chaffered for half an hour before acquiring his ~⟩ **b :** an advantageous purchase **:** something whose value to the purchaser considerably exceeds its cost ⟨at that price the house is a ~⟩ **4 :** a transaction, situation, or event regarded in the light of its good or bad consequences or results ⟨make the best of a bad ~⟩ — **in the bargain** *or* **into the bargain :** over and above what is agreed on or might be anticipated **:** BESIDES ⟨singers . . . subdued and colorless, often naturally mediocre and conspicuously untrained *in the bargain* —H.F.Mooney⟩ ⟨destroyed the Popular Front and ruined the Spanish Republic *into the bargain* —*Times Lit. Supp.*⟩

²bargain \"\ *vb* -ED/-ING/-S [ME *bargaynen*, fr. MF *bargaignier*, fr. OF, of Gmc origin; akin to OE *borgian* to borrow — more at BURY] *vi* **1 :** to negotiate over the terms of an agreement or contract **:** haggle esp. over a purchase price ⟨nosegays bought from the urchins who ~*ed* on the carriage roads —Jean Stafford⟩ ⟨~*ed* for the use of the property⟩ ⟨considered the possibility of ~*ing* with the enemy⟩; *specif* **:** to engage in collective bargaining ⟨ask that both management and labor ~ in good faith⟩ **2 :** to agree to certain terms or conditions **:** come to terms ⟨~*ed* on setting me ashore tonight⟩ ~ *vt* **1 a :** to bring (a price) to a desired level by bargaining ⟨~ the price of meat down⟩ **b :** to sell or dispose of by bargaining ⟨~ his services to the highest bidder —*Springfield (Mass.) Daily News*⟩ **:** BARTER, TRADE ⟨~ one horse for another⟩ **c :** to resolve or settle (as differences) by bargaining ⟨~*ed* out the remaining obstacles to an agreement⟩ **d :** to bring (a party) to a specific agreement by bargaining ⟨tried . . . to ~ Britain out of her share of this region —R.W.Van Alstyne⟩ **2 :** to give assurances or make a commitment **:** PLEDGE — usu. used with clause as object ⟨I couldn't ~ that my mind should remain suggestive at that age —O.W.Holmes †1935⟩ ⟨I ~ that he'll be there on time⟩ — **bargain for :** to expect or plan for **:** count on in advance ⟨find mountain climbing harder than one *bargained for*⟩ — often used in negative construction ⟨they had not *bargained for* anything on so large a scale —Jean Stafford⟩ — **bargain on :** to count on **:** EXPECT ⟨*bargain on* making a fortune early in life⟩ ⟨hadn't *bargained on* so cold a reception⟩

bar·gain·a·ble \-nəbəl\ *adj* **:** subject to bargaining; *esp* **:** legitimately subject to collective bargaining ⟨a ~ contract⟩

bargain and sale *n, law* **:** a conveyance by which the vendor contracts for a consideration paid to convey the lands to the vendee and becomes by such contract a trustee for and seized to the use of the vendee — see BARGAINEE, BARGAINOR

bargain basement *n* **:** a section of a store (as the basement) where merchandise is sold at bargain prices

bargain–basement \ˈ⸗⸗ˈ⸗⸗\ *adj* [*bargain basement*] **:** markedly cheap or inexpensive ⟨a bill to . . . sell it to them at *bargain-basement* rates — A.J.Liebling⟩

bargain counter *n* **:** a counter where merchandise is sold at bargain prices

bargain–counter \ˈ⸗⸗ˈ⸗⸗\ *adj* [*bargain counter*] **:** BARGAIN-BASEMENT ⟨*bargain-counter* divorces —Morris Ploscowe⟩

bar·gain·ee \ˌ⸗gəˈnē\ *n* -S [²*bargain* + *-ee*] **:** the vendee in a bargain and sale

bar·gain·er \-nə(r)\ *n* -S [ME *bargayner*, fr. *bargaynen* to bargain + *-er*] **:** one that bargains

bargain hunter *n* **:** one that goes shopping for bargains

bargaining power *n* **:** the relative capacity of each of the parties to a negotiation or dispute to compel or secure agreement on its own terms ⟨widespread unemployment is adding to employers' *bargaining power* in their talks with the unions⟩

bargaining unit *n* **:** the group of employees on whose behalf a union seeks to negotiate a collective agreement

bar·gain·or \ˌ⸗gəˈnȯ(ə)r, -ȯə, ˈ⸗gənə(r)\ *n* -S **:** the vendor in a bargain and sale

bargain plea *n, slang* **:** a plea of guilty to one usu. the least of several charges allowed by the prosecution when the prosecution stands to gain thereby (as where an offer of prosecution under a lesser charge is useful in persuading an offender to turn state's evidence)

¹barge \ˈbärj, ˈbȧj\ *n* -S [ME, fr. OF, fr. LL *barca*] **1** *obs* **:** a sailing vessel; *specif* **:** one next larger than the balinger **:** BARK **2 :** any of various boats: as **a :** a roomy usu. flat-bottomed boat used principally in harbors or inland waterways though often sea-going for the transport of goods (as coal, oil, lumber, or grain) and sometimes passengers and usu. propelled by towing **b :** a large boat formerly a double-banked rowboat but now a powerboat supplied to a naval flagship for the use of a flag officer **c :** a roomy pleasure boat; *esp* **:** a boat of state elegantly furnished and decorated **d :** a racing boat somewhat broader and heavier than a shell and often used for practice purposes **e :** a towed or self-propelled boat used to transport freight cars over or across water routes not provided with bridges **3 :** ²KEEL 1b **4 :** a tub or box for bread for the crew's mess on a ship **5** *chiefly NewEng* **:** a large horse-drawn omnibus usu. used for excursions or the transportation of groups (as from a railroad station to a hotel)

²barge \"\ *vb* -ED/-ING/-S *vt* **:** to carry by barge ⟨ore will be *barged* down the Orinoco —*Newsweek*⟩ ⟨have already *barged* out the virgin forests in the form of lumber —*Sat. Eve. Post*⟩ ~ *vi* **1 :** to move or charge in a lumbering, ponderous, or clumsy manner ⟨he was a particularly cheeky saurian and soon came *barging* along to inspect us —Francis Birtles⟩ or in a headlong, impetuous, heedless, or aimless fashion ⟨a bat flew in the front door, *barged* around for 20 minutes until finally knocked down —*Time*⟩ **2 :** to thrust oneself unceremoniously (as into a place where one is unwanted) — used with *in* or *into* ⟨~ in on some friends while they are eating dinner⟩

³barge \ˈbärj, ˈbȧj\ *vt* -ED/-ING/-S [E dial. (Ireland), *barge* shrewish woman, fr. IrGael *bàirseach*] *dial Brit* **:** SCOLD, REBUKE ⟨she could have *barged* me all night telling me I was a cur and a coward —D'Arcy Niland⟩

bargeboard \ˈ⸗ˌ⸗\ *n* [origin unknown] **:** a piece of board often elaborately ornamented that conceals roof timbers projecting over gables

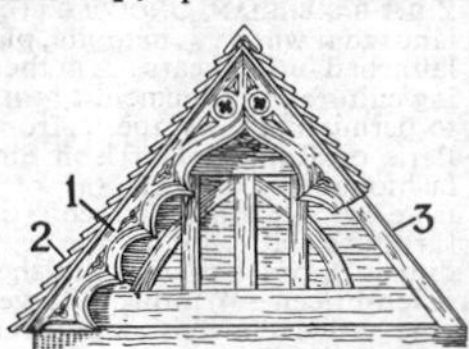

1 bargeboard, cut away at right to show *2* barge course; *3* barge couple

barge couple *n* [origin unknown] **:** one of the two rafters in a gable that project beyond the gable wall and carry the overhanging part of the roof

barge course *n* [origin unknown] **1 :** a part of the tiling on the sloping edges of a gable roof usu. projecting beyond the principal rafters or the bargeboards **2 :** the course of bricks laid on edge to form the coping of a wall

barg·ee \(ˈ)bärˈjē, (ˈ)bȧˈ-\ *n* -S [¹*barge* + *-ee*] *Brit* **:** BARGEMAN

barge·man \ˈbärjmən, -ȧj-\ *n, pl* **bargemen** [ME, fr. ¹*barge* + *man*] **:** the master or a deckhand of a barge

bar gemel *or* **bar gemelle** *n, pl* **bars gemel** *or* **bars gemels** *or* **bars gemelles** *heraldry* **:** a pair of narrow bars borne close together — called also *gemel*

barge pole *n* [¹*barge*] **:** a long pole used on a barge for propelling, for fending off objects, or with an attached hook for holding onto a wharf

barg·er \ˈbärjər, ˈbȧjə(r\ *n* -S [¹*barge* + *-er*] **:** BARGEMAN

barge spike *n* [¹*barge*] **:** a long square spike used in heavy timber construction — called also *boat spike*

barge stone *n* [origin unknown] **:** one of the stones that make the sloping edge of a gable

bar·gham \ˈbärfəm, -rkəm\ *n* -S [ME, perh. fr. OE *beorgan* to protect + *hama* covering — more at BURY, HAME] *now dial Eng* **:** a horse collar

bar·ghest *also* **bar·guest** \ˈbärgəst\ *n* -S [perh. fr. E dial. *bar*, *bargh* ridge (fr. ME *bergh* hill) + E dial. *ghest*, alter. of *ghost* — more at BARROW] *dial Eng* **:** a ghost or goblin believed to portend misfortune and sometimes appearing in the shape of a large dog

bar graph *n* [¹*bar*] **:** BAR CHART

barhal *var of* BHARAL

bar–headed goose \ˈ⸗ˌ⸗⸗-\ *or* **barhead goose** \ˈ⸗ˌ⸗-\ *n* [¹*bar*] **:** an Asiatic goose (*Anser indicus*) having a white head with two black bars on the occiput

barhop \ˈ⸗ˌ⸗\ *vi* **barhopped**; **barhopped**; **barhopping**; **barhops** [¹*bar* (counter) + *hop*] **:** to visit and usu. to drink at a series of bars esp. in one evening staying only a short time in any one bar ⟨to spend a vacation *barhopping* in Paris and London⟩ **:** PUB-CRAWL

¹ba·ri \ˈbärē\ *n, pl* **bari** *or* **baris** *usu cap* **1 a :** a Nilotic Negro people in the Sudan near Gondokoro **b :** a member of the Bari people **2 :** a Nilotic language of the Bari

²bari \"\ *adj, usu cap* [fr. *Bari*, Italy] **:** of or from the city of Bari, Italy **:** of the kind or style prevalent in Bari

ba·ria \bəˈrēə\ *n* -S [AmerSp *baria*] **:** PRINCEWOOD 1

ba·ri·ba \bəˈrēbə, ¦bärē¦bä\ *n, pl* **bariba** *or* **baribas** *usu cap* **1 a :** a Negro people of northern Dahomey, West Africa **b :** a member of such people **2 :** a Gur language of the Bariba people

bar·ic \ˈbarik\ *adj* [NL *barium* + E *-ic*] **:** of or relating to barium

ba·ri·lla \bəˈrēlyə, -ē(y)ə\ *n* -S [modif. of Sp *barrilla*] **1 a :** either of two European saltworts (*Salsola kali* and *S. soda*) **b :** an Algerian plant (*Halogeton souda*) formerly burned as a source of sodium carbonate **2 :** an impure sodium carbonate made from the ashes of barillas formerly used esp. in making soap and glass

bar·ing \ˈba(a)riŋ, ˈber-, -rēŋ\ *n* -S **:** something that is removed in making bare: as **a :** the surface soil removed from ore or rock **b barings** *pl* **:** the small coal made in undercutting coal seams

ba·ri·o·lage \ˌbarēō¦läzh\ *n* -S [F, fr. MF, fr. *barioler* to variegate (prob. blend of *barrer* to cross out, streak, bar + *rioler* to cross out, streak, fr. *riole* rule, ruler, fr. L *regula*) + *-age* — more at BAR, RULE] **1 :** MEDLEY **2 :** a cadenza for a solo musical instrument; *specif* **:** a special effect in violin playing obtained by playing in rapid alternation upon open and stopped strings

bar iron *n* [¹*bar*] **:** wrought iron in the form of bars

ba·ris \ˈbärəs\ *n, pl* **baris** [native name in Bali] **:** a Balinese spear dance or warriors' dance with angular movements depicting a sham battle

bar·i·sal guns \ˈbarəˌsȯl-\ *n pl, cap* B [fr. *Barisal*, town in East Bengal, Pakistan] *meteorol* **:** brontides heard near the town of Barisal on a mouth of the Ganges

bar·ish \ˈba(a)rish, ˈber-\ *adj* [¹*bare* + *-ish*] **:** rather bare **:** scant in furnishings, equipment, or contents **:** thinly covered (as with hair or tree growth)

ba·rit \bəˈrēt\ *n* -S [Tag] **:** a stoloniferous marsh grass (*Leersia hexandra*) of the Philippines that is used as horse fodder

bar·ite *or* **bar·yte** \ˈbaˌrīt *also* ˈbe-\ *or* **ba·ry·tes** \bəˈrīd·ēz, ˈbarəˌtēz\ *n, pl* **barites** *or* **barytes** [Gk *barytēs* weight, fr. *barys* heavy — more at GRIEVE] **:** a white, yellow, or colorless mineral consisting of native barium sulfate $BaSO_4$ occurring in orthorhombic and generally tabular crystals, in granular form, or in compact massive forms resembling marble (sp. gr. 4.3–4.6) — called also *heavy spar*

bar·i·ten·or \ˈbarəˌtenə(r)\ *n* -S [blend of *baritone* and *tenor*] **1 :** a baritone singing voice with virtually a tenor range **2 :** a singer having a baritenor voice

bar·i·tone *or* **bar·y·tone** \ˈbarəˌtōn *also* ˈber-\ *n* -S *often attrib* [F *baryton* or It *baritono*, fr. Gk *barytonos*, adj., deep sounding, fr. *bary-* + *tonos* tone — more at TONE] **1 a :** a male singing voice of medium compass between bass and tenor and partaking somewhat of the quality of both **b :** one having such a voice **2 :** VIOLA BASTARDA **3 :** the saxhorn intermediate in size between althorn and tuba

baritone oboe *n* **:** HECKELPHONE

bar·i·um \ˈba(a)rēəm, ˈber-, ˈbār-\ *n* -S [NL, fr. *bar-* + *-ium*] **:** a silver-white malleable toxic bivalent metallic element of the alkaline-earth group that tarnishes rapidly in air, that occurs only in combination esp. as barite and witherite, that is made by reduction of barium oxide or by electrolysis of a fused salt (as barium chloride), and that is used in the form of alloys chiefly as a getter in electron tubes — symbol *Ba*; see ELEMENT table

barium carbonate *n* **:** a water-insoluble toxic salt $BaCO_3$ occurring in nature as witherite, made artificially by precipitation as a white powder, and used chiefly in making other barium compounds, in removing sulfates from aqueous solutions, in ceramics as a flux, and in optical glass

barium chloride *n* **:** a water-soluble toxic salt obtained usu. as colorless crystals $BaCl_2.2H_2O$ by treating barium sulfide with hydrochloric acid and used chiefly as a raw material (as for blanc fixe) and a reagent in analysis

barium chromate *n* **:** a yellow crystalline toxic salt $BaCrO_4$ used chiefly as a pigment

barium enema *n* **:** a suspension of barium sulfate injected into the lower bowel to render it radiopaque, usu. followed by injection of air to inflate the bowel and increase definition, and used in the roentgenographic diagnosis of intestinal lesions

barium hydroxide *n* **:** a strong toxic base $Ba(OH)_2.8H_2O$ obtained usu. as colorless crystals by dissolving barium oxide in water and used chiefly in making lubricating greases and esp. formerly in recovering sugar from molasses

barium meal *n* **:** a solution of barium sulfate that is swallowed by a patient to facilitate fluoroscopic or roentgenographic diagnosis

barium nitrate *n* **:** a colorless crystalline toxic salt $Ba(NO_3)_2$ used chiefly in pyrotechnics (as in green lights) and in explosives

barium oxide *n* **:** any oxide of barium; *esp* **:** the monoxide BaO obtained usu. as a white to grayish toxic powder by heating

barium carbonate or barium sulfate with carbon and used chiefly in making barium hydroxide and barium peroxide, in coating cathodes of electron tubes, and as a drying agent
barium peroxide *also* **barium dioxide** *n* **:** a compound BaO_2 obtained as a grayish white toxic powder by heating barium monoxide in air or oxygen and used chiefly in making hydrogen peroxide and in pyrotechnics
barium sulfate *n* **:** a colorless crystalline insoluble salt $BaSO_4$ occurring in nature as barite, obtained artificially by precipitation, and used chiefly as a pigment and extender, as a filler, and as a radiopaque substance — see BLANC FIXE, LITHOPONE
barium sulfide *n* **:** any sulfide of barium; *esp* **:** the colorless crystalline toxic monosulfide BaS obtained usu. as a gray to black substance by reducing barite with coal and used chiefly in making other barium compounds, pigments (as lithopone), and luminous paints
barium titanate *n* **:** a white crystalline compound $BaTiO_3$ characterized by ferroelectric and piezoelectric properties and used in hearing aids, phonograph pickups, and ceramic transducers
barium yellow *n* **1 :** barium chromate used as a pigment **2 :** a pale to light yellow — called also *colonial buff*
¹bark \ˈbärk, ˈbȧk-\ *vb* -ED/-ING/-S [ME *berken*, fr. OE *beorcan*; akin to ON *berkja* to bark, Lith *burgėti* to growl, quarrel] *vi* **1 a** *of a dog* **:** to emit or utter its characteristic short loud explosive cry **b :** to make a noise resembling a bark ⟨a fox ~*ed* far away —Ellen Glasgow⟩ ⟨a squirrel ~*ed* at him from a beech tree —Edwin Granberry⟩ ⟨a seal ~*s*⟩ ⟨a solitary cannon ~*ed* —Louis Bromfield⟩ **2 :** to speak in a curt loud or explosive and usu. angry tone **:** SNAP ⟨Mr. Webb . . . alternately ~*ing* at his "son" and accusing his wife of an unforgivable breach of taste —Hollis Alpert⟩ ⟨~*ing* at his crew⟩ ⟨spends his life ~*ing* into phones —J.S.Sandoe⟩ ~ *vt* **1 :** to utter in a curt loud usu. angry tone ⟨he would suddenly ~ out harsh, bitter, and coarse sayings —V.S.Pritchett⟩ ⟨~*ed* orders into the telephone for coffee and food —Barnaby Conrad⟩ **2 :** to advertise (goods for public sale or use) by loud persistent outcry ⟨newsboys will be found ~*ing* their wares on the . . . steps —*Brit. Books of the Month*⟩
²bark \ˈ"\ *n* -S **1 a :** the short loud explosive sound made by a dog; *also* **:** a similar sound made by some other animals **b :** any other similar sound (as a cough or a pistol shot) **2 :** a short sharp peremptory tone of speech or utterance ⟨the . . . ~ of the coxswain —W.H.Mansfield⟩
³bark \ˈ"\ *n* -S [ME *barke*, fr. ON *bark-*, *bǫrkr*; akin to MD & MLG *borke* bark and prob. to ON *björk* birch tree — more at BIRCH] **1 a :** the exterior dead cellular covering of woody roots and stems, often rough when older, that consists at first mainly of cork layers and cortical parenchyma together with epidermis, pericycle, and phloem of which only phloem and cork persist indefinitely, and is considered to include (1) all tissues outside the true cambium or (2) only those tissues external to the innermost cork cambium — compare PERIDERM **b :** the outer layer or covering; *specif* **:** the human skin ⟨fell, knocking all the ~ off his shins⟩ **2 a :** TANBARK **b :** CINCHONA BARK **3 :** a dark olive brown — called also *mocha*
⁴bark \ˈ"\ *vt* -ED/-ING/-S [ME *barken*, fr. *barke*, n.] **1 :** to treat with an infusion of tanbark **:** TAN **2 :** to strip the bark from; *specif* **:** ²GIRDLE 3 **3 :** to rub a portion of skin off or break the skin of usu. by banging or rubbing sharply against a rough or sharp object ⟨they kept on colliding with the cabinet in the dark, bruising their elbows and ~*ing* their shins —Hamilton Basso⟩ **4 :** to bring down or kill (a squirrel in a tree) by striking the bark of the tree with a bullet
⁵bark *or* **barque** \ˈ"\ *n* -S [ME *bark*, fr. MF *barque*, fr. OProv *barca*, fr. LL] **1 a :** any small sailing ship (as a fishing smack or pinnace) **b :** ROWBOAT **2 :** a three-masted vessel with her foremast and mainmast square-rigged and her mizzenmast fore-and-aft rigged — compare FOUR-MASTED BARK **3 :** a craft of any size or character propelled by sails or oars ⟨some lone ~ buoy'd on the dense marine —Walt Whitman⟩

bark 2

bark beetle *n* [³*bark*] **:** any of numerous beetles constituting the family Scolytidae, boring under bark of trees both as larvae and adults, and including certain destructive pests of conifers — see DENDROCTONUS
bark canker *n* [³*bark*] any of various cankers of woody plants; *specif* **:** a canker of rubber trees caused by a fungus (*Phytophthora faberi*)
bark cloth *n* [³*bark*] **1 :** a papery fabric made by primitive peoples from the bark of certain trees usu. by retting and beating; *specif* **:** TAPA CLOTH **2 :** a loosely woven cotton or rayon cloth resembling linen but with a heavier fiber and used for drapes, slipcovers, or bedspreads
bark cloth tree *n* **:** any of various trees (as the paper mulberry or members of the genera *Ficus* and *Brachystegia*) having a strong fibrous inner bark from which bark cloth is made
bark disease *n* [³*bark*] **:** CHESTNUT BLIGHT
barked *past of* BARK
bar keel *n* [¹*bar*] **:** a solid keel of rectangular section in an iron or steel ship — distinguished from *plate keel* and *trough keel* — see SHIP illustration
barkeeper \ˈ=,==\ *or* **barkeep** \ˈ=,=\ *n* -S **:** one that keeps or tends a bar for the sale of alcoholic beverages
¹bark·en \ˈbärkən, ˈbȧk-\ *vb* -ED/-ING/-S [³*bark* + *-en*] *dial Brit* **:** to dry into a crust **:** ENCRUST
²barken \ˈbärkən, ˈbȧk-\ *adj* [³*bark* + *-en*] **:** made of bark
bar·ken·tine *or* **bar·kan·tine** *also* **bar·quen·tine** *or* **bar·quan·tine** \ˈbärkən,tēn\ *n* -S [⁵*bark*, *barque* + *-entine*, *-antine* (as in *brigantine*)] **:** a three-masted ship having the foremast square-rigged and the mainmast and mizzenmast fore-and-aft rigged
¹bark·er \ˈbärkər, ˈbȧkə(r\ *n* -S [¹*bark* + *-er*] **:** one whose work requires or involves the use of loud voluble glib speech or patter: as **a :** one whose occupation is to attract a crowd (as for a sales talk at a fair booth) or patrons (as for a circus sideshow) **b :** a sightseeing guide — called also *spieler* **c :** a theater employee who stands outside to announce attractions and answer questions about the availability of seats and the time and length of the show
²barker \ˈ"\ *n* -S [⁴*bark* + *-er*] **1 a :** one that removes bark **:** ROSSER; *specif* **:** one that removes bark and dirt from logs and pulpwood by subjecting them to water pressure in a stream barker or to tumbling in a drum barker — called also *power barker* **b** *in tanning* **:** one that prepares or shovels bark **2 a :** a machine used esp. in pulp mills to remove bark from logs **b :** BARK SPUD
bar·ke·vik·ite \ˈbärkə,vi,kīt, ,==ˈ=,=\ *n* -S [Norw *barkevikit*, fr. *Barkevik*, Norway, its locality + Norw *-it* -ite] **:** a mineral consisting of a velvet-black amphibole resembling arfvedsonite (sp. gr. 3.43) — **bar·ke·vik·it·ic** \;==(,)viˈkid·ik\ *adj*
bark graft *n* [³*bark*] **:** a plant graft made by slitting or slipping the bark of the stock and inserting the scion beneath it and used esp. in topworking and frameworking where two or more scions are inserted in the end of each truncated branch of the stock — compare CROWN GRAFT
bark grafting *n* **:** grafting by bark grafts
barkhan *var of* BARCHAN
bark·hau·sen effect \ˈbär,kau̇zᵊn-, -rk,hau̇-\ *n*, *cap B* [after Heinrich *Barkhausen* †1956 Ger. physicist and electrical engineer] **:** the series of abrupt changes or jumps in the magnetization of a substance when the magnetizing field is gradually altered
barkhausen-kurz oscillation \-ˈ;ku̇rts-\ *or* **barkhausen oscillation** *n*, *usu cap B&K* [after H.*Barkhausen* & K.*Kurz*, 20th cent. Ger. scientists] **:** ultrahigh-frequency oscillation produced in a triode oscillator by means of a positively biased grid that causes the cathode electrons passing through it to oscillate at a frequency characteristic of the tube and applied voltages
barking *pres part of* BARK
barking bird *n* [fr. pres. part. of ¹*bark*] **:** any of several birds with harsh discordant notes likened to the barking of a dog
barking deer *n* **:** MUNTJAC
barking drum *n* [fr. pres. part. of ⁴*bark*] **:** a revolving drum in which pulp logs are placed for loosening and removing bark by repeated impacts
barking fits *n pl but sing in constr* [fr. pres part. of ¹*bark*] **:** CANINE HYSTERIA
barking iron *n* [fr. pres. part. of ⁴*bark*] **:** BARK SPUD
barking squirrel *n* [fr. pres. part. of ¹*bark*] **:** PRAIRIE DOG
bar·kle \ˈbarkəl, ˈbȧk-\ *vb* -ED/-ING/-S [freq. of ⁴*bark* "to cover with bark"] *dial Eng* **:** ENCRUST, CAKE
bark·less \ˈbärkləs, ˈbȧk-\ *adj* **:** having no bark
bark louse *n* [³*bark*] **:** any of a number of small insects living on the bark of plants (as certain psocids, scales, and aphids)
bark·ly·ite \ˈbärklē,īt\ *n* -S [Sir Henry *Barkly* †1898 Eng. colonial administrator + E *-ite*] **:** a magenta-colored nearly opaque variety of corundum found in Australia
bark mill *n* [³*bark*] **1 :** a machine for removing bark from pulpwood usu. by means of rotating knives **2 :** a mill in which bark is ground (as for tanning)
bark·om·e·ter \bärˈkäməd·ər\ *n* -S [³*bark* + *-o-* + *-meter*] **:** a hydrometer with a special scale for determining the strength of tanning liquor
barkpeel \ˈ=,=\ *vi* -ED/-ING/-S [³*bark* + *peel*] **:** to peel the bark from a tree — **barkpeeler** \ˈ=,==\ *n* -S
bark pocket *n* [³*bark*] **:** a patch of bark partially or wholly enclosed in the wood of the tree
barks *pres 3d sing of* BARK, *pl of* BARK
bark scorch *n* [³*bark*] **:** sunscald usu. following sudden exposure to sunlight
bark spud *n* [³*bark*] **:** a tool for peeling off bark
bark·stone \ˈ=,=\ *n* [³*bark* + *stone*] **:** ¹CASTOR 2
bark tree *n* [³*bark*] **1 :** CINCHONA 2 **2 :** BARK CLOTH 1
barky \ˈbärkē, ˈbȧk-, -ki\ *adj* -ER/-EST [³*bark* + *-y*] **:** covered with or resembling bark ⟨from one ~ post to another⟩ ⟨a diamondback rattlesnake . . . ruffles his ~ scales —Marjory S. Douglas⟩
bar-le-duc \ˌbärlə;d(y)ük, -du̇k\ *n* -S *often cap* [F, fr. *Bar-le-Duc*, commune in Meuse dept., northeastern France] **1 :** a preserve of whole white currants from which the seeds have been removed **2 :** any preserve of whole fruit (as berries)
bar·less \ˈbärləs, ˈbȧl-\ *adj* **:** being without a bar
¹bar·ley \ˈbärlē, ˈbȧlē, -li\ *n* -S [ME *barly*, fr. OE *bærlic* of barley, fr. *bær-* (akin to OE *bere* barley) + *-lic* -ly; akin to ON *barr* barley, Goth *barizeins* of barley, L *far* spelt] **1 :** any cereal grass of the genus *Hordeum* cultivated since prehistoric times and widely adaptable being grown for forage and as a nurse or a smother crop **2 :** the seed or grain of barley and its many varieties (esp. *Hordeum vulgare*) commonly used in the manufacture of malt beverages and also in breakfast foods and as feed for stock — see SIX-ROWED BARLEY

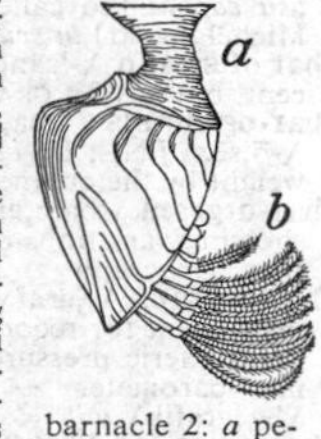
barley head

²barley \ˈ"\ *n* -S [prob. by folk etymology fr. *parley*] **:** TRUCE, RESPITE — used in children's games ⟨save oneself from being caught by crying ~⟩
bar·ley-break *also* **bar·ley-brake** \-,brāk\ *n* -S [prob. fr. ²*barley* + *break*] **:** an old British group game in which one couple or player stationed in a defined area called "hell" or the "barley field" tries to catch the others as they venture into it
barley-bree *also* **barley-broo** \ˈ==,=\ *n* -S [¹*barley* + *bree* or *broo* (liquor)] **1** *chiefly Scot* **:** WHISKEY **2** *chiefly Scot* **:** BEER, ALE
barley broth *n*, *dial Brit* **:** BARLEY-BREE
barley candy *n* **:** BARLEY SUGAR
barley coal *also* **barley** *n* **:** anthracite coal of a small size number 3 buckwheat coal — see ANTHRACITE table
barleycorn \ˈ==,=\ *n* -S [ME *barly corn*] **1 :** a grain of barley **2 :** an old unit of length equal to the average length of a grain of barley **:** the third part of an inch **3 :** a basket weave with an allover design of small geometric figures **4 :** a pointed front gunsight common in British military rifles that appears like a triangle with the sharp point at the top when the rifle is aimed
barley feed *n* **:** by-products from the manufacture of pearl barley used for feed
barley fork *n* **:** a pitchfork with a guard at the base of the handle used to gather up barley or other short-stemmed grains
barley grass *n* **:** WALL BARLEY
barley itch *n* **:** GROCER'S ITCH
barley jointworm *n* **:** a jointworm (*Harmolita hordei*) attacking the stems of barley and sometimes extremely destructive to crops in eastern Canada
barley pearler *n* **:** a device containing a revolving abrasive stone that rubs the hull, bran, and germ from the barley kernel to produce pearled barley, small models being used to test the density of the kernels of barley, wheat, and other grains
barley reel *n* **:** a machine having a rotating reel of corrugated woven-wire screen for separating wild oats from tame oats and barley and pin oats from wheat
barley scald *n* **:** a disease of barley caused by an imperfect fungus (*Rhynchosporium secalis*) producing bluish green to yellow blotches, often with brown margins, and blighting of the foliage
barley smut *n* **:** either of two diseases of barley: **a :** a naked or loose smut caused by a fungus (*Ustilago nuda*) **b :** a covered smut caused by a related fungus (*U. hordei*)
barley stripe *n* **:** a disease of barley caused by a fungus (*Helminthosporium gramineum*) and characterized by green or pale yellow and finally dark brown and frayed-out stripes on the leaves
barley sugar *or* **barley candy** *n* **:** a transparent brittle confection produced by melting and then cooling cane sugar
barley water *n* **:** a decoction of barley used esp. in diarrheal disorders of infants
barley wine *n* **:** an ale of more than average strength
bar lift *n* [¹*bar*] **:** J-BAR LIFT, T-BAR LIFT
bar line *n* [¹*bar*] **:** BAR 6a
bar lock *n* [¹*bar*] **:** a door lock consisting of a lug or lugs on the doorframe and a bar fitting into them
bar·low \ˈbär,lō, ˈbȧ,lō\ *n* -S [after Russell *Barlow*, 18th cent. Englishman, its maker] **:** a large sturdy 1- or 2-bladed jackknife with a long bolster
barlow's plate *n*, *usu cap B* [after Peter *Barlow* †1862 Eng. mathematician] **:** an iron plate formerly used on a ship to compensate for the action of part of the ship's magnetism on the compass — compare FLINDERS BAR
barm \ˈbärm, ˈbȧm\ *n* -S [ME *berme*, fr. OE *beorma*; akin to MLG *barm* yeast, L *fermentum* yeast, *fervēre* to boil — more at BURN] **:** yeast formed during the fermentation of alcoholic beverages
bar magnet *n* [¹*bar*] **:** a magnet in the shape of a bar with poles at its ends
barmaid \ˈ=,=\ *n* [¹*bar* (counter) + *maid*] *chiefly Brit* **:** a female bartender
barman \ˈbärmən, ˈbȧm-\ *n*, *pl* **barmen** [¹*bar* (counter) + *man*] **1 :** BARTENDER **2 :** a metalworker who makes or prepares bars
bar·mas·ter \ˈ=,==\ *n* [alter. of earlier *bargh-master*, prob. part modif., part trans. of G *bergmeister*, fr. *berg-* mining (fr. *berg* mountain, fr. OHG) + *meister* master — more at BARROW] **1 :** a local official arbiter or judge among English miners **2 :** an officer of the barmote who presides at meetings, collects dues, and acts as manager
barm·brack \ˈbärm,brak\ *n* -S [IrGael *bairghean breac*, lit., speckled cake, fr. *bairghean* cake, loaf (fr. OIr *bairgen* bread) + *breac* speckled, fr. OIr *brecc*; akin to L *perca* perch — more at FARRAGO, PERCH] *Irish* **:** a rich currant bun or cake
bar·me·ci·dal \ˌbärməˈsīdᵊl\ *or* **bar·me·cide** \ˈ==,sīd\ *adj*, *usu cap* [*Barmecide* a member of a wealthy Persian family *fl* 752–803 (fr. Ar *barmok* chief priest) + E *-al*] **:** providing only the illusion of plenty or abundance **:** UNREAL, ILLUSORY ⟨he could persuade his guests that they had eaten well, though the meal had really been a ~ one —Hesketh Pearson⟩ ⟨a *Barmecide* room, that always had a great dining table in it and never had a dinner —Charles Dickens⟩ ⟨it was the first crumb of proof he had obtained after a long *Barmecide* banquet on pure theory —Fletcher Pratt⟩
bar mitz·vah \(ˈ)bärˈmitsvə, -(,)vä\ *n*, *pl* **bar mitzvahs** \-vəz, -(,)väz\ *or* **bar mitz·vot** *or* **bar mitz·voth** \-,vōth, -ōt,-ōs\ *often cap B & M* [Heb *bar miṣwāh*, lit., son of the (divine) law or precept] **1 :** a Jewish boy who has reached his 13th birthday and has attained the age of religious duty and responsibility — compare BATH MITZVAH **2 :** the initiatory synagogue ceremony recognizing a boy as a bar mitzvah
barmkin *n* -S [ME, perh. alter. of *barbican*] *obs* **:** BARBICAN
bar money *n* [¹*bar*] **:** money in the form of bars of metal; *esp* **:** the stamped copper bars issued 1796–1818 for use as money in the Dutch East Indies
bar·mote \ˈbär,mōt\ *n* -S [alter. of earlier *barghmoot*, prob. modif. of G *berg-* mining + E *moot* (meeting) — more at BARMASTER] **:** a court held in Derbyshire, England, for deciding controversies between miners
bar movement *n* [¹*bar*] **:** an old type of watch movement in which the upper pivot bearings are in separate bridges instead of in a full top plate — called also *Geneva movement*
barm·skin \ˈbärmz,kin, -m,sk-\ *n* -S [ME *barm-skin*, fr. *barm* bosom, lap (fr. OE *bearm*) + *skin*; akin to OHG *barm* bosom, ON *barmr*, Goth *barms*, OE *beran* to bear — more at BEAR] *dial Brit* **:** a leather apron
barmy \ˈbärmē, ˈbȧmē, -mi—ˈbȧmē *or* -mi *is also* -R *pronunc for* "*balmy*" (*see sense 2*)\ *adj* -ER/-EST [*barm* + *-y*] **1 :** full of froth or ferment **2 :** BALMY 2
¹barn \ˈbärn, ˈbȧn\ *n* -S [ME *bern*, fr. OE *beręrn*, fr. *bere* barley + *ærn* place — more at BARLEY, REST] **1 a :** a usu. large farm building orig. for the storage of farm products and feed (as grain and hay) but now used as a general storage building (as for hay, drying tobacco, and farm equipment or vehicles) and usu. for the housing of farm animals typically in separated sections **b :** the section of such a building that is used for the housing of farm animals (as horses or cows) and their feed **c :** a building for the housing of cattle or horses and their feed ⟨stabling accommodations for nearly nine hundred horses in ~*s* of the latest type —*New Yorker*⟩ **d :** a large building for the housing of a fleet of vehicles (as trolley cars or trucks) — compare CARBARN **e :** an unusually large and usu. bare building ⟨a great ~ of a hotel with roomy porches —W.A.White⟩ **2** *railroad slang* **:** ROUNDHOUSE **3** [so called fr. its having been considered "as big as a barn" with respect to nuclear bombardment] **:** a unit of area that equals 10^{-24} sq. cm. used in nuclear physics for measuring cross section
²barn \ˈ"\ *vt* -ED/-ING/-S **:** to store (a crop) in a barn
³barn \ˈbȧn\ *var of* BAIRN
bar·na·bite \ˈbärnə,bīt\ *n* -S *usu cap* [It *barnabita*, fr. Santa *Barnaba*, monastery in Milan where the order was founded + It *-ita* -ite (fr. L)] **:** REGULAR CLERK OF ST. PAUL
bar·na·by bright \-ˌbē-\ *or* **barnaby day** *n*, *usu cap 1st B* [after St. *Barnabas* (Acts 4:36-37), whose feast day is June 11] **:** June 11 Old Style, the longest day in the year — called also *St. Barnabas' day*; contrasted with *Lucy light*
bar·na·by's thistle \ˈbärnəbēz-\ *n*, *usu cap B* [fr. *Barnaby* (*day*), the time of its flowering] **:** any of several weeds of the genus *Centaurea*; *esp* **:** a European herb (*C. solstitialis*) adventive in the eastern U.S. and having a winged stem and tomentose leaves
¹barnacle \ˈbärnəkəl, ˈbȧn-, -nēk-\ *n* -S [ME *bernak*, *bernacle*, fr. OF *bernac*] **1 a barnacles** *pl* **:** an instrument for restraining a horse by pinching his nose **b :** a conventionalized heraldic representation of a pair of barnacles — sometimes used in pl. **2** *obs* **:** an instrument of torture resembling a pair of barnacles — usu. used in pl. **3 barnacles** *pl*, *dial Eng* **:** SPECTACLES
²barnacle \ˈ"\ *n* -S [ME *barnakylle*, alter. of *bernekke*, *bernake*, of Celt origin; akin to W *brenig* limpets, Corn *brennyk*, Bret *bernic* barnacle, MIr *bairnech* limpet; fr. a popular belief in the Middle Ages that the goose grew from the shellfish; prob. akin to MIr *bern* cleft, L *forare* to bore — more at BORE] **1 :** BARNACLE GOOSE **2 :** any of numerous marine crustaceans constituting the order Cirripedia, being free-swimming in the larval state but permanently fixed as adults and protected by a calcified shell of several pieces, and having usu. six pairs of biramous feathery cirri that are modified limbs and are protruded and drawn back with a grasping motion serving to catch the food that floats within reach — see ACORN BARNACLE, GOOSE BARNACLE **3 a :** a person who clings tenaciously (as to an easy or comfortable job) or who sticks close to another against his will ⟨forced to avoid predatory people and ~ friends —Corra Harris⟩ **b :** anything (as a venerable trait, institution, or vestige from the past) that mars or hinders (as progress of any kind) ⟨the judicial process is clumsy and covered with ~*s* —T.W.Arnold⟩

barnacle 2: *a* peduncle, *b* cirri

³barnacle *vt* **barnacled; barnacled; barnacling** \-k(ə)liŋ\ **barnacles :** to fasten or attach (oneself) securely or persistently to ⟨there are the legends, the "scandals" . . . which ~ such a public figure —Trevor Allen⟩ **:** cover with something so that it clings persistently ⟨the ancient Egyptians . . . *barnacled* their heads with lumps of hard —D.W.Dresden⟩
bar·na·cled \-kəld\ *adj* **:** covered with barnacles ⟨the ~ hull of a wrecked ship⟩ ⟨foundations have occasionally become so ~ with steady pensioners . . . that they have lost almost all freedom of maneuver —Dwight Macdonald⟩
barnacle goose *n* **:** a European goose (*Branta leucopsis*) breeding in the far north that is related to but larger than the brant
barnacle scale *n* **:** a soft scale (*Ceroplastes cirripediformis*) attacking orange and quince trees in Florida and having a scale that resembles a sessile barnacle in form
bar·na·ul \ˌbärnəˈu̇l\ *adj*, *usu cap* [fr. *Barnaul*, U.S.S.R.] **:** of or from the city of Barnaul, Altai territory, U.S.S.R. **:** of the kind or style prevalent in Barnaul
barn·brack \ˈbärn,brak\ *var of* BARMBRACK
barn dance *n* **1 :** a rollicking American social dance held in a barn with square dances, certain round dances, and traditional music and calls **2 :** an American ballroom dance developed in England early in the 20th century that is similar to the schottische but characterized by three running steps and a hop
barn door *n* **:** a hinged opaque panel mounted usu. in a pair on a motion-picture or TV studio lamp and used to screen light from an area or from the camera
barn-door fowl \ˈ=;=-\ *n* **:** BARNYARD FOWL
barn-door skate *n* **:** a large No. American skate (*Raja laevis*) growing four feet or more long
barn-dry *or* **barn-finish** *vt* **:** to complete the drying of (partly cured hay stored in a barn) by forced ventilation often with heated air ⟨*barn-dried* hay⟩
barne \ˈbarn, ˈbȧn\ *dial Brit var of* BAIRN
barned *past of* BARN
bar·nett effect \(ˈ)bärˈned·-, -net-\ *n*, *usu cap B* [after Samuel J. *Barnett* †1956 Am. physicist] **:** magnetization produced by rotating a body the direction of the magnetization being that of the rotation axis — compare EINSTEIN-DE HAAS EFFECT
bar·ne·veld·er \ˈbärnə,veldər\ *n* -S *usu cap* [D, fr. *Barneveld*, commune of eastern Netherlands + D *-er*] **:** a Dutch breed of large dual-purpose fowls laying numerous deep-brown eggs
bar·ney \ˈbärnē, ˈbȧn-, -ni\ *n* -S [perh. fr. the name *Barney*] **1** *Brit* **a :** a noisy argument **:** ALTERCATION, ROW ⟨what's the big ~ about⟩ **b :** a boisterous good time **2 :** a small car attached to a cable used to push cars up a slope in a mine
barn·ful \ˈbärn,fu̇l, ˈbȧn-\ *n* -S **:** the amount or number that fills a barn
barn grass *var of* BARNYARD GRASS
barn gun \ˈbärn,gən\ *n* [E dial. *barn* (alter. of *burn*) + dial. *gun*, *gund* scab, fr. OE *gund-* matter, pus; akin to OHG *gunt* pus, Norw *gund* dandruff, scab, Goth, *gaceson* tumor, and prob. to Gk *kanthylē* swelling, tumor] *dial Eng* **:** a skin eruption: *specif* **:** SHINGLES
barning *pres part of* BARN
barn itch *n* **:** any contagious irritation of the skin of livestock (as sarcoptic mange or ringworm)
barn lantern *n* **:** a portable kerosine lantern similar to a standard kerosine lamp but having also a tubular frame with handle and guard encircling the chimney — see LANTERN illustration
barn lot *n*, *chiefly South & Midland* **:** BARNYARD
barn·man \-mən, -,man\ *n*, *pl* **barnmen :** one who takes care of cows and the barn and usu. does the milking
barn owl *n* **:** a nearly cosmopolitan owl (*Tyto alba*, syn. *Strix flammea*) having plumage mottled with buff brown and gray

above and chiefly white below and frequenting barns and other buildings where it is an important factor in rodent control
barn raising *n* **:** a gathering for the purpose of erecting a barn — compare ¹BEE 3a
barn red *n* **:** a variable color averaging a moderate reddish brown that is stronger and slightly redder and lighter than mahogany, yellower and stronger than roan, and stronger and slightly redder than oxblood
barns *pres 3d sing of* BARN, *pl of* BARN
barns-break·ing \ˈbärnz,brākən\ *n* -s *Scot* **:** MISCHIEF **:** idle play
barn·storm \ˈbärn,stȯrm, ˈbȧnz,tȯ(ə)m, -n,st-\ *vb* -ED/-ING/-S *vi* **1 :** to tour through rural districts staging theatrical performances in barns or makeshift theaters usu. in one-night stands ⟨traveled with Will Benbon's road show . . . ~*ing* through Mississippi —*Tomorrow*⟩ **2 :** to travel from one town or locality to another making brief stops (as in campaigning or in the course of a concert or exhibition tour) ⟨the candidates ~*ed* through the Eastern states last week⟩ ⟨~*ing* in Boston, Chicago, and Manhattan lecture halls —*Time*⟩ **3 :** to pilot one's airplane in sightseeing flights with passengers or in exhibition stunts in an unscheduled itinerant course esp. in rural districts ⟨his ~*ing* plane was forced down in a Minnesota swamp —Grace H. Flandrau⟩ ~*vt* **:** to travel across while barnstorming ⟨figure-skating troupes that ~ the country —*Amer. Guide Series: Minn.*⟩ — **barn·storm·er** \-mə(r)\ *n* -s
barn swallow *n* **:** the common European swallow (*Hirundo rustica*) or its No. American variety (*H. r. erythrogaster*) both usu. attaching their nests to beams and rafters of barns
barny \ˈbärnē\ *adj* -ER/-EST **:** like or suggesting a barn esp. in size, shape, or characteristic smell
¹**barnyard** \ˈ≈,≈\ *n* [ME *bernyerde*, fr. *bern* barn + *yerde* yard] **:** a usu. fenced area adjoining a barn — compare FARMYARD
²**barnyard** \"\ *adj* **:** EARTHY, SMUTTY, SCATOLOGICAL ⟨the ~ school of novelists⟩ ⟨~ humor⟩
barnyard fowl *n* **:** the common domestic fowl; *esp* **:** the mongrel fowl allowed to pick up its living casually about the farmstead
barnyard golf *n, slang* **:** the game of horseshoes
barnyard grass *also* **barn grass** *or* **barnyard millet** *n* **:** a coarse annual grass (*Echinochloa crusgalli*) that has terminal panicles of one-sided flower clusters resembling spikes, is near cosmopolitan as a weed in cultivated ground, and is occas. used for hay or grazing — see JAPANESE MILLET
baro- — see BAR-
barocco *var of* BAROQUE
baro·cy·clon·om·e·ter \ˌbarō,sī,klōˈnämәd·ә(r)\ *n* -s [*bar-* + *cyclone* + *-o-* + *-meter*] **:** a form of aneroid barometer used in conjunction with a dial having adjustable arrows to determine the location and movement of a tropical cyclone
ba·ro·da \bəˈrōdə\ *adj, usu cap* [fr. *Baroda*, India] **:** of or from the city of Baroda, India **:** of the kind or style prevalent in Baroda
baro·dynamic \ˌbarō+\ *adj* [*bar-* + *dynamic*] **:** of or relating to barodynamics
bar·o·dynamics \"+\ *n pl but sing in constr* **:** mechanics applied to the behavior of heavy structures (as bridges, dams, and mine shafts) liable to failure because of their own weight
bar off *vi* [²*bar*] **:** to move soil from each side of row plants usu. in a cropped field and usu. with a turn plow or similar implement so as to leave the plant roots in a high narrow bed
bar of mi·chel·an·ge·lo \-,mīkəˈlanjə,lō, -,mik- *also* -,mēk-\ *usu cap M* [so called from its prominence in the statues of Michelangelo] *in sculpture* **:** SUPERCILIARY RIDGE
bar of sa·nio \-ˈsänē,ō\ *usu cap S* [after Carl *Sanio*, 19th cent. botanist] **:** CRASSULA
bar·og·no·sis \ˌba,rägˈnōsəs, ˌbarəg-\ *n, pl* **barognoses** \-ō,sēz\ [NL, fr. *bar-* + *-gnosis*] *psychol* **:** the perception of weight by the cutaneous and muscle senses
bar·o·gram \ˈbarə,gram\ *n* -s [ISV *bar-* + *-gram*] **:** a tracing showing variations of atmospheric pressure that is usu. made by a barograph
bar·o·graph \-,graf\ *n* -s [ISV *bar-* + *-graph*] **:** an automatic instrument for recording variations of atmospheric pressure **:** a self-registering barometer — **bar·o·graph·ic** \ˌ≈≈ˈgrafik\ *adj*

barograph

ba·rom·e·ter \bəˈrämәd·ә(r), -ətə-\ *n* -s [*bar-* + *-meter*] **1 :** an instrument for determining the pressure of the atmosphere and hence for assisting in judgment as to probable weather changes and for determining the height of an ascent — see ANEROID BAROMETER, CUP BAROMETER, SIPHON BAROMETER **2 :** something that serves to register accurately changes in fluctuating activity or state (as in public opinion) ⟨retail sales, perhaps the most sensitive ~ of general prosperity —*Time*⟩
barometer crab *n* **:** a crab (*Carpillius maculatus*) of the Great Barrier reef that is lilac colored with 11 symmetrically placed blood-red spots that are said to change in appearance with the state of the weather
bar·o·met·ric \ˌbarəˈme·trik,-rēk *also* ˌber-\ *also* **bar·o·met·ri·cal** \-rəkəl, -rēk-\ *adj* [*barometer* + *-ic, -ical*] **:** relating to the barometer **:** made or indicated by a barometer — **bar·o·met·ri·cal·ly** \-rək(ə)lē, -rēk-, -li\ *adv*
barometric gradient *n, meteorol* **:** the rate of fall in atmospheric pressure between two stations **:** the slope of an isobaric surface
barometric pressure *n* **:** the pressure of the atmosphere usu. expressed in terms of the height of a column of mercury — compare BAROMETER
barometric surface *n* **:** a surface having the same barometric pressure at all points **:** an isobaric surface
barometric tendency *n* **:** the change of atmospheric pressure during the last few (generally three) hours before a regular observation
barometric tide *n* **:** a regular daily fluctuation in barometric pressure
barometric wave *n* **:** a change of atmospheric pressure that occurs progressively over an area
bar·o·met·ro·graph \ˌbarəˈme·trə,graf\ *n* -s [*barometro-* (fr. *barometer*) + *-graph*] **:** a self-recording barometer **:** BAROGRAPH
ba·rom·e·try \bəˈrämə·trē, -i\ *n* -ES **:** the science or process of making barometric measurements
bar·on \ˈbarən *also* ˈber-\ *n* -s [ME *barun, baroun, baron*, fr. OF *baron*, of Gmc origin; akin to OHG *baro* man, freeman, prob. akin to ON *berjask* to fight, OE *borian* to bore — more at BORE] **1 a :** one of a class of tenants in chief of a feudal superior holding his rights and title by military or other honorable service **b :** one of a class of tenants in chief of the king summoned by writ to the central council of the king's tenants in chief **c** *from the time of Henry III* **:** one of the king's tenants in chief personally summoned to Parliament — called also *baron by writ, great baron* **d :** a lord of the realm **:** NOBLE, PEER **2 a :** a member of the fifth and lowest grade of the peerage in Great Britain being entitled to be addressed as "Lord" and to sit in the House of Lords **b :** a nobleman on the continent of Europe whose rank and status vary from country to country **c :** a member of the lowest order of nobility in Japan **3 :** one of the former freemen of London, York, and other places who were bound to attendance upon and service to the king as homagers **4 :** a joint of meat consisting of two loins or sirloins not cut apart at the backbone ⟨a ~ of beef⟩ **5 :** a man of great or overweening power or influence in some field of activity (as business or industry) — usu. used with a specifying noun adjunct ⟨coal ~⟩ ⟨oil ~⟩ ⟨lumber ~⟩ ⟨cattle ~⟩ **6 :** HUSBAND — used in law and heraldry usu. with the correlative term *feme* ⟨an escutcheon per pale ~ and feme⟩
bar·on·age \-nij\ *n* -s [ME *barnage, barunage*, fr. OF *barnage*, fr. *baron* + *-age*] **:** the whole body of barons or peers **:** NOBILITY 2
baron bailie *n* **:** a Scottish magistrate of a barony or burgh
baron court *n* **:** COURT BARON
bar·on·du·ki *also* **bar·an·du·ki** *or* **bar·un·du·ki** \ˌbarənˈdükē\ *or* **bu·run·du·ki** \ˌbu̇r-\ *n* -s [Russ *burunduk*] **1 :** a Siberian ground squirrel (*Eutamias asiaticus* or *E. sibiricus*) with 5 conspicuous dark stripes down its back **2 :** the fur or pelt of the baronduki
bar·on·ess \ˈbarənəs *also* ˈber-\ *n* -ES [ME *barnesse*, fr. MF, fr. *baron* + *-esse* -ess] **1 :** the wife or widow of a baron **2 a :** a woman who holds a baronial title in her own right

¹**bar·on·et** \ˌbarəˈnet (*apparently infrequent in Brit*), ˈbarənət, -,net *also* -ber-; *usu* -d·+V\ *n* -s [ME, fr. *baron* + *-et*] **1** *obs* **a :** a young or a lesser baron **b** *in Ireland* **:** the holder of a small barony **c :** ¹BANNERET 1 **2 :** the holder of a dignity or degree of honor, the lowest that is hereditary, ranking immediately below a baron but having precedence of all orders of knights except those of the garter
²**baronet** \"\ *vt* -ED/-ING/-S **:** to raise to the baronetcy
bar·on·et·age \-d·ij,-tij\ *n* -s [¹*baronet* + *-age*] **1 :** the rank of a baronet **2 a :** the whole body of baronets **b :** a list or record of baronets
bar·on·et·cy \-tsē, -i\ *n* -ES [¹*baronet* + *-cy*] **1 :** the rank or position of a baronet **2 :** the possession of a baronetcy
bar·on·et·i·cal \ˌ≈≈ˈned·əkəl\ *adj* [¹*baronet* + *-ical*] **:** of or belonging to a baronet or baronetcy
ba·rong \bəˈrȯŋ, bäˈ-, -räŋ\ *n* -s [native name in the Philippines] **:** a broad-bladed knife or sword with thick back and thin edge used by the Moros
ba·rong-ba·rong \≈ˈ≈≈ˈ≈\ *n* -s [Tag] *Philippines* **:** a makeshift dwelling **:** HUT, SHANTY
barong ta·ga·log \-təˈgä-ləg\ *n* -s *sometimes cap T* [Tag *barò tagalog* Tagalog shirt] **:** a light loose long-sleeved man's shirt, the national dress shirt of the Philippines, that is frequently made of piña, ramie, or similar fiber, often embroidered on the collar and facing, and worn with the tails not tucked in

barong and sheath

baroni *var of* BARANI
ba·ro·ni·al \bəˈrōnēəl, -nyəl\ *adj* [*barony* + *-al*] **1 :** of or relating to a baron or the baronage **2 :** SPLENDID, STATELY, SPACIOUS, AMPLE ⟨a ~ room⟩ ⟨the logs are of ~ dimensions —George Santayana⟩ **3** *of an envelope* **:** being smaller and squarer than envelopes used for ordinary commercial purposes and designed esp. for short social or personal correspondence or business announcements
ba·ronne \bəˈrän, ba-, -ȯn\ *n* -s [F, fr. OF, fem. of *baron*] **:** BARONESS
bar·on·ry \ˈbarənrē, -ri *also* ˈber-\ *n* -ES [ME *barunrie*, fr. MF *baronerie*, fr. *baron* + *-erie* -ery] **1 :** the domain, rank, or dignity of a baron **2 :** the body of barons
barons *pl of* BARON
bar·ony \ˈbarənē, -ni *also* ˈber-\ *n* -ES [ME *baronie*, fr. OF, fr. *baron* baron + *-ie* -y — more at BARON] **1 a :** the fee or domain of a baron **b :** the rank or dignity of a baron **2 a** *in Ireland* **:** a division of a county roughly corresponding to an English hundred **b** *in colonial So. Carolina* **:** a large tract of land of 12,000 acres granted to a landgrave or cacique **c** *in Scotland* **:** an extensive freehold **3 :** a vast or extensive private landholding ⟨to operate and maintain this ~, the billionaire employed some 350 people —Andrew Tully⟩ ⟨a cotton ~⟩ **4 :** a region or field of activity under the unchecked or predominant control or sway of a single individual or family ⟨the power of . . . the last of the nation's old-fashioned political *baronies* is perceptibly ebbing —Gladwin Hill⟩
bar opal *n* **:** jade-colored opal
baro·phil·ic \ˌbarōˈfilik\ *adj* [*bar-* + *-philic*] **:** thriving under high environmental pressures — used of deep-sea organisms
¹**ba·roque** \bəˈrōk, ba-; baˈräk, bə-; *also* baˈrȯk *or* bə- *sometimes* ˈba,r-\ *adj* [F, fr. Pg *barrôco* irregularly shaped pearl] *of a pearl* **:** irregular in form
²**baroque** \"\ *n* -s [F] **:** a baroque pearl
³**baroque** \"\ *adj* [F, fr. It *barocco*, perh. after Federigo *Barocci* or *Baroccio* †1612 Ital. painter] **1** *also* **ba·roc·co** \bəˈrä(,)kō, -rō-\ **:** of, relating to, or having the characteristics of a style of artistic expression prevalent esp. in the 17th century: as **a** (1) **:** of, relating to, or being a style of art and architecture prevalent from the latter part of the 16th century to the latter part of the 18th century, marked by dynamic opposition and energy, by the use of curved and plastic figures, and esp. in its later phases by elaborate and sometimes grotesque ornamentation, and represented typically by the sculpture of Bernini and the painting of Rubens (2) **:** ROCOCO ⟨many writers draw no distinction between the words *rococo* and ~, which are far from synonymous —M.S.Briggs⟩ **b** (1) **:** of, relating to, or being a style of musical composition prevalent from about 1600 to 1750, marked by elaborate ornamentation and improvisation, the use of contrasting effects, and the creation of powerful tensions and climaxes, and culminating in the work of J.S.Bach and Handel (2) *of an organ* **:** built according to the specifications of the time of J.S.Bach **c :** of, relating to, or being a style of literary composition prevalent from the late 16th century to the early 18th century and marked typically by complexity and elaborateness of form and by the use of bizarre, calculatedly ingenious, and sometimes intentionally ambiguous imagery — compare EUPHUISM, GONGORISM **2 :** characterized by grotesqueness, extravagance, or flamboyance ⟨a truly ~ act of sabotage —G.N.Shuster⟩ **syn** see ORNATE
⁴**baroque** *n* -s **:** baroque work or style
ba·roque·ly *adv* [³*baroque* + *-ly*] **:** in a baroque manner
bar·o·scope \ˈbarə,skōp\ *n* [*bar-* + *-scope*] **:** an apparatus for showing that the loss of weight of an object in air equals the weight of the air displaced by it
ba·ros·ma \bəˈräzmə\ *n, cap* [NL, fr. *bar-* + *-osma*] **:** a genus of southern African strong-scented evergreen shrubs (family Rutaceae) having small pentamerous flowers — see BUCHU
bar·o·stat \ˈbarə,stat\ *n* -s [ISV *bar-* + *-stat*] **:** a usu. automatic device for maintaining a constant pressure (as in an airplane cabin or in a pressure cooker)
bar·o·switch \ˈ≈≈+\ *n* [*bar-* + *switch*] **:** an electrical switching device in the radiosonde that is operated by the atmospheric pressure and used to switch temperature and humidity measuring elements alternately into the circuit
bar·o·tac·tic \ˈbarō,taktik\ *adj* **:** of, relating to, or being a barotaxis
bar·o·tax·is \ˌ≈≈ˈtaksəs\ *n, pl* **barotaxes** [NL, fr. *bar-* + *-taxis*] **:** a taxis in which pressure is the orienting stimulus
bar·o·taxy \ˈ≈≈,≈sē\ *n* -ES [ISV *bar-* + *-taxy*] **:** BAROTAXIS
bar·o·thermograph \ˌbarō+\ *n* -s [ISV, blend of *barograph* and *thermograph*] **:** an instrument for recording both pressure and temperature (as of the atmosphere)
bar·o·ther·mo·hygrograph \ˌbarəˈthərmō+\ *n* -s [blend of *barograph, thermograph* and *hygrograph*] **:** an instrument for automatically recording on the same sheet of paper the pressure, temperature, and humidity of the atmosphere
ba·ro·to \bəˈrōd·(,)ō\ *n* -s [PhilSp] *Philippines* **:** a dugout canoe that is larger and heavier than a banca
bar·o·trauma \"+\ *n, pl* **barotraumata** [NL, fr. *bar-* + *trauma*] **:** injury of a part or organ as a result of changes in barometric pressure; *specif* **:** AERO-OTITIS MEDIA
ba·rot·se \bəˈrätsə\ *n, usu cap* **1** *pl* **barotse** *or* **barotses** **:** LOZI **2 :** a breed of large long-horned African cattle
ba·rouche \bəˈrüsh, ba-\ *n* -s [modif. of G *barutsche*, fr. It *baroccio, biroccio*, fr. (assumed) VL *birotium* two-wheeled vehicle, fr. LL *birotus* two-wheeled, fr. L *bi-* ¹bi- + *rota* wheel — more at ROLL] **:** a four-wheeled shallow carriage with a driver's seat high in front, two double seats inside, one facing back and the other front, and a folding top over the back seat, the entire carriage being suspended on C springs

barouche

ba·rou·chet \ˌba(,)rüˈshā\ *or* **ba·rou·chette** \-shet\ *n* -s **:** a light barouche
bar pilot *n* [¹*bar*] **:** a pilot who navigates a ship from a pilot station over a bar and often into the harbor or to the docks
bar pin *n* [¹*bar*] **:** a long narrow ornamental pin
bar pit \ˈbär,-\ *n* [by alter.] *chiefly West* **:** BARROW PIT
bar plate *n* [¹*bar*] **:** a drawbar follower on a railroad car
bar point *n* [¹*bar*] **:** the backgammon point nearest the bar on each player's outer table **:** the player's seventh point

barque *var of* BARK
bar·quen·tine *also* **bar·quan·tine** *var of* BARKENTINE
bar·qui·si·me·to \ˌbärkəsəˈmād·(,)ō\ *adj, usu cap* [fr. *Barquisimeto*, Venezuela] **:** of or from the city of Barquisimeto, Venezuela **:** of the kind or style prevalent in Barquisimeto
barr *abbr* barrister
bar·ra·ble \ˈbärəbəl, ˈbȧr-\ *adj* [²*bar* + *-able*] **:** capable of being barred esp. by legal process
bar·ra·bo·ra \ˌbarəˈbōrə\ *n* -s [origin unknown] **:** an Eskimo earth lodge below the surface of the ground with a roof of sod or dirt shaped like a dome — compare KEEKWILEE-HOUSE
¹**bar·rack** \ˈbarək *also* ˈber- *or* -rik *or* -rēk\ *n* -s [F *baraque*, fr. MF, fr. OCatal *barraca*] **1 :** a hut used for temporary shelter esp. for soldiers ⟨he lodged in a miserable hut or ~ composed of dry branches and thatched with straw —Edward Gibbon⟩ **2** *or* **barracks** *pl but sing or pl in constr* **a :** an often permanent building or set of buildings used esp. for lodging soldiers in garrison ⟨stepped into the ~ and blew his whistle —L.M.Uris⟩ ⟨the dormitory where I was quartered was like an army ~s —John Cheever⟩ **b :** the regular quarters of the Salvationists **3** *or* **barracks** *pl but sing or pl in constr* **a :** a building or a group of buildings often like a shed or barn in structure and appearance that provides temporary housing (as for a group of workmen) ⟨the construction gang occupied a wooden ~ on the site of the job⟩ ⟨accommodated in a barely furnished ~s for commercial travelers —William Sansom⟩ **b :** a large building or set of buildings housing a number of people (as a crowded tenement house) that is characterized by extreme plainness or an air of dreary uniformity ⟨the big house on the hill . . . and the factory ~s in the valley —W.A.White⟩ ⟨the grim, toploftу ~s that we are now building —Lewis Mumford⟩ **4** *Northeast* **:** a structure with a movable roof sliding on four posts used to cover a hay or straw rick
²**barrack** \"\ *vt* -ED/-ING/-S **:** to lodge in barracks ⟨buildings . . . used to ~ George Washington's troops in 1775 —*Official Register of Harvard Univ.*⟩
³**barrack** \"\ *vb* -ED/-ING/-S [origin unknown] *vi, chiefly Austral* **:** to shout usu. at a person or team engaged in a contest: **a :** JEER, HECKLE ⟨had to undergo some ~*ing* for playing slowly —P.F.Warner⟩ **b :** ROOT, CHEER ⟨his game would lose a lot of its venom if the crowd were not ~*ing* for him —Jack Crawford⟩ ~ *vt, chiefly Austral* **:** to shout at derisively or sarcastically ⟨the crowd started to ~ me and shout for me to kick the ball clear —*Irish Digest*⟩
bar·rack·er \-kə(r)\ *n* -s *chiefly Austral* **:** one that barracks **:** a noisy partisan
barracks bag *n* **:** a heavy cotton bag in which a soldier carries personal equipment (as uniforms) except in the field
bar·ra·coon \ˌbarəˈkün\ *n* -s [Sp *barracón*, aug. of *barraca* hut, fr. Catal] **:** an enclosure or barrack formerly used for temporary confinement of slaves or convicts
bar·ra·cou·ta \ˌbarəˈküd·ə, -ütə *also* ˌber-\ *also* **bar·ra·cou·da** \-üdə\ *n, pl* **barracouta** *or* **barracoutas** [modif. of AmerSp *barracuda* (*Sphyraena barracuda*)] **:** a large marine food fish (*Thyrsites atun*) related to the escolar and common on the coasts of Australia, New Zealand, and southern Africa — called also *snoek*
bar·ra·cu·da \ˌbarəˈküdə *also* ˌber-\ *also* **bar·ra·cou·ta** \-üd·ə,-ütə\ *n, pl* **barracuda** *or* **barracudas** [AmerSp *barracuda*] **1 :** any of several voracious pikelike marine mugiloid fishes related to the gray mullets, constituting the genus *Sphyraena* and family Sphyraenidae cosmopolitan in warm seas, and including excellent food fishes as well as forms regarded as toxic — see GREAT BARRACUDA **2 :** a large scombroid food and game fish (*Scomberomorus commersonii*) of the warmer Indo-Pacific seas
¹**bar·rage** \ˈbärij, ˈbȧr-, -rēj\ *n* -s [F, fr. *barrer* to bar + *-age* — more at BAR] **1 :** the act or the result of barring; *specif* **:** an artificial dam placed in a river or watercourse to increase the depth of water or to divert it into a channel for navigation or irrigation **2 :** the application of the forefinger of the left hand across some or all of the strings (as of a guitar) to change their pitch **3 :** a space between two masses of mycelium caused by lack of compatibility between them
²**bar·rage** \bəˈrä\|zh, -ä\| *also* \|j *sometimes* ba-, *Brit usu* ˈba,räzh\ *n* -s [F (*tir de*) *barrage* barrier fire] **1 a :** a barrier of fire esp. of artillery and mortar fire laid on a line close to friendly troops to screen and protect them by inflicting losses on the enemy and by impeding or preventing enemy movement and fire; *broadly* **:** a heavy bombardment of artillery fire — see BOX BARRAGE, EMERGENCY BARRAGE, NORMAL BARRAGE, ROLLING BARRAGE, STANDING BARRAGE **b :** a screen of antiaircraft artillery fire **c :** a barrier consisting of a series of barrage balloons — called also *aerial barrage* **d :** a barrier of mines preventing the passage of ships **e :** a barrier created by nonexplosive weapons ⟨the bowmen . . . laid down a ~ of arrows from the flanks —G.H.Fathauer⟩ **f :** a massive concentrated and usu. continuous discharge or shower (as of missiles or blows) ⟨killed by a ~ of stones . . . by sardonic townspeople —*Springfield (Mass.) Union*⟩ **2 :** a rapid-fire massive or concentrated delivery or outpouring (as of speech or writing) ⟨a ~ of footnotes —Geoffrey Bruun⟩ ⟨speakers kept up an oratorical ~ —*N.Y.Times*⟩
³**barrage** \"\ *vt* -ED/-ING/-S **:** to deliver a barrage against **:** attack with or subject to a barrage ⟨the besiegers immediately *barraged* the enemy stronghold with a torrent of rifle fire —*Sericana Quarterly*⟩ ⟨patrons . . . *barraged* the Post Office Department with letters of complaint —*Newsweek*⟩
barrage balloon *n* [²*barrage*] **:** a small captive balloon used to support wires or nets as protection against air attacks
barrage reception *n* [¹*barrage*] **:** a system of radio reception in which interference from one or more directions is prevented (as by directional properties of antennas)
barragudo *var of* BARRIGUDO
bar·ra·mun·da \ˌbarəˈməndə\ *or* **bar·ra·mun·di** \-dē\ *n, pl* **barramunda** *or* **barramundas** *or* **barramundi** *or* **barramundis** *or* **barramundies** [native name in Australia] **:** any of several Australian fishes: **a :** a large red-fleshed lungfish (*Neoceratodus* or *Ceratodus forsteri*) of Australian rivers that attains a length of 6 feet and is highly esteemed as food — called also *Burnett salmon, salmon* **b :** a river fish (*Scleropages leichhardtii*) esteemed as food **c** *in northern Australia* **:** BEGTI
bar·ran·ca \bəˈraŋkə\ *or* **bar·ran·co** \-ŋ(,)kō\ *n* -s [Sp, of non-IE origin] **1 :** a deep gulley or arroyo with steep sides **2 :** a steep bank or bluff
bar·ran·dite \bəˈran,dīt, ˈbarən-\ *n* -s [F *barrandite*, fr. Joachim *Barrande* †1883 Fr. geologist + F *-ite*] **:** a mineral $(Fe,Al)PO_4.2H_2O$ consisting of a pale-gray hydrous phosphate of iron and aluminum belonging to the isomorphous series strengite-variscite
bar·ran·qui·lla \ˌbarənˈkē(y)ə\ *adj, usu cap* [fr. *Barranquilla*, Colombia] **:** of or from the city of Barranquilla, Colombia **:** of the kind or style prevalent in Barranquilla
bar·ra·tor *also* **bar·ra·ter** *or* **bar·re·tor** \ˈbarəd·ə(r)\ *n* -s [ME *baratour*, fr. MF *barateor* deceiver, fr. *barater* to deceive, barter + *-eor* -or] **:** one who engages in barratry
bar·ra·trous \-rə·trəs\ *adj* [*barratry* + *-ous*] **:** tainted with or constituting barratry — **bar·ra·trous·ly** *adv*
bar·ra·try \-rə·trē\ *n* -ES [ME *barratrie*, fr. MF *baraterie* deception, fr. *barater* + *-erie* -ery] **1 :** the purchase or sale of office or preferment in church or state **:** SIMONY **2 :** a fraudulent breach of duty or willful act of known illegality on the part of a master of a ship or of the mariners to the injury of the owner of the ship or cargo and without his consent (as running away with the ship, sinking or deserting her, or embezzling the cargo) **3 :** the practice of exciting and encouraging or maintaining lawsuits or quarrels **:** the persistent incitement of litigation
¹**bar·ré** \bäˈrā\ *n* -s *often attrib* [F, fr. past part. of *barrer* to bar — more at BAR] **1 :** a weftwise bar or striped pattern in fabrics **2 :** a defect in the weaving, knitting, or printing process that causes a weftwise streak
²**bar·ré** \(ˈ)bä\|ˈrā\ *adv (or adj)* [F, fr. past part. of *barrer*] **:** with all strings stopped by the forefinger laid across them — compare ¹BARRAGE 2
³**barre** \ˈbär, ˈbȧ(r\ *n* -s [F] **:** ¹BAR 1d(2)
¹**barred** \ˈbärd, ˈbȧd\ *adj* [¹*bar* +*-ed*] **:** having, marked by, or divided off by bars; *specif, of a bird* **:** having alternate bands of different color crossing the feathers

2barred \"\ *adv (or adj)* [trans. of F *barré*] : BARRÉ
barred owl *n* : a large American owl (*Strix varia* or *Syrnium varium*) with bars of dark brown on the breast
barred perch *n* : a silvery sea perch (*Amphistichus argenteus*) that is barred and spotted with brassy olive along the sides and is a valued game fish along the California coast
barred pickerel *n* : REDFIN PICKEREL
barred rock *n, often cap R* : a barred Plymouth Rock
barred spiral *n* : a spiral galaxy whose arms apparently spring from the extremities of a luminous bar that extends across the nucleus giving the object somewhat the appearance of a letter S
barred stamp *n* : a postage stamp that is a canceled remainder
1bar·rel \'barəl *also* 'ber-\ *n* -s [ME *barell, barel,* fr. MF *baril*] **1** : a round bulging vessel of greater length than breadth that is usu. made of staves bound with hoops and has flat ends of equal diameter **2 a** : a barrel with its contents **b** : the contents of a barrel **c** : the amount contained in a barrel **d** : any of various units of capacity or volume: as (1) : a U.S. unit of liquid measure equal to 31½ gallons; *also* : a unit of measure for fermented beverages equal to 31 gallons (2) : a unit of measure for petroleum equal to 42 gallons (3) : a unit of dry measure (as for fruits or vegetables) equal to 105 dry quarts or about 3.9 bushels; *also* : a measure for cranberries equal to about 87 quarts or about 2.7 bushels — abbr. *bbl.* **e** : a great quantity : LOT ⟨have a ~ of fun⟩ **3** : a drum or cylinder or similar round part: as **a** : the body of a windlass or capstan about which the cable winds **b** : the tube of a gun from which the projectile is discharged **c** : the revolving cylinder of a barrel organ **d** : the flat cylindrical metal box that encloses the mainspring of a timepiece **e** : the upper inside part of a bell **f** : the large cylindrical part of a locomotive boiler containing the tubes **g** : the core of various cylindrical devices (as a spool or bobbin) on which yarn or cloth is wound **h** : the cylindrical part of a clarinet connecting the mouthpiece with the first joint **i** : the part of a fountain pen or of a pencil containing the writing fluid or the lead **j** : a cylindrical or tapering housing containing the optical components of a photographic-lens system and the iris diaphragm usu. equipped with a flange on the outside for mounting on a camera **k** : a revolving hollow cylinder or drum within which metal may be cleaned by tumbling with abrasive material or may be dissolved from ore by mixing with a leaching solution **l** : the cylinder in which a piston travels **m** : the fuel outlet from the carburetor on a gasoline engine **4** : the trunk of a quadruped esp. of a domestic animal — see COW illustration

barrel: *H* hoop, *S* stave, *B* bunghole

2barrel \"\ *vb* **barreled** *or* **barrelled; barreled** *or* **barrelled; barreling** *or* **barrelling; barrels** [ME *barellen,* fr. *barell,* n.] *vt* **1** : to put or pack in a barrel **2** : to clean or otherwise treat (metal) in a barrel **3 a** : to transport at a high speed ⟨~s heavy loads up steep hills⟩ **b** : to cause (as an automobile) to travel fast ⟨~ed the convertible for a distant roadhouse⟩ **4** : to fit (a firearm) with a barrel ~ *vi* : to travel at a high speed ⟨~ing along in excess of the speed limit⟩
bar·rel·age \-lij\ *n* -s : amount in barrels
barrel arch *n* : an arch resembling a segment of a barrel in that its length is considerable compared to its span
barrel band *n* : 1BAND 3f
barrel bolt *n* : a door or sash bolt made to slide into a cylindrical socket
barrel cactus *n* : a cactus of the genus *Ferocactus*
barrel ceiling *n* : a ceiling that is semicircular in cross section and resembles a segment of a barrel
barrel chair *n* : an upholstered easy chair with a high solid rounded back suggestive of a barrel with a section removed
barrel chest *n* : the enlarged rounded thorax with fixed horizontal position of the ribs occurring in chronic pulmonary emphysema
barrel–chested \¦==¦==\ *adj* : having a large rounded chest ⟨he was powerful and *barrel-chested* —Alan LeMay⟩
barrel clover *or* **barrel medic** *n* : a clover (*Medicago tribuloides*) native to Australia and used there and elsewhere for pastures esp. on alkaline soil
barrel cuff *n* : a single soft unfolded cuff on a shirt usu. fastened by a button — distinguished from *French cuff*
barrel distortion *n* : distortion (as by an optical instrument or television receiver) in which the image of a straight line appears to be curved convexly away from the axis — compare PINCUSHION DISTORTION
barreled *adj, of an arrow* : tapered toward both ends
bar·rel·ful \'barəl,fu̇l *also* 'ber-\ *n, pl* **barrel·fuls** \-əl,fu̇lz\ *or* **barrels·ful** \-əlz,fu̇l\ [ME *barel ful*] : BARREL 2c
barrelhead \'==,=\ *n* : the flat end of a barrel — **on the barrelhead** *adv (or adj)* : asking for or granting no credit : in cash ⟨was paid for, cash *on the barrelhead* —*Time*⟩ ⟨prepared to pay *on the barrelhead* for what it needs —*Newsweek*⟩
barrel helm *n* : a cylindrical helmet with flat top worn esp. in the 13th century
1barrelhouse \'==,=\ *n* [so called fr. the row of barrels sometimes stacked along its walls] **1** : a cheap drinking establishment usu. with facilities for dancing and sometimes for gambling and lodging **2** : a style of jazz characterized by a very strongly accented beat, syncopation, dissonance, free improvisation, and when performed by a group continuous simultaneous improvisation by each member throughout an entire number
2barrelhouse \'==,hau̇s, -au̇z\ *vb* -ED/-ING/-S : BARREL ⟨every crow in hearing distance will come *barrelhousing* in, gang up, and drive this most hated enemy from the neighborhood —Eugene Kinkead⟩
barrel key *n* : PIPE KEY
barrel knot *n* : either of two knots used for tying fishing leaders together: **a** : a knot made by twisting the ends of two standing parts one around the other usu. two or three times and then pushing the ends back through the center twist — called also *blood knot* **b** : a knot made by tying double or triple overhand knots with each end around the opposite standing part — called also *double Englishman's knot, double fisherman's knot, grapevine knot*

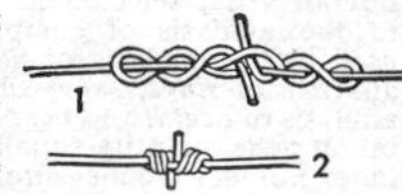

barrel knot a: *1* before, and *2* after ends are pulled tight

barrel organ *n* **1** : an instrument used chiefly by street musicians for producing music by the action of a revolving cylinder studded with pegs upon a series of valves that admit air from a bellows to a set of pipes **2** : a church organ operated like a barrel organ
barrel palm *n* : BOTTLE PALM
barrel plating *n* : the electroplating of objects placed in a revolving perforated barrel
barrel process *n* : a process of extracting gold or silver by treating the ore in a revolving barrel with mercury, chlorine, cyanide solution, or other reagent
barrel pump *n* : a hand pressure pump attached to a barrel containing a liquid spray
barrel quartz *n* : the quartz of certain folded gold-bearing quartz veins (as in Nova Scotia) whose outcrops resemble barrels
barrel roll *n* : an aerial maneuver in which a complete revolution about the longitudinal axis is made while the direction of flight is approximately maintained
barrel roof *n* **1** : a roof like the interior of a barrel vault **2** : BARREL VAULT
barrels *pl of* BARREL, *pres 3d sing of* BARREL
barrel saw *n* : a saw of cylindrical shape used to cut such rounded pieces as barrel staves, chair backs, and brush backs
barrel scale *n* : CYLINDER SCALE
barrel spindle *n* : a thick removable spindle for the turntable of a record player designed esp. for adapting the turntable to play 45 r.p.m. records with large center holes
barrel vault *n* : a semicylindrical vault having parallel abutments and the same section throughout; *also* : a similar vault that is curved in plan or rampant — see VAULT illustration
barrel vaulting *n* : vaulting consisting of barrel vaults

bar·re·mi·an \bə'rāmēən, -rēm-\ *adj, usu cap* [F *barrémien,* fr. *Barrême,* town in southeast France + F *-ien* -an] : of or relating to a subdivision of the European Cretaceous
1bar·ren \'barən *also* 'ber-\ *adj, often* -ER/-EST [ME *bareyne,* fr. OF *baraine,* fem. of *barain, brehaing,* prob. of non-IE origin; akin to the source of Alb *beronjë* sterile] **1 a** : having produced or borne no young : seemingly incapable of pregnancy or reproduction : STERILE ⟨spinsters and ~ women were not allowed to benefit under wills at all and their loss was the gain of their fruitful sisters —Robert Graves⟩ **b** *of an animal* : not with young : not pregnant at the usual season **c** *of a plant* : not bearing fruit or seed **d** *of land or a region* : deficient in producing vegetation : BARE, DESOLATE ⟨obtain wretchedly poor crops . . . from the ~ soil immediately round their cabins —Anthony Trollope⟩ **e** : producing ore in too small quantities to be commercially profitable ⟨a ~ mine⟩ **2** : DEVOID, LACKING — used with *of* ⟨~ of all love —John Keats⟩ ⟨a sea ~ of seals —Jack London⟩ ⟨~ of troublesome conventions and artificialities —Mark Twain⟩ **3** : providing little or no aesthetic or intellectual stimulation or gratification : lacking interest, information, or charm ⟨nameless millions performing ~ office routines —Edmund Wilson⟩ ⟨religion . . . buried under an even narrower and more ~ scholasticism —J.H.Randall⟩ **4** : unproductive of results or gain : lacking the intended effect or force : FRUITLESS, UNPROFITABLE ⟨a ~ conquest which brought him no special repute —John Buchan⟩ ⟨a high-sounding but ~ title, which gratified the Duke's vanity and signified nothing —J.L.Motley⟩ **5** : lacking inspiration or ideas : DULL, UNRESPONSIVE ⟨a dull suspicion in leaden, opaque, and ~ minds that wit, brilliancy, and imagination are incompatible with great mental power and solidity of judgment —J.J.Ingalls⟩ **syn** see BARE, STERILE
2barren \"\ *n* -s **1** : a tract of barren land **2 barrens** *pl* : an extent of usu. level land that lacks trees, has an inferior growth of trees, or has little vegetation of any kind whether due to natural factors (as climate or poor soil) or to accident (as fire) ⟨covered largely with stunted pine woods — the famous pine ~s —*Amer. Guide Series: N.J.*⟩
barren brome grass *or* **barren brome** *n* : a feathery Eurasian grass (*Bromus sterilis*) adventive in waste places in No. America
bar·ren·er \-nə(r)\ *n* -s [1*barren* + *-er*] *Brit* : a barren or a relatively infertile cow
barren–ground \¦==¦=\ *adj, usu cap B&G* : of or living in the Barren Grounds of northern Canada
barren ground bear *n, usu cap 1st B&G* : a peculiar bear that inhabits the Barren Grounds of northern Canada and is believed to be a variety of the grizzly bear
barren ground caribou *n, usu cap B&G* : any of several rather small caribou of the Barren Grounds of No. America and Greenland
bar·ren·ly *adv* [1*barren* + *-ly*] : in a barren manner ⟨a time when technical philosophy seems ~ timid —M.R.Cohen⟩
bar·ren·ness \'barənnəs\ *n* -ES [ME *bareynesse,* fr. *bareyne* barren + *-nesse* -ness — more at BARREN] : the quality or state of being barren
barren oak *or* **barrens oak** *n* **1** : BLACKJACK 5 **2** : BEAR OAK
barren strawberry *n* **1** : a low herb (*Waldsteinia fragarioides*) resembling a strawberry and having yellow flowers and dry fruits **2 a** *Brit* : a cinquefoil (*Potentilla fragariastrum*) with hairy carpels **b** : ROUGH CINQUEFOIL
barrenwort \'==,=\ *n* -s [so called fr. the belief that it causes sterility] : any of certain plants of the genus *Epimedium* having or believed to have sudorific properties: as **a** : a European herb (*E. alpinum*) often cultivated and having bitter leaves **b** : a Japanese herb (*E. diphyllum*) with small bluish flowers **c** : an herb (*E. hexandra*) of the Pacific coast of No. America having ternate leaves and small nodding flowers on a scapelike stalk
bar·rer \'bärər, bȧrə(r\ *n* -s [2*bar* + *-er*] : a shoeworker who stitches in parallel rows across parts of shoe uppers that need to be strengthened
bar·rera \bə'rerə, bä-\ *n* -s [Sp, fr. *barra* bar] **1** : the red wooden fence surrounding a bullring **2** : the first row of seats in the amphitheater of a bullring
bar·ret \'barət, bə'ret\ *also* **bar·rette** \bə'ret\ *n* -s [F *barrette,* fr. It *berretta* — more at BIRETTA] : a small cap; *esp* : BIRETTA
barretor *var of* BARRATOR
bar·rette \bä'ret, bə-\ *n* -s [F, dim. of *barre* bar] : a clip or pin shaped like a bar and used to hold a woman's hair in place

barrettes

bar·ret·ter \bə'redə(r)\ *n* -s [modif. of OF *bareter* to exchange] : an early form of radio detector operating by increased resistance when subjected to the influence of electric waves
1bar·ri·cade \'barə,kād, ,==' *also* -er-\ *vt* -ED/-ING/-S [MF *barricader,* fr. *barricade*] **1** : to block off or stop up (as a street or passage) with a barricade esp. in order to prevent the advance of an enemy : BLOCKADE ⟨angry workers *barricaded* the narrow streets with furniture, carriages, and piles of lumber⟩ **2** : to prevent access to by means of a barricade ⟨*barricaded* myself behind my study door—Bentz Plagemann⟩
2barricade \"\ *n* -s [F, fr. MF, fr. *barriquer* to barricade, fr. *barrique* barrel (a typical component of barricades, fr. dial. —Gascon— *barrico*) + *-ade;* akin to OF *barril* barrel] **1 a** : an obstruction or rampart hastily improvised and thrown up across some way or passage (as in revolutionary street fighting) to check the advance of the enemy — usu. used in pl. ⟨men, women, and children manned the ~s⟩ **b** : material barrier or obstacle that prevents passage ⟨a man behind a floor-to-ceiling concrete ~ was looking through a glass porthole —Stanley Frank⟩ **2** : a nonmaterial barrier or protective shield ⟨sat stiff as a poker behind his flimsy ~ of silence —Claud Cockburn⟩ ⟨guarded by . . . legal ~s —W.P.Webb⟩ **3** : a field of disagreement, dispute, or combat ⟨would die upon the literary ~ of defending the noble proportions of "War and Peace" —Ellen Glasgow⟩
1bar·ri·ca·do \,==¦kā(,)dō\ *vt* **barricadoed; barricadoed; barricadoing; barricadoes** *also* **barricados** [modif. of F *barricade*] *archaic* : BARRICADE
2barricado \"\ *n, pl* **barricadoes** *also* **barricados** *archaic* : BARRICADE
bar·ri·co \bə'rē(,)kō, *Brit often* 'brākə\ *n, pl* **barricoes** *also* **barricos** [modif. of Sp *barrica*] : a small cask : KEG
1bar·ri·er \'barēə(r) *also* 'ber-\ *n* -s [ME *barrere,* fr. MF *barriere,* fr. *barre* bar] **1** *obs* : BARRICADE; *esp* : an outer defense to impede or stop an enemy **2** : a material object or set of objects that separates, keeps apart, demarcates, or serves as a unit or barricade: as **a** : the palisades that enclosed the lists in medieval tournaments — usu. used in pl. **b** (1) *or* **barrier beach** *also* **barrier bar** : a long narrow sandy island lying parallel to a shore and built up by the action of waves, currents, and wind — called also *offshore bar;* see BARRIER ISLAND (2) *sometimes cap* : an extension of the antarctic continental ice sheet into the sea resting partly on the bottom **c** : the gate where customs duties are collected at the boundaries of some European countries **d** : a railing or other separation between the station building and train platforms in some European countries with openings to permit the passage of arriving and departing passengers **e** (1) : POTENTIAL BARRIER (2) : a movable net or structure serving in an emergency to halt a landing airplane esp. on an aircraft carrier when the tail hook has failed to engage the arresting gear **f** : a porous partition (as a thin sheet of silver-zinc alloy from which the zinc has been dissolved out) used in atmolysis **g** *in packaging* : a flexible material that can be formed into a container preventing or limiting the entrance of moisture, retaining flavors or oils, and otherwise protecting its contents **h** : a solid usu. white or yellow warning line painted between traffic lanes of a highway **3 barriers** *pl, often cap* : a medieval war game in which combatants fought on foot with a fence or railing between them — often used in the phrase *at barriers* **4 a** : the starting point in an ancient racecourse **b** : the movable gate or device at the starting line in a modern racetrack which is opened to signal the start of a race **5** : something intangible or immaterial that acts as a barrier (as by impeding or separating) ⟨psychological and social ~s to increased agricultural production —G.P. Wibberley⟩ ⟨the ~ between the craft and scholarly traditions —S.F.Mason⟩ **6** : a factor (as a topographic feature or a physical or physiological quality) that tends to restrict the free movement and mingling of individuals or populations — compare ISOLATING MECHANISM
2barrier \"\ *vt* -ED/-ING/-S : to obstruct or confine by a barrier
barrier berg *n* : a usu. large flat-topped iceberg that has broken from the antarctic barrier
barrier cell *n* : a barrier-layer cell
barrier chain *n* : a series of barriers extending along a considerable length of coast
barrier cream *n* : any of several cosmetic creams applied to the skin as a protective measure against dermatitis caused by chemical irritants
barrier ice *n* : floating freshwater ice of the antarctic barrier
barrier island *n* : a barrier so broadened as to be much more than a barrier beach; *also* : a long series of such barriers
barrier layer *n* : the surface of contact between a semiconductor (as cuprous oxide) and a metal (as copper) that acts as an alternating current rectifier or photovoltaic cell when included in a circuit
barrier line *n* : a line painted or otherwise marked on a roadway as a guide to traffic; *esp* : such a line that is not to be crossed by vehicles
barrier reef *n* **1** : a coral reef roughly parallel to a shore and separated from it by a lagoon **2** : limestone produced by the consolidation of materials in a barrier reef
barrier spit *n* : a barrier connected at one end to the mainland
barries *pl of* BARRY
bar·ri·gu·da \,barə'güdə\ *n* -s [Pg, fr. fem. of *barrigudo*] : a large Brazilian thatch palm (*Iriartea ventricosa*) having its trunk much swollen between the top and the ground
bar·ri·gu·do *also* **bar·ra·gu·do** \,=='=(,)dō\ *n* -s [Pg *barrigudo,* fr. *barrigudo* big-bellied, fr. *barriga* belly, barrel] : WOOLLY MONKEY
1bar·ring \'bäriŋ, 'bȧr-, -rēŋ\ *pres part of* BAR
2barring \"\ *n* -s [ME, fr. gerund of *barren* to mark with bars, to bar — more at BAR] : BARS; *esp* : the arrangement of bars ⟨the curious ~ on a raccoon's back⟩
3barring \"\ *prep* [ME, fr. pres. part. of *barren* to bar] : excluding by exception : EXCEPTING ⟨they knew that, ~ a miracle, they would never be able to save the large cash outlay required —Warner Olivier⟩
barring–out \¦=='=\ *n, pl* **barrings–out** : the shutting out of a schoolmaster from the schoolroom as a prank or to win certain concessions
bar·ring·to·nia \,bariŋ'tōnēə, -nyə\ *n, cap* [NL, fr. Daines *Barrington* †1800 Eng. judge and naturalist + NL *-ia*] : a genus of tropical trees (family Lecythidaceae) with alternate leaves often crowded toward the branch ends and large white flowers in spikes or racemes
bar·rio \'bärē,ō\ *n* -s [Sp, fr. Ar *barrī* of the open country, fr. *barr* exterior, outside, open country] **1** : a ward, quarter, or district of a city or town in Spanish-speaking countries **2** : a village or rural community unit in Latin America and the Philippines — see POBLACIÓN, SITIO **3** : a Spanish-speaking quarter or neighborhood in a city or town in the U.S. esp. in the Southwest
bar·ris·ter \'barəstə(r)\ *n* -s [1*bar* + *-i-* + *-ster*] **1** : a counsel admitted to plead at the bar and undertake the public trial of causes in an English superior court : COUNSELOR-AT-LAW — distinguished from *solicitor;* see LAWYER; compare ADVOCATE, ATTORNEY **2** : LAWYER, ATTORNEY
barrister–at–law \'====\ *n, pl* **barristers–at–law** : BARRISTER — used chiefly as a formal title
bar·ris·te·ri·al \¦barə¦stirēəl\ *adj* : of or relating to a barrister
bar roller *n* [1*bar*] : a roller that consists of one or more rotating cylinders whose surfaces are made up of horizontal tubular bars with spaces between and that is used for crushing clods and packing surface soil without leaving a smooth surface
barroom \'=,=\ *n* [1*bar* + *room*] : a room or establishment whose main feature is a bar for the sale of liquor : TAPROOM, SALOON
1bar·row \'ba(,)rō, -,rə *also* 'be- *often* -,rəw+V; *dial or sporadic & old-fash* 'bä-\ *n* -s [ME *berwe, bergh,* fr. OE *beorg;* akin to OHG *berg* mountain, ON *berg* rock, Goth *bairgahei* hill country, Skt *bṛhant* high] **1** : MOUNTAIN, HILL, MOUND — now used only in the names of hills in England ⟨Cadon Barrow⟩ **2** : a large mound of earth or stones over the remains of the dead and often enclosing a sepulchral cell or an apartment built of large rocks : TUMULUS — see LONG BARROW, ROUND BARROW
2barrow \"\ *n* -s [ME *barow,* fr. OE *bearg;* akin to OHG *barug* barrow, ON *bǫrgr,* Russ *borov* barrow, OE *borian* to bore — more at BORE] : a male hog castrated before it reaches sexual maturity
3barrow \"\ *n* -s [ME *barew, barowe,* fr. OE *bearwe* basket, handbarrow; akin to OFris *bare* handbarrow, LG *berwe,* ON *barar* bier, OE *beran* to carry — more at BEAR] **1 a** : HANDBARROW **b** : WHEELBARROW **2** : a cart with a shallow box body, two wheels, and shafts for pushing it : PUSHCART ⟨street vendors pushing their ~s⟩
barrow boy *also* **bar·row·man** \-mən, -,man\ *n* [3*barrow* + *boy* or *man*] : COSTERMONGER
bar·row·ist \'barəwəst\ *n* -s *usu cap* [Henry *Barrow* or *Barrowe* †1593 Eng. church reformer + E *-ist*] : a follower of Henry Barrow, a founder of Congregationalism in England who was executed for nonconformity
barrow pit \'barō-, 'bä- *also* 'be-\ *n* [by alter.] *chiefly West* : BORROW PIT; *esp* : a ditch dug along a roadway to furnish fill and provide drainage
bar·row's goldeneye \'barōz-, -rəz *also* 'be-\ *n, usu cap B* [after Sir John *Barrow* †1848 Eng. traveler and admiralty official] : a No. American goldeneye (*Bucephala islandica*) distinguished from the American goldeneye by the somewhat more crested head and white patch shaped like a crescent in front of the eye of the male
bar·ru·let \'bar(y)ələt\ *n* -s [1*bar* + *-ule* + *-et*] *heraldry* : a diminutive of the bar usu. half to a fourth as wide
bar·ru·ly \'bar(y)əlē\ *also* **bar·ru·lé** *or* **bar·ru·lée** \¦bar(y)ə¦lā\ *adj* [ME *berle,* prob. modif. of MF *burelé,* fr. OF — more at BURELLY] *heraldry* : divided into a large number of horizontal bars
1bar·ry \'bärē, 'ba-\ *adj* [ME, fr. AF *barré,* fr. OF *barre* bar — more at BAR] *heraldry* : divided into an even number of horizontal bars of two tinctures arranged alternately
2bar·ry \'barē\ *n* -ES [by shortening and alter.] : BARRACUDA
bar·ry–bendy \¦bärē¦bendē, ¦bar-\ *adj* [1*barry* + *bendy*] *heraldry* : divided by bars and bends with tinctures alternate — see BENDY
barry–nebuly \¦==¦===\ *adj* [1*barry* + *nebuly*] *heraldry* : composed of bars having nebuly bounding lines — compare BARRY-WAVY
barry–pily \¦==¦==\ *adj* [1*barry* + *pily*] *heraldry* : divided into equal piles arranged horizontally — see PILY
barry–wavy \¦==¦==\ *adj* [1*barry* + *wavy*] *heraldry* : divided into an even number of wavy bars — compare BARRY-NEBULY
bars *pl of* BAR, *pres 3d sing of* BAR
bar·sac \'bär,sak\ *n* -s *usu cap* [fr. *Barsac,* dept. Gironde, France] : a white semisweet Bordeaux wine produced near the Garonne river in the department of Gironde, France
bar screen *n* [1*bar*] : a screen or sieve with parallel uniformly spaced bars instead of wire mesh — see GRIZZLY
bars gemel *or* **bars gemels** *pl of* BAR GEMEL
bar share *n* [1*bar*] : a plowshare welded to the landside
bar shoe *n* [1*bar*] : a horseshoe having a flat piece across the usual opening at the heel to protect a tender frog from injury
bar sight *n* [1*bar*] : a rear sight on a firearm consisting of a movable bar with an open notch or peep
bar sinister *n* [1*bar*] **1** : a supposed heraldic charge widely believed to be a mark of bastardy **2** : the fact or condition of being of illegitimate birth ⟨started with the initial handicap of the *bar sinister* —G.D.Brown⟩ **3** : an enduring stigma, stain, or reproach (as of improper conduct or irregular status) ⟨the loyalty determinations presented a special situation involving the imposition of a *bar sinister* —N.L.Nathanson⟩ ⟨a number of the great universities still ignore ecology or accord it the *bar sinister* —*Amer. Naturalist*⟩
bar soap *n* [1*bar*] : soap sold in the form of solid oblong cakes commonly for laundry purposes

bar·som \'bärsəm\ n -s [Per barsam, fr. MPer barsum, fr. Av barəsman; akin to Skt barhis sacrificial grass, brhati he plucks] : a bundle of sacred twigs or metal rods used by priests in Zoroastrian ceremonies

bar spade n [1bar] : a trenching spade with a cutting blade welded across the ends of three parallel bars for use in spading wet sticky soil

bar·spoon \'=,=\ n [1bar (counter) + spoon] : a spoon equivalent to a teaspoon that is used in measuring ingredients for mixed drinks

bar·stool \'=,=\ n [1bar (counter) + stool] : a high stool that usu. has a round seat fixed permanently on a central post

bart \'bärt, 'bät\ n -s often cap [by abbr.] : BARONET

bar tack n [1bar] : a reinforcement for points of strain in clothing consisting of a bar-shaped line of small stitches worked across several threads — **bartacked** \'=,=\ adj

bar-tailed godwit \'=,=-\ n : a godwit (Limosa lapponica) that has a slightly curved bill, a closely barred tail, and relatively short legs and that breeds in extreme northern Europe and Asia and winters chiefly in Africa and Australasia

bar·tangi \bär'täŋē\ n, pl bartangi or bartangis usu cap [fr. the Bartang river valley, Tadzhik S.S.R., U.S.S.R.] 1 : an Iranian people from the Bartang river valley in the western Pamirs 2 : a member of the Bartangi people

bar·tend \'bär,tend, 'bä,-\ vi -ED/-ING/-S [back-formation fr. bartender] : to act as a bartender esp. professionally

bar·tend·er \-ə(r)\ n -s [1bar (counter) + tender] : one that serves alcoholic beverages at a bar : BARKEEPER

1bar·ter \'bär|d·ər, 'bȧ|, |tə(r)\ vb bartered; bartered; bartering \|d·əriŋ, |təriŋ also |·triŋ\ barters [ME bartren, fr. MF barater to cheat, exchange] vi 1 : to trade by exchanging one commodity for another ⟨~ed for furs with tobacco and rum⟩ : TRUCK ⟨stores ~ing with farmers⟩ 2 : to trade in intangible or nonmaterial values ⟨~ for success at the price of happiness⟩ ~ vt 1 : to trade or exchange by bartering ⟨Indians . . . ~ed their services for "ironmongery" —C.B.Hitchcock⟩ 2 : to trade or exchange (as an ideal or intangible value) for a material or unworthy consideration — often used with away ⟨would cheerfully ~ away all the social gains of the last century for one first-class new symphony —Hunter Mead⟩

2barter \"\ n -s 1 : the act or practice of carrying on trade by bartering : an exchange of goods for goods ⟨the former system of ~ has virtually ceased to exist, replaced by money economy —H.S.Tschopik⟩ 2 : the thing given in exchange in bartering ⟨the trinkets were ~ for food and manual service from the natives⟩

1barth·ian \'bärd·ēən, -rthē-\ adj, usu cap [Karl Barth †1968 Swiss theologian + E -ian] : of or relating to Barth or to his theology which has exercised a formative influence in the development of the neoorthodox school of Protestant theology

2barthian \"\ n -s usu cap : a follower or adherent of the theology of Karl Barth

barth·ian·ism \-,nizəm\ n -s usu cap : the Barthian crisis theology or dialectical theology that rejects theological liberalism and its emphasis on empirical methods and stresses instead reliance on supernatural revelation

barth·ite \'bär,thīt, -rd-,īt\ n -s [G barthit, fr. Barth, 20th cent. mining engineer in southwestern Africa + G -it -ite] : CONICHALCITE

bar·tho·lin·itis \,bärthələ'nīd·əs, -rtᵊl-\ n, pl **bartholin·ites** \-ī,tēz\ sometimes cap [NL, fr. ISV (glands of) Bartholin + NL -itis] : inflammation of the glands of Bartholin

bartholin's gland n, usu cap B : GLAND OF BARTHOLIN

bar·ti·zan \'bärd·əzən, ¦==¦zan\ n -s [alter. of ME bretasynge, fr. bretasce parapet — more at BRATTICE] : a small structure (as a turret) overhanging or projecting from a building near an entrance for lookout or defense or for support for a flagpole — **bar·ti·zaned** \-nd\ adj

bartizans

bar·ton \'bärtᵊn\ n -s [ME berton, fr. OE beretūn threshing floor, barn, fr. bere barley + tūn enclosure — more at BARLEY, TOWN] 1 dial Eng : a large farm; esp : a demesne farm or the demesne lands of a manor 2 dial Eng a : a farmyard or the outbuildings behind a farmhouse b : a poultry yard or hen coop

bar·ton·el·la \,bärtᵊn'elə\ n [NL, fr. A.L.Barton fl1909 Peruvian physician + NL -ella] 1 cap : the type genus of Bartonellaceae including the causative organism of Oroya fever and verruga peruana in man 2 -s sometimes cap : any member of the genus Bartonella

bar·ton·el·la·ce·ae \,bärtᵊn,elə'lāsē,ē\ n pl, cap [NL, fr. Bartonella, type genus + -aceae] : a family of microorganisms (order Rickettsiales) that invade blood and tissue cells of man and other vertebrates and are often transmitted by blood-sucking arthropods

bar·ton·el·lo·sis \-'lōsəs\ n, pl **bartonello·ses** \-ō,sēz\ sometimes cap [NL, fr. Bartonella + -osis] : a disease of man and other mammals orig. in the valleys of the Andes of Peru but now in other parts of So. America characterized by severe anemia and high fever followed by an eruption like warts on the skin and caused by an organism (Bartonella bacilliformis) like rickettsia that invades the red blood cells and is transmitted by sandflies (genus Phlebotomus)

1bar·to·nia \bär'tōnēə\ [NL, fr. Benjamin S. Barton †1815 Amer. botanist + NL -ia] syn of MENTZELIA

2bartonia \"\ n [NL, fr. B.S.Barton + NL -ia] 1 -s : MENTZELIA 2a 2 cap : a genus of very small herbs (family Gentianaceae) with scalelike leaves and small yellow flowers

bar tracery n [1bar] : decorative architectural tracery that is formed by the curves and intersections of the molded bars of mullions

bar·tra·mia \bär'trāmēə\ n, cap [NL, fr. William Bartram †1823 Am. naturalist + NL -ia] : a genus (the type of the family Bartramiaceae) of acrocarpous mosses with globular capsules which dry in ridges and folds

bar·tra·mi·an sandpiper or **bartramian plover** \(')bär-¦trāmēən-\ n, usu cap B [William Bartram + E -ian] : UPLAND PLOVER

bar·tram oak \'bärtrəm-\ n, usu cap B [after John Bartram †1777 Am. botanist] : an oak (Quercus heterophylla) of the eastern U.S. usu. considered a natural hybrid between the northern red oak and the willow oak

bartram's sandpiper n, usu cap B [after William Bartram] : UPLAND PLOVER

bartree \'=,=\ n -s [1bar + tree] : WARPING BOARD

barts pl of BART

bart·sia \'bärtsēə\ n [NL, irreg. fr. Johann Bartsch †1738 Ger. physician in Surinam + NL -ia] 1 cap : a small genus of partly parasitic herbs (family Scrophulariaceae) of the northern hemisphere with opposite leaves and showy irregular flowers in terminal leafy spikes — see ALPINE BARTSIA 2 -s : any plant of the genus Bartsia

ba·rukh·zy \bə'rüksē\ also **barukhzy hound** n -ES often cap B [Russ, fr. Pashto Bārakzi people of Afghanistan] : AFGHAN HOUND

barunduki var of BARONDUKI

barway \'=,=\ n [1bar + way] : a gateway closed by bars usu. fitting into posts

bar winding n [1bar] : an armature winding consisting of a series of metallic bars connected at their extremities

bar·wing \'=,=\ n [so called fr. the wide white wing stripe] Austral : WHITE-EYED DUCK

bar·wise \'=,wīz\ also **bar·ways** \-,wāz\ adv [1bar + -wise or -ways] 1 heraldry : in the direction of a bar : HORIZONTALLY 2 heraldry : in a line in the direction of a bar — used of two or more charges esp. when not across the middle of the field; compare in fess at FESS

barwood \'=,=\ n [1bar + wood] : a hard red dyewood of tropical Africa from a tree of the genus Pterocarpus but supposed by some to be camwood; also : redwood from any of several other African trees

bar-wound \'=,=\ adj : made with bar winding

bary- comb form [Gk bary-, fr. barys — more at GRIEVE] : heavy ⟨barylite⟩ ⟨barysphere⟩

bar·y·cen·ter \'barə,sentə(r)\ n -s [part trans. of G baryzentrum, fr. bary- + zentrum center] : CENTER OF MASS — **bar·y·cen·tric** \,==='sentrik, -ēk\ adj

bar·ye \'barē\ n -s [F, fr. Gk barys heavy] : 7BAR 2

bar·y·lambda \,barə'lamdə\ n, cap [NL, fr. bary- + Gk lambda, the letter; fr. the shape of the upper molars] : a genus of large powerful herbivorous mammals (order Pantodonta) from the upper Paleocene of Colorado that have tails like kangaroos and small heads

bar·y·lite \'barə,līt\ n -s [ISV bary- + -lite; orig. formed as G barylit] : a mineral $BaBe_2Si_2O_7$ consisting of rare silicate of barium and beryllium occurring in colorless prismatic crystals (hardness 7, sp. gr. 4.03)

ba·ryp·o·da \bə'ripədə\ [NL, fr. bary- + -poda] syn of EMBRITHOPODA

ba·rys·i·lite \bə'risə,līt, ,barə'si,līt\ n -s [Sw barysil (fr. bary- + silikon silicon) + E -ite] : a rare lead silicate $Pb_3Si_2O_7$ occurring in white cleavable masses

bar·y·sphere \'barə,sfi(ə)r, -iə\ n -s [ISV bary- + -sphere] : the heavy interior portion of the earth within the lithosphere

baryt- or **baryto-** comb form [ISV, fr. baryta] : baryta : barytic ⟨barytocalcite⟩

ba·ry·ta \bə'rīd·ə\ n -s [alter. of barytes — more at BARITE] : any of several compounds of barium; esp : barium monoxide

baryta paper n : paper that is coated with a preparation of barium sulfate in gelatin and used after calendering as a support for the light-sensitive emulsion used in photography

baryta water n : an aqueous solution of barium hydroxide

baryta white n : barium sulfate used as a pigment or extender

baryta yellow n : BARIUM YELLOW 2

baryte or **barytes** var of BARITE

ba·ryt·ic \bə'rid·ik\ adj [baryta + -ic] : of or relating to baryta

bar·y·tine \'barə,tēn\ n -s [F, fr. baryte barite + -ine] : BARITE

ba·ry·to·cal·cite \bə,rīd·ō+\ n -s [baryt- + calcite] : a mineral $BaCa(CO_3)_2$ consisting of white monoclinic barium calcium carbonate (hardness 4, sp. gr. 3.66)

bar·y·ton \'barə,tän\ n -s [F — more at BARITONE] 1 : BARITONE 2, 3 2 [G, fr. It baritono — more at BARITONE] : a tenor vox humana organ stop of 16- or 8-foot pitch

1bar·y·tone \'barə,tōn\ adj [Gk barytonos, lit., deep-sounding — more at BARITONE] : having an unaccented final syllable — used esp. in Greek grammar

2barytone \"\ n -s : a barytone word (as Greek philos "dear" contrasted with sophós "wise")

3barytone var of BARITONE

1bas pres 3d sing of BA, pl of BA

2bas \'bəs\ adv [Hindi bas, fr. Per] India : ENOUGH, STOP — often used interjectionally

bas abbr basso

ba·sad \'bā,sad\ adv [1base + -ad] : toward the base ⟨with small bony processes lying ~ to the true fin rays⟩

1ba·sal \'bāsəl also -āz-\ adj [1base + -al] 1 : relating to, situated at, or forming the base; specif : 1RADICAL 1a(2) ⟨~ leaves⟩ 2 a : of or relating to the foundation, base, or essence : FUNDAMENTAL, BASIC, ESSENTIAL ⟨~ texts in reading⟩ b : of, relating to, or essential for maintaining the fundamental vital activities of an organism (as respiration, heartbeat, or excretion) : MINIMAL ⟨~ diet⟩ — see BASAL METABOLISM 3 : serving as or serving to induce an initial comatose or unconscious state that forms a basis for further anesthetization ⟨~ narcosis⟩ ⟨~ anesthetic⟩ — **ba·sal·ly** \-əlē,-əli\ adv

2basal \"\ n -s : a basal part or structure; esp : a basal plate of an echinoderm

basal age n : the mental age level at which all the items on an intelligence test can be creditably passed

basal area n : the area of a breast-high cross section of a tree or of all the trees in a stand

basal body n 1 : a minute distinctively staining cell organelle found at the base of a flagellum or cilium and resembling a centriole in structure — called also blepharoplast 2 : KINETOPLAST

basal cell n : one of the innermost cells of the Malpighian layer of the skin

basal-cell carcinoma n : a skin cancer derived from and preserving the form of the basal cells of the skin

basal cleavage n : cleavage parallel to the base of a crystal or to the plane of the lateral axes

basal complex n : FUNDAMENTAL COMPLEX

basal conglomerate n : a conglomerate that resting on a surface of erosion and consequently marking an unconformity forms the bottom member of a sedimentary series

basal disk n : an expanded basal portion by which certain stalked sessile organisms are attached to the substrate

ba·sa·le \bə'sa(,)lē, -za-, -ā(,)lē, -ä(,)lē\ n, pl **ba·sa·lia** \-lēə\ [NL, fr. E basal] : the proximal one of the two or more cartilaginous or bony portions in the axis of any of the paired fins of a fish — compare BASIPTERYGIUM

basal ganglion n : any of four deeply placed masses of gray matter within each cerebral hemisphere comprising the caudate nucleus, the lenticular nucleus, the amygdaloid nucleus, and the claustrum — usu. used in pl.

basal granule n : BASAL BODY 1

ba·sa·lis \-ləs\ n, pl **basa·les** \-,lēz\ [NL, fr. E basal] : the basal part of the endometrium that is not shed during menstruation

basal lamina n : the part of the gray matter of the embryonic neural tube from which the motor nerve roots arise

basal length n, anthrop : distance from gnathion to basion

basal metabolic rate n : the rate at which heat is given off by an organism at complete rest usu. determined 12 to 15 hours after ingestion of food and expressed in large calories per square meter of body surface per hour and as a percentage above or below a standard value

basal metabolism n : the metabolism of an organism in the fasting and resting state when it uses just enough energy to maintain vital cellular activity, respiration, and circulation as measured by the basal metabolic rate

basal-nerved \'==¦=\ adj, of a leaf : having the veins radiating from the base

basal plane n 1 : a plane parallel to the lateral or horizontal axis 2 : a basal pinacoid

basal plate n : an underlying structure: as a : the ventral portion of the neural tube b : the part of the decidua of a placental mammal that is intimately fused with the placenta c : the part of a coral corallium immediately below the polyp d : any of certain chiefly ventral skeletal plates of an echinoderm

basal ration n : a ration furnishing the necessary energy but lacking in one or more accessory food substances (as vitamins) that may be added in varying proportion for the study of their effects

basal rot n : a rot affecting the basal parts of a plant; specif : a rot of narcissus bulbs due to a fungus (Fusarium bulbigemum)

ba·salt \bə'sȯlt, 'bā,sȯlt, 'ba,sȯlt also 'bā,zȯlt sometimes 'basəlt or 'bazəlt\ n -s [alter. of earlier basaltes, fr. L, MS var. of basanites touchstone, fr. Gk basanitēs, fr. basanos touchstone (fr. Egypt bḫnw) + -itēs -ite] 1 : a dark-gray to black dense to fine-grained igneous rock that is the extrusive equivalent of gabbro, that consists of basic plagioclase, augite, and usu. magnetite with olivine or basalt glass or both sometimes present, that is often vesicular the cavities sometimes being filled with secondary minerals, and that sometimes has a prismatic parting (as in the basalts of the Giant's Causeway, Northern Ireland) and occas. a pillow or ellipsoidal structure 2 usu **ba·sal·tes** \bə'sȯl(,)tēz\ n : a hard fine-grained black stoneware introduced by Josiah Wedgwood in 1768

basalt dome n : a broad rounded dome-shaped volcano formed almost exclusively of basaltic lava — compare SHIELD VOLCANO

basalt glass n : a black glassy form of basalt — called also hyalobasalt, vitrobasalt

ba·sal·tic \bə'sȯltik\ adj : relating to, formed of, containing, or resembling basalt ⟨~ lava⟩

ba·sal·ti·form \bə'sȯltə,fȯrm\ adj [basalt + -iform] : like basalt in form : COLUMNAR

basalt-porphyry n : a basalt characterized by prominent phenocrysts of olivine or augite

bas·aluminite \'bās+\ n -s [basic + alumin- + -ite] : a mineral $Al_4(SO_4)(OH)_{10}.5H_2O$ consisting of a basic hydrated aluminum sulfate found in veinlets in siderite at Irchester and Brighton Hill, England, and in France

basal wall n, bot : the primary wall in archegoniates that divides the oospore into an anterior and a posterior half

bas·a·nite \'basə,nīt, -azə-\ n -s [L basanites — more at BASALT] 1 : TOUCHSTONE 1 2 : an extrusive-igneous rock composed of plagioclase, augite, olivine, and either nephelite or leucite

bas bleu \bäblœ\ n, pl **bas bleus** \-œ(z)\ [F bas-bleu, fr. bas stocking + bleu blue] : BLUESTOCKING 1

bas·cart \'ba,skärt\ n [blend of basket and cart] : a waist-high wire basket or pair of baskets on wheels into which shoppers in supermarkets gather their purchases

bas·cine or **bas·sine** \bə'sēn\ adj [F bassine, lit., pan, fr. bassin basin, fr. OF bacin — more at BASIN] of a watchcase : having a flush joint that is barely visible

bascinet var of BASINET

bas·col·o·gist \ba'skäləjəst\ n -s usu cap : a specialist in the Basque language or culture

bas·col·o·gy \-əjē\ n -ES usu cap [Basco- (fr. Basque) + -logy] : the study of the Basque language or culture

bas·cule \'ba,skyül\ n -s [F, seesaw, fr. MF, alter. (influenced by bas low) of earlier bacule, fr. baculer to punish by beating the buttocks against the ground, fr. bas low + cul buttocks — more at BASE, CULET] : an apparatus or structure in which one end is counterbalanced by the other on the principle of the seesaw or by weights (as in a bascule bridge)

bascule bridge n : a counterpoised or balanced drawbridge

bascule escapement n : the detent escapement in which the detent is pivoted, the tension being supplied by a small hairspring

1base \'bās\ n, pl **bas·es** \'bāsəz\ [ME, fr. MF, fr. L basis, fr. Gk, step, stepping, base, pedestal, fr. bainein to go, step — more at COME] 1 a : the bottom of something considered as its support : that on which something rests or stands : FOUNDATION ⟨the ~ of the lamp⟩ ⟨the ~ of the pyramid⟩ ⟨the ~ of the mountain⟩ b (1) : the lower part of a wall, pier, or column considered as a separate architectural feature (2) : the lower part of a complete architectural design (as of a monument) c : one of the lines or surfaces of a geometrical figure from which an altitude is or is thought to be constructed ⟨the ~ of a triangle⟩ d : that part of a bodily organ by which it is attached to another more central structure of the organism ⟨the ~ of the thumb⟩ e (1) : the part on, to, or in which the frame and operating parts of a mechanism are fastened (2) : the part (as a panelboard) upon which other parts (as buses, switches, terminal and contact parts) are mounted (3) : the insulated part of a lamp bulb or electron tube through which its intervals make electrical connection with the circuit associated with it f : 1BLOCK 4g 2 : the main ingredient ⟨an exotic drink with a rum ~⟩: as a (1) : an essential ingredient of an explosive — compare DOUBLE-BASE POWDER, SINGLE-BASE POWDER (2) : the predominating substance held in solution in a crude petroleum or left as a residue on refining ⟨mixed-base crudes⟩ — see ASPHALT-BASE, NAPHTHENE-BASE, PARAFFIN-BASE b (1) : an inert supporting or carrying ingredient : an absorbent or adsorbent (as kieselguhr in dynamite) : CARRIER 9 — compare DOPE 3a (2) : an active supporting ingredient (as wood pulp mixed with an oxidizing agent in dynamite) c (1) : the usu. inactive ingredient of a preparation serving as the vehicle for the active medicinal principle ⟨the fatty ~ of an ointment⟩ (2) : the chief active ingredient of a preparation — called also basis d (1) : a transparent support for photographic film (2) : the paper support used for photographic paper 3 a : the fundamental part of something : basic principle : ESSENCE, FOUNDATION, BASIS, GROUNDWORK ⟨tried to furnish criticism with a psychological ~ —C.I.Glicksberg⟩ ⟨rejuvenating the moral ~ of a society—Herbert Agar⟩ b (1) : the fundamental unit or pattern of a rhythm or one of its component parts or the norm of this unit (2) : the nuclear pattern in a complex rhythmic figure or system (3) : BASIS 5 4 bases pl, archaic : a skirt often of velvet or brocade and sometimes of mailed armor that reaches from the waist to the knees 5 : the lower or back part of something without reference to its function as a support: as a : the lower part of an heraldic field — usu. used in the phrase in base; compare ESCUTCHEON 1 b : the lowest part of the hilt of a saber c : the pavilion of a cut gem d : the underside of a cloud ⟨fly below the cloud ~⟩ 6 a : the point or line from which a start is made in an action or undertaking ⟨plans to make this city his ~ of operation for six to eight weeks —J.A.Loftus⟩ b : a line in a survey which when accurately determined in length and position serves as the origin for computing the distances and relative positions of remote points and objects by triangulation c (1) : the locality or the installations on which a military force relies for supplies or from which it initiates operations ⟨a large naval ~⟩ ⟨an advanced ~⟩ (2) : the element on which a military movement or formation is regulated d : a number (as 5 in $5^{6.44}$ or 5^7) that is raised to a power; esp : the number that when raised to a power equal to the logarithm of a number yields the number itself ⟨the logarithm of 100 to the ~ 10 is 2 since $10^2=100$⟩ e : a number equal to the number of units in a given digit's place that for a given system of writing numbers is required to give the numeral 1 in the next higher place ⟨the decimal system uses a ~ of 10⟩; also : such a system of writing numbers using an indicated base ⟨convert from ~ 10 to ~ 2⟩ f (1) historical and comparative linguistics : ROOT, STEM, THEME; esp : one reconstructed from words or from the relationships among words in several languages (as assumed Indo-European bher- "to carry" reconstructed from Greek pherein, Latin ferre, Old English beran, and their cognates) (2) descriptive linguistics : the word or morpheme, which may be a bound form but not an affix, selected as a convenient point of departure in the analysis of complex words or derivatives (as play used in the analysis of played and playful, sing used in the analysis of sings, sang, sung, and song, or acet- used in the analysis of acetal and acetate) g : the basal pinacoid of a crystal h : the quantity equaling 100 from which variations in an index number are measured ⟨the 1946–49 profit ~⟩ 7 a : the starting place or goal in various games b obs : PRISONER'S BASE c : any one of the four stations at the corners of a baseball infield ⟨was thrown out at first ~⟩ 8 a : a compound (as lime, ammonia, a caustic alkali, or an alkaloid) capable of reacting with an acid to form a salt either with or without the elimination of water, its aqueous solutions if it is water-soluble having an acrid brackish taste and turning litmus blue : a compound (MOH) containing the hydroxide ion (OH^-) or hydroxyl group (OH) that is capable of yielding in aqueous solution a hydroxyl ion together with the cation (M^+), the degree of ionization in dilute solutions of strong bases (as sodium hydroxide, calcium hydroxide, and choline) being virtually complete and that of weak bases (as ammonium hydroxide and many organic bases) being in the neighborhood of one percent or less b according to the Brønsted-Lowry system : a molecule (as ammonia) or ion (as hydroxyl or nitrate) that can take up a proton from an acid : a proton acceptor ⟨the chloride ion is the conjugate ~ of hydrogen chloride⟩ c according to the G.N.Lewis system : a compound (as ammonia, ether, or benzene) or a negative ion (as hydroxyl) capable of giving up to an acid an unshared pair of electrons which then form a covalent chemical bond — called also Lewis base 9 : the least number of natural cards that will form a canasta when a required number of natural or wild cards is added — **off base** 1 : completely or absurdly mistaken ⟨any man who said such a thing is certainly off base⟩ 2 : by surprise : UNAWARES ⟨the sudden question caught him off base⟩

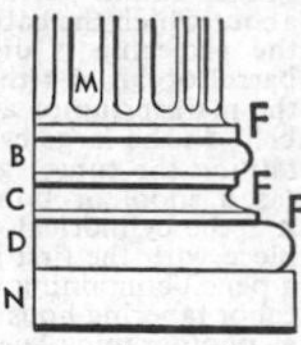

base of a column: B upper torus; C scotia; D lower torus; F, F, F, fillets; M shaft; N plinth

2base \"\ vb -ED/-ING/-S vt 1 a : to make or form a foundation for ⟨great roots based the tree columns —George Macdonald⟩ b : to serve as a base for ⟨these carriers can ~ 100 planes⟩ c : to establish or maintain a base for ⟨would be necessary to ~ them at specially designated . . . strategic points —Vera M. Dean⟩ 2 : to use as a base or basis for : ESTABLISH, FOUND — used with on or upon ⟨~s his position on a wide and shrewd scrutiny of man —A.L.Locke⟩ ⟨basing her life-sized portrait . . . on contemporary evidence —Harry Levin⟩ ~ vi 1 : to become based — used with on or upon ⟨the value of diamonds ~s on the gem value —G.S.Brady⟩ 2 : to establish or maintain one's base ⟨would fly on to Luzon after the attack and ~ there overnight —Fletcher Pratt⟩

syn BASE, FOUND, GROUND, BOTTOM, STAY, and REST can mean, in common, to provide with or serve as a basis. BASE now usu. applies to what underlies a belief, a system of thought, a judgment, a hope, and so on ⟨a conviction not *based* on any ascertainable fact⟩ ⟨a tax *based* on prospective earnings⟩ ⟨a religion *based* on faith as much as principle⟩ FOUND is very close to BASE but usu. adds the idea of something consciously advanced as support (of an opinion, a judgment, and so on) ⟨an opinion *founded* on a careful written analysis of facts⟩ ⟨this criticism is *founded* in misconception —B.N.Cardozo⟩ ⟨the terrible old mythic story on which the drama was *founded* —Matthew Arnold⟩ GROUND implies or connotes an implanting (as in the ground) to give solidity and firmness ⟨a love *grounded* in understanding and trust⟩ ⟨*grounded* all his work as a novelist on the faithful study of human nature —M.P.Linehan⟩ ⟨America was *grounded* not in the overthrow of the feudal past but in escape from it —Richard Hofstadter⟩ BOTTOM, rarer in this sense than the other terms, implies a broad and strong base ⟨his report was *bottomed* on sober statistics —*Time*⟩ ⟨*bottomed* on ideas to which everyone subscribes today —C.G.Bowers⟩ STAY implies a support that keeps upright or prevents from falling ⟨*stay* a tipping barn with heavy supporting timbers on one side⟩ ⟨his nature looked coldly upon its early faith and sought to *stay* itself with rational knowledge —H.O.Taylor⟩ REST stresses reliance upon something as a base or fundamental support, usu. figurative ⟨continuing progress based on science and technology . . . the foundation upon which our prosperity and our increasing standard of living *rest* —H.H.Curtice⟩ ⟨their academic reputations *rest*, quite largely, upon their academic power —C.W.Mills⟩ ⟨the cultures of the ancient empires of the Near East, of Greece and Rome, and of medieval Europe, all *rest* on the technical achievements of the Neolithic Age —Benjamin Farrington⟩

³**base** \"\ *adj* [¹*base*] **1 :** constituting or serving as a base ⟨are now setting up a string of ~ camps —*Time*⟩ **2 :** BASIC ⟨the right to work is a ~ right —Ira Mosher⟩

⁴**base** \"\ *adj* -ER/-EST [ME *bas*, fr. MF, fr. ML *bassus* fat, short, low] **1** *archaic* **:** of little height : not high or tall ⟨the cedar stoops not to the ~ shrub's foot —Shak.⟩ **2** *obs* **:** low in place or position ⟨fall to the ~ earth from the firmament —Shak.⟩ **3** *obs* **:** ³BASS **4** *archaic* **a :** of humble birth or position **:** LOWLY, PLEBEIAN, POOR ⟨~ in kind and born to be a slave —William Cowper⟩ **b :** of illegitimate birth **:** BASTARD ⟨Edmund the ~ shall top the legitimate —Shak.⟩ **5 a :** like a villein **:** SERVILE ⟨a ~ tenant⟩ **b :** held by villenage ⟨~ tenure⟩ **6 :** of inferior quality **:** SHABBY, COARSE, DEBASED: as **a** (1) **:** alloyed with inferior metal ⟨~ gold⟩ (2) **:** made of inferior metal ⟨~ coins of aluminum⟩ **b** *of language* **:** not classical ⟨~ Latin⟩ **7 :** having no dignity of sentiment or trustworthiness **:** LOW-MINDED, MEANSPIRITED, SHAMEFUL, IGNOBLE, UNWORTHY ⟨seemed a ~ betrayal of idealism —L.M.Sears⟩ **8 :** lacking higher values **:** DEGRADING, MENIAL ⟨citizens go on existing with a ~ mechanical kind of life like that of insects —Stephen Spender⟩ **9 :** of comparatively little value **:** not precious — compare BASE METAL

syn LOW, VILE: BASE stresses the ignoble; it may suggest cruelty, treachery, greed, or grossness ⟨all those features which distinguish the errors of magnanimous and intrepid spirits from *base* and malignant crimes —T.B.Macaulay⟩ ⟨*base* self-centered indulgence and selfish ambition —W.R.Inge⟩ LOW may connote crafty cunning, vulgarity, or immorality ⟨a man who by exercising a *low* sort of cunning, has managed to grab three or four millions of money selling bad whiskey —G.B. Shaw⟩ ⟨some sporting events of a *low* type, such as setting on men, women, or animals to fight —G.M.Trevelyan⟩ VILE, the most extreme of these three words, often suggests depravity or filth ⟨a jeering intention in his meanly unctuous tone, something more *vile* than mere cruelty —Joseph Conrad⟩ ⟨*vile* abuse and unbelievable blasphemies poured from her snarling lips —W.H.Wright⟩ ⟨the jail was a *vile* place, in which most kinds of debauchery and villainy were practiced, and where dire diseases were bred —Charles Dickens⟩ or, unlike BASE and LOW, is often used as a strong synonym for *objectionable* or *poor* ⟨curses . . . for the *vile* drinks he had been the means of introducing there —W.M.Thackeray⟩

⁵**base** [⁴*base*] *obs var of* ²BASS

base angle *n* [³*base*] **:** the horizontal angle between the base line and the orienting line in artillery fire measured from the base line in the same direction as angles are measured by the sight on the gun

base·ball \'ˌ,ˌ\ *n, often attrib* [¹*base* (goal) + *ball*] **1 :** a game played with a ball, bat, and gloves between 2 teams of 9 players each on a large field centering upon 4 bases that form the corners of a square 90 feet on each side, each team having a turn at bat and in the field during each of the 9 innings that constitute a normal game, the winner being the team that scores the most runs — see BALL 3a, b, STRIKE, OUT; FAIR BALL, FOUL BALL; INFIELD, OUTFIELD **2 :** a ball having a cork or rubber center wound tightly with twine and covered with two pieces of bleached white horsehide stitched together, officially from 5 to 5¼ ounces in weight and from 9 to 9¼ inches in circumference **3 :** a form of seven-card stud poker in which nines and threes are wild and threes and fours when dealt face up give the recipient certain special privileges

baseball field: *1* pitcher, *2* catcher, *3* first baseman, *4* second baseman, *5* third baseman, *6* shortstop, *7* left fielder, *8* center fielder, *9* right fielder, *a* first base, *b* second base, *c* third base, *d* home plate, *e* batter's box, *f* catcher's line, *g* foul line, *h* coach's box

baseball stitch *n* **:** a stitch for making two edges just meet worked under and over from the inside outward and used esp. in seaming baseball covers and mending tears in sails

baseboard \'ˌ,ˌ\ *n* [¹*base* + *board*] **:** a board situated at or forming the base of something ⟨the ~ of a camera⟩; *specif* **:** a protecting or finish molding of board or other material covering the joint of a wall and the adjoining floor

baseboard heating *n* **:** panel heating by means of baseboards

baseborn \'ˌ,ˌ\ *adj* [⁴*base* + *born*] **1 a :** of humble birth **:** LOWLY **b :** of illegitimate birth **:** BASTARD **2 :** MEANSPIRITED, IGNOBLE

base box *n* **:** a unit of area for tin plate and terneplate equal to 31,360 square inches or 217.78 square feet or 20.232 square meters corresponding to the area covered by 112 plates of 14 by 20 inches each

base broom *n* **:** WOODWAXEN

base bullion *n* [⁴*base*] **:** crude lead containing silver or gold and silver

base burner *n* [¹*base*] **:** a stove in which the fuel is fed from a hopper as the lower layer is consumed

base circle *n* [¹*base*] **:** the circle of an involute gear wheel from which the involute forming the outline of the tooth face is generated

base coat *n* [³*base*] **1 :** the plaster underlying the finish coat and consisting of a single coat or of separately applied scratch coat and brown coat **2 :** PRIMING 1b(2)

base course *n* [³*base*] **1 a :** the first or lowest course of a wall (as of a foundation wall or of the wall of a building above the basement) **b :** the bottom layer of material laid down in the construction of a pavement **2** *of a ship* **:** a straight-line course ⟨the destroyer turned back to *base course*⟩

base-court \'ˌ,ˌ\ *n* [MF *basse-court*, fr. *basse* (fem. of *bas* low) + *court* — more at *base*] **1 a :** the lower or outer court of a castle or mansion **:** BAILEY **b :** the rear courtyard of a farmhouse **2 :** an English inferior court of law

based \'bāst\ *adj* [¹*base* + *-ed*] **:** having a base or having as a base ⟨firmly ~ ice⟩ ⟨a soundly ~ argument⟩

ba·se·dow's disease \'bäzə,dōz-\ *n, usu cap B* [after Karl von *Basedow* †1854 Ger. physician] **:** EXOPHTHALMIC GOITER

base elbow *n* [¹*base*] **:** a cast-iron pipe bend having a flange or pad cast on it as a seat for a supporting column or bracket

base esquire *n* [⁴*base*] *heraldry* **:** the lower of the halves of a canton divided diagonally

base exchange *n* [¹*base*] **:** CATION EXCHANGE

base fee *or* **base fee simple** *n* [³*base*] **1 :** a determinable fee; *broadly* **:** a defeasible fee-simple estate (as a conditional fee) **2** *obs* **a :** an estate held by a tenant at the will of his lord or superior **b :** the status of an estate conveyed by a tenant in tail out of possession as a fee simple without proper adherence to the relevant rules of law

basehearted \'ˌ;ˌ\ *adj* **:** having a base heart

base hit *n* [¹*base*] **:** a hit in baseball that enables the batter to reach base safely with no error being made and no base runner being forced out on the play

base horehound *n* [⁴*base*] **1 :** WHITE DEAD NETTLE **2 :** a common European woundwort (*Stachys germanica*) with ashy gray foliage and pinkish white flowers

base knob *n* [¹*base*] **:** a knob often made partly of rubber and fastened to a baseboard to prevent a door from striking the wall

ba·sel \'bäzəl, 'bäz-\ *adj, usu cap* [fr. *Basel*, Switzerland] **:** of or from the city of Basel, Switzerland **:** of the kind or style prevalent in Basel

base·less \'bāslǝs\ *adj* [¹*base* + *-less*] **:** having no base **:** GROUNDLESS ⟨a ~ fear⟩ — **base·less·ly** *adv* — **base·less·ness** *n* -ES

¹**baselevel** \'ˌ;ˌˌ\ *n* [¹*base* + *level*] **:** the level below which a land surface cannot be reduced by running water

²**baselevel** \"\ *vt* **:** to reduce to or toward the condition of a plain at baselevel

baselevel plain \'ˌ,ˌˌ-\ *n* **:** a plain produced by the degradation of a region to its baselevel — compare PENEPLAIN

base line *n* [¹*base*] **:** a main line taken as or representing a base: as **a :** BASE 6b; *specif* **:** a line extending east and west from a chosen reference point on a principal meridian and forming with the meridian a pair of coordinate axes for locating township and section corners — used in U.S. public-land surveying **b :** the line joining the base piece and the base point in artillery fire **c :** the lowest horizontal line in a profile drawing of a ship used as a base for vertical measurements **d** *of a perspective drawing* **:** the line formed by the intersection of the ground plane and the picture plane **e :** the area within which a baseball player must keep when running between bases **f :** the back line at each end of a tennis court — see TENNIS illustration **g :** the lower horizontal guideline for aligning capitals in freehand lettering **h :** a known quantity used as a control for further experimentation

base·lin·er \'bā,slīnə(r)\ *n* -S [*base line* + *-er*] **:** a tennis player who usu. plays near the base line

ba·sel·la \bə'selə, -'zе-\ *n, cap* [NL, prob. fr. a native name in India] **:** a genus of herbaceous annual or biennial vines (the type of the family Basellaceae) having sessile flowers on thickened pedicels and being natives of tropical Asia and Africa where they are used as potherbs — see MALABAR NIGHTSHADE

bas·el·la·ce·ae \,basə'lāsē,ē, -azə-\ *n pl, cap* [NL, fr. *Basella*, type genus + *-aceae*] **:** a small family of usu. climbing herbs (order Caryophyllales) sometimes included in the Chenopodiaceae but distinguished by having the calyx and corolla dissimilar — **bas·el·la·ceous** \ˌ;ˌˌ;ˌshəs\ *adj*

base·ly *adv* [⁴*base* + *-ly*] **:** in a base manner **:** DISHONORABLY, IGNOBLY, SHAMEFULLY ⟨few . . . have been clearly and ~ faithless to their society —C.W.deKiewiet⟩

base·man \'bāsmən\ *n, pl* **basemen :** a man stationed at a base

base map *n* [³*base*] **:** a map having only essential outlines and used for the plotting or presentation of specialized data of various kinds

base·ment \'bāsmənt\ *n* -S *often attrib* [prob. fr. ¹*base* + *-ment*] **1 :** the architectural member that serves as a pedestal or substructure for the main order; *specif* **:** the ground floor facade in Renaissance architecture **2 a :** the part of a building that is wholly or partly below ground level; *esp* **:** such a room having overlaid or hard-surface flooring and housing a furnace — compare CELLAR **b :** the interior at ground level in a basement house or in a building having a basement facade **3 :** the lowest or fundamental part of anything ⟨the ~ of the fountain —Charles Dickens⟩ **4 a :** BASEMENT COMPLEX **b :** a compact firm rock underlying less firmly consolidated earth materials ⟨atolls can grow on various types of ~s —F.P.Shepard⟩ **5** *chiefly New Eng* **:** an indoor school toilet or washroom ⟨the boy's ~⟩

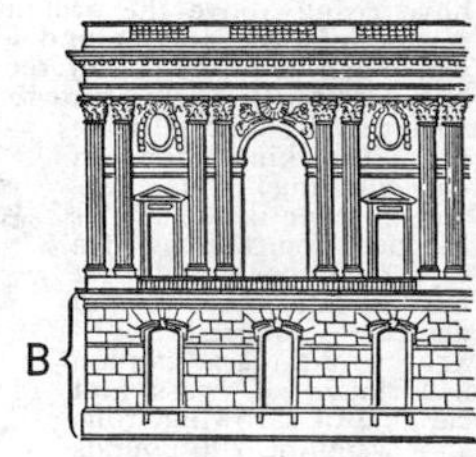

B basement

basement complex *n* **1 :** the assemblage of metamorphic and igneous rocks underlying stratified rocks in a particular region **2 :** the Archean rocks — compare FUNDAMENTAL COMPLEX

basement house *n* **:** a dwelling in which the principal drawing rooms are located at least one story above ground level with the main entrance at ground level or one story above and reached by exterior steps

basement membrane *n* **:** a delicate connective tissue membrane commonly composed of a single layer of flat cells and underlying the epithelial cells of many organs

base metal *n* [⁴*base*] **1 :** a metal or alloy (as zinc, lead, or brass) of comparatively low value and relatively inferior in certain properties (as resistance to corrosion) — opposed to *noble metal* **2 :** the metal to which a coating or plating is applied **:** the metal existing underneath a coating or plating **3 :** the chief constituent of any alloy **4 :** the metal composing parts to be welded

base molding *n* [¹*base*] **:** a molding along the upper margin of a baseboard or other plinth

bas·en·dite \'bā'sen,dīt\ *n* -S [¹*base* + *endite*] **:** either of a pair of lobes attached at the end of each of the specialized paired appendages of a crustacean — compare ENDITE, EXITE

base·ness \'bāsnǝs\ *n* -ES [⁴*base* + *-ness*] **1 :** the quality or state of being base ⟨moral ~⟩ **2 :** a base act or trait ⟨perpetrate a ~ so unmixed —Robert Browning⟩

base net *n* [¹*base*] **:** a system of triangles and quadrilaterals including and immediately adjacent to a base line in a triangulation system

ba·sen·ji \bə'senjē\ *n* [of Bantu origin; akin to Lingala & Tshiluba *basenji*, pl. of Lingala *mosenji*, Tshiluba *musenji* native, inhabitant of the hinterland] **1** *usu cap* **:** an African breed of small compact curly-tailed chestnut-brown dogs that rarely bark **2** *-s sometimes cap* **:** any dog of the Basenji breed

base of fire [¹*base*] **:** an element of one or more military units that give supporting fire to an attacking unit

base on balls [¹*base*] **:** an advance to first base given to a baseball player who during his time at bat receives four pitches outside the strike zone ⟨was given an intentional *base on balls* in the seventh inning⟩ — called also *pass, walk*

base paper *or* **base stock** *n* [¹*base*] **:** BODY PAPER

base path *n* [¹*base*] **:** the area between the bases of a baseball field used by a base runner

base pay *or* **base salary** *or* **base wage** *n* [³*base*] **:** BASIC WAGE; *specif* **:** the minimum pay for a given rank or grade of a member of the armed forces ⟨retired for life upon three-quarters of his *base pay* —Nancy B. Shea⟩

base period *n* [³*base*] **:** a period of business or economic activity used as a basis or reference point esp. for indexing, calculating, estimating, or adjudicating prices, taxes, compensation, income, and production

base piece *n* [³*base*] **:** the piece of a gun battery for which the initial firing data are computed

baseplate \'ˌ,ˌ\ *n* [³*base* + *plate*] **1 :** a plate that serves as a base or support: as **a :** the foundation plate of heavy machinery (as of a steam engine) **:** BEDPLATE **b :** the steel or cast-iron plate on which a column rests **c :** the metal plate that serves as a base and firing support for the breech end of a mortar **2 a :** the portion of an artificial denture in contact with the jaw **b :** the sheet of plastic material used in the making of trial denture plates

baseplug \'ˌ,ˌ\ *n* [¹*base* + *plug*] **:** an electric wall receptacle; *esp* **:** one in or near the baseboard

base price *n* [³*base*] **1 :** a price for a standard commodity from which variations are readily computed (as by a formula) **2 :** a price before discounts and extras

baser *comparative of* BASE

base rate *n* [³*base*] **:** an established and usu. guaranteed rate of pay per unit of time (as per hour or day) or for production at the standard rate

base right *n* [³*base*] **:** the right in Scots law acquired by a disponee taking feudal property to hold as subvassal

base ring *n* [¹*base*] **1 :** a projecting band of metal around the breech of a muzzle-loading cannon — see CANNON illustration **2 :** the circular base of a heavy gun carriage

base rocker *or* **base rocking chair** *n* [¹*base*] **:** a rocking chair fastened upon a base that is usu. mounted on casters

base runner *n* [¹*base*] **:** a baseball player of the team at bat who is on base or is attempting to reach a base — **base·running** \'ˌ,ˌˌ\ *n*

bases *pl of* BASE *or of* BASIS, *pres 3d sing of* BASE

base shoe *n* [¹*base*] **:** a narrow molding often of quarter round joining the bottom of a baseboard and the floor

basest *superlative of* BASE

base stock method *n* [³*base*] **:** an accounting method of valuing inventories by carrying on the books a minimum quantity of a commodity at the same low fixed price from year to year and valuing the quantity in excess of the minimum at a separate price which is usu. the lower of cost or market value — compare LAST IN, FIRST OUT

base stone *n* [³*base*] **:** FOOTING STONE

base surge *n* [¹*base*] **:** the cloud of mist, water, and debris that spreads outward from the surface point of an underwater atomic explosion

base time *n* [³*base*] **:** the time calculated as the normal time required by a qualified individual working at normal pace for completion of a given work cycle with no allowance for delay or fatigue and personal needs

¹**bash** \'bash, -aa(ə)-,-ai-\ *vb* -ED/-ING/-S [origin unknown] *vt* **:** to strike violently **:** BEAT, KNOCK ⟨~ him on the head with a club⟩ **:** smash by a blow — often used with *in* ⟨the tree ~*ed* in the roof⟩ ~ *vi* **1 :** CRASH ⟨the car ~*ed* into a tree⟩ **2** *Brit* **:** HIT, KNOCK ⟨a branch ~*ing* against the window⟩; *also* **:** to punch with the fist — **bash one's ear** *chiefly Austral* **:** to talk long and insistently to one

²**bash** \"\ *n* -ES **1** *chiefly Brit* **:** a forceful blow **2** *slang Brit* **:** a good time **:** ENTERTAINMENT

ba·sha \bä'shä, 'ˌ(,)ˌ\ *n* -S [Assamese] **:** an Assamese hut typically made of bamboo and grass

bash·am's mixture \'bashəmz-\ *n, usu cap B* [after William R. *Basham* †1877 Eng. physician] **:** an aromatic solution of iron and ammonium acetate formerly used as a hematinic

bashaw *often cap, var of* PASHA

bash·er \'bashə(r), -aash-,-aish-\ *n* -S [¹*bash* + *-er*] **:** one that bashes; *esp, chiefly Austral* **:** a criminal who beats and robs his victims

bash·ful \'bashfəl, -aash-, -aish-\ *adj* [obs. *bash* to be abashed (fr. ME *basshen*, short for *abasshen*) + *-ful* — more at ABASH] **1 :** inclined to shrink from public attention **:** socially shy or timid **:** SELF-CONSCIOUS, DIFFIDENT ⟨he hesitated, awkward and ~, shifted his weight from one leg to the other —Jack London⟩ ⟨they considered themselves a tough outfit and weren't ~ about letting anybody know it —F.B. Gipson⟩ **2 :** characterized by, showing, or resulting from extreme sensitiveness, self-consciousness, or shyness ⟨found that ~ words tumbling from his tongue's end really spelled themselves out into sensible talk —Carl Sandburg⟩ **syn** see SHY

bashful billy *n, usu cap 2d B* **:** LORIS 1b

bash·ful·ly \-fəlē, -li\ *adv* **:** in a bashful manner

bash·ful·ness \-fəlnəs\ *n* -ES **:** the quality or state of being bashful

bashi-ba·zouk \,bashēbə'zük\ *n* -S [Turk *başı bozuk* irregular soldier, fr. *baş* head, leader + *bozuk* depraved, corrupt] **1 a :** a member of an irregular ill-disciplined auxiliary of the Ottoman Empire **b :** IRREGULAR **2 :** a turbulent ill-disciplined person

bashing *n* -S [fr. gerund of ¹*bash*] **:** BEATING ⟨they have both had a ~⟩

bash·kir \(')bash¦ki(ə)r\ *n, pl* **bashkir** *or* **bashkirs** *usu cap* [Russ, of Turkic origin; akin to Jagatai *badžkyr* Bashkir, Chuvash *puškərt*] **1 a :** a Turkic-speaking Muslim people between the Volga and the Ural mountains regarded as tatarized Finns **b :** a member of the Bashkir people **2 :** the language of the Bashkirs

bash·lyk *also* **bash·lik** \(')bash¦lik\ *n* -S [Russ *bashlyk*, fr. Turk *başlık* hood, fr. *baş* head] **:** a protective hood with long ends for use as a scarf worn esp. by the Russian military

ba·si \'bäsē\ *n* -S [native name in the Philippines] **:** a fermented beverage prepared by natives of the Philippines

basi- *in pronunciations below* ¦ˌˌ = ¦bāsē *(bef vowels or consonants) or* -sə *(bef consonants)*\ *also* **baso-** *comb form* [ISV, fr. L *basis*] **1 a :** base **:** lower part ⟨*basipetal*⟩ **b :** at or near the base ⟨*basifixed*⟩ ⟨*basiglandular*⟩ **c :** of or belonging to the base of ⟨*basicranial*⟩ **2 a :** chemical base ⟨*basify*⟩ **b :** subsilicic and ⟨*basiophitic*⟩

ba·si·al \'bāsēəl\ *adj* [*basi-* + *-al*] **:** of or relating to the basion

¹**ba·si·branchial** \¦ˌˌ *at* BASI- + \ *adj* [*basi-* + *branchial*] **:** of, relating to, or being a median bone or cartilage at the ventral point of a branchial arch

²**basibranchial** \"\ *n* -S **:** a basibranchial bone or cartilage

ba·si-bregmatic height \¦ˌˌ+ . . . -\ *var of* BASION-BREGMA HEIGHT

¹**ba·sic** \'bāsik, ¦ēk *sometimes* -āz|\ *adj* [¹*base* + *-ic*] **1 :** of, relating to, or forming the base or essence **:** FUNDAMENTAL, ESSENTIAL, IRREDUCIBLE ⟨a ~ fact⟩ ⟨a ~ argument⟩ ⟨~ truths⟩ **2 :** constituting or serving as the basis or starting point ⟨a ~ house⟩ **3 a :** of, relating to, or characteristic of a base ⟨~ groups⟩ ⟨~ nitrogen⟩ — compare ALKALINE **b :** having an alkaline reaction ⟨~ compounds⟩ ⟨a ~ catalyst⟩ **c** *of salts* **:** derived by partial neutralization ⟨~ lead carbonate⟩ ⟨~ bismuth chloride⟩ **d :** containing or involving the use of alkaline material ⟨a furnace with a ~ lining⟩ — see BASIC PROCESS **e :** base-forming ⟨lime is a ~ oxide⟩ **4** *of rocks* **:** containing relatively little silica **:** SUBSILICIC — opposed to *acid* **5 :** relating to or made by a basic process ⟨~ steel⟩ ⟨~ rails⟩ **6** *of language* **:** having a vocabulary that consists of a very small number of words but that can be used to convey a wide range of ideas or information ⟨~ French⟩ **7 :** assigned for general duties within a military organization ⟨a ~ private⟩ **8 :** prescribed and nominal — used of standards (as of size) that are the basis for the calculation of allowances and tolerances

²**basic** \"\ *n* -S **1 :** something that is basic **:** FUNDAMENTAL — usu. used in pl. ⟨the ~s of honesty⟩ ⟨the ~s of sewing⟩ **2 :** BASIC TRAINING ⟨took his ~ at Keesler Field⟩

basic airman *n* **:** an airman undergoing basic training in the U.S. Air Force

ba·si·cal·ly \¦ək(ə)lē, ¦ēk-, -li\ *adv* **:** FUNDAMENTALLY, ESSENTIALLY

basic anxiety *n, psychol* **:** a feeling of helplessness and personal isolation

basic crew *n* **1 :** the group or number of employees considered necessary for continuous operation (as of a business or factory) **2 :** a limited number or prescribed group of employees subject to guaranteed wage provisions in a labor contract

basic crop *or* **basic commodity** *n* **:** an agricultural product deemed of sufficient economic or political importance to be designated by the U.S. Congress for special production controls or price supports

basic dress *n* **:** a simple classic dress usu. of a solid color and adaptable to many occasions by a change of accessories

basic dye *or* **basic color** *n* **:** any of various chiefly synthetic dyes reacting as bases because of the presence of certain nitrogen-containing groups (as amino groups), producing clear brilliant colors that are not very fast to light, and being used in the form of water-soluble salts in the dyeing of textiles and as histological stains or as water-insoluble free bases as the coloring ingredient of certain products (as inks, plastics, or shoe polishes) — see DYE table I

basic english *also* **basic** *n* -s *cap B&E* **:** a copyrighted system of simplified English consisting of the 850 words considered most essential and of a short list of grammatical rules and designed to serve both as an auxiliary language and as an introduction to English

basic fuchsin *n* **:** a complex red phenyl methane dye important as a biological stain

ba·si·chromatic \¦== *at* BASI- +\ *adj* [*basi-* + *chromatic*] **1 :** capable of being stained with basic dyes **2** [*basichromatin* + *-ic*] **:** composed of basichromatin **:** BASICHROMATINIC

ba·si·chromatin \"+\ *n* -s [ISV *basi-* + *chromatin;* orig. formed in G] **:** basophilic chromatin — **ba·si·chromatinic** \"+\ *adj*

basic iron *n* **:** pig iron that contains a high percentage of phosphorus and is used for making steel by a basic process that removes the phosphorus

ba·sic·i·ty \bā'sisəd·ē\ *n* -ES [*basic* + *-ity*] **1 :** the quality, state, or degree of being a base ⟨the ~ of a slag⟩ **2 :** the power of an acid to react with one or more equivalents of a base according to the number of replaceable hydrogen atoms contained in the acid

basic lime *n* **:** a superphosphate to which enough lime has been added to change water-soluble phosphate to the citrate= soluble form

basic–lined \¦=¦=\ *adj, of a metallurgic furnace* **:** lined with basic material (as dolomite, magnesite, or basic slag)

basic nitrogen *n* **:** nitrogen present in the form of a base; *specif* **:** nitrogen or the proportion of the total nitrogen present in protein or its products of hydrolysis in predominantly basic radicals (as in arginine, histidine, and lysine) as distinguished from nitrogen in radicals whose basicity is modified by adjacent acidic radicals

basic pay *n* **:** pay that includes the base pay and longevity of a member of the armed forces

basic pilot training *n* **:** the second stage of flying training in the U.S. Air Force in which students qualify to solo single-engine jet fighter aircraft or multi-engine aircraft and at the conclusion of which they receive pilot ratings and, if cadets, commissions as second lieutenants

basic process *n* **:** a process (as in steelmaking) carried on in a furnace lined with basic material (as magnesite, dolomite, lime, or iron oxide) and under a slag that is dominantly basic — opposed to *acid process;* compare BESSEMER PROCESS

basic proposition *or* **basic statement** *n* **:** PROTOCOL STATEMENT

ba·si·cranial \¦== *at* BASI- +\ *adj* [*basi-* + *cranial*] **:** of or relating to the base of the skull

basic rate *n* **:** BASE RATE

basic science *n* **:** any one of the sciences (as anatomy, physiology, bacteriology, pathology, or biochemistry) fundamental to the study of medicine

basic size *n* **:** a sheet size used as a standard in the paper industry (as 17 x 22 in. for ledger, bond, and writing papers)

basic slag *n* **:** a slag low in silica and high in base-forming oxides; *specif* **:** a slag that is used to remove phosphorus and other elements from pig iron in the basic process of steelmaking and that contains sufficient phosphorus after such use to be used as a fertilizer

basic stain *n* **:** a basic dye used as a stain

basic steel *n* **:** steel made by a basic process

basic training *n* **:** the initial period of training of a military recruit

basic wage *or* **basic salary** *n* **1 :** a wage or salary based on the cost of living and used as a standard for calculating rates of pay **2 :** a rate of pay for a standard work period exclusive of such additional payments as bonuses and overtime

basic weight *also* **basic substance weight** *n* **:** BASIS WEIGHT

basic yield *n* **:** the rate of return in interest or dividends upon the actual amount of an investment

basidi- *or* **basidio-** *comb form* [NL, fr. *basidium*] **:** basidium **:** basidial ⟨*basidio*spore⟩ ⟨*Basidio*mycetes⟩

basidia *pl of* BASIDIUM

ba·sid·i·al \bə'sidēəl\ *adj* [NL *basidium* + E *-al*] **:** relating to, characterized by, or consisting of a basidium or basidia ⟨a ~ layer⟩

ba·si·dig·i·ta·le \¦== *at* BASI- + ˌdijə'ta(ˌ)lē, -ä(ˌ)lē, -ä(ˌ)lē\ *n, pl* **basidigita·lia** \-lēə\ [NL, fr. *basi-* + L *digitalis* pertaining to the fingers — more at DIGITAL] **:** a cartilage or bone at the base of a digit **:** METACARPAL, METATARSAL

ba·sid·io·carp \bə'sidēōˌkärp, -ēə,-\ *n* -s [*basidi-* + *-carp*] **:** the basidium-bearing fruiting body of a basidiomycete

ba·sid·io·lichen \=¦===+\ *n* [NL *Basidiolichenes*] **:** a lichen of the group Basidiolichenes — compare ASCOLICHEN, DISCOLICHEN

ba·sid·io·lichenes \=,===+\ *n pl, cap* [NL, fr. *basidi-* + *Lichenes*] **:** a group of lichens consisting of the few genera in which the component fungus is a basidiomycete — compare ASCOLICHENES

ba·sid·io·my·cete \=,===+'mīˌsēt,mī'sēt\ *n* -s [NL *Basidiomycetes*] **:** a fungus of the Basidiomycetes

ba·sid·io·my·ce·tes \"+mī'sēd·ˌēz\ *n pl, cap* [NL, fr. *basidi-* + *-mycetes*] **:** a large class of higher fungi distinguished by having septate hyphae and bearing the spores on a basidium produced either directly from the mycelium or as an outgrowth of a spore — see HETEROBASIDIOMYCETES, HOMOBASIDIOMYCETES; compare PROMYCELIUM — **ba·sid·io·my·ce·tous** \=¦===+mī¦sēd·əs\ *adj*

ba·sid·io·phore \=¦===+ˌfō(ə)r\ *n* -s [*basidi-* + *-phore*] **:** a sporophore bearing basidia

ba·sid·io·spore \=¦===ˌspō(ə)r\ *n* -s [*basidi-* + *spore*] **:** a spore produced by a basidium — **ba·sid·io·spo·rous** \=¦===¦spōrəs, =¦==¦äspərəs\ *adj*

ba·sid·i·um \bə'sidēəm\ *n, pl* **basid·ia** \-ēə\ [NL, fr. *basi-* + *-idium*] **:** a structure on a basidiomycete in which nuclear fusion occurs followed by meiosis and on which usu. four basidiospores are borne — compare HEMIBASIDIUM, PROMYCELIUM

ba·si·facial \¦== *at* BASI- +\ *adj* [*basi-* + *facial*] **:** of or relating to the lower part of the face

ba·si·fi·ca·tion \ˌbāsəfə'kāshən\ *n* -s **:** the act or process of basifying

ba·si·fixed \¦== *at* BASI-+\ *adj* [*basi-* + *fixed*] *bot* **:** attached at or near the base ⟨a ~ anther⟩ — compare VERSATILE 3b

ba·sif·u·gal \(')bā¦sif(y)əgəl\ *adj* [*basi-* + *-fugal*] **:** ACROPETAL

ba·si·fy \'bāsəˌfī\ *vt* -ED/-ING/-ES [¹*base* + *-ify*] **:** to convert into a base **:** make alkaline

¹**ba·si·hy·al** \¦== *at* BASI- + ¦hīəl\ *adj* [ISV *basi-* + *hyoid* + *-al*] **1 :** of, relating to, or being a median element or bone at the ventral point of the hyoid arch that in man forms the body of the hyoid bone **2 :** HYPOHYAL

²**basihyal** \"\ *n* -s **:** a basihyal bone

ba·si·hyoid \¦== *at* BASI- +\ *adj or n* [*basi-* + *hyoid*] **:** BASIHYAL

¹**bas·il** \'bazəl *also* 'bās- *or* 'bas- *or* 'bāz-\ *n* -s [MF *basile,* fr. LL *basilicum,* fr. Gk *basilikon,* fr. neut. of *basilikos* royal — more at BASILICA] **:** any of several aromatic plants: as **a :** any plant of the genus *Ocimum; esp* **:** SWEET BASIL — see BUSH BASIL **b :** MOUNTAIN MINT 1

²**basil** \"\ *n* -s [modif. of F *basane,* fr. Prov *bazana,* fr. Sp *badana,* fr. Ar *biṭānah,* lit., lining] **:** sheepskin tanned with bark — distinguished from *roan*

³**bas·il** \'bazəl\ *n* -s [by alter.] **:** BEZEL 1

bas·i·lar \'basələ(r)\ *also* **bas·i·lary** \-ˌlerē\ *adj* [irreg. fr. *basis* + *-ar, -ary*] *biol* **:** of, relating to, or situated at the base

basilar artery *n* **:** an unpaired artery formed by the uniting of the two vertebrals, running forward within the skull just under the pons, dividing into the two posterior cerebrals, and supplying the pons, cerebellum, posterior part of the cerebrum, and the internal ear

basilar groove *n* **:** the depression in the upper surface of the basilar process on which the medulla rests

basilar index *n* **:** the ratio of the distance between the basion and the alveolar point to the total length of the skull multiplied by 100

basilar membrane *n* **:** a supporting membrane; *specif* **:** the membrane that extends from the margin of the bony shelf of the cochlea to the outer wall and that supports the organ of Corti

basilar meningitis *n* **:** a usu. tuberculous inflammation of the meninges at the base of the brain

basilar plate *n* **:** a cartilaginous plate formed of the fused parachordals and anterior notochord that gives rise to the ethmoid and certain other bones of the vertebrate skull

basilar process *n* **:** an anterior median projection of the occipital bone in front of the foramen magnum articulating in front with the body of the sphenoid by the basilar suture

basil balm *n* [¹*basil*] **1 :** a perennial herb (*Monarda clinopodia*) of eastern No. America with aromatic foliage and whitish or yellowish pink flowers **2 :** a fragrant European mint (*Satureia acinos*) naturalized esp. in eastern No. America

ba·si·leus \ˌbäsə'leůs\ *n, pl* **basi·leis** \-'lās\ [Gk] **:** a ruler of the Eastern Roman Empire

¹**ba·sil·ian** \bə'zilēən, -lyən *also* -'si-\ *adj, usu cap* [St. *Basil* †*ab* A.D.379 Cappadocian church father + E *-ian*] **:** of or relating to St. Basil or to the order following his monastic rule

²**basilian** \"\ *n* -s *usu cap* **:** one who follows the Basilian rule

basilian rule *n, usu cap B* **:** a series of ascetic precepts for cenobites of either sex written by St. Basil and forming the basis of the statutes of practically all monasteries in the Eastern churches

¹**ba·sil·ic** \bə'silik, -lēk *also* -'zi-\ *also* **ba·sil·i·cal** \-ləkəl, -ēk-\ *adj* [L *basilicus,* fr. Gk *basilikos*] **:** of great importance **:** KINGLY, ROYAL

²**basilic** \"\ *n* -s [F *basilique,* fr. L *basilica*] **:** BASILICA

³**basilic** \"\ *also* **basilical** \"\ *adj* **:** BASILICAN

ba·sil·i·ca \bə'siləkə, -lēkə *also* -'zi-\ *n, pl* **basilicas** \-kəz\ *also* **basili·cae** \-ˌkī, -ˌsē, -ˌchā\ [L, fr. Gk *basilikē,* fr. fem. of *basilikos* royal, fr. *basileus* king + *-ikos* -ic] **1 :** an oblong building typically with a broad nave flanked by colonnaded aisles or porticoes and ending in a semicircular apse used in ancient Rome esp. for a court of justice and place of public assembly **2** [LL, fr. L] **:** an early Christian church building consisting of nave and aisles with clerestory, sometimes a narthex, and a large high transept from which an apse projects and in its simplest form having a wooden roof, brick walls, and decorations usu. in mosaic or interior painting **3 :** a Roman Catholic church or cathedral having certain liturgical privileges — used as a canonical title ⟨the church was raised to the rank of ~⟩

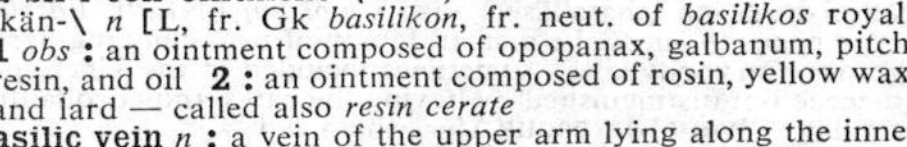

basilica 2: *1* narthex, *2* nave, *3* aisle, *4* altar, *5* bema, *6* apse, *7* transept

ba·sil·i·can \-kən\ *adj* [ML *basilicanus,* fr. LL *basilica* + L *-anus* -an] **:** of, relating to, or resembling a basilica **:** having nave and aisles with clerestory ⟨churches of the ~ form⟩

ba·sil·i·con ointment \-kən-, -lə-, -ˌkän-\ *n* [L, fr. Gk *basilikon,* fr. neut. of *basilikos* royal] **1** *obs* **:** an ointment composed of opopanax, galbanum, pitch, resin, and oil **2 :** an ointment composed of rosin, yellow wax, and lard — called also *resin cerate*

basilic vein *n* **:** a vein of the upper arm lying along the inner border of the biceps muscle, draining the whole limb, and opening into the axillary vein

¹**bas·i·lid·i·an** \ˌbasə¦lidēən, -azə-\ *adj, usu cap* [*Basilides* †*ab* A.D.140 gnostic of Alexandria + E *-ian*] **:** of, relating to, or taught by Basilides, a Gnostic of Alexandria

²**basilidian** \"\ *n* -s *usu cap* **:** a follower of Basilides

bas·i·lis·cus \ˌbasə'liskəs, -azə-\ *n, cap* [NL, fr. L, basilisk] **:** a genus of active carnivorous lizards (family Iguanidae) that have rising above the occiput a membranous pouch which can be inflated with air and along the back a movable crest which can be raised or lowered at will — see BASILISK 3

¹**bas·i·lisk** \'basəˌlisk, -azə- *sometimes* -āsə-\ *n* -s [ME, fr. L *basiliscus,* fr. Gk *basiliskos,* lit., little king, dim. of *basileus* king] **1 :** a legendary reptile that is hatched from the egg of a 7-year-old cock and that has a fatal breath and glance — compare COCKATRICE **2 :** a large cannon usu. made of brass and capable of throwing stone shot weighing 200 pounds **3 :** any of several tropical American lizards (genus *Basiliscus*) noted for their activity and ability to run at high speed upon their hind legs

basilisk 3

²**basilisk** \"\ *adj* **:** like a basilisk **:** SPELLBINDING, FATAL ⟨the eyes fell full upon me with all their blaze of ~ horror —Bram Stoker⟩

basil mint *n* [¹*basil*] **:** a mountain mint (*Pycnanthemum virginianum*) of eastern No. America with narrow leaves and inconspicuous greenish white flowers

basil oil *n* [¹*basil*] **:** a yellowish essential oil obtained from the flowering tops of sweet basil and used as a flavoring material and in perfumery — called also *sweet basil oil*

bas·i·lo·sau·rus \ˌbasəlō'sȯrəs\ *n, cap* [NL, fr. Gk *basileus* king + NL *-o-* + *-saurus*] **:** a genus (the type of the family Basilosauridae) of large slender-bodied Eocene whales that are found most abundantly in Alabamian and Floridian rocks and that have serrated posterior teeth with two roots — see ZEUGLODONTIA

basils *pl of* BASIL

basil thyme *n* [¹*basil*] **:** any of several fragrant herbs or shrubs: as **a :** BASIL BALM 2 **b :** FIELD BASIL 1

basilweed \'==,=\ *n* [¹*basil*] **:** WILD BASIL

¹**ba·sin** \'bās³n\ *n* -s [ME *basin,* fr. OF *bacin,* fr. LL *bacchinon,* fr. (assumed) VL *bacca* water vessel, perh. of non-IE origin; akin to the source of L *baca* berry — more at BAY] **1 a :** an open usu. circular vessel or dish with sloping or curving sides and wider than its depth used typically for holding water for washing **b :** a container of similar shape: as (1) **:** the scalepan of a balance (2) **:** a tank or reservoir used for the treatment of liquids **c :** the quantity contained in a basin **2 a** (1) **:** a dock built in a tidal river or harbor and used esp. for ships discharging or loading cargo, floodgates serving to keep the water level constant ⟨constructing ships in ~*s* resembling drydocks from which they float out on completion —*Time*⟩ (2) **:** a part of a river or canal widened and provided with wharves **b** (1) **:** a water area enclosed or partly enclosed by land and suitable for anchorage of ships **:** a landlocked harbor **:** a little bay ⟨a ~ . . . provides mooring space for eighty yachts —*Amer. Guide Series: Md.*⟩ (2) **:** a water area artificially enclosed or partly enclosed (as by jetties) that is designed to shelter small craft ⟨rates for mooring boats at boat ~*s* —*N. Y. Herald Tribune*⟩ **3 a** (1) **:** a large or small depression in the surface of the land, the lowest part often being occupied by a lake or pond ⟨the ~ of Lake Michigan⟩ (2) **:** a similar depression in the ocean floor ⟨some 2000 fathoms down, but it still separates broad eastern and western ~*s* —R.E.Coker⟩ **b :** an area that does not drain to the ocean **c :** an area largely enclosed by higher lands but having an outlet and being drained ⟨the Big Horn ~⟩ **d :** the entire tract of country drained by a river and its tributaries — called also *river basin* ⟨appropriations for flood control in the Missouri ~ —*New Republic*⟩ **e :** a great depression in the surface of the lithosphere occupied by an ocean ⟨the ~ now filled by the Pacific ocean —Waldemar Kaempffert⟩ — called also *ocean basin* **4 a :** a broad area of the earth beneath which the strata dip usu. from the sides toward the center ⟨the Richmond coal ~⟩ — called also *structural basin, synclinal basin* **b :** a depression of the earth in which sedimentary materials accumulate or have accumulated usu. characterized by continuous deposition over a long period of time ⟨a salt ~⟩ **c :** rocks of such composition and having such structural and topographic relations as to facilitate the presence of artesian water ⟨an artesian ~⟩ **5 :** the depression at the apex of an apple or similar fruit **6 a :** an area enclosed so as to be flooded for subsequent cultivation ⟨a ~ for irrigation⟩ **b :** a hollow or enclosure made about the base of a tree to receive water for moistening the roots **c :** a small depression or pocket made (as with a basin lister) in a field to check water runoff

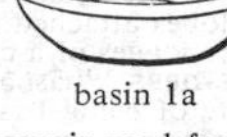
basin 1a

²**basin** \"\ *vb* **basined; basined; basining** \-s(³)niŋ\ **basins** *vt* **:** to bend down (a part of the earth's crust) in the form of a basin ⟨the rocky surface of Greenland is actually ~*ed* as if by the weight of the existing icecap —R.A.Daly⟩ ~ *vi* **:** to form a basin by erosion

ba·sin·al \-s³n³l,-snəl\ *adj* [*basin* + *-al*] **:** of or relating to a basin ⟨thick ~ deposits⟩ ⟨~ facies⟩ — **ba·sin·al·ly** \-³lē,-əlē\ *adv*

ba·sined \'bās³nd\ *adj* [¹*basin* + *-ed*] **:** enclosed in a basin

bas·i·net *or* **bas·ci·net** *also* **bas·si·net** \¦basə¦net\ *n* -s [ME *bacinet,* fr. OF, dim. of *bacin* basin — more at BASIN] **:** a light often pointed steel helmet orig. open and worn under the battle helmet but subsequently made with a visor

basing *pres part of* BASE

basing point *n* [fr. pres. part. of ²*base*] **:** a location agreed upon by sellers from which they compute transportation charges so that all customers in an area pay uniform delivery charges regardless of the exact distance to the sellers

basing point system *n* **:** a pricing system using one or more basing points

basin irrigation *n* **:** irrigation of land by surrounding it with embankments to form a basin and flooding it with water

basin range *n* [fr. the Great *Basin,* region of the western U.S.] **:** a mountain range that owes its present elevation essentially to faulting and tilting **:** a tilted fault block

basin stand *n* **:** a light table usu. made to fit into a corner to hold a basin **:** WASHSTAND

¹**ba·si·occipital** \¦== *at* BASI- +\ *adj* [*basi-* + *occipital*] **:** relating to or being a bone in the base of the cranium immediately in front of the foramen magnum, represented in man by the basilar process of the occipital

²**basioccipital** \"\ *n* -s **:** the basioccipital bone

ba·si·on \'bāsēˌän *also* -zē-\ *n* -s [NL, irreg. fr. L *basis* base — more at BASE] **:** the midpoint of the anterior margin of the foramen magnum

basion–bregma height \'==,='==-\ *or* **basi–bregmatic height** \¦== *at* BASI- + . . . -\ *n* **:** the distance between basion and bregma

basion–prosthion line *n* **:** a line from the basion to the prosthion

ba·si·ophthalmite \¦== *at* BASI- +\ *n* -s [*basi-* + *ophthalmite*] **:** the lowest joint of the eyestalk of certain crustaceans — **ba·si·oph·thal·mous** \"+¦äf'thalməs\ *adj*

ba·sip·e·tal \(')bā¦sipəd·³l\ *adj* [ISV *basi-* + *-petal*] **:** from the apex toward the base or from above downward ⟨~ differentiation of an inflorescence or leaf primordium⟩ ⟨~ movement of dissolved materials in a plant body⟩ — compare ACROPETAL — **basipetally** *adv*

ba·sip·o·dite \=¦==ˌdīt\ *n* -s [ISV *basi-* + *-podite*] **1 :** the proximal joint of the arthropod limb **2 :** the second joint, next succeeding the coxopodite, of certain limbs of crustaceans (as the ambulatory limbs of a decapod). — **ba·sip·o·dit·ic** \=¦==did·ik\ *adj*

ba·sip·ter·yg·i·al \(¦)bāˌsiptə¦rij(ē)əl\ *adj* [NL *basipterygium* + E *-al*] **:** of, relating to, or being a basipterygium

ba·sip·ter·yg·i·um \-jēəm\ *n, pl* **basipteryg·ia** \-jēə\ [NL, fr. *basi-* + Gk *pterygion* fin, lit., small wing — more at PTERYGIUM] **:** a basal bone or cartilage forming a support of one of the paired fins of a fish: **a :** a large cartilage supporting the radialia in ganoids and selachians **b :** a large bone supporting the rays of a pelvic fin in teleosts **c :** the posterior member of a group of three such supporting elements in certain fishes — compare MESOPTERYGIUM, METAPTERYGIUM, PROPTERYGIUM

ba·si·rhinal \¦== *at* BASI- +\ *or* **ba·sir·rhi·nal** \"\ *adj* [ISV *basi-* + *rhinal*] **:** situated at the base of the rhinencephalon

ba·si·rostral \¦== *at* BASI- +\ *adj* [ISV *basi-* + *rostral*] **:** related to or at the base of the bill of a bird

¹**ba·sis** \'bāsəs\ *n, pl* **ba·ses** \-āˌsēz\ [L — more at BASE] **1 a :** the bottom of anything considered as a foundation for the parts above **:** BASE, FOOT **b** *obs* **:** the pedestal of a column, pillar, or statue ⟨if no ~ bear my rising name —Alexander Pope⟩ **c :** any of certain anatomical structures that function as bases: as (1) **:** the membranous or calcareous base by which a barnacle is attached to the substrate (2) **:** BASIPODITE (3) **:** the articulated proximal part of the capitulum of a tick — called also *basis capituli* **2 :** the principal component of anything **:** fundamental ingredient **:** BASE ⟨a combination of fruit or fruit juices and sugar is the fundamental ~ of jelly⟩ **3 :** something that supports or sustains anything immaterial **:** ESSENCE ⟨his argument rested on a ~ of conjecture⟩ **4 a :** something on which anything is constructed or established ⟨Indian trails . . . were the ~ for many of their roads —*Amer. Guide Series: N.C.*⟩ **:** the basic principle **:** GROUNDWORK ⟨the frustrating task of putting international affairs on a permanent ~ of law and order —A.E.Stevenson †1965⟩ **b :** FOOTING 6 ⟨a club where everyone was on a first-name ~ —J.P.Marquand⟩ **5 a :** a rhythmic unit constituted by a given proportion of arsis to thesis without reference to the order or placement of long and short elements ⟨trochaic and iambic feet represent the same ~⟩ **b :** a free first foot in some ancient verse that admits more variation from the norm of the line than appears in subsequent feet **6 :** a glassy or felsitic noncrystalline granular material that is a last product of solidification of a volcanic rock and that forms a cement for earlier minerals **7 a :** the price difference between a specified grade of a commodity and a designated futures delivery **b :** the actual yield on an investment in bonds **c :** the original cost of property used in computing capital gains or losses for income tax purposes

²**basis** \'bāˌsēz\ *pl of* BASI

ba·si·scop·ic \¦== *at* BASI- +\ *adj* [*basi-* + *-scopic*] *bot* **:** facing or on the side toward the base ⟨the sori of most ferns are ~⟩ — compare ACROSCOPIC

¹**ba·si·sphenoid** \¦== *at* BASI- +\ *also* **ba·si·sphenoidal** \"+\ *adj* [ISV *basi-* + *sphenoid, sphenoidal*] **:** relating to or being the part of the base of the cranium that lies between the basioccipital and the presphenoid and that usu. ossifies separately and becomes a part of the sphenoid only in the adult

²**basisphenoid** \"\ *n* **:** the basisphenoid bone

basis point *n* **:** one hundredth of one percent in the yield of an investment

basis rate *n* **:** the amount of premium per unit of insurance assumed and used as a starting point for computing the specific rates to be charged to policyholders

ba·si·sternum \¦== *at* BASI- +\ *n* [NL, fr. *basi-* + *sternum*] **:** the anterior of the two sternal skeletal plates of insects

ba·si·style \"+\ *n* [*basi-* + *style*] **:** either of a pair of more or less flexible processes on the hypopygium of certain male two= winged flies

basis weight *n* **1 :** the weight in pounds of a 500-sheet ream of paper cut to a basic size — called also *basic weight, substance, substance number* **2 :** the weight of a sheet of paper expressed in terms of the weight of a ream of that paper

ba·si·tarsus \"+\ *n* [NL, fr. *basi-* + *tarsus*] **:** the basal segment of an arthropod tarsus being often conspicuously enlarged or differentiated from other segments

¹**ba·si·temporal** \"+\ *adj* [ISV *basi-* + *temporal*] **:** of, relating to, or being one of a pair of membrane bones of the skull of birds underlying and uniting with the part of the true cranium formed by the basisphenoid and basioccipital bones

²**basitemporal** \"\ *n* **:** a basitemporal bone

ba·si·vertebral \¦== *at* BASI- +\ *adj* [ISV *basi-* + *vertebral*] **:** of or relating to the centrum of a vertebra

bask \'bask, -aa(ə)-,-ai-,-á-\ *vb* -ED/-ING/-S [ME *basken,* fr. ON *bathask,* refl. of *batha* to bathe — more at BATHE] *vi* **1 :** to lie in or expose oneself to a pleasant warmth or atmosphere **:** LUXURIATE ⟨pretend that I'm still ~*ing* on the beach —Hamilton Basso⟩ ⟨the house ~*ed* in the moonlight —Agatha Christie⟩ ⟨spent 10 days in the capital, ~*ing* in civilization's comfort—*Nat'l Geographic*⟩ **2 :** to take pleasure or derive enjoyment — usu. used with *in* ⟨he ~*ed* in the smiles of the girls and was patted and complimented by the old men —Stephen Crane⟩ ~ *vt, obs* **:** to warm by continued exposure to heat ⟨~*s* at the fire his hairy strength —John Milton⟩

¹**bas·ket** \ˈbaskət, -aas-,-ais-,-ȧs-, *usu* -d·+V\ *n* -s [ME, prob. fr. (assumed) ONF *baskot* (akin to F dial. *bâchot* wicker basket), fr. (assumed) ONF *baskou, baskoue* (akin to OF *baschoue* wooden or wicker vessel), fr. L *bascauda* dishpan, of Celt origin; akin to MIr *basc* necklace — more at FASCIA] **1 a :** a receptacle made of interwoven osiers, cane, rushes, splints, or other flexible material **b :** any of various lightweight usu. wood containers in which berries, fruits, or vegetables are packed, shipped, or sold **c :** the quantity contained in a basket ⟨fishing upstream, I have sometimes in my youth had good ~*s* with the red worm —John Buchan⟩ **2** *archaic* **:** CHARITY **3 :** anything that resembles a basket esp. in shape or use: as **a** *Brit* **:** the two back seats facing one another on the outside of a stagecoach **b :** a shallow receptacle sometimes with a bail handle used to serve cake, bread, or rolls **c :** the perforated container for the ground coffee through which heated water seeps in a coffee maker **d :** a metal liner of coarse mesh made to fit into a deep fat fryer and used to hold the food for frying and to lift it from the fryer **e :** the typebars of a typewriter taken as a unit **f :** the perforated metal container in a centrifugal for holding material being processed **4 :** the box, cage, or other vessel suspended from a balloon to carry passengers, ballast, and equipment **5 a :** a net of white cord that is 15 to 18 inches long, open at the bottom, and suspended from a metal ring 18 inches in diameter and that constitutes the goal in basketball **b :** the score made by putting the ball through the basket in basketball; *esp* **:** FIELD GOAL ⟨an occasional game is won with more points scored on fouls than ~*s* —Jimmy Jemail⟩ **6 :** a square dance pattern formed by the raised interlocking arms of concentric circles of men and women

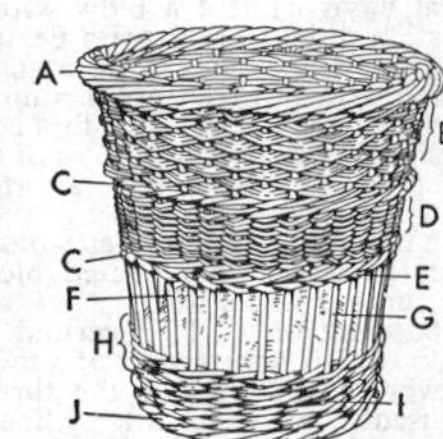

a form of basket: *A* border, *B* slew, *C* wale, *D* rand, *E* fitch, *F* stake, *G* by-stake, *H* upset, *I* end of by-stake, *J* foot

²**basket** \"\ *vt* -ED/-ING/-S **:** to put or throw into a basket ⟨the pigeons were ~*ed* and sent to several race points⟩

³**basket** \"\ *adj* **1 :** made like a basket **:** made of basketwork ⟨a ~ carriage⟩ **2 :** used for baskets or basketmaking ⟨~ osiers⟩ **3 :** with provisions brought in a basket ⟨an old-fashioned ~ picnic⟩

basket ash *n* **:** ¹BLACK ASH 1

basketball \ˈ⸗⸗,⸗\ *n, often attrib* **1 :** a game played with a ball between 2 teams of 5 players each, 6 in a women's game, on a rectangular court usu. indoors, each team attempting to throw the ball through its own basket and to prevent the other team from scoring, the winner being the team that scores the most points — see FIELD GOAL, FOUL **2 :** a spherical ball made of an airtight rubber case covered with leather officially from 29 to 30 inches in circumference and from 20 to 22 ounces in weight

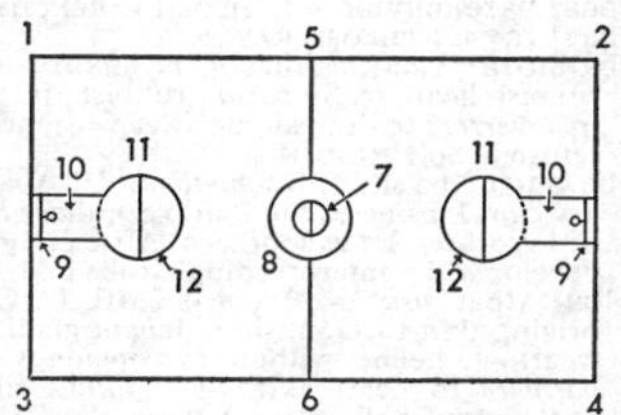

basketball court: *1 2, 3 4* sidelines, *1 3, 2 4* end lines, *5 6* division line, *7* center circle, *8* restraining circle, *9* backboard and basket, *10* free throw lane, *11* free throw line, *12* free throw circle

basket capital *n* **:** a capital of the Byzantine style with interlaced bands like those of a basket

basket case *n* **:** one who has all four limbs amputated ⟨rumors have been heard in this country about the large number of *basket cases* among our war casualties —Bruce Bliven b.1889⟩

basket cell *n* **:** any of the cells in the molecular layer of the cerebellum whose axis-cylinder processes pass inward and end in a basketlike network around the cells of Purkinje

basket chair *n* **:** a deep low wicker armchair with back and arms in one and rounded at the top

basket clam *n* **:** BASKET SHELL 1

basket cloth *n* **1 :** cloth with a basket weave **2 :** book cloth with an embossed wicker pattern

basket dance *n* **:** a women's vegetation dance of certain peoples of medieval Europe and certain Indians of the southwestern U.S., a basket serving as the focal prop

bas·ke·teer \ˌ⸗kə¦ti(ə)r\ *n* -s [*basket*ball + *-eer*] **:** a basketball player

basket fern *n* **1 :** MALE FERN **2 :** a tropical American sword fern (*Nephrolepis pectinata*) often cultivated for its finely divided grayish green foliage

basket–fired \ˈ⸗⸗,⸗\ *adj, of Japanese longleaf tea* **:** fired in baskets rather than metal pans or other containers

basket flower *n* **1 :** an annual plant (*Centaurea americana*) of the southwestern U.S. often cultivated for its purple-rayed flower heads with involucres like baskets **2 :** a spider lily (*Hymenocallis calathina*) having umbels of two to four flowers, each with linear perianth segments

bas·ket·ful \ˈ⸗⸗,fu̇l\ *n, pl* **basketfuls** *also* **basketsful** \-t,fu̇lz, -t,sfu̇l\ **1 :** as much or as many as a basket will hold ⟨a ~ of apples⟩ **2 :** a considerable quantity ⟨a whole ~ of allegories —Thomas Wood †1950⟩ ⟨a ~ of ironic commentary on contemporary truths —Henry Hewes⟩

basket grass *n* **:** TURKEY BEARD

basket–handle arch *n* **:** a low-crowned elliptical arch drawn from three or more centers — see ARCH illustration

basket hilt *n* **:** a hilt with a guard wrought like basketwork to protect the hand

basket–hilted \¦⸗⸗¦⸗⸗\ *adj* **:** having a basket hilt

basketing *pres part of* BASKET

basket maker *n, usu cap B&M* **1 :** any of three stages of an ancient culture of the plateau area of southwestern U.S. that preceded and formed one cultural development with the Pueblo, was characterized by excellent basketry and use of the spear thrower, and was marked by development from an initial nomadic preagricultural state through a cave-dwelling phase with limited agriculture to a village economy with semi-subterranean houses, agriculture, the beginnings of pottery, and use of bow and arrow **2 :** a member of the people who produced the Basket Maker culture

basketmaking \ˈ⸗⸗,⸗⸗\ *n* **:** the making of baskets

basket mast *n* **:** an obsolete type of mast formerly used on some battleships and composed of a number of straight elements of steel tubing arranged as a hyperboloid of revolution — called also *cage mast*

basket meeting *n* **:** a usu. all-day meeting esp. for religious purposes to which food is brought in baskets

basket oak *n* **:** a rather large oak (*Quercus prinus*) of the southeastern and central U.S. having a durable wood that is used as timber and often split and woven into baskets — called also *cow oak, swamp chestnut oak*

basket–of–gold \¦⸗⸗⸗¦⸗\ *n* **:** a European perennial herb (*Alyssum saxatile*) widely cultivated esp. in rock gardens and having grayish foliage and yellow flowers in compact clusters that elongate in fruit — called also *golden tuft*

basket osier *n* **:** either of two European osier willows (*Salix purpurea* and *S. viminalis*)

basket phaeton *n* **:** a phaeton carriage with a body of wickerwork

basket plant *n* **:** a trailing plant (as Kenilworth ivy) that can be grown in a hanging basket

basket rummy *n* **:** CANASTA 1

bas·ket·ry \-kətrē, -ri\ *n* -ES **1 :** the art or craft of assembling slender elongated elements (as reeds, osiers, wooden splints, or metal ribbons) into baskets or other objects (as chair seats, mats, or boats) usu. by weaving, braiding, or sewing **2 :** objects or any fabrication produced by basketry ⟨delicate ~ panels⟩

baskets *pl of* BASKET, *pres 3d sing of* BASKET

basket salt *n* **:** salt that has drained from baskets after being drawn from the evaporating pans

basket shell *n* **1 :** a bivalve mollusk of a family (Corbulidae) having unequal valves, the right usu. larger, and a single large hinge tooth on each valve — called also *basket clam* **2** *also* **basket whelk :** any of several marine snails (family Nassariidae) living on muddy bottoms and feeding on other mollusks

basket sponge *n* **:** GLASS SPONGE; *specif* **:** VENUS'S-FLOWER-BASKET

basket star *also* **basket fish** *n* **:** any of numerous ophiuroids (order Euryalida) having slender complexly branched interlacing arms that serve to entrap the fish on which they feed — called also *sea spider*

basket weave *n* **1 :** a textile weave with two or more adjacent warp and weft threads worked as one in plain-weave manner resembling the checkered pattern of a plaited basket **2** *radio* **:** a type of coil winding in which the windings of successive layers are woven in and out of one another

basket willow *n* **:** OSIER 1

basketwork \ˈ⸗⸗,⸗\ *n* **:** BASKETRY 2

basking *pres part of* BASK

basking shark *n* **1 :** one of the largest of sharks (*Cetorhinus maximus*) attaining a length of 40 feet, commonly lying at the surface of the water basking in the sun and feeding on plankton which it strains from the water by means of gill rakers, the water straining out through very long gill slits and the minute teeth being nearly functionless, and being of commercial interest because of its immense liver which yields large quantities of oil **2 :** WHALE SHARK

basks *pres 3d sing of* BASK

bas mitzvah *var of* BATH MITZVAH

baso– — see BASI-

ba·so·cellular \¦bāsō¦⸗⸗⸗\ *adj* [*baso-* + *cellular*] **:** of, relating to, or derived from basal cells

ba·so·cyte \ˈ⸗⸗,sīt\ *n* -s [*baso-* + *-cyte*] **:** BASOPHIL

¹**bas·oid** \ˈbā,sȯid\ *adj* [¹*base* + *-oid*] *of certain soil substances* **:** potentially basic — compare ACIDOID

²**basoid** \"\ *n* -s **:** a basoid substance

ba·som·ma·toph·o·ra \bə,sämə'täf(ə)rə\ *n pl, cap* [NL, fr. *baso-* + ISV *ommatophore*] **:** a suborder of Pulmonata comprising snails that have the eyes at the base of the nonretractile tentacles and including many common pond snails — **ba·som·ma·toph·o·rous** \⸗¦⸗⸗¦täf(ə)rəs\ *adj*

bason \ˈbāsᵊn\ *var of* BASIN — now used chiefly in the Church of England

ba·so·nym \ˈbāsə,nim, -sō-\ *n* -s [*baso-* + *-onym*] **:** the earliest validly published name of a taxon, being in the case of a binomial or trinomial the source of the valid specific or subspecific epithet when the taxon is transferred to a new combination and in technical usage always accompanied by the name of the original author ⟨*Crataegus spicata* Lamarck is the ~ of *Amelanchier spicata*⟩

ba·so·phil \ˈ⸗⸗,fil\ *or* **ba·so·phile** \-,fīl\ *n* -s **:** a basophilic substance or structure: as **a :** a white blood cell with basophilic cytoplasmic granules **b :** a secretory cell of the anterior lobe of the pituitary with similar granules

basophile \"\ *also* **ba·soph·i·lous** \(ˈ)bā¦säfələs\ *adj* [*baso-* + *-phile, -philous*] **:** attracted to or growing best in alkaline soils ⟨~ plants⟩

ba·so·phil·ia \,bāsō'filēə\ *n* -s [NL, fr. *baso-* + *-philia*] **1 :** tendency to stain with basic dyes ⟨cytoplasmic ~⟩ **2 :** an abnormality of which increased basophilia of some tissue element is a feature: as **a :** leukocytosis in which the number of circulating basophils is elevated **b :** the presence of basophilic granules in red blood cells (as in lead poisoning) — called also *punctate basophilia*

ba·so·phil·ic \¦⸗⸗¦filik\ *also* **ba·soph·i·lous** \(ˈ)bā¦säfələs\ *or* **ba·so·phile** \ˈbāsō,fīl\ *or* **ba·so·phil** \-,fil\ *adj* [ISV *baso-* + *-philic, -philous, -phile, -phil*] *biol* **:** staining readily with basic stains

ba·soph·i·ly \bā'säfəlē\ *n* -ES **:** the condition of being basophilic

¹**basque** \ˈbask, -aa(ə)-,-ai- *also* -ȧ-\ *n* -s [F, fr. L *Vasco*] **1** *cap* **:** one of a people inhabiting from pre-Roman times the region of the western Pyrenees on the Bay of Biscay in Spain and France, being of obscure origin but believed by some authorities to represent a pre-Aryan people, and constituting a distinct people become distinctive through long isolation **2** *cap* **:** the language of the Basques, of unknown relationship though attempts have been made to connect it with the Caucasic languages, the Berber languages, Etruscan, or Iberian — called also *Euskarian* **3** [F, fr. MF, alter. (influenced by *Basque,* the people) of *baste,* fr. OProv *basta* seam, tuck] **a** (1) **:** a short skirtlike continuation of a man's doublet (2) **:** a similar continuation of a woman's bodice **b :** any of various tight-fitting bodices for women copied from the Basque costume

²**basque** \"\ *adj, usu cap* [F, fr. *basque,* n.] **1 a :** of, relating to, or characteristic of the Basque provinces **b :** of, relating to, or characteristic of the Basque people **2 :** of, relating to, or characteristic of the Basque language

basque shirt *n* **:** a pullover sweaterlike shirt often of knitted cotton and usu. having a round ribbed neck and a design of horizontal stripes

bas·quine \(ˈ)ba¦skēn\ *n* -s [F, fr. MF, fr. OSp *basquiña,* fr. OPg *vasquinha,* fr. *vasco* Basque, fr. L *Vasco*] **1 :** a tightly fitting corsetlike underbodice of heavy material worn esp. in the 16th century **2 :** a rich outer petticoat worn by Basque and Spanish women

bas·ra *or* **bas·rah** \ˈbäːsrə, ˈbəl, ˈbal, ˈzrə\ *adj, usu cap* [fr. *Basra,* Iraq] **:** of or from Basra, Iraq **:** of the kind or style prevalent in Basra

bas–relief \ˌbä, ˌbá+⸗¦⸗ *sometimes* ˈbas *or* ˈbaas *or* ˈbais+\ *n* -s [F (trans. of It *bassorilievo*), fr. *bas* low + *relief* raised work — more at BASE, RELIEF] **1 :** sculptural relief in which the projection from the surrounding surface is slight and no part of the modeled form is undercut ⟨heraldic emblems carved in *bas-relief*⟩ — compare HIGH RELIEF **2 :** sculpture or a sculptural form executed in bas-relief ⟨an early Wedgwood *bas-relief*⟩ **3 :** a photographic print having the appearance of sculpture made from a positive transparency and its negative in contact but with the images not quite coinciding

¹**bass** \ˈbas, -aa(ə)-,-ai- *sometimes in NE* -ȧ-\ *n, pl* **bass** *or* **basses** [ME *bace, base,* alter. of OE *bærs;* akin to MHG *bars* perch, OE *byrst* bristle — more at BRISTLE] **1 a :** a European perch (*Perca fluviatilis*) **b :** any of numerous edible spiny-finned freshwater and marine fishes esp. of the families Centrarchidae and Serranidae — see SEA BASS, BLACK BASS, CHANNEL BASS, KELP BASS, SAND BASS, STRIPED BASS, WHITE BASS **2 :** the flesh of any bass used as food

²**bass** \ˈbās\ *n* -ES [alter. (influenced by F *basse* & It *basso*) of ⁵*base*] **1 :** a deep or grave tone **:** low-pitched sound **2 a** (1) **:** the lowest part in polyphonic or harmonic music; *specif* **:** the lowest tone of a chord — distinguished from *root* (2) **:** the lower half of the whole vocal or instrumental tonal range — contrasted with *treble* **b** (1) **:** the lowest male singing voice (2) **:** a person having such a voice **c :** the lowest member in range of a family of instruments: as (1) **:** CONTRABASS (2) **:** a bass tuba

³**bass** \ˈbās\ *adj* [alter. (influenced by F *basse* & It *basso*) of ⁴*base*] **:** deep or grave in tone **:** of low pitch ⟨a ~ voice⟩ ⟨a ~ lute⟩

⁴**bass** \ˈbas, -aa(ə)-,-ai- *sometimes* -ȧ-\ *n* -ES [alter. of *bast*] **1 a :** the usu. coarse tough fiber found on the sheathing leaf bases or leafstalks of many palms **b :** any of various articles (as a mat or basket) made of bast or similar material **2 :** BASSWOOD 1

¹**bas·sa** \ˈbäsə\ *n, pl* **bassa** *or* **bassas** *usu cap* **1 a :** a seafaring people of Liberia **b :** a member of such people **2 :** a Kwa language of the Bassa people

²**bassa** \"\ *adj* [It, fem. of *basso* low — more at BASSO] **:** OTTAVA BASSA

bas·sa·lia \bə'sālēə\ *n, usu cap* [NL, fr. LL *bassus* thick, short, low + NL *-alia* — more at BASE] **:** ABYSSAL ZONE

bas·sa·li·an \bə'sālēən\ *adj, usu cap B* [NL *bassalia* + E *-an*] **:** ABYSSAL

bas·sa·nel·lo \,basə'ne(,)lō, ,bäs-\ *n, pl* **bassanel·li** \-(,)lē\ [It, from Giovanni *Bassani* †1716 Ital. composer] **:** a 17th century double-reed woodwind instrument

bas·sa·nite \bə'sä,nīt\ *n* -s [It, fr. Francesco *Bassani,* 20th cent. Ital. geologist + It *-ite*] **:** a mineral $CaSO_4·½H_2O$ consisting of calcium sulfate found in white opaque crystals in blocks ejected from Vesuvius in 1906 (sp. gr. 2.69-2.76) — compare PLASTER OF PARIS

bas·sa·ris·cus \,basə'riskəs\ *n, cap* [NL, fr. Gk *bassaris* fox + NL *-iscus* (dim. suffix)] **:** a genus of carnivorous mammals that comprises the cacomistles of western No. America, is usu. included with the raccoons in the family Procyonidae, but is sometimes made type of a separate family

bas·sa·risk \ˈbasə,risk\ *n* -s [modif. of NL *Bassariscus*] **1 :** CACOMISTLE **2 :** the fur or pelt of the cacomistle

bass–bar \ˈbās,⸗\ *n* [²*bass*] **:** an oblong piece of wood attached lengthwise to the top or belly within the body of instruments of the violin class for withstanding the pressure at the bridge

bass broom *n* [⁴*bass*] **:** a broom made from piassava fiber

bass bug *n* [¹*bass*] **:** an artificial floating lure used usu. with a fly rod in fishing for bass

bass clarinet *n* [³*bass*] **:** a large clarinet that is lower in pitch by an octave than the ordinary B-flat clarinet

bass clef *n* [³*bass*] **1 :** F CLEF **2 :** the bass staff

bass drum *n* [³*bass*] **:** a large drum having a cylindrical body with two heads and giving a booming sound of low indefinite pitch — see DRUM illustration

basse–cour \(ˈ)bä¦sku̇(ə)r\ *n, pl* **basse–cours** \-r(z)\ [F, fr. MF *basse-court* — more at BASE-COURT] **:** BASE-COURT 1

basse danse \(ˈ)bäs¦däⁿs\ *n, pl* **basses danses** \-äⁿs(əz)\ [F *basse-danse, danse basse,* lit., low dance] **:** a stately 15th century court dance that was ancestor to the minuet

basse–lisse \(ˈ)bä¦slēs\ *adj* [F, fr. *basse* low (fem. of *bas*) + *lisse* warp — more at BASE, LISSE] **:** LOW-WARP

basses *pl of* BASS

¹**bas·set** \ˈbasət, *usu* -əd·+V\ *or* **basset hound** *n* [F *basset,* fr. MF, fr. *basset,* adj., short, low, fr. *bas* low — more at BASE] **1** *often cap B* **:** a long-established French breed of short-legged slow-moving hunting dogs that have very long ears, crooked front legs, and a typical hound coat, are used chiefly on hares and rabbits, and are noted for the depth and quality of their voice when trailing **2** -s **:** any dog of the basset breed

bass clarinet

²**basset** \"\ *n* -s [F *bassette,* fr. It *bassetta,* fr. *basso* low — more at BASSO] **:** a game at cards that resembles faro and was popular in the 18th century

³**basset** \"\ *n* -s [perh. fr. obs. F, low stool, fr. *basset,* adj., short, low] **:** the outcropping edge of a geological stratum

⁴**basset** \"\ *vi* -ED/-ING/-S **:** to appear at the surface **:** crop out ⟨a seam of coal ~*s*⟩

basse–taille \(ˈ)bä¦stī\ *adj* [F, lit., a low cutting, fr. *basse* (fem. of *bas* low) + *taille* act of cutting — more at BASE, TAIL (tax)] **:** having a background carved in low relief — used of an enameling technique in which translucent enamels are applied over such a background or of objects enameled by this method ⟨a *baisse-taille* silver brooch⟩

bas·set horn \ˈbasət-\ *n* [prob. fr. G *bassetthorn,* fr. It *bassetto* (dim. of *basso* bass) + G *horn* (fr. OHG) — more at BASSO, HORN] **:** a tenor clarinet in F pitched lower than the normal clarinet

bas·set·ite \ˈbasəd·,īt\ *n* -s [*Basset* mines, Redruth, Cornwall, England + E *-ite*] **:** a mineral that consists of a yellow phosphate of calcium and uranium and that is close to autunite in composition

basset oboe *n* [It *bassetto*] **:** HECKELPHONE

bass fiber *n* [⁴*bass*] **:** any of several strong bast fibers: as **a :** fiber from a West African palm (*Raphia vinifera*) **b :** piassava fiber

bass fiddle *n* [³*bass*] **:** the contrabass esp. as used in jazz orchestras

bass flute *n* [³*bass*] **1 :** ALTO FLUTE **2 :** an organ stop in the pedal division

bass fly *n* [¹*bass*] **:** any of certain large artificial flies used in fishing for bass

bass horn *n* [³*bass*] **1 :** a former wind instrument shaped like the bassoon but having a cup-shaped mouthpiece and a metal bell — compare SERPENT 7a **2 :** TUBA

bassi *pl of* BASSO

¹**bas·sia** \ˈbasēə\ *n, cap* [NL, fr. Ferdinando *Bassi* †1774 Ital. naturalist + NL *-ia*] **:** a small genus of European herbs (family Chenopodiaceae) that have corolla lobes without appendages, sepals usu. in two pairs, and seeds without endosperm and that are naturalized locally in eastern No. America

²**bassia** \"\ [NL, fr. F *Bassi* + NL *-ia*] *syn of* MADHUCA

bas·sie \ˈbasi, ˈbä-\ *n* -s [perh. irreg. fr. ¹*basin* + *-ie*] *Scot* **:** a wooden bowl

¹**bas·sine** \(ˈ)ba¦sēn\ *n* -s [⁴*bass* + *-ine*] **:** the coarse leaf fiber of the palmyra palm used esp. in the manufacture of brushes and brooms

²**bassine** *var of* BASCINE

¹**bassinet** *var of* BASINET

²**bas·si·net** *also* **bas·si·nette** \ˌbas-ə¦net, *usu* -ed·+V\ *n* -s [prob. modif. (influenced by ¹*bassinet*) of F *barcelonnette,* dim. of *berceau* cradle] **1 :** an infant's bed made of wickerwork, plastic, or other material and often having a hood over one end **2 :** CRIB **3 :** an infant's bed in a hospital usu. as representative of the equipment and services required to care for one infant in an obstetrical service — compare BED 1j **4 :** a perambulator that resembles a bassinet

bass·ing \ˈbasiŋ, ˈbaas-, ˈbais-, -sēŋ *sometimes in NE* ˈbȧs-\ *n* -s [²*bass* + *-ing*] **:** fishing for bass (as striped bass) particularly with rod and reel ⟨night ~⟩

bassinet 1

bass·ist \ˈbāsəst\ *n* -s [²*bass* + *-ist*] **1 :** a contrabass player **2 :** a bass singer

bass·ly \ˈbāslē\ *adv* **:** in a bass manner

bass·ness \ˈbāsnəs\ *n* -ES **:** the quality or state of being bass

bas·so \ˈba(,)sō, ˈbaa-, ˈbai-, ˈbä-, ˈbȧ-\ *n, pl* **bassos** \-ōz\ *or* **bas·si** \-ä(,)sē, -ȧ-\ [It, fr. ML *bassus,* fr. *bassus,* adj., fat, short, low] **1 :** a bass singer; *esp* **:** an operatic bass **2 :** a bass part (as in a chorus or opera)

basso oboe *n* **:** HECKELPHONE

basso buf·fo \¦⸗(,)⸗¦bü(,)fō\ *n, pl* **bassi buf·fi** \-(,)fē\ *or* **basso buffos** \-(,)fōz\ [It, lit., comic bass] **:** a bass singer of comic roles in opera

basso can·tan·te \¦⸗(,)⸗kən'tantē, -(,)kän'täntē, -tän-,tā\ *n, pl* **bassi cantan·ti** \-ntē, -n-,tē\ [It, lit., singing bass] **:** a bass voice with a well-developed upper range ⟨a *basso cantante* . . . he combines baritone agility with bass sonority and boom —*Time*⟩ — compare BASSO PROFUNDO

basso continuo *n, pl* **basso continuos** [It, lit., continuous bass] **:** CONTINUO

basso da ca·me·ra \-də'kam(ə)rə, -'kaamrə,-'kämərə\ *n, pl* **bassi da camera** [It, lit., chamber bass] **:** a small contrabass esp. for use in ensemble playing

bas·son russe \bäsōⁿrüs\ *n, pl* **bassons russes** \"\ [F, lit., Russian bassoon] **:** BASS HORN 1

bas·soon \bə'sün, ba's- *sometimes* bə'zün\ *n* -s [F *basson*, fr. It *bassone*, fr. *basso* bass — more at BASSO] **1 :** a tenor or bass double-reed woodwind instrument having a long doubled conical wooden body connected to the mouthpiece by a thin metal tube **2 :** a 16-foot pipe organ stop imitating the bassoon in tone

bassoon

bas·soon·ist \-nəst\ *n* -s **:** a bassoon player

basso osti·na·to \-,ästə'näd·(,)ō, ,ōs-, ,ós-\ *n, pl* **basso ostinatos** [It, lit., obstinate bass] **:** GROUND BASS

basso pro·fun·do \-prə'fən(,)dō, -ün-,-ün-\ *n, pl* **bassi profun·di** \-(,)dē\ *or* **basso profundos** \-(,)dōz\ [It *basso profondo*, lit., deep bass] **1 :** a deep heavy bass voice with a compass extending to about C below the bass staff — compare BASSO CANTANTE **2 :** a person having a basso profundo voice

bas·so·ra gum \'bas(ə)rə-, 'bəs-\ *n, often cap B* [fr. *Bassorah* (Basra), Iraq] **:** STERCULIA GUM; *esp* **:** a gum derived from an Asiatic tree (*Cochlospermum gossypium*)

bas·so-re·lie·vo *also* **bas·so-ri·lie·vo** \¦ba(,)sōrē-'lē(,)vō, ¦baa-, ¦bai-, ¦bä-, ¦bá-; ¦bä(,)sōrēl'yä-, ¦bá-, -ye-\ *n, pl* **basso-relievos** \-vōz\ *or* **bas·si-ri·lie·vi** \¦bä(,)sērēl'yä(,)vē, ¦bá-, -ye-\ [It *basso-rilievo*, fr. *basso* low + *rilievo* relief, fr. *rilevare* to raise, fr. L *relevare* — more at BASSO, RELIEVE] **:** BAS-RELIEF

bas·so·rin \'basərən, 'bəs-\ *n* -s [ISV *bassor-* (fr. *Bassora gum*) + *-in*] **:** a substance obtained from certain gums (as tragacanth) that is insoluble in water but swells to form a gel — compare TRAGACANTHIN

bass player *n* [²*bass*] **:** a performer on a bass musical instrument (as the contrabass) ⟨allows the pianist, the *bass player*, and the drummer to get in a few licks —*New Yorker*⟩

bass·ra locust \'basrə-, 'bəs-\ *n* [origin unknown] **:** ANGELIQUE 1a

bass reflex *n* [²*bass*] **:** a vent arrangement in the front surface of a loudspeaker enclosure designed to improve the reproduction of low-pitched tones

bass trumpet *n* [³*bass*] **:** a valve trumpet sounding usu. an octave lower than the ordinary trumpet and often considered to be a valve trombone

bas·sus \'basəs\ *n, pl* **bassi** [ML — more at BASSO] **:** the bass part in early polyphonic music

bass viol *n* [³*bass*] **1 :** VIOLA DA GAMBA **2 :** CONTRABASS

¹basswood \'=,=\ *n* [⁴*bass* + *wood*] **1 a :** a tree of the genus *Tilia* (esp. *T. americana*) — called also *bass, linden*; see TREE illustration **b :** the wood of any of these trees **2 a :** TULIP TREE **b :** the wood of this tree

²basswood \"\ *adj* **:** of or relating to a basswood **:** made of basswood

bast \'bast, -aa(ə)-,-ai-\ *n* -s [ME, fr. OE *bæst*; akin to OHG & ON *bast*] **1 :** PHLOEM **2** *or* **bast fiber :** any of certain strong woody fibers obtained chiefly from the phloem but also sometimes from the pericycle or cortex of various plants and used esp. in the manufacture of ropes, cordage, matting, and fabrics

bas·ta \'bastə, -äs-\ *or* **bas·to** \-stō\ *n* -s [Sp *basto*, fr. *bastón* stick — more at BASTINADO] **:** the third-highest trump in various card games: as **a :** the ace of clubs in omber **b :** the queen of spades in solo

bas·taard \'bastə(r)d, 'baas-,'bais-, -,stärd, -tàd\ *or* **bas·tard** \-,stə(r)d\ *n* -s *cap* [obs. Afrik *Bastaard* (now *Baster*), lit., bastard, fr. MD *bastaert*, fr. OF *bastard*] **:** GRIQUA 2

¹bas·tard \'bastə(r)d, 'baas-,'bais- *also* 'bàstəd\ *n* -s [ME, fr. OF *bastart, bastard*, fr. *bast*, perh. meaning "barn" (in *fils de bast* bastard, perh. of Gmc origin; akin to Goth *bansts* barn) + *-art, -ard* — more at BOOSE] **1 :** one born out of wedlock **:** an illegitimate child — compare LEGITIMATE, NULLIUS FILIUS **2 :** a sweet Spanish wine resembling muscatel that was esp. popular in England in Elizabethan times **3 :** something that is spurious, irregular, inferior, or of questionable origin ⟨the . . . residence is a ~ of the architectural era which followed the building of the Imperial Hotel —Hugh Byas⟩ **4 :** HYBRID — now used chiefly to imply inferior quality or to indicate a product of chance interbreeding **5 :** writing paper 16x20 inches in size **6 :** an inferior brown sugar made from the syrups that have already had several boilings **7 a :** an obnoxious or mean overbearing person — used as a generalized term of abuse ⟨they made him an officer and right away he became the biggest ~ you ever saw —T.O. Heggen⟩ **b :** an unfortunate victim ⟨once the sequence of events was set going the poor ~ never had a chance —Samuel Yellen⟩ **c :** FELLOW — used as a generalized term of approval ⟨the nicest thing an Aussie can call you is a bloody fine ~ —*Life*⟩

²bastard \"\ *adj* [ME, fr. OF *bastart, bastard*, fr. *bastart, bastard*, n.] **1 :** born out of wedlock **:** ILLEGITIMATE ⟨the ~ son of a rich old noble —J.T.Farrell⟩ **2 :** of inferior breed or stock **:** MONGREL, HYBRID, LOWBRED ⟨~ dogs⟩ ⟨~ oats⟩ **3 a :** of abnormal shape or irregular size **:** of unusual make or proportions ⟨a sash and door catalog with its fifty or more ~ sizes of doors and windows —R.E.Flanders⟩ — usu. used in technical phrases ⟨~ car⟩ ⟨~ connection⟩ ⟨~ bolt⟩ **b** *of printing type* (1) **:** having a face of one size and a body of another size (2) **:** not cast on the point system (3) **:** of a size arbitrarily classed as nonstandard **4 :** having the appearance of **:** resembling to some extent **:** being an inferior kind of ⟨~ sugar⟩ ⟨~ marble⟩ ⟨~ measles⟩ **5 :** lacking genuineness or authority **:** SPURIOUS, DEBASED, FALSE ⟨a ~ poetic form⟩ ⟨houses of ~ design⟩ ⟨the indiscriminate use of Greek letters by ~ groups not connected with the higher learning —C.W. Ferguson⟩

bas·tar·da \ba'stärdə, bä-\ *n* -s [It, fr. OIt, fr. *bastardo* bastard, fr. OF *bastart, bastard*] **:** a Gothic script used in France and Germany in the 14th and 15th centuries having mixed cursive and book hand features and characterized by flourishes and hairlines

bastard alkanet *n* **:** CORN GROMWELL

bastard aloe *n* **1 :** a Mexican century plant (*Agave vivipara*) cultivated for its fiber **2 :** the fiber of bastard aloe

bastard apple *n* **:** a bastard box (*Eucalyptus cambagei*)

bastard asphodel *n* **:** BOG ASPHODEL

bastard bar *n* **:** BATON 3b

bastard box *n* **:** any of several Australian or New Caledonian trees of the genera *Eucalyptus* (esp. *E. goniocalyx* and *E. cambagei*) and *Tristania* (esp. *T. neriifolia*) with strong hard wood that resembles boxwood

bastard bullet tree *n* **:** any of several tropical American timber trees of the genus *Humiria* (esp. *H. floribunda*)

bastard canna *n* **:** SAFFLOWER 1

bastard cedar *n* **:** any of several trees: as **a :** INCENSE CEDAR **b :** SEQUOIA **c :** SPANISH CEDAR **d :** CHINABERRY 2 **e :** a medium-sized West Indian tree (*Guazuma ulmifolia*) that is used for forage and timber and yields a cordage fiber **f :** RIBBONWOOD 3

bastard cherry *n* **1 :** a shrub (*Ehretia tinifolia*) bearing small black edible berries **2 :** GROUND-CHERRY 2

bastard chinaroot *n* **:** a prickly-stemmed No. American vine (*Smilax pseudo-china*) resembling the chinaroot

bastard cress *n* **1 :** FIELD CRESS **2 :** PENNYCRESS

bastard-cut \'=,=\ *adj* **:** TANGENT-SAWED

bastard dittany *n* **1 :** a European mint (*Ballota pseudodictamnus*) **2 :** FRAXINELLA

bastard dogwood *n* **:** an Australasian shrub or small tree (*Pomaderris apetala*)

bastard eigne *or* **bastard elder** *n* **:** a bastard son of parents who afterward marry each other and have a legitimate son — compare MULIER PUISNE

bastard elm *n* **:** a hackberry (*Celtis occidentalis*)

bastard feverfew *n* **:** a tropical American annual weed (*Parthenium hysterophorus*) with small radiate heads of white flowers that is adventive in the southern U.S.

bastard file *n* **:** a file having teeth of a grade next finer than coarse

bastard gemsbok *n* **:** ROAN ANTELOPE

bastard gentian *n* **1 :** a No. American gentian (*Gentiana acuta*) **2 :** ORANGE GRASS

bastard grain *n* **:** grain appearing when the angle of cut is such that the growth rings of a timber form angles of 30 to 60 degrees with the face of a board cut from the timber

bastard granite *n* **:** GNEISS

bastard halibut *n* **:** CALIFORNIA HALIBUT

bastard hartebeest *n* **:** SASSABY

bastard hellebore *n* **1 :** HELLEBORINE **2 :** ARETHUSA 2 **3 :** GREEN HELLEBORE 2

bastard hemp *n* **1 :** either of two herbs of the genus *Datisca*: **a :** an Asiatic herb (*D. cannabina*) **b :** an American herb (*D. glomerata*) **2 :** HEMP AGRIMONY **3 :** HEMP NETTLE

bastardies *pl of* BASTARDY

bastard indigo *n* **1 :** FALSE INDIGO 1 **2 :** an East Indian shrub (*Tephrosia purpurea*)

bastard ipecac *n* **1 :** FEVERROOT **2 :** an ipecac from the roots of a milkweed (*Asclepias curassavica*)

bastard ironwood *n* **1 :** a small prickly tree (*Zanthoxylum fagara*) of the southern U.S. and tropical America **2 :** a tropical American tree (*Trichilia hirta*) with odd-pinnate leaves and pendulous flower clusters

bas·tard·i·za·tion \,bastə(r)də'zāshən, ,baas-, ,bais- *also* ,bàstəd-\ *n* -s **:** the act or process of bastardizing ⟨~ of the chief principle of which they had the custody —Philip Wylie⟩

bas·tard·ize \'==,dīz\ *vb* -ED/-ING/-S [¹*bastard* + *-ize*] *vt* **1 :** to stigmatize as or prove to be a bastard **:** declare or decide legally to be illegitimate ⟨they can therefore ~ the issue of the second marriage —Morris Ploscowe⟩ **2 :** to reduce from a higher to a lower state or condition **:** DEBASE ⟨decide whether we want to propagate opera or ~ it —Irving Kolodin⟩ ~ *vi* **:** to become debased **:** DEGENERATE, DETERIORATE

bastard jasmine *n* **1 :** MATRIMONY VINE **2 :** a plant of the genus *Cestrum*

bastard jute *n* **:** KENAF

bastard lignum vitae *n* **1 :** a tropical American tree (*Guaiacum sanctum*) yielding a wood similar to the lignum vitae **2 :** a West Indian shrub (*Badiera diversifolia*)

bastard locust *n* **:** ANGELIQUE 1a, 1b

bas·tard·ly \'stə(r)dlē, -li\ *adj* [¹*bastard* + *-ly*] **1 :** of no worth or value **:** CONTEMPTIBLE, MEAN — usu. a generalized term of abuse ⟨quarts of that ~ stuff —Calder Willingham⟩ ⟨I'm not just doing it to be ~ —James Jones⟩ **2** *obs* **:** of no authority **:** SPURIOUS, CORRUPT ⟨apocryphal and ~ canons which they father upon the Apostles —John Donne⟩

bastard mahogany *n* **1 a** *also* **bastard jarrah** (1) **:** an Australian tree (*Eucalyptus botryoides*) — called also *bangalay, woolly butt* (2) **:** the timber of this tree that is hard and durable though inferior to the other so-called mahoganies of the continent **b :** JARRAH 1 **2 :** a West Indian tree (*Ratonia apetala*) of the family Sapindaceae

bastard mar·ga·ret \-'märg(ə)rət\ *n* **:** a ronco (*Haemulon parra*)

bastard marjoram *n* **:** WILD MARJORAM

bastard mouse-ear *n* **:** an Italian hawkweed (*Hieracium tenoreanum*)

bastard myall *n* **:** any of several Australian wattles (esp. *Acacia glaucescens* and *A. acuminata*)

bastard oak *n* **1 :** SCARLET OAK **2 :** a moderate-sized oak (*Quercus durandii*) of the south-central U.S. with rather small ovoid acorns — called also *bastard white oak, pin oak*

bastard parsley *n* **:** BUR PARSLEY

bastard pennyroyal *n* **:** BLUE CURLS 1

bastard pimpernel *n* **:** CHAFFWEED

bastard pine *n* **1 :** LOBLOLLY PINE 1 **2 :** POND PINE **3 :** CARIBBEAN PINE **4 :** WHITE FIR 1a(1)

bastard plantain *n* **1 :** WILD PLANTAIN **2 :** MUDWORT

bastard quartz *n* **:** massive quartz with no accessory minerals and valueless as an ore — called also *bull quartz*

bastard quince *n* **:** a European shrub (*Sorbus chamaemespilus*) with pink flowers and red inedible fruit

bastard rosewood *n* **1 :** an Australian tree (*Synoum glandulosum*) of the family Meliaceae **2 :** the valuable hard timber of bastard rosewood — called also *Australian rosewood*

bastards *pl of* BASTARD

bastard saffron *n* **:** CARTHAMUS RED

bastard sandalwood *n* **1 :** FALSE SANDALWOOD **2 :** any of several trees of the family Myoporaceae: as **a** (1) **:** either of two small shrubby Australian trees (*Myoporum platycarpum* and *M. tenuifolium*) with pleasantly scented wood (2) **:** NAIO **c b :** an aromatic shrub or shrubby tree (*Eremophila mitchelli*) of Australia **3 :** a small tree (*Zelkova abelicea*) of Crete **4** *New Zeal* **:** AKEAKE

bastard-saw \'==¦=\ *vt* **:** TANGENT-SAW

bastard sensitive plant *n* **:** a tropical American herb (*Aeschynomene americana*) the leaves of which are sensitive like those of mimosas

bastard spikenard *n* **:** a European matgrass (*Nardus strictus*) adventive in Newfoundland and Massachusetts

bastard strangles *n pl but sing or pl in constr* **:** atypical strangles in which abscess formation occurs elsewhere than in the cervical lymph glands

bastard thread *n* **:** BUTTRESS THREAD

bastard title *n* **:** HALF TITLE 1

bastard toadflax *n* **1** *Brit* **:** a plant of the genus *Thesium* **2 :** a plant of the genus *Comandra* (esp. *C. umbellata* and *C. pallida*)

bastard tree *n* **:** REDWOOD 3a

bastard trout *or* **bastard weakfish** *n* **:** SILVER SQUETEAGUE

bastard turtle *n* **:** RIDLEY

bastard white oak *n* **:** BASTARD OAK 2

bastard wing *n* **:** the process of a bird's wing corresponding to the thumb and bearing a few short quills — called also *alula*

bas·tardy \'bastə(r)dē, 'baas-,'bais- *also* 'bàs-\ *n* -ES [ME *bastardie*, fr. OF, fr. *bastart, bastard* bastard + *-ie* -y] **1 :** the quality or state of being a bastard **:** ILLEGITIMACY ⟨acutely conscious of his ~ —*Time*⟩ **2 :** the begetting of an illegitimate child

bastard yellowlegs *n* **:** STILT SANDPIPER

¹baste \'bāst\ *vt* -ED/-ING/-S [ME *basten*, fr. MF *bastir* to build, baste, of Gmc origin; akin to OHG *besten* to patch, mend, fr. *bast* — more at BAST] **:** to sew (as a garment) by hand or machine with long loose stitches in order to hold in place during fittings or for final stitching

²baste \"\ *vb* -ED/-ING/-S [origin unknown] *vt* **:** to moisten (foods, esp. meat) at intervals with melted butter, fat, pan drippings, or other liquids esp. during the cooking process to prevent drying and to add flavor ⟨~ a roast every half hour⟩ ~ *vi* **:** to become moistened with fat, drippings, or other liquids during cooking

³baste \"\ *n* -s **:** the liquid used in basting food during cooking

⁴baste \"\ *vt* -ED/-ING/-S [prob. fr. ON *beysta*; akin to ON *bauta* to beat — more at BEAT] **1 :** to beat severely or soundly **:** CUDGEL, THRASH **2 :** to scold vigorously **:** BERATE, DENOUNCE **syn** see BEAT

bas·tel house *or* **bas·tle house** \'bast°l-, -səl-\ *n* [ME *bastel*, *bastile* tower, fortress, fr. MF *bastile* — more at BASTILLE] **:** a fortified house esp. on the English and Scottish border usu. having its lowest floor vaulted

bast·en \'bastən, -aas-,-ais-\ *adj* [OE *bæsten*, fr. *bæst* bast + *-en* — more at BAST] **:** made of bast

¹bast·er \'bāstə(r)\ *n* -s [¹*baste* + *-er*] **:** one that bastes garments, parachutes, or other articles by hand or machine

²baster \"\ *n* -s [²*baste* + *-er*] **:** one that bastes foods; *specif* **:** a device that consists of a large glass tube fitted with a rubber bulb at one end and is used in basting meat

bast fiber *n* **:** BAST 2

bas·tide \(')ba¦stēd\ *n* -s [MF, fr. OProv *bastida* — more at BASTILLE] **1 :** a village or town in medieval France built esp. for defense and usu. laid out according to a definite geometric plan **2 :** a small country house in the south of France

¹bas·tille *or* **bas·tile** \(')ba¦stēl, -aa¦-, -ai¦-\ *n* -s [F *bastille*, fr. the *Bastille*, tower in Paris used as a prison, fr. MF *bastille* tower, fortress, modif. of OProv *bastida*, fr. *bastir* to build, of Gmc origin; akin to OHG *besten* to patch, mend] **:** a place of detention or imprisonment **:** PRISON, JAIL ⟨found that the ~ harbored as many drunkards and fighting men as before she began her campaign —Herbert Asbury⟩

²bas·tille *or* **bas·tile** \"\ *vt* -ED/-ING/-S **:** to confine in or as if in a bastille **:** IMPRISON

bastille day *n, usu cap B&D* [after *Bastille*, the fortress-prison in Paris] **:** July 14, the anniversary of the fall of the Bastille in 1789, observed in France as a national holiday

¹bas·ti·na·do \,bastə'nā(,)dō, -nä-\ *or* **bas·ti·nade** \¦bastə¦nād, -äd\ *n, pl* **bastinadoes** *or* **bastinades** [modif. of Sp *bastonada*, fr. *bastón* stick (fr. LL *bastum*) + *-ada* -ade — more at BASTON] **1 :** a blow with a stick or cudgel **2 a :** a beating esp. with a stick **:** CUDGELING **b :** a form of corporal punishment practiced in Asia that consisted of beating the soles of the culprit's feet with a stick **3 :** STICK, CUDGEL

²bastinado \"\ *vt* -ED/-ING/-S **:** to subject to repeated blows **:** BLUDGEON, BEAT

bastinado 2b

¹basting *n* -s [fr. gerund of ¹*baste*] **1 :** the action of a sewer who bastes **2 a :** the thread used by a baster **b :** the line of stitching made by a baster

²basting *n* -s [fr. gerund of ²*baste*] **1 :** the action of one that bastes food **2 :** the liquid used by a baster

bas·tion \'baschən *also* -stēən *sometimes* -styən *or* -schēən\ *n* -s [MF, fr. *bastille* fortress — more at BASTILLE] **1 :** a projecting part of a fortification ⟨the old fort with a ~ at each of its five corners⟩ **2 :** a fortified area or position ⟨planes disrupted surface communications and bombed island ~s⟩ **3 :** something that is considered a stronghold **:** BULWARK, SAFEGUARD ⟨one of the main ~s of order in a world so badly in need of them —D.W.Brogan⟩ ⟨responsible for weakening the final and greatest ~ of civil liberty —R.K.Carr⟩ **4 :** a pronounced salient of rock projecting from the wall of a glaciated valley and most commonly formed where a tributary joins a trunk glacier

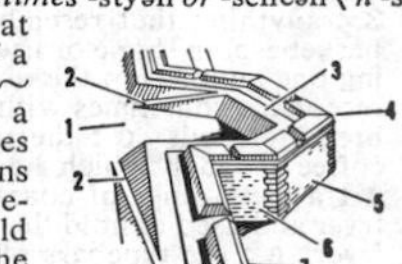

bastion: *1* gorge, *2* ramp, *3* banquette, *4* salient angle, *5* face, *6* flank, *7* curtain

bas·tioned \-nd\ *adj* **:** having or defended by a bastion

bas·tite \'ba,stīt, 'bä-\ *n* -s [G *bastit*, fr. *Baste*, town near Harzburg, Germany + G *-it* -ite] **:** SCHILLER SPAR

bastle house *var of* BASTEL HOUSE

bast·naes·ite *or* **bast·näs·ite** \'bastnə,sīt\ *n* -s [Sw *bastnäsit*, fr. *Bastnäs*, Riddarhyttan dist., Västmanland, Sweden + Sw *-it* -ite] **:** a mineral consisting of a fluocarbonate of the cerium metals that is wax-yellow to reddish brown

basto *var of* **basta**

bas·ton \'bastən\ *n* -s [ME, fr. OF, fr. LL *bastum* stick, staff, prob. fr. (assumed) VL *bastare* to carry, fr. Gk *bastazein* to lift, carry] **1 :** BATON 3 **2 :** a convex round molding **:** TORUS

bast parenchyma *n* **:** PHLOEM PARENCHYMA

bast ray *n* **:** PHLOEM RAY

ba·su·ral \,bä(,)sü'räl\ *n, pl* **basura·les** \-ä,läs\ [AmerSp, rubbish heap, fr. Sp *basura* rubbish, fr. (assumed) VL *versura*, fr. L *verrere* to drag along, sweep — more at WAR] **:** an ancient refuse heap **:** MIDDEN

ba·su·to \bə'süd·(,)ō *sometimes* -'zü-\ *n, pl* **basuto** *or* **basutos** *usu cap* **1 :** one of the Bantu Southern Sotho-speaking people of Lesotho **2 :** a southern African breed of hardy ponies developed by interbreeding Arabs and Barbs

¹bat \'bat, *usu* -d·+V\ *n* -s [ME, fr. OE *batt*, prob. of Celt origin; akin to Gaulish andabata gladiator that fought while wearing a helmet without eye openings and to the source of L *battuere* to beat; akin to L *fatuus* silly, Russ *bat* cudgel] **1 :** a stout solid stick **:** CLUB, CUDGEL **2 :** a sharp blow **:** STROKE ⟨getting only one halfhearted ~ on his ear and a small scratch on his cheek —A.B.Mayse⟩ **3 a :** a wooden implement used for hitting the ball in various games (as baseball or cricket) **b :** a racket used in various games (as squash or badminton) **c :** the short whip used by a jockey **4 a :** BATSMAN ⟨a handy ~ and a good fast bowler⟩ **b :** the act of batting esp. in baseball **:** a turn at batting — usu. used in the phrase *at bat* ⟨the second baseman was at ~⟩ **5 a :** a part of a brick with one end whole and the other broken off **b :** a sun-dried brick **c** (1) **:** a flat round slab of clay or plaster esp. as representing the first stage in plate or saucer making (2) **:** a flat slab of fired clay serving as a kiln shelf (3) **:** the flat plaster disk supporting clay on the potter's wheel **6 a** *or* **batt** \"\ **:** BATTING 2 — usu. used in pl. **b** *or* **batt :** a continuous sheet of cotton or wool fiber prepared for carding or for layering in felt making **c** *also* **batt :** a layer of felt as used in making hats **7** *Brit* **:** rate of speed **:** CLIP, GAIT ⟨it can travel at a fair ~ —Alan Marshall⟩ **8 :** a drinking bout **:** SPREE, BINGE ⟨went off on a monumental ~ —Robert Wilder⟩ **9 :** a corrugation across the face of a masonry stone having a tooled finish — **go to bat for :** to give active support or assistance to **:** DEFEND, CHAMPION ⟨many friends stepped forward to *go to bat for* him and try to get him reinstated —James Jones⟩ — **off one's own bat :** through one's own efforts **:** on one's own account ⟨able to win the war *off its own bat* —George Orwell⟩ — **off the bat** *adv* **:** without delay **:** at once **:** IMMEDIATELY ⟨lock these people up right *off the bat* without letting them run around —Clare Hoffman⟩

²bat \"\ *vb* **batted; batted; batting; bats** [ME *batten*, fr. *bat*, n.] *vt* **1 :** to strike or hit with or as if with a bat **:** BEAT, CUDGEL ⟨~ each of the studio audience over the head —Richard Maney⟩ ⟨easily *batted* down the opposition's arguments⟩ **2** *in baseball* **a :** to advance (a base runner) by batting **:** DRIVE — see BAT IN **b :** to have a batting average of **:** HIT ⟨some players are never able to ~ .300⟩ **c :** to send to bat **d :** to lead to victory by batting ⟨*batted* his team to a 2-1 win last night⟩ **3 :** to compose esp. in a casual, careless, or hurried manner — usu. used with *out* ⟨*batted* out the first draft of the document —Charles Michelson⟩ **4 :** to discuss at length **:** consider in detail — usu. used with *around* or *back and forth* ⟨the plan was *batted* around for weeks⟩ ⟨we *batted* the subject back and forth —C.E. LeMay⟩ ~ *vi* **1 a :** to strike or hit a ball with a bat **:** HIT ⟨he ~s unusually well for a pitcher⟩ **b :** to take one's turn at bat (as of a player or a team) ⟨the shortstop was *batting* when the rain began⟩ **2 :** to travel from one place to another esp. in an aimless fashion **:** WANDER ⟨almost convinced myself that I was ready to ~ around the mountains with the snake nooses and cameras and guns —Saul Bellow⟩ **3 :** to strike repeatedly **:** BEAT ⟨the moths *batted* and trembled on the screens —Hamilton Basso⟩

³bat \"\ *n* -s [alter. of ME *bakke*, prob. of Scand origin; akin to OSw nattbakka bat] **1 :** any one of the numerous flying mammals that constitute the order Chiroptera, the only mammals capable of true flight, having the forelimbs modified to form wings, the metacarpals and finger bones except those of the thumb being greatly elongated and supporting like the ribs of an umbrella a cutaneous membrane that also extends a little in front of the arm and embraces the hind limbs except the feet and sometimes the whole length of the tail;

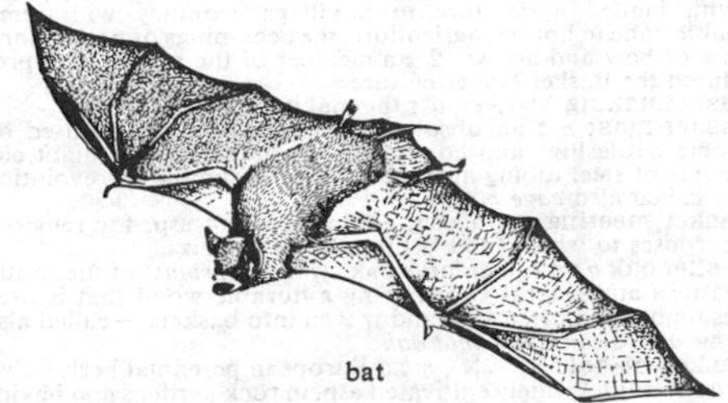
bat

having a thumb and toes with claws by which the animal suspends itself often head downward when at rest; being nocturnal in habit and among the most perfectly aerial of all animals, locomotion other than by flight being comparatively difficult for it; occurring most abundantly and attaining the largest size in warm countries; and being mostly insectivorous though some are frugivorous (as the flying fox) and a few suck the blood of other mammals — see VAMPIRE **2** *in the West Indies* **:** any of certain large moths and butterflies **3 :** IRON GRAY **4** *slang* **a :** PROSTITUTE **b :** an unattractive usu. unpleasant woman — often used as a generalized expression of abuse ⟨we ain't got around to telling the old ~ we're married yet —Maxwell Griffith⟩ — **have bats in the belfry :** to be foolish, eccentric, or insane

⁴**bat** \"\ *adj* [ME *batt*, fr. MF *bat, bast*, n., packsaddle, fr. (assumed) VL *bastum*, fr. (assumed) VL *bastare* to carry — more at BASTON] **:** for carrying a packsaddle or baggage ⟨~ mules⟩ ⟨a ~ and forage allowance⟩

⁵**bat** \"\ *vt* **batted; batted; batting; bats** [prob. alter. of ²*bate*] **1 a :** WINK ⟨*batting* her eyelids⟩ ⟨the son-in-law had begun to ~ his eyes rapidly —William Faulkner⟩ **b :** FLUTTER ⟨she *batted* mascaraed eyelashes foolishly —Lael Tucker⟩ **2 :** to show surprise or emotion by or as if by blinking (the eyes) **:** blink (the eyes) in or as if in surprise ⟨no one would have *batted* an eye had Bruce admitted to ten years more —Jane Woodfin⟩

⁶**bat** \"\ *n* -s [Hindi *bāt* speech, language, news, fr. Skt *vārttā* news, fr. *vartate* it turns, happen — more at WORTH (to become)] **:** the colloquial language of a foreign country **:** LINGO — used esp. in the phrase *sling the bat*

⁷**bat** *var of* BAHT

ba·taan \bə'tan, -ăn\ *n* -s [fr. *Bataan* province, Luzon, Philippines] **:** a valuable Philippine timber tree (*Shorea polysperma*) that yields a resin

¹**ba·tak** \bə'tăk, bä-\ *n, pl* **batak** *or* **bataks** *usu cap* [Tagbanuwa *Baták*] **1 :** a small predominantly pagan native group inhabiting northern Palawan Island, Philippines **2 :** a member of the Batak group

²**ba·tak** \'bä,tăk\ *also* **bat·tak** \"\ *n, pl* **batak** *or* **bataks** *usu cap* [Malay] **1 a :** an Indonesian ethnic group inhabiting the highlands of Sumatra **b :** a member of this group **2 :** an Austronesian language of the Batak people

bataleur *var of* BATELEUR

ba·ta·mote \,bäd·ə'mōt, -mōd·(,)ā\ *n* -s [AmerSp] **:** WATER WALLY

ba·tan \bə'tăn\ *n, pl* **batan** *or* **batans** *usu cap* **:** IVATAN

ba·tan·gan \bə'taŋgən, -tăŋg-\ *n, pl* **batangan** *or* **batangans** *usu cap* [Tag *Batángan*] **1 :** a small pagan group inhabiting central Mindoro, Philippines **2 :** a member of the Batangan group

bâ·tarde \bə'tärd\ *n* -s [F, fr. fem. of *bâtard* bastard, fr. OF *bastard, bastart* — more at BASTARD] **:** a French round handwriting developed in the early 17th century and modified by the current English commercial cursive

ba·ta·ta \bə'täd·ə\ *n* -s [Sp, fr. Taino] **:** SWEET POTATO

ba·ta·tas \bə'tā,tas\ [NL, fr. Sp *batata* sweet potato] *syn of* IPOMOEA

ba·ta·ti·lla \,bäd·ə'tēyə, -tilə\ *n* -s [AmerSp, dim. of Sp *batata*] *in the West Indies* **:** any of numerous plants of the genus *Ipomoea*

ba·ta·via cassia *or* **batavia cinnamon** \bə'tāvēə-, -vyə-\ *n, usu cap B* [fr. *Batavia*, now Djakarta, Java] **:** FAGOT CINNAMON

¹**ba·ta·vi·an** \-vēən,-vyən\ *n* -s *cap* [L *Batavi*, ancient inhabitants of the Low Countries + E *-an*] **1 :** one of an ancient people of the Low Countries **2** [NL *Batavia* Holland + E *-an*] **:** DUTCHMAN

²**batavian** \"\ *adj, usu cap* **1 :** of, relating to, or characteristic of the ancient Batavians **2 :** of, relating to, or characteristic of the Netherlands

³**batavian** \"\ *adj, usu cap* [*Batavia*, Java + E *-an*] **1 :** of, relating to, or characteristic of the city of Batavia, now Djakarta, Java **2 :** of, relating to, or characteristic of Batavians

⁴**batavian** \"\ *n* -s *cap* **:** a native or resident of the city of Batavia (now Djakarta) Java

bat bolt *n* [³*bat*] **:** a bolt that is barbed or jagged at its butt or tang

bat boy *n* [¹*bat*] **:** a boy who looks after the bats and other equipment of a baseball team

bat bug *n* [³*bat*] **:** any of a family (Polyctenidae) of small flattened elongated hairy bugs related to the bedbug that are ectoparasites of bats

¹**batch** \'bach\ *n* -ES [ME *bache* process of baking, batch of bread; akin to OE *bacan* to bake — more at BAKE] **1 :** the quantity (as of bread) baked at one time **:** BAKING ⟨the first ~ of cookies⟩ **2 a :** the quantity of material prepared or required for one operation; *specif* **:** a quantity of properly proportioned and mixed raw materials ready for fusion into glass **b :** the quantity (as of beer or concrete) produced at one operation ⟨a detailed record of all ~*es* manufactured⟩ **3 :** a quantity or number of persons or things considered as a group **:** LOT, SET, GROUP ⟨taken out in ~*es* to a firing squad —Green Peyton⟩ ⟨a ~ of childish braggarts who marry nasal bossy women —Claudia Cassidy⟩ ⟨a uniformed official stamped a ~ of yellow passes —Andy Logan⟩ ⟨my report on the latest ~ of office buildings —Lewis Mumford⟩ ⟨a great ~ of rules and regulations —St. Clair McKelway⟩; *specif* **:** a lumber raft made up of a number of units fastened together

²**batch** \"\ *adj* **1 :** by the batch **:** in a batch or batches ⟨a qualitative and quantitative analysis on a *batch*-sampling basis —*Science*⟩ **2 :** of, relating to, or intended for use in a batch ⟨the ~ materials must be as inexpensive as possible —C.J.Phillips⟩

³**batch** \"\ *vt* -ED/-ING/-ES **1 a :** to bring together (a quantity or number of things) for processing at one time **b :** to put (a quantity or number of things) through a manufacturing process at one time **2 :** to measure out (the material required for a batch) ⟨concrete was ~*ed* at a conveniently located plant⟩

⁴**batch** \"\ *var of* BACHE

⁵**batch** \"\ *var of* BACH

batch·er \-chə(r)\ *n* -s [³*batch* + *-er*] **:** one that batches: as **a :** one who operates a batching plant — called also *batching man, batch man* **b :** a machine that weighs the materials for batches of concrete **c :** BAGGER b

batching plant *n* [fr. pres. part. of ³*batch*] **:** an assemblage of bins, conveyers, and weighing equipment arranged for the purpose of weighing the materials entering into a batch of concrete

batch mixer *n* **:** a mixer into which the ingredients for one batch are placed, mixed, and discharged before another batch is introduced — opposed to *continuous mixer*

batchwise \'=,=\ *adv (or adj)* [¹*batch* + *-wise*] **:** by the batch **:** in a batch or batches ⟨data were obtained ~⟩ ⟨~ production⟩

¹**bate** \'bāt, *usu* -d·+V\ *vb* -ED/-ING/-S [ME *baten*, short for *abaten* to abate (beat down)] *vt* **1 :** to reduce the force or intensity of **:** MODERATE, RESTRAIN ⟨the *bated* his breath⟩ **2 :** to take away **:** DEDUCT, SUBTRACT ⟨that grave and orderly senior was not going to ~ a jot of his dignity —George Eliot⟩ **3** *archaic* **:** to lower esp. in amount or estimation **:** DIMINISH, LESSEN ⟨and I shall have to ~ my price —A.E.Housman⟩ **4** *archaic* **:** to make dull the point or edge of **:** BLUNT ⟨and now I have *bated* your curiosity —J.F.Cooper⟩ **5 :** to leave out of consideration **:** EXCEPT, OMIT ⟨*bating* their jewels . . . I would not give three souş —Laurence Sterne⟩ **6** *archaic* **:** DEPRIVE ⟨when baseness is exalted do not ~ the place its honor for the person's sake —George Herbert⟩ ~ *vi, dial* **:** to fall off **:** DIMINISH, DECREASE ⟨the wind is *bating*⟩

²**bate** \"\ *vi* -ED/-ING/-S [ME *baten*, fr. MF *batre* to beat, fr. L *battere, battuere* — more at BAT] *of a falcon* **:** to beat the wings suddenly **:** flutter wildly downward from the fist or perch

³**bate** \"\ *n* -s [prob. of Scand. origin; akin to Sw *beta* to macerate; akin to OHG *beiza* maceration — more at BAIT] **:** a bath used by tanners after liming to remove the lime and soften the hides — compare PUER

⁴**bate** \"\ *vt* -ED/-ING/-S **:** to steep (as hides) in bate

⁵**bate** *var of* BAIT 5

⁶**bate** *var of* BETE

⁷**bate** *dial Brit past of* BITE

ba·tea \bə'tēə, -tāə\ *n* -s [Sp, perh. fr. Ar *bāṭiyah* tub] **1 :** a large shallow pan of wood or iron used for washing sand and gravel to recover gold or valuable minerals **2 :** a painted or lacquered tray made of wood or from gourds

bat ear *n* [³*bat*] **:** an ear (as of certain dogs) that is large, erect, and rounded at the tip and resembles that of a bat

ba·teau *also* **bat·teau** \ba'tō, bə-, 'ba(,)tō\ *n, pl* **ba·teaux** \-tōz,-tō\ [CanF, fr. F, boat, fr. OF *batel*, fr. OE *bāt* + OF *-el* (dim. suffix) — more at BOAT] **:** any of various small craft used esp. in the U.S. and Canada; *esp* **:** a flat-bottomed boat with raked bow and stern, flaring sides, strong sheer, and rockered bottom used esp. on rivers by lumbermen

a Canadian bateau

bateau bridge *n* **:** a pontoon bridge supported on bateaux

bateau neck *or* **bateau neckline** *n* **1 :** a wide neckline that follows the line of the collarbone and is high in front and back **2 :** any of various high or low necklines that extend toward the tips of the shoulders

bateless *adj* [¹*bate* + *-less*] *obs* **:** that cannot be blunted

ba·te·leur *or* **ba·ta·leur** \,bad·ᵊl;ər(·)\ *or* **bateleur eagle** *n* -s [F *bateleur*, fr. OF *bastelleur* juggler, puppet player, fr. *baastel* puppet] **:** a short-tailed African eagle (*Terathopius ecaudatus*) that is basically black with ruddy chestnut back, reddish tail, legs, bill, and cheeks, a silver-gray patch at the bend of each wing, and a white undersurface with a black margin along the hind edge of the wing

bate·ment light \'bātmənt-\ *n* [short for *abatement*; fr. the reduced line of the window] **:** a window or one division of a window having vertical sides but with the sill curved or inclined (as where it follows the rake of a staircase)

bat·er \'bād·ə(r), -ātə-\ *n* -s [⁴*bate* + *-er*] **:** one that bates; *specif* **:** a tannery worker who treats hides in bate to remove lime that was used for unhairing

-bates \bəd·,ēz, bə,tēz\ *n comb form* [NL, fr. Gk *-batēs* one that goes, fr. *bainein* to go, walk — more at COME] **:** walker — in generic names of animals ⟨Hydro*bates*⟩ ⟨Pelo*bates*⟩

bates·i·an mimicry \'bātsēən-\ *n, usu cap B* [Henry Walter *Bates* †1892 Eng. naturalist + E *-ian*] *zool* **:** resemblance of an innocuous species to another that is protected from predators by unpalatability or other qualities

ba·te·te \bə'tād·(,)ā\ *n* -s [native name in the Philippines] **1 :** a Philippine tree (*Kingiodendron alternifolium*) of the family Leguminosae with an aromatic sap used in making incense **2 :** the reddish brown oily wood of batete used in cabinetwork and furniture

batfish \'=,=\ *n* [³*bat* + *fish*] **:** any of several fishes having more or less winglike processes: as **a :** any of the flattened fishes constituting a family Ogcocephalidae of the Pediculati (as a common West Indian form *Ogcocephalus vespertilio*) **b :** the flying gurnard (*Dactylopterus volitans*) of the Atlantic **c :** a California stingray (*Aetobatus californicus*)

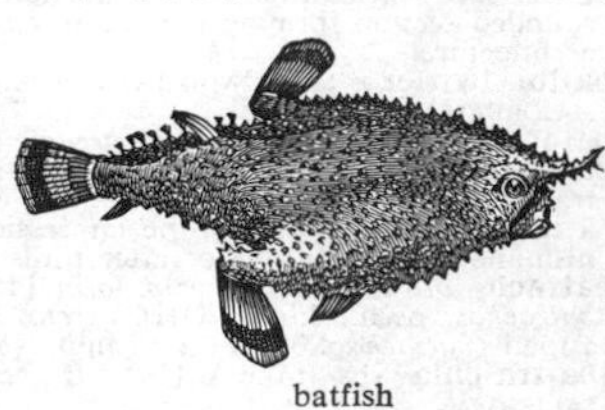
batfish

bat fly *n* [³*bat*] **:** any of numerous small flies constituting the families Streblidae and Nycteribiidae, being ectoparasitic on bats, and having larvae completely developed in the body of the mother

batfowl \'=,=\ *vi* [ME *batfowlyn*, fr. *bat* + *fowlyn, foulen* to fowl — more at FOWL] **:** to catch birds at night by blinding them with a light and knocking them down with a stick or netting them ⟨he taught them to throw flies and bait crawfish nets, to ~, and ferret for rabbits —Thomas Hughes⟩

¹**bath** \'bath, -aa(ə)th,-aith,-àth\ *n, pl* **baths** \-t͟hz,-ths\ [ME, fr. OE *bæth*; akin to OHG *bad* bath, ON *bath*, OHG *bāen* to warm — more at BAKE] **1 :** a washing or soaking of all or part of the body (as in water, steam, mud, or sunshine) ⟨a cool ~ refreshed him⟩ ⟨he took sun ~*s* for his health⟩ ⟨a mud ~⟩ **2 a :** water or any other medium used for bathing ⟨told her maid to draw her a ~⟩ ⟨baby played in its ~⟩ **b :** a contained liquid for a special purpose (as for immersion of something to be acted upon in dyeing, metallurgy, or photography) ⟨a mercury ~⟩ ⟨a fixing ~ containing a small amount of silver⟩ **c :** a medium (as water, air, sand or oil) for regulating the temperature of something placed in or on it **3 a :** a room where one may bathe **:** BATHROOM ⟨went into the ~ to take a shower⟩ **b** (1) **:** a building containing an apartment or a series of rooms designed for bathing ⟨went twice a week to the public ~⟩ (2) **:** one of the elaborate bathing establishments of the ancients — usu. used in pl. ⟨the Roman ~*s* in this quarter were found covered by an old burying ground —Tobias Smollett⟩ **c :** a place resorted to esp. for medical treatment by bathing **:** SPA — usu. used in pl. ⟨spent the summer at the ~*s*⟩ **d :** SWIMMING POOL ⟨the sound of swimmers diving into ~*s* —William Sansom⟩ **4 :** the quality or state of being covered with a liquid ⟨his head all over in a ~ of sweat —Bernard Mandeville⟩ **5 a :** a receptacle for water in which to bathe **:** BATHTUB ⟨cast-iron ~*s* were introduced during the early 19th century —J.E. Gloag⟩ **b :** a receptacle for holding a liquid preparation in which something is immersed (as in dyeing, metallurgy, or photography) **c :** a vessel containing a medium for regulating the temperature of something placed in or on it and used esp. in chemistry

²**bath** \'bath\ *vb* -ED/-ING/-S *vt, Brit* **:** to give a bath to ⟨you'll have your little girl to ~ and put to bed —Richard Llewellyn⟩ ~ *vi, Brit* **:** to take a bath ⟨he was expected to shave, expected to ~ —H.G.Wells⟩

³**bath** \'bath\ *n* -s [Heb] **:** an ancient Hebrew unit of capacity for liquids equal to ¹⁄₁₀ homer or about 10 gallons and corresponding to the ephah of dry measure

bath- *or* **batho-** *comb form* [ISV, fr. Gk *bathos*, fr. *bathys* deep — more at BATHY-] **1 :** depth ⟨*bath*ic⟩ ⟨*batho*lith⟩ ⟨*batho*meter⟩ ⟨*batho*phobia⟩ **2 :** downward **:** lower ⟨*batho*chrome⟩

bath asparagus \'bath-, 'bàth-\ *n* [fr. *Bath*, city and county borough, England] **:** the edible young shoots of a European star-of-Bethlehem (*Ornithogalum pyrenaicum*)

bath brick *n, usu cap 1st B* [fr. *Bath*, England] **:** an unfired brick of siliceous material used as a scourer and polisher of metals

bath bun *n, usu cap 1st B* [fr. *Bath*, England] **:** a round bun made of sweet yeast dough containing eggs, butter, and currants and usu. decorated with sugar, nuts, or pieces of candied fruit

bath chair *n, sometimes cap B* [fr. *Bath*, England] **:** a hooded and sometimes glassed wheeled chair used esp. by invalids that is drawn by a horse or pushed by an attendant; *sometimes* **:** WHEELCHAIR

bath coup *n, usu cap B* [fr. *Bath*, England] **:** the refusal by a bridge or whist player holding the ace, jack, and at least one other card of a suit to take a king led by the opponent on his left

¹**bathe** \'bāt͟h\ *vb* -ED/-ING/-S [ME *bathen*, fr. OE *bathian*; akin to OHG *badōn* to bathe, ON *batha*, OE *bæth* bath — more at BATH] *vt* **1 :** to wash in water or another liquid esp. for the purpose of cleanliness, refreshment, or health **:** give a bath to ⟨shall wash his clothes and ~ himself in water —Lev 15:5 (RSV)⟩ ⟨hurried upstairs to ~ the baby⟩ **2 :** to moisten or suffuse with water or another liquid **:** WET ⟨and let us ~ our hands in Caesar's blood —Shak.⟩ **3 :** to apply water or a liquid medicament to ⟨was advised to ~ the eye with warm water⟩ **4 :** to touch in flowing **:** flow along the edge of **:** LAVE ⟨the lake which *bathed* the foot of the Alban mountain —Thomas Arnold⟩ **5 :** to suffuse with or as if with light **:** COVER, OVERSPREAD ⟨the sunlight *bathing* the ragged lawn —Ellen Glasgow⟩ ⟨the refulgent glow which ~*s* this story of an English mansion —John Barkham⟩ ~ *vi* **1 :** to take a bath **:** bathe oneself ⟨after dinner at the New York Café he *bathed* and dressed —Carson McCullers⟩ **2 :** to swim for pleasure **:** go in bathing ⟨he could ~ and lie in the sun for long hours —W.G.MacCallum⟩ **3 :** to become suffused as if with water **:** become immersed or absorbed ⟨our two ladies were privileged to ~ in those luscious strains each Sunday —Osbert Sitwell⟩

²**bathe** \"\ *n* -s **1** *Brit* **:** ¹BATH 1 ⟨a ~ in blood like that can change the world —H.J.Laski⟩ **2** *Brit* **:** SWIM, DIP ⟨you walk right out of the front door on to the sands and into the sea for a ~ —William Aspden⟩

bath·er \'bāt͟hə(r)\ *n* -s **1 :** one that bathes **2** *Brit* **:** SWIMMER **3** *Austral* **:** a bathing suit — usu. used in pl.

ba·thet·ic \bə'thed·ik, -etik, -ēk\ *adj* [*bathos* + *-etic* (as in *pathetic*)] **:** characterized by bathos ⟨neither could his stout rationality lapse into ~ extravagance —Douglas Bush⟩ — **ba·thet·i·cal·ly** \-ək(ə)lē, -ēk-, -li\ *adv*

bath·house \'=,=\ *n* **1 :** a house or building equipped and used for bathing ⟨though it was not Saturday he went early to the ~ with his sons —Hope Muntz⟩ **2 :** a building (as at the seashore) containing dressing rooms for bathers ⟨resembled a ~ under a cliff —Sinclair Lewis⟩

Bath·i·nette \,=thə'net\ *trademark* — used for a portable bathtub for babies

bath·ing \'bāt͟hiŋ, -ēŋ\ *n* -s [fr. gerund of *bathe*] **1 :** the act or sport of one who bathes ⟨the chief attraction of the resort is ~⟩ **2 :** the conditions (as the temperature of the water and the safeness of the beach) under which one may bathe and swim ⟨the ~ is good on the east coast⟩

bathing beauty *n* **:** an attractive woman in a bathing suit; *esp* **:** one who competes in a beauty contest

bathing box *n, chiefly Brit* **:** a small detached building in which bathers dress and undress ⟨clothes were lying all about as in a *bathing box* —Robert Lynd⟩

bathing dress *n, now chiefly Brit* **:** BATHING SUIT ⟨a middle-aged woman and her husband were sitting in *bathing dresses* in deck chairs —Nevil Shute⟩

bathing machine *n* **:** a small bathhouse on wheels which is capable of being driven into the water and in which bathers dress and undress ⟨*bathing machines* are ranged along the beach —Tobias Smollett⟩

bathing suit *n* **:** a one-piece or two-piece garment worn esp. by swimmers

bath kol \,bät'kōl, ,bä'sk-\ *n* -s [Heb *bath qōl*] *in Jewish tradition* **:** a divine revelation given in the postprophetic age to certain Jewish teachers

bath·less \'=ləs\ *adj* **1 :** without a bath **:** not having or not having had a bath ⟨they went ~ for a week⟩ **2 :** without a bathroom ⟨an old ~ farmhouse⟩

bath mat *n* **:** a mat that is usu. made of a washable material and is used in a bathroom

bath·mic \'bathmik, -ēk\ *adj* [*bathmism* + *-ic*] **:** of or relating to bathmism

bath·mism \'=,mizəm\ *n* -s [Gk *bathmos* step (fr. *bainein* to go) + *-ism* — more at COME] **:** a hypothetical growth force — compare ÉLAN VITAL

bath mitz·vah \(')bäth'mitsvə, -ät'-,-äs'-, -(,)vä\ *or* **bas mitzvah** \-äs-\ *also* **bat mitzvah** \-ät-\ *n, often cap B & M* [Heb *bath miṣwāh* daughter of the (divine) law or precept] **1 :** a Jewish girl who at about 13 years of age assumes religious duties and responsibilities — compare BAR MITZVAH **2 :** the initiatory synagogue ceremony recognizing a girl as a bath mitzvah

bath·mo·trop·ic \;bathmə;träpik\ *adj* [Gk *bathmos* step + E *-tropic*] **:** modifying the degree of excitability of the cardiac musculature — used esp. of the action of the cardiac nerves

bath·mot·ro·pism \=ˈmä·trə,pizəm\ *n* -s **:** the state of being bathmotropic

batho- — see BATH-

bath·o·chrome *also* **bath·y·chrome** \'bathə·,krōm\ *n* -s [G *bathychrom*, fr. *bathy-* + *-chrom* -chrome] **:** an atom or group that when introduced into a compound (as a dye) causes a visible deepening of color (as from yellow toward green) — contrasted with *hypsochrome* — **bath·o·chro·mic** \;==;krōmik\ *adj*

bath·o·lith *also* **bath·o·lyth** *or* **bath·y·lith** \'bathə,lith\ *or* **bath·o·lite** *or* **bath·y·lite** \-,līt\ *n* -s [ISV *bath-* or *bathy-* + *-lith* or *-lite*; orig. formed as G *batholith*] **:** a great mass of intruded igneous rock that for the most part stopped in its rise a considerable distance below the surface and that extends downward to unknown depth ⟨the Sierra Nevada ~⟩ ⟨the Boulder ~ of Montana⟩ — **bath·o·lith·ic** *also* **bath·y·lith·ic** \;==;lithik\ *or* **bath·o·lit·ic** *or* **bath·y·lit·ic** \-;lid·ik\ *adj*

bath ol·i·ver \-'äləvə(r)\ *n, usu cap B&O* [fr. *Bath*, England and William *Oliver* †1764 Eng. physician who invented the biscuit] **:** an unsweetened biscuit

ba·thom·e·ter \bə'thämad·ə(r)\ *n* [*bath-* + *-meter*] **:** an instrument for measuring depths in water

bat·horse \'bat+,-\ *n* [part trans. of F *cheval de bât* packhorse, fr. *bât* packsaddle, fr. OF *bast* — more at BAT] **:** a horse that carries baggage (as of an officer) during a military campaign

ba·thos \'bā,thäs, -ōs,-ōs *also* 'ba-\ *n* -ES [Gk, depth, fr. *bathys* deep — more at BATHY-] **1 :** the lowest phase **:** BOTTOM, NADIR ⟨the very ~ of stupidity —Frederick Marryat⟩ **2 a :** the sudden or unexpected appearance of the commonplace in writing or speaking otherwise elevated in style or content ⟨this habit of cultivating ~ . . . has become one of modern poetry's most persistent vices —D.J.Enright⟩ **b :** ANTICLIMAX, COMEDOWN ⟨spring was the real apex of the year. Summer was ~ —Jan Struther⟩ **3 :** exceptional commonplaceness **:** TRITENESS, FLATNESS ⟨some have deplored the aridity and attributed to it the ~ and prosing of the less successful ballads —Roger Sharrock⟩ ⟨its relentless conformity . . . filled him at first with a deep feeling of ~ —Fred Majdalany⟩ **4 :** insincere or overdone pathos **:** excessive sentimentality **:** SENTIMENTALISM, MAUDLINISM ⟨the ~ of the "my old mammy" theme —Lillian Smith⟩

bathrobe \'=,=\ *n* **:** a loose ankle-length or knee-length garment usu. of a warm or absorbent material that is worn before and after bathing and sometimes as a dressing-gown

bathroom \'=,=\ *n* **1 :** a room containing a bathtub or shower and usu. a washbowl and toilet **2 :** TOILET

bath salts *n pl* **:** a usu. colored crystalline compound for perfuming and softening bath water

bath sponge *n* **1 :** a sponge used in or for bathing **2 :** any of several fairly large sponges (family Spongidae) lacking spicules and having elastic skeletons of spongin that are gathered commercially in the Mediterranean, the Caribbean, and the Gulf of Mexico

bath stone *n, usu cap B* [fr. *Bath*, England, near which it was quarried] **1 :** an oolitic limestone used for building **2 :** FREESTONE 3

bath towel *n* **:** a towel usu. large and with a rough nap used after a bath

bathtub \'=,=\ *n* **1 :** a tub that is usu. permanently fixed in a bathroom and in which a bath can be taken **2 :** SITZMARK

bathtub gin *n* **:** a usu. strong liquor made often illicitly and under makeshift conditions from spirits flavored with essences and essential oils so as to resemble gin ⟨the speakeasies, the *bathtub gin*, the gangsters —Carl Jonas⟩

bath·urst burr \'bathə(r)st-\ *n, usu cap 1st B* [fr. *Bathurst*, New South Wales, Australia] **:** a plant of the genus *Xanthium*; *esp, Austral* **:** SPINY CLOTBUR

bath·vill·ite \'bathvə,līt\ *n* -s [*Bathville*, West Lothian, Scotland + E *-ite*] **:** an oxygenated hydrocarbon occurring as brown porous lumps in coal

bath white *n, usu cap B & often cap W* **:** a European pierid butterfly (*Pontia daplidice*) that is largely white but with green marbling the undersurface of the wings

bathy- *comb form* [ISV, fr. Gk, fr. *bathys* deep; akin to W *boddi* to drown, Skt *gāhate* he dives into] **1 :** deep ⟨*bathy*seism⟩ **:** depth ⟨*bathy*thermograph⟩ **2 :** deep-sea ⟨*bathy*pelagic⟩ ⟨*bathy*plankton⟩ ⟨*bathy*sphere⟩ **3 :** inner parts of the body ⟨*bathy*esthesia⟩

bathy·al \'bathēəl\ *also* **bathy·al·ic** \;==;alik\ *adj* [*bathy-* + *-al* or *-alic* (fr. *-al* + *-ic*)] **:** of or relating to the deeper parts of the ocean esp. between 100 and 1000 fathoms **:** DEEP-SEA

bathyal zone *or* **bathyal district** *n* **:** the slope from the continental shelf at 100 fathoms to the abyssal zone at 1000 fathoms
ba·thyb·ic \bə'thibik\ *or* **ba·thyb·i·al** \-bēəl\ *adj* [NL *bathy*bius + E *-ic* or *-ial*] **:** of, relating to, or living in the deepest parts of the sea
ba·thyb·i·us \-bēəs\ *n* -ES [NL, fr. *bathy-* + Gk *bios* life — more at QUICK] **:** a gelatinous substance precipitated by alcohol from mud dredged from the Atlantic and orig. regarded as free-living protoplasm but now recognized as a form of calcium sulfate
bathychrome *var of* BATHOCHROME
bathy·clinograph \ˈbathə+\ *n* [*bathy-* + *clinograph*] **:** an instrument for measuring vertical currents in the deep sea
bathy·er·gi·dae \ˌbathēˈərjəˌdē\ *n pl, cap* [NL, fr. *Bathyergus*, type genus (fr. Gk *bathyergein* to plow deeply, fr. *bathy-* + *ergein* to plow) + *-idae*] **:** a family of aberrant hystricomorph rodents that includes the mole rats and sand rats of Africa
bathy·gram \ˈbathəˌgram\ *n* -S [*bathy-* + *-gram*] **:** a record obtained from sonic sounding instruments
bath·yl \ˈbathəl\ *adj* [by alter.] **:** BATHYAL
bathy·limnetic \ˈbathə+\ *adj* [*bathy-* + *limnetic*] **:** relating to or inhabiting a bathylimnion
bathy·limnion \ˈbathə+\ *n, pl* **bathylimnia** [NL, fr. *bathy-* + *-limnion*] **:** the deeper part of the hypolimnion distinguished by rather constant rates of heat absorption at different depths — compare CLINOLIMNION
bathylith *or* **bathylite** *var of* BATHOLITH
bathy·mas·ter·i·dae \ˌbathə(ˌ)maˈsterəˌdē\ *n pl, cap* [NL, fr. *Bathymaster*, type genus (fr. *bathy-* + Gk *mastēr* seeker, fr. *masteuein* to seek) + *-idae*] **:** a family of percoid fishes comprising the ronquils
ba·thym·e·ter \bəˈthimәd·ə(r)\ *n* -S [*bathy-* + *-meter*] **:** a device for the sounding of depths
bathy·metric *or* **bathy·metrical** \ˈbathə, -thē+\ *adj* [*bathymetric* ISV *bathy-* + *-metric*; orig. formed as F *bathymétrique*; *bathymetrical* fr. *bathy-* + *metrical*] **1 :** relating to the measurement of depths of water in oceans, seas, and lakes **2 :** relating to the contour of the bottoms of oceans, seas, and lakes ⟨a ~ map⟩ **3 :** relating to the distribution in depth of marine or lacustrine organisms ⟨~ range⟩ — **bathy·metrically** \"+\ *adv*
ba·thym·e·try \bəˈthimə·trē\ *n* -ES [ISV *bathy-* + *-metry*; orig. formed as F *bathymétrie*] **:** the measurement of depths of water in oceans, seas, and lakes; *also* **:** the information derived from such measurements
bathy·orographical \ˈbathē+\ *adj* [*bathy-* + *orographical*] **:** of or relating to ocean depths and mountain heights ⟨a ~ map⟩
bathy·pelagic \ˈbathə+\ *adj* [*bathy-* + *pelagic*] **:** of, relating to, or living in the deeper waters of the ocean, esp. those several hundred feet below the surface — distinguished from *abyssal*, *pelagic*
bathy·pi·tot·me·ter \ˌbathəpēˈtōˌmēd·ə(r)\ *n* -S [*bathy-* + Henri *Pitot* †1771 Fr. physicist and engineer + E *-meter*] **:** an instrument designed to record the current velocity and water temperature at indicated depths below the surface of a sea or lake — compare BATHYTHERMOGRAPH
bathy·scaphe \ˈbathəˌskaf, -thē- *also* -āf\ *n* -S [ISV *bathy-* + Gk *skaphē* light boat; orig. formed in F] **:** a navigable submersible ship that is used for deep-sea exploration, has a spherical watertight cabin attached to its underside, and uses gasoline and shot for ballast
bathy·seism \ˈbathəˌsīzəm\ *n* [*bathy-* + *-seism*] **:** an earthquake of deep origin recordable at seismographic stations the world over
ba·thys·mal \bəˈthizməl\ *adj* [Gk *bathysma* deep place (fr. *bathys* deep) + E *-al*] **:** of or relating to the bottom of the deeper parts of the sea, esp. those parts between 100 and 1000 fathoms deep
bathy·sophical *also* **bathy·sophic** \ˈbathə+\ *adj* [*bathy-* + *sophical*, *sophic*] **:** of or relating to a knowledge of the depths of the sea or of the things found there
bathy·sphere \ˈbathə, -thē+ˌ-\ *n* [*bathy-* + *sphere*] **:** a strongly built steel diving sphere used for deep-sea observation and study
bathy·thermogram \"+\ *n* [*bathy-* + *thermogram*] **:** a record obtained with a bathythermograph
bathy·thermograph \"+\ *n* [ISV *bathy-* + *thermograph*] **:** an instrument designed to record the temperature of sea or fresh water as a function of depth
bathy·ther·mo·sphere \ˌbathəˈthərmə+ˌ-\ *n* -S [*bathy-* + *therm-* + *sphere*] **:** BATHYTHERMOGRAPH
bathy·vessel \ˈbathə+ˌ-\ *n* [*bathy-* + *vessel*] **:** a ship (as a submarine or a bathysphere) designed for exploration of or navigation in water far below the surface of a sea or lake
bat·i·a·tor root \ˈbad·ēˈād·ə(r)-\ *n* [origin unknown] **:** the root of a tropical African shrub (*Vernonia nigritiana*) that yields vernonin
ba·ti·cu·lin *or* **ba·ti·ku·lin** \bəˌtēkəˈlēn\ *or* **ba·ti·cu·ling** *or* **ba·ti·ku·ling** \-ˈliŋ\ *n* -S [Tag *batikuling*] **:** any of several Philippine timber trees of the family Lauraceae (esp. *Litsia robusta*) that yield a wood much used for carvings and cabinetwork
bat·i·da·ce·ae \ˌbad·əˈdāsēˌē\ *n pl, cap* [NL, fr. *Batid-*, *Batis*, type genus + *-aceae*] **:** a family of low straggling dioecous shrubs (order Caryophyllales) having succulent opposite leaves and a conelike inflorescence — see BATIS — **bat·i·da·ceous** \ˌ=ˌ=ˈdāshəs\ *adj*
ba·tik \bəˈtēk; ˈbad·ik, -atik, -ēk *also* ˈbä-\ *n* -S [Malay, fr. Jav, painted] **1 a :** an Indonesian method of hand-printing textiles by coating parts of the fabric with wax to resist dye, dipping in a cold dye solution, boiling off the wax, and repeating the process for each color used **b :** a design so executed **2 a :** a fabric printed by the batik method **b :** an imitation of such a fabric
bat in *vt* **:** to bring about (a run) by batting
bat·ing \ˈbād·iŋ, -ātiŋ, -ēŋ\ *prep* [fr. pres. part. of [1]*bate*] **:** with the exception of **:** EXCEPTING
ba·ti·no \bəˈtē(ˌ)nō\ *n* -S [Tag] **:** a Philippine tree (*Alstonia macrophylla*) that yields a moderately valuable timber
ba·tis \ˈbād·əs\ *n, cap* [NL, fr. L, samphire, fr. Gk] **:** a genus of plants constituting the family Batidaceae and characterized by flowers in scaly spikes — see SALTWORT 3
ba·tiste \bəˈtēst, baˈ-\ *n* -S [F, fr. MF (*toile de*) *baptiste*, prob. after *Baptiste* of Cambrai, 13th cent. Fr. textile maker, its inventor] **:** a fine soft sheer fabric of plain weave made of any of the principal fibers (as cotton, linen, rayon, silk, or wool) and used esp. for clothing
ba·ti·ti·nan \ˌbäd·əˈtēˌnän\ *n* -S [Tag] **:** a Philippine tree (*Lagerstroemia pyriformis*) yielding a grayish or brown wood
bat·lan *or* **bat·lon** \ˈbätˈlän, -ōn, ˈ=ˌ=\ *n, pl* **batla·nim** *or* **batlo·nim** \=ˈlänəm, -lōn-, -ēm\ [Heb *baṭlān*] **:** an unemployed Jewish man who spends most of his time in the synagogue or study hall or who is available for making up the number required for religious services or for singing prayers in memory of the dead
[1]**bat·man** \ˈbatmən\ *n* -S [Turk] **:** any of various old Persian or Turkish units of weight: as **a :** a Tabriz unit equal to 6.5 pounds **b :** a Turkish unit equal to 16.96 pounds
[2]**batman** \ˈbatmən\ *n, pl* **batmen** [[4]*bat* + *man*] **1 :** one in charge of a bathorse and its load **2 :** the personal military servant of an officer in the British forces **:** ORDERLY
bat mitzvah *var of* BATH MITZVAH
batn *abbr* battalion
ba·toc·ri·nus \bəˈtä·krənəs\ *n, cap* [NL, fr. Gk *batos* skate (fish) + NL *-crinus*] **:** a genus (the type of the family Batocrinidae) of extinct crinoids esp. well represented in Lower Carboniferous rocks
bat·o·den·dron \ˌbad·əˈdendrən\ *n, cap* [NL, fr. Gk *batos* bramble + *-dendron*] *in some classifications* **:** a genus of recent and fossil shrubs usu. included in *Vaccinium*
ba·toi·dea \bəˈtȯidēə\ *n pl, cap* [NL, fr. *Batis*, genus of fish (fr. Gk, a flat fish) + *-oidea*] **:** Batoidei when considered a suborder of Hypotremata
ba·toi·dei \bəˈtȯidēˌī\ *n pl, cap* [NL, fr. *Batis* + *-oidei*] **:** an order or suborder of Hypotremata comprising somewhat dorsoventrally flattened elasmobranch fishes including the skates, rays, guitarfishes, sawfishes, and sometimes torpedoes
ba·to·ko plum \bəˈtō(ˌ)kō-\ *n* [origin unknown] **:** INDIAN PLUM
ba·tol·o·gist \bəˈtäləjəst\ *n* -S [Gk *batos* bramble + E *-logy* + *-ist*] **:** one who specializes in the study of brambles
[1]**ba·ton** \bəˈtän, baˈ-, -ˈtäⁿ,-tōⁿ *sometimes* -tōn; *also* ˈba,= *or US sometimes and Brit usu* ˈbatᵊn\ *n* -S [F *bâton*, fr. OF *baston* — more at BASTON] **1 :** a club used as a weapon **:** CUDGEL, TRUNCHEON; *esp* **:** a policeman's billy **2 :** a staff borne as a symbol of office ⟨the ~ of a field marshal⟩ **3** *heraldry* **a :** a narrow bend **b :** a narrow bend with the ends cut off that is borne sinister and used as a mark of illegitimate descent in English heraldry **4 :** a stick or wand with which a leader directs a band or orchestra **5** *also* **baton de com·man·de·ment** \bätōⁿdəkōmäⁿd(ə)mäⁿ, bätōⁿtk-\ **:** an artifact of Aurignacian and later paleolithic times consisting of a reindeer or stag horn having one or more perforations and usu. engraved or carved and possibly used as a shaft straightener — compare ARROW STRAIGHTENER **6 :** a hollow wooden, paper, or plastic cylinder carried by each member of a relay team and passed to the succeeding runner in the exchange zone **7 a :** a long loaf of bread **b :** a thin short stick made of bread or pastry dough and sometimes flavored (as with cheese) **8 :** a smooth staff weighted with a ball at one end for balance and carried by a drum major or baton twirler

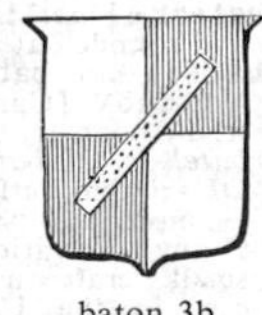
baton 3b

[2]**bat·on** \ˈbatᵊn\ *vt* **batoned; batoned; batoning** \ˈbat(ᵊ)niŋ\ **batons :** to beat or strike with a baton **:** CUDGEL ⟨threatened to ~ him to death —Sir Walter Scott⟩
[3]**ba·ton** \bəˈtän, baˈ- *sometimes* -ˈtōn *also* ˈba,=\ *vi* -ED/-ING/-S **:** to lead a band or orchestra **:** CONDUCT
ba·ton·eer \bəˌtäˈni(ə)r, baˌ-, =ˈ=ˌ=\ *n* -S [[1]*baton* + *-eer*] **:** a leader of an orchestra or band
ba·ton·ist \bəˈtänəst, baˈ-\ *n* -S [[1]*baton* + *-ist*] **:** one who uses a baton **:** CONDUCTOR
ba·ton·is·tic \ˈba(ˌ)tälˈnistik, ˈbatᵊnˈis-\ *adj* **:** relating to the use of the conductor's baton and to the art of conducting ⟨~ experience⟩
ba·ton·né paper \ˈbätᵊnˈā-, ba-, -tōˈnā-, -tō-\ *n* [part trans. of F *papier batonné* ruled paper, fr. *papier* paper + *batonné* ruled, crossed out, past part. of *bâtonner* to rule, cross out, fr. *bâton*] **:** a paper watermarked with widely spaced parallel lines and used esp. by philatelists
ba·ton·nier \ˌbätōˈnyā, ˌba-, -tō-\ *n* -S [F *bâtonnier*, fr. MF *bastonnier*, fr. *baston* staff — more at BASTON] **:** the chief of the advocates of a court or bar
bat·on rouge \ˌbatᵊnˈrüzh\ *adj, usu cap B&R* [fr. *Baton Rouge*, La.] **:** of or from Baton Rouge, the capital of Louisiana ⟨a *Baton Rouge* residence⟩ **:** of the kind or style prevalent in Baton Rouge
bâ·tons rom·pus \bätōⁿrōⁿpüe, ba-\ *n pl* [F, broken sticks] **:** the short straight billets or portions of molding usu. of rounded section forming the zigzag molding in Romanesque architecture
ba·ton twirler *n* **:** one who twirls a baton — compare DRUM MAJORETTE
batoon *n* -S [modif. of F *bâton*] *archaic* **:** BATON
bat printing *n* [[1]*bat*] **:** a mode of printing on glazed ware by transferring the impression from the engraving to the ware on a thin slab of gelatin with the impression being taken in varnish and dusted with color after transfer
batrach- *or* **batracho-** *comb form* [ISV, fr. Gk, frog, fr. *batrachos*; perh. akin to OHG *kreta*, *krota* toad] **1 :** frog **:** toad ⟨*batracho*phobia⟩ **2 :** ranula ⟨*batracho*plasty⟩
[1]**ba·tra·chia** \bəˈtrākēə\ [NL, fr. *batrach-* + *-ia*] *syn of* SALIENTIA
[2]**batrachia** \"\ [NL, fr. *batrach-* + *-ia*] *syn of* AMPHIBIA
[3]**batrachia** \"\ *n pl, sometimes cap* [NL, fr. *batrach-* + *-ia*] **1 :** SALIENTIANS — usu. used collectively **2 :** members of the class Amphibia
[1]**ba·tra·chi·an** \bəˈtrākēən\ *adj* [F *batracien*, fr. *batrachbatrach-* + *-ien* -ian] **1 :** of or relating to the Batrachia **2 :** relating to or having the characteristics of frogs and toads
[2]**batrachian** \"\ *n* -S **:** one of the Batrachia
ba·tra·chi·ate \-kēət\ *adj* [NL [1]*Batrachia* + E *-ate*] **:** SALIENTIAN
ba·trach·i·dae \bəˈtrakəˌdē\ [NL, fr. *Batrachus*, genus of amphibians (fr. Gk *batrachos* frog) + *-idae*] *syn of* BATRACHOIDIDAE
ba·tra·chi·um \-ˈtrākēəm\ *n, cap* [NL, fr. L *batrachion*, a medicinal plant, fr. Gk, fr. *batrachos* frog + *-ion* (dim. suffix)] **:** a genus of aquatic or marsh herbs (family Ranunculaceae) having finely dissected or lobed leaves, small white flowers, and wrinkled achenes
[1]**bat·ra·choid** \ˈba·trəˌkȯid\ *adj* [*batrach-* + *-oid*] **:** like a frog or toad
[2]**batrachoid** \"\ *adj* [NL *Batrachoididae*] **:** of or relating to the Batrachoididae
bat·ra·choi·di·dae \ˌ=ˈkȯidəˌdē\ *n pl, cap* [NL, fr. *Batrachoides*, type genus (fr. Gk *batrachos* frog + NL *-oides*) + *-idae*] **:** a family of marine fishes (order Haplodoci) having the head large and depressed and the mouth very wide and including the common toadfishes
bat·ra·choph·a·gous \ˌ=ˈkäfəgəs\ *adj* [*batrach-* + *-phagous*] **:** feeding on frogs
bat·ra·cho·sper·mum \ˈba·trə(ˌ)kōˈspərməm\ *n, cap* [NL, fr. *batrach-* + *-spermum*] **:** a genus (the type of the family Batrachospermaceae) of red algae of the order Nemalionales found in slow-moving fresh waters and having a thallus that consists of a conspicuous central axis bearing transverse whorls of short branches at regular intervals
-bat·ra·chus \ˈbatrəkəs\ *n comb form* [NL, fr. Gk *batrachos*] **:** batrachian — in generic names of animals ⟨Megalo*batrachus*⟩
bat ray *or* **bat stingray** *n* [[3]*bat*] **:** BATFISH c
[1]**bats** *pl of* BAT, *pres 3d sing of* BAT
[2]**bats** \ˈbats\ *adj* [by alter.] *slang* **:** BATTY 2 ⟨nothing to do but sweat out the old degree and try not to go ~ —Theodore Morrison⟩
bats·man \ˈbatsmən\ *n, pl* **batsmen 1** [*bats* (gen. of [1]*bat*) + *man*] **:** BATTER — the usual term in cricket; see CRICKET illustration **2** [*bats* (pl. of [1]*bat*) + *man*] **:** a man who guides aircraft with a pair of bats; *esp* **:** one who guides incoming aircraft in this manner from the deck of a carrier
batsman's ground *n* **:** GROUND 5h (2)
bats·man·ship \-ˌship\ *n* -S **:** ability at bat esp. in cricket
batt *var of* BAT
batt *abbr* **1** battalion **2** batten **3** battery **4** battle
[1]**bat·ta** \ˈbad·ə, -atə\ *n* -S [Hindi *bhattā* allowance for food, fr. Skt *bhakta* allotted, something distributed or enjoyed, food, fr. *bhajati* he distributes, allots & *bhajate* he receives, enjoys — more at BAKSHEESH] **1** *India* **:** subsistence money (as for a witness or prisoner) **:** maintenance or traveling expenses of an employee **2** *India* **:** extra pay; *esp* **:** an extra allowance on special grounds to British officers, soldiers, and others serving in India
[2]**batta** \"\ *n* -S [Hindi *baṭṭā*] **1** *India* **:** rate of exchange **:** AGIO **2** *India* **:** discount on uncurrent coins
bat·tail·ous \ˈbad·ᵊləs\ *adj* [ME *batailous*, fr. MF *bataillos*, fr. *bataille* battle + *-os* -ous — more at BATTLE] *archaic* **:** ready for battle **:** WARLIKE
battak *usu cap, var of* [2]BATAK
bat·ta·lia \bəˈtälyə, -tal-\ *n* -S [It *battaglia* company of soldiers, battle — more at BATTALION] **1** *obs* **:** a large body of men in battle array **2** *archaic* **:** order of battle **:** battle array
bat·tal·ion \bəˈtalyən\ *n* -S [MF *bataillon*, fr. OIt *battaglione*, aug. of *battaglia* company of soldiers, battle, fr. LL *battalia* combat — more at BATTLE] **1 :** a considerable body of troops organized to act together **:** ARMY **2 :** a tactical military unit composed basically of a headquarters and two or more companies, batteries, or similar units **3 :** a large group of persons or things usu. marked by similarity of characteristics, condition, or purpose ⟨a ~ of instructors teaching elementary composition to freshmen —Douglas Bush⟩ — often used in pl. ⟨summoned new ~*s* to the service of the liberal ideal —M.W.Straight⟩ **4 :** a fire department unit made up of several fire companies **5 :** the headquarters of a military battalion ⟨someone . . . up from ~ —W.C.Fridley⟩
batteau *var of* BATEAU
batted *past of* BAT
[1]**bat·tel** \ˈbad·ᵊl, -atᵊl\ *n* -S [perh. fr. [5]*battle*] **:** the account for college expenses at Oxford University; *specif* **:** the account for board and provisions supplied from the college kitchen — usu. used in pl. ⟨Father would have the money put by for my first year's ~*s* —Thomas Wood †1950⟩
[2]**battel** \"\ *vi* -ED/-ING/-S **:** to have an account with or to be supplied with provisions from a college kitchen or buttery at Oxford University
bat·tel·er *or* **bat·tler** \-lə(r)\ *n* -S **:** one that battels
bat·te·ment \bätmäⁿ, ˈbatmənt\ *n* -S [F, fr. *battre* to beat + *-ment* — more at BAT] *ballet* **:** an extension of the free foot in any direction followed by a beat against the supporting foot
[1]**bat·ten** \ˈbatᵊn\ *vb* **battened; battened; battening** \ˈbat(ᵊ)niŋ\ **battens** [prob. fr. ON *batna* to improve; akin to ON *betr* better — more at BETTER] *vi* **1 a :** to grow fat **:** thrive by feeding ⟨skepticism ~*ing* at the vitals of belief —C.J.Rolo⟩ **b :** to feed gluttonously **:** glut oneself — usu. used with following *on* or *upon* ⟨foreigners who had been ~*ing* on the carcass of the peninsula —G.C.Sellery⟩ **2 :** to grow prosperous **:** thrive esp. at the expense or to the detriment of another ⟨the pilgrim . . . was expected to serve the state, not ~ on it —Agnes Repplier⟩ ~ *vt* **:** to cause to thrive by feeding **:** FATTEN ⟨we drove afield . . . ~*ing* our flocks with the fresh dews of night —John Milton⟩
[2]**batten** \"\ *n* -S [F *bâton* stick — more at BATON] **1 a :** a strip of sawed timber that is usu. seven inches wide, less than four inches thick, and more than six feet long and is used esp. for flooring — compare BOARD 3a **b** *dial Eng* **:** a deal less than seven inches wide **2 a :** a strip of wood used for nailing across two other pieces (as to hold them together or to cover a crack) **b** (1) **:** a strip usu. of wood used to strengthen or to help seal a structure (2) **:** a reinforcing strip usu. of wood attached to the end or base of a box, a barrelhead, or a crate (3) **:** a piece of wood used to hold and strengthen loads in freight handling **3 a :** a strip of light wood sewed into a ship's sail at approximately right angles to the leech to make it set flat **b :** an iron bar used to stretch and hold a tarpaulin over the hatch covers or gratings of a ship **c :** a strip of wood nailed or clamped around the edges of the covering of a ship's hatchway to hold it in place **d :** a strip of wood used to keep cargo away from the steel hull of a ship or to prevent it from shifting — see SHIP illustration **4 :** a stripped log less than 11 inches in diameter at the small end **5 a :** a thin strip usu. of wood used in fairing a ship's lines in the mold loft **b :** a thin strip usu. of wood used as an auxiliary for reference or measurement in erecting structures during the building of a ship or in setting up a dry dock to receive a ship **6 a :** a length of wood or pipe suspended from the gridiron and used to support the scenery or lighting instruments in a theater **b :** a strip of lumber usu. 1x3 inches used in the construction of stage scenery **c :** a strip of wood fastened to the top and bottom of a stage drop
[3]**batten** \"\ *vb* -ED/-ING/-S *vt* **1 :** to furnish with battens ⟨the wall had to be ~*ed*⟩ **2 :** to fasten by or as if by means of battens — often used with *down* ⟨had ~*ed* down his hatches long before the first gale winds began to blow —Bennett Cerf⟩ ~ *vi* **:** to make oneself secure by or as if by battens — often used with *down* ⟨we ~*ed* down at the first hurricane warning⟩
[4]**batten** \"\ *n* -S [origin unknown] *dial Eng* **:** a bundle of straw
[5]**batten** \"\ *n* -S [F *battant*, fr. pres. part. of *battre* to beat — more at BAT] **:** the movable bar carrying the reed of a loom that strikes home each filling thread as it is interlaced with the warp by the passage of the shuttle
[6]**batten** \"\ *dial var of* BATTING
bat·ten·berg lace \ˈbatᵊnˌbərg-\ *n, usu cap B* [fr. *Battenberg*, village in Prussia, Germany] **:** RENAISSANCE LACE
batten door *n* [[2]*batten*] **:** a door made of usu. narrow boards set lengthwise and secured by battens nailed crosswise
bat·ten·er \ˈbat(ᵊ)nə(r)\ *n* -S [[3]*batten* + *-er*] **:** one that battens; *specif* **:** a person who attaches cleats to packing cases
batten plate *n* [[2]*batten*] **:** a short plate used to connect two parallel parts of a built-up structural-steel member of a bridge or building
[1]**bat·ter** \ˈbad·ə(r), -atə-\ *vb* -ED/-ING/-S [ME *bateren*, prob. freq. of *batten* to bat — more at BAT] *vt* **1 a :** to beat with successive blows **:** beat repeatedly and violently so as to bruise, shatter, or demolish ⟨he's got sense enough not to ~ his head against a stone wall for a lost cause —Mary Deasy⟩ ⟨they ~*ed* open the door —E.E.Shipton⟩ **b :** to assail orig. with a battering ram but now esp. with an artillery bombardment so as to break down or demolish **:** BOMBARD ⟨they ~*ed* down with cannon the beautiful apartment houses —Sinclair Lewis⟩ **2 a :** to subject to strong, overwhelming, or repeated attack ⟨the English professional class has been ~*ed* by change —V.S.Pritchett⟩ **b :** to drive by strong, overwhelming, or repeated attack ⟨the constant change of theme soon ~*s* the reader into exhaustion —A.J.P.Taylor⟩ **3 :** to wear or damage by blows or hard usage ⟨the raincoat and the hat were now ~*ed* by weather out of their former glossiness —John Buchan⟩ ⟨seems so much cruder in sensibility and expression as well as rather ~*ed* in appearance —Willa Cather⟩ ~ *vi* **:** to strike heavily and repeatedly **:** BEAT, POUND ⟨flies ~*ed* against and buzzed around the electric-light bulbs —D.B.Chidsey⟩ **syn** see MAIM
[2]**batter** \"\ *n* -S [ME *bater*, prob. fr. *bateren*] **1 :** a mixture (as for cake or waffles) that consists of flour, liquid, and other ingredients and is thin enough to pour or drop from a spoon — compare DOUGH **2** *Scot* **:** a paste of flour and water **3 :** the act or result of battering: as **a :** a damaged area on a printing surface (as a plate or type) **b** (1) **:** the wear on the surface of a railhead at or near a track joint (2) **:** a deviation from the vertical in the upright members forming a trestle bent
[3]**batter** \"\ *vb* -ED/-ING/-S [origin unknown] *vi* **:** to have a receding upward slope ~ *vt* **:** to give a receding upward slope to (as a wall)
[4]**batter** \"\ *n* -S **:** a receding upward slope of the outer face of a wall or other structure usu. causing a decrease in thickness as it ascends
[5]**batter** \"\ *n* -S [[2]*bat* + *-er*] **1 :** one that bats; *esp* **:** the player (as in baseball or cricket) whose turn it is to bat **2 a** *or* **batter-out** \ˈ=ˌ=ˈ=\ (1) **:** a pottery worker who shapes balls of soft clay and throws them into the hollow molds used in forming wares — called also *baller*, *cup baller* (2) **:** a pottery worker who spreads bats for plates or similar dishes and throws them upon the center of the mold **b :** a plaster block with a handle used in ceramics in making bats
batter board *n* [[4]*batter*] **:** one of a pair of horizontal boards nailed to posts set near the corners of an excavation for a building and used by the builders to indicate a desired level and also as a fastening for stretched strings to mark outlines
batter brace *n* [[4]*batter*] **:** an inclined brace at the end of a truss used to give added strength and support — called also *batter post*
batter bread *n* [[2]*batter*] *chiefly Midland* **:** SPOON BREAD
battercake \ˈ=ˌ=ˌ=\ *n* [[2]*batter* + *cake*] *chiefly South&Midland* **:** GRIDDLE CAKE
batter head *n* [[1]*batter*] **:** the upper head of a snare drum — compare SNARE HEAD
bat·te·rie *like* BATTERY, *or* (as F) bȧtrē\ *n* -S [F, fr. *battre* to beat + *-erie* -ery — more at BATTERY] **1 :** a ballet movement consisting of beating together the feet or calves of the legs during a leap **2 :** BATTERY 12
battering ram *n* [fr. pres. part. of [1]*batter*] **1 :** a military siege engine that consisted of a large wooden beam with a head of iron and was used in ancient times to beat down the walls of a besieged place **2 :** a heavy metal bar with handles that is used (as by firemen) to batter down doors and to breach brick walls
batter pile *n* [[4]*batter*] **:** a pile driven at an angle with the vertical to resist a lateral force

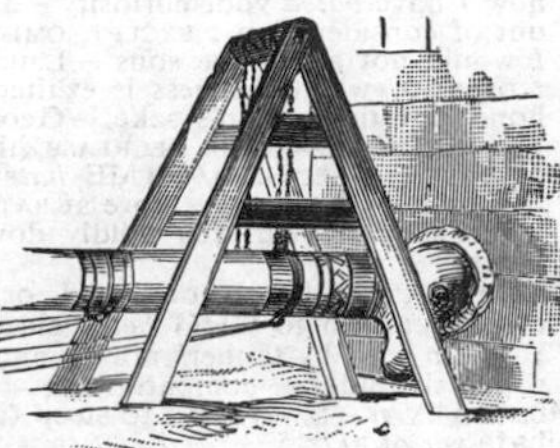
battering ram 1

batter post *n* [⁴*batter*] **1 :** BATTER BRACE **2 :** a post set at the corner of a building or at one side of a gateway as protection against damage by vehicles
batter pudding *n* [²*batter*] **:** an unsweetened pudding of flour, eggs, and milk or cream baked or boiled
batter rule *n* [⁴*batter*] **:** an instrument consisting of a rule or frame and a plumb line and bob and used to regulate the batter of a wall in building
batters *pres 3d sing of* BATTER, *pl of* BATTER
batter's box *n* [⁵*batter*] **:** the rectangular area on either side of home plate in which the batter stands while at bat
bat·ter·sea enamel \'bad-ə(r)sē-, -atə-, -si-\ *n, usu cap B* [fr. *Battersea,* metropolitan borough of London, England] **:** 18th century English decorative enamel work with painted or transfer designs on a usu. white background
bat·tery \'bad-ərē, -atərē, -a·trē, -ri\ *n* -ES [MF&F *batterie,* fr. OF, beating, fr. *battre* to beat — more at BAT] **1 :** metal or metal articles esp. of brass or copper wrought by hammering; *specif* **:** metallic kitchen utensils **2 a :** the act of battering or beating **b :** the unlawful beating of another including every willful, angry and violent, or negligent unlawful touching of another's person or clothes or anything attached to his person or held by him — compare ASSAULT 3a **c** *obs* **:** BOMBARDMENT ⟨keep the bulwark fronts from ~ —Christopher Marlowe⟩ **3 a :** a temporary grouping (as of mortars or searchlights) for tactical purposes **b** (1) **:** the entire armament of a warship (2) **:** a group of a warship's guns ⟨the starboard ~⟩ ⟨the main ~⟩ **4 a :** an emplacement where artillery is mounted ⟨a fortress crowned with *batteries* —S.P.B.Mais⟩ **b** (1) **:** SINK-BOX (2) **:** a blind usu. of turf used on English and Scottish moors esp. by grouse shooters **5 :** the basic tactical and administrative artillery unit usu. consisting of from two to six pieces with the necessary personnel, transportation, communications, and equipment — compare COMPANY **6 a :** a combination of apparatus for producing a single electrical effect ⟨a ~ of dynamos⟩ **b** (1) **:** a group of two or more cells connected together to furnish electric current (2) **:** a single voltaic cell **7 a :** a number of similar articles, devices, or machines arranged, connected, or used together **:** SET, SERIES, GROUP ⟨a ~ of files⟩ ⟨a ~ of roman candles⟩ ⟨a ~ of coke ovens⟩ ⟨a ~ of exhausted brooms and mops leaned against the rail —Philip Wylie⟩: as (1) **:** a group or series of tests esp. of intelligence or personality given to a subject as an aid in psychological analysis (2) **:** a series of cages or compartments for raising or fattening poultry (3) **:** a closely packed group of nematocysts on the tentacle of a coelenterate **b :** an imposing series or group of similar things **:** ARRAY ⟨has equipped his book with . . . a formidable ~ of prepublication comments —Robert Bierstedt⟩ **c :** an impressive group of persons having similar characteristics, occupations, or interests ⟨a ~ of specialists . . . all testified that the bill was too high —Milton Silverman⟩ **d :** a group of bulls kept for breeding **8 a :** the position of readiness (of a gun) for firing ⟨the breechblock failed to close and the gun would not return to ~ —*Infantry Jour.*⟩ ⟨in ~⟩ ⟨out of ~⟩ **b :** the part of a flintlock the flint strikes against in firing **9 a :** a series of usu. five stamps operated in one box or mortar for crushing ores **b :** the box in which such stamps are operated **10 :** a tank with its electrical and chemical accessories in which an electrotype shell is formed by electrodeposition **11 :** the pitcher and catcher of a baseball team **12 :** the percussion section of an orchestra
battery acid *n* **:** dilute sulfuric acid for use in storage batteries — called also *electrolyte acid*
battery charger *n* **:** CHARGER 1c
battery eliminator *n* **:** a device to supply voltage to electron tubes from electric power supply mains — compare A POWER SUPPLY, B POWER SUPPLY, C POWER SUPPLY
battery indicator *n* **:** a small direct-current ammeter that continuously indicates the net charging or discharging current of an automobile battery
battery jar *n* **:** a glass container that has straight sides and a round, square, or rectangular bottom and is entirely open at the top and that is used esp. in biology and chemistry laboratories
bat·tery·man \-mən\ *n, pl* **batterymen 1 :** one who charges and repairs storage batteries — called also *chargeman, charger* **2 :** an electrotyper who works at the battery **3 :** one who tends the battery cells in which sugar is extracted from beets
battier *comparative of* BATTY
battiest *superlative of* BATTY
bat·ting \'bad-iŋ, -atiŋ, -ēŋ; *in sense 2 sometimes* -tᵊn *by speakers who usu pronounce* ng ŋ *in* -ing *words*\ *n* -S [fr. gerund of ²*bat*] **1 :** the act of one who bats: as **a :** the use of a bat in beating raw cotton or wool to separate and clean it **b :** the use of or ability with a bat (as in baseball or cricket) **:** HITTING **2 :** layers or sheets usu. of raw cotton or wool used esp. for lining quilts or for stuffing or packaging
batting average *n* **1 a :** the average (as of a baseball batter) determined by dividing the number of official times at bat into the number of base hits ⟨ended the season with a *batting average* of .312⟩ **b :** the ratio of runs scored by a batsman in cricket to innings completed **2 :** a record of achievement or accomplishment ⟨has maintained an almost unbelievably high *batting average* in gaining and holding the friendship of the home folk —G.S.Perry⟩
batting block *n* **:** a solid block of plaster on which the batter beats out the clay in making a bat
batting cage *n* **:** CAGE 9a
batting crease *n* **:** POPPING CREASE
batting eye *n* **:** visual judgment by a baseball batter of balls thrown by a pitcher ⟨the coach's suggestion greatly improved the rookie's *batting eye*⟩
¹**bat·tle** \'bad-ᵊl, -atᵊl\ *n* -S *often attrib* [ME *bataile, batel,* fr. OF *bataille* battle. battalion, fr. LL *battalia* combat, alter. of *battualia* fencing exercises, fr. L *battuere* to beat, of Celt origin; akin to Gaulish anda*bata* gladiator that fought while wearing a helmet without eye openings — more at BAT] **1 :** a general fight or encounter between armies, ships of war, or aircraft **:** a general and prolonged military engagement **:** COMBAT ⟨the 4-month ~ at Anzio⟩ **2 :** a combat between two persons; *specif* **:** the combat by which disputes were legally decided — see TRIAL BY BATTLE **3 :** participation in armed conflict **:** WARFARE ⟨and drunk delight of ~ with my peers —Alfred Tennyson⟩ **4** *archaic* **:** a body of troops composing an army or one of its chief divisions; *esp* **:** BATTALION **5 :** an extended contest, struggle, or controversy (as between athletic teams or political parties) **:** WAR ⟨the advocates of the old classical education have been . . . fighting a losing ~ for over half a century —W.R.Inge⟩ ⟨a ~ for control of the railroad⟩ **6** *obs* **:** the main body of a military force esp. as distinct from the van and rear
²**battle** \"\ *vb* **battled; battled; battling** \-d-ᵊliŋ, -t(ᵊ)l-\ **battles** [ME *batailen,* fr. MF *bataillier,* fr. *bataille*] *vi* **1 :** to engage in battle **:** FIGHT ⟨the king will bid you ~ presently —Shak.⟩ **2 :** to contend with full strength, vigor, craft, or other resources **:** STRUGGLE ⟨*battled* like an avenging angel for the seamen's rights —Van Wyck Brooks⟩ ⟨like one who having *battled* with the waves —L.G.White⟩ ~ *vt* **1 :** to engage in battle with **:** fight against ⟨when the nobles rebelled the king *battled* them⟩ **2 :** to engage in an extended contest, struggle, or controversy with **:** FIGHT ⟨for three years he *battled* factions of both parties —Oscar Handlin⟩ ⟨they are *battling* tremendous odds —Henry Hewes⟩ **3 :** to force, thrust, or drive by contending or resolute battling ⟨a small boy *battled* his way through the crowd —Virginia Woolf⟩ **syn** see CONTEND
³**battle** \"\ *vt* -ED/-ING/-S [ME *batailen,* fr. MF *bataillier* to fortify, fr. OF, fr. *bataille* fortifying tower, battle] *archaic* **:** to fortify with battlements ⟨beneath the *battled* tower —Alfred Tennyson⟩
⁴**bat·tle** \'bā-,'be-\ *var of* BAITTLE
⁵**battle** *vb* -ED/-ING/-S [perh. of Scand origin; akin to ON *beit* pasture land — more at BAIT] *vt, obs* **:** to feed well **:** NOURISH ~ *vi, obs* **:** to feed well **:** THRIVE
⁶**bat·tle** *like* ¹BATTLE\ *vt* -ED/-ING/-S [prob. freq. of ²*bat*] *chiefly South & Midland* **:** to beat (clothes) with a stick or paddle during laundering
¹**battle-ax** *or* **battle-axe** \'⸗⸗,⸗\ *n* [ME *bataile-axe,* fr. *bataille* battle + *axe*] **1 :** a broadax formerly used as a weapon of war **2** *slang* **:** a quarrelsome, irritable, domineering woman ⟨was a formidable old *battle-ax* —G.W.Johnson⟩
²**battle-ax** *or* **battle-axe** \"\ *adj, usu cap B&A* **:** of or belonging to a Neolithic culture of northern Europe characterized by the decoration of pottery with cord impressions and the depositing of perforated stone battle-axes in graves
battle bill *n* **:** a list of battle assignments on a warship

battle-axes

battle-board tennis *n* **1 :** modified tennis in which opponents play side by side on a half court with the net hung at one end in front of a board from which the ball rebounds **2 :** a practice tennis game for one player in which the rebound from a board simulates a return shot from an opponent
battle chess *n* **:** chess in which each player places his men in a permissible arrangement of his own choosing on the first three ranks of his side of the board, a screen separating the two opponents until play begins
battle clasp *n* **:** CLASP 1c(1)
battlecraft \'⸗⸗,⸗\ *n* **:** skill in the technics of military combat and in the procedures of living under battle conditions
battle cruiser *n* **:** a warship of battleship size and of the highest speed and heaviest battery but without the heavy armor protection of the battleship and designed for high-speed cruising, scouting, and long-range fighting
battle cry *n* **1 :** a war cry of forces engaged in battle **2 :** a slogan used esp. in a campaign or contest **:** CATCHWORD ⟨the *battle cry* of freedom⟩
battled *adj* [ME *batailed,* fr. past part. of *batailen* to battle] **:** EMBATTLED 2
battle dance *n* **:** WAR DANCE 1
bat·tle·dore \'bad-ᵊl,dō(ə)r, -atᵊl-, -ó(ə)r,-ōə,-ó(ə)\ *n* -S [ME *batyldore,* prob. modif. of OProv *batedor* beating instrument, fr. *batre* to beat, fr. L *battere, battuere* — more at BATTLE] **1 a :** a beetle or bat that is used in washing or smoothing clothes **b :** a tool with a long flat blade with a square end that is used in glassworking to flatten the bottoms of vessels **c :** a long-handled paddle that is used for placing loaves in an oven **2 a :** a light flat bat or racket that is used in striking a shuttlecock **b :** BATTLEDORE AND SHUTTLECOCK **3 :** a child's primer usu. made of two or three pages of stiff cardboard on which were printed or impressed the alphabet, numerals, and other rudimentary material and used esp. in the 17th and 18th centuries
battledore and shuttlecock *n* **:** a game of ancient Oriental origin that evolved into badminton
battle dress *n* **:** military uniform that is designed for field service
battle fatigue *n* **:** COMBAT FATIGUE
battlefield \'⸗⸗,⸗\ *n* **:** BATTLEGROUND
battlefield flower *n* **:** JOHNNY-JUMP-UP
battlefront \'⸗⸗,⸗\ *n* **:** the region where armed forces face the enemy
battle game *n* **:** a variety of tenpins in which a score of 12 can be made by knocking down all of the pins except the kingpin 3 balls being rolled to the frame, 4 or 6 frames constituting a game, and strikes and spares not being counted
battleground \'⸗⸗,⸗\ *n* -S **1 :** the territory on which a battle is waged **2 :** an area of conflict ⟨human nature as a ~ between the forces of evil and the forces of good —F.B.Millett⟩
battle group *n* **:** a military unit that is normally a fifth part of a division and is normally made up of five companies
battle jacket *n* **1 :** a waist-length woolen jacket worn by members of the armed forces **2 :** any jacket cut like a battle jacket
battle lantern *n* **:** one of the lanterns on a naval vessel; *esp* **:** a portable battery-powered electric light for emergency use on such a vessel ⟨he fumbled through the dim glow of the *battle lanterns* —Keith Wheeler⟩
battle light *n* **:** a special low-intensity red light used inside a warship at night
battle line *n* **1 :** a line along which a battle is waged **2 :** battleships, cruisers, and supporting warships organized to function as a fighting unit
bat·tle·ment \'bad-ᵊlmənt, -atᵊl-\ *n* -S [ME *batelment,* fr. MF *bataille* fortifying tower + ME *-ment* — more at BATTLE] **1 a :** a parapet that consists of alternate solid parts and open spaces, that surmounts a wall, and that is used in fortified buildings for purposes of defense and in other edifices (as a church) for decoration ⟨pinnacles on the ~s are frequent but not universal —Nikolaus Pevsner⟩ **2 :** an embattled roof or platform

battlements: *A* merlon: *B* crenel, *C* machicolations

bat·tle·ment·ed \-,mentəd, *esp Brit* -,mən-\ *adj* **:** furnished with or as if with battlements
battle piece *n* **:** a work (as a painting, musical composition, or poem) concerned with or descriptive of a battle
battleplane \'⸗⸗,⸗\ *n* **:** WARPLANE
battle police *n pl* **:** military policemen detailed to prevent straggling during battle
battle position *n* **:** a defensive position on which is concentrated the main effort of the defense
¹**bat·tler** \'batlə(r), -ad-ᵊl-,-atᵊl-\ *n* -S [²*battle* + *-er*] **:** one that battles; *esp* **:** a dogged fighter
²**battler** *var of* BATTELER
battle range *n* **:** the range for which the sights of a military weapon are adjusted when in the normal or carrying position — compare BATTLE SIGHT
battle royal *n, pl* **battles royal** *or* **battle royals 1 a :** a fight participated in by more than two combatants ⟨he tells of seeing a *battle royal* among five, each gashing, slashing, and puncturing the nearest to him until only one was left alive —J.W. Lippincott⟩; *esp* **:** such a contest in which the last man in the ring or on his feet is declared the winner **b :** a fight to the finish **:** a violent struggle ⟨after a *battle royal* the cops hauled Jack off to jail —*Sat. Eve. Post*⟩ **2 :** a heated discussion, disagreement, or dispute ⟨these *battles royal* between him and Lady Henry were not uncommon —Mrs. Humphry Ward⟩
battles *pl of* BATTLE, *pres 3d sing of* BATTLE
battleship \'⸗⸗,⸗\ *n* [short for *line-of-battle ship*] **1 :** a warship of the largest and most heavily armed and armored class usu. having at least 10-inch armor and carrying in the main battery guns of 12-inch or larger caliber **2** *slang* **:** a large railroad locomotive **3 :** BATTLESHIP GRAY **4 battleships** *pl but sing in constr* **:** SALVO 4

battleship

battleship gray *n* **:** a nearly neutral slightly bluish medium gray that is darker than pearl — called also *Denver*
battle sight *n* **:** an arrangement of sights that makes possible the rapid aiming of a firearm at short ranges
bat·tle·some \'bad-ᵊlsəm, -atᵊl-\ *adj* [*battle* + *-some*] **:** inclined to battle **:** QUARRELSOME ⟨the young fellows were tough and the girls ~ —Saul Bellow⟩
battlewagon \'⸗⸗,⸗⸗\ *n* **1 :** BATTLESHIP 1 **2 :** a large heavily armored and heavily armed bombing plane or tracked vehicle
battlewise \'⸗⸗,⸗\ *adj* **:** having knowledge of or experience in battle ⟨~ troops⟩
battling *pres part of* BATTLE
battling stick *n* [fr. pres. part. of ⁶*battle*] *chiefly South & Midland* **:** a paddle or stick used to battle clothes
bat tree *n* [³*bat*] **:** EVERGREEN MAGNOLIA
¹**batts** \'bats\ *n pl* [origin unknown] *Scot* **:** COLIC
²**batts** *pl of* BATT
bat·tu \bàtüe, ba'tü, ba·'tyü\ *adj* [F, past part. of *battre* to beat] *of a ballet movement* **:** BEATEN — see ¹BEAT 1c
bat·tue \ba'tü, ba·'tyü, *Fr* bàtüe\ *n* -S [F, fr. fem. of *battu,* past part. of *battre* to beat, fr. OF *batre,* fr. L *battere, battuere* — more at BATTLE] **1 a :** the driving or drawing out of game from cover esp. by beating woods and bushes **b :** a hunt in which this procedure is used ⟨I never cared much for a ~ of pheasants or a grouse drive —John Buchan⟩ **2 :** a concerted action by a number of persons performed with bustle ⟨once a year a grand ~ is organized when every nook and cranny of the church is raked from roof to floor —Richard Free⟩ **3 :** indiscriminate slaughter ⟨a huge prison ~ was ordered . . . on the principle that many should pay for one —Bernard Pares⟩
bat·ture \ba'tü(ə)r, ba-'tyü-, *Fr* bàtüer\ *n* -S [LaF, fr. F *battre* to strike + *-ure* — more at BATTUE] **:** the alluvial land between a river at low-water stage and a levee — used esp. of such land along the lower Mississippi river
bat·tu·ta \bə'tüd-ə\ *n* -S [It, fr. fem. of *battuto,* past part. of *battere* to beat, fr. L *battere, battuere* — more at BATTLE] **1 :** the beat of a musical composition **2 :** MEASURE 4c(1)
bat·ty \'bad-ē, -atē, -i\ *adj, usu* -ER/-EST [³*bat* + *-y*] **1 :** belonging to or resembling a bat **:** like a bat's ⟨large ~ wings⟩ **2** *slang* **:** mentally unstable **:** CRAZY, INSANE ⟨undoubtedly the *battiest* critical judgment of the year —Wolcott Gibbs⟩
ba·tu \bə'tü\ *n* -S [Malay, lit., stone] **:** a yellow to brown or black hard semifossil dammar resin derived from any of certain trees of the genus *Agathis* (esp. *A. dammara*)
ba·tu·que \bə'tükə\ *n* -S [Pg, prob. fr. a native name in Africa] **:** an impassioned Brazilian Negro courtship dance of African origin
ba·twa \'bä,twä\ *n, pl* **batwa** *or* **batwas** *usu cap* **1 a :** a Bantu-speaking pygmy people of the Kasai region and elsewhere in Africa **b :** a member of such people **2 :** any African pygmy or pygmoid
batwing \'⸗,⸗\ *adj* [³*bat* + *wing*] **:** shaped like the wing or wings of a bat ⟨the ~ doors of a saloon⟩ ⟨a ~ collar⟩: as **a** *of a necktie* **:** worn in a bowknot and having ends of equal length ⟨a black ~ tie for evening wear⟩ **b** *of a sleeve* **:** made with a deep armhole ⟨the ~ sleeves of a knitted blouse⟩ **c** *of chaps* **:** having wide flared sides and snap or buckle fastenings ⟨he picked up the scarred ~ chaps —W.V.T.Clark⟩
batyl alcohol \'bad-əl-\ *n* [ISV *bat-* (fr. NL *Batis,* genus of fish) + *-yl* — more at BATOIDEA] **:** a colorless crystalline alcohol $C_{18}H_{37}OCH_2CH(OH)CH_2OH$ obtained esp. from many shark-liver oils and ray-liver oils and from the yellow marrow of cattle bones; glycerol α-octadecyl ether
batz \'bäts\ *n, pl* **batz·en** \-sən\ [G (now usu. *batzen*), fr. *batz, batzen* lump, fr. *batzen* to stick together, freq. of *backen* to stick together, bake, fr. OHG *backan* to bake — more at BAKE] **1 :** an old base silver coin of southern Germany and Switzerland worth four kreuzers **2 :** a unit of value equivalent to one batz ⟨in Switzerland ½-*batz* and 10-*batzen* and 40-*batzen* coins were issued⟩
baubee *var of* BAWBEE
bau·ble \'bȯbəl, 'bäb-\ *n* -S [ME *babel,* fr. MF *babel, baubel*] **1 :** something that is bright, showy, sometimes expensive, and usu. of little use **:** TRINKET, GEWGAW, PLAYTHING ⟨he affixed the ~, with a kiss, upon her middle finger —Elinor Wylie⟩ **2 :** a fool's scepter ⟨the licensed jester . . . brandished his ~ —Sir Walter Scott⟩ **3 :** a child's toy ⟨a child asleep with a ~ —R.P.Warren⟩ **4 a :** something that is considered childish, foolish, or worthless **:** TRIFLE ⟨the Right Honorable before my name is a ~ —T.B.Macaulay⟩ **b** *obs* **:** a childish, foolish, or worthless person ⟨thither comes the ~ and falls me thus about my neck —Shak.⟩

bauble 2

bau·bling \-bliŋ\ *adj* [*bauble* + *-ing*] *archaic* **:** INSIGNIFICANT, CONTEMPTIBLE
bauch \'bák, 'bȯk\ *adj* [perh. of Celt origin; akin to ScGael *beag* little, short, disagreeable, trifling, OIr *becc, bec* small, W *bach,* Bret *biban*] *chiefly Scot* **:** INFERIOR, SUBSTANDARD — **bauch·ly** *adv*
bauch·le \'bákəl, 'bȯk-\ *n* -S [perh. fr. *bauch* + *-le*] **1** *Scot* **:** an old shoe; *esp* **:** one worn down at the heel **2** *Scot* **:** something useless, worn out, or worthless ⟨a ~ of a creature⟩
bauck·ie \'bák-, 'bȯ-\ *or* **bauckiebird** \'⸗⸗,⸗\ *n* -S [alter. of ME *bakke* bat + E *-ie* — more at BAT] *Scot* **:** ³BAT 1
baud \'bȯd\ *n* -S [after J.M.E. *Baudot* †1903 Fr. inventor] **:** a unit equal to one dot per second or the equivalent interval per second and used in measuring the speed of signaling in telegraphic code
bau·de·kin \'bȯdēkn\ *n* -S [ME, fr. MF *baudequin, baldequin* — more at BALDACHIN] **:** BALDACHIN 1
bau·drons \'badrənz, -athr-\ *n* -ES [ME] *chiefly Scot* **:** CAT, PUSS, KITTY ⟨and ~ was watching a rathole⟩
bau·era \'bau̇ərə\ *n* [NL, after Ferdinand *Bauer* †1826 and Franz A. *Bauer* †1840 Austrian botanical painters] **1** *cap* **:** a small genus of evergreen shrubs (family Saxifragaceae) native to eastern Australia with pink or purple long-stalked flowers resembling single roses **2** *pl* **bauera :** a plant of the genus *Bauera*
bau·haus \'bau̇,hau̇s\ *adj, usu cap* [fr. G *Bauhaus,* lit., architecture house, an academy of the arts founded in Weimar, Germany, in 1919, fr. *bau-* architecture (fr. *bauen* to build) + *haus* house] **:** of, relating to, or influenced by a school of design founded by Walter Gropius at Weimar in 1919 and noted for its association with functional architecture, abstract art, innovation in the use of building materials, and the absence of applied ornament in design and for a program that synthesized technology, craftsmanship, and design esthetics and disregarded the distinction between fine and applied art ⟨*Bauhaus* furniture⟩ ⟨the *Bauhaus* point of view⟩
bau·hin·ia \bō'inēə, -'hin-, bȯ'-\ *n* [NL, fr. Jean *Bauhin* †1613 and Gaspard *Bauhin* †1624 Swiss botanists + NL *-ia*] **1** *cap* **:** a large genus of tropical trees, shrubs, or lianas (family Leguminosae) with leaves that are usu. bifoliolate and tough fibrous bark — see MOUNTAIN EBONY **2** *pl* **bauhinia** *or* **bauhinias :** a plant of the genus *Bauhinia* ⟨the trees on the street . . . are to be ~s, an Asiatic variety that puts out mauve blooms in the fall —Christopher Rand⟩
bauk \'bák, 'bȯk\ *dial var of* BALK
bauld \'bȯl(d), 'bȯl-\ *chiefly Scot var of* BOLD
¹**baule** \,bäu̇'lā, '⸗(,)⸗\ *n, pl* **baule** *or* **baules** *usu cap* **1 :** a people of the Ivory Coast region of West Africa linguistically related to Ashanti and other peoples eastward and renowned for their carved statuary in wood **2 :** a member of the Baule people
²**baule** \'bȯl, 'bōl\ *n* -S [origin unknown] **:** the theoretical amount of nitrogen or other essential mineral constituent necessary to produce one-half of the maximum possible yield of a crop
baulk *var of* BALK
bau·mé *also* **bau·me** *or* **beau·mé** \bō'mā, '⸗(,)⸗\ *adj, usu cap* [after Antoine *Baumé* †1804 Fr. chemist] **:** according to a Baumé scale ⟨a hydrometer indicating degrees *Baumé*⟩ **:** calibrated in accordance with a Baumé scale ⟨*Baumé* hydrometer⟩
bau·mer \'bōmə(r)\ *adj, usu cap* [fr. the name *Baumer*] **:** of or belonging to an ancient culture of southern Illinois and adjacent areas characterized by fabric-impressed flat-based pottery, stone implements and ornaments, and permanent villages with large square houses
baumé scale *n, usu cap B* [after Antoine *Baumé*] **:** either of two arbitrary hydrometer scales, one for liquids lighter than water and the other for liquids heavier than water, that indicate specific gravity in degrees, the intervals between the degree graduations being of equal length, readings on the scale being approximately reducible to specific gravities by the following formulas given by the U.S. Bureau of Standards (*n* in each case being the reading on the Baumé scale): (a) for liquids heavier than water, sp. gr. = 145÷(145 − *n*) at 60° F; (b) for liquids lighter than water, sp. gr. = 140 ÷ (130 + *n*) at 60° F
baum·hau·er·ite \(')bau̇m¦hau̇ə,rīt, (')bau̇m,hau̇-\ *n* -S [H.A. *Baumhauer* †1926 Swiss mineralogist + E *-ite*] **:** a mineral $Pb_4As_6S_{13}$ consisting of a lead thioarsenite and occurring in metallic gray monoclinic crystals
bau·mier \bōm'yā\ *n* -S [F, fr. *baume* balm, fr. OF *basme* — more at BALM] **1 :** BALSAM POPLAR **2 :** BALSAM FIR 1 **3 :** any of several plants of the genera *Ocimum, Amyris,* and *Trigonella*
baum marten \'baum,-\ *n* [part trans. of G *baummarder,* fr. *baum* tree (fr. OHG *boum*) + *marder* marten — more at BEAM] **:** the pelt or fur of the European pine marten

bau·no \bä'ü(,)nō, 'bau̇-\ *n, pl* **baunoes** *or* **baunos** [Cebuan & Taw-sug] **:** a wild mango (*Mangifera verticillata*) found in the Philippines having a juicy rich subacid fruit

bau·ple nut \'bȯpəl-,-\ *n* [origin unknown] **:** MACADAMIA 2

bauré \bau̇'rā\ *n, pl* **bauré** *or* **baurés** *usu cap* [Sp, of AmerInd origin] **1 a :** an Arawakan people living in the Baures river valley in northeastern Bolivia **b :** a member of such people **2 :** the language of the Bauré people

bau·sching·er effect \'bȯ(,)shiŋə(r)-\ *n, usu cap B* [after Johann *Bauschinger* †1893 Ger. technologist] **:** the phenomenon by which plastic deformation of a metal increases the yield strength in the direction of plastic flow and decreases the yield strength in the opposite direction

bau·son \'bȯsᵊn\ *n* -s [ME *bausen*, fr. MF *baucent*, fr. *baucent*, adj., spotted] *archaic* **:** BADGER

bau·sond \'bäsənd, 'bȯ-\ *adj* [ME *bausand*, fr. MF *baucent*, perh. fr. L *balteus* belt, prob. fr. Etruscan] *dial Brit, of an animal* **:** having a white spot or streak on a dark ground esp. on the forehead or face

bau·ta \'bau̇də\ *n* -s [modif. of ON *bautasteinn*, fr. *bauta* (meaning and origin unknown) + *steinn* stone] **:** a prehistoric upright gravestone or memorial stone sometimes 20 feet high that was often placed at the summit of a barrow — compare MENHIR

ba·ut·ta \bä'üd·ə\ *n* -s [It, fr. It dial. (Venice) *bauta*, prob. fr. *bava* slobber, fr. (assumed) VL] **:** a black cloak with a hood that falls so as to mask the face esp. for masquerades

baux·ite \'bȯk,sīt, 'bäk,s-, -k,z- *sometimes* 'bō,zīt, *usu* -d·+V\ *also* **beaux·ite** \'bō,zīt, *usu* -d·+V\ *n* -s [F *bauxite*, fr. Les *Baux*, near Arles, Dept. Bouches-du-Rhône, France + F *-ite*] **:** an impure mixture of earthy hydrous aluminum oxides and hydroxides that commonly contains similar compounds of iron and occas. of manganese, usu. has a concretionary or oolitic structure, and is the principal source of aluminum used in commerce and industry

baux·it·ic \(')bȯk¦sid·ik, (')bäk¦-, -k¦z- *sometimes* (')bō¦zi-\ *adj* **:** containing or resembling bauxite ⟨~ clay⟩

ba·var·dage \,bavə(r)'däzh, '==,=\ *n* -s [F, fr. *bavarder* to gossip, chatter (fr. MF, fr. *bavard* chatterbox, fr. *bave* slobber, fr. — assumed — VL *bava*) + *-age*] **:** SMALL TALK, CHITCHAT

[1]ba·var·i·an \bə'verēən, -va(a)r-, -vār-\ *adj, usu cap* [*Bavaria*, region of Germany + E *-an*] **1 :** of, relating to, or characteristic of Bavaria **2 :** of, relating to, or characteristic of Bavarians **3 :** of, relating to, or characteristic of the Bavarian dialect

[2]bavarian \"\ *n* -s *cap* **1 :** a native or inhabitant of Bavaria **2 :** the High German dialect of Bavaria and Austria

bavarian cream *also* **bavarian** *n* -s *usu cap B* **:** a dessert of a flavored whipped gelatine mixture into which whipped cream is folded

ba·ve·nite \bə'vē,nīt, -vā-\ *n* -s [It, fr. *Baveno*, on Lake Maggiore, Italy + It *-ite*] **:** a mineral $Ca_4BeAl_2Si_9O_{24}(OH)_2$ consisting of a basic calcium beryllium aluminosilicate, belonging to the zeolite group, and occurring in radiated groups of white fibrous crystals (hardness 5.5, sp. gr. 2.7)

ba·vi·an \'bävēən, -vyən\ *n* -s [obs. G or D; obs. G *bavian* (now *pavian*), fr. D *baviaan*, alter. of *babiaen* — more at BABIANA] **:** CHACMA

bav·in \'bavən\ *n* -s [origin unknown] *Brit* **:** a bundle of brushwood or kindling used for fuel or in fences or drains

baw·bee *or* **bau·bee** \'bȯ(,)bē, 'bō- =¦=\ *n* -s [prob. after Alexander Orrok, laird of Sille*bawbe*, appointed mintmaster 1538] **1 :** an old Scottish billon coin issued by James V and Mary, Queen of Scots, at three halfpence **2 :** a Scottish copper coin worth sixpence issued by Charles II and William III **3 :** a unit of value equivalent to a bawbee coin ⟨half-*bawbee* coins were made⟩ **4 :** an English halfpenny **5 :** something of small value **:** TRIFLE ⟨no Scotsman who can write worth a ~ is ever quite happy until he has done a book about his glorious native tipple —Clifton Fadiman⟩

baw·cock \'bȯ,käk\ *n* -s [by folk etymology fr. F *beau coq*, fr. *beau* fine + *coq* fellow, cock (bird)] **:** a fine fellow ⟨how now, my ~ —Shak.⟩

[1]bawd \'bȯd\ *n* -s [ME *bawde*, perh. fr. MF *baud* (fem. *baude*) bold, merry, of Gmc origin; akin to OHG *bald* bold — more at BOLD] **1** *obs* **:** GO-BETWEEN, PANDER **2 a :** one who keeps a house of prostitution **:** MADAM **b :** PROSTITUTE ⟨there will be ~*s* aplenty when we reach Saint-Domingue —Frank Yerby⟩

[2]bawd \'bȧd, 'bȯd\ *n* -s [perh. short for *baudrons*] *chiefly Scot* **:** HARE

bawd·i·ly \'bȯdᵊlē, -dəlē, -li\ *adv* **:** in a bawdy manner

bawd·i·ness \-dēnə̇s\ *n* -ES **:** the quality or state of being bawdy ⟨his ribaldry and ~⟩

bawd·ry \'bȯdrē, -ri\ *n* -ES [ME *bawderie*, fr. *bawde* + *-erie* -ery] **1** *obs* **:** the practice or business of a bawd **2** *obs* **:** illicit intercourse **:** UNCHASTITY ⟨we must be married or we must live in ~ —Shak.⟩ **3 :** offensively suggestive, coarse, or obscene language **:** BAWDINESS ⟨smoking-room ~⟩

[1]bawdy \'bȯdē, -di\ *adj, usu* -ER/-EST [[1]*bawd* + *-y*] **:** of, relating to, or having the characteristics of a bawd **:** OBSCENE, LEWD, INDECENT, SMUTTY ⟨a ~ woman⟩ ⟨a ~ story⟩

[2]bawdy \"\ *n* -ES [prob. fr. [1]*bawdy*] **:** BAWDRY 3 ⟨how can that . . . coachman talk so much ~ to that lean horse —Laurence Sterne⟩

bawdy house \'==,=\ *n* [[2]*bawdy* + *house*] **:** BROTHEL

[1]bawl \'bȯl\ *vb* -ED/-ING/-S [ME *baulen*, prob. of Scand origin; akin to Icel *baula* to low, LG *bölen*, and prob. to ON *bylja* to resound — more at BELLOW] *vi* **1 :** to cry out loudly and unrestrainedly **:** YELL, BELLOW ⟨as the circle of sage lessened the steers began to ~ —Zane Grey⟩ ⟨Herr Direktor ~*ed* at them, worked them to weariness, and reduced Tania to nervous exhaustion —Winifred Bambrick⟩ **2 :** to cry loudly or lustily esp. from distress **:** WEEP, WAIL ⟨he collapsed in an armchair in the lobby and ~*ed* . . . uncontrollably —E.J.Kahn⟩ ~ *vt* **:** to cry out at the top of one's voice **:** SHOUT, PROCLAIM ⟨the sergeant ~*ing* commands⟩ ⟨a hawker ~*ing* his wares⟩ **syn** see ROAR

[2]bawl \"\ *n* -s **:** a loud prolonged cry **:** OUTCRY ⟨despite all political ~*s* and bellows about cattle prices —*Time*⟩

baw·ley \'bȯlē, -li\ *or* **bawley boat** *n* -s [origin unknown] **:** a broad-beamed shallow-draft cutter-rigged fishing boat used esp. for shrimping around the Thames and Medway estuaries

bawl out *vt* **:** to reprimand loudly or severely **:** REBUKE, REPROVE ⟨he *bawled* me *out* for letting such dangerously infectious material get on my fingers —Fredric Wertham⟩ **syn** see SCOLD

bawn \'bȯn\ *n* -s [IrGael *badhūn* enclosure, bulwark, fr. MIr *bōdhūn*, fr. *bō* cow + *dūn* enclosure, fr. OIr, castle, fortified town; akin to OE *cū* cow — more at COW, TOWN] **:** an enclosure usu. of mud or stone walls about a farmhouse or castle in Ireland: as **a :** the fortified court of a castle **b :** a fold for livestock, esp. cattle

baw·neen \'bȧ,nēn\ *n* -s [IrGael *bāinīn* flannel, white flannel jacket, fr. *bāin-*, *bān* white (fr. OIr *bān*) + *-īn* (dim. suffix); akin to Skt *bhāti* he shines — more at FANCY] **:** a man's work jacket of homemade undyed wool flannel worn esp. in Ireland

bax·ter \'bakstə(r)\ *n* -s [ME *bakestre*, *baxtere*, fr. OE *bæcestre*, fr. *bæcere* baker + *-stre* -ster — more at BAKER] **:** BAKER ⟨the excelling stewards, cunning ~*s*, excellent cooks —Sir Walter Scott⟩

[1]bax·te·ri·an \(')bak¦stirēən\ *adj, usu cap* [Richard *Baxter* †1691 Eng. Puritan scholar and writer + E *-ian*] **:** of or relating to Richard Baxter or his doctrines which sought to promote tolerance and restrain fanaticism by emphasizing certain fundamental tenets — **bax·te·ri·an·ism** \-ə,nizəm\ *n* -s

[2]baxterian \"\ *n* -s *usu cap* **:** an adherent or follower of Richard Baxter

[1]bay \'bā\ *adj* [ME, fr. MF *bai*, fr. L *badius*; akin to OIr *buide* yellow] **:** reddish brown **:** chestnut-colored — usu. used of a horse ⟨a ~ mare⟩

[2]bay \"\ *n* -s **1 :** an animal of a bay color; *specif* **:** a horse having a reddish brown body color with mane, tail, and points black ⟨a dashing pair of ~*s*⟩ — compare CHESTNUT **2 :** a moderate brown that is deeper and slightly redder than auburn, redder, stronger, and slightly darker than chestnut brown, lighter, stronger, and very slightly redder than tobacco, and darker and slightly yellower and less strong than toast brown — called also *Malabar*, *mummy brown*, *Trotteur tan*

[3]bay \"\ *n* -s [ME, weir, millrace] **:** a bank to keep back water **:** DAM

[4]bay \"\ *vt* -ED/-ING/-S **:** DAM — usu. used with *up* or *back* ⟨~ water up⟩

[5]bay \"\ *n* -s [ME *baye*, fr. MF *baie*, fr. L *baca*, prob. of non-IE origin; akin to the source of Gk *Bakchos* Bacchus, a name of Dionysus, god of fruits including esp. the grape] **1** *obs* **:** a berry esp. of the laurel **2 a :** LAUREL 1a **b :** any of several shrubs or trees esp. of the genera *Magnolia*, *Myrica*, and *Gordonia* resembling the laurel **3 a :** a garland or crown esp. of laurel given as a prize for victory or excellence — often used in pl. **b :** HONOR, FAME, RENOWN — usu. used in pl. ⟨the patriot's honors and the poet's ~*s* —John Trumbull⟩

[6]bay \"\ *n* -s [ME, fr. MF *baée* open part, opening, fr. OF *baee*, fr. fem. of *baé*, past part. of *baer* to be open, gape — more at ABEYANCE] **1 :** a principal compartment of the walls, roof, or other part of a building or of the whole building ⟨in a Gothic cathedral the transverse arches and adjacent piers of the arcade divide the building into ~*s* —Helen Gardner⟩ **2 :** a main division of any structure: as **a :** a compartment in a barn ⟨chaff packed into a whole ~ of the barn —Adrian Bell⟩ **b :** BAY WINDOW **c :** a straight section of trench between two adjacent traverses **d :** the length of bridge between center and center of adjacent pontoons in a pontoon bridge **e :** the forward part of a ship on each side between decks often used as a ship's hospital **f** (1) **:** a longitudinal portion of an elongated structure (as a truss or wing) lying between two adjacent transverse members or walls (as uprights or ribs) of an airship (2) **:** any of several compartments in the fuselage of an aircraft; *esp* **:** BOMB BAY **3 a :** a vertical support or group of such supports on which various pieces of electronic apparatus are mounted — used esp. of radio and telephone equipment **b :** one of the units including a dipole and a reflector that comprise an antenna array

[7]bay \"\ *vb* -ED/-ING/-S [ME *baien*, alter. of *abaien*, fr. OF *abaiier*, of imit. origin] *vi* **1** *of a dog* **:** to bark (as at a thief or at the game that is pursued) esp. with deep prolonged tones ⟨the wakeful dogs did never cease to ~ —Edmund Spenser⟩ **2 :** to cry out loud and long **:** SHOUT ⟨the prosecutor ~*ed* for a death penalty —*Time*⟩ ~ *vt* **1 :** to bark at **:** set upon with barking ⟨the dogs ran mad and ~*ed* the sky — Clinton Scollard⟩ **2 :** to bring to bay **:** hold at bay ⟨hounds jumping a fox . . . run it down and ~ it —Hart Stilwell⟩ **3 :** to pursue with barking ⟨killed by the aid of dogs ~*ing* and driving him up a tree —C.R.Darwin⟩ **4 :** to utter in deep prolonged tones ⟨a deep voice ~*ed* a question —Anne Green⟩

[8]bay \"\ *n* -s [ME *bay*, *abay*, fr. OF *abai*, fr. *abaier*, v.] **1 :** the position of one (as an animal) forced to face an antagonist ⟨a handsome young huntsman facing a furious boar at ~ —H.A.Overstreet⟩ **2 :** the position of one checked (as in pursuit, growth, or development) ⟨such infections can be kept at ~ if a wound is kept clean —C.L.Boltz⟩ **3 :** the barking of dogs; *esp* **:** a deep prolonged barking of dogs closing in on their quarry ⟨in full ~ the hounds followed the trail⟩

[9]bay \"\ *n* -s *often attrib* [ME *baye*, fr. MF *baie*, perh. alter. of *baiée* open part, opening, fr. OF *baiee*, fr. *baee*] **1 a :** an inlet of the sea or other body of water usu. smaller than a gulf but of the same general character **b :** a large tract of water around which the land forms a curve **c :** a recess or inlet between capes or headlands **2 :** a small body of water set off from the main body: as **a :** a compartment containing water for a wheel **b :** the portion of a canal just outside the gates of a lock **3 :** any of various terrestrial formations felt to resemble a bay of the sea: as **a :** a recess of plain within a curve in a range of hills **b :** an opening of prairie in the edge of a forest **c :** CAROLINA BAY **d :** a recess (as in the forepart of a shrubbery) for the display of specimen or accent plants

[10]bay *n* -s [back-formation fr. earlier *bayse*, fr. MF *baies*, pl. — more at BAIZE] *obs* **:** BAIZE — usu. used in pl.

ba·ya \'bīyə, bī'yä\ *or* **baya weaver** *n* -s [Hindi *bayā*, *baiyā*] **:** an East Indian weaverbird (*Ploceus philippinus*) that feeds on seeds and insects and is sometimes destructive to grain crops

bayacura root *var of* BIACURU

baya·dere \'bī(y)ə,di(ə)r, -de(ə)r\ *n* -s [fr. *bayadere* Hindu dancing girl, fr. F *bayadère*, fr. Pg *bailadeira* female dancer, fr. *bailar* to dance, fr. LL *ballare* — more at BALL] **1 :** a fabric made with a design of horizontal stripes in strongly contrasted colors **2 a :** a design of horizontal stripes in strongly contrasted colors **b :** decoration applied in horizontal stripes (as in a printed pattern on textiles)

ba·ya·mo \bə'yä(,)mō\ *n* -s [fr. *Bayamo*, Cuba] **:** a violent thundersquall that occurs on the south coast of Cuba esp. near Bayamo, the gusts being modified foehn winds

bay antler \'bā-\ *or* **bes antler** \'bes-, 'bās-\ *or* **bez antler** \'bez-, 'bāz-\ *n* [*bay antler* by folk etymology fr. *bes antler*, *bez antler*; *bes antler*, *bez antler* fr. *bes-*, *bez-* secondary (fr. ME *bes-*, fr. MF, fr. L *bis-* twice) + E *antler* — more at BIS-] **:** the second tine from the base of a stag's antler — called also *bay point*; see ANTLER illustration

bay bar *or* **bay barrier** *n* [[9]*bay*] **:** a bank of sand or of sand and gravel deposited by waves and currents across the mouth of a bay so that the bay is no longer connected or is connected only by a narrow outlet with the main body of water — called also *baymouth bar*

bay-bay \bī'ē,bī, 'bī,bī\ *n* -s [Island Carib *bai-bai*] **:** a tropical American shrub or small tree (*Byrsonima spicata*) with racemose flowers and fleshy fruits

bay bean *n* **1 :** a tropical vine (*Canavalia lineata*) growing on the seashore **2 :** one of the brown seeds of bay bean

bayberry \'=(,)==, '== — *see* BERRY\ *n* [[5]*bay* + *berry*] **1 a :** a West Indian tree (*Pimenta acris*) that is closely related to the allspice tree and that is a source of bay oil — called also *bay rum tree*, *Jamaica bayberry*, *wild cinnamon*; see BAY RUM **b :** the fruit of the bay tree **2 a :** any of several plants of the genus *Myrica* (esp. the eastern *M. pensylvanica*) common mostly near No. American coasts **b :** the fruit of wax myrtle **3 :** a variable color averaging a grayish green that is bluer, lighter, and stronger than slate green and yellower and lighter than average blue spruce

bayberry bark *n* **:** the bark of the root of either of two trees (*Myrica cerifera* and *M. pensylvanica*) used as a tonic and astringent — called also *candleberry bark*

bayberry family *n* **:** MYRICACEAE

bayberry gray *n* **:** a pale green that is bluer and very slightly duller than celadon gray, bluer and duller than spray green, and bluer and duller than aloes green

bayberry wax *or* **bayberry tallow** *n* **:** a deep fragrant green waxlike fat obtained from the wax myrtle and used esp. in making candles

bay bird *n* [[9]*bay*] **:** any of various limicoline birds that frequent the shores of bays and inlets

baybolt \'=,=\ *n* [[6]*bay* + *bolt*] **:** a bolt with a barbed shank

bay-breasted warbler \'=¦==-\ *n* [[1]*bay*] **:** an American warbler (*Dendroica castanea*) having the breast and crown of the head of the male a rich chestnut brown

baybush \'=,=\ *n* [[5]*bay* + *bush*] **:** SWEET GALE

bay camphor *n* [[5]*bay*] **:** LAURIN

bay cat *n* [[1]*bay*] **:** a wildcat (*Felis bodia*) of Borneo and adjacent regions

bay cedar *n* [[5]*bay*] **1 :** a common Central American timber tree (*Guazuma ulmifolia*) with wood not unlike that of the American elm **2 :** any of several plants of the genus *Suriana* (esp. the tropical *S. maritima*) with alternate entire leaves and yellow flowers — called also *tassel plant*

bay-ce·dar family \'=¦==-\ *n* **:** SURIANACEAE

bay coot *n* [[9]*bay*] **:** an American scoter: as **a :** SURF SCOTER **b :** an immature or female white-winged scoter

bayed *past of* BAY

bay·er·ite \'bāə,rīt, 'bīə,-\ *n* -s [fr. the name *Bayer* + E *-ite*] **:** an artificially prepared compound $Al(OH)_3$ that is a polymorph of gibbsite

bay·er process \'bāə(r)-, 'bīə-\ *n, usu cap B* [after Karl J. *Bayer* †1904 Ger. chemist] **:** a process for producing alumina from bauxite by digesting it in hot sodium hydroxide solution

bay·er's acid \'bīə(r)z-\ *n, usu cap B* [after Friedrich *Bayer* †1880 Ger. industrialist] **:** CROCEIN ACID

bay·er 205 \'bīə(r)¦tü,ō'fīv\ *n, usu cap* [after Friedrich *Bayer* and Co., 19th cent. Ger. chemical company] **:** SURAMIN

baye·ta \bī'ād·ə, -'yā-\ *n* -s [Sp, prob. fr. obs. F *baïette*, fr MF, dim. of *baie* baize — more at BAIZE] **1 :** BAIZE 1 **2 :** an imitation of baize woven by the Navahos

bay floe *n* [[9]*bay*] **:** a floe of bay ice

baygall \'=,=\ *n* [[9]*bay* + *gall*] **1 :** RED BAY **2 :** a tract of swampy land; *esp* **:** a low-lying tract of boggy or spongy land in the southern U.S. usu. overgrown with the inkberry and with bay trees

bay grass *n* [[9]*bay*] **:** LOVE GRASS

bayhead \'=,=\ *n* [[9]*bay* + *head*] **:** the part of a bay that is most remote from the larger body of water with which the bay is confluent

bayhead bar *or* **bay head barrier** *n* **:** a bank of sand or of sand and gravel deposited across a bay near its head often with a narrow breach to serve as outlet of the nearly confined water

bayhead beach *n* **:** a beach at the head of a bay

bay ice *n* [[9]*bay*] **:** sea ice that is formed in the shelter of a bay in the arctic or antarctic and that is relatively smooth since it is not subjected to wind or pressure

baying *pres part of* BAY

bay laurel *n* [[5]*bay*] **1 :** BAY TREE **2 :** OLEANDER **3 :** CHERRY LAUREL 1 **4 :** CALIFORNIA LAUREL

bay lavender *n* [[9]*bay*] **:** a fleshy shrub (*Mallotonia gnaphalodes*) of the family Boraginaceae of Florida, Central America, and the West Indies having silky gray leaves in clusters near the ends of the branches

bayl·don·ite \'bāldə,nīt\ *n* -s [John *Bayldon*, 19th cent. Englishman + E *-ite*] **:** a mineral $(Cu,Pb)_2(AsO_4)(OH)$ consisting of a lead copper arsenate and occurring in mammillary green masses

bay leaf *n* [[5]*bay*] **:** the dried leaf of the bay tree (*Laurus nobilis*) used as an herb in cooking

bay-leaf willow *or* **bay-leaved willow** \'=,=-\ *n* **:** BAY WILLOW 1

bay·ley·ite \'bālē,īt\ *n* -s [William S. *Bayley* †1943 Am. geologist + E *-ite*] **:** a mineral $Mg_2(UO_2)(CO_3)_3.18H_2O$ consisting of a rare hydrous magnesium uranyl carbonate of yellow color found in Arizona

bay lynx *n* [[1]*bay*] **:** a wildcat (*Lynx rufus*) that is the common wildcat of the eastern U.S. — see DESERT CAT

bay mackerel *n* [[9]*bay*] **:** a Spanish mackerel (*Scomberomorus maculatus*)

bay·man \'bāmən\ *n, pl* **baymen** [[9]*bay* + *man*] **:** one who lives or works on or about a bay

bay·mouth bar \'bā,mau̇th-\ *n* [[9]*bay* + *mouth*] **:** BAY BAR

bay myrtle *n* [[5]*bay*] **:** WAX MYRTLE

bay oak *n* [[5]*bay*] **:** ENGLISH OAK

bay·o·gou·la \,bī(y)ō'gülə, -(y)ə'-\ *n, pl* **bayogoula** *or* **bayogoulas** *usu cap* [Choctaw *Bayuk-ókla*, lit., bayou people] **1 :** an extinct Muskogean people of southern Louisiana **2 :** a member of the Bayogoula people

bay oil *n* [[5]*bay*] **1 :** a yellow aromatic antiseptic essential oil obtained from the leaves of the West Indian bayberry and used in perfumes and esp. in bay rum — called also *myrcia oil* **2 :** a light-yellow essential oil obtained from the leaves of the California laurel — called also *California bay oil*

ba·yok \(')bī¦(y)ōk\ *also* **ba·yog** \-¦(y)ōg\ *n* -s [Tag *bayok*] **:** any of several Philippine timber trees of the genus *Pterospermum* (esp. *P. diversifolium*) the bark of which yields an inferior fiber and a dye

[1]bay·o·net \'bāənə̇t, -,net, ¦bāə'net, *usu* -d·+V\ *n* -s *often attrib* [F *baïonnette*, fr. *Bayonne*, France, where first made + F *-ette*] **1 :** a steel blade made to be attached to or at the muzzle end of a shoulder arm and used esp. for stabbing and slashing in hand-to-hand combat **2 :** a pin that plays in and out of holes made to receive it and serving to engage or disengage parts (as of machinery) ⟨~ joint⟩ ⟨~ lamp base⟩

[2]bayonet \"\ *vb* **bayoneted** *also* **bayonetted**; **bayoneted** *also* **bayonetted**; **bayoneting** *also* **bayonetting**; **bayonets** *vt* **1 :** to stab with a bayonet ⟨we found their bodies *bayoneted* right through the blankets —Burtt Evans⟩ **2 :** to compel or drive by or as if by the bayonet ⟨troops to sabre and to ~ us into a submission —Edmund Burke⟩ ~ *vi* **:** to use a bayonet ⟨taught soldiers to ~ and to survive hand-to-hand combat⟩

bayonets 1

bayonet gauge *n* **:** a graduated stick or rod esp. for testing the depth of oil in a crankcase

bayonet grass *n* **:** a pale-green sedge (*Scirpus paludosus*) of alkaline marshes and shores chiefly of western No. America with ovoid to cylindric spikelets in clusters

bayonet mount *n* **:** a mount in which prongs or bayonets on the rim of the lens or lens accessory of a camera fit into slots in the camera to facilitate quick attachment (as in interchanging lenses)

bayonet plant *n* **:** YUCCA; *esp* **:** an Adam's needle (*Yucca filamentosa*)

bayonet stack *n* **:** an exhaust pipe whose open end is cut off diagonally and partly flattened and has the edges curved inward to increase the muffling effect

bay·ong \bī'ȯŋ, -'yȯŋ\ *also* **bay·on** \-'ȯn, -'yōn\ *n* -s [Tag & Bisayan *bayóng*, *bay-óng*] **:** a coarse sack of woven strips of pandanus or palm leaves used esp. in the Philippines

bay·ott \(')bī¦ät, -¦yät\ *n* -s [origin unknown] **:** PALOSAPIS

bay·ou \'bī,(y)ü; *S usu* -,(y)ō, *esp La also* -(y)ə *or sometimes* bāyü\ *n* -s [LaF, fr. Choctaw *bayuk*] **1 :** a creek, secondary watercourse, or minor river that is tributary to another river or other body of water **2 :** any of various bodies of water: as **a :** a large stream or creek or a small river that is characterized by a slow or imperceptible current; *esp* **:** a sluggish stream that follows a tortuous course through alluvial lowlands, swamps, or plantations **b :** a clear brook or rivulet that rises in the hills esp. of northern Arkansas or southern Missouri **c :** an effluent usu. sluggish or stagnant branch of a main stream: as (1) **:** a natural canal connecting two bodies of water (2) **:** a by-channel of a river enclosing a low island (3) **:** a branch of a river discharging through a delta **d :** an intermittent, partly closed, or disused watercourse that is sluggish or stagnant: as (1) **:** a partly closed channel of a river delta (2) **:** *or* **bayou lake :** a lake or pool in an abandoned channel of a stream (3) **:** a swampy or miry offshoot of a lake or river subject to overflow (4) **:** an outlet for a coastal lake or swamp (5) **:** a slough in a salt marsh (6) **:** a shallow or stagnant inlet opening into a bay, lake, or river **e** (1) **:** an estuarial creek or inlet on the Gulf coast (2) **:** a small bay, open cove, or harbor (3) **:** a lagoon, lake, or bay esp. in a sea marsh or among salt-marsh islands **f** (1) **:** a passage connecting two bodies of open water (as bays) (2) **:** a navigable channel through sandbars or mud flats

bayou bass *n* **:** LARGEMOUTH BLACK BASS

bay plum *n* [[9]*bay*] **:** GUAVA 1, 2

bay point *n* [*bay* (antler)] **:** BAY ANTLER

bay poplar *n* [[5]*bay*] **1 :** TUPELO GUM **2 :** the wood of tupelo gum

bay rum *n* [[5]*bay*] **:** a fragrant liquid used for cosmetic and medicinal purposes, the original from the West Indies being prepared by distilling the leaves of the bayberry (*Pimenta acris*) with rum and that of the National Formulary being prepared from bay oil (sense 1), orange oil (sense a), pimenta oil, alcohol, and water

bay-rum tree \'=¦=,=\ *n* **:** BAYBERRY 1a

bays *pl of* BAY, *pres 3d sing of* BAY

bay salt *n* [[9]*bay*] **:** SOLAR SALT

bay scallop *n* [[9]*bay*] **:** a small delicate-flavored scallop (*Pecten irradians*) formerly abundant in shallow water from Maine to the Gulf of Mexico but now greatly reduced by excessive commercial fishing

bay shark *n* [[9]*bay*] **:** a common shark (*Carcharhinus lamiella*) widespread in shallow waters of warm or temperate seas and very destructive to nets and fishes

bay shilling *n, usu cap B* [fr. Massachusetts *Bay* Colony, where it was coined] **:** PINE TREE SHILLING

bay stall *n* [[6]*bay*] **:** a seat fixed in a window bay

bay stater *n, usu cap B&S* [*Bay State*, nickname for Massachusetts + E *-er*] **:** a native or resident of Massachusetts — used as a nickname

bay stone *n* [perh. alter. of *base stone*] **:** a stone laid on the ground as part of a surface foundation for a structure

bay-top palmetto \'ˌ=ˌ=-\ *n* [⁵*bay*] **:** a tropical American thatch palm (*Coccothrinax argentea*) with silvery leaves and black fruit

bay tree *n* [⁵*bay*] **1 :** LAUREL 1a **2 :** CALIFORNIA LAUREL **3 :** BAYBERRY 1a

bay willow *n* [⁵*bay*] **1 :** a European willow (*Salix pentandra*) with shining coriaceous leaves **2 :** FIREWEED b

bay window *n* [ME *baye wyndowe*, fr. *baye, bay* bay (compartment)] **1 :** a window or series of windows forming a bay or recess in a room and projecting outward from the wall in a rectangular, polygonal, or curved form — compare BOW WINDOW, ORIEL **2 :** a large protruding stomach esp. of a man **:** PAUNCH, POTBELLY ⟨men with weak hearts and *bay windows*⟩

bay window

bay-winged bunting \'=ˌ=-\ *n* [¹*bay*] **:** VESPER SPARROW

bay·wood \'bā+ˌ-\ *n* [*Bay* of Campeche, Mexico + E *wood*] **:** MAHOGANY 1a (2)

ba·zaar *also* **ba·zar** \bə'zär, -'zà(r\ *n* -s [Per *bāzār*, alter. of MPer *bāchār*, fr. OPer *abēcharish*] **1 :** an Oriental market place or market that usu. consists of rows of shops or stalls where all kinds of goods are offered for sale ⟨the mock Rajah is reduced to going about the ~ and the villages soliciting alms —J.G.Frazer⟩ **2 a :** a place or establishment (as a large hall) for the sale of goods (as fine fabrics and odd knickknacks) ⟨days were spent in the big ~*s* where already the Christmas stocks were beginning to fill the counters —Winifred Bambrick⟩ **b :** a departmentalized retail store **:** DEPARTMENT STORE ⟨the great city ~ crushed its country rivals with branch stores —Edward Bellamy⟩ **3 :** a fair for the sale of useful and ornamental articles esp. for charitable or religious ends ⟨one of those nabobs . . . first thought of helping the local church by means of a ~ —Ernest Weekley⟩

ba·ze·ries cylinder \ˌbaz(ə)'rē,-, '=(=),=-\ *n, usu cap B* [after Etienne *Bazeries* †1931 Fr. cryptographer credited with its invention] **:** a cryptographic cylinder assembled of disks that can be rotated on a common shaft, each disk having on its periphery a different mixed alphabet and used for multiple substitution

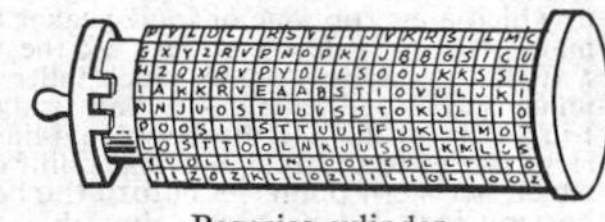
Bazeries cylinder

ba·zi·gar \ˌbäzə'gär\ *n, pl* **bazigar** *or* **bazigars** *usu cap* [Hindi *bāzīgar*, fr. Per, lit., player] **1 :** a gypsylike nomadic Muslim people in India **2 :** a member of the Bazigar people

ba·zoo \bə'zü\ *n* -s [origin unknown] **1 :** KAZOO **2** *slang* **:** MOUTH ⟨she's always blowing off her ~ —J.T.Farrell⟩ **3 :** a sound of disapproval **:** RASPBERRY ⟨the British ~ is higher and clearer than the Madison Square Garden variety —*Newsweek*⟩

ba·zoo·ka \bə'zükə\ *n* -s [fr. *bazooka*, a crude musical instrument made of pipes and a funnel and used by Bob Burns †1956 Am. comedian, prob. fr. *bazoo*] **1 :** a light portable usu. crew-served shoulder weapon consisting of an open-breech smooth-bore firing tube and used esp. to launch armor-piercing rockets **2 :** a rocket launcher placed on the underside of the wing of a warplane

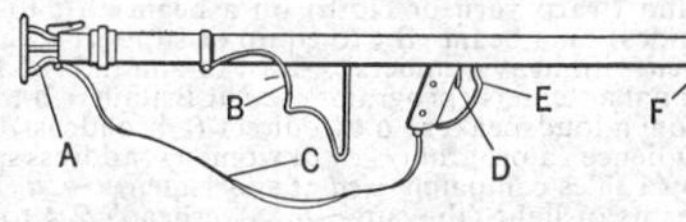

bazooka: *A* breech guard, *B* shoulder rest, *C* strap for carrying, *D* trigger *E* guard, *F* muzzle

ba·zoo·ka·man \-ˌman,-maa(ə)n\ *n, pl* **bazookamen :** a man armed with a bazooka

baz·zite \'baˌzīt, 'bät,sīt\ *n* -s [It, fr. Alessandro E. *Bazzi* †1929 Ital. engineer + It *-ite*] **:** a mineral consisting of a silicate of scandium and other rare-earth metals and occurring in small azure-blue hexagonal prisms

bb \'bēbē\ *or* **beebee** \"\ *n* -s *usu cap both Bs* [prob. fr. the letter *b*] **1 :** a shot pellet 0.18 inch in diameter for use in shotgun cartridges **2 :** a shot pellet 0.175 inch in diameter for use in a BB gun

BB *abbr, often not cap* **1** bail bond **2** ball bearing **3** balloon barrage **4** bankbook **5** base on balls **6** bearer bond **7** best of breed **8** bill book **9** blessed **10** blue book **11** break bulk

b battery \'bē,-\ *n, usu cap 1st B* **:** an electric battery connected in the plate circuit of an electron tube to cause flow of electron current in the tube — called also *plate battery*; compare A BATTERY, C BATTERY

bbb *abbr* **1** bed, breakfast, and bath **2** *usu cap all 3 Bs* better business bureau

bbc *abbr, often cap both Bs&C* **1** baseball club **2** basketball club

bb cap \'bēbē,-\ *n, usu cap both Bs* **:** a .22 caliber metallic cartridge about 0.43 inch long overall that consists of a rimfire case and a small (as about 20 grain) round-nose lead bullet and in which orig. the primer served as the propellant

bb gun *n, usu cap both Bs* **:** a smooth-bore air gun actuated by a spring-loaded plunger that upon release from the cocked position compresses the air behind the pellet and propels it from the tube — compare AIR RIFLE 1

bbl *abbr* barrel

BBT *abbr* basal body temperature

BC *abbr* **1** [It *basso continuo*] thorough bass **2** battery commander **3** before Christ **4** bicycle club **5** board of control **6** boat club **7** borough council **8** bowling club **9** broadcast

BCD *abbr* bad conduct discharge

BCE *abbr* before the Common Era

BCG *abbr* bacillus Calmette-Guérin

bcg vaccine \ˌbē,sē'jē-\ *n, usu cap B&C&G* **:** a vaccine prepared from a living attenuated strain of tubercle bacilli and used to vaccinate human beings against tuberculosis

bch *abbr* bunch

BCL \ˌbē,sē'el\ *abbr or n* -s **:** a bachelor of civil law

BCL *abbr* broadcast listener

bcn *abbr* beacon

b complex \'bē,-\ *n, usu cap B* [by shortening] **:** VITAMIN B COMPLEX

bc soil \(')bē'sē,-\ *n, usu cap B&C* **:** a soil with a profile having only B-horizons and C-horizons

bd *abbr* **1** band **2** board **3** bond **4** bound **5** boundary **6** brindled **7** bundle

BD *abbr or n* -s **:** a bachelor of divinity

BD *abbr, often not cap* **1** back dividend **2** bank draft **3** barrels per day **4** bills discounted **5** bomb disposal **6** brought down

bde *abbr* brigade

bdell- *or* **bdello-** *comb form* [F & NL, fr. Gk, fr. *bdella*] **:** leech ⟨*Bdelloura*⟩ ⟨*Bdelloida*⟩ ⟨*bdellotomy*⟩

-bdel·la \-b+'delə\ *n comb form* -s [NL, fr. Gk *bdella*] **:** leech — esp. in generic names in helminthology ⟨*Malacobdella*⟩

bdel·li·dae \'delə,dē\ *n pl, cap* [NL, fr. *Bdella*, type genus (fr. Gk *bdella* leech) + *-idae*] **:** a family of mites (order Acarina) comprising the snout mites that feed on insects and on other mites

bdel·li·um \'delēəm, -lyəm\ *n* -s [ME, fr. L, fr. Gk *bdellion*, perh. of Semitic origin; akin to Heb *bĕdhōlah*] **:** a gum resin obtained from various trees of the genus *Commiphora* that is similar to myrrh and used for the same purposes — compare BISABOL

bdel·lod·ri·lus \de'lädrələs\ *n, cap* [NL, fr. *bdell-* + Gk *drilos* earthworm] **:** a genus of small leechlike oligochaete worms parasitic on the gills of crayfishes

¹**bdel·loid** \'de,lȯid\ *adj* [*bdell-* + *-oid*] **:** like or relating to a leech

²**bdelloid** \"\ *n* -s **:** LEECH

bdel·loi·da \de'lȯidə\ [NL, fr. *bdell-* + *-oida*] *syn of* BDELLOIDEA

bdel·loi·dea \-'lȯidēə\ *n pl, cap* [NL, alter. of *Bdelloida*] **:** an order of Rotifera comprising forms that swim freely by means of the ciliated disk and also creep like leeches

bdel·lo·nemertea \ˌdelō+\ *n pl, cap* [NL, fr. *bdell-* + *Nemertea*] **:** an order of Nemertea (class Enopla) comprising short thick-bodied forms with a large posterior sucker and no eyes or cerebral organ — see MALACOBDELLA

bdel·lo·nys·sus \ˌdelə'nisəs\ *n, cap* [NL, fr. *bdell-* + *-nyssus* (fr. Gk *nyssein, nyttein* to prick, sting) — more at NUMEN] **:** a genus of mites (family Dermanyssidae) parasitic on vertebrates and including serious pests (as *B. bursa* and *B. sylviarum*) of domestic fowl and the tropical rat mite

bdel·lou·ra \de'lürə, -'laù-\ *n, cap* [NL, fr. *bdell-* + Gk *oura* tail; akin to Gk *orrhos* buttocks — more at ASS] **:** a genus (the type of the family Bdellouridae) of triclad flatworms that live in the gills of the horseshoe crab

bdg *abbr* binding

BDI *abbr, often not cap* **1** both dates inclusive **2** both days inclusive

bdl *abbr* bundle

bdr *abbr, often cap B* **1** bombardier **2** brigadier

bdry *abbr* boundary

BDS *abbr* bomb disposal squad

bdy *abbr* boundary

¹**be** \(ˌ)bē, ˌbi\ *vb, past 1st & 3d sing* **was** \(ˌ)wəz, (ˌ)wäz *also* (ˌ)wȯz\ *or dial* **were** *see below*\ *or* **war** \(ˌ)wär\; *2d sing* **were** \ˌwə(r); ˌwər, + V ˌwər-, ˌwə̄, + V " *or* ˌwər- *also* ˌwər; *archaic or Brit* (ˌ)w|a(a)(ə)r *or* |e(ə)r *or* |a(a)ə *or* |eə\ *or dial & archaic* **was** *or dial* **war** (with *you*) *or archaic* **wast** (with *thou*) \ˌwəst, (ˌ)wäst *also* (ˌ)wȯst\ *or* **wert** (with *thou*) \ˌwə(r)t, ˌwər|t, (ˌ)wə̄|t, (ˌ)wəi|t, *usu* |d·+V\ *pl* **were** *or substand & archaic* **was** *or dial* **war**; *past subjunctive* **were** *or substand & archaic* **was** *or archaic 2d sing* **wert** (with *thou*); *past part* **been** \(ˌ)bin, ˌbən; ben (*in standard speech more often unstressed or with secondary stress than with primary stress*); *Brit usu & US sometimes* (ˌ)bēn\ *or dial* **ben** \(ˌ)ben\ *pres part* **be·ing** \ˈbēiŋ, ˈbēŋ, *rapid* (ˌ)bēŋ\ *or dial Brit & archaic* **been** \(ˌ)bēn, ˈbēən\ *pres 1st sing* **am** \ˌəm, (ˌ)am *also* (ˌ)aa(ə)m; *after "I" often* m\ *or dial* **is** *or* **be**; *2d sing* **are** (with *you*) \ˌə(r), (ˌ)är, (ˌ)å(r; *after a vowel-final pronoun often* r\ *or archaic* **art** (with *thou*) \ˌə(r)|t, (ˌ)är|t, (ˌ)å|t, +V *usu* |d·\ *or dial* **be** *or* **is** (with *you*) *or dial Brit* **beest** (with *thou*) \(ˌ)bēst, ˈbēəst\ *or* **bist** (with *thou*) \(ˌ)bist\ *3d sing* **is** \(ˌ)iz, əz; *after vowels & after voiced consonants other than* z, zh, & j: *often* z; *after voiceless consonants other than* s, sh, & ch: *often* s\ *or dial Brit* **be**, *pl* **are** *or substand* **is** *or dial & archaic* **be** *or archaic* **been** *the last like past part* BEEN\ *pres subjunctive* **be** *or obs 2d sing* **beest** (with *thou*) [ME *been*, fr. OE *bēon*; akin to OHG *bim* am, ON *būa* to live, dwell, Goth *bauan*, L *fui* I have been, *futurus* about to be, *fieri* to become, Gk *phyein* to bring forth, *phynai* to be born, be, Skt *bhavati* he is] *vi* **1 a :** to equal in meaning **:** have the same connotation (sense 3) as ⟨*God is* love⟩ ⟨January *is* the first month⟩ ⟨let *x* ~ 10⟩ **:** represent symbolically ⟨the seven lampstands *are* the seven churches —Rev 1:20 (RSV)⟩ **b :** to constitute the same idea or object as **:** have individual identity with ⟨the first person I met *was* my brother⟩ ⟨the pianist himself *was* the composer of the piece⟩ ⟨$50 *was* all I had⟩ **c :** to constitute the same class as ⟨these three books *are* the authoritative works on the president's life⟩ **d :** to have a meaning that includes or implies the meaning of ⟨fish *are* vertebrates⟩ ⟨red *is* a color⟩ **:** have a (specified) qualification or characterization ⟨the leaves *are* green⟩ ⟨this book *is* heavy⟩ **e :** to belong as an individual to the class of ⟨the fish you caught *was* a trout⟩ **f :** to belong as a class to the larger class of ⟨some animals with horns and divided hoofs *are* graminivorous animals⟩ — used regularly in senses 1a through 1f as the copula of simple predication **g :** SIGNIFY **:** amount to ⟨her death *was* nothing to him⟩ **h :** to show oneself as an outstanding example of — used with main stress in spoken sentences ⟨the doctor pleased the parents by commenting, "That *is* a baby"⟩ **i :** to constitute genuinely **:** actualize well the type of ⟨one of the few great elegies which *are* elegies —Douglas Bush⟩ **j :** to seem to consist of **:** show oneself gripped or dominated by (a feeling) ⟨she *was* all scorn at the proposition⟩ **:** become completely covered with ⟨road *was* all mud⟩ **2 a :** to exist either absolutely or in relations or under conditions specified **:** have an objective existence **:** have reality or actuality **:** LIVE ⟨Thee, which *wert* and *art* and evermore shalt *be* —Reginald Heber⟩ ⟨I think, therefore I *am*⟩ — often used with *there* ⟨once upon a time there *was* a knight⟩ ⟨there *is* a wreck ahead⟩ **b :** to have, maintain, or occupy a place, situation, or position **:** show a certain characteristic — often used with a prepositional phrase ⟨the book *is* on the table⟩ ⟨he *was* at ease⟩ **c :** to remain unmolested, unbothered, or uninterrupted — used only in infinitive form ⟨let him ~ ; stop pestering him⟩ **d :** HAPPEN, OCCUR **:** take place ⟨the concert *was* last night⟩ ⟨where will the meeting ~⟩ **e** *archaic* **:** BELONG, PERTAIN ⟨to thine and Albany's issue ~ this perpetual —Shak.⟩ **f** (1) **:** to come or go **:** JOURNEY ⟨we will ~ on our way shortly⟩ ⟨have you *been* home since Christmas⟩ (2) **:** to make a stay **:** show oneself or be present ⟨they will ~ in town all week⟩ ⟨*was* your sister at the party last night⟩ — not used in the present; use of the past tense followed by *to* ⟨I *was* to town yesterday⟩ often considered nonstandard **g :** to come around in due course often in following a schedule or appointed round — used only in perfect forms ⟨has the postman *been* this morning⟩ **h** *substand* **:** ACT — used only in the perfect; used as an intensive ⟨see what you have *been* and done⟩ **3** *now dial Brit* **:** to stand good for expense (as in a treat) ⟨offering to ~ his friend's dinner⟩ ~ *verbal auxiliary* **1 :** to undergo an action — used with the past participle of transitive verbs as a passive-voice auxiliary ⟨the money *was* found⟩ ⟨German *is* spoken here⟩ ⟨the house is *being* built⟩ **2 :** to perform a continuous action **:** be supposed to perform a future action — used as the auxiliary of the present participle in the so-called progressive tenses, usu. expressing continuous action ⟨he *is* reading⟩ ⟨I have *been* sleeping⟩ ⟨the house *is* being built⟩ but sometimes in present-tense form expressing future noncontinuous action ⟨he *is* leaving tomorrow⟩ **3 :** to have changed place or condition as a result of completing an action — used with the past participle of certain intransitive verbs as an auxiliary forming archaic perfect tenses ⟨Christ *is* risen from the dead —1 Cor 15:20 (DV)⟩ ⟨the minstrel boy to the war *is* gone —Thomas Moore⟩ **4 :** become supposed **:** become destined — used with the infinitive with *to* to express futurity, arrangement in advance, or obligation ⟨I *am* to interview him today⟩ ⟨he *was* to become one of the most famous men of his century⟩ ⟨you *are* to repay the loan in monthly installments⟩ — usu. not used in the form of an infinitive or participle **5 :** to undergo a continuous action **:** be in the process of — used in a passive sense with the present participle or with the gerund preceded by the prefix *a-* or the preposition *a* ⟨while the ark *was* building —1 Pet 3:20 (NCE)⟩ ⟨when the ark *was* a building —1 Pet 3:20 (DV)⟩; now usu. replaced by the passive construction with *being* followed by the past participle, as in 1 and 2 — **be oneself :** to act, talk, or comport oneself in a usual or fitting manner **:** show that one has attained to a suitable self-realization — **to be sure :** GRANTED, ADMITTEDLY

²**be** *var of* BEE

be- *prefix* [ME, fr. OE *be-, bi-*; akin to OE *bī* by, near, OHG *bi-* be-, *bī* by, near, Goth *bi-* be-, *bi* by, about, at — more at BY] **1 :** on **:** around **:** over ⟨*be*daub⟩ ⟨*be*smear⟩ **2 :** to a great or greater degree **:** thoroughly — esp. in intensive verbs formed from simple verbs ⟨*be*cudgel⟩ ⟨*be*fuddle⟩ ⟨*be*smite⟩ ⟨*be*spatter⟩ ⟨*be*rate⟩ **3 :** excessively **:** ostentatiously — in intensive verbs formed from simple verbs ⟨*be*deck⟩ ⟨*be*laud⟩ and in adjectives based on adjectives ending in *-ed* ⟨*be*ribboned⟩ ⟨*be*furbelowed⟩ **4 :** about **:** to **:** at **:** upon **:** against **:** across — in transitive verbs formed from intransitive simple verbs ⟨*be*stride⟩ ⟨*be*speak⟩ ⟨*be*croak⟩ **5 :** make **:** cause to be **:** treat as — in verbs formed from adjectives or nouns ⟨*be*little⟩ ⟨*be*numb⟩ ⟨*be*fool⟩ ⟨*be*friend⟩ **6 :** call or dub esp. excessively — in verbs formed from nouns ⟨*be*lady⟩ ⟨*be*rascal⟩ ⟨*be*doctor⟩ **7 :** affect, afflict, treat, provide, or cover with esp. excessively — in verbs formed from nouns ⟨*be*famine⟩ ⟨*be*devil⟩ ⟨*be*glue⟩ ⟨*be*blood⟩ and sometimes only in the form of a past participle or adjective ending in *-ed* ⟨*be*capped⟩ ⟨*be*cobwebbed⟩

Bé *abbr* Baumé

BE *abbr* **1** band elimination **2** bill of entry **3** bill of exchange **4** board of education **5** Buddhist Era

Be *symbol* beryllium

¹**beach** \'bēch\ *n* -ES [origin unknown] **1 :** shore pebbles **:** SHINGLE **2 a :** a gently sloping shore of an ocean, sea, or lake or the bank of a river that is covered by sand, sand and gravel, or larger rock fragments, is usu. orig. water-borne, and is typically devoid of much vegetation **:** STRAND; *also* **:** the deposit of sand, gravel, or rock fragments along a shore **b :** a seashore area ⟨a vacation at the ~⟩ **c** *in New Jersey* **:** a low sand island along the coast **d :** a stretch of sand placed beside a bathing area for the bathers' pleasure and recreation ⟨putting in a ~ by the pool⟩ **e :** naval or mercantile offices or instrumentalities ashore ⟨the ~ handed over the sealed orders to the captain⟩ **f :** an African trading or shopping center not necessarily located near a shoreline **3 :** a light olive gray to light grayish olive that is very slightly redder and paler than sage gray — called also *chip, smoke yellow* — **on the beach 1 :** UNEMPLOYED, DOWN-AND-OUT **:** badly needing money or work **:** STRANDED **2 :** assigned to a post ashore ⟨a living allowance for officers *on the beach*⟩

²**beach** \"\ *vt* -ED/-ING/-ES **1 :** to run or haul (a ship) ashore or aground esp. when mooring, anchoring, or docking is unfeasible or when quick landing of supplies and personnel is required ⟨the mutineers ~*ed* the ship on the island⟩ ⟨~*ing* the landing craft in the assault⟩ **2 a :** to force or drive ashore or aground usu. with considerable damage ⟨the storm ~*ed* half the fleet⟩ ⟨sinking one enemy ship and ~*ing* another⟩ **b :** to draw ashore or moor and relegate to desuetude

³**beach** \"\ *adj* **:** on, of, or relating to a beach; *often* **:** designed for wear on a beach ⟨lounging casually in a ~ shirt⟩

beach apple *n* **1 :** a fig marigold (*Carpobrotus chilensis* syn. *Mesembryanthemum chilense*) native to southern Africa — called also *beach strawberry, sea fig* **2 :** the fruit of the beach apple plant

beach aster *n* **:** SEASIDE DAISY

beach ball *n* **:** a large inflated ball for use at the beach

beach bird *n* **:** any of various limicoline birds (as the knot) that frequent beaches

beachboy \'=ˌ=\ *n* **:** a male beach attendant; *esp* **:** an entertainer and instructor in surfing and swimming

beach buggy *n* **:** a motor vehicle with oversize tires for use on sand beaches

beach·comb \'=+ˌkōm\ *vb* [back-formation fr. *beachcomber*] *vi* **:** to live or act as a beachcomber **:** engage in a beachcomber's activities or lack of them ~ *vt* **:** to search (an area) as a beachcomber **:** find by a beachcomber's procedure

beach·comb·er \-mə(r)\ *n* -s **1 :** a casual often in So. Pacific areas who may ship as a short-haul sailor or engage in short-term work or irregular ventures in coastal areas ashore **2 a :** a disreputable unemployed or derelict seaman **:** a drifter or loafer usu. along the seacoast; *esp* **:** a white man (as an American or Britisher) leading a bum's existence in the So. Pacific **b :** a seashore lounger or vacationist **c :** a hanger-on in Bohemian circles **3 :** one who searches along a shore for worthwhile flotsam, refuse, or specimens; *sometimes* **:** WRECKER

beach crab *n* **:** any of various crabs living on seabeaches; *esp* **:** a common tropical American grapsoid (*Sesarma ricordi*)

beach cusp *n* **:** sand and gravel deposits formed by wave action into points that project seaward along a coast

beach flea *n* **:** any of numerous amphipod crustaceans of the family Orchestiidae living on seabeaches and leaping like fleas

beach fly *n* **:** any of certain two-winged flies that frequent beaches; *esp* **:** any biting fly (as a horsefly) encountered in such an area

beach gear *n* **:** rope, winches, and other equipment for handling boats on a beach

beach goldenrod *n* **:** SEASIDE GOLDENROD

beach grass *n* **:** any of several tough strongly rooted grasses that grow on exposed sandy shores; *esp* **:** a perennial European grass (*Ammophila arenaria*) with hard creeping rhizomes that is widely planted to bind sandy blowing slopes — called also *marram grass, sand reed*

beach·head \'bēch,hed\ *n* **1 :** an area on a hostile shore seized and defended to secure further landing of troops and supplies **2 :** an initial advance position or foothold to be used as vantage ground for extending to new areas

beach heather *n* **:** a plant of the genus *Hudsonia*; *esp* **:** a small heathlike plant (*H. tomentosa*) growing on beaches in northeastern No. America

beaching gear *n* **:** a wheeled cradle that may be attached to the hull of a seaplane for hauling it ashore and moving it on land

beach-la-mar \ˌbēchlə'mär\ *n* -s *usu cap* [by folk etymology] **:** BÊCHE-DE-MER 2

beach·less \'bēchləs\ *adj* **:** being without a beach

beachline \'=ˌ=\ *n* **:** shoreline esp. if marked by a series of well-developed beaches

beach·man \'=mən, -ˌman\ *n, pl* **beachmen 1 :** a person who works (as at odd jobs) on a beach **2 :** a worker who hauls flying boats from the water by means of special beaching gear

beachmaster \'=ˌ==\ *n* **1 :** an officer in charge of disembarkation of troops and munitions **2 :** a bull fur seal on its breeding ground

beach morning glory *n* **:** a creeping fleshy glabrous herb (*Ipomoea pes-caprae*) occurring on sandy beaches throughout the tropics and subtropics and having rounded leaves notched at the apex and purple flowers

beach mouse *n* **:** a pale buff-colored field mouse (*Peromyscus polionotus*) occurring as distinct subspecies on sandy beaches of the Florida east coast and adjacent islands

beach pea *n* **:** a wild pea (*Lathyrus maritimus*) with long tough roots and purple flowers that is found along seashores of the north temperate zone and that is useful as a sand binder

beach pine *n* **:** LODGEPOLE PINE a

beach plover *n* **:** any of certain plovers or sandpipers that frequent beaches (as the sanderling)

beach plum *n* **1 :** a shrub (*Prunus maritima*) of the seacoast of northeastern No. America with showy white flowers and edible fruit often used for jam **2 :** the dark purple fruit of the beach plum

beach pool *n* **:** a pool of water between two beaches or two beach ridges **:** a more or less transitory pool that adjoins a lake and is often the result of wave action — compare TIDE POOL

beach ridge *n* **:** a ridge of sand and gravel built up along the beach by wave action

beach robin *n* **:** ³KNOT

beach-sap \'bēch,sap\ *n* **:** a sea rocket (*Cakile chapmani*) with pale purple flowers and jointed pods that is found along the Gulf coast

beach seine *n* **:** a long net that is made fast to the shore at one end and then circled about a school of fish and drawn ashore

beach strawberry *n* **1 :** BEACH APPLE **2 :** CHILEAN STRAWBERRY

beach tan *n* **:** SEDGE 3

beach umbrella *n* **:** a large umbrella used to shade part of a beach, patio, or recreation area

beach wagon *n* **:** STATION WAGON

beach wormwood *n* **:** an herb (*Artemisia stelleriana*) with greyish foliage found along the eastern coast of the U.S. and used as an ornamental plant — called also *dusty miller*

beachy \'bēchē\ *adj* -ER/-EST **:** covered with pebbles, shingle, or sand

¹**bea·con** \'bēkən\ *n* -s [ME *beken*, fr. OE *bēacen* sign; akin to OHG *bouhhan* sign and perh. to Gk *phainein* to show — more at FANCY] **1 :** a signal fire commonly on a hill, tower, or pole **2 a :** a lighthouse or other signal mark ashore or in shoal water usu. to guide mariners **b :** an unattended light or other signaling device for the guidance of aviators **c :** a fixed automatic radio transmitter emitting characteristic signals for the guidance of aircraft **d :** a traffic light or other signal serving a similar purpose **3 a** *Brit* **:** a high hill with a conspicuous outlook **b** *Brit* **:** a watchtower or signaling station **c :** a pole that marks **4 :** a very clear or conspicuous signal or indication **:** a monumental indication often serving as a source of

light and inspiration ⟨the ~ to the oppressed of all countries —Adrienne Koch⟩ ⟨a ~ for creative artists the world over —A.R.Katz⟩ **5** *heraldry* **:** a fire basket usu. depicted inflamed set up on a pole against which a ladder leans **:** CRESSET

2**beacon** \"\ *vb* -ED/-ING/-S *vt* **1 a :** to light as a beacon ⟨fires where the hedgers had been at work ~*ed* the darkness —Adrian Bell⟩ **b :** to give light to **:** inspire and guide **:** summon to achievement ⟨one truth would dimly ~ me —Robert Browning⟩ **2 :** to furnish or mark with a beacon ⟨~ the headland⟩ ~*vi* **:** to shine as a beacon ⟨then Adventure ~*ed* from far off, and his heart leapt —Maurice Hewlett⟩

bea·con·age \-(,)nij\ *n* -S **:** charges levied for the maintenance of beacons

bea·con·ite \-,nīt\ *n* -S *usu cap* [*A Beacon* to the Society of Friends, book by Isaac Crewdson †1844 Eng. religious leader + E *-ite*] **:** a member of an English party of Quakers that were led by Isaac Crewdson to secede from other English Quakers in 1836 on the basis that the doctrines of the latter were scripturally unsound

bea·con·less \'bēkənləs\ *adj* **:** being without a beacon

bea·con·ry \'bēkənrē\ *n* -ES **:** the technique of using radio beacons

1**bead** \'bēd\ *n* -S *often attrib* [ME *bede* prayer, prayer bead, fr. OE *bed, gebed* prayer; akin to OHG *beta* request, *gibet* prayer, Goth *bida* prayer, OE *biddan* to entreat, pray — more at BID] **1 a** *obs* **:** PRAYER, SUPPLICATION — usu. used in pl. **b beads** *pl* **:** a series of prayers and devotional meditations made with the use of a rosary ⟨saying his ~*s* in solitude⟩ **2 :** a small often round piece of stone, glass, shell, wood, metal, or other material that is pierced for threading on a string or wire ⟨the ~*s* of the necklace⟩ ⟨~*s* for trade with the natives⟩ ⟨children stringing ~*s*⟩; *specif* **:** a bead of a rosary **3 beads** *pl* **a :** ROSARY ⟨~*s* blessed by the bishop⟩ **b :** a necklace of beads or pearls **4 :** a drop like a bead or a small body shaped like a ball ⟨letting the ~*s* of lead pour as easily as sand —Kay Boyle⟩: **a :** a drop of sweat or blood ⟨~*s* of pain broke out on her forehead —Ellen Glasgow⟩ **b :** a minute bubble formed in or on a beverage; *specif* **:** the bubbles that are formed on the surface of a distilled beverage when it is shaken and that by their number and duration may indicate proof and quality ⟨this whiskey holds a good ~⟩ **c :** a small knob of metal on a firearm near the muzzle used for a front sight in aiming ⟨to draw a ~ on a target⟩ **:** AIM ⟨to take a ~ on a man⟩ **d :** a blob of weld metal or a continuous deposit of weld metal blobs **e :** the globule of precious metal obtained by the cupellation process in assaying **f :** a glassy drop of flux (as borax or microcosmic salt) used as a solvent and color test for several metallic oxides and salts (as of iron, manganese) that is formed by fusion in the loop of a usu. platinum wire **g :** one of a series of tiny bosses or raised dots on a coin, token, medal, or plate **5 :** a projecting rim, band, or molding: **a :** a small salient molding of rounded surface, continuous or broken, the section being usu. an arc of a circle — compare ASTRAGAL 1 **b :** any of various pieces or members (as a parting strip) usu. having a section somewhat like such a molding **c :** a similarly rounded or cordlike projecting band (as the exposed portion of the headband of a book or a projecting band round a metal box) **d :** one of the strips around the inner periphery of a pneumatic tire shaped often with external ridge or rounded fold for engaging the rim of a wheel **e :** a wood or metal strip embedded in the plaster at a salient corner of a wall and serving as a guide and support for the plaster **f :** an extended rounded rim or flange (as on a pot or kettle) **g :** a ledge below the finish on a glass jar or bottle to aid in removal of pry-off closure **h :** a groove or rounded elevation on the surface of a metal can, fiber drum, glass jar, or metal closure to improve appearance and to stiffen **i :** the outer edge of circled heading that fits into the croze of barrel staves **j :** a raised ridge on sheet metal

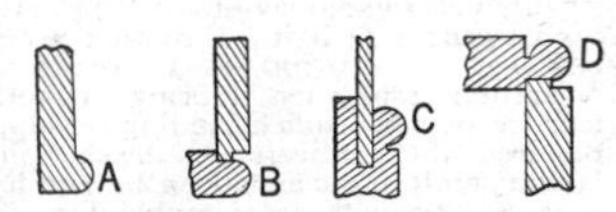

beads 5a: *A* cock bead; *B, C* quirk beads; *D* double-quirked bead

2**bead** \"\ *vb* -ED/-ING/-S *vt* **1 :** to trim, furnish, or adorn with beads or beading **:** cover with beads **2 :** to string together like beads ⟨row houses ~*ed* together⟩ **3 :** to cause beads to develop on ⟨her face was flushed and rosy, ~*ed* with small particles of rain —Thomas Wolfe⟩ ⟨tears were ~*ing* Dorinda's lashes —Ellen Glasgow⟩ **4 :** to form a bead on (as sheet metal) ~ *vi* **1 :** to form into a bead **:** develop as beads ⟨sweat ~*ed* on his forehead —Hartley Howard⟩ **2 :** to take aim ⟨the major ~*ed* too low⟩

bead and butt *n* **:** framing in which the panels are flush, having beads stuck or run upon the two edges with the grain

bead and flush *n* **:** beadflush work

bead and reel *n* **:** a round convex molding with disks alternating singly or in pairs with oblong beads

bead chain *n* **:** a chain formed of small hollow metal spheres connected by short dumbbell-shaped metal links that is used esp. in electric pull sockets and switches

bead and reel

bead curtain *n* **:** a curtain formed of vertical strands threaded with beads

bead·ed \'bēdəd\ *adj* **:** having the edges skived thin and turned in to present a finished edge — used of shoes

beaded esker *n* **:** an esker with numerous expansions and contractions in width

beaded lightning *also* **bead lightning** *n* **:** a streak of lightning that seems to be broken up into short segments

beaded lizard *n* **:** GILA MONSTER

beaded ribs *n pl* **:** ribs with beading (sense f)

bea·del \'bēdᵊl\ *archaic var of* BEADLE

bead·er \'bēdə(r)\ *n* -S **1 a :** a tool or machine for making a bead (as about the end of a boiler tube) **b :** BEADING PLANE **2 :** a worker who attaches beads or finishes with beading **3 a :** one that sews together pieces of leather or fabric on a machine which sews with a zigzag stitch **b :** one that machine-sews around collar neckbands to make the seam between collar and neckband flat **c :** one that sews beads by hand onto dresses and other articles of theatrical wardrobes

bead·flush \'bēd fləsh\ *adj, of a panel or paneling work* **:** surrounded by a bead usu. worked in the edges of the frame so that panel, bead, and frame are flush at their front faces

beadier *comparative of* BEADY

beadiest *superlative of* BEADY

bead·i·ly \'bēdᵊlē, -dəlē\ *adv* [*beady* + *-ly*] **:** in a beady manner

beading *n* -S [1*bead* + *-ing*] **:** a part or piece consisting of a bead or beads **:** beaded material **:** BEADS **:** the result of beading: **a :** a molding or rounded projecting bead **b :** an edging of small loops used on lace or ribbon **c :** an insertion or edging with openings through which ribbon, tape, or elastic may be laced **d :** decorative bead trimming on fabric or leather **e :** a bead design on a coin, token, or medal **f :** the beadlike nodules occurring in rickets at the junction of the ribs with their cartilages — called also *rachitic rosary*

beading plane *n* **:** a carpenter's plane with a cutter having a semicircular concave edge for making beads on molding

bea·dle \'bēdᵊl\ *n* -S [ME *bedel, bidel, budel*, fr. OE *bydel*; akin to OHG *butil* bailiff, OE *bēodan* to offer, command — more at BID] **1 :** a herald or messenger esp. in the service of a law court **2 :** a parish officer whose duties include ushering and preserving order at church services **3 :** a synagogue officer who maintains order

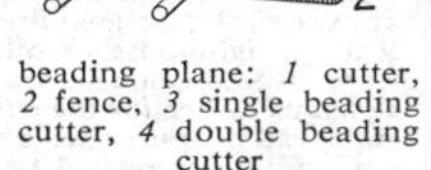

beading plane: *1* cutter, *2* fence, *3* single beading cutter, *4* double beading cutter

bea·dle·dom \-ldəm\ *n* -S **:** the characteristics felt to mark beadles as a class; *usu* **:** stupid officialism

bead plant *n* **:** a creeping herb (*Nertera depressa*) of the southern hemisphere cultivated for its tiny leaves and orange-colored fruit

bead pointing *n* **:** masonry pointing that forms a protruding bead

beadroll \'=,=\ *n* [1*bead* + *roll*] **1** *archaic* **:** a list of persons for whom prayers were to be said **2 :** an often long list or series of names **:** CATALOG ⟨the ~ of substantive and noteworthy poems in English —George Saintsbury⟩ **3 :** ROSARY **4 :** a bookbinder's finishing roll designed to impart a bead pattern

bead-ruby \'=,=,=\ *n* **:** FALSE LILY OF THE VALLEY

beads *pl of* BEAD, *pres 3d sing of* BEAD

bead saw *n* **:** a short saw with a curved blade and backward-pointing teeth that is used for scoring grooves in window and door frames in preparation for weatherstrips

beads·man *also* **bedes·man** \'bēdzmən\ *or* **bede·man** \-dmən\ *n, pl* **beadsmen** [ME *bedeman*, fr. *bade* prayer, prayer bead + *man* — more at BEAD] **1** *archaic* **:** one who prays for the soul of another — used until the 17th century in England in letters as a complimentary close ⟨your grace's ~ and servant⟩ **2 a :** an almshouse inmate usu. charged with praying for the souls of his benefactors **b :** a licensed beggar in Scotland ⟨a king's ~ being given a blue gown on the king's birthday⟩

bead snake *n* [so called fr. its markings resembling beads] **:** the common venomous coral snake (*Micrurus fulvius*) of southeastern No. America

bead tree *n* [so called fr. its bright scarlet seeds, used for necklaces] **1 :** CHINABERRY 2 **2 :** NECKLACE TREE **3 :** RED SANDALWOOD 2

beadwork \'=,=\ *n* **1 :** ornamental work in beads **2 :** joinery beading

beady \'bēdē, -di\ *adj* -ER/-EST **1 :** seeming to resemble beads **:** small, round, prominent, and intent esp. with interest or greed ⟨a look of avid interest crept into the ~ eyes of the priest —T.B.Costain⟩ **2 :** marked by bubbles or beads ⟨a ~ liquor⟩

1**bea·gle** \'bēgəl\ *n* -S [ME *begle*] **1 :** a small short-legged smooth-coated hound said to have originated as a definite breed in England at least four centuries ago, being about 12 to 15 inches high with pendulous ears and coat of hound colors, the tricolor being common **2 :** CONSTABLE **:** sheriff's officer **:** SPY **:** a zealous aide given to ferreting ⟨the senator's ~*s* probing the deal⟩ **3** *usu cap* **:** VIRGINIAN — used as a nickname

2**beagle** \"\ *vi* **beagled; beagled; beagling** \-g(ə)liŋ\ **beagles** **:** to hunt game with a beagle or a pack of beagles

bea·gler \-g(ə)lə(r)\ *n* -S **:** one that beagles

bea·gling *n* -S **:** hunting with beagles

1**beak** \'bēk\ *n* -S [ME *bec*, fr. OF, fr. L *beccus*, fr. Gaulish] **1 a :** the bill of a bird; *sometimes* **:** the bill of a bird of prey adapted for striking and tearing — often distinguished from *bill* **b :** the long projecting sucking mouth of some insects and other invertebrates (as in the typical bugs) **c :** the bill of some other animals (as the turtle and octopus) **d** (1) **:** the tip of the umbo of a bivalve shell or a brachiopod (2) **:** the prolongation of certain univalve shells containing the canal **e :** the human nose ⟨his face, with small ~ and the pricked skin of smallpox —Saul Bellow⟩ **f :** the projecting bony elements of the jaws of a fish (as in the pike) or of the upper jaw only (as in swordfish or sawfish) or of the lower jaw alone (as in the halfbeak) **2 :** a pointed structure, formation, or construction: **a :** PEAK **b :** a beam shod or armed with a metal head or point projecting from the bow of an ancient galley for piercing the ship of an enemy **c :** PROMONTORY **d** (1) **:** the spout of a vessel (as a teakettle) (2) **:** the tapering tube of a retort **e :** one of the jaws of a forceps or pliers **f :** a continuous slight architectural projection ending in an arris or narrow fillet **:** the part of a drip from which water is thrown off — see MOLDING illustration **g :** a process terminating the fruit or other parts of a plant and somewhat resembling the beak of a bird; *esp* **:** a short awn on the outer chaff of wheat **h :** the mouthpiece of a musical instrument (as the flageolet, clarinet, or flûte à bec) **3 a** *chiefly Brit* **:** MAGISTRATE, JUSTICE OF THE PEACE **b :** a master at certain British public schools

2**beak** \"\ *vt* -ED/-ING/-S [ME *beken*, fr. OF *bequer, bequier*, fr. *bec*] **:** PECK **:** peck at **:** strike or seize with the beak

beaked \'bēkt, 'bēkəd\ *adj* [1*beak* + *-ed*] **1 :** having a beak: **a :** ROSTRATE ⟨a ~ fruit⟩ **b :** having a mouth or proboscis resembling a beak **2 a :** resembling a beak ⟨a gaunt, grizzled man of middle age, with a ~ nose —Ellen Glasgow⟩ **b :** having a beaked nose ⟨a gaunt, ~ lady of eighty-odd —Frances G. Patton⟩

beaked cockle *n* **:** a mollusk of the genus *Nuculana* or family Nuculanidae — called also *elongate nut shell*

beaked hazel *or* **beaked hazelnut** *n* **:** an American hazel (*Corylus cornuta*) with involucral bracts that enclose the nut and form a tubular beak

beaked nightshade *n* **:** BUFFALO BUR

beaked parsley *n* **:** CHERVIL 1

beaked salmon *n, Austral* **:** SANDFISH

beaked whale *n* **:** a toothed whale of the family Ziphiidae

1**beak·er** \'bēkə(r)\ *n* -S [ME *biker*, fr. ON *bikarr*, prob. fr. OS *bekari*; akin to OHG *behhari* beaker; both fr. a prehistoric OHG-OS word derived fr. ML *bicarius* goblet, beaker, fr. Gk *bikos* earthen jug, prob. of non-IE origin] **1 :** a large drinking cup without handles that has a wide and often flaring mouth and is sometimes supported on a foot or standard **2 :** a deep openmouthed thin vessel (as of glass, porcelain, or metal) that often has a projecting lip for pouring and is used esp. by chemists and pharmacists **3 :** a breaker or other storage vessel esp. for water on shipboard

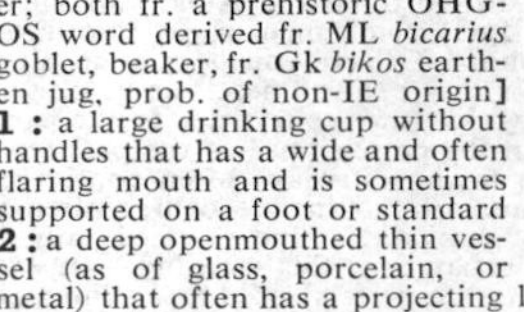
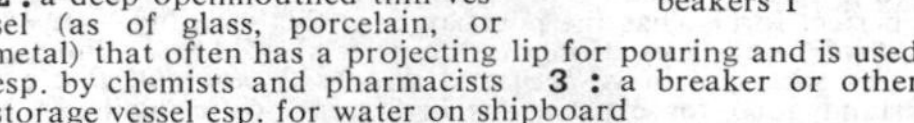
beakers 1

2**beaker** \"\ *adj, usu cap* **:** of or relating to the beaker folk

beaker folk *also* **beaker people** \'bēkə(r)-\ *or* **beaker·men** \-mən,-,men\ *n pl, often cap B* **:** a prehistoric people living in Europe in the early Bronze Age whose culture was characterized by bell beakers buried with their dead in round barrows

beak flute *n* [trans. of F *flûte à bec*] **:** FIPPLE FLUTE

beakhead \'=,=\ *n* **1 a :** a ship's beak **b :** a space forward of a forecastle containing latrines for crewmen **2 :** an architectural ornament resembling a head with a beak used in some Norman doorways

beak·horn stake *n* [1*beak* + *horn*] **:** a stake or small bench anvil having a slender horn on one side — see STAKE illustration

beak·ing joint \'bēkiŋ-\ *n* **:** a joint formed by the meeting in a continuous line of several heading joints

beak·iron \'bikə(r)n, 'bē,kīə(r)n\ *n* [by folk etymology (influence of E *beak* & *iron*) fr. earlier *bickern, bycorne* — more at BICKIRON] **:** BICKIRON

beak molding *n* **:** an architectural molding whose profile resembles a beak — see MOLDING illustration

beak rush *or* **beaked rush** *or* **beak sedge** *n* **:** a sedge of the genus *Rhynchospora* having a tubercle like a beak crowning the fruit

beak wattle *n* **:** one of the fleshy outgrowths at the base of both mandibles of carrier pigeons

beak willow *or* **beaked willow** *n* **:** a No. American shrub or small tree (*Salix bebbiana*) with broad leaves and long conic capsules

beaky \'bēkē\ *adj* -ER/-EST **:** having a beak, esp. a noticeable one **:** resembling a beak ⟨his overcivilized, prim, finely drawn, ~ profile —Christopher Isherwood⟩

1**beal** \'bē(ə)l\ *vi* -ED/-ING/-S [prob. fr. obs. E *beal* boil, fr. ME *bele*, prob. var. of *bile* — more at BOIL] *now dial* **:** to swell and become infected **:** SUPPURATE, FESTER

2**beal** \"\ *vi* -ED/-ING/-S [perh. alter. of 3*bell*] *dial Eng* **:** BELLOW, ROAR ⟨a bull ~*ing*⟩

bealing *n* -S [fr. gerund of 1beal] *now dial* **:** BOIL, SUPPURATION

beal·lach *also* **beal·ach** \'be,läk\ *n* -S [IrGael *bealach* road, path, mountain pass, fr. MIr *belach* gap, pass] *Scot & Irish* **:** a mountain pass

be-all and end-all \'bē,ōl . . . 'en,dōl\ *n* **:** prime cause **:** essential element **:** dominant or definitive factor; *sometimes* **:** WHOLE, TOTALITY ⟨the *be-all and end-all* of the detective story is to conceal the identity of the criminal —*Times Lit. Supp.*⟩

bealtine *usu cap, var of* BELTANE

1**beam** \'bēm\ *n* -S [ME *beem*, fr. OE *bēam* tree, beam; akin to OHG *boum* tree, ON *bathmr*, Goth *bagms*, and perh. to Gk *phyma* growth, *phyein* to bring forth — more at BE] **1 a** *obs* **:** a sizable metal bar **b :** a long piece of heavy often squared timber suitable for use in house construction **c** (1) **:** a large cylinder of wood or metal on which yarns comprising a warp are wound before weaving or warp knitting or on which woven or knitted cloth is wound as it is made (2) **:** a hand-weaving loom part over which warp yarns travel up and forward during the weaving process **d :** the part of a plow to which handles, standard, and colter are attached and by which the implement is drawn — see PLOW illustration **e :** the crossbar of a balance from the ends of which scales or weights are suspended; *sometimes* **:** the whole balance **f** *obs* **:** the shaft of a chariot **g :** a structural member (as an iron girder) usu. supported at the two ends that is laid horizontally to bear a load and brace a frame **:** a horizontal supporting span (as between opposite foundation walls of a building) **h** (1) **:** a horizontal structural member supporting the deck of a ship and aiding in holding her sides in place — see SHIP illustration (2) **:** the extreme width of the hull of a ship including projecting structures **:** the widest part of a ship; *also* **:** the maximum width of a seaplane float or hull measured between the chines — see SHIP illustration (3) **:** the side of a ship **:** the direction outward from the side **i :** a lever having an oscillating motion on a central axis and connected at one end with an engine piston rod from which it receives motion and at the other with the crank or its equivalent **j :** a sloping board or frame upon which hides are worked in tanning **k :** a long structural member not supported everywhere along its length and subject to the force of flexure (as a rod resting on supports at the ends and bearing a weight at the center) **:** SPAR, BOOM, LEVER **2 a :** a light ray **:** a radiating line (as of light or color) ⟨how far that little candle throws his ~*s* —Shak.⟩ **:** a shaft of light rays from a lamp ⟨the ~*s* from the searchlights⟩ **b :** a collection of nearly parallel rays (as of light or X rays) or of particles (as electrons) **c :** GLANCE **d :** a gleam or other emanation or manifestation **e** (1) **:** a directional radio signal transmitted in quadrants from a radio range station audible as a continuous tone or whine as long as an aircraft proceeds directly on the proper course but audible as dot-dash or dash-dot as it veers to left or right (2) **:** the exact course indicated by a radio beam **f** (1) **:** stream of electrons in a vacuum tube flowing from an emitting electrode to a collecting electrode (2) **:** a directed flow of a radio signal in space **g :** the zone in which a microphone or loudspeaker functions best **3 :** the main stem of a deer's antler **4 :** the width of the buttocks **:** RUMP ⟨a massive woman, much taller than her husband and immensely broad in the ~ —Ann Bridge⟩ — **abaft the beam :** in an arc of the horizon between a line that crosses a ship at right angles to the keel and that point of the compass toward which her stern points — **before the beam :** in an arc of the horizon included between a line that crosses a ship at right angles to the keel and that point of the compass toward which the ship heads — **off the beam :** not following a guiding beam **:** proceeding on a wrong course **:** deviating from the normal or true ⟨truly *off the beam* and wandering in a Stygian darkness —Peggy Bennett⟩ — **on the beam :** following a guiding beam **:** proceeding correctly **:** following the normal or true **:** operating well — **the beam in one's own eye :** a fault as palpable as a house beam ⟨cast *the beam* out of *thine own eye* —Matt 7:5 (AV)⟩

2**beam** \"\ *vb* -ED/-ING/-S [ME *beemen*, fr. *beem*, n.] *vt* **1 :** to send out, radiate, or project in beams or as a beam **2 a :** to wind (warp yarn or cloth) on a beam **b :** to dress or work (hides) on a beam **3 :** to equip or support with beams ⟨a roof ~*ed* with heavy timbers⟩ **4 a :** to aim (a broadcast) by directional antennas ⟨programs ~*ed* at Britain⟩ **b :** to aim (sound) from a loudspeaker **c :** to direct (a broadcast) to a particular audience ⟨a program ~*ed* to women⟩ **:** address special attention to ⟨a sales campaign ~*ed* at sportsmen⟩ ~ *vi* **1 :** to send out beams of light ⟨the sun ~*ing* overhead⟩ **2 :** to smile broadly or blandly with unreserved satisfaction, pleasure, or joy ⟨~*ing* with good nature —R.L.Stevenson⟩

3**beam** \"\ *adj* [1*beam*] **1 :** moving toward or directed at a ship's beam ⟨a ~ sea⟩ ⟨a ~ wind⟩ **2 :** relating to wave transmission in a fairly well-defined beam as distinguished from substantially uniform transmission in all directions ⟨~ antenna⟩

beam·age \'bēmij\ *n* -S [1*beam* + *-age*] **:** a deduction for loss by evaporation of weight in a freshly dressed animal carcass cooling on a beam

beam anchor *n* **:** a building anchor used to tie walls firmly to floors

beam and scales *n* **:** BALANCE

beam antenna *n* **:** ANTENNA ARRAY

beam arm *n* **1 :** a forked timber bolted to a beam next to a deck opening — called also *fork beam* **2 :** a split end of a steel deck beam bent over so as to be bolted to the frame where it forms a knee

beambird \'=,=\ *n* **:** SPOTTED FLYCATCHER

beam board *n* **:** the platform of a steelyard or balance

beam bracket *n* **:** a riveted or welded steel plate connecting a ship's beam to its frame

beam caliber *n* **1 :** CALIPER SQUARE **2** *or* **beam divider :** a trammel fitted with caliper legs

beam ceiling *n* **:** a ceiling with exposed beams

beam compass *n* **:** a compass that consists of a beam with sliding sockets which carry steel or pencil points and that is used for drawing large circles

beamed *past of* BEAM

beam-ends \'=,=\ *n pl* **:** ends of beams usu. on a ship — **on her beam-ends :** inclined so much on one side that beams approach a vertical position with danger of capsizing — **on one's beam-ends 1 :** laid up **2 :** at the end of one's material resources **:** in extremities

beam·er \'bēmə(r)\ *n* -S [1*beam* + *-er*] **1 a :** a machine for winding yarn or cloth on a beam **b :** an operator of such a machine — compare WARPER a **2 :** a leather worker who scrapes wet hides with a beaming knife to remove flesh and traces of hair **3 :** a bone implement like a drawknife found in Mississippi sites and in later cultural stages of the southwestern U.S., usu. made from metapodal bones of deer or elk, and having cutting and scraping edges midway between the handles

beam·fill·ing \'bēm,filiŋ\ *n* **1 :** masonry placed between the ends of beams in a wall **2 :** cargo that is or can be stowed between beams

beamhouse \'=,=\ *n* **:** a tannery section where hides are prepared for tanning

beam·i·ly \'bēməlē\ *adv* **:** in a beamy manner

beaming *adj* **1 :** marked by, emitting, or reflecting strong or clear rays of light ⟨the ~ sun above⟩ **2 :** marked by or expressive of extreme and unreserved joy, happiness, or satisfaction ⟨~ parents watching a baby⟩ ⟨quiet, confident, bright, and smiling eyes, ~ with a consciousness of being associated with a cause far higher —Sir Winston Churchill⟩ **syn** see BRIGHT

beaming knife *or* **beam knife** *n* **:** a tanner's 2-handled knife used to shave hides stretched over a beam

beam·ing·ly *adv* **:** with radiance **:** RADIANTLY

beaming machine *n* **1 :** a machine for working hides to remove hair roots — compare SCUD **2 :** a machine for filling beams with yarn or cloth

beam·ish \'bēmish\ *adj* **:** beaming and bright with optimism, promise, or achievement ⟨those ~ young men you encounter on . . . recruiting posters —John McCarten⟩

beam knee *n* **1 :** a knee supporting a ship's beam **2 :** BEAM ARM

beam·less \'bēmləs\ *adj* **:** being without a beam or ray

beam light *n* **:** a candle kept burning before the rood in a church

beam pump *n* **:** an oil-well pump actuated by a walking beam

beam-rider \'=,=,=\ *n* **:** a missile guided along a radio beam

beams *pl of* BEAM, *pres 3d sing of* BEAM

beams·man \'bēmzmən\ *n, pl* **beamsmen :** a worker at a tannery beam

beam splitter *n* **:** a mirror that is sometimes built into a prism, that reflects part of a beam of light and transmits part, and that is used for diverting a portion of the beam to one side in color separation cameras, in photomicrography, and for superposition of images in special cameras or printers

beam·ster \'bēmstə(r)\ *n* -S [1*beam* (for tanning) + *-ster*] **:** one that beams

beam trawl *n* **:** a trawl net with its mouth spread by a beam — compare OTTER TRAWL

beam-trawl \ˈ=,=\ *vi* [*beam trawl*] **:** to fish with a beam trawl
beam trawler *n* **:** a fishing boat equipped with a beam trawl
beam tree *n* **:** WHITEBEAM
beam tube *n* **:** a power amplifier vacuum tube in which the flow of electrons is channeled by means of beam-forming plates and similarly spaced control and screen grids
beam well *n* **:** an oil well having a beam pump
beamy \ˈbēmē\ *adj* -ER/-EST [ME *beemy*, fr. *beem* beam + *-y*] **1 a :** marked by, emitting, or reflecting beams of light **:** BRIGHT, RADIANT **b :** radiantly joyful **:** flushed with optimism or marked by happy benignness **2 :** resembling a beam in size and weight **:** MASSIVE, BROAD **3 :** having horns or antlers ⟨~ stags —John Dryden⟩ **4 :** notably broad in the beam ⟨a ~ cargo ship⟩ **syn** see BRIGHT
¹bean \ˈbēn\ *n* -S *often attrib* [ME *bene*, fr. OE *bēan*; akin to OHG *bōna* bean, ON *baun*, and prob. to L *faba* bean, Gk *phakos* lentil] **1 a :** BROAD BEAN **b :** the seed of any of various other erect or climbing leguminous plants esp. of the genera *Phaseolus, Dolichos*, and *Vigna* — see KIDNEY BEAN, LIMA BEAN, SIEVA BEAN, SNAP BEAN **c :** a plant bearing beans **d :** a bean pod used when immature as a vegetable **2 a :** a valueless item ⟨not worth a ~⟩ **b** *slang Brit* **:** a sovereign or a guinea **c :** a small amount of money ⟨he didn't have a ~ when they were married⟩ ⟨haven't spent a ~ on it in years⟩ **d** *slang* **:** DOLLAR **e beans** *pl* **:** an appreciable amount ⟨he doesn't know *beans* about it⟩ ⟨I haven't heard *beans* about the matter lately⟩ **3 a :** any of various seeds or fruits that resemble beans ⟨a coffee ~⟩ ⟨catalpa ~*s* littering the walk⟩ **b :** any of several plants producing such beans — usu. used in combination ⟨a field of castor ~*s*⟩; see BLACK BEAN, CORAL BEAN **4 a :** a bean used in balloting **b :** a man that becomes leader of Twelfth Night festivities through having drawn a piece of cake containing a bean **5 :** something felt to resemble a bean: as **a :** a protuberance on the upper mandible of waterfowl (as of certain geese) — see GOOSE illustration **b :** a nipple or similar device placed in an oil-well line to restrict the flow of the oil **c :** a hardened mass of fatty secretion in the sheath of a stallion or gelding that if allowed to accumulate may block the urethra causing colicky pain and impeding urination **6** *slang* **a beans** *pl* **:** BEATING, PUNISHMENT, PAIN, CENSURE — usu. used with *give* ⟨giving the enemy ~*s* when they came within range⟩ ⟨giving the opposition ~*s* in a stinging speech⟩ **b :** HEAD, SKULL, BRAIN ⟨every whim and caprice which enters his ~ —Henry Miller⟩
²bean \"\ *vt* -ED/-ING/-S [¹*bean* (head)] **:** to strike typically with a hurled or propelled object and on the head ⟨a caddie ~*ed* by a wild shot⟩; *specif* **:** to hit (a baseball batter) esp. on the head with a pitched ball
bean anthracnose *n* **:** a disease of the bean caused by an imperfect fungus (*Colletotrichum lindemuthianum*) producing pinkish or brown lesions on the pod and seed and rusty to black discolorations on the veins on the lower leaf surface — see BEAN BLIGHT
bean aphid *also* **bean aphis** *n* **:** an aphid attacking bean plants; *specif* **:** a dull black or dark green aphid (*Aphis fabae* or *A. rumicis*) that feeds in great numbers on succulent parts of many cultivated and native plants
beanbag \ˈ=,=\ *n* **1 :** a cloth bag partly filled with dried beans or comparable small firm objects and used (as for tossing or passing) in many games **2 :** a game played with one or more beanbags
beanball *n* **:** a baseball deliberately pitched at a batter's head
bean beetle *n* **:** MEXICAN BEAN BEETLE
bean blight *n* **:** a disease caused by a bacterium (*Xanthomonas phaseoli*) distinguished from bean anthracnose by more irregular diffuse extended and water-soaked lesions on stem, leaf pod, and seed that later become yellowish brown
bean cake *n* **:** oil cake made from soybeans
bean caper *n* **:** any of several perennial plants constituting the genus *Zygophyllum* and having usu. ill-smelling foliage and flower buds that are used as capers; *esp* **:** a small shrub or tree (*Z. fabago*) of the eastern Mediterranean region and southwestern Asia that has yellow 5-petaled flowers brick red at the base
bean-caper family \ˈ=,==-\ *n* **:** ZYGOPHYLLACEAE
bean clam *n* **:** a small wedge-shaped clam (*Donax gouldii*) of southern California and Mexico
bean curd *also* **bean cheese** *n* **:** a soft vegetable cheese extensively eaten in the Orient that is prepared by treating soybean milk with magnesium chloride, dilute acids, or other coagulants and draining and pressing
bean cutworm *n* **:** a pinkish brown larval noctuid moth (*Loxagrotis albicosta*) that feeds on developing bean pods and seeds
bean-eater \ˈ=,==\ *n*, *sometimes cap B&E* **1 :** BOSTONIAN — used as a nickname **2 :** MEXICAN — used as a nickname
bean·ery \ˈbēnərē\ *n* -ES **:** a restaurant often of the cheaper class
beanfeast \ˈ=,=\ *n* **1** *Brit* **:** an annual dinner given to employees by their employers **2** *chiefly Brit* **:** a festive occasion often including an outing and a meal
bean flour *n* **:** a ground meal made of dried ripe beans
bean fly *n* **:** a small dark fly (*Agromyza phaseoli*) having larvae that are leaf miners esp. in the leaves of beans and are a serious pest of cultivated crops in Australia and adjacent regions
bean goose *n* **:** a common brownish Eurasian wild goose (*Anser fabalis*) having a bean-shaped mark on the bill
bean harvester *n* **:** a machine consisting of a cutting device of two long horizontal knives inclined to the rear for cutting bean plants and a raking device for gathering them into cocks or windrows
bean hole *n* **:** a hole in the ground sometimes lined with stones or bricks that is heated to serve as a slow-baking oven esp. for beans
bean huller *n* **:** BEAN THRESHER
bean·ie *also* **beany** \ˈbēnē\ *n*, *pl* **beanies** [prob. fr. ¹*bean* (head) + *-ie, -y*] **1 :** a small round tight-fitting skullcap worn esp. by schoolboys and collegians **2 :** a woman's small round hat worn off the face
bean king *n* **:** BEAN 4b
bean leaf beetle *n* **:** a reddish or yellowish beetle (*Cerotoma trifurcata*) that as an adult feeds on the leaves of beans and peas and sometimes other legumes
bean leaf roller *n* **:** a larval skipper butterfly (*Urbanus proteus*) that sometimes injures the foliage of beans, peas, and related plants in the southeastern U.S.
bean mosaic *n* **:** a virus disease of the bean transmitted by plant lice and by the seed and characterized by light green and dark green mottling and puckering of the leaves
¹beano \ˈbē(,)nō\ *n* -S [alter. of *beanfeast*] **1** *slang chiefly Brit* **:** BEANFEAST **2** *slang chiefly Brit* **:** a noisy good time
²beano \"\ *n* -S [by alter. (influenced by *bean*)] **:** BINGO
bean oil *n* **:** SOYBEAN OIL
bean-pod borer \ˈ=,=-\ *n* **:** a larval pyralid moth (*Etiella zinckenella*) that feeds in the developing seeds of beans and other legumes
bean pole *n* **1 :** a pole up which bean vines may climb **2 :** a tall thin person
bean pot *n* **1 :** a covered pot of heavy crockery made esp. for the slow cooking of beans **2 :** any crockery or metal pot or utensil used in the slow cooking of foods (as beans) ⟨an electric *bean pot*⟩ ⟨individual *bean pots* of brown pottery⟩
beans *pl of* BEAN, *pres 3d sing of* BEAN
bean·shooter \ˈ=,==\ *n* **1 :** PEASHOOTER **2 :** SLINGSHOT
bean sprouts *n pl* **:** the sprouts of bean seeds esp. of the mung bean germinated in humid darkness and used as food
beanstalk \ˈ=,=\ *n* **:** the stem of a bean plant
be·ant \ˈbēənt\ [by alter. & contr.] *dial* **:** be not
bean thresher *n* **:** a thresher that removes beans from pods by a combination of a low-speed cylinder that threshes out dry pods and two high-speed cylinders that thresh out damp or green pods
bean·town·er \ˈbēn,taůnə(r)\ *n* -S *usu cap* [fr. *Bean Town*, nickname for Boston, Mass. + *-er*; fr. the proverbially famous Boston baked beans] **:** BOSTONIAN — used as a nickname
bean tree *n* **:** any of several trees having fruits that are held to resemble a bean pod: as **a :** an Australian leguminous tree (*Castanospermum australe*) with bright yellow flowers, large pods containing three or four seeds like chestnuts, and dark strong wood — called also *Moreton Bay chestnut* **b :** CATALPA 2
bean trefoil *n* **1 :** a shrub (*Anagyris foetida*) of southern Europe with trifoliolate leaves and yellow flowers **2 :** BUCKBEAN **3 :** CORAL TREE **4 :** LABURNUM 2
bean-vine \ˈ=,=\ *n* **:** a perennial climbing American herb (*Phaseolus perennis*) with minutely pubescent stem and slender racemes or panicles of purple or whitish flowers
bean weevil *n* **:** any of several small weevils that deposit their eggs in the pods of beans and peas, the larva burrowing in and feeding on the seed; *specif* **:** a mottled olive-brown weevil (*Acanthoscelides obtectus*) native to America but now a cosmopolitan pest of growing and stored beans
¹beany \ˈbēnē\ *adj* -ER/-EST **1 :** METTLESOME, SPIRITED **2** *of an oil* **:** marked by an off-flavor suggestive of that of beans
²beany *var of* BEANIE
be·aproned \(ˈ)bē+\ *adj* [*be-* + *aproned*] **:** wearing an apron
¹bear \ˈbe(ə)r, ˈba(a)(ə)r, ˈbeə, ˈba(a)ə\ *n* -S *see sense 1, often attrib* [ME *bere*, fr. OE *bera*; akin to OHG *bero* bear, Lith *bėras* brown, OE *brūn* — more at BROWN] **1** *or pl* **bear a :** an animal of the family Ursidae (order Carnivora) of large heavy mammals having long shaggy hair, rudimentary tail, and plantigrade feet, feeding largely on fruit and insects as well as on flesh, and though ordinarily slow and clumsy moving very fast for short distances esp. on rough or steep ground — see GRIZZLY BEAR, POLAR BEAR **b** *Austral* **:** KOALA **c :** the fur or pelt of any bear **2 a :** a person felt to resemble a bear esp. in surly irascibility, coarse uncouthness, or shambling burliness ⟨bad-tempered and demanding, he was a perfect ~ all morning⟩ ⟨a lumbering good-natured ~ of a man⟩ **b :** a person having a special aptitude, excellence, or enthusiasm ⟨a ~ at mathematics⟩ **:** one showing resolution or ruggedness in enduring ⟨a ~ for punishment⟩ **3** [prob. fr. *bear* as used in the proverb about *selling the bearskin before catching the bear*] **a** *obs* **:** a stock or commodity sold short **b :** one that sells short **:** one interested in price decline **:** one who wishes or expects a fall in stock prices — compare BULL **4 :** a mat or matting-covered block esp. for scouring decks; *sometimes* **:** HOLY STONE **5 :** a small invertebrate animal felt to resemble a bear: as **a :** WATER BEAR **b :** ANT BEAR **c :** WOOLLY BEAR **6 :** a nearly neutral slightly brownish dark gray — called also *Chaetura drab* **7 :** a cub scout of the third rank who is at least nine years old
²bear \"\ *vt* -ED/-ING/-S **:** to lower prices in or at **:** DEPRESS ⟨attempts to ~ the stock market⟩
³bear \ˈbe(ə)r, ˈbe(ə)r\ *n* -S [ME *bere*, fr. OE — more at BARLEY] *chiefly Scot* **:** BARLEY
⁴bear \ˈbe(ə)r, ˈba(a)(ə)r, ˈbeə, ˈba(a)ə\ *vb* **bore** \ˈbō(ə)r, ˈbȯ(ə)r, ˈbōə, ˈbȯ(ə)\ *or archaic* **bare** *pronounced like* BEAR\ **borne** \ˈbō(ə)rn, ˈbȯ(ə)rn, ˈbōən, ˈbȯ(ə)n\ *also* **born** \ˈbȯ(ə)rn, ˈbȯ(ə)n\ (*see vt 2a,d,e,f*) *or dial* **bore** *pronounced like* BORE *above*\ **bearing; bears** [ME *beren*, fr. OE *beran*; akin to OHG *beran* to carry, ON *bera*, Goth *bairan*, L *ferre*, Gk *pherein*, Skt *bharati* he carries] *vt* **1 a :** to move while holding up or supporting often with effort or special care **:** CARRY ⟨let four captains ~ Hamlet, like a soldier to the stage —Shak.⟩ ⟨~*ing* gifts to the newborn prince⟩ **b :** to be accoutered or fitted out with **:** carry as equipment ⟨the right to ~ a sword in the king's presence⟩ **c :** to harbor or entertain mentally or emotionally; *sometimes* **:** CHERISH ⟨~*ing* malice in his heart⟩ ⟨the love he *bore* his mother⟩ **d :** to carry as a communication and usu. to relate ⟨killing the runner ~*ing* the orders⟩ ⟨constantly ~*ing* tales⟩ **e :** BEHAVE, CONDUCT, DEPORT — used reflexively ⟨~*ing* himself well in battle⟩ **f** *archaic* **:** MANAGE, WIELD, EXERCISE ⟨~ his power wisely⟩ ⟨~*ing* the rule in the land⟩ **g :** to have as an attribute, feature, or characteristic ⟨~*ing* a likeness to the suspect⟩ ⟨~*ing* the scars of old wounds⟩ **:** be capable of (as meaning or significance) ⟨a word ~*ing* many meanings⟩ **h :** to adduce in testifying ⟨~*ing* false witness⟩ ⟨~ testimony⟩ **i :** to have attached to one by way of identification, characterization, or evaluation ⟨~*ing* the name of John Doe⟩ ⟨~*ing* a good local reputation⟩ ⟨~*ing* a high price⟩ **j :** to use as an armorial emblem ⟨~*ing* the family coat of arms⟩ **k :** to have as a bodily part ⟨~*ing* a good pair of eyes⟩ **l** *obs* **:** WIN **:** prevail in — used only with *it* ⟨~ it by speaking a great word —Francis Bacon⟩ **m :** LEAD, ESCORT ⟨~ the officer to his quarters⟩ **n :** RENDER, GIVE, TENDER ⟨~ a hand in helping⟩ **o :** TRANSPORT ⟨goods *borne* in neutral ships⟩ ⟨*airborne* troops⟩ **2 a :** to give birth to (offspring) **:** bring forth (young) — *borne* is the usual past participle form in active uses ⟨she has *borne* several children⟩ and is commonly used in passives seeming to suggest the action of giving birth esp. as used with *by* ⟨several children *borne* by her⟩; *born* is the usual form in passives indicating the fact of birth ⟨a son *born* to her⟩ ⟨he was *born* in the city⟩ and in adjective uses indicating condition or status often with durative aspect ⟨new-*born* kittens⟩ ⟨a suitor lowly *born* —W.S.Gilbert⟩ **b :** PRODUCE **:** send forth as yield esp. as leaf, flower, or fruit ⟨a tree ~*ing* late pears⟩ ⟨a bush ~*ing* red flowers⟩ **c :** AFFORD: (1) **:** to permit growth of often readily ⟨this soil ~*s* good cotton⟩ (2) **:** to contain in quantity and form permitting extraction ⟨oil-*bearing* shale⟩ (3) **:** to yield to the owner ⟨a bond that ~*s* interest⟩ **d :** to call into being — used only in the passive; *born* is the usual past participle form ⟨with this discovery a new age was *born*⟩ **e :** to give birth to or to develop with a special predisposition or bent — used only in the passive; *born* is the usual past participle form ⟨he loved teaching; he had been *born* to it⟩ **f :** EXTRUDE — used mainly in the passive; *born* is the usual past participle form ⟨after the lamb's head was *born*⟩ **3 a :** SUSTAIN **:** support or hold up without moving **b** (1) **:** TOLERATE **:** sustain with opposing or resisting — usu. used in negative constructions ⟨a nuisance not to be *borne* longer⟩ (2) **:** to endure esp. without giving way, collapsing, or succumbing ⟨~*ing* his sorrows as best he could⟩ ⟨pain more than he could ~⟩ (3) **:** to tolerate without discomfort or distaste **:** come to accept the presence of — usu. used in negative constructions ⟨he could not ~ his sister-in-law⟩ **c** (1) **:** ASSUME, ACCEPT ⟨he must ~ the blame⟩ (2) **:** to incur and defray ⟨~ by himself the whole cost of the arrangement⟩ **d :** to hold up **:** keep from falling ⟨columns that ~ the roof⟩ — often used with *up* ⟨a support that ~*s* up the weight⟩ **e :** to hold above, on top, or aloft — usu. used with adverb or prepositional phrase ⟨a banner *borne* aloft⟩ ⟨a table ~*ing* several vases⟩ **f :** to endure with ill will, resentment, or grievance **:** experience with bitterness or other deep unpleasant feeling — usu. used with *hard* or *heavy* ⟨he *bore* it hard to be ignored⟩; obs. with a personal object ⟨Ligarius doth ~ Caesar hard —Shak.⟩ **g** (1) **:** to show as written, inscribed, or otherwise displayed on a surface ⟨a cornerstone ~*ing* a Latin inscription⟩ ⟨a letter ~*ing* the date of 1900⟩ ⟨a shield ~*ing* strange symbols⟩ (2) **:** to enter on a list **:** ENROLL, REGISTER — used passively ⟨inactive personnel still *borne* on the rolls⟩ **h** (1) **:** to allow or admit of **:** be capable of sustaining without violence or wrenching ⟨a style that can ~ adornment⟩ ⟨a work that will not ~ close scrutiny⟩ (2) **:** SUGGEST, PROVOKE, INVITE ⟨his book *bore* heavy praise⟩ ⟨the answer of this witness will ~ examination⟩ **i** *archaic* **:** PURPORT, IMPORT, SIGNIFY ⟨her sentence *bore* that she should stand a certain time upon the platform —Nathaniel Hawthorne⟩ **j :** TAKE, PLAY ⟨~*ing* only a secondary part⟩ **4 :** THRUST, DRIVE, PRESS **:** impel with force ⟨the defenders being *borne* backward⟩ ⟨a canoe *borne* down the rapids⟩ ~ *vi* **1 a :** to force one's way **:** make way against resistance **:** PRESS ⟨*bear* back that the prince may pass⟩ **b :** to be situated, often as to compass direction ⟨the land ~*s* N by E⟩ ⟨the fleet ~*ing* directly off the point⟩ **c :** to extend or continue usu. along a direction indicated or implied ⟨a stream ~*ing* south for several miles⟩ **d :** to show a certain direction, range, or aim **:** to have a position commanding an objective (as an enemy position) — used with *on* or *upon* ⟨to bring guns to ~ upon a target⟩ **e :** GO, PROCEED ⟨nearer and nearer the foe are ~*ing*⟩; *often* **:** to direct or take a course (in an indicated way) esp. with a slight veering or inclination rather than a right-angle turn ⟨the road ~*s* west beyond the lake⟩ ⟨~ right into the outer lane at the next corner but do not turn⟩ **2 a :** to relate or have relevance **:** APPLY, PERTAIN ⟨facts ~*ing* on the question⟩ **b :** to exert influence or force **:** AFFECT, SWAY **:** put into effect ⟨to bring pressure to ~⟩ ⟨how this discovery will ~ on later developments⟩ ⟨legislation brought to ~ directly upon industry —Harriet Martineau⟩ **c :** to exert pressure or repose weight **:** push on or against something ⟨the wall ~*ing* on the floor⟩ ⟨an arch ~*ing* against piers⟩ **3 a :** to become subjected to a strain esp. in a structure **:** withstand a strain ⟨a wall added later that does not ~⟩ ⟨these small joists will not ~⟩ **b** *obs* **:** to hold good **:** be convincing **c :** to support a person's or a vehicle's weight without cracking or breaking ⟨wondering if the thawing ice would still ~⟩ **4 :** to produce as fruit **:** be fruitful **:** YIELD ⟨plants that ~ well⟩
syn PRODUCE, YIELD, TURN OUT: BEAR in the sense here involved usu. implies a giving birth to or a bringing forth naturally ⟨*bearing* children⟩ ⟨a sow may *bear* litters of over a dozen⟩ ⟨these fruit trees *bear* very well⟩ PRODUCE is very wide in its application and is used for any act of bringing forth or making ⟨the tree will *produce* no fruit⟩ ⟨a pair will *produce* over a hundred offspring⟩ ⟨the factory is *producing* more silk than ever⟩ ⟨he *produced* a book on the subject at the publisher's request⟩ ⟨not until the end of the tenth century did the English *produce* a truly notable prose writer —Kemp Malone⟩ ⟨George was dead. This death *produced* no effect of sadness on me at all —Arnold Bennett⟩ YIELD may center attention on the fact of giving forth or out of something within ⟨the farms *yielded* a variety of fruit, vegetables, poultry, and cattle —*Amer. Guide Series: N.J.*⟩ ⟨these areas *yield* about one hundred thousand barrels of oil a day —*Current Biog.*⟩ TURN OUT indicates production or result of previous labor or effort ⟨the factory is now *turning out* more automobiles⟩
syn ENDURE, SUFFER, ABIDE; TOLERATE, STAND: BEAR is likely to indicate the power of sustaining an affliction onerous or difficult without breaking or flinching ⟨*bear* the brunt of the fighting⟩ ⟨*bear* the major part of the loss⟩ ⟨*bear* the pain of the illness⟩ ⟨his decency, which has made him *bear* prolonged and intolerable humiliation with control and courtesy —Marya Mannes⟩ ⟨a hardy crew, these men who *bore* the hardships of the lumbering industry —*Amer. Guide Series: Wash.*⟩ ENDURE indicates the fact of lasting without succumbing, of continuing unbroken or firm through trials and difficulties ⟨he had endured, and was to *endure* again, a life of tragic penury —W.B. Yeats⟩ ⟨an element of the austere which has allowed him to *endure* the miseries of prison life with indifference —*Times Lit. Supp.*⟩ ⟨Chinese culture has *endured* many conquerors but has always managed to absorb them —Stuart Chase⟩ SUFFER indicates the experiencing of affliction, or what is felt to be like affliction, sometimes with voluntary acceptance ⟨identify himself so thoroughly with the cause of the exploited Indian that he denounced his Puritan fellows and *suffered* exile —H.A.Overstreet⟩ ⟨braves *suffered* their hands and noses to be cut off for their defiance of Spanish authority —*Amer. Guide Series: Fla.*⟩ ⟨for a moment the girl *suffered* the caress; almost she seemed to nestle closer to the Dowager's shoulder —Rafael Sabatini⟩ ABIDE may refer notably to looking forward to afflictive circumstances or agencies as well as trying to endure them with patience and stoicism ⟨I had been grossly wrong, and must *abide* the consequences —Jane Austen⟩ ⟨he fled to Sicily, with a tacit confession that he dared not *abide* his trial —J.A.Froude⟩ ⟨she was a professional do-gooder, a professional busybody; Hawthorne could not *abide* her —H.S.Commager⟩ TOLERATE suggests an enduring or countenancing conditioned in part by individual characteristics or inclinations ⟨the Father of all mankind seems always to have *tolerated* a diversity of views among His children —M.R. Cohen⟩ ⟨children have been found quite able to *tolerate* eyeglasses at the age of fifteen months —Morris Fishbein⟩ ⟨Arnold swallowed an injustice which others would not have *tolerated* —R.G.Adams⟩ STAND, which sometimes has informal suggestion, may apply to bearing with steady firmness, without discomposure or flinching ⟨his wife could not have *stood* another winter here —Owen Wister⟩ ⟨this interference, is more than we can *stand* —W.S.Gilbert⟩ **syn** see in addition CARRY, PRESS
— **bear a hand :** to extend help **:** join in and help out **:** PARTICIPATE — **bear arms 1 :** to carry or possess arms ⟨the right of the people to keep and *bear arms* —*U.S. Constitution*⟩ **2 :** to serve as a soldier — **bear arms against :** to fight against **:** wage war on — **bear date :** to have the date of execution (as of a document) written down explicitly ⟨a letter *bearing date* of 1800⟩ — **bear fruit :** to come to satisfying fruition, production, or development repaying expenditure or compensating for quiescence ⟨his conduct in the primary election *bore fruit* in November⟩ — **bear in hand 1 :** MANAGE, CONTROL **2 :** MAINTAIN, ASSERT, CHARGE ⟨*bearing in hand* that he is guilty⟩; *sometimes* **:** PROMISE ⟨*bear in hand* to marry the princess⟩ **3** *obs* **:** to deceive or gull with pretenses or false promises ⟨how you were *borne in hand*, how crossed —Shak.⟩ — **bear in mind :** to think of esp. as a cautionary or reservation **:** REMEMBER ⟨*bear in mind* that your supplies are limited⟩ — **bear in with :** to run or tend toward ⟨a ship *bears in with* the land⟩ — **bear low sail** *archaic* **:** to comport oneself humbly — **bear with :** to be indulgent, patient, or forbearing with **:** ENDURE ⟨*bear with* the old bore for a while longer⟩
bear·a·ble \-rəbəl\ *adj* [⁴*bear* + *-able*] **:** capable of being borne or endured **:** TOLERABLE — **bear·a·bly** \-rəblē, -bli\ *adv*
bear animalcule *n* **:** one of the Tardigrada **:** WATER BEAR
bear away *vt* **:** to carry off or attain to in victory ⟨*bear away* the spoils⟩ ~ *vi* **:** to change course so as to sail with the wind farther aft
bear·baiting \ˈ=,==\ *n* -S [ME *berebaiting* fr. *bere* bear + *baiting*, fr. gerund of *baiten* to bait — more at BEAR, BAIT] **:** the former practice of setting dogs on a chained bear
bearberry \ˈ=- — *see* BERRY\ *n* [¹*bear* + *berry*] **1 :** any of several plants of the genus *Arctostaphylos* (esp. *A. uva-ursi*) with astringent foliage and glossy red berries **2 :** AMERICAN CRANBERRY **3 :** a deciduous shrub (*Ilex decidua*) of the southern U.S. with green flowers and red fruit **4 :** CASCARA BUCKTHORN
bearberry willow *n* **:** a dwarf prostrate shrub (*Salix uva-ursi*) of the arctic and alpine regions of northeastern No. America with deep green elliptical leaves that taper toward their base
bear·bine \ˈ=,=\ *n* [¹*bear* + *bine*] **1** *or* **bear·bind** \-,bīnd\ **:** any of various European plants of the genus *Convolvulus* (as *C. arvensis* and *C. soldanella*) **2 :** BLACK BINDWEED 1
bear brush *n* **:** a shrub (*Garrya fremonti*) of the western U.S. with oblong shining leaves and dark purple berries — called also *California feverbush*
bear bush *n* **:** INKBERRY 1
bear cat *n* **1 :** BINTURONG **2 :** PANDA **3 :** a person or thing that is marked by especial power or force ⟨obviously this new skipper was a *bear cat*, at least insofar as getting into action with the enemy was concerned —E.L.Beach⟩ ⟨mosquitoes that are regular *bear cats* in action⟩
bear caterpillar *n* **:** WOOLLY BEAR
bear clover *n* **:** MOUNTAIN MISERY
bear corn *n* **:** AMERICAN HELLEBORE
¹beard \ˈbi(ə)rd, ˈbi(ə)d\ *n* -S [ME *berd*, fr. OE *beard*; akin to OHG *bart* beard, L *barba*, OSlav *brada*] **1 :** the hair on the chin, lips, and adjacent parts of the human face usu. of an adult male ⟨he has a very light ~ and does not shave every day⟩: **a :** such hair esp. on cheek and chin permitted to grow until capable of being shaped or trimmed ⟨wearing a ~ to conceal the scar on his chin⟩ **b :** hair growing over the face except that on the upper lip — compare MOUSTACHE, WHISKER **2 :** any of certain appendages of animals felt to resemble a beard: as **a :** a tuft or fringe of hair about the mouth or chin of certain mammals (as some dogs or the goat) **b :** any of various groups of processes about the mouth (as of barbels on catfish or hairy feathers at the base of the bill of some birds) **c :** any of certain groups, tufts, or clusters of hairs, filaments, or processes located on the bodies of animals elsewhere than about the mouth (as the gills of certain bivalve mollusks or the tuft of coarse hair on the breast of adult male turkeys) **3 a :** bristlelike often barbed hairs on plants; *esp* **:** the awns of a head of grain **b beards** *pl* **:** the bristly hairs on the acorn cup of the valonia oak used in tanning **4 :** a projecting element: **a :** a barb or point projecting backward or outward (as on a crochet hook) **b :** a spring piece on the back of a lock bolt to prevent rattling **c :** a crosspiece fastened below the upper lip of a flue pipe of an organ to aid in promptness of speech **d :** BEVEL 1e; *sometimes* **:** the bevel plus the shoulder — see TYPE illustration **5 :** the tail of a comet often when preceding the nucleus **6 :** a noticeable error in performance in a broadcast **:** a word misread or mispronounced **:** FLUFF **7 :** a person who diverts attention

or suspicion from another; *esp* : a person employed to place bets for another whose reputation might affect the odds — **to one's beard** : to one's face : in open defiance

²**beard** \"\ *vt* -ED/-ING/-S [ME *berden*, fr. *berd*, n.] **1** : to cause to have a beard — usu. used in adjective uses of the past participle ⟨letters that may be ~*ed*⟩; *specif* : to cut barbs on (fishhooks) **2 a** : to remove the gills of (a shellfish) **b** : to bevel or round the edges of (timber) to a required angle or curve **3** : to confront and oppose with boldness and resolution often to the point of affronting or defying a powerful or secure opponent ⟨no . . . subject on which he has not taken a clear and open stand even to the point of ~*ing* selfish groups —John Steinbeck⟩ **syn** see FACE

bear dance *n* : a rhythmic animal dance among No. American Indians imitating the bear and primarily propitiatory for aid in hunting or in effecting cures or in connection with totemic worship

bearded *adj* [ME *berded*, fr. *berd* beard + *-ed*] **1** : having a beard ⟨a ~ meteor⟩ ⟨a ~ man⟩ — often used in names of animals and plants **2** : awned or having a growth of hairs **3** : having a jagged point like a fishhook : BARBED

bearded argali *n* : AOUDAD

bearded darnel *n* : a weedy annual grass (*Lolium temulentum*) with very long awns on the glumes and seeds sometimes considered poisonous that often occurs in grainfields and other cultivated land — called also *cheat*

bearded iris *n* : any of numerous wild or cultivated irises with bearded falls — compare BEARDLESS IRIS; see GERMAN IRIS

bearded lizard *also* **bearded dragon** *n* : JEW LIZARD

bearded needle *n* : SPRING NEEDLE

bearded pig *n* : a wild swine (*Sus barbatus*) of Borneo and Malaya with short rounded ears, a wartlike outgrowth between the nostril and eye, and curly whitish whiskers covering the cheeks

bearded seal *n* : a large grayish or yellowish arctic seal (*Erignathus barbatus*) having a tuft of flattened bristles on each side of the muzzle

bearded tit *also* **bearded titmouse** *n* : a small long-tailed European titlike bird (*Panurus biarmicus*) that frequents reedy places, is largely orange-brown, black, and white, and in the male has a tuft of black feathers on each side of the face — called also *reedling*

bearded tongue *var of* BEARD TONGUE

bearded tortoise *n* : MATAMATA

bearded vulture *n* : LAMMERGEIER

bearded wheatgrass *n* : a wheatgrass (*Agropyron subsecundum*) with straight terminal awns on the lemmas

beard·er \-də(r)\ *n* -S : one that beards; *also* : one that tends a bearding machine

beard grass *n* **1** : a grass of the genus *Polypogon* (esp. *P. monspeliensis*) with a densely bearded spike **2** : any of several common grasses of the genus *Andropogon* (as *A. scoparius*) **3** : NEEDLEGRASS 2 **4** : any perennial grass of the genus *Gymnopogon* (family Gramineae) with short rigid leaves and numerous slender flower spikes **5** : PLUME GRASS 1

beard hair *n* : coarse medullated hair of many mammals that grows through and partly covers shorter wool or down (as in goats or seals) : KEMP, GUARD HAIR

beard·ie \ˈbirdē\ *n* -S [*beard* + *-ie*; fr. its bristly gills] **1** : an Australian codlike fish (*Lotella callarias*) with a barbel beneath the lower lip **2** : a small vigorous shaggy collielike sheep dog of Scottish origin

bearding *n* -S [¹*beard* + *-ing*] **1** : a beardlike growth **2 a** : the beveling of a timber to fit the angle of a ship's side **b** : the forward edge of a rudder : the corresponding edge of a sternpost

bearding line *n* : a line on the side of the stem, deadwoods, keel, and sternpost of a ship marking the intersection of the outer face of the frames with these members

bearding machine *n* : a machine that barbs fishhooks

beard·less \ˈ=+ləs\ *adj* [ME *berdles*, fr. *berd* beard + *-less*] **1** : lacking a beard ⟨~ barley⟩ **2 a** : too young to have a beard **b** : YOUTHFUL, INEXPERIENCED, CALLOW — **beard·less·ness** *n* -ES

beardless iris *n* : any of numerous wild or cultivated irises having no beard on the falls — compare BEARDED IRIS; see JAPANESE IRIS

beardless wheat *n* : a wheat in which the outer glumes are without prominent awns — see WHEAT illustration

beard lichen *or* **beard moss** *n* : a greenish gray pendulous lichen (*Usnea barbata*) growing on trees

bear dog *n* [¹*bear*] : any of several massive carnivorous extinct mammals of *Amphicyon* and related genera (family Canidae) that suggest but were probably not ancestral to the bears

bear down *vt* [⁴*bear*] **1 a** : to subdue in battle or contention : OVERWHELM ⟨the castle defenders were *borne down*⟩ **b** : to overcome in argument or discussion ⟨*borne down* by the weight of evidence⟩ **2** : to weigh down : drag down ⟨branches of the tree *borne down* by the large yield⟩ ~ *vi* **1 a** : to sail esp. with the wind **b** *of ships* : to sail toward each other **2** : to be arduous and zealous : exert full strength and concentrated attention ⟨to hold his place he had to *bear down*⟩ ⟨the pitcher *bore down* in the pinches and won the game⟩ **3** : to contract the abdominal muscles and the diaphragm during childbirth —**bear down on** *or* **bear down upon** **1** : to sail toward often in force or with hostile intent ⟨an enemy frigate *bearing down on* the sloop⟩ : proceed toward esp. impressively, awesomely, or forcibly **2** : to give major attention to : STRESS ⟨a lecture that *bore down on* economic causes⟩ **3** : to weigh heavily on : AFFLICT, BURDEN : treat in a noticeably demanding way ⟨a tax that *bore down on* the poorer groups⟩ ⟨*bear down on* a man whose work has fallen off⟩

beards *pl of* BEARD, *pres 3d sing of* BEARD

beards·lee trout \ˈbirdzlē-\ *n, usu cap B* [after Rear Admiral L.A. *Beardslee* †1903 Am. naval officer] : BLUEBACK TROUT b

beard·tongue *also* **beards·tongue** \ˈ=,=\ *or* **bearded tongue** *n* : PENTSTEMON

beardy \ˈbirdē\ *adj* -ER/-EST : BEARDED

beared *past of* ²BEAR

¹**bear·er** \ˈberə(r), ˈba(a)r-\ *n* -S [ME *berere*, fr. *beren* to carry + *-er* — more at BEAR] **1 a** : one bearing a communication to or involving another ⟨rewarding the ~ before reading the note⟩ **b** : one who holds a check, note, draft, or other order for the payment of money; *specif* : the person in possession of a check payable to bearer whether so drawn or having become so by being last endorsed in blank **2 a** : one that bears: as (1) : CARRIER, PORTER ⟨the ~*s* stopped at the door⟩ (2) : a man carrying baggage and supplies for travelers in a situation in which other means of transport are lacking ⟨native ~*s* serving the safari⟩ **b** : one that aids actually or symbolically in carrying a dead person in a funeral proceeding : PALLBEARER **c** : a palanquin bearer **d** *India* : a personal or household servant **e** : a military corpsman who carries stretchers and attends the wounded **3** : one that affords, yields, produces, or supplies ⟨trees that are good ~*s*⟩ **4 a** : one that holds or enjoys an indicated rank, office, or endowment; *specif* : INCUMBENT ⟨an office-*bearer*⟩ **b** : one marked by a distinctive cultural tradition ⟨the invasion of Mexico by Spanish culture ~*s*⟩ **5 a** : one that supports or upholds : one that bears a weight ⟨posts, walls, and other ~*s*⟩ : a small member (as one of a series) used primarily to support another member or structure (as one of the short pieces of quartering supporting the winders of winding stairs) **b** : something that protects a printing surface from excessive pressure (as from an inking or impressing mechanism) or prevents the inking of a blank part: as (1) : one of the pieces of type-high material placed near the corners of the bed of a handpress (2) : a track on the bed of a press against which cylinder or rollers rotate (3) : type-high material placed in the blank parts of a form or left on the face of an engraving or plate to protect it during molding

²**bearer** \"\ *adj* **1** : freely negotiable by the holder ⟨a ~ check⟩ **2** : not registered with full title being transferred merely by delivery ⟨~ securities⟩

bear family *n* : URSIDAE

bear garden *n* **1** : an establishment for bearbaiting or similar practices or entertainment **2** : a scene or procedure marked by unruly rowdy disturbance : HURLY-BURLY

bear grape *var of* BEAR'S-GRAPE

bear grass *n* **1** : any of several liliaceous plants chiefly of the southern and western U.S. that have foliage which resembles coarse blades of grass: as **a** : any of several yuccas (esp. *Yucca glauca* and *Y. filamentosa*) **b** : SOUR GRASS 2 **c** : a plant of the genus *Nolina* native to desert regions of the southwestern U.S. and Mexico and sometimes cutivated as greenhouse succulents **2 a** : a needle grass (*Stipa setigera*) **b** : a bur grass (*Cenchrus pauciflorus*)

bear huckleberry *n* **1** : any of certain low huckleberries of eastern No. America (esp. *Gaylussacia ursina* and *G. baccata*) **2** : a low blueberry (*Vaccinium hirsutum*) of the southeastern U.S.

bear hug *n* : a rough tight embrace; *specif* : a wrestling hold in which a contestant facing his opponent locks his arms around the opponent's back and forces him backwards to the mat

¹**bear·ing** \ˈberiŋ, ˈba(a)r-, -rēŋ\ *n* -S [ME *bering*, fr. gerund of *beren* to bear — more at BEAR] **1 a** : the manner in which one bears oneself : CARRIAGE ⟨a man of erect and soldierly ~⟩ **b** : the manner in which one comports oneself : BEHAVIOR, MIEN ⟨a sedate and dignified ~⟩ ⟨a confident and cheerful ~ —Sheridan LeFanu⟩ **c** : pleasing, impressive, or assured carriage or mien ⟨a man of ~⟩ **2 a** : the act of bringing forth young ⟨weakened by this succession of child-*bearings*⟩ ⟨an older woman past ~⟩ **b** : the action or fact of bringing forth fruit, flowers, or other yield : CROP ⟨three ~*s* in a year⟩ **3** : PRESSURE, THRUST **4 a** : an object, surface, or point that supports : supporting power : point of support **b** : the act or fact of carrying or supporting **c** : a machine part in which a journal, gudgeon, pivot, pin, or other part revolves, oscillates, or slides — see BALL BEARING, NEEDLE BEARING, ROLLER BEARING, THRUST BEARING **5 a** : a single charge in a coat of arms ⟨the lion is a frequent heraldic ~⟩ **b bearings** *pl* : COAT OF ARMS ⟨the ~*s* of Scrope are: azure a bend or⟩ **6 bearings** *pl* **a** : the widest part of a ship below plank-sheer **b** : the line of flotation of a ship when properly trimmed **7 a** : relative situation or position : the situation of one point with respect to another or its direction from another **b bearings** *pl* : relative positions or directions (as in reference to the compass or to landmarks) **c** : the horizontal direction of an object or point from an observer (as on a ship or aircraft) usu. measured clockwise from a reference direction and expressed in degrees from 0° to 360° : AZIMUTH 1b — see COMPASS BEARING, MAGNETIC BEARING, RELATIVE BEARING, TRUE BEARING **d** : an examination or determination of one's position or situation ⟨let's take a ~⟩ **e bearings** *pl* : comprehension or appreciation of one's position, environment, or situation : perception aiding orientation ⟨time for a newcomer to get his ~*s*⟩ ⟨to lose your ~*s*⟩ **f** : RELATION, CONNECTION : full consequence ⟨to consider the matter in all its ~*s*⟩ : RELATIONSHIP, INFLUENCE ⟨the question had no ~ on the outcome⟩ **g** : PURPORT, SIGNIFICANCE ⟨the ~ of a remark⟩ **8 a** : the part of any member of a building that rests upon its supports ⟨a lintel or beam with 4 inches of ~ upon the wall⟩ **b** : an unsupported span ⟨the beam has 20 feet of ~ between its supports⟩ **9 a** *sometimes pl* : the genital tract of a female domestic animal; *often* : its uterus **b bearings** *pl* : eversion of the vagina at parturition in the ewe; *also* : the everted part

²**bearing** \"\ *adj* [ME *bering*, fr. pres. part. of *beren* to bear] **1** : producing or yielding ⟨an interest-*bearing* note⟩ ⟨fruit-*bearing* trees⟩ : marked by or fit for producing or yielding ⟨a good ~ year⟩ ⟨a *bearing*-age tree⟩ **2** *of a structural member* : SUPPORTING : withstanding a weight, thrust, or strain ⟨a ~ partition⟩

bearing arrow *n* [¹*bearing*] : a war arrow

bearing block *n* [²*bearing*] **1** : a block of material acting as a bearing plate **2** *or* **bearing box** [¹*bearing*] : JOURNAL BOX

bearing brass *n* [¹*bearing*] : a brass or bronze step, bushing, or lining for a bearing

bearing cloth *n* [¹*bearing*] : a cloth with which a child is covered when carried to baptism

bearing off spar *n* [fr. pres. part. of ⁴*bear*] : a spar to keep two boats apart

bearing pile *n* [²*bearing*] : a pile driven into the ground so as to carry a vertical load

bearing plate *n* [²*bearing*] : a plate placed under one end of a truss beam, girder, or column to distribute the load

bearing rein *n* [²*bearing*] : CHECKREIN 1a

bearing robe *n* [¹*bearing*] : a garment used as a bearing cloth formerly given to a child by his sponsors

bearing value *n* [¹*bearing*] : the compression a rivet will stand

bear·ish \ˈberish, ˈba(a)rish, -rēsh\ *adj* **1** : felt to resemble a bear in roughness, gruffness, irascibility, or surliness ⟨disappointed and ~ this morning⟩ **2 a** : marked by or tending to a decline in stock prices : DECLINING ⟨present trends are ~⟩ ⟨a ~ effect on the market⟩ **b** : expecting a decline : investing on the notion that prices will fall : dubious or pessimistic about developments ⟨a ~ stock-market operator⟩ ⟨~ about the new issues of the company⟩ — **bear·ish·ly** *adv*

bear leader *n* [¹*bear*, fr. the way trained bears were led around on a chain by their masters] : one that takes charge of a young man on cultural travels : a traveling tutor ⟨sent with a *bear leader* to the continent for years to be ripened —P.E.More⟩

bear mat *n* : MOUNTAIN MISERY

bear moss *n* : a haircap moss (*Polytrichum juniperinum*)

béar·naise \ˌberˈnāz, ˌba(a)rˈ-, ˌbāərˈ-, -ˈnez\ *or* **béarnaise sauce** *n* -S *sometimes cap B* [F *béarnaise*, fem. of *béarnais* of Béarn, region of southwestern France] : hollandaise sauce seasoned (as with minced shallots, tarragon, and chervil) and served with meat or fish

bear oak *n* [so called fr. its acorns' serving as food for bears and other wildlife] : a shrubby evergreen oak (*Quercus ilicifolia*) of the southeastern U.S. forming dense thickets

bear off *vb* [⁴*bear*] *vt* **1 a** : to ward off **b** : to remove to a distance : to keep off or clear from rubbing against anything ⟨*bear off* a boat⟩ **2** : GAIN : carry off (as a prize) ~ *vi* **1** : to steer away **2** : to remove the backgammon men finally from the board after they are all home

be around *vi* : to have experience : become sophisticated; *sometimes* : to have sexual experience — used only in perfect tenses ⟨he'll know how to act; he's *been around*⟩

bear out *vt* [⁴*bear*] : CORROBORATE, CONFIRM, SUBSTANTIATE ⟨recent discoveries that have *borne out* his theory⟩ ⟨history will *bear* his prediction *out*⟩

bear-paw \ˈ=,=\ *n* [¹*bear*] : a snowshoe typically blunt and tailless that is suitable for use in mountains or on rocky terrain

bear pig *n* [¹*bear*] : HOG-NOSED BADGER

bear raid *n* [¹*bear*] : concerted selling of securities usu. by short sellers to force down prices

bears *pl of* BEAR, *pres 3d sing of* BEAR

bear's-bed \ˈ=,=\ *n, pl* **bear's-beds** : the soft cushionlike tuft or mat of certain mosses (as *Polytrichum commune*)

bear's-breech \ˈ=,=\ *n, pl* **bear's-breeches** : either of two prickly European herbs (*Acanthus mollis* and *A. spinosus*) having rough-pubescent leaves

bear's-bush \ˈ=,=\ *var of* BEAR BUSH

bear's-ear \ˈ=,=\ *also* **bear's-ears** \ˈ=,=\ *n, pl* **bear's-ears** : AURICULA 1

bear's-foot \ˈ=,=\ *n, pl* **bear's-foots** : a hellebore (*Helleborus foetidus*) with digitate leaves, an acrid taste, an offensive odor, and irritant qualities when taken internally

bear's-grape \ˈ=,=\ *also* **bear grape** *n, pl* **bear's-grapes** *also* **bear grapes** : BEARBERRY 1

bear's grease *or* **bear's oil** *n* : the rendered fat of the bear

bear's-head \ˈ=,=\ *n, pl* **bear's-heads** : an edible fungus (*Hydnum caput-medusae*) growing on trees in irregular masses

bear·skin \ˈ=,=\ *n* **1** : an article (as a rug) made of the skin of a bear **2** : an often large full-dress military hat made of bearskin **3** : a coarse shaggy woolen cloth used for making overcoats

bear's-paw \ˈ=,=\ *n, pl* **bear's-paws** : the shell of a large East Indian clam (*Hippopus hippopus*)

bear's-weed \ˈ=,=\ *n, pl* **bear's-weeds** : YERBA SANTA

bear-trap dam \ˈ=,=\ *n* : a movable dam usu. consisting of two leaves that is used to deepen shallow parts in a river

bear up *vb* [⁴*bear*] *vt* : SUPPORT, ENCOURAGE : check from sinking, flagging, or becoming discouraged ⟨aid that should *bear* them *up*⟩ ⟨*borne up* in adversity by his faith⟩ ~ *vi* **1** : to summon up courage, resolution, morale, or strength : find stamina to cope or resist ⟨*bearing up* under the long strain⟩ ⟨she *bore up* well during her convalescence⟩ **2** : to check a horse's head with a checkrein **3** : to put the helm to windward and so change the ship's course to leeward : take a leeward course ⟨the ship *bore up*⟩ **4** : to keep pace ⟨fain he would *bear up* with his neighbors in that —John Milton⟩ — **bear up for** : to sail toward esp. on a leeward course

bearwalker \ˈ=,==\ *n* [¹*bear* + *walker*] : a person powerful and malevolent and believed able to assume the shape of a bear or other animal — compare WEREWOLF

bear wallow *n* : a declivity or sink in the ground made or capable of having been made by bears

bear·ward \ˈ=+,wȯrd\ *n* [ME *bereward*, fr. *bere* bear + *ward* keeper] : a bear keeper

bearwood \ˈ=,=\ *n* : CASCARA BUCKTHORN

beas·lings \ˈbēzlənz, -liŋz\ *dial var of* BEASTINGS

beast \ˈbēst\ *n* -S *often attrib* [ME *beest*, *beste*, fr. OF *beste*, fr. L *bestia*; perh. akin to Lith *dvasas* spirit, breath — more at DUST] **1 a** : a living creature : animal as distinguished from plant **b** : any lower animal as distinguished from man **c** : a 4-footed mammal as distinguished on the one hand from man and on the other from birds and lower vertebrates (as fishes and reptiles) and from invertebrates **d** (1) *obs* : any domesticated mammal (2) : a game mammal (3) : a wild mammal fierce by nature; *esp* : a carnivorous wild mammal (4) : an animal used for riding or draft; *esp* : HORSE (5) : a domestic bovine; *esp, Brit* : a fat or fattening butcher's steer **2 a** : a person arousing contempt or loathing for any of a number of traits (as folly, great stupidity, coarseness, vileness, degradation, lust, or insensate brutality) ⟨called me a ~ and a satyr and asked me whether I had gone mad —Robert Graves⟩ **b** : a thing, situation, or condition felt to be hateful or offensive ⟨a ~ of a day, bleak, cold, and rainy⟩ **3** *slang* : GIRL : young woman; *esp* : a coarse or unattractive woman

beast epic *n* : a long verse narrative with climactic epic construction comprising stories of animals represented as acting with human feelings and motives

beast fable *n* : a prose or verse fable or short story which usu. points a moral and in which animal characters are represented as acting with human feelings and motives

beast god *n* : a god represented wholly or partly in animal form

beastial *obs var of* BESTIAL

beast·ie \ˈbēstē, -ti\ *n* -S [*beast* + *-ie*] : ANIMAL ⟨the buffalo were stubborn ~*s* —W.F.Harris⟩; *often* : a small creature ⟨rats and other small ~*s* —W.H.Hudson †1922⟩

beast·i·ly \ˈbēstəlē\ *adv* : BESTIALLY

beast·ings *or* **beest·ings** \ˈbēstiŋz, -stənz\ *also* **beast·lings** \-liŋz, -lənz\ *n pl but sing or pl in constr* [ME *bestynge*, fr. OE *bȳsting*, fr. *bēost* beastings; akin to OHG *biost* beastings, ON *beysti* ham — more at BOAST] : COLOSTRUM; *esp* : the colostrum given by a cow after calving

beast·li·ly \ˈbēstləlē\ *adv* : in a beastly manner

beast·li·ness \ˈbēstlēnəs\ *n* -ES [ME *beestlynesse*, fr. *beestly* + *-nesse* -ness] : the quality or state of being beastly : brutal or disgusting behavior

¹**beast·ly** \-lē, -li\ *adj* -ER/-EST [ME *beestly*, *bestly*, fr. *beest*, *beste* beast + *-ly*] **1** : like a beast : marked by the traits of an animal and by lack of man's dignity or refinement; *often* : lustful or brutal ⟨a ~ froth of rage —Robert Browning⟩ ⟨the abstentious and ~ crudeness of the battlefield —Lewis Mumford⟩ **2** : like, characteristic of, or relating to animals as opposed to man ⟨~ divinities and droves of gods —Matthew Prior⟩ **3** : ABOMINABLE, DISGUSTING, DISTASTEFUL, UNPLEASANT ⟨~ weather⟩ ⟨the ~ stench almost made him faint —W.S.Maugham⟩ ⟨the ~ dullness of the village⟩ **syn** see BRUTAL

²**beastly** \"\ *adv* -ER/-EST [ME *beestly*, *bestly*, fr. *beestly*, *bestly*, adj.] : to a beastly degree or in a beastly manner : ABOMINABLY, EGREGIOUSLY ⟨~ vulgar —Henry James †1916⟩

beast·man \ˈbēstmən, -ˌman\ *n, pl* **beastmen** **1** *Brit* : HERDSMAN **2** : a low or brutal person

beast of burden : an animal employed to carry heavy material or to perform other heavy work (as pulling a cart or a plow)

beast of chase **1** : any of the animals (as fallow deer, roe deer, fox, marten) that might be kept in or hunted under a chase in medieval England — compare *beast of venery*, *beast of warren* **2** : a game mammal — not used technically

beast of prey : a carnivorous animal

beast of venery : any of the animals (as red deer, boar, wolf, hare) that might be hunted in the forests (sense 1) in medieval England — called also *beast of the forest*; compare BEAST OF CHASE, BEAST OF WARREN

beast of warren : either the hare or the coney when kept and hunted in a warren (sense 1) — compare BEAST OF CHASE, BEAST OF VENERY

beast tale *n* : a prose or verse narrative similar to the beast fable but usu. without a moral

¹**beat** \ˈbēt, *usu* -d·+V\ *vb* **beat** \"\ **beaten** \ˈbētᵊn\ *also* **beat** \ˈbēt, *usu* -d·+V\ *or now dial* **bet** \ˈbet\ **beating; beats** [ME *beten*, fr. OE *bēatan*; akin to OHG *bōzan* to beat, ON *bauta*, L *-futare* to beat, *fustis* club] *vt* **1** : to strike repeatedly: **a** : to hit repeatedly with hand, fist, weapon, or other instrument so as to inflict pain (as in order to punish or warn) often cruelly or oppressively ⟨arrested for ~*ing* his wife⟩ ⟨~*ing* the dog for barking at night⟩ ⟨*beaten* by thugs⟩ **b** : to walk on : TREAD ⟨~*ing* the streets looking for work⟩ **c** : to strike (part of one's own body) repeatedly in the throes of emotion ⟨the wedding guest he ~ his breast —S.T.Coleridge⟩ or in accordance with musical rhythm ⟨the natives watching the dance, ~*ing* their thighs⟩ **d** : to strike directly against forcefully and repeatedly : dash against ⟨a house *beaten* by repeated storms⟩ **e** *obs* : to assail or importune with repeated sounds ⟨~*ing* our ears with his endless complaints⟩ **f** : to flail, flap, or thrash at futilely ⟨the trapped bird ~*ing* the air⟩ **g** (1) : to strike, lash, or poke at (as in order to rouse game animals or birds) ⟨~*ing* the hedgerow for rabbits⟩ : range over in quest of game ⟨~ the woods and rouse the bounding prey —Matthew Prior⟩ : SEARCH, SCOUR ⟨~*ing* the woods for the lost child⟩ (2) : to sweep a net across to dislodge and capture insects ⟨~*ing* the limb for injurious insects⟩ (3) : to hit repeatedly in order to knock something off or out ⟨~*ing* the olive trees and picking up the fruit⟩ ⟨~*ing* the dirty rugs⟩ **h** : to mix together or to bring about frothing in by mixing with air by means of repeated strong turning, stirring, whirling, or agitating : WHIP ⟨~*ing* eggs⟩ ⟨~*ing* pancake batter⟩ **i** : to strike repeatedly to produce musical, rhythmical, or meaningful sound ⟨~*ing* a drum⟩ ⟨~*ing* a gong⟩ **2** : to effect by or as if by repeated striking or hitting: **a** : to drive, force, or impel by blows ⟨*beaten* back by the defenders of the castle⟩ ⟨~*ing* off the savage dogs with a club⟩ **b** (1) : to pound into a powder, paste, or pulp ⟨pebbles *beaten* to a fine dust⟩ (2) *papermaking* : to subject (fibrous materials) to a mechanical process (as in a beater) causing disintegration, cutting, bruising, and fraying out **c** : to force or drive home by repeated strong admonition or injunction ⟨trying to ~ some sense into these dolts⟩ **d** : BATTER : bring or make by hard or crushing blows ⟨*beaten* to the ground by a series of blows⟩ ⟨*beaten* black-and-blue⟩ ⟨*beaten* to death by the mob⟩ ⟨a beached ship *beaten* to pieces in the storm⟩ — used in a number of metaphoric phrases such as *to beat the daylights out of, to beat the tar out of, to beat the devil out of, to beat the life out of, to beat the ears off* **e** : to make by repeated treading, walking, or driving over ⟨~ a path through the thicket⟩ ⟨the trail he used was *beaten* into a road by the feet and wagons of the first homesteaders —*Amer. Guide Series: Mich.*⟩ **f** (1) : to dislodge by repeated hitting ⟨~*ing* dust from the carpet⟩ (2) : to lodge securely by repeated striking ⟨~*ing* the stakes into the ground⟩ **g** : to shape by beating ⟨~ swords into plowshares⟩; *esp* : to flatten out by hammer blows sometimes into leaf thinness ⟨gold *beaten* into strips⟩ : make ornamental dents in by beating ⟨*beaten* pewter⟩ **h** (1) : to sound by drumming ⟨~*ing* a martial tune⟩ ⟨rain ~ a tattoo on the roof⟩ : give a signal for or express a wish for by beat of drum or sound of other instrument ⟨~ an alarm⟩ ⟨~*ing* a charge⟩ ⟨~*ing* the reveille⟩ ⟨~*ing* a parley⟩ (2) *of a drum* : to express or signify when beaten ⟨the drums ~ a merry tune⟩ ⟨drums ~*ing* a march⟩ **i** : to flatten (book leaves) by hammering **j** : to ink (a printing surface) by dabbing with ink

balls **3 :** to cause to beat, strike, or flap repeatedly ⟨a bird ~*ing* its wing⟩ ⟨~ his foot nervously on the ground —Charles Dickens⟩ ⟨~*ing* their hands in time to the music⟩ **4 :** OVERCOME, DEFEAT: **a :** to achieve victory over **:** conquer, vanquish, or subdue in a battle, contest, strife, race, game, or other competition ⟨~*ing* the insurgents in a bloody battle⟩ ⟨Central ~*ing* Suburban in football⟩ ⟨~*ing* his rival in the election⟩ **:** bring about the defeat of ⟨his own great wealth ~ him in the election⟩ ⟨*beaten* in the game by their own mistakes⟩ **b :** SURPASS, TOP, EXCEL **:** be or be judged superior to ⟨a meal hard to ~⟩ ⟨for loveliness it would be hard to ~ —Matthew Arnold⟩ ⟨this dog ~ the others for the blue ribbon⟩ **:** outdo and supersede ⟨his performance ~*s* the record⟩ — used in a number of phrases sometimes adverbially: *to beat hell, to beat the cars, to beat the band, to beat the devil, to beat the Dutch* ⟨I lay down and cried to ~ the band all afternoon —Scott Fitzgerald⟩ **c** *archaic* **:** to beat down **:** endeavor to bring down in price or terms ⟨~*ing* the bargain⟩ **d :** to get the better of, win against, or prevail over or despite ⟨~*ing* the bank with his system⟩ ⟨~*ing* the odds against him⟩ **e** (1) **:** CHECK **:** defy all efforts of (one) at solving ⟨a problem that ~ the engineers⟩ (2) **:** MYSTIFY, BEWILDER, PERPLEX, BAFFLE ⟨it ~*s* me how he does it⟩ (3) **:** to be too canny to outwit or too capricious to outguess **f :** FATIGUE, EXHAUST — used mostly in passives and adjective uses of the past participle ⟨feeling completely ~ after the race⟩ **g :** CHEAT, DEFRAUD ⟨~*ing* him out of his due return⟩ **h :** to check and leave dispirited, irresolute, or hopeless ⟨a failure at fifty, a *beaten* man⟩ **i :** to escape the possible consequences of **:** defeat or check the effect of **:** NULLIFY, VITIATE, SURMOUNT **:** prevail over ⟨~*ing* the sultry weather⟩ ⟨~*ing* the inflationary trend⟩ **j :** to report a news item in advance of or to the exclusion of (competing newsmen or news media) **k :** ELUDE **:** break through **:** get past ⟨the batsman was *beaten* and bowled by an inswinger⟩ **5 a :** FORESTALL, ANTICIPATE **:** get ahead of **:** take important or decisive action before ⟨he was going to bid at the auction but I ~ him⟩ **b :** to act ahead of usu. so as to forestall or make ineffective the engaging in a like action of (another) ⟨~*ing* his enemy to the draw⟩ ⟨he ~ his opponent to the punch⟩ **c :** to act or to complete an act before (a determined final point in time) ⟨~ the deadline⟩ **d :** to come to, arrive at, or sojourn at before ⟨another man ~ me to the empty chair⟩ **:** arrive at a goal or destination before ⟨the fielder's throw ~ the baserunner⟩ **e :** to start or to do something before (an official signal to begin) ⟨~ the gun⟩ ⟨leaving early and ~*ing* the whistle⟩ **f :** CIRCUMVENT **:** surmount or escape from by devious procedure ⟨no system can be devised that cannot be *beaten* by collusion —*Jour. of Accountancy*⟩ **6 :** to indicate by one's motions (a musical beat or tempo) ⟨a young conductor will ~ wildly almost any tempo —Warwick Braithwaite⟩ **~** *vi* **1 a :** DASH, STRIKE **:** become forcefully impelled **:** fall violently ⟨waves ~ against the shore⟩ ⟨rain ~*ing* on the roof⟩ **b :** to glare with continuing oppressive intensity ⟨burning hot weather, with the sun ~*ing* down —G.W.Talbot⟩ **:** become projected steadily with unpleasant force or intensity ⟨the heat in the shadeless fields ~*s* down on the steaming black earth —Marjory S. Douglas⟩ **c :** to sustain violent or strident activity with a demanding distracting effect ⟨the turbulence of the Renaissance and the quarrels of England and Spain ~*ing* about his head —Douglas Stewart⟩ **d :** to make a succession of strokes on a drum ⟨the drummers ~ to call soldiers to their quarters⟩ **2 a :** to course or operate with perceptible strokes **:** PULSATE ⟨my pulse ~ so quickly and hardly that I felt the palpitation of every artery —Mary W. Shelley⟩ **b :** to throb with animation **:** pulsate strongly; *often* **:** to demand attention with agitating exigency ⟨her dominant will ~ so strongly within her —Hugh Walpole⟩ ⟨his breathing was hard and . . . the blood ~ in his ears and eyes —Robertson Davies⟩ ⟨a question was ~*ing* unanswered at the back of her brain —Ellen Glasgow⟩ **c** *of a timepiece* **:** to operate audibly **:** TICK ⟨the ~*ing* of the clock⟩ **d** (1) **:** to sound upon being struck ⟨the drums ~⟩ (2) **:** to become sounded by or as if by drums ⟨before the assembly ~*s* —W.M.Thackeray⟩ **e :** to result in beats (as produced by two simultaneous tones of slightly different frequencies) ⟨the B ~*s* unpleasantly with the C⟩ **3 a :** to strike repeatedly **:** inflict repeated blows **:** knock or pound vigorously or loudly ⟨their air attack still ~*ing* upon us —Sir Winston Churchill⟩ ⟨~*ing* on the door of the cabin⟩ **b** *of a hare* **:** to tap the ground as a mating gesture **c :** to strike the air **:** FLAP ⟨the wings of the bird ~*ing* feebly⟩ **d :** to strike bushes or other cover to rouse game; *also* **:** to range or scour for or as if for game **4 :** to progress with changes of direction or procedure: **a :** to make progress to windward by sailing in a zigzag line (as by tacking) **b :** to sail with much tacking ⟨~*ing* along the coast⟩ **c :** to make one's way persistently and often arduously usu. by a series of expedient choices ⟨the castaways ~*ing* inland⟩ **5 :** WIN ⟨our team will ~⟩

syn POUND, PUMMEL, THRASH, THRESH, BUFFET, BASTE, BELABOR: BEAT is a general word to designate repeated striking ⟨*beat* a carpet⟩ ⟨*beat* a child, hitting him repeatedly⟩ ⟨a savage *beating*⟩ POUND may apply to beating with heavier, more massive, damaging, or crushing blows ⟨a tropical hurricane *pounded* the island with giant waves —Martin Gardner⟩ ⟨the artillery and the dive bombers *pounded* the defense —S.L.A. Marshall⟩ PUMMEL may apply to a continuous shower of blows not massive but fairly heavy and damaging ⟨with Dick fastened on him, *pummeling* away most unmercifully —Samuel Lover⟩ ⟨the piers are *pummelled* by the waves —W.H.Auden⟩ THRASH and THRESH apply to repeated striking as with a flail, stick, or whip ⟨*thrashing* grain⟩ ⟨*thrash* a child or servant⟩ ⟨Indians paddle into the swamp, two men in each canoe; while one rows the other *threshes* the rice heads into the boat with two sticks —*Amer. Guide Series: Minn.*⟩ BUFFET, often used figuratively, implies a repeated striking, heavy slapping, cuffing to and fro ⟨Sung Yung was shoved about and *buffeted* by angry hands —T.B.Costain⟩ ⟨the two hands of Madame Defarge *buffeted* and tore her face —Charles Dickens⟩ ⟨*buffeted* by the bewildering passions and divided loyalties —C.J.Rolo⟩ BASTE may imply a thorough cudgeling, thrashing, or beating ⟨if you will give me the loan of a horsewhip, I'll *baste* the backs of these lazy fellows of yours —J.H. Wheelwright⟩ BELABOR suggests a prolonged beating or drubbing ⟨a group of demonstrating Egyptians being *belabored* by police —R.C.Doty⟩ **syn** see in addition CONQUER, PULSATE

— **beat about the bush** *also* **beat around the bush :** to fail or refuse to come to the point in discourse — **beat a retreat :** to retreat or retire often in haste or with loss of dignity — **beat goose** *or* **beat the booby :** to thrust the hands under the armpits to warm them — **beat hollow** *or* **beat all hollow :** to defeat or surpass utterly ⟨*beat* his opponents *hollow*⟩ ⟨this movie *beats* that one *all hollow*⟩ — **beat it 1 :** to hurry away **:** get out in a rush **:** SCRAM ⟨the youngsters *beat it* when the police came⟩ **2 :** HURRY, RUSH ⟨the reporter *beat it* to a telephone to call in the news⟩ — **beat one's brains out** *or* **beat one's brains :** to cudgel one's brain **:** try continually and energetically to think out something difficult — **beat one's breast** *or* **beat one's chest :** to declaim often vaingloriously or vauntingly and usu. in vindicating oneself — **beat one's gums :** to talk continually or excessively; to talk with little effect — **beat one's time :** to surpass one's understanding **:** leave one puzzled or mystified — **beat one's way :** to make one's way usu. against difficulties by a series of resourceful expedients or varied means ⟨*beating his way* across country doing odd jobs —Elmer Davis⟩ ⟨*beating his way* on foot, muleback, raft, and canoe⟩ — **beat the air :** to flail away at nothing — **beat the bounds :** to survey the bounds of an English parish by marching in procession and marking them at various points by switching with boughs — **beat the bushes :** to scour or search through all likely or possible areas ⟨*beating the bushes* for promising talent⟩ — **beat the drum** *also* **beat a drum :** to declaim as meritorious or esp. significant **:** publicize or argue noisily ⟨publicity men *beating the drum* about the new star⟩ ⟨*beat the drum* for him as a candidate⟩ — **beat the rap :** to escape or evade the penalties connected with an accusation or charge ⟨he was charged with arson but he *beat the rap*⟩ — **beat the time of :** to cut out esp. with a date **:** court and win the choice of (another suitor) — **beat time :** to measure or mark off musical time by strokes or taps — **beat to leeward :** to sail before the wind with mainsail and headsails trimmed for a broad reach at an angle to the course first on one side of the course and then after jibbing on the other — **beat to windward :** BEAT *vi* 4a

²beat \" \ *n* -s **1 a :** a single stroke, blow, or pulsation; *also* **:** the sound so produced **b :** a stroke in a series or a set of strokes as on a drum; *also* **:** the sound so given **c :** the driving impact of or as if of steady blows ⟨the full force of the surf ~ —Joyce Allan⟩ ⟨the fierce ~ of the eastern sun —T.B.Costain⟩ **d :** the number of strokes per minute rowed by a racing crew or completed by a swimmer ⟨the cox lifted the ~ to 36⟩ **2 a :** one swing of the pendulum or the balance of a timepiece **b :** the tick or other sound made as a tooth of the escape wheel in a timepiece engages a pallet face of the escapement **3 :** each of the pulsations of amplitude recurring at regular intervals produced by the union of sound waves, radio waves, or electric currents having different frequencies, the frequency of the beats being the sum or difference between the frequencies of the waves or currents **4 a :** a sharp tap delivered on a fencing opponent's blade esp. to open up a line of attack **b :** an accented stroke in dancing (as of one leg or foot against the other, one prop against another, or the hand against a part of the body) **5 a :** a recurring stroke **:** THROB, PULSATION ⟨a heart ~⟩; *also* **:** the sound of such a throb **b :** the sound of a steady sequence of blows or strokes ⟨the ~ of the waves on the rock⟩ **:** a steady sequence of sounds **c :** an effect of rhythmical repetition ⟨the ~ of a poet's verse⟩ **:** metrical or rhythmical stress **6 a :** a grace or ornament in early English music probably equivalent to a mordent **b :** the recurring periodic accent that constitutes the basis of meter in all metrical music **c :** the unit of time or tempo measurement indicated to the performer (as by a movement of a conductor's hand or baton or by the tick of a metronome) **d :** the pronounced and swinging rhythm that is characteristically the generating or driving force in jazz music and jazz bands ⟨that band has a fine ~⟩ **e :** a noteworthy rhythmical effect ⟨the irregular ~ of city life⟩ **7 a :** a round, course, or stretch frequently gone over **:** an habitual range or resort **:** an area frequently traversed esp. in the course of work or duty ⟨a policeman's ~⟩ **b :** a tract with more or less definite bounds over which sportsmen customarily range for game **c** (1) **:** a scouring of a tract of land to rouse or drive out game (2) **:** those engaged in a beat **d :** the area of one's special duty, responsibility, or jurisdiction **e :** a group of news sources that a reporter covers regularly **f :** one's special range of knowledge or interests **8 :** the part of a valve surface that contacts the seat when the valve is closed **9 a :** an administrative subdivision of a county in Alabama or Mississippi — called also *supervisor district* **b :** an election precinct in Alabama or Mississippi **10 a :** something that excels or surpasses ⟨I have never seen the ~ of it⟩ **b :** the reporting of an important news story ahead of or to the exclusion of one's competitors; *broadly* **:** an action defeating or checking a competitor **11 a :** DEADBEAT **2 b :** one that fails to make returns **c :** a shiftless character **:** LOAFER **12 a :** an act of beating to windward **b :** one of the reaches in the zigzag course so traversed **:** TACK — **in beat :** in a condition in which a timepiece pendulum or balance receives its impulses when at equal distances from the dead point — **off one's beat :** out of one's accustomed sphere or scope — **off the beat** *or* **off beat :** out of tempo **:** showing irregularity **:** off the beam — **out of beat :** in a condition in which a pendulum or balance receives its impulses at unequal distances from the dead point

³beat \" \ *adj* [ME *bete*, fr. *bete*, *beten*, past part. of *beten* to beat] **1 :** EXHAUSTED **:** used up **:** completely tired ⟨so ~ that I'd flop down and go to sleep fully dressed —Polly Adler⟩ **2 :** BEATEN 3 **3 :** marked by injury or weakness brought about by the jarring impacts incident to working with a pick ⟨a miner with a ~ hand⟩ **4 :** of, relating to, or having the characteristics of beatniks ⟨~ jargon⟩ ⟨~ generation⟩ ⟨~ poet⟩

⁴beat \" \ *n* -s **:** BEATNIK

⁵beat \'bēt, 'bāt\ *dial Brit var of* ³BEET

⁶beat \" \ *n* -s [origin unknown] *Brit* **:** turf pared from fallow land for spreading and burning on cropland as a fertilizer

be·a·ta \bā'äd·ə, -ätə,-äd·(,)ä,-ä(,)tä *sometimes* bē'äd·ə, -ätə\ *n, pl* **bea·tae** \bā'äd·(,)ä, -ä(,)tä *sometimes* bē'äd·(,)ē, -ä(,)tē, -äd·,ī,-ä,tī\ *also* **beatas** \-əz,-äz\ [L, fr. fem. of *beatus* happy — more at BEATIFY] *Roman Catholic Church* **:** a woman or girl who has been beatified

beat about *vi* **1 :** to range about in quest or search **2 :** to change course repeatedly **:** TACK; *esp* **:** to experiment to find an expedient course

beat back *vt* **:** REPULSE, REPEL **:** drive back ⟨*beat back* the enemy⟩

beat board *n* [²*beat*] **:** a short slanted platform used as a takeoff in vaulting and broad jumping

beat down *vt* **1 :** to harass, subdue, or crush the spirit of ⟨he *beat down* the arrogance of a heretic —H.O.Taylor⟩ **:** VANQUISH ⟨the enemy was *beaten down*⟩ **2 a :** to haggle for a reduction of **:** force down by haggling ⟨*beating* the price *down*⟩ **:** cause lowering of **b :** to force esp. by haggling into accepting a lower price or more advantageous arrangement ⟨we *beat* him *down* to a dollar⟩

beat·em·est *also* **beat·'em·est** \'bētəməst\ *adj* [prob. alter. of *beatingest*, fr. superl. of *beating*, pres. part. of ¹*beat*] *dial* **:** BEST **:** most outstanding or powerful

beaten *adj* [ME *beten*, fr. past part. of *beten* to beat] **1 :** wrought by hammering **:** hammered into shape **:** hammered thin or fine ⟨~ gold⟩; *sometimes* **:** REPOUSSÉ **2 a :** much trodden and worn smooth or bare; *sometimes* **:** FAMILIAR, WELL-KNOWN ⟨a ~ path⟩ **b** *archaic* **:** TRITE **3 :** defeated or checked and sapped of strength, resolution, and morale ⟨too ~ to pull himself out of the latest mess —Laurent Le Sage⟩ **4 a :** ³BEAT 1 **b :** worn out **:** exhausted of fertility ⟨~ soil⟩ **c :** much worn **:** BATTERED, TATTERED, DILAPIDATED ⟨one of my most precious volumes is a ~ old volume —Christopher Morley⟩

beaten biscuit *n* **:** a biscuit made of a dough of flour, water, and shortening lightened by beating and folding

beaten-up \'==,=\ *adj* **:** WORN, BATTERED, DILAPIDATED ⟨a *beaten-up* old car⟩

beaten zone *n* **:** the elliptical ground area struck by the fire of automatic weapons or by artillery projectiles

beater \'bēd·ə(r), -ētə\ *n* -s [ME *beter*, fr. *beten* to beat + *-er*] **1 :** one that beats: as **a :** a plasterer's staff for beating mortar **b :** a tool for packing tamping on a charge of powder in a blasthole **c :** MAUL **d :** a device like a fan placed at the back of the cylinder in a grain thresher for directing straw to straw racks **e :** DOWN-BEATER **f :** an attachment to the discharge end of a manure spreader for pulverizing the manure as it passes from the spreader **g :** the part of a flail that strikes the grain in threshing **h :** a revolving cylinder bearing chains or flails that chop up standing cornstalks, potato vines, brush, or sugar-beet tops **i :** a tailor's paddle used in pressing **j :** a kitchen utensil used for beating, stirring, or whipping **k :** a device on a cotton picker or opener for separating raw cotton **l :** a knife for breaking flax or hemp **m :** the lay of a loom for driving the weft from the shed into the cloth **n :** a machine consisting essentially of a tank equipped with adjustable cutting elements between which paper stock passes to be cut or beaten and in which coloring, loading, and sizing are sometimes done — compare HOLLANDER **o :** a heavy iron for beating basketwork into compactness **p :** a worker who spreads filler material evenly in quilts or mattresses **2 a :** one that beats up game in hunting ⟨engaged a native ~⟩ **b :** an advance publicity agent **3** *in Newfoundland* **:** a young harp seal on its first journey northward from the breeding area

beater 1 j

beater chest *n* **:** a reservoir into which paper pulp is discharged from beaters

beat·er·man \'==mən, -,man\ *n, pl* **beatermen :** one in charge of a beater in paper manufacturing

beater roll *n* **:** a rotating roller in a papermaking beater that is faced with a series of parallel bars or knives that brush against similar bars in the bedplate

beater-size \'==,=\ *vt* **:** to make (paper) from pulp mixed with a sizing agent in a beater — compare SURFACE-SIZE, TUB-SIZE

beati *pl of* BEATUS

be·a·tif·ic \,bēə¦tifik\ *also* **be·a·tif·i·cal** \-fəkəl\ *adj* [L *beatificus*, fr. *beatus* happy (fr. past part. of *beare* to bless, make happy) + *-i-* + *-ficus* -fic; akin to L *bonus* good — more at BOUNTY] **1 :** of, possessing, or imparting beatitude **2 :** marked by an appearance of complete bliss or utter benignity **:** SAINTLY, ANGELIC, SERAPHIC — **be·a·tif·i·cal·ly** \-fək(ə)lē, -li\ *adv*

be·a·tif·i·cate \,bēə'tifə,kāt, bē'ad·əfə,-, *usu* -ād· + V\ *vt* -ED/-ING/-S [It *beatificato* (past part. of *beatificare*), fr. LL *beatificatus*, past part. of *beatificare*, fr. L *beatificus*] **:** BEATIFY

be·at·i·fi·ca·tion \bē,ad·əfə'kāshən, -,atəf-\ *n* -s [LL *beatification*, *beatificatio*, fr. *beatificatus* + L *-ion-*, *-io* -ion] **1 :** the act of beatifying **2 :** the state of being beatified

beatific vision *n* **:** the immediate sight of God in the glory of heaven **:** the direct intuition of God

be·at·i·fy \bē'ad·ə,fī, -'atə,fī\ *vt* -ED/-ING/-ES [MF *beatifier*, fr. LL *beatificare*] **1 :** to make supremely happy **:** endow with beatitude and bliss **2** *Roman Catholicism* **:** to declare (a deceased person) to have attained the blessedness of heaven and authorize the title "Blessed" and limited public religious honor for — compare CANONIZE

beat·in'·est *or* **beat·in·est** *also* **beat·en·est** \'bētᵊnəst\ *adj* [alter. of *beatingest*, fr. superl. of *beating*, pres. part. of ¹*beat*] *chiefly South & Midland* **:** surpassing all others **:** most unusual or surprising

beating *n* -s [ME *beting*, fr. gerund of *beten* to beat] **:** a material or immaterial injury, impairment, or detriment like the bruising of heavy blows ⟨taking a ~ in the stock market⟩

beating engine *n* **:** BEATER 1n

beating reed *n* **:** a reed covering an air opening in a musical instrument so as to vibrate against the edge of an air slot (as in a clarinet or organ pipe) — compare FREE REED

be·at·i·tude \bē'ad·ə,tüd, -'atə,-, -ə-,tyüd\ *n* -s [L *beatitudo*, fr. *beatus* happy + *-tudo* -tude] **1 :** the quality or state of being blessed **:** consummate bliss **2 :** transcendent happiness **3 :** a declaration of a specific condition for being blessed or gaining a kind of bliss **4 :** BEATIFICATION **5 :** a patriarch in either the Eastern or Western Orthodox Church **:** the head of any of certain autocephalous Eastern churches — used mostly as a title ⟨his ~ the Patriarch⟩ **syn** see HAPPINESS

beat man *n* [²*beat*] **:** a newsman with a regular beat

beat·nik \'bētnik, -nēk\ *n* -s [³*beat* + *-nik* (as in *nudnik*)] **:** a person having a predilection for unconventional behavior and dress and often a preoccupation with exotic philosophizing and self-expression

beat off *vt* **:** REPEL, REPULSE **:** drive back

beat·om·est \'bētəməst\ *var of* BEATEMEST

beat out *vt* **1 :** to make or perform by or as if by beating ⟨*beating out* pewter ware⟩ **:** accomplish by beating ⟨*beat out* a path⟩ **2 :** to prevail over (a rival or competitor) ⟨*beat out* another firm in bidding⟩ ⟨*beat out* others for a job⟩ **3 :** EXHAUST, WEARY **4 a :** to mark or accompany by beating ⟨*beat out* the rhythm strongly⟩ **b :** PLAY ⟨*beat out* jazz⟩ **5 :** to turn (a ground ball) into a hit in baseball by fast running to first base

beat-out *adj* [fr. past part. of *beat out*] **:** WEARY, EXHAUSTED **:** ³BEAT 1 ⟨too *beat-out* to think, even about home —L.M.Uris⟩

beats *pres 3d sing of* BEAT, *pl of* BEAT

beat up *vi* **1 :** to sail or attempt to sail against adverse winds or currents ⟨*beating up* for hours trying to enter the harbor⟩ **2 :** to go about zealously seeking ⟨*beat up* for likely recruits⟩ **~** *vt* **1 :** DISTURB, ALARM, AROUSE ⟨urgent messengers *beating up* the general's quarters⟩ **2 :** to muster up ⟨*beating up* volunteers for the corps⟩ **3 :** to bring to froth or mix thoroughly by repeated beating, stirring, or whipping **:** ¹BEAT 1h ⟨*beat up* an egg⟩ **4 :** to beat soundly with fists or clubs or other weapons **:** THRASH ⟨thugs and brutes who *beat up* their victims without compunction —J.H.Plumb⟩ ⟨*beat up* a scab⟩ **5 :** to remove (a depression or mark) from the face of an engraver's plate by striking the back **6 :** to drive (the filling) into its proper position in a fabric being woven **7 :** to force (as by haggling) into acceptance of a higher price or offer

¹beat-up \'=¦=\ *adj* [fr. past part. of *beat up*] **:** worn or damaged by hard or long use or by neglect **:** DILAPIDATED, EXHAUSTED ⟨a *beat-up* car fifteen years old⟩ ⟨a *beat-up* piano⟩

²beat-up *n* -s [*beat up*] **:** tufts per inch warpwise in Axminster and chenille carpeting

be·a·tus \bā'äd·əs, -ätəs,-äd·(,)üs,-ä(,)tüs *sometimes* bē'äd·əs, -ätəs\ *n, pl* **bea·ti** \bā'äd·(,)ē, -ä(,)tē *sometimes* bē'äd·,ī, -ä,tī\ [L, blessed, happy — more at BEATIFIC] *Roman Catholicism* **:** a man or boy who has been beatified

beat your neighbor *n* **:** a form of poker in which a player must drop unless his exposed cards form a higher-ranking combination than the exposed cards of the player to his right

¹beau \'bō\ *adj* [ME, fr. MF] **:** FAIR, GOOD, GALLANT

²beau \" \ *n, pl* **beaux** \'bōz, 'bō\ *or* **beaus** \'bōz\ [F, fr. *beau* fine, beautiful, fr. OF *biau*, *bel*, fr. L *bellus* pretty — more at BEAUTY] **1 :** a man who shows careful, meticulous, or vain addiction to the latest fashions in dress, bearing, and etiquette **:** DANDY — formerly used as an epithet or sobriquet ⟨the magnificent ~, dancing to the light of chandeliers —T.L.Peacock⟩ **2 a :** a man or boy who goes frequently or steadily with a woman or girl **:** ESCORT, STEADY **b :** a man or boy in an intimate relationship with a woman or girl **:** LOVER, SWEETHEART ⟨her ~'s gone and left her —William Faulkner⟩

³beau \" \ *vt* -ED/-ING/-S **:** go with **:** act as beau to **:** ESCORT ⟨all of us ~*ed* the girls to the little dances —W.A.White⟩

beau brum·mel *also* **beau brummell** \(')bō'brəməl\ *n, pl* **beau brummels** *also* **beau brummells** *usu cap both B's* [after *Beau Brummell*, nickname of George B. Brummell †1840 Eng. dandy] **1 :** a typical or extreme dandy **2 :** a man's dressing table of 18th century design with an adjustable mirror, side leaves, and many small drawers or compartments

beaufet *archaic var of* ³BUFFET

beau·fort cipher \'bōfə(r)t-\ *n, usu cap B* [after Sir Francis *Beaufort* †1857 Eng. naval officer and hydrographer] **:** a system of polyalphabetic substitution equivalent to Vigenère cipher with a reversed normal cipher sequence, the keying formula of which is P+C=K

beaufort scale *n, usu cap B* [after Sir Francis *Beaufort*] **:** a

BEAUFORT SCALE

BEAUFORT NUMBER	NAME	MILES PER HOUR	DESCRIPTION
0	Calm	Less than 1	Calm; smoke rises vertically
1	Light air	1–3	Direction of wind shown by smoke but not by wind vanes
2	Light breeze	4–7	Wind felt on face; leaves rustle; ordinary vane moved by wind
3	Gentle breeze	8–12	Leaves and small twigs in constant motion; wind extends light flag
4	Moderate breeze	13–18	Raises dust and loose paper; small branches are moved
5	Fresh breeze	19–24	Small trees in leaf begin to sway; crested wavelets form on inland waters
6	Strong breeze	25–31	Large branches in motion; telegraph wires whistle; umbrellas used with difficulty
7	Moderate gale	32–38	Whole trees in motion; inconvenience in walking against wind
8	Fresh gale	39–46	Breaks twigs off trees; generally impedes progress
9	Strong gale	47–54	Slight structural damage occurs; chimney pots and slates removed

(*Continued*)

BEAUFORT SCALE — *continued*

BEAUFORT NUMBER	NAME	MILES PER HOUR	DESCRIPTION
10	Whole gale	55–63	Trees uprooted; considerable structural damage occurs
11	Storm	64–72	Very rarely experienced; accompanied by widespread damage
12	Hurricane	73–82	Devastation occurs
13	Hurricane	83–92	Devastation occurs
14	Hurricane	93–103	Devastation occurs
15	Hurricane	104–114	Devastation occurs
16	Hurricane	115–125	Devastation occurs
17	Hurricane	126–136	Devastation occurs

wind scale in which the force of the wind is indicated by a series of numbers from 0 to 17, orig. from 0 to 12, with corresponding descriptive terms, these terms being commonly used by the U.S. Weather Bureau

beau geste \(ˈ)bōˈzhest\ *n, pl* **beaux gestes** *or* **beau gestes** \"\ [F, lit., beautiful gesture] **1 :** a graceful pleasing fine or magnanimous gesture **2 :** a gracious conciliatory insubstantial or ineffectual gesture

beau greg·o·ry \(ˈ)bōˈgregərē\ *also* **beau gre·goire** \-greˈgwär\ *n, pl* **beau gregories** \-(ˌ)rēz\ *also* **beau gregoires** \-ˈgwärz\ *often cap B&G* [¹*beau* + the name *Gregory*] **:** a small blue-and-gold pomacentrid fish (*Eupomacentrus leucostictus*) found along the coasts of Florida and the West Indies

beau ideal \(ˈ)bō,īˈdēl, *esp bef pause or cons* -ēəl\ *n* [F *beau idéal* ideal beauty] **1** *pl* **beaus ideal** \(ˈ)bō,zī-\ *or* **beaux ideal** \" *also* (ˈ)bō,ī-\ **:** ideal or perfect beauty **2** *pl* **beau ideals** \(ˈ)bō,īdē(ə)lz\ **:** the perfect type or model **:** a type attaining to highest excellence ⟨the *beau ideal* of all that was romantic, exquisite, and passionate —Harrison Smith⟩ **syn** see MODEL

beau·jo·lais \ˌbōzhəˈlā\ *n, pl* **beaujolaises** \-āz\ *usu cap* [F, fr. *Beaujolais*, region of central France] **:** a red Burgundy table wine from grapes grown between the Loire and Saône around Beaujeu in the department of Rhone, France

beaumé *usu cap, var of* BAUMÉ

beau monde \(ˈ)bō¦mȯnd, -ˈmänd\ *n, pl* **beau mondes** *or* **beaux mondes** [F, lit., fine world] **:** the world of high society and fashion

beau·mon·tage \bōˈmäntij\ *n* -s [origin unknown] **:** a composition used by artisans to fill and conceal holes or cracks in wood or metal

beau·mon·tia \bōˈmänsh(ē)ə, -tēə\ *n, cap* [NL, fr. Diana *Beaumont* †1831 Englishwoman + NL *-ia*] **:** a small genus of East Indian woody vines (family Apocynaceae) having very large showy fragrant white flowers and being grown as ornamental climbers in warm regions

beau·mont root \ˈbō(ˌ)mänt-, -ōmənt-\ *n, usu cap B* [prob. fr. the name *Beaumont*] **:** CULVER'S ROOT

beaune \ˈbōn\ *n* -s *usu cap* [F, fr. *Beaune*, France] **:** a usu. red table wine produced in the department of Côte d'Or, France

beaus *pl of* BEAU, *pres 3d sing of* BEAU

beau sa·breur \ˌbōsaˈbrər\ *n, pl* **beau sabreurs** \-rz\ *or* **beaux sabreurs** \ˌbōsaˈ-\ [F, lit., handsome swordsman] **:** a dashing adventurer

¹**beau·sé·ant** \ˌbōsāˈäⁿ\ *n* -s [MF *beaucéant*, fr. OF *baucent* spotted with white — more at BAUSOND] **:** the black-and-white banner of the Knights Templars

²**beauséant** \"\ *interj* — used as a battle cry by the Knights Templars

beaut \ˈbyüt, usu -d·+V\ *n* -s [short for *beauty*] *slang* **:** a beautiful, outstanding, or egregious example **:** BEAUTY

beau·te·ous \ˈbyüdēəs, -ütēəs, -ü·tyəs *sometimes* ÷ ˈüchəs\ *adj* [ME, fr. *beaute* + *-ous*] **:** replete with beauty **:** commanding rapt appreciation for sensuous beauty ⟨~ even where beauties most abound —Lord Byron⟩ **syn** see BEAUTIFUL

beau·te·ous·ly *adv* [ME, fr. *beauteous* + *-ly*] **:** in a beauteous manner

beau·te·ous·ness *n* -ES **:** the quality or state of being beauteous

beau·ti·cian \byüˈtishən\ *n* -s [*beauty* + *-ician*] **:** COSMETOLOGIST

beau·ti·fi·ca·tion \ˌbyüdəfəˈkāshən, -ütəf-\ *n* -s **:** BEAUTIFYING

beau·ti·fi·er \ˈ==,fī(ə)r\ *n* -s **:** one that beautifies

¹**beau·ti·ful** \ˈbyüdəfəl, -yütə- *also* -yüd·ef-, -yütēf-\ *adj, sometimes* -ER/-EST [*beauty* + *-ful*] **1 :** marked by beauty: **a :** keenly delighting the senses as approaching perfection or the ideal in form, proportion, arrangement, grace, color, or sound ⟨seldom have I seen . . . so ~ a face. She was a blonde, golden-haired, blue-eyed —A. Conan Doyle⟩ ⟨the Song of Songs, ~, orientally sensuous, too glowing perhaps for western taste —H.O.Taylor⟩ ⟨a ~ sonorous and flexible language —H.T.Buckle⟩ **b :** delighting with a higher, more exalted appeal **:** calling forth great spiritual, intellectual, and aesthetic appreciation **:** lofty in effect ⟨an Aquinas in his cell before a crucifix or a Narcissus . . . equally ~ —W.H.Mallock⟩ **2 a :** attractive or impressive through expressing or suggesting fitness, order, regularity, rhythm, cogency, or perfection of structure ⟨this most ~ system of the sun, planets, and comets —Isaac Newton⟩ ⟨the deep canyon of Broadway, between those vast structures, ~ but sinister —P.E.More⟩ ⟨his arguments were ~ and deserved to be true —Francis Galton⟩ **b :** perfect, nearly perfect, or extremely attractive through such qualities as honesty, devotion, charity, or self-sacrifice ⟨young children not infrequently have an exquisitely ~ saintliness of character —W.R.Inge⟩ **c :** marked by practically perfect unerring art, skill, finesse, technique, or polish ⟨he made a ~ shot on that leopard —Ernest Hemingway⟩ ⟨its accurate and ~ record of folk dialect —*Amer. Guide Series: Ind.*⟩ ⟨a ~ book so technically perfect that the professional writer stands in awe of it —*Saturday Rev.*⟩ **d :** perfect as an illustration **:** outstanding as a type or model ⟨a case of disease may be so typical in its exhibition of characteristic relations as to be called ~ —John Dewey⟩ **3 :** generally pleasing **:** FINE, EXCELLENT, DELECTABLE **:** superlatively good **:** lacking anything detracting from enjoyment ⟨~ weather⟩ ⟨a ~ friendship⟩ ⟨a ~ roast turkey⟩

syn LOVELY, BEAUTEOUS, PULCHRITUDINOUS, PRETTY, COMELY, BONNY, FAIR, HANDSOME, GOOD-LOOKING: BEAUTIFUL, wide in its application and extreme in praise, describes a close approach to an ideal and indicates a quite keen delight in contemplation ⟨O Cynthia, ten times bright and fair! . . . too divine art thou, too keen in beauty . . . how *beautiful* thou art —John Keats⟩ ⟨after nursery rhymes they should learn equally *beautiful* songs —Bertrand Russell⟩ ⟨the Deanery is now a *beautiful* private residence with herbaceous borders —E.V. Lucas⟩ LOVELY suggests sensuous or emotional delights ⟨Freydis now showed as the most *lovely* of womenkind. She had black plaited hair, and folds of crimson silk were over her white flesh, and over her shoulders was a black coat embroidered with little gold stars —J.B.Cabell⟩ BEAUTEOUS, a rather literary word, and PULCHRITUDINOUS, a relatively new word uncommon outside journalism, stress rich appeal ⟨young maidens came, *beauteous* and calm, like shapes of living stone, clothed in the light of dreams —P.B.Shelley⟩ PRETTY suggests presence of grace, charm, vivacity, daintiness, or petiteness, an absence of perfection, ideality, stateliness, and dignity ⟨she was *pretty* at all times . . . with her light-brown ringlets, her delicately tinged but healthful cheek, her sensitive, intelligent, yet most feminine and kindly face. But every few moments, the *pretty* and girlish face grew beautiful and striking, as some inward thought and feeling brightened, rose to the surface —Nathaniel Hawthorne⟩ ⟨as a *pretty* household toy, Pussy was carried from Africa to Europe —Agnes Repplier⟩ COMELY and BONNY, which has a Scotch suggestion, stress pleasant wholesomeness and fitness ⟨a quick brunette, well molded, falcon-eyed. . . . '*Comely*, too, by all that's fair' —Alfred Tennyson⟩ ⟨your *bonny* face sae mild and sweet his honest heart enamors —Robert Burns⟩ FAIR, less common as a synonym for BEAUTIFUL in today's English, may suggest lightness or freshness ⟨the girl was certainly *fair* to look upon. Many heavens were in her sunny eyes, and the outline of that arm of hers . . . was the very curve of beauty —Herman Melville⟩ The words preceding refer more commonly to women than to men; HANDSOME and GOOD-LOOKING refer about equally to men, women, and things. HANDSOME suggests a pleasing appearance, due proportions, and a measure of dignity and taste ⟨Cleveland was . . . a he-man, *handsome* with a certain bull-like pulchritude, which was the outer symbol of his inner courage —W.A.White⟩ ⟨she was very *handsome;* a bold beauty, with shining black hair, red lips, and eyes not afraid of men —George Meredith⟩ ⟨*handsome* houses rich in mahogany, plate, and pier glasses —Allan Nevins & H.S.Commager⟩ GOOD-LOOKING is less expressive and is not rich in especial connotations ⟨a *good-looking* young fellow of twenty-five. His cheeks were dyed with fine Saxon red . . . his blue eye opened well, and a profusion of fair hair curled over a well-shaped head —Herman Melville⟩

²**beautiful** \"\ *n* -s **:** the abstract or ideal essence or principle of that which appeals to aesthetic tastes and dispositions — used with *the* ⟨studying the ~⟩

beautiful letters *n pl* [trans. of F *belles-lettres*] **:** BELLES LETTRES

beau·ti·ful·ly \-f(ə)lē, -li\ *also substand* **beautiful** *adv* **:** in a beautiful manner

beau·ti·ful·ness \-fəlnəs\ *n* -ES **:** the quality or state of being beautiful

beau·ti·fy \ˈbyüdə,fī, -yütə-\ *vb* -ED/-ING/-ES [*beauty* + *-fy*] *vt* **:** to make beautiful: as **a :** adorn in order to mask or transform the plain or unpleasant **:** EMBELLISH ⟨plants and flowers used to ~ all public parks and buildings —*Amer. Guide Series: Minn.*⟩ **b :** to grace with pleasurable, worthy, or ennobling attributes ⟨a scholarly formula for ~*ing* the corporation way of life —Norman MacKenzie⟩ ⟨religious faith . . . not only stabilizes one's life; it *beautifies* and consecrates it —Rufus Jones⟩ ~ *vi* **:** to grow beautiful ⟨her face ~*ing* at the encouraging answer⟩ **syn** see ADORN

¹**beau·ty** \ˈbyüdē, -yütē, -i\ *n* -ES *often attrib* [ME *beaute*, *bealte*, fr. OF *biauté*, *belté*, fr. *biau*, *bel* beautiful (fr. L *bellus* pretty) + *-té* -ty; akin to L *bonus* good — more at BOUNTY] **1 a :** extreme physical attractiveness and loveliness **:** perfect combination of characteristics pleasurable to see ⟨the ~ of the actress⟩ ⟨the ~ of the scenery⟩ **b :** a characteristic or combination of characteristics affording great sensory pleasure ⟨the ~ of the sonata⟩ **c** (1) **:** one notably marked by beauty ⟨the new car was a ~⟩ ⟨fishing for trout and catching several *beauties*⟩; *esp* **:** a person so marked ⟨a bold ~, with shining black hair, red lips, and eyes not afraid —George Meredith⟩ (2) **:** the aggregate of those marked by beauty ⟨the ~ and chivalry of the county were gathered there —Raymond Weeks⟩ **d** (1) **:** a particular grace, adornment, or excellence **:** a single characteristic or attribute marked by beauty ⟨he had two great *beauties*, the pale flat white of his skin, and his great shaggy mass of dark hair —Dorothy C. Fisher⟩ (2) **beauties** *pl* **:** passages of literature strongly marked by beauty ⟨a collection of the poet's *beauties*⟩ **e :** a trait or combination of traits calling forth admiration, praise, or respect ⟨the ~ of his character⟩ ⟨the ~ of this mathematical demonstration⟩ **f :** a brilliant, extreme, or egregious example or instance ⟨the goalie's save was a ~⟩ ⟨his bruise after the fall was a ~⟩ ⟨this mistake in strategy was a ~⟩ **g :** most cogent feature **:** characteristic insuring effectiveness **:** climactic detail ⟨the ~ of it is that everyone can play⟩ ⟨the ~ of the scheme is that the trickster is defrauded⟩ **2 a :** perfection that excites admiration or delight for itself rather than for its uses **:** a quality in a consummate thing that induces immediate and disinterested pleasure **:** something that is beautiful as determined by subjective awareness and by such reactions as delightful sensation, moral exaltation, or reverie ⟨the ~ of a silent eve —John Keats⟩ **b :** the characteristic value of a beautiful thing apart from any effect it produces **:** perfection of form attained through the flawless sensible manifestation of an artist's conception or by an independent self-subsistent product of the creative imagination **c** (1) **:** the absolute perfection of the ideal or idea as suggested by or reflected in the relative sensuous perfection of works of art (2) **:** the ideal itself apprehended through the medium of a beautiful thing

²**beauty** \"\ *vt* -ED/-ING/-ES [ME *beautien*, fr. *beaute*, n.] *archaic* **:** BEAUTIFY

beauty-berry \ˈ==- — see BERRY\ *n* **:** a plant of the genus *Callicarpa* — see FRENCH MULBERRY, JAPANESE BEAUTY-BERRY

beauty bush *n* **:** a Chinese shrub (*Kolkwitzia amabilis*) with yellow-throated pinkish flowers and a fruit covered with bristles that is often planted as an ornamental

beauty contest *n* **:** an assemblage of girls or women at which judges select the most beautiful

beauty culture *n* **:** COSMETOLOGY

beauty-fruit \ˈ==,=\ *n* **:** any of several plants of the genus *Callicarpa*; *esp* **:** FRENCH MULBERRY

beauty operator *n* **:** COSMETOLOGIST

beauty shop *or* **beauty parlor** *n* **:** an establishment or a department in an establishment where hairdressing, facials, and manicures are done

beauty sleep *n* **:** sleep before midnight

beauty spot *n* **1 :** ¹PATCH 2 **2 a :** NEVUS **b :** a minor blemish — called also *beauty mark* **3 :** a beautiful scenic area

beau·vais \(ˈ)bō¦vā\ *adj, usu cap* [fr. *Beauvais*, commune, Oise dept., France] **:** of or relating to fine tapestry and embroidery originating at Beauvais, France and noted for its delicate floral designs

beau·ve·ria \bōˈvirēə\ *n, cap* [NL] **:** a genus of imperfect fungi (order Moniliales) that is sometimes included in the genus *Botrytis* and that comprises several fungi used in biological control of insects — see CALCINO

beaux *pl of* BEAU

¹**beaux arts** \(ˈ)bōˈzär, -ˈzȧ(r\ *n pl* [F *beaux-arts*] **:** FINE ARTS

²**beaux arts** \"\ *adj* **1** *archit* **:** characterized by formalism, the reapplication of historic forms and details, and a tendency toward monumental conception ⟨a *beaux arts* design⟩ **2 :** relating to a method of architectural education esp. prominent in the 19th century in which hypothetical problems are solved by individual students working in an atelier under a master critic and the solutions are judged by a jury of architects that rates them on a competitive basis

beaux esprits *pl of* BEL ESPRIT

beauxite *var of* BAUXITE

beaux mondes *pl of* BEAU MONDE

beaux sabreurs *pl of* BEAU SABREUR

¹**bea·ver** \ˈbēvə(r)\ *n, pl* **beaver** *or* **beavers** *often attrib* [ME *bever*, fr. OE *beofor;* akin to OHG *bibar* beaver, ON *bjōrr*, L *fiber*, Lith *bebrus* beaver, Skt *babhru* large ichneumon, *babhru* reddish brown — more at BROWN] **1 a :** either of two large semiaquatic rodents having webbed hind feet and a broad flat tail, feeding chiefly on bark and twigs, being remarkable for ingenuity in the construction of lodges and dams, and yielding valuable fur and castor: (1) **:** an Old World rodent (*Castor fiber*) formerly abundant over much of northern Europe and Asia (2) **:** a New World congener (*C. canadensis*) whose skins were a major factor in the exploration and settlement of much of No. America and served in early times as a basic standard of exchange **b :** any of certain other rodents that resemble beavers; *esp* **:** MOUNTAIN BEAVER **2 a :** the fur or pelt of the beaver **b :** the fur or pelt of any of various animals processed to resemble that of the beaver — often used with a qualifying word **3 a :** a hat with a tall approximately cylindrical crown made of beaver fur or a fabric imitation of beaver ⟨tall men wearing ~*s*⟩ **b :** SILK HAT **4** *also* **beaver cloth a :** a thick woolen coating in twill weave made with a deep nap to resemble beaver fur **b :** a cotton cloth for clothing napped on both sides **c :** plush used for millinery **5 a :** MADE-BEAVER **b :** one of the 5-dollar or 10-dollar gold coins with the picture of a beaver on the obverse that were issued by the state of Oregon in 1849 **6** *or* **beaver brown :** a grayish brown that is yellower, less strong, and slightly lighter than chestnut, less strong and slightly yellower and lighter than coconut, and less strong and slightly lighter than new cocoa — called also *mushroom*, *starling* **7** [approximate trans. of Beaver *Tsattine*, lit., dwellers among the beavers] *usu cap* **a :** an Athapaskan people of the Peace river valley in Alberta **b :** a member of such people **8 :** the language of the Beaver people **9 a :** a full beard **b :** a man wearing a full beard **c :** a game in which one shouts "beaver" when he sees a bearded man **10 :** EAGER BEAVER

²**beaver** \"\ *n* -s [ME *baviere*, fr. MF, beaver, bib, fr. *bave* slobber — more at BAVARDAGE] **1 :** a piece of armor protecting the lower part of the face **2 :** a helmet visor ⟨saw you not his face? O, yes, my lord; he wore his ~ up —Shak.⟩

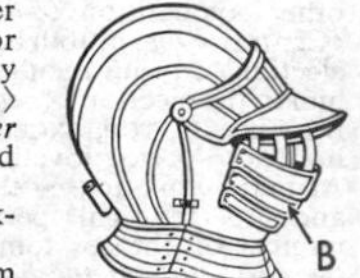

B beaver 1

beaverboard \ˈ==,=\ *n* [fr. *Beaver Board*, a trademark] **:** a fiberboard used for partitions and ceilings

beaver bundle *n* [¹*beaver*] **:** a Blackfoot Indian medicine bundle

beaver dam *n* [¹*beaver*] **1 :** a dam built by beavers **2 :** the pond formed behind a beaver dam

beaver eater *n* [¹*beaver*] **:** WOLVERINE

bea·ver·ette \ˌbēv(ə)ˈret\ *n* -s [¹*beaver* + *-ette*] **:** rabbit fur dyed and processed to imitate beaver

beaver gray *n* [¹*beaver*] **:** a dark gray to brownish gray that is darker and slightly yellower than hair brown

bea·ver·ite \ˈbēvə,rīt\ *n* -s [*Beaver* co. Utah + E *-ite*] **:** a mineral $Pb(Cu,Fe,Al)_3(SO_4)_2(OH)_6$ consisting of a hydrous sulfate of copper, lead, and iron occurring in microscopic canary-yellow plates

beaver lily *n* [¹*beaver*] **:** SPATTERDOCK 1

beaverpelt \ˈ==,=\ *n* [¹*beaver* + *pelt*] **:** NUTRIA 2

beaver poison *n* [¹*beaver*] **:** WATER HEMLOCK

beaver rat *n* [¹*beaver*] **:** a golden Australian water rat (*Hydromys chrysogaster*) with an elongated flattened body, broad flat head, short limbs, large feet, and a short heavy white-tipped tail

beaverroot \ˈ==,=\ *n* [¹*beaver*] **1 :** SPATTERDOCK 1 **2 :** a water lily (*Nymphaea odorata*) with fragrant flowers

beaver stone *n* [¹*beaver*] **:** either of a pair of glandular pouches in the groin of a beaver that secrete castor

beaver tail *n* [¹*beaver*] **:** a prickly-pear cactus (*Opuntia basilaris*) of southwestern U.S. and adjacent Mexico often cultivated for its showy purple, reddish, or white flowers

beavertail \ˈ==,=\ *n* [so called fr. its flat, wide shape] **:** a rifle or shotgun fore-end made wider than standard to afford a better grip and improve the balance

bea·ver·teen \ˌbēvə(r)ˈtēn, ˈ==,=\ *n* -s [¹*beaver* + *-teen* (as in *velveteen*)] **:** a heavy twilled cotton cloth made with an uncut pile and a short nap

beaver trade *n* [¹*beaver*] *obs* **:** trade with the Indians; *specif* **:** trade in beaver skins

beaver tree *n* [¹*beaver*] **:** SWEET BAY 2

beaverwood \ˈ==,=\ *n* [¹*beaver* + *wood*] **1 :** a hackberry (*Celtis occidentalis*) **2 :** SWEET BAY 2

bea·very \ˈbēv(ə)rē\ *n* -ES [blend of *beaver* and *-ry*] **:** a place in which beavers live or are kept

beb \ˈbeb\ *chiefly Scot var of* ¹BIB

bebb willow \ˈbeb-\ *n, often cap B* [after Michael S. *Bebb* †1895 Amer. botanist] **:** BEAK WILLOW

be·bee·rine \bəˈbi,rēn, -ˌrən; ˈbebə,rēn\ *also* **bi·bi·rine** \bəˈbi,rēn, -ˌrən; ˈbibə,rēn\ *n* -s [G *bebeerin*, fr. *bebeerubaum* bebeeru tree (fr. Sp & Pg *bibirú*) + *-in* -ine] **:** a crystalline alkaloid $C_{36}H_{38}N_2O_6$ known in two optically different forms; *esp* **:** the dextrorotatory form obtained from the bark of the bebeeru and the pareira — see CURINE

be·bee·ru \bəˈbi(ˌ)rü, ¦bebə¦rü\ also **bi·bi·ru** \bəˈbi(ˌ)rü, ¦bibə¦rü\ *n* -s [Sp & Pg *bibirú*, of Cariban origin; akin to Macusi *bibiru*] **:** a tropical So. American evergreen tree (*Nectandra rodioei*) — called also *greenheart*

be·bi·za·tion \ˌbābəˈzāshən\ *n* -s [G *bebisation*, irreg. fr. *be*, one of the notes of this scale + *-isation* -ization] **:** an obsolete musical solmization using the syllables *la, be, ce, de, me, fe, ge*

be·bop \ˈbē,bäp\ *n* -s [imit. of a staccato 2-tone phrase distinctive in this music] **:** ³BOP

be·bop·per \-pə(r)\ *n* -s **:** BOPPER

be·bouldered \bə̇, bē+\ *adj* [*be-* + *bouldered*] **:** strewn with boulders

be·bung \ˈbā(ˌ)bu̇ŋ\ *n, pl* **be·bung·en** \-ŋən\ [G, lit., trembling, fr. *beben* to tremble (fr. OHG *bibēn*) + *-ung* -ing (fr. OHG *-unga*); akin to OE *bifian* to tremble, ON *bifa*, L *foedus* ugly, Gk *pithēkos* ape, Skt *bhayate* he is afraid; basic meaning: fearing] **:** a tremolo effect that is similar in sound to a violin vibrato and is produced on the clavichord by sustaining a varying pressure on the key after striking a note

bec *abbr* because

be·call \bə̇, bē+\ *vt* -ED/-ING/-S [*be-* + *call*] **:** to call names **:** MISCALL

be·calm \bə̇, bē+\ *vt* -ED/-ING/-S [*be-* + *calm*, adj. or v.] **1 a :** to keep from motion or stop the progress of by lack of wind ⟨the fleet was ~*ed*⟩ **b :** to bring about a cessation of the work, progress, or activity of ⟨a ~*ed* movie industry would not keep up their standard of living —Martin Kasindorf⟩ **2 :** to make calm **:** SOOTHE, TRANQUILIZE ⟨~ an agitated mind⟩

became *past of* BECOME

be·card \bāˈkärd\ *n* -s [F *bécarde*, fr. *bec* beak — more at BEAK] **:** any of several large-billed tropical American birds of the family Cotingidae

be·casse \bāˈkås\ *n* -s [F *bécasse*, fr. OF *becaz*, fr. *bec* beak — more at BEAK] **:** WOODCOCK 1a

be·cas·sine \bākåˈsēn\ *n* -s [F *bécassine*, fr. *bécasse* + *-ine*] **:** SNIPE; *esp, in Louisiana* **:** any of several American snipes

be·cause \bə̇ˈkȯz, bē-, -(¦)kəz, *chiefly in substand speech* -ȯs\ *conj* [ME, fr. *be*, *bi* by + *cause*] **1 :** SINCE **:** for the reason that **:** on account of the cause that — used to introduce dependent clauses ⟨we stopped at the filling station ~ we needed gasoline⟩ **2** *obs* **:** in order that **:** to the end that ⟨"Why laugh you?" "*Because* you should see my teeth" —John Lyly⟩ **3 a :** THAT **:** the fact that — used to introduce a noun clause serving as the subject or the complement of a sentence ⟨one of the reasons why it has seemed to me to be desirable to speak on this subject is ~ it may contribute —E.N.Griswold⟩ ⟨~ men are still incapable of being angels is no good reason why they should be ants —E.A.Mowrer⟩; in reputable use though disapproved by some **b :** on account of being ⟨a rather stuffily written book, but the material is interesting ~ firsthand —A.W.Long⟩

because of *prep* **:** by reason of **:** on account of ⟨the game was postponed *because of* rain⟩ ⟨*because of* losses the unit was not at full strength⟩ — in reputable use though sometimes disapproved in constructions complementary to expressions of the notion of reason or cause ⟨the reason we do not now have such a trained reserve . . . is *because of* lack of foresight and energy —*N.Y.Times*⟩

bec·ca·fi·co \ˌbekəˈfē(ˌ)kō\ *n, pl* **beccaficos** *or* **beccaficoes** [It, fr. *beccare* to peck (fr. *becco* beak, fr. L *beccus*) + *fico* fig, fr. L *ficus* — more at BEAK] **:** any of various European songbirds esteemed as a table delicacy when fat on fruit and grains in autumn; *specif* **:** GARDEN WARBLER

be·cer·ris·ta \ˌbāsəˈrēstə, -āthə-\ *n* -s [Sp, fr. *becerro* yearling bull (fr. OSp *bezerro*, prob. fr. a word cognate to the non-IE source of L *ibex* chamois) + *-ista* -ist] *in bullfighting* **:** one who fights calves

bé·cha·mel \ˌbāshəˈmel\ *or* **béchamel sauce** *n* -s *sometimes cap B* [F (*sauce*) *béchamelle*, after Louis de *Béchamel* (Béchameil) †1703 Fr. courtier] **:** a white sauce sometimes enriched with cream

bé·champ reduction \(ˈ)bāˈshäⁿ-\ *n, cap B* [after Pierre J. A. *Béchamp* †1908 Fr. physician, surgeon, and chemist] **:** a method of reducing aromatic nitro compounds to amines by means of iron usu. in acid solution

be·chance \bə̇, bē+\ *vb* -ED/-ING/-S [*be-* + *chance* (v.)] *vi, archaic* **:** HAPPEN, BEFALL ~ *vt, obs* **:** to happen to ⟨my sons — God knows what hath *bechanced* them —Shak.⟩

be·charm \bə̇, bē+\ *vt* [ME *becharmen*, fr. *be-* + *charmen* to charm] **:** to hold under or as if under a spell

be·chatter \bə̇, bē+\ *vt* [*be-* + *chatter* (v.)] **:** to oppress with chatter

bêche-de-mer \ˌbeshdəˈme(ə)r, ˌbā-\ *n* [F, lit., sea grub] **1** *pl* **bêche-de-mer** \"\ *or* **bêches-de-mer** \-sh(əz)d-\ **:** TREPANG **2** *usu cap B&M* [so called fr. the trepang's having been an important commercial item in these islands, its designation thus becoming a type-word to designate the pidgin]

: a pidgin based on English and used as a lingua franca in New Guinea, the Bismarck archipelago, the Solomon islands, and other islands nearby

bech·tel crab \ˈbektᵊl-\ *or* **bech·tel's crab** \-ᵊlz-\ *n, usu cap B* [after Ernst A. *Bechtel*, 19th cent. Am. nurseryman] : a flowering crab derived from the Iowa crab apple and having very large double pink flowers

bech·te·rew's nucleus \ˈbektə,refs-, -,revz-\ *n, usu cap B* [after V. M. Bekhterev (*Bechterew*) †1927 Russ. neuropathologist] : the upper part of the vestibular nucleus

bech·u·a·na \,bech(ə)ˈwänə\ *n, pl* **bechuana** *or* **bechuanas** *usu cap* : a member of one of the various Bantu-speaking Negro peoples dwelling between the Orange and Zambezi rivers esp. in Botswana, So. Africa

¹**beck** \ˈbek\ *n* -s [ME *bek*, fr. ON *bekkr;* akin to OE *bæc* brook, OHG *bah*, MIr *búal* flowing water] *Brit* : a small stream usu. with a stony bed

²**beck** \"\ *vb* -ED/-ING/-S [ME *becken*, alter. of *beknen* — more at BECKON] *vi* **1** *archaic* : GESTURE, SIGNAL **2** *chiefly Scot* : BOW, CURTSY ~ *vt, archaic* : to signal to : BECKON

³**beck** \"\ *n* -s [ME, fr. *becken*] **1** *chiefly Scot* : a gesture of salutation or respect : BOW, CURTSY, NOD ⟨coming into the parlor with a low ~⟩ **2 a** (1) : a gesture or signaling motion (2) : a nod, wave, or other signal summoning or commanding **b** (1) : an indication whereby one gives a command or expresses a desire (2) : full and absolute control — **at beck and call** : in obedient readiness to obey any command or fulfill any wish ⟨a thousand servants and a huge palace *at* his *beck and call* —Robert Keable⟩

⁴**beck** \"\ *n* -s [prob. alter. (influenced by ¹*beck*) of ⁵*back*] : a large vat : ⁵BACK; *esp* : a vat used in dyeing by hand

⁵**beck** \"\ *n* -s [back-formation fr. *beckiron*] : the beak of an anvil

beck·e·lite \ˈbekə,līt\ *n* -s [Friedrich *Becke* †1931 Austrian mineralogist + E *-lite*] : a mineral $Ca_3(Ce,La,Y)_4(SiZr)_3O_{15}$ consisting of the cerium metals and calcium and occurring in wax-yellow isometric crystals (hardness 5, sp. gr. 4.15)

beck·en \ˈbekən\ *n pl* [G, lit., basin, fr. OHG *beckīn*, fr. LL *bacchinon* — more at BASIN] : CYMBALS

¹**beck·et** *also* **beck·ett** \ˈbekət\ *n* -s [origin unknown] : a simple device for holding something in place: as **a** : a small grommet or a loop of rope with a knot at one end to catch in an eye at the other **b** : a ring of rope or metal **c** : BRACKET **d** : POCKET **e** : HOOK

²**becket** \"\ *vt* -ED/-ING/-S : to secure by beckets : provide with beckets

becket bend *n* : SHEET BEND

becke test \ˈbekə-\ *n, usu cap B* [after Friedrich *Becke* — more at BECKELITE] : a method of determining with a microscope the relative indices of refraction of a transparent particle (as a plant or animal cell or a mineral) immersed in or in contact with a standard medium of known refractive index

beck·iron \ˈbek·+,-\ *n* -s [by folk etymology fr. earlier *bickern*, fr. *bycorne*, fr. MF *bigorne*, fr. (assumed) VL *bicornia*, fr. L *bicornis* with two horns — more at BICORN] : a horned anvil; *esp* : a cooper's anvil used in clinching nails or rivets

beck·ite \ˈbek,īt\ *n* -s [by alter.] : BEEKITE

beck·mann rearrangement \ˈbekmən-, -,män-\ *n, usu cap B* [after Ernst O. *Beckmann* †1923 Ger. chemist] : a rearrangement by which a ketoxime [as the oxime $(C_6H_5)_2C{:}NOH$ of benzophenone] changes into an amide derivative (as benzanilide) on treatment usu. with phosphorus pentachloride or an acid

beckmann thermometer *n, usu cap B* [after Ernst O. *Beckmann*] : a very sensitive thermometer that has a small range adjustable for any desired values and that is used for determining accurately small differences in temperature (as the change in freezing point or boiling point of a liquid when some substance is dissolved in it)

beck·mes·ser \ˈbek,mesə(r)\ *n* -s *usu cap* [G, after Sixtus *Beckmesser*, pedantic musical philistine in the opera *Die Meistersinger von Nürnberg* (1867) by Richard Wagner †1883 Ger. composer] : a critic or teacher of music characterized by timid and excessive reliance upon rules : PEDANT

¹**beck·on** \ˈbekən\ *vb* **beckoned; beckoned; beckoning** \-k(ə)niŋ\ **beckons** [ME *beknen*, fr. OE *bīecnan*, fr. *bēacen* sign — more at BEACON] *vi* **1** : to gesture or signal typically with a wave, nod, or other motion in summons or command ⟨he . . . *~ed* to the other generals to come and stand where he stood —H.E.Scudder⟩ **2** : to appear inviting : offer strong attraction or allure ⟨Australian goldfields *~ed*, and he sailed —L.R.Hafen⟩ ⟨sending his ships wherever profit *~ed* —*Time*⟩ ~ *vt* **1** : to signal to typically with a wave in summons or request to approach or follow ⟨my guide *~ed* me off the narrow path —John Connell⟩ ⟨they *~ed* us to come⟩ **2** : to seem to invite : extend attraction, interest, allure, or appeal to ⟨it *~s* men . . . into the calm of the absolute and eternal —John Dewey⟩

²**beckon** \"\ *n* -s : a signaling gesture esp. to approach

beck·on·ing *adj* : inviting by or as if by attraction or allure : APPEALING ⟨myth reveals beauty in ~ imagery —J.P. Anton⟩ — **beck·on·ing·ly** *adv*

beckoning crab *n* : FIDDLER CRAB

becks *pres 3d sing of* BECK, *pl of* BECK

be·clad \bə̇, bē+\ *adj* [*be-* + *clad*] *archaic* : CLOTHED

be·clip \bə̇, bē+\ *vt* [ME *beclippen*, fr. OE *beclyppan*, fr. *be-* + *clyppan* to clasp, embrace — more at CLIP] *archaic* : EMBRACE, CLASP, ENCIRCLE

be·cloud \bə̇, bē+\ *vt* -ED/-ING/-S [*be-* + *cloud*, v, or n.] **1** : to cover over with a cloud : OBSCURE, MASK ⟨the ink of the cuttlefish *~ing* the water⟩ **2 a** : to confuse and check from incisive thought ⟨scrambling up the issues and *~ing* the minds and memories of witnesses —R.H.Rovere⟩ **b** : to muddle and prevent clear perception or realization of ⟨disputes . . . threatened to ~ the real issues —M.J.Adler⟩ **syn** see OBSCURE

be·come \bə̇ˈkəm, bē-\ *vb* **be·came** \-ˈkām\ **become; becoming; becomes** [ME *becomen*, fr. OE *becuman*, *becuman* to come to, approach, happen, befit (akin to OHG *biqueman* to come to, meet, Goth *biquiman* to come to) fr. *be-* + *coman*, *cuman* to come — more at COME] *vi* **1 a** *obs* (1) : COME (2) : GO ⟨where is Warwick then ~ —Shak.⟩ **b** (1) : to come to exist or occur (2) : to emerge as an entity : grow to manifest a certain essence, nature, development, or significance ⟨we do not know our own identity since we are always in a state of *becoming* —J.D.Adams⟩ ⟨what *~s* has duration —A. N.Whitehead⟩ **c** *archaic* : to come to experience — used with an infinitive **2 a** : to pass from a previous state or condition and come to be : grow or change into being through taking on a new character or characteristic ⟨as the pain *~s* more intense⟩ ⟨that they might rest and ~ warm —T.B.Costain⟩ **b** : to take on a new role, essence, or nature and come to be ⟨he *became* the nation's first president⟩ ⟨his former foes *becoming* loyal allies⟩ ⟨materials formerly wasted *becoming* profitable by-products⟩ **c** : to come to be — used as an auxiliary in passive constructions ⟨she *became* influenced by these ideas⟩ ⟨men *becoming* hurt in the battle⟩ **3 a** : HAPPEN ⟨it sometimes *~s* that these accounts are misleading⟩ **b** : to ensue by way of fate, destiny, or disposition — usu. used with *of* ⟨he wondered what had ~ of his boyhood friends⟩ ⟨investigating what *became* of the missing ship⟩ ~ *vt* **1 a** : to accord with : be suitable to : lack jarring contrast to or incongruity with ⟨rough clothes *becoming* their lowly condition⟩ ⟨brash confidence ill *becoming* his record of failures⟩ **b** : to suit with propriety : be quite proper for ⟨dignity *becoming* a lord⟩ ⟨the humility that *~s* the amateur —B.N.Cardozo⟩ **2** : GRACE: **a** : to adorn or look well on while befitting or according with ⟨a hat that *~s* her⟩ **b** : to occupy, use, or wear with suitable bearing or pleasing grace ⟨he *~s* his high office⟩

becomed *adj* [fr. obs. past part. of *become*] *obs* : BECOMING, DECOROUS

¹**becoming** *adj* [fr. pres. part. of *become*] **1** : marked by fitness or propriety : SUITABLE, SEEMLY ⟨~ modesty⟩ ⟨~ respect and obedience⟩ ⟨monks for whom self-effacement is ~ —H.O. Taylor⟩ **2** : having an attractive effect : tending to grace or adorn ⟨a fashionable ~ dress⟩ ⟨a hairdo ~ to her⟩

²**becoming** *n* -s [fr. gerund of *become*] **1** *obs* **a** : the action of befitting **b** : something that befits or becomes **2 a** : a coming into being : emergence into change that leads to a distinct stage or condition ⟨life is a constant ~: all stages lead to the beginning of others —G.B.Shaw⟩ **b** : a process in which the new appears : a passage of events in time : CHANGE ⟨there is a constant ~; there was no beginning, there can be no ending —John Burroughs⟩ — **be·com·ing·ly** *adv*

be·com·ing·ness \-nə̇s\ *n* -ES **1** : the quality or state of being becoming **2** : the character or fact of becoming ⟨that ultimate ~ which is the creative advance of nature —A.N.Whitehead⟩

be·coom \bə̇ˈküm, bē-\ *vt* -ED/-ING/-S [*be-* + *coom* soot] *Brit* : to begrime with smut or soot

bec·que·rel effect \(ˈ)beˈkrel-, ¦bekəˈrel-\ *n, usu cap B* [after Antoine H. *Becquerel* †1908 Fr. physicist] : a photovoltaic electromotive force manifested by certain electrolytic cells with identical but unequally illuminated electrodes

bec·que·rel·ite \beˈkre,līt, ,bekəˈre-\ *n* -s [F *becquerelite*, fr. A. H. *Becquerel* + F *-ite*] : a mineral $UO_3.2H_2O$ consisting of uranium hydroxide and occurring in small yellow crystals and crusts on pitchblende from Shaba, Zaire

becquerel ray *n, usu cap B* [after A. H. *Becquerel*] : a ray emitted by a radioactive substance — used before adoption of the terms *alpha ray, beta ray, gamma ray*

be·crime \bə̇, bē+\ *vt* -ED/-ING/-S [*be-* + *crime*] : to make guilty of crime

be·cross \bə̇, bē+\ *vt* [*be-* + *cross* (n.)] **1** : ²CROSS *vt* 3a **2** : to decorate with a cross

be·crush \bə̇, bē+\ *vt* [*be-* + *crush*] : to crush utterly or repeatedly

bec–scie \F beksē\ *n* -s [CanF *bec-scie* (trans. of E *sawbill*), fr. F *bec* beak + *scie* saw, fr. *scier* to saw, fr. L *secare* to cut — more at BEAK, SAW] : MERGANSER

be·cui·ba *or* **bi·cu·hy·ba** \bə̇ˈkwēbə\ *or* **bi·cu·hy·bao** \-ē,baů\ *or* **bi·cui·ba** \-ēbə\ *n* -s [Pg *becuiba*, fr. Tupi *bicuiba*] : a Brazilian timber tree (*Virola becuhyba*) of the family Myristicaceae with nuts that yield a wax

be·cu·na \bāˈkünə\ *or* **be·cune** \-ün\ *n* -s [F & Sp; F *bécune*, fr. Sp *becuna*] : GREAT BARRACUDA

be·curl \bə̇, bē+\ *vt* [*be-* + *curl* (n. or v.)] : to furnish or adorn with curls

¹**bed** \ˈbed\ *n* -s *often attrib* [ME, fr. OE *bedd;* akin to OHG *betti* bed, ON *bethr*, Goth *badi* bed, L *fodere* to dig, Lith *besti*] **1 a** : a piece of furniture on or in which one may lie down and sleep often including bedstead, legs or supports, spring, mattress, and bedding **b** (1) : a place of marital sex relations (2) : marital relationship ⟨dishonoring her ~ with a lover⟩ **c** : any improvised place or arrangement for sleeping ⟨hikers making their *~s* under the trees⟩ **d** (1) : a place of procreation (2) : marital union ⟨the eldest son of his second ~ —Edward Hyde⟩ (3) : PROGENY **e** : situation or fact of being in bed : SLEEP, SLEEPING : time for sleeping ⟨taking a walk before ~⟩ **f** : place of repose : REPOSE ⟨the bugle calling them from their *~s*⟩ **g** : a flat sack or mattress filled with some soft material in distinction from the bedstead on which it is placed ⟨a feather ~⟩; *also* : a mattress and bedclothes **h** : BEDSTEAD **i** : lodging for the night with accommodations for sleeping ⟨getting a ~ at the inn⟩ **j** : a measure of the equipment and services needed in a hospital to care for one hospitalized patient or in a hotel to care for one guest ⟨a new wing of 200 *~s*⟩ **2** : a flat or level surface: as **a** (1) : a plot in a garden or lawn often a little raised above the adjoining ground : the plants growing in such plot; *also* : HOTBED (2) : an area in a greenhouse or conservatory in which plants are grown (3) : a cluster or concentration of plants ⟨a ~ of ferns⟩ **b** : the bottom of a watercourse or of any other body of water; *esp* : an area of sea bottom supporting a heavy growth of a particular kind of organism ⟨a kelp ~⟩ ⟨an oyster ~⟩ **c** : the surface of a bowling alley along which the ball is bowled **d** : the surface on which the cloth of a billiard table is fastened **e** : the canvas surface of a trampoline upon which a gymnast performs **3** : a grave as a place of last sleep ⟨digging out his narrow ~⟩ **4** : SUPPORT, REST: **a** : the supporting part of a gun carriage **b** (1) : an extended base : MATRIX (2) : a layer of specialized or altered tissue; *often* : such a layer or zone separating dissimilar structures ⟨a ~ of vigorous granulation tissue is essential for a satisfactory skin graft⟩ — see VASCULAR BED **c** : a framework or support on or in which a piece of machining or carpentry work rests **d** : the cradle of a ship on the stocks **e** : a foundation for a machine or apparatus ⟨the ~ of an engine⟩ : the rigid part of a machine serving to support or secure **f** : the superficial earthwork that supports the ballast and track of a railroad **g** : the body, box, or supporting frame of a vehicle (as a wagon, truck, or trailer); *sometimes* : the floor or bottom of a truck or trailer **h** : the inclined piece of a carpenter's plane against which the plane iron bears **i** : the lower die of a punching machine **j** : the surface on which the printing form is locked on a flatbed press **k** *or* **bed ladder** : the lower section of an aerial ladder **l** : a drawer or layer supporting a typewriter in an office desk **m** : the base of a bellows camera usu. including the focusing guide rails **5** : a nest of small animals crowded together ⟨a ~ of snakes⟩ **6** : a layer esp. if placed with something above ⟨salad served on a ~ of lettuce⟩: as **a** : a rock stratum; *esp* : a bedding plane of stratified rock **b** (1) : a horizontal surface of a brick or stone in position ⟨in the upper ~⟩ (2) : a course of stone or brick in a wall (3) : the place or material in which a block or brick is laid (4) : the lower surface of a brick, slate, or tile (5) : BED JOINT **c** : a layer containing a concentration of paleontological or anthropological evidence (as bones) **d** : FILTER BED **e** : FIRE BED **7** : the place where an animal sleeps; *esp* : a place arranged or covered for a domestic or farm animal to sleep **8 a** : a mass or heap felt to resemble a bed ⟨a ~ of ashes⟩ ⟨the judging tent floor was a deep ~ of sawdust —Christopher Rand⟩ **b** : a mass of solid catalyst or solid chemical reactant that may be either in a fixed state or in a moving fluidized state **c** : a stack of raw hides or skins spread flat and salted for curing and preserving **9 a** : a water solution of gum tragacanth used as a couch in the process of marbling book edges **b** : the impression base used by bookbinders in stamping, graining, or embossing covers or materials

²**bed** \"\ *vb* **bedded; bedded; bedding; beds** [ME *bedden*, *beddien*, fr. OE *beddian*, fr. *bedd* bed] *vt* **1 a** : to furnish with a bed : accommodate with sleeping quarters ⟨the innkeeper was unable to ~ all the guests⟩ — sometimes used with *down* ⟨a garrison of about seventy, which the captain *bedded* down in the ground floor —Earle Birney⟩ **b** : to put to bed ⟨getting the children *bedded*⟩ **c** : to put (a couple) to bed — used with the implication that sex relations will ensue **d** : to furnish (an animal) with a bed or bedding : settle (an animal) in sleeping quarters ⟨*bedding* the mare —Ellen Glasgow⟩ — often used with *down* ⟨~ down the cattle —Andy Adams⟩ **e** : to take to bed for sexual intercourse : have sex relations with ⟨when he had *bedded* his wife and . . . had left her bed —B.A.Williams⟩ **f** : to put to bed with an illness — used mostly in the passive ⟨*bedded* for a week with influenza⟩ **2 a** : EMBED : place, sink, bury, or cover over securely in an enclosed place or situation ⟨the tremendous mortar . . . was *bedded* in the great timbers of her foredeck —Frank Yerby⟩ ⟨edges *bedded* in rabbets⟩ **b** : to plant or arrange in beds : set or cover esp. in a bed of soft earth ⟨*bedding* roots in mold⟩ ⟨~ out geraniums⟩ — often used with *up, down,* or *out* **c** : BASE, ESTABLISH **d** : to fit (a rifle barrel) to a fore-end **3 a** : to lay or embed in a layer : lay flat ⟨*bedding* bricks in the mortar⟩ ⟨*bedding* metal plates together to test them⟩ **b** : to dress the bearing surface of a brick or stone block **c** : to form (soil) into a bed or ridge (as for cotton) by plowing two or more furrows together — often used with *up* **d** : to spread or strew in a layer ⟨the floor of the pen being *bedded* with straw⟩ **e** : to prepare the ground about a tree by leveling and other means so as to lessen the chances of its shattering when felled **f** : to lay, place, or set (something) in a plastic bedding material (as masonry units in mortar or glass in putty) **4** : to place (oysters) in beds for setting ~ *vi* **1 a** : to find or make sleeping accommodations — often used with *down* ⟨*bedding* down in a sleeping bag —Hamilton Basso⟩ ⟨halted beside a haystack and told to ~ down —E.J.Kahn⟩ **b** : to go to bed with opportunity for sex relations or in order to have sex relations : have sex coition ⟨the couple *bedded* that night at the inn⟩ — used with *with, down with, up with* ⟨man may ~ with slaves, concubines, mistresses —H.M.Parshley⟩ **c** *of an animal* : to make its bed or lair — often used with *down* ⟨the deer *bedded* down on the slope⟩ **d** : to go to bed to sleep : RETIRE ⟨accustomed to ~ early⟩ **e** : to burrow into a mud bottom ⟨the side of the lake where the eels ~⟩ **2** : to form a layer usu. compact — often used with *down* ⟨litter in the hen coop *~s* down if it is not raked⟩ **3** : to lie or be placed on or as if on a bed in a mechanical operation : lie flat or flush against another part ⟨countersunk rivets ~ well against a flat plate⟩

be·dabble \bə̇, bē+\ *vt* -ED/-ING/-S [*be-* + *dabble*] : to wet or soil by dabbling ⟨clothes *bedabbled* with blood⟩

be·dad \bə̇ˈdad, bē-\ *interj* [euphemism for *by God*] *Irish* — used as a mild oath

be·damn \bə̇, bē+\ *vt* [*be-* + *damn*] : to swear at : DAMN

bed and board *n* : sleeping quarters and meals esp. in marital cohabitation ⟨his wife has left his *bed and board*⟩

be·dash \bə̇, bē\ *vt* [*be-* + *dash*] **1** : DASH; *esp* : to splash with color or rain **2** : to dash against **3** : RUIN ⟨hopes *~ed*⟩

be·daub \bə̇, bē+\ *vt* [*be-* + *daub*] **1** : to daub over : besmear or soil with anything thick, dirty, or sticky ⟨*~ed* with clay⟩ **2** : to ornament with vulgar excess : BEDIZEN

be·daux system \bə̇ˈdō-\ *also* **bedaux plan** *n, usu cap B* [after Charles E. *Bedaux* †1944 Fr. efficiency engineer in U.S.] : POINT SYSTEM

be·da·wi *or* **ba·da·wi** \bəˈdäwē\ *n, pl* **beda·win** \-,wēn\ *or* **bedawis** \-(,)wēz\ *or* **bada·win** \-,wēn\ *or* **ba·da·wis** \-(,)wēz\ *often cap* [Ar *badāwī* — more at BEDOUIN] : BEDOUIN

be·daze \bə̇ˈdāz, bē-\ *vt* [*be-* + *daze*] : DAZE, STUN, CONFUSE — **be·daze·ment** \-mənt\ *n* -s

be·dazzle \bə̇, bē+\ *vt* [*be-* + *dazzle*] **1** : to confuse by a strong light : DAZZLE **2** : to impress awesomely or most forcefully and take away power to think or notice : ENCHANT ⟨*bedazzled* by the mountains and the ranch —Jean Stafford⟩ — **be·dazzle·ment** \"+\ *n* -s

bed board *n* : a stiff thin wide board inserted usu. between bedspring and mattress

bed bolt *n* : a metal bolt with a tapered square head

bed book *n* : a book typically light and interesting for reading in bed

bedbug \ˈ=,=\ *n* **1 a** : a wingless bloodsucking bug (*Cimex lectularius*) sometimes infesting houses and esp. beds and feeding on human blood **b** : any other bloodsucking bug of the genus *Cimex* **2** : CONENOSE

common bedbug

bedbug hunter *n* : a bug (*Reduvius personatus*) of the family Reduviidae that is said to prey esp. on bedbugs

bedchamber \ˈ=,==\ *n* : BEDROOM

bedchamber woman *n* : WOMAN OF THE BEDCHAMBER

bed check *n* : a night inspection to check the presence of persons (as soldiers) required by regulations to be in bed or in quarters

bedclothes \ˈ=,=\ *n pl* [ME, fr. ¹*bed* + *clothes*] : sheets, blankets, or other coverings used on a bed

bedclothing \ˈ=,==\ *n* [*bed* + *clothing*] : BEDCLOTHES

bedcord \ˈ=,=\ *n* [*bed* + *cord*] : a rope drawn from one side of a bedstead to another to support a mattress

bedcover \ˈ=,==\ *n* **1** : BEDSPREAD **2** : ²COVER 2g

bed–curtain \ˈ=,==\ *n* : a curtain hung from a bed canopy

beddal *Scot var of* BEADLE

bed·da nut \ˈbedə-\ *n* [Marathi *behḍā*] : NUT OF BAHERA

bed·ded \ˈbedə̇d\ *adj* [¹*bed* + *-ed*] *geol* : deposited in layers : STRATIFIED

bed·der \ˈbedə(r)\ *n* -s [¹·²*bed* + *er*] **1** : one that makes up beds esp. in an English university **2** : one that places or fixes something in a bed: as **a** : a pottery worker who arranges greenware in piles with sand and clay between to protect and support the pieces during biscuit firing **b** : a leatherworker who salts hides and piles them in beds to preserve them **3 a** : a bedding plant : a plant grown in a bed for ornamental purposes (as a rose, begonia, or geranium) **4** *Brit* : BEDROOM **5 a** : a device for adjusting contact between rifle barrel and fore-end consisting of one or more adjustable contact points mounted in the forearm by means of which compensation may be made for error in initial fit of forearm to barrel, minor stock warpage due to weather conditions, and barrel vibration under given powder loads

¹**bed·ding** \ˈbediŋ, -ēŋ\ *n* -s [ME, fr. OE, fr. *bedd* bed + *-ing*] **1** : BEDCLOTHES **2** : a bottom layer : FOUNDATION **3** : litter (as straw or wood chips) for livestock **4** : the arrangement of rock in layers : STRATIFICATION **5** : a layer of soft material (as jute yarn) put on an electric cable underneath its armor **6** : the mortar, putty, or other substance used to bed building units (as bricks or glass)

²**bedding** \"\ *n* -s [fr. gerund of ²*bed*] **1** : the act of putting or taking a bride to bed **2** : the storing of different ores in thin layers or beds for future reclamation as a nearly uniform mixture

³**bedding** \"\ *adj* [fr. gerund of ²*bed*] : appropriate or adapted for culture in beds in the open air; *specif* : adapted to produce a massed effect for decoration, ⟨a ~ plant⟩ ⟨a ~ geranium⟩

bedding course *n* : CUSHION 3

bedding fault *n* : a displacement along or parallel to a bedding plane

bedding plane *n* : the surface that separates each successive layer of a stratified rock from its preceding layer : a depositional plane : a plane of stratification

bedding–slip \ˈ==,=\ *n* : a bedding fault with slight displacement

be·deck \bə̇, bē+\ *vt* [*be-* + *deck*] : to deck out : ornament profusely : decorate in a showy manner ⟨*~ed* in fine silks and laces⟩ **syn** see ADORN

be·deen \bə̇ˈdēn\ *adv* [ME *bedene*] *chiefly Scot* : STRAIGHTWAY, FORTHWITH, ANON

bed·e·guar *or* **bed·e·gar** \ˈbedə̇,gär\ *n* -s [MF *bedegard*, fr. Per *bādāward*] : gall like a moss produced on rosebushes (as the sweetbrier or eglantine) by a gall wasp (*Rhodites rosae* or related species)

be·del *or* **be·dell** \bəˈdel, be-\ *n* -s [ME *bedel* — more at BEADLE] : an English university officer who walks at the head of processions of officers and students — usu. spelled *bedel* at Oxford, *bedell* at Cambridge

bed·er·al \ˈbed(ə)rəl\ *n* -s [by alter.] *Scot* : BEADLE 2

bedesman *or* **bedeman** *var of* BEADSMAN

be·devil \bə̇, bē+\ *vt* **bedeviled** *or* **bedevilled; bedeviled** *or* **bedevilled; bedeviling** *or* **bedevilling; bedevils** [*be-* + *devil*] **1** : to possess with or as if with a devil : BEWITCH **2** : to change for the worse ⟨a room *~ed* by a poor decorator⟩ : SPOIL, CORRUPT **3 a** : to treat diabolically : torment and abuse or maltreat **b** : to drive frantic with or as if with care and worry **c** : HARASS, VEX, ANNOY, PESTER ⟨*~ing* city officials in little matters —Green Peyton⟩ ⟨hard to hold the horses on a straight course with the insects *~ing* them —H.L.Davis⟩ **d** : to make worse often by obscuring or muddling : confuse and aggravate ⟨racial tensions that ~ politics —*Times Lit. Supp.*⟩ ⟨how tendentious maps can ~ an international problem —G.R.Crone⟩

be·dev·il·ler \-lə(r)\ *n* -s : one that bedevils

be·dev·il·ment \-lmənt\ *n* -s **1** : a situation or condition that bedevils : CONFUSION, DISORDER, VEXATION, TROUBLE **2** : possession by a devil ⟨mad conduct and other signs of ~⟩

be·dew \bə̇, bē+\ *vt* -ED/-ING/-S [ME *bedewen*, fr. *be-* + *dewen* to wet with dew — more at DEW] : to moisten with dew or with something felt to resemble dew (as tears or sweat) ⟨sympathetic tears my cheeks ~ —W.S.Gilbert⟩

bedfast \ˈ=,=\ *adj* [¹*bed* + *fast* (fixed)] : confined to bed because of sickness or weakness : BEDRIDDEN

bedfellow \ˈ=,=(,)=\ *n* [ME *bedfelawe*, fr. *bed* + *felawe* fellow] **1** : a person sharing one's bed **2** : one found in proximity to or cooperation with another ⟨the press, like politics, makes strange *~s* — *Newsweek*⟩ : ASSOCIATE, ALLY

bed·fel·low·ship \ˈ=,=,=,ship\ *n* : the condition of being bedfellows

bedflower \ˈ=,==\ *n* : YELLOW BEDSTRAW

bed·ford \ˈbedfə(r)d\ *adj, usu cap* [fr. *Bedford*, England] : of or from the municipal borough of Bedford, England : of the kind or style prevalent in Bedford

bedford cord *n, usu cap B* : a plain or twill-weave clothing fabric with wide or narrow lengthwise ribs made in various weights of cotton, wool, or other fibers singly and in combination

bed·ford·shire \ˈbedfərd,shi(ə)r, -fəd,shiə(r, -fə(r)dshə(r)\ *or*

bedford \-fə(r)d\ *adj, usu cap* [fr. *Bedfordshire* or *Bedford* county, England] **:** of or from the county of Bedford, England **:** of the kind or style prevalent in Bedford
bed fuel *n* **:** the bottom layer of fuel in a cupola furnace
bedgery *var of* PITURI
bedgown \ˈ=,=\ *n* **1 :** NIGHTGOWN **2** *dial Brit* **:** a woman's short loose jacket formerly worn for general work
bed-ground \ˈ=,=\ *n* **:** an area on which a drove of cattle or sheep sleep for a night
bedhead \ˈ=,=\ *n* [¹*bed* + *head*] **:** the head of a bed
be·dias·ite \bēˈdī,zīt\ *n* -s [fr. *Bedias*, town in Grimes county, Texas + E *-ite*] **:** TEKTITE
be·dight \bəˈdīt, bē-\ *vt* **bedighted** *or* **bedight; bedighted** *or* **bedight; bedighting; bedights** [ME *bedighten*, fr. *be-* + *dighten* to put in order — more at DIGHT] *archaic* **:** EQUIP, ACCOUTER, ARRAY, BEDECK
be·di·kah \bə(ˌ)dēˈkä, =ˈ=(ˌ)=\ *n, pl* **bedikahs** \-äz\ *or* **bedikoth** \=(ˌ)=ˈkōt, -ōth,-ōs\ [Heb *bĕdhīqāh* inspection] **:** the ritual inspection (as of a ceremonial act, person, or object) to ascertain fitness or unfitness according to rabbinical law
be·di·kath ha·metz \bə(ˌ)dēˈkätkōˈmäts,-ˈdē,kät-,-äthk-,-äsk-,-ˈkō,mets\ *or* **be·di·kat hametz** \-kät-,-käs-\ *n* [Heb *bĕdhīqath hāmēṣ* search for leaven] **:** the Jewish ceremony of searching for leaven in the home on the evening before Passover
be·dim \bə, bē+\ *vt* **bedimmed; bedimmed; bedimming; bedims** [*be-* + *dim* (v. or adj.)] **:** to make less bright or lustrous by or as if by covering ⟨clouds ~ the sun⟩ ⟨the surface was *bedimmed* by exposure to air⟩ **:** DIM **:** make indistinct or confused **syn** see OBSCURE
be·dimple \bə, bē+\ *vt* [*be-* + *dimple*] **:** to mark with dimples
be·di·zen \bəˈdīzᵊn, bē-, -ˈdiz-\ *vt* -ED/-ING/-S [*be-* + *dizen*] **:** to dress or adorn with gaudy and meretricious vulgarity ⟨a bold and shameless creature, *~ed*, painted and overdressed —Kenneth Roberts⟩
be·di·zen·ment \-mənt\ *n* -s **:** vulgar gaudy ornamentation ⟨*~s* of purple, scarlet, and apricot —Osbert Sitwell⟩
bed jacket *n* **:** a short lightweight jacket worn over a nightgown often when sitting up in bed
bed joint *n* **1 :** a horizontal joint in masonry **2 a :** a horizontal crack or fissure in massive rock **b :** one of a set of cracks or fissures parallel with the bedding of a rock
bedkey \ˈ=,=\ *n* [¹*bed* + *key*] **:** a wrench for adjusting the nuts and bolts or the ropes of a bedstead
bed ladder *n* **:** ¹BED 4k
¹**bed·lam** \ˈbedləm\ *n* -s [fr. *Bedlam*, popular name for the Hospital of St. Mary of Bethlehem, London, England, an insane asylum, fr. ME *Bedlem, Bethlem*, alter. of *Bethlehem*, town of Palestine] **1** *obs* **a :** MADMAN, LUNATIC **b** *sometimes cap* **:** a discharged often imperfectly cured patient of an asylum who is licensed to beg **2** *archaic* **:** a hospital for the insane **:** a lunatic asylum **3 a :** a place or scene of wild mad uproar ⟨after the speech the meeting became a ~⟩ **b :** an extremely confused scene **:** a situation making for confusion ⟨the ~ of roads, crescents, drives and avenues that forms the suburbs —*Irish Digest*⟩
²**bedlam** \"\ *adj* **:** MAD, LUNATIC **:** of or appropriate to an insane asylum
bed·lam·er \ˈbedləmə(r)\ *n* -s [origin unknown] **:** an immature harp or hooded seal
¹**bed·lam·ite** \ˈbedlə,mīt\ *n* -s *sometimes cap* [¹*bedlam* + *-ite*] **:** MADMAN, LUNATIC
²**bedlamite** \"\ *adj* **:** MAD, LUNATIC ⟨the ~ yells of carnival in the street —Joseph Conrad⟩
bed lathe *n* **:** a lathe whose bed extends to the floor
bed·less \ˈbedləs\ *adj* **:** being without a bed
bed linen *n* **:** linen or cotton articles for a bed; *esp* **:** sheets and pillowcases
bed·ling·ton terrier \ˈbedliŋtən-\ *n, usu cap B* [fr. *Bedlington*, Eng.] **:** a swift rough-coated terrier of a breed originating in Northumberland, England, being of light build with arched loin, roached back, and tapering neck and tail, and weighing from 22 to 24 pounds
bed load *n* **:** sediment not in suspension rolled or dragged along a stream bottom
bed·man \ˈbedmən\ *n, pl* **bedmen :** one who prepares sand beds in which pig iron is cast
bedmate \ˈ=,=\ *n* **:** one that shares one's bed; *sometimes* **:** MISTRESS, CONCUBINE, WIFE
bed molding *or* **bed mold** *n* **:** the molding of a cornice immediately below the corona and above the frieze; *also* **:** a molding below a deep projection
be·doctor \bə, bē+\ *vt* [*be-* + *doctor* (n.)] **1 :** to confer a doctoral degree upon **2 :** to address as doctor
bed of roses : a place or situation of agreeable ease **:** a relaxed carefree luxurious situation
be·dog \bə, bē+\ *vt* [*be-* + *dog* (n. & v.)] **1 :** to call (a person) a dog **2 :** ²DOG *vt* **1**
¹**bed·ou·in** *also* **bed·u·in** \ˈbedəwən, -dwən,-də,win,-də,wēn\ *or* **bed·oui** \ˈbedə(,)wē\ *n, pl* **bedouin** *or* **bedouins** *also* **beduin** *or* **beduins** *or* **bedouis** *often cap* [F *bédouin*, fr. Ar *badāwi* (colloq. Ar *bidwān*), pl. of *badawi, badwi* desert dweller] **:** a nomadic Arab of the Arabian, Syrian, or No. African deserts
²**bedouin** *also* **beduin** \"\ *adj, often cap* **:** of or relating to the bedouin
bedpan \ˈ=,=\ *n* **1** *obs* **:** WARMING PAN **2 :** a shallow vessel so constructed that it can be used by a person in bed for urination or defecation
bed piece *n* **1 :** a skid piece placed under a pile of lumber **2 :** a bank-note engraving die consisting of a flat hardened hand-engraved steel plate from which the printing plates are made by transference
bed plane *n* **:** BEDDING PLANE
bedplate \ˈ=,=\ *n* **:** a plate or framing used as a bed or support for something: as **a :** the heavy foundation framing or plate giving support and stability to the lighter parts in a machine ⟨an engine ~⟩ **b :** a stationary set of mounted knives or bars in a papermaking beater against which corresponding knives of the beater roll brush as they rotate
bedpost \ˈ=,=\ *n* **1 :** the usu. turned or carved post of a bed **2 :** the 7-10 split in bowling — usu. used in pl.
bedpost clock *n* **:** LANTERN CLOCK
be·drabble \bə, bē+\ *vt* -ED/-ING/-S [*be-* + *drabble*] **:** to wet and dirty with rain and mud
be·draggle \bə, bē+\ *vt* -ED/-ING/-S [*be-* + *draggle*] **:** to wet thoroughly ⟨little ducklings suffering from being *bedraggled*⟩
be·drag·gled \-gəld\ *adj* **1 :** left wet and limp or dragging by or as if by rain ⟨the ~ flags after the shower⟩ **2 :** soiled and stained by or as if by trailing in mud ⟨the ~ clothes of the beggar⟩ **3 :** lacking all former impressiveness **:** DILAPIDATED, DECREPIT, SOILED, WORN ⟨the ~ buildings of the slums⟩
bed·ral \ˈbedrəl\ *n* -s [by alter.] *Scot* **:** BEADLE 2
be·dress \bə, bē+\ *vt* [*be-* + *dress*] **:** to dress up
bed rest *n* **:** continuous confinement of a sick person to bed (as in treatment of tuberculosis or certain nerve disorders)
bed·rid·den \ˈbe,dridᵊn\ *also* **bed·rid** \-id\ *adj* [alter. of ME *bedrede, bedreden*, fr. OE *bedreda, bedrida*, fr. *bedreda, bedrida*, n., one who is confined to bed, fr. *bedd* bed + *-reda, -rida* rider (fr. *rīdan* to ride) — more at RIDE] **1 :** confined to one's bed by illness, injury, or weakness ⟨a ~ invalid⟩ **2 :** DECREPIT, WORN-OUT, ENERVATED ⟨~ notions⟩
¹**bedrock** \ˈ=ˈ=\ *n* [¹*bed* + *rock*] **1 :** the solid rock underlying the soil and other unconsolidated materials or appearing at the surface where these are absent — called also *ledge* **2 a :** lowest point **:** NADIR, MINIMUM **:** least quantity ⟨his resources were at ~⟩ **b :** BASIS, FOUNDATION ⟨a ~ of elementary learning on which an intermediate teacher could build⟩ **:** basic situation or consideration after matters adventitious have been stripped away
²**bedrock** \"\ *adj* **:** stripped of nonessential matter obscuring or adorning **:** BASIC, FUNDAMENTAL **:** SOLID, FACTUAL ⟨the great advantage of reality is its hard, ~, concrete quality —Lionel Trilling⟩
bedrock valley *n* **:** a valley eroded in bedrock
bedroll \ˈ=,=\ *n* [¹*bed* + *roll*] **:** bedding often of blankets only that is rolled up for ready carrying
¹**bedroom** \ˈ=,=\ *n* **1 :** a room furnished with a bed and intended primarily for sleeping **2 :** a private room on a railroad sleeping car larger than a roomette and smaller than a compartment and containing toilet facilities and usu. two berths
²**bedroom** \"\ *adj* **1 :** dealing with, suggestive of, or inviting to sex relations usu. illicit ⟨a ~ farce concerning a wife and her lover⟩ ⟨~ eyes which caressed the female on whom he looked —Ethel Wilson⟩ **2 :** inhabited or used by commuters ⟨a fringe of ~ towns around the city⟩
bedroom slipper *n* **:** a fabric or soft leather house slipper often without heel or counter
be·drop \bə, bē+\ *vt* **bedropped; bedropped; bedropping; bedrops** [*be-* + *drop* (n.)] **:** to sprinkle with or as if with drops
bed rot *n* **:** DAMPING-OFF
beds *pl of* BED, *pres 3d sing of* BED
bed setter *n* **:** one that arranges blocks of granite on a bed of wooden beams and levels them in preparation for polishing of the tops — called also *setter*
¹**bedside** \ˈ=,=\ *n* [ME *bedside, beddes side*, fr. *bed* or *beddes* (gen. of *bed*) + *side*] **:** the side of a bed **:** a place beside a bed (as a sickbed or a deathbed) ⟨by her ~ when she died⟩
²**bedside** \"\ *adj* **1 :** relating to or conducted at the bedside of a patient ⟨~ teaching⟩ ⟨a ~ diagnosis⟩ **2 :** suitable for reading in bed esp. in short bits; *sometimes* **:** light and entertaining ⟨a ~ book⟩ ⟨~ literature⟩
bedside manner *n* **:** the manner often solicitous and sympathetic that a physician assumes toward his patients
bed-sitter \ˈ=,=\ *n* [by shortening and alter.] **:** BED-SITTING-ROOM
bed-sitting-room \ˈ=ˈ==,=\ *n, Brit* **:** a one-room apartment serving as both bedroom and sitting room
bed slat *n* **:** a board supporting bedsprings usu. extending from side to side of a bedstead
bedsore \ˈ=,=\ *n* **:** an ulceration of tissue deprived of nutrition by prolonged pressure; *specif* **:** ulceration of tissue covering a prominent bony point (as the spine or a hipbone) in patients bedfast or animals recumbent for long periods
bedspread \ˈ=,=\ *n* **:** a large usu. ornamental cloth used as a cover for a bed
bedspring \ˈ=,=\ *n* **:** a spring supporting a mattress
bedstaff \ˈ=,=\ *n* **:** BED SLAT
bed·stead \ˈbed,sted *sometimes* -,stəd\ *n* -s [ME *bedstede*, fr. *bed* + *stede* stead, place — more at STEAD] **:** a framework of a bed usu. including a head with legs, a foot with legs, and connecting sides or rails
bed steps *n pl* **:** steps used to climb into a quite high bed
bedstock \ˈ=,=\ *n* [ME *bedstoke*, fr. *bed* + *stoke, stok* stock — more at STOCK] *dial Eng* **:** a structure supporting bed slats that runs either from side to side or from head to foot
bed stone *n* **1 :** a large foundation stone **2 :** the stationary lower stone of a pair of millstones
bedstraw \ˈ=,=\ *n* [ME, fr. *bed* + *straw*] **1 :** straw used in place of a mattress **:** straw used to fill a mattress **2 :** an herb of the genus *Galium*
bed tester *n* **:** fittings about the head of a bed; *sometimes* **:** CANOPY
bedtick \ˈ=,=\ *n* **:** TICK
bedticking \ˈ=,==\ *n* **:** TICKING
bed timber *n* **:** a foundation timber
bedtime \ˈ=,=\ *n* [ME, fr. *bed* + *time*] **:** time to go to bed
bedtime story *n* **:** a simple story for young children often about animals
be·du \ˈbe(,)dü\ *n, pl* **bedu** *sometimes cap* [Ar *badāwi* — more at BEDOUIN] **:** BEDOUIN
beduin *var of* BEDOUIN
bed up *vt* **:** to plow (two or more furrows) together to form a ridge on which a crop (as cotton or sweet potatoes) is grown
bed vein *n* **:** a vein that runs parallel to a bedding plane in a rock formation
bed wagon *n* **:** a wagon carrying bedding and supplies on a cattle roundup
bed·ward \ˈbedwə(r)d\ *or* **bed·wards** \-dz\ *adv* [ME *bedward*, fr. ¹*bed* + *-ward*] **1 :** toward bed **2** *obs* **:** towards bedtime
bed warmer *n* **:** a covered pan containing hot coals used to warm a bed
bedway \ˈ=,=\ *n* **1 :** the bed of a child's slide **2 :** one of the rails or guides on the bed of a lathe
be·dwell \bə, bē+\ *vt* [*be-* + *dwell*] **:** to dwell in **:** INHABIT
bed wetter *n* **:** a person that habitually urinates in bed during sleep
bed-wetting \ˈ=,==\ *n* **:** ENURESIS
¹**bee** \ˈbē\ *n* -s *often attrib* [ME, fr. OE *bēo*; akin to OHG *bini, bīa* bee, ON *bȳ*, W *bydaf* beehive, Lith *bitis* bee] **1 :** a social colonial hymenopterous insect (*Apis mellifera*) often maintained in a state of domestication for the sake of the honey that it produces and for use as a pollinator **:** HONEYBEE; *broadly* **:** any of numerous membranous-winged noncarnivorous insects constituting a superfamily (Apoidea) of the order Hymenoptera that differ from the closely related wasps in possession of a heavier hairier body and sucking as well as chewing mouthparts, feed on pollen and nectar and store both and often also honey, the fertile females and workers usu. having functional stings **2 :** an eccentric, fantastic, or delusive notion **:** WHIM, FANCY ⟨he has a new ~ that he'd like to be an actor⟩ **3** [perh. alter. of E dial. *been, bean* voluntary help given by neighbors toward the accomplishment of a particular task, prob. fr. ME *bene* boon, prayer, fr. OE *bēn* prayer — more at BOON] **a :** a usu. social gathering of people to accomplish cooperatively a specific purpose — often used in combinations ⟨husking ~⟩ ⟨quilting ~⟩ **b :** PARTY 10a ⟨a square-dancing ~⟩ **c :** SPELLING BEE **4 :** a lump of a yeast (*Saccharomyces pyriformis*) intermittently rising and releasing bubbles in brew — usu. used in pl. — **bee in one's bonnet :** ¹BEE 2 ⟨he has the presidential *bee in his bonnet* —O.W.Holmes †1935⟩
²**bee** \"\ *or* **bee block** *n* -s [ME *beghe, beh* ring, bracelet, fr. OE *bēag, bēah*; akin to OHG *boug* ring, bracelet, ON *baugr*, Skt *bhoga* coil (of a snake), OE *būgan* to bend, bow — more at BOW] **:** a piece of hard wood bolted to the side of a bowsprit sometimes with metal sheaves to reeve fore-topmast stays through
³**bee** *also* **be** \"\ *n* -s **:** the letter *b*
be-east \bē+\ *prep* [ME (northern dial.) *be est, be eist*, fr. *be* by (fr. OE *be, bi, bī*) + *est, eist* east — more at BY, EAST] **:** east of
bee·ball \ˈbē+,-\ *n* **:** a game that combines elements of rugby and soccer and is played on a football field between two teams of nine players using a leather ball slightly smaller than a soccer ball
bee balm *n* **1 :** LEMON BALM **2 :** either of two common monardas: **a :** OSWEGO TEA **b :** a wild bergamot (*Monarda fistulosa*)
¹**bee·bee** *var of* BIBI
²**beebee** *var of* BB
bee bird *n* **:** any of several birds reputed to eat bees (as the European flycatchers and the kingbird)
beebread \ˈ=,=\ *n* **:** bitter yellowish brown pollen stored up in honeycomb cells and used mixed with honey by bees as food
bee brush *n* **:** a soft brush for removing bees from the honeycomb
bee-butt \ˈbē,bət\ *n* [¹*bee* + E dial. *butt* straw beehive, fr. OCorn] *dial Eng* **:** BEEHIVE
bee candy *n* **:** sugar with another substance (as honey) incorporated in it for feeding bees
bee cellar *n* **:** a cellar where bees are kept through the winter
¹**beech** \ˈbēch\ *n, pl* **beeches** *or* **beech** [ME *beche*, fr. OE *bēce*; akin to OE *bōc* beech, OHG *buohha*, ON *bōk*, L *fagus* beech, Gk *phēgos* oak, and perh. to Russ *buzina* elder] **1 :** any tree of the genus *Fagus* characterized by smooth gray bark, hard fine-grained wood, deep green foliage, and small sweet-flavored edible triangular nuts enclosed in burs — see AMERICAN BEECH, COPPER BEECH, EUROPEAN BEECH; TREE illustration **2 :** the wood of the beech **3** *Austral* **:** any of numerous trees resembling the true beech esp. in their timber — compare FLINDOSA **4 :** a tree of the genus *Nothofagus*
²**beech** \"\ *adj* [ME *beche*, fr. *beche*, n.] **1 :** of or relating to the beech **2 :** made of beech
beech agaric *n* **:** a white glutinous edible mushroom (*Armillaria mucida*) that is a wound parasite on the beech
beech bark disease *n* **:** a disease of beech esp. destructive in eastern Canada and northern U.S. that is due to the combined activities of the beech scale (*Cryptococcus fagi*) and a fungus (*Nectria coccinea faginata*) and causes destruction of living bark, wilting of foliage, and finally death of the tree
beechdrops \ˈ=,=\ *n pl but sing or pl in constr* **1 :** a low wiry plant (*Epifagus virginiana*) parasitic on the roots of beeches **2 :** SQUAWROOT
beech·en \ˈbēchən\ *adj* [ME *bechen*, fr. OE *bēcen*, fr. *bēce*, n. + *-en*] **:** consisting or made of beech **:** derived from or belonging to the beech
beech family *n* **:** FAGACEAE
beech fern *n* **:** either of the two ferns (*Dryopteris phegopteris* and *D. hexagonoptera*) that grow frequently in beechwoods — see BROAD BEECH FERN
beech fungus *n* **:** a So. American edible fungus — see CYTTARIA
beech leaf snake *n, dial* **:** COPPERHEAD
beech marten *n* **:** STONE MARTEN
beech mast *n* **:** beechnuts esp. as they lie under trees
beech·nut \ˈbēch,nət *sometimes* -,nat\ *n* **:** the nut of the beech
beech scale *n* **:** a destructive European scale (*Cryptococcus fagi*) now established in the northeastern U.S. and adjacent parts of Canada where it is destructive to stands of native beech
beech seal *n, in Vermont* **:** a beech rod **:** a flogging with beech rods
beech-tree \ˈ=,=\ *n* [ME *bech-tre*, fr. *beche* beech + *tre* tree] **:** BEECH 1
beechy \ˈbēchē\ *adj* -ER/-EST **:** of, relating to, or abounding in beeches
bee-eater \ˈ=,==\ *n* **:** any of numerous brightly colored chiefly tropical Old World birds constituting the family Meropidae and distinguished by a strong graceful flight like that of a swallow
bee-escape \ˈ==,=\ *n* **:** a device to permit the escape of bees but prevent their return (as from a compartment of a hive)
¹**beef** \ˈbēf\ *n, pl* **beefs** \-ēfs\ *or* **beeves** \-ēvz\ *also* **beef** *see numbered senses* [ME, fr. OF *buef* ox, beef, fr. L *bov-, bos* head of cattle — more at COW] **1 :** the flesh of a steer, cow, or other adult bovine animal when killed for food **2 a** *pl* **beeves** *also* **beefs** *or* **beef :** an ox, cow, or bull in a full-grown or nearly full-grown state; *esp* **:** a steer or cow fattened for food ⟨*beeves* of quality —P.A.Rollins⟩ ⟨Texan *beefs* were loaded in the Abilene yards —R.A.Billington⟩ ⟨a herd of *beef* —E.C.Abbott & Helena Smith⟩ **b** *pl* **beeves** *also* **beefs :** the dressed carcass of a beef animal ⟨*beeves* hanging in the slaughterhouse⟩ **c :** beef animals ⟨growing ~ on the range⟩ **3 a :** muscular flesh **:** BRAWN, WEIGHT **:** bulky strength ⟨a heavyweight wrestler with a great deal of ~⟩ **b :** strength and power ⟨an engine with added ~⟩ **c :** ARGUMENT, QUARREL, BRAWL, FIGHT **4** *pl* **beefs** [fr. the verb] **a** *slang* **:** PROTEST, OBJECTION **:** grievance or ground for complaint **:** point at issue ⟨*~s* and grumbling by disappointed contestants —Bennett Cerf⟩ **b** *slang* **:** COMPLAINT, ACCUSATION **:** criminal charge ⟨parole officer said he was going straight — no *~s* anywhere —Thurston Scott⟩

A. wholesale cuts of beef: *1* shank; *2* round (with rump and shank cut off); *3* rump; *4* sirloin; *5* short loin; *6* flank; *7* rib; *8* chuck; *9* plate; *10* brisket; *11* shank B. retail cuts of beef: *a* heel pot roast; *b* round steak; *c* rump roast; *d* sirloin steak; *e* pinbone steak; *f* short ribs; *g* porterhouse steak; *h* T-bone steak; *i* club steak; *j* flank steak; *k* rib roast; *m* blade rib roast; *n* plate; *o* brisket; *p* crosscut shank; *q* arm pot roast; *r* boneless neck; *s* blade roast

²**beef** \"\ *vb* -ED/-ING/-S *vt* **1 :** to add weight, strength, force, or power to — usu. used with *up* ⟨de-emphasize their navy and ~ up their army —*Fortune*⟩ ⟨the inspector general's office would be *~ed* up with additional investigators —*Time*⟩ **2 :** to fatten or kill (a beef animal) for food ~ *vi* **1 :** to complain, object, or protest often angrily or emphatically ⟨seamen can always find something to ~ about —S.E.Morison⟩ **2** *slang* **a :** to make a complaint **b :** to inform or give evidence ⟨if the mark *~s* and goes to the police —D.W.Maurer⟩ **syn** see COMPLAIN
³**beef** \"\ *adj* **1 :** of, from, or relating to the ox kind ⟨~ blood⟩ ⟨~ serum⟩ **2 :** raised for or suitable for beef ⟨a ~ animal⟩
beef bacon *n* **:** beef plate or brisket cured in the same way as pork bacon
beef boat *n* **:** a supply ship or boat
beef bread *n* **:** the pancreas of a mature animal (as a beef) used for food
beef breed *n* **:** any breed of cattle developed primarily for the efficient production of meat (as the Angus, Hereford, or Shorthorn) and characterized by capacity for rapid growth, heavy rectangular well-fleshed body, and comparatively short stocky neck and legs — compare DAIRY BREED
beef·burg·er \ˈbēf,bərgər\ *n* -s [¹*beef* + *hamburger*] **:** HAMBURGER
beefcake \ˈ=,=\ *n, slang* **:** display (as in photographs featuring bare chests) of robust or vigorous masculine physique — compare CHEESECAKE
beef cattle *n* **:** cattle suitable for beef; *esp* **:** cattle of one of the beef breeds
beef cow *n* **:** a cow of a beef breed
beef critter *n, dial* **:** a mature beef
beefeater \ˈ=,==\ *n* **1 :** a yeoman of the guard that forms part of an English monarch's train on state occasions **2 :** a warder of the Tower of London uniformed like a beefeater
¹**beef·er** \ˈbēfə(r)\ *n* -s [¹*beef* + *-er*] **:** an animal of the ox kind produced for meat
²**beefer** *n* -s *slang* **:** one that beefs ⟨was a constant ~; nothing ever pleased him⟩
beef extract *n* **:** an extract of the soluble constituents of beef or beef blood used to stimulate gastric secretion — compare BEEF TEA
beefheaded \ˈ=ˈ==\ *adj* **:** STUPID ⟨resented the ~ ward heelers —John Fischer⟩
beef juice *n* **:** the juice of beef extracted by pressure rather than by cooking
beef·less \ˈbēfləs\ *adj* **:** being without beef ⟨this hungry, thirsty . . . ~ land —Richard Ford⟩
beeflower \ˈ=,=\ *n* **:** BEE PLANT
bee fly *n* **1 :** any of numerous flies constituting a family (Bombyliidae) having many members resembling bees **2 :** a fly (*Heterostylum robustum*) that parasitizes wild bees by laying its eggs in the nesting cells

beefeater 1

beef measles *n pl but sing or pl in constr* **:** the infestation of beef muscle by cysticerci of the beef tapeworm which make oval white vesicles giving a measly appearance to beef
beefs *pl of* BEEF
beef's blood *n* **:** OXBLOOD
beefsteak \ˈ=,=\ *n* **:** a steak of beef usu. cut from the hindquarter and suitable for broiling or frying
beefsteak begonia *or* **beefsteak geranium** *n* **:** a rhizomatous begonia (*Begonia feastii*) with round fleshy leaves reddish colored beneath
beefsteak fungus *also* **beefsteak mushroom** *n* **:** a fungus (*Fistulina hepatica*) of the family Polyporaceae growing on dead trees in bright-red shelving masses and esteemed as a table delicacy — called also *beeftongue*

beefsteak plant *n* **:** any of several plants having red or purple foliage: as **a :** an ornamental foliage plant (*Perilla frutescens crispa*) **b :** a wood betony (*Pedicularis canadensis*) **c :** a plant of the genus *Begonia; esp* **:** BEEFSTEAK BEGONIA

beef tapeworm *n* **:** an unarmed tapeworm (*Taenia saginata*) that infests the human intestine as an adult, has a cysticercus larva that develops in cattle, and is contracted by man through ingestion of the larva in raw or rare beef

beef tea *n* **:** a beverage prepared by extracting finely cut lean beef with hot water or by dissolving commercial beef extract in boiling water — compare BEEF EXTRACT, BOUILLON

beeftongue \'ˌ\ *n* **:** BEEFSTEAK FUNGUS

beef–witted \'ˌ\ *adj* **:** STUPID

beefwood \'ˌ\ *n* **1 :** any of several hard heavy reddish chiefly tropical woods including some that are used for cabinetwork **2 :** any tree yielding beefwood: as **a :** any of several casuarinas; *esp* **:** a common Australian tree (*Casuarina equisetifolia*) now widely grown as an ornamental in warm regions — called also *Australian pine* **b :** either of two Australian silk oaks (*Grevillea striata* and *Stenocarpus salignus*) **c :** BLOLLY 1 **d :** a bully tree (*Manilkara bidentata*)

beefwood family *n* **:** CASUARINACEAE — compare CASUARINA

beefy \'bēfē, -fi\ *adj* -ER/-EST [¹*beef* + *-y*] **1 :** brawny or fleshy with suggestions of grossness **:** THICKSET, HEAVY ⟨coarsened and ~, with a neck like a bull's and a rapidly spreading girth —Ellen Glasgow⟩ ⟨~ and sturdy, with heavy legs —Joseph Bennett⟩ **2 a :** promising a good yield of beef ⟨~ cattle⟩ **b :** coarsely overfleshed **:** obesely heavy

bee·ger·ite \'bēgəˌrīt\ *n* -S [Hermann *Beeger*, 19th cent. Amer. metallurgist + E *-ite*] **:** a mineral $Pb_6Bi_2S_9$ consisting of massive gray sulfide of lead and bismuth

bee glue *n* **:** PROPOLIS

bee gum *n* **1** *chiefly South & Midland* **:** a hollow gum tree in which wild bees hive **2** *chiefly South & Midland* **:** a beehive made from sections of a hollow tree; *broadly* **:** BEEHIVE **3** *chiefly South & Midland* **:** a tall silk hat

beeheaded \'ˌ\ *adj* **:** ECCENTRIC, CRAZY

beehive \'ˌ\ *n* [ME, fr. ¹*bee* + *hive*] **1 :** a hive for bees **2 :** something felt to resemble a hive for bees: as **a :** a rounded conical shape ⟨a ~ hut⟩ **b :** a scene of swarming buzzing activity **3 :** SHAPED CHARGE

beehive coke *n* **:** coke that is made in a beehive oven and is usu. of large size and hard stringy structure

beehive kiln *n* **:** a circular brick kiln with a domed roof

beehive oven *n* **:** a now little used arched coke oven in which heat is supplied by partial combustion of the coal within the oven chamber and no by-products are recovered

old-fashioned beehive

beehive tomb *n* **:** a tomb shaped like a beehive cut in a hillside and usu. approached by a horizontal passage, distinctive of the Mycenaean age in Greece

beehouse \'ˌ\ *n* **:** a house for bees **:** APIARY

beek \'bēk\ *vb* -ED/-ING/-S [ME *beken*] *chiefly Scot* **:** WARM ⟨~ before a fire⟩ **:** BASK

beekeeper \'ˌ\ *n* **:** one that engages in beekeeping esp. as a means of livelihood

beekeeping \'ˌ\ *n* **:** the branch of agriculture concerned with the production of and caring for bees and honey **:** APICULTURE

bee killer *n* **:** a large robber fly that feeds on or is supposed to feed on bees

beek·ite \'bēˌkīt\ *n* -S [Henry *Beeke* †1837 dean of Bristol, who first called attention to it + E *-ite*] **:** a pseudomorph of chalcedony after coral or shell

¹**beeline** \'ˌ\ *n* [¹*bee* + *line;* fr. the belief that nectar-laden bees return to their hives in a direct line] **:** a straight line: a straight direct course traversed rapidly — usu. used with *make* ⟨make a ~ to safer quarters⟩

²**beeline** \"\ *vi* -ED/-ING/-S **:** to go fast over the straightest quickest course — sometimes used with *it* ⟨ambulances *beelining* it for the hospital⟩

bee–lin·er \'bēˌlīnə(r)\ *n* [blend of ¹*beeline* and *liner*] **:** a self-propelled diesel railroad car

bee louse *n* **:** a minute wingless fly (*Braula coeca*) parasitic on honeybees

beel·ze·bub \bē'elzəˌbəb, 'bēl-,'bel-\ *n* -S [after *Beelzebub*, called "prince of the devils" in Mt 12:24, fr. L, fr. Gk *Beelzeboub*, fr. Heb *Ba'al Zěbhūbh*, lit., lord of flies] **1** *sometimes cap* **:** DEVIL **2 :** a So. American howler monkey (*Alouatta beelzebul*)

bee·man \'bēmən, -ˌman\ *n, pl* **beemen :** BEEKEEPER

bee–martin \'ˌ\ *n* **:** KINGBIRD

beemaster \'ˌ\ *n* **:** BEEKEEPER

bee moth *n* **:** a dull brownish or ashen moth (*Galleria mellonella*) whose larva feeds on the wax of the combs of the honeybee fouling the honey and injuring the brood and sometimes destroying weak colonies of bees — called also *wax moth*

been *past part of* BE, *dial Brit & archaic pres pl of* BE

bee·na marriage \'bēnə-\ *n* [Ar *binah* distinct, separate] **:** a marriage in parts of India and Ceylon in which the husband enters the wife's kinship group and has little authority in the household — compare MUTA

bee nettle *n* **1 :** HEMP NETTLE **2 :** HENBIT

bee orchis *or* **bee orchid** *n* **:** a European orchid (*Listera apifera*) whose flowers bear a resemblance to bees, flies, or other insects

¹**beep** \'bēp\ *n* -S [imit.] **1 :** a sound from a horn on a moving vehicle (as an automobile, boat, or locomotive) serving as a signal or warning **2 :** a short high-pitched note as if from a reed instrument sounded esp. as a time signal in radio broadcasting or as an indication that a telephone conversation is being recorded or that a recording has been made by telephone

²**beep** \"\ *vb* -ED/-ING/-S *vi* **1 :** to sound a horn ⟨drivers *~ing* behind us⟩ **:** make a beep ⟨horns *~ing*⟩ **~** *vt* **1 :** to cause (a horn) to sound **2 :** to make by sounding — sometimes used with *out* ⟨*~ing* out a warning⟩

beep·er \-pə(r)\ *n* -S **1 :** a device emitting beep signals esp. to pilotless aircraft **2 :** one that governs the flight of pilotless aircraft by remote control

bee plant *n* **:** a plant much frequented by bees for nectar: as **a :** a heavy-scented herb (*Cleome serrulata*) with numerous pink flowers **b :** any of various plants of the genus *Scrophularia* **c :** BEE BALM

¹**beer** \'bi(ə)r, -iə\ *n* -S *often attrib* [ME *ber*, fr. OE *bēor;* akin to OHG *bior* beer and perh. to OE *bȳsting* beastings — more at BEASTINGS] **1 :** a malted and hopped somewhat bitter alcoholic beverage; *specif* **:** such a beverage brewed by bottom fermentation — compare ALE, BOCK BEER, LAGER, PORTER **2 :** a carbonated nonalcoholic or a fermented slightly alcoholic beverage with flavoring derived from roots and other plant parts — used chiefly in compounds; see BIRCH BEER, GINGER BEER, ROOT BEER, SPRUCE BEER **3 :** fermented mash **:** WASH **4 :** a drink of beer ⟨order a ~⟩

²**beer** \"\ *also* **bier** \"\ *n* -S [perh. fr. ¹*bier*] **:** one of the groups in weaving usu. consisting of 40 threads into which the threads of the warp are divided; *also* **:** the corresponding group of dents on the reed consisting usu. of 20

beer·age \'biriǰ\ *n* -S [blend of *beer* and *peerage*] **:** the British peerage — usu. used disparagingly

beer and skittles *n* **:** drink and play **:** easygoing enjoyment

beer barrel *n* **:** a large common tun shell (*Tonus cerevisina*) of the Australian coast

beer cellar *n* **1 :** a cellar for storing beer **2 :** RATHSKELLER

beer gallon *n* **:** ALE GALLON

beer garden *n* **:** a garden where beer and other liquors are served at tables

beer hall *n* **:** an establishment featuring beer and sometimes offering entertainment

beerhouse \'ˌ\ *n, Brit* **:** a public house licensed to sell only malt liquors

beer·i·ly \'birəlē\ *adv* **:** in a beery and esp. a muddled or maudlin way ⟨they may sound as ~ nostalgic . . . at 2:00 a.m. —*Saturday Rev.*⟩

beerpull \'ˌ\ *n* **:** BEER PUMP; *also* **:** its handle

beer pump *n* **:** a pump for drawing up beer from casks (as from cellar to bar)

beer's law \'bāərz-\ *n, usu cap B* [after August *Beer* †1863 Ger. physicist] **:** a law in physics: the absorption of light by different concentrations of the same solute dissolved in the same solvent is an exponential function of the concentration provided the thickness of the absorbing medium remains constant

beer stone *also* **beer scale** *n* **:** a grayish brown scale composed of calcium oxalate and organic substances forming on the inside surfaces of brewing apparatus

beery \'birē, -ri\ *adj* -ER/-EST **1 :** inspired or influenced by beer drinking **:** convivial, mellowed, muddled, or maudlin ⟨~ song⟩ ⟨~ reminiscenses⟩ **:** affected or conditioned by beer ⟨a ~ face⟩ ⟨~ voices⟩ **2 a :** smelling of beer ⟨a ~ tavern⟩ **b :** mixed or flavored with beer

bees *pl of* BEE

bee sage *n* **:** a shrub (*Hyptis emorgi*) of the family Labiatae of southwestern U.S. and Mexico with aromatic white woolly foliage and purple flowers

bee smoker *n* **:** a device for blowing smoke into a hive to quiet bees before working on or about the hive

bee space *n* **:** a space a little less than ¼ inch that provides for the passage of bees in a hive

¹**beest** \'bēst\ *n* -S [by shortening] **:** BEASTINGS

²**beest** *dial Brit pres 2d sing of* BE, *obs pres subjunctive 2d sing of* BE

bee·sting \'bēˌstiŋ\ *n* [¹*bee* + *sting*] **1 :** the burning itching swollen lesion produced by the stinging of a bee **2** *or* **bee's sting :** the modified ovipositor of a bee that is typically associated with a venom gland and that serves as the bee's chief weapon

beest·ings \'bēˌstiŋz, -ˌstēnz\ *var of* BEASTINGS

¹**bees·wax** \'bēzˌwaks\ *n* [*bee's* (gen. of ¹*bee*) + *wax*] **1 :** WAX 1a **2 a :** a wax obtained as a yellow to brown solid by melting a honeycomb with boiling water, straining, and cooling and used esp. in polishes, modeling, and making patterns — called also *yellow wax* **b :** bleached yellow wax used esp. in cosmetics, ointments, and cerates and in church candles — called also *white wax* **3 :** a moderate yellowish brown that is slightly lighter than Bismarck brown or antique bronze, yellower and slightly lighter and stronger than cinnamon brown, darker than maple sugar, and redder and lighter than bronze — called also *linoleum brown, wax brown*

²**beeswax** \"\ *vt* -ED/-ING/-ES **:** to rub, coat, or polish with beeswax

beeswax flint *n* **:** a paleolithic flint of the color of beeswax

bees·wing \'bēzˌwiŋ\ *n* [*bee's* (gen. of ¹*bee*) + *wing*] **1 :** a film of shining scales of tartar formed in port and some other wines after long keeping **2 :** very thin filmy pieces of bran — **bees·winged** \-ŋd\ *adj*

¹**beet** \'bēt, *usu* -ēd·+V\ *n* -S *often attrib* [ME *bete*, fr. OE *bēte*, fr. L *beta*] **1 :** any biennial plant of the genus *Beta* (esp. *B. vulgaris*) with large thick leaves used esp. when young as greens and with a bulbous root **2 :** the enlarged root of the beet cultivated as a garden vegetable or as a source of sugar or for forage — usu. used in pl. when referring to a table vegetable; see CHARD, MANGEL, SUGAR BEET

²**beet** \"\ *vt* -ED/-ING/-S [ME *beten, beeten* to improve, amend, kindle or feed a fire, fr. OE *bētan;* akin to OHG *buozzen* to improve, amend, ON *bœta*, Goth *gabotjan*, all causatives fr. the root of OE *bōt* help, relief — more at BOOT] *dial Brit* **:** to add fuel to (a fire) **:** FEED

³**beet** \"\ *n* -S [ME *bete, beite*] **:** a tied bundle or sheaf of fiber flax plants

beet armyworm *n* **:** an armyworm (*Spodoptera exigua*) that eats the foliage of beets, alfalfa, and vegetables

bee·tewk \bē'tyük\ *n, usu cap* [Russ *bityug, bityuk*, prob. fr. the *Bityug* river, Russia] **:** a Russian breed of heavy draft horses

bee·tho·ve·nian \ˌbāˌtōˌ'vēnēən, -nyən *also* -ād·ˌō- *or* -ād·ō'v-\ *adj, usu cap* [Ludwig van *Beethoven* †1827 German composer + E *-ian*] **:** of, relating to, or characteristic of Ludwig van Beethoven or his musical style or works ⟨possessed of a *Beethovenian* genius⟩

¹**bee·tle** \'bēd·ᵊl, -ētᵊl\ *n* -S [ME *bityl, betylle*, fr. OE *bitula*, fr. *bītan* to bite — more at BITE] **1 :** an insect of the order Coleoptera — sometimes distinguished from *weevil* **2 :** any of various insects (as cockroaches) more or less resembling those of the order Coleoptera esp. in being of large size and dark color — not used technically

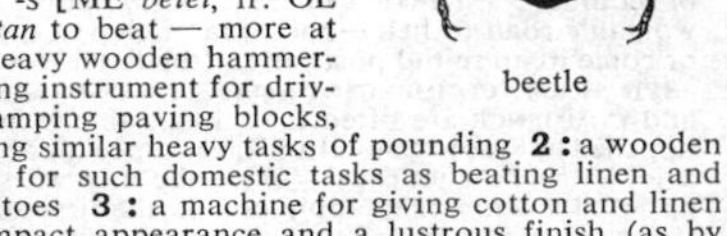

beetle

²**beetle** \"\ *vi* **beetled; beetled; beetling** \-ēd·ᵊliŋ, -ēt(ᵊ)liŋ\ **beetles :** to scuttle like a beetle either with speed or with awkward bumbling ⟨while the heavy buses ~ past —Thomas Wolfe⟩

³**beetle** \"\ *n* -S [ME *betel*, fr. OE *bīetel*, fr. *bēatan* to beat — more at BEAT] **1 :** a heavy wooden hammering or ramming instrument for driving stakes, tamping paving blocks, and performing similar heavy tasks of pounding **2 :** a wooden pestle or bat for such domestic tasks as beating linen and mashing potatoes **3 :** a machine for giving cotton and linen fabrics a compact appearance and a lustrous finish (as by hammering over rollers)

⁴**beetle** \"; *for pres part see* ²BEETLE\ *vt* -ED/-ING/-S **:** to flatten and compact (a fabric) in a beetle

⁵**beetle** \"\ *adj* [ME *bitel-* (as in *bitel-browed* beetle-browed)] **:** prominent and overhanging — usu. used of eyebrows with suggestion of lowering sullenness

⁶**beetle** \"; *for pres part see* ²BEETLE\ *vi* -ED/-ING/-S **:** to project, overhang, jut, or loom often ominously or threateningly ⟨the dark heavy brows *beetling* in a frown —Ellen Glasgow⟩ ⟨spending my strength in vain to scale the *beetling* crags —R.L.Stevenson⟩ **syn** see BULGE

beet leafhopper *n* **:** a destructive homopterous insect (*Circulifer tenellus*) widely distributed in the western U.S. where it serves as a vector of curly top on a large number of crop and ornamental plants

beetled *adj* [fr. past part. of ⁶*beetle*] **:** BEETLE

beetle green *n* **:** an iridescent color that under normal viewing is a deep yellowish green

beetlehead \'ˌ\ *n* [³*beetle* + *head*] **1 :** a stupid person **2 :** BLACK-BELLIED PLOVER

beetleheaded \'ˌ\ *adj* **:** STUPID

beetle mite *n* [so called fr. their hard, shining bodies] **:** any of numerous free-living mites (superfamily Oribatoidea) that are abundant and widespread in soil and that include several important intermediate hosts of tapeworms of domestic animals

bee·tler \'bēd·ᵊlə(r), -ēt(ᵊ)lə(r)\ *n* -S [⁴*beetle* + *-er*] **:** one that beetles cloth

beetleweed \'ˌ\ *n* [prob. fr. ¹*beetle* + *weed*] **:** GALAX 2

beet puller *or* **beet lifter** *n* **:** an implement that lifts sugar beets out of soil at harvest time

beet pulp *n* **:** wet or dried slices of sugar beet after the sugar has been extracted used as a stock feed

bee tree *n* **1 :** a hollow tree in which honeybees have a nest **2 :** BASSWOOD 1

beetroot \'ˌ\ *n* -S **1** *chiefly Brit* **:** BEET 2 **2 :** a pigweed (*Amaranthus retroflexus*) with stem base of a reddish color

beets *pl of* BEET, *pres 3d sing of* BEET

beet sugar *n* **:** sugar made from sugar beets by extraction of juice from the finely sliced roots, evaporation of excess water, and crystallization of the resulting syrup

beet webworm *n* **:** the green or yellowish larva of a small brownish pyralidid moth (*Loxostege sticticalis*) that feeds on and defoliates garden beets and sugar beets and many other cultivated plants

beeve \'bēv\ *n* -S [back-formation fr. *beeves*, pl. of *beef*] **:** ¹BEEF 2a

bee veil *n* **:** a protective device of fine fabric or wire mesh worn about the head by beekeepers when working with bees

beeves *pl of* BEEF *or of* BEEVE

beev·ish \'bēvish\ *adj* [*beeve* + *-ish*] **:** resembling or suggesting cattle

beeware \'ˌ\ *n* [¹*bee* + *ware*] **:** materials used by beekeepers

beeway \'ˌ\ *n* [¹*bee* + *way*] **:** BEE SPACE

beeweed \'ˌ\ *n* [¹*bee* + *weed*] **:** any of several bee plants; *esp* **:** an American woodland aster (*Aster cordifolius*)

beeyard \'ˌ\ *n* [¹*bee* + *yard*] **:** APIARY

bee·zer \'bēzə(r)\ *n* -S [perh. blend of *beak* and *sneezer*] *slang* **:** NOSE

bef *abbr* before

be·fall \bə'fȯl, bē-\ *vb* **be·fell** \-fel\ **be·fall·en** \-fȯlən, *also in poetry & sometimes + V in prose* -fōln\ **befalling; befalls** [ME *befallen*, fr. OE *befeallan* (akin to OHG *bifallan* to fall), fr. *be-* + *feallan* to fall — more at FALL] *vi* **1** *archaic* **:** to fall due **:** PERTAIN ⟨taking only what *befell* to him⟩ **2 :** to take place esp. as if by the prompting of destiny or fate **:** come to pass ⟨these things *befell* —George Santayana⟩ **3** *obs* **:** BECOME — used with *of* **~** *vt* **:** to happen or occur to esp. in the course of events ⟨the saddest thing that ~s a soul is when it loses faith —Alexander Smith⟩ **syn** see HAPPEN

be·fettered \bə, bē+\ *adj* [*be-* + *fettered*] **:** ENSLAVED

be·fezzed \bə'fezd, bē-\ *adj* [*be-* + *fez* + *-ed*] **:** wearing a fez

be·fit \bə'fit, bē-, *usu* -id·+V\ *vt* **befitted; befitted; befitting; befits** [ME *befitten*, prob. fr. *be-* + *fit*, adj.] **1 :** to accord with **:** be in harmony with **:** be proper or becoming to **:** SUIT ⟨clothing that ~s his position⟩ ⟨as *befitted* his New England background he was a staunch protectionist —Broadus Mitchell⟩ **2** *obs* **:** to fit out

befitting *adj* **1 :** SUITABLE, APPROPRIATE ⟨the matter was written in ~ prose⟩ ⟨the ~ elegance of a royal court⟩ **2 :** in harmony with moral, ethical, or social norms **:** PROPER, DECENT ⟨act in a ~ manner⟩ — **be·fit·ting·ly** *adv* — **be·fit·ting·ness** *n* -ES

be·flagged \bə'flagd, bē-, -aa(ə)gd, -aigd\ *adj* [*be-* + *flag* + *-ed*] **:** decorated with or as if with flags ⟨the ~ balcony⟩

be·flatter \bə, bē+\ *vt* -ED/-ING/-S [*be-* + *flatter*] **1 :** to dupe by flattery **2 :** to flatter greatly

be·flour \bə, bē+\ *vt* -ED/-ING/-S [*be-* + *flour*, n.] **:** to dust over with or as if with flour ⟨bees *~ed* with yellow⟩

be·flowered \bə, bē+\ *adj* [*be-* + *flower* + *-ed*] **:** adorned with flowers

be·flum \bə'fləm, bē-\ *vt* **beflummed; beflummed; beflumming; beflums** [*be-* + *flum;* perh. influenced by Sc *blaflum* to cajole] *chiefly Scot* **:** to deceive esp. by flattery

be·flustered \bə, bē+\ *adj* [*be-* + *flustered*] **:** much flustered

be·fog \bə, bē+\ *vt* **befogged; befogged; befogging; befogs** [*be-* + *fog*, n.] **1 :** to obscure with or as if with fog ⟨*befogged* roads⟩ ⟨cigar smoke *befogged* the room⟩ ⟨television . . . *befogged* with zigging and zagging lines —Philip Hamburger⟩ **2 a :** to make indistinct, vague, or confused ⟨the issue was *befogged* with bias⟩ **b :** to lessen or impair the clarity, perceptivity, or sensitivity of ⟨drink *befogged* his senses⟩ **c :** to throw into a state of uncertainty, indecision, or confusion **:** PUZZLE ⟨questions of rising or not and shaking hands or not ~ many people —Agnes M. Miall⟩ **syn** see OBSCURE

be·fool \bə, bē+\ *vt* -ED/-ING/-S [*be-* + *fool*, n.] **1 a :** to make a fool of **:** cause to appear foolish ⟨*~ing* a pedant with questions⟩ **b :** to lead on or astray esp. into something foolish or stupid **c :** to cause to believe something false **:** DECEIVE ⟨the masses . . . browbeaten and *~ed* by bureaucrats —A. R.Williams⟩ **2** *obs* **:** to call (a person) a fool **syn** see DUPE

¹**be·fore** \bə'fō(ə)r, bē-, -ō(ə)r,-ōə,-ō(ə)\ *adv* [ME *before, beforen*, adv. & prep., fr. OE *beforan*, fr. *be-* + *foran* before, fr. *fore* — more at FORE] **1 :** in advance **:** AHEAD ⟨racing on ~ to give warning⟩ ⟨the army encamped with its tanks covering the rear and some infantry units ~⟩ **2 :** in time past ⟨he had known it ~⟩ **:** PREVIOUSLY ⟨two weeks ~⟩ **:** ALREADY ⟨the names ~ mentioned⟩ — often used with *go* ⟨in terms of the experience that has gone ~ —C.E.Kellogg⟩ **3 :** in the future **:** to come ⟨forgetting the things that are behind, and stretching forth myself to those that are ~ —Phil 3:13 (DV)⟩ **4 :** EARLIER, SOONER **:** until then ⟨you'll get it tomorrow, not ~⟩ ⟨he was surprised at the news and said he hadn't known it ~⟩

²**before** \ˌ\ *prep* [ME *before, beforen*] **1 a :** preceding (a point, turn, or incident in time) **:** earlier than ⟨20 minutes ~ 12⟩ ⟨returning ~ dark⟩ ⟨making up his mind long ~ the meeting⟩ **b :** preceding (something or someone in a chronological series) ⟨he lived in New York as did his father ~ him⟩ **2 a :** in the presence of ⟨speaking ~ the conference⟩ **:** in sight or notice of **b :** face to face with **:** CONFRONTING ⟨powerless ~ such restrictions⟩ **c :** in defiance of **:** in firm opposition to ⟨~ successful crime he stood unmoved . . . the inflexible judge of its manifest wrong —W.L.Sullivan⟩ **3 a :** in advance of (someone or something moving in the same direction) **:** ahead of ⟨destroyers zigzagging ~ a convoy⟩ ⟨the captain going ~ his troops⟩ **b :** driven in front by ⟨refugees ~ barbarian armies⟩ **:** harassed by ⟨fleeing ~ a storm⟩ **c :** in the same direction as the main force of ⟨a ship running ~ a heavy sea⟩ ⟨sailing ~ the wind⟩ **4 a :** in a position facing, opposing, or close to **:** in front of ⟨stand ~ the fire⟩ **b :** just preceding (as in a spatial series) **:** next to ⟨the road to the left ~ the junction⟩ **:** just in front of **5 a :** at the disposal of **:** available to ⟨the six candidates ~ the people⟩ ⟨great sums of money were placed ~ the scientists⟩ **b :** in store for **:** AWAITING ⟨still thirty years of life ~ him —H.O.Taylor⟩ ⟨a whole glorious summer was ~ the children⟩ **6 a :** in the estimation of ⟨make the Europeans lose face ~ the common people —Peggy Durdin⟩ **b :** according to the precepts, doctrines, or views emanating from or associated with ⟨man and wife ~ God⟩ ⟨a crime ~ the law⟩ **7 a :** to be judged or acted on by ⟨the case went ~ the court⟩ ⟨a bill coming up ~ Congress⟩ **b :** under the official or formal consideration of ⟨in order that there may be a debate, a definite proposal . . . must ordinarily be ~ the House —C.J.Friedrich⟩ **8 :** occupying, inviting, or compelling the attention of ⟨the problems ~ the American public⟩ **9 a :** in greater esteem, significance, or value than ⟨thou shalt have none other gods ~ me —Deut 5:7 (AV)⟩ ⟨put profits ~ conscience⟩ **b :** more important than — used with *else* ⟨he is ~ all else a gentleman⟩ **10 :** in advance of **:** superior to ⟨~ all nations in cheap-car production⟩ **11 :** as a result of **:** in consequence of ⟨forests have dwindled ~ ax and saw —*Amer. Guide Series: Wash.*⟩ ⟨these archaic people . . . disappeared suddenly, evidently ~ the pressure of a new people —R.W. Murray⟩ **12 :** up to but not including or taking into account **:** exclusive of ⟨his yearly income ~ taxes⟩

³**before** \"\ *conj* [ME *before, beforen*, fr. *before, beforen*, prep.] **1 :** earlier than the time when ⟨~ the year was out⟩ — sometimes used archaically with a postpositive *that* ⟨it is not the custom of the Romans to give up any man, ~ that the accused have the accusers face to face —Acts 25:16 (ASV)⟩ **2 :** sooner than ⟨he will starve ~ he will steal⟩

beforehand \ˌ\ *adv (or adj)* [ME *before hand, beforen hand*, fr. *before, beforen* before + *hand*] **1 a :** in anticipation **:** so as to be prepared ⟨all equipment must be in the trucks ~⟩ ⟨taken . . . pains to inform himself ~ concerning the subject matter —Vera M. Dean⟩ **b :** in advance ⟨demanding his fee ~⟩ ⟨payment ~⟩ **2 :** BEFORE, PREVIOUSLY ⟨the city had ~ borne a different name⟩; *specif* **:** before the appointed time ⟨he arrived at the meeting place ~⟩ **3 a :** in a sound financial state **:** possessing enough or somewhat more than enough ⟨he was ever a little ~ and never lived precariously⟩ **b** *of money* **:** in reserve or excess ⟨having nothing ~⟩ **4 :** in a position to or being able to forestall or anticipate something — used with *with* ⟨a general ever ~ with his enemy⟩

be·fore·ness \ˌ\ *n* -ES **:** the condition of having existed previously **:** PREEXISTENCE **:** the quality or state of having been before

beforetime \ˌ\ *also* **be·fore·times** \-ˌtīmz\ *adv* [ME *beforetime*, fr. *before, beforen* + *time*] **:** FORMERLY ⟨neither shall the children of wickedness afflict them any more as ~ —2 Sam 7:10 (AV)⟩

be·fortune \bə, bē +\ *vb* -ED/-ING/-S [*be-* + *fortune*] *archaic* **:** BEFALL ⟨good things *befortuned* him⟩

be·foul \bə, bē +\ *vt* -ED/-ING/-S [ME *befoulen*, alter. (influenced by *foul*) of *befilen* to befoul, fr. OE *befȳlan*, fr. *be-* + *fȳlan* to foul — more at FILE] **1 :** to make foul with or as if with dirt or filth ⟨a building *~ed* with soot⟩ ⟨mudslinging *~ed* his speeches⟩ **2 a :** SLANDER, CALUMNIATE ⟨*~ing* his reputation⟩ **b :** DISGRACE, BLACKEN, DENIGRATE ⟨scandals that *~ed* the administration⟩

be·friend \bə, bē+\ *vt* -ED/-ING/-S [*be-* + *friend*, n.] **:** to act as a friend to **:** show kindness, sympathy, and understanding to ⟨~ a helpless person⟩

be·frilled \bə'frild, bē-\ *adj* [*be-* + *frill* + *-ed*] **:** furnished with frills

be·fringe \bə̇, bē +\ *vt* -ED/-ING/-S [*be-* + *fringe*, n.] **:** to border with a fringe

be·frogged \bə̇'frȯgd, bē-, -ägd\ *adj* [*be-* + *frog* + *-ed*] **:** adorned with frogging

be·fuddle \bə̇, bē +\ *vt* -ED/-ING/-S [*be-* + *fuddle*] **1 :** to dull, muddle, or stupefy ⟨a mind *befuddled* with fatigue⟩ ⟨the old doctor is *befuddled* with drink all the time —Ellen Glasgow⟩ **2 :** to throw into confusion or perplexity **:** PUZZLE ⟨the problem *befuddled* the experts⟩ — **be·fud·dle·ment** \-mənt\ *n* -s

be·furred \bə̇'fərd, bē-, -fə̄d\ *adj* [*be-* + *fur* + *-ed*] **:** adorned with fur

[1]**beg** \'beg, 'bāg — *some who have* ā *in* "*leg*" *and* "*egg*" *have* e *in* "*beg*"\ *vb* **begged; begged; begging; begs** [ME *beggen*, perh. alter. of OE *bedecian*; akin to Goth *bidagwa* beggar, OE *biddan* to entreat — more at BID] *vt* **1 :** to ask for as a charity esp. habitually or from house to house ⟨~ his bread from door to door⟩ **2 :** to ask earnestly for **:** request warmly or humbly **:** ENTREAT ⟨~ forgiveness⟩ — often used in expressions of polite deference ⟨I ~ your pardon⟩ ⟨I ~ leave to disagree⟩ **3 a :** EVADE, SIDESTEP ⟨Maynard ~*s* the difficulties set . . . by designating its principles as "simply Christian" —C.T.Harrison⟩ **b :** to assume the fact of established solution, settlement, or proof of (a question or issue) ⟨grave danger that these questions may be *begged* —Walter Moberly⟩ — compare PETITIO PRINCIPII **4 :** to obtain release of esp. by entreaty — used with *off* ⟨~ a person off from a duty⟩ ~ *vi* **1 :** to ask for alms or charity ⟨*begging* from door to door⟩ **:** live by asking for charity ⟨a license to ~⟩ **2 :** to ask earnestly **:** entreat humbly ⟨~ for mercy⟩ — often used as a term of polite deference ⟨I ~ to state⟩ **3** *of a dog or other pet animal* **:** to make a formalized gesture of request; *esp* **:** to sit erect on the haunches with the forepaws raised **4 :** DECLINE, RENEGE **:** back out — used with *off* ⟨men of stern morality ~ off from all discussions of . . . morality —R.H.Rovere⟩ **5 :** to reject the turned-up trump in the game of all fours thereby giving the dealer certain privileges

syn IMPLORE, ENTREAT, BESEECH, SUPPLICATE, ADJURE, IMPORTUNE: these seven verbs are closely related in all signifying the making of an appeal in some way. BEG is often used in certain forms of politeness ⟨I *beg* leave to return tomorrow⟩ Otherwise it suggests strongly the personal urgency of the appeal, often to the point of a certain self-abasement of the doer ⟨now that you're through, you come *begging* me to marry you —Barnaby Conrad⟩ ⟨turning to Foley he *begged* silently for some help —Morley Callaghan⟩ ⟨we watched the fat, lazy squirrels lollop inquisitively round us *begging* the crumbs —Wilfred Fienburgh⟩ ⟨he, casting himself prostrate on the ground, implored her forgiveness and *begged* to know her will —W.H.Hudson⟩ IMPLORE usu. emphasizes even more strongly than BEG personal urgency and earnestness although usu. implying more dignity in the doer ⟨how she pleaded, and *implored* me to wait —George Meredith⟩ ⟨the last look of my dear mother's eyes, which *implored* me to have mercy —Charles Dickens⟩ ⟨the one thing the doctor *implored* him to avoid was that kind of exertion —J.C.Powys⟩ ENTREAT suggests the earnestness of a persuasive petition, implying generally less personal, emotional involvement than do BEG or IMPLORE ⟨smooth-tongued barkers *entreat* passerby to stop and inspect bargains —*Amer. Guide Series: Tenn.*⟩ ⟨he did not *entreat* or plead; he announced —Margaret Deland⟩ ⟨he earnestly *entreated* her to name the day that was to make him the happiest of men —Jane Austen⟩ BESEECH, not as strong as ENTREAT in the suggestion of personal urgency, sometimes stresses an earnestness arising from anxiety or solicitude ⟨a Cape captain, whose bride *beseeched* him to write while he was away —R.W.Hatch⟩ ⟨the girl *besought* her so earnestly that Lady Drum was driven into warm language to defend herself —William Black⟩ ⟨a beggar *beseeches* him in the name of Allah —Jean & Franc Shor⟩ SUPPLICATE emphasizes the humbleness of the doer, suggesting strongly a respectful or prayerful attitude ⟨invite, entreat, *supplicate* them to accompany you —Earl of Chesterfield⟩ ⟨to visit the governor and *supplicate* for more welfare aid⟩ ADJURE usu. suggests a certain seriousness or solemnity of request, an invocation of duty or responsibility or of something bindingly sacred ⟨the wives and daughters . . . rushed about the camp . . . *adjuring* their countrymen to save them from slavery —J.A.Froude⟩ ⟨the student who seeks a closer acquaintance with the playwrights mentioned . . . is *adjured* to make any contact he can achieve with the living theater —W.Bridges-Adams⟩ ⟨"You must give the people an example of poverty, misery and denial," he sometimes *adjures* his disciples —*Time*⟩ IMPORTUNE implies an insistence, esp. in repetition, of appeal or request, usu. to the point of annoyance or irritation ⟨they are *importuned* to spread the official gospel throughout the community via their patients to the utmost of their ability —J.H.Means⟩ ⟨she knew how to look after him without ever imposing herself on him or *importuning* him —Edmund Wilson⟩

[2]**beg** \'beg\ *n* -s [Russ *beg*, *bek*, of Turkic origin; akin to Jagatai *bäg* beg, Turk *bey*] **:** a central Asian, Turkish, or Mogul Indian chieftain or official — often used as a title; compare BEY

beg *abbr* begin; beginning

be·gad \bə̇'gad, bē-, -gaa(ə)d\ *interj* [euphemism for *by God*] — a mild oath

be·gam \'bēgəm, 'bā-\ *var of* BEGUM 1

began *past of* BEGIN

be·gar \'bā,gär\ *n* -s [Hindi *begār*, fr. Per] *India* **:** forced labor

be·ga·ri \bā'gä(,)rē\ *n* -s [Hindi *begārī*, fr. Per, fr. *begār*] *India* **:** a forced laborer

begass *or* **begasse** *var of* BAGASSE

begat *archaic past of* BEGET

be·gats \bə̇'gats, bē-\ *n pl* [*begat* + *-s*; fr. its frequent use in the Bible, esp. Gen 5] **1** *slang* **:** a genealogical list ⟨the Old Testament ~⟩ **2** *slang* **:** OFFSPRING ⟨some ~ . . . died without issue —*Time*⟩

be·gaud \bə̇,bē+\ *vt* -ED/-ING/-S [*be-* + *gaud*] **:** to make gaudy

be·gem \bə̇, bē+\ *vt* **begemmed; begemmed; begemming; begems** [*be-* + *gem*, n.] **:** to adorn with or as if with gems ⟨a *begemmed* sword hilt⟩ ⟨morning sun *begemmed* the lake⟩

be·get \bə̇'get, bē-, *usu* -ed·+V\ *vt* **be·got** \-gät, *usu* -äd·+V\ *or archaic* **be·gat** \-gat, *usu* -ad·+V\ **be·got·ten** \-gät^ən\ *or* **begot; begetting; begets** [ME *begeten*, alter. (influenced by *geten* to get) of *beyeten*, fr. OE *begietan* to get, beget, fr. *be-* + *gietan* to get — more at GET] **1** *obs* **:** to acquire esp. through effort **2 a :** to procreate as the father **:** SIRE ⟨and Mehujael *begat* Methusael and Methusael *begat* Lamech —Gen 4:18 (AV)⟩ ⟨no conquering race ever lived . . . among a tributary one without *begetting* children on it —A.T.Quiller-Couch⟩ **b :** to give birth to **:** BREED ⟨excellent cows do not ~ only excellent daughters —V.A.Rice & F.N.Andrews⟩ **3** *obs* **:** to make (a woman) pregnant **4 :** to produce usu. as an effect or as a natural outgrowth ⟨economic dependency ~*s* a moral subserviency —J.M.Morse⟩ ⟨emotionally *begotten* rationalizations —Ernest & Pearl Beaglehole⟩

be·get·tal \-ged·ᵊl, -et^ᵊl\ *n* -s **:** the act or fact of being begotten

be·get·ter \-ged·ə(r), -etə(r)\ *n* -s [ME *begetere*, fr. *begeten* + *-ere* -er] **:** one that begets

[1]**beg·gar** \'begə(r), -ägə-\ *n* -s [ME *beggare*, *beggere*, fr. *beggen* to beg + *-are*, *-ere* -er — more at BEG] **1 a :** one that begs; *esp* **:** one that lives by asking for gifts **b :** one that asks (as for a gift) earnestly or humbly ⟨he must be a good ~ — money raiser the vestries call it —Nelson Rightmyer⟩ **2 :** a poor or impoverished person ⟨this system only created ~*s*, completely dependent on outside help —Darcy Ribeiro⟩ **3 :** FELLOW ⟨the poor little ~*s* in the orphanages⟩ ⟨a good-hearted ~⟩

[2]**beggar** \"\ *vt* **beggared; beggared; beggaring** \-g(ə)riŋ\ **beggars 1 :** to reduce to beggary **:** IMPOVERISH ⟨wars that ~ a nation⟩ **:** reduce the value of ⟨~*ing* the very policy he was advocating —*Time*⟩ **2 :** to reduce to inadequacy **:** exceed the resources of ⟨the costumes of the performers almost ~ description —Bess A. Garner⟩

beg·gar·li·ness \-gə(r)lēnə̇s, -lin-\ *n* -ES **:** the quality or state of being beggarly

[1]**beg·gar·ly** \-gə(r)lē, -li\ *adv* [ME, fr. *beggare* + *-ly*] *archaic* **:** in a mean, servile, or despicable manner ⟨entreated them ~ for alms⟩

[2]**beggarly** \"\ *adj* [[1]*beggar* + *-ly*] **1 :** befitting or like a beggar **:** marked by low mean inferior unrelieved poverty ⟨~ starved-out paupers —Anthony Trollope⟩ **2 :** meriting or arousing contempt or disdain esp. by being mean, scant, or paltry ⟨the poorest and most ~ things . . . in the whole range of criticism —George Saintsbury⟩ **syn** see CONTEMPTIBLE

beggar-my-neighbor \¦==(,)='==\ *n* **:** a game of cards in which the object is to gain all the opponent's cards

beggar's-buttons \¦==,==\ *n pl but sing or pl in constr* **:** BURDOCK; *esp* **:** its flower heads

beggar's dance *or* **begging dance** *n* **1 :** a dance of India and Central Europe performed for the purpose of obtaining gifts **2 :** an American Indian dance consisting largely of a masked procession and performed for the purpose of obtaining gifts

beggar's-lice *or* **beggar-lice** \'==,=\ *n pl but sing or pl in constr* **1 :** any of several plants esp. of the genera *Lappula*, *Desmodium*, and *Galium* bearing prickly or adhesive fruits that cling to clothing **2 :** the fruit of beggar's-lice

beggar's needle *n* **:** LADY'S-COMB

beggar-ticks *or* **beggar's-ticks** \'==,=\ *n pl but sing or pl in constr* **1 :** a plant of the genus *Bidens* **2 :** the fruit of beggar-ticks (sense 1) **3 :** BEGGAR'S-LICE **4 :** a plant of the genus *Agrimonia* **5 :** the fruit of beggar-ticks (sense 4)

beg-gar-ticks 2

beggarweed \'==,=\ *n* **1 :** any of various plants that grow in waste ground (as knotweed, spurry, and dodder) **2 :** any of several tick trefoils of the genus *Desmodium*; *esp* **:** a West Indian forage plant (*D. tortuosum*) cultivated in the southern U.S.

beg·gary \'begərē, 'bäg-, -gəri\ *n* -ES [ME *beggarie*, fr. *beggare* beggar + *-ie* -y] **1 :** the quality or state of being impoverished **:** PENURY ⟨the ~ to which the . . . tribesmen have been reduced —M.J.Herskovits⟩ **2 :** the class or occupation of beggars **3 :** the act of begging esp. as a livelihood **:** MENDICANCY ⟨suffered the bitterest privation, and were even . . . threatened with ~ —H.E. Barnes & H.P.Becker⟩ **4 :** BASENESS, CONTEMPTIBLENESS ⟨the ~ of his lies⟩ **5 :** mean impoverished appearance **:** DISREPUTABLENESS ⟨shabby and unshaven almost to the point of ~ —Edmund Wilson⟩

begged *past of* BEG

beg·giatoa \bə̇'jad·əwə, ,bejə'tōə\ *n*, *cap* [NL, fr. F. S. *Beggiato*, 19th cent. Ital. botanist] **:** a genus (the type of the family Beggiatoaceae) of colorless filamentous sulfur bacteria of the order Beggiatoales that in form and motility resemble algae of the family Oscillatoriaceae and that often form thick mats of unsheathed filaments in swamps, sulfur springs, and seawater — **beg·giato·a·ceous** \bə̇¦jad·ə¦wāshəs, ¦bejə,tō¦ā-\ *adj*

beg·giat·o·a·les \bə,jad·ə'wā(,)lēz\ *n pl*, *cap* [NL, fr. *Beggiatoa* + *-ales*] **:** an order of free-living bacteria having relatively large rigid cells often in filaments, lacking flagella and moving by gliding like some of the blue-green algae, and often containing sulfur granules within or on the surface of the cells — see BEGGIATOA

begging *pres part of* BEG

beg·ging·ly *adv* **:** in a begging manner

beg·hard \'be,gärd, -eg,härd,-egərd\ *n* -s *usu cap* [ML *Beghardus*, *Begardus*, prob. fr. OF *begard*] **:** a member of one of many semimonastic associations of laymen founded in the 13th century in the Low Countries in imitation of the Beguines and eventually proscribed as heretical by the medieval church and in the 14th century all but extinct

be·gild \bə̇, bē+\ *vt* [*be-* + *gild*] **:** to gild esp. to excess

be·gin \bə̇'gin, bē-\ *vb* **be·gan** \-'gan, -aa(ə)n\ *or dial* **be·gun** \-'gən\ **begun; beginning; begins** [ME *beginnen*, fr. OE *beginnan*, fr. *be-* + *-ginnan* to begin; akin to OE *onginnan* to begin, OHG *biginnan*, Goth *duginnan*] *vi* **1 a :** to perform or execute the first part of an action, activity, or procedure **:** START **:** set about or enter on some course or operation ⟨after the introduction, the speaker *began*⟩ ⟨the night shift ~*s* at five o'clock⟩ **b :** COMMENCE **:** show occurrence or performance of first steps or stages ⟨work on the project *began* in May⟩ **2 a :** to come into existence **:** ARISE **:** originate or be called into being ⟨World War I *began* in 1914⟩ ⟨the organization *began* at a discussion meeting⟩ **b :** to have initial or starting point ⟨the alphabet ~*s* with *A*⟩ **3 :** to do or succeed in the least degree **:** make an appreciable approach to doing ⟨can't even ~ to describe the beauty of the scene⟩ ~ *vt* **1 a :** to set about **:** go into activity of ⟨they *began* the attack at dawn⟩ — often used with the infinitive or gerund ⟨*beginning* to study⟩ ⟨he *began* to speak⟩ ⟨the children *began* laughing⟩ ⟨~ doubting his comments⟩ **b :** to perform the first steps or stages of **:** do or perform the first actions or activities of **:** enter on ⟨he *began* his career as a teacher⟩ ⟨he *began* his collection in early summer⟩ **2 a :** to found or call into being **:** bring about a start or establish an origin for ⟨he *began* the movement with a series of magazine articles⟩ ⟨~ a dynasty⟩ **b :** start on a way or course **:** INITIATE ⟨where I *began* poor Nell upon the woman's road to hell —John Masefield⟩ **c :** to come first in or come in an initial position in ⟨the letter *A* ~*s* the alphabet⟩

syn START, COMMENCE, INITIATE, INAUGURATE: BEGIN, START, and COMMENCE are often interchangeable in meaning. BEGIN, opposed to *end*, is general and lacks especial connotation ⟨*begin* a job⟩ ⟨*begin* a journey⟩ ⟨*begin* the day with hope⟩ START, opposed to *stop*, may apply esp. to the first actions, steps, or stages of a course, career, or progression ⟨the conversation stopped, and it refused to *start* again —Arnold Bennett⟩ ⟨the movement recently *started* by such psychoanalysts —H.J.Muller⟩ COMMENCE is sometimes more formal than BEGIN or START, more bookish in suggestion ⟨they sat down and tried to *commence* a conversation —George Meredith⟩ ⟨things never began with Mr. Borthrop Trumbull; they always *commenced* —George Eliot⟩ INITIATE always suggests taking or facilitating first steps or preliminary measures culminating in an actual start, without suggesting any necessary continuation ⟨the art of recording thought, invented ages ago, *initiated* history —A.C.Morrison⟩ ⟨a third section called Ardencroft was *initiated* by Frank Stephens, but was not developed —*Amer. Guide Series: Del.*⟩ INAUGURATE indicates a starting or a bringing into effect or operation with some formality, seriousness, notion of significance, sweep, utility, or service ⟨since it was *inaugurated* in 1894 the May Festival has presented numerous important American and world premieres —*Amer. Guide Series: Mich.*⟩ ⟨the New Light theology *inaugurated* by Jonathan Edwards —T.D.Bacon⟩ ⟨a passionately modern mind who feels that science has *inaugurated* a new era —J.C.Powys⟩ ⟨not until 1786 was a ferry *inaugurated* between the two towns —Green Peyton⟩

be·gin·ner \-'ginə(r)\ *n* -s [ME, fr. *beginnen* + *-er*] **:** one that begins anything; *specif* **:** a young or inexperienced person **:** TYRO

beginner's luck *n* **:** the good fortune felt to attend one's first ventures (as at gambling, hunting, or fishing)

[1]**be·gin·ning** \bə̇'giniŋ, bē-, -nēŋ\ *n* -s [ME, fr. gerund of *beginnen*] **1 :** the point at which something begins to exist ⟨the ~ of the world⟩ ⟨the ~ of the war fell in May⟩ **2 :** the first part **:** initial section or division ⟨the first few chapters at the ~ of a novel⟩; *specif* **:** the first third ⟨the ~ of the play was good but the middle and end were dull⟩ **3 :** anything that has given rise to something **:** ORIGIN, SOURCE ⟨nobody knows what the ~ of the feud was⟩ **4 a :** rudimentary stage **:** early period ⟨this small ~ political corruption was to grow to tremendous proportions —Carol L. Thompson⟩ — often used in pl. ⟨Canada has had a dramatic and colorful history, particularly in her ~*s* —J.D.Adams⟩ **b :** anything that is undeveloped, only partially realized, or far from completion ⟨the Alaska highway system . . . is still incomplete and still only a ~ —Harold Griffin⟩ **5 :** the act or action of calling or being called into existence ⟨ascribing the blame for the ~ of a war⟩ **6 :** the first principle or basic assumption ⟨the ~ of justice is the capacity to generalize and make objective one's private sense of wrong —Earl Warren⟩

[2]**beginning** \"\ *adj* [fr. pres. part. of *begin*] **1 :** just called into existence **:** INCIPIENT ⟨elected president of the ~ organization⟩ **2 a :** of the introductory part or first third ⟨the ~ chapters of a book⟩ **b :** very first **:** INITIAL ⟨the ~ canto of an epic —*New Yorker*⟩ **:** ORIGINAL ⟨he quickly modified his ~ plan⟩ **3 a :** treating the rudiments or basic elements of ⟨a course in ~ chemistry⟩ **b :** just becoming familiar with the rudiments, skills, practice, or routine ⟨a ~ machinist⟩ ⟨the ~ fisherman⟩ ⟨a ~ dentist⟩

beginning rhyme *n* **1 :** rhyme at the beginning of successive lines of verse **2 :** ALLITERATION

be·gird \bə̇, bē+\ *vt* **begirt** *also* **begirded; begirt; begirding; begirds** [ME *begyrden*, fr. OE *begyrdan*, fr. *be-* + *gyrdan* to gird — more at GIRD] **1 :** to bind about or around ⟨a warrior *begirt* with sword and dagger⟩ **2 :** to surround, envelop, or encompass ⟨*begirt* by wilderness enemies —V.L.Parrington⟩ ⟨we are *begirt* with spiritual laws —R.W.Emerson⟩

be·girdle \bə̇, bē+\ *vt* -ED/-ING/-S [*be-* + *girdle*] **:** to surround as if with a girdle

be·glamour \bə̇, bē+\ *vt* -ED/-ING/-S [*be-* + *glamour*, n.] **1 :** to impart glamour to **:** GLAMORIZE **2 :** to impress or deceive with glamour

beg·ler·beg \'beglə(r),beg\ *also* **beg·ler·bey** \-,bā\ *or* **beyler·bey** \'bālə(r),bā\ *n* -s [Turk *beylerbeyi*, fr. *beyler-* (pl. of *bey* prince) + *bey* + *-i* (possessive suffix)] **:** a governor of a province of the Ottoman Empire next in dignity to the grand vizier

be·gloom \bə̇, bē+\ *vt* [*be-* + *gloom*, n. or v.] **:** to make gloomy

be·gnaw \bə̇, bē+\ *vt*, *past part* **begnawn** [*be-* + *gnaw*] *obs* **:** to gnaw at ⟨the worm of conscience still ~ thy soul! —Shak.⟩

be·gob \bə̇'gäb, bē-\ *or* **be·gobs** \-bz\ *interj* [euphemism for *by God*] *Irish* — a mild oath

be·god \bə̇, bē+\ *interj* [euphemism for *by God*] — a mild oath

be·goggled \bə̇, bē+\ *adj* [*be-* + *goggle* + *-ed*] **:** wearing goggles

be·gone \bē, bə̇+\ *vi* [ME, fr. *be* (imper. of *been* to be) + *gone* — more at BE] **:** to go away **:** DEPART — used in the infinitive ⟨he was ordered to ~⟩ and esp. in the imperative ⟨gather up your gold now, and ~ from my sight —J.M.Synge⟩

be·go·nia \bə̇'gōnyə, -nēə, bē-\ *n* [NL, fr. Michel *Bégon* †1710 Fr. governor of Santo Domingo + NL *-ia*] **1** *cap* **:** a large genus of succulent herbs or rarely subshrubs (family Begoniaceae) native to the tropics but widely cultivated with asymmetrical leaves and monoecious flowers succeeded by 3-winged capsular fruit **2** -s **:** a plant of the genus *Begonia* — see FIBROUS-ROOTED BEGONIA, REX BEGONIA, TUBEROUS BEGONIA **3** -s **:** a deep pink that is bluer, lighter, and stronger than average coral (sense 3b), bluer than fiesta, and bluer and stronger than sweet william — called also *gaiety*

be·go·ni·a·ce·ae \=,=nē'āsē,ē\ *n pl*, *cap* [NL, fr. *Begonia*, type genus + *-aceae*] **:** a family of monoecious plants (order Parietales) distinguished by the asymmetrical leaves and consisting of five tropical genera of which *Begonia* is much the largest — **be·go·ni·a·ceous** \=¦=¦āshəs\ *adj*

begonia rose *n* **:** a moderate red that is bluer and lighter than cerise, claret (sense 3a), or average strawberry (sense 2a)

be·good *or* **be·goud** \bə̇'güd\ [ME (northern dial.) *begouthe*, alter. (influenced by *couthe* could, past of *can*) of *began*, past of *beginnen*] *chiefly Scot past of* BEGIN

be·gor·ra \bə̇'gȯrə, -är-, bē-\ *or* **be·gor·ry** \-rē, -ri\ *also* **be·gor** \-ȯ(ə)r, -är\ *interj* [euphemism for *by God*] *Irish* — a mild oath

begot *past of* BEGET

begotten *past part of* BEGET

be·gowk \bə̇, bē+\ *vt* [*be-* + Sc *gowk*, n.] *Scot* **:** to make a fool of

be·grime \bə̇, bē+\ *vt* -ED/-ING/-S [*be-* + *grime*] **1 :** to make dirty with grime ⟨*begrimed* streets⟩ **2 :** SULLY, TARNISH, CORRUPT ⟨graft had *begrimed* the town's politics⟩

be·grudge \bə̇'grəj, bē-\ *vt* -ED/-ING/-S [ME *begrucchen*, fr. *be-* + *grucchen*, *gruggen* to murmur, grudge — more at GRUDGE] **1 a :** to give reluctantly ⟨the government did not ~ the millions spent on flood control⟩ **b :** to yield or concede with displeasure ⟨they *begrudged* every minute taken from their work⟩ **2 a :** to look upon or acknowledge with reluctance, hesitation, or disapproval ⟨we shall not ~ this exquisite soul the pleasure of his sensations —C.I.Glicksberg⟩ **b :** to be annoyed by or take little pleasure in ⟨he *begrudged* reading newspapers because it meant taking "time from Tacitus and Horace" —E.W. Parks⟩ **3 :** to envy the pleasure or enjoyment of ⟨no one . . . has ever *begrudged* his recreations —J.E.Sayers⟩

be·grudg·ing·ly *adv* **:** in a begrudging manner **:** GRUDGINGLY

be·grutch \bə̇'grəch, -rüch\ [ME *begrucchen*] *now dial var of* BEGRUDGE

be·grut·ten \bə̇'grət^ən\ *adj* [*be-* + Sc *grutten*, alter. of ME *graten*, *greten*, fr. OE *grēten*, *grǣten*, past part. of *grǣtan*, *grētan* to weep — more at GREET] *Scot* **:** TEAR-STAINED

begs *pres 3d sing of* BEG, *pl of* BEG

beg·ti \'begtē, -ek-\ *also* **bek·ti** \-ek-\ *n* -s [Bengali] **:** a large percoid fish (*Lates calcifer*) of river mouths and brackish waters of eastern and southern Asia, New Guinea, and northern Australia that is esteemed as food and in India often reared in ponds — called also *cockup*, *giant perch*

be·guile \bə̇'gīl, bē, *esp bef pause or cons* -īəl\ *vb* -ED/-ING/-S [ME *begilen*, fr. *be-* + *gilen* to guile, deceive — more at GUILE] *vt* **1 a :** to lead or draw by deception ⟨*beguiled* into ambush⟩ **b :** to lead away **:** DIVERT ⟨*beguiled* from these prejudices only by the president's prestige⟩ **2 a :** DECEIVE, HOODWINK ⟨*beguiled* by vague promises⟩ **b :** to deprive by guile **:** CHEAT — used with *of* or *out of* ⟨worries ~ him of sleep⟩ **3** *obs* **:** to cause to fail **:** DISAPPOINT, SHATTER **4 :** to cause to dwindle or vanish painlessly or without notice ⟨*beguiling* sorrow with music⟩ ⟨the seven poems were written to ~ the tedium of a sea voyage —V.L.Parrington⟩ **5 :** to gain the notice of by the use of wiles **:** CHARM ⟨her ways *beguiled* him⟩ ~ *vi* **:** to deceive by wiles **:** CHARM ⟨all her intent was to ~⟩ **syn** see DECEIVE

be·guil·er \-īlə(r)\ *n* -s [ME *begiler*, fr. *begilen* + *-er*] **:** one that beguiles

beguiling *adj* **:** provoking pleased interest and diverting from concern or vexation **:** ATTRACTIVE, PLEASING, INTRIGUING — **be·guil·ing·ly** *adv*

bé·guin \bāgaⁿ\ *n* -s [F, lit., hood of a beguine (influenced in meaning by *s'embéguiner* to become infatuated, fr. *béguin* hood), fr. MF, fr. *béguine*] **:** INFATUATION ⟨the girl has a ~ for you —W.S.Maugham⟩

[1]**be·guine** \'bā,gēn, 'be-, =¦=; bə'g-\ *n* -s *usu cap* [MF, fr. OF] **:** a member of one of a number of semimonastic associations for women not bound by the vows of a religious but interested in devotional life and works of charity

[2]**be·guine** \bə̇'gēn, bā-\ *n* -s [AmerF *béguine*, fr. F *béguin* flirtation] **:** a vigorous popular dance of the islands of Saint Lucia and Martinique somewhat like the rumba

be·gum \'bēgəm, 'bā-\ *n* -s [Hindi *begam*, fr. a Turkic word akin to the fem. of Jagatai *bäg* beg — more at BEG] **1** *India* **:** a Muslim queen, princess, or lady of high rank **2** *Brit* **:** an Anglo-Indian heiress

be·gummed \bə̇, bē+\ *adj* [*be-* + *gum* + *-ed*] **:** smeared or clogged with or as if with gum

begun *dial past of* BEGIN, *past part of* BEGIN

be·gunk \bə̇'gəŋk\ *n* -s [*be-* + Sc *gunk*] *chiefly Scot* **:** a piece of deception **:** TRICK

be·half \bə̇'ha|f, bē-, -aa(ə)|f,-ai|f,-å|f,-ä|f\ *n*, *pl* **be·halves** \|vz\ [ME, fr. *be* by (fr. OE *be*, *bi*, *bī*) + *half* side — more at BY, HALF] **1** *archaic* **:** RESPECT, QUARTER — used as the object of *in* ⟨more can be said in this ~⟩ **2 :** INTEREST, BENEFIT, SUPPORT — used as the object of *in* or *on* and with a possessive noun or pronoun ⟨a good word in a friend's ~⟩ ⟨the senator who is now stumping the state on his own ~⟩ ⟨intervening in her ~ —Warren Beck⟩ — **in behalf of** *or* **on behalf of** *prep* **:** in the interest of **:** as the representative of **:** for the benefit of ⟨this letter is written in *behalf* of my client⟩

behari *usu cap*, *var of* BIHARI

be·hatted \bə̇, bē+\ *adj* [*be-* + *hat* + *-ed*] **:** wearing a hat **:** adorned with a hat

be·have \bə̇'hāv, bē-\ *vb* -ED/-ING/-S [ME *behaven*, fr. *be-* + *haven* to have — more at HAVE] *vt* **1 a :** to bear or comport (oneself) in a particular way ⟨the plaintiff *behaved* himself with great composure⟩ **b :** to conduct (oneself) in a correct, obedient, or proper manner ⟨he *behaved* himself, got good marks, never made a fuss, was always right —G.W.Brace⟩ **2** *obs* **:** RESTRAIN, REGULATE ~ *vi* **1 a :** to act or react in a particular way ⟨he *behaved* to the emperor as an equal —Edith Sitwell⟩ ⟨under fire the troops *behaved* admirably⟩ **b :** to conform to the accepted patterns of society ⟨his conscience that is trying to make him ~ —Weston La Barre⟩ **:** do the right thing or what one is told ⟨children who won't ~⟩ **2 a :** to perform or function in a particular way ⟨all vehicles *behaved* well on their test runs⟩ **b :** to react under stimulus in a particular way ⟨the alloy *behaved* unpredictably under intense heat⟩

syn CONDUCT, COMPORT, DEMEAN, DEPORT, ACQUIT, QUIT: BEHAVE indicates performing various actions or saying various things in the manner indicated by modifiers ⟨one must keep one's contracts, and *behave* as persons of honor and breeding should behave —Rose Macaulay⟩ ⟨you will bitterly reproach him in your own heart, and seriously think that he has *behaved* very badly to you —Oscar Wilde⟩ Used without modifiers, it indicates action and conduct adjudged proper and seemly; in this use it is common in relation to children and adolescents ⟨the average parent is likely to say that the child *behaves* if the child conforms to what the parent thinks is right —Morris Fishbein⟩ CONDUCT often applies to actions showing direction or control of one's actions or bearing with command, will, knowledge, and resolution ⟨he *conducted* himself with patience and tact, endeavoring to enforce the laws and to check any revolutionary moves —W.E.Stevens⟩ COMPORT, in this sense always reflexive, is somewhat more formal than BEHAVE and CONDUCT but lacks any other special suggestion ⟨the missionaries . . . *comported* themselves in a way that did not rouse general antagonism or they could have been easily ousted —E.H.Spicer⟩ ⟨a man is judged now by how well he *comports* himself in the face of danger —J.W.Aldridge⟩ ⟨after having seen him thus publicly *comport* himself, but one course was open to me — to cut his acquaintance —W.M.Thackeray⟩ In this sense DEMEAN and DEPORT are close synonyms for COMPORT; the former is becoming rare ⟨it shall be my earnest endeavor to *demean* myself with grateful respect towards her —Jane Austen⟩ The latter may suggest deportment according to a code ⟨Dido and Aeneas, in the "Roman d'Eneas", *deport* themselves in accordance with the strictest canons of courtly love —J.L.Lowes⟩ ACQUIT and QUIT, the latter archaic, are always used reflexively in this sense; they are likely to apply to action deserving praise or meeting expectations ⟨I trust we *acquit* ourselves worthily as custodians of this sacred mystery —Elinor Wylie⟩ ⟨he then *acquitted* himself well as a hard-working and level-headed chairman of the judiciary committee of the House —C.C.Pearson⟩ ⟨the endless heroes of life and death who still bravely meet their separate hours . . . and *quit* themselves like men —*Yale Rev.*⟩ **syn** see in addition ACT

be·hav·ior \bə'hāvyə(r), bē-\ *n* -S *see -or in Explan Notes* [alter. (influenced by *havior*) of earlier *behavour*, fr. ME, fr. *behaven* to behave + *-our* -or] **1 a :** the manner in which a person behaves in reacting to social stimuli ⟨his flustered ~ before women⟩ or to inner need ⟨his ~ under the impress of loneliness⟩ or to a combination thereof ⟨hunger and poverty left their mark on her adult ~⟩ **b :** an activity of a defined organism; *esp* **:** observable activity when measurable in terms of quantifiable effects on the environment whether arising from internal or external stimulus **c** (1) **:** anything that an organism does that involves action and response to stimulation (2) **:** the response of an individual, group, or species to the whole range of factors constituting its environment **2 a :** the treatment shown by a person toward another or others esp. in its conformity with or divergence from the norms of good manners or social decorum ⟨the gracious ~ of the hostess⟩ ⟨loyal ~ toward his brothers⟩ **b** *obs* **:** good manners **3 :** the peculiar reaction of (a thing) under given circumstances ⟨the ~ of a new car⟩ ⟨the ~ of dyes in certain weathers⟩ ⟨the ~ of steel under stress⟩

be·hav·ior·al \-yərəl\ *adj* **:** of or relating to behavior ⟨~ similarities⟩ ⟨~ disturbances⟩ — **be·hav·ior·al·ly** \-yərəlē, -li\ *adv*

be·hav·ior·al·ist \-yərələst\ *n* -S **:** one who studies, accepts, or observes the point of view of behavioristics

behavioral science *n* **:** a science (as psychology, sociology, or anthropology) dealing with human action and aiming at the establishment of generalizations of man's behavior in society —compare SOCIAL SCIENCE

behavior disorder *n* **:** a mental usu. functional disorder

be·hav·ior·ism \-yə,rizəm\ *n* -S **1 :** the doctrine that the data of psychology consist exclusively of the observable evidences of organismic activity esp. when expressible in operational or physicalistic terms — compare BEHAVIOR 1b, INTROSPECTIONISM, MENTALISM **2 :** the application of principles of behavioral science to industry, personality evaluation, the arts, or literary criticism **3 :** the characteristic behavior of a defined organism or group under defined conditions

¹be·hav·ior·ist \-yərəst\ *n* -S **:** one who accepts or assumes the point of view of behaviorism

²behaviorist \"\ *or* **be·hav·ior·is·tic** \¦⸗⸗¦ristik, -ēk\ *adj* **:** of or belonging to behaviorism ⟨~ psychology⟩ — **be·hav·ior·is·ti·cal·ly** \-tək(ə)lē, -ēk-, -li\ *adv*

be·hav·ior·is·tics \⸗,⸗⸗'⸗tiks, -ēks\ *n pl but sing in constr* **:** a physicalistic science of individual and social behavior wherein an organism's responses to its environment are studied

behavior problem *n* **1 :** symptomatic expression of emotional or interpersonal maladjustment esp. in children (as by nail-biting, enuresis, negativism, or by overt hostile or antisocial acts) **2 :** an individual evidencing maladjustment by indulging in behavior problems; *esp* **:** a child indulging in such problems

behavior psychology *n* **:** BEHAVIORISM

be·head \bə'hed, bē-\ *vt* -ED/-ING/-S [ME *beheden, beheveden*, fr. OE *beheāfdian*, fr. *be-* + *hēafdian* to behead, fr. *hēafod* head —more at HEAD] **1 :** to sever the head or crown from **:** DECAPITATE ⟨~ a prisoner⟩ ⟨~ a tree⟩ **2 a :** to divert the headwaters of (a stream) into another drainage system by stream piracy — compare BETRUNK **b :** to remove the upper part of the drainage area of (a stream) by wave erosion

be·head·al \-dᵊl\ *n* -S **:** BEHEADING

beheld *past of* BEHOLD

¹be·he·moth \bə'hēməth, bē'hēməth *also* 'bēə,mōth *sometimes* ⸗'⸗,mōth *or* ⸗'⸗,māth *or* '⸗⸗,māth *or* '⸗⸗,mōth\ *n* -S [ME *bemoth, behemoth*, fr. L *behemoth*, fr. Heb *bĕhēmōth*, pl. (expressing magnitude) of *bĕhēmāh* beast] **1** *often cap* **:** an animal, prob. the hippopotamus, described in Job 40: 15–24 (RSV) **2 :** something of oppressive or monstrous size ⟨a ~ of a book⟩ or power ⟨a ~ of a tractor⟩ or appearance ⟨he stood there, a dirty and unshaven ~⟩

²behemoth \"\ *adj* **:** very large **:** MONSTROUS ⟨~ football linesmen⟩ — **be·he·moth·i·an** \¦bē¦mōthēən, -māth-, -mōth-\ *adj*

behen *var of* BEN

be·hen·ate \bə'he,nāt, bə'hē,n-, 'bāə,n-, 'bēə,n-\ *n* -S [ISV *behenic* + *-ate*] **:** a salt or ester of behenic acid

be·hen·ic acid \bə'henik, -ēn-\ *n* [ISV *behen* (var. of ⁷*ben*) + *-ic*; prob. orig. formed as F *béhénique*] **:** a crystalline fatty acid $CH_3(CH_2)_{20}COOH$ occurring in the form of esters esp. in the fats and oils from seeds (as ben oil, peanut oil) and in some waxes — called also *docosanoic acid*

be·hest \bə'hest, bē-\ *n* -S [ME, fr. OE *behǣs*, fr. *behātan* to promise, fr. *be-* + *hātan* to promise, command, call — more at HIGHT] **1** *obs* **:** PROMISE ⟨the land of ~⟩ **2 a :** COMMAND ⟨at divine ~⟩ ⟨signs of imperfect obedience to military ~s —A.M. Young⟩ **b :** a strong often authoritative request **:** DEMAND ⟨at the ~ of Congress an investigation was made⟩ **c :** urgent prompting **:** insistent desire ⟨at the ~ of friends he would sometimes read his own poems aloud⟩

be·hight *vt, past or past part* **behight** *or* **behighted** *also* **be·hote**; *pres 3d sing* **behighteth** [ME *behighten, beheten*, alter. (influenced by *behight, behet*, past of *beheten*) of *beheten*, fr. OE *behātan*] **1** *obs* **:** PROMISE **2** *obs* **:** COMMAND **3** *obs* **:** CALL, NAME

¹be·hind \bə'hīnd, bē-\ *adv (or adj)* [ME *behinde, behinden*, fr. OE *behindan*, fr. *be-* + *hindan* from behind, behind — more at HIND] **1 :** in the place or situation left (as by someone or some thing gone or departed) ⟨leaving much unfinished work ~⟩ ⟨only a small group stayed ~⟩ ⟨little residue remained ~ after evaporation⟩ **2** *archaic* **:** to come **:** UNREALIZED ⟨his heritage that is yet ~⟩ **3 a :** in arrears ⟨~ with the rent⟩ ⟨~ in his dues⟩ **b :** in a secondary or inferior position ⟨lag ~ in competition⟩ **:** REMISS ⟨~ in his work⟩ — often used with a negative ⟨the opposition was not ~ in the use of bitter words⟩ **c :** SLOW ⟨the clock was ~⟩ ⟨the train was an hour ~⟩ **4 a :** in back ⟨the car ~⟩ **:** to the rear ⟨the men in poor condition fell ~ early in the march⟩ **b :** toward the back **:** BACKWARD ⟨to look ~⟩ **5 :** in the past **:** gone by ⟨the drab days in a furnished room in Rome seem well ~ —*Time*⟩ **6 :** BEYOND **:** on the other or far side of ⟨the stream, slowing through broad meadows, has the Green mountains ~ —H.E.McDaniel⟩

²behind \"\ *prep* [ME *behinde, behinden*, fr. *behinde, behinden*, adv.] **1 a** *of something having a front and back* **:** at the back of ⟨a garden ~ a house⟩ ⟨taking cover ~ barricades⟩ — sometimes used with a reflexive object ⟨he looked ~ him⟩ **b** — used as a function word to indicate anything that lies or intervenes between or as if between one thing (as an observer) and another ⟨hills hidden ~ clouds⟩ ⟨~ his friendly manners was maliciousness⟩ ⟨drop ~ the horizon⟩ **2 a** — used as a function word to indicate someone who has departed or is at a distance ⟨the staff remained ~ the troops⟩; often used with a reflexive object ⟨they left wives and children ~ them⟩ ⟨left ~ him a great reputation⟩ **b :** as past experience for ⟨believe that . . . we have ~ us, at least in most parts of the country, the crudest of the pioneering period —M.Eucharista⟩ ⟨with several generations of devoted service to the church ~ him —M.H.Thomas⟩ **c :** not in prospect for **:** gone by for ⟨his best jobs are all ~ him⟩ **3 a** (1) **:** FOLLOWING ⟨there was rain ~ the wind —H.D.Skidmore⟩ ⟨~ the band marched the infantry⟩ (2) **:** in pursuit of ⟨a fox with a pack of hounds ~ him⟩ **b** (1) **:** BELOW ⟨way ~ his last year's average⟩ **:** inferior to ⟨sales were only a few percentage points ~ those for the previous year⟩ **:** retarded in relation to ⟨~ the times⟩ ⟨with theory running ~ practice, we will not be surprised to meet some inconsistencies —Hunter Mead⟩ (2) **:** not up to but competing with ⟨the firm was close ~ the leader in the field⟩ (3) *of a pitcher in baseball* **:** in the situation of having thrown more balls than strikes to ⟨the pitcher was ~ the batter⟩ (4) *of a batter in baseball* **:** in the situation of having a count of more strikes than balls **4 a :** later than understood or stipulated ⟨a train ~ schedule⟩ ⟨~ time in his appointments⟩ **b** — used as a function word to indicate anything that belongs in a period later than or subsequent to another ⟨looking back ~ the vast technological superstructure of western civilization to a quieter day —H.J.J.Winter⟩ **5 a :** in the background of **:** as an ever-present quality or feature of ⟨~ United States-Mexican relations lies the constant question of unsettled damage claims —H.E.Davis⟩ **b :** out of the mind or consideration of ⟨he put unpleasant memories ~ him⟩ **c :** BEYOND ⟨an analysis of the story ~ the news⟩ **:** PAST ⟨whenever possible he has gone ~ the printed book to the manuscript —*Times Lit. Supp.*⟩ **6 a :** on the side of **:** SUPPORTING ⟨in a crisis Latin America would probably be ~ the U.S.⟩ **b :** serving as a foundation for or basis of **:** UPHOLDING, BACKING ⟨~ his arguments are years of experience⟩ ⟨a good picture . . . must have intelligent thinking ~ it —F.L.Mott⟩ **7 a :** serving as motivation for **:** PROMPTING, PROVOKING ⟨economic pressure was ~ the thievery⟩ ⟨the real reasons ~ his actions⟩ **b :** in control of **:** GUIDING, REGULATING ⟨the person ~ the wheel of a car⟩ ⟨~ the throttle of a locomotive⟩

³behind \"\ *n* -S [¹*behind*] **1 :** the back side (as of a garment) **2 :** BUTTOCKS — sometimes considered vulgar

behindhand \⸗'⸗,⸗\ *adv (or adj)* [²*behind* + *hand*] **1 :** in arrears **:** in debt ⟨a company that has been run ~ for years⟩ ⟨to live ~⟩ **2 :** REMISS ⟨were ~ in providing aid⟩ ⟨she was ~ in courtesy to Mrs. Andersen —Willa Cather⟩ **:** after the fact ⟨wise only ~⟩ **3 a :** behind the times **:** BACKWARD ⟨a country usually so ~ in matters of art⟩ **b :** in an inferior position **:** BEHIND ⟨men . . . are not in the least ~ with women in their love of flattery —Earl of Chesterfield⟩ **c :** behind schedule **:** not caught up ⟨~ with what one wants to do⟩ **syn** see TARDY

behind-the-scenes \⸗¦⸗⸗¦⸗\ *adj* **:** kept or made in secret or private **:** not revealed ⟨a *behind-the-scenes* conference⟩ ⟨the colonel has actually held *behind-the-scenes* power since 1949 —J.S.Roucek⟩

behite *past of* BEHIGHT

behither *prep* [*be-* + *hither*] *obs* **:** on this side of

behmenism *cap, var of* BOEHMENISM

be·hold \bə'hōld, bē-\ *vb* **be·held** \-'held\ **beheld** \"\ *or archaic* **be·hold·en** \-hōldən\ **beholding; beholds** [ME *beholden* to hold, keep, behold, fr. OE *behaldan, behealdan*, fr. *be-* + *haldan, healdan* to hold — more at HOLD] *vt* **1** *obs* **:** to look at **:** examine closely **:** WATCH **2 :** to receive the impression of through or as if through visual means **:** see intently and fully **:** APPREHEND, EXPERIENCE ⟨the author ~s life on earth as molded by forces that are blindly mechanical⟩ ⟨a truth . . . so central that it shall commend itself to the eye at whatever angle *beholden* —R.W.Emerson⟩ **~** *vi* **1** *obs* **:** LOOK **2** — used in the imperative as an interjection esp. to call attention ⟨~, he cometh with the clouds, and every eye shall see him —Rev 1: 7 (AV)⟩ **syn** see SEE

beholden \bə'hōldən, bē'-\ *adj* [ME, fr. *beholden*, past part. of *beholden*, fr. OE *behealden*, past part. of *behealdan*] **1 :** being under obligation to return a favor or gift ⟨getting support without becoming ~ for it⟩ **2 :** indebted (as for aid or inspiration) ⟨no poet likes to acknowledge that he is ~ to an older — or a contemporary one —O.S.J.Gogarty⟩ **3 :** DEPENDENT — usu. used with *to* ⟨domesticated animals are plainly dominated by and ~ to adult human beings —Weston La Barre⟩ ⟨politically ~ to the industrial strength of the state —R.E. McGill⟩

be·hold·er \-də(r)\ *n* -S [ME, fr. *beholden* + *-er*] **:** one that beholds

be·hold·ing \-dən\ *adj* [alter. of *beholden*] *now dial Brit* **:** OBLIGED, BEHOLDEN

be·hoof \bə'hüf, bē-\ *n, pl* **be·hooves** \-üvz\ [ME *behof*, fr. OE *behōf*; akin to OFris *behōf* advantage, MHG *behuof* something useful, business, purpose, ON *hōf* correct measure, OE *hebban* to raise — more at HEAVE] **:** ADVANTAGE, PROFIT — used in prepositional phrases ⟨spending the money directly for his own ~ —George Eliot⟩ ⟨diversions of public money to their own use and ~ —A.J.Nock⟩

be·hoove \bə'hüv, bē-\ *or* **be·hove** \-hōv\ *vb* -ED/-ING/-S [ME *behoven*, fr. OE *behōfian*, fr. *behōf*] *vt* **1** *obs* **:** to have need of **:** REQUIRE **2 a :** to be morally or ethically necessary for — usu. used impersonally ⟨it ~s the archaeologist as a scientist to work objectively —G.W.Brainerd⟩ **b :** to be fitting or proper for ⟨he played the piano well, as *behooved* the son of a musical father⟩ — usu. used impersonally ⟨it *behooved* Punch to fold up his clothes neatly on going to bed —Rudyard Kipling⟩ **3 :** to be worthwhile, advantageous, or profitable for — chiefly used impersonally ⟨it would ~ us to examine our motives⟩ **~** *vi* **1 :** to be necessary, fit, or proper — used esp. with *it* as the subject ⟨it *behoved* to pass these points swiftly and unobtrusively —John Buchan⟩ **2** *now Scot* **:** to be in duty bound **:** be obliged ⟨we ~ to rejoice at it —E.B.Ramsay⟩

be·hoove·ful *or* **be·hove·ful** \-fəl\ *adj* [ME *behofful, behoveful*, fr. *behof* + *-ful*] *archaic* **:** ADVANTAGEOUS, PROFITABLE, NEEDFUL

be·hoov·ing·ly *adv* **:** in a behooving manner

behote *past of* BEHIGHT

be·howl \bə, bē+\ *vt* -ED/-ING/-S [*be-* + *howl*] **:** to howl at (as in lamentation)

be·hung \bə, bē+\ *adj* [fr. past part. of obs. *behang* to hang around, fr. ME *behangen*, fr. OE *behōn*, fr. *be-* + *hōn* to hang — more at HANG] **:** HUNG, DRAPED — used with *with* ⟨a hall ~ with decorations⟩

bei·del·lite \bī'de,līt\ *n* -S [*Beidell*, locality in Colo. + E *-ite*] **:** a mineral ideally $Ca_{0.16}Al_3Si_{3.17}O_{10}(OH)_2$ that is a common constituent of certain clays and consists of basic aluminosilicate with exchangeable calcium, sodium, or other cation

¹beige \'bāzh\ *n* -S [F, perh. fr. It *bambagia* cotton, fr. ML *bambac-, bambax*, fr. MGk *bambak-, bambax*, prob. fr. a Turkish word represented now by Turk *pamuk* cotton, prob. of Per origin; akin to Per *pamba* cotton] **1 :** cloth (as dress goods) made of natural undyed wool **2 a :** a variable color averaging light grayish yellowish brown **b :** a pale to grayish yellow

²beige \"\ *adj* [F, fr. *beige*, n.] **1 :** of the color beige **2 :** having the natural color — used of fabrics made of undyed or unbleached wool

beige brown *n* **:** a grayish yellowish brown to light olive brown — called also *mist brown*

beige gray *n* **:** MOUSE 4a

bei·gnet \(')bān¦yā\ *n, pl* **beignets** \-ā(z)\ [F, fr. MF *bignet, buignet*, fr. *buigne* bump, bruise] **:** FRITTER

bein \'bēn\ *var of* BIEN

¹be·ing \'bēiŋ, 'bē·ēŋ, *rap.* 'bēŋ\ *n* -S [ME, fr. gerund of *been, beon* to be — more at BE] **1 a :** the quality or state of existing **:** material or immaterial existence ⟨artistic form comes into ~ only when two elements are successfully fused —Carlos Lynes⟩ **b** (1) **:** something that is more abstract and has less intension than existence, nonexistence, or any other predicate ⟨pure ~ is the empty absolute —W.T.Harris⟩ — used esp. by Hegelians (2) **:** something that is logically conceivable and hence capable of existence **:** something that has or may have reality (3) **:** something that exists as an actuality or entity in time or space or in idea or matter (4) **:** the totality comprising the possible and the actual **:** something that is common to the objects within a class and to the objects not included in the same class **c :** conscious or mortal existence **:** LIFE ⟨the mother who gave him his ~⟩ **2 :** the complex of physical and spiritual qualities that constitute an individual ⟨it thus enlarges our ~ and gives us strength —M.R.Cohen⟩ **:** PERSONALITY ⟨one of history's most enigmatic ~s⟩ **3 a** *now dial Eng* (1) **:** LIVELIHOOD, LIVING (2) **:** dwelling place **:** HOME **b** *archaic* **:** station in life **:** STANDING **4 :** ESSENCE ⟨an analysis that probes the very ~ of religion⟩ **5 a :** HUMAN, PERSON ⟨always a well-dressed ~⟩ **b :** INDIVIDUAL ⟨a human ~⟩ ⟨the incredible ~s you see in the circus⟩

²being \"\ *pres part of* BE

³being \"\ *adj* [ME, fr. pres. part. of *been, beon* to be] **:** PRESENT — used postpositively with *time* ⟨enough for the time ~⟩

⁴being \" *or more often* 'bēən *or* 'bēn; "*being as*" *is often* 'bēənz *or* 'bēnz\ *conj, now dial* **:** SINCE, BECAUSE ⟨~ I'm late already⟩ — often used with *as* or *that* ⟨~ that he's your cousin⟩ ⟨~ as it's you⟩

be·ing·less *pronunc at* ¹BEING + ləs\ *adj* **:** having no being **:** not existing ⟨to be meaningless is to be ~ —J.H.Muirhead⟩

be·ing·ness *n* **:** the quality of having existence

bei·ra *also* **bai·ra** \'bīrə\ *n* -S [native name in Africa] **:** a small antelope (*Dorcatragus megalotis*) of Somaliland that is purplish black and brightly marked with yellowish fawn

bei·rut \(')bā¦rüt, *usu* -üd·+V\ *adj, usu cap* [fr. *Beirut*, Lebanon] **:** of or from Beirut, the capital of Lebanon **:** of the kind or style prevalent in Beirut

bei·sa \'bāzə, -,zä\ *n* -S [Amharic *be'zā*] **:** an antelope (*Oryx beisa*) found in Somaliland and northeastern Africa

be·ja \'bājə\ *n, pl* **beja** *or* **bejas** *usu cap* **1 a :** a nomadic pastoral people living between the Nile and the Red sea — compare BENI AMER, BISHARIN, HADENDOA **b :** a member of such people **2 :** the Cushitic language of the Beja people

be·jab·bers \bə'jabə(r)z\ *also* **be·ja·bers** \-jā-\ *interj* [euphemism for *by Jesus*] — a mild oath; used in noun function virtually without meaning ⟨beat the ~ out of him⟩

bejade *vt* -ED/-ING/-S [*be-* + *jade*] *obs* **:** to tire out **:** JADE

be·jan \'bējən\ *or* **be·jant** \'bējənt\ *also* **ba·jan** \'bājən\ *n* -S [F *béjaune*, fr. MF *becjaune* beak of young birds, fr. *bec* beak + *jaune* yellow — more at BEAK, JAUNDICE] **:** a freshman at certain Scottish universities

bej·el \'bejəl\ *n* -S [Ar *bajlah*] **:** a disease that is chiefly endemic in children in northern Africa and Asia Minor, is marked by bone and skin lesions, and is caused by a spirochete of the genus *Treponema*

be·jesuit \bə, bē+\ *vt* -ED/-ING/-S [*be-* + *jesuit*] **:** to make Jesuitic

be·je·sus \bə'jēzəs, bē- *also* -zəz; *esp by speakers subject to Irish influence* -jā-\ *interj* [alter. of *by Jesus*] — a mild oath; used in noun function virtually without meaning ⟨kick the ~ out of him⟩

be·jewel \bə, bē+\ *vt* [*be-* + *jewel*] **:** to ornament with or as if with jewels

be·ju·co \bə'hü(,)kō\ *n* -S [Sp, fr. Taino] **1 :** a climbing woody vine of the tropics with the habit of a liana **2** *Philippines* **:** RATTAN

be·juggle \bə, bē+\ *vt* [*be-* + *juggle*] **:** to deceive as if by sleight of hand **:** DELUDE, CHEAT

be·kah *or* **be·ka** \'bā(,)kä, -kə\ *n* -S [Heb *beqa'*] **:** an ancient Hebrew unit of weight equal to half a shekel

be·kiss \bə, bē+\ *vt* [*be-* + *kiss*] **:** to kiss intensely or excessively

be·knave \"+\ *vt* -ED/-ING/-S [*be-* + *knave*, n.] **:** to call knave **:** treat as a knave

bek·ra \'bekrə\ *n* -S [prob. native name in India] **:** FOUR-HORNED ANTELOPE

bekti *var of* BEGTI

¹bel \'bel\ *also* **bael** \", 'bāl, 'bīl\ *n* -S [Hindi *bel* fruit of the bel, fr. Skt *bailva*, fr. *bilva* bel tree, of Dravidian origin; akin to Tamil *vilā, viḷavu* bel tree] **1 :** a thorny tree (*Aegle marmelos*) of India **2 :** the aromatic edible fruit of the bel tree — called also *Bengal quince, golden apple*

²bel \'bel\ *n* -S [after Alexander Graham *Bell* †1922 Scottish-Am. inventor of the telephone] **:** ten decibels — abbr. *b*

bel *abbr* below

be·labor \bə, bē+\ *vt, see -or in Explan Notes* [*be-* + *labor*] **1 a** *obs* **:** to work diligently on or at **b :** to work on or at to absurd lengths ⟨~ an argument⟩ ⟨~ the obvious⟩ **2 a :** to beat soundly **b :** ASSAIL, ATTACK ⟨she ~s the foibles of grandparents, great-aunts, uncles, and cousins —Virgilia Peterson⟩ **syn** see BEAT

be·lah \'bēlə\ *also* **be·lar** \-lə(r)\ *n* -S [native name in Australia] **1 :** a beefwood (*Casuarina glauca*) of Australia **2 :** a tall forest tree (*Acacia excelsa*) of Queensland with oblong phyllodia and globular heads of flowers

belamour *n* -S [MF *bel amour* fair love, fr. *bel* fair, beautiful + *amour* love — more at BEAUTY, AMOUR] *obs* **:** one who is loved

belanda *cap, var of* BLANDA

be·late \bə, bē+\ *vt* -ED/-ING/-S [*be-* + *late*, adj.] *archaic* **:** to retard or make late **:** DELAY

be·lat·ed \bə'lādəd, bē-, -ātəd\ *adj* **1** *archaic* **:** overtaken by night **:** BENIGHTED **2 a :** delayed beyond the usual time ⟨one of the men was ~ and did not join us at all —B.A.Botkin & A.F.Harlow⟩ **b :** staying, existing, or appearing past the normal time or season ⟨nothing but an occasional rabbit and a ~ heron —John Buchan⟩ **c :** OUT-OF-DATE, PASSÉ ⟨his ideas are now quite ~⟩ — **be·lat·ed·ly** *adv* — **be·lat·ed·ness** *n* -ES

be·laud \bə, bē+\ *vt* [*be-* + *laud*] **:** to praise esp. unduly or excessively

¹be·lay \bə'lā, bē-\ *vb* -ED/-ING/-S [ME *beleggen*, fr. OE *belecgan*, fr. *be-* + *lecgan* to lay — more at LAY] *vt* **1** *obs* **:** ORNAMENT, ADORN **2** *obs* **a :** BESIEGE **b :** WAYLAY **c :** to occupy (a place) for the purpose of intercepting or guarding **3 a :** to secure (as a rope or cable) by one or more figure-eight turns around a cleat, pin, or bitt **b :** to make fast **:** fasten down ⟨~*ing* ammunition on deck⟩ **4** *naut* **:** STOP **:** hold back on ⟨~ that last order⟩ **:** CANCEL, DISREGARD **5 a :** to secure (a person) at the end of a rope ⟨our guides ~*ed* us and accepted belays from us —*Appalachia*⟩ ⟨~*ing* each other over the difficult places —*Nat'l Geographic*⟩ **b :** to secure (a rope) to a person or to a firm object **~** *vi* **1** *chiefly naut* **:** to be made fast ⟨knowing where each rope ~s on deck⟩ **2** *naut* **:** STOP, QUIT — used in the imperative ⟨~ there⟩ **3 :** to make fast by belaying ⟨he kept going when he ought to have ~*ed*⟩

²belay \"\ *n* -S **1 :** the obtaining of a hold (as for a rope) during mountain climbing ⟨~s are more difficult to secure on ice and snow than on rock —K.A.Henderson⟩ **2 :** a method of obtaining a hold or anchor (as for a rope) during mountain climbing **3 :** something to which a mountain climber's rope is anchored (as a projection of rock or an embedded piton)

belaying pin *n* **1 :** a pin around which ropes on shipboard are belayed to make them fast **2 :** a rock projection used by mountain climbers to belay a rope

belaying pin 1

bel can·to \(')bel 'kän,tō, -ȧn-\ *n* [It, lit., beautiful singing] **:** operatic singing originating in 17th century and 18th century Italy and stressing ease, purity, and evenness of tone production and an agile and precise vocal technique

¹belch \'belch\ *vb* -ED/-ING/-S [ME *belchen*, fr. OE *bealcian*] *vi* **1 :** to expel gas suddenly from the stomach through the mouth **2 :** to erupt, explode, or detonate violently ⟨artillery growled and ~*ed* on the horizon —Earle Birney⟩ **3 :** to issue forth spasmodically **:** GUSH ⟨the wind ~*ing* down the narrow alleys —G.G.Carter⟩ ⟨obscenities ~*ed* out of him —Albert Morgan⟩ **~** *vt* **1 a :** to throw out or cast forth violently **:** EJECT ⟨smokestacks of rumbling smelters ~ forth their fumes —Tom Marvel⟩ **b :** to vent forcibly **:** EMIT, EJACULATE ⟨~*ing* blasphemies⟩ **2 a :** to expel (gas) from the stomach suddenly **:** ERUCT **b :** to burp (a baby)

²belch \"\ *n* -ES **1 :** an act or instance of belching **:** ERUCTATION

2 : a sudden violent gush ⟨a ~ of flame⟩ ⟨a ~ of angry words⟩ **3 :** beer of poor quality

¹bel·cher \'belchə(r)\ *n* -s [after James *Belcher* †1811 Eng. pugilist] **1 :** a blue neckerchief having large white spots with dark blue spots at their centers **2 :** a multicolored handkerchief worn about the neck

²belcher \"\ *adj, often cap* [fr. the name *Belcher*] **:** BROAD — used of jewelry (as of rings and the links of chains)

beld \'beld\ *Scot var of* ¹BALD

bel·dam \'beldəm, -,dam, -,daa(ə)m\ *or* **bel·dame** \-,dəm, -,dām\ *n* -s [ME *beldam*, fr. MF *bel* fair, beautiful + ME *dam, dame* lady, mother — more at BEAUTY, DAME] **1** *obs* **:** GRANDMOTHER **2 :** a woman of advanced age ⟨old Lady Shropshire and some other old ~ —Edith Sitwell⟩ **3 a :** an old and loathsome woman **:** HAG **b :** a raging woman **:** VIRAGO ⟨performed in an opera house with a posse of fat ~s throwing themselves about the stage —H.L.Mencken⟩

be·lea·guer \bə'lēgə(r), bē-\ *vt* **beleaguered; beleaguered; beleaguering** \-g(ə)riŋ\ **beleaguers** [D *belegeren*, fr. *be-* + *leger* camp, fr. MD *lēgher*; akin to OHG *legar* couch, lair — more at LAIR] **1 :** to surround with an army so as to prevent escape **:** BESIEGE, BESET ⟨~ a town⟩ **2 :** to hem in **:** bottle up **3 :** to subject to oppressive or grievous forces **:** HARASS ⟨pests that ~ Alberta wheat farmers —*Lamp*⟩ ⟨~*ed* parents⟩

be·lecture \bə, bē+\ *vt* [*be-* + *lecture*] **:** to subject to much lecturing

belee *vt, past part* **beleed** [*be-* + *lee*, n.] *obs* **:** to cut off from or as if from favorable wind ⟨I . . . must be *beleed* and calmed —Shak.⟩

be·lém *or* **be·lem** \bə'lem\ *adj, usu cap* [fr. *Belém* or *Belem*, Brazil] **:** of or from the city of Belém, Brazil **:** of the kind or style prevalent in Belém

bel·em·nite \'beləm,nīt, bə'lem-\ *n* -s [F *bélemnite*, fr. Gk *belemnon* dart + F *-ite*; akin to Gk *belos* arrow, *ballein* to throw — more at DEVIL] **:** a conical calcareous Mesozoic fossil tapering to a point at the lower extremity, having a conical cavity at the other end that is usu. broken but when perfect contains a small chambered phragmocone prolonged on one side into a delicate concave blade, and being the internal shell of any of numerous extinct cephalopods (family Belemnitidae) related to the surviving spirulas — compare THUNDERSTONE — **bel·em·nit·ic** \¦beləm¦nid·ik, -,lem-\ *adj*

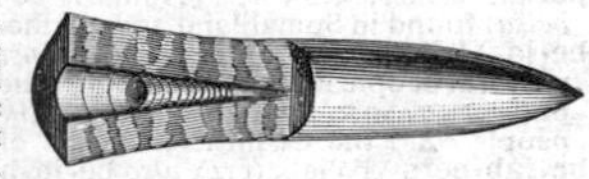
belemnite (partly in section)

bel·em·nit·i·dae \,beləm'nid·ə,dē\ *n pl, cap* [NL, fr. *Belemnites*, type genus (fr. F *bélemnite* or E *belemnite*) + *-idae*] **:** a family of extinct Mesozoic dibranchiate cephalopods comprising the belemnites

¹bel·em·noid \'beləm,nȯid, bə'lem-\ *adj* [Gk *belemnon* dart + E *-oid*] **1 :** shaped like a dart **2** [NL *Belemnoidea*] **:** of, relating to, or like the Belemnoidea

²belemnoid *n* -s **:** a belemnite or a closely related cephalopod

bel·em·noi·dea \,beləm'nȯidēə\ *n pl, cap* [NL, fr. *Belemnites* + *-oidea*] **:** an order or other division of Dibranchiata comprising the belemnites and sometimes the genus *Spirula*

belemnoid process *n* **:** STYLOID PROCESS

beleper *vt* [*be-* + *leper*] *obs* **:** to affect with or as if with leprosy

bel es·prit \,bel,e'sprē, ,belə's-\ *n, pl* **beaux es·prits** \,bō,ze'sprē, ,bōzə's-\ [F, lit., fine mind] **:** a person with a fine and gifted mind ⟨as a *bel esprit* she despised pedantry whether in a man or in a bluestocking —Robert Halsband⟩

bel étage \belātäàzh\ *n* [F, lit., beautiful story] **:** the chief story of a house

be·letter \bə, bē+\ *vt* [*be-* + *letter* (of the alphabet)] **:** to decorate the name of (a person) by appending abbreviations of official or academic rank ⟨the most academic and ~*ed* conventionalist —Joseph Macleod⟩

bel·fast \'bel,fast, 'beu̇,f-, -aa(ə)st,-aist,-ast; *in Belfast often, in US also* ='=; *in US also* 'belfəst\ *adj, usu cap* [fr. *Belfast*, Ireland] **:** of or from Belfast, the capital of Northern Ireland **:** of the kind or style prevalent in Belfast

bel·fry \'belfrē, -ri\ *n* -ES [ME *belfray* tower, bell tower, alter. (influenced by ME *belle* bell or ML *belfredus* tower) of *berefreid, berfrey*, fr. OF *berfrei*, fr. MHG *bervrit*, prob. fr. ML *berfredus, belfredus, balfredus*, perh. fr. an (assumed) L word derived fr. Gk *pyrgos phorētos* movable war tower] **1 a :** BELL TOWER; *esp* **:** one surmounting or attached to another structure — compare CAMPANILE, CARILLON **b** *obs* **:** the bell ringer's floor or room under the bells in a tower **c** (1) **:** a room in which the bell is hung in a tower (2) **:** a cupola, turret, or framework designed to enclose a bell **d :** the framing by which a ship's bell is suspended **2** *slang* **:** HEAD **:** mental capacities ⟨man's cocksureness that he was master of his own ~ —*Newsweek*⟩ — see ³BAT

belfry 1a

bel·ga \'belgə\ *n* -s [F, fr. L *Belga* a member of the Belgae] **:** a former unit of value in Belgium equivalent to five francs and used esp. in foreign exchange; *also* **:** a coin worth one belga

bel·gae \'bel,jē, -l,gī\ *n pl, usu cap* [L] **:** a people occupying northern France and Belgium in Caesar's time who were prob. of Celtic stock and may have been the ancestors of the modern Belgians

belgard *n* -s [It *bel guardo*] *obs* **:** a loving look

¹bel·gian \'beljən *sometimes* -jēən\ *adj, usu cap* [*Belgium*, country of Europe + E *-an*] **1 :** of, relating to, or characteristic of Belgium **2 :** of, relating to, or characteristic of the Belgians

²belgian \"\ *n* **1** -s *cap* **:** a native or inhabitant of Belgium — compare FLEMING, WALLOON **2** *usu cap* **:** a Belgian breed of heavy draft horses that are usu. roan or chestnut in color and have massive compact deep bodies and esp. well-developed hindquarters

belgian block *n, usu cap 1st B* **:** a stone paving block cut as a truncated pyramid with base 5 to 6 inches square, depth 7 to 8 inches, and the face opposite the base not more than 1 inch smaller than the base; *also* **:** any stone paving block

belgian endive *n, usu cap B* **:** ENDIVE 2

belgian fence *n, usu cap B* **:** a trellis with diamond-shaped openings used to support espaliered fruit trees

belgian hare *n, usu cap B* **:** a rabbit of a breed of slender long-legged long-eared domestic rabbits of a dark red or mahogany color

belgian pansy *n, usu cap B* **:** the common pansy with blended, blotched, or streaked petals

belgian sheepdog *or* **belgian shepherd** *n, usu cap B* **:** a dog of a breed of hardy working dogs developed in Belgium esp. for herding sheep, being about 23 inches in height and over 50 pounds in weight, and occurring in two varieties — see GROENENDAEL, MALINOIS

bel·gic \'beljik\ *adj, usu cap* [L *Belgicus*, fr. *Belgae* + *-icus* -ic] **1 :** of, relating to, or characteristic of the Belgae **2 :** BELGIAN

bel·gium \'beljəm *sometimes* -jēəm\ *adj, usu cap* [fr. *Belgium*, country of Europe] **:** of or from Belgium **:** of the kind or style prevalent in Belgium **:** BELGIAN

belgo- *comb form, cap* [*Belgium* + *-o-*] **1 :** Belgium **:** Belgian ⟨*Belgo*phile⟩ **2 :** Belgium and ⟨*Belgo*-Luxembourg⟩ **:** Belgian and ⟨*Belgo*-Dutch⟩

bel·grade \'bel,grād *also* -ād *or* -ad *or* -ȧd *or* -aa(ə)d *or* ='=\ *adj, usu cap* [fr. *Belgrade*, Yugoslavia] **:** of or from Belgrade, the capital of Yugoslavia **:** of the kind or style prevalent in Belgrade

bel·gra·via \bel'grāvēə, -vyə\ *n* -s *usu cap* [*Belgrave* Square, London, center of a fashionable residential section in the 19th cent.] **:** a fashionable residential section — **bel·gra·vian** \(')=¦=vēən, -vyən\ *adj, usu cap*

be·lial \'bēlēəl, -lyəl\ *n* -s *usu cap* [Heb *bĕlīya'al*, prob. fr. *bĕlī* without + *ya'al* use] **:** worthlessness or wickedness — often personified in the Old Testament ⟨children of *Belial* —Deut 13:13 (DV)⟩

be·libel \bə, bē+\ *vt* [*be-* + *libel*] **:** to attack with libels **:** CALUMNIATE

be·lie *also* **be·ly** \bə'lī, bē-\ *vt* **belied; belied; belying; belies** [ME *belien*, fr. OE *belēogan*, fr. *be-* + *lēogan* to lie — more at LIE] **1** *archaic* **:** to tell lies about **:** defame by lies ⟨~ a person shamefully⟩ **2** *obs* **:** to deny the authority, presence, or validity of **:** REJECT **3 a :** to give a false impression of ⟨the rasping and combative voice . . . which *belied* him because he was really friendly and good-humored —J.J.Mallon⟩ **b** (1) **:** to stand in contrast to ⟨a hard pair of eyes that *belied* his unmanly, almost effeminate face —Barnaby Conrad⟩ (2) **:** to present an appearance that is not in agreement with ⟨the imperturbable gentlemen . . . nearly all ~ their origins —Bill Wolf⟩ **4 a :** to prove false ⟨the event has *belied* this reasoning —Walter Moberly⟩ **b :** to run counter to **:** CONTRADICT ⟨at first sight Home Term Court . . . appeared to ~ all the rosy things I had heard about it —Katherine T. Kinkead⟩ **5 :** to cover up **:** HIDE, DISGUISE ⟨an air of rural charm . . . ~s the community's industrial activity —*Amer. Guide Series: Pa.*⟩ **syn** see MISREPRESENT

be·lief \bə'lēf, bē-, *rap.* 'blēf\ *n* -s [alter. (influenced by such pairs as E *grief: grieve*) of ME *beleve, beleave*, prob. alter. (influenced by *beleven* to believe) of OE *gelēafa*, fr. *ge-*, collective prefix + *lēafa* belief; akin to *lēfan, lȳfan* to allow, believe — more at CO-, BELIEVE] **1 :** a state or habit of mind in which trust, confidence, or reliance is placed in some person or thing **:** FAITH **2 a :** something believed; *specif* **:** a statement or body of statements held by the advocates of any class of views **b :** trust in religion **:** persuasion of the validity of religious ideas ⟨the war of ~ against unbelief —Thomas Carlyle⟩ **:** a statement of religious doctrines believed **:** CREED **3 a :** conviction of the truth of some statement or the reality of some being or phenomenon esp. when based on an examination of the grounds for accepting it as true or real **:** reflective assurance **:** intellectual assent ⟨~ in the validity of logical propositions and scientific statements⟩ **b :** a statement or a state of affairs on the basis of which one is willing to act; *specif* **:** a deliberate habitual readiness to act in a certain manner under appropriate conditions **4 :** immediate assurance or feeling of the reality of something ⟨~ in sensation⟩

syn FAITH, CREDENCE, CREDIT: BELIEF signifies mental acceptance of or assent to something offered as true, with or without certainty ⟨we tend to speak of faith when we are designating the less sure *beliefs*. We believe our eyes, and we believe the proposition that twice two are four —G.W.Allport⟩ ⟨the *belief* that the dead shall rise and live again is purely a matter of faith with which reason has nothing to do directly —Frank Thilly⟩ FAITH applies to full and certain assent, often on grounds other than those afforded by the senses and reason and often with a complete trust or confidence ⟨the *faith* that human science and freedom would advance hand in hand to usher in an era of indefinite human perfectibility —John Dewey⟩ ⟨he's still touchingly full of *faith*, even after all that has happened, in a new heaven and a new earth —Rose Macaulay⟩ CREDENCE suggests the fact of intellectual assent without implying anything about grounds for assent; it may refer to less intimately significant matters than FAITH and BELIEF ⟨we are not now concerned with the finality or extent of truth in this judgment. The point is that it gained a widespread *credence* among the cultured class in Europe —C.D.Lewis⟩ ⟨the colonial office statement is too pitiably thin for *credence* —*New Statesman & Nation*⟩ CREDIT suggests that a notion is held worthy of trusting consideration although it practically never connotes certainty or conviction in acceptance ⟨giving no *credit* to such reports⟩ **syn** see in addition OPINION

be·li·er \bəlīə(r), bē-\ *n* -s [*belie* + *-er*] **:** one that belies

be·liev·a·bil·i·ty \bə,lēvə'biləd·ē, bē-\ *n* -ES **:** the quality or state of being believable ⟨advertising exists basically on a foundation of ~ —C.B.Larrabee⟩

be·liev·a·ble \='=vəbəl\ *adj* [ME *belevable*, fr. *beleven* + *-able*] **:** capable of instilling faith, trust, or acceptance ⟨a ~ explanation⟩ ⟨a ~ portrayal of the doctor's character⟩

be·liev·a·bly \-vəblē, -li\ *adv* **:** in a believable manner

be·lieve \bə'lēv, bē- *rap.* 'blēv\ *vb* -ED/-ING/-S [ME *bileven, beleven*, fr. OE *belēfan*, *belȳfan*, fr. *be-* + *lēfan*, *lȳfan* to allow, believe; akin to OE *gelȳfan* to believe, *alȳfan* to allow, OHG *gilouben* to believe, *irlouben* to allow, ON *leyfa* to allow, Goth *galaubjan* to believe, *uslaubjan* to allow, OE *lēof* dear — more at LOVE] *vi* **1 a :** to have a firm or wholehearted religious conviction or persuasion — usu. used with *in* ⟨~ in the Scriptures⟩ and sometimes with *on* ⟨and many *believed* on him there —Jn 10:42(AV)⟩ **b :** to receive in faith or trust **:** ACCEPT ⟨a story that divided the audience into those who *believed* and those who didn't⟩ — often used with *in* ⟨serfs incapable of *believing* in the sincerity of a master who desired to help them —E.J.Simmons⟩ ⟨because of its sincerity . . . this is the kind of play one would like to ~ in —*Punch*⟩ **2** *obs* **:** to give credence **:** TRUST — used with *to* ⟨~ to your own virtues⟩ **3 :** to have a firm conviction as to the beneficial, genuine, or good quality of something — used with *in* ⟨~ in physical culture⟩ **4 :** THINK, SUPPOSE ⟨inclined to ~ in accordance with her husband⟩ ~ *vt* **1 a :** to take (a statement or person making a statement) as true, valid, or honest **:** give credence to ⟨~ the reports⟩ **b :** to accept or receive as genuine, valid, or good ⟨a bland assumption that all scientists . . . decide and publish what science ~s —R.M.Weaver⟩ **2** *obs* **:** to assume the existence of as true or valid ⟨~ a God⟩ **3 :** to be of the opinion **:** SUPPOSE, SUSPECT. ⟨~ it will rain⟩ ⟨the dye is *believed* to be a complex acid⟩

be·liev·er \-və(r)\ *n* -s [ME *biliver*, fr. *bileven* to believe + *-er*] **1 :** one that believes ⟨a ~ in the power of words⟩ **2 :** one who professes a religious faith; *esp* **:** one who believes in the saving power of the Christian faith

believer's baptism *n* **:** baptism administered (as among Baptists) only to those old enough to make an independent profession of faith

be·like \bə, bē +\ *adv* [ME, fr. *be-* (fr. *bi* by) + *like*, adj.] *archaic* **:** most likely **:** PROBABLY ⟨a tale one told to me — for a jest ~ —Rudyard Kipling⟩

belime *vt* [*be-* + *lime*] *obs* **:** BIRDLIME

bel·i·nu·rus \,belə'n(y)u̇rəs\ *n, cap* [NL, irreg. fr. Gk *belonē* needle + NL *-urus*] **:** a genus (the type of the family Belinuridae) of Devonian and Carboniferous arthropods related to the modern king crab

be·li·sha beacon \bə¦lēshə-\ *n, usu cap 1st B* [after Leslie Hore-*Belisha* †1957 Eng. political leader] **:** an orange traffic signal for the protection of pedestrians at street crossings in English cities

be·lite \'bē,līt\ *n* -s [Sw *belit*, fr. *be* (name of the letter *b*) + Sw *-lit* -lite] **:** larnite found as a constituent of portland-cement clinker

be·littered \bə, bē +\ *adj* [*be-* + *littered*] **:** strewn with litter

be·lit·tle \bə'lid·ᵊl, bē-, -itᵊl\ *vt* **belittled; belittled; belittling** \-itliŋ, -id·ᵊl-,-itᵊl-\ **belittles** [*be-* + *little*] **1 :** to make small or make appear as small ⟨the bulk of the warehouse *belittles* the houses around it⟩ **2 :** to speak of slightingly **:** DISPARAGE, DEPRECIATE ⟨~ a person's efforts⟩ **syn** see DECRY

be·lit·tle·ment \-id·ᵊlmənt. -itᵊl-\ *n* -s **:** the act of belittling

be·lit·tler \-itlə(r), -id·ᵊl-,-itᵊl-\ *n* -s **:** one that belittles

be·live \bə'līv, bē-\ *adv* [ME *bilive*, fr. *bi* by + *live*, dat. of *lif* life — more at LIFE] **1** *now Scot* **:** SPEEDILY, QUICKLY **2** *now Scot* **:** in due time **:** by and by

¹bell \'bel\ *n* -s *often attrib* [ME *belle*, fr. OE; akin to MLG *belle* bell, ON *bjalla* bell, OE *bellan* to roar — more at BELLOW] **1 a :** a cup-shaped, saucer-shaped, or hollow spherical metallic device that vibrates and gives forth a ringing sound when struck by a clapper or hammer or by a loose ball inside — see CHIME, GONG, SLEIGH BELL **b :** DOORBELL ⟨the ~ began to chime more frequently —A.R.Foff⟩ **2 :** the ringing or sound of a bell as a signal ⟨school ~⟩ or summons ⟨dinner ~⟩ or warning ⟨fire ~⟩ **3 a :** a bell (as of a clock) rung to tell the hour **b :** the stroke of such a bell esp. on shipboard — often used in pl. **c :** the time so indicated **d** *naut* **:** a half hour — compare WATCH (see column 3) **e :** a signal to a ship's engine room given orig. by striking a bell **f :** the gong sounded at the beginning and end of a round in boxing **4 :** a mark of superiority or merit **:** AWARD, PRIZE — used in such phrases as *to bear the bell, to carry away the bell*

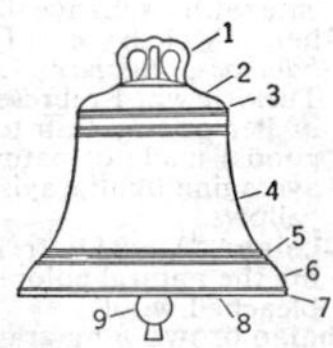

bell 1a: *1* crown, *2* head, *3* shoulder, *4* waist, *5* bead lines, *6* sound bow, *7* lip, *8* mouth, *9* clapper

SHIP'S BELLS

NO. OF BELLS	HOUR (A.M. OR P.M.)		
1	12:30	4:30	8:30
2	1:00	5:00	9:00
3	1:30	5:30	9:30
4	2:00	6:00	10:00
5	2:30	6:30	10:30
6	3:00	7:00	11:00
7	3:30	7:30	11:30
8	4:00	8:00	12:00

5 : something having the form of a bell: as **a :** the cup or corolla of a flower ⟨in a cowslip's ~ I lie —Shak.⟩ **b :** a hollow inverted vessel (as a diving bell or bell jar) **c :** a bell-shaped organ or part (as the umbrella of a jellyfish or the nectocalyx of a siphonophore) **d :** a small pouch of hairy skin that hangs from the neck of a deer **e :** the part of the capital of a column between the abacus and neck molding; *esp* **:** the nearly bell-shaped naked core assumed to exist within the leafage of a Corinthian capital **f :** a flaring mouth (as of a trumpet or other musical wind instrument or of an old firearm) **g :** a bell-shaped cover of metal or glass placed over food in cooking or serving — called also *cloche* **h :** the cone-shaped part in a bell and hopper **i :** the enlarged end of a section of pipe that receives the spigot end of the adjoining section **j :** the cup-shaped endpiece of a stethoscope that is placed against a body area (as the chest) **6 a :** a musical percussion instrument consisting of a number of metal bars or tubes of various graded lengths that when struck with a hammer give out tones resembling those of different-sized bells — usu. used in pl.; called also *chimes* **b :** GLOCKENSPIEL **7 bells** *pl* **:** heel clicks performed in the air in tap dancing — **with bells on** *adv* **:** in full party dress and spirits **:** with readiness and zeal **:** in full force **:** with clear superiority

²bell \"\ *vb* -ED/-ING/-S *vt* **1 :** to put a bell upon **:** provide with a bell ⟨camels had got away from them in the dark and . . . were not ~*ed* —Myrtle R. White⟩ **2 a :** to ring a bell for ⟨~ the man to come up⟩ **b :** to cause to ring ⟨the ground, so hard it hurt our brittle feet, ~*ed* the iron rakes —Whitney Balliett⟩ **3 :** to make bell-mouthed ⟨~ out the end of a tube⟩ **4 :** to cover by a bell or bell jar ⟨artificial fruit . . . the stuff your grandmother ~*ed* under glass —Walter de la Mare⟩ ~ *vi* **1 :** to ring a bell or bells ⟨trams ~ against motors and drays —William Sansom⟩ **2 :** to make a sound suggestive of a bell ⟨a great ~*ing* chorus of thrushes —H.E.Bates⟩ **:** RING ⟨his head ~*ing* with interrupted sleep —D.C.Peattie⟩ **3 a :** to take the form of a bell **:** swell up or puff out into the shape of a bell ⟨~*ing* sleeves⟩ ⟨~*ed* flowers⟩ ⟨skirts inclined to ~ at the hemline —*Women's Wear Daily*⟩ **b :** to develop bells or corollas **:** BLOSSOM ⟨hops ~*ing* at the end of August⟩ — **bell the cat :** to do a daring or risky deed ⟨everybody made suggestions but no one actually offered to *bell the cat*⟩

³bell \"\ *vi* -ED/-ING/-S [ME *bellen*, fr. OE *bellan* — more at BELLOW] **:** to make a resonant bellowing or baying sound ⟨the bobcat . . . was ahead of the ~*ing* hounds —William Faulkner⟩ **:** BELLOW, ROAR ⟨the distant ~*ing* of the herds of deer —Sacheverell Sitwell⟩

⁴bell \"\ *n* -s **:** the noise of one that bells **:** BELLOW, ROAR ⟨the ~ of a stag⟩

bel·la \'belə\ *n* -s [It, *bella*, adj., fem. of *bello*, fr. L *bellus* — more at BEAUTY] **:** the king and queen of trumps given a special scoring value in European card games

bel·la·bel·la \¦belə¦belə\ *n, pl* **bellabella** *or* **bellabellas** *usu cap* [alter. of *Millbank*, Brit. Columbia, Canada] **1 a :** a Wakashan people or group of peoples of the coast of British Columbia **b :** a member of the Bellabella people or group of peoples **2 :** the language of the Bellabella people

bel·la·coo·la \,belə'külə\ *n, pl* **bellacoola** *or* **bellacoolas** *usu cap* [Kwakiutl *Bilxula*] **1 a :** a Salishan people of the vicinity of Queen Charlotte Sound, British Columbia **b :** a member of such people **2 :** the language of the Bellacoola people

bel·la·don·na \,belə'dänə\ *n* -s [It, lit., fine lady, fr. *bella*, fem. of *bello* beautiful (fr. L *bellus*) + *donna* lady; fr. its use as a cosmetic — more at BEAUTY, DONNA] **1 :** a European poisonous plant (*Atropa belladonna*) which is extensively grown in the U.S., which has reddish bell-shaped flowers and shining black berries, and from the root and leaves of which atropine is produced — called also *deadly nightshade* **2 :** a medicinal extract from the belladonna plant **3 :** BELLADONNA LILY

belladonna lily *n* **:** a southern African bulbous plant (*Amaryllis belladonna*) often cultivated for its fragrant usu. white or rose-colored flowers which resemble lilies

belladonna ointment *n* **:** an official ointment containing belladonna extract, wool grease, yellow wax, and petrolatum

bell and hopper *n* **:** an apparatus at the top of a blast furnace consisting of a large hopper closed by a cone which is pulled up from below by the apex and through which the charge may be introduced without escape of the gases

bell-and-spigot joint *n* **:** a pipe joint formed by the insertion of the spigot end of one length of pipe into the bell end of the next length

bell animalcule *n* **:** any of many bell-shaped stalked ciliated infusorians of *Vorticella* and related genera

bell apple *n* **:** JAMAICA HONEYSUCKLE

bell arch *n* **:** a round arch on two corbels faced convexly to a wider space below

bel·lar·mine \¦belər¦mēn, -,lär-; 'belərmən\ *n* -s [after Roberto Cardinal *Bellarmine* (Bellarmino) †1621 Ital. prelate whom such jugs orig. caricatured] **:** a narrow-necked large-bellied stoneware drinking jug typically adorned with the figure of a bearded man

bell beaker *n* **:** a bell-shaped pottery vessel of the prehistoric Beaker folk

bell·bind \'bel,bīnd\ *or* **bell·bind·er** \-ndə(r)\ *or* **bell·bine** \-n\ *n* -s **1 :** FIELD BINDWEED **2 :** HEDGE BINDWEED

bellbird \'=,=\ *n* [so called fr. its bell-like note] **:** any of several birds whose notes are likened to the sound of a bell: as **a :** a loud-voiced white So. American bird (*Procnias nivea*) having a fleshy caruncle on the head or a related bird **b :** a honey eater (*Manorina melanophrys*) of Australia or a honey eater (*Anthornis melanura*) of New Zealand **c :** a western Australian bird (*Oreoica cristata*) **d :** WOOD THRUSH 1

bellbird a

bell book *n* [so called fr. the shipboard use of bells for signals] **:** a book in which a ship's engineer records speeds, directions, and engine data

bell boot *n* [so called fr. its shape] **:** a rubber covering fitted over the hoof of a horse to protect the hoof surface

bell-bottom \'=,=\ *also* **bell-bottomed** \(')=¦==\ *adj, of trousers* **:** having legs with wide flaring bottoms ⟨sailors wearing *bell-bottom* pants⟩

bell-bottoms \(')=¦==\ *n pl* **:** a pair of bell-bottom trousers

bellboy \'=,=\ *n* **1 :** a hotel or club employee who escorts guests to their rooms, assists them with their luggage, and is available for running errands — called also *bellhop, bellman* **2 :** a logging signalman who uses a bell system

bell buoy *n* **:** a buoy with a bell that rings by the action of the waves and usu. marks a shoal or rocks

bell button *n* **1 :** a push button to ring a bell **2 :** a bell-shaped button used esp. on some dress uniforms

bell cage *n* **:** a timber frame constructed to support a large bell

bell canopy *n* **1 :** BELL GABLE **2 :** an open-roofed structure for protecting a bell

bell captain *n* **:** ¹CAPTAIN 1m(2)

bell center punch *n* **:** a center or prick punch mounted on the axis of a hollow cone that when placed over the end of round stock and struck marks the center of the stock

bell cord *n* **:** a cord that rings a bell when pulled (as in a room for summoning a servant or on a railroad car for giving a signal)

bell cot *or* **bell cote** *n* **:** a small or subsidiary construction frequently corbeled out from the walls of a structure and used to contain and support one or more bells

bell cow *n* **1 :** a cow with a bell attached to its neck; *esp* **:** a lead cow **2** *slang* **:** LEADER ⟨the *bell cow* in county politics —James Street & J.S.Childers⟩
bell crank *n* [so called fr. the bell wires used to transfer motion] **:** a lever having its fulcrum at the apex of the angle formed by its two arms
bell crown *n* **:** a silk hat or a beaver with a crown shaped like an inverted bell
bell deck *n* **:** the floor of a belfry serving as a roof to the rooms below

bell crank

belle \'bel\ *n* -s [F, fr. fem. of *beau* beautiful, handsome — more at BEAU] **:** a girl or woman who is popular and beautiful or attractive **:** a girl or woman whose charm and beauty make her a favorite ⟨the ~ of the ball⟩
bell ear *n* **:** a rabbit's ear with a large lopped tip that is rated as a disqualifying fault in show stock
belled \'beld\ *adj* [¹*bell* + *-ed*] **:** having bell-shaped flowers ⟨the ~ hyacinth⟩
bel·leek \bə'lēk\ *n* -s [*Belleek*] **:** CHAMPAGNE 3
Belleek \"\ *trademark* — used for a thin translucent often ornately decorated porcelain covered with a lustrous often iridescent glaze
belle isle cress \(')be¦lī(ə)l-\ *n*, *usu cap B&I* [prob. fr. *Belle Isle*, Orange county, Fla.] **:** WINTER CRESS
bel·ler \'belə(r)\ *dial var of* BELLOW
bel·ler·ic \bə'lerik\ *n* -s [F, fr. Ar *balīlaj*, fr. Per *balīlah*] **:** the fruit of the bahera — compare MYROBALAN
bel·ler·o·phon \bə'lerə,fän, -,fon\ *n*, *cap* [NL, fr. *Bellerophon*, mythological character who slew the Chimera with the help of Pegasus, fr. L, fr. Gk *Bellerophōn*] **:** a genus (the type of the family Bellerophontidae) of extinct Palaeozoic gastropod mollusks having a somewhat loosely coiled plain spiral shell and often placed in the superfamily Bellerophontacea of the Aspidobranchia — **bel·ler·o·phont** \-,fänt\ *adj or n*
belles let·tres \bel(l)etr(ᵊ), -le·tr(ə)\ *n pl but sing in constr* [F *belles-lettres*, lit., beautiful letters] **:** literature that is an end in itself (as most poetry, fiction, and drama) and not practical or purely informative ⟨a magazine more concerned with public affairs than *belles lettres*⟩; *specif* **:** light entertaining literature often of a facile or sophisticated nature ⟨the *belles lettres* fragrance that clings to the humanities repelled the social scientists —A.L.Guérard⟩
bell·et·er \'belə̇d·ə(r)\ *n* -s [¹*bell* + *-eter* (fr. obs. *yeter* metal caster, fr. OE *gēotere*, fr. *gēotan* to cast, pour + *-ere* -er) — more at ⁵FOUND] **:** a bell founder
bel·le·trism *or* **belles-let·trism** \bel'le·,trizəm\ *n* -s [*belles lettres* + *-ism*] **:** an interest in belles lettres to the neglect of more practical or informative literature **:** literary aestheticism ⟨emphasis upon ~ . . . is an educational luxury in this chaotic era —W.L.Moore⟩
bel·le·trist *also* **belle-let·trist** \-le·trə̇st\ *n* -s [*belles lettres* + *-ist*] **:** a writer of or a person devoted to belles lettres
bel·le·tris·tic *also* **bel·let·tris·tic** \¦belə¦tristik\ *adj* **:** belonging to or suggestive of belles lettres ⟨~ writing⟩ ⟨a ~ trifler⟩ ⟨~ qualities⟩
bellflower \'=,=\ *n* **1 :** any of several plants having bell-shaped flowers: as **a :** a plant of the genus *Campanula* or a closely related genus **b :** CHILEAN BELLFLOWER **c :** BALLOONFLOWER **2 :** MAZARINE BLUE
bellflower family *n* **:** CAMPANULACEAE
bell gable *n* **:** a piece of walling pierced with openings that are usu. arched and arranged for the hanging of large bells and are often upward prolongations above the roof of a gable wall (as of a church or chapel)
bell gamba *n* **:** CONE GAMBA
bell glass *n* **:** BELL JAR
bellhanger \'=,==\ *n* **:** one who hangs, puts up, or repairs bells esp. as a trade
bell harp *n* **:** an 18th century musical instrument consisting of a psaltery mounted in a triangular frame and plucked with plectra attached to the thumbs
bell heather *n* **1 a :** a European heather (*Erica tetralix*) with rose-colored flowers **b :** a European heather (*E. cinerea*) with purple flowers — called also *heather bell* **2 :** an alpine plant (*Cassiope mertensiana*) of western No. America found in wet places and resembling a heath
¹bell·hop \'bel,häp\ *n* -s [short for *bell-hopper*, fr. ¹*bell* + *hopper*] **1 :** BELLBOY **2 :** one who does messenger service within a bank
²bellhop \"\ *vi* **:** to work as a bellhop
bellhouse \'=,=\ *n* [ME *bellhous*, fr. OE *bellhūs*, fr. *belle* bell + *hūs* house] **:** a structure for containing a bell (as a detached building or a belfry)
bel·li·cist \'beləsə̇st\ *n* -s [L *bellicus* of war + E *-ist*] **:** one who advocates war — opposed to *pacifist*
bel·li·cose \'belə̇,kōs, -lē-\ *adj* [ME, fr. L *bellicosus*, fr. *bellicus* (fr. *bellum* war — fr. OL *duellum* — + *-icus* -ic) + *-osus* -ose — more at DUEL] **:** WARLIKE ⟨~ young officers⟩ **:** favoring or inclined to favor war or strife **:** inclined to foment contention and quarrels **:** AGGRESSIVE, COMBATIVE **syn** see BELLIGERENT
bellicosely *adv* **:** in a bellicose manner
bel·li·cos·i·ty \,=='käsəd·ē, -ətē, -i\ *n* -ES **:** showy, demonstrative, or arrant truculence or aggressiveness ⟨confuse courage with ~ —*Yale Rev.*⟩
bel·lied \'belēd, -lid\ *adj* [¹*belly* + *-ed*] **1 :** possessed of a belly ⟨a man ~ like a hog⟩ — often used in combination ⟨a great-*bellied* person⟩ ⟨empty-*bellied* children⟩; *specif* **:** possessing a large or pronounced belly ⟨to produce long, fine, not too ~ animals —Poul Vestbirk⟩ **2 :** possessing a convex, rounded, or bulging surface ⟨a ~ sail⟩ ⟨a ~ file⟩
bellies *pl of* BELLY, *pres 3d sing of* BELLY
bel·lig·er·ence \bə'lij(ə)rən(t)s *sometimes* bē-\ *n* -s **:** an attitude, atmosphere, or disposition distinguished by aggressiveness or truculence ⟨to circumvent ~ and reduce suspicion of adult control —*Newsweek*⟩
bel·lig·er·en·cy \-rənsē, -si\ *n* -ES **1 :** the state of being at war or in conflict; *specif* **:** the status whereby a recognized military force is granted the protection of the international laws and usages of war (as those laid down by the Hague Convention in 1899) **2 :** BELLIGERENCE ⟨over against this persistent ~ of the German militarists stood the ideology of British pacifism —*Hibbert Jour.*⟩
¹bel·lig·er·ent \-rənt\ *adj* [irreg. fr. L *belligerant-, belligerans*, pres. part. of *belligerare* to be at war, fr. *belliger* waging war, fr. *bellum* war + *gerere* to wage — more at CAST] **1 :** waging war **:** carrying on war ⟨~ factions⟩ ⟨~ powers⟩; *specif* **:** belonging to or recognized as an organized military power protected by and subject to the laws of war ⟨~ embassies in neutral countries⟩ ⟨a ~ nation⟩ — often used of a party in revolt after its establishment of and recognition as a de facto government **2 :** inclined to or exhibiting assertiveness, hostility, truculence, or combativeness ⟨an obnoxious, ~, argumentative adolescent —Hannah Smith⟩ ⟨such ~ verbalizing as makes peaceful action more difficult to achieve —H.A.Overstreet⟩
syn BELLICOSE, PUGNACIOUS, COMBATIVE, CONTENTIOUS, QUARRELSOME: BELLIGERENT may describe a country or group actually at war ⟨a truce of six months between the *belligerent* parties —W.H.Prescott⟩ Less legalistically, it indicates an aggressive, truculent attitude and connotes very hostile feelings ⟨still fighting some of the battles . . . and he is at times unnecessarily *belligerent* —H.S.Commager⟩ ⟨and the most *belligerent* of all . . . she who at tea heroically slaughtered not only German men but all their women and viperine children —Sinclair Lewis⟩ BELLICOSE likewise suggests a pronounced inclination to fight ⟨Calhoun joined with Clay in driving through Congress a war policy. In this he seems to have represented his constituents, whose patriotism was always somewhat *bellicose* —V.L. Parrington⟩ ⟨they were a *bellicose* people, wielding axes, spears, and clubs against their enemies —John Murra⟩ PUGNACIOUS indicates ready and pleasurable willingness to fight ⟨their *pugnacious* dispositions are well known, and they are not only fight among themselves but are incessantly quarreling with their neighbors —John Burroughs⟩ ⟨a certain *pugnacious* virtue that would inculcate righteousness by means of a broken head — V.L.Parrington⟩ COMBATIVE may indicate either pertaining to combat or, more positively, willingly ready for combat ⟨combat in the field of sports, contests in various forms of games . . . are generally approved. The *combative* impulses in human nature may thus find an expression —M.R.Cohen⟩ ⟨on Mary's face there was . . . something *combative* and alert as well. She was still fighting, but Will was obviously beaten —Dorothy Sayers⟩ PUGNACIOUS and COMBATIVE may lack unpleasant connotation; CONTENTIOUS implies a perverse and irritating fondness for arguments and strife ⟨ideal wives are thought to be like sisters or mothers, cherishing and submissive; others are considered *contentious* —A.L.Kroeber⟩ ⟨his experience with the *contentious* Dominion council led him often abruptly to silence lengthy and unprofitable debates —Viola F. Barnes⟩ QUARRELSOME suggests a fretful ill-natured disposition to quarrel for petty ill-grounded reasons ⟨you also feel very *quarrelsome*, and you swear at each other in hoarse whispers —J.K. Jerome⟩ ⟨she was such a confounded *quarrelsome* high-bred jade —W.M.Thackeray⟩
²belligerent \"\ *n* -s **:** a belligerent nation, state, or person ⟨recognized the Confederacy as a ~ —W.C.Ford⟩
belligerently *adv* **:** in a belligerent manner
¹bell·ing \'beliŋ, -lēŋ\ *n* -s [ME, fr. gerund of *bellen* to roar — more at BELL] **:** the crying or bellowing of animals (as the baying of foxhounds or the sound made by deer in rutting season)
²belling \"\ *n* -s [fr. gerund of ²*bell*] *chiefly Midland* **:** SHIVAREE
bel·linger·ite \'beliŋə,rīt, -lənjə,r-\ *n* -s [Herman C. *Bellinger* †1940 metallurgist + E *-ite*] **:** a mineral $3Cu(IO_3)_2.2H_2O$ consisting of a light-green hydrous copper iodate found at Chuquicamata, Chile
bel·li·ni's duct *also* **bellini's tube** *or* **bellini's tubule** \bə'lēnēz-\ *n*, *cap B* [after Lorenzo *Bellini* †1704 Ital. anatomist] **:** any of the excretory ducts of the kidney — usu. used in pl.
bel·lip·o·tent \(')be¦lipəd·ənt\ *adj* [L *bellipotent-, bellipotens*, fr. *bellum* war + *potent-, potens* powerful — more at BELLICOSE, POTENT] **:** mighty in war
bel·lis \'belə̇s\ *n*, *cap* [L, white daisy, perh. fr. *bellus* pretty — more at BEAUTY] **:** a small genus of scapose herbs (family Compositae) having solitary heads of ray flowers with involucral bracts that are nearly equal — see DAISY 1, WESTERN DAISY
bell jar *n* **:** a bell-shaped usu. glass vessel designed to cover and protect objects, to contain gases, or to enclose a vacuum
bell-less \'belləs\ *adj* **:** being without a bell
bell-lyra \(')=¦==\ *or* **bell lyre** *n* **:** a glockenspiel mounted in a portable lyre-shaped frame and used esp. in marching bands
bell-ma·gen·die law \'bel,mä,zhaⁿ 'dē-\ *n*, *usu cap B & M* [after Sir Charles *Bell* †1842 Scottish anatomist & François *Magendie* †1855 Fr. physiologist] **:** BELL'S LAW

bell jar

bell magpie *n* [so called fr. its bell-like call note] **:** CURRAWONG
bell·man \'belmən *also* -,man *or* -,maa(ə)n\ *n*, *pl* **bellmen** [ME, fr. *belle* bell + *man*] **1 :** a man who rings a bell (as a town crier or a night watchman) **2 :** one who assists a diver by checking his equipment and pulling in or letting out the lifeline according to his instructions **3 :** BELLBOY **4 :** a construction-crew signalman who uses a bell
bell mare *n* **:** a female horse, mule, or ass wearing a bell and serving as leader of a packtrain or herd
bellmaster \'=,==\ *n* **:** CARILLONNEUR
bell metal *n* **:** bronze that consists usu. of three to four parts of copper to one of tin and is used for making bells
bell-metal ore *n* **:** STANNITE
bell-mouthed \'=,=\ *adj* **:** flaring at the mouth
bell olive tree *n* [so called fr. the shape of the flowers] **:** SILVER BELL
bello·ta *also* **bello·te** \bə'lōd·ə, bə'yō-\ *n* -s [MexSp *bellota*, fr. Sp, acorn, fr. Ar *ballūṭa*] **1 :** GAMBEL OAK **2 :** the acorn of the gambel oak
¹bel·low \'be(,)lō, -lə, *often* -ləw+V\ *vb* -ED/-ING/-S [ME *belwen*, fr. OE *bylgian*; akin to OE & OHG *bellan* to roar, ON *belja* to bellow, *bylja* to resound, Skt *bhāṣate* he talks] *vi* **1 :** to emit a loud deep hollow prolonged sound (as of a bull) **2 :** to speak or shout in a deep voice and unrestrained manner **:** BAWL ⟨~*ing* with hoarse merriment —Kenneth Roberts⟩ ~ *vt* **:** to utter in a bellowing manner **:** BAWL ⟨the captain ~*ed* out commands⟩ ⟨the cannon ~*ed* forth their salvos⟩ **syn** see ROAR
²bellow \"\ *n* -s **:** a loud deep forceful reverberating outcry; *typically* **:** the roaring of a bull
¹bel·lows \'be(,)lōz, -,lə z, *formerly often & still sometimes esp in S* -ləs\ *n pl but sing or pl in constr* [ME *bely*, *belowe* belly, bellows — more at BELLY] **1 :** an instrument or machine that by alternate expansion and contraction or by rise and fall of the top draws in air through a valve or orifice and expels it more or less forcibly through a tube; *also* **:** any of various forms of rotary and other blowers — compare BLOWER 5 **2 :** LUNGS ⟨the yell from the deep ~ of the man —Barnaby Conrad⟩ **3 :** the pleated expansible part of leather, cloth, or similar material in a camera making a light-tight passage between the lens and the light-sensitive material at the back of the camera — see CAMERA illustration **4 :** any of various enclosures of variable volume with walls like those of an accordion (as in sealed expansion joints and thermostats)

bellows 1

²bellows *vt* -ED/-ING/-ES *obs* **:** to blow with or as if with bellows
bellows fish *n* **1 :** any of several fishes (family Macrorhamphosidae) having a deep compressed body and long tubular snout — called also *snipefish*, *trumpet fish* **2 :** ANGLER 2a **3 :** a globefish (*Sphoeroides maculatus*)
bellows pocket *n* **:** a pocket with an expansion pleat applied to the outside of a garment
bellows tongue *n* **:** a wide folding tongue of a shoe or boot (as of a blucher) attached at the sides to the uppers so as to make the shoe watertight
bellows top *n* **:** a folding top of a carriage
bell pepper *n* [so called prob. fr. the shape] **:** SWEET PEPPER
bellpull \'=,=\ *n* **:** a handle or knob attached to a cord or wire by which one rings a bell; *sometimes* **:** the cord itself
bell push *n* **:** a button that is pushed to ring a bell
bell ringer *n* **1 :** one that rings a bell: as **a :** CARILLONNEUR **b :** one that rings a church bell; *esp* **:** one that takes part in change ringing **c :** a performer on musical hand bells **2 :** something that succeeds or makes a hit
bell ringing *n* **:** the art or occupation of playing a chime, carillon, or other set of musical bells
bell rope *n* **:** a rope attached to a bell or to the tongue of a bell
bells *pl of* BELL, *pres 3d sing of* BELL
bell scraper *n* **:** a flattened bell-shaped metal instrument with sharpened edges used for scraping the hair from hog carcasses as they come from the scalding vat
bell shape *n* **:** the shape in full or in outline of vertical section of an inverted cup with flaring rim and convex crown — compare CAMPANIFORM
bell's law \'belz-\ *n*, *usu cap B* [after Sir Charles *Bell* †1842 Scot. anatomist] **:** a statement in physiology: the roots of the spinal nerves coming from the ventral portion of the spinal cord are motor in function and those coming from the dorsal portion are sensory — called also *Bell-Magendie law*
bells of ireland *usu cap I* [so called fr. the green bell-shaped calyx] **:** MOLUCCA BALM
bell's palsy *n*, *usu cap B* [after Sir Charles *Bell*] **:** paralysis of the facial nerve producing distortion of one side of the face
bell sparrow *or* **bell's sparrow** *n*, *often cap B* [after J.G.*Bell* †1889 Am. physician and ornithologist] **:** a California desert sparrow (*Amphispiza belli belli*) that is brownish gray above and white below with a black tail and yellowish wing margins
bell's vireo *n*, *usu cap B* [after J.G.*Bell*] **:** a vireo (*Vireo bellii bellii*) of the central U. S. with a brownish olive back, white throat, and yellow underparts
belltail \'=,=\ *n* **:** RATTLESNAKE
bell toad *n* **:** a small drab upland toad (*Ascaphus truei*) of the northwestern U. S.
bell tone *n* **1 :** the tone or timbre peculiar to a bell (as a church bell) and composed of a unique series of harmonics beginning 1 : 2 : 2 : 4 : 3 : 4 **2 :** a musical tone (as produced on a trumpet) characterized by a strong initial accent followed by a sharp diminuendo similar in dynamics to a tone struck on a bell
belltopper \'=¦==\ *n* [so called fr. its bell-shaped crown] *chiefly Austral* **:** a tall silk hat
bell tower *n* **:** a tower either freestanding or surmounting a civil or religious building that supports or shelters a bell — compare BELFRY, CAMPANILE, CARILLON
bell trap *n* **:** a bell-shaped trap below the inlet of a floor drain
bell tree *n* **:** SILVER BELL
bell turret *n* **:** a turret (as of a small church or chapel having no bell tower) where a bell is hung
bel·lum \'beləm\ *n* -s [modif. of Per *balam*] **:** a Persian-gulf boat holding about eight persons and propelled by paddles or poles
bell vine *n* [so called fr. the bell-shaped corolla] *New Zeal* **:** HEDGE BINDWEED
bellwaver \'=,==\ *vi* **:** to wander aimlessly **:** FLUCTUATE, RAMBLE ⟨with a ~*ing* air —Muriel Rukeyser⟩
bellwether \'=¦==\ *n* [ME, fr. *belle* bell + *wether*] **1 :** a belled wether or sheep **2 :** one that takes the lead or initiative **:** LEADER ⟨distinguished for his outstanding work as a ~ bomber pilot —R.G.Hubler & J.A.DeChant⟩ ⟨California, traditional ~ of the canning industry —*Wall Street Jour.*⟩
bell wire *n* **:** a small-size wire insulated with paraffin-coated cotton and used esp. for electric bell circuits
bellwood \'=,=\ *n* **:** SILVER BELL
bellwort \'=,=\ *n* -s **1 :** a plant of the family Campanulaceae **2 :** a plant of the genus *Uvularia* having yellow flowers shaped like bells
¹bel·ly \'belē, -li\ *n* -ES [ME *bely, baly*, fr. OE *belg, bælg* bag, skin; akin to OHG *balg* bag, skin, ON *belgr*, Goth *balgs* wineskin, Skt *upabarhaṇa* cushion, L *flare* to blow — more at BLOW] **1 a** (1) **:** the front part of the human body between the breast and the thighs enclosing the abdominal viscera **:** ABDOMEN (2) **:** the underpart of an animal's body corresponding to the human belly; *also* **:** the hide from the underside of an animal — see HIDE illustration **b :** WOMB, UTERUS **c :** the internal cavity of the body **:** the abdominal cavity **d :** the part of a garment that covers a person's belly **e :** the piece of wool from the sheep's belly — usu. used in pl. **2 :** the internal cavity of something **:** INTERIOR ⟨a boat carrying a half dozen freight cars in its ~⟩ **3 :** APPETITE ⟨thoughts that rose little above his ~⟩ **:** satisfaction of hunger ⟨always intent on his ~⟩ **4 :** a surface or object so curved or rounded as to resemble or suggest the human or animal belly ⟨the ~ of a flask⟩ ⟨the ~ of an airplane⟩ ⟨a cold ~ of fog advancing down the street⟩ **5 a :** the convex inner side of an archer's bow **b :** the part of a sail that swells out when filled with wind **c :** the enlarged fleshy body of a muscle between the usu. slender points of attachment **d :** the side of a piece of printer's type opposite the back and having the nick — see TYPE illustration **e :** the part of a blast furnace at the top of the bosh where the diameter is greatest **f** (1) **:** the front or upper plate of the sound box of instruments of the violin and lute classes — called also *table* (2) **:** the soundboard of a piano
²belly \"\ *vb* -ED/-ING/-ES *vt* **1 :** to round out **:** SWELL, FILL ⟨wind ~*ing* the sails⟩ **2** *Austral* **:** to remove the wool on the belly of (a sheep) before shearing **3 :** to disable the treads of (an army tank) esp. in such a way as to expose the underside to enemy fire (*bellied* by concrete blocks) **~** *vi* **1 :** to swell out **:** bulge out ⟨his blouse *bellied* out round him —F.M. Ford⟩ **2 :** to move along on the belly ⟨the patrol *bellied* across the field under enemy fire⟩ or with the belly foremost ⟨the cowboys *bellied* up to the bar⟩
¹bellyache \'==,=\ *n* [¹*belly* + *ache*] **:** pain in the abdomen and esp. in the bowels **:** COLIC
²bellyache \"\ *vi* **:** to complain and find fault whiningly or with disgruntled peevishness ⟨*bellyached* about small matters —Stanley Walker⟩ **syn** see COMPLAIN
bellyache-bush *or* **bellyache-weed** \'==,=,=\ *n* **:** a shrub (*Jatropha gossipiifolia*) of the southeastern U.S. that is reputedly poisonous and has seeds with purgative properties
bellyband \'=,=\ *n* **:** a band that passes around or across the belly: as **a :** a band that goes around or under the belly of a horse and holds the saddle, harness, or shafts in place **:** GIRTH — see HARNESS illustration **b :** a strengthening band of canvas sewed across a sail below the lower reef band **c :** a strip of fabric worn around the abdomen; *esp* **:** BAND 4b(2)
belly brace *n* **:** a vertical steel plate that is used to secure a locomotive boiler to a casting that binds together the frames of a locomotive at a point just in front of the firebox — compare WAIST SHEET
belly bump *also* **belly bumper** *n or adv or vi*, *chiefly NewEng* **:** BELLY FLOP
belly bunt *n or adv or vi*, *NewEng* **:** BELLY FLOP
belly bust *or* **belly buster** *n or adv or vi* **:** BELLY FLOP
belly button *n* **:** NAVEL 1
bellycheer *n* **1** *obs* **:** gratification of the belly **:** GLUTTONY **2** *obs* **:** FOOD
belly dance *n* **:** a dance emphasizing movement of the abdominal muscles — called also *danse du ventre*
¹belly flop *also* **belly flopper** *n* **:** a dive (as into water or in coasting prone on a sled) in which the front of the body strikes flat against another surface
²belly flop *adv* **:** with a belly flop **:** on the belly **:** PRONE ⟨slide *belly flop* downhill⟩
³belly flop *vi* **:** to execute a belly flop
belly-footed \'==¦==\ *adj* **:** of or having to do with a gastropod mollusk
bel·ly·ful \'belē,fu̇l, -li-\ *n* -s **:** an amount over and above what can be stood with comfort ⟨a ~ of advice⟩
belly-god \'==,=\ *n*, *archaic* **:** GLUTTON
belly-gun \'==,=\ *n* **:** an easily concealed short-barreled revolver used only at very close range
belly gut \'==,=\ *also* **belly gut·ter** \¦==¦gəd·ə(r)\ *n or adv or vi*, *dial* **:** BELLY FLOP
belly in *vi* [²*belly*] **:** to crash-land an aircraft with landing gear retracted **:** BELLY-LAND
bellying *pres part of* BELLY
belly-land \¦==¦=\ *vi* [¹*belly* + *land* (v.)] **:** to land an airplane without use of landing gear — **belly landing** *n*
belly laugh *n* **:** a deep hearty laugh
bel·ly·man \'belē,man\ *n*, *pl* **bellymen :** a worker who assembles and adjusts the soundboard of a piano
belly offal *n* **:** hide from the belly that does not measure up to the standard of that from other parts
belly robber *n*, *slang* **:** COOK, STEWARD
belly tank *n* **:** an auxiliary jettisonable fuel tank mounted under the belly of an airplane
belly whop *also* **belly whopper** *n or adv or vi* **:** BELLY FLOP
be·lo hor·i·zon·te \¦bā(,)lō,hȯrə'zäntē, ¦be-\ *adj*, *usu cap B &H* [fr. *Belo Horizonte*, Brazil] **:** of or from the city of Belo Horizonte, Brazil **:** of the kind or style prevalent in Belo Horizonte
be·loid \'bē,lȯid\ *adj* [Gk *belos* dart, arrow + E *-oid*; akin to Gk *ballein* to throw — more at DEVIL] **1 :** having a shape like that of an arrow **2** *of a skull or head* **:** having a contour broad in the occipital and narrow in the frontal regions when viewed from above
bel·o·man·cy \'belə,man(t)sē\ *n* -ES [Gk *belos* dart, arrow + E *-mancy*] **:** divination by drawing arrows at random from a container
bel·o·mys \'belə,mis\ *n*, *cap* [NL, fr. Gk *belos* dart + NL *-mys*] **:** a genus of Asiatic flying squirrels
bel·o·ne \'belə,nē\ *n*, *cap* [NL, fr. L, fr. Gk *belonē* needle, a sea fish, fr. *belos* dart; prob. akin to Gk *ballein* to throw — more at DEVIL] **:** a genus (the type of the family Belonidae) of needlefishes — **bel·o·nid** \'belənə̇d, -,nid\ *n or adj*
be·long \bə̇'lȯŋ, bē- *also* -läŋ\ *vi* -ED/-ING/-S [ME *belongen*, fr. *be-* + *longen* to belong — more at LONG (to be suitable)] **1 a :** to be suitable, appropriate, or advantageous (for a person or thing) ⟨strong meat *belongeth* to them that are of full age — Heb 5:14 (AV)⟩ ⟨a dictionary ~*s* in every office⟩ **b :** to be in a proper, rightful, or fitting place, situation, or connection ⟨books placed where they don't ~⟩ ⟨a man of his ability ~*s* in business⟩ **2** *archaic* **:** to have relation or reference (to a person or thing) — used with *to* or *unto* **3 a :** to be the property of a person or thing — used with *to* ⟨the money ~*s* to him⟩ ⟨buildings ~ to the government⟩ **b :** to become attached or bound (as to a person, group, or organization) by birth, allegiance, residence, or dependency — used with *to* ⟨soldiers ~*ing* to a famous regiment⟩ **c** (1) **:** to be a member of a club

or similar association — used with *to* ⟨~ to the golf club⟩ (2) **:** to have the social qualifications or ability to be a member of a group, circle, or society ⟨she's smart and jolly and everything, but she just doesn't ~ —Edna Ferber⟩ **4 :** to be an attribute, part, adjunct, or function (of a person or thing) — used with *to* ⟨good humor and wit ~ to his personality⟩ **5** *chiefly South & Midland* **:** to become accustomed **:** OUGHT ⟨he ~s to come at 8 o'clock⟩ **6 :** to be properly classified ⟨whales ~ among the mammals⟩

belonging *n* -s **1 belongings** *pl* **:** relative matters, circumstances, or features **:** ADJUNCTS ⟨reality or its ~s⟩ **2 :** POSSESSION ⟨favorite ~⟩ — usu. used in pl. ⟨left all his ~s to his brother⟩ **3 belongings** *pl* **:** RELATIVES ⟨followed his female ~s up the aisle —Dorothy Sayers⟩ **4 :** close or intimate relationship **:** mutual loyalty ⟨each member had a sense of ~⟩

be·long·ing·ness \-nəs\ *n* -ES **:** the quality or state of being essential, integral, or important ⟨a feeling of ~ through participation in the discussion —K.H.Recknagel⟩

bel·o·nite \ˈbelə,nīt\ *n* -s [G *belonit,* fr. Gk *belonē* needle + G *-it* -ite — more at BELONE] **:** an elongated crystallite with rounded or pointed ends

bel·o·noid \ˈbelə,nȯid\ *adj* [Gk *belonoeidēs,* fr. *belonē* needle + *-eidēs* -oid] **:** needlelike in shape **:** STYLOID

1be·lo·russian \ˌbelō+\ *also* **bielo·russian** *or* **byelo·russian** \bēˌelō, ˌbye- +\ *n* -s *cap* [*Belorussia, Bielorussia, Byelorussia,* region of the U.S.S.R. (fr. Russ *Byelorussiya,* fr. *byelo-* white — fr. *byely* — + *Russiya* Russia) + E *-an;* akin to Skt *bhāti* he shines — more at FANCY] **1 :** a native or inhabitant of Belorussia, U.S.S.R. — called also *White Russian* **2 :** the Slavic language of the Belorussians

2belorussian \"\ *also* **bielorussian** *or* **byelorussian** \"\ *adj, usu cap* **1 a :** of, relating to, or characteristic of Belorussia **b :** of, relating to, or characteristic of Belorussians **2 :** of, relating to, or characteristic of the Belorussian language

bel·o·stom·a·tid \ˌbeləˈstäməd·əd\ *n* -s [NL *Belostomatidae*] **:** a bug of the family Belostomatidae

bel·o·sto·mat·i·dae \ˌbeləstōˈmad·ə,dē\ *n pl, cap* [NL, fr. *Belostomat-, Belostoma,* type genus (fr. Gk *belos* dart + NL *-stomat-, -stoma*) + *-idae* — more at BELONE] **:** a family of large predaceous water bugs with piercing and sucking mouthparts that may be very destructive to young fishes

bel·o·stom·i·dae \ˌbeləˈstämə,dē\ [NL, fr. *Belostoma,* type genus + *-idae*] *syn of* BELOSTOMATIDAE

be·lote *or* **be·lotte** \bəˈlät\ *n* -s [F *belote,* after F. *Belot,* 20th cent. Frenchman] **:** a card game played with a 32-card pack similar to klaberjass and very popular in France

belouga *var of* BELUGA 1

1be·loved \bəˈləvd, bē— *compare* 2BELOVED *and* 3BELOVED\ *past part* [ME, past part. of *beloven* to love, fr. *be-* + *loven* to love — more at LOVE] **:** LOVED — used as a passive transitive with *of* or *by* ⟨I was ~ of the Italian and Chinese —Eve Langley⟩

2be·loved \-v(ə)d — *usu* -vd *when modified by an adverb of degree other than "dearly"; after "dearly" and when there is no adverb of degree both pronunciations are frequent, the frequency of* -vəd *after "dearly" prob being due to the analogy of the noun "dearly beloved", for which* -vəd *is usual*\ *adj* [ME, fr. 1*beloved*] **:** dear to the heart **:** dearly loved ⟨his ~ aunt⟩ ⟨a well-*beloved* novel⟩ ⟨a post ~ to old soldiers⟩

3be·lov·ed *usu* -vəd\ *n* -s **:** one who is loved; *esp* **:** SWEETHEART

1be·low \bəˈlō, bē-\ *adv* (or *adj*) [*be-* + *low* (adv.)] **1 a** (1) **:** at a lower level ⟨the pencil rolled off the desk and fell on the floor ~⟩ **:** further down (as along a river, valley, or slope) ⟨several houses ~ on the right bank of the stream⟩ (2) **:** directly under **:** down under ⟨the elevator was let down to pick up the men on the floor ~⟩ — sometimes used interjectionally to express warning ⟨in spite of a shout "*Below!*" an engineer was hit on the shoulder —John May⟩ **b** (1) **:** on earth ⟨if man is born in sin . . . improvements in conditions here ~ can be of only secondary importance —*Times Lit. Supp.*⟩ (2) **:** in Hades or hell ⟨the fiends ~⟩ **2 a :** lower in rank **:** in a lower station ⟨the kindergarten ~⟩ **b :** in or to a court or tribunal of inferior jurisdiction ⟨the learned judge ~ did not distinguish —*Amer. Jour. of International Law*⟩ **3 :** inside or into the superstructure of a boat or down from an upper deck or structure (as a bridge or pilothouse) to a lower deck ⟨set his course, and went ~ to sleep —*Saturday Rev.*⟩ **4 a :** below zero ⟨20 ~⟩ **b :** BELOW-THE-LINE

2below \"\ *prep* **1 a :** downward from ⟨flower boxes ~ the windows⟩ **b :** further down from ⟨a river barge moored a mile ~ town⟩ **:** at a lower level than ⟨lava beds lying ~ the volcanic cone⟩ **c :** at the bottom of **:** directly underneath ⟨the caption ~ a picture⟩ **d :** farther south than ⟨Richmond is ~ Washington⟩ **2 :** BENEATH ⟨he thought manual labor ~ him⟩ **3 :** inferior to **:** lower down the scale than ⟨fairly high in the scale of animal life and only a little ~ the vertebrates —R.E.Coker⟩ **4 :** covered, concealed, or hidden by ⟨the real reason ~ the mass of pretexts⟩ ⟨~ the sod⟩

3below \"\ *n* -s **1 :** matter located lower on the same page or on a following page ⟨the ~ is iambic⟩ **2 a :** a lower class (as of people) ⟨churches have always drawn their recruits from ~ —A.W.Long⟩ **b :** a lower region (as of a building interior, land, or water)

4below \"\ *adj* **:** located lower on the same page or on a following page ⟨the ~ list contains about 500 names⟩

belowdecks \ˈ=ˌ=ˌ=\ *adv* [2*below* + *decks,* pl. of *deck*] **:** 1BELOW 3 ⟨stayed ~ all afternoon⟩

belowground \ˈ=ˌ=ˌ=\ *adj* [2*below* + *ground*] **1 :** under the ground ⟨~ storage⟩ **2 :** dead and buried ⟨most of his friends are now ~⟩

1belowstairs \ˈ=ˌ=ˌ=\ *adv* [2*below* + *stairs*] **:** DOWNSTAIRS ⟨many works . . . kept ~ . . . are accessible only on demand —Denys Sutton⟩

2belowstairs \"\ *adj* **1 :** on a lower floor ⟨the servants' quarters are ~⟩ **2 :** COMMON, UNREFINED ⟨a ~ love affair⟩

below-the-line \ˈ=ˌ=ˌ=\ *adv* (or *adj*) **1 :** in that part of the score sheet in bridge reserved for the trick score **2 :** classified as an unusual or nonrecurring expense or revenue item rather than as a current expense or asset

Bel Pa·e·se \ˌbelpäˈāzē\ *trademark* — used for a mild soft creamy cheese in a firm rind

bels *pl of* BEL

belsire *n* -s [ME *belsyre,* fr. *bel* fair, beautiful (fr. OF) + *syre* sire — more at BEAUTY] *obs* **:** GRANDFATHER, ANCESTOR

belswagger *n* [origin unknown] **1** *obs* **:** PIMP **2** *obs* **:** BULLY

1belt \ˈbelt\ *n* -s [ME, fr. OE; akin to OHG *balz* belt, ON *belti;* all fr. a prehistoric Gmc word borrowed fr. L *balteus* girdle, belt] **1 a :** a strip of flexible material (as leather, plastic, cloth) used in a circular form with or without a buckle or other closing and for wear generally around the waist (as a support for trousers, a decoration for dresses, or a means of carrying weapons, tools, or ornaments) ⟨sword ~⟩ **b :** a similar article worn as a corset or as a protection for the body (as a medical bandage or support) or for safety (as by airplane passengers or telephone linemen) **c :** a mark or symbol of distinction in the form of a belt ⟨the championship ~ of heavyweight boxing⟩ **2 :** a continuous band of tough flexible material (as leather, rubber, fabric, wire) for transmitting motion and power from one pulley to another or for conveying materials — see CHAIN BELT illustration **3 a :** an area distinctively characterized by its species or forms of life ⟨a pine ~⟩ ⟨a forest ~⟩ **b :** an elongated area characterized by some particular geologic feature or occurrence and generally not so extensive as a zone ⟨mountain ~⟩ ⟨~ of volcanoes⟩ ⟨coal ~⟩ ⟨oil ~⟩ **c :** a region marked by the prevalence of some type of inhabitant or noteworthy condition ⟨the goiter ~⟩ ⟨the vacationland ~⟩ **4 :** a horizontal band of brick or stone running across a face of a masonry wall or pier **5** [Dan *bælt;* akin to MHG *Beltemeer* Baltic sea] **:** a strait leading to the Baltic sea **6 :** one of several roads or routes arranged concentrically **:** BELT HIGHWAY — **below the belt** *adv* **1 :** in the area below the waistline ⟨a boxer disqualified for hitting *below the belt*⟩ **2 :** in an unfair or cowardly manner ⟨most of the criticism hit *below the belt*⟩ — **under one's belt 1 :** in one's stomach ⟨a couple of drinks *under his belt*⟩ **2 :** in one's possession ⟨with four flourishing papers *under their belts* —*Newsweek*⟩ **:** as part of one's past or experience ⟨she now had three great classic roles *under her belt* —Agnes de Mille⟩

A belt 2

2belt \"\ *vb* -ED/-ING/-S [ME *belten,* fr. *belt,* n.] *vt* **1 a :** to encircle, girdle, or fasten with a belt ⟨a cord ~*ing* a gown⟩ ⟨paraphernalia ~*ed* together⟩ **b :** to gird on ⟨~ on a gun and ammunition⟩ **c :** to invest (a person) with a distinction or title ⟨~ a squire with the rank of knight⟩ **2 a :** to beat with or as if with a belt **:** THRASH **b :** to strike vigorously **:** HIT ⟨~ a person in the jaw⟩ — often used with *out* ⟨~*ing* out a triple⟩ **3 :** to mark with or as if with a band ⟨all equipment to be sold was ~*ed* in green⟩ ⟨~*ed* with a shining porch of enormous pillars —Robinson Jeffers⟩; *specif* **:** GIRDLE 3a ⟨~ a tree⟩ **4 :** to sing in a very loud forceful manner or style ⟨the hoydenish numbers are ~*ed* across effectively —Bill Simon⟩ — usu. used with *out* ⟨~ out a high note⟩ **~** *vi* **:** to move, act, or perform in a vigorous or violent manner ⟨~ along in a car⟩ ⟨waves ~*ing* over a ship⟩

3belt \"\ *n* -s **1 :** a jarring blow **:** JOLT, WHACK ⟨gave the ball a terrific ~⟩ ⟨a ~ of lightning⟩ **2** *slang* **:** a strong emotional reaction ⟨get a terrific ~ out of this tale —*New Republic*⟩

belt ammunition *n* **:** ammunition of usu. small caliber loaded in web or metallic link belts for an automatic weapon

bel·tane \ˈbel(ˌ)tān, -ˌtin\ *also* **beal·ti·ne** \ˈbyaültənə\ *n* -s *usu cap* [ME, fr. ScGael *bealltainn;* akin to MIr *beltene*] **1 :** the first day of May in the old Scottish calendar **2 :** the May Day festival once widely celebrated in Celtic lands with bonfires on the hills, dancing, and various rites

belt conveyor *n* **:** CONVEYER 2a(1)

belt course *n* **:** a horizontal band forming part of an interior or exterior architectural composition (as around pillars or engaged columns) — called also *band course*

B belt course

belted *adj* [ME, fr. past part. of *belten*] **1 :** wearing or encircled by a belt; *esp* **:** girded by a king in an investiture ⟨the son of a ~ earl —Sir Walter Scott⟩ **2 :** marked or furnished with a band (as about the body of an animal) ⟨a ~ hog⟩

belted cattle *n* **:** cattle of any breed characterized by a white band about the body

belted coastal plain *n* **:** a coastal plain on which there are two or more roughly parallel cuestas

belted galloway *n, usu cap B&G* **:** a breed of black or dun-colored cattle developed from the Galloway and having a white band about the body

belted kingfisher *n* **:** a No. American kingfisher (*Ceryle,* or *Megaceryle, alcyon*) that is about a foot long and slate-blue above and white below with a chestnut band across the breast and is sometimes a pest about fish hatcheries

bel·ter \ˈbeltə(r)\ *adj, often cap* [after John H. *Belter* †1863 Ger.-Am. cabinetmaker] **:** belonging to or suggestive of a style of richly carved 19th century furniture ⟨a ~ chair⟩

belt-fed \ˈ=ˌ=\ *adj* **:** using belt ammunition ⟨*belt-fed* weapons⟩

belt highway *n* **:** a highway skirting an urban area — called also *beltway, ring road*

belt·ian \ˈbeltēən\ *adj, usu cap* [Big *Belt* & Little *Belt* Mountains, Montana + E *-ian*] **:** of or relating to a division of Proterozoic geologic era in No. America region — see GEOLOGIC TIME table

1belting *n* -s [1*belt* + *-ing*] **1 :** BELTS **2 :** material for belts: as **a :** a firm narrow fabric usu. of cotton made in various weights and thicknesses **b** *or* **belting leather :** heavy cattlehide leather used for power transmission belts

2belting *n* -s [fr. gerund of 2*belt*] **:** THRASHING, BEATING

bel·tir \ˈbel,ti(ə)r\ *n, pl* **beltir** *or* **beltirs** *usu cap* **1 :** a turkicized Samoyed people of Yeniseisk province, Siberia **2 :** a member of the Beltir people

belt leather *n* **:** leather used to make waist belts — compare 1BELTING 2b

beltline \ˈ=ˌ=\ *n* **1 :** production line ⟨manufacture requiring only simple ~ operations⟩ **2 :** WAISTLINE

belt line *n* **1 a :** a railroad going wholly or partly around a city for the interchange of traffic between trunk lines or for handling traffic to off-trunkline terminals **b :** a transport line that makes a fairly complete circuit (as around a city) **2 :** a line of rope carried at the belt by a fireman for use in emergency

belt loom *n* **:** a primitive loom consisting usu. of two parallel sticks supporting the warp, one being attached to a tree or post and the other to the weaver's belt

belt·man \ˈbeltmən, -ˌman\ *n, pl* **beltmen :** a worker who tends and repairs machine belts

belt of cementation : the portion of the zone of fracture in which mineral matter is commonly deposited in cracks, fissures, intergranular spaces, and other openings of the earth

belt of fire : an area of active volcanoes

bel·ton \ˈbeltᵊn *also* -tən\ *n* -s [fr. *Belton,* Northumberland, Eng.] **1 :** a blended, flecked, or finely mottled combination orig. of gray and yellow but now of any two colors including esp. white — used of the coats of dogs (as of certain setters) ⟨blue ~⟩ ⟨orange ~⟩ **2 :** a dog with a belton coat

belt pulley *n* **:** a pulley designed to drive or be driven by a belt

belt punch *n* **:** a punch for making holes (as in leather)

belt railroad *n* **:** BELT LINE 1a

belts *pl of* BELT, *pres 3d sing of* BELT

belt sander *n* **:** a machine for belt-sanding

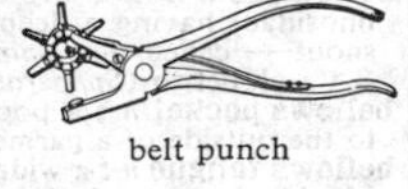

belt punch

belt-sanding \ˈ=ˌ==\ *n* **:** the sanding or smoothing of a flat wood surface by means of a mechanically driven abrasive belt

belt shifter *n* **:** a device for placing a belt on a pulley or for shifting a belt from one pulley to another

belts·ville small white \ˈbelts,vil-, *esp S* - vəl-\ *n, usu cap B&S&W* [fr. *Beltsville,* Maryland] **:** a small white domestic turkey of a variety developed by the U.S. Department of Agriculture to meet the demand for a smaller table bird

belt tightening *n* **:** the curbing of unnecessary expenditure

beltway \ˈ=ˌ=\ *n* **:** BELT HIGHWAY

beltwise \ˈ=ˌ=\ *adv* [1*belt* + *-wise*] **:** in the manner of a belt

beltwork \ˈ=ˌ=\ *n* **:** an operation in which power from a stationary tractor is applied to other machines through a pulley and belt

beluchi *var of* BALUCHI

beluchistan *usu cap, var of* BALUCHISTAN

be·lu·ga *also* **be·lou·ga** \bəˈlügə\ *n* -s [Russ *byeluga,* fr. *byely* white; akin to OSlav *bělŭ* white, Skt *bhāti* he shines — more at FANCY] **1 :** a white sturgeon (*Acipenser huso*) of the Black sea, Caspian sea, and their tributaries that reaches a length of 18 feet and has a swim bladder that is used to make isinglass and roe that is made into caviar **2** [Russ *byelukha,* fr. *byely* white] **:** a cetacean (*Delphinapterus leucas*) of the family Delphinidae becoming about 10 feet long and white when adult and occurring chiefly in northern seas and esp. in the lower St. Lawrence river — called also *white whale*

1bel·ve·dere *also* **bel·vi·dere** \ˈbelvə,di(ə)r, ˌ==ˈ=\ *n* -s [It *belvedere,* lit., beautiful view, fr. *bel, bello* beautiful (fr. L *bellus*) + *vedere* view, fr. *vedere* to see, fr. L *vidēre* — more at BEAUTY, WIT] **:** a structure (as a cupola or a summerhouse) designed to command a view

2belvedere *also* **belvidere** \"\ *n* -s [It *belvedere* (alter. of It dial. — Tuscany — *bedduvidiri*), fr. *bel* + *vedere*] **:** SUMMER CYPRESS

bely *var of* BELIE

belying *pres part of* BELIE

be·lyve *var of* BELIVE

bel·ze·buth \ˈbelzə(ˌ)bəth, -ˌbüth\ *n* -s [NL (specific epithet of *Ateles belzebuth*) prob. alter. of *Beelzebub*] **:** a Brazilian spider monkey (*Ateles belzebuth*)

be·ma \ˈbēmə\ *n* -s [LL & LGk; LL, fr. LGk *bēma,* fr. Gk, step, tribune, fr. *bainein* to step, go — more at COME] **1 :** the part of an early Christian and modern Eastern Orthodox church that contains the altar and synthronon and corresponds to the sanctuary of Western churches — see BASILICA illustration **2 :** ALMEMAR

bemad *vt* [*be-* + *mad*] *archaic* **:** to make insane or frantic

be·master \bə, bē+\ *vt* [*be-* + *master*] **:** to master thoroughly **:** bring under control

be·maul \bə, bē+\ *vt* [*be-* + *maul*] **:** to maul thoroughly

be·mazed \bəˈmāzd, bē-\ *adj* [ME *bemased,* fr. past part. of *bemasen* to stupefy, fr. *be-* + *masen* to stupefy — more at MAZE] *archaic* **:** BEWILDERED, STUPEFIED

bem·ba \ˈbembə\ *n, pl* **bemba** *or* **bembas** *usu cap* **1 a :** a prominent primarily agricultural Bantu-speaking people in northern Rhodesia **b :** a member of the Bemba people **2 :** a Bantu language of the Bemba people

1bembex \ˈbem,beks\ [NL, alter. of *Bembix*] *syn of* BEMBIX

2bembex \"\ *n* -ES [NL, fr. 1*Bembex*] **:** a bembicid wasp

bem·bi·cid \ˈbembəsəd, -ˌsid\ *adj* [NL *Bembicidae,* fr. *Bembic-, Bembix,* type genus + *-idae*] **:** of or relating to the genus *Bembix* or the family Bembicidae

bem·bix \ˈbembiks\ *n, cap* [NL, fr. Gk, buzzing insect, top, whirlpool, cyclone; akin to Gk *bombos* booming or humming sound — more at BOMB] **:** a genus (the type of the family Bembicidae) of wasps comprising the large solitary or gregarious burrowing sand wasps

be·mean \bəˈmēn, bē-\ *vt* -ED/-ING/-S [*be-* + *mean* (adj.)] **:** DEBASE, LOWER

be·med·aled *or* **be·med·alled** \bəˈmedᵊld, bē-\ *adj* [*be-* + *medal* + *-ed*] **:** wearing or decorated with medals esp. in excessive numbers

bemeet *vb* [*be-* + *meet*] *obs* **:** MEET

be·ment·ite \ˈbēmənt,īt\ *n* -s [C.S. *Bement* †1923 Am. manufacturer and mineral collector + E *-ite*] **:** a mineral consisting of a hydrous silicate of manganese occurring in grayish yellow radiated masses

be·mire \bə, bē+\ *vt* [*be-* + *mire* (n.)] **1 :** to cover or soil with or as if with mud or dirt ⟨surveyed his extended leggings, his immense *bemired* boots —F.M.Ford⟩ **2 :** to drag through, encumber with, or sink in mire ⟨*bemired* in a ditch⟩

be·mist \bə, bē+\ *vt* [*be-* + *mist* (n.)] **:** to envelop, involve, or obscure in or as if in mist ⟨a ~*ed* mind⟩

be·moan \bə, bē+\ *vt* [alter. (influenced by *moan*) of ME *bemenen,* fr. OE *bemǣnan,* fr. *be-* + *mǣnan* to moan — more at MOAN] **1 a :** to express grief over **:** LAMENT ⟨she ~*ed* her brother's death⟩ **b** *archaic* **:** to subject (oneself) to lamentations ⟨people grieve and ~ themselves, but it is not half so bad with them as they say —R.W.Emerson⟩ **2** *obs* **:** to express pity or sorrow for ⟨they ~*ed* him and comforted him over all the evil . . . brought upon him —Job 42:11 (AV)⟩ **3 :** to look upon with regret, displeasure, or disapproval ⟨the governmental control which industrialists ~ so consistently —Douglas McGregor⟩ **syn** see DEPLORE

be·moan·ing·ly *adv* **:** in a bemoaning manner

be·mock \bə, bē+\ *vt* [*be-* + *mock*] **:** to mock or mock at

bemoil *vt* [*be-* + *moil*] *obs* **:** to soil or encumber with mud and dirt

be·monster \bə, bē+\ *vt* -ED/-ING/-S [*be-* + *monster* (n.)] **1** *obs* **:** to make ugly or vicious as a monster **2 :** to address or refer to as a monster

be·mouth \bəˈmau̇th, bē-\ *vt* [*be-* + *mouth*] **:** to talk bombastically about **:** put into a specified condition by bombastic talk

be·mud \bə, bē+\ *vt* [*be-* + *mud* (n.)] **1** *archaic* **:** to cover or spatter with mud **2 :** MUDDLE ⟨*bemudded* thought⟩

be·muffled \bə, bē+\ *adj* [*be-* + *muffled*] **:** muffled up

be·muse \bəˈmyüz, bē-\ *vt* [*be-* + *muse*] **1 :** to make confused or muddled ⟨he drinketh strong waters which do ~ a man —W.S.Gilbert⟩ **:** BEWILDER ⟨the extraordinary dialect used in this case . . . would have *bemused* the acutest jury —Malcolm Muggeridge⟩ **2 :** to cause to dream or muse **:** induce a state of reverie in ⟨there is another theory that ~s the pilots in the islands —Corey Ford⟩ **syn** see DAZE

be·mused \-ˈmyüzd\ *adj* **1 :** marked by confusion or bewilderment **:** DAZED ⟨he was fumbling with the sheets and looking down at them with a slightly ~ expression —R.P.Warren⟩ **2 :** lost in thought or reverie **:** ABSTRACTED ⟨as distant and ~ as a professor emeritus listening to the prattling of his freshman class —M.W.Straight⟩ — **be·mus·ed·ly** \-zədlē, -li\ *adv*

be·muse·ment \-zmənt\ *n* -s **:** the quality or state of being bemused ⟨this ~ by superficial ideas —H.L.Mencken⟩

1ben \ˈben\ *adv* [ME *ben, binne, binnen,* fr. OE *binnan,* fr. *be-* + *innan* within, from within, fr. *in* — more at IN] *Scot* **:** in or into the inner part or parlor of the house **:** INSIDE, WITHIN ⟨with kindly welcome Jenny brings him ~ —Robert Burns⟩ — opposed to *but*

2ben \"\ *prep, Scot* **:** in or into the inner room of **:** WITHIN ⟨~ the house⟩

3ben \"\ *adj, Scot* **:** situated in the inner part of a house **:** INNER, INTERIOR

4ben \"\ *n* -s *Scot* **:** the inner room or parlor of a house (as of a but-and-ben) — compare 6BUT

5ben \"\ *n* -s [ScGael *beann* peak, horn; akin to MIr *benn* peak, horn, W *ban* peak — more at PIN] *Scot* **:** a high hill **:** MOUNTAIN — often used in place names ⟨*Ben* Nevis⟩ ⟨*Ben* Lomond⟩

6ben *dial past part of* BE

7ben \ˈben\ *also* **be·hen** \bəˈhen, ˈbāən, ˈbēən\ *n* -s [Ar *bān*] **:** the seed of any tree of the genus *Moringa* — see BEN OIL

bena \ˈbenə\ *n, pl* **bena** *or* **benas** *usu cap* **1 :** an African Bantu-speaking people north of Lake Nyasa **2 :** a member of the Bena people

be·nab \bəˈnab\ *n* -s [prob. native name in Guiana] **:** a native hut or shelter in Guiana

Ben·a·dryl \ˈbenədrəl, -ˌdril\ *trademark* — used for diphenhydramine

be·na·mi *also* **be·na·mee** \bəˈnämē\ *adj* [Hindi *benāmī,* fr. Per *banām* in the name of + *-ī*] **:** made, held, done, or transacted in the name of (another person) — used in Hindu law to designate a transaction, contract, or property that is made or held under a name that is fictitious or is that of a third party who holds as ostensible owner for the principal or beneficial owner

benares *usu cap, var of* BANARAS

be·nasty \bə, bē+\ *vt* [*be-* + *nasty*] *dial* **:** to make nasty **:** SOIL

ben·ben \ˈben,ben\ *n* -s [alternate transliteration of Egypt *bnbn*] **:** an Egyptian stone of pyramidal shape

bence-jones protein \ˈben(t)s,jōnz-\ *n, usu cap B&J* [after Henry *Bence-Jones* †1873 Eng. physician and chemist] **:** a globulin or a group of globulins found in the blood serum and urine in multiple myeloma and occas. in other bone diseases and usu. characterized by coagulation at 50-60°C with partial redissolving at higher temperatures

1bench \ˈbench\ *n* -ES [ME, fr. OE *benc;* akin to OHG *bank* bench, ON *bekkr*] **1 a :** a long usu. wooden seat often for two or more persons and sometimes with a back ⟨a park ~⟩ **b :** a thwart or seat in a boat **c** (1) **:** a seat on which members of an athletic team sit while awaiting a turn or an opportunity to play (2) **:** the reserve players of a team **2 a :** the seat where a judge sits in court **:** the seat of justice **b :** the office or dignity of a judge ⟨a recent appointment to the ~⟩ **c :** the place where justice is administered **:** COURT **d :** the persons who sit as judges — see COURT OF KING'S BENCH **3 a :** a seat or seat and table or desk for an official **b :** the office or dignity of such an official ⟨he aspires to the civic ~⟩ **c :** the officials occupying such a bench ⟨the bishops' ~ in the House of Lords⟩ **4 a :** a long worktable having a level top ⟨a carpenter's ~⟩ **b :** a usu. metal table forming part of a machine **c :** any of various machines (as for drawing wires or tubes) that are developments of the simple workbench **5 :** TERRACE, SHELF: as **a :** an area of level or gently sloping land with steep slopes above and below formed by differential erosion of rocks of varying resistance or by a change of base-level erosion **b :** a former wave-cut shore of a sea or lake or floodplain of a river **c :** a shelf formed in working an open excavation on more than one level **d :** a shelf or ledge made in a mine tunnel or working when an upper section is cut back **e** (1) **:** a stratum of coal forming part of a seam (2) **:** one of two or more portions of a coal seam often separated (as by slate) **6 a** (1) **:** a platform with wooden sides and back and often a heavy screen top and front on which a dog is placed at a dog show (2) **:** a public exhibition of dogs **b :** a raised platform with sides that is used for supporting potted plants or for holding soil in which plants are grown (as in a greenhouse or conservatory) **7 a :** a group of retorts in an oven or furnace for generating coal gas **b :** the complete oven or furnace containing a set or group of retorts — **on the bench** **1 :** sitting as a judge **2 a :** awaiting a turn or opportunity to play **b :** temporarily out of a game

²**bench** \"\ *vb* -ED/-ING/-ES [ME *benchen*, fr. *bench*, n.] *vt* **1 :** to furnish with benches **2 a :** to seat on a bench (as of justice or honor) **b :** to remove (a player) from a game or keep (a player) on the bench ⟨the infielder was ~*ed* for poor fielding⟩ **c :** to set out (plants) in greenhouse benches or beds **3 a :** to exhibit (dogs or other show animals) in a bench show **b :** to arrange the bench for (a dog or other animal show) **4 :** to cut ledges or steps in (as an embankment) ~ *vi* **1** *obs* **:** to sit on a seat of justice **2 :** to form a bench by natural processes ⟨the soil showed a tendency to ~ off levelly between the tree rows —Russell Lord⟩

benchboard \'ˌ=ˌ=\ *n* **:** a horizontal or slightly inclined switchboard with or without vertical instrument sections

bench·er \'benchə(r)\ *n* -S [¹*bench* + -*er*] **:** one that sits on, works at, or presides at a bench: as **a :** one that sits on an official bench (as a judge) — see BACK BENCHER, FRONT BENCHER **b :** one of the senior and governing members of an Inn of Court

ben chervil \'ben+,-\ *n* [origin unknown] **:** HEDGE PARSLEY

¹**bench graft** *n* [¹*bench* + *graft*] **:** a plant propagated by bench grafting

²**bench graft** *vt* **:** to graft indoors (as on a greenhouse bench during the winter) ⟨cherries were *bench grafted* successfully⟩

bench hardening *n* **:** the hardening of wire by drawing after annealing

bench hook *n* **:** any of various hook-shaped stops on a bench against which work may be pushed (as while planing or chiseling)

benching *n* -S [¹*bench* + -*ing*] **1 :** benches esp. around a room **2 :** ¹BENCH 6a(1)

bench jockey *n* **:** a baseball player who heckles the members of the opposing team ⟨all the *bench jockeys* on the circuit were quickly counting ten on every pitch Lefty made —G.S.Cochrane⟩

bench key *or* **bench winder** *n* **:** a watchmaker's adjustable clock or watch key

bench knife *n* **:** an adjustable stop with a projecting knife or hook that holds a piece of work on the bench

benchland \'ˌ=ˌ=\ *n* **1 :** a bench esp. along a river **2 :** a land surface composed largely of benches

bench lathe *n* **:** a lathe mounted on a workbench

bench-legged \'bench¦leg(ə)d\ *adj* [*bench leg* + -*ed*] **:** having the legs spread wide apart ⟨a *bench-legged* pony⟩

bench-made \'ˌ=ˌ=\ *adj* **:** made on a bench usu. by hand **:** HANDMADE — used esp. of shoes

bench·man \'benchmən\ *n, pl* **benchmen :** one that works at a bench: as **a :** a repairer of shoes **b :** one that cleans, fits, assembles, tests, or repairs component parts of a product **c :** a bakery worker who prepares dough for baking by kneading, shaping, weighing, and placing in pans **d :** a chemist who performs laboratory tests during the processing of sugar

bench mark *n* **1 :** a mark on a fixed and enduring object (as on an outcropping of rock or a concrete post set into the ground) indicating a particular elevation and used as a reference in topographical surveys and tidal observations **2** *usu* **benchmark** \'ˌ=ˌ=\ **:** a point of reference from which measurements of any sort may be made ⟨the fact is a ~ to measure our progress toward . . . culmination of the war —*New Republic*⟩

bench plane *n* **:** a plane (as a jack plane or smoothing plane) used by a carpenter or joiner in benchwork

bench press *n* **:** a small punch press mounted on a workbench

benchrest \'ˌ=ˌ=\ *n* **:** a sturdy table on which a heavy target rifle is cradled usu. by means of sandbags and a pedestal so as to ensure maximum steadiness when it is aimed and fired

bench saw *n* **:** a circular saw mounted on a bench

bench screw *n* **:** a long wood or iron screw used in operating the jaws of a bench vise or clamp

bench show *n* **:** an exhibition of small animals in competition for prizes on the basis of points of physical conformation and condition — compare FIELD TRIAL

bench table *n* **:** a projecting course at the base of a wall (as in a church) or round a pillar sufficient to form a seat

bench terrace *n* **:** an artificial land terrace with flat top and often nearly vertical side and used esp. in series to convert mountainous slopes to arable land (as in certain Old World vineyards)

bench warmer *n* **:** one that sits on a bench; *specif* **:** a substitute player on an athletic team

bench warrant *n* **:** a warrant issued by a presiding judge or by a court against a person guilty of some contempt or indicted for some crime — compare JUSTICE'S WARRANT

benchwork \'ˌ=ˌ=\ *n* **:** work done at a bench

benchy \'benchē\ *adj* [¹*bench* + -*y*] **:** occurring in benches or tending to split horizontally — used esp. of a bed of coal or stone

¹**bend** \'bend\ *n* -S [ME, fr. OE *bend* bend, chain, fetter & MF *bende, bande* band, ring, stripe — more at BAND] **1** *obs* **:** a thin flat strip (as of iron) used for strengthening **2** *heraldry* **:** a diagonal band **3 :** the half of a butt or a hide trimmed of the thinner parts and containing the best quality of sole leather — see HIDE illustration **4 :** a knot by which one rope is fastened to another or to some object — **in bend 1 :** in a line in the direction of a bend — used of two or more heraldic charges **2 :** BENDWISE — **in bend dexter :** in bend — used only in contrast with *in bend sinister*

²**bend** \"\ *vb* **bent** \-nt\ *or archaic* **bended; bent** *or archaic* **bended; bending; bends** [ME *benden*, fr. OE *bendan*; akin to ON *benda* to bend, OE *bend* fetter — more at BAND] *vt* **1 a :** to constrain or strain to tension (as a bow) **b** *archaic* **:** to strain, brace, or bring into a tense condition **2 a :** to turn, press, or force with stress concentrated at specific points from straight, level, or even to curved, angular, uneven, or cambered ⟨~ a pipe⟩ ⟨a *bent* glass tube⟩ **b :** to press or force back to an original straight, level, or even condition ⟨~ a crooked bar straight again⟩ **c :** to force, prize, or crush from a proper, intended, or usable shape ⟨he *bent* the can opener⟩ **3 :** FASTEN ⟨~ one rope to another⟩ ⟨~ a sail to its yard⟩ ⟨~ a cable to the ring of an anchor⟩ **4 :** to make submissive **:** SUBDUE ⟨natives unwilling to be *bent* by colonial power⟩ **5 :** to determine usu. after considerable thought **:** RESOLVE — used in passive and with *on* or *upon* ⟨they were *bent* on self-destruction⟩ **6 a :** to cause to turn at an angle or on a curve from a straight line, course, or pattern **:** DEFLECT ⟨*bent* rays emerging from a prism⟩ **b :** to guide or turn toward **:** DIRECT ⟨Tictocq ~*s* his rapid steps in the direction of the headquarters of the Paris gendarmerie —O.Henry⟩ ⟨Santayana ~*s* his genius . . . to deal with the concrete facts of actual political life —*Times Lit. Supp.*⟩ **c :** INCLINE, DISPOSE, PREDISPOSE **:** induce a liking, inclination, or partiality or a distaste or antipathy in ⟨ignoring other peoples and ~*ing* their minds to the Buddhist concept of eternity —Christopher Rand⟩ **d :** to influence or constrain from a usual, expected, or individual course or pattern ⟨how society ~*s* its individual members to function in conformity with its needs —A.N.Whitehead⟩ **7 a** *obs* **:** to direct (as a weapon) with hostile intent **b :** to direct strenuously or with interest ⟨~ their efforts to the task⟩ **:** APPLY ⟨*bent* themselves to the work at hand⟩ **c** *Scot* **:** DRINK, GUZZLE ~ *vi* **1 :** to curve over or away from a vertical line or position; *specif* **:** to incline the body often in token of submission or reverence ⟨*bent* to the queen⟩ **2 a :** to move out of a straight line **:** be or become curving **:** CROOK, BOW ⟨trees ~*ing* under the weight of snow⟩ **b :** to have a direction or inclination away from a straight line **:** CURVE, TREND ⟨beyond the rocks the coastline *bent* west⟩ **3** *archaic* **:** to direct oneself **:** take one's course **:** TURN **4 :** INCLINE, LEAN, TEND ⟨an individual who always ~*s* toward his own tastes⟩ **5 :** to work vigorously ⟨sailors ~*ing* to the oars⟩ **6** *Scot* **:** to drink hard **syn** see CURVE — **bend an ear :** to listen closely ⟨*bend an ear* toward how the man in the street feels about this business —*Frontier*⟩ — **bend one's ear :** to talk to someone at length esp. to the point of boredom ⟨Humphrey *bent the ear of* . . . Charles Murphy for nearly two hours —*Newsweek*⟩ — **bend over backward :** to make extreme efforts at concession

³**bend** \'bend\ *n* -S **1 a :** the act or action of bending ⟨a quick ~ of the body⟩ **b :** the quality or state of being bent or curved ⟨the graceful ~*s* of Gothic windows⟩ **2 :** something that is bent or curved: as **a :** a curved part of a stream, lake, inlet, or coastline **b :** the thickest and strongest planks in the sides of a wooden ship **:** WALES — usu. used in pl. **c :** a curved piece of pipe **d :** the part of a fishhook lying between the shank and the barb **3 bends** *pl but sing or pl in constr* **:** CAISSON DISEASE, AEROEMBOLISM; *specif* **:** the form of aeroembolism that is marked by intense pain in muscles and joints due to formation of gas bubbles in the tissues — usu. used with preceding *the* **4 :** the distance between a bow braced ready for use and its string **5 :** a stylistic effect produced by varying the pitch of a sustained note and commonly employed by brass-wind instruments in jazz bands

bend \'bē¦end\ *n, usu cap B* **:** the end of a railway car on which the hand brake is located

bend·a·ble \'bendəbəl\ *adj* [²*bend* + -*able*] **:** capable of being bent

¹**ben·day** \(')ben¦dā\ *vt* -ED/-ING/-S [fr. *Ben Day* process, after *Benjamin Day* †1916 Am. printer] **:** to produce or prepare by the benday process ⟨~ a plate⟩ ⟨a ~*ed* area⟩

²**benday** \"\ *adj, often cap B* [fr. *Ben Day* process] **:** involving or used in a method of adding tints made up of dots, lines, or other patterns to original copy, negatives, or plates for reproduction as line engravings

bended *archaic past of* BEND — **on bended knee :** kneeling or as if kneeling in supplication

bend·er \'bendə(r)\ *n* -S [ME, fr. *benden* + -*er*] **1 :** one that bends or folds: as **a :** an instrument or power-driven machine for bending **b :** a factory worker who bends and shapes wooden or metal parts by hand or by machine; *specif* **:** one that shapes wooden parts of furniture that have been made flexible by steaming **c :** a paper-products worker who folds blanks (as for boxes or bags) along scored lines to prepare them for further processing or to collapse them for shipment **d :** a paperboard suitable for folding — called also *bending board* **2 :** SPREE ⟨go out on a ~⟩ **3** *slang Brit* **:** SIXPENCE **4** *dial chiefly Eng* **:** an extraordinary specimen ⟨it's a ~ of a night —Rudyard Kipling⟩ **5 benders** *pl* **:** BENDER COTTON

bend·er cotton \'bendə(r)-\ *n* [³*bend* + -*er*] **:** cotton grown on land partly enclosed by the bends of the Mississippi river

ben·der gestalt test \'bendə(r)-\ *n, usu cap B&G* [after Lauretta *Bender* *b*1897 Am. psychiatrist] **:** a performance test requiring reproduction of the configuration in line drawings

bending *pres part of* BEND

bending moment *n, physics* **:** the resultant moment about the neutral axis of any cross section of a rod or beam of the system of forces that produce bending

bending shackle *n* **:** a shackle joining a chain cable to an anchor

bending slab *n* **:** a slab consisting of several large cast-iron blocks with holes for pins around which frames and other structural members of ships are bent

bend·let \'bendlət\ *n* -S [¹*bend* (in heraldry) + -*let*] *heraldry* **:** a narrow bend

bends *pl of* BEND, *pres 3d sing of* BEND

bend sinister *n* [¹*bend*] *heraldry* **:** a bend drawn from sinister chief to dexter base — **in bend sinister 1 :** in a line in the direction of a bend sinister — used of two or more heraldic charges **2 :** BENDWISE SINISTER

bend sinister

bend-sin·is·ter-wise \(')ˌ=¦===,wīz\ *also* **bend-sin·is·ter-ways** \-,wāz\ *adv* **:** BENDWISE SINISTER

¹**bend·wise** \'ben,dwīz\ *also* **bend·ways** \-wāz\ *adv* [¹*bend* + -*wise*] *heraldry* **:** in the direction of a bend **:** DIAGONALLY

²**bendwise** \"\ *adj* **:** having the direction of a bend in a coat of arms **:** DIAGONAL

bendwise sinister *adv* **:** in the direction of a bend sinister

¹**bendy** \'bendē\ *adj* [ME, fr. ¹*bend* + -*y*] *heraldry* **:** divided into an even number of bends, usu. six

²**ben·dy** \"\ *n* -S [Hindi *bhiṇḍī*] **:** OKRA

ben·dy tree \"-\ *n* [Marathi *bhēḍī*] **:** PORTIA TREE

bendy-wavy \¦==¦==\ *adj* [¹*bendy*] *heraldry* **:** composed of an even number of wavy bends

bene *var of* BENNE

be·neaped \bə̇, bē+\ *adj* [*be-* + *neaped*] **:** NEAPED

¹**be·neath** \bə̇'nēth, bē-\ *adv (or adj)* [ME *benethe, benethen*, adv. & prep., fr. OE *beneothan*, fr. *be-* + *neothan* below; akin to OFris *nitha* below, OHG *nidana*, ON *nethan* — more at NETHER] **1 a :** directly under ⟨look at the illustration and read what is ~⟩ **b :** underneath esp. in relation to something screening, sheltering, surmounting ⟨an awning with chairs and tables ~⟩ ⟨the sky above and the earth ~⟩ **c :** in a low position (as in relation to something else) **:** lower down ⟨the mountains and the little towns ~⟩ **2 :** lower in rank, dignity, or quality ⟨a man intolerant of those above and merciless to those ~⟩ **3 :** on the further side **:** beyond what intervenes ⟨slashes in the glaze to show the beige pottery ~ —*New Yorker*⟩

²**beneath** \"\ *prep* [ME *benethe, benethen*] **1 a :** unworthy of **:** unbecoming or lowering to ⟨an occupation ~ his dignity⟩ **b :** too low, vile, or wretched for **:** far below ⟨his words were ~ contempt⟩ **2 a** (1) **:** at or to a level lower than ⟨the sun sank ~ the horizon⟩ **:** further down from ⟨a town located a mile ~ the crest of a hill⟩ (2) **:** at the foot or base of ⟨a chair ~ a wall⟩ ⟨a camp ~ a hill⟩ (3) **:** immediately under **:** UNDERNEATH ⟨the floor echoed ~ his tread⟩ ⟨a cellar ~ the first floor⟩ **b :** lower than (as in rank, dignity, excellence) **:** BELOW ⟨he in turn became something of a bully to the men ~ him —Sherwood Anderson⟩ **3 :** overhung, shaded, or screened by **:** BELOW ⟨~ an umbrella⟩ **4 :** under esp. in relation to something that exerts pressure, influence, control ⟨trees bent down ~ their weight of fruit⟩ ⟨the Higher Order ~ which men carry on their fantastic mummeries —W.L.Sullivan⟩ **5 a :** concealed by **:** covered by ⟨wearing a vest ~ his coat⟩ **b :** on the other side of **:** below the surface of **:** BEYOND ⟨detected moral truth ~ the veil of antique fable⟩

¹**be·ne·di·ci·te** \,benə'disəd·ē, -səd·i,-sə(,)tē, -'dikə,tā, -'dēchə,tā, ,bānā'dēchē,tā *Brit usu* ,beni'dīsiti\ *n* -S [ME, fr. LL, bless ye] **:** an invocation of a blessing ⟨the friar answered his reverend greeting with a paternal ~ —Sir Walter Scott⟩

²**benedicite** \"\ *interj* [ME, fr. LL, bless ye, imper. pl. of *benedicere* to bless — more at BENEDICTION] *obs* — used to express a wish ⟨grace go with you, ~ —Shak.⟩

¹**benedict** *adj* [LL *benedictus*, past part. of *benedicere* to bless] *obs* **:** BLESSED, BENIGN, MILD

²**ben·e·dict** \'benə,dikt\ *also* **ben·e·dick** \-ik\ *n* -S *sometimes cap* [after *Benedick*, newly married man in Shakespeare's *Much Ado about Nothing*] **:** a married man; *esp* **:** a newly married man who has long been a bachelor ⟨he had married our great-aunt . . . shortly before the death of our parents and so became our guardian while still a ~ —Mary McCarthy⟩

¹**ben·e·dic·tine** \,benə'dik,tēn, -tən — *the second is the usu pronunc in the order*\ *n* -S *usu cap* [after St. *Benedict* of Nursia †*ab* 543, who founded it] **:** a member of a monastic order founded in the sixth century and noted esp. for its liturgical worship and its scholarly activities

²**benedictine** \¦==¦=(,)=\ *adj, usu cap* **1 :** of or relating to St. Benedict of Nursia **2 :** of or relating to the Benedictines

ben·e·dic·tin·ism \,==¦=tə̇,nizəm, -,tē,n-\ *n* -S *usu cap* **:** the state, system, or practices of Benedictines

ben·e·dic·tion \,benə'dikshən\ *n* -S [ME *benediccioun*, fr. LL *benediction-, benedictio*, fr. *benedictus* (past part. of *benedicere* to bless, fr. L *bene dicere* to praise, speak well, fr. *bene* well + *dicere* to say) + L -*ion*, -*io* -ion — more at BOUNTY, DICTION] **1 :** an expression or utterance of blessing or good wishes ⟨departing with his parents' ~⟩ ⟨yearning for the ~ of the New York critics —*Time*⟩ **2 :** the invocation of a blessing on persons or things being dedicated to God: as **a :** the short blessing pronounced by a clergyman with which public worship is concluded **b :** the blessing before or after meals **c :** the Roman Catholic rite of solemnly blessing and hallowing (as a person or house) or of solemnly blessing and dedicating (as bells or vestments intended for sacred use) **3 :** a Roman Catholic service consisting of the exposition of the eucharistic Host in the monstrance, the incensing of the exposed Host, at least one prescribed hymn, sometimes a prayer, and the blessing of the people by a formal sign of the cross made with the monstrance containing the Host **4 :** something that blesses or promotes goodness, well-being, or betterment ⟨the Mexican sun is no pleasant ~ like our northern sun —Gertrude Diamant⟩ **5 :** a prayer or scripture passage pronounced to dismiss a meeting

¹**ben·e·dic·tion·al** \-shənᵊl,-shnəl\ *n* -S [ML *benedictionale*, fr. neut. of *benedictionalis* of a benediction (in *benedictionalis liber* book of benedictions), fr. LL *benediction-, benedictio* + L -*alis* -al] **:** a book of benedictions

²**benedictional** \¦==¦=(=)=\ *adj* [*benediction* + -*al*] **:** of or relating to benediction ⟨the ~ attitude of the child —Herbert Read⟩

ben·e·dic·tive \¦==¦=iv\ *adj* [LL *benedictus* (past part. of *benedicere* to bless) + E -*ive*] *of a set of verb forms* **:** expressing a wish **:** PRECATIVE — used of an aorist optative in Sanskrit and of moods with similar grammatical meaning in other languages — **ben·e·dic·tive·ly** *adv*

ben·e·dic·to·ry \-t(ə)rē\ *adj* [*benediction* + -*ory*] **:** of or expressing benediction ⟨a ~ prayer⟩

ben·e·dict's test \'benə,dik(t)s-\ *n, usu cap B* [after Stanley R. *Benedict* †1936 Am. physiological chemist] **:** a test for the presence of a reducing sugar in a solution (as urine) made by heating with a complex reagent containing sodium carbonate and citrate and copper sulfate, a colored precipitate being indicative of the presence of a reducing sugar

ben·e·dight \'benə,dīt\ *adj* [ME, fr. LL *benedictus* — more at BENEDICTION] *archaic* **:** BLESSED

ben·e·fact \'benə,fakt\ *vt* -ED/-ING/-S [back-formation fr. *benefactor*] **:** to act as a benefactor of

ben·e·fac·tion \'benə,fakshən, ,==¦==\ *n* -S [LL *benefaction-, benefactio*, fr. L *benefactus*, past part. of *benefacere* to do good to (fr. *bene* well + *facere* to make, do) + -*ion*, -*io* -ion — more at BOUNTY, DO] **1 :** an act or action of doing good esp. by generous donation ⟨the ~*s* of the American GIs to the . . . children of Korea —*Hartford (Conn.) Times*⟩ **2 :** a charitable donation **:** GRANT, GIFT ⟨this ~ totals almost $5 million —*Americana Annual*⟩

¹**ben·e·fac·tive** \¦==¦=tiv\ *adj* [L *benefactus* + E -*ive*] *of a linguistic form* **:** indicating that someone is benefited — used esp. of affixes and verb forms in various American Indian languages

²**benefactive** \"\ *n* -S **:** a benefactive form or set of forms in a language

ben·e·fac·tor \'benə,faktə(r), ,==¦== *sometimes* ,==¦=,tō(ə)r *or* -,tō(ə)\ *n* -S [LL, fr. L *benefactus* + -*or*] **:** one that gives help or confers a benefit ⟨a ~ of mankind⟩; *specif* **:** one that makes a gift or bequest ⟨his endowments . . . placed him high among the ~*s* of the convent —Jane Austen⟩

ben·e·fac·tress \'==,_trə̇s, ,==¦==\ *or* **ben·e·fac·trix** \-triks\ *n, pl* **benefactresses** \-trə̇sə̇z\ *or* **benefactrixes** \-triksə̇z\ *or* **benefactri·ces** \,==¦faktrə,sēz, -,fak'trī(,)sēz\ [*benefactor* + -*ess* or -*trix*] **:** a female benefactor

be·nef·ic \bə̇'nefik, be-\ *adj* [L *beneficus*, fr. *bene* well + -*ficus* (fr. *facere* to make, do) — more at BOUNTY, DO] **:** of, having, or exerting a favorable or beneficent influence ⟨a ~ star⟩ ⟨a ~ force⟩

¹**ben·e·fice** \'benəfə̇s\ *n, pl* **benefic·es** \-fə̇sə̇z, -,fis-\ [ME (also, "favor, advantage, benefit"), fr. MF, fr. ML, LL, & L; ML *beneficium* ecclesiastical and feudal benefice, LL, right, benefit, fr. L, kindness, favor, support, promotion, fr. *beneficus* + -*ium*] **1 :** an ecclesiastical post or office to which property or a determined revenue is attached (as a rectory, vicarage, or perpetual curacy) **2 :** a feudal estate in lands **:** FIEF; *specif* **:** an estate granted for life only and held on the mere good pleasure of the donor **3 :** GIFT ⟨a ~ of love —Amy Lowell⟩

²**benefice** \"\ *vt* **beneficed; beneficed; beneficing** \-fə̇siŋ, -,fis-\ **benefic·es** [ME *beneficen*, fr. *benefice*, n.] **:** to endow or invest with a benefice ⟨a *beneficed* clergyman⟩

be·nef·i·cence \bə̇'nefəsən(t)s\ *n* -S [L *beneficentia*, fr. *beneficus* + -*entia* -ence] **1 :** the quality or state of being beneficent **:** active goodness or kindness ⟨men who might be more profitably employed in works of a wider ~ —Clive Bell⟩ **2 :** a beneficent act or gift **:** BENEFACTION ⟨bestow your ~*s* generously but as though no such thing as gratitude existed —W.L.Sullivan⟩

be·nef·i·cent \-nt\ *adj* [fr. *beneficence*, after such pairs as E *benevolence: benevolent*] **1 :** doing or producing good ⟨a ~ influence⟩; *specif* **:** performing acts of kindness and charity ⟨a ~ king⟩ **2 :** productive of benefit ⟨~ bacteria⟩ — **be·nef·i·cent·ly** *adv*

beneficia *pl of* BENEFICIUM

ben·e·fi·cial \¦benə¦fishəl\ *adj* [*benefice* (in obs. sense "advantage, benefit") + -*ial*] **1 :** conferring benefits **:** contributing to a good end **:** HELPFUL, ADVANTAGEOUS ⟨~ animals⟩ ⟨a ~ organization⟩ ⟨~ effects⟩ — often used with *to* ⟨moist, cool summers, which are not ~ to such crops as maize —P.E. James⟩ **2 :** receiving or entitling one to have or receive in one's own right and for one's own benefit an advantage, use, or benefit that need not be monetary ⟨the ~ owner of securities⟩ ⟨a ~ interest in an estate⟩ — see CESTUI QUE TRUST; compare TRUSTEE

syn ADVANTAGEOUS, PROFITABLE: BENEFICIAL, the most general of the three words, may describe anything conducive to well-being, esp. to personal health and feeling and to social welfare ⟨only his daughter had the power of charming this black brooding from his mind . . . the touch of her hand had a strong *beneficial* influence with him almost always —Charles Dickens⟩ ⟨the relative ability of individuals and public bodies to make a *beneficial* use of the money —J.A.Hobson⟩ ADVANTAGEOUS stresses a choice or preference for the thing referred to over something else or over its lack or absence ⟨primitive rules of moral action . . . are all more or less *advantageous* and helpful on the road of primitive life —Havelock Ellis⟩ ⟨the republican government found it to be very *advantageous* to pay its troops promptly, for thereby a discipline was secured that surprised the Spaniards —J.L.Motley⟩ PROFITABLE suggests a pleasing return or remuneration in matters financial or in matters of education and character development ⟨the war boom demonstrated positively that mass production and distribution in books are both feasible and highly *profitable* —J.T.Farrell⟩ ⟨give . . . yourselves to *profitable* meditation at home —Robert Browning⟩

beneficial improvement *n* **:** an improvement on land that enhances the value of a property but is not necessary to prevent deterioration

ben·e·fi·cial·ly \-shəlē, -li *also* -shl-\ *adv* **:** in a beneficial manner

ben·e·fi·cial·ness \-shəlnə̇s\ *n* -ES **:** the quality or state of being beneficial

¹**ben·e·fi·cia·ry** \,benə'fishē,erē, -shərē, -ri\ *n* -ES [ML *beneficiarius* (influenced in meaning by ML *beneficium*), fr. L, privileged soldier, fr. *beneficium* favor + -*arius* -ary — more at BENEFICE] **1 a :** one who holds a feudal benefice **:** FEUDATORY, VASSAL **b :** one who holds an ecclesiastical benefice **2 :** one who receives something: as **a :** the person designated to receive the income of a trust estate **b :** the person named (as in an insurance or annuity policy) as the one who is to receive proceeds or benefits accruing **c :** a person in whose favor a letter of credit is issued entitling him to draw a draft or bill of exchange

²**beneficiary** \¦==¦=-\ *adj* [ML *beneficiarius* (influenced in meaning by ML *beneficium*), fr. L, of a favor, fr. *beneficium* + -*arius* -ary] **:** arising from, held as, or having a benefice ⟨~ services⟩ ⟨a ~ baron⟩

beneficiary heir *n, Scots law* **:** an heir who enters upon the estate of his predecessor with the benefit of an inventory that determines the exact limits of his liability for the predecessor's debts

ben·e·fi·ci·ate \,benə'fishē,āt\ *vt* -ED/-ING/-S [Sp *beneficiar* to benefit, to derive profit from working land or a mine, to beneficiate (fr. *beneficio* benefit, fr. LL *beneficium*) + E -*ate*] **:** to process (as a raw material) so as to improve the physical and chemical properties: as **a :** REDUCE ⟨~ ores⟩ **b :** to concentrate or otherwise prepare for smelting (as iron ore) esp. by drying, sintering, or magnetic concentration — **ben·e·fi·ci·a·tion** \-,fishē'āshən\ *n* -S

ben·e·fi·ci·um \,benə'fikēəm, -kē,ùm, -fishēəm\ *n, pl* **benefi·cia** \-ikēə, -kē,ä, -ishēə\ [LL — more at BENEFICE] *Roman & civil law* **:** RIGHT, BENEFIT, PRIVILEGE, BENEFICE

beneficium abs·ti·nen·di \-,äbztə'nen(,)dē, -,äpst-; -,abztə'nen(,)dē, -,dī\ *n* [LL, privilege of refusing] **:** POTESTAS ABSTINENDI

beneficium ce·den·da·rum ac·ti·o·num \-,kā,den'därəm-,äktē'ōnəm, -ä,rü-, -ō,nüm; -,sē,den'da(a)rə,makshē'ōnəm\ *n*

[LL, right of yielding the suits] *Roman & civil law* **:** the right of a surety before paying his principal's debt to a creditor to insist that the creditor's cause of action against the debtor or any cosurety first be assigned to the surety making the payment
beneficium cler·i·ca·le \-,klerə'kālē, -ä,lā,-alē,-ālē\ *n* [ML] **:** BENEFIT OF CLERGY 1
beneficium com·pe·ten·ti·ae \-,kämpə'tentē,ī, -tenchē,ē\ *n* [ML, right to a competency] **1** *Roman law* **:** the right of a defendant debtor bearing to plaintiff a special relationship (as ascendant, patron, husband, former partner, or one who has promised but not delivered a gift or dowry) to a judgment that will not deprive him of the means of existence **2 a** *civil law* **:** the right of a gratuitous grantor to reserve if indigent a competency to himself out of the subject of his grant **b** *Scots law* **:** this right extended to fathers and grandfathers with respect to provisions granted to their children
beneficium di·vi·si·o·nis \-də,wēsē'ōnəs, -də,vizhē'ō-\ *n* [LL, right of division] *Roman, civil, & Scots law* **:** the right of a surety sued by a creditor to compel the creditor also to sue the cosureties; *also* **:** the right of such surety to be held liable only for his proportionate share, with other solvent sureties, of the debt
beneficium ex·cus·si·o·nis \-(,)ek,skūsē'ōnəs, -,skəs(h)ē'ō-\ *or* **beneficium dis·cus·si·o·nis** \-də,skūsē'ōnəs, -,skəs(h)ē'ō-\ *or* **beneficium or·di·nis** \-'ȯrdᵊnəs\ *n* [*beneficium excussionis* fr. ML, right of discussion; *beneficium discussionis* fr. LL, right of discussion; *beneficium ordinis* fr. LL, right of rank] *Roman, civil, & Scots law* **:** the right granted to a surety or cautioner to compel a creditor suing him first to sue the principal debtor — called also *benefit of discussion*
beneficium in·ven·ta·rii \-,in,wen'tärē,ē, -,in,ven·'ta(a)rē,ī\ *n* [LL] **:** BENEFIT OF INVENTORY
beneficium se·pa·ra·ti·o·nis \-,sepə,räd·ē'ōnəs, -,rāshē'ō-\ *n* [LL, right of separation] **:** SEPARATIO BONORUM
[1]**ben·e·fit** \'benə,fit, *US sometimes* -,fət, *S sometimes* -ni- *or* -nē-, *Brit usu* -ni,fit; *US usu* -d·+V\ *n* -S [ME *benefet, benefit*, alter. (influenced by L *bene*) of *benfet*, fr. AF, fr. L *bene factum*, fr. neut. of *bene factus*, past part. of *bene facere* to do good, benefit, fr. *bene* well (adv. of *bonus* good) + *facere* to do — more at BOUNTY, DO] **1** *archaic* **:** an act of kindness **:** good deed **:** BENEFACTION ⟨bless the Lord, O my soul, and forget not all his ~s —Ps 103:2 (RSV)⟩ **2 a :** something that guards, aids, or promotes well-being **:** ADVANTAGE, GOOD ⟨no voice is louder than that of business in affirming the ~s of political democracy —W.H.Whyte⟩ **b :** useful aid **:** HELP, MEANS, AGENCY — used esp. in the phrase *without benefit of* ⟨the attack proceeded without ~ of artillery —P.W.Thompson⟩ **3 :** PAYMENT, GIFT: as **a :** financial help in time of sickness, old age, or unemployment — see BENEFIT SOCIETY **b** *obs* **:** a winning ticket or prize in a lottery **c :** a cash payment or service provided for under an annuity, pension plan, or insurance policy **4** *obs* **:** a natural advantage ⟨disable all the ~s of your own country —Shak.⟩ **5 :** an entertainment or social event to raise funds for a person, public program, or cause ⟨a ~ luncheon⟩; *specif* **:** a theatrical performance whose proceeds are given to a particular actor or a designated cause
[2]**benefit** \"\ *vb* **benefited** *or* **benefitted** \-,fid·əd, -,fitəd, *Brit usu* -,fitid\ **benefited** *or* **benefitted** \"\ **benefiting** *or* **benefitting** \-,fid·iŋ, -,fitiŋ, *Brit usu* -,fitiŋ\ **benefits** \-,fits, *US sometimes* -,fəts, *Brit usu* -,fits\ *vt* **:** to be useful or profitable to **:** AID, ADVANCE, IMPROVE ⟨medicines that ~ mankind⟩ ~ *vi* **:** to receive benefit **:** become protected, aided, or advanced ⟨~ from experience⟩ ⟨a novel that would ~ by revision⟩
benefit of clergy [trans. of ML *beneficium cléricale*] **1 :** the privilege claimed by the medieval church of demanding a trial and punishment by an ecclesiastical court for a member of the clergy accused of crime before a temporal court **2 :** the ministration or sanction of the church — used chiefly of the marriage rite ⟨a man and a girl living together without *benefit of clergy* —Wolcott Gibbs⟩
benefit of discussion [trans. of LL *beneficium discussionis*] **:** BENEFICIUM EXCUSSIONIS
benefit of inventory [trans. of LL *beneficium inventarii*] *Roman & civil law* **:** the right of an heir to have an inventory of his ancestor's estate made in the presence of a notary and representatives of the creditors of the estate upon the heir's election within 30 days after notice that he was instituted as an heir; *also* **:** the right to be liable for debts and legacies only to the amount of three fourths of the estate, the remaining one fourth being for the use of the heir
benefit of the doubt : the advantage derived from doubt about guilt, a possible error, or the weight of evidence
benefit society *n* **:** an association by which life insurance, sick allowances, the payment of funeral expenses, provision for old age, or other similar benefits are secured by means of regular dues or special assessments paid by its members
benefit theory of taxation : the theory that taxes should be considered as payments for services rendered by the state to the taxpayers and so proportioned
benefit year *n* **:** a one-year period during which workers may collect unemployment insurance benefits
ben·e·lux \'benᵊl,əks\ *adj, usu cap* [*Belgium* + *Netherlands* + *Luxembourg*] **:** of or relating to the countries of Belgium, the Netherlands, and Luxembourg esp. with reference to their customs union formed in 1947
be·net \bə, bē+\ *vt* [*be-* + *net*] **:** to ensnare with or as if with a net ⟨a man *benetted* by a woman's charms⟩
ben·e·ven·tan \,benə¦ventᵊn, -ntən\ *adj, usu cap* [It *beneventano*, fr. ML *Beneventanus*, fr. *Beneventum* Benevento, province of Italy + L *-anus* -an] **:** LOMBARDIC 2
be·nev·o·lence \bə'nevələn(t)s\ *n* -S [ME, fr. L *benevolentia*, fr. *benevolent-, benevolens* + *-ia*] **1 :** benevolent feeling **:** kindly disposition to do good and promote the welfare of others **:** GOODWILL ⟨we shook hands and I again glowed with ~ to my fellow men —Richard Aldington⟩ **2** *archaic* **:** personal regard or affection ⟨his dislike of application and control prevented his acquiring the ~ of his superiors —James Mill⟩ **3 :** an expression of benevolence: **a :** an act of kindness **b :** a generous gift **4 :** a compulsory contribution or tax formerly levied by certain English kings with no other authority than the claim of prerogative
be·nev·o·lent \-lənt\ *adj* [ME, fr. L *benevolent-, benevolens*, fr. *bene* well + *volent-, volens*, pres. part. of *velle* to will, wish — more at WILL] **1 :** marked by a kindly disposition to promote the happiness and prosperity of others or by generosity in and pleasure at doing good works ⟨a ~ donor⟩ **2 :** marked by or suggestive of goodwill or benign feelings **:** lacking any hostility ⟨a ~ judge⟩ ⟨a ~ smile⟩ **3 :** arising from or prompted by motives of charity or a sense of benevolence **:** PHILANTHROPIC ⟨a ~ society⟩ — **be·nev·o·lent·ly** *adv* — **be·nev·o·lent·ness** *n* -ES
[1]**ben·gal** \(')ben¦gȯl, -eŋ¦-, -¦gäl, '=,gəl\ *adj, usu cap* [fr. *Bengal*, region of the Indian subcontinent] **:** of or from the region of Bengal in northeastern India and East Pakistan **:** of the kind or style prevalent in Bengal **:** BENGALESE, BENGALI
[2]**bengal** \"\ *n* -S *usu cap* [fr. *Bengal* (region)] **:** any of various fabrics: as **a :** a silk or striped cotton woven in Bengal **b :** an imitation of such a fabric
bengal bean *n, usu cap 1st B* [*Bengal* (region)] **:** an annual plant (*Mucuna aterrima*) with long trailing stems used esp. in Brazil, Australia, and Ceylon for forage
bengal catechu *n, usu cap B* **:** CATECHU 1a
ben·gal·ee *like* BENGALI\ *n* -S *usu cap* [fr. *Bengali, Bengalee* native of Bengal] **:** any of several small tropical songbirds commonly kept as cage birds: as **a :** CORDON BLEU **b** *also* **bengalese :** SOCIETY FINCH
ben·gal·ese \¦bengə¦lēz, -eŋg-, -ēs; ben'gȯ,l-, beŋ-, -'gä,-\ *n, pl* **bengalese** *cap* [*Bengal* (region) + E *-ese*] **:** a native or resident of Bengal, India
[2]**bengalese** \"\ *adj, usu cap* **1 :** of, relating to, or characteristic of Bengal **2 :** of, relating to, or characteristic of the Bengalese
bengal gram *n, usu cap B* **:** CHICK-PEA
bengal grass *n, usu cap B* **:** FOXTAIL MILLET
bengal hemp *n, usu cap B* **:** SUNN
[1]**ben·gali** *also* **ben·gal·ee** \(')ben¦gȯlē, (')beŋ-, -¦gä-, -lī; 'bengə,lē, -eŋg-\ *n, pl* **bengali** *or* **bengalis** *also* **bengalee** *or* **bengalees** *cap* [Hindi *baṅgālī*, fr. *baṅgāl* Bengal, fr. Skt *vaṅga*] **1 :** a native or resident of Bengal **2 :** the modern Indic language of Bengal
[2]**bengali** *also* **bengalee** *adj, usu cap* **1 a :** of, relating to, or characteristic of Bengal **b :** of, relating to, or characteristic of the Bengali people **2 :** of, relating to, or characteristic of the Bengali language
ben·ga·line \'beŋgə,lēn, -eŋg-, ,==ˈ=\ *n* -S [F, fr. *Bengal* (region) + *-ine*] **:** a drapery and clothing fabric woven with a pronounced crosswise rib and made from the major textile fibers or a combination of these
bengal isinglass *n, usu cap B* **:** AGAR 1a
bengal kino *n, usu cap B* **:** BUTEA GUM
bengal light *or* **bengal fire** *n, usu cap B* **1 :** a bluish white light composed usu. of a mixture of potassium nitrate, sulfur, and realgar and used formerly in signaling and for illumination (as in theaters) — called also *Indian fire* **2 :** any of various colored lights or flares ⟨red and blue *Bengal lights* flared up —J.G.Frazer⟩
bengal monkey *n, usu cap B* **:** RHESUS MONKEY
bengal quince *n, usu cap B* **:** BEL
bengal rose *n, usu cap B* **:** CHINA ROSE 1a
bengal sage *n, usu cap B* **:** a camphor-scented medicinal mint (*Meriandra bengalensis*) of India
bengal tiger *n, usu cap B* **:** the southern short-haired tiger
ben·ga·si *or* **ben·ga·zi** *or* **ben·gha·zi** \(')ben¦gäzē, -gazē\ *adj, usu cap* [fr. *Bengasi, Bengazi, Benghazi*, Libya] **:** of or from Bengasi, joint capital of Libya **:** of the kind or style prevalent in Bengasi
ben·go·la \ben'gōlə, beŋ\ *or* **bengola light** *n, usu cap B* [irreg. fr. *Bengal*, the region] **:** BENGAL LIGHT
beni *usu cap, var of* BINI
beni amer \,benē'ämər\ *n, pl* **beni amer** *usu cap B&A* **1 :** a pastoral Tigre-speaking Hamitic people belonging to the same racial group as the Bisharin and Hadendoa **2 :** a member of the Beni Amer people
be·night \bə, bē+\ *vt* -ED/-ING/-S [*be-* + *night*, n.] **1 :** to overtake by darkness or night esp. before the end of a journey — usu. used in the passive ⟨there was no fear of our being ~*ed*, for in Norway at this season it never gets dark —Frances Pitt⟩ **2 :** to envelop in intellectual, moral, or social darkness ⟨what men . . . call religion now ~*ing* half the earth —John Wilson †1854⟩ — usu. used in the passive **3 :** to make dark esp. by depriving of light **:** OBSCURE ⟨the cliffs were so high that the bay itself was already ~*ed* —Clemence Dane⟩
benighted *adj* **1 :** overtaken by darkness or night ⟨~ travelers . . . have seen his midnight candle glimmering —W.B. Yeats⟩ **2 :** in a state of intellectual, moral, or social darkness **:** UNENLIGHTENED ⟨to some ~ souls even antiquarians seem peculiar —*Antiques*⟩ ⟨how long have you been in this ~ country —Charles Beadle⟩ — **be·night·ed·ness** *n* -ES
be·nign \bə'nīn, bē-\ *adj* [ME *benigne*, fr. MF, fr. L *benignus*, fr. *bene* well + *-ignus* (fr. *genere, gignere* to produce, beget) — more at KIN] **1 :** of a kind and gentle disposition **:** GRACIOUS ⟨a ~ teacher⟩ **2 a :** acting or appearing kind, gracious, or gentle ⟨an ominous frown gathered upon Mr. Littlepage's ~ forehead —Ellen Glasgow⟩ **b :** arising from or prompted by generous or gracious kindliness ⟨~ contributions⟩ ⟨~ actions⟩ **3 a :** tending to promote or indicative of happiness, goodness, or favorable outcome **:** SALUTARY, WHOLESOME ⟨a ~ balance between firmness and laxity⟩ ⟨a ~ rather than a malevolent phenomenon —Margaret Halsey⟩ **b :** FAVORABLE, PROPITIOUS ⟨born under a ~ planet⟩ **c :** of a mild type or character **:** not threatening health or life ⟨~ malaria⟩ ⟨a ~ tumor⟩ **:** having a good prognosis ⟨a ~ psychosis⟩ — opposed to *malignant* **4 :** forgivingly or understandingly tolerant ⟨viewed the antagonism shown his eccentricities with ~ complacency —Alvin Redman⟩ **syn** see FAVORABLE, KIND
be·nig·nan·cy \bə'nignənsē, bē-, -si\ *n* -ES **:** benignant quality ⟨filled with a special, protective ~ for her —Elizabeth Bowen⟩
be·nig·nant \-gnənt\ *adj* [*benign* + *-ant* (as in *malignant*)] **1 :** KINDLY, MILD, GENTLE ⟨a ~ face⟩ ⟨a ~ counselor⟩ **2 :** FAVORABLE, BENEFICIAL ⟨a ~ power⟩ **syn** see KIND
be·nig·nant·ly *adv* **:** in a benignant manner
be·nig·ni·ty \-nignəd·ē, -ətē, -i\ *n* -ES [ME *benignite*, fr. MF *benignité*, fr. L *benignitat-, benignitas*, fr. *benignus* benign + *-itat-, -itas* -ity] **1 :** the quality or state of being benign ⟨the angelic spinster . . . smiled with soft ~ —Arnold Bennett⟩ ⟨the ~ or malignancy of the tumor —*Biol. Abstracts*⟩ **2** *archaic* **:** a kind or generous deed, gift, or manifestation **:** KINDNESS
be·nign·ly \-nīnlē, -li\ *adv* [ME *benignely*, fr. *benigne* + *-ly*] **:** in a benign manner ⟨~ help a person in distress⟩ ⟨look upon his criticisms ~⟩ ⟨a ~ growing foreign trade⟩
beni-israel \,benē +\ *n, pl* **beni-israel** *usu cap B&I* [Ar *banī Isrā'īl* the children of Israel] **1 :** a people of Jewish descent living in the neighborhood of Bombay, India, and known to history at least as early as the 12th century A.D. **2 :** a member of the Beni-Israel people
ben·in·ca·sa \,benən'kāsə\ *n, cap* [NL, after Giuseppe *Benincasa*, 16th cent. Italian who developed the botanical garden at Pisa] **:** a small genus of Asiatic herbaceous vines (family Cucurbitaceae) with large yellow flowers and fleshy fruit that is used for pickles —see WAX GOURD
ben·i·son \'benəsən, -əzən\ *n* -S [ME *beneson, benesoun*, fr. OF *beneiçon, beneïçun*, fr. LL *benediction-, benedictio* benediction — more at BENEDICTION] **1 :** BLESSING ⟨with no help except their hands and the ~ of God —A.E.Stevenson b.1900⟩ **2 :** the pronouncing of a blessing **:** BENEDICTION ⟨the prelate's ~⟩
bé·ni·tier \bānē·tyā\ *n* -S [F, fr. OF *beneoitier*, fr. *beneoit*, past part. of *beneïr* to bless, fr. LL *benedicere* — more at BENEDICTION] **:** a holy-water stoup
be·ni·to·ite \bə'nēd·ə,wīt, -ēd·ō,ī, -ī\ *n* -S [San *Benito* co., Calif. + E *-ite*] **:** a mineral $BaTiSi_3O_9$ consisting of sapphire-blue crystallized barium titanosilicate sometimes used as a gem
[1]**ben·ja·min** \'benjəmən\ *n* -S [by folk etymology fr. MF *benjoin* — more at BENZOIN] **1 :** BENZOIN 1 **2 :** any of several plants of the genus *Trillium* **3 :** BALSAM 4
[2]**benjamin** \"\ *n* -S [prob. fr. the name *Benjamin*] *slang* **:** a man's close-fitting overcoat
benjamin bush *n* [[1]*benjamin*] **:** SPICEBUSH
ben·ja·min·ite \-mə,nīt\ *n* -S [Marcus *Benjamin* †1932 Am. museum official + E *-ite*] **:** a mineral Pb (Cu, Ag) Bi_2 S_4 consisting of sulfobismuthite of lead, silver, and copper occurring in gray masses
benjamin tree *n* [[1]*benjamin*] **1 :** BENZOIN 3 **2 :** SPICEBUSH
ben·ja·mite \-,mīt\ *or* **ben·ja·min·ite** \-mə,nīt\ *n* -S *usu cap* [*Benjamin*, youngest of Jacob's 12 sons in the Bible (Gen 35) + E *-ite*] **:** a member of the Hebrew tribe of Benjamin
ben·jy \'benji\ *n* -ES [perh. fr. *Benjy*, dim. of the name *Benjamin*] **1** *slang Brit* **:** [2]BENJAMIN **2** *slang Brit* **:** [1]BENNY 1
ben marcato \¦ben+,-\ *adv* (*or* adj) [It, well-marked] **:** MARCATO — used as a direction in music
ben·ne *also* **ben·ni** *or* **bene** \'benē, -ni\ *n* -S [of African origin; akin to Wolof & Mandingo *bĕne* sesame, Bambara *bene*] **:** SESAME 1, 2
benne cake *n* **:** a candy consisting of a small flat cake of benne seeds boiled with sugar
ben·net \'benət\ *n* -S [short for *herb bennet*] **1 :** HERB BENNET **2 :** either of two American avens (*Geum virginianum* or *G. canadense*) **3** *in the writings of early herbalists* **a :** HEMLOCK **b :** GARDEN HELIOTROPE **4 :** DAISY 1a **5 :** BURNET SAXIFRAGE
ben·net·ti·ta·ce·ae \bə,ned·ə'tāsē,ē\ *n pl, cap* [NL, fr. *Bennettites*, type genus + *-aceae*] **:** a family of fossil gymnospermous plants of the order Bennettitales having strobili usu. bisexual and the female sporophyll more reduced than that of the male — **ben·net·ti·ta·ceous** \=¦==¦shəs\ *adj*
ben·net·ti·ta·le·an \=¦==¦tālēən\ *adj* **:** of, relating to, or characteristic of the order Bennettitales
ben·net·ti·ta·les \=,==¦tā(,)lēz\ *n pl, cap* [NL, fr. *Bennettites* + *-ales*] **:** an order of fossil gymnospermous plants first known from the Carboniferous and probably becoming extinct during the Cretaceous that appear to have derived from the seed ferns but have megasporophylls aggregated into cones and with little resemblance to foliage leaves, that are in general structurally similar to the cycads from which they differ chiefly in having the reproductive organs on the trunk embedded in a thick external covering of persistent leaf bases, and that have been considered as possible ancestors of the angiosperms — see BENNETTITACEAE
ben·net·ti·tes \,benə'tīd·ēz\ *n, cap* [NL, fr. John Joseph *Bennett* †1876 Eng. botanist + L *-ites* -ite] **:** a genus of fossil gymnospermous plants (family Bennettitaceae) known only from seeds and parts of the fruits and often considered not demonstrably distinct from *Cycadeoidea*
ben·ni·seed *also* **beni·seed** \'benē,sēd, -ni-\ *n* [*benni* + *seed*] **:** SESAME 2
ben nut *n* [[7]*ben*] **:** [7]BEN
[1]**ben·ny** \'benē, -ni\ *n* -ES [prob. fr. the name *Benny*] **1** *slang* **:** a low-crowned broad-brimmed straw hat **2** *slang* **:** OVERCOAT — compare BENJAMIN
[2]**benny** \"\ *n* -S [by alter. and shortening fr. *benzedrine*] *slang* **:** a tablet of amphetamine taken as a stimulant to the central nervous system
be·no *or* **bi·no** \'bē(,)nō\ *n* -ES [modif. of Sp *vino* wine, fr. L *vinum* — more at WINE] **:** a strongly alcoholic drink of the Philippines distilled from the fermented sap of certain palms — compare [3]TUBA
ben oil *also* **behen oil** *n* [[7]*ben, behen*] **:** a fatty oil or semisolid fat that is obtained from ben and used esp. in cosmetics and in cooking
be·no·ni \bə'nōnē\ *adj, usu cap* [fr. *Benoni*, Union of So. Africa] **:** of or from Benoni, Union of So. Africa **:** of the kind or style prevalent in Benoni
be·north \bi'nȯrt(h)\ *prep* [ME *benorth*, fr. OE *be northan*, fr. *be* by (fr. *bi, bī*) + *northan* from the north, fr. *north* — more at BY, NORTH] *Scot* **:** north of
be·note \bə, bē+\ *vt* [*be-* + *note*] **:** to annotate excessively or absurdly
ben·rath line \'ben,rät-, -ät-\ *n, usu cap B* [trans. of G *benrather linie*, fr. *Benrath*, Germany, near which the isogloss dividing HG *machen* "to make" from LG *maken* crosses the Rhine] **:** one of a bundle of isoglosses crossing Germany roughly from Aachen and Düsseldorf to Frankfurt an der Oder and dividing High German to the south, with fricatives and affricates for proto-Germanic *p, t, k*, from the rest of the West Germanic speech area to the north and northwest, with proto-Germanic *p, t, k* remaining intact (as in E *pipe*, *that*, *to*, *make*, contrasted with G *pfeife*, *das*, *zu*, *machen*)
[1]**ben·sel** *also* **ben·sil** \'ben(t)səl, -nzəl\ *n* -S [prob. of Scand origin; akin to ON *benzl* bent state of a bow, fr. *benda* to bend — more at BEND] *chiefly Scot* **:** sudden violent motion or action
[2]**bensel** *also* **bensil** \"\ *vt* **benseled** *or* **bensell̇ed; benseled** *or* **benselled; benseling** *or* **benselling; bensels** *chiefly Scot* **:** to strike violently **:** BEAT
bensh \'bench\ *vb* -ED/-ING/-S [Yiddish *bentshen*, fr. LL *benedicere* to bless — more at BENEDICTION] *vt* **:** BLESS ~ *vi* **:** to say a blessing **:** recite prayers
[1]**bent** \'bent\ *n* -S [ME, grassy place, bent grass, fr. OE *beonot-* (in place names); akin to OHG *binuz* rush] **1 a :** an unenclosed pastureland **:** FIELD, MOOR ⟨curlews crying over the snow-patched ~ —John Buchan⟩ **b** *archaic* **:** HILLSIDE, SLOPE **2 a** (1) **:** a reed, rush, or reedlike grass ⟨a coastline grown over with sedge and ~⟩ (2) **:** a stalk of stiff coarse grass ⟨his spear a ~, both stiff and strong —Michael Drayton⟩ **b :** a beach grass (*Ammophila arenaria*) **c :** DOGSTAIL 1 **d** *or* **bent grass :** any grass of the genus *Agrostis; esp* **:** any of several important pasture and lawn grasses that are typically perennial, rhizomatous, resistant to adverse conditions, and noted for their fine velvety or wiry herbage — see CREEPING BENT
[2]**bent** \"\ *adj* [ME, fr. past part. of *benden* to bend — more at BEND] **1 a :** changed by bending or being bent so as to be no longer in an original straight, level, or even condition ⟨a boy fishing with a ~ pin⟩ ⟨a ~ automobile fender⟩ ⟨a ~ head and sloping shoulders⟩ **b :** braced by being bent ⟨a ~ bow⟩ **c :** CURVED ⟨~ glass⟩ **2 a :** strongly inclined **:** RESOLVED, DETERMINED — used with *on* or *upon* ⟨a country ~ upon world domination⟩ **b :** actively engaged or occupied — used with *on* or *upon* ⟨housewives ~ on spring cleaning⟩
[3]**bent** \"\ *n* -S [fr. *bend*, v., after such pairs as E *descend: descent*] **1** *obs* **:** something curved or crooked **:** BEND **2 a :** particular inclination or tendency **:** strong interest conducive to bias **:** BIAS ⟨the ~ of his mind . . . was at all times much to metaphysical theology —William Wordsworth⟩ **b :** a special and often inherent inclination, disposition, or capacity; *esp* **:** one facilitating ready and easy learning or mastery ⟨a decided ~ for language⟩ **3** *archaic* **:** a curved state or form **:** CURVATURE **4 :** capacity of endurance ⟨they fool me to the top of my ~ —Shak.⟩ **5 :** a framework transverse to the length of a structure (as a trestle, bridge, or long shed) usu. designed to carry lateral as well as vertical loads **syn** see GIFT
be'nt \(')bēnt\ *var of* BEANT
ben·tang \'ben,taŋ\ *n* -S [Wolof *benteng, bentengi*] **:** CEIBA 2a
ben·teak \'ben·,tēk\ *n* -S [origin unknown] **:** the wood of an East Indian tree (*Lagerstroemia lanceolata*)
bent grass *n* [[1]*bent*] **:** [1]BENT 2d
ben·tham·ic \(')ben¦thamik\ *adj, usu cap* [J. *Bentham* + E *-ic*] **:** of or belonging to Benthamism
ben·tham·ism \'ben(t)thə,mizəm, -ntə,m-\ *n* -S *usu cap* [Jeremy *Bentham* †1832 Eng. jurist and philosopher + E *-ism*] **:** the utilitarian philosophy of Bentham and his followers; *esp* **:** the theory that the morality of actions is estimated and determined by their utility and that pleasure and pain are both the ultimate standard of right and wrong and the fundamental motives influencing human desires and actions
ben·tham·ite \-,mīt\ *n* -S *usu cap* [J. *Bentham* + E *-ite*] **:** one that adheres to Benthamism
ben·thic \'ben(t)thik *or* **ben·thal** \-thəl\ *adj* [*benthos* + *-ic* or *-al*] **1 :** of, relating to, or occurring on the bottom underlying a body of water ⟨mud-dwelling ~ mollusks⟩ **2 :** of, relating to, or occurring in the depths of the ocean or the bottom underlying these depths
ben·tho·graph \'benthə,graf\ *n* -S [*benthos* + *-graph*] **:** an instrument consisting of a hollow steel sphere that contains cameras and lighting equipment and is designed for underwater photographic exploration at great depths
ben·thon \'ben,thän\ *n* -S [*benthos* + *-on* (as in *plankton*)] **:** organisms dwelling in the benthos — compare PLANKTON
ben·thon·ic \(')ben¦thänik\ *adj* [irreg. fr. Gk *benthos* + E *-ic*] **:** BENTHIC 1
ben·thos \'ben,thäs\ *n* -ES [Gk, depth; akin to *bathys* deep — more at BATHY-] **1 :** the bottom of the sea esp. in the deep parts of the oceans **2** [G, fr. Gk] **:** organisms that live on or in the bottom of bodies of water
ben·tho·scope \'benthə,skōp\ *n* -S [*benthos* + *-scope*] **:** a deep-sea diving instrument consisting of a hollow steel sphere capable of carrying an observer to depths of several thousand feet
ben·tinck \'benti(ŋ)k\ *n* -S *usu cap* [after John A. *Bentinck* †1775 Brit. naval officer, its inventor] **:** a triangular sail superseded by the storm staysail
bentinck boom *n, usu cap 1st B* [after J.A.*Bentinck*, its inventor] **:** a boom used to stretch the foot of the foresail in some small square-rigged ships
bent leg *n* [[2]*bent*] **:** a bowed condition of the forelegs of lambs suggesting and possibly being a form of rickets
ben·ton·ite \'bentᵊn,īt, -tə,nīt\ *n* -S [Fort *Benton*, Montana + E *-ite*] **1 :** a soft porous moisture-absorbing rock composed essentially of clayey minerals often of volcanic origin **2 :** any of numerous variously colored clay deposits containing montmorillonite as the essential mineral, characterized either by the ability to swell in water or by the ability to be slaked and to be activated by acid, and used chiefly in oil-well drilling muds, as fillers and plasticizers (as in paint and soap), as suspending agents (as in pharmaceutical preparations), and as carriers for agricultural chemicals — **ben·ton·it·ic** \¦bentᵊn¦id·ik, -tə¦ni-\ *adj*
ben tro·va·to \,ben·trō'vä,tō\ *also* **ben tro·va·ta** \-ä(,)tä\ *adj* [It, lit., well found, well thought up] **:** characteristic or appropriate but not true ⟨of Baudelaire, who was a bit overfond of shocking, is told this tale, which is probably *ben trovato* —C.H.Grandgent⟩
bents *pl of* BENT
bentwood \'=,=\ *adj* [[2]*bent* + *wood*] **:** made of wood that is bent and not cut into shape ⟨a ~ chair⟩
benty \'bentē\ *adj* [[1]*bent* + *-y*] **1 :** of, relating to, or suggestive of bent ⟨the herb had a ~ stalk⟩ **2 :** abounding in bent ⟨a wide ~ moor —John Buchan⟩
be·numb \bə, bē+\ *vt* -ED/-ING/-S [ME *benomen*, fr. *benome, benomen* (past part. of *benimen* to take away, deprive), fr. OE *benumen*, past part. of *beniman* to take away, fr. *be-* + *niman* to take — more at NIMBLE] **1 :** to make inactive **:** DEADEN, STUPEFY ⟨a spirit of the blindest imitation . . . ~*ed* the intel-

lectual faculties —Van Wyck Brooks⟩ **2 :** to make numb esp. by cold **:** deprive of sensation ⟨the fearful cold that overtakes and ~*s* the traveler —John Burroughs⟩ **syn** see DAZE

be·numb·ing·ly *adv* **:** in a benumbing manner

ben·weed \ˈben,wēd\ *n* [origin unknown] *chiefly Scot* **:** TANSY RAGWORT

benz- *or* **benzo-** *comb form* [ISV, fr. *benzoin;* prob. orig. formed in F] **1 :** related to benzene or benzoic acid ⟨*benz*azide⟩ ⟨*benzo*pinacol⟩ **2 :** containing a benzene ring fused on one side to one side of another ring ⟨*benz*acridine⟩ ⟨*benzo*pyrone⟩

ben·zal \ˈben,zal\ *n* -s [ISV *benz-* + *aldehyde*] **:** the bivalent radical $C_6H_5CH=$ derived from benzaldehyde by removal of the oxygen atom — called also *benzylidene*

benzal chloride *n* **:** a colorless highly refractive liquid compound $C_6H_5CHCl_2$ made by chlorinating toluene and used esp. in the synthesis of benzaldehyde; α,α-dichloro-toluene — called also *benzylidene chloride*

benz·al·de·hyde \benz+\ *n* -s [G *benzaldehyd,* fr. *benz-* + *aldehyd* aldehyde] **:** a colorless nontoxic liquid aldehyde C_6H_5CHO that has an odor like that of bitter almond oil, that occurs in many essential oils (as bitter almond oil and peach-kernel oil) and is usu. made from toluene, and that is used chiefly in flavoring and perfumery, in pharmaceutical preparations, and in synthesis (as of dyes) — called also *artificial bitter almond oil;* see AMYGDALIN

ben·zald·ox·ime \,benzalˈdäk,sēm, -,sȯm\ *n* -s [ISV *benzaldehyde* + *oxime*] **:** a crystalline oxime $C_6H_5CH{=}NOH$ derived from benzaldehyde and known in two stereoisomeric forms usu. distinguished as *syn-benzaldoxime* and *anti-benzaldoxime* — compare STRUCTURAL FORMULA

$C_6H_5-\underset{\Vert}{C}-H$ / N-OH — *syn*-benzaldoxime; $C_6H_5-\underset{\Vert}{C}-H$ / HO-N — *anti*-benzaldoxime

ben·zal·ko·ni·um \-ˈkōnēəm\ *n* -s [*benz-* + *alkyl* + *ammonium*] **:** a mixture of alkyl-benzyl-dimethyl-ammonium radicals $C_6H_5CH_2N(CH_3)_2R$ in which the alkyl groups range from C_8H_{17} to $C_{18}H_{37}$

benzalkonium chloride *n* **:** a white or yellowish white salt obtained as a bitter aromatic powder or gelatinous pieces that is used as an antiseptic and germicide

benz·am·ide \benˈza,mīd, -məd, ˈbenzə,mīd\ *n* -s [G *benzamid,* fr. *benz-* + *amid* amide] **:** a colorless crystalline compound $C_6H_5CONH_2$ obtained usu. by the action of ammonia on benzoyl chloride; the amide of benzoic acid

benzamido- *comb form* [ISV, fr. *benzamide* + *-o-*] **:** containing the univalent radical C_6H_5CONH- derived from benzamide ⟨α-*benzamido*cinnamic acid⟩

ben·za·mine brown 3GO \ˈbenzə,mēn . . . ˈthrē,gēˈō\ *n, usu cap both Bs* **:** a direct dye — see DYE table I (under *Direct Brown 1*)

benz·anilide \benz+\ *n* [ISV *benz-* + *anilide*] **:** a white crystalline compound $C_6H_5CONHC_6H_5$ made from benzoic acid and aniline and used in the manufacture of pharmaceuticals and dyes

benz·anthracene \"+\ *n* [ISV *benz-* + *anthracene*] **:** a crystalline feebly carcinogenic cyclic hydrocarbon $C_{18}H_{12}$ that is isomeric with naphthacene and is found in small amounts in coal tar — called also *1,2-benzanthracene, benz[a]anthracene*

benz·anthrone \"+\ *n* [ISV *benz-* + *anthrone*] **:** a pale yellow crystalline ketone $C_{17}H_{10}O$ made from anthraquinone and glycerol and used as a dye intermediate

Ben·ze·drine \ˈbenzə,drēn *sometimes* benˈzedrən\ *trademark* — used for amphetamine

ben·zene \ˈben,zēn, ,=ˈ=\ *n* -s [ISV *benz-* + *-ene*] **:** a colorless volatile flammable toxic liquid aromatic hydrocarbon C_6H_6 that burns with a luminous flame, that is usu. obtained commercially from the carbonization of coal(as from the light oil from coke-oven gas) or from certain petroleum fractions by catalytic dehydrogenation, and that is used chiefly in organic synthesis (as of styrene, phenol, aniline, and cyclohexane), as a solvent, and as a motor fuel (as for blending with gasoline) — called also *benzol*

ben·zene·di·a·zo·ni·um \,ben,zēn,dīəˈzōnēəm\ *n* -s [*benzene* + *diaz-* + *-onium*] **:** a univalent cation $C_6H_5N_2^+$ known best in the form of crystalline explosive salts (as the chloride $C_6H_5N_2Cl$ made by reaction of aniline hydrochloride and nitrous acid)

benzene hexachloride *n* **:** a compound $C_6H_6Cl_6$ occurring in several stereoisomeric forms, obtained usu. as a white to grayish musty powder containing some of these forms by chlorinating benzene in the presence of actinic light, and used as an insecticide — see LINDANE

benzene ring *or* **benzene nucleus** *n* **:** the structural arrangement of atoms believed to exist in benzene and other aromatic compounds showing six carbon atoms in planar symmetrical hexagonal fashion numbered 1 to 6 for convenience in designating the location of substituting groups and linked by alternate single and double bonds with each carbon attached to hydrogen in benzene itself or to other atoms or groups in substituted benzenes of which there is but one variety for each monosubstituted product (as toluene, phenol) but three for each disubstituted product — see META- 4b, ORTH- 3b, PARA- 2b(1); compare CYCLOHEXANE, PYRIDINE, STRUCTURAL FORMULA

Kekulé formula for benzene (three methods of representation, the plain hexagon without double bonds being acceptable only when it cannot be mistaken for cyclohexane)

benzene series *n* **:** a series of liquid and solid aromatic hydrocarbons containing the benzene ring of which benzene is the simplest member and toluene the next higher member and from which hydrocarbons with condensed rings (as naphthalene) are sometimes excluded

ben·zene·sulfonate \ˈben,zēn+\ *n* [ISV *benzene* + *sulfonate*] **:** a salt or ester of benzenesulfonic acid

ben·zene·sulfonic acid \ˌ=,=+. . .-\ *n* [ISV *benzene* + *sulfonic*] **:** a colorless crystalline acid $C_6H_5SO_3H$ made by sulfonating benzene and used chiefly in organic synthesis and in the form of derivatives as detergents

ben·ze·noid \ˈbenzə,nȯid\ *adj* [*benzene* + *-oid*] **:** like benzene esp. in structure or linkage **:** of the benzene series — sometimes contrasted with *alicyclic, naphthalenoid, quinonoid*

ben·zes·trol \benˈze,strōl, -,strȯl\ *n* -s [*benz-* + *estrogen* + *-ol*] **:** a crystalline estrogenic diphenol $C_{20}H_{26}O_2$ derived from diphenyl-propane

benz·hydrol \benz+\ *also* **ben·zo·hydrol** \,benzō+\ *n* -s [ISV *benz-* + *hydrol*] **:** a colorless crystalline secondary alcohol $(C_6H_5)_2CHOH$ made usu. by reduction of benzophenone and used in organic synthesis

ben·zi·dine \ˈbenzə,dēn, -dən\ *n* -s [prob. fr. G *benzidin,* blend of *benzin* benzine and *-id* -ide] **:** a white or reddish gray crystalline base $NH_2C_6H_4C_6H_4NH_2$ made usu. by a series of reactions from nitrobenzene and used chiefly in making dyes (as Congo red), in chemical analysis, and in the detection of blood; 4,4′-biphenyl-diamine

benzidine yellow *n* **:** any of several azo pigments — see DYE table I (under *Pigment Yellow 12*)

ben·zil \ˈben,zil, -zəl, =ˈzil\ *n* -s [F, fr. *benzoin* + *-il*] **:** a yellow crystalline diketone $C_6H_5COCOC_6H_5$ made by oxidizing benzoin

ben·zil·ic acid \(ˈ)benˈzilik\ *n* [F *benzilique,* fr. *benzil* + *-ique* -ic] **:** a white crystalline acid $(C_6H_5)_2C(OH)COOH$ obtained by warming benzil with alcohol and alkali; diphenyl-glycolic acid

benz·imidazole \,benz+\ *or* **benz·iminazole** \"+\ *n* -s [ISV *benz-* + *imidazole or iminazole*] **:** a crystalline base $C_7H_6N_2$ made by reaction of *ortho*-phenylenediamine with formic acid; *also* **:** a derivative of this base

ben·zine \ˈben,zēn, =ˈ=, ˈ=zən\ *also* **ben·zin** \ˈbenzən\ *n* -s [G *benzin,* fr. *benz-* + *-in*] **1 :** BENZENE — not used scientifically **2 :** any of various volatile flammable petroleum distillates that are lighter than kerosene, consist of mixtures chiefly of aliphatic hydrocarbons, and are used esp. as solvents or as motor fuels: as **a :** LIGROIN **b :** GASOLINE — see PETROLEUM BENZIN

benzine cup *n* **:** a watermark-detector tray used in stamp collecting

ben·zin·er \ˈben,zēnə(r)\ *n* -s [*benzine* + *-er;* fr. the use of *benzine* in dry cleaning] **:** DRY CLEANER

benzo- — see BENZ-

ben·zo·ate \ˈbenzə,wāt, *usu* -ād.+V\ *n* -s [*benz-* + *-ate*] **:** a salt or ester of benzoic acid

benzoate of soda : SODIUM BENZOATE

ben·zo·caine \ˈbenzō,kān\ *n* -s [ISV *benz-* + *-caine*] **:** a white crystalline ester $NH_2C_6H_4COOC_2H_5$ used as a local anesthetic; ethyl *para*-aminobenzoate — called also *ethyl aminobenzoate*

ben·zo·dioxan \ˌben(,)zō+\ *or* **ben·zo·dioxane** \"+\ *n* -s [ISV *benz-* + *dioxan, dioxane*] **:** a compound containing a benzene ring fused to a dioxane ring; *esp* **:** PIPEROXAN

ben·zo dye \"+\ *n, usu cap B* [*benzo* fr. *benz-*] **:** any of numerous direct dyes — see DYE table I (under *Direct*)

ben·zo·flavine \"+\ *n* -s [ISV *benz-* + *flavine*] **:** a basic acridine dye that dyes leather yellow

ben·zo·furan \"+\ *n* -s [*benz-* + *furan*] **:** COUMARONE

ben·zo·hydrol \"+\ *var of* BENZHYDROL

ben·zo·ic acid \(ˈ)benˈzōik-\ *n* [ISV *benz-* + *-ic*] **:** a lustrous white crystalline acid C_6H_5COOH occurring in benzoin and other resins, in cranberries, and combined in the urine of herbivorous animals, made chiefly by decarboxylation of phthalic acid and by oxidation of toluene, and used esp. as a preservative of foods, pharmaceuticals, and cosmetics, in medicine for the treatment of ringworm, and in organic synthesis

benzoic aldehyde *n* **:** BENZALDEHYDE

benzoic sulfimide *n* **:** SACCHARIN

ben·zoin \ˈbenzəwən, -,wēn, -,zōin, =ˈzōən\ *n* [MF *benjoin,* fr. OCatal *benjui,* fr. Ar *lubān jāwī* frankincense of Java (prob. confused with Sumatra)] **1** -s **:** a balsamic resin that is obtained from various trees of the genus *Styrax* growing esp. in Sumatra, Java, and Thailand, that appears in commerce in yellowish to brown hard brittle tears or masses having a fragrant odor, and that is used chiefly in treating irritations of the skin, as a stimulating expectorant, as a fixative in perfumes, and as incense **2** -s **:** a white crystalline hydroxy ketone $C_6H_5COCHOHC_6H_5$ made usu. by condensation of two molecules of benzaldehyde in the presence of potassium cyanide **3** -s **:** a tree yielding benzoin **4 a** *cap, in some classifications* **:** a genus of aromatic shrubs comprising the American spicebush and certain other plants often included in the genus *Lindera* **b** -s **:** a plant of the genus *Benzoin; esp* **:** SPICEBUSH 1

ben·zoi·nat·ed \ˈbenzəwəˌnād·əd, -ˈzōəˌn-, -ˈzōiˌn-\ *adj* **:** containing or impregnated with benzoin resin ⟨~ lard⟩

ben·zol \ˈben,zōl, -ōl\ *also* **ben·zole** \-ōl\ *n* -s [G, fr. *benz-* + *-ol*] **:** BENZENE; *also* **:** a mixture containing other aromatic hydrocarbons as well as benzene ⟨motor ~⟩ — usu. used commercially

ben·zo·lize \ˈbenzə,līz\ *vt* -ED/-ING/-S [*benzol* + *-ize*] **:** to treat with benzene

ben·zo·ni·trile \ˌben(,)zōˈnī·trəl\ *n* -s [G *benzonitril,* fr. *benz-* + *nitril* nitrile] **:** a colorless toxic oily compound C_6H_5CN of almond-oil odor made by fusing a mixture of sodium cyanide and sodium benzenesulfonate and in other ways and used chiefly as a solvent for synthetic resins — called also *cyanobenzene, phenyl cyanide*

ben·zo·phe·none \,=(,)=fəˈnōn, -ˈfē,nōn\ *n* -s [ISV *benz-* + *-phenone*] **:** a colorless crystalline ketone $C_6H_5COC_6H_5$ with a roselike odor made by the pyrolysis of calcium benzoate or from benzene and carbon tetrachloride by the Friedel-Crafts reaction and used chiefly in perfumery — called also *diphenyl ketone*

ben·zo·purpurine \ˌben(,)zō+\ *also* **ben·zo·purpurin** \"+\ *n* -s *often cap* [ISV *benz-* + *purpurine, purpurin*] **:** any of several closely related direct disazo red dyes: as **a** *or* **benzopurpurine 4B :** a red dye made from *ortho*-tolidine and naphthionic acid and used on cellulosic textiles and as an indicator and plasma stain — see DYE table I (under *Direct Red 2*) **b** *or* **benzopurpurine 10B :** a carmine-red dye made from *ortho*-dianisidine and naphthionic acid — see DYE table I (under *Direct Red 7*)

ben·zo·pyrene \"+\ *or* **benz·pyrene** \benz+\ *n* -s [ISV *benz-* + *pyrene*] **:** a yellow crystalline cancer-producing hydrocarbon $C_{20}H_{12}$ found in coal tar

ben·zo·quinone \ˌben(,)zō+\ *n* -s [ISV *benz-* + *quinone*] **:** QUINONE 1

ben·zo·sul·fi·mide \ˈben(,)zōˈsəlfə,mīd\ *n* -s [*benz-* + *sulf-* + *imide*] **:** SACCHARIN

ben·zo·thiazole \ˌben(,)zō+\ *n* -s [ISV *benz-* + *thiazole*] **:** a liquid compound C_7H_5NS made by cyclization from *ortho*-amino-thiophenol and formaldehyde well known as a parent compound of mercaptobenzothiazole and many dyes

ben·zo·thiophene \"+\ *n* -s [ISV *benz-* + *thiophene*] **:** THIANAPHTHENE

ben·zo·triazole \"+\ *n* -s [ISV *benz-* + *triazole*] **:** a white crystalline compound $C_6H_5N_3$ made by the action of nitrous acid on *ortho*-phenylenediamine and used in photographic developing solutions as an antifoggant

ben·zo·trichloride \"+\ *n* -s [ISV *benz-* + *trichloride*] **:** a colorless highly refractive liquid compound $C_6H_5CCl_3$ made by the action of chlorine on boiling toluene and used chiefly in the manufacture of dyes; α,α,α-trichloro-toluene

benzoxy- *comb form* [ISV *benz-* + *oxy-*] **:** containing the benzoate radical C_6H_5COO-; benzoyl-oxy ⟨*benzoxy*acetanilide⟩

ben·zo·yl \ˈbenzəwəl, -,wēl\ *n* -s [G — more at -YL] **:** the radical C_6H_5CO- of benzoic acid — compare -YL

benzoyl acetyl peroxide *n* **:** ACETYL BENZOYL PEROXIDE

ben·zo·yl·ate \ˈbenzōə,lāt, ,=ˈ==,=\ *vt* -ED/-ING/-S [*benzoyl* + *-ate*] **:** to introduce benzoyl into (a compound) — **ben·zo·yl·a·tion** \,=(,)==ˈlāshən\ *n* -s

benzoyl chloride *n* **:** a colorless very pungent liquid compound C_6H_5COCl made by partial hydrolysis of benzotrichloride and in other ways and used chiefly in organic synthesis (as of dyes)

ben·zo·yl·glycine \ˌbenzəwəl, -,wēl+\ *n* -s [*benzoyl* + *glycine*] **:** HIPPURIC ACID

benzoyl peroxide *n* **:** a white crystalline flammable compound $(C_6H_5CO)_2O_2$ made usu. by reaction of benzoyl chloride with sodium peroxide and used chiefly in initiating vinyl-type polymerizations and in bleaching (as flour, fats, oils)

benz·pyr·in·i·um \,benzpəˈrinēəm\ *n* -s [*benz-* + *pyridinium*] **:** the substituted pyridinium ion $[C_6H_5CH_2NC_5H_4OOCN(CH_3)_2]^+$ derived by benzylation of dimethyl-carbamoyl-oxypyridinium; *also* **:** a salt containing this radical (as the bromide used to relieve postoperative urinary retention)

ben·zyl \ˈben,zēl, -zil\ *n* -s [ISV *benz-* + *-yl*] **:** the univalent radical $C_6H_5CH_2$ derived from toluene by removal of one hydrogen atom from the side chain

benzyl acetate *n* **:** a colorless fragrant liquid ester $CH_3COOCH_2C_6H_5$ occurring in jasmine oil and other essential oils, made synthetically, and used chiefly in perfumery

benzyl alcohol *n* **:** a colorless liquid primary alcohol $C_6H_5CH_2OH$ occurring free and in the form of esters in many essential oils, made usu. by hydrolysis of benzyl chloride, and used chiefly as a solvent and in making esters

ben·zyl·amine \ˌben,zil, -zēl+\ *n* -s [ISV *benzyl* + *amine*] **:** a colorless liquid base $C_6H_5CH_2NH_2$ made synthetically (as by the action of ammonia on benzyl chloride)

ben·zyl·ate \ˈbenzə,lāt\ *vt* -ED/-ING/-S [*benzyl* + *-ate*] **:** to introduce benzyl into (a compound) — **ben·zyl·a·tion** \,==ˈlāshən\ *n* -s

benzyl benzoate *n* **:** a colorless oily ester $C_6H_5COOCH_2C_6H_5$ occurring esp. in balsams (as balsam of Peru), made synthetically, and used chiefly in medicine as an antispasmodic and in the form of a lotion as a scabicide and in perfumery as a fixative and solvent

benzyl cellulose *n* **:** any of various white granular thermoplastic substances made by benzylating alkali cellulose and used similarly to ethyl cellulose

benzyl chloride *n* **:** a colorless pungent lacrimatory liquid compound $C_6H_5CH_2Cl$ made usu. by treating boiling toluene with chlorine and used chiefly in organic synthesis (as of pharmaceuticals and dyes); α-chloro-toluene

benzyl cinnamate *n* **:** an aromatic white crystalline ester $C_{16}H_{14}O_2$ found in balsam of Peru, balsam of Tolu, and storax and used in perfumery — called also *cinnamein*

benzyl cyanide *n* **:** an oily aromatic compound $C_6H_5CH_2CN$ found in some essential oils (as of garden peppergrass) and also made synthetically; phenyl-acetonitrile

ben·zyl·ic \(ˈ)benˈzilik, -ēk\ *adj* [ISV *benzyl* + *-ic*] **:** relating to benzyl

ben·zyl·i·dene \benˈzilə,dēn\ *n* -s [ISV *benzyl* + *-idene*] **:** BENZAL

benzylidene chloride *n* **:** BENZAL CHLORIDE

ben·zyl·oxy \ˌbenzəˈläksē\ *adj* [*benzyloxy-*] **:** relating to or containing the radical $C_6H_5CH_2O-$

benzyloxy- *comb form* [ISV *benzyl* + *oxy-*] **:** containing the univalent radical $C_6H_5CH_2O-$ composed of benzyl united with oxygen ⟨*benzyloxy*amine⟩

ben·zyl·penicillin \ˌbenzəl, -(,)zēl+\ *n* [*benzyl* + *penicillin*] **:** PENICILLIN 2b

benzyl violet *n, often cap B&V* **:** a basic dye — see DYE table I (under *Basic Violet 13*)

be·o·thuk \ˈbāə,thu̇k\ *n, pl* **beothuk** *or* **beothuks** *usu cap* **1 a :** an extinct Indian people of Newfoundland **b :** a member of such people **2 :** a language of the Beothuk people that is of unknown relationship — **be·o·thuk·an** \ˈ==,=kən\ *adj*

be·paint \bə̇, bē+\ *vt* [*be-* + *paint*] **1** *archaic* **:** to paint esp. heavily or gaudily **:** smear with paint ⟨~*ed* Indians⟩ **2** *archaic* **:** to tinge with color ⟨the ~*ed* sky of dawn⟩

be·paper \bə̇, bē+\ *vt* [*be-* + *paper*] **:** to cover with paper **:** encumber with papers

be·patched \bə̇, bē+\ *adj* [*be-* + *patched*] **1 :** covered with patches **:** wearing patched clothing **2 :** wearing an ornamental patch or patches on the face

be·picture \bə̇, bē+\ *vt* [*be-* + *picture,* n.] **1 :** to adorn with or as if with a picture or pictures **2 :** to show in or as if in a picture

be·plaster \bə̇, bē+\ *vt* [*be-* + *plaster*] **:** to plaster over **:** cover profusely ⟨a uniform ~*ed* with medals⟩ **:** smear thickly ⟨~*ing* her cheeks with cosmetics⟩

be·powder \bə̇, bē+\ *vt* [*be-* + *powder*] **:** to cover with powder

be·praise \bə̇, bē+\ *vt* [*be-* + *praise*] **:** to praise greatly, repeatedly, or excessively

be·pranked \bə̇, bē+\ *adj* [*be-* + *pranked*] **:** showily dressed or adorned

be·puffed \bə̇, bē+\ *adj* [*be-* + *puffed*] **1 :** praised unduly **2 :** very puffy or swollen

be·puzzle \bə̇, bē+\ *vt* [*be-* + *puzzle*] **:** to puzzle greatly — **be·puzzlement** \"+\ *n* -s

be·queath \bə̇ˈkwēth, -ēth, bē-\ *vt* -ED/-ING/-S [ME *bequethen* to say, assign, allot, bequeath, fr. OE *becwethan,* fr. *be-* + *cwethan* to say — more at QUOTH] **1 a :** to give or leave by will **:** give by formal declaration so that the thing given passes into the ownership of the recipient after the death of the donor **:** give by testament — used esp. of personalty; compare DEVISE **b :** to hand down (as to successors or posterity) **:** TRANSMIT ⟨politicosocial myths ~*ed* to us by the 19th century —Ignazio Silone⟩ **2** *archaic* **:** to consign trusting that the recipient will accept and take care of that which is consigned **:** ENTRUST, COMMEND **3** *obs* **:** to assign or make over by formal declaration so as to give the recipient immediate possession **:** transfer ownership of **syn** see WILL

be·queath·al \-əl\ *n* -s **:** BEQUEST

be·queath·ment \-mənt\ *n* -s **:** BEQUEST

be·quest \bə̇ˈkwest, bē- *sometimes* ˈbē,k-\ *n* -s [ME *bequeste,* irreg. fr. *bequethen* to bequeath] **1 :** the action of bequeathing **2 :** something (as personal property) bequeathed **:** LEGACY

ber \ˈbe(ə)r\ *n, pl* **ber** *also* **bers** [Hindi, fr. Skt *badara*] **:** JUJUBE 1

be·rai·rou \bəˈrī,rau̇\ *n* -s [prob. native name in New Zealand] **:** RED KAURI

be·ra·kah *or* **be·ra·chah** \bəˈrä(,)kä, =,=ˈ=\ *n, pl* **bera·koth** *or* **bera·choth** \-kōth, -ōt,-ōs\ *or* **bera·kot** *or* **bera·chot** \-ōt,-ōs\ [Heb *bĕrākhāh* blessing] *Jewish relig* **:** BENEDICTION, BLESSING ⟨the kiddush is a well-known ~⟩

be·rat *or* **ba·rat** \bəˈrät\ *n* -s [Turk *berat,* fr. Ar *barā'ah*] **:** a formal authorization granting a privilege or conferring a dignity issued by a sovereign in the Near East

be·rate \bə̇ˈrāt, bē-, *usu* -ād.+V\ *vt* -ED/-ING/-S [*be-* + *rate* (to chide)] **:** to heap reproaches on **:** criticize vigorously ⟨hearing Ed Hall ~ a farmer who doubted the practicability of the machine —Sherwood Anderson⟩ **:** scold or chide vehemently ⟨an Italian shrew *berating* her unemployed husband —John McCarten⟩ **syn** see SCOLD

berattle *vt* [*be-* + *rattle*] *obs* **:** to scold at **:** cry down

be·raun·ite \bəˈrau̇,nīt, bäˈr-, ˈbä,r-\ *n* -s [G *beraunit,* fr. *Beraun* (Beroun), Czechoslovakia + G *-it* -ite] **:** a mineral consisting of a hydrous basic iron phosphate commonly in brown or dark red druses or radiated globules

berav *vt* -ED/-ING/-S [*be-* + *ray* (soil)] *obs* **:** to spatter with dirt or filth; *esp* **:** to defile with excrement

ber·ba·mine \ˈbərbə,mēn, -,mən\ *n* -s [ISV *berberine* + *amine;* orig. formed as G *berbamin*] **:** a crystalline alkaloid $C_{37}H_{40}N_2O_6$ found esp. in barberry

ber·ber \ˈbərbər; ˈbəbə(r), ˈbəib-\ *n* -s *cap* [Ar *Barbar*] **1 :** a member of a Caucasoid people of northern Africa west of Tripoli closely related to southern Europeans, Egyptians, and Ethiopians **2 :** a branch of the Afro-Asiatic language family comprising languages spoken by minorities in No. Africa and the Sahara **3 :** any one of the Berber languages or the whole group considered as one language with numerous dialects

ber·beri \ˈbərbərē\ *n, pl* **berberi** *or* **berberis** *usu cap* **1 :** a people of Mongol origin in the Afghan-Iran frontier region **2 :** a member of the Berberi people

ber·ber·i·da·ce·ae \,bərbərəˈdāsē,ē, bər,ber-\ *n pl, cap* [NL, fr. *Berberid-, Berberis,* type genus + *-aceae*] **:** a family of shrubs or herbs (order Ranales) having the sepals and petals imbricated in several series and the fruit either a berry or a capsule

ber·ber·i·da·ceous \ˌbərbərəˈdāshəs, bərˌber-\ *adj* [NL *Berberidaceae* + E *-ous*] **:** of or relating to the Berberidaceae

[1]**ber·ber·ine** \ˈbərbə,rēn, -,rən\ *n* -s [G *berberin,* fr. NL *Berberis* + G *-in* -ine] **:** a bitter crystalline yellow alkaloid $C_{20}H_{19}NO_5$ obtained from the roots of the barberry, goldenseal, and other plants and used as a tonic and antiperiodic

[2]**berberine** \"\ *also* **berberine tree** *n* -s **:** an African tree (*Xylopia polycarpa*) yielding a yellow dye containing berberine

[3]**ber·ber·ine** \ˈbərbə,rēn, -,rīn\ *adj, usu cap* [*Berber* + *-ine*] **:** of or relating to the Berbers or their languages

ber·ber·is \ˈbərbərə̇s\ *n* [NL, alter. of ML *barbaris* barberry, fr. Ar *barbārīs*] **1** *cap* **:** a large genus of shrubs (family Berberidaceae) natives of the north temperate zone and of the Andes to Tierra del Fuego having prickly stems and yellow flowers succeeded by red berries — see BARBERRY **2** -ES **:** the dried rhizome and roots of certain barberries of the genus *Mahonia* that contain the alkaloids berberine, oxyacanthine, and berbamine — called also *Oregon graperoot*

berberry *or* **berbery** *var of* BARBERRY

ber·ceuse \berˈsə(r)z, -sœz; beəˈsœz\ *n, pl* **berceuses** \-z(əz)\ [F, fr. *bercer* to rock] **1 :** CRADLESONG **2 :** a vocal or instrumental composition of a tranquil or soothing character

ber·che·mia \(,)bərˈkēmēə\ *n, cap* [NL] **:** a genus of widely distributed woody vines (family Rhamnaceae) having bright green foliage — see SUPPLEJACK

ber·cy \(ˈ)berˈsē\ *also* **bercy sauce** *n* -ES *usu cap B* [fr. *Bercy,* quarter of Paris, France] **:** velouté sauce with minced shallots, parsley, lemon juice, white wine, and butter

ber·dache \bə(r)ˈdash\ *n* -s [F *bardache* homosexual male — more at BARDASH] **:** an American Indian transvestite assuming more or less permanently the dress, social status, and role of a woman

be·re·an \bəˈrēən\ *n* -s *usu cap* [*Berea* or *Beroea,* ancient name for Veroia, town in Macedonia, Greece; Bire, Palestine; and Alep, Syria + E *-an*] **:** a native or inhabitant of the ancient city Beroea

be·reave \bə̇ˈrēv, bē-\ *vt* **bereaved** \-vd\ *or* **be·reft** \-ˈreft\ **bereaved** *or* **bereft** *or archaic* **be·reav·en** \-ˈrēvən\ **bereaving; bereaves** [ME *bereven,* fr. OE *berēafian,* fr. *be-* + *rēafian* to rob — more at REAVE] **1 :** to deprive esp. by death **:** STRIP, DISPOSSESS — used with *of* before that which is taken away ⟨the war *bereaved* them of their three sons⟩ ⟨*bereft* of all hope⟩

⟨*bereft* of their senses⟩ **2** *obs* **:** to take away (a cherished or valued possession) esp. by force or violence **syn** see DEPRIVE
be·reave·ment \-ēvmənt\ *n* -s **:** the state or fact of being bereaved **:** DEPRIVATION; *esp* **:** loss of a loved one by death
berendo *var of* BERRENDO
ber·en·gar·i·an \ˌberən'ga(a)rēən\ *n* -s *usu cap* [*Berengarius* (Bérenger de Tours) †1088 Fr. ecclesiastic + E *-an*] **:** one who follows Bérenger de Tours in denying transubstantiation
ber·en·ge·lite \ˌberən'gäˌlīt\ *n* -s [San Juan de *Berengela*, Peru + E *-ite*] **:** a brown resinous substance used in caulking ships
be·res·o·vite \bə'resəˌvīt\ *n* -s [F, fr. *Beresov*, Ural mts., U.S.S.R., its locality + F *-ite*] **:** a mineral perhaps $Pb_6(CrO_4)_3(CO_3)O_2$ consisting of a deep red lead chromate-oxide-carbonate
be·ret \bə'rā, be-\ *n* -s [F *béret*, fr. Prov *berret*, fr. OProv, cap — more at BIRETTA] **1 :** a soft flat visorless cap of woolen material orig. worn by Basque peasants **2 :** a woman's hat the design of which is based on the beret

beret 2

beretta *var of* BIRETTA
berettina *var of* BERRETTINO
berewick *n* -s [OE *berewīc*, lit., barley-village, fr. *bere* barley + *wīc* village — more at BARLEY, WICK] **:** a detached portion of farmland that belonged to a medieval manor and was reserved for the lord's own use
¹berg \'bərg, -ēg, -əig\ *n* -s [by shortening] **:** ICEBERG
²berg \'berk\ *n* -s [Afrik, fr. MD *bergh*, *berch*; akin to OHG *berg* mountain — more at BARROW] *chiefly Africa* **:** MOUNTAIN
berg adder *n* [²*berg*] **:** a small venomous snake (*Bitis atropos*) inhabiting the highlands of the Transvaal and the southern African uplands
ber·ga·ma \'bərgəmə, 'ber-, bər'gämə\ *or* **ber·ga·mo** \ˌbergə'mō\ *or* **ber·ga·mot** \ˌbergə'mō\ *n* -s *usu cap* [fr. *Bergama*, town in western Turkey] **:** a rug of long loose pile, strong geometric designs, and rich vivid colors
ber·ga·mo \'bergəˌmō\ *adj, usu cap* [fr. *Bergamo*, Italy] **:** of or from the city of Bergamo, Italy **:** of the kind or style prevalent in Bergamo
ber·ga·mot \'bərgəˌmät, -mət, *usu* -d·+V\ *or* **bergamot orange** *n* -s [F *bergamote*, fr. It *bergamotta*, fr. a Turkic word akin to Turk *bey-armudu*, lit., prince's pear] **1 a :** an orange (*Citrus bergamia*) with a pear-shaped fruit whose rind yields an essential oil much used in perfumery; *also* **:** its fruit **b :** any of several mints (esp. *Mentha aquatica*, *Mentha citrata*, *Monarda fistulosa*, and *Monarda didyma*) **2 :** the oil or perfume made from bergamot fruit **3 :** a snuff scented with bergamot perfume
bergamot camphor *n* **:** BERGAPTEN
bergamot mint *n* **:** a bergamot (*Mentha citrata*) with thick flower spikes and mostly ovate or elliptic obtuse leaves
bergamot oil *n* **:** a greenish or brownish yellow fragrant essential oil expressed from the rind of the fruit of a tree (*Citrus bergamia*) and used chiefly as a perfume (as in colognes)
ber·gan *or* **ber·gen** \'bərgən\ *n* -s *usu cap* [fr. *Bergen*, Norway] **:** a rucksack supported by a wooden frame and having a belt to fasten around the waist
ber·gan·der \bə(r)'gandə(r)\ *n* -s [origin unknown] *chiefly Brit* **:** the common European sheldrake
ber·gap·ten \bə(r)'gaptən\ *or* **ber·gap·tene** \-ˌtēn\ *n* -s [ISV *bergamot* + *-pten* -*ptene* (as in *eleoptene*)] **:** a crystalline lactone $C_{12}H_8O_4$ that separates from crude bergamot oil on standing — called also *bergamot camphor*
berg crystal \'bərg-\ *n* [part trans. of G *bergkristall*, fr. *berg* mountain (fr. OHG) + *kristall* crystal — more at BARROW] **:** ROCK CRYSTAL **:** transparent quartz
berg·da·ma \'bergˌdämə\ *or* **berg·dam·a·ra** \-ˌdamərə, -ˌdəˌmärə\ *n, pl* **bergdama** *or* **bergdamas** *or* **bergdamara** *or* **bergdamaras** *usu cap* [Afrik, fr. *berg* mountain + *Dama*, *Damara* — more at BERG] **:** a branch of the Damara
ber·gen \'bərgən, 'ber-\ *adj, usu cap* [fr. *Bergen*, Norway] **:** of or from the city of Bergen, Norway **:** of the kind or style prevalent in Bergen
ber·ge·nia \(ˌ)bər'gēnēə, -nyə\ *n, cap* [NL, fr. Karl A. von *Bergen* †1760 Ger. physician and botanist + NL *-ia*] **:** a genus of perennial spring-blooming herbs (family Saxifragaceae) often included in the genus *Saxifraga* but having large thick rootstocks that produce typical colonies or clumps of plants with very thick heavy leaves
ber·gère \(')ber¦zhe(ə)r\ *n* -s [F, lit., shepherdess, fem. of *berger* shepherd, fr. OF *bergier*, fr. (assumed) VL *berbicarius*] **:** an upholstered armchair of a style fashionable in the 18th century
ber·ge·rette \ˌberzhə'ret\ *n* -s [F, dim. of *bergère* shepherdess] **1 :** a 16th century pastoral song or dance **2 :** an 18th century French song or other composition resembling the pastoral form
ber·ger rhythm \'bərgər-, 'ber-\ *n, usu cap B* [after Hans *Berger* †1944 Ger. neurologist] **:** ALPHA RHYTHM
berg·haan \'berkˌhän, -ān\ *n* -s [Afrik, fr. *berg* mountain (fr. MD *berch*, *bergh*) + *haan* cock, fr. MD *hāne*; akin to OHG *berg* mountain and to OHG *hano* cock — more at BARROW, HEN] **:** any of several southern African eagles; *esp* **:** BATELEUR
berg ice *n* [¹*berg*] **:** the ice of a broken iceberg
ber·gi·ni·za·tion \ˌbergənə'zāshən, -ˌnī'z-\ *n* -s [*Bergius* (*process*) + connective *-n-* + *-ization*] **:** subjection to the Bergius process
ber·gi·us process \'bergēəs-\ *n, usu cap B* [after Friedrich *Bergius* †1949 Ger. chemist] **:** a process of hydrogenating usu. powdered coal mixed with oil and a catalyst under heat and high pressure in order to obtain chiefly liquid products (as fuel oil and gasoline)
berg·mann's rule \'bərgmənz, 'berg-\ *n, usu cap B* [after Karl *Bergmann* †1865 Ger. biologist] **:** a statement of the principle that within a polytypic wide-ranging species of warm-blooded animals the average body size of members of each geographic race varies inversely with the mean environmental temperature
berg·schrund \'berkˌshrůnt\ *n* -s [G, fr. *berg* mountain (fr. OHG) + *schrund* crack, fr. OHG *scrunta*; akin to MD *schronde* crack, OFris *schran* sharp, Norw *skrunda* wooden box, OHG *scrintan* to crack open, OPruss *skrundos* shears — more at BARROW] **:** a deep and often broad crevasse or series of such crevasses frequently occurring near the head of a mountain glacier
¹berg·so·nian \(')berg¦sōnēən, -nyən\ *adj, usu cap* [Henri *Bergson* †1941 Fr. philosopher + E *-ian*] **:** of or relating to Bergson or Bergsonism
²bergsonian \"\ *n* -s *usu cap* **:** an adherent of Bergsonism
berg·so·nian·ism \⸗'⸗nēəˌnizəm, -nyə-\ *n* -s *usu cap* **:** BERGSONISM
berg·son·ism \'bergsəˌnizəm\ *n* -s *usu cap* [F *bergsonisme*, fr. H. *Bergson* + F *-isme* -ism] **:** the theories of the philosopher Bergson according to whom the world is a process of creative evolution in which the novelty of successive phenomena rather than the constancy of natural law is the significant fact, reality being regarded as time or duration that is the same as free motion and that is the expression of a vital impetus or creative force while the space world of science and common sense is taken to be an interpretation put upon sense images in the interest of practical activity and as a falsification of free-moving reality so that a true apprehension of reality is to be gained not by the analytic procedures of mathematics and science but by that intuition that can grasp wholes as such
berg·stock \'bərgˌstäk, *Ger* 'berkˌshtōk\ *n* -s [G, fr. *berg* mountain (fr. OHG) + *stock* staff, fr. OHG *stoc* — more at BARROW, STOCK] **:** ALPENSTOCK
berg till \'bərgˌtil\ *n* [¹*berg*] **:** lacustrine clay with boulders and other glacial debris dropped in it by melting icebergs
bergy bit \¦bərgē-\ *n* [¹*berg* + *-y*] **:** a great chunk of ice broken free of a large ice body (as an iceberg)
ber·gylt \'bergəlt\ *n* -s [Sw or Norw *berggylta*, fr. *berg* rock (fr. ON *berg*) + *gylta* sow (pig), fr. ON — more at BARROW, GILT] **:** ROSEFISH
be·rhyme *or* **be·rime** \bə, bē+\ *vt* [*be-* + *rhyme*, *rime*] *archaic* **:** to use as the subject of a rhyme; *esp* **:** to lampoon in rhyming verse
be·rib·boned \bə'ribənd, bē-\ *adj* [*be-* + *ribbon* + *-ed*] **:** adorned with ribbons ⟨dressed in a child's shorts, blouse, socks, and ~ sailor hat —John Buchan⟩
beri·beri \¦berē'berē\ *n* -s [Sinhalese *bæribæri*] **:** a deficiency disease marked by inflammatory or degenerative changes involving the nerves, digestive system, and heart and caused by a lack of or inability to assimilate vitamin B_1
ber·ing·ite \'beriŋˌīt, 'bir-\ *n* -s [G *beringit*, fr. *Bering* island, Kamchatka, U.S.S.R. + G *-it* -ite] **:** a melanocratic alkali-trachyte rock composed of barkevikite, albite, and orthoclase
ber·ing sea \'beriŋ-, 'bir-\ *adj, usu cap B&S* [fr. *Bering Sea*, part of the northern Pacific] **:** OLD BERING SEA
bering time *or* **bering standard time** *n, cap B* **:** the time of the former 11th time zone west of Greenwich that included western Alaska and the Aleutian islands and was six hours slower than eastern time
be·rith *or* **brith** *or* **be·rit** *also* **briss** *or* **bris** \bə'rith, 'bri-, -it,-is\ *n, pl* **beriths** *also* **brisses** [Heb *bĕrīth* covenant] **1 :** BERITH MILAH **2 :** the Jewish rite or ceremony of circumcision performed on the male child on the eighth day after his birth
berith mi·lah \-'mē(ˌ)lä\ *n* [Heb *bĕrīth mīlāh*] *Jewish relig* **:** the covenant of circumcision
¹berke·le·ian *or* **berke·ley·an** \'bär(ˌ)klēən, bär'klēən; 'bər(ˌ)klēən, ˌbər'k-, *Brit. usu* 'bä(ˌ)k- *or* bä'k-\ *adj, usu cap* [George *Berkeley* †1753 Irish philosopher + E *-ian*] **:** of or relating to Bishop Berkeley or his system of philosophical idealism
²berkeleian *or* **berkeleyan** \'⸗ ⸗⸗, (ˌ)⸗'⸗⸗\ *n* -s *usu cap* **:** one who believes in or advocates Berkeleianism
berke·le·ian·ism *or* **berke·ley·an·ism** \'⸗ ⸗⸗ˌnizəm, (ˌ)⸗'⸗⸗-\ *n* -s *usu cap* **:** a system of philosophical idealism first taught by George Berkeley maintaining that so-called material things exist only in being perceived and that the physical universe is not independent reality but exists as a perception of the divine mind and also partially as perceived by the finite minds of men
berke·ley \'bərklē\ *adj, usu cap* [fr. *Berkeley*, Calif.] **:** of or from the city of Berkeley, Calif. ⟨*Berkeley* stores⟩ **:** of the kind or style prevalent in Berkeley
berke·ley·ism \'bərklēˌizəm, *Brit usu* 'bäk-\ *n* -s *usu cap* [G. *Berkeley* + E *-ism*] **:** BERKELEIANISM
berke·ley·ite \-ˌīt\ *n* -s *usu cap* [G. *Berkeley* + E *-ite*] **:** BERKELEIAN
berke·li·um \'bərklēəm (*the coiners' pronunc*), ˌbər'kēl-\ *n* -s [NL, fr. *Berkeley*, Calif., location of the Univ. of Calif., where it was discovered + NL *-ium*] **:** a radioactive metallic element discovered by bombarding americium 241 with helium ions — symbol *Bk*; see ELEMENT table
ber·ko·vets \'berkəˌvets\ *n, pl* **berkov·tsi** \-kəf,tsē\ [Russ *berkovets*, fr. ORuss *birkovĭskŭ*, *berkovĭskŭ*, fr. OSw *Biærkö* Björkö (Koivisto), fortress of Vyborg, U.S.S.R.] **:** a Russian unit of weight equal to 361.13 pounds
¹berk·shire \'bərkˌshi(ə)r, -iə, -ˌshə(r), *Brit usu* 'bäk-\ *adj, usu cap* [fr. *Berkshire*, England] **:** of or from Berkshire, England **:** of the kind or style prevalent in Berkshire
²berkshire \"\ *n* -s *usu cap* [fr. *Berkshire*, England, where the breed originated] **1 :** a breed of medium-sized swine black with white markings **2 :** a Berkshire swine
ber·le·se funnel \bə(r)'lāzē-, -āsē-\ *n, cap B* [after Antonio *Berlese* †1927 Ital. entomologist] **:** an apparatus that separates and preserves small insects found in ground litter and consists of a sieve placed over a funnel connected at the bottom to a preserving bottle
ber·ley \'bərlē\ *n* -s [origin unknown] *Austral* **:** GROUND BAIT
¹ber·lin \bə(r)'lin; ˌbər'l-,bə̄'l-,bəi'l-, '⸗,⸗\ *adj, usu cap* [fr. *Berlin*, Germany] **:** of or from the city of Berlin, Germany **:** of the kind or style prevalent in Berlin
²ber·lin \bə(r)'lin, ˌbər'l-,bə̄'l-,bəi'l-\ *also* **ber·line** \", -'lēn; ber'lēn, beə'l-\ *n* -s [F *berline*, fr. *Berlin*, Germany, where it was fashionable in the late 17th & 18th cent.] **1 a** *sometimes cap* **:** a 4-wheeled 2-seated covered carriage with a hooded rear seat **b :** an enclosed automobile body having at the rear of the driver's seat a glass partition with usu. one movable window **2** [by shortening] *sometimes cap* **a :** BERLIN WOOL **b :** something (as a glove) made of Berlin wool
berlin black *n, often cap 1st B* [¹*berlin*] **:** a black varnish that dries with an almost dead surface and is used for coating the better kinds of ironwork
berlin blue *n, often cap 1st B* **1 :** any of various iron-blue pigments **2 :** PRUSSIAN BLUE 2
berlin brown *n, often cap 1st B* **:** a grayish red that is yellower and duller than livid brown, bluer and duller than Pompeian red, and duller and slightly yellower than bois de rose — called also *iron minium*
ber·lin·er \bə(r)'linə(r), ˌbər'l-,bə̄'l-,-bəi'l-\ *n* -s *cap* [G *berliner*, fr. *Berlin*, Germany] **:** a native or inhabitant of Berlin, esp. Berlin, Germany
ber·lin·ite \(ˌ)bər'liˌnīt, 'bərlə,n-\ *n* -s [Sw *berlinit*, fr. N. H. *Berlin*, 19th cent. Swedish pharmacologist + Sw *-it* -ite] **:** a mineral $AlPO_4$ consisting of a hydrous aluminum phosphate occurring in colorless to rose-red masses (sp. gr. 2.6)
berlin porcelain *n, usu cap B* [¹*berlin*] **:** a hard paste porcelain made at Berlin since about 1750
berlin red *n, often cap B* **:** ²BOLE 3
berlin ware *n, usu cap B* **:** Berlin-porcelain ware
berlin wool *n, usu cap B* **:** a fine worsted yarn for knitting and embroidery
berlin work *n, usu cap B* **:** embroidery (as cross-stitch and needlepoint) usu. done with Berlin wool on canvas
ber·lock dermatitis \bər'läk-, 'bər,l-\ *n* [F *berloque*, *breloque*, lit., charm for a watch or bracelet; fr. the pattern of the discoloration] **:** a brownish discoloration of the skin that develops on exposure to sunlight after the use of perfume containing ethereal oils
ber·loque \bər'läk, -lōk\ *n* -s [F *berloque*, *breloque* (also, charm for a watch or bracelet)] **:** a drumbeat in which one stick beats twice to the other's once and which is used as a signal for certain fatigue duties (as at breaking ranks); *also* **:** a corresponding trumpet call
berm *or* **berme** \'bərm\ *n* -s [F *berme*, fr. D *berm* strip of ground along a dike; akin to ON *barmr* edge, brim — more at BRIM] **:** a narrow shelf, edge, or path typically at the bottom or top of a slope or along a bank: as **a :** a ledge between the foot of the exterior slope and the top of the scarp of a fortification **b :** a narrow shelf near the top of a trench or dugout to prevent dirt slides and to provide supports for beams **c :** the level space between the edge of a ditch and the bank of earth excavated from it **d :** the bank of a canal opposite the towpath ⟨poorly constructed sections of the canal's ~ and towpath . . . were dangerously vulnerable to muskrat burrowings and flood pressure —S.H.Adams⟩ **e :** the shoulder of a road ⟨deer . . . were feeding on the ~ of the highway between the concrete and the guardrails —Norman Erickson⟩ **f :** the nearly horizontal portion of a beach generally bounded on one side or other by a beach ridge or beach scarp ⟨waves wash across the beach to the ~ —W.C.Krumbein & R.L.Miller⟩ **g :** BENCH 5a **h** *North & Midland* **:** TREE BELT
ber·man·ite \'bərməˌnīt\ *n* -s [Harry *Berman* †1944 Am. mineralogist + E *-ite*] **:** a mineral $(Mn,Mg)_5(Mn,Fe)_8(PO_4)_8(OH)_{10}.15H_2O(?)$ consisting of a reddish brown basic hydrous phosphate of manganese, iron, and magnesium
¹ber·mu·da \bə(r)'myüdə, *S also* -mü-; *attrib sometimes* 'bər,m- *or* 'bə̄,m- *or* 'bəi,m-\ *adj, usu cap* [fr. *Bermuda* islands, western No. Atlantic] **:** of or from Bermuda **:** of the kind or style prevalent in Bermuda **:** BERMUDIAN
²bermuda \"\ *n* -s *often cap* [fr. *Bermuda* islands] **1 :** GERANIUM PINK **2 2 bermudas** *pl* **:** BERMUDA SHORTS
bermuda arrowroot *n, usu cap B* **1 :** arrowroot obtained from a maranta (*Maranta arundinacea*) **2 :** the plant that yields Bermuda arrowroot
bermuda buttercup *n, usu cap 1st B* **:** a southern African bulbous wood sorrel (*Oxalis cernua*) cultivated for its showy yellow flowers
bermuda cedar *n, usu cap B* **:** a juniper (*Juniperus bermudiana*) endemic in Bermuda that has tough hard wood, scalelike leaves, and dark blue fruit
bermuda chub *n, usu cap B* **:** a gray percoid fish (*Kyphosus sectatrix*) striped with blue or yellow that is a common food and game fish of the warmer waters of the western Atlantic esp. about the Florida keys and Bermuda
bermuda cress *n, usu cap B* **:** WINTER CRESS
bermuda grass *n, usu cap B* **:** a grass (*Cynodon dactylon*) of trailing and stoloniferous habit native to southern Europe but now widely distributed in warm countries and used for lawns and pasture esp. in the southern U.S. and in India — called also *Bahama grass*, *devil grass*, *doob*, *scutch grass*
bermuda high *n, usu cap B* **:** a semipermanent system of high atmospheric pressure near Bermuda in the Atlantic ocean found particularly well developed in the summer
bermuda lily *n, usu cap B* **:** a lily that is a variety (*Lilium longiflorum eximium*) of the white trumpet lily with flowers green tinged toward the base and with a long narrow tube the upper part of which flares like a trumpet formerly much cultivated in Bermuda and sold as an Easter lily
bermuda lobster *n, usu cap B* **:** a large brightly colored spiny lobster (*Panulirus argus*)

Bermuda grass

bermuda maidenhair *n, usu cap B* **:** a delicate endemic Bermudian fern (*Adiantum bellum*) with a creeping rootstock
bermuda mulberry *n, usu cap B* **:** FRENCH MULBERRY 1
bermuda olivewood bark *n, usu cap B* **:** an endemic Bermudian evergreen tree (*Elaeodendron laneanum*) with dioecious axillary flowers and roundish white-fleshed fruit
bermuda onion *n, usu cap B* **:** a large flat yellow-skinned mild-flavored onion that probably originated in Italy or the Canary islands and is now widely grown in southern Texas; *broadly* **:** any of several long-season onions that differ from the Bermuda onion chiefly in skin color
bermuda rig *or* **bermudian rig** *n, usu cap B* **:** a fore-and-aft rig marked by a triangular sail and a mast with an extreme rake
bermuda shorts *n pl, usu cap B* **:** knee-length walking shorts worn by men and women
¹ber·mu·di·an \bə(r)'myüdēən, *S also* -mü-; *attrib sometimes* 'bər,m- *or* 'bə̄,m- *or* 'bəi,m-\ *or* **ber·mu·dan** \-d³n\ *adj, usu cap* [*Bermuda* islands + E *-ian* or *-an*] **1 :** of, relating to, or characteristic of Bermuda **2 :** of, relating to, or characteristic of Bermudians
²bermudian \"\ *n* -s *cap* **:** a native or resident of Bermuda
bern *or* **berne** \'bərn, 'be(ə)rn\ *adj, usu cap* [fr. *Bern* or *Berne*, Switzerland] **:** of or from Bern, the capital of Switzerland **:** of the kind or style prevalent in Bern **:** BERNESE
¹ber·nard·ine *R* 'bərnə(r)ˌdēn, *-R* 'bə̄nəˌd- *or* 'bəinəˌd-\ *adj, usu cap* [F *bernardin*, fr. St. *Bernard* of Clairvaux †1153 Fr. ecclesiastic + F *-in* -ine] **1 :** of or relating to St. Bernard of Clairvaux **2 :** of or relating to the branch of the Cistercian order instituted by St. Bernard of Clairvaux
²bernardine \"\ *n* -s *usu cap* **:** a nun of one of several non-Cistercian congregations following a rule modeled on the original Cistercian observance
ber·ne \'bernə\ *n* -s [Pg] **:** TORSALO
¹bern·ese \¦bər¦nēz, (')ber-, -ēs\ *adj, usu cap* [*Bern*, city and canton in Switzerland + E *-ese*] **1 :** of, relating to, or characteristic of Bern, a city and canton in Switzerland **2 :** of, relating to, or characteristic of the Bernese
²bernese \"\ *n, pl* **bernese** *cap* **:** a native or resident of Bern
bernese mountain dog *n, usu cap B & sometimes cap M&D* **:** one of a Swiss breed of large powerful long-coated black dogs that have deep tan or russet-brown markings on the legs and over the eyes, that often have a blaze, white feet, and white chest mark, and that were formerly used for draft
ber·ni·cla \'bərnəklə, (ˌ)bər'nik-\ [NL, fr. F *bernicle* barnacle (goose and shellfish), fr. Bret *bernic* — more at BARNACLE] *syn of* BRANTA
ber·ni·cle \'bərnəkəl\ *or* **bernicle goose** *n* -s [MF] **:** BARNACLE GOOSE
ber·noul·li distribution \bər¦nülē-, ¦berˌnü¦lē-\ *n, usu cap B* [after Jacques *Bernoulli* †1705 Swiss mathematician] **:** BINOMIAL DISTRIBUTION
ber·noul·li effect \"-\ *n, usu cap B* [after Daniel *Bernoulli* †1782 Swiss mathematician and scientist] **:** an effect observed in hydrodynamics: the pressure in a stream of fluid is reduced as the speed of flow is increased — compare BERNOULLI'S THEOREM 2
bernoulli's theorem *n, usu cap B* **1** [after Jacques *Bernoulli*] **:** a basic principle of statistics: as the number of independent trials of an event of theoretical probability *p* is indefinitely increased, the observed ratio of actual occurrences of the event to total trials approaches *p* as a limit; — called also *law of averages* **2** [after Daniel *Bernoulli*] **:** a law of hydrodynamics: in a stream of liquid the sum of the elevation head, the pressure head, and the velocity head remains constant along any line of flow provided no work is done by or upon the liquid in the course of its flow and decreases in proportion to the energy lost in viscous flow — see HEAD 14b
ber·oë \'berəˌwē\ *n, cap* [NL, fr. L, a nymph] **:** a widely distributed genus that is coextensive with the class Nuda and comprises delicately iridescent thimble-shaped ctenophores
be·ro·i·da \bə'rōədə\ *n pl, cap* [NL, fr. *Beroë* + *-ida*] **:** an order of ctenophores coextensive with the class Nuda
be·rok \bə'räk\ *n* -s [origin unknown] **:** PIG-TAILED APE
be·rouged \bə, bē + \ *adj* [*be-* + *rouged*] **:** obviously or thickly rouged
ber·ren·do *or* **be·ren·do** \bə'ren(ˌ)dō\ *n* -s [Sp, fr. *berrendo*, adj., spotted] *Southwest* **:** PRONGHORN
berretta *var of* BIRETTA
ber·ret·ti·no \ˌberə'tē(ˌ)nō\ *or* **ber·et·ti·na** \-ēnə\ *n* -s [It, dim. of *berretta* biretta — more at BIRETTA] **:** a cardinal's scarlet skullcap
ber·ri·chon \berēshōⁿ\ *n* -s *usu cap* [F, fr. *Berry*, region of central France] **:** a native or inhabitant of the former province of Berry in central France
ber·ried \'berēd, -rid\ *adj* **1 :** furnished with berries **:** BACCATE **2 :** bearing eggs ⟨a ~ lobster⟩
ber·ri·gan \'berəgən\ *n* -s [native name in Australia] **:** EMU BUSH
ber·ru·ga·te \ˌberə'gäd·ē\ *n* -s [prob. fr. AmerSp *verrugato*, fr. Sp *verruga* wart (fr. L *verruca*) + *-ato* -ate — more at WART] **:** a tripletail fish (*Verrugato pacificus*) found at Panama and used for food
¹ber·ry \'berē, -ri; *in compounds in which a stressed syllable immediately precedes*, ˌb(ə)rē *or* ˌb(ə)ri *is usual in Brit speech and is used by some US speakers esp in compounds that are well known and that are in attrib position (as in "strawberry jam"); in compounds in which an unstressed syllable immediately precedes (as "huckleberry"), this pronunc is less freq in Brit speech and is little heard in US speech*\ *n* -ES [ME *berye*, fr. OE *berie*; akin to OHG *beri* berry, ON *ber*, Goth *weinabasi* grape] **1 a :** a pulpy and usu. edible fruit of small size irrespective of its structure (as the strawberry, raspberry, checkerberry, and hip of the rose) **b** *dial Brit* **:** GOOSEBERRY **c :** any simple fruit that has a pulpy or fleshy pericarp (as the currant, grape, gooseberry, cranberry, tomato, or banana) **d :** the dry seed or kernel of certain plants ⟨a coffee ~⟩ ⟨a wheat ~⟩ **2 :** one of the eggs of a fish or lobster **3 :** the black knob on the bill of the mute swan — **in berry :** carrying ova or spawn — used of lobsters and crabs
²ber·ry \'berē, -ri\ *vi* -ED/-ING/-ES **1 :** to bear or produce berries ⟨a ~*ing* shrub⟩ **2 :** to gather berries **:** pick berries
berry alder *n* **:** ALDER BUCKTHORN
berry basket *or* **berry box** *or* **berry cup** *n* **:** a small nesting container of wood veneer, paper, or plastic usu. in standard sizes of ½ pint, 1 pint, or 1 quart used for berries or other small fruit
berry cone *n* **:** the ripened berrylike fruit of certain conifers (as the juniper) in which the fleshy cone scales are fused together
ber·ry·less \-ləs\ *adj* **:** having no berries
ber·ry·like \'⸗⸗,⸗\ *adj* **1** *of a fruit* **:** resembling a berry esp. in size or structure **2 :** small and rounded **:** COCCOID
berry pepper *n* **:** BIRD PEPPER
berry spoon *n* **:** a large spoon with a broad deep bowl used in serving berries, salad, and other juicy foods
berry sugar *n* **:** finely granulated sugar **:** CASTOR SUGAR
berry tree *n* **:** GOOSEBERRY 1b
berry wax *n* **:** a wax obtained from the berries of a southern

African shrub (*Myrica cordifolia*) and used in making polishes and soap

bers *pl of* BER

ber·sag horn \'bər,sag-\ *n, usu cap B* [*Bersag*lieri] **:** a bugle with one valve on which a diatonic scale may be played

ber·sa·glie·re \,bersəl'yerē, -ye(,)rā\ *n, pl* **bersaglie·ri** \-e(,)rē\ *often cap* [It, fr. *bersaglio* target, fr. OIt, fr. OF *bersail*, fr. *berser* to shoot, hit] **:** a member of the Italian army infantry corps organized about 1850 as sharpshooters or riflemen

ber·seem \bər'sēm\ *or* **berseem clover** \(')==-\ *or* **ber·sim** \bər'sēm\ *or* **ber·sine** \-'sēn\ *n* -s *sometimes cap B* [Ar *barsīm, birsīm*, fr. Copt *bersīm*] **:** a clover (*Trifolium alexandrinum*) generally more succulent than alfalfa or other clovers and extensively cultivated as a forage plant and green-manure crop in the alkaline soils of the Nile valley and to some extent in the southwestern U.S. — called also *Egyptian clover*

ber·serk *R* bər'sərk, ,bər-, -'zərk *also* bə'sərk *or* bə'zərk *or* 'bər,sərk *sometimes* 'bər,sə(r)k *or* 'bər,zərk; *-R* bə's|ək, |əik, bə's|ək, bəi's|əik, -'z| *also* 'bə,sək *or* 'bəi,səik *sometimes* 'bə,sək *or* 'bəi,sək *or* 'bə,zək *or* 'bəi,zəik\ *also* **ber·serk·er** *R* -kər, *-R* -kə(r\ *adj* **:** marked by a display of violent erratic behavior indicative of extreme excitement or agitation and suggestive of sudden mental unbalance **:** FRENZIED, CRAZED, MAD, WILD ⟨attacked the fish with ~ fury —Claude Dredge⟩ ⟨a machinist's mate went ~ with a knife —F.J.Bell⟩

berserker \"\ *or* **berserk** \"\ *n* -s [ON *berserkr*, from *ber-* (stem of *björn* bear) + *serkr* shirt — more at BEAR, SARK] **1 :** an ancient Scandinavian warrior reputed to be invulnerable, of enormous strength, and filled with wild frenzy in battle **2 :** one whose actions are marked by a headstrong intractable spirit or by reckless defiance (as of orthodox views or attitudes) ⟨a political ~ whose course was completely unpredictable⟩

ber·tat \bər'tat\ *n, pl* **bertat** *or* **bertats** *usu cap* **1 :** an agricultural Negro people of the Shangalla group dwelling along the tributaries of the Blue Nile **2 :** a member of the Bertat people

ber·te·roa \,bərtə'rōə, (,)bər'terəwə\ *n, cap* [NL, after Carlo G. *Bertero* †1831 Ital. botanist] **:** a small genus of Eurasian herbs (family Cruciferae) with narrow entire leaves, white racemose flowers, and oblong or nearly round pods — see HOARY ALYSSUM

¹berth \'bərth, 'bəth, 'bəith\ *n, pl* **berths** \-ths *sometimes* -thz\ *n* -s [prob. fr. ⁴*bear*, after E *birth*: ⁴*bear*] **1 a :** convenient sea room **:** sufficient or safe distance for maneuvering maintained between a ship and another object ⟨keep a clear ~ of the shoals⟩ ⟨give the lighthouse a wide ~⟩ **b :** distance preserved for the sake of safety — used esp. with *wide* ⟨an orderly place to which outlaws and criminals gave wide ~ —S.H.Holbrook⟩ **2 a :** the place where a ship lies when at anchor or at a wharf ⟨an ocean liner riding quietly at her ~⟩ **b :** the place in a shipyard where a ship is built **:** SHIPWAY **c :** a space designed to accommodate an automotive vehicle (as a truck or train or plane) at rest for a specific purpose (as loading) ⟨plenty of room for 20 parking ~s⟩ **3 a** *archaic* **:** a room in which a number of the officers of a ship or the ship's company mess and reside **b :** a place to sit or sleep **:** ACCOMMODATION ⟨vainly looked for a ~ in the crowded bus⟩ ⟨helped him find a ~ during his visit to town⟩ **4 a :** a billet on board ship ⟨waiting for a ~ as a ship's surgeon —Bernard Keelan⟩ **b :** JOB, POSITION, SITUATION, POST ⟨dissatisfied with his prewar truck driving ~ —*Newsweek*⟩ ⟨the sales department is an excellent ~ for a young man —Jo Ranson & R.M.Pack⟩ ⟨high-school seniors having difficulty in locating ~s in leading colleges⟩; *specif* **:** a playing position on a team ⟨won a regular first-string ~⟩ ⟨the left-field ~⟩ **5 :** a sleeping accommodation (as on a ship, train, or plane) that consists typically of a shelf or frame fixed to a wall or of unfolded facing seats and is provided with a mattress and bedding **syn** see ROOM, WHARF — **on the berth :** properly moored so as to be ready to load or unload cargo

²berth \"\ *vb* -ED/-ING/-S *vt* **1 a :** to bring to anchorage **:** MOOR **:** maneuver to a suitable place for anchoring or docking ⟨tugs when ~*ing* a ship sometimes work by pushing with their bow against the ship's side —D.W.Pye⟩ **b :** to put or maneuver (as a bus) into a berth ⟨~*ing* the plane in the hangar⟩ ⟨~*ed* the car in the space reserved for it⟩ **2 :** to allot a berth to **:** furnish with a berth ⟨a cabin with 16 bunks in it to ~ the crew⟩ **~** *vi* **1 :** to come into a position suitable for mooring **:** arrive at a berth **:** stop at a berth ⟨the ship glided in and effortlessly ~*ed*⟩ **2 :** to have a berth or a lodging place ⟨~*ed* beside him —Frederick O'Brien⟩

ber·tha \'bərthə, -əthə, -əithə\ *n* -s [in sense 1, fr. F *berthe*, after *Berthe* (Bertha) †783 queen of the Franks, noted for her modesty; in sense 2, fr. G *Bertha*, after Frau *Bertha* Krupp von Bohlen und Halbach †1957 proprietress of the Krupp Works, Essen, Germany — more at BIG BERTHA] **1 a :** a woman's shoulder cape **b :** a wide round collar covering the shoulders (as for a dress or blouse) **2** *usu cap* **:** BIG BERTHA

bertha 1b

bertha armyworm *n* [prob. fr. the name *Bertha*] **:** a destructive climbing cutworm (*Mamestra configurata*) feeding on a variety of cultivated crops in the north-central states and adjacent parts of Canada

berth·age \-thij\ *n* -s **1 :** accommodation for mooring or anchoring; *specif* **:** space (as at a wharf) reserved to take care of shipping **2 :** a toll for anchorage **:** berthing duties **:** DOCKAGE

berth cargo *n* **:** cargo taken by a ship at less than the regular line rates to fill surplus cargo space

berth deck *n* **1 :** the deck on which the hammocks on a warship were formerly swung **2 :** a space containing the crew's sleeping quarters

berthe \'be(ə)rt\ *n* -s [F — more at BERTHA] **:** BERTHA 1

ber·thi·er·ite \'bərthēə,rīt\ *n* -s [F *berthierite*, after Pierre *Berthier* †1861 Fr. chemist + F *-ite*] **:** a mineral $FeSb_2S_4$ consisting of a sulfide of antimony and iron of a dark steel-gray color (sp. gr. 4.0)

¹berth·ing \'bərthiŋ, 'bəth-, 'bəith-, -thēŋ\ *n* -s [fr. gerund of ²*berth*] **:** BERTHAGE 1

²berthing \"\ *n* -s [fr. gerund of obs. *berth* to cover with boards, perh. of Scand origin; akin to ON *byrthi* side of a ship, fr. *borth* border, side of a ship — more at BOARD] **:** the planking outside of a wooden ship above the sheer strake; *also* **:** the upright planking of the sides and partitions

ber·thol·le·tia \,bərthə'lēsh(ē)ə\ *n, cap* [NL, after Comte Claude L. *Berthollet* †1822 Fr. chemist + NL *-ia*] **:** a genus of tall So. American trees (family Lecythidaceae) having flowers with six petals and a 2-parted deciduous calyx succeeded by hard-shelled capsules — see BRAZIL NUT

ber·thol·lide \'bərthə,līd; (,)bər'thä,līd, -,lə̇d\ *n* -s [C.L. *Berthollet* + E *-ide*] **:** a solid chemical compound (as some metallic hydrides and the tungsten bronzes) that does not conform to the law of definite proportions **:** a nonstoichiometric compound — distinguished from *daltonide*

ber·thon boat \'bər,thän-\ *n, often cap 1st B* [after Edward L. *Berthon* †1899 Eng. ecclesiastic and physician, its inventor] **:** a collapsible lifeboat often carried on small ships

berths *pl of* BERTH, *pres 3d sing of* BERTH

ber·tia \'bərd·ēə, 'ber-\ [NL, fr. Paul *Bert* †1886 Fr. physiologist and politician + NL *-ia*] *syn of* BERTIELLA

ber·ti·el·la \,=d·ē'elə\ *n, cap* [NL, fr. P. *Bert* + NL *-i-* + *-ella*] **:** a genus of medium-sized taeniid tapeworms parasitizing apes, monkeys, and in rare instances man

ber·til·lon·age \'bərd·ᵊlə,näzh, bertēyōnázh\ *n* -s [F, fr. Alphonse *Bertillon* + F *-age*] **:** BERTILLON SYSTEM

ber·til·lon system \'bərd·ᵊl,än-, bertēyōⁿ-\ *n, usu cap B* [after Alphonse *Bertillon* 1914 Fr. criminologist] **:** a system for the identification of persons by a physical description based on anthropometric measurements, standardized photographs, notation and classification of markings, color, bodily anomalies, thumb line impressions, and other data that has been largely superseded by fingerprinting

bertin's column *n, usu cap B* **:** COLUMN OF BERTIN

ber·to·lo·nia \,bərd·ᵊl'ōnyə, -nēə\ *n, cap* [NL, fr. Antonio *Bertoloni* †1869 Ital. botanist + NL *-ia*] **:** a small genus of ornamental Brazilian herbs (family Melastomaceae) having showy leaves and white, rose, or purple flowers in one-sided racemes

ber·trand curve \'ber·,tränd-, ber·träⁿ-\ *n, usu cap B* [after Joseph L. F. *Bertrand* †1900 Fr. mathematician] **:** either of two twisted curves having the property that the principal normals to one of them are also principal normals to the other

ber·trand·ite \'bər·trən,dīt\ *n* -s [F, fr. E. *Bertrand*, 19th cent. Frenchman who first described it + F *-ite*] **:** a mineral $Be_4Si_2O_7(OH)_2$ consisting of a beryllium silicate occurring in hard colorless or pale-yellow prismatic crystals (hardness 6–7, sp. gr 2.59–2.60)

bertrand lens *n, usu cap B* [prob. after Joseph L. F. *Bertrand*] **:** an auxiliary removable lens in the tube of a polarizing microscope used to obtain interference figures

ber·wick·shire \'berik,shi(ə)r, -shər\ *or* **ber·wick** \'berik\ *adj, usu cap* [fr. *Berwickshire*, Scotland] **:** of or from the county of Berwick, Scotland **:** of the kind or style prevalent in Berwick

be·ryc·i·dae \bə'risə,dē\ *n pl, cap* [NL, fr. *Beryc-, Beryx*, type genus + *-idae*] **:** a family of fishes that have a narrow compressed body and thoracic ventral fins, are usu. black or bright scarlet, and live chiefly in rather deep water

ber·y·coid \'berə̇,kȯid\ *n* -s [NL *Berycoidei*] **:** a fish of the group Berycoidei or the order Berycomorphi

ber·y·coi·dei \,==='kȯidē,ī\ *n pl, cap* [NL, fr. *Beryc-, Beryx*, genus of fishes + *-oidei*] *in some classifications* **:** a suborder or other division of Acanthopterygii comprising a number of marine fishes possessing an orbitosphenoid bone and other primitive features

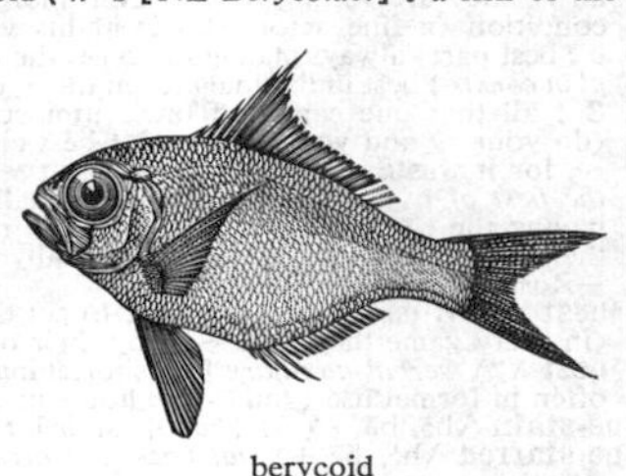

berycoid

be·ry·co·mor·phi \bə,rīkō'mȯr,fī\ *n pl, cap* [NL, fr. *Beryc-, Beryx* + *-o-* + *-morphi*] **:** an order of spiny-rayed fishes that is nearly coextensive with Berycoidei and that includes a number of families of marine chiefly deepwater fishes intermediate in some respects between clupeoid fishes and the Percomorphi, some of which (as the Australian red snapper) are of considerable commercial value

ber·yl \'berəl, -(,)ril\ *n* -s [ME, fr. OF *beril*, fr. L *beryllus*, fr. Gk *bēryllos*, of Indic origin; akin to Skt *vaidūrya* cat's-eye gem] **1 :** a mineral $Be_3Al_2Si_6O_{18}$ consisting of a silicate of beryllium and aluminum of great hardness and occurring in green, bluish green, yellow, pink, or white hexagonal prisms **2 :** a light greenish blue that is bluer and deeper than average aqua, greener than average robin's-egg blue (sense 1), bluer and paler than average turquoise blue, and greener and deeper than beryl blue

beryl blue *n* **:** a light greenish blue that is bluer and paler than beryl or average turquoise blue and bluer and slightly paler than average aqua

beryl green *n* **:** a light bluish green that is greener and deeper than average aqua green (sense 1), greener and slightly lighter than average turquoise green, and bluer and stronger than robin's-egg blue (sense 2)

ber·yl·late \bə'ri,lāt, -,lət; 'berə,lāt\ *n* -s [ISV *beryll-* (fr. NL *beryllia*) + *-ate*] **:** a salt formed by the reaction of a strong alkali with beryllium oxide ⟨sodium ~⟩

be·ryl·lia \bə'rilēə\ *n* -s [NL, fr. *beryllium*] **:** BERYLLIUM OXIDE

ber·yl·line \'berə,līn, -lēn\ *adj* [*beryl* + *-ine*] **:** like beryl esp. in color

be·ryl·li·o·sis \bə,rilē'ōsə̇s\ *also* **ber·yl·lo·sis** \,berə'lō-\ *n, pl* **beryllio·ses** \-ō,sēz\ *or* **beryllo·ses** \-lō-\ [NL, fr. *beryllium* + *-osis*] **:** poisoning resulting from exposure to fumes and dusts of beryllium compounds or alloys and occurring chiefly as an acute pneumonitis or as a granulomatosis involving the lungs or other organs or tissues

be·ryl·li·um \bə'rilēəm\ *n* -s [NL, fr. Gk *bēryllion*, dim. of *bēryllos* beryl — more at BERYL] **:** a steel-gray light strong brittle toxic bivalent metallic element having high electric conductivity and high permeability to X rays that occurs in combination (as in beryl, chrysoberyl, and phenakite), that is produced by reduction of its compounds (as by electrolysis), and that is used chiefly as a hardening agent in alloys (as with copper), as windows in X-ray tubes, and as a moderator and reflector in nuclear reactors — symbol *Be;* called also *glucinium;* see ELEMENT table

beryllium oxide *n* **:** a white amorphous compound BeO having high thermal conductivity and high electrical resistance that is usu. obtained by treatment of beryl ore and is used chiefly as a high-temperature refractory (as in crucibles) and in phosphors (as for television screens, X-ray equipment, and formerly fluorescent lamps)

ber·yl·loid \'berə,lȯid\ *n* -s [ISV *beryll-* (prob. fr. L *beryllus*) + *-oid;* fr. the frequent occurrence of beryl crystals in this form] **:** a form consisting of a double 12-sided pyramid **:** the dihexagonal dipyramid

be·ryl·lo·nite \bə'rilə,nīt\ *n* -s [NL *beryllium* + E *-on* + *-ite*] **:** a mineral $NaBePO_4$ consisting of sodium beryllium phosphate occurring in light-colored topazlike orthorhombic crystals (hardness 5.5–6, sp. gr. 2.85)

berylloid

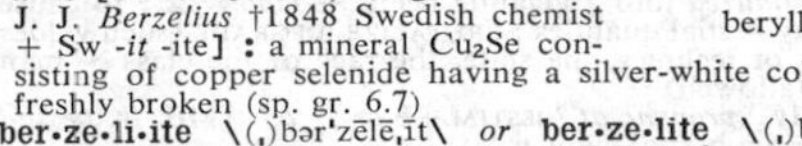

ber·ze·lian formula \(,)bər'zēlyən-, -lēən-\ *n, usu cap B* [Jöns J. *Berzelius* †1848 Swedish chemist + E *-an*] **:** DUALISTIC FORMULA

ber·ze·lian·ite \(,)bər'zēlyə,nīt, -lēə,-\ *n* -s [Sw *berzelianit*, irreg. fr. Baron J. J. *Berzelius* †1848 Swedish chemist + Sw *-it -ite*] **:** a mineral Cu_2Se consisting of copper selenide having a silver-white color when freshly broken (sp. gr. 6.7)

ber·ze·li·ite \(,)bər'zēlē,īt\ *or* **ber·ze·lite** \(,)bər'zē,līt, 'bərzə,-\ *n* -s [G *berzeliit*, fr. Baron J. J. *Berzelius* + G *-it -ite*] **:** a mineral $(Mg,Mn)_2(Ca,Na)_3(AsO_4)_3$ consisting of a bright yellow arsenate of calcium, magnesium, and manganese (sp. gr. 4.03)

bes *pl of* BE

be·sa \'bäsə\ *n, pl* **be·se** \-(,)sā\ *or* **besas** [It] **1 a :** a bronze coin issued 1909–21 for use in Italian Somaliland where it was worth ¹⁄₁₀₀ of a rupee **b :** a corresponding unit of value ⟨the circulation of 2-*besa* and 4-*besa* coins⟩ **2 a :** a copper coin formerly used in Ethiopia where it was worth ¹⁄₁₀₀ of a talari **b :** a corresponding unit of value ⟨a ½-*besa* coin was struck⟩

besant *var of* BEZANT

bes antler *var of* BAY ANTLER

be·scattered \bə̇, bē+\ *adj* [*be-* + *scattered*] **:** sparsely covered **:** BESPRINKLED, BESTREWED

be·screen \bə̇, bē+\ *vt* [*be-* + *screen*] *archaic* **:** SCREEN

be·scribble \bə̇, bē+\ *vt* [*be-* + *scribble*] **1 :** to scribble very illegibly **2 :** to scribble about **:** scribble upon

besee *vt* **besaw; beseen; beseeing; besees** [ME *beseen*, fr. OE *besēon*, fr. *be-* + *sēon* to see — more at SEE] *obs* **:** to treat well or badly **:** provide or furnish with

¹be·seech \bə̇'sēch, bē-\ *vb* **be·sought** \-sȯt, *usu* -ȯd·+V\ *or* **beseeched; besought** *also* **beseeched; beseeching; beseeches** [ME *besechen*, fr. *be-* + *sechen* to seek — more at SEEK] *vt* **1 :** to ask earnestly for **:** BEG, SOLICIT ⟨*besought* their collaboration in the work of reform⟩ **2 :** to address oneself earnestly to **:** call upon **:** IMPLORE, ENTREAT, SUPPLICATE ⟨a Cape captain whose bride ~*ed* him to write while he was away —R.W.Hatch⟩ **~** *vi* **:** to make supplication **:** engage in entreaty **syn** see BEG

²beseech *n* -ES *obs* **:** ENTREATY, PETITION

beseeching *adj* **:** marked by earnest entreaty **:** SUPPLICATING ⟨he met her gaze with a look of ~ intensity —J.C.Powys⟩ — **be·seech·ing·ly** *adv* — **be·seech·ing·ness** *n* -ES

be·seem \bə̇'sēm, bē-\ *vb* -ED/-ING/-S [ME *besemen*, fr. *be-* + *semen* to seem — more at SEEM] *vi* **1** *archaic* **:** SEEM **2** *archaic* **:** to be in accordance with what is proper **:** be fitting **:** be becoming ⟨with such embellishment as well ~s —William Wordsworth⟩ **~** *vt, archaic* **:** to be suitable to the nature or appearance of **:** BECOME, BEFIT ⟨as might ~ so bright a dame —S.T. Coleridge⟩

beseeming *adj, archaic* **:** SUITABLE, PROPER — **be·seem·ing·ly** *adv, archaic* — **be·seem·ing·ness** *n* -ES *archaic*

be·set \bə̇'set, bē-, *usu* -ed·+V\ *vt* **beset; beset; besetting; besets** [ME *besetten*, fr. OE *besettan*, fr. *be-* + *settan* to set — more at SET] **1 a :** to set at intervals **:** stud esp. with ornaments ⟨leaves whose edges were *beset* with thorns —J.G.Frazer⟩ ⟨a crown *beset* with pearls⟩ **b :** to cover esp. with plant growth ⟨*beset* with tangled vegetation —Xavier Herbert⟩ **:** fill or strew esp. with impediments ⟨the road is *beset* with dragons and evil magicians —T.B.Costain⟩ **2 :** PLAGUE, TROUBLE, HARASS **:** weigh down **:** DOG, BEDEVIL ⟨subject to none of the pressures that ~ American and English papers —F.L.Mott⟩ ⟨distrust of himself had always *beset* and hampered him —S.H. Adams⟩ **3 a :** to set upon **:** attack repeatedly **:** ASSAIL ⟨throughout the long trek the settlers were *beset* by savages⟩ **b :** to lay siege to **:** surround so as to compel surrender **:** BESIEGE ⟨enemy troops *beset* the fortress⟩ **c :** to occupy, take possession of, or overrun in such a way as to prevent free passage **:** choke off **:** BLOCKADE ⟨a screaming mob *beset* every road into the town⟩ **d** (1) **:** to close or hem in **:** ENCOMPASS, SURROUND ⟨a town *beset* with towering mountains⟩ (2) **:** to surround (as a task or problem) with immaterial or nonphysical perils or obstacles ⟨his task was *beset* with many difficulties⟩ (3) **:** to surround (as a ship) on all sides with ice so that free movement is totally checked — used of ice fields ⟨in danger of being *beset* by the worst pack we'd ever seen —Glen Jacobsen⟩

be·set·ment \-tmənt\ *n* -s **1 :** the action of besetting or the condition of being beset ⟨would invite ~ in the frozen sea —Glen Jacobsen⟩ **2 :** something by which one is beset **:** TROUBLE, VEXATION ⟨the small ~s and annoyances of life⟩; *esp* **:** a besetting sin, weakness, or failing

besetting *adj* **:** constantly in evidence **:** persistent or deeply rooted **:** PRINCIPAL, DOMINANT ⟨the ~ sin of woman, her passion to discuss her private affairs with anyone who is willing to listen —W.S.Maugham⟩ **:** OBSESSIVE, HAUNTING ⟨a ~ idea⟩ ⟨a strange ~ desire to know what to do when the time came —Charles Dickens⟩

be·shawled \bə̇'shȯld, bē-\ *adj* [*be-* + *shawl* + *-ed*] **:** wearing a shawl ⟨a ~ woman⟩

be·show \bə̇'shō\ *n* -s [Makah *bishowk*] **:** SABLEFISH

be·shrew \bə̇, bē+\ *vt* -ED/-ING/-S [ME *beshrewen*, fr. *be-* + *shrewen* to curse — more at SHREW] *archaic* **:** CURSE — often used in mild imprecations ⟨~ all them that are in love untrue —William Wordsworth⟩

¹be·side \bə̇'sīd, bē-\ *adv* [ME *beside, besiden*, adv. & prep., fr. OE *be sīdan* at or to the side, fr. *be* at, by (fr. *bī*) + *sīdan*, dat. & acc. of *side* side — more at BY, SIDE] **1** *archaic* **:** in a nearby position **:** close by **:** ALONGSIDE **2** *archaic* **:** BESIDES ⟨myself and divers gentlemen ~ —Shak.⟩

²beside \"\ *prep* [ME *beside, besiden*] **1 a :** at or by the side of ⟨walk ~ me⟩ **:** along or on one side of ⟨the ditch ~ the road⟩ ⟨the road leads ~ a branch of the White river —Bernard DeVoto⟩ **b :** close to **:** NEAR **:** next to ⟨there's an orchard ~ the house, about a half mile off⟩ **c :** in comparison with ⟨a writer needs to be a Walt Whitman if his faults of technique are to be rated unimportant ~ the vigor of his personality —Douglas Stewart⟩ **d :** on a par with ⟨a musical achievement that can be ranked ~ that of the masters⟩ **2 :** BESIDES 1 ⟨~ being taken into a world of escapist literature a thoughtful reader can go somewhat further —J.P.Marquand⟩ **3 :** BESIDES 2 ⟨many creatures ~ man live in communities —Stuart Chase⟩ **4 a** *obs* **:** outside of **b :** away from (as through irrelevance) **:** wide of ⟨~ the point⟩ **c** *archaic* **:** beyond the range of **:** contrary to — **beside oneself :** carried out of oneself (as through extreme excitement) **:** out of one's wits or senses ⟨*beside* himself with embarrassment —Sherwood Anderson⟩ ⟨filled them with such delirious emotions that they were *beside* themselves —Liam O'Flaherty⟩

¹be·sides \bə̇'sīdz, bē-\ *adv* [ME, adv. & prep., fr. *beside* + *-s*] **1 a :** in addition **:** over and above ⟨possessing a wealth of printed material and many original manuscripts ~⟩ **b :** MOREOVER, FURTHERMORE ⟨the play is excellent, and ~ the tickets cost very little⟩ **2 :** OTHERWISE, ELSE ⟨knows the rules of grammar, but very little ~⟩

²besides \"\ *prep* [ME] **1 :** in addition to ⟨~ being a model of scholarly thoroughness, the biographical chapters are vivid and engrossing —C.J.Rolo⟩ **2 :** other than **:** EXCEPT ⟨there's nothing you can do ~ making the best of the situation⟩

be·siege \bə̇'sēj, bē-\ *vt* -ED/-ING/-S [ME *besegen*, fr. *be-* + *sege* siege — more at SIEGE] **1 a :** to surround (as a city) with armed forces for the purpose of compelling surrender **:** lay siege to **b :** to surround closely **:** hem in **:** crowd upon or around ⟨I was *besieged* by four small Bedouin children —A.J. Liebling⟩ ⟨on Saturday nights the "picture house" in the town is *besieged* by eager young men and women —J.M.Mogey⟩ ⟨the land offices . . . were *besieged* daily by dozens of new settlers —*Amer. Guide Series: Ind.*⟩ **2 a :** to press esp. with requests **:** IMPORTUNE ⟨hungry for jobs and patronage, they *besieged* the president from morning to night —H.F.Wilkins⟩ ⟨*besieging* the royal ministers with petitions —T.B.Costain⟩ ⟨I was constantly *besieged* for an opinion —Henry Miller⟩ **b :** ASSAIL, BESET — used of fears or other troubling ideas or sensations ⟨such doubts and hesitations ~ one now and again —B.N.Cardozo⟩ ⟨a kind of loneliness . . . that ~s us —J.A.Pike⟩ **be·sieg·er** \-jə(r)\ *n* -s

be·sieg·ing·ly *adv* **:** in a besieging manner

be·silver \bə̇, bē+\ *vt* -ED/-ING/-S [*be-* + *silver*] **:** to cover with or as if with silver

be·sing \bə̇, bē+\ *vt* [*be-* + *sing*] **1 :** to sing about **:** celebrate esp. in song or poetry **2 :** to sing to

be·slabber \bə̇, bē+\ *vt* **:** BESLOBBER

beslave \bə̇, bē+\ *vt* -ED/-ING/-S [*be-* + *slave*] **1** *obs* **:** ENSLAVE **2** *obs* **:** to address as a slave **3 :** to fill with slaves

be·slobber \bə̇, bē+\ *vt* [*be-* + *slobber*] **1 :** to slobber upon **:** smear with or as if with slobber **2 :** to praise fulsomely

be·slubber \bə̇, bē+\ *vt* [*be-* + *slubber*] **:** to besmear esp. with something thick or oily

be·smear \bə̇, bē+\ *vt* [ME *bismerwen*, fr. OE *be- smierwan*, fr. *be-* + *smierwan* to smear — more at SMEAR] **1 :** to smear with any thick, sticky, or greasy substance ⟨savages whose faces and bodies were ~*ed* with war paint⟩ **2 :** TARNISH, SULLY ⟨~*ing* the reputation of a distinguished scholar⟩

be·smirch \bə̇, bē+\ *vt* [*be-* + *smirch*] **:** to lessen the purity, luster, or beauty of **:** SULLY, SOIL, TARNISH, STAIN ⟨high ideals were ~*ed* by cruelty and greed —R.A.Newhall⟩ ⟨having his name ~*ed* in a litigation —M.R.Cohen⟩

be·smirch·ment \-mənt\ *n* -s **:** the action or an instance of besmirching **:** the condition of being besmirched ⟨a ~ of all that had gone before —Richard Joseph⟩

be·smoke \bə̇, bē+\ *vt* [ME *besmoken*, fr. *be-* + *smoken* to smoke — more at SMOKE] **1 :** to soil with smoke **2 :** to fill with smoke **3 :** to cure (as bacon) by smoking

be·soil \bə̇, bē+\ *vt* [ME *besoilen*, fr. *be-* + *soilen* to soil — more at SOIL] **:** to make very dirty

be·som \'bēzəm, 'biz-, 'bis-, 'bəz-\ *n* -s [ME *beseme*, fr. OE *besma;* akin to OHG *besmo, besamo* broom] **1 :** BROOM; *esp* **:** a broom made with a bundle of twigs **2 a :** BROOM 1a **b** *dial Eng* **:** a heath of the genus *Erica* **3** *dial Brit* **:** WOMAN; *esp* **:** a woman of slovenly, shrewish, or morally unacceptable character — usu. a generalized term of disparagement

besom moss *n* **:** HAIRCAP MOSS

¹besort *vt* -ED/-ING/-S [*be-* + *sort*] *obs* **:** to be suitable to

²besort *n* -s *obs* **:** suitable company

be·sot \bə̇'sät, bē-, *usu* -äd·+V\ *vt* **besotted;** **besotted** *also* **besot; besotting; besots** [*be-* + *sot* (to befool)] **:** to make or cause to be besotted ⟨the king . . . was *besotted* by her purely carnal attractions —*Times Lit. Supp.*⟩ ⟨*besot* by rhythm, visual . . . as well as auditory —Agnes de Mille⟩ ⟨*besotted* as we are by names —William Wordsworth⟩ ⟨permitted . . . to ~ themselves in the company of their favorite revelers —T.B.Macaulay⟩

besotted *adj* **1 :** characterized by a condition of blind doting affection **:** utterly fascinated **:** INFATUATED, OBSESSED ⟨~ with a dancing girl —W.E.Allen⟩ ⟨seemed absolutely ~ about the damned woman —Agatha Christie⟩ ⟨only the most ~ classicist would prefer the smell of ancient Athenians to the smell of his compatriots —Katharine F. Gerould⟩ **2 a :** STUPID, DULL-WITTED, DOLTISH, DAZED, MUDDLED ⟨the empress was not so ~ as to take his . . . word for it —A.M.Young⟩ ⟨half-starved and . . . frequently idle, ~ and fever-stricken —Van Wyck Brooks⟩ ⟨his ~ confidence, his sober radiant face . . . made them uncomfortable —Willa Cather⟩ **b :** intoxicated or stupefied esp. with drink ⟨the ~ fool had been drinking steadily for weeks⟩

besought *past of* BESEECH

be·soul \bə̇, bē+\ *vt* -ED/-ING/-S [*be-* + *soul*, n.] **:** to endow with a soul

be·spangle \bə̇, bē+\ *vt* -ED/-ING/-S [*be-* + *spangle*] **:** to adorn with spangles **:** dot or sprinkle with brilliantly sparkling or glittering objects ⟨the grass . . . is all *bespangled* with dewdrops —William Cowper⟩

be·spatter \bə̇, bē+\ *vt* [*be-* + *spatter*] **1 :** to spatter esp. with muck ⟨in his little room with the dingy walls . . . *~ed* with printer's ink —Van Wyck Brooks⟩ **2 a :** to heap (as abuse or criticism) upon ⟨*~ed* him with all the vitriolic language at her command⟩ **:** cover with abuse **:** SLANDER ⟨no man in public life had ever been so foully *~ed*⟩ **b :** to render less attractive or valuable **:** MAR, SPOIL ⟨the slick, heartless, elegant phrases of the past still ~ the poetry —J.H.Plumb⟩ ⟨the meaningless abstractions which ~ history books —*Times Lit. Supp.*⟩

bespawl *vt* -ED/-ING/-S [*be-* + *spawl*] *obs* **:** to spatter with or as if with saliva

1be·speak \bə̇'spēk, bē-\ *vb* **be·spoke** \-pōk\ *or archaic* **be·spake** \-pāk\ **be·spo·ken** \-pōkən\ *or archaic* **bespoke; bespeaking; bespeaks** [ME *bespeken*, fr. OE *bespecan, besprecan* to speak about, accuse of, complain, fr. *be-* + *specan, sprecan* to speak — more at SPEAK] *vi, archaic* **:** SPEAK ⟨and thus *bespake* sweet Christabel —S.T.Coleridge⟩ **~** *vt* **1 :** to arrange for in advance **:** hire or engage beforehand **:** ORDER ⟨if the place is not *bespoken* you will be welcome —O.W.Holmes †1935⟩ ⟨the taxi *bespoken* by cousin Francis to drive him back again to the station —Elizabeth Bowen⟩ **:** lay claim to beforehand ⟨the Rockefellers, the Fricks, the Morgans entered the North Star Country . . . *~ing* the ore "forever" —Meridel Le Sueur⟩ **2 :** to speak to esp. with some formality **:** ADDRESS ⟨sends one of his friends to ~ the girl to whom he has been betrothed —A.H.J.Prins⟩ ⟨we were *bespoken* through public address megaphones and told what to do —Christopher Morley⟩ **3 a** *obs* **:** to request or engage (a person) to do something **b :** REQUEST **:** ask for ⟨~ a favor⟩ ⟨he *bespoke* me a job with Flood the next time he met him —Andy Adams⟩ ⟨*~ing* Federal assistance in the problem —*N.Y. Times*⟩ **:** request to know **:** ask about ⟨the letter Sir Austin lifted his head from to ~ his son's wishes —George Meredith⟩ **4 a :** to give evidence of **:** testify to **:** INDICATE, SIGNIFY, REVEAL ⟨noise is the loud laugh that *~s* the empty mind —O.S.J.Gogarty⟩ ⟨shrugged in that faint way which *bespoke* total indifference —Marcia Davenport⟩ ⟨these names ~ the quality and sincerity of this compilation —J.C.Smith⟩ **b :** to speak of or show beforehand **:** FORETELL, PORTEND ⟨murmurings that *bespoke* imminent rebellion⟩ **syn** see INDICATE

2bespeak \"\ *n* -S **1 :** a request (as by an actor's patrons) for the presentation of a particular play to be given usu. as a benefit performance **2** *Brit* **:** a request made to a lending library by a borrower for the loan of a book when it is available

be·speckle \bə̇, bē+\ *vt* [*be-* + *speckle*] **:** SPECKLE, BESPRINKLE

be·spectacled \bə̇, bē+\ *adj* [*be-* + *spectacle* + *-ed*] **:** wearing spectacles

be·spell \bə̇, bē+\ *vt* -ED/-ING/-S [*be-* + *spell*, n.] **:** to cast a spell on **:** ENCHANT

bespete *vt; past* **bespet;** *past part* **bespate** [ME *bespeten*, fr. *be-* + *speten* to spit — more at SPET] *obs* **:** to spit upon **:** spatter with saliva

be·spoke \bə̇'spōk, bē-\ *or* **be·spo·ken** \-kən\ *adj* [fr. past part. of *bespeak*] **1** *Brit* **a :** CUSTOM-MADE **:** made to order — used esp. of wearing apparel ⟨~ suits⟩ **b :** dealing in or producing custom-made articles ⟨~ dressmaking⟩ ⟨a ~ tailor⟩ **2** *dial* **:** ENGAGED; *esp* **:** engaged to be married

be·spot \bə̇, bē+\ *vt* [ME *bespotten*, fr. *be-* + *spotten* to spot — more at SPOT] *archaic* **:** to mark with or as if with spots

be·spread \bə̇, bē+\ *vt* [ME *bespreden*, fr. *be-* + *spreden* to spread — more at SPREAD] *archaic* **:** OVERSPREAD ⟨a region that is *bespread* with lush vegetation⟩

be·sprent \bə̇'sprent, bē-\ *adj* [ME *bespreynt*, fr. *bespreynt, besprenged*, past part. of *besprengen* to besprinkle, fr. OE *besprengan*, fr. *be-* + *sprengan* to scatter, sprinkle, burst, causative fr. the root of *springan* to spring — more at SPRING] *archaic* **:** sprinkled over ⟨glistening grass ~ with raindrops⟩

be·sprinkle \bə̇, bē+\ *vt* [ME *besprengeln*, freq. of *besprengen*] **:** to sprinkle over **:** SPRINKLE ⟨white and yellow flowers *besprinkled* the banks —Van Wyck Brooks⟩ ⟨the surnames of authors quoted ~ the text —F.L.M.Dawson⟩

1bes·sa·ra·bi·an \¦besə¦rābēən\ *adj, usu cap* [*Bessarabia*, region of southeastern Europe + E *-an*] **1 :** of, relating to, or characteristic of Bessarabia, **2 :** of, relating to, or characteristic of Bessarabians

2bessarabian \"\ *n* -S *cap* **:** a native or inhabitant of Bessarabia

bess-bug \'bes,bəg\ *or* **bes·sy·bug** \-sē,-\ *also* **bess beetle** *n* [prob. of imit. origin] **:** any of various gregarious flattened dark-colored beetles constituting a family (Passalidae) and living in decaying wood

bes·sel function \'besəl-\ *n, usu cap B* [after Friedrich W. *Bessel* †1846 Prussian astronomer] **:** one of a class of transcendental functions expressible as infinite series and occurring in the solution of the differential equation $x^2\frac{d^2y}{dx^2}+x\frac{dy}{dx}=(n^2-x^2)y$

besselian elements *n, usu cap B* [F.W. *Bessel* + E *-ian*] **:** mathematical-astronomical data employed by Bessel for facilitating precise prediction of a solar eclipse at any place on the earth

bes·sel's day numbers \'besəlz-\ *or* **bessel's star numbers** *n pl, usu cap B* [after F.W. *Bessel*] **:** four numbers, *A, B, C, D*, constant for all stars, whose logarithms are tabulated for different dates and used in calculating the apparent change in right ascension and declination for any date from any date

bes·se·mer \'besəmə(r)\ *or* **bessemer converter** *n* -S *usu cap B* [after Sir Henry *Bessemer* †1898 Eng. engineer and inventor] **:** the type of furnace used in the Bessemer process

bessemer copper *n, often cap B* [after H. *Bessemer*] **:** BLISTER COPPER

bessemer iron *or* **bessemer pig** *n, usu cap B* [after H. *Bessemer*] **:** a cast iron that contains not more than 0.10 percent of phosphorus and is suitable for the manufacture of Bessemer steel by the acid process

bes·se·mer·ize \-mə,rīz\ *vt* -ED/-ING/-S *often cap* [*Bessemer (process)* + *-ize*] **:** to treat with a blast of air (as in the Bessemer process)

bessemer process *n, usu cap B* [after H. *Bessemer*] **1 :** a process of making steel from pig iron by burning out carbon and other impurities through the agency of a blast of air that is forced through the molten metal, the blowing usu. being continued until nearly all the carbon is removed, the desired proportion being restored together with manganese by adding ferromanganese while the blown metal is being poured into a large ladle from which the ingot molds are filled **2 :** a process of refining copper matte by burning out the sulfur in a similar way

bessemer steel *n, usu cap B* **:** steel made by the Bessemer process

bes·sy \'besē, -si\ *n* -ES *usu cap* [fr. the name *Bessy*] **:** a stock character in English folk dances and plays played by a man dressed as a woman

bes·sy cer·ka \¦besē'sərkə, ¦besi-\ *n, usu cap B* [perh. by folk etymology fr. AmerSp *pejepuerco*] **:** QUEEN TRIGGERFISH

1best \'best\ *adj, superlative of* GOOD [ME, adj. & adv., fr. OE *betst*; akin to OHG *bezzist* best, ON *beztr*, Goth *batista*; superlative of the root found in OE *bōt* remedy, compensation — more at BETTER] **1** *of a person* **a :** excelling all others (as in moral, intellectual, or physical qualities) ⟨the ~ boxer in his class⟩ ⟨the ~ teacher of the subject I ever knew⟩ ⟨the ~ person in the community — kind, gentle, and understanding⟩ **b :** excelling or leading all others in social and usu. financial standing — used esp. in the phrases *the best families* or *the best people* ⟨the ~ people, alas, were no longer always the people with money —Brian Glanville⟩ ⟨the rich and arrogant, the traditional "~ families" —Bess A. Garner⟩ **2** *of a thing* **:** excelling or surpassing all others of its kind in inherent quality or according to some standard **:** most productive of good **:** providing or offering the greatest advantage, utility, or satisfaction ⟨ready to receive ideas and to devote life's ~ energies to developing . . . their implications —M.R.Cohen⟩ ⟨what is the ~ thing to do⟩ ⟨a luxurious yet practical material, the ~ you can buy⟩ ⟨the ~ road⟩ ⟨the ~ way to make coffee⟩ ⟨the ~ of Shakespeare's plays⟩ **3 :** LARGEST, MOST ⟨they passed the ~ part of the three weeks at the seashore⟩

2best \"\ *adv, superlative of* WELL [ME] **1 :** in the best way **:** to the most advantage **:** with the most success, ease, profit, benefit, or propriety ⟨of his many roles, he appears ~ as Hamlet⟩ ⟨adjusted to the situation as ~ they could⟩ **2 :** to the highest degree **:** to the fullest extent **:** MOST ⟨my *best*-loved friend⟩ ⟨those ~ able to fight⟩

3best \"\ *n* -S [ME, fr. *best*, adj.] **1 :** something that is best: as **a :** the point or circumstance that is best ⟨the ~ of it all is, they are willing to give even more⟩ **b :** best state or condition ⟨a fine actor who is at his very ~ in this play⟩ **c :** best part ⟨always managing to get the ~ out of life⟩ **2** *usu pl in constr* **:** best individuals ⟨even the ~ of us make mistakes⟩ **3 :** all that one can do **:** one's utmost or maximum effort ⟨do your ~ and you'll win⟩ **4 :** best clothes ⟨wearing their ~, for it was Sunday⟩ **5** ADVANTAGE — used in the phrase *the best of it* ⟨in the 3d round the challenger seemed to be having the ~ of it⟩ ⟨when it comes to ridin' pitchin' horses them little bench-legged fellows usually has all the ~ of it —Ross Santee⟩

4best \"\ *vt* -ED/-ING/-S [*1best*] **:** to get the better of **:** OUTDO ⟨in every game they were *~ed* by their opponents⟩

5best \"\ *verbal auxiliary* [by shortening] **:** had best — not often in formal use ⟨you ~ get home in a hurry⟩

be·stain \bə̇, bē+\ *vt* [*be-* + *stain*] **:** to stain thoroughly

be·starred \bə̇, bē+\ *adj* [*be-* + *starred*] **:** decorated with stars

best-ball foursome *n* **:** a golf match of two players against two others, the best score of the two on each side being the one counted on each hole

best-ball match *n* **:** a golf match in which one player competes against the best ball of two or more players

best bet *n* **:** safest or most reliable course of action **:** surest means to a desired end **:** most advantageous approach **:** most satisfactory choice ⟨the pilot's *best bet* was to make an emergency landing⟩ ⟨the *best bet* for stabilizing the national economy⟩

best bib and tucker *n* **:** best clothes — not often in formal use ⟨strutting in their *best bib and tucker* —C.G.Bowers⟩

best bower *n* **:** a ship's spare anchor about the same size as the bowers usu. used and often about 15 percent heavier

1be·sted *also* **be·sted** \bə̇'sted, bē-\ *adj* [ME *bested, bestad*, fr. *be-* + *sted, stad*, past part. of *steden* to place, stead — more at STEAD] **1** *archaic* **:** PLACED, VESTED ⟨my faith [is] *bestead* in the love of my own land —W.R.Benét⟩; *esp* **:** placed in a difficult or hazardous situation ⟨thank you for sending your knights . . . when we were really hard *bestead* —Charles Kingsley⟩ **2** *archaic* **:** HARASSED, ENDANGERED

2bestead \"\ *vt* **besteaded; bestead; besteading; besteads** [*be-* + *stead*] **1** *archaic* **:** to be of assistance to **:** HELP ⟨so long as they are behoveful, they may ~ each other —Sir Richard Burton⟩ **2** *archaic* **:** to be useful to **:** AVAIL

best foot *n* **:** one's most prepossessing or favor-winning appearance or traits ⟨there was no reason for him to concentrate on putting his *best foot* forward —Hamilton Basso⟩

best girl *n* **:** a favorite girl sweetheart

best gold *n* **:** the shot nearest the exact center of the bull's-eye in an archery contest

1bes·tial \'bestyəl\ *n* -S [ME *bestaile, bestial*, fr. OF & ML; OF *bestail*, fr. ML *bestialia*, fr. L, adj., neut. pl. of *bestialis*] *Scot* **:** a domestic animal esp. of the bovine kind; *collectively* **:** CATTLE, LIVESTOCK

2bes·tial \'bes(h)chəl, 'bēs-, *Brit usu & US sometimes* -styəl *or* -stiəl\ *adj* [ME, fr. MF, fr. L *bestialis*, fr. *bestia* beast + *-alis* -al — more at BEAST] **1 a :** of or relating to a beast ⟨in their ~ form the dead men extend a benign protection to their living human kinsfolk —J.G.Frazer⟩ **:** like or resembling a beast in form or appearance ⟨things of ~ shape and with hideous voices —Oscar Wilde⟩ **b** *of a sign of the zodiac* **:** represented by the figure of an animal **2 a :** lacking intelligence or reasoning power **:** moved by unthinking prejudice or passion **:** BRUTISH, BARBAROUS ⟨the ~ man has no sense of right and wrong —J.E.Hankins⟩ ⟨some historians, to prove their immunity from ~ prejudice . . . are prone to treat the American Revolution almost apologetically —C.G.Bowers⟩ **b :** marked by, indicating, or gratifying base, inhuman, or immoderate instincts or desires **:** BRUTAL, DEPRAVED ⟨the ~ commander of a notorious concentration camp⟩ ⟨~ lust⟩ ⟨supplied an abundance of wine and brandy, and a scene of ~ intoxication was the natural consequence —Herman Melville⟩ **syn** see BRUTAL

bes·ti·al·i·ty \,bes(h)chē'alədē, bes(h)'chal-, -ēs-, -lətē, -i *Brit usu & US sometimes* ,ᵻstī'al-\ *n* -ES [ME *bestialite*, fr. MF *bestialité*, fr. *bestial* + *-ité* -ity — more at BESTIAL] **1 :** the condition of being a beast (sense 1b) ⟨all this which marks the difference between ~ and humanity . . . is because man remembers, preserving and recording his experiences —John Dewey⟩ **2 a :** the display, gratification, or an instance of bestial traits or impulses ⟨the ~ and degradation that war brings —Drew Middleton⟩ ⟨the calculated *bestialities* of sadistic conquerors⟩ **b :** a debased brutalized condition of life ⟨the ~ of existence in a tenement jungle is well portrayed⟩ **3 :** sexual relations between a human being and a lower animal

bes·tial·ize *pronunc at* 2BESTIAL+,īz\ *vt* -ED/-ING/-S [*2bestial* + *-ize*] **1 :** to change into a beast (sense 1b) ⟨a man who has been *bestialized* into a gigantic beetle —*Time*⟩ **2 :** to cause to display bestial qualities **:** BRUTALIZE, DEGRADE ⟨such values as those of technics, the state, the race or the class ~ man —J.H.Hallowell⟩

bes·tial·ly *pronunc at* 2BESTIAL+ē *or* i\ *adv* [ME, fr. *bestial* + *-ly*] **:** in a bestial manner

bes·ti·a·rist \-s(h)chēərəst, 'bēs-, -stēər-\ *n* -S **:** a writer of bestiaries

bes·ti·ary \-s(h)chē,erē, -stē,-\ *n* -ES [ML *bestiarium*, fr. L, neut. of *bestiarius* of beasts, fr. *bestia* beast + *-arius* -ary — more at BEAST] **1 :** a medieval often illustrated work in verse or prose describing with an allegorical moralizing commentary the appearance and habits of real and fabled animals **2 :** the sculptured or painted representation of a group of real or imaginary animals (as in a medieval cathedral) often vested with a symbolical significance

bes·ti·culture \'bestə, 'bēs- +,-\ *n* [L *bestia* beast + E *culture*] **:** exploitation and utilization of wild animals (as by hunting and fishing)

besting *pres part of* BEST

be·stir \bə̇, bē+\ *vt* [ME *bestiren, besteren*, fr. *be-* + *stiren, steren* to stir — more at STIR] **:** to stir up **:** rouse into brisk vigorous action ⟨she had grown fat because she no longer *bestirred* herself —Elizabeth Taylor⟩

best man *n* **:** the principal groomsman at a wedding

best·ness \'bes(t)nə̇s\ *n* -ES **:** the quality or state of being best

be·stow \bə̇'stō, bē-\ *vt* -ED/-ING/-S [ME *bestowen*, fr. *be-* + *-stowen* (fr. *stowe* place) — more at STOW] **1 a :** to put to use **:** APPLY, DEVOTE ⟨hours quite as well *~ed* as hours spent in golfing —A.C.Benson⟩ **b** *obs* **:** to lay out (money) **:** SPEND **2 a :** to set in a given place, position, or situation **:** PUT, PLACE, LOCATE ⟨they saw her down the path and *~ed* in her car with tender solicitude by the chauffeur —Frances Towers⟩ **b :** to put away (as in storing) **:** deposit for safekeeping **:** STOW ⟨parcels which she *~ed* in the corners of the vehicle —Arnold Bennett⟩ ⟨without pausing to take breath till the whole cargo was *~ed* —R.L.Stevenson⟩ **3** *obs* **:** to give in marriage **:** marry off **4 :** to provide with a lodging place **:** put up **:** QUARTER ⟨*~ed* Clotilde in lodgings of her own —Rayner Heppenstall⟩ **5 :** to present as a gift **:** GIVE, GRANT, CONFER ⟨a favor that the Roman was pleased to ~ —L.C.Douglas⟩ — usu. used with *on* or *upon* ⟨he *~s* on them more praise than critical judgment —R.A.Cordell⟩ **6** *obs* **:** to conduct or acquit (oneself)

be·stow·al \-ōəl\ *n* -S **1 :** the act of bestowing or conferring **:** PRESENTATION ⟨conditions for ~ of a name —Leslie Spier⟩ **:** an instance of bestowing **:** GIFT ⟨viewed these afflictions as God's *~s* upon his saints⟩ **2 :** the act or an instance of bestowing in a given place or position **:** the condition of being bestowed **:** STORAGE ⟨an odor of mothballs that told of long ~ —Marguerite Steen⟩

be·stow·er \-ō(ə)r, -ōə\ *n* -S **:** one that bestows

be·stow·ing \-ōiŋ\ *n* -S **:** a casing of burned brick on the upper part of a brickmaking clamp

be·stow·ment \-ōmənt\ *n* -S **:** BESTOWAL

bestraught *adj* [*be-* + *straught*, short for *distraught*] *archaic* **:** DISTRAUGHT

be·streak \bə̇, bē+\ *vt* [*be-* + *streak*] **:** to cover with streaks

be·strew \bə̇, bē+\ *vt* **bestrewed** *or archaic* **bestrowed; bestrewed** *also* **bestrewn** *or archaic* **bestrowed** *also* **bestrown; bestrewing** *or archaic* **bestrowing; bestrews** *or archaic* **bestrows** [ME *bestrowen, bestrewen*, fr. OE *bestrēowian*, fr. *be-* + *strēowian, strewian* to strew — more at STREW] **1 :** to cover with objects lying scattered about **:** STREW ⟨with some flowers my grave ~ —Robert Herrick †1674⟩ ⟨a sea of blood *~ed* with wrecks —S.T.Coleridge⟩ **2 :** to lie or be scattered over (as an area) ⟨the isolated farmhouses of today which so liberally ~ Ordnance Survey maps —J.H.G.Lebon⟩

be·stride \bə̇, bē+\ *vt* **bestrode** *also* **bestrid; bestridden** *also* **bestrid** *or* **bestrode; bestriding; bestrides** [ME *bestriden*, fr. OE *bestrīdan*, fr. *be-* + *strīdan* to stride — more at STRIDE] **1 a :** to ride astride ⟨I saw fair boys *bestriding* steeds —R.W.Emerson⟩ **:** MOUNT ⟨*bestrode* his precious bike, and . . . went roaring out —Elizabeth Goudge⟩ **b :** to sit astride ⟨two small boys *bestriding* a fallen log⟩ **c :** to lie on either side of **:** STRADDLE ⟨one rather formal consultation about a dead balsam that *bestrode* the property line —A.B. Mayse⟩ **:** SPAN ⟨a bridge *bestriding* the torrential river⟩ **2 a :** to stand astride (as a fallen man) **:** stand over **b :** to dominate absolutely **:** have unquestioned control over **:** tower over ⟨*~s* the new Democratic Congress as . . . in the past —W.S.White⟩ **3** *archaic* **:** to stride across

bests *pres 3d sing of* BEST, *pl of* BEST

best seller *n* **1 a :** a book or other publication whose sales are among the highest of its class **b :** an article of merchandise whose sales are among the highest of its class **2 :** the author of a best-selling book or other publication; *also* **:** the maker of a best-selling phonograph record ⟨the band has been a *best seller* in the record shops for weeks⟩

best·sell·er·dom \(ˈ)bes(t)'selə(r)dəm\ *n* -S **:** the category of a best seller **:** the condition of being a best seller ⟨wrote obscurely . . . before he came into ~ —*Saturday Rev.*⟩

best-selling \'⸗¦⸗⸗\ *adj* **:** ranking among best sellers

be·stud \bə̇, bē+\ *vt* [*be-* + *stud*] **:** to set (a surface) with or as if with studs

be·su·go \bə̇'sü(,)gō\ *n* -S [Sp] **:** a European red porgy (*Pagrus pagrus*)

1bet \'bet, *usu* -ed·+V\ *n* -S [origin unknown] **1 a** (1) **:** something that is laid, staked, or pledged typically between two parties on the outcome of a contest or any contingent issue **:** WAGER ⟨a ~ on the game⟩ ⟨lay a ~ on a racehorse⟩ (2) **:** a sum put into a poker pot requiring other players to stay or drop; *esp* **:** the first such sum put in after a deal or draw — compare 2ANTE, 2CALL 8, 2RAISE **b :** the act of giving or promising such a pledge **2 :** something on which one lays a bet **:** a thing to wager on ⟨the gray horse is the best ~ to win the race⟩ **3 :** a choice decided on with consideration of probabilities ⟨your best ~ is to avoid short cuts if you do not know the route⟩ ⟨he is a poor ~ for the job⟩

2bet \"\ *vb* **bet** *or* **betted; bet** *also* **betted; betting; bets** *vt* **1 :** to stake (money) on the outcome of an issue or the performance of a contestant ⟨*betting* $2 on the race⟩ ⟨*betting* $100 on the election⟩ **2 a :** to maintain with or as if with a bet ⟨I will ~ that he will be elected⟩ **b :** to make a bet with or against (a person) ⟨I ~ him on the game⟩ **c :** to lay a bet on ⟨he ~ the track favorite to place⟩ **~** *vi* **:** to lay a bet

3bet *now dial past of* BEAT

4bet *var of* BETH

bet *abbr* between

1be·ta \'bād·ə, -ātə *also* 'bē-\ *n* -S [Gk *bēta*, of Sem origin; akin to Heb *bēth-* — more at BETH] **1 :** the second letter of the Greek alphabet — symbol B or β; see ALPHABET table **2 :** BETA PARTICLE, BETA RAY

2beta *or* **β-** \"\ *adj* **1 :** of or relating to one of two or more closely related chemical substances ⟨β-yohimbine⟩ — used somewhat arbitrarily to specify ordinal relationship or to specify a particular physical form, esp. an allotropic modification (as in β-iron), or an isomeric or sometimes polymeric or stereoisomeric form (as in β-D-glucose); abbr. sometimes *b-* **2 :** second in position in the structure of an organic molecule from a particular group or atom or having a structure characterized by such a position ⟨the ~ positions of furan⟩ ⟨β-hydroxy acids⟩ ⟨β-naphthol⟩ **3 :** producing a zone of decolorization when grown on blood media — used of certain hemolytic streptococci or of the hemolysis they cause **4 :** second in order of brightness — used of a star in a constellation

3be·ta \'bēd·ə, -ētə\ *n, cap* [NL, fr. L, beet — more at BEET] **:** a small genus of glabrous succulent herbs (family Chenopodiaceae) having greenish flowers and aggregate fruits — see BEET, CHARD, SEA BEET

betabacterium \¦⸗⸗+\ *n* [NL, fr. *3Beta* + *bacterium*] **1** *cap* **:** a genus or subgenus of heterofermentative lactobacilli **2** *pl* **betabacteria :** a member of the genus *Betabacterium* **:** a heterofermentative lactobacillus

beta brass *n* [*2beta*] **:** a copper-zinc alloy with a copper content of approximately 50 to 55 percent

beta cell *n* [*2beta*] **:** any of certain secretory cells distinguished by their basophilic staining characters: as **a :** a pituitary basophil **b :** an insulin-secreting cell of the islets of Langerhans

beta cellulose *n* [*2beta*] **:** CELLULOSE 2c

be·ta·cism \'bād·ə,sizəm *also* 'bē-\ *n* -S [NL *betacismus*, fr. L *beta* (fr. Gk *bēta*) + LL *-cismus* (as in *iotacismus* iotacism)] **:** loss of distinction between the sounds of *b* and *v* in a language or dialect

1be·ta·coc·cus \'bēd·ə,käkəs\ [NL, fr. L *beta* beet + NL *coccus*] *syn of* LEUCONOSTOC

2betacoccus \"\ *n, pl* **betacoc·ci** \-ä,kī, -ä,kē, -äk,sī, -äk,sē\ [NL, fr. L *beta* beet + NL *coccus*] **:** a heterofermentative streptococcus

bet·a·fite \'bed·ə,fīt\ *n* -S [F, fr. *Betafo*, Madagascar, its locality + F *-ite*] **:** a mineral consisting of an oxide of niobium, titanium, and uranium occurring as greenish black isometric crystals near Betafo, Madagascar

beta gauge *n* [*1beta*] **:** a device for measuring the thickness of a material by its absorption of beta rays

beta globulin *n* [*2beta*] **:** any of several globulins of human or animal plasma or serum that have electrophoretic mobilities intermediate between those of the alpha globulins and gamma globulins — see LIPOPROTEIN

beta hemolysis *n* [*2beta*] **:** a sharply defined clear colorless zone of hemolysis surrounding colonies of certain streptococci on blood agar plates

beta-hypophamine \¦⸗⸗+\ *n* [*2beta*] **:** a polypeptide hormone that is secreted together with oxytocin by the posterior lobe of the pituitary, that is also obtained synthetically, that increases blood pressure in mammals and exerts an antidiuretic effect, and that is used esp. in treating diabetes insipidus

be·ta·ine \'bēd·ə,ēn\ *n* -S [ISV *beta-* (fr. NL *Beta*) + *-ine*; prob. orig formed as G *betain*] **1 a :** a crystalline sweet-tasting quaternary ammonium salt that occurs in beet juice and other plant substances and in some marine animals and that is regarded as an inner salt or as a dipolar ion $(CH_3)_3N^+CH_2COO^-$ derived from glycine by methylation or from choline by oxidation; *also* **:** the hydrated form $(OH)(CH_3)_3NCH_2COOH$ **b** *or* **betaine hydrochloride :** the chloride $Cl(CH_3)_3NCH_2COOH$ of the hydrated form used as a source of hydrochloric acid esp. in medicine **2 :** any of several quaternary ammonium salts analogous in structure to betaine ⟨alanine trimethyl*betaine* $(CH_3)_3N^+CH(CH_3)COO^-$⟩

beta iron *n* [*2beta*] **:** the nonmagnetic form of iron that exists between 768° and 910°C and that is identical with alpha iron except that alpha is magnetic — compare ALPHA IRON, GAMMA IRON

be·take \bə̇, bē+\ *vb* **betook; betaken; betaking; betakes** [ME *betaken,* fr. *be-* + *taken* to take — more at TAKE] *vt* **1** *obs* **:** to deliver over **:** give for disposal **:** give up **:** GRANT ⟨Phoebe to a nymph her babe *betook* —Edmund Spenser⟩ **2** *archaic* **:** OCCUPY, COMMIT ⟨they *betook* themselves to a short debate —John Bunyan⟩ **3 :** to cause (oneself) to go ⟨he *betook* himself to the steamship offices —C.G.D. Roberts⟩ **~** *vi, obs* **:** to take oneself **:** have recourse **:** GO ⟨then to her . . . wagon she ~*s* —Edmund Spenser⟩

beta–naphthol \ˌ≈≈+\ *n* [²*beta*] **:** NAPHTHOL 1b

beta–naphthyl \ˌ≈≈+\ *n* [²*beta*] **:** NAPHTHYL b

be·ta·nin \ˈbēd·ənən\ *n* -s [blend of NL *Beta* and E *cyanin*] **:** a nitrogen-containing anthocyanin constituting the chief coloring matter of garden beets

beta oxy naphthoic acid *n* **:** HYDROXYNAPHTHOIC ACID a

beta particle *n* [¹*beta*] **:** an electron or positron emitted by the nucleus of an atom during radioactive decay

beta ray *n* **1 :** BETA PARTICLE **2** *or* **beta radiation :** a stream of beta particles

beta rhythm *or* **beta wave** *n* [¹*beta*] **:** a brain wave current having a frequency of more than 10 pulsations per second

betas *pl of* BETA

be·tassel \bə̇, bē+\ *vt* [*be-* + *tassel*] **:** to adorn with or as if with tassels

beta test *n* [¹*beta*] **:** a nonverbal group intelligence test used in the U.S. Army during World War I

be·ta·tron \ˈbād·əˌträn, -ātə- *also* ˈbē-\ *n* -s [ISV ¹*beta* + *-tron*] **:** an accelerator in which electrons are propelled by the inductive action of a rapidly varying magnetic field

betch·er·y·gah \ˈbecharēˌgä, -gā\ *n* -s [native name in Australia] **:** BUDGERIGAR

¹**bete** \ˈbāt\ *adj* [prob. fr. F *bête,* lit., blockhead, beast (in *faire la bête* to pass in a card game), fr. OF *beste* beast — more at BEAST] *in certain card games* **:** subject to a penalty for failure to fulfill one's contract; *also* **:** DOWN, BEATEN

²**bete** \"\ *n* -s **:** failure by the bidder (as in auction pinochle) to fulfill his contract; *also* **:** the penalty for such failure

beteem *vt* -ED/-ING/-S **1** *obs* **:** VOUCHSAFE, GRANT, ACCORD, CONCEDE **2** *obs* **:** ALLOW, PERMIT

be·tel \ˈbēd·ᵊl, -ētᵊl\ *or* **betel pepper** *n* -s [Pg *betel, betle,* fr. Tamil *verrilai*] **:** a climbing pepper (*Piper betle*) whose leaves are wrapped around or mixed with a whole betel nut or scrapings from it together with lime made from burnt coral and chewed as a stimulant masticatory esp. by southeastern Asians

betel nut *n* [so called fr. its being chewed with betel leaves] **:** the astringent seed of the betel palm used as a vermifuge and myotic and in the East for chewing — called also *areca nut*

betel palm *n* [*betel* nut] **:** an Asiatic pinnate-leaved palm (*Areca catechu*) having a slender ringed trunk and an orange-colored pungent astringent drupe with an outer fibrous husk — see BETEL NUT; compare BETEL

betel phenol *n* **:** CHAVIBETOL

bête noire *also* **bête noir** \ˌbetnəˈwär, betˈnw-, -āt-, -wȧ(r\ *n, pl* **bêtes noires** *also* **bêtes noirs** \-är(z),-äz,-ȧ(r\ [F *bête noire,* lit., black beast] **:** a person or thing usu. strongly and persistently detested, feared, or avoided ⟨an idiosyncratic driver whose *bête noir* was the left turn—Marylin Bender⟩

beth \ˈbāth, -āt,-ās\ *also* **bet** \-āt,-ās\ *n* -s [Heb *bēth-,* construct form of *bayith,* lit., house] **1 :** the second letter of the Hebrew alphabet — symbol ב; see ALPHABET table **2 :** the letter of the Phoenician or of any of various other Semitic alphabets corresponding to Hebrew beth

be·thab·a·ra \beˈthabərə\ *n* -s [origin unknown] **:** any of several British Guiana timber trees of the genus *Tabebuia* yielding dense hard wood

beth din *or* **bet din** \≈ˈdin, -ˈdēn\ *n* [Heb *bēth dīn,* lit., house of judgment] **1 :** a Jewish court in ancient times composed of three or four judges **2 :** a judicial body composed of a rabbi and two or more assistants having jurisdiction in matters of Jewish law

beth·el \ˈbethəl\ *n* -s [Heb *bēth'ēl* house of God] **:** HOUSE OF WORSHIP: as **a :** a chapel for nonconformists **b :** a place of worship for seamen

beth·ell process \ˈbethəl-\ *n, usu cap B* [after John *Bethell,* 19th cent. Am. inventor] **:** a method of preserving wood with creosote under pressure

be·thes·da \bə̇ˈthezdə, be-\ *n* -s [fr. *Bethesda,* Biblical pool believed to have curative powers (Jn 5:2–4), fr. Gk *Bēthesda*] **:** a hallowed place **:** CHAPEL; *esp* **:** BETHEL a

beth ha·mi·drash \ˌbāth,hämiˈdrāsh, ˌbāth·häˈmi,drāsh, -āt-,-ās-\ *or* **bet hamidrash** \-āt-,-ās-\ *n* [Heb *bēth hammidhrāsh,* lit., house of study] **:** a hall or school where Jews esp. in eastern Europe study the Bible, the Talmud, and later Hebrew literature

beth ha·se·pher *or* **bet ha·se·fer** \ˌ≈ häˈsāfər\ *n* [Heb *bēth hassēpher* house of the book] **:** a Jewish elementary school

beth ha·tef·fil·lah *or* **bet ha·te·fil·lah** \ˈ≈ˌhätəˈfilə, -təfiˈlä\ *n* [Heb *bēth hattĕphillāh* house of prayer] **:** a Jewish house of worship **:** SYNAGOGUE

be·think \bə̇, bē+\ *vb* **bethought; bethought; bethinking; bethinks** [ME *bethinken, bethenken, bethenchen,* fr. OE *bethencan,* fr. *be-* + *thencan* to think — more at THINK] *vt* **1 a** *archaic* **:** to call to mind **:** REMEMBER ⟨~ how those of old . . . clove to their word —Edwin Arnold⟩ **b :** to cause (oneself) to call something to mind ⟨he *bethought* him of his responsibility as head of the house —Mary Webb⟩ **2** *obs* **a :** to consider with a view to decision or action **:** think over ⟨~ what clemency . . . they would desire —Francis Bland⟩ **b :** to cause (oneself) to consider something with a view to decision or action ⟨may find the grace . . . to ~ themselves and recover —John Milton⟩ **3 :** to give (oneself) up to reflection **:** devote (oneself) to thought ⟨Rip *bethought* himself a moment —Washington Irving⟩ **4** *obs* **:** to contrive as a result of thought **:** DEVISE ⟨we ~ a means to break it off —Shak.⟩ **5 :** to bring (oneself) to a conclusion **:** RESOLVE ⟨has *bethought* himself of joining profit and pleasure together —Richard Steele⟩ **~** *vi* **:** to engage in thought **:** CONSIDER ⟨~ ere thou dismiss us —Lord Byron⟩ **syn** see REMEMBER

beth·le·hem \ˈbethlə,hem, -lē,h-, ˈbethlēəm, *rapid* ˈbethləm, ÷ -lə,ham *or* ÷ -lē,ham\ *n* -s *usu cap* [fr. the Hospital of St. Mary of *Bethlehem,* London, England] *archaic* **:** ¹BEDLAM 2

beth·le·hem·ite \-,mīt\ *n* -s *cap* [*Bethlehem,* Palestine + E *-ite*] **:** a native or inhabitant of Bethlehem

bethlehem sage *n, usu cap B* **:** a European herb (*Pulmonaria saccharata*) with white or reddish violet flowers shaped like bells

bethlehem's–star \ˌ≈ . . . ˈ≈\ *n, pl* **bethlehem's–stars** *usu cap B* **:** STAR-OF-BETHLEHEM 1

beth·root \ˈbeth+,-\ *n* -s [alter. of *birthroot*] **1 :** BIRTHROOT **2 :** TRILLIUM 2

be·thumb \bə̇, bē+\ *vt* [*be-* + *thumb*] **:** to wear or soil with or as if with thumbs

be·thump \bə̇, bē+\ *vt* [*be-* + *thump*] **:** to beat or pelt soundly

be·thwack \bə̇, bē+\ *vt* [*be-* + *thwack*] **:** to beat, thrash, or pelt thoroughly

beth·y·lid \ˈbethələd, -,lid\ *adj* [NL *Bethylidae*] **:** of or relating to the family Bethylidae

be·thyl·i·dae \bəˈthilə,dē\ *n pl, cap* [NL, fr. *Bethylus,* type genus (fr. Gk *bēthylos,* a kind of bird) + *-idae*] **:** a family of small wasps the females of which oviposit on other insects that they sting and paralyze

be·tide \bə̇ˈtīd, bē-\ *vb* **betided** \-tīdə̇d\ *also archaic* **be·tid** \-tid\; **betided** *also archaic* **betid; betiding; betides** [ME *betiden,* fr. *be-* + *tiden* to happen — more at TIDE] *vt* **1 :** to happen to **:** BEFALL — now used chiefly in the expression *woe betide* ⟨woe ~ the man who recognizes no law⟩ ⟨woe ~ our enemies⟩ **2 :** FOREBODE, PRESAGE ⟨such omens ~ no good⟩ **~** *vi* **1 :** BEFALL, HAPPEN ⟨hope . . . must abide with all of us, whate'er ~ —William Wordsworth⟩ **2** *obs* **:** to be the fate or end — used with *of* or *on* ⟨if he were dead, what would ~ on me —Shak.⟩ **3 :** BETOKEN, FOREBODE **syn** see HAPPEN

betime *adv* [ME, fr. *be-* + *time*] *obs* **:** BETIMES

be·times \bə̇ˈtīmz, bē-\ *adv* [ME, fr. *betime* + *-s*] **1 :** in good season or time **:** SEASONABLY, EARLY ⟨that Friday morning Stephen awoke ~ with a sense that something was to happen —Winston Churchill⟩ **2** *archaic* **:** in a short time **:** SOON, SPEEDILY ⟨my father and sister very ~ took their leave —Samuel Pepys⟩ **3** *chiefly dial* **:** at times **:** OCCASIONALLY ⟨to write local items ~ —W.A.White⟩

be·tis \ˈbēd·əs\ *n* -ES [Sp, fr. Tag *bitis*] **:** a Philippine tree (*Payena betis*) of the family Sapotaceae the fruit of which yields an illuminating oil

bê·tise \bāˈtēz\ *n, pl* **bê·tises** \-z(əz)\ [F, fr. *bête* foolish, fr. *bête* blockhead, beast — more at BETE] **1 :** FOLLY, STUPIDITY, IGNORANCE ⟨one more exhibition of the ~ of an audience when confronted with something fresh —Arnold Bennett⟩ **2 :** an act of foolishness or stupidity ⟨he had committed as many literary as ideological ~*s* and he was soundly chastised for both —D.U.McDowell⟩

be·title \bə̇, bē+\ *vt* [*be-* + *title*] **1 :** to give a title to ⟨a *betitled* elder statesman⟩ **2 :** to call by a title **:** call by the title of ⟨*betitled* "king of the Anglo-Saxons" in some charters⟩

be·toil \bə̇, bē+\ *vt* [*be-* + *toil*] **:** to oppress or exhaust with toil

be·to·ken \bə̇ˈtōkən, bē-\ *vt* **betokened; betokened; betokening** \-k(ə)niŋ\ **betokens** [ME *betacnien, betokenen,* fr. *be-* + *tacnien, tokenen* to token — more at TOKEN] **1 a** *obs* **:** to be a symbol of **:** signify visibly **:** REPRESENT ⟨in the cloud a bow ~*ing* peace from God —John Milton⟩ **b :** to show esp. by signs or tokens **:** give evidence of ⟨thin, tall, and of that ash-gray color which ~*s* constant sleeplessness —Osbert Sitwell⟩ ⟨an elderly man, of . . . strong, square features, ~*ing* a steady soul —Nathaniel Hawthorne⟩ **2 :** FORESHOW, PRESAGE ⟨no sighing in the woods to ~ a big weather change —John Muir⟩ **syn** see INDICATE

be·ton·i·ca \bə̇ˈtänəkə\ *n, cap* [NL, fr. L *betonica, vettonica* betony] *in some esp. former classifications* **:** a small genus of Eurasian herbs (family Labiatae) often included in *Stachys* having the corolla tube greatly exceeding the calyx

bet·o·ny \ˈbetᵊnē\ *n* -ES [ME *betone,* fr. OF *betoine,* fr. L *betonica, vettonica,* fr. *Vettones,* an ancient people inhabiting the Iberian peninsula] **1 :** any of several woundworts formerly included in the genus *Betonica; esp* **:** PURPLE BETONY **2 :** any of several plants of the genus *Teucrium; esp* **:** AMERICAN GERMANDER

betook *past of* BETAKE

be·toss \bə̇, bē+\ *vt* [*be-* + *toss*] **:** to toss violently **:** AGITATE

be·to·yan \bäˈtōyən, -tȯi(y)ən\ *n* -s *usu cap* [*Betoya,* a So. American Indian people, the language of the Betoya (fr. Sp *betoya, betoy, betoye,* of AmerInd origin) + E *-an*] **1 :** a language family of Chibchan stock in eastern Colombia **2 :** TUCANO 1b

be·trample \bə̇, bē+\ *vt* [*be-* + *trample*] **:** to mark or dirty by trampling

be·tray \bə̇ˈtrā, bē-\ *vb* -ED/-ING/-S [ME *betrayen,* fr. *be-* + *trayen* to betray, fr. OF *traïr,* fr. L *tradere* to betray, deliver — more at TRAITOR] *vt* **1 :** MISLEAD: as **a :** to lead astray (as into error, sin, or danger) ⟨a peaceful man ~*ed* by anger into violence⟩ ⟨their heroes are still victims ~*ed* by circumstances into criminal follies that lead to disasters —Malcolm Cowley⟩ **b :** to lead astray and abandon (a girl or woman) **:** SEDUCE ⟨a girl ~*ed* in her teens by a much older man⟩ **2 :** to deliver into the hands of an enemy by treachery or fraud in violation of trust ⟨~ a citadel by opening its gates in the night to enemy forces⟩ **3 :** to prove faithless or treacherous to **:** fail or desert esp. in time of need ⟨~ his own people by going over to the enemy⟩ ⟨use the poor as a stepping-stone to power, and then to ~ them —*Encounter*⟩ **4 :** REVEAL: as **a :** reveal unintentionally (as something more prudently concealed) **:** DISCLOSE ⟨even his best writings ~ a limited imagination and a sour view of life⟩ **b :** to show or indicate (as something not obvious on the surface) ⟨only a tension of mouth muscles ~*ed* his uneasiness⟩ ⟨his best columns ~ . . . the philosophical bent of his mind —John Mason Brown⟩ **c :** to disclose in violation of confidence ⟨~ government secrets⟩ **~** *vi* **:** to prove false ⟨when lovely woman stoops to folly and finds too late that men ~ —Oliver Goldsmith⟩ **syn** see DECEIVE, REVEAL

be·tray·al \-ā(ə)l\ *n* -s **:** the act of betraying or fact of being betrayed ⟨his ~ of that trust by his unthinking egotism —Mark Schorer⟩ ⟨the hesitation was a ~ of his uncertainty⟩

be·trim \bə̇, bē+\ *vt* [*be-* + *trim*] **:** to adorn on both or all sides

be·troth \bə̇ˈträth, bē-, -ˈtrōth, -ˈtrōth, *or with* th \ *vt* -ED/-ING/-S [ME *betreuthen, betrouthen,* fr. *be-* + *treuthe, trouthe* truth, troth — more at TRUTH] **1** *archaic* **:** to promise to take in marriage **:** plight one's troth to **2 a :** to promise in marriage **:** AFFIANCE ⟨a daughter ~*ed* to a rising young lawyer⟩ ⟨two children of noble blood ~*ed* almost from birth⟩ **b** *obs* **:** PLEDGE ⟨a fool that ~*s* himself to unquietness —Shak.⟩ **3 :** to give or pledge in religious faith and affiliation

be·troth·al \-ˈthəl, -ˈtrōth-, -ˈtrōth-\ *n* -s [*betroth* + *-al*] **:** the act of betrothing or fact of being betrothed **:** a mutual promise or contract for a future marriage — called also *espousal*

be·trothed \-tht,-thd *sometimes* -thəd *or* -thəd\ *n* -s **:** one betrothed; *esp* **:** the person to whom one is betrothed

be·troth·ment \-th-\ *n* -s **:** BETROTHAL

be·trousered \bə̇, bē+\ *adj* [*be-* + *trousers* + *-ed*] **:** wearing trousers

be·trunk \bə̇ˈtrəŋk, bē-\ *vt* -ED/-ING/-S [*be-* + *trunk* (to truncate)] **:** to remove the lower part of the course of (a stream) esp. by submergence of a valley or by recession of the land along a shore — compare BEHEAD

betrust *vt* [*be-* + *trust*] *obs* **:** TRUST

bets *pres 3d sing of* BET, *pl of* BET

bet·sey bug *or* **bet·sy bug** \ˈbetsē-\ *also* **betsy beetle** *n, sometimes cap 1st B* [by folk etymology] **:** BESS-BUG

bet·si·mi·sar·a·ka \ˌbetsēməˈsarəkə\ *n, pl* **betsimisaraka** *or* **betsimisarakas :** a native of the east coast of Madagascar of predominantly Malay blood and type — compare MALAGASY

bet·ta \ˈbed·ə\ *n* [NL] **1** *cap* **:** a genus of small brilliantly colored long-finned freshwater anabantid fishes of southeastern Asia related to the climbing perch **2** -s *sometimes cap* **:** any fish of the genus *Betta; esp* **:** one (*B. splendens*) often kept in the tropical aquarium — called also *Siamese fighting fish*

betted *past of* BET

¹**bet·ter** \ˈbed·ə(r), -etə-\ *adj, comparative of* GOOD [ME *bettre,* fr. OE *betera;* akin to OHG *bezziro* better, ON *betri,* Goth *batiza;* comparative (with the suffix represented by OE *-ra*) of the root found in OE *bōt* remedy, compensation, *batian* to get better, OHG *bazzēn,* ON *batna* to get better, Goth *gabatnan* to receive as a benefit, Skt *bhadra* fortunate, good — more at -ER] **1 :** more than half; *esp* **:** much more than half ⟨waiting the ~ part of an hour⟩ **2 :** improved in health ⟨the patient is much ~ after a good night's rest⟩ **3 :** of higher quality (as in breeding, style, or workmanship) ⟨a ~ class of people⟩ ⟨a ~ line of yard goods⟩ ⟨a ~ type of car⟩ — **bet·ter·ly** *adv* — **bet·ter·ness** *n* -ES

²**better** \"\ *adv, comparative of* WELL [ME *bettre,* fr. *bettre,* adj.] **1 a :** in a superior or more excellent manner ⟨he writes ~ than I do⟩ **b :** more desirably **:** PREFERABLY ⟨things ~ left unsaid⟩ **2 a :** to a higher or greater degree ⟨he knows the story ~ than you do⟩ **b :** MORE ⟨it is ~ than 10 miles to the lake⟩ ⟨the book was published ~ than 50 years ago⟩

³**better** \"\ *n* -s [ME *bettre,* fr. *bettre,* adj.] **1 a :** something better ⟨I expected ~⟩ ⟨I never looked for ~ at his hands —Shak.⟩ **b :** one who has a claim to precedence **:** a superior esp. in merit or rank ⟨the common man has been put and kept in his place by his ~*s* —C.G.Benjamin⟩ ⟨I like novels to be about my ~*s,* in body, wit, energy, breeding, or bank balance —W.H. Auden⟩ **2 :** superior position **:** ADVANTAGE, VICTORY — usu. used with *of* ⟨have the ~ of an argument⟩ ⟨get the ~ of a rival⟩ — **for the better :** so as to produce improvement ⟨making alterations *for the better* in the design of a house⟩

⁴**better** \"\ *vb* -ED/-ING/-S [ME *bettren,* fr. *bettre,* adj.] *vt* **1 :** make better **:** IMPROVE: as **a :** AMELIORATE ⟨strive toward ~*ing* the condition of the slum dwellers⟩ **b :** to advance or make sounder the condition or circumstances of ⟨as time goes by and we ~ our acquaintance —A.T.Quiller-Couch⟩ ⟨closer proofreading would have ~*ed* the book —M.B.Emeneau⟩ ⟨~ his lot⟩ **2 :** to surpass in excellence **:** EXCEED, EXCEL ⟨ran the mile in four minutes flat, ~*ing* his own previous record by several seconds⟩ ⟨industrial production this year considerably ~*ed* that of last year⟩ **3 :** to increase (a previous bet) in certain card games **:** RAISE **~** *vi* **:** become better **:** IMPROVE ⟨the general condition . . . must be ~*ing* instead of worsening —Thomas Carlyle⟩ ⟨the cattle . . . , though they doubled in weight and shortened their horns, but little ~*ed* in temper —P.A.Rollins⟩ **syn** see IMPROVE

⁵**better** \"\ *verbal auxiliary* **:** had better — not often in formal use ⟨the boy felt he ~ go before the fight started⟩

⁶**better** *var of* BETTOR

Better Business Bureau *trademark* — used for a bureau maintained by businessmen in a town or city for keeping up local standards of honesty in business transactions

better half *n, pl* **better halves :** SPOUSE; *esp* **:** WIFE

bettering house *n, archaic* **:** ²REFORMATORY

bet·ter·ment \ˈbed·ə(r)mənt, -etə-\ *n* -s **1 :** a making or becoming better **:** IMPROVEMENT: as **a :** an improvement of an estate (as by the addition of new buildings) that makes it better and more valuable than mere repairing would do **b :** an improvement (as of a highway, railroad, or business establishment) that does more than restore to a former good condition **c :** the replacement in accounting of an existing asset with one of greater cost or superior value **2 :** the sum of money assessed, required, or used for a betterment ⟨~*s* for street construction⟩; *specif* **:** an expenditure that adds greater worth (as extended life or increased capacity) to a fixed asset

bet·ter·most \-,mōst\ *adj* **1** *now chiefly dial* **:** BEST ⟨my lady might wear some of her ~ gowns —Emily Eden⟩ **:** SUPERIOR ⟨the ~ person who shows her superiority by wearing kid gloves —Flora Thompson⟩ **2** *now chiefly dial* **:** GREATER ⟨the ~ part of the time⟩

better nature *or* **better self** *n* **:** the more virtuous, amiable, or kindly instincts of a person

better 'ole \ˌbed·əˈ(r)ōl\ *n* ['*ole* alter. of ¹*hole*] **:** the more tolerable of two undesirable things

¹**better–to–do** \ˌ≈≈≈\ *adj* [intended as comparative of *well-to-do*] **:** in prosperous economic circumstances **:** better off ⟨many of the *better-to-do* urban Frenchmen acquire homes in the country —S.K.Padover⟩

²**better–to–do** \"\ *n, pl* **better–to–do :** one who is better-to-do ⟨the *better-to-do* on whom the burden of the expense of the liberal program had fallen —C.L.Jones⟩

betting *pres part of* BET

betting machine *n* **:** PARI-MUTUEL

bet·tong \ˈbe,tȯŋ, -äŋ\ *also* **bet·ton·ga** \-ŋgə\ *n* -s [native name in Australia] **:** any of several kangaroos of the genus *Bettongia*

bet·ton·gia \beˈtäŋgēə\ *n, cap* [NL, fr. E *bettong* + NL *-ia*] **:** a common Australian genus of small leaping rat kangaroos

bet·tor *or* **bet·ter** \ˈbed·ə(r), -etə-\ *n* -s **:** one that bets

betts' process \ˈbets(əz)-\ *n, usu cap B* [after Anson G. *Betts* b1876 Am. metallurgist] **:** an electrolytic process for refining lead, the electrolyte being a solution of lead fluosilicate $PbSiF_6$ and fluosilicic acid

bet·ty \ˈbedē, ˈbetē, -i\ *n* -ES *usu cap* [short for *brown Betty*] **:** a dessert made of alternate layers of fruit and buttered crumbs, sugar, and spices baked in a large baking dish or in individual dishes ⟨cranberry ~⟩; *specif* **:** BROWN BETTY

betty lamp \"-\ *n, usu cap B* [prob. fr. the name *Betty*] **:** a lamp consisting of a shallow lidded metal vessel with a small spout for a coarse wick, fueled by tallow, grease, or oil, usu. hung by a hook and chain, and used esp. in the American colonies

Betty lamp

bet·u·la \ˈbechələ\ *n, cap* [NL, fr. L *betula, betulla* birch, fr. Gaulish *betulla;* akin to MIr *bethe, beithe* box (tree), W *bedw* birch, and to the (prob. Celtic) source of L *bitumen* mineral pitch; fr. the use of the birch tree as a source of tar — more at CUD] **:** a genus of north-temperate and arctic trees and shrubs (family Betulaceae) comprising the birches and having hard close-grained wood, alternate toothed leaves, monoecious flowers in catkins, the fruiting bracts 3-lobed or entire, thin, and deciduous, and the fruit a small samara

bet·u·la·ce·ae \ˌbechəˈlāsē,ē\ *n pl, cap* [NL, fr. *Betula,* type genus + *-aceae*] **:** a family of trees and shrubs (order Fagales) having simple leaves, monoecious or rarely dioecious flowers, and one-seeded nutlike fruits and comprising the birches and certain related plants (as alders, hornbeams, and hazels) — **bet·u·la·ceous** \ˌ≈≈ˈlāshəs\ *adj*

betula oil *n* **:** BIRCH OIL 2

bet·u·lin \ˈbechələn\ *n* -s [ISV *betul-* (fr. NL *Betula,* genus name of *Betula alba*) + *-in*] **:** BETULINOL

bet·u·lin·ic acid \ˌbechəˈlinik\ *n* [ISV *betulin* + *-ic*] **:** a crystalline triterpenoid acid $C_{29}H_{46}(OH)COOH$ found in various plants (as flowering dogwood) and obtained from betulinol by oxidation

bet·u·lin·ol \-lə,nȯl, -ōl\ *n* -s [*betulin* + *-ol*] **:** a crystalline triterpenoid alcohol $C_{30}H_{48}(OH)_2$ occurring esp. as the white pigment of the outer bark of the European birch (*Betula alba*)

bet·u·li·tes \ˌbechəˈlīd·(ˌ)ēz\ *n, cap* [NL, fr. *Betula* + L *-ites* -ite] **:** a genus of extinct Cretaceous trees resembling the genus *Betula*

be·turbaned \bə̇, bē+\ *adj* [*be-* + *turban* + *-ed*] **:** wearing a turban

be·twat·tled \bə̇ˈtwäd·ᵊld, bē-\ *adj* [*be-* + *twattled,* past part. of *twattle*] *dial* **:** ADDLED, CONFUSED

¹**be·tween** \bə̇ˈtwēn, bē-\ *prep* [ME *betwene,* prep. & adv., fr. OE *betwēonum,* fr. *be-* + *-twēonum* (dat. pl. of an old distributive numeral akin to Goth *tweihnai* two each); akin to OE *twēgen, twā, tū* two — more at TWO] **1 a :** involving the reciprocal action of **:** involving as participants **:** jointly engaging ⟨the job was completed ~ the two of them⟩ ⟨two years of quiet talks ~ the three —*Time*⟩ **b :** shared by ⟨there are many interrelationships, and many mutual interests, ~ linguistics, philosophy, and psychology —J.B.Carroll⟩ **c :** by giving a portion of the total to each of ⟨the fortune was divided ~ the four grandchildren⟩ ⟨the food was shared ~ three families⟩ **2 a :** in the time interval that separates ⟨the two days ~ Monday and Thursday⟩ ⟨~ bites of food, they talked to their teacher⟩ **b :** in the space that separates **:** BETWIXT ⟨an alleyway ~ two tall buildings⟩ ⟨a vacuum ~ two electrodes⟩ **:** in the midst of **:** surrounded by ⟨a lion rampant ~ eight crosses⟩ **c :** in intermediate relation to in respect to quantity, quality, or degree ⟨weighing somewhere ~ a pound and a pound and a half⟩ ⟨a grade ~ passing and failing⟩ **3 a :** from one to the other of ⟨air service ~ the two cities⟩ **b :** JOINING, CONNECTING ⟨a passageway ~ two rooms⟩ **c :** in common to **:** in the joint possession, action, or agency of ⟨an agreement ~ states⟩ ⟨there is no continuity of mood ~ the three books —F.A.Swinnerton⟩ ⟨mutual understanding ~ the brothers⟩ **d :** SEPARATING, DISTINGUISHING **:** setting apart ⟨the lines ~ different new media —F.L.Mott⟩ ⟨a distinction must be drawn ~ the . . . three functions of authority —Abram Kardiner⟩ **4 :** after a comparison of **:** in point of comparison of ⟨there is not much to choose ~ the two coats⟩ **5 :** in confidence restricted to ⟨a secret ~ ourselves⟩ ⟨there's nothing private ~ you and me —Walter de la Mare⟩ **6 :** taking together the total effect of (a series of things) ⟨~ making beds, washing dishes, sewing, cleaning, and raising her children, she was kept busy⟩

²**between** \"\ *adv* [ME *betwene*] **1 a :** in an intermediate position in relation to two other objects ⟨two desks with a wastebasket ~⟩ **b :** filling the space limited by two objects ⟨two buildings with a parking area ~⟩ **2 :** in the interval **:** in intervals ⟨two short movies with a newsreel ~⟩ ⟨dancing all the dances with very little rest ~⟩ **3 :** through a space limited by two objects ⟨since he could not go around the two strolling men, he went ~⟩

³**between** \"\ *n* -s **:** the time, space, state, or way between

betweenbrain \≈ˈ≈,≈\ *n* -s [²*between*] **:** DIENCEPHALON

¹**between decks** \≈ˈ≈,≈, ≈ˈ≈ˈ≈\ *adv* [¹*between*] **:** in the space on a ship between decks **:** BELOWDECKS **:** below the main deck

²**between decks** \≈ˈ≈,≈\ *n pl but sing in constr* **1 :** the space belowdecks **:** the space below the main deck **2 :** a deck below the main deck; *specif* **:** a raised deck in the hold of a cargo ship

betweenmaid \≈ˈ≈,≈\ *n* -s [²*between*] *Brit* **:** a maidservant whose work supplements that of cook and housemaid

be·tween·ness \-ēnnə̇s\ *n* -ES **:** the quality or state of being between two others in an ordered series

between-the-lens shutter *n* : DIAPHRAGM SHUTTER

between the lines *adv* : by implication : in an indirect way ⟨made it clear, *between the lines*, that he would be in line for J's present job —W.S.Carlson⟩ : INFERENTIALLY ⟨read *between the lines*⟩

between the sheets *n* : a cocktail consisting of equal parts of rum, an orange-flavored liqueur, and brandy and flavored with lime or lemon juice

be·tween·times \-'-,tīmz\ *adv* : at or during intervals ⟨spent the bulk of his time writing but ~ worked as a janitor and a car salesman⟩

be·tween·whiles \-'-,(h)wīlz\ *adv* : BETWEENTIMES

¹be·twixt \bə·'twikst, bē·-\ *prep* [ME *betwix, betwixte*, fr. OE *betwuh, betweox, betwyxt*, fr. *be-* + *-tweoh, -tweox, -twyxt* (fr. an old distributive numeral akin to Goth *tweihnai* two each); akin to OE *twēgen, twā, tū* two — more at TWO] : BETWEEN ⟨~ the eyes⟩

²betwixt \"\ *adv* [ME *betwix, betwixte*, fr. *betwix, betwixte*, prep.] : ²BETWEEN

betwixt and between *adv* : in a midway position : neither one thing nor the other ⟨wrote . . . in such wise that he seemed more or less *betwixt and between* —*Amer. Guide Series: Pa.*⟩

betz cell \'bet(s),s-\ *n, usu cap B* [after Vladimir A. *Betz* †1894 Russ. anatomist] : a very large pyramidal nerve cell of the motor area of the cerebral cortex

beu·dant·ite \'byüd^ən,tīt, byü'dan-\ *n* -s [F *beudantite*, fr. François S. *Beudant* †1852 Fr. mineralogist + F *-ite*] : a mineral $PbFe_3(AsO_4)(SO_4)(OH)_6$ consisting of a basic ferric lead arsenate and sulfate occurring in green to black rhombohedral crystals

beuk \'byük\ *chiefly Scot var of* BOOK

beurre \'bər\ *n* -s [F, fr. L *butyrum* — more at BUTTER] : BUTTER — usu. used in the phrase *au beurre* ⟨peas au ~⟩

beurre noir \,bərn(ə)'wär\ *n, pl* **beurres noirs** \-är(z)\ [F, lit., black butter] : butter browned and seasoned with vinegar and parsley

BEV *abbr, often not cap* billion electron volts

¹bev·el \'bevəl\ *adj* [fr. (assumed) MF *bevel*, n.] : having the slant of a bevel : OBLIQUE, BEVELED ⟨a ~ edge⟩

²bev·el \"\ *n* -s [fr. (assumed) MF *bevel* (whence MF *béveau, biveau*), fr. OF *baif* with open mouth, fr. *baer* to gape + *-if* -ive (fr. L *-ivus*) — more at ABEYANCE] **1 a** : the angle that one surface or line makes with another when they are not at right angles **b** : the slant or inclination of such a surface or line **c** : the surface or line at such a slant or inclination **d** : FLEAM 2 **e** : the part of a piece of printer's type extending from the face to the shoulder — compare BEARD 4d; see TYPE illustration **2** *or* **bevel square** : an instrument consisting of two rules or arms jointed together and opening to any angle for drawing angles or adjusting the surfaces to be given a bevel **3** : BEVEL WHEEL 2 **4** : the direction in which the bolt of a lock tapers

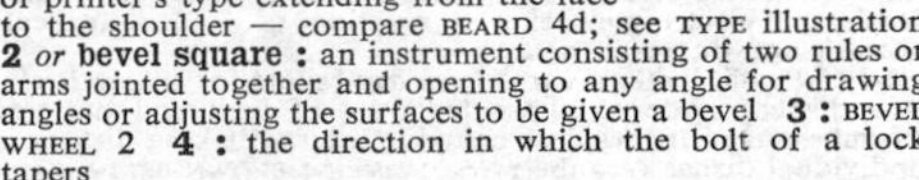

A bevel 1c

³bevel \"\ *vb* **beveled** *or* **bevelled**; **beveled** *or* **bevelled**; **beveling** *or* **bevelling** \-v(ə)liŋ\ **bevels** *vt* **1** : to cut or shape to a bevel : slope the edge or surface of : put a bevel on ⟨a carpenter must often ~ the bottom edge of a door to fit a slanting sill⟩ ⟨a printer ~s a rule in a mitering machine⟩ ⟨an engraving or electrotype is ~*ed* for fastening to patent bases⟩ **2** *geol* : to cut across ⟨the waves ~*ed* a volcanic island⟩ ⟨the erosion surface ~*s* an anticlinal structure⟩ ~ *vi* : to deviate or incline so as not to be at right angles with a line or surface : SLANT

bevel chisel *n* : a wood carver's chisel with a cutting edge that makes an oblique angle with the sides

beveled *or* **bevelled** *adj* **1** *mineralogy* : replaced by two planes inclining equally upon the adjacent planes ⟨a ~ edge⟩ **2** *mineralogy* : having its edges replaced by sloping planes

bev·el·er *or* **bev·el·ler** \-v(ə)lə(r)\ *n* -s : one that bevels: as **a** : one that bevels and smooths the edges of optical glass by means of an abrasive wheel **b** : one that files and sands slabs of slate for building purposes

bevel gauge *n* : ²BEVEL 2

bevel gear *n* : one of a pair of toothed wheels whose working surfaces are inclined to nonparallel axes

bevel pinion *n* : the smaller of a pair of bevel gears

bevel protractor *n* : a protractor with an arm pivoted so that it serves also as a bevel — see PROTRACTOR illustration

bevel siding *n* : siding tapered or beveled so that its upper edge is thinner than its lower and lapped in laying to cover the horizontal joint between adjoining pieces

bevel wheel *n* : **1** : a bevel gear **2** : a wheel having a conical surface that rolls in contact with a disk or another bevel wheel

bevel gears

¹bever *obs var of* BEAVER

²bev·er \'bevə(r), 'bi-,'bā-\ *vi* -ED/-ING/-S [freq. of ME *biven* to tremble, fr. OE *beofian* — more at BEBUNG] *dial chiefly Brit* : SHIVER, TREMBLE

³bever \"\ *n* -s *dial chiefly Brit* : TREMBLING ⟨all of a ~ with cold⟩

⁴be·ver \'bēvə(r), 'bā-\ *n* -s [ME, drinking, potation, fr. MF *beivre*, fr. *beivre* to drink] *chiefly dial* : a light lunch eaten between regular meals

bev·er·age \'bev(ə)rij, -ēj\ *n* -s [ME, fr. MF *bevrage*, fr. *beivre* to drink, fr. L *bibere* — more at POTABLE] **1** : liquid for drinking; *esp* : such liquid other than water (as tea, milk, fruit juice, beer) usu. prepared (as by flavoring, heating, admixing) before being consumed **2** *archaic* : any of several prepared drinks: as **a** : a drink made by passing water through pressed grapes **b** : weak beer **c** : diluted cider **3** *dial Brit* : a drink or drink money esp. when exacted from someone wearing manifestly new clothes

beverage room *n, Canad* : a hotel barroom that serves only beer

bev·er·en \'bev(ə)rən, 'bāv-\ *n, usu cap* [fr. *Beveren*, commune of Belgium] **1** : a breed of blue-eyed rabbits of Belgian origin raised for meat, fur, and show **2** -s : a rabbit of the Beveren breed

be·vue \bā'vü\ *n* -s [F *bévue*, fr. *bé-*, pejorative prefix (fr. L *bis* twice) + *vue* sight, view, fr. OF *veue* — more at BIS, VIEW] : an error due to ignorance or inadvertence

bevy \'bevē, -vi\ *n* -ES [ME *bevey, bevie*] **1 a** : a usu. large group or collection ⟨amorous involvement with a ~ of young women —Rex Lardner⟩ ⟨a ~ of balloons filling the sky⟩ ⟨a ~ of nature activities —*Ford Times*⟩ **b** : ¹BEE 3a **2** : a number of animals (as birds) together — used chiefly of quail

be·wail \bə̇, bē +\ *vb* -ED/-ING/-S [ME *bewailen*, fr. *be-* + *wailen* to wail — more at WAIL] *vt* **1** : to express deep sorrow for : wail over : LAMENT ⟨~ your injuries or losses⟩ ⟨a servant ~*ing* her hard luck —W.A.White⟩ **2** : to express deep regret for : DEPLORE ⟨he ~*ed* the breaches of the Constitution —H.D.Jordan⟩ ~ *vi* : to express grief : LAMENT **syn** see DEPLORE

be·wail·ing·ly *adv* : in a bewailing manner

be·wail·ment \-l(ə)lmənt\ *n* -s : the act or the sound of bewailing : LAMENTATION

be·ware \bə̇'wa(a)(ə)r, bē-, -we(ə)r,-wa(a)ə,-weə\ *vb* -ED/-ING/-S [ME *been war*, fr. *been* to be + *war* careful — more at BE, WARE] *vi* **1** : to be on one's guard : be cautious : take care — usu. used with *of* or *lest* and now chiefly in imperative or infinitive ⟨~ of straying into . . . absurdities —*Manchester Guardian Weekly*⟩ **2** *obs* : to have a special regard : pay heed ⟨~ of him and obey his voice —Exod 23:21 (AV)⟩ ~ *vt* **1** : to take care of : have a care for — now chiefly in imperative or infinitive ⟨~ your pocketbook when he is around⟩ **2** : to be wary of — used chiefly in imperative or infinitive constructions ⟨~ the exceedingly tenuous generalization —Matthew Lipman⟩

be·weep \bə̇, bē+\ *vt* **bewept**; **bewept**; **beweeping**; **beweeps** [ME *bewepen*, fr. OE *bewēpan*, fr. *be-* + *wēpan* to weep — more at WEEP] *archaic* : to weep over : LAMENT

be·west \bi'west\ *prep* [ME, fr. OE *be westan*, fr. *be* by, at (fr. *bi, bī*) + *westan* from the west, fr. *west* west, westward — more at BY, WEST] *Scot* : to the west of

bewet *vt* [ME *beweten*, fr. *be-* + *weten* to wet — more at WET] *obs* : WET

be·whisker \bə̇, bē +\ *vt* -ED/-ING/-S [*be-* + *whisker*] : to put whiskers on

bewhiskered *adj* **1** : wearing whiskers **2** : staled by repetition : OLD ⟨a ~ joke⟩

bewhore *vt* -ED/-ING/-S [*be-* + *whore*, n.] **1** *obs* : to call or name (a woman) a whore **2** *obs* : to make a whore of

bew·ick's swan \'byüik(s)'s-\ *also* **bewick swan** *n, usu cap B* [after Thomas *Bewick* †1828 Eng. wood engraver who illustrated a book about birds] : a white swan (*Cygnus bewickii*) of northern Asia and northeastern Europe that occas. appears in western Europe in winter and is smaller than the whooper swan with a smaller and more orange patch of naked skin in front of the eye

bewick's wren \-iks'r-\ *n, usu cap B* [after T. *Bewick*] : a brown wren (*Thryomanes bewickii*) common in the southern half of the U.S.

be·wig \bə̇, bē +\ *vt* **bewigged**; **bewigged**; **bewigging**; **bewigs** [*be-* + *wig*, n.] : to furnish with a wig ⟨hatless but *bewigged* and protected by flowing baronial robes —*Amer. Guide Series: Va.*⟩

bewigged *adj* : clothed in or marked by official dignity or importance ⟨the Age of Reason, with its ~ platitudes —L.P. Smith⟩

be·wil·der \bə̇'wildə(r), bē-\ *vb* **bewildered**; **bewildered**; **bewildering** \-d(ə)riŋ\ **bewilders** [*be-* + *wilder*] *vt* **1** : to cause to lose one's bearings : perplex or confuse by revealing no clear or right path to follow ⟨~*ed* by the maze of streets in the town⟩ **2** : to perplex, confuse, or lead mentally astray esp. by a complexity, variety, or multitude of objects or considerations ⟨so many questions ~ him⟩ ⟨events which have caused ~*ed* and angry anxiety —Thomas Cadett⟩ ~ *vi* : CONFUSE ⟨the ~*ing* expansion of science during the last century —C.H. Grandgent⟩ ⟨a complexity of logic that ~*s* and confuses⟩ **syn** see PUZZLE

be·wil·dered·ly \-ldə(r)dlē, -li\ *adv* : in a bewildered manner

be·wil·dered·ness \-də(r)dnə̇s\ *n* -ES : the quality or state of being bewildered

be·wil·der·ing·ly \-ld(ə)riŋlē, -ŋli\ *adv* : in a way that bewilders ⟨a ballet which is ~ beautiful —Stephen Graham⟩ ⟨~ rapid conquests —J.P.Baxter b.1893⟩

be·wil·der·ment \-ldə(r)mənt\ *n* -s **1** : the quality or state of being bewildered ⟨his complete ~ as to what had really taken place —F.W.Crofts⟩ **2** : a bewildering tangle or confusion ⟨led his now grumbling men . . . into a ~ of headwaters, beaver ponds, mountains, and unfriendly Indians —Ralph Gray⟩

bew·it *or* **bew·et** \'byüə̇t\ *n* -s [ME *bewette*, fr. MF *buie, beue* fetter (fr. L *bojae*, pl., neck-collar, fr. (assumed) Gk *boeiai*, fr. fem. pl. of *boeios* of an ox, fr. *bous* ox, cow) + ME *-ette* -et — more at COW] : a slip of leather by which bells are fastened to a hawk's legs in falconry

be·witch \bə̇'wich, bē-\ *vb* -ED/-ING/-ES [ME *bewicchen*, fr. *be-* + *wicchen* to witch — more at WITCH] *vt* **1 a** : to influence or control by witchcraft : dominate by witchcraft : affect (as injuriously) by charms or incantations ⟨look how I am ~*ed*; behold, mine arm is like a blasted sapling withered up —Shak.⟩ ⟨charged with ~*ing* a girl, who had been seized with a sudden illness that the doctor could not diagnose —*Amer. Guide Series: Tenn.*⟩ **b** : to cast a spell over ⟨the spotlight was on them, and the spell, and they stood there ~*ed* and helpless —Dorothy Baker⟩ **2** : to attract or please to such a degree as to take away all power of resistance or considered reservation : ENCHANT, CHARM, FASCINATE ⟨she ~*ed* King James no less than her first lover —*N.Y.Times*⟩ ⟨that time-honored privilege of saying foolish things in the grand manner which seems to have ~*ed* our gallant forefathers —Norman Douglas⟩ ~ *vi* : to act in a way that bewitches : CHARM, FASCINATE ⟨a book that ~*es* and enchants as it teaches —*Americas*⟩ **syn** see ATTRACT

be·witchedness \-chə̇dnə̇s, -ch(t)n-\ *n* -ES : the quality or state of being bewitched

be·witch·ery \-ch(ə)rē, -ri\ *n* -ES : BEWITCHMENT 1 ⟨a great ~ in the idea —Nathaniel Hawthorne⟩

be·witch·ing·ly *adv* : in a bewitching manner : to a bewitching degree ⟨a ~ beautiful girl⟩

be·witch·ing·ness *n* -ES : the quality or state of being bewitching

be·witch·ment \-chmənt\ *n* -s **1 a** : the act or power of bewitching : FASCINATION ⟨the ~ of forbidden pleasures⟩ **b** : a spell that bewitches **2** : the state of being bewitched ⟨the ~ of a young man in love⟩

bewpers *n, pl* **bewpers** [perh. fr. *Beaupréau*, near Cholet, Maine-et-Loire dept., France] *obs* : a fabric prob. of linen used for flags

be·wrap \bə̇, bē +\ *vt* [ME *bewrappen*, fr. *be-* + *wrappen* to wrap — more at WRAP] : to wrap up : clothe in a wrap

¹be·wray \bə̇'rā, bē-\ *vt* -ED/-ING/-S [ME *bewreyen*, fr. *be-* + *wreyen* to accuse, inform on, fr. OE *wrēgan*; akin to OHG *ruogen* to accuse, ON *rægja* to defame, Goth *wrōhjan* to accuse, and prob. to Lith *rėkti* to cry out] **1** *archaic* : to make known : DIVULGE, DISCLOSE; *esp* : to reveal (as a secret) to one's disadvantage often unintentionally **2** *archaic* : to reveal the true character of **syn** see REVEAL

²beway \"\ *vt* -ED/-ING/-S [alter. (influenced by ¹*bewray*) of *beray*] *archaic* : BERAY

be·wray·er \-āə(r)\ *n* -s [ME *bewreyer*, fr. *bewreyen* + *-er*] : one that bewrays ⟨a ~ of secrets —Joseph Addison⟩

be·wreath \bə̇'rēth, bē-, -th\ *vt* -ED/-ING/-S [*be-* + *wreath*] : to decorate with wreaths

be·write \bə̇, bē +\ *vt* **bewrote**; **bewritten**; **bewriting**; **bewrites** [*be-* + *write*] : to write about ⟨a public figure who has been much *bewritten* in the newspapers⟩

be·wusst·seins·la·ge \bə'vůst,zīn(t)s,lägə, -zīnz,l-, -lägə\ *n, pl* **bewusstseinsla·gen** \-gən\ *usu cap* [G, fr. *bewusstsein* consciousness (fr. *bewusst* conscious — past part. of *bewissen* to know, fr. *be-* + *wissen* to know, fr. OHG *wizzan* — + *sein* being, fr. *sein* to be, fr. OHG *sīn*) + *lage* situation, fr. OHG *lāga* act of laying; akin to OHG *ligen* to lie — more at WIT, IS, LIE] *psychol* : a state of consciousness or a feeling devoid of sensory components

bey \'bā\ *n* -s [Turk, gentleman, chief, prince] **1 a** : the governor of a district or minor province in the Ottoman Empire **b** : the sovereign of the former kingdom of Tunis **c** : the native and often nominal sovereign of the former monarchy of Tunisia **2** : the bearer of a title of courtesy or honor formerly used in Turkey and Egypt

be·yant \-'(y)ănt, -an-\ *chiefly Irish var of* BEYOND

bey·er·ite \'bīə,rīt\ *n* -s [Adolph *Beyer* †1805 Ger. mining engineer and mineralogist + E *-ite*] : a mineral $Ca(BiO)_2(CO_3)_2$ consisting of a rare calcium bismuth oxide and carbonate occurring in yellow crystals

beylerbey *var of* BEGLERBEG

bey·lic *or* **bey·lik** \'bālik\ *n* -s [Turk *beylik*, fr. *bey* + *-lik* (suffix used to form abstract nouns)] : the territory ruled by a bey : the jurisdiction of a bey — **bey·lic·al** \-kəl\ *adj*

¹be·yond \bē'ănd *also* bē'yä- *or* bə̇'yä- *sometimes* -'(y)ȯ- *or* -'(y)ə-\ *adv* [ME *beyonde*, adv. & prep., fr. OE *begeondan*, fr. *be-* + *geondan* beyond, fr. *geond* yond, yonder — more at YOND] **1 a** : farther away or farther along in space, time, or any developing temporal activity ⟨along the road through the valley and ~ to town⟩ ⟨the class lasts until four o'clock and seldom goes ~⟩ ⟨through the secondary school and ~⟩ **b** : on the farther side ⟨a hayfield with a pond ~⟩ **2** : in addition : FURTHER ⟨to provide the essentials but nothing ~⟩

²beyond \"\ *prep* [ME *beyonde*] **1** : on or to the farther side of : in the same direction as but farther on or farther away ⟨a house ~ a field and a small wood⟩ ⟨traveling ~ the larger cities to a village on the same route⟩ ⟨he made his native town his home, never journeying many miles ~ its borders —H.E. Starr⟩ **2 a** : out of the reach or sphere of ⟨then we grew ~ it —H.A.Overstreet⟩ : greater than the grasp or power of ⟨a task ~ his strength⟩ ⟨a sick man far ~ medical help⟩ ⟨the job was clearly ~ him —Merle Miller⟩ **b** : in a degree or amount surpassing ⟨angry ~ measure⟩ ⟨beautiful ~ expression⟩ **c** : out of or passing the comprehension of ⟨his reasoning is ~ us⟩ ⟨God's ways are ~ us —M.R.Cohen⟩ **3** : in addition to : OVER AND ABOVE, BESIDES ⟨decided to make traffic control their personal business ~ their regular duties —*Lamp*⟩ ⟨without any treatment ~ sedatives and rest —Stuart Chase⟩

³beyond \"\ *n* -s [¹*beyond*] **1** : something that lies beyond ⟨a river for small boats for twenty miles back into the ~ —R.W.Hatch⟩ **2** *sometimes cap* : something that lies outside the scope of ordinary experience ⟨there's a ~ that the mind can't see, and that's where the answers are —Robert Nathan⟩; *specif* : ²HEREAFTER

be·yond·ness \-nə̇s\ *n* -ES : the quality or state of being beyond ⟨their dream of ~ was forgotten in the immediacy of the sky, breeze, and turf of actual experience —Viola Meynell⟩

be·yont \-n(t)\ *or* **be·yonst** \-nzt,-n(t)st\ *dial var of* BEYOND

bez·ant *also* **bes·ant** \'bez^ənt, bə̇'zant\ *or* **byz·ant** \'biz^ənt, bə̇'zant\ *n* -s [ME *besand, besant*, fr. OF *besant*, fr. ML *Byzantius* Byzantine, fr. *Byzantium*, ancient city (now Istanbul, Turkey)] **1** : the Byzantine gold solidus as designated in western Europe where it circulated up to the 16th century **2** : a flat disk used in architectural ornament sometimes as one of many overlapping circular scales arranged in a single row (as in a molded jamb or archivolt) **3** *heraldry* : a roundel or

¹be·zan·tée *or* **be·zan·té** \bə̇'zantē, ¦bez^ən¦tā\ *also* **be·zan·ty** \bə̇'zantē\ *adj* [F *besanté*, fr. *besant*] **1** : set with bezants **2** *heraldry* : semé of bezants

²be·zan·tee \bə̇'zantē\ *n* -s : BEZANT 2

bez antler [OF *bes* twice, fr. L *bis* — more at BIS] *var of* BAY ANTLER

¹be·zel *or* **be·zil** \'bēzəl, 'bez-\ *n* -s [prob. fr. a dial form of F *biseau*, perh. fr. L *bis* twice — more at BIS] **1** : a sloping edge or face esp. on a cutting tool — called also *basil* **2** *also* **biz·el** \'bizəl\ **a** : the top part of a ring that may be a flat table or hold a gem, bear an intaglio, or have some other ornamentation **b** : the oblique side or face of a cut gem; *specif* : the upper faceted portion of a brilliant projecting from the setting between the table and the girdle : CROWN — compare PAVILION; see BRILLIANT illustration **c** : the grooved rim that holds the crystal on a watch **d** : a similar rim that holds a glass or plastic covering (as on a clock dial or headlight)

²be·zel *or* **be·zil** \"\ *vt* **bezeled** *or* **bezelled** *or* **beziled** *or* **bezilled**; **bezeled** *or* **bezelled** *or* **beziled** *or* **bezilled**; **bezeling** *or* **bezelling** *or* **beziling** *or* **bezilling** \-z(ə)liŋ\ **bezels** *or* **bezils** : to form the edge of to an angle : BEVEL

be·zique \bə̇'zēk\ *n* -s [F *bésique*] **1** : a card game similar to pinochle that is played with a pack of 64 cards and in which the points are made chiefly by winning tricks (as those containing brisques) and thereupon declaring any of certain combinations in the hand (as a marriage, a sequence, or four of a kind) **2** : a combination of a queen and a jack (as the queen of spades and jack of diamonds) in bezique commonly scored as 40 but counting as 500 when doubled

be·zoar \'bēzō(ə)r\ *or* **bezoar stone** *n* -s [MF *bézoard*, fr. Sp *bezoar*, fr. Ar *bāzahr, bādizahr*, fr. Per *bād-zahr, pād-zahr*, fr. *pād* protecting (against) + *zahr* poison] : any of various concretions found in the alimentary organs (esp. of certain ruminants) formerly believed to possess magical properties and used in the Orient as a medicine or pigment — see GERMAN BEZOAR, ORIENTAL BEZOAR, PHYTOBEZOAR, TRICHOBEZOAR, WESTERN BEZOAR

bezoar antelope *n* : BLACK BUCK 1

bezoar goat *n* : the wild goat (*Capra aegagrus*) of Iran and adjacent regions

be·zold-brücke phenomenon \¦bāt,sȯlt'brikə-, -rœkə-\ *n, usu cap both Bs* [after Wilhelm von *Bezold* †1907 Ger. meteorologist and Ernst W. von *Brücke* †1892 Ger. physiologist] : the shift in the hue of colors that occurs when the intensity of the corresponding energy stimulus is materially increased, except in the case of the stimuli for certain invariable hues approximating the psychologically primary hues

be·zo·ni·an \bə̇'zōnēən, bē-, -nyən\ *n* -s *sometimes cap* [modif. (influenced by E *-ian*) of It *bisogno* recruit from Spain, lit., need, fr. ML *bisonium*] **1** *archaic* : a military recruit **2** *archaic* : a mean dishonest person : SCOUNDREL

bez·po·po·vets \,bespə'pȯvəts, ,bezp-\ *n, pl* **bezpo·pov·tsy** \-ōftsē\ *usu cap* [Russ, fr. *bez* without (fr. ORuss) + *popov-* (pl. stem of *pop* priest, fr. OHG *pfaffo*, fr. Goth *papa*, fr. LGk *papas*, fr. Gk, father) + *-ets*, agent suffix; akin to OSlav & Pol *bez* without, Lith *bė*, Skt *bahis* outside — more at POPE] : a member of a Raskolnik priestless sect in Russia — compare POPOVETS

bez tine *n* [OF *bes* twice — more at BAY ANTLER] : BAY ANTLER

bez·zle \'bezəl\ *vb* -ED/-ING/-S [ME *besilen*, fr. MF *besillier* to destroy, kill] *vt, dial chiefly Brit* : WASTE, PLUNDER ~ *vi, dial chiefly Brit* : to drink or eat to excess

bf *abbr* **1** boldface **2** brief

BF *abbr* **1** beat frequency **2** *often not cap* board foot **3** brought forward

b flat \'-'-\ *n, usu cap B* **1** : the keynote of B-flat major or B-flat minor **2** : the tone a half step below B

b-flat major \'-,'-'--\ *n, usu cap B* : the major musical key having a signature of two flats

b-flat minor \'-,'-'--\ *n, usu cap B* : the minor musical key having a signature of five flats

BFO *abbr* beat-frequency oscillator

bg *abbr* **1** bag **2** background **3** being

BG *abbr* **1** bonded goods **2** brigadier general

bght *or* **bgt** *abbr* bought

b-girl \'bē+,-\ *n, usu cap B* [prob. fr. *bar* + *girl*] : a woman employed frequently on a commission basis to entertain and listen to bar patrons and encourage them to spend freely

BH *abbr* **1** base hospital **2** bill of health

bha·bar \'bäbə(r)\ *n* -s [Hindi *bhābar*] **1** : a valuable Indian fiber grass (*Ischaemum angustifolium*) used for making mats, rope, and paper — called also *baib grass* **2** : a sedge (*Eriophorum comosum*) found with bhabar and used for the same purposes

bha·don \'bä,dōn\ *n* -s *usu cap* [Hindi *bhādō*, fr. Skt *bhādrapada*, fr. *Bhadrapadā*, either of two lunar asterisms, fr. fem. of *bhadrapada* having fortunate steps or feet, fr. *bhadra* fortunate + *pada* step, foot; akin to Skt *pad* foot — more at BETTER, FOOT] : a month of the Hindu year — see MONTH table

bha·gat \'bəgət\ *n* -s [Hindi *bhagat*] : a Hindu saint or religious devotee

bha·ga·vat \'bəgəvət\ *n, usu cap* [Skt, lit., possessing good fortune, fr. *bhaga* good fortune; akin to Skt *bhajati* he grants, allots — more at BAKSHEESH] : blessed one : LORD — used chiefly as an epithet of deities in Hinduism and Buddhism

bha·ga·va·ta \,bägə'vəd·ə\ *n* -s [Skt *bhāgavata* relating to the blessed one, fr. *bhagavat*] : a devotional worshiper of a deity, esp. of Vishnu : BHAKTA

bhai \'bäē\ *n* -s [Hindi *bhāī* brother, fr. Skt *bhrātṛ* — more at BROTHER] *India* : BROTHER, FRIEND — used in address as an expression of friendship

bhak·ta \'bəktə\ *n* -s [Skt, one who resorts or is devoted to (a god), belonging to, allotted — more at BATTA] *Hinduism* : a religious devotee : WORSHIPER — compare BHAKTI

bhak·ti \'bəktē\ *n* -s [Skt, lit., portion, share, fr. *bhajati* he grants, allots] *Hinduism* : religious devotion : love directed toward a personal deity — **bhak·tic** \'baktik, 'bək-\ *adj*

bhak·ti-mar·ga \¦bəktē¦märgə\ *n* [Skt *bhaktimārga*, fr. *bhakti* + *mārga* path, fr. *mṛga* deer, gazelle] *Hinduism* : approach to salvation by way of ardent devotion to a deity — compare KARMA-MARGA

bhakti yoga *n* [Skt *bhaktiyoga*, fr. *bhakti* + *yoga*] : devotional yoga

bha·lu \'bä,lü, -'-\ *n* -s [Hindi *bhālū*, fr. Skt *bhallūka*, fr. *bhalla* bear; akin to OE *bera* bear — more at BEAR] : BEAR; *specif* : SLOTH BEAR

bhang *also* **bang** \'baŋ, 'bäŋ\ *n* -s [Hindi *bhāg*, fr. Skt *bhaṅga*; akin to Per *bang* hemp] **1 a** : HEMP 1 **b** : the leaves and flowering tips of hemp, esp. of the female plant : CANNABIS — compare GANJA, HASHISH, MARIJUANA **2** : any of several narcotic and intoxicant products obtained from bhang: as **a** : an Asian decoction of bhang usu. fermented in milk or water **b** : MAJOON **c** : a resinous extractive rich in narcotic principles

bhan·gi *or* **bhun·gi** \'bəŋ(,)gē\ *n* -s [Hindi *bhaṅgī*, lit., one addicted to bhang, fr. *bhāg*] : a Hindu sweeper or scavenger being a member of one of the lowest untouchable castes

bhar \'bär\ *n, pl* **bhar** *or* **bhars** *usu cap* **1** : a caste of agricultural laborers in India linguistically of the Kol group inhabiting central India **2** : a member of the Bhar caste

bhar·al *also* **barh·al** *or* **burh·el** *or* **burrh·el** \'bərəl\ *n* -s [Hindi *bharal*] : a wild sheep (*Pseudois nahoor*) having downcurved horns and living at high elevations in the Himalayas and Tibet

bhar·a·ta \'bärəd·ə, -rətə\ *n* -s *cap* [Skt *bhārata* inhabiting India, of India, descended from Bharata, of Bharata, fr. *Bharata*, a legendary monarch of India whose descendants are the principal characters in the Mahabharata, one of the two great Sanskrit epics] **:** an inhabitant of India

bhar·a·ta na·tya \¦bərəd·ə'nä·tyə, -rətə'-\ *or* **bharata na·tyam** \-·tyəm\ *n* [Skt *bharatanātya*, lit., Bharata's dancing, fr. *Bharata*, a sage reputed to be the author of the Natyashastra, a manual of dramatic art + *nātya* dramatic art, dancing — more at NATYA] **:** a traditional Indian dance formerly exclusively performed by devadasis — compare KATHAK, KATHAKALI, MANIPURI

bhar·a·ti \'bärəd·ē, -rətē, -i\ *adj, usu cap* [Skt *bhārati*, fem. of *bhārata*] **:** of or relating to India **:** INDIAN

bhar·ti \'bär|d·ē, 'bȧ|d·ē, |tē, -i\ *n* -s [native name in India] *India* **:** BARNYARD GRASS

bhat \'bät\ *n* -s [Hindi *bhāt*, fr. Skt *bhaṭṭa*] **:** a member of an Indian caste of bards or entertainers

bhat·pa·ra \(')bät¦pärə\ *adj, usu cap* [fr. *Bhatpara*, India] **:** of or from the city of Bhatpara, India **:** of the kind or style prevalent in Bhatpara

bhav·na·gar \(')baù¦nəgə(r)\ *adj, usu cap* [fr. *Bhavnagar*, India] **:** of or from the city of Bhavnagar, India **:** of the kind or style prevalent in Bhavnagar

BHC *abbr* benzene hexachloride

bhd *abbr* bulkhead

bhees·ty *or* **bhees·tie** *or* **bhis·ti** \'bēstē, -ti\ *n, pl* **bhees·ties** *or* **bhistis** [Hindi *bhistī*, fr. Per *bihishtī* heavenly one] *India* **:** a water carrier esp. of a household or a regiment

bher tree \'be(ə)r-, 'ba(a)(ə)r-\ *n* [Hindi *ber*, fr. Skt *badara*] **:** CHINESE JUJUBE

bhik·ku \'bi(,)kü, -ikə\ *n* -s [Pali, fr. Skt *bhikṣu*] **:** a Buddhist monk or religious mendicant — compare BONZE

bhik·shu \'bikshə\ *n* -s [Skt *bhikṣu*, fr. *bhikṣate* he desires, begs, desiderative of *bhajati* he grants, allots — more at BAKSHEESH] **:** a Hindu or Buddhist monk or religious mendicant

bhil \'bē(ə)l\ *n, pl* **bhil** *or* **bhils** *usu cap* [Hindi *Bhīl*, fr. Skt *Bhilla*] **1 :** a hill people of west central India having a bow-and-arrow culture **2 :** a member of the Bhil people

bhil·a·wan nut \'bilə,wän-, 'bēl-, -,wən-\ *n* [prob. fr. *Bhilawan*, *Bhilwara*, district in central India] **:** MARKING NUT

bhi·li \'bēlē\ *n* -s *cap* [Hindi *Bhīlī*, fr. *Bhīl*] **:** the Indic language of the Bhil people

BHN *abbr* Brinell hardness number

bhoj·pu·ri \'bäjpə,rē\ *n* -s *cap* [Hindi *Bhojpurī*, fr. *Bhojpur*, village in Shahabad district, western Bihar, India] **:** the dialect of Bihari spoken in western Bihar and the eastern United Provinces, India

bho·kra \'bōkrə\ *n* -s [Gujarati] **:** FOUR-HORNED ANTELOPE

bhoo·sa *also* **bhu·sa** \'büsə, -(,)sä\ *n* -s [Hindi *bhus*, *bhūsā*, fr. Prakrit *bhusa*; akin to Skt *busa* chaff] *India* **:** the broken straw and husks from the threshing floor used as fodder **:** CHAFF

bho·ra \'bōrə, -rä\ *or* **bo·ho·ra** \bō'hōr-\ *n, pl* **bhora** *or* **bhoras** *or* **bohora** *or* **bohoras** *usu cap* [Hindi *bohrā*] **:** a modern Shi'ite sect of western India retaining some Hindu elements

b-horizon \'bē-¦--\ *n, usu cap B* **:** the soil layer immediately beneath the A-horizon from which it obtains humic and other organic matter chiefly by illuviation and is usu. distinguished by less weathering — see C-HORIZON

bho·tan pine \(')bō¦tan-, -tän-\ *also* **bhu·tan pine** \(')bü¦-\ *n, often cap B* [fr. *Bhotan*, *Bhutan*, country in eastern Himalayas] **:** a very resinous pine (*Pinus excelsa*) that resembles the American white pine and is native to the Himalayas but grown in Australia for timber and turpentine

bho·tia *also* **bho·ti·ya** \'bōd·ē(y)ə, -ōtē-, -ē(,)yä\ *or* **bhu·tia** \'büd·ē-, -ütē-\ *n, pl* **bhotia** *or* **bhotias** *also* **bhotiya** *or* **bhotiyas** *or* **bhutia** *or* **bhutias** *usu cap* [Skt *bhoṭiya* Tibetan (adj.), fr. *Bhoṭa* Tibet] **1 a :** the peoples of southern Tibet and Bhutan **b :** a member of such peoples **2 a :** TIBETAN **b :** any or all of the Sino-Tibetan languages spoken in Tibet or in the Himalayan region

b'hoy \bə'hȯi\ *n* -s [alter. (representing Irish pronunc.) of *boy*] *slang* **:** ROWDY, TOUGH

bhp *abbr* bishop

BHP *abbr* brake horsepower

bhpric *abbr* bishopric

bhui·ya \'büē(y)ə, -(,)(y)ä\ *n, pl* **bhuiya** *or* **bhuiyas** *usu cap* **1 :** a people in the Orissa and Bengal regions of India **2 :** a member of the Bhuiya people

bhu·mi·dar \¦bümē¦där\ *n* -s [Hindi *bhūmidār*, fr. *bhūmi* earth, land (fr. Skt) + *-dār* holder (fr. Per); akin to Skt *bhavati* he is and to Skt *dhārayati* he holds, possesses — more at BE, FIRM] *India* **:** a landholder having full title to his land

bhu·mij \'bümij\ *n, pl* **bhumij** *usu cap* [Hindi *bhūmij*, lit., earth-born, fr. Skt *bhūmija*, fr. *bhūmi* earth + *-ja* born; akin to Skt *janati* he begets — more at KIN] **1 a :** a Munda people of Chota Nagpur, India **b :** a member of this people **2 :** the Munda language of the Bhumij people

bhunder *var of* BANDAR

bhungi *var of* BHANGI

bhut \'büt, *usu* -d.+V\ *n* -s [Hindi *bhūt*, fr. Skt *bhūta*, lit., having come into being, fr. *bhavati* he becomes, is — more at BE] *India* **:** an esp. malevolent spirit **:** GHOST, DEMON, GOBLIN

bhu·tan \(')bü¦tan, -tän\ *adj, usu cap* [fr. *Bhutan*, country in eastern Himalayas] **:** of or from Bhutan **:** of the kind or style prevalent in Bhutan **:** BHUTANESE

bhutan cypress *n, usu cap B* **:** a lofty East Indian cypress (*Cupressus torulosa*) venerated by the natives

¹bhu·ta·nese \¦büt³n¦ēz\ *adj, usu cap* **1 a :** of, relating to, or characteristic of Bhutan **b :** of, relating to, or characteristic of the people of Bhutan **2 :** of, relating to, or characteristic of the Bhutanese language

²bhutanese \"\ *also* **bhu·ta·ni** \bü'tanē, -tä-\ *or* **bho·ta·ni** \bō'-\ *n, pl* **bhutanese** *or* **bhutani** *or* **bhutanis** *or* **bhotani** *or* **bhotanis** *usu cap* **1 a :** a Tibetan Mongolian people of Bhutan **b** (1) **:** a member of the Bhutanese people (2) **:** an inhabitant of Bhutan **2 :** the Tibetan language of Bhutan

bhu·ta·ta·tha·ta \,büd·əd·ə'tə,tä\ *n* -s [Skt *bhūtatathatā*] **:** the essence of suchness in Buddhism

¹bhutia *usu cap, var of* BHOTIA

²bhu·tia \'büd·ēə\ *n* -s *usu cap* **:** any of a breed of chiefly gray riding ponies native to Nepal and adjacent regions

¹bi- *prefix* [ME, fr. L; akin to OE *twi-* — more at TWI-] **1 a :** two ⟨*bi*muscular⟩ ⟨*bi*cycle⟩ ⟨*bi*racial⟩ **b :** lasting two **:** coming or occurring every two ⟨*bi*ennial⟩ ⟨*bi*monthly⟩ ⟨*bi*weekly⟩ **c :** into two parts ⟨*bi*sect⟩ **2 a :** twice **:** doubly **:** on both sides ⟨*bi*conic⟩ ⟨*bi*convex⟩ ⟨*bi*serrate⟩ **b :** coming or occurring two times ⟨*bi*diurnal⟩ ⟨*bi*quarterly⟩ ⟨*bi*weekly⟩ — often disapproved in this sense because of the likelihood of confusion with sense 1b; compare SEMI- **3** *anat* **:** between, involving, or affecting two (specified) symmetrical parts ⟨*bi*gonial⟩ ⟨*bi*-iliac⟩ **4** *chem* **a :** containing one (specified) constituent in double the proportion of the other constituent or in double the ordinary proportion — esp. in names of acid salts formed with twice as much acid as is required for a normal salt ⟨*bi*urate⟩ **b :** DI- 2 — esp. in names of organic compounds to denote the doubling of a radical or molecule ⟨*bi*tolyl⟩ ⟨*bi*phenol⟩

²bi- *or* **bio-** *comb form* [Gk, fr. *bios* mode of life — more at QUICK] **1 :** life ⟨*bio*blast⟩ **:** living organisms or tissue ⟨*bio*psy⟩ ⟨*bio*dynamics⟩ **2 :** biology **:** biological ⟨*bio*psychology⟩

Bi *symbol* bismuth

-bia \bēə, *sometimes US and usu Brit* byə\ *n comb form* [NL, fr. fem. sing. and neut. pl. of *-bius* having a (specified) mode of life — more at -BIUS] **:** one or ones having a (specified) mode of life — in generic names as a singular ⟨*Bryobia*⟩ and in descriptive biological group names as a plural ⟨*aerobia*⟩ ⟨*coenobia*⟩

bi·acetyl \¦bī, (')bī+\ *n* [ISV ¹*bi-* + *acetyl*] **:** a greenish yellow liquid diketone $(CH_3CO)_2$, with an odor like that of quinone that is found in some essential oils (as bay oil), that is chiefly responsible for the flavor of butter and also contributes to the aroma of coffee and tobacco, and that is made synthetically and used as a flavoring agent in foods (as margarine); 2,3-butane-dione — called also *diacetyl*

bi·acromial \¦bī+\ *adj* [ISV ¹*bi-* + *acromial*] **:** of, relating to, or between the two acromion processes ⟨~ diameter⟩

bi·a·cu·ru \,bī(y)əkə'rü, '---+,-\ *or* **ba·ya·cu·ra root** \¦bī-(y)ə¦kùrə-\ *n* -s [Pg *bayucuru*, fr. Tupi] **:** the powerfully astringent root of a So. American herb (*Limonium brasiliense*); *also* **:** the plant itself

bi·a·jai·ba \,bēə'hībə\ *n* -s [AmerSp] **:** LANE SNAPPER

bi·ak \bē'(y)äk\ *n, pl* **biak** *or* **biaks** *usu cap* **1 a :** a Papuan people of western New Guinea inhabiting the islands of Biak, Numfor, and Japen **b :** a member of such people **2 :** the language of the Biak people

bi·alate \(')bī+\ *adj* [¹*bi-* + *alate*] **:** having two wings **:** DIPTEROUS

bia·ly·stok \byä'wi,stȯk, ,bēə'-, -'li,s-\ *adj, usu cap* [fr. *Bialystok*, Poland] **:** of or from the city of Bialystok, Poland **:** of the kind or style prevalent in Bialystok

bian·chi \'byäŋkē, bē'äŋ-\ *n pl, usu cap* [It, lit., whites, pl. of *bianco* white, of Gmc origin; akin to OHG *blanch* shining, white — more at BLANK] **:** a political faction of the Guelphs in Tuscany, Italy, about 1300 opposed to the Neri

bi·an·chite \bē'aŋ,kīt\ *n* -s [It, fr. Angelo *Bianchi* b1892 Ital. mineralogist + It *-ite*] **:** a rare mineral $(Zn,Fe)SO_4.6H_2O$ consisting of hydrous sulfate of zinc and iron occurring as white crystalline crusts

bian·co so·pra bianco \¦byäŋ(,)kō¦sōprə¦-, bē¦äŋ-\ *n* [It, white on white] **:** a technique of porcelain decoration using white glaze in floral or scroll designs on a near-white usu. pale gray or blue ground

bi·anisidine \¦bī+\ *n* -s [¹*bi-* + *anisidine*] **:** any of several isomeric compounds $C_{14}H_{16}N_2O_2$ the molecule of which is a doubled anisidine molecule; *esp* **:** the white crystalline ortho isomer derived from benzidine, made by reducing *ortho*-nitro-anisole, and used as an intermediate for many azo dyes — called also *dianisidine*

bi·annual \(')bī+\ *adj* [¹*bi-* + *annual*] **:** occurring, appearing, or being made, done, or acted upon twice a year; *sometimes* **:** BIENNIAL — compare SEMIANNUAL — **bi·annually** \"+\ *adv*

bi·articular \¦bī+\ *adj* [¹*bi-* + *articular*] *anat* **:** of or relating to two joints

bi·articulate *or* **bi·articulated** \¦bī+\ *adj* [¹*bi-* + *articulate* or *articulated*] *biol* **:** having or consisting of two joints

¹bi·as \'bīəs\ *n, pl* **bi·as·es** \-əsəz\ [MF *biais*, fr. OProv, perh. irreg. fr. Gk *epikarsios* athwart, oblique, fr. *epi* on + *-karsios* (as in *enkarsios* athwart, oblique); akin to Lith *skersas* oblique, Russ *cherez* over, across] **1 :** a line diagonal to the grain of a fabric; *esp* **:** a line at a 45° angle to the selvage producing a cut with some stretchability and often utilized in the cutting of garments for smoother fit **2 a :** an inclination of temperament or outlook ⟨a strong liberal ~⟩; *often* **:** such prepossession with some object or point of view that the mind does not respond impartially to anything related to this object or point of view ⟨the most pernicious kind of ~ consists in falsely supposing yourself to have none —Walter Moberly⟩ **:** PREJUDICE **b :** BENT, TENDENCY, TREND ⟨a panel of experts of psychiatric ~⟩ ⟨the present ~ of trade in our favor⟩; *sometimes* **:** INCLINATION ⟨my brother had a strong ~ toward the scholarly life⟩ **c** *statistics* **:** a tendency of an estimate to deviate in one direction from a true value (as by reason of nonrandom sampling) **3** *now dial Eng* **:** established procedure **:** settled way or course ⟨there is no putting him out of his ~. He is a regular piece of clockwork —Samuel Richardson⟩ **4** *archaic* **:** anything tending to influence one in a particular direction **:** a determining influence **5** *lawn bowling* **a :** a peculiarity in the shape of a bowl that causes it to swerve when rolled on the green **b :** a tendency of the bowl to swerve; *also* **:** the impulse causing this tendency **c :** the swerve of the bowl **6 :** an unvarying component of the electric potential difference between a given element of an electron tube and the cathode — see GRID BIAS **syn** see PREDILECTION — **on the bias 1 :** diagonally to the grain — used of cloth **2 :** OBLIQUELY, ASKEW

²bias \"\ *adj* **1 :** DIAGONAL, SLANTING, OBLIQUE ⟨a ~ light⟩ ⟨trimmed with ~ bands of velvet⟩ — used chiefly of fabrics and their cut; compare ¹BIAS 1 **2** *obs* **:** swelled or weighted on one side **3 :** of, relating to, or exhibiting bias — **bi·as·ness** *n* -ES

³bias \"\ *adv* [²*bias*] **1 :** in a slanting manner **:** OBLIQUELY, DIAGONALLY ⟨cut cloth ~⟩ **2** *obs* **:** AWRY, AMISS

⁴bias \"\ *vt* **bi·ased** *or* **bi·assed; biased** *or* **biassed; bi·as·ing** *or* **bi·as·sing; bi·as·es** *or* **bi·as·ses** ['bīəs] **1 :** to give a bias to **:** give a settled and often prejudiced outlook to **:** INFLUENCE, PREPOSSESS ⟨fixed ideas may ~ observation of events⟩ ⟨his background ~*es* him against foreigners⟩ **2 :** to apply a slight negative or positive voltage to (as a vacuum tube grid)

bias binding *or* **bias tape** *n* **:** a narrow strip of cloth cut on the bias, folded once or twice, and used chiefly for finishing and decorating clothing

biased *or* **biassed** *adj* **:** exhibiting or characterized by bias ⟨a ~ estimate of the book's worth⟩ — **biasedly** *adv*

bi·as·ter·ic \¦bīa¦sterik, -tir-\ *adj* [¹*bi-* + *asterion* + *-ic*] **:** of, relating to, or between the two asterions

bias·wise \'--+,wīz\ *adv* **:** OBLIQUELY, ASKEW

biaural *var of* BINAURAL

bi·auricular \¦bī +\ *adj* [¹*bi-* + *auricular*] **1 :** BIAURICULATE **2 a :** of or relating to the two auditory openings **b :** joining the two auricular points ⟨the ~ diameter of the skull⟩

bi·auriculate \¦bī +\ *adj* [¹*bi-* + *auriculate*] **:** having two auricles — used esp. of the heart of mammals, birds, and reptiles

bi·axial *also* **bi·axal** *or* **bi·axiate** \(')bī +\ *adj* [¹*bi-* + *axial* or *axal* or *axiate*] **:** having two axes ⟨~ crystals⟩ — **bi·axiality** \¦bī +\ *n* -ES — **bi·axially** \(')bī +\ *adv*

¹bib \'bib\ *vb* **bibbed; bibbed; bibbing; bibs** [ME *bibben*, perh. fr. L *bibere* to drink — more at POTABLE] **:** DRINK, TIPPLE

²bib \"\ *n* -s **1 a :** a piece of cloth worn across the chest and often tied around the neck to protect a child's clothing **b :** a similar part of an adult's dress or costume that is usu. for decoration **c :** the part of a garment (as an apron) rising above the waist **d :** a canvas throat protector attached to a fencing mask **e :** a patch of differently colored feathers or fur immediately below the chin of a bird or mammal **f :** a leather shield fitting behind the lower jaw and attached to the halter of a horse to prevent interference (as with blanket or bandages) while permitting eating and drinking **2 :** a small cod (*Gadus luscus*) of European coasts having on the head a distensible membrane like a bib **3** *or* **bibb** \"\ **a :** BIBCOCK **b :** BIB NOZZLE **4 :** a long projection of land sloping gradually into the sea

bib *abbr* **1** *often cap* Bible **2** biblical

bi·ba·cious \bə'bāshəs, (')bī¦b-\ *adj* [L *bibac-*, *bibax* bibulous (fr. *bibere* to drink) + E *-ious* — more at POTABLE] **:** addicted to drinking **:** BIBULOUS

bi·bac·i·ty \-'basəd·ē\ *n* -ES [L *bibac-*, *bibax* + E *-ity*] *archaic* **:** addiction to drink **:** TIPPLING

bib and tucker *n* **:** an entire outfit of clothing — usu. used in the phrase *best bib and tucker*

bi·ba·tion \bī'bāshən, bī-\ *n* -s [¹*bib* + *-ation*] **:** TIPPLING, IMBIBING

¹bibb \'bib\ *n* -s [alter. of ²*bib*] **:** a side piece of timber bolted to the hounds of a ship's mast to support the trestletrees

²bibb *var of* BIB

bibbed \'bibd\ *adj* [²*bib* + *-ed*] **:** having a bib ⟨a ~ apron⟩

bib·ber \'bibə(r)\ *n* -s [¹*bib* + *-er*] **:** one addicted to drinking **:** TIPPLER — often used in combination ⟨wine*bibber*⟩ — **bib·bery** \-b(ə)rē\ *n* -ES

bib·ble \'bibəl\ *vb* [freq. of ¹*bib*] *now dial* **:** TIPPLE

bib·ble–babble \¦bibəl+¦-\ *n* [redupl. of ²*babble*] **:** idle talk **:** BABBLE

bib·bler \'bib(ə)lə(r)\ *n* -s *archaic* **:** TIPPLER

bib·by \'bibē\ *n* -ES *often cap* [after the *Bibby* Line, Ltd., on whose ships (between England and India) such rooms were first used] **:** a stateroom on a passageway of a ship

bibcock \'-,-\ *also* **bibb cock** *n* [²*bib* + *cock*] **:** a stopcock or faucet having a bent-down nozzle

bi·be·lot \'bēbə,lō, 'bē(,)blō, 'bi-; bēblō\ *n, pl* **bibelots** \-,lō(z)\ [F] **1 :** a small household ornament or decorative object **:** TRINKET **2 :** a miniature book esp. of elegant design or format

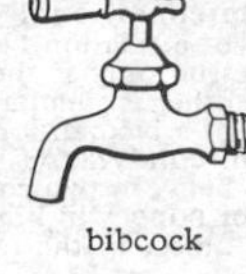
bibcock

bi·be·ron \'bibə,rän, -,rən, bēbrōⁿ\ *n* -s [F, fr. L *bibere* to drink — more at POTABLE] **:** a drinking vessel with an elongated spout as its only opening formerly used for invalids, travelers, or children

bi·bi \'bē(,)bē\ *n* -s [Hindi *bībī*, fr. Per] *India* **:** a lady usu. of a European country; *sometimes* **:** the Hindu mistress of a house **:** WIFE — used as a term of respect

bib·i·on·id \'bibēənəd\ *adj* [NL *Bibionidae*] **:** of or relating to the family Bibionidae

bib·i·on·i·dae \,bibē'änə,dē\ *n pl, cap* [NL, fr. *Bibion-*, *Bibio*, type genus (fr. L *bibion-*, *bibio* small insect found in wine) + *-idae*; perh. akin to L *bibere*] **:** a family of two-winged flies (suborder Nematocera) comprising the March flies and having larvae that feed on the roots of grasses and other plants

bi·bi·ri \bə'bērē\ *n* -s [Sp & Pg *bibiri bibirú* — more at BEBEERU] **:** BEBEERU

bibirine *var of* BEBEERINE

bibiru *var of* BEBEERU

bib·i·to·ry \'bibə,tōrē, -tȯrē\ *adj* [ML *bibitorius*, fr. L *bibitus* (past part. of *bibere*) + *-orius* -ory] **1 :** concerned with or relating to drinking ⟨a ~ muscle⟩ **2 :** capable of taking up moisture ⟨~ papers⟩

bi–bivalent \¦bī, (')bī +\ *adj* **:** relating to or being an electrolyte that dissociates into two bivalent ions

bibl *abbr* **1** biblical **2** bibliography

¹bi·ble \'bībəl\ *n* -s *often attrib* [ME, Bible, book, fr. OF, Bible, fr. ML *biblia*, fr. Gk, pl. of *biblion* book, dim. of *biblos*, *byblos* book, papyrus, fr. *Byblos* (now Jubayl), Phoenician city from which papyrus was exported] **1** *usu cap* **a :** the book composed of writings generally accepted by Christians as inspired by God and of divine authority **b :** the portion of this book that antedates the Christian era **:** an integrated segment of this earlier work (as the Torah) **c :** a book containing the sacred writings of a religion ⟨the Koran is the Muslim *Bible*⟩ **2** *obs* **:** BOOK **3** *obs* **:** a library or collection of books **4** *usu cap* **:** a copy or an edition of the Bible **5 :** a publication likened to the Bible esp. in authoritativeness or in the regularity with which it is consulted: as **a :** an outstanding or definitive reference work in any field ⟨Blackstone was the lawyer's ~ in those days⟩ **b :** a publication regularly read and regarded as indispensable ⟨the ~ of show business⟩ **c :** a book of rules **6 :** something suggesting a book: as **a :** a small holystone **b :** OMASUM **c :** a piece of whale blubber sliced into leaves like those of a book to facilitate heating in the try-pot

²bible \"\ *vt* -ED/-ING/-S **:** to supply with Bibles ⟨~ a hotel⟩

bible belt *n, usu cap both Bs* **:** an area chiefly in the southern portion of the U.S. supposedly holding uncritical allegiance to the literal accuracy of the Bible; *broadly* **:** any area characterized by an ardent fundamentalism

bible box *n, usu cap 1st B* **:** a miniature chest of the 17th century or earlier with flat top and with or without a till

bible church *n, usu cap B&C* **:** a Christian congregation that lays special emphasis on the Bible as the basis of faith and the inerrant word of God — used frequently in names of churches that hold such doctrines and do not have other denominational affiliations

bible class *n, often cap B* **:** a Sunday-school or church-school class devoted to the study of the Bible

bible clerk *n, usu cap B* **:** one of certain scholars who read the lessons in chapel or say grace in hall at some colleges of Oxford University

bible college *or* **bible institute** *n, usu cap B* **:** a Christian college offering courses in religion and specializing in training students as ministers and religious workers

bible leaf *n* **1 :** COSTMARY **2 :** one of the thin segments making up a bible of whale blubber

bible oath *n, usu cap B* **:** a solemn oath; *esp* **:** one sworn upon the Bible

bible paper *n, usu cap B* **:** INDIA PAPER

bible school *n, usu cap B* **:** SUNDAY SCHOOL, CHURCH SCHOOL 2

bible society *n, usu cap B* **:** an association for securing the wide distribution of the Christian Bible

bib·less \'bibləs\ *adj* **:** being without a bib

bi·blia a·bi·blia \¦biblēə(')ā¦biblēə\ *n pl* [NL, books that are no books] **:** volumes of no humanist interest or worth

biblia pau·pe·rum \'biblē(,)ä'paùpə,rùm, -blēə'p-, -'pȯpərəm\ *n pl, usu cap B* [NL, lit., Bible of the poor] **:** one of a class of biblical picture books that depicted important scriptural events and were used in medieval and somewhat later times as a means of instructing large numbers of people in the Christian faith

biblic- *or* **biblico-** *comb form, often cap* [obs. *biblic* biblical (prob. fr. ML *biblicus*, fr. *biblia* Bible + L *-icus* -ic) + E *-o-*] **:** Bible ⟨*biblic*ist⟩ **:** biblical and ⟨*biblico*literary⟩

bib·li·cal \'biblәkəl, -blēk-\ *adj, sometimes cap* [obs. *biblic* + E *-al*] **1 :** of, relating to, derived from, or in accord with the Bible **2 :** like that of the Bible ⟨a ~ inevitability⟩ ⟨~ styles in writing⟩; *sometimes* **:** like that of the time and region where the Bible was produced ⟨~ costume⟩ ⟨a beard of ~ proportions⟩ — **biblically** *adv, sometimes cap*

biblical hand *n, usu cap B* **:** a book hand of the Byzantine period (about A.D. 300–650) characterized by squarish uncials of somewhat heavy appearance

biblical hebrew *n, usu cap B&H* **:** the Hebrew language of the Old Testament — see AFRO-ASIATIC LANGUAGES table

bib·li·cal·i·ty \,biblə'kaləd·ē\ *n* -ES **:** biblical quality or something embodying it

biblical theology *n, often cap B* **:** theology based on the Bible; *specif* **:** theology that seeks to derive its categories of thought and the norms for its interpretation from the study of the Bible as a whole

bib·li·cism \'biblə,sizəm\ *n* -s *often cap* [*biblic-* + *-ism*] **:** narrow or exclusive use of the Bible; *specif* **:** adherence to the letter of the Bible

bib·li·cist \-,səst\ *n* -s [*biblic-* + *-ist*] **1** *often cap* **:** one that adheres to or practices biblicism **2 :** a Bible scholar

biblio- *comb form* [MF, fr. L, fr. Gk, fr. *biblion* book — more at BIBLE] **:** book ⟨*biblio*graphy⟩ ⟨*biblio*mania⟩

bib·lio·clast \'biblēə,klast, -blēō,-\ *n* -s [*biblio-* + *-clast*] **:** a destroyer or mutilator of books

bib·lio·film \'---+,-\ *n* [*biblio-* + *film*] **:** a microfilm used esp. for photographing pages of books

bib·lio·genesis \¦---+\ *n* [*biblio-* + *genesis*] **:** BIBLIOGONY

bib·li·og·nost \'biblēəg,näst\ *n* -s [F *bibliognoste*, fr. *biblio-* + *-gnoste* (fr. Gk *gnōstēs* one who knows, fr. *gignōskein* to know) — more at KNOW] **:** one that has comprehensive knowledge of books and bibliography — **bib·li·og·nos·tic** \¦---¦nästik\ *adj*

bib·li·og·o·ny \,biblē'ägənē\ *n* -ES [*biblio-* + *-gony*] **:** production of books — called also *bibliogenesis*

bib·lio·graph \'biblēə,graf, -lēō,-\ *vt* -ED/-ING/-S [back-formation fr. *bibliographer*, *bibliographic*, & *bibliography*] **1 :** to enter in a bibliography **2 :** to provide (as a book) with a bibliography **3 :** to compile a bibliography of

bib·li·og·ra·pher \,biblē'ägrəfə(r)\ *n* -s [F *bibliographe* bibliographer (prob. back-formation fr. *bibliographie*) + E *-er*] **1 :** one that writes about or is informed about books, their authorship, format, publication, and similar details **2 :** a compiler of bibliography

bib·lio·graph·ic \¦biblēə¦grafik, -lēō¦-, -fēk\ *also* **bib·lio·graph·i·cal** \-¦grafəkəl, -fēk-\ *adj* [*bibliographic* fr. F *bibliographique*, fr. *bibliographie* + *-ique* -ic; *bibliographical* fr. F *bibliographique* + E *-al*] **:** of, relating to, or dealing with bibliography — **bib·lio·graph·i·cal·ly** \-fək(ə)lē, -fēk-, -li\ *adv*

bib·lio·graph·i·ca \,---'grafəkə\ *n pl* [NL, fr. neut. pl. of *bibliographicus* bibliographic, fr. ISV *bibliographic*] **:** bibliography esp. when bearing on a particular subject, period, or author

bib·li·og·ra·phy \,biblē'ägrəfē, -fi\ *n* -ES [prob. fr. F *bibliographie*, prob. fr. NL *bibliographia*, fr. *biblio-* + L *-graphia* -graphy, fr. Gk] **1 a :** the history, identification, or analytical and systematic description or classification of writings or publications considered as material objects **b :** the investigation or determination of the relationships of varying texts or multiple editions of a single work or a related group of works — called also *analytic bibliography*, *descriptive bibliography* **2 :** a list or catalog, often with descriptive or critical notes, of writings relating to a particular subject, period, or author ⟨a ~ of modern poetry⟩ ⟨a ~ of the 17th century⟩; *also* **:** a list of works written by an author or printed by a publishing house ⟨the ~ of Walt Whitman⟩ ⟨a publisher's ~⟩ **3 :** a list of the source material (as books and articles) used in the preparation of a work or referred to in the text ⟨a bibliography with a ~ of over 400 items⟩ **4 :** the study of bibliography or bibliographic methods ⟨an intensive course in ~⟩

bib·lio·klept \'biblēə,klept, -lēō,-\ n -s [biblio- + -klept] : one who steals books
bib·li·ol·a·ter \,biblē'äləd·ə(r)\ also **bib·li·ol·a·trist** \-'älə-·trəst\ n -s [biblio- + -later] : one characterized by bibliolatry : a book worshiper
bib·li·ol·a·trous \¦==¦älə·trəs\ adj [bibliolatry + -ous] : given to bibliolatry
bib·li·ol·a·try \,==ʼälə·trē\ n -ES [biblio- + -latry] **1** : extravagant devotion to or concern with books **2** : excessive veneration of or absolute dependence on a group of sacred writings as infallible; specif : worship of the Bible
bib·li·ol·o·gy \-'äləjē\ n -ES [biblio- + -logy] **1** : the history and science of books as physical objects in all aspects : bibliography in its widest sense **2** often cap : the study of the theological doctrine of the Bible
bib·lio·man·cy \'biblēə,man(t)sē, -lēō,-\ n -ES [biblio- + -mancy] : divination by books, esp. the Bible
bib·lio·mane \-,mān\ n -s [F, back-formation fr. bibliomanie] : BIBLIOMANIAC
bib·lio·mania \,biblēə, ,biblēō +\ n [modif. (influenced by E mania) of F bibliomanie, fr. biblio- + manie mania, fr. LL mania] : extreme preoccupation with books, esp. with their acquisition and possession
¹bib·lio·maniac \" +\ n [fr. bibliomania, after E mania: maniac] : one affected with bibliomania; esp : an avid book collector
²bib·lio·maniac also **bib·lio·maniacal** \¦=== +\ adj : characteristic of bibliomania; also : characterized by or noted for bibliomania
bib·lio·peg·ic \-¦pejik, -pēj-\ adj [bibliopegist + -ic] : relating to bookbinding — **bib·lio·peg·i·cal·ly** \-jək(ə)lē\ adv
bib·li·op·e·gist \,biblē'äpəjəst\ n -s [perh. fr. obs. F bibliopégiste, fr. F biblio- + obs. F -pégiste (fr. Gk pēgnynai to fasten together + F -iste -ist) — more at PACT] : BOOKBINDER
bib·li·op·e·gis·tic \¦==¦==¦jistik\ also **bib·li·op·e·gis·ti·cal** \-tәkәl\ adj : BIBLIOPEGIC
bib·li·op·e·gy \,biblē'äpəjē\ n -ES [bibliopegist + -y] : the art of binding books
bib·lio·phage \'biblēə,fāj, -lēō,-\ n -s [ISV biblio- + -phage] : BOOKWORM — **bib·li·oph·a·gous** \,biblē¦äfəgəs\ adj
bib·lio·phile \'biblēə,fīl, -lēō,-\ n -s [F, fr. biblio- + -phile (fr. Gk philos friend)] : a lover of books esp. for beautiful or rare qualities of format; also : a book collector — **bib·lio·phil·ic** \¦===¦filik, -lēk\ adj
bib·li·oph·i·lism \,biblē'äfə,lizəm\ n -s : love of books ⟨a center of good music, serious art, ~, the ballet —William Manchester⟩
bib·li·oph·i·list \-ləst\ n -s : BIBLIOPHILE — **bib·li·oph·i·lis·tic** \¦==¦==¦listik, -tēk\ adj
bib·li·oph·i·ly \-'äfəlē, -li\ n -ES [F bibliophilie, fr. bibliophile + -ie -y] : the love of books characteristic of the bibliophile
bib·lio·phobe \'biblēə,fōb, -lēō,-\ n -s [ISV biblio- + -phobe] : a person with bibliophobia
bib·lio·pho·bia \,===ʼfōbēə\ n -s [biblio- + -phobia] : strong dislike of books
bib·lio·pole \'===,pōl\ or **bib·li·op·o·list** \,biblē'äpələst\ n -s [L bibliopola bookseller, fr. Gk bibliopōlēs, fr. biblio- + -pōlēs (fr. pōlein to sell) — more at MONOPOLY] : a dealer in books (as secondhand, rare, or curious books) — **bib·lio·pol·ic** \¦biblēə¦pälik, -lēō¦-, -¦pä-\ adj
bib·lio·taph also **bib·lio·taphe** \'biblēə,taf, -lēō,-\ n -s [F bibliotaphe, fr. biblio- + -taphe (fr. Gk taphos tomb) — more at EPITAPH] : one that hides away or hoards books — **bib·lio·taph·ic** \¦===¦tafik\ adj
bib·lio·the·ca \,===ʼthēkə\ n, pl **bibliothecas** \-kəz\ or **bibliothe·cae** \-ē(,)kē,-ē(,)sē,-ē,kī,-ē,sī\ [L bibliotheca collection of books, fr. Gk bibliothēkē, fr. biblio- + thēkē case, chest; akin to Gk tithenai to put, place — more at DO] **1** archaic : BIBLE 1a **2** : a library or collection of books **3** : a list or catalog of books — **bib·lio·the·cal** \¦===¦thēkəl\ adj
bib·lio·the·car·i·al \¦===thə'ka(a)rēəl, ¦biblē,äth-\ adj [L bibliothecarius librarian (fr. bibliotheca + -arius -ary) + E -al] : of or related to a library
bib·lio·therapeutic \¦biblēə, ¦biblēō +\ adj [biblio- + therapeutic] : of, relating to, or involving bibliotherapy
bib·lio·therapist \" +\ n -s [bibliotherapy + -ist] : one skilled in bibliotherapy
bib·lio·therapy \" +\ n [ISV biblio- + therapy] : the use of selected reading materials as therapeutic adjuvants in medicine and in psychiatry; also : guidance in the solution of personal problems through directed reading
bib·li·ot·ic \¦biblē¦äd·ik\ adj [fr. bibliotics, after such pairs as E aesthetics : aesthetic] : of or relating to bibliotics
bib·li·ot·ics \-ks\ n pl but sing or pl in constr [biblio- + connective -t- + -ics] : the scientific study of handwriting, documents, and writing materials esp. for determining genuineness or authorship — **bib·lio·tist** \'biblēəd·əst, -lēō-, -təst\ n -s
bi·blism \'bībə,lizəm also 'bī,bli- sometimes 'bi,bli-\ n -s often cap [bible + -ism] : adherence to the Bible as the sole rule of faith
bi·blist \in sense 1 'bibləst also and in sense 2 usu 'bībələst, 'bībləst\ n -s often cap [bible + -ist] **1** : a biblical scholar **2** : one who practices or advocates biblism
bib·lus \'bibləs\ also **bib·los** \", -,läs\ n -ES [Gk & L; L biblus, fr. Gk biblos, byblos — more at BIBLE] : PAPYRUS 2
bib nozzle n [²bib] : a bent-down nozzle of a cock or faucet often threaded for attachment of a hose
bi·borate \(')bī + \ n [¹bi- + borate] : TETRABORATE
biborate of soda : BORAX — not used scientifically
bi·bos \'bī,bäs, -,bōs\ n, cap [NL, prob. fr. Bison + Bos] : a genus of Asiatic wild oxen (family Bovidae) comprising the gaur and related animals — **bi·bo·vine** \'bībə,vēn, -,vīn, -vən\ adj
bib pout n : ²BIB 2
bibs pl of BIB, pres 3d sing of BIB
bib·u·los·i·ty \,bibyə'läsəd·ē\ n -ES [bibulous + -osity] : state of being bibulous
bib·u·lous \'bibyələs\ adj [L bibulus, fr. bibere to drink — more at POTABLE] **1** : readily taking up fluids or moisture ⟨the ~ paper with which the dentist keeps his working area dry⟩ **2 a** : inclined to drink : addicted to tippling **b** : of, relating to, or affected by tippling ⟨a ~ farewell⟩ **c** : of or relating to drink ⟨the ~ history of wine country⟩ — **bib·u·lous·ly** adv
bi·cameral \(')bī+\ adj [¹bi- + camera + -al] **1 a** : consisting of two chambers ⟨the ~ heart of a fish⟩ **b** : having or made up of two distinct legislative bodies ⟨the Congress is ~, consisting of the Senate and the House of Representatives⟩ **2** : based on or involving legislative bicameralism ⟨the evident advantages of the ~ system⟩ — **bi·camerally** \"+\ adv
bi·cameralism \(')bī+\ n -s : bicameral organization of a legislative body
bi·cameralist \(')bī+\ or **bi·cam·er·ist** \(')bī¦kamərəst\ n -s : an advocate of bicameralism
bi·canine \(')bī+\ adj [¹bi- + canine] : between the outer borders of the canine teeth of a jaw ⟨the ~ width of the chimpanzee⟩
bi·capsular \(')bī+\ adj [prob. fr. F bicapsulaire, fr. bi- ¹bi- + capsulaire capsular] **1** biol : having two capsules **2** biol : having a bilocular capsule
bi·carb \(')bī'kärb, -kəb\ n -s [short for bicarbonate] : SODIUM BICARBONATE
bi·carbonate \(')bī+\ n [ISV ¹bi- + carbonate] : an acid carbonate : a hydrogen carbonate — see ¹BI- 4
bicarbonate of soda : SODIUM BICARBONATE — not used scientifically
bi·carinate \(')bī+\ adj [fr. (assumed) NL bicarinatus, fr. NL ¹bi- + L carinatus carinate] : having two projections like keels ⟨the strongly ~ shell of certain marine snails⟩
bi·caudal also **bi·caudate** \(')bī+\ adj [NL bicaudalis & (assumed) NL bicaudatus, fr. NL ¹bi- + caudalis caudal & caudatus caudate] : having or terminating in two tails
bice blue \'bīs\ n [ME bis, fr. bis (adj.) dark gray, fr. MF; akin to OProv bis dark gray, It bigio] : AZURITE BLUE
bice green n : MALACHITE GREEN 2
bi·cellular \(')bī+\ adj [¹bi- + cellular] : having or composed of two cells
bi·centenary \,bī, (')bī+\ adj or n [¹bi- + centenary] : BICENTENNIAL
¹bi·centennial \¦bī+\ n -s [¹bi- + centennial] : a 200th anniversary or its celebration
²bi·centennial \"+\ adj : relating to a 200th anniversary
bi·centric \(')bī+\ adj [¹bi- + centric] **1 a** of a taxon : having two centers of origin ⟨it is doubtful that Zea is ~⟩ ⟨Limulus is an outstanding example of a ~ genus⟩ **b** : having or involving two centers ⟨the ~ distribution of certain Scandinavian plants⟩ ⟨a lichen of ~ origin⟩ **2** : having two centromeres — **bi·centricity** \¦bī+\ n -ES
bi·cep \'bī,sep\ n -s [back-formation fr. biceps, taken as a plural] : BICEPS
bi·cephalous \(')bī+\ or **bi·cephalic** \¦bī+\ adj [¹bi- + -cephalous or -cephalic] : having two heads
bi·ceps \'bī,seps\ n, pl **biceps** also **bi·ceps·es** \-,sepsəz\ [NL bicipit-, biceps, fr. L, two-headed, fr. ¹bi- + -cipit-, -ceps (fr. capit-, caput head) — more at HEAD] : a muscle having two heads or origins: as **a** : the large flexor muscle of the front of the upper arm arising by its short head from the coracoid process and by its long head from the upper margin of the glenoid cavity and being inserted into the tuberosity of the radius — called also biceps brachii, biceps humeri, biceps flexor cubiti **b** : a muscle that arises by its long head from the ischial tuberosity and by its short head from the shaft of the femur, that is inserted into the head of the fibula, its tendon forming the outer hamstring, and that flexes the leg on the thigh and extends the thigh on the trunk — called also biceps femoris, biceps flexor cruris
bich·ir \'bichə(r)\ n -s [F] : a large primitive fish (Polypterus bichir) of the order Cladistia found in the upper Nile and certain neighboring waters and esteemed as food

bichir

bi·chloride \(')bī +\ or **bichloride of mercury** n [ISV ¹bi- + chloride] : MERCURY CHLORIDE b
bi·chord \'bī +,-\ adj [¹bi- + chord] : having two strings in unison for each note ⟨the mandolin is a ~ instrument⟩
bi·chromate \(')bī +\ n [¹bi- + chromate] : DICHROMATE — used chiefly commercially and esp. of the dichromates of sodium and potassium
bichromate cell n : a zinc-carbon cell having an acid bichromate solution as electrolyte and developing an electromotive force of about two volts
bi·chromated \(')bī +\ adj : treated or combined with a bichromate ⟨~ gelatin⟩
bi·chromatic \¦bī +\ adj [¹bi- + chromatic] : DICHROMATIC
bi·chromatized \(')bī +\ adj [fr. past part. of (assumed) bichromatize to treat or combine with a bichromate, fr. bichromate + -ize] : BICHROMATED
bi·chrome \'bī +,-\ adj [¹bi- + -chrome] : two-colored : having two colors
bi·ciliate or **bi·ciliated** \(')bī +\ adj [¹bi- + ciliate or ciliated] : having two cilia
bi·cip·i·tal \(')bī¦sipəd·əl\ adj [NL bicipit-, biceps + E -al] **1 a** of certain muscles : having two heads or origins **b** : of or relating to a biceps muscle **2** bot : dividing into two parts at one extremity
bicipital fascia n : an aponeurosis given off from the tendon of the biceps of the arm and continuous with the deep fascia of the forearm
bicipital groove n : a furrow on the upper part of the humerus occupied by the long head of the biceps
bicipital tuberosity n : the rough eminence which is on the anterior inner aspect of the neck of the radius and into which the tendon of the biceps is inserted
bi·circular \(')bī +\ adj [ISV ¹bi- + circular] : consisting of or like two circles
bick \'bik\ n -s [ON bikkja — more at BITCH] Scot : BITCH
¹bick·er \'bikə(r)\ n -s [ME biker] **1 a** : an act of bickering : CONTENTION, ALTERCATION : petulant quarreling **b** : a sound of or as if of bickering ⟨the ~ and plash of the fountain⟩ **2** Scot : TUSSLE, BRAWL, FRACAS
²bick·er \"\ vb **bickered**; **bickered**; **bickering** \-k(ə)riŋ\ **bickers** [ME bikeren; akin to ME biker] vi **1** archaic : to skirmish esp. with missiles : FIGHT **2** : to contend in petulant or petty altercation : WRANGLE ⟨America . . . ~s with the Asian countries about the price of rubber —Mochtar Lubis⟩ ⟨they had ~ed so long as to quite forget the original quarrel⟩ **3** : to move quickly and unsteadily often with a rapidly repeated noise ⟨water ~ing over stones⟩ : QUIVER, FLICKER ⟨a wistful smile ~ed across her face⟩ **4** Scot : to make a quick short run : SPRINT ~ vt, archaic : to attack or assail with (as missiles) ⟨if we're going to ~ adverbs —Christopher Morley⟩
³bicker \"\ n -s [ME biker beaker — more at BEAKER] **1** chiefly Scot : a drinking vessel esp. of wood **2** chiefly Scot : a porridge dish often made of wooden staves
bickering n -s [ME bikeringe skirmishing, fr. bikeren + -inge -ing] : petty and petulant quarreling esp. when prolonged or habitual ⟨the factional ~ that has wrecked many a well-meaning organization⟩; sometimes : an instance of this ⟨those childish ~s that are part of growing up⟩ **syn** see QUARREL
bick·er·ment \-mənt\ n -s [²bicker + -ment] now dial Eng : BICKERING
bick·er·ton·ite \'bikə(r)tə,nīt\ n -s usu cap [William Bickerton 19th cent. Am. religious leader, who founded the denomination + -ite] : a member of the Church of Jesus Christ founded 1862 in Pennsylvania
bick·ford fuse \'bikfə(r)d-\ n, usu cap B [after William Bickford †1834 Eng. leather merchant, its inventor] : SAFETY FUSE 1
bick·iron \'bikə(r)n, -,kīə(r)n\ n [by folk etymology (influence of E iron) fr. earlier bickern, bycorne taper end of an anvil, anvil with two taper ends, modif. of MF bigorne anvil with two taper ends, fr. L bicornia, neut. pl. of bicornis] : the taper end of an anvil
bick·nell's thrush \'biknəlz-, -,nelz-\ also **bicknell thrush** \-nəl-, -,nel-\ n, usu cap B [prob. after Eugene P. Bicknell †1925 Am. botanist and ornithologist] : a small slender-billed thrush (Hylocichla minima bicknelli) of upland areas of northeastern No. America that is olive-brown above and buffy-white below
bi·clin·i·um \bī'klinēəm\ n, pl **biclin·ia** \-nēə\ [L, fr. bi- ¹bi- + -clinium (fr. Gk -klinion — as in triklinion triclinium)] : an ancient Roman dining couch for the use of two persons
bicol usu cap, var of BIKOL
bi·collateral \¦bī +\ adj [ISV ¹bi- + collateral] of a vascular bundle : having the phloem both external and internal to the xylem — compare COLLATERAL — **bi·collaterality** \" +\ n -ES
bi·colligate \(')bī +\ adj [fr. (assumed) NL bicolligatus, fr. NL ¹bi- + L colligatus bound together, past part. of colligare to bind together — more at COLLIGATE] of certain birds : having the three anterior toes connected by webs
¹bi·color also **bi·colored** \(')bī +\ adj [bicolor fr. L bicolor, fr. bi- ¹bi- + color; bicolored fr. ¹bi- + colored] : having or marked with two colors ⟨a ~ jonquil⟩ : printed in two colors (as of a postage stamp)
²bicolor \"\ n -s : a bicolor individual (as a postage stamp or a flower)
bicolor lespedeza n : an Asian shrub (Lespedeza bicolor) that has conspicuous purple flowers in axillary racemes and is now widely used as an ornamental, as a source of wild-bird food, and in erosion control
bi·col·or·ous \(')bī¦kələrəs\ adj [L bicolor + E -ous] : BICOLOR
bi·concave \(')bī, ¦bī +\ adj [ISV ¹bi- + concave] : concave on both sides : CONCAVO-CONCAVE ⟨~ vertebrae⟩ ⟨a ~ lens⟩ —see LENS illustration — **bi·concavity** \¦bī +\ n -ES
bi·conditional \¦bī +\ n [¹bi- + conditional] **1** : a statement of a relation between a pair of propositions such that one is true only if the other is simultaneously true, or false if the other is simultaneously false **2** : the symbolic representation of a biconditional — called also sentential connective
bi·condylar \(')bī +\ adj [¹bi- + condylar] : of, relating to, or between two condyles ⟨the ~ breadth of the jaw⟩
bi·cone \'bī,kōn\ n [prob. back-formation fr. biconical] : an object in the form of two cones with their bases placed together; specif : a bead having this form found among Sumerian and early Egyptian jewelry
bi·conical \(')bī +\ adj [ISV ¹bi- + conical] : having the form of a bicone
bi·conjugate \(')bī +\ adj [fr. (assumed) NL biconjugatus, fr. NL ¹bi- + L conjugatus joined together — more at CONJUGATE] : twice paired (as when each branch of a forking petiole bears a pair of leaflets)
bi·consonantal also **bi·consonantic** \(')bī +\ adj [¹bi- + consonantal or consonantic] : of or containing two consonants
bi·convex \(')bī +\ adj [ISV ¹bi- + convex] : convex on both sides : CONVEXO-CONVEX ⟨a ~ lens⟩ — see LENS illustration
bi·corn \'bī,kȯrn\ or **bicorned** \-nd\ also **bicornous** \(')bī¦kȯrnəs\ adj [bicorn fr. L bicornis, fr. bi- ¹bi- + -cornis (fr. cornu horn); bicorned fr. L bicornis + E -ed; bicornous fr. L bicornis + E -ous — more at HORN] : two-horned : like a crescent
bi·corne also **bi·corn** \'bī,kȯrn\ n -s [F bicorne, fr. L bicornis two-horned] : COCKED HAT 1b
bi·cor·nu·ate \(')bī¦kȯrnyü,āt, -yüət\ also **bi·cor·nate** \-,nāt, -,nət\ or **bi·cor·nu·ous** \-nyüəs\ adj [bicornuate fr. ¹bi- + L cornu horn + E -ate; bicornate fr. L bicornis two-horned + E -ate; bicornuous fr. ¹bi- + L cornu + E -ous] : having two horns or horn-shaped processes ⟨a ~ uterus⟩
bi·corporal \(')bī +\ adj [¹bi- + corporal] of a sign of the zodiac : represented by two figures
bi·costate \(')bī +\ adj [¹bi- + costate] of a leaf : having two principal ribs running longitudinally
bi·cris·tal \(')bī¦kristəl\ adj [¹bi- + L crista crest + E -al — more at CREST] : of, relating to, or between the iliac crests
bi·crural \(')bī +\ adj [¹bi- + crural] : having two legs
bicuhyba or **bicuhybao** or **bicuiba** var of BECUIBA
bi·cultural \(')bī +\ adj [¹bi- + cultural] : combining two distinct cultures ⟨a recognition of . . . Canada's ~ character —Dict. of Canadian Biog.⟩
bi·cur·sal \(')bī¦kərsəl\ adj [¹bi- + L cursus course + E -al — more at COURSE] : having two paths, one for each of two moving points — used of a curve (as a hyperbola); opposed to unicursal
¹bi·cuspid also **bi·cuspidate** \(')bī +\ adj [bicuspid fr. NL bicuspid-, bicuspis, fr. ¹bi- + L cuspid-, cuspis point; bicuspidate fr. (assumed) NL bicuspidatus, fr. NL ¹bi- + L cuspidatus pointed, past part. of cuspidare to make pointed, fr. cuspid-, cuspis] : having two points or prominences : ending in two points ⟨~ teeth⟩ ⟨~ leaves⟩
²bicuspid \bī +\ n -s [NL bicuspid-, bicuspis, fr. ¹bi- + L cuspid-, cuspis point] : either of the two double-pointed teeth that intervene in man between the canines and the molars on each side of each jaw : PREMOLAR — see DENTITION illustration
bicuspid valve n : the mitral valve of the heart
¹bi·cy·cle \'bī,sikəl, -,sək-,-,sēk- sometimes -,sīk-\ n -s [F, fr. bi- ¹bi- + -cycle (as in tricycle)] **1** : a vehicle that has two wheels one behind the other, a steering handle, and a saddle seat or seats and is usu. propelled by the action of the rider's feet upon pedals **2** : a traveling block used on a cable in skidding logs **3** [so called fr. the picture of the ace, two, three, four, and five of hearts formerly printed on the container of a pack of Bicycle brand playing cards] : the best possible hand in lowball comprising ace, two, three, four, and five of mixed suits **4** : a literal translation : PONY

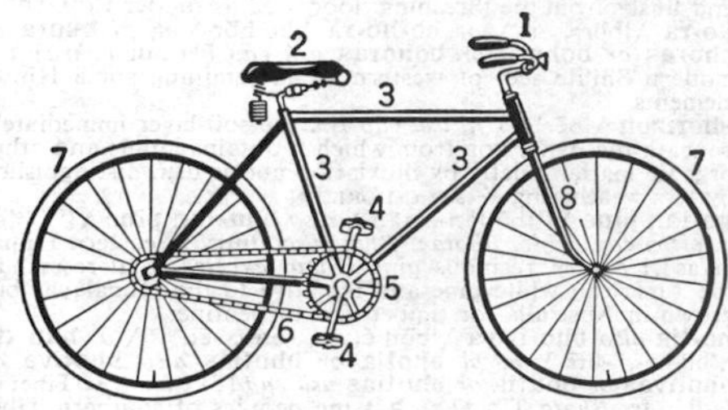

bicycle: 1 handlebar, 2 saddle, 3 frame, 4 pedal, 5 sprocket wheel, 6 chain, 7 tire, 8 fork

²bicycle \"\ vb **bicycled**; **bicycled**; **bicycling** \-k(ə)liŋ\ **bicycles** vi **1** : to ride a bicycle **2** West : to spur a bucking horse repeatedly, alternately on the right and on the left side ~ vt : to send (a recorded radio, television, or motion-picture program) directly from one broadcasting or exhibition point to another to facilitate distribution or to avoid payment of fees — **bi·cy·cler** \-k(ə)lə(r)\ n -s
bicycle gear n : a landing gear configuration in airplanes in which the main wheels or sets of wheels are placed under the center of the fuselage to take the main weight of the airplanes and are supplemented by small outrigger wheels under the wings
bi·cy·clic \(')bī¦sīklik, -¦sik-\ also **bi·cy·cli·cal** \-kləkəl\ adj [ISV ¹bi- + cyclic or cyclical] **1** : consisting of or arranged in two cycles or circles ⟨a ~ flower with the petals in two whorls⟩ **2** : containing two usu. fused rings in the structure of the molecule (as in naphthalene) ⟨a ~ terpene⟩
bi·cy·clist \'bī,sikləst, -sək-,-sēk- sometimes -,sīk-\ n -s : one that rides a bicycle; specif : a bicycle racer
bicyclo- comb form [ISV, fr. bicyclic] chem : bicyclic ⟨bicycloalkane⟩
bi·cylindrical \¦bī +\ adj [¹bi- + cylindrical] : having two cylindrical surfaces usu. with their axes parallel ⟨certain lenses are ~⟩
¹bid \'bid\ vb **bade** \'bad, 'baa(ə)d\ or **bid** or archaic **bad** \'bad\ **bidden** \'bid°n\ or **bid** also **bade**; **bidding**; **bids** [partly fr. ME bidden to entreat, pray, invite, command, fr. OE biddan to entreat, pray, command; akin to OHG bitten to entreat, ON bithja, Goth bidjan to entreat, ask for, Skt bādhate he presses, harasses; partly fr. earlier bede to invite, command, fr. ME beden to offer, proclaim, invite, command, fr. OE bēodan to offer, proclaim, command; akin to OHG biotan to offer, ON bjōtha to offer, command, Goth anabiudan to command, Gk pynthanesthai to learn by inquiry, Skt bodhati, bodhate he wakes, is awake, observes] vt **1 a** archaic : to ask for insistently : BESEECH, ENTREAT, PRAY **b** : to issue an order to either mildly and without especial emphasis or authoritatively or peremptorily ⟨the servant did as he was bidden⟩ ⟨they bade him enter⟩ **c** : to request to come : INVITE ⟨as many as ye shall find, ~ to the marriage —Mt 22:9 (AV)⟩ **2 a** obs : to make known : DECLARE, REVEAL, PROCLAIM **b** : to give expression to (as a greeting, a farewell, or a wish) to someone ⟨she bade me a tearful farewell⟩ **3 a** : OFFER — obs except in the phrase to bid defiance **b** (1) : to offer (a price) whether for payment or acceptance ⟨~ $10,000 less than his nearest competitor⟩ ⟨surely you can afford to ~ one dollar⟩ (2) : to obtain (goods) by offering a price or premium ⟨bidding scarce goods away from the open market⟩ (3) : to make (a bid) to someone ⟨I'll ~ you 50 cents and not one penny more⟩ **c** past or past part **bid** : to make a bid of or in ⟨~ hearts⟩ ⟨he bid one spade⟩ **d** : to enter a claim for (a vacant job) on the basis of seniority ~ vi **1** : to make a bid: as **a** : to state what one will pay or take **b** : to try to obtain or attain something — usu. used with for ⟨bidding for the support of special-interest groups⟩ **c** : to enter a claim for a vacant job on the basis of seniority — usu. used with in or for ⟨he bid in the operation of the big crane⟩ **2** : SEEM, APPEAR — usu. used with fair (sense 8a(1)) and now with a complementary infinitive ⟨his effort ~s fair to succeed⟩ though formerly also with for **syn** see COMMAND
²bid \"\ n -s **1 a** : the act of one who bids : an offer of a price (as at an auction) : a statement of what one will give or do for something to be received or will take for something to be done or furnished **b** : something offered as a bid **2** : an opportunity to bid ⟨the ~ is with you, sir⟩ : one's turn at bidding ⟨it's your ~⟩ **3** : INVITATION ⟨a ~ to join a sorority⟩ **4** card games **a** : an announcement of willingness to attempt to accomplish a certain result under specified conditions (as

to take a stated number of tricks in bridge if a stipulated suit is trumps) **b :** the amount of such a bid ⟨a 3-heart ~⟩ ⟨a 350 bid⟩ **c :** a bridge hand on which one may reasonably bid ⟨I haven't had a ~ in the last three hands⟩ **5 :** an attempt or effort to win, achieve, or attract ⟨he made a strong ~ for the championship⟩; *sometimes* **:** an appeal or plea esp. for sympathy

[3]**bid** *archaic past part of* BIDE

BID *abbr* [L *bis in die*] twice a day

bi·dac·tyl \(ˈ)bīˌdaktəl\ *or* **bi·dac·tyle** \", -ˌtīl\ *also* **bi·dac·ty·lous** \-ˌdaktələs\ *adj* [*bidactyl* & *bidactyle* fr. F *bidactyle*, fr. *bi-* [1]*bi-* + *-dactyle* -dactylous (fr. Gk *-daktylos*); *bidactylous* fr. *bidactyl* + *-ous*] **:** DIDACTYL

bi·dai \ˈbēˌdī\ *n, pl* **bidai** *or* **bidais** *usu cap* [prob. fr. Caddo *bidai* brushwood] **1 :** an Atakapan people of the Trinity river valley, Texas **2 :** a member of the Bidai people

bid ale *n* [ME *bede ale*, fr. *bede, beden*, past part. of *bidden* to invite + *ale* — more at BID] *obs* **:** a feast commonly held in past centuries in England for the benefit of a destitute person

bid–and–asked \ˌ==ˈ=\ *adj* **1** *of market quotations* **:** showing both the least price acceptable to a seller and the highest price acceptable to a buyer **2** *of a market or exchange* **:** functioning on the basis of bid-and-asked quotations

bi·dar *also* **bai·dar** \bīˈdär\ *n* -s [Russ *baidara;* akin to Russ *baidak* boat, Ukrainian *bajdak* boat, canoe] **:** a large skin-covered boat used chiefly by the Aleuts

bi·dar·ka *also* **bai·dar·ka** \bīˈdärkə\ *or* **bi·dar·kee** \-kē\ *n* -s [Russ *baidarka*, dim. of *baidara*] **:** a portable boat made of skins stretched over wood frames and widely used by Alaskan coastal natives and Aleuts

bid bond *n* **:** a surety bond often required of contractors bidding on construction work to provide that the bidder, if successful, shall furnish a satisfactory bond ensuring completion of the work — called also *proposal bond*

bid·da·bil·i·ty \ˌbidəˈbiləd·ē, -i\ *n* **:** the state or quality of being biddable **:** DOCILITY

bid·da·ble \ˈbidəbəl\ *adj* **1 :** OBEDIENT, DOCILE **2** *of a hand or suit at cards* **:** capable of being bid **:** strong enough to warrant a bid **syn** see OBEDIENT

bid·da·bly \ˈbidəblē, -bli\ *adv* **:** OBEDIENTLY, DOCILELY

bid·dance \ˈbidᵊn(t)s\ *n* -s **:** the act of bidding **:** INVITATION, COMMAND

bidden *past part of* BID, *archaic past part of* BIDE

bid·der \ˈbidə(r)\ *n* -s [ME *biddere*, fr. OE, *petitioner*, fr. *biddan* to entreat + *-ere* -er — more at BID] **:** a person who bids: as **a :** one that commands or orders **b :** the giver of an invitation **c :** the maker of a bid (as at an auction or in a card game)

bid·der's ganglion \ˈbidə(r)z-\ *n, usu cap B* [after Friedrich H. *Bidder* †1894 Ger. physician] **:** a nerve-cell ganglion in the vicinity of the atrioventricular groove in frogs

bidder's organ *n, usu cap B* **:** a rudimentary ovary present near the fat body in both sexes of some toads sometimes becoming functional in old males

bid·dery \ˈbid(ə)rē\ *var of* BIDRI

bid·ding \ˈbidiŋ, -dēŋ\ *n* -s [ME *biddinge, bidding*, fr. *bidden* to entreat, pray, command + *-inge*, *-ing* -ing] **1** *archaic* **:** ENTREATY, PRAYER **2 a :** the act of making bids; *also* **:** the period during which bids are made (as in a card game or at an auction) **b :** an offer of a price **3 :** COMMAND, INJUNCTION, ORDER, BEHEST, DIRECTION, SUMMONS ⟨I shall give up all the joys of life at your ~⟩ ⟨writing only at the ~ of a deep love of nature⟩; *sometimes* **:** INVITATION ⟨we gathered at his ~⟩

bidding prayer *n* **1 :** a prayer said in English churches down to the Reformation for those living and dead whose names were on the list of persons to be prayed for **2 :** a prayer taking the form of a series of petitions for specified objects or classes of persons said esp. in Anglican churches before the sermon

bid·dul·phia \bəˈdəlfēə\ *n, cap* [NL, prob. fr. G. *Biddulph*, 19th cent. Eng. botanist + NL *-ia*] **:** a large genus (the type of the family Biddulphiaceae) of rectangular diatoms having winglike or hornlike projections at the corners of the valves and being locally abundant in the marine plankton

[1]**bid·dy** \ˈbidē, -di\ *n* -ES [perh. of imit. origin] **1 a :** an adult female domestic fowl — often used as a call **b :** a young chicken ⟨a hen and her *biddies*⟩ **2 :** any of various wild fowls in some respect suggesting a domestic hen

[2]**biddy** \"\ *also* **biddie** *n* -ES [dim. of *Bridget* (the name)] **1 :** a hired girl or maidservant; *esp* **:** an elderly impoverished or cleaning woman in a dormitory **2 :** WOMAN: **a :** an elderly and often gossipy or dissolute woman — used disparagingly **b :** a young woman — often used disparagingly **c** *slang* **:** a female school teacher **3 :** a toothless old ewe **:** GUMMER

biddy–bid \ˈbidēˌbid\ *also* **biddy–biddy** \ˈ==ˌ==\ *or* **bid–a–bid** \ˈbidəˌbid\ *n* -s [modif. of Maori *piripiri*] **1** *NewZeal* **:** PIRIPIRI **2** *NewZeal* **:** the bur of piripiri

bide \ˈbīd\ *vb* **bode** \ˈbōd\ *or* **bided** \ˈbīdəd\ *also* **bade** \ˈbad, ˈbaa(ə)d\ *or archaic* **bad; bided** *or archaic* **bid** *or* **biden** *or* **bidden; biding; bides** [ME *biden*, fr. OE *bīdan;* akin to OHG *bītan* to wait, ON *bītha*, Goth *beidan* to wait, L *fidere* to trust, Gk *peithesthai* to believe, be persuaded, obey, Russ *beda* misfortune] *vi* **1 :** to continue in some state or condition ⟨~ still until you feel better⟩ **2 a :** WAIT, TARRY — used esp. with an expression of time ⟨~ yet a little⟩ **b** *of things* **:** to await one's pleasure **:** be left unchanged ⟨let the matter ~⟩ **3 :** ABIDE, SOJOURN, DWELL ⟨the old man still ~*s* in the shanty though the mill has fallen to ruin⟩ ~ *vt* **1** *past usu* **bided :** to wait for ⟨their ready answer suggested that they had long *bided* that demand⟩ — now used chiefly in the phrase *bide one's time* **2** *archaic* **:** to encounter and resist **:** WITHSTAND, FACE ⟨the ships that ~ the storm⟩ **3** *now chiefly dial* **:** to put up with **:** TOLERATE, ENDURE ⟨couldn't ~ children on his place —J.W.Riley⟩ ⟨aggregated power does not readily ~ legal restraints —M.O.Hudson — **bide by** *archaic* **:** abide by

bi·dens \ˈbīˌdenz\ *n, cap* [NL, fr. L, having two teeth, 2-pronged, fr. *bi-* [1]*bi-* + *dent-, dens* tooth — more at TOOTH] **:** a large genus of herbs (family Compositae) native to the warmer parts of both hemispheres that have divided or compound leaves and yellow flowers and the usu. flattened achenes armed with barbed awns — see BEGGAR-TICKS, BUR MARIGOLD, SPANISH NEEDLE

bi·dent \ˈbīdᵊnt\ *n* -s [L *bident-, bidens*, fr. *bident-, bidens* 2-pronged] **:** a 2-pronged instrument

bi·dentate \(ˈ)bī+\ *adj* [fr. (assumed) NL *bidentatus*, fr. NL [1]*bi-* + *-dentatus* -dentate] **:** having two teeth or two processes suggestive of teeth

bi·denticulate \(ˈ)bī+\ *adj* [[1]*bi-* + *denticulate*] *biol* **:** having two small teeth

bid·er \ˈbīdə(r)\ *n* -s **:** one that bides

bi·det \bēˈdet, bəˈ-, ˈdā\ *n* -s [F, fr. MF, fr. *bider* to trot] **1 :** a small horse esp. in pack or courier service in an army **2 :** a vessel about the height of the seat of a chair that often has fixtures for running water and is used esp. for bathing the external genitals and the posterior parts of the body

bi·di \ˈbē(ˌ)dē\ *var of* BIRI

bi·di–bi·di \ˌbēdēˌbēdē\ *n* -s [modif. of Maori *piripiri*] **:** PIRIPIRI

bi·digitate \(ˈ)bī+\ *adj* [fr. (assumed) NL *bidigitatus*, fr. NL [1]*bi-* + L *digitatus* digitate] **:** having two fingers or digitate projections or parts

bi·dimensional \(ˈ)bī+\ *adj* [[1]*bi-* + *dimensional*] **:** having or perceived in terms of two dimensions — **bi·dimensionality** \(ˌ)bī+\ *n* -ES

bid in *vt* **:** to retain (property offered at auction) by overbidding the highest offer of a bona fide customer

bid·ing \ˈbīdiŋ\ *n* -s [ME *bidinge, biding*, fr. OE *bīding*, fr. *bīdan* to bide + *-ung, -ing* -ing] **1** *archaic* **:** an awaiting or remaining **:** STAY, RESIDENCE **2** *obs* **:** a lodging place **:** ABODE

biding place *n, archaic* **:** a place of abode **:** lodging place

bi·directional \(ˈ)bī+\ *adj* [[1]*bi-* + *directional*] **:** reactive or functioning in two usu. opposite directions; *esp of a microphone* **:** having two sensitive areas

bid off *vt* **:** to receive (property offered at auction) immediately upon one's bid

bid price *n* **:** the price that a buyer offers to pay

bid·ri \ˈbidrē\ *n* -s [Hindi *bidrī*, fr. *Bidar*, town in India] **:** a pewter formerly used in India for making ware inlaid with gold or silver; *also* **:** BIDRI WARE

bidri ware *n* **:** the ware made by inlaying bidri

bids *pl of* BID, *pres 3d sing of* BID

bid up *vt* **:** to raise the price of (as property at auction) by a succession of offers ⟨the dealer clique *bid up* everything worth having to shut out the amateurs⟩; *also* **:** to raise (the price of something) by such means ⟨they *bid* the prices *up* sky-high to maintain their monopoly⟩

bid whist *n* **:** whist in which the players bid for the privilege of naming the suit to be trump

bie·ber·ite \ˈbēbəˌrīt\ *n* -s [G *bieberit*, fr. *Bieber*, town in Hesse, Germany + G *-it* -ite] **:** a mineral $CoSO_4.7H_2O$ consisting of hydrous cobalt sulfate occurring esp. in pale red crusts and stalactites

bie·brich scarlet \ˈbēˌbrik-\ *n, usu cap B & often cap S* [prob. trans. of G *biebricher scharlach*, fr. *Biebrich*, former city (now part of Wiesbaden), Prussia, Germany] **:** PONCEAU 3RB

[1]**bie·der·mei·er** \ˈbēdə(r)ˌmīə(r)\ *adj, usu cap* [after Gottlieb *Biedermeier* ("Papa Biedermeier"), satirical name for a simple, fussy, uninspired Ger. bourgeois, the imaginary author of poems by Adolf Kussmaul †1902, Ludwig Eichrodt †1892, and others] **1** *of furniture* **:** of a type developed in Germany between 1815 and 1848, derived from French Empire styles but at once simpler in detail and weaker and heavier in design **2 :** artistically, intellectually, or socially staid, conventional, humdrum, limited; *also* **:** bourgeois or Philistine ⟨*Biedermeier* writers⟩ ⟨a comfortable *Biedermeier* pastor⟩

[2]**biedermeier** \"\ *n* -s *usu cap* **:** one that is Biedermeier ⟨the story was a nice piece of *Biedermeier*⟩

bielby *var of* BILBY

[1]**bield** \ˈbē(ə)l(d)\ *vt* [ME *belden* to assist, encourage, protect, fr. OE *beldan, byldan* to encourage, denominative fr. the stem of OE *bald, beald* bold — more at BOLD] *now chiefly Scot* **:** SHELTER, PROTECT

[2]**bield** \"\ *n* -s [ME *belde* shelter, confidence, boldness, fr. OE *beldo, byldo* boldness; akin to OHG *baldī* boldness, Goth *balthei*; derivative fr. the stem of OE *bald, beald* bold] **1** *chiefly Scot* **:** SHELTER, PROTECTION **2** *chiefly Scot* **a :** a place affording shelter **:** REFUGE **b :** a habitation for man or beast

bieldy \-ldē\ *adj* [[2]*bield* + *-y*] *chiefly Scot* **:** SHELTERING

bie·le·feld \ˈbēləˌfelt\ *adj, usu cap* [fr. *Bielefeld*, Germany] **:** of or from the city of Bielefeld, Germany **:** of the kind or style prevalent in Bielefeld

bielorussian *usu cap, var of* BELORUSSIAN

bien \ˈbēn\ *adj* [ME *bene* pleasant, comfortable, in good condition] **1** *Scot* **a :** COMFORTABLE, COZY, SNUG **b :** PROSPEROUS, WELL-TO-DO **2** *obs slang* **:** GOOD, FINE

[1]**bi·en·ni·al** \(ˈ)bīˌenēəl, -nyəl\ *adj* [L *biennium* period of two years (fr. *bi-* + *-ennium*, fr. *annus* year) + E *-al* — more at ANNUAL] **1 :** occurring, appearing, or being made, done, or acted upon every two years — compare BIANNUAL **2 :** continuing or lasting for two years — used specif. of plants (as the parsnip) that require two growing seasons in which to go from seed to seed; compare ANNUAL

[2]**biennial** \"\ *n* -s **:** something that is biennial (as an exhibition or examination); *esp* **:** a biennial plant

biennial bearing *n* **:** the production of a heavy crop one year followed by a light or no crop the next (as in certain varieties of apple trees) — called also *alternate bearing*

bi·en·ni·al·ly \-əlē, -li\ *adv* **:** every two years

bi·en·ni·um \(ˈ)bīˌenēəm\ *n, pl* **bienniums** \-mz\ *or* **bien·nia** \-nēə\ [L] **:** a period of two years

bien·ve·nue *also* **bienvenu** \byaⁿv(ə)nü\ *n* -s [ME *bienvenue*, fr. MF, fr. OF, fr. *bienvenu* welcome (adj.), fr. *bien* well (fr. L *bene*, adv. of *bonus* good) + *venu*, past part. of *venir* to come, fr. L *venire* — more at BOUNTY, COME] **1 :** WELCOME — formerly common in English but now usu. a conscious borrowing from the French **2** *obs* **:** a fee demanded of a new workman by his fellows

[1]**bier** \ˈbi(ə)r, ˈbiə\ *n* -s [ME *bere*, fr. OE *bǣr, bēr;* akin to OS & OHG *bāra* bier; derivative fr. the stem of OE *beran* to carry — more at BEAR] **1** *archaic* **:** a framework (as a litter or stretcher) for carrying; *also* **:** HANDBARROW **2 :** a stand on which a corpse or coffin is placed or carried to the grave; *sometimes* **:** a coffin and the stand on which it is placed **3** *archaic* **:** the place where someone is buried **:** GRAVE, SEPULCHER

[2]**bier** *var of* BEER

bier·mer's anemia \ˈbirmərz-\ *also* **biermer's disease** *n, usu cap B* [after Anton *Biermer* †1892 Ger. physician] **:** PERNICIOUS ANEMIA

bier right *n* **:** an ordeal formerly used to test the guilt of one accused of murder by requiring him to vindicate himself in the presence of the corpse, the victim's wounds being believed to bleed afresh if the body were touched by the murderer

bier·stu·be \ˈbirˌs(h)tübə\ *n, pl* **bierstubes** \-bəz\ *or* **bier·stu·ben** \-bən\ [G, fr. *bier* beer (fr. OHG *bior*) + *stube* room (fr. OHG *stuba* heated room) — more at BEER, STOVE] **:** a room or other place (as in a German or German-style tavern) used primarily for the serving of beer

biestings *var of* BEASTINGS

bi·face *also* **bi·facial** \ˈbī+ˌ-\ *n* [*biface* prob. back-formation fr. *bifacial*, adj.; *bifacial*, n. fr. *bifacial*, adj.] *archaeol* **:** a stone tool usu. of flint made from a core flattened on both sides **:** HAND AX

bi·facial \(ˈ)bī+\ *adj* [[1]*bi-* + *facial*] **:** having opposite surfaces alike (as of certain chipped flint tools or some leaves); *sometimes* **:** having two fronts ⟨a representation of the Roman Janus is ~⟩

bifacially \(ˈ)bī+\ *adv* **:** on two sides

bi·fanged \(ˈ)bī+\ *adj* [[1]*bi-* + *fanged*] *of a tooth* **:** having two roots

bif·a·ra \ˈbifərə\ *n* -s [perh. fr. It *bifara, bifra*] **:** an organ stop of 8-foot or 4-foot pitch in which each pipe has two mouths of which one is cut a little higher than the other, causing a gentle vibrato effect; *also* **:** a similar stop with two ranks of pipes one of which is slightly sharped to produce a comparable vibrato effect

bi·far·i·ous \(ˈ)bīˈfa(a)rēəs\ *adj* [L *bifarius*, fr. *bifariam* in two ways, fr. *bi-* [1]*bi-* + *-fariam* (akin to Skt root *dhā* in *dvidhā* in two ways, *dadhāti* he places, sets) — more at DO] *archaic* **:** TWOFOLD, AMBIGUOUS ⟨some strange, mysterious verity in old ~ prophesy —Ned Ward⟩ — **bi·far·i·ous·ly** *adv*

[1]**biff** \ˈbif\ *n* -s [prob. imit.] *slang* **:** WHACK, BLOW

[2]**biff** \"\ *vt* -ED/-ING/-S **1** *slang* **:** to deal a blow to **:** WHACK, SOCK **2** *chiefly Austral* **:** THROW

bif·fin \ˈbifən\ *n* -s [earlier *beefen*, fr. obs. *beefin* ox for slaughter, fr. ME, fr. (assumed) ME *beefing*, fr. ME *beef* + *-ing* one of a (specified) kind; fr. its deep-red color — more at -ING] **1 :** an English apple of a variety often sold after being dried in the oven **2** *Brit* **:** an apple that has been baked and flattened into a cake

bif·fy \ˈbifē\ *n* -ES [origin unknown] *slang* **:** TOILET; *often* **:** OUTHOUSE, PRIVY

bi·fid \ˈbīˌfid, -ˌfəd\ *adj* [L *bifidus*, fr. *bi-* [1]*bi-* + *-fidus* (fr. the stem of L *findere* to split) — more at BITE] **1 :** divided into two equal lobes or parts by a median cleft ⟨a ~ leaf⟩ ⟨claws ~⟩ **2** *of a cipher alphabet* **:** constructed by matching the letters of the alphabet with 2-unit equivalents of such a nature that exactly as many of them can be constructed as there are letters of the alphabet (as by using the 25 possible pairs made up of combinations of one or more of the numerals 1,2,3,4, and 5 for a 25-letter alphabet) — compare FRACTIONAL SUBSTITUTION — **bi·fid·i·ty** \bīˈfidəd·ē\ *n* -ES — **bi·fid·ly** *adv*

bi·filar \(ˈ)bī+\ *adj* [ISV [1]*bi-* + *fil-* (fr. L *filum* thread) + *-ar* — more at FILE] **1 :** composed of or employing two threads or wires ⟨a ~ suspension of a waving part of an instrument⟩ **2 :** composed of or employing a single thread or wire doubled back upon itself ⟨~ winding of a resistance coil⟩ — **bi·filarly** *adv*

bi·flabellate \ˌbī+\ *adj* [fr. (assumed) NL *biflabellatus*, fr. NL [1]*bi-* + (assumed) NL *flabellatus* flabellate] *of an insect antenna* **:** having short joints with long flattened processes on opposite sides

bi·flagellate \(ˈ)bī+\ *adj* [[1]*bi-* + *flagellate*] **:** having two flagella ⟨a ~ zoospore⟩

bi·fluoride \(ˈ)bī+\ *n* -s [ISV [1]*bi-* + *fluoride*] **:** an acid fluoride of the formula MHF_2 (as lithium bifluoride $LiHF_2$)

[1]**bi·focal** \(ˈ)bī+\ *adj* [ISV [1]*bi-* + *focal*] **1 a :** having two focal lengths **b** *of an eyeglass lens* **:** having one part that corrects for near vision and one for distant vision **2 :** marked by two distinct often seemingly incompatible approaches or points of view ⟨the ~ nature of medieval historiography with its mixture of myth and history —Keith Spalding⟩ ⟨an Indian, educated in England and America, and hence able to give a sort of ~ view of the people and problems of Asia —*Nation*⟩

[2]**bifocal** \"\ *n* -s **1 :** a bifocal glass or lens **2 bifocals** *pl* **:** eyeglasses with bifocal lenses

bi·fold \(ˈ)bī+\ *adj* [[1]*bi-* + *-fold*] **:** TWOFOLD, DOUBLE

bi·foliate \(ˈ)bī+\ *adj* [fr. (assumed) NL *bifoliatus*, fr. NL [1]*bi-* + L *foliatus* leaved — more at FOLIATE] **1 :** two-leaved **2 :** BIFOLIOLATE

bi·foliolate \(ˈ)bī+\ *adj* [fr. (assumed) NL *bifoliolatus*, fr. NL [1]*bi-* + LL *foliolum* foliole + L *-atus* -ate — more at FOLIOLE] *of compound leaves* **:** having two leaflets

bi·follicular \ˌbī+\ *adj* [[1]*bi-* + *follicular*] **:** having two follicles or twin pods esp. of milkweed

bi·fo·rate \(ˈ)bīˌfōˌrāt, ˈbīfə-, ˈbifə-, (ˈ)bīˈfōrət\ *adj* [fr. (assumed) NL *biforatus*, fr. NL [1]*bi-* + L *foratus* pierced, bored, past part. of *forare* to bore — more at BORE] *biol* **:** having two perforations

bi·forked \(ˈ)bī+\ *adj* [[1]*bi-* + *forked*] **:** so forked as to have two branches or peaks

bi·form \ˈbī+ˌ-\ *adj* [*biform* fr. L *biformis*, fr. *bi-* [1]*bi-* + *-formis* (fr. *forma* form); *biformed* fr. L *biformis* + E *-ed* — more at FORM] **1 :** combining the qualities or forms of two distinct kinds of individuals ⟨a ~ crystal⟩ ⟨the ~ body of a satyr⟩ **2 :** having or appearing in two dissimilar guises — used of characters in classical mythology that appeared to mortals in other than their customary bodily form ⟨whence Europa fled with ~ Jove⟩

biformed *obs var of* BIFORM

bi·fo·rous \ˈbifərəs, ˈbīf-\ *adj* [L *biforus* having two doors, fr. *bi-* [1]*bi-* + *-forus* (fr. *fores* door) — more at DOOR] **:** BIFORATE

bi·front \ˈbī+ˌ-\ *or* **bi·fronted** \(ˈ)bī+\ *adj* [L *bifront-, bifrons*, fr. *bi-* [1]*bi-* + *front-, frons* forehead; *bifronted* fr. L *bifront-, bifrons* + E *-ed* — more at BRINK] *archaic* **:** having two faces or fronts

bi·furcal \(ˈ)bī+\ *adj* [L *bifurcus* 2-pronged (fr. *bi-* [1]*bi-* + *-furcus*, fr. *furca* fork) + E *-al* — more at FORK] **:** BIFURCATE

[1]**bi·fur·cate** \ˈbīfə(r)ˌkāt, (ˈ)bīˌfərˌkāt, -ˌfə-, *usu* -d·+V\ *vb* -ED/-ING/-S [ML *bifurcatus*, past part. of *bifurcare* to bifurcate, fr. L *bifurcus*] *vi* **:** to branch or separate into two parts — often used with *into* ⟨the stream *bifurcated* into two narrow winding channels⟩ ~ *vt* **:** to cause to branch or separate into two parts ⟨it might be possible to ~ the beam of light⟩ **syn** see BRANCH

[2]**bifurcate** \ˈbīfə(r)ˌkāt, -kət; (ˈ)bīˌfərkət, -ˌfək-, -ˌkāt, *usu* -d·+V\ *adj* [ML *bifurcatus*, past part. of *bifurcare*] **:** divided into two branches **:** DICHOTOMOUS — used chiefly of physical objects — **bi·furcately** *adv*

bifurcate collateral *adj, of kinship name classes* **:** distinguishing collateral relatives both from lineal relatives of the same generation and from one another on the basis of the sex of connecting relatives

bifurcated *adj* [fr. past part. of [1]*bifurcate*] **1 :** BIFURCATE **2 :** combining or made up of two aspects, factors, or parts ⟨a ~ E layer in the ionosphere⟩ ⟨socially ~ populations⟩; *sometimes* **:** BIFOCAL 2 ⟨Freneau's peculiarly ~ view of the Indian, his agrarianism and primitivism, his warm humanitarianism —J.T.Flanagan⟩

bifurcate merging *adj, of kinship name classes* **:** identifying collateral relatives with lineal relatives of the same sex and generation when the connecting relative is of the same sex but distinguishing them when the connecting relative is of the opposite sex ⟨in a *bifurcate merging* terminology a father's brother would be identified as father but a mother's brother as uncle⟩

bi·furcation \ˌbī+\ *n* -s [F *bifurcation*, prob. fr. NL *bifurcation-, bifurcatio*, fr. ML *bifurcatus* + L *-ion-, -io* -ion] **1 :** separation or branching into two parts, areas, aspects, or connected segments ⟨the Cartesian ~ of reality into mind and matter⟩ **2 :** the point at which bifurcation occurs — used almost wholly of physical objects ⟨inflammation may occlude the ~ of the trachea⟩ **3 :** either member of a pair produced by bifurcation **:** BRANCH ⟨the left ~ of the common iliac artery⟩ ⟨a ~ of the Japan current that carries warmth and moisture to the Alaska coastline⟩

[1]**big** \ˈbig\ *adj* **bigger; biggest** [ME, prob. of Scand origin; akin to Norw dial. *bugge* important man — more at BOAST] **1 a** *obs* **:** of great physical strength **:** powerful in body ⟨Sir Launcelot was ~ and strong again —Thomas Malory⟩ **b :** of great force or vehemence **:** VIOLENT ⟨farewell the ~ wars that make ambition virtue —Shak.⟩ — now used only of natural phenomena ⟨the night of the ~ blow⟩ **2 :** LARGE 4a: **a :** large in physical dimensions, bulk, or mass ⟨a ~ bag of potatoes⟩ ⟨the ~ white house on the hill⟩ **b :** of great extent ⟨a ~ tract of open country⟩ **c :** large in magnitude ⟨a ~ change from our simple country life⟩; *also* **:** large in quantity, number, or amount ⟨a ~ fleet⟩ **d :** formed or conducted on a large scale ⟨~ government⟩ ⟨a ~ merchandising combine⟩ **e :** having the largeness of — used chiefly in the comparative ⟨a little fish scarcely *bigger* than a mosquito larva⟩ **3 :** FULL: **a :** PREGNANT; *esp* **:** nearly ready to give birth — usu. used with *with* ⟨a white heifer ~ with calf⟩ **b :** full to bursting **:** FILLED, BRIMMING, SWELLING, TEEMING — usu. used with *with* ⟨eyes ~ with tears⟩ ⟨~ with rage⟩ ⟨no period *bigger* with opportunity for the daring man⟩ **c** *of the voice* **:** full and resonant **4 :** conspicuous or noteworthy in some respect: **a :** CHIEF, LEADING, PREEMINENT ⟨the ~ issue of this campaign⟩ ⟨the ~ shopping center is on 10th Avenue⟩ **b :** NOTORIOUS, BAD — used esp. in the superlative ⟨the *biggest* rascal on two feet⟩ **c :** OUTSTANDING, PROMINENT ⟨a ~ banker⟩; *esp* **:** outstandingly worthy or able ⟨a truly ~ man⟩ ⟨the *bigger* they are the harder they fall⟩ **d :** of importance, moment, or significance **:** IMPRESSIVE ⟨the ~ moment of his life⟩ ⟨a ~ piece of news⟩ **e :** IMPOSING, HIGH-SOUNDING, PRETENTIOUS ⟨such ~ words to put abroad such petty thoughts⟩; *often* **:** BOASTFUL, POMPOUS, THREATENING ⟨his ~ words were never backed by deeds⟩ **f :** having or showing greatness of spirit **:** MAGNANIMOUS, GENEROUS ⟨a heart ~ enough to hold no grudges⟩ ⟨he can be trusted to do the ~ thing⟩ — **too big for one's breeches** *also* **too big for one's pants** *or* **too big for one's boots :** exhibiting self-approval not justified by circumstances **:** above oneself

[2]**big** \"\ *adv* **1 :** to a large amount or extent **:** LARGELY ⟨pay ~ for a privilege⟩ ⟨I eat ~ in the mornings⟩ **2 :** in a big manner **:** to a marked degree: **a** *slang* **:** so as to bring notable success or advantage ⟨if the new line goes ~ he should clean up a fortune⟩ **:** with pronounced effect ⟨the only one to score ~ was George S. Kaufman —*Time*⟩ **b :** POMPOUSLY, PRETENTIOUSLY ⟨to talk ~⟩ **c :** BRAVELY, COURAGEOUSLY ⟨taking his losses ~⟩ **3** *dial* **:** VERY, EXTREMELY ⟨~ rich⟩ ⟨~ lazy⟩

[3]**big** \"\ *vt* **bigged; bigged; bigging; bigs** *chiefly Midland* **:** IMPREGNATE **:** make pregnant

[4]**big** \"\ *n* -s **:** an individual or organization of outstanding importance or power ⟨competition with the ~s of the aviation industry⟩

[5]**big** \"\ *vt* **bigged; bigged; bigging; bigs** [ME *biggen* to build, dwell, inhabit, fr. ON *byggja;* akin to OE *bēon* to be — more at BE] *dial Brit* **:** BUILD, CONSTRUCT, ERECT ⟨~ a new house⟩

BIG *abbr* best in group

bi·ga \ˈbē(ˌ)gä, ˈbī-, -gə\ *n, pl* **bi·gae** \ˈbēˌgī, -(ˌ)gē,-(ˌ)jē; ˈbī(ˌ)jē\ [L, fr. *bi-* [1]*bi-* + *-ga* (fr. *jugum* yoke) — more at YOKE] **:** a two-horse chariot of ancient Mediterranean countries

big·a·mist \ˈbigəməst\ *n* -s [*bigamy* + *-ist*] **:** one that practices bigamy; *esp* **:** one that has two wives or mates at the same time — **big·a·mis·tic** \ˌ==ˈmistik, -tēk\ *adj*

big·a·mize \ˈ==ˌmīz\ *vi* -ED/-ING/-S [*bigamy* + *-ize*] **:** to commit bigamy

big·a·mous \ˈbigəməs\ *adj* [*bigamy* + *-ous*] **1 :** guilty of bigamy ⟨a ~ man⟩ **2 :** involving bigamy ⟨a ~ marriage⟩ — **big·a·mous·ly** *adv*

big·a·my \-mē, -mi\ *n* -ES [ME *bigamie*, fr. ML *bigamia*, fr. L *bi-* [1]*bi-* + LL *-gamia* -gamy, fr. Gk, fr. *gamos* marriage + *-ia* -y; akin to L *gener* son-in-law, Skt *jāmi* being a brother or sister, *jāmī* daughter-in-law] **1** *criminal law* **a :** unlawful polygamy **b :** the statutory offense of entering into a ceremonial marriage with one person while still legally married to another **2** *canon law* **:** any of several offenses that disqualify one from holding ecclesiastical office or entering holy orders: **a :** the offense of marrying two persons successively whether the first spouse be dead or divorced or of marrying a widow — called also *real bigamy* **b :** the offense of marrying one already carnally known by another — called also *interpretative bigamy* **c :** the offense of one in holy orders or under a vow of continence in marrying anyone

big apple *n, often cap B&A* **:** a jazz dance combining circular group formations with improvised solos and duets

big·a·rade \'bigə,räd\ *n* -s [F, fr. Prov *bigarrado*, fr. past part. of *bigarra* to variegate, fr. (assumed) OProv *bigarrar*, prob. fr. MF *bigarrer*] **:** SOUR ORANGE ⟨roast duck with a sauce ~⟩

big·ar·reau cherry \,bigə¦rō-\ *also* **bigarreau** *n* -s *usu cap B* [F *bigarreau*, fr. MF, fr. *bigarrer* to variegate, fr. *bi-* ¹bi- + *-garrer* (fr. *garre* variegated)] **:** any of several cultivated sweet cherries with rather firm, often light-colored globular fruits — compare DUKE 5, HEART CHERRY

big bedbug *n* **:** CONENOSE

big bertha *n, usu cap both Bs* [approximate trans. of G *dicke Bertha*, lit., fat Bertha, after Frau *Bertha* Krupp von Bohlen und Halbach †1957 proprietress of the Krupp Works, Essen, Germany, where during the First World War a particularly celebrated and effective 42-centimeter mortar was made] **1 :** a German gun of large bore or of long range used in World War I **2 a :** something large or cumbersome of its kind — used esp. of machines or tools **b :** something effective at long range — used esp. of cameras and photographic lenses

bigbloom \'=,=\ *n* **:** LARGE-LEAVED MAGNOLIA

big bluegrass *n* **:** a grass (*Poa ampla*) used in the Pacific Northwest for forage and pasture having flat leaf blades, glabrous sheaths, and spikelets that are little compressed and have the lemma obscurely keeled

big bluestem *n* **:** BLUESTEM 1a

big board *n, often cap both Bs, often attrib* **:** a quotation board for securities listed on the New York Stock Exchange; *also* **:** the exchange

big–boned \'=¦=\ *adj* **:** having the skeletal structure large and rugged in comparison to the fleshy parts **:** somewhat rawboned

big–bore \'=¦=\ *adj* **1** *of firearms* **:** having a large or relatively large caliber — distinguished from *small-bore* **2 :** of, relating to, or involving the use of big-bore firearms ⟨*big-bore* shooting⟩

big boss *n* **:** the person ultimately in charge of an enterprise (as the active head of a business enterprise or the officer in charge of a military organization)

big boy *n* **:** a man of prominence in some organization or field of endeavor

big brother *n* **1 :** an older brother **2 :** one that is like or likened to an older brother: **a :** a man who befriends a delinquent or friendless boy **b** *often cap both Bs* [*Big Brother*, a personification of the power of the state in *1984* (1949) by George Orwell (Eric Blair) †1950 Eng. author] (1) **:** the leader of an authoritarian state or movement (2) **:** such a state or movement — called also *Big Brotherism*

big brown bat *n* **:** a rather large widely distributed No. American bat (*Eptesicus fuscus*) having soft loose brown fur, naked flight membranes, and moderately short rounded ears

big bud *n* **1 :** any of several diseases of plants characterized by abnormal swelling of the buds: as **a :** such a condition in currants caused by a gall mite (*Eriophyes ribis*) **b :** a virus disease of the tomato **2** *also* **big–bud hickory :** MOCKERNUT

big bug *n, slang* **:** a person of consequence **:** BIGWIG

big business *n* **1 :** large aggregations of capital and business organizations; *esp* **:** monopolies or trusts regarded collectively — often used derogatorily **2 :** any business having a large turnover and income **3 :** an institution of prominence or importance; *sometimes* **:** a nonbusiness organization unpleasantly suggestive in its methods or acts of big business (sense 1)

big casino *n, in casino* **:** the ten of diamonds for winning which a score of two is earned

big cat *n* **:** a hand recognized in some poker games that consists of king, queen, jack, ten, and eight, contains no pairs, includes cards from two or more suits, and ranks next below a flush — compare LITTLE CAT

big cheese *n, slang* **:** a person of consequence **:** BIGWIG

big chief *n, slang* **:** an important or influential person

big–city \'=¦==\ *adj* **:** typical of or restricted to large urban areas ⟨*big-city* delinquency problems⟩

big–cone pine \'=,=-\ *n* **:** COULTER PINE

big–cone spruce *n* **:** an evergreen tree (*Pseudotsuga macrocarpa*) of the western U.S. having cones 4 to 7½ inches long with their bracts protruding little beyond the scales — compare DOUGLAS FIR

big crab *n* **:** DUNGENESS CRAB

big dick *n, usu cap B&D, in craps, slang* **:** a throw of 10

big ditch *n* **:** a large artificial water channel (as the Erie Canal or the main channel of an irrigation system) — usu. cap. when designating a particular channel ⟨when the *Big Ditch* finally joined the Atlantic and Pacific oceans⟩

big drum *n* **:** BLACK DRUM

big–eared bat \'=,=-\ *n* **:** any of numerous bats having exceptionally large ears (as members of a No. American genus *Corynorhines* or of an Old World tropical family Megadermatidae)

big–eared fox *n* **:** LONG-EARED FOX

big·e·lowia \,bigə'lōēə\ *n* [NL, fr. Jacob *Bigelow* †1879 Am. physician and botanist + NL *-ia*] **1** *cap* **:** a genus of herbaceous or shrubby plants (family Compositae) with alternate linear or lanceolate leaves and flower heads arranged in corymbs **2** -s **:** a plant of the genus *Bigelowia*

big·em·i·nal \(')bī¦jemənəl\ *adj* [LL *bigeminus* doubled (fr. L *bi-* ¹bi- + *geminus* twofold, twin) + E *-al* — more at GEMINI] **:** DOUBLE, PAIRED ⟨the ~ optic parts of the brain in fishes⟩

bigeminal pulse *n, med* **:** a pulse characterized by two beats close together with a pause following each pair of beats

bi·geminate *also* **bi·geminated** \(')bī+\ *adj* [*bigeminate* fr. (assumed) NL *bigeminatus*, fr. NL ¹*bi-* + L *geminatus* geminate; *bigeminated* fr. (assumed) NL *bigeminatus* + E *-ed*] **:** twice geminate **:** having two pairs: **a :** BICONJUGATE **b** *mineralogy* **:** having two pairs of crystal forms

bi·gem·i·ny \bī'jeməne\ *n* -ES [ISV *bigemin-* (fr. LL *bigeminus* doubled) + *-y*] **:** the state of being bigeminal; *specif* **:** that of having a bigeminal pulse

big end *n* **:** the crankpin end of an engine connecting rod

bi·ge·ner \'bījənə(r)\ *n* -s [L, hybrid (adj.), fr. *bi-* ¹bi- + *gener-, genus* kind, race — more at KIN] **:** a bigeneric hybrid

bi·generic \¦bī+\ *adj* [*bigener* + *-ic*] **:** of, relating to, or involving two genera ⟨a ~ hybrid is produced by interbreeding members of species belonging to different genera and is rare in nature⟩

big·eye \'bi,gī\ *n* **:** either of two small widely distributed catalufas (*Priacanthus cruentatus* and *P. arenatus*) that are reddish to silvery and esteemed as food in areas where they are abundant

bigeye bass *or* **big–eyed bass** *n* **:** a small percoid fish (*Xenistius californiensis*) of the coast of California sometimes used as bait or for food

big–eyed \'=¦=\ *adj* **:** having big eyes; *also* **:** ASTONISHED **:** deeply impressed **:** WONDERING ⟨*big-eyed* with delight⟩

big–eyed bug *n* **:** a lygaeid bug; *esp* **:** any of certain bugs of the genus *Geocoris* that suck the juices from and destroy large numbers of leafhoppers

big–eyed herring *n* **1 :** TENPOUNDER **2 :** an alewife (*Pomolobus pseudoharengus*)

big–eyed mackerel *n* **:** CHUB MACKEREL

big–eyed scad *or* **bigeye scad** *n* **:** a small carangid fish (*Trachurops crumenophthalmus*) with large prominent eyes that is widely distributed in tropical seas and in some areas is an important food fish — called also *akule, goggler*

big four yellow *n, often cap B&F* **:** a strong to vivid orange that is slightly yellower and lighter than Navaho and redder than orpiment orange

bigg \'big\ *var of* ⁵BIG

²bigg \"\ *n* -s [ME *byge*, fr. ON *bygg* barley; akin to OE *bēow* barley and perh. to Gk *phyein* to bring forth — more at BE] *dial Brit* **:** FOUR-ROWED BARLEY

biggah *var of* BIGHA

big–gait·ed \'=¦==\ *adj, of a horse* **:** having a long easy stride

big game *n* **1 :** the large animals sought or taken by hunting or fishing for pleasure rather than profit ⟨*big game* angling is not without its risks⟩ **2 :** an important object of quest; *esp* **:** one involving risk

bigged *past of* BIG

big·gen \'bigən\ *vi* -ED/-ING/-S [¹*big* + *-en*] *now dial Brit* **:** to become big **:** increase in size

bigger *comparative of* BIG

biggest *superlative of* BIG

big·gety *or* **big·gity** \'bigəd·ē, -ətē, -i\ *adj* [prob. fr. ¹*big* + *-ety* or *-ity* (as in *persnickety* or *persnickity*)] **1** *South & Midland* **:** CONCEITED, VAIN **2** *South & Midland* **:** rudely self-important **:** assertively independent **:** IMPUDENT ⟨all that ~ talk of his⟩ ⟨a little authority and some folks act mighty ~⟩

big·gie *also* **big·gy** \'bigē\ *n* -s [¹*big* + *-ie* or *-y*] *slang* **1 :** one that is big **2 :** a person of consequence **:** BIG SHOT, BIGWIG

¹big·gin *or* **big·ging** \'bigən\ *n* -s [ME *bigginge, bigging*, fr. *biggen* to build, dwell, inhabit + *-inge, -ing* — more at ⁵BIG] *dial Brit* **:** any of certain buildings: as **a :** HOUSE **b :** OUTBUILDING

²biggin \"\ *n* -s [MF *beguin*, fr. *beguine* Beguine, fr. OF] *now dial Brit* **:** CAP, HOOD: **a :** a child's cap **b :** NIGHTCAP

³biggin \"\ *n* -s [after Mr. *Biggin* *fl*1800 its inventor] **:** a coffee percolator used in the early 19th century; *also* **:** a pot with stand and lamp used in the same period for keeping coffee warm

bigging *pres part of* BIG

big·gish \'bigish, -gēsh\ *adj* [¹*big* + *-ish*] **:** somewhat big **:** comparatively big

big goldenrod *n* **:** a stout coarse goldenrod (*Solidago squarrosa*) of eastern No. America with the tips of its involucral bracts squarrose

big·go·net \'bigə,net\ *n* -s [irreg. fr. ²*biggin* + *-et*] *chiefly Scot* **:** a woman's cap or coif of linen

big gun *n* **:** a person or factor of outstanding importance esp. in some particular relation ⟨a *big gun* in the diplomatic corps⟩ ⟨ecology may be the *big gun* in the battle to keep the world's wild animals alive —W.A.Bridges⟩

bi·gha *or* **big·gah** \'bēgə\ *n, pl* **bigha** *or* **bighas** *or* **biggah** *or* **biggahs** [Hindi *bighā*, fr. Skt *vigraha* division, fr. *vigrhṇāti* he separates, divides, fr. *vi* apart + *grhṇāti* he seizes — more at WITH, GRAB] **:** any of various Indian units of land area varying between ⅓ acre and 1 acre

bighead \'=,=\ *n* -s **1 :** any of several diseases of animals: as **a :** equine osteoporosis **b :** an acute photosensitization of sheep and goats that follows the ingestion of certain plants and is characterized by subcutaneous edema of the head, ears, and neck, by impairment of vision, and by fever **c** *Austral* **:** a malignant edema of rams due to infection of head wounds with a bacterium (*Clostridium novyi*) causing gelatinous infiltration of the head and neck usu. followed by death **2 :** an exaggerated opinion of one's worth or importance **:** CONCEIT, POMPOSITY — **big·head·ed** \'=¦==\ *adj*

big-headed gurnard *n* **:** a sea robin (*Prionotus tribulus*) of the So. Atlantic and Gulf coasts of the U.S.

bighearted \'=¦==\ *adj* **:** generous and kindly **:** OPENHANDED, LIBERAL — **bigheartedly** *adv*

big hole *n, railroading, slang* **:** emergency application of brakes

big hook *n, railroading, slang* **:** a wrecking crane

bighorn \'=,=\ *also* **bighorn sheep** *n, pl* **bighorn** *or* **bighorns :** a usu. grayish brown wild sheep (*Ovis canadensis*) of mountainous western No. America resembling the Asiatic argali but smaller and with less massive horns — compare DALL SHEEP

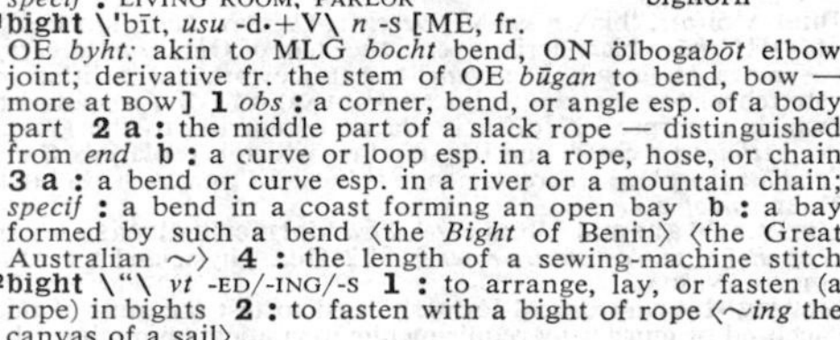
bighorn

big house *n, often cap B&H* **1 :** the outstanding residence of a locality; *esp* **:** the seat of the local magnate ⟨mother worked for years in the kitchen of the *big house*⟩ **2** *slang* **:** PENITENTIARY **3** *South & Midland* **:** the social or living area of a house; *specif* **:** LIVING ROOM, PARLOR

¹bight \'bīt, *usu* -d·+V\ *n* -s [ME, fr. OE *byht*; akin to MLG *bocht* bend, ON *ölbogabōt* elbow joint; derivative fr. the stem of OE *būgan* to bend, bow — more at BOW] **1** *obs* **:** a corner, bend, or angle esp. of a body part **2 a :** the middle part of a slack rope — distinguished from *end* **b :** a curve or loop esp. in a rope, hose, or chain **3 a :** a bend or curve esp. in a river or a mountain chain; *specif* **:** a bend in a coast forming an open bay **b :** a bay formed by such a bend ⟨the *Bight* of Benin⟩ ⟨the Great Australian ~⟩ **4 :** the length of a sewing-machine stitch

²bight \"\ *vt* -ED/-ING/-S **1 :** to arrange, lay, or fasten (a rope) in bights **2 :** to fasten with a bight of rope ⟨~*ing* the canvas of a sail⟩

big idea *n, slang* **:** PURPOSE, INTENT

big if *n, slang* **:** something that is both important and uncertain **:** a fundamental question

big inch *n* **:** a very long oil or gas pipeline 24 inches in diameter

big jaw *n* **:** actinomycosis of the jaw of cattle **:** LUMPY JAW

big joker *n* **:** JOKER 2b(1) — used in certain card games (as canasta) in which other wild cards of lower scoring value also take the name of *joker*; compare LITTLE JOKER

big knife *n, usu cap B&K* **:** an American colonist esp. of Virginia — used orig. by the Indians to distinguish established settlers from the English; called also *Long Knife*

big laurel *n* **1 :** EVERGREEN MAGNOLIA **2 :** a large large-leaved evergreen rhododendron (*Rhododendron maxima*) of eastern No. America having the leaves hairy below and rosy bell-shaped flowers more or less speckled with green — called also *great laurel, rosebay*

big–leaf maple \'=,=-\ *n* **:** OREGON MAPLE

big league *n* **1** *often cap B&L* **a :** MAJOR LEAGUE **b :** any comparable sports association **2 :** something or some group that is outstanding of its kind (as in stature, quality, or worth) ⟨there is only one commercially sponsored dramatic program in the *big league*—*New Republic*⟩ ⟨*big league* politics⟩

big–leagu·er \'bi'glēgə(r)\ *n* **:** one that belongs to or plays in a big league

big leg *n* **:** an acute lymphangitis of equines usu. affecting the hind legs, accompanied by severe pain and high fever, and commonly the result of overfeeding though sometimes due to local infection

big lie *n, sometimes cap B&L* [trans. of G *grosse lüge*] **:** untruth on a large scale consciously used as a propaganda technique on the assumption that it is more likely to compel belief than untruth on a modest scale

big·lip sucker \'=,=-\ *n* **:** COLUMBIA RIVER SUCKER

big liver disease *n* **:** that form of avian leukosis in which the liver is greatly enlarged and infiltrated with white blood cells; *broadly* **:** AVIAN LEUKOSIS COMPLEX

big·ly \'biglē, -li\ *adv* [ME, fr. ¹*big* + *-ly, -liche* -ly] **:** in a big manner: as **a :** with great scope **:** LARGELY, COMPREHENSIVELY ⟨few things done, but those done ~⟩ **b** *archaic* **:** in a swelling blustering manner **:** HAUGHTILY, POMPOUSLY

big man *n, slang* **:** LEADER; *esp* **:** an unlawful wholesale dealer in narcotics

big meeting *n* **:** a series of revival meetings held successively in one locality

bigmitt \'=,=\ *n* [¹*big* + *mitt*; fr. the use of sleight of hand] **:** a confidence game involving dishonest card play

¹bigmouth \'=,=\ *n* **1 :** any of various fishes having noticeably large mouths: as **a :** LARGEMOUTH BLACK BASS **b :** WARMOUTH **c :** SQUAWFISH **d :** the common buffalo fish **2 :** a loudmouthed, talkative, and often maliciously gossipy person

²bigmouth \"\ *adj* **:** BIGMOUTHED

bigmouth buffalo *or* **bigmouth buffalo fish** *n* **:** the largest of the suckers (*Megastomatobus cyprinella*) that inhabits large rivers, bayous, and oxbows in central No. America and sometimes exceeds 3 feet in length and 50 pounds in weight

bigmouthed \'=¦=\ *adj* **1 :** having a large mouth **2 :** LOUDMOUTHED, LOUD, BOISTEROUS; *often* **:** indiscreetly talkative ⟨a gossipy, ~ spreader of tales⟩

big name \'=¦=\ *n* **:** a big-name performer or personage ⟨the *big name* is the one you read about on page one —N.M. Loomis⟩ ⟨get some *big names* for the show⟩

big–name \'=¦=\ *adj* **1 :** of top rank in popular recognition **:** NOTABLE ⟨a *big-name* industrialist⟩ ⟨a *big-name* university⟩ ⟨*big-name* guests at a hotel⟩ **2 :** of or involving a big-name person, organization, or product ⟨a *big-name* committee⟩ ⟨a *big-name* novel⟩

big neck *n* **:** goiter of livestock

big–neck clam \'=,=-\ *n* **:** a large gaper (*Schizothaerus nuttallii*) of the Pacific coast of No. America

big·ness \'bignəs\ *n* -ES **1 :** quality or state of being big **2 :** size, whether great or small ⟨a painful lump having the ~ of a pea⟩ **3 :** broadness of outlook or scope; *sometimes* **:** POMPOSITY **:** self-assertive quality ⟨the ~ of their bandied words⟩

big noise *n, slang* **:** a person of consequence **:** BIGWIG

big·no·nia \big'nōnēə\ *n, cap* [NL, fr. J.P.*Bignon* †1743 French royal librarian + NL *-ia*] **:** a small genus of American and Japanese woody vines (family Bignoniaceae) climbing by small disks at the ends of tendrils and having compound leaves and showy somewhat irregular tubular flowers in axillary cymes — see CROSS VINE

big·no·ni·a·ce·ae \-,nē'āsē,ē\ *n pl, cap* [NL, fr. *Bignonia*, type genus + *-aceae*] **:** a family of trees, shrubs, woody vines, or occas. herbs (order Polemoniales) growing widely in the tropics, a few in temperate regions, and having opposite or occas. alternate leaves and irregular showy flowers with 2 or 4 stamens — **big·no·ni·a·ceous** \-¦=¦āshəs\ *adj*

big·no·ni·ad \big'nōnē,ad\ *n* -s [NL *Bignonia* + E *-ad*] **:** a plant of the family Bignoniaceae or the genus *Bignonia*

big one *n* **:** WHOPPER

big·o·net \'bigə,net\ *var of* BIGGONET

bi·go·ni·al \(')bī¦gōnēəl\ *also* **bi·go·ni·ac** \-nē,ak\ *adj* [¹*bi-* + *gonial* or *goniac*] **:** of, relating to, or joining the two gonia

bigonial diameter *also* **bigonial** *n* -s *anthrop* **:** the distance between the gonia

¹big·ot \'bigət, *usu* -d·+V\ *n* -s [MF, bigot, hypocrite, fr. OF *bigot* Norman] **1** *obs* **:** HYPOCRITE; *esp* **:** a superstitious religious hypocrite **2 :** one obstinately and irrationally, often intolerantly, devoted to his own church, party, belief, or opinion **syn** see ENTHUSIAST

²bigot \"\ *adj* **:** BIGOTED

big·ot·ed \'bigəd·əd, -ətəd\ *adj* **:** obstinately and blindly attached to some creed, opinion, or practice **:** unreasonably devoted to a system or party and illiberal, often intolerant, toward others' opinions — **big·ot·ed·ly** *adv*

big·ot·ry \'bigətrē, -ri\ *n* -ES [F *bigoterie*, fr. MF, fr. *bigot* + *-erie* -ery] **:** state of mind of a bigot **:** obstinate and unreasoning attachment to one's own belief and opinions with intolerance of beliefs opposed to them; *also* **:** behavior or beliefs ensuing from such a condition

big·ot·ty \'bigəd·ē, -ətē, -i\ *var of* BIGGETY

big pine *n* **1 :** PONDEROSA PINE **2 :** SUGAR PINE

bi·gram \'bī,gram\ *n* [¹*bi-* + *-gram*] *cryptography* **:** DIGRAPH

big·root \'=,=\ *n* **:** an herbaceous California vine (*Echinocystis fabacea*) with an enormous tuberous root

bigs *pl of* BIG, *pres 3d sing of* BIG

big sagebrush *n* **:** SAGEBRUSH

big shellbark *or* **big shellbark hickory** *also* **big shagbark** *n* **:** a hickory (*Carya laciniosa*) of the eastern U.S., resembling the shagbark but having a much larger nut — called also *king nut*

big shot *n* **:** a person of consequence or prominence ⟨a *big shot* in gambling circles⟩ ⟨what's your problem, *big shot*⟩

big sister *n* **1 :** an older sister **2 :** one that is like an older sister: as **a :** a woman who befriends a delinquent or friendless girl **b :** a girl in an upper class at college who acts as adviser to a girl in the freshman class

big skunk *n* **:** a skunk of the genus *Mephitis*

big stick *n* **1 :** coercive power, esp. military or political ⟨we must speak softly but carry a *big stick* —Theodore Roosevelt⟩ **2** *slang* **:** a long ladder; *esp* **:** AERIAL LADDER

big talk *n* **:** boastful talk **:** BLUSTER

big thing *n* **:** something that is prominent, important, or in wide use ⟨tweed is the *big thing* this fall⟩

big–ticket \'=¦==\ *adj* **:** high-priced **:** having a large initial cost ⟨credit buying of *big-ticket* items such as refrigerators is on the increase⟩

big–time \'=¦=\ *adj* **1 :** of or relating to the big time **2 :** OUTSTANDING, PROMINENT, TOP-NOTCH, FIRST-CLASS ⟨her presentation was definitely *big-time*⟩

big time *n* **1 :** any high-paying vaudeville circuit requiring only two performances a day **2 :** the top rank of professional performance or of large-scale enterprise esp. as indicated by high income or great popular prestige ⟨a prizefighter may have a long wait before breaking into the *big time*⟩

big–tim·er \'big,tīmə(r), =¦==\ *n* **:** one who has reached the big time ⟨a television *big-timer*⟩

big toe *n* **:** the innermost and largest digit of the foot

bigtooth aspen *or* **bigtoothed aspen** \'=,=\ *n* **:** LARGE-TOOTHED ASPEN

bigtooth maple *n* **:** WESTERN SUGAR MAPLE

big top *n* **1 :** the main tent of a circus ⟨the glamour of the *big top*⟩ **2 :** CIRCUS 1c

big tree *n* **1 :** a California evergreen (*Sequoiadendron giganteum*) that sometimes exceeds 270 feet in height and 80 feet in girth — called also *giant sequoia* **2 :** NOBLE FIR

big–tree plum \'=,=-\ *n* **:** a small tree (*Prunus mexicana*) of the southeastern U.S. that is sometimes cultivated for ornament, that has glandless, abruptly acuminate, coarsely serrate leaves broadly rounded at the base and softly pubescent beneath, and that produces a purplish red fruit

big trefoil *n* **:** a European perennial legume (*Lotus uliginosus*) used in the U.S., chiefly in the Northwest, as a forage crop esp. on acid and wet soil

bi·gua·nide \(')bī¦gwä,nīd, -,nəd\ *n* -s [ISV ¹*bi-* + *guan-* (fr. *guanidine*) + *-ide*] **:** a strong amorphous base $NH[C(=NH)NH_2]_2$ some of whose derivatives (as aryl derivatives) find use as antimalarial drugs or as precipitants for dyes in color photography

bi·guttate \(')bī+\ *adj* [¹*bi-* + *guttate*] **:** having a pair of droplike spots

big vein *or* **big vein disease** *n* **:** a soil-borne virus disease of lettuce characterized by strikingly enlarged light-yellow leaf veins and more or less stunting of the plants

big wheel *n, slang* **:** a person of consequence or authority **:** BOSS, BIGWIG

big·wig \'big,wig\ *n* **:** a person of consequence or self-importance; *esp* **:** one of high official position ⟨a couple of senators and some other political ~s⟩

bi·ha·ri *or* **be·ha·ri** \bē'hä(,)rē\ *n, pl* **bihari** *or* **biharis** *or* **behari** *or* **beharis** *usu cap* [Hindi *bihārī*, fr. *Bihār* Bihar, state in northeastern India] **1 :** a native or inhabitant of Bihar, India **2 :** a group of Indic dialects spoken by the inhabitants of Bihar

bi·har tree \bē'här-\ *n* [prob. fr. *Bihar*, state in northeastern India] **:** LACQUER TREE

bi–iliac \(')bī+\ *adj* [¹*bi-* + *iliac*] **:** of, relating to, or between the two most prominent points of the crests of the iliac bones ⟨a large *bi-iliac* diameter⟩

bi·ischial \(')bī+\ *also* **bi·ischiadic** *or* **bi·ischiatic** \(¦)bī+\ *adj* [¹*bi-* + *ischial* or *ischiadic* or *ischiatic*] **:** of, relating to, or between both ischia

bi·ja \'bējə\ *n* -s [short for *bijasal*] *India* **:** KINO 2

bi·jar \bə'jär\ *n* -s [fr. *Bijar*, town in northwest Iran] **:** a thick-piled Persian rug of very close weave and variable design produced in Bijar

bi·ja·sal \'bējə,säl\ *n* -s [prob. fr. an Indic word akin to Skt *bīja* seed and *śāla* sal tree] **:** BIJA

¹bi·jou \'bē,zhü, =¦=\ *n, pl* **bi·joux** \-üz, -ü\ [F, fr. Bret *bizou* ring, fr. *biz* finger; akin to W *bys* finger, OCorn *bis, bes*] **:** TRINKET, JEWEL **:** a small dainty usu. ornamental piece of delicate workmanship and fine material

²bijou \"\ *adj* **:** small of its kind and usu. marked by fine detail and workmanship ⟨can Americans be persuaded to pay out dollars for ~ cars⟩ — used esp. of buildings ⟨a ~ theater with delicate rococo decorations⟩

bi·jou·te·rie \bē'zhütə,rē, *F* bēzhütrē\ *n* -s [F, fr. *bijou*] **1 a :** a collection of trinkets or ornaments ⟨proud of his Gothic ~⟩; *collectively* **:** TRINKETS, JEWELS **b :** jewelry in which delicate or intricate metalwork contributes more to the value than do the constituent materials **2 :** an apt turn of phrase **:** BON MOT

bi·ju·gate \'bījə,gāt; (')bī¦jügət, -,gāt\ *also* **bi·ju·gous** \-gəs\ *adj* [*bijugate* fr. ¹*bi-* + *jugate*; *bijugous* fr. ¹*bi-* + L *jugum* yoke + E *-ous* — more at YOKE] *of a pinnate leaf* **:** having two pairs of leaflets

bik·a·ner \,bikə¦ne(ə)r, ¦bē-, -¦ni(ə)r\ *adj, usu cap* [fr. *Bikaner*, India] **:** of or from the city of Bikaner, India **:** of the kind or style prevalent in Bikaner

bik·a·neri \,bikə'nerē, ,bē-, -nirē\ *also* **bik·a·ner** \-'ne(ə)r,

-ni(ə)r\ *n* -s *usu cap* : a sheep of an Indian breed of wool-type sheep having the body white and the face usu. colored

¹bike \ˈbīk\ *n* -s [ME] **1** *chiefly Scot* : a nest of wild bees, wasps, or hornets **2** *chiefly Scot* : a crowd or swarm of people ⟨the busy ~ of the city —R.L. Stevenson⟩

²bike \"\ *n or vb* [by shortening and alter.] : BICYCLE — **bik·er** \-kə(r)\ *n* -s

bikh \ˈbik\ *n* -s [Hindi, fr. Skt *viṣa* poison — more at VIRUS] *India* : a poison extracted from certain plants of the genus *Aconitum*

bikh·a·con·i·tine \ˌbikəˈkänəˌtēn, -ˌtən\ *n* -s [ISV *bikh*] + *aconite* + *-ine*] : a toxic crystalline alkaloid $C_{36}H_{51}NO_{11}$ obtained from the root of certain plants of the genus *Aconitum*

bi·ki·ni \bəˈkēnē\ *n* -s [F, fr. *Bikini*, atoll of the Marshall islands in the northern Pacific, site of atomic bomb tests of 1946; fr. the comparison of the effects wrought by a scantily clad woman to the effects of an atomic bomb] : a woman's abbreviated two-piece bathing suit

bi·ki·ni·an \-nēən,-nyən\ *n* -s *usu cap* [*Bikini* + E *-an*] : a native of the Marshallese island Bikini

bik·ku·rim \bi,küˈrēm, -ˈkurim\ *n pl* [Heb *bikkūrīm* first fruits] **1** : the first ripe fruits offered in thanks to God on the altar of the Temple in ancient Palestine **2** *in modern Israel* : the products of the orchards and fields gathered and sold to further the Jewish National Fund

bi·kol *also* **bi·col** \bēˈkōl\ *n, pl* **bikol** *or* **bikols** *also* **bicol** *or* **bicols** *usu cap* [Bikol & Tag] **1 a** : a Christianized people in southeastern Luzon and adjacent islands of the Philippines **b** : a member of such people **2** : the Austronesian language of the Bikol people

bi·la·an \bēˈlä,än, -ˈlän\ *n, pl* **bilaan** *or* **bilaans** *usu cap* [Bisayan *Bilaan*, fr. Bilaan *Blaan*] **1 a** : a predominantly pagan people inhabiting southern Mindanao and the Sarangani islands, Philippines **b** : a member of such people **2** : the Austronesian language of the Bilaan people

¹bi·labial \(ˈ)bī+\ *adj* [ISV ¹*bi-* + *labial*] **1** *of a consonant* : produced with both lips ⟨\p\ and \b\ and \m\ are ~ consonants⟩ — compare LABIAL **2 a** : of, relating to, or between the lips **b** *anthrop* : between the highest point on the upper lip and the lowest point on the lower lip

²bilabial \"\ *n* -s : a bilabial consonant

bi·labiate \(ˈ)bī+\ *adj* [¹*bi-* + *labiate*] : having two lips ⟨a ~ corolla of a flower⟩

bi·laminate *or* **bi·laminated** *also* **bi·laminar** \(ˈ)bī+\ *adj* [¹*bi-* + *laminate* or *laminated* or *laminar*] : formed of or having two laminae

bil·an·der \ˈbiləndə(r), ˈbī-\ *n* -s [obs. D *billander* (now *bijlander*), alter. of (assumed) obs. D *binlander*, fr. obs. D *bin* inside (fr. MD, alter. of *binnen*, fr. *be-* + *innen* inside) + D *land* + *-er*; akin to OE, OHG & ON *innan* from the inside, Goth *innana*, OE *in*, and to OHG *lant* land — more at IN, LAND] : a small 2-masted merchant ship

bi·lat·er·al \(ˈ)bī¦lad·ərəl, -lat(ə)rəl\ *adj* [¹*bi-* + *lateral*] **1** : having two sides ⟨a problem that poses a ~ difficulty⟩ **2** : affecting reciprocally two sides or two parties ⟨a ~ contract⟩ ⟨a ~ treaty⟩; *specif* : of or relating to bilateralism in trade ⟨~ trade policies⟩ **3** *biol* **a** : of or relating to the right and left sides of a central area, organ, or plane **b** : possessing bilateral symmetry **4** : related or tracing descent through both maternal and paternal ancestors — contrasted with *unilateral* **5** : of or relating to a system of tolerance specification that allows variation both above and below the basic size — **bi·lat·er·al·ly** \-lad·ərəlē, -lat(ə)rəlē, -li\ *adv*

bi·lat·er·al·ism \-ə,lizəm\ *n* -s **1** : the state of being bilateral; *esp* : BILATERAL SYMMETRY **2** : the practice of advancing trade between two countries by concluding agreements governing such factors as the volume and composition of trade, the price of commodities, and the settling of accounts — contrasted with *multilateralism*

bi·lat·er·al·is·tic \-ə¦listik\ *adj* : BILATERAL 2

bi·lat·er·al·i·ty \ˌbī,lad·əˈraləd·ē, -latəˈ-, -ralətē, -i\ *n* -ES : BILATERALISM

bilateral monopoly *n* : a market condition in which only one buyer or one group of associated buyers confronts only one seller or one group of associated sellers

bilateral symmetry *n* : the condition of having the right and left sides (as of the body) counterparts one of the other — compare RADIAL SYMMETRY

¹bi·la·te·ria \ˌbīləˈtirēə\ [NL, fr. ¹*bi-* + L *later-*, *latus* side + NL *-ia* — more at LATERAL] *syn of* EXOCYCLOIDA

²bilateria \"\ *also* **bi·lat·er·a·lia** \ˌbī,lad·əˈrālēə\ *n pl, cap* [*bilateria*, NL, fr. ¹*bi-* + L *later-*, *latus* side + NL *-ia*; *bilateralia*, NL, fr. ¹*bi-* + L *lateralis*, neut. pl. of *lateralis* lateral — more at LATERAL] : bilaterally symmetrical animals

bil·bao \(ˈ)bilˈbä(,)ō, -ˈbau *also* -ˈbā(,)ō\ *adj, usu cap* [fr. *Bilbao*, Spain] : of or from the city of Bilbao, Spain : of the kind or style prevalent in Bilbao

bil·bao glass \"-\ *also* **bilboa** \ˈbil(,)bō(ə)\ *n* -s : a mirror with a marble or marble and mahogany frame frequently ornamented in filigree

bil·ber·ry \ˈbil- — *see* BERRY\ *n* [*bil-* (prob. of Scand origin; akin to Dan *bølle* whortleberry) + *berry*; akin to ON *beyla* hump — more at BILE] **1** : any of certain plants of the genus *Vaccinium* that differ from the typical blueberries in having their flowers solitary or in very small clusters and arising from axillary buds: **a** : WHORTLEBERRY 1 **b** : any of several chiefly alpine or boreal No. American plants (as *V. membranaceum*, *V. caespitosum*, or *V. uliginosum*) **2** : the sweet edible blue or bluish black fruit of a bilberry **3 a** : a bearberry (*Arctostaphylos uva-ursi*) **b** : a withe rod (*Viburnum nudum*)

¹bil·bo \ˈbil(,)bō\ *or* **bil·boa** \-(,)bō(ə)\ *n, pl* **bilboes** *or* **bilbos** *or* **bilboas** [fr. *Bilboa*, earlier form of *Bilbao*, Spain] : a finely tempered sword

²bilbo \"\ *n* -ES [earlier *bilbowe*, perh. fr. *Bilboa*, Spain] : a long bar of iron with sliding shackles and a lock at the end that is used to confine the feet of prisoners esp. on shipboard

bil·bo·quet \ˌbilbəˈket\ *n* -s [F, fr. MF *billeboquet*, fr. *bille* ball (of Gmc origin; akin to MHG *bickel* die, ankle) + *bouquer* to thrust, fr. *bouc* male goat, of Celt origin; akin to OIr *bocc* male goat — more at BUCK] : a device having a cup or spike at the top of a stick to which is attached a ball on a string; *also* : the game of maneuvering the device so as to catch the ball in the cup or on the spike — compare CUP AND BALL

bil·by *also* **bil·bi** \ˈbilbē, -bi\ *or* **biel·by** \ˈbēl-\ *n, pl* **bilbies** *also* **bilbis** *or* **bielbies** [native name in Australia] : the rabbit bandicoot of Australia

bil·cock \ˈbil,käk\ *n* -s [origin unknown] *Brit* : WATER RAIL

bil·dar \bilˈdär\ *n* -s [Hindi *beldār*, fr. Per *bēldār*, fr. *bēl* spade + *-dar* holder] *India* : DIGGER, EXCAVATOR

bil·dungs·ro·man \ˈbil,dün(k)srō,män, -ünzr-\ *n, pl* **bildungsroma·ne** \-nə\ *or* **bildungsromans** *usu cap* [G, fr. *bildung* education, culture + *roman* novel] : a novel about the usu. early development or spiritual education of the main character ⟨a long, detailed *Bildungsroman*⟩

¹bile \ˈbī(ə)l\ *n* -s [ME, fr. OE *bȳl*; akin to OHG *būlla* boil, ON *beyla* hump, growth, Goth *ufbauliths* swollen with pride, Serb *buljiti* to stare with goggle eyes — more at BOAST] *dial* : ¹BOIL

²bile \ˈbīl, *esp bef pause or cons* -īəl\ *n* -s [F, fr. L *bilis*; akin to W *bustl* bile] **1 a** : a yellow or greenish viscid alkaline fluid secreted by the liver from which it passes into the duodenum where it mixes with the duodenal and pancreatic secretions, aids in the digestive processes by emulsifying fats and otherwise assisting in their digestion and absorption, and may also aid in neutralizing the acid chyme from the stomach, in promoting peristalsis, and in reducing putrefactive action **b** : HUMOR 1b(1) : (1) : YELLOW BILE (2) : BLACK BILE **2** : proneness to anger : ILL HUMOR, IRASCIBILITY, SPLEEN ⟨the villain in every novel gives you somebody "to shoot at", rather than firing your stored-up ~ at yourself —T.V.Smith⟩

³bile \ˈbī(ə)l\ *vb* -ED/-ING/-S [by alter.] *dial* : ²BOIL

⁴bile \"\ *n* -s [by alter.] *dial* : ³BOIL

bile acid *n* : any of several acids (as cholic acid) that occur in bile usu. in the form of sodium salts of the acids conjugated with glycine or taurine (as in glycocholic acid or taurocholic acid), that are formed in the body from cholesterol and belong to the class of steroids, that promote the digestion of fats and other lipides by their emulsifying and solubilizing actions, and that aid in the absorption of many water-insoluble organic substances by forming soluble complexes with them; *also* : any conjugated bile acid

bilection *var of* BOLECTION

bile cyst *n* : GALLBLADDER

bile duct *n* : an excretory duct of the liver — see COMMON BILE DUCT

bile fluke *n* : CHINESE LIVER FLUKE

bile pigment *n* : any of several coloring matters (as bilirubin or biliverdin) in the bile that pass on oxidation through a succession of colors useful as tests for the pigments

bile salt *n* **1** : a salt of a bile acid; *esp* : a naturally occurring sodium salt of a conjugated bile acid **2 bile salts** *pl* : a dry mixture of the principal salts of ox gall consisting of sodium glycocholate and sodium taurocholate in varying proportions used as a liver stimulant and laxative

bile vessel *n* : any of numerous fine channels within the liver that conduct bile

¹bilge \ˈbilj\ *n* -s [origin unknown] **1 a** : the point of largest circumference of a cask or barrel usu. located at the middle **b** : the difference in width between the midsection of a barrel stave and the end **2 a** : the part of the underwater body of a ship lying between the flat of the ship's bottom and the straight vertical topsides; *specif* : the point of greatest curvature **b** : the lowest point of a ship's inner hull adjacent to the keelson **3 a** : BILGE WATER **b** : stale, offensive, or worthless remarks or ideas ⟨all his sanctimonious ~ —John Buchan⟩

²bilge \"\ *vb* -ED/-ING/-S *vt* **1** : to fracture or otherwise damage the bilge of (a ship) : stave in the bottom of ⟨the boat was *bilged* by a snag —W.S.Campbell⟩ **2** *slang* : to require to resign (as from a naval academy) because of failure in studies ⟨a couple of midshipmen got *bilged*⟩ ~ *vi* **1 a** : to undergo a fracture or other damage in the bilge : spring a leak through damage to the bilge ⟨the ship *bilged* when it struck the reef⟩ **b** : to rest on the bilge (as after running aground) ⟨for three hours the ship lay *bilging* on the sand bar⟩ **2** *slang* : to fail in one's studies and resign under compulsion ⟨he *bilged* out⟩

bilge block *n* : one of the blocks supporting the bilge of a ship at the turn of the bilge while in a dry dock or under construction

bilge·board \ˈ=,=\ *n* **1** : a plane of wood or metal sliding in a case like a centerboard but built into each bilge of a ship **2** : LIMBER BOARD

bilge keel *also* **bilge piece** *n* : a steel plate or other longitudinal projection like a fin secured for a distance along a ship near the turn of the bilge on either side to check rolling — called also *rolling chock*; see SHIP illustration

bilge keelson *n* : a keelson located near the turn of the bilge

bilge log *n* : one of the logs of the bilge ways

bilge saw *n* : a saw similar to a barrel saw but having the diameter at the middle greater than at the ends

bilge strake *n* : one of the strakes at the turn of the bilge

bilge water *n* **1** : water that collects by seepage or leakage in the bilge of a ship or other vessel **2** : BILGE 3b

bilge ways *n pl but sometimes sing in constr* **1** : heavy timbers that rest on the ground ways and carry the weight of a vessel in launching — compare DOGSHORE **2** : transverse timbers or supports on which the bilge blocks travel

bilgy \ˈbiljē, -i\ *adj, usu* -ER/-EST : suggestive of or like bilge water; *esp* : highly offensive in odor

¹bil·har·zia \bilˈhärzēə\ [NL, fr. Theodor *Bilharz* †1862 Ger. helminthologist + NL *-ia*] *syn of* SCHISTOSOMA

²bilharzia *n* -s [NL, fr. T. *Bilharz* + NL *-ia*] **1** : SCHISTOSOME **2** : SCHISTOSOMIASIS — **bil·har·zi·al** \(ˈ)=¦=zēəl\ *or* **bil·har·zic** \-zik\ *adj* — **bil·har·zi·al·ly** \-zēəlē\ *adv*

bil·har·zi·a·sis \ˌbilhärˈzīəsəs\ *or* **bil·har·zi·o·sis** \(,)bil-,härzēˈōsəs\ *n, pl* **bilharzia·ses** \-ə,sēz\ *or* **bilharzio·ses** \-ˈō,s-\ [NL, fr. ¹*Bilharzia* + *-iasis* or *-osis*] : SCHISTOSOMIASIS

bili- *comb form* [MF, fr. L, fr. *bilis* — more at BILE] **1** : bile ⟨*bilic*⟩ **2** : derived from bile ⟨*bilirubin*⟩

bil·i·ary \ˈbilē,erē, -lyər-, -i\ *adj* [F *biliaire*, fr. *bili-* + *-aire* -ary] **1 a** : of or relating to bile, the bile ducts, or the gallbladder ⟨~ acids⟩ **b** : conveying bile ⟨~ ducts⟩ **2** *archaic* : BILIOUS

biliary calculus *n* : GALLSTONE

biliary canal *n* : a passage for the bile : HEPATIC DUCT

biliary dyskinesia *n* : pain or discomfort in the epigastric region resulting from spasm esp. of the sphincter of Oddi following cholecystectomy

biliary fever *n* : piroplasmosis esp. of dogs and horses

biliary tract *n* : the bile ducts and gallbladder

bil·ic \ˈbilik\ *adj* [²*bile* + *-ic*] : of, relating to, or derived from bile

bil·i·cy·a·nin \ˌbiləˈsīənən\ *n* -s [ISV *bili-* + *cyan-* (fr. Gk *kyanos* dark blue) + *-in*] : a blue pigment found in gallstones and formed by oxidation of biliverdin or bilirubin

bil·i·fi·ca·tion \ˌbiləfəˈkāshən, ˌbī-\ *n* -s [*bili-* + *-fication*] : formation and excretion of bile

bil·i·fus·cin \ˌ=¦=ˈfəsən\ *n* -s [*bili-* + *fusc-* (fr. L *fuscus* dark) + *-in* — more at DUSK] : a brown pigment found in human gallstones and in old bile and formed by oxidation of biliverdin

bi·lim·bi \bəˈlimbē\ *or* **bi·lim·bing** \-ˈlim(,)biŋ\ *n* -s [Konkani & Malay; Konkani *bilimbī*, fr. Malay *bělimbing*] **1** : an East Indian evergreen tree (*Averrhoa bilimbi*) resembling the carambola **2** : the very acid fruit of the bilimbi that is used for preserves or pickles — compare CARAMBOLA

biliment *n* -s [short for habiliment] *obs* : an ornamental part of women's dress (as a jeweled headdress or special lace) esp. in the 16th century

bi·lin \bəˈlēn\ *n* -s *usu cap* : the Cushitic language of the Bogos — compare HAMITIC LANGUAGES

bi·linear \(ˈ)bī +\ *adj* [¹*bi-* + *linear*] **1** : of or relating to two lines ⟨~ coordinates⟩ **2** : of or relating to an algebraic form each term of which involves one variable to the first degree from each of two sets of variables

biling *pres part of* BILE

¹bi·lin·gual \(ˈ)bī¦liŋgwəl\ *adj* [L *bilinguis* (fr. *bi-* ¹*bi-* + *lingua* tongue) + E *-al* — more at TONGUE] **1** : containing or expressed in two written languages ⟨a ~ inscription⟩ ⟨a ~ street sign⟩ : involving the use of two languages ⟨books printed in ~ form⟩ : having reference to two languages written, spoken, or manual ⟨~ study⟩ ⟨the ~ deaf⟩ **2** : having or using two languages esp. as spoken with the fluency characteristic of a native speaker ⟨a practically ~ control of French and English⟩ ⟨a ~ speaker⟩ — **bi·lin·gual·ly** \-gwəlē, -li\ *adv*

²bilingual \"\ *n* -s **1** : an inscription in two languages **2** : a person using two languages esp. habitually and with a control like that of a native speaker

bi·lin·gual·ism \bīˈliŋgwə,lizəm\ *also* **bi·lin·gual·i·ty** \ˌ=¦=ˈgwaləd·ē\ *n, pl* **bilingualisms** *also* **bilingualities** : the quality or state of being a bilingual; *also* : the use (as by a community) of two languages

bil·i·nite \ˈbilə,nīt\ *n* -s [Czech *bilinit*, fr. *Bílina*, Czechoslovakia + Czech *-it* -ite] : a mineral $FeSO_4.Fe_2(SO_4)_3.22H_2O$ consisting of a hydrous iron sulfate occurring in yellowish radiating fibers

bil·ious \ˈbilyəs *sometimes* -lēəs\ *adj* [MF *bilieux*, fr. L *biliosus*, fr. *bilis* bile + *-osus* -ose — more at BILE] **1 a** : of or relating to bile **b** : marked or accompanied by disordered liver function ⟨a ~ attack⟩; *broadly* : due to or associated with excessive secretion of bile ⟨suffered three years with a ~ ague⟩ **c** : affected by a bilious disorder ⟨a ~ patient⟩ **d** : appearing as though affected by a bilious disorder ⟨a sickly ~ face⟩ — compare JAUNDICE **2** : of a peevish ill-natured disposition : marked by a glum and morosely sour attitude : fretfully irascible : CHOLERIC ⟨a ~ disagreeable old skinflint⟩ ⟨looking at life with a ~ eye⟩ **3** : sickeningly unpleasant : of a kind that makes one queasy : NAUSEATING, REVOLTING ⟨utterly ~ weather⟩ ⟨with clapboards painted red and ~ yellow —Sinclair Lewis⟩ — **bil·ious·ly** *adv* — **bil·ious·ness** *n* -ES

bil·i·ru·bin \ˌbiləˈrübən, ˌbī-\ *n* -s [ISV *bili-* + L *ruber* red + ISV *-in* — more at RED] : a reddish yellow crystalline pigment $C_{33}H_{36}N_4O_6$ occurring in bile, blood, urine, and gallstones sometimes in combination with protein and formed by reduction of biliverdin

bil·i·ru·bi·ne·mia *or* **bil·i·ru·bi·nae·mia** \ˌ=¦=ˌ=ˈnēmēə\ *n* -s [NL, fr. ISV *bilirubin* + NL *-emia*, *-aemia*] : the presence of bilirubin in the blood in excess of the normal slight quantity

bil·i·ru·bi·nu·ria \-ˈn(y)urēə\ *n* -s [NL, fr. ISV *bilirubin* + NL *-uria*] : excretion of bilirubin in the urine

bi·literal \(ˈ)bī+\ *adj* [¹*bi-* + *literal*] **1** : consisting of or employing two letters or types of letters: as **a** : having two root consonants ⟨Semitic ~ nouns⟩ **b** : written in two different alphabets **2** *cryptography* **a** : composed of or employing a cover text in which two letter forms or type faces are used in significant combinations — see BACON BILITERAL CIPHER **b** : representing one letter by two

bi·lith \ˈbī,lith\ *or* **bi·lith·on** \bīˈli,thän\ *n* -s [¹*bi-* + *-lith*, *-lithon* (fr. Gk *lithos* stone)] : a prehistoric monument composed of two stones usu. constituting a pillar capped by a slab

bil·i·ver·din \ˌbiləˈvərdən, ˌbī-\ *n* -s [Sw, fr. *bili-* + obs. F *verd* green (now *vert*) + Sw *-in* — more at VERDANT] : a green crystalline pigment $C_{33}H_{34}N_4O_6$ occurring as the chief bile pigment of amphibians and birds and chiefly as a precursor of bilirubin in man and carnivorous mammals and formed at least in part by the breakdown of hemoglobin

¹bilk \ˈbilk\ *vt* -ED/-ING/-S [perh. alter. of ²*balk*] **1** : to block the free development, functioning, or fulfillment of : BALK, CHECK ⟨whatever measures one suggests are bound to be resisted if not ~*ed* —*Saturday Rev.*⟩ **2 a** : to cheat out of what is due : DEFRAUD ⟨~*ed* insurance companies of more than $1,000,000 —Henry La Cossitt⟩ **b** *archaic* : to evade payment of or for ⟨don't intend to ~ my lodgings —Henry Fielding⟩ **3 a** *archaic* : to slip away from **b** : AVOID, SHUN ⟨~*ed* the problem of slavery by making Heaven democratic —Waldo Frank⟩

²bilk \"\ *n* -s : an untrustworthy tricky individual : CHEAT

¹bill \ˈbil\ *n* -s [ME *bile*, fr. OE; akin to OE *bill* sword]

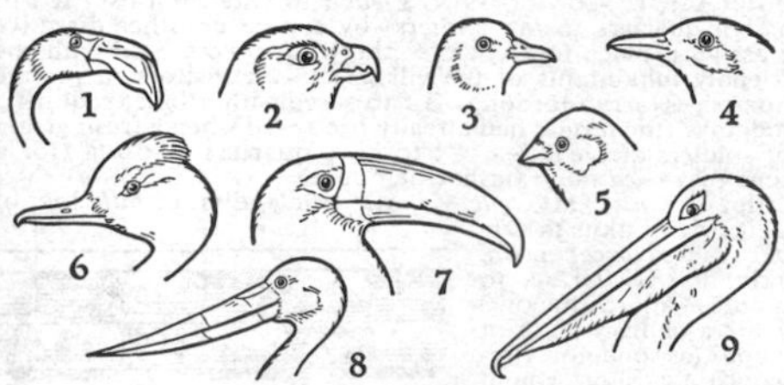

bills: *1* flamingo, *2* hawk, *3* pigeon, *4* thrush, *5* finch, *6* duck (merganser), *7* toucan, *8* saddle-bill, *9* pelican

1 : the jaws of a bird together with their horny covering, the whole varying greatly in form according to the food and habits of the various kinds : BEAK, NIB **2 a** : any mouthpart similar to or likened to a bill (as the horny jaws of a turtle, the elongated snout of a marlin, or the sensitive skin-covered beak of a platypus) **b** : a thin flattened part of the shell margin of the broad end of an oyster **3** : a projection of land like a beak : PROMONTORY, HEADLAND **4** : the point of the end of an anchor fluke or of a yard — see ANCHOR illustration **5** : the prong of the metal hook of a pompier ladder **6** : one of the blades of a pair of scissors **7** : the visor of a cap

²bill \"\ *vb* -ED/-ING/-S [ME *bilen*, fr. *bile*, n.] *vi* **1** *obs* : PECK **2** : to touch and rub bill to bill ⟨a pair of doves gently ~*ing*⟩ **3** : to show affection through fondling and kissing ⟨lovers ~*ing* and cooing⟩ ~ *vt* : to catch or pick up with the bill ⟨swift birds ~*ing* insects on the wing⟩

³bill \"\ *n* -s [ME *bil*, fr. OE *bill*; akin to OHG *bill* pickax, ON *bīldr* instrument for letting blood, Gk *phitros* log, OSlav *biti* to strike] **1** : a weapon used up to the 17th century mainly by infantry and up to the 18th by civic guards that consisted of a long staff terminating in a hook-shaped blade usu. with pikes at the back and top — compare HALBERD **2** : BILLHOOK

head of a bill

⁴bill \"\ *n* -s [ME *bille*, fr. ML *billa*, alter. of *bulla* document, seal, fr. L *bulla* bubble, boss, stud, amulet — more at POLL (head)] **1** : a written or printed statement: as **a** : a written document **b** : MEMORANDUM **c** : LETTER **2** *obs* : a formal and usu. written petition : SUPPLICATION **3** : a draft of a law presented to a legislature for enactment : a proposed or projected law ⟨a new ~ was set before Congress⟩ — compare ¹ACT 3, ¹STATUTE **4** : a declaration in writing stating some wrong a complainant has suffered from a defendant or stating a breach of law by some person — used chiefly in various phrases (as *bill of complaint*) **5 a** : a written list : a paper carrying a statement of particulars ⟨a ~ of quantities containing specifications of building materials⟩ **b** *obs* : a list of drugs : medical prescription **c** : a list of men and their duties esp. as part of a ship's crew : a chart or organization sheet listing functions or assignments ⟨watch quarter and station ~⟩ **d** : a list of a complete correctly proportioned assortment of printer's type of one size and style; *also* : the assortment itself : FONT ⟨a ~ of pica⟩ **6 a** : an itemized account that states the separate costs of goods sold, services rendered, or work done : INVOICE ⟨the ~ accompanying a large consignment of furniture⟩ **b** : a statement in gross of a creditor's claim : statement of account : total amount indicated as due : total charge ⟨last month we had a huge grocery ~⟩ **c** : a statement of charges for food or drink consumed (as in a restaurant) : CHECK ⟨ask the waiter to bring the ~⟩ **7** *obs* : LABEL **8 a** : a written or printed advertisement that is posted or otherwise distributed to announce an event (as an exhibition or an auction) of interest to the public : PLACARD, POSTER, HANDBILL; *esp* : a written or printed announcement of a theatrical entertainment : PLAYBILL ⟨~*s* about the new play were in nearly every store window⟩ **b** : a programmed presentation (as a motion picture, play, lecture, concert) : the entertainment or other event of interest presented on a given program ⟨the newly built theater was offering a wonderful ~ that evening⟩ **9 a** : a piece of paper money ⟨a 10-dollar ~⟩ **b** : an individual or commercial note ⟨~*s* receivable⟩ ⟨a discounted ~⟩

⁵bill \"\ *vt* -ED/-ING/-S [ME *billen*, fr. *bille*, n.] **1 a** : to enter in a book of accounts : prepare a bill of (charges to customers or clients) ⟨~*ing* each month's purchases⟩ **b** : to submit a bill of charges to ⟨the company ~*s* its customers every other month⟩ **c** : to enter (as passengers or freight) in a waybill : consign to a destination : BOOK **d** : to issue a bill of lading to or for **2 a** : to advertise esp. by posters or placards ⟨the circus was ~*ed* well in advance of its arrival in town⟩ **b** : to present or arrange for the presentation of (an event or attraction of interest to the public, as a motion picture, lecture, or concert) ⟨the theater is ~*ing* the play for three weeks⟩ **c** : to present or arrange for the presentation of (as an entertainer or group of entertainers) : bring before the public : offer on a program ⟨an astute producer who ~*ed* the country's leading actress in the new play⟩ ⟨they were ~*ed* as a brilliant dance team⟩; *esp* : to allot a specific part (as a role in a play) to : CAST ⟨for three consecutive seasons he was ~*ed* in leading roles⟩

⁶bill \"\ *n* -s [by alter.] *Scot* : ¹BULL 1

⁷bill \"\ *n* -s [alter. of ⁴*bell*] : the cry of the bittern ⟨the bittern's hollow ~ was heard —William Wordsworth⟩

bil·la·bong \ˈbilə,bȯŋ, -,bäŋ\ *n* -s [native name in Australia] *Austral* **1 a** : a blind channel leading out from a river **b** : a stream bed usu. dry but filled seasonally **2** : a backwater caused by overflow from a river and forming a stagnant pool

billback \ˈ=,=\ *n* [⁴*bill* + *back*] : a charge to members of a marketing group when the commodity sells for less than the sum advanced to members

billbeetle \ˈ=,=\ *n* [¹*bill* + *beetle*] : BILLBUG

billbergia \bilˈbərjēə\ *n* [NL, fr. J.G.*Billberg* †1844 Swedish botanist + NL *-ia*] **1** *cap* : a genus of tropical American epiphytes (family Bromeliaceae) with stiff spiny-edged leaves and showy flowers **2** -s : a plant of the genus *Billbergia*

¹billboard \ˈ=,=\ *n* [¹*bill* (point of an anchor fluke) + *board*] : a projection or ledge fixed on the bow of a vessel for the anchor to rest on

²billboard \"\ *n* [⁴*bill* + *board*] **1** : a flat surface (as of a panel, wall, or fence) on which notices are posted; *specif* : a large panel designed to carry outdoor advertising and mounted on a building or framework near a road **2** : an announcement at the beginning of a television or radio program that lists starring performers or other features

bill broker *n* [⁴*bill* + *broker*] *chiefly Brit* **:** one who negotiates the discount of bills of exchange either as agent or usu. by buying and selling them or buying them and carrying them with money borrowed upon them as security — compare NOTE BROKER — **bill·brok·ing** \ˈbil,brōkiŋ, -ēŋ\ *n* -s

billbug \ˈ≈,≈\ *n* [¹*bill* + *bug*] **:** any of numerous weevils (as members of the genus *Calendra*) having larvae that are destructive to the roots of grasses and cereal crops

billed \ˈbild\ *adj* [ME *biled,* fr. *bile* + *-ed*] **:** having a bill ⟨a thick-*billed* bird⟩ ⟨a long-*billed* cap⟩

bill·er \ˈbilə(r)\ *n* -s [⁵*bill* + *-er*] **:** one that bills: as **a :** a clerk who makes out bills; *esp* **:** a billing-machine operator **b :** BILLING MACHINE **c :** a worker in a planing mill who having calculated from blueprints or shop drawings designates on shop orders the wood to be used in making such units as sashes and doors

¹**bil·let** \ˈbilət, *usu* -d·+V\ *n* -s [ME *bylet,* fr. MF *billette, bullette,* dim. of *bulle* document, fr. ML *bulla* — more at BILL] **1** *archaic* **:** a brief usu. informal letter **:** NOTE **2 a :** an official order directing that a member of a military force be provided with board and lodging (as in a private home) ⟨the townspeople received ~*s* ordering them to lodge the regiment overnight⟩ **b :** quarters assigned (as by a billet) **:** a lodging place ⟨the old mansion served as the soldiers' ~ for nearly a week⟩ **3 a :** POSITION, JOB, POST, APPOINTMENT ⟨he landed a lucrative ~ with a New York publishing house⟩ **b :** a place allotted **:** DESTINATION ⟨every bullet has its ~⟩

²**billet** \"\ *vb* -ED/-ING/-S *vt* **1** *obs* **:** to enter in a list **2 :** to assign quarters to (as soldiers) by a note or other directive **:** assign a place to **:** LOCATE ⟨the troops were ~*ed* with the friendly inhabitants of the village⟩ ⟨~*ing* visitors in private homes —Harry Gordon⟩ **3 :** to serve with a billet requiring lodgings ⟨the farmer had already been ~*ed* when a fresh group of soldiers arrived⟩ ~ *vi* **:** to have quarters **:** LODGE ⟨for a time they ~*ed* in a ramshackle house⟩

³**billet** \"\ *n* -s [ME *bylet,* fr. MF *billete,* dim. of *bille* log, of Celt origin; akin to OIr *bile* sacred tree; prob. akin to L *florēre* to bloom — more at BLOW] **1 a :** a chunky piece of wood (as one for firewood) **:** a short round log **:** a section obtained by halving, quartering, or otherwise splitting or sawing logs lengthwise **b** *obs* **:** a thick usu. knobbed stick **:** CUDGEL **2 a :** a strap that enters a buckle (as the ends of harness reins or of the cheek pieces that buckle on the bit) **b :** a loop that receives the end of a buckled strap **3 :** a heraldic bearing in the form of an upright rectangle **4 a :** a bar of metal (as of gold or iron) **b :** a piece of semifinished iron or steel nearly square in section made by rolling an ingot or bloom until it has been reduced in size to 1½ to 6 in. square **c :** a section of nonferrous metal ingot hot-worked by forging, rolling, or extrusion **d :** a nonferrous metal casting suitable for rolling or extrusion **5 :** an ornament in Norman moldings that resembles a billet of wood of rounded or sometimes polygonal cross section

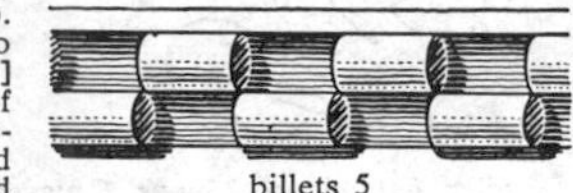
billets 5

⁴**billet** \"\ *n* -s [prob. alter. of earlier *billard* coalfish] *chiefly Brit* **:** a young pollack or coalfish

bil·let-doux \ˌbilāˈdü, -lē-, *F* bēyādü\ *n, pl* **billets-doux** \-ˈdüz, *F* bēyādü\ [F *billet doux,* lit., sweet letter] **:** LOVE LETTER

billethead \ˈ≈≈,≈\ *n* [³*billet* + *head*] **1 :** a round piece of timber at the bow or stern of a whaleboat around which a harpoon line may be run out **2 :** a scroll or ornamental carving used in place of a figurehead on a ship

billet rolls *n pl* [³*billet*] **:** ROUGHING ROLLS

billets *pl of* BILLET, *pres 3d sing of* BILLET

billetwood \ˈ≈≈,≈\ *n* [³*billet* + *wood*] **:** a tropical African timber tree (*Diospyros dendo*) with wood similar to ebony

bil·lety *also* **bil·let·ty** \ˈbilə̇d·ē, -ətē, -i\ *or* **bil·let·té** \ˌbiləˈtā, *F* bēyətā\ *adj* [F *billeté,* fr. *billette* billet — more at BILLET (log)] **:** charged or studded with heraldic billets

billfish \ˈ≈,≈\ *n* [¹*bill* + *fish*] **:** any of numerous fishes having long slender jaws like a bird's bill (as the saury, the marine and freshwater gars, the spearfish, the sailfish)

billfold \ˈ≈,≈\ *n* -s [short for earlier *billfolder*] **1 :** a folding pocketbook for paper money about the size of bills that will fit into it without previous folding and usu. carried in a pocket or larger pocketbook **2 :** WALLET 2b

billhead \ˈ≈,≈\ *n* [⁴*bill* + *head*] **:** a printed form commonly headed with the seller's name and address on which accounts of money owed are rendered

billholder \ˈ≈,≈≈\ *n* [⁴*bill* + *holder*] **1 :** one that holds a bill or acceptance **2 :** a device by means of which bills are held

billhook \ˈ≈,≈\ *n* [³*bill* + *hook*] **1 :** a cutting tool consisting of a blade with a hooked point fitted with a handle and used in pruning and similar work **2 :** KNOTTING BILL

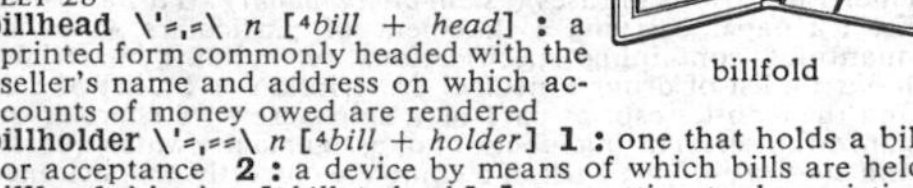
billfold
billhook 1

bil·li·an \ˈbilēən, -lyən\ *n* -s [Malay (*pokok*) *bĕlian,* lit., sorcerer's tree, fr. *pokok* tree + *bĕlian* sorcerer] **:** a valuable timber tree (*Eusideroxylon zwageri*) of the family Lauraceae of Borneo having heavy hard antproof wood

bil·liard \ˈbilyə(r)d, ˈbiy-\ *n* -s [back-formation fr. *billiards*] **1 :** CAROM 1 **2 :** a tobacco pipe with slightly rounded sides

billiard ball *n* [*billiards*] **:** one of the balls used in playing billiards

billiard cloth *n* **:** the smooth green woolen cloth thoroughly shrunk and felted that is used to cover billiard and pool tables

billiard green *n* **:** a deep yellowish green

bil·liard·ist \-də̇st\ *n* -s **:** one who plays billiards esp. professionally

billiard room *or* **billiard hall** *or* **billiard parlor** *or* **billiard saloon** *n* **:** a room in which billiards is played **:** POOLROOM

bil·liards \ˈbilyə(r)dz, ˈbiy-\ *n pl but usu sing in constr* [MF *billard* curved stick used in certain games, billiard cue, billiards, fr. *bille* log — more at BILLET] **:** any of several games played on an oblong table in which small balls are driven against one another or into pockets by means of a cue; *specif* **:** a game in which one scores by causing a cue ball to hit in succession two object balls — see CAROM BILLIARDS, POOL 2b

billiard table *n* **:** a table having a slate bed covered with billiard cloth and surrounded by cushioned rails on which billiards is played; *also* **:** any similar table provided with six pockets for the playing of pool or English billiards

bil·lie *also* **bil·ly** \ˈbili\ *n, pl* **billies** [prob. fr. the name *Billie, Billy*] **1** *chiefly Scot* **:** COMRADE, COMPANION ⟨my old school ~⟩ **2** *chiefly Scot* **:** BROTHER **3** *chiefly Scot* **:** LAD, FELLOW, BOY ⟨when chapman *billies* leave the street —Robert Burns⟩

billies *pl of* BILLIE *or of* BILLY

bil·lie·tite \ˈbil(ē)ə,tīt, bəˈlē,t-\ *n* -s [F, fr. Valère Louis *Billiet* †1945 Belg. mineralogist] **:** a mineral consisting of a hydrous barium uranium oxide closely related to becquerelite

bil·li·ken \ˈbilə̇kən\ *n* -s *often cap* [prob. fr. the name *Billy* + *-ken* (alter. of *-kin*)] **:** a squat smiling comic figure used as a mascot

bill in aid of an execution : a creditor's bill filed to reach assets subject to execution but fraudulently transferred

bill in equity : the process instituting an action or proceeding in a suit in equity setting forth the plaintiff's cause of action

bill·ing \ˈbiliŋ, -ēŋ\ *n* -s [fr. gerund of ⁵*bill*] **1 :** the making out or forwarding of customer invoices and bills ⟨a battery of clerks to take care of the firm's monthly ~⟩ **2 a :** advertising (as by posters or placards) ⟨a widely publicized product that lived up to its advance ~⟩ **b :** presentation (as of an actor or play) to the public ⟨he spent much time arranging for the ~ of the controversial production⟩ **3 :** total amount of business or investments (as of an advertising agency) within a given period ⟨~*s* of leading agencies for a one-year period hit a record high⟩ **4 :** the relative prominence given a name (as of an actor) in publicizing, advertising, or other promotional programs ⟨the marquee of every theater gave him top ~⟩

billing machine *n* **:** a machine designed specif. for some or all of the mechanical operations (as typing, adding or computations, and sometimes duplicating) usu. involved in filling out and providing a record of customer invoices or bills

bil·lings·gate \ˈbiliŋz,gāt, -,git\ *n* -s *sometimes cap* [fr. *Billingsgate,* old gate and fish market, London, England, noted for the abusive language used there] **:** condemnatory language marked by the coarse or offensive and scornfully abusive or contentious ⟨the ~ common to the lower political quarreling —H.R.Warfel⟩ ⟨a kind of ~ Falstaff at his worst never approached —Edith Hamilton⟩ **syn** see ABUSE

bil·lion \ˈbilyən, ˈbiy-\ *n* -s *often attrib* [F, fr. *bi-* ¹bi- + *-illion* (as in *million*) — more at MILLION] **1** — see NUMBER table **2 :** a very large number

bil·lion·aire \ˌbilyəˈna(ə)(ə)r, ,biy-, -ne(ə)r, -na(a)ə, -neə, ˈ≈≈,≈\ *n* -s [*billion* + *-aire* (as in *millionaire*)] **:** one whose wealth is about a billion dollars or other monetary units

bil·lion-dol·lar grass \ˈ≈≈ˈ≈≈-\ *n* **:** JAPANESE MILLET

¹**bil·lionth** \ˈbilyən(t)th, ˈbiy-\ *adj* [*billion* + *-th*] **1 :** being number one billion in a countable series — see NUMBER table **2 :** being one of a billion equal parts into which anything is divisible

²**billionth** \"\ *n, pl* **billionths** \-yən(t)s,-yən(t)ths\ **1 :** number one billion in a countable series **2 :** the quotient of a unit divided by one billion **:** one of a billion equal parts of anything

¹**bill·man** \ˈbilmən\ *n, pl* **billmen** [³*bill* + *man*] **:** one using or armed with a bill

²**billman** \"\ *n, pl* **billmen** [⁴*bill* + *man*] **:** one that posts advertising bills **:** BILLPOSTER

bill of attainder : a bill or statute attainting a person

bill of complaint : COMPLAINT 1c

bill of costs : COST 4b

bill of credit 1 : LETTER OF CREDIT **2 :** a bill issued by a state (as in the American colonial period) involving the faith and credit of the state and designed to circulate as money on the credit of the state

bill of divorce *or* **bill of divorcement** *Jewish law* **:** a written document prepared according to prescribed form and given by the husband to his wife by which the marriage relation is dissolved — called also *get*

bill of entry : a written account of goods entered at the customhouse whether imported or intended for exportation

bill of exceptions : a statement of exceptions to the rulings or decision of a judge in the trial of a cause made for the purpose of a writ of error or an appeal to a superior court

bill of exchange : an unconditional written order addressed by one person to another and signed by the person giving it that requires the person to whom it is addressed to pay on demand or at a fixed or determinable future time a certain sum of money to or to the order of a specified person or to bearer, the drawee not being liable on it until he has accepted it — usu. used of foreign transactions; see ACCEPTANCE 4; compare DRAFT 14a(1); ACCEPTOR, DRAWER, PAYEE; NEGOTIABLE

bill of fare 1 : a printed or written list of the dishes that may be ordered (as in a restaurant) or of specially prepared dishes that are to be served (as at a banquet) **:** MENU **2 :** a listing of something offered to customers, clientele, or audience

bill of goods : a consignment of merchandise

bill of health : a duly authenticated certificate of the state of health of a ship's company and of a port with regard to infectious diseases, the bill being given to the ship's master at the time of leaving the port; *broadly* **:** a usu. satisfactory report about a condition or situation ⟨getting a clean *bill of health* in the loyalty investigation⟩

bill of indictment : an indictment before it is found or ignored by the grand jury

bill of interpleader : INTERPLEADER

bill of lading 1 : a written account of goods shipped by any person signed by the agent of the owner of the ship or by its master and acknowledging the receipt of the goods and promising to deliver them safe at the place directed, dangers of the sea excepted **2 :** a written document issued by a common carrier acknowledging the receipt of the goods named and setting forth the terms of the contract of carriage

bill of mortality : a periodical official statement of the number of deaths (later also of births) within a given time formerly issued in districts of London and vicinity

bill of pains and penalties : a legislative act imposing upon those who have previously committed a certain designated act or acts punishment or disability by which the act was not punishable at the time of its commission — compare EX POST FACTO LAW

bill of parcels : an account given by the seller to the buyer of the several articles purchased with their prices

bill of particulars : a detailed statement of the items of a plaintiff's demand in an action or of the defendant's setoff or counterclaim

bill of peace : a bill in equity to secure relief from repeated vexatious litigation

bill of rights *often cap B&R* **:** a summary of certain fundamental rights and privileges guaranteed to a people against violation by the state — used esp. of the first 10 amendments to the U.S. Constitution

bill of sale : a formal instrument for the conveyance or transfer of title to goods and chattels

bill of sight : a form of entry at the customhouse by which goods respecting which the importer is not possessed of full information may be provisionally landed for examination

bill of store 1 : a license formerly granted at the customhouse to merchants to carry stores and provisions necessary for a voyage custom free **2 :** a license permitting the reimportation of exported dutiable goods

bill of sufferance : a license to load and discharge cargo at specified ports without paying duty

bil·lon \ˈbilən\ *n* -s [F, fr. MF, ingot, billon, fr. *bille* log — more at BILLET] **1 :** an alloy of silver containing more than 50 percent by weight of copper **2 :** gold or silver alloyed with a considerable amount of some less valuable metal

¹**bil·low** \ˈbi(,)lō, -lə, *often* -lәw+V\ *n* -s [prob. fr. ON *bylgja;* akin to MHG *bulge* billow, MLG *bülge,* ON *belgr* bag — more at BELLY] **1 a :** a large swelling wave of water esp. in the open sea ⟨the ~*s* rose and fell, flashing in the sunlight⟩ **b :** a marked undulation of water ⟨the small boat cut swiftly through the lake's quiet ~*s*⟩ **2 :** a rolling or swirling surge ⟨~*s* of flame swept through the forest⟩ **:** an undulating or swelling mass ⟨~*s* of marching regiments wound through the valley⟩

²**billow** \"\ *vb* -ED/-ING/-S *vi* **1 :** to rise or roll in waves or surges **:** SURGE, UNDULATE ⟨the restless ~*ing* sea⟩ ⟨the smoke from the houses thickened and spread, bellied out, ~*ed* up —Kenneth Roberts⟩ **2 :** to bulge or swell out in billows (as through the action of the wind) ⟨~*ing* clouds⟩ ⟨the flags in front of the Supreme Court building ~*ed* out in pride —G.B. Oxnam⟩ ⟨the girl flashed on, her pretty skirt ~*ing* —Irwin Shaw⟩ ~ *vt* **:** to cause to billow ⟨a high wind was blowing from the west, ~*ing* the sleeves and skirts of women's dresses —Ellen Glasgow⟩ ⟨a field of burning grass ~*ing* thick black clouds of smoke into the sky —Donald Windham⟩

billow cloud *n* **:** a long narrow cloud or usu. a series of such clouds roughly parallel to each other caused by the flow of one layer of air over another producing waves at their interface the relatively cold crests of which are cloud-capped and their relatively warm troughs clear when the humidity is just right

bil·low·i·ness \ˈbilәwēnə̇s, -win-\ *n* -ES **:** the quality or state of being billowy

bil·lowy \ˈbilәwē, -wi\ *adj, sometimes* -ER/-EST **1 :** characterized by billows ⟨the ~ sea⟩ **2 :** suggestive of billows ⟨the ~ prairie⟩

billposter \ˈ≈,≈≈\ *n* **1 :** one that posts advertising bills **2 :** an advertising bill **:** POSTER

billposting \ˈ≈,≈≈\ *n* [⁴*bill* + *posting* (gerund of *post*)] **:** the action or occupation of posting advertising bills

bill quia timet \-ˈkwēəˈtē(,)met, -kwīəˈtī-\ *n* [L *quia timet* because he fears] **:** a bill by which a petitioner asks aid to prevent a wrong that he fears he may suffer from an act or an omission of another

bill rate *n* [⁴*bill*] **:** the rate of return on bills: **a :** the interest rate at which treasury bills are allotted in the weekly auction **b :** the rates at which outstanding bill issues are traded in the bill market

bills *pres 3d sing of* BILL, *pl of* BILL

billsticker \ˈ≈,≈≈\ *n* [⁴*bill* + *sticker*] **:** BILLPOSTER 1

billsticking \ˈ≈,≈≈\ *n* [⁴*bill* + *sticking*] **:** BILLPOSTING

¹**billy** *var of* BILLIE

²**bil·ly** \ˈbilē, -li\ *n, pl* **billies** *also* **billys** \-(,)lēz, -liz\ [prob. fr. the name *Billy*] **1 :** a slubbing frame **2 :** a heavy usu. wooden weapon for delivering blows **:** CLUB; *esp* **:** a policeman's club **3** [by shortening] **:** BILLY GOAT

³**billy** \"\ *n* -ES [prob. back-formation fr. *billycan*] *chiefly Austral* **:** a cylindrical container usu. made of metal or enamelware, having a set-in lid and a wire bail and often used for outdoor cooking or for carrying food or liquid ⟨tea fresh from the ~⟩

billyboy \ˈ≈≈,≈\ *n* [prob. fr. the name *Billy* + *boy*] *Brit* **:** a flat-bottomed bluff-bowed river or coasting boat usu. rigged as a ketch or sloop and carrying leeboards

billycan \ˈ≈≈,≈\ *n* [by folk etymology fr. *billa* water (a native name in Australia) + E *can*] **:** ³BILLY

billy club *n* [²*billy*] **:** ²BILLY 2

billycock \ˈ≈≈,käk\ *also* **billycock hat** *n* [origin unknown] *Brit* **:** DERBY 2a

billy gar *n* [¹*bill* + *-y*] **:** LONG-NOSED GAR

billy gate *n* [²*billy*] **:** the moving carriage in a slubbing machine

billy goat *n* [fr. the name *Billy*] **:** a male goat

billy-goat weed \ˈ≈≈,≈-\ *n* **:** a tropical American annual low herb (*Ageratum conyzoides*) widely cultivated as a border and bedding plant for its bluish or white flowers

billy owl *n, often cap B* [prob. fr. the name *Billy*] **:** BURROWING OWL

billy webb \-ˈweb\ *n, usu cap B&W* [origin unknown] **:** a tropical American timber tree (*Sweetia panamensis*) of the family Leguminosae with hard brown wood

bil·ly·wix \ˈ≈≈,wiks\ *n* -ES [origin unknown] *dial Eng* **:** TAWNY OWL

bi·lo \ˈbē(,)lō\ *n* -s [Serbo-Croatian] **:** an area of wide and roughly parallel ridges in the Karst topography of the Dinaric region of the Balkan peninsula

bi·lobate *also* **bi·lobated** \(ˈ)bī+\ *adj* [¹*bi-* + *lobate*] **:** divided into two lobes

bi·lobed \ˈbī+\ *adj* [¹*bi-* + *lobe* + *-ed*] **:** BILOBATE

bi·lobular \(ˈ)bī+\ *adj* [¹*bi-* + *lobular*] **:** having or divided into two lobules

bi·location \ˌbī+\ *n* [¹*bi-* + *location*] **:** the state or power of being in two places at the same time

bi·loc·u·lar \(ˈ)bīˈläkyələ(r)\ *adj* [¹*bi-* + NL *loculus* + E *-ar*] **:** divided into two cells or compartments

bi·loc·u·late \(ˈ)bīˈläkyələt, -,lāt\ *adj* [¹*bi-* + *loculate*] **:** BILOCULAR

bi·loc·u·li·na \bī,läkyəˈlīnə\ *n, cap* [NL, fr. ¹*bi-* + *loculus* + *-ina*] **:** a genus of calcareous imperforate foraminiferans extraordinarily abundant in the North sea where their remains form much of the ooze covering the bottom

bi·loc·u·line \(ˈ)bīˈläkyə,līn, -,lən\ *adj* [¹*bi-* + NL *loculus* + E *-ine*] **1 :** having two chambers **2** [NL *Biloculina*] **:** relating to the genus *Biloculina*

bi·loph·o·dont \(ˈ)bīˈläfə,dänt, -lōf-\ *adj* [¹*bi-* + *lophodont*] *zool* **:** having two transverse ridges or crests ⟨the molar teeth of the tapirs are ~⟩ — **bi·loph·o·dont·ism** \(ˈ)≈ˈ≈≈,dän,tizəm\ *n* -s

bilos *pl of* BILO

bi·loxi \bəˈläksē\ *n, pl* **biloxi** *or* **biloxis** *usu cap* **1 a :** a Siouan people in the lower Pascagoula river valley, Mississippi **b :** a member of the Biloxi people **2 :** the language of the Biloxi people

bil·sted \ˈbil,sted\ *n* -s [origin unknown] **:** SWEET GUM

bil·ston \ˈbilstən\ *n* -s *usu cap* [fr. *Bilston,* urban district, Staffordshire, England] **:** a type of English enameled ware often characterized by rich ground colors and gilding

bilt·more ash \ˈbilt,mō(ə)r-, -ō(ə)r-, -ōə-, -ó(ə)-\ *n, usu cap B* [from the *Biltmore* estate, Asheville, N.C.] **:** a medium-sized tree (*Fraxinus biltmoreana*) of the southeastern U.S. resembling and closely related to the white ash

biltmore stick *n, usu cap B* **:** a graduated rule used by timber estimators in determining tree diameters

bil·tong \ˈbil,tȯŋ, -äŋ\ *n* -s [Afrik, fr. *bil* buttock (fr. MD *bille*) + *tong* tongue, fr. MD *tonghe;* fr. its source & its tonguelike appearance; akin to OHG *arspelli* buttock, G dial. *bille* penis, OE *bealloc* testicle, and to OHG *zunga* tongue — more at BULL, TONGUE] *Africa* **:** jerked meat; *esp* **:** jerked beef, venison, or ostrich

bim *n* -s [origin unknown] *slang* **:** WOMAN; *esp* **:** a woman of loose morals

BIM *abbr* best in match

bi·maculate *also* **bi·maculated** \(ˈ)bī+\ *adj* [¹*bi-* + *maculate*] **:** marked with two maculae

bi·mah *also* **bi·ma** \ˈbēmə\ *n* -s [Yiddish *bime,* fr. Russ *bima* bema, fr. LGk *bēma* — more at BEMA] **:** ALMEMAR

bima·na \ˈbimənə, bīˈmānə\ *also* **bima·nes** \-,nēz\ *or* **bima·nus** \-,nəs\ *n pl* [NL, fr. F *bimane* two-handed, fr. *bi-* ¹bi- + *-mane* (fr. L *manus* hand) — more at MANUAL] *zool* **:** man considered as sole representative of a group distinguished by having hands unlike the feet — compare QUADRUMANA — **bi·mane** \ˈbī,mān\ *adj or n*

bima·nal \ˈbimənᵊl, (ˈ)bīˈmān-\ *or* **bima·nous** \-nəs\ *adj* [F *bimane* + E *-al* or *-ous*] **:** having two hands **:** TWO-HANDED

bi·manual \(ˈ)bī+\ *adj* [¹*bi-* + *manual*] **:** done with two hands **:** requiring the use of both hands ⟨a machine designed for ~ operation⟩ — **bi·manually** \(ˈ)bī+\ *adv*

bi·mas·tic \(ˈ)bīˈmastik\ *adj* [¹*bi-* + *mast-* + *-ic*] **:** having two mammae — **bi·mas·tism** \bīˈma,stizəm\ *n* -s — **bi·mas·ty** \ˈbī,mastē\ *n* -ES

bi·mastoid \(ˈ)bī+\ *adj* [¹*bi-* + *mastoid*] **:** of, relating to, or joining the two mastoid processes

bi·maxillary \(ˈ)bī, ˌbī+\ *adj* [¹*bi-* + *maxillary*] **1 :** of or relating to the two halves of the maxilla **2** *anthrop* **:** of or relating to the distance between the lower margins of the sutures of the maxilla and malar bones

bim·bo \ˈbim(,)bō\ *n, pl* **bimbos** *or* **bimboes** [origin unknown] **1** *slang* **:** MAN, FELLOW — often a generalized expression of disparagement ⟨a couple of ~*s* slouching down the street⟩ **2** *slang* **:** WOMAN; *esp* **:** a woman of loose morals

bime·by \(ˈ)bīmˈbī, ˌbīəmˈbī, ,bəmˈbī\ *adv* [by alter.] *chiefly dial* **:** by and by

bime·ler·ite \ˈbīmlə,rīt\ *n* -s *usu cap* [Joseph M. *Bimeler* (Bäumler) †1853 German-American founder of Separatist Society of Zoar, Ohio + E *-ite*] **:** ZOARITE

bi·mes·ter \(ˈ)bīˈmestə(r)\ *n* -s [¹*bi-* + *-mester* (as in semester)] **:** a period of two months

bi·mes·tri·al \-trēəl\ *adj* [L *bimestris* (fr. *bi-* ¹bi- + *-mestris,* fr. *mensis* month) + E *-al* — more at MOON] **:** continuing two months **:** BIMONTHLY

¹**bi·metal** \(ˈ)bī+\ *adj* [by shortening] **:** BIMETALLIC

²**bimetal** \"\ *n* -s **:** a bimetallic material or device

¹**bi·metallic** \ˌbī+\ *adj* [F *bimétallique,* fr. *bi-* ¹bi- + *métallique* metallic — more at METALLIC] **1 :** relating to, based on, or using bimetallism **2** [¹*bi-* + *metallic*] **:** composed of two different metals: as **a :** formed of two different metals or alloys (as in sheets, layers, or strips) bonded together (as by fusing, welding, plating, or riveting) — often used of devices in which a change in temperature causes bending of a part composed of two metals that expand differently **b** *of offset printing plates* **:** surfaced with two metals, one grease-repellent and one grease-receptive — compare LITHOGRAPHY

²**bimetallic** \"\ *n* -s **:** BIMETAL

bi·met·al·lism \(ˈ)bīˈmed·ᵊl,izəm, -etᵊl-\ *n* -s [F *bimétallisme,* fr. *bi-* ¹bi- + *métal* metal + *-isme* -ism — more at METAL] **:** the policy or practice of using two metals (as gold and silver) jointly as a monetary standard by specifying that both constitute legal tender at a predetermined ratio

bi·met·al·list \-ᵊlə̇st\ *n* -s [prob. fr. F *bimétalliste,* fr. *bi-* ¹bi- + *métal* + *-iste* -ist] **:** an advocate of bimetallism — **bi·met·al·lis·tic** \(ˌ)≈ˌ≈ᵊlˈistik\ *adj*

¹**bi·millenary** \(ˈ)bī, ˌbī+\ *or* **bi·millennial** \ˌbī+\ *n, pl* **bimillenaries** *or* **bimillennials** [¹*bi-* + *millenary* or *millennial*] **1 :** a period of 2000 years **2 :** a 2000th anniversary or its celebration

²**bimillenary** \"\ *adj* **:** of or relating to a bimillenary

bi·millennium \ˌbī+\ *n, pl* **bimillenniums** *also* **bimillennia** [NL, fr. ¹*bi-* + *millennium*] **:** BIMILLENARY

bim·li·pa·tam hemp \ˌbimlēpəˈtam-, -ˈtäm-\ *or* **bim·li hemp** \ˈbimlē-\ *or* **bimlipatam jute** *or* **bimli jute** *n, usu cap B* [fr.

Bimlipatam, Bimlipatnam, city in northeastern Madras, India] : KENAF
bim·me·ler \'bim(ə)lə(r)\ *n* -s *usu cap* [after J.M. *Bimeler* — more at BIMELERITE] : ZOARITE
bi·modal \(')bī+\ *adj* [1*bi-* + *modal*] : possessing two statistical modes — **bi·modality** \¦bī+\ *n* -ES
bi·molecular \¦bī+\ *adj* [ISV 1*bi-* + *molecular*] : relating to or formed from two molecules ⟨~ reaction⟩ : being two molecules thick ⟨~ layers⟩ — **bi·mo·lec·u·lar·ly** *adv*
1**bi·monthly** \(')bī+\ *adj* [1*bi-* + *monthly*] : occurring, appearing, or done every two months; *sometimes* : occurring, appearing, or done twice a month ⟨a ~ magazine⟩ — compare SEMIMONTHLY
2**bimonthly** \"\ *n* -ES : a bimonthly publication
3**bimonthly** \"\ *adv* : once every two months; *sometimes* : twice a month
bi·morph \'bī,mȯrf\ *n* -S [1*bi-* + *-morph*] : a device consisting of two layers of a crystal (as Rochelle salt) cemented together and often used in a phonograph pickup because of the ability to convert the vibration of the needle into electrical voltage
bi·morphemic \¦bī+,-\ *adj* [1*bi-* + *morphemic*] : consisting of two morphemes (sense 2) ⟨the ~ word *tied*⟩ : involving two morphemes
bi·motored \(')bī+\ *adj* [1*bi-* + *motored*] : equipped with two separate motors — used esp. of airplanes
bims *pl of* BIM
bi·muscular \(')bī+\ *adj* [1*bi-* + *muscular*] : having two adductor muscles ⟨most bivalves are ~⟩
1**bin** \'bin\ *n* -S [ME *binne,* fr. OE *binn, binne* manger, basket, prob. of Celt origin; akin to Gaulish *benna* two-wheeled cart with a wicker body; akin to Gk *phatnē* manger, OE *bindan* to bind — more at BIND] : a box, frame, crib, or enclosed place used for storage ⟨coal ~⟩ ⟨apple ~⟩ ⟨grain ~⟩
2**bin** \"\ *vt* **binned; binned; binning; bins** : to put into a bin; *esp* : to stow and age (bottled wine) in a bin
3**bin** \'bēn\ *n* -S [Hindi *bīn,* fr. Skt *vīṇā*] : VINA
4**bin** \"\ *n* -S [modif. (influenced by 3*bin*) of Hindi *ben,* fr. Skt *venu* bamboo, flute] : PUNGI
bin- *comb form* [ME, fr. LL, fr. L *bini* two by two; akin to OE *twin* twine — more at TWINE] **1** : two : two by two : two at a time ⟨*bin*ary⟩ ⟨*bin*ate⟩ ⟨*bin*aural⟩ **2** *chem* : BI- 4 ⟨*bin*oxalate⟩ ⟨*bin*oxide⟩ — in some words of which the last constituent begins with a vowel; compare BI-
bina *var of* VINA
1**bi·na·ry** \'bīnərē, -ri *sometimes* -,ner-\ *adj* [LL *binarius,* fr. L *bini* two by two + *-arius* -ary] **1** : compounded or consisting of two things or parts : characterized by two : DUAL, DOUBLE **2** : composed of two chemical elements, of an element and a radical that acts as an element, or of two such radicals ⟨a ~ compound⟩ ⟨~ salts⟩ **3 a** : of, relating to, or being a system of numbers having two as its base **b** : involving two variables ⟨a ~ form⟩ **4** *logic* : relating two arguments or terms (of functions and propositions) ⟨a ~ relation⟩ **5 a** : having two musical subjects or two divisions or sections one complementary to the other ⟨a song in ~ form⟩ **b** : DUPLE — used of measure or rhythm
2**binary** \"\ *n* -ES [ME *binarie,* fr. ML *binarius,* fr. LL, consisting of two] : something that is constituted of two figures, things, or parts; *specif* : BINARY STAR
binary color *n* : a color made by mixing two primary colors : SECONDARY COLOR
binary combination *or* **binary name** *n* : 3BINOMIAL
binary digit *n* **1** : either of the two digits, conventionally 0 and 1, used in a binary system of numeration **2** : 7BIT 1
binary fission *n* : reproduction of a cell by division into two approximately equal parts ⟨the *binary fission* of protozoans⟩
binary granite *n* : a granite composed only of quartz and feldspar or one containing two kinds of mica
binary nomenclature *n* : a system of nomenclature in which the designation of a species consists of two parts that may or may not be single names — compare BINOMIAL NOMENCLATURE
binary opposition *n, phonetics* : one of a number of pairs of diametrically opposed characteristics (as voicedness or voicelessness) taken as a basis for the classification of speech sounds
binary star *also* **binary system** *n* : a system of two stars that revolve around each other under their mutual gravitation and falling into one or more of three classes — compare ECLIPSING VARIABLE, SPECTROSCOPIC BINARY, VISUAL BINARY
binary system *n* : a system having two components
binary theory *n* : DUALISM 4
1**bi·nate** \'bī,nāt, *usu* -ād.+V\ *adj* [*bin-* + *-ate*] *bot* : growing in pairs or couples : DOUBLE — **bi·nate·ly** *adv*
2**binate** \"\ *vi* -ED/-ING/-S [NL *binatus,* past part. of *binare,* prob. fr. L *bini* two by two — more at BIN-] : to celebrate two masses on the same day
bi·na·tion \bī'nāshən\ *n* -S [NL *bination-, binatio,* prob. fr. *binatus* + *-ion-, -io* -ion] : celebration of mass twice on the same day by the same priest
bi·national \(')bī+\ *adj* [1*bi-* + *national*] : composed of, belonging to, or connected with two nations or nationalities
bin·aural \(')bī¦n+,-\ *adj* [ISV *bin-* + *aural*] **1** *also* **bi·aural** \(')bī+\ : of or relating to two ears ⟨~ perception of sound⟩ : involving the use or function of both ears ⟨a ~ stethoscope⟩ **2** : of, relating to, or characterized by directional techniques and systems that utilize the actual placement of sound sources (as in sound transmission and recording) to achieve in sound reproduction an effect on the listener of hearing the sound sources in their original positions, so creating the illusion of added dimension and fuller fidelity ⟨~ broadcasting⟩ ⟨a ~ tape recorder⟩ — usu. limited to techniques and systems using two separate transmission or recording paths and sometimes limited in sound reproduction to the use of earphones; compare STEREOPHONIC — **binaurally** *adv*
bin·auricular \'bī,n, ¦bi,n+\ *adj* [*bin-* + *auricular*] : BIAURICULAR
bin-burn \'=,=\ *vi* [1*bin*] *of cereal grains* : to become discolored and poor in quality through heat generated and moisture accumulated in bin storage
binche lace \'baⁿsh-, -anch-\ *n, usu cap B* [fr. *Binche,* Belgium, where it was originally made] : a bobbin lace of Flemish origin having flat designs of floral scrolls on a coarse mesh ground with a scattered snowflake pattern
1**bind** \'bīnd\ *vb* **bound** \'baund\ **bound** *or archaic* **bounded; binding; binds** \'bīn(d)z\ [ME *binden,* fr. OE *bindan;* akin to OHG *bintan* to bind, ON *binda,* Goth *bindan,* Gk *peisma* cable, Skt *badhnāti* he binds] *vt* **1 a** : to make secure by tying (as with a cord) ⟨they *bound* his hands⟩ **b** : to confine with or as if with chains or other bonds so as to deprive of liberty : make captive ⟨he was *bound* and thrown into prison⟩ ⟨she was not wholly *bound* in mind by her middle-class existence —Delmore Schwartz⟩ **c** : to hold in check : keep in place : RESTRAIN ⟨a sense of fair play ~*s* them and preserves their open-mindedness⟩ **d** : to hamper the free movement of : exert an uncomfortably restrictive and chafing force upon ⟨tight-fitting clothes that ~ the hiker⟩ **e** : to put under an obligation (as by making, accepting, or exacting a solemn promise) ⟨the knight *bound* himself with an oath to serve faithfully⟩ **f** : to constrain with legal authority : ⟨the court's decision ~*s* them to pay the fine⟩ **2 a** : to wrap around so as to cover (as with cloth) : SWATHE ⟨a broad sash *bound* her waist⟩ **b** : to wrap up (an injury) with a cloth : BANDAGE ⟨~*ing* up the gash with clean gauze⟩ **3** : to fasten round about : ENCIRCLE, GIRD, WREATHE ⟨a statue of a poet, laurel *bound* about the head⟩ **4** : to tie together (as stalks of wheat) ⟨~*ing* the reaped grain into sheaves⟩ **5 a** : to cause (particles) to stick together in a usu. hard mass ⟨wet sand that had been baked and *bound* by the sun⟩ **b** : to cause to cohere : unite into a cohesive whole ⟨~ the chopped celery and apples with mayonnaise⟩ : give a moist or thickened consistency to ⟨~ poultry dressing with beaten eggs⟩ **c** : to take up and hold usu. by chemical forces : combine with ⟨cellulose ~*s* water⟩ **6** : to make costive : CONSTIPATE **7** : to make firm or sure : SETTLE ⟨~*ing* our agreement with a friendly handshake⟩ **8** : to protect, strengthen, or decorate by a band or binding ⟨a carpet *bound* with a yellow edging⟩ **9 a** : to apply the parts of the cover to (a book) in successive stages (as in hand binding) **b** : CASE *vt* 1d **10** : INDENTURE, APPRENTICE ⟨he was *bound* out to the tailor for one year⟩ **11** : to cause to be attached (as by gratitude or affection) ⟨some gracious instinct ~*s* her to her home —Agnes Repplier⟩ **12** : to fasten together : CONNECT, UNITE ⟨a jeweled pin *bound* the ends of the scarf⟩ **13** : to move (a fencing opponent's blade) from one line to another by exerting pressure against **14** : to effect (an insurance policy) by means of an oral commitment or by a binder **15** *logic* : to convert (a free variable in a statement or formula) into a bound variable by prefixing a quantifier or other operator — compare QUANTIFICATION ~ *vi* **1 a** : to form a usu. hard lump or mass ⟨heat causes clay to ~⟩ **b** : to form a cohesive mass ⟨a little milk added to the ingredients will quickly make the mixture ~⟩ **2** : to hamper free movement : exert an uncomfortably restrictive and chafing force ⟨shorts that are guaranteed not to ~⟩ **3** : to become hindered from free operation : become blocked or jammed ⟨rust caused the door to ~ in its frame⟩ **4** : to exert a restraining, compelling, or uniting influence ⟨a promise that ~*s*⟩ **5** *falconry* : to close with or grapple quarry in the air **6** *printing* : to lock up improperly ⟨oversize cuts caused the form to ~⟩
2**bind** \" *but* 'bin(d) *in sense 2*\ *n* -S [ME *binde,* fr. *binden,* v.] **1** : something that binds or ties : the act of binding : a place where binding occurs : the state or an instance of being bound **2** : BINE **3** *Scot* : capacity esp. for drink : LIMIT **4 a** : TIE **b** : SLUR **5** : the action of forcing a fencing opponent's blade from one line to another by means of pressure against his blade **6** : a position that restricts an opponent's freedom of action (as in chess) ⟨White gets a ~ on Black's position⟩ — **in a bind** *slang* : in distress : in trouble
bind·er \'bīndə(r)\ *n* -S [ME, fr. *binden* + *-er*] **1** : one that binds: as **a** : BOOKBINDER **b** : BUNCHER **c** : a worker who stitches decorative or reinforcing bindings to wearing apparel, household furnishings, or upholstery **2 a** : something that is used in binding (as a fillet, band, or cord) **b** : a broad bandage applied (as about the chest or abdomen) for support ⟨breast ~⟩ ⟨obstetrical ~⟩ **c** : a detachable cover or other device for holding together sheets of paper or similar material (as sheet music or magazines) in loose-leaf form — see POST BINDER, RING BINDER, SPRING BINDER **d** : the sheet of tobacco that binds the filler in a cigar next to the wrapper **e** : a band (as of straw) used for binding sheaves of grain; *also* : a band (as of wire) used for binding bales **f** : a series of extra warp or weft threads that hold together the face and back of a cloth (as a double cloth) by interweaving without disturbing the surface patterns **g** *North* : RUBBER BAND **3 a** : something (as tar or cement) that produces or promotes cohesion in loosely assembled substances **b** : the nonvolatile portion of a paint vehicle **c** : a substance (as flour or cornstarch) used in cooking as a thickening agent or as an agent to improve consistency (as of a sauce) **d** : a fibrous material used in plaster and stucco to increase their cohesiveness while in the plastic state **e** : an adhesive used in a coated paper or a material used in the paper stock to make the paper firmer and less fuzzy **f** : a substance (as cereal, oil, clay, resin, or pitch) that causes cohesion of the grains of sand in foundry molds or cores **g** : a substance added to metal powder to assist in cohesion of the metal particles during sintering **h** : a substance (as glucose or acacia) used in pharmacy to hold together the ingredients of a compressed tablet **4** : a mechanical device used in binding: as **a** : a sewing-machine attachment for putting on bindings **b** : a harvesting machine that cuts grain and binds it into bundles **c** : a single machine designed to perform several operations in the construction of a book **5 a** : a beam, girder, or frame used to bind together the parts of a structure **b** : a springy pole used for tightening a chain binding together a load of logs **c** *weaving* : a lever in a shuttle box that prevents the rebound of the shuttle **d** : BONDSTONE, HEADER **e** : one of the fibers connecting the staples so as to form a piece or fleece of wool **6 a** : a written instrument used when an insurance policy cannot be immediately issued to evidence that the insurance coverage attaches at a specified time and continues subject to a maximum limitation until the policy is issued or the risk is declined and notice thereof given **b** : BINDING RECEIPT **7** : a receipt for money paid to the owner or his agent to secure the right to purchase a piece of real estate upon agreed terms; *also* : the money itself **8** : BINDER LINE
binder course *n* : a coarse aggregate bound with bitumen between the foundation and the wearing course of an asphalt pavement
binder line *n* : a large-type identifying line that heads an esp. long newspaper story or group of related stories carried on an inside page
binder's board *also* **binder board** *n* : a smooth hard tough pulpboard much used in covers by bookbinders
binder's cloth *n* : cotton fabric with a finish suitable for book covers — compare BOOK CLOTH
binder's title *n* : the title printed or stamped by the binder on the outside of the cover of a book
binder twine *n* : a coarse slack-twisted twine or thin rope (as of sisal or henequen) used in binding esp. of grain after cutting
bind·ery \'bīnd(ə)rē, -ri\ *n* -ES [1*bind* + *-ery*] : a place where books are bound
bind·heim·ite \'bint,hī,mīt\ *n* -S [G *bindheimit,* fr. Johann J. *Bindheim* †1825 Ger. chemist + G *-it* -ite] : a mineral $Pb_2Sb_2O_6(O,OH)$ consisting of hydrous lead antimony oxide produced from the alteration of other ores
bin·di-eye \'bindē,ī\ *n* [origin unknown] : a grayish perennial Australian herb (*Calotis cuneifolia*) of the family Compositae with globular fruiting heads resembling burs
1**bind·ing** \'bīndiŋ, -dēŋ\ *n* -S [ME, fr. gerund of *binden*] **1** : the action of one that binds **2** : a material or device used to bind: as **a** : the fastening of the sections of a book; *esp* : this fastening and the cover **b** : a narrow fabric (as tape) or a narrow piece of fabric (as bias fabric) used to finish, strengthen, or decorate raw edges (as of a garment, carpet, or blanket) **c** : a band of masonry so laid as to fasten together or strengthen adjoining parts **d** : an ingredient (as flour, eggs, or starch) used in cooking to give cohesion or a richer or thicker consistency (as to a sauce) **e** : the set of ski fastenings for holding the toe of the boot firm on the ski
2**binding** \"\ *adj* [ME, fr. pres. part. of *binden*] **1** : that binds or causes to bind : tending to bind **2** : imposing an obligation, duty, or responsibility ⟨a solemnly ~ promise⟩ **3** : requiring submission, conformity, or obedience ⟨the ~ force of wise laws⟩ — **bind·ing·ly** *adv* — **bind·ing·ness** *n* -ES
binding course *n* : a row (as of bricks) set across an inner and an outer course to bind them together
binding edge *n* : the edge (as of an insert or leaf) that is bound into a book, pamphlet, or magazine
binding energy *n* : the energy required to break up a molecule, an atom, or an atomic nucleus completely into its constituent particles; *also* : the portion of the energy acquired by one part when separated from the rest, being in the case of nuclear disintegration large enough to give a measurable change in mass — compare MASS DEFECT
binding joist *n* : a joist framed into the girders of a double-framed floor to support the bridging joists
binding post *n* **1** : a metallic post attached to electrical apparatus for convenience in making connections **2** : any of the posts holding the sheets in place in a loose-leaf binder
binding rafter *n* : a longitudinal timber (as a purlin) between the plate and the ridge of a roof for the support of rafters
binding receipt *n* : a receipt given to an applicant for life insurance when he signs the application and pays his first premium stipulating that the insurance shall go into effect immediately if the risk proves to be acceptable irrespective of the date of delivery of the policy and providing for return of the money if risk is declined — called also *binder, conditional receipt*
binding screw *n* : a setscrew used to hold parts together (as for making a firm electrical connection or for clamping a glass lampshade in place)
binding strake *n* : a heavy strake of planking next to and under the sheer strake
binding tape *n* : FRICTION TAPE
bin·dle \'bindᵊl\ *n* -S [prob. alter of *bundle*] **1** *slang* **a** : a bundle usu. containing clothing and cooking utensils **b** : BLANKET ROLL 1, BEDROLL **2** *slang* : a small package, envelope, or paper containing a narcotic (as morphine, heroin, or cocaine); *also* : a usu. small quantity of a narcotic : a narcotic dose
bindle stiff *n, slang* : a transient usu. carrying a bundle (as of clothing or bedding): as **a** : a migratory worker **b** : TRAMP, HOBO
bind off *vt* : to decrease (stitches) in knitting in order to form an edge by slipping the first of two stitches over the second and repeating across
bind over *vt* : to put under bonds to do something (as to appear at court) ⟨he was *bound over* to the grand jury⟩
binds *pres 3d sing of* BIND, *pl of* BIND
bindweed \'=,=\ *n* [1*bind* + *weed;* fr. their twining habit] : any of numerous plants of more or less twining habit and dense or prickly form that tend to mat together or interlace with plants among which they grow: as **a** : any of several plants of the genus *Convolvulus* — see FIELD BINDWEED, HEDGE BINDWEED, ROUGH BINDWEED **b** : knotgrass or a closely related plant (as black bindweed)
bindweed nightshade *n* : ENCHANTER'S NIGHTSHADE
bine \'bīn\ *n* -S [alter. of 2*bind*] : a twining stem or flexible shoot: as **a** : the stem of common hop varieties **b** : BINDWEED **c** : WOODBINE 1
bi·negation \¦bī+\ *n* -S [1*bi-* + *negation*] : JOINT DENIAL
bi·nervate \(')bī+\ *adj* [1*bi-* + *nervate*] : TWO-NERVED
bi·net age \bē'nā-, bi-\ *n, usu cap B* [after A. *Binet*] : mental age as determined by the Binet-Simon test
binet-si·mon test \-sē'mōⁿ-\ *n, usu cap B & S* [after Alfred *Binet* †1911 and Théodore *Simon* †1961, Fr. psychologists] : an intelligence test consisting orig. of tasks graded in difficulty from the level of the average 3-year-old to that of the average 12-year-old but later revised and extended in range — called also *Binet test;* see STANFORD-BINET TEST
1**bing** \'biŋ\ *n* -S [ME, of Scand origin; akin to ON *bingr* divided space, bin, OSw *binge* storage room, Icel *bingur* heap; akin to OHG *bungo* tuber — more at BUNCH] **1** *dial Brit* **a** : a heap or pile for storage ⟨a ~ of potatoes⟩ **b** : a storage bin **2** *slang* : a solitary-confinement prison cell
2**bing** \"\ *vi* [origin unknown] *archaic* : GO
3**bing** \"\ *interj* [imit.] — used to suggest a sharp ringing sound
1**binge** \'binj\ *vb* -ED/-ING/-S [origin unknown] *vt, dial Brit* : to soak (a wooden vessel) so as to swell the wood and prevent leakage ~ *vi, dial Brit* : to stand soaking so as to swell and prevent leakage ⟨putting vats to ~⟩
2**binge** \"\ *n* -S [E dial. *binge* to drink heavily, fr. 1*binge*] **1 a** : uninhibited and usu. excessive indulgence esp. in alcoholic beverages : CAROUSAL ⟨bleary-eyed from a week-end ~⟩ **b** : unreserved and often riotous indulgence in or abandonment to any form of activity : a riotous display : ORGY, RAMPAGE, SPLURGE ⟨a buying ~⟩ ⟨an emotional ~⟩ **2 a** : social gathering : PARTY ⟨fancy-dress ~*s* have always been my dish —P.G.Wodehouse⟩ ⟨the intimate ~ or book tea —R.G.G. Price⟩
bin·gee *also* **bin·gy** \'binjē\ *n, pl* **bingees** *also* **bingies** [native name in Australia] *Austral* : STOMACH, BELLY
bing·hi \'biŋ,ī\ *n* -S *often cap* [native name in Australia] *slang Austral* : ABORIGINE
1**bin·gle** \'biŋgəl\ *n* -S [prob. alter. (influenced by 3*bing*) of *single*] : BASE HIT
2**bingle** \"\ *n* -S [*bob* + *shingle*] : a woman's short bob partly shingled at the back
bing·ley terrier \'biŋlē-\ *n, usu cap B* [fr. *Bingley,* Yorkshire, England] : AIREDALE TERRIER
1**bin·go** \'biŋ(,)gō\ *interj* [alter. of 3*bing*] **1** — used to point up the occurrence of a sudden or unexpected event **2** — used in the game of bingo to indicate that one has completed a 5-number row
2**bingo** \"\ *n* -S *sometimes cap* [1*bingo,* the winner's exclamation] **1 a** : a game resembling lotto or keno, the card used being a grid on which five numbers that are covered in a row in any direction constitute a win, the center square being counted as an already drawn number — called also *beano* **b** : a social gathering at which bingo is played **2** : a dice game with usu. petty merchandise as stakes
binh dinh \'bin,din\ *adj, usu cap B&D* [fr. *Binh Dinh,* So. Vietnam] : of or from the city of Binh Dinh, So. Vietnam : of the kind or style prevalent in Binh Dinh
bi·ni *also* **be·ni** \bə'nē\ *n, pl* **bini** *or* **binis** *usu cap* : EDO
bin·io·dide \(')bī¦n, (')bi¦n+,-\ *n* [*bin-* + *iodide*] : DIIODIDE ⟨mercury ~⟩
biniou \bē'nyü, bi'-\ *n* -S [F, fr. Bret] : the Breton bagpipe consisting of one drone and a chanter with seven finger holes
bi·nit \'bīnət\ *n* -S [*binary digit*] : BINARY DIGIT
bink \'biŋk\ *n* -S [ME (northern dial.) *bink, benk,* fr. OE *benc* — more at BENCH] **1** *chiefly Scot* : a bench to sit on **2** *chiefly Scot* : an open rack of shelves for dishes **3** *chiefly Scot* : a bank of earth
bin·man \'binmən\ *n, pl* **binmen** [1*bin* + *man*] : a worker who fills hoppers or tends the flow of material through bins connected by conveyors
bin·na \'binə\ *conj* [*be,* pres. subjunctive of *be,* v.i. + *na* (adv.)] *Scot* : UNLESS
1**bin·na·cle** \'binəkəl, -nēk-\ *n* -S [alter. (perh. influenced by *bin*) of earlier *bittacle,* fr. ME *bitakle,* fr. OPg *bitácola,* or OSp *bitácula,* fr. L *habitaculum* dwelling place, fr. *habitare* to dwell — more at HABIT] : a case, box, or stand containing a ship's compass and a lamp
2**binnacle** \"\ *also* **bin·ne·kill** \"\ *n* -S [D *binnenkil,* fr. *binnen* within + *kil* channel — more at BILANDER, KILL] *in New York & Pennsylvania* : a secondary channel of a stream
binnacle list *n* : a sick list posted at or near the binnacle for the use of the officer of the deck
binned *past of* BIN
binning *n* -S [fr. gerund of 2*bin*] : the action of putting into a bin; *esp* : the stowing and aging of bottled wine in a bin
bin·ny \'binē\ *n* -ES [NL *bynni,* specific epithet of *Barbus bynni*] : a very large cyprinid fish (*Barbus bynni*) common in the Nile river and sometimes used as food
bino *var of* BENO
1**bin·oc·u·lar** \(')bī¦näkyələ(r) *also* bə'n-\ *adj* [*bin-* + *ocular*] **1** : of or relating to both eyes ⟨~ infection⟩ **2** : employing both eyes at once; *specif* : producing an appearance of solidity or depth because of the slight difference in the two retinal images due to the angle from which each eye views an object ⟨~ vision⟩ **3** : adapted to the use of both eyes ⟨a ~ microscope⟩ — **bin·oc·u·lar·i·ty** \(,)bī,näkyə'larəd.ē *also* bə,n-\ *n* -ES — **bin·oc·u·lar·ly** \(')bī¦näkyələ(r)lē, bə'n-\ *adv*
2**binocular** \bə'näkyələ(r) *also* bī-\ *n, pl* **binoculars** *but sometimes sing in constr* : an optical instrument composed of two refracting telescopes mounted on a single frame and containing erecting systems usu. with both focusing tubes simultaneously adjustable by means of a single screw ⟨a 6-power ~⟩ ⟨the ~*s* are in that leather case⟩ — usu. used in pl. and often with *pair* ⟨a pair of ~*s*⟩

binocular

binocular rivalry *n* : RETINAL RIVALRY
bin·oculate \(')bī¦n, bə'n+,-\ *adj* [*bin-* + *oculate*] : having two eyes
bin·oc·u·lus \bī'näkyələs, bə'-\ *n* -ES [NL, fr. *bin-* + L *oculus* eye — more at EYE] : the two eyes and their central nervous connections regarded as a functional whole
bi·nodal \(')bī+\ *adj* [1*bi-* + *nodal*] : consisting of or having two nodes ⟨a ~ stem of a plant⟩ ⟨a ~ quartic curve⟩
bin·o·kid \'binəkəd, ,==kid\ *n* -S *usu cap* [of Philippine origin; akin to Bisayan *bukidnon* — more at BUKIDNON] : BUKIDNON 2
bi·no·men \(')bī¦nōmən\ *n, pl* **binom·i·na** \-'nämənə\ [NL, fr. 1*bi-* + L *nomen* name — more at NAME] : a binomial naming a species ⟨*Canis latrans* is the ~ of the coyote⟩
bi·no·men·cla·ture \'bī'nōmən,klāchə(r)\ *n* -S : BINOMIAL NOMENCLATURE
1**bi·no·mi·al** \bī'nōmēəl\ *n* -S [NL *binomium* (fr. neut. of ML *binomius*) + E *-al*] : a mathematical expression consisting of two terms connected by a plus sign or minus sign (as $a+b$ or $7-3$)
2**binomial** \(')=¦===\ *adj* [ML *binomius* having two names (alter. of L *binominis,* fr. *bi-* 1*bi-* + *-nominis,* fr. *nomin-, nomen* name) + E *-al* — more at NAME] **1** [1*binomial*] : relating to binomials **2** : consisting of two terms or names — **bi·no·mi·al·ly** \-ēəlē, -li\ *adv*
3**binomial** \=¦===\ *n* -S : a species name consisting of two terms — see BINOMIAL NOMENCLATURE

binomial coefficient *n* : the coefficient of any term resulting from the expansion of the binomial $(x+y)^n$
binomial distribution *n* : a frequency distribution of the probability that an attribute that occurs with a given probability among the members of a population will occur a certain number of times in a succession of samples of the population — called also *Bernoulli distribution*
binomial expansion *n* : the expansion of a binomial
bi·no·mi·al·ism \bī'nōmēə,lizəm\ *n* -s : the theory or use of binomial nomenclature
binomial law *n* : a theorem in mathematics: the probability of an event whose probability on each trial is *p* occurring *r* times in *n* trials is given by the term containing p^r in the binomial expansion of $(p+q)^n$ in which $q=1-p$
binomial nomenclature *n* : a system of nomenclature in which each species of plant or animal receives a name of two terms of which the first identifies the genus to which it belongs and the second the species itself and which was first standardized by Linnaeus about the middle of the 18th century — compare LINNAEAN
binomial theorem *n* : a theorem in mathematics: a binomial may be raised to any power according to $(x+y)^n = x^n + nx^{n-1}y + \frac{n(n-1)}{1\cdot2}x^{n-2}y^2 + \frac{n(n-1)(n-2)}{1\cdot2\cdot3}x^{n-3}y^3 + \ldots$
bi·nominal \(ˈ)bī+\ *adj* [L *binominis* having two names + E *-al* — more at BINOMIAL] : using a combination of two names : BINOMIAL
bi·normal \bī+\ *n* -s [1*bi-* + *normal*] : the normal to a twisted curve at a point of the curve that is perpendicular to the osculating plane of the curve at that point
bin·ovular \(ˈ)bī¦n+-\ *adj* [*bin-* + *ovular*] : BIOVULAR
bin·oxalate \(ˈ)bī¦n, (ˈ)bi¦n +-\ *n* -s [*bin-* + *oxalate*] : an acid oxalate (as sodium binoxalate $NaHC_2O_4$) formed from oxalic acid by the replacement of half the acid hydrogen
bin·oxide \"+-\ *n* -s [*bin-* + *oxide*] : DIOXIDE
bins *plural of* BIN, *pres 3d sing of* BIN
bint \ˈbint\ *n* -s [Ar, girl, daughter] *slang Brit* : WOMAN, GIRL ⟨my regular Thursday night ~, a married woman of twenty-nine, so she said —Bill Naughton⟩
bin·tang·or \bin'taŋə(r)\ *n* -s [Malay *bĕntangor*] : POON
bin·tu·rong \bin·'tü,rȯŋ\ *n* -s [Malay *bĕnturong, binturong, binturon*] : an Asiatic prehensile-tailed civet (*Arctictis binturong*)
bi·nuclear *or* **bi·nucleate** *or* **bi·nucleated** \(ˈ)bī+\ *adj* [1*bi-* + *nuclear* or *nucleate* or *nucleated*] : having two nuclei
bi·nucleolate \¦bī, (ˈ)bī+\ *adj* [1*bi-* + *nucleolate*] : having two nucleoli
bio \ˈbī(,)ō\ *n* -s [by shortening] : BIOGRAPHY
bio- — see 2BI-
bio·acoustic \¦bī(,)ō+\ *adj* [2*bi-* + *acoustic*] : of or relating to the relation between living beings and sound
bio·acoustician \"+\ *n* [*bioacoustics* + *-ian*] : a specialist in bioacoustics
bio·acoustics \"+\ *n pl but sing in constr* [fr. *bioacoustic*, after such pairs as E *acoustic: acoustics*] : a branch of science that deals with the relation between living beings and sound
bio–aer·a·tion \¦bī(,)ō+\ *n* [2*bi-* + *aeration*] : the activation of sewage by mechanical means
1**bio·assay** \¦bī(,)ō+\ *n* [*biological assay*] : determination of the relative effective strength of a substance (as a vitamin, hormone, or drug) by comparing its effect on a test organism with that of a standard preparation; *also* : a particular test of this kind ⟨do a ~ on the sample⟩
2**bio·assay** \¦bī(,)ō+\ *vt* : to perform a bioassay on
bio·bibliographical \¦bī(,)ō+\ *adj* : of, relating to, or being a biobibliography
bio·bibliography \¦bī(,)ō+\ *n* [2*bi-* + *bibliography*] : a bibliography with biographical notes about the author or authors listed; *also* : a usu. short biography esp. concerned with the bibliography of the biographee
bi·o·blast \ˈbīō,blast\ *n* -s [ISV 2*bi-* + *-blast*; orig. formed in G] : ALTMANN'S GRANULE — **bioblastic** \¦==¦=stik\ *adj*
bio·catalyst \,bīō+\ *n* [2*bi-* + *catalyst*] : ENZYME 1 — **bio·catalytic** \¦bīō+\ *adj*
bi·ocel·late \¦bī, (ˈ)bī+\ *adj* [1*bi-* + *ocellate*] : having two ocelli
bi·o·ce·nol·o·gy *also* **bi·o·coe·nol·o·gy** \,bī(,)ōsə'näləjē\ *n* -ES [2*bi-* + *coen-* + *-logy*] : a branch of biology concerned with the study of natural communities and the interaction of the members of such a community — compare ECOLOGY
bi·o·ce·no·sis *or* **bi·o·coe·no·sis** \,bīōsə'nōsə̇s\ *or* **bi·o·ce·nose** *also* **bi·o·coe·nose** \-'sē,nōs\ *n, pl* **bio·ceno·ses** *or* **biocoeno·ses** \-sə'nō,sēz, -'sē,nōsə̇z\ [NL *biocenosis, biocoenosis*, fr. 2*bi-* + Gk *koinōsis* sharing (fr. *koinoun* to make common, fr. *koinos* common) — more at COEN-] : an assemblage of diverse organisms inhabiting a common biotope : a biotic community — **bi·o·ce·not·ic** *or* **bi·o·coe·not·ic** \¦==sə¦nädik\ *adj*
bio·centric *also* **bio·central** \¦bīō+\ *adj* [2*bi-* + *centric* or *central*] : centering in life : taking life as a central fact — **bio·cen·trist** \"+¦sen·trə̇st\ *n*
1**bio·chemical** *also* **bio·chemic** \¦bīō, ¦bīə+\ *adj* [ISV 2*bi-* + *chemical* or *chemic*; orig. formed as G *biochemisch*] : of or relating to biochemistry : characterized by, produced by, or involving chemical reactions in living organisms ⟨~ mutants⟩ — **bio·chemically** \"+\ *adv*
2**biochemical** \"\ *n* : a biochemical product
biochemical oxygen demand *n* : the oxygen used in meeting the metabolic needs of aerobic microorganisms in water rich in organic matter (as water polluted with sewage) — called also *biological oxygen demand*
bio·chemist \¦bīō, ¦bīə+\ *n* [2*bi-* + *chemist*] : one trained in or engaged in biochemistry
bio·chemistry \"+\ *n* [ISV 2*bi-* + *chemistry*; orig. formed as G *biochemie*] 1 : the chemistry of plant and animal life : biological chemistry or physiological chemistry 2 : chemistry in relation to life processes ⟨~ of chlorophyll⟩ ⟨~ of microorganisms⟩
bio·chemor·phol·o·gy \¦bīō¦ke(,)mȯr¦fäləjē\ *n* [2*bi-* + blend of *chem-* and *morphology*] : the study of the relationship between the chemical structure of a compound and its biological action
bi·o·chore \ˈbīō,kō(ə)r\ *n* -s [ISV 2*bi-* + *-chore*] : a group of similar biotopes (as temperate forests)
bi·o·chrome \-,krōm\ *n* -s [2*bi-* + *-chrome*] : a coloring matter that can be extracted from a plant or animal : a natural pigment
bi·o·chron \-,krän\ *n* -s [2*bi-* + *-chron* (fr. Gk *chronos* time)] : a fossil fauna or flora of relatively short time range
bi·o·cide \ˈbīə,sīd\ *n* -s [2*bi-* + *-cide*] : PESTICIDE
bi·o·clas·tic \¦bīō¦klastik\ *adj* [2*bi-* + *-clastic*] *of rock or similar material* : attaining its present form through the action of living organisms ⟨concrete, like the consolidated muds of certain coral reefs, may be considered a ~ substance⟩
bio·climatic \¦bī(,)ō+\ *adj* [2*bi-* + *climatic*] : of, relating to, or concerned with the relations of climate and living matter ⟨~ research⟩ ⟨~ peculiarities of desert regions⟩
bioclimatic law *n* : a statement in ecology: phenological events in temperate No. America are generally altered about 4 days for each change of 5° of latitude northward, 5° of longitude eastward, or 400 feet of altitude upward, the vernal alteration being retardation (as of flowering), the autumnal being acceleration (as of leaf fall)
bio·cli·mat·ics \¦bī(,)ō,klī'mad·iks\ *n pl but sing or pl in constr* : BIOCLIMATOLOGY
bio·cli·mat·o·graph \¦bī(,)ō,klī¦mad·ə,graf\ *n* -s [2*bi-* + *climatograph* climograph (fr. *climate* + *-o-* + *-graph*)] : a climograph constructed to show the relation between climatic conditions and some living organism and used esp. to determine the points most susceptible to attack in the life cycle of various pests and parasites
bio·climatological \¦bī(,)ō+\ *adj* [2*bi-* + *climatological*] : of, relating to, or involving the methods of bioclimatology ⟨~ research⟩
bio·climatologist \"+\ *also* **bio·cli·ma·ti·cian** \¦bī(,)ō-,klīmə¦tishən\ *n* [*bioclimatologist* fr. *bioclimatology* + *-ist*; *bioclimatician* fr. *bioclimatics* + *-ian*] : a specialist in bioclimatology
bio·climatology \¦bī(,)ō+\ *n* [2*bi-* + *climatology*] 1 : a branch of knowledge concerned with the direct and indirect impact of climate or sometimes other geophysical factors on living matter 2 : the interrelation of an organism and climate
biocoenology *var of* BIOCENOLOGY
biocoenosis *also* **biocoenose** *var of* BIOCENOSIS
bio·colloid \¦bīō+\ *n* -s [2*bi-* + *colloid*] : a colloid or colloidal mixture of plant or animal origin — **bio·colloidal** \¦bī(,)ō+\ *adj*
bio·cycle \ˈbīō+,-\ *n* [2*bi-* + *cycle*] : a group of related biochores constituting a major division of the biosphere ⟨the ~s usu. recognized are saltwater, freshwater, and terrestrial⟩
bi·o·cy·tin \,bīō'sītᵊn\ *n* -s [blend of *biotin* and *cyt-*] : a colorless crystalline peptide $C_{16}H_{28}N_4O_4S$ occurring naturally (as in yeast) and yielding biotin and lysine on hydrolysis
bio·dynamic \¦bī(,)ō+\ *adj* [ISV 2*bi-* + *dynamic*] 1 : of, relating to, or concerned with the dynamic relation between organisms and their environment ⟨~ concepts in psychology⟩ 2 : of, relating to, or being a system of farming that depends wholly on organic materials for fertilizing and soil conditioning ⟨~ agriculture⟩
bio·dynamics \"+\ *n pl but sing or pl in constr* [ISV 2*bi-* + *dynamics*] : biodynamic state, factors, or condition ⟨the ~ of a watercourse⟩ ⟨the ~ of sewage purification⟩
bio·ecological *also* **bio·ecologic** \¦bīō+\ *adj* : of or relating to bioecology
bio·ecologist \"+\ *n* : a specialist in bioecology
bio·ecology \"+\ *n* [2*bi-* + *ecology*] : general ecology : ecology dealing with the interrelation of plants and animals with their common environment — sometimes opposed to *biocenology*
bio·electric *also* **bio·electrical** \¦bī(,)ō+\ *adj* [2*bi-* + *electric, electrical*] : of or relating to electrical phenomena in plants or animals — **bio·electricity** \¦bīō+\ *n*
bio·energetic \¦bīō+\ *adj* [2*bi-* + *energetic*] : of or relating to bioenergetics or bioenergy
bio·energetics \"+\ *n pl but sing or pl in constr* [2*bi-* + *energetics*] : the branch of biology that deals with the energy relations in and the energy changes produced by living organisms
bio·energy \"+,-\ *n* [2*bi-* + *energy*] : energy available for the bodily work of the living organism
bio·engineering \"+\ *n* [2*bi-* + *engineering*] : engineering relating to the biosynthesis or processing of animal or plant products; *specif* : engineering relating to fermentation processes
bio·facies \"+,-\ *n* [NL, fr. 2*bi-* + *facies*] *geol* : a part of a stratigraphic unit in which the fossil fauna or flora differs significantly from that found elsewhere in the same unit
bio·filter \"+,-\ *n* [2*bi-* + *filter*] : a filter bed in which sewage is subjected to the action of microorganisms that assist in decomposing it
bio·filtration \¦bī(,)ō+\ *n* [2*bi-* + *filtration*] : the process of treating sewage by passing it through a biofilter
bio·flavonoid \¦bīō+\ *n* [2*bi-* + *flavonoid*] : a flavonoid compound (as rutin) having in mammals biological activity related to its reducing and chelating properties and its effect on the functioning of minute blood vessels but in many cases (as some such compounds obtained commercially from citrus fruits) not having nutritional functions — called also *vitamin P*
bi·o·gen \ˈbīəjən\ *n* -s [ISV 2*bi-* + *-gen*; orig formed in G] : a hypothetical ultimate living unit of which cells are built up : BIOPHORE
bio·genesis \¦bīō+\ *n* [NL, fr. 2*bi-* + L *genesis*] 1 : the development of life from preexisting life — opposed to *abiogenesis* 2 : the supposed tendency for stages in the evolutionary history of a race to briefly recur during the development and differentiation of an individual of that race — compare RECAPITULATION THEORY
bio·gen·e·sist \"+¦jenəsə̇st\ *n* -s [irreg. fr. NL *biogenesis* + E *-ist*] : a student or protagonist of biogenesis
bio·ge·net·ic *also* **bio·ge·net·i·cal** \¦bī(,)ō+\ *adj* [F *biogénétique*, fr. *bi-* 2*bi-* + *génétique* genetic, genetical] 1 : of, relating to, or produced by biogenesis 2 : BIOGENOUS — **bio·ge·netically** \"+\ *adv*
biogenetic law *n* : RECAPITULATION THEORY
bi·o·gen·ic \¦bīō¦jenik\ *adj* [2*bi-* + *-genic*] 1 : produced by the action of living organisms ⟨~ rocks⟩ 2 : essential to life and its maintenance ⟨sleep, food, and water are among the ~ needs of the organism⟩
bi·og·e·nous \(ˈ)bī¦äjənəs\ *adj* [2*bi-* + *-genous*] 1 : produced from living organisms (as by growing on them) 2 : BIOGENIC
bi·og·e·ny \-jənē\ *n* -ES [2*bi-* + *-geny*] : BIOGENESIS
bio·geo·chemical \,bīō,jēō+\ *adj* [2*bi-* + *ge-* + *chemical*; trans. of Russ *biogeokhimicheskiy*] : of or relating to biogeochemistry ⟨~ prospecting⟩
bio·geo·chemistry \"+\ *n* -ES [2*bi-* + *ge-* + *chemistry*; trans. of Russ *biogeokhimiya*] : the science that deals with the relation of earth chemicals to plant and animal life in an area : chemistry in relation to geology and plant and animal life ⟨~ of iron⟩
bio·geographic *or* **bio·geographical** \¦bīō+\ *adj* [2*bi-* + *geographic, geographical*] : of, relating to, or involved with biogeography — **bio·geographically** \"+\ *adv*
bio·geography \"+\ *n* -ES [ISV 2*bi-* + *geography*] : a branch of biology that deals with the geographical distribution of animals and plants and includes both zoogeography and phytogeography — compare ECOLOGY, GEOGRAPHY
bi·og·no·sis \,bī,äg'nōsə̇s\ *n, pl* **biogno·ses** \-ō,sēz\ [NL, fr. 2*bi-* + *-gnosis*] : the scientific investigation of life
bi·o·graph \ˈbīə,graf, -raa(ə)f, -raif, -räf\ *vt* -ED/-ING/-S [back-formation fr. *biographer, biography*] : to write a life or biographical sketch of ⟨after ~*ing* the painter⟩
bi·og·ra·phee \(,)bī¦ägrə¦fē *also* bē¦äg- *sometimes* ¦bīə,gra¦fē\ *n* -s [*biography* + *-ee*] : the person about whom a biography is written
bi·og·ra·pher \bī'ägrəfə(r) *also* bē'ä-\ *n* -s [*biography* + *-er*] : a writer of a biography or of biography
bi·o·graph·i·cal \¦bīə¦grafə̇kəl, -fēk- *sometimes* ¦bēə-\ *or* **bi·o·graph·ic** \-fik, -fēk\ *adj* [*biography* + *-ical, -ic*] 1 : of, relating to, or being biography ⟨~ material⟩ ⟨a ~ interest⟩ ⟨a ~ work⟩ 2 : consisting of biographies or biographical matter ⟨a ~ dictionary⟩ ⟨a ~ novel⟩ — **bi·o·graph·i·cal·ly** \-fə̇k(ə)lē, -fēk-, -li\ *adv*
bi·og·ra·phize \bī'ägrə,fīz *also* bē'ä-\ *vt* -ED/-ING/-S [*biography* + *-ize*] : 2BIOGRAPHY
1**bi·og·ra·phy** \bī'ägrəfē, -fi *also* bē'ä-\ *n* -ES [LGk *biographia*, fr. Gk *bio-* 2*bi-* + *-graphia* -graphy] 1 : a usu. written history of a person's life 2 : biographical writings in general; *esp* : such writings considered as a genre ⟨the field of ~⟩ 3 : an account in biographical form of the life of something (as an animal, a coin, or a building) ⟨the ~ of the commonwealth⟩
2**biography** \"\ *vt* -ED/-ING/-ES : to write a biography of
bi·o·herm \ˈbīō,hərm\ *n* -s [2*bi-* + Gk *herma* sunken rock, reef — more at WART] : a body of rock built up by or composed mainly of sedentary organisms (as corals, algae, or mollusks) and enclosed or surrounded by rock of different origin — compare BIOSTROME — **bi·o·her·mal** \¦==¦hərməl\ *adj*
bioi *pl of* BIOS
bi·o·lith \ˈbīō,lith\ *also* **bi·o·lite** \-,līt\ *n* -s [ISV 2*bi-* + *-lith* or *-lite*; orig formed as G *biolith*] : a rock of organic origin : a rock produced directly by the activities of organisms
1**bi·o·log·ic** \¦bīə¦läjik, -jēk\ *or* **bi·o·log·i·cal** \-jə̇kəl, -jēk-\ *adj* [ISV *biology* + *-ic, -ical*] 1 : of or relating to biology or to life and living things : belonging to or characteristic of the processes of life — compare PHYSIOLOGICAL 2 : used in or produced by practical application of biology ⟨*biological* methods⟩ ⟨~ supplies⟩ — **bi·o·log·i·cal·ly** \-jə̇k(ə)lē, -jēk-, -li\ *adv*
2**biologic** \"\ *or* **biological** \"\ *n* -s : a biological product (as a globulin, serum, vaccine, antitoxin, or antigen) used in the prevention or treatment of disease
biological assay *n* : BIOASSAY
biological balance *n* : a dynamic equilibrium existing between members of any relatively stable natural community and being the resultant of all the effects (as in food chains, parasitism, or pollinization) of the constituent organisms on one another
biological control *n* : attack upon noxious organisms (as insects) by interference with their ecological adjustment (as by the introduction of parasites not previously present)
biological dye *or* **biological stain** *n* : STAIN 4b
biological efficiency *n* : the relative ability of a protein or protein foodstuff to meet adequately the metabolic needs of an animal — compare BIOLOGICAL VALUE
biological environment *n* : the natural biological factors (as wild animals and plants or bacteria) that affect human life (as in a particular place or period)
biological geography *n* : BIOGEOGRAPHY
biological half-life *n* : the time that a living body requires to eliminate one half the quantity of an administered substance (as a radioisotope) through its normal channels of elimination
biological method *or* **biological test** *n* : a method or test involving experiment on organisms — compare BIOASSAY
biological oceanography *n* : a science that deals with the animal and plant inhabitants of ocean waters
biological oxygen demand *n* : BIOCHEMICAL OXYGEN DEMAND
biological product *n* : a complex pharmaceutical substance, preparation, or agent of organic origin depending for its action on the processes effecting immunity and used esp. in diagnosis and treatment of disease (as a vaccine or pollen extract); *also* : any such complex product of organic or synthetic origin obtained or standardized by biological methods or assay (as arsphenamine, pituitary extract, or insulin) : BIOLOGIC
biological race *n* : PHYSIOLOGIC RACE — used esp. of insects
biological species *n* : PHYSIOLOGIC RACE
biological value *n* : a measure of the efficiency of the protein in a foodstuff for the maintenance and growth of the bodily tissues of an individual usu. computed as the percentage of protein intake actually utilized in the body but sometimes as the percentage of digestible protein assimilated from a foodstuff
biological warfare *n* : warfare involving the use of living organisms (as disease germs) and toxic substances produced by them against men, animals, or plants; *also* : warfare involving the use of synthetic chemicals harmful to plants
biological zone *n* : ZONE 3b
biologic false-positive *n* : a positive serological reaction for syphilis given by blood of a nonsyphilitic person
bi·ol·o·gism \bī'älə,jizəm\ *n* -s [*biology* + *-ism*] 1 a : a doctrine or system formulated from the biological point of view or based on biological modes of explanation b : adherence to such a doctrine, system, or point of view; *esp* : preoccupation with biological explanations in the analysis of social situations 2 : the use of scientific phraseology peculiar to biologists; *also* : an expression peculiar to biologists
bi·ol·o·gist \-jə̇st\ *n* -s [*biology* + *-ist*] : a specialist in biology
bi·ol·o·gis·tic \¦bī,älə¦jistik, bī¦ä-\ *adj* : of or relating to biologism — **bi·ol·o·gis·ti·cal·ly** \-tə̇k(ə)lē\ *adv*
bi·ol·o·gize \bī'älə,jīz\ *vb* -ED/-ING/-S [*biology* + *-ize*] *vi* : to engage in biological investigations esp. superficially or amateurishly ~ *vt* : to treat (as a problem) biologistically
bi·ol·o·gy \bī'äləjē, -ji\ *n* -ES *often attrib* [G *biologie*, fr. *bi-* 2*bi-* + *-logie* -logy] 1 a : the science of life : a branch of knowledge that deals with living organisms and vital processes broadly including zoology, botany, morphology, genetics, embryology, and allied sciences but commonly being restricted to consideration of principles of wide application to the origin, development, structure, functions, and distribution of living matter as represented by plants and animals and to the generally recurrent phenomena of life, growth, and reproduction b : ECOLOGY 2 a : the plant and animal life of a particular region or environment considered as a unit ⟨the ~ of the plains⟩ b : the laws and phenomena relating to an organism or group ⟨the ~ of the honeybee⟩ ⟨the ~ of parasitic worms⟩ 3 : a treatise on biology
bio·luminescence \,bī(,)ō+\ *n* [ISV 2*bi-* + *luminescence*] : the emission of light from living organisms as the result of internal oxidative changes; *also* : the light so produced — compare PHOSPHORESCENCE — **bio·luminescent** \¦bī(,)ō+\ *adj*
bi·ol·y·sis \bī'äləsə̇s\ *n, pl* **bioly·ses** \-ə,sēz\ [NL, fr. 2*bi-* + *-lysis*] 1 : death and the bodily disintegration that follows 2 : decomposition by living organisms of sewage and other complex materials — **bi·o·lyt·ic** \¦bīə¦lid·ik\ *adj*
biolytic tank *n* : a chamber having a hopper bottom in which the oxidation of organic matter is hastened by agitating the sludge with raw sewage
bio·mass \ˈbīō+,-\ *n* [2*bi-* + *mass*] : the amount of living matter in the form of one or more kinds of organisms present in a particular habitat usu. expressed as weight of organisms per unit area of habitat or as volume or weight of organisms per unit volume of habitat
bio·mathematical \¦bīō+\ *adj* [2*bi-* + *mathematical*] : of or relating to biomathematics
bio·mathematics \"+\ *n pl but usu sing in constr* [2*bi-* + *mathematics*] : the principles of mathematics that are of special use in biology and medicine
bi·ome \ˈbī,ōm\ *n* -s [2*bi-* + *-ome*] : an ecological formation considered in terms of both plants and animals of the area concerned and usu. identified in terms of characteristic vegetation forms
bio·mechanical \¦bī(,)ō+\ *adj* [2*bi-* + *mechanical*] : of, relating to, or involving biomechanics
bio·mechanics \"+\ *n pl but sing or pl in constr* [2*bi-* + *mechanics*] : the mechanical bases of biological, esp. muscular, activity; *also* : the study of the principles and relations involved
bio·meteorological \"+\ *adj* : of or relating to biometeorology
bio·meteorology \"+\ *n* -ES [2*bi-* + *meteorology*] : a science that deals with the relationship between living beings and atmospheric phenomena
bi·om·e·ter \bī'äməd·ə(r)\ *n* -s [ISV 2*bi-* + *-meter*] : a device for measuring carbon dioxide given off by living matter
bi·o·met·ric \,bīō'me·trik\ *also* **bi·o·met·ri·cal** \-trə̇kəl\ *adj* [back-formation fr. *biometrics*] : of, relating to, or concerned with biometrics — **bi·o·met·ri·cal·ly** \-rə̇k(ə)lē\ *adv*
bi·o·me·tri·cian \,bīōmə'trishən, ,bī,ämə-\ *also* **bi·o·met·ri·cist** \,bīō'me·trəsə̇st\ *n* -s [*biometrics* + *-ian* or *-ist*] : a specialist in biometrics
bi·o·met·rics \,bīō'me·triks\ *n pl but sing or pl in constr* [ISV *biometry* + *-ics*; prob. orig. formed as F *biométrique*] : the statistical study of biological observations and phenomena
bi·om·e·try \bī'ämə·trē\ *n* -ES [ISV 2*bi-* + *-metry*] : BIOMETRICS
bio·microscope \,bīō+\ *n* [2*bi-* + *microscope*] : a low-power binocular microscope placed horizontally and used with a slit lamp for detailed examination of the anterior part of the eye
bio·microscopic \¦bīō+\ *adj* : of, relating to, or by means of biomicroscopy or the biomicroscope — **bio·microscopically** \"+\ *adv*
bio·microscopy \"+\ *n* [2*bi-* + *microscopy*] : the microscopic examination and study of living cells and tissues; *specif* : examination of the living eye with the biomicroscope
bio·molecule \"+\ *n* [2*bi-* + *molecule*] : a hypothetical living molecule — compare BIOGEN, BIOPHORE
bi·o·mor·phic \¦bīō¦mȯrfik\ *adj* [2*bi-* + *morphic*] : related to, derived from, or incorporating the forms of living beings — used esp. of primitive and abstract art
bio·negative \¦bīō+\ *adj* [2*bi-* + *negative*] : DISRUPTIVE, RETROGRESSIVE; *specif* : relating to the phase of radiation damage to living tissue in which organization is disrupted
bi·o·nom·ic \,bīə¦nämik\ *or* **bi·o·nom·i·cal** \-mə̇kəl\ *adj* [prob. fr. F *bionomique*, fr. *bionomie* bionomy + *-ique* -ic, -ical] : of or relating to ecology — **bi·o·nom·i·cal·ly** \-mə̇k(ə)lē\ *adv*
bi·o·nom·ics \-miks\ *n pl but sing or pl in constr* : ECOLOGY
bi·on·o·mist \bī'änəmə̇st\ *n* -s : ECOLOGIST
bi·on·o·my \-mē\ *n* -ES [2*bi-* + *-nomy*] 1 : PHYSIOLOGY 2 : ECOLOGY
bi·ont \ˈbī,änt\ *n* -s [2*bi-* + *-ont*] : a discrete unit of living matter : ORGANISM
-bi·ont \ˈbī,änt, ,bē,änt\ *n comb form* -s [prob. fr. G, modif. of Gk *biount-, biōn* living, pres. part. of *bioun* to live, fr. *bios* mode of life — more at QUICK] : one having a (specified) mode of life ⟨aero*biont*⟩
bi·on·tic \(ˈ)bī¦äntik\ *adj, biol* : INDIVIDUAL — opposed to *phyletic* — **bi·on·ti·cal·ly** \-tə̇k(ə)lē\ *adv*
bi·operculate \¦bī+\ *adj* [1*bi-* + *operculate*] : having two opercula
bi·oph·a·gous \(ˈ)bī¦äfəgəs\ *adj* [2*bi-* + *-phagous*] : using living organisms as food ⟨a ~ plant⟩ — **bi·oph·a·gy** \bī'äfəjē\ *n* -ES

bi·oph·i·lous \(ˈ)bī¦äfələs\ *adj* [²*bi-* + *-philous*] **:** PARASITIC 2a

bi·o·phore \ˈbīə,fō(ə)r, -ó(ə)r\ *also* **bi·o·phor** \-fó(ə)r\ *n* -S [G *biophor*, fr. *bio-* ²bi- + *-phor* -phore] **:** the ultimate supramolecular vital unit in Weismann's theory of life processes, being conceived as the basic building block of living structures — see DETERMINANT 5a, ID

bio·photogenesis \,bī(,)ō +\ *n* [NL, fr. ²*bi-* + *photogenesis*] **:** production of bioluminescence

bio·photometer \" +\ *n* [²*bi-* + *photometer*] **:** an instrument for measuring the rate and efficiency of dark adaptation of the eye used esp. in detecting vitamin A deficiency

bio·physical \¦bīō +\ *adj* [²*bi-* + *physical*] **1 :** of or relating to biophysics **2 :** involving biological and physical factors or considerations

bio·physicist \" +\ *n* [²*bi-* + *physicist*] **:** a specialist in biophysics

bio·physics \" +\ *n pl but sing or pl in constr* [ISV ²*bi-* + *physics*] **:** the physics of living organisms **:** the application of physical principles and methods to biological problems

bio·physiography \" +\ *n* [²*bi-* + *physiography*] **:** descriptive zoology and botany

bio·physiologist \" +\ *n* [²*bi-* + *physiologist*] **:** a specialist in general physiology

bio·physiology \" +\ *n* [²*bi-* + *physiology*] **:** GENERAL PHYSIOLOGY

bi·o·pic \ˈbīō,pik\ *n* -S [*bio*graphical *pic*ture] **:** a biographical motion picture

bi·o·plasm \ˈbīō,plazəm\ *n* -S [²*bi-* + *-plasm*] **:** living protoplasm as distinguished from ergastic substances — **bi·o·plas·mic** \¦bīō¦plazmik\ *adj*

bi·o·plast \ˈbīō,plast\ *n* -S [²*bi-* + *-plast*] **1 :** ALTMANN'S GRANULES **2 :** a functional unit of living protoplasm **:** CELL

bio·positive \¦bīō +\ *adj* [²*bi-* + *positive*] **:** REGENERATIVE; *specif* **:** relating to the phase of radiation damage to living tissue in which repair of previously disrupted tissue takes place (as in the replacing of X-ray-destroyed tumor cells by connective tissue)

bio·potency \" +\ *n* [²*bi-* + *potency*] **:** capacity to function in a biological system ⟨the ~ of a synthetic hormone⟩

bio·potential \" +\ *n* [*bio*electric *potential*] **:** a bioelectric potential

bio·precipitation \" +\ *n* [²*bi-* + *precipitation*] **:** precipitation brought about by biological agents (as in the activated-sludge process for sewage treatment)

bi·op·sy \ˈbī,äpsē, ˈbīəp-, -si\ *n* -ES [ISV ²*bi-* + *-opsy*; orig. formed as F *biopsie*] **:** the removal of tissue, cells, or fluids from the living body for examination or study; *also* **:** the examination of such material esp. for diagnostic purposes

bio·psychic *also* **bio·psychical** \¦bīō +\ *adj* [²*bi-* + *psychic*, *psychical*] **:** of, relating to, or involving both psychic and biological phenomena **:** relating to the place of mind in life

bio·psychological \" +\ *adj* **:** of, relating to, or involving biology and psychology ⟨the human ~ makeup⟩

bio·psychology \" +\ *n* [²*bi-* + *psychology*] **:** psychology as related to biology or as a part of the vital processes

bi·o·pyr·i·bole \,bīō¦pīrə,bōl\ *adj* [*bi*otite + *py*roxene + amphi*bole*] *of igneous rocks* **:** composed of biotite, pyroxene, or amphibole

bi·orbital \(ˈ)bī + \ *adj* [¹*bi-* + *orbital*] **:** of or relating to the two orbits; *specif* **:** relating to a measure taken between the outer borders of the bony orbits on the skull or between the outer corners of the eyes on the living

¹**bi·os** \ˈbī,äs\ *n* -ES [NL, fr. Gk, mode of life — more at QUICK] **1 a :** living beings **b :** organic nature **2** [F, fr. Gk] **:** a mixture of vitamins of the B complex including biotin, *meso*-inositol, and pantothenic acid extracted from various yeasts and essential for the optimum growth of these yeasts

²**bios** *pl of* BIO

bi·o·scope \ˈbīə,skōp\ *n* -S [²*bi-* + *-scope*] **1 :** a motion-picture projector **2** *chiefly Brit* **:** a motion-picture theater

bi·ose \ˈbī,ōs\ *n* -S [ISV ¹*bi-* + *-ose*] **1 :** DISACCHARIDE **2 :** DIOSE

bio·seston \ˈbīō+,-\ *n* [²*bi-* + *seston*] **:** the living constituents of seston

-bi·o·sis \,bī¦ōsəs\ *n comb form, pl* **-bioses** [NL, fr. Gk *biōsis*, fr. *bioun* to live, fr. *bios* mode of life) + *-ōsis* -osis] **:** mode of life ⟨aero*biosis*⟩ ⟨necro*biosis*⟩

bio·social \¦bīō+\ *adj* [²*bi-* + *social*] **:** of, relating to, or involving the interaction of the biological and the social **:** of or relating to animal or human aspects of social life as affected by biological principles or processes ⟨speech is a ~ activity⟩ **:** viewing the organism and environment as a complex unity

biosocial environment *n* **:** domesticated plants and animals as a factor affecting human life

bio·sociological \"+\ *adj* [²*bi-* + *sociological*] **:** BIOSOCIAL

bio·sociology \"+\ *n* [²*bi-* + *sociology*] **:** the study of social interaction in terms of analogy with the vital processes of the living organism

bi·o·some \ˈbīə,sōm\ *n* -S [²*bi-* + *-some*] **:** a self-perpetuating organized unit within protoplasm (as a chromonema)

bio·sphere \ˈbīə+,-\ *n* -S [²*bi-* + *sphere*] **1 :** the part of the world in which life can exist including parts of the lithosphere, hydrosphere, and atmosphere **2 :** living beings together with their environment

bio·statistical \¦bī(,)ō+\ *adj* **:** relating to or according with biostatistics

bio·statistician \,bīō+\ *n* -S **:** a specialist in biostatistics

bio·statistics \"+\ *n pl but sing in constr* [²*bi-* + *statistics*] **:** statistical processes and methods applied to the analysis of biological phenomena

bio·stratigraphic *also* **bio·stratigraphical** \¦bīō+\ *adj* **:** of or relating to biostratigraphy **:** employing the methods of biostratigraphy

biostratigraphic unit *n* **:** a group of geologic strata characterized by a particular fossil fauna or flora rather than by lithologic features

bio·stratigraphy \¦bī(,)ō+\ *n* [²*bi-* + *stratigraphy*] **:** the part of paleontology that is directly related to the conditions and order of deposition of the sedimentary rocks **:** stratigraphic paleontology

bi·o·stromal \¦bīə¦strōməl\ *adj* **:** of or relating to a biostrome

bi·o·strome \ˈbīə,strōm\ *n* -S [²*bi-* + LL *stroma* coverlet, fr. Gk *strōma* bed, mattress] **:** a distinctly bedded or broadly lenticular body of rock composed mainly of the remains of sedentary organisms (as shell beds, crinoid beds, or coral beds) — compare BIOHERM

bio·synthesis \,bīō+\ *n* [NL, fr. ²*bi-* + *synthesis*] **:** the production of a chemical compound by a living organism by either synthesis or degradation (as of adrenaline by vertebrates or of alcohol by yeasts) — **bio·synthetic** \¦bī(,)ō+\ *adj* — **bio·synthetically** \"+\ *adv*

bio·systematic \¦bīō+\ *adj* **:** of or relating to biosystematy

bio·systematics \"+\ *n pl but sing or pl in constr* **:** BIOSYSTEMATY

bio·systematist \"+\ *n* -S **:** a specialist in biosystematy

bi·o·sys·tem·a·ty \¦bīōsə'stemədē\ *n* -ES [²*bi-* + Gk *systēmat-*, *systēma* system + E *-y* — more at SYSTEM] **:** experimental taxonomy esp. as based on cytogenetics

¹**bi·o·ta** \bīˈōd·ə, ˈbīəd·ə\ *n* -S [NL, fr. Gk *biotē* way of life, sustenance, fr. *bios* life — more at BIOTIC] **:** the animal and plant life of a region **:** living things **:** flora and fauna

²**biota** \"\ *n, cap* [NL, fr. Gk *biotē*] *in some classifications* **:** a genus of evergreen shrubs or small trees having branchlets in vertical planes and that is often included in *Thuja*

bio·technic *also* **bio·technical** \¦bīō+\ *adj* [²*bi-* + *technic*, *technical*] **:** of or relating to biotechnics; *also* **:** concerned with the adaptation of technology to the betterment of human life

bio·technics \"+\ *n pl but sing or pl in constr* [²*bi-* + *technics*] **1 :** the control and adaptation of living organisms to the needs and ends of man **2 :** the application of natural forms to problems of design and engineering

bio·technological \"+\ *adj* **:** of or relating to biotechnology

bio·technology \¦bī(,)ō+\ *n* [²*bi-* + *technology*] **1 :** applied biological science (as the synthesis of enzymes, genes, and antibodies for medical use) **2 :** ERGONOMICS

bio·test \ˈbīə+,-\ *n* [²*bi-* + *test*] **:** BIOASSAY

bio·therapy \¦bīō+\ *n* [²*bi-* + *therapy*] **:** treatment of disease with products produced by living organisms (as vaccines, antisera, toxoids, or antigens)

¹**bi·ot·ic** \(ˈ)bī¦äd·|ik, -ät|, |ēk *also* bēˈä-\ *also* **bi·ot·i·cal** \|əkəl, |ēk-\ *adj* [*biotic* fr. Gk *biōtikos* of life, fr. *biōtos* livable, worth living (fr. *bioun* to live, fr. *bios* life) + *-ikos* -ic; *biotical* fr. Gk *biōtikos* + E *-al*] **:** of or relating to life **:** BIOLOGIC ⟨a ~ community⟩ **:** induced or caused by the action of living beings ⟨~ alteration of a habitat⟩

²**biotic** \"\ *n* -S [by shortening] **:** ANTIBIOTIC

-biotic \(,)=¦==\ *adj comb form* [prob. fr. NL *-bioticus*, fr. Gk *biōtikos*] **1 :** relating to life **:** having life ⟨anti*biotic*⟩ **2 :** having a (specified) mode of life ⟨aero*biotic*⟩ ⟨necro*biotic*⟩

biotic climax *n* **:** an ecological climax primarily due to the action of living organisms

biotic formation *n* **:** BIOME

biotic potential *n* **1 :** the inherent capacity of an organism or species to reproduce and survive, being usu. expressed in terms of numbers that could be produced under optimum conditions and in the absence of environmental resistance **2 :** CARRYING CAPACITY

biotic province *n* **:** a geographic region characterized by the presence of one or more ecological associations that differ at least quantitatively from those of adjoining provinces and marked by a tendency to act as a center of ecological dispersion

bi·o·tin \ˈbīətən\ *n* -S [ISV *biot-* (fr. Gk *biotos* life, sustenance, fr. *bios* life, way of life) + *-in*; orig. formed in G] **:** a colorless crystalline growth vitamin $C_{10}H_{16}N_2O_3S$ of the vitamin B complex that occurs widely (as in yeast, liver, and egg yolk) usu. in combined form, that is inactivated by combination with avidin in the case of egg-white injury, and that is involved in the fixation of carbon dioxide (as by pyruvate to form oxalacetate) in mammals and bacteria

bi·o·tite \ˈbīə,tīt\ *n* -S [G *biotit*, fr. Jean B. *Biot* †1862 Fr. mathematician + G *-it* -ite] **:** a generally black or dark green form of mica $K_2(Mg,Fe,Al)_6(Si,Al)_8O_{20}(OH)_4$ forming a constituent of crystalline rocks and being a silicate of iron, magnesium, potassium, and aluminum (hardness 2.5-3) — **bi·o·tit·ic** \¦bīə¦tid·ik\ *adj*

bi·o·tit·ize \ˈbīə,tīd·,īz, -ətə,tīz\ *also* **bi·o·tize** \ˈbīə,tīz\ *vt* -ED/-ING/-S **:** to transform (a metamorphic rock) into biotite by replacement of other components

bi·o·tope \ˈbīə,tōp\ *n* -S [²*bi-* + Gk *topos* place — more at TOPIC] **:** a region uniform in environmental conditions and in its populations of animals and plants for which it is the habitat

biot-sa·vart law \¦bē,ōsə¦vär-, ¦byōsə-\ *n, usu cap B&S* [after Jean B. *Biot* †1862 Fr. mathematician and Félix *Savart* †1841 Fr. physician & physicist] **:** a statement in electromagnetism: the magnetic intensity at any point due to a steady current in an infinitely long straight wire is directly proportional to the current and inversely proportional to the distance from point to wire — compare AMPERE'S LAW

bi·o·type \ˈbīə,tīp\ *n* -S [ISV ²*bi-* + *type*; orig. formed as G *biotypus*] **1 :** all the organisms sharing a specified genotype; *also* **:** the genotype so shared or the peculiarity distinguishing such a genotype ⟨the silver ~ in red foxes⟩ ⟨the species may be considered a complex assemblage of ~s⟩ **2 :** a group of individuals sharing many psychological traits — **bi·o·typ·ic** \¦==¦tipik\ *adj*

bi·o·ty·po·gram \¦bīə¦tīpə,gram\ *n* [*biotype* + *-o-* + *-gram*] **:** a set of diagrams or test scores reflecting the basic physical and psychological characteristics of an individual

bi·o·ty·pol·o·gy \,bīə,tīˈpäləjē\ *n* -ES [*biotype* + *-o-* + *-logy*] **:** the study of biotypes

bi·ovular \(ˈ)bī+\ *adj* [¹*bi-* + *ovular*] **:** derived from two ova — used of fraternal twins or their characteristic state; compare MONOVULAR

bi·oxalate \(ˈ)bī+\ *n* [¹*bi* + *oxalate*] **:** BINOXALATE

bio·zone \ˈbīō+,-\ *n* [²*bi-* + *zone*] **:** the temporal and stratigraphic range of a kind of organism (as of a species) as reflected by its occurrence in fossiliferous rocks

bi·pack \ˈbī+,-\ *n* -S [¹*bi-* + *pack*] **:** a pair of films each sensitive to a different color that are used in color photography by simultaneous exposure one through the other usu. with the emulsion surfaces in contact — compare TRIPACK

bi·pa·li·um \bīˈpālēəm\ *n, cap* [NL, fr. L, double mattock, fr. *bi-* ¹bi- + *pala* shovel, spade + *-ium*] **:** a genus (the type of the family Bipaliidae) of terrestrial mostly large triclad flatworms occurring in tropical countries and having the head end expanded into a semicircular plate

bi·palmate \(ˈ)bī+\ *adj* [¹*bi-* + *palmate*] **:** palmate with the segments again palmate ⟨some compound leaves are ~⟩

bi·parasitic \¦bī+\ *adj* [¹*bi-* + *parasitic*] **:** parasitic upon or in a parasite

bi·parental \"+\ *adj* [¹*bi-* + *parental*] **:** of, relating to, involving, or derived from two parents ⟨~ reproduction⟩ — **bi·parentally** \"+\ *adv*

bi·parietal \"+\ *adj* [ISV ¹*bi-* + *parietal*] *anthrop* **:** of or relating to the parietal bones; *specif* **:** being a measurement between the most distant opposite points of the two parietal bones

bip·a·rous \ˈbipərəs\ *adj* [¹*bi-* + *-parous*] **1 :** bringing forth two young at a birth **2** *of a plant part* **:** having branches or axes dichotomous ⟨a ~ cyme⟩

bi·par·ti·ent \(ˈ)bī¦pärd·ēənt\ *adj* [L *bipartient-*, *bipartiens*, pres. part. of *bipartire* to divide into two parts, fr. *bi-* ¹bi- + *partire*, *partiri* to divide — more at PART] **:** dividing into two parts **:** dividing twice

bi·parting \ˈbī+,-\ *adj* [¹*bi-* + *parting*] *of a door or gate* **:** composed of two sections that open away from each other

bi·partisan *also* **bi·partizan** \(ˈ)bī+\ *adj* [¹*bi-* + *partisan*, *partizan*] **:** representing or composed of members of two parties; *specif* **:** marked by or involving accord and cooperation between two major political parties ⟨a ~ foreign policy⟩ ⟨~ support for the bill⟩

bi·partisanism \"+\ *n* -S **:** the quality or state of being bipartisan

bi·partisanship \"+\ *n* -S **:** a bipartisan relation; *esp* **:** formulation of governmental policy by compromise and agreement between two major political parties esp. in respect to foreign affairs

bi·par·tite \(ˈ)bī¦pär|,tīt, -pä| *also* |d·,īt, *usu* īd· +V\ *adj* [L *bipartitus*, past part. of *bipartire* to divide into two parts] **1 :** being in two parts **:** having two correspondent parts one for each party ⟨a ~ contract⟩ ⟨~ writing⟩ **:** shared by two ⟨a ~ treaty⟩ **2 :** divided into two parts almost to the base ⟨~ leaf⟩ **:** consisting of two subdivisions — **bi·par·tite·ly** *adv*

bi·par·ti·tion \,bī(,)pärˈtishən, ,bīpər-\ *n* [L *bipartitus* + E *-ion*] **:** the act of dividing or state of being divided into two parts, esp. two corresponding parts

bi·party \(ˈ)bī+\ *adj* [¹*bi-* + *party*] **:** TWO-PARTY

bi·paschal \"+\ *adj* [¹*bi-* + *paschal*] **:** including two Passover feasts — used of a theory that regards Christ's public ministry as of only about one year's duration

bi·pectinate \"+\ *adj* [¹*bi-* + *pectinate*] **1** *also* **bi·pecti·nated** \"+\ **:** having two margins toothed like a comb — used esp. of the antennae of certain moths **2 :** branched like a feather on both sides of a main shaft ⟨the organ of smell in certain snails is ~⟩

¹**bi·ped** \ˈbī,ped *sometimes* -,pəd\ *adj* [L *biped-*, *bipes*, fr. *bi-* ¹bi- + *ped-*, *pes* foot — more at FOOT] **:** two-footed

²**biped** \-,ped\ *n* -S **1 :** a two-footed animal (as man) **2 :** any two of the legs of a horse or other quadruped — called also according to the legs involved *anterior biped*, *diagonal biped*, *lateral biped*, *posterior biped*

bi·ped·al \(ˈ)bī¦pedᵊl *also* -¦pē- *sometimes* ˈbipədᵊl\ *adj* [¹*bi-* + *pedal*] **1 :** having two feet **:** BIPED **2 :** of or relating to a biped

bi·ped·al·ism \(ˈ)bī¦pedᵊl,izəm *also* -¦pēd- *sometimes* ˈbipəd-\ *or* **bi·pe·dal·i·ty** \,bīpəˈdaləd·ē *sometimes* ,bip-\ *n, pl* **bipedalisms** *or* **bipedalities :** the condition of having but two feet or of using only two for locomotion if more are present ⟨the ~ of some desert lizards⟩

bi·peltate \(ˈ)bī+\ *adj* [¹*bi-* + *peltate*] **1** *zool* **:** having a shell or covering like a double shield **2** *bot* **:** having two shield-shaped parts

bi·penniform \"+\ *adj* [¹*bi-* + *penni-* + *-form*] **:** resembling a feather barbed on both sides — used of certain muscles from the arrangement of their fibers

bi·phasic \"+\ *adj* [¹*bi-* + *phasic*] **:** having two phases; *specif* **:** having both a sporophytic and a gametophytic phase in the life cycle

bi·phenyl \(ˈ)bī+\ *n* [ISV ¹*bi-* + *phenyl*] **:** a white crystalline hydrocarbon $C_6H_5C_6H_5$ obtained usu. by heating vapors of benzene to about 800°C and used chiefly in a mixture with phenyl ether as an industrial heat-transfer medium — called also *diphenyl*

bi·phonemic \¦bī+\ *adj* [¹*bi-* + *phonemic*] **:** constituting, consisting of, or standing for two phonemes

bi·phosphate \(ˈ)bī+\ *n* [¹*bi-* + *phosphate*] **:** an acid phosphate (as sodium acid phosphate) **:** a monobasic phosphate

bi·phyletic \¦bī+\ *adj* [¹*bi-* + *phyletic*] **:** descended or evolved in two branches from common ancestry — **bi·phyletically** \"+\ *adv*

bi·pin \ˈbī,pin\ *adj* [¹*bi-* + *pin*] **:** having two terminal pins that fit into corresponding sockets — used of certain lamp or vacuum-tube bases and cable terminals

bi·pin·nar·ia \,bīpəˈna(a)rēə\ *n* -S [NL, fr. ¹*bi-* + L *pinna* feather + NL *-aria* — more at FIN] **:** a bilaterally symmetrical free-swimming larva of certain starfishes that swims by means of ciliated bands

bi·pinnate \(ˈ)bī+\ *adj* [¹*bi-* + *pinnate*] **:** twice pinnate — **bi·pinnately** \"+\ *adv*

bi·pinnatifid \¦bī+\ *adj* [¹*bi-* + *pinnatifid*] **:** pinnatifid with the segments or divisions also pinnatifid

bi-place \ˈ=,=\ *adj* [¹*bi-* + *place*] *of an airplane* **:** having space for two occupants

bi·planar \(ˈ)bī+\ *adj* [¹*bi-* + *planar*] **:** lying in two planes

¹**bi·plane** \ˈbī+,-\ *n* [¹*bi-* + *plane*] **:** an airplane with two main supporting surfaces usu. placed one above the other

²**biplane** \"\ *adj* [¹*bi-* + *plane*] **:** acting in or taking place from two planes ⟨a ~ examination of the hip joint⟩ ⟨~ fluoroscopy⟩ **:** having parts arranged in two planes esp. at right angles to one another ⟨a ~ filament lamp⟩

biplane fluoroscope *n* **:** an X-ray machine by means of which examinations and roentgenograms can be made in the horizontal and the vertical planes

biplane

bipli·cate \(ˈ)bīˈplī,kāt, ˈbipləkət\ *adj* [¹*bi-* + *plicate*] **:** twice folded

bi·pod \ˈbī,päd\ *n* -S [¹*bi-* + *-pod* (as in *tripod*)] **:** a two-legged mount (as for an automatic rifle) or support (as for a mast)

bi·polar \(ˈ)bī+\ *adj* [¹*bi-* + *polar*] **1 a :** having or involving the use of two poles ⟨a ~ dynamo⟩ ⟨~ encephalograph leads⟩ **b** *of a neuron* **:** having an afferent and an efferent process **2 :** relating to or associated with the polar regions ⟨certain marine organisms have a ~ distribution and are found only north and south of an equatorial or median zone⟩ **3 :** having or marked by two mutually repellent forces or two diametrically opposed natures, qualities, or views

bi·polarity \¦bī+\ *n* -ES [ISV *bipolar* + *-ity*] **:** the quality or state of being bipolar: as **a :** identity or similarity between fauna of northern regions and that of southern, the fauna of the intervening regions being different **b :** AMBIVALENCE

bi·po·lar·ize \(ˈ)bī+ˈ-\ *vt* **:** to bring into a bipolar state

bi·post \ˈbī,pōst\ *adj* [¹*bi-* + *post*] **:** BIPIN — used esp. of a high-power lamp base having heavy pins

bi·potential \¦bī+\ *adj* [¹*bi-* + *potential*] *biol* **:** having potentiality for development in either of two mutually exclusive directions ⟨the larva of *Bonellia* is ~ for sex⟩

bi·potentiality \"+\ *n* **:** capacity to function as male or female **:** HERMAPHRODITISM

bi·prism \ˈbī+,-\ *n* [¹*bi-* + *prism*] **:** a triangular prism with vertex angle of nearly 180° used to obtain images of a single source in observing the interference of light — called also *Fresnel biprism*

¹**bi·propellant** \¦bī+\ *n* [¹*bi-* + *propellant*] **:** a rocket propellant consisting of separate fuel and oxidizer that come together only in a combustion chamber; *also* **:** either of these substances — compare MONOPROPELLANT

²**bipropellant** \"\ *adj* **:** of, relating to, or employing a bipropellant

bi·punctal *or* **bi·punctual** \(ˈ)bī+\ *adj* [¹*bi-* + *punctal* or *punctual*] **:** having or relating to two points

bi·punctate \"+\ *adj* [¹*bi-* + *punctate*] *bot* **:** marked with two spots

bi·pyramid \(ˈ)bī+\ *n* [¹*bi-* + *pyramid*] **:** DIPYRAMID

bi·pyramidal \¦bī+\ *adj* [¹*bi-* + *pyramidal*] **:** DIPYRAMIDAL

¹**bi·quadratic** \"+\ *adj* [¹*bi-* + *quadratic*] **:** of or relating to the fourth power in mathematics

²**biquadratic** \"\ *n* **1 :** a fourth power in mathematics **2 :** a biquadratic equation

biquadratic equation *n* **:** an algebraic equation of the fourth degree — called also *quartic equation*

bi·quarterly \(ˈ)bī+\ *adj* [¹*bi-* + *quarterly*] **:** occurring twice every three months

bi·quartz \ˈbī+,-\ *n* [¹*bi-* + *quartz*] **:** a quartz plate made up of a dextrorotatory and a levorotatory half and used in detecting polarization

bi·quintile \(ˈ)bī+\ *n* [¹*bi-* + *quintile*] **:** an aspect of the planets when their positions are twice the fifth part of a great circle apart or at an angle of 144 degrees

bi·racial \(ˈ)bī+\ *adj* [¹*bi-* + *racial*] **:** of, relating to, or involving members of two races ⟨~ strife⟩ ⟨~ organizations⟩; *esp* **:** concerned with the separate coexistence of white and Negro populations ⟨a ~ school system⟩ — **bi·racialism** \"+\ *n* -S

bi·radial \(ˈ)bī+\ *adj* [¹*bi-* + *radial*] **:** having both bilateral and radial symmetry ⟨a ~ ctenophore⟩ — see CTENOPHORA

bi·radiate *also* **bi·radiated** \(ˈ)bī+\ *adj* [¹*bi-* + *radiate*] **:** having two rays

bi·radical \(ˈ)bī+\ *n* [¹*bi-* + *radical*] **:** a free radical or compound (as sulfur monoxide ·SO·) with two unpaired electrons

bi·ramous *also* **bi·ramose** \(ˈ)bī+\ *adj* [¹*bi-* + *ramous*, *ramose*] **:** having or consisting of two branches ⟨a ~ antenna⟩

¹**birch** \ˈbərch, ˈbəch, ˈbəich\ *n* -ES *often attrib* [ME *birche*, *birk*, fr. OE *birce*, *beorc*; akin to OHG *birka* birch, ON *björk* birch, L *fraxinus* ash tree, Skt *bhūrja* birch, OE *beorht* bright — more at BRIGHT] **1 a :** a tree of the genus *Betula* — see PAPER BIRCH, RIVER BIRCH, SWEET BIRCH, WHITE BIRCH, YELLOW BIRCH **b** *Austral* **:** PIRIPIRI **c** *NewZeal* **:** any of various trees resembling those of the genus *Betula* (as the kamahi or the native beeches) **d :** GUMBO-LIMBO **2 :** the wood or timber of the birch **3 :** a birch rod or a bundle of twigs for whipping an offender **:** SWITCH **4 :** BIRCHBARK

²**birch** \"\ *vt* -ED/-ING/-ES **:** to beat with or as if with a birch **:** CANE, WHIP **:** punish (as a schoolboy) by caning or whipping

birchbark \ˈ=,=\ *n* **:** a canoe made of birch bark

birch beer *n* **:** a sweetened effervescent beverage including oil of birch or oil of wintergreen among its flavoring ingredients and prepared by carbonating or fermenting

birch borer *n* **:** an insect larva that bores in the wood of birch trees; *esp* **:** BRONZE BIRCH BORER

birch·en \-chən\ *adj* [ME *birchen*, *birken*, fr. *birche*, *birk* + *-en*] **:** of or relating to birch

birch family *n* **:** BETULACEAE

birching *n* -S **:** a beating with a birch **:** CANING, WHIPPING

birch-leaf mahogany \ˈ=,=-\ *n* **:** a hardtack (*Cercocarpus betuloides*)

birch leaf miner *n* **:** a small black sawfly (*Fenusa pusilla*) native to Europe but now established in much of eastern No. America with a larva that mines in the leaves of various birches often causing serious defoliation

birch oil *n* **1 :** BIRCH-TAR OIL **2 :** an essential oil obtained from the bark or twigs of the sweet birch that resembles wintergreen oil in consisting chiefly of methyl salicylate and is used similarly to methyl salicylate — called also *sweet-birch oil*

birch partridge *n* **:** RUFFED GROUSE

birch rod *n* **:** BIRCH 3

birch skeletonizer *n* **:** a small tineoid moth (*Bucculatrix canadensisella*) whose larva attacks birch leaves

birch-tar oil \ˈ=,=-\ *n* **:** a brown toxic phenolic oil obtained by destructive distillation of the bark and wood of the European white birch and used in finishing Russia leather to which it gives the characteristic odor and sometimes in ointments for skin diseases (as eczema) — called also *birch oil*

birchwood \ˈ=,=\ *n* **1 :** BIRCH 2 **2 :** a wood or grove of birch trees

[1]bird \ˈbərd, ˈbəd, ˈbəid\ *n* -s [ME *brid, bird* young bird, bird, fr. OE *bridd* young bird] **1 a** *archaic* **:** the young of a feathered vertebrate (as a chick, eaglet, or duckling) **:** NESTLING **b :** any young animal as: (1) *obs* **:** CHILD, YOUNGSTER (2) *chiefly Brit* **:** a girl or young woman ⟨struggling to make it with the ~~—Adam Faith⟩ **2 a :** a member of the class Aves all differing from the ancestral reptiles in possession of a covering of feathers instead of scales, a completely four-chambered heart served by a single (the right) aortic arch, fully separate systemic and pulmonary circulations, a warm-blooded metabolism, and large eggs with hard calcareous shells, and all recent forms having the forelimbs modified into wings, the jaws without teeth and enclosed in horny sheaths, and usu. the breastbone enlarged by a ventral keel for the attachment of the pectoral muscles that control the action of the wings **b :** an adult of any variety of domestic poultry ⟨a table ~⟩ ⟨a show ~⟩ ⟨housing for 3000 ~s and 1000 poults⟩ **3 :** GAME BIRD; *esp* **:** PARTRIDGE **4 :** a saucer (as of pottery) made to be thrown from a spring trap and used in skeet and as a substitute for a live bird in trapshooting **:** CLAY PIGEON **5** *slang* **a :** FELLOW, CHAP; *esp* **:** a peculiar or inconsequential one — usu. used somewhat patronizingly ⟨a queer ~⟩ ⟨a gay old ~⟩ **b** (1) **:** a notably clever or accomplished person — often used ironically ⟨her grandfather really is a ~⟩ (2) **:** something admirable of its kind ⟨a ~ of a filly⟩ ⟨a ~ of a scheme⟩ **6 :** SHUTTLECOCK 1a **7 :** a hissing or jeering expressive of disapproval ⟨the crowd gave him the ~⟩; *also* **:** dismissal from employment ⟨I've got to get busy if I don't want to get the ~⟩ **8 :** a small thin piece of meat rolled up with stuffing and skewered, browned, and braised — see VEAL BIRD **9 :** GUIDED MISSILE — **bird in the hand** [from the proverb "a bird in the hand is worth two in the bush"] **:** something assured or definite rather than the merely possible — **for the birds :** WORTHLESS, RIDICULOUS, NONSENSICAL ⟨that's *for the birds*⟩

bird (waxwing): *1* bill, *2* forehead, *3* crown, *4* crest, *5* auricular region, *6* throat, *7* breast, *8* abdomen, *9* under tail coverts, *10* tail, *11* primaries, *12* secondaries, *13* upper wing coverts, *14* scapulars

feet of birds: *1* swift, *2* cuckoo, *3* fowl, *4* finch, *5* kingfisher, *6* hawk, *7* stork, *8* ostrich, *9* duck, *10* sandpiper, *11* grebe, *12* coot, *13* pelican

[2]bird \"\ *vi* -ED/-ING/-S **:** to observe or identify wild birds in their natural environment

bird–alane \ˈbərdəˌlān\ *var of* BURD-ALANE

birdbander \ˈ=,==\ *n* **:** one that bands birds — **birdbanding** \ˈ=,==\ *n*

birdbath \ˈ=,=\ *n* **1 :** a usu. ornamental vessel provided esp. in gardens for birds to bathe in **2** *also* **birdbath dish :** a small usu. oval saucedish used esp. formerly for the serving of individual portions of vegetables

bird–batting \ˈ=,==\ *n, now dial* **:** BATFOWLING

bird bell *n* **:** RATTLESNAKE ROOT a

birdberry \ˈ=- — *see* BERRY\ *n* **:** PEPPER VINE 2

bird bills *n pl* [so called fr. the shape of the flowers] **:** SHOOTING STAR 2

bird–bolt \ˈ=,=\ *n* **:** a short blunt missile (as a blunt arrow) formerly used for killing birds without piercing them

bird box *n* **:** a box for wild birds to nest in **:** BIRDHOUSE

birdbrain \ˈ=,=\ *n* **:** a flighty thoughtless person **:** SCATTERBRAIN **:** a stupid person — **bird–brained** \ˈ=ˈ=\ *adj*

birdcage \ˈ=,=\ *n* [ME, fr. *bird* + *cage*] **1 :** a cage for confining birds **2 :** something resembling a birdcage (as a wire cage for dice) **3 :** CHUCK-A-LUCK **4** *Brit* **:** a paddock in which horses are saddled at a racecourse **5 :** a double-block construction to allow the top of a tilt-top table to revolve as well as to tip up when not in use

birdcage clock *n* **:** LANTERN CLOCK

birdcall \ˈ=,=\ *n* **1 :** the note or cry of a bird or a sound made in imitation of it **2 :** an instrument (as a whistle) used in imitating a birdcall

bird cherry *n* **1 :** any of several small-fruited cherry trees frequented or fed on by birds: as **a :** EUROPEAN BIRD CHERRY **b :** PIN CHERRY 1 **2 :** the fruit of a bird cherry

bird–claw \ˈ=ˌ=\ *adj* **:** like the claw of a bird esp. in gauntness and lack of flesh ⟨trembling *bird-claw* hands⟩

bird colonel *n* [so called fr. the eagle of the insignia] *slang* **:** a colonel as distinguished from a lieutenant colonel

bird dog *n* **1 :** a gundog trained to locate or to retrieve birds for the hunter **2 :** one that seeks out or locates: as **a :** CANVASSER; *esp* **:** one who locates prospects for a salesman **b :** a talent scout esp. in sports **c :** one (as a detective) who pries after information **d :** one who steals another's date

bird–dog \ˈ=,=\ *vb* [*bird dog*] *vi* **:** to play the part of a bird dog **:** watch closely ~ *vt* **:** to seek out **:** follow and detect **:** FERRET, DOG

birded *past of* BIRD

bird·er \-də(r)\ *n* -s [ME, fr. *bird* + *-er*] **1 :** a catcher or hunter of birds; *esp* **:** a person who kills birds in quantity for market **2 :** an observer or identifier of wild birds in their natural surroundings

birdeye \ˈ=,=\ *n* [so called fr. the spot resembling an eye in the flower's center] **:** a partially woody herb (*Caperonia castaneaefolia*) of the spurge family occurring in wet soils of the southeastern U.S. and having alternate toothed leaves and flowers in elongate interrupted spikelike clusters — called also *Mexican weed*

bird–eyed \ˈ=ˌ=\ *adj* **1 :** having eyes like a bird **:** having something (as spots) suggesting the eyes of a bird ⟨a *bird-eyed* tissue⟩ **2 :** easily frightened **:** SKITTISH — used chiefly of horses

bird flower *n* **1 :** BIRD-OF-PARADISE **2 :** any of several flowers the pollination of which is accomplished by birds (usu. hummingbirds): as **a :** OSWEGO TEA **b :** CARDINAL FLOWER **3 :** BIRD PLANT

bird font *n* **:** BIRDBATH

bird–foot *var of* BIRD'S-FOOT

bird–foot delta *n* **:** a delta (as that of the Mississippi river) having many levee-bordered channels extending seaward like outstretched claws

bird grape *n* **:** a wild grape (*Vitis munsoniana*) of Florida, Georgia, and the Bahamas closely related to the muscadine

bird grass *n* **1 :** KNOTGRASS 1 **2 :** ROUGH BLUEGRASS

birdhouse \ˈ=,=\ *n* **1 :** an artificial nesting site (as a box or other container) for birds **2 :** an enclosure or building where birds are confined and exhibited **:** AVIARY

[1]**bird·ie** \-dē,-di\ *n* -s [[1]*bird* + *-ie*] **1 :** a little bird — often used as a pet name **2 :** a golf score of one stroke less than par on a hole **3 :** any of various sounds suggesting the chirp or trill of a bird

[2]**birdie** \"\ *vt* -ED/-ING/-S **:** to shoot (a hole in golf) in one stroke under par ⟨*birdied* the 18th hole to win the match⟩

birdie in the cage *or* **bird in the cage :** a square-dance figure in which three members of a two-couple team encircle the fourth dancer

birdier *comparative of* BIRDY

birdiest *superlative of* BIRDY

birding *pres part of* BIRD

bird–in–the–bush \ˌ===ˈ=\ *n* **:** PRICKLY POPPY

bird knotgrass *n* **:** KNOTGRASS 1

bird·less \-dləs\ *adj* **:** being without a bird

birdlife \ˈ=,=\ *n* **:** AVIFAUNA; *also* **:** the activities and habits of the constituent birds ⟨~ of this state⟩

bird·like \ˈ=,=\ *adj* **:** resembling or suggestive of a bird esp. in alertness or in voice

[1]**birdlime** \ˈ=,=\ *n* [ME *birdlim, bridlim*, fr. *bird, brid* bird + *lim* lime — more at BIRD, LIME] **1 :** an extremely adhesive sticky substance usu. made from the bark of the holly (*Ilex aquifolium*) but also from other plants (as the European mistletoe or the breadfruit) and used esp. formerly to entrap small birds by smearing twigs where they are accustomed to perch **2 :** something that entraps or ensnares ⟨a ~ of words⟩ **3 :** CLEAVERS

[2]**birdlime** \"\ *vt* **:** to smear with or as if with birdlime **:** catch with birdlime **:** ENSNARE

bird·ling \ˈ= + (ˌ)liŋ, (ˌ)lēŋ\ *n* -s [[1]*bird* + *-ling*] **:** a little bird **:** NESTLING, FLEDGLING

bird louse *n* **:** any of numerous wingless insects of the order Mallophaga mostly parasitic on birds, a few on mammals, all having mouths adapted to biting, not sucking, and feeding on the feathers, hair, or skin of the host often causing injury — called also *biting louse*

bird malaria *n* **:** a febrile disease of wild birds and poultry that is physiologically comparable to human malaria and caused by related protozoan parasites of *Plasmodium* and related genera

bird·man \ˈ= + mən, -ˌman, ˌmaa(ə)n; *in sense 2 usu* + mən\ *n, pl* **birdmen 1 :** one that deals with birds (as a fowler or an ornithologist) **2 :** AVIATOR, AIRMAN; *sometimes* **:** an airplane passenger

bird mite *n* **:** any of numerous small mites parasitic upon birds; *esp* **:** CHICKEN MITE

bird of freedom : BALD EAGLE; *also* **:** a representation of it (as on the coat of arms and coins of the U.S.)

bird of jove *usu cap J* [after *Jove* (Jupiter), ancient Roman divinity — more at JOVE] **:** EAGLE

bird of ju·no \-ˈjünō\ *usu cap J* [after *Juno*, ancient Roman goddess, consort of Jupiter, fr. L] **:** PEACOCK

bird of minerva *usu cap M* [after *Minerva*, ancient Roman goddess] **:** OWL

bird of night : OWL

bird of paradise 1 : any of a number of birds of the family Paradisaeidae inhabiting New Guinea and the adjacent islands notable for the brilliant colors, graceful plumes, and often remarkably developed tail feathers of the adult males, the females and young being without plumes and plainly colored **2 :** in *New South Wales* **:** LYREBIRD

bird of paradise

bird–of–paradise \ˌ==ˈ==(ˌ)=\ *or* **bird–of–paradise flower** *n* [*bird of paradise*] **1 :** an ornamental bananalike plant (*Strelitzia reginae*) having scapes of orange and purple flowers suggestive of a bird **2 :** a poinciana (*Poinciana gilliesii*) with colorful red and yellow flowers

bird of passage 1 : a migratory bird **2 :** a person who moves freely from one place to another and usu. has no permanently fixed abode **:** ROLLING STONE; *sometimes* **:** an immigrant laborer temporarily in a country

bird of prey : any of various carnivorous birds that feed wholly or chiefly on meat taken by hunting as opposed to carrion and including most members of the orders Falconiformes and Strigiformes (as hawks, eagles, and owls)

bird of wonder : PHOENIX

bird–on–the–wing \ˌ===ˈ=\ *n* [so called fr. the shape of the flower] **:** GAYWINGS

bird peck *n* **:** a small spot of distorted grain or a hole in wood attributed to damage by birds

bird pepper *n* **:** a pepper having very small oblong red fruits that are among the most pungent of all peppers, commonly occurring wild or spontaneously in warm countries, and being considered to constitute the type of a species (*Capsicum frutescens*) or to be a variety (*C. frutescens baccatum*) of this species

bird pest *or* **bird plague** *n* **:** FOWL PLAGUE

bird plant *n* **:** a Mexican herb (*Heterotoma lobelioides*) having yellow-and-purple flowers that suggest the form of a bird — called also *bird flower, canarybird flower*

bird pox *n* **:** FOWL POX

bird rattle *n* **:** a device for scaring birds away from fields or gardens by making a rattling noise

bird–ringer \ˈ=,==\ *n, Brit* **:** BIRDBANDER — **bird–ringing** \ˈ=,==\ *n* -s

birds *pl of* BIRD, *pres 3d sing of* BIRD

bird's–beak \ˈ=,=\ *n, pl* **bird's–beaks 1 :** an architectural molding with a section resembling a beak **2** [so called fr. the shape of the flower] **:** a California herb of the genus *Cordylanthus* (family Scrophulariaceae)

bird's–bread \ˈ=,=\ *n, pl* **bird's–breads :** a stonecrop (*Sedum acre*)

birdseed \ˈ=,=\ *n* **1 :** a mixture of small seeds (as those of hemp, millet, and certain grasses) used chiefly for feeding cage birds **2 :** the common groundsel (*Senecio vulgaris*)

birdseed grass *n* **:** CANARY GRASS 1

bird's–egg green \ˈ=,=-\ *n* **:** ROBIN'S-EGG BLUE

[1]**bird's–eye** \ˈ=,=\ *n, pl* **bird's–eyes 1 :** any of numerous plants with bright-colored flowers: as **a :** a primrose (*Primula farinosa*) having a pale lilac flower with a yellow eye **b** *Brit* (1) **:** GERMANDER SPEEDWELL (2) **:** PHEASANT'S-EYE (3) **:** BIRD'S-FOOT TREFOIL (4) **:** HERB ROBERT **2 a :** an allover geometric pattern for textiles consisting of a small diamond with a center dot resembling a bird's eye **b :** a fabric esp. of cotton, linen, or worsted woven with this pattern **3 :** a small spot with the wood fibers arranged around it in the form of an ellipse in some lumber **4 :** a spot on coated paper caused by a particle of grease in the coating mixture

[2]**bird's–eye** \"\ *adj* **1 a :** seen from above as if by a flying bird **:** PANORAMIC ⟨a *bird's-eye* view⟩ **b :** GENERAL, CURSORY, SUPERFICIAL ⟨a *bird's-eye* survey of American politics⟩ **2 :** marked with spots resembling birds' eyes ⟨*bird's-eye* diaper⟩ ⟨a *bird's-eye* scarf⟩ **3 :** [*bird's-eye* (*maple*)] **:** made of bird's-eye maple ⟨a *bird's-eye* chest⟩ ⟨*bird's-eye* veneer⟩

bird's–eye maple *n* **:** wood of the sugar maple in which a wavy grain causes eyelike markings

bird's–eye primrose *n* **:** any of several bright-flowered primroses; *esp* **:** BIRD'S-EYE 1a

bird's–eye rot *n* **:** anthracnose of the grape caused by a fungus (*Elsinoe ampelina*) and manifested by small sunken dark fruit spots with light centers

bird's–eyes \ˈ=,=\ *n pl but sing or pl in constr* **:** an erect annual garden herb (*Gilia tricolor*) with dissected leaves and corolla having a yellowish tube, a purple-marked throat, and violet or lilac lobes

bird's–eye spot *n* **:** a disease of plants characterized by round dark spots with lighter surrounding tissue suggesting the appearance of a bird's eye: as **a :** a disease of tea leaves caused by a fungus (*Cercospora theae*) **b :** a leaf spot of the Hevea rubber tree caused by a fungus (*Helminthosporium heveae*)

bird's–foot *also* **bird–foot** \ˈ=,=\ *n, pl* **bird's–foots** *also* **bird–foots :** any of numerous plants having leaves or flowers resembling the foot of a bird; *specif* **:** a plant of the genus *Ornithopus* having bent and jointed pods or of the related genera *Lotus* and *Trigonella*

bird's–foot clover *n* **:** BIRD'S-FOOT TREFOIL

bird's–foot fern *n* **:** a rock brake (*Pellaea ornithopus*) of the Pacific coast of No. America having some of the lower pinnules replaced by secondary pinnae each consisting of three sessile pinnules arranged so as to suggest a bird's foot

bird's–foot trefoil *n* **1 :** a plant of the genus *Lotus*: as **a :** a European plant (*L. corniculatus*) having claw-shaped pods and now widely used esp. in the U. S. as a forage and fodder plant — called also *babies'-slippers* **b :** PRAIRIE BIRD'S-FOOT TREFOIL **2 :** a glabrous annual or perennial prostrate Old World herb (*Trigonella ornithopodioides*) related to fenugreek

bird's–foot violet *also* **bird–foot violet** *n* **:** a common violet (*Viola pedata*) of the eastern U.S. with pedate leaves and large pale blue or purple flowers that resemble pansies — see PANSY VIOLET

bird shot *n* **:** shot of small size for shooting birds

birds–in–the–bush \ˌ===ˈ=\ *n* **:** PRICKLY POPPY

bird skin *n* **:** the skin of a bird; *specif* **:** the external part of a bird prepared for study or display by removing most parts internal to the skin and replacing them with cotton or tow

bird's knotgrass *n* **:** KNOTGRASS 1

bird's–mouth \ˈ=,=\ *n, pl* **bird's–mouths :** an interior angle of notch cut across the end of a piece of timber to receive the edge of another piece

bird snake *n* **:** a back-fanged tree snake (*Thelotornis kirtlandii*) of tropical and southern Africa having a slender body and a green head that allow it to be mistaken for a liana by the birds and lizards on which it preys

bird's nest *n* **1 :** the nest in which a bird lays eggs and hatches young **2 a :** EDIBLE BIRD'S NEST; *also* **:** a substitute used in the preparation of soup **b :** any of several dishes commonly containing nuts or fruit (as an apple dumpling or a cobbler) **3 :** any of several plants having a real or fancied resemblance to a bird's nest; *esp* **:** WILD CARROT **4 :** CROW'S NEST 1a **5 :** a snarl of fishing line at the reel **:** BACKLASH

bird's–nest \ˈ=,=\ *vi* [*bird's nest*] **:** to hunt for or take birds' nests or their contents — **bird's–nester** \ˈ= ==\ *n*

bird's–nest cactus *n* **:** BALL CACTUS

bird's–nest fern *n* **1 :** an Australian epiphytic fern (*Asplenium nidus*) frequently forming tufts in tree crotches **2 :** a fern (*Pycnodoria vittata*) of the southern U.S. having prostrate rosettes

bird's–nest fungus *n* **:** a fungus of the family Nidulariaceae

bird's–nest moss *n* **:** a Mexican club moss (*Selaginella lepidophylla*)

bird's–nest orchid *or* **bird's–nest orchis** *n* **:** a European orchid (*Neottia nidusavis*) having closely matted roots

bird's–nest plant *n* **1 :** INDIAN PIPE **2 :** BIRD'S NEST 3

birdsong \ˈ=,=\ *n* **:** the song of a bird; *also* **:** sound suggesting the singing of birds

bird's–pep·per \ˈ=,==\ *n, pl* **bird's–peppers :** a wild peppergrass (*Lepidium virginicum*) with nearly orbicular seed pods

bird spider *n* **:** any of a number of large hairy spiders (family Theraphosidae) chiefly of tropical America that are reputed to capture small birds in their strong webs

bird·stone \ˈ=,=\ *n* **:** a stone artifact known only from archaic sites in midwestern and eastern No. America that resembles a bird and is thought to have been an atlatl weight — compare BANNERSTONE, BOATSTONE

bird's–tongue \ˈ=,=\ *n, pl* **bird's–tongues** [so called fr. the shape of the leaves] **1 :** JOINT GRASS 1 **2 :** SCARLET PIMPERNEL **3 :** a common European maple (*Acer campestre*) used as an ornamental **4 :** a stitchwort (*Alsine holostea*)

birds·ville disease \ˈbərdzˌvil-, ˈbədz-, -ˌvəl\ *n, usu cap B* [fr. *Birdsville*, village and cattle region in Queensland, Australia] **:** a disease of Australian horses marked by drowsiness, emaciation, incoordination, and labored breathing, frequently ending fatally in 7 to 10 days, and being of uncertain etiology, both poisonous forage and heavy worm burdens having been suggested as possible causes

bird tick *n* **1 :** a fly of the family Hippoboscidae parasitic on birds **2 :** any of several ticks (family Argasidae) attacking birds

bird vetch *n* **:** TUFTED VETCH

birdvine \ˈ=,=\ *n* **:** a plant of the genus *Loranthus*

bird walk *n* **:** a walk usu. by a group of people and often under the guidance of a skilled leader for the purpose of observing and identifying wild birds in their natural surroundings

bird–watch \ˈ=,=\ *vi* [back-formation fr. *bird watcher*] **:** [2]BIRD

bird watcher *n* **:** BIRDER 2

birdweed \ˈ=,=\ *n* **:** KNOTGRASS 1

bird wheat *n* **:** PIGEON-WHEAT

bird–wing butterfly \ˈ=,=-\ *also* **bird wing** *n* **:** any of various very large often brilliantly colored butterflies (family Papilionidae) of southeast Asia, the East Indies, and tropical Australia

bird–wit·ted \ˈ=ˌ==\ *adj* **:** FLIGHTY **:** lacking capacity for prolonged attention

birdy \-dē\ *adj, often* -ER/-EST [[1]*bird* + *-y*] **1 :** like or like that of a bird ⟨~ curiosity⟩ **2 a :** abounding in birds, esp. game birds ⟨quartering an upland slope that should have been very ~⟩ **b** *of a gun dog* **:** skilled at finding game birds

bi·rectangular \(ˈ)bī + \ *adj* [[1]*bi-* + *rectangular*] **:** having two right angles ⟨a ~ spherical triangle⟩

bi·refracting \ˌbī + \ *adj* [[1]*bi-* + *refracting*] **:** BIREFRINGENT

bi·refraction \ˌbī + \ *n* -s [[1]*bi-* + *refraction*] **:** DOUBLE REFRACTION

bi·refractive \ˌbī + \ *adj* [[1]*bi-* + *refractive*] **:** BIREFRINGENT

bi·refringence \ˌbī + \ *n* -s [ISV [1]*bi-* + *refringence*] **:** DOUBLE REFRACTION

bi·refringent \ˌbī + \ *adj* [[1]*bi-* + *refringent*] **:** having or characterized by double refraction

bi·reme \ˈbīˌrēm\ *n* -s [L *biremis*, fr. *bi-* [1]bi- + *-remis* (fr. *remus* oar) — more at REMI-] **:** a galley with two banks of oars common in the early classical period — compare TRIREME

bi·ret·ta *also* **ber·ret·ta** *or* **be·ret·ta** \bəˈredə, -etə\ *n* -s [It *berretta, berretto*, fr. OProv *berret* cap, irreg. fr. LL *birrus* cloak with a hood, of Celt origin; akin to MIr *berr* short, W *byr*] **:** a square head covering worn by ecclesiastics that has three or four projections above the crown, often with a tassel at the top, and is red, purple, or black to correspond to the rank of cardinal, bishop, or priest

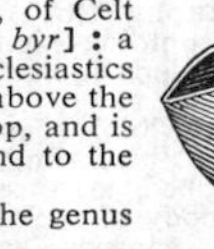

biretta

bir·gus \ˈbərgəs\ *n, cap* [NL] **:** the genus containing the purse crab

birh·or \ˈbiˌrȯr\ *n, pl* **birhor** *or* **birhors** *usu cap* **1 :** a Dravidian people in the plateau jungles in east-central India **2 :** a member of the Birhor people

bi·ri \ˈbē(ˌ)rē\ *n* -s [Hindi *bīṛī, bīṛī* betel quid, cigar, fr. Skt *viṭikā* betel quid] *India* **:** a cheap locally made cigarette

bi·ri·ba \ˌbirēˈbä\ *n* -s [Pg *biribá*, fr. Tupi] **:** a Brazilian tree (*Rollinia deliciosa*) whose fruit resembles the custard apple

bi·rimose \(ˈ)bī + \ *adj* [[1]*bi-* + *rimose*] *bot* **:** opening by two slits (as of an anther)

birk \ˈbi(ə)rk, ˈbərk\ *n* -s [ME — more at BIRCH] *chiefly Scot* **:** BIRCH

birk·en \-kən\ *adj* [ME — more at BIRCHEN] *chiefly Scot* **:** BIRCH, BIRCHEN

bir·ken·head \ˈbərkənˌhed\ *adj, usu cap* [fr. *Birkenhead*, England] **:** of or from the county borough of Birkenhead, England **:** of the kind or style prevalent in Birkenhead

bir·ke·nia \bərˈkēnēə\ *n, cap* [NL, fr. *Birkenhead* Burn, Lanark county, Scotland + NL *-ia*] **:** a genus (the type of the family Birkeniidae of the order Anaspida) of Upper Silurian ostracoderms having no cephalic armor and having the body covered with small scales

birk·ie \ˈbirki, ˈbər-\ *n* -s [origin unknown] **1** *Scot* **:** a lively smart assertive person ⟨a gay stout ~⟩ **2** *Scot* **:** FELLOW, BOY

birl \ˈbərl, ˈbərəl; *in sense 1 usu* ˈbir(ə)l\ *vb* -ED/-ING/-S [ME *birlen*, fr. OE *byrelian*; akin to OE *byrele* cup-bearer, OS *biril* basket, and perh. to OE *beran* to bear — more at BEAR] *vt* **1** *also* **birle** \ˈbir(ə)l, ˈbər(ə)l\ *chiefly Scot* **a :** POUR ⟨come ~ the ale, lass⟩ **b :** to ply with drink ⟨she ~ed him with strong beer⟩ **2 :** to revolve or cause to revolve: **a :** to cause (a floating log) to rotate by treading (as in log driving or in a logrolling contest) **b :** SPIN ⟨~ a coin on the table⟩ ~ *vi* **1** *chiefly Scot* **:** to drink in company **:** CAROUSE **2 :** to progress with a curved or rotary motion **:** SPIN, WHIRL **3 :** to birl a log esp. in competition — **birl the bawbee** *Scot* **:** to spend freely esp. for drink

birl·er \-lə(r)\ *n* -s **:** one that birls; *esp* **:** a person who birls logs

bir·lie·man \'birlēmən\ *var of* BYRLAWMAN

¹bir·ling \'birliŋ\ *or* **birlinn** \-lən\ *n* -s [ScGael *birlinn*, prob. (like MIr *birling*), fr. ON *byrthingr* merchant ship, fr. *byrth-* (akin to *borth* board) + *-ingr* -ing — more at BOARD] **:** a chieftain's galley or barge used about the Hebrides

²birl·ing \'bərliŋ\ *n* -s [fr. gerund of *birl*] **:** the sport of logrolling

bir·ma \'bərmə\ *n* -s [origin unknown] **:** SANTA MARIA TREE

birman *usu cap, var of* BURMAN

bir·ming·ham *see separate senses*\ *adj, usu cap* [fr. *Birmingham*, England] **1** \'bərmiŋəm *sometimes* -ŋ,ham\ **:** of or from the city of Birmingham, England **:** of the kind or style prevalent in Birmingham — compare BRUMMAGEM **2** \'bərmiŋ,ham *sometimes* -ŋəm\ [fr. *Birmingham*, Alabama] **:** of or from the city of Birmingham, Ala. ⟨a *Birmingham* industry⟩ **:** of the kind or style prevalent in Birmingham

birn \'bərn\ *n* -s [G (now usu. *birne*), lit., pear, fr. MHG *bir*, fr. OHG *bira*, fr. ML *pira* — more at PEAR] **:** the pear-shaped socket of an instrument of the clarinet class into which the mouthpiece is fitted

bir·ne \'birnə\ *n* -s [G, lit., pear] **:** ⁴BOULE

bir·nirk \(')bir¦ni(ə)rk\ *adj, usu cap* [fr. *Birnirk*, locality near Point Barrow, Alaska] **:** of or belonging to an Eskimo culture centered around Point Barrow in northeastern Alaska, intermediate between Old Bering Sea and Thule, dated about A.D. 600–1000, and characterized by toggle harpoon heads and elements suggesting Asiatic derivation

bi·rotation \¦bī +\ *n* -s [ISV ¹*bi-* + *rotation*] **:** MUTAROTATION

bi·rot·u·lar \(')bī¦räl(chələ(r), -rōl, |·tyə-\ *or* **bi·rot·u·late** \-lət, -,lāt\ *adj* [*birotular* fr. ¹*bi-* + *rotular*; *birotulate* fr. ¹*bi-* + L *rotula* little wheel + E *-ate* — more at ROLL] **:** being or resembling a birotulate

bi·rot·u·late *like adj*\ *or* **bi·ro·tule** \'bīrə,tyül, -rō·,-\ *n* -s [*birotulate* fr. *birotulate*, adj.; *birotule* prob. back-formation fr. *birotulate*, adj.] **:** a sponge spicule having two wheel-shaped ends

¹birr \'bər, 'bə̄\ *n* -s [ME *bir, birr* strong wind, force, attack, fr. OE *byre* strong wind and ON *byrr* favoring wind; both akin to OE *beran* to bear — more at BEAR] **1 a :** force esp. of the wind or of an onslaught in battle **:** onward rush **:** IMPETUS; *also* **:** ENERGY, VIGOR ⟨full of ~ and go⟩ **b :** BLOW, THRUST, PUSH **2 :** a whirring sound (as of a spinning wheel) **:** BURR

²birr \'bi(ə)r, 'bər\ *vi* -ED/-ING/-S *chiefly Scot* **:** to make a whirring sound

bir·rus *or* **byr·rus** \'birəs\ *n, pl* **bir·ri** *or* **byr·ri** \-(,)rē, -,rī\ [LL — more at BIRETTA] **:** a woolen cape or cloak usu. with a hood worn by the Romans and by members of the poorer classes in the middle ages

birse \'bi(ə)rs, 'bərs\ *n* -s [fr. (assumed) ME *birst*, fr. OE *byrst* — more at BRISTLE] **1** *chiefly Scot* **:** a bristle or tuft of bristles **2** *chiefly Scot* **:** ANGER, IRRITATION

bir·sle \'birsəl, 'bər-\ *vb* -ED/-ING/-S [origin unknown] *Scot* **:** BROIL, TOAST, DRY ⟨*birsled* peas⟩ ⟨~ yourselves at the fire⟩

birsy \'birsi\ *adj* [*birse* + *-y*] *Scot* **:** BRISTLY, IRRITABLE

¹birth \'bərth, 'bə̄th, 'bəith\ *n, pl* **births** \-ths *sometimes* -t͟hz\ *often attrib* [ME *birthe, burthe*, fr. ON *byrth*; akin to OE *gebyrd* birth, OHG *giburt*, Goth *gabaurths*, ON *bera* to bear — more at BEAR] **1 a :** the act of coming forth from the womb **:** the condition of being born **:** the emergence of a new individual from the body of its parent; *specif* **:** the period during which and processes by which the mammalian fetus becomes established as an individual physically independent of its mother's body ⟨several years after the ~ of the princess⟩ ⟨the ~ of the head was delayed⟩ ⟨a child sickly from ~⟩ **b :** the act or process of bringing forth young from the womb ⟨she had a very hard ~ after a prolonged labor⟩ **2 a :** the condition or position that falls to a person as a result of being born esp. at a particular time or place or into a particular kinship ⟨a Frenchman by ~⟩ ⟨marriage between those unequal in ~ and ability is risky⟩ **b :** high or noble status dependent on birth ⟨a lady of ~ descended from the Kings of Ireland⟩ **c** *obs* **:** NATIVITY 4 **3** *obs* **:** FETUS **4 a** *archaic* **:** one that is born **:** CHILD, OFFSPRING, YOUNG **b :** a coming into existence **:** BEGINNING, START ⟨the ~ of an idea⟩

²birth \"\ *vb* -ED/-ING/-S *vt* **1** *now chiefly dial* **:** to bring forth (as a child) **2 :** to give rise to **:** ORIGINATE, PRODUCE ⟨provided the weapons that won the war and . . . ~*ed* the Atomic Age —Philip Wylie⟩ ~ *vi, dial* **:** to bring forth a child or young ⟨two women due to ~ 'bout the same time —Ralph Ellison⟩

birth canal *n* **:** the channel formed by the cervix, vagina, and vulva through which the mammalian fetus is expelled during parturition

birth certificate *n* **:** a certificate embodying a copy of an official record of the date and place of birth and parentage of a person

birthcoat \'=,=\ *n* **:** the dense coat of wool of a newborn lamb

birth control *n* **:** control or limitation of the number of children born esp. by preventing or lessening the frequency of impregnation (as by the use of contraceptive measures or by avoiding coitus when ovulation is likely to occur) **:** CONTRACEPTION

birth controller *n* **:** an advocate of birth control

birth·day \'=(,)dā, -,dē,-di\ *n* [ME *birthe day*, fr. *birthe* birth + *day*] **1 a :** the day on which a person is born **b :** a day of origin or commencement **2 a :** an anniversary of one's birth; *also* **:** a celebration of an anniversary of it **b :** YEAR — chiefly in figurative or poetic use

birthday cake *n* **:** a cake for a birthday celebration

birthday honor *n* **:** recognition (as a title) bestowed by the British sovereign at the celebration of the ruler's official birthday — usu. used in pl.

birthday suit *n* **:** unclothed skin — used chiefly in the phrase *in one's birthday suit*

birth·dom \'=dəm\ *n* -s [*birth* + *-dom*] *obs* **:** domain by birthright **:** native land

birth flower *n* **:** a flower considered as appropriate to or symbolic of the month of one's birth

birthing *n* -s [fr. gerund of ²*birth*] **1** *chiefly dial* **:** the act of giving birth **:** BEARING ⟨on tenterhooks like she was the one that had to go through ~ —Conrad Richter⟩ **2 :** BIRTH

birth·land \'=,land, -,lənd\ *n* **:** the land where someone or something is born

birth·less \'=ləs\ *adj* **1 :** ABORTIVE, FRUITLESS **2 :** having unknown or unimportant parents or ancestors

¹birthmark \'=,=\ *n* [¹*birth* + *mark*] **1 :** an unusual mark or blemish on the skin at birth **:** NEVUS **2 :** a distinguishing characteristic or quality ⟨words sang for him, and that is the ~ of a poet —Dylan Thomas⟩

²birthmark \"\ *vt* **:** to fix a birthmark on — usu. used passively

birthnight \'=,=\ *n* **:** the night in which a person is born **:** the anniversary of that night in any succeeding year; *specif* **:** the celebration formerly held on the evening of a royal birthday

birth pang *n* **1 :** one of the regularly recurrent pains that are characteristic of childbirth — usu. used in pl. **2 birth pangs** *pl* **:** disorder and distress incident to a major organizational or social change ⟨the *birth pangs* of civilization⟩

birth phantasy *n, psychoanalysis* **:** a primitive or childish notion of the process of childbirth

birthplace \'=,=\ *n* **1 :** the place (as a house or town) where a person is born **2 :** the place of origin of something ⟨the ~ of freedom⟩

birthrank \'=,=\ *n* **:** order of birth among siblings

birthrate \'=,=\ *n* **:** the ratio between number of births and number of individuals in a specified population and period of time often expressed as number of live births per hundred or per thousand population

birthright \'=,=\ *n* **:** a right, privilege, or possession to which a person is entitled by birth (as an estate or as civil liberty guaranteed under a constitution); *esp* **:** the inheritance of the firstborn ⟨to sell his ~ for a mess of pottage⟩ **syn** see RIGHT

birthroot \'=,=\ *n* [so called fr. its use to ease childbirth] **:** any of several trilliums having astringent roots that were formerly used in folk medicine; *esp* **:** PURPLE TRILLIUM

births *pl of* BIRTH, *pres 3d sing of* BIRTH

birth sin *n* **:** ORIGINAL SIN

birthstone \'=,=\ *n* **:** a precious stone considered as appropriate to or symbolizing the influences due to the month of one's birth

birth·stool \'=,=\ *n* **:** a seat formerly used by women in childbirth

birth trauma *n* **:** the physical injury or emotional shock sustained by an infant in the process of birth

birthwort \'=,=\ *n* -s **1 :** any of several plants of the genus *Aristolochia* (as *A. longa, A. pistolochia, A. clematitis*, or *A. serpentaria*) the aromatic roots of which are reputed to aid in parturition **2 :** either of two European herbs (*Corydalis fabacea* and *C. tuberosa*) whose roots are reputed to aid in parturition **3 :** BIRTHROOT

birthwort family *n* **:** ARISTOLOCHIACEAE

bis \'bis\ *adv* [F, fr. L, twice, fr. OL *dvis*; akin to MHG *zwis* twice, OHG *zwiro*, ON *tvisvar* twice, Goth *twis-* apart, Gk *dis* twice, Skt *dvis* twice, L *duo* two — more at TWO] **1 :** AGAIN — used to direct repetition of a passage of music or to request an encore **2** [L] **:** TWICE — used to call attention to the occurrence of an item twice (as in an account or an address)

bis- *comb form* [L, fr. *bis*] **1 a :** both **:** of or belonging to both — chiefly in anatomical or medical words of which the second constituent begins with a vowel ⟨*bis*ischiatic⟩ **b :** two ⟨*bis*marine⟩ **2 :** twice **:** doubled — esp. in complex chemical expressions ⟨*bis*dimethylamino-⟩ ⟨*bis*quarternary⟩

bis *abbr* bissextile

BIS *abbr* best in show

bis·a·bol \'bisə,bōl, -bōl\ *or* **bisabol myrrh** *also* **bis·sa·bol** *like first form*\ *n* [of African origin; akin to Wolof *bisap u ala*, a Senegambian tree] **:** a gum resin that resembles true myrrh and is obtained from two African trees (*Commiphora kataf* and *C. erythraea*) — called also *opopanax*

bis·a·bol·ene \,bisəbə'lēn, '==,=\ *n* -s [ISV *bisabol* + *-ene*] **:** a colorless oily sesquiterpene $C_{15}H_{24}$ derived from cyclohexene and found in many essential oils (as oil of bisabol and lime oil)

bi·sag·re \bə'sa(,)grē, bi'sä(,)grā\ *n* -s [MexSp] **:** a small spiny cactus (*Echinocactus horizonthalonius*) of Mexico and southwestern U. S. that is sometimes cut into slices and candied

bi·sal·tae \bə'sal(,)tē\ *n pl, usu cap* [L, fr. Gk *Bisaltai*] **:** a people of ancient Thrace

bi·sa·yan \bə'sī(y)ən\ *also* **bi·sa·ya** \-(y)ə\ *n, pl* **bisayan** *or* **bisayans** *also* **bisaya** *or* **bisayas** *usu cap* [*Bisayan* fr. Bisayan *Bisayâ* + E *-an*; *Bisaya* fr. Bisayan *Bisayâ*] **1 a :** any of several Christianized peoples in the Visayan islands, Philippines **b :** a member of any of such peoples **2 :** the Austronesian language of the Bisayan peoples; *collectively* **:** the Bisayan languages — see AKLAN, CEBUAN, HANTIK, HILIGAYNON, SAMAR-LEYTE

bis·azo \(')bis+\ *adj* [*bisazo-*, fr. *bis-* + *-az-*] **:** DISAZO

bis·bi·glian·do \,bisbēl¦yän(,)dō\ *or* **bis·bi·glia·to** \-¦yäd·-(,)ō, -ä(,)tō\ *adj* [*bisbigliando* fr. It, verbal of *bisbigliare* to whisper, of imit. origin; *bisbigliato* fr. It, past part. of *bisbigliare*] **:** very light and murmuring — used as a direction in music for a fingered tremolo on the harp

biscacha *var of* VIZCACHA

¹bis·cay·an \(')bis¦kā(y)ən\ *n* -s *cap* [*Biscay* or *Biscaya*, province of Spain (fr. Sp *Vizcaya*) + E *-an*] **1 :** a native or resident of Biscay province, Spain **:** BASQUE **2 a :** the Basque language **b :** the westernmost dialect of Basque spoken in the Spanish province of Biscay

²biscayan \"\ *adj, usu cap* **:** BASQUE

bis·cay green \'bi(,)skā-\ *n, often cap B* [fr. *Biscay, Biscaya*, province of Spain] **:** a moderate yellow green that is greener and lighter than average moss green, yellower and less strong than average pea green, and yellower and duller than apple green (sense 1)

bis·cay·ner \'bi(,)skānər\ *also* **bis·cay·neer** \,=='ni(ə)r\ *n* -s *usu cap* [obs. *Biskaine, Biscayne* Biscayan (fr. *Biscay*, province of Spain) + *-er* or *-eer*] **:** a seaman or ship from Biscay

bisch·of·ite \'bishə,fīt, -,vīt\ *n* -s [G *bischofit*, fr. Gustav *Bischof* †1870 Ger. geologist + G *-it* -ite] **:** a mineral $MgCl_2.6H_2O$ composed of hydrous magnesium chloride

bis·cuit \'biskət, *usu* -d·+V\ *n, pl* **biscuits** *also* **biscuit** [ME *bisquite, besquite*, fr. MF *bescuit*, fr. (*pain*) *bescuit* twice-cooked bread, fr. *pain* bread + *bescuit* twice-cooked, fr. *bes-* bis- (fr. L *bis-*) + *cuit* past part. of *cuire* to cook, fr. L *coquere* — more at COOK] **1 :** any of certain hard or crisp dry baked products: **a** *Brit* (1) **:** CRACKER 4 (2) **:** COOKIE 1 **b :** PILOT BISCUIT **c :** DOG BISCUIT **2 :** unglazed clayware (as porcelain or tile) permanently hardened by the dehydrating and vitrifying effect of heat **3 a :** a quick bread made in a small shape from dough that has been rolled and cut or dropped and that is raised in the baking by a leavening agent other than yeast ⟨baking-powder ~*s*⟩ **b :** ROLL 2d(1) **4 a :** ALMOND 6a **b :** a grayish yellow **5 :** a flat rounded cake of crude rubber (as Para rubber) or of synthetic rubber **6 a :** a small piece of plastic suitable for the pressing of a single disc record; *also* **:** plastic stock from which such pieces are prepared **b** *slang* **:** a phonograph record

biscuit beetle *n* **:** DRUGSTORE BEETLE

biscuit cutter *n* **:** a circular device for cutting out biscuits from rolled dough

buscuit fire *n* **:** the fire or firing that converts ceramic greenware to biscuit — called also *bisque fire*

bis·cuit·ing \'biskəd·iŋ, -ətiŋ\ *n* -s **:** a first firing of ceramic greenware that converts it to biscuit

biscuit leaves *n pl but sing or pl in constr* [so called fr. the edible leaves] **:** a greenbrier (*Smilax rotundifolia*)

biscuit plant *n* **:** a greenbrier (*Smilax rotundifolia*)

biscuit-root \'==,=\ *n* [so called fr. their being used for meal by the Indians] **1 :** CAMAS 1 **2** *West* **:** a plant of the genus *Lomatium*

biscuit shooter *n, slang* **:** a cook or waiter esp. in a camp or on a ranch

biscuit tortoni \bēskwē- *also* 'biskət-\ *n* **:** tortoni frozen and served in a paper cup

biscuit ware *n* **:** unglazed porcelain or pottery

bis·diapason \¦bis+\ *n* -s [*bis-* + *diapason*] **:** a musical interval of two octaves

bise \'bēz\ *n* -s [ME, fr. OF, of Gmc origin; akin to OHG *bīsa* north wind, OS *bīsa* whirlwind, D dial. *bijs* gust of wind, OHG *bisōn* to run around in confusion, OSw *bisa* to run, and perh. to OHG *bibēn* to tremble — more at BEBUNG] **:** a cold wind; *esp* **:** a cold dry north wind of southern France, Switzerland, and Italy

¹bi·sect \(')bī¦sekt\ *vb* -ED/-ING/-S [¹*bi-* + *-sect*] *vt* **1 :** to divide into two usu. equal parts **2 :** to cut (a postage stamp) into two or occas. more pieces each representing a corresponding fraction of the postage value of the whole — used chiefly as a participial adjective ⟨~*ed* copies of some stamps are very valuable⟩ ~ *vi* **:** SEPARATE; *also* **:** CROSS, INTERSECT — used chiefly of roads and ways

²bisect \'=,=\ *n* -s **1 :** one of the pieces of a bisected stamp **2 a :** examination of the lateral and vertical dimensions of the above-ground and below-ground parts of plants by means of a cross-section through soil exposing the profile of underground parts (as roots, tubers, rhizomes) **b :** a graphic representation of the findings of such an examination

bi·sec·tion \(')bī¦sekshən\ *n* -s **:** division into two usu. equal parts

bi·sec·tion·al \-nəl\ *adj* **:** of or relating to bisection **:** that bisects — **bi·sec·tion·al·ly** \-nəlē\ *adv*

bi·sec·tor \(')bī¦sektə(r)\ *n* -s **:** one that bisects; *esp* **:** a straight line that bisects an angle or a line segment

bi·sec·trix \-,triks\ *n, pl* **bisectri·ces** \,=='trī(,)sēz\ [*bisec-* (fr. *bisector*) + *-trix*] **:** BISECTOR; *specif* **:** a line bisecting the angle between the optic axes of a biaxial crystal

bi·segmentation \¦bi+\ *n* [¹*bi-* + *segmentation*] **:** complete or partial division into two parts

bi·sel·li·um \bī'selēəm\ *n, pl* **bisel·lia** \-lēə\ [L, fr. *bi-* ¹bi- + *-sellium* (fr. *sella* seat, chair, saddle) — more at SELLATE] **:** an ancient Roman seat of honor for occupancy by two persons

bi·serial \(')bī+\ *adj* [¹*bi-* + *serial*] **:** arranged or characterized by an arrangement in two rows or series — **bi·serially** *adv*

bi·seriate \(')bī+\ *adj* [¹*bi-* + *seriate*] **:** BISERIAL — **bi·seriately** *adv*

bi·serrate \(')bī+\ *adj* [¹*bi-* + *serrate*] **1 :** doubly serrate **:** having the serrations serrate ⟨~ leaves⟩ **2 :** serrate on both sides ⟨~ antennae⟩

bi·setose *also* **bi·setous** \(')bī+\ *adj* [¹*bi-* + *setose, setous*] *biol* **:** having two bristles

bi·sexed \'bī,sekst\ *adj* [¹*bi-* + *sex* + *-ed*] **:** BISEXUAL 1a

¹bi·sexual \(')bī+\ *adj* [¹*bi-* + *sexual*] **1 a :** HERMAPHRODITIC **:** possessing characters (as mental and behavioral qualities) typical of both sexes **b :** having sexual desire commonly on an unconscious level for members of both sexes **2 :** relating to, consisting of, or involving two sexes ⟨a ~ hormone⟩ ⟨~ progeny⟩ ⟨~ reproduction⟩ — **bi·sexuality** \¦bī+\ *n* -ES — **bi·sexually** \(')bī+\ *adv*

²bisexual \"\ *n* -s **:** a bisexual person, animal, or plant

bish·a·rin *also* **bish·a·reen** \,bishə'rēn\ *n pl, usu cap* **:** one of the three main divisions of the Beja

¹bish·op \'bishəp\ *n* -s [ME *bisshop*, fr. OE *bisceop, biscop*; akin to OS *biskop* bishop, OHG *biscof*, MD *bisskop*; all fr. a prehistoric WGmc word borrowed fr. (assumed) VL *biscopus, ebiscopus*, fr. LL *episcopus* bishop, overseer, fr. Gk *episkopos*, fr. *epi* on, over + *skopos* watcher; akin to Gk *skeptesthai* to view — more at EPI-, SPY] **1 :** a chief priest of a non-Christian religion **2 :** a clergyman of the highest order in Christian churches usu. charged with an administrative function such as the supervision of a diocese and in certain communions held to be ordained in direct succession from the apostles **3 :** OVERSEER; *esp* **:** a spiritual guide and overseer **4 :** one of two pieces in a set of chessmen that move diagonally across any number of unoccupied squares **5 :** a mulled beverage with a base of port wine flavored with roasted orange and cloves **6 :** a bustle worn in 18th and 19th century America **7** *or* **bishop bird :** any of various African weaverbirds the males of which are scarlet and black or orange and black **8 :** a Mormon high priest ordained and set apart as the administrative and executive officer of a ward and head of the Aaronic priesthood

²bishop \"\ *vt* -ED/-ING/-S [ME *bisshopen*, fr. OE *bisceopian*, fr. *bisceop*, n.] **1** *archaic* **a :** to administer the sacrament of confirmation to **:** CONFIRM **b :** to approve formally **:** SANCTION **2 :** to appoint as bishop **:** to make a bishop of **3** *dial Eng* **:** to burn or scorch while cooking ⟨the milk is ~*ed*⟩

³bishop \"\ *vt* -ED/-ING/-S [fr. the name *Bishop*] **:** to make (a horse) seem younger by operating on the teeth

bishop coadjutor *n* **1 :** a Roman Catholic bishop assisting a diocesan and usu. having the right of succession **2 a :** a Church of England bishop appointed or consecrated to assist an infirm diocesan in matters of jurisdiction as well as in the performance of purely episcopal duties **b :** a Protestant Episcopal bishop elected as assistant to a diocesan with right of succession upon the latter's death or resignation

bish·op·dom \-dəm\ *n* -s **:** the episcopal body of bishops

bish·oped \'bishəpt\ *adj* [origin unknown] *of pigeons* **:** having white shoulder patches or wing margins

bish·op·ess \-pəs\ *n* -ES [¹*bishop* + *-ess*] **:** the wife of a bishop

bishop in par·ti·bus in·fi·de·li·um \-,in'pärd·əbə,sinfə'dālēəm\ [part trans. of ML *episcopus in partibus infidelium* bishop in infidel parts] **:** TITULAR BISHOP

bish·op·less \-pləs\ *adj* **:** being without a bishop

bishop pine *or* **bishop's pine** *n* [so called fr. its discovery near the mission of San Luis Obispo de Tolosa, Calif., lit., "Saint Louis, bishop of Toulouse"] **:** a California pine (*Pinus muricata*) having a spreading flattened crown and small prickly cones that remain attached to the tree for many years

bish·op·ric \'bishə(,)prik\ *n* -s [ME *bisshopriche, bisshoprike*, fr. OE *bisceoprice*, fr. *bisceop* bishop + *rīce* realm; akin to OE *rīce* rich, powerful — more at RICH] **1 :** the administrative area under the jurisdiction of a bishop; *specif* **:** DIOCESE **2 :** the office of a bishop **3 :** a Mormon administrative body of a ward consisting of a bishop and two high priests as counselors

bishops *pl of* BISHOP, *pres 3d sing of* BISHOP

bishop's apron *n* **:** a shortened cassock formerly worn by Anglican clergy out of doors but now used by bishops, deans, and archdeacons only

bish·op's-cap \'==,=\ *n, pl* **bishops'-caps** [so called fr. the shape of the seedpod] **1 :** MITERWORT **2 :** STAR CACTUS

bishop's-leaves \'==,=\ *n pl but sing or pl in constr* **:** WATER BETONY

bishop sleeve *n* **:** a long full sleeve usu. gathered on a wristband and adapted from a bishop's robe

bishop's length *n* **:** an artist's canvas measuring 58 by 94 inches

bishop's-miter \'==;==\ *n, pl* **bishops'-miters :** a miter shell — compare MITRA

bishop's purple *n* **1 :** a violet glaze occurring in Oriental porcelain — called also *aubergine purple* **2 :** BISHOP'S VIOLET

¹bishop's ring \'bishəps-\ *n* **:** a ring worn by bishops on the third finger of the right hand signifying that the bishop is wedded to his diocese

²bishop's ring \'==-\ *n, usu cap B* [after Sereno E. *Bishop* †1909 Am. missionary in Hawaii, who first explained it] **:** a faint reddish brown corona due to the sun's shining through fine dust in the atmosphere

bishop's staff *n* **:** CROSIER

bishop's stone *n* **:** AMETHYST

bishop·stool \'==,=\ *n* [ME *bisshopstol*, fr. OE *bisceopstōl*, fr. *bisceop* bishop + *stōl* stool, throne, see — more at BISHOP, STOOL] *archaic* **:** a bishop's seat or see

bishop suffragan *n* **:** a Church of England bishop consecrated with the title of some town or see usu. within the diocese where he assists the diocesan in duties purely episcopal — compare SUFFRAGAN 1a

bishop's violet *n* **:** a moderate reddish purple that is bluer, stronger, and slightly lighter than heliotrope (sense 4b) and bluer and duller than eupatorium purple — called also *bishop's purple*

bishop's-weed *also* **bishop-weed** \'==,=\ *n, pl* **bishops'-weeds** *also* **bishop-weeds 1 :** a plant of the genus *Ammi* **2 :** GOUTWEED **3 :** WATER MINT

bis·hy·droxy·coumarin \,bis,hī,dräksē+\ *n* -s [*bis-* + *hydroxy-* + *coumarin*] **:** DICOUMAROL — not used systematically

bi·silicate \(')bī+\ *n* [¹*bi-* + *silicate*] **:** METASILICATE

bi·sinuate \(')bī+\ *adj* [¹*bi-* + *sinuate*] **:** having two sinuate edges — **bi·sinuation** \¦bī+\ *n* -s

bisk *var of* BISQUE

bisk·op \'biskəp\ *n* -s [Afrik, lit., bishop, fr. MD *bisscop*; fr. the supposed grave appearance of the head — more at BISHOP] **:** either of two large sparid marine food and sport fishes of southern Africa — called also *musselcracker, steenbras*; see BLACK BISKOP, WHITE BISKOP

¹bis·marck \'biz,märk, 'bi,sm-\ *n* -s [prob. after Prince Otto Edward Leopold von *Bismarck*-Schönhausen †1898 Ger. chancellor] **1** [short for *Bismarck brown*] *often cap* **:** a moderate reddish brown that is yellower, stronger, and slightly lighter than roan and lighter and stronger than mahogany **2** *sometimes cap* **:** a raised doughnut shaped like a ball with filling usu. of jelly

²bis·marck \'biz,-\ *adj, usu cap* [fr. *Bismarck*, North Dakota] **:** of or from Bismarck, the capital of North Dakota **:** of the kind or style prevalent in Bismarck

bismarck brown \'biz,-, 'bi,sm-\ *n* [trans. of G *bismarckbraun*, after Prince Otto von *Bismarck*-Schönhausen] **1** *often cap 1st B* **:** a moderate yellowish brown that is yellower and very slightly stronger than cinnamon brown, darker and very slightly yellower than maple sugar, redder and lighter than bronze, and very slightly less strong than antique bronze — called also *bunny, Havana* **2** *often cap both Bs* **:** either of two basic diazo dyes: **a :** a dye made from *meta*-phenylenediamine that dyes wool, silk, and leather brown — called also *Bismarck Brown G*; see DYE table I (under *Basic Brown 1*) **b :** a dye made from *meta*-tolylenediamine that dyes wool, jute, and leather reddish brown — called also *Bismarck Brown R*; see DYE table I (under *Basic Brown 4, Pigment Brown 3*, and *Solvent Brown 12*)

bismarck herring *n, usu cap B* [trans. of G *bismarckhering*, after Prince Otto von *Bismarck*-Schönhausen] **:** filleted salt herring marinated in wine, vinegar, and spices and served cold with raw onion and lemon

bis·marck·i·an \(')biz¦märkēən, (')bi¦sm-\ *adj, usu cap* [Prince Otto von *Bismarck*-Schönhausen + E *-ian*] **:** of, relating to, or characteristic of Bismarck who was noted for his aggressiveness, executive capacity, relentlessness, and far-sighted diplomacy — **bis·marck·i·an·ism** \-kēə,nizəm\ *n* -s *usu cap*

bis·mil·lah \bi'smilə\ *interj* [Ar *bismi 'llāh* in the name of Allah] — a Muslim invocation

bis·mite \'biz,mīt, 'bi,sm-\ *n* -s [*bismuth* + *-ite*] **:** bismuth trioxide Bi_2O_3 occurring as a straw-yellow earth

bis·mo·clite \'bizmō,klīt, 'bism-\ *n* -s [*bismuth* + *O* (symbol for oxygen) + *Cl* (symbol for chlorine) + *-ite*] **:** a bismuth oxychloride BiOCl isomorphous with daubreelite

bismut- *or* **bismuto-** *comb form* [G *bismut-, bismuto-*, fr. *bismut* (now *wismut*)] **:** bismuth ⟨*bismut*ite⟩ ⟨*bismuto*plagionite⟩

bis·muth \'bizməth, 'bism-\ *n* -s [obs. G *bisemutum, bismut* (now *wismut*), modif. of *wismut*, fr. *wise* meadow (fr. OHG *wisa*) + *mut* claim to a mine, fr. *muten* to claim, fr. OHG *muotōn*, fr. *muot* mind; akin to OE *wāse* mire, marsh — more at OOZE, MOOD] **:** a heavy brittle highly diamagnetic chiefly trivalent metallic element resembling arsenic and antimony chemically, crystallizing usu. in grayish white rhombohedrons with a pinkish tinge and high luster, characterized by low melting point, expansion on solidification, low thermal conductivity and electric conductivity, occurring widely but sparingly both native in veins (as in arborescent, foliated, or granular forms) and in combination (as in bismuthinite, bismite, and bismutite), but being usu. recovered as a by-product from ores of other metals (as lead, copper, or tin), and used chiefly in making fusible alloys, casting alloys, and bismuth compounds for chemical and pharmaceutical use — symbol *Bi;* see ACTINIUM SERIES, THORIUM SERIES, URANIUM SERIES; ELEMENT table

bis·muth·al \'bizməthəl, 'bism-, -ma*th*əl; (')biz¦mə-, -¦myü-\ *adj* **:** of or relating to bismuth

bis·muth·ate \'bizmə,thāt, 'bism-, -,*th*at, -,thət,-*th*ət\ *n* -s [*bismuth* + *-ate*] **:** a salt (as sodium bismuthate $NaBiO_3$) containing pentavalent bismuth in the anion

bismuth blende *n* **:** EULYTITE

bismuth glance *n* **:** BISMUTHINITE

bis·muth·ic \(')bizmə,thik, (')bism-; (')biz¦məth-, (')bi¦sm-, -myü-; -*th*ik, -ēk\ *adj* **:** of, relating to, or containing bismuth ⟨~ oxide Bi_2O_5⟩ — used esp. of compounds in which this element is pentavalent

bis·muth·ine \'bizmə,thēn, 'bism-, -mə,*th*ēn,-məthən,-mə*th*ən\ *n* -s [F, fr. *bismuth* + *-ine*] **1 :** BISMUTHINITE **2 :** an unstable gaseous hydride of bismuth BiH_3 of which stable organic derivatives [as trimethyl-*bismuthine* $Bi(CH_3)_3$] are known; *also* **:** any of such derivatives ⟨the aliphatic ~*s*⟩

bis·muth·in·ite *n* -s \'bizməthə,nīt, 'bism-, -mə*th*ə-; (')biz¦mə-, -myü-\ [*bismuthine* + *-ite*] **:** a mineral Bi_2S_3 consisting of native bismuth sulfide usu. in foliated or fibrous masses of lead-gray color and metallic luster

bis·muth·ite \'bizmə,thīt, 'bism-, -,*th*īt\ *n* -s [G *bismutit, bismut* bismuth + *-it* -ite] **:** a nitrate of bismuth: as **a :** the normal nitrate $Bi(NO_3)_3.5H_2O$ obtained as colorless lustrous hygroscopic crystals by the action of nitric acid on bismuth and used chiefly in making other bismuth compounds **b :** BISMUTH SUBNITRATE

bismuth ocher *n* **:** BISMITE

bismuth oxide *n* **:** an oxide of bismuth; *esp* **:** the trioxide Bi_2O_3 occurring naturally as bismite, obtained synthetically as a yellow powder, and used chiefly in painting porcelain

bismuth oxychloride *n* **:** a white crystalline basic salt approximately BiOCl made usu. by reaction of an acid solution of bismuth nitrate with a solution of sodium chloride and used chiefly as a pigment and a cosmetic

bismuth spar *n* **:** BISMUTITE

bismuth subcarbonate *n* **:** a basic salt obtained as a white powder of varying composition by reaction of a carbonate with a bismuth salt (as bismuth subnitrate) and used chiefly in treating gastrointestinal disorders and in cosmetics

bismuth subchloride *n* **:** BISMUTH OXYCHLORIDE

bismuth subgallate *n* **:** a basic salt obtained as a bright yellow powder usu. by reaction of hydrated bismuth oxide with gallic acid and used chiefly as a dusting powder in treating skin diseases (as eczema)

bismuth subnitrate *n* **:** a basic salt or usu. a mixture of basic salts obtained as a white powder from normal bismuth nitrate (as by reaction with sodium bicarbonate) and used similarly to bismuth subcarbonate and also in ceramics

bismuth subsalicylate *or* **bismuth salicylate** *n* **:** a basic salt obtained as a white or nearly white powder of varying composition and sometimes used as an adjuvant to penicillin in the treatment of syphilis

bismuth white *n* **1 :** bismuth oxychloride used as a pigment **2 :** BISMUTH SUBNITRATE

bismuth yellow *n* **1 :** bismuth chromate used as a pigment **2 :** bismuth trioxide used as a pigment

bis·muth·yl \'bizmə,th¦il, 'bis-, -,*th*¦ēl; -məth¦əl, -məth¦\ *n* -s [ISV *bismuth* + *-yl*] **:** a univalent radical BiO regarded as existing in some basic salts of bismuth

bismuthyl chloride *n* **:** BISMUTH OXYCHLORIDE

bis·mut·ite \'bizməd·,īt, 'bism-, -mə,tīt'\ *n* -s [G *bismutit*, fr. *bismut-* + *-it* -ite] **:** a mineral $(BiO)_2CO_3$ consisting of an earthy and amorphous basic bismuth carbonate usu. dull white or yellowish

bismuto- — see BISMUT-

bis·mut·o·tantalite \,bizməd·ə, ,bizmətə, ,bis-+\ *n* -s [*bismut-* + *tantalite*] **:** a mineral $Bi(Ta,Cb)O_4$ consisting of an oxide of bismuth and tantalum commonly with some columbium

bis·na·ga *also* **biz·na·ga** \bi'snägə\ *n* -s [Sp *biznaga*, prob. by folk etymology (influence of *biznaga* parsnip, fr. Ar *bastināj, bashnāqah*, fr. L *pastinaca*) fr. earlier *vitznauac*, fr. Nahuatl *huitz-nahuac*, lit., surrounded by thorns, fr. *huitztli* thorn + *nahuac* around — more at PARSNIP] **:** any of several thorny cacti of the genera *Ferocactus* and *Echinocactus* (esp. *F. peninsulae* of Lower California and adjacent regions)

bi·sociation \¦bī+\ *n* -s [¹*bi-* + *association*] **:** the simultaneous mental association of an idea or object with two fields ordinarily not regarded as related ⟨the pun is perhaps the simplest form of ~⟩

bi·sociative \(')bī+\ *adj* **:** of, or relating to bisociation

bi·son \'bīsᵊn, 'bīzᵊn\ *n* [L *bisont-, bison*, of Gmc origin; akin to OE *wesend* aurochs, OHG *wisant, wisunt*, ON *vīsundr*; akin to OPruss *wis*sambrs aurochs and perh. to L *virus* slimy liquid, poison, stench; fr. its musky odor — more at VIRUS] **1** *pl* **bison** *also* **bisons a :** any of several large shaggy-maned usu. gregarious recent or extinct bovine mammals constituting the genus *Bison* and having a large head with short horns and heavy forequarters surmounted by a large fleshy hump formed by the withers and supported by prolonged spinous processes of the ribs **b :** a recent member of this group: (1) **:** WISENT (2) **:** BUFFALO 1c **2** *cap* **:** the genus of Bovidae comprising bison and sometimes being regarded as a subgenus of *Bos* **3** *pl* **bison :** any of certain Asiatic wild oxen; *specif* **:** GAUR **4** -s **:** a dark grayish yellowish brown that is stronger and slightly yellower and lighter than seal, slightly redder and lighter than sepia brown, and very slightly yellower and paler than lama

bi·son·tine \-ᵊn,tīn, -,tən\ *adj* [L *bisont-, bison* + E *-ine*] **:** of, relating to, or characteristic of bison

bi·sphenoid \(')bī+\ *n* -s [¹*bi-* + *sphenoid*] **:** DISPHENOID

bi·spi·nous *or* **bi·spi·nose** \(')bī+\ *adj* [¹*bi-* + *spinous, spinose*] **:** having two spines

bi·spo·ran·gi·ate \¦bīspə¦ranjēət, -jē,āt\ *adj* [¹*bi-* + NL *sporangium* + E *-ate*] **:** having two different kinds of sporangia — compare MONOCLINOUS

bi·spore \'bī+,-\ *n* -s [¹*bi-* + *spore*] **:** an asexual spore produced in pairs by certain red algae — compare TETRASPORE — **bi·sporous** \(')bī+\ *adj*

¹**bisque** *also* **bisk** \'bisk\ *n* -s [F *bisque*] **:** odds allowed an inferior player in certain games: **a :** a point to be taken when desired in a set of tennis **b :** an extra turn in croquet **c :** one or more strokes to be deducted from the whole or part score in golf

²**bisque** *also* **bisk** \"\ *n* -s [F *bisque*] **1 :** a thick cream soup made of crayfish or other shellfish or of the flesh of birds or rabbits; *also* **:** a cream soup of pureed vegetables ⟨tomato ~⟩ **2 :** ice cream containing powdered nuts or macaroons

³**bisque** \"\ *n* -s **1 :** a variable color that is brownish pink, light grayish yellowish brown, and pale orange yellow to yellowish gray **2 :** a light grayish brown esp. used in textiles

⁴**bisque** \"\ *n* -s [by shortening & alter.] **:** BISCUIT 2; *esp* **:** unglazed ceramic ware that is not to be glazed but is hard-fired and vitreous ⟨Sèvres ~⟩

bisque fire *n* [⁴*bisque*] **:** BISCUIT FIRE

bissabol *var of* BISABOL

bis·sex·tile day \(')bī, bə+\ *n* [ML *bissextilis, bisextilis* of a bissextus, fr. LL *bissextus, bisextus*, an intercalary day in the Julian calendar, fr. *bi-* ¹bi or *bis-* + *sextus* sixth; fr. its following Feb. 24, the 6th day before the calends of March — more at SIXTH] **:** LEAP DAY

bissextile year *n* **:** leap year in the Julian or Gregorian calendar

bisson *adj* [ME *bisen*, fr. OE *bisene*] *obs* **:** BLIND, PURBLIND; *also* **:** BLINDING

bist *dial Brit pres 2d sing of* BE

bi·state \'≤¦≤\ *adj* [¹*bi-* + *state*] **:** of two states **:** established and maintained by two states acting as a unit ⟨a ~ water commission⟩

bis·ter *or* **bis·tre** \'bistə(r)\ *n* -s [F *bistre*] **1 a :** an artist's medium for use with brush or pen made with a brown extract obtained from the soot of wood after the soot has been soaked or boiled in water and ranging in color from yellowish brown to dark brown **b :** a watercolor medium having the general color characteristics of bister **2 :** MANGANESE BROWN **3 :** SOOT BROWN

bis·tered *also* **bis·tred** \-tə(r)d\ *adj* **:** colored with or as if with bister; *esp, of skin* **:** SWARTHY

bister green *n* **:** a dark grayish to dark yellow that is slightly darker than pyrite yellow and very slightly duller than sulphine yellow

bis·tort \'bi,stȯrt, bi's-\ *n* -s [MF *bistorte*, fr. (assumed) ML *bistorta*, fr. L *bis-* + *torta*, fem. of *tortus*, past part. of *torquēre* to twist — more at TORTURE] **:** any of several plants of the genus *Polygonum*; *esp* **:** either a European herbaceous plant (*P. bistorta*) or a related American form (*P. bistortoides*) the twisted roots of which are used as astringents

bis·tour·nage \'bistə(r),nij\ *n* -s [F, fr. *bistourner* to twist (fr. MF, fr. OF *bestourner*, fr. *bes-* — fr. L *bis-* — + *tourner* to turn) + *-age* — more at TURN] **:** castration by torsion of the spermatic cord

bis·tou·ry \'bistərē\ *n* -ES [F *bistouri*, fr. MF *bistorie, bistorit* dagger] **:** a small slender straight or curved surgical knife sharp-pointed or probe-pointed

bi·stratal \(')bī+\ *adj* [¹*bi-* + *stratal*] **:** having or belonging to two layers

bi·striate \(')bī+\ *adj* [¹*bi-* + *striate*] **:** marked with two parallel striae

bi·stro *also* **bi·stro** \'bē(,)strō, 'bi(,)-\ *n* -s [F] **1 :** a small or unpretentious European wineshop or restaurant **2 a :** a usu. small and often out-of-the-way bar, tavern, or other place selling drinks and often food to patrons and marked by an atmosphere of extreme casualness **b :** NIGHTCLUB — **bi·stro·ic** \(')≤¦strōik\ *adj*

bi·sulcate \(')bī+\ *adj* [¹*bi-* + *sulcate*] *of a hoof or foot* **:** CLOVEN

bi·sulfate \(')bī+\ *n* [ISV ¹*bi-* + *sulfate*] **:** an acid sulfate (as potassium bisulfate $KHSO_4$) **:** a hydrogen sulfate — see ¹BI- 4

bi·sulfide \(')bī+\ *n* [ISV ¹*bi-* + *sulfide*] **:** DISULFIDE 1 — used chiefly commercially in the term *carbon bisulfide*

bi·sulfite \(')bī+\ *n* [F, fr. *bi-* ¹bi + *sulfite*] **:** an acid sulfite (as potassium bisulfite $KHSO_3$) **:** a hydrogen sulfite — see ¹BI-4

bisulfite of lime : CALCIUM BISULFITE

bi·syllabic \¦bī+\ *adj* [¹*bi-* + *-syllabic*] **:** DISYLLABIC

¹**bit** \'bit, *usu* -d·+V\ *n* -s [ME *bitt*, fr. OE *bite*; akin to OE *bītan* to bite — more at BITE] **1** *obs* **:** the action of biting; *also* **:** GRAZING, EATING **2 :** something that is bitten or held with the teeth: **a** *obs* **:** ²BITE 5 **b :** the part of a usu. steel bridle that is inserted in the mouth of a horse together with its appendages (as the rings to which the reins are fastened) — see BAR 1e (3), BRIDOON, CURB, SNAFFLE, BRIDLE illustration **c :** the rimmed mouth end on the stem of a pipe or a cigar or cigarette holder ⟨a fishtail ~⟩ **3 a :** the biting or cutting edge or part of a tool (as of an ax, adz, or rock drill); *also* **:** a replaceable part of a compound tool that actually performs the function (usu. some form of cutting) for which the whole tool is designed (as a screwdriver blade or boring tool for use with a brace, an inserted saw tooth, a plane iron, or the copper head of a soldering iron) **b bits** *pl* **:** the jaws or nippers of tongs or pincers **4 :** something that curbs or imposes a restraint on something or someone ⟨folly curbed by honor's ~⟩ **5 :** the part of a key which enters the lock and in which are cut the wards that act upon the bolt and tumblers **6 :** a triangular earmark (as for identifying cattle) — see EARMARK illustration **7 :** a piece of wire or brass fixed to a dandy roll to make a watermark in paper — **bit in one's teeth :** control of affairs esp. on a headlong or willful course — used chiefly with *get* or *take* ⟨he took the *bit in his teeth* and soon dissipated his fortune⟩

bits 2b: *A* bar bit, *B* snaffle, *C* curb, *D* Pelham

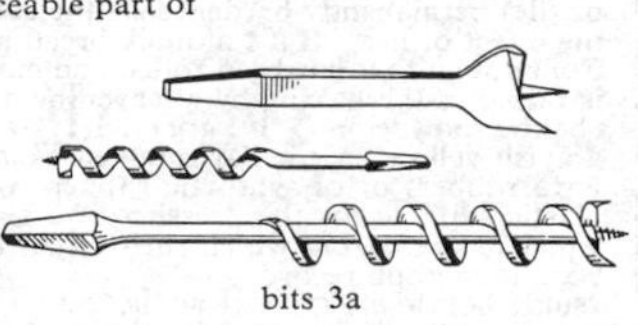

bits 3a

²**bit** \"\ *vt* **bitted; bitted; bitting; bits; 1 a :** to put a bit in the mouth of (a horse) **b :** to accustom (a horse) to the bit **c :** to control with or as if with a bit **:** CURB, CHECK **2 :** to form a bit on (a key)

³**bit** \"\ *n* -s [ME, fr. OE *bita*; akin to OE *bītan* to bite — more at BITE] **1 :** a small quantity of food: **a** *obs* **:** a piece of food such as may be bitten off at once **:** BITE **b :** MORSEL; *esp* **:** a small delicacy **c :** fragment of food **:** SCRAP, LEAVING — usu. used in pl. ⟨we can make supper from the ~*s*⟩ **2 :** a small piece, portion, or quantity of some material thing: as **a** (1) *chiefly Scot* **:** PLACE, SPOT ⟨may I never stir from the ~ —Sir Walter Scott⟩ **:** (2) *of land or lands* **:** a small or relatively small amount ⟨planting the level ~*s* to grain and terracing the hills for their vineyards⟩ ⟨a ~ of the old country set down in the midst of this American state⟩ **b** (1) **:** an old one-real piece worth ⅛ of a Spanish peso (2) **:** a unit of value equivalent to ⅛ of a Spanish peso — used esp. in designating the value of a piece of cut money ⟨each piece of a peso cut into four parts was worth two ~*s*⟩ (3) **:** a unit of value equal to ⅛ of a dollar (12½ cents) — used only of even multiples ⟨four ~*s*⟩ ⟨six ~*s*⟩ (4) **:** a unit of value equal to ⅕₀₀ of a daler ⟨2½-, 5-, 10-, 25-, and 50-*bit* coins were issued⟩ — used in the Virgin islands of the U.S. when they were the Danish West Indies (5) *in British Guiana* **:** FOURPENCE; *also* **:** a corresponding unit of value equal to ⅙ of a florin (6) *Brit* **:** any particular small coin ⟨a threepenny ~⟩ ⟨a sixpenny ~⟩ **c :** a small piece of hot glass gathered on an iron rod ready to be attached to a glass vessel (as to form a foot or handle) **d** *ceramics* **:** a loose material (as flint fragments) sprinkled over the bottom of a sagger to prevent glazed pieces (as cups) from adhering to it — called also *bitstone* **e :** a section of rootstock or rhizome (as of bananas) used in propagation **3** *chiefly of immaterial objects* **:** something small or unimportant of its kind: as **a** *of time* (1) **:** a brief period **:** WHILE ⟨rest a ~ longer⟩ (2) *chiefly Scot* **:** the exact or critical moment ⟨he came just at the ~⟩ (3) *slang* **:** a term of imprisonment **b :** SOMEWHAT **:** some degree or extent — used chiefly in the phrase *a bit of* ⟨there is a ~ of the cad in all men⟩ ⟨a ~ of a mystery⟩ **c :** the smallest or an insignificant amount or degree **:** WHIT, MITE — often used adverbially with *a* ⟨the sauce is a ~ too sweet⟩ ⟨she felt a ~ better after her nap⟩ **d :** one's contribution however small to a cause — used chiefly in the phrase *do one's bit* **e :** a sketch or incident in a literary work or in a theatrical performance ⟨leafing the pages seeking the ~*s* that had brightened his childhood⟩ ⟨one of the best ~*s* was the bawdy exchange between the two brothers in the second act⟩; *often* **:** a sketch forming a unit in a burlesque or nightclub show **f :** a small part usu. with some spoken lines in a theatrical performance — compare WALK-ON **4** *slang* **:** a young woman **:** GIRL — sometimes used disparagingly — **a bit of all right** *chiefly Brit* **:** something or someone regarded with full and hearty approval

⁴**bit** \"\ *adj, chiefly Scot* **:** SMALL ⟨a ~ lassie⟩ ⟨~ portraits of worthies like Rob Roy —*New Yorker*⟩

⁵**bit** \"\ *past or substand past part of* BITE

⁶**bit** \"\ *Scot var of* BUT

⁷**bit** \"\ *n* -s [*binary digit*] **1 :** a unit of information equivalent to the result of a choice between two equally probable alternatives — used esp. in communication and information theory **2 :** a unit of memory corresponding to the ability to store the result of a choice between two alternatives — used esp. in connection with digital computing devices

bit·a·ble *also* **bite·a·ble** \'bīd·əbəl, 'bītə-\ *adj* [¹*bite* + *-able*] **:** that may be bitten

bi·tan·hol \,bē,tän'hōl\ *n* -s [Tag *bitanhól*] **:** a tropical tree (*Calophyllum blancoi*) common in the Philippines with bark and seeds that yield an aromatic resin and a bitter oil

bi·tartrate \(')bī+\ *n* -s [ISV ¹*bi-* + *tartrate*; prob. orig. formed in F] **:** an acid tartrate (as sodium bitartrate $NaHC_4H_4O_6$) **:** a hydrogen tartrate — see ¹BI- 4

bitbrace \'≤,≤\ *n* [¹*bit* + *brace*] **:** ¹BRACE 4

bit by bit *adv* **:** PIECEMEAL **:** little by little **:** by degrees

¹**bitch** \'bich\ *n* -ES [ME *bicche*, fr. OE *bicce*; akin to ON *bikkja* female dog, OE *bæc* back — more at BACK] **1 a :** the female of the dog or of a closely related animal (as the wolf or fox) **b :** the female of certain other carnivorous mammals (as the ferret or otter) **2 a :** a lewd or immoral woman **:** TROLLOP, SLUT — a generalized term of abuse **b :** a malicious, spiteful, and domineering woman **3 :** any of several mechanical devices designed to grasp and hold something in position **4 :** a makeshift lamp consisting of a can or cup of grease with a wick of twisted rag much used in pioneer western and northwestern No. America **5** *slang* **:** something regarded as outstanding of its kind esp. in unpleasantness ⟨we'll have a ~ of a time getting home at this hour⟩ **6** *slang* **:** COMPLAINT, GRUMBLING

²**bitch** \"\ *vb* -ED/-ING/-ES *vt* **1** *slang* **:** SPOIL, BOTCH — often used with *up* ⟨someone had really ~*ed* things up for fair —R.H.Newman⟩ **2** *slang* **:** to complain of (someone or something) **:** gripe about **3** *slang* **:** CHEAT, DO, DOUBLECROSS ~ *vi, slang* **:** COMPLAIN, GROUSE

bitch chain *n* **:** a short logging chain with hook and ring used for fastening the lower end of a gin pole to a sled or car when loading logs

bitch·ery \'bich(ə)rē, -ri\ *n* -ES **:** behavior of or like that of a bitch

bitch goddess *n* **:** SUCCESS; *esp* **:** material or worldly success

bitch·i·ly \'bichəlē, -li\ *adv* **:** in a bitchy manner

bitch·i·ness \'bichēnəs, -chin-\ *n* -ES **:** the quality of being bitchy or of acting like a bitch

bitchy \'bichē, -chi\ *adj* -ER/-EST **1 :** suggestive of a bitch esp. in malice or arrogance **2** *of a male dog* **:** EFFEMINATE

¹**bite** \'bīt, *usu* -d·+V\ *vb* **bit** \'bit, *usu* -d·+V\ *or dial Brit* **bate** \'bāt\ *or* **bote** \'bōt\ **bitten** \'bitᵊn\ *or substand* **bit; biting; bites** [ME *biten*, fr. OE *bītan*; akin to OHG *bīzan* to bite, ON *bíta*, Goth *beitan* to bite, L *findere* to split, Skt *bhedati* he splits] *vt* **1 a** (1) **:** to seize with the teeth so that they enter, grip, or wound ⟨the dogs *bit* the child savagely⟩ (2) **:** to remove (a part of something) with the teeth ⟨a piece was *bitten* from the apple⟩ **:** sever by biting ⟨she *bit* the thread in two⟩ **b :** to seize, pinch, or sever with the jaws (as of a snapping turtle) or with a jawlike organ (as the claw of a lobster) **c :** STING: (1) **:** to pierce with any of certain sharp-pointed buccal organs (as the proboscis of a mosquito or the fangs of a snake) (2) **:** to pierce with any of certain other pointed organs not associated with the mouth (as the stinger of a bee) — not used technically **2 :** CUT, PIERCE — used of edged weapons or their wielders ⟨the sword cleft his armor and *bit* him to the bone⟩ **3** *obs* **:** EAT, NIBBLE, CHEW **:** GRAZE **4 :** to cause sharp pain or stinging discomfort to ⟨the wind howling, the sleet *biting* our necks⟩ **5 a :** to take hold of **:** hold fast ⟨the scored jaws of a vise help it ~ the work⟩ **b :** to act like teeth or jaws in removing (part of something) ⟨the giant shovels *bit* 5-yard chunks from the hill⟩ **c :** affect profoundly **:** IMPRESS **6 :** to eat into **:** CORRODE ⟨acid ~*s* an etcher's plate⟩; *sometimes* **:** to etch with acid ⟨he *bit* and printed his lithographs —Margery Allingham⟩ **7 a :** to cheat, trick, or take in; *esp* **:** to borrow with little intention of repaying ⟨he *bit* me for a fiver⟩ **b :** to catch as with teeth by a sudden turn of events — usu. used in passive ⟨he was badly *bitten* on the market⟩ **8** *slang* **:** PERTURB, WORRY, DISTRESS ⟨well, what's *biting* him today⟩ ~ *vi* **1 a :** to seize something with the teeth or jaws **:** wound with the teeth **:** pierce or sting esp. with proboscis or fang ⟨the mosquitoes *bit* fiercely all evening long⟩ **b :** to have the habit of so doing ⟨does that dog ~⟩ **2** *of a weapon or tool* **:** to cut, pierce, or take hold — used esp. with reference to power or quality ⟨this saw ~*s* well⟩ **3 :** to cause an irritation or smarting ⟨his words *bit* deeply into our spirit⟩ **:** be pungent ⟨the sauce is a bit too sharp, it really ~*s*⟩ **4 :** SNAP, SNARL, CARP — usu. used with *at* ⟨why are you always *biting* and bickering at one another⟩ **5** *of a chemical* **:** PENETRATE ⟨few dyes will ~ until the wool has been boiled with some mordant —Karis E. Legge⟩; *specif* **:** CORRODE, EAT ⟨if the acid fails to ~ well, the fault may be with the metal of the etcher's plate⟩ **6 :** to produce an impression **:** have an effect ⟨such thoughts ~⟩ **7 a** *of fish* **:** to take a bait **b** *chiefly slang* **:** to respond so as to be caught by something (as a trick or deceit) used as bait **8 :** to take or maintain a firm hold ⟨be sure the anchor ~*s* well⟩ **9** *printing* **:** to cause a bite **10 :** to grip the surface of the ground momentarily esp. so as to rebound in a manner influenced by a previously imparted spin — used of a bowled ball in cricket — **bite one's lip** *or* **bite one's tongue :** to hold back a remark one would like to make — **bite the dust** *also* **bite the ground 1 :** to fall dead esp. in a battle ⟨many a redskin *bit the dust* that day⟩ **2 a :** to fall from a horse **b :** to come a cropper **:** suffer humiliation or defeat — **bite the hand that feeds one :** to injure a benefactor maliciously — **bite the thumb at :** to insult provocatively **:** JEER

²**bite** \"\ *n* -s [ME, fr. *biten*, v.] **1 a :** the act of seizing with the teeth or mouth or of bringing the teeth together as in seizing **b :** the act of wounding or separating with the teeth or mouth **c :** a seizure (as of a bait) with the teeth or mouth **d :** the act (as of some insects) of puncturing or abrading with the mouth parts **2 :** FOOD, VICTUALS: **a :** the amount of food taken at a bite **:** MORSEL ⟨I couldn't eat another ~⟩ **b :** a small amount of food **:** SNACK ⟨we had just a ~ at tea⟩ **c :** a meal esp. if impromptu ⟨why not have a ~ of dinner now and finish the work later⟩ **d :** herbage for grazing **3 :** an unintended blank area on a printed sheet caused by the accidental covering (as by foreign matter) of part of the inked surface during printing **4** *archaic* **:** CHEAT, TRICK; *also* **:** SHARPER, CHEATER **5 :** a wound made by biting ⟨the ~ became infected⟩ **6 :** the hold or grip by which friction is created or purchase obtained (as the hold of the short end of a lever upon the thing to be lifted or of one part of a machine upon another) **7 :** a surface that creates friction or is brought into contact with another for the purpose of obtaining a hold; *specif* **:** the holding surfaces of the jaws of a chuck **8 :** the keen incisive quality or the smart, tang, or penetrating effect of a sharply impinging sensation ⟨the ~ of raw whiskey⟩ ⟨the ~ of his words was sharp⟩ ⟨the ~ of wind on our cheeks⟩ **9 :** the corroding of an etcher's plate by acid; *also* **:** a period during which the plate is exposed to the action of the acid **10 :** the distance between the point and the bottom of the bend of a fishhook **11 :** an amount (as of money) taken usu. in one operation for one purpose **:** CUT, SLICE, SHAVE ⟨the tax ~⟩ ⟨a 10 percent ~ for his manager⟩

biteable *var of* BITABLE

bite block *n* **:** a device used chiefly in dentistry for recording the spatial relation of the jaws esp. in respect to the occlusion of the teeth

bi·teg·mic \(')bī¦tegmik\ *also* **bi·teg·mi·nous** \-¦tegmənəs\ *adj* [¹*bi-* + NL *tegmin-, tegmen* + E *-ic* or *-ous*] *bot* **:** having two integuments ⟨~ ovules⟩

bite in *vt* **:** to corrode or eat (lines or figures) into an etcher's plate by means of an acid

bi·temporal \(')bī+\ *adj* [*bi-* + *temporal*] **:** relating to, involving, or joining the two temporal bones or the areas that they occupy

bite off *vt* **1 :** to remove by or as if by biting ⟨great chunks of the countryside *bitten off* for cheap housing⟩ **2 a :** to eliminate (as music or dialogue) from a radio program while it is being broadcast **b :** to cut short (a program) — **bite off more than one can chew :** to undertake more than one can perform

bit·er \'bīd·ə(r), 'bītə-\ *n* -s [ME, fr. *biten* + *-er*] **1 :** one that bites; *esp* **:** one that is inclined to bite or bites habitually ⟨a dog that is a known ~⟩ **2** *obs* **:** one that cheats **:** SHARPER

bi·ternate \(')bī + \ *adj* [*bi-* + *ternate*] **:** doubly ternate — used esp. of a ternate leaf in which each division is also ternate — **bi·ternately** *adv*

bites *pres 3d sing of* BITE, *pl of* BITE

bite-wing \'=,=\ *n* **:** a dental X-ray film designed to show the crowns of the upper and lower teeth simultaneously and having a fin for the teeth to bite upon and hold the film in place during exposure

bit extension *n* [¹*bit*] **:** a metal rod with a tang at one end and a socket at the other and used for increasing the effective length of an auger bit

bit-gatherer \'=,===\ *n* [³*bit*] **:** a glassworker who gathers bits

bit gauge *n* [¹*bit*] **:** a device attached to the shank of a drilling or boring bit to control the depth of the hole

bi·theism \'bī(,)thē,izəm, ,bī'th-\ *n* -s [*bi-* + *-theism*] **:** belief in the existence of two gods (as one good and one evil)

bi·thyn·ia \bə'thinēə\ [NL, fr. *Bithynia*, Asia Minor] *syn of* BULIMUS

¹**bi·thyn·i·an** \-nēən\ *adj, usu cap* [*Bithynia*, ancient country of northwestern Asia Minor (fr. L, fr. Gk) + E *-an*] **1 :** of, relating to, or characteristic of Bithynia in Asia Minor **2 :** of, relating to, or characteristic of Bithynians

²**bithynian** \"\ *n* -s *usu cap* **:** a native or inhabitant of ancient Bithynia

biting *adj* [ME, fr. pres. part. of *biten*] **:** that bites or tends to bite esp. with the production of mental or physical discomfort **:** SHARP, CUTTING, CAUSTIC ⟨a ~ acid odor⟩ ⟨~ sarcastic words⟩ ⟨chill ~ winds⟩ **syn** see INCISIVE

biting crowfoot *n* **:** BULBOUS BUTTERCUP

biting fly *n* **:** a fly (as the mosquito, midge, or horsefly) having mouthparts adapted for piercing and biting man and other vertebrates

biting housefly *n* **:** STABLE FLY

biting knotweed *n* **:** WATER PEPPER

biting louse *n* **:** BIRD LOUSE

bit·ing·ly *adv* [ME, fr. *biting* + *-ly*] **:** in a biting manner

biting midge *n* **:** a midge of the family Ceratopogonidae

bit·ing·ness *n* -ES **:** the quality or state of being biting

biting stonecrop *n* **:** a stonecrop (*Sedum acre*)

bi·tis \'bīd·əs\ *n, cap* [NL] **:** a genus of African vipers including the Old World puff adder, the Gaboon viper, and a few other heavy-bodied rather sluggish venomous snakes

bit key *n* [¹*bit*] **:** a key having a wing bit (as for lever tumbler locks)

bi·to \'bēd·(,)ō\ *or* **bito tree** *n* -s [origin unknown] **:** a small scrubby tree (*Balanites aegyptiaca*) that grows in dry regions of tropical Africa and Asia and has bark that yields a fish poison and seeds that yield a medicinal oil — called also *desert date*; see BALANITES

bi·tonal \(')bī + \ *adj* [¹*bi-* + *tonal*] **:** using two musical tonalities simultaneously — **bi·tonality** \¦bī + \ *n* -ES

bi·tot's spots \(')bē¦tōz,-\ *n pl, usu cap B* [after Pierre A. *Bitot* †1888 Fr. physician] **:** shiny pearly spots of triangular shape occurring on the scleras in severe vitamin A deficiency esp. in children

bit part *n* [³*bit*] **:** ³BIT 3f

bit pincers *n pl* [¹*bit*] **:** pincers having curved jaws

bi·trochanteric \(')bī + \ *adj* [*bi-* + *trochanteric*] **:** of, relating to, or between the two trochanters or trochanterions

bits *pl of* BIT, *pres 3d sing of* BIT

bit·stock *also* **bit·stalk** \'=,=\ *n* [¹*bit* + *stock* or *stalk*] **:** a handle or other device for holding and turning a bit by hand; *specif* **:** a carpenter's brace

bit·stone \'=,=\ *n* [³*bit* + *stone*] **:** ³BIT 2d

bit·sy \'bitsē\ *adj* [prob. alter. of *bitty*] *dial* **:** TINY

¹**bitt** \'bit, *usu* -d· + V\ *n* -s [perh. fr. ON *biti* beam, thwart — more at BOAT] **1 :** a single or double post of metal or wood fixed on the deck of a ship and around which mooring lines or other lines are made fast **2 :** BOLLARD 1a

²**bitt** \"\ *vt* -ED/-ING/-s **:** to make (a cable) fast about the bitt of a ship (as in mooring)

bit·ta·ci·dae \bə'tasə,dē\ *n pl, cap* [NL, fr. *Bittacus*, type genus (fr. Gk *bittakos, psittakos* parrot) + *-idae*] **:** a family of chiefly tropical predacious red-and-black flies (order Mecoptera) comprising the scorpion flies

bit·ta·cle \'bid·əkəl\ *archaic var of* BINNACLE

bitted *past of* BIT *or of* BITT

bitten *past part of* BITE

bitten-leaf disease \'==¦=-\ *n* **:** LEAF BITE

¹**bit·ter** \'bid·ə(r), 'bitə-\ *adj, usu* -ER/-EST [ME, fr. OE *biter*; akin to OHG *bittar* bitter, ON *bitr* sharp, biting, Goth *baitrs* bitter, OE *bītan* to bite — more at BITE] **1 a :** indicating or inducing the one of the four basic taste sensations that is mediated by end organs in the circumvallate papillae, is produced chiefly by organic compounds (as alkaloids and certain glucosides), and when strongly developed is markedly unpleasant and lingering ⟨the medicine left a ~ taste in her mouth⟩ — compare SALT, SOUR, SWEET **b :** distasteful to the mind **:** distressing to contemplate **:** UNPALATABLE, GALLING ⟨~ truths⟩ ⟨a ~ sense of shame⟩ **2 :** marked by intensity or severity **:** RIGOROUS: **a :** accompanied by severe pain or suffering of mind or body **:** difficult to bear ⟨a ~ death⟩ ⟨there was a ~ moment when they parted for the last time⟩ **b :** VEHEMENT, RELENTLESS, DETERMINED ⟨a ~ partisan⟩ ⟨the ~ struggle for economic freedom⟩; *often* **:** exhibiting intense animosity ⟨~ enemies⟩ **c** *obs* **:** cruel and oppressive **d** (1) *of modes of expression* **:** harshly reproachful **:** sharp and resentful **:** BITING ⟨~ complaints⟩ (2) *of a person or attitude* **:** marked by cynicism and rancor **:** intensely unfriendly ⟨~ contempt⟩ ⟨a ~ answer⟩ **e** *of weather or its manifestations* **:** intensely unpleasant esp. in coldness or rawness **:** PIERCING, RAW ⟨a ~ wind whistled about our ears⟩ **3** *obs* **:** causing or designed to cause pain or anguish **4 :** caused by or expressive of severe pain, grief, or regret ⟨~ tears shed too late⟩

syn ACRID stresses astringent effects accompanying strong, pungent, unpleasant tastes or penetrating or suffocating odors ⟨in its green state, it is exceedingly *acrid*, but boiled or baked, had the sweetness of the sugarcane —Herman Melville⟩ ⟨there was an *acrid* musty smell; the raw air was close with breathing —Rose Macaulay⟩ BITTER, a more general and often less extreme word, indicates a marked pungent taste, usu. unpleasant, and an absence of sweetness or mildness ⟨*bitter* as aloes, it parched my tongue —Elinor Wylie⟩ ⟨McCoy had made some beer, once, with ti roots . . . It was *bitter* stuff and fair gagged ye to get it down —C.B.Nordhoff & J.N.Hall⟩ Sometimes, as with BITTER chocolate, BITTER winter cress and tonics, and flavors called bitters, the unpleasant suggestion is lacking. Both words refer to acid, misanthropic temperaments. ACRID suggests malevolent, caustic sarcasm ⟨the thin, angular woman, with her haughty eye and her *acrid* mouth —Lytton Strachey⟩ BITTER may add to this the suggestion of cynicism ⟨the good-humoured, affectionate-hearted Godfrey Cass was fast becoming a *bitter* man, visited by cruel wishes —George Eliot⟩

syn SORE, GRIEVOUS: BITTER applies to that which may hurt by or as if by stinging or biting and to that which is unpleasant or unpalatable in the extreme because galling, chagrining, inducing sharpest regret ⟨a *bitter* winter⟩ ⟨a *bitter* period of frustration⟩ ⟨no act of Caesar's showed more sagacity than the introduction of Gallic nobles into the Senate; none was more *bitter* to the Scipios and Metelli, who were compelled to share their august privileges with these despised barbarians —J.A.Froude⟩ ⟨one had a *bitter* sense of waste when one read how tuberculosis had taken him at last up in Switzerland —Rebecca West⟩ In descriptions of persons and their moods, utterances, and activities, BITTER indicates deep, virulent, implacable resentment and hate ⟨an ugly story of low passion, delusion, and waking from delusion, which needs not to be dragged from the privacy of Godfrey's *bitter* memory —George Eliot⟩ SORE applies to what occasions severe trial, tribulation, or painful affliction ⟨Baltimore's tribulations were indeed *sore*; there was no peace for him day nor night —Herman Melville⟩ ⟨an exceptionally long history of struggle and suffering has left many *sore* and sensitive spots in the body of Israel —M.R.Cohen⟩ Applied to persons SORE may indicate either painful sensitivity or smarting resentment ⟨the worst of suffering such as hers was that it left one *sore* to the gentlest touch —Edith Wharton⟩ ⟨many of the delegates were *sore* and angry about places in the Constitution that they didn't like and had worked hard to cut out —Dorothy C. Fisher⟩ GRIEVOUS, rather archaic in effect, applies to the painfully onerous or sorely lamentable ⟨though his hurts were many and *grievous*, and his lifeblood ebbing fast —William Morris⟩ ⟨Europe had suffered *grievous* losses of men and materials —Vera M. Dean⟩

²**bitter** \"\ *adv* [ME, fr. OE *bitere*, fr. *biter*, adj.] **1 :** BITTERLY — used esp. in the phrase *bitter cold* **2** *dial Eng* **:** EXTREMELY, VERY ⟨this drug is wanted ~ bad, sir —R.L.Stevenson⟩

³**bitter** \"\ *n* -s [ME, fr. *bitter*, adj.] **1 a :** something bitter; *also* **:** bitter quality ⟨take the ~ with the sweet⟩ **b :** a bitter taste sensation ⟨the medicine has a ~ all its own⟩ **2 a bitters** *pl* **:** a usu. alcoholic liquor prepared by maceration or distillation of a bitter herb, leaf, fruit, seed, or root and used as a mild tonic or stimulant to increase the appetite and improve digestion and as a flavoring agent esp. in cocktails and sauces **b** *Brit* **:** a very dry heavily hopped ale usu. sold on draft

⁴**bitter** \"\ *vt* -ED/-ING/-s [ME *bitteren*, fr. OE *biterian*, fr. *biter*, adj.] **:** to make bitter ⟨~*ed* ale⟩ **:** EMBITTER

⁵**bitt·er** \"\ *n* -s [¹*bitt* + *-er*] **:** a turn of cable round the bitts

bitter almond *n* **:** an almond that has a very bitter seed and forms a variety (*Amygdalus communis amara*) of the common almond; *also* **:** the seed of this plant

bitter almond oil *n* **1 :** ALMOND OIL 1b, 2 **2 :** BENZALDEHYDE

bitter aloes *n pl* **:** ALOE 4

bitter apple *n* **:** COLOCYNTH

bitter ash *n* **1 :** BITTERWOOD 1a **2 :** ²WAHOO a

bitterbark \'==,=\ *n* **1 :** any of several woody plants having bitter bark: as **a** *Austral* (1) **:** a woody shrub (*Alstonia constricta*) with a bark sometimes used as a febrifuge (2) **:** NATIVE QUINCE (3) **:** a shrub or small tree (*Tabernaemontana orientalis*) having evergreen leaves, sweet-scented flowers with slender tubes, and orange-colored fruit **b :** FEVER TREE b **c :** CASCARA BUCKTHORN **2 :** the bark from a bitterbark esp. when used medicinally

bitterbloom \'==,=\ *n* **:** an American centaury (*Sabbatia angularis*)

bitterbrush \'==,=\ *n* **:** a much-branched silvery shrub (*Purshia tridentata*) with 3-toothed leaves and yellow flowers that is common in arid regions of western No. America and valuable for winter forage — called also *antelope bitterbrush, antelope brush*

bitter bugle *n* **:** either of two mints of the genus *Lycopus* (*L. americanus* and *L. europaeus*) with bitter foliage

bitterbush \'==,=\ *n* **1 :** BEAR OAK **2 :** a tropical American shrub or small tree (*Picramnia pentandra*) with red berries

bitter buttons *n pl but sing or pl in constr* **:** a tansy (*Tanacetum vulgare*)

bitter cassava *n* **:** a cassava (*Manihot utilissima*) commonly used to make cassiri and other intoxicating drinks

bitter cherry *n* **:** a wild cherry (*Prunus emarginata*) of the western U.S. with bitter fruit

bitter chocolate *n* **:** CHOCOLATE 1

bitter clover *n* **:** a yellow-flowered Eurasian annual sweet clover (*Melilotus indica*) used as a cover crop in the western U.S. and now naturalized there and eastward

bitter cress *n* **1 :** a plant of the genus *Cardamine* (as the European *C. amara* and the American *C. hirsuta*) **2 :** WINTER CRESS

bitter cucumber *n* **:** COLOCYNTH

bitter damson *n* **:** MARUPA

bitter dock *n* **:** a European dock (*Rumex obtusifolius*) having broad obtuse leaves and bitter rootstocks that is very common as a weed in the U.S. — called also *broad-leaved dock, yellow dock*

bitter dogbane *n* **:** a No. American dogbane (*Apocynum androsaemifolium*) with pink flowers

¹**bitt·er end** *n* [⁵*bitter*] **:** the inboard end of a ship's anchoring cable or line

²**bit·ter end** *n* [prob. fr. ¹*bitter*] **:** the last extremity however painful, distasteful, or calamitous ⟨to the *bitter end*⟩

bitter-ender \'=='==\ *n* -s [²*bitter end* + *-er*] **:** one who inflexibly rejects opportune compromising or yielding on any part of an effort or policy **:** EXTREMIST, DIEHARD

bitterer *comparative of* BITTER

bitterest *superlative of* BITTER

bitter gourd *n* **1 :** COLOCYNTH **2 :** an edible gourd of Australia and Asia that is prob. identical with a snake gourd (*Trichosanthes anguina*)

bitterhead \'==,=\ *n* **1 :** BLACK CRAPPIE **2 :** GOLDEN SHINER

bitter herb *n* **1 :** an annual centaury (*Centaurium umbellatum*) with purplish rose flowers in dense clusters **2 :** TURTLEHEAD **3 :** a salad usu. of horseradish and sometimes supplemented by cos lettuce eaten during the seder of Passover as maror ⟨with *bitter herbs* they shall eat it —Exod 12:8 (AV)⟩

bit·ter·ish \'bid·ərish, 'bitə-, -rēsh\ *adj* [¹*bitter* + *-ish*] **:** somewhat bitter

bitter lake *n* **:** a lake the water of which contains in solution large quantities of sodium sulfate as well as lesser amounts of the carbonates and chlorides ordinarily found in salt lakes

bit·ter·less \-ləs\ *adj* [¹*bitter* + *-less*] **:** without a bitter taste — used of pharmaceutical preparations in which the bitter principle is masked or eliminated ⟨~ syrup of quinidine⟩

bit·ter·ling \'bid·ə(r)liŋ\ *n* -s [G, fr. *bitter* (fr. OHG *bittar*) + *-ling* — more at BITTER] **:** a small European cyprinid fish (*Rhodeus amarus*) introduced and locally common about New York that is much used in bioassay of mammalian hormones — see BITTERLING TEST, JAPANESE BITTERLING

bitterling test *n* **:** a test for human pregnancy based on response of the female Japanese bitterling to substances excreted in pregnant urine and made by adding test urine to the water containing the fish, a positive test being reported if the ovipositor enlarges markedly

bit·ter·ly *adv* [ME, fr. OE *biterlice*, fr. *biter* + *-lice* -ly] **:** in a bitter manner ⟨spoke ~⟩ **:** to a bitter degree ⟨~ exhausted⟩

¹**bit·tern** \'bid·ə(r)n, 'bitə-\ *n* -s [ME *bitoure, botor*, fr. MF *butor*, perh. fr. (assumed) VL *butitaurus*, fr. L *butio* bittern (prob. of imit. origin) + *taurus* ox, bull — more at STEER] **:** any of various small or medium-sized herons of *Botaurus* and related genera that frequent reedy bogs and swamps, nest on the ground, are nocturnal in habit, and have soft streaked and speckled plumage and a characteristic booming cry — see LEAST BITTERN, STAKE DRIVER

European bittern

²**bittern** \"\ *n* -s [irreg. fr. ¹*bitter*] **1 :** the bitter mother liquor that remains in saltworks after the salt has crystallized out and that contains other salts (as magnesium chloride, magnesium sulfate, bromides, and iodides) **2 :** a very bitter mixture of quassia and other drugs formerly used in adulterating beer

bit·ter·ness \'bid·ə(r)nəs, 'bitə-\ *n* -ES [ME *bitternesse*, fr. OE *biternes*, fr. *biter* bitter + *-nes* -ness — more at BITTER] **1 :** the quality or state of being bitter **2 :** something bitter

bitter nightshade *n* **:** BITTERSWEET 2a

bit·ter·nut \'==,=\ *or* **bitternut hickory** *n* **:** a hickory (*Carya cordiformis*) of the eastern U.S. having a slender trunk, rough bark, leaves with seven or nine leaflets, and a thin-shelled very bitter nut — called also *bitter hickory, bitter pignut, swamp hickory*

bitter orange *n* **:** SOUR ORANGE

bitter orange oil *n* **:** ORANGE OIL b

bitter osier *n* **:** PURPLE WILLOW

bitter pecan *n* **:** WATER HICKORY

bitter pepper *n* **:** an Asiatic tree (*Evodia daniellii*) with compound deciduous leaves, white flowers, and black fruit

bitter pill *n* **:** an extreme vexation or humiliation; *esp* **:** one constituting a punishment, retribution, or unavoidable expedient ⟨having to seek his foe's aid was a *bitter pill* to take⟩

bitter pit *n* **:** a nonparasitic disease of the apple, pear, and quince of uncertain etiology but suspected of being caused by upset in the water balance between leaves and fruit and producing spots of dead brown tissue in the flesh of the fruit and discolored depressions on its surface — called also *Baldwin spot, stippen*

bitter principle *n* **:** any of various neutral substances of strong bitter taste (as aloin) extracted from plants

bitterroot \'==,=\ *n* **1 :** a succulent plant (*Lewisia rediviva*) of the Rocky mountains with fleshy farinaceous roots and pink flowers **2 :** DOGBANE 1

bitter rot *n* **1 :** a very destructive disease of apples, grapes, and other fruit caused by a fungus (*Glomerella cingulata*) and producing cankers on the twigs, limbs, and fruit spurs and a spotting or blistering and decay of the fruit characterized by bitterness of the pulp — called also *anthracnose, ripe rot* **2 :** a rot of ripening grapes caused by an imperfect fungus (*Melanconium fuligineum*)

bitter rubberweed *n* **:** an erect herb (*Actinea odorata*) of the family Compositae of the southwestern U.S. having alternate leaves often sprinkled with resinous globules and chiefly yellow terminal flower heads and causing poisoning of livestock

bitters *pl of* BITTER

bitter salt *n* **:** EPSOM SALTS

bitter spar *n* **:** DOLOMITE

¹**bittersweet** \¦==¦=\ *n* [ME *bitterswete*, fr. *biter* bitter + *swete* sweetness — more at SWEET] **1 :** something that is bittersweet **:** pleasure alloyed with pain ⟨all the ~ of their long separation —Christopher Morley⟩ **2 a :** a sprawling Old World poisonous plant (*Solanum dulcamara*) that is common as a weed in America and has purple flowers and oval coral-red berries and a taste at first sweetish and then bitter **b :** a No. American ornamental woody vine (*Celastrus scandens*) having clusters of small greenish flowers succeeded by yellow capsules that burst open when ripe disclosing the scarlet aril — called also *climbing bittersweet, false bittersweet*; see EVERGREEN BITTERSWEET, JAPANESE BITTERSWEET **3 a :** a deep orange that is deeper than bittersweet orange **b :** a dark to deep reddish orange — called also *lobster*

²**bittersweet** \"\ *adj* **1 :** at once bitter and sweet ⟨a ~ apple⟩; *esp* **:** pleasant but attended by elements or twinges of suffering or regret ⟨~ hunger of desire —Hamlin Garland⟩ **2 :** of or relating to a prepared chocolate containing little sugar; *also* **:** of or relating to syrups and candy coatings made of this chocolate or confections covered with such coatings

bittersweet orange *n* **:** a deep orange that is paler than bittersweet — called also *neutral orange*

bittersweet pink *n* **:** a strong yellowish pink that is yellower and darker than salmon pink, yellower than peach red, and yellower and slightly lighter than average salmon — called also *Du Barry*

bitter thistle *n* **:** BLESSED THISTLE 1

bitter vetch *n* **:** any of several reputedly bitter or toxic vetches: as **a :** ERS **b :** CHICKLING **c :** an erect glabrous European vetch (*Lathyrus montanus*) with creeping and tuberous rhizomes **d :** a western No. American vetch (*Lathyrus lanszwertii*) with narrow coriaceous leaflets and pale lavender to pinkish violet flowers

bitter waternut *n* **:** NUTMEG HICKORY

bitterweed \'==,=\ *n* **1 :** any of several American plants containing a bitter principle: as **a :** RAGWEED 2 **b :** HORSEWEED **c :** SNEEZEWEED 1a **d :** any of several trees of the genus *Xylopia*; *esp* **:** a West Indian tree (*X. glabra*) **:** BITTER RUBBERWEED **2 :** the wood of a bitterweed tree

bitter willow *n* **:** PURPLE WILLOW

bitterwood \'==,=\ *n* -s **1 a :** a West Indian tree (*Picrasma excelsum*) of the family Simaroubaceae that yields Jamaica quassia **b :** PARADISE TREE 1 **2 :** QUASSIA 2

bitterworm \'==,=\ *n* [so called fr. the creeping scaly root and the bitter principle contained in the plant] **:** BUCKBEAN

bitthead \'=,=\ *n* [¹*bitt* + *head*] **:** the upper end of a bitt

¹**bit·tie** *var of* BITTY

²**bittie** \"\ *n* [³*bit* + Sc *-ie* (dim. suffix)] *Scot* **:** ³BIT

³**bittie** \"\ *adj, Scot* **:** LITTLE

¹**bitting** *pres part of* BIT *or of* BITT

²**bit·ting** \'bid·iŋ, 'bitiŋ\ *n* -s [¹*bit* + *-ing*] **:** the shape of the bit of a key that causes it to fit or actuate the lock

bit·ti·um \'bid·ēəm\ *n, cap* [NL] **:** a genus of rather small marine snails (family Arithiidae) having elongated spiral shells with a granulated sculpture

bit·tock \'bitək\ *n* -s [³*bit* + *-ock*] *chiefly Scot* **:** a little bit

bitt pin *n* **:** a pin thrust through the bitthead to keep the cable from slipping off

bitts *pl of* BITT, *pres 3d sing of* BITT

¹**bit·ty** *or* **bit·tie** \'bid·ē, 'bitē\ *adj, often* -ER/-EST [³*bit* + *-y*, *-ie*] **:** made up of bits **:** SCRAPPY; *also* **:** containing particulate matter

²**bitty** *or* **bittie** \"\ *adj* [(*little*) *bitty*, prob. fr. *little bit* + *-y*, *-ie*] *dial* **:** SMALL, TINY — used esp. in the phrase *little bitty*

bitty cream *n* [¹*bitty*] **:** sweet cream curdled by bacteria that survive pasteurization — compare ¹BROKEN 2j

bi·tubercular \¦bī + \ *adj* [¹*bi-* + *tubercular*] *of a tooth* **:** having two cusps

bi·tu·mas·tic \,bī·tyü'mastik\ *n* -s [fr. *Bitumastic*, a trademark] **:** a composition of asphalt and filler (as asbestos shorts) used chiefly as a protective coating on structural metals exposed to weathering or corrosion

bi·tu·men \bī·'t(y)ümən, bə·'-, -(,)men; *US sometimes and Brit usu* 'bityü-\ *n* -s [ME *bithumen* mineral pitch, fr. L *bitumen*, prob. of Celt origin; akin to MIr *bethe, beithe* box (tree), W *bedw* birch; fr. the use of the birch tree as a source of tar — more at CUD] **1 a :** an asphalt of Asia Minor used in ancient times as a cement and mortar **b :** any of various mixtures of hydrocarbons (as asphalt, crude petroleum, or tar) often together with their nonmetallic derivatives that are usu. dark brown or black and occur naturally or are obtained as residues from naturally occurring substances by heat refining; *specif* **:** such a mixture soluble in carbon disulfide — see ASPHALTENE **c :** a roadbed or other surface faced with bitumen **2 :** CONGO 4

bitumen process *n* **:** a photographic process in which advantage is taken of the fact that prepared bitumen is rendered insoluble in benzene or other organic solvents by exposure to light (as in photolithography)

bi·tu·mi·ni·za·tion \bī·,t(y)ümənə'zāshən, bə·,-\ *n* -s **1 :** treatment with bitumen **2 :** the natural development of oil shale from ordinary shales

bi·tu·mi·nize *also* **bi·tu·men·ize** \=¹==,nīz\ *vt* -ED/-ING/-s [L *bitumin-*, *bitumen* + E *-ize*] **:** to prepare or treat with bitumen

bi·tu·mi·noid *also* **bi·tu·men·oid** \-,nȯid\ *adj* [L *bitumin-*, *bitumen* + E *-oid*] **:** like bitumen

bi·tu·mi·nous \(')bī·'t(y)ümənəs, bə·'t-\ *adj* [F or L; F *bitumineux*, fr. MF, fr. L *bituminosus*, fr. *bitumin-*, *bitumen* + *-osus* -ous] **1 a :** having the qualities of bitumen **b** *of a mineral* **:** having an odor of bitumen **2 :** impregnated with, infiltrated by, or containing bitumen ⟨~ shale⟩ ⟨~ paint⟩ ⟨a stretch of ~ road⟩ **3 :** of or relating to bituminous coal ⟨the ~ production of the U.S.⟩

bituminous coal *n* **:** a coal that yields when heated considerable volatile bituminous matter — called also *soft coal*

bituminous grout *n* **:** a grout that has bituminous material as a binder and sandy mineral matter as an aggregate and that can be poured when heated

bituminous macadam *n* **:** a pavement constructed by spreading two or more layers of crushed stone on a suitable base and pouring a bituminous binder on each

bit-wise \'=,=\ *adj* [¹*bit* + *-wise*] *of a saddle horse* **:** responsive to pressure on the bit

bi·typic \(')bī+\ *adj* [¹*bi-* + *typic*] *of a genus* **:** consisting of two species

-bi·um \bēəm\ *n comb form, pl* **-bia** [NL, fr. neut. of *-bius*] **:** organism or group having a (specified) mode of life — in taxonomic names ⟨*Anobium*⟩ and group names ⟨*coenobium*⟩ in biology

bi·unguiculate \ˈbī+\ *adj* [ˈ*bi-* + *unguiculate*] **:** of or having a double claw ⟨the ~ leg of a crustacean⟩

bi·u·ni·al \(ˈ)bī¦yünēəl\ *also* **bi·une** \ˈbī,yün\ *adj* [*biunial* fr. ˈ*bi-* + L *unus* one + E *-ial*; *biune* fr. ˈ*bi-* + L *unus* — more at ONE] **:** combining two in one

bi·u·ret \,bīyəˈret, ˈ==,=\ *n* -s [ISV ˈ*bi-* + *-uret*] **:** a white crystalline compound $NH_2CONHCONH_2$ formed by heating urea — called also *allophanamide*

biuret reaction *n* **:** a reaction shown by biuret, proteins, and most peptides on treatment in alkaline solution with copper sulfate, resulting in a violet color, and used esp. in testing for proteins

-bi·us \bēəs\ *n comb form* [NL, fr. *-bius* having a (specified) mode of life, fr. Gk *-bios*, fr. *bios* mode of life — more at QUICK] **:** one that has a (specified) mode of life — chiefly in generic names in zoology ⟨Entero*bius*⟩

bi·valence *or* **bi·valency** \(ˈ)bī+\ *n, pl* **bivalences** *or* **bivalencies** [ˈ*bi-* + *valence*; trans. of G *zweiwertigkeit*] **:** the quality or state of being bivalent

ˈ**bi·valent** \(ˈ)bī+\ *adj* [ˈ*bi-* + *valent*; trans. of G *zweiwertig*] **1 :** having a valence of two **2 :** DOUBLE — used of homologous chromosomes associated in pairs in synapsis **3 a** *of an antigen, hapten, or antibody* **:** having two sites for combination with antibody or antigen **b** *of an antibody* **:** capable of producing agglutination or precipitation under ordinary experimental conditions

²**bivalent** \"\ *n* -s **:** a pair of synaptic chromosomes

ˈ**bi·valve** *also* **bi·valved** \(ˈ)bī+\ *adj* [ˈ*bi-* + *valve* or *valved*] **1 :** having a shell composed of two usu. movable valves that open and shut ⟨~ oysters⟩ ⟨~ clams⟩ **2** *of a shell or capsule* **:** having two valves ⟨the ~ wall of a diatom⟩ **3 :** consisting of two corresponding movable pieces suggesting the shells of mollusks ⟨a ~ speculum⟩

²**bivalve** \"\ *n* -s **:** an animal with a 2-valved shell; *esp* **:** a mollusk of the class Lamellibranchia (as a clam, mussel, or oyster) — compare UNIVALVE

³**bivalve** \"\ *vt* [ˈ*bi-* + *valve*] **:** to split (a cast) along one or two sides (as to renew surgical dressings or to restore circulation)

bi·val·via \bīˈvalvēə\ *n pl, cap* [NL, fr. E ²*bivalve* + NL *-ia*] *in former classifications* **:** the Lamellibranchia and Brachiopoda considered as a natural group; *sometimes* **:** LAMELLIBRANCHIA

bi·variant \(ˈ)bī+\ *adj* [ˈ*bi-* + *variant*] **:** capable of twofold variation **:** having two degrees of freedom — used of a system in which the number of components equals the number of phases — compare PHASE RULE

bi·variate \(ˈ)bī+\ *adj* [ˈ*bi-* + *variate*] **:** of, relating to, or involving two variables ⟨a ~ frequency distribution⟩

bi·vascular \(ˈ)bī+\ *adj* [ˈ*bi-* + *vascular*] **:** having two blood or other body vessels

bi·venter \(ˈ)bī+\ *n* [NL, fr. ˈ*bi-* + *venter*] **:** a muscle with two fleshy bellies

bi·ventral \(ˈ)bī+\ *adj* [ˈ*bi-* + *ventral*] **:** having two bellies **:** DIGASTRIC

bi·verbal \(ˈ)bī+\ *adj* [ˈ*bi-* + *verbal*] **:** relating to or involving two words or expressions; *also* **:** PUNNING

bi·vinyl \(ˈ)bī+\ *n* [ISV ˈ*bi-* + *vinyl*] **:** BUTADIENE

bi·visible \(ˈ)bī+\ *n* [ˈ*bi-* + *visible*] **:** a dry fly tied from hackles of contrasting colors so that it may be seen readily by both fish and angler

bi·vittate \(ˈ)bī+\ *adj* [ˈ*bi-* + *vittate*] *zool* **:** having two longitudinal stripes

biv·i·um \ˈbivēəm, ˈbīv-\ *n, pl* **bivia** [NL, fr. L, crossroads, fr. neut. of *bivius* having two roads, fr. *bi-* ˈ*bi-* + *-vius* (fr. *via* road, way) — more at VIA] **:** the two rays of a starfish between which is the madreporite — opposed to *trivium*

bi·vol·tine \bīˈvōl,tēn, (ˈ)=ˈ=,tᵊn\ *also* **bi·vol·tin** \-ˈtᵊn\ *adj* [F *bivoltin*, fr. *bi-* ˈ*bi-* + It *volta* time, instance (fr. — assumed — VL *volvita*, fr. L *volvere* to turn) + F *-in* -ine — more at VOLUBLE] **1 :** producing two broods in a season — used esp. of silkworms **2** *of insects* **:** having two generations a year, a summer generation without diapause and a winter generation with diapause — **bi·vol·tin·ism** \-ˈtᵊn,izəm\ *n* -s

bi·vol·tin·ize \=ˈ=tə,nīz\ *vt* -ED/-ING/-S **:** to treat (silkworm eggs) so as to produce bivoltine products

ˈ**biv·ouac** \ˈbiv,wak *also* -və,w-\ *n* -s [F, fr. LG *biwake*, fr. *bi* at, by (fr. MLG *bī*) + *wake* guard; akin to OHG *bī* by, at and to OHG *wahha* guard, *wahhēn*, *wahhōn* to wake — more at WAKE] **1 a** *obs* **:** the watch of a whole army by night when in danger of surprise or attack **b :** an encampment under little or no shelter usu. for a short time; *also* **:** the site of such encampment **2 :** a camping out for a night; *also* **:** a temporary or casual shelter or settlement

²**bivouac** \"\ *vi* **bivouacked**; **bivouacked**; **bivouacking**; **bivouacks** *also* **bivouacs 1 :** to encamp with little or no shelter ⟨the troops *bivouacked* there for a week⟩ **2 a :** to spend the night in the open **b :** to put up temporarily **:** make a casual or temporary settlement ⟨the troupe . . . *bivouacked* at a three-story house —Milton Esterow⟩

bivouac sheet *n* **:** ZDARSKY TENT

biv·ver \ˈbivə(r)\ *dial chiefly Brit var of* ²BEVER

bivvy *also* **bivy** \ˈbivē\ *n or vb* [by shortening & alter.] *slang* **:** BIVOUAC

bi·wa \ˈbē(,)wä\ *n* -s [Jap] **:** a 4-stringed Japanese lute

ˈ**bi·weekly** \(ˈ)bī+\ *adj* [ˈ*bi-* + *weekly*] **1 :** occurring or appearing every two weeks **:** having a 2-week interval between recurrences **:** FORTNIGHTLY — now usu. used with this meaning in respect to publication dates; compare SEMIWEEKLY **2 :** occurring or appearing twice a week **:** SEMIWEEKLY — used esp. of transportation schedules

²**biweekly** \"\ *adv* **1 :** every two weeks **2 :** twice a week

³**biweekly** \"\ *n* -ES **1 :** a publication issued every two weeks **2 :** SEMIWEEKLY

bixa \ˈbiksə\ *n, cap* [NL, fr. AmerSp *bija*, *bixa* achiote, fr. Taino *bixa*] **:** an American genus (the type of the family Bixaceae) of trees with cordate leaves and large pink or rose flowers — see ANNATTO TREE

bix·a·ce·ae \bikˈsāsē,ē\ *n pl, cap* [NL, fr. *Bixa*, type genus + *-aceae*] **:** a family of tropical shrubs or trees (order Parietales) having alternate leaves, perfect flowers, a superior ovary, and valvate capsules — **bix·a·ceous** \-ˈsāshəs\ *adj*

bix·by·ite \ˈbiksbē,īt\ *n* -s [Maynard *Bixby*, 19th cent. American who discovered it + E *-ite*] **:** a mineral $FeO.MnO_2$ consisting of an iron manganese oxide occurring in black isometric crystals

bix·in \ˈbiksən\ *n* -s [ISV *bix-* (fr. NL *Bixa*, genus name of *Bixa orellana*) + *-in*] **:** a red-brown carotenoid acid ester $HOOCC_{22}H_{26}COOCH_3$ constituting the chief coloring matter of annatto and used similarly

bi·yearly \(ˈ)bī+\ *adj* [ˈ*bi-* + *yearly*] **1 :** BIENNIAL **2 :** BIANNUAL

biz \ˈbiz\ *n* [by shortening & alter.] *slang* **:** BUSINESS

ˈ**bizarre** \bəˈzär, bēˈz-, -zȧ(r\ *adj* [F, fr. It *bizzarro*] **:** being strikingly out of the ordinary or at variance with some standard real or implied: as **a :** not suited to the situation; *esp* **:** being at variance with good taste or accepted standards (as of fashion, design, or color) ⟨a ~ little house, fit home for a troll⟩ ⟨her ~ hanging sleeves⟩ **b :** odd, extravagant, or eccentric in style or mode ⟨the ~ fur forms of the early 20th century⟩ ⟨he became increasingly ~ in speech⟩ **c :** involving sensational contrasts or marked incongruities **:** FANTASTIC ⟨the ~ assurance of this mousy little man⟩ **d :** not falling within the bounds of what is recognized as normal **:** ATYPICAL ⟨~ bone formation⟩ ⟨the ~ test scores indicated a schizophrenic tendency⟩ **syn** see FANTASTIC

²**bizarre** \"\ *n* -s **:** any of certain flowers with atypical striped markings: **a :** a carnation with white or yellowish flowers striped and flecked with two or more other colors **b :** a yellow tulip with stripes and blotches of usu. scarlet or brown

bi·zarre·ly *adv* **:** in a bizarre manner

bi·zarre·ness *n* -ES **:** the quality or state of being bizarre

bi·zar·re·rie \bə,zärəˈrē, bē,z-\ *n* -s [F, fr. *bizarre* + *-erie* -ery] **1 :** bizarre quality **2 :** something bizarre

bizel *var of* BEZEL

bizen *var of* BYZEN

bi·zet \bəˈzet\ *n* -s [prob. by alter.] **:** BEZEL 2b

biznaga *var of* BISNAGA

bi·zonal \(ˈ)bī+\ *adj* [ˈ*bi-* + *zonal*] **:** of, relating to, or concerned with the combined affairs of two administrative areas — often cap. when referring to the British and American occupied zones in Germany after World War II ⟨*Bizonal* currency⟩

bi·zone \ˈbī+,-\ *n* -s [prob. back-formation fr. *bizonal*] **:** a bizonal area; *specif* **:** a zone governed or administered by two powers acting together

ˈ**bi·zygomatic** \(ˈ)bī+\ *adj* [ˈ*bi-* + *zygomatic*] **:** of or relating to the two cheekbones; *specif* **:** relating to a measure of facial width taken between the most lateral points on the external surfaces of the zygomatic arches

²**bizygomatic** \"\ *n* -s **:** the bizygomatic width of the face

bizz \ˈbiz\ *dial var of* BUZZ

biz·zar·ro \bətˈsä(,)rō\ *adj* [It] **:** BIZARRE — used as a direction in music

bk *abbr* **1** backwardation **2** balk **3** bank **4** bark **5** black **6** block **7** book **8** brake **9** brook

Bk *symbol* berkelium

bkcy *abbr* bankruptcy

bkg *abbr* **1** banking **2** bookkeeping **3** breakage

bkgd *abbr* background

bkp *abbr* bookplate

bkpg *abbr* bookkeeping

bkpr *abbr* bookkeeper

bkpt *abbr* bankrupt

bkry *abbr* bakery

bks *abbr* **1** backstrip **2** barracks

bkt *abbr* **1** basket **2** bracket

bl *abbr* **1** bale **2** barrel **3** black **4** blessed **5** block **6** blue

BL *abbr or n* -s **1 :** a bachelor of laws **2 :** a bachelor of letters

BL *abbr* **1** base line **2** bill of lading **3** black letter **4** breadth-length **5** breech-loading **6** building line

blaa *or* **blaa-blaa** *var of* BLAH

blaas·op \ˈblä,säp\ *n* -s [Afrik, fr. *blaas* (imper. of *blaas* to blow, fr. MD *blāsen*) + *op* up, fr. MD; akin to OHG *blāsan* to blow and to OHG *ūf* up — more at BLAST, UP] *Africa* **:** GLOBEFISH

blaauwbok *var of* BLAUBOK

blaauw wildebeest \ˈblō-\ *n* [obs. Afrik (now *blouwildebees*), lit., blue wildebeest] *Africa* **:** BRINDLED GNU

ˈ**blab** \ˈblab, -aa(ə)b\ *n* -s [ME *blabbe*; akin to ME *blaberen* to blabber] **1 :** one that blabs ⟨who will open himself to a ~ or a babbler —Francis Bacon⟩ **2 :** idle or excessive talk **:** the telling of secrets **:** CHATTER **3 :** a word or series of usu. high sounding or pretentious words, that is empty of meaning or too vague in meaning to serve as a basis of discussion ⟨"that's just ~", came the rude interruption⟩ — **blab·by** \-ē, -i\ *adj*

²**blab** \"\ *vb* **blabbed**; **blabbed**; **blabbing**; **blabs** *vt* **:** to reveal (as a secret) esp. by talking without reserve or discretion ⟨confessions made to him are rarely . . . *blabbed* —Christopher Morley⟩ — often used with *out* ⟨expect me to ~ out my private feelings —Robertson Davies⟩ ~ *vi* **1 :** to reveal a secret esp. by talking without reserve or discretion ⟨he will be sure to ~, and it will be all over the town in no time —Joseph Conrad⟩ **2 :** to talk idly or thoughtlessly **:** CHATTER, GAB

³**blab** \"\ *n* -s [origin unknown] *West* **:** a thin piece of board attached to a calf's nose to prevent suckling

⁴**blab** \"\ *vt* **blabbed**; **blabbed**; **blabbing**; **blabs** *West* **:** to attach a blab to **:** wean with a blab

ˈ**blab·ber** \ˈblabə(r)\ *vb* **blabbered**; **blabbered**; **blabbering** \-b(ə)riŋ\ **blabbers** [ME *blaberen*, prob. of imit. origin like OHG *blabbizōn* to babble, ON *blabbra*] *vi* **:** to talk indiscreetly, excessively, or nonsensically **:** BABBLE ~ *vt* **:** to say or utter indiscreetly or foolishly — often used with *out* ⟨he ~*ed* out some kind of reply⟩

²**blabber** \"\ *n* -s **:** indiscreet, excessive, or nonsensical talk

³**blabber** \"\ *archaic var of* ³BLUBBER

⁴**blabber** \ˈblabə(r), -laab-\ *n* -s [²*blab* + *-er*] **:** one that blabs

⁵**blabber** \"\ *n* -s [by alter.] **:** BLUBBERER 2

blabbermouth \ˈ=,=\ *n* -s [²*blabber* + *mouth*] **:** one that talks too much **:** BLABBER

blabmouth \ˈ=,=\ *n* -s [ˈ*blab* + *mouth*] **:** BLABBERMOUTH

blab school *n* [²*blab*] **:** a school common in the U.S. during pioneer days in which pupils study their lessons by repeating them aloud separately or in chorus until one is called forward to recite

ˈ**black** \ˈblak\ *adj* -ER/-EST [ME *blak*, fr. OE *blæc*; akin to OHG *blah* black, ON *blakra* to blink, L *flagrare* to burn, Gk *phlegein*, Skt *bharga* radiance, OE *bæl* fire, pyre — more at BALD] **1 a :** of the color black **:** having the color of soot or coal ⟨~ cloth⟩ ⟨as ~ as ebony⟩ **b :** very dark in color ⟨his face ~ with rage —T.B.Costain⟩ **c** *of written or printed letters* **:** characterized by thickness of form and consequent intense contrast with the white of a page ⟨a heavy ~ type⟩ **d :** covered or darkened with numerous dark objects close together ⟨the . . . ceiling was . . . ~ with flies —Ann Bridge⟩ ⟨the boxcars going north would be ~ with harvesters sitting on the top —Meridel Le Sueur⟩ **2 a** *of human beings* (1) **:** having darkly pigmented skin, hair, and eyes **:** dark-complexioned **:** BRUNET ⟨whether the writer . . . be a ~ or a fair man —Joseph Addison⟩ (2) **:** dark in comparison to the average complexion of a group **:** SWARTHY ⟨a ~ Irishman⟩ (3) **:** being a member of a group or race characterized by dark pigmentation ⟨organized Negro regiments commanded by ~ officers⟩; *esp* **:** NEGROID — compare BROWN 2a, COLORED, WHITE, YELLOW **b :** of, belonging to, consisting of, or connected with black, esp. negroid, people ⟨~ Africa⟩ ⟨~ races⟩; *esp* **:** having a large Negro population ⟨a ~ belt⟩ **c :** advocating more rights for Negroes — used esp. in reference to the slavery controversy of the 19th century in the U.S. ⟨~ abolitionist⟩ ⟨~ Republican⟩ **3 a :** characterized by wearing black clothes or black armor ⟨the ~ knight⟩ **b :** of, belonging to, or being a member of a group characterized or formerly characterized by wearing black: as (1) **:** clerical in politics (2) **:** FASCIST ⟨the red and ~ totalitarians —Mark Starr⟩ — see BLACKSHIRT **4 :** soiled with dirt **:** DIRTY ⟨how ~ your hands are⟩ ⟨the pot calls the kettle ~⟩ **5 a :** characterized by the absence of light or the presence of very little light ⟨a ~ night⟩ **:** reflecting or transmitting little or no light ⟨~ water⟩ ⟨~ glass⟩ **b** *of coffee* **:** served without cream or milk and sometimes also without sugar **6 a :** outrageously wicked **:** deserving unmitigated condemnation ⟨a ~ deed⟩ ⟨a ~ heart⟩ ⟨a ~ villain⟩ ⟨a moralist to whom everything is either ~ or white⟩; *sometimes* **:** DISHONORABLE, DISCREDITABLE **b :** expressing or indicating disgrace, dishonor, discredit, or guilt sometimes through symbolic use of an object that is black in color ⟨a ~ mark for tardiness⟩ ⟨with evidence so ~ against him —Charlotte Armstrong⟩ **7 :** connected with some baneful aspect of the supernatural, esp. the devil ⟨a ~ curse⟩ ⟨~ magic⟩ ⟨the ~ art⟩ **8 a :** unrelievedly sad, gloomy, or calamitous ⟨~ despair⟩ ⟨things are looking ~⟩ ⟨the autumn of 1776 was a ~ season for the Continental Army —J.D.Hart⟩ **b** *sometimes cap, of a day* **:** marked by the occurrence of a disaster ⟨on September 24, 1869, when Jay Gould, James Fisk, Jr., and their associates effected the partial corner in gold that ended so disastrously in the panic of ~ Friday —S.A.Nelson⟩ **9 :** expressing or characterized by menace or angry discontent **:** SULLEN, HOSTILE ⟨he gave me a ~ look⟩ ⟨~ resentment filled his heart —Miriam James⟩ **10 :** being such to the greatest possible extent **:** EXTREME, UNQUALIFIED, UTTER ⟨it was a ~ born fool I had for a son —J.M.Synge⟩ ⟨they were all ~ strangers to me —Mary Deasy⟩ **11 :** constituting, committing, or connected with a violation of an official quota, price ceiling, rationing restriction, or other public regulation **:** ILLICIT, ILLEGAL ⟨the ~ market⟩ ⟨~ gasoline⟩ **12** [short for ˈ*blackleg*] *chiefly Brit* **:** subject to boycott by trade-union members as employing or favoring nonunion workmen or as operated, conducted, or made under conditions considered unfair by trade-union members ⟨a ~ ship⟩ ⟨declare a pub ~⟩ **13 :** marked by or as if by a black section on a map or chart as being affected by some undesirable condition (as infection or a high rate of unemployment) ⟨the polio situation is improving but there are still some ~ areas⟩ **14 :** covered with a dark scale of oxide **:** not galvanized ⟨~ iron pipe⟩ **15 a** *of propaganda* **:** conducted so as to appear to originate within an enemy country and designed to weaken enemy morale — opposed to *white* **b :** characterized by or connected with the use of black propaganda ⟨~ psychological warfare⟩ ⟨~ radio⟩

²**black** \"\ *n* -s [ME *blak* black color, black particle, black material, fr. OE *blæc* ink, fr. *blæc*, adj.] **1 :** any of various substances (as bone black, carbon black, lampblack) containing elemental carbon usu. as the chief constituent **2 a :** the neutral or achromatic object color of least lightness **:** the darkest gray **:** the achromatic color bearing the least resemblance to white **b :** the one of the six psychologically primary colors that is characteristically perceived to belong to objects that neither reflect nor transmit an appreciable fraction of the incident light **c :** any object color of very low lightness and saturation ⟨the painter's ~s and browns⟩ **3 :** a black part or area **:** a black speck or stain **4 :** a black material or substance: **a :** black clothing ⟨~ is becoming to her⟩ esp. as worn as a sign of mourning ⟨wear ~ for her father⟩ **b :** a black garment esp. as worn as a sign of mourning or by men on formal occasions ⟨the lawyer . . . in his ~s and his silk hat —G.K.Chesterton⟩ ⟨uncomfortable in his wedding ~s —Edna Ferber⟩ — usu. used in pl. **5 :** a Negro, Negrito, or Australian aborigine **:** a person belonging to a darkly pigmented race **:** a person whose appearance shows that some of his ancestors belonged to a darkly pigmented race **6 :** a poacher in 18th century England who operated as a member of a band disguised by blackened faces **7 :** the dark-colored pieces in a two-handed board game; *also* **:** the player by or the side of the board from which these pieces are played **8 a :** a black animal: as (1) **:** a black horse (2) **:** an Aberdeen Angus (3) **:** a Norfolk turkey **b :** an individual of a black or melanistic variety of certain common mammals (as squirrel or skunk) **9** *usu cap* **:** one of the Neri **10 :** the black circle of a target; *also* **:** a shot that hits it **11** *usu cap* **:** a member or adherent of a group characterized or formerly characterized by wearing black: as **a :** a member or adherent of a clerical political party **b :** FASCIST **12 :** something deserving unmitigated condemnation ⟨pure whites and seamy ~s of character, inviting sighs and hisses —Leslie Rees⟩ ⟨the tendency to think only in terms of ~ or white —D.K.Berninghausen⟩ **13** *print* **:** BOLDFACE 2 **14 :** total or nearly total absence of light **:** DARKNESS ⟨the ~ of night⟩ **15** [fr. the bookkeeping practice of entering credit items in black ink] **:** the condition of making a profit — usu. used with *the* ⟨the company is now operating in the ~⟩; opposed to *red*

³**black** \"\ *vb* -ED/-ING/-S [ME *blaken*, fr. *blak*, n.] *vi* **1 :** BLACKEN — often used with *over* ⟨the sky ~*ed* over⟩ **2 :** to put black coloring matter on one's face in preparation for playing the role of a Negro — used with *up* ⟨~ up for the minstrel show⟩ ~ *vt* **1 a :** BLACKEN 1 **b :** to bruise and discolor (an eye) by a blow ⟨say that again and I'll ~ your eye⟩ **2 :** BLACKEN 2 **3 :** to apply black coloring matter to: as **a :** to make black and shiny by applying blacking to ⟨who will ~ these shoes⟩ ⟨they ~*ed* the stove⟩ **b :** to put black coloring matter on in preparation for playing the role of a Negro ⟨the makeup man ~*ed* the actor's face⟩ — often used with *up* ⟨he ~*ed* himself up for the next performance⟩ **c :** to obliterate with or as if with black ink **:** BLOT **:** delete or suppress through censorship — used with *out* ⟨ordered the passage ~*ed* out from all copies in the school libraries —Upton Sinclair⟩ **d :** to treat (a ship's rigging) with tar or with a mixture containing a black oil or grease — used with *down*

⁴**black** \"\ *adv* [ˈ*black*] *dial Brit* **:** EXTREMELY ⟨~ afraid⟩ **:** UTTERLY, COMPLETELY ⟨the fire was ~ out⟩

black abalone *n* **:** a comparatively small dark-shelled abalone (*Haliotis cracherodii*) feeding on plankton along the coast from Oregon to Lower California

black acacia *n* **:** LOCUST 3a(2)

blackacre \ˈ=,==\ *n, law* **:** a particular piece of land esp. in distinction from whiteacre — used as an arbitrary name

black alder *n* **1 :** a shrub (*Ilex verticillata*) with clusters of axillary flowers — called also *winterberry* **2 :** an alder (*Alnus glutinosa*) with broadly oval leaves and with very glutinous young parts

black alkali *n* **:** alkali containing carbonates that dissolve organic matter and blacken soil or crusts **:** soil blackened by such alkali

black·a·moor \ˈblakə,mu̇(ə)r *also* -mō(ə)r *or* -mȯ(ə)r\ *n* -s [alter. of earlier *black More*, fr. *black* + *More*, earlier form of *Moor*] **:** a dark-skinned person **:** a person belonging to a darkly pigmented race; *esp* **:** NEGRO

black-and-blue \¦=¦=¦=\ *adj* **:** darkly discolored **:** livid or bluish black from a bruise causing rupture of blood vessels and effusion of blood in the tissues

black-and-tan \¦=¦=¦=\ *adj* **1** *of a dog's coat* **:** having a dominant color pattern that occurs typically in the dachshund, doberman, bloodhound, Manchester terrier, and several other breeds, the body being black with deep tan or rusty red on feet, breeching, and cheek patches, above eyes, and inside ears **2** *often cap B & T* **:** favoring or practicing proportional representation of whites and Negroes in politics ⟨in the campaign of 1912 the Roosevelt supporters in the southern states broke away from the *black-and-tan* regulars and excluded Negroes from the bolting conventions —D.D.McKean⟩ — opposed to *lily-white* **3 :** frequented by both Negroes and whites ⟨a *black-and-tan* bar⟩

black and tan \"\ *n* [*black-and-tan*] **1** *often cap B & T* **:** a black-and-tan dog; *specif* **:** a black-and-tan hound **2** *usu* **black-and-tan :** a nightclub frequented by both Negroes and whites **3** *often cap B & T* **:** a member of the black-and-tan faction of the Republican party in the southern U.S. — opposed to *lily-white* **4** *cap B & T* **:** a recruit enlisted in England in 1920–21 for service in the Royal Irish Constabulary against the armed movement for Irish independence

black-and-tan coonhound *n* **:** a strong vigorous American coonhound having a black-and-tan coat and commonly regarded as constituting a distinct breed

black and white *n* **1 :** WRITING, PRINT ⟨the facts have been set down in *black and white*⟩ **2 :** a drawing or print executed in black or a dark pigment on a white or light ground or in a light pigment on a dark ground **:** the mode or practice of executing such drawings or prints **3 :** a monochrome printed reproduction of a work of art; *also* the mode or practice of executing such reproductions **4 :** monochrome reproduction of visual images (as by photography or television)

black-and-white \¦=¦=¦=\ *adj* [*black and white*] **1 :** being in writing or print ⟨a *black-and-white* statement of the true situation⟩ **2 :** partly black and partly white in color ⟨a *black-and-white* desert hawk —Zane Grey⟩ **3 a :** executed in black or a dark pigment on a white or light ground or in a light pigment on a dark ground ⟨a *black-and-white* sketch⟩ ⟨*black-and-white* work⟩ **b :** working with such pigment on such a ground ⟨a *black-and-white* artist⟩ **4 a :** printed in ink of one color only ⟨a *black-and-white* map⟩ **b :** characterized by the reproduction or transmission of visual images in tones of gray rather than in colors ⟨*black-and-white* photography⟩ ⟨*black-and-white* television⟩ **5 :** sharply divided into good and evil groups, camps, or sides ⟨a *black-and-white* world where a guy is either your pal or probably a bum —Hal Boyle⟩ **:** evaluating things as altogether bad or good ⟨*black-and-white* morality⟩ ⟨a *black-and-white* judgment⟩

black-and-white warbler *also* **black-and-white creeper** *n* **:** an eastern No. American warbler (*Mniotilta varia*) that is streaked with black and white and that creeps about on trunks and stems

black-and-white work *n* **:** timber framework the interstices of which are filled in with rough masonry or coarse plastering

black-and-yellow warbler \¦=¦=¦=-\ *n* **:** MAGNOLIA WARBLER

black angelfish *n* **:** a large dark-colored angelfish (*Pomacanthus arcuatus*) of the warm western Atlantic sometimes used as a food fish

black angelica *n* **:** BLACK HOREHOUND

black ape *n* **:** a sooty black monkey (*Cynopithecus niger*) of Celebes having an extremely short tail and a long muzzle and being intermediate in several characteristics between the macaques and the baboons

black apple *n* **1 :** an Australian tree (*Sideroxylon australe*) — called also *brush apple, native plum, wild plum* **2 :** the large plumlike fruit of the black apple

black apricot *n* **:** PURPLE APRICOT

black archangel *n* **:** BLACK HOREHOUND

blackarm \ˈ=,=\ *also* **blackarm disease** \(ˈ)=¦=-\ *n* **:** a form of angular leaf spot producing dark lesions on the stem and petioles of cotton

ˈ**black ash** *n* [*ash* (tree)] **1 :** a No. American ash (*Fraxinus nigra*) having dark brown heavy wood — called also *basket ash, brown ash, hoop ash* **2 :** an Australian eucalyptus (*Eucalyptus stellulata*) **3 :** BOX ELDER

²**black ash** *n* [*ash* (combustion product)] **1 :** any of various

dark-colored crude products obtained in industrial processes: as **a :** crude sodium carbonate obtained in the Leblanc process **b :** crude barium sulfide **2 :** a black mass containing chiefly soda in the form of sodium carbonate and usu. also sodium sulfide with some carbon and produced esp. for recovery of its soda content by concentrating and burning black liquor (sense 2) in rotary furnaces

black-a-vised \ˈblakə,vīst, -,vīzd,-,vēst\ *also* **black-a-viced** \-st\ *adj* [¹*black* + F *à vis* as to face + E *-ed*] **:** DARK-COMPLEXIONED

blackback \ˈ⸗,⸗\ *n* **1 :** any of certain black-backed fishes: as **a :** MENOMINEE WHITEFISH **b :** WINTER FLOUNDER **2 :** any of certain black-backed birds (as the black-backed gull)

black-backed gull \ˈ⸗,⸗-\ *n* **:** any of several gulls having the back and upper surface of the wings of a very dark slate or black color as adults — see GREAT BLACK-BACKED GULL, LESSER BLACK-BACKED GULL

black-backed jackal *n* **:** a common So. African jackal (*Canis mesomelas*) with a dark dorsal saddle mark — called also *saddle-backed jackal*

black bag *n* **:** BLUE BAG 2

¹**blackball** \ˈ⸗,⸗\ *vt* -ED/-ING/-S [¹*black* + *ball*] **1 a :** to prevent from becoming a member of an organization by casting an adverse vote esp. by putting a black ball into a ballot box or urn ‹if he applies for membership, I'll ~ him› **b :** to vote against **:** make impossible by casting an adverse vote **:** VETO ‹~*ed* the membership applications of some candidates of unsavory character› **2 :** to exclude socially **:** OSTRACIZE ‹he was ~*ed* by all his former friends› **:** exclude from normal professional or economic relations **:** BLACKLIST, BOYCOTT ‹an advertisement inviting the population at large to ~ me —Victor Ross› **syn** see EXCLUDE

²**blackball** \ˈ⸗,⸗\ *n* [¹*black* + *ball*] **1 :** a small black ball that may be put into a ballot box or urn to constitute a vote against admitting someone to membership in an organization **2 :** an adverse vote esp. as excluding an applicant from membership in an organization

black bamboo *n* **:** a small Asiatic bamboo (*Phyllostachys nigra*) having black branches

blackband \ˈ⸗,⸗\ *n* **:** the mineral siderite when occurring mixed with clay, sand, and considerable carbonaceous matter and frequently being associated with coal

black-banded snake \ˈ⸗,⸗⸗-\ *n* **:** a small brownish back-fanged snake (*Coniophanes imperialis*) with three black bands extending along its back and sides that is native to Mexico and southern Texas

black-banded sunfish *n* **:** a small yellowish gray sunfish (*Mesogonistius chaetodon*) with vertical black bars that is sometimes kept in the aquarium

black bass *n* **1 :** any of several widely distributed and highly prized freshwater game fishes (genus *Micropterus*) of the family Centrarchidae that is native to eastern and central No. America and has been introduced into several western states — see LARGEMOUTH BLACK BASS, SMALLMOUTH BLACK BASS, SPOTTED BLACK BASS **2 :** any of several dark-colored fishes: as **a :** BLACK SEA BASS 1 **b :** PRIESTFISH **c :** BLACK CROAKER a

black-bead \ˈ⸗,⸗\ *n, chiefly Brit* **:** CAT'S-CLAW 1b

black bean *n* **1 :** the seed or wood of Moreton Bay chestnut **2 :** HYACINTH BEAN **3 :** any of several black-seeded beans of the genus *Phaseolus* used esp. in So. America for food

black bear *n* **1 :** the common American bear (*Ursus americanus* or *Euarctos americanus*) known in a number of color phases from typical black through various shades of brown or gray to white **2 :** an Asiatic bear (*Selenarctos thibetanus* or *Ursus thibetanus*) that is usu. black and larger than the American black bear

black bearberry *n* **:** a depressed arctic-alpine shrub (*Arctostaphylos alpinus*) with evergreen leaves and black fruit

black beast *n* [trans. of F *bête noire*] **:** BÊTE NOIRE

black bee *n* **:** a dark-colored ill-tempered honeybee of a race supposedly of German origin — called also *German bee*

black beech *n* **1 :** AMERICAN HORNBEAM **2** *NewZeal* **:** a forest tree (*Nothofagus solanderi*) having entire leaves

black beetle \ˈ⸗,⸗\ *n* **:** either of two glossy black burrowing beetles that are very destructive to turf and certain cultivated plants in Australia: **a :** a beetle (*Heteronychus sanctae-helenae*) that was accidentally introduced from Africa **b :** a native beetle (*Metanastes vulgivagus*)

blackbeetle \ˈ⸗,⸗⸗\ *n, chiefly Brit* **:** ORIENTAL COCKROACH

black-bellied plover \ˈ⸗,⸗⸗-\ *n* **:** a large plover (*Squatarola squatarola* or *Charadrius squatarola*) highly esteemed as a game bird that breeds in the arctic regions of both continents but winters in Africa and So. America and differs from related birds in its jet-black throat and underparts when in breeding plumage

black-bellied sandpiper *n* **:** RED-BACKED SANDPIPER

black-bellied snake *n* **:** a common slightly venomous snake (*Denisonia signata*) widely distributed in eastern Australia that is olive or brownish above with the underparts very dark gray or black

black-berried elder \ˈ⸗,⸗⸗-\ *n* **:** ELDERBERRY 1b

¹**blackberry** \ˈ⸗(,)⸗⸗, ˈ⸗⸗ — *see* BERRY\ *n* [ME *blakberie*, fr. OE *blæcberie*, fr. *blæc* black + *berie* berry — more at BLACK, BERRY] **1 a :** any of various usu. black or dark purple juicy but seedy and sweet to somewhat bitter edible berries that technically are aggregate fruits consisting of numerous small drupes crowded upon a fleshy receptacle to which, unlike those of the closely related raspberries, they usu. adhere even when fully ripe **b :** any of various trailing or erect usu. prickly brambles of the genus *Rubus* that bear blackberries, are usu. considered to constitute a distinct subgenus, readily form complex hybrids, and include numerous forms cultivated for their fruits **2 :** any of various plants or their black or dark berrylike fruits: as **a :** WHORTLEBERRY 1 **b :** BLACK CURRANT **c :** CROWBERRY 1a

²**blackberry** \"\ *vi* -ED/-ING/-ES **:** to pick blackberries — usu. used in the form *blackberrying* ‹they went ~*ing*›

blackberry bark *n* **:** the dried bark of the rhizome and roots of any species of blackberry (genus *Rubus*) used as an astringent in diarrhea

blackberry lily *n* **:** a garden plant (*Belamcanda chinensis*) of the family Liliaceae with lilylike leaves and flower clusters whose capsule discloses when ripe a mass of seeds resembling a blackberry

blackberry liqueur *n* **:** a dark red liqueur made from blackberry juice often with the addition of red wine and alcohol

blackberry mite *n* **:** a minute mite (*Aceria essigi*) infesting the fruit of blackberries and interfering with their ripening

blackberry wine *n* **:** a variable color averaging a dark purplish red that is bluer and duller than pansy purple, redgrape, raisin, or Bokhara and bluer and less strong than dahlia purple (sense 1)

blackberry winter *n, South & Midland* **:** a period of cold weather in late spring when the blackberries are in bloom

black bile *n* [trans. of L *atra bilis*, prob. trans. of Gk *melaina cholē*] *in medieval physiology and natural philosophy* **:** a humor (sense 1b(1)) believed to be secreted by the kidneys or spleen and to cause gloominess

black-billed cuckoo \ˈ⸗,⸗-\ *n* **:** a common No. American cuckoo (*Coccyzus erythropthalmus*) that constructs a nest and hatches its own eggs and is grayish brown above with a circle of bare red skin about the eye and a solid-black bill

black bindweed *n* **1 :** a twining herb (*Polygonum convolvulus*) naturalized in America from Europe and frequently troublesome as a weed **2 :** BLACK BRYONY

blackbine \ˈ⸗,⸗\ *n* **:** BLACK BINDWEED 1

black birch *n* **1 :** SWEET BIRCH **2 :** any of several western birches; *esp* **:** RIVER BIRCH **3 :** BEECH 4

¹**blackbird** \ˈ⸗,⸗\ *n* [ME *blakbrid*, fr. *blak* black + *brid*, *bird* bird] **1 :** any of various birds of which the males are largely or entirely black: as **a** *Brit* **:** a common and familiar thrush (*Turdus merula*) that is black with orange bill and eye rim — called also *merl* **b :** any of several American birds of the family Icteridae: as (1) **:** REDWING BLACKBIRD (2) **:** PURPLE GRACKLE (3) **:** RUSTY BLACKBIRD **2 :** a Kanaka kidnaped for use as a plantation laborer esp. in Australia

²**blackbird** \"\ *vb* -ED/-ING/-S *vi* **:** to kidnap Kanakas for use or sale as laborers esp. in Australia — usu. used in the form *blackbirding* ‹that . . . man who became the terror of the Pacific in the lawless days of ~*ing* and piracy —*Times Lit. Supp.*› ~ *vt* **:** to kidnap (Kanakas) for use or sale as laborers

black·bird·er \-də(r)\ *n* **1 :** a person that blackbirds **2 :** a ship used in blackbirding

black biskop *n* **:** a large biskop (*Cymatoceps nasutus*) sometimes exceeding 100 pounds in weight that is dark mottled gray above and white below with blackish fins and a bulbous snout that overhangs the lower lip

black blight *n* **:** any of several tropical plant diseases caused by superficial sooty molds

black blister beetle *n* **:** an all-black blister beetle (*Epicauta pennsylvanica*) widespread in eastern No. America that feeds destructively on the foliage of potatoes and certain other cultivated plants as an adult

black blizzard *n* **:** a dust storm esp. in the dust-bowl area of the U.S.

black blowfly *n* **:** a rather large dark greenish black typically cold-weather blowfly (*Phormia regina*) breeding chiefly in carrion but also in open wounds of sheep and other animals including man

black blueberry *n* **1 :** a shrub (*Vaccinium atrococcum*) of the eastern U.S. having nearly black fruit without a bloom **2 :** the fruit of the black blueberry

blackboard \ˈ⸗,⸗\ *n, often attrib* **:** a thin broad piece of a hard material with a smooth surface formerly always black but now often white or tinted and used esp. in a classroom for chalk writings and drawings that are to be made visible to a group — called also *chalkboard*

blackbody \ˈ⸗ˈ⸗⸗\ *n* **:** an ideal body or surface that completely absorbs all radiant energy of any wavelength falling upon it with no reflection of energy, the temperature on the absolute scale being determined by measuring the intensity and spectral distribution of the radiated energy

blackbody radiation *n* **:** the characteristic thermal radiation emitted by a blackbody when heated — called also *Planckian radiation*; compare PLANCK RADIATION LAW 2

black bone *n, often cap both Bs* **1 :** a member of the Nosu ruling class — distinguished from *white bone* **2 :** a Kazak commoner — distinguished from *white bone*

black bonito *n* **:** COBIA

black bonnet *n, Scot* **:** REED BUNTING 1

black book *n* **:** a book listing persons that have committed offenses against morality, law, or any set of regulations or giving an account of the offenses of a person or group ‹six of the exile governments, which have indicted thousands of quisling and Axis culprits in detailed, documented *black books* —*Newsweek*› — **in one's black books :** out of one's favor **:** in disgrace with one

black-bordered oyster \ˈ⸗,⸗⸗-\ *n* **:** a large edible oyster (*Saxostrea gradiva*) of northern Australia with a bluish black shell

black bottle *n* **:** a bottle from which according to folklore a dose of poison is administered to unwanted patients in hospitals

black bottom *n* **1** *sometimes cap both Bs* **:** a tract of low-lying land with black soil **2** *often cap both Bs* [prob. fr. *black bottom* "low-lying Negro section of a southern town"] **:** an American dance popular from 1926 to 1928 with sinuous movements of the hips and rocking steps

black-bottom \ˈ⸗ˈ⸗⸗\ *vi* -ED/-ING/-S [*black bottom*] **:** to dance the black bottom

black box *n* **:** any of several Australian eucalypts with dark foliage (as *Eucalyptus bicolor, E. baueriana, E. boormani*)

blackboy \ˈ⸗,⸗\ *n* **1** *Austral* **:** BLACKFELLOW **2** *Austral* **:** GRASS TREE 1

blackboy gum *n* **:** ACAROID RESIN

black brant *n* **:** a small brownish black goose (*Branta nigricans*) having a white bar across the front of the neck and white on belly, flanks, and tail coverts, breeding along the north coast of No. America, and wintering along the west coast from Puget Sound to Lower California

black bread *n* **:** dark-colored bread; *esp* **:** a close-grained sour rye bread of central and northern Europe

black bream *n* **1** *Austral* **:** any of several dark-colored edible fishes: as **a :** an important percoid food and game fish (*Chrysophrys australis*) **b :** LUDERICK **2** *Africa* **:** GALJOEN

blackbreast \ˈ⸗,⸗\ *n* **1 :** RED-BACKED SANDPIPER **2 :** PLOVER; *esp* **:** BLACK-BELLIED PLOVER

black-browed \ˈ⸗ˈ⸗\ *adj* **:** SCOWLING, GLOOMY, FORBIDDING

black-browed albatross *n* **:** a large albatross (*Diomedea melanophrys*) with a dark mark above the eye

blackbrush \ˈ⸗,⸗\ *n* **1 :** TARBUSH 3 **2 :** a desert shrub (*Coleogyne ramosissima*) of the family Rosaceae of the southwestern U.S. with spiny twigs and solitary apetalous flowers

black bryony *n* **:** a common European twining vine (*Tamus communis*) with tuberous roots and cordate leaves

black buck *n* **1 :** the common medium-sized antelope (*Antilope cervicapra*) of India having in the male long spirally twisted closely ringed horns **2 :** SABLE ANTELOPE

black buffalo *n* **1 :** a buffalo fish (*Ictiobus niger*) chiefly of the southern part of the Mississippi valley **2 :** CAPE BUFFALO

black bullhead *n* **:** a small dusky greenish brown to black bullhead (*Ameiurus melas*) having a flattened head and plump body and being widely distributed chiefly in sluggish waters in much of temperate No. America — called also *horned pout*

black bunch grass *n* **:** GALLETA GRASS

black-burn \ˈblak(,)bərn, -,bən,-,bən\ *adj, usu cap* [fr. *Blackburn*, England] **:** of or from the county borough of Blackburn, England **:** of the kind or style prevalent in Blackburn

black·burn·ian \blakˈbərnēən\ *or* **blackburnian warbler** \(ˈ)⸗ˈ⸗⸗⸗-\ *n* -S *often cap B* [Mrs. Hugh *Blackburn*, 18th cent. Englishwoman + E *-ian*] **:** a No. American warbler (*Dendroica fusca* syn. *blackburniae*) strongly marked in the male with orange, yellow, and black on the head and neck and with an orange-yellow breast

blackbush \ˈ⸗,⸗\ *n* **:** BLACKBRUSH 2

blackbutt \ˈ⸗,⸗\ *n* **:** any of several Australian timber trees of the genus *Eucalyptus* (esp. *E. pilularis*) in which the bark of the lower part of the trunk resembles charred wood

black cabbage tree *n* **:** a tree (*Melanodendron integrifolium*) of the family Compositae of the island of St. Helena having dark alternate oblong or lanceolate leaves and a campanulate involucre about the flower head

black caiman *n* **:** a very large So. American reptile (*Caiman niger*) that is related to the typical crocodiles but has the snout rounded like that of the alligator and is abundant in parts of the Amazon drainage

black calabash *n* **:** a tree (*Crescentia ovata*) of tropical America having a thin-shelled gourdlike fruit

black calla *n* **:** an ornamental aroid (*Arum palaestinum*) cultivated in greenhouses for its dark purple or almost black spathe somewhat resembling that of the calla

black cancer *n* **:** MELANOMA

black canker *n* **1** *archaic* **:** severe diphtheria **2 :** any of several plant diseases characterized by dark-colored cankers: as **a :** INK DISEASE **b :** a disease of willows caused by a fungus (*Physalospora miyabeana*) — called also *willow blight*

blackcap \ˈ⸗,⸗\ *n* **1** *also* **blackcap raspberry :** a black-fruited raspberry (*Rubus occidentalis*) native to eastern No. America that is the source of several cultivated varieties — called also *black raspberry* **2 :** any of several birds with black heads or crowns: as **a :** a small European warbler (*Sylvia atricapilla*) with a black crown **b :** CHICKADEE **c :** WILSON'S WARBLER **3 :** the common cattail (*Typha latifolia*)

black cap *n* **:** the black cap worn by a British judge when passing sentence of death

black-capped \ˈ⸗ˈ⸗\ *adj, of a bird* **:** having the top of the head black

black-capped chickadee *n* **:** CHICKADEE; *esp* **:** the common chickadee (*Parus atricapillus* or *Penthestes atricapillus*) of northern and eastern No. America having the throat and crown of the head jet black — called also *willow tit*

black-capped petrel *n* **:** a heavy-bodied petrel (*Pterodroma hasitata*) with a dark crown and whitish nape, neck, forehead, and tail coverts that is now rare and that has unknown breeding grounds

black-capped vireo *n* **:** a vireo (*Vireo atricapillus*) of western No. America having the top and sides of the head black

black caraway *n* **:** an herb (*Nigella sativa*) of the Mediterranean region having pungent seeds that are used like those of caraway — called also *black cumin*

black carib *n, usu cap B&C* **:** a member of an ethnic group of mixed Negro and Carib ancestry, Arawakan speech, and Caribbean-Arawakan culture that originated on St. Vincent Island but was deported in the late 18th century to Roatán Island and now lives chiefly along the Caribbean coast of Honduras, Guatemala, and British Honduras

black carpet beetle *n* **:** CARPET BEETLE b

black cat *n* **:** FISHER 2

black catechu *n* **:** CATECHU 1a

black cattle *n, archaic* **:** beef cattle of any color

black cayuga *n, usu cap B&C* [fr. *Cayuga*, lake and county, N.Y.] **:** CAYUGA DUCK

black chaff *n* **:** a disease of wheat caused by a bacterium (*Xanthomonas translucens undulosa*) and producing dark stripes running lengthwise of the chaff

black chalk *n* **:** a dark carbonaceous clay, shale, or slate used as a pigment or crayon

black chamber *n, usu cap B&C* [trans. of F *chambre noire*] **:** a government office or department engaged in cryptographic work, esp. cryptanalysis

black chaser *n* **:** BLACK SNAKE 1a

black check *n* **:** a defect common in western hemlock characterized by pockets in the bark containing resin

black cherry *n* **1 :** SWEET CHERRY **2 a :** a large American wild cherry (*Prunus serotina*) with dark bark, thick oval leaves, white flowers in racemes, and black astringent fruits — called also *rum cherry* **b :** the strong reddish brown wood of this tree used esp. for cabinetwork **3 :** any cultivated cherry having black fruit

black cherry aphid *n* **:** a large black shiny aphid (*Myzus cerasi*) feeding on and causing curling and distortion of the terminal growth of various cherries

black cherry fruit fly *n* **:** a small black fruit fly (*Rhagoletis fausta*) having a larva that burrows in and feeds on the fruit of native and cultivated cherries in western No. America — compare APPLE MAGGOT

black-chinned hummingbird \ˈ⸗,⸗-\ *n* **:** a hummingbird (*Archilochus alexandri*) of western No. America, the male being greenish above with the upper part of the throat velvety black, the lower a brilliantly iridescent violet, and the under parts of the body dull white

black chokeberry *n* **:** a shrub (*Pyrus melanocarpa*) of eastern No. America with white flowers like those of the pear and nearly black fruit

black choler *n* **:** BLACK BILE

black cinnamon *n* **:** BAYBERRY 1

black citrus aphid *n* **:** a black aphid (*Toxoptera aurantii*) widely distributed in warm regions that feeds on a number of cultivated plants and is considered to be a vector of tristeza disease of citrus in Brazil

black-clawed crab \ˈ⸗,⸗-\ *n* **:** a small active crab (*Lophopanopeus bellus*) having claws with black tips that is common along rocky shores of Puget Sound and adjacent areas

black clergy *n* **:** monks of the Russian Orthodox Church — distinguished from *white clergy*

black coal *n* **:** BITUMINOUS COAL

blackcoat \ˈ⸗,⸗\ *n* **1 :** CLERGYMAN — usu. used disparagingly **2** *Brit* **:** a member of the black-coated class

black-coated \ˈ⸗ˈ⸗⸗\ *adj, Brit* **:** WHITE-COLLAR

blackcock \ˈ⸗,⸗\ *n* [ME *blakcok*, fr. *blak* black + *cok* cock] **:** BLACK GROUSE; *specif* **:** the male black grouse

black cockatoo *n* **:** any of several Australian cockatoos (genus *Calyptorhynchus*) that are chiefly rusty black but distinguished by different bright colors of their tail feathers

black cod *n* **:** SABLEFISH

black code *n, often cap B&C* [fr. *Black Code*, a code of laws promulgated in Louisiana in the 18th cent. to define the status of the Negro, trans. of F *Code Noir*] **:** a code of laws esp. as adopted by some southern states of the U.S. shortly after the Civil War limiting the rights of Negroes

black cohosh *n* **:** a bugbane (*Cimicifuga racemosa*)

black comb *n* **:** a disease of Australian pullets resembling and perhaps identical with blue comb

black copper *n* **1 :** MELACONITE **2 :** a product containing usu. 70 to 99 percent of copper formed in smelting copper ores direct to metal without first forming matte or by remelting old or scrap copper and copper alloys

black coral *n* **:** an antipatharian coral having a black horny axis

black core *n* **:** a flaw in ceramic ware attributed to the decomposition of iron pyrites

black cosmos *n* **:** a Mexican perennial herb (*Cosmos atrosanguineus*) grown for its dark purplish red flowers

black cotton *or* **black cotton soil** *n* [so called fr. its suitability for growing cotton] **:** a soil formed in the Deccan region of India by the disintegration of a black lava

black cottonwood *n* **1 :** a tree (*Populus trichocarpa*) of the Pacific coast of No. America with dark green leaves shining above and rusty or silvery beneath **2 :** SWAMP COTTONWOOD

black cow *n* **:** a dark carbonated drink (as root beer) with ice cream in it

black crab *n* **:** a brilliantly marked edible land crab (*Gecarcinus ruricola*) of southern Florida and the West Indies that is noted for its annual mass migrations to the sea for the hatching of the eggs and is considered a great delicacy

black crappie *n* **:** a common sunfish (*Pomoxis nigro-maculatus*) that is black-mottled on a silvery ground, widely distributed throughout the Mississippi drainage and much of the eastern U.S., and regarded as both a food and game fish through most of its range — called also *calico bass*

black-crested monkey \ˈ⸗ˈ⸗⸗-\ *n* **:** SIMPAI

black-crested titmouse *n* **:** a titmouse (*Parus atricristatus*) of the southwestern U.S. and Mexico

black croaker *n* **:** any of several marine fishes of the Pacific coast of America: **a :** a croaker (*Sciaena saturna*) that is dusky blue or blackish above and silvery below **b :** SPOTFIN CROAKER **c :** SARGO 2

black crowberry *n* **:** CROWBERRY 1a

black-crowned night heron \ˈ⸗,⸗-\ *n* **:** a No. American night heron (*Nycticorax nycticorax hoactli*)

black cumin *n* **:** BLACK CARAWAY

black curlew *n* **:** the Old World glossy ibis (*Plegadis falcinellus*)

black currant *n* **1 :** a European currant (*Ribes nigrum*) with loosely flowered drooping racemes of yellow flowers and black aromatic fruit **2 :** WILD BLACK CURRANT **3 :** NORTHERN BLACK CURRANT

black-currant rust *n* **:** the white pine blister rust in its uredinial and telial stages

black cutworm *n* **:** an abundant almost cosmopolitan cutworm (*Agrotis ypsilon*) of dark color and waxen appearance — called also *greasy cutworm*

black cyanide *n* **:** CALCIUM CYANIDE

black cypress *n* **:** a bald cypress (*Taxodium distichum*)

black cypress pine *n* **:** an Australian evergreen coniferous tree (*Callitris calcarata*) having small flattened scales as leaves and being valued for its timber and resin

black dammar *also* **black damar** *n* **:** a resin obtained mostly from an East Indian tree (*Canarium strictum*)

blackdamp \ˈ⸗,⸗\ *n* [¹*black* + *damp* (gas)] **:** a nonexplosive mine gas that is heavier than air, that consists of a mixture of carbon dioxide and other gases, and that will not support life or flame — called also *chokedamp*; compare FIREDAMP

black death *n, sometimes cap B&D* **:** a form of plague that was epidemic in Asia and Europe in the 14th century and was marked by hemorrhages into the skin forming large dark patches

black diamond *n* **1 black diamonds** *pl* **:** ¹COAL 3a **2 :** ³CARBONADO **3 :** dense black hematite that takes a polish like metal and is sometimes used for intaglios

black disease *n* **:** a rapidly fatal toxemia of sheep characterized by liver necrosis and subcutaneous hemorrhage resulting from growth of an anaerobic toxin-producing bacterium (*Clostridium novyi* or *Clostridium oedematiens*) in liver tissue damaged by the common liver fluke — compare BLACKLEG, BRAXY, LIVER ROT, MALIGNANT EDEMA

black dog *n* **1 :** a coin made of base silver or pewter **2 :** depression of spirits **:** BLUES, DEJECTION, MELANCHOLY, DESPONDENCY ‹shake the *black dog* from your back —J.B.Cabell›

black dogwood *n* **:** ALDER BUCKTHORN

black dot *n* **:** DARTROSE

black draft *n* **1 :** an infusion of senna with magnesium sulfate used as a purgative **2 :** BLACK DRINK

black drink *n* **:** a drink prepared from the leaves of the yaupon by the Indians of the southeastern U.S. as a medicine and ceremonial beverage

black drongo *n* **:** a small-billed purplish black drongo (*Dicrurus macrocercus*) having a long deeply forked tail and being common in India and southeastern Asia

black drop *n* **1 :** VINEGAR OF OPIUM **2 :** an optical phenomenon observed in transits of Mercury and Venus near the instant of internal contact when the planet seems for the moment attached to the sun's limb by a dark ligament that is probably due to irradiation and the imperfections of the telescope — called also *black ligament*

black drum *n* **:** a large sluggish gray or coppery croaker (*Pogonias cromis*) of the eastern coast of No. America that is usu. considered inferior as a food or sport fish

black duck *n* **:** any of various ducks that are predominantly black or dusky in color: as **a :** a common duck (*Anas rubripes*) of the northeastern U.S. and Canada related to the mallard but having in both sexes plumage that is chiefly dusky brown with lighter edging to the feathers **b :** SCOTER; *esp* **:** BLACK SCOTER **c :** RING-NECKED DUCK **d :** a brownish duck (*Anas superciliosa*) of Australia, New Zealand, and Polynesia highly regarded as a game and table bird

black eagle *n* **1 :** a young golden eagle — used esp. when the bird is supposed to be a representative of a separate species **2 :** a large powerful eagle (*Aquila verreauxii*) of mountainous parts of southern and eastern Africa that is chiefly black but has white tail coverts and a V-shaped band across the shoulders

black-eared bushtit \'=,=\ *n* **:** a bushtit that has conspicuously black cheek patches (as members of several races of the southwestern U.S., Mexico, and Central America)

black-ears \'=,=\ *n pl but sing or pl in constr* **:** LONGEAR SUNFISH

black earth *n* **:** CHERNOZEM

black east indian *n, usu cap B&E&I* **:** a small domestic duck of a breed having black plumage with greenish reflections and an olive-green bill

black ebony *n* **:** the black or nearly black wood of any of several ebony trees (genus *Diospyros*); *usu* **:** the heartwood of such a tree

blacked *past of* BLACK

black elderberry *n* **1 :** BLUE ELDER **2 :** a common elder (*Sambucus canadensis*) of central and eastern No. America

black·en \'blakən\ *vb* **blackened; blackened; blackening** \-k(ə)niŋ\ **blackens** [ME *blaknen*, fr. *blak* black + *-enen* -en — more at BLACK] *vi* **1 :** to become black **2** *of paper* **:** to become darker in color than intended because of improper calendering ~ *vt* **1 :** to make black ⟨the house burned down, leaving only a ~*ed* chimney⟩ ⟨mosquitoes capable of ~*ing* a man with their bodies within a minute —E.T.Gilliard⟩ ⟨the shadow of the possibility of famine ~*ed* everybody's life —G.E.Fussell⟩ **2 :** to speak evil of ⟨~ the past rather than to report it faithfully —Ernest Beaglehole⟩ **:** make infamous ⟨he ~*s* opponents by giving them . . . names such as Barbarian and Philistine —*Times Lit. Supp.*⟩ **3 :** [3]BLACK 3a, 3b, 3d

black end *n* **1 :** a nonparasitic disease of the pear characterized by a blackening of the epidermis and flesh of the calyx end and believed to be caused by a disturbed water relation aggravated by uncongenial stocks **2 :** a disease of the banana caused by fungi (esp. *Gloeosporium musarum*) and characterized by a discoloration or rot of the fruit stem

black·en·er \-k(ə)nə(r)\ *n* -s **:** a leather worker that brushes blackening compound onto the grain side of tanned hides — called also *blacker*

blackening *n* -s [ME *blakning*, fr. gerund of *blaknen* to blacken] **1 :** BLACKING **2 :** DENSITY 5b

[1]**black·er** \'blakə(r)\ *comparative of* BLACK

[2]**blacker** \"\ *n* -s [[3]*black* + *-er*] **:** any of several workers that apply blacking to articles: as **a :** BOOTBLACK **b :** BLACKENER

blackest *superlative of* BLACK

blackey *var of* BLACKIE

black eye *n* **1 a :** a darkening of the skin about the eye resulting from a bruise **b** (1) **:** a severe defeat **:** SETBACK, REBUFF ⟨voters gave the administration a *black eye*⟩ (2) **:** a discrediting **:** a bad reputation ⟨pleasant views may greet visitors instead of sore spots which might give the community a *black eye* —*N.Y. Times*⟩ ⟨the word "aristocracy" in this country has a *black eye* —A.N.Whitehead⟩ **2 :** an eye with a very dark iris

blackeye \'=,=\ *or* **blackeye bean** *or* **black-eyed bean** \'=,=-\ *n* [so called fr. its black hilum] **:** COWPEA 1

black-eyed pea *also* **blackeye pea** *n* **1 :** COWPEA 1 **2** *black-eyed pea* **:** a tropical vine (*Dolichos sphaerospermus*) having a seed that is used in the West Indies for food

black-eyed su·san \-'süz°n\ *n, usu cap S* [*black-eyed* (fr. [1]*black* + *eyed*) + *Susan* (the name)] **1 :** either of two coneflowers, one (*Rudbeckia hirta*) of central and eastern No. America and one (*R. serotina*) of the southeastern U.S., having flower heads with deep yellow to orange rays and dark conical disks **2 :** FLOWER-OF-AN-HOUR **3** *also* **black-eyed susan vine :** a tropical African vinelike herb (*Thunbergia alata*) with yellow flowers having a dark purple center

blackface \'=,=\ *n, often attrib* **1 :** a sheep with a black face; *esp* **:** one of the Scottish Blackface breed **2 a :** makeup for Negro roles, esp. comic ones ⟨he appeared in ~⟩ ⟨a ~ comedian⟩ **b :** an actor that plays a comic Negro role esp. in a minstrel show **3 :** BOLDFACE 2

black-faced \'='=\ *adj* **:** BOLD-FACED 3

black-faced highland *n, usu cap B&H* **:** SCOTTISH BLACKFACE

black-fast \'='=\ *vi* **:** to undergo a black fast

black fast *n* **:** a fast of the most severe kind

blackfeet *pl of* BLACKFOOT

blackfellow \'=,=(,)=\ *n* **:** an Australian aborigine

blackfellows' bread *n* **:** the usu. large sclerotium of an Australian pore fungus (*Polyporus mylittae*) used as food by the aborigines

black fever *n* **:** any of various febrile diseases characterized by a hemorrhagic rash: as **a :** KALA-AZAR **b :** ROCKY MOUNTAIN SPOTTED FEVER **c :** TYPHUS 1a

black fiber *n* **:** KITTUL

black fig *n* **1 :** a West Indian tree (*Ficus laurifolia*) with thick leathery leaves and inedible fruit **2 :** MORETON BAY FIG

[1]**black-figure** \'=,=\ *or* **black-figured** \'='=\ *adj* **:** of, belonging to, or constituting a style of ceramic painting practiced by or in imitation of Greeks of the 6th century B.C. in which the decoration is in black with occasional added details in white slip on the red body clay of the vessel and in which the subjects are usu. drawn from mythology, athletic events, or the hunt in an archaic and stiff style ⟨a *black-figure* vase⟩ ⟨*black-figure* ware⟩ — compare POLYCHROME, RED-FIGURE

[2]**black-figure** \'='=\ *n* [*black-figure*] **:** black-figure ware

blackfin \'=,=\ *also* **blackfin cisco** *n* **:** a whitefish (*Leucichthys nigripinnis*) of the Great Lakes valued as a food fish

blackfin shark *n* **:** BLACKTIP SHARK

blackfin snapper *n* **:** a common West Indian market fish (*Lutjanus buccanella*)

blackfire \'=,=\ *n* **:** a disease of tobacco caused by a bacterium (*Pseudomonas angulata*) and characterized by angular leaf spots without a surrounding halo that are at first dark green but become zonate and turn grayish, tan, or dark brown and may drop out leaving ragged holes — compare WILDFIRE

blackfish \'=,=\ *n* **1 :** any of several dark-colored fishes: as **a :** the female salmon just after spawning **b :** a deep-sea stromateoid fish (*Centrolophus niger*) of the Atlantic, esp. of the European coast **c :** TAUTOG **d :** RIVER BLACKFISH **e :** BLACK SEA BASS 1 **f :** a small but important food fish (*Dallia pectoralis*) common in shallow freshwaters (as sphagnum swamps) of Alaska and Siberia and noted for its resistance to cold **g :** a California cyprinid fish (*Orthodon microlepidotus*) **h :** any of several marine Australian bass-type food fishes of the genus *Girella*; *esp* **:** LUDERICK **i** *Austral* **:** a food and game fish of Australia that is either identical with or closely related to the Bermuda chub **j :** any of several small serranid fishes (genus *Dinoperca*) of the Indian ocean that are highly esteemed as food **k :** GALJOEN **l :** BOWFIN **2 :** any of several small toothed whales (genus *Globicephala*) related to the dolphins and found in all the warmer seas

blackfisher \'=,==\ *n* [*blackfish* + *-er*] *Scot* **:** one that engages in blackfishing

blackfishing \'=,==\ *n* [*blackfish* + *-ing*] *Scot* **:** the illegal catching of blackfish (sense 1a)

black flag *n* **:** a flag black in color or having a device on a black field (as a pirate flag) — see JOLLY ROGER

black flower *n* **:** a bunchflower (*Melanthium virginicum*) of the eastern and southern U.S.

black flux *n, metallurgy* **:** a reducing flux composed of powdered carbon and alkali-metal carbonate

blackfly \'=,=\ *n* **:** any of several black or dark-colored insects: as **a :** a small two-winged biting fly of *Simulium* and related genera whose larvae live in flowing usu. clear streams — called also *buffalo gnat* **b :** BEAN APHID **c :** CITRUS BLACKFLY **d :** GREENHOUSE THRIPS

[1]**blackfoot** \'=,=\ *n, pl* **blackfeet** *sometimes sing in constr, or* **blackfoot** *usu cap* [trans. of Blackfoot *Siksika*] **1 a :** an Indian confederacy comprising the Siksika (sense 1a), the Bloods, and the Piegan ⟨the *Blackfeet* were the toughest —Chad Oliver⟩ ⟨gave the *Blackfoot* their present home —Edward Sapir⟩ — called also *Siksika* **b :** a member of a people belonging to the Blackfoot confederacy ⟨the heart of a *Blackfoot* —Washington Irving⟩ ⟨the official . . . calls himself a *Blackfeet* —Marcus Rosenblum⟩ **c :** the Algonquian language of the Blackfeet **2 :** SIKSIKA 1 **3 :** SIHASAPA 2

[2]**blackfoot** \"\ *n* [[1]*black* + *foot*] *Scot* **:** a lovers' go-between

black-footed albatross \'=,==-\ *n* **:** an albatross (*Diomedea nigripes*) of the Pacific that is chiefly blackish with dusky bill and black feet and legs — called also *gooney*

black-footed cat *n* **:** a southwestern African desert wildcat (*Felis nigripes*) that resembles a dwarf serval, that is colored cream or grayish faun and mottled and striped with black or dark brown, and that is the smallest of the true cats and readily hybridizes with domesticated cats

black-footed ferret *n* **:** an American weasel (*Mustela nigripes*) related to the European polecat and resembling a yellow mink with dark feet, tail, and mask

black fox *n* **1 a :** a melanistic red fox **b :** the fur or pelt of a melanistic red fox at one time much prized because of its rarity and the beauty of its pure-black fur **2 :** SILVER FOX 1a

black friar *n, often cap B&F* [so called fr. the black mantle worn by Dominicans] **:** a Dominican friar

black frost *n* **:** frost or cold so intense as to blacken vegetation and usu. unaccompanied by hoarfrost

black fungus *n* [so called fr. the production of dark excrescences that look like charred spots] **:** FIRE FUNGUS 1

black game *n* **1 :** BLACK GROUSE **2 :** one of a black variety of the old English Game fowl

black gang *n* [so called fr. the grime traditionally associated with them] **:** the stokers or the engineer's crew on a ship

black garget *n* [so called fr. the dark color of the udder in the late stages of the disease] **:** BLUE BAG 2

black ginger *n* **:** the rootstock of ginger dried and unscraped — called also *coated ginger, unpeeled ginger, unscraped ginger;* distinguished from *white ginger*

black gold *n* **:** a dark-colored product containing gold or resembling gold in value: as **a :** MALDONITE **b :** PETROLEUM

black gown *n* **:** a Jesuit missionary to the Indians of the western U.S. esp. in the 19th century

black gram *n* **1 :** HORSE GRAM **2 :** URD

black grama *n* **1 a :** HAIRY GRAMA **b :** a grama (*Bouteloua eriopoda*) important as a forage grass esp. of the plains and western coastal region of No. America — compare BLUE GRAMA **2 :** GALLETA GRASS

black granite *n* **:** a dark-colored intrusive rock (as diorite or gabbro) — not used technically

black grass *n* **1 :** a grasslike rush (*Juncus gerardi*) of salt marshes that is good for hay **2 :** SLENDER FOXTAIL **3 :** SPINY ROLLING GRASS **4 :** BLACK MEDIC

black greasewood *n* **:** GREASEWOOD 1

black grouper *n* **1 :** BLACK JEWFISH **2 :** a large dark grouper (*Mycteroperca bonaci*) having a protruding jaw and widely distributed in the warmer waters of the Atlantic **3 :** SPOTTED JEWFISH

black grouse *n* **:** a large grouse (*Lyrurus tetrix*) widely distributed in western Asia and Europe including most of the heath districts of England and Scotland of which the male is chiefly black with white wing patches and outwardly curved tail feathers and the female has barred and mottled plumage — see BLACKCOCK, GRAY HEN

black growth *n* **:** a forest or woods consisting largely of conifers (as hemlock, pine, and spruce)

black grub *n* **:** a larval fluke (family Strigeidae) encysted in the flesh of fish (as black bass)

black grunt *n* **1 :** TRIPLETAIL 1a **2 :** any of several grunts with dark coloration; *esp* **:** a grunt (*Haemulon bonariense*) widely distributed in the western Atlantic from Florida to Argentina

[1]**black·guard** \'blagə(r)d, -aigə-, -a,gärd, -ai,gärd, -ak,gärd, -,gäd\ *n* [[1]*black* + *guard*] **1** *obs* **a :** the kitchen servants of a noble or royal household **b :** the servants and hangers-on of an army **c :** a black, black-clothed, or villainous retinue **d :** street urchins esp. as employed in blacking shoes, carrying torches, or running errands **e :** the criminal element of a community **2** *obs* **:** a vagabond child **:** a street urchin esp. as employed in blacking shoes, carrying torches, or running errands **3 a :** one whose conduct or character is disgraceful **:** a contemptible scoundrel — a generalized term of abuse **b :** a foulmouthed person **4 :** [5]SNUFF 1a **syn** see VILLAIN

[2]**blackguard** \"\ *adj* **1** *obs* **:** of or relating to a shoeblack or street urchin **2 :** BLACKGUARDLY ⟨my schoolfellows were a very ~ set —George Borrow⟩ ⟨~ talk⟩

[3]**blackguard** \"\ *vb* -ED/-ING/-S *vi* **1 :** to act in a ruffianly or scoundrelly manner **:** engage in disorderly behavior **:** run riot ⟨~*ing* about the streets till he got his head cut and his clothes torn —Charles Lever⟩ **2 :** to talk obscenely ~ *vt* **:** to talk about or address in abusive or obscene terms ⟨he ~*ed* the war, and the people that started it —Mark Twain⟩

black·guard·ery \-d(ə)rē, -ri\ *or* **black·guard·ry** \-dr-\ *n* -ES **:** behavior characteristic of a blackguard (sense 3a)

black·guard·ism \-,dizəm\ *n* -S **:** behavior characteristic of a blackguard (sense 3a); *esp* **:** use of abusive language

black·guard·ly \-,dlē, -li\ *adj* **:** being, belonging to, or characteristic of a ruffian or scoundrel ⟨~ street rows —Rudyard Kipling⟩ ⟨a ~ fellow⟩; *esp* **:** SCURRILOUS ⟨~ language⟩

black guava *n* **:** a tree (*Guettarda argentea*) of Jamaica and Guiana with black edible fruit

black guillemot *n* **:** a small red-footed guillemot (*Cepphus grylle*) that is black with white wing patches in summer and largely mottled with white in winter — called also *white guillemot*

black gum *n* **1 :** either of two trees of the genus *Nyssa*: **a :** a tree (*Nyssa sylvatica*) of the eastern, central, and southern U.S. having close-grained wood, entire obovate or ovate leaves, and small blue-black drupaceous fruits with nearly ribless stones — called also *pepperidge, sour gum, tupelo* **b :** a tree (*N. biflora*) of the southern U.S. with spatulate leaves and ribbed stones **2 :** WHITE FIR 1a(1) **3 :** BLACK SALLY

black gyrfalcon *n* **:** a very dark slaty gyrfalcon (*Falco rusticolus obsoletus*) of northern No. America

black hand *n, often cap B&H* [fr. *Black Hand*, a lawless Sicilian and Italian-American secret society of the late 19th and 20th centuries, an imitation of an Andalusian anarchist society of the 19th century, trans. of It *Mano Nera*, trans. of Sp *Mano Negra*; fr. the black hand on their emblem] **:** a lawless secret society practicing terrorism, extortion, or other crimes

black-hand·er \'=,=də(r)\ *n* **1 :** a member of a black hand society **2 :** EXTORTIONER

black harry *n, often cap H* **:** BLACK SEA BASS 1

black haw *n* **1 :** a shrub (*Viburnum prunifolium*) bearing cymes of white flowers and bluish black drupes **2 a :** SOUTHERN BUCKTHORN **b :** FALSE BUCKTHORN **3 :** either of two trees (*Bumelia tenax* and *B. lanuginosa*) of the southern U.S. **4** *also* **black hawthorn :** a hawthorn (*Crataegus douglasii*) of the western U.S.

black hazel *n* **:** HOP HORNBEAM

[1]**blackhead** \'=,=\ *n* **1 :** any of various birds with more or less black about the head; *esp* **:** SCAUP DUCK **2 :** COMEDO **3 :** a destructive disease of turkeys and in a milder form of chickens and other related birds caused by a protozoan (*Histomonas meleagridis*) that invades the intestinal ceca and liver causing tissue destruction and necrosis and intense systemic reaction and that is commonly transmitted from bird to bird by fecal contamination but maintained in nature by intermediate stages developed in the cecal worm (*Heterakis gallinae*) from which it may pass directly to the bird — called also *enterohepatitis, infectious enterohepatitis* **4 :** a glochidium larva of a freshwater clam or mussel attached to the skin or gills of any of several freshwater fishes and with the cells of its host growing around it in a blackish mass

[2]**blackhead** \"\ *adj* **:** having a black head

blackhead disease *n* **1 :** a disease of the banana caused by eelworms of the family Tylenchidae **2 :** a rot of the banana rootstock caused by a fungus (*Thielaviopsis paradoxa*)

black-headed budworm \'='==-\ *n* **:** the bright green brownish headed (black when young) larva of a small variably marked grayish moth (*Acleris variana*) that is a serious pest of hemlock, spruce, and fir throughout much of the northern U.S. and Canada feeding on the new foliage and webbing it into mats

black-headed grosbeak *n* **:** a grosbeak (*Pheucticus melanocephalus*) of western No. America that in the adult male has the head black, the neck, rump, and underparts orange-brown, and the belly and under-wing parts yellow, the female being chiefly brown

black-headed gull *n* **:** any of certain small gulls with a black head

blackhead minnow *n* **:** FATHEAD MINNOW

blackhead persian *n, often cap B & usu cap P* **:** a sheep of an African breed having the head and neck black and the body white that is much used in crossing to introduce superior mutton quality or hardiness into other breeds

blackheart \'=,=\ *n* **1 :** a heart cherry having a dark flesh and skin **2 :** WHORTLEBERRY 1 **3 :** any of several plants of the genus *Polygonum* having black seeds **4 :** RED-BACKED SANDPIPER **5 :** a plant disease in which the central tissues blacken; *specif* **:** a disease of potato tubers caused by high temperature or poor ventilation **6 :** a dark coloration of undetermined cause in the wood of certain hardwoods (as maple and ash)

blackhearted \'='==\ *adj* **:** having a wicked disposition **:** MALIGNANT

black heat *n* **:** a heat just below a dull-red heat at which iron or steel turns black

black heath *n* **:** a European heath (*Erica cinerea*)

black hellebore *n* **1 :** either of two hellebores: **a :** an herb (*Helleborus orientalis*) with greenish to dark purple flowers **b :** CHRISTMAS ROSE **2 :** the root of black hellebore **3 :** BLACK SANICLE 1

black hemlock *n* **:** MOUNTAIN HEMLOCK

black henbane *n* **:** HENBANE 1a

black hickory *n* **1 :** any of several hickories: as **a :** MOCKERNUT **b :** any of several pignut trees (esp. *Carya glabra*) **2 :** BLACK WALNUT 1

black hills beetle *n, usu cap B&H* [fr. *Black Hills*, mountains in So. Dak. and Wyo.] **:** a bark beetle (*Dendroctonus ponderosae*) of the Rocky mountain area that feeds chiefly on mature ponderosa pine destroying the cambium and causing the death of great numbers of valuable timber trees

black hills spruce *n, usu cap B&H* **:** a compact tree (*Picea glauca densata*) of central No. America that is used for ornament and hedges and has bright green or bluish green leaves

black hole *n, sometimes cap B&H* [fr. *Black Hole (of Calcutta)*, a military lockup in Calcutta, India, where 146 Europeans were disastrously incarcerated in 1756] **:** a place of confinement for punishment; *specif* **:** a military lockup

black hollander *n, usu cap H* **:** ALMOND WILLOW 1

black horehound *n* **:** an ill-smelling European herb (*Ballota nigra*) with ovate rugose leaves and whorls of dark purple flowers — called also *black archangel, fetid horehound, stinking horehound*

black horse *n* **:** HOG SUCKER

black house *n, Scot* **:** a low windowless cottage

black huckleberry *n* **1 :** a rather low shrub (*Gaylussacia baccata*) of eastern No. America that produces a shining black somewhat acid drupe and that is the best known of the huckleberries **2 :** the fruit of the black huckleberry; *broadly* **:** any huckleberry black in color — compare DANGLEBERRY

black hu·ron *n* **:** LARGEMOUTH BLACK BASS

black hurts *n pl* [*hurts*, pl. of *hurt* (hurtleberry)] **:** the fruit of any plant of the genus *Gaylussacia*

black ice *n* **:** dark-colored glacial ice formed by freezing of silt-laden water — compare BLUE ICE, WHITE ICE

black·ie *also* **black·ey** *or* **blacky** \'blakē, -ki\ *n, pl* **blackies** *also* **blackeys** *or* **blackies :** one that is black: as **a :** a person belonging to a darkly pigmented race; *esp* **:** NEGRO **b :** any of several largely black or dark-colored birds: as (1) *Brit* **:** BLACKBIRD 1a (2) **:** RING-NECKED DUCK (3) **:** CANADA GOOSE (4) **:** BLACK DUCK a

black indian hemp *n, usu cap I* **:** INDIAN HEMP 1

blacking *n* -S [fr. gerund of [3]*black*] **:** a substance that is applied to objects and makes them black: as **a :** a paste or liquid used in shining black shoes **b :** a carbon facing for foundry molds or cores usu. consisting of charred wood, coal, coke, or graphite ground to a powder

black ipecac *n* **1 :** a tropical American shrub (*Psychotria emetica*) **2 :** the powerfully emetic root of the black ipecac

black ironwood *n* **1 :** a shrub or small tree (*Krugiodendron ferreum*) of the family Rhamnaceae of southern Florida and the West Indies having hard dark very heavy wood **2 :** a southern African timber tree (*Olea laurifolia*) with dark wood

black·ish \'blakish, -kēsh\ *adj* [ME *blakish*, fr. *blak* black + *-ish*] **:** somewhat black

black italian poplar *n, usu cap I* **:** a rapid-growing hybrid poplar produced by crossing an Old World black poplar (*Populus nigra*) with the cottonwood of eastern No. America and widely used in screen plantings, often being treated by the nursery trade as a separate species (*P. serotina*)

black ivory *n* **:** Negroes subject to economic exploitation esp. in plantation industry; *specif* **:** Negro slaves ⟨the old rich traffic in *black ivory* is no more —Lawrence & Sylvia Martin⟩

[1]**black·jack** \'blak,jak\ *n* -S [[1]*black* + *jack* (jacket)] *archaic Scot* **:** a black leather jerkin

[2]**blackjack** \"\ *n* -S **1** [[1]*black* + *jack* (vessel)] **:** a capacious vessel for beer or ale usu. of tar-coated leather **2** *or* **black jack** [[1]*black* + *jack* (man); fr. its presence in lead ore, considered by the miners an impish intrusion of a worthless substance] **:** SPHALERITE **3** [[1]*black* + *jack* (bird)] **:** any of several dark-colored No. American ducks: as **a :** SCAUP DUCK **b :** BLACK DUCK a **c :** RUDDY DUCK **4** [[1]*black* + *jack* (instrument)] **:** a small striking weapon typically consisting at the striking end of a leather-enclosed piece of lead or other heavy metal and at the handle end of a strap or springy shaft that increases the force of impact **5** *or* **blackjack oak** [so called fr. the club-shaped leaves] **:** a common often somewhat scrubby oak (*Quercus marilandica*) of the southeastern and southern U.S. that has a black bark, broad-ovate leaves, and a rather large ovoid-oblong acorn and that tends to form dense thickets — called also *scrub oak* **6** [[1]*black* + *jack* (knave of cards)] **a :** TWENTY-ONE **b :** a card game identical with twenty-one except that additional rules make it possible for any player to become the dealer **c :** an ace and a face card or ten received by a player as his first two cards in the game of blackjack (sense 6a or 6b) — called also *natural*

[3]**blackjack** \"\ *vt* -ED/-ING/-S **1 :** to strike with a blackjack **2 :** to coerce by threats or pressure

blackjack pine *n* [[1]*black* + *jack* (*pine*)] **:** JACK PINE 1

black jew *n, often cap B&J* **1 :** a member of a community of persons professing Judaism as their religion but belonging to the same darkly pigmented biological type as their neighbors who do not profess Judaism; *esp* **:** FALASHA **2 a :** one of a Negro Christian sect called the Church of God and Saints of Christ that holds the Negro race to be descended from the ten lost tribes of Israel, observes the Jewish Sabbath, and practices immersion and foot washing **b :** COMMANDMENT KEEPER

black jewfish *n* **:** a very large grouper (*Garrupa negrita*) sometimes weighing several hundred pounds and widely distributed in the warmer parts of the western Atlantic

black kernel *or* **black kernel disease** *n* **:** a disease of rice caused by a fungus (*Curvularia lunata*) and characterized by a dark discoloration of the kernels

black kingfish *n* : COBIA
black kirghiz *n, usu cap B&K* : KARA KIRGHIZ
black kite *n* [so called fr. its dark color] : a large brown hawk (*Milvus migrans*) that feeds chiefly on carrion and is an important scavenger over much of the Old World
black knot *n* **1** : a destructive disease of plum and cherry trees characterized by black excrescences on the branches and caused by a fungus (*Dibotryon morbosa*) **2** : a destructive disease of the gooseberry characterized by black excrescences on the branches and caused by a fungus (*Dibotryon ribesia*) **3** : a disease of the filbert and hazel characterized by black warty excrescences on the bark and caused by a fungus (*Cryptosporella anomala*) **4** : a cane infection of the grape caused by the crown-gall bacterium
black lady *n* **1** : the queen of spades **2** : a variety of hearts in which the queen of spades counts as 13 hearts
blackland \ˈ=,land\ *n* : a heavy sticky black soil such as that covering extensive areas in Texas
black land crab *n* : a large active burrowing land crab (*Gecarcinus lateralis*) that is widely distributed on the Caribbean islands and the northern coast of So. America
blackland plow *n* : a plow built with a low front and a moldboard and share so shaped that the plow penetrates and sheds sticky heavy soil
black larch *n* : a tamarack (*Larix laricina*)
black latten *n* : LATTEN 1
black laurel *n* **1** : LOBLOLLY BAY 1 **2** : an evergreen fetterbush (*Leucothoe davisiae*) of springy wet places in the western U.S. that in some areas causes stock poisoning
black lead \ˈ=ˈled\ *n* : ¹GRAPHITE 1
blacklead \"\ *vt* [*black lead*] : to apply graphite to; *esp* : to cover the face of (matter to be molded for electrotyping) with graphite to prevent adhesion of wax or the face of (a wax mold) with graphite to induce electrodeposition
¹**blackleg** \ˈ=,=\ *n* [¹*black* + *leg*] **1** : an enzootic usu. fatal toxemia of young cattle and less commonly of sheep, goats, and swine characterized by high fever and crackling discolored swellings under the skin and caused by toxins produced by an anaerobic soil bacterium (*Clostridium feseri* syn. *C. chauvoei*) usu. entering the tissues through minor wounds or abrasions — called also *black quarter, symptomatic anthrax;* compare MALIGNANT EDEMA **2** : a professional gambler : SHARPER, SWINDLER **3** *chiefly Brit* : a worker hostile to trade unionism or acting in opposition to union policies : STRIKEBREAKER, SCAB **4 a** : a destructive disease of cabbage and other plants esp. of the family Cruciferae caused by certain fungi (as *Phoma lingam*) and characterized by lesions in the stem near the soil surface that become sunken and dark and may girdle the stem **b** : a disease of potato plants caused by a bacterium (*Erwinia atroseptica*) that rots the bases of the stems with subsequent yellowing, wilting, and sometimes rotting of the tubers
²**blackleg** \"\ *vb* **blacklegged; blacklegged; blacklegging; blacklegs** *chiefly Brit, vt* : to act as a blackleg (sense 3) against ~ *vi* : to act as a blackleg (sense 3)
black·leg·gery \ˈ=,=ərē\ *n* -ES : behavior characteristic of a blackleg (sense 2)
black·leg·ism \-,gizəm\ *n* -S : BLACKLEGGERY
black lemur *n* : a large dark lemur (*Lemur macaco*)
black leopard *n* : a melanistic variety of the common leopard
black letter *n* : a style of type or lettering characterized by a heavy face and angular outlines and used chiefly by the earliest European printers or sometimes for the printing of German — called also *Gothic, Old English*
black level *n* : the instantaneous amplitude of a television signal that corresponds to a black area in the transmitted image
black ligament *n* : BLACK DROP 2
black light *n* : invisible ultraviolet or infrared light
black lignite *n* : low-grade coal that is intermediate between ordinary lignite and bituminous coal
black lily *n* : either of two bulbous plants (*Fritillaria biflora* and *F. camschatcensis*) of the Pacific coast of No. America that have a dark purple perianth
black line *n* : a nonparasitic disease of walnuts esp. of English varieties grafted onto black walnuts that appears to be associated with incompatibility between certain stocks and is characterized by a black line of dead tissue at the graft union, later dying of the bark below, and subsequent decline and death of the tree
black linn \-ˈlin\ *n* : CUCUMBER TREE 1
black lip *n* : a pearl oyster (*Pinctada margaritifera*) that has valves with a black margin
black liquor *n* **1** : IRON LIQUOR **2** : the dark-colored alkaline waste liquor which comes from the sulfate and soda processes of making cellulosic pulp and from which tall oil and lignin are recovered — compare ²BLACK ASH 2
¹**blacklist** \ˈ=,=\ *n* [¹*black* + *list*] : a list of persons that are disapproved of or are to be punished or discriminated against: as **a** : an employers' privately circulated list of workers that are to be refused employment because they are reputed to hold opinions or engage in actions contrary to the employers' interests **b** : a union list of employers that are to be boycotted because they are reputedly unfair to workers **c** : a list of firms and individuals with whom the nationals of a belligerent country are forbidden to trade because of their reputed contribution to the economic strength of the enemy **d** : a public or privately circulated list often used to screen for employment applicants suspected of or charged with holding views or engaging in activities subversive of the national interest
²**blacklist** \"\ *vt* -ED/-ING/-S : to put on a blacklist
black locust *n* **1** : LOCUST 3a(2) **2** : HONEY LOCUST 1a(1)
black lotion *n* : BLACK WASH 1
black·ly *adv* : in a black manner
black lye *n* : BLACK LIQUOR 2
black mahogany *n* : a Mexican mahogany (*Swietenia humilis*) that has harder, heavier, and darker wood than the common mahogany
black maidenhair *n* **1** : VENUSHAIR **2** : BLACK SPLEENWORT
¹**black·mail** \ˈblak,māl\ *n* -S [¹*black* + *mail* (tribute)] **1** : a tribute of money or commodities exacted in the 16th and early 17th centuries in the north of England and south of Scotland by freebooting chiefs for protection or immunity from pillage **2** : extortion of money or anything of value by threats esp. of subjecting someone to criminal prosecution or revealing something injurious to his reputation : something of value extorted by such threats
²**blackmail** \"\ *vt* -ED/-ING/-S : to extort money or anything of value from by threats esp. of subjecting someone to criminal prosecution or revealing something injurious to his reputation ⟨his former mistress tried to ~ him⟩ : compel to act in a particular way by threats ⟨~ a government employee into giving secrets to the enemy⟩ — **black·mail·er** \ˈ=,=ə(r)\ *n*
black maire *n* **1** : a New Zealand tree (*Olea cunninghamii*) with coriaceous leaves and stout flower clusters **2** : the dense hard light brown wood of the black maire
black mallard *n* : BLACK DUCK a
black mamba *n* : a mamba in its black phase
black man *n* **1** : BLACK 5 **2** : an evil spirit : BOOGEYMAN, DEVIL
black manganese *n* : PYROLUSITE
black mangrove *n* **1** : a mangrove (*Avicennia marina*) of the West Indies and the southern Florida coast that usu. occurs in dense thickets and that has numerous short roots that bend up or away from the ground **2** : an Australian plant (*Aegiceras majus*) of the family Verbenaceae that resembles the black mangrove of the West Indies and Florida
blackman reaction *n, cap B* [after Frederick F. *Blackman* †1947 Eng. botanist] : the secondary part of the process of photosynthesis involving only chemosynthesis
black maple *n* **1** : a sugar maple (*Acer nigrum*) having black bark and dark soft leaves **2** : the wood of the black maple
black margate *n* : ²POMPON
black ma·ria \-məˈrīə\ *n, usu cap B&M* [prob. fr. the name *Maria*] **1** : PATROL WAGON **2** : BLACK LADY
black market *n* : trading activity in violation of public regulations (as price ceilings, rates of exchange, tax laws, or rationing); *also* : a place where such activity is carried on
black–market \ˈ=ˈ=,=\ *vb* [*black market*, n.] *vi* : to buy or sell goods in the black market ~ *vt* : to sell in the black market
black mar·ke·teer \,=,=ˈ=\ *n* [*black market* + *-eer*] : one that sells goods in the black market
black–marketeer \"\ *vi* -ED/-ING/-S [*black marketeer*] : to sell goods in the black market
black mar·ket·er \ˈ=ˈ===\ *n* [*black market* + *-er*] : BLACK MARKETEER
black marlin *n* : either of two Pacific ocean game fishes (*Makaira mazara* and *M. marlina*) that may attain a weight of 1000 pounds and a length of 14 feet
black mass *n* **1** *usu cap B&M* : a travesty of the Christian mass ascribed to the reputed worshipers of Satan — compare SATANISM **2** : a mass for the dead in which the priest's vestments are black : a requiem mass
black measles *n* **1 a** : hemorrhagic measles **b** : ROCKY MOUNTAIN SPOTTED FEVER **2** : a disease of grapevines in California of obscure and undetermined cause characterized by black spotting of the skin of the berries and browning and drying up of the leaf tissue between the veins and often developing suddenly and severely, the leaves dropping and the canes dying back from the tips in a few days — called also *apoplexy*
black medic *n* : a prostrate herb (*Medicago lupulina*) with heads of small yellow flowers and curved black pods — called also *yellow trefoil*
black mercury *n* : POISON IVY 1
black miao *n, pl* **black miao** *or* **black miaos** *usu cap B&M* [part trans. of Chin *hei*⁴ *miao*²] : HEI-MIAO
black mica *n* : BIOTITE
black mint *n* : a peppermint with dark green stems and foliage that is widely cultivated for its oil — compare WHITE MINT
black mold *n* **1** : a mold or fungus like a mold with dark mycelium or spores: as **a** : a fungus of the order Mucorales; *esp* : the common bread mold (*Rhizopus stolonifer*) — compare ⁵MOLD **b** : a sooty mold of the families Perisporiaceae and Capnodiaceae **c** : an imperfect fungus of the family Dematiaceae **2** : a diseased and blackened condition produced by a black mold; *esp* : a disease of roses that is caused by a fungus (*Chalaropsis thielavioides*) and that causes serious losses in rose grafts esp. on Manetti stock by growing over the cut surface of the scion and thus preventing proper union
black mollie *or* **black mollienisia** *n* -S [*black mollie* by shortening fr. *black mollienisia*] : a small jet-black poeciliid fish (*Mollienisia sphenops*) from Yucatan that is often kept in the tropical aquarium
black monday *n, usu cap B&M* [ME *blak Monunday*] *obs* : EASTER MONDAY
black money *n* : base coin; *esp* : the coins issued as silver but containing a high alloy of base metal that were current in England esp. in the 14th century
black monk *n, often cap B&M* [ME *blak monek;* fr. the color of the habit] : a Benedictine monk
black moss *n* : SPANISH MOSS
blackmouth \ˈ=,=\ *also* **blackmouth salmon** *n* : a king salmon esp. when immature
black mulberry *n* **1** : a European mulberry (*Morus nigra*) with dark foliage and fruit **2** : the purplish to black fruit of the black mulberry **3** : RED MULBERRY
black muskrat *n* : a melanistic muskrat fur or pelt
black mustard *n* [so called fr. the dark-colored testae] : a much-branched annual Eurasian herb (*Brassica nigra*) now widespread as a weed that is the principal source of table mustard and that has small bright yellow flowers and a thin-beaked seed pod which is closely appressed to the stem — compare WHITE MUSTARD
black muzzle *n* : HEAD SCAB
black myrobalan *n* : CHEBULE
blackneb \ˈ=,=\ *n* **1** *Brit* : a black-billed bird; *esp* : CARRION CROW **2** *Scot* : a sympathizer with the French Revolution **3** *Brit* : ¹BLACKLEG 3
black–neck \ˈ=,=\ *n* : SCAUP DUCK
black–necked cobra \ˈ=,=-\ *n* : a venomous and aggressive elapid snake (*Naja nigricollis*) common and widely distributed in Africa that rarely bites but discharges by spitting a venom that is harmless to the intact skin but may cause blindness if it enters the eyes — called also *spitting cobra*
black–necked grebe *n* : EARED GREBE
black–necked stilt *n* : a stilt (*Himantopus mexicanus*) that ranges from the western and southern U.S. to northern So. America and that has the characteristic black mantle extended forward along the back of the neck to the crown of the head and about the eyes
black·ness *n* -ES [ME *blaknes,* fr. *blak* black + *-nes* -ness] : the quality or state of being black
black nightshade *n* : a cosmopolitan weed (*Solanum nigrum*) with hairy poisonous foliage, white flowers, and edible black berries
black·nob \ˈblak,näb\ *n* [¹*black* + *knob*stick] *Brit* : ¹BLACKLEG 3
black nonesuch *n* : BLACK MEDIC
black norway pine *n, usu cap N* : a pitch pine (*Pinus rigida*) with slightly curved and twisted needles in threes
blacknose \ˈ=,=\ *n* : a physiological disease of the date that is characterized by darkening, cracking, and shriveling of the distal end of the fruit
blacknose dace *also* **black–nosed dace** \ˈ=,=-\ *n* : a common No. American dace (*Rhinichthys atronasus* or *Atratulus atronasus*) with a black stripe along either side passing from the base of the tail to the tip of the nose — called also *striped dace*
black oak *n* **1** : any of several American oaks having dark bark or foliage (as blackjack or scarlet oak); *esp* : a large timber tree (*Quercus velutina*) of the eastern and central U.S. that has foliage resembling that of the red oak and a yellow inner bark that is used for tanning — called also *quercitron* **2** *Austral* : SHE-OAK 1
black oat *n* : an annual European oat (*Avena strigosa*) with a lemma having two long apical bristles
black oat grass *n* : an oat grass (*Stipa avenacea*) of the eastern U.S. that has a spikelet with a black third scale
black ocher *n* : ⁵WAD 2
black oil *n* : any of various dark-colored oils obtained esp. from petroleum (as heavy crude lubricating oils)
black oldwife *n* : a plectognath fish of the genus *Melichthys; esp* : GALAFATE
black olive *n* **1** : a tropical American tree (*Bucida buceras*) of the family Combretaceae with dark-colored very durable wood and a fruit that is a one-seeded drupe **2** : a dark grayish olive to olive-green color
black onyx *n* : chalcedony that is artificially colored black
black opal *n* : a dark-colored opal showing usu. red or green internal reflections
black out *vi* **1 a** : to turn off the stage lighting in order to indicate the end of a theatrical performance or of a scene in a play **b** : to become enveloped in darkness ⟨as the heroine speaks this line the scene *blacks out*⟩ ⟨astronomers have observed that stars sometimes *black out*⟩ **2 a** : to undergo a transient dulling or loss of vision or consciousness as a result of temporary impairment of cerebral circulation or retinal anoxia, traumatic emotional blows, or an alcoholic bout ⟨an airplane pilot may *black out* while pulling out of a dive⟩ **b** : to have a lapse of memory **c** : to lose consciousness ⟨became ill and *blacked out* behind the wheel —*Springfield (Mass.) Union*⟩ **3 a** : to make an object or area invisible or less conspicuous by extinguishing or screening all lights for protection esp. against air attack ⟨my orders are to *black out* at sunset⟩ **b** : to become invisible or less conspicuous by the extinguishing or screening of all lights for protection esp. against air attack : become blacked out ⟨I have a truck to sleep in . . . It can . . . *black out*, and has a huge map board so one can work at night —G.S.Patton⟩ **4** : to become inoperative or ineffectual : cease to exist or act ⟨shortwave radio transmission *blacked out* because of a sunspot⟩ ⟨telephones *blacked out* over a wide area⟩ ~ *vt* **1 a** : to envelop in darkness ⟨power failure *blacked out* the city⟩; *esp* : to make (an object or area) invisible or less conspicuous by extinguishing or screening all lights for protection against air attack ⟨the city was *blacked out*⟩ **b** : to extinguish or screen esp. in order to make an object or area invisible or less conspicuous for protection against air attack ⟨the lights were *blacked out*⟩ ⟨we had to *black out* all our windows⟩ **c** : to debar from transmitting or receiving information and ideas ⟨a nation that had been *blacked out* from the rest of the world — Sigrid Arne⟩ **2** : to silence or jam (radio transmission) effectively **3** : to make inoperative, ineffectual, or temporarily nonexistent or insignificant : DESTROY ⟨falling trees *blacked out* several electric power lines⟩ ⟨some intercollegiate sports were *blacked out* by the war⟩ ⟨the newspaper was *blacked out* by insolvency⟩ ⟨relief emergencies . . . must not *black out* the longer task of recovery —*Air Transport*⟩ **4** : to cause (a person) to undergo transient dulling or loss of vision or consciousness ⟨the first drag at the cigarette had nearly *blacked* him *out* —J.A.Phillips⟩ **5** : to restrict or forbid the telecasting of (a program to which admission is charged) esp. in the area of origination in order to protect gate receipts ⟨a program *blacked out* in the city⟩ : prohibit such telecasting in ⟨the city is *blacked out* for this game⟩
blackout \ˈ=,=\ *n* -S *often attrib* [*black out*] **1 a** : a turning off of the stage lighting for the purpose of separating scenes in a play or of closing a skit in a revue, burlesque show, or musical comedy **b** : a skit that ends with a blackout **2 a** : transient dulling or loss of vision or consciousness resulting from temporary impairment of cerebral circulation **b** : a lapse of memory **c** : a loss of consciousness **3** : an action of blacking out (as through the interruption of electrical power) an object or area : a condition or period of being blacked out **4** : a blotting out, suppression, obscuring, or cessation esp. when temporary ⟨a ~ of waterfront commerce over the whole North Atlantic coast —A.H.Raskin⟩ ⟨unless a ~ on science be decreed in every land —A.J.Carlson⟩ **5** : a condition of severe loss of radio signal during intense phases of magnetic storms **6** : a restriction or prohibition of the telecasting of a program to which admission is charged esp. in the area of origination
black ox *n* **1** : bad luck **2** : old age ⟨the *black ox* has trod on his foot⟩
black oyster catcher *n* : a blackish brown oyster catcher (*Haematopus bachmani*) of the Pacific coast of No. America
black palm *n* **1** : an Australian palm tree (*Areca normanbyi*) **2** : any palm tree of the genus *Astrocaryum*
black partridge *n* : a francolin (*Francolinus francolinus*) that is now restricted to southern Asia though formerly extending into southern Europe and that is distinguished by the black plumage of the male
black patch *n* : a disease of red clover caused by an unidentified sterile fungus and characterized by groups of blackened plants resulting from the spread of the disease
black pea *n* : a European bitter vetch (*Lathyrus niger*) with foliage that turns black in drying
black peach aphid *n* : an aphid (*Brachycaudus persicaecola*) having the adult shiny black and the young reddish brown, wintering on the roots of peach trees, and feeding during the growing season on the leaves and young fruit
black pear *n* : BLACK CHOKEBERRY
black pepper *n* **1** : a pungent condiment consisting of the fruit of an East Indian plant (*Piper nigrum*) ground with the black husk still on **2** : the black pepper plant
black peppermint *n* : BLACK MINT
black perch *n* : any of various dark-colored saltwater or freshwater fishes: as **a** *chiefly Midland* : SMALLMOUTH BLACK BASS **b** : BLACK SEA BASS 1 **c** : TRIPLETAIL 1a **d** : a common surf fish (*Embiotoca jacksoni*) of the Pacific coast
black petrel *n* : a rather large common sooty to brownish black petrel (*Oceanodroma melania*) of the coast of southern California and Mexico
black phoebe *n* : a phoebe (*Sayornis nigricans*) of the southwestern U.S. and Mexico that is chiefly dull or slaty black with a pure-white abdomen
black pigment *n* : coal-tar lampblack used chiefly in printer's ink
black pilot *n* **1** : BEAU GREGORY **2** : BLACK RUDDER FISH
black pine *n* **1** : any of several American pines having dark-colored bark: as **a** : LOBLOLLY 3 **b** : LODGEPOLE PINE b **c** : JEFFREY PINE **d** : POND PINE **e** : JACK PINE 1 **2 a** : AUSTRIAN PINE **b** : CORSICAN PINE **3** *Austral* : any of several coniferous trees: as **a** : either of two podocarps of New Zealand (*Podocarpus ferruginea* and *P. spicata*) **b** : BLACK CYPRESS PINE **c** : CAMPHORWOOD 2 **4** : JAPANESE BLACK PINE
black pit *n* **1** : a spot disease of lemons and less frequently of other citrus fruits that is caused by a bacterium (*Erwinia citrimaculans*) — compare CITRUS BLAST **2** : a disease of peas that is prevalent in the Netherlands and that produces black spots in the seeds
black plantain *n* : a common ribgrass (*Plantago lanceolata*)
black plate *n* : sheet steel or sheet iron that has not yet been made into tin plate by being coated with tin or that is used uncoated where the protection afforded by tin is unnecessary (as in certain cans)
black plum *n* **1** : an Australian date plum (*Diospyros microcarpa*) **2** : JAVA PLUM **3** : a purplish black that is redder and less strong than mulberry (sense 2b)
black pod *n* : a pod rot of cacao caused by a fungus (*Phytophthora faberi*)
black point *n* : a worldwide disease of wheat and other cereal grains that is caused by various bacteria and fungi esp. of the genera *Alternaria* and *Helminthosporium* and that blackens the embryo ends of the grains, sometimes impairs germination, and lowers the market value of the grain
black poison *or* **black poisonwood** *n* : a West Indian poisonous tree (*Metopium brownei*) of the family Anacardiaceae that has alternate pinnate leaves and small greenish flowers
black–poll warbler \ˈ=,=-\ *also* **blackpoll** \ˈ=,=\ *n* : a No. American warbler (*Dendroica striata*) having the top of the head of the male bird black when in full plumage
black·pool \ˈblak,pül\ *adj, usu cap* [fr. *Blackpool*, England] : of or from the county borough of Blackpool, England : of the kind or style prevalent in Blackpool
black pope *n, usu cap B&P* [so called fr. the habit of the order and the great power its leader had during the papacy of Pius IX] : the head of the Jesuits
black poplar *n* **1** : a European poplar (*Populus nigra*) of which the Lombardy poplar is a variety **2 a** : SWAMP COTTONWOOD **b** : the wood of the swamp cottonwood **3** : BALSAM POPLAR **4** : a European aspen (*Populus tremula*) with petioles strongly compressed laterally
blackpot \ˈ=,=\ *n* **1** *archaic* : a beer or ale mug **2** *dial Eng* : BLOOD SAUSAGE
black pottery *n* : a fine thin black Chinese pottery burnished and made on a wheel that is characteristic of the ancient Ch'eng-tzu-yai culture
black powder *n* : an explosive consisting of black gunpowder now used chiefly as an ignition charge and primer, as a propellant in older guns fired as a hobby, and in pyrotechnics; *also* : a similar explosive consisting of a mixture of sodium nitrate instead of potassium nitrate and charcoal and sulfur used chiefly in blasting — see BLASTING POWDER
black prairie *n* : prairie land having rich black soil
black pudding *n* : BLOOD SAUSAGE
black purslane *n* : SPOTTED SPURGE
black quahog *n* : ¹QUAHOG 2
black quarter *n* : ¹BLACKLEG 1
black racer *n* : an American black snake of a typical subspecies (*Coluber constrictor constrictor*) common in the eastern U.S.
black rail *n* : a small dark No. American rail (*Laterallus*, or *Creciscus, jamaicensis*) with a short bill and tail and a chestnut-brown patch on the back
black rain *n* : rain blackened by gathering in its fall particles of smoke, black fungus spores, or atmospheric dust
black raspberry *n* : BLACKCAP 1
black rat *n* : a rat (*Rattus rattus*) of a species that infests houses
black rattlesnake *n* : MASSASAUGA a
black rent *n, Eng law* : rent paid in grain, meat, or the lowest coin — opposed to *white rent*
black rhinoceros *n* : a rhinoceros (*Diceros bicornis*) of the species that is most common in Africa
black ring *also* **black ring spot** *n* **1** : a virus disease of cabbage and other members of the cabbage family (Cruciferae) that is characterized by necrotic, dark, and often sunken rings on the leaf surface **2** : a virus disease of the tomato that is characterized in its initial stage by numerous small black rings on young leaves
black robe *n* : a Roman Catholic priest; *esp* : a Roman Catholic missionary to the American Indians
black rock cod *n* **1** : a large Australian grouper (*Epinephelus*

damelii) **2 :** either of two common rockfishes: **a :** BLACK ROCKFISH 1b **b :** PRIESTFISH

black rockfish *n* **1 :** either of two common rockfishes: **a :** PRIESTFISH **b :** a common dark-colored scorpaenid food fish (*Sebastodes melanops*) of the Pacific coast of No. America **2 :** BLACK GROUPER 2

black rod *n* [so called fr. his staff of office] **1 :** an officer of the Order of the Garter that is also usher to the British House of Lords and that has as one of his duties the occasional summoning of the Commons and their speaker to the House of Lords to hear a speech from the throne **2 :** an usher in the legislature of some of the British dominions or colonies

black root *n* **1 :** any of several plants or their dark-colored roots: as **a :** a perennial plant (*Pterocaulon undulatus*) of the southern U.S. that has large black rootstocks **b :** CULVER'S ROOT **c :** COLICROOT 1 **d :** a common comfrey (*Symphytum officinale*) with the upper part of the stem and inflorescence densely hispid **2 :** any of several plant diseases characterized by dark discoloration of roots: as **a :** COTTON WILT 1 **b :** a disease of radishes, beets, and sugar beets caused by fungi (genus *Aphanomyces*) and producing brown or black lesions on the roots, deformation of the roots, and a damping off of seedlings

black root rot *n* **:** any of several diseases of plants marked by dark often confluent lesions of the root and sometimes the crown often involving the whole cortex: as **a :** a disease of apples caused by a fungus (*Xylaria mali*) **b :** a disease of tobacco and various other plants caused by a fungus (*Thielaviopsis basicola*)

black rot *n* **:** any of various diseases of cultivated plants caused by fungi or bacteria and producing dark brown discoloration and decay: as **a :** a disease of the apple, pear, and quince caused by a fungus (*Physalospora cydoniae*) **b :** a disease of the grape caused by a fungus (*Guignardia bidwellii*) — see GRAPE ROT **c :** a disease of cabbage and related plants caused by a bacterium (*Xanthomonas campestris*) **d :** a disease of the sweet potato caused by a fungus (*Ceratostomella fimbriata*) **e :** a disease of the potato caused by a bacterium (*Erwinia atroseptica*)

black rouge *n* **:** chemically precipitated magnetite used as a polishing agent and pigment

black rudder fish *n* **:** a blackish stromateoid fish (*Palinurichthys perciformis*) that is common off the New England coast

black ruff *n* **1 :** BLACKFISH 1b **2 :** a stromateoid fish closely related to the blackfish (sense 1b)

black runner *n* **:** BLACK SNAKE 1a

black rush *n* **1 :** GREAT BULRUSH **2 :** PIASSAVA 1

black rust *n* **1 :** a plant rust producing black discoloration; *esp* **:** BLACK STEM RUST **2 :** STEM RUST 2; *esp* **:** the uredostage of this fungus

blacks *pres 3d sing of* BLACK, *pl of* BLACK

black sage *n* **1 :** a woolly-leaved plant (*Trichostema lanatum*) native to southern California and Mexico **2 :** any of several plants of the genus *Cordia; esp* **:** an introduced weed (*C. macrostachya*) that is a serious pest in sugar plantations on Mauritius **3 :** a common highly inflammable California sage (*Salvia mellifera*) that is the chief source of sage honey **4 :** either of two sagebrushes (*Artemisia arbuscula* and *A. tridentata*) of the western U.S. **5 :** a California herb (*Audibertia stachyoides*)

black salamander *n* **:** ALPINE SALAMANDER

black sally \-ˈsalē\ *n* **:** an Australian tree (*Eucalyptus stellulata*) having rough dark-colored bark near the butt and yielding a red kino

black salmon *n* **:** any of several dark-colored salmons or similar fishes: as **a :** COBIA **b :** KING SALMON

black salsify *n* **:** a European herb (*Scorzonera hispanica*) cultivated for the edible root and for winter greens

black salt *also* **black salts** *n* **:** crude potassium carbonate obtained from wood ashes or in the Leblanc process

black saltwort *n* **:** SEA MILKWORT

black samp·son \-ˈsam(p)sən\ *n* **:** PURPLE CONEFLOWER

black sanctus *n, archaic* **:** confused singing or speaking by several persons at one time without regard to each other **:** a burlesque of a hymn

black sand *adj, usu cap B&S* [so called fr. the glacial sand of the Illinois river flood plain near Liverpool, Ill., where remains were found] **:** of or relating to a component of Woodland culture and a physical type first found in central Illinois

black sanicle *n* **1 :** a sanicle (*Sanicula marylandica*) of the eastern U.S. with thickish leaves and a thick rhizome **2 :** MASTERWORT b

black sapote *n* **:** a Mexican persimmon (*Diospyros ebenaster*) with an almost seedless dark-fleshed fruit

black sassafras *n* **:** OLIVER'S BARK

black scab *n* **:** POTATO WART

black scale *n* **1 :** a large dark brown or black unarmored scale (*Saissetia oleae*) destructive to olive, citrus, and other cultivated plants **2 :** a serious disease of Easter lilies caused by a fungus (*Colletotrichum lilii*) that produces black lesions on the bulb scales

black scoter *n* **:** a common European scoter (*Oidemia nigra*) having the adult male completely black and the female and young birds largely dark brown above and mottled brown and white below

black scour *n, pl* **black scours** *sing or pl in constr* **:** a hemorrhagic enteritis of sheep, swine, and cattle that affects esp. young animals and is usu. associated with a heavy worm burden but sometimes results from bacterial infection or improper feeding

black scour worm *n* **:** a small nematode worm (genus *Trichostrongylus*) parasitizing the small intestine and fourth stomach of sheep

black scrub oak *n* **:** BEAR OAK

black scurf *n* **:** RHIZOCTONIA DISEASE 2

black sea bass *n* **1 :** an abundant and important food fish (*Centropristes striatus*) of the Atlantic coast of the U.S. that is dark bluish with black bands and more or less varied with small white spots and blotches — called also *sea bass* **2 :** GIANT BASS

black sea devil *n* **:** a fish of the family Ceratiidae

blackseed \ˈ⸗,⸗\ *n* **1 :** SMUT GRASS **2 :** BLACK MEDIC

black shank *n* **:** a disease of tobacco caused by a fungus (*Phytophthora parasitica nicotianae*) and producing a black rot of the stem, brown blotches on the leaves, and damping off of seedlings

black shark *n* **1 :** BLACKTIP SHARK **2 :** a small dark-colored shark (*Scymnorhinus licha*) widely distributed in warm seas

black sheep *n* **1 :** a recessive black-fleeced individual in a flock of normally white-fleeced sheep — compare MELANISM 1a **2 :** a member of a group that stands in conspicuous and unfavorable contrast to the other members esp. by reason of socially undesirable characteristics or behavior ⟨he's the *black sheep* of his family⟩

black·shirt \ˈ⸗,⸗\ *n, usu cap* **:** a member of a fascist organization having a black shirt as a distinctive part of its dress or uniform; *esp* **:** a member of the Italian Fascist party

black·shop \ˈ⸗,⸗\ *n* **:** the part of an electrotyping plant where blackleading is done

black-shouldered kite \ˈ⸗,⸗⸗-\ *n* **:** a common Asiatic and African hawk (*Elanus caeruleus*) that is chiefly bluish gray above and white below with a black patch on each shoulder

black·side darter *n* **:** a small darter (*Hadropterus maculatus*) of the upper Mississippi drainage that is greenish yellow with dark blotches along the sides

black silver *n* **:** STEPHANITE

black skimmer *n* **:** a black-and-white skimmer (*Rhynchops nigra*) that has a bright red bill tipped with black and is widely distributed along the east coast of No. America

black slash pine *n* **:** LOBLOLLY PINE 1

black sloe *n* **:** a wild plum (*Prunus umbellata*) of the southern U.S. that has small sour fruits

black smallpox *n* **:** a highly fatal form of smallpox characterized by cutaneous hemorrhages

blacksmith \ˈ⸗,⸗\ *n* [ME *blaksmith*, fr. *blak* black + *smith*; fr. his working with iron, known as black metal] **1 a :** a smith who works in iron with a forge — sometimes distinguished from *whitesmith* **b :** a blacksmith who shoes horses — called also *farrier, horseshoer* **c :** one who makes metal into tools, machine parts, and other objects by heating it in a forge and hammering it into shape on an anvil — called also *smith, striker* **2 :** an edible blackish pomacentrid fish (*Chromis punctipinnis*) of the Pacific coast **3** *or* **blacksmith plover :** a spur-winged plover (*Hoplopterus armatus*) of Africa

black·smith·ery \-(ə)rē\ *n* **:** BLACKSMITHING

black·smith·ing \-iŋ\ *n* **:** the craft or job of a blacksmith

blacksmith shop *or* **blacksmith's shop** *n* **:** the workshop of a blacksmith

blacksmith welding *n* **:** forge welding by manual hammering

black snake \ˈ⸗,⸗\ *n* **1 :** any of several snakes predominantly dark or black in color: as **a :** a widely distributed colubrid snake (*Coluber constrictor*) of No. America that may reach a length of six feet **b :** PILOT BLACK SNAKE **c :** a colubrid snake (*Ocyophis ater*) of Jamaica **d :** any of several venomous elapid snakes of Australia: as (1) **:** a venomous elapid snake (*Pseudechis porphyriacus*) that is black above with a cherry-red belly (2) **:** TIGER SNAKE 1 **2** *usu* **blacksnake** *or* **blacksnake whip :** a long tapering braided whip of rawhide or leather ending in a leaf-shaped piece that serves as a snapper

blacksnake \"\ *vb* -ED/-ING/-S [*blacksnake*, n. (whip)] **:** to whip with a blacksnake

black snakeroot *n* **1 :** a bugbane (*Cimicifuga racemosa*) **2 :** SANICLE a **3** *or* **black snakeweed :** WILD GINGER 2a

black snapper *n* **:** any of several dark-colored marine fishes: as **a :** SCHOOLMASTER 3 **b :** PRIESTFISH

black snowbird *n* **:** SLATE-COLORED JUNCO

black southern beech *n* **:** BLACK BEECH 2

black spanish *n, usu cap B&S* **:** an old Mediterranean breed of glossy black domestic fowls with blue legs and white faces

black speck *n* **1 :** RHIZOCTONIA DISEASE 2 **2 :** DARTROSE

black spleenwort *n* **:** a European spleenwort (*Asplenium adiantum-nigrum*) having foliage that resembles that of the maidenhair and yielding an astringent

black sponge *n* **:** a commercial sponge that has not been cleaned or trimmed

black spot *n* **1 :** any of several plant diseases characterized by black spots or blotches: as **a :** APPLE SCAB **b :** APPLE ANTHRACNOSE **c :** a common destructive disease of roses caused by a fungus (*Diplocarpon rosae*) and characterized by black spots or blotches on the leaves, yellowing of the remaining portions, and premature falling of the leaves **d :** a disease of citrus fruits caused by an imperfect fungus (*Phoma citricarpa*) **e :** a disease of peaches and plums caused by a bacterium (*Xanthomonas pruni*) **f :** a disease of beets caused by boron deficiency in the soil **2 :** a spotting of frozen meat caused by an imperfect fungus (*Cladosporium herbarum*) **3 :** BLACK GRUB

black-spotted trout \ˈ⸗,⸗⸗-\ *n* **:** CUTTHROAT TROUT

black spruce *n* **1 :** a spruce (*Picea mariana*) of northeastern No. America that grows chiefly in wet boggy areas and has inferior wood, spreading branches, deep green and very dense foliage, and oval persistent cones — see TREE illustration **2 :** DOUGLAS FIR

black squall *n* **:** a squall accompanied by dark clouds — compare WHITE SQUALL

black squirrel *n* **:** a squirrel that is black or exceptionally dark in color; *esp* **:** a fox squirrel with such coloring typically found in the southern and western parts of its range

black stem *n* **:** any of various diseases of plants characterized by darkening of the stem: as **a :** a disease of alfalfa caused by a fungus (*Ascochyta imperfecta*) **b :** a disease of cabbage and cauliflower caused by a fungus (*Phoma lingam*)

black stem rust *n* **:** stem rust in the teliospore stage

blackstick \ˈ⸗,⸗\ *n* **:** quinoidine molded into sticks

black stinkwood *n* **:** a stinkwood (*Ocotea bullata*)

black stock *n* **:** the dark-colored material that in papermaking is discharged from a digester at the end of an alkaline cook of wood chips and contains the fiber, the alkali, and about half the weight of the wood in solution

black stork *n* **:** an Old World stork (*Ciconia nigra*) that is glossy black above and white below

blackstrap \ˈ⸗,⸗\ *n* [*black* + *strap*] **1 :** a common red wine of the Mediterranean **2 :** a drink consisting of a mixture of rum and molasses **3** *or* **blackstrap molasses a :** the final molasses that is obtained in the last of successive processes of raw sugar manufacture and used as a constituent of many mixed cattle feeds and as a raw material for the production of industrial alcohol **b :** any thick and very dark molasses **4 :** a dark heavy oil used esp. for lubricating mine-car wheels

black streak *n* **:** BLACK CHECK

black stripe *n* **1 :** BLACK STRAP 2 **2** *or* **black stripe canker :** BLACK THREAD

black sucker *n* **:** any of several suckers; *esp* **:** HOG SUCKER

black sugar *n* **:** Spanish licorice or its juice

black sugar maple *n* **:** BLACK MAPLE

black sumac *n* **:** DWARF SUMAC

black swallower *n* **:** a small dark deep-sea percoid fish (*Chiasmodon niger*) that is remarkable for the distensibility of its stomach and body

black swallowtail *n* **:** a common butterfly (*Papilio polyxenes*) of eastern No. America that is black with yellow spots and has a larva that often feeds on the foliage of carrots, parsley, and related plants

black swallow-wort *n* **:** a European perennial twining herb (*Cynanchum nigrum*) that is occas. cultivated and sometimes escaped in No. America and has purple-brown or dark purple flowers with triangular ovate petals

black swan *n* **:** an Australian swan (*Cygnus atratus*) that is black with white wing tips and red bill

black sweetwood *n* **:** a tropical American evergreen tree (*Ocotea floribunda*) with dioecious greenish flowers

blacktail \ˈ⸗,⸗\ *n* **1** *also* **blacktail deer :** BLACK-TAILED DEER **2 a :** a young salmon trout **b :** DASSIE 2 **3 :** BLACK-TAILED GODWIT

black-tailed deer \ˈ⸗,⸗-\ *n* **1 :** a deer (*Odocoileus columbianus*) of British Columbia, Oregon, and Washington that is in many respects intermediate between the mule deer and the Virginia deer **2 :** MULE DEER

black-tailed gnatcatcher *n* **:** a gnatcatcher (*Polioptila melanura californica*) of southern California and Lower California

black-tailed godwit *n* **:** a long-legged European godwit (*Limosa limosa*) with a long straight bill and a broad black band on the white tail

black-tailed jackrabbit *n* **:** a jackrabbit (*Lepus californicus*) of the southwestern U.S. and Mexico that has a tail with a black upper surface

black-tailed native cat *n* **:** a native cat (*Dasyurus geoffroyi*) distinguished from the common native cat by possession of a distinct hallux

black-tailed rattlesnake *n* **:** a medium-sized black-tailed heavy-bodied rattlesnake (*Crotalus molossus*) of Texas, Arizona, and northern Mexico

black-tailed shrimp *n* **:** a dark-colored edible shrimp (*Crago nigricauda*) common from California to Alaska in relatively shallow water

black tamarind *n* **1 :** VELVET TAMARIND **2 :** a tropical American timber tree (*Pithecolobium arboreum*)

black tang *n* **:** BLADDER WRACK 1

black tea *n* **:** tea that is dark in color due to the leaf's being fully fermented before firing

black tellurium *n* **:** NAGYAGITE

black tern *n* **:** any of several very small short-tailed terns with largely dark gray or black plumage that breed in marshes and constitute a genus (*Chlidonias*) of nearly cosmopolitan distribution

blackthorn \ˈ⸗,⸗\ *n* [ME *blakthorn*, fr. *blak* black + *thorn*] **1 a :** a European spiny tree or shrub (*Prunus spinosa*) that has hard wood and bears small white flowers before the leaves and small purplish or blue black astringent fruits — see SLOE **b :** a cane made of the wood of this tree or shrub **c** *or* **blackthorn cocktail :** a cocktail variously made from sloe gin or rye whiskey and French or Italian vermouth flavored with bitters and occas. anisette **2 :** PEAR HAW

blackthorn winter *n, chiefly Brit* **:** cold weather in spring when the blackthorn is in bloom

black thread *n* **:** a disease of the tapped area of the Para rubber tree that is caused by a fungus (*Phytophthora meadii*) and that is characterized by black lines extending through the exposed bast into the cambium or wood — called also *black stripe, stripe canker*

black thrips *n, Austral* **:** GREENHOUSE THRIPS

black-throated blue warbler \ˈ⸗,⸗⸗-\ *n* **:** a common warbler (*Dendroica caerulescens*) of eastern No. America the male of which has a conspicuously black throat and breast and bluish upper parts

black-throated bunting *n* **:** DICKCISSEL

black-throated gray warbler *n* **:** a grayish warbler (*Dendroica nigrescens*) of western No. America that has black markings on head, throat, and sides

black-throated green warbler *n* **:** a common warbler (*Dendroica virens*) of eastern No. America the male of which has a black throat, yellow sides of the head, and olive-green upperparts

black tie *n* **1 :** the black bow tie worn with men's semiformal evening dress — compare WHITE TIE **2 :** semiformal evening dress for men ⟨a *black-tie* dinner⟩

black tip *n* **1 :** any of several plant diseases characterized by dark-colored necrotic areas at the end of the fruit or seed: as **a :** a nonparasitic disease of the mango that is of undetermined cause and is characterized by a dark area at the distal end of the fruit **b :** BLACK POINT **2 :** BLACKTIP SHARK

blacktip shark *or* **black-tipped shark** \ˈ⸗,⸗-\ *n* **:** a small grayish shark (*Carcharias limbatus*) with black-tipped fins that is widely distributed in warm seas

black titi *n* **:** ¹TITI 1a

blacktongue \ˈ⸗,⸗\ *n* **1 :** a dark discoloration of the tongue that is sometimes associated with a fungous growth **2 a :** STUTTGART DISEASE **b :** a disease of dogs that is characterized by ulcers in the mouth, inflammation of the alimentary canal, erythema, and severe nervous symptoms and that results from certain deficiencies in the diet and has been found to be identical with pellagra in man

black tooth *n* **1 :** NEEDLE TOOTH **2 :** a mottled condition of the teeth caused by excess fluorides in the drinking water of growing children

¹blacktop \ˈ⸗,⸗\ *n, often attrib* [¹*black* + *top*] **1** *also* **blacktopping** \ˈ⸗,⸗⸗\ **:** a blackish bituminous material used esp. for surfacing roads, playgrounds, and airport runways and spread while in a plastic state over a base course of crushed rock, concrete, or an existing surface in need of resurfacing **2 :** an area (as a road) surfaced with blacktop

²blacktop \"\ *vt* **:** to surface (a road) with a blacktop coating

blacktracker \ˈ⸗,⸗⸗\ *n, Austral* **:** an aborigine employed to help police in the backcountry find fugitives and lost people

blacktree \ˈ⸗,⸗\ *n* **:** BLACK MANGROVE 1

black tree fern *n* **:** SILVER TREE FERN

black trevally *n* **:** a small spiny-finned fish (*Siganus nebulosus*) occurring on the coast of New South Wales

black tupelo *n* **:** BLACK GUM 1

black turkey *n* **:** NORFOLK TURKEY

black turnstone *n* **:** a common turnstone (*Arenaria melanocephala*) of the Pacific coast of No. America that has a black back with a bronzy-green sheen and white underparts

black turpentine beetle *n* **:** a bark beetle (*Dendroctonus terebrans*) that is extremely destructive to pines esp. of the southeastern U.S.

black twinberry *n* **:** a fly honeysuckle (*Lonicera involucrata*) of western No. America with bitter black fruit

black udder *n* **:** BLUE BAG 2

black-varnish tree *n* **:** a Burmese tree (*Melanorrhoea usitata*) that yields a black varnish — called also *theetsee*

black velvet *n* **1** *Austral* **:** an aboriginal girl or woman; *collectively* **:** aboriginal girls or women **2 :** a drink that is half champagne and half stout — compare VELVET

black vetchling *n* **:** BLACK PEA

black vine weevil *n* **:** a small elongated dull-black flightless weevil (*Brachyrhinus sulcatus*) of which the adult feeds on foliage and the larva on the roots of many crop and ornamental plants

black vomit *n* **1 a :** vomitus consisting of dark-colored matter (as broken-down blood) seen in yellow fever and cancer of the stomach — called also *coffee-ground vomit* **b :** a condition characterized by such vomitus; *esp* **:** YELLOW FEVER **2 :** HEMATEMESIS

black vulture *n* **:** an American vulture (*Coragyps atratus*) that is smaller than the turkey buzzard and heavier in flight

black·wall hitch \ˈblak‚wȯl-\ *n, usu cap B* [fr. *Blackwall*, shipyard in Poplar district, London, England] **:** a hitch used for temporarily securing a line to a hook and made by passing the end of the line round the shank of the hook and crossing it under the standing part in the mouth of the hook

Blackwall hitch

black walnut *n* **1 a :** a tall timber tree (*Juglans nigra*) of eastern No. America that has hard strong heavy dark brown wood much used for furniture and implements and that bears oily edible roughly spherical nuts — see TREE illustration **b :** the wood of this tree **c :** one of the nuts of this tree **2 :** an aromatic timber tree (*Cryptocarya palmerstonii*) of Australia **3 :** CALIFORNIA BLACK WALNUT

black wart *n* **:** POTATO WART

blackwash \ˈ⸗,⸗\ *vt* **1 :** to color with blackwash **2 :** ¹DEFAME 2 — contrasted with *whitewash*

black wash \"\ *n* **1 :** a lotion of calomel and lime water used on syphilitic sores — called also *black lotion* **2** *usu* **blackwash a :** a wash that colors a surface black — compare WHITEWASH **b :** DEFAMATION 2 **3 :** a wash of blacking and other ingredients used for coating foundry molds and cores to prevent their being burned by the molten metal

blackwater \ˈ⸗,⸗⸗\ *n* **:** any of several diseases of animals or man that are characterized by dark-colored urine: as **a :** RED WATER 1b **b :** BLACKWATER FEVER **c :** TEXAS FEVER **d :** azoturia of horses

blackwater fever *n* [so called fr. the blackish or dark red urine passed during the disease] **:** a febrile condition occurring after repeated attacks of malaria (as falciparum malaria) and marked by destruction of blood cells with hemoglobinuria and extensive kidney damage

black wattle *n* **:** any of several Australian acacias (esp. *Acacia mollissima*) that yield tanning materials

black waxy *also* **black wax** *n, West* **:** a black soil that is sticky when moist

blackweed \ˈ⸗,⸗\ *n* **:** RAGWEED 2a

black weevil *n* **:** RICE WEEVIL

black whale *n* **1 :** SOUTHERN RIGHT WHALE **2 :** SPERM WHALE

black wheatear *n* **:** a large European wheatear (*Oenanthe leucura*) having the plumage black with the rump, under tail coverts, and sides of the tail white

black-whiskered vireo \ˈ⸗,⸗⸗ \ *n* **:** a vireo (*Vireo altiloquus barbatulus*) of Florida and the West Indies that has black markings on the sides of the head

black widow *n* **1 :** a venomous New World spider (*Latrodectus mactans*) that is black with an hourglass-shaped red mark on the underside of the abdomen; *broadly* **:** any other spider of the genus *Latrodectus* **2 :** BLACK LADY

black wildebeest *n* **:** WHITE-TAILED GNU

black will \-ˈwil\ *n* **:** BLACK SEA BASS 1

black willow *n* **1 :** any of several willows with dark bark; *esp* **:** an American tree (*Salix nigra*) with linear leaves that grows close to streams and lakes **2 :** MULE FAT

black-winged stilt \-‚wiŋd-\ *n* **:** a stilt (*Himantopus himantopus*) of southern Europe, Africa, and Asia that is distinguished by very long pinkish red legs and plumage largely white but with black wings and upper parts

black witch *n* **:** a very large noctuid moth (*Erebus odora*) having dark mottled-brown wings with an eyespot in each and being native to tropical America but migrating as far north as Canada in summer

black wolf *n* **1 :** a melanistic color phase of the European wolf once common in the Pyrenees **2 :** a melanistic color phase of the American gray wolf **3 :** KARAKURT

blackwood \ˈ⸗,⸗\ *n* **:** any of several hardwood trees or their dark-colored wood: as **a :** BLACK MANGROVE 1 **b :** an East Indian tree (*Dalbergia latifolia*) having a useful dark purple wood — called also *East Indian rosewood* **c :** LOGWOOD 1 **d :** LIGHTWOOD 2a

black·wood convention \ˈblak‚wu̇d-\ *n, usu cap B* [after Easley F. *Blackwood*, 20th cent. American who devised it] **:** a bidding method used in reaching slam contracts in contract bridge and consisting of the use of four no-trump as an asking bid to which the bidder's partner is supposed to respond five clubs if he holds no ace, five diamonds if he holds one ace, five hearts if he holds two aces, five spades if he holds three aces, or five no-trump if he holds four aces and the use of five no-trump as an asking bid to which the bidder's partner is supposed to respond six clubs with no king, six diamonds with one king, six hearts with two, six spades with three, or six no-trump with four

black·work \'=,=\ *n* **1 :** metal products (as forgings or rolled work) that have not undergone a process (as pickling or machining) that gives a bright finish **2 :** embroidery worked in black thread on white material

black wrack *n* **:** a rockweed (*Fucus serratus*) common in the No. Atlantic

¹**blacky** \'blakē, -ki\ *adj* [¹*black* + *-y*] **:** somewhat black **:** BLACKISH

²**blacky** *var of* BLACKIE

black yeast *n* **:** any of various yeasts or similar organisms (as of the genera *Torula* and *Monilia*) that form colonies of a characteristic black color

blacky-white \¦==¦=\ *n* **:** ²ANGLO-INDIAN 2 — usu. used disparagingly

¹**blad** \'blad, -ȧd\ *vt* **bladded; bladded; bladding; blads** [origin unknown] **1** *chiefly Scot* **:** slap hard **:** STRIKE **2** *chiefly Scot* **:** to beat against **:** BUFFET ⟨the wind *bladding* the young trees⟩

²**blad** \"\ *n* -s **1** *Scot* **:** SLAP, BLOW **2** *Scot* **a :** PORTION **b :** SELECTION, FRAGMENT

¹**blad·der** \'bladə(r)\ *n* -s [ME *bladdre*, fr. OE *blǣdre* bladder, blister; akin to OHG *blātara* bladder, ON *blathra* blister, OE *blāwan* to blow — more at BLOW] **1 a :** a membranous sac in animals that serves as the receptacle of a fluid or contains gas ⟨urinary ~⟩ ⟨gall ~⟩ — usu. used of the urinary bladder when unqualified; see AIR BLADDER **b :** a vesicle or pouch forming part of an animal body ⟨the ~ of a larval tapeworm⟩ **c :** VESICLE **c 2 a :** a urinary bladder dressed and used for some purpose, esp. as a container ⟨a ~ of lard⟩ **b :** a man-made flexible and elastic container (as a toy balloon or the rubber lining of an inflatable ball) suggesting such a bladder **3 :** something resembling a bladder esp. in being inflated, empty, or unsound; *specif* **:** a pretentious self-important person

²**bladder** \"\ *vb* -ED/-ING/-S *archaic* **:** to puff up **:** swell out **:** INFLATE

bladder-and-string \¦===¦=\ *n* **:** an ancient burlesque bass fiddle consisting of a string stretched on a pole and over a bladder and bowed with a notched stick — called also *bumbass*

bladder campion *n* **1 :** any of several plants of the genus *Silene* having a much-inflated calyx; *esp* **:** a bluish green herb (*S. latifolia*) **2 :** an alpine plant (*Wahlbergella apetala*) of the Rocky mountain region having a calyx in shape suggestive of a Chinese lantern

bladder catchfly *n* **:** a bladder campion (*Silene latifolia*)

bladder cell *n* **:** any of numerous large vacuolated cells conspicuous in the outer layers of the tunic of certain tunicates

blad·der·et \¦bladə¦ret\ *n* -s [¹*bladder* + *-et*] *archaic* **:** a little bladder

bladder fern *n* **:** a fern of a genus (*Cystopteris*) characterized by a hooded or bladderlike indusium; *esp* **:** a common No. American fern (*C. fragilis*) with finely dissected fronds

bladder fucus *n* **:** BLADDER WRACK 1

bladder green *n* **:** SAP GREEN 2b

bladder kelp *n* **:** any of various brown algae with prominent floats**:** as **a :** BLADDER WRACK 1 **b :** SEA-OTTER'S-CABBAGE

bladder ket·mia \-'ketmēə\ *n* **:** FLOWER-OF-AN-HOUR

bladderlike \'==,=\ *adj* **1 :** similar to a bladder esp. in form or distensibility ⟨the ~ float of a Portuguese man-of-war⟩ **2 :** inflated like a bladder **:** BLADDERY 1

bladdernose \'==,=\ *n* [so called fr. the inflatable sac on the head] **:** HOODED SEAL

bladdernut \'==,=\ *n* **1 :** a shrub or small tree of the genus *Staphylea* **2 :** the bladderlike seed pod of any bladdernut shrub or tree

bladdernut family *n* **:** STAPHYLEACEAE

bladderpipe \'==,=\ *n* **:** a primitive bagpipe with an animal's bladder used for the bag

bladder plum *n* **:** PLUM POCKET

bladderpod \'==,=\ *n* **:** any of certain plants having inflated pods**:** as **a :** an American herb of the genera *Physaria* and *Lesquerella* **b :** INDIAN TOBACCO **c :** a European plant of the genus *Vesicaria* **d :** a California shrub (*Isomeris arborea*) of the family Capparidaceae **e :** BAGPOD

bladderseed \'==,=\ *n* **:** a plant of a European genus (*Physospermum*) of the family Umbelliferae with seeds that are somewhat inflated and have large oil tubes

bladder senna *n* **1 :** any of several leguminous shrubs of the genus *Colutea*; *esp* **:** a yellow-flowered European shrub (*C. arborescens*) cultivated for its flowers and bladdery pod and as a source of wildlife food **2 :** a southern African shrub (*Sutherlandia frutescens*) with a much-inflated pod

bladder snout *n* **:** BLADDERWORT

bladder tree *n* **:** BLADDERNUT 1

bladderweed \'==,=\ *n* **:** a seaweed (as the bladder wrack) with air bladders in the fronds

bladder worm *n* **1 :** a saclike or bladderlike tapeworm larva (as a cysticercus, a coenurus, or a hydatid) **2 :** a parasitic worm infesting the urinary bladder; *esp* **:** a nematode (*Capillaria plica*) of the bladder of many carnivores

bladderwort \'==,=\ *n* -s **:** any of several aquatic plants of the genus *Utricularia* having bladderlike floats; *broadly* **:** any of numerous members of the family (Lentibulariaceae) to which *Utricularia* belongs

bladderwort family *n* **:** LENTIBULARIACEAE

bladder wrack *n* **1 :** a common black rockweed (*Fucus vesiculosus*) used in preparing kelp and as a manure **2 :** a seaweed (*Ascophyllum nodosum*) closely related to bladder wrack and often found intermingled with it

blad·dery \'bladərē, -ri\ *adj* **1 a :** resembling a bladder esp. in being swollen but empty **b :** PUFFY, INFLATED ⟨a fruit with ~ pulp⟩ **2 :** having or characterized by bladders ⟨certain ~ kelps⟩

¹**blade** \'blād\ *n* -s [ME, fr. OE *blæd*; akin to OHG *blat* leaf, ON *blath*, L *folium*, Gk *phyllon* leaf, OE *blōwan* to blossom — more at BLOW] **1 a :** a leaf of a plant; *esp* **:** a leaf of an herb or more narrowly of a grass ⟨~*s* of stunted grass⟩ **b** *chiefly Scot* **:** a leaf that is broad and flat ⟨a ~ of rhubarb⟩ **c (1) :** the expanded portion of a leaf or a plant organ resembling a leaf **:** LAMINA 2b(1) — distinguished from *petiole* (2) **:** the broad terminal part of certain petals — distinguished from *claw* **2 :** an object or part of an object resembling the blade of a leaf esp. in broadness and flatness**:** as **a :** the broad flattened part of an oar or paddle that exerts force against the water to propel a boat **b :** something with an action basically similar to that of the blade of an oar**:** as (1) **:** a fluke of a whale (2) **:** a float of a paddle wheel (3) **:** an arm of a screw propeller, centrifugal fan, or steam turbine (4) **:** an airfoil used as a propeller to produce thrust or as a part of the lift-producing system of a rotary-wing aircraft **c :** a broad flat bone (as one of the rami of a mandible); *specif* **:** SCAPULA — now used chiefly in naming cuts of meat ⟨a ~ chop⟩; see BEEF illustration **d :** a piece of mace **e :** the part of the arm of an anchor behind the palm **f :** the expanded rear portion of the comb of a single-comb fowl — see COCK illustration **g :** the striking surface of a golf club or a hockey stick **h** *phonetics* (1) **:** the portion of the tongue immediately behind the tip and lying approximately opposite the teethridge when the tongue is at rest (2) **:** this portion of the tongue together with the tip **i :** the light-obstructing portion of the shutter of a camera **j :** an inclined metal slab that functions as an ink reservoir in the fountain mechanism of a printing press **k :** the broad, flat, or concave part of a road grader, bulldozer, or snowplow that comes into direct contact with the material to be moved **3 :** an object or part of an object resembling a blade of grass**:** as **a :** the cutting part of an instrument ⟨the ~ of a sword⟩ ⟨well-set saw ~*s*⟩ **b :** an edged instrument**:** as (1) **:** SWORD (2) **:** a stone tool similar to a knife and having one or more sharp cutting edges **c :** the runner of an ice skate **d :** the long arm of a T square or carpenter's square **e :** a single plate of baleen from a right whale **f :** one of the movable conducting bars of an electrical switch **g :** a slat esp. in a venetian blind, louver, or shutter **4 :** a human being**: a :** SWORDSMAN **b :** a sharp-witted, dashing, wild, or reckless fellow ⟨such a gay ~ of a fellow⟩ **c :** WOMAN ⟨the old ~ shouldn't last much longer⟩ **5 :** one of the principal rafters of a roof

²**blade** \"\ *vb* -ED/-ING/-S [ME *bladen*, fr. *blade*, n.] *vt* **1 :** to furnish with a blade **2** *chiefly Scot* **:** to pluck leaves from (a plant) ⟨*blading* cabbages for market⟩ **3 :** to remove (as gravel or dirt) with machinery having a blade (as a grader or bulldozer) ~ *vi* **1 :** to leaf out **:** put forth leaves **2 :** to remove typically gravel, dirt, or muck with machinery having a blade

³**blade** \"\ *adj* [¹*blade*] *of speech sounds* **:** articulated with or involving the participation of the blade of the tongue ⟨\s\ and \z\ are ~ consonants⟩

blade angle *n* **:** the angle between the chord of a propeller or rotor blade and a plane normal to the axis of rotation, its value varying along the span and decreasing from root to tip because of blade twist

blade apple *n* **:** BARBADOS GOOSEBERRY

blade back *n* **:** the surface of a propeller or rotor blade that corresponds to the upper surface of a lifting airfoil

bladebone \'=,=\ *n* -s **1 :** SCAPULA **2 :** a cut of meat containing part of the bladebone

blad·ed \'blādəd\ *adj* [¹*blade* + *-ed*] *of a mineral* **:** composed of plates shaped like knife blades

blade face *n* **:** the surface of a propeller or rotor blade that corresponds to the lower surface of a lifting airfoil — called also *driving face, thrust face*

blade harrow *n* **:** ACME HARROW

blade loading *n* **:** the gross weight of a rotary-wing aircraft divided by the total area of the rotor blades

blade plate *n* **:** a metal plate consisting of a shank terminated by a blade at an angle used in correcting and holding fractures in the upper end of the femur

blade-point \'=,=\ *adj, of a speech sound* **:** articulated with or involving the participation of the blade and raised tip of the tongue ⟨\sh\ is a *blade-point* sound with many speakers⟩

blad·er \'blādə(r)\ *n* -s [¹*blade* + *-er*] **1 :** a bladed implement or vehicle **2 :** a worker who fits blades on turbines

blades *pl of* BLADE, *pres 3d sing of* BLADE

blade section *n* **:** a cross section of a propeller blade in a plane parallel to that containing the axis of rotation

bladesmith \'=,=\ *n* **:** a cutler who makes blades

blad·ing \'blādiŋ\ *n* -s [¹*blade* + *-ing*] **:** a set of blades (as of a cutter bar or in a turbine)

blads *pres 3d sing of* BLAD, *pl of* BLAD

blady \'blādē\ *adj* -ER/-EST [¹*blade* + *-y*] **1 :** having or made up of blades ⟨coarse ~ fodder⟩ **2 :** like a blade ⟨~ elbows⟩

bladygrass \'=,=\ *n, Austral* **:** COGON

blae \'blā\ *adj* [ME *bla* (northern dial.), *blo* (southern dial.), fr. ON *blār* — more at BLUE] *chiefly Scot* **:** dark blue or bluish gray **:** BLUISH**: a** *of the skin* **:** livid or lead-colored (as from a bruise) **b** *of weather* **:** DARK, BLEAK, CHEERLESS ⟨the ~ east wind⟩

blae·ber·ry \'blā- — *see* BERRY\ *n* [ME (northern dial.) *blaberie*, fr. *bla* blae + *berie* berry] *chiefly Scot* **:** BILBERRY

blae·wort \'blāwərt\ *var of* BLAWORT

blaf·fert \'bläfə(r)t\ *n* -s [MHG] **:** a base silver coin of Switzerland and Germany in the 15th century — called also *plappert*

blaf·lum \'blaf(l)əm, blə'f(l)əm\ *n* -s [origin unknown] *chiefly Scot* **:** empty talk **:** HOAX

blag·gard *n* -s [by alter.] **:** BLACKGUARD

¹**blague** \'bläg, -ȧg\ *n* -s [F] **:** HUMBUG, CLAPTRAP, RAILLERY

²**blague** \"\ *vi* -ED/-ING/-S **:** to talk pretentiously and usu. inaccurately **:** lie boastfully

¹**blah** \'blä, -ȧ\ *also* **blah-blah** \'=,=\ *or* **blaa** \'blä, -ȧ\ *or* **blaa-blaa** \'=,=\ *n* -s [prob. fr. *blah-blah*, interj. used as a derogatory comment on meaningless chatter, of imit. origin] **:** silly or pretentious nonsense **:** BUNKUM, HOKUM ⟨this week a record is being made in the output of ~, bunkum, and hypocrisy —Raymond Moley⟩

²**blah** \"\ *adj* **:** dull and unattractive ⟨when the dormitory fare gets too ~ to bear —*Mademoiselle*⟩ **:** without verve or originality ⟨she was just ~ but her friend wasn't so bad⟩

blah-blah \'blä,blä, 'blȧ,blȧ\ *also* **blah** *vb* -ED/-ING/-S [prob. fr. *blah-blah*, interj.] *vi* **:** to utter blah ~ *vt* **:** REPEAT, MOUTH ⟨*blah-blahing* their outworn slogans⟩

blain \'blān\ *n* -s [ME *blein*, fr. OE *blegen*; akin to MLG *bleine* blain, OSw *blena* blain, OE *blāwan* to blow — more at BLOW] **:** an inflammatory swelling or sore **:** BULLA, PUSTULE, BLISTER — now used chiefly of animals

blake \'blāk\ *adj* [ME, pale, fr. OE *blāc* — more at BLEACH] *dial Eng* **:** YELLOW — often used of foodstuffs ⟨fine ~ butter⟩

blake·ite \'blā,kīt\ *n* -s [William P. *Blake* †1910 Am. geologist & mineralogist + E *-ite*] **:** a mineral consisting of an iron tellurite found sparingly in the mines at Goldfield, Nev.

bla·lock-taus·sig operation \¦blā,läk'tausig-\ *n, usu cap B&T* [after Alfred *Blalock* b1899 & Helen B. *Taussig* b1898 Am. physicians who devised it] **:** surgical correction of the congenital malformation of the heart known as tetralogy of Fallot — called also *blue-baby operation*

blam·a·ble *also* **blame·a·ble** \'blāməbəl\ *adj* [ME *blamable*, fr. *blamen* + *-able*] **:** deserving reproach, blame, or censure **:** REPREHENSIBLE ⟨the most ~ act of his life⟩ **syn** see BLAMEWORTHY

blam·a·bly *also* **blame·ably** \-məblē, -li\ *adv* **:** in a blamable manner

¹**blame** \'blām\ *vt* -ED/-ING/-S [ME *blamen*, fr. OF *blamer*, *blasmer*, fr. (assumed) VL *blastemare*, alter. of LL *blasphemare* to revile, blaspheme, fr. Gk *blasphēmein* to speak ill of, blaspheme, fr. *blasphēmos* evil-speaking, fr. *blas-* (perh. akin to Gk *meleos* futile, unhappy) + *-phēmos* (fr. *phanai* to say); akin to MIr *mell* error, Lith *melas* lie, Av *mairya* deceitful — more at BAN] **1 :** to express disapproval of **:** find fault with **:** REPROACH ⟨Aristotle, while *blaming* the man who is unduly passionate, ~*s* equally the man who is insensitive —G.L.Dickinson⟩ **2 a :** to attribute responsibility to **:** make answerable — usu. used with *for* ⟨the *blamed* himself for the failure on the agricultural front —T.P.Whitney⟩ **b :** to ascribe responsibility for **:** account for by placing culpability — usu. used with *on* ⟨dimly conscious that something was wrong, he *blamed* it on his father —E.L.Acken⟩ **3** *obs* **:** to bring reproach upon **:** LOWER, ABASE **4 :** BLAST, DAMN — used in the imperative as a mild imprecation ⟨~ this rainy weather⟩ **syn** see CRITICIZE — **to blame :** deserving blame **:** at fault **:** RESPONSIBLE ⟨the conductor was *to blame* for the accident⟩ ⟨I know the cucumbers were *to blame* for his upset⟩

²**blame** \"\ *n* -s [ME, fr. MF *blame*, fr. *blamer*] **1 :** expression of disapproval or reproach **:** REPROOF, CENSURE ⟨saying nothing . . . either in the way of ~ or praise —R.L.Stevenson⟩ **2 a :** CULPABILITY, FAULT ⟨acknowledge the world as a world of common ~ —Muriel Rukeyser⟩ **b** *archaic* **:** GUILT, CRIME, SIN ⟨that we should be holy and without ~ before him —Eph 1:4 (AV)⟩ **3 :** responsibility for something that deserves or is felt to deserve censure ⟨the low-tax lobby at home must share the ~ for starving local and state governments —K.F.Zeisler⟩ **4** *obs* **:** HURT, INJURY

¹**blamed** \'blām(d)\ *also* **blame** \-m\ *adj* **:** DARNED, BLASTED, CONFOUNDED — used as a mild imprecation ⟨it's a ~ shame⟩

²**blamed** \"\ *or* **blame** \"\ *adv, dial* **:** EXCEEDINGLY, DEUCEDLY, VERY ⟨a ~ cold winter⟩

blame·ful \-mfəl\ *adj* [ME, fr. ²*blame* + *-ful*] **:** deserving disapproval, blame, or punishment **:** GUILTY ⟨by our peculiar double standard the taker of the bribe is considered more ~ than the giver —Estes Kefauver⟩ — **blame·ful·ly** \-fəlē, -li\ *adv*

blame·less \-mləs\ *adj* [ME, fr. ²*blame* + *-less*] **:** free from blame or fault **:** IRREPROACHABLE ⟨has lived a ~ life and . . . has prospered —Green Peyton⟩ — **blame·less·ly** *adv* — **blame·less·ness** *n* -ES

blam·er \-mə(r)\ *n* -s [ME, fr. *blamen* + *-er*] **:** one that blames

blameworthiness \'=,===\ *n* -ES **:** the quality or state of being blameworthy

blameworthy \'=,==\ *adj* [ME, fr. ²*blame* + *worthy*] **:** deserving blame **:** at fault **:** CENSURABLE

syn BLAMABLE, GUILTY, CULPABLE**:** BLAMEWORTHY and BLAMABLE, wide in application and lacking specific suggestions, are used when GUILTY and CULPABLE are too severe ⟨anyone in any party who falls below the level of the high spirit of national unity which alone can give national salvation is *blameworthy* —Sir Winston Churchill⟩ ⟨a *blamable* or at least questionable, lack of such doings —G.G.Coulton⟩ GUILTY usually refers to serious offenses ⟨in old German law infanticide was treated as the murder of a relative. The *guilty* mother was buried alive in a sack —W.G.Sumner⟩ It may indicate legal proof or conviction of guilt ⟨tried, all five, found *guilty*, and put to death —Robert Browning⟩ It may indicate a state of mind or the expression of it ⟨the woman's face was *guilty* —Arnold Bennett⟩ CULPABLE suggests less stringent blame than GUILTY and connotes malfeasance or errors of omission, negligence, or ignorance ⟨a most urgent telegram was dispatched to you from London by Godfrey Staunton at six-fifteen yesterday evening — a telegram which is undoubtedly associated with his disappearance — and yet you have not had it. It is most *culpable* —A. Conan Doyle⟩ ⟨the prevailing abuses, *culpable* stupidity, common dishonesty and empty political buncombe, which too often passes for statesmanship —J.H.Robinson †1936⟩

blam·ing·ly *adv* **:** in a blaming manner

blanc \'blaŋk, -ai-, 'bläⁿ\ *also* **blank** \'blaŋk, -ai-\ *n* -s [F *blanc*, fr. OF, fr. *blanc*, adj., white — more at BLANK] **:** a French coin of the 14th to 18th centuries orig. of silver but later debased

blanc de chine \¦bläⁿdə¦shēn\ *n* [F, lit., white of China] **:** a white Chinese porcelain made at Te-hua and often decorated with embossed ornament but without color

blanc fixe \bläⁿ 'fēks\ *n* [F, lit., fixed white] **:** barium sulfate obtained as a fine heavy white precipitate from aqueous solutions of a soluble barium compound (as barium sulfide) and sodium sulfate

¹**blanch** \'blanch, -aa(ə)n-,-ain-,-ȧn-\ *adj* [ME *blaunche*, *blanche*, fr. MF *blanche*, fem. of *blanc* white — more at BLANK] **1** *Eng law* **:** of or relating to a white rent **2** *or* **blench** \-len-\ *Scots law* **:** of or relating to a nominal duty paid as a quitrent or the tenure held by payment of such rent

²**blanch** \"\ *vb* -ED/-ING/-ES [ME *blaunchen*, fr. MF *blanchir*, fr. OF, fr. *blanche*] *vt* **1 :** to take the color out of and make white **:** BLEACH ⟨~*ing* linen on the grass⟩ ⟨age has ~*ed* his hair⟩**: a :** to bleach by excluding light; *esp* **:** to bleach (the leaves or stalks of plants) by earthing, boarding, or wrapping **b :** to scald or parboil (foods) in boiling water or steam in order to remove the skin from (as almonds), whiten (as kidney), or stop enzymatic action in (as fruits or vegetables for canning or freezing) **c :** to clean (a coin blank) in an acid solution **d :** to cover (sheet iron or steel) with a coating of tin **2 :** to make ashen or pale ⟨fear ~*es* the cheek and stills the heart⟩ **3 :** to give a favorable appearance to **:** WHITEWASH, GLOSS — often used with *over* ~ *vi* **:** to become pale **:** WHITEN **:** grow pallid or ashen ⟨his face ~*ed* with horror⟩ ⟨some red roses ~ in the direct sun⟩

³**blanch** \"\ *vb* -ED/-ING/-ES [alter. of ¹*blench*] *vt* **:** to cause to turn aside or back **:** HEAD 5b ⟨crashed through the brush and ~*ed* a deer⟩ ~ *vi* **:** to flinch or shrink back

¹**blanch·er** \-nchə(r)\ *n* -s [²*blanch* + *-er*] **:** one that blanches something (as foods, metals, linens)

²**blancher** *n* -s [³*blanch* + *-er*] *obs* **:** a person or object stationed for turning driven game in the desired direction

blanching *adj* [fr. pres. part. of ²*blanch*] **:** destructive of color — **blanch·ing·ly** *adv*

blanc·mange \blə'mänj, -äⁿzh\ *n* -s [alter. of ME *blancmanger*, fr. MF *blanc manger*, fr. *blanc* white (fr. OF) + *manger* food, fr. OF *mangier*, fr. *mangier* to eat, fr. L *manducare* to chew, eat — more at BLANK, MANGER] **:** a dessert made from gelatinous or starchy substances and milk usu. sweetened, flavored, and shaped in a mold

blancmanger *n* -s [ME] *archaic* **:** BLANCMANGE

blan·co \'blaŋ(,)kō\ *vt* -ED/-ING/-ES [*Blanco*] **:** to whiten with Blanco whitening

Blanco \"\ *trademark* — used for a substance used to whiten belts or other equipment esp. in the British army

¹**bland** \'bland, -aa(ə)nd\ *adj, usu* -ER/-EST [L *blandus*] **1 a :** smooth and soothing in manner **:** GENTLE, SUAVE, INGRATIATING ⟨~ approval⟩ ⟨a ~ smile⟩ **b :** exhibiting no personal concern or embarrassment **:** UNCONCERNED, UNPERTURBED ⟨the criminal made a ~ confession⟩ **2 a :** having soft and soothing qualities **:** not drastic or irritating **:** not stimulating or vigorous ⟨a ~ oil⟩ ⟨a simple ~ diet⟩ ⟨the ~ climate of the southern coast⟩ **b :** FLAT, DULL, INSIPID, WISHY-WASHY ⟨a ~ pudding⟩ ⟨he submits and becomes ~ and tasteless —Norman Kelman⟩ **3 :** not infected ⟨a ~ infarct⟩ **syn** see SOFT, SUAVE

²**bland** \"\ *n* -s [ON *blanda*, fr. *blanda* to mix — more at BLEND] **:** a drink of the Orkney and Shetland islands consisting of buttermilk and water

blan·da \'bländə\ *or* **be·lan·da** \bə'ländə, 'bl-\ *n* -s *cap* [Malay *bĕlanda*, fr. a Dravidian word derived fr. Pg *Holanda* Holland] **:** DUTCHMAN — used esp. in the Malay peninsula

bland dollar \'bland-, -aa(ə)nd-\ *n, usu cap B* [after Richard P. *Bland* †1899 U.S. congressman] **:** the U.S. silver dollar of 412½ grains troy coined under the Bland-Allison Act of 1878 that provided for the free coinage of silver

bland·for·dia \blan'fȯrdēə\ *n, cap* [NL, fr. George, Marquis of *Blandford*, 19th cent. Englishman + NL *-ia*] **:** a genus of Australian tuberous-rooted plants (family Liliaceae) having large orange or crimson flowers

blan·ding's turtle \'blandiŋz-\ *n, usu cap B* [after William *Blanding*, 19th cent. Am. herpetologist] **:** a freshwater turtle (*Emys blandingii*) of the northeastern U.S. and Canada having a black or dark olive shell with small yellow spots

blan·din's gland \bläⁿ'daⁿz-, 'blandənz-\ *n, usu cap B* [after Philippe F. *Blandin* †1849 Fr. surgeon] **:** ANTERIOR LINGUAL GLAND

blan·dish \'blandish, -aan-, -dēsh, *esp in pres part* -dəsh\ *vb* -ED/-ING/-ES [ME *blandishen*, fr. MF *blandiss-*, stem of *blandir*, fr. L *blandiri*, fr. *blandus* mild, flattering] *vt* **:** to flatter with soft words or affectionate actions **:** COAX, CAJOLE ⟨found herself being ~*ed* by millionaires —Lee Rogow⟩ ~ *vi* **:** to act or speak in a flattering manner

blan·dish·er \-shə(r)\ *n* -s **:** one that blandishes **:** FLATTERER, CAJOLER

blandishing *adj* [ME, fr. pres. part. of *blandishen*] **:** FLATTERING, CAJOLING — **blan·dish·ing·ly** *adv*

blan·dish·ment \-shmənt\ *n* -s [*blandish* + *-ment*] **:** speech, action, or device that flatters and tends to coax or cajole **:** ALLUREMENT — often used in pl. ⟨he refuses to yield to their ~*s* —Irving Babbitt⟩

bland·ly *adv* [¹*bland* + *-ly*] **:** in a bland manner

¹**blank** \'blaŋk, -aiŋk\ *adj, usu* -ER/-EST [ME, fr. MF *blanc*, of Gmc origin; akin to OHG *blanch* shining, bright, white, OE *blanca* white horse, ON *blakkr*; akin to L *flagrare* to burn — more at BLACK] **1** *archaic* **:** of a white or pale color **:** lacking color **2 a** *archaic* **:** lacking resource or answer **:** DISCONCERTED **:** taken aback **:** ABASHED ⟨the Damsel of Burgundy at sight of her own letter was soon ~ —John Milton⟩ **b** *of emotions* **:** OVERMASTERING, INTENSE, SHEER **:** lacking relief or break ⟨watched with ~ awe⟩ ⟨~ terror gripped them⟩ **c** *of expressions* **:** lacking animation as though dazed, confounded, or nonplused ⟨her face ~ with wonder⟩ **3 a :** devoid of interest or event, of variety or change, or of affections or hopes ⟨a ~ prospect⟩ ⟨if it is a bad day, he can occupy his ~ hours looking at the scenery —Michael Warr⟩ **b :** devoid of covering or content **:** UNOCCUPIED, UNFILLED ⟨a ~ space⟩ **c :** free from writing or marks — used of paper or other substances normally written on ⟨give me a ~ sheet to do my sums⟩ **d :** having an empty space or spaces to be filled in with some special writing ⟨a ~ application form⟩ ⟨a ~ check⟩ **e :** BLIND 6d **f** (1) **:** lacking some critical ingredient ⟨a ~ solution used as a control⟩ (2) **:** involving the use of such a blank substance (as in analysis or pharmacological experimentation) ⟨a ~ test⟩ ⟨a ~ run⟩ **g** (1) **:** lacking any card **:** VOID ⟨a ~ suit⟩ ⟨he was ~ in spades⟩ (2) **:** containing no valuable cards **:** WORTHLESS ⟨a ~ hand⟩ **4 :** ABSOLUTE, DOWNRIGHT, UNMIXED, ⟨the ~ impossibilities of Lilliput —Thomas De Quincey⟩ **5 :** having a plain or unbroken surface where an opening, finish, or other interruption of continuity is usual**:** as **a** *of a key* **:** not yet having had the slots made **b** *of an architectural feature* **:** lacking the opening that is characteristic of such a feature ⟨a ~ arch⟩ ⟨~ window over a stair well⟩ **6 :** of a kind denoted euphemistically or for the occasion by a blank (sense) 4 — often used as a

substitute for an abusive or imprecatory epithet ⟨you ~ idiot⟩ or for something (as a date or address) that one cannot or is unwilling to supply ⟨when the ~ regiment was transferred to Ireland⟩ **syn** see EMPTY

²blank \"\ *n* -s **1 a :** an empty space on a paper or in any written or printed instrument ⟨leave a ~ for his signature⟩ **b :** a paper with spaces left to be filled with desired or appropriate data (as names, dates, descriptions); *esp* **:** a paper containing the substance of a document or legal instrument (as a deed, release, or charter) with spaces to be filled in before execution ⟨a deed made out in ~⟩ **c :** a sheet, card, leaf, or other object without printing, writing, or other impression on it ⟨this machine turns out few ~*s*⟩ **2 a :** an empty form without substance or significance ⟨he is a mere ~ of what he once was⟩ **b :** an empty place or space ⟨my mind became a ~ when I heard the question⟩ **c :** an empty interval; *esp* **:** a period devoid of consciousness, interest, action, or result ⟨a long ~ in American history between the decline of the Mayans and the Aztec civilization⟩ ⟨they say I talked rationally enough but for me the time after the accident was a total ~⟩ **d :** something useless, valueless, or undesirable; *specif* **:** a lottery ticket that does not win a prize — usu. used as object of *draw* **3 :** something aimed at; *specif* **:** the bull's-eye of a target **4 :** a dash written or printed as a substitute for an omitted word — see ¹BLANK 6 **5** *archaic* **:** BLANK VERSE ⟨and rhyme and ~ maintain an equal race —Lord Byron⟩ **6 :** something in an unfinished or incomplete state that is designed for further working or manipulation: as **a :** a piece of flint or shell roughly blocked out for later shaping into a prehistoric tool **b :** a wooden gunstock before it is cut to receive the metal parts **c :** a piece of material prepared to be made into something (as a coin, key, screw, tile, or container) by a further operation; *esp* **:** a small segment (as one produced by punching, sawing, or cleaving a large sheet, block, or billet) suitable for the production of a single finished piece (as a dowel, key, or button) **d :** an unrecorded lacquer disc **7 :** BLANK DETERMINATION **8 :** any of certain cardboards made in standard thicknesses with a white or colored liner and combining stiffness and printability **9 :** an old moneyers' unit of weight equal to $\frac{1}{24}$ perit or $\frac{1}{230400}$ grain **10 a :** something lacking a critical element and used (as in experimental medicine or chemical analysis) to provide a control for comparison with the complete material; *esp* **:** a solution for use in a blank determination **b :** BLANK CARTRIDGE **11 :** a domino without any spots on one of its halves **12 a :** an instance of having no cards in a specified suit **:** VOID ⟨a ~ in spades⟩ **b :** CARTE BLANCHE

³blank \"\ *vb* -ED/-ING/-S *vt* **1** *archaic* **:** NONPLUS, FOIL, DISCONCERT **b :** to make void or ineffective **:** FRUSTRATE **2 a :** OBSTRUCT, OBSCURE, BLOT — usu. used with *out* ⟨an announcement apparently timed to ~ out their opponents' claims of progress⟩ **b :** to seal (as an oil sand, a tunnel, or part of a pipeline) against the unwanted flow of oil or water — used with *off* **c :** to make (a radio or television signal) undetectable at the output for short periods of time in order to avoid undesirable effects (as return traces in a television receiver) **3 a :** to indicate by a written or printed dash — compare ²BLANK 4 **b :** DAMN ⟨~ him! that is just like him —Charles Reade⟩ **4 :** to keep (an opposing team) from scoring **5 :** to cut with a die from a sheet or flat piece of stock **:** form into blanks — often used with *out* ⟨levers ~*ed* out of strip steel⟩ **6 :** to fill out with space (as a short line of type, a column, a page, or the nonprinting areas of a form) — often used with *out* **7 :** ²BLIND 4 ~ *vi* **1 :** to become obscure or tenuous **:** FADE — usu. used with *out* ⟨laughter and music that ~*ed* out as he passed on his way⟩ **2 :** to become confused or distrait **:** black out ⟨her mind seemed to have ~*ed* out —Peggy Bennett⟩

⁴blank *var of* BLANC

blank bar *n* **:** COMMON BAR

blankbook \ˈ=ˌ=\ *n* -s [¹*blank* + *book*] **:** a book of mostly blank pages or of printed forms; *esp* **:** one in a strong flat easily opened style of binding

blank cartridge *n* **:** a cartridge having instead of a projectile a wadding (as of paper) sealed in the mouth of the case

blank charter *n* **: 1** *obs* **:** a charter given to a crown agent in Richard II's time with liberty to fill it out as he pleased **2 :** liberty to do as one pleases ⟨our substitutes at home shall have *blank charters* —Shak.⟩

blank check *n* **1 :** a check signed by the maker but with the amount left to the discretion of the recipient **2 :** complete control or freedom of action **:** CARTE BLANCHE

blank determination *n* **:** a determination in analytical chemistry made as nearly as possible under the same conditions as a true determination but with the omission of the substance to be tested for the purpose of ascertaining the effect due to associated factors (as impurities in the reagents) — compare CONTROL EXPERIMENT

blank endorsement *n* **:** an endorsement of commercial paper that omits the name of a person in whose favor the endorsement is made and makes the paper payable to the bearer and that is usu. made by simply writing the name of the endorser on the back of the paper

blank·er \-kə(r)\ *n* -s [³*blank* + *-er*] **:** one that blanks; *specif* **:** a worker who cuts or punches blanks from sheet metal or other stock

¹blan·ket \ˈblaŋkət, -aiŋ-, *usu* -əd.+V\ *n* -s [ME, fr. OF *blanqete*, fr. *blanc* white + *-et* (dim. suffix) — more at BLANK] **1 a** *archaic* **:** a white or undyed woolen cloth **b :** a cloth woven with samples of various designs usu. used as a display sample or for experimental purposes **c** *or* **blanket cloth** (1) **:** a heavy reversible cotton fabric often with jacquard figures and usu. with a dense nap used for blankets and clothing (as bathrobes) (2) **:** a similar woolen cloth in solid colors used for coats **2 :** a sheet of fabric adapted to a particular purpose: as **a :** a piece of warm fabric for use as a bed covering being of wool, cotton, or synthetic yarns and usu. oblong and napped on both sides — compare QUILT, ROBE, SHEET **b :** a similar piece of fabric used as a body covering (as for a horse or dog) or among certain primitive peoples as a cloak **c :** a band of fabric running beneath the cloth in a cloth-printing machine and forming the covering of a slasher cylinder **d** (1) **:** a heavy cloth used to catch fine gold or valuable minerals (as in blanket sluices or on concentrating tables (2) **:** the permeable cloth sheet or membrane used in flotation cells in ore dressing **e** (1) **:** a sheet of wool, felt, or rubber in the packing of an impression cylinder to soften the impression or reduce make-ready in printing (2) **:** a rubber sheet in an offset press that receives the inked impression from the plate and transfers it to the surface being printed **3 :** a covering layer or sheet ⟨a ~ of clouds⟩ ⟨the still-white snow ~⟩: as **a :** a covering (as of sauce, chopped vegetable, bacon) on a service of food (as of meat or fish) ⟨a thick ~ of glutinous cream sauce⟩ **b :** a thin surface formed by one or more coats of bituminous material on a roadway **c :** a thin widespread geologic deposit ⟨a ~ ore deposit⟩ ⟨an alluvial ~⟩ — compare TABULAR **d :** a streak or layer of blubber in whales **e :** a floral display for a funeral designed to be spread over the coffin like a bed blanket **f :** a layer of a fire-extinguishing agent (as foam or gas) spread over a burning surface in order to smother the fire **g :** a layer of less active material surrounding the highly reactive core of an atomic reactor **h :** insulating or shock-absorbing material formed into batts or sheets for ease of application **4 :** a large pelt; *esp* **:** a beaver pelt of the largest market size **5 :** something that covers and encloses ⟨a ~ of gloom descended on us⟩ or serves to guard, isolate, and protect ⟨the airfield was under security ~*s*⟩ ⟨the vast Civil Service ~*s* which Presidents Roosevelt and Truman threw over Federal personnel —Arthur Krock⟩

²blanket \"\ *vt* -ED/-ING/-S **1 :** to cover with or as if with a blanket ⟨new green grass ~*ing* the slopes⟩ ⟨designed to ~ the Iron Curtain countries and other critical areas with powerful standard broadcasts —*N.Y.Times*⟩ **2** *archaic* **:** to toss in a blanket (as by way of punishment) **3 :** to cover so as to obscure, interrupt, suppress, or extinguish: as **a :** to cover (food) with a blanket **b :** to interfere with or stop (the fire of friendly forces) by coming into the line of fire or interposing friendly forces in the line of fire **c :** to make (radio receiving sets) ineffective by powerful signals or interference **d :** to take the wind out of the sails of by sailing to windward of (another ship) **e :** to control or extinguish (a fire) by means of a foam or gas blanket **f :** EXCLUDE, ELIMINATE — usu. used with *out* ⟨using an inert gas to ~ out corrosive fumes⟩ **4 a :** to cover or apply to uniformly despite wide separation or diversity among the elements included ⟨legislation ~*ing* subversive acts⟩ ⟨freight rates that ~ a region⟩ **b :** to cause to belong **:** cause to be included — often used with *into* or *in* ⟨every area . . . had automatically been ~*ed* into the San Jose Unified School District —*Fortnight*⟩ ⟨will result in ~*ing* additional millions into the old-age pension system⟩

³blanket \"\ *adj* **1 a :** including or covering a group or class without any individual apportionment ⟨~ insurance coverage⟩ ⟨a ~ wage increase⟩ **b :** effective or applicable in all instances or contingencies ⟨a ~ price⟩ ⟨~ rules⟩ ⟨a ~ complaint⟩ **2 a :** of, relating to, or suggestive of a blanket **b :** having contestants extremely close together — used of the finish of a race **3 :** consisting of one or more large sheets of newsprint folded once to make four pages each — often used in distinguishing the modern large newspaper from the tabloid

blanket ballot *n* **:** a single ballot listing all the offices to be filled and candidates to be voted upon and sometimes containing legislative proposals — called also JUNGLE BALLOT, LONG BALLOT; compare SHORT BALLOT

blanket bond *n* **1 :** an insurance policy covering a wide variety of risks (as loss from dishonesty of employees, burglary, misplacement, damage, or destruction of property) **2 :** a fidelity bond covering all or all of a category of the employees of the insured

blanket chest *n* **:** a piece of case furniture with hinged lid, a deep well, and one or two drawers underneath

blanket–coat \ˈ==ˌ=\ *n* **:** a heavy short coat of blanket material **:** MACKINAW

blanket cylinder *n* **1** *archaic* **:** IMPRESSION CYLINDER **2 :** the cylinder of an offset press that carries the rubber blanket

blanket deposit *n* **:** MANTO 2a

blanket fish *also* **blanket ray** *n* **:** MANTA 3

blanketflower \ˈ==ˌ=\ *n* **:** a flower or plant of the genus *Gaillardia* — compare INDIAN BLANKET

blanket indian *n, usu cap I* **:** an Indian who retains or returns to tribal costume and custom

blanketing *n* -s [¹*blanket* + *-ing*] **1 :** cloth for blankets **2 :** supply of blankets

blanket leaf *or* **blanket plant** *n* **:** MULLEIN

blanket mortgage *n* **:** a mortgage that covers a group or class of things or properties instead of one or more things mentioned individually (as a mortgage that secures various debts as a group or subjects a group or class of different pieces of property to one general lien)

blanket moss *n* **:** a felted scum of dead algae (as members of the genera *Spirogyra* or *Cladophora*) often found stranded after high water; *also* **:** an alga that is a constituent of such scum

blanket piece *n* **:** one of the large strips into which blubber is cut in removing it from a whale

blanket policy *n* **:** an insurance policy in which various items or classes of property (as buildings and contents) are covered

blanket rate *n* **1 :** GROUP RATE **2 a :** an insurance rate applying to two or more risks of a similar character but at different locations **b :** the insurance rate applying under a blanket policy

blanket roll *n* **1 :** a cylindrical pack made up of kit or accessories rolled in bedding and often in an outer water-resistant cover (as a shelter half or poncho) and used esp. by hikers and the military **2 :** a method of cheating at craps involving the throwing of the dice so that they will rotate only on their horizontal axes

blanket shawl *n* **:** a shawl made of blanketing or heavy woolen cloth

blanket sheet *n* **1 :** a newspaper of blanket size **2 :** a bed sheet or thin blanket of cotton having a nap on both sides

blanket stiff *n* **:** an itinerant usu. unskilled workman who travels with a blanket roll

blanket stitch *n* **:** a buttonhole stitch with spaces of variable width between the stitches

blanket–stitch \ˈ==ˌ=\ *vt* [*blanket stitch*] **:** to sew or finish with blanket stitches

blanketweed \ˈ==ˌ=\ *n* -s **:** a green alga of the genus *Cladophora* that often forms felted sheets along the shoreline

¹blank·ety–blank \ˌblaŋkəd·ēˈblaŋk, -aiŋkəd-\|dˈblaiŋk, -kət\|, \|ˌ-\ *also* **blankety** \ˈ===\ *adj (or adv)* [redupl. of ¹*blank*] **:** DAMNED — used as a generalized expression of disapproval ⟨the interruptions for those *blankety-blank* . . . commercials —Jack Gould⟩ ⟨do what he *blankety-blank* well pleases —Gerard Smith⟩

²blankety–blank \"\ *n* **:** WRETCH, FOOL — used as a generalized expression of disapproval ⟨that *blankety-blank* can't make up his mind whether he's for us or against us —*Newsweek*⟩

blanking *pres part of* BLANK

blanking die *n* **:** a cutting die that in conjunction with a blanking punch cuts out flat pieces of stock

blanking punch *n* **:** a punch used in conjunction with a blanking die

blank·ly *adv* [¹*blank* + *-ly*] **1 :** in a blank manner **:** without expression **:** VACUOUSLY ⟨gaze ~ at one⟩ **2 :** UTTERLY, COMPLETELY ⟨contains little that is not ~ medieval —H.O.Taylor⟩

blank·ness *n* -ES **:** the quality or state of being blank

blanks *pl of* BLANK, *pres 3d sing of* BLANK

blank signature *n* **:** a signature appended to a document (as a blank bill or note) that still has essential parts to be added and usu. authorizing any person to whom the document is delivered to fill it up as a bill for any amount subject to any limits stated in or on the instrument

blank tooling *n* **:** BLIND TOOLING

blank verse *n* **:** unrhymed verse; *specif* **:** the unrhymed iambic pentameter verse used esp. in English dramatic and narrative poetry

blank wall *n* **:** an impenetrable obstacle or barrier ⟨they suddenly saw a *blank wall* raised between government and a man —Vannevar Bush⟩

blanky \ˈblaŋkī\ *adj* [¹*blank* + *-y*] *Brit* **:** BLANKETY-BLANK

blanquette \blänˈket\ *n* -s [F, prob. fr. Prov *blanqueto*, fr. *blanc* white, of Gmc origin; akin to OHG *blanch* white — more at BLANK] **:** a light meat (as veal or breast of chicken) in a white sauce

blan·qui·llo \bläŋˈkē(ˌ)(y)ō\ *n* -s [Sp, fr. *blanco* white (fr. OSp, fr. OF *blanc*) + *-illo*, dim. suffix — more at BLANK] **:** a marine fish of the percoid family Branchiostegidae including several important food fishes (as the ocean whitefish and the tilefish)

blan·quism \ˈbläŋˌkizəm\ *n* -s *usu cap* [Louis-Auguste *Blanqui* †1881 Fr. socialist + E *-ism*] **:** the revolutionary doctrine that a socialist state could be established only by an immediate seizure of power by the workers themselves

blan·quist \-kəst\ *n* -s *usu cap* [Louis-Auguste *Blanqui* + E *-ist*] **:** an advocate of Blanquism

¹blare \ˈbla(a)(ə)r, -le(ə)r,-la(a)ə,-leə\ *vb* -ED/-ING/-S [ME *bleren, bloren*; akin to MHG *blēren, blerren* to bleat, *brüelen* to bellow, moo, OE *blǣtan* to bleat — more at BLEAT] *vi* **1** *now dial* **:** to utter a prolonged cry ⟨the calf *blared* for its mother⟩ **2 :** to sound with or as if with the loud and somewhat harsh tone characteristic of a trumpet ⟨radios *blaring* in the night⟩ **3** *of lights* **:** to shine forth brilliantly and often garishly **:** GLARE ~ *vt* **1 a :** to sound loudly and usu. harshly or vehemently ⟨sat *blaring* the car horn⟩ **b :** to proclaim loudly or announce sensationally or flamboyantly ⟨headlines *blared* his disgrace⟩ **2 :** to give off (light) brilliantly or garishly **:** GLARE ⟨the chandelier . . . *blared* light like a trumpet —Eleanor Clark⟩

²blare \"\ *n* -s **1 :** the loud and somewhat harsh sound of a trumpet **2 a :** a sound felt to resemble the blast of a trumpet ⟨an automobile passed before the house, its horn giving off a ~ —Hamilton Basso⟩ **b :** sound that is loud and often harsh ⟨the jukebox filled the room with ~⟩ **3 :** dazzling and often garish brilliance ⟨tunnels with their sudden ~ of daylight —Osbert Sitwell⟩ **4 :** sensationalism or flamboyance that often exceeds good taste ⟨for general ~ and blarney and pandemonium —C.L.Becker⟩; *also* **:** an instance of this ⟨a ~ of publicity⟩ **5 :** tar mixture used in caulking

bla·ri·na \bla(a)ˈrīnə, -ˈrēnə\ *n* [NL, perh. irreg. fr. *Blair*, Nebr. + NL *-ina*] **1** *cap* **:** a genus of short-tailed shrews widely distributed in No. America **2** -s *also* **blarina shrew :** any shrew of the genus *Blarina*

¹blar·ney \ˈblärnē, -ȧn-, -ni\ *vb* **blarneyed; blarneyed; blarneying; blarneys** *vt* **:** to influence or gain by smooth talk **:** WHEEDLE ⟨demagogues who pleasingly ~ the electorate —B.I.Bell⟩ ~ *vi* **:** to use flattering speech ⟨then would she wheedle and laugh and ~ —Nathaniel Hawthorne⟩

²blarney \"\ *n* -s [fr. *Blarney stone*, a stone in Blarney castle, near Cork, Ireland, reputed to bestow talent for eloquent cajolery upon those who kiss it] **:** smooth wheedling talk **:** FLATTERY ⟨made fun of his gift for ~, his adroitness in playing up to whatever an audience or a situation demanded of him —Eleanor Dark⟩

blart \ˈblät\ *n or vb* [prob. of imit. origin] *dial Eng* **:** CRY, BLEAT, BLARE

blas \ˈblas, -äs\ *n* -ES [D, fr. *blazen* to blow, fr. MD *blāsen*; akin to OHG *blāsan* to blow — more at BLAST] **:** a supposed emanation from the stars

bla·sé \(ˈ)bläˈzā, -lȧ- *also* -la-\ *adj* [F] **:** apathetic to pleasure or life esp. as a result of excessive indulgence or enjoyment **:** SOPHISTICATED ⟨the ~ traveler likes to refer to the ocean he has crossed as "the pond" —R.E.Coker⟩ **:** WORLD-WEARY ⟨the ~ indifference of . . . the people —Jack Belden⟩

¹blash \ˈblash\ *n* -ES [prob. of imit. origin] **1** *dial Brit* **:** a splash of liquid or mud **2** *dial Brit* **:** a shower of rain or sleet

²blash \"\ *vb* -ED/-ING/-ES *dial Brit* **:** SPLASH, SPLATTER

blashy \-shi\ *adj* [¹*blash* + *-y*] **1** *dial Brit* **:** RAINY, GUSTY, SPLASHY **2** *dial Brit, of food* **:** THIN, WATERY

blas·pheme \(ˈ)blasˈfēm, -laa-,-lai-\ *vb* -ED/-ING/-S [ME *blasfemen*, fr. LL *blasphemare* — more at BLAME] *vt* **1 :** to speak of or address with irreverence **:** revile impiously ⟨and when he reproved them they *blasphemed* all the saints in the calendar —W.H.Hudson †1922⟩ **2 :** to speak evil of **:** REVILE, ABUSE ⟨he has been *blasphemed* more than he deserves —*Wildlife Rev.*⟩ ~ *vi* **:** to utter blasphemy

blas·phem·er \-mə(r) *sometimes* ˈ=ˌsfəmə(r)\ *n* -s [ME *blasfemer*, fr. *blasfemen* + *-er*] **:** one that blasphemes

blaspheme–vine \ˈ=ˌ=ˌ=\ *n* **:** a greenbrier (*Smilax laurifolia*) of the southeastern U.S. with thick coriaceous leaves

blas·phe·mous \ˈblasfəməs, -laa-,-lai-, *now chiefly in substand speech* (ˈ)=ˈsfēməs\ *adj* [LL *blasphemus*, fr. Gk *blasphēmos* evil-speaking — more at BLAME] **1 :** speaking or writing blasphemy **:** impiously irreverent ⟨the ~ Swinburne is a very good though hardly a great poet —H.N.Fairchild⟩ **2 :** constituting blasphemy ⟨observing stiffly that such audacious claims were ~ —M.L.Bach⟩ **:** PROFANE ⟨a ~ epithet⟩ **syn** see IMPIOUS

blas·phe·mous·ly *adv* **:** in a blasphemous manner

blas·phe·my \ˈblasfəmē, -laa-,-lai-, -mi\ *n* -ES [ME *blasphemie*, fr. LL *blasphemia*, fr. Gk *blasphēmia*, fr. *blasphēmos* evil-speaking + *-ia* -y] **1 :** irreverence toward God ⟨the crime of ~ in 17th century England was the crime of dissenting from whatever was the current religious dogma —T.C.Clark⟩: **a** *Jewish law* (1) **:** the cursing or reviling of God or the king (2) **:** the pronouncing of the forbidden name of God — compare TETRAGRAMMATON **b** (1) **:** indignity offered to God in speaking, writing, or signs ⟨~ . . . is now an offense against the common law —R.C.Mortimer⟩ (2) **:** the act of claiming the attributes or prerogatives of deity ⟨for a mere man to suggest that he was both messiah and divine could only be viewed . . . as ~ —John Bright †1889⟩ **2 :** irreverence toward something considered sacred or held in high regard ⟨an outraged House of Commons officer sourly viewing the breach of precedent, muttered: "This is ~" —*Time*⟩ **syn** see PROFANATION

¹blast \ˈblast, -aa(ə)st, -aist,-ȧst\ *n* -s [ME, fr. OE *blǣst*; akin to OHG *blāst* blast, *blāsan* to blow, ON *blāstr* blast, *blāsa* to blow, Goth *ufblesan* to inflate with self-importance, OE *blāwan* to blow — more at BLOW] **1 a :** a violent gust of wind ⟨heavy ~*s* whistling about our ears⟩ **b :** a blowing or battering of winds ⟨this prosperous handsome town has withstood the ~ of hurricanes —G.S.Perry⟩ **c :** something borne by a gust of wind ⟨a ~ of sleet⟩ ⟨the drizzle became a ~ and then a deluge —John Buchan⟩ **2 a :** the sound produced from a horn or whistle at one breath **b :** the sound produced by a steam whistle or any comparable mechanical instrument ⟨the ~ of an auto horn⟩ **c :** a signal made by a ship's whistle **d :** an inadvertent loud sound so intense as to overload a sound-recording or sound-transmission system and produce a discordant effect **3 :** something resembling a gust of wind: as **a :** BREATH; *esp* **:** air exhaled in breathing or coughing **b :** a violent or vigorous outburst or onslaught ⟨let out a great ~ of mirth —Marcia Davenport⟩ ⟨the senator's angry ~ against special privilege⟩ **c :** the continuous blowing to which one charge of ore or metal is subjected in a furnace ⟨melt so many tons of iron at a ~⟩ **d** (1) **:** the exhaust steam from a steam engine that drives a column of air up the smokestack and thus creates an intense draft through the fire (2) **:** the draft thus created **e :** the exhaust from an internal-combustion engine or a rocket or jet engine **f** *chiefly Scot* **:** a smoke of tobacco **:** PIPE ⟨a quiet cup and a peaceful ~ by the fire⟩ **4 a :** a sudden pernicious influence or effect ⟨virtue preserved from fell destruction's ~ —Shak.⟩ ⟨the ~ of a great pestilence⟩ **b :** any of certain diseases (as erysipelas) that suggest the effect of a noxious wind or that spread as though distributed by wind; *esp* **:** a disease of plants that causes the foliage or flowers to appear as though dried by a hot wind, that is sometimes marked by spotting and cracking and in some crops (as rice) by rotting of the neck or (as in oats) by failure of the buds or flowers to open, and that is caused by infection (as with bacteria or fungi) or by environmental conditions (as drought) **5 a :** an explosion or violent detonation: as (1) **:** the discharge of a shot or series of shots of an explosive (as dynamite) used to break rock and other solid material; *also* **:** the charge used for this purpose (2) **:** an explosion of gas or dust in a mine (3) **:** muzzle blast **b :** the violent effect produced in the vicinity of an explosion that consists of a wave of increased atmospheric pressure followed by a wave of decreased atmospheric pressure **6 :** a season's run from a particular furnace in glass manufacturing **7 :** ACTIVITY, OPERATION, CAPACITY, SPEED — usu. used in phrases to indicate relative degree or level of activity ⟨the new educational system going full ~⟩ ⟨the plant had run at half ~ for several months⟩ **syn** see WIND

²blast \"\ *vb* -ED/-ING/-S [ME *blasten*, fr. *blast*, n.] *vi* **1 :** to give out blasts; *specif* **:** to produce sounds of undesired loudness ⟨a good voice marred by a tendency to ~ when before a microphone⟩ **2** *dial Eng, of an animal* **:** BLOAT **3 a :** to employ an explosive to shatter or open something **b :** to employ the most vigorous means to attain an end ⟨you'll have to ~ to make her change her mind⟩ **4 a :** to fire a gun **:** SHOOT ⟨as we walked in they started ~*ing*⟩ **b :** to attack with vigor — often used with *away* ⟨he ~*ed* away at the false idealism of his opponents⟩ **5 :** to hit a golf ball out of a sand trap with an explosion shot — usu. used with *out* ⟨it was a poor lie but he ~*ed* out successfully⟩ **6** *slang* **:** to smoke marijuana ~ *vt* **1 :** to injure by or as if by the action of wind ⟨seedlings ~*ed* by the hot dry wind⟩ **:** stop or check from growth or fruit bearing ⟨we'll have no peaches; frost ~*ed* the blossoms this year⟩ **:** WITHER, STUNT, BLIGHT, SHRIVEL **2 :** to affect with some violence, plague, calamity, or blighting influence that thwarts or destroys **:** WRECK, RUIN ⟨time has ~*ed* his ambition⟩ **3** *obs* **:** to confound by a blast or as if of trumpets **4 :** to denounce vigorously ⟨his own lack of hesitation in . . . ~*ing* any and all dignitaries —J.T.Farrell⟩ **:** CURSE, DAMN ⟨I am not making this up, ~ you; it is all in the book —Samuel Grafton⟩ **5 a :** to shatter (as rock) by an explosive agent **b :** to remove (as an obstruction) or open (as a ditch) by blasting — often used with *away* or *out* ⟨set himself to ~ away these barriers to progress —Elmer Davis⟩ ⟨they ~*ed* out a new course for the stream⟩ **c :** to kill by shooting or bombing — often used with *down* ⟨when the senator rose to speak the conspirators ~*ed* him down⟩ **6 a :** to apply a forced draft to (as a fuel bed) **b :** to blow particles of abrasive against (a metal object) for the purpose of cleaning the surface **7 a :** to defeat (as an opposing team) decisively ⟨they ~*ed* the home team by a score of 12 to 2⟩ **b :** to hit vigorously and effectively (as in baseball) ⟨~*ed* a homer over the right-field wall⟩

blast– *or* **blasto–** *comb form* [G *blast-*, *blasto-*, fr. Gk, fr. *blastos*] **1 :** bud **:** budding **:** germ **:** embryo in its early stages ⟨*blasto*derm⟩ **2 :** metamorphic and ⟨*blasto*granitic⟩

-blast \ˌblast, -aa(ə)st, -aist\ *n comb form* -s [NL *-blastus*, fr. Gk *blastos*; akin to OE *molda* top of the head, Gk *blōthros* tall!, *melathron* roof, Skt *mūrdhan* head, Toch A *malto* first] **1** *biol* **a :** germ : shoot : sprout **b :** embryonic or formative cell — in names of formative cells corresponding to names of fully developed cells ending in *-cyte* ⟨erythro*blast*⟩ **c :** germ layer : formative layer of cells ⟨splanchno*blast*⟩ **d :** formative constituent unit of living matter ⟨idio*blast*⟩ **2** *geol* **:** crystal formed during metamorphism ⟨porphyro*blast*⟩

blas·taea \bla'stēə\ *n* -s [NL, irreg. fr. Gk *blastos*] **:** a hypothetical metazoan ancestral form corresponding in organization to the blastula — **blas·tae·al** \(')≡ˈstēəl\ *adj*

blast burner *n* **:** a gas burner in which combustion is intensified by means of a controlled blast of air or oxygen — called also *blast lamp*

blast cleaning *n* **:** the removal of sand or scale from metal objects by the impinging action of a current of abrasive material (as sand, shot, or grit)

blasted *adj* [fr. past part. of ²*blast*] **1 :** BLIGHTED, WITHERED ⟨upon this ~ heath —Shak.⟩ **2 :** CONFOUNDED, ACCURSED, DETESTABLE — often used as a mild imprecation ⟨if I ever get out of this ~ mess⟩ **3 :** cleft, torn, or injured by or as if by an explosive, lightning, or the wind ⟨an old ~ apple tree⟩

blas·te·ma \bla'stēmə\ *n, pl* **blastemas** \-məz\ *or* **blaste·ma·ta** \-məd·ə\ [NL, fr. Gk *blastēma* offspring, offshoot, fr. *blast-* + *-ēma* -eme] **:** a mass of living substance capable of growth and differentiation: **a :** the protoplasmic portion of a fertilized egg **b :** a mass of undifferentiated embryonic cells from which an organ or definitive structure will develop : ANLAGE **c :** undifferentiated tissue that is capable in an emergency (as loss of a body part) of renewed growth and differentiation sometimes (as in salamanders) to the extent of restoring a missing part — **blas·te·mal** \(')bla'stēməl\ *or* **blas·te·mat·ic** \ˌ≡stəˈmad·ik, -stē-\ *or* **blas·tem·ic** \(')≡ˈstēmik, -ste-\ *adj*

blast·er \ˈblastə(r), -aas-,-ais-,-ȧs-\ *n* -s **:** one that blasts: as **a :** one whose work is blasting with an explosive — called also *chargeman, firer, shooter* **b :** a golf club with a broad face and rounded base

blast-freeze \ˈ≡,≡\ *vt* **:** to quick-freeze by rapidly circulating cold air

blast furnace *n* **:** a furnace in which combustion is forced by a current of air under pressure; *specif* **:** such a furnace for obtaining iron by the reduction of the ore with suitable fuel and fluxes at a high temperature

cross section of a typical blast furnace: *A* coke, *B* ore, *C* limestone, *D* hot blast, *E* charging hopper, *F* downcomer, *G* slag, *H* molten iron

blast gate *n* **:** a damper (as of the butterfly-valve type) used for controlling the volume of a blast of air or exhaust gases

blast heater *n* **:** a heating unit (as a coil of steam pipes) through or over which air is driven by a fan and then circulated through the rooms to be heated

blasthole \ˈ≡,≡\ *n* -s **1 :** a hole in the bottom of a pump stock through which water enters **2 :** the hole into which a blasting charge is inserted

blas·tic \ˈblastik, -laa-,-lai-, -tēk\ *adj* [Gk *blastikos* budding, fr. *blast-* + *-ikos* -ic] **:** involving growth of new constituents in metamorphic rocks

-blastic \ˈ≡≡\ *adj comb form* [ISV, fr. *-blast* + *-ic*] **:** sprouting or germinating (in a specified way) ⟨hetero*blastic*⟩ **:** having (such or so many) sprouts, buds, or germ layers ⟨calypto*blastic*⟩ ⟨mono*blastic*⟩

blas·tid \ˈ≡təd\ *n* -s [*blast-* + *-id*] **:** an echinoderm or fossil of the class Blastoidea

blast·ie \ˈblastē\ *n* -s [Sc *blast* to curse, wither (fr. ²*blast*) + *-ie*] *Scot* **:** an ill-favored little being (as a dwarf or elf)

blastier *comparative of* BLASTY

-blasties *pl of* -BLASTY

blastiest *superlative of* BLASTY

blasting *n* -s [fr. gerund of ²*blast*] **1 :** BLIGHT **2 :** the practice or occupation of breaking up heavy masses (as of rock) by means of explosives **3 :** abrasion or attrition effected by the impact of fine particles moved against or past a stationary body — often used in combination ⟨sand*blasting* by the wind⟩

blasting cap *n* **:** a small usu. metal or plastic tube closed at one or both ends, containing a detonating agent together with other charges (as a priming composition), and used in detonating high explosives

blasting gelatin *n* **:** a translucent tough rubbery very powerful explosive consisting chiefly of nitroglycerin and lower-nitrated cellulose nitrate and used esp. in submarine work — compare GELATIN DYNAMITE

blasting machine *n* **:** a hand-operated magneto or dynamo for firing explosives by electricity

blasting powder *n* **:** black powder usu. containing sodium nitrate manufactured in grains or pellets and used esp. for blasting soft materials (as in coal mines) — called also *black blasting powder*

blast injury *n* **:** the harmful effects on the body of sudden changes in pressure produced by explosion

blast lamp *n* **1 :** BLAST BURNER **2 :** BLOWTORCH

blast main *n* **:** BLAST PIPE

blast·man \-stmən, -ˌman\ *n, pl* **blastmen :** SANDBLASTER c

blast·ment \-stmənt\ *n* -s **:** a blasting process or influence : BLIGHTING

blas·to- — see BLAST-

blas·to·car·pous \ˌblastōˈkärpəs, -təˈ-\ *adj* [*blast-* + *-carpous*] **:** germinating in the pericarp

blas·to·chyle \ˈ≡≡+ˌkīl\ *n* -s [*blast-* + *chyle*] **:** the fluid that fills the blastocoel

blas·to·cla·dia \ˌ≡≡ˈklādēə\ *n, cap* [NL, fr. *blast-* + *clad-* + *-ia*] **:** a genus of fungi (family Blastocladiaceae) lacking false septa and having cylindrical sporangia with one collar

blas·to·cla·di·a·ce·ae \ˌ≡≡ˌdēˈāsēˌē\ *n pl, cap* [NL, fr. *Blastocladia*, type genus + *-aceae*] **:** a family of saprobic fungi (order Blastocladiales) having resistant sporangia with walls that are often conspicuously pitted

blas·to·cla·di·a·les \-ˈā(ˌ)lēz\ *n pl, cap* [NL, fr. *Blastocladia* + *-ales*] **:** an order of fungi (subclass Oomycetes) having a eucarpic thallus and carrying out asexual reproduction by thick-walled often punctate resting spores that produce zoospores upon germination

blas·to·coel *or* **blas·to·coele** *also* **blas·to·cele** \ˈ≡≡ˌsēl\ *n* -s [ISV *blast-* + *-coel, -coele, -cele*] **:** the cavity of a blastula — called also *segmentation cavity*; see BLASTULA illustration — **blas·to·coel·ic** \ˌ≡≡ˈsēlik\ *adj*

blas·to·col·la \ˌ≡≡ˈkälə\ *n* -s [NL, fr. *blast-* + Gk *kolla* glue] **:** the gummy or balsamic varnish on certain buds (as of the horse chestnut)

blas·to·cone \ˈ≡≡+ˌ-\ *n* -s [*blast-* + *cone*] **:** an incomplete blastomere; *esp* **:** one at the periphery of an egg undergoing discoidal cleavage

blas·to·cyst \"+ˌ-\ *n* [*blast-* + *-cyst*] **1 :** the modified blastula characteristic of placental mammals **2** [NL *Blastocystis*] **:** a yeast of the genus *Blastocystis*

blas·to·cys·tis \ˌ≡≡+\ *n, cap* [NL, fr. *blast-* + *-cystis*] **:** a cosmopolitan genus of commensal yeasts common in human feces and a frequent source of confusion in fecal examinations for the detection of pathogenic protozoans

blas·to·cyte \ˈ≡≡ˌsīt\ *n* -s [*blast-* + *-cyte*] **1 :** an undifferentiated embryonic cell **2 :** a residual undifferentiated cell capable of replacing lost or damaged tissues esp. in certain lower animals — compare BLASTEMA

blas·to·derm \ˈ≡≡ˌdərm\ *n* -s [G, fr. *blast-* + *-derm*] **1 :** a blastodisc after completion of cleavage and formation of the blastocoel **2 :** the part of insect and certain other invertebrate embryos corresponding to the vertebrate blastoderm — **blas·to·der·matic** *or* **blas·to·der·mic** \ˌ≡≡+\ *adj*

blastodermic vesicle *n* **:** BLASTOCYST 1

blas·to·disc *also* **blas·to·disk** \ˈ≡≡+ˌ-\ *n* [*blast-* + *disc, disk*] **:** the embryo-forming portion of a megalecithal egg with discoidal cleavage, usu. appearing as a small disc on the upper surface of the yolk mass — called also *germinal disc*; see EGG illustration

blast off *vi* **:** to take off : begin to travel — used esp. of rocket-propelled missiles and vehicles

blast-off \ˈ≡ˌ≡\ *n* -s [*blast off*] **:** the action of blasting off — used esp. of rocket-propelled missiles and vehicles

blas·to·genesis \ˌ≡≡+\ *n* [NL, fr. *blast-* + L *genesis*] **1 :** reproduction by budding **2 :** the transmission of inherited characters through the germ plasm — opposed to *pangenesis*

blas·to·genetic \ˌ≡≡+\ *adj* [*blast-* + *genetic*] **1 :** of or relating to blastogenesis **2 :** BLASTOGENIC 1a

blas·to·genic \"+\ *adj* [*blast-* + *-genic*] **1 a** *of somatic characters* **:** originating in the germ plasm — compare SOMATOGENIC **b** *of castes of social insects* **:** determined genetically — opposed to *trophogenic* **2 :** promoting or initiating tissue proliferation

blas·tog·e·ny \blaˈstäjənē\ *n* -ES [*blast-* + *-geny*] **:** BLASTOGENESIS

¹**blas·toid** \ˈblaˌstȯid\ *n* -s [NL *Blastoidea*, fr. *blast-* + *-oidea*] **:** an echinoderm or fossil of the class Blastoidea

²**blastoid** \"\ *adj* **:** of, relating to, or like the Blastoidea

blas·toi·dea \blaˈstȯidēə\ *n pl, cap* [NL, fr. *blast-* + *-oidea*] **:** a class, formerly considered a division of Crinoidea, of extinct Paleozoic short-stemmed or stemless pelmatozoan echinoderms shaped somewhat like a flower bud and having five ambulacral areas with slender appendages along their margins and flattened tubes along their internal surface — **blas·toi·de·an** \(')≡ˈdēən\ *adj or n*

blas·to·kinesis \ˌblastō, ˌblastə+\ *n* [NL, fr. *blast-* + *kinesis*] **:** movement of the developing embryo in some insect eggs into the yolk mass usu. involving partial revolution of the body — **blas·to·kinetic** \ˌ≡≡+\ *adj*

blas·to·mere \ˈ≡≡ˌmi(ə)r\ *n* -s [ISV *blast-* + *-mere*] **:** a cell produced during cleavage : a blastula cell — **blas·to·mer·ic** \ˌ≡≡ˈmerik\ *adj*

blas·to·my·ces \ˌ≡≡ˈmīˌsēz\ *n, cap* [NL, fr. *blast-* + *-myces*] *in some classifications* **:** a genus of yeastlike fungi coextensive with the group Blastomycetes

blas·to·my·cete \ˌ≡≡ˈmīˌsēt, -ˌmīˈsēt\ *n* -s [NL *Blastomycetes*] **:** a fungus of the group Blastomycetes

blas·to·my·ce·tes \ˌ≡≡ˌmīˈsēdˌēz\ *n pl, cap* [NL, fr. *blast-* + *-mycetes*] *in some classifications* **:** a group of pathogenic fungi growing typically like yeasts by budding but sometimes forming mycelium and conidia on artificial media and being usu. classed among the Moniliales or formerly sometimes made synonymous with Saccharomycetaceae

blas·to·my·ce·tic \ˌ≡≡ˌ≡ˈsēd·ik\ *adj* [NL *Blastomycetes* + E *-ic*] **1** *also* **blas·to·my·ce·tous** \-ˈsēd·əs\ **:** of or relating to the group Blastomycetes ⟨~ fungi⟩ **2 :** of, relating to, or caused by blastomycetes ⟨~ dermatitis⟩

blas·to·my·co·sis \ˌ≡≡ˌ≡ˈkōsəs\ *n, pl* **blastomyco·ses** \-ō,ˌsēz\ [NL, fr. *Blastomycetes* + *-osis*] **:** a disease of man and less often of other animals caused by infection with any of several blastomycetes and involving invasion of the skin, mucous membrane, lymph nodes, or internal organs — see NORTH AMERICAN BLASTOMYCOSIS, SOUTH AMERICAN BLASTOMYCOSIS — **blas·to·my·cot·ic** \ˌ≡≡ˌkäd·ik\ *adj*

blas·to·neuropore \ˌ≡≡+\ *n* -s [*blast-* + *neuropore*] **:** a temporary opening formed by the union of the blastopore and neuropore in some embryos

blas·toph·a·ga \blaˈstäfəgə\ *n* [NL, fr. *blast-* + *-phaga*] **1** *cap* **:** a common genus of fig wasps essential to the pollination of Smyrna figs **2** *pl* **blastophaga** *or* **blastophagas :** a wasp of the genus *Blastophaga*

blas·to·phore \ˈ≡≡ˌfō(ə)r\ *n* -s [*blast-* + *-phore*] **1 :** the residual cytoplasm detached during transformation of a spermatid to a spermatozoon **2 :** an amorphous cytoplasmic core that holds together the cells of the male morula of developing oligochaete germ cells and is produced by segregation of part of the cytoplasm of each spermatoblast of the morula — **blas·to·phor·ic** \ˌ≡≡ˈfórik\ *adj*

blas·toph·tho·ria \ˌblastəfˈthōrēə\ *also* **blas·toph·tho·ry** \blaˈstäfthərē\ *n, pl* **blastophthorias** *also* **blastophthories** [NL *blastophoria*, fr. *blast-* + Gk *phthoria* decay, fr. *phtheirein* to destroy — more at PHTHIRIASIS] **:** degeneration of the germ cells believed to be due to chronic poisoning (as by alcohol) or to disease — **blas·toph·thor·ic** \ˌblastəfˈthórik\ *adj*

blas·to·po·ral \ˌblastō, ˌblastə + ˈpōrəl\ *or* **blas·to·por·ic** \"+ˈpórik\ *adj* **:** of, relating to, or involving a blastopore

blas·to·pore \ˈ≡≡+ˌ-\ *n* -s [*blast-* + *-pore*] **:** the mouth or opening of the archenteron — see GASTRULA

blas·to·porphyritic \ˌ≡≡+\ *adj* [ISV *blast-* + *porphyritic*; orig. formed as G *blastoporphyritisch*] *of rocks* **:** having a palimpsest texture showing traces of the original porphyritic texture

blas·to·sphere \ˈ≡≡+ˌ-\ *n* -s [*blast-* + *sphere*] **:** BLASTULA; *esp* **:** BLASTOCYST — **blas·to·spheric** \ˌ≡≡+\ *adj*

blas·to·spore \"+ˌ-\ *n* -s [*blast-* + *spore*] **:** a fungous spore that is produced by budding and that acts as a resting spore or (as in yeasts) gives rise to another spore or a hypha while still attached to the parent cell and without an intervening dormant period

blas·to·style \"+ˌstīl\ *n* -s [*blast-* + *-style*] **:** a process in certain hydroids that may be regarded as a zooid without mouth or tentacles whose function is to produce medusoid buds

blas·tot·o·my \blaˈstäd·əmē\ *n* -ES [*blast-* + *-tomy*] **:** separation of cleavage cells during early stages of embryonic development ⟨both polyembryony and identical twinning may be explained in terms of ~⟩

blas·to·zooid \ˌblastə+\ *n* -s [*blast-* + *zooid*] **:** a zooid or individual produced by budding — distinguished from *oozooid*

blast pipe *n* **:** a pipe delivering steam or air so as to cause a blast — called also *blast main*

blast roasting *n* **:** the process of roasting finely divided ores by means of a blast maintaining internal combustion in the charge (as in desulfurizing ores of lead or copper) — called also *roast sintering*

blasts *pl of* BLAST, *pres 3d sing of* BLAST

-blasts *pl of* -BLAST

blas·tu·la \ˈblaschələ\ *n, pl* **blastulas** \-ləz\ *or* **blastu·lae** \-ˌlē\ [NL, fr. *blast-* + *-ula*] **:** an early metazoan embryo typically having the form of a hollow fluid-filled rounded cavity bounded by a single layer of cells — compare GASTRULA, MORULA — **blas·tu·lar** \-lə(r)\ *adj*

section of blastula: *c* blastocoel, *ma* macromere, *mi* micromere, *a* animal pole, *v* vegetal pole

blas·tu·la·tion \ˌ≡≡ˈlāshən\ *n* -s [NL *blastula* + E *-ation*] **:** formation of a blastula

blast wall *n* **:** a protective work designed to minimize blast damage to buildings or other structures exposed to bombing or other types of explosions

blasty \ˈblastē, -laa-,-lai-,-lȧ-, -ti\ *adj, usu* -ER/-EST [¹*blast* + *-y*] **1 :** subject to or marked by blasts esp. of wind : GUSTY ⟨this bleak and ~ shore —Nathaniel Hawthorne⟩ **2 :** causing or impaired by blast ⟨a good recording but a bit ~ at times⟩

-blas·ty \ˌblastē, -laa-,-lai-, -ti\ *n comb form* -ES [ISV, fr. *-blastic* + *-y*] **:** manner or condition of germinating ⟨hetero*blasty*⟩

¹**blat** \ˈblat, *usu* -d·+V\ *vb* **blatted; blatted; blatting; blats** [imit.] *vi* **1 :** to cry esp. like a calf or sheep : BELLOW, BLEAT ⟨the calf *blatted* in fear as it was borne to the ground —F.D. Davison⟩ **2 a :** to make a senseless or raucous noise ⟨like an oboe *blatting* . . . inside a barrel of feathers —R.P.Warren⟩ **b :** to talk loudly and often foolishly ⟨someone has to be constantly *blatting* around the house —Wilder Hobson⟩ ~ *vt* **:** to utter (as an opinion) loudly and often foolishly or unthinkingly : BLURT ⟨you don't want to go *blatting* this all over town —Mary S. Watts⟩

²**blat** \"\ *n* -s **1 :** a bleat or bleatlike cry ⟨the thin ~ of a sheep beneath the barn —Mary E. Waller⟩ **2 :** a senseless or raucous noise ⟨the never-ending ~ of airhorns piercing the dusk —E.L.DeGolyer⟩

bla·tan·cy \ˈblātᵊnsē, -si\ *n* -ES **1 :** the quality or state of being blatant ⟨human-interest stories . . . may be ruined by ~ —F.L. Mott⟩ **2 :** something blatant ⟨attacks the *blatancies* of our culture in a series of oracular essays —*New Yorker*⟩

bla·tant \ˈblātᵊnt\ *adj* [perh. fr. L *blatire* to chatter, gossip + E *-ant*; perh. of imit. origin like MLG *pladderen* to chat, gossip, Sw *pladder* loose gossip, Dan *bladre* to gossip, L *blaterare* to chatter, bleat, croak] **1 :** noisy esp. in a vulgar or offensive manner : loud and clamorous ⟨an enormous ~ jukebox —Dan Wickenden⟩ **2 :** obtrusive in an offensive manner: **a :** conspicuous or enforcing attention in a vulgar manner (as by gaudy pretense) ⟨the predominant tendency toward a coarse and ~ westernization —Harold Strauss⟩ **b :** completely or crassly obvious : PROMINENT ⟨loathed the squalor and ~ poverty —Willard Robertson⟩; *esp* **:** BRAZEN ⟨found this ~ form of intellectual seduction irresistible —Anthony West⟩ **syn** see VOCIFEROUS

bla·tant·ly *adv* **:** in a blatant manner

¹**blate** \ˈblāt\ *adj* [ME, prob. fr. OE *blāt* pale; akin to OHG *bleizza* pallor, OSlav *blědŭ* pale, Gk *phalos* white — more at BALD] **1** *chiefly Scot* **:** BASHFUL, TIMID, SHY ⟨you are not ~ — you will never lose fair lady for faint heart —Sir Walter Scott⟩ **2** *chiefly Scot* **:** DULL, SLOW

²**blate** \"\ *vb* -ED/-ING/-S [by alter] **:** BLEAT

¹**blath·er** \ˈblat͟hə(r)\ *also* **bleth·er** \ˈblet͟h-\ *vi* **blathered; blathered; blathering** \-t͟h(ə)riŋ\ **blathers** [ON *blathra* to talk unintelligibly; akin to MHG *blōdern* to chatter, gurgle, prob. of imit. origin] **:** to talk foolishly or nonsensically ⟨he ~*s* about goodness and beauty and his own genius —Herman Wouk⟩

²**blather** \"\ *n* -s [ON *blathr* nonsense, fr. *blathra* to talk unintelligibly] **1 a :** voluble, foolish, or nonsensical talk ⟨sensible people can get up . . . and talk such ~ —Francis Neilson⟩ **b :** bubbling sound ⟨the ~ that the water made —Wallace Stevens⟩ **2 :** ADO, STIR, COMMOTION ⟨out of all this ~ will come a demand . . . to rewrite the . . . law —*New Republic*⟩

³**blather** \ˈblät͟hər\ *Scot var of* BLADDER

blath·er·er \ˈblat͟h(ə)rə(r)\ *n* -s [¹*blather* + *-er*] **:** one that blathers

blath·er·skite \ˈblat͟hə(r)ˌskīt\ *n* -s [alter. of earlier *bletherskate*, fr. ¹*blether* + *skate* (fish)] **1 :** a blustering, talkative, and often incompetent person ⟨elect fewer cowards . . . and fewer ~*s* who will do anything for publicity —Elmer Davis⟩ **2 :** NONSENSE, BLATHER ⟨your literary fakers . . . talk ~ about Celtic poetry —Thomas Beer⟩ **3 :** RUDDY DUCK

blat·ta \ˈblad·ə\ *n, cap* [NL, fr. L, cockroach, chafer, moth; perh. akin to Lith *blakts* bedbug, Latvian *blãkē*] **:** a genus (the type of the family Blattidae) of cockroaches including the common Oriental cockroach that infests buildings in America and most other parts of the world

blat·tar·ia \bləˈta(a)rēə, -ter-\ *n pl, cap* [NL, fr. *Blatta* + *-aria*] **:** an order of medium to large-sized broadly oval flattened cursorial insects consisting of the roaches and having the head concealed from above beneath the pronotum, strong chewing mouthparts, long many-jointed antennae, two pairs of wings when present with the forewings membranous and veined, prominent jointed cerci at the end of the abdomen, incomplete metamorphosis, and eggs produced in an ootheca

blat·tar·i·ae \-rē(ˌ)ē\ *syn of* BLATTARIA

blatted *past of* BLAT

blat·tel·la \bləˈtelə\ *n, cap* [NL, fr. L *blatta* + NL *-ella*] **:** a genus of cockroaches including the abundant small domestic croton bug

¹**blat·ter** \ˈblad·ə(r), -atə-\ *vi* -ED/-ING/-S [perh. fr. L *blaterare* to chatter — more at BLATANT] **1** *dial* **:** to talk noisily and fast : PRATTLE ⟨he ~*ed* along and managed to inquire about pretty much everybody —Mark Twain⟩ **2** *chiefly Scot* **:** PATTER, BEAT ⟨the rain that ~*ed* in my face⟩

²**blatter** \"\ *n* -s *chiefly Scot* **:** a clatter of repetitive sounds : a prattle of words or sounds ⟨listening to the ~ of snow and wind —*Nat'l Geographic*⟩

¹**blat·tid** \ˈblad·əd, -atəd\ *adj* [NL Blattidae] **:** of or relating to the family Blattidae

²**blattid** \"\ *n* -s [NL *Blattidae*] **:** an insect of the family Blattidae; *broadly* **:** ROACH

blat·ti·dae \ˈblad·əˌdē\ *n pl, cap* [NL, fr. *Blatta*, type genus + *-idae*] **:** a family of Blattaria including domestic pest roaches

blat·ti family \ˈblad·ē-\ *n* [Malayalam *plātti*] **:** SONNERATIACEAE

blatting *pres part of* BLAT

blat·to·dea \bləˈtōdēə\ [NL, fr. *Blatta* + *-odea*] *syn of* BLATTARIA

blau·bok *or* **blaauw·bok** \ˈblau̇ˌbäk\ *n, pl* **blaubok** *or* **blauboks** [obs. Afrik *blauwbok* (now *bloubok*), fr. *blauw* blue (fr. MD *blā, blau*) + *bok* male antelope, male goat, fr. MD *boc*; akin to OHG *blāo* blue and to OHG *boc* male goat — more at BLUE, BUCK] **1 :** a southern African antelope (*Hippotragus leucophaeus*) closely related to the sable antelope but now exterminated **2 :** BLUE DUIKER

blaud \ˈblad, ˈblȯd\ *var of* BLAD

blaud's pill \ˈblōdz-,ˈblō(d)z-\ *n, usu cap B* [after Pierre *Blaud* †1858 Fr. physician] **:** a pill consisting essentially of ferrous carbonate used in the treatment of anemia

blaue rei·ter \ˌblau̇əˈrītə(r)\ *adj, usu cap B & R* [G, n. pl., blue riders] **:** of, relating to, or characteristic of a short-lived group of German artists concerned esp. with the emotional use of color in primarily nonrepresentational art

blau gas \ˈblau̇-\ *n* [fr. *Blaugas*, a trademark] **:** an oil gas consisting chiefly of a mixture of lower saturated and unsaturated hydrocarbons supplied in liquid form under pressure and used esp. formerly for heating and lighting and as a motor fuel — distinguished from *blue gas*

bla·ver \ˈblävə(r)\ *n* -s [origin unknown] **1 :** CORN POPPY **2 :** CORNFLOWER 1b

blaw \ˈblä, ˈblō\ *vb* **blawed; blawn; blawing; blaws** [ME (northern dial.) *blawen*, fr. OE *blāwan* — more at BLOW] *chiefly Scot* **:** BLOW

bla·wort *or* **blae·wort** \ˈblawərt, -lāw-\ *n* [Sc *bla* + E *wort* — more at BLAE] **1** *chiefly Scot* **:** CORNFLOWER 1b **2** *chiefly Scot* **:** HAREBELL 1

¹**blay** \ˈblā\ *n* -s [fr. (assumed) ME, fr. OE *blǣge*; akin to MD *blei* bleak, MLG *blei, bleig*] **:** ²BLEAK

²**blay** \"\ *adj* [alter. of *blae*] *Irish* **:** UNBLEACHED ⟨~ linen⟩

¹**blaze** \ˈblāz\ *n* -s [ME *blase*, fr. OE *blæse* torch, firebrand; akin to MHG *blas* bald, Icel *blesa* blaze on a horse's face, OE *bǣl* fire, pyre — more at BALD] **1 a :** a bright and lambent flame ⟨with what a ~ the lamp shines forth⟩ **b :** intense direct light often accompanied by heat ⟨the ~ of noon⟩ **2 a :** FIRE: (1) **:** a freely burning flaming fire ⟨we'll have a good ~ in a minute⟩ (2) **:** a fire that flares up suddenly and spreads rapidly ⟨fires would appear in the most distant places from the main ~ —Mary H. Vorse⟩ **b :** an instance of blazing : a burning with brightness and flame ⟨the crackle and ~ of dry oak logs⟩ — compare SMOLDER **3 :** something suggesting or resembling a flame or fire: as **a :** a display of or as if of light ⟨the Christmas ~ of shops —Saul Bellow⟩; *esp* **:** a striking or brilliant display ⟨hills covered with a ~ of flowers⟩ ⟨a ~ of love, and extinction, was better than a lantern glimmer of the same —Thomas Hardy⟩ **b :** a bursting forth or active display of some quality ⟨a great ~ of patriotism⟩ : OUTBURST ⟨her words came in a ~ of fury⟩ **c :** BRILLIANCE, BRIGHTNESS ⟨the ~ of his auburn hair⟩ **d :** HELL — usu. used in pl. ⟨go to ~*s*⟩ often as an intensive with *in* ⟨where in ~*s* have you been⟩ **4 a :** a hand or combination of cards in certain old card games containing only face cards **b :** such a hand in some poker games where it ranks between two pairs and three of a kind

²**blaze** \"\ *vb* -ED/-ING/-S [ME *blasen*, fr. *blase*, n.] *vi* **1 a :** to burn with bright flame ⟨he stirred the fire and the logs *blazed* up⟩ **b :** to burn with fervor or passion ⟨his eyes *blazed* with anger⟩ **c :** to flare up like a fire ⟨must this old conflict ~ up again⟩ **2 a :** to send forth or reflect glowing or brilliant light ⟨the sun *blazing* overhead⟩ **b :** to be or become conspicuous or resplendent ⟨an intellect that *blazed* above his fellows like a meteor⟩ ⟨the air was frosty, the ridges *blazing* with color⟩ **3 a :** to shoot esp. rapidly and repeatedly — usu. used with *away* ⟨any but the best would have lost their nerve and *blazed*

away —Fred Majdalany⟩ **b** : to do or continue to do something vigorously; *esp* : to utter arguments or reproaches with great intensity ⟨they keep *blazing* away about ideals and principles —John Buchan⟩ ⟨she *blazed* out in anger and disgust⟩ ~ *vt* **1 a** : to cause to blaze : BURN ⟨the forests were *blazed* by the contemptuous use of wood fuel —Bernard Pares⟩ **b** : to cause the surface of (a food) to flame ⟨a pudding *blazed* with brandy⟩ **2 a** : to shine with : be resplendent with ⟨the sugar maples ~ their orange glory —L.S.Gannett⟩ **b** : to show forth : call attention to ⟨he *blazed* his wrath to all who would listen⟩ ⟨the stalls and stores *blazing* their bargains⟩

syn FLAME, FLARE, GLARE, GLOW: BLAZE implies great activity in burning, with suggestions of leaping flame or of radiation of intense heat. Figuratively, it applies to what commands notice by fervency, marked activity, or intensity ⟨the pine branches were soon *blazing*⟩ ⟨the sun *blazing* down on the prairie⟩ ⟨Cobbett, the tough, bluff Englishman . . . lived in the United States from 1792 to 1800 and made the country too hot to hold him by *blazing* antirevolutionary propaganda —Gilbert Highet⟩ ⟨Conkling, eyes *blazing*, rose to reply and lashed out with all the oratorical fury and savage invective at his command —Sidney Warren⟩ ⟨after the heavy rains which come at infrequent intervals, the desert *blazes* with colorful flowers —*Amer. Guide Series: Calif.*⟩ FLAME calls attention to leaping or darting tongues of fire, perhaps with less steadiness, intensity, and effectiveness than BLAZE ⟨the paper fire *flamed* up⟩ ⟨discontent with harsh treatment and long hours without pay *flamed* into open protest —*Amer. Guide Series: Ark.*⟩ ⟨she *flamed* forth in public life as an embodiment of democracy, as the hope and cheer of common men —Marvin Lowenthal⟩ ⟨the windowpanes, which *flamed* with a reflected glow —Ellen Glasgow⟩ FLARE may suggest single flames or fires darting up with sudden light or similar lighting effects or sudden bursts of activity or feeling ⟨torches *flared* in the darkness —F.V.W. Mason⟩ ⟨the shore shut off the bottom of the tower. You could only see the top, the white tapering over the brown sand until it *flared* into the red crown that held the light which mariners on a tall bridge could see for more than thirty miles in the night —Wirt Williams⟩ ⟨national guardsmen stand ready to move in if violence should *flare* between the trigger-tempered factions —H.H.Martin⟩ ⟨on the Republican side of the aisle tempers *flared* and fighting words were hurled —*N.Y.Times*⟩ GLARE suggests a quite bright or dazzling steady light that compels notice and often becomes unpleasant; in figurative uses it may apply to the egregious or flagrant or may connote antipathy or malevolence ⟨the sun *glaring* on the snow⟩ ⟨an unshielded light bulb *glaring* in his eyes⟩ ⟨this injustice was peculiarly *glaring* —T.B.Macaulay⟩ ⟨watch a pair of cats, crouching on the brink of a fight. Balefully the eyes *glare* —Aldous Huxley⟩ GLOW stresses emission of light without flame and may suggest steadiness, luminousness, and duration; in extensions it may indicate showing strong bright color or diffused strong feeling ⟨the sun was low in the west, and the sky was *glowing* —Charles Dickens⟩ ⟨the beauty of hills *glowing* purple with heather —O.S.Nock⟩ ⟨what mattered . . . was the fire that burned within him,that *glowed* with so strange and marvelous a radiance in almost all he wrote —Aldous Huxley⟩

³**blaze** \"\ *vt* -ED/-ING/-S [ME *blasen* to blow (an instrument), to proclaim, fr. MD *blāsen* to blow; akin to OHG *blāsan* to blow — more at BLAST] **1** : to make public or conspicuous : PROCLAIM, DISSEMINATE ⟨~ those virtues which the good would hide —Alexander Pope⟩ — often used with *abroad* ⟨people who ~ abroad each new bit of scandal⟩ **2** *obs* : BLAZON 2

⁴**blaze** \"\ *n* -s [G *blas,* fr. OHG *plas;* akin to MD & MLG *bles* blaze, Sw *bläs* blaze, horse with a blaze, ON *blesōttr* with a blaze, MLG *blare* blaze, OE *blæse* torch — more at BLAZE (fire)] **1 a** : a white mark on the face of a horse, cow, or other animal; *esp* : a white stripe running down the face to the lips **b** : a facial pattern in certain cats in which two colors (as red and black) meet along a line down the nose **c** : a white or gray streak in the hair of the head; *esp* : one clearly demarked and extending back from the forehead **2 a** : a mark made on a tree usu. by chipping off a piece of the bark **b** : a trail or road marked out by blazes **c** : something serving as a clew to or identification of a course or way to be followed ⟨she must try to find her way by the ~*s* of former emotion —Kathleen Sproul⟩ **3** : ¹PATCH 5

⁵**blaze** \"\ *vt* -ED/-ING/-S **1** : to mark (a tree) usu. by chipping off a piece of bark ⟨go through the lot and ~ the trees to be cut this winter⟩ **2 a** : to mark out (as a path) by making blazes on trees ⟨*blazed* a trail through the mountains⟩ **b** : to lead or pioneer in some direction or activity ⟨the new Russia promised, for a time, to follow the liberal democratic path the United States had *blazed* —Oscar Handlin⟩ ⟨we ~ open a vast new territory of enjoyment —John Gassner⟩

¹**blaz·er** \'blāzə(r)\ *n* -s [ME *blasour,* fr. *blasen* to proclaim + *-our* -or] *obs* : one who spreads reports ⟨babblers of folly and ~*s* of crime —Edmund Spenser⟩

²**blazer** \"\ *n* -s [²*blaze* + *-er*] **1** : a single-breasted sports jacket of flannel or other fabric in bright stripes or solid color made usu. with a notched collar, patch pockets, and sometimes decorated edges **2** *slang* : an overheated railroad-car journal with its packing afire

blazer

³**blazer** \"\ *n* -s [⁵*blaze* + *-er*] : one that blazes trees to mark them for cutting or to mark a path

blaze-up \'⸗,⸗\ *n* -s [fr. *blaze up,* v.] : FLARE-UP

blaz·ing·ly *adv* : in a blazing manner

blazing star *n* **1** *archaic* : COMET 1 **2** *archaic* : one that is a center of attraction : CYNOSURE **3** : any of several plants with showy inflorescence: as **a** : a plant of the genus *Liatris* **b** : a plant of the genus *Chamaelirium* **c** : a colicroot (*Aletris farinosa*) **d** : TRITONIA 2 **e** : a plant of the genus *Mentzelia; esp* : a yellow-flowered biennial herb (*M. laevicaulis*) of California

¹**bla·zon** \'blāz°n\ *n* -s [ME *blason,* fr. MF] **1 a** : COAT OF ARMS : ARMORIAL BEARINGS **b** : the proper description or representation of heraldic or armorial bearings **2** : DESCRIPTION, REPRESENTATION ⟨let me set forth a ~ of her charms⟩; *esp* : ostentatious display ⟨obtruding the ~ of their accomplishments on all present⟩

²**blazon** \"\ *vt* -ED/-ING/-S **1** [prob. influenced in meaning by ³*blaze*] : to make public : publish far and wide : PROCLAIM ⟨I'll ~ it to high heaven from every street corner in this town —Kenneth Roberts⟩; *esp* : to boast of ⟨the entertainment world daily ~*s* a new play or film as "the epic to end all epics" —*English Digest*⟩ **2 a** : to describe (heraldic or armorial bearings) in proper technical language **b** : to represent (armorial bearings) in drawing or engraving : EMBLAZON **3 a** : to depict or inscribe in colors **b** : to exhibit conspicuously : DISPLAY ⟨carry photographs of their girls ~*ed* on their planes —Dixon Wecter⟩ **4** : to cover as if with blazons : DECK, EMBELLISH ⟨permitted the Communist Party to ~ Indonesia with hammer and sickle posters —*Time*⟩

bla·zon·er \'blāz(°)nə(r)\ *n* -s : one that blazons; *esp* : one that blazons coats of arms

bla·zon·ing \'blāz(°)niŋ\ *n* -s **1** : the act or process of blazoning **2** : heraldic or armorial bearings

bla·zon·ry \'blāz°nrē\ *n* -ES **1** : BLAZON 1b **2** : BLAZON 1a **3 a** : artistic or brilliant representation or display **b** : a superficial finish or ornamental covering ⟨for she did look remarkably young, despite her ~ of makeup —Mary McCarthy⟩

blazy \'blāzē\ *adj, often* -ER/-EST [¹*blaze* + *-y*] : that blazes

blc *abbr* balance

bldg *abbr* building

bldr *abbr* builder

¹**bleach** \'blēch\ *vb* -ED/-ING/-ES [ME *blechen, fr.* OE *blǣcean,* causative-denominative fr. the root of OE *blāc* pale; akin to MHG *bleichen* to make pale, OHG *bleih* pale, ON *bleikja* to bleach, *bleikr* pale, Lith *blizgėti* to glitter, shine, OE *bǣl* fire, pyre — more at BALD] *vt* **1 a** : to remove the color or stains from (as natural fibers, cellulosic pulp, or fats) esp. by chemical means (as by oxidizing agents or less often by reducing agents) — compare BLANCH, DECOLORIZE **b** : PURIFY **c** : to whiten esp. by an oxidizing agent ⟨~*ing* flour⟩ **d** : to lighten the shade of (hair) by use of a chemical (as hydrogen peroxide) that removes color **2 a** *archaic* : to cause to whiten : make pale as from fear ⟨liberty . . . ~*ed* the tyrant's cheek —Tobias Smollett⟩ **b** : to make pure and decent ⟨~*ing* the barroom stories for polite use⟩ **c** : to make pallid and dull : remove the emotional intensity from ⟨~*ing* the affect⟩ **3** : to remove the original silver image from (a photographic negative or positive) ~ *vi* **1** *of a material object* : to grow white : lose color **2** *of the countenance* : to become pale : BLANCH

²**bleach** \"\ *n* -ES **1** : the act or process of whitening or lightening the color of something ⟨this cloth is still stained; you'll have to give it another ~⟩ **2** : a chemical or preparation used in bleaching ⟨peroxide is a common ~ for the hair⟩ **3** : the result of bleaching : the color or degree of whiteness obtained by bleaching ⟨a perfect ~ is seldom attained in one treatment⟩

bleach·a·ble \-chəbəl\ *adj* : capable of being bleached

bleached ginger *n* : LIMED GINGER

bleached rattler *or* **bleached rattlesnake** *n* : a moderate-sized pale-colored rattlesnake (*Crotalus mitchellii*) of desert areas of the southwestern U.S.

bleach·er \-chə(r)\ *n* -s **1 a** : one that bleaches or is used in bleaching; *specif* : a worker who works at the bleaching of materials (as flour, cloth, or certain leathers) **b** : one that carries out bleaching and often also preliminary and subsequent treatments **c** : a vessel (as a tank or bin) used in bleaching **2 a** *usu* **bleachers** *pl but sometimes sing in constr* : a stand of tiered planks providing relatively inexpensive and usu. unreserved undivided seating space for spectators (as in a ball park) usu. in a section without protection from sun or weather and affording a less advantageous view than that afforded by a grandstand ⟨*bleacher* seats available⟩; *also* : a similarly constructed stand erected elsewhere (as in a gymnasium) ⟨in front of a ~*s* filled with VIPs —K.M.Dodson⟩ **b bleachers** *pl* : all these seats of a particular place (as of a stadium) **c bleachers** *pl* : the occupants of the bleachers ⟨the ~*s* booed the umpire⟩

bleach·er·ite \'blēchə,rīt\ *n* -s [*bleacher* + *-ite*] : one seated in the bleachers

bleach·ery \-ch(ə)rē\ *n* -ES [¹*bleach* + *-ery*] : a place or an establishment where bleaching is done

bleachfield \'⸗,⸗\ *n* [²*bleach* + *field*] *Brit* : an area where textiles are exposed to the sun for bleaching

bleaching *n* -s : the act or process of bleaching; *esp* : the process of improving the whiteness of a textile material by other means than scouring only

bleaching clay *or* **bleaching earth** *n* : an adsorbent clay or earth (as activated clay) used for removing the coloring matter from liquids (as oils)

bleaching powder *n* : a nearly white powder made by passing chlorine gas over hydrated lime, believed to consist chiefly of compounds or mixtures of calcium hydroxide, calcium chloride, and calcium hypochlorite with varying contents of available chlorine and of water, and used as a bleaching agent, disinfectant, and deodorant — called also *chloride of lime, chlorinated lime;* compare TROPICAL BLEACH

bleach liquor *n* : a liquid for bleaching; *usu* : a solution of calcium hypochlorite or of bleaching powder used esp. for bleaching paper pulp and textile materials — compare LIQUID BLEACH

bleach-out process \'⸗,⸗-\ *n* : any of several processes of color photography in which light-sensitive dyes are bleached directly by the action of light — distinguished from *dye-bleach process*

¹**bleak** \'blēk\ *adj* -ER/-EST [ME *bleke* pale, prob. alter. (influenced by ME *blok* pale, fr. OE *blāc*) of *bleche,* fr. OE *blǣc;* akin to OE *blāc* pale — more at BLEACH] **1** *dial Eng* : lacking color : PALE **2** : lacking vegetation : exposed and barren and often windswept ⟨~ alkali soils⟩ ⟨watching the sunset from the ~ crest of the ridge⟩ **3** : COLD, RAW : bitter and chilling ⟨the snow was deep, the wind ~⟩ ⟨on a ~ November evening⟩ **4 a** : lacking in warmth or kindliness : DRAB, FRIGID, CHEERLESS, GRIM ⟨the ~*est* woman I ever knew⟩ ⟨with the ~ dogmas of election and reprobation put away, with the God of wrath dethroned —V.L.Parrington⟩ **b** : lacking likelihood of favorable termination or solution : wholly distressing : DEPRESSING ⟨these desires . . . stand in ~ contradiction to our central proposals —J.R.Oppenheimer⟩ ⟨a ~ outlook⟩ ⟨~ facts⟩ **c** : lacking petty or softening detail : severely simple : AUSTERE ⟨some who have been repelled by the ~ isolation of the mystic's final climb —W.R.Inge⟩ ⟨I like ~ thinking, as I like austerity in religion —H.L.Stuart⟩ ⟨the brittle, ~ photography . . . is a lesson in realism —J.P.Lyford⟩ **syn** see DISMAL

²**bleak** \"\ *n* -s [ME *bleke,* prob. alter. (influenced by *bleke* pale) of OE *blǣge* — more at BLAY] : a small European cyprinid river fish (*Alburnus lucidus*) having silvery pigment lining its scales that is used in making artificial pearls — see PEARL ESSENCE

bleak·ly *adv* : in a bleak manner

bleak·ness *n* -ES : the quality or state of being bleak

bleaky \'blēkē\ *adj* : somewhat bleak

¹**blear** \'bli(ə)r, 'bliə\ *vb* -ED/-ING/-S [ME *bleren;* perh. akin to LG *bleer*-oged, blear-eyed] *vi* : to look or observe dully with or as if with watery eyes ⟨young men ~*ing* at suffering with no understanding in their eyes —Bruce Marshall⟩ ~ *vt* **1 a** : to make (the eyes) sore or watery ⟨wind gluing coats to bodies, ~*ing* eyes, ripping at corners —Stanford Whitmore⟩ **b** : DIM, BLUR ⟨~*ed* sight⟩ **2** *archaic* : DECEIVE, HOODWINK, TRICK — usu. used in the phrase *to blear the eyes of* ⟨the king was crafty and cautious; he sought to ~ the eyes of the world before he struck⟩

²**blear** \"\ *adj* [ME *blere;* akin to *bleren* to blear] **1** : dim with water or tears — used of the eyes **2** : DULL, DIM, CLOUDY

³**blear** \"\ *n* -s **1** : a bleared state or appearance **2** : a film or other impediment that causes the eyes to be bleared

bleared \'bli(ə)rd, -iəd\ *adj* [ME *blered,* fr. past part. of *bleren*] **1** *of the eyes* : dimmed esp. by a watery secretion or a covering film **2** : BLURRED : indistinct as though seen through bleared eyes ⟨a dull ~ old voice⟩

blear-eyed \'⸗¦⸗\ *adj* [ME *bleereyed*] **1** : having blear eyes **2** : STUPID, DULL-WITTED; *sometimes* : SHORT-SIGHTED

blear-eyed herring *n* : ALEWIFE 1a

blear·i·ly \'blirəlē, -li\ *adv* : in a bleary manner

blear·i·ness \-rēnəs\ *n* -ES : the state of being bleary

blear-witted \'⸗¦⸗⸗\ *adj* : dull of mind

bleary \'blirē, 'blērē, -ri\ *adj, often* -ER/-EST [²*blear* + *-y*] **1** *of the eyes or vision* : partially or temporarily blear : dull or dimmed esp. from fatigue or sleep **2** : poorly outlined or defined : DIM ⟨the world had had the ~ white look of a country seen through a train window —Josephine Pinckney⟩ **3** : tired to the point of exhaustion : WORN-OUT ⟨after 12 hours of conferences the ~ aide staggered home to bed⟩

bleary-eyed \'⸗¦⸗\ *adj* [by alter.] : BLEAR-EYED

¹**bleat** \'blēt, *usu* -d.+V\ *vb* -ED/-ING/-S [ME *bleten,* fr. OE *blǣtan;* akin to OHG *blāzan* to bleat, L *flēre* to weep, Russ *bleyat'* to bleat, OE *bellan* to roar — more at BELLOW] *vi* **1 a** *of a sheep or goat or sometimes a calf* : to utter its natural cry **b** : *of various animals or man* : to make a sound suggestive of the call of a sheep; *sometimes* : WHIMPER, WHINE ⟨a dog cringing and ~*ing* in the cold⟩ **2 a** : to talk complainingly or with a whine **b** : to talk without due consideration : BLATHER ⟨we ~ once a year about peace on earth and goodwill to men —G.B.Shaw⟩ ~ *vt* : to utter as though a bleat ⟨~*ing* their good-nights at the door⟩; *often* : to utter in a bleating manner ⟨the bigwigs in the Capitol are ~*ing* their fears —*Wall Street Jour.*⟩

²**bleat** \"\ *n* -s **1 a** : the cry of a sheep, goat, or calf **b** : any sound similar to or imitative of this cry **2** : whining or foolish talk : BLATHER

bleat·er \'blēd·ə(r), -ētə-\ *n* -s **1** : one that bleats; *specif* : SHEEP **2** : SNIPE 1a

bleating *n* -s [ME *bleting,* fr. gerund of *bleten*] : BLEAT; *also* : the uttering of bleats

bleat·ing·ly *adv* : in a bleating manner

bleaty \'blēd·ē\ *adj* [²*bleat* + *-y*] : like a bleat

ble·aunt \'blēənt\ *n* -s [ME *bleaunt, blihand,* fr. MF *bliaud, bliaut,* fr. OF *bliaut, blialt*] : BLIAUT

bleb \'bleb\ *n* -s [perh. alter. of *blob*] **1** : a small circumscribed elevation of the cuticle usu. containing serum : a small blister — compare BULLA **2** : a bubble esp. in water or glass; *also* : a small bit or particle of distinctive material (as of mercury ore in quartzite) — **bleb·by** \'blebē\ *adj*

blebbed \'blebd\ *adj* : covered with or full of blebs

¹**blech·noid** \'blek,nȯid\ *adj* [NL *Blechnum* + E *-oid*] : of or resembling the genus *Blechnum*

²**blechnoid** \"\ *n* -s : a fern of the genus *Blechnum*

blech·num \-nəm\ *n, cap* [NL, fr. L *blachnon, blechnon,* a fern, fr. Gk *blēchnon*] : a genus of chiefly tropical ferns (family Polypodiaceae) having rather stiff pinnate leaves with the sori linear and parallel to the midvein of the pinnae

¹**bleck** \'blek\ *n* -s [ME *blek* ink, fr. *blæc,* fr. OE *blæc* black — more at BLACK] **1** *now chiefly Scot* : a black substance as: **a** : shoe blacking **b** : black grease **c** : SOOT, SMUT **2** *Scot* : NEGRO **3** *Scot* : BLACKGUARD, SCOUNDREL

²**bleck** \"\ *vt* [ME *blecken,* fr. *blek,* n.] *dial Brit* : BLACKEN

bled \'bled\ *n* -s [Ar *bilād* land] : a prairie or treeless plain in northern Africa; *also* : open country : COUNTRYSIDE, HINTERLAND

bled ingot \'bled-\ *n* : an ingot or casting from the interior of which, while cooling, liquid steel has escaped through a rupture

blee \'blē\ *n* -s [ME *ble, bleo,* fr. OE *blēo;* akin to OS & OFris *blī* color, OE *blīthe* happy — more at BLITHE] **1** *archaic* : COLOR, HUE, COLORATION ⟨under a banner of mingled ~⟩ **2** *archaic* : COMPLEXION, COLORING — used chiefly in the phrase *bright of blee* ⟨three fair sisters bright of ~⟩

¹**bleed** \'blēd\ *vb* **bled** \'bled\ *obs* **bleeded; bled** *obs* **bleeded; bleeding; bleeds** [ME *bleden,* fr. OE *blēdan,* fr. *blōd* blood — more at BLOOD] *vi* **1 a** : to emit blood ⟨the wound *bled* freely⟩ : to lose blood ⟨hemophiliacs often ~ severely from the slightest scratch⟩ **b** : to lose blood from wounds : to sacrifice one's blood (as in battle) ⟨men who fought and *bled* along this rocky coast⟩ **2 a** : to feel anguish, pain, or sympathy ⟨his heart ~*s* for the distress of his fellows⟩ **b** : to be in grave distress or seriously disordered circumstances ⟨the human race . . . ~*ing* in its uneasy sleep —Irwin Shaw⟩ **c** : to become upset or bothered ⟨only steak and four eggs for breakfast? I ~ for you⟩ **3 a** : to ooze, drop, or flow from or as though from a wound ⟨grease ~*ing* through a wrapper⟩; *also* : to escape by such a process ⟨pitch ~*s* freely from any little break in the bark⟩ **b** *of life or its phenomena* : to terminate as a result of bleeding — usu. used with *away* ⟨retaining but a quantity of life, which ~*s* away —Shak.⟩ **c** : to give up some constituent or content by bleeding ⟨fruits sulfured at high temperatures . . . ~ more readily than when sulfured at lower temperatures —*Experiment Station Record*⟩ **4** : to exude something : DISCHARGE: as **a** : to exude water or sap from a wounded surface (as of a tree) **b** : to diffuse or run when wetted — used chiefly of textile dyes or dyed fabrics **c** : to diffuse into and show through a covering layer — used of various pigments or of the paints, enamels, or varnishes into which they are incorporated **5** *dial Brit, of grain crops* : to yield well **6 a** : to pay out or give money ⟨willing to ~ freely for the cause⟩ **b** : to have money drawn or extorted ⟨hang those city fellows, they must ~ —W.M.Thackeray⟩ **7** : to be printed so as to run off one or more edges of a printed page or sheet after trimming — often used with *off* ⟨the halftones ~ off all round the edges of the 4-page spread⟩ **8** : to separate from a mixture — used esp. of oils (as from grease) **9** : to exude bituminous material — used of pavements or creosoted timber bound or impregnated with such material ~ *vt* **1** : to remove or draw blood from ⟨at one time the surgeon *bled* the patient for any or every ill⟩ ⟨the meat will keep better if the carcass is *bled* immediately and thoroughly⟩ **2 a** : to obtain money from esp. by improper or unlawful methods ⟨the company . . . had *bled* consumers in western Mississippi of $2 to $3 million a year in excessive rates —*New Republic*⟩ **b** : to take away : EXTRACT ⟨mobilization plans call for ~*ing* just as much metals out of the durable-goods industries as they can stand —*Newsweek*⟩ **3** : to draw the sap from (a tree) **4** : to drain or empty of liquid, gas, or other contents esp. slowly: as **a** : to empty of accumulated water (as a steam cylinder, air reservoir, or a leaking buoy in which water has accumulated) **b** : to let out the air from (a reservoir or other container) so as to diminish pressure **c** : to let out grain from (a sack) by slitting (as in stowing a cargo) **d** : to draw off or extract (low-pressure steam) from any of the stages of the expansions of a steam turbine for heating buildings, for boiler feed water, for process work, or for other purposes **5** : to cause (as a printed illustration) to bleed; *also* : to trim (as a page) so that some of the printing bleeds **6** *of a dyed article* : to give up (dye or color) when wetted — **bleed white** : to drain or be drained of blood or resources

²**bleed** \"\ *n* -s **1** *print* : something that bleeds or is bled (as an illustration or a page); *also* : the part trimmed off in bleeding or the corresponding area of the printing plate **2** : a stain discoloration showing on a surface resulting from diffusion of coloring matter from a substance **3 a** : BLEEDER 4a **b** : a narrow opening in the surface of an air inlet through which low-energy boundary-layer air is bled off from the main stream

bleed·er \'blēdə(r)\ *n* -s **1** : one that draws blood: **a** : a person (as a barber-surgeon) who draws blood for medical reasons **b** : BLOODLETTER **b** : STICKER **2** : one that gives up blood: **a** : HEMOPHILIAC **b** : a large blood vessel divided during surgery **c** : a prizefighter who cuts and bleeds easily in the ring **d** : a horse or other animal immunized against some pathogen and regularly bled for the production of serums **3 a** : one that bleeds another of money or resources : SPONGE, PARASITE **b** *slang* : ROGUE, RASCAL — often used as a deprecatory or affectionate term of address ⟨you old ~, you⟩ **4 a** : a device or arrangement that permits bleeding (as an escape valve or the device controlling the extraction of steam from a turbine) **b** : an electrical resistor connected across a power supply in parallel with the load and of such value that normal variations in load resistance have little effect on the terminal voltage

bleeder turbine *n* : a steam turbine from the casing of which steam is drawn at one or more points to be used for heating of feedwater or industrial fluids or for district steam heating

¹**bleeding** *adj* [ME *bleding* fr. pres. part. of *bleden*] **1** : that bleeds or appears to bleed ⟨a ~ wound⟩ **2** : feeling anguish or compassion **3** — used as a generalized intensive ⟨a ~ idiot⟩; compare BLOODY 6

²**bleeding** \"\ *n* -s [ME *bleding,* fr. gerund of *bleden*] : an act, instance, or result of being bled or the process by which something is bled: as **a** : the escape of blood from vessels : HEMORRHAGE; *also* : the operation or an instance of performing the operation of bleeding a person medically : BLOODLETTING **b** : the diffusion of pigment or other materials to alter an overlying surface (as in leather) **c** : the exudation of bituminous material (as from pavements or creosoted lumber) **d** : extraction of steam from a turbine for use in heating or low pressure pump operation **e** : the autogenous flow of mixing water within freshly mixed concrete or mortar or its emergence therefrom

bleeding bread *n* : bread containing reddish patches produced by a bacterium (*Serratia marcescens*)

bleeding canker *n* : a disease of hardwoods (as of maples) caused by a fungus (*Phytophthora cactorum*), characterized by the exudation of a reddish ooze from small cracks in cankers on the trunk and branches, and leading to wilting and branch dieback

bleeding disease *n* : a disease of the coconut palm caused by a fungus (*Ceratostomella paradoxa*) and characterized by a reddish brown or rusty liquid exudation from cracks in the stem

bleeding heart *n* **1** : any of several plants of the genus *Dicentra; esp* : a garden plant (*D. spectabilis*) with racemes of deep-pink drooping heart-shaped flowers **2** *dial Eng* : a wallflower (*Cheiranthes cheiri*) **3** *Austral* : CORAL PEA **4** *South* : ²WAHOO a **5** *West Indies* **a** : TARO **b** : CALADIUM **2 6 a** : a person who makes a show of great concern for any group or individual that can be made to appear persecuted

bleeding-heart pigeon \'⸗⸗¦⸗-\ *n* : a Philippine pigeon (*Gallicolumba luzonica*) with a greenish blue back, a white throat, and a patch of stiff crimson feathers on the breast

bleeding time *n* : a period of time of usu. about 2½ minutes during which a small wound (as a pinprick) continues to shed blood

bleeding tooth *n* : a marine gastropod mollusk (*Nerita peloronta*) of the Caribbean area having projections resembling teeth reddish about the base on the inner wall of the aperture; *also* : any of several related mollusks some of which lack the colored projections

blees *pl of* BLEE

¹**bleeze** \'blēz, ,blāz\ *Scot var of* ¹BLAZE, ²BLAZE

²**bleeze** \"\ *vi* -ED/-ING/-S [alter. of ³*blaze*] *chiefly Scot* : BRAG : talk officiously

blel·lum \'bleləm\ *n* -s [perh. blend of Sc *bleber* to babble (alter. of *blabber*) and *skellum* rascal] *Scot* : a lazy talkative person

1blem·ish \'blemish, -mēsh\ *vt* -ED/-ING/-ES [ME *blemisshen*, fr. MF *blemiss-*, *blesmiss-*, stem of *blemir, blesmir* to make pale, wound, of Gmc origin; akin to G *blass* pale, MHG *blas* bald — more at BLAZE] **:** to produce flaws in ⟨too much heat will ~ the glass⟩: **a :** to spoil by a flaw (as something well formed or excellent) **:** IMPAIR ⟨these little singularities . . . rather set off than ~ his good qualities —Joseph Addison⟩ **b :** SULLY, STAIN, TAINT **c** *archaic* **:** DISCREDIT, DEFAME ⟨whether a man should be permitted to ~ himself, by pleading his own insanity —William Blackstone⟩

2blemish \"\ *n* -ES **1 :** a flaw of character or spirit **:** a moral defect **:** TAINT, STAIN ⟨I suppose that human character will never free itself entirely from the ~ of prejudice —A.E. Stevenson b. 1900⟩ **2 :** a mark of physical deformity or injury ⟨a calf and a lamb, both a year old without ~, for a burnt offering —Lev 9:3 (RSV)⟩: as **a :** any small mark on the skin (as a pimple or birthmark) ⟨~*es* on the adolescent skin may be a symptom of acne —*Today's Health*⟩ **b :** a defect of an animal (as a horse) that detracts from its appearance but does not interfere with its usefulness — compare UNSOUND **c :** any flaw in wood that mars its appearance without necessarily impairing its strength or durability — compare DEFECT **3 :** a fault or imperfection esp. of workmanship or art ⟨he played his minor role without ~ if without distinction —C.L.Becker⟩

syn DEFECT, FLAW: BLEMISH applies to a marring external or superficial spot or to something likened thereto ⟨he studiously perfected nature by correcting all the little *blemishes* of manner and little weaknesses of character in order to produce an immaculate effect —V.L.Parrington⟩ ⟨they assure you that complete, 99 percent waterproof, governmentally organized thought control in China is just a temporary pimple, a passing *blemish* —Peggy Durdin⟩ DEFECT applies to an imperfection or incompleteness, superficial or not, impairing value or operation ⟨a *defect* in the machine⟩ ⟨a *defect* in his hearing⟩ ⟨the moral *defects* of the thinker are such as make him unfaithful to his work, e.g. laziness or prejudice —Samuel Alexander⟩ ⟨the Spartan state, in fact, by virtue of that excellence which was also its *defect* —the specializing of the individual on the side of discipline and rule — carried within it the seeds of its own destruction —G.L.Dickinson⟩ FLAW may refer to defect in continuity or cohesion (as a crack, fissure, or break) or to something compared to a break or weak spot ⟨we have already seen *flaws* in the great structure, which were to widen into breaches —John Buchan⟩ ⟨we most enjoy, as a spectacle, the downfall of a good man, when the fall is justified by some *flaw* in his being —A.L.Guérard⟩ ⟨while Milton's work is immaculate, Wordsworth's is full of *flaws* —Richard Garnett †1906⟩

blem·ish·er \'blemәshә(r), -mēsh-\ *n* -S [ME *blemissher*, fr. *blemisshen* + *-er*] **:** one that blemishes

blem·my·es \'blemē,ēz\ *n pl, usu cap* [L, fr. Gk] **:** an ancient Ethiopian Hamitic people dwelling between the Nile and the Red sea

1blench \'blench\ *vb* -ED/-ING/-ES [ME *blenchen* to deceive, blench, fr. OE *blencan* to deceive; akin to ON *blekkja* to impose on; prob. causative fr. the root of E *blink*] *vi* **:** to draw back or turn aside from lack of courage or resolution **:** FLINCH, QUAIL, SHRINK ⟨though sometimes you do ~ from this to that —Shak.⟩ ~ *vt* **1** *obs* **:** BAFFLE, DISCONCERT, FOIL **2** *archaic* **:** to draw back from **:** AVOID, EVADE **syn** see RECOIL

2blench \"\ *vb* -ED/-ING/-ES [alter. (influenced by *1blench*) of *2blanch*] **:** PALE, BLEACH, WHITEN

3blench *var of* BLANCH

blenching *adj* [fr. pres. part. of *2blench*] **:** PALING, BLEACHING, WHITENING — **blench·ing·ly** *adv*

1blend \'blend\ *vt* **blend** \"\ *or* **blent** \'blent\ **blend·ed; blending; blends** [ME *blenden*, lit., to blind, fr. OE *blendan*; akin to OHG *blenten* to blind, OFris *blenda*. causatives fr. the root of E *blind*] *archaic* **:** BEDAZZLE, BLIND, DECEIVE ⟨a villainous affair . . . and will one day so ~ and confound us —Laurence Sterne⟩

2blend \"\ *vb* **blended** \'blendәd\ *also* **blent** \'blent\ **blended** *also* **blent; blending; blends** [ME *blenden*, modif. of ON *blanda*; akin to OE *blandan* to mix, OHG *blantan* to mix, Goth *blandan* to associate, Lith *blandus* thick (of soup), Skt *bradhna* pale red, ruddy; basic meaning: obscure, indistinct] *vt* **1 :** MIX, MINGLE; *esp* **:** to mingle, combine, or associate so that the separate constituents or the line of demarcation cannot be distinguished ⟨the new North Africa, in order to endure, must successfully ~ the cultures of East and West —*Lamp*⟩ ⟨~*ing* flour with broth to thicken a gravy⟩ **2 :** to prepare (as whiskey, flour, tobacco, or tea) by mixing and thoroughly intermingling different varieties or grades whether for purposes of adulteration or of standardization and improvement of qualities **:** make by mixing or blending **3 :** to darken the hairs, (as the tips of the hairs) of (a fur) with dye **4 :** to cause (paints or pigments) to mingle and shade into each other **5 :** to reduce the bulk of (a turned seam) by trimming one edge ~ *vi* **1 a :** to mingle intimately **:** pass or shade insensibly into one another ⟨that vein of contempt for the crowd, which runs across Leonardo's writings, ~*ed* . . . with his vein of human sweetness —Havelock Ellis⟩ **b :** to combine into an integrated whole **:** UNITE ⟨various traditional dishes ~ into a distinctive and tasty meal⟩ **2 :** to produce a harmonious effect **:** agree with or balance one another **:** HARMONIZE — used esp. of color, design, or objects in which these are of prime importance ⟨how well the new curtains ~ with the rug⟩ ⟨pick a color that will ~ with your skin⟩ **3** *biol* **:** to exhibit or possess a character that does not directly show the result of mendelian dominance or segregation but is intermediate between contrasting characters of the parents — compare BLENDING INHERITANCE **syn** see MIX

3blend \"\ *n* -S **:** something produced by blending: as **a :** a product (as a whiskey, a flour, or a tobacco) prepared by blending **b :** a congruous mixture of articles, qualities, or characteristics ⟨the little sketch . . . is a wonderful ~ of charm and gentle sadness —Bergen Evans⟩; *often* **:** the harmonious product of such a mixture ⟨associated with a racial ~ that was henceforth to be distinctively English —Herbert Read⟩ **c :** a merging of one color or musical timbre into another ⟨a little more concern for tonal quality and ~ would have been welcome —Irving Kolodin⟩ **d :** a word composed of parts of two words (as *chortle* from *chuckle* and *snort*), all of one word and part of another (as *bookmobile* from *book* and *automobile*), or two entire words and characterized invariably in the latter case and frequently in the two former cases by single occurrence of one or more sounds or letters that appear in both the component words (as *motel* from *motor hotel*, *camporee* from *camp* and *jamboree*, *aniseed* from *anise seed*) — compare CONTAMINATION 3

☞ In this dict. the term *blend* is used in etymologies only when the entry word is characterized by single occurrence of one or more sounds or letters that appear in both the component words or by infixation of all or part of one component word within all or part of the other

e *biol* **:** a blending character; *also* **:** an individual exhibiting such a character — compare BLENDING INHERITANCE **f :** a compound of two or more elementary sensations that is experienced as a homogeneous unit ⟨the color orange is a ~ of red and yellow⟩ **g :** MIXTURE 2d

blende \'blend\ *n* -S [G, fr. *blenden* to blind, fr. OHG *blenten* — more at BLEND] **1 :** SPHALERITE **2 :** any of several minerals, chiefly metallic sulfides, with somewhat bright but nonmetallic luster

blended whiskey *n* **:** whiskey consisting of either a blend of two or more straight whiskeys or a blend of whiskey and neutral spirits with the proof adjusted by addition of distilled water

blend·er \-dә(r)\ *n* -S [*2blend* + *-er*] **:** one that blends: as **a :** an instrument (as a blunt brush) used in blending colors **b :** a worker who blends various materials or grades of material to produce a finished product (as a whiskey, a flour, a tobacco, or a gasoline) of a desired quality or flavor **c :** a machine or device by which materials are blended ⟨a pastry ~⟩; *sometimes* **:** BLENDOR

blending *n* -S [fr. gerund of *2blend*] **:** a product resulting from blending **:** BLEND

blending inheritance *n* **:** inheritance by the progeny of characters intermediate between those of the parents that is now usu. explained on a mendelian basis by use of the multiple factor hypothesis — compare BLOOD 2, MULTIPLE FACTORS, PARTICULATE INHERITANCE, QUANTITATIVE INHERITANCE

blen·dor \-dә(r)\ *n* -S [*2blend* + *-or*] **:** a mechanical device for producing a fine uniform suspension or blend

blend–word \'⸗,⸗\ *n* **:** *3*BLEND d

blen·heim spaniel \'blenәm-\ *n, usu cap B* [fr. *Blenheim* Palace, seat of the Duke of Marlborough, in England] **:** a spaniel of a red and white variety of the English toy spaniel

blen·ni·idae \ble'nīә,dē\ *n pl, cap* [NL, fr. *Blennius*, type genus (fr. L, a sea fish) + *-idae* — more at BLENNY] **:** a large family of small carnivorous marine fishes comprising the typical blennies and with related forms constituting a suborder of the Percomorphi — see BLENNIOIDEA

1blen·ni·oid \'blenē,ȯid\ *adj* [NL *Blennioidea*] **:** of or relating to the suborder Blennioidea

2blennioid \"\ *n* -S [NL *Blennioidea*] **:** a blennioid fish

blen·ni·oi·dea \,blenē'ȯidēә\ *n pl, cap* [NL, fr. *Blennius* + *-oidea*] **:** a suborder of Percomorphi that includes the Blenniidae and other families of blennies and comprises marine fishes with the pectoral fins large but the pelvic fins reduced or absent, scales partially or wholly lacking, and a usu. elongated body often specialized for tide pool existence

blen·ni·oi·dei \-dē,ī\ [NL, fr. *Blennius* + *-oidei*] *syn of* BLENNIOIDEA

blen·noid \'ble,nȯid\ *adj* [Gk *blennos* mucus + E *-oid*] **:** resembling mucus **:** MUCOID

blen·nor·rhea *also* **blen·nor·rhoea** \,blenә'rēә\ *n* -S [NL, fr. Gk *blennos* mucus + NL *-o-* + *-rrhea, -rrhoea*] **:** an excessive secretion and discharge of mucus — **blen·nor·rheal** *also* **blen·nor·rhoeal** \¦⸗⸗¦rēәl\ *adj*

blen·ny \'blenē\ *n* -ES [L *blennius*, a sea fish, fr. Gk *blennos*] **:** any of numerous usu. small fishes belonging to Blenniidae and related families having a usu. elongate, often scaleless body tapering to a more or less rounded tail with the ventral fins jugular or wanting and the dorsal and anal fins long, living about rocky shores of all regions and occas. in fresh water, and often having protective coloration

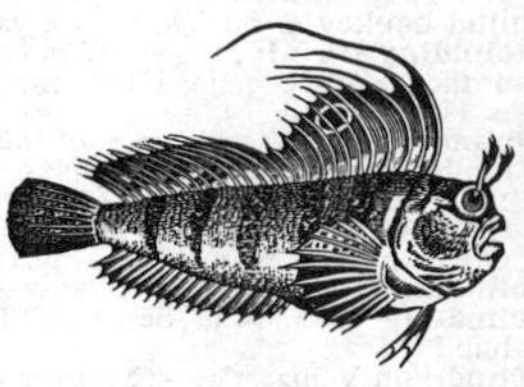

European blenny

blent *past of* BLEND

blephar- *or* **blepharo-** *comb form* [NL, fr. Gk, fr. *blepharon*] **1 :** eyelid ⟨*blephar*itis⟩ ⟨*blepharo*spasm⟩ **:** of the eyelid and ⟨*blepharo*conjunctivitis⟩ **2 :** cilium **:** flagellum ⟨*blepharo*plast⟩

bleph·a·ra \'blefәrә\ *n, pl* **blepharae** \-,rē,-,rī\ [NL, fr. Gk *blepharon* eyelid] **:** one of the peristome teeth of a moss

bleph·a·ral \-rәl\ *adj* [*blephar-* + *-al*] **:** of or relating to the eyelids

bleph·a·ri·glottis \,blefәrә +\ [NL, fr. Gk *blepharis* eyelash + *glōttis* tongue — more at GLOTTIS] *syn of* HABENARIA

bleph·a·rism \'blefә,rizәm\ *n* -S [ISV *blephar-* + *-ism*] **:** spasm of the eyelids

bleph·a·risma \,⸗⸗'rizmә\ *n, cap* [NL, fr. *blephar-* + *-isma* (fr. L *-ismus* -ism)] **:** a genus of large ovoid or pyriform frequently rose-colored free-living ciliates (order Spirotricha) having the peristome highly developed

bleph·a·ri·tis \-'rīd·әs\ *n, pl* **blepharit·i·des** \-'rid·ә,dēz\ [NL, fr. *blephar-* + *-itis*] **:** inflammation of the eyelids, esp. of the margins

bleph·a·ro·conjunctivitis \¦blefә(,)rō, ¦blefәrә + \ *n* [NL, fr. *blephar-* + *conjunctivitis*] **:** inflammation of the eyelid and conjunctiva

bleph·a·ro·plast \" + ,plast\ *n* -S [*blephar-* + *-plast*] **:** a basal granule or kinetoplast — usu. used in botany or by cytologists when the nature of the body is uncertain — **bleph·a·ro·plastic** \" + ¦plastik\ *adj*

bleph·a·rop·to·sis \,blefәrәp'tōsәs\ *n* [NL, fr. *blephar-* + *-ptosis*] **:** a drooping or abnormal relaxation of the upper eyelid

bleph·a·ro·spasm \'blefә(,)rō, -,rә + ,-\ *n* [NL *blepharospasmus*, fr. Gk *blephar-* + L *spasmus* spasm] **:** spasmodic winking from involuntary contraction of the orbicular muscle of the eyelids

ble·phil·ia \blә'filēә\ *n, cap* [NL, irreg. fr. Gk *blepharis* eyelash] **:** a small genus of No. American herbs (family Labiatae) with opposite hairy leaves and purplish or bluish flowers in dense clusters

bles·bok \'bles,bäk\ *also* **bles·buck** \-,bәk\ *n, pl* **blesbok** *or* **blesboks** [Afrik *blesbok*, fr. *bles* blaze (fr. MD) + *bok* male antelope, male goat, fr. MD *boc*; akin to OHG *boc* male goat — more at BLAZE, BUCK] **:** a So. African antelope (*Damaliscus albifrons*) resembling the bontebok and having a large white spot on a face divided by a dark crossbar between the eyes

bles·mol \'bles,mȯl, -mōl\ *or* **bles mole** \'bles,mōl\ *n* -S [Afrik *blesmol*, fr. *bles* blaze + *mol* mole, fr. MD — more at MOLE] **:** any of several grayish burrowing southern African rodents of *Bathyergus* and related genera that are very destructive to root crops

1bless \'bles\ *vb* **blessed** \'blest\ *also* **blest** \"\ **blessed** \"\ *also* **blest** \"\ **blessing; blesses** [ME *blessen*, fr. OE *bletsian, blētsian, blēdsian*, fr. *blōd* blood; fr. the use of blood in consecration or sacrifice — more at BLOOD] *vt* **1 :** to consecrate or hallow by religious rite or word **:** make or pronounce holy ⟨and God ~*ed* the seventh day, and sanctified it —Gen 2:3 (AV)⟩ ⟨this little touch of ceremony . . . seemed to ~ the union —Margaret A. Barnes⟩ **2 :** to make the sign of the cross upon or over — often used reflexively ⟨they shivered and ~*ed* themselves as they passed the gloomy opening⟩ **3 :** to invoke divine care for ⟨then the bishop shall ~ them —*Bk. of Com. Prayer*⟩ **:** pray for ⟨we may as well ~ our enemies; they are too many to fight⟩ **4 a :** PRAISE, GLORIFY **:** to extol for excellences ⟨~ the Lord, O my soul —Ps 103:1 (RSV)⟩ **b :** to regard with great favor **:** approve highly ⟨your cameraman may ~ you because he can go all out for atmosphere —Richard Harrison⟩ **5 :** to make happy **:** give good fortune or satisfaction to **:** confer prosperity upon ⟨a child soon ~*ed* the union⟩ ⟨the whole region is ~*ed* with good soil and abundant water⟩ **6 :** GUARD, PROTECT, KEEP, PRESERVE — formerly usu. used with *from* and often reflexively ⟨~ me from marrying a usurer —Shak.⟩ ⟨he ~*ed* himself from such customers —Tobias Smollett⟩; now used almost wholly in exclamations ⟨God ~ me, what's happened now⟩ **7 :** FAVOR, ENDOW ⟨few persons have been ~*ed* as he has in his every endeavor⟩ — usu. used with *with* ⟨a man ~*ed* with a happy nature and a healthy appetite⟩ **:** to give approval to ⟨the president would ~ the reopening of this issue⟩ **8** *archaic* **:** to account happy **:** FELICITATE — used reflexively ⟨the nations shall ~ themselves in him —Jer 4:2 (AV)⟩ **9 :** CURSE, DAMN, CONDEMN — usu. used in the first person present ⟨I'm ~*ed* if I know what went wrong⟩ or future ⟨I'll be ~*ed* if I do⟩ or absolutely ⟨~*ed* if I care⟩ ~ *vi* **:** to offer thanksgivings or ask for blessings ⟨if you ~ with the spirit —1 Cor 14:16 (RSV)⟩ ⟨his historic sense would have *blest* and feasted —*Atlantic*⟩

2bless *vt* [origin unknown] *obs* **:** WAVE, BRANDISH

1blessed \'blesәd *sometimes esp for meter's sake or when imperative "be" follows* -est\ *or* **blest** \-est\ *adj, sometimes* **blesseder** *sometimes* **blessedest** [ME, fr. past part. of *blessen*] **1 :** HALLOWED, CONSECRATED, HOLY ⟨the ~ death of the martyr⟩; *also* **:** worthy of blessing or adoration **:** held in adoration ⟨the ~ Trinity⟩ **2 :** highly favored (as with blessings or divine care) **:** existing in or enjoying happiness ⟨the ~ saints⟩ **3 :** bringing pleasure or contentment **:** PLEASING, ENJOYABLE, DELIGHTFUL ⟨that extra ~ quarter hour in bed —A.C.Spectorsky⟩; *sometimes* **:** FORTUNATE ⟨a ~ state of unquestioning trust⟩ ⟨traveled about Amazonia with greater ease than most who have been so ~ —*Geog. Jour.*⟩ **4 :** enjoying or relating to spiritual contentment ⟨cast out from God and ~ vision —John Milton⟩ **5** *Roman Catholicism* **:** BEATIFIED **6 :** CURSED, DAMNED, DARNED, DOGGONE, DRATTED — used as an intensive ⟨not a ~ drop of rain⟩ ⟨will those ~ bells never stop ringing⟩

2bless·ed \'blesәd\ *n, pl* **blessed** *also* **blesseds :** a person beatified by the Roman Catholic Church

blessed bread \'blest-\ *n, Eastern Church* **:** ANTIDORON

bless·ed event \-sәd-\ *n* **:** the birth of a baby

bless·ed·ly \-esәdlē, -li\ *adv* **:** in a blessed manner

bless·ed·ness \'blesәdnәs\ *n* -ES [ME, fr. *blessed* + *-ness*] **:** the quality or state of being blessed **syn** see HAPPINESS

bless·ed sacrament \-sәd-\ *n, usu cap B&S* **:** the consecrated Host

bless·ed thistle \-sәd-\ *n* **1 :** an annual pubescent herb (*Cnicus benedictus*) with large heads of yellow flowers **2 :** MILK THISTLE 1

blessed word \-sәd-\ *n* **:** CATCHWORD, SHIBBOLETH

blessing *n* -S [ME, fr. OE *blētsung*, fr. *blētsian* to bless — more at BLESS] **1 a :** act of one that blesses **b :** words used in such an act **c :** BENEDICTION 1 **d :** APPROVAL, ENCOURAGEMENT ⟨presumably had the ~ . . . of the British government —*Time*⟩ ⟨tried to obtain the president's ~ for higher steel prices⟩ **2 a :** a thing conducive to happiness or welfare ⟨able to appreciate the ~ of peace⟩ **b :** a present or gift accorded as a token of esp. divine favor **3 :** PRAISE, WORSHIP; *esp* **:** grace said at a meal ⟨father will ask the ~⟩ **4** *chiefly Midland* **:** CURSING, SCOLDING; *esp* **:** a severe or wordy rebuke — often with *out* ⟨I'll give her a real ~ out when she gets home⟩

bless·ing·ly *adv* **:** in a blessing manner

blessing way *n, usu cap B&W* **:** a Navaho rite intended to attract good fortune by establishing harmony with good spirits

bless out *vt, chiefly Midland* **:** to rebuke sternly **:** SCOLD

1blest *past of* BLESS

2blest *var of* BLESSED

1blether *var of* BLATHER

2bleth·er \'bleth̲ә(r)\ *dial Brit var of* BLADDER

bleth·er·a·tion \,bleth̲ә'rāshәn\ *n* -S [*1blether* + *-ation*] *chiefly Scot* **:** NONSENSE

blethernose \'⸗,⸗,⸗\ *n* [*2blether* + *nose*] **:** HOODED SEAL

bleth·ers \'bleth̲ərz\ *n pl* [*1blether*] *Scot* **:** foolish talk

ble·tia \'blēsh(ē)ә, -ēd·ēә\ *n, cap* [NL, fr. Luis *Blet*, 18th cent. Span. pharmacist and botanist + NL *-ia*] **:** a genus of terrestrial cormose orchids of tropical America with linear plicate leaves and a slender scape of large purple or pink flowers — see BLETILLA

ble·til·la \blә'tilә\ *n, cap* [NL, alter. of *Bletia*] **:** a small genus of chiefly Asiatic terrestrial orchids that resemble those of the genus *Bletia* and include one (*B. striata*) that is cultivated in several horticultural forms in the open in mild climates or in the cool greenhouse

blet·ting \'bled·iŋ\ *n* -S [fr. gerund of *blet* to become overripe, fr. F *blettir*, fr. *blet* overripe, fr. OF] **:** the ripening and softening of certain fruits in storage

bleu cheese \'blü-\ *n* [part trans. of F *fromage bleu*, fr. *fromage* cheese + *bleu* blue, of Gmc origin; akin to OHG *blāo* blue — more at BLUE] **:** BLUE CHEESE

bleu de ly·on \blœtlēō"\ *n, pl* **bleus de lyon** \"\ *often cap L* [F, lit., Lyons blue, fr. *Lyons* (Lyon), France] **:** NATIONAL BLUE

bleu de roi \blœd(ә)·rwä\ *n, pl* **bleus de roi** \"\ [F, lit., king's blue] **:** SÈVRES BLUE 2b (2)

bleu lou·ise \blœlü(w)ēz\ *n, pl* **bleus louise** \"\ *often cap L* [F, lit., Louise blue] **:** EMAIL 2

bleu pas·sé \blœpäsā\ *n, pl* **bleus passés** \"\ [F, lit., faded blue] **:** OLD BLUE

1blew *obs var of* BLUE

2blew *past of* BLOW

blew·its \'blüәts\ *n* -ES [prob. irreg. fr. *blue*] **:** an edible agaric (*Tricholoma personatum*) that is pale lilac when young

bli·aut *or* **bli·aud** \'blē(,)ō\ *n* -S [F, fr. OF *bliaut, blialt*] **:** a close-fitting often laced medieval tunic with long skirts and sleeves

blickey *or* **blickie** *also* **blicky** \'blikē\ *n, pl* **blickeys** *or* **blickies** [D *blikje*, dim. of *blik* pail, tin, fr. MD *blic, blec*; akin to OHG *bleh* tin, ON *blik* gleam, OE *blice* act of becoming visible, OHG *bleih* pale — more at BLEACH] *North* **:** a small pail; *esp* **:** a covered metal lunch pail

1blight \'blīt, *usu* -d·+V\ *n* -S [origin unknown] **1 a :** any disease, symptom of disease, or injury of plants characterized by or resulting in withering, cessation of growth, and a more or less general death of parts (as leaves, flowers, and stems) without rotting and caused by fungi or bacteria, viruses, unfavorable climatic conditions, or insect attack — often used with a qualifying word that describes the disorder ⟨black ~*s* of various plants⟩ or that names the plant or plant affected **b :** any organism causing blight; *esp* **:** an insect (as the woolly apple aphid) that causes such a condition **2 :** something that frustrates one's plans or withers one's hopes ⟨suffering the pervading ~ of poverty⟩ **3 a :** something that impairs or destroys ⟨the censorship . . . has brought under its ~ Ireland's greatest poets, dramatists, and scholars —Paul Blanshard⟩ **b :** a condition or influence that lowers the value of real estate ⟨industrial expansion may create urban ~⟩; *often* **:** the state resulting from such a condition ⟨congested slums and decaying areas of ~ which are the outstanding disgrace of American city life —*Pencil Points*⟩ **4** *chiefly Brit* **:** APHID; *esp* **:** WOOLLY APPLE APHID **5** *Austral* **:** an inflammation of the eye in which the eyelids discharge a thick mucous substance that often seals them up for days and minute granular pustules develop inside the lid — called also *sandy blight*

2blight \"\ *vb* -ED/-ING/-S *vt* **1 :** to affect (as a plant) with blight **:** BLAST ⟨last night's hard frost ~*ed* the late flush of growth⟩ **2 :** to cause to deteriorate **:** RUIN, FRUSTRATE ⟨some human beings ruin and ~ themselves by old-fashioned sex suppression while others ruin and ~ themselves by new-fashioned sex excess —J.C.Powys⟩ ~ *vi* **:** to suffer from or become affected with blight **:** become blasted ⟨our potatoes ~*ed*⟩

blightbird \'⸗,⸗\ *n* **:** any of several silvereyes of Australia and New Zealand that feed freely on various insect pests

blight canker *n* **:** a phase of fire blight characterized by cankers

blight·ed \'blīd·әd, -ītәd\ *adj* **1** *slang* **:** BLASTED 2 **2 :** affected by blight ⟨a ~ rose⟩; *esp, of real estate* **:** marked by termination of healthy growth and development accompanied by deterioration and decline of property values ⟨the ~ areas that are the shame of every metropolis⟩

blight·er \'blīd·ә(r), -ītә-\ *n* -S **1 :** one that blights **2** *slang Brit* **a :** a worthless or contemptible person **b :** FELLOW, GUY ⟨we're for you against the other ~*s* —John Buchan⟩

blight·ing \'blīd·iŋ, -ītiŋ\ *adj* **:** causing blight — **blight·ing·ly** *adv*

blighty \'blītī\ *n* -ES [by folk etymology fr. Hindi *bilāyatī, wilāyatī* foreign country, England, fr. Ar *wilāyat* province, country] **1** *often cap, slang Brit* **:** one's native land (as England) **2** *slang Brit* **a :** a wound whereby a member of the armed forces is invalided home **b :** FURLOUGH

blij·ver \'blīvә(r)\ *n* -S [D, one that remains, fr. *blijven* to remain (fr. MD *blīven*) + *-er*; akin to OE *belīfan* to remain — more at LEAVE] **:** a European typically of mixed blood who is a permanent resident of the Netherlands Indies

blim·bing \'blimbiŋ\ *n* -S [Tag *balimbing, bilimbing* + Malay *bĕlimbing*] **:** CARAMBOLA

bli·mey *also* **bli·my** \'blīmī\ *interj* [by shortening] *chiefly Brit* **:** GORBLIMEY

blimp \'blimp\ *n* -S [perh. fr. (*type*) *B* + *limp*] **1 a :** a nonrigid airship **b :** a fat person **2 :** a soundproof housing for a motion-picture camera used in taking pictures with sound **3** [after Col. *Blimp*, character created by David Low *b*1891 British cartoonist] *often cap* **:** a diehard of ultraconservative nationalistic outlook and complacent stupidity

blimp·ish \-pish,-pēsh\ *adj, often cap* **:** in the manner of or resembling a blimp ⟨the pig-headed ~ obstinacy with which Britain clung to the imperial defense plan —*Sydney (Australia) Daily Telegraph*⟩ — **blimp·ish·ly** *adv*

blin \'blin\ *n, pl* **blini** *or* **bliny** \'blinē\ *or* **blinis** [Russ — more at BLINTZE] **:** BLINTZE

1blind \'blīnd\ *adj, usu* -ER/-EST [ME, fr. OE; akin to OHG *blint* blind, ON *blindr*, Goth *blinds* blind, OE *blandan* to mix — more at BLEND] **1 a :** lacking the sense of sight by natural defect or by deprivation **b :** not having an eye or having an eye that does not see ⟨that horse will shy if you come up on his ~ side⟩ **c :** deficient in or lacking a physical sense other than sight — usu. with a qualifying term ⟨taste-*blind*⟩ **d :** for sightless persons ⟨~ care⟩ ⟨~ home⟩ **2 a :** not having the faculty of discernment **:** lacking in intellectual light **:** unable or unwilling to judge rationally ⟨~ to his own defects⟩ **b :** unsupported by evidence or plausibility **:** not substantially based ⟨~ faith⟩ **3 a :** without regard to rational discrimination, guidance, or restriction ⟨if they persist in such a ~ choice they must suffer for it⟩ **b** *of an impersonal force* **:** lacking any directing or controlling consciousness ⟨our fate is in the hands of ~ chance⟩ **c :** marked by complete insensibility ⟨lying helpless in a ~ stupor⟩; *esp* **:** drunken to the point of insensibility **:** DEAD-DRUNK **4 :** made or done without sight of objects or knowledge of facts comprising the chief or usual means of guidance or judgment ⟨a ~ purchase⟩: as **a :** performed solely by the aid of data given by instruments within an airplane and without direct sight of landmarks ⟨a ~ landing⟩ ⟨~ flying⟩ **b** *in card games* **:** made without seeing some relevant factor (as one's own hand or the dummy) ⟨a ~ lead⟩ **c :** made or done from psychological test data without reference to other case material ⟨~ analysis⟩ ⟨~ interpretation⟩ **5 :** DEFECTIVE, INCOMPLETE, ABORTIVE: **a** *of plants or plant parts* (1) **:** SUPPRESSED (2) **:** lacking a growing point (3) **:** failing to produce flowers or seeds — used esp. of buds and bulbs **b** *music* **:** having alternate tones in different registers ⟨a ~ trill⟩ ⟨a ~ octave series⟩ **c :** incapable of producing a print — used of a lithographic surface ⟨the plate went ~ after 10,000 impressions⟩ **6 a** *archaic* **:** lacking in light or brightness **:** DARK ⟨the little ~ bedchamber —Samuel Pepys⟩ **b** *obs* **:** UNLIGHTED ⟨a ~ candle⟩; *also* **:** having its light concealed ⟨a ~ lantern⟩ **c :** DULL **:** lacking in brightness or luster; *esp* **:** not polished or brought to a high gloss **:** finished dull ⟨a mellow ~ finish to the paneling⟩ **d :** impressed or tooled without gilding, inking, or coloring ⟨~ lettering⟩ ⟨~ scoring⟩ **7 :** difficult to discern, make out, or discover **:** hard to locate or identify **:** OBSCURE, HIDDEN: as **a** *archaic* **:** out of the way; *also* **:** SECRET ⟨a ~ meeting place⟩ **b** *archaic, of a track or way* **:** dim and ill-defined; *also* **:** not easily followed or traced **:** INVOLVED, INTRICATE ⟨the ~ mazes of this tangled wood —John Milton⟩ **c** (1) *of writing* **:** ILLEGIBLE; *esp, of mail* **:** lacking a complete or legible address (2) **:** concerned with the handling of blind mail **d** *of the sense of a passage* **:** unintelligible or uncertainly determinable **e** *of material objects* **:** constructed or arranged so as to be hidden from sight **:** COVERED ⟨a ~ veneer⟩ ⟨~ seams in a shoe⟩: as (1) *of a ditch or other water channel* **:** consisting of a cut in the soil filled loosely with stones between which water can trickle or percolate (2) *of minerals and lodes and strata* **:** not appearing in an outcrop at the surface ⟨a ~ vein⟩ (3) *of roads, driveways, and crossings* **:** screened from the view of oncoming drivers or engineers ⟨a ~ crossroad⟩ **8 a :** having but one opening or outlet **:** closed at one end **:** not permitting passage or flow all the way through ⟨a ~ alley⟩ ⟨~ sockets⟩ ⟨the ~ gut⟩ **b** *of a rivet or other fastener* **:** designed to be inserted and made fast from one side **c** *geol* **:** terminating abruptly where it might be expected to continue ⟨a ~ joint in rocks⟩ ⟨a ~ valley that ends downstream where drainage disappears underground⟩ **9 :** having no opening for light or passage **:** BLANK ⟨a ~ wall⟩: as **a** *of a hedge* **:** too thick to see through or pass through **b** *of a structural member* **:** made without an opening but like a member that normally has an opening ⟨a ~ arch⟩ ⟨a ~ window over the stairs⟩ **10** *railroading* **:** turned edgewise — used of a target or of its position

[2]blind \"\ *vt* -ED/-ING/-S [ME *blinden*, fr. *blind*, adj.] **1 :** to make blind: **a :** to deprive of the sense of sight ⟨his right eye was ~*ed* when he was a child⟩ **b :** to deprive of insight or understanding ⟨prejudice usually ~*s* judgment⟩ **c :** DECEIVE, FOOL, BEDAZZLE **d :** to deprive temporarily or partially of vision **:** make seeing difficult for or painful to **:** DAZZLE ⟨the hot glare ~*ed* her as she stepped into the street⟩ **2 a :** to withhold light from **:** DARKEN ⟨shrubbery ~*ing* all their windows⟩ **b :** HIDE, CONCEAL **c :** to make dim by comparison **:** OUTSHINE, ECLIPSE ⟨torches that ~ the candles⟩ **d :** to render nonlustrous **:** DULL ⟨a synthetic fabric may need to be ~*ed* in the finishing process⟩ **3 :** to fill the interstices of **:** CLOG: as **a :** to cover (a newly paved road) with a coating of sand and gravel in order that joints may be filled **b :** to cover (drain tiles) with earth while the trench is being filled **4 :** to stamp (as a book cover) without gilding or coloring — often used with *in* **5 :** to protect with blindages or with blinds

[3]blind \"\ *n* -S **1 :** something to hinder sight or keep out light: as **a :** a screen used to deflect or redirect light or to restrict observation from without: as (1) **:** WINDOW SHUTTER (2) **:** a roller window shade (3) **:** VENETIAN BLIND (4) *chiefly Brit* **:** AWNING (5) **:** BRISE-SOLEIL (6) **:** a shutter for a porthole **b :** BLINDER **c :** a cloth covering for the eyes used esp. in games **2 :** a place or means of concealment **:** AMBUSH 1; *esp* **:** a concealing enclosure from which a person may shoot game or observe wildlife **3 a :** something put forward to screen or cover another object or design **:** SUBTERFUGE, DECEPTION ⟨the holding company was a ~ for out-of-state interests⟩ ⟨his helpful offer is no more than a ~⟩ **b** (1) **:** a person serving as an agent for another who keeps under cover (2) **:** one who acts as a decoy or distraction **4 :** hand tooling without gilding or coloring ⟨bindings decorated in ~⟩ **5 a :** BLINDAGE **b :** a strong frame of uprights and crosspieces used to support a blindage **6** *card games* **a :** an obligatory opening bet in some forms of draw poker made by the player at the dealer's left before the cards are dealt and often constituting a raise of the ante **b :** the player who makes this bet **c :** WIDOW 3 **7** *railroading* **a :** BLIND BAGGAGE **b :** the platform of a blind baggage immediately behind the tender — usu. used in pl. **8** *slang Brit* **:** a noisy usu. drunken party **:** BRAWL

[4]blind \"\ *adv* [[1]*blind*] **:** BLINDLY: as **a :** to the point of insensibility ⟨~ drunk⟩ **b :** without the aid of visual or other indicators that are usu. a source of guidance or judgment ⟨learning to fly ~⟩ **c :** RECKLESSLY, HEEDLESSLY ⟨I'd rather go it ~ than not get home at all⟩

blind advertisement *n* **:** an advertisement that does not disclose the name of the advertiser

blind·age \'blīndij\ *n* -S [F, fr. *blinder* to screen, protect (fr. *blinde* blind to screen military operations, fr. G *blende*, fr. *blenden* to blind, fr. OHG *blenten*) + *-age* — more at BLIND] **:** an overhead protection: as **a :** an earth-covered screen supported by a blind for an advanced trench or approach **b :** a large deep dugout often with bunks and other fittings

blind alley *n* **:** something that offers no opportunity for progress or advancement

blind area *n* **:** a wholly or partly covered area outside the wall of a building to keep moisture from the wall

blind attic *n* **:** a closed unfinished dead space immediately beneath the roof of a building

blind baggage *n* **:** a railway baggage, express, or postal car that has no door or opening at one end; *esp* **:** one immediately behind a tender

blind blocking *n* **:** BLIND 4

blind bond *n* **:** a masonry bond in which the headers extend only halfway through the tier of face brick all of which are stretchers and some of which are split lengthwise to accommodate the ends of the headers

blind bridle *n* **:** a bridle provided with blinders

blind catch *n* **:** BLINDFAST

blind date *n* **1 :** a date arranged by a third person between two persons of opposite sex who have not previously met **2 :** either participant in a blind date

blinded *adj* **1 :** made blind **:** DAZZLED, OBSCURED, DARKENED **2 :** furnished with a blind or blinds ⟨green-*blinded* windows⟩ **3 :** having the window blinds closed

blind eel *n* **1 :** CONGO SNAKE **2 :** seaweed accidentally hauled up in a net — used esp. by fishermen

[1]blinder *comparative of* BLIND

[2]blind·er \'blīndə(r)\ *n* -S **1 :** either of two flaps on a horse's bridle to prevent sight of objects at his sides **2 blinders** *pl* **:** an obstruction to sight or discernment **:** an impediment to clear thinking

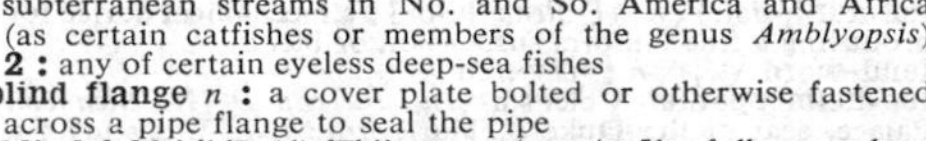

b blinder

blindest *superlative of* BLIND

blind·eyes \'=,=\ *n pl but sing or pl in constr* **1 :** CORN POPPY **2 :** a scarlet-flowered poppy (*Papaver dubium*) often occurring as a weed in cultivated fields and waste ground

blindfast \'=,=\ *n* -S [[3]*blind* + *fast*] **:** a window-blind fastener

blindfish \'=,=\ *n* **1 :** any of several small fishes with vestigial and functionless eyes found usu. in the waters of caves and subterranean streams in No. and So. America and Africa (as certain catfishes or members of the genus *Amblyopsis*) **2 :** any of certain eyeless deep-sea fishes

blind flange *n* **:** a cover plate bolted or otherwise fastened across a pipe flange to seal the pipe

[1]blind·fold \'blīn(d),fōld\ *vt* -ED/-ING/-S [by folk etymology fr. ME *blindfelden*, alter. of *blindfellen* to strike blind, to blindfold, fr. *blind* + *fellen* to fell, strike down — more at FELL] **1 :** to cover the eyes of with or as if with a bandage **2 :** to hinder from seeing; *esp* **:** to keep from comprehension

[2]blindfold \"\ *adj* [by folk etymology fr. ME *blindfeld*, *blindfelled*, fr. past part. of *blindfellen*] **1 :** having the eyes covered **2 a :** lacking mental vision or understanding **b :** lacking consideration **:** HEEDLESS, RECKLESS ⟨a ~ fury⟩

[3]blindfold \"\ *n* **1 :** a bandage for covering the eyes and shutting out light or vision **2 :** something that acts as a blindfold esp. in obscuring mental or physical vision ⟨do not let the wool grow down into a ~ that interferes with grazing⟩ ⟨his arrogance was a ~ shutting him away from his fellows⟩

blindfold chess *n* **:** chess played without sight of the board

blind·fold·ed·ness *n* -ES **:** the quality or state of being blindfolded

blind gentian *n* **:** CLOSED GENTIAN

blind goby *n* **:** PINKFISH

blind gut *n* [so called fr. its having only one opening] **:** CECUM

blind head *n, obs* **:** a cover without outlet for a retort or other distilling vessel; *also* **:** the whole apparatus of which the cover is a part

blind header *n* **:** a masonry header in the interior of a wall; *also* **:** SNAP HEADER

blind hookey *n, card games* **:** a variety of banker and broker

[1]blinding *n* -S [ME, fr. gerund of *blinden*] **1 :** the act of making or the fact of becoming blind **2 :** the sand and fine gravel used to blind a road

[2]blinding *adj* [fr. pres. part. of [2]*blind*] **1 :** making blind or as if blind: **a :** depriving of sight **b :** depriving of understanding **:** CONFUSING **c :** brilliant with light or color **:** DAZZLING **d :** OBSCURING ⟨~ tears⟩ **2** *slang* **:** DARNED, BLAMED, BLASTED ⟨what are you in such a ~ hurry over⟩ — **blind·ing·ly** *adv*

blinding tree *n* **:** BLIND-YOUR-EYES

blind·ish \'blīndish, -dēsh\ *adj* [[1]*blind* + *-ish*] **:** somewhat blind

blind·ism \-,dizəm\ *n* -S **:** a form of behavior characteristic of blind persons

blind·less \-dləs\ *adj* [[3]*blind* + *-less*] **:** having no blind

blind lift *n* **:** a catch for raising or lowering a window blind

blind-loaded \'=¦==\ *adj* **1 :** containing no bursting charge but loaded with sand so as to come up to service weight — used of a shell **2 :** not having a fuse, the bursting charge being exploded by the heat of impact — used of a shell

blind·ly *adv* [ME, fr. [1]*blind* + *-ly*] **:** in a blind way ⟨groping ~ in the dark passage⟩: **a :** without reason or understanding **:** without comprehension or consideration ⟨let no one follow me ~⟩ **b :** without conscious purpose **:** MECHANICALLY ⟨toying ~ with the ringlet on her neck⟩ **c :** without an opening or outlet ⟨the path ended ~ at a high brick wall⟩

blind·man \-dmən\ *n, pl* **blindmen** [*blind* (*mail*) illegible or insufficiently addressed mail + *man*] *chiefly Brit* **:** BLIND-READER

blind·man's buff \'blīn(d),manz-, -,maa(ə)nz-\ *n* [*blind man* + *buff* (buffet)] **1 :** a group game in which a blindfolded player tries to catch and identify any other member of the group **2 :** something concerted with trickery and bedazzlement or carried out without awareness of the facts and issues involved

blindman's holiday \"-\ *n* [*blind man*] *archaic* **:** TWILIGHT

blind mortise *n* **:** a mortise that does not extend entirely through the material in which it is cut

blind-nail \'=,=\ *vt* **:** to nail in such a way that nailheads are not visible on the face of the work

blind·ness \'blīnnəs\ *n* -ES [ME, fr. [1]*blind* + *-ness*] **1 :** want of discernment esp. with reference to some particular object or matter **:** failure to exercise understanding, judgment, or discrimination **2 a :** the quality or state of being blind; *specif* **:** that of having less than $\frac{1}{10}$ of normal vision in the more efficient eye when refractive defects are fully corrected by suitable lenses — compare COLOR BLINDNESS **b :** psychic inability to perceive visual images although the visual receptors are functional — called also *mental blindness, mind blindness, psychic blindness* **c :** lack of sensory perception involving all or part of some sense other than sight ⟨taste ~⟩ ⟨smell ~⟩ **3 a** *obs* **:** CONCEALMENT **b :** OBSCURITY **4** *of plants* **:** failure to produce a growing tip or flowers or to develop vegetative parts — compare [1]*blind* 5a

blind nettle *n* [ME *blind netyll*, fr. OE *blindnetle*, fr. *blind* + *netle* nettle — more at NETTLE; fr. its lack of sting] **1 :** WHITE DEAD NETTLE **2 :** HENBIT

blind officer *n* [*blind* (*mail*) illegible or insufficiently addressed mail] *chiefly Brit* **:** BLIND-READER

blind P \-'pē\ *n* [so called fr. the fact that the loop is inked in] **:** the paragraph mark ⟨¶ is one form of *blind P*⟩

blind pig *n, slang* **:** BLIND TIGER

blind pit *n, bot* **:** a pit lacking a complementary pit and commonly found opposite an intercellular space — see PIT-PAIR

blind pocket *also* **blind pocket psorosis** *n* **:** a phase of psorosis of citrus trees characterized by a creasing of the trunk of the tree that results in a fluted effect

blind pool *n* **:** a pool of funds placed at the discretion of the manager

blind pull *n* **:** BLIND LIFT

blind pulley *n* **:** DEADEYE

blind-punch \'=¦=\ *vt* **:** to punch (as metal) only a part of the way through

blind rat *n* **:** MOLE RAT

blind-reader \'=,==\ *n* [*blind* (*mail*) illegible or insufficiently addressed mail] *chiefly Brit* **:** a post-office clerk whose duty is the deciphering of illegible or insufficient addresses

blind robin *n* **:** a smoked herring

blinds *pl of* BLIND, *pres 3d sing of* BLIND

blind-seed disease \'=¦=-\ *also* **blind seed** *n* **:** a disease of forage grasses (as rye grass and fescue) caused by an ascomycetous fungus (*Phialea temulenta*) and resulting in abortion of the seed

blind set *n* **:** an unbaited trap hidden in the runway or burrow of an animal — compare BAIT SET

blind shaft *n* **:** WINZE

blind shell *n* **1 a :** a blind-loaded shell **b :** [1]DUD 5 **2** [so called fr. the closing of the apex at maturity] **:** a mollusk of the family Caecidae

blind side *n* **1 :** the side on which one that is blind in one eye cannot see **2 :** an aspect of a matter in which one can see no fault **3 :** the ground on the side of a rugby scrum opposite to the side the referee stands on

blind siding *n* **:** a railroad siding located at a point where there is no agent or means of communication

blind snake *n* **1 :** a snake of the family Typhlopidae or of the related Leptotyphlopidae — called also *worm snake* **2 :** any of various limbless burrowing lizards

blind snipe *n* **:** WOODCOCK 1a(2)

blind spot *n* **1 a :** the point in the retina not sensitive to light where the optic nerve passes through the inner coat of the eyeball — see EYE illustration **b :** a portion of a field not seeable or inspectable with available equipment ⟨one limitation of radar is the existence of *blind spots* at low levels⟩ **2 :** an area in which one fails to exercise understanding, judgment, or discrimination **3 :** a locality in which radio reception is markedly poorer than in the surrounding area

blind staggers *n pl but sing or pl in constr* **1 a :** [2]STAGGER 1a **b :** SELENOSIS; *esp* **:** a severe acute form of this condition **2 a :** dizziness accompanied by staggers **b :** extreme drunkenness

blind stamp *n* **:** an impression made by blind stamping

blind-stamp \'=,=\ *vt* [*blind stamp*] **:** to stamp (as the cover of a book) without gilding or coloring

blind stitch *n* **:** a sewing stitch so made as to be invisible on the right side and often nearly invisible on the wrong side

blind·stitch \'=,=\ *vt* [*blind stitch*] **:** to sew with blind stitches

blind·story \'=,==\ *n* **:** a story without windows; *specif* **:** the triforium of a Gothic church without windows in the outer wall

blind teat *n* **:** a teat that does not permit passage of milk (as an occluded or inverted teat)

blind tiger *n* [prob. so called fr. the evasion of prohibition laws by selling liquor in establishments disguised as halls for exhibiting natural curiosities] *slang* **:** a place that sells intoxicants illegally **:** SPEAKEASY

blind tire *n* **:** BALD TIRE

blind-tool \'=,=\ *vt* **:** to hand-tool (as the cover of a book) without gilding or coloring — compare BLIND-STAMP

blindworm \'=,=\ *n* [[1]*blind* + *worm*] **1 :** a small burrowing limbless lizard with minute eyes; *esp* **:** a small-scaled European lizard (*Anguis fragilis*) that feeds on grubs and worms and is popularly believed to be blind — called also *slowworm* **2** *archaic* **:** ADDER

blind-your-eyes \¦==¦=\ *n, pl* **blind-your-eyes** [so called fr. its volatile juice] **:** an Australian tree (*Excoecaria agallocha*) — called also *milky mangrove, poison tree*

bling·er \'bliŋə(r)\ *n* -S [origin unknown] *slang* **:** a superlative example of its kind ⟨his cold was a real ~⟩

blini *or* **blinis** *pl of* BLIN

[1]blink \'bliŋk\ *vb* -ED/-ING/-S [ME *blinken* to open one's eyes; prob. akin to MD & G *blinken* to glitter, shine, OHG *blanch* shining, bright, white — more at BLANK] *vi* **1 a** *obs* **:** to look glancingly **:** PEEP, GLANCE **b :** to look with half-shut winking eyes (as when roused from sleep or dazzled by strong light) ⟨seated in her obscure corner ~*ing* at the fire⟩ ⟨the glare on the snow made us ~⟩ **c :** to open and shut the eye repeatedly or rapidly **:** wink involuntarily ⟨one eye ~*ing* and twitching⟩ **2** *of light or a source of light* **a :** to shine intermittently **:** FLICKER, TWINKLE **b :** to shine dimly or uncertainly ⟨sun ~*ing* through the strands of fog⟩ **3 a :** to look evasively **:** look with ignoring or condoning — usu. used with *at* ⟨modern popular philosophy ~*s* at these facts —M.R.Cohen⟩ **b :** to look with surprise **:** become startled, amazed, or dismayed — used with *at* ⟨a professional statistician might ~ at the methods though the results seem reasonable⟩ ~ *vt* **1** *obs* **:** to cause to sour **:** make sour (as milk or beer) **2** *of a sporting dog* **:** to refuse to see and point (game) ⟨his dog *blinked* the first bevy of the day⟩ **3 a :** to close and open (the eye) involuntarily **:** WINK ⟨he ~*ed* his tired eyes⟩ **b :** to remove (as tears) from the eye by blinking **4** *chiefly Scot* **:** to put the evil eye on **:** BEWITCH **5 a :** to deny recognition to **:** deliberately evade **:** IGNORE — often used in negative constructions ⟨there was no ~*ing* the fact that she had been worried —Helen Howe⟩ or with *away* ⟨truths that at the turn of the century were firmly ~*ed* away —*Saturday Rev.*⟩ **b :** to be aware of **:** RECOGNIZE ⟨if we ~ the truth we must admit our share of responsibility⟩ **6 a :** to cause to emit flashes or twinkles of light ⟨he ~*ed* his flashlight to show us the way⟩ **b :** to signal by a blinker

[2]blink \"\ *n* -S **1** *chiefly Scot* **:** GLIMPSE, GLANCE ⟨a view on a bit of empty road, houses, and a ~ of sea —R.L.Stevenson⟩ **2 a :** a brief show of light **:** GLEAM, GLIMMER, SPARKLE ⟨a ~ of bright flame⟩ **b :** a brief period of time **:** INSTANT, MOMENT, TRICE **3 :** an involuntary shutting and opening of the eye **:** WINKING **4** *dial* **:** milk that is slightly sour **5 a :** a whitish or mottled appearance of the sky about the horizon caused by the reflection of light from an ice field or from scattered ice — compare ICEBLINK **b :** a dark appearance of the sky about the horizon caused by the absence of reflected light due to open water — compare WATER SKY — **on the blink** *adv* (*or adj*) **:** in or into a disabled or useless condition **:** INDISPOSED **:** out of order

[3]blink \"\ *adj* **:** BLINK-EYED

[4]blink \"\ *n* -S [by shortening] **:** BLINKER 3

blink·ard \'bliŋkə(r)d\ *n* -S [[1]*blink* + *-ard*] **1** *archaic* **:** one that blinks with or as if with weak eyes **2 :** a stupid, slow-witted, or obtuse person

blink comparator *n* **:** an optical instrument by means of which two pictures identical in all but a few details may be registered in a single visual field and viewed alternately in rapid succession

blinked *adj* [fr. past part. of [1]*blink*] **:** affected with blinking

[1]blink·er \'bliŋkə(r)\ *n* -S [[1]*blink* + *-er*] **1 :** one that blinks: as **a** *archaic* **:** COQUETTE **b :** a sporting dog that refuses to see and point game or to hold to a point and flush his game **c** (1) **:** a device consisting essentially of a light that can be flashed on and off regularly as a warning (as at a railway crossing) (2) **:** a traffic light arranged to blink rather than show a color for a sustained period **d** (1) **:** a device consisting essentially of a light that can be flashed on and off in a sequence of coded intervals for signaling a message (as from ship to ship) (2) **:** a message sent by means of a blinker **2 a** (1) **:** BLINDER 1 (2) **:** a cloth hood with shades projecting at the sides of the eye openings used on skittish racehorses — usu. used in pl. **b :** something that impairs mental or moral perception **3** *also* **blink :** a young or undersized mackerel smaller than a tinker

[2]blinker \"\ *vt* **blinkered; blinkered; blinkering** \'bliŋk(ə)riŋ\ **blinkers 1 :** to put blinders or blinkers on ⟨they ~*ed* themselves against the facts⟩; *specif* **:** HOODWINK ⟨a person ill-equipped for his task, ~*ed* as he is by long association with partisan groups⟩ **2 :** to send (a message) by means of a blinker ⟨~*ed* a breakfast invitation from shore —*Newsweek*⟩

blinkered *adj* **:** NARROW, OBTUSE, LIMITED

blinker tube *n* **:** a tube for confining signals by blinker to a single direction

blink-eyed \'=¦=\ *adj* **:** habitually winking

blinking *adj* [fr. pres. part. of [1]*blink*] *slang Brit* **1 :** DAMNED, BLASTED ⟨a ~ nuisance⟩ **2 :** COMPLETE, UTTER ⟨a ~ fool⟩

blink·ing·ly *adv* **:** with blinking eyes **:** EVASIVELY

blink microscope *n* **:** a blink comparator in which the compared images are magnified

[1]blinks *pres 3d sing of* BLINK

[2]blinks *n, pl* **blinks** [fr. pl. of [2]*blink;* fr. the fact that the flowers do not open fully] **:** a small herb (*Montia lamprosperma*) of northern regions — called also *blinking chickweed, water chickweed*

blinky \'bliŋkē, -ki\ *adj, usu* -ER/-EST [[1]*blink* + *-y*] **1 :** BLINKING, BLINK-EYED **2** *dial* **:** slightly sour — used esp. of milk or beer

blin·ter \'blintə(r)\ *vi* -ED/-ING/-S [prob. freq. of obs. Sc *blent* to gleam, glance, fr. ME (northern dial.) *blenten*, fr. *blent*, *blenked* past part. of *blenken* to deceive, swerve, gleam, glance, fr. OE *blencan* to deceive — more at BLENCH] **1** *Scot* **:** FLICKER, GLIMMER ⟨the firelight ~*ed* on her face⟩ **2** *Scot* **:** BLINK

blin·tze \ blintsə\ *or* **blintz** \'blints\ *n, pl* **blintzes** [Yiddish *blintse*, fr. Russ *blinets*, dim. of *blin* pancake, fr. ORuss *mlinŭ;* akin to Russ *molot'* to grind, OHG *malan* — more at MEAL] **:** a thin rolled pancake with a filling usu. of cream cheese

bliny *pl of* BLIN

[1]blip \'blip\ *n* -S [imit.] **1 :** a short crisp sound ⟨the ~ of a switch button⟩ **2 :** an image on a radar screen

[2]blip \"\ *vb* **blipped; blipped; blipping; blips** *vt* **:** to strike or slap ~ *vi* **:** to make or cause a blip

blirt \'bli(ə)rt, 'blərt\ *Scot var of* BLURT

bliss \'blis\ *n* -ES [ME *blis, blisse*, fr. OE *bliss, blīths;* akin to OS *blīdsea* bliss; derivative fr. the root of E *blithe*] **1 :** a state of complete or ecstatic happiness ⟨they lived in perfect loving ~⟩ ⟨the ~ of complete understanding can only come to the equally endowed⟩ **2 a :** the perfect and exalted joy of saved souls **:** BEATITUDE 1 **b :** the place where such joy is experienced **:** PARADISE, HEAVEN **c :** the state of enjoying such joy **3** *archaic* **:** a cause of happiness **syn** see HAPPINESS

bliss·ful \'=fəl\ *adj* [ME *blisful*, fr. *blis* + *-ful*] **1 :** full of, marked by, or causing bliss **:** very happy ⟨a ~ couple of young lovers⟩ **2 :** content with things as they are **:** oblivious of existing incongruities, improprieties, or inequities ⟨Meddling's ~ lack of sensitivity to other people's feelings —Gordon Merrick⟩ ⟨new regulations issued in ~ ignorance of the real situation⟩ — **bliss·ful·ly** \-fəlē, -li\ *adv* — **bliss·ful·ness** \fəlnəs\ *n* -ES

bliss·less \-ləs\ *adj* **:** being without bliss

blissom *vb* [ME *blissomen*, of Scand origin; akin to ON *blæsma* in heat (said of goats); akin to ON *blāsa* to blow — more at BLAST] *vt, obs, of a ram* **:** TUP ~ *vi, obs, of a ewe* **:** to be in heat

[1]blis·ter \'blistə(r)\ *n* -S [ME *blester*, *blister*, modif. of OF or MD; OF *blostre* boil, pustule, fr. MD *bluyster* blister; akin to OE *blǣst* blast — more at BLAST] **1 :** an elevation of the epidermis containing watery liquid or serum : BLEB, BULLA **2** : an enclosed raised spot on the surface of an organism caused by the separation of skin or other covering (as one resulting from a bruise on a plant) **3** : an agent that causes a blister (as a blistering plaster) **4** : a flaw on a surface caused by nonadherence or by separation of an applied substance: as **a** : a nodule on a painted surface filled with air, solvent, or water **b** : an elevated layer of rock resulting from the flow of molten rock into low wet areas and the generation of steam pockets **c** : BLISTER PEARL **d** : a fault in plywood or veneer resulting from failure to obtain uniform binding of the surface layer **e** : a large bubble in glass **f** : a spot of emulsion in a photographic film or plate loosened from its base in processing **g** : a rounded elevation on the surface of metal caused by expansion of gas within or through the subsurface metal while it is hot or plastic **5** : an oyster smaller than a quarter dollar **6** : BLISTER COPPER **7 a** : a disease of plants caused by ascomycetous fungi (genus *Taphrina*) that produce large swollen patches on the leaves (as that of the pear caused by *T. bullata*) **b** : any of various similar diseases (as a nonparasitic disorder of the apple) — see BLISTER BLIGHT, BLISTER CANKER, BLISTER SPOT **8** : any of various structures that bulge out from the main mass of which they are part: as **a** : a watertight compartmented structure applied to the hull of certain vessels esp. below the waterline to offer added protection (as against torpedoes or mines) **b** : a gunner's or observer's compartment protruding from the fuselage of an airplane and often covered by a transparent dome **c** : a glass observation dome built into and protruding above the roof of a railroad car **d** : a housing for a radar antenna — see RADOME **9** *slang* : PERSON; *esp* : 1BAG 5 — usu. used disparagingly

2blister \"\ *vb* **blistered; blistered; blistering** \'blist(ə)riŋ\ **blisters** [ME *blisteren*, fr. *blister*, n.] *vi* **1 a** : to become affected with blisters ⟨lips will ~ and chap in the wind⟩ **b** : to raise a blister ⟨that sauce is hot; it positively ~*s*⟩ **2** : to have or take on the form of a blister ⟨the trumpeter's cheeks were ~*ing* like a child's balloon⟩ ~ *vt* **1 a** : to raise a blister on ⟨she ~*ed* her hand with her grease⟩ : cause a blister to form on ⟨the hot sun will ~ the paint⟩ **b** : to treat by blistering or by means of blisters — now usu. restricted to veterinary usage ⟨the doctor physicked him, and bled him, and ~*ed* him, but he lived all the same⟩ **2** : to affect as if to the point of raising blisters: **a** : to administer severe physical punishment to esp. by whipping or beating ⟨get in here this minute or I'll ~ your bottom when you do⟩ **b** : to scorch with words (as in anger or contempt) : censure harshly : EXCORIATE ⟨the sergeant ~*ed* the men and set them to drilling again⟩

blister beetle *n* : any of certain beetles (as the Spanish fly) that when dried and powdered are used to raise blisters on the skin (as in the relief of certain forms of neuritis); *broadly* : any of numerous soft-bodied beetles that constitute the family Meloidae, have a complex metamorphosis, and include the blister beetles and some that as adults are destructive pests of economic plants

blister blight *n* **1** : a blister disease affecting the leaves of the tea plant caused by a fungus (*Exobasidium vexans*) **2** : a disease of Scotch pine caused by a rust (*Cronartium asclepiadeum*) that causes lesions like blisters on the twigs and gradually kills them

blister canker *n* : a disease of the apple tree caused by an ascomycetous fungus (*Nummularia discreta*) producing roughened and blackened cankers on the trunk and larger limbs — called also *apple pox*

blister cone *n* : a small cone produced by the expansion and escape of gas or vapor from liquid lava

blister copper *n* : metallic copper of a black blistered surface, being the product of converting copper matte and being about 98.5 to 99.5 per cent pure — called also *Bessemer copper*

blister cress *n* : any of certain pungent cresses (esp. of the genera *Erysimum* and *Cheiranthus*)

blister disease *var of* BLISTER

blistered *adj* **1** : affected with blisters : having the surface irregular and often pebbled, nodular, or covered with blisters ⟨certain fabrics are ~⟩ **2** : having slashes or openings through which cloth of another material or color shows or is drawn in puffs — used of a 16th century decoration esp. of doublets, breeches, and sleeves

blister figure *n* : an uneven appearance in some woods caused by irregular depressed and elevated rounded areas in the annual rings

blister fly *or* **blistering fly** *n* : BLISTER BEETLE

blister gas *n* : VESICANT

blistering *adj* **1** : extremely hot : hot enough to blister ⟨a ~ sun⟩ **2** *slang* : BLAMED, DARNED, DAMNED **3** : ACRIMONIOUS, WITHERING, SCATHING ⟨a ~ letter⟩ **4** : SEVERE, INTENSE ⟨the troops fell back under a ~ assault from the enemy⟩ ⟨invest human existence with something more . . . than a ~ misery —Norman Cousins⟩ **5** : very rapid : such as might be expected to cause blistering from frictional heat : SCORCHING, GRUELING ⟨the leader set a ~ pace⟩ **6** : of pressing and immediate importance ⟨a ~ local issue⟩ — **blis·ter·ing·ly** *adv*

blistering cerate *n* : a cerate composed of cantharides, glacial acetic acid, oil of turpentine, yellow wax, rosin, and benzoinated lard — called also *cantharides cerate*

blister mite *n* : any of several mites esp. of the genus *Eriophyes* producing a gall on leaves (as the pear-leaf blister mite)

blister pearl *n* : a pearly excrescence on the inside of the shell of a mollusk (as the oyster) commonly enclosing a foreign body (as a bit of mud or a parasite)

blister plant *or* **blister flower** *n* : a crowfoot (*Ranunculus acris*)

blister rust *n* : any of several diseases of pines caused by rust fungi (genus *Cronartium*) in the aecial stage, affecting the sapwood and inner bark and producing blisters externally; *often* : WHITE-PINE BLISTER RUST

blisters *pl of* BLISTER, *pres 3d sing of* BLISTER

blister spot *n* : a disease of the apple caused by a bacterium (*Pseudomonas papulans*) and characterized by dark brown blisters on the fruit and rough bark cankers on the limbs

blister steel *n* : crude steel formerly formed from wrought iron by cementation

blis·tery \'blist(ə)rē, -ri\ *adj* [1*blister* + -*y*] : having, full of, or marred by blisters

blite \'blīt\ *n* -s [ME, fr. L *blitum* orach, fr. Gk *bliton*] : any of several herbs of the family Chenopodiaceae: **a** : STRAWBERRY BLITE **b** : SEA BLITE **c** : GOOD-KING-HENRY

1blithe \'blīth, 'blīth\ *adj* -ER/-EST [ME, fr. OE *blīthe*; akin to OHG *blīdi* kind, joyous, ON *blīthr* gentle, Goth *bleiths* merciful, Lith *blyvas* violet-blue, OE *bǣl* fire, pyre — more at BALD] **1** : of a happy contented character or disposition : JOYFUL, GLAD, CHEERFUL; *also* : exhibiting light-hearted gaiety **2** : without due thought, consideration, or knowledge : LIGHT-MINDED : CASUAL, HEEDLESS ⟨a ~ disregard of the rights of others⟩ ⟨acting in ~ ignorance of historic precedent⟩ **syn** see MERRY

2blithe \"\ *adv* [ME, fr. OE *blīthe*, fr. *blīthe*, adj.] : BLITHELY

blithe·ful \-fəl\ *adj* [ME *blithful*, fr. *blithe* + -*ful*] : GAY, JOYOUS — **blithe·ful·ly** *adv*

blithe·ly *adv* [ME *blithely*, *blitheliche*, fr. OE *blīthelīce*, fr. *blīthe* + -*līce* -ly] : in a blithe manner

blithe·meat \'blīth+,-\ *n* [*blithe* + *meat*] *chiefly Scot* : food prepared for a feast to celebrate the birth of a child

blith·en \'blīthən, -īth-\ *vt* -ED/-ING/-S [1*blithe* + -*en*] : to make blithe

blithe·ness \-thnəs, -th-\ *n* -ES [ME *blitheness*, fr. OE *blīthnes*, fr. *blīthe* + -*nes* -ness] : the quality or state of being blithe

1blith·er \'blithə(r)\ *vi* -ED/-ING/-S [by alter.] : BLATHER — used chiefly in the present participle form ⟨a ~*ing* idiot⟩

2blither \"\ *n* -s [by alter.] : BLATHER

blith·ered \'blithə(r)d\ *adj*, *Austral* : DRUNK

blithe·some \'blīthsəm, -īth-\ *adj* [1*blithe* + -*some*] : CHEERY, GAY, MERRY — **blithe·some·ly** *adv*

blit·ter \'blitər\ *n* -s [perh. alter. of *bleater*] *Scot* : the common Old World snipe (*Capella gallinago*)

1blitz \'blits\ *n* -ES [short for *blitzkrieg*] **1 a** : BLITZKRIEG 1 **b** : an intensive all-out aerial attack or campaign; *also* : AIR RAID ⟨Hitler's ~*es* in 1941 —*Time*⟩ **2** : a fast intensive nonmilitary campaign ⟨the top GOP strategists . . . can hold the Senate by a last-minute ~ —*Newsweek*⟩ ⟨a ~ of spot announcements introduced the new models⟩

2blitz \"\ *vt* -ED/-ING/-ES **1 a** : to subject to a blitz ⟨the district was ~*ed* regularly —*Reader's Digest*⟩ **b** : to make a vigorous attack on ⟨an army of doctors ~*ed* the disease⟩ **2** : to damage by or as if by blitz ⟨Congress ~*ed* them last month by cutting their budgets —*Newsweek*⟩ — used chiefly as a past participle ⟨not one English city, no matter how badly ~*ed* —Elmer Davis⟩ **3** : HUSTLE, PUSH, MOVE ⟨I was ~*ed* off my lunch-counter seat —*Collier's*⟩; *also* : to cause to act without due consideration : STAMPEDE ⟨a drive to ~ the Chicago convention into an early ballot —*Christian Science Monitor*⟩

3blitz \"\ *adj* **1** : of, resulting from, typical of, or used in a blitz ⟨~ tactics⟩ ⟨~ ground units⟩ **2** : like a blitz esp. in speed and effectiveness ⟨making a ~ tour of Europe⟩ **3** : involving the offer of unusual discounts or other advantages to stimulate immediate volume sales — used chiefly in the retail automobile trade ⟨clearing last year's models in a ~ sale⟩

blitz can *n* : the standard U. S. government issue 5-gallon container used esp. to transport water or gasoline

blitzed *adj* : subjected to blitz

1blitz·krieg \'ˌ=ˌkrēg\ *n* -s [G, lit., lightning war, fr. *blitz lightning* + *krieg* war] **1** : war conducted with great speed and force; *specif* : a violent surprise offensive by massed air forces and mechanized ground forces in close coordination, and with objectives (isolation of bodies of troops, disruption of communications, and capture of matériel) such that mobility may be exploited to the fullest **2** : any sudden overpowering bombardment (as with propaganda)

2blitzkrieg \"\ *vt* -ED/-ING/-S : to subject to or overpower with a blitzkrieg

blitzweed \'=ˌ=\ *n* [1*blitz* + *weed*; fr. its use in England during World War II to cover areas devastated by bombing] *Brit* : FIREWEED b

bliz·zard \'blizə(r)d\ *n* -s [origin unknown] **1** *archaic* : a shot or volley of shots **2 a** : a severe and prolonged snowstorm **b** : an intensely strong cold wind filled with fine snow **3** : something likened to a blizzard of snow ⟨a ~ of volcanic ash⟩; *esp* : a sudden outbreak : unexpected occurrence : RASH ⟨a ~ of damage suits⟩ ⟨the ~ of bureaus that swirls around our nation's capital —T.W.Arnold⟩

blizzard head *n* : a woman television performer having hair so blond as to require special lighting to prevent a flare or halo from appearing

bliz·zar·dy \-dē,-di\ *also* **bliz·zard·ly** \-lē,-li\ *adj* : marked by blizzard ⟨a ~ day⟩ : tending to become or produce a blizzard ⟨the wind picked up, the storm became ~⟩

blk *abbr* **1** black **2** blank **3** block **4** bulk

blkd *abbr* bulkhead

blo \'blō\ *adj* [ME — more at BLAE] *dial Eng* : BLUE-BLACK

bloak *var of* BLOKE

1bloat \'blōt, *usu* -d·+V\ *adj* [alter. (prob. influenced by obs. *bloat* cured in such a way as to be comparatively soft and moist) of earlier *blowt*, fr. ME *blout*, prob. fr. ON *blautr* soft, weak, soaked; akin to OE *blēat* miserable, *blēath* timid, OHG *blōz* proud, MHG *blōz* naked, OHG *blōdi* timid, ON *blauthr* timid, Goth *blauthjan* to annul, Gk *phlydan* to be too moist, become soft, OE *blāwan* to blow — more at BLOW] : BLOATED, PUFFY, STUFFED

2bloat \"\ *vb* -ED/-ING/-S *vt* **1** : to make turgid (as with water or air): **a** : to cause swelling of the cellular tissue of by accumulation of serous fluid : produce edema in **b** : to cause or result in accumulation of gas in the digestive tract of ⟨cucumbers sometimes ~ me⟩ **2 a** : to fill to capacity or overflowing : INFLATE, STUFF **b** : to puff up : make vain ⟨encourage him and ~ him up with praise —John Dryden⟩ ~ *vi* : to become turgid : puff out : SWELL

3bloat \"\ *n* -s [2*bloat*] **1 a** : one that bloats or is bloated **b** *slang* : DRUNKARD **2 a** : distention of the rumen of ruminant mammals with gases from fermenting foodstuffs that is usu. associated with feeding on wet legumes but sometimes involves anaphylactic reactions and is esp. common in domestic cattle but sometimes also affects sheep and goats **b** : any flatulent digestive disturbance of domestic animals

bloat colic *n* : BLOAT — used esp. of a horse

1bloat·ed \'blōd·əd, -ōtəd\ *adj* [fr. past part. of obs. *bloat* to cure (a herring) by a process that leaves it comparatively soft and moist, fr. obs. *bloat*, adj., cured in such a way as to be comparatively soft and moist, fr. ME *blote* soft and moist, prob. of Scand origin; akin to ON *blotna* to become soft, lose courage, *blautr* soft, weak, soaked] *of a fish* : cured by a process involving salting and smoking that leaves it comparatively soft and moist

2bloated \"\ *adj* [fr. past part. of 2*bloat*] **1** *of living things* : distended beyond the natural size by fluid (as serum or gas) : EDEMATOUS; *also* : excessively or unhealthily fat : GROSS, PAUNCHY, STUFFED **2 a** : enlarged beyond usual or expected bounds : SWOLLEN ⟨a river ~ by bursting dams and heavy rains⟩ ⟨increases in the already ~ defense budget⟩ **b** : giving an effect of swollen clumsiness ⟨the ~ side-wheelers that he had seen all his life —Marcia Davenport **3** : puffed up with pride : POMPOUS

bloated clay *n* [2*bloated*] : clay caused to swell naturally or by gas-forming additives and used esp. as insulation in concrete because of its porosity and lightness

bloat·ed·ness *n* -ES : the quality or state of being bloated

1bloat·er \'blōd·ə(r), -ōtə-\ *n* -s [obs. *bloat* to cure + -*er*] : one that is bloated: as **a** : a large fat herring lightly salted and smoked for a short time so that it remains plump and moist **b** : a large fat mackerel similarly cured or suitable for such curing

2bloater \"\ *vt* -ED/-ING/-S : to process (as herrings) into bloaters

3bloater \"\ *n* -s [2*bloat* + -*er*] **1** : a fruit or vegetable containing hollow spaces as a result of gaseous fermentation during processing **2** : a small but common cisco (*Leucichthys hoyi*) of the Great lakes formerly of no importance but now often marketed with related larger forms

1blob \'bläb\ *n* -s [ME] **1** *now dial Brit* : BLISTER, BUBBLE **2 a** : a small drop, globule, or lump of something viscid or thick ⟨a ~ of melting butter⟩ **b** : a spot of color ⟨candles burned in a golden ~ —Bruce Marshall⟩; *also* : DAUB 4 ⟨to the uninitiated his paintings were mere ~*s*, rich in color but meaningless⟩ **c** : something ill-defined or amorphous ⟨small ~*s* and faint glimmers of satire —*Time*⟩ ⟨a ~ of land looming up in the dusk⟩ — sometimes used of persons when considered only as shapes viewed ⟨a big sluggish ~⟩ **3** : an imperfect or harsh note on a wind instrument **4** : MILLER'S-THUMB 1 **5** : a score of zero in cricket : GOOSE EGG **6** *NewEng* : BLOSSOM

2blob \"\ *vt* **blobbed; blobbed; blobbing; blobs** [ME (northern dial.) *bloben*, fr. *blob*, n.] : to mark with blobs : SPLOTCH, BLOT

blobbed \'bläbd\ *adj* : SPOTTED, SPECKLED

blob·ber \'bläbə(r)\ *dial or archaic var of* BLUBBER

blob·by \'bläbē, -bi\ *adj* -ER/-EST **1** : covered or filled with blobs **2** : made up of blobs; *also* : like a blob

bloc \'bläk\ *n* -s *often attrib* [F, lit., block, fr. MF — more at BLOCK] **1 a** : a temporary combination of parties in a legislative assembly; *esp* : one organized to support the government in power in a country having a multiparty system **b** : a group of legislators in a U.S. legislative assembly who act together for some common purpose irrespective of party lines ⟨the farm ~⟩ **2 a** : a combination of persons, groups, or nations forming a unit with a common interest or purpose : UNION **b** : a group of nations united by treaty or agreement for mutual support or joint action ⟨the Western ~⟩ ⟨a middle course between the two power ~*s*⟩; *esp* : a group of nations whose currencies are so linked as to be convertible into each other at fixed rates and usu. freely transferable within the group ⟨the sterling ~⟩ ⟨the dollar ~⟩

blo·cage \blō'käzh, -äj\ *n* -s [F, fr. *bloc* block + -*age*] : rough cheap masonry usu. with a facing built up of irregular usu. small stones laid in mortar

bloch wall \'bläk-, 'blȯk-\ *n*, *usu cap B* [after Felix *Bloch* b1905 Swiss-Amer. physicist] : the boundary between two domains in a magnetic material marked by a layer wherein the direction of magnetization is assumed to change gradually from one domain to the other

1block \'bläk\ *n* -s [ME *blok*, fr. MF *bloc*, fr. MD *blok*; akin to OHG *bloh* block, MIr *blog* fragment, and perh. to OHG *bliuwan* to beat — more at BLOW (stroke)] **1** : a compact usu. solid piece of substantial material (as wood, stone, or metal) ⟨a fine ~ of marble⟩; *esp* : one worked or altered from its natural or rough state to serve a particular purpose: as **a** : a bulky piece of strong hard wood usu. having the upper surface dressed and serving as a base on which some operation (as the cutting of firewood) is performed: as (1) : such a block on which a butcher cuts meat (2) : the piece of wood on which a person condemned to be beheaded lays his neck for execution **b** : a mold or form upon which articles or materials are shaped or displayed: as (1) : a wooden form upon which hats are shaped; *also* : the pattern or style of a hat (2) : a hollow wooden or metal device in which a gather of glass is shaped (3) : a cast or turned plaster form around which plaster is cast to make a potter's mold **c** : HORSE BLOCK **d** : a piece of stone or other natural or artificial composition dressed or formed usu. to uniform size for use as a structural unit ⟨paving ~*s*⟩; *esp* : a hollow rectangular building unit of terracotta, concrete, glass, burned clay, or gypsum — compare BRICK, TILE **e** : BLOCK COAL **f** : a piece of solid material used to strengthen, support, or retain in position: as (1) : CHOCK 1 ⟨put a ~ behind the rear wheel⟩ (2) : a piece of wood or other material glued into an interior angle to strengthen a joint (3) : a support placed behind a wainscot to hold it out from the wall (4) : BREECHBLOCK (5) : SPRING BLOCK (6) : BRAKE BLOCK (7) : one of the supports on which the keel of a ship is laid (8) : a rectangular prism of wood placed to support a vessel in dry dock (as under its keel or under any stiffened part between keel and turn of the bilge) **g** : a percussion musical instrument consisting of a hollow slotted block of wood played usu. with a drumstick — called also *wood block* **h** : a cylinder that revolves drawing an attached wire through a die and coiling it **i** : a lightweight usu. cubical and solid wooden or plastic toy that is typically decorated on each face with a letter or picture and is usu. provided in sets permitting varied arrangement and building activities — called also *building block* **j** : the casting that contains the cylinders of an internal-combustion engine — called also *cylinder block* **2** : something (as a person or a body part) suggesting or likened to a piece of wood: **a** : a stupid doltish person **b** : a harsh inconsiderate hard-hearted person **c** *now slang* : HEAD 1 ⟨knock his ~ off⟩ **d** : a dressed and trimmed carcass (as of beef) **3** : an obstruction or cause of obstruction : STUMBLING BLOCK, HINDRANCE, OBSTACLE, STOP, CHECK, IMPEDIMENT: as **a** : something interfering with free passage (as a military roadblock or a traffic jam) **b** : any of several kinds of or procedures for interference (as with other contestants or players) in sports: (1) : the obstruction with the hand or arm of a punch in boxing (2) : BLOCK BALL (3) : the checking of a player in football by using one's body esp. to keep him out of the path of the ball carrier ⟨a rolling ~⟩ ⟨a shoulder ~⟩ (4) : GUARD 5b (5) : BLOCKHOLE **c** : a situation in various card and other games (as checkers or dominoes) in which no player can make a further legal move and which in most games results in a draw but in checkers wins the game for the player making the last move **d** : interruption of normal physiological function of a tissue or organ (as by fatigue or the presence of a chemically abnormal environment) ⟨respiratory ~ due to carbon monoxide⟩ ⟨mucosal ~ may accompany certain gastrointestinal disorders⟩; *esp* : HEART BLOCK **e** (1) : BLOCK ANESTHESIA (2) : NERVE BLOCK **f** : an instance or the result of psychological blockage or blocking **g** : DIAPAUSE **4** : a base, platform, or supporting frame: **a** : a wooden or metal case enclosing one or more pulleys, provided with a hook, eye, or strap by which it may be attached to an object, and used to change the direction of motion of the object or, when two or more pulleys are compounded, to change the rate of motion or exert increased force **b** : a platform from which slaves or other property are displayed for sale at auction; *broadly* : sale at auction — used chiefly with *on* **c** : a permanent base for mounting a device or machine (as for exhibition, testing, or support) **d** : PEDESTAL, PLINTH 2 **e** : a frame for supporting a log while sawing it **f** : a base commonly of wood or metal on which a relief printing plate is mounted — compare PATENT BASE **g** : a bookbinder's stamp too large for handwork **h** : GAGE BLOCK **5** : a whole made up of like or unlike elements esp. when itself a part of some greater whole : AGGREGATE: **a** : a quantity, number, or section of things dealt with as a unit ⟨a large ~ of shares⟩ ⟨the experimental ~ of trees was far more productive than the control⟩ **b** : 1PAD 7 **c** [prob. trans. of D *blok*] (1) : a large building divided into separate functional units (as shops or offices) (2) : a line of row houses (3) : a group of neighboring buildings (as houses built by a single agency) (4) : a part of a building or integrated group of buildings distinctive in some respect (as in function, origin, or styling); *sometimes* : WING — used almost entirely of large complex structures ⟨a ~ of classrooms⟩ ⟨the laboratory ~ is nearing completion⟩ ⟨a magnificent refectory was then designed in one ~ of the palace⟩ (5) : CELLBLOCK **d** : something of a convenient or appropriate size (as for handling, working, using, or considering) ⟨a ~ of questions⟩ ⟨a design for a quilt ~⟩ **e** [prob. trans. of D *blok*] : a portion of land: as (1) : a usu. rectangular space (as in a city) enclosed usu. by streets but sometimes by other bounds (as rivers or railroads) and occupied by or intended for buildings ⟨a factory covering an entire ~⟩ (2) : the distance along one of the sides of such a block ⟨living only two ~*s* from the bus⟩ ⟨walked 10 ~*s*⟩ : the side of a block abutting on a street (3) : an area of land ⟨four ~*s* of woodland⟩; *esp* : a tract of land leased for drilling a wildcat oil well (4) : a part of the earth's crust bounded by faults and behaving as a unit in earth movements due to faulting (5) *chiefly Austral* : one of the large lots of public land divided by the government and opened to settlers (6) *often cap*, *Austral* : a street or quarter of a city; *often* : a section popular as a promenade — usu. used with *the* **f** [F *bloc*] : BLOC **g** : a group of four or more attached stamps in square or rectangular arrangement — contrasted with *strip* **h** : a length of railroad track of defined limits the use of which is governed by block signals **i** : a group of points considered together in determining transportation rates **j** : two or more lines of type set flush left and right **6 a** : CUT 3k(1); *esp* : WOODCUT **b** : material (as linoleum or rubber) mounted (as on wood or plywood) and having on its surface a hand-cut design from which impressions are to be printed — see BLOCK PRINT *vt* 1a

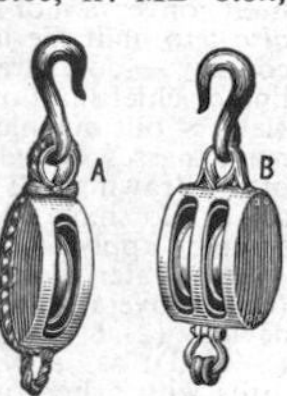

blocks 4a: *A* with single sheave; *B* with double sheave

2block \"\ *vb* -ED/-ING/-S *vt* **1 a** : to render (as a way) unsuitable for passage or progress by obstruction ⟨they ~*ed* the road with a barricade⟩ — sometimes used with *up* ⟨if grease ~*s* up the pipe⟩ ⟨my nose is all ~*ed* up⟩ **b** *archaic* : BLOCKADE, INVEST ⟨a city . . . besieged and ~*ed* about —John Milton⟩ **c** : to obstruct the passage, progress, or accomplishment of (someone or something) esp. by a positive obstacle ⟨they made every effort to ~ his election⟩ ⟨the ambulance was ~*ed* by traffic⟩ ⟨his brother ~*ed* him at every turn⟩ **d** : to interfere usu. legitimately with (an opponent's action or equipment) in various games or sports (as by use of a block): as (1) : to end (as a game of dominoes) with a block (2) : to check the play of (as a piece in checkers) by suitable arrangement of pieces or a suit in bridge by withholding a high card of the suit from play) (3) : to halt or impede the progress of (a ball) usu. in a particular manner (as in cricket, volleyball, or football) (4) : to obstruct or interfere with (an opponent, his play, or his movement) by bodily contact; *specif* : to so impede the progress of (a basketball player who does not have the ball) **e** : to prevent normal functioning of (a bodily element) ⟨~ the reticuloendothelial system with trypan blue⟩ ⟨~ a nerve with novocaine⟩ **f** : to stop the output of alternating current from (an electron tube) by overloading the input **g** *chem* : to obstruct the effect of : render inactive : HINDER, MASK ⟨a carboxyl group ~*ed* by esterification⟩ **h** : to prohibit conversion of (foreign-held funds) into foreign exchange; *also* : to limit the use to be made of (such funds) within the country — compare FREEZE **2** : to mark or indicate the outline or chief lines of — usu. used with *out,* sometimes with *in* ⟨let's ~ out our plan of action⟩ ⟨it's a good idea to ~ in the main masses of light and shade before touching any details of the drawing⟩ **3** : to shape on, with, or as if with a block: as **a** : to shape or restore (as a garment) to original dimensions by applying steam and adjusting sometimes over a form ⟨~ a sweater to a person's measurements⟩ **b** (1) : to emboss (book covers) with a frame or block containing the entire device (2) : [1]STAMP 3e **4** : to form or divide into blocks ⟨~ coal⟩: as **a** : to remove (as sugar-beet seedlings) from drills with a hoe or other tool so as to leave small bunches for thinning later to single plants **b** : to set (two or more lines of type) flush left and right **c** : to separate (hair) into squared-off sections for waving **d** : to divide (beef) into wholesale cuts **5 a** : to secure, support, provide, or raise with a block ⟨~*ing* a plate for printing⟩ — often used with *up* ⟨~ up one rear wheel⟩ **b** : to secure (as two boards at their angles of intersection) by pieces of wood glued to each **c** : to raise the walls of (a log cabin) — used with *up* **6** : to run (trains) by the block system **~** *vi* **1** : to make or commit a block (as in football, boxing, basketball) : block an opponent **2** *of paper* : to stick together under the influence of heat and pressure **3** : to experience or exhibit psychological blocking or blockage **4** *of a photographic print or negative* : to lack halftones or gradations in highlights or shadows — usu. used with *up* **syn** see HINDER

[3]**block** \"\ *adj* **1 a** : made or taken in the block ⟨a ~ sum⟩ **b** : formed (as by pressing) into a block ⟨~ rubber⟩ **c** : of or forming block or a block : formed of blocks **2** *of an address, heading, or paragraph* : forming a block without an indentation at the left **3** : resembling a block : BLOCK-UNIVERSE

[1]**block·ade** \(ˈ)bläˈkād\ *n* -S *often attrib* [[2]*block* + *-ade*] **1 a** : a measure of war involving the isolation by a belligerent of a particular area vital to the interests of an enemy through deployment of any part of its armed forces so as to effectively hamper ingress and egress and harass the enemy by cutting off trade, communications, and supplies, being commonly agreed as legal against neutral nations only after due notice has been given and when carried on with such force as required to make passage through the area a real hazard but when so established and maintained permitting the seizure, detention, or sometimes destruction of neutral property found in the area; *broadly* : any restrictive measure or measures designed to obstruct the commerce and communications of an unfriendly nation whether or not a formal state of war exists **b** : something that acts in the manner of a blockade to prevent free and normal exchange (as of ideas) ⟨only clear thinking can free us from our emotional ~ and dissipate our prejudices⟩ **2 a** : something that constitutes an obstacle to passage; *esp* : a blocking of a pass or way (as by snow) **b** : [1]BLOCK 3b, 3c **c** : the filling of the receptive cells of the reticulo-endothelial system with material that is expected to prevent their taking up any new antigenic material — compare BLOCKING ANTIBODY **3** *chiefly Midland* : MOONSHINE 3

[2]**blockade** \"\ *vt* -ED/-ING/-S **1** : to effect a blockade of (as a port, coast, or fleet) : subject (as a nation) to a blockade : INVEST **2** : to close with obstructions : BLOCK, OBSTRUCT

block·ad·er \-dә(r)\ *n* -S **1** : one that blockades; *specif* : a ship employed in blockading a port **2** *South & Midland* : MOONSHINER

blockade-runner \(ˈ)ˌ=ˈ=ˌ==\ *n* : a ship or person that runs or attempts to run through a blockade — **blockade-running** \(ˈ)=ˈ=ˌ==\ *n*

block·ad·ing \(ˈ)=ˈ=diŋ\ *n* -S *South & Midland* : the distilling of moonshine

block·age \ˈbläkij, -ēj\ *n* -S [[2]*block* + *-age*] : an act or instance of obstructing : the state of being blocked: as **a** : BLOCKADE 1a, 2c **b** : [1]BLOCKING 4 **c** : internal resistance of an individual to understanding a communicated idea, to learning new material, or to adopting a new mode of response because of existing habitual ways of thinking, perceiving, and acting — compare BLOCKING 3

block and block *adj* : CHOCKABLOCK

block and tackle *also* **block and fall** *or* **block and falls** *n* : pulley blocks with associated rope or cable for hoisting or hauling : TACKLE

block anesthesia *n* : anesthesia of an area produced by interruption of the flow of impulses along a nerve trunk (as by the injection of an anesthetic near it) — compare REGIONAL ANESTHESIA

block ball *n* : a batted or thrown baseball interfered with when in play by a person not a player

blockboard \ˈ=ˌ=\ *n* : a plywood board in which veneer layers used in the core are replaced by blocks of wood, the direction of grain of the blocks running at right angles to that of the adjacent veneer

block bond *n* **1** : FLEMISH BOND **2** : ENGLISH BOND

block book *n* : a book in which the entire text and illustrations are block printed

block booking *n* : the licensing for exhibition of motion-picture films in a block or group, the licensee being compelled to take an entire group of films or none

block brake *n* : a friction brake consisting of one or more shoes (as wooden blocks) to be pressed against a wheel or other moving part

blockbuster \ˈ=ˌ==\ *n* [[1]*block* (space in a city) + *buster,* fr. *bust,* v. + *-er*] **1** : a huge high-explosive demolition bomb usu. several tons in weight designed to be dropped from an airplane **2** : something or someone notably outstanding, effective, or violent ⟨they predict the new show will be a ~⟩ ⟨his speech was a real ~⟩

block-busting \ˈ=ˌ==\ *adj* : suggesting the action of a blockbuster esp. in vigor or effectiveness

block capital *n* : a square bold capital letter without serifs — compare BLOCK LETTER

block-caving \ˈ=ˌ==\ *n* -S : a mining in which sections of a large ore body are undercut by working places and then permitted to cave in, the ore so crushed being recovered through drifts

block chain *n* : a drive chain (as on a bicycle) made up of alternate transverse blocks or cylinders and side links held together by pins, the blocks engaging the driving-wheel teeth and the pins and side links giving flexibility

block chain

block chords *n pl* : a succession of musical chords produced by the component voices or parts moving in the same rhythm

block coal *n* : very coarse lump coal

block coefficient *n* : the ratio of the volume of the displacement of a ship to that of a rectangular block having the same length, breadth, and draft

block dance *n* : a public dance commonly featuring folk and other specialty dancing that is held outdoors (as in a street temporarily closed to traffic) — compare BLOCK PARTY

block diagram *n* **1** : a perspective diagram of a three-dimensional object used orig. for physiographic illustration of parts of the earth's surface but later adapted to other uses (as demonstration of the relation of cells in tissue) **2** : a drawing in which labeled squares, rectangles, and other arbitrary figures represent the relative position and function of the parts of an apparatus ⟨a *block diagram* of a radio receiving set⟩

block dissection *n* : the operation of dissecting out and removing all the lymph nodes that provide lymphatic drainage for a cancerous area in an effort to prevent lymphatic spread of cancer cells

block down *vt* : to force (sheet metal) into a die esp. by covering with a thick blanket of lead and then hammering

blocked *adj* **1** : OUTLINED; *also* : shaped, supported, or stamped with or as if with a block ⟨finely ~ linens⟩ **2** : closed by or as if by a block or blocks : OBSTRUCTED, OCCLUDED **3** *of money or other assets* **a** : not available for international circulation esp. by reason of the action of a monetary bloc ⟨~ accounts limit the free exchange of goods between nations⟩ **b** : not available to the owner by reason of government action ⟨the ~ assets of enemy nationals are administered by a special office⟩

blocked ball *n* : BLOCK BALL

block·er \ˈbläkә(r)\ *n* -S : one that blocks: as **a** : a tool or device used in blocking or blocking out something; *esp* : a forging die used for giving a forging approximately its final shape — compare BREAKDOWN 5, FULLER **b** : a worker who blocks something or whose work is done on or with blocks: as (1) : one that blocks clothing (as hats or knitted garments) (2) : one that operates the blocks in wiredrawing (3) : [2]BRACER 1c **c** : a football player who engages in or is esp. proficient in blocking **d** : BLOCKING ANTIBODY **e** : CASER 2 **f** : one who blocks out with water colors the imperfections or unwanted parts of negatives to be used in photoengraving

block faulting *n* : geological faulting that produces blocks

block figure *n* : a sculpture in which natural form is expressed as a composition of geometric solids

block·flö·te \ˈbläk,flœd·ә, -flәrd·ә\ *n, pl* **blockflö·tes** \-d·әz\ *or* **blockflö·ten** \-d·әn\ *usu cap* [G, fr. *block* block of wood (fr. LG, fr. MLG) + *flöte* flute, fr. MHG *vloite, flöute,* fr. MD *flūte, fleute, fluite,* fr. OF *flaüte, fleute;* akin to OHG *bloh* block — more at BLOCK, FLUTE] **1** : RECORDER 3a **2** : a flute organ stop of 16-, 8-, 4-, or 2-ft. pitch tonally similar to the recorder

block foot *n* : a furniture foot in the shape of a cube generally used with a square untapered leg — see FOOT illustration

blockfront \ˈ=ˌ=\ *n* **1** : a front (as of a chest of drawers or a desk) characterized by a sunken center panel flanked on either side by a raised panel **2** : the frontage of a block : one side (as the main side) of a block with a portion of land abutting esp. when considered as the site of a single building ⟨the structure is going on the north ~ of the street⟩

block grant *n* : a fixed grant of money made by the British parliament to local governing authorities

blockhead \ˈ=ˌ=\ *n* **1** *obs* **a** : a wooden head serving as a block for hats or wigs **b** : a head dull and wanting in intelligence **2** : a dull and stupid person : one deficient in understanding or intellect

blockhead board *n* : a device that consists of a pair of conspicuously numbered boards one of which rises while the other falls and that is used as a detector on a jacquard loom to show if the cards are working correctly

blockheaded \ˈ=ˌ==\ *adj* : STUPID, DULL, UNINTELLIGENT — **block·head·ed·ly** *adv* — **block·head·ed·ness** *n* -ES

block·head·ism \ˈ=ˌ=ˌizәm\ *n* -S : the stupidity of or that might be expected of a blockhead

[1]**blockhole** \ˈ=ˌ=\ *n* : a light indentation in the ground just behind the popping crease and in front of the wicket made by a batsman in cricket with the end of his bat to mark the position of his guard

[2]**blockhole** \"\ *vt* : to shatter (a boulder) by drilling a hole and exploding dynamite in it — **block·hol·er** \ˈ=ˌ=ә(r)\ *n*

blockhouse \ˈ=ˌ=\ *n* [[1]*block* (impediment) + *house*] **1** *obs* : a detached fort blocking or covering access (as to a landing, bridge, or pass) **2 a** : a structure of heavy timbers or logs formerly used for military defense having its sides loopholed and pierced for gunfire and often an upper story projecting over the lower or so placed upon it as to have its sides make an angle with the sides of the lower story, thus enabling the defenders to fire downward and in all directions **b** : a small defensible wood, iron, or concrete building usu. partially dug in that gives protection from enemy fire and provides a firing base for defense **3** : a house of squared logs **4** : a building usu. more or less hemispherical and formed of reinforced concrete as a shelter against and observation point of certain dangerous operations likely to be accompanied by heat, blast, or radiation hazard

blockhouse 2a

blockier *comparative of* BLOCKY

blockiest *superlative of* BLOCKY

block·i·ly \-kәlē\ *adv* [*blocky* + *-ly*] : in a blocky manner

block-in-course \ˈ==ˌ=\ *n* : squared stone masonry with good close joints to give great strength and soundness

block-in-course bond *n* : a bond used in brick arches in which the arch is divided into sections similar in shape to the voussoirs of stone arches with the brick in each section laid with any desired bond but with the radial joints between sections continuous from intrados to extrados

blocking *n* -S **1** : the act of one that blocks: as **a** : the act of obstructing, supporting, shaping, or stamping with or as if with a block or blocks **b** : the act or process of signaling by the block system **2 a** : blocks in quantity ⟨stack the ~ to one side⟩ **b** : a wooden block, jack, or other device used as a temporary support esp. in structural and machine erecting operations and in shipping; *broadly* : material used to secure or brace something (as freight in a car) **3** *psychol* : interruption of a trend of associative thought by the arousal of a countertrend or through the welling up into consciousness of a complex of unpleasant ideas — compare BLOCKAGE c **4** : adhesion between sheets of paper in a pile or in a roll in storage or use that can result in damage or loss — compare [2]BLOCK *vi* 2 **5** : an atmospheric process that is often produced by a deep well-developed anticyclone and that deflects strong westerlies and eastward-moving storms from their usual paths

blocking antibody *n* : an antibody that combines with an antigen without producing visible reaction but preventing another antibody from later combining with or producing its usual effect on that antigen — called also *incomplete antibody, univalent antibody*

blocking course *n* : the finishing course of a wall showing above a cornice usu. serving as a solid parapet and forming a small architectural attic

blocking layer *n* : BARRIER LAYER

blocking patent *n* : FENCING PATENT

blocking press *n Brit* : a press for stamping titles and designs on book covers

block interlocking system *n* : BLOCK SYSTEM 2

block·ish \-kish, -kēsh\ *adj* [[1]*block* + *-ish*] : like a block : lacking in intellect and understanding : STUPID, DOLTISH — **block·ish·ly** *adv*

block lava *n* : AA

block letter *n* : a letter of the alphabet written or printed in sans serif; *also* : sans-serif type or lettering

blocklike \ˈ=ˌ=\ *adj* : like a block

block·man \ˈ=mәn, -ˌman, -ˌmaa(ә)n\ *n, pl* **blockmen** **1** : a workman who makes blocks (as of stone) or works with or at a block **2** : a manufacturer's representative acting as a district agent and intermediary between the company and its local agents in an assigned block of territory — used esp. in the field of agricultural supplies and equipment

block mold *n* **1** : the original mold for a pottery form made directly from the model and used only for making working molds **2** : a one-piece unjointed mold for pressed glassware (as tumblers, saucers, or bowls)

block mountain *n* : a mountain caused by faulting and uplifting or tilting — compare BASIN RANGE

block operator *n* : a railroad worker who operates block signals manually

block out *vt* **1** : to shut from view : SCREEN ⟨that vine on the porch *blocks out* all the sunlight⟩: **a** : to prevent (a part of a photographic negative) from printing by painting over with opaque or a comparable substance **b** : to cancel (printed matter) by overprinting with a solid patch of ink **2 a** : to excavate (as ore and gravel) by making a drive in the wall and taking out the material in blocks or strips along the sides of the drive **b** : to subdivide (a lode) into blocks in advance of the working stopes by shafts, winzes, and intersecting drives or levels so as to be ready for stoping and to keep a known amount of reserve ore in sight

blockout \ˈ=ˌ=\ *n* -S [*block out*] : a reproduction (as a photographic negative or a halftone) of which a part has been blocked out

block paper *n* : paper printed with a pattern usu. in color from blocks (as of wood or linoleum) and used esp. as wallpaper or for endpapers or box covers

block paragraph *n* : a paragraph (as in a news story) written as an independent unit to allow its deletion or rearrangement in the order of paragraphs without loss of coherence

block party *n* : a public party held in the open air (as in a stretch of street temporarily barred to traffic) commonly under the auspices of a public figure or organization — compare BLOCK DANCE

block plan *n* : an outline sketch : a plan in which only broad general features are indicated

block plane *n* : a small plane having the iron set at a lower pitch than other planes and used chiefly on end grains of wood — see PLANE illustration

[1]**block print** *vt* **1 a** : to print (as books) from hand-cut wooden blocks — used chiefly of printers' practice before the general adoption of movable types **b** : to print from blocks ⟨a linen scarf *block printed* in black⟩ **2** : to write in block letters ⟨it may be easier to *block print* the lessons at first⟩

[2]**block print** *n* **1** : a large founding core print the impression of which receives a core that also replaces a part of the mold **2** : a print produced by block printing

blockprinter \ˈ=ˌ==\ *n* : one that block prints; *esp* : a designer and user of blocks for decorative printing (as of textiles)

block programming *n* : the arrangement of programs on radio or television so that several items of one general class (as soap operas or popular music) occur in sequence

block rate *n* **1** : a certain price charged for the first definite number of units (as of electricity) used : a successively lower price for each additional block used **2** : GROUP RATE

blocks *pl of* BLOCK, *pres 3d sing of* BLOCK

block salt *n* : salt often with accompanying trace elements or medicaments that is pressed into blocks for salting livestock

block-saw \ˈ=ˌ=\ *vt* : to slab (a log) on four sides so as to form a block

block·ship \ˈ=ˌ=\ *n* [[1]*block* (impediment) + *ship*] : a ship intended to be sunk in a channel or fairway to block its use

block shot *n* : HALF VOLLEY

block signal *also* **block signal system** *n* : a fixed signal at the entrance of a block to govern railroad trains entering and using that block — compare BLOCK SYSTEM 2

blocks·man \ˈbläksmәn\ *n, pl* **blocksmen** : a worker who shapes highway curbs or lays paving blocks

block station *n* : a place at which railroad manual block signals are displayed

block sugar *n* : CUBE SUGAR

block system *n* **1** : a system of mountain ranges composed of tilted or uplifted fault blocks — compare BASIN RANGE **2** : a system by which a railroad track is divided into short sections (as of three or four miles) and trains are so run by the guidance of electric or combined electric and pneumatic signals that (1) no train enters a section or block until the preceding train has left it or that (2) a train may be allowed to follow another into a block as long as it proceeds with extreme caution — called also respectively (1) *absolute blocking,* (2) *permissive blocking* **3** : a method of betting in draw poker comprising a 19-chip ante by the dealer, a 2-chip blind, and a 4-chip straddle

block teeth *n pl* : two or more artificial teeth in one piece

block test *n* : a test of an internal-combustion engine in which it is mounted on a block and checked as to workmanship and performance

block tin *n* : commercial tin cast into blocks and partly refined but containing small quantities of various impurities (as copper, lead, iron, or arsenic) : solid tin as distinguished from tin plate

block-universe \ˈ=ˌ===\ *n* : the universe conceived as resembling a block in being a closed system, monistic and without any real novelty, plurality, and individuality

block vote *n* : a method of voting (as at a convention) by which each delegate's vote has a value proportional to his representation; *also* : such a vote

blockwood \ˈ=ˌ=\ *n* : LOGWOOD 1a

block worker *n* : a person who actively campaigns on the most local level (as a city block) as one of the organized workers of a political party or pressure group

blocky \-kē,-ki\ *adj* -ER/-EST **1 a** : like a block in form or massiveness ⟨the hood lines of these car models are high and ~⟩ **b** *of a body or its parts* : heavily or sturdily built : somewhat square or boxy : CHUNKY ⟨a fine ~ steer⟩ ⟨a ~ tireless man⟩ ⟨a terrier with a ~ head⟩ **2** : filled with or made up of blocks or blocklike parts ⟨a ~ soil aggregate⟩; *often* : full of or marked with patches esp. of light and shadow : DAPPLED

bloe·dite \ˈblō,dīt\ *also* **blö·dite** \", ˈblәr,d-, ˈblœ,d-\ *or* **blo·dite** \ˈblō,d-\ *n* -S [G *blödit,* fr. Carl A. *Bloede* †1820 Ger. chemist + G *-it* -ite] : a mineral $Na_2Mg(SO_4)_2.4H_2O$ consisting of a hydrous sodium magnesium sulfate that is colorless or white when pure and occurs in monoclinic crystals or massive

bloed·pens \ˈblüt,pen(t)s\ *n pl but sing or pl in constr* [Afrik, fr. *bloed* blood (fr. MD *bloet*) + *pens* belly, paunch, fr. MD *pense, panse,* fr. OF *pance;* akin to OE *blōd* blood — more at BLOOD, PAUNCH] *Africa* : enterotoxemia of lambs

bloem·fon·tein \ˈblümfәnˌtān\ *adj, usu cap* [fr. *Bloemfontein,* Union of So. Africa] : of or from the city of Bloemfontein, Union of So. Africa : of the kind or style prevalent in Bloemfontein

bloke *or* **bloak** \ˈblōk\ *n* -S [origin unknown] *chiefly Brit* : MAN, CHAP, FELLOW — used informally and commonly implying mild disrespect when applied to a superior and slight or affected deprecation when used of oneself ⟨the admiral was a jolly old ~ but no administrator⟩ ⟨I'm a peaceful sort of a ~ if folks let me alone⟩

blol·ly \ˈblälē\ *n* -ES [short for *loblolly*] **1** : a shrub or small tree (*Torrubia longifolia*) of southern Florida and the West Indies with smooth oval leaves and bright red fruit **2** : a low shrub (*Chiococca alba*) of southern Florida and the West Indies with yellow flowers and white fruit

blom·strand·ine \ˈblämstrәn,dēn, -ˌdәn\ *n* -S [C.W.*Blomstrand* †1897 Swedish chemist + E *-ine*] : PRIORITE

[1]**blond** *also* **blonde** \ˈbländ\ *adj, sometimes* -ER/-EST [F *blond* (masc.), *blonde* (fem.), prob. of Gmc origin; akin to OE *blondenfeax, blandenfeax* gray-haired, old, fr. *blondan, blandan* to mix — more at BLEND] **1 a** *of human hair* : flaxen, golden, light auburn, or pale yellowish brown **b** *of human skin* : pale white or rosy white **c** *of persons* : having blond hair and skin and usu. blue or gray eyes **d** *of peoples* : consisting of blond individuals ⟨a ~ tribe from the northern hills⟩ **2 a** : light-colored ⟨~ long-furred pelts will be preferred this year⟩ **b** : of the color blond **c** *of wood and wood products* : rendered light-colored by bleaching ⟨a table of ~ oak⟩ — **blond·ness** *also* **blonde·ness** \-n(d)nәs\ *n* -ES

[2]**blond** *or* **blonde** \"\ *n* -S **1** [F *blonde,* fr. *blonde,* adj.] *usu* **blonde lace** *also* **blond lace** : a silk bobbin lace orig. unbleached and now bleached white or dyed black made with a mesh ground of fine thread and floral patterns of a soft heavy thread **2** : a blond person : a person with fair complexion and light hair and eyes; *sometimes* : a person of noticeably lighter coloring than that typical of the population to which he belongs **3** : a light yellowish brown to dark grayish yellow

blond beast *n, sometimes cap both Bs* : the blond type of primitive man of northern Europe often regarded (as by Nietzsche) as a splendid animal, a superior or ideal physical type, or a predatory creature; *broadly* : anyone who acts in a predatory manner

blonde *or* **blonde ray** *n* -S : a large sluggish ray (*Raja blanda*) of the French and English coasts that is sometimes used as food

[1]**blondine** \(ˈ)blänˈdēn\ *n* -S [F, fr. *blond* + *-ine*] **1** : a bleach for the hair; *also* : a person with bleached hair **2 a** : BLOND 3 **b** : WOODBARK

[2]**blondine** \"\ *vt* -ED/-ING/-S : to bleach (hair) to a blond color

blondined *adj* **1** *of hair* : BLEACHED **2** *of a person* : having bleached hair

blond·i·nette \ˌbländәˈnet\ *n* [F, young blond girl, dim. of *blondine*] **1** *usu cap* : a breed of small plump show pigeons that are bred in several colors usu. with the plumage more or less laced with white and with the feathers somewhat frilled **2** -S *sometimes cap* : a bird of the Blondinette breed

blond·ish \ˈbländish, -dēsh\ *adj* : somewhat blond : nearer blond than brunet; *esp* : rather light in color ⟨a . . . chemical can turn ~ pine to the flaming red of cherry —*Geog. School Bull.*⟩

blond·ism \-ˌdizәm\ *n* -S : the state of being blond; *specif* : the occurrence of blond traits in a predominantly dark or colored population

[1]**blood** \ˈblәd\ *n* -S *see sense 9, often attrib* [ME, fr. OE *blōd;* akin to OHG *bluot* blood, ON *blōth,* Goth *blōth,* and prob. to OE *blōwan* to bloom — more at BLOW] **1 a** : the fluid that

circulates in the principal vascular system of vertebrate animals carrying nourishment and oxygen to all parts of the body and bringing away waste products for excretion and that consists of a liquid plasma containing dissolved nutrients, waste products, and other substances and suspended red blood cells, leukocytes, and blood platelets — see CIRCULATION, RESPIRATION; COAGULATION **b :** any fluid of similar function and comparable composition in an invertebrate animal usu. containing a respiratory pigment dissolved in the plasma and one or more kinds of cells often amoeboid **c :** any fluid suggestive of or likened to vertebrate blood esp. in color or in vital quality (as the juice of the grape or the sap of a plant) **2 a :** blood regarded as a vital principle **:** LIFEBLOOD; *broadly* **:** LIFE **b :** human blood regarded as a hereditary differentiating factor typical of and specific to a given family, stock, lineage, or race ⟨English ~⟩; *esp* **:** the national blood royal — used with *the* ⟨a prince of the ~⟩ **c :** the whole body of physical traits passed from parent to offspring whether in man, animals, or plants **d :** relationship by descent from a common ancestor ⟨the Delaware grape shows a strong strain of vinifera ~⟩ **:** KINSHIP, CONSANGUINITY ⟨~ is thicker than water⟩ **e :** persons related through a common familial or racial descent **:** KINDRED, LINEAGE, STOCK, RACE; *also, obs* **:** KINSMAN, RELATIVE **f :** honorable birth or descent; *often* **:** aristocratic or high birth or lineage ⟨a gentleman of ~ and breeding —Shak.⟩ **g** *of animals or plants* **:** descent from parents of recognized breed or pedigree; *specif, of horses* **:** descent from Thoroughbred ancestors — see HALF BLOOD **3 a :** blood shed in the taking of life esp. in sacrifice; *specif* **:** the blood shed in the atonement offered by Christ ⟨the ~ of the Lamb⟩ **b** *cap* **:** the wine or its equivalent in the sacrament of the Lord's Supper, held by some to be and by others to represent the blood of Jesus Christ **4 a :** the shedding of blood; *also* **:** the taking of life **:** MURDER, MANSLAUGHTER ⟨~ ever demands revenge⟩ **b :** murderous habit or deed ⟨a man of ~⟩ **c** *archaic* **:** BLOODGUILT ⟨His ~ be on us and on our children —Mt 27:25 (RSV)⟩ **5 a :** blood regarded as the seat of the emotions **:** TEMPER, PASSION ⟨when you perceive his ~ inclined to mirth —Shak.⟩ ⟨he was no mean adversary when his ~ was up⟩ — compare HUMOR, SANGUINE; see BAD BLOOD, COLD BLOOD **b** *obs* **:** bodily passion **:** animal appetite **:** LUST **c :** a gay showy foppish man **:** one unduly preoccupied with the trivia of fashionable life and lacking restraint or regard for proprieties **:** BUCK, DANDY, RAKE **6 :** PERSONNEL — used regularly with a qualifying term implying new and additional ⟨we need young ~ in this office⟩ ⟨give me enough new ~ and we'll get everything straightened out⟩ **7 :** a measure of the fineness of wool fiber based on Merino wool as full blood with others in decreasing order of fineness (as three-quarter blood, half blood, quarter blood) — now used without any implication as to the breeding of the sheep producing the wool **8** *Brit* **:** a lurid work of fiction: *esp* **:** a cheap and ill-written book of adventure or crime **9** *or pl* **blood** *usu cap* **a :** a people that comprise a division of the Blackfeet **b :** a member of such people — **in blood** *obs, of an animal* **:** full of life **:** abounding in vigor — **in one's blood :** acting as a fundamental factor or guiding principle in one's life — used esp. of something that may be construed as having such influence because of family or ancestral association ⟨religion is *in his blood;* both his father and his uncle are ministers⟩ — **out of blood** *obs, of an animal* **:** lacking in vigor **:** spiritless and sluggish

²blood \"\ *vt* -ED/-ING/-S **1** *archaic* **:** to let the blood of **:** BLEED **2 :** to stain, smear, or wet with blood **:** BLOODY; *esp* **:** to mark the face of (an inexperienced fox hunter) with blood of the prey when a hunt is successful **3 a :** to familiarize (a hunting dog) with its intended prey by exposing it to sight, scent, or taste of the blood of this prey **b :** to give (soldiers) experience in battle; *broadly* **:** to give (a novice) experience in any field **c :** to use (a new weapon) in conflict **4 :** to heat the blood of **:** EXASPERATE

blood albumin *n* **1 :** SERUM ALBUMIN **2 :** soluble dried blood

blood-al·bu·min glue \'⸗¦⸗⸗-\ *n* **:** BLOOD GLUE

blood alley *n* **:** an alley used in the game of marbles that is spotted or streaked with red

bloodalp \'⸗,⸗\ *n* -S [*blood* + *alp* (bullfinch)] *dial Eng* **:** a male bullfinch

blood-and-feather-dressed \¦⸗⸗¦⸗⸗,⸗\ *adj* **:** NEW YORK DRESSED

blood-and-guts \¦⸗⸗¦⸗\ *adj* **:** marked by vigor and attention to fundamentals **:** INTENSIVE ⟨few people ever get down to real *blood-and-guts* self-criticism⟩

blood and iron *n* [trans. of G *blut und eisen*] **:** reliance on and use of force; *esp* **:** the use of military power rather than normal diplomatic means

blood and thunder *n* **:** violence and uproar such as characterizes melodrama ⟨novels full of *blood and thunder*⟩

blood bank *n* **:** a place for storage of or an institution storing blood or plasma; *also* **:** blood so stored

bloodbath \'⸗,⸗\ *n* **:** a great slaughter **:** MASSACRE — compare PURGE

blood bay *n* **:** a dark reddish bay color; *often* **:** a horse of this color

bloodberry \'⸗- — *see* BERRY\ *n* **:** a tropical American herb (*Rivina humilis*) with racemes of red berries resembling those of pokeweed

bloodbird \'⸗,⸗\ *n* **:** an Australian honey eater (*Myzomela sanguinolenta*) having the head, neck, breast, and back bright scarlet, the wings and tail black, and the under parts buff

blood blister *n* **:** a blister containing blood or bloody serum usu. caused by an injury

blood bond *n* **:** the familial bond of common descent or of a similarly close relationship established by adoption or other ceremony

blood brother *n* **1 :** a brother by birth **2 :** one that is bound by a blood bond by virtue of a ceremony (as of the mingling of blood) **3 :** something viewed as basically related to some other often apparently incongruous item ⟨the social idealist is declared to be *blood brother* to the snake-oil practitioner —M.B.Smith⟩ ⟨soldiering and drinking have always been *blood brothers* —James Jones⟩

blood brotherhood *n* **:** a solemn friendship established between usu. unrelated men by a ceremonial use of each other's blood

blood cancer *n* **:** LEUKEMIA

blood cell *n* **:** any cell present in blood (as a leukocyte) **:** HEMOCYTE

blood clam *n* **:** a clam of a genus (*Arca*) of widely distributed red-blooded clams with a thick equivalve shell, pointed foot, and numerous marginal compound eyes on the mantle

blood corpuscle *n* **:** BLOOD CELL

blood count *n* **1 :** the determination of the blood cells in a definite volume of blood by partial enumeration and extrapolation — compare RED COUNT, WHITE COUNT; DIFFERENTIAL BLOOD COUNT **2 :** the number of blood cells in a definite volume of the blood of an individual as determined by a blood count, a figure that varies with sex, physiologic state, and health but in normal man approximates 5,000,000 red cells and 7000 white cells per cubic millimeter, the latter divided among 55 percent or more neutrophils, about 30 percent lymphocytes, and small percentages of eosinophils, monocytes, and basophils

blood crisis *n* **:** a sudden appearance of large numbers of nucleated red blood cells in the circulation presumably due to stimulation of the erythropoietic tissues

blood crystal *n* **:** one of the crystals obtained by heating a hemoglobin solution with acetic acid containing a little common salt, the form of the crystal differing according to the animal from which the hemoglobin was obtained

blood cup *n* **1 :** a cup-shaped ascomycetous fungus of a widely distributed genus (*Peziza*); *esp* **:** a scarlet European fungus (*P. coccinea*) **2 :** a heavy elongated metal vessel attached to the jaw of a table bird to catch the blood during dressing

bloodcurdler \ ⸗,⸗(⸗)⸗\ *n* -S **:** one that is bloodcurdling; *specif* **:** a lurid melodramatic theatrical or literary production

bloodcurdling \'⸗,⸗(⸗)⸗\ *adj* **:** such as might be expected to congeal the blood through fear or horror ⟨a ~ scream⟩ ⟨recovering slowly from the shock of that ~ experience⟩

blood disease *n* **:** an important vascular disease of the banana in the Celebes probably caused by a bacterium (*Xanthomonas celebensis*) and characterized by blighting of the leaves and reddish brown rot of the fruits

blood disk *n* **:** a mammalian red blood cell

blood donor *n* **:** a person who gives blood for use in transfusion

blooddrop \'⸗,⸗\ *n* **:** a terebellid bloodworm

blooddrops \'⸗,⸗\ *n pl but sing or pl in constr* [so called fr. its bright red flowers] **:** WIND POPPY

blood dust *n* **:** HEMOCONIA

blood dyscrasia *n* **:** an abnormal condition or disease of the blood

blooded *adj* [ME *bloded,* fr. ¹*blood* + *-ed*] **1 :** entirely or largely of pure blood ⟨~Jerseys⟩ **:** of the best stock ⟨good ~ animals⟩ **2 :** having blood of a specified kind — used in combination ⟨low-*blooded*⟩ ⟨warm-*blooded*⟩

blood feud *n* **:** a feud between the members of different clans or families arising out of a crime of violence (as a killing) committed by a member of one upon a member of the other and requiring a continuing series of alternative retaliations in kind — called also *vendetta;* compare BLOOD MONEY, WERGILD

bloodfin \'⸗,⸗\ *n* **:** a small So. American characin (*Aphyocharax rubripinnis*) with silvery body and deep-red fins often kept in the tropical aquarium

blood fine *n* **:** a fine for shedding blood **:** BLOODWITE, WERGILD

blood flour *n* **:** finely ground blood meal

bloodflower \'⸗,⸗⸗\ *n* **1 :** a tropical herb (*Asclepias curassavica*) with orange-red flowers **2 :** BLOOD LILY

blood fluke *n* **:** SCHISTOSOME

blood gill *n* **:** one of the thin-walled fimbriated blood-filled evaginations more or less completely free from tracheae that are characteristic of certain chiefly aquatic insects and may be concerned with respiratory or osmotic activity

blood gland *n* **:** ENDOCRINE GLAND

blood glue *n* **:** an adhesive made chiefly from blood, esp. soluble dried blood, and used because of its water resistance in making plywood

blood groove *n* **:** a longitudinal groove on the shaft of an arrow or spear or on the blade of a bayonet or knife said to have been introduced to cause increased bleeding of a wound produced and possibly actually facilitating withdrawal of bayonet or knife by preventing suction

blood group *n* **1 :** a group of persons related by a blood bond **2 :** one of the classes into which human beings can be separated on the basis of their possession or nonpossession of certain antigens, the classical ABO antigens subdividing human blood into four groups: O, A, B, and AB — compare ISOANTIBODY, RH FACTOR

blood grouping *n* **:** the act of determining to what blood group a sample of blood belongs

bloodguilt \'⸗,⸗\ *also* **bloodguiltiness** \'⸗,⸗⸗⸗\ *n* **:** guilt resulting from the shedding of blood; *esp, anthrop* **:** a formal state of guilt produced by killing human beings (as in war) and subject to removal by suitable ritual acts

bloodguilty \'⸗,⸗⸗\ *adj* **:** guilty of murder or bloodshed; *esp* **:** affected with bloodguilt

blood heat *n* **:** a temperature approximating that of the human body and being usu. taken as about 98° Fahrenheit — used esp. of fluids the temperature of which is estimated by dropping a portion on the skin and noting the sensation of relative warmth or chill ⟨heat the baby's bottle to *blood heat*⟩

blood horse *n* **1 :** THOROUGHBRED **2 :** any purebred horse

¹bloodhound \'⸗,⸗\ *n* [ME *bloodhound, bloodhund,* fr. *blood* + *hound, hund* hound] **1 a :** a large powerful hound of a breed (Bloodhound) originated in European monasteries but largely developed in England, distinguished by long smooth pendulous ears, long head, and wrinkled face and by remarkable acuteness of smell, and used formerly in tracking game but now almost entirely in tracking criminals or lost persons **b :** any hound hunting by scent and used for tracking humans **2 :** a person keen or relentless in pursuit

bloodhound

²bloodhound \"\ *vt* **:** to pursue (as an aim) relentlessly or keenly

bloodied *past of* BLOODY

bloodier *comparative of* BLOODY

bloodies *pres 3d sing of* BLOODY

bloodiest *superlative of* BLOODY

blood·i·ly \'blədᵊlē, -dəlē, -li\ *adv* **:** in a bloody manner

blood·i·ness \-dēnəs, -din-\ *n* -ES **:** the quality or state of being bloody

blooding *pres part of* BLOOD

blood island *also* **blood islet** *n* **:** any of the reddish areas in the extraembryonic mesoblast of developing vertebrate eggs where blood cells and vessels are forming

blood kin *n* **:** RELATIVES **:** those that are kin by reason of common ancestry; *also* **:** a group united by blood bond

blood knot *n* **1 :** a multiple overhand knot esp. when tied in a cat-o'-nine-tails **2** *Brit* **:** BARREL KNOT a

bloodleaf \'⸗,⸗\ *n* **:** any of several plants of the family Amaranthaceae having colored foliage; *esp* **:** a member of either of two genera (*Iresine* and *Aerva*) including several that are used as ornamental and bedding plants

blood·less \'blədləs\ *adj* [ME *blodles,* fr. OE *blōdlēas,* fr. *blōd* blood + *-lēas* -less — more at BLOOD] **1 a :** lacking or apparently lacking blood **:** free from blood ⟨the meat must be made completely ~⟩ ⟨a ~ surgical field⟩; *often* **:** PALE, PALLID, BLANCHED ⟨a wan and ~ countenance⟩ **b :** LIFELESS ⟨the ~ carcass of my Hector sold —John Dryden⟩ **2 :** not accompanied by bloodshed or slaughter ⟨a ~ victory⟩ ⟨a ~ revolution⟩ **3 :** lacking in spirit or vitality ⟨a ~ descendant of a noble race⟩; *also* **:** lacking in originality or vigor ⟨the ~ art of the mid-19th century⟩ ⟨make his novels and dramas rather ~ exercises in abstract morality —F.B.Millett⟩ **4 :** lacking in human feeling **:** COLD-HEARTED, UNEMOTIONAL, UNFEELING ⟨a batch of ~ statistics —F.L.Allen⟩ ⟨a curious ~ attempt to examine and pry into the lives of his fellows⟩ — **blood·less·ly** *adv* — **blood·less·ness** *n* -ES

bloodless surgery *n* **1 :** manipulative procedures for the correction of deformities or reduction of fractures or dislocations **2 :** surgery performed with a minimum effusion of blood (as by electrocoagulation or with the patient in a state of hypothermia)

bloodletter \'⸗,⸗⸗\ *n* -S [ME *bloodletere,* fr. OE *blōdlǣtere,* fr. *blōd* blood + *-lǣtere* -letter (fr. *lǣtan* to let + *-ere* -er) — more at BLOOD, LET] **:** one that engages in bloodletting: **a :** a practitioner of venesection **b :** a warlike or bloodthirsty person

bloodletting \'⸗,⸗⸗\ *n* -S [ME *bloodleting,* fr. *blood* + *leting,* gerund of *leten* to let — more at LET] **1 a :** VENESECTION **b :** a draining away (as of strength or character) ⟨the intellectual ~ Germany has suffered, owing to the emigration of many of her greatest writers —H.F.Garten⟩ **2 :** BLOODSHED

bloodlike \'⸗,⸗\ *adj* **:** like or like that of a Thoroughbred ⟨a trim horse with small ~ head and well-set ears⟩

blood lily *n* **:** any of various southern African plants (genus *Haemanthus*) of the family Amaryllidaceae; *esp* **:** one of a species (*H. coccineus*) having brilliant red flowers and often cultivated

bloodline \'⸗,⸗\ *n* **1 :** a sequence of direct ancestors esp. in a pedigree regarded as transmitting the distinctive traits or characters of the sequence ⟨there's a sound young bull of proven performance and with the best of ~s behind him⟩ **2 :** a group of individuals linked by ancestry and usu. by distinctive qualities ⟨a ~ outstanding in productivity and finish through several generations⟩ **:** FAMILY, STRAIN

bloodlust \'⸗,⸗\ *n* [*blood* + *lust*] **:** desire for bloodshed

bloodlusting *adj* **:** desiring bloodshed

blood meal *n* **:** the ground dried blood of animals characterized by a high protein content and used for feeding livestock and as a nitrogenous fertilizer

blood·mo·bile \'⸗mō,bēl, -mə,-, -,bil\ *n* -S [*blood* + *-mobile*] **:** an automobile staffed and equipped for the purpose of collecting blood from donors

blood money *n* **1 :** money or other benefit obtained as the price or at the cost of another's life or sometimes of his happiness, good name, or welfare — used esp. of a reward for supporting a capital charge, of money received for betraying a fugitive or for committing murder, or of the price obtained by sale of something that will destroy the purchaser **2 :** money paid by a manslayer or members of his family, clan, or tribe to the next of kin of a person killed by him — compare WERGILD

blood·noun \'bləd,naůn\ *n* -S [imit.] *South & Midland* **:** BULLFROG

blood orange *n* **:** any of several varieties of the sweet orange with deep-red pulp

blood pheasant *n* **:** any of several pheasants (genus *Ithaginis*) of the mountains of India and China remarkable for the bright red colors of their throat and breast

blood picture *n* **:** the condition and quality of the blood as indicated by a blood count, hemoglobin determination, and various other chemical and physical tests

blood pink *n* **:** a perennial pink (*Dianthus cruentus*) of southern Europe with dense clusters of bloodred flowers

blood plasma *n* **:** the fluid portion of whole blood — compare BLOOD SERUM

blood platelet *n* **:** one of the minute protoplasmic disks occurring in vertebrate blood, playing a role in blood clotting, and believed to originate as bits of cytoplasm pinched off the megakaryocytes

blood poisoning *also* **blood poison** *n* **:** SEPTICEMIA

blood poor *adj* **:** very poor **:** POVERTY-STRICKEN

blood pressure *n* **:** pressure exerted by the blood upon the walls of the blood vessels varying with the muscular efficiency of the heart, the blood volume and viscosity, the age of the individual, and the state of the vascular wall, being usu. measured on the radial artery by means of a sphygmomanometer and expressed in millimeters of mercury either as a fraction having as numerator the maximum pressure that follows systole of the left ventricle of the heart and as denominator the minimum pressure that accompanies cardiac diastole ⟨a *blood pressure* of $\frac{120}{80}$⟩ or as a whole number representing the first value only ⟨a *blood pressure* of 120⟩, tending to increase normally with age and excessively with certain vascular kidney and endocrine disorders and decreasing in hemorrhage, hypothyroidism, and various debilitating diseases — compare DIASTOLIC PRESSURE, PULSE PRESSURE, SYSTOLIC PRESSURE; HYPERTENSION, HYPOTENSION; ARTERIOSCLEROSIS

blood price *n* **:** BLOOD MONEY 2

bloodproof paper \'⸗,⸗-\ *n* **:** BUTCHER PAPER

blood pudding *n* **:** BLOOD SAUSAGE

blood purge *n* **:** the elimination en masse by massacre or execution of individuals considered to constitute an untrustworthy or undesirable element within a party or movement

blood rain *n* **:** rain colored red by dust from the air

bloodred \'⸗¦⸗\ *adj* [ME, fr. OE *blōdrēad,* fr. *blōd* blood + *rēad* red — more at BLOOD, RED] **:** having the color of blood **:** bright red ⟨~ tomatoes⟩

blood red *n* **:** a moderate to strong red that is yellower and darker than camellia — called also *cadmium vermilion, para red, Parma red, perma red, permanent red, scarlet lake*

blood-relationship \'⸗⸗'⸗⸗,⸗\ *n* **:** CONSANGUINITY

blood revenge *n* **:** BLOOD VENGEANCE

bloodroot \'⸗,⸗\ *n* **1 :** a scapose woods plant (*Sanguinaria canadensis*) having a red root and red sap, bearing a solitary lobed leaf and white flower in early spring, and having acrid emetic properties and a rootstock that is used as a stimulant expectorant — called also *bloodwort, Indian paint, puccoon, redroot, tetterwort, turmeric* **2** *Brit* **:** TORMENTIL

blood royal *n* **:** royal family; *specif* **:** those members of the royal family by birth ⟨a prince of the *blood royal*⟩

bloods *pl of* BLOOD, *pres 3d sing of* BLOOD

blood sacrifice *n* **:** a religious rite involving bloodshed

blood sausage *n* **:** sausage containing a large proportion of blood so that it is very dark in color

blood scours *n pl but sing or pl in constr, Austral & New Zeal* **:** a bloody diarrhea of calves prob. due to intestinal infection following malnutrition and lowered resistance

blood serum *n* **:** blood plasma from which the fibrin has been removed (as by clotting or defibrinating)

bloodshed \'⸗,⸗\ *n* -S [ME, fr. *blood* + *-shed* (fr. *sheden* to shed) — more at SHED] **1 :** the shedding or spilling of blood **:** act of shedding human blood **2 :** the taking of life (as in war or murder) **:** SLAUGHTER, CARNAGE

bloodshedder \'⸗,⸗⸗\ *n* **:** one that sheds blood **:** MURDERER

bloodshedding \'⸗,⸗⸗\ *n* [ME *bloodsheding,* fr. *blood* + *sheding,* gerund of *sheden* to shed] **:** BLOODSHED

blood·shot \'⸗,⸗\ *adj* [alter. of earlier *bloodshotten*] **1** *of an eye* **:** red and inflamed **:** suffused with blood or having the vessels turgid with blood (as when the conjunctiva is inflamed or irritated) **2 :** INFLAMING, CHALLENGING, TENSE ⟨another thought came in mad ~ pursuit —Liam O'Flaherty⟩

blood·shot·ten \'bləd¦shätᵊn\ *adj* [*blood* + *shotten,* obs. past part. of *shoot*] *now dial* **:** BLOODSHOT

blood spavin *n* **:** distention of the saphenous vein of a horse in the vicinity of the hock causing a soft swelling

bloodspilling \'⸗,⸗⸗\ *n* [*blood* + *spilling*] **:** BLOODSHED

blood sport *n* **:** a sport (as hunting) involving bloodshed

blood spot *n* **:** a clot of blood in a hen's egg due to hemorrhage within the ovarian follicle during the growth of the egg

bloodspotting \'⸗,⸗⸗\ *n* -S **:** the occurrence of blood spots **:** the tendency to produce blood spots, which appears to be inherited in certain strains of fowls

bloodstain \'⸗,⸗\ *n* [*blood* + *stain*] **:** a discoloration caused by blood

bloodstained \'⸗,⸗\ *adj* **:** stained or soiled with blood **:** BLOODY; *esp* **:** BLOODGUILTY

blood·stanch \'⸗,⸗\ *n* -ES **:** HORSEWEED 1

blood star *also* **blood starfish** *n* **:** a small bright red starfish (*Henricia sanguinolenta*) lacking pedicellaria and widely distributed in shallow seas

blood·stock \'⸗,⸗\ *n* **:** horses of Thoroughbred breeding; *esp* **:** such horses when used for or considered in relation to racing

blood·stone \'⸗,⸗\ *n* **1 :** a stone consisting of green chalcedony sprinkled with red spots resembling blood and resulting from oxidizing of the green — called also *heliotrope* **2 :** HEMATITE

bloodstream \'⸗,⸗\ *n* [ME *bloodstreme,* fr. *blood* + *strem* stream — more at STREAM] **1 :** the flowing blood in a circulatory system **2 :** something regarded as comparable to the living bloodstream esp. in pervasive or vital quality ⟨the influence of communism had entered the ~ of national politics in southeast Asia —*N.Y. Times*⟩ ⟨Lancashire might be in thriving health if its ~ of labor had not been so ruthlessly tapped during the war —*Economist*⟩

bloodsucker \'⸗,⸗⸗\ *n* [ME *blood soukere,* fr. *blood* + *soukere* sucker — more at SUCKER] **1 :** an animal that sucks blood; *esp* **:** LEECH **2 :** a person who bleeds another preying upon his money, ideas, or other resources **:** SPONGER, EXTORTIONER; *sometimes* **:** a rapacious and exacting master, landlord, or moneylender **3 a :** any of several Indian lizards (genus *Calotes*) having the throat blotched with red **b :** any of several Australian lizards

bloodsucking \'⸗¦⸗⸗\ *adj* **:** that draws blood from the body of another by or as if by sucking ⟨the plague of ~ insects⟩; *broadly* **:** that behaves as a bloodsucker

bloodsucking bat *n* **:** VAMPIRE 3

blood sugar *n* **1 :** the glucose in the blood; *also* **:** the amount or proportion of such sugar, normally from 0.08 to 0.11 percent but much increased in certain diseases, esp. diabetes mellitus **2 :** a determination of the amount of glucose in the blood ⟨some days we may do a dozen *blood sugars,* others not one⟩

blood test *n* **:** a test of the blood (as to determine parentage or ascertain the nature of an infection); *specif* **:** a serologic test for syphilis

blood-test \'⸗¦⸗\ *vt* [*blood test*] **:** to make a blood test on ⟨chicks from *blood-tested* stock⟩

bloodthirst \'⸗,⸗\ *n* [*blood* + *thirst*] **:** desire for bloodshed

bloodthirstily \'⸗,⸗⸗⸗\ *adv* **:** in a bloodthirsty manner

bloodthirstiness \'⸗,⸗⸗⸗\ *n* -ES **:** the quality or state of being bloodthirsty

bloodthirsty \'⸗,⸗⸗\ *adj* **1 :** eager for the shedding of blood **:** SANGUINARY; *also* **:** MURDEROUS **2 :** vehement in partisan-

ship or antagonism as though seeking the shedding of blood ⟨the ~ yells of the fans⟩
blood transfusion *n* : TRANSFUSION
blood tree *n* **1** : a small West Indian tree (*Croton draco*) yielding a red kino **2** : an Australian bloodwood (*Eucalyptus corymbosa*)
blood type *n* : BLOOD GROUP
blood–type \'ₛ,ₛ\ *vt* [*blood type*] : to determine the blood group of (an individual)
blood–vascular \'ₛ;ₛₛₛ\ *adj* : of, relating to, or involving blood vessels ⟨the *blood-vascular* system⟩ ⟨a serious *blood-vascular* lesion⟩
blood vengeance *n* : vengeance for bloodshed requiring bloodshed in return — compare BLOOD FEUD
blood vessel *n* : a vessel or canal in an animal in which blood circulates : ARTERY, VEIN, CAPILLARY
blood–warm \'ₛ;ₛ\ *adj* : as warm as blood in the living body; *specif* : warmed to blood heat
bloodwealth \'ₛ,ₛ\ *n* [*blood* + *wealth*] : an indemnity for murder paid in some African tribes to the family of the victim
bloodweed \'ₛ,ₛ\ *n* **1** : BLOOD LILY **2** : BLOODFLOWER 1 **3** : GREAT RAGWEED
bloodwite *also* **bloodwit** \'ₛ,ₛ\ *n* [ME, fr. OE *blōdwīte*, fr. *blōd* blood + *wīte* punishment — more at WITE] **1** *early English law* **a (1)** : a fine or amercement for the shedding of blood payable to the king, lord, or other superior in compensation for the breach of his peace — compare WERGILD **(2)** : a penalty for murder **b (1)** : the right to levy such a fine **(2)** : exemption from payment of such a fine **2** *Scots law* : a broil or riot in which blood is spilled
bloodwood \'ₛ,ₛ\ *n* : any of numerous trees having a red juice or red wood: as **a** *Austral* **(1)** : any of several eucalypts (as *Eucalyptus corymbosa*) **(2)** : a tree (*Baloghia lucida*) the sap of which is used as a paint **b** *in tropical America* **(1)** : LOGWOOD **(2)** : FALSE LOGWOOD **(3)** : any of several plants of the genus *Pterocarpus* **(4)** : a tree of the genus *Vismia* **c** *in the East Indies* : QUEEN'S CRAPE MYRTLE
bloodworm \'ₛ,ₛ\ *n* **1** : any of certain annelid worms that are more or less red in color: **a** : any of several small reddish earthworms used as bait **b** : any of several red-blooded polychaete worms: **(1)** : a soft-bodied terebellid worm of the genus *Polycirrus* **(2)** : a common intertidal worm (*Glycera dibranchiata*) common on the east coast of Canada and used for bait **2** : the red aquatic larva of certain midges of the family Tendipedidae **3** : PALISADE WORM
bloodwort \'ₛ,ₛ\ *n* [ME *bloodwurt*, fr. *blood* + *wurt, wort* wort — more at WORT] **1** : a plant of the family Haemodoraceae the members of which contain a deep red coloring matter in the roots **2 a** : a European dock (*Rumex sanguineus*) with red-veined leaves **b** : WATER DOCK **3 a** : European elder (*Sambucus ebulus*) **4** : a centaury (*Centaurium umbellatum*) **5** : SALAD BURNET **6** : YARROW **7** : BLOODROOT **8** : HERB ROBERT
bloodwort family *n* : HAEMODORACEAE
[1]**bloody** \'blədē, -di\ *adj* -ER/-EST [ME, fr. OE *blōdig*, fr. *blōd* blood + *-ig* -y — more at BLOOD] **1 a** : containing or made up of blood ⟨a ~ boil⟩ ⟨a ~ sweat⟩ **b** : of or in the blood ⟨lust is but a ~ fire —Shak.⟩ **2 a** : smeared or stained with blood ⟨your scarf is all ~⟩ **b** : dripping blood : BLEEDING ⟨too many minor arguments were ending in ~ noses⟩ **3 a** : portending or calling for bloodshed ⟨a ~ augury⟩ ⟨I do begin to have ~ thoughts —Shak.⟩ **b** : accompanied by or involving bloodshed, often cruel or needless bloodshed : SANGUINARY ⟨a bitter ~ quarrel⟩; *esp* : marked by great slaughter ⟨a ~ battle was once fought here⟩ **4 a** : given or tending to the shedding of blood : MURDEROUS ⟨there was no escape from this ~ rule⟩ **b** : having a cruel savage disposition : MERCILESS, CRUEL ⟨a foul ~ villain⟩ **5** : suggesting or like blood in color : BLOODRED ⟨maples ~ at the touch of Jack Frost⟩ **6** *Brit* — used as a generalized expression of intensification ⟨a ~ rascal⟩ often losing all force ⟨pass the ~ salt⟩; often considered vulgar
[2]**bloody** \"\ *vt* -ED/-ING/-ES : to make bloody ⟨let me alone or I'll ~ your nose⟩; *esp* : to stain or redden with or as if with blood ⟨autumn already ~*ing* the dwarf shrubs of the plain —Farley Mowat⟩ ⟨the battles that have *bloodied* this sacred soil⟩
[3]**bloody** \"\ *adv*, *Brit* — used as an intensive ⟨a ~ good lot⟩ ⟨he can ~ well get his own dinner⟩; often considered vulgar
bloody–back \'ₛₛ,ₛ\ *n*, *archaic* : a British soldier : REDCOAT
bloody bark *n* : a showy Australian woody vine (*Lonchocarpus blackii*) with rusty red twigs and foliage and purple flowers in drooping racemes
bloodybone *n* -S *obs* : BLOODYBONES
bloody•bones \'ₛₛ,ₛ\ *n pl but sing or pl in constr*, *archaic* [alter. of earlier *bloodybone*] : HOBGOBLIN, SPECTER — used esp. in the phrase *rawhead and bloodybones*
bloody bread *n* : BLEEDING BREAD
bloody clam *n* : BLOOD CLAM
bloody dock *n* : BLOODWORT 2
bloody fingers *n pl but sing or pl in constr* **1** : FOXGLOVE 1 **2** : MALE ORCHIS
bloody flux *n* **1** : a diarrhea in which blood is mixed with the intestinal discharge — now archaic when used of man **2** : SWINE DYSENTERY
bloody hand *n* **1** : a hand stained with deer's blood being sufficient evidence in old English forest laws of a man's trespass in the forest against venison **2** *heraldry* : a red hand (as in the arms of Ulster) that is now the distinguishing mark of a baronet of the United Kingdom or of Ireland
bloody man's fingers *n pl but sing or pl in constr* : FOXGLOVE 1
bloody mary \-'merē, -ma(a)rē, -mārē, -ri\ *n*, *often cap B&M* [prob. after *Bloody Mary*, nickname for Mary I †1558 queen of England, notorious for her persecution of Protestants; fr. the red color] : a beverage consisting of vodka and tomato juice to which is usu. added seasoning and sometimes lemon juice
bloody murder *adv* : as though face to face with a gory murder ⟨he thought of screaming *bloody murder* so that they would let him get out of the car —Jean Stafford⟩
bloody murrain *n* : TEXAS FEVER
bloody–nosed beetle \'ₛₛ;ₛ-\ *n*, *Brit* : a dull blue Old World chrysomelid beetle (*Timarcha tenebricosa*) that exudes a drop of reddish fluid from its head when disturbed
bloody•noun \'blədē,naůn, -di,-\ *var of* BLOODNOUN
bloody scours *n pl but sing or pl in constr* : a bloody diarrhea of domestic animals; *also* : a disease characterized by such a diarrhea (as swine dysentery or coccidiosis of calves)
bloody shirt *n* : the blood-stained shirt of a slain man used to incite vengeance for his death; *broadly* : a symbol used to inflame to anger or to retaliative action — used specif. in the U.S. after the Civil War of any means employed to stir up or revive party or sectional animosity esp. in the phrase *wave the bloody shirt*
bloo•ey *also* **bloo•ie** \'blüē\ *adj* [origin unknown] *slang* : out of order : AWRY : incomprehensibly wrong — used chiefly with *go* ⟨the ladder slipped, then everything went ~⟩
[1]**bloom** \'blüm\ *n* -S [ME *blome* lump of metal, fr. OE *blōma*] **1** : a mass of wrought iron from the Catalan forge or from the puddling furnace deprived of its dross and shaped in the form of an oblong block by shingling **2** : a semifinished mass of steel usu. nearly square in section and not smaller than 6 by 6 inches formed directly from an ingot by hot rolling — compare BILLET, SLAB **3** : a mass of iron or steel formed by consolidating scrap at a high temperature by hammering or rolling
[2]**bloom** \"\ *n* -S [ME *blome*, fr. ON *blōm*, *blōmi*; akin to OHG *bluomo* flower, blossom, Goth *blōma* lily, OE *blōma* mass, lump of metal, *blōwan* to bloom — more at BLOW] **1 a** : the flower of a seed plant : an individual flower : BLOSSOM 1a; *collectively* : flowers or amount of flowers esp. of a plant or a season ⟨look at the ~ on that bush⟩ ⟨the apples had a very light ~ this spring⟩ **b** : the flowering state ⟨the roses are all in ~⟩ **c** : a period or instance of flowering ⟨there are usually two ~s, a heavy one in May and another in late September⟩ ⟨the spring ~ in the park⟩ **2 a** : one (as a girl) that is estimable, outstanding, or lovely ⟨it is hard to accept the frailty of so fair a ~⟩ **b** : a state or time of beauty, freshness, and vigor ⟨the ~ of youth⟩; *also* : highest development : PERFECTION, PEAK, CULMINATION ⟨if automation comes into fuller ~ —J.I.Snyder⟩ ⟨a world that has become sufficiently relaxed to allow its tendencies toward a diversification of manners to reach their ~ —Irving Howe & Eliezer Greenberg⟩ **c** : a period of development or improvement (as in quality or standing) ⟨the clavichord had . . . a second ~ almost unique in history —Curt Sachs⟩ **3** : a surface coating or appearance: as **a** : the delicate powdery coating on certain fresh fruits (as grapes or plums) and leaves (as of cabbage or carnation); *also* : the waxy material that forms such a coating **b** : a rosy appearance of the cheeks : FLUSH ⟨recovered all her health and ~⟩; *broadly* : an outward evidence of freshness or healthy vigor : GLOW ⟨a new, fresh world, with all the ~ upon it —W.M.Thackeray⟩ **c** : a deposit or coating of ellagic acids that appears on leather **d** : the grainy or powdery surface of a newly minted coin **e** : the fluorescence of petroleum or its products or of rosin oil **f** : the cloudy appearance often observed on a film of varnish or lacquer **g** : a milky appearance on the surface of glass produced by slight decomposition **h** : luster or brightness of textile fibers or materials esp. when dyed ⟨wool with a fine ~⟩ ⟨the soft ~ of silk velvets⟩ **i** : WATER BLOOM **j** : the surface appearance characteristic of freshness and quality in dressed meat and poultry **k** : the protective cuticle of an eggshell **l** : a healthy well-kept appearance of the coat and skin of a domestic animal; *also* : FATNESS, FINISH **m** : a grayish discoloration on chocolates resulting from the deposit of microscopic crystals of fat or sugar on the surface of the coating **n** : glare caused by an object reflecting too much light into a television camera **o** : an appearance of brightness on dyed material ⟨a red ~ on indigo navy⟩ **4** : a mineral that is frequently found as an efflorescence ⟨cobalt ~⟩ ⟨antimony ~⟩ **5** : the characteristic aroma of a wine : BOUQUET 4a
[3]**bloom** \"\ *vb* -ED/-ING/-S [ME *blomen*, fr. *blome*, n.] *vi* **1** : to produce or yield blossoms : flower or be in flower : BLOSSOM ⟨bulbs that ~ in the spring⟩ ⟨that bush will ~ soon⟩ **2 a** : to attain, undergo, or acquire bloom; *esp* : to flourish esp. in youthful beauty, freshness, or excellence ⟨the arts ~*ed* in this heady environment⟩ ⟨we could not believe that scrawny child had ~*ed* into such a lovely lass⟩ **b** : to become affected or marred with bloom ⟨a beautiful finish but it ~s so easily⟩ **c** : to exhibit bloom : shine out : GLOW ⟨the stove ~*ed* warm and bright in the dark room⟩ **d** : to cause bloom ⟨this polish does not ~ or become sticky⟩ **3** : to come out like a bloom on a plant; *esp* : to appear or occur unexpectedly or in surprising quantity or degree ⟨subscription selling ~*ed* splendidly —Bernard Kalb⟩ ⟨the senator ~*ed* as an enthusiastic liberal⟩ **4** : to become densely populated with microorganisms and esp. with plankton — used of bodies of water ~ *vt* **1** *obs* : to cause to bloom; *esp* : to make flourishing **2** : to give bloom or a bloom to: as **a** : to make glowing or radiant : BRIGHTEN ⟨while barred clouds ~ the soft-dying day —John Keats⟩ **b** : to cloud or mar with a bloom ⟨dampness can ~ the best of varnishes⟩ **c** *Brit* : to coat (a photographic lens) with a thin layer of low-refracting material to reduce surface reflection
[1]**bloom•er** \-mə(r)\ *n* -S [[3]*bloom* + *-er*] **1** : a plant that blooms; *sometimes* : a person that reaches full competence, skill, or maturity ⟨some youngsters are late ~s⟩ **2** : a workman who removes bloom (as a leather scourer) **3** : a workman or a rolling mill that shapes blooms **4** *slang chiefly Brit* : a gross error : a stupid blunder : BONER, BLOOPER
[2]**bloomer** \"\ *n* -S [after Mrs. Amelia *Bloomer* †1894 Am. pioneer in social reform who advocated such clothing] **1** : a costume for women introduced about 1850 consisting of a short skirt and long loose trousers gathered closely about the ankles and usu. with a coat and broad-brimmed hat **2 a bloomers** *pl* : the trousers of a bloomer costume **b** : full loose trousers gathered at the knee formerly worn by women for athletics — usu. used in pl. **c** : underpants of similar design but less bulk worn chiefly by girls — usu. used in pl. **3** : a woman wearing a bloomer (sense 1); *esp* : one adopting such a costume as an indication of adherence to the fight for the rights and freedom of women during the 19th century
bloo•me•ria \blü'mirēə\ *n*, *cap* [NL, fr. H. G. *Bloomer*, 19th cent. Amer. botanist + NL *-ia*] : a genus of bulbous Californian plants (family Liliaceae) with grasslike leaves and showy orange flowers — see GOLDEN STAR 3
bloomer pit *n* [[1]*bloomer*] : TAN VAT
bloom•ery *also* **bloom•a•ry** \'blümərē\ *n* -ES [[1]*bloom* + *-ery* or *-ary*] : a furnace and forge in which wrought-iron blooms were formerly made directly from the ore or more rarely from cast iron
bloom•field•ian \(')blüm¦fēldēən\ *n* -S *usu cap* [Leonard *Bloomfield* †1949 Am. linguist + E *-ian*] : a follower of the principles of linguistic analysis taught by Leonard Bloomfield
bloom•i•ness \'blümēnəs\ *n* -ES : the state of having the surface covered with bloom
[1]**blooming** *adj* [fr. pres. part. of [3]*bloom*] **1** : having blooms unfolding : FLOWERING ⟨a ~ violet⟩; *also* : attaining full development or improved status **2** : thriving in health, beauty, and vigor : exhibiting the freshness and beauties of youth or health **3** [prob. euphemism for *bloody*] *slang* — used as a generalized intensive ⟨a ~ fool⟩; compare BLOODY 6 — **bloom•ing•ly** *adv* — **bloom•ing•ness** *n* -ES
[2]**blooming** \"\ *n* -S [fr. gerund of [3]*bloom*] **1** : BLOOM **2** : the process of coating the surface of glass (as of a lens) with a film designed to increase transmission of light through the glass by reducing loss due to reflection
[3]**blooming** \"\ *n* -S [[1]*bloom* + *-ing*] *metallurgy* : the process of making blooms
blooming mill *n* [[3]*blooming*] : a rolling mill in which blooms are produced from ingots in steel manufacture : ROUGHING MILL, COGGING MILL
blooming sal•ly \-'salē\ *also* **blooming willow** *n* [[1]*blooming*] : GREAT WILLOW HERB
bloom•less \'blümləs\ *adj* : lacking bloom; *sometimes* : incapable of flowering ⟨a ~ apple tree⟩
bloom poison *n* : either of two poisonous Australian shrubs (*Gastrolobium ovalifolium* and *Oxylobium retusum*) of the family Leguminosae — compare POISON BUSH
blooms *pl of* BLOOM, *pres 3d sing of* BLOOM
blooms•bury \'blümz,berē, -zb(ə)rē, -ri\ *adj*, *usu cap* [fr. *Bloomsbury*, district of London, England] : cultivating or displaying literary and artistic interests flourishing among an informal group of intellectuals associated with the residential district of Bloomsbury ⟨the *Bloomsbury* group⟩ ⟨he is more *Bloomsbury* than the British Museum —Harvey Breit⟩
bloom side *n* : the hair side of a skin or hide
bloom spray *n* : a pesticidal orchard spray applied when 90 percent or more of the flowers are in full bloom
bloomy \'blümē\ *adj*, *often* -ER/-EST **1** : full of or characterized by flowers : FLOWERY ⟨a ~ sunlit slope⟩ **2** : covered with bloom (sense 3) **3** *archaic* : FLOURISHING; *esp* : exhibiting youthful beauty and vigor ⟨but all the ~ flush of life is fled —Oliver Goldsmith⟩
[1]**bloop** \'blüp\ *vb* -ED/-ING/-S [imit.] *vi* : to make a howling noise : operate a radio receiving set that makes such a noise — see BLOOPER 1 ~ *vt* **1** : to silence bloops in by the application of a mask or by electrical cutoff of the sound output **2** : to hit (a blooper) in baseball
[2]**bloop** \"\ *n* -S **1** : an unpleasing sound; *specif* : the noise made when the beam of light in a sound reproducer is interrupted in its passage through the film by a splice or other unwanted abrupt change in the density of the film **2** : a special mask applied over a splice in a film to prevent a bloop
bloop•er \'blüpə(r)\ *n* -S **1** : a radio receiving set that generates current of radio frequency thus causing radiation from the receiving antenna and under certain circumstances causing nearby sets to bloop **2** : an embarrassing public blunder ⟨his prize ~ was introducing the speaker by the wrong name⟩ **3** *baseball* **a** : a high pitch lobbed to the batter with backspin **b** : a lofting fly ball hit barely beyond the infield
blooth \'blüth\ *var of* BLOWTH
[1]**blore** \'blō(ə)r, -ō(ə)\ *vi* [ME *bloren* — more at BLARE] *dial Eng* : BELLOW, LOW — used of cattle or those (as children) that cry out loudly
[2]**blore** \'blō(ə)r\ *n* -S [ME; perh. akin to ME *blowen* to blow — more at BLOW] *archaic* : a roaring wind : BLAST, BLUSTER
blos•my \'bläs(ə)mē\ *adj* [ME — more at BLOSSOMY] *archaic* : BLOSSOMY
[1]**blos•som** \'bläsəm\ *n* -S [ME *blosme*, fr. OE *blōstm*, *blōstma*; akin to MHG *bluost* blossom, OE *blōwan* to bloom — more at BLOW] **1 a** : the flower of a seed plant : [2]BLOOM 1a — used esp. of flowers having a colored or conspicuous perianth, rarely of apetalous flowers, and often preferred to *flower* or *bloom* when the reference is to plants producing edible fruits ⟨the scent of apple ~s mingled with that of woodland flowers⟩ **b** : the mass of bloom on a single plant ⟨this tree had an excellent ~ this year⟩; *also* : the state of bearing flowers ⟨those plums are in full ~ now⟩ **2** : a period or stage of development analogous to the unfolding of a flower ⟨in the ~ of one's youth⟩ **3** : something resembling a blossom esp. in freshness, loveliness, or rich promise ⟨a ~ of literature⟩ ⟨my babe, my ~, ah, my child —Alfred Tennyson⟩ **4** : the weathered outcrop of a coal or ore deposit **5** : a moderate pink that is yellower and duller than arbutus pink, yellower and less strong than blossom pink, stronger than chalk pink, and deeper than hydrangea pink — called also *Venetian pink*
[2]**blossom** \"\ *vi* -ED/-ING/-S [ME *blosmen*, fr. OE *blōstmian*, fr. *blōstm*, *blōstma*] **1 a** *of plants* : to put forth flowers : come into bloom : FLOWER ⟨this lily ~s very early⟩ **b** *of places* : to be or become full of flowers ⟨during its short season the desert ~s gloriously⟩ **2** : to unfold like a blossom ⟨smoke ~*ed* out from the cracks⟩: as **a** : to flourish and prosper ⟨the romance . . . ~*ed* for six or seven months and then wilted —Saxe Commins⟩ **b** : DEVELOP, EVOLVE, EXPAND — often used with *into*, sometimes with *out* ⟨the town ~*ed* into a metropolis⟩ ⟨genuine culture often ~s tardily⟩ ⟨he started small and ~*ed* out as he gained experience⟩ **c** : to come into being : put in an appearance : APPEAR ⟨under rental control trickery and connivance ~*ed*⟩ ⟨new industries can ~ overnight if we find an outlet for their products⟩ **d** *of a parachute* : to open and expand **3** : to be or become changed by or notable for the appearance or addition of something — usu. used with *with* or *out* ⟨the ward had ~*ed* out in shiny plaster casts —Earle Birney⟩ ⟨Apple Valley ~s with dude ranches —Ralph Friedman⟩
blossombill \'ₛₛ,ₛ\ *n* [so called fr. the colored spot on the bill] : SURF SCOTER
blossom bud *n* : FLOWER BUD; *esp* : a flower bud of a fruit tree that is formed during one growing season but develops during the next
blossomed *adj* [ME *blossumed*, fr. *blossum*, *blosme* blossom + *-ed*] : bearing blossoms : FLOWERING ⟨a fully ~ rose⟩; *often* : having blossoms of a specified kind — used in combination ⟨scarlet-*blossomed*⟩ ⟨double-*blossomed*⟩
blossom–end rot \'ₛₛ,ₛ-\ *n* **1** : any fruit rot originating at the blossom end **2** : a common physiological disease of the tomato attributed to great fluctuation in available moisture and characterized by slightly sunken leathery areas around the tip end of the fruit that appear water-soaked or colored lead to brown
blossomhead \'ₛₛ,ₛ\ *n* : SURF SCOTER
blossom–headed parakeet \'ₛₛ¦ₛₛ-\ *n* : a common parakeet (*Psittacula cyanocephala*) of India and southeast Asia, having a green back, a greenish yellow breast, and a red head with bluish iridescence
blos•som•less \'bläsəmləs\ *adj* : being without a blossom
blossom pink *n* : a moderate pink that is yellower and deeper than arbutus pink, bluer and stronger than chalk pink, and bluer and deeper than hydrangea pink — called also *cherry pink*
blos•som•ry \'bläsəmrē\ *n* -ES : BLOSSOMS
blos•somy \'bläsəmē, -mi\ *adj* [alter. of earlier *blosmy*, fr. ME, fr. *blosme* blossom + *-y*] : full of blossoms : like a blossom : FLOWERY
[1]**blot** \'blät, — *usu* -d·+V\ *n* -S [ME *blot*, *blotte*, perh. fr. MF *blotte*, *bloste*, *blostre* clod, perh. of Gmc origin; akin to MD *bluyster* blister — more at BLISTER] **1 a** : a soiling or disfiguring mark, spot, or stain (as of ink or earth) ⟨a letter full of ~s⟩ **b** : something resembling such a spot or mark esp. in detracting from the excellence or beauty of the whole of which it is a part ⟨these filthy streets are a ~ on our city⟩ **2** : a spot on a reputation : a moral flaw : DISGRACE, REPROACH, BLEMISH **3** *archaic* : a deliberate obliteration of something written or printed; *specif* : a mark covering something unwanted in a piece of writing
[2]**blot** \"\ *vb* **blotted**; **blotted**; **blotting**; **blots** [ME *bloten*, *blotten*, fr. *blot*, *blotte*, n.] *vt* **1** : to spot, stain, or bespatter with some discoloring substance ⟨her tears *blotted* the page as she wrote⟩ **2** *obs* : to spoil (as paper) with bad writing : write ineptly or clumsily **3** : to make obscure or indistinct : blot out : ECLIPSE **4** *obs* **a** : to cause flawing of : MAR, SOIL, IMPAIR ⟨it ~s thy beauty, as frosts do bite the meads —Shak.⟩; *esp* : to stain with infamy : DISGRACE ⟨to do me honor in that very thing, wherein these men thought to have *blotted* me —John Milton⟩ **b** : CALUMNIATE, STIGMATIZE ⟨there's a good mother, boy, that ~s thy father —Shak.⟩ **5 a** : to dry (as writing) with blotting paper or other absorbing agent ⟨she hastily *blotted* her letter⟩ **b** : to remove (an unwanted deposit) by blotting with an absorbent material — often used with *up* ⟨with a paper towel she carefully *blotted up* the ink she had spilled⟩ ~ *vi* **1** : to make a blot or blots ⟨this pen ~s badly⟩; *sometimes* : to make an erasure **2** : to become marked with a blot : take a blot ⟨this paper ~s easily⟩ — **blot one's copybook** : to do something that spoils one's record (as for probity or good sense)
[3]**blot** \"\ *n* -S [origin unknown] **1** : a backgammon man exposed to capture by being placed or left alone on a point **2** *archaic* : a weak point : FAILING; *also* : an exposed point or mark ⟨he is too great a master of his art to make a ~ which may be so easily hit —John Dryden⟩
[1]**blotch** \'bläch\ *n* -ES [prob. alter. (influenced by *blister* or *blain*) of *botch* swelling] **1 a** : IMPERFECTION, BLEMISH ⟨face covered with ~*es*⟩; *sometimes* : a moral flaw : FAULT **b** : a spot or mark (as of color or ink) esp. when large or irregular **2** : a disease of plants characterized by dark, irregular, and often diffusely margined spots on the leaves or fruit: **a** : a disease of apples caused by an imperfect fungus (*Phyllosticta solitaria*) producing small dark spots on the leaves and fruit and cankers on the tree **b** : BLACK SPOT 1c — see NET BLOTCH, SPOT BLOTCH
[2]**blotch** \"\ *vt* -ED/-ING/-ES : to mark or mar with blotches ⟨the mimosa ~*ed* the faces of the hills as monotone and pale as mustard —Elizabeth Bowen⟩ ⟨an elder man, stout, and ~*ed* with scurvy —Sheridan Le Fanu⟩
[3]**blotch** \"\ *adj*, *of textile printing* : involving production of a black or colored ground
blotchy \'bläche, -chi\ *adj* -ER/-EST **1** : having or marked with blotches **2** : like a blotch
blot•less \'blätləs\ *adj* : free from blots or spots : IMMACULATE
blot on the escutcheon : a disgrace in a family record : a stain in reputation
blot out *vt* **1 a** : to alter (as writing) by covering with a blot : correct or cancel (something written) by blotting ⟨my name be *blotted out* from the book of life —Shak.⟩ **b** : to render insignificant or inconsequential : withdraw from awareness or need for consideration ⟨time will *blot out* these bitter memories⟩ ⟨one act like this *blots out* a thousand crimes —John Dryden⟩ **2** : to make obscure or invisible ⟨mist slowly *blotted out* the hills⟩ : HIDE, CONCEAL, DARKEN ⟨acquired prejudices . . . can spread a fog over verbal messages, *blotting out* common meanings, distorting common experiences —Stuart Chase⟩ **3** : DESTROY, ANNIHILATE, KILL ⟨*blot out* the nations of men —Lewis Mumford⟩ **syn** see ERASE
blot•ter \'blăd·ə(r), -ătə-\ *n* -S **1** : one that blots; *esp* : a piece of blotting paper **2** : a book in which entries (as of transactions or occurrences) are made temporarily pending their transfer to permanent record books ⟨a police ~⟩ **3** *slang* : a person who blots up liquor : DRUNK, SOT **4** [so called fr. its having been made of blotting paper] : a disk of compressible material (as a cloth or felt gasket in the mounting of a grinding wheel) for avoidance of excessive pressure by clamping nuts **5** : a coat of gravel, crushed rock, or crushed slag spread over a layer of bituminous material with which it consolidates to form a bonded road surface **6** *West* : a cattle thief who attempts to conceal his depredations by altering the brands of stolen cattle
blot•tesque \(')blä¦tesk\ *adj* [[1]*blot* + *-esque* (as in *grotesque*)] : painted with heavy touches or blotlike brushwork
blotting *n* -S [by shortening] : BLOTTING PAPER
blotting book *n* : a book of blotting paper

blot·ting·ly *adv* **:** with blots **:** in a blotting style or manner
blotting pad *n* **:** a pad of blotting paper
blotting paper *n* **:** a soft spongy unsized paper used to absorb ink from freshly written manuscript
blot·to \ˈblä(ˌ)tō, -ä(ˌ)tō\ *adj* [prob. irreg. fr. ²*blot*] **1** *slang* **:** completely drunk **:** made unconscious by drink **2** *slang* **:** CONFUSED, DISORDERED, UNCONSCIOUS
blot·ty \ˈbläd-ē, -ätē\ *adj, often* -ER/-EST [¹*blot* + -*y*] **:** covered or disfigured with blots **:** DAUBY
blou·bis·kop \ˈblau̇ˌbiskəp\ *n* -s [Afrik, fr. *blou* blue (fr. MD *blā, blau*) + *biskop;* akin to OHG *blāo* blue — more at BLUE] *Africa* **:** BLACK BISKOP
¹**blouse** \ˈblau̇z\ *var of* BLOWZE
²**blouse** \ˈblau̇s, ˈblau̇z\ *n, pl* **blouses** \ˈblau̇səz, -au̇zəz\ [F] **1 :** a loose overgarment like a shirt or smock, hiplength to calf-length, belted or unbelted, and worn esp. by workmen, artists, and peasants **2 :** the dress and undress uniform coat of the U.S. Army; *also* **:** the upper outer garment of any uniform ⟨a postman's gray ~⟩ **3 :** a usu. loose-fitting garment covering the body from the neck to the waist or just below, made with or without a collar, sleeves, or belt, and worn over or tucked inside a waistband (as of a skirt) **4 :** a bloused draping of cloth (as in a coat or dress)
³**blouse** \"\ *vi* -ED/-ING/-S **1 :** to fall in folds like those of a loose blouse when closely belted — used of textiles and garments ⟨the new coats ~ gracefully above the hipline⟩ **2 :** DROOP, BAG ⟨sails bellying and *blousing* in a fitful breeze⟩
bloused \ˈblau̇st, -au̇zd\ *adj* **1 :** wearing a blouse **2 :** made with fullness like that of a blouse **3 :** having a bulge or droop similar to the effect of a blouse belted at the waist

Russian blouse

blous·ette \blau̇ˈset, -ˈzet\ *n* -s [²*blouse* + -*ette*] **:** a woman's sleeveless blouse
¹**blousy** *var of* BLOWSY
²**blousy** *also* **blous·ey** \ˈblau̇sē, -au̇zē, -i\ *adj* **blousier; blousiest** [¹*blouse* + -*y*] **:** like a blouse **:** BLOUSED
blou·wil·de·bees·oog \ˈblau̇ˌvildəˌbāˌsōk\ *n* -s [Afrik, fr. *blouwildebees* brindled gnu + *oog* eye, fr. MD *ōghe;* akin to OE *ēage* eye — more at BLUE WILDEBEEST, EYE] *Africa* **:** a disease marked by exophthalmos, blindness, and frequently rupture of the eyeball occurring in sheep that come in contact with the gnu and prob. due to an unidentified infective agent
blo·vi·ate \ˈblōvēˌāt\ *vi* -ED/-ING/-S [prob. irreg. fr. *blow* + -*i*- + -*ate*] **:** to orate verbosely and windily
¹**blow** \ˈblō\ *vb* **blew** \ˈblü\ *or dial* **blowed** \ˈblōd\ **blown** \ˈblōn\ *or dial* **blowed; blowing; blows** [ME *blowen,* fr. OE *blāwan;* akin to OHG *blāen* to blow, inflate, L *flare* to blow, *follis* bellows, Gk *phallos* penis, Skt *bhāṇḍa* pot; basic meaning: to swell] *vi* **1** *of air or air currents* **:** to move with speed or force ⟨the wind *blew* in gusts⟩ — often used with *it* as an impersonal nominative ⟨let it ~, we're snug and warm⟩ **2 a :** to produce a current of air (as by expelling it forcibly from the lungs through the mouth) ⟨never ~ on your soup to cool it⟩ **b :** to drive air or other gas ⟨the fan is ~*ing* on my neck⟩ **c :** to escape (as of natural gas or oil) from a region of high pressure **3 a :** to make a sound by or as if by blowing **:** HISS, WHISTLE, TOOT ⟨the train *blew* for the crossing⟩ **b :** to play a wind instrument; *also, slang* **:** to play jazz on any instrument **c** *of a wind instrument* **:** SOUND ⟨there let the pealing organ ~ —John Milton⟩ **d** *of an animal* **:** SNORT ⟨the horse stood stamping and ~*ing* restlessly in the cold⟩ **4 a :** to talk emptily **:** BOAST ⟨he kept us awake half the night ~*ing* about his family⟩ **b :** STORM, BLUSTER, FULMINATE; *also* **:** to be or become enraged **:** blow up ⟨when he heard what they had done he really *blew*⟩ **5 a :** to breathe hard or rapidly **:** PANT, PUFF, GASP ⟨my, those stairs make me ~⟩ **b** *of whales and other cetaceans* **:** to eject moisture-laden air from the lungs through the blowhole **6** *obs, of flies* **:** to lay eggs **7 a :** to move or be carried by or as if by wind ⟨the echo of a lost world ~*s* through her sparkling prose —Beatrice Washburn⟩ ⟨the soil is ~*ing* badly all along the hedge⟩ **b :** to flutter, billow, or flap in a current of air ⟨curtains ~*ing* out the open window⟩ **:** to be carried by the wind ⟨the kite *blew* away⟩ **8 :** to be damaged in a manner involving swelling or expansion: **a :** to become destroyed by explosion **:** EXPLODE ⟨if this old blunderbuss doesn't ~ we may have duck for dinner⟩ **b** *of cement* **:** to swell and crack due to imperfect preparation and curing **c** *of foods* **:** to become swollen by the products of abnormal fermentation ⟨certain bacteria cause cheeses to ~⟩ **d** *of an electrical fuse* **:** to melt when overloaded ⟨an overloaded outlet often causes fuses to ~⟩ **e** *of a pneumatic tire* **:** to release its air through a spontaneous rupture **:** blow out **f** *of pottery* **:** to blow apart from too rapid heating in the kiln **g** *of paper* **:** to blister esp. from air entrapped between the wet sheet and the felt or from too sudden drying on the cylinder; *also, of paperboard* **:** to blister from air entrapped between two plies **9** *slang* **:** to move off **:** clear out **:** DEPART ⟨~ now, nobody wants the likes of you around here⟩ **10** *of a horse or mule* **:** to pause for breath ⟨let the mare ~ at the end of the furrow⟩ ~ *vt* **1 a :** to drive (gas or vapor) from a region of greater to a region of lower pressure ⟨use the bellows to ~ air on the forge⟩; *specif* **:** to eject (breathed air) from the lungs during normal or forced exhalation ⟨don't ~ your breath in my face⟩ **b :** to set (gas or vapor) in motion (as by the action of a fan) ⟨the fan *blew* the hot air about our heads⟩ **c :** to force a current of gas or vapor upon, through, or into, usu. to produce a particular effect (as of warming, cooling, drying) ⟨come on out, let the breeze ~ your hair dry⟩ ⟨~ the fire into a good blaze⟩ ⟨oil being *blown* with air and oxygen⟩ **d** (1) **:** to force air through (molten metal) to refine (as in a Bessemer or other converter) (2) **:** to force air into (as a blast furnace) to support the combustion of coke **2 a :** to play on (a wind instrument); *also, slang* **:** to play jazz on (any instrument) **b :** to sound a signal for (as an assault or retreat) on a wind instrument **c :** to sound (as a note or blast) on or with a wind instrument **d** *of a wind instrument* **:** SOUND **e :** to direct (hunting dogs) with the sound of a horn **f :** to play (jazz) on an instrument **3 a :** to spread by report **:** noise abroad **:** make public **:** DISCLOSE ⟨through the court his courtesy was *blown* —John Dryden⟩ — now usu. used with *about* or *abroad* ⟨they have *blown* all sorts of silly rumors about⟩ **b** *obs* **:** to give utterance to **:** UTTER — used esp. of emotional expression **c** *archaic* **:** to inform against (a person) or inform a person of (as an act or secret) **:** BETRAY — formerly used with *up;* now only in the phrase *blow the gaff* **d :** DARN, DAMN, BLAST ⟨~ it, my watch has stopped⟩; *often* **:** pay no attention to **:** put aside from consideration **:** IGNORE, DISREGARD ⟨~ the expense⟩ ⟨risk be *blowed*⟩ **4 a :** to drive, activate, or act upon with a current of gas or vapor ⟨the storm *blew* the boat aground⟩ **b :** to clear of contents by the passage of such a current: (1) **:** to free (the nose) of mucus and debris by forcible exhalation (2) **:** to empty (an egg) by forcing out the contents through one small hole with a current of air introduced through another small hole (3) **:** to expel (the contents of a wood-pulp digester) by relief of pressure at the completion of a cook **5 a :** to distend with or as if with gas **:** blow up **:** BLOAT ⟨his face *blown* out like a bladder⟩ ⟨small boys ~*ing* their balloons⟩ **b** *obs* **:** to puff up with pride ⟨look how imagination ~*s* him —Shak.⟩ **c :** to expand and shape (glass) by the action of injected air **d :** to produce or shape (as a glass vessel) by the action of blown or injected air ⟨~*ing* iridescent soap bubbles⟩ ⟨the wind *blew* a hollow on the edge of the dune⟩ **6** *of insects* **:** to deposit eggs or larvae on or in — now used only of blowflies and flesh flies ⟨wounds *blown* by flies often healed faster than supposedly clean wounds⟩ **7 :** to shatter, burst, or destroy by explosion — used commonly with *out, in,* or *up* ⟨be ready to charge when we ~ in the gate⟩ or with phrases expressing degree of damage ⟨they were *blown* to bits⟩ **8 a :** to put out of breath **:** cause to pant with fatigue ⟨take it easy on the hills or you'll ~ your horse⟩ **b :** to let (as a horse) pause to catch the breath — often used with *out* **c** *of a saddle horse* **:** to keep the chest of expanded by holding the breath while being girthed — used with *out* ⟨the stud frequently *blew* himself out⟩ **9 a :** to spend (money) recklessly or extravagantly **:** SQUANDER ⟨he *blew* his pay at the gambling tables⟩ **b :** to treat with unusual or lavish expenditure — used with *to* ⟨come on, I'll ~ you to a steak⟩ ⟨I may live on beans for a month, but I'm going to ~ myself to a really good handbag now⟩ **10 :** to cause (a fuse) to blow **11 :** to rupture (as a seal or cover) by too much pressure ⟨the engine *blew* a head gasket⟩ **12** *slang* **:** to lose control of (a winning position) **:** toss away **:** MISPLAY, MUFF ⟨two chances to win and he *blew* them both⟩ ⟨~ an easy putt⟩ **13 :** to leave esp. hurriedly ⟨he *blew* town after running up huge bills⟩ — **blow a fuse** *or* **blow a gasket** *slang* **:** to exhibit anger **:** become enraged **:** make a big fuss ⟨when he saw what they had done he like to *blew a fuse*⟩ — **blow great guns** *of wind* **:** to blow furiously and with roaring gusts — **blow hot and cold :** to be favorable at one moment and adverse the next **:** react or respond both favorably and unfavorably **:** SHILLY-SHALLY — **blow into** *slang* **:** to appear or arrive at casually or unexpectedly ⟨he just *blew into* town last night⟩ — **blow one's horn** *or* **blow one's own horn :** to praise oneself **:** boast of one's achievements — **blow one's lines 1** *theater* **:** to forget one's lines or make an error in speaking them **2 :** to deviate from an announced or prescribed course **:** fall into inconsistency **:** FALTER ⟨before the week was out he had *blown his lines* as president and perhaps blown the Democratic party out of office —*Time*⟩ — **blow one's top** *or* **blow one's lid** *or* **blow one's stack** *slang* **:** to lose control of oneself: **a :** to become furiously angry **:** be incoherent with rage **b :** to go crazy **:** become insane — **blow the lid :** to expose something to view — usu. used with *off* ⟨this book *blew the lid* off the secret corruption and gangsterism in these unions⟩ — **blow the whistle** *slang* **:** BETRAY, INFORM — **blow upon :** to bring into disrepute or discredit **:** render unsavory or worthless **:** BLEMISH, TAINT, DEFAME ⟨the reputation of her house, which was never *blown upon* before, was utterly destroyed —Henry Fielding⟩
²**blow** \"\ *n* -s **1 a :** a blowing of wind esp. when strong or violent **:** WINDSTORM, GALE ⟨recurrent ~*s* sweep the coastal islands bare⟩ **2 :** the act of certain insects of depositing eggs or larvae; *sometimes* **:** a larva so deposited (as in a wound) — used chiefly of blowflies and flesh flies **3 a :** BOASTING, BRAG **b** *slang* **:** BOASTER **4 a :** an act or instance of forcing air through or from some instrument ⟨give the fire a ~ with the bellows⟩ ⟨a single loud ~ of his horn⟩ **b :** forcible ejection of air from the body (as in freeing the nose of mucus and debris) ⟨Junior, give your nose a good ~ before we start⟩ **5 :** the spouting of a whale **6 a :** a short rest **:** BREATHING SPELL, BREATHER **b :** a brief stop (of a horse) for rest **7 a :** PARISON **b :** the vacuity in the stem of certain blown-glass vessels **8 :** HUFF 5 **9** *slang* **:** a social affair; *esp* **:** BLOWOUT, BINGE, SPREE **10 :** BLOAT 2 — usu. pl. but sing. or pl. in constr. **11 a :** a leak in the packing of a valve or cylinder (as of a steam locomotive) **b :** the failure of a cofferdam or dike causing a sudden inrush of water through or under the structure **12 :** BLOWHOLE **13 a :** the period in the manufacture of water gas in which a blast of air is admitted to the ignited fuel bed for heating the bed by combustion before the run **b :** the blowing of gas from an open well **c** (1) **:** the blast of air forced through molten metal to refine it (as in a Bessemer or other converter) (2) **:** the time during which air is being forced through molten metal to refine it (3) **:** the quantity of metal refined during that time
³**blow** \"\ *vb* **blew; blown** *or obs* **blowe; blowing; blows** [ME *blowen,* fr. OE *blōwan;* akin to OHG *bluoen* to bloom, L *florēre* to bloom, *flos* flower, *folium* leaf, Gk *phyllon*] *vi* **:** FLOWER, BLOSSOM, BLOOM ⟨I know a bank where the wild thyme ~*s* —Shak.⟩ ~ *vt* **1** *archaic* **:** to cause to blossom **2** *obs* **:** to put forth (blossoms or flowers) ⟨banks that ~ flowers —John Milton⟩
⁴**blow** \"\ *n* -s **1 a :** a display of flowers ⟨the south border made a fine ~ this spring⟩ **b :** ²BLOOM 1b — used chiefly in the phrases *in blow, in full blow* ⟨the old lilac by the fence is in full ~⟩ **c** *archaic* **:** an individual flower **2 :** full and perfect development **:** ²BLOOM 2b **3 a :** BLOSSOM 4 **b :** BLOWOUT 8
⁵**blow** \"\ *n* -s [ME (northern dial.) *blaw;* perh. akin to OHG *bliuwan* to beat, ON *blegthi* wedge, Goth *bliggwan* to beat, OE *bealu* evil — more at BALE] **1 a :** a forcible stroke delivered with a part of the body (as the fist or head) or with an instrument (as a hammer) **:** BUFFET, PUNCH, SLAP **b** *Austral* **:** a single stroke in shearing sheep **c** *slang* **:** BASE HIT **2 :** a hostile act or state **:** COMBAT, FIGHTING — usu. used in pl. and used esp. in the phrase *come to blows* ⟨nations like small boys have come to ~*s* over the most trivial issues⟩ **3 :** a forcible, determined, or sudden and unexpected act or effort **:** IMPACT, ASSAULT ⟨such a language . . . would solve many of his . . . difficulties at a single ~ —Edward Sapir⟩ ⟨shall we not support the downtrodden in their ~ for freedom⟩ **4 :** a severe and usu. sudden misfortune or calamity ⟨hail at this season was like a ~ from heaven⟩ **:** something that suddenly or unexpectedly produces mental, physical, or financial suffering or loss ⟨the loss of her husband was a ~ from which she never recovered⟩ **5** *sports* **:** MISPLAY; *specif* **:** failure to bowl a spare when no split exists — **at a blow :** SUDDENLY **:** at one effort **:** by a single vigorous act
blow accordion *n* **:** an accordion in which the air is furnished by the player's lungs
blow away *vt* **:** to dissipate or remove (something) as if with a current of air ⟨the whole well-ordered system has been *blown away* —Roger Fry⟩ ⟨even this caution . . . might well be *blown away* by the rush of buying . . . before the holiday —*Newsweek*⟩
blowback \ˈ=ˌ=\ *n* -s *often attrib* [*blow back,* v.] **1 :** an act of blowing back; *esp* **:** escape backward of imperfectly burned gunpowder after a shot **2 :** the action of a recoil-operated automatic or semiautomatic weapon that uses in its operation no locking or inertia mechanism to delay the rearward motion of the slide or breechblock; *also* **:** a weapon using such an action
blowball \ˈ=ˌ=\ *n* **:** a fluffy seed ball (as of the dandelion); *also* **:** a plant bearing such a ball
blow-by \ˈ=ˌ=\ *n* -s [*blow by,* v.] **:** leakage of gas or liquid between a piston and its cylinder during operation
blow-by-blow \ˌ=ˌ=ˈ=\ *adj* **:** minutely detailed ⟨a *blow-by-blow* account of the campaign⟩
blowcase \ˈ=ˌ=\ *n* **:** ACID EGG
blow down *vt* **:** to blow off
blowdown \ˈ=ˌ=\ *n* -s [*blow down*] **1 a :** the action of blowing down something **b :** a severe wind storm that blows over trees or structures **c :** WINDFALL **:** an area in which trees have been blown down **2 a :** the act or process of blowing off **b :** an apparatus for blowing off steam or gas
blowdown tunnel *n* **:** an intermittent wind tunnel in which the air flow is produced by the rapid discharge of a high-pressure storage tank or by suction from an evacuated reservoir
blowdown turbine *n* **:** a turbine driven by the escaping exhaust gases of a reciprocating internal-combustion engine
blowed *dial past of* BLOW
blow·en \ˈblōən, ˈblau̇ən\ *n* -s [origin unknown] **:** WENCH, STRUMPET
blow·er \ˈblōə(r)\ *n* -s [ME, fr. OE *blāwere,* fr. *blāwan* to blow + -*ere* -er — more at BLOW] **1 :** one that blows; *specif* **:** a worker who blows something (as furs), produces something (as glassware) by blowing, or operates a blowing machine or blowing equipment (as a blast furnace) **2 :** PUFFER 4a **3 a :** a boastful person **:** BRAGGART **4** *slang* **a :** a communication system; *esp* **:** a closed or private system (as between police headquarters and cruisers on duty or between bookmakers and their representatives at a track) **b :** the receiving device of such a system **5 :** a device for producing a current of air or gas (as to increase the draft of a furnace, ventilate a building or shaft, cool electronic equipment, or move or raise hay, silage, grain, or sawdust pneumatically)
blowfish \ˈ=ˌ=\ *n* **1 :** PUFFER 4a **2** *South* **:** WALLEYED PIKE
blowfly \ˈ=ˌ=\ *n* **:** any of various two-winged flies (family Calliphoridae) that deposit their eggs or maggots on meat and other foodstuffs or in wounds on living creatures; *esp* **:** the widely distributed bluebottle (*Calliphora vicina*) that is larger than the housefly and has a dark steel-blue abdomen and hairy thorax — compare STRIKE
blow gas *n* **:** gas leaving the generator during a blow period in the manufacture of water gas
blowgun \ˈ=ˌ=\ *n* **1 :** a tube (as of cane or reed) generally about 10 feet long through which a projectile (as a poisoned dart) may be impelled by the force of the breath **2 :** a device used for cleaning or spraying with a blast (as of air or liquid)
blowhard \ˈ=ˌ=\ *n* -s [¹*blow* + *hard* (adv.)] **:** BRAGGART
blowhole \ˈ=ˌ=\ *n* -s **1 :** a hole in a metal ingot or casting caused by a bubble of gas captured in the solidifying metal and constituting a flaw or defect **2 :** a nostril in the top of the head of a whale or other cetacean, there being two in the whalebone whales and only one in the toothed whales and related forms **3 :** a hole or fissure in rocks along a shore through which incoming waves force air to rush upward or water to spout intermittently **4 :** a hole in the ice to which aquatic mammals (as whales or seals) come to breathe
blowier *comparative of* BLOWY
blowiest *superlative of* BLOWY
blow in *vi* **1** *slang* **:** to appear or arrive casually or unexpectedly ⟨he *blew in* last night about eight⟩ **2** *of gas or an oil well* **:** to come into production **:** start discharging oil and gas ~ *vt* **:** to start (a blast furnace) in operation — opposed to *blow out*
blow·ing \ˈblōiŋ, -ēŋ\ *n* -s [ME, fr. OE *blāwung,* fr. *blāwan* to blow + -*ung* -ing — more at BLOW] **1 :** a noise caused by the forcible ejection of air, steam, or gas **2 :** a sound that is habitually produced by the vibration of the nostrils in some horses during breathing and is not considered an unsoundness or associated with roaring **3 :** a step in the processing of textile fibers, fabrics, or furs in which air or steam is forced through the material **4 :** a process of forming hollow wares (as of plastic) by use of internal pressure (as of compressed air) to press the material against the inside of a mold — called also *blow molding*
blowing adder *or* **blowing viper** *n* [so called fr. its habit of distending the surface of its head before striking] **:** HOGNOSE SNAKE
blowing agent *n* **:** a substance (as sodium bicarbonate) that produces gas used in making expanded cellular or spongy products (as of rubber)
blowing cave *or* **blowing cavern** *n* **:** a cave into or from which a strong current of air passes
blowing charge *n* **:** a small charge of powder or of a mixture of powder and coal dust having just sufficient strength to blow out the fuse plug of a shell without rupturing the shell
blowing cone *n* **:** a small volcanic cone built up of congealed drops of lava from which steam or other vapors escape — compare DRIBLET CONE
blowing iron *n* **:** BLOWPIPE 4
blowing machine *n* **:** a machine for blowing bottles and other hollow glassware
blowing pipe *or* **blowing tube** *n* **:** BLOWPIPE 4
blowing–up \ˌ==ˈ=\ *n, pl* **blowings–up** [fr. gerund of *blow up*] **:** a violent scolding
blow·iron \ˈblō+ˌ-\ *n* **:** BLOWPIPE 4
blowlamp \ˈ=ˌ=\ *n* **:** BLOWTORCH
blow land *n* **:** land subject to wind erosion
blowline \ˈ=ˌ=\ *n* **:** a fishing line so light that the wind will carry it with the lure out over the stream
blow·mo·bile \ˈblōmōˌbēl, -məˌ-, -ˌbil\ *n* [blend of ¹*blow* and *snowmobile*] **:** a sledge driven by an airplane propeller
blow mold *n* **:** a usu. hinged mold in which a glass article may be shaped as it is blown
blow molding *n* **:** BLOWING 4
¹**blown** *adj* [ME *blowen,* fr. OE *geblōwen,* fr. past part. of *blōwan* to blossom — more at BLOW] **1** *of a flower* **:** OPEN **2** *of a place or plant* **:** covered with flowers **:** FLOWERY
²**blown** *adj* [ME *blowen,* fr. past part. of *blowen* to blow — more at BLOW] **1 :** SWOLLEN, INFLATED, DISTENDED: **a** *of animals* **:** having the stomach distended (as with food that develops gas) **:** afflicted with bloat **b** *of a sealed food container* **:** swollen or misshapen by pressure resulting from spoilage of the contents **2 :** moved or acted upon by moving air or vapor ⟨~ clouds⟩ ⟨~ soil mounded on window sills⟩ **3 a :** SPOILED, TAINTED — used esp. of food **b :** infested with fly larvae **:** FLY-BLOWN ⟨caring for ~ sheep⟩ **4 :** out of breath **:** TIRED, EXHAUSTED ⟨their horses much ~ —Sir Walter Scott⟩ **5 :** destroyed or broken to pieces by explosion ⟨troops delayed by a ~ bridge⟩
³**blown** *n* -s **:** BLOAT 2
blown glass *n* **:** glassware shaped by forcing air into a ball of molten glass
blown–in–the–bottle \ˌ===ˌ==\ *adj* **:** GENUINE, INDUBITABLE
blown joint *n* **:** a plumbing joint formed in soft metal (as lead) by means of a blowtorch
blown–molded \ˈ=ˌ==\ *also* **blown–mold** \ˈ=ˌ=\ *adj, of glassware* **:** produced by blow molding
blown oil *n* **1 :** a thickened oil obtained by blowing a fatty oil (as linseed oil or a fish oil) and used in paints and varnishes as a drying oil and in lubricants — called also *oxidized oil;* compare BODIED OIL **2 :** a semisolid or solid substance (as an asphalt) obtained by blowing fluid bitumens or residual oils from the distillation of petroleum and used in paints and protective coatings
blown–out shot \ˈ=ˌ=-\ *n* **:** a blast in which the explosive action breaks little or no coal or rock
blown pattern *n* **:** the unevenly distributed pattern of shotgun pellets that results from the charge of shot overtaking the front wadding of the shell and being disrupted in flight
blown three–mold \ˈ=ˌ=ˌ=\ *adj, of glassware* **:** produced by blow molding in a mold of two or more pieces and designed to simulate hand-cut glass
blown–up \ˈ=ˌ=\ *adj* **:** ENLARGED ⟨a *blown-up* photograph⟩ **:** BLOATED ⟨a *blown-up* person⟩ **:** pointlessly or artificially elaborated ⟨a *blown-up* part in a play⟩
blow off *vi* **1 :** to let steam escape through a passage provided for the purpose ⟨the engine is *blowing off*⟩ **2** *slang* **a :** COMPLAIN, GRIPE ⟨always *blowing off* about his superiors⟩ **b :** to speak earnestly and forthrightly ~ *vt* **1 a :** to empty (a boiler) of water through the blowoff pipe while under steam pressure **b :** to eject (steam, water, or sediment) from a boiler **2 :** to relieve (as emotional tension) by vigorous speech or action ⟨all the repressed eagerness of his young years must now be *blown off* —Donn Byrne⟩ ⟨having *blown off* his indigestion⟩ **3 :** to clean (a dusty place) with an air blast ⟨all looms are *blown off* three times each week — *Textiles Industries*⟩ — **blow off steam :** to relieve physical or emotional tension, ill temper, or resentment by vigorous activity or talk; *specif* **:** to talk freely on the topic of one's grievance
blowoff \ˈ=ˌ=\ *n* -s [*blow off*] **1 a :** a blowing off of or as if of steam, water, or other fluid (as from a boiler); *sometimes* **:** something that is blown off ⟨the drought has made the soil ~ very bad this year⟩ **b :** SPREE, BINGE **2 :** a device for blowing off steam or gas or for discharging water or accumulated matter from pipe lines and sewers **3 :** a climax esp. when marked by a shift from relative passivity to vigorous action ⟨the ~ had come when he had lodged his thousandth complaint about the food —Don Tracy⟩ **:** a strong reaction to an existent condition ⟨upset the military balance of the area, and made some kind of ~ inevitable —*Time*⟩ **4** *slang* **:** a main or featured attraction **:** DRAWING CARD; *esp* **:** a special usu. vulgar performance that follows the main performance in some carnivals and side shows
blow out *vi* **1** *of a flame* **:** to be extinguished by a gust (as of wind) **2 :** to be driven out by the expansive force of a gas or vapor ⟨a spark plug may *blow out*⟩ **3 a** *of a pneumatic tire* **:** to rupture spontaneously in service usu. at a point previously weakened or damaged **b** *of an oil or gas well* **:** to erupt out of control **4** *of a storm* **:** to dissipate by blowing **5** *of an electric fuse* **:** to melt under an excess of current **6 :** to explode without doing any useful work (as of a shot in a drill hole in mining) ~ *vt* **1 :** to extinguish (a flame) by a gust or puff (as of air) ⟨with one puff *blew out* the candle she was wishing on⟩ **2 a :** to clear of contents by blowing **:** clean (as a pipeline) by a current of air **b :** to remove (as dirt or an occlusion) by the action of a current of gas or vapor ⟨keep the pressure up until you have *blown* all the oil *out* of the line⟩ **3 :** to put (a blast furnace) out of operation — opposed to *blow in* **4 :** to walk or exercise (a horse) either to loosen his muscles for further exertion or to prevent chilling and stiffening after a hard workout **5 :** to dissipate (itself) by blowing — used of storms of which wind is a marked feature ⟨many hurricanes *blow* themselves *out* over the sea⟩ ⟨you'll have to stay here until the blizzard *blows* itself *out*⟩ **6 :** to cause (a pneumatic tire or other container)

to burst because of internal pressure ⟨*blew out* a tire⟩ **7 :** to cause (an electric fuse) to blow out **8 :** to deflect and extinguish (an arc or spark) ⟨the magnetic field *blows out* an arc⟩
blowout \ˈ⸗,⸗\ *n* -s [*blow out*] **1** *slang* **:** a big social affair **:** a convivial party or celebration typically featuring abundant food and drink **2 :** an outburst of temper or disorder **:** ROW **3 a :** a bursting of a container caused by the weight or pressure of the contained material (as of a cofferdam by the weight of water, of a tube pipe by the expansive force of contained gas, or of a pneumatic tire by pressure of the contained air on a weak spot) **b :** the hole made in the container by such bursting **c :** the sudden escape of air from the working chamber of a pneumatic caisson **d :** SAND BOIL **e :** an uncontrolled eruption of an oil or gas well due to excessive natural pressure **4 :** a valley or depression blown out by the wind in areas of shifting sand or of light cultivated soil **5 a** *of an electric fuse* **:** the action of blowing out or the condition of being blown out **b :** MAGNETIC BLOWOUT **6 :** a toy or novelty device consisting essentially of a flexible rolled tube that straightens and extends suddenly when the breath is blown into its open end **7 :** eversion or prolapse of the oviduct of domestic poultry through the vent, being a frequent disorder of heavy-laying hens **8 :** the irregular surface outcrop of certain mineral deposits **9 :** FLAMEOUT **10 :** the lateral thrust of an explosion, being of the extent of its horizontal range of effectiveness
blowout grass \"-\ *n* **:** any of several grasses growing on interior sand dunes in the western U.S. (esp. *Redfieldia flexuosa* and *Muhlenbergia pungens*)
blow over *vi* **:** to pass away without effect **:** DISSIPATE, SCATTER ⟨it looked like rain but the clouds have all *blown over* now⟩ ⟨be patient, your troubles will soon *blow over*⟩
blowpipe \ˈ⸗,⸗\ *n* **1 :** a small tubular instrument for directing a jet of air or other gas into a flame so as to concentrate and increase the heat, used esp. in analysis in which the nature of a substance is studied by means of its characteristic behavior (as with respect to fusibility, flame coloration, or formation of volatile coatings) when exposed to the flame **2 a :** a small simple tubular instrument tapered to a straight or slightly curved tip used in anatomy and zoology for revealing or cleaning a cavity **b :** a blowgun for ejecting compressed air **3 :** BLOWGUN 1 **4** *or* **blowing pipe :** a long metal tube on the end of which a glassmaker gathers a quantity of molten glass and through which he blows to expand and shape it **5 :** BLOWTORCH; *esp* **:** one using acetylene and oxygen (as for cutting metal or welding)
blowpit \ˈ⸗,⸗\ *n* **:** a pit or tank into which the contents of a digester are blown at the completion of a cook in papermaking
blowpoint \ˈ⸗,⸗\ *n* **:** an old game prob. of blowing arrows at a mark
blow·proof \ˈ⸗;⸗\ *adj* **:** proof against failure by blowing out ⟨a ~ gasket⟩
blow run *n* **:** an operation sometimes performed in the making of water gas in which part or all of the blow gas is recovered
blows *pl of* BLOW, *pres 3d sing of* BLOW
blowse \ˈblau̇z\ *var of* BLOWZE
blowsed *var of* BLOWZED
blows·i·ly *or* **blowz·i·ly** \ˈblau̇zəlē, -li\ *adv* **:** in a blowsy manner
blow snake *n* [so called fr. its habit of distending the surface of its head before striking] **:** HOGNOSE SNAKE
blow steam *n* **:** the steam escaping from a digester charge when it is blown in papermaking
blowsy *also* **blowzy** *or* **blousy** \ˈblau̇zē, -zi\ *adj* -ER/-EST [*blowse* or *blowze* or *blouse* + -*y*] **1** *of a person* **:** coarse and ruddy-faced **:** fat and ruddy **:** high-colored and well-fed **2 :** DISHEVELED, FROWSY ⟨a careless ~ wench⟩ ⟨lived in a series of ~ rooms⟩; *often* **:** giving an effect of dishevelment (as by reason of imperfect planning, inattention to detail, or omission of needed polish and finish) ⟨~ novels⟩ ⟨~ metaphysical abstractions —Brendan Gill⟩ **syn** see SLATTERNLY
blow tank *n* **:** BLOWPIT
blowth \ˈblōth\ *n* -s [fr. ³*blow*, after E *grow: growth*] *now dial* **:** the stage of blossoming **:** BLOOM ⟨the bushes were in the ~⟩
blowtorch \ˈ⸗,⸗\ *n* **:** a small portable blast burner either supplied with gaseous fuel and air or oxygen through tubes or including a fuel tank (as for kerosene or gasoline) that is pressurized by a hand pump, used esp. in plumbing — called also *blast lamp, blowlamp*

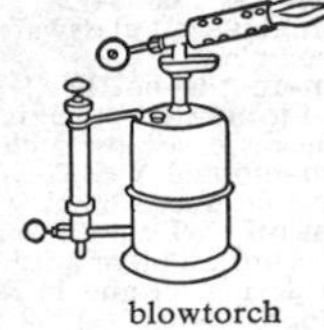
blowtorch

blowtube \ˈ⸗,⸗\ *n* **1 :** BLOWGUN 1 **2 :** BLOWPIPE 4
blow up *vt* **1 :** to rend apart, shatter, or destroy by explosion — compare BLOW *vt* 7 **2 a :** to destroy or damage as if by explosion ⟨many biographies have cruelly *blown up* the reputations of some of the great men in history⟩; *esp* **:** to impair the validity, credibility, or significance of ⟨these facts completely *blew up* the case against him⟩ **b :** to reprimand sharply or harshly **3 a :** to fill with or as if with air ⟨*blowing up* a balloon⟩ **b :** to inflate esp. with pride or self-conceit ⟨they *blew him up* to ridiculous proportions with their childish adulation⟩ **c :** to expand (as a relatively minor issue) to unreasonable proportions ⟨it is easy to *blow up* the medical school out of all proportion to its place in the university structure —Morley Callaghan⟩ **4 a :** to bring into existence (bad weather) — usu. used with *it* as an impersonal nominative ⟨it looks as though it may *blow up* a storm by nightfall⟩ **b** *archaic* **:** to stir up (as animosity, discord, anger) **:** EXCITE, AROUSE **5 a :** to make an enlargement of (as a photograph) **b :** to enlarge an image of a motion-picture film by optical printing from (a smaller one) ⟨he *blew up* an 8 mm to a 16 mm film⟩ **c :** to enlarge (as original copy or cuts) photographically ~ *vi* **1 a** *of explosives* **:** EXPLODE ⟨all the charges *blew up* at once⟩ **b :** to be disrupted by explosion ⟨it looked as though half the town had *blown up*⟩ **2 a :** to be destroyed as if by explosion ⟨saw his academic career *blow up* in a tabloid scandal —*Time*⟩ **b :** FAIL, COLLAPSE; *esp* **:** to fail to stand up under careful scrutiny or stress ⟨on further investigation the case *blew up*⟩ ⟨many an experienced player *blows up* in his lines on opening night⟩ **c :** to lose self-control; *esp* **:** to become violently angry or abusive ⟨he finally *blew up* and fairly screamed with rage⟩ **3 a :** to become filled with or as if with air **:** SWELL ⟨this tire won't *blow up*, the valve must be blocked⟩ **b :** to become expanded esp. to unreasonable proportions ⟨this matter could *blow up* out of sight if someone doesn't set it straight⟩ **4 a** *of bad weather* **:** to come in on or as if on a blowing of wind — often used with *it* as an impersonal nominative ⟨it's going to *blow up* cold⟩ **b :** to come to the fore **:** appear suddenly or unexpectedly **:** arise without warning ⟨where will the next international crisis *blow up*⟩ ⟨a foolish argument *blew up*⟩ — **blow up in one's face :** to fail completely and publicly esp. in such a way as to embarrass ⟨his whole scheme *blew up in his face*⟩
blowup \ˈ⸗,⸗\ *n* -s [*blow up*] **1 :** a blowing up: as **a :** EXPLOSION **b :** an outburst of temper **c :** a photographic enlargement (as of original art work, engravings, or type proofs); *sometimes* **:** the production of such blowups **2 :** failure (of a pavement) involving heaving due to excessive expansion **3 :** a tank where crude sugar is dissolved; *also* **:** one in which a solution of crude sugar is clarified
blowy \ˈblōē, -i\ *adj* -ER/-EST [²*blow* + -*y*] **1 :** WINDY ⟨a chill ~ day⟩ **2 :** subject to the action of wind ⟨~ sloping land⟩; *esp* **:** readily blown about ⟨soft full ~ skirts⟩
blowze \ˈblau̇z\ *n* -s [origin unknown] **1** *now dial Eng* **:** WENCH; *esp* **:** a beggar wench **2** *now dial Eng* **:** a coarse or untidy woman **3** *now dial Eng* **:** a wild girl **:** HOYDEN
blowzed *also* **blowsed** \ˈblau̇zd\ *adj* [*blowze* or *blowse* + -*ed*] **:** BLOWSY
blowzily *var of* BLOWSILY
blowzy *var of* BLOWSY
blr *abbr* boiler
BLR *abbr* breech-loading rifle
BLs *pl of* BL
blst *abbr* ballast
blt *abbr* built
blub \ˈbləb\ *vi* **blubbed; blubbed; blubbing; blubs** [by shortening] **:** BLUBBER 2
¹**blub·ber** \ˈbləbə(r)\ *n* -s [ME *bluber, blober* bubble, foam, prob. of imit. origin] **1 :** a large sea nettle or medusa **2 :** fat which lies between the skin and muscular flesh of whales and other large marine mammals, which serves as an insulating layer, and from which oil is obtained **3 :** superfluous fat on a person or animal **4** [²*blubber*] **:** the act or sound of blubbering
²**blubber** \"\ *vb* **blubbered; blubbered; blubbering** \-b(ə)riŋ\ **blubbers** [ME *blubren, blobren,* fr. *bluber, blober,* n.] *vi* **1 :** to make a bubbling sound **:** issue with a bubbling sound — often used with *up* or *out* **2 :** to weep noisily and excessively **:** SOB ⟨she wept, she ~*ed*, and she tore her hair —Jonathan Swift⟩ ~ *vt* **1 :** to swell or distort with weeping **:** wet with tears ⟨her face all ~*ed* from weeping⟩ **2 :** to utter haltingly while weeping **:** pour out (words) in tearful broken phrases ⟨he ~*s* all his troubles to the world⟩
³**blubber** \"\ *adj* [ME *blaber-* (in *blaber-lipped* blubber-lipped), prob. of imit. origin like ME *bluber, blober* bubble] **:** puffed out **:** THICK ⟨full ~ lips⟩ ⟨*blubber*-cheeked⟩
⁴**blubber** \ˈbləbə(r)\ *adj* [¹*blubber*] **1 :** used for removing blubber esp. in whaling ⟨~ hook⟩ ⟨~ spade⟩ **2 :** using blubber as a fuel ⟨~ lamp⟩ ⟨~ stove⟩
blub·ber·er \ˈbləbərə(r)\ *n* -s **1 :** one that blubbers **2 :** one that scrapes blubber from sealskins
blubber finger *n* [¹*blubber*] **:** SEAL FINGER
blubbering *n* -s [fr. pres. part. of *blubber*] **:** noisy weeping
blub·ber·ing·ly *adv* **:** in a blubbering manner
blubber oil *n* [⁴*blubber*] **:** oil obtained from blubber; *esp* **:** WHALE OIL
¹**blub·bery** \ˈbləb(ə)rē, -ri\ *adj* [³*blubber* + -*y*] **:** ³BLUBBER ⟨her lips grew broader and more ~ —David Garnett⟩
²**blubbery** \"\ *adj* [¹*blubber* + -*y*] **:** having or characterized by large or excessive amounts of blubber or fat ⟨a coarse ~ individual for whom he formed an instant dislike⟩
blu·cher \ˈblükə(r), -üchə(r)\ *n* -s [after G.L.von *Blücher* †1819 Prussian field marshal] **1 :** a shoe having the tongue and vamp cut in one piece and the quarters lapped over the vamp and laced together for closing **2 :** the highest bid in the game of napoleon

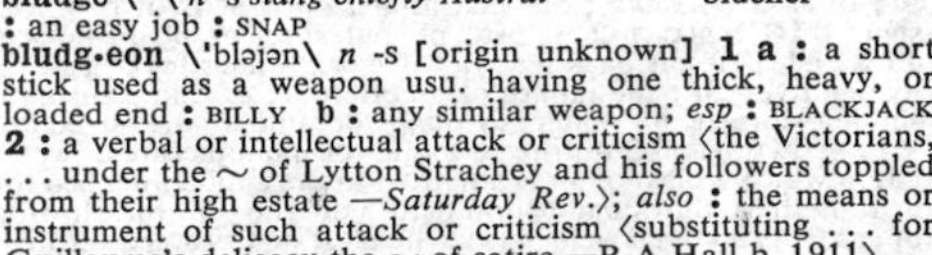
blucher

blude \blüd\ *Scot var of* BLOOD
¹**bludge** \ˈbləj\ *vb* -ED/-ING/-S [prob. back-formation fr. *bludger*] *vi, slang chiefly Austral* **:** to avoid responsibilities or hard work ~ *vt, slang chiefly Austral* **:** to take advantage of **:** impose on
²**bludge** \"\ *n* -s *slang chiefly Austral* **:** an easy job **:** SNAP
¹**bludg·eon** \ˈbləjən\ *n* -s [origin unknown] **1 a :** a short stick used as a weapon usu. having one thick, heavy, or loaded end **:** BILLY **b :** any similar weapon; *esp* **:** BLACKJACK **2 :** a verbal or intellectual attack or criticism ⟨the Victorians, . . . under the ~ of Lytton Strachey and his followers toppled from their high estate —*Saturday Rev.*⟩; *also* **:** the means or instrument of such attack or criticism ⟨substituting . . . for Guillaume's delicacy the ~ of satire —R.A.Hall b. 1911⟩
²**bludgeon** \"\ *vt* **bludgeoned; bludgeoned; bludgeoning** \-j(ə)niŋ\ **bludgeons 1 :** to hit with a bludgeon **:** BEAT ⟨~*ed* to death⟩ **2 :** to overcome by aggressive argument **:** OVERBEAR, BULLY ⟨we do not talk — we ~ one another with facts and theories —Henry Miller⟩ ⟨conversationally ~*s* his way through the world —Wyndham Lewis⟩ **3 :** COERCE ⟨~*ed* into learning grammatical rules⟩
bludg·er \ˈbləjə(r)\ *n* -s [fr. earlier *bludger* pimp, prob. contr. of *bludgeoner* pimp, bully, fr. ²*bludgeon* + -*er*] *chiefly Austral* **:** LOAFER, SHIRKER
¹**blue** \ˈblü\ *adj, usu* -ER/-EST [ME *bleu, blew,* fr. OF *blo, blou,* of Gmc origin; akin to OHG *blāo* blue, ON *blār* dark blue, livid; akin to L *flavus* yellow, OE *bǣl* fire, pyre — more at BALD] **1 a :** of the color blue ⟨~ violets⟩ ⟨as ~ as a sapphire⟩ **b :** having the color of the clear sky or the deep sea ⟨the ~ firmament⟩ ⟨the ~ ocean⟩ **2 a :** tinged with blue **:** BLUISH ⟨the ~ haze of tobacco smoke⟩ ⟨~ as a vein⟩ ⟨the ~ mountains⟩ ⟨the milk was ~⟩ ⟨the candle burned ~⟩ ⟨~ lightning⟩ **b** *of the skin* **:** livid esp. with cold or from a blow ⟨a face ~ from the damp —T.B.Costain⟩ **c** *of the coat of an animal* **:** bluish gray ⟨a short-haired ~ cat⟩ **3 a :** low in spirits **:** MELANCHOLY, DEPRESSED ⟨she was ~ and lonesome and half sick —J.B.Benefield⟩ **b :** productive of low spirits **:** UNPROMISING, DEPRESSING ⟨things looked ~ for them⟩ **4 a :** wearing blue ⟨the painting is called "The Blue Boy"⟩ **b :** having blue as a distinguishing color ⟨the ~ team defeated the red team⟩ **c :** of or relating to a blue lodge of Freemasons ⟨~ Masonry⟩ **5** *of a woman* **:** really or affectedly learned **:** INTELLECTUAL ⟨the ladies were very ~ and well-informed —W.M. Thackeray⟩ **6 :** characterized by or derived from rigid morals **:** PURITANICAL ⟨a ~ Sunday city by local option —James Street⟩ **7 a :** characterized by indecency or obscenity **:** OFF-COLOR, RISQUÉ ⟨the same joke each time — and a bit *bluer* than anything Charlie had ever heard before in mixed company —J.B.Priestley⟩ **b :** characterized by or filled with cursing and swearing **:** PROFANE ⟨~ language⟩ ⟨shop owners turned the air ~ at a mass meeting —*Time*⟩ **8 :** EXTREME, COMPLETE — used as an intensive ⟨the very name . . . put her in a ~ fear —R.L.Stevenson⟩ **9 :** relating to, suggesting, or suited to blues singing or playing ⟨*blue*-voiced⟩ ⟨a ~ song⟩ — **blue in the face :** in a state of extreme anger or exasperation ⟨argued until he was *blue in the face*⟩
²**blue** \"\ *n* -s [ME *bleu, blew,* fr. *bleu, blew,* adj.] **1 a :** a color whose hue is that of the clear sky or that of the portion of the color spectrum lying between green and violet **b :** the one of the four psychologically primary hues that is evoked in the average normal observer under normal conditions by radiant energy of the wavelength 475 millimicrons **c :** one of the six psychologically primary object colors **2 a :** any of certain varieties of gray having a bluish appearance — used esp. of pelage or plumage colors in dogs, cats, and poultry **b :** an animal having a coat of such a blue **3 a :** a pigment or dye that colors blue **b :** BLUING 2 **4 a :** blue clothing or cloth ⟨the boys in ~⟩ **b :** one wearing blue or belonging to an organization or party whose uniform or badge is blue ⟨next time you see the ~ ashore —Rudyard Kipling⟩ **5 a** (1) **:** SKY ⟨boomerangs that were once hurled into the ~ —A.J.Toynbee⟩ (2) **:** the far distance **:** SPACE ⟨chuck up Seville and go off somewhere into the ~ —William Sansom⟩ **b :** SEA, OCEAN ⟨the Marianas were right out in the ~ —Fletcher Pratt⟩ **6 :** an object that is blue in color or that belongs to a group whose characteristic color is blue ⟨pieces of Nanking ~⟩ ⟨the poker player bought a stack of ~*s*⟩ **7** [by shortening] **:** BLUESTOCKING **8 a :** a student who represents Oxford or Cambridge University in athletic contests and is awarded the right to wear the university color ⟨was an Oxford ~ in cricket⟩ **b :** the right to wear such a university color ⟨won his ~ in tennis at Cambridge⟩ **9 :** any of numerous small chiefly blue butterflies of the family Lycaenidae **10 a :** the blue third circle of an archery target **b :** a shot that hits such a circle **11 :** first place or first prize **:** BLUE RIBBON ⟨won the ~ at the horse show⟩ **12 :** BLUE CHEESE **13** *Austral* **:** an argument or fight ⟨he got mixed up in a ~⟩ — **out of the blue :** without preliminary warning **:** UNEXPECTEDLY ⟨the job was offered to me *out of the blue* —F.A.Swinnerton⟩
³**blue** \"\ *vb* **blued; blued; blueing** *or* **bluing; blues** [¹*blue*] *vt* **1 :** to make blue in color: as **a :** to dye or paint blue **b :** to apply bluing to **c :** to make blue (as steel, rifle barrels, or razor blades) by heating in air, steam, or appropriate chemicals — see BLUE HEAT **2** *slang Brit* **:** to spend lavishly or wastefully **:** SQUANDER ⟨while they've got money they ~ it —Ngaio Marsh⟩ ~ *vi* **:** to turn blue
blue acara *n* **:** a small brightly marked acara (*Aequidens latifrons*) of northern So. America having each scale blotched with bright blue and being a popular tropical aquarium fish
blue alert *n* **:** the second stage of alert (as for a threatened air attack or an approaching storm) during which emergency preparations are carried out according to plan; *also* **:** the signal for this — compare RED ALERT, WHITE ALERT, YELLOW ALERT
blue andalusian *n, usu cap A&B* **:** a blue-gray domestic fowl produced by interbreeding black and white Andalusians
blue-and-yel·low macaw \ˌ⸗ˌ⸗ˌ⸗-\ *n* **:** a So. American macaw (*Ara ararauna*) predominantly blue and yellow
blue anemone *n* **:** SQUIRREL CUP
blue angel *or* **blue angelfish** *n* **:** a common chaetodont angelfish of Florida and the West Indies
blue ant *n* **:** a large solitary metallic blue or purple Australian wasp (*Diamma bicolor*) with red legs and antennae, the female being without wings but having a powerful sting
blue asbestos *n* **:** CROCIDOLITE
blue ash *n* **:** an ash (*Fraxinus quadrangulata*) of the central and southern U.S. having bluish green foliage and hard brown wood
blue ashes *n pl but usu sing in constr* **:** AZURITE BLUE
blue baby *n* **:** an infant with a bluish or dusky tint from birth; *specif* **:** one with a congenital defect of the heart in which the flow of venous blood to the lungs is impeded, resulting in the mingling of venous and arterial blood and deficient oxygenation of the hemoglobin
blue-baby operation \ˈ⸗ˈ⸗⸗-\ *n* **:** BLALOCK-TAUSSIG OPERATION
blueback \ˈ⸗,⸗\ *n* **1 :** any of various fishes (as lake herring or glut herring) having a blue or bluish color on the back **2** [so called fr. the contrast of the blue ink used on its back to the green ink used on the back of the Northern greenback] *archaic* **:** a paper note of Confederate money **3 :** a bluish discoloration of the backs of turkeys resulting from dissemination of feather pigment through the skin when immature feathers are broken **4** [so called fr. the color of the coat] **:** a young hooded seal
blueback mullet *n* **:** LEBRANCHO
blueback salmon *n* **:** a salmon of a species (*Oncorhynchus nerka*) that includes the landlocked kokanee and the sockeye
blueback trout *n* **:** a trout somewhat bluish above: as **a :** OQUASSA **b :** a rainbow trout of a variety restricted to Crescent Lake, Wash.
blue bag *n* **1 :** a barrister's brief bag made of blue material **2 :** gangrenous mastitis of sheep — called also *black bag, black garget, black udder*
blue ball *n* **:** BLUE SCABIOUS
blue basic lead sulfate *n* **:** BLUE LEAD 2
blue bass \-ˈbas\ *n* **:** any of various somewhat blue marine or freshwater fishes (as the black sea bass, the sargo, or the green sunfish)
bluebead \ˈ⸗,⸗\ *also* **bluebead lily** *n* [so called fr. the beadlike blue fruit] **:** YELLOW CLINTONIA
blue bear *n* **:** GLACIER BEAR
¹**bluebeard** \ˈ⸗,⸗\ *n* [after *Bluebeard*, a fairy-tale character who murdered six wives, trans. of F *Barbe-Bleue*, the best-known literary version being by Charles Perrault †1703 Fr. writer] **:** a man who marries and kills one wife after another
²**bluebeard** \"\ *adj* [after *Bluebeard*, the fairy-tale character; fr. his having hidden the bodies of his murdered wives in a room which his seventh wife was forbidden to enter] **:** not to be entered or explored **:** FORBIDDEN ⟨the ~ room of the house —Thomas De Quincey⟩
³**bluebeard** \"\ *n* -s [¹*blue* + *beard*; fr. the appearance of the flower] **:** a shrub of the genus *Caryopteris*; *esp* **:** an autumn-blooming Asiatic ornamental (*C. incana*) with blue flowers suggesting those of a spirea — called also *blue spirea*
blue beardtongue *n* **:** a Rocky Mountain penstemon (*Pentstemon virens*) having bluish foliage and deep-blue flowers with conspicuous yellow-bearded sterile stamens
blue beech *n* **:** AMERICAN HORNBEAM
bluebell \ˈ⸗,⸗\ *n* **1 :** a plant of the genus *Campanula*, many species of which bear flowers shaped like bells; *esp* **:** HAREBELL 1 **2 :** either of two European plants having racemes of drooping blue flowers shaped like bells: **a :** WOOD HYACINTH **b :** GRAPE HYACINTH **3 :** any of a number of American plants having blue flowers shaped somewhat like bells (as *Viorna crispa, Mertensia virginica, Polemonium reptans, Veronica americana*) **4 :** GARDEN COLUMBINE **5** *NewZeal* **:** any of several plants of the genus *Wahlenbergia* of the bellflower family; *esp* **:** a low tufted plant (*W. gracilis*) that has blue flowers that are shaped like bells
bluebells-of-scotland \ˈ⸗,⸗⸗ˈskätlənd\ *n pl, cap S* **:** HAREBELL 1
blue·ber·ry \ˈblü,berē, -b(ə)rē, -ri — *see* BERRY\ *n* **1 a :** the sweet edible blue or blackish berry of any of several plants of the genus *Vaccinium* — see HUCKLEBERRY **b :** any plant that bears this fruit **2 a** (1) **:** the edible berry of an Australian tree (*Myoporum serratum*) — called also *native currant, palberry* (2) **:** the tree that bears this fruit — called also *cockatoo bush, native juniper, native myrtle* **b :** the fruit of the blueberry ash
blueberry ash *or* **blueberry tree** *n* **:** any of several Australian trees of the genus *Elaeocarpus* (as *E. obovatus* and *E. reticulatus*) that yield a strong white wood and bear an edible drupe
blue·ber·ry·ing \ˈblü,berēiŋ\ *n* **:** the act of gathering or looking for blueberries
blueberry maggot *n* **:** the larva of a trypetid fly (*Rhagoletis mendax*) that is similar in habits to the apple maggot but usu. attacks blueberries
blueberry root *n* **:** BLUE COHOSH
blueberry thrips *n* **:** a thrips insect (*Frankliniella vacinii*) prevalent in commercial blueberry areas of eastern Canada feeding on and causing twisting and curling of the leaves and sometimes loss of fruit
blue bice *n* **:** AZURITE BLUE
bluebill \ˈ⸗,⸗\ *n* **:** any of various American ducks: as **a :** SCAUP DUCK **b :** WIDGEON **c :** RUDDY DUCK
blue billy *n* [prob. fr. the name *Billy*] **:** a petrel (*Pachyptila desolata*) of the southern oceans with a bluish back and white underparts
blue bindweed *n* **:** BITTERSWEET 2a
blue birch *n* **:** a small tree (*Betula caeruleo-grandis*) growing in dry soils of northeastern No. America and having ovate to deltoid sharply serrate leaves and catkin scales with widely divergent lateral lobes
bluebird \ˈ⸗,⸗\ *n* **1 :** any of several small No. American songbirds (genus *Sialia*) which are related to the robin and the males of which are conspicuously blue above, the male of the common migratory species (*S. sialis*) of the eastern and central U. S. having a blue back and reddish breast — see MOUNTAIN BLUEBIRD, WESTERN BLUEBIRD **2 :** FAIRY BLUEBIRD **3 :** a moderate blue that is greener and duller than average copen and redder and deeper than azurite blue, Dresden blue, or pompadour
blue bird *n* **:** a member of the Blue Birds, the junior program of Camp Fire Girls for girls aged 7, 8 and 9
blue biskop *n* **:** BLACK BISKOP
blue-black \ˈ⸗ˈ⸗\ *adj* **:** extremely dark; *esp* **:** black with a tinge of blue
blue black *n* **1 :** a pigment of a blue-black color (as a vegetable black or a carbon black) **2 :** a dye producing a blue-black color
blue blazer *n, often cap both Bs* [so called fr. the blue flame of the ignited whiskey] **:** a cocktail made of ignited Scotch whiskey and boiling water with sweetening and lemon peel added
blue blazing star *n* **:** a blazing star (*Liatris squarrosa*) with purplish blue flowers
blue blindness *n* **:** TRITANOPIA
blue blood *n* [trans. of Sp *sangre azul*] **1 :** the blood of noble, aristocratic, or socially prominent families **2 a :** a member of a noble, aristocratic, or socially prominent family ⟨a *blue blood* . . . related to half the noble families in the British isles —*Time*⟩ **b :** the nobility or aristocracy **:** the upper classes ⟨one of high rank and birth, of the *blue blood* —Maria Edgeworth⟩ — **blue-blood·ed** \ˈ⸗ˈ⸗⸗\ *adj*
blueblossom \ˈ⸗,⸗⸗\ *n* **:** a blue-flowered California shrub (*Ceanothus thyrsiflorus*) — called also *blue myrtle, California lilac*
blue boneset *n* **:** MISTFLOWER
bluebonnet \ˈ⸗,⸗⸗\ *n* **1 a :** a wide flat round cap of blue wool formerly worn in Scotland **b :** one that wears such a cap; *specif* **:** SCOT **2 a :** BLUE TIT **b :** an Australian parrot (*Psephotus haematogaster*) with bright blue on its forehead, face, and shoulders **3 a :** CORNFLOWER 1b **b :** a low-growing annual lupine of Texas with silky foliage and blue flowers that is now usu. considered to constitute a single somewhat variable species (*Lupinus subcarnosus*) but is sometimes felt to be divisible into two closely related species (*L. subcarnosus* and *L. texensis*) that differ chiefly in habitat and distribution — called also *buffalo clover* **c :** BLUE SCABIOUS
blue book *n* **1** *often cap both Bs* **:** a government publication providing information on any topic (as a manual or register of

officials); *esp* **:** a usu. detailed government report (as the report of a department or commission) ⟨the U.S. Department of State issued . . . a heavily documented 40,000-word *Blue Book* —F.A.Magruder⟩ **2 :** a nongovernmental directory or register esp. of persons of social prominence ⟨the renowned cast that read like the *Blue Book* of the London theatre —Brooks Atkinson⟩ **3 a :** a blank blue-covered booklet used in colleges for writing examinations **b :** a college examination

blue·bot·tle \ˈ=,==\ *n* **1a :** CORNFLOWER 1b; *broadly* **:** any plant of the genus *Centaurea* **b :** GRAPE HYACINTH **2** *Brit* **:** a person wearing a blue uniform; *esp* **:** POLICEMAN ⟨turns out to be the village ~ —P.G.Wodehouse⟩ **3 :** any of several blowflies that are larger than the houseflies, have the abdomen or the whole body iridescent blue in color, and make a loud buzzing noise in flight **4** *chiefly Austral* **:** PORTUGUESE MAN-OF-WAR

blue brant *n* **:** BLUE GOOSE

blue bream *n* **:** BLUEGILL

bluebreast darter \ˈ=,=-\ *or* **blue-breasted darter** \ˈ=,==-\ *n* **:** a brilliantly colored darter (*Poecilichthys camurus*) of clear swift streams from Lake Erie to Tennessee

blue-breasted quail *n* **:** PAINTED QUAIL 1b

blue brick *n* **:** SEWER BRICK

blue brush *n* **:** BLUEBLOSSOM

bluebuck \ˈ=,=\ *n* [trans. of Afrik *bloubok*] **:** BLAUBOK

blue bug *n* **:** CHICKEN TICK

blue bull *n* **:** NILGAI

blue bunch grass *also* **bluebunch fescue** \ˈ=,=-\ *n* **:** a fescue grass (*Festuca idahoensis*) of the western U.S. used as forage

bluebunch wheatgrass *n* **:** a tufted grass (*Agropyron spicatum*) of western No. America used for forage and pasture and having stiff pale leaves and strongly compressed spikelets

blue bur *n* [so called fr. the pale blue flowers] **:** STICKSEED

bluebush \ˈ=,=\ *n* **1 :** a Mexican shrub (*Ceanothus coeruleus*) bearing a profusion of blue flowers **2** *Austral* **:** any of various plants: as **a :** a tomentose saltbush (*Kochia pyramidata*) with short linear leaves **b :** a wattle (*Acacia brachybotrya*) with rather broad phyllodia and linear to narrowly elliptic pods

bluecap \ˈ=,=\ *n* **1 :** BLUEBONNET 1b **2 a :** BLUE TIT **b :** an Australian fairy wren (*Malurus cyaneus*) of which the male is largely bright blue and black in summer plumage **3 a :** FIELD SCABIOUS **b :** CORNFLOWER 1b

blue cardinal flower *n* **:** GREAT LOBELIA

blue cat *or* **blue catfish** *or* **blue channel cat** *or* **blue channel catfish** *n* **:** a large bluish catfish (*Ictalurus furcatus*) of the Mississippi valley that may exceed 100 pounds in weight and is an important food fish

blue cheese *n* [trans. of F *fromage bleu*] **:** a cheese usu. made of cow's milk and marked with veins of greenish blue mold

blue chip *n* **1 a :** a blue-colored poker chip usu. of high value **b :** a valuable asset; *esp* **:** one that can be readily used when needed (as in negotiations) ⟨we've got the *blue chips* in the form of our airplanes and ships and fighting men —*Saturday Rev.*⟩ **2 a :** a stock issue esp. of a well-established corporation with substantial assets that usu. commands a high price in relation to its earnings and to the prices of other stocks as a result of public acceptance and confidence in its stability **:** a quality common stock **b :** a venture, investment, or enterprise that is considered to be among the most secure or consistently profitable or successful in its class ⟨the council's drive is supported by the *blue chips* in the advertising field —*N.Y. Times*⟩

blue-chip \ˈ=;=\ *adj* [*blue chip*] **1 :** of or relating to a blue chip ⟨with the *blue-chip* stocks at record levels, many companies were paying dividends amounting to only 3 percent of their stock purchase price —*Time*⟩ **2 :** being among the leaders in some class **:** being among the most consistently profitable or successful in some field of activity ⟨the *blue-chip* organizations of the electrical world —*Iron Age*⟩ ⟨*blue-chip* farm lands —*Wall Street Jour.*⟩

bluecoat \ˈ=,=\ *n* **:** one that wears a blue coat: as **a :** a soldier esp. of the U.S. during the Civil War **b :** POLICEMAN

bluecoat boy *n* **:** a student at a bluecoat school

bluecoat school *n* **:** any of certain English charity schools whose students wear long blue coats or gowns

blue cod *n* **1 :** any of several marine fishes of the Pacific coast of No. America: as **a :** LINGCOD **b :** CABEZON 1a **c :** SABLEFISH **2 :** a common marine spiny-finned fish (*Parapercis colias*) of New Zealand

blue cohosh *n* **:** a tall herb (*Caulophyllum thalictroides*) of eastern No. America and Asia having triternate leaves, small greenish yellow or purplish flowers, large blue fruits like berries, and a thick knotty rootstock that was formerly used as an antispasmodic and emmenagogue — called also *blueberry root, papooseroot, squawroot*

blue-collar \ˈ=;==\ *adj* [so called fr. the contrast of the typically blue collars of work shirts to the typically white collars of dress shirts] **:** belonging or relating to a broad class of wage earners whose duties call for the wearing of work clothes or protective clothing ⟨warehousemen, longshoremen, farmers, miners, mechanics, construction workers, and other *blue-collar* workers —W.J.Hudson⟩ — compare WHITE-COLLAR

blue comb *also* **blue comb disease** *n* [so called fr. its discoloring effect on the combs of fowls] **:** a severe disease of domestic fowl and certain other birds that resembles Bright's disease of man and is due to unknown causes, although both a virus and excessive consumption of common salt have been implicated and hereditary factors may play a part

blue copperas *n* **:** COPPER SULFATE

blue copper ore *n* **:** AZURITE 1

blue coral *n* **:** a massive coral (*Heliopora coerulea*) with a lamellated calcareous skeleton colored blue by iron salts that is widely distributed in the Indian and southwest Pacific oceans and is the sole recent form of a once abundant order (Coenothecalia)

blue crab *n* **1 :** any of several largely blue swimming crabs of

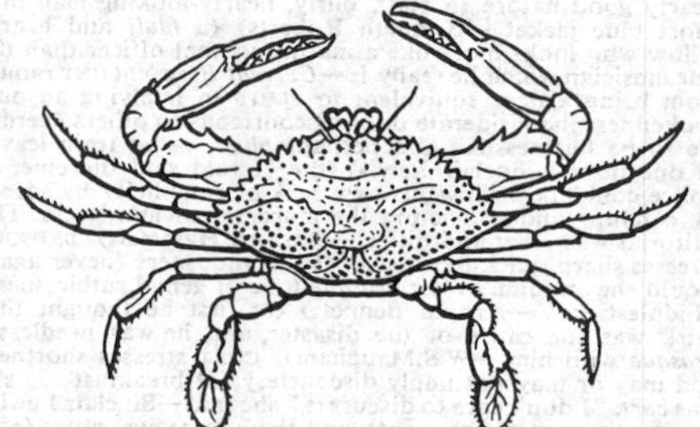

blue crab 1

the genus *Callinectes* of the Atlantic and Gulf coasts of the U.S.; *esp* **:** a crab (*C. sapidus*) that is particularly common from Texas to Delaware and is used extensively as food, providing the soft-shelled crabs of the markets **2** *Austral* **:** an important edible crab (*Portunus pelagicus*)

blue crane *n* **:** GREAT BLUE HERON

blue creeper *n* **:** an Australian vine (*Bredemeyera volubilis*) with showy blue flowers

blue crevally *also* **blue crevalle** *n* **:** a large black-spotted cavalla (*Caranx stellatus*) widely distributed in warmer parts of the Pacific ocean

bluecup \ˈ=,=\ *n* **:** CORNFLOWER 1b

blue curls *n pl but sing or pl in constr* **1 :** a plant of the genus *Trichostema*: as **a :** a plant (*T. dichotomum*) of the eastern U.S. — called also *bastard pennyroyal* **b :** a plant (*T. lanceolatum*) of California **2 :** SELF-HEAL

blued *past of* BLUE

blue daisy *n* **1 :** an Australian herb (*Felicia amelloides*) with blue-rayed flowers resembling the marguerite **2** *Brit* **:** MICHAELMAS DAISY **3 :** CHICORY

blue dandelion *n* **:** CHICORY

blue darner *n* **:** any of certain large strong-flying often chiefly blue dragonflies of the genus *Aeschna*

blue darter *n* **:** any of several hawks (as the sharp-shinned hawk or the Cooper's hawk) having darting erratic flight rather than soaring

blue devil *n* **1 blue devils** *pl* **:** low spirits **:** DESPONDENCY, MELANCHOLY **2 a :** a common blue-rayed aster (*Aster lowrieanus*) of the eastern U.S. **b :** BLUEWEED 1 **3 a :** either of two Australian percoid fishes (*Paraplesiops gigas* and *P. meleagris*) brightly marked with light blue dots **b :** a small brilliantly marked blue fish (*Pomacentrus fuscus*) of the West Indies

blue dicks \-ˈdiks\ *n pl but sing or pl in constr* **:** a wild hyacinth (*Brodiaea capitata*) of the western U.S.

blue discharge *n* **:** a discharge on blue paper formerly issued by the U.S. Army or Air Force to one considered undesirable (as through inefficiency or incompatibility)

blue disease *n* **1 :** CYANOSIS **2 :** ROCKY MOUNTAIN SPOTTED FEVER

blue doe *n* [so called fr. its bluish pelt] **:** a female red kangaroo — called also *blue flier*

blue dog *n* **1 :** SMOOTH DOGFISH **2 :** SAND SHARK a

blue dogwood *n* **:** a shrub or small tree (*Cornus alternifolia*) of eastern No. America with small white flowers and blue fruit — see TREE illustration

blue duck *n* **:** a New Zealand duck (*Hymenolaimus malacorhynchos*) with mostly lead-blue plumage

blue duiker *n* **:** any of several small bluish gray antelopes (genus *Cephalophus*) of southern and equatorial Africa of about the same size and weight as a large hare

blue earth *n* **:** KIMBERLITE

blue elder *or* **blue elderberry** *n* **:** a shrub or small tree (*Sambucus caerulea*) of the western U.S. with white flowers and blue berries covered with a whitish bloom

blue ensign *n* **:** a nautical ensign with a blue field borne by various classes of vessels in British government service other than the Royal Navy, under certain conditions by merchantmen commanded by retired officers of the Royal Navy or by officers of the Royal Naval Reserve, and by many British yacht clubs and yachts — see ENSIGN 1

blue-eye \ˈ=,=\ *n* **1 :** an Australian honey eater (*Entomyzon cyanotis*) **2 :** a small Australian silversides (*Pseudomugil signifer*) used locally in mosquito control and widely known as an aquarium fish **3 :** a faulty or defective eye of a horse; *esp* **:** WALLEYE **4 :** a disease of Indian corn caused by fungi of the genus *Penicillium* and characterized by a rotting and darkening of the germ often after harvesting

blue-eyed \ˈ=;=\ *adj* **1 :** having blue eyes ⟨*blue-eyed* children⟩ **2 :** FAVORED, PREFERRED ⟨the *blue-eyed* boy can do no wrong⟩

blue-eyed babies *n pl* **:** BLUETS

blue-eyed grass *n* **:** a plant of the genus *Sisyrinchium* having grasslike foliage and delicate blue flowers

blue-eyed mary \-ˈmerē, -ma(a)rē,-mārē, -ri\ *n, usu cap M* [fr. the name *Mary*] **1 :** a European navelwort (*Omphalodes verna*) with small blue flowers **2 :** INNOCENCE 3b(1) **3 :** BLUE-EYED GRASS **4 :** a common erect spiderwort (*Tradescantia virginiana*) with blue flowers

blue-faced booby \ˈ=,=-\ *n* **:** a booby (*Sula dactylatra*) of tropical seas that is white with blackish brown tail and wing tips

blue false indigo *n* **:** a wild indigo (*Baptisia australis*) of the eastern U.S. with racemes of blue flowers

blue fescue *n* **:** a variety (*Festuca ovina glauca*) of sheep's fescue with silvery blue foliage

blue field madder *n* **:** FIELD MADDER

blue fig *n* **:** BRISBANE QUANDONG

bluefin \ˈ=,=\ *n* **1 :** a deep-water cisco (*Leucichthys cyanopterus*) of Lake Superior **2** *also* **bluefin tuna :** a very large tuna (*Thunnus thynnus*) with short pectoral fins that is widely distributed in temperate seas

bluefish \ˈ=,=\ *n* **1 :** a very active and voracious fish (*Pomatomus saltatrix*) related to the Carangidae but usu. regarded as constituting a separate family (Pomatomidae) that is distributed in many seas and that is an important food fish on the Atlantic coast of the U.S. **2 :** any of various somewhat dark or bluish fishes: as **a :** ARCTIC GRAYLING **b :** POLLACK **c :** BLACK SEA BASS

blue flag *n* **:** a blue-flowered iris; *esp* **:** a common herb (*Iris versicolor*) the dried rhizome of which has been used as a cathartic and emetic

blue flax *n* **1 :** FLAX 1a **2 :** a perennial flax (*Linum lewisii*) of the desert and mountain regions of No. America and esp. California with blue flowers in loose corymbose clusters

blue flier *n* **:** BLUE DOE

¹blue flower *n, sometimes cap B&F* [trans. of G *blaue blume,* symbol of poetry in *Heinrich von Ofterdingen* (1802), fragmentary novel by Baron Friedrich von Hardenberg (Novalis) †1801 German poet] **:** the mystic vague object of romanticist longing esp. in the 19th century — usu. used with preceding *the* ⟨always in search of the *blue flower* —Willi Apel⟩

²blue flower *n* [ˈ*blue* + *flower*] **:** a pale blue that is redder, lighter, and stronger than average powder blue or Sistine and greener, lighter, and stronger than average cadet gray

blue-footed booby \ˈ=;==-\ *n* **:** a Pacific coast booby (*Sula nebouxi*) that is brownish flecked with white above and white below and has bright blue feet and legs

blue fox *n* **1 a :** a color phase of the arctic fox in which the coat remains blue gray in winter **b :** the typical arctic fox in summer pelage **c :** the pelt or fur of one of these foxes often imitated by dyeing white fox pelts **2 :** a dark reddish gray that is lighter and very slightly yellower than average mauve taupe and less strong and slightly bluer and darker than average rose taupe

blue-fronted jay \ˈ=;==-\ *n* **:** a variety (*Cyanocitta stellere frontalis*) of Steller's jay occurring in the mountains of California

blue gall *n* **:** a small high quality green gall

blue gas *n* **:** uncarbureted water gas burning with a blue nonluminous flame that is used chiefly as a synthesis gas and as a source of hydrogen — distinguished from *blau gas*

blue gentian *n* **1 :** any of several blue-flowered gentians: as **a :** FRINGED GENTIAN **b :** SOAPWORT GENTIAN **c :** CLOSED GENTIAN **2 :** FALSE PENNYROYAL **3 :** an herb (*Eustoma russellianum*) of central No. America with opposite leaves and large purplish flowers

bluegill \ˈ=,=\ *n* *also* **bluegill bream** *or* **bluegill sunfish** *n* **:** a common sunfish (*Lepomis macrochirus*) of the Mississippi drainage, the Great lakes region, and much of the southeastern U.S. that is an excellent panfish and often stocked in artificial ponds to provide both food and sport

blue ginseng *n* **:** BLUE COHOSH

blue glede *n* **:** HEN HARRIER

blue goose *n* **:** a wild goose with a white head and dark plumage that is a genetic color variant of the snow goose (*Chen caerulescens*)

bluegown \ˈ=,=\ *n* [so called fr. the blue gown worn as the badge of office] **:** BEADSMAN 2b

blue grama *n* **:** a grama (*Bouteloua gracilis*) that is an important forage grass in the plains area of No. America and that has the rachis not extended as a point beyond the spikelet — compare BLACK GRAMA

blue grape *n* **:** a native grape (*Vitis aestivalis argentifolia*) of the eastern U.S. with bluish glaucous stems, 3-lobed leaves, and sour bluish black berries

bluegrass \ˈ=,=\ *n, often attrib* [so called fr. the bluish green color of the culms] **1 :** any of several grasses of the genus *Poa* of which some have bluish green culms: as **a :** KENTUCKY BLUEGRASS **b :** WIRE GRASS a **2** *New Zeal* **:** a grass (*Agropyron scabrum*) having leaves usu. scabrous on both sides **3** *Austral* **:** any of several grasses of the genus *Andropogon* **4 :** DUCK GREEN

blue-gray \ˈ=;=\ *n* **:** the offspring of a mating of a white Shorthorn bull with an Aberdeen Angus cow or a Galloway cow, having a mixture of black and white hairs that gives it a bluish appearance and being highly esteemed as a beef animal

blue-gray gnatcatcher *n* **:** a common gnatcatcher (*Polioptila caerulea caerulea*) of the eastern U.S. of which the male is bluish gray above

blue-green alga \ˈ=;=-\ *n* **:** an alga of the division Cyanophyta

blue grosbeak *n* **:** a grosbeak (*Guiraca caerulea*) that is represented by several subspecies in the U.S. and that has the male very dark blue with two chestnut bars on the wing

blue ground *n* [trans. of Afrik *blougrond*] **:** KIMBERLITE

blue grouse *n* **:** any of several obscurely mottled predominantly slaty gray grouses (genus *Dendragapus*) of western No. America; *esp* **:** DUSKY GROUSE

blue gularis *n* **:** GULARIS

blue gum *n* **1 :** any of several Australian timber trees of the genus *Eucalyptus; specif* **:** a tree (*E. globulus*) now much cultivated esp. in California **2 :** a bluish gum held in American Negro folklore to be characteristic of a Negro whose bite is fatally poisonous

blue hawk *n* **:** HEN HARRIER

blue-headed vireo \ˈ=;==-\ *n* **:** a common vireo (*Vireo solitarius solitarius*) of northeastern No. America with the top and sides of the head a bluish slaty gray

bluehearts \ˈ=,=\ *n pl but sing or pl in constr* **:** an American herb (*Buchnera americana*) with rough hairy foliage and blue flowers

blue heat *n* **:** a temperature (as 550° to 600° F) at which iron or steel becomes bluish — compare TEMPER COLOR

blue heeler *n* **:** AUSTRALIAN CATTLE DOG

blue hen's chickens *n pl, usu cap B&H&C* [prob. fr. a nickname for a Delaware regiment in the Revolutionary War, known earlier as *Caldwell's gamecocks,* fr. *blue hen,* a kind of hen reputed to breed good gamecocks] **:** DELAWAREANS

blue heron *n* **:** any of certain herons with somewhat bluish or slaty plumage — see GREAT BLUE HERON, LITTLE BLUE HERON

blue huckleberry *n* **:** DANGLEBERRY

blue ice *n* **1 :** clean compact ice formed in glaciers by recrystallization of snow, often in bands presumably along shear zones **2 :** coarsely crystallized ice on the surface of some seas and lakes — compare BLACK ICE, WHITE ICE

blue indigo *n* **:** BLUE FALSE INDIGO

blueing *var of* BLUING

blueish *var of* BLUISH

blue·jack \ˈblü,jak\ *also* **bluejack oak** *n* [ˈ*blue* + *-jack* (as in *blackjack oak*); fr. the ashy appearance of the foliage] **:** an oak (*Quercus cinerea*) of the southern U.S. with entire cuneate leaves and numerous small acorns

bluejacket \ˈ=,==\ *n* **:** an enlisted man in the navy **:** SAILOR

blue jasmine *or* **blue jessamine** *n* **:** a clematis (*Clematis crispa*) of the southern U.S. with bluish purple flowers

blue jay *n* **1 a :** the common jay (*Cyanocitta cristata*) of eastern No. America with a handsome crest and the plumage of the upper parts chiefly bright blue **b :** any of several related largely blue birds of the western U.S. with crests (genus *Cyanocitta*) or without crests (genus *Aphelocoma*) **2 :** ROAD MONKEY

blue jay 1a

blue jeans *n pl* **:** work pants or overalls usu. made of jean or denim and blue in color **:** DENIMS

blue john \ˈ=,=\ *n* [fr. the name *John*] **1 :** a fibrous or columnar variety of fluorite found in Derbyshire, England and used esp. for vases **2** *sometimes cap J, dial* **:** SKIM MILK; *esp* **:** milk that is just beginning to sour

bluejoint \ˈ=,=\ *n* **1 :** an American forage grass (*Calamagrostis canadensis*) growing in tussocks and having soft flat often involute leaves **2 :** WESTERN WHEATGRASS 1

bluejoint turkeyfoot *n* **:** LITTLE BLUESTEM

blue kite *n* **:** HEN HARRIER

blue krait *n* **:** a black or blue-black Indian krait (*Bungarus caeruleus*) more or less banded with white

blue lace flower *also* **blue lace** *n* **:** a delicate Australian annual herb (*Trachymene coerulea*) of the family Umbelliferae having flat umbels of tiny blue flowers and used as an ornamental

blue land crab *n* **:** BLACK CRAB

blue lavender *n* **:** ONTARIO VIOLET

blue law *n* [ˈ*blue* (puritanical)] **1 :** one of numerous extremely rigorous laws designed to regulate morals and conduct in colonial New England **2 :** a statute regulating work, commerce, and amusements on Sundays

¹blue lead \-ˈlēd\ *n* [*lead* (gravel deposit)] **:** tertiary gold-bearing gravel deposits of the Sierra Nevada

²blue lead \-ˈled\ *n* [*lead* (metal)] **1 :** GALENA **2 :** a slate-gray pigment produced by subliming lead ore with coal or coke and used esp. in rust-resistant paints — called also *blue basic lead sulfate, sublimed blue lead*

blue lettuce *n* **:** a plant of the genus *Lactuca* (as *L. pulchella*) with blue-rayed flower heads

blue light *n* [so called fr. the allegation of Commodore Stephen Decatur †1820 American naval officer that on the night of Dec. 12, 1813 American Federalists traitorously signaled to the British by means of blue lights on either end of the mouth of the harbor at New London, Conn.] **:** a member of that wing of the American Federalist party that bitterly opposed the War of 1812 — usu. used disparagingly

blue lily *n* **:** BLUE FLAG

blue line *n* **1 :** ¹LEAD LINE 1 **2 :** either of two lines colored blue and showing through the ice that divide the defensive zones from the center ice area of an ice-hockey rink

blue lips *n pl but sing or pl in constr* **:** any of several blue-flowered herbs of the genus *Collinsia* of the western U.S.

blue lobelia *n* **:** GREAT LOBELIA

blue lodge *n, usu cap B&L* [so called from the color of the decorations of these degrees] **:** a masonic lodge in which the first three degrees are conferred — compare ENTERED APPRENTICE, FELLOWCRAFT, MASTER MASON

blue lotus *n* **:** either of two blue-flowered cultivated water lilies: **a :** a lotus (*Nymphaea stellata*) of India **b :** a lotus (*N. caerulea*) of Egypt

blue louse *n* **:** any of several sucking lice that infest cattle and sheep

blue lucy *n, often cap L* [fr. the name *Lucy*] **:** SELF-HEAL

blue lupine *or* **blue lupin** *n* **:** a blue-flowered plant of the genus *Lupinus* (as *L. perennis* and *L. angustifolius*) of eastern No. America, useful for forage and for soil-building purposes

blue·ly *adv* **1 :** with a blue or bluish color or tinge **2 :** in a blue manner

blue magnolia *n* **:** CUCUMBER TREE

blue mahoe *or* **blue mahogany** *n* **:** MAJAGUA b

blue mallow *n* **:** DWARF MALLOW

blue marguerite *n* **:** BLUE DAISY 1

blue marlin *n* **:** a very large marlin (*Makaira nigricans*) widely distributed in warm seas

blue mass *n, pharmacy* **:** a pilular preparation containing finely divided mercury — called also *blue pill, mass of mercury*

blue melilot *n* **:** an erect branching annual (*Trigonella coerulea*) grown for its blue and white flowers borne in long-stalked heads — see SAPSAGO

blue metal *n* **:** broken bluestone or basalt used in macadamizing

blue mold *n* **1 :** a fungus of the genus *Penicillium; esp* **:** a mold that produces blue or blue-green surface growths on bread and other foods — compare GREEN MOLD **2** *also* **blue mold rot :** a plant disease caused by a blue-mold fungus **3 :** a serious fungous disease of tobacco seedlings caused by a fungus (*Peronospora tabacina*) and characterized by yellowish spots and a bluish gray mildew on the underside of the leaves — called also *downy mildew*

blue monday *n, often cap B & usu cap M* **:** a Monday that is depressing or trying esp. because of the return to work and routine after a weekend

blue moon *n* **1 :** a very long period of time — usu. used in the phrase *once in a blue moon* ⟨such people happen along only once in a *blue moon* —*Saturday Rev.*⟩ **2 :** the rare blue appearance of the moon that is due to dust particles in the high atmosphere

blue mountain tea *n, usu cap B&M* [fr. the *Blue mountains,* range in Pennsylvania] **:** a goldenrod (*Solidago odora*) of the eastern U.S. from whose aromatic dried leaves a medicinal tea is sometimes made

bluemouth sunfish \ˈ=,=-\ *or* **blue-mouthed sunfish** \ˈ=,=-\ *n* **:** BLUEGILL

blue mud *n* **:** a marine sediment that owes its color to organic matter and iron sulfide

blue myrtle *n* **1 :** BLUEBLOSSOM **2 :** PERIWINKLE
blue·ness \ˈblünəs\ *n* -ES **:** the quality or state of being blue
blue nevus *also* **blue naevus** *n* **:** a small blue or bluish black spot on the skin, sharply circumscribed, rounded, and flat or slightly raised that is usu. benign but often mistaken for a melanoma
blue nightshade *n* **:** BITTERSWEET 2a
blue norther *n* [so called fr. the color of the accompanying cloud bank] **:** a cold wind from the north that brings rapidly falling temperatures to the Kansas, Oklahoma, Texas region
bluenose \ˈ⸗ˌ⸗\ *n* **1** [[1]*blue* (puritanical) + *nose*] **:** one who advocates a rigorous moral code esp. in matters of individual conscience or personal conduct **:** PURITAN ⟨once the ~s were in power they put down all strong language with a brutal hand —H.L.Mencken⟩ **2** *often cap* [perh. so called fr. the extreme cold of the winters in the Maritime Provinces] **:** a native or resident of the Canadian Maritime Provinces; *esp* **:** a native or resident of Nova Scotia — used as a nickname
bluenosed \ˈ⸗ˌ⸗\ *adj* **:** having the characteristics of a bluenose **:** STRAITLACED
blue note *n* [[1]*blue* (of blues singing)] **1 :** a minor interval (as at the third and seventh degree) occurring in a melody or harmony where a major would be expected **2 :** a wrong, off-pitch, or badly sounded note
blue nurse *or* **blue nurse shark** *n* **:** a large viviparous gray or bluish shark (*Carcharias tricuspidatus*) of the Indian and western Pacific oceans often taken for its fins and oily liver
blue oak *n* **:** an oak of the genus *Quercus* (*Q. douglasii*) that occurs on sunny dry foothills and slopes up to about 3000 feet in the California coastal range, has smooth whitish bark, usu. ovoid acorns maturing in one year, and stiff bluish-green deciduous leaves usu. with irregular lobes, and grows to a height of 50 to 75 feet
blue ointment *n* **:** mercurial ointment containing 10 percent of mercury
blue oxalis *n* **:** SHAMROCK PEA
blue palm *n* **1 :** a dwarf fan palm (*Sabal adansonii*) of the southern U.S. having a subterranean stem, spineless petioles, and glaucous leaves **2 :** a fan palm (*Erythea armata*) of Lower California with very glaucous leaves and the leaf segments clothed with white filaments
blue palmetto *n* **:** a dwarf fan palm (*Rhapidophyllum hystrix*) of the southern U.S. having a creeping stem that is clothed with fibrous leaf sheaths and occasional spines and leaves that are long-stalked and somewhat glaucous
blue panic *n* **:** a robust glabrous leafy perennial grass (*Panicum antidotale*) of southeastern U.S. with spikelets that are black at maturity
blue parrot fish *n* **1 :** either of two large chiefly West Indian parrot fishes (*Scarus caeruleus* and *Sparisoma chrysopterum*) **2 :** either of two Australian labrid food fishes (*Choerodon ommopterus* and *C. cyanodus*)
blue pea *n* **:** a tropical vine (*Clitoria ternatea*) with pinnate leaves and bright-blue yellow-centered flowers
blue pelt *n* [so called fr. the bluish tinge of the leather side] **:** a pelt taken before priming is complete
blue pencil *n* **:** any instrument (as a blue pencil) with which an editor makes deletions; *also* **:** the act or an instance of deleting ⟨the book is a good one; vigorous use of a *blue pencil* would have made it better —Keith Hutchison⟩
blue-pencil \ˈ⸗ˈ⸗⸗\ *vt* [*blue pencil*] **:** to edit, delete, or revise with or as if with a blue pencil (as in order to eliminate wordiness or irrelevant material or with the aim of censorship) ⟨used to look over Hemingway's early manuscripts . . . and returned them, mercilessly *blue-penciled*, the adjectives gone —*Time*⟩ ⟨bludgeoned by high-ranking officers into *blue-penciling* everything except vague generalities —*Infantry Jour.*⟩
blue perch *n* **:** any of various bluish fishes: as **a :** CUNNER **b :** PRIESTFISH **c :** HALF-MOON
blue peter *n* [fr. the name *Peter*] **1 :** a blue signal flag with a white square in the center used to indicate that a merchant vessel is ready to sail **2 a :** PURPLE GALLINULE b **b** *Midland* **:** AMERICAN COOT
blue phlox *n* **:** WILD BLUE PHLOX
blue pigeon *n* **:** a dove-gray Australian cuckoo shrike (*Coracina novae-hollandiae*) with black markings on head, throat, wings, and tail
blue pike *n* **1 :** WALLEYE; *also* **:** any other pike perch (genus *Stizostedion*) **2 :** MUSKELLUNGE
blue pill *n* **1 :** a pill of prepared mercury used esp. as an aperient **2 :** BLUE MASS
blue pimpernel *n* **:** MAD-DOG SKULLCAP
blue pine *n* **1 :** BHOTAN PINE **2 :** CANARY PINE
blue plantain-lily *n* **:** a day lily (*Hosta ventricosa*) having blue flowers with a corolla tube that widens suddenly into a bell
blue plate *n* **1 :** a restaurant dinner plate divided into compartments for serving several kinds of food as a single order **2 :** a main course (as of meat and vegetable) served as a single menu item
blue plum *n* **1 :** an Australian tree (*Notelaea quadristaminea*) having an edible fruit like a plum **2 :** a variable color averaging a dark violet that is stronger and slightly lighter than plum purple (sense 2) and redder and less strong than Derby blue
bluepoint \ˈ⸗ˌ⸗\ *n* [fr. *Blue Point*, Long Island] **:** a small oyster typically from the south shore of Long Island and often served on the half shell — compare LYNNHAVEN
blue point *n* [[1]*blue* + *point*] **:** a Siamese cat having a bluish cream body and dark gray points
blue pointer *n* **1** *Austral* **:** BONITO SHARK **2 :** GREAT WHITE SHARK
blue pop *n* **1 :** BLUE GROSBEAK **2 :** INDIGO BUNTING
blue poplar *n* **:** TULIP TREE
blue poppy *n* **:** any of several species of the genus *Meconopsis* (family Papaveraceae) of the north temperate zone
blue powder *n* **:** a mixture of finely divided and partly oxidized metallic zinc formed by the condensation of zinc vapor into droplets; *also* **:** any similar zinc by-product (as dross, skimmings, or sweepings)
[1]**blueprint** \ˈ⸗ˌ⸗\ *n* [[1]*blue* + *print*] **1 a :** a photographic print in white on a bright blue ground made usu. on paper or cloth sensitized with potassium ferricyanide and a ferric salt, developed after exposure by washing in plain water, and used esp. for copying maps, mechanical drawings, and architects' plans — called also *cyanotype* **b :** a photographic print (as of a map, mechanical drawing, or architect's plans) in white and black or other color (as a vandyke) **2 a :** detailed, thoroughly coordinated plan or program of action for effecting some policy or achieving some goal or solution ⟨had drawn up ~s for educating the boys in winter quarters —Dixon Wecter⟩ **3 :** any pattern of action or statement of views, principles, or rules regarded as a guiding program for the achievement of some large objective or objectives ⟨the political leaders of the two countries are guided by the same political ~s —Aneurin Bevan⟩ ⟨books on the American Constitution . . . have guided . . . legislatures in drafting their own national ~s —D.M.Lacy & Paul Hill⟩ **4 :** a body of experience or a completed project or experiment regarded as a model ⟨a workable ~ . . . is afforded by the reclamation projects . . . which have regenerated Palestine —C.J.Rolo⟩
[2]**blueprint** \"\ *vt* **1 :** to make a blueprint of **2 :** to work out (as a program or plan) **:** outline in detail **:** DEVISE, ORGANIZE, FORMULATE ⟨the purpose was to ~ a concrete program for bolstering world prosperity —*Newsweek*⟩
blueprinter \ˈ⸗ˌ⸗⸗\ *n* **:** one that makes blueprints
blueprint paper *n* **:** sensitized paper used in making blueprints
blue quail *n* **1 :** SCALED QUAIL **2 :** a small African quail (*Coturnix adansonii*) or an Asiatic or Australian congener
[1]**bluer** *comparative of* BLUE
[2]**blu·er** \ˈblüə(r)\ *n* -S [[3]*blue* + *-er*] **:** one that works at or supervises bluing: as **a :** a worker who colors the metal parts of guns by immersing them in bluing chemicals or by heat-treating **b :** an auto worker who tests the seating of valves by rotating them after smearing them with a blue compound that will show up high spots
blue racer *n* **:** an American blacksnake of a bluish green subspecies (*Coluber constrictor flaviventris*) occurring in the U.S. from Ohio to Texas
blue rail *n, in Louisiana* **:** GALLINULE
blue ribbon *n* **1 a :** a blue ribbon usu. with appropriate words or markings awarded the first-place winner in a competition **b :** an honor, distinction, or award gained for preeminence in some field ⟨this prize was the *blue ribbon* in mathematical research —*Atlantic*⟩ **2 :** a blue ribbon worn by members of certain temperance organizations
blue-ribbon \ˈ⸗ˈ⸗⸗\ *adj* [*blue ribbon*] **:** of the highest quality **:** carefully selected **:** OUTSTANDING ⟨the *blue-ribbon* event of the social season⟩ ⟨a *blue-ribbon* investigating commission⟩
blue-ribbon jury *n* **:** SPECIAL JURY 2
blue rider *adj, usu cap B&R* [trans. of G *blauer Reiter*, noun phrase] **:** BLAUE REITER
[1]**blue-roan** \ˈ⸗ˈ⸗\ *adj* [[1]*blue* + *roan*] **:** of a roan color produced by mingling of black and white hairs
[2]**blue-roan** \"\ *n* **:** a blue-roan individual (as a horse or dog)
blue rock *n* **:** any of certain somewhat bluish wild or domestic pigeons: as **a** *or* **blue rock pigeon :** ROCK PIGEON **b :** RED-BILLED PIGEON **c :** a blue-barred homing pigeon
blue rot *n* **:** a disease of conifers caused by certain fungi (genus *Ceratostomella*) and producing a blue coloration of the wood — called also *bluing*
blue runner *n* **:** an excellent carangid food fish (*Caranx crysos*) of the warmer parts of the western Atlantic that is bluish green above and golden yellow or silvery below
[1]**blues** *pl of* BLUE, *pres 3d sing of* BLUE
[2]**blues** \ˈblüz\ *n pl but sometimes sing in constr* **1 :** low spirits **:** mental depression **:** DESPONDENCY, MELANCHOLY — usu. used with *the* ⟨staying in this dull place was enough to give anyone the ~ —Joseph Conrad⟩ **2 :** a song sung or composed in a style originating among the American Negroes, characterized typically by the use of three-line stanzas in which the words of the second line repeat the first, expressing a mood of longing or melancholy, and marked by the continual occurrence of blue notes in melody and harmony **3 :** the blue uniform of the U.S. Navy ⟨put on his ~ and went ashore⟩ **4 :** unreserved seats at the two far ends of a circus tent usu. painted blue **syn** see SADNESS
blue sage *n* **1 :** any of several blue-flowered sages of the genus *Salvia*: as **a :** a plant (*S. farinacea*) of Texas **b :** a plant (*S. lancifolia*) of the western U.S. **c :** a plant (*S. azurea*) esp. of dry prairies in the eastern U.S. **2 :** SAGEBRUSH
blue-sail·ors \ˈ⸗ˌ⸗⸗\ *n pl but sing or pl in constr* **:** CHICORY
blue scabious *n* **:** a European herb (*Succisa pratensis*) with opposite leaves and blue flowers
blue sclera *or* **blue sclerotic** *n* **:** FRAGILITAS OSSIUM; *also* **:** the bluish whites of the eyes characteristic of this condition
blue shark *n* **1 :** a voracious and very active pelagic shark (*Prionace glauca*) that may become 20 to 25 feet long and is reputed to be a man-eater **2 :** any of various other sharks; *esp* **:** REQUIN
blue sheep *n* **:** BHARAL
blue shirt *n* **:** one who wears a blue shirt; *esp* **:** a professional fire fighter
bluesides \ˈ⸗ˌ⸗\ *n* **:** a young harp seal
blue skullcap *n* **:** MAD-DOG SKULLCAP
[1]**blue-sky** \ˈ⸗ˈ⸗\ *adj* [so called fr. the emptiness of the sky] **1 :** having little or no value **:** UNSOUND, UNSECURED ⟨*blue-sky* stock⟩ **2 :** ill-defined, grandiose, or excessive in scope or object **:** UNREALISTIC, VISIONARY ⟨mass movements, especially of the *blue-sky* variety —Robert Shaplen⟩
[2]**blue-sky** \"\ *vt* [*blue-sky (law)*] **:** to qualify a security issue for sale in a state under its blue-sky law
blue-sky law \ˈ⸗ˈ⸗-\ *n* [[1]*blue-sky*] **:** a law providing for the regulation and supervision of the sale of stocks, bonds, or other securities
blue slate *n* **:** SLATE BLUE
blue smelt *n* **:** JACKSMELT
blue spirea *n* **:** [3]BLUEBEARD
blue spot *n* **:** a bluish pigmented area near the base of the spine present at birth esp. in infants of Mongoloid ancestry — called also *Mongolian spot*
blue sprat *n* **:** a small clupeoid fish (*Stolephorus robustus*) important as a major food source for the larger sport and food fishes of Australian seas
blue spruce *n* **1 a :** COLORADO SPRUCE; *often* **:** a spruce belonging to a horticultural variety derived from the Colorado spruce **b :** BLACK SPRUCE 1 **2 a :** a variable color averaging a grayish green that is bluer and darker than average bayberry and bluer, lighter, and stronger than slate green **b :** a moderate green that is bluer and paler than average myrtle (sense 3 a) or average laurel green (sense 1) and less strong than sea green (sense 1 a)
blues scale *n* **:** a musical scale having intervals that mutate between major and minor and used esp. in jazz
bluest *superlative of* BLUE
blue stain *also* **blue sap stain** *n* **:** a bluish discoloration of sapwood caused in many trees and esp. conifers by any of various fungi (as of the genera *Ceratostomella, Penicillium*, or *Fusarium*) — compare BLUE ROT
blue star *n* **:** a star of spectral type *O* or *B* having a high surface temperature and a bluish white color (as Rigel)
bluesteel \ˈ⸗ˈ⸗\ *n* **:** a grayish blue that is redder and duller than electric, greener and duller than copenhagen or old china, and redder and darker than Gobelin
blue·stem \ˈ⸗ˌ⸗\ *n* **1 a :** a tall grass (*Andropogon furcatus*) with smooth bluish leaf sheaths and slender spikes borne in pairs or clusters used in the western U.S. for hay **b** *or* **bluestem wheatgrass :** WESTERN WHEATGRASS **1 2 a :** a disease of raspberries and blackberries in the Pacific coast region of northwestern No. America caused by a fungus (*Verticillium alboatrum*) and characterized by bluish black discoloration of the stem, stunting, reduction of vigor, and curling of the leaflets **b :** a similar disease of raspberries in the eastern U.S. believed to be caused by a virus — called also *eastern bluestem*
bluestock·ing \ˈ⸗ˌ⸗⸗\ *n* **1** [after *Bluestocking* society, 18th cent. literary clubs, some of whose members wore informal attire often including blue worsted stockings] **:** a woman having or pretending to have intellectual interests or literary tastes **:** a female scholar ⟨she was sensitive, percipient, but in no sense a ~ —George Mallaby⟩ **2** [so called from the color of its legs] **:** the avocet (*Recurvirostra americana*) of No. America
[1]**bluestone** \ˈ⸗ˌ⸗\ *n* [[1]*blue* + *stone*] **1 :** the hydrated copper sulfate $CuSO_4.5H_2O$ **2 :** a building or paving stone of bluish gray color; *specif* **:** a sandstone quarried near the Hudson river
[2]**bluestone** \"\ *vt* **:** to treat (as a net or a stream) with copper sulfate
blue·ston·er \ˈblüˌstōnə(r)\ *n* **:** one that stains with bluestone
blue·ston·ing \ˈblüˌstōniŋ\ *n* **:** a color effect in clay wares caused by reduction of iron oxide
blue streak *n* **1 :** something that moves very fast ⟨ran like a *blue streak*⟩ **2 :** a constant stream of words **:** a seemingly endless flow ⟨talked a *blue streak*⟩
blue·striped grunt \ˈ⸗ˌ⸗-\ *n* **:** YELLOW GRUNT
blue stuff *n* **:** KIMBERLITE
blue succory *n* **:** a So. European plant (*Catananche coerulea*) having heads of flowers with flat blue rays
blue sunfish *n* **:** BLUEGILL
blue swedish *n* **1** *usu cap B&S* **:** a breed of ducks resembling the Pekins but typically smaller and of a blue-gray color **2** *often cap B&S* **:** a duck of the Blue Swedish breed
blue swimming crab *n* **:** BLUE CRAB
blu·et \ˈblüət\ *n* [prob. fr. [1]*blue* + *-et*] **1 a** *dial Eng* **:** CORNFLOWER **1 b b :** FARKLEBERRY **c** (1) **:** a delicate plant (*Houstonia caerulea*) of the U.S. with 4-parted bluish flowers and tufted stems — often used in pl; called also *innocence, quaker-ladies* (2) **:** a Texas plant (*Houstonia patens*) often only 1 to 2 inches high with a single blue flower **2 :** a light to moderate blue that is redder and stronger than king's blue (sense 1)
blue-tailed skink *or* **blue-tailed lizard** \ˈ⸗ˌ⸗-\ *n* **:** a harmless widely ranging No. American scincoid lizard (*Eumeces fasciatus* syn. *quinquelineatus*) having the under surface of the tail bright azure — called also *five-lined lizard, redheaded lizard, scorpion*
blue tangle *n* **:** DANGLEBERRY
blue thistle *n* **1 :** BLUEWEED 1 **2** *Austral* **:** PRICKLY POPPY
bluethroat \ˈ⸗ˌ⸗\ *n* **:** a singing bird (*Erithacus svecicus*) of northern Europe and Asia
blue·tick \ˈ⸗ˌ⸗\ *n, sometimes cap* **:** a very speedy American hound having a white coat blotched and flecked with bluish gray and sometimes considered a distinct breed
blue tick *n* **:** a southern African tick (*Boophilus decoloratus*) that feeds on cattle, horses, and other domestic animals and transmits several important diseases (as red water and anaplasmosis)
blue tit *n* **:** a widely distributed European titmouse (*Parus caeruleus*) having the crown of the head, wings, and tail bright cobalt blue
blue toadflax *n* **:** a weed (*Linaria canadensis*) of sandy soil on coastal plains esp. in southeastern U.S. with violet or purple flowers
bluetongue \ˈ⸗ˌ⸗\ *n* [trans. of Afrik *bloutong*] **1 :** an African horse sickness in which the lesions are most marked about the head — called also *thickhead* **2 :** a serious virus disease of African sheep that is marked by hyperemia, cyanosis, and punctate hemorrhages and by swelling and sloughing of the epithelium esp. about the mouth and tongue, that sometimes affects goats and in a milder form often simulating foot-and-mouth disease occurs in cattle, that is localized in low-lying or marshy areas, and that is thought to be transmitted by biting midges
blue-tongue *or* **blue-tongued lizard** *n* **1 :** BLUE-TONGUED SKINK **2 :** a lizard (*Tiliqua nigrolutea*) of Tasmania
blue-tongued skink *n* **:** a large and stoutly built Australian scincoid lizard (*Tiliqua scincoides*) often kept as a pet
bluetop \ˈ⸗ˌ⸗\ *n* **1 :** HORSE NETTLE **2 bluetops** *pl* **:** KNAPWEED **3 :** BLUEJOINT 1
blue turquoise *n* **:** a light greenish blue that is bluer, lighter, and stronger than average turquoise blue, bluer and paler than average turquoise (sense 2a), and bluer and deeper than average aqua
blue tussock *n* **:** a valuable grazing grass (*Poa colensoi*) native to New Zealand
blue ultramarine ash *n* **:** a strong to vivid greenish blue
blue verditer *n* **1 :** AZURITE BLUE **2 :** a highly basic copper carbonate used as a blue pigment — compare BREMEN BLUE, MINERAL BLUE 1a
blue vervain *n* **:** a tall weed (*Verbena hastata*) of the eastern U.S. with hastate leaves and slender spikes of blue flowers
blue vetch *n* **:** TUFTED VETCH
blue vi·en·na \-vēˈenə\ *n* **1** *usu cap B&V* **:** a breed of blue-coated rabbits resembling and largely derived from New Zealands **2** *often cap B&V* **:** a rabbit of the Blue Vienna breed
blue vine *n* **:** SAND VINE
blue vinny *n, often cap B&V* **:** a white cheese made of cow's milk and characterized by blue veining — called also *Dorset*
blue vitriol *n* **:** the hydrated copper sulfate $CuSO_4.5H_2O$
blue water *n* **:** the open sea ⟨talk to the swart men just in from *blue water* —D.C.Peattie⟩
blue water gas *n* **:** BLUE GAS
blue water lily *n* **1 :** BLUE LOTUS **2 :** a blue-flowered African water lily (*Nymphaea capensis zanzibariensis*)
blue-wattled crow \ˈ⸗ˌ⸗⸗-\ *n* **:** a passerine bird (*Callaeas wilsoni*) of New Zealand that resembles a starling
blue wavey *n* **:** BLUE GOOSE
blue waxweed *n* **:** WAXWEED
blueweed \ˈ⸗ˌ⸗\ *n* **1 :** a coarse prickly weed (*Echium vulgare*) of Europe that has been naturalized in the U.S. and that has blue flowers in scorpioid spikes — called also *blue devil, blue thistle, viper's bugloss* **2 :** CHICORY **3** *in Texas* **:** a Mexican weed (*Larrea densiflora*) introduced as a range plant for alkali soils **4 :** a small perennial (*Helianthus ciliaris*) that is native in southwestern U.S. and often troublesome as a weed and that has blue-green or gray-green foliage
blue whale *n* **:** a rorqual (*Sibbaldus musculus*) common in the northern and southern oceans and sometimes exceeding 80 feet in length
blue wheat grass *n* **:** BLUEGRASS 2
blue-white \ˈ⸗ˈ⸗\ *adj, of a diamond* **:** colorless and of the highest quality
blue wildebeest *n* [trans. of Afrik *blouwildebees*, fr. *blou* blue + *wildebees* wildebeest — more at WILDEBEEST] **:** BRINDLED GNU
blue wild rye *n* **:** a tufted perennial No. American grass (*Elymus glaucus*) having very long awns on the lemmas and often cultivated for ornament and in northwest U.S. as a forage crop
bluewing \ˈ⸗ˌ⸗\ *n* **:** BLUE-WINGED TEAL
blue-winged goose \ˈblüˌwiŋd-\ *n* **:** an African sheldrake (*Cyanochen cyanopterus*) that superficially resembles a goose
blue-winged teal *n* **:** an American teal (*Anas discors*) resembling the green-winged teal but having blue wing coverts and a large white crescent on each cheek
blue-winged warbler *n* **:** a warbler (*Vermivora pinus*) greenish above, bright yellow below, and with a narrow black line through the eye, found esp. in the east-central U.S.
bluewood \ˈ⸗ˌ⸗\ *n* **1 :** a chaparral shrub (*Condalia obovata*) of western Texas and northern Mexico **2 :** LOGWOOD 2
blue wood aster *n* **:** a common perennial No. American herb (*Aster cordifolius*) with basal cordate leaves and numerous heads of bluish purple flowers
blue wren *n* **:** BLUECAP
[1]**bluey** \ˈblüē\ *adj* [[1]*blue* + *-y*] **:** BLUISH
[2]**bluey** \"\ *n* -S **1** [so called fr. the blue blanket that was commonly used to wrap the bundle] *Austral* **:** a swagman's bundle **2 :** BLUE CRAB 2 **3 :** any of several Australian lizards
blue-yellow blindness \ˈ⸗ˌ⸗⸗-\ *n* **:** TRITANOPIA
[1]**bluff** \ˈbləf\ *adj* -ER/-EST [obs. D *blaf* flat, broad; akin to MLG *blaff* smooth, even] **1 a :** having a broad flattened front ⟨the ~ bows of a ship⟩ **b :** rising steeply with a broad front either flat or rounded ⟨the ~ banks of the river⟩ **2** *dial Eng* **:** SURLY, ROUGH **3 :** having a good-naturedly abrupt, frank, and outspoken manner **:** heartily blunt ⟨a ~ and rugged natural leader with impulsive determination and an explosive personality —John Warner⟩ ⟨a ~ aggressive manner⟩
syn BLUNT, BRUSQUE, CURT, CRUSTY, GRUFF: BLUFF, the only completely complimentary one of these terms, implies a rough, hearty good nature ⟨a *bluff*, burly, hearty-looking man in a short blue jacket —Kenneth Roberts⟩ ⟨a *bluff* and hearty fellow who looks more like a marine combat officer than the fine musician which he really is —*Current Biog.*⟩ BLUNT ranges from being a near equivalent to BLUFF to implying an outspokenness inconsiderate of or discourteous to others ⟨permit me to be businesslike and perhaps *blunt*, as my train leaves in one hour —Sinclair Lewis⟩ ⟨the Herald said the chief of police could best show his own lack of complicity by speedily catching and convicting the murderer or murderers. The editorial was *blunt* and bitter —Dashiell Hammett⟩ BRUSQUE stresses sharp quickness and unceremoniousness ⟨never again would she exclaim, in her *brusque* tone of genial ruthlessness: "Fiddlesticks" —Arnold Bennett⟩ ⟨at first he thought that Dirk was the cause of the disaster, and he was needlessly *brusque* with him —W.S.Maugham⟩ CURT stresses shortness and may or may not imply discourtesy ⟨at breakfast . . . she was *curt*. "I don't care to discuss it," she said —Sinclair Lewis⟩ ⟨it was the first of the month and there were *curt* notes from the water company —John Steinbeck⟩ CRUSTY suggests a harsh, uncivil, irascible manner, sometimes concealing an inner kindliness ⟨the lashing tongue of a *crusty* disciplinarian —F.V.W.Mason⟩ ⟨this *crusty* old lawyer, who had made no bones about his contempt for the tetrarch —L.C.Douglas⟩ GRUFF also implies a harsh surly manner and curt, perhaps guttural, utterance ⟨a man's voice, ill-tempered and *gruff*, rose through the shadowy room —Louis Bromfield⟩ ⟨"Fool" said the sophist, in an undertone *gruff* with contempt —John Keats⟩
[2]**bluff** \"\ *n* -S **1 :** a high steep bank (as by a river or the sea or beside a ravine or plain) **:** a cliff with a broad face ⟨a fort on the ~ overlooking the junction of the rivers⟩ **2** *North* **:** a clump of trees on the open plain **:** GROVE
[3]**bluff** \"\ *vb* -ED/-ING/-S [prob. fr. D *bluffen* to boast, play a kind of card game, fr. MD, to strike, beat, to swell up, alter. of *buffen, boffen*, fr. *buf, bof* blow, swollen face; prob. of imit. origin] *vt* **1** *obs* **:** BLINDFOLD **2 :** to deceive (an opponent in cards) by a bold bet on an inferior hand with the result that the opponent drops a winning hand — often used with *out* **3 a :** to deter, dissuade, or frighten by pretense or a mere show of strength **:** frighten off ⟨with the power of England behind him had ~*ed* the Hamburg merchants out of participating —W.P.Webb⟩ **b :** to cause to believe what is not true **:** MISLEAD, DECEIVE ⟨wanted to ~ them into thinking that the route of

the railroad had been changed⟩ **c** : to make a pretense of : FEIGN ⟨the catcher ~*ed* a throw to first base⟩ ~ *vi* **1 a** : to bet boldly on a poor hand in the hope that an opponent will drop **b** : to make any show of strength not justified by the hand held in a card game with the intention of deceiving an opponent **2** : to make use of pretense, a mere show of strength, or deception : SHAM ⟨it is destructive of public goodwill to ~ or fake when you cannot give the information requested —Lou Smyth⟩

[4]**bluff** \"\ *n* -s **1** : a blinder or blinker esp. for a horse **2** : STRAIGHT POKER **3 a** : an act or instance of bluffing ⟨having . . . nothing to support his pretensions he decided to put up a ~ —Sherwood Anderson⟩ ⟨he put on a good ~⟩ ⟨it was all a ~⟩ **b** : the practice of bluffing ⟨the agreement had been reached after weeks of ~ and haggle —*Time*⟩ **4** : one that bluffs ⟨he was pretty much of a ~⟩

bluff–bowed \ˈ=ˌbau̇d\ *adj* [[1]*bluff*] *of a ship* : having a broad flat bow

bluff·er \ˈbləfə(r)\ *n* -s [[3]*bluff* + *-er*] : one that bluffs

bluff formation *n* [[1]*bluff*] : LOESS

bluff–headed \ˈ=¦==\ *adj* [[1]*bluff*] : BLUFF-BOWED

bluff·ly *adv* [[1]*bluff* + *-ly*] : in a bluff manner

bluff·ness *n* -ES : the quality or state of being bluff

bluffy \ˈbləfē\ *adj, often* -ER/-EST [[2]*bluff* + *-y*] : having or resembling bluffs : STEEP

bluft \ˈbləft\ *vt* -ED/-ING/-S [alter. of [3]*bluff*] *dial Eng* : BLINDFOLD

blug·gy \ˈbləgē\ *adj* [euphemism for [1]*bloody*] : BLOODY

bluid \ˈblüd\ *Scot var of* BLOOD

blu·ing *or* **blue·ing** \ˈblüiŋ\ *n* -s [fr. gerund of [3]*blue*] **1** : the act of making blue ⟨the ~ of steel⟩ **2** : something that gives a bluish tint: as **a** : a rinse for gray or white hair **b** : a preparation of blue or violet dyes used in laundering to counteract the yellowish tinge of white linen or cotton **3** : BLUE ROT

blu·ish *or* **blue·ish** \ˈblüish, -üēsh\ *adj* [ME *blewish*, fr. *bleu, blew* blue + *-ish* — more at BLUE] : somewhat blue : having a tinge of blue ⟨a ~ green⟩ ⟨~ air⟩ — **blu·ish·ness** *or* **blue·ish·ness** *n* -ES

blume \ˈblüm\ *Scot var of* BLOOM

blu·mea \ˈblümēə\ *n, cap* [NL, fr. Karl L. *Blume* †1862 Ger. botanist] : a genus of tropical Australasian and African herbs or shrubs (family Compositae) with simple alternate leaves and discoid purple or yellow flower heads

[1]**blun·der** \ˈbləndə(r)\ *vb* -ED/-ING/-S [ME *blundren, blondren*] *vi* **1** : to move unsteadily, confusedly, or blindly : FLOUNDER, STUMBLE ⟨the cabman ~*ed* up and downstairs with trunks —Arnold Bennett⟩ ⟨in their exhaustion they often ~*ed* against each other —Norman Mailer⟩ **2** : to come or happen by or as if by accident : STUMBLE — usu. used with *on* or *upon* ⟨evidence which I ~*ed* upon in a manuscript —Charlton Laird⟩ **3** : to make a mistake or commit an error usu. as a result of stupidity, ignorance, mental confusion, or carelessness ⟨while he often ~*ed* he usually won his case by sheer energy and persistence —Edward Preble⟩ ~ *vt* **1** *now dial Eng* : to mix up : MUDDLE, ROIL **2** : to utter stupidly, confusedly, or thoughtlessly : BLURT — usu. used with *out* ⟨he ~*ed* out an apology⟩ **3** : to lose usu. by stupidity, carelessness, or thoughtlessness : THROW — usu. used with *away* ⟨it maddens me to see people ~*ing* away thousands of pounds —G.B.Shaw⟩ **4** : to make a stupid, careless, or thoughtless mistake in : BOTCH, BUNGLE, MISMANAGE ⟨the risk we run of ~*ing* matters through ignorance —Rafael Sabatini⟩

[2]**blunder** \"\ *n* -s [ME *blunder, blonder*] : an error or mistake resulting usu. from stupidity, ignorance, mental confusion, or carelessness ⟨the building of light-draft monitors was a costly ~ —H.K.Beale⟩ ⟨his chief ~ is his misconception of Aristotle —H.O.Taylor⟩ **syn** see ERROR

blun·der·bush \ˈbləndərˌbu̇sh\ *dial var of* BLUNDERBUSS

blun·der·buss \ˈbləndə(r)ˌbəs\ *n* -ES [by folk etymology fr. obs. D *donderbus*, fr. *donder* thunder (fr. MD *donder, donre*) + obs. D *bus* gun, fr. MD *busse, bosse* box, tube, gun, fr. LL *buxis* box; akin to OHG *thonar* thunder — more at THUNDER, BOX] **1** : an obsolete short gun or firearm that had a large bore and usu. a bell muzzle, was capable of holding a number of balls, and was intended for shooting at close quarters without exact aim **2** : a blundering person

blunderbuss

blun·der·er \ˈblənd(ə)rə(r)\ *n* -s [ME, fr. *blundren* to blunder + *-er*] : one that blunders; *esp* : one that makes a stupid, careless, or thoughtless mistake

blunderhead \ˈ=ˌ=ˌ=\ *n* [prob. alter. (influenced by [1]*blunder*) of *dunderhead*] : a blundering person — **blun·der·head·ed** \¦==¦==\ *adj*

blundering *adj* : characterized by or given to making blunders : BUNGLING ⟨a ~ attempt to capture the fort⟩ ⟨a ~ lawyer⟩ — **blun·der·ing·ly** *adv*

blunge \ˈblənj\ *vt* -ED/-ING/-S [prob. blend of *blend* and *plunge*] : to amalgamate and blend : beat up or mix in water (as clay to form slip)

blung·er \ˈblənjə(r)\ *n* -s : one that blunges; *specif* : a vat with mechanical stirrers for mixing clay and water into slip

[1]**blunt** \ˈblənt\ *adj* -ER/-EST [ME; perh. akin to ON *blunda* to doze, OE *blind* — more at BLIND] **1 a** : dull or deficient in feeling or perception : INSENSITIVE ⟨served his time by showing how ~ the eyes and ears of writers generally are —Norman Foerster⟩ **b** : slow or obtuse in understanding or discernment : DULL ⟨this consideration will make it evident to a ~*er* discernment than yours —Edmund Burke⟩ **2** : having a thick edge or point : not sharp or keen ⟨the murderous knife was dull and ~ —Shak.⟩ **3** *archaic* : lacking refinement or polish : RUDE, ROUGH ⟨though ~ my tale —Alexander Pope⟩ **4** : abrupt in speech or manner : outspokenly frank : not suave : PLAIN ⟨you are entirely too ~ in your human relations —W.J.Reilly⟩ ⟨the petition was rejected in a ~ one-sentence letter of refusal —Paul Blanshard⟩ **syn** see BLUFF, DULL

[2]**blunt** \"\ *vb* -ED/-ING/-S [ME *blonten* fr. *blunt, blont*, adj.] *vt* **1 a** : to make (as an edge or point) less sharp : DULL ⟨~*ed* the swords⟩ **b** : to make (as an acid or corrosive) less sharp : DILUTE ⟨~*s* the acidity of vinegar⟩ **2** : to make (as the senses or mental faculties) dull or sluggish : DEADEN ⟨diminished men's sense of wonder and ~*ed* their sensitiveness to the great mystery —Aldous Huxley⟩ **3** : to lessen or destroy the force or effectiveness of : WEAKEN ⟨their zeal was quickly ~*ed* by the yawn of habit around them —Bruce Marshall⟩ ⟨the attack was ~*ed*⟩ ~ *vi* : to become dull or less sharp ⟨its edges will never ~ —John Bunyan⟩

[3]**blunt** \"\ *n* -s [[1]*blunt*] **1** : something blunt; *specif* : BLUNT ARROW **2** *slang* : ready cash : MONEY

blunt arrow *n* : an arrow with a blunt head used to kill birds and small game without mangling

blunt dissection *n* : surgical separation of tissue layers by means of an instrument without a cutting edge or by the fingers

blunt file *n* : a file having parallel edges

blunt–head \ˈ=ˌ=\ *n* : a snake of the family Amblycephalidae

blunt·ie \ˈbləntē\ *n* -s [[1]*blunt* + *-ie*] *Scot* : a stupid person

blunt·ly *adv* : in a blunt manner ⟨he is ready to say ~ what every one else is afraid to say —T.S.Eliot⟩

blunt·ness *n* -ES [ME *bluntnes*, fr. *blunt* + *-nes* -ness] : the quality or state or being blunt

blunt–nosed crab \ˈ=¦=ˌ=\ *n* : a large pinkish spider crab (*Hyas lyratus*) of the northwest coast of No. America

[1]**blur** \ˈblər + V -ər-; ˈblə, + V -ər- *also* -ər\ *n* -s [perh. akin to ME *bleren* to blear] **1** : a moral stain or blot : BLEMISH ⟨these ~*s* are too apparent in his life —John Milton⟩ **2** : a smear or stain that obscures but does not efface (as one made with ink on paper) : BLOT ⟨the letter was full of ~*s*⟩ **3 a** : a vague, dim, or confused appearance : INDISTINCTNESS ⟨the ~ of spring foliage in the southeast —Ellen Glasgow⟩ **b** : something seen or perceived as vague or lacking definite outline ⟨picked up his book and pretended to read, turning the pages and staring at a dim ~ of words —Josephine Johnson⟩ **4** : an indistinct somewhat confused sound : HUM ⟨his voice came clearly through the ~ of engines —Vincent McHugh⟩

[2]**blur** \"\ *vb* **blurred**; **blurred**; **blurring**; **blurs** *vt* **1** : to obscure, soil, or blemish by smearing (as with ink) : SMEAR ⟨his damp fingers *blurred* the manuscript⟩ **2** : SULLY, STAIN, BLOT ⟨his reputation was *blurred*⟩ : BLEMISH ⟨an act that ~*s* the grace and blush of modesty —Shak.⟩ **3** : to make dim, indistinct, or vague in outline or character ⟨the needs of association *blurred* the peculiarities among Dane and Swede and Norwegian —Oscar Handlin⟩ ⟨with memory *blurring* out all but the high light —Ernest Beaglehole⟩ **4** : to make dim, imperfect, or confused (as the senses or mental faculties) : DIM, DARKEN ⟨in her nineties time had begun to ~ her senses —W.A.White⟩ ~ *vi* **1** : to make blurs ⟨the moths tapped and *blurred* at the window screen —R.P.Warren⟩ **2** : to become vague, indistinct, or indefinite : DIM ⟨the distinctions of politics in both countries tend to ~ —Frank Gorrell⟩

[1]**blurb** \ˈblərb, ˈbləb, ˈbləib\ *n* -s [coined 1907 by Gelett Burgess †1951 Am. humorist & illustrator] : a short highly commendatory and often extravagant publicity notice; *esp* : such a notice printed on the dust jacket of a book ⟨this book fails to give what the ~ describes —O.G.S.Crawford⟩

[2]**blurb** \"\ *vt* -ED/-ING/-S **1** : to publicize in or by means of a blurb ⟨whom they now ~ as "the Canadian Mark Twain" —*Time*⟩ **2** : to advertise in the extravagant manner often characteristic of a blurb ⟨was ~*ed* as a great novel⟩

blurb·ist \-bəst\ *n* -s : a writer of blurbs ⟨I have no doubt that the ~ was Walt himself —H.S.Canby⟩

blur circle *n* : CIRCLE OF CONFUSION

blurred \ˈblərd, ˈbləd, ˈbləid\ *adj* [fr. past part. of [2]*blur*] **1** : smeared with or as if with ink ⟨~ sheets of paper⟩ **2** : characterized by dimness, indistinctness, or obscurity ⟨the ~ names on the gravestones⟩ ⟨a ~ photograph⟩ : VAGUE, CONFUSED ⟨the ~ aims of the group⟩ ⟨people of ~ and divided minds⟩ — **blur·red·ly** \ˈblərədlē *also* ˈblər-\ *adv*

blur·ry \ˈblərē, -ri *also* ˈblər-\ *adj, sometimes* -ER/-EST [[1]*blur* + *-y*] : BLURRED ⟨a ~ snapshot⟩

[1]**blurt** \ˈblərt, ˈblət, ˈbləit, *usu* d.+V\ *vb* -ED/-ING/-S [prob. of imit. origin] *vt* : to utter abruptly and impulsively : divulge unadvisedly : EJACULATE — usu. used with *out* ⟨you don't leave me any alternative to ~*ing* it out like this —Lester Atwell⟩ ~ *vi* **1** *obs* : to make a contemptuous puffing grimace with the lips **2** : to speak impulsively ⟨while Henry was ~*ing* and Wolsey thundering —Francis Hackett⟩ **syn** see EXCLAIM

[2]**blurt** \"\ *n* -s : an abrupt impulsive utterance ⟨loudly and lengthily denied his undiplomatic ~ —*Time*⟩

[1]**blush** \ˈbləsh\ *vb* -ED/-ING/-ES [ME *blusshen, blisshen*, fr. OE *blyscan* to redden, fr. *blȳsa* flame, torch; akin to MLG *blūs* torch, ON *blys* light, flame, OHG *bluhhen* to burn brightly] *vi* **1** : to become red in the face esp. from shame, modesty, or confusion : FLUSH, COLOR ⟨Clara looked at her aunt and ~*ed* —Sherwood Anderson⟩ ⟨~*ing* more scarlet than ever, slunk off . . . deeply humiliated —Samuel Butler †1902⟩ **2** : to feel shame : be embarrassed ⟨the grossly injurious suspicions which she must ever ~ to have entertained —Jane Austen⟩ ⟨no man ought ever to be called upon to ~ for his wife —W.M.Thackeray⟩ **3 a** : to become red : have a red or rosy color ⟨the skies yet ~*ing* with departing light —Alexander Pope⟩ **b** : to have a fresh color : BLOOM ⟨full many a flower is born to ~ unseen —Thomas Gray⟩ **4** : to assume a cloudy appearance — used of varnish or lacquer films; compare [3]BLOOM 2b ~ *vt* **1** : to make red : REDDEN ⟨a shielded scutcheon ~*ed* with blood of queens and kings —John Keats⟩ **2** *archaic* : to make known by blushing

[2]**blush** \"\ *n* -ES [ME, prob. fr. *blusshen*, v.] **1** : appearance, view, or consideration — used esp. in the phrase *at first blush* ⟨at first ~ the answer seems simple enough —Margaret Mead⟩ **2** : a reddening of the face esp. from shame, modesty, or confusion : FLUSH ⟨a ~ revealed his embarrassment⟩ **3 a** : a red or reddish color ⟨light's last ~*es* tinged the distant hills —George Lyttelton⟩ **b** : a rosy glow : BLOOM ⟨are meant to amuse while the ~ is on them —Charlton Laird⟩ **4 a** : a light brown that is stronger and slightly redder and darker than alesan, lighter and slightly redder than French beige, and redder and lighter than cork — called also *Josephine, rose blush* **b** : an undesirable whitish or milky appearance of films (as of varnish or lacquer), resins, or plastics — compare [2]BLOOM 3f

blushed \ˈbləsht\ *adj* : suffused with a tone of red ⟨the ~ and green sides of apples⟩

blush·er \-shə(r)\ *n* -s **1** : one that blushes **2** *or* **blushing mushroom** : a yellowish edible agaric (*Amanita rubescens*) that usu. turns red when touched

blush·ful \-fəl\ *adj* **1** : full of, given to, or provoking blushes ⟨a ~ flirtation⟩ **2** : blush-colored : RUDDY, ROSY ⟨~ mists⟩ — **blush·ful·ly** \-fəlē\ *adv*

[1]**blushing** *n* -s **1** : the act or process of blushing **2** : BLUSH 4b

[2]**blushing** *adj* : marked by blushes — **blush·ing·ly** *adv*

blush rose *n* : a grayish red that is bluer and duller than bois de rose or Pompeian red, yellower and duller than appleblossom, and bluer and deeper than livid brown

blushy \ˈbləshē\ *adj, often* -ER/-EST : BLUSHFUL

[1]**blus·ter** \ˈbləstə(r)\ *vb* **blustered**; **blustered**; **blustering** \-st(ə)riŋ\ **blusters** [ME *blustren*, prob. fr. MLG *blüsteren* to storm; prob. akin to OHG *blāsan* to blow — more at BLAST] *vi* **1** : to blow in stormy noisy gusts ⟨with clouds spitting snow and wind ~*ing* off the lake —T.W.Duncan⟩ : be windy and boisterous ⟨when autumn ~*s* and the orchard rocks —Robert Browning⟩ **2** : to talk and act with noisy, swaggering, and often empty threats : play the bully : STORM, RAGE ⟨it pleased a people who bragged and ~*ed* but felt themselves outsiders in the world of nations —J.D.Hart⟩ ~ *vt* **1** : to utter with noisy swaggering self-assertiveness ⟨~*ing* I know not what of insolence and love —Alfred Tennyson⟩ **2** : to drive or force by blustering : BULLY, HECTOR ⟨a hurricane ~*ing* its wild way across quiet country —W.S.Maugham⟩ ⟨trying to ~ us into the belief that they are much better than they look —F.A. Swinnerton⟩ **syn** see ROAR

[2]**bluster** \"\ *n* -s **1** : a violent boisterous blowing : STORM, BLAST ⟨the strong breeze driving them was setting up a ~ on the water —Rose Thurburn⟩ **2** : boisterous noise or violent commotion ⟨they do their work without ~ or ostentation —Stanley Walker⟩ **3** : noisy, violent, or threatening talk : boastful empty speech ⟨I don't count his ~ worth a cent —Winston Churchill⟩

blus·ter·er \ˈbləst(ə)rə(r)\ *n* -s : one that blusters

blustering *adj* **1** : blowing boisterously : STORMY, TUMULTUOUS ⟨less violent and ~ than the wind of Patagonia —P.E.James⟩ **2** : uttering noisy often empty threats : SWAGGERING, BULLYING ⟨the ~ army officer appeared with an unruly following —R.A.Billington⟩ — **blus·ter·ing·ly** *adv*

blus·ter·ous \ˈbləst(ə)rəs\ *adj* [[2]*bluster* + *-ous*] : BLUSTERING — **blus·ter·ous·ly** *adv*

blus·tery \ˈbləst(ə)rē, -ri\ *adj* [[2]*bluster* + *-y*] **1** : blowing boisterously : STORMY ⟨a cold ~ day⟩ **2** : noisily self-assertive : SWAGGERING ⟨a brusque ~ man⟩

blut·wurst \ˈblütˌvu̇rst\ *n* -s [G, fr. *blut* blood (fr. OHG *bluot*) + *wurst* sausage, fr. OHG; akin to OHG *werran* to confuse — more at BLOOD, WAR] : BLOOD SAUSAGE

blvd *abbr* boulevard

blype \ˈblīp\ *n* -s [origin unknown] *Scot* : a piece or shred of skin

blythe process \ˈblīth-\ *n, usu cap B* [fr. the name *Blythe*] : a wood-preservative process by which carbolic acid or tar is injected into dried timber

bm *abbr* beam

BM \ˈbēˈem\ *abbr or n* -s : a bowel movement

BM *abbr* **1** basal metabolism **2** [L *beatae memoriae*] of blessed memory **3** bench mark **4** bill of material **5** bishop and martyr **6** board measure **7** brigade major **8** bronze medal **9** burgomaster

b major \(ˈ)bē-\ *n, usu cap B* : the major musical key having a signature of five sharps

BMEP *abbr* brake mean effective pressure

b minor \(ˈ)bē-\ *n, usu cap B* : the minor musical key having a signature of two sharps

BMOC *abbr* big man on campus

BMR *abbr* basal metabolic rate

BMV *abbr* [LL *Beata Maria Virgo*] Blessed Mary the Virgin

bn *abbr* **1** baron **2** battalion **3** beacon **4** been

BN *abbr* bank note

bnd *abbr* **1** band **2** bound

bnss *abbr* baroness

[1]**bo** *var of* BOO

[2]**bo** *also* **boe** \ˈbō\ *n, pl* **boes** [by shortening] *slang* : HOBO

[3]**bo** \"\ *n* -s [prob. short for *bozo* or *hobo*] *slang* : FELLOW, BUDDY — used chiefly in informal address ⟨the truth is, ~, that the man's got a good name —Geoffrey Household⟩

[4]**bo** \"\ *n* -s [Singhalese *bō* — more at BO TREE] : PIPAL

BO *abbr* **1** back order **2** blackout **3** body odor **4** box office **5** branch office **6** broker's order **7** brought over **8** buyer's option

boa \ˈbōə\ *n* [NL, fr. L, a water snake] **1** *cap* : a genus (the type of the family Boidae) of nonvenomous snakes of tropical America **2** -s : a large snake that crushes its prey (as the boa constrictor, anaconda, or python) **3** -s : a long fluffy scarf of fur, feathers, or delicate fabric **4** -s : NILE GREEN

bo·a·bab \ˈbōəˌbab\ *n* -s [by alter.] : BAOBAB

boa constrictor *n* **1** : a tropical American boid snake (*Constrictor constrictor*) that is light brown in color and barred or mottled with darker brown, reaches a length of 10 feet or more, is at home on land or in the water, and climbs freely in search of its prey (as small animals) which it kills by constriction and swallows whole **2** : a large constrictor (as the anaconda or python)

boal \ˈbōl\ *dial var of* [3]BOLE 1

boar \ˈbō(ə)r, -ó(ə)r, -ōə, -óə\ *n* -s [ME *bor*, fr. OE *bār*; akin to OHG & OS *bēr* boar] **1 a** : the uncastrated male of swine **b** : a wild hog (*Sus scrofa*) — see WILD BOAR **2** : the male of any of various mammals (as the guinea pig) ⟨the first coon, a big old ~, came trundling into my camp —Hugh Fosburgh⟩

[1]**board** \ˈbō(ə)rd, -ó(ə)rd, -ōəd, -óəd\ *n* -s [ME *bord* piece of sawed lumber, table, shield, ship's side, border, fr. OE; akin to OHG *bort* ship's side, ON *borth* piece of sawed lumber, table, ship's side, Goth *fotubaurd* footstool, Skt *bardhaka, vardhaka*, adj., cutting off, *bardhaka, vardhaka*, n., carpenter, and perh. to Gk *perthein* to destroy] **1** *obs* : BORDER, SIDE, EDGE **2 a** : the side of a ship **b** : the stretch that a ship makes on one tack in beating to windward : TACK 3e **3 a** : a piece of sawed lumber of little thickness but considerable surface area usu. being rectangular and of a length greatly exceeding its width, in technical specifications of a thickness not exceeding 2½ inches and a width of from 6 to 12 inches, and designated according to thickness ⟨a half-inch ~⟩ ⟨a 2-inch ~⟩ — compare BATTEN; see [4]DEAL, PLANK **b boards** *pl* (1) : STAGE 2b(1) ⟨as good an actor as ever trod the ~*s*⟩ (2) : STAGE 2b(3) ⟨if intellectual ideas were to vanish from the ~*s* I am not sure that my heart would break —Max Beerbohm⟩ **c boards** *pl, slang* : SKIS **4 a** *archaic* : TABLE 3a (1) **b** : a table on which food is customarily served esp. when spread with a meal ⟨bade the fellow call help to clear the ~, where still was set their interrupted noontide meal —Rafael Sabatini⟩ ⟨a feast spread upon the ~⟩ **c** : food in the form of daily meals often provided as payment for services ⟨room and ~⟩ ⟨~ was the most expensive item in his budget⟩ ⟨the job gave him bed, ~, and 10 dollars a week to spend⟩ **d** : a table at which a council or the magistrates of a court sit ⟨sit as a guest at the council ~⟩ **e** : a number of persons appointed or elected to sit in council for the management or investigation of a public or private business, trust, or other organization or institution ⟨a ~ of advisers to the mayor⟩ ⟨~ of directors⟩ ⟨a university examining ~⟩ **f** : LEAGUE, ASSOCIATION ⟨the local ~ of underwriters⟩ **g** : an examination given by an examining board — often used in pl. ⟨passed his ~*s*⟩ **h** (1) : the exposed hands of all the players in a stud poker game (2) : an exposed dummy hand in bridge **5 a** : a flat usu. rectangular piece of material (as wood) often marked off or provided with pegs and used for some special purpose (as the playing of certain games or the providing of a flat or hard surface on which to cut food or set dishes) ⟨a gaming ~⟩ ⟨a molding ~⟩ — see BACKBOARD, SIDEBOARD, SPRINGBOARD, WARPING BOARD **b** : a wall or a specially constructed flat usu. rectangular device attached to a wall or free standing used for varied purposes (as the posting of notices, the listing of stock-market quotations, or the display of theater advertisements esp. where they may be seen by groups or by the general public) ⟨quotations on the ~ of a brokerage house⟩ ⟨~*s* with playbills in front of a theater⟩ **c** : a panel (as of wood) in which electrical circuit components (as jacks) may be inserted **d** : PARI-MUTUEL MACHINE **e** : any of various forms used in finishing fabrics and knitted garments (as hosiery) — see [2]BOARD 8 **f** (1) : a device that is used in bridge for holding the four hands of a deal in their original form so that they may be played more than once (as in duplicate bridge) and that consists usu. of a flat oblong container with four pockets for the hands dealt and is marked on its face to show which player is dealer and who is vulnerable — called also *tray* (2) : the particular distribution of cards in duplicate bridge constituting any one deal as contained in such a board : a deal in duplicate whist or bridge (3) : the entire process of bidding and playing such a deal (4) : the score accruing to the winning side when such a deal is played; *esp* : one match point (5) : the greatest number of match points that can be scored on any deal in duplicate bridge **6 a** : any of various wood pulps or composition materials formed or pressed into somewhat stiff or rigid flat usu. rectangular sheets; *specif* : material of the same general composition as paper but stiffer and usu. thicker, being in one classification at least 12/1000 inch thick — compare PAPER **b** : the stiff foundation piece for the side of a book cover ⟨bound in ~*s*⟩ ⟨~ binding⟩ **c** : PRESSING BOARD **7** *chiefly Austral* **a** : the part of a woolshed where sheep are sheared **b** : the sheep about to be sheared **c** : the crew of shearers **8** : an organized exchange providing facilities for buying and selling securities or commodities **9** : a fixed signal governing the movement of trains ⟨a slow ~⟩ ⟨a clear ~⟩ — **board on board** *or* **board and board** *or* **board by board** *archaic, of ships* : side by side : close beside each other — **go by the board 1** : to go or be carried by force over the side of a ship ⟨in the storm the masts *went by the board*⟩ **2** : to go or be thrown into discard : be passed by and beyond recall — **on board** : ABOARD

[2]**board** \"\ *vb* -ED/-ING -S [ME *borden*, fr. *bord* piece of sawed lumber, table, shield, ship's side, border] *vt* **1** *archaic* : to come up against or alongside of (a ship) usu. for the purpose of attacking **2** : ACCOST, ADDRESS ⟨he ~*ed* me with some light remark —W.A.White⟩ **3 a** : to go on board of or enter (a ship) **b** : ENTER ⟨~ a train⟩ ⟨~ an airplane⟩ : MOUNT ⟨~ a motorcycle⟩ **4** : to cover with boards or boarding ⟨store owners taped and ~*ed* their windows —*Springfield (Mass.) Daily News*⟩ — usu. used with *up* ⟨~*ing* up the windows of the empty house⟩ **5 a** : to provide with regular meals or with regular meals and lodging usu. for a compensation ⟨the question is, will she ~ as well as lodge her guest —Clara Morris⟩ ⟨~*ing* students⟩ **b** : to place where board or board and shelter or other accommodations are provided usu. for a compensation ⟨~ a horse at a livery stable⟩ **6** : to haul (the tack of a course on a sailing vessel) down to the deck or to the bumpkin **7** : to work or rub with a board (as in graining leather) **8** : to shape (knitted garments) by processing on special forms ~ *vi* **1** : TACK *vi* 1 **2** : to have one's regular meals or regular meals and lodging provided usu. for a compensation ⟨having ~*ed* for a time at the Rutledge Tavern —Ruth P. Randall⟩

[3]**board** *var of* BORD

board·a·ble \-d(ə)bəl\ *adj* : capable of being boarded ⟨the ship was not ~ in such a rough sea⟩

board–a–match \¦=ə¦=\ *adj* : being or relating to a method of scoring used in duplicate bridge whereby each board played between two teams of four counts one point for the team making the higher score on the board and ½ point for each team if they make the same score

board–and–batten \¦=ə=¦==\ *also* **board–and–batt** \¦=ə=¦=\ *n* : wall construction that gives the appearance of wide vertical strips with intervening recesses or projections by means of (1) wide boards rabbeted on transverse edges and lapped not to the entire width of the rabbet on one side or (2) wide boards alternating with narrow and thin battens usu. fitting into grooves in the wide boards or (3) wide boards covered at the seams by narrow usu. 2-inch battens

board around *vi* : to board at a succession of houses in a community as part of one's compensation ⟨in the early U.S. country teachers and ministers used to *board around*⟩

board boy *n* : one who marks up-to-date information on a stock quotations board

board check *n* **:** a body check of an opponent in ice hockey against the rink sideboards

board cloth *n, dial Eng* **:** TABLECLOTH

board company *n* **:** a company having membership in an insurance trade association (as one which makes rates and recommends forms and underwriting rules for the guidance of its members)

board drop hammer *n* **:** a drop hammer in which the ram is raised by means of one or more boards that pass between two friction rollers at the top of the hammer

boarded *adj* **1 :** covered with boards or boarding ⟨a ~ window⟩⟨a pine-*boarded* cellar⟩ **2 :** made of boards ⟨a ~ walk across the lawn⟩

board·er \'bōrdər, 'bȯr-, 'bōədə, 'bȯ(ə)də\ *n* -s **1 :** one that boards: **a :** one (as a man) that is provided with regular meals or regular meals and lodging **:** one (as a horse) that is provided with food and shelter **b :** one that boards or is sent to board a ship (as an enemy ship) **c :** GRAINER 1d **2 :** one that boards knitted garments (as hosiery) **3 :** a cow or chicken that does not produce enough to pay for its keep; *also* **:** an animal (as a dog) that is not worth its keep

board foot *n* **:** a unit of quantity for lumber equal to the volume of a board 12 x 12 x 1 inches — abbr. *bd ft*

board game *n* **:** a game of strategy (as checkers, chess, or backgammon) played by moving pieces on a board; *broadly* **:** a game played on a board

board hole *n* **:** a notch cut in a tree by lumbermen to hold the springboard on which the faller works

boardier *comparative of* BOARDY

boardiest *superlative of* BOARDY

boarding *n* -s [in sense 1, fr. [1]*board* + *-ing*, in sense 2, fr. gerund of [2]*board*] **1 a :** a quantity of boards **b :** a covering made of boards **2 :** the act or an instance of boarding a ship ⟨hundreds of ~s by guardsmen all along the coast to enforce the use of safety equipment —John Bunker⟩

boarding home *n* [fr. gerund of [2]*board* (to have regular meals)] **:** a home for foster children

boardinghouse \'==,=\ *n* [fr. gerund of *board* (to have meals) + *house*] **:** a house that provides board and sometimes rooms

boarding nettings *n pl* **:** a strong network of cords or ropes formerly erected at the side of a ship to prevent an enemy from boarding it

boarding officer *n* **:** a naval officer detailed to board an incoming ship to provide local information (as to the ceremonies or honors expected, uniforms required, or facilities available)

boarding pike *n* **:** a pike formerly used by sailors in boarding a ship or in repelling boarders

boarding school *n* [fr. gerund of [2]*board* (to have meals)] **:** a school in which pupils are boarded and lodged as well as taught

board lot *n* [[1]*board* (wall)] **:** the usual stock-exchange trading unit determined by the rules of the particular exchange (as, in New York, 100 shares of stock) — called also *full lot*

board·man \'=mən, ,man,-maa(ə)n\ *n, pl* **boardmen 1 :** one who works at a board: as **a :** one who sorts glazed tile on a large inclined board and marks it according to shade **b :** a motion-picture studio electrician who arranges the lighting and operates control boards during the shooting of scenes **2 :** SANDWICH MAN **3 :** a member of a stock-exchange firm who does the trading on the exchange floor

board measure *n* **:** lumber measurement by the board foot — abbr. *bm*

board mill *n* **:** a sawmill specializing in the cutting of 1-inch and 2-inch lumber — compare TIMBER MILL

board of commissioners : a county administrative board in many states of the U.S. consisting usu. of three, five, or seven elected county commissioners

board of education : a board controlling an educational system or a unit of it; *esp* **:** a board of citizens controlling esp. the elementary and secondary public-school education in a state, county, city, or town — compare SCHOOL BOARD

board of elections : a local bipartisan board in each of the counties of New York state appointed to supervise political elections

board of estimate : a board that is responsible for the direction of fiscal affairs of a city (as New York) and usu. consists of the mayor, the president of the council, and the chief fiscal officer

board of supervisors : a county governing board in many states of the U.S. often having as many as 50 members elected proportionally from the county's cities, towns, townships, or wards — compare BOARD OF COMMISSIONERS

board of trade 1 : a board or an organization that regulates, promotes, supervises, or protects commercial or business enterprises or interests: as **a :** a committee of the English privy council formerly appointed to consider matters relating to trade and the colonies **b :** an English administrative department concerned with the government's commercial and industrial policies **c :** an organization or league of businessmen for the protection and promotion of business interests — compare CHAMBER OF COMMERCE **2 :** a commodities exchange ⟨the Chicago *Board of Trade*⟩

board out *vt, chiefly Brit* **:** to discharge from the service on medical grounds

boardroom \'=,=\ *n* **1 :** a room that is designated for meetings of a board and usu. contains a large conference table ⟨the board of directors convened once a month in the ~⟩ **2 :** a room (as in a broker's office or stock exchange) containing a board for the listing of transactions or prices

board rule *n* **:** a measuring stick bearing various scales for computing board feet

boards *pl of* BOARD, *pres 3d sing of* BOARD

board school *n* **:** one of various former elementary schools established in Great Britain during the late 19th century that were maintained out of local taxes and controlled by a locally elected school board

board tree *n* **:** a tree suitable for cutting up into boards; *esp* **:** a pine tree

board wages *n pl* **1 :** wages (as of a domestic servant) paid in the form of board and lodging **2 :** an allowance for food or for food and lodging provided to an employee esp. as part of wages

boardwalk \'=,=\ *n* **1 :** a low wooden platform providing a walk (as over sand or a worn or slippery area of floor) ⟨bungalows approached by a ~ over the long marsh of the yard —Saul Bellow⟩ ⟨the slatted ~ on the floor behind the bar —Harry Sylvester⟩ **2 :** a promenade along a beach usu. wholly, partly, or orig. consisting of a boardwalk ⟨the ~ . . . of steel and concrete construction overlaid with pine planking —*Amer. Guide Series: N.J.*⟩ ⟨a 1000-foot concrete ~ along its ocean front —C.E.Wright⟩

boardy \-dē\ *adj, often* -ER/-EST [[1]*board* + *-y*] *of fabrics* **:** not pliable **:** HARD, STIFF

boarfish \'=,=\ *n* **:** any of several fishes that have a projecting snout like that of a hog: as **a :** a deep-bodied zeomorph fish (*Capros aper*) of the Mediterranean and sometimes related forms **b :** any of a number of chiefly tropical percoid fishes (family Histiopteridae)

boar grunt *n* [so called fr. the shape of the snout] **1 :** WHITE GRUNT **2 :** YELLOW GRUNT

boarhound \'=,=\ *n* **:** a large dog used in hunting wild boars

boar·ish \'bō(ə)rish, -ȯ(ə)r-, -rēsh\ *adj* **:** of or relating to a boar **:** resembling a boar **:** CRUEL, LECHEROUS

boar's nest *n, slang* **:** living quarters esp. in a camp in which there are only men

boart *var of* BORT

boarwood \'=,=\ *n* **1 :** a tropical American timber tree (*Symphonia globulifera*) of the family Guttiferae **2 :** the hard greenish brown lustrous wood of boarwood

boas *pl of* BOA

bo·as·i·an \bō,asēən\ *adj, usu cap* [Franz Boas †1942 Ger.-Am. anthropologist + E *-ian*] **:** of or relating to the anthropologist Boas or his anthropological theories

[1]**boast** \'bōst\ *n* -s [ME *boost, bost;* prob. akin to OE *bȳl* boil, OHG *būsi* bad, MHG *būsch* cudgel, ON *beysti* ham, Norw dial. *bugge* important man, Gk *phōides* blisters (pl.), Skt *bhūri* abundant; basic meaning: to swell, inflate] **1 :** the act of boasting or an instance of boasting **:** VAUNT, BRAG ⟨the man's constant ~ was that he had an infallible memory for names⟩ **2 :** a cause of boasting **:** a reason for pride ⟨the university's ~ was its high standard of scholarship⟩

[2]**boast** \"\ *vb* -ED/-ING/-S [ME *bosten,* prob. fr. *boost, bost,* n.] *vi* **1 :** to say or tell something intended to give others a high opinion of one **:** BRAG **:** puff oneself up in speech **:** vaunt oneself ⟨~ of her accomplishments or family line⟩ **2** *archaic* **:** GLORY, EXULT ⟨in God we have ~*ed* continually —Ps 44:8 (RSV)⟩ ~ *vt* **1 a :** to speak of or assert boastfully or in an excessively prideful manner ⟨~ that you have been in every state of the union⟩ ⟨~ their skill at tennis⟩ **b :** to proclaim (oneself) boastfully ⟨~ myself a patriot⟩ ⟨~ himself to be a better man than his neighbor⟩ **2** *now Scot* **:** THREATEN **3** *obs* **:** to display pridefully or vaingloriously **4 a :** to possess usu. conspicuously something one is proud of ⟨the city ~s a campanile and a new city hall⟩ **b :** HAVE, POSSESS ⟨the office ~s only one desk⟩

syn BOAST, BRAG, VAUNT, CROW, GASCONADE signify, in common, to give oral expression to one's pride in oneself or in something produced by, belonging to, or related to oneself, as one's family, connections, race, or accomplishments. Although BOAST means commonly to claim with a certain pride ⟨the town *boasts* an excellent school system⟩ it can also point to a self-pride often to the point of conceit, ostentation, or exaggeration ⟨childishly anxious to *boast* that he had walked the whole of the six or seven miles —Compton Mackenzie⟩ ⟨*boast* of past triumphs long forgotten⟩ ⟨annoy the company with an incessant *boasting* of one's wealth and position⟩ BRAG, more common in speech than BOAST, suggests a crude self-glorification ⟨a *bragging* politician⟩ ⟨*brag* of one's importance to the community⟩ VAUNT, more literary than BRAG or BOAST, implies more pomp and bombast than BOAST and less crudity than BRAG ⟨a poem . . . in which a peasant sings octaves *vaunting* the beauty of the beloved —R.A.Hall b. 1911⟩ ⟨pamphlets *vaunting* the region's unique opportunities —*Amer. Guide Series: Minn.*⟩ ⟨ashamed of *vaunting* ourselves to claim credit where credit is due —Robert Moses⟩ CROW, most common in speech, is more contemptuous than the others, suggesting an exultant but petty and unbecoming boasting or blatant bragging esp. over an opponent regarded as defeated in some way ⟨the barrister *crowed* with triumph but the professor was in no way put out —Cyril Kersh⟩ ⟨boasted, gloated, and *crowed* —W.E.Buckler⟩ ⟨advocates of the plane against the capital ship *crowed,* "I told you so" —J.P.Baxter b.1893⟩ GASCONADE, a rare term, implies an habitual and extravagant self-glorification ⟨an enlightened statesman, and not a *gasconading* militarist —C.G.Bowers⟩ ⟨the horn, intended for who knows what sonorous *gasconading,* uttering instead a few piteous bleats —*New Yorker*⟩

[3]**boast** \"\ *vt* -ED/-ING/-S [origin unknown] **1 :** to shape (stone) roughly with a broad chisel in sculpture and stonecutting in preparation for finer work to follow **2 :** to finish (the face of a building stone) by making or cutting several cross rows of parallel corrugations

[4]**boast** \"\ *vt* -ED/-ING/-S [prob. modif. of F *bosse* protuberance, place where the ball hits the wall when boasted, fr. OF *boce* — more at BOSS] **1** *court tennis or squash* **:** to return in play by striking (the ball) against either of the side walls or against the end wall on the striker's side **2 :** to make (a stroke) in boasting

[5]**boast** \"\ *n* -s **:** the stroke made in boasting in court tennis or squash

[1]**boast·er** \'bōstə(r)\ *n* -s [ME *boster,* fr. *bosten* to boast + *-er*] **:** one who boasts **:** BRAGGART

[2]**boaster** *n* -s [[3]*boast* + *-er*] **:** DROVE 4a

boast·ful \-fəl\ *adj* [ME *boostful, bostful,* fr. *boost, bost* boast + *-ful*] **:** given to or marked by boasting ⟨silly young officers, who talked in bellicose and ~ terms —*Times Lit. Supp.*⟩ — **boast·ful·ly** \-fəlē, -li\ *adv* — **boast·ful·ness** \-fəlnəs\ *n* -ES

boast·ing·ly *adv* **:** in a boasting manner

boast·less \-stləs\ *adj* **:** having no boast

[1]**boat** \'bōt, *usu* -d·+V\ *n* -s [ME *boot,* fr. OE *bāt;* akin to ON *beit* boat, *biti* beam, and prob. to OE *bītan* to bite, L *findere* to split; prob. fr. the practice of making a boat by hollowing out a tree trunk — more at BITE] **1 :** a small vessel with or without a deck propelled by oars or paddles or by sail or power — see CANOE, CRUISER, DINGHY, SLOOP **2 a :** SHIP ⟨packet ~⟩ ⟨came from England in the last ~⟩ **b :** SUBMARINE **3 :** a utensil or device shaped like a boat: as **a :** GRAVY BOAT **b :** an ecclesiastical vessel for incense **c :** an open long narrow usu. small receptacle (as of porcelain or nickel) for holding a substance to be heated or burned esp. in chemical analysis by combustion **4 :** a wooden device used in weaving to obtain a strong selvage — **in the same boat :** in the same situation or predicament

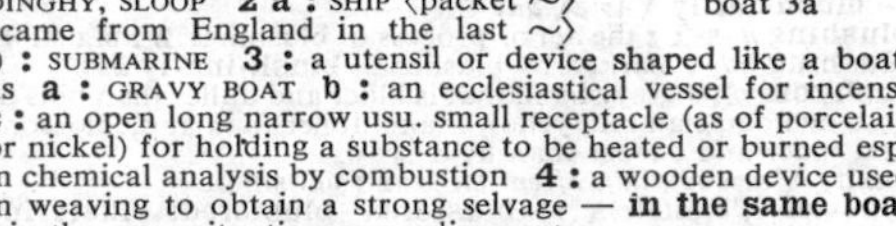

boat 3a

[2]**boat** \"\ *vb* -ED/-ING/-S *vt* **1 a :** to place in a boat or ship ⟨the oarsmen ~*ed* their oars when we touched shore⟩ **b :** to bring (a hooked fish) toward and into a boat ⟨I've almost worn out my wrists ~*ing* a 30-pound halibut —Fred Beck⟩ **2 :** to transport by boat ⟨a company of soldiers ~*ed* across a river⟩ ~ *vi* **:** to go by boat **:** ride in a boat often as a pastime ⟨the company ~*ed* to the island⟩ ⟨was ~*ing* on the river last Sunday afternoon⟩

boat·a·ble \'bōd·əbəl, -ōtə-\ *adj* **:** navigable for boats, esp. small river craft ⟨the canal will be ~ for your ark while the others are still mudfast —S.H.Adams⟩

boat·age \'bōd·ij\ *n* -s **1 :** transportation (as of merchandise) by boat **2 :** a charge for boatage

boatbill \'=,=\ *n* **1** *or* **boat-billed heron** \'=;=-\ **:** a wading bird (*Cochlearius cochlearius*) of tropical America related to the night herons and distinguished by a broadly convex bill suggesting an overturned boat **2 :** BROADBILL 2

boatbill 1

boat boom *n* **:** a spar at right angles to the side of a vessel at anchor to which small boats can be attached

boat bug *n* **1 :** any of numerous aquatic hemipterous insects (family Corixidae) having one pair of legs that resemble long oarlike paddles **2 :** BACK SWIMMER

boatbuilder \'=,==\ *n* **:** one that builds boats

boatbuilding *n* **:** the occupation of building boats

boat cloak *n* **:** a long black naval uniform cloak now optional and worn infrequently with evening dress uniforms

boat deck *n* **:** a ship's upper deck on which lifeboats are stored — see DECK illustration

boat drill *n* **:** drill aboard ship in the launching and manning of lifeboats

boat·er \'bōd·ə(r), -ōtə-\ *n* -s **1 :** one that rows a boat for a livelihood or as a pastime ⟨~s on the river⟩ **2** [so called fr. its having been worn typically by boaters] *chiefly Brit* **:** a man's stiff straw hat with a flat crown, ribbon band, and straight brim **3 :** a woman's hat adapted from the man's boater

boat fall *n* **:** a tackle used to hoist or lower a ship's boat from or to the davits — usu. used in pl.

boat form *n* **:** one of the stereochemical conformations of a strainless 6-membered ring (as a cyclohexane ring) in which two atoms directly opposite each other in the ring are above the plane containing the other four atoms — compare CHAIR FORM

boatheader \'=,==\ *n* **:** one that is in charge of a whaleboat or a small boat putting off from a larger boat in the cod or halibut fisheries; *esp* **:** an officer who stands in the stern sheets of a whaleboat and manipulates the steering oar and lances the harpooned whale

boathook \'=,=\ *n* **:** a hook with a point or knob on the back

boathook

fixed on a pole handle and usu. used to pull or push a boat, raft, or log into place

boathouse \'=,=\ *n* **1 :** a building usu. built partly over water for the housing or storing of boats and often provided with accommodations for gear or general storage and often with rooms for social activity (as of a sailing club) **2 :** a building near water for the social or club activities of a group owning boats or interested in boats

boathouse rum *n* **:** a variety of rummy in which a player if he takes the top card of the discard pile may then draw another card

boating *n* -s **:** the act or sport of one who boats ⟨an afternoon of ~⟩

boat knot *n* **:** MARLINESPIKE HITCH

boat·less \'bōtləs\ *adj* **:** having no boat

boat line *n* **:** GUEST ROPE

boat livery *n* **:** a boathouse or dock where boats are let out for hire

boatload \'=;=\ *n* **1 :** a boat's full load or an amount or number equivalent to such a load ⟨a ~ of passengers arrived on the dock⟩ ⟨a ~ of grain⟩ **2 :** an indefinitely large number ⟨brought in a ~ of books for my entertainment⟩ ⟨dumped a whole ~ of gifts in the boy's lap⟩

boat·man \'=mən, -,man,-maa(ə)n\ *n, pl* **boatmen 1 :** one who earns his livelihood by the management or use of a boat or raft: as **a :** DECKHAND **b :** one who operates a tender to carry passengers and supplies between shore and anchored terminals of transoceanic airplanes **c :** a sawmill worker who works from a flatboat or raft and uses a pike pole to shift and sort logs in the pond — called also *poler* **2 :** BOAT BUG

boat·man·ship \'bōtmən,ship\ *n* -s **:** the ability to handle or skill in handling a boat, esp. a small one

boat nail *n* **:** a nail usu. 3 to 10 inches long made with a large oval or round head or often a rosehead and of soft galvanized iron or of copper usu. with a rectangular shaft tapering to a blunt or chisel point and capable of being effectively clinched

boat neck *or* **boat neckline** *n* **:** BATEAU NECK

boat plant *n* **:** OYSTER PLANT 3

boat plug *n* **:** a wood or metal plug stopping up the drainage hole near the keel of a boat and removable when the boat is dry-docked to drain out bilge water

boat rod *n* **:** a fishing rod of rugged construction usu. jointed and used in saltwater trolling

boat rope *n* **:** a rope by which a smaller boat may make fast to a larger boat or which a crew can grasp when leaving or getting aboard

boats *pl of* BOAT, *pres 3d sing of* BOAT

boat-shaped \'=;=\ *adj* **:** resembling the hull of a boat

boat shell *n* **1 :** SLIPPER LIMPET **2 :** MELON SHELL

boats·man \'bōtsmən\ *n, pl* **boatsmen :** one who manages, uses, or works at boats

boat spike *n* **:** BARGE SPIKE

boat·steerer \'=,=,=\ *n* **:** a crewman in a whaling boat who pulls the harpoon oar, harpoons the whale, and then steers while his superior officer lances the whale

boat-stone \'=,=\ *n* **:** a stone artifact known only from archaic sites in midwestern and eastern No. America that is shaped like a dugout canoe and is thought to have been an atlatl weight — compare BANNERSTONE, BIRDSTONE

boat·swain \'bōsᵊn *sometimes* 'bōt,swān\ *also* **bo·s'n** *or* **bo'·s'n** *or* **bo·sun** *or* **bo'·sun** \'bōsᵊn\ *n* [ME *bootswein,* fr. *boot* boat + *swein* young man, servant — more at BOAT, SWAIN] **1 a :** a petty officer on a merchant ship having immediate supervision of the deck force, of boat crews, and of work parties engaged in maintenance of the hull, anchors, boats, and related equipment **b :** a warrant officer in the U.S. Navy who under the first lieutenant is in charge of the hull and all related equipment (as anchors and boats) **2 a :** JAEGER 3 **b :** TROPIC BIRD

boatswain's chair *n* **:** a wooden board slung by a rope and used to sit on while at work aloft or over the side of a ship

boatswain's locker *n* **:** a ship's locker for the small equipment (as tackle) used by the deck force

boatswain's mate *n* **1 :** an assistant to the boatswain **2 :** a petty officer in the U.S. Navy whose specialty is seamanship and who has supervisory duties in the operation of the deck force and the maintenance of equipment

boatswain's pipe *or* **boatswain's whistle** *also* **boatswain's call** *n* **1 :** a silver whistle used by a boatswain's mate (as in relaying orders to the crew or giving orders to winch and crane operators) **2 :** the note or notes sounded on the boatswain's pipe

boatswain's pipe

[1]**boattail** \'bō(t),tāl\ *n* **1 :** BOAT-TAILED GRACKLE **2 :** the part of an artillery projectile in the rear of the rotating band when shaped like the inverted frustum of a cone

[2]**boattail** \"\ *also* **boat-tailed** \'=;=\ *adj* **1 :** tapered at the back end like the stern of a boat ⟨a ~ bullet⟩ ⟨a ~ ski⟩ **2** [[1]*boattail*] *of,* relating to, or having a boattail ⟨bullets of the ~ type⟩

boat-tailed grackle *n* **:** a large grackle (*Cassidix mexicanus*) of the southern U.S. and Mexico having a tail that is keel-shaped when spread or when the bird is in flight

boat train *n* **:** a train scheduled to connect with a boat

boat truck *n* **:** a low platform with casters for moving a heavy, clumsy, or large piece of stage scenery that must be changed quickly during a play

boat-truck \'=,=\ *n* **:** [5]DUCK

boat·yard \'bōt+\ *n* **:** a yard near the water with facilities (as docks and rails) for the building, repair, and storage of small boats and yachts

[1]**bob** \'bäb\ *vb* **bobbed; bobbed; bobbing; bobs** [ME *bobben,* perh. of imit. origin] *vt* **1 a** *obs* **:** STRIKE, POMMEL, BUFFET **b :** to strike with a quick light blow **:** TAP, RAP **2 a :** to move with a bob **:** cause to move down and up or up and down in a short quick movement ⟨~ the head⟩ **b :** to move with any sudden quick movement (as back and forth or in and out) ⟨~ your head in and out of the window⟩ **3 :** to polish with a bob **:** BUFF ~ *vi* **1 a** (1) **:** to move down and up or up and down suddenly and briefly and often repeatedly ⟨a cork *bobbing* in the water⟩ ⟨a child *bobbing* along on a pogo stick⟩ (2) **:** to emerge, arise, or appear suddenly or unexpectedly ⟨a few minutes later it *bobbed* free of the boiling water —*Time*⟩ — usu. used with *up* ⟨the same question ~s up at each town meeting⟩ ⟨after months in hiding he *bobbed* up in Paris⟩ **b :** to nod the head or curtsy briefly ⟨a little girl *bobbing* before a visitor⟩ **c :** to try to seize with the teeth (as an apple floating in a tub of water or hanging on a string) — used with *for* ⟨~ for apples at a Halloween party⟩ **d :** to move with any sudden quick movement ⟨he *bobbed* to the telephone like a puppet —Carolyn Hannay⟩ **e :** to move or go from place to place fitfully — often used with *around* ⟨*bobbing* around town for a day or two⟩ ⟨small birds *bobbing* all over the yard⟩ **2** *Scot* **:** to dance a bob

[2]**bob** \"\ *n* -s **1 a :** a short quick down-and-up motion ⟨a ~ of the head⟩ ⟨her curtsy was a mere ~⟩ **b** *Scot* **:** any of several dances **2** *obs* **:** a blow, jog, tap, or rap esp. with the fist **3** *obs* **:** TAUNT, GIBE **4 a :** a modification of the coursing order in change ringing **b :** a method of change ringing using a bob ⟨~ major⟩ **5 :** a small polishing wheel of solid felt or leather with rounded edges

[3]**bob** \"\ *vt* **bobbed; bobbed; bobbing; bobs** [ME *bobben,* fr. MF *bober* to deceive, fr. *bobe* deceit] **1** *obs* **:** DECEIVE, FOOL, CHEAT **2** *obs* **:** to take by fraud **:** FILCH

[4]**bob** \"\ *n* -s [ME *bobbe,* perh. of Celt origin; akin to IrGael *baban* tassel, tuft, ScGael, bobbin] **1 a :** a bunch or cluster: as (1) *Scot* **:** a small bouquet of flowers **:** NOSEGAY (2) *now chiefly dial* **:** a bunch of leaves, flowers, or fruit ⟨red clover ~s⟩ ⟨a ~ of grapes⟩ (3) **:** a wad of rags, bait, feathers, or hooks used in angling **b :** a knob, knot, twist, or curl esp. of ribbons, yarn, or hair **c :** a wig with tight horizontal or loose vertical curls **d :** a horse's docked tail **:** BOBTAIL **e :** a

very short to shoulder-length haircut on a woman or child **2** *archaic* **:** a grub, worm, or beetle esp. as used for bait in angling **3 :** a ball or weight esp. at the end of something: as **a** *archaic* **:** a pendant worn as an ornament (as in an earring or attached to a necklace) **b :** the weight at the bottom end of a pendulum **c :** the weight on a plumb line **d :** ¹FLOAT 4 **e :** any weighting matter attached to the tail of a kite to steady it **4 a** *archaic* **:** the refrain of a song; *specif* **:** a short and abrupt refrain often of two syllables **b :** a single very short line usu. of two or three syllables occurring in a series of longer lines in English verse **5 a :** CLIPPING ⟨the animal would be earmarked; that is, assorted crops, bits, and ~*s* would have been carved out of his long ears —W.F.Harris⟩ **b :** a small usu. insignificant piece **:** TRIFLE ⟨the ~*s* and trinkets of criticism —Laurence Sterne⟩

⁵bob \"\ *vi* **bobbed; bobbed; bobbing; bobs** [⁴*bob* (grub)] **:** to angle with a bob esp. through the ice

⁶bob \"\ *vt* **bobbed; bobbed; bobbing; bobs** [⁴*bob* (knob of hair, bobtail)] **1 :** to cut shorter **:** DOCK, CROP — sometimes used with *off* ⟨a show horse with a beribboned mane and *bobbed* tail⟩ ⟨~ off a dog's tail⟩ ⟨prune and ~ shrubbery⟩ **2 :** to cut (hair) in the style of a bob

⁷bob \"\ *n, pl* **bob** [perh. fr. *Bob,* nickname for the name *Robert*] *slang Brit* **:** SHILLING

⁸bob \"\ *n* -s [back-formation fr. *bobsled*] **1 :** a single pair of sled runners on which the forward ends of logs may be loaded in logging **2** (by shortening) **:** BOBSLED

⁹bob \"\ *vb* **bobbed; bobbed; bobbing; bobs** *vi* **1 :** to ride on a bobsled as a recreation **2 :** to transport logs on a bob ~ *vt* **:** to transport (as logs) on a bob

¹⁰bob \"\ *n* -s [by shortening] **:** BOBWHITE

bo·bac *also* **bo·back** \'bō,bak\ *n* -s [Pol *bobak*] **:** a marmot (*Marmota bobak*) of eastern Europe and Asia

bobache *var of* BOBECHE

bob·a·chee \'bäbə,chē\ *n* -s [Hindi *babarcī,* fr. Per *bāwarchī*] *India* **:** a male cook

bob·a·dil \'bäbə,dil\ *n, usu cap* [after Captain *Bobadil,* a character in *Every Man in His Humor* by Ben Jonson †1637 Eng. dramatist] **:** BRAGGART; *esp* **:** a cowardly braggart — **bob·a·dil·ian** \¦=='dilēən\ *adj* — **bob·a·dil·ish** \-lish\ *adj*

bob and wheel *or* **bob wheel** *n* [⁴*bob*] **:** a bob refrain to a stanza or a bob followed by rhyming lines

bobbed *past of* BOB

bob·be·jaan \'bäbə,yän\ *n* -s [Afrik, baboon, fr. obs. D *babiaen* — more at BABIANA] **:** CHACMA

¹bob·ber \'bäbə(r)\ *n* -s [¹*bob* + *-er*] **:** one that bobs: as **a** *angling* (1) **:** FLOAT (2) **:** BOBFLY (3) **:** DROPPER **b :** RUDDY DUCK **c** *logging* **:** DEADHEAD

²bobber \"\ *n* -s [⁹*bob* + *-er*] **:** one that rides on a bobsled; *esp* **:** a member of a bobsled team

¹bob·bery \'bäb(ə)rē, -ri\ *n* -ES [Hindi *bāp re,* lit., oh father, an exclamation] **:** a noisy disturbance **:** ROW, BRAWL

²bobbery \"\ *adj* [prob. fr. ¹*bobbery*] *of hounds* **:** of miscellaneous or uncertain breed and of mediocre quality

bob·bie \'bäbē, -bi\ *var of* BOBBY

bobbies *pl of* BOBBY

bob·bin \'bäbən\ *n* -s [origin unknown] **1 a :** any of various small, round, or cylindrical devices usu. of bone, wood, or metal on which threads are wound for working bobbin lace **b :** a cylinder or spindle with a flange at one or both ends and a hole through the center of its length on which slubbing, roving, yarn, or thread is wound in machinery for roving, spinning, twisting, weaving, or sewing or for making lace — called also *cop, pirn, quill, reel, spool* **c :** the little rounded piece of wood at the end of a latchstring **d :** a coil of insulated wire or the reel round which it is wound **e :** an assembly of the carbon electrode with the depolarizer molded around it in dry-cell construction **2 :** a narrow cotton cord formerly used by dressmakers for piping

bobbin and fly frame *n* **1 :** a machine in cotton spinning that draws and twists the sliver and winds the roving on a bobbin **2 :** a cotton-spinning machine that converts the roving into yarn

bob·bi·net *also* **bob·i·net** \¦bäbə¦net — *usu* -ed·+V\ *n* -s [blend of *bobbin* and *net*] **:** a machine-made net usu. with a hexagonal mesh made of cotton, silk, or nylon and used plain or appliquéd (as for dresses, curtains, veils)

bobbinet (enlarged)

bobbing *pres part of* BOB

bob·bing joan \'bäbiŋ¦jōn\ *n, usu cap J* [fr. the pres. part. of ¹*bob* + the name *Joan*] *dial Eng* **:** a lively rustic dance

bobbin lace *n* **:** a handmade lace made by intertwisting threads wound on bobbins and worked over a pillow on which the pattern is marked out by pins

bobbin line *n* **:** a line of rope carried in a pouch by a fire fighter and used in various emergencies

bob·bish \'bäbish\ *adj* [perh. fr. ¹*bob* + *-ish*] *slang Brit* **:** being in good spirits **:** HEARTY

¹bob·ble \'bäbəl\ *vb* **bobbled; bobbled; bobbling** \-b(ə)liŋ\ **bobbles** [freq. of ¹*bob*] *vi* **1 :** ¹BOB *vi* 1 a (1) ⟨a basketball *bobbling* on the rim of the basket for a moment before dropping in⟩ ⟨laughed . . . so that her black wig *bobbled* —M.F.K.Fisher⟩ **2 :** to make an error or mistake (as in baseball or football) **:** FUMBLE ⟨the catcher *bobbled* at a crucial point⟩ ~ *vt* **:** MUFF, FUMBLE ⟨~ an easy infield grounder⟩

²bobble \"\ *n* -s **1 :** a repeated bobbing movement ⟨the ~ of the cork in the rough water⟩ **2 :** a small ball; *esp* **:** one in a series of tiny yarn balls used on an edging **3 :** ERROR, MISTAKE ⟨a man who can laugh at his own ~*s* and stick to his job —*Time*⟩; *esp* **:** an error consisting of momentarily juggling the ball in baseball or fumbling it in football ⟨lost the game because of two ~*s* by a single ball carrier⟩

bob·by \'bäbē, -bi\ *n* -ES [fr. *Bobby,* nickname fr. *Robert,* after Sir *Robert* Peel †1850 Eng. statesman who organized the London police force] *Brit* **:** POLICEMAN

bobby calf *also* **bobby** *n* -ES [E dial. *bob* young calf (prob. fr. the name *Bob*) + *-y*] *Austral, NewZeal, & Africa* **:** a young calf; *specif* **:** one of less than 100 pounds live weight

bob·by pin \'bäbē-, -bi-\ *n* [⁴*bob* + *-y*] **:** a flat wire hairpin with prongs that press close together used esp. for bobbed hair — see HAIRPIN illustration

bob·by sock \'bäbē-, -bi-\ *n, pl* **bobby socks** *or* **bobby sox** \-¦säks\ [fr. the name *Bobby* (influenced by *bobby pin*)] **:** a sock reaching above the ankle and usu. worn by teen-age girls and children

bobby-sock *or* **bobby-socks** *or* **bobby-sox** \'==,=\ *adj* **:** consisting or of relating to bobby-soxers ⟨the *bobby-sox* audience —Ruth Inglis⟩ ⟨the *bobby-sock* brigade⟩ ⟨young wives, only a few years away from their *bobby-socks* days —Lois & Don Thorburn⟩

bob·by-sox·er \'==,säksə(r)\ *or* **bob·by-sock·er** \-,säkə(r)\ *n* -s **:** an adolescent girl

bob·cat \'bäb,kat\ *n, pl* **bobcats** *also* **bobcat** [⁴*bob* + *cat;* fr. the stubby tail] **1 :** BAY LYNX **2** *pl* **bobcats :** a beginning cub scout who has not advanced to the rank of wolf

bo·beche \bō'besh, -'bash\ *or* **bo·bache** \-'bash\ *n* -s [F *bobèche*] **1 :** a slightly cupped collar (as of glass or plastic) that is placed above a candle socket to catch candle drippings **2 :** an ornamental collar that is fitted to a candlestick, lamp, or chandelier and from which glass prisms are often suspended

bobfly \'=,=\ *n* [²*bob* + *fly*] **:** a fishing fly attached to the leader some distance above the tail fly

bob–haired \'=¦=\ *adj* [⁴*bob*] **:** having bobbed hair ⟨a *bob-haired* teenager⟩

bob–house \'=,=\ *n* [⁸*bob*] **:** a small shack usu. on runners and used for fishing through the ice (as for smelt or lake trout)

bo·bi·er·rite \'bōbēə,rīt\ *n* -s [F fr. Pierre A. *Bobierre* †1881 Fr. chemist + F *-ite*] **:** a mineral $Mg_3(PO_4)_2.8H_2O$ consisting of hydrous magnesium phosphate occurring massive or in crystals in guano

bo·bi·za·tion \,bōbə'zāshən\ *n* -s [G *bobisation,* irreg. fr. *bo,* one of the notes of this scale + *-isation* -ization] **:** an obsolete Flemish system of musical solmization using the syllables *bo, ce, di, ga, lo, ma, ni*

bob·let \'bäblət\ *n* -s [⁸*bob* + *-let*] **:** a 2-man bobsled

bob·o·link \'bäbə,liŋk\ *n* -s [fr. earlier *Bob-o-Lincoln, bob-lincon,* of imit. origin] **1 :** a common American songbird (*Dolichonyx oryzivorus*) of the family Icteridae with the breeding plumage of the male chiefly black and white and the plumage of the female and eclipse male streaky brown above and yellowish brown below that migrates over a wide range, breeds in No. America well north into Canada where it is noted for its rollicking musical song, passes southward in the fall in great flocks toward its winter range south of the Amazon river, and constitutes a serious pest in rice-growing areas through which it passes though formerly regarded as a table delicacy — called also *reedbird, ricebird* **2 :** DEER 4

bo·bo·tie *or* **bo·bo·tee** \bə'bōd·ē, ¦bōbəd·¦ē\ *n* -s [Afrik *bobotie*] **:** a dish of minced meat with curry and condiments esp. popular in southern Africa

bobs *pl of* BOB, *pres 3d sing of* BOB

¹bobsled \'=,=\ *also* **bobsleigh** \'=,=\ *n* -s [⁴*bob* + *sled* or *sleigh*] **1 :** a short sled usu. used as one of a pair joined by a coupling **2 :** a compound sled formed of two bobsleds and a coupling or a common seat — called also *double-ripper*

bobsled

²bobsled \"\ *also* **bobsleigh** \"\ *vi* **:** to ride or coast on a bobsled

bob·sled·der \'=,=də(r)\ *n* **:** one that rides or coasts on a bobsled esp. as a winter sport

bobsledding *n* **:** the act, skill, or sport of riding or racing on a bobsled

bob·stay \'=,=\ *n* [²*bob* + *stay*] **:** a rope, chain, or bar extending from the stem of a ship to the end of the bowsprit — see SHIP illustration

¹bobtail \'=,=\ *n* [⁴*bob* + *tail*] **1 :** a bobbed tail **2 :** something with a short or shortened tail: as **a :** OLD ENGLISH SHEEPDOG **b** *also* **bobtail coat** *obs* **:** a man's coat with short skirts as contrasted to one with tails **c :** a switching locomotive **3 :** a bobtailed arrow **4 :** something curtailed, shortened, or abbreviated **5** *slang* **:** a dishonorable discharge from one of the armed services **6 :** a bobtail straight or flush in poker **7 a :** a motortruck with a short wheelbase **b :** the tractor of a trailer truck

²bobtail \"\ *adj* **1 :** having a bobtail **2 a :** SHORTENED, CURTAILED, ABBREVIATED **b :** SHORT; *esp* **:** shorter than usual or common **c :** DEFICIENT **3 a** *poker* **:** requiring either of two ranks of cards to make into a straight **:** open at both ends — used of four cards in a sequence **b :** requiring one more card of the same suit to become a flush — used of four cards of the same suit

³bobtail \"\ *vt* -ED/-ING/-S **1 :** to dock the tail of **2 :** to cut short **:** CURTAIL, ABBREVIATE

bobtail drawbridge *n* **:** a drawbridge that rotates about a pivot near one end

bobtailed \'=¦=\ *adj* **1 :** BOBTAIL **2** *of an arrow* **:** decreasing in thickness from the tip to the nock

bobtailed disease *n* [so called fr. the loss of caudal hair accompanying this disease] **:** ALKALI DISEASE 3

bob veal *n* [E dial. *bob* young calf — more at BOBBY] **:** the veal of a very young or unborn calf

bob wheel *var of* BOB AND WHEEL

bob·white \(')bäb¦(h)wīt, *usu* -d·+V\ *also* **bobwhite quail** *n* -s [imit.] **:** any quail of the genus *Colinus* of which the best-known species (*C. virginianus*) includes a favorite game bird of the eastern and central U.S. that is replaced in Cuba, Texas, and Mexico by members of related varieties and species, all being about 10 inches long and mottled above with gray, rufous, and whitish, the male having the head striped with black and white and a white throat patch — called also *quail, partridge*

bob wig *n* [⁴*bob*] **:** a short wig with bobs worn in British courts

bob wire *n* [by alter. fr. *barbed wire*] **:** BARBED WIRE

bobwood \'=,=\ *n* [¹*bob* + *wood*] **:** BALSA 1

bo·ca \'bōkə\ *n* -s [Sp, lit., mouth, fr. L *bucca* cheek, mouth — more at POCK] **:** a river mouth **:** a harbor entrance (as of a So. American seaport)

bo·cac·cio \bō'kä,chō, bə'-\ *n* -s [perh. by folk etymology (influence of Giovanni *Boccaccio* †1375 Ital. writer) fr. an AmerSp word derived fr. Sp *bocacha* big mouth, aug. of *boca* mouth] **:** a large olive to brown red-flushed rockfish (*Sebastodes paucispinis*) of the Pacific coast from British Columbia to southern California being an important market fish in the southern part of its range

bo·ca·chi·ca \,bōkə'chēkə\ *n* -s [modif. of AmerSp *bocachico,* prob. alter. of Sp *boca de chico* boy's mouth, fr. *boca* mouth + *de* of + *chico* boy, fr. *chico* small — more at CHICO] **:** any of several small So. American freshwater fishes (family Characidae)

bo·cage \bō'käzh\ *n* -s *often attrib* [F, fr. OF *boscage* — more at BOSCAGE] **:** countryside or landscape (as of western France) marked by intermingling patches of woodland and heath, small fields, tall hedgerows, and orchards

bo·cal \'bōkəl, bō'kal\ *n* -s [F, a kind of vase, mouthpiece, fr. It *boccale,* a kind of vase, fr. LL *baucalis,* fr. Gk *baukalis*] **:** CROOK 4b(2)

boc·ca \'bōkə, 'bäkə\ *n* -s [It, mouth, fr. L *bucca* cheek, mouth — more at POCK] **1 :** the mouth of a glass furnace **2 :** a vent on the side or near the base of an active volcano from which lava issues

bo·ca·ro \'bükə,rō, 'bäk-\ *n* -s [prob. modif. of Pg *búcaro* clay vase, fr. OPg *púcaro,* fr. Ar dial., fr. L *poculum* cup; akin to L *potare* to drink — more at POTABLE] **:** a usu. dark red and often ornately modeled stoneware produced in I-hsing, China, and introduced into Europe in the 17th century

boc·cie *or* **boc·ci** *or* **boc·ce** *also* **boc·cia** \'bächē\ *n pl but usu sing in constr* [It *bocce,* pl. of *boccia* ball, fr. (assumed) VL *bottia* — more at BOSS] **:** a bowling game of Italian origin in which balls are rolled or tossed down a long court to stop as close as possible to a smaller target ball

¹boc·co·nia \bō'kōnēə\ *n* [NL, fr. Paolo *Boccone* †1704 Sicilian botanist + NL *-ia*] *syn of* MACLEAYA

²bocconia \"\ *n* -s [NL, fr. P. *Boccone* + NL *-ia*] **:** a garden plant of the genus *Macleaya; esp* **:** PLUME POPPY

boce \'bōs\ *n* -s [L *boc-, box,* a sea fish, fr. Gk *bōk-, bōx*] **:** a brightly colored European fish (*Box vulgaris*) of the family Sparidae having a compressed body

¹boche *or* **bosche** \'bäsh, 'bòsh, 'bōsh\ *n, pl* **boches** *or* **boche** *or* **bosches** *or* **bosche** *usu cap* [F *boche,* prob. short for *alboche,* fr. *allemand* German + *-boche* (as in *caboche* cabbage, squarehead) — more at CABBAGE] *slang* **:** GERMAN — usu. used disparagingly ⟨the place is still thick with *Boche* —Fred Majdalany⟩

²boche *or* **bosche** \"\ *adj, usu cap, slang* **:** GERMAN — usu. used disparagingly ⟨the *Boche* air force⟩ ⟨his hotel here filled . . . with the *Boche* military on leave —Kay Boyle⟩

bocht \'bòkt\ *Scot var of* BOUGHT

bo·chum \'bōkùm\ *adj, usu cap* [fr. *Bochum,* Germany] **:** of or from the city of Bochum, Germany **:** of the kind or style prevalent in Bochum

bochur *also* **bocher** *var of* BAHUR

¹bock \'bäk\ *var of* BOKE

²bock \"\ *n* -s [Hindi *bok* he-goat] **:** leather made from sheepskin and sometimes substituted for morocco in bookbinding

bock beer \'bäk-\ *or* **bock** *n* [*bock beer* part trans. of G *bockbier,* by folk etymology (influence of *bock* he-goat) & shortening fr. *Einbecker bier,* lit., beer from Einbeck, fr. *Einbeck,* town in Hannover, Germany; *bock* fr. G, short for *bockbier*] **:** a heavy dark rich beer usu. sold in the early spring

bock·ing \'bäkiŋ\ *n* -s [fr. *Bocking,* village in Essex, England] **:** a coarse woolen fabric used esp. as a floor covering

bocks·beu·tel \'bäks,bòid·ᵊl\ *n* -s [G, fr. *bock* he-goat (fr. OHG *boc*) + *beutel* bag, purse, scrotum, fr. OHG *būtil;* fr. the similarity of its shape to the testes of a goat — more at BUCK, BUD] **:** a short-necked bulbous bottle for white wine produced along the Main river in Germany or for similar wine

bocland *n* [OE *bōcland* — more at BOOKLAND] *archaic* **:** BOOKLAND

bo·co \'bō(,)kō\ *n* -s [F, fr. a native name in the Guianas] **:** a large brightly colored deepwater crab (*Cancer porteri*) from the west coast of Central and So. America

bo·con \bō'kōn\ *n* -s [Sp *bocón,* fr. *bocón* big-mouthed, fr. *boca* mouth — more at BOCA] **:** any of several Caribbean anchovies; *esp* **:** an anchovy (*Cetengraulis edentulis*) common about the West Indies

bo·cor *also* **bo·kor** \bō'kò(ə)r\ *n* -s [Haitian Creole] **:** a Haitian witch doctor and magician

¹bod *var of* BOTT

²bod \'bäd\ *n* -s [prob. short for *body*] *Brit* **:** FELLOW, GUY

BOD *abbr* biochemical oxygen demand; biological oxygen demand

bo·dach \'bōdək, 'bäd-\ *n* -s [IrGael & ScGael] **1** *Scot & Irish* **:** a boorish old man **2** *Scot & Irish* **:** GOBLIN, BUGABOO

bo·da·cious \(')bō¦dāshəs\ *adj* [prob. back-formation fr. *bodaciously*] **1** *South & Midland* **:** complete and unmitigated **:** UNMISTAKABLE **2** *South & Midland* **:** REMARKABLE, NOTEWORTHY

bo·da·cious·ly *adv* [fr. earlier *bodyaciously,* perh. fr. *body* + *-aciously* (as in *graciously*)] *South & Midland* **:** in a bodacious manner **:** THOROUGHLY, UNQUESTIONABLY, EXTREMELY

bo·dan·sky unit \bə'dan(t)skē-, bō'-, -dän-\ *n, usu cap B* [after Aaron *Bodansky* †1960 Amer. (Russ.-born) biochemist] **:** a unit based on the activity of phosphatase toward sodium beta-glycerophosphate and used as a measure of phosphatase concentration (as in the blood) esp. in the diagnosis of various pathological conditions, the normal value for the blood averaging about 7 for children and about 4 for adults

bodark \'bō,därk -dək,-dăk\ *var of* BODOCK

boddhisattva *var of* BODHISATTVA

boddice *var of* BODICE

¹bode \'bōd\ *n* -s [ME, fr. OE *boda;* akin to OHG *boto* messenger, ON *bothi,* OE *bēodan* to command, proclaim — more at BID] *archaic* **:** MESSENGER, HERALD

²bode \"\ *vt* -ED/-ING/-S [ME *boden,* fr. OE *bodian;* akin to ON *botha* to proclaim, presage; derivative fr. the root of OE *boda* messenger; akin to OE *bēodan* to proclaim, command — more at BID] **1 a** *archaic* **:** to announce beforehand **:** FORETELL **b :** to indicate by signs (as a future event) **:** be the omen of **:** PORTEND, PRESAGE ⟨her little face puckered up into an expression that *boded* tears —W.H.Hudson †1922⟩ ⟨watched the weather very anxiously, for it *boded* snow —Mary Webb⟩ **2 :** to give promise of ⟨this controversy . . . will ~ ill for both of us —A.H.Lowe⟩ **syn** see FORETELL

³bode \"\ *n* -s [ME, fr. OE *bod, gebod;* akin to OHG *gabot* command, ON *both,* OE *bēodan* to command — more at BID] **1** *archaic* **:** OMEN, FORESHADOWING **2** *chiefly Scot* **:** BID, OFFER

⁴bode *past of* BIDE

bode·ful \'bōdfəl\ *adj* [³*bode* + *-ful*] **:** PORTENTOUS, OMINOUS

bo·de·ga \bō'dāgə, -'dēgə\ *n* -s [Sp, fr. L *apotheca* storehouse — more at APOTHECARY] **1 a :** a storehouse for wine esp. above ground **b :** WINE CELLAR **c :** WAREHOUSE **2 a :** WINESHOP **b :** a combined wineshop and grocery store **c :** ¹BAR 5 a, 5 b

bo·de·gon \,bōdā'gōn\ *n* -ES **:** a Spanish genre or still-life painting

bode·ment \'bōdmənt\ *n* -s [³*bode* + *-ment*] **1 :** OMEN, FOREBODING, PRESENTIMENT **2 :** PREDICTION, PROPHECY

bo·den \'bōdᵊn\ *adj* [ME *bodin,* prob. fr. ON *bothinn* ready, past part. of *bjōtha* to bid — more at BID] *chiefly Scot* **:** EQUIPPED, PROVIDED

bo·de's law \'bōdəz-\ *n, usu cap B* [after Johann E. *Bode* †1826 Ger. astronomer] **:** an empirical rule of astronomy: the approximate relative distances of most of the planets (excluding Mercury and Neptune but including the asteroid Ceres) from the sun are given in terms of the astronomical unit by means of the formula $D=0.3(2)^{(n-1)}+0.4$ where D is the distance and n is the number of the planet in order outward from the sun (as Venus=1)

bode·wash \'bōd,wòsh, -wäsh\ *n* -ES [by folk etymology fr. AmerF *bois de vache* — more at BOIS DE VACHE] *North & West* **:** BUFFALO CHIPS

¹bodge \'bäj\ *n* -s [origin unknown] **:** an English unit of capacity equal to about ½ peck and out of use since the 17th century

²bodge \"\ *vt* -ED/-ING/-S [by alter.] **:** ²BOTCH

³bodge \"\ *n* -s *chiefly dial* **:** ³BOTCH

bodg·er \'bäjə(r)\ *n* -s [origin unknown] *Brit* **:** a wood-carver or woodturner; *specif* **:** a turner who makes chairs of beech wood

bo·dhi \'bōdē\ *n* -s [Skt, fr. *bodhati* he wakes, is awake — more at BID] **:** the state of enlightenment attained by a Buddhist who has practiced the Eightfold Path and achieved salvation

bo·dhi·satt·va *or* **bod·dhi·satt·va** \,bōdə'satwə\ *also* **bo·dhi·satta** \-tə\ *n* -s [Skt *bodhisattva* one whose essence is enlightenment, fr. *bodhi* enlightenment + *sattva* being, essence — more at SATTVA] *Buddhism* **:** a being that compassionately refrains from entering nirvana in order to save others **:** a future Buddha; *specif* **:** one worshiped as a deity in Mahayana Buddhism

bodhi tree *n* [Skt *bodhi,* lit., enlightenment] **:** PIPAL

bo·di·a·nus \,bōdē'ānəs, -anəs\ *n, cap* [NL] **:** a genus of stout-bodied chiefly tropical percoid fishes (family Labridae) that is sometimes made the type of a separate family (Bodianidae)

bod·ice \'bädəs\ *n* -s [fr. earlier *bodies,* pl. of ¹*body* (part of a garment)] **1 :** an undergarment stiffened with whalebone and resembling a corset **:** STAYS **2 a :** the attached or separate waist of a woman's dress **b :** a tight-fitting sleeveless waist or a very wide girdle often laced and worn over or forming part of a dress

¹bod·ied \'bädēd, -did\ *adj* [¹*body* + *-ed*] **1 :** having a body **:** having such a body ⟨full-*bodied*⟩ **2 :** invested with a body **:** INCARNATE

²bodied \"\ *adj* [fr. past part. of ²*body*] **:** thickened or made viscous usu. by heating ⟨~ paint⟩

bodied oil *n* **:** an oil thickened by bodying; *esp* **:** a drying oil whose drying properties have been improved in the process — compare BLOWN OIL, BOILED OIL

bo·di·e·ron \,bōdē'irən\ *n* -s [origin unknown] **:** the California sea trout or a related greenling

¹bodies *pl of* BODY, *pres 3d sing of* BODY

²bodies *obs var of* BODICE

bodi·less *or* **body·less** \'bädēləs, -dᵊl-\ *adj* [ME, fr. ¹*body* + *-less*] **:** having no body: as **a :** having no trunk or main part ⟨a ~ head⟩ **b :** lacking substance **:** INCORPOREAL ⟨~ ghosts⟩

¹bodi·ly \'bädᵊlē, -dəlē, -li\ *adj* [ME, fr. *body* + *-ly*] **1 :** having a body or a material form **:** PHYSICAL, CORPOREAL ⟨a ghostlike figure with ~ form⟩ **2 a :** of or relating to the body ⟨~ comfort⟩ **b :** concerning the body ⟨~ fear⟩ **3** *obs* **:** ACTUAL, REALIZED

syn PHYSICAL, CORPOREAL, CORPORAL, SOMATIC: these words agree in referring to the human body and differ so little that they are often interchangeable. BODILY contrasts with *mental* or *spiritual* ⟨*bodily* illness is more easy to bear than mental —Charles Dickens⟩ ⟨if from any *bodily* or mental defect the eldest son is disqualified for ruling —J.G.Frazer⟩ PHYSICAL, in this sense, may be somewhat milder and less explicit than BODILY ⟨even if he dreads no *physical* betrayal, he suffers from terror and morbid sensitiveness at every hint of mental estrangement —George Santayana⟩ ⟨her emotional breakdown had probably more to do with *physical* exhaustion than with any eloquence of his —A.T.Quiller-Couch⟩ CORPOREAL stresses substance and may contrast either with *spiritual* or with *immaterial* ⟨the spiritual life commences where the *corporeal* existence terminates —J.G.Frazer⟩ ⟨we saw . . . the woman, with a *corporeal* body as real at that moment as our own, pass in through the interstice —Bram Stoker⟩ CORPORAL, now less common in these uses than the others, is likely to refer to things which affect the body unpleasantly ⟨*corporal* punishment⟩ In some contexts as "*corporal* works of mercy" it contrasts with *spiritual.* SOMATIC, meaning of or relating to the body, is almost entirely scientific in suggestion ⟨language is produced through the action of definite body parts and is thus a *somatic* function —*Psychoanalytic Rev.*⟩

²bodily \"\ *adv* [ME, fr. *bodily,* adj.] **1 :** in the body **:** in the flesh **:** in person ⟨the Savior walking ~ among men⟩ **2 :** as a body **:** as a whole **:** ALTOGETHER, ENTIRELY ⟨the first of 160 homes to be moved ~ from this village —*N.Y.Times*⟩

bodily injury liability insurance *or* **bodily injury insurance** *n* **:** insurance against loss from legal liability of the insured for bodily injury to others esp. when caused by accident

bodily oath *n* **:** CORPORAL OATH

bod·i·ment \'bädēmənt, -dəm-\ *n* -s [¹*body* + *-ment*] **:** EMBODIMENT

boding *n* -s [ME, fr. gerund of *boden* to bode, announce — more at BODE] **1 :** OMEN, FOREBODING ⟨laughed at signs and ~*s* —Mary Webb⟩ **2 :** a prediction usu. of evil

bod·ing·ly *adv* [*boding* (fr. pres. part. of ²*bode*) + *-ly*] **:** OMINOUSLY, FOREBODINGLY

[1]**bod·kin** \'bädkən\ *n* -s [ME *bodekin, boidekin*] **1 a :** DAGGER, PONIARD, STILETTO **b :** a small slender instrument with a sharp point for making holes in cloth and leather and for picking out bastings **c :** an ornamental hairpin shaped like a stiletto **2 :** a blunt needle with a large eye for drawing tape or ribbon through a casing, beading, or hem **3 :** a compositor's sharp-pointed tool used chiefly to push out a character from set type when making corrections **4** *chiefly Brit* **:** a person closely wedged between two others ⟨a ~ squeezed and sweating on a bus⟩

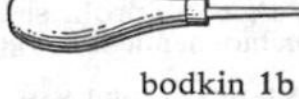
bodkin 1b

[2]**bodkin** \"\ *adv, chiefly Brit* **:** in the position of a bodkin (sense 4) ⟨sitting ~ on the crowded train⟩ ⟨too fat to ride ~ between two friends⟩

bod·le \'bäd^əl, 'bōd-\ *n* -s [origin unknown] **:** a small copper coin that was issued in Scotland in the 17th century and was worth two Scotch pence

bod·lei·an \(')bäd¦lēən\ *adj, usu cap* [Sir Thomas *Bodley* †1613 Eng. scholar (who restored the Oxford library) + E *-ian*] **:** belonging to the Bodleian Library of Oxford University

[1]**bo·do** \'bō,dō\ *n, pl* **bodo** *or* **bodos** *usu cap* **1 a :** a group of peoples living in Assam chiefly along the north bank of the Brahmaputra river as far eastward as the Darrang district and working typically in clannish groups as laborers in tea plantations — called also *Cachari* **b :** a member of such people **2 :** the language of the Bodo people

[2]**bodo** \"\ *n, cap* [NL] **:** a genus (the type of the family Bodonidae) of minute ovoid but plastic biflagellate protozoans (order Protomonodina) common in stagnant water or coprozoic and comprising numerous intestinal commensals of vertebrates as well as sewage organisms

bo·dock \'bō,däk\ *n* -s [by folk etymology fr. AmerF *bois d'arc* — more at BOIS D'ARC] *chiefly South & Midland* **:** OSAGE ORANGE

bo·do·ni \bə'dōnē, -dänē\ *n* -s *cap* [after Giambattista *Bodoni* †1813 Ital. printer] **1 :** a book printed by the printer Bodoni **2 :** a text type based on original designs by Bodoni — see MODERN

bo·do·nid \'bōd^ənəd, bō'dän-\ *n* -s [NL *Bodonidae*, family of protozoans, fr. *Bodon-, Bodo*, type genus + *-idae*] **:** any protozoan of the genus *Bodo* or family Bodonidae

bod-pa \'bōd'pä, bə'pä\ *n pl* [Tibetan *Bod* Tibet + *-pa* (suffix used in individual and family names)] **:** the Tibetans of southern central Tibet

bods *pl of* BOD

bod-skad \'bōd'skäd, bə'käd\ *n* -s *cap B* [Tibetan, fr. *Bod* Tibet + *skad* speech] **:** the Tibetan language

bod stick *var of* BOT STICK

[1]**body** \'bädē, -di\ *n* -ES [ME, fr. OE *bodig*; akin to OHG *botah* body] **1 a :** the total organized physical substance of an animal or plant **:** the aggregate of tissues **:** the physical organism: as (1) **:** the material part or nature of man (2) **:** the dead organism **:** CORPSE (3) **:** the person of a human being **b :** PERSON **:** human being ⟨a feckless ~ who hasn't the faintest idea how to run a house —C.F.Brockington⟩ **2** *relig* **a :** the bread in the sacrament of the Lord's Supper held by some to be and by others to represent Christ's body **b :** the Christian church conceived as a mystical living being of which Christ is the head **c :** the form assumed by man after the resurrection of the dead **3 :** the trunk (as of a person, animal, plant) without appendages **:** the main, central, or principal part of something: as **a :** the nave of a church **b** (1) **:** the bed or box of a vehicle on or in which the load is placed (2) **:** the enclosed or partly enclosed part of an automobile usu. not including the hood and fenders **c :** the part of a garment covering the body or trunk **d** (1) **:** the main part of a document, speech, or literary composition as distinguished from the title, preamble, preface, conclusion, or appendixes (2) **:** the text of a book as distinguished from the front matter, footnotes, and back matter (3) **:** the main part of a social or business letter as distinguished from the heading, salutation, and close **e :** the hull of a ship **f :** the sound box or pipe of a musical instrument **g :** the dominant part of a fortification **h :** TUBE 3a **i :** the statement of a plaintiff's case in a legal action **j :** the main or the larger part of a tool ⟨the ~ of a square is its larger arm⟩ **k :** the fuselage of an aircraft **l** *in printing* (1) **:** text or ordinary reading matter esp. as distinguished from headlines, display lines, footnotes, or tables ⟨a good ~ type⟩ ⟨~ matter⟩ (2) **:** the main matter of a table exclusive of the headings **m :** the largest part of a container; *esp* **:** the part forming the side walls in a metal can body **n :** the main casing of a projectile; *specif* **:** the part of a projectile between the bourrelet and the rotating band **4 a :** a mass or portion of matter esp. distinct in its totality from other masses ⟨a ~ of cold air⟩ ⟨a ~ of water⟩ ⟨no definite proof that the *bodies* found were nitrogen bubbles —H.G.Armstrong⟩ **b** *obs* **:** the real as opposed to the symbolical **:** the substance as opposed to the shadow **c :** one of the seven planets of the old astronomy — called also *celestial body, heavenly body* **d :** one of the seven metals corresponding to the seven planets of the old astronomy — called also *terrestrial body* **e :** a solid figure in geometry **f :** a kind or form of matter **:** a material substance ⟨combining chemical elements to form compound *bodies*⟩ **g :** AMOUNT, QUANTITY **:** BULK, EXTENT **h :** something that embodies, realizes, or gives concrete reality to a thing ⟨see how his theory works in the solid ~ of a novel —C.C.Walcutt⟩ ⟨his intuitions of the future may still give ~ to a better world —*N.Y. Times*⟩; *specif* **:** something that is perceptible or realizable as exhibited in space, that has sensible qualities, or that is the cause of sensation **i** *obs* **:** ENTITY, SUBJECT **j :** ORE BODY **5** *archaic* **:** a vessel for distilling **:** CUCURBIT **6 :** a group or number of persons or things: as **a :** a fighting unit **:** FORCE ⟨a ~ of cavalry⟩ **b :** a group of individuals united by a common tie or organized for some purpose **:** a collective whole or totality **:** CORPORATION ⟨a legislative ~⟩ ⟨a clerical ~⟩ ⟨the student ~ of the university⟩ ⟨a solid ~ of educated readers —V.S.Pritchett⟩ **c :** a number of particulars regarded as forming a system or embodied in a comprehensive and systematic presentation ⟨a ~ of facts⟩ ⟨a ~ of law⟩ ⟨a ~ of learning⟩ ⟨a ~ of precedents⟩ **7 a :** VISCOSITY, CONSISTENCY — used esp. of oils and grease ⟨a paint with considerable ~ is needed to hide the light undercoating⟩ ⟨oil used in machinery that heats up must have a good deal of ~⟩ **b :** compactness or firmness of texture in cloth **c :** fullness or resonance of a musical tone ⟨his baritone has ~ and richness⟩ **d :** fullness or richness of flavor — used of a beverage **e :** IMPORT, SIGNIFICANCE, MEANINGFULNESS — usu. used of a literary or dramatic work ⟨a play with very little ~ but quite amusing⟩ **f :** strength in intermediate cards (as tens, nines, and eights) in a bridge hand additional to strength in higher cards **8 a :** a clay or a mixture (as of clay and frit or ground rock) from which clayware is made **b :** a piece of ceramic ware distinct from its glaze **9 a :** the part of an attachment plug that screws into a lamp holder **b** (1) **:** the part of a lamp holder or receptacle that contains the contacts (2) **:** a lamp holder and its outer shell **c :** the part of a flexible cord connector that receives the attachment plug cap **10** *of printer's type* **a :** the part extending from foot to shoulder **:** all that underlies the bevel ⟨a kerned letter extends beyond the edge of the ~⟩ — called also *shank;* see TYPE illustration **b :** the distance from belly to back — used as a dimension ⟨a 10-point face on a 12-point ~⟩

[2]**body** \"\ *vt* -ED/-ING/-ES [ME *bodien*, fr. [1]*body*] **1 :** to furnish with a body **:** give material form or shape to **:** EMBODY ⟨believed the sovereign state *bodied* a divine idea⟩ **2 :** to give form or shape to in imagination or art **:** REPRESENT, SYMBOLIZE, INDICATE — often used with *forth* ⟨never been a poet who enjoyed the sensuous world with more gusto . . . or who more solidly *bodied* it forth —Edmund Wilson⟩ ⟨an allegorical figure ~*ing* forth the plight of modern man⟩ **3 :** to give strength, substance, or body to; *specif* **:** to increase the viscosity of (an oil) usu. by heating with resulting polymerization — see BODIED OIL

body blow *n* **1 :** a usu. hard blow in boxing that lands between the neck and the waistline **2 :** a serious setback or defeat ⟨the committee has already delivered a *body blow* to wage stabilization —*New Republic*⟩

body brush *n* **:** a stiff bristle brush used in grooming an animal esp. to remove loose scurf and dander from the coat

body brussels *n, usu cap 2d B* [fr. *Brussels*, Belgium] **:** BRUSSELS CARPET 1

body-build \'≈,≈\ *n* **:** the distinctive physical makeup of a human being **:** CONSTITUTION 3a

body cavity *n* **:** a cavity within an animal body; *specif* **:** the more or less complete space intervening in all higher animals between the body wall and the digestive tract and in mammals and birds divided by the diaphragm into an anterior thoracic cavity that contains heart, lungs, and esophagus and a peritoneal cavity that contains the remainder of the digestive system, the internal parts of the reproductive system, and certain other organs — see COELOM

body cell *n* **1 :** SOMATIC CELL — opposed to *germ cell* **2 :** the one of two cells produced by division of the generative cell in the pollen grain of certain gymnosperms that in turn divides to produce two male nuclei or cells

body-centered \'≈¦≈≈\ *adj, of a space lattice* **:** having like points at both ends of every vector parallel and equal to that between the corner and the center of the unit cell **:** having identical atoms or atomic groupings at and about the corners and the center of the unit cell

[1]**body check** *n* **:** a blocking of an opponent with the body in ice hockey and lacrosse

[2]**body check** *vb* [[1]*body check*] **:** to block with a body check

body clothes *n pl* **:** clothing for the body; *esp* **:** UNDERCLOTHES

body coat *n* **:** a coat of opaque paint laid on before translucent coats (as in automobile painting)

body color *n* **1 :** the color of the body of absorbing substances (as gems) due to transmitted light — opposed to *surface color* **2 a :** a pigment that imparts opacity or hiding power to a paint **b :** an opaque coat of paint **c :** the predominant color of a house or other object as contrasted with the color of the trim

body corporate *n, pl* **bodies corporate :** CORPORATION

body english *n, usu cap E* **:** the instinctive attempt of a player to control the movement of a ball or puck after it has been thrown, batted, stroked, or bowled by contorting his body in the desired direction

body fluid *n* **:** a fluid or fluid secretion (as lymph) of the body

bodyguard \'≈,≈\ *n* [*body* + *guard*] **:** a usu. armed attendant who travels with an individual to protect him from bodily harm

body harness *n* **:** the part of a horse's harness worn on or hanging down from the trunk and hindquarters and including saddle, bellybands, crupper, and breeching

body heat *n* **:** ANIMAL HEAT

body image *n* **:** a subjective picture of one's own physical appearance established both by self-observation and by noting the reactions of others

bodying agent *n* **:** an agent that gives body to a material (as a paint, a plastic, or a cosmetic) with which it is mixed or with which it coalesces

body·kins \'bädəkənz, -dēk-\ *interj* [*body* + *-kin* + *-s*] *obs* — a mild oath used esp. in the phrase *God's bodykins*

bodyless *var of* BODILESS

body-line \'≈,≈\ *or* **body-line bowling** *n* **:** bowling in cricket aimed generally at the leg stump esp. when fast, pitched short, and made to rise sharply — compare LEG THEORY

body louse *n* **:** a louse primarily feeding on the body as distinguished from the extremities or head or from the plumage, pelage, or other modified part of the body; *esp* **:** the sucking louse (*Pediculus humanus humanus*) feeding on the body and breeding in the clothing of man

body mark *or* **body stroke** *or* **body line** *n* **:** the downstroke of a letter

body odor *n* **1 :** the characteristic odor of a living animal body **2 :** an unpleasant odor from a perspiring or unclean person

body out *vt* **:** to make more ample **:** fill out ⟨*body out* the sketchy account of the campaign⟩

body paper *or* **body stock** *n* **:** paper that is to be further processed (as by coating, gumming, impregnating, or vulcanizing) — called also *base paper, raw stock*

body pew *n* **:** a quadrangular enclosed area in the body of a church for a group of worshipers (as a family)

body pigment *n* **:** the chief pigment constituent of a paint

body plan *n* **:** an end elevation in shipbuilding showing the contour of the sides or the transverse vertical cross sections of a ship at certain points of her length

body plasm *n* **:** SOMATOPLASM

body politic *n, pl* **bodies politic 1** *archaic* **:** CORPORATION 2 **2 :** the whole people organized and united under a single political authority **:** a politically organized society **:** STATE

body post *n* **:** STERNPOST

body press *n* **:** a wrestling hold in which one contestant attempts to pin the other on his back by lying on top of him

body rappel *n* **:** a technique of rappelling in which a doubled rope running from the rappel point is passed between the climber's legs, beneath the left buttock, up and around the left hip, across the chest, over the right shoulder, and across the back to the left hand, the right hand grasping the rope above at about shoulder height — called also *Dülfer rappel*

body release *or* **body shutter release** *n* **:** a lever on the body of a camera connected mechanically to the shutter and permitting the shutter to be released easily when the camera is held at eye level

body servant *n* **:** a valet or personal maid

body shop *n* **:** a shop at which automotive bodies are made or repaired

body slam *n* **:** a wrestling throw in which the opponent's body is lifted and brought down hard to the mat

body snatcher *n* **:** one who without authority takes corpses from graves usu. for purposes of dissection or for sale for such purposes **:** RESURRECTIONIST

body stalk *n* **:** the mesodermal cord that connects a fetus with its chorion and through which course the umbilical vessels

body track *n* **:** each of the parallel tracks in a railroad yard upon which cars are switched or stored

body type *n* **:** the type commonly used for the text of a piece of printed matter (as an article, newspaper, or book) as distinguished from the varying type used for such items as headlines, appendixes, footnotes, or advertisements

body varnish *n* **:** RUBBING VARNISH

body wall *n* **:** the external surface of the body in all animals consisting of original ectoderm and mesoderm and enclosing the body cavity

body wave *n* **:** an earthquake vibration transmitted through the earth's interior — contrasted with *surface wave*

body whorl *n* **:** the last and outer whorl of a univalve shell

body·wood \'≈,≈\ *n* **:** cordwood cut from the bole of a tree

bodywork \'≈,≈\ *n* **1 :** a vehicle body **2 a :** the act or process of making vehicle bodies **b :** the act or process of repairing vehicle bodies

boe *var of* BO

boea \'büə\ *n* -s [native name in the East Indies] **:** a hard alcohol-soluble Manila copal obtained in the East Indies usu. as a fossil resin

boe·bera \'bōbərə\ [NL, after J. von *Boeber* †1820 Ger. botanist] *syn of* DYSSODIA

boeck's sarcoid \'beks-\ *also* **boeck's disease** *n, usu cap B* [after Caesar P. M. *Boeck* †1917 Norw. dermatologist] **:** SARCOIDOSIS

boe·del·hou·der \'büd^əl,haudə(r)\ *n* -s [D, fr. *boedel* property (fr. MD) + *houder* holder, fr. *houden* to hold (fr. MD) + *-er;* akin to ON *bōl* farm, abode and to OHG *holtan* to hold — more at BUILD, HOLD] **:** an administrator or a trustee of a boedelhouding

boe·del·hou·ding \-diŋ\ *n* -s [D, fr. *boedel* property + *houding* holding, fr. *houden* to hold + *-ing*] *Roman Dutch law* **:** the holding by an administrator or trustee of the community property of husband and wife as still subject to the community rights after the decease of either

boe·del·schei·ding \'büd^əl,skādiŋ\ *n* -s [D, fr. *boedel* property + *scheiding* separation, fr. *scheiden* to separate (fr. MD *sceiden, scēden*) + *-ing;* akin to OHG *sceidan* to separate — more at SHED] *Roman Dutch law* **:** partition of an estate

boeh·men·ism *or* **beh·men·ism** \'bāmə,nizəm\ *n* -s *usu cap* [after Jakob *Böhme* (*Boehme* or in England *Behmen*) †1624 Ger. theosophist & mystic] **:** the mystical teaching of Böhme which exerted an influence on George Fox and Quakerism

boeh·men·ist \-nəst\ *also* **boeh·men·ite** \-,nīt\ *or* **boehmist** \'bāməst\ *n* -s *usu cap* [after J. Böhme (*Boehme*)] **:** an adherent of Boehmenism

boeh·me·ria \bā'mirēə, bō'm-\ *n, cap* [NL, fr. G.R.*Boehmer* (Böhmer) †1803 Ger. botanist + NL *-ia*] **:** a large and widely distributed genus of trees, shrubs, and herbs (family Urticaceae) with glomerate flowers in spikes — see RAMIE

boehm·i·an \'bāmēən\ *adj, usu cap* [fr. J.Böhme (*Boehme*) †1624 + E *-ian*] **:** of or relating to Boehmenism

boehmite *also* **böhmite** \'bā,mīt, 'bō,m-\ *n* -s *sometimes cap* [G *böhmit*, fr. J.*Böhm* (Boehm), 20th cent. Ger. scientist + G *-it* -ite] **:** a mineral consisting of an orthorhombic form of aluminum oxide and hydroxide AlO(OH) found in bauxite

boehm system \'bām-, 'bōm-\ *n usu cap B* [after Theobald Böhm (*Boehm*) †1881 Ger. musician, its inventor] **:** an improved system of keys and fingering invented for the flute and later adapted to other woodwind instruments

boe·ken·hout \'bükən,haut\ *n* -s [Afrik, fr. *boeken-* beech (fr. MD *boeke, bouke*) + *hout* wood, fr. MD; akin to OHG *buohha* beech and to OHG *holz* wood — more at BEECH, HOLT] **:** a small tree (*Faurea saligna*) of the family Proteaceae of the savanna forests of West Africa with durable wood that is yellowish brown to reddish in color

boe·o·tarch \'bēə,tärk, bē'ō,t-\ *n* -s *sometimes cap* [Gk *Boiōtarchēs*, fr. *Boiōtia* Boeotia + *-archēs* -arch] **:** one of the body of chief magistrates elected in ancient times by the cities of central Greece comprising the Boeotian Confederacy

[1]**boe·o·tian** \(')bē¦ōshən\ *adj* [*Boeotia*, district in ancient Greece (fr. L, fr. Gk *Boiōtia*) + E *-an*] **1** *usu cap* **a :** of, relating to, or characteristic of the ancient district of Boeotia in east central Greece **b :** of, relating to, or characteristic of Boeotians **2** *often cap* **:** marked by stupidity and philistinism **:** crudely obtuse **:** DULL, LOUTISH ⟨a ~ distaste for art⟩

[2]**boeotian** \"\ *n* -s **1** *cap* **a :** a native or inhabitant of Boeotia **b :** an Aeolic dialect of ancient Greek used by the Boeotians **2 :** *often cap* **:** a dull obtuse individual **:** a boorish opponent of art and letters **:** PHILISTINE, BOOR

boer \'bō(ə)r, 'bȯ(ə)r, -ōə, -ȯ(ə) *also* bů(ə)r, bůə\ *n* -s *usu cap, often attrib* [D, lit., farmer — more at BOOR] **:** a South African of Dutch or Huguenot descent; *esp* **:** a rural descendant of the early Dutch settlers

boer·haa·via \bůr'hävēə\ [NL, fr. Hermann *Boerhaave* †1738 Dutch physician + NL *-ia*] *syn of* BOERHAVIA

boer·ha·via \bůr'hāvēə, -'häv-\ *n, cap* [NL, alter. of *Boerhaavia*] **:** a genus of widely distributed pubescent or glandular tropical herbs (family Nyctaginaceae) having small apetalous flowers and club-shaped ribbed fruit

boes *pl of* BO

boe·thu·si·an \,bōə'thüzh(ē)ən\ *n* -s *usu cap* [*Boethus*, 1st cent. B.C. Jewish high priest, founder of the sect + E *-ian*] **:** a member of a Jewish sect associated in Jewish tradition with the Sadducees

boet·i·nese \,büt^ən'ēz, -ēs\ *n, pl* **boetinese** *or* **boetineses** *usu cap* [irreg. fr. *Boeton, Boetong, Buton*, island of Indonesia + E *-ese*] **1 :** a Papuan people of Netherlands New Guinea **2 :** a member of the Boetinese people

B of E \¦bē'vē\ *abbr* board of education

boff \'bäf\ *n* -s [perh. fr. *box office*] *slang* **1 :** BELLY LAUGH **2 :** a gag or line designed to produce a belly laugh **3 :** HIT 2b **4 :** [2]PUNCH 3

bof·fin \'bäfin\ *n* -s [origin unknown] *slang Brit* **:** a scientific expert

boff·o·la \bä'fōlə, bə'f-\ *n* -s [irreg. fr. *boff*] **1** *slang* **:** BOFF 1, 2 **2** *slang* **:** HIT 2b

B of H \¦bēə¦vāch\ *abbr* board of health

bo·fors gun \'bō,fȯrz-, -rs-\ *n, usu cap B* [fr. *Bofors*, munition works in Sweden where it was first made] **:** a double-barreled 40 mm. automatic antiaircraft gun firing an explosive projectile 120 times per minute

B of T \¦bēəv¦tē\ *abbr* board of trade

[1]**bog** \'bäg, 'bȯg\ *n* -s *often attrib* [of Celt origin; akin to IrGael & ScGael *bog* soft (respectively fr. & akin to OIr *bocc*), ScGael *boglach* swamp, IrGael *bogach;* akin to OE *būgan* to bend — more at BOW] **1 a :** wet spongy ground where a heavy body is likely to sink **:** QUAGMIRE, MORASS; *esp* **:** an inadequately drained area rich in plant residues, usu. acid in reaction, frequently surrounding a body of open water, and having a characteristic flora (as of sedges, heaths, and sphagnum) — compare MARSH, MEADOW, SWAMP **b :** low-lying land having a thick layer of peat **2 :** land making up a bog

[2]**bog** \"\ *vb* **bogged; bogged; bogging; bogs** *vt* **:** to cause to sink into or as if into a bog **:** submerge in a bog **:** MIRE, IMPEDE **:** slow up ⟨treacherous ground in which you can easily get *bogged*⟩ ⟨too much pedantry ~*s* what might otherwise have some interest⟩ — often used with *down* ⟨the book is the result of much careful research, but it is not *bogged* down by it —John Gould⟩ ~ *vi* **:** to become sunk in or as if in a bog **:** become impeded and slowed up — usu. used with *down* ⟨work on the new highway *bogged* down for lack of cement⟩ ⟨the attack would ~ down sooner or later —Norman Mailer⟩

bo·gach *also* **bo·gash** \(')bō¦gash\ *n* -ES [Ar] **1 :** a subsidiary unit of value in Yemen **2 :** a coin representing one bogach

bo·gan \'bōgən\ *n* -s [of Algonquian origin; akin to Malecite *pecelaygan* stopping place] *dial* **:** POKELOGAN

bog asphodel *n* **:** either of two bog herbs (*Narthecium ossifragum*) of Europe and (*N. americanum*) of the U.S.

bo·ga·tyr \,bōgə'ti(ə)r, '≈≈,≈\ *n, pl* **bogatyrs** \-rz\ *or* **bogaty·ri** \-irē\ [Russ *bogatyr'* hero, athlete, warrior, fr. ORuss *bogatyrĭ*, of Turkic origin; akin to Turk *batur* brave] **:** one of the legendary medieval heroes of Russia

bogbean \'≈,≈\ *n* **:** BUCKBEAN

bog bilberry *n* **:** an evergreen shrub (*Vaccinium uliginosum alpinum*) with coriaceous leaves and one to three nearly sessile 4-parted flowers from a scaly bud

bog birch *n* **1 :** YELLOW BUCKTHORN **2 :** SCRUB BIRCH

bog blitter *n, chiefly Scot* **:** the European bittern

bog borer *n* **1 :** WOODCOCK 1a(2) **2 :** an instrument for sampling vegetation below the surface of a bog

bogbuttons \'≈,≈≈\ *n* **:** HAIRY PIPEWORT

bog cotton *n* **:** any of several bog sedges of the genus *Eriophorum* with plumose cottony heads

bog cress *n* **:** BITTER CRESS 1

bog crook *n, Irish* **:** chronic aphosphorosis of cattle

bog deal *n* **:** BOG PINE

bog earth *n* **:** a soil composed mostly of fine siliceous matter and partly decomposed vegetable fiber

[1]**bo·gey** *or* **bo·gy** *or* **bo·gie** \'bōgē, -gi; *in senses 2&3 often and in the other senses sometimes* 'bůg- *or* 'büg-\ *n, pl* **bogeys** *or* **bogies** [prob. alter. of *bogle*] **1** *usu cap, archaic* **:** DEVIL 1 **2 a :** GOBLIN **b :** SPECTER, PHANTOM **3 a :** an object of dread, fear, or loathing ⟨the ~ of war⟩ **b :** a source of annoyance, perplexity, or harassment ⟨the necessity of grueling study was a ~ he could not escape⟩ **4 :** an unidentified aircraft detected visually or by radar **5** *golf* **a** *chiefly Brit* **:** the number of strokes for each hole set as normally required by an average player **b :** one stroke over par on a hole **6 :** a numerical standard of performance set up as a mark to be attained (as in a contest) **7 a :** a quota, budget, or other estimated figure set up by management in preplanning **b :** a quota restricting output maintained by informal agreement among employees

[2]**bo·gey** \'bōgē, -gi *sometimes* 'bůg- *or* 'büg-\ *vt* **bogeyed; bogeyed; bogeying; bogeys :** to shoot (a hole in golf) in one over par ⟨~*ed* the 17th hole⟩

[3]**bo·gey** \"\ *n* -s [prob. fr. Sc, outhouse, cooking galley on a fishing boat] **:** a small stove

[4]**bogey** *var of* BOGIE

bo·gey·man \'bōgē,man, 'bůg-,'büg-, -gə-, -,maa(ə)n\ *n, pl* **bogey·men** \-,men\ [*bogey* + *man*] **:** a monstrous imaginary figure used in threatening children; *broadly* **:** a terrifying person or thing **:** MENACE

bogfern \'≈,≈\ *n* **1 :** a chain fern (*Woodwardia virginica*) **2 :** MASSACHUSETTS FERN

bog garden *n* **:** an ornamental garden in an artificially created or natural bog

bog·gart \'bägə(r)t\ *n* -s [earlier *boggard, buggard*, fr. [1]*bug* + *-ard*] **1** *dial chiefly Brit* **a :** GOBLIN **b :** a specter or ghost; *esp* **:** one that is believed to be malicious **2** *dial chiefly Brit* **:** SCARECROW

bog gentian *n* **:** a New Zealand herb (*Gentiana townsoni*) with wiry stems, mostly basal leaves, and white flowers

[1]**bog·gle** \'bägəl\ *vb* **boggled; boggled; boggling** \'bäg(ə)liŋ\ **boggles** [perh. fr. [3]*boggle*] *vi* **1 a :** to make a sudden jerky movement (as of alarm) **:** start with fright **:** SHY ⟨the prisoner *boggled* at the sight of the gallows⟩ **b :** to be startled (as with

amazement or surprise) : be overwhelmed : be set reeling ⟨the reporters *boggled* over the president's sensational press statement⟩ ⟨the imagination ~*s* at the thought of interstellar distances⟩ **2 a :** to move hesitatingly or evasively : hold back from decisive action (as through doubt, fear, or scruples) : show indecision : SHILLY-SHALLY ⟨his responsibilities coupled with his marked ineptitude caused him to be perpetually *boggling*⟩ **b :** to raise objections usu. minor or petty : hang back from full acceptance or agreement : DEMUR, STICKLE, HAGGLE ⟨no matter how good the argument, he would always pick out something to ~ about⟩ **3 :** to perform an action awkwardly : work unskillfully : make clumsy efforts ⟨uses only one epithet, but it is the right one, and never ~*s* and patches —Leslie Stephen⟩ : BUNGLE, BLUNDER ⟨*boggling* along through the job⟩ **~ vt 1 a :** to overwhelm with wonder or bewilderment **b** *dial Brit* : EMBARRASS, PERPLEX ⟨*boggled* by his father's unexpected return⟩ **2 :** to attend to in an awkward clumsy manner : BUNGLE ⟨*boggling* the little affairs of his own life —Paul de Kruif⟩ **syn** see DEMUR

²**boggle** \"\ *n* -S **1 :** the action of boggling **2** *archaic* : a difficult, unpleasant, or bungled situation

³**boggle** \"\ *var of* BOGLE

bog grass *n* : any grass or sedge that grows in a bog; *specif* : a sedge of the genus *Carex*

bog·gy \'bägē, 'bȯgē, -gi\ *adj* -ER/-EST [¹*bog* + -*y*] **1 :** consisting of, containing, or being a bog : SWAMPY **2** *med* : marked by sponginess and turgidity ⟨~ edema of the mucous membrane of the nose in hay fever⟩

bog harrow *n* : a disc harrow with extra-large notched discs for breaking up rank vegetation or hard soil

bog·head coal \'bäg,hed-\ *also* **boghead** *n, often cap B* [fr. *Boghead*, West Lothian, Scotland] : a cannel coal in which algal remains predominate and which is valuable as a source of paraffin oils and gas

boghole \'⸗,⸗\ *n* : a hole or depression in a land surface having a miry or spongy bottom

¹**bo·gie** *also* **bo·gey** *or* **bo·gy** \'bōgē, -gi *sometimes* 'bùg-, 'büg-\ *n, pl* **bogies** *also* **bogeys** [origin unknown] **1 :** a low strongly built truck or cart **2 a** *chiefly Brit* (1) : a swiveling axle or truck on which the leading wheels of a locomotive are fixed (2) : a four-wheel swiveling truck supporting a railroad car **b** *chiefly Brit* : a locomotive or car equipped with a bogie **c :** a swiveling truck including two or more pairs of wheels and used at the end of a vehicle (as a gun carriage) **d :** the drive-wheel assembly and undercarriage of a 6-wheel truck comprising the rear four wheels so mounted as to adjust themselves to sharp curves and road irregularities **3 :** one of the weight-carrying wheels on the inside perimeter of the tread of a tank serving to keep the treads in line

²**bogie** \"\ *n* -S [fr. *Bogie* river, Aberdeenshire, Scotland] : tobacco in small twisted ropes

³**bogie** *var of* BOGEY

bogie engine *n* [¹*bogie*] *chiefly Brit* : a locomotive with one or both ends mounted on a bogie

bo·gie·man \'bōgē,man, 'bùg-, 'büg-, -gə̇-, -,maa(ə)n\ *var of* BOOGEYMAN

bogie roll *n* [²*bogie*] : ²BOGIE

bogie wagon *n* [¹*bogie*] *chiefly Brit* : a railroad car with one or both ends mounted on a bogie

bo·gi·ji·ab \,bōgē'jhē,ab, -gē'jē,-\ *n, pl* **bogijiab** *or* **bogijiabs** *usu cap* **1 :** an Andaman people of So. Andaman Island **2 :** a member of the Bogijiab people

bog iron ore *or* **bog iron** *n* : a porous variety of limonite

bog kalmia *or* **bog laurel** *n* : SWAMP LAUREL

bog lake *n* : a lake with bogs around its margins

bog·land \'bäg, 'bȯg + ,land\ *n* : BOG 2

bo·gle \'bōgəl, 'bäg-\ *n* -S [E dial. (Sc & northern) *bogill, boggle, bogle* terrifying apparition, goblin; akin to ME *bugge* scarecrow — more at BUG] **1** *also* **bog·gle** \'bäg-\ *dial Brit* : a goblin or specter : any object of dread, fear, or loathing : BOGEY **2** *also* **boggle** *dial Brit* : SCARECROW **3** *chiefly Scot* : HIDE-AND-GO-SEEK

bog lemming *n* : a lemming mouse (*Synaptomys cooperi*) that ranges as far south as the U.S.

bog·let \'bäglət\ *n* -S [¹*bog* + -*let*] : a little bog

bog lime *n* : earthy impure calcium carbonate deposited in lakes and ponds largely through the chemical action of aquatic plants

bog manganese *n* : a mineral of variable composition being chiefly hydrous manganese oxide : WAD

bog mine *or* **bog-mine ore** \'⸗,⸗-\ *n* : BOG ORE

bog moss *n* **1 :** a moss of the genus *Sphagnum* **2 :** a plant of the genus *Mayaca*

bog myrtle *n* **1 :** SWEET GALE **2 :** BUCKBEAN

bo·go \'bō(,)gō\ *n* -S [Hiligaynon, Sugbuhanon, & Magindanao] : a Philippine tree (*Garuga abilo*) of the family Burseraceae with pinnate leaves and fleshy fruits

bog oak *n* : oak that has become dark from long burial in a peat bog

bo·go·do lama \bə'gō(,)dō-\ *n, pl* **bogodo lamas** *usu cap B&L* [Tibetan] : TESHU LAMA

bo·go·mil \'bägə,mil\ *also* **bog·o·mile** \-,mīl\ *n* -S *usu cap* [Russ *bogomil*, after *Bogomilŭ*, 10th cent. Bulgarian priest, founder of the sect] : one of a Bulgarian sect about 1000–1400 which held that the Creator had two sons, Satanaël or Satan, and Christ or Logos

bog·o·mil·ism \'bägəmə̇,lizəm\ *n* -S *usu cap* : the distinctive doctrines of the Bogomils

bo·gong moth \'bō,gȯŋ-, -gäŋ-\ *or* **bu·gong moth** \'bü,-\ *n* [fr. Mount *Bogong*, highest peak of Victoria, Australia] : an Australian noctuid moth (*Agrotis infusa*) that is made into a paste and eaten by the aborigines when the moths aestivate in huge clusters in rocky mountains to which they migrate from the breeding grounds many miles away

bog onion *n* **1 :** JACK-IN-THE-PULPIT 1 **2** [so called fr. its onion-shaped corm] : ROYAL FERN **3** [so called fr. the onion odor sometimes present in the timber] : an Australian tree (*Owenia venosa*) having foliage with an odor like garlic

bog orchid *n* : any of several orchids growing in bogs; *esp* : a small European orchid (*Malaxis paludosa*) with inconspicuous green flowers

bog ore *n* **1 :** BOG IRON ORE **2 :** BOG MANGANESE

bo·go·tá *or* **bo·go·ta** \,bōgə'tä, -'tō\ *adj, usu cap* [fr. *Bogotá*, Colombia] : of or from Bogotá, the capital of Colombia : of the kind or style prevalent in Bogotá

bog owl *n* : SHORT-EARED OWL

bog pimpernel *n* : a small creeping European herb (*Anagallis tenella*) with delicate pink flowers

bog pine *n* : the wood of pine preserved in peat bogs

bog rose *n* : WILD PINK 2

bog rosemary *n* : a shrub of the genus *Andromeda* — called also *moorwort*

bog rush *n* **1 :** any rush of the genus *Juncus*, growing in bogs **2 :** any of several sedges of the genus *Schoenus* (esp. *S. nigricans*)

bogs *pl of* BOG, *pres 3d sing of* BOG

bogsha *var of* BUQSHA

bog soil *n* : an intrazonal group of poorly drained dark peat or muck soils underlain by peat and developed under swamp or marsh types of vegetation

bog spavin *n* : a soft swelling usu. on the inner surface of the hock of horses resulting from chronic inflammation of the hock joint with accumulation of fluid in the synovial capsule

bog spruce *n* : BLACK SPRUCE 1

bog star *n* : GRASS-OF-PARNASSUS; *esp* : an herb (*Parnassia palustris*) found in wet places in mountainous or northern regions in the northern hemisphere

bog stitchwort *n* : a bog or marsh chickweed (*Stellaria uliginosa*) with weak stems and tiny white flowers

bog strawberry *n* : MARSH CINQUEFOIL

bog·sucker \'bäg+,-\ *n* : WOODCOCK 1a(2)

bog timber *n* : BOGWOOD

bog torch *n* **1 :** GOLDEN CLUB **2 :** SNOWY ORCHID

bog·trotter \'bäg+,-\ *n* **1 :** a native or resident of Ireland — usu. used disparagingly **2 a :** SHORT-EARED OWL **b :** AMERICAN BITTERN

¹**bogue** \'bōg\ *vi* -ED/-ING/-S [origin unknown] *dial* : to move aimlessly or slowly ⟨just *boguing* around⟩

²**bogue** \"\ *also* **bogue bream** *n* -S [F, fr. MF, fr. OProv *boga*, fr. L *boca*, fr. Gk *boak-, boax*, a sea fish] : BOCE

³**bogue** \"\ *n* -S [LaF, fr. Choctaw *bok, bouk* stream, creek] *chiefly South & Midland* : a passage of water : STREAM

¹**bo·gus** \'bōgəs\ *adj* [fr. *bogus*, a machine for making counterfeit money, perh. irreg. fr. *bogle*] **1 a :** not genuine : COUNTERFEIT, FORGED ⟨~ currency⟩ ⟨~ documents⟩ : being a spurious imitation of or substitute for the genuine ⟨imitation rosewood or oak panels, false parquetry, ersatz beams, ~ gilt dadoes —Janet Flanner⟩ : SHAM, PRETENDED ⟨a ~ king⟩ **b :** pretending to the possession of qualities or character not actually possessed ⟨wrote with ~ elegance —Malcolm Cowley⟩ : false and artificial in tone ⟨a ~ literary flavor⟩ **2** *of a postage stamp, coin, or note* : made privately for fraudulent purposes to appear to be a genuine issue but not in exact imitation of any particular official issue — often distinguished from *counterfeit* **3 :** having qualities like those of a specified paper or board but made partially or wholly of substitute or inferior materials ⟨~ bristol⟩ ⟨~ manila⟩ **syn** see COUNTERFEIT

²**bogus** \"\ *n* -ES [fr. *bogus*, a machine for making counterfeit money] **1** *archaic* : counterfeit money **2 a** *slang* : FILLER 1d(1) **b :** printing type or copy set usu. by union requirement in duplication of something that is already typeset and that may have been molded for stereotyping

³**bogus** \"\ *n* -ES [short for *calibogus*] : a liquor made of rum and molasses

bog violet *n* : a butterwort (*Pinguicula vulgaris*) with violet-colored flowers

bog whortleberry *n* : BOG BILBERRY

bog willow *n* : a pussy willow (esp. *Salix discolor* and *S. pedicellaris*)

bogwood \'⸗,⸗\ *n* : the wood of trees preserved in peat bogs and used chiefly for ornamental purposes

¹**bogy** *var of* BOGEY

²**bogy** *var of* BOGIE

bo·gy·man \'bōgē,man, 'bùg-,'büg-, -gə̇-, -,maa(ə)n\ *var of* BOOGEYMAN

¹**boh** \'bō\ *n* -S [Burmese *bō*] *India* : a leader of dacoits

²**boh** *var of* BOO

bo·hai \bō'hī\ *n, pl* **bohai** *or* **bohais** *usu cap* **1 :** an ancient people of northeast Asia once occupying the Sea of Japan coast of the present Soviet Far East **2 :** a member of the Bohai people

¹**bo·hai·ric** \bō'hīrik\ *n* -S *usu cap* [fr. *Bohair*ah Lower Egypt (fr. Ar *buhairah* lake) + E -*ic*] : a Coptic dialect formerly spoken in the northwestern Nile delta region including Alexandria and surviving in Coptic Christian liturgical use and as the language of the official Bible version of the Coptic Church

²**bohairic** \(')⸗¦⸗⸗\ *adj, usu cap* : of, relating to, being, or composed in Bohairic

bo·hea \bō'hē\ *n* -S *often cap* [Chin (Pek) *wu*[3]-*i*[2], hills in China where it was grown] : BLACK TEA — used in the 18th century of the best China black tea and now usu. of inferior grades of black tea

bo·he·mia \bō'hēmēə\ *n* -S *often cap* [fr. *Bohemia*, formerly a kingdom, now a province of western Czechoslovakia, thought of as the home of the gypsies; trans. of F *bohème*] : a community of bohemians : the world of bohemians

¹**bo·he·mi·an** \bō'hēmēən, -myən\ *n* -S [*Bohemia* + E -*an*] **1** *cap* **a :** a native or inhabitant of Bohemia in central Europe **b :** the group of dialects of Czech used in Bohemia **2** *often cap* [trans. of F *bohème*] **a :** one who wanders about not having a definite home: as (1) : VAGABOND (2) : GYPSY **b :** a follower of art, literature, or similar pursuits who adopts an individualistic, easygoing, and sometimes eccentric way of living that reflects protest against or indifference to social conventions

²**bohemian** \(')⸗¦⸗(⸗)⸗\ *adj* **1** *usu cap* **a :** of, relating to, or characteristic of the province of Bohemia **b :** of, relating to, or characteristic of the natives or inhabitants of the province of Bohemia **2** *usu cap* : of, relating to, or constituting Bohemian **3** *often cap* [trans. of F *bohème*] : of, relating to, or characteristic of bohemians : UNCONVENTIONAL

bohemian bole *n, usu cap 1st B* [*bole* (clay)] : a clay that is a yellow variety of bole

bohemian brethren *n pl, usu cap both Bs* : a Christian body organized in 1467 at Kunwald in Bohemia by followers of Peter of Cheltshic, reformist writer — see MORAVIAN

bohemian earth *n, often cap B* [prob. trans. of G *böhmische erde*] : TERRE VERTE 2

bohemian glass *n, usu cap B* **1 :** ornamental glass noted for its rich colors and incised or engraved patterns **2 :** a hard resistant potash-lime glass much used as a material for chemical ware

bo·he·mi·an·ism \-ə,nizəm\ *n* -S *often cap* : the outlook and way of living typical of bohemians

bohemian ruby *n, usu cap B* [prob. trans. of G *böhmischer rubin*] : a red variety of rock crystal

bohemian waxwing *n, usu cap B* [*bohemian* (gypsy); fr. its extensive and irregular wanderings] : a large waxwing (*Bombycilla garrula pallidiceps*) of northern No. America that closely resembles the smaller cedar waxwing

bo·reen *or* **bohi·reen** \bō'rēn, ,bōə'r-\ *var of* BOREEN

böhmite *sometimes cap, var of* BOEHMITE

bo·hor \'bō,hȯr\ *n* -S [Amharic *behōr*] : a small fawn-colored eastern African reedbuck (*Redunca bohor*)

bohora *usu cap, var of* BHORA

bohr atom \'bō(ə)r-, 'bȯ(ə)r-\ *n, usu cap B* [after Niels H. D. Bohr †1962 Dan. physicist] : the atom as described by the Bohr theory

bohr magneton *n, usu cap B* : a magneton based on quantum theory equal to about 9.273×10^{-21} centimeter dyne per gauss per particle

bohr orbit *n, usu cap B* : the hypothetical path of an electron about the nucleus of the Bohr atom

bohr radius *n, usu cap B* : the radius of the smallest or ground-state electron orbit in the hydrogen atom, equal to about 5.29×10^{-9} centimeter — compare BOHR THEORY

bohr theory *n, usu cap B* : a theory of the structure of the hydrogen atom that was later elaborated to apply to atoms of other elements: the hydrogen atom is conceived as a positively charged nucleus with an electron revolving around it in one of many possible circular orbits, each corresponding to a distinct energy state

bo·hunk \'bō,həŋk\ *n* -S [*Bohemian* + *Hunk* central European of the working class, prob. fr. *Hungarian*] **1 a** *often cap* : an eastern or southeastern European (as a Bohemian, Hungarian, or Czech) esp. of the working class — often taken to be offensive **b** *sometimes cap* : a usu. unskilled laborer esp. of foreign origin and usu. of eastern European or southeastern European parentage — often taken to be offensive **2** *slang* **a :** a rough-looking often illiterate or semiliterate individual : LOUT **b :** FELLOW, CHAP

boiar *var of* BOYAR

bo·id \'bōə̇d\ *n* -S [NL *Boidae*] : one of the Boidae

bo·i·dae \'bōə̇,dē\ *n pl, cap* [NL, fr. *Boa*, type genus + -*idae*] : a family of sometimes very large nonvenomous snakes having teeth in both jaws and rudiments of hind limbs in the form of hooks or spurs and preying chiefly on warm-blooded animals which they kill by crushing, the family being usu. regarded as including the boas, anacondas, and related snakes of the New World tropics in addition to the Old World pythons — see PYTHONIDAE

bo·i·ga \'bȯigə\ *n, cap* [NL] : the type genus of Boigidae

¹**bo·ig·id** \bō'ijə̇d\ *adj* [NL *Boigidae*] : of or relating to the family Boigidae

²**boigid** \"\ *n* -S : any snake of the family Boigidae

bo·i·gi·dae \bō'ijə̇,dē\ *n pl, cap* [NL, fr. *Boiga*, type genus + -*idae*] : a widely distributed family (type genus *Boiga*) consisting of somewhat venomous opisthoglyph snakes of which a few (as the African boomslang) are dangerous to man and being sometimes considered a subfamily of Colubridae — see CAT SNAKE

boii \'bȯi,ī, 'bōē,ī\ *n pl, usu cap* [L *Boi, Boii*] : a Celtic people from transalpine Gaul settled partly in northern Italy and partly on the Danube in the region called after them Bohemia

¹**boil** \'bȯil, *esp bef pause or cons* 'bȯiəl\ *n* -S [alter. (prob. influenced by ²*boil*) of ME *bile* — more at BILE] **1 :** FURUNCLE **2 :** SEED 4a

²**boil** \"\ *vb* -ED/-ING/-S [ME *boilen, boillen*, fr. OF *boillir*, fr. L *bullire* to bubble, boil, fr. *bulla* bubble — more at POLL (head)] *vi* **1 a :** to generate through the action of heat bubbles of vapor that rise and agitate the mass : be agitated by ebullition — used of a liquid **b :** to come to the boiling point ⟨a watched kettle never ~*s*⟩ ⟨the coffee ~*ed* up quickly⟩ **2 a :** to be agitated and tossed about in a manner suggestive of boiling water : bubble or foam violently : SEETHE, CHURN ⟨the sound of the river ~*ing* along the banks —C.S.Forester⟩ **b :** to move in a swirling eddying mass ⟨dust motes ~*ed* up in a ray of light —Archie Binns⟩ ⟨a great cloud of dust ~*ed* up past the windows —Hamilton Basso⟩ ⟨black smoke ~*ed* up from the burning warehouse⟩ **3 :** to be moved or excited (as with indignation or anger) : be intensely stirred up ⟨his blood ~*s* at the mention of it⟩ **4 a :** to rush tumultuously or headlong ⟨they ~*ed* through the door in pursuit of the fleeing bandit⟩ ⟨the insects would come ~*ing* out of the swamps —R.P.Warren⟩ **b :** to break forth : gush up or out : ERUPT ⟨the sensational news ~*ed* into headlines and bulletins⟩ **c** *of a fish* : to rise swiftly (as in striking) **5 :** to undergo the action of a boiling liquid ⟨the beans must ~ for some time⟩ **~ vt 1 :** to subject to the action of a boiling liquid (as in cooking or cleaning) ⟨the potatoes will need to be ~*ed* longer⟩ **2 :** to heat to the boiling point : cause (a liquid) to bubble with heat ⟨the water must be ~*ed* before use⟩ **3 :** to form or separate (as sugar or salt) by boiling or by evaporation involving ebullition ⟨they carefully ~*ed* the salt out of the water⟩ — **boil the pot 1 :** to provide the means of living ⟨he works 10 hours a day to *boil the pot* for his family⟩ **2 :** to turn out hackwork : produce potboilers ⟨a once-gifted writer who now simply *boils the pot*⟩

³**boil** \"\ *n* -S **1 :** the act or state of boiling : AGITATION **2 a :** a swirling upheaval of water; *esp* : one at the surface of a river, a large spring, a pool below a dam, or the sea **b :** the swirl made by a fish moving at or near the surface esp. when feeding **3 :** a disturbance in the surface soil caused by the escape of water under a water-excluding structure (as a levee or cofferdam) **4 :** a stage during which the metal bath in a steelmaking furnace seems to boil as a result of the escape of gas

boil disease *n* [¹*boil*] : a disease of freshwater fish caused by a myxosporidian protozoan (*Myxobolus pfeifferi*) that invades connective tissue and muscles forming large tumorous masses and commonly causing the death of the host

boil down *vt* **1 :** to reduce in bulk by boiling ⟨*boil down* syrup⟩ **2 :** CONDENSE ⟨*boil down* a narrative⟩; *also* : SIMPLIFY ⟨*boil down* the facts to a short statement⟩ **~ vi 1 :** to become reduced in bulk by boiling ⟨the syrup *boils down* in a very short time⟩ **2 :** to be adaptable to condensation ⟨the story *boils down* easily⟩ **3 :** to be equivalent : AMOUNT ⟨the facts *boil down* to very little significance⟩

boildown \'⸗,⸗\ *n* -S [*boil down*] : CONDENSATION, ABRIDGMENT

boiled *adj* [ME, fr. past part. of *boilen*] **1 :** subjected to boiling : cooked, cleaned, or otherwise acted upon by boiling ⟨~ beef⟩ ⟨~ clothes⟩ **2** *slang* : very drunk : INTOXICATED

boiled dinner *n* : a dinner of boiled meat (as corned beef or ham) prepared and served with boiled vegetables (as potatoes, cabbage, and turnips)

boiled-off silk \'⸗,⸗-\ *n* : silk with the gum removed by boiling in a soap solution

boiled oil *n* : any fatty oil (as linseed oil) whose drying properties have been improved by heating usu. with driers (as lead soaps); *also* : any drying oil made by treating a raw oil with driers in the cold — compare BODIED OIL

boiled shirt *n* : a man's dress shirt with a starched front

boiled sweets *n pl, Brit* : HARD CANDY

boil·er \'bȯilə(r)\ *n* -S [²*boil* + -*er*] **1 :** one that boils: as **a :** one that boils ingredients (as of candy, paint, soap) as part of a manufacturing process **b :** a worker who boils fabric **2 a :** a vessel (as a kettle or evaporator) used for boiling **b :** the part of a steam generator in which water is converted into steam and which consists usu. of metal shells, headers, and tubes that form the container for the steam and water under pressure **c :** a tank in which water is heated or hot water is stored (as for domestic use) **3 :** something that is capable of boiling or that is esp. suitable for boiling ⟨milk is a quick ~⟩ ⟨these chickens are good ~*s*⟩ **4 :** a submerged reef; *esp* : a coral reef where the sea breaks

boiler compound *n* : any chemical added to feedwater for boilers (as for preventing corrosion, foaming, or the formation of scale)

boiler deck *n* : the deck directly above the boilers of a steamer

boiler horsepower *n* : a unit for measuring the power of a steam boiler, being the equivalent of 34.5 pounds of steam evaporated from and at 212°F per hour

boil·er·less \-ləs\ *adj* : being without a boiler

boilermaker \'⸗⸗,⸗⸗\ *n* **1 :** one that performs any or all of the operations in the making, assembling, or repairing of boilers and other objects made of heavy metal plates **2 :** whiskey with a beer chaser — **boilermaking** \'⸗⸗,⸗⸗\ *n* -S

boiler plate *n* **1** *or* **boiler iron** : flat-rolled steel usu. about a quarter to a half inch thick used esp. for making boilers and tanks and for covering ships **2 a :** syndicated material supplied esp. to weekly newspapers in matrix or plate form **b :** hackneyed or unoriginal writing **3 a :** a relatively smooth surface (as of flush or overlapping slabs of rock) on a cliff affording little or no foothold **b :** a frozen crusty surface of snow

boiler room *n* **1 :** a room in which one or more steam boilers are located **2 :** a room equipped with many telephones and used for high-pressure selling of stock securities that are often without real value

boiler scale *n* : scale formed on the walls and tubes of a steam boiler

boiler shop *n* : a shop for the manufacture or repair of boilers

boiler suit *n* : COVERALL

boil·ery \'bȯil(ə)rē\ *n* -ES [²*boil* + -*ery*] : a place where boiling is carried on ⟨salt *boileries*⟩

¹**boiling** *adj* [ME, fr. pres. part. of *boilen*] **1 a :** heated to the boiling point : bubbling from the action of heat **b :** intensely hot : TORRID ⟨under a ~ sun⟩ **2 a :** violently agitated : marked by swirling and eddying : SEETHING ⟨winds whipped the ~ sea⟩ **b :** intensely moved or stirred up ⟨~ with anger⟩ — **boil·ing·ly** *adv*

²**boiling** *adv* **1 :** to a boiling degree ⟨some ~ hot coffee⟩ **2 :** EXTREMELY, VERY ⟨~ mad⟩ ⟨they got ~ drunk⟩

³**boiling** *n* -S [ME, fr. gerund of *boilen*] **1 :** the action of boiling : subjection to boiling **2** *archaic* : GROUP, BATCH, LOT ⟨the handsomest woman of her day, and the cleverest, the nicest, the best of the whole ~ —George Meredith⟩

boiling flask *n* : FLORENCE FLASK

boiling-house \'⸗⸗,⸗\ *n* : a building specially equipped for boiling; *esp* : a building in which sap is boiled to syrup

boiling point *n* : the temperature at which a liquid boils; *specif* : the temperature at which the vapor pressure of a liquid is equal to the external pressure, the boiling point thus decreasing with a decrease in pressure (as 100°C for water at a pressure of 760 mm. of mercury and 51°C at 100 mm.)

boiling spring *n* **1 :** a natural pool of hot water through which bubbles of steam or volcanic gas rise to the surface often with much force **2 :** a spring in which water rises swiftly developing strong vertical eddies

boiling stone *n* : a small object (as a stone or piece of porcelain) used in a boiling liquid to prevent bumping

boil off \'⸗,⸗\ *vt* **1 :** to degum (silk) by boiling **2 :** to remove (gum, sizing, wax, dye) from fabric by boiling in a solution

boil-off *n* -S [*boil off*] : the process of removing impurities (as size or gum) by boiling fabrics in a scouring solution

boil out *vt* : to boil off

boil over *vi* **1 :** to overflow while boiling ⟨the milk was on the fire too long and *boiled over*⟩ ⟨use a deep saucepan that won't easily *boil over*⟩ **2 :** to become so excited (as with anger or indignation) as to lose self-control ⟨if you're the least bit late the boss *boils over*⟩

boilover \'⸗,⸗⸗\ *n* -S [*boil over*] : the action or process of boiling over : overflow of boiling liquid

boils *pres 3d sing of* BOIL, *pl of* BOIL

boil smut *n* [¹*boil*] : the common smut of Indian corn caused by a fungus (*Ustilago maydis*) and characterized by grayish white swellings that rupture to expose a black spore mass

¹**boing** \'bȯiŋ\ *n* -S [imit.] : a reverberating metallic sound made by or as if by a spring

²**boing** \"\ *vi* : to make a boing

bois blanc \bwä'bläⁿ\ *n, pl* **bois blancs** \"\ [CanF, lit., white wood] : AMERICAN BASSWOOD

bois brû·lé \,bwäbrü'lā\ *n, pl* **bois brûlés** \-'lā(z)\ *often cap both Bs* [CanF, lit., burnt wood] **1** : a Canadian half-breed; *esp* : one of French and Indian blood **2** : BRÛLÉ

bois co·te·let \-,kōd·ᵊl'ā\ *or* **bois co·te·lette** \-'et\ *n, pl* **bois cotelets** \-ā(z)\ *or* **bois cotelettes** \-et(s)\ [F *bois côtelet*, lit., fiddlewood wood] *West Indies* : FIDDLEWOOD 1

bois d'arc \'bō,därk, -dȧk,-dȧk\ *n, pl* **bois d'arcs** \-ks\ *or* **bois d'arc** *like sing.*\ [LaF, lit., bow wood] : OSAGE ORANGE

bois de fer \,bwädə'fa(ə)r, bwät'f-, -fe(ə)r\ *n, pl* **bois de fers** \-rz\ *or* **bois de fer** *like sing*\ [CanF, lit., iron wood] : HOP HORNBEAM

bois de rose \,bwäd(ə)'rōz\ *n, pl* **bois de roses** \-ōzəz\ *or* **bois de rose** *like sing.*\ [F, lit., rose wood] **1 a** : an important tropical American yellow timber derived chiefly from a tree (*Aniba panurensis*) of French Guiana **b** : any tree yielding bois de rose **2** : a grayish red that is yellower, lighter, and stronger than blush rose, yellower and deeper than apple-blossom, bluer and deeper than Pompeian red, and yellower and stronger than livid brown

bois de rose oil *n* : a colorless to yellow essential oil obtained from bois de rose and used in perfumery and as a source of linalool — called also *Brazilian bois de rose oil, Cayenne linaloe oil, rosewood oil*

bois de vache \,bwäd(ə)'vash\ *n* [AmerF, lit., cow's wood] : BUFFALO CHIPS

boi·se \'bȯisē, -zē\ *adj, usu cap* [fr. *Boise*, Idaho] : of or from Boise, the capital of Idaho ⟨*Boise* shops⟩ : of the kind or style prevalent in Boise

boi·se·an \-ēən\ *n* -s *cap* [*Boise*, Idaho + E -*an*] : a native or resident of Boise, Idaho

boi·se·rie \,bwäzə¦rē, (ˈ)bwäz¦rē\ *n* -s [F, fr. *boiser* to adorn with wood (fr. *bois* wood, fr. OF, forest, wood, of Gmc origin; akin to OHG *busc* bush) + -*erie* -ery — more at BUSH] : carved wood paneling

bois im·mor·tel \,bwä,zimȯr'tel, -zēm-\ *n, pl* **bois immortels** \-tel(z)\ [AmerF, lit., immortal wood] *West Indies* : a tropical American shrub or tree (*Erythrina umbrosa*) used to shade young cacao plantations

bois in·con·nu \-,zaⁿkə'nü, -'nue\ *n, pl* **bois inconnus** \-nü(z), -nue\ [LaF, lit., unknown wood] : HACKBERRY 1

bois pu·ant \,bwäpü'ant, -pue'äⁿ\ *n, pl* **bois puants** \-pü'ants, -pue'äⁿ\ [LaF, lit., stinking wood] **1** : HARDY CATALPA **2** : SYCAMORE 3a

boist \'bȯist\ *n* -s [prob. fr. ME, box, fr. OF *boiste*, fr. ML *buxida*, fr. Gk *pyxida*, acc. of *pyxis* box — more at BOX] *dial* : a rough shelter

bois·ter·ous \'bȯist(ə)rəs\ *adj* [ME *boistrous* rough, coarse, alter. of *boistous*, perh. fr. OF *boisteos* lame, rough (said of a road), fr. *boister* to limp (fr. *boiste* knee joint, box) + -*eos* -ous] **1** *obs* **a** : of a strong durable quality ⟨the leathern outside, ~ as it was, gave way —John Dryden⟩ **b** : painfully rough ⟨love . . . is too rough, too rude, too ~ —Shak.⟩ **c** : MASSIVE, CUMBROUS ⟨his ~ club —Edmund Spenser⟩ **2 a** : noisily turbulent : loudmouthed and rough in behavior : ROWDY, BRAWLING, CLAMOROUS ⟨a ~ mob⟩ ⟨the ~ shantytowns of gold-rush days —*Amer. Guide Series: Calif.*⟩ **b** : full of exuberant uninhibited and often excessive animal spirits : completely unrestrained ⟨~ laughter⟩ ⟨children enjoying a ~ play period⟩ **3 a** : rough, stormy and agitated : marked by tumultuous violence and fury : not calm ⟨~ winds and waves⟩ **b** *obs* : savagely fierce : TRUCULENT ⟨your indecent and ~ treatment of this man —Alexander Pope⟩ **syn** see VOCIFEROUS

bois·ter·ous·ly *adv* : in a boisterous manner

bois·ter·ous·ness *n* -ES : the quality or state of being boisterous

boîte \'bwät, 'bwȧt\ *or* **boîte de nuit** \¦=dənü'ē, -nue'wē\ *n, pl* **boîtes** \'bwät(s), 'bwȧt\ *or* **boîtes de nuit** [*boîte* fr. F, lit., box, fr. OF *boiste*; *boîte de nuit* fr. F, lit., night box] : NIGHTCLUB

bo·ka·dam \'bōkədəm\ *n* -s [prob. native name in the East Indies] : an East Indian aquatic venomous snake (*Hurria*, syn. *Cerberus, rhynchops*)

¹boke \'bōk\ *vb* -ED/-ING/-S [ME *bolken*; prob. akin to OE *bealcian* to belch — more at BELCH] **1** *chiefly Scot* : VOMIT, RETCH **2** *chiefly Scot* : BELCH, BURP

²boke \"\ *n* -s [ME *bolke*, fr. *bolken* v.] **1** *chiefly Scot* : RETCHING, VOMITING **2** *chiefly Scot* : BELCH, BURP

bo·kha·ra \bō'kärə, -karə\ *also* **bu·kha·ra** \bü'-\ *n* -s [fr. *Bokhara, Bukhara*, region in Uzbek S.S.R., U.S.S.R.] **1** *often cap* : astrakhan from Bukhara in central Asia **2** *usu cap* : a Turkoman rug in small and large sizes coming from the region of Bukhara, distinguished generally by very fine knotting, geometric allover designs (as octagons, diamonds, angular shrubs, and flowers), and by its prevailing colors of mulberry red with touches of dark blue, vermilion, and ivory white **3** *often cap* : a dark purplish red that is redder and duller than red-grape or pansy purple, redder and deeper than raisin, and redder, stronger, and slightly lighter than dahlia purple

bokhara clover *n, usu cap* [fr. *Bokhara*, the region] : WHITE SWEET CLOVER

bokharan *usu cap, var of* BUKHARAN

bo·kie \'bōkē\ *Scot var of* BOGEY

bok·ma·kier·ie \,bäkmə'kirē\ *n* -s [Afrik, of imit. origin] : a short-winged shrike (*Telophorus zeylonus*) of southern Africa

bo·ko \'bō(,)kō\ *n* -s [origin unknown] *slang Brit* : NOSE

bokor *var of* BOCOR

¹bo·la \'bōlə\ *or* **bo·las** \-ləs, -,läs\ *n, pl* **bolas** \-ləz\ *also* **bolases** \-ləsəz\ [AmerSp *bolas*, pl. of Sp *bola* ball, fr. OSp, fr. OProv, fr. L *bulla* bubble, ball — more at POLL (head)] : a weapon that consists of two or more usu. stone or iron balls attached to the ends of a cord and that is used for hurling at and entangling an animal

bola

²bola \'bō(,)lä\ *n* -s [Bengali *bolā*, perh. of Dravidian origin; akin to Malayalam & Kanarese *pollu* hollow] *India* : MAJAGUA a

bo·lar \'bōlə(r)\ *adj* [²*bole* + -*ar*] : of or relating to bole : CLAYEY

bol·bo·phyl·lum \¦bälbə¦filəm, ¦bōl-\ *n* [NL, fr. Gk *bolbos* bulb + NL -*phyllum* — more at BULB] **1** *cap* : a large genus of epiphytic orchids having small pseudobulbs, stiff leaves, and racemose or solitary showy flowers with a jointed lip, being native chiefly to the Old World tropics, and including a few forms in cultivation **2** -s : a plant or flower of the genus *Bolbophyllum*

¹bold \'bōld\ *adj, usu* -ER/-EST [ME, fr. OE *bald, beald*; akin to OHG *bald* bold, ON *ballr* frightful, Goth *balthaba* boldly, and prob. to OE *blāwan* to blow — more at BLOW] **1 a** : fearless in meeting danger or difficulty : aggressively daring : not shrinking from risk : INTREPID, VENTURESOME ⟨~ settlers on some foreign shore —William Wordsworth⟩ **b** : showing or reflecting a courageous daring spirit and contempt of danger ⟨a ~ speech⟩ ⟨a ~ plan⟩ **2** : presumptuously confident and self-reliant : taking undue liberties : lacking modesty and restraint : FORWARD, RUDE, IMPUDENT ⟨~ triflers with the unknown⟩ ⟨a ~ little urchin⟩ **3** *obs* : wholly assured : CONFIDENT **4 a** : of great strength or intensity : FIERCE ⟨the howling of ~ winds⟩ ⟨~ flames leaping to the sky⟩ **b** : full-flavored : HEADY ⟨~ brandy⟩ : piquant, pungent, or nippy ⟨~ aromatic peppers⟩ **c** : fully developed : MATURE, RIPE ⟨~ fields of grain⟩ **d** : well filled out : PLUMP ⟨a laughing girl with a ~ lithe figure⟩ **5** : rising, sloping, or dropping abruptly : SHEER, STEEP ⟨where some of the ~*est* chalk cliffs of England rise from the waters of the Atlantic —Richard Joseph⟩ **6** : marked by departure from convention or tradition : FREE, DARING ⟨a ~ thinker⟩ ⟨a ~ art design⟩ ⟨this ~ modern trend toward loose behavior in love —Ellen Glasgow⟩ **7** : standing out prominently : markedly conspicuous : EYE-CATCHING, ARRESTING : fully delineated ⟨~ letters scrawled across the wall⟩ ⟨~ newspaper headlines⟩ ⟨a figure carved in ~ relief⟩ **8** : being or composed of large pieces (as of fossil resin in commerce) **9** : BOLD-FACED 3 **syn** see BRAVE

²bold \"\ *vb* -ED/-ING/-S [ME *bolden*, fr. OE *bealdian*, fr. *beald* bold] *vi, obs* : to be or become bold ~ *vt, obs* : EMBOLDEN

³bold \"\ *n* -s [by shortening] : BOLDFACE

bol·da·cious \(ˈ)bōl¦dāshəs\ *adj* [prob. blend of *bold* and *audacious*] *dial Brit* : BRAZEN, IMPUDENT

bold·en \'bōldən\ *vb* -ED/-ING/-S [¹*bold* + -*en*] *vt, now dial Brit* : EMBOLDEN ~ *vi, now dial Brit* : to take courage

bold·face \'=,=\ *n* **1** *archaic* : a forward and usu. impudent individual **2** : a typeface with downstrokes or all strokes wide producing a relatively heavy impression; *also* : boldface print ⟨a paragraph set in ~⟩ ⟨~ letters⟩ — compare LIGHTFACE

bold–faced \'=¦=\ *adj* **1** : having a bold face **2** : bold in manner or expression : FORWARD, IMPUDENT ⟨*bold-faced* ruffians⟩ **3** : having the character of boldface : set in boldface

boldhearted \'=¦==\ *adj* : having a bold heart

bol·dine \'bäl,dēn, -,dən\ *n* -s [ISV *boldo* + -*ine*] : a poisonous bitter crystalline alkaloid $C_{19}H_{21}NO_4$ found in leaves of the boldo

bold·ly \'bōl(d)lē, -li\ *adv* [ME, fr. OE *baldlīce, bealdlīce*, fr. *bald, beald* bold + -*līce* -ly — more at BOLD] : in a bold manner : with assurance : DARINGLY

bold·ness \-l(d)nəs\ *n* -ES [ME *boldnesse*, fr. *bold* + -*nesse* -ness] : the quality or state of being bold

bol·do \'bäl(,)dō\ *n* -s [AmerSp, fr. Araucan *boldu*] : a Chilean evergreen shrub (*Peumus boldus*) with sweet edible fruit

boldo family *n* : MONIMIACEAE

bol·du \'bäl,dü\ [NL, fr. AmerSp *boldú* boldo, fr. Araucan *boldu*] *syn of* PEUMUS

¹bole \'bōl\ *n* -s [ME, fr. ON *bolr*; akin to MLG *bole* plank, OE *bula* bull — more at BULL] **1** : the trunk of a tree; *esp* : the lower merchantable portion of such a trunk **2** : any cylindrically shaped object or mass ⟨massive ~*s* of stone⟩

²bole \"\ *n* -s [ME, fr. MF, fr. LL *bolus* clod, large pill, fr. Gk *bōlos* lump, clod; perh. akin to L *bulla* bubble — more at POLL (head)] **1** : any of several varieties of friable earthy clay usu. colored red by iron oxide and consisting essentially of hydrous silicates of aluminum or less often of magnesium **2** *archaic* : BOLUS 1 **3** : a moderate reddish brown that is yellower, lighter, and stronger than roan, mahogany, or oxblood, redder, lighter, and stronger than rustic brown, and redder and stronger than russet tan — called also *Antwerp red, Armenian bole, bole Armoniac, oriental bole, red bole, red chalk, red ocher, ruddle, terra Lemnia, terra pozzuoli, terra rosa, terra sigillata, Venice red*

³bole \"\ *n* -s [origin unknown] **1** *chiefly Scot* : a small recess or cupboard in a wall **2** *chiefly Scot* : an opening in a wall for light and air usu. closed with a wooden shutter

⁴bole \"\ *n* -s [prob. var. of *bowl*] : a site of an ancient smelter in Derbyshire, England

bole armoniac *n, often cap A* [ME *bol armoniak*, fr. (assumed) ML *bolus Armeniacus*, lit., Armenian bole, fr. LL *bolus* + L *Armeniacus* Armenian, fr. *Armenia*, ancient country in Asia Minor] : ARMENIAN BOLE 1

bo·lec·tion \bō'lekshən\ *or* **bi·lec·tion** \bī'-\ *n* -s [origin unknown] : a molding or group of moldings separating two planes (as a stile from a panel) and projecting beyond the surface of both — **bo·lec·tioned** \-shənd\ *adj*

PANEL STILE

typical bolection molding

boled \'bōld\ *adj* [¹*bole* + -*ed*] : characterized by or having a bole ⟨a forest of straight-*boled* trees⟩ ⟨a cottage with two ~ walls⟩

bo·le·ite \bō'lā,īt, -'lē,-\ *n* -s [F *boleite*, fr. *Boleo*, village near Santa Rosalia, Lower California, Mexico + F -*ite*] : a mineral $Pb_9Cu_8Ag_3Cl_{21}(OH)_{16}.2H_2O$ consisting of a basic and hydrous lead copper silver chloride

bo·le·ro \bə'la(a)(,)rō, bō'-, -le(,)-, -lā(,)-\ *n* -s [Sp, perh. fr. *bola* ball — more at BOLA] **1 a** : a Spanish dance to music in ¾ time and characterized by sharp turns and revolutions of the body and stamping of the feet in syncopated rhythm **b** : a West Indian derivative of the Spanish bolero in ¾ time **2** : music for or suited to the bolero **3** : a jacket of Spanish origin characteristically of waist-length or shorter made with or without sleeves, lapels, and collar and usu. worn open

bo·le·ta·ce·ae \,bōlə'tāsē,ē\ *n pl, cap* [NL, fr. *Boletus*, type genus + -*aceae*] : a family of pore-bearing fleshy fungi (order Agaricales) usu. having the pores easily separating from the pileus and often from each other

bo·le·ta·ceous \¦==¦tāshəs\ *adj* [NL *Boletaceae* + E -*ous*] : of or relating to the family Boletaceae

bo·lete \bō'lēt, bə'-\ *n* -s [NL *Boletus*] : any fungus of the family Boletaceae

bo·le·tus \bō'lēd·əs, bə'-, -ētəs\ *n, cap* [NL, fr. L, a fungus, fr. Gk *bolitēs*] : a genus (the type and principal representative of the family Boletaceae) of soft early-decaying pore fungi some of which are poisonous and others edible

bo·lide \'bō,līd, -ləd\ *n* -s [F, fr. L *bolid-, bolis* arrow-shaped meteor, fr. Gk, lit., missile, javelin, fr. *ballein* to throw — more at DEVIL] : an exploding or exploded meteor or meteorite

bo·li·ta \bə'lēd·ə, bō'-\ *also* **bo·li·to** \-ēd·(,)ō\ *n* -s [AmerSp (Cuba) *bolita*, fr. Sp, little ball, dim. of *bola* ball — more at BOLA] **1** : a game of chance having the character of a lottery in which a bag of small numbered balls is tossed about until only one remains or until one is grasped at random, the ball so selected being considered as bearing the winning number **2** : a numbers game in which one attempts to guess a variously determined 2-digit number

bo·li·var \'bälәvər, bō'lē,vär\ *n, pl* **bolivars** \-rz\ *or* **bo·li·va·res** \bō'lēvə,räs, -vä,-\ [AmerSp *bolívar*, after Simón *Bolívar* †1830 So. Amer. liberator] **1** : the basic monetary unit of Venezuela — see MONEY table **2** : a silver coin representing one bolivar

bo·li·var·i·an \¦bälә¦verēən, ¦bäl-, -va(a)r-\ *adj, usu cap* [Sp *bolivariano*, fr. S. *Bolívar*, who helped liberate these countries from the rule of Spain + Sp -*iano* -ian] : of or relating to the So. American republics of Colombia, Venezuela, Peru, Ecuador, and Bolivia

¹bo·liv·ia \bō'livēə, bə-\ *adj, usu cap* [fr. *Bolivia*, country in So. America] : of or from Bolivia : of the kind or style prevalent in Bolivia : BOLIVIAN

²bolivia \"\ *n* -s **1** [prob. so called fr. the use of Bolivian alpaca in its composition] : a twilled woolen fabric for outwear with a surface like plush in diagonal or vertical lines **2** *often cap* [fr. *Bolivia*, the country] **a** : a form of canasta in which sequences and wild cards may be melded **b** : a 7-card meld of wild cards in the game of bolivia

¹bo·liv·i·an \-vēən\ *adj, usu cap* [Sp *boliviano*, adj. & n., fr. *Bolivia* + -*ano* -an] **1** : of, relating to, or characteristic of Bolivia **2** : of, relating to, or characteristic of Bolivians

²bolivian \"\ *n* -s *cap* [Sp *boliviano*] : a native or resident of Bolivia

bolivian coca *n, usu cap B* : COCA 2a

bo·liv·i·a·no \bō,livē'ä(,)nō, bə-\ *n* -s [Sp, fr. *boliviano*, adj.] **1** : a former basic monetary unit of Bolivia **2** : a coin or note representing one boliviano

¹boll \'bōl\ *n* -s [ME, prob. var. of *bolle* bowl — more at BOWL] **1** : any of various old units of capacity used in Scotland and northern England varying from two to six Winchester bushels; *also* : a Scottish unit of weight equal to 140 pounds **2** : the pod or capsule of a plant esp. of flax or cotton : a pericarp of a globular form

²boll \"\ *vt* -ED/-ING/-S : to strip bolls from (cotton)

bol·land·ist \'bäləndəst\ *n* -s *usu cap* [Jean de *Bolland* †1665 Flem. Jesuit hagiologist who began the work + E -*ist*] : any of the Jesuit editors of the *Acta Sanctorum*, a collection of biographies of Christian saints and martyrs based on critical evaluation of the sources

bol·lard \'bälə(r)d\ *n* -s [perh. irreg. fr. ¹*bole* + -*ard*] **1 a** : a single or double post of metal or wood fixed on a pier or wharf and around which mooring lines are thrown : DOLPHIN **b** : ¹BITT 1 **2** *Brit* : any of a series of short posts set at intervals to exclude motor vehicles from an area

bollard timber *n* : KNIGHTHEAD 1

bolled \'bōld\ *adj* [¹*boll* + -*ed*] *archaic* : producing bolls : having bolls ⟨the barley was in the ear, and the flax was ~ —Exod 9:31 (AV)⟩

bol·ley's green \'bälēz-\ *n, usu cap B* [fr. the name *Bolley*] : a green copper borate used as a pigment

boll hull *n* [¹*boll*] : the bur of cotton

bol·ling·er body \'bälinjə(r)-\ *n, usu cap 1st B* [after Otto von *Bollinger* †1909 Ger. physician] : one of the inclusion bodies that occur in epithelial cells of birds affected with fowl pox

¹bol·lix *also* **bol·ix** \'bäliks, -lēks,-ləks\ *vt* -ED/-ING/-ES [fr. *bollocks, ballocks*, pl. of *bollock, ballock* testicle, fr. ME *ballok*, fr. OE *beallue*; akin to ON *böllr* ball — more at BALL] **1** : to throw into disorder : involve in bewildering entanglements — usu. used with *up* ⟨~*ing* up the life of everyone he met⟩ **2** : to perform or carry out badly : BOTCH, BUNGLE ⟨the pilot ~*ed* his takeoff⟩ — often used with *up* ⟨he ~*ed* up his final exams⟩

²bollix *also* **bolix** \"\ *n* -ES : a confused jumble : HODGEPODGE, MESS ⟨a hybrid art form that at least is earnestly ambitious, at worst is a humorless ~ —*Time*⟩

bol·lo \'bä(,)lō, 'bäl(,)yō\ *n* -s [AmerSp, fr. Sp, bun, muffin, fr. L *bulla* bubble, ball — more at POLL (head)] : a fritter made of black-eyed-pea flour and seasonings

bol·lock \'bälək\ *n* -s [by shortening & alter.] : BULLOCK BLOCK

boll rot *n* : a common rot of cotton bolls caused by various fungi (as *Glomerella gossypii* or *Diplodia gossypii*)

boll weevil *n* : a grayish weevil (*Anthonomus grandis*) about ¼ inch long that infests the cotton plant puncturing and laying its eggs in the squares and bolls, the larvae living in and feeding on the interior substance of the buds and bolls and doing great damage to developing cotton

bollworm \'=,=\ *n* **1** : CORN EARWORM — used chiefly when the larva is feeding on cotton bolls **2** : any of several noctuid moth larvae other than the corn earworm — usu. used in combination ⟨red ~⟩

bolly \'bōlē\ *n* -ES [¹*boll* + -*y*] **1** : a cotton boll that has remained unopened or partly opened usu. as a result of frost injury; *also* : a quantity of such bolls usu. cracked and ginned **2** : cotton ginned from undeveloped bolls

bol·ly gum \'bälē-\ *also* **bol·ly·wood** \'bälē,wu̇d\ *n* [origin unknown] **1** : an Australian tree (*Litsea reticulata*) of the family Lauraceae with scaly bark, alternate oval leaves, and racemose flowers **2** : the wood of bolly gum

¹bo·lo \'bō(,)lō\ *n* -s [Sp, prob. fr. a native name in the Philippines] : a long and usu. rather heavy Philippine single-edged knife resembling a machete

²bolo \"\ *vt* -ED/-ING/-S : to cut, hack, or kill with a bolo

³bolo \"\ *n* -s : BOLO PUNCH

⁴bolo \"\ *n* -s [perh. fr. Malay *bulu* hairy or feathery covering] : a parasitic Malayan plant (*Rafflesia schadenbergii*) with enormous flowers

⁵bolo \"\ *n* -s [fr. *Bolo* Pascha †1918, assumed name of a German agent in France who was convicted of treason] **1** *usu cap* : DEFEATIST; *esp* : one acting traitorously **2** *usu cap, slang* : BOLSHEVIST **3** *slang* **a** : a soldier who fails to qualify on the rifle range **b** : an incompetent or unreliable soldier : SAD SACK

⁶bolo \"\ *vi* -ED/-ING/-S : to fail to qualify on the rifle range

bolo

bo·lo–bo·lo \¦bōlō¦bōlō\ *n* -s [of African origin; akin to Bini *bo¹lo³* to peel or strip (as bark from a tree)] **1** : a West African fiber somewhat resembling jute and derived from the bast of a tree (*Honckenya ficifolia*) of the family Tiliaceae **2** : the tree that yields bolo-bolo

¹bo·lo·gna \bə'lōnyə *also* -nə\ *adj, usu cap* [fr. *Bologna*, Italy] : of or from the city of Bologna, Italy : of the kind or style prevalent in Bologna

²bo·lo·gna \bə'lōnē, -ni *sometimes* -nə *or* -nyə\ *n* -s [short for *Bologna sausage*, trans. of It *mortadella di Bologna*] **1** *or* **bologna sausage** \"-\ *also* **bo·lo·ney** *or* **ba·lo·ney** \bə'lōnē, -ni\ *sometimes* **Bologna** : a large moist sausage usu. made of beef, veal, and pork that is chopped fine, seasoned, enclosed in a casing, boiled, and smoked red **2** *slang* : BALONEY

bologna bull *also* **bologna** *n, sometimes cap 1st B* [²*bologna*] : a low-grade bull supplying beef of inferior quality

bologna flask *or* **bologna phial** *or* **bologna vial** *n, usu cap B* [¹*Bologna*] : a bottle of unannealed glass that will fly into pieces when scratched — compare RUPERT'S DROP

¹bo·lo·gnan \bə'lōnyən *also* -ōnən\ *or* **bo·lo·gnian** \-ōnyən\ *adj, usu cap* [*Bologna*, Italy + E -*an*, -*ian*] : BOLOGNESE

²bolognan *or* **bolognian** \"\ *n* -s *cap* : BOLOGNESE

bologna phosphorus *or* **bolognian phosphorus** *n, usu cap B* [*Bologna* (*stone*)] : a phosphorescent sulfide of barium made by reducing Bologna stone or other barium sulfate

bologna stone *or* **bolognan stone** *n, usu cap B* [¹*Bologna* or ¹*Bolognan*; fr. its discovery near Bologna, Italy] : the mineral barite when found in roundish masses composed of radiating fibers, being phosphorescent when calcined with charcoal

¹bo·lo·gnese \,bōlən¦yēz, -ēs, bə'lōn,y- *also* ¦bōlə¦nē-\ *adj, usu cap* [It, adj. & n., fr. *Bologna* + -*ese*] **1** : of, relating to, or characteristic of Bologna, Italy **2** : of, relating to, or characteristic of the Bolognese **3** : having to do with painting in Bologna during the 15th and 16th centuries or with the eclectic late 16th century painters of the Bolognese school

²bolognese \"\ *n, pl* **bolognese** *cap* : a native or resident of Bologna

bo·lo·gram \'bōlə,gram\ *n* -s [Gk *bolē* stroke, cast, beam of light (fr. *ballein* to throw) + E -*o-* + -*gram* — more at DEVIL] : BOLOGRAPH

bo·lo·graph \-,graf\ *n* -s [Gk *bolē* + E -*o-* + -*graph*] : the record made by a bolometer — **bo·lo·graph·ic** \¦=¦=¦fik\ *adj*

bo·lo·ism \'bōlō,izəm, -lə,wi-\ *n* -s *usu cap* [*Bolo* Pascha + E -*ism* — more at BOLO] : defeatist activities and propaganda favoring an enemy country

bololo *var of* PALOLO

bo·lo·man \'bōlō,man\ *n, pl* **bolomen** [¹*bolo* + *man*] : a man armed with a bolo

bo·lom·e·ter \bō'lämәd·ә(r), bә'-\ *n* -s [Gk *bolē* beam of light, stroke, cast (fr. *ballein* to throw) + E -*o-* + -*meter* — more at DEVIL] : a very sensitive resistance thermometer used in the detection and measurement of feeble thermal radiation and esp. adapted to the study of infrared spectra — **bo·lo·met·ric** \¦bōlō¦me·trik, -lə¦-\ *adj* — **bo·lo·met·ri·cal·ly** \-trәk(ә)lē\ *adv*

bolometric magnitude *n* : the magnitude of a star based upon its total radiation in all wavelengths — compare BOLOMETER

¹boloney *var of* BOLOGNA

²boloney *var of* ²BALONEY

bolo punch *n* [³*bolo*] : a usu. long uppercut that is started with a downward swing

bolos *pl of* BOLO

¹bol·she·vik \'bōlshә,vik, 'bäl-, -,vēk *also* 'bȯl- *sporadically* 'bәl-\ *n, pl* **bolsheviks** \-ks\ *also* **bol·she·vi·ki** \-,vikē, -,vēkē\ [Russ *bol'shevik*, fr. *bol'she* larger (comp. of *bol'shoi* large, great) + -*vik* (nominal suffix); fr. their forming the majority group of the Russian Social Democratic party in 1903; akin to Gk *belteros* better — more at DEBILITY] **1** *usu cap* **a** : a member of the wing of the Russian Social Democratic party that favored revolutionary tactics to achieve full socialization and seized supreme power in Russia during the Revolution (1917–20) for the purpose of setting up a workers' state **b** : a member of the Russian Communist party **2** *often cap* : an extreme radical opposed to an existing social, political, and economic order : REVOLUTIONARY ⟨began as a literary ~ but ended as a conservative⟩ **3** *usu cap* : COMMUNIST

²bolshevik \"\ *adj, usu cap* : of, relating to, favoring, or characteristic of bolshevism or Bolsheviks

bol·she·vism \-,vizәm\ *n* -s [¹*Bolshevik* + -*ism*] **1** *often cap* : the doctrine or program of the Bolsheviks advocating violent overthrow of the political and economic institutions of capitalism and the establishment of a socialist state controlled by the workers **2** : communism esp. as developed and practiced by Russian Bolsheviks

¹bol·she·vist \-shә,vist, -,vәst\ *n* -s *usu cap* [*Bolshevik* + -*ist*] : a supporter or adherent of bolshevism : BOLSHEVIK

²bolshevist \"\ *adj, usu cap* : BOLSHEVIK

bol·she·vi·za·tion \,=shәvә'zāshәn, -,vī'z-\ *n* -s *sometimes cap* : the process of bolshevizing or the fact of being bolshevized

bol·she·vize \'==,vīz\ *vt* -ED/-ING/-S *see -ize in Explan Notes, sometimes cap* [¹*Bolshevik* + -*ize*] : to make Bolshevist in character or principle : convert (a country) to a Bolshevist form of government : bring under the domination of Bolshevists

¹bol·shie *or* **bol·shy** \'=shē\ *n, pl* **bolshies** *usu cap* [by shortening & alter.] *slang* : BOLSHEVIK

²bolshie *or* **bolshy** \"\ *adj, sometimes cap, slang* : BOLSHEVIK

bol·son \ˈbōl,sōn\ *n* -s [AmerSp *bolsón*, aug. of Sp *bolsa* purse, pouch, fr. ML *bursa* — more at PURSE] : a flat-floored desert valley that drains to a playa

¹bol·ster \ˈbōlstə(r)\ *n* -s [ME, fr. OE; akin to OHG *bolstar* bolster, ON *bolstr* bolster, OE *belg* bag — more at BELLY] **1 a :** a long pillow or cushion that is used to support the head of a person lying on a bed and that usu. extends across the bed and is placed under the pillows and often under the sheets **b :** any soft pad, padding, cushion, or support resembling a bolster **2 a :** a structural part of a mechanism designed to eliminate friction between moving parts, reduce pressure, deaden noise, or accomplish similar cushioning effects **b :** any structural part designed to afford support or give a bearing: as (1) **:** a transverse bar above the axle of a wagon on which the bed of the wagon rests (2) **:** a plate often with a hole in the center or T slots on its surface bolted to the top of a punch-press bed (3) **:** the spindle bearing in the rail of a support or spinning frame and the support for the drafting rolls (4) **:** the crossbeam forming the bearing piece of the body of a railroad car **:** the central and principal crossbeam of a railroad-car truck (5) **:** a short timber or block set horizontally upon a post so as to secure a structural advantage (as attaining a greater bearing surface for girders, shortening their span, or allowing erection of an upper post between their ends) (6) **:** the horizontal connection between the volutes of an Ionic capital (7) **:** one of the small pieces of scantling nailed across the outer curve of the centering for an arch and taking the weight of the arch masonry (8) **:** a crosspiece connecting the ribs of the centering that supports the voussoirs of an arch **3 :** any contrivance that prevents chafing; *specif* **:** a block of wood or a stuffed canvas used on shipboard to reduce or eliminate chafing between ropes or other rigging **4 a :** the part of a knife blade that abuts upon the handle **b :** the metallic end of a pocketknife handle **5 :** ²BUNK 2a **6 a :** the slight excrescence at the junction of branch and stem or of the leafstalk and its axis **b :** the cupule of the hazelnut **c :** the husk of the English walnut

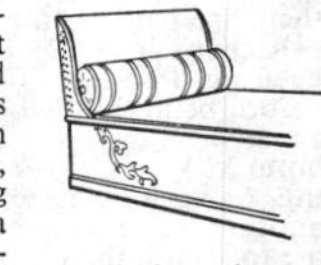
bolster 1a

²bolster \"\ *vb* **bolstered; bolstered; bolstering** \-st(ə)riŋ\ **bolsters** *vt* **1 :** to support with or as if with a bolster — often used with *up* ⟨the sick man lay ~*ed* up in his bed⟩ **2 a :** to give a strong support or foundation to **:** give additional strength to **:** give a boost to **:** REINFORCE, UPHOLD ⟨a convincing argument that was ~*ed* still more by the speaker's respected position⟩ ⟨extra men will ~ already augmented dock details —Stanley Levey⟩ ⟨~*ed* his faltering courage⟩ ⟨~*ing* superstition and prejudice⟩ **b :** to supply for the deficiencies of **:** SUPPLEMENT ⟨a diet that needs to be ~*ed* with more vitamin-rich foods⟩ **3 :** to cause to be increased (as in size, bulk, or intensity) through the addition or presence of something **:** to fill out **:** EXPAND, PAD ⟨a mattress that was ~*ed* to the bursting point⟩ **:** HEIGHTEN, INTENSIFY ⟨a moonless night that ~*ed* the gloom of the forest⟩ **~** *vi, obs* **:** to lie on the same bolster **syn** see SUPPORT

bolster plate *n* **:** a circular metal plate bolted to the front axle of a wagon on which the front bolster is pivoted so that the front wheels can be turned

¹bolt \ˈbōlt\ *n* -s [ME, fr. OE; akin to OHG *bolz* crossbow bolt, Lith *beldėti* to knock, beat] **1 a :** a shaft or missile designed to be shot from a crossbow or catapult; *esp* **:** a short stout usu. blunt-headed arrow **b :** a concentrated flow of usu. atmospheric electricity **:** a lightning stroke **:** THUNDERBOLT **2 a :** a bar or other usu. cylindrically shaped length of metal, wood, or other strong material that moves through guides (as iron staples) attached to a door or other movable frame the end being received into an adjoining fixed socket (as one attached to the jamb or lintel) **b :** the part of a lock that is shot or withdrawn by the key **3 a :** a roll of cloth of specified length **b :** a bundle (as of osiers or straw) **c :** a roll of wallpaper of specified length usu. including two or three separate sections **4** *obs* **:** SHACKLE, FETTER **5 a :** any of several herbs of the genus *Ranunculus*; *esp* **:** BULBOUS BUTTERCUP **b :** a globeflower (*Trollius europaens*) having lemon-yellow flowers with incurving sepals **6 :** a rod or heavy pin (as one made of steel) designed to fasten two or more objects (as metal plates) together or to hold one or more objects in place often having a head at one end and a screw thread cut upon the other end and being usu. secured by a nut or by riveting **7 a :** a block of timber to be sawed or cut (as into shingles or staves) **b :** a short round section of a log **c :** a bundle of boards joined by an end not sawed through **8 :** a usu. large quantity of matter often like a jet in form or movement ⟨~*s* of water gushing over the dam⟩ ⟨flaming ~*s* erupting from the surface of the sun⟩ **9 :** the breech closure of breech-loading rifles that is designed like a door bolt, has a back-and-forth movement that opens and closes the bore, and is locked in position usu. through rotation; *also* **:** a small-arm breech closure however designed **10 :** the uncut folded paper at the head, fore edge, and foot of a signature (as of a book)

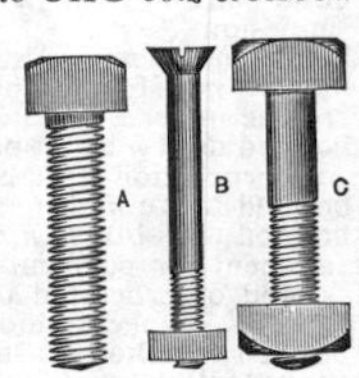

bolts 6: *A* tap bolt, *B* stove bolt, *C* machine bolt

²bolt \"\ *vb* -ED/-ING/-S [ME *bolten, bulten*, fr. *bolt*, n.] *vi* **1 :** to move suddenly or nervously (as from surprise or fright) often involuntarily **:** move with a sudden jerk from one position to another **:** START, SPRING — usu. used with *up* or *upright*, ⟨anger energized me and I ~*ed* upright in bed —Robert Hazel⟩ ⟨the Judge had ~*ed* upright from the pillows —Sir Winston Churchill⟩ **2 :** to move rapidly **:** dart forward **:** DASH ⟨he completely lost his head, ~*ed* out of the yard into the road, and ran up the street —J.C.Powys⟩ **3 a :** to dart off or away (as when fleeing) **:** suddenly make off **:** rush away **:** run off **:** ESCAPE ⟨two sullen-faced aides ~*ed* from the farmhouse and ran —Kenneth Roberts⟩ ⟨a young woman ~*ing* from too much domesticity —E.A.Weeks⟩ **b :** to emerge (as from a lair) and flee ⟨the fox ~*ed*⟩ **c :** to break away from control **:** dash violently aside or off a set course ⟨the horse shied and ~*ed*⟩ ⟨the well-trained bird dog rarely ~*s*⟩ **4** *obs* **:** to fall suddenly like a stroke of lightning ⟨his cloudless thunder ~*ed* on their heads —John Milton⟩ **5 :** to loose an arrow too soon after the draw **6 a :** to produce seed prematurely ⟨the cultivated carrot is a biennial but it may sometimes ~ —J.M. Hector⟩ **b :** to produce a flowering stalk ⟨the lettuce will ~⟩ **7 :** to break away from a political party and go over to the opposition **:** refuse to support the party platform or candidate ⟨many party members were indignant and promptly ~*ed*⟩ **~** *vt* **1** *obs* **:** to put into irons **:** FETTER **2 a** *archaic* **:** to let fly (as a missile) **:** SHOOT, DISCHARGE ⟨~*ing* the arrows straight at the target⟩ **b** *archaic* **:** to drive out by force **:** EXPEL ⟨to have been ~*ed* forth, thrust out abruptly into Fortune's way —William Wordsworth⟩ **c :** to cause to emerge into the open (as from a lair) **:** DISLODGE ⟨they used ferrets to ~ the rabbits⟩ **3 :** to utter explosively or impulsively **:** give voice to or express hastily and usu. with little or no reflection **:** BLURT ⟨~*ing* the word out as if he had restrained it with difficulty until this moment —Virginia Woolf⟩ **4 a :** to secure (as a door) with a bolt **b :** to cause to be shut up or excluded (as by bolting a door) ⟨~*ing* the prisoners in their cells⟩ ⟨keeping prowlers ~*ed* out⟩ **5 a :** to attach or fasten together with bolts ⟨steel plates ~*ed* together⟩ **b :** to furnish or stud with bolts ⟨the newly ~*ed* hull of the ship⟩ **6 :** to consume (as food or drink) hastily or greedily **:** gobble or gulp down **:** eat with little or no chewing **:** swallow whole **:** swallow with spasmodic gulps ⟨tearing the food from one another and ~*ing* what they could keep with convulsive haste —T.B.Costain⟩ ⟨I struggled out of bed, pried open my eyes, shaved and showered, and ~*ed* down some breakfast —H.A.Smith⟩ ⟨~*ing* a cup of coffee⟩ **7 a :** to cut (timber) into bolts ⟨logs that were ~*ed* into 18-inch blocks⟩ **b :** to make up (as lengths of cloth) into bolts **8 :** to break away from or refuse to support (as a political party or candidate) ⟨~*ed* the national ticket⟩

³bolt \"\ *adv* [ME, fr. *bolt*, n.] **1 :** in a rigidly erect or straight-backed position **:** PERPENDICULARLY — usu. used with *upright* ⟨she, sitting ~ upright, paused —Elizabeth Bowen⟩ **2** *archaic* **:** DIRECTLY, STRAIGHT ⟨Mrs. Berry . . . ran ~ out of the house —George Meredith⟩

⁴bolt \"\ *n* -s [²*bolt*] **:** an act or instance of bolting: as **a :** a quick dash or flight ⟨a ~ for shelter⟩ **b :** refusal to support or repudiation of a political party, candidate, or platform ⟨fear of a widespread ~ by party members⟩

⁵bolt \"\ *vt* -ED/-ING/-S [ME *bulten*, fr. OF *buleter*, of Gmc origin; akin to MHG *biuteln* to sift, fr. *biutel* bag, fr. OHG *būtil* — more at BUD] **1 :** to sift (as meal or flour) usu. through fine-meshed cloth; *also* **:** to refine or purify (as meal or flour) through any process **2** *archaic* **:** to examine and separate as though by sifting ⟨time and nature will ~ out the truth of things —Roger L'Estrange⟩

⁶bolt \"\ *n* -s [ME *bult*, fr. *bulten*, v.] **:** ¹BOLTER a

bolt action *n* [¹*bolt*] **:** a rifle action in which the breechblock takes the form of a manually operated sliding rod

bolted *past of* BOLT

bol·tel \ˈbōltəl\ *also* **bow·tel** *or* **bow·tell** *or* **bou·tell** \ˈbōd-ᵊl\ *n* -s [ME, perh. fr. ¹*bolt* + *-el*] **1 :** a torus or ovolo; *esp* **:** one just below the abacus in the Tuscan and Roman Doric capital **2 :** one of the shafts of a clustered pier

bol·ten·ia \bōlˈtēnēə, -tēn-\ *n, cap* [NL, fr. Johannes *Bolten* †1796 Ger. naturalist and physician + NL *-ia*] **:** a genus of simple ascidians related to *Tethyum* but distinguished by a 4-lobed branchial aperture — compare SEA PEAR

¹bolt·er \ˈbōltə(r)\ *n* -s [ME *bulter*, fr. *bulten* to bolt (sift) + *-er*] **:** one that bolts: as **a :** a machine for bolting (as flour or meal) **b :** an operator of a machine for bolting

²bolter \"\ *n* -s [²*bolt* + *-er*] **:** one that bolts: as **a :** a horse or bird dog given to suddenly breaking away from control **b :** a voter who bolts his party **c :** a plant (as a sugar beet) producing seed prematurely **d :** a machine consisting of one or more circular ripsaws for cutting dimension lumber **e** *also* **bolterman :** a sawmill worker who bolts slabs and short logs into sizes suitable for fuel or by-product conversion — called also *splitterman*

bolt eye *n* [¹*bolt*] **:** a device like a clevis used to terminate a suspension rod or bolt

bolt face *n* [¹*bolt*] **:** the surface of the rifle-bolt end that makes contact with the base of the cartridge case

bolt from the blue [¹*bolt*] **1 :** lightning from a clear sky **2 :** a complete and stunning surprise

bolt handle *n* [¹*bolt*] **:** the projecting lever or knob by which a rifle bolt is manually operated

bolt head *n* [ME *bolthed*, fr. ¹*bolt* + *hed* head] **1 :** the head of a bolt **2 :** MATRASS **3 :** the end of a rifle bolt that seats the cartridge in the chamber

bolt-hole \ˈ=,=\ *n* [⁴*bolt*] **:** a place or way of escape; *specif* **:** a hole through which an animal may flee when pursued into its den

bolt hook *n* [¹*bolt*] **:** a hook having a screw and nut so that it can be used like a bolt

bol·ti *also* **bol·ty** \ˈbōltē\ *or* **bul·ti** \ˈbu̇l-\ *n, pl* **boltis** *also* **bolties** [Ar *bulṭī*] **:** a cichlid food fish (*Tilapia nilotica*) of the Nile and other rivers of Africa and Asia Minor

bolt·in \ˈbōltin\ *n* -s [¹*bolt* (bundle) + *-in* (alter. of *-ing*)] *dial Eng* **:** a bundle of straw

¹bolting *n* -s [ME *bulting*, fr. gerund of *bulten* to bolt (sift) — more at BOLT] **1 :** the action or process of bolting (as flour or meal) **2 boltings** *pl* **:** the coarser portion (as of flour or meal) separated from the rest by bolting

²bolting *adj* [fr. pres. part. of ²*bolt*] *of an eye* **:** prominent (as in certain pigeons)

bolting cloth *n* [¹*bolting*] **:** a firm fabric now usu. of silk woven in various mesh sizes for bolting (as flour) or for use in screen printing, needlework, or photographic enlargements

bolt·less \ˈbōltləs\ *adj* **:** having no bolt

bol·ton \ˈbōltən\ *adj, usu cap* [fr. *Bolton*, England] **:** of or from the county borough of Bolton, Lancashire, England **:** of the kind or style prevalent in Bolton

bol·to·nia \bōlˈtōnēə\ *n, cap* [NL, fr. James *Bolton*, 18th cent. Eng. botanist + NL *-ia*] **:** a genus of tall leafy perennial eastern American and eastern Asiatic herbs (family Compositae) with white ray flowers like asters

bol·ton·ite \ˈbōltə,nīt\ *n* -s [*Bolton*, Mass., its locality + E *-ite*] **:** a greenish granular variety of forsterite

bol·ton thumb \ˈbōltən-\ *n, often cap B* [alter. of *Boulton*, a glove-manufacturing firm] **:** a thumb whose gusset is formed in the main part of a glove

boltrope \ˈ=,=\ *n* [¹*bolt* + *rope*] **1 :** a strong usu. hemp rope stitched to the edges of a sail to strengthen it **2 :** any rope of superior quality (as of strength)

bolts *pres 3d sing of* BOLT, *pl of* BOLT

boltz·mann's constant \ˈbōltsmənz-, -,mänz-\ *n, usu cap B* [after Ludwig *Boltzmann* †1906 Austrian physicist] **:** the ideal gas constant per molecule being the ratio of the molar gas constant to the number of molecules of a substance in a gram molecule and having a value of about 1.3803×10^{-16} ergs per degree C

bol·us \ˈbōləs\ *n* -ES [LL — more at BOLE] **1 :** a rounded mass: as **a :** a large pill (as one used in veterinary practice) **b :** a soft mass of chewed food **2 :** ²BOLE 1 **3 :** ²BOLE 3

bolus al·ba \-ˈalbə\ *n* [NL, white clay] **:** KAOLIN

bom \ˈbōm\ *or* **bo·ma** \-mə\ *var of* ABOMA

bom *abbr* bombardier

bo·ma \ˈbōmə\ *n* -s [Swahili] **1 a :** an enclosure (as a barrier of thorn brush or a palisade) erected about a village, camp, or animal pen in central Africa and designed chiefly as a protection against wild beasts **b :** a place of concealment usu. protected (as with thorn brush) and camouflaged (as with foliage) and used by hunters or by animal photographers in central Africa **:** a hunter's blind **2 a :** a police post in central Africa **b :** the office of a district commissioner in central Africa

bo·mar·ea \bōˈma(a)rēə, -mer-\ *n, cap* [NL, after J.C.Valmont de *Bomare* †1807 Fr. naturalist] **:** a large genus of tropical American herbaceous vines (family Amaryllidaceae) with showy and often spotted umbellate flowers — see SALSILLA

¹bomb \ˈbäm; *sometimes esp South and chiefly archaic* ˈbəm\ *n* -s [F *bombe*, fr. It *bomba*, prob. fr. L *bombus* deep hollow sound, fr. Gk *bombos*; of imit. origin like ON *bumba* drum, Lith *bambėti* to hum, buzz, Alb *bumbulit* it is thundering] **1 :** a projectile or other device carrying an explosive charge fused to detonate under certain conditions (as upon impact or through a timing contrivance) and that is hurled (as by a mortar), dropped (as from an aircraft), or merely set into position at a given point (as by dynamite) with varying effects (as concussion, or fire-flinging, or the release of gases) depending upon the type used ⟨spangle ~*s* for fireworks displays⟩; *also* **:** any container (as of propaganda leaflets or food) designed to be dropped from aircraft in the manner of an aerial bomb **2 :** a vessel (as a steel cylinder) for compressed gases: as **a :** a pressure vessel for conducting chemical experiments at high temperature and high pressure **b :** a small manually operated dispenser that releases a substance stored under pressure (as an insecticide, a fire-extinguishing liquid, or paint) in the form of a vapor, spray, or gas **3 :** the combustion chamber of a bomb calorimeter **4 :** a mass of lava exploded from a volcanic vent and shaped while viscous by passage through the air into a rounded form ranging from a few inches to many feet in diameter **5 :** an explosive head on a harpoon **6 :** BOMBE **7 :** a lead-lined container for radioactive material used esp. in the radiation treatment of cancer ⟨a cobalt ~⟩ **8 :** BOMBSHELL 2

²bomb \"\ *vt* -ED/-ING/-S **:** to attack with or as if with bombs **:** drop bombs upon **:** hurl bombs at **:** blow up with bombs **:** BOMBARD

bom·ba·ca·ce·ae \,bämbəˈkāsē,ē\ *n pl, cap* [NL, fr. *Bombac-*, *Bombax*, type genus + *-aceae*] **:** a widely distributed family of tropical trees (order Malvales) with palmate leaves and large dry or fleshy fruit containing usu. woolly seeds

bom·ba·chas \bəmˈbächəz, bōm'-\ *n pl* [AmerSp, pl. of *bombacha*, fr. fem. of Sp *bombacho*, adj.; bomb-shaped, fr. *bomba* bomb, fr. It] **:** loose baggy trousers gathered tightly at the ankle and worn esp. in Argentina and Uruguay for riding and outdoor work

bom·ba·cop·sis \,bämbəˈkäpsəs\ *n* [NL, fr. ML *bombac-*, *bombax* cotton + NL *-opsis* — more at BOMBAST] **1** *cap* **:** a genus of large trees (family Bombacaceae) with capsular fruits that burst when dry or release a soft brown wool surrounding the small brown seeds **2** *pl* **bombacopses :** any tree of the genus *Bombacopsis*

bom·ba·je palm \bōmˈbäzhə-\ *n* [Pg *bombaje*] **:** JIPIJAPA

¹bom·bard \ˈbäm,bärd, -bȧd\ *n* -s [ME *bumbard*, *bombarde* fr. MF *bombarde*, prob. fr. L *bombus* deep hollow sound — more at BOMB] **1 :** a late medieval cannon that hurled large stone balls **2** *obs* **:** a leather jug or bottle **3 :** a large shawm

²bombard \(ˈ)bäm¦bärd, -bȧd *also* (ˈ)bəm-\ *vt* -ED/-ING/-S [MF *bombarder*, fr. *bombarde*] **1 :** to attack with explosive projectiles or other explosive weapons **:** assault with cannon and other heavy ordnance; *esp* **:** BOMB **2 :** to assail vigorously or persistently (as with questions or petitions) ⟨~*ing* the governor with pleas for leniency⟩ **3 :** to subject (a body or substance) to the impact of rapidly moving particles (as electrons or alpha rays) **syn** see ATTACK

bom·barde \(ˈ)bōm¦bärd, (ˈ)bäm-\ *n* -s [F, prob. fr. It *bombarda*, lit., bombard, fr. OIt, fr. MF *bombarde*] **:** a powerful reed stop of 32-foot or 16-foot pitch in a pipe organ; *also* **:** the manual containing such a stop

bom·bar·dier \¦bämbər¦di(ə)r, *-R & R often* -bəˈd-, *-R* -diə; *sometimes* ¦bəm\ *n* -s [MF, one in charge of a bombard, fr. *bombarde* bombard] **1 a** *archaic* **:** ARTILLERYMAN **b :** a noncommissioned officer in the British artillery **2 :** a bomber-crew member whose duty it is to guide the airplane in the run over the target by means of the bombsight and to release the bombs

bombardier beetle *n* **:** any of numerous carabid beetles of *Brachinus* or related genera that when disturbed discharge audibly a pungent and corrosive vapor from the anal glands

bom·bard·ment \(ˈ)bäm¦bärdmənt, -bȧd- *also* (ˈ)bəm-\ *n* -s **1 :** the act or an instance of bombarding or the state of being bombarded **2 :** a sustained attack (as with guided missiles, aircraft bombs, or artillery)

bom·bar·do \bōmˈbär(,)dō\ *n, pl* **bombar·di** \-(,)dē\ *or* **bombardoes** \-,dōz\ [It, alter. of *bombarda* bombarde] **:** BOMBARDON 1

bom·bar·don \bämˈbärdən, ˈbämbər-\ *n* -s [F, fr. It *bombardone*, aug. of *bombardo*] **1 :** the bass member of the shawm family **2 :** a bass tuba; *esp* **:** HELICON

bombasine *var of* BOMBAZINE

¹bom·bast \ˈbäm,bast, -baa(ə)st\ *n* -s [modif. of MF *bombace*, fr. ML *bombac-*, *bombax* cotton, alter. of L *bombyc-*, *bombyx* silkworm, silk, fr. Gk *bombyk-*, *bombyx* silkworm, silk garment, prob. of Per origin; akin to Per *pamba* cotton] **1** *obs* **:** cotton or any soft fibrous material used as padding or stuffing **2 :** a pretentious inflated style of speech or writing ⟨adolescent ~ about Destiny and Youth⟩

syn RHAPSODY, RANT, FUSTIAN, RODOMONTADE: BOMBAST indicates a verbose grandiosity or pretentious inflation of language and style disproportionate to thought ⟨the rant and *bombast* and sentimental cant of politics —Florence Converse⟩ ⟨in the days when a more decorated style was fashionable in many quarters, *bombast* and extravagance were common in the press —F.L.Mott⟩ RHAPSODY may suggest ecstatic effusiveness, extravagant and often incoherent ⟨a *rhapsody* of enchanting images which "led to nothing" —*Times Lit. Supp.*⟩ ⟨his characters, because of the intensity of his feeling about them, are excellently drawn, but he writes as though he had uncovered a new religion and thought it deserved a *rhapsody*, at least —*New Yorker*⟩ RANT is likely to suggest sustained violence of expression ⟨Williams, in a characteristic prose *rant*, writes as if free verse were one of the inalienable rights for which the American Revolution was fought —Irving Howe⟩ ⟨the hoarse *rant* of that demagogue fills the air and distracts the people's minds —Max Ascoli⟩ FUSTIAN suggests or may suggest a filling or padding with the sonorous or grandiloquent but inane ⟨lines of Jonson, detached from their context, look like inflated or empty *fustian* — T.S.Eliot⟩ ⟨condemned as literary because its characters speak the *fustian* of pretentious books —C.E.Montague⟩ RODOMONTADE may suggest the bluster or swaggering rant of the mountebank, braggart, or demagogue ⟨the brothers set about abusing each other in good round terms and with each intemperate sally their phrases became more deeply colored with the tincture of Victorian *rodomontade* —Ngaio Marsh⟩

²bombast \(ˈ)=¦=; *sometimes* bəmˈ=\ *vt* -ED/-ING/-S **1** *archaic* **:** PAD, STUFF **2 :** to make speciously impressive **:** INFLATE **:** make bombastic ⟨a book ~*ed* with attempts at wit⟩

³bombast \ˈbäm,=\ *adj, archaic* **:** PRETENTIOUS, INFLATED

bom·bast·er \(ˈ)=¦=stə(r) *sometimes* bəmˈ==\ *n* -s **:** one given to bombast ⟨a town that had no use for long-winded orators and other ~*s*⟩

bom·bas·tic \(ˈ)=¦=stik, -ēk *sometimes* bəmˈ==\ *adj* **:** marked by or given to bombast ⟨a wearisome speech, theatrical and ~⟩ ⟨a ~ writer⟩ — **bom·bas·ti·cal·ly** \-stək(ə)lē, -li\ *adv*

bombastry *n* -ES *obs* **:** BOMBAST

bom·bax \ˈbäm,baks\ *n* [NL, fr. ML, cotton — more at BOMBAST] **1** *cap* **:** a large genus of trees (family Bombacaceae) chiefly of So. America, a few of India, and one of Africa having digitate leaves and showy white or scarlet flowers — compare CEIBA **2** -ES **:** any tree of the genus *Bombax*

bombax cotton *or* **bombax floss** *n* **:** a fiber obtained from the bombax

bom·bay \(ˈ)bäm¦bā\ *adj, usu cap* [fr. *Bombay*, India] **:** of or from the city of Bombay, India **:** of the kind or style prevalent in Bombay

bombay aloe *n, usu cap B* **:** BASTARD ALOE

bombay duck *n, usu cap B* **1 :** a small marine Asiatic lizard fish (*Harpodon nehereus*) the flesh of which is dried and used in India as a relish **2** *India* **:** dried fish eaten with curry

bombay hemp *n, usu cap B* **1 :** SUNN **2 :** KENAF

bombay lamb *n, usu cap B* **:** the gray-dyed pelt of an Indian lamb

bombay senna *n, usu cap B* **:** the leaves of the Indian senna

bombay sumbul *n, usu cap B, pharmacy* **:** the root of an Asiatic perennial herb (*Dorema ammoniacum*) of the family Umbelliferae that is used as a substitute for true sumbul

bom·ba·zet *or* **bom·ba·zette** \¦bämbə¦zet\ *n* -s [*bombazine* + *-et*, *-ette*] **:** a thin plain or twill-woven worsted cloth with smooth finish used for dresses and coats

bom·ba·zine \¦bämbə¦zēn\ *also* **bom·ba·sine** \", -¦sēn\ *or* **bom·ba·zeen** \-¦zēn\ *n* -s *often attrib* [MF *bombasin*, fr. ML *bombacinum*, alter. of *bombycinum* silken, fr. L, neut. of *bombycinus* silken, fr. *bombyc-*, *bombyx* silk + *-inus* -ine — more at BOMBAST] **1 :** a silk fabric in twill weave dyed black for mourning wear **2 :** a twilled fabric with silk warp and worsted filling that is dyed various colors

bomb bay *n* **:** a bomb-carrying compartment on the underside of a combat airplane fuselage usu. with down-swinging doors through which bombs are dropped

¹bombe \ˈbäm(b), ˈbōⁿb\ *n* -s [F, lit., bomb — more at BOMB] **:** a frozen dessert consisting of two or more mixtures packed into a round or melon-shaped mold

²bom·bé \(ˈ)bäm¦bā, (ˈ)bōⁿ¦-\ *adj* [F, fr. *bombe*] **:** having an outward swelling curve (as at front, sides or base) — used chiefly of furniture ⟨a ~ chest of drawers⟩

bombed *past of* BOMB

bomb·er \ˈbämə(r)\ *n* -s **:** one that bombs; *specif* **:** an airplane specially designed for use in bombing

bomb fly *n* **:** the adult of the northern cattle grub

bom·bic·cite \bämˈbē,chīt\ *n* -s [It, fr. L. *Bombicci* 19th cent. Ital. geologist + It *-ite*] **:** a colorless hydrocarbon mineral found in Tuscan lignite

bom·bi·dae \ˈbämbə,dē\ *n pl, cap* [NL, fr. *Bombus*, type genus + *-idae*] *in some classifications* **:** a family of medium to very large robust usu. black and yellow hairy bees comprising the bumblebees now often included with honeybees and related bees in the family Apidae

bom·bi·la·tion \,==ˈlāshən\ *n* -s [L *bombilatus* (past part. of *bombilare* to buzz, hum, fr. *bombus* deep hollow sound) + E *-ion* — more at BOMB] **:** a buzzing droning sound

bom·bil·la \bōmˈbē(l)yə\ *n* -s [AmerSp (Argentina), dim. of Sp *bomba* pump, perh. fr. L *bombus* deep hollow sound — more at BOMB] **:** a small tube with a strainer at one end used in drinking maté

bom·bi·nate \ˈbämbə,nāt, usu -d-+V\ *vi* -ED/-ING/-S [NL *bombinatus*, past part. of *bombinare*, alter. of L *bombilare* — more at BOMBILATION] **:** BUZZ, DRONE — **bom·bi·na·tion** \,==ˈnāshən\ *n* -s

bombing *pres part of* BOMB

bomb run *n* : BOMB RUN

bomb ketch *n* : a small strongly built ketch having mortars mounted for use in naval bombardments

bomb lance *n* : a harpoon with an explosive head

bomb·line \ˈ=,=\ *n* -s : a demarcation line established in a combat area beyond which aircraft can attack (as by bombing) without danger to their own ground troops

bomb·load \ˈ=,=\ *n* : the quantity of bombs carried by an aircraft and measured by weight, by number, or (as for nuclear bombs) by kilotons or megatons of equivalent TNT

bombo *var of* BUMBO

bom·bonne \ˈbäm,bän\ *n* -s [F, fr. Prov *boumbouno*, fr. *boumbo* large ball, fr. L *bombus* deep hollow sound — more at BOMB] : a large globular bottle; *specif* : an earthenware Woulff bottle

bomb out *vt* **1** : to subject (as an industrial center) to bombing so that continued operation or inhabitation of the bombed objective is impossible ⟨a munitions factory which was *bombed out* early in the war⟩ ⟨a once beautiful city that was now *bombed out*⟩ **2** : to force out of a dwelling or place of business by bombing : make homeless by bombing ⟨millions of people were *bombed out*⟩

bomb pilot *n* : a map or drawing of a bombed target annotated with the location of each bomb hit

¹bombproof \ˈ=ˈ=\ *adj* : so constructed or placed as to be relatively secure against the explosive force of bombs or shells ⟨a ~ cellar⟩

²bombproof \ˈ=ˈ=\ *n* : a bombproof shelter

bomb release line *n* : the point on the ground ahead of the target over which an aircraft must release its bombs to get a hit on the target

bomb run *n* : the portion of a bomber's attack during which the actual sighting for and release of bombs occurs and which is flown usu. straight and level so that the bombardier's computations may be accurate

bombs *pl of* BOMB, *pres 3d sing of* BOMB

bomb·shell \ˈ=,=\ *n* **1** : BOMB 1 **2 a** : something that stuns, amazes, or is shatteringly upsetting: as (1) : a devastating surprise : a totally unexpected occurrence ⟨her arrival was a ~ in the previously tranquil town⟩ (2) : an unprecedented and often revolutionary idea or action ⟨a new theory that was a ~ to conservative thinkers⟩ **b** : one who is the cause and object of sensational and usu. widespread attention, excitement, or attraction ⟨a writer who is a literary ~⟩ ⟨a film featuring a stunning actress who can best be described as a blond ~⟩

bombsight \ˈ=,=\ *n* : a sighting device for aiming bombs; *specif* : a combined optical aiming and calculating mechanism and gyroscopic control for dropping aerial bombs from high altitudes

bomb up *vt* : to load (an aircraft) with bombs ⟨can be *bombed up* more or less like loading a clip of cartridges —*Science News Letter*⟩ ~ *vi* : to take on a load of bombs

bom·bus \ˈbämbəs\ *n, cap* [NL, fr. L, deep hollow sound, buzzing — more at BOMB] : a genus of bees comprising the typical bumblebees — compare BOMBYLIIDAE

¹bom·by·cid \ˈbämbəsəd, -,sid\ *adj* [NL *Bombycidae*] : of or relating to the family Bombycidae or to silkworms

²bombycid \"\ *n* -s : one of the Bombycidae : a silkworm or silkworm moth

bom·byc·i·dae \bäm'bisə,dē\ *n pl, cap* [NL, fr. *Bombyc-*, *Bombyx*, type genus + *-idae*] : a family of chiefly Asiatic moderate-sized moths having larvae that feed on leaves and spin cocoons of commercially usable silk and including the domesticated silkworms (genus *Bombyx*) and a few related forms but formerly including many other moths

bom·by·cil·la \,bämbə'silə\ *n, cap* [NL, blend of L *bombyc-, bombyx* silkworm, silk and NL *Motacilla* — more at BOMBAST] : a genus (the type of the family Bombycillidae) of passerine birds comprising the waxwings

bom·by·cine \ˈbämbə,sīn, -,sən\ *adj* [L *bombyc-, bombyx* silkworm + E *-ine*] : of or relating to silkworms

bom·by·li·i·dae \,bämbə'līə,dē\ *n pl, cap* [NL, fr. *Bombylius*, type genus (fr. Gk *bombylios* buzzing insect, bumblebee, fr. *bombos* deep hollow sound) + *-idae* — more at BOMB] : a family of hairy-bodied often brightly colored two-winged flies many of which resemble bees and are called bee flies

bom·byx \ˈbäm(,)biks\ *n, cap* [NL, fr. L, silkworm — more at BOMBAST] : the type genus of Bombycidae including the domestic silkworm moth (*Bombyx mori*) — see SILKWORM

¹bon \ˈbän\ *n* -s [perh. fr. D *boon* bean, fr. MD *bōne*; akin to OHG *bōna* bean — more at BEAN] **1** : BROAD BEAN **2** [perh. another word] : KIDNEY BEAN

²bon \ˈbōn\ *n -s usu cap* [Jap] : a great popular festival of Japan held July 13 to 16 when the spirits of ancestors are supposed to revisit the household altars — called also *Feast of Lanterns*

³bon \"\ *n -s cap* [Tibetan *bön*] : the pre-Buddhist animistic religion of Tibet

⁴bon \ˈbän\ *n* -s [origin unknown] : CHINA GRASS

bo·na \ˈbōnə\ *n pl* [L, fr. neut. pl. of *bonus* good] : PROPERTY — used in Roman and civil law of real and personal property of any kind but chiefly of real property in Roman law and usu. only of movables in common law

bona ad·ven·ti·tia *or* **bona ad·ven·ti·cia** \-,advən'tish(ē)ə\ *n pl* [L *bona adventicia* adventitious goods] *Roman Law* : all the property that is acquired by a person by his own labor or from persons other than his father and which he is permitted to keep as his own subject to the right of his father to enjoy its usufruct — called also, in post-Roman times, *peculium adventicium*; compare BONA MATERNA

bo·na·ci \,bōnə'sē\ *n* -s [Sp *bonasí*] : the black grouper (*Mycteroperca bonaci*) or a related marine food fish (as the gag)

bona con·fis·ca·ta \-,känfə'skād·ə\ *n pl* [L, confiscated goods] : property (as that forfeited for felony) appropriated to the fiscus under Roman law

bona fide \÷'bōnə,fīd, ÷'bänə,fīd, ˈ==ˈfīdē, ˈ==ˈfīdə\ *adj* [L, in good faith] **1** : made in good faith without fraud or deceit ⟨a *bona fide* contract⟩ : legally valid ⟨truth of such persons to place of *bona fide* residence —*U.S. Code*⟩ **2** : SINCERE ⟨the only *bona fide* friends of democracy and self-determination —Sinclair Lewis⟩ : made with earnest or wholehearted intent ⟨a *bona fide* proposal⟩ **3** : not specious or counterfeit : GENUINE ⟨just what a *bona fide* United States flag looked like —E.J.Kahn⟩ ⟨*bona fide* dinosaur eggs⟩ ⟨*bona fide* pockets below the waistline —*Women's Wear Daily*⟩ **syn** see AUTHENTIC

bona fide holder *n* : a holder of negotiable paper who before it reached maturity acquired title in the ordinary course of business and without actual or constructive notice of any defect in title or of lack of consideration

bona fide purchaser *n* : a purchaser who buys in good faith without notice of any defect and for a valuable consideration

bona fi·des \,==ˈfī,dēz, -fē,dās\ *n* [L] : good faith ⟨a claimant whose *bona fides* is unquestionable⟩ : lack of deceit or fraud ⟨the *bona fides* of a transaction⟩ : SINCERITY ⟨lays himself open to suspicion as to his *bona fides* and as to his knowledge by his remarks —F.W.Rolfe⟩

bon·aght \ˈbänəkt\ *n* -s [IrGael *buannacht*, fr. *buanna* soldier] : a tax formerly imposed by Irish chieftains upon their people for the quartering of soldiers

bon·ail·ie \bä'nālī\ *n* -s [ME (Scottish dialect), alter. (influenced by MF *bon* good) of MF *bien alee* parting felicitation, gift, or repast, fr. *bien* (fr. L *bene*, adv. of *bonus* good) + *alee*, fr. fem. of *alé*, past part. of *aler* to go — more at BOUNTY, ALLEY] *Scot* : a parting drink : STIRRUP CUP

bona ma·ter·na \,bōnəmə'tərnə\ *n pl* [L, maternal property] *Roman law* : all the property a son subject to paternal power acquires from his mother — compare BONA ADVENTITIA

bo·nang \bō'naŋ\ *n* -s [Jav] : a Javanese musical instrument consisting of a series of tuned gongs

bo·na no·ta·bi·lia \,bōnə,nōd·ə'bilēə\ *n pl* [L, notable goods] *obs* : the goods of a deceased person held in a diocese other than his own at the time of his death that according to older English probate law required consideration by the courts if of or exceeding the value of five pounds

bo·nan·za \bə'nanzə, bō'-\ *n* -s *often attrib* [Sp, lit., calm, fair weather, prosperity, rich mine, fr. ML *bonacia*, alter. (influenced by L *bonus* good) of L *malacia* calm at sea, fr. Gk *malakia*, lit., softness — more at BOUNTY, MALACIA] **1 a** : an exceptionally large and rich ore shoot or pocket in veins carrying gold and silver **b** : a mine having such an ore shoot or pocket; *also* : the yield of such a mine ⟨a ~ worth millions⟩ **2 a** : something that yields an often unexpectedly large profit ⟨a ~ enterprise⟩ ⟨put the full resources of his studio behind the picture . . . and achieved a box-office ~ —Al Hine⟩ **b** : an extremely large amount ⟨the ~ paid to foreign countries to help them keep out of debt⟩ ⟨a ~ of Socialist sympathy —*Time*⟩ **c** : something excessively rich, lush, or rewarding ⟨the ~ farms of the middle west —Lewis Mumford⟩ ⟨a ~ era⟩ — **in bonanza** *of a mine* : producing heavily and profitably

bo·na·parte's gull \ˈbōnə,pärts-\ *or* **bo·na·parte gull** \-rt-\ *n, usu cap B* [after C.L.J.L.*Bonaparte* †1857 Fr. naturalist in U.S.] : a No. American black-headed gull (*Larus philadelphia*) about the size of a pigeon

bonaparte's sandpiper *n, usu cap B* [after C.L.J.L.*Bonaparte*] : WHITE-RUMPED SANDPIPER

bonaparte's weasel *n, usu cap B* [after C.L.J.L.*Bonaparte*] : a small weasel (*Mustela cicognanii*) of northern No. America, slightly larger than a chipmunk, short-tailed, and chocolate-brown turning white in winter

bo·na·part·ism \ˈbōnəˌpärd·,izəm, -pȧd·,-, -är,tiz-, -ȧ,tiz-, ˈ===,==\ *n* -s *usu cap* [prob. fr. F *bonapartisme*, fr. Napoléon *Bonaparte* (Napoleon I) †1821 Fr. emperor + F *-isme* -ism] **1** : the policy of Bonaparte **2** : a policy advocating or supporting dictatorial rule by a popular leader who has ostensibly received a mandate from the people ⟨it has been a socialist and Communist tradition to be wary of *Bonapartism* —Aneurin Bevan⟩

¹bo·na·part·ist \ˈ==ˈ=əst\ *n* -s *usu cap* [prob. fr. F *bonapartiste*, fr. *Bonaparte* + F *-iste* -ist] : one attached to the policy or family of Bonaparte

²bonapartist \"\ *adj, usu cap* : of, relating to, or supporting Bonaparte or Bonapartism

bo·na per·i·tura \ˈbōnə,perə'tùrə\ *n pl* [L] *law* : perishable property

bo·na·ro·ba \ˈbōnəˈrōbə, ˈbän-\ *n* -s [It *bona roba* good material, good property, fr. *bona* (var. of *buona*, fem. of *buono* good, fr. L *bonus*) + *roba* property, material, of Gmc origin; akin to OHG *roub* booty, something stolen — more at BOUNTY, ROBE] : COURTESAN, PROSTITUTE

bo·na·sa \bō'nāzə, -āsə\ *n, cap* [NL, prob. alter. of L *bonasus* aurochs; fr. the similarity of its characteristic drumming sound to the bellowing of a bull] : a genus of birds (family Tetraonidae) containing only the ruffed grouse

bo·na·sus \bō'nāsəs\ *n, pl* **bonasi** \-,sī\ [L, fr. Gk *bonasos*, *bonassos*] *archaic* : WISENT

bona va·can·tia \ˈbōnəvə'kansh(ē)ə\ *n pl* [L, ownerless goods] *law* : goods without an apparent owner (as shipwrecks or the property of an intestate with no next of kin)

bon·a·ven·ture \,bänə'venchə(r), ˈ==,==\ *also* **bonaventure mizzen** *n* -s [prob. fr. It *buonaventura* good luck, fr. *buona* good + *ventura* luck, fortune, short for *avventura*, fr. L *adventura* — more at BONA-ROBA, ADVENTURE] : a sail hoisted on the fourth mast of a medieval boat; *also* : the mast itself

bon·a·vist \ˈbänəvəst, -,vist\ *also* **bonavist bean** *n* -s [prob. fr. It *buona vista* fine sight, fr. *buona* good + *vista* sight — more at VISTA] : HYACINTH BEAN

bona wa·vi·a·ta \,bōnə,wāvē'ād·ə\ *n pl* [ML, waived goods] : WAIFS

bon·bon \ˈbän,bän\ *n* -s [F, (baby talk), redupl. of *bon* good, fr. L *bonus*] **1** : a piece of candy; *specif* : a small chocolate-coated or fondant-covered candy with a center of sugar fondant to which fruits and nuts are sometimes added **2** : something cloying and insubstantial ⟨newsstands . . . plastered with gory thrillers, romantic ~*s*, and pornography —Michael Scully⟩

bon·bon·nière \,bänbə'ni(ə)r, ,bōⁿbən'ya(a)(ə)r\ *n* -s [F, fr. *bonbon*] : a small fancy box or dish for bonbons

bonbon spoon *n* : a spoon with a flat perforated bowl for bonbons and nuts

bonce \ˈbän(t)s\ *n* -s [origin unknown] *dial Eng* : a boys' game played with marbles; *also* : a large marble

¹bond *n* -s [ME *bonde* peasant, serf, fr. OE *bōnda*, *bunda* householder, husband, fr. ON *bōndi*, alter. of *būandi*, fr. pres. part. of *būa* to live, dwell, have a household — more at BOWER] *obs* : BONDMAN

²bond *adj* [ME *bonde*, fr. *bonde*, n.] : being in a state of serfdom, servitude, or slavery : BOUND ⟨by one spirit are we all baptized into one body . . . whether we be ~ or free —1 Cor 12:13(AV)⟩

³bond \ˈbänd\ *n* -s [ME *band*, *bond* — more at BAND] **1 a** : something that confines or restrains (as a fetter or chain) : SHACKLE — usu. used in pl. ⟨you may chain the law down with all manner of clamps and ~*s* —B.N.Cardozo⟩ **b** *archaic* : IMPRISONMENT, CONFINEMENT — usu. used in pl. **2** : an agreement binding one or more parties ⟨a ~ between two governments to aid each other in war⟩ : COVENANT, CHARTER ⟨the principles of friendship and ethics as espoused in the ~ of Phi Delta Theta —P.F.Connolly⟩ **3 a** : a hoop, band, or cord used to hold something down or together (as wheat, fagots, thatch) ⟨master the trick of tying the sheaf with its ~ —H.E.Bates⟩ **b** : a piece of building material (as a timber, brick, stone) that serves to bind or unite **c** : a device for binding together the armor or lead sheaths of two or more adjacent cables or for anchoring a cable to the earth **d** : a conductor that provides a continuous path for electric current between adjacent metal parts of a structure: as (1) : a conductor between the abutting rails of a track (2) : the connection between water mains and gas mains (3) : the grounded return of an electric railway system **e** : a mechanism by means of which atoms, ions, or groups of atoms are held together in a molecule or crystal, being usu. represented in chemical formulas by a line, a dot, or a pair of dots or lines denoting paired electrons — called also *link*, *linkage*; see COVALENT BOND, DOUBLE BOND, ELECTROSTATIC BOND, ELECTROVALENT BOND, HYDROGEN BOND, METALLIC BOND, TRIPLE BOND, VALENCE **f** : an adhesive that binds different ingredients together: as (1) : a cementing material that holds abrasive grains together (as in grinding wheels) or that binds the grains to the backing in coated abrasives (as sandpaper) (2) : the lime in silica brick (3) : a fusible ingredient that imparts strength to fired ceramic ware **4 a** : a uniting or binding element or force : TIE ⟨the ~ of fellowship⟩ — often used in pl. ⟨his wish to strengthen the ~*s* between Colombia and the U.S. —*Current Biog.*⟩; *specif* : a linkage between a stimulus and a reaction or between one idea and an associated idea ⟨the ~ theory of learning⟩ **b** : the state, result, or an instance of being bonded (as by an adhesive) : COHESION ⟨it is impossible to secure the proper ~ of coating to metal when the slightest particle of rust is present —*advt*⟩ **c** : resistance to slipping (as between the major components of a structure) provided by adhesion or friction ⟨precautions were taken to prevent ~ between the concrete roadway and the structural steel beneath it so that the concrete could shorten under the compression —N.J. Sollenberger⟩ **5 a** (1) : a writing under seal by which a person binds himself to pay a certain sum on or before an appointed day and usu. containing a condition that if the obligator shall do or abstain from doing a certain act on or before a time specified the obligation shall be void but otherwise shall remain in full force; *also* : the amount of money so guaranteed — often used with *give* ⟨each must give ~ for his appearance before the court⟩; compare BAIL, PENAL SUM (2) : one who acts as bail or surety **b** : an interest-bearing document giving evidence of a long-term debt and issued by a government body or corporation sometimes secured by a lien on property and often designed to take care of a particular financial need — see CALLABLE, COLLATERAL TRUST BOND, COUPON BOND, DEBENTURE, EQUIPMENT BOND, HIGHWAY BOND, REGISTERED BOND, SAVINGS BOND, SERIAL BOND, SINKING-FUND BOND, TAP BOND **c** : an insurance agreement pledging surety for financial loss caused to another by the act or default of a third person or by some contingency over which the third person may have no control **6** : a connection or system of connections in which adjacent parts of a structure are made to overlap so as to be tied or bound together; *specif* : the systematic lapping of brick in a wall ⟨the brickwork is unusually fine and the ~ used on the south front of the house is different from that on the other sides —*Amer. Guide Series: La.*⟩ — see AMERICAN BOND, BLIND BOND, BLOCK-IN-COURSE BOND, CHAIN BOND, CROSS-AND-ENGLISH BOND, CROSS BOND, DIAGONAL BOND, DOG'S-TOOTH BOND, ENGLISH BOND, ENGLISH CROSS BOND, FLEMISH BOND, FLYING BOND, HERRINGBONE BOND, IN-AND-OUT BOND, PLUMB BOND, RANGING BOND, RUNNING BOND, SPLIT BOND **7** : the state of goods being manufactured, stored, or transported under the care of bonded agencies until the duties or taxes on them are paid ⟨you may leave . . . tobacco in ~ with customs —Richard Joseph⟩ **8** : a 100-proof straight whiskey that has been aged at least four years under government supervision before being bottled — called also *bonded whiskey* **9** : BOND PAPER

⁴bond \"\ *vb* -ED/-ING/-S *vt* **1** : to bind or tie (a wall, a building, or various masonry units) usu. by lapping one unit over another **2** : to place under the conditions of a bond: as **a** : to secure the payment of the duties and taxes on (goods or merchandise being manufactured, warehoused, or transported) by giving a bond **b** : to mortgage or issue bonds secured by mortgage upon (property) **c** : to convert into a debt secured by bonds **d** : to give or secure an option upon (as a mine or other property) by a bond tying up the property till the option has expired **e** : to provide a bond (sense 5c) for or cause to provide such a bond ⟨~ a trustee⟩ ⟨~ an employee⟩ ⟨~ an official⟩ **3** : to bind together or connect by or as if by bonds: as **a** : to cause to adhere firmly (as metal to glass or plastic) **b** : to make secure and adequate electrical connection between (two or more conductors) either to ensure free passage of current ⟨a railroad track with ~*ed* joints⟩ or to maintain uniformity of electric potential (as of water and gas piping or the sheaths of electric cables) — compare ³BOND 3d **c** : to embed in a matrix ⟨abrasive material ~*ed* in a resinous binder to form a grinding wheel⟩ — compare ³BOND 3f **d** : to hold together in a molecule or crystal by means of chemical bonds ~ *vi* : to hold together or solidify by or as if by means of a bond or a binder ⟨a cement failing to make materials ~⟩; *specif* : to cohere (as the fibers in paper, the coating of the surface of paper, the elements in laminated board) ⟨the coatings ~ tightly to many surfaces —*Graphic Arts Monthly*⟩ — **bond·a·ble** \-dəbəl\ *adj*

bond·age \ˈbändij, -dēj\ *n* -s [ME, fr. ML *bondagium*, fr. ME *bonde* peasant, serf + L *-agium* -age] **1 a** : the tenure or service of a villein, serf, or slave **b** *chiefly Scot* : services due from a tenant farmer to his proprietor or from a cottager to the farmer **2** : the quality or state of being bound: as **a** : restraint of personal liberty by compulsion : SERFDOM, CAPTIVITY ⟨the ~ of the Hebrews in Egypt⟩ **b** : voluntary subjugation (as to some service or duty) ⟨she had gone into ~ among the aristocracy as a governess —Virginia Woolf⟩ **c** : servitude or subjugation (as to someone superior or dominating or to some power, motive, or appetite) ⟨with the House of Representatives in ~ to its leaders —Lindsay Rogers⟩ ⟨the ~ of specialization⟩ ⟨the obvious and painful ~ of shyness —Helen Howe⟩ **d** *linguistics* : the state of being a bound form

bond·ag·er \-jə(r)\ *n* -s **1** : one that performs bondage service **2** *chiefly Scot* : one obligated to perform certain services on a farm; *specif* : a woman engaged by a tenant farmer or cotter under his agreement with the proprietor to do field work on the farm

bon·dar \ˈbän,där\ *n* -s [prob. fr. Bengali or Hindi *bãda* monkey — more at BANDAR] : a palm civet (*Paradoxurus hermaphrodytus*) of India

bond clay *n* [³*bond*] : a plastic ceramic clay that gives strength to dry but unfired ware

bond coat *n* [³*bond*] : a coat (as of plaster or paint) to ensure adhesion

bond course *n* [*bond*stone] : a course of masonry bondstones

bonded *adj* [fr. past part. of ⁴*bond*] : in, operating under, or placed under a bond ⟨a ~ carrier⟩ ⟨~ goods⟩

bonded debt *n* : that part of the indebtedness of a government or corporation represented by bonds — called also *funded debt*

bonded store *n, Brit* : BONDED WAREHOUSE

bonded warehouse *n* **1** : a warehouse under bond to the government for payment of customs duties and taxes on goods stored or processed there **2** : a warehouse insured against loss or damage to goods stored therein

bonded whiskey *n* : ³BOND 8

¹bon·der \ˈbändə(r)\ *n* -s [⁴*bond* + *-er*] **1** : one that bonds: as **a** : an assembler of electromagnet laminations **b** : a worker who welds copper bonds between the joints of rails **2** : BONDSTONE 1

²bond·er \"\ *n* -s [modif. of Norw *bonde* and Icel *bōndi* householder, fr. ON *bōndi* — more at BOND] : a Norwegian or Icelandic farmer or peasant landowner

bond·er·ize \ˈbändə,rīz\ *vt* -ED/-ING/-S [back-formation fr. *Bonderized*, a trademark] : to coat (steel) with a patented phosphate solution for protection against corrosion

bondholder \ˈ=,==\ *n* [³*bond* + *holder*] : a person who holds a bond (as of a government or corporation)

bon·dieu·se·rie \bōn,dyüzə'rē\ *n* -s [F, fr. *bon Dieu* dear Lord (fr. *bon* good + *dieu* god, fr. L *deus*) + connective *-s-* + *-erie* -ery — more at BONNY, DEITY] : banal and often shoddy religious art; *also* : a piece of bondieuserie (as a statue or picture)

bonding *n* -s [fr. gerund of ⁴*bond*] : electrical interconnection between parts (as of an airplane) to minimize differences of voltage

bonding company *n* [fr. pres. part. of ⁴*bond*] : a company issuing fidelity and surety bonds : SURETY COMPANY

bonding course *n* : BOND COURSE

bonding plaster *n* : BOND PLASTER

bond·less \ˈbändləs, *rapid* -nl-\ *adj* : being without a bond

bond·maid \ˈbän(d),mād\ *n, archaic* : a female slave or bond servant

bond·man \ˈbän(d)mən\ *n, pl* **bondmen** [ME *bondeman* peasant, serf, fr. *bonde* peasant, serf + *man* — more at BOND] : one who is bound : SLAVE, SERF, VILLEIN

bond miner *n* [³*bond*] : a contractor hewer

bon·do \ˈbän(,)dō\ *n, pl* **bondo** *or* **bondos** *usu cap* **1** : a people of the hill country of the Koraput district in India **2** : a member of the Bondo people

bond of indemnity [³*bond*] : an indemnification agreement filed with a carrier relieving it from liability for something that it would otherwise be liable for

bon·don \(ˈ)bōⁿ'dōⁿ\ *also* **bondon cheese** *n* -s [F *bondon*, lit., bung, fr. *bonde* bung, fr. (assumed) Gaulish *bunda*; akin to MIr *bond*, *bonn* sole of the foot, L *fundus* bottom — more at BOTTOM] : a cheese resembling a bung in form and made in Neufchâtel, France

bond paper *n* [³*bond*] : a strong durable paper of a type orig. made for documents (as government bonds) and now commonly used for letterheads and other stationery

bond plaster *n* [³*bond*] : a plaster with high adhesive properties made esp. for use as a first coat on interior concrete surfaces

bonds *pl of* BOND, *pres 3d sing of* BOND

bondslave \ˈ=,=\ *n* [²*bond* + *slave*] : a person in slavery : BONDMAN, SLAVE

¹bonds·man \ˈbän(d)zmən\ *n, pl* **bondsmen** [by alter.] : ¹BONDMAN

²bonds·man \"\ *n, pl* **bondsmen** [³*bond* + *-s* + *man*] : one who assumes the responsibility of a bond : SURETY

³bondsman \"\ *n, pl* **bondsmen** *usu cap* [Afrik, fr. *Bond* (short for *Afrikanerbond*, lit., alliance of Afrikaners, fr. *Afrikaner* + *bond* alliance, fr. MD, bundle, alliance) + *man*, fr. MD; akin to OE *bundel* bundle and to OE *man*, *mon* man — more at BUNDLE, MAN] : a member of the Afrikanerbond, an organization founded in 1880 to achieve unification and independence of the states and colonies of So. Africa

bondstone \ˈbän,stōn\ *n* [³*bond* + *stone*] **1** : a stone running through a masonry wall to bind it together **2** : a stone that joins the coping above a gable to the upper surface of a wall

bond timber *n* [³*bond*] : a timber built horizontally into a masonry wall to which battens and laths are fastened — compare CHAIN BOND

bon·duc \ˈbän,dək\ *n* -s [F, fr. Ar *bunduq* hazelnut, filbert] **1** : NICKER NUT **2** *also* **bonduc tree** : any of several trees of the genus *Caesalpinia* (as *C. bonduc*) with large prickly pods enclosing beanlike seeds **3** : KENTUCKY COFFEE TREE

bond·wom·an \ˈbän,dwůmən\ *also* **bonds·wom·an** \-n(d)z-,w-\ *n, pl* **bondwom·en** *also* **bondswom·en** \-,wimən\ [ME *bondewoman*, fr. *bonde* bond (adj.) + *woman* — more at BOND] : a female slave

1bone \'bōn\ *n* -s *often attrib* [ME *boon, bon,* fr. OE *bān;* akin to OHG & ON *bein* bone] **1 a :** one of the hard parts of the skeleton of a vertebrate ⟨shoulder ~⟩ ⟨the ~s of the arm⟩ — compare CARTILAGE **b :** any of various hard animal substances or structures akin to or resembling bone (as baleen, ivory, the internal calcareous shell of the cuttlefish) **c :** the hard tissue of which the adult skeleton of most vertebrates is largely composed, being a dense form of connective tissue, hard and rigid from its inorganic matter of chiefly calcium phosphate, and being externally of compact tissue covered except on the articular surfaces with a fibrous coat of vascular connective tissue and internally porous and containing cavities of various sizes — see BONE CELL, CANALICULUS, HAVERSIAN CANAL, LAMELLA, OSSIFICATION, PERIOSTEUM **2 :** ESSENCE, CORE ⟨chilled to the ~⟩ ⟨lying was in his very ~s⟩ ⟨cut expenses to the ~⟩ **3 bones** *pl* **a** (1) **:** the skeleton ⟨reduced to skin and ~s by hunger⟩ or other framework resembling a skeleton ⟨vessels lost on the lakes, many of whose ~s are still . . . along the shores —*Amer. Guide Series: Mich.*⟩ (2) **:** BODY ⟨running as fast as his old ~s would carry him⟩ (3) **:** the more enduring parts of a dead body **:** mortal remains ⟨inter a person's ~s⟩ **b :** the essential design or framework (as of a story, novel, picture, or other work of art) **4 :** MATTER, SUBJECT ⟨a ~ of contention⟩ **5 :** something orig. or usu. made of bone: as **a bones** *pl* **:** thin bars of bone, ivory, or wood held in pairs between the fingers and used to produce musical rhythms **:** CLAPPERS, KNACKERS **b :** a strip of whalebone, steel, featherbone, or plastic inserted into a casing to stiffen a garment (as a corset or dress) **c bones** *pl* **:** DICE **d :** DOMINO **6 :** the bow wave of a ship when under way or esp. when traveling at good speed — usu. used with the phrase *in her teeth* ⟨the ship all sails set, was roaring along with a ~ in her teeth⟩ **7 bones** *pl but sing in constr, often cap* **:** an end man in a minstrel show who often performs on the bones — compare TAMBO **8 a :** a layer or fragments of shale, slate, or other rock in a coal seam or in coal **b** *or* **bone coal :** slaty coal often of such a high ash content that it cannot be used in the ordinary ways **:** carboniferous shale — called also *bony, slate* **9** *slang* **:** DOLLAR — **bone to pick :** a point of contention **:** a cause for complaint **:** a matter to argue or complain about ⟨a *bone to pick* with the sales manager over defective merchandise⟩

2bone \"\ *vb* -ED/-ING/-S [ME *bonen,* fr. *bon, boon,* n.] *vt* **1 :** to remove the bones from ⟨~ a fish⟩ ⟨~ a turkey⟩ ⟨the ribs can be *boned* out and the meat rolled for roasting⟩ **2 :** to provide (a garment) with stays ⟨~ a corset⟩ ⟨a *boned* camisole⟩ **3 :** to rub (as a boot) with a piece of bone in order to remove scratches and smooth the surface **4 :** to sight along (an object or set of objects, as rods or sticks) to arrive at a straight line or ascertain a level ~ *vi* **1 :** to study hard or ploddingly **:** GRIND ⟨~ away at premedical courses⟩ ⟨*boning* through law school⟩ **2 :** to attempt to master necessary or required information in a short time (as in preparation for an examination) **:** CRAM — usu. used with *up* ⟨~ up on a problem⟩ ⟨~ up on Latin⟩; compare SWOT

3bone \"\ *adv* [*1bone* (as in *bone-dry, bone-tired*)] **:** EXTREMELY ⟨a ~ lazy fellow⟩ **:** ABSOLUTELY ⟨a novel ~ clean of sentimentality⟩ **:** UTTERLY ⟨he gets ~ tired and edgy —S.E.Fletcher⟩ **:** DESPERATELY ⟨~ poor⟩ ⟨the poor are ~ hungry —Margaret Shedd⟩

4bône \"\ *or* **bone** *adj, usu cap* [fr. *Bône* or *Bone* (now *Annaba*), Algeria] **:** of or from the city of Bône, Algeria **:** of the kind or style prevalent in Bône

bone–ace *n, obs* **:** a card game in which the highest third card took half the stake; *also* **:** the ace of diamonds which was the highest card

bone age *n, usu cap B&A* **:** a prehistoric period characterized by the use of bone and antler implements **:** the period of Magdalenian culture

bone ash *n* **:** the white porous residue containing chiefly tribasic calcium phosphate from bones calcined in air and used esp. in making cupels, pottery, and glass and in cleaning jewelry; *also* **:** synthetic tribasic calcium phosphate used similarly

bone bed *n* **:** any terrestrial or marine stratum in which bones or bone fragments are abundant

bone black *or* **bone char** *n* **:** the black substance containing chiefly tribasic calcium phosphate and carbon into which crushed defatted bones are converted by carbonization in closed vessels and which is used esp. as a black pigment and as a decolorizing adsorbent — called also *animal black, animal charcoal;* compare ACTIVATED CARBON, CARBON BLACK, DROP BLACK, IVORY BLACK

bonebreaker \'=,==\ *n* **:** any of several large birds (as the giant petrel, the lammergeier, or the osprey)

bone breccia *n* **:** a deposit of fragments of bones of vertebrates often mixed with earth, sand, and calcium carbonate

bone brown *n* **1 :** a pigment similar to bone black made by partially carbonizing bones **2 :** a moderate to dark olive brown — called also *bracken, ivory brown*

bone cell *n* **1** *or* **bone corpuscle :** any of the cells occupying the lacunae of bone **:** OSTEOBLAST **2 :** OSTEOSCLEREID

bone china *n* **:** a very white translucent ceramic ware developed in England about the beginning of the 19th century that has a body of kaolin, china stone, and bone ash and is fired at temperatures intermediate between those of soft-paste and hard-paste porcelain; *broadly* **:** any porcelain containing bone ash

bone coal *n* **:** 1BONE 8b

bone conduction *n* **:** the transmission of sound waves to the inner ear through the bones of the skull

boned \'bōnd\ *adj* [ME, fr. *boon, bon* bone (n.) + *-ed* — more at BONE] **1 :** having bones of a specified type ⟨she is slender, erect, and exquisitely ~ —Joseph Mitchell⟩ **2 :** with bones removed ⟨a ~ fish⟩ ⟨a ~ rib roast⟩ **3 :** manured with bone ⟨~ land⟩ **4 :** provided or strengthened with stays ⟨her long neck wrapped in its high ~ collar —Marcia Davenport⟩

bone–dry \'=¦=\ *adj* **1 a :** dry as a weathered bone **:** very dry **:** absolutely dry ⟨fire hazards present in *bone-dry* leaves⟩ **b** *of clay* **:** completely dried but not fired **2 :** opposed to or being without intoxicating beverages ⟨a *bone-dry* luncheon⟩

bone dust *n* **:** BONE MEAL

bone earth *n* **:** BONE ASH

bone–eater \'=,==\ *n* [by folk etymology fr. *bonito*] **:** ATLANTIC BONITO

bo·neen \bə'nēn, bə'-\ *n* -s [IrGael *banabhin,* dim. of *banbh,* fr. OIr *banb;* akin to obs. W *banw* young pig, Breton *bano* sow with a litter, OCorn *baneu* sow] *Irish* **:** a young pig

bone fat *n* **:** the fatty matter in bones obtained by boiling, steaming, or extracting with solvents and used chiefly in candles, cheap soap, and lubricating greases

bone felon *n, dial* **:** 3FELON 2

bonefish \'=,=\ *n* [so called fr. its many small bones] **1 :** any of several slender silvery small-scaled fishes of the family Albulidae; *esp* **:** an outstanding game and food fish (*Albula vulpes*) of warmer seas that sometimes exceeds 10 pounds in weight — called also *banana fish* **2 :** TENPOUNDER

bone glass *n* **:** a glass of a milky white color due to the presence of bone ash or other form of calcium phosphate

bonehead \'=,=\ *n* **:** a stupid or slow-thinking person **:** NUMSKULL, BLOCKHEAD ⟨you got ~s running business nowaday —Ira Wolfert⟩ ⟨a ~ play by the shortstop⟩ — **bone·headed** \'=¦=\ *adj*

bone lace *n* [so called fr. the fact that it was made by bone bobbins] **:** BOBBIN LACE

bone·less \'bōnləs\ *adj* [ME *banles,* fr. OE *bānlēas,* fr. *bān* bone + *-lēas* -less — more at BONE] **1 :** being without a bone ⟨jellyfish are ~⟩ **:** having the bone or bones removed ⟨~ roasts of beef⟩ **2 :** lacking character, strength, or vigor ⟨the sentences are occasionally ~ —J.N.Hall⟩

bone·let \-lət\ *n* -s **:** a small bone **:** OSSICLE

bo·nel·lia \bō'nelēə, bə-\ *n, cap* [NL, fr. Francesco A. *Bonelli* †1830 Ital. naturalist + NL *-ia*] **:** a genus of marine worms (group Echiuroidea) that exhibit marked dimorphism and size disparity between the sexes, the male living parasitically in the nephridium of the female and that have what appears to be a unique mechanism of sex determination, the indifferent larva becoming a male if it settles on the proboscis of a mature female and becoming a female if it develops independently on the sea bottom

bone marrow *n* **:** MARROW 1

bone meal *n* **:** bone crushed or ground usu. after extraction of fat and gelatin and used chiefly as a fertilizer but also in the feed of farm animals

bone oil *n* **1 :** a dark-colored ill-smelling oil obtained by carbonizing bones (as in making bone black) that contains hydrocarbons and many nitrogen compounds (as pyrrole and pyridine bases) and is used esp. in sheep dips and in denaturing alcohol — called also *animal oil, Dippel's oil* **2 :** the liquid portion of bone fat used as a lubricant and in leather manufacture

bone phosphate *n* **:** tribasic calcium phosphate from bones

bone picker *n* **:** an American Indian who follows a burial custom of cleaning the flesh from the bones of corpses prior to burial

bone–pointing \'=,==\ *n* **:** the practice (as among Australian aboriginals) of pointing a sharpened bone at an enemy and uttering incantations conjuring his illness, disability, or death

bone porcelain *n* **:** BONE CHINA

bon·er \'bōnə(r)\ *n* -s [*2bone* + *-er*] **1 :** one that puts bones into garments (as corsets) — called also *stayer, steeler* **2 :** a low-grade beef animal suitable only for boning out (as for the preparation of canned meats or sausage) **3** [*1bone* + *-er*] **a :** a ridiculous and usu. embarrassing or painful mistake or slip often arising from a sudden and fortuitous lapse of understanding, tact, or decorum — often used with *pull* **b :** a grammatical, logical, or factual blunder in a piece of writing often producing a humorous effect ⟨a few historical ~s . . . such as dinosaurs surviving until medieval times —Coulton Waugh⟩ ⟨~s in student themes⟩ **syn** see ERROR

bones *pl of* BONE, *pres 3d sing of* BONE

bone·set \'bōn,set, *usu* -d·+V\ *n* **1 :** any of several American herbs of the genus *Eupatorium* (esp. *E. perfoliatum*) distinguished by opposite perfoliate leaves and white-rayed flower heads and formerly used as a household remedy — called also *agueweed, thoroughwort* **2 :** CLIMBING HEMPWEED **3 :** COMMON COMFREY

bonesetter \'=,==\ *n* [ME *boone setter,* fr. *boone, boon* bone + *setter*] **:** a person usu. not a licensed physician who sets broken or dislocated bones — **bonesetting** \'=,==\ *n*

bone·shaker \'bōn,shākə(r)\ *n, slang* **:** a dilapidated, uncomfortable, or outmoded vehicle (as a bicycle of an early model without rubber tires)

bone shark *n* [so called fr. its gill rakers resembling whalebones] **:** BASKING SHARK

bone·shave \'bōn,shāv\ *also* **bone·shaw** \-,shȯ\ *n* [ME *boneschawe*] *archaic* **:** SCIATICA

bone skin *n* **:** PERIOSTEUM

bone spavin *n* **:** a new growth of bone on the hock of the horse that is the result of inflammation and hereditary predisposition and that causes somewhat severe lameness

bone spirit *n* **:** an ammoniacal liquid obtained along with bone oil in the carbonization of bones

bone·tail \'=,=\ *n* **:** FER-DE-LANCE

bone tankage *n* **:** DIGESTER TANKAGE

bone–throwing \'=,==\ *n* **:** the throwing of pieces of bone or wood practiced by some primitive peoples for purposes of divination or diagnosis

bone turquoise *n* **:** ODONTOLITE

bone whale *n* **:** a whalebone whale; *esp* **:** RIGHT WHALE

bonewood \'=,=\ *n* [so called fr. its ivory color and hardness] **:** CHEESEWOOD

boney *var of* BONY

bone·yard \'=,=\ *n* **1 a** *slang* **:** CEMETERY **b :** a place where domestic animals are disposed of or their bones collected **c :** a restricted area where the bones of wild animals have accumulated ⟨a caribou ~⟩ **2 :** a place where worn-out, obsolete, or irreparably damaged ships, airplanes, or automobiles are collected to await ultimate disposal **3 :** the dominoes remaining after each player has drawn a hand — called also *stock*

bon·fire \'bän + ,-\ *n* [ME *bonefyre,* fr. *bone, bon* bone + *fyre* fire — more at BONE, FIRE] **1 a** *obs* **:** a large public fire in which bones or bones and wood were traditionally burned **b** *obs* **:** a funeral pyre **c** *archaic* **:** a fire in which heretics or officially proscribed articles (as books or religious objects) were publicly burned **2 :** a great open-air fire kindled to mark a religious anniversary (as the eves of St. Peter and St. John) or to highlight some public event (as a political rally, a community outing, a victory celebration, the birthday of a famous person) **3 :** an open-air fire in which waste paper, leaves, brush, or other rubbish is burned

1bong \'bȯŋ, 'bäŋ\ *n* -s [imit.] **:** the deep resonant sound of a bell or one resembling that of a bell ⟨a spittoon slid against the bar with a dull ~ —W.D.Overholser⟩

2bong \"\ *vb* -ED/-ING/-S **:** RING ⟨the clock ~*ed* out the hour⟩ ⟨the clerk . . . ~*ed* the call bell —John Selby⟩

bonga \'bȯŋə, 'bȯŋə\ *also* **bunga** \'büŋə\ *n* -s [Tag & Bisayan *bunga*] **1** *Philippines* **:** BETEL PALM **2** *Philippines* **:** BETEL NUT

bon·gar \'bəŋ(,)gär\ *n* -s [native name in India] **:** a poisonous snake of India of the genus *Bungarus*

1bon·go \'bäŋ(,)gō, 'bȯŋ-\ *n, pl* **bongo** *or* **bongos** *usu cap* **1 :** a Negro people of eastern Sudan who are agriculturists and efficient metalworkers and are distinguished by their reddish skin — called also *Dor* **2 :** a member of the Bongo people

2bongo \"\ *n, pl* **bongo** *or* **bongos** [of African origin; akin to Lingala *mongu,* an antelope] **:** a large forest antelope (*Tragelaphus eurycerus* syn. *Boocercus euryceros*) of central Africa that is reddish or chestnut brown with narrow white stripes

3bongo *var of* BONGO

4bon·go \'bäŋ(,)gō, 'bȯŋ-\ *n* -s [AmerSp] **:** a tropical American timber tree (*Cavanillesia platanifolia*) of the family Bombacaceae that yields a light soft wood resembling balsa

5bongo \", ='=\ *or* **bongo drum** *n, pl* **bongos** *also* **bongoes** [AmerSp *bongó*] **:** one of a pair of small tuned drums played with the fingers and used esp. in Cuban bands

6bongo \"\ *n* -s [AmerSp] **:** a sensuous Trinidad Negro dance secularized from an original funeral ritual

bon·grace \'bän,grās\ *n* -s [obs. E, projecting brim for a bonnet, fr. (assumed) MF *bonne-grace* (whence F *bonne-grâce,* a cloth), fr. *bonne* (fem. of *bon* good) + *grâce* grace, favor — more at BONNY, GRACE] *archaic* **:** a hat or bonnet with a brim projecting in front

bon·ham \'bänəm\ *n* -s [modif. of IrGael *banbh* — more at BONEEN] *chiefly Irish* **:** a young pig

bon·heur du jour \bə,nərdü'jü(ə)r, -də'-\ *n, pl* **bonheurs du jour** *like sing.*\ [F, lit., happiness of the day; fr. its tremendous popularity in 18th cent. France] **:** a small desk or writing table with a cabinet top

bon·ho·mie *also* **bon·hom·mie** \'bänə,mē, ,==='=\ *n* -s [F *bonhomie* (formerly *bonhommie*), fr. *bonhomme* good-natured man (fr. *bon* good + *homme* man, fr. L *homo*) + *-ie* -y — more at BONNY, HOMAGE] **:** good-natured easy friendliness **:** warm open geniality **:** atmosphere of good cheer ⟨Christmas ~⟩ ⟨the ~ of a fraternity reunion⟩ ⟨an undying ~ radiated from her —Jean Stafford⟩

bon·ho·mous \'bänəməs\ *adj* **:** full of bonhomie **:** warmly genial ⟨a ~ master of ceremonies⟩ ⟨stories that can be told only in ~ moments⟩

bo·ni \'bō(,)nē\ *n, pl* **boni** *or* **bonis** *usu cap* [F, of Amerind origin] **1 :** a Bush Negro people of the interior of French Guiana **2 :** a member of the Boni people

bon·ie \'bänī\ *archaic Scot var of* BONNY

bonier *comparative of* BONY

bonies *pl of* BONY

boniest *superlative of* BONY

bon·i·face \'bänəfəs, -,fās\ *n* -s *sometimes cap* [fr. *Boniface,* jovial innkeeper in *The Beaux' Stratagem* (1707) by George Farquhar †1707 Irish dramatist] **:** the proprietor of a hotel, nightclub, or restaurant ⟨local ~s preparing to accommodate a political convention⟩

bon·i·fi·ca·tion \,bänəfə'kāshən\ *n* -s [F, fr. ML *bonificatus* (past part. of *bonificare* to ameliorate, fr. L *boni-* — fr. *bonus* good — + *-ficare,* fr. *facere* to do, make) + F *-ion* — more at BOUNTY, DO] **:** betterment of housing conditions and farming practices in a particular area (as a malarial area)

bon·i·form \'bänə,fȯrm\ *adj* [NL *boniformis* (trans. of Gk *agathoeidēs*), fr. L *bonus* good + *-iformis* -iform] *archaic* **:** promoting, perceiving, or akin to good ⟨the ~ powers of knowledge⟩ ⟨man's ~ faculty⟩

bon·ing \'bōniŋ, -nēŋ\ *n* -s [*1bone* + *-ing*] **:** bones used to stiffen garments

boning knife *n* **:** a short knife with narrow blade and sharp point for boning meat

bon·i·tar·i·an \,bänə'terēən, -ta(a)r-\ *or* **bon·i·tary** \'==,terē\ *adj* [L *bonitas* goodness (fr. *bonus* good + *-itas* -ity) + E *-arian* or *-ary* — more at BOUNTY] **1** *Roman law* **:** beneficial or equitable rather than statutory, civil, or quiritarian **2** *Roman law* **:** of or relating to ownership or possession protected not by the jus civile but by praetorian edict

bo·ni·to \bə'nēd·ō, bō'-, -ētō, -ə\ *also* **bo·ni·ta** \-ə\ *n, pl* **bonitos** *or* **bonito** *also* **bonitas** *or* **bonita** [Sp *bonito,* fr. *bonito,* adj., pretty, nice, fr. L *bonus* good + Sp *-ito* (dim. suffix)] **1 :** any of various medium-sized scombroid fishes intermediate in size and in other characteristics between the smaller mackerels and the larger tunas — compare CHILE BONITO, FRIGATE MACKEREL, SKIPJACK **2 :** any of various other fishes somewhat resembling bonitos

bonito shark *n* **:** a common blue or blue-gray mackerel shark (*Isurus glaucus*) of the Pacific ocean notable as a sport fish in the southwest Pacific and sometimes used for food — called also *blue pointer, mako*

bon·jean curves \'bän,jēn-\ *n pl, usu cap B* [origin unknown] **:** curves of areas of transverse sections and their moments about the base line of a ship used in making calculations (as to determine the force of buoyancy during launching)

bonk \'bäŋk\ *n* -s [D, lit., bone, mass (as of flesh), fr. MD *bonc, bonke* bone, jawbone — more at BUNCH] **:** a piece of the old copper bar money of the Dutch East Indies of which pieces worth ½, 1, 2, and 8 stivers were issued

bon mot \bōⁿmō\ *n, pl* **bons mots** *or* **bon mots** \bōⁿmō(z)\ [F, lit., good word] **:** a clever usu. witty remark **:** WITTICISM ⟨his *bons mots* were being repeated . . . from coast to coast —W.J.Fisher⟩

bonn \'bän, 'bȯn\ *adj, usu cap* [fr. *Bonn,* Germany] **:** of or from Bonn, the capital of the West German Federal Republic **:** of the kind or style prevalent in Bonn

bon·naz \bə'naz\ *n* -s *usu cap* [after *J.Bonnaz,* 19th cent. Fr. inventor] **:** embroidery (as chain stitch or appliqué) made with a sewing machine

bonne \'bȯn, 'bən\ *n* -s [F, fr. fem. of *bon* good — more at BONNY] **:** a French maidservant

bonne bouche \bȯn'büsh, bən'-\ *n, pl* **bonnes bouches** *or* **bonne bouches** *like sing.*\ [F, lit., good mouth] **1 :** something supremely delicious or appetizing **:** a choice morsel **:** DELICACY ⟨there was no profusion of unmeaning dishes; each was a *bonne bouche* — Charles Reade⟩ **2 :** a final, unexpected, or supreme delight **:** TREAT ⟨reprints as a *bonne bouche* . . . a delightful and characteristic essay —*Saturday Rev.*⟩

bonne femme \(')bȯn¦fam, (')bən-, -fäm\ *adj* [F (*à la*) *bonne femme* in the manner of a good housewife] **:** prepared as in home cooking — often used postpositively ⟨filet of sole *bonne femme*⟩

bonne projection \'bȯn-, 'bən-\ *n, usu cap B* [after Rigobert *Bonne* †1795 Fr. cartographer] **:** a modified conical equal-area map projection having one standard parallel and all meridians curved except the central meridian which is a straight line

1bon·net \'bänət, *usu* -d· + V\ *n* -s [ME *bonet,* fr. MF *bonet, bonnet,* fr. ML *abonnis*] **1 a** (1) *chiefly Scot* **:** a man's or boy's cap (2) **:** a brimless Scotch cap of seamless woolen fabric having usu. an ample soft crown and a snug headband — compare BALMORAL, TAM-O'-SHANTER **b** (1) **:** a woman's head covering of cloth or straw usu. tied under the chin with ribbons or strings and made with or without a brim, formerly fashionable but now worn chiefly by children or as part of a uniform or habit — see POKE BONNET, SUNBONNET (2) **:** a woman's hat **c :** any bizarre, out-of-the-ordinary, or out-of-fashion headgear ⟨the 19th century ~ of a German infantryman⟩ ⟨the steeple-shaped ~ worn by women in medieval times⟩ **d :** WARBONNET **2 :** something shaped like or suggestive of the shape of a bonnet and used to cover, protect, or enclose: as **a :** an additional piece of canvas laced to the foot of a jib or foresail **b** (1) **:** the second stomach of a ruminant — compare RETICULUM (2) **:** a horny excrescence on the head of the southern right whale **c** *chiefly Midland* (1) **:** SPATTERDOCK — usu. used in pl. (2) **:** the infolded cornucopia-shaped leaf of the southern spatterdock **d** (1) **:** the cover or roof of a mine cage (2) **:** a projecting hood over the platform of a railroad car (3) *Brit* **:** HOOD 3h(2) (4) **:** the parasol-shaped appliance that protects the valve of an airship or balloon against rain **e** (1) **:** a spark arrester for a locomotive funnel (2) **:** the metal shield or cover for the gauze of a miner's safety lamp (3) **:** a cover for an open fireplace or a cowl or hood to increase the draft of a chimney (4) **:** the usu. slightly tapered upper part of the casing of a hot-air furnace from which the hot-air ducts project — called also *hood* **f** (1) **:** a metal covering for valve chambers, hydrants, or ventilators (2) **:** a cap placed over wooden piles to prevent their brooming esp. when being driven **3** *Brit* **:** SHILL

bonnet 1b

2bonnet \"\ *vb* -ED/-ING/-S *vi* **:** to remove the bonnet in token of respect ~ *vt* **1 :** to provide with or dress in a bonnet ⟨a mother ~*ing* her children⟩ ⟨~*ed* highlanders⟩ **:** to furnish with or as if with a bonnet ⟨all residences . . . are white, ~*ed* with red tile —Aubrey Drury⟩ **2 :** to crush (a person's) hat down around the head ⟨getting drunk and ~*ing* a policeman on Boat Race night —*Atlantic*⟩

bonnet gourd *n* **:** DISHCLOTH GOURD

bonnet grass *n* **1 :** a redtop (*Agrostis alba*) **2 :** POVERTY GRASS 1b

bonnet·head \'==,=\ *or* **bonnethead shark** *n* **:** a shark (*Sphyrna tiburo*) of warm seas related to the hammerhead shark but smaller and having the lobes of the head less developed — called also *bonnet shark, shovelhead*

bonnet laird *n* **:** a petty Scottish landowner wearing a bonnet like the humbler folk

bon·net·less \-ləs\ *adj* **:** having no bonnet

bonnet limpet *or* **bonnet shell** *n* [so called fr. the shape of its shell] **:** a snail of *Calyptraea* or a related genus

bonnet monkey *or* **bonnet macaque** *n* [so called fr. the bonnetlike tuft of hair on its head] **:** a monkey (*Macaca radiata*) of the southern part of the Indian subcontinent related to but larger and darker than the toque macaque — called also *capped macaque, crown monkey*

bonnet pepper *n* **:** PIMIENTO; *sometimes* **:** SWEET PEPPER

bonnet piece *n* **:** a Scottish gold coin issued 1539–40 by James V that represented him wearing a bonnet

bon·net rouge \bȯnāruzh\ *n, pl* **bonnet rouges** *or* **bonnets rouges** *like sing.*\ [F, lit., red cap] **:** the red cap adopted by extremists in the French Revolution — compare LIBERTY CAP

bonnets *pl of* BONNET, *pres 3d sing of* BONNET

bonnet shark *n* **:** BONNETHEAD

bonnet skate *n* **1 :** LITTLE SKATE **2 :** a large stingray (*Aetobatus narinari*) common and widespread in tropic seas and an important food fish

bonnet top *n* **:** a broken-arch top in cabinet furniture and doorheads common between 1730 and 1780 with the break extending the entire depth of the top and the center often ornamented with a bust or urn and the corners with urns

highboy with bonnet top

bon·ni·ly \'bän³lē, -nəlē\ *adv* [*bonny* + *-ly*] **:** in a bonny manner

bon·ni·ness \-ēnēs, -ēnin-\ *n* -ES **:** the quality or state of being bonny

bon·ny *also* **bon·nie** \'bänē, -ni\ *adj* -ER/-EST [ME *bonie,* fr. OF *bon* good (fr. L *bonus*) + ME *-ie* -y — more at BOUNTY] **1** *chiefly Brit* **:** having a pleasing appearance: **a** *of a person* **:** attractive esp. as suggesting health, charm, sweetness, and liveliness ⟨as fair art thou, my ~ lass, so deep in love am I —Robert Burns⟩ **b** *of a place* **:** pleasant esp. through the appeal of the mild, placid, and rural **2 a** *chiefly Brit* **:** of considerable degree, size, or quantity ⟨a ~ fighter, who . . . never fought better than when he championed a losing side —Thomas Wood †1950⟩ **b** *Brit* (1) **:** in good health ⟨at the end of three weeks he was . . . ~ . . . and the mother too was . . . recovering —Ruth Mitchell⟩ (2) **:** PLUMP **3** *archaic* **:** HAPPY, GAY **4** *Brit* **:** very pleasant **:** FINE, EXCELLENT — a generalized term of approbation sometimes used ironically ⟨well, my ~ lad, they found you out⟩ **syn** see BEAUTIFUL

bon·ny·clab·ber \ˈbänē,klabə(r)\ *also* **bon·ny·clap·per** \-apə(r)\ *n* [IrGael *bainne clabair*, fr. *bainne* milk (fr. MIr, drop, milk) + *clabair*, gen. of *clabar* sour thick milk; MIr *bainne* akin to Skt *bindu* drop] *North & Midland* **:** ¹CLABBER

bo·no·rum pos·ses·sio \bəˈnōrəmpəˈzesē(,)ō, bō'-, -ˈses-\ *n* [L, possession of goods] *Roman law* **:** the right of possession of the property of a deceased person; *specif* **:** the effective right to succeed, which changed the order of succession of the older jus civile, given by the praetor to emancipated children along with descendants in power, to cognatic after agnatic relatives, and last to the surviving spouse

bon·pa \bōnˈpä, -ˈpō\ *n* -S *usu cap* [Tibetan] **:** an adherent of the Bon religion

bons *pl of* BON

bon·sai \(ˈ)bōnˈsī, (ˈ)bän-\ *n, pl* **bonsai** [Jap] **:** a potted plant (as a tree) dwarfed by special methods of culture (as by limiting the space for and pruning of roots and by training of shoots by pruning and esp. by coiling wire around the branches); *also* **:** the art of growing such a plant — compare MINIASCAPE

bon–seki \(ˈ)bänˈsakē, ˈbōn-\ *n* -S [Jap, fr. *bon* tray + *seki* stone] **:** a landscape constructed of sand and stones on a tray; *also* **:** the art of constructing such a landscape

bon·spiel \ˈbän,spēl\ *n* -S [perh. fr. D *bond* league (fr. MD *bont*) + *spel* game, fr. MD — more at BUND, SPIEL] **:** a match or tournament between curling clubs

bon·te·bok \ˈbäntə,bäk\ *also* **bon·te·buck** \-,bək\ *n, pl* **bontebok** *or* **bonteboks** [Afrik *bontebok, bontbok*, fr. *bont* spotted (fr. MD, prob. fr. ML *punctus* dotted) + *bok* male antelope, male goat, fr. MD *boc;* akin to OHG *boc* male goat — more at POINT, BUCK] **:** a southern African antelope (*Damaliscus dorcas dorcas* syn. *D. pygargus*) that is now extinct except in semidomestication and is of a purplish red color with a white face and rump

bon·te quagga \ˈbäntə-, -tē-\ *n* [obs. Afrik (now *bontkwagga*), fr. *bont* spotted + *quagga* — more at QUAGGA] **:** BURCHELL'S ZEBRA

bon·tok *also* **bon·toc** \bänˈtäk\ *n, pl* **bontok** *or* **bontoks** *also* **bontoc** *or* **bontocs** *usu cap* [native name in northern Luzon] **1 a :** a predominantly pagan people inhabiting northern Luzon, Philippines — compare IGOROT **b :** a member of such people **2 :** the Austronesian language of the Bontok people

bon ton \bōⁿˈtōⁿ, (ˈ)bänˈtän\ *n, pl* **bon tons** [F, lit., good tone] **1 :** STYLISHNESS, FASHIONABLENESS ⟨the worldliness and *bon ton* of the characters . . . held me spellbound —S.J.Perelman⟩ **2 :** the fashionable or proper thing ⟨the *bon ton* here is to be grave and learned —Horace Walpole⟩ **3 :** a fashionable social set

bont tick \ˈbänt-\ *n* [Afrik *bont* spotted + E *tick* — more at BONTEBOK] **:** a southern African tick (*Amblyomma hebraeum*) attacking livestock, birds, and sometimes man and transmitting heartwater disease of sheep, goats, and cattle; *broadly* **:** any African tick of the genus *Amblyomma*

¹**bo·nus** \ˈbōnəs\ *n* -ES [L, good — more at BOUNTY] **1 :** something given or received that is over and above what is expected ⟨as a ~ she got the day off from school⟩ ⟨a ~ of five days of beautiful weather⟩; *specif* **:** a gift given (as to a person) for complying with the donor's wishes **2 a** *Brit* **:** DIVIDEND 1c **b** (1) **:** money or an equivalent given in addition to the usual compensation ⟨surplus profits distributed among the workers as a ~⟩ (2) **:** the payment made by the employer under a bonus system **c :** a premium (as of stock) given by a corporation to a purchaser of its securities, to a promoter, or to an employee in recognition of his services **d** (1) **:** a government subsidy to an industry ⟨the mills closed down because the city did not provide a $100,000 ~ to keep them operating —*Amer. Guide Series : Mich.*⟩ (2) **:** a government payment to all ex-servicemen of a war often viewed as compensation for decreased earnings during time spent in the service **e :** a sum in excess of salary given a baseball player for signing with a team ⟨a ~ pitcher⟩ **3 :** a sum of money in addition to interest or royalties charged for the granting of a loan, for the granting of a charter or other privilege to a company, or for the lease or transfer of property (as oil lands) **4 a :** a score in a card game that does not count toward winning: as (1) **:** the score in bridge for honors, for making a doubled or redoubled contract, for a slam, or for winning the rubber — called also *premium* (2) **:** the score in gin rummy for each hand won or game won **b :** an extra amount received in poker for holding an unusually good hand (as a straight flush) — called also *premium, royalty*

²**bonus** \"\ *vt* -ED/-ING/-ES **:** to give a bonus to ⟨~*ing* each family having more than three children⟩ **:** SUBSIDIZE ⟨the enterprise . . . was heavily ~*ed* with land and a certain amount of cash —B.K.Sandwell⟩

bonus system *also* **bonus plan** *n* **:** wage payment whereby a worker is paid an additional amount for accomplishing more than a specified measure of work

bon vi·vant \;bänvēˈvänt, bōⁿvēväⁿ\ *n, pl* **bons vivants** *or* **bon vivants** \-vän(t)s, bōⁿvēväⁿ\ [F, lit., good liver] **:** a person having cultivated or refined tastes esp. in food and drink **:** HIGH LIVER, GOURMET ⟨a prodigious worker, a hard and frequent *bon vivant* —Arthur Krock⟩ **syn** see EPICURE

bon vi·veur \;bänvēˈvər, bōⁿvēvœr\ *n, pl* **bons viveurs** *or* **bon viveurs** \-vər, bōⁿvēvœr\ [F, lit., good liver] **:** a person who lives high and well **:** MAN-ABOUT-TOWN

bon vo·yage \,bänvwīˈäzh, ,bōn-, bōⁿvwäyäzh\ *n* [F] **:** a good trip ⟨delegates came to wish the explorers *bon voyage*⟩ **:** FAREWELL ⟨*bon voyage* baskets of fruit and flowers —I.V.Morris⟩ — often used as a parting phrase ⟨"*bon voyage* and a happy return," she said formally —Joseph Conrad⟩

bonx·ie \ˈbäŋksē\ *n* -S [perh. of Scand origin; akin to Norw *bunke* heap, corpulent woman, dumpy body, ON *bunki* heap, pile — more at BUNCH] *Scot* **:** GREAT SKUA

¹**bony** *or* **bon·ey** \ˈbōnē, -ni\ *adj* **bonier; boniest** [¹*bone* + *-y*] **1 a :** consisting of bone ⟨a ~ substance⟩ **:** made up of bones ⟨the ~ framework of the body⟩ **b :** resembling bone ⟨a ~ tumor⟩ **2 a :** full of bone or bones ⟨a ~ roast⟩ ⟨bass aren't so ~ as pickerel⟩ **b :** having prominent bones ⟨a ~ face⟩ ⟨a ~ horse⟩ **3 a :** SKINNY, SCRAWNY ⟨poor underfed ~ children⟩ **b :** BARREN, LEAN, SPARE ⟨brown and ~ mountains —Norman Cousins⟩ ⟨~, close-mouthed prose —John Woodburn⟩

²**bony** \"\ *or* **bony coal** *n* -ES **:** BONE 8b

bony bream *n* **:** any of several bony Australian freshwater fishes (genus *Nematalosa*) of the herring family (Clupeidae)

bony-fish \ˈ==,=\ *n* **1 :** MENHADEN **2 :** TENPOUNDER **3 :** BONEFISH

bony fish *n* **:** any of the higher fishes having usu. a well ossified skeleton **:** one of the Teleostomi — compare CARTILAGINOUS FISH

bony labyrinth *n* **:** the cavity in the petrous portion of the temporal bone that contains the membranous labyrinth of the inner ear

bonytail \ˈ==,=\ *or* **bonytail chub** *n* **:** a minnow (*Gila robusta*) of the Colorado river system that is now rarely seen

bonze \ˈbän(d)z\ *n* -S [F, fr. Pg *bonzo*, fr. Jap *bonsō*, fr. *bon-* (prob. fr. Chin — Pek — *fan*⁴ Buddhist, Sanskrit) + *sō* monk, priest, prob. trans. of Chin (Pek) *fan*⁴ *sêng*¹] **:** a Buddhist monk of the Far East

bon·zer \ˈbän(d)zə(r)\ *also* **bonza** \-zə\ *adj* [perh. alter. of *bonanza*] *slang Austral* **:** FIRST-RATE, EXCELLENT

¹**boo** \ˈbü\ *also* **bo** *or* **boh** \", ˈbō\ *interj* [ME *bo*] — used to express contempt or disapproval or to startle or frighten

²**boo** \ˈbü\ *n* -S **1 :** a shout of disapproval **:** a cry of contempt ⟨the unpopular speaker was greeted by ~*s* and hisses⟩ **2 :** any sound at all esp. when uttered in protest or when silence is expected ⟨the baby was good as gold and didn't say ~ all through church⟩

³**boo** \"\ *vb* -ED/-ING/-S *vi* **:** to deride and jeer esp. by uttering or shouting *boo* ⟨the crowd ~*ed* for five minutes⟩ ~ *vt* **:** to boo at **:** express disapproval of or dissatisfaction with (as a person, a performance, an idea) by booing ⟨the play was ~*ed* unmercifully by the gallery —Celia Johnson⟩

¹**boob** \ˈbüb\ *n* -S [short for ¹*booby*] **1 :** a stupid awkward person **:** SIMPLETON, DOPE ⟨the big ~ doesn't know enough to come in out of the rain⟩ **2 :** an ignorant insensitive person who is extremely gullible **:** PHILISTINE ⟨compared to the civilized and educated European, the American seemed a ~ —J.T.Farrell⟩

²**boob** \"\ *vb* -ED/-ING/-S *vi*. *Brit* **:** to make a mistake **:** GOOF ~ *vt*. *Brit* **:** to make a fool of **:** DUPE

³**boob** \"\ *n* -S [short for *booby* jail, short for *booby hutch*, prob. alter. of *booby hatch*] *chiefly Austral* **:** JAIL

boob·i·ly \ˈbübəlē, -li\ *adv* **:** in the manner of a booby

boo·boi·sie \,bübwäˈzē, -bwə'-\ *n* -S [¹*boob* + *-oisie* (as in *bourgeoisie*)] **:** the class composed of all who are considered boobs ⟨Mencken began his linguistic crusade as part of his attack on middle-class stupidity and the ~ —W.C.Greet⟩

boo–boo \ˈbü,bü\ *n* -S [prob. baby-talk alter. of *boohoo*] **1** *dial* **:** a usu. minor physical injury (as a bruise or scratch) esp. on a child ⟨he fell down and he's got a *boo-boo* on his forehead⟩ **2** *slang* **:** a foolish or embarrassing error **:** a stupid or careless mistake **:** BLUNDER, BONER ⟨committed a *boo-boo* at his press conference⟩

boobook owl \ˈbü(,)bůk-, -(,)bük-\ *also* **boobook** *n* -S [imit.] **:** a small owl (*Ninox novae-seelandiae*) of Australia, New Zealand, New Guinea, and some associated Pacific islands

¹**boo·by** \ˈbübē, -bi\ *n* -ES [modif. of Sp *bobo*, fr. L *balbus* stammering; akin to L *babulus* babbler — more at BABBLE] **1 :** an awkward foolish person **:** DOPE **2 :** any of several gannets (genus *Sula*) of tropical seas resembling the common gannet but smaller — see BLUE-FOOTED BOOBY, RED-FOOTED BOOBY **3 :** any of several American ducks; *esp* **:** RUDDY DUCK **4 :** the poorest of a group of performers or contestants **:** the player with the lowest score (as in a card game)

²**booby** \ˈbübē, -bi\ *n* -ES [alter. of *bubby*] **:** BREAST — sometimes considered vulgar

boo·by·al·la *or* **boo·bi·al·la** \,bübēˈalə\ *n* -S [native name in Australia] **1 :** an Australian wattle (*Acacia longifolia*) — called also *native willow* **2 :** any of several Australian trees of the genus *Myoporum* having alternate leaves and flowers in clusters (esp. *M. acuminatum*)

booby hatch \ˈbübē-\ *n* [perh. fr. *booby* (bird) + *hatch;* fr. its being a favorite resting place of these birds aboard ship] **1 :** a raised framework with a sliding cover over a small hatch; *specif* **:** a hatch in the stern leading to quarters below the deck **2** [influenced in meaning by *booby* (dunce)] **a :** an insane asylum ⟨the pressure drove him into the *booby hatch*⟩ **b :** a place felt to resemble an insane asylum (as in frantic or purposeless activity or in zany characters)

booby hutch *n* [¹*booby*] **:** a covered horse-drawn vehicle used esp. in the 18th century

booby prize *n* [¹*booby*] **1 :** an award for the poorest score or performance in a game or competition **2 :** an acknowledgement or recognition of notable inferiority ⟨he takes the *booby prize* for bad manners⟩

booby trap *n* [¹*booby*] **1 :** a trap for the unwary or unsuspecting: **a :** a trap laid to play a trick on an unwary person ⟨*booby traps* with buckets of water suspended over doors —Robert Graves⟩ **b :** a concealed explosive device usu. attached to some harmless-looking object ⟨the *booby trap* exploded when he touched the doorknob⟩ **c :** an object wired to set off an explosion when touched ⟨the car, which they suspected might be a *booby trap* —*Combined Operations*⟩ **2 :** a critical or potentially dangerous aspect (as of a problem or situation) **:** PITFALL ⟨words and expressions which are *booby traps* when used in the other language —Richard Joseph⟩

booby–trap *vt* **:** to provide with a booby trap ⟨drivers should be trained thoroughly in careful driving through mined and *booby-trapped* roads —*Infantry Jour.*⟩ ⟨Congress . . . *booby-trapped* the bill with unworkable provisions —*Time*⟩

boo·die \ˈbüdē\ *n* -S [modif. of ScGael *bodach* old man, churl, miser, ghost, fr. *bod* penis; akin to OIr *bot* penis, Corn & W *both* nave of a wheel, boss of a shield, OSlav *gvozdĭ* nail] *Scot* **:** HOBGOBLIN

¹**boo·dle** \ˈbüdᵊl\ *n* -S [D *boedel* estate, property, stock, lot (now usu. *boel* in sense "lot"), fr. MD; akin to OS *bōdlos* entire estate, OFris *bōdel* inheritance, ON *būth* booth — more at BOOTH] **1 :** a collection or lot of persons ⟨a big ~ of kids⟩ **:** PACK, CABOODLE **2 a** *slang* **:** counterfeit money **b :** money paid or taken for votes or political favors **:** bribe money ⟨the lobbyist can pocket the money earmarked for bribing and tell his client he passed on the ~ —Jack Lait & Lee Mortimer⟩ **c :** a large amount esp. of money ⟨he's got a ~ hidden away somewhere⟩ **d :** plunder or swag of any sort ⟨the ~ picked up by beachcombers after the storm⟩ **3 :** the game of Michigan

²**boodle** \"\ *vb* **boodled; boodled; boodling** \ˈbüd(ᵊ)liŋ\ **boodles** *vi* **:** to obtain money through bribery or swindling ~ *vt* **:** SWINDLE, DEFRAUD

boodle card *n* [¹*boodle*] **:** a playing card displayed as part of a layout in various card games (as Michigan) on which an extra stake is placed to be won by the player who holds or plays that card

boo·dler \ˈbüd(ᵊ)lə(r)\ *n* -S **:** a political grafter

boo·dling \ˈbüd(ᵊ)liŋ\ *n* -S **:** graft and fraud esp. in politics

booed *past of* BOO

boof \ˈbůf, ˈbüf\ *n* -S [imit.] **:** the sound made by a dog **:** BARK

¹**booger** *var of* BUGGER

²**boog·er** \ˈbůgə(r)\ *or* **bug·ger** \" *also in sense 1* ˈbəg-\ *n* -S [alter. (prob. influenced by *booger* bugger) of *boggart*] **1 :** BOOGEYMAN **2** *dial* **:** a piece of dried nasal mucus

³**booger** \"\ *vb* **boogered; boogered; boogering;** \ˈbůg(ə)riŋ\ **boogers** *vi, of an animal* **:** to take fright **:** SHY ⟨this horse ~*s* a little at gunfire⟩ ~ *vt, West* **:** to frighten or startle (an animal) into shying or running wild ⟨the cattle were already through the pasture gate when something ~*ed* them —Ross Santee⟩

⁴**booger** \"\ *n* -S [prob. alter. (influenced by *booger* boogeyman) of *bug*] *chiefly Midland* **:** HEAD LOUSE

booger dance *n* [²*booger*] **:** a grotesque masked dance included in a satirical mimetic episode of Cherokee Indian winter festivals

boo·gey·man \ˈbůgē,man, ˈbüg-, ˈbōg-, -gə̇-, -ma(a)(ə)n *also* ,mən\ *or* **boo·ger·man** \-gə(r),-\ *also* **boo·gie·man** \-gē,-, -gə̇,-\ *n, pl* **boogeymen** *or* **boogermen** *also* **boogiemen** [*boogey, boogie* (alter. of ²*booger*) or ¹*booger* + *man*] *dial* **:** a monstrous imaginary figure used in threatening children ⟨be good or the ~ will get you⟩

boog·ie *also* **boogy** \ˈbůgē, ˈbügē, -gi\ *n, pl* **boogies** [prob. alter. of *booger* (boogeyman)] *slang* **:** NEGRO — usu. used disparagingly

¹**boog·ie–woog·ie** \ˌbůgēˈwůgē, ˌbügēˈwü-\ *also* **boogie** *n* -S [origin unknown] **1 a :** a percussive style of playing blues on the piano characterized by a persistent rhythmic ground bass and florid figurations of a simple melody **b :** a piece so played **2 :** a jitterbug dance danced to boogie-woogie music in a sway-backed posture with motions throughout the body, the basic step being a double side step with toe-heel accent

²**boogie–woogie** \"\ *vi* -ED/-ING/-S **:** to dance the boogie-woogie

boo·gum \ˈbügəm\ *or* **boo·jum** \-üjəm\ *n* -S [perh. fr. *boojum*, an imaginary creature in *The Hunting of the Snark* by Lewis Carroll (C.L.Dodgson) †1898 Eng. mathematician & writer; fr. its grotesque appearance] **:** a spiny tree (*Idria columnaris*) of the family Fouquieriaceae chiefly of Lower California sometimes arching over and rooting at its tips

boo·hoo \büˈhü, ˈ=,=\ *vi* -ED/-ING/-S [imit.] **:** to weep loudly and with sobs ⟨he ~*ed* when he skinned his knee⟩

bo·oi·dea \bōˈöidēə\ [NL, alter. of *Bovoidea*] *syn of* BOVOIDEA

booing *pres part of* BOO

¹**book** \ˈbůk\ *n* -S [ME, fr. OE *bōc;* akin to OHG *buoh* book, ON *bōk*, Goth *bōka* letter, OE *bōc* beech; prob. fr. the early Germanic use of beech wood as a medium for the carving of runic characters — more at BEECH] **1 a** *obs* **:** a formal written document; *esp* **:** a deed of conveyance of land — see BOOKLAND **b** (1) **:** a collection of written sheets of skin or tablets of wood or ivory (2) **:** a continuous roll of parchment or a strip of parchment creased between columns and folded like an accordion **c :** a collection of written, printed, or blank sheets fastened together along one edge and usu. trimmed at the other edges to form a single series of uniform leaves; *specif* **:** a collection of folded sheets bearing printing or writing that have been cut, sewn, and usu. bound between covers into a volume **d** (1) **:** a stack of sheets of paper interleaved alternately with

BOOK SIZES

The names of book sizes are based on the old system still widely used of considering the size of a page as a fraction of the large sheet of paper on which it was printed. This system is illustrated in Table I below. In printing books an even number (as 4, 8, 16, 24, 32, 48, 64) of pages is printed on each side of a single large sheet which is then folded so that the pages are in proper sequence and the outside edges are cut so that the book will open. Except for the largest size, the folio, the name of the size indicates the fractional part of the sheet one page occupies (as octavo "eighth"). In this system, since the fractional name alone cannot denote an exact size, the name of the sheet size precedes the fractional name. Thus, *royal octavo* is understood to designate a page one-eighth the size of a royal sheet, *medium octavo* a page one-eighth the size of a medium sheet, and *crown octavo* one-eighth the size of a crown sheet. But paper is cut into many sheet sizes and even the terms *crown, medium,* and *royal* do not always designate sheets of the same dimensions. Three of the more common sheet sizes have been selected: royal 20 x 25 inches, medium 18 x 23 inches, and crown 15 x 19 inches. Actual page sizes run a little smaller than calculations since the sheets, when folded to page size, are trimmed at top, outside, and bottom, the inside edge becoming part of the binding. British sheet size sometimes differs slightly from American.

Table II illustrates the size names as they are used by the American Library Association, with only the octavo sizes including the name of a sheet size. The dimensional limits given in the table remain standard for this system.

Table III gives equivalent terms and symbols for the size names.

TABLE I

SIZE NAME	TIMES SHEET FOLDED	LEAVES TO SHEET	PAGES TO SHEET	SIZE OF PAGE IN INCHES
royal folio	1	2	4	20 x 12½
royal quarto	2	4	8	12½ x 10
royal octavo	3	8	16	10 x 6¼
royal sixteenmo	4	16	32	6¼ x 5
royal thirty-twomo	5	32	64	5 x 3⅛
royal sixty-fourmo	6	64	128	3⅛ x 2½
medium folio	1	2	4	18 x 11½
medium quarto	2	4	8	11½ x 9
medium octavo	3	8	16	9 x 5¾
medium sixteenmo	4	16	32	5¾ x 4½
medium thirty-twomo	5	32	64	4½ x 2⅞
medium sixty-fourmo	6	64	128	2⅞ x 2¼
crown folio	1	2	4	15 x 10
crown quarto	2	4	8	10 x 7½
crown octavo	3	8	16	7½ x 5
crown sixteenmo	4	16	32	5 x 3¾
crown thirty-twomo	5	32	64	3¾ x 2½
crown sixty-fourmo	6	64	128	2½ x 1⅞

TABLE II

SCALE OF THE AMERICAN LIBRARY ASSOCIATION

SIZE NAME	SYMBOL	OUTSIDE HEIGHT[1]	APPROX. SIZE[2] IN INCHES
folio	F	over 30 cm	12 x 19
quarto	Q	25–30 cm	9½ x 12
octavo	O	20–25 cm	6 x 9
imperial octavo	O		8¼ x 11½
super octavo	O		7 x 11
royal octavo	O		6½ x 10
medium octavo	O		6⅛ x 9¼
crown octavo	O		5⅜ x 8
duodecimo	D	17.5–20 cm	5 x 7⅜
duodecimo (large)	D	17.5–20 cm	5½ x 7½
sextodecimo	S	15–17.5 cm	4 x 6¾
octodecimo	T	12.5–15 cm	4 x 6½
trigesimo-secundo	Tt	10–12.5 cm	3½ x 5½
quadragesimo-octavo	Fe	7.5–10 cm	2½ x 4
sexagesimo-quarto	Sf	less than 7.5 cm	2 x 3

[1]Outside height refers to the head-to-foot dimension of the book's cover.
[2]Approximate size refers to the front cover's rectangular dimensions.

TABLE III

SIZE NAMES AND THEIR EQUIVALENTS

OLD	MODERN—PREFERRED BY PRINTERS	ABBR	SYMBOL[1]
folio	folio	fo *or* f	
quarto	quarto	4to	4°
sexto	sixmo	6to *or* 6mo	6°
octavo	octavo	8vo	8°
duodecimo[2]	twelvemo	12mo	12°
sextodecimo	sixteenmo	16mo	16°
octodecimo	eighteenmo	18mo	18°
vincesimo-quarto / vigesimo-quarto	twenty-fourmo	24mo	24°
trigesimo-secundo	thirty-twomo	32mo	32°
quadragesimo-octavo	forty-eightmo	48mo	48°
sexagesimo-quarto	sixty-fourmo	64mo	64°

[1]Note also in Table II the symbols used by the American Library Association.
[2]For the terms duodecimo, sextodecimo, etc., printers often use "twelve" or "twelves," "sixteen" or "sixteens," etc. (as in "an ordinary *sixteen*"; "a sheet of *sixteens*")

the material whose finish the paper acquires after it passes through the plater — called also *form* (2) **:** the printed but unfolded and uncut sheets for a book **e :** a long systematic literary composition **f :** a major division of a treatise or literary work ⟨an epic in 12 ~*s*⟩ **g :** any of the records (as the daybook, cashbook, salesbook, journal, ledger) in which a systematic record of business transactions may be kept — often used in pl. ⟨their ~*s* show a profit⟩ **h** *in U.S. copyright law* **:** any of various written or printed materials: as (1) **:** a bound volume (2) **:** a private letter (3) **:** a telephone or trade directory (4) **:** an article in an encyclopedia **i :** a magazine or publication in magazine format **2** *cap* **:** BIBLE ⟨he swore on the *Book* that it was so⟩ **3 a** *obs* **:** LEARNING, STUDY, SCHOLARSHIP **b books** *pl, chiefly Midland* **:** school or the time spent in school ⟨~*s* took up at 8 o'clock —H.E.Giles⟩ **4 a :** something felt to be a source of enlightenment or instruction ⟨drew his knowledge from the great ~ of nature⟩ ⟨her face was an open ~⟩ **b** (1) **:** a particular set of facts, circumstances, or ideas ⟨this past is an open ~⟩ (2) **:** an area of experience or knowledge ⟨calculus was a closed ~ to him⟩ **c :** the total available knowledge and experience that can be brought to bear on a task or problem ⟨tried every trick in the ~ to win the election⟩ **5 :** an official or personal set of standards, rules, or policies ⟨mules did not, according to the ~, scratch their heads with their hind feet —Herbert Hoover⟩ ⟨the sergeant ran his squad by the ~⟩ **6 a :** the aggregate charges that can be made or pressed against an accused person — usu. used with *throw* ⟨he thought he'd get off with just a reprimand, but they threw the ~ at him⟩ **b :** a position from which one must answer for certain acts **:** ACCOUNT — usu. used with *bring* or *call* ⟨our system of bringing the guilty to ~ —Felix Frankfurter⟩ **7 a :** a libretto esp. of an opera or musical comedy **b :** the script of a play **c :** the repertory of an orchestra or a musician **8 :** a packet of commodities bound together for convenient dispensing and usu. removed and used one at a time ⟨a ~ of stamps⟩ ⟨a ~ of matches⟩; *specif* **:** a bundle of skeins of raw silk often 30 in number **9 a** (1) **:** BOOKMAKER (2) **:** a bookmaker's business or base of operations **b :** an event or contingency on which a bookmaker will accept bets together with the odds offered **c :** the record kept by a bookmaker of bets placed with him ⟨he makes ~ on dog races⟩ **d :** a participant or onlooker in a game (as craps) who accepts bets on its contingencies **e :** BANKER 2c **f :** ³POOL 1b **10 a :** the number of tricks a cardplayer or side must win before any trick can have scoring value: (1) *whist* **:** six tricks (2) *bridge* **:** six tricks for declarer and for his opponents the greatest number declarer can lose without being defeated **b :** a set of cards having scoring value (as all four cards of one kind in authors) **c** *archaic* **:** a deck of cards **11 :** the omasum of a ruminant **12 :** a thick aggregate of mica usu. consisting of a single crystal of considerable dimension in the direction perpendicular to the cleavage **13 :** a stack of half leaves of tobacco from which the stems have been cut **14 :** flat sections of stage scenery joined by hinges ⟨a ~ ceiling⟩ **15 :** a record of membership esp. in a union — **in one's bad books :** in disfavor with one — **in one's book :** in one's own opinion ⟨a trainer of the old school — and *in my book*, there's no better school —G.F.T.Ryall⟩ — **in one's good books :** in favor with one — **one for the book :** an act or occurrence worth recording **:** a notable performance **:** RECORD ⟨that play is *one for the book*⟩ — **on the books :** on the records **:** ENROLLED — **without book 1 :** without authority **2 :** from memory or by rote

²**book** \"\ *vb* -ED/-ING/-S [ME *boken*, fr. OE *bōcian*, fr. *bōc* book] *vt* **1** *obs* **:** to convey or grant (land or property) by charter **2 :** to enter, write, or register (as a name, an act, or an intention) in a record, book, or list: **a :** to engage transportation or conveyance for ⟨a load of eggs ~*ed* for Chicago⟩ ⟨he is ~*ed* to sail Monday⟩ **b :** to schedule a program of engagements for ⟨the orchestra was ~*ed* for a week at the hotel⟩ **c :** to set aside time for **:** SCHEDULE ⟨the president ~*ed* a strategy meeting⟩ **d :** to reserve in advance — chiefly Brit. in all but past participial use and often used with *up* ⟨he paid the dinner bill and stopped to ~ cinema seats⟩ ⟨sorry, but we're all ~*ed up*⟩ **3 :** to enter the name of and tentative charges against (a person) usu. in a police register ⟨they ~*ed* him on suspicion⟩ **4 :** to accept (bets) as a bookmaker ~ *vi* **1 :** to express in advance a desire for something in order to reserve it ⟨we should have ~*ed*⟩ **2 :** *chiefly Brit* **:** to register in a hotel — usu. used with *in* ⟨we went to a hotel and ~*ed in*⟩

³**book** \"\ *adj* **1 a :** put down in writing **:** FORMAL **b :** BOOKISH **2 a :** derived from or based on the matter in a book ⟨an ounce of mother-wit . . . is worth a stone of *book*-knowledge —F.T.Palgrave⟩; *specif* **:** theoretical as opposed to practical ⟨~ farming⟩ **b :** correct or advisable according to a book accepted as authoritative ⟨a ~ bid in bridge⟩ **3 :** shown by a system of accounting ⟨~ value⟩ ⟨the ~ strength of the enemy⟩

book·a·ble \-kəbəl\ *adj, chiefly Brit* **:** that may be booked or reserved in advance ⟨all seats ~ for matinee⟩

book account *n* **:** CURRENT ACCOUNT 1a

book agent *n* **:** a book salesman

bookbinder \'=,==\ *n* [ME, fr. *book* + *binder*] **:** one that binds or repairs books — called also *binder*

bookbindery \'=,=(=)=\ *n* -ES **:** a place where bookbinding is done

bookbinding \'=,==\ *n* -S **1 :** the binding of a book **2 :** the trade or art of a bookbinder

book boat *n* **:** a boat fitted with bookshelves and used as a mobile branch library

book burning *n* **:** destruction of writings or pictures regarded as politically or socially harmful or subversive or produced by persons whose ideas or acts are so regarded

book card *n* **:** a record card retained by the library when a book is lent

bookcase \'=,=\ *n* **1 :** a case for books; *esp* **:** one having several shelves often with doors **2 :** ²CASE 2e

book clamp *n* **:** a clamp to hold or press books (as for binding or marbling)

book cloth *n* **:** any of several specially woven fabrics (as cotton) prepared for use in covering books

book club *n* **1 a :** a group of people who buy books for circulation among the group **b :** a club of booklovers or of people with literary interests **2 :** a commercial organization that offers selected new books often of a particular kind to its members at regular intervals often at a discount

book code *n* **:** a code based on an ordinary book or dictionary, the plaintext words being identified by page and line

book corner *n* **:** a protective cap for the corner of a book

bookdealer \'=,==\ *n* **:** one who deals in books

book debt *n* **:** the amount owed on a current account

booked *adj* **1 :** entered, registered, or otherwise placed in a book **2 a :** engaged or contracted for **b** *Brit, of tickets* **:** SOLD, RESERVED

bookend \'=,=\ *n* **:** a supporting device placed at the end of a row of books

book·er \-kə(r)\ *n* -S **:** one that books: as **a :** one that schedules or secures reservations for a traveler or engagements for a performer **b :** BOOKMAKER **c :** one that removes the stems from tobacco leaves by machine and arranges the half leaves into books **d :** a worker in a rubber-goods factory who puts strips of rubber or rubberized material between layers of cloth to facilitate handling

bookends

book·ery \'bu̇k(ə)rē\ *n* -ES **1** *archaic* **:** LIBRARY **2 :** BOOKSTORE

book·e·te·ria *also* **book·a·te·ria** \,bu̇kə'tirēə\ *n* -S [*booketeria* fr. ¹*book* + *-eteria* (as in *cafeteria*); *bookateria*, alter. of *booketeria*] **1 :** a self-service bookstore **2 :** a self-service free lending library carrying books owned by a public library but housed elsewhere (as at a supermarket)

bookfair \'=,=\ *n* **1 :** a display or exhibit of books typically by a group of publishers or bookdealers for promoting sales and stimulating interest **2 :** a fair or bazaar at which books are sold or auctioned to raise money for some worthy cause

book fell *n* [ME, fr. OE *bōcfell*, fr. *bōc* book + *fell* skin — more at BOOK, FELL] **:** a sheet or manuscript of vellum or parchment

book-fold \'=,=\ *n* **:** a method of folding cloth so that it can be opened like the pages of a book

book gill *n* **:** a gill found in the king crabs that consists of membranous folds arranged like the leaves of a book

book hand *n* **:** the handwriting designed primarily for legibility and beauty and ordinarily used in officially transcribing manuscripts intended for preservation before printing became common — compare MINUSCULE, RUSTIC CAPITAL, UNCIAL

bookholder \'=,==\ *n* **:** a device that supports a book — compare BOOKRACK, BOOKREST

bookhunter \'=,==\ *n* **:** one that looks for books to be bought

book·ie \'bu̇kē, -ki\ *n* -S [by shortening & alter.] **:** BOOKMAKER 2

bookier *comparative of* BOOKY

bookiest *superlative of* BOOKY

booking *n* -S **1 :** the act of one that books **2 :** an engagement or scheduled performance ⟨she has ~*s* to sing several concerts next fall⟩ **3 :** RESERVATION; *esp* **:** one for transportation, entertainment, or lodging ⟨the porter will help with ticket and theatre ~*s*⟩ **4 :** ORDER 3b(2) — usu. used in pl.

booking clerk *n* **1 :** one who registers passengers, baggage, or freight for conveyance **2 :** a ticket seller

booking hall *n, Brit* **:** a room or hall in a railway station that contains the ticket office

booking office *n, chiefly Brit* **:** a ticket office; *esp* **:** one in a railroad station

book inventory *n* **:** an inventory (as of stock or goods) shown on the books of account—distinguished from *physical inventory;* compare PERPETUAL INVENTORY

book·ish \'bu̇kish, -kēsh\ *adj* **1 a :** of or relating to books ⟨a ~ pastime⟩ ⟨a ~ career⟩ ⟨a ~ life⟩ **b :** fond of books and reading ⟨a ~ farmer who carried favorite volumes in his saddle bags—Will Irwin⟩ **2 a :** inclined to rely on knowledge obtained from books as opposed to that gained from practical experience ⟨a ~ approach to life⟩ ⟨a ~ cast of mind⟩ **b** (1) **:** literary and formal as opposed to colloquial and informal ⟨a ~ way of speaking⟩ (2) **:** affectedly learned or pedantic ⟨a ~ writer overly bent on giving his sources and authority⟩ — **book·ish·ly** *adv*

bookit *var of* BOUKIT

book jacket *n* **:** JACKET 3f(1)

bookkeeper \'=,==\ *n* **:** one who keeps accounts **:** one whose business or vocation is bookkeeping — distinguished from *accountant*

bookkeeping \'=,==\ *n* **1 :** a branch of accounting that deals with the systematic classification, recording, and summarizing of business and financial transactions in books of account **2 :** the act or practice of keeping books of account

bookkeeping machine *n* **:** a key-operated business machine designed esp. for keeping and posting office records and for performing computational functions

book label *n* **:** a book owner's identification label that is usu. small and of distinctive design and is affixed inside the front cover of a book — compare BOOKPLATE

bookland \'bu̇,kland\ *n* [trans. of OE *bōcland*] **:** land granted by a book or charter in Anglo-Saxon England

book·lear \'bu̇,kler\ *n* [¹*book* + Sc *lear* learning — more at LEAR] *Scot* **:** BOOK LEARNING

book-learned *in sense 1* '=;lərnəd, -lə̄n-; *in sense 2* '=;lərnd, -lə̄nd\ *adj* **1 a :** marked by book learning **b :** BOOKISH **2 :** learned through books rather than from practical experience or application

book learning *n* **1 :** learning acquired from books as distinguished from practical knowledge **2 :** formal education **:** SCHOOLING

book·less \'bu̇kləs\ *adj, archaic* **:** UNLEARNED, UNSCHOLARLY

book·let \-lət\ *n* -S **1 :** a usu. paper-covered publication in book format ranging in size from a few pages to a small-scale edition of a book **2 :** STAMP BOOKLET

booklet pane *or* **booklet leaf** *n* **:** PANE 3b

booklift \'=,=\ *n* **:** a small usu. electric and automatic lift for moving books from tier to tier in a library

booklist *n* **:** a reading list of books having some unifying feature

book·lore \'=,=\ *n* [alter. (influenced by *lore*) of Sc *booklear*] **:** BOOK LEARNING

book louse *n* **:** any of several minute wingless insects of the order Corrodentia; *usu* **:** an insect of the family Atropidae (esp. *Liposcelis divinatorius*) that is injurious to books and papers — called also *deathwatch*

booklover \'=,==\ *n* **:** one fond of books — compare BIBLIOPHILE

book lung *n* **:** a saccular breathing organ occurring in many arachnids that contains numerous thin folds of membrane arranged like the leaves of a book through which gaseous exchange takes place

bookmaker \'=,==\ *n* **1 :** one that makes books: as **a :** a printer, binder, or designer of books **b :** one that compiles books from the writings of others **2 :** one that determines odds and receives and pays off bets

bookmaking \'=,==\ *n* [ME, fr. *book* + *making*] **1 :** the making of books — used to include design, illustration, typography, materials, and production **2 :** the business of a bookmaker

book·man \'bu̇kmən, -,man\ *n, pl* **bookmen 1 :** one having to do with books: as **a :** MAN OF LETTERS, SCHOLAR ⟨the ~ . . . appreciates, enjoys, he communicates pleasure —Van Wyck Brooks⟩ **b :** a bookdealer or book salesman **2 :** the clerk of a tobacco auction

bookmark \'=,=\ *or* **bookmarker** \'=,==\ *n* **:** a narrow strip of material (as an attached ribbon, an insertable card, or a leather slip) to mark a place in a book

book-match \'=,=\ *vt* [so called fr. the resemblance of two book-matched pieces of veneer to two opposing pages of a book] **:** to match the grains of (a pair of sheets of veneer or plywood) for symmetrical effect in such a way that one sheet seems to be the mirrored image of the other

book match *n* **:** one of the matches in a matchbook

book·mo·bile \'bu̇kmō,bēl\ *n* -S [¹*book* + *-mobile*] **:** an autotruck with shelves of books that serves as an itinerant library or bookstore

book mold *n* **:** a split foundry mold hinged at the side

book muslin *n* **1 :** muslin used to strengthen the backbone construction of books **2 :** a thin muslin formerly used for women's dresses

book number *n* **:** a combination of letters and figures used to distinguish an individual book from all others having the same library classification number

book of account 1 : LEDGER **2 :** a book or record essential to a system of accounts

book of hours *sometimes cap B&H* **:** a book containing prayers or offices appointed to be said at the canonical hours

book of original entry 1 : JOURNAL **2 :** any one of the books of account in which a transaction is first recorded

book palm *n* **:** an East Indian palm (*Corypha taliera*) whose leaves furnish a substitute for paper — called also *taliera*

book paper *n* **:** a paper suitable for printing books, magazines, and advertising matter including many grades of plain and coated papers but excluding newsprint

bookplate \'=,=\ *n* **1 :** a book owner's identification label that is usu. engraved or printed, has a distinctive design, and is pasted to the inside front cover of a book — called also *ex libris;* compare BOOK LABEL **2 :** the plate from which a bookplate is printed

book post *n, chiefly Brit* **:** a postal service providing special low rates for books

book profit *n* **:** profit as shown in or according to books of account

bookrack \'=,=\ *n* **:** a rack for holding books

book rate *n* **:** the reduced rate at which books may be sent through the mails

bookrest \'=,=\ *n* **:** a support that holds a book while it is being read

book review *n* **1 :** a descriptive and critical or evaluative account of a book **2 :** a newspaper supplement or magazine devoted chiefly to book reviews ⟨a typical book campaign in eight important *book reviews —Publishers' Weekly*⟩

book reviewer *n* **:** one who reviews books esp. for a magazine or newspaper

books *pl of* BOOK, *pres 3d sing of* BOOK

book scorpion *n* [so called because some species are often found in old papers] **:** any of various minute arachnids of the order Pseudoscorpiones that feed on small insects, mites, or other minute animals

bookseller \'=,==\ *n* **:** one whose business is dealing in books; *esp* **:** the proprietor of a bookstore

book sewer \'=,==\ *n* **:** one that sews sections together to form books

book-sewing \'=,==\ *adj* **:** of or relating to the sewing of books

bookshelf \'=,=\ *n, pl* **bookshelves 1 :** an open shelf for holding books **2 :** a small collection of books

book square *n* **:** SQUARE 13

bookstack \'=,=\ *n* **:** STACK 7

bookstall \'=,=\ *n* **1 :** a stall where books are sold **2** *chiefly Brit* **:** NEWSSTAND ⟨bought a copy of *Punch* at the ~ in the station⟩

book stamp *n* **1 :** a metal plate or die for stamping book covers **2 :** a postage stamp printed for or included in a stamp booklet

bookstore *also* **bookshop** \'=,=\ *n* **:** a place of business where books are the chief stock in trade

book support *n* **:** BOOKEND

booksy \'bu̇ksē\ *adj* **:** affectedly or pretentiously intellectual ⟨a ~ crowd⟩

book table *n* **:** a table with shelves beneath for books

book tile *n* **:** a flat clay building tile that has hollow sections, that is usu. 2 to 3 inches thick, 12 inches wide, and from 16 to 24 inches long, and that is shaped roughly like a closed book so that adjoining pieces fit into each other

book truck *n* **1 :** a small wheeled vehicle typically with two or three shelves used esp. in libraries for moving books **2 :** BOOKMOBILE

book value *n* **:** the value of something as shown in or according to the books of account of a business; *specif* **:** the value of capital stock as indicated by the excess of assets over liabilities — distinguished from *market value*

book van *n, Brit* **:** BOOKMOBILE

book wagon *n* **:** BOOKMOBILE

book word *n* **:** a word learned solely or principally from reading and often understood without knowledge of its customary pronunciation ⟨*eleemosynary* is a *book word*⟩ ⟨fine *book words* and long sentences —Charles Kingsley⟩

bookwork \'=,=\ *n* **1 :** the manufacture of books as distinct from newspaper or magazine printing or from job work **2 :** work that involves the use of books: as **a :** SCHOOLWORK **b :** PAPER WORK

bookworm \'=,=\ *n* **1 :** the larva of any of various moths or beetles (as the drugstore beetle) that injures books by feeding on the binding and paste and often piercing the leaves **2 :** one unusually devoted to reading or studying books

book wrapper *n* **:** JACKET

booky \'bu̇kē\ *adj, often* -ER/-EST **:** BOOKISH

¹**bool** \'bü(ə)l\ *dial var of* BOWL

²**bool** \"\ *n* -S [ME (Scottish dial.) *bowl*, prob. fr. MD *boghel* bow, hoop; akin to MLG *bogel* hoop, OE *būgan* to bend — more at BOW] **1** *dial Brit* **:** any of various objects with a curve or bend (as a semicircular handle, the bow of a key or scissors) **2** *dial Brit* **:** a wooden hoop forming part of the framework of a basket **3 :** a hoop for rolling

³**bool** \"\ *n* -S [ME *boule* ball — more at BOWL] *Scot* **:** a child's marble

bool·e·an *also* **bool·i·an** \'bülēən\ *adj, usu cap* [George *Boole* †1864 Eng. mathematician and logician + E *-an, -ian*] **:** of, relating to, or being a logical system (as Boolean algebra) that represents symbolically relationships (as those implied by *and, or,* and *not* used as logical operators) between entities (as sets, propositions, or on-off computer circuit elements) ⟨~ expression⟩ ⟨~ search strategy for information retrieval⟩

boolean algebra *n, usu cap B* **:** a set that is closed under two commutative binary operations and that can be described by any of various systems of postulates all of which can be deduced from the postulates that an identity element exists for each operation, that each operation is distributive over the other, and that for every element in the set there is another element which when combined with the first under one of the operations yields the identity element of the other operation ⟨under the operations of taking intersections and unions, the subsets of a given set form a *Boolean algebra*⟩

bool·ie \'bülē, -li\ *var of* ¹BOWLY

boo·ly \'bülē, -li\ *n* -ES [IrGael *buaile* cattle pen, fr. OIr *būale*, prob. fr. L *bovile, bubile* cattle stall, fr. *bov-, bos* head of cattle — more at COW] **1 :** a temporary enclosure once common in Ireland for the shelter of cattle or their keepers **2 :** a company of herdsmen wandering with their cattle

¹**boom** \'büm\ *vt* -ED/-ING/-S [D *bomen*, fr. *boom* tree, pole, beam] **1 :** to extend, move, or manipulate with a boom — usu. used with *off* or *out* ⟨~ out a sail⟩ **2 a :** to confine (logs) by means of a boom **b :** to supply (a body of water) with a boom or booms **3 :** to lift and position (a load attached to a derrick) by raising and swinging the boom

²**boom** \"\ *n* -S *often attrib* [D, tree, pole, beam, fr. MD; akin to OHG *boum* tree — more at BEAM] **1 :** a long spar projecting from a ship used variously to extend the foot of a sail or facilitate handling of cargo or mooring — see SHIP illustration **2 :** any of various devices resembling a ship's boom in appearance or function used usu. to maneuver a piece of equipment into a desired position: as **a :** a long beam projecting from the mast of a derrick to support or guide the body to be lifted or swung **b :** a long more or less horizontal supporting arm or brace (as for holding a microphone) **3 :** a 2-masted sailing ship used for coastal trade and pearling in the eastern Mediterranean and Indian ocean **4 a :** a line of connected floating timbers across a river or enclosing an area of water to keep saw logs together; *also* **:** the enclosed logs **b :** an obstruction formed of floating logs that retards the flow of a stream **c :** a similar construction arranged to guide floating logs in a certain direction **5 :** a long wooden bar of more or less elliptical cross section supported horizontally and adjustable as to height and used as a support in executing gymnastic stunts and exercises **6 :** a chain cable or line of spars extended across a river or the mouth of a harbor to defend it by obstructing navigation **7 :** a spar or outrigger connecting the tail surfaces and the main supporting structure of an airplane — called also *tail boom*

³**boom** \"\ *vb* -ED/-ING/-S [imit.] *vi* **1 a :** to make a deep hollow sound ⟨the cannon ~*ed* from the deck⟩ ⟨surf ~*ing* on the distant shore⟩ **b :** to utter a deep resonant cry with a hollow note (as of a bird) ⟨in some deep canyon a night owl started ~*ing* —F.B.Gipson⟩ **c :** to make a sonorous humming or croaking sound (as of an insect or animal) ⟨two frogs ~*ed* again, close at hand —William Beebe⟩ **2 a :** to move swiftly and with a booming sound (as of a ship under full sail) **b** *of a person* **:** to move about from place to place idly **:** BUM, TRAMP **3 a** *of a river* **:** to rise suddenly (as during a spring freshet); *specif* **:** to reach a height sufficient to float logs **b** *of logs* **:** to float down a river that is booming **4 a :** to have a sudden increase in popular esteem or importance often occasioned by a compelling exhortation or appeal ⟨the movement to elect him president began to ~ early in the convention⟩ **b :** to experience a sudden rapid growth and expansion usu. including or implying an increase in market value ⟨business was ~*ing*⟩ ⟨stocks began to ~⟩ **c :** to develop rapidly in population and importance often as a result of location or connection with a feature that draws people to the region ⟨California began to ~ when gold was discovered there⟩ ~ *vt* **1 :** to sound forth or give out with a resonant or booming sound — often used with *out* ⟨a 21-gun salute ~*ed* out by the artillery⟩ **2 a :** to cause a rapid growth or increase of (as in price, sales, commercial development, influence, prestige) ⟨skyrocketing rates and unregulated bookings are ~*ing* the market —Eliot Janeway⟩ **b :** to work for and encourage such growth or increase in ⟨real estate operators hopefully tried to ~ the area —*Amer. Guide Series: Conn.*⟩ **:** PUSH, BOOST ⟨enthusiasts ~*ed* the old soldier —E.T.Folliard⟩

⁴**boom** \"\ *n* -S **1 :** a booming sound: as **a :** a roar esp. of waves **b :** the cry of a bird or animal that booms ⟨the ~ of a bittern⟩ **2 :** a strong rapid expansion movement: as **a :** advocacy and progression into favor of a candidate for office **b :** rapid settlement and development of a town or district often through the efforts of promoters ⟨the Klondike ~ came with the gold rush⟩ **c :** an expansion of economic activity that is characterized by optimistic expectations, increased employment, rising prices and production, and credit expansion ⟨in the midst of an $8,500,000 building ~ —*N.Y. Times*⟩ **d :** the period during which such expansion occurs ⟨during the ~, tremendous tasks of production and administration are performed —Philip Klein⟩

⁵**boom** \"\ *adj* **:** participating in, arising from, or maintained by an economic boom ⟨the ~ days of lumbering⟩ ⟨~ prices⟩

boom·age \-mij\ *n* -S [²*boom* + *-age*] **:** a tax or toll formerly paid for the use of a log boom

boom-and-bust \;=;=\ *n* [⁴*boom*] **:** an alternation of prosperity and depression; *specif* **:** alternate periods of high and low levels of economic activity in the business cycle ⟨we're in for the biggest *boom-and-bust* . . . that we've ever seen —Hal Borland⟩

boom cat *n* [²*boom*] **1 :** a derrick mounted on a caterpillar tractor **2 :** one who operates a power shovel at a strip mine to remove overlying ground and load coal into cars

boom crutch *n* [²*boom*] **:** a movable prop to support the free end of a ship's boom when it is not in use

boom·das·sie \'büm,dasē\ *n* -S [Afrik *boomdas*, fr. *boom* tree (fr. MD) + *dassie*, dim. of *das* badger, fr. MD; akin to OHG *boum* tree and to OHG *dahs* badger — more at BEAM, TECHNICAL] **:** any of several African arboreal coneys (genus *Dendrohyrax*) **:** TREE HYRAX

boomed *past of* BOOM

¹**boom·er** \'bümə(r)\ *n* -S *often attrib* [³*boom* + *-er*] **1 :** one that booms **2 :** one that joins a rush of settlers to a boom area **3 :** a person who moves around the country and works at his trade wherever he happens to be usu. keeping a job for a relatively short period ⟨~*s* who have drifted in from such places as Greenland or Morocco run dredges, build railroads, drive piles —*Time*⟩ **4 a :** MOUNTAIN BEAVER **b :** a large male kangaroo; *specif* **:** GIANT KANGAROO **c** *South & Midland* **:** RED SQUIRREL 1 **5 :** a seller of Salvation Army literature

²**boomer** *n* -S [²*boom* + *-er*] **:** a lever-operated device for tightening chains that hold a load (as of logs or pipe) on a truck — called also *load binder*

1boo·mer·ang \'bümə,raŋ\ *n* -s *often attrib* [native name in Australia] **1 :** a bent or angular throwing club usu. somewhat flat which can be thrown so as to return near the starting point **2 :** a statement or action that backfires on its originator ⟨such crude methods of conquest would serve as a ~ —Paul Blanshard⟩ **3** [influenced in meaning by *2boom*] **a :** a movable platform for supporting painters of theater scenery at various convenient heights **b :** a movable stand or arm for supporting stage lights at various levels

2boomerang \"\ *vi* -ED/-ING/-S **1 :** to return in the manner of a boomerang **2 :** to produce by word or deed a result directly opposed to that intended; *esp* **:** to injure the originator (as of a policy) instead of the intended target **:** BACKFIRE ⟨his . . . policy had ~*ed* disastrously —*U.N. World*⟩

boomerangs

boom hoist *n* [*2boom*] **:** a hoist having a spar projecting from the mast to support and guide the load **:** DERRICK

boom·i·ness \'büménəs\ *n* -ES [*boomy* + *-ness*] **:** an excessive amount of bass in the sound reproduced by a loudspeaker

1booming *adj* -ER/-EST [fr. pres. part. of *3boom*] **1 :** making or performing an action with a booming sound ⟨his ~ voice⟩ ⟨the ~ river⟩ **2 :** increasing or growing rapidly ⟨a ~ railroad center⟩ ⟨~ wheat prices⟩ — **boom·ing·ly** *adv*

2booming *n* -s [fr. gerund of *3boom*] **1 :** the sound or act of one that booms **2 :** the process of discharging water behind a dam down a hillside or gorge to wash out deposits of gold

booming ground *n* **:** an area in which the male of certain grouse (as the prairie chicken) takes his stand during the breeding season and performs his characteristic nuptial display accompanied by booming or drumming sounds produced by vibrating the wings in air

boomkin *var of* BUMPKIN

boom·less \'bümləs\ *adj* **:** being without a boom

boom·let \'bümlət\ *n* -s [*4boom* + *-let*] **:** a small boom; *specif* **:** a short-term increase in economic activity

boom man *n* [*2boom*] **1 :** one who operates the controls of a loading boom or crane **2 :** POLEMAN 2 **3 :** RAFTER

boom pole *n* [*2boom*] **:** 2BOOM 2a

booms *pl of* BOOM, *pres 3d sing of* BOOM

boom shot *n* [*2boom*] **:** a motion-picture or television shot; *esp* **:** a traveling shot taken with a camera mounted on a boom

boom·slang \'büm,slaŋ, -laŋ\ *n, pl* **boom·slange** \-ŋə\ *or* **boomslangs** [Afrik, fr. *boom* tree + *slang* snake, fr. MD *slanghe;* akin to OS & OHG *slango* snake, OHG *slingan* to wind — more at BOOMDASSIE, SLING] **:** a large boigid tree snake (*Dispholidus typus*) of southern Africa variously colored green or brownish black and having retiring ways and a back-fanged mouth that render it practically harmless to man despite its powerful venom

boom·ster \'bümstə(r)\ *n* -s [*4boom* + *-ster*] **:** BOOMER

boom stick *n* [*2boom*] **:** any of the timbers chained end to end to form a boom in logging

boom table *n* [*2boom*] **:** a structure around the lower part of a ship's mast to which booms are attached

boom tackle *n* [*2boom*] **:** a tackle used on or with a boom

boomtown \'=,=\ *n* [*4boom* + *town*] **:** a town that has experienced sudden growth as the result of a boom

boomy \'bümē\ *adj, often* -ER/-EST [*4boom* + *-y*] **:** having the quality of a boom; *specif, of reproduced sound* **:** having an excessive accentuation on the tones of lower pitch

1boon \'bün\ *n* -s [ME *boone, bone,* fr. ON *bōn* petition; akin to OE *bēn* prayer, *bannan* to summon — more at BAN] **1** *obs* **:** an order or command in the form of a request **2 :** BENEFIT, FAVOR; *esp* **:** one that is specif. asked for or is given as the result of a request ⟨told he would be granted any ~ he asked⟩ **3 :** an often timely and gratuitous benefit received and enjoyed **:** BLESSING ⟨the rain was a ~ to parched crops⟩

2boon \"\ *adj* [ME *bon, bone,* fr. MF *bon* good — more at BONNY] **1** *obs* **:** GOODLY, FAVORABLE, PROSPEROUS **2 :** BOUNTEOUS, BENIGN ⟨~ nature⟩ **3 :** MERRY, JOVIAL, CONVIVIAL, INTIMATE ⟨a ~ companion, loving his bottle —John Arbuthnot⟩

3boon \"\ *n* -s [ME *bone, bunne,* prob. fr. OE *bune* reed — more at BUN] **:** the woody portion of the stem of flax or hemp after the removal of the fiber by retting, braking, and scutching

boon·dock·ers \'bün,däkə(r)z\ *n pl, slang* **:** field shoes

boon·docks \'bün,däks\ *also* **bundocks** \", 'bün-, 'bən-\ *n pl* [Tag *bundok* mountain] **1** *also* **boon·dock** \k\ -s *slang* **:** rough country **:** dense brush **:** JUNGLE — usu. used with *the* **2** *slang* **:** rural backcountry **:** STICKS

1boon·dog·gle \'bün,dägəl\ *n* -s [coined 1925 by Robert H. Link *b*1897 Am. scoutmaster] **1 :** a handicraft article esp. of leather or wicker fashioned for utility **2 :** an impracticable or useless project wasteful of time and money

2boondoggle *vi* **boondoggled; boondoggled; boondoggling** \-g(ə)liŋ\ **boondoggles 1 :** to engage in making boondoggles **2 :** to engage in useless or frivolous occupations — **boon·dog·gler** \-g(ə)lə(r)\ *n* -s

boong \'büŋ, 'bö,äŋ\ *n* -s [native name in Australia] *slang Austral* **1 :** ABORIGINE **2 :** a native of New Guinea

boon·ga·ry \'büŋgərē\ *n* -ES [native name in Australia] **:** a small tree wallaby (*Dendrolagus lumholtzi*) native to Queensland

boon·less \'bünləs\ *adj* **:** being without a boon

bo·oph·i·lus \bō'äfələs\ *n, cap* [NL, fr. Gk *boo-* (fr. *bous* head of cattle) + NL *-philus* — more at COW] **:** a genus of ticks some of which are pests of cattle and other ruminants and vectors of disease — see CATTLE TICK

1boor \'bü(ə)r, 'büə\ *n* -s [D *boer* peasant, farmer, short for MD *gheboer, ghebuur,* fr. *ghe-* co- + *-boer, buur* dweller; akin to OHG *gi-* co- and to OE *gebūr* dweller, farmer, OHG *gibūro* peasant, fellow countryman, OE & OHG *būan* to dwell — more at BOWER (dwelling)] **1 :** a small farmer **:** PEASANT, HUSBANDMAN **2 :** BOER **3 a :** a rustic or peasant typically rough, crude, insensitive, uncommunicative, or dull **:** YOKEL ⟨a kind of heroic ~ devoid of civilized graces and refinements —F.R.Leavis⟩ **b :** a rude, clumsy, insensitive, or boring individual ⟨an ill-mannered ~⟩

syn CHURL, LOUT, CLOWN, BUMPKIN, CLODHOPPER, HICK, YOKEL, RUBE: BOOR, orig. applicable to any small farmer, now strongly implies rudeness, insensitivity, or dullness; it is an antonym to *gentleman* ⟨he that is rude to a pretty girl when she offers him wine is too great a *boor* to understand —Charles Kingsley⟩ ⟨love makes gentlemen even of *boors* —Henry Adams⟩ CHURL, orig. a rustic or villein, is now more likely to suggest ill-bred surly meanness in general than that associated with rural backgrounds ⟨magic . . . that this divine sweet creature could be allied with that old *churl* —George Meredith⟩ LOUT is applicable to any crude and hulking oaf, rural or urban ⟨a stupid *lout,* seemingly a farmer's boy —Sir Walter Scott⟩ CLOWN, orig. a field worker, now suggests ill-bred clumsiness or gaucheness, perhaps laughable ⟨any *clown,* ignorant of the usages of the house —T.B.Macaulay⟩ BUMPKIN suggests an awkward, gauche, and naive rustic ⟨awkward lads with shy, red faces . . . poor *bumpkins* —James Hilton⟩ CLODHOPPER suggests a shambling heaviness and a cloddish lack of information or urbanity ⟨*clodhoppers* gaping at the stores on Saturday night⟩ HICK is a less forceful term for an unsophisticated simple native ⟨*hicks* in the hinterlands disliking city candidates⟩ YOKEL and RUBE may suggest either rustic lack of polish or gullible obtuseness ⟨like a listener in a country store to wondrous tales . . . his mouth was agape in *yokel* fashion —Stephen Crane⟩ Many of these terms are interchangeable ⟨not worthy to be a knight — a *churl,* a *clown* —Alfred Tennyson⟩ ⟨he got off with scorn — he was a *hick,* a *rube* . . . , a rustic, a *boor* or a hillbilly —Bergen Evans⟩

2boor \"\ *Scot var of* BOWER

boo·rach \'bürək\ *var of* BOUROCK

boord·ly \'bürdlē\ *var of* BUIRDLY

boor·ish \'bürish, -rēsh\ *adj* **:** characteristic of or relating to a boor **:** unrefined and insensitive **:** RUDE ⟨~ remarks⟩ — **boor·ish·ly** *adv* — **boor·ish·ness** *n* -ES

boors *pl of* BOOR

boort *var of* BORT

boor·tree \'bür,trē\ *var of* BOURTREE

boos *pl of* BOO, *pres 3d sing of* BOO

1boose \'büs\ *n* -s [ME *boos;* akin to OE *bōsig* cow stall, ON *bās,* Goth *bansts* barn, OE *bindan* to bind — more at BIND] *dial Brit* **:** a stall for a horse or a cow

2boose *var of* BOOZE

1boost \'büst\ *vt* -ED/-ING/-S [origin unknown] **1 :** to push or shove from below to or towards a higher level ⟨they ~*ed* him up so he could climb the oak tree⟩ **2 a :** to increase (as a price) by a numerically expressible amount **:** RAISE ⟨plans to ~ production by 30 percent next year⟩ **b :** to aid or assist esp. towards progress or increase ⟨an extra holiday to ~ morale⟩ **3 :** to promote the cause or interests of (as a person, city, idea) with enthusiasm and determination **:** recommend vigorously **:** PLUG ⟨they began to ~ him for the presidency early⟩ ⟨an advertising program to ~ local products abroad⟩ **4 a** (1) **:** to raise the voltage of or across (an electric circuit) (2) **:** to charge (a storage battery) at a high rate for a short time **b :** to augment (as by a supercharger) the natural supply of air to (an internal-combustion engine) **c :** to increase the pressure of (as a fluid) **d :** to control or regulate by increase of pressure **5** *slang* **:** STEAL; *esp* **:** SHOPLIFT **syn** see LIFT

2boost \"\ *n* -s **1 :** an act of boosting **:** a push upwards ⟨give him a ~ so he can climb over the fence⟩ **2 :** an increase esp. of prices, wages, production ⟨a ~ in potato acreage⟩ ⟨a bass ~ on an amplifier⟩ **3 :** assistance or commendation that betters position or enhances reputation ⟨music criticism . . . was given a ~ as an academic subject —*Saturday Rev.*⟩ **4 :** an uplift or encouragement ⟨gave the free world a tonic ~ —*New Yorker*⟩

boost·er \-tə(r)\ *n* -s *often attrib* **1 :** one that boosts **2 :** an enthusiastic supporter or backer ⟨a great ~ for his home town⟩ **3 :** an auxiliary device for increasing force, power, or pressure esp. for the purpose of moving an object: as **a :** an additional locomotive on a train **b :** a hydraulic brake servomechanism **4** *also* **booster pump :** a pump used to increase the pressure of fluids **5 :** a transformer for regulating or modifying a fluctuating or sagging voltage in an electric circuit **6 :** a high explosive charge usu. in the form of one or more pressed pellets in a cup or tube sensitive enough to be set off by a detonator and powerful enough to set off the main charge in a shell, mine, bomb, or other explosive device; *also* **:** a device (as a tube) containing this charge **7 :** a radio-frequency amplifier for intensifying signals picked up by a radio or television antenna before passing them on to the regular receiving set used esp. where reception would otherwise be weak **8 :** an auxiliary part of the propulsive system of a pilotless airplane or missile used to supply a part or all of the thrust during the launching and initial stage of flight **:** the first stage of a multistage rocket **9 :** a pressure blower that draws in air or gas and expels it through an outlet pipe at a higher pressure **10 :** a substance or dose used to renew or increase the effect of a drug or immunizing agent: as **a :** an injection of antigen given after completion of a primary course of immunization ⟨the child was given a ~⟩ ⟨a ~ shot of diphtheria toxoid⟩ — called also *recall dose* **b :** SYNERGIST 2 ⟨a chemical acting as a ~ to sulfa drugs⟩ **11** *slang* **a :** THIEF; *esp* **:** SHOPLIFTER **b :** SHILL

booster battery *n* **:** a battery used to maintain a certain voltage across a crystal detector to increase the sensitivity of the detector by adjusting conditions for increased response for a given input

boost·er·ism \-tə,rizəm\ *n* -s **:** the activities and attitudes typical of boosters (sense 2) ⟨natives deeply in love with their environment with more sincerity than ~ —Al Hine⟩

booster rocket *n* **:** RATO

boost pressure *n* **:** the pressure in the induction system of an aircraft engine in excess of the standard sea-level atmospheric pressure

boosy \'büzē\ *n* -ES [fr. (assumed) ME, fr. OE *bōsig* — more at BOOSE] **:** BOOSE

1boot \'büt, *usu* -üd.+V\ *n* -s [ME *boote, bote,* fr. OE *bōt* remedy, compensation; akin to OHG *buoza* change for the better, ON *bōt* remedy, compensation, Goth *bōta* advantage, gain, OE *betera* better — more at BETTER] **1** *archaic* **a :** help or relief esp. in time of peril or great want **:** DELIVERANCE **b :** a person or thing that brings such help **2** *now chiefly dial* **:** something to equalize an exchange ⟨give me your sow and $10 ~ or the trade is off for the heifer —Frank Neefe⟩ **3** *obs* **:** profit or advantage towards the accomplishment of an end **:** AVAIL, USE ⟨then talk no more of flight, it is no ~ —Shak.⟩ — **to boot** *adv* **:** in addition **:** over and above **:** BESIDES **:** as a compensation for the difference of value between things bartered ⟨he traded and gave $10 *to boot*⟩

2boot \"\ *vb* -ED/-ING/-S [ME *booten, boten,* fr. *boote, bote*] *vi, archaic* **:** to be of help, profit, or advantage **:** AVAIL ⟨it ~s not to look backwards —Thomas Arnold⟩ ~ *vt, obs* **:** BENEFIT, ENRICH

3boot \"\ *n* -s [ME, fr. MF *bote*] **1 a :** a covering for the foot and leg that is usu. made of leather or rubber and is of varying height between the ankle and hip **b** *Brit* **:** a shoe reaching to the ankle **c :** a rubber overshoe **2 :** an instrument of torture applied to the leg and tightened so as to crush the leg and foot **3 :** a sheath or casing resembling a boot that provides a protective covering for the leg: as **a** *obs* **:** a piece of leg armor **b :** a partial covering for the hoof and leg of a horse designed to prevent injury from interference **c :** the feathers on the shank and toes of certain domestic fowls **d :** the part of a stocking between the top and the foot **e :** a canvas or skin mitten used to protect the feet of working dogs from snow or ice **4 :** a protective sheath or casing typically of an object or part resembling a leg: as **a :** the sheath near the uppermost leaves on the stems of grains and many palms that encloses the inflorescence which swells within it **b :** the metal casing and flange fitted about a pipe where it passes through a roof **c :** the box or compartment that contains the reed of a reed pipe of an organ **d :** a large thick patch for the inside of a tire casing **5 a** *obs* **:** a built-in compartment on a horse-drawn coach used orig. as a seat for the coachman and later for storage **b** *Brit* **:** the storage compartment at the rear of an automobile **:** TRUNK **6 :** a usu. leather article that resembles a boot: as **a :** a leather drinking vessel **b :** a leather carrying case for a rifle ⟨with the adoption of the bolt-action Krag . . . a long ~ came into use, covering the entire carbine, up to the stock —W.F. Harris⟩ **c** *aeronautics* **:** a pneumatic rubber cell or tube used for deicing a wing or tail surface **7 a :** the box in which the lower pulley of a grain elevator runs **b :** the chamber and housing at the base of a bucket elevator **8 a :** a blow delivered by or as if by a booted foot **:** KICK **b :** a usu. unexpected and often rude discharge or dismissal — often used with *the* ⟨she gave him the ~ and married another man⟩ ⟨he got the ~ after 14 years and had to find a new job⟩ **c :** pleasure or enjoyment esp. of a momentary sort **:** BANG, KICK ⟨I get a big ~ out of his jokes⟩ **9 :** a fumble in baseball **10 a :** a recruit undergoing basic training in the U. S. Navy or Marines **b :** NOVICE, TRAINEE, APPRENTICE **11** *in glass manuf* **:** a clay receptacle suspended in the nose of a tank furnace to exclude scum and to allow working of the glass without direct contact with heat and gases **12 :** a drain cock in the bottom of a tank car or oil tank

boot 1a

4boot \"\ *vb* -ED/-ING/-S [ME *booten,* fr. *boot* — more at 3BOOT] *vt* **1 a :** to put boots on (oneself or another) **b :** to supply with boots ⟨this firm . . . has ~*ed* and spurred every British monarch from George II on —*New Yorker*⟩ **2 a :** to send off or propel with force **:** KICK **b :** to eject or discharge summarily — used often with *out* ⟨he has been quietly ~*ed* out as chief —*Newsweek*⟩ **3 :** to make an error on (a baseball batted on the ground) **:** FUMBLE ⟨he ~*ed* an easy grounder and another run scored⟩ **4** *slang* **:** to ride (a horse) in a race ⟨after a 24-year career in which he ~*ed* home nearly 150 stakes winners⟩ ~ *vi* **:** to put on one's boots

5boot \"\ *n* -s [*1boot* (influenced in meaning by *booty*)] *archaic* **:** BOOTY, PLUNDER

bootblack \'=,=\ *n* **:** one who shines shoes and boots

bootboy \'=,=\ *n* **:** BOOTS

boot camp *n* **:** a station for the basic training of newly enlisted seamen or marines

bootcatcher *n, obs* **:** BOOTS

booted *adj* [fr. past part. of *4boot*] **1 :** wearing boots; *specif* **:** equipped for riding ⟨~ and spurred⟩ **2 :** having a continuous horny covering somewhat resembling a boot — used of the tarsus of some birds in distinction from those covered with plates, scales, or soft skin **3 :** having the shanks and toes feathered — used of certain domestic fowls and pigeons

booted eagle *n* **:** a rather small slender Old World eagle (*Hieraetus pennatus*) that breeds in Europe and western Asia and winters in Africa and southern Asia

boo·tee *or* **boo·tie** \(')bü¦tē\ *in sense 2 usu* 'büd.ē *or* 'büte *or* -i\ *n* -s [*3boot* + *-ee* or *-ie*] **1 :** a boot with a short leg: as **a :** a boot with a front extending from the throat of the vamp over the instep to the ankle **b :** a slipper with the upper extending to or nearly to the ankle **2 :** an infant's sock of knitted or crocheted wool usu. of half-leg length with a tie at the ankle

bootee 2

boot·er \'büd.|ə(r), -üt|\ *n* -s [*4boot* + *-er*] **:** one that boots; *specif* **:** a soccer player

boot·ery \|ərē\ *n* -ES [*3boot* + *-ery*] **:** a shoe store

booth \'büth, *Brit usu* -th\ *n, pl* **booths** \-üthz,-üths *sometimes* -üz\ [ME *bothe,* of Scand origin; akin to ON *būth* booth; akin to MHG *buode* booth, OE & OHG *būan* to dwell, inhabit — more at BOWER] **1 :** a simple roofed structure often built of any material at hand and used as a temporary shelter for livestock or field workers ⟨in harvest time ~s in fields and vineyards were occupied even at night by some member of the family —Madeleine S. Miller & J.L.Miller⟩ **2 a :** a temporary structure (as at a fair) where articles may be placed for sale or display or where exhibits may be shown ⟨the 4-H ~ at the county fair was a soil conservation exhibit⟩ **b :** a totally or partially enclosed structure often inside a building; *esp* **:** a small enclosure designed to hold one person at a time usu. to afford privacy or to separate its occupant from patrons or customers ⟨a telephone ~⟩ ⟨a voting ~⟩ ⟨the information ~ in the bus station⟩ **c :** a seating and eating accommodation much used in restaurants and bars that consists of a table placed between two backed benches ⟨they sat in the ~ and talked for an hour⟩ **3 :** an enclosure of varying size and construction designed to isolate an area and to prevent the functions carried on within it from being interfered with by the surrounding area ⟨a broadcasting ~ in the ball park⟩

boothale *vb* [*5boot* + *hale*] *vi, obs* **:** to forage for booty **:** PLUNDER ~ *vt, obs* **:** PILLAGE, PLUNDER

boot·heel \'=,=\ *n* **1 :** the heel of a boot **2 :** something resembling a bootheel in shape; *esp* **:** a land formation in the shape of a bootheel ⟨the ~ of Missouri⟩

boot hill *n, sometimes cap B&H* [so called fr. the supposition that most persons buried there died with their boots on] *West* **:** a burial-ground esp. for men killed in gunfights ⟨as a wild town in early days, it had its *boot hill* and knew . . . notorious gunfighters —*Amer. Guide Series: Texas*⟩

booth·ite \'bü,thīt, *Brit usu* -th-\ *n* -s [Edwin *Booth* †1917 Am. chemist + E *-ite*] **:** a mineral $CuSO_4.7H_2O$ consisting of a hydrous copper sulfate occurring in indistinct monoclinic blue crystals

boot hook *n* **:** a long cross-handled hook for pulling on riding boots by the straps

boot·hose \'=,=\ *n pl* **:** stockings or protective overstockings worn with or in place of boots

bootjack \'=,=\ *n* [*3boot* + *jack*] **1 :** a metal or wood device shaped like the letter V and used in pulling off boots **2 bootjacks** *pl* [so called fr. the flat two-awned achenes] **:** BEGGAR-TICKS 1, 2 **3** *mining engin* **:** a fishing tool consisting of two wings and a latch used in well boring for grabbing bailers

bootlace \'=,=\ *n* **1 :** a lace for a boot **2** *Brit* **:** SHOELACE

1bootleg \'=,=\ *n* [*3boot* + *leg*] **1 a :** the upper part of a boot **b :** an object shaped or used like a bootleg; *specif* **:** a protective cover for railroad track wires where the wires leave the conduit or ground **2 :** a large locking lever in a spinning mule **3 :** something bootlegged; *specif* **:** MOONSHINE

2bootleg \"\ *vb* **bootlegged; bootlegged; bootlegging; bootlegs** *vt* **1 a :** to carry (alcoholic liquor) on one's person illegally **b :** to manufacture, sell, or transport for sale (alcoholic liquor) contrary to law ⟨*bootlegged* corn whiskey during Prohibition⟩ **2 a :** to produce or obtain for sale or distribution or to sell or distribute illicitly without such inspection, permission, or approval as may be required by law or by existing private agreements ⟨register the number . . so that any watch can be traced should it be *bootlegged* through unscrupulous outlets —*Jewelers' Circular-Keystone*⟩ **b :** SMUGGLE ~ *vi* **1 :** to engage in bootlegging **2 :** to separate and slip — used of the plies of a machine belt

3bootleg \"\ *adj* **1 :** sold or distributed illicitly or surreptitiously **:** produced, procured, or transported for illicit sale or distribution ⟨~ coal taken from abandoned mines and trucked to the city for sale⟩ ⟨the hills were full of ~ whiskey⟩ **2 :** clandestine or surreptitious esp. in order to avoid laws or regulations ⟨a ~ radio station⟩ ⟨~ wage increases that violated contracts⟩ **3 :** characterized by the presence of, participation in, or dealing with bootlegging ⟨a ~ town⟩

boot·leg·ger \'=,=ə(r)\ *n* -s **:** one that bootlegs esp. alcoholic liquor

bootlegging *n* **:** the act or practice of a bootlegger

bootleg play *n* **:** a football play in which the quarterback fakes giving the ball to a teammate, conceals it on his hip, and runs with it behind interference

boot·less \'bütləs\ *adj* [ME *bootelees,* fr. OE *bōtlēas* inexpiable, fr. *bōt* remedy, compensation + *-lēas* -less — more at 1BOOT] **1** *archaic* **:** without remedy **:** INCURABLE **2 :** to no advantage or avail **:** fruitless and frustrating ⟨no guides were to be found, and in the next summer the young man returned from his ~ errand —Francis Parkman⟩ — **boot·less·ly** *adv* — **boot·less·ness** *n* -ES

1boot·lick \'=,=\ *vb* -ED/-ING/-S [*3boot* + *lick*] *vt* **:** to fawn on **:** cultivate the favor of through obsequious speech or actions ⟨always beholden to the favor of kings and princes, ~*ing* bishops for a pittance, courting fair ladies for a few crowns —Corra Harris⟩ ~ *vi* **:** to act as a bootlicker **:** play the sycophant

2bootlick \"\ *n* -s **:** BOOTLICKER **syn** see PARASITE

boot·lick·er \-ə(r)\ *n* -s **:** SYCOPHANT, TOADY **syn** see PARASITE

boot·man \'bütmən, -,man\ *n, pl* **bootmen 1 :** a worker who shapes the sheet-metal fairing for aircraft **2 :** a road worker who applies oil to roads from a specially equipped truck

1boots *pres 3d sing of* BOOT

2boots \'büts\ *n pl but sing in constr* [fr. pl. of *3boot*] *Brit* **:** SERVANT; *esp* **:** a hotel employee whose main duty is to shine boots and shoes

boots and saddles *n pl but sing in constr* **:** the bugle call preceding assembly for mounted formations

1boot·strap \'=,=\ *n* **1 :** a looped strap sewed at the side or the rear top of a boot to help in pulling it on **2 bootstraps** *pl* **:** unaided efforts — often used in the phrase *by one's bootstraps* ⟨"well, George, . . . pull yourself up by your own ~s and start in to be a man" —Helen Eustis⟩

2bootstrap \"\ *adj* **:** based on or carried out with minimum resources or advantages **:** relying on its own efforts ⟨the city recovered from the flood by the ~ method⟩ ⟨a ~ operation⟩

boot top *n* **1 :** the upper part or top of a boot **2 :** a lace ruffle formerly worn so as to conceal the top of the boot

boot topping *n* **1 :** the part of a ship's hull between the light line and the load water line **2** *also* **boot top :** a paint used on the boot topping to prevent corrosion and fouling

boot tree *n* **1 :** SHOE TREE **2 :** BOOTJACK 1

boo·ty \'büd.ē, -üte, -i\ *n* -ES [modif. (influenced by *boot* profit) of MF *butin,* fr. MLG *būte* exchange, distribution] **1 a :** PLUNDER, SPOILS; *esp* **:** loot taken in war **b :** *international law* **:** spoils taken on land as distinguished from that captured on the high seas — compare PRIZE **2 :** REWARD, PRIZE, GAIN ⟨I made ~ of a great bunch of . . . flowers and scarlet raspberries —Rachel Henning⟩

boo·ty·less *adj* **:** being without booty **:** yielding no booty

booza *var of* BOZA

1booze *also* **boose** \'büz\ *vi* -ED/-ING/-S [alter. (perh. influenced by Flem *boezen* to tipple) of earlier *bouse,* fr. ME *bousen,* fr. MD or MFlem *būsen;* akin to MLG *būsen* to tipple, MHG *būs* swelling, fullness and prob. to OHG *buosam* bosom — more at BOSOM] **:** to drink intoxicating liquor esp. habitually or to excess ⟨he still *boozed* till daylight and dozed into the afternoon —G.O.Trevelyan⟩

²**booze** *also* **boose** \"\ *n* -s *often attrib* [alter. (perh. influenced by Flem *boezen* to tipple) of earlier *bouse*, fr. ME *bous*, fr. *bousen*] **1 :** intoxicating drink; *esp* **:** hard liquor ⟨a bottle of ~⟩ **2 :** a drinking bout or spree **:** DRUNK ⟨went on a ~⟩

booze fighter *n* **:** BOOZEHOUND

booze·hound \'⸗,⸗\ *n* **:** a heavy or habitual drinker ⟨a violent and lecherous ~ —Joseph Cannata⟩

booz·er \'büzə(r)\ *n* -s **1 :** one that boozes **2** *slang Brit* **:** a drinking place **:** PUB

booz·i·ly \'büzəlē, -li\ *adv* **:** in a boozy manner

boozy \-zē,-zi\ *adj, usu* -ER/-EST **1 :** affected by or showing the influence of liquor **:** slightly drunk **2 :** DRUNK

¹**bop** \'bäp\ *vt* **bopped; bopped; bopping; bops** [imit.] **:** to strike esp. with the fist or a club **:** SOCK, HIT ⟨he reached out and *bopped* me over the head with a rolled-up newspaper —Leslie Ford⟩

²**bop** \"\ *n* -s **:** a blow esp. with the fist or a club **:** SOCK, HIT ⟨I gave him a ~ that laid him out⟩

³**bop** \"\ *n* -s *often attrib* [short for *bebop*] **:** jazz characterized by rhythmic harmonic complexity and innovation, lengthened melodic line, and usu. fast tempos and loud bravura execution

bo-peep \bō'pēp\ *n* -s ['*boo* + *peep*] **:** PEEKABOO

bop·per \'bäpə(r)\ *also* **bop·pist** \-pəst\ *or* **bop·ster** \-pstə(r)\ *n* -s **1 a :** one that plays bop **:** a musician skilled at playing bop **b :** a vocalist that sings with bop accompaniment **2 :** a devotee of bop

bo·pyr·id \bō'pīrəd\ *n* -s [NL *Bopyridae*] **:** an isopod of the family Bopyridae

bo·pyr·i·dae \-rə,dē\ *n pl, cap* [NL, fr. *Bopyrus*, type genus (prob. fr. a proper name *Bopyrus*) + *-idae*] **:** a large family of isopod crustaceans that live as parasites on shrimps and other decapods, the large females attaching themselves to their host by hooked legs, often causing parasitic castration of the host, and themselves becoming extremely degenerated while the minute males live on or near the females and in large measure retain their isopod characters

BOQ *abbr or n* -s bachelor officers' quarters

bor \'bō(r)\ *n* -s [prob. alter. of ¹*boor*] *dial Brit* **:** NEIGHBOR, FRIEND — used in address

bor- *or* **boro-** *comb form* [ISV, fr. *boron*] **:** boron ⟨*borism*⟩ ⟨*boryl*⟩ ⟨*boroarsenate*⟩

bor *abbr* borough

¹**bo·ra** \'bōrə, 'bȯrə\ *n* -s [It dial. (Venetian), fr. L *boreas* — more at BOREAS] **:** an occasional violent cold north to northeast wind that blows over the northern Adriatic from the interior highlands

²**bora** \"\ *n* -s [Australian, fr. *bōr, būr* girdle, circle] **:** a rite in which Australian aborigine boys are initiated into manhood

³**bora** *usu cap, var of* BORO

borachio *n* -s [modif. of Sp *borracho* drunkard, intoxicated, irreg. fr. L *burrus* red, flushed with food or drink, fr. Gk *pyrrhos* red, tawny — more at PYRRH-] *obs* **:** DRUNKARD

bo·rac·ic \bə'rasik, bō'-, -raas-\ *adj* [ISV *borac-* (fr. ML *borac-, borax*) + *-ic*] **:** BORIC

boracic acid *n* **:** BORIC ACID a — not used scientifically

bo·ra·cite \'bōrə,sīt, 'bȯr-\ *n* -s [G *borazit*, fr. ML *borac-, borax* + G *-it* -ite] **:** a mineral $Mg_3B_7O_{13}Cl$ consisting of a borate and chloride of magnesium that is strongly pyroelectric and occurs in hard glassy crystals and in softer white masses (hardness 7, sp. gr. 2.9)

bor·age \'bȯrij, 'bär-, 'bərij\ *n* -s [ME, fr. MF *bourache, bourage*, prob. fr. (assumed) VL *burrago*, fr. LL *burra* shaggy cloth; fr. the hairy leaves — more at BUREAU] **:** a rough-hairy blue-flowered European herb (*Borago officinalis*) used esp. in France as a demulcent and diaphoretic and also as a salad herb and widely naturalized as a weed

borage family *n* **:** BORAGINACEAE

bo·rag·i·na·ce·ae \bə,rajə'nāsē,ē\ *n pl, cap* [NL, fr. *Boragin-, Borago*, type genus + *-aceae*] **:** a family of herbs, shrubs, or trees (order Polemoniales) of wide distribution distinguished mainly by circinate inflorescence and nutlike fruit

bo·rag·i·na·ceous \bə¦rajə¦nāshəs\ *adj* [NL *Boraginaceae* + E *-ous*] **:** of, relating to, or like the Boraginaceae

bo·ra·go \bə'rā(,)gō, -rä-\ *n, cap* [NL, fr. ML *borago, borrago* borage, prob. fr. (assumed) VL *burrago*] **:** a small genus of perennial herbs (family Boraginaceae) that are natives of the Mediterranean region and distinguished by a rotate corolla and large scar at the base of the nutlet

bor·ak \'bȯrək, 'bär-\ *n* [native name in New South Wales, Australia] *Austral* **:** FUN, RIDICULE — used esp. in the phrase *poke borak at* ⟨one of the crowd was poking *borak* and said something pretty bad to him —*Blackwood's*⟩

bor·al \'bōr,al, 'bȯ,ral, -,ral\ *n* -s [ISV *bor-* (fr. *borate*) + *-al* (fr. *aluminum*)] **:** a fine white astringent powder consisting of a borate and tartrate of aluminum

bo·ran \bə'ran, -rän\ *n, usu cap* [prob. fr. *Borana, Boran*] **:** an East African breed of cattle of the zebu type

bo·rana \bə'ranə, -ränə\ *also* **bo·ran** \-n\ *n, pl* **borana** \-nə\ *or* **boranas** \-nəz\ *also* **boran** \-n\ *or* **bo·rani** \-nē\ *usu cap* [native name in East Africa] **1 :** a widely distributed Hamitic people of southern Ethiopia and northeast Uganda **2 :** a member of the Borana people

bo·rane \'bōr,ān, 'bȯ,rān\ *n* -s [ISV *bor-* + *-ane*] **1 :** a compound of boron and hydrogen; *specif* **:** BORINE 1 — compare DIBORANE **2 :** a derivative (as methyl-diborane) of a borane

boras *pl of* BORA

bo·ras·ca *also* **bor·ras·ca** \bə'raskə\ *or* **bo·ras·co** \-(,)skō\ *or* **bo·rasque** \-rask\ *n* -s [Sp *borrasca*, fr. LL *borras* north wind, fr. Gk *borras, boreas* — more at BOREAS] **1 :** a squall often attended with a thunderstorm occurring esp. in the Mediterranean **2** [MexSp *borrasca* unproductiveness (of a mine), fr. Sp, squall] **a :** a mine section or an entire mine that is largely oreless **:** an unproductive mine **b :** unproductiveness esp. of a mine; *also* **:** PENURY, WANT

bo·ras·sus \bə'rasəs\ *n, cap* [NL, fr. Gk *borassos* date palm spadix with immature fruit] **:** a monotypic genus of sugar palms native to tropical Africa and naturalized throughout the tropics and having fan-shaped leaves and very hard wood — see PALMYRA

bo·rate \'bōr,āt, 'bȯ,rāt *also* -,rət; *usu* -d.+V\ *n* -s [ISV *bor-* + *-ate* (n. suffix)] **:** a salt or ester of a boric acid

bo·rat·ed \-ād·əd\ *adj* [*bor-* + *-ate* (vb. suffix) + *-ed*] **:** mixed or impregnated with borax or boric acid ⟨~ cream of tartar⟩

¹**bo·rax** \'bōr,aks, 'bȯ,ra-, -,rəks\ *n* -ES [alter. (influenced by ML *borax*) of earlier *boras*, fr. ME, fr. MF, fr. ML *borac-, borax*, fr. Ar *bawraq, būraq*, fr. Per *būrah*] **:** the best-known sodium borate $Na_2B_4O_7.10H_2O$ crystallizing usu. in large monoclinic prisms that occurs naturally in this form as a mineral, that is also obtained from other minerals (as kernite or tincalconite) or from the boric acid of fumaroles by reaction with soda, and that is used chiefly in glass and ceramics, in agricultural chemicals, as a flux, as a cleansing agent and water softener, and as a preservative and fire retardant (as for wood) — called also *sodium tetraborate*

²**borax** \"\ *n* -ES **:** cheap shoddy flashy merchandise; *esp* **:** cheap poorly constructed ostentatious furniture of a nondescript or hybrid style ⟨to develop guides for telling high quality from ~ —*Money*⟩

³**borax** \"\ *adj* **1 :** characterized by cheapness, shoddy construction, flashiness, and nondescript or hybrid design ⟨~ furniture⟩ ⟨buying ~ goods on the installment plan⟩ **2 :** of, relating to, or dealing in cheap shoddy flashy merchandise, esp. furniture ⟨a ~ credit store⟩; *also* **:** marked by the ballyhoo and high-pressure salesmanship usu. associated with the promotion and sale of such merchandise ⟨~ advertising⟩

borax bead *n* **:** a bead (sense 4f) having borax as the flux

borax carmine *n* **:** an alkaline staining fluid composed of borax, carmine, and water and used with dilute hydrochloric acid in microscopy to produce a permanent red nuclear stain

borax glass *n* **:** a transparent anhydrous glassy solid formed by fusing borax

borax honey *n* **:** a medicinal mixture of borax, glycerin, and purified honey

borax lake *n* **1 :** a lake whose shores are encrusted with borax⸗rich deposits **2 :** a dry lake bed rich in borax

bor·azole \'bōrə,zōl, 'bȯr-; bə'ra,zōl\ *or* **bor·azine** \-zēn\ *n* -s [*bor-* + *azole* or *azine*] **:** a colorless volatile liquid compound $B_3N_3H_6$ that is formed by heating diborane and ammonia and has a structure like that of benzene with alternating boron and nitrogen atoms in a ring — called also *triborine triamine*

Bor·a·zon \'bōrə,zän, 'bȯr-\ *trademark* — used for a boron nitride abrasive

bor·bo·ryg·mic \¦bȯrbə¦rigmik\ *also* **bor·bo·ryg·mat·ic** \-(,)rig¦mad·ik\ *adj* [*borborygmic* fr. *borborygmus* + *-ic*; *borborygmatic* fr. NL *borborygmat-, borborygma* borborygmus (alter. of *borborygmus*) + E *-ic*] **:** of, relating to, resembling, or affected with borborygmus

bor·bo·ryg·mus \,bȯrbə'rigməs\ *also* **bor·bo·ryg·my** \'bȯrbə,rigmē\ *n, pl* **borboryg·mi** \-'rig,mī\ *also* **borboryg·mies** \-,rigmēz\ [*borborygmus*, NL, fr. Gk *borborygmos*, fr. *borboryzein* to rumble, of imit. origin; *borborygmy* fr. Gk *borborygmos* + E *-y*] **:** a rumbling sound made by the movement of gas in the intestine

bord \'bō(ə)rd\ *also* **board** \'bō(ə)rd, 'bȯ-\ *n* -s ['*board*; prob. fr. the former practice of laying boards in mine passageways to form a relatively smooth surface along which the coal was dragged in sledges] **:** a straight road or passageway driven at right angles to the main cleavage of the coal in a coal mine

bor·dage \'bȯrdij\ *n* -s [OF & MF, fr. OF *borde* hut, cabin + *-age*] **:** the tenure or services of a bordar

bord alexander \,bȯrd, -ō(ə)d+\ *n, usu cap A* [alter. (influenced by the name *Alexander*) of ME *borde alisaundre*, perh. fr. MF *bourde*, a cloth + ME *Alisaundre* Alexander or *Alisaundre* Alexandria] **:** ²ALEXANDER

bord-and-pillar \¦⸗⸗¦⸗⸗\ *adj* **:** of or relating to a system of coal mining in which tunnels are driven in a checkerboard pattern having massive square pillars between them which are gradually cut away as the work proceeds

bor·dar \'bȯrdər\ *n* -s [ML *bordarius*, fr. *borda* hut, cabin (fr. OF *borde*) + L *-arius* -ary] **:** a feudal tenant holding a cottage and usu. a few acres of land at the will of his lord and bound to menial service

¹**bor·deaux** \(')bȯr¦dō, -ō(ə)¦dō\ *n, pl* **bordeaux** \-ō(z)\ *usu cap* [fr. *Bordeaux*, capital of Gironde dept., France] **1 :** a red or white table wine or white dessert wine from vineyards in the Gironde department of France **2** *or* **bordeaux red** *usu cap B* **:** any of several red acid and direct azo dyes; *esp* **:** FAST RED b — see DYE table I (under *Acid Red 17, Direct Red 44*) **3** *or* **bordeaux red** *usu cap B* **:** CLARET 3a **4 :** BORDEAUX MIXTURE

²**bordeaux** \"\ *adj, usu cap* **:** of or from the city of Bordeaux, France **:** of the kind or style prevalent in Bordeaux

bordeaux mixture *n, often cap B* [trans. of F *bouillie bordelaise*] **:** a fungicide made by reaction of copper sulfate, lime, and water

bordeaux turpentine *n, usu cap B* [trans. of F *térébenthine de Bordeaux*] **:** GALIPOT

bor·del \'bȯrdᵊl\ *n* -s [ME, fr. MF, brothel, hut, fr. OF, fr. *borde* hut, cabin, of Gmc origin; akin to OE *bord* board — more at ¹BOARD] *archaic* **:** BROTHEL

bor·de·laise \¦bȯrdᵊl¦āz\ *also* **bordelaise sauce** *n* -s *usu cap B* [F *bordelaise*, fem. of *bordelais* of Bordeaux, fr. *Bordeaux*] **:** a brown sauce flavored with Bordeaux wine

bor·del·lo \bȯr'de(,)lō\ *n* -s [It, fr. OF *bordel*] **:** BROTHEL

¹**bor·der** \'bȯrdər, 'bō(ə)də(r)\ *n* -s *often attrib* [ME *bordure*, fr. MF, fr. OF, fr. *border* to border, fr. *bort* border, ship's side, of Gmc origin; akin to OHG *bort* ship's side — more at BOARD] **1 a :** an outer part or edge **:** the part that parallels the boundary or outline of something **:** MARGIN ⟨at the ~s of the forest is a lake⟩ **b :** a surrounding arrangement (as of material or objects) ⟨a grass plot with a cement ~ running about it⟩ ⟨a roast with a ~ of browned potatoes⟩ **2 a :** a region lying along the edge of a country or territory **:** frontier country ⟨the ~s of the republic are notable for the vast forests there⟩ **b :** a boundary line ⟨travelers crossing the ~ suddenly find themselves in a totally new world⟩ **3 :** a long and usu. narrow bed used for continuous planting; *also* **:** a strip of planted ground or of plants along or around the edge of a garden, bed, or walk ⟨shrub ~s⟩ ⟨a ~ of perennials⟩ **4 a :** an ornamental stripe, print, or other design on or paralleling an edge (as of a fabric, garment, or rug) **b :** a distinctive or functional edging **5 a :** a narrow strip of painted cloth hung above a stage set to conceal the lights and flies **b :** BORDERLIGHT **6 :** a plain or decorative band around or at an edge of printed matter; *also* **:** the type or other material used to produce such a band **7 :** BORDURE 1

syn MARGIN, VERGE, EDGE, RIM, BRIM, BRINK: BORDER indicates either a boundary line or the thin strip just within a boundary line; it may indicate a strip superimposed over an ending or dividing line to emphasize it ⟨the *border* of a flower bed⟩ ⟨the *borders* of the forest⟩ ⟨crossing the *border* between the U.S. and Mexico⟩ ⟨the *border* of a handkerchief⟩ MARGIN may denote a border having definite width and definitely differing in some way from the interior surface ⟨the *margin* of the page⟩ ⟨the nether *margin* of the heath, where it became marshy —Thomas Hardy⟩ VERGE may indicate a very narrow margin area or a boundary line marking an extreme limit; it is more often used figuratively than literally ⟨tethered the horse for half an hour on the *verge* of the road —H.E. Bates⟩ ⟨like two nations which reluctantly accept the fact that a seemingly trivial border incident has brought them to the *verge* of war —Louis Auchincloss⟩ ⟨the entire expedition was on the *verge* of being surrounded and exterminated —John Mason Brown⟩ EDGE indicates a sharply defined terminating line, sometimes between two levels or planes ⟨the *edge* of the precipice⟩ ⟨the *edge* of the shelf⟩ ⟨flat-topped or rolling upland with a steep high *edge* to the west and a long gentle slope to the east —L.D. Stamp⟩ RIM usu. designates a curving or round edge ⟨the *rim* of a wheel⟩ ⟨new *rims* for his glasses⟩ ⟨the *rim* of the canyon⟩ ⟨a *rim* of mountains around the town⟩ BRIM may apply to the upper rim of a vessel or container or whatever else retains a liquid ⟨the *brim* of a goblet⟩ ⟨filling the tub up to the *brim*⟩ ⟨their host predicted that a rain would follow on the heels of the calm and fill the cisterns to the *brim* —Jean Stafford⟩ BRINK may indicate a steep or abrupt edge or brim; it is often figurative ⟨the *brink* of the cliff⟩ ⟨the *brink* of the canyon⟩ ⟨the *brink* of disaster⟩ ⟨the lineaments of that girl on the *brink* of death were those of the woman already dead —Edith Sitwell⟩ ⟨on the *brink* of a horrible danger —Oscar Wilde⟩

²**border** \"\ *vb* **bordered; bordered; bordering** \-d(ə)riŋ\ **borders** [ME *borduren*, fr. *bordure*, n.] *vt* **1 :** to make a border for **:** furnish with a border **:** put a border on ⟨~*ing* the cloth with lace⟩ **2 a :** to form a border or boundary to **:** BOUND ⟨shade trees ~*ing* the streets of the town⟩ **b** *obs* **:** to confine within bounds **:** LIMIT ⟨that nature which contemns its origin cannot be ~*ed* —Shak.⟩ **3 :** to touch upon the border or boundary of **:** be contiguous or adjacent to **:** ADJOIN ⟨an airport ~*s* the city on the south⟩ ~ *vi* **1 :** to lie on the border **:** be in an adjacent position to ⟨Iowa ~*s* on Missouri⟩ **2 :** to come to be closely similar to a specified thing **:** approach closely the nature or character of a specified thing **:** VERGE — usu. used with *on* ⟨training nurses to practice what ~*s* on medicine —Leonard Gross⟩

border collie *n* **:** a medium-sized black or gray farm dog with white and tan markings that is usu. not recognized as a definable breed though the majority of sheep and herd dogs of the English-Scottish borderlands conform to the type

bor·de·reau \¦bȯrdə¦rō\ *n, pl* **bordereaux** \-ō(z)\ [F, fr. MF, fr. *bord* border, fr. OF *bort* — more at BORDER] **1 :** a detailed note or memorandum of account; *esp* **:** one containing an enumeration of documents **2 :** a paper setting forth a description of reinsured risks that is prepared by an original underwriter for the information of the reinsuring company

bordered *adj* **:** having a border: as **a :** having a margin differentiated by its structure or marking — used esp. of a leaf **b :** having a border of a specified tincture — used in heraldry

bordered pit *n* [*bordered*, past part. of ²*border*] **:** a wood-cell pit (as of gymnosperm tracheids) having the secondary cell wall arched over the pit cavity

border effect *n, photog* **:** an adjacency effect characterized by a faint dark line just within the high-density side of the margin lying between a lightly exposed and a heavily exposed area

bor·der·er \'bȯ(r)dərə(r)\ *n* -s [ME, fr. *border, bordure* border + *-er, -ere* -er] **1 :** an inhabitant of a border ⟨valiant ~*s* who built their log huts in the woods —Van Wyck Brooks⟩; *specif* **:** an inhabitant of the border between England and Scotland **2** *archaic* **a :** one that is located nearby **:** NEIGHBOR **b :** one that verges ⟨~*s* on the savage state —William Hazlitt⟩ **3** [²*border* + *-er*] **:** one that makes or applies a border

bordering *n* -s [fr. gerund of ²*border*] **:** something that serves as a border **:** EDGING

border irrigation *n* **:** irrigation controlled or directed by short dikes around areas treated

¹**bor·der·land** \'bȯ(r)də(r),land, -laa(ə)nd\ *n* **1 a :** territory at or near a border **:** FRONTIER ⟨rugged folk of the ~⟩ **b :** an outlying region; *esp* **:** fringe area ⟨living from hand to mouth on the ~ of society⟩ **c :** the farthest point proper to or within the scope of a given state, condition, or field of activity **:** BOUNDARY, LIMITS ⟨going beyond the ~ of science⟩ **2 :** a vague region or condition that lacks precise demarcation **:** TWILIGHT ZONE ⟨the ~ between the area of undisputed rights and that of undisputed wrongs —F.L.Mott⟩

²**borderland** \"\ *adj* **:** BORDERLINE

border leicester *n, usu cap B&L* **:** a strain or variety of the Leicester breed of sheep used in England and Scotland chiefly in the production of superior mutton through crossbreeding esp. with the Cheviot

bor·der·less *adj* **:** being without a border

borderlight \'⸗⸗,⸗\ *n* **:** a long striplight hung above a theater stage for general illumination

border line *n* **:** a line of demarcation **:** a boundary line

borderline \'⸗⸗,⸗\ *adj* **1 :** situated at or near a border line ⟨a ~ town⟩ **2 a :** situated between two points or states **:** INTERMEDIATE ⟨mental ~ states between dream and wakefulness —Józef Wittlin⟩ **b :** verging on one or the other place or state without being definitely assignable to either one **:** MARGINAL ⟨a ~ district that was neither opulent nor impoverished⟩; *esp* **:** not quite average, standard, or normal ⟨a person of ~ intelligence⟩ **c :** not quite meeting or conforming to accepted patterns (as of good taste or morality); *esp* **:** verging on the indecent or obscene ⟨a ~ joke⟩ ⟨a ~ book⟩ **d :** not clearly fixed or convincing **:** subject to challenge or debate **:** DUBIOUS, QUESTIONABLE ⟨in their opinion the new theory is of ~ validity⟩ **e :** manifesting typical but not altogether conclusive characteristics **:** apparently existent but lacking definitive development ⟨a patient with ~ diabetes⟩ ⟨attempting some sort of ~ economy⟩

border pen *n* **:** a drawing pen designed for the drawing of ornamental borders

border ruffian *n, often cap B&R* **:** one of a group of proslavery Missourians during the period from 1854 until the beginning of the Civil War who used to cross the border into Kansas to vote illegally, make raids, and intimidate the antislavery settlers

borders *pl of* BORDER, *pres 3d sing of* BORDER

border state *n* **1** *sometimes cap B&S* **a :** a state (as Delaware, Maryland, Virginia, Kentucky, or Missouri) bordering on an antislavery state and favoring slavery before the Civil War **b :** a state (as Maryland, West Virginia, Kentucky, Missouri, Oklahoma, or Tennessee) just north of the Solid South and traditionally voting Democratic **c :** a state (as Montana or No. Dakota) bordering on Canada **2 :** a small country (as Poland) bordering on a larger more powerful country; *esp* **:** such a country lying between two larger more powerful countries **:** BUFFER STATE

border stone *n* **:** a boundary stone **:** CURBSTONE

border terrier *n, usu cap B & often cap T* **:** a small terrier of a breed originating in the border area between England and Scotland with a harsh and dense coat and close undercoat and colored variously red, grizzle and tan, blue and tan, or wheaten

border warrant *n, usu cap B* **:** a writ of arrest issued on one side of the Scottish border for execution on the other side

bor·det-gen·gou \¦bȯr¦dā¦zhäⁿ¦gü\ *adj, usu cap B&G* [Jules J.B.V. *Bordet* b1870 Belgian bacteriologist and Octave *Gengou* †1957 Belgian bacteriologist] **:** of, relating to, or for use in connection with the Bordet-Gengou bacillus ⟨*Bordet-Gengou* media⟩

bordet-gengou bacillus *n, usu cap 1st B&G* **:** a small ovoid bacillus (*Hemophilus pertussis*) held to cause whooping cough

bordet-gengou test *n, usu cap B&G* **:** COMPLEMENT FIXATION TEST; *specif* **:** WASSERMANN TEST

bordroom \'⸗,⸗\ *n* **:** a space off a bord from which the coal is being or has been mined — compare BORD-AND-PILLAR

bords *pl of* BORD

bordun *var of* BOURDON

bor·dure \'bȯrjər, 'bȯrdyər, bȯr'dü(ə)r, *F* bȯrdüer\ *n* -s [ME, fr. MF — more at BORDER] **1 :** a border about the field often used esp. in Scottish heraldry to difference the arms of a cadet from those of the chief of the family **2 :** BORDER 1; *specif* **:** a border used as a garnish (as around meat, fish, or desserts) ⟨chicken giblets with a ~ of rice⟩

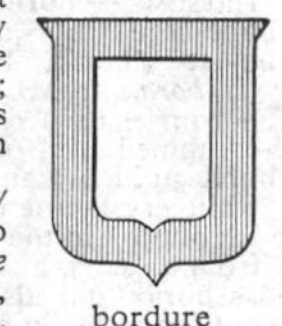

bordure

¹**bore** \'bō(ə)r, 'bȯ(ə)r,'bōə,'bȯ(ə)\ *vb* -ED/-ING/-s [ME *boren*, fr. OE *borian*; akin to OHG *borōn* to bore, ON *bora*, L *forare* to bore, *ferire* to strike, Gk *pharos* plow, Russ *borona* harrow] *vt* **1 :** to pierce esp. by or as if by means of a rotatory tool (as a drill, auger, or gimlet) ⟨*boring* a plank at 5-inch intervals⟩ **:** make a cylindrical opening in or through by removal of material ⟨a tree with its center *bored out*⟩ **:** make a hole in or through **:** PENETRATE **2 a :** to form or construct by boring ⟨a tunnel was *bored* through the mountain⟩ **:** sink (as a mine shaft or a well) by boring **b :** to hollow out evenly **:** enlarge (a roughly formed hole) and finish true to size and center by internal turning against a boring tool **3** *of a horse* **:** to push or thrust aside ⟨the leading racehorse *bored* the closest competitor off course⟩ ~ *vi* **1 a :** to make a hole by boring ⟨insects that ~ into trees⟩ **:** sink a mine shaft, well, or other cylindrical opening by boring ⟨~ for oil⟩ **b :** to become pierced or penetrated by an instrument that cuts as it turns ⟨this timber does not ~ well⟩ **2 a :** to make one's way laboriously ⟨we *bored* through the jostling crowds⟩ **b :** to move ahead steadily **:** push forward with constant irresistible force ⟨in spite of furious antiaircraft fire, waves of planes *bored* in over the city⟩ **3** *of a horse* **:** to thrust the head forward and downward putting weight on the bit **4 :** to stare with a fixed penetrating gaze ⟨his eyes were still *boring* into vacancy —William DuBois⟩ **syn** see PERFORATE — **bore from within :** to undermine something insidiously and treacherously ⟨infiltrating the government and *boring from within*⟩

²**bore** \"\ *n* -s [ME, fr. *boren*, v., and ON *bora* hole made by boring (akin to ON *bora* to bore)] **1 :** a hole made by or as if by boring: as **a** *Scot* **:** CREVICE, CHINK **b** (1) **:** a deep vertical hole (as a mine shaft or well) (2) *Austral* **:** a water hole for cattle **c :** a surface opening or outlet (as of a geyser) **d :** TUNNEL **2 a :** an interior cylindrical opening usu. running the entire or nearly the entire length of an object ⟨the ~ of a thermometer⟩ ⟨the ~ of an artery⟩ **b :** the interior tube of a gun: (1) **:** the interior tube of old muzzle-loading ordnance including cylinder and, if present, chamber and the part connecting cylinder and chamber — see CANNON illustration (2) **:** the interior tube of modern breech-loading ordnance; *esp* **:** that between the muzzle and the forward end of the chamber **3 a :** the size of a hole **b :** the interior diameter of a tube (as of a hypodermic needle or a gun barrel) **:** CALIBER, GAUGE **c :** the diameter of an engine cylinder **4 :** a tool (as an auger) for boring

³**bore** \"\ *past or dial past part of* BEAR

⁴**bore** \"\ *n* -s [fr. (assumed) ME *bore* wave, fr. ON *bāra*; prob. akin to OE *beran* to carry — more at BEAR] **:** a tidal flood that regularly or occas. rushes with a roaring noise into certain rivers (as the Amazon in So. America) or narrow bays (as the Bay of Fundy) of peculiar configuration or location and proceeds in one or more waves that often present a very abrupt front of considerable height dangerous to shipping

⁵**bore** *vt* -ED/-ING/-s [perh. alter. of obs. *bourd* to make a fool of, jest with, jest, fr. ME *bourden* to jest, fr. MF *bourder, border*, fr. OF, fr. *bourde, borde* jest] *obs* **:** to make a fool of **:** TRICK

⁶**bore** *like* ¹BORE\ *n* -s [origin unknown] **:** a cause of ennui: **a :** a dull tiresome annoying person ⟨a loquacious self-centered ~⟩ **b :** something that is monotonous, wearisome, and te-

diously devoid of interest ⟨an evening that turned out to be one long ~⟩
⁷bore \"\ *vt* -ED/-ING/-S : to afflict with ennui : depress, weary, and annoy by dullness : crush with irksome tediousness ⟨*bored* by the same old facts —Marston Bates⟩
bo·re·al \'bōrēəl, 'bȯr-\ *adj* [ME *boriall*, fr. LL *borealis*, fr. L *boreas* north wind, *Boreas*, Greek god of the north wind + *-alis* -al] **1** : of, relating to, or located in northern regions **2** : NORTHERN: as **a** *usu cap* : of, relating to, or constituting a terrestrial biogeographic division comprising the northern and mountainous parts of the northern hemisphere in which mean temperature during the six hottest weeks does not exceed 64.4°F and being equivalent to the Holarctic region exclusive of the Sonoran and Transition zones and corresponding Old World areas; *esp* : NEARCTIC **b** *usu cap* : of or relating to a terrestrial biogeographic zone between the Arctic and the Transitional zone and made up of Hudsonian and Canadian zones **c** : of or relating to the northern biotic area characterized by dominance of coniferous forests and tundra **3** : of, relating to, or marked by qualities associated with Boreas : COLD, ICY, FROSTY, WINTRY ⟨~ snows and never-thawing ice —J.A.Hillhouse⟩ **4** : relating to or constituting a period in postglacial times when Europe and No. America had a cooler climate like that of the present Boreal region
bo·re·al·i·za·tion \,ˌ==ələ'zāshən\ *n* -S : adaptation (as of plants) to life in more northerly regions
boreal sign *n* : one of the signs of the zodiac from Aries to Virgo that lie wholly or in part north of the celestial equator
bo·re·as \'bōrēəs, 'bȯr- *also* -ē,as *or* -,aa(ə)s\ *n* -ES [ME, fr. L *boreas* north wind, *Boreas*, Greek god of the north wind, fr. Gk; perh. akin to OSlav *gora* mountain, Skt *giri*] : the north wind or wind north by east
bore bit *n* : a bit for drilling rock
bore·cole \'bōr,kōl, 'bȯr-\ *n* -S [modif. of D *boerenkool*, fr. *boeren-* (fr. *boer* peasant) + *kool* cabbage; akin to OE *cāl* cabbage — more at BOOR, COLE] : KALE
bored *adj* [fr. past part. of ⁷*bore*] : filled with or characterized by boredom ⟨had never been more ~ in her life⟩ ⟨strolled through the gallery with a ~ air⟩
bore·dom \'bōrdəm, 'bȯrd-,'bōəd-,'bȯ(ə)d-\ *n* -S [⁶*bore* + *-dom*] **1** : the state of being bored : ENNUI ⟨jaundiced actors suffering from total ~⟩ **2** : a cause or instance of boredom : BORE ⟨every meal with the family was an unmitigated ~⟩
¹**boree** *n* -S [modif. of F *bourrée* — more at BOURRÉE] *obs* : BOURRÉE
²**bor·ee** \'bōrē\ *n* -S [Australian (Queensland) *booreah*, lit., fire] *Austral* : any of several wattle trees (as *Acacia pendula* and *A. glaucescens*) — see MYALL
bo·reen \bō'rēn\ *n* -S [IrGael *bóithrín*, dim. of *bóthar* road, fr. OIr, prob. fr. *bó* ox, cow; akin to L *bos* cow — more at COW] *Irish* : a narrow country road or lane esp. in hilly country
bor·e·gat \'bȯrə,gat\ *n* -S [origin unknown] : CALIFORNIA SEA TROUT
borehole \'=,=\ *n* : a hole made by boring; *esp* : WELL
bore·le \'bȯrə,lā\ *n* -S [Tswana *bodile*] : BLACK RHINOCEROS
bore·mat·ic \bōr'mad·ik\ *n* -S [²*bore* + *-matic* (as in *automatic*)] : an automatic machine for boring that uses a single-point tool
bore meal \'=,=\ *n* : the crushed debris brought up by boring (as through rock)
bor·er \'bōrə(r), 'bȯr-\ *n* -S [ME, fr. *boren* to bore + *-er*, *-ere* -er, fr. OE *-ere* — more at ¹BORE, -ER] **1** : one that bores: as **a** : a worker who bores holes **b** : a tool (as a drill) used for boring **2** : any of various animals that burrow in wood or other substances: as **a** : SHIPWORM **b** : any of various bivalve mollusks (as those of the genera *Saxicava* and *Lithophaga*) that bore in limestone rock — compare PIDDOCK **c** : ⁵DRILL 4a **d** : any of numerous insects of different orders (as Lepidoptera and Coleoptera) that as larva or adult bore in the woody parts (as bark, stem or roots) of plants **3** : HAGFISH **4** : ACCRETION BORER
bores *pres 3d sing of*, *pl of* BORE
bore·scope \'bōr,skōp\ *n* -S [²*bore* + *-scope*] : a device usu. consisting of either a prism or a tube with a small mirror at one end and used to inspect a cylindrical cavity (as the bore of a gun or the inside of a hydraulic cylinder)
boresight \'=,=\ *vt* **1** : to bring into proper parallel alignment (the bore and sights of a gun) by sighting on a distant point through the bore and adjusting the sights on that same point **2 a** : to aim at (a target) by sighting through the bore **b** : to aim at (a target) very accurately
bore·some \'bō(ə)rsəm, 'bȯ(ə)rs-,'bōəs-,'bȯ(ə)s-\ *adj* : causing or tending to cause boredom : TEDIOUS, MONOTONOUS, TIRESOME — **bore·some·ly** *adv*
bore·tree \'bōr-,trē\ *var of* BOURTREE
bo·ric \'bōrik, 'bȯr-, -rēk\ *adj* [F *borique*, fr. *bore* boron (fr. *borax*, fr. ML) + *-ique* -ic] : of, relating to, or derived from boron — used esp. of compounds in which this element is combined with oxygen
boric acid *n* : any acid derived from boric oxide: as **a** : a white crystalline toxic weak acid H_3BO_3 that occurs naturally in solution in the fumaroles of Tuscany, that is easily obtained from its salts, and that is used for many of the same purposes as borax and also in electroplating and formerly as a weak antiseptic (as in eyewashes) — called also *boracic acid, orthoboric acid* **b** : METABORIC ACID **c** : TETRABORIC ACID
bor·ick·ite \'bȯrə,kīt *sometimes* 'bȯrzhət,sk-\ *n* -S [Emanuel *Bořický* †1881 Czech petrographer + E *-ite*] : a mineral consisting of a reddish brown compact hydrous basic phosphate of iron and calcium of uncertain composition
boric oxide *also* **boric anhydride** *n* : the trioxide B_2O_3 of boron obtained usu. as a transparent glassy solid by fusing boric acid
bo·ride \'bōr,īd, 'bȯ,rīd, -,rəd\ *n* -S [ISV *bor-* + *-ide*] : a binary compound of boron usu. with a more electropositive element or radical
bo·rine \'bōr,ēn, 'bȯ,rēn, -,rən\ *n* -S [*bor-* + *-ine*] **1** : a borane BH_3 known only in the form of derivatives **2** : a derivative [as trimethyl-borine $(CH_3)_3B$] of borine
¹**boring** *n* -S [ME *boringe*, fr. *boren* to bore + *-inge*, *-ing* -ing, fr. OE *-ung*, *-ing* — more at BORE, -ING] **1** : the action or process of one that bores ⟨a successful ~ for oil⟩ ⟨the ~ of wood by insects⟩ **2 a** : an inner cavity (as of a tube) : BORE ⟨the ~ of a shotgun⟩ **b** : BOREHOLE **3** : the residue (as shavings or chips) left after the process of boring — usu. used in pl.
²**boring** *adj* [fr. pres. part. of ¹*bore*] : that bores : PIERCING ⟨a ~ tool⟩
³**boring** *adj* [fr. pres. part. of ⁷*bore*] : causing boredom : TIRESOME, TEDIOUS ⟨a long ~ wait⟩ — **bor·ing·ly** *adv* — **bor·ing·ness** *n* -ES
boring bar *n* : a cylindrical cutter bar to which a boring tool or cutter is securely attached
boring bit *n* : a steel cutter bit to be supported by a boring bar inside a hole (as the bore of a large gun) in process of enlargement
boring block *n* **1** : a slotted block for holding work to be bored **2** : the cutter holder on a boring rod
boring clam *n* : any of several marine clams that bore into or dissolve away rock, cement, clay, or mud, making chambers in which they live
boring head *n* : the cutting end of a boring tool: as **a** : the cutterhead of a diamond drill **b** : the cutter holder on a boring rod
boring machine *n* : a machine essentially like a drill press but designed primarily for boring holes in wood with an auger bit
boring mill *n* [¹*boring*] : a large machine tool essentially a lathe but commonly with rotating work table, fixed cutting tools, and a vertical axis
boring mussel *n* [²*boring*] : DATE MUSSEL
boring rod *n* : a rod made up of segments carrying at its lower end a tool for earth boring or rock drilling — compare AUGER STEM
boring sponge *n* : any sponge of *Cliona* or related genera that penetrates the substance of shells, some species (as *C. celata*) of the Atlantic coast being injurious to oysters
boring tool *n* : a boring bit with its supporting boring bar and arbor, used to enlarge and accurately finish a large bore previously formed by casting or otherwise
boring tube *n* [¹*boring*] : WELL CASING

bo·rin·que·ño \,bȯriŋ'kān(,)yō\ *n* -S *cap* [Sp, fr. *Borinquén*, *Boriquén*, old name for Puerto Rico, fr. Taino *Boriquen*] **1** : a native or resident of Puerto Rico **2** : one of the extinct aboriginal Indians of Puerto Rico — compare ARAWAK
bor·i·ty \'bȯrəd·ē\ *n* -ES [Swahili *boriti*] *East Africa* : a mangrove pole
¹**born** \'bȯ(ə)rn, -ȯ(ə)n\ *adj* [ME *born*, *yborn*, fr. OE *boren*, *geboren*; akin to OHG *giboran* born, carried, ON *borinn*, Goth *baurans*, *gabaurans*; past part. of the verb represented by OE *beran* to bear, carry — more at BEAR] **1 a** : brought forth by or as if by birth ⟨a newly ~ baby⟩ ⟨a recently ~ idea⟩ **b** : by birth : NATIVE ⟨American-*born*⟩ : having as place of birth ⟨Maine-*born*⟩ **c** : having origin in or from ⟨sea-*born* breezes⟩ ⟨a country-*born* boor⟩ : deriving or resulting from ⟨poverty-*born* crime⟩ **2 a** : having from or as if from birth specified or implied qualities ⟨a ~ leader⟩ or status ⟨a ~ aristocrat⟩ or character or makeup ⟨a ~ criminal⟩ — sometimes used postpositively ⟨though a fisherman ~, he did not want to fish now —Frank Gallagher⟩ **b** : being in specified circumstances from or as if from birth ⟨~ to riches⟩ ⟨nobly ~⟩ **3** : not acquired : NATURAL, INNATE ⟨her ~ dignity⟩ ⟨a ~ respect for old age⟩ **4** : destined from or as if from birth ⟨~ to succeed⟩ **5** *chiefly dial* : existing or elapsed from the time of one's birth — used chiefly in the phrase *born days* ⟨I never saw anything like it in all my ~ days⟩
²**born** \"\ *vt* **borned** *or* **born**; **borned** *or* **born**; **borning**; **borns** **1** *dial* : to give birth to : BEAR ⟨look at what'll ~ *ed*, and thinking no harm at the time —Maristan Chapman⟩ **2** *dial* : to assist at the birth of : DELIVER ⟨I seen him ~ twin calves from a cow —Helen Eustis⟩
bor·na disease \'bȯrnə-\ *n*, *usu cap B* [trans. of G *bornasche krankheit*, fr. *Borna*, Saxony, Germany, where the disease was esp. prevalent in the 1890s] : a virus disease of equines related to sleeping sickness that occurs as an acute infectious inflammation of the brain and spinal cord usu. giving rise to violent trembling, unsteady gait, inability to swallow, great excitement and signs of pain, or to stupor
bor·nane \'bȯr,nān\ *n* -S [ISV *born-* (fr. *borneol*) + *-ane*] : a crystalline saturated terpene $C_{10}H_{18}$ that may be regarded as the parent compound of borneol, camphor, and related compounds; 1,7,7-trimethyl-norbornane — called also *camphane*
¹**borne** *past part of* BEAR
²**bor·né** \(')bȯr¦nā\ *adj* [F, past part. of *borner* to limit, fr. OF *borner*, *bonner* to delimit, fr. *borne*, *bonne* limit, boundary — more at BOUND] : LIMITED : lacking scope, depth, or variety esp. in breadth of vision or variety of interests : NARROW-MINDED, HIDEBOUND, PROVINCIAL ⟨his slow methodical ~ mind —Walter Bagehot⟩
¹**bor·ne·an** \'bȯ(r)nēən\ *adj*, *usu cap* [*Borneo*, island in the Malay archipelago + E *-an*] **1** : of, relating to, or characteristic of the island of Borneo **2** : of, relating to, or characteristic of the people of Borneo
²**bornean** \"\ *n* -S *cap* : a native or inhabitant of Borneo
bor·née \(')bȯr¦nā\ *adj* [F, fem. of *borné*] *of a woman* : BORNÉ ⟨a rather ordinary girl, ~, perhaps stupid —E.R.Bentley⟩
bor·neo camphor \'bȯ(r)nē,ō-\ *n*, *usu cap B* : a camphor that occurs in masses in a tree (*Dryobalanops aromatica*) of the family Dipterocarpaceae and is used as an incense and in embalming; dextrorotatory borneol — called also *Malay camphor, Sumatra camphor*
bor·ne·ol \-ē,ȯl, -ōl\ *n* -S [*Borneo* + ISV *-ol*] : a crystalline cyclic terpenoid alcohol $C_{10}H_{17}OH$ known in three optically different forms distinguished as dextrorotatory borneol, levorotatory borneol, and racemic borneol, found in many essential oils (as pine oils), formed by reduction of camphor, and used chiefly in the form of esters (as the acetate) in perfumery — called also *bornyl alcohol*; *see* ISOBORNEOL
borneo tallow *n*, *usu cap B* : a hard brittle greenish fat obtained esp. from nuts of trees of the genus *Shorea* growing in the Malay archipelago and used as a substitute for cocoa butter
born·holm disease \'bȯrn,hō(l)m-\ *n*, *usu cap B* [*Bornholm*, Danish island in the Baltic sea, where it has been observed] : EPIDEMIC PLEURODYNIA
borning *n* -S [fr. gerund of ²*born*] *dial* : BIRTH 1
born·ite \'bȯr,nīt, *usu* -īd·+V\ *n* -S [G *bornit*, fr. Ignaz von *Born* †1791 Austrian mineralogist + G *-it* -ite] : a valuable brittle metallic-looking sulfide of copper and iron Cu_5FeS_4 usu. brownish on fresh fracture (hardness 3, sp. gr. 4.9-5.4) — called also *erubescite, horseflesh ore, purple copper ore* — **born·it·ic** \(')bȯr¦nid·ik\ *adj*
bor·nyl \'bȯrnᵊl, -,nil, -,nēl\ *n* -S [ISV *born-* (fr. *borneol*) + *-yl*] : a univalent radical $C_{10}H_{17}$ derived from borneol by removal of hydroxyl — called in full *2-bornyl*
bornyl alcohol *n* : BORNEOL
boro- — see BOR-
¹**bo·ro** \'bōr(,)ō\ *n* -S [Hindi, fr. Skt *vorava*] *India* : rice harvested in spring
²**boro** \"\ *or* **bo·ra** \'bōrə\ *n*, *pl* **boro** *or* **boros** *or* **bora** *or* **boras** *usu cap* [Sp, of AmerInd origin] **1 a** : a Witotoan people of southeastern Colombia, northeastern Peru, and adjacent areas in Brazil **b** : a member of such people **2** : the language of the Boro people
bo·ro·fluoric acid \¦bōrō, ¦bȯ+...-\ *n* [ISV *bor-* + *fluoric*] : FLUOBORIC ACID
bo·ro·fluoride \"+\ *n* [ISV *bor-* + *fluoride*] : FLUOBORATE
bo·ro·glyceride \"+\ *n* [*bor-* + *glyceride*] : a compound of boric acid and glycerol formerly used as an antiseptic
bo·ro·hydride \"+\ *n* [*bor-* + *hydride*] : any of a class of compounds containing the anion BH_4— (as sodium borohydride $NaBH_4$) that are useful reducing agents — called also *hydroborate, tetrahydroborate*
bo·ron \'bōr,än, 'bȯ,rän\ *n* -S [*borax* + *-on* (as in *carbon*)] : a high-melting trivalent metalloid element that is known both in an extremely hard shiny black crystalline form and in the form of a greenish yellow or brown amorphous powder, that occurs in nature only in combination (as in borax and boric acid and as a trace element in plants and animals), that is usu. obtained by electrolysis of fused potassium fluoborate and potassium chloride or by thermal reduction of other compounds (as boric oxide), and that is used chiefly in metallurgy (as for increasing the hardenability of steel) and in nucleonics because of its high absorption of neutrons — symbol *B*; see ELEMENT table
bo·ro·na·tro·cal·cite \¦bōrō¦nā·trō'kal,sīt\ *n* -S [G *boronatrokalzit*, fr. *bor-* + *natro-* natr- + *kalz-* calc- + *-it* -ite] : ULEXITE
boron carbide *n* : any binary compound of boron and carbon; *esp* : a refractory shiny black crystalline solid B_4C ranking next to the diamond in hardness made usu. by heating boric oxide and coke in an electric furnace and used chiefly as powdered and molded abrasives
bo·ro·nia \bə'rōnēə\ *n* [NL, fr. Francesco *Borone* 18th cent. Ital. servant + NL *-ia*] **1** *cap* : a large genus of Australian aromatic shrubs (family Rutaceae) with highly scented red, purple, or white flowers **2** -S : a plant of the genus *Boronia*
bo·ron·ic \(')bō¦ränik, (')bȯ¦rä-, bə'rä-\ *adj* : of or relating to boron
boron nitride *n* : any binary compound of boron and nitrogen; *esp* : a fluffy white crystalline powder BN made in various ways (as by the reaction of ammonia and fused boric oxide) and used chiefly as a lubricant and electric insulator
boron trifluoride *n* : a colorless pungent gas BF_3 that fumes in moist air, that is made usu. by reaction of a boron compound (as borax) with a fluoride (as hydrogen fluoride) and then sulfuric acid, and that is used chiefly as an acidic catalyst in organic reactions (as alkylations and polymerizations)
bo·ro·ro \¦bōrə¦rō\ *n*, *pl* **bororo** *or* **bororos** *usu cap* [Pg *Bororó*, of AmerInd origin] **1 a** : a people of southern Brazil **b** : a member of such people **2** : the language of the Bororo people constituting the Bororoan language family of the Bororo-tuke stock — called also *Coroado* — **bo·ro·ro·an** \-ən\ *adj*, *usu cap*
bo·ro·silicate \¦bōrō, ¦bȯ-+\ *n* [ISV *bor-* + *silicate*] : a silicate (as datolite) containing boron in the anion
borosilicate glass *n* : a silicate glass having at least 5 percent of boric oxide and used esp. in heat-resistant glassware
bo·ro·tu·ke \¦bōr,ōd·ə¦kā\ *n*, *usu cap* [blend of *Bororo* and *Otuke*] : a language stock of Brazil and Paraguay comprising the Bororo and Otuke
bo·ro·tungstic acid \¦bōrō, ¦bȯ-+...-\ *n* [ISV *bor* + *tungstic*]

: any of several complex acids of boron and tungsten (as a colorless crystalline acid $H_5BW_{12}O_{40}{\cdot}xH_2O$) — called also *tungstoboric acid*
bor·ough \'bər·(,)ō, 'bər·ə, 'bə·(,)rō, 'bə·rə, *often* -r·əw *or* -·rəw+V\ *n* -S [ME *burgh*, *burwe*, *borugh*, fr. OE *burg*, *burh* fortified town, fortress; akin to OHG *burg* fortified place, ON *borg* wall, fortification, Goth *baurgs* city, MIr *brí* hill, Av *bərəz-* high, OE *beorg* mountain, hill, mound — more at BARROW] **1 a** : a medieval fortified group of houses (as in Great Britain) forming a town with special duties and privileges, having in its later form its own courts, the right of burgherhood inheritable, representatives in the national council or parliament, and holding a charter from the king **b** : a town or urban constituency in Great Britain that sends a member or members to Parliament; *also* : an organized part of such a constituency sharing in the election of a member **c** : an urban area in Great Britain incorporated for purposes of self-government — see ¹COUNTY 3c, METROPOLITAN BOROUGH, MUNICIPAL BOROUGH **d** : an incorporated town in Scotland : BURGH; *specif* : one returning or contributing to return a member to Parliament **2 a** : a municipal corporation proper in some states (as Connecticut, Pennsylvania, New Jersey, and Minnesota) corresponding in general to the incorporated town or village of the other states **b** : one of the five constituent political divisions of New York City **3** : a village, township, or town in New Zealand having a special governing body **4 a** : a town area in New So. Wales in Australia as incorporated by an act of Parliament of 1857 or holding a special charter from the crown — compare MUNICIPALITY, SHIRE **b** : a municipal area in Australia of a minimum size and population
borough-english \¦==¦==\ *n*, *usu cap E* [earlier *burghenglish*, part trans. of AF *burgh engloys*, fr. *burgh* borough (fr. ME) + *engloys* English] : a former custom in some cities and boroughs in Great Britain by which estates descended to the youngest son or sometimes to the youngest daughter or collateral heir
borough-holder \'==,==\ *n* **1** : one holding property by burgage in certain Yorkshire boroughs in England **2** : BORSHOLDER
boroughmonger \'==,==\ *n*, *archaic* : one who buys or sells the parliamentary seats of boroughs in England
boroughreeve \'==,=\ *n* : the chief municipal officer in certain unincorporated English municipalities before 1835
bor·ra·cha \bə'räshə\ *n* -S [Pg, lit., leather wine bottle, prob. fr. Sp, fr. *borracho* intoxicated — more at BORACHIO] **1** : any of several grades of crude Para rubber **2** : any of several Brazilian latex-producing trees; *also* : their coagulated gum (as balata, Ceará rubber, mangabeira rubber, sorva)
borrasca *var of* BORASCA
borrel *adj* [ME *borel*, *burel*, fr. *borel*, *burel* coarse woolen cloth, fr. OF *burel* — more at BUREAU] **1** *obs* : belonging to the laity **2** *archaic* : UNLETTERED, UNPOLISHED ⟨a coarse, ignorant, ~ man —Sir Walter Scott⟩
bor·rel body \bə'rel-, bō'-\ *n*, *usu cap 1st B* [after Amédée *Borrel* †1936 Fr. bacteriologist] : one of the particles included in a Bollinger body, believed to be actual units of the virus of fowl pox
bor·rel·ia \bə'relēə, -rēl-, -lyə\ *n* [NL, fr. Amédée Borrel + NL *-ia*] **1** *cap* : a genus of small flexible spirochetes (family Treponemataceae) parasitic upon man and warm-blooded animals, having three to five large wavy spirals and a terminal filament, and including several important pathogens (as *B. anserina*, the cause of septicemia in chickens, *B. recurrentis*, the cause of European relapsing fever, and *B. duttoni*, the cause of the relapsing fever of Africa) **2** -S : a spirochete of the genus *Borrelia*
bor·rel·o·my·ce·ta·ce·ae \bə¦relō,mīsə'tāsē,ē, -¦rēl-\ *n pl*, *cap* [NL, fr. Amédée *Borrel* + NL *-o-* + *mycet-* + *-aceae*] *in some classifications* : a group of microorganisms coextensive with Mycoplasmataceae
bor·rel's blue \bə'relz-, bō'-\ *n*, *usu cap 1st B* [after Amédée *Borrel*] : a stain made by adding methylene blue to silver oxide and used in parasitology
bor·re·ria \bə'rirēə\ *n*, *cap* [NL, fr. William *Borrer* †1862 Eng. botanist + NL *-ia*] : a genus of herbs or shrubs (family Rubiaceae) found in warm or tropical regions with opposite entire leaves and small funnel-shaped flowers
bor·rich·ia \bə'rikēə\ *n*, *cap* [NL, fr. Olaus *Borrichius* †1690 Dan. medical writer + NL *-ia*] : a small genus of low shrubby American herbs (family Compositae) having coriaceous or fleshy opposite leaves and solitary heads of yellow flowers with blackish anthers
¹**bor·row** \'bä(,)rō, -,rə *also* 'bȯ-; *often* -,rəw+V; *chiefly in substand speech* -,rē *or* -,ri\ *vb* -ED/-ING/-S [ME *borwen*, fr. OE *borgian*; akin to OHG *borgēn* to take heed, give security, ON *borga* to go bail, OE *beorgan* to preserve, defend — more at BURY] *vt* **1** : to receive temporarily from another, implying or expressing the intention either of returning the thing received or of giving its equivalent to the lender : obtain the temporary use of ⟨he returned the pen that he had ~*ed* from her⟩; *specif* : to receive (a book, magazine, or other circulating material) from a lending library for temporary use outside the library premises ⟨these books may be ~*ed* for two weeks⟩ **2 a** : to appropriate (something not capable of being returned) for one's own esp. immediate or temporary use ⟨the speaker ~*ed* a metaphor from Shakespeare⟩ ⟨the books from which he has ~*ed* his opinions —G.B.Shaw⟩ **b** : to derive (as authority) from another : have by a right that is not inherent ⟨~*ing* prestige from the ability of his predecessor⟩ **c** : to derive from an alien source, somewhat radically adapting and modifying the thing so obtained ⟨voodoo practices are frequently blended with rituals ~*ed* from established Christian denominations —*Amer. Guide Series: La.*⟩ **3** *obs* : to be surety for : set free by or as if by ransom ⟨if thou be taken prisoner . . . I will not ~ thee —John Palsgrave⟩ **4** : to take (one) from a digit of the minuend in arithmetical subtraction in order to add as 10 to the digit holding the next lower place when the latter digit is less than the corresponding one of the subtrahend when subtraction is performed ⟨~ 1 from 4 in the number 42 to add as 10 to the 2 in order to carry out the subtraction 42 minus 25 equals 17⟩ **5** : to introduce (as a word) into one language from another ⟨English *kindergarten* was ~*ed* from German⟩ — see LOANWORD **6** : to remove (fill) from a borrow pit ⟨~*ing* earth to make a fill⟩ **7** *dial* : LEND ⟨~ me your pencil⟩ **8** : to bring in (organ pipes) from a stop in another division ~ *vi* **1** : to receive, appropriate, or derive something (as by way of a loan) from another ⟨a mixed people freely ~*ing* from others in religion, language, laws, and manners —M.R. Cohen⟩ **2** : to make a stop or part of a stop in one division of a pipe organ available in another division **3** : to putt to the left or right of the cup in golf so as to allow for the slant or roll of the green — **borrow trouble** : to take upon oneself needless trouble or anxiety ⟨if you just stick to your own job you won't be *borrowing trouble*⟩
²**borrow** *n* -S [ME *borwe*, fr. OE *borg*, *borh*, prob. back-formation fr. *borgian*] **1** *obs* : something deposited as security : PLEDGE **2** *obs* **a** : SURETY **b** : HOSTAGE
³**borrow** *like* ¹BORROW\ *n* -S [¹*borrow*] **1** *archaic* **a** : the act of borrowing **b** : something borrowed **2** : material (as earth or gravel) taken from one location (as a borrow pit) to be used for fill at another location
borrow ditch *n* : a ditch dug along a roadway to furnish fill and provide drainage
borrowed light *n* : reflected light; *specif* : light entering an interior and otherwise dark room or passage from an adjoining space having windows or skylights
borrowed time *n* : an unexpected or artificially contrived extension of time usu. of uncertain and limited duration ⟨an old, old man who was merely living on *borrowed time*⟩
bor·row·er \-,rəwə(r)\ *n* -S [ME *borwere*, fr. *borwen* to borrow + *-ere* -er] : one that borrows ⟨neither a ~ nor a lender be —Shak.⟩
borrowing *n* -S [fr. gerund of ¹*borrow*] **1 a** : the act of one that borrows **b** : something borrowed; *esp* : a word or phrase adopted from one language into another ⟨English is full of foreign-language ~*s*⟩ **2 a** : adoption (as of a custom) from a neighboring people ⟨extensive Indian ~ of material culture —E.H.Spicer⟩ **b** : something (as a custom) adopted from a neighboring people ⟨cultural ~*s* from Italy —R.W.Murray⟩
borrowing days *n pl*, *Scot* : the last three days of March, Old Style

borrow pit *n* **:** an excavated area where material (as earth) has been borrowed to be used as fill at another location
bors *pl of* BOR
borsch *or* **borscht** *or* **borsht** *or* **bortsch** *or* **borshch** \'bȯ(ə)rsh(t) *sometimes* -rshch *or* -rch\ *n, pl* **borsches** *or* **borschts** *or* **borshts** *or* **bortsches** *or* **borshches** [Russ *borshch* cow parsnip (*Heracleum sphondylium*), borsch; fr. the soup's being originally made of cow parsnips; akin to Pol *barszcz* cow parsnip, borsch, Latvian *burkšis* cow parsnip, Skt *bhṛṣṭi* spike, point, OHG *burst* bristle — more at BRISTLE] **:** a soup having fermented or fresh red beet juice as the foundation, sour cream or sour milk often being added when the soup is served
borsch circuit *or* **borscht circuit** *n* **:** the summer theaters and nightclubs associated with the Jewish summer camps and resort hotels of the Catskills
bors·hold·er \'bȯ(r)s,hōldə(r), 'bȯ(r),sō-\ *n* -s [by folk etymology (influence of *holder*) fr. earlier *borsolder*, fr. (assumed) ME *borwes alder, borghes alder* (whence AF *borghesaldre*), fr. (assumed) ME *borwes, borghes* of a tithing (fr. ME *borwes, borghes,* of a pledge, gen. of *borwe, borgh* pledge) + ME *alder* leader, chief, fr. OE *aldor, ealdor* chief, parent, head of a family — more at BORROW, ALDERMAN] **1 :** the head person of a tithing **2 :** a parish officer in Great Britain corresponding to the petty constable
¹bor·stal *or* **bor·stall** \'bərst°l, 'bȯr-\ *n* -s [fr. (assumed) ME *borstall*, fr. OE *borgsteall, borhsteall*, fr. (assumed) OE *borg, borh* protection, refuge (fr. OE *borg, borh* pledge, surety) + OE *steall* place; prob. fr. the use of steep hills as places of refuge in war — more at BORROW, STALL] *dial Eng* **:** a pathway up a steep hill
²borstal \'bȯrst°l, 'bȯ(ə)s-\ *or* **borstal institution** *n* -s *often cap B* [fr. *Borstal*, village in Kent, England] **:** one of a group of British reform schools for delinquents between the ages of 16 and 23 that follows a system stressing occupational training, special attention to the individual, and highly organized supervision after dismissal
bort \'bȯ(ə)rt\ *n* -s [prob. fr. D *boort*, perh. fr. MF *bourt* bastard, fr. L *burdus* hinny] **1** *also* **boart** *or* **boort** \'bō(ə)rt, 'bȯ(-\ **:** a diamond of inferior quality **:** a diamond not of gem quality; *collectively* **:** material consisting of imperfectly crystallized diamonds or of fragments produced in cutting diamonds used for dressing and truing grinding wheels and in making abrasive diamond powder — called also *bortz* **2 :** ³CARBONADO
bortz \'bȯ(ə)rts\ *n* -ES [alter. of *borts*, pl. of *bort*] **:** BORT 1
bo·ru·ca \bə'rükə\ *n, pl* **boruca** *or* **borucas** *usu cap* [Sp, of AmerInd origin] **1 :** a Chibchan people on the Pacific coast in southeastern Costa Rica in Central America **2 :** a member of the Boruca people
bo·run \bō'rün\ *n* -s *usu cap* [native name] **:** BOTOCUDO
bo·run·duk \'bȯrən,dük\ *n* -s [Russ *burunduk*] **:** BARONDUKI
bo·rus·sian \bō'rəshən, -rəshən\ *n or adj, usu cap* [NL *Borussia* Prussia, historical region at the eastern end of the south shore of the Baltic sea + E -*an*] **:** PRUSSIAN
bor·zi·cactus \,bȯrzə+\ *n, cap* [NL, fr. Antonio *Borzi* Ital. botanist + NL *Cactus*] **:** a small genus of cylindrical cacti found in the Andes with well-marked ribs, stout spines, and orange or scarlet flowers
bor·zoi \'bȯr,zȯi *also* ='=\ *n* [Russ *borzoĭ*, fr. *borzoĭ* swift; akin to OSlav *brŭzŭ* swift, Pol *bardzo* very, Lith *burzdùs* agile, L *festinare* to make haste] **1** *usu cap* **:** a breed of tall slender long-haired dogs of greyhound type developed in Russia esp. for pursuing wolves **2** -s *often cap* **:** a dog of the Borzoi breed — called also *Russian wolfhound*
¹bos \'bäs, 'bōs,\ *n, cap* [NL, fr. L, ox, cow — more at COW] **:** a genus of ruminant mammals including the wild and domestic cattle and sometimes the water buffaloes and related forms, distinguished by a stout body and by hollow curved horns standing out laterally from the skull
²bos *pl of* BO
bo·sa *also* **bo·za** \'bōzə\ *or* **boo·za** *or* **bou·za** \'büzə\ *n* -s [Turk *boza*] **:** a drink of the Egyptians and Arabs resembling beer; *esp* **:** an acidulated fermented drink made from millet
bo·sal \bō'sal\ *n* -s [MexSp, fr. Sp, muzzle, bells on a halter, fr. *bozo* mouth, nose of a horse, halter, fr. L *bucca* mouth, cheek — more at POCK] *Southwest* **:** NOSEBAND
bos·cage *also* **bos·kage** \'bäskij\ *n* -s [ME *boskage*, fr. MF *boscage*, fr. OF, fr. *bosc, bois* forest (perh. of Gmc origin; akin to OHG *busc* forest) + -*age* — more at BUSH] **:** a growth of trees or shrubs **:** GROVE, THICKET, UNDERWOOD
bosch·bok *also* **bosh·bok** \'bäs(h),bäk\ *n* -s [obs. Afrik *boschbok* (now *bosbok*), fr. *bosch* (now *bos*) forest (fr. MD *bosch, busch* — akin to OHG *busc*) + *bok* male antelope, he-goat, fr. MD *boc;* akin to OHG *boc* he-goat — more at BUCK] **:** BUSHBUCK
bosche *usu cap, var of* BOCHE
bosch·vark *or* **bosh·vark** \'bäs(h),värk\ *n* -s [obs. Afrik *boschvark* (now *bosvark*), fr. *bosch* (now *bos*) + *vark* pig, fr. MD *varken;* akin to OHG *farh* little pig — more at FARROW] **:** a southern African bushpig
bosch·veld \'bäs(h),felt\ *n* -s [obs. Afrik (now *bosveld*), fr. *bosch* (now *bos*) + *veld* field, fr. MD *velt;* akin to OHG *feld* field — more at FIELD] **:** BUSHVELD
bose \'bōs\ *vt* -ED/-ING/-s [prob. fr. E dial. *boss* to bang] *archeol* **:** to test (ground) by noting the sound of percussion from the blow of a heavy rammer
bose-ein·stein statistics \'bō'sīnz,|tīn-, -īn,s| *sometimes* -īn,sh|\ *also* **bose statistics** \'bōs-\ *n pl but sing or pl in constr, usu cap B&E* [after Satyendra Nath *Bose* b1894 Indian physicist and Albert *Einstein* †1955 Am. physicist born in Germany] **:** quantum-mechanical statistics according to which subatomic particles of a given class (as photons and pi-mesons) have a quantum-mechanical symmetry that in cases of thermal equilibrium tends to cause an accumulation of many particles of the same kind in each of the possible low-energy quantum-mechanical states — called also *Einstein-Bose statistics;* compare FERMI-DIRAC STATISTICS
bo·sel·a·phus \bō'seləfəs\ *n, cap* [NL, fr. L *bos* ox, cow + Gk *elaphos* deer — more at ELK] **:** a genus of Asiatic antelopes including only the nilgai
bo·sey \'bōzē, -zi\ *n* -s [irreg. fr. B. J. T. *Bosanquet* †1936 Eng. cricketer + E -*y*] *chiefly Austral* **:** GOOGLY
¹bosh \'bäsh\ *n* -ES [perh. fr. G dial. *bosch* grass-covered slope; akin to OHG *busc*] **1 :** the lower sloping part of a blast furnace where the diameter increases to a maximum above the tuyeres **2 :** a trough used in forging and smelting in which tools and ingots are cooled **3 :** a tank of boiling soda water in which metal parts are washed
²bosh \"\ *n* -ES [Turk *boş* empty, useless] **1 :** absurd or empty talk, actions, ideas, or opinions **:** pretentious nonsense **:** SILLINESS ⟨what he would say would be utter ~ —Joseph Conrad⟩ ⟨all the trappings and ~ which goes to make up the autarchic state —*Times Lit. Supp.*⟩ — often used interjectionally to express disapproval or disbelief **2 :** something worthless or trifling ⟨~ consisting of corny short stories, on the gangster or Western pattern —J.B.Priestley⟩
bo·shas \bō'shäs\ *n, pl* **boshas** \-äz\ *usu cap* **1 :** a Gypsy people of the Caucasus living among the Armenians **2 :** a member of the Boshas
bosh·er \'bäshə(r)\ *n* -s **:** a worker who transfers metal sheets to a bosh
bos·jes·man \'bäshəsmən, 'bōsh-, -shəzm-\ *n, pl* **bosjes·men** \-mən\ *usu cap* [obs. Afrik *Bossiesman* (now *Boesman*), fr. Afrik *bossies-* (fr. *bossie* bush, shrub, dim. of *bos* bush, forest, fr. MD *bosch, busch*) + *man*, fr. MD; akin to OHG *man* — more at MAN] **:** BUSHMAN 1
bosk *or* **bosque** \'bäsk\ *n* -s [prob. back-formation fr. *bosky* (wooded)] *archaic* **:** a small woods **:** wooded area
bos·ker \'bäskə(r)\ *or* **bosh·ter** \'bäshtə(r)\ *adj* [origin unknown] *slang Austral* **:** FIRST-RATE, EXCELLENT
bos·ket *or* **bos·quet** \'bäskət\ *n* -s [F *bosquet*, fr. It *boschetto*, dim. of *bosco* forest, perh. of Gmc origin; akin to OHG *busc* forest — more at BUSH] *archaic* **:** THICKET
bos·kop man *or* **boskop race** \'bä,skäp-\ *n, usu cap B* [fr. *Boskop*, locality in the Transvaal, Union of So. Africa, where remains were found] **:** a late Pleistocene southern African man of moderate stature with a dolichocephalic skull, vertical forehead, orthognathous face, and large brain, this form being orig. described as a separate species (*Homo capensis*) but now commonly regarded as an early strain of *Homo sapiens*, prob. ancestral to modern Bushmen and Hottentots
bos·kop·oid \'bä,skä,pȯid, -,skə-,-\ *adj, usu cap* **1 :** belonging or related to Boskop man **2 :** resembling Boskop man; *esp* **:** showing skull features similar to those of the skull of Boskop man
¹bosky \'bäskē, -ki\ *adj, usu* -ER/-EST [E dial. *bosk* bush (fr. ME) + E -*y* — more at BUSH] **1 :** marked by an abundant growth of woods, bushes, or thickets ⟨the thousand red roofs of a ~ suburb —V.S.Pritchett⟩ **:** richly verdant **:** WOODED ⟨the still, ~ side of the mountain —Joseph Hergesheimer⟩ **2 :** typical or suggestive of a woods **:** like a forest ⟨cool, ~ shade⟩
²bosky \"\ *adj, usu* -ER/-EST *chiefly Brit* **:** TIPSY, DRUNK
bos·mi·na \bäz'mīnə, -mēnə\ *n, cap* [NL] **:** a genus of water fleas resembling in profile microscopic elephants
bos'n *var of* **bo's'n** *var of* BOATSWAIN
bos·ni·ac *or* **bos·ni·ak** \'bäznē,ak\ *adj or n, usu cap* [prob. modif. (influenced by *Bosnia*) of Serbo-Croatian *bošnjak*, fr. *Bosna* Bosnia, region of central Yugoslavia] **:** BOSNIAN
¹bos·ni·an \'bäznēən\ *adj, usu cap* [*Bosnia* + E -*an*] **1 a :** of, relating to, or characteristic of Bosnia, central Yugoslavia **b :** of, relating to, or characteristic of Bosnians **2 :** of, relating to, or characteristic of the Bosnian language
²bosnian \"\ *n* -s *cap* **1 :** a native or inhabitant of Bosnia in central Yugoslavia, a region predominantly Serbian in language and ethnic affiliation **2 :** the Serbo-Croatian language of the Bosnians
¹bos·om \'bůzəm *also* 'büz-\ *n* -s *often attrib* [ME, fr. OE *bōsm;* akin to OHG *buosam* bosom, Skt *bhūri* abundant — more at BOAST] **1 a :** the fore part of the chest of a human being **:** BREAST **b :** either or both of the breasts; *usu* **:** the female breasts ⟨slipping a quilted housecoat over her broad erect shoulders, pinning it across her ample ~ —Viola G. Liddell⟩ **2 a** *archaic* **:** the breast considered as the center of cherished and secret thoughts **b :** the breast considered as the center of emotions **:** HEART ⟨she has the ability to melt and chill your ~ —Stanley Kauffmann⟩ **c** *obs* **:** DESIRE, WISH ⟨you shall have your ~ on this wretch —Shak.⟩ **d :** a close or intimate relationship usu. marked by affection and protectiveness **:** EMBRACE ⟨for years she lived in the ~ of her family⟩ **:** inner circle ⟨he was accepted into the ~ of the organization⟩ **3 a :** a broad expansive surface ⟨the heaving ~ of the sea —Tom Marvel⟩ **b :** any supporting surface ⟨resting on the ~ of the earth⟩ **c :** an inmost recess **:** intimate center **:** INTERIOR ⟨hiding in the very ~ of the cave⟩ **4 a :** the part of a garment covering the breast; *esp* **:** a distinctive or decorative part of a garment ⟨the pleated ~ of a man's dress shirt⟩ **b :** the space between the breast and the undersurface of whatever garment covers the breast ⟨she seized the letter and thrust it into her ~⟩ **5 a :** the inside of an angle bar **b :** a depression round the eye of a millstone — **in abraham's bosom** *usu cap A* **:** DEAD; *specif* **:** in the realm of the blessed dead
²bosom \"\ *vb* -ED/-ING/-s [ME *bosomen*, fr. *bosom*, n.] *vi* **:** to swell out **:** BELLY ⟨her profuse skirt ~*ed* out with the gusts —Adrian Bell⟩ ~ *vt* **1 :** to put into the bosom ⟨she ~*ed* her letter —E.P.O'Donnell⟩ **2** *archaic* **a :** to take to the bosom **:** EMBRACE **b :** to keep (as a secret) to oneself **c :** to take to heart **:** mull over **3 :** to enclose in or as if in an embrace **:** EMBOSOM ⟨a Gothic, moss-grown structure, half ~*ed* in trees —T.L.Peacock⟩
³bosom \"\ *adj* [¹*bosom*] **:** very intimate or dear ⟨a ~ friend⟩
bos·omed \-md\ *adj* **1 :** kept in the bosom **:** HIDDEN **2 :** having (such) a bosom ⟨full-*bosomed*⟩
bosom-pin \'==,=\ *n* **:** BREASTPIN
bos·omy \-zəmē, -mi\ *adj* **1 :** swelling upward or outward **:** expanding in a curved outline **:** BALLOONING ⟨~ hills⟩ ⟨old ~ trees —Frances G. Patton⟩ **2 a :** having a prominent bosom ⟨a ~ dowager in gray satin —Lewis Mumford⟩; *esp* **:** having prominent and well-developed breasts ⟨a brawny hero and a ~ heroine —P.S.Nathan⟩ **b :** featuring bosomy women ⟨~ photographs⟩ ⟨~ book jackets⟩
bos·on \'bō,sän\ *n* -s [S. N. *Bose* + E -*on* — more at BOSE-EINSTEIN STATISTICS] **:** a particle (as a photon, meson, or alpha particle) having zero spin or an integral number of quantum units of spin and conforming to the Bose-Einstein statistics
bos·po·ran \'bäsp(ə)rən\ *adj, usu cap* [L *bosporanus* of the Bosporus, fr. *Bosporus, Bosphorus* Bosphorus, strait connecting the Sea of Marmara with the Black sea, strait connecting the Sea of Azov with the Black sea (fr. Gk *Bosporos*) + -*anus* -an] **1 :** of or relating to the Bosporus **2 :** of or relating to Kerch strait
bos·po·ran·ic \,bäspə¦ranik\ *or* **bos·po·ri·an** \(')bä¦spōrēən, -pȯr-\ *adj, usu cap* [*bosporanic* fr. L *bosporanus* + E -*ic;* *bosporian* fr. Gk *bosporios* of the Bosporus + E -*an*] **:** BOSPORAN
bos·po·rus \'bäsp(ə)rəs\ *or* **bos·pho·rus** \-sf(-\ *n, pl* **bosporuses** *or* **bosphoruses** \-səz\ *also* **bospo·ri** \-pə,rī\ *or* **bospho·ri** \-fə,rī\ [L *Bosporus, Bosphorus*] **:** a strait or a narrow sea connecting two seas or connecting a lake and a sea
bos·que \'bä(,)skā\ *n* -s [Sp, woods, perh. of Gmc origin; akin to OHG *busc* forest — more at BUSH] *chiefly Southwest* **:** a dense growth of trees and underbrush **:** a clump of trees
²bosque *var of* BOSK
bosquet *var of* BOSKET
¹boss \'bäs, 'bȯs\ *n* -ES [ME *boce*, fr. OF, fr. (assumed) VL *bottia* (whence also It *bozza* boss, swelling, *boccia* bubble, Romanian *boț* lump)] **1 a :** protuberant part **:** a round swelling part or body **:** a knoblike process **:** HUMP ⟨~*es* on the horns of an animal⟩ **b :** a raised ornamentation shaped (as by hammering or carving) from the material of the object it ornaments ⟨a metal plaque with ~*es* along its edges⟩ or made of other material ⟨glittering ~*es* on a leather bridle⟩ **:** an ornamental stud or knob ⟨a beautifully wrought ~ on a shield⟩ **c :** an ornamental projecting block or mass used in architecture (as at the intersection of ribs in Gothic vaulting or at the centers of ceiling panels); *also* **:** a block left in the rough to be carved in position **2 a :** a protuberant and often dome-shaped mass of igneous rock congealed beneath the surface of the earth and laid bare by erosion **b :** a smooth mound or hillock of bedrock usu. bare of soil or vegetation **3 :** a soft pad (as of soft leather, corduroy, or silk) used in ceramics and glassmaking for smoothing or making uniform the oil upon which color is to be dusted (as in decorating porcelain) or for cleaning surfaces (as of gilded work) **4 a :** the enlarged part of a shaft on which a wheel is keyed **b :** a flange at the end of a shaft where it is coupled to another shaft **:** a small projection above the general surface of a part to form a seating or reinforcement for another part **c :** a raised rim around a hole (as about the axle hole in a wheel) **:** a hub esp. of a propeller **d :** a projecting part of a screw-steamer sternpost, enclosing the propeller shaft **e :** the part of a ship's propeller to which the blades are attached **f :** a projection on a forging or casting to facilitate handling or to provide extra metal for a test

boss 1c

²boss \"\ *vt* -ED/-ING/-ES [ME *bocen*, fr. MF *bocer*, fr. OF *bocier*, fr. *boce*, n.] **1 :** to ornament with bosses **:** furnish with bosses **:** EMBOSS ⟨a ~*ed* book cover⟩ **2 :** to treat (as the surface of porcelain) with a boss
³boss \'bäs\ *adj* [origin unknown] *dial Brit* **:** HOLLOW, EMPTY
⁴boss \'bȯs, 'bäs\ *n* -ES [perh. fr. obs. D *bosse* box (now *bus*), fr. LL *buxis* — more at BOX] **:** a wooden vessel for the mortar used in tiling or masonry that is hung by a hook from the laths or from the rounds of a ladder
⁵boss \'bȯs *also* 'bäs\ *n* -ES [D *baas* master, fr. MD *baes;* akin to Fris *baes* master] **1 :** a chief workman or superintendent (as a foreman, director, or manager) **2 :** someone who exercises control or authority; *esp* **:** a top executive **3 a :** a professional politician who controls a large number of votes in a party organization or who unofficially dictates appointments or legislative measures **b :** a top official regarded as having dictatorial authority over an organization that has wide public contacts ⟨a labor ~⟩
⁶boss \"\ *adj* **1 :** being in charge **:** having authority **:** PRINCIPAL, MASTER ⟨a ~ printer⟩ **2** *slang* **:** marked by superiority **:** EXCELLENT, CHAMPION, FIRST-RATE ⟨she's really a ~ cook⟩
⁷boss \"\ *vt* -ED/-ING/-ES **:** to act as chief workman or superintendent of ⟨we need a good man to ~ that job⟩ **:** exercise control or authority over ⟨wasn't going to have her ~*ing* this show —D.H.Lawrence⟩
⁸boss \'bäs\ *n* -ES [perh. fr. D *bos* bundle (as of straw), bush, forest, fr. MD *bosch, busch* bush, forest — more at BUSH] **1** *now dial Brit* **:** a low seat or hassock; *esp* **:** one made of straw **2 :** the straw back of an archery target made by coiling and sewing straw into a compact round mat
⁹boss \'bȯs, 'bäs *sometimes* 'bəs\ *n* -ES [E dial. *buss, boss* young calf] **:** a cow or other bovine animal — used chiefly in calling
boss·age \'bäsij, 'bȯs-\ *n* -s [F, fr. *bosse* boss (fr. OF *boce*) + -*age* — more at ¹BOSS] **:** the bosses in a piece of architecture considered as a feature of the architecture; *also* **:** such bosses left in the rough for carving in position
boss·dom \'bȯsdəm, -stəm *also* 'bäs-\ *n* -s **1 :** the state of being a political boss **2 :** the power or influence of a political boss **:** control of politics by a boss
bosse \(')bä¦sā, 'bäs, 'bȯs\ *n* -s [F *bossé*] **1 :** an African tree (*Guarea cedrata*) having glabrous oblong pointed leaflets and small blue flowers **2 :** the pinkish to reddish brown wood of the bosse tree used esp. for plywood
bossed *adj* [fr. past part. of ²*boss*] **:** having bosses **:** EMBOSSED
bos·se·lat·ed \'bäsə,lād·əd, 'bȯs-\ *adj* [modif. of F *bosselé* (after such pairs as F *élevé* elevated: E *elevated*), fr. OF *bosselé* covered with protuberances, fr. past part. of *boceler* to ornament with bosses, fr. *boce* boss] **:** marked or covered with small bosses ⟨a ~ tumor⟩
bosses *pl of* BOSS, *pres 3d sing of* BOSS
bos·set \'bäsət, 'bȯs-\ *n* -s [F *bossette*, fr. OF *bocete, bocette* small protuberance, fr. *boce* boss + -*ete, -ette* -ette] **:** the rudimentary antler of a young male red deer
boss-eyed \'bȯ¦sīd, 'bä¦-\ *adj* [perh. fr. ¹*boss*] **:** CROSS-EYED
boss·i·ness \'bȯsēnəs *also* 'bäs-\ *n* -ES **:** the quality or state of being bossy
boss·ing \'bäsiŋ, 'bȯs-\ *n* -s [ME *bocinge*, fr. *bocen* to boss + -*inge, -ing* -ing — more at ²BOSS] **:** a boss or a swelling resembling a boss
boss·ism \'bȯs,izəm *also* 'bä,-\ *n* -s **:** the rule, practices, or system of bosses esp. in politics
bos·si work \'bȯsē-, 'bäsē-\ *n, usu cap B* [prob. after *Bossi*, 18th cent. Irish artisan] **:** marble inlay
boss plate \'bäs-, 'bȯs-\ *n* **:** one of the after plates on each side of a single-screw ship, covering the boss for the stern tube
boss-ship \'bȯs(h),ship *also* 'bäs(h)-\ *n* -s **:** rule by a political boss
¹bossy \'bäsē, 'bȯsē, -si\ *adj, usu* -ER/-EST [¹*boss* + -*y*] **1 a :** marked by a swelling or roundness resembling a boss **b** *of a dog* **:** having the shoulder muscles overdeveloped **2 :** marked by bosses **:** STUDDED
²bossy \'bȯsē, 'bäsē, -si *sometimes* 'bəs-\ *n* -ES [E dial. *buss, boss* young calf + E -*y*] **:** a cow or calf
³bossy \'bȯsē, -si *also* 'bäs-\ *adj, usu* -ER/-EST [⁵*boss* + -*y*] **:** inclined to domineer **:** DICTATORIAL ⟨childish braggarts who marry nasal, ~ women —Claudia Cassidy⟩
bos·tan·ji *or* **bos·tan·gi** \bō'stanjē\ *n* -s [Turk *bostancı*, lit., gardener, fr. *bostan* garden, fr. Per *bustān* flower or herb garden, fr. *bō* fragrance + -*stān* place, fr. OPer *stāna;* akin to L *stare* to stand — more at STAND] **:** one of the imperial guards of Turkey whose duties included protecting the palace and its grounds, rowing the sultan's barge, and acting as imperial gardeners
bos·thoon \bäs'thün\ *n* -s [IrGael *bastūn*, lit., switch of green rushes, fr. AF *bastun* stick, staff, fr. LL *bastum* — more at BASTON] *Irish* **:** BOOR, DOLT
¹bos·ton \'bȯstən *sometimes* 'bäs-, *rap. sometimes* -s°n\ *adj, usu cap* [fr. *Boston*, capital of Massachusetts] **:** of or from Boston, the capital of Massachusetts **:** of the kind or style prevalent in Boston **:** BOSTONIAN
²boston \"\ *n* -s [F, fr. *Boston*, capital of Massachusetts] **1** *usu cap* **:** a variant of whist popular in the late 18th and early 19th centuries in which the players bid for the right to name trumps **2** *often cap* **:** a bid in the game of Boston to win five tricks
³boston \"\ *n* -s *usu cap* [fr. *Boston*, capital of Massachusetts] **1 :** a waltz characterized by a hold of two beats on one foot and an occasional dipping turn **2 :** BOSTON TERRIER
boston bag *n, usu cap 1st B* **:** a traveling bag or general-utility bag that is oblong at the bottom and is tapered or folded in at either end toward a top opening held together by two handles
boston baked beans *n, usu cap 1st B* **:** beans (as navy beans) seasoned with molasses and salt pork and baked for a long time at a low temperature
boston bluefish *n, usu cap 1st B* **:** POLLACK
boston brown bread *n, usu cap 1st B* **:** BROWN BREAD 1c
boston bull *also* **boston bulldog** *or* **boston bull terrier** *n, usu cap 1st B* **:** BOSTON TERRIER
boston butt *n, usu cap 1st B* **:** the upper portion of a pork shoulder containing a small piece of the shoulder blade and characterized by leanness
boston crab *n, usu cap B* **:** a professional wrestling hold in which the aggressor sits on the buttocks of a prone opponent and pulls upward on the opponent's legs
boston cracker *n, usu cap B* **:** a round thick unsalted cracker usu. served split
boston cream pie *n, usu cap B* **:** a round cake that is split and then filled with a custard or cream filling
bos·ton·er \-nə(r)\ *n* -s *cap* **:** BOSTONIAN
¹bos·ton·ese \,bȯstə¦nēz, -ēs *sometimes* 'bäs-; *rap. sometimes* -s°n¦ē-\ *n, pl* **bostonese** *cap* **1 :** BOSTONIAN **2 :** the speech of Boston and the immediately surrounding region marked by certain features (as the use of \ȧ\ for the *a* in *ask*) that set it off sharply from most other speech patterns of the U.S.
²bostonese \"\ *adj, usu cap* **:** BOSTONIAN
boston fern *n, usu cap B* **:** a luxuriant fern (*Nephrolepis exaltata bostoniensis*) often with drooping foliage and much-divided and delicate or crested fronds of which scores of varieties have been produced since it was first cultivated in 1895
¹bos·to·nian \(')bȯ¦stōnēən, -nyən *sometimes* (')bä¦-\ *adj, usu cap* **1 :** of, relating to, or characteristic of Boston, the capital of Massachusetts **2 :** of, relating to, or characteristic of the people of Boston
²bostonian \"\ *n* -s *cap* **:** a native or resident of Boston
boston ivy *n, usu cap B* **:** a woody Chinese and Japanese vine (*Parthenocissus tricuspidata*) with 3-lobed leaves that is commonly used as a wall cover and climber — called also *Japanese ivy*
boston ledger *n, usu cap B* **:** a columnar ledger in which the account names and money columns are vertically arranged to facilitate the horizontal calculation of daily or periodic balances
boston lettuce *n, usu cap B* **:** any of several butterhead lettuces
boston pink *n, usu cap B* **:** SOAPWORT
boston rocker *n, usu cap B* **:** a rocking chair that is a modification of the Windsor chair, having a wooden seat curved up to meet the spindles of the notably high back, the spindles being held at the top by a usu. flat stenciled headrail

Boston rocker

boston rod *n, usu cap B* **:** a light leveling rod
boston round *n, usu cap B* **:** a cylindrical narrow-necked glass bottle of various sizes, its height being about 2¼ times its diameter
boston terrier *n, usu cap B* **:** a dog of a breed of small smooth-coated terriers originating in Massachusetts about 1890 from a crossing of the bulldog and the bullterrier and being brindle or black in color with white markings
boston two-step *n, usu cap B* **:** a slow two-step incorporating a low jump
¹bos·try·chid \'bästrəkəd, -,kid\ *adj* [NL *Bostrychidae*] **:** of or relating to the family Bostrychidae
²bostrychid \"\ *n* -s **:** a beetle of the family Bostrychidae
bos·trych·i·dae \bä'strikə,dē\ *n pl, cap* [NL, fr. *Bostrychus*, type genus (fr. Gk *bostrychos* curl — or, a winged insect) + -*idae*] **:** a family of small cylindrical beetles having a hoodlike

thorax and boring both as larvae and adults in wood, stored products, and lead cables

bos·tryx \'bästriks\ *n, pl* **bostry·ces** \-rə,sēz\ *or* **bostryxes** \-riksəz\ [NL, irreg. fr. Gk *bostrychos* curl; akin to OHG *questa* apron of leaves, OSw *kvaster, koster* tuft, brush, Norw *kvas* small branches when cut off, L *vespices* thick shrubbery, Alb (Gheg) *ghethi* leaf, Skt *guspita* accumulation] **:** a cyme with all the flowers on one side of the rachis usu. causing it to curl — called also *helicoid cyme*

bosun *or* **bo'sun** *var of* BOATSWAIN

bo·sun bird \'bōsᵊn-\ *n* [perh. so called fr. its whistle] **:** TROPIC BIRD

bos·well \'bäz,wel, -,wəl\ *n* -s *usu cap* [after James *Boswell* †1795 Scottish lawyer and biographer; fr. the wealth of first-hand detail in Boswell's life (1791) of Samuel Johnson †1784 Eng. lexicographer, critic, and conversationalist] **1 a :** one who out of admiration or hero worship records in detail and usu. contemporaneously the life, conversation, intimate moods, and personal relationships esp. of a famous or otherwise significant contemporary ⟨a *Boswell* to a man of letters⟩ **b :** one who writes with love for and intimate knowledge of any subject ⟨a *Boswell* of the sea⟩ ⟨nature's *Boswell*⟩ **2 :** one who stays in almost constant attendance upon another out of great admiration or hero worship, often in a voluntarily servile position ⟨a faithful and mistreated *Boswell*⟩

bos·well·ia \bäz'welēə\ *n, cap* [NL, perh. fr. James *Boswell* †1795 + NL *-ia*] **:** an important genus of incense-yielding trees (family Burseraceae) of northern Africa and India having triangular 3-celled fruit with winged seeds — see FRANKINCENSE, SALAI

bos·well·ian \(')bäz¦welēən\ *adj, usu cap* [James *Boswell* †1795 + E *-ian*] **1 :** relating to or characteristic of Boswell **2 :** characteristic of a Boswell or the writings of a Boswell ⟨a *Boswellian* biography⟩

bos·well·ize \'bäzwə,līz\ *vb* -ED/-ING/-S *often cap, vi* **:** to write a biographical account or other study with the method or manner of a Boswell ⟨*boswellizing* for several pages⟩ ~ *vt* **:** to write of in the manner of a Boswell ⟨an author who *boswellized* the American foot soldier⟩

¹bot *also* **bott** \'bät\ *n* -s [perh. modif. of ScGael *boiteag* maggot] **:** the larva of the botfly, esp. of the species infesting the horse

²bot \"\ *n* -s *Austral* **:** a constant borrower **:** CADGER, SPONGER

³bot \"\ *vi* **botted; botted; botting; bots** [²*bot*] *Austral* **:** to borrow with little or no intention of repaying **:** CADGE, SPONGE

⁴bot *n* -s [OE *bōt* — more at ¹BOOT] *obs* **:** COMPENSATION

bot *abbr* **1** botany **2** bottle **3** bottom **4** bought

BOT *abbr* board of trade

bo·tal·lack·ite \bō'talə,kīt\ *n* -s [*Botallack* mine, Saint Just, Cornwall, England + E *-ite*] **:** a rare bluish green basic chloride of copper prob. $Cu_2(OH)_3Cl.H_2O$

¹bo·tan·i·cal \bə'tanəkəl, -nēk- *also* bō'- *or* bä'-\ *also* **bo·tan·ic** \-nik,-nēk\ *adj* [*botanical* fr. *botanic* + *-al; botanic* fr. F *botanique,* fr. Gk *botanikos* of herbs, fr. *botanē* pasture, herb, fr. *boskein* to feed; akin to Lith *gauja* herd and prob. to L *bos* cow — more at COW] **1 a :** of or relating to plants **b :** relating to botany **2 :** composed of, derived from, or employing vegetable remedial substances **3 :** occurring naturally or in cultivation more or less unchanged from the original wild form ⟨a ~ tulip⟩ — compare HORTICULTURAL — **bo·tan·i·cal·ly** \-nək(ə)lē, -nēk-, -li\ *adv*

²botanical \"\ *also* **botanic** \"\ *n* -s **:** a crude vegetable drug consisting of roots, herbs, leaves, bark, or other plant material as distinguished from a refined or prepared vegetable product **:** a botanical drug as opposed to an animal drug or mineral drug

botanical garden *n* **:** a garden often with greenhouses that is used for the culture and study of plants collected and grown for scientific and display purposes

bot·a·nist \'bät(ᵊ)nəst\ *n* -s [fr. *botanical,* after such pairs as E *chemical: chemist*] **:** a specialist in botany or in a branch of botany **:** a professional student of plants

bot·a·nize \-tᵊn,īz\ *vb* -ED/-ING/-S [*botany* + *-ize*] *vi* **:** to collect plants for botanical investigation **:** study plants esp. on a field trip ~ *vt* **:** to explore for botanical purposes

¹bot·a·ny \'bät(ᵊ)nē, -ni\ *n* -ES [fr. *botanical,* after such pairs as E *astronomical: astronomy*] **1 :** the science of plants **:** the branch of biology dealing with plant life **2 a :** plant life (as of a given region) ⟨the ~ of this section⟩ **b :** the properties and life phenomena exhibited by a plant, plant type, or plant group ⟨the ~ of the orchid⟩ **3 :** a botanical treatise or study; *esp* **:** a particular system of botany ⟨carefully analyzing the earliest *botanies*⟩

²botany \"\ *or* **botany wool** *n* -ES [*Botany* Bay, New South Wales, Australia] **:** a fine grade of usu. merino wool for yarns and fabrics and obtained chiefly from Australia

botany bay greens *n pl but sing or pl in constr, usu cap both Bs* [*Botany Bay,* New South Wales, Australia] **:** an Australasian seashore plant (*Atriplex cinerea*) with an almost woody stem and scurfy foliage

botany bay gum *n, usu cap both Bs* **:** yellow acaroid resin

botany bay kino *n, usu cap both Bs* **:** EUCALYPTUS GUM

botany bay oak *n, usu cap both Bs, chiefly Brit* **:** the wood or timber of the she-oak

botany bay olive *n, usu cap both Bs* **:** an Australasian shrub or small tree (*Olea apetala*) with evergreen leaves and red fruits

bo·tau·rus \bō'tórəs\ *n, cap* [NL, modif. (influenced by L *bos* cow and L *taurus* bull) of ME *botor* bittern & OF *butor* bittern; ME *botor* fr. MF *butor,* fr. OF — more at BITTERN, COW, STEER] **:** a genus of birds (family Ardeidae) comprising the typical bitterns

¹botch \'bäch\ *n* -ES [ME *boche,* fr. ONF, fr. (assumed) VL *bottia* protuberance, hump — more at BOSS] **1** *obs* **:** a noninflammatory swelling (as a tumor) **2 a :** an inflammatory sore spot (as a boil or ulcer) **b :** a condition marked by a profusion of boils, ulcers, or other sore spots ⟨the Lord will smite thee with the ~ of Egypt —Deut 28: 27 (AV)⟩

²botch \"\ *vt* -ED/-ING/-ES [ME *bocchen*] **1 :** to repair, mend, or patch usu. in a bungling clumsy inept way ⟨a pair of old trousers that had been ~*ed* up with blue patches⟩ **:** make over, redo, adjust, or alter usu. unskillfully ⟨my best suit had been ~*ed,* and I could no longer wear it⟩ **2 :** to make a mess of through clumsiness, stupidity, or lack of ability **:** foul up hopelessly **:** BUNGLE, SPOIL, RUIN ⟨one of those natural incompetents who ~*es* whatever he puts his hand to —Farley Mowat⟩ **3 :** to assemble, construct, or compose in a makeshift or bungling way ⟨the rest of the report was a patchwork of data ~*ed* together —Dwight Macdonald⟩ ⟨~*ing* up jingles to produce what he fondly thought was a poem⟩

³botch \"\ *n* -ES **1 :** a botched place or part **:** DEFECT, FLAW, BLEMISH ⟨the ~*es* of a poorly constructed building⟩ **2 a :** something that is botched **:** MESS ⟨they made a real ~ of that job⟩ **b :** a bungled piece of work **:** clumsy or careless work ⟨that kind of ~ is worse than no work at all⟩ **c :** a jumbled mixture **:** PATCHWORK, HODGEPODGE, MISHMASH ⟨the script was as often as not a ~ of stolen scenes —Arthur Miller⟩ ⟨a miserable ~ of falsehoods —A.M.Schlesinger b. 1917⟩ **3** *archaic* **:** something used for patching or filling out **:** patching material

botched \'bächt\ *adj* [¹*botch* + *-ed*] **:** afflicted with or as if with boils, ulcers, or other sore spots ⟨the ~ and unfit —H.L. Mencken⟩

¹botch·er \'bächə(r)\ *n* -s [ME *bocchere,* fr. *bocchen* to botch + *-ere, -er* -ed] **:** one that does bungling makeshift work; *esp* **:** an incompetent writer ⟨the unconscionable compromises of the artist with the ~ —F.R.Leavis⟩

²botcher \"\ *n* -s [origin unknown] **:** a young salmon **:** GRILSE

botch·ery \'bäch(ə)rē\ *n* -ES **:** ³BOTCH 2

botchwork \'⸗,⸗\ *n* **:** clumsy or careless work ⟨a clumsy craftsman surrounded by his ~ —Samuel Yellen⟩

¹botchy *adj, usu* -ER/-EST [ME *bochy,* fr. *boche* botch + *-y* — more at ¹BOTCH] *obs* **:** having the character of a boil, ulcer, or similar sore spot

²botchy \'bächē, -chi\ *adj, usu* -ER/-EST [³*botch* + *-y*] **:** full of defects **:** poorly done ⟨a ~ piece of work⟩

bote *dial Brit past of* BITE

bo·te·te \bō'tād·ē\ *n* -s [AmerSp] **:** GLOBEFISH

bot·fly \'bät,flī\ *n* **:** any of various medium to large-sized stout two-winged flies with small mouth opening and vestigial mouthparts usu. constituting a group (Oestroidea) of muscoid flies with segmented larvae that are parasitic in cavities or tissues of various mammals including man — see HORSE BOTFLY, HUMAN BOTFLY, SHEEP BOTFLY

¹both \'bōth\ *adj* [ME *bothe, bathe,* fr. ON *bāthir,* adj. & pron.; akin to OHG *beide, bēde* both; both fr. a prehistoric NGmc-WGmc compound whose first constituent is akin to OE *bēgen, bā, bū* both, Goth *bai, ba,* L *ambo,* Gk *amphō,* Skt *ubhau* both, Gk *amphi* around, and whose second constituent is a demonstrative pronoun or definite article (whence E *the*) — more at BY, THE] **:** being the two **:** involving the one and the other — used prepositively with an unmodified noun ⟨~ planes⟩ or with a noun modified by a demonstrative pronoun ⟨~ these armies⟩ or a possessive ⟨~ his eyes⟩ or other attributive word

²both \"\ *pron* [ME *bothe, bathe,* fr. ON *bāthir,* adj. & pron.] **:** the one and the other **:** the two without excepting either **:** the one as well as the other — used (1) alone ⟨I want ~⟩ or (2) with *of* and a pronoun ⟨~ of us⟩ or noun ⟨~ of the books⟩ though with a noun many prefer instead the adjectival form for formal use ⟨~ books⟩ or (3) appositionally with a pronoun ⟨we were ~ happy⟩ or noun ⟨English and French are ~ widely used⟩

³both \"\ *conj* [ME *bothe, bathe,* fr. *bothe, bathe,* adj.] — used as a function word to indicate and stress the inclusion of each of two or more things specified by coordinated words, phrases, or clauses, its position being usu. before the first element while the last element is usu. preceded by *and* ⟨~ New York and London⟩ ⟨speaking ~ with kindness and with understanding⟩ ⟨they were happy ~ when you arrived and when you left⟩ ⟨~ a musician, an archaeologist, and an anti-Fascist —Cyril Connolly⟩

¹both·er \'bäthə(r)\ *vb* **bothered; bothered; bothering** \'bäth(ə)riŋ\ **bothers** [perh. fr. IrGael *bodhar* deaf, bothered, annoyed, fr. OIr *bodar;* akin to W *byddar* deaf and prob. to Skt *badhira*] *vt* **1 a :** to put into a state of agitation **:** put into a flutter **:** cause to be nervous **:** FLUSTER, EXCITE ⟨just the sight of him ~*ed* her and set her heart beating⟩ **b :** to cause to be undecided, uneasy, or perplexed **:** PUZZLE, MYSTIFY ⟨the complexities of life ~*ed* him⟩ **2 a :** to annoy, anger, or upset esp. by petty provocations **:** VEX, IRRITATE, IRK ⟨he would be . . . excessively ~*ed* with details and complaints —Brian Crozier⟩ **b :** to intrude upon **:** force unwelcome attention or company on **:** PESTER, DISTURB ⟨don't ~ me while I'm taking my nap⟩ ⟨they could hardly walk down the street without being ~*ed*⟩ **c :** to cause to be mildly anxious or concerned **:** WORRY, TROUBLE ⟨rest and recovery from what's been ~*ing* you —Richard Joseph⟩ ⟨without ~*ing* their heads about a lot of newfangled nonsense —Green Peyton⟩ ⟨she didn't ~ herself to lower her voice⟩ **d :** to cause to suffer mild discomfort ⟨the sun did not ~ him —Richard Sale⟩ **:** give trouble to ⟨his stomach's been ~*ing* him⟩ — sometimes used as a mild imprecation or interjection expressing annoyance, disagreement, or impatience ~ *vi* **1 :** to feel mild concern or anxiety ⟨she needed help, but they didn't ~ about that⟩ **:** become concerned or interested ⟨I haven't time to ~ with such things⟩ **:** devote time, energy, or attention **2 :** to take pains **:** take the trouble ⟨don't ~ to lock the door⟩ ⟨he did not even ~ to be polite —Fitzroy Maclean⟩ **3 :** to stir up petty trouble **:** make a fuss **syn** see ANNOY, WORRY

²bother \"\ *n* -s **1 a :** a state of petty discomfort, annoyance, or worry ⟨when scenery gets mixed up with our personal ~*s* all the virtue goes out of it —Edith Wharton⟩ **b :** something that causes petty discomfort, annoyance, or worry **:** TROUBLESOMENESS, VEXATION ⟨she valued his gifts by the ~ they cost him —H.G.Wells⟩ **2 :** unnecessary and vexatious fussing ⟨all the ~ of trying to follow this rule —Evelyn Barkins⟩

both·er·ate \'bäthə,rāt\ *vt* -ED/-ING/-S [fr. *botheration,* after such pairs as E *creation: create*] *chiefly Midland* **:** BOTHER

both·er·a·tion \,bäthə'rāshən\ *n* -s **1 :** the act of bothering or the state of being bothered **2 :** something that bothers ⟨I fear that I have been too much of a ~ already —Hamilton Basso⟩ — often used as a mild imprecation

botherheaded \¦⸗⸗¦⸗⸗\ *adj* **:** MUDDLEHEADED

both·er·ment \'bäthə(r)mənt\ *n* -s **:** BOTHER, BOTHERATION ⟨beefing about the ~*s* which pester those in my spot —James Cagney⟩ — not often in formal use

both·er·some \-(r)səm\ *adj* **:** causing trouble or annoyance

both·i·dae \'bäthə,dē\ *n pl, cap* [NL, fr. *Bothus,* type genus + *-idae*] **:** a widely distributed family of flatfishes (order Heterosomata) having large scales and the eyes on the left side of the body

both·ie \'bäthi, 'bōthi\ *var of* BOTHY

¹both·ni·an \'bäthnēən\ *adj, usu cap* [*Bothnia,* region about the Gulf of Bothnia, northern arm of the Baltic sea + E *-an*] **1 :** of, relating to, or characteristic of Bothnia, a onetime province of Sweden **2 :** of, relating to, or characteristic of the people of Bothnia

²bothnian \"\ *n* -s *cap* **:** a native or inhabitant of Bothnia

both·nic \-nik\ *adj, usu cap* [*Bothnia* + *-ic*] **:** BOTHNIAN

bothr- *or* **bothro-** *comb form* [NL, fr. Gk, fr. *bothros*] **:** trough **:** pit ⟨*bothr*enchyma⟩ — chiefly in generic names ⟨*Bothro*dendron⟩ ⟨*Bothr*ops⟩

bothri- *or* **bothrio-** *comb form* [NL, fr. *bothrium*] **:** bothrium ⟨*bothri*othorax⟩ ⟨*Bothrio*lepis⟩

bo·thrid·i·um \bō'thridēəm\ *n, pl* **bothrid·ia** \-ēə\ *or* **bothridiums** [NL, fr. *bothr-* + *-idium*] **:** one of the outgrowths from the head of tapeworms of the order Tetraphyllidea that act as holdfasts

both·rio·ceph·a·lus \,bäthrēō'sefələs\ *n, cap* [NL, fr. *bothri-* + *-cephalus*] **:** a genus of pseudophyllidean tapeworms with two bothria that is sometimes considered to include the common fish tapeworm of man — see DIPHYLLOBOTHRIUM

both·rio·cid·a·ris \-'sidərəs\ *n, cap* [NL, fr. *bothri-* + *Cidaris*] **:** a genus (coextensive with the family Bothriocidaridae and order Bothriocidaroida) of extinct primitive simple sea urchins that somewhat resemble Cystoidea and are known from the Ordovician of the Russo-Baltic area

both·ri·ol·e·pis \,bäthrē'äləpəs\ *n, cap* [NL, fr. *bothri-* + *-lepis*] **:** a genus of Devonian ostracoderms (family Asterolepidae)

both·ri·um \'bäthrēəm\ *n, pl* **both·ria** \-ēə\ *or* **bothriums** [NL, fr. Gk *bothrion* small pit, dim. of *bothros* pit] **:** a slit, groove, or depression esp. on the holdfast of a pseudophyllidean tapeworm

both·ro·den·dron \,bäthrō'dendrən\ *n, cap* [NL, fr. *bothr-* + *-dendron*] **:** a genus (the type of the family Bothrodendraceae) of Paleozoic plants somewhat resembling present-day club mosses of the genus *Lycopodium* and having characters intermediate between those of the fossil genera *Lepidodendron* and *Sigillaria*

bo·throp·ic \bō'thräpik\ *adj* [NL *Bothrop-, Bothrops* + E *-ic*] **:** of, relating to, or produced by the genus *Bothrops*

bo·throps \'bō'thräps\ *n, cap* [NL, fr. *bothr-* + *-ops*] **:** a genus of venomous pit vipers (family Crotalidae) including the fer-de-lance (*B. atrox*) and palm viper (*B. nigroventris*) of Central and So. America, their hemolytic venom causing the breakdown of blood cells and small blood vessels with consequent interstitial hemorrhage

both·ros \'bäthrəs\ *n, pl* **both·roi** \-,thrói\ *also* **bothroses** [Gk; perh. akin to L *fodere* to dig — more at BED] *archeol* **:** a hole or pit into which drink offerings to the nether gods were poured by the ancient Greeks

bothy \'bäthi, 'bōthi\ *n* -ES [Sc, prob. fr. obs. Sc *both* booth (fr. ME *bothe*) + E *-y* — more at BOOTH] *chiefly Scot* **:** a rude dwelling **:** HUT: as **a :** a shepherd's or hunter's shelter **b :** quarters for unmarried farm laborers

bo·to·cu·do \,bōd·ə'kü(,)dō\ *n, pl* **botocudo** *or* **botocudos** *usu cap* [Pg, fr. *botoque* wooden plug, alter. of *batoque* plug, bunghole, prob. fr. MF *bartoc* plug, bung; fr. the large cylindrical wooden plugs they wear in their ear lobes and lower lips] **1 :** a So. American labret-wearing people (as the Tupian Indians of eastern Brazil) **2 :** a member of a Botocudo people **3 :** the language of the Botocudo people

bo·tog·e·nin \bō'täjənən, ,bōd·ə'jenən\ *n* -s [*boto-* (perh. irreg. fr. Sp *batata* sweet potato) + *-genin* — more at POTATO] **:** a crystalline steroidal sapogenin $C_{27}H_{40}O_4$ obtained from a yam (*Dioscorea mexicana*)

bot·o·née *or* **bot·on·née** \'bätᵊn¦ā\ *or* **bot·on·ny** *or* **bot·to·ny** \'bätᵊnē\ *adj* [MF *botonné,* fr. OF *botoné,* past part. of *botoner* to bud, furnish with buttons, fr. *boton* bud, button — more at BUTTON] *of a cross* **:** having a cluster of three balls or knobs at the end of each arm — see CROSS illustration

bo tree \'bō-\ *n* [Singhalese *bō,* fr. Skt *bodhi* — more at BODHI] **:** PIPAL

botry- *or* **botryo-** *comb form* [Gk, fr. *botrys*] **1 :** bunch of grapes ⟨*botry*ose⟩ **2 :** botryoid ⟨*botryo*lite⟩

bo·trych·i·um \bō'trikēəm\ *n, cap* [NL, fr. Gk *botrychos* stalk of a bunch of grapes (fr. *botrys* bunch of grapes) + NL *-ium;* fr. the grapelike cluster of sporangia] **:** a small widely distributed genus of low fleshy ferns (family Ophioglossaceae) comprising the grape ferns and having a lobed or compound sterile leaf and sporophyll bearing distinct sporangia in spikes or panicles

bo·tryd·i·um \-idēəm\ *n, cap* [NL, fr. Gk *botrydion* small cluster, dim. of *botrys* bunch of grapes] **:** a genus (the type of the family Botrydiaceae of the order Heterosiphonales) of coenocytic yellow-green algae that occur on moist earth as round or pear-shaped vesicles — see PROTOSIPHON

¹bo·tryl·lid \bō'triləd\ *adj* [NL *Botryllidae,* fr. *Botryllus,* type genus + *-idae*] **:** of or relating to the genus *Botryllus* or the family Botryllidae

²botryllid \"\ *n* -s **:** a tunicate of the genus *Botryllus* or the family Botryllidae

bo·tryl·lus \-ləs\ *n, cap* [NL, irreg. fr. Gk *botrys*] **:** a genus (the type of the family Botryllidae) of colonial incrusting tunicates with zooids resembling rays arranged about a common excurrent atrium — see GOLDEN STAR

bot·ry·o·gen \'bätrēə,jen\ *n* -s [G, fr. *botry-* + *-gen,* fr. Gk *-genēs* born — more at -GEN] **:** a mineral $MgFe(SO_4)_2(OH).7H_2O$ consisting of a hydrous sulfate of iron and magnesium that is deep red or deep yellow and usu. botryoid

bot·ry·oid \'bätrē,óid\ *n* -s [*botryoid,* adj.] **:** a formation (as of calcium carbonate on the walls of caves) resembling a bunch of grapes

bot·ry·oi·dal \,⸗⸗¦óidᵊl\ *also* **bot·ry·oid** \'⸗⸗,óid\ *adj* [*botryoidal* fr. *botryoid,* adj. + *-al; botryoid* fr. Gk *botryoeidēs,* fr. *botry-* + *-oeidēs* -oid] **:** having the form of a bunch of grapes ⟨a ~ mineral structure⟩ ⟨~ growths⟩

bot·ry·o·my·co·ma \,⸗⸗(,)ō,mī'kōmə\ *n, pl* **botryomycomas** \-ōməz\ *or* **botryomycoma·ta** \-ōməd·ə\ [NL, fr. *Botryomyces* + *-oma*] **:** one of the vascular granulomatous masses occurring in botryomycosis

bot·ry·o·my·co·sis \-ōsəs\ *n, pl* **botryomyco·ses** \-ō,sēz\ [NL, fr. *Botryomyces,* former genus name of an organism believed to cause the infection (fr. *botry-* + *-myces*) + *-osis*] **:** a bacterial and prob. always micrococcal infection of domestic animals and man marked by the formation of usu. superficial vascular granulomatous masses, associated esp. with castration or other wounds, and sometimes followed by metastatic visceral tumors — **bot·ry·o·my·cot·ic** \¦⸗⸗(,)⸗,mī¦käd·ik\ *adj*

bot·ry·op·ter·i·da·ce·ae \,bätrē,äp,terə'dāsē,ē\ *n pl, cap* [NL, fr. *Botryopterid-, Botryopteris,* type genus (fr. *botry-* + *-pterid-, -pteris*) + *-aceae*] **:** a family of three or four genera of primitive ferns found in Devonian and Carboniferous rocks of Europe and having the stem strand of xylem surrounded by phloem and the petioles with characteristic single W-shaped vascular bundle

bot·ry·ose \'bätrē,ōs\ *adj* [prob. modif. (influenced by *racemose* or *cymose*) of G *botrytisch,* irreg. fr. *botry-* (fr. Gk) + *-isch* -ish, fr. OHG *-isc*] **1 :** RACEMOSE **2 :** BOTRYOIDAL

bo·try·tis \bō'trīd·əs\ *n, cap* [NL, irreg. fr. Gk *botrys*] **:** a form genus of imperfect fungi (family Moniliaceae) having the conidia in bunches like grapes on branched conidiophores and several of them causing serious plant diseases

botrytis disease *n, usu cap B* **:** any of several plant diseases caused by fungi of the genus *Botrytis* and typically characterized by a soft rotting

bots *pl of* BOT, *pres 3d sing of* BOT

bot·swa·na \bät'swänə, bət-\ *adj, usu cap* [fr. *Botswana,* country in southern Africa] **:** of or from the country of Botswana **:** of the kind or style prevalent in Botswana

¹bott *var of* BOT

²bott \'bät\ *or* **bod** \'bäd\ *n* -s [perh. alter. of ¹*bat*] **:** a plug of clay for closing the taphole of a cupola in founding

botted *past of* BOT

bot·te·ga \bō'tägə, bə'-\ *n, pl* **bottegas** \-gəz\ *also* **botteghe** \-gē, -(,)gā\ [It, artist's studio, shop, fr. L *apotheca* warehouse — more at APOTHECARY] **:** the studio or workshop of a major artist in which other artists may participate in the execution of the projects or commissions of the major artist

bot·tery tree \'bäd·ərē-\ *n* [*bottery* alter. of *bourtree*] **:** BOURTREE

bött·ger ware \'betgə(r)-\ *n, usu cap B* [after Johann F. *Böttger* †1719 Ger. maker of porcelains who originated it] **:** a fine reddish brown stoneware

bot·tine \bə'tēn, bä'-\ *n* -s [F, fr. MF *botine,* dim. of *bote* boot] **:** a woman's light boot

botting *pres part of* BOT

¹bot·tle \'bäd·ᵊl, 'bätᵊl\ *n* -s *often attrib* [ME *botel,* fr. MF *boteille, bouteille,* fr. ML *butticula,* dim. of LL *buttis* cask — more at BUTT (cask)] **1 a :** a rigid or semirigid container made typically of glass or plastic, having a round and comparatively narrow neck or mouth that is usu. closed with a plug, screw top, or cap, and having no handle — contrasted with *jar, jug* **b :** a nonrigid container resembling a bag, made of skin, and usu. closed by tying at one end ⟨nomads storing wine in goatskin ~*s*⟩ **c :** the quantity held by a bottle ⟨drank a ~ of wine⟩ **2 a :** intoxicating drinks **:** LIQUOR ⟨fond of the ~⟩ **b :** liquid food usu. consisting of milk and supplements that is fed from a bottle (as to an infant) in place of mother's milk **3 a :** a metal container for holding gas

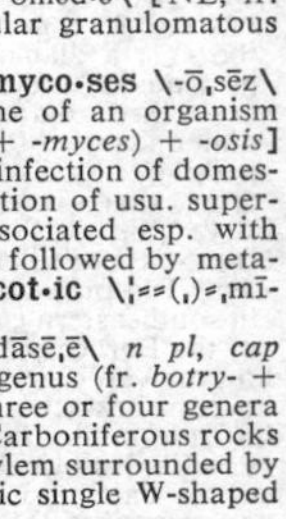

chemical bottles: *1* reagent, *2* weighing, *3* dropping, *4* and *5* washing: *4* for precipitates, *5* for gases

²bottle \"\ *vt* **bottled; bottled; bottling** \-d·ᵊliŋ, -t(ᵊ)liŋ\ **bottles 1 a :** to put into a bottle ⟨*bottling* the wine⟩ **b** *Brit* **:** to preserve (as fruit) by canning in glass jars **:** CAN ⟨she helped to ~ raspberries⟩ **2 a :** to confine as if in a bottle **:** CHECK, RESTRAIN — usu. used with *up* ⟨*bottling* up the anger they felt⟩ **b :** to put or keep in a position or situation that makes escape or free activity impossible **:** CORNER — usu. used with *up* ⟨they successfully *bottled* up the enemy troops in the mountains⟩

³bottle \"\ *n* -s [ME *botel,* fr. MF, dim. of *bote* bundle, fr. MD *bōte* bundle of flax; akin to MD *bōten* to beat, OHG *bōzan* — more at BEAT] *dial Brit* **:** a bundle usu. of straw or hay

bottle baby *n* **:** a baby fed chiefly or wholly on the bottle as contrasted with a baby that is chiefly or wholly breast-fed

bottlebird \'⸗⸗,⸗\ *n* **:** any of various weaverbirds that build nests shaped like a bottle

bottlebrush \'⸗⸗,⸗\ *n* [so called fr. the shape of the flower] **1 a :** any of certain Australian shrubs or trees of the family Myrtaceae that are widely cultivated in warm regions esp. for their spikes of brightly colored flowers: (1) **:** any plant of the genus *Callistemon* (2) *or* **bottlebrush tea tree :** HONEYMYRTLE **b :** AUSTRALIAN HONEYSUCKLE **2** *or* **bottlebrush grass :** a grass of the genus *Hystrix; esp* **:** a No. American grass (*H. patula*)

bottlebrush buckeye *n* **:** a spreading shrub (*Aesculus parviflora*) of the southeastern U.S. that has pinkish flowers

bottlebrush squirreltail *n* **:** SQUIRRELTAIL 1

bot·tle-butt·ed \¦⸗⸗¦bəd·əd\ *adj* **:** SWELL-BUTTED

bottle club *n* **:** an establishment (as a private club) at which patrons are served intoxicating drinks after legal closing hours from the supplies that they have previously purchased or reserved

bot·tled \'bäd·ᵊld, 'bätᵊld\ *adj* [¹*bottle* + *-ed*] **1** *archaic* **:** shaped like a bottle **2 :** kept in or as if in a bottle

bottled gas *n* [*bottled* fr. past part. of ²*bottle*] **:** gas under pressure in portable cylinders; *esp* **:** LIQUEFIED PETROLEUM GAS

bottled in bond *adj, of whiskey* **:** bottled unblended at 100 proof under U. S. government warehouse supervision after aging at least four years and being free of taxation until removal from the bonded warehouse

bottle fern *n* **:** FRAGILE FERN

bottle fly *n* **:** BLUEBOTTLE 3

bot·tle·ful \'==,fu̇l\ *n* -s **:** BOTTLE 1c

bottle gentian *n* [so called fr. the shape of its flower] **:** CLOSED GENTIAN

bottle glass *n* **:** glass from which containers (as bottles or jars) are made: as **a :** GREEN GLASS **b :** soda-lime glass that is clear, white, or colored

bottle gourd *n* **:** a common cultivated gourd (*Lagenaria siceraria*) whose shell is used as a bottle — called also *calabash*

bottle graft *n* **:** an approach graft in which the scion is a detached branch protected from wilting by keeping its base in a bottle of water until union is achieved

bottle grass *n* **1 :** a foxtail of the genus *Setaria* **2 :** RABBIT-FOOT CLOVER

bottle green *n* **:** a variable color averaging a dark green that is bluer and less strong than forest green (sense 1) and yellower than evergreen

bottlehead \'==,=\ *n, pl* **bottleheads** *or* **bottlehead 1 :** any of several small whales (as the beaked whale or blackfish) **2 :** BLACK-BELLIED PLOVER

bottleholder \'==,==\ *n* **1 :** a rack or other device for holding bottles **2** [so called fr. the custom of having water held in readiness for boxers by their seconds] **:** one that assists or supports another **:** SECOND

bottle jack *n* **:** a jackscrew somewhat resembling a bottle or jug in shape

bottle jaw *n* **:** a pendulous edematous condition of the tissues under the lower jaw in sheep and cattle resulting from infestation with bloodsucking parasites esp. stomach worms

bottle kiln *n* **:** a circular ceramic or lime kiln in which the walls of the hovel are drawn up into a bottle shape

1bottleneck \'==,=\ *n* **1 a :** a narrow entrance or passageway ⟨entering the harbor through the ~ formed by the reefs⟩ **b :** a narrow stretch of road **:** narrow route ⟨widened streets are gradually taking the place of the city's ~*s*⟩ **c :** a point of traffic obstruction or congestion ⟨at five o'clock in the afternoon the downtown streets are a series of ~*s*⟩ **2 a :** a condition or situation that obstructs, slows down, or halts free movement and progress ⟨breaking the twin ~*s* of ignorance and prejudice⟩ **b :** the state of blocked activity resulting from a bottleneck **:** state of checked, frustrated, or paralyzed action **:** IMPASSE ⟨lack of outside sympathy and understanding leaves the group in an apparently inescapable ~⟩

2bottleneck \"\ *vb* -ED/-ING/-S *vt* **:** to obstruct, slow down, or halt by or as if by causing or being a bottleneck **:** produce a bottleneck in **:** THROTTLE, CHECK, FRUSTRATE, PARALYZE ⟨their stupidity ~*ed* all freedom of expression⟩ ~ *vi* **1 :** to be or cause a bottleneck ⟨obstructing progress by constant ~*ing*⟩ **2 :** to become obstructed or checked by or as if by a bottleneck ⟨production of material has ~*ed*⟩ **3 :** to become narrow or confined like a bottleneck ⟨supply routes run along the rivers, ~*ing* in some spots —*Newsweek*⟩

3bottleneck *or* **bottlenecked** \'==,=\ *adj* **1 a :** shaped like or suggesting the neck and shoulders of a bottle ⟨~ gun cartridges⟩ **b :** narrow or confined like a bottleneck ⟨~ streets⟩ **2 :** obstructed or checked by or as if by a bottleneck ⟨progress has unfortunately entered a ~ phase⟩

bottle nose *n* **:** a swollen or protuberant and sometimes ruddy nose

bottle–nosed \¦==¦=\ *adj* **:** having a bottle nose ⟨a large, shapeless man, *bottle-nosed* and evidently no ascetic at table —G.B. Shaw⟩

bottle–nosed diver *n* **:** SURF SCOTER

bottle–nosed dolphin *or* **bottle–nose dolphin** *also* **bottle–nosed porpoise** *or* **bottle–nose porpoise** \'==¦=-\ *or* **bottle–nose** \'==¦=\ *n* **:** any of certain moderately large stout-bodied toothed whales that are usu. all included in the genus *Tursiops*, have a prominent beak and falcate dorsal fin, and are most common in warm seas; *esp* **:** a nearly cosmopolitan dolphin (*T. truncatus*)

bottle–nosed whale *n* **:** BOTTLEHEAD 1

bottle palm *n* **:** any of several palms (as *Colpothrinax wrightii* of Cuba and *Hyophorbe amaricaulis* of the Mascarene islands in the Indian ocean) that have trunks marked by a swelling shaped like a bottle — called also *barrel palm*

bottle party *n* **1 :** a private party to which the guests bring their own liquor **2 :** BOTTLE CLUB

bottle pool *n* **:** pool played with a cue ball, two object balls, and a leather bottle placed upside down, points being scored for caroming, pocketing an object ball, or overturning the bottle after hitting an object ball; *broadly* **:** any pool game in which a leather bottle is used on the table

bot·tler \'bäd·ᵊl(ə)r, 'bät(ᵊ)l-\ *n* -s **:** one that bottles: as **a :** a worker or machine that puts up goods in bottles **b :** a concern that makes and bottles beverages, esp. carbonated beverages

bottles *pl of* BOTTLE, *pres 3d sing of* BOTTLE

bottle spring *n* [so called fr. the fact that fresh water may be secured by submerging a stopped bottle directly over the spring and then removing the stopper] **:** a freshwater spring issuing through the floor of a saline lake or pool

bottle swallow *n* [so called fr. the shape of its nest] **:** FAIRY MARTIN

bottle tit *n* [so called fr. the shape of its nest] **:** LONG-TAILED TIT

bottle tree *n* [so called fr. the swollen trunk] **:** an Australian tree of the genera *Brachychiton* and *Sterculia* (esp. *S. rupestris*) — see KURRAJONG

bottling *n* -s [fr. gerund of ²*bottle*] **:** the act or process of putting goods (as beverages) into bottles

1bot·tom \'bäd·əm, -ätəm\ *n* -s [ME *botme*, fr. OE *botm*; akin to OHG *bodam* bottom, ON *botn*, L *fundus*, Gk *pythmēn*, Skt *budhna*] **1 a :** the under surface as opposed to the top surface **:** the side lying underneath **:** UNDERSIDE ⟨the ~ of a box⟩ ⟨the ~ of a plank⟩; *specif* **:** the underside on which a thing normally stands or rests ⟨the ~ of a vase⟩ **b :** a surface facing upwards (as the seat of a chair or the floor of a room) and designed to support something resting on it or to serve as a functional termination of the thing of which it forms a part **c :** the posterior end of the trunk **:** BUTTOCKS, RUMP **2 :** the continuous and gently curved or somewhat flat surface (as of earth, sand, or rock) on which a body of water (as a river, lake, or sea) lies **:** BED ⟨the ship sank to the ~ of the ocean⟩ **3** *obs* **:** a very deep place **:** ABYSS **4 a :** the hull of a boat; *esp* **:** the part of the hull that lies below the water **b :** BOAT, SHIP — used chiefly of cargo ships ⟨cargo . . . carried by foreign ~*s* —Virginia A. Oakes⟩ **5 a** (1) **:** the lower or lowest part as opposed to the upper or topmost part ⟨at the ~ of the mountain⟩ (2) **:** the lower or lowest section, point, region, or level ⟨the ~ of the page⟩ ⟨the ~ of the graph⟩ ⟨traveling to the ~ of the world⟩ ⟨starting out on his career from the ~⟩ (3) **:** the worst possible level (as of misery, destitution, or degradation) ⟨falling to the ~ of disillusionment⟩ **b :** the farthest removed or inmost point of a recess ⟨sailing to the ~ of the bay⟩ **c :** a position marked by the least dignity or honor ⟨demoted to the ~ of the ranks⟩; the lowest or last place in point of precedence ⟨marching at the ~ of a procession⟩ **d** (1) **:** the undermost part of the sole of a shoe; *esp* **:** the part of the sole extending from the breast of the heel to the toe (2) **:** the lower part of a garment or a garment worn on the lower part of the body; *esp* **:** the trousers of pajamas — usu. used in pl. **e :** the card at the bottom of a deck of cards ⟨he cheated by dealing ~*s*⟩ **f :** the last half of an inning of baseball **6 :** low-lying land; *esp* **:** low-lying grassland and fields along a watercourse — usu. used in pl. ⟨the Mississippi river ~*s*⟩ **7** *obs* **:** CLEW 1 **8 a :** something used underneath or as if underneath another thing to support and strengthen it or to give it an advantageous point from which to develop **:** FOUNDATION, BASIS ⟨the ~ of a hypothesis⟩ **b :** a solid underlying structure (as of a work of literature) marked by unity and a convincing acceptance and interpretation of reality **:** SUBSTANCE ⟨their writing lost all grip and ~ —Van Wyck Brooks⟩ **9 :** intrinsic nature **:** ESSENCE **:** basic character **:** HEART, CENTER, SOURCE ⟨the ~ of the trouble lay deeper —G.M.Trevelyan⟩ ⟨he tackles problems, tries to get to the ~ of them —H.A.Overstreet⟩ **10 a :** a heavy residuum of impure metal (as in copper smelting) **b :** a residue left in a still (as in refining petroleum) **11 :** vigorous physical qualities combined with stamina **:** capacity to endure strain **:** SPIRIT — used esp. of horses and dogs ⟨a breed of dogs outstanding for ~⟩ **12 :** the main plowing mechanism of a plow comprising the moldboard, share, frame, and landside **13** *Austral* **:** a gutter in mining **14 :** a color applied as a foundation before the dyeing of textile fibers — **at bottom** *also* **at the bottom :** BASICALLY, REALLY, ESSENTIALLY **:** in reality ⟨he was *at bottom* modest and cautious —H.J.Muller⟩ ⟨a world familiar and close but *at bottom* unknown —Carlo Levi⟩ — **at the bottom of :** being the cause, source, or originator of **:** BEHIND ⟨they are *at the bottom of* every such scheme⟩ — **at the bottom of one's heart :** within one's own mind **:** in one's heart ⟨*at the bottom of his heart* he welcomed the news⟩ — **from the bottom of one's heart :** with unreserved sincerity ⟨he speaks *from the bottom of his heart* of something that has impressed and moved him —Stewart Cockburn⟩ — **from the bottom up :** from the very beginning **:** COMPLETELY ⟨the job will have to be done all over again *from the bottom up*⟩

2bottom \"\ *vb* -ED/-ING/-S *vt* **1 :** to furnish (as a chair or shoe) with a bottom **2** *obs* **:** to wind up (as a ball of thread) **3 :** to provide a foundation for **:** BASE, FOUND, ESTABLISH — usu. used with *on* or *upon* ⟨men who wanted to ~ the dreams of the Romantics on a solid basis —Bonamy Dobrée⟩ **4 :** to bring to the bottom ⟨they ~*ed* the submarine on the ocean floor⟩ **5 :** to get to the bottom of **:** figure out **:** PLUMB, FATHOM ⟨a mystery they hadn't ~*ed*⟩ **6 :** to treat with a foundation hue or a mordant preparatory to dyeing ⟨cloth may be ~*ed* with a pale shade of indigo⟩ **7 a :** to underrun (as a gold deposit that is to be worked by the hydraulic method) with a level for drainage **b :** FINISH ⟨~ a borehole or shaft⟩ **c :** EXHAUST ⟨~*ed* the ore in the mine⟩ ~ *vi* **1 :** to rest as an ultimate support **:** become based or grounded — usu. used with *on* or *upon* ⟨find on what foundation any proposition ~*s* —John Locke⟩ **2 :** to reach the bottom **:** strike against the bottom ⟨~*ing* on the bed of the sea⟩; *specif* **:** to touch bottom so as to impede free action (as when the point of a gear tooth strikes the bottom of a space between two other teeth, a piston strikes the end of a cylinder, or a die forces material solidly into a matrix in coining) **3 :** to develop a turf — used of a grass **4** *bot* **:** to develop a bulb or similar enlargement **syn** see BASE

3bottom \"\ *adj* **1 a :** of, relating to, or situated at the bottom ⟨~ rock⟩ **b :** lower or lowest ⟨the ~ part of the building⟩ ⟨~ prices⟩ **c :** frequenting the bottom ⟨~ fish⟩ **2 :** FUNDAMENTAL, BASIC ⟨the ~ reason⟩ ⟨~ ideas⟩

bottom board *n* **1 :** the base or floor of a beehive **2 bottom boards** *pl* **:** removable boards inside a boat at the bottom to protect the outer planking

bottom bracket *n* **:** BRACKET 2b

bottom break *n* **:** a branch or shoot arising from the base of a plant without being developed from an axillary bud on a branch and occurring either on grafted or on own-root plants — used esp. of roses

1bottom–chrome \'==,=\ *adj* [¹*bottom* + *chrome*, n. (in attrib. use)] **:** CHROME-MORDANT

2bottom–chrome \¦==¦=\ *vt* **:** to dye by the chrome-mordant method

bottom dealer *n* **:** one that deals illegally from the bottom of a deck of cards

bottom disease *n* **:** any poisoning of stock (as crotalism or Winton disease) caused by the eating of bottomland plants

bottom dog *n* **:** UNDERDOG

bottom dollar *n* **:** last dollar ⟨you can bet your *bottom dollar*⟩

bottom drawer *n, chiefly Brit* **:** a drawer (as in a dresser) used as a hope chest

bottomed *past of* BOTTOM

bot·tom·er \'bäd·əmə(r), -ätəm-\ *n* -s **:** one that bottoms: as **a :** a worker who finishes the bottom part of shoes preparatory to stitching or cementing on the outsoles **b :** a worker who nails bottoms to wooden box frames or makes the bottoms of other containers **c :** a worker stationed at the bottom of a mine shaft or haulage slope to direct the raising of loaded cars to the surface — called also *footman*, *foot tender*

bottom fermentation *n* **:** a slow alcoholic fermentation during which the yeast cells collect at the bottom of the fermenting liquid, which takes place at a temperature of 4 to 10° C and which occurs in the production of lager beer and of wines of low alcohol content — compare TOP FERMENTATION

bottom fishing *n* **:** fishing designed to catch bottom fish in which natural bait is usu. used and the sinker or hook rests on or near the bottom

bottom gear *n, Brit* **:** LOW SPEED **:** first gear ⟨he put the car in *bottom gear*⟩

bottom grass *n* **1 :** grass growing on bottomlands **2 :** any grass of low stature grown in mixtures for turf or sod **3 :** TEXAS MILLET

bottom heat *n* **:** supplemental heat applied beneath greenhouse benches or plant frames to induce rooting of cuttings or to benefit heat-loving plants

bottom–hole \'==,=\ *adj* **:** at or relating to the bottom of a drilled well ⟨*bottom-hole* temperature⟩

bottom ice *n* **:** ANCHOR ICE

1bottoming *n* -s [fr. gerund of ²*bottom*] **:** the process of attaching the outsole of a shoe to the insole and upper and performing subsequent finishing work on the outsole

2bottoming *n* -s [¹*bottom* + *-ing*] **:** material (as broken stone) suitable for the bottom coat of a paved road

bottoming drill *n* **:** a drill designed to form a flat base at the bottom of a drilled hole

bottoming hole *n* **:** the furnace opening at which a globe of crown glass is exposed in glass manufacture to soften it — called also *glory hole*

bottoming tap *n* **:** a hand tap cutting a full thread to the bottom of a hole — see TAP illustration

bot·tom·land \'==,land, -laa(ə)nd\ *n* **:** BOTTOM 6

bot·tom·less \-ləs\ *adj* [ME *botmelees*, fr. *botme* bottom + *-lees* -less] **1 a :** having no bottom ⟨a ~ chair⟩ **b :** lacking a foundation **:** BASELESS ⟨~ arguments⟩ **2 a :** extremely deep ⟨the ~ sea⟩ **b :** incapable of being plumbed to the depths **:** UNFATHOMABLE ⟨a ~ mystery⟩ **:** PROFOUND ⟨~ gloom⟩ **c :** BOUNDLESS, UNLIMITED, INEXHAUSTIBLE ⟨a man whose charity seemed ~⟩ — **bot·tom·less·ly** *adv* — **bot·tom·less·ness** *n* -ES

bot·tom·most \-m,mōst, *esp Brit also* -mməst\ *adj* **1 a** (1) **:** that is at the very bottom ⟨a village at the ~ part of the mountain⟩ **:** farthest down **:** LOWEST ⟨sitting on the ~ step⟩ (2) **:** that is closest to the end ⟨the ~ part of the day —Alfred Kazin⟩ **b** (1) **:** DEEPEST ⟨the ~ depths of the sea⟩ (2) **:** most profound ⟨pangs of ~ grief⟩ **2 :** most fundamental **:** most basic ⟨the ~ problems facing the world⟩

bottom plate *n* **1 :** the horizontal beam on which the studs of a partition rest **2 :** a plate supporting a foundry mold

bottom rake *n* **:** CLEARANCE 2e

bottom–road bridge *n* **:** a bridge having its roadway carried on a floor system at the level of the lower chord in a truss bridge or at the bottom in a tubular bridge — called also *through bridge*

bottom–rooted \¦==¦==\ *adj* **:** having roots in the soil of a pool or pond ⟨*bottom-rooted* water lilies⟩

bottom rot *n* **1 :** a disease of lettuce caused by a fungus (*Corticium solani*) that first rots the lower leaves and then spreads upward **2 :** a decay of the basal portion of a tree trunk by any of various pore fungi (as *Polyporus schweinitzii*)

bottom round *n* **:** the part of a round steak situated on the outside of the round — compare TOP ROUND

1bot·tom·ry \'bäd·əmrē, -ätəm-, -ri\ *n* -ES [alter. (influenced by *-ry*) of earlier *bottomary*, modif. (influenced by ¹*bottom*) of D *bodemerij*, fr. *bodem* bottom, ship + *-erij* -ery, fr. OF *-erie*; akin to OHG *bodam* bottom — more at BOTTOM] **:** a contract in the nature of a mortgage by which either the owner of a ship or the master as his agent hypothecates and binds the ship and sometimes the accruing freight as security for the repayment of money advanced or lent for the use of the ship with the lender losing his money if the ship is lost by the perils of the sea but receiving with his loan the interest or premium stipulated if the ship arrives safe — compare RESPONDENTIA

2bottomry \"\ *vt* -ED/-ING/-S **:** to pledge by a bottomry bond

bottoms *pl of* BOTTOM, *pres 3d sing of* BOTTOM

bottom sawyer *n* **:** a worker at a saw pit who stands below the timber — called also *pit sawyer*; compare TOP SAWYER

bottomset beds \'==,=-\ *n pl* **:** layers of sedimentary material lying along the bottom of a body of water near the point of entry of a stream, the material having been carried to the area by the entering stream and being subsequently covered by foreset beds and topset beds in the formation of a delta

bottom shellbark *or* **bottom shellbark hickory** *n* **:** BIG SHELLBARK

bottom stope *n* **:** a stope for ore lying on the floor

bottom tool *n* **1 :** a tool held under a piece of work and used in conjunction with another tool working on top (as the lowermost of a pair of dies or fullers) **2 :** a tool for machining the bottom of a hole

bottom water *n* **:** the water immediately underlying oil or gas in productive formations — compare TOP WATER

bottom yeast *n* **:** a yeast that is present in the manufacture of wine and lager beer and that separates after fermentation on the bottom of the fermenting vessel

bottony *var of* BOTONÉE

bot·trop \'bä,träp\ *adj, usu cap* [fr. *Bottrop*, city in Germany] **:** of or from the city of Bottrop, Germany **:** of the kind or style prevalent in Bottrop

bott stick *also* **bod stick** *n* [²*bott*] **:** a rod about 10 feet long on the end of which a bott is placed when closing a taphole

bot·tu \'bä(,)tü\ *n* -s [Kanarese-Telugu *bottu*] *India* **:** an ornamental or sectarian mark (as a dot on the forehead)

bot·u·li·form \'bächələ,fȯrm; bə'tül-,bə'tyül-\ *adj* [*botuli-* (fr. L *botulus* sausage) + *-form* — more at BOWEL] **:** shaped like a sausage

bot·u·lin \'bächələn\ *n* -s [prob. fr. NL *botulinus*] **:** a toxin that is formed by a bacterium (*Clostridium botulinum*) and that is the direct cause of botulism — called also *botulinus toxin*, *botulismus toxin*

bot·u·li·nal \¦bächə¦līnᵊl\ *adj* [NL *botulinus* + E *-al*] **:** of, relating to, or produced by the botulinus

bot·u·lin·ic \-¦linik\ *adj* [ISV *botulin-* (fr. NL *botulinus*) + *-ic*] **:** BOTULINAL

bot·u·li·nus \,bächə'līnəs, *attrib* ¦=¦==\ *also* **bot·u·li·num** \-nəm\ *n, pl* **botulinuses** *also* **botulinums** *often attrib* [*botulinus* fr. NL, fr. L *botulus* + *-inus* -ine; *botulinum* fr. NL, neut. of *botulinus*] **:** a bacterium (*Clostridium botulinum*) that causes botulism — compare BOTULIN

bot·u·lism \'bächə,lizəm\ *n* -s [ISV *botul-* (fr. L *botulus*) + *-ism*; orig. formed as G *botulismus*] **:** acute food poisoning in man, various mammals, and birds caused by ingestion of food containing the toxin secreted by a spore-forming bacterium (*Clostridium botulinum*), characterized by muscle weakness and paralysis, disturbances of vision, swallowing, and speech, and marked by a high mortality rate — see DUCK SICKNESS, LIMBERNECK

bot·u·lis·mus toxin \¦bächə¦lizməs-\ *n* [G *botulismus* + E *toxin*] **:** BOTULIN

bou·bou \'bü(,)bü\ *also* **boubou shrike** *n* -s [origin unknown] **:** any of several African shrikes (genus *Laniarius*)

boucan *var of* BUCCAN

bou·chal \'büəkəl\ *n* -s [Ir *buachaill*, fr. MIr, cowherd; akin to W *bugail* shepherd, Bret *bugel*; all fr. a prehistoric Celt compound whose first and second constituents respectively are akin to Gk *bous* cow and to L *colere* to cultivate — more at COW, WHEEL] *chiefly Irish* **:** young man **:** BOY; *specif* **:** HERDBOY

bou·charde \bü'shärd\ *n* -s [F] **:** a tool for roughening or furrowing the surface of marble

1bouche \'büsh\ *n* -s [ME, fr. MF, lit., mouth, fr. L *bucca* cheek, mouth — more at POCK] **1** *obs* **:** an allowance of food and drink for retinue in a royal or noble household **2 :** a slit in the edge of a medieval shield for a sword blade or a rounded opening for the shaft of a lance

2bouche \"\ *n* -s [prob. alter. (influenced by F *boucher* to stop up) of *bush* (bushing)] **:** BUSHING

3bou·ché \(')bü¦shā\ *adj* [F, fr. past part. of *boucher* to stop up, fr. OF, fr. (assumed) OF *bouche* bunch, sheaf (whence MF *bouche*), perh. of Gmc origin; akin to OHG *busc* bush, forest — more at BUSH] **:** stopped with the hand — used as a direction in music in horn playing

bou·chée \bü'shā\ *n* -s [F, lit., mouthful, fr. (assumed) VL *buccata*, fr. L *bucca* + LL *-ata* (fr. L, fem. of *-atus* -ate)] **:** a very small patty or cream-puff shell filled with creamed meat or fish

bouche fer·mée \¦büsh,fer¦mā\ *adv (or adj)* [F, lit., mouth closed] **:** with the mouth closed — used as a direction in music

bou·che·rie process \¦büshə¦rē-, (')bü¦shrē-, 'büsh(ə)rē-\ *n, cap B* [after Auguste *Boucherie* †1871 Fr. chemist] **:** a method of preserving wood involving impregnation with copper sulfate under pressure

bou·chon \(')bü¦shän, -shōⁿ\ *n* -s [F, bouchon, cork, sheaf, fr. MF, cork, sheaf, fr. *bouche* bunch, sheaf] **1 :** a bushing pressed into a bridge or plate of a timepiece **2 :** the plug and fuze assembly of a grenade

bou·clé *or* **bou·cle** \(')bü¦klā\ *n* -s [F *bouclé* curly, having a curly appearance (as fabrics), fr. past part. of *boucler* to curl, fr. *boucle* curl, buckle — more at BUCKLE] **1** *also* **bouclé yarn :** an uneven yarn of three plies one of which forms loops at intervals that is made in various weights of the principal clothing fibers **2 :** a textile fabric that is used for clothing or decorating, has a rough looped surface, and is knitted or woven of bouclé yarns

bou·din \(')bü¦dan, -aⁿ\ *n* -s [F] **1 :** BLOOD SAUSAGE **2 :** forcemeat shaped like a sausage and served as an entree **3 :** an individual unit in a boudinage

bou·di·nage \,büdᵊn¦äzh, -äj\ *n* -s [F, fr. *boudin* + *-age*] **:** a structure which is sometimes present in metamorphic rocks apparently as a result of tension and in which a competent bed is thinned and thickened so that it resembles in cross section a string of sausages

bou·doir *R* 'bü,dwä(r), 'bu̇,-, ==*also* -wȯ(ə)r; *–R* -wå(r *also* -wȯ(ə)(r\ *n* -s *often attrib* [F, fr. *bouder* to pout, be sulky, prob. of imit. origin] **:** a woman's dressing room, bedroom, or private sitting room

boudoir chair *n* **:** a small fully upholstered chair

boudoir lamp *n* **:** a small ornamental table lamp for a woman's dressing table

bou·et \'büət\ *n* -s [ME *bowett*, *bowat*, perh. fr. MF *boete* box, fr. OF *boete*, *boite*, *boiste*, fr. (assumed) VL *buxita*, irreg. fr. LL *buxis* — more at BOX] *Scot* **:** a small hand lantern

bouf·fan·cy \'büfənsē\ *n* -ES **:** an effect of fullness in women's clothing usu. achieved by voluminous skirts

bouf·fant \(')bü¦fänt, -äⁿ\ *adj* [F, fr. MF, fr. pres. part. of *bouffer* to swell, puff, of imit. origin] **:** puffed out **:** VOLUMINOUS, FLARING ⟨~ hairdos⟩ — used esp. of very full skirts with tight waistbands

bouffe \'büf\ *n* [by shortening] **:** OPÉRA BOUFFE

bouf·fon \(')bü¦fän, -fōⁿ\ *n* -s [F, buffoon — more at BUFFOON] **1 :** MATACHIN **2 :** a dancing buffoon in modern Spanish and Mexican fiestas

bou·gain·vil·laea \,bügən'vilyə, ,bōg-, -vē(y)ə,-vēlyə,-vilēə, -vilaya\ *n* [NL, fr. Louis Antoine de *Bougainville* †1811 Fr. navigator] **1** *cap* **:** a small genus of ornamental tropical American woody vines (family Nyctaginaceae) with brilliant red or purple floral bracts **2** -s **:** ²BOUGAINVILLEA

1bou·gain·vil·lea \"\ [NL, alter. of *Bougainvillaea*] *syn of* BOUGAINVILLAEA

2bougainvillea \"\ *n* -s **:** a vine of the genus *Bougainvillaea*

bou·gain·vil·lia \"\ *n* [NL, fr. Louis Antoine de *Bougainville* + NL *-ia*] **1** *cap* **:** a widely distributed genus of marine hydrozoans forming arborescent colonies and having polyps with a single whorl of tentacles **2** -s **:** ²BOUGAINVILLEA

bou·gar \'bü,gär, -,gər\ *n* -s [origin unknown] *chiefly Scot* **:** a rafter or cross spar of a roof esp. of a cottage — usu. used in pl.

bouge \'büj\ *now dial var of* BULGE

bougee *var of* BURGEE

bou·get \'büjət\ *n* -s [MF *bougette* leather pouch or wallet — more at BUDGET] **:** WATER BOUGET 2

bough \'bau̇\ *n* -s [ME *bow*, *bough* bough, shoulder, fr. OE *bōg*, *bōh*; akin to OHG *buog* shoulder, ON *bōgr* shoulder, bow of a ship, Gk *pēchys* forearm, Skt *bāhu* forearm, front foot, Toch A *poke* arm] **1 :** a branch of a tree; *esp* **:** a main branch **2** *archaic* **:** GALLOWS

boughed \'bau̇d\ *adj* [ME *bowed*, fr. *bow*, *bough* + *-ed*] **:** having boughs **:** covered with boughs **:** having such boughs ⟨heavy-*boughed* oaks⟩

bough·less *adj* **:** being without a bough

bough·pot *also* **bow·pot** \'bau̇,pät\ *n* [*bough* + *pot*] **1 :** a vase for cut flowers or boughs; *also* **:** BOUQUET **2 :** an ornamental design representing a conventionalized vase of flowers — compare ANTHEMION

¹bought [ME *boughte* (past), *bought, ybought* (past part.), fr. OE *bohte* (past), *boht, geboht* (past part.); akin to Goth *bauhta* bought (past), *bauhts* bought (past part.) — more at BUY] *past of* BUY

²bought *adj* [fr. past part. of *buy*] **:** not homemade **:** PURCHASED, READY-MADE ⟨unable to let a ~ sauce go by undoctored —*New Yorker*⟩ ⟨~ Christmas cards⟩

³bought \'bȯkt, 'bəkt\ *n* -s [ME (Sc) *bowcht*, prob. fr. MD *bocht, bucht* pen for animals; akin to OE *byht* bend — more at BIGHT] *chiefly Scot* **:** a shelter of any kind; *esp* **:** one for animals

⁴bought *n* -s [ME, perh. fr. MLG *bucht, bocht;* akin to OE *byht*] **1** \'bükt, 'bȯkt\ *chiefly Scot* **:** BEND, CURVE ⟨the ~ of his elbow⟩ **2** *archaic* **:** TWIST, TURN, COIL

bought-and-sold note *n* **:** SALE NOTE

bought·en \'bȯtᵊn\ *adj* [*bought* (past part. of *buy*) + *-en* (as in *forgotten*)] *now dial* **:** ²BOUGHT ⟨my red sled, and my ~ wagon —W.A.White⟩

bou·gie \'bü,zhē, -üjē *sometimes* bü'zhē\ *n* -s [F, fr. *Bougie*, seaport in Algeria from which these candles were first imported into Europe] **1 :** a wax candle **2 :** a candle-shaped filter **3 a :** a tapering cylindrical medical instrument (as of rubber, waxed silk, or metal) for introduction into tubular passages (as the urethra or anus) to facilitate dilation or exploration or to serve as guide for the passage of other instruments **b :** SUPPOSITORY

bou·gi·nage *or* **bou·gie·nage** \¦büzhē¦näzh\ *n* -s [*bougie* + connective *-n-* + *-age*] **:** the dilation of a tubular cavity (as a constricted esophagus) with a bougie

bou·guer's halo \(')bü¦ge(ə)rz-\ *n, usu cap B* [after Pierre *Bouguer* †1758 Fr. mathematician] **:** a faint white halo of about 32 degrees minimum radius around the antisolar point

bouguer's law *n, usu cap B* **:** LAMBERT'S LAW b

bouil·la·baisse \¦büyə¦bās *sometimes* ¦bül(y)ə-\ *n* -s [F, fr. Prov *boui-abaisso*, fr. *boui* (sing. imper. of *bouie* to boil, fr. L *bullire*) + *abaisso* (sing. imper. of *abeissa* to lower, fr. — assumed — VL *abbassiare*) — more at BOIL, ABASE] **:** a fish stew made of at least two and usu. five or six kinds of fish, seasoned with onions and herbs, and flavored and colored with saffron

bouil·li \(')bü¦yē\ *n* -s [F, fr. MF, fr. past part. of *bouillir* to boil, fr. OF *boillir*] **:** boiled meat and esp. beef

bouil·lon \'bü,yän *also* 'bu̇- *or* =¦=; 'bu̇l,yän *also* 'bü- *or* =¦=; 'bu̇lyən; bü'yōⁿ, '=,=\ *n* -s [F, fr. OF *boillon*, fr. *boillir* to boil — more at BOIL] **:** a broth made by slow boiling of meat and esp. beef in water; *specif* **:** clarified and seasoned stock served as a soup and made from lean beef unless otherwise stated ⟨clam ~⟩ — compare BEEF TEA, MEDIUM

bouil·lon blanc \büyōⁿbläⁿ\ *n* [F, fr. MF, fr. (assumed) MF *bouillon* mullein (modif. — influenced by MF *bouillon* broth — of LL *bugillon-, bugillo*, a plant, prob. of Celt origin and akin to OIr *buge*, a plant with a blue flower) + MF *blanc* white — more at BLANK] **:** MULLEIN

bouillon cube *n* **:** a cube of evaporated seasoned meat extract

bouillon cup *n* **:** a small cup with two handles for serving bouillon

bouillon spoon *n* **:** a round-bowled spoon somewhat smaller than a soup spoon

bouil·lotte \bü'yät\ *n* -s [F, fr. *bouillir;* prob. fr. the rapidity of the game] **:** BRELAN 1

bou·in's fluid *or* **bouin's solution** \(')bü¦anz-, -aⁿz-; 'bwaⁿz-\ *also* **bouin** \-an,-aⁿ\ *n, usu cap B* [after Paul *Bouin*, 20th cent. Fr. histologist] *biol* **:** a fixing and preserving solution consisting of picric acid, formaldehyde, and glacial acetic acid

¹bouk *in sense 1* 'bük, *in sense 2* 'bu̇k\ *n* -s [ME, belly, body, fr. OE *būc* belly — more at BUCKET] **1** *chiefly Scot* **a :** the body of a person **b :** an animal carcass ⟨a mutton ~⟩ **2 :** OMASUM

²bouk \'bük\ *dial Brit var of* BULK

³bouk \"\ *Scot var of* ⁷BUCK

bouk·it \'bükət\ *adj* [²*bouk* + Sc *-it* -ed] *chiefly Scot* **:** FORMED, BUILT — usu. used with a qualifier ⟨a lad who was wee ~⟩

boul \'bül\ *chiefly Scot var of* BOOL

boul *abbr* boulevard

bou·lan·gère \¦bü,läⁿzhe(ə)r\ *adj* [F, female baker, baker's wife, fr. OF *boulengiere*, fem. of *boulengier* baker, fr. ONF *boulenc* baker (fr. MD *bolle* round loaf of bread + OF *-enc*, n. suffix, of Gmc origin and akin to OHG *-ing* one belonging to) + OF *-ier* -er; prob. akin to OE *bolla* bowl — more at BOWL, -ING] **:** cooked with sliced onions in a casserole

bou·lan·ger·ite \bü'lanjə,rīt\ *n* -s [G *boulangerit*, fr. C.L. *Boulanger* †1849 Fr. mining engineer + G *-it* -ite] **:** a bluish gray metallic-looking mineral $Pb_5Sb_4S_{11}$ consisting of antimony lead sulfide occurring usu. in plumose masses (hardness 2.5–3, sp. gr. 5.75–6.0)

¹boul·der *also* **bowl·der** \'bōldə(r)\ *n* -s [short for *boulder stone*, fr. ME *bulder ston*, part trans. of a word of Scand origin; akin to Sw dial. *bullersten* large stone in a stream, fr. *buller* noise (fr. OSw *bulder*) + *sten* stone; akin to MLG *balderen* to make a noise, Dan *buldre*, Lith *bildėti*, OE *bellan* to bellow — more at BELLOW] **:** a detached and rounded or much-worn mass of rock from 8 or 10 inches to 10 or more feet in diameter typically carried some distance from the parent rock by natural forces and worn by a stream, ocean waves, or glacier or by weathering in situ — see ³COBBLE 1

²boulder *also* **bowlder** \"\ *vt* **bouldered; bouldered; boulder·ing** \'bōld(ə)riŋ\ **boulders 1 :** to make into boulders — used chiefly in past participial form **2 :** to smooth (a revolving polishing wheel) by crushing against a quartz stone or boulder

boulder beach *n* **:** a beach deposit consisting largely of boulders

boulder belt *n* **:** a line or zone of glacial boulders

boulder clay *n* **:** an unassorted glacial deposit containing much clay in the matrix surrounding pebbles, boulders, and other rock fragments **:** TILL

boulder fern *n* **:** HAY-SCENTED FERN

boulderhead *also* **bowlderhead** \'==,=\ *n* **:** a row of piles before a dike to protect it from wave erosion

boul·der·ing *also* **bowl·der·ing** \'bōld(ə)riŋ\ *n* -s **:** pavement of or paving with small boulders

bouldering stone *n* **:** pebbles of smooth flint used in abrading or crushing the faces of emery wheels and glazers

boulder pavement *n* **:** a concentration of boulders as a result of removal of finer particles of a glacial deposit by water

boulder raspberry *n* **:** a shrub (*Rubus deliciosus*) native to the Rocky mountains and having dark purple fruit

boulder train *n* **:** a line or fan-shaped spread of glacial boulders that extends from the original rock outcrop often for many miles in the direction of glacial movement

boul·dery *also* **bowl·dery** \'bōld(ə)rē\ *adj* **:** characterized by boulders

¹bou·le \'bü(,)lē, bü'lā\ *n* -s [Gk *boulē*, lit., will, fr. *boulesthai* to wish, be willing; perh. akin to Gk *ballein* to throw — more at DEVIL] **:** a legislative council of ancient Greece consisting in Homeric times of an aristocratic body of princes and leaders merely advisory to the king and in Athens in Solon's time of an elective senate acting as a check on the popular assembly and later extending its functions to include certain matters of administration and supervision

²boule *var of* BOULLE

³boule \'bül\ *n* -s [F, ball — more at BOWL (ball)] **:** a game similar to roulette in which a ball is put in motion in a bowl and players bet on the numbered compartment it will come to rest in

⁴boule \"\ *n* -s [F, ball] **:** a pear-shaped mass of some substance (as sapphire, spinel, rutile) formed synthetically in the Verneuil furnace with the atomic structure of a single crystal but with crystallographic axes generally in a random position with respect to its length

⁵boule \"\ *n* -s [F, ball] **:** a log sawed into slabs that are reassembled with spacer strips to form an oval stack resembling the original log

bou·leu·te·ri·on \,bü,lü'tirē,än, ,bül,yü-\ *n, pl* **bouleute·ria** \-ēə\ [Gk *bouleutērion*, fr. *bouleuein* to advise, take counsel, fr. *boulē* counsel, council, will] **:** an ancient Greek council chamber

¹bou·le·vard \'bu̇lə,värd, -vȧd *also* 'bül-\ *n* -s [F, modif. of MD *bolwerc* — more at BULWARK] **1 a :** a broad thoroughfare; *esp* **:** one more pretentious than an ordinary street or avenue often having grassplots with trees along the center or between curbings and sidewalks **b :** a grassed or landscaped strip in the center or between the curbings and sidewalks of a boulevard **2 :** MOUSE GRAY

²boulevard \"\ *vt* -ED/-ING/-S **:** to make into a boulevard **:** provide with boulevards

bou·le·var·dier \¦bül,värd¦yā; ¦bu̇lə,vär¦di(ə)r, ¦bül-\ *n, pl* **boulevardiers** \-yā(z),-i(ə)rz\ [F, fr. *boulevard* + *-ier* -er] **:** a frequenter of the Parisian boulevards **:** a sophisticated man of fashion; *also* **:** BON VIVANT, FLANEUR, TRIFLER

boulevard light *n* **:** a tall ornamental streetlight with a luminaire like a lantern at the top used chiefly on parkways and principal thoroughfares

boulevard stop *n* **:** a traffic stop required of vehicles before entering or crossing a through street

boule·verse·ment \bülversəmäⁿ\ *n* -s [F, fr. MF, fr. *bouleverser* to overturn (fr. *boule* ball + *verser* to overturn, fr. L *versare* to turn, overturn + *-ment* — more at VERSATILE] **:** OVERTURNING, REVERSAL; *also* **:** CONVULSION, DISORDER

-boulia — see -BULIA

-boulic — see -BULIC

boulimia *var of* BULIMIA

boulle *or* **buhl** *also* **boule** \'b(y)ül\ *n* -s [after André Charles *Boulle* †1732 Fr. cabinetmaker] **:** inlaid decoration developed under Louis XIV by André Charles Boulle in which tortoiseshell, yellow metal, and white metal are inlaid in cabinetwork, forming scrolls or cartouches

bou·lon·nais \¦bülə¦nā\ *n* [F, fr. *boulonnais* of Boulogne, fr. *Boulogne*, seaport city in northern France] **1** *usu cap* **:** a French breed of very large quick-maturing draft horses **2** *pl* **boulon·naises** \-āz\ *often cap* **:** a horse of the Boulonnais breed

boult *obs var of* BOLT

boul·ter \'bōltə(r)\ *n* -s [origin unknown] **:** a long stout fishing line to which many hooks are attached and which is used for bottom fishing esp. in deep water

boul·ter·er \-tərə(r)\ *n* -s **:** one who fishes with a boulter

¹boun \'bün, 'bau̇n\ *chiefly dial var of* ¹BOUND

²boun \"\ *var of* BOWN

¹bounce \'bau̇n(t)s\ *vb* -ED/-ING/-S [ME *bounsen*, prob. of imit. origin] *vt* **1** *obs* **:** BEAT, BELABOR **2 a :** to cause to rebound ⟨~ a ball off a wall⟩ **:** cause to be reflected ⟨~ a light ray off a reflector⟩ **b :** to throw about **:** handle violently **3** *chiefly Brit* **a :** to bluff or bully with big talk **b :** SCOLD, BROWBEAT **4 a :** to discharge from a post or employ esp. peremptorily and unceremoniously ⟨the old mess sergeant had been *bounced* on recommendation of the mess officer —H.H.Arnold & I.C.Eaker⟩ **b :** to expel or eject esp. precipitately from a room or place or from membership or participation ⟨if the college would only ~ him for something that wasn't too much his fault —Theodore Morrison⟩ ~ *vi* **1** *obs* **:** to make a loud sudden noise **:** bang or knock loudly **2 :** to strike and rebound ⟨*bouncing* from rock to rock⟩ ⟨the ball will hardly ~ at all⟩ ⟨the car *bounced* all over the road⟩ **3 :** to recover from a blow or a defeat quickly or vigorously — usu. used with *back* **4 a** *of a check* **:** to be returned by a bank as no good (as because of lack of funds) **b :** RECOIL, BOOMERANG ⟨a tendency, which could ~ uncomfortably back on them, to come out and boldly blame the press for everything —Mollie Panter-Downes⟩ **5 a :** to leap or spring suddenly, violently, or noisily **:** BOUND ⟨*bounced* into the room⟩ ⟨*bouncing* on his seat with ecstasy⟩ **b :** to walk with springing steps **6** *chiefly Brit* **:** to talk big **:** BLUSTER, SWAGGER, BOAST **syn** see DISMISS

²bounce \"\ *n* -s **1** *obs* **:** a heavy sudden often noisy blow or thump; *also* **:** the sound of an explosion **:** BANG **2 :** a sudden leap or bound **:** a rebound esp. of a ball **3 :** BLUSTER, BRAG, SWAGGER **:** an impudent lie or boast **4 :** LIVELINESS, RESILIENCE, VERVE ⟨full of ~ and enthusiasm⟩ **5** *slang* **:** a peremptory discharge or expulsion ⟨he got the ~⟩ **6 :** a pronounced beat characterizing a style of playing jazz usu. in a medium or moderate tempo

bounce·able \-səbəl\ *adj, now dial chiefly Eng* **:** BUMPTIOUS, PUGNACIOUS — **bounce·ably** \-səblē\ *adv*

bounce back *n* [*bounce back*, v.] **1 :** ECHO, REFLECTION ⟨locating submarines by the sonar *bounce back*⟩ **2 :** COMEBACK

bounce pass *n* **:** a basketball pass in which the ball is caromed off the floor

bounc·er \'bau̇n(t)sə(r)\ *n* -s **1** *Brit* **a :** BOASTER, BULLY, LIAR **b :** LIE, WHOPPER **2 :** something big **:** a good stout example of the kind ⟨that baby is a ~⟩ **3 :** one that ejects disorderly persons (as at a dance hall, gambling house, or barroom) or keeps gate-crashers out (as at a party or ceremony) **4** *slang* **:** CABOOSE

bounc·i·ly \-sȯlē, -li\ *adv* [*bouncy* + *-ly*] **:** with verve **:** JAUNTILY, SPRINGILY

bouncing *adj* [fr. pres. part. of ¹*bounce*] **1 :** LUSTY, HUSKY ⟨a ~ baby boy⟩ **:** HEALTHY, VIGOROUS ⟨a ~ young woman⟩ **2 :** LIVELY, ANIMATED ⟨a ~ disposition⟩ — **bounc·ing·ly** *adv*

bouncing bet \-'bet\ *or* **bouncing bess** \-'bes\ *n, often cap 2d B* [*bouncing* + *Bet* or *Bess*, nickname for *Elizabeth*] **:** SOAPWORT 1

bouncing-pin indicator *n* **:** an instrument that indicates knocking in a gasoline engine by the electrically recorded jumps made by a steel pin resting on a steel plate

bouncing putty *n* **:** any of various soft elastic silicone polymers that usu. increase in elasticity with rate of application of force and that are used esp. as centers of golf balls, as muscle exercisers in occupational therapy, and as shock-absorbent padding around instruments in high-speed aircraft and rockets

bouncy \'bau̇n(t)sē, -si\ *adj* -ER/-EST [²*bounce* + *-y*] **1 :** BOUNCING, BUOYANT, LIVELY **2 :** RESILIENT ⟨~ chair cushions⟩

¹bound \'bau̇nd\ *adj* [alter. of *boun*, fr. ME, fr. ON *būinn*, past part. of *būa* to live, dwell, make ready — more at BOWER] **1** *archaic* **:** PREPARED, READY, DRESSED **2 :** intending to go **:** on the way toward **:** GOING — used with *to* or *for* or with an adverb of motion ⟨a ship ~ for Gibraltar⟩ ⟨homeward ~⟩

²bound \"\ *n* -s [ME *bounde, bunne, bonne*, fr. OF *bodne, bonne, borne*, fr. ML *bodina*] **1 a :** the external or limiting line of an object, space, or area ⟨the ~*s* of a forest reserve⟩ ⟨set ~*s* on a property⟩ — usu. used in pl. **b :** something that limits or restrains **:** LIMIT ⟨beyond the ~*s* of reason⟩ ⟨set a lower ~ to a temperature range⟩; *specif* **:** limits beyond which military personnel are forbidden to go ⟨out of ~*s*⟩ **2** *usu pl* **a :** BORDERLAND **b :** the land within certain bounds **:** DOMAIN ⟨woodland ~*s* —William Wordsworth⟩ **3 :** a number greater than or equal to every number in a set (as the values of a function over an interval); *also* **:** a number less than or equal to every number in a set

³bound \"\ *vb* -ED/-ING/-S [ME *bounden*, fr. *bounde*] *vt* **1 :** to set limits or bounds to **:** to establish the bounds of **:** confine within limits ⟨fields ~*ed* by tall hedges⟩ ⟨art . . . is always greater than the rules with which we may attempt to ~ it —C.S. Kilby⟩ **2 :** to form the limits of or lie along the borders of ⟨the sea ~*s* it on three sides⟩ **:** CIRCUMSCRIBE, ENCLOSE ⟨the stream that ~*s* this land⟩ **3 :** to name the boundaries of ⟨the class was asked to ~ their country⟩ ~ *vi, archaic* **:** to form a common boundary — often used with *with*

⁴bound \"\ *adj* [ME *bounden*, fr. past part. of *binden* to bind — more at BIND] **1 a :** fastened by or as if by a band **:** CONFINED ⟨desk-*bound*⟩ **b :** compelled or constrained esp. by logical necessity **:** CERTAIN, SURE — used postpositively ⟨such a plan is ~ to fail⟩ ⟨we are ~ to have a frost soon⟩ **2 :** under legal or moral restraint or obligation **:** OBLIGED — usu. used postpositively ⟨~ to pay his wife's debts⟩ ⟨~ by sacred vows⟩ ⟨honor-*bound*⟩ ⟨duty-*bound*⟩; *specif* **:** APPRENTICED ⟨a ~ girl⟩ **3 :** CONSTIPATED, COSTIVE — used postpositively **4** *of a book* **a :** secured to its covers by cords or tapes ⟨a ~ volume⟩ **b :** cased in **5 a :** RESOLVED ⟨~ and determined to have his way⟩ **b :** ASSURED — often used as if spoken under oath ⟨you're a . . . first-rate seaman, I'll be ~ —W.S.Gilbert⟩ **6 :** held in chemical or physical combination **:** COMBINED ⟨some vitamins occur in ~ forms⟩ — opposed to *free* **7** *of a linguistic form* **:** always occurring in combination with another linguistic form (as *splend-* in *splendor* and *splendid*, *un-* in *unknown*, *-s* in *hats*, *-er* in *speaker*) ⟨a ~ form⟩ ⟨a ~ allomorph⟩ — opposed to *free*

⁵bound \"\ *vt, South & Midland* **:** BET, WAGER — used chiefly in assertions and affirmations ⟨I ~ you he'll like it⟩

⁶bound \"\ *n* -s [MF *bond*, fr. *bondir*] **1 :** a leap or spring usu. made easily and lightly ⟨cleared the hedge at a ~⟩ **:** one of a continuous series of such springs **2 :** BOUNCE, REBOUND **3 :** one of a series of relatively short movements by a military unit or by elements of it alternately from one preselected point on the ground to the next **syn** see JUMP

⁷bound \"\ *vi* -ED/-ING/-S [MF *bondir* to leap, bound, resound, fr. (assumed) VL *bombitire* to hum, irreg. fr. L *bombus* deep hollow sound — more at BOMB] **1 :** to move with a spring or leap or with a succession of springs or leaps **2 :** REBOUND ⟨an elastic ball ~*s*⟩ **:** BOUNCE **syn** see JUMP

bound·a·ry \'bau̇nd(ə)rē, ri\ *n* -ES [²*bound* + *-ary*] **1 :** something that indicates or fixes a limit or extent **:** something that marks a bound (as of a territory or a playing field) **:** a bounding or separating line **2** *cricket* **:** a hit that sends the ball to or across the boundary **3** *Midland* **:** a tract of land esp with timber on it

boundary condition *n, physics* **:** a condition which a quantity that varies throughout a given space or enclosure must fulfill at every point on the boundary of that space esp. when the velocity of a fluid at any point on the wall of a rigid conduit is necessarily parallel to the wall

boundary layer *n* **:** the region of retarded flow in a fluid (as air) close to the surface of a body (as an airplane wing) which moves through the fluid or past which the fluid flows with the retardation being greatest close to the surface of the body and being due to viscosity of the fluid and its adhesion to the surface

boundary light *n* **:** any light used to indicate the limits of the landing area of an airport

boundary marker *n* **:** a usu. cone-shaped orange marker that indicates the boundary of an area available for the landing of an airplane

boundary rider *n, Austral* **:** one that rides around the boundaries of a station and keeps the fences in order

bound bailiff *n* [alter. (influenced by ⁴*bound*) of *bumbailiff*] **:** a bonded sheriff's officer who serves writs and makes arrests

bound charge *n* [⁴*bound*] **:** the portion of the electrical charge on a conductor that because of the inductive action of a neighboring charge will not escape to the earth when the conductor is grounded

bounded *past of* BOUND, *archaic past part of* BIND

bound·ed·ness *n* -ES **:** the quality or state of being bounded

bounded noun *n* [*bounded* fr. past part. of ³*bound*] **:** a noun (as *book, letter, window*) that in the singular is always accompanied by a determiner

bound·en \'bau̇ndən\ *adj* [ME — more at ⁴BOUND] **1** *archaic* **:** BOUND **:** fastened by bonds **:** in bondage **2** *archaic* **:** under obligation (as for a favor) **:** OBLIGED, BEHOLDEN ⟨~ to political supporters⟩ **3 :** made obligatory **:** imposed as a duty **:** BINDING ⟨our ~ duty⟩

¹bound·er \-də(r)\ *n* -s [³*bound* + *-er*] *archaic* **:** BOUNDARY

²bounder \"\ *n* -s [⁷*bound* + *-er*] **1** *slang Brit* **a :** DOGCART **b :** a 4-wheeled cab **2** *chiefly Brit* **:** a man of objectionable manners, taste, or other form of social behavior **:** OUTSIDER, CAD ⟨a big, jolly fellow, with a touch of the ~ about him —D.H.Lawrence⟩ — often used in general disparagement ⟨almost offensive, the old ~ had been —Norman Douglas⟩ **3 :** a batted ball that bounces along the ground **:** GROUNDER

bound·er·ish \'bau̇ndərish\ *adj* **:** resembling or typical of a bounder

bounding *pres part of* BOUND

bound·ing·ly *adv* **:** in a bounding manner

bound·less \'bau̇n(d)ləs\ *adj* [²*bound* + *-less*] **:** having no boundaries or limits ⟨~ ocean⟩ ⟨the ~ prairie⟩ **:** IMMEASURABLE, VAST ⟨~ heavens⟩ **:** without restraining limits ⟨~ joy⟩ ⟨~ optimism⟩ — sometimes distinguished from *infinite* ⟨a spherical surface is ~ but not infinite in extent⟩ — **bound·less·ly** *adv* — **bound·less·ness** *n* -ES

bound·ness *n* -ES **:** the quality or state of being bound

bounds *pl of* BOUND, *pres 3d sing of* BOUND

bound up *adj* **:** inseparably connected or associated ⟨his career is *bound up* with the fortunes of the enterprise⟩; *also* **:** deeply involved **:** wrapped up ⟨he is *bound up* in his family⟩

bound variable *n* [⁴*bound*] *logic* **:** a variable occurring within the scope of a quantifier and so no longer available for substitution by a constant **:** an apparent variable

bound water *n* [⁴*bound*] **:** water that is an essential component of various materials (as animal and plant cells or soils) from which it cannot be removed without changing their structure or composition and distinguishable from free water in such ways as by its inability to dissolve sugar or to form ice crystals

boun·te·ous \'bau̇ntēəs *esp Brit sometimes* -nchəs\ *adj* [ME, alter. (influenced by *bounte* bounty) of *bountevous*, fr. MF *bontif* kind, benevolent (fr. OF, fr. *bonté* goodness, kindness + *-if* -ive) + ME *-ous*] **1 :** characterized by bounty **:** giving or disposed to give freely **:** GENEROUS, LIBERAL **2** *obs* **:** abounding in goodness **3 :** liberally bestowed **:** AMPLE, BOUNTIFUL, PLENTIFUL ⟨a ~ yield of corn⟩ ⟨his ~ good looks —J.D.Salinger⟩ **syn** see LIBERAL

boun·te·ous·ly *adv* **:** in a bounteous manner

boun·te·ous·ness *n* -ES [ME *bounteousnesse*, fr. *bounteous* + *-nesse* -ness] **:** the quality or state of being bounteous

boun·tied \'bau̇ntēd, -tid\ *adj* **1 :** having the benefit of a bounty ⟨a ~ export⟩ **2 :** rewarded or rewardable by a bounty ⟨a ~ animal pelt⟩

boun·ti·ful \'bau̇ntəfəl, -tēf-\ *adj* **1 :** full of bounty **:** free in giving **:** liberal in bestowing gifts and favors **:** GRACIOUS **2 :** ABUNDANT, PLENTIFUL ⟨a ~ supply of food⟩ **syn** see LIBERAL

boun·ti·ful·ly \-f(ə)lē, -li\ *adv* **:** in a bountiful degree **:** GENEROUSLY, PLENTIFULLY

boun·ti·ful·ness *n* -ES **:** the quality or state of being bountiful

boun·tith \'büntəth\ *n* -s [ME, fr. MF *bontet, bonté* goodness, kindness] *Scot* **:** a supplement to regular wages **:** BONUS

boun·ty \'bau̇ntē, -ti\ *n* -ES [ME *bounte*, fr. OF *bonté, bunté*, fr. L *bonitat-, bonitas*, fr. *bonus* good (fr. OL *dvenos*) + *-itat-, -itas* -ity; akin to OE *langtwīdig* granted for a long time, MHG *zwīden* to grant, OIr *den* strong, Skt *duvas* gift, reverence] **1** *obs* **:** GOODNESS, KINDNESS, VIRTUE **2 :** liberality in bestowing gifts or favors **:** gracious or liberal giving **:** GENEROSITY, MUNIFICENCE **3 :** something that is given generously or liberally **4 :** yield esp. of a crop **5 :** a reward, premium, or subsidy esp. when offered or given by a government: as **a :** an extra allowance to induce entry into the armed services **b :** a grant to encourage an industry **c :** a grant of land to encourage settlement **d :** a payment to encourage the destruction of noxious animals ⟨a ~ on wildcats⟩

bounty hunter *n* **1 :** one that hunts predatory animals for the reward offered **2 :** one that tracks down and captures outlaws for whom a reward is offered

bounty jumper *n* **:** one who during the Civil War enlisted in the U.S. service to get a bounty and then deserted

boun·ty·less *adj* **:** being without a bounty

bou·quet \(')bō¦kā, (')bü¦k- *sometimes* bu̇'k- *or* bə'k-; (')bō- *is less freq for sense 4 than for the other senses*\ *n* -s [F, fr. MF, bouquet, thicket, fr. ONF *bosquet* thicket, fr. OF *bosc, bois* forest (perh. of Gmc origin and akin to OHG *busc* forest) + *-et* — more at BUSH] **1 :** flowers picked and fastened together in a bunch **:** NOSEGAY **2 :** COMPLIMENT ⟨~*s* and brickbats⟩ **3 :** BOUQUET GARNI **4 a :** the distinctive fragrance (as of a wine or brandy) derived from the processes of fermentation and aging — compare AROMA 2 **b :** a distinctive subtle quality (as of an artistic performance) **syn** see FRAGRANCE

bouquet gar·ni \-,gär'nē\ *n, pl* **bouquets garnis** \-kā(z). . .nē\ [F, lit., garnished bouquet] **:** a tied bunch of herbs (as parsley, bay leaf, and thyme) used in soups and other savory dishes

bouquet larkspur *n* **:** any of several cultivated larkspurs derived from a species (*Delphinium grandiflorum*) having finely cut leaves and flowers with spurs straight or nearly so

bou·qui·niste \bükēnēst\ *n, pl* **bouquinistes** \"\ [F, fr. *bouquin* old book (fr. obs. D *boeckin* little book, dim. of D *boek* book) + *-iste* -ist; akin to OHG *buoh* book — more at BOOK] **:** a dealer in secondhand books

bour \'bür\ *Scot var of* BOWER

bou·rach \'bürək\ *var of* BOUROCK

bour·bon \'bu̇r|bən, 'bōr|,'bȯr|,'bu̇ə|,'bōə(|),'bȯ(ə)|; 'bər| *or* 'bə| *is usual for sense 4 and sometimes occurs for the other senses*\ *n* -s [*Bourbon*, seigniory in central France] **1** *cap* **:** a member of a French family founded in 1272 by Robert, Count of Clermont, to which belonged the rulers of France from 1589 (Henry IV) to 1793 and from 1814 to 1830, of Spain from 1700 (Philip V) to 1808, from 1814 to 1868, from 1875 to 1931, and from 1975, of Naples from 1735 (Charles III) to 1805, and of the Two Sicilies from 1815 (Ferdinand I) to 1860 **2** *usu cap* [after *Bourbon*, French royal family, fr. *Bourbon*, seigniory in central France] **:** a person who clings obstinately to the social and political ideas of the old order of things **:** REACTIONARY, CONSERVATIVE; *specif* **:** an extremely conservative member of the Democratic party of the U.S. ⟨the *Bourbons* refused to consider the proposal⟩ **3** *or* **bourbon rose** [*Bourbon* (now Réunion), French island in the Indian ocean, after *Bourbon*, French royal family] **a :** a rose (*Rosa borboniana*) that is generally considered an accidental hybrid between the China rose and the French rose and is of compact upright growth with shining leaves, prickly branches, and clustered flowers **b :** any of various cultivated roses derived from the bourbon rose and typically being hardy and recurrent-blooming **4** *or* **bourbon whiskey** [*Bourbon* county, Kentucky] **:** a whiskey distilled from corn mash; *specif* **:** a whiskey distilled from a mash containing at least 51 percent corn, the rest being malt and rye, and aged in new charred oak containers — compare CORN WHISKEY **5** [perh. fr. *Bourbon* (now Réunion)] **:** a Santos coffee of a superior grade

bour·bon·al \ˈbərbəˌnal\ *n* -S [perh. fr. *Bourbon*, French royal family + *-al* (aldehyde)] **:** ETHYL VANILLIN

bourbon cotton *n, usu cap B* [*Bourbon* (now Réunion), French island in the Indian ocean] **:** a cotton derived from a West Indian cotton plant (*Gossypium purpurascens*)

bour·bon·ism \ˈbu̇rbəˌnizəm\ *n* -S *often cap* **1 :** support of the Bourbons (sense 1) **:** LEGITIMISM **2 :** adherence to the Bourbons (sense 2)

bourbon red *n, usu cap B&R* [prob. fr. *Bourbon* county, Kentucky] **:** a variety of domestic turkey of medium size and reddish brown color

bourbon tea *n, usu cap B* [*Bourbon* (now Réunion)] **:** FAHAM

bour·don \ˈbu̇rdᵊn, -ȯr-,-ər-\ *also* **bor·dun** \ˈbȯr-\ *n* -S [ME *burdoun*, fr. MF *bourdon* bass horn, of imit. origin] **1 :** ³BURDEN 1 **2 a :** a drone bass (as in a bagpipe or a hurdy-gurdy) **b :** a pipe-organ stop of a droning or buzzing quality usu. of 16-foot pitch **c :** the lowest bell (as in a carillon) in a ring of bells

bour·don gauge \ˈbu̇rˌdōⁿ-\ *n, usu cap B* [after Eugène *Bourdon* †1884 Fr. engineer and inventor] **:** a pressure gauge having a Bourdon tube as its sensitive element

bour·don lace \"-\ *n* [F *bourdon* cord edging on lace, staff of a fish net, pilgrim's staff, fr. LL *burdon-*, *burdo* hinny, fr. L *burdus*] **:** a net lace with edge and pattern outlined by cording

bour·don·née \ˌbu̇rdᵊnˈā\ *adj* [F *bourdonné*, fr. *bourdon* pilgrim's staff; fr. the knob-shaped handle characteristic of a pilgrim's staff] **:** POMMÉE

bour·don spring \ˈbu̇rˌdōⁿ-\ *n, usu cap B* [after Eugène *Bourdon*] **:** a Bourdon tube coiled into a flat spiral spring

bourdon tube *n, usu cap B* **:** a thin-walled flattened tube of elastic metal bent into a circular arc whose application to certain pressure gauges and thermometers depends upon the fact that increase of pressure inside the tube tends to straighten it — see BOURDON GAUGE, BOURDON SPRING

bou·rette *also* **bour·rette** \bu̇ˈret, bəˈ\ *n* -S [F *bourrette* coarse silk on the outside of a cocoon, fr. MF, fr. *bourre* (silk) waste, padding (fr. LL *burra* shaggy cloth) + *-ette* — more at BUREAU] **1 :** an irregular slubbed yarn made usu. of silk waste **2 :** a plain-woven fabric that has a rough uneven appearance and is made from bourette yarn

bourg \ˈbu̇(ə)r(g)\ *n* -S [ME, fr. MF, fr. OF *borc*, fr. L *burgus* fortified place, of Gmc origin; akin to OHG *burg* fortified place — more at BOROUGH] **:** TOWN, VILLAGE: as **a :** one neighboring a castle **b :** MARKET TOWN

bour·gade \bu̇rˈgäd\ *n* -S [F, prob. fr. OProv *borgada* village, suburb, fr. *borc* fortified place, fr. L *burgus*] **:** a village of scattered dwellings **:** an unfortified town

¹**bour·geois** \ˈbu̇rzh,wä, ˈbu̇ȯzh,wä, ˈbu̇əzh,wä *sometimes* ˈbüzh-; *sometimes* ⸗ˈ⸗; *in sense 4* (ˌ)bərˈjȯis *or* bəˈj- *or* bōˈj-\ *n, pl* **bourgeois** [MF, fr. OF *borjois*, fr. *borc*] **1 a :** BURGHER **b :** a middle-class person **:** one of the social class whose income derives from the profits of commercial and industrial enterprise esp. as distinguished from the landed gentry, the wage earners and farmers, and sometimes the professions **:** SHOPKEEPER, BUSINESSMAN **2 :** one whose social behavior and political views are determined or influenced by private-property interest **:** CAPITALIST **3 bourgeois** *pl* **:** BOURGEOISIE ⟨the talk of disheartened ~ and elated intellectuals —J.A. Schumpeter⟩ **4 :** an old size of type (approximately 9 point) between brevier and long primer — compare POINT SYSTEM **5 :** one formerly in charge of a trading post in the fur trade of the American Northwest

²**bourgeois** \"\ *adj* [F, fr. OF *borjois*, fr. *borjois*, n.] **1 :** of, belonging to, or characteristic of the townsman or of the social middle class ⟨a solid ~ family⟩ ⟨the ~ virtues of thriftiness, forethought and a serious attitude toward life —Gilbert Cadoffre⟩ ⟨~ culture⟩ **2 :** characterized by selfish concern for material comfort and well-being, by preoccupation with moneymaking or property accumulation, by anxiety about social respectability, and by a tendency toward safe mediocrity in matters of thought, feeling, and artistic taste **:** PHILISTINE — usu. used in disparagement **3** *of a nation* **:** dominated by commercial and industrial interest **:** CAPITALISTIC

bour·geoise \-äz,-āz\ *n* -S [F, fem. of *bourgeois*] **1 :** a wife or daughter of a bourgeois **:** a woman of the middle class **2 :** BOURGEOIS

bour·geoi·sie \ˌ⸗,wäˈzē, -,wȧ-\ *n* -S [F, fr. *bourgeois*] **1 :** MIDDLE CLASS **2 :** a social order dominated by bourgeois ⟨civilized society is one huge ~; no nobleman dares now shock his greengrocer —G.B.Shaw⟩

bourgeon *var of* BURGEON

bour·gui·gnon \ˌbu̇r(ˌ)gēnˈyōⁿ\ *n* -S *cap* [F, fr. *Bourgogne* (Burgundy), region in east central France] **:** ¹BURGUNDIAN 2

bourkha *var of* BURKA

¹**bourn** *or* **bourne** \ˈbō(ə)rn, -ȯ(ə)rn, -u̇(ə)rn\ *n* -S [ME *bourne*, fr. OE *burn*, *burna*, *burne*; akin to OHG *brunno* spring of water, ON *brunnr*, Goth *brunna*, Gk *phrear* well, L *fervēre* to boil — more at BURN] **:** STREAM, BROOK, RIVULET; *specif* **:** an intermittent stream on chalk downs

²**bourn** *or* **bourne** \"\ *n* -S [MF *bourne*, *borne*, fr. OF *bodne*, *bonne*, *borne* — more at BOUND] **1** *archaic* **:** BOUND, BOUNDARY, LIMIT **2** *archaic* **:** a terminal point aimed at **:** GOAL, DESTINATION ⟨sole ~, sole wish, sole object of my song —William Wordsworth⟩

bourne·mouth \-nməth\ *adj, usu cap* [fr. *Bournemouth*, England] **:** of or from the county borough of Bournemouth, England **:** of the kind or style prevalent in Bournemouth

bour·non·ite \ˈbȯrnəˌnīt, ˈbȯr-, ˈbu̇r-\ *n* -S [Count J.L.de *Bournon* †1825 Fr. mineralogist + E *-ite*] **:** a mineral $PbCuSbS_3$ consisting of a steel-gray or black metallic-looking sulfide of antimony, lead, and copper occurring in orthorhombic crystals, and also massive — see WHEEL ORE

bou·rock \ˈbürək\ *n* -S [prob. fr. *bour* + *-ock*] **1** *Scot* **:** a rude hut; *esp* **:** one used by shepherds **2** *Scot* **a :** MOUND, KNOLL **b :** HEAP, MASS; *specif* **:** a stone heap **3** *Scot* **:** CROWD, GROUP

bourout *usu cap, var of* BURUT

bour·rée \(ˈ)bu̇ˈrā\ *n* -S [F, perh. fr. fem. of *bourré*, past part. of *bourrer* to stuff, beat, fr. MF, fr. *bourre* (silk) waste, padding, fr. LL *burra* shaggy cloth — more at BUREAU] **1 :** a lively old French dance tune usu. in duple time and beginning with an upbeat; *also* **:** a musical composition with the rhythm of such a dance **2 a :** a clogging peasant dance of Auvergne and Berry **b :** a 16th century French court dance with crossing steps **3 :** a ballet combination that consists of small crossing steps

bour·re·let \ˌbu̇rəˈlā\ *n* -S [F — more at BURLET] **1 :** BURLET **2 :** a cloth wreath or turban worn on a helmet **3 :** the raised portion of an artillery projectile between the ogive and the body

bourrette *var of* BOURETTE

bour·sault rose \ˈbu̇rˌsō-\ *n, usu cap B* [prob. fr. the name *Boursault*] **:** a climbing hybrid rose (*Rosa lheritierana*) with purplish double flowers

bourse \ˈbu̇(ə)rs, -u̇əs\ *n* -S [F, lit., purse, fr. ML *bursa* — more at PURSE] **1 :** a place where merchants, bankers, and brokers meet for business at certain hours **:** MARKET, EXCHANGE **2 :** a sale of numismatic or philatelic items carried on by a number of dealers displaying their wares on tables (as at a convention)

bour·tree \ˈbu̇r·(ˌ)trē, ˈbü·(ˌ)-\ *n* [ME *burtre*, *bourtre*, perh. fr. *bour* bower + *tre*, *tree* tree] *Brit* **:** the common large black-fruited elder (*Sambucus nigra*) of Europe and Asia formerly esteemed as a source of dyestuffs and of several folk remedies

¹**bouse** \ˈbüz, ˈbau̇z\ *archaic var of* BOOZE

²**bouse** *or* **bowse** \ˈbau̇z\ *vb* -ED/-ING/-S [origin unknown] *vt, naut* **:** to pull or haul by means of a tackle; *also* **:** to haul well taut and belay (as a purchase) — usu. used with *taut* ~ *vi, naut* **:** to bouse something — usu. used with *taut*

bouser \ˈbüzə(r), ˈbau̇z-\ *archaic var of* BOOZER

bous·sin·gaul·tia \ˌbüsᵊnˈgōltēə\ *n, cap* [NL, fr. J.B.J.D. *Boussingault* †1887 Fr. chemist + NL *-ia*] **:** a small genus of graceful succulent perennial vines (family Basellaceae) found in tropical America with pedicellate flowers in axillary and terminal spikelike racemes — see MADEIRA VINE

bous·sin·gaul·tite \-lˌtīt\ *n* -S [F, fr. J.B.J.D.*Boussingault* + F *-ite*] **:** a mineral $(NH_4)_2Mg(SO_4)_2.6H_2O$ consisting of a crystallized magnesium ammonium sulfate first found in boric-acid fumaroles of Tuscany, Italy

bou·stro·phe·don *also* **bou·stro·phei·don** *or* **bu·stro·phe·don** *or* **bu·stro·phei·don** \ˌbüstrəˈfēˌdän, -ēdᵊn, ˌ⸗⸗ˈfēˌdän; büˈsträfəˌdän\ *n* -S [Gk *boustrophēdon*, adv., turning like oxen in plowing, fr. *bou-* (fr. *bous* ox, cow) + *-strophēdon* (fr. *strephein* to turn) — more at COW, STROPHE] **:** the writing of alternate lines in opposite directions, one line from left to right and the next from right to left — **bou·stro·phe·don·ic** \ˌbüstrəfēˈdänik, (ˈ)büˌsträfəˈ-\ *adj*

¹**bout** \ˈbau̇t, ˈbət\ *prep* [ME, fr. OE *būtan* without, except — more at BUT] *dial Eng* **:** WITHOUT ⟨he came ~ a hat⟩

²**bout** \ˈbau̇t, *usu* -au̇d·+V\ *n* -S [alter. of *bought* (bend)] **1 a** *dial Brit* **:** a trip going and returning in plowing or mowing **:** TURN **b :** a course or round of knitting **c** *dial chiefly Eng* **:** TIME, OCCASION ⟨won't be caught napping this ~⟩ **2 :** a spell of activity or a period of action having a definite beginning and end: as **a :** a contest or match esp. of boxing, wrestling, fencing **:** TURN ⟨a ~ at cudgels⟩ **b :** OUTBURST, ATTACK, SIEGE ⟨~s of bad temper⟩ ⟨drinking ~⟩ ⟨a ~ of fever⟩ **c :** SESSION ⟨long ~s of stubborn argument⟩ **3 :** one of the six sections or ribs comprising the side walls of the body of a stringed instrument (as a violin); *sometimes* **:** the waist section only

³**bout** \"\ *vt* -ED/-ING/-S **:** to plow (a field) by bouts

bou·tade \büˈtäd\ *n* -S [F, fr. MF, fr. *bouter* to thrust + *-ade* — more at BUTT] **1 a :** an outbreak or burst esp. of temper **b :** CAPRICE, WHIM ⟨no need to take his little ~s seriously⟩ **2 a :** an 18th century French dance of impromptu character **b :** an instrumental musical composition similar to the Italian capriccio in an impromptu fanciful style

boutefeu *n* -S [MF, lit., linstock, fr. *bouter* to thrust, put, set + *feu* fire, fr. L *focus* hearth — more at FOCUS] *obs* **:** one who causes contention **:** FIREBRAND

boutell *var of* BOLTEL

bou·te·loua \ˌbüd·ᵊlˈüə, ˌbōd·ᵊlˈōə\ *n, cap* [NL, irreg. fr. Claudio *Boutelou* †1848 Span. botanist] **:** a large genus of No. American forage grasses distinguished by the one-sided spikes of the inflorescence — see GRAMA

bou·tique \büˈtēk\ *n* -S [F, prob. fr. OProv *botica*, fr. Gk *apothēkē* warehouse — more at APOTHECARY] **1 :** a small retail store; *esp* **:** a specialty shop dealing in ladies' fashionable ready-to-wear clothes and accessories **2 :** a utilitarian or luxury item lavishly decorated (as with gilt, sequins, jewels)

bou·to \ˈbōˌtü\ *n* -S [Pg *boto*, lit., wineskin, fr. LL *buttis* cask; fr. its shape — more at BUTT (cask)] **:** a river dolphin (*Inia geoffrensis*) that is peculiar to the Amazon and has a long snout

bou·ton \(ˈ)büˈtōⁿ\ *or* **bouton ter·mi·nal** \-ˌtermə'nal\ *n, pl* **boutons** \-ōⁿ\ *or* **boutons termi·naux** \-ˈnō\ [F *bouton terminal*, lit., terminal button] **:** a terminal club-shaped enlargement of a nerve fiber lying in contact with the body or dendrites of another neuron — called also *end bulb*, *end foot*

bou·ton·neuse fever \ˈbütᵊnˌüz-, -ə(r)z-, -ˌəz-\ *n* [part trans. of F *fièvre boutonneuse*, fr. *fièvre* fever + *boutonneuse*, fem. of *boutonneux* pimply, fr. *bouton* pimple, button, bud] **:** a disease prevalent in the Mediterranean area that is characterized by headache, pain in muscles and joints, and an eruption over the body including palms and soles and is caused by a rickettsia (*Rickettsia conorii*) which is transmitted by the bite of a tick

bou·ton·niere \ˌbütᵊnˈi(ə)r, -iə also -tᵊnˈe(ə)r *or* -tənˈye(ə)r *or* -eə\ *n* -S [F *boutonnière* buttonhole, fr. MF *boutonniere*, fr. *bouton* button] **:** a flower or bouquet worn in a buttonhole; *also* **:** BOUQUET

bou·ton pearl \(ˈ)büˈtōⁿ-\ *or* **but·ton pearl** \ˈbətᵊn-\ *n* [F *bouton* button — more at BUTTON] **:** a pearl flat on one side

bou·tre \ˈbütr(ᵊ), -t(rə)\ *n* -S [F] **:** a small Arabian coasting boat of the eastern African coast

bouts-ri·més \ˌbü(ˌ)rēˈmā(z)\ *n pl* [F, lit., rhymed ends] **:** rhyming words or syllables to which verses are to be written; *also* **:** verses so composed

bou·var·dia \büˈvärdēə\ *n* [NL, fr. Charles *Bouvard* †1658 Fr. physician + NL *-ia*] **1** *cap* **:** a genus of tropical American herbs and shrubs (family Rubiaceae) with corymbs of showy tubular red, scarlet, yellow, and white flowers **2** -S **:** a plant or flower of the genus *Bouvardia*

bou·veault-blanc reduction \ˌbüˌvōˈbläⁿ-\ *n, cap both Bs* [after Louis *Bouveault* †1909 and Gustave *Blanc* *fl*1903 French chemists] **:** a method for the preparation of alcohols from esters and of amines from oximes or nitriles by reduction with metallic sodium in solution in an alcohol (as ethyl alcohol)

bou·vier des flan·dres \büvyādəˈflaⁿdr(ᵊ), -d(rə)\ *n, usu cap B&F* [F, lit., cowherd of Flanders] **1 :** a breed of large powerfully built rough-coated dogs originating in Belgium and used esp. for herding and in guard and police work, having a slightly tousled appearance, with definite eyebrows, a mustache, and a beard, and ranging in color from fawn to black, through pepper-and-salt, and gray and brindle **2** *pl* **bouvier des flandres** \"\ **:** a dog of this breed

bouw \ˈbau̇, ˈbōu̇\ *n* -S [D, lit., tillage; akin to OE *bū* dwelling, OHG *bū* tillage, dwelling, ON *bū* household, OE *būan* to dwell — more at BOWER] **:** an Indonesian unit of land area equal to 1.75 acres

bouza *var of* BOSA

bouze \ˈbüz\ *archaic var of* BOOZE

bo·va·rism *or* **bo·va·rysm** \ˈbōvəˌrizəm\ *n* -S [F *bovarysme*, fr. Madame Bovary (principal character in the novel *Madame Bovary* by Gustave Flaubert †1880 Fr. novelist) + *-isme* -ism] **:** a conception of oneself as other than one is to the extent that one's general behavior is conditioned or dominated by the conception; *esp* **:** domination by such an idealized, glamorized, glorified, or otherwise unreal conception of oneself that it results in dramatic personal conflict (as in tragedy), in markedly unusual behavior (as in paranoia), or in great achievement

bo·va·rist \-ˌrəst\ *n* -S [F, fr. *bovarism*, after such pairs as E *romanticism*: *romanticist*] **:** a person subject to bovarism ⟨a religious ~⟩ — **bo·va·ris·tic** \ˌbōvəˈristik\ *adj*

bo·vate \ˈbōˌvāt\ *n* -S [ML *bovata*, fr. L *bov-*, *bos* cow, ox] **:** an old English unit of land area equal to ⅛ carucate

bov·ey coal \ˈbəvē-\ *n, usu cap B* [*Bovey*, parish in Devonshire, England, its locality] **:** a lignite of the Miocene period found esp. at Bovey, England

bovi- *comb form* [LL *bovi-*, fr. L *bov-*, *bos*] **:** cattle ⟨*boviculture*⟩

bo·vic·o·la \bōˈvikələ\ *n, cap* [NL, fr. *bovi-* + *-cola*] **:** a genus of biting lice (order Mallophaga) including the red louse of cattle and several other lice infesting the hair of domestic mammals

¹**bo·vid** \ˈbōvəd\ *adj* [NL *Bovidae*] **:** belonging to the family Bovidae

²**bovid** \"\ *n* -S **:** an animal of the family Bovidae

bo·vi·dae \ˈbōvəˌdē\ *n pl, cap* [NL, fr. *Bov-*, *Bos*, type genus + *-idae*] **:** a large family of ruminants containing the true antelopes, oxen, sheep, and goats, distinguished from the deer family by the polycotyledonary placenta, the hollow nondeciduous unbranched horns, and by the nearly universal presence of a gallbladder

¹**bo·vine** \ˈbōˌvīn, -ēn *also* ⸗ˈ⸗\ *adj* [LL *bovinus*, fr. L *bov-*, *bos* ox, cow + *-inus* -ine — more at COW] **1 :** of or belonging to the genus *Bos* **:** relating to or resembling the ox or cow **2 :** having qualities characteristic of oxen or cows **:** sluggish and patient **:** DULL ⟨a ~ temperament⟩ — **bo·vine·ly** *adv* — **bo·vin·i·ty** \bōˈvinəd·ē\ *n* -ES

²**bovine** \"\ *n* -S **:** an animal of *Bos* or of a closely related genus of the family Bovidae

bovine farcy *n* **:** FARCY 2

bovine malaria *n* **:** TEXAS FEVER

bovine mastitis *n* **:** inflammation of the cow's udder resulting from injury or bruising or more commonly from bacterial infection and being a major source of loss to the dairy industry both through direct damage to the animals and through loss of milk — see STREPTOCOCCAL MASTITIS, SUMMER MASTITIS

bovine staggers *n pl but sing in constr* **:** a disease of cattle in southern Africa characterized by staggering, inflammation, emaciation, and finally paralysis and caused by eating a poisonous herb (*Matricaria nigellaefolia*)

bo·vis·ta \bōˈvistə\ *n, cap* [NL, fr. G *bofist*, *bovist* puffball, alter. of MHG *vohenvist*, fr. *vohe* she-fox (fr. OHG *foha*) + *vist*, *vīst* emission of gas from the colon — more at FOX, FEIST] **:** a genus of basidiomycetes (family Lycoperdaceae) including various puffballs having a thin peridium at maturity

bo·vo \ˈbō(ˌ)vō\ *n* -S [It] **:** a lateen-rigged masted fishing boat of Genoa

bo·void \ˈbōˌvȯid\ *adj* [L *bov-*, *bos* + E *-oid*] **:** like or belonging to the genus *Bos* or family Bovidae **:** BOVINE

bo·voi·dea \bōˈvȯidēə\ *n pl, cap* [NL, fr. *Bov-*, *Bos* genus of ruminant mammals including the wild and domestic cattle + *-oidea*] **:** a superfamily or other division of horned ruminant mammals (order Artiodactyla) comprising the families Antilocapridae and Bovidae and distinguished by possession of hollow horns that are deciduous in the former family but permanent in the latter

¹**bow** \ˈbau̇\ *vb* -ED/-ING/-S [ME *bowen*, fr. OE *būgan*; akin to OHG *biogan* to bend, ON *boginn* bent, *beygja* to bend, Goth *biugan* to bend, Skt *bhujati* he bends] *vi* **1** *archaic* **a :** BEND, CURVE **b :** to bend down **:** STOOP **c :** TURN, SWERVE, WEND **2 :** to give in **:** cease from independent resolution, competition, or resistance through courtesy, cooperation, subjugation, admission of defeat, or inferior position **:** DEFER, YIELD ⟨a man who good-humoredly ~*ed* to the inevitable —Willa Cather⟩; *specif* **:** to suffer defeat in a contest ⟨~*ed* to the champion in a close match⟩ **3 :** to bend the head or the body or the knee as an expression of reverence, submission, or shame ⟨~ and scrape⟩ — often used with *down* ⟨~*ing* down before false gods⟩ **4 :** to incline the head or body in salutation ⟨~*ing* to acquaintances⟩ or as a sign of assent (as to a request or order) or to acknowledge applause ~ *vt* **1 :** to cause to incline **:** BEND ⟨the wind ~*s* the treetops⟩ **2** *obs* **:** TURN, INCLINE ⟨may God ~ their hearts to our cause⟩ **3 :** to bend or incline (the head, neck, body, or knee) esp. as a sign or token of respect, submission, surrender, or self-abasement ⟨the whole nation ~*ed* their necks to tyranny —W.H.Prescott⟩ **4 :** to crush with or as if with a heavy burden ⟨whose heavy hand hath ~*ed* you to the grave —Shak.⟩ **5 a :** to express or signal by bowing ⟨he ~*ed* his thanks⟩ **b :** to usher in or out with a bow ⟨~*ed* in by a footman⟩ **syn** see YIELD

²**bow** \"\ *n* -S **:** a bending of the head or body as an expression of reverence, respect, submission, or assent or as a salutation **:** OBEISANCE — **make one's bow :** to make a first public appearance or, formerly, a final appearance

³**bow** \ˈbō\ *n* -S [ME *bowe*, fr. OE *boga*; akin to OHG *bogo* bow, ON *bogi*, OE *būgan* to bend] **1 a :** something bent into a simple curve **:** BEND, ARCH ⟨perfect ~*s* above her eyes⟩ ⟨*bow-backed*⟩ **b :** RAINBOW ⟨I do set my ~ in the cloud —Gen 9:13 (AV)⟩ **c :** a curved or polygonal part projecting from a straight wall of a building **2 :** a weapon made of a strip of wood, metal, or other flexible material with a cord that connects the two ends so as to hold the strip bent in an arc under tension and used to propel an arrow by nocking the arrow on the string and drawing it back against the tension so that upon release it is propelled through the air **3 :** BOWMAN, ARCHER ⟨he was high ~ in the meet⟩ **4 :** SADDLEBOW **5 a** *dial* **:** a U-shaped piece embracing the neck of an ox and fastening it to the yoke; *also* **:** an ox yoke **b** *now dial Brit* **:** an arch esp. of a bridge or gateway ⟨four-and-twenty ~*s* on the old bridge of Callander⟩ **c :** a bentwood support used in furniture **d :** an early nautical quadrant for measuring arcs, chiefly the sun's altitude **e :** a metal ring or loop forming a handle (as of a key or a pair of scissors) or encircling the winding crown of a pocket watch for attaching a chain **f :** the guard of a sword hilt or trigger **g :** a bent piece of wood or metal supporting the top or cover of a vehicle **:** BAIL **h :** a knot (as an ornamental slipknot) formed by doubling a ribbon or string into two or more loops which usu. can be readily drawn through the knot in untying; *also* **:** BOW TIE **i :** a frame for the lenses of eyeglasses; *also* **:** the curved sidepiece passing over the ear to support eyeglasses **j :** the frame of a snowshoe **6 a :** a resilient wooden rod orig. having a convex curve but from the late 18th century on being slightly concave with a number of horsehairs stretched from end to end and used in playing on a musical instrument of the viol or violin family **b :** a stroke of the bow in playing a stringed instrument ⟨the up ~⟩ **7 :** a contrivance that consists of a bent elastic rod with ends connected by a string and is employed for various purposes (as for giving reciprocating motion to a drill, for wood turning, and for preparing and arranging the hair and fur used by hatters) **8 :** a bent rod or piece in basketmaking; *esp* **:** a rod bent twice at right angles so as to form three sides of a rectangle **9 :** a warping along the length of a piece of lumber — compare CROOK

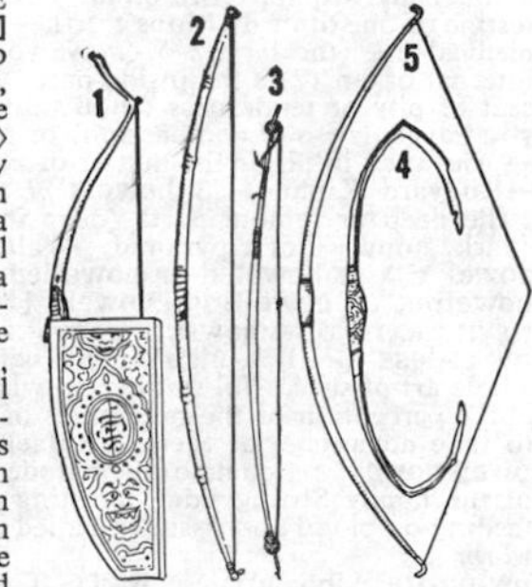

bow 2: *1* Chinese bow in quiver, *2* African cane bow, *3* Brazilian Indian bow, *4* Hindu bow, *5* modern bow; see also CUPID'S BOW illustration

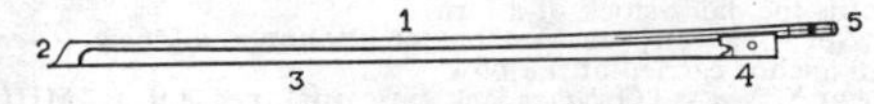

violin bow: *1* stick, *2* head, *3* hair, *4* frog, *5* screw

⁴**bow** \"\ *vb* -ED/-ING/-S *vi* **1 :** to bend into a curve **:** bend out of line ⟨the wall ~*s* inward⟩ **2 :** to play a stringed musical instrument with a bow; *also* **:** to perform with or manage the bow ~ *vt* **1 :** to make or bend into a curve ⟨a desk with a ~*ed* front⟩ **2 :** to separate and distribute (cotton fibers for felting) by a bow **3 :** to play (a stringed instrument) with a bow

⁵**bow** \ˈbau̇\ *n* -S [prob. fr. Dan *bov* bow, shoulder, fr. ON *bōgr* — more at BOUGH] **1 :** the forward part of a ship **:** the part where the sides curve inward to terminate in the stem ⟨the ~ lights⟩ — often used in pl. ⟨passed under her ~*s*⟩ ⟨~*s* under⟩ — see SHIP illustration **2 :** one that rows in the forward end of a boat **:** BOW OAR — **on the bow** *adv (or adj)* **:** on that part of the horizon bearing within 4 points of 45 degrees on either side of the line ahead

⁶**bow** \ˈbō, ˈbü\ *n* -S [by alter.] **:** ¹BOLL 1

bow-arm \ˈ⸗,⸗\ *n* **:** the arm that holds the bow in archery or in playing a musical instrument of the violin family

bow-backed \ˈ⸗,⸗\ *adj* [³*bow*] **:** having the upright spindles held in place by a bow-shaped piece of wood ⟨a *bow-backed* chair⟩

bow bearer *n* [³*bow*] **:** an underofficer of the forest in old England who looked after trespasses affecting vert and venison

bow cap *n* [⁵*bow*] **1 :** a cap of metal or fabric used to reinforce the extreme forward ends of the bow stiffeners of an airship **2 :** the conical or cap-shaped structure at the bow of a rigid airship to which the longitudinal girders are attached and which supports the bow mooring spindle

bow chaser *n* [⁵*bow*] **:** a gun so placed as to be able to fire ahead (as at a ship being chased)

bow china \ˈbō-\ *n, usu cap B* [Stratford-le-*Bow*, town near London, England, where it was made] **:** china made at Stratford-le-Bow, near London, in the 18th century

bow compass *n* [³*bow*] **:** a small pair of compasses one leg of which carries a pencil, pen, or point, its legs being connected by a bow-shaped spring instead of by a joint

bow compass

bow·darc *or* **bow·dark** \'bō,dä(r)k, -dȧk\ *var of* BODOCK

bow·den \'bōdᵊn\ *vi* -ED/-ING/-S [earlier Sc *boldin*, fr. ME (Sc) *boldnen*, alter. of ME *bolnen*, modif. of ON *bolgna*; akin to OE & OHG *belgan* to be angry, ON *bolginn* swollen, *belgja* to cause to swell, OE *belg*, *bælg* bag, skin — more at BELLY] *Scot* **:** SWELL; *specif* **:** BLOAT

bow·den cable *or* **bowden wire** \'bōdᵊn, 'bau̇d-\ *n, usu cap B* [after E.M.*Bowden*, 19th cent. Eng. inventor] **:** spring steel wire enclosed in a spiral wire casing for transmitting longitudinal motion at a distance esp. (as in a hand brake) around curves

bow·dich·ia \bau̇'dichēə\ *n, cap* [NL, fr. Thomas E. *Bowdich* †1824 Eng. traveler + NL -*ia*] **:** a genus of large tropical So. American trees (family Leguminosae) with odd-pinnate leaves, blue or white flowers, and very hard wood

bow·ditch \'bau̇(ˌ)dich\ *n* -ES *usu cap* [after Nathaniel *Bowditch* †1838 Am. mathematician and astronomer] **:** a navigation manual

bow divider *n* **:** a bow compass with two divider points

bowd·ler·ism \'bōdlə,rizəm, 'bau̇d-\ *n* -S [T. *Bowdler* + E -*ism*] **:** BOWDLERIZATION, EXPURGATION

bowd·ler·i·za·tion \ˌbōdlərə'zāshən, ˌbau̇d-, -lə,rī'z-\ *n* -S **:** the act or result of bowdlerizing

bowd·ler·ize \'bōdlə,rīz, 'bau̇d-\ *vt* -ED/-ING/-S *see -ize in Explan Notes, sometimes cap* [Thomas *Bowdler* †1825 Eng. editor of an expurgated Shakespeare + E -*ize*] **1 :** to remove matter considered indelicate or otherwise objectionable from by expurgation or alteration ⟨~ a text⟩ ⟨a *bowdlerized* version of the scene⟩ ⟨*bowdlerized* the manuscript⟩ **2 :** to alter (something) by removing forceful elements **:** EMASCULATE ⟨~ a philosophy⟩

bow·dock \'bō,dȧk\ *var of* BODOCK

bow drill *n* **:** a drill worked by a bow and string to bore holes or make fire

¹**bowed** \'bau̇d\ *adj* [ME, fr. past part. of *bowen* to bend — more at ¹BOW] **:** bent down **:** with the head inclined — **bowed·ness** *n* -ES

²**bowed** \'bōd\ *adj* [ME, fr. *bowe* bow + -*ed* — more at ³BOW] **:** furnished with a bow **:** shaped like a bow — **bowed·ness** *n* -ES

bowed cotton *n* [*bowed*, past part. of ⁴*bow*; fr. the practice of separating the fiber from the seeds by blows of a bowstring] **:** UPLAND COTTON

bowed tendon *n* [*bowed*, past part. of ⁴*bow*] **:** a suspensory ligament of a horse that has ruptured and shortened in healing, assuming a bowed appearance; *also* **:** the resulting condition of lameness

¹**bow·el** \'bau̇(ə)l, *esp S* -au̇wəl\ *n* -S [ME, fr. OF *boel*, *boiel*, fr. ML *botellus*, fr. L, small sausage, dim. of L *botulus* sausage; prob. akin to OE *cwith* belly, womb, OHG *quiti* vulva, ON *kvithr* belly, womb, Goth *qithus* stomach, womb] **1 :** the intestine or one of its divisions **:** GUT — usu. used in pl. except in medical use ⟨the large ~⟩ ⟨move your ~*s*⟩ **2 a** *obs* (1) **:** an internal organ (2) **:** the inside parts together **b** *archaic* **:** the seat of pity or tenderness ⟨thou thing of no ~*s* —Shak.⟩ ⟨if you have any ~*s* of compassion⟩ or of courage **:** GUTS, HEART — usu. used in pl. ⟨in the matter of backbone, brains, and ~*s* —Rudyard Kipling⟩ **3 bowels** *pl* **:** the interior parts; *esp* **:** the deep or remote parts ⟨deep in the ~*s* of the earth⟩ ⟨dark, stony ~*s* of a pyramid —Walter de la Mare⟩

²**bowel** \"\ *vt* **boweled** *or* **bowelled; boweled** *or* **bowelled; boweling** *or* **bowelling; bowels** [ME *bowelen*, fr. ¹*bowel*] **:** EVISCERATE, DISEMBOWEL ⟨hanging and ~*ing* their enemies⟩

bow·el·less \-əl(l)əs.-ùlləs\ *adj* **:** being without bowels ⟨the whole art of successful trading, in whatsoever degree, lies in a quick perception of the necessities of others and ~ readiness to take advantage of them —Rafael Sabatini⟩

bowel worm *n* **:** a common nematode worm (*Chabertia ovina*) of the family Strongylidae infesting the colon of sheep and feeding on blood and tissue — called also *large-mouthed bowel worm*

bow·en·ite \'bōə,nīt\ *n* -S [G.T.*Bowen*, 19th cent. Am. mineralogist who analyzed it + E -*ite*] **:** a mineral consisting of a hard compact light green serpentine resembling nephrite (hardness 5.5–6)

bow·en's disease \'bōənz-\ *n, usu cap B* [after John T. *Bowen* †1940 Am. dermatologist] **:** a precancerous lesion of the skin or mucous membranes characterized by small solid elevations covered by thickened horny tissue

¹**bow·er** \'bau̇(ə)r, -au̇ə, *esp S* -au̇wə(r\ *n* -S [ME *bour* bedroom, dwelling, fr. OE *būr*; akin to OE & OHG *būan* to dwell, inhabit, cultivate, OHG *būr* dwelling, ON *būa* to prepare, live, dwell, *būr* pantry, Goth *bauan* to live, dwell, OE *bēon* to be — more at BE] **1 :** a rustic cottage **:** an attractive dwelling or retreat **2 :** a lady's private apartment in a medieval hall or castle **3** *also* **bow·ery** \'bau̇(ə)rē, -ri\ -ES [*bowery* alter. (prob. influenced by *bough* & -*ery*) of *bower*] **:** a shelter or covered place in a garden made with boughs of trees or vines twined together **:** ARBOR

²**bower** \"\ *vb* -ED/-ING/-S *vt* **:** EMBOWER, ENCLOSE ~ *vi* **1** *obs* **:** LODGE, DWELL **2** *of branches* **:** to form bowers

³**bow·er** \'bōər, 'būər\ *n* -S [Sc *bow* herd of cattle on a farm (fr. ME, fr. ON *bū* livestock, household) + E -*er* — more at BOUW] *Scot* **:** one that rents or manages for a share of the profits the dairy stock of a farm

⁴**bow·er** \'bau̇(ə)r, -au̇ə\ *or* **bower anchor** *n* -S [⁵*bow* + -*er*] **:** an anchor carried at the bow

⁵**bower** \"\ *n* -S [G *bauer* jack (in cards), peasant, fr. MHG *būre* peasant, fr. *gebūre*, fr. OHG *gibūro*, lit., fellow-countryman — more at BOOR] **:** the jack of trumps or of the other suit of the same color in euchre and five hundred — compare LEFT BOWER, RIGHT BOWER

bower actinidia *n* [¹*bower*] **:** a high-climbing Asiatic vine (*Actinidia arguta*) that is sometimes cultivated for its ornamental long-petioled finely serrate leaves, white flowers, and globose greenish yellow edible fruits — called also *tara vine*

bow·er–barff process \'bau̇(ə)r'bärf-\ *n, usu cap both Bs* [after George and A.S.*Bower* and F.S.*Barff*, 19th cent. Am. engineers] **:** a process for producing upon iron or steel an adhering coating of iron oxides to resist atmospheric corrosion

bowerbird \'⸗,⸗\ *n* **:** any of a group of large usu. brightly colored passerine birds (family Paradiseidae) of the Australian region that build chambers or passages which are arched over with twigs and grasses and often adorned with bright-colored objects (as shells or feathers) and are used as playhouses or to attract the females rather than as nests — compare BIRD OF PARADISE; see GREAT BOWERBIRD, SATIN BOWERBIRD

bow·er·ly \'bȯə(r)lē\ *adj* [prob. alter. of *burly*] *dial Eng* **:** STOUT, BURLY

bowermaiden \'⸗,⸗⸗\ *n* [ME *bourmaiden*, fr. *bour* bedroom + *maiden*] *archaic* **:** a lady's maid **:** MAID-IN-WAITING

bower plant *n* **:** an Australian woody vine (*Pandorea jasminoides*) cultivated for its large pink-and-white flowers

bowerwoman \'⸗,⸗⸗\ *n, pl* **bowerwomen** [ME *bourwoman*, fr. *bour* bedroom + *woman*] *archaic* **:** CHAMBERMAID

¹**bow·ery** \'bau̇(ə)rē, -ri\ *adj* [¹*bower* + -*y*] **:** like a bower **:** full of bowers

²**bowery** \"\ *var of* ¹BOWER 3

³**bowery** \"\ *n* -ES [D *bouwerij*, fr. *bouwer* farmer (fr. *bouwen* to till — fr. MD *bouwen*, *būwen* — + -*er* — akin to OE -*ere* -er) + -*ij* -y, fr. MD -*ie*, fr. OF -*ie*; akin to OHG *būan* to dwell, cultivate] **1 :** a colonial Dutch plantation or farm (as in early New York or in So. Africa) **2** [The *Bowery*, street in New York City] **:** a city street or district notorious for cheap saloons and homeless derelicts

bow·et \'bau̇ət\ *var of* BOUET

bow fast *n* **:** a mooring line at the bow of a ship

bowfin \'⸗,⸗\ *n* -S [³*bow*] **:** a voracious dull-green iridescent ganoid fish (*Amia calva*) of little value as food that is found in the fresh waters of the Great lakes, Mississippi valley, and adjacent areas and is the sole surviving representative of a genus known from the Paleocene and formerly widespread in both New and Old Worlds — called also *mudfish*

bowfront \'⸗,⸗\ *adj* [³*bow*] **1** *of a case piece of furniture* **:** having an outward curving front **2** *of a house* **:** having a bow window in front

bow·grace \'bau̇,grās\ *n* -S [perh. by folk etymology (influence of ⁵*bow*) fr. obs. *bongrace* bowgrace, lit., projecting brim for a bonnet — more at BONGRACE] **:** a fender of rope or waste for protecting a ship from injury by floating ice

bow hair *n* **:** the horsehairs of a bow used in playing a stringed musical instrument — see BOW illustration

bow hand *n* **1 :** the left hand **:** left direction — used esp. in archery in the phrase *on the bow hand* **2 :** the hand that draws the bow of a stringed musical instrument ⟨a light *bow hand*⟩

bowhead \'⸗,⸗\ *n* [³*bow*] **:** GREENLAND WHALE

bow–hough'd \'bō,häkt\ *adj* [³*bow* + *hough* + -'*d*] *Scot* **:** BOWLEGGED

¹**bow·ie** \'bōē\ *n* -S [prob. fr. Sc *bow* bowl (fr. ME *bolle*) + -*ie*] **1** *Scot* **:** a wooden barrel; *esp* **:** one for water or ale **2** *Scot* **:** any of various shallow wooden bowls or dishes **3** *Scot* **:** a bucket or pail made of wood

²**bow·ie** \'büē, 'bōē\ *or* **bowie knife** *n* -S [after James *Bowie* †1836 Am. soldier, who first used such a knife, probably invented by his brother Rezin P. Bowie †1841 Am. pioneer] **:** a large hunting knife adapted esp. for knife-fighting and common in western frontier regions and having a guarded handle and a strong single-edge blade typically 10 to 15 inches long with its back straight for most of its length and then curving concavely and sometimes in a sharpened edge to the point

bowie knife

bowing *n* -S [fr. gerund of ⁴*bow*] **:** the act or art of managing the bow in playing a stringed musical instrument; *specif* **:** the manner of articulating or grouping the notes of a given phrase or passage with the bow

bowing acquaintance *n* **:** acquaintance limited to bowing in recognition; *also* **:** a person with whom one has such acquaintance

bow·ing·ly *adv* **:** in a bowing manner

bowk \'bük, 'bōk\ *vt* -ED/-ING/-S [ME *bouken* — more at BUCK (to soak)] **:** to steep (textile materials) often with boiling in a bath usu. containing lime, soda, or soap in order to cleanse before bleaching

bow·kail \'bō,kāl\ *n* -S [prob. fr. ³*bow* + *kale*; fr. its rounded shape] *Scot* **:** CABBAGE

bowknot \'⸗,⸗\ *n* [³*bow*] **:** a knot with decorative loops; *esp* **:** a square knot or granny knot in which the second half-knot is tied with loops instead of ends

¹**bowl** \'bōl\ *n* -S [ME *bolle*, fr. OE *bolla*; akin to OHG *bolla* blister, ON *bolli* bowl, OE *blāwan* to blow — more at BLOW] **1 :** a rounded hollow vessel usu. nearly hemispherical in form and generally deeper than a basin and larger or heavier than a cup; *specif* **:** a drinking vessel of this shape ⟨come and fill the flowing ~⟩ **2 :** the contents of a bowl **3 :** a bowl-shaped or concave part: as **a :** the hollow of a spoon, oar, tobacco pipe, flagon, candlestick **b :** the part or parts of such letters as O, b, d, p, q, g, B that are closed curves; *also* **:** the space enclosed by the closed curves **c :** the receptacle of a toilet **4 a :** a natural formation (as a valley) or geographical region shaped like a bowl ⟨the Western dust ~⟩ **b :** a bowl-shaped structure (as an amphitheater) often formed by excavation; *esp* **:** an athletic stadium **c :** a postseasonal football game between specially invited teams ⟨a ~ invitation⟩ ⟨~ squad⟩ **d :** a floor surface sloping toward a center (as in a theater)

²**bowl** \"\ *n* -S [ME *boule*, *bowle*, fr. MF *boule*, fr. L *bulla* bubble — more at POLL (head)] **1 a** *obs* **:** SPHERE, GLOBE **b :** a usu. lignum vitae ball that is weighted or shaped so as to give it a bias when rolled in lawn bowling **c bowls** *pl but sing in const* **:** LAWN BOWLING **d bowls** *pl but sing in constr, Scot* **:** MARBLES **2 :** a cast or delivery of the ball down the green or alley (as in bowling); *also* **:** a turn in the game of bowling **3 :** a cylindrical roller or drum variously used (as for an antifriction wheel or bearing or in pairs as a means of drawing or pressing fabrics in manufacture)

³**bowl** \"\ *vb* -ED/-ING/-S [ME *bowlen*, fr. *boule*, *bowle*] *vi* **1 :** to participate in the game of bowls or any of various bowling games (as tenpins) **2 :** to roll a ball down the alley (as in tenpins) or along the green (as in lawn bowling) **3 :** to move on or as if on wheels esp. smoothly and rapidly — usu. with *along* ⟨~*ing* along the highway in a bus⟩ **4 :** to deliver a cricket ball from behind the bowling crease to the batsman with a smooth movement of the arm ~ *vt* **1 a :** to send rolling along the ground or down a green or an alley **b :** to complete by bowling ⟨~ a string⟩ **:** achieve by bowling ⟨~ a 300 game⟩ **:** score by bowling ⟨~*s* a steady 150⟩ **2 :** to deliver (a cricket ball) to the batsman **3 a :** to strike with or as if with a swiftly rolling object esp. so as to displace ⟨~*ed* over by a runaway horse⟩ ⟨~*ed* aside by a man dashing blindly for the exit⟩ **b :** to overwhelm or stun esp. with surprise **:** dismay suddenly **:** DISCONCERT — usu. used with *over* ⟨he was completely ~*ed* over by the news⟩ **4 a :** to put out (a cricket batsman) with a bowled ball that breaks the wicket — often used with *out* **b** *chiefly Brit* **:** to put out of action **:** defeat finally or utterly — often used with *out* or *down* ⟨~*ed* out only by death itself⟩ ⟨~ down an opponent in a debate⟩ — **bowl over the wicket** *cricket* **:** to deliver a ball with the stumps on the same side as one's bowling arm and usu. while standing quite close to the stumps — **bowl round the wicket** *cricket* **:** to deliver a ball from the side of the bowling crease corresponding to the bowling arm (as right for a right-hand bowler) usu. while standing somewhat away from the stumps

bowlder *var of* BOULDER

bowled *past of* BOWL

bowleg \'⸗,⸗\ *n* [³*bow*] **:** a leg bowed outward at or below the knee usu. from disease

bow·legged *esp US* 'bō¦legəd, *esp Brit* -gd\ *adj* **:** having legs bowed outward

¹**bowl·er** \'bōlə(r)\ *n* -S [³*bowl* + -*er*] **:** one that bowls; *specif* **:** the player who delivers the ball to the batsman in cricket

²**bow·ler** \"\ *or* **bowler hat** *n* -S [after *Bowler* *fl*1861 Eng. hatmaker] **:** DERBY 2a

bow·less \'bōləs\ *adj* [³*bow* + -*less*] **:** being without a bow

bow light *n* [⁵*bow*] **:** the white light displayed forward by a ship at anchor or by a power ship under way

bow·line \'bōlən, -,līn\ *n* [ME *bouline*, *bowelyne*, perh. fr. *bowe* bow + *line* — more at ³BOW, LINE] **1 :** a rope fastened near the middle of the perpendicular edge of a square sail and used to keep the weather edge of the sail taut forward when the ship is close-hauled **2** *or* **bowline knot :** a loop knot that neither slips nor jams used esp. for mooring and hoisting — see PORTUGUESE BOWLINE, RUNNING BOWLINE, SPANISH BOWLINE

bowline knot

bow line \'bau̇,līn\ *n* [⁵*bow*] **:** the line of intersection of a fore-and-aft vertical plane with the fore-body of a ship

bowline bridle *n* **:** a rope by which the bowline is connected to the leech of the sail — see BOWLINE CRINGLE; SAIL illustration

bowline cringle *n* **:** a loop or eye in the leech of a sail for attaching the bowline bridle

bowline on a bight : a bowline knot with a double loop tied in the bight of a rope

bowling *n* -S [fr. gerund of ³*bowl*] **:** any of several games in which balls are rolled on a green outdoors or down an alley indoors at an object or group of objects; *esp* **:** a game in which pins are set up in a usu. triangular pattern at one end of an alley and balls rolled at them from the other end, the object being to knock down as many pins as possible with each ball — see CANDLEPINS, DUCKPINS, LAWN BOWLING, NINEPINS, TENPINS; compare BOCCIE, SKITTLES

bowling analysis *n* **:** a tabulation of the work of the bowlers in a cricket match or innings showing balls bowled, wickets taken, and runs scored

bowling average *n* **:** the ratio in cricket obtained by dividing the number of runs scored by the number of wickets taken by a bowler

bowling crease *n* **:** one of two lines with wickets pitched in the center of each from or behind which the cricket ball must be bowled

bowling green *n* **:** a level piece of ground for lawn bowling

bowling on the green : LAWN BOWLING

bowling stump *n* **:** a stump marking the cricket bowler's position when a single wicket is used

bowls *pl of* BOWL, *pres 3d sing of* BOWL

¹**bow·ly** \'bōlē, 'bülē\ *adj* [perh. fr. *bool* + -*y*] *Scot* **:** CROOKED, BENT ⟨~ legs⟩

²**bow·ly** \'bōlē\ *n* -ES [Hindi *bāwlī*, fr. Skt *vāpī* pond] **:** a large usu. rectangular sunken pool or well in India that serves as a public water supply and a resting place and is usu. provided with terraces and shaded recesses

¹**bow·man** \'bōmən\ *n, pl* **bowmen** [ME *boweman*, fr. *bowe* bow + *man* — more at ³BOW] **:** ARCHER

²**bow·man** \'bau̇mən\ *n, pl* **bowmen** [⁵*bow*] **:** a boatman, oarsman, or paddler stationed in the front of a boat: as **a :** BOW OAR **b :** a logger who sits in the front of the boat to guide floating logs with a pike pole or peavey

bow·man's capsule \'bōmənz-\ *n, usu cap B* [after Sir William *Bowman* †1892 Eng. surgeon] **:** a thin membranous double-walled capsule surrounding the glomerulus of a vertebrate nephron

bowman's glands *n pl, usu cap B* **:** branching tubular glands in the olfactory mucous membrane

bowman's membrane *n, usu cap B* **:** the thin condensed outer layer of the substantia propria of the cornea immediately underlying the epithelium

bow·man's root \'bōmənz-\ *also* **bowman root** *or* **bowman** *n, sometimes cap B* [by folk etymology fr. *beaumont root*] **1 :** CULVER'S ROOT **2 :** FLOWERING SPURGE **3 :** INDIAN PHYSIC 1

bown \'bau̇n, 'bün\ *vb* -ED/-ING/-S [ME *bounen*, fr. *boun* ready — more at ¹BOUND] **1** *chiefly Scot* **:** to make ready **2** *chiefly Scot* **:** GO

bow net *n* [³*bow*] **1 :** a trap for lobsters consisting of a wickerwork cylinder with a funnel-shaped entrance at one end **2 :** a net attached to a wooden bow for catching birds

bow oar *n* [⁵*bow*] **1 :** the oar used by the rower nearest the bow; *sometimes* **:** the foremost oar but one in a whaleboat **2 :** one who pulls the bow oar

bow on *adv* **:** head on

bow out *vi* [¹*bow*] **:** to retire or withdraw esp. from a contest ⟨*bowed out* after tiring in the 6th inning⟩ ⟨*bowed out* of the race for governor⟩ **:** work at one's job for the last time **:** make a final appearance at one's post **:** step down ⟨*bowed out* with a great performance⟩ ⟨*bowed out* after 40 years of railroading⟩

bow pen *n* **:** a bow compass for drawing small circles in ink

bow pencil *n* **:** a bow compass provided with a pencil point

bowpin \'⸗,⸗\ *n* [³*bow*] **:** a cotter for the bows of an ox yoke

bowpot *var of* BOUGHPOT

bow priest *n* [³*bow* + *priest*; fr. the fact that he is also a leader in war] **:** a Zuñi ceremonial group leader and high-ranking member of the religious hierarchy

bow pulpit *n* [⁵*bow*] **:** PULPIT 4

bow rudder *n* [⁵*bow*] **1 :** one of the forward diving rudders of a submarine — usu. used in pl. **2 :** a steering stroke that is used by a bow paddler to turn a canoe sharply and is executed by bracing the shaft of the paddle against the gunwale while pointing the blade diagonally forward at slight depth

bows *pl of* BOW, *pres 3d sing of* BOW

bow saw *n* [³*bow*] **:** a saw that has a narrow blade held under tension by a light bow-shaped frame and is used for pruning and sawing medium-sized logs

bow saw

¹**bowse** \'bau̇z, 'büz\ *archaic var of* BOOZE

²**bowse** *var of* BOUSE

bow·ser \'bau̇zə(r)\ *n* -S [fr. *Bowser*, a trademark] *chiefly Austral* **:** a pump usu. at a service station for dispensing liquid fuels, esp. gasoline

bowshot \'⸗,⸗\ *n* [ME *boweshot*, fr. *bowe* bow + *shot* — more at ³BOW] **:** the distance traversed by an arrow shot from a bow **:** the effective range of a bow ⟨waiting for the foe to come within ~⟩

bow shot *n* [³*bow*] **:** a shot in squash racquets that is hit into a sidewall from rear court, rebounds to the opposite sidewall, and then rebounds to the front wall

bow sight *n* [³*bow*] **:** a device usu. of pins set in a calibrated frame attachable to a shooting bow for aid in aiming for distance

bows·man \'bau̇zmən\ *n, pl* **bowsmen** [by folk etymology (influence of ⁵*bow*) fr. F *bosseman*, prob. fr. obs. LG *bossman*, alter. of (assumed) LG *bootsman*, fr. *boots* (gen. of *boot* boat, fr. MLG, fr. ME) + *man*, fr. OS; akin to OHG *man* — more at BOAT, MAN] **:** a crew member of a small boat who is usu. stationed in the bow, not assigned to an oar, and usu. has some supervisory status

bow's notation \'bōz-\ *n, usu cap B* [after R.H.*Bow*, 19th cent. Eng. engineer] **:** a method of lettering the cells and outside spaces formed by the directions of the stresses in and loads on a framed structure so that these stresses and loads can be traced by similar letters in the reciprocal diagram

bow·sprit \'bau̇,sprit, 'bō,-\ *n* -S [ME *bouspret*, prob. fr. MLG *bōchsprēt*, fr. *bōch* bow (akin to OE *bōg* shoulder, bough) + *sprēt* pole; akin to OE *sprēot* pole, MHG *spriez* twig, OE *sprūtan* to sprout — more at BOUGH, SPROUT] **:** a large spar projecting forward from the stem of a ship to carry sail forward and to support the masts by stays — see SHIP illustration

bowsprit bed *n* **:** the part of the stem on which the bowsprit rests

bowsprit cap *n* **:** an iron band fitted to the outer end of the bowsprit with a ring on top for the jibboom to run through — compare CRANCE; see SHIP illustration

bowsprit shrouds *n pl* **:** ropes, chains, or rods from the head of the bowsprit to the ship's bows — see SHIP illustration

bows·sen \'bau̇sᵊn\ *vt* -ED/-ING/-S [modif. of Corn *beuzi*, *bedhy*, *būdhy* to drown, submerge; akin to OIr *bāidim* I drown (transitive), W *boddi* to drown — more at BATHY-] *in Cornwall* **:** to duck in water as a treatment for insanity

bow·stave \'bō,stāv\ *n* [back-formation fr. *bowstaves*, pl. of obs. *bowstaff* bowstave, fr. ME *bowestaf*, fr. *bowe* bow + *staf* staff — more at BOW, STAFF] **:** a trimmed rod of wood to be made into a shooting bow

bow·ster \'bōstər\ *chiefly Scot var of* BOLSTER

bow stiffener *n* [⁵*bow*] **:** one of the rigid members attached to the bow of a nonrigid or semirigid envelope of an airship to reinforce it against pressure caused by the motion of the ship — called also *nose stiffener*

bow street runner *also* **bow street officer** \'bō-\ *n, usu cap B & S* [fr. *Bow Street*, London, England] **:** a London policeman attached to the Bow Street police court; *specif* **:** one of the officers appointed about 1805 to act as detectives in London and elsewhere in England

¹**bowstring** \'⸗,⸗\ *n* [ME *bowestring*, fr. *bowe* bow + *string*, *streng* string — more at ³BOW, STRING] **:** a waxed or sized cord usu. of hemp or linen threads joining the ends of a shooting bow ⟨nerves taut as a ~⟩

²**bowstring** \"\ *vt* **bowstringed** *or* **bowstrung; bowstringed** *or* **bowstrung; bowstringing; bowstrings :** to strangle with a bowstring

bowstring beam *or* **bowstring girder** *or* **bowstring truss** *n* **:** a beam or girder consisting of an arched beam strengthened by a tie connecting its two ends

bowstring bridge *n* **:** a bridge with bowstring girders

bowstring hemp *n* **1 :** any of various Asiatic and African plants of the genus *Sansevieria* — see AFRICAN BOWSTRING HEMP, IFE, MURVA, PANGANE **2 :** the soft tenacious leaf fiber of bowstring hemp used in making bowstrings, cordage, and cloth and in packing **3 :** MUDAR

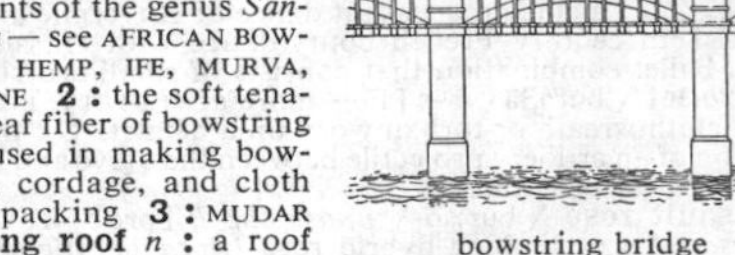

bowstring bridge

bowstring roof *n* **:** a roof with bowstring beams

bowtel *or* **bowtell** *var of* BOLTEL

bow tie \bō\ *n* **:** a short necktie tied in a bowknot

bow trolley *n* [³*bow* + *trolley*; fr. its shape] **:** a bow-shaped member for collecting current by sliding contact with an overhead trolley wire

bow up *vi* [⁴*bow*] *dial* **:** to reach the limit of one's patience and rebel **:** BALK ⟨the chore of it fell to me until I finally *bowed up* —Ross Santee⟩
bow wave \ˈbau̇\ *n* **1 :** the wave on either side of the bow of a ship under way **2 :** SHOCK WAVE
bow weight *n* **:** the force expressed in pounds that is required to draw a bow the length of its arrow
bow window *n* [³*bow*] **:** BAY WINDOW; *esp* **:** one with a curved ground plan
bowwood \ˈ=,=\ *n* **1 :** any of several woods suitable for making archery bows **2 :** OSAGE ORANGE
bow·wow \ˈbau̇,wau̇; ("*bark*") ˈ=¦= *or* =ˈ=\ *n* -S [imit.] **1 :** the bark of a dog; *also* **:** DOG **2 :** noisy clamor or protest **3 :** arrogance or dogmatism of manner ⟨remarks delivered in the big ~ style⟩ **4 bowwows** *pl* **:** RUIN, PERDITION **:** the dogs ⟨headed for the ~*s*⟩ ⟨gone to the ~*s*⟩
bowwow theory *n* **:** a theory that language originated in imitations of natural sounds (as those of birds, dogs, or thunder) — compare DINGDONG THEORY, POOH-POOH THEORY
bow·yang \ˈbō,yaŋ\ *n* -S [alter. of E dial. *bowy-yanks* (pl.) leather leggings] *Austral* **:** a cord or strap tied around a workman's trousers just below the knee — usu. used in pl.
bow·yer \ˈbōyə(r)\ *n* -S [ME *bowyere*, fr. *bowe* bow + *-ere* -er — more at ³BOW] **:** one that makes shooting bows
bowyer's knot *n* **:** TIMBER HITCH
¹**box** \ˈbäks\ *n, pl* **box** *or* **boxes** [ME *box*, fr. OE, fr. L *buxus*, fr. Gk *pyxos*] **1 :** an evergreen shrub or small tree of the genus *Buxus*; *esp* **:** a widely cultivated typically large shrub (*B. sempervirens*) that is extensively used for hedges, borders, and topiary figures because of its slow growth and compact habit — see BOXWOOD **2** *Austral* **a :** any of several trees of the genera *Alyxia*, *Eucalyptus*, *Tristania*, and *Murraya* which have timber resembling boxwood **b :** NATIVE BOX
²**box** \"\ *n* -ES [ME, fr. OE, fr. LL *buxis*, fr. Gk *pyxis*, fr. *pyxos* boxtree] **1 a :** a rigid typically rectangular receptacle often with a lid or cover in which something nonliquid is kept or carried ⟨shoe ~⟩ ⟨money ~⟩ ⟨take along a ~ lunch⟩ **b :** something constructed of a flat bottom and four upright solid sides (as the carrying part of a wagon) ⟨a ~ of growing seedlings⟩ ⟨playing in the sand ~⟩ ⟨the ~ of a pickup truck⟩ **:** FRAME, FLASK 2 **c :** the contents of a box as a measure of quantity ⟨5 cents a ~⟩ **d :** a closed receptacle to hold contributions (as of money, letters, ballots) **e** *Brit* **:** the money contained in a box **:** FUND **f :** the driver's seat on a carriage or coach **g** *slang* **:** GUITAR, BANJO, FIDDLE **2** *Brit* **:** a gift (as at Christmas) in a box ⟨have you given the postman his ~⟩ — see BOXING DAY **3 a** *in a theater* **:** a space with chairs enclosed by partitions except toward the stage ⟨the royal ~⟩; *also* **:** the occupants of such a space ⟨a favorite of the ~*es*⟩ **b :** a group of spectator seats in a grandstand enclosed by railings **c :** a railed or partitioned enclosure provided for the jury or for witnesses in a courtroom **d :** a space partitioned off in a tavern or public eating house **:** BOOTH **e :** BOX STALL; *also* **:** HORSE BOX **4 a :** a closed case or container for storing or shipping merchandise or belongings **b** *Brit* **:** TRUNK **5 a :** a boxlike protective covering, housing, or mechanical part (as for a bearing or bushing) ⟨gear ~⟩ ⟨journal ~⟩ **b :** an apparatus (as for sending a signal or fire alarm) with its enclosing case ⟨police ~⟩ **c :** the receptacle for a shuttle at the end of a loom lay **6 :** a square or oblong division or compartment: as **a :** any of the compartments in a type case **b :** a cell or pigeonhole in a wall or rack for holding mail **:** POST-OFFICE BOX **7 :** a square or oblong hollow space or recess: as **a :** a recess cut into a tree to collect sap or resin **b :** the part of a window frame for sash windows in which the weight to counterpoise the sash moves up and down **c :** a recess in a window trim into which the shutters may fold **d :** a socket on a doorjamb for the bolt **e :** the portion of a gemstone setting that surrounds the precious stone; *also* **:** a style of such setting **8 a :** a small simple sheltering or enclosing structure (as for a sentry or a watchman) **b** *chiefly Brit* **:** a simple cabin or cottage ⟨a shooting ~⟩ **c :** SINKBOX **d** *Brit* **:** TELEPHONE BOOTH **9 a :** printed matter set off by being enclosed or partly enclosed by rules or white space; *also* **:** the rules or white space enclosing such matter **b :** a hollow rectangle in which a check mark is to be made ⟨please check the ~ that applies to you⟩ **c :** a single unit of a comic strip **d :** LINE 12b **e** *or* **box step :** a combination of ballroom dance steps describing a rectangle on the floor **10 a** *baseball* (1) **:** the space where the pitcher stands formerly outlined with rectangular lines but now marked only by the pitcher's plate (2) **:** a space on either side of the home plate within which the batter must stand while batting (3) **:** either of the rectangular spaces 15 feet from the diamond and opposite first base and third base respectively within which the coaches are required to stand (4) **:** a triangular space behind the home plate in which the catcher must take his stand before every pitch — see BASEBALL illustration **b :** GULLY 4 **11 a :** boarded leather **b :** BOX CALF **12 :** a difficult situation **:** tight corner **:** FIX, PICKLE ⟨I must take some blame on myself for getting into this ~ —Walter H. Page⟩ **13 :** a case that holds a pack of cards so that they may be dealt one by one in the game of faro — called also *dealing box* **14 :** VULVA — usu. considered vulgar — **in the box :** accepting the bets of all the other players on the result of a game with the captain — used of a chouette player

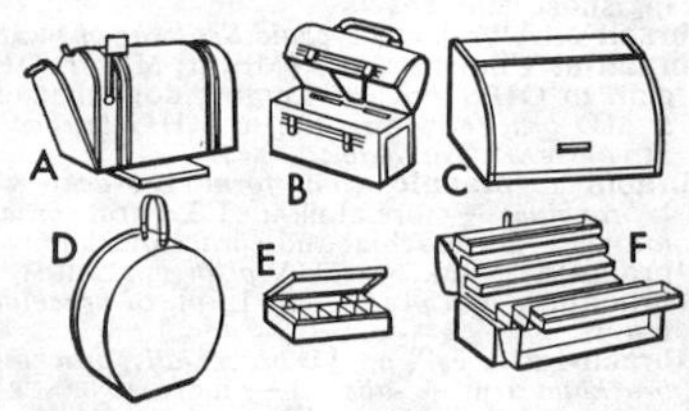

various boxes: *A* rural mailbox; *B* lunch box; *C* bread box; *D* hatbox; *E* cashbox; *F* toolbox

³**box** \"\ *vt* -ED/-ING/-S **1 a** *obs* **:** CUP 1 **b :** to cut a hole into (a tree) to collect sap or resin **2 a :** to furnish (as a wheel hub) with a box **b** *Brit* **:** to give a Christmas box to **3 :** to enclose in or as if in a box ⟨~*ed* cigars⟩ ⟨a ~*ed* newspaper story⟩ **:** STOW — often with *up* ⟨~*ed* up and put away⟩ **4 :** BOXHAUL **5 :** to enclose with boarding or lathing so as to bring to a required form — usu. used with *out* or *up* **6** *English & Scots law* **:** to file (a document) with a court of law **7** *Austral* **:** to mix up **:** CONFUSE, BEFUDDLE — orig. used of sheep; often used with *up* **8 :** to mix (paint, varnish) by pouring back and forth between two containers **9 :** to hem in (an opponent or a competitor) — usu. used with *in*, *out*, or *up* ⟨~*ed* out the opposing tackle⟩ ⟨~*ed* in by a horse to his right⟩ **10 :** to stack (ceramic ware) in a kiln **11 :** to bet on (a specified number to win) in certain games and lotteries; *specif* **:** to bet on each of the 6 permutations of (a 3-digit number) in the numbers game — **box the compass 1 :** to name the 32 points of the compass in their order **2 :** to make a complete turn or reversal (as in policy, opinion) — **box the heart :** to cut slabs or boards in sawmilling from the outside of a log leaving a timber containing the heartwood
⁴**box** \"\ *n* -ES [ME] **:** a blow with the fist **:** BUFFET; *specif* **:** a cuff on the ear
⁵**box** \"\ *vb* -ED/-ING/-S *vt* **1 a** *obs* **:** to hit with the hand or fist **b :** to slap smartly in the region of (the ears) ⟨~*ed* his ears⟩ **2 :** to engage in boxing with (a person) ~ *vi* **:** to fight with the fists **:** engage in boxing **syn** see STRIKE
box and cox \ˌbäksənˈkäks\ *adv* (*or adj*), *usu cap B&C* [*Box and Cox*, farce (1847) by John M. Morton †1891 Eng. playwright, and *Cox and Box*, comic opera (1867) with text by Sir Francis C. Burnand †1917 Eng. playwright and music by Sir Arthur S. Sullivan †1900 Eng. composer, adapted from Morton's farce; fr. the arrangement in the farce and opera whereby the same room is rented to two men named Box and Cox, one occupying it by day and one by night without either's knowing about the other] *Brit* **:** in turn **:** ALTERNATING
box barberry *n* [¹*box*] **:** a dwarf Japanese barberry (*Berberis thunbergii minor*) used for low hedges
box barrage *n* [²*box*] **1 :** a barrage on three sides of a given area to prevent escape or reinforcement of the enemy or to cover the front and flanks of a friendly force **2 :** a barrage of antiaircraft fire intended to block off invaders from a given objective
box beam *n* **:** BOX GIRDER
box bed *n* **1 :** a bed built into an alcove or enclosed with panels **2 :** a bed that folds up into the form of a box
boxberry \ˈ=- — see BERRY\ *n* [¹*box*] **1 :** WINTERGREEN 2a **2 :** PARTRIDGEBERRY 1
box bill *n* [²*box*] **:** a fishing tool used in well drilling to recover tools lost in the hole
boxboard \ˈ=,=\ *n* **:** a board from which cardboard boxes are made
box bolt *n* **:** a barrel bolt square or rectangular in cross section
box brier *n* **:** a tropical American spiny shrub (*Randia mitis*) with black fruits and leaves like those of the box — called also *inkberry, wild box*
boxbush \ˈ=,=\ *n* [¹*box*] **:** BURBARK 2
box caisson *n* **:** a heavy-timber watertight box open at the top, floated over a position prepared by dredging, and sunk by building a masonry pier within it
box calf *n* [²*box* + *calf*; fr. the square markings] **:** chrome-tanned calfskin having square markings on the grain because of being rolled lengthwise and then crosswise — compare BOARD *vt* 7
box camera *n* **:** a camera of simple box shape with a simple lens and rotary shutter
box canyon *n* [²*box*] **:** a canyon with approximately vertical walls and typically closed upstream with a similar wall
¹**boxcar** \ˈ=,=\ *n* **1 :** a roofed freight car with enclosed sides and usu. with sliding doors in the sides for the conveyance of lading that must be protected from the weather or pilferage **2 boxcars** *pl but sometimes sing in constr* **:** a throw of 12 in the game of craps **3 :** a truck trailer resembling a railway boxcar in size and shape
²**boxcar** \"\ *adj* **:** very large ⟨billboards with ~ letters⟩
box chisel *n* **:** a chisel with a notched edge used for prying open nailed wooden boxes — see CHISEL illustration
box cloth *n* [²*box* + *cloth*; prob. fr. its use in making box coats] **:** a heavy feltlike woolen coating made dense and almost waterproof by considerable fulling and shrinking and given a hard smooth face
box coat *n* [²*box* + *coat*; fr. its use by coachmen riding on the box exposed to all kinds of weather] **1 :** a heavy overcoat with or without shoulder capes formerly worn esp. by coachmen and coach passengers **2** *also* **box jacket** [prob. so called fr. its shape] **:** a loose straight-lined single-breasted or double-breasted coat or jacket usu. fitted at the shoulders
box couch *n* **:** a couch with a built-in storage box
box coupling *n* [²*box*] **1 :** a metal collar and tapered key for uniting the ends of shafts or other parts in machinery **2 :** a pipe coupling with threads on the inside
box crab *n* [so called fr. the way the legs fold against the carapace, resembling a box] **1 :** a crab of the tropical oxystomatous family Calappidae **2 :** a large rough anomuran crab (*Lopholithodes foraminatus*) of the Pacific coast of No. America — called also *shamefaced crab*
box culvert *n* **:** a reinforced concrete culvert of rectangular cross section
box day *n* [²*box*] *Scots law* **:** one of the days in vacation appointed for depositing papers with the Court of Sessions
box defense *n* **:** a defensive formation in football in which the players behind the line are arranged in a rectangle
box ditch *n* [²*box*] **:** a wooden irrigation flume resting on the ground and used to replace an earthen head ditch
box dolly *n* **:** a lumber-carrying truck with a single wide-tired wheel in the center of the box frame
box drain *n* **:** a drain that is rectangular in cross section
box drawer *n* **:** a desk drawer divided into compartments resembling boxes
boxed *past of* BOX
boxed heart *n* [*boxed*, past part. of ³*box*] **:** a sawn timber enclosing within its faces the heart of a log
boxed seam *n* **:** a decorative seam having the welt on the outside and made similar to a French seam
box elder *n* [¹*box*] **:** a maple (*Acer negundo*) widely distributed in the central and eastern U. S. and represented to the westward by distinct varieties that has compound leaves and is used as a shade tree because of its rapid growth — called also *ash-leaved maple*; see CALIFORNIA BOX ELDER
box–elder aphid *n* **:** a pale green hairy aphid (*Periphyllus negundinis*) that infests box elder and certain other maple trees
box–elder bug *n* [so called fr. its preference for the box elder] **:** a red-and-black sap-sucking bug (*Leptocoris trivittatus*) of the family Coreidae that sometimes feeds on fruit and hibernates in a partially dormant state often in buildings
box·en \ˈbäksən\ *adj, archaic* **:** of, like, or relating to boxwood or the box
¹**box·er** \ˈbäksə(r)\ *n* -S [⁵*box* + *-er*] **:** one that engages in the sport of boxing **:** one with ability to box rather than merely punch ⟨more of a ~ than a fighter⟩
²**boxer** \"\ *n* -S [³*box* + *-er*] **1 :** a worker who boxes trees to collect sap or resin **2 :** one that makes boxes or one that packs things in boxes by hand or by machine
³**boxer** \"\ *n* -S *usu cap* [approx. trans. of Chin *i*⁴ *hê*² *ch'üan*², lit., righteous harmonious fist, alter. of *i*⁴ *hê*² *t'uan*² righteous harmonious band (the original name of the society)] **:** a member of a secret society that in 1900 attempted by violence to drive foreigners out of China and to force native converts to renounce Christianity — **box·er·ism** \-ə,rizəm\ *n* -S *usu cap*
⁴**boxer** \"\ *n* -S [prob. fr. ²*box* + *-er*] *Austral* **:** DERBY HAT
⁵**boxer** \"\ *n* -S *often cap* [G, fr. E ¹*boxer*; fr. its fighting habits] **:** a medium-sized square-built short-haired dog of a breed originating in Germany with fawn, brindle, or an intermediate coloring, a black mask, and often some white on face, chest, and feet
boxer shorts *n pl* [¹*boxer*] **:** men's underwear shorts characterized by loose fit, a continuous elastic waistband, and an overlapping fly that does not fasten
boxer–up \ˈ=ˈ=\ *n* -S [³*box* + *-er*] **:** a hooper that assembles cylinders and heads of kegs and drums
boxes *pl of* BOX, *pres 3d sing of* BOX
box family *n* [¹*box*] **:** BUXACEAE
boxfish \ˈ=,=\ *n* **:** any of a number of small bright-colored fishes (family Ostraciontidae) of tropical seas that are related to the triggerfishes but have the body and head enclosed in a hard carapace of hexagonal bony plates — called also *trunkfish*
box frame *n* [²*box*] **:** a frame with boxlike members; *specif* **:** a window frame having hollow spaces for sash weights
box girder *n* [²*box*] **:** a girder or beam of rectangular cross section with two or more webs
box green *n* [¹*box*] **:** a moderate yellow green that is greener and deeper than average moss green, yellower and darker than average pea green, and yellower and duller than apple green (sense 1)
box groove *n* [²*box*] **:** a closed groove formed in metalworking by a collar on one roll fitting between collars on another
boxhaul \ˈ=,=\ *vt* [³*box* + *haul*] **:** to put (a square-rigger) on the other tack by luffing and then veering under sternway by bracing the head yards abox
boxhead \ˈ=,=\ *or* **box heading** *or* **boxed head** *n* **:** a printed head or subhead set within a box (as in display composition or at the head of a column in an account book or of figures in a table)
boxholder \ˈ=,==\ *n* **1 :** one having title to a box (as in a theater, opera house, or racetrack) **2 a :** a renter of a post-office box **b :** a holder of a mailbox ⟨folders were sent to ~*s*⟩
box hook *n* **:** a hook with a transverse handle used in handling heavy boxes or crates
box huckleberry *n* [¹*box*] **:** a rare prostrate evergreen shrub (*Gaylussacia brachycera*) of the southeastern U.S. with shiny leaves like those of the box
boxier *comparative of* BOXY
boxiest *superlative of* BOXY
box·i·ness \ˈbäksēnəs, -sin-\ *n* -ES [*boxy* + *-ness*] **:** the quality of having unadorned or unrelieved square corners and edges ⟨avoids the barren ~ . . . so often encountered in modern designs —L.G.White⟩
¹**boxing** *n* -S [partly fr. gerund of ³*box*, partly fr. ²*box* + *-ing*] **1 :** a square or oblong enclosure or recess **:** CASING: as **a** *archit* **:** the external case of thin material used to bring a structural member to a required form **b :** a form for poured concrete **2 :** material for making boxes **3 :** the scarf joint uniting the stem and keel of a ship **4 boxings** *pl* **:** coarse flour separated in bolting **5 :** a stiffening material (as leather, wire, shellacked canvas) used in toes of shoes — compare TOE BOX, TOE CAP, TOE PUFF **6 :** a straight strip for joining two sections of a slipcover, bedspread, or upholstery at an angle; *esp* **:** an allowance for the thickness of a cushion or chairback **7 :** FORM 6d
²**boxing** *n* -S [fr. gerund of ⁵*box*] **:** the art of attack and defense with the fists practiced as a sport
boxing day *n, usu cap B&D* [*boxing*, gerund of ³*box*] **:** the first weekday after Christmas observed as a legal holiday in England, Wales, northern Ireland, Australia, New Zealand, and the Union of So. Africa and celebrated by the giving of Christmas boxes to postmen and other service workers
boxing glove *n* [²*boxing*] **:** one of a pair of leather mittens heavily padded on the back and worn in boxing

boxing gloves

boxing night *n, usu cap B&N* **:** the night of Boxing Day
boxing shutter *n* **:** one of a set of shutters made to fold back into an oblong recess
box iron *n* [²*box*] **:** a hollow flatiron that is heated by inserting a hot iron core
box jacket *n* **:** BOX COAT
box jig *n* **:** a jig in which work is rigidly held so that it can be drilled or machined from different angles at a single setting depending on which face of the jig is turned toward the tool
boxkeeper \ˈ=,==\ *n* **:** an attendant in charge of the boxes in a theater
box key *n* **:** a T-shaped wrench with a socket in the end of the shank to fit over a nut or bolt head
box kite *n* **:** a kite without a tail much used formerly in meteorology and consisting of two or more open-ended connected boxes — called also *cellular kite, Hargrave kite, tetrahedral kite*

box kite

box–length \ˈ=ˈ=\ *n* **:** the approximately 12-foot length of a placer gold-mining sluice box
box level *n* **:** a spirit level in which a glass-covered box is used instead of a tube — called also *circular level*
boxlike \ˈ=,=\ *adj* **:** resembling a box esp. in shape **:** rectangular and hollow
box lock *n* [²*box*] **:** an encased lock for surface mounting
box–loom \ˈ=ˈ=\ *n* **:** a loom with more than one shuttle box on one or both sides for weaving with two or more shuttles
box magazine *n* **:** a magazine for a repeating firearm which consists of a detachable metal box that fits into the receiver and from which the cartridges are fed into the chamber by the action of the piece
box maker's certificate *n* **:** a statement printed on a shipping container giving test values, rule compliance, the box maker, and other information
box·man \ˈbäksmən\ *n, pl* **boxmen 1 a :** one who takes care of the boxes in which different sizes of coal are washed **b :** a weigher of blast-furnace charges **2 :** CEMENT MIXER 2 **3** *slang* **:** SAFECRACKER
box myrtle *n* [¹*box*] **:** an Asiatic shrub (*Myrica nagi*) whose leaves yield a yellow crystalline dye — see MYRICETIN
box nail *n* **:** a slender wire nail used in making boxes
box nut *n* [²*box*] **:** a nut with a blind hole — called also *cap nut*
box oak *n* **:** BOX WHITE OAK
box off *vt* [³*box*] **:** to turn the bow of (a ship) by bracing the head yards aback
box office *n* [²*box*] **1 :** the office in a theater, auditorium, or stadium where tickets of admission are sold **2 :** success (as of a show, program, or performer) in attracting ticket buyers often in distinction from critical praise **:** popular appeal **:** DRAWING POWER; *also* **:** something that enhances drawing power ⟨almost any sort of publicity may be good *box office*⟩
box oyster *n* [²*box* + *oyster*; fr. being shipped in boxes rather than in barrels] **:** a choice large oyster
box pew *n* **:** an old-fashioned church pew walled in like a box
box pleat *n* [²*box* + *pleat*; fr. its rectilinear form] **1 :** a pleat made by forming two folded edges one facing right and the other left on the front side so that an inverted pleat is formed on the reverse side **2 :** INVERTED PLEAT
box press *n* **:** a device for drawing the covers of boxes into place for nailing
boxroom \ˈ=,=\ *n, Brit* **:** a storeroom (as for trunks) in a house
box score *n* [²*box* + *score*; fr. the compact arrangement of the summaries in a newspaper box] **:** the complete score of a game (as baseball) giving the names and positions of the players and a record of the play arranged in tabular form; *broadly* **:** total count **:** SUMMARY
box seat *n* **1 :** a built-in chest whose top forms a seat; *specif* **:** the driver's seat on a coach **2 a :** a seat in a theater or grandstand box **b :** a position esp. favorable for viewing something
box set *n* **:** a stage set realistically representing three walls and the ceiling of a room
box settle *n* **:** a settle with an enclosed foundation the cover of which forms the seat
box shell *n* **:** ARK SHELL
box shutter *n* **:** BOXING SHUTTER
box sill *n* **:** a sill that is constructed of brick or concrete enclosed in planks and that is used in frame house construction
box social *or* **box sociable** *or* **box party** *or* **box supper** *n* **:** a fund-raising affair at which box lunches or suppers prepared individually by the women are auctioned so that the highest bidder on each box may then share it with its donor
box spanner *n* **:** BOX WRENCH
box spring *n* **:** a bedspring that consists of spiral springs attached to a foundation and enclosed in a cloth-covered frame
box stall *n* **:** an individual enclosure within a barn or stable in which an animal may move about freely without tethering or other restraining device — called also *loose-box*
box staple *n* **:** the box for the bolt of a lock
box step *n* **:** ²BOX 9e
box stirrup *n* **:** a wide stirrup closed at the forward end
box stool *n* **:** a stool with hinged seat that acts as cover to a compartment beneath
box strike *n* **:** a door strike with the socket enclosed to prevent access from the other side of the door
box string *n* [²*box*] **:** CLOSE STRING
box taler *n* **:** a hollow taler the obverse and reverse of which fit or screw together to form a thin box
box tenon *n* [²*box*] **:** an angle tenon (as in a corner post)
boxthorn \ˈ=,=\ *n* [¹*box*] **1 :** MATRIMONY VINE **2** *Austral* **:** NATIVE BOX
box toe *n* **:** a toe of a shoe made with a rigid or a flexible reinforcement
box tool *n* **:** a tool holder that partially surrounds the work piece in an automatic lathe or screw machine and supports it against the pressure of the cutting tool
box tortoise *or* **box turtle** *n* **:** any of three No. American land tortoises (genus *Terrapene* syn. *Cistudo*) that can withdraw entirely within the shell and close it by hinged joints in the lower shell
box trap *n* **:** a trap made of a wooden box supported by an often baited trigger so that the box will drop over an animal seeking the bait
boxtree \ˈ=,=\ *n* [ME, fr. OE *boxtrēow*, fr. *box* + *trēow* tree — more at ¹BOX, TREE] **:** ¹BOX
box truck *n* **1 :** a low flat truck for boxes or bales **2 :** a large light box or crate mounted on casters and used in transferring materials or merchandise in factories or stores
box wagon *n* **1 :** an open wagon with an oblong body with or without seats **2** *Brit* **:** BOXCAR
box·wal·lah \ˈbäk,swälə\ *n* -S [Hindi *bakswālā*, fr. E ²*box* + Hindi *-wālā* man — more at WALLAH] *India* **:** PEDDLER
box white oak *n* [¹*box*] **:** a post oak (*Quercus stellata*) —called also *box oak*
boxwood \ˈ=,=\ *n* [¹*box*] **1 a :** the very hard tough close-

grained heavy white to yellow wood of the box that is used in wood-engraving and in the making of musical instruments, rules, inlays, and other fine delicate woodwork — see TURKISH BOXWOOD **b** : any of several other woods having properties and uses similar to those of boxwood — often with a qualifying term ⟨West Indian ~⟩ **2** : a plant producing boxwood: as **a** : ¹BOX 1 **b** : FLORIDA BOXWOOD **c** : ZAPATERO 2 **d** : FLOWERING DOGWOOD **e** : SHITTIMWOOD 3

boxwood leaf miner *n* : a minute orange two-winged fly (*Monarthropalpus buxi*) having a larva that mines in and causes blistering and browning of the foliage of boxwood

boxwork \ˈ=,=\ *n* : a mineral-aggregate structure having plates or septa that are often coated with crystals and that intersect at various angles and enclose angular spaces

box wrench *n* [²*box*] : a wrench with a socket or a closed ring that fits over the bolt head or nut

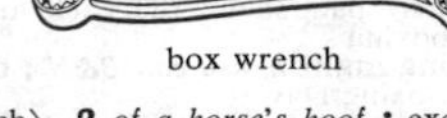
box wrench

boxy \ˈbäksē, -si\ *adj* -ER/-EST [²*box* + -*y*] **1** : like a box : SQUARISH — usu. used in disparagement ⟨a ~ automobile design⟩ ⟨a ~ church⟩ **2** *of a horse's hoof* : excessively small and contracted **3** : having an unfitted square straightlined appearance ⟨a jacket of ~ cut⟩

boy \ˈbȯi\ *n* -S *often attrib* [ME; akin to Fris *boi* boy and prob. to OE *Bōia, Bōfa* (masculine proper names), OHG *Buobo* (masculine proper name), MHG *buobe* boy; all perh. fr. prehistoric WGmc words derived by baby talk fr. the WGmc word corresponding to OE *brōthor* brother — more at BROTHER] **1 a** : a male child from birth to puberty ⟨~ baby⟩ **b** : SON : male offspring ⟨this is my little ~⟩ **c** : a male person not fully matured or not felt to be mature : LAD, YOUTH ⟨a job that separates the men from the ~s⟩ ⟨~ scientist⟩ ⟨~ wonder⟩ **d** : SWEETHEART, BEAU : young social partner ⟨she is never seen with a ~⟩ : FAVORITE ⟨the fair-haired ~ of the department⟩ **e** : PUPIL, STUDENT ⟨college ~s⟩ ⟨day ~⟩ **2 a** : one native to or orig. belonging to a given place ⟨a country ~ at heart⟩ ⟨a local ~ who made good in the big city⟩ **b** : a member of a group, gang, or any kind of association of equals ⟨wait till the ~s back home hear this⟩ ⟨the ~s at the office⟩ : CONFORMIST — usu. used in pl. ⟨trying to be just one of the ~s⟩ **c** *slang* : one classed or identified with a particular profession or specialty ⟨what the science ~s have discovered⟩ ⟨the ~s in the drafting room⟩ or doctrine ⟨the hard-money ~s⟩ ⟨the happiness ~s⟩ or faction ⟨controlled by the big-business ~s⟩ — usu. used with some degree of ridicule, hostility, or contempt; usu. used in pl. **3** *obs* : RASCAL, KNAVE, VARLET **4 a** : a male servant ⟨house ~⟩ ⟨stable ~⟩ **b** : one who does light work esp. in the service fields ⟨I'll send a ~ over with it⟩ — usu. used in combinations ⟨delivery ~⟩ **c** : a male member of a race felt to be inferior ⟨hiring ~s for a safari⟩ **5** : MAN, FELLOW — used in affection or admiration or familiarity ⟨a nice old ~⟩ ⟨the boss is quite a ~⟩ ⟨cheer up, old ~⟩

bo·yar *also* **bo·yard** *or* **bo·iar** \bōˈyär, -yä\ *n* -S [Russ *boyarin*, fr. ORuss, fr. OSlav *boljarinŭ*, prob. fr. OTurk *boila*] **1** : a member of a Russian aristocratic order that was next in rank to the ruling princes and was possessed of many exclusive privileges until its abolition by Peter the Great **2** : a member of a privileged landholding class in Romania

¹**boy·cott** \ˈbȯi,kät, *usu* -äd·+V; *esp Brit* -,kət\ *vt* -ED/-ING/-S [Charles C. *Boycott* †1897 Eng. land agent in County Mayo, Ireland, who was ostracized in 1880 for refusing to reduce rents] **1** : to combine against (a person, employer, a group of persons, or a nation) in a policy of nonintercourse for economic or political reasons : withhold wholly or partly social or business intercourse from as an expression of disapproval or means of coercion ⟨a threat to ~ the Security Council⟩ **2** : to engage in a concerted refusal to have anything to do with the products or services of (an employer) in order to force acceptance of certain conditions desired by a union ⟨agreed to ~ all uncooperative manufacturers⟩

²**boycott** \"\ *n* -S : the process or an instance of boycotting — see SECONDARY BOYCOTT

boy·er \ˈbȯiə(r)\ *n* -S [D *boeier*, fr. MD *boeyer, boyer*, fr. *boeyen, boyen* to plank up the side of a ship (perh. fr. *boeye, boye* fetter, chain, fr. OF *buie, boie*, fr. L *boia* shackle for the neck) + -*er* -er (akin to OE -*ere* -er)] : a small Flemish sailing boat

boyfriend \ˈ=,=\ *n* **1** : a male friend **2** : a frequent, regular, or favorite escort or male companion of a girl or woman **3** : the male partner in an intimate or esp. an illicit relationship : LOVER, PARAMOUR

boyg \ˈbȯig\ *n* -S *usu cap* [Norw *bøig* bugbear, ogre, bend, curve; akin to ON *beygja* to bend — more at ¹BOW] : a formless or pervasive obstacle, problem, or enemy (as despair or public apathy or popular ignorance) ⟨battling against the great amorphous *Boyg* —Graham Greene⟩

boy·hood \ˈbȯi,hu̇d\ *n* -S **1** : the state or period of being a boy **2** : boyish nature : BOYISHNESS **3** : BOYS ⟨outstanding service to ~⟩

boy·ish \ˈbȯiish, ˈbȯiēsh\ *adj* : like or belonging to a boy : IMMATURE **syn** see YOUTHFUL

boy·ish·ly *adv* : in a boyish manner

boy·ish·ness *n* -ES : the quality or state of being boyish

boy·ism \ˈbȯi,izəm\ *n* -S **1** : boy nature : a boyish trait or feature **2** : a puerile notion or expression

boy·la \ˈbȯilə\ *n* -S [native name in Australia] *Austral* : a native sorcerer

boyle's law \ˈbȯi(ə)lz-\ *n, usu cap B* [after Robert *Boyle* †1691 Brit. physicist, its formulator] : a statement in physics: the product of the pressure and the specific volume of a gas at constant temperature is constant — called also *Mariotte's law*

boyo \ˈbȯi(,)ō\ *n* -S [*boy* + -*o*] *Irish* : BOY, LAD ⟨"keep out of this, ~", he said grimly —John Fountain⟩

boys *pl of* BOY

boys-and-girls \ˈ=;==\ *n pl but sing or pl in constr* **1** : DUTCHMAN'S-BREECHES **2** : a slender annual American weed (*Mercurialis annua*) with branching stems

boy scout *n* **1** : a boy member of the Boy Scouts, a movement founded in Great Britain in 1908 and in the U.S. in 1910 for carrying out among boys a program of outdoor and educational activities aimed at developing good citizenship and healthy useful living — compare GIRL GUIDE, GIRL SCOUT **2** : a member of the Boy Scouts who is 11, 12, or 13 years old as distinguished from a cub scout or an explorer

boy·sen·ber·ry \ˈbȯizᵊn-, ˈbȯisᵊn- —*see* BERRY\ *n* [after Rudolph *Boysen* *fl*1923 Am. horticulturist, its originator] **1** : a very large bramble fruit with a flavor like a raspberry esp. valued for canning and preserving **2** : the trailing hybrid bramble that bears boysenberries that was developed in California by hybridization from several blackberries and raspberries

boy's-love \ˈ=,=\ *n, pl* **boy's-loves** [so called fr. its use to promote the growth of beard] **1** *dial Eng* : SOUTHERNWOOD **2** : WORMWOOD

boza *var of* BOSA

bo·zal \bōˈsal, -ˈzal\ *var of* BOSAL

bozine *var of* BUSINE

bo·zo \ˈbō(,)zō\ *n* -S [origin unknown] *slang* : FELLOW, GUY

boz·zet·to \bätˈsed·(,)ō, bəˈze-\ *n, pl* **bozzet·ti** \-ed·(,)ē\ [It, dim. of *bozzo* sketch, rough stone, alter. of *bozza*, lit., swelling — more at ¹BOSS] : a small rough clay study for a larger sculpture — used esp. of baroque sculpture

bp *abbr* **1** baptized **2** birthplace **3** *often cap* bishop **4** boiling point

BP *abbr* **1** band pass **2** before present **3** below proof **4** bill of parcels **5** bills payable **6** blood pressure

BPB *abbr* bank post bill

BPD *abbr* barrels per day

BPH *abbr* barrels per hour

B Phil *abbr or n* -S : a bachelor of philosophy

bpl *abbr* birthplace

b power supply *n, usu cap B* : a battery or transformer and rectifier supplying electric power in the plate circuit of an electron tube to maintain the electron current in the tube — compare A POWER SUPPLY, C POWER SUPPLY; B BATTERY

bq *or* **bque** *abbr* barque

br *abbr* **1** branch **2** brand **3** brass **4** bridge **5** brief **6** brig **7** brigade **8** broché **9** bronze **10** brother **11** brown **12** brush

BR *abbr* **1** bank rate **2** bedroom **3** bill of rights **4** bills receivable **5** builder's risk

Br *symbol* bromine

bra \ˈbrä, -à *sometimes* -ó\ *n* -S [by shortening] : BRASSIERE

brab·an·çon \ˈbrabən,sän, brəˈban(t)sən\ *n* -S *usu cap* [F, lit., Brabantine, fr. *Brabant*] **1** : a Belgian breed of heavy powerful draft horses noted for their quiet temperament **2** : a horse of the Brabançon breed

bra·bant rose \brəˈbant-\ *n, usu cap B* [fr. *Brabant*, province of central Belgium] : a cut (as of a diamond) similar to a Dutch rose but having 12 facets or less — see ROSE illustration

¹**brab·ble** \ˈbrabəl\ *vi* **brabbled**; **brabbled**; **brabbling** \-b(ə)liŋ\ **brabbles** [MD *brabbelen* to quarrel, stammer, jabber, of imit. origin] : to talk noisily or captiously : SQUABBLE ⟨the desultory *brabbling* between the Western Powers and the Russians —*Time*⟩

²**brabble** \"\ *n* -S **1 a** : ALTERCATION, QUARREL ⟨the ~s of the law courts⟩ **b** *obs* : a noisy fight : BRAWL ⟨in private ~ did we apprehend him —Shak.⟩ **2 a** : BABBLE ⟨a ~ of voices⟩ : CHATTER ⟨I'm not to be mollified by any woman's ~ —P.L.Ford⟩ **b** : a discordant continued murmuring ⟨a fresh nor'-westerly breeze had sprung up . . . and there was a heavy ~ alongshore —G.G.Carter⟩

brab·bler \ˈbrab(ə)lə(r)\ *n* -S : one that brabbles

brac·cae \ˈbrä,kī, ˈbra,kē, -ak,sē\ *also* **bra·cae** \ˈbrä,kī, ˈbrā,sē\ *n pl* [L *bracae*, pl. of *braca*, fr. Gaulish *brāca*, of Gmc origin; akin to OHG *bruoh* pair of breeches — more at BREECHES] : shapeless trousers of wool or skin tied at the waist and ankles by cords worn chiefly by the ancient Gauls

brac·cio \ˈbrä(,)chō, -,chē,ō\ *n, pl* **brac·cia** \-(,)chä, -,chē,ä\ [It, lit., arm, fr. L *brachium*] : an Italian unit of length varying between 15 and 39 inches

¹**brace** \ˈbrās\ *n, pl* **braces** *also* **brace** *see sense 2* [ME, fr. MF, two arms, fr. L *bracchia, brachia*, pl. of *bracchium, brachium* arm, modif. of Gk *brachiōn*, fr. *brachys* short — more at BRIEF] **1** *obs* **a** : armor esp. for the arm **b** : an arm of water : INLET **2** *pl* **brace** *or* **braces** : two of a kind ⟨a ~ of hounds⟩ ⟨several ~ of quail⟩ : a pair esp. of things usu. kept together ⟨a ~ of dueling pistols⟩ **3** [ME, prob. influenced in meaning by ME *bracen* to embrace, clasp] *archaic* : a clasp, a buckle, or a similar binding or encompassing device **4** : a crank-shaped instrument with handles and a chuck for holding and turning auger bits **5** : something that transmits, directs, resists, or supports weight or pressure: as **a** : a piece of material that divides a frame or truss into triangular parts and serves as a tie or strut to bear transverse strains and prevent distortion **b** : one of the slides on the cords of a drum used to tighten the drumhead **c** [perh. influenced in meaning by F *bras*, lit., arm, fr. L *brachium*] : a rope rove through a block at the end of a yard of a square-rigged ship and used to swing and trim the yard horizontally — see SHIP illustration **d** : one of the leather straps used to suspend the body of a horse-drawn carriage from the springs **e** **braces** *pl* : SUSPENDERS **f** : an appliance that gives support to movable parts (as a joint or a fractured bone), to weak muscles (as in paralysis), or to strained ligaments (as of the lower back) **g** : an endpiece by which the outer end of the mainspring of a timepiece is attached to the barrel **h** : something (as a chock) used to secure goods and containers during shipment **i** : a device (as a bar or an angle bracket) used to provide stiffness or rigidity : REINFORCEMENT **6 a** : a mark { or } or ⏟ used to connect words or items to be considered together, equal, or in pairs or to enclose items of which only one is to be chosen **b** : this mark connecting two or more musical staffs and indicating that the parts on these staffs are to be performed simultaneously; *also* : the group of staffs so connected ⟨the upper ~⟩ **c** : one of the pair of such marks used as signs of aggregation in mathematics **d** : BRACKET 4a **7** : an exaggerated position of attention or of rigidly erect bearing (as while drilling or on parade) ⟨on review, his uniform and ~ were technically correct —*Time*⟩ **8** : something that arouses energy, increases power of exertion, or strengthens or helps in recovering morale

brace 4

²**brace** \"\ *vb* -ED/-ING/-S [ME *bracen*, fr. MF *bracier* to embrace, fr. *brace*] *vt* **1** *archaic* : to fasten tightly : BIND, TIE **2 a** *obs* : EMBRACE **b** *archaic* : ENCIRCLE, SURROUND **3 a** : to prepare for use by making taut ⟨~ a drum⟩; *esp* : to place the string of (a bow) in the nocks **b** : to prepare esp. for a struggle, enterprise, shock : STEEL ⟨~ his will⟩ ⟨no other country was so . . . *braced* for empire and for glory —Mary S. Douglas⟩ ⟨the class *braced* itself for the examination⟩ — sometimes used with *up* ⟨hearing the words "bad news", the family *braced* itself up⟩ **c** : INVIGORATE, FRESHEN, ENLIVEN ⟨wind ~*ing* the air⟩ — often used with *up* ⟨I took the shower and it *braced* me up a bit —Raymond Chandler⟩ **4** [¹*brace* (rope at the end of a yard)] : to turn (a sail yard) by means of a brace **5** [¹*brace*] **a** : to prop up or support with braces ⟨~ a sagging floor⟩ ⟨a well-*braced* trestle⟩ ⟨the 29-year-old . . . woman, heavily *braced* because of polio —*Springfield (Mass.) Union*⟩ **b** : STRENGTHEN, REINFORCE ⟨the sides were *braced* by tar paper, chicken wire, and timber —S.W.Matthews⟩ ⟨nerves . . . *braced* by long familiarity with danger —T.B.Macaulay⟩ **6 a** : to make rigid : STIFFEN ⟨Constance was *braced* into a moveless anguish —Arnold Bennett⟩ **b** : to put or plant firmly ⟨he . . . *braced* his hand on the stone . . . and . . . sprang lightly up —Kay Boyle⟩ **7 a** : to waylay esp. with demands or questions : CONFRONT ⟨when *braced*, Willie had naturally denied his identity —*Time*⟩ ⟨he *braced* the owners for a raise —N.M.Clark⟩ **b** : to harry with repeated and abusive questions or criticism : dress down : BADGER, GRILL, HOUND ⟨the police *braced* him on the charge⟩ ~ *vi* **1** : to take heart : buck up — used with *up* ⟨if you don't ~ up and do something —Upton Sinclair⟩ **2** : to get ready : prepare quickly (as for an attack) **3** : to assume a brace (sense 7) ⟨today, the plebe need never ~ in public and physical hazing is forbidden —*Newsweek*⟩ **syn** see SUPPORT

³**brace** \"\ *archaic var of* ³BRASS

brace about *or* **brace around** *vt* : to turn (a yard of a square-rigged ship) about for the opposite tack

brace bit *n* : a bit for use in a brace

brace bumpkin *n* : ²BUMPKIN b

brace comb *n* : honeycomb built in small pieces by bees to bridge spaces

braced *adj* [fr. past part. of ²*brace* (to embrace, clasp)] *of two or more heraldic bearings* : INTERLACED ⟨three chevrons ~⟩

braced arch *n* : a truss (as of steel or concrete) in the form of an arch

braced frame *n* : a building frame in which the timbers are heavy enough to be mortised and in which diagonal bracing is used — compare BALLOON FRAME

braced framing *n* : the method of building that employs the braced frame

brace drill *n* : a drill provided with a tang at the end of the shank to fit the chuck of a brace

brace game *n* [¹*brace* (pair); fr. its original application to collusion between the dealer and casekeeper in faro] : a gambling game organized for the purpose of swindling

brace head *or* **brace key** *n* : an attachment (as a long-handled wrench) for turning a boring rod

brace in *vt* : to turn (a ship's yard) more thwartwise by hauling in the weather brace

brace·let \ˈbrāslət\ *n* -S [ME, fr. MF, dim. of *bras* arm, fr. OF *braz*, fr. L *brachium* — more at BRACE] **1** : an ornamental band, ring, or chain worn around the wrist **2** : something that in position or appearance suggests a bracelet: as **a** : HANDCUFF — usu. used in pl. **b** : a chain for securing an identification tag to the wrist **c** : one of the dark bands of fur ringing the forelegs of a well-marked tabby cat — compare NECKLACE **d** : ANKLE STRAP ⟨a ~ sandal⟩ **e** : RASCETTE **3** : a piece of armor (as the vambrace) for the wrist or arm

bracelet watch *n* : a small wristwatch; *esp* : one for a woman

bracelet wood *n* : a small West Indian tree (*Jacquinia armillaris*) of the family Myrsinaceae with hard seeds that are used to make bracelets

bracemate \ˈ=,=\ *n* [¹*brace* (pair) + *mate*] : one of two hunting dogs that are shown or worked as a pair

brace molding *n* : a molding composed of two ogees connected so as to resemble in outline a printer's brace

brace pendant *n* : a rope or chain by which a brace block is attached to a yard

¹**brac·er** \ˈbrāsə(r)\ *n* -S [ME, fr. MF *braciere*, fr. OF, fr. *braz* arm — more at BRACELET] : an arm or wrist protector (as one used by a fencer or a ballplayer); *esp* : a guard usu. of leather worn by an archer to shield the left wrist from the snap of the bowstring

²**brac·er** \"\ *n* -S [²*brace* + -*er*] : one that braces, binds, or makes firm: as **a** (1) : a drink taken as a tonic or stimulant; *esp* : a drink of liquor (2) : something that acts as a freshener, revitalizer, or reviver ⟨the news was a ~ for us all⟩ **b** : SHORER; *specif* : TIMBERMAN **c** : a worker who puts blocks, bracing, and strapping into freight cars and trucks to prevent shifting of load in transit — called also *blocker* **d** : a worker who attaches uppers to the soles of shoes

bra·ce·ro \brəˈse(,)rō\ *n* -S [Sp, laborer, fr. *brazo* arm, fr. L *brachium* — more at BRACE] : a Mexican laborer admitted to the U.S. under immigration treaties for chiefly seasonal contract labor in agriculture or industry — compare WETBACK

brace root *n* : PROP ROOT

braces *pl of* BRACE, *pres 3d sing of* BRACE

brace to *vt* : to brace in

brace up *vt* : to turn (a yard) nearer to the fore-and-aft position by hauling in the lee brace ⟨*braced* sharp *up*⟩

brace wrench *n* : a wrench with a crank-shaped handle and socket head

brach \ˈbrach\ *n* -ES [ME *brache*, a kind of hound, back-formation fr. *braches, brachez*, pl., fr. MF, fr. OF, pl. of *brachet* — more at BRACHET] *archaic* : a bitch hound

brach·el·y·trous \(ˈ)braˈkelə·trəs\ *adj* [Gk *brachys* short + *elytron* covering, shard of a beetle's wing (fr. *eilyein* to enwrap) + E -*ous* — more at BRIEF, VOLUBLE] *of a beetle* : having short wing covers

brach·en \ˈbrakən\ *archaic Scot var of* BRACKEN

brach·et \ˈbrachət\ *n* -S [ME, fr. MF, fr. OF, of Gmc origin; akin to OHG *braccho* hunting dog (that uses scent), MLG & MD *bracke*; prob. akin to MHG *bræhen* to smell — more at FRAGRANT] *archaic* : BRACH

brachi- *or* **brachio-** *comb form* [L *brachi-* & NL *brachio-*, fr. L *brachium* — more at BRACE] **1** : arm ⟨*brachi*ferous⟩ ⟨*brach*iotomy⟩ **2** : brachial and ⟨*brachio*facial⟩

¹**brach·ia** \ˈbrakēə, -rāk-\ *pl of* BRACHIUM

²**brachia** \"\ *n pl* [NL, fr. L, pl. of *brachium* arm] : LOPHOPHORE

¹**brach·i·al** \-ēəl\ *adj* [L *bracchialis, brachialis*, fr. *bracchium, brachium* arm + -*alis* -al — more at BRACE] : of or relating to the arm or a process like an arm

²**brachial** \"\ *n* -S : a brachial part (as a scale or plate)

brachial artery *n* : the chief artery of the upper arm, being a direct continuation of the axillary artery and dividing into the radial and ulnar arteries just below the elbow

brachial cavity *n* : the anterior space inside the valves of brachiopods into which the brachia are withdrawn

brach·i·al·is \,brakēˈāləs, -ˈal-, -ˈäl-\ *or* **brachialis an·ti·cus** \-lə,sanˈtēkəs, -ˈtīk-\ *n* -ES [*brachialis*, NL, fr. L, adj., brachial; *brachialis anticus*, NL, front brachialis] : a flexor muscle lying in front of the lower part of the humerus whence it arises and being inserted into the ulna

brachial ossicle *n* : a small bone of the pectoral fin of a fish

brachial plexus *n* : a complex network of nerves that is formed chiefly by the lower four cervical and first thoracic nerves, lies partly within the axilla, and supplies nerves to the chest shoulder, and arm

brachial vein *n* : one of a pair of veins accompanying the course of the brachial artery and uniting with each other and with the basilic vein to form the axillary vein

¹**brach·i·ate** \ˈbrakē,āt, -rāk-, -ēət\ *adj* [L *bracchiatus, brachiatus*, fr. *bracchium, brachium* arm + -*atus* -ate] **1** : having widely spreading branches arranged in alternating pairs ⟨the maple is ~⟩ — compare DECUSSATE **2** *zool* : having arms

²**brachiate** \-ē,āt\ *vi* -ED/-ING/-S [*brachi-* + -*ate*] : to progress by swinging from one hold to another by the arms (as of the gibbon)

brach·i·a·tion \,==ˈāshən\ *n* -S : the act or practice of brachiating

brach·i·a·tor \ˈ==,ād·ə(r)\ *n* -S : a brachiating animal

bra·chid·i·um \brəˈkidēəm, brəˈ-\ *n, pl* **brachid·ia** \-ēə\ [NL, fr. *brachi-* + -*idium*] : the calcareous support of the lophophore of certain brachiopods

brach·io·ganoidei \ˈbrakē(,)ō+\ [NL, fr. *brachi-* + *Ganoidei*] *syn of* CROSSOPTERYGII 1

bra·chi·o·la \brəˈkēələ, brəˈ-, -kīə-, ,brakēˈōlə\ *n* -S [NL, fr. *brachi-* + L -*ola* (fem. dim. suffix)] : one of the three processes of the brachiolaria

brach·i·o·lar·i·a \,brakēōˈla(a)rēə\ *n, pl* **brachiolar·i·ae** \-rē,ē\ [NL, fr. *brachiola* + -*aria*] : a transitional larva of certain starfishes that develops from the bipinnaria and is distinguished by possession of three anterior processes homologous with those of the adult starfish —**brach·i·o·lar·i·an** \;==;=ˈ=rēən\ *adj*

brach·ion·ich·thy·i·dae \,brakēə,nikˈthīə,dē\ *n pl, cap* [NL, fr. *Brachionichthys*, type genus (fr. Gk *brachion-, brachiōn* arm + *ichthys* fish) + -*idae* — more at BRACE, ICHTHUS] : a family of pediculate fishes comprising the handfishes and distinguished by highly modified pectoral fins that resemble hands

¹**brach·i·o·pod** \ˈbrakēə,päd\ *adj* [NL *Brachiopoda*] : BRACHIOPODOUS

²**brachiopod** \"\ *n* -S : an animal of the phylum Brachiopoda

brach·i·op·o·da \,brakēˈäpədə\ *n pl, cap* [NL, fr. *brachi-* + -*poda*] : a phylum of invertebrates that has persisted with reduced numbers from the Lower Cambrian to the present and that consists of sedentary unsegmented marine animals with well-developed coelom and hemocoel, a lophophore, and often a fleshy stalk extending into the substrate, the body being enclosed in a bivalve chitinophosphatic or calcareous shell the valves of which are unequal, bilaterally symmetrical, and usu. regarded as dorsal and ventral

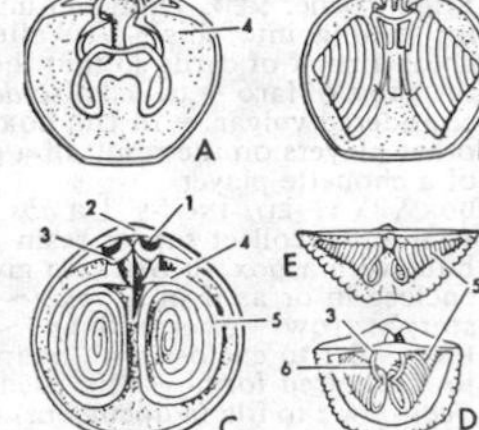

brachiopod shells: looped brachidia, *A*; athyroid, *B*; atrypoid, *C*; spiriferoid, *D* and *E*; *1* dental socket, *2* cardinal process, *3* crura, *4* jugal process, *5* spiralium, *6* primary lamella

brach·i·op·o·dist \-dəst\ *n* -S [NL *Brachiopoda* + E -*ist*] : one who specializes in the study of Brachiopoda

brach·i·op·o·dous \;brakē;äpədəs\ *adj* [NL *Brachiopoda* + E -*ous*] : of or belonging to the Brachiopoda

brach·io·ra·di·al·is \,brakē(,)ō,rādēˈāləs, -ˈal-, -ˈäl-\ *n, pl* **brachioradial·es** \-,lēz\ [NL, fr. *brachi-* + ML *radialis* radial, fr. L *radius* + -*alis* -al — more at RADIUS] : a flexor of the radial side of the forearm arising from the lateral epicondylic ridge of the humerus and inserted into the styloid process of the radius

brach·i·o·saur \ˈbrakēə,sȯ(ə)r\ *n* -S [NL *Brachiosaurus*] : a dinosaur of the genus *Brachiosaurus*

brach·i·o·sau·rus \,brakēəˈsȯrəs\ *n, cap* [NL, fr. *brachi-* + -*saurus*] : a genus of huge dinosaurs (suborder Sauropoda) of the Upper Jurassic having longer forelegs than hind legs

bra·chis·to·cephalic *also* **brachistocephalous** \brəˈkistō, brəˈ-+\ *adj* [Gk *brachistos* (superlative of *brachys* short) + E -*cephalic*, -*cephalous* — more at BRIEF] : brachycephalic with a cephalic index of 85 or more — compare EURYCEPHALIC — **bra·chis·to·ceph·a·ly** \"+ˈsefəlē\ *n* -ES

bra·chis·to·chrone \brəˈkistə,krōn, brəˈ-\ *n* -S [fr. Gk *brachistos* shortest + *chronos* time] : a curve in which a body starting from a point and acted on by an external force will reach another point in a shorter time than by any other path — **bra·chis·to·chron·ic** \=;=;=ˈkränik\ *adj*

bra·chi·um \'brākēəm, -rak-\ *n, pl* **bra·chia** \-ēə\ [L *bracchium, brachium* arm, forearm — more at BRACE] **1 :** the upper segment of the arm or forelimb from the shoulder to the elbow **2 :** any of certain processes similar to an arm: as **a :** a ray of a crinoid **b :** a tentacle of a cephalopod **c :** a tentaculiferous process in certain jellyfishes **d :** either of the coiled muscular paired appendages that together constitute the lophophore of a brachiopod

brachium con·junc·tiv·um \-kən¦jəŋktəvəm\ *n* [NL, fr. L, lit., connective arm] **:** a cerebellar peduncle that connects the cerebellum with the midbrain

brachy- *comb form* [Gk, fr. *brachys* — more at BRIEF] **1 :** short ⟨*brachy*cephalic⟩ **2 :** brachydiagonal — in terms in crystallography ⟨*brachy*dome⟩

brachy·axis \¦brakē+\ *n* [*brachy-* + *-axis*] **:** the shorter lateral axis of an orthorhombic or triclinic crystal

brach·y·blast \'brakə,blast, -kē,-\ *n* -s [ISV *brachy-* + *-blast*] **:** a short shoot often bearing leaves in clusters (as in the pines)

brachy·catalectic \¦brakē+\ *adj* [Gk *brachykatalēktos* (fr. *brachy-* + — assumed — *katalēktos*, verbal of *katalēgein* to leave off, stop, fr. *kata-* cata- + *lēgein* to stop, cease, leave off) + E *-ic;* akin to Gk *lagaros* slack, thin — more at SLACK] *prosody* **:** characterized by or due to brachycatalexis

brachy·catalexis \"+\ *n* [LL, modif. of Gk *brachykatalēxia*, fr. *brachykatalēktos* + *-ia* -y] *Greek & Latin prosody* **:** omission of two syllables at the end of a verse composed of the larger metrical units (as dipodies)

brachy·ceph·al \,brakə'sefəl, -kē'-\ *n* -s [NL *brachycephalus*, fr. *brachy-* + *-cephalus*] **:** a brachycephalic person

brachy·cephalic \¦brakə, -kē+\ *adj* [NL *brachycephalus* + E *-ic*] **:** short-headed or broad-headed with a cephalic index of over 80 — see CEPHALIC INDEX illustration

brachy·ceph·a·lid \,brakə'sefələd, -kē'-\ *n* -s [NL *Brachycephalidae*] **:** a toad of the family Brachycephalidae

brachy·ce·phal·i·dae \-,sə'falə,dē\ *n pl, cap* [NL, fr. *Brachycephalus*, type genus (fr. *brachy-* + *-cephalus*) + *-idae*] **:** a large family of small Neotropical toads (suborder Procoela) having partial or complete median fusion of the shoulder girdle

brachy·ceph·a·lism \-'sefə,lizəm\ *n* -s [*brachycephalic* + *-ism*] **:** BRACHYCEPHALY

brachy·ceph·a·li·za·tion \-,sefələ'zāshən, -,lī'z-\ *n* -s [*brachycephalic* + *-ization*] **:** transition toward a more brachycephalic condition ⟨the increasing ~ of Europe⟩

brachy·ceph·a·ly \-lē\ *n* -ES [ISV *brachycephalic* + *-y*] **:** the quality or state of being brachycephalic

bra·chyc·era \brə'kisərə, brə'-\ *n pl, cap* [NL, fr. *brachy-* + *-cera*] **:** a suborder of Diptera including the more highly specialized flies which have palpi with one or two joints and usu. short antennae with one or never more than six joints (as the horsefly, robber fly, and housefly) — compare NEMATOCERA

brachy·cerebral \¦brakē+\ *adj* [*brachy-* + *cerebral*] **:** possessing a round or rather short brain

bra·chyc·er·ous \brə'kisərəs, brə'-\ *adj* [NL *Brachycera* + E *-ous*] **:** having short antennae; *specif* **:** of or relating to the Brachycera

brachy·chi·ton \,brakə'kītᵊn, -akē'-\ *n, cap* [NL, fr. *brachy-* + Gk *chitōn* covering, case, tunic — more at CHITON] **:** a genus of Australian trees (family Sterculiaceae) that are grown in warm regions for ornament and have flowers with numerous stamens and woody fruits — see BOTTLE TREE

bra·chyc·o·me \brə'kikə(,)mē, brə'-\ *n, cap* [NL, fr. *brachy-* + Gk *komē* hair] **:** a genus of mostly Australian herbs (family Compositae) with basal or alternate leaves and solitary or loosely corymbose flower heads

brachy·cranial \¦brakē+\ *adj* [*brachy-* + *cranial*] **:** short-skulled or broad-skulled with a cranial index of 80 and above — **brachy·cranic** \"+\ *adj* — **brachy·cra·ny** \'brakē-,krānē\ *n* -ES

brachy·cranium \¦brakē+\ *n* [NL, fr. *brachy-* + *cranium*] **:** a brachycranial skull

brachy·dac·ty·lism \,brakē'daktə,lizəm\ *n* -s [*brachydactylous* + *-ism*] **:** a brachydactylous condition or a tendency toward brachydactyly

brachy·dac·ty·lous \¦==¦==ləs\ *adj* [*brachy-* + *-dactylous*] **:** of or relating to brachydactyly

brachy·dac·ty·ly \-lē\ *also* **brachy·dac·tyl·ia** \,===='tilyə, -lēə\ *n, pl* **brachydactylies** *also* **brachydactylias** [NL *brachydactylia*, fr. *brachy-* + *dactyl-* + *-ia*] **:** abnormal shortness of the digits (as when the fingers have but two joints)

[1]**brachy·diagonal** \¦brakē+\ *adj* [*brachy-* + *diagonal*] **:** of or relating to the brachyaxis

[2]**brachydiagonal** \"\ *n* -s **:** BRACHYAXIS

brach·y·dod·ro·mous \¦brakə¦dädrəməs\ *adj* [by alter.] **:** BROCHIDODROMOUS

brachy·dome \'brakə,dōm\ *n* [*brachy-* + *dome*] **:** the dome of a crystal having planes parallel to the shorter lateral axis — compare CLINODOME, MACRODOME, ORTHODOME

brachy·dont \-,dänt\ *also* **brachy·odont** \'brakēō,d-\ *adj* [*brachy-* + *-odont*] **1** *of teeth* **:** having short crowns, well-developed roots, and only narrow canals in the roots (as in man) — compare HYPSODONT **2 :** having brachydont teeth

brachy·facial \¦brakē+\ *adj* [*brachy-* + *facial*] **:** having a short or broad face

brachy-form \'brakē+,-\ *n* [*brachy-* + *-form*] **:** a rust that does not produce aecia — compare EU-FORM

bra·chyg·na·tha \brə'kignəthə, brə'-\ *n pl, cap* [NL, fr. *brachy-* + *-gnatha*] **:** a division of the tribe Brachyura comprising the Brachyrhyncha and Oxyrhyncha and including the majority of the true crabs with the mouth field more or less square, sternal female openings, and the last pair of legs usu. normal in size and position

[1]**bra·chyg·na·than** \-thən\ *adj* [NL *Brachygnatha* + E *-an*] **:** of or relating to the Brachygnatha

[2]**brachygnathan** \"\ *n* -s **:** a crab of the division Brachygnatha

bra·chyg·ra·phy \-grəfē\ *n* -ES [Gk *brachy-* + E *-graphy*] **:** SHORTHAND

brach·y·lae·mus \,brakə'lēməs\ [NL, alter. of *Brachylaima*] *syn of* BRACHYLAIMA

brach·y·lai·ma \-'līmə\ *n, cap* [NL, fr. *brachy-* + *-laima* (fr. Gk *laimos* throat, gullet)] **:** a genus (the type of the family Brachylaimidae) of elongated digenetic trematodes including parasites of gallinaceous birds and of swine

[1]**brach·y·lai·mid** \¦brakə¦līməd\ *also* **brach·y·lae·mid** \-lēm-\ *adj* [NL *Brachylaima* or *Brachylaemus* + E *-id*] **:** of or relating to the genus *Brachylaima*

[2]**brachylaimid** \"\ *also* **brachylaemid** \"\ *n* -s **:** a trematode of the genus *Brachylaima*

bra·chyl·o·gy \brə'kiləjē, brə'-\ *n* -ES [Gk *brachylogia*, fr. *brachy-* + *-logia* -logy] **:** conciseness of expression; *also* **:** a condensed expression

brachy·meiosis \¦brakē+\ *n* [NL, fr. *brachy-* + *meiosis*] **:** a second reduction division following the usual two meiotic divisions reputed to occur in the ascus of certain fungi; *also* **:** the entire meiotic process when involving double reduction that has been suggested as an explanation of the restoration of the haploid condition in fungi in which double fertilization has produced a tetraploid primary ascus nucleus

brachy·meiotic \"+\ *adj* [fr. NL *brachymeiosis*, after such pairs as NL *hypnosis:* E *hypnotic*] **:** marked by or relating to brachymeiosis

brachy·mor·phic \¦brakə¦mȯrfik\ *adj* [*brachy-* + *-morphic*] **:** ENDOMORPHIC, PYKNIC — opposed to *dolichomorphic* — **brachy·mor·phy** \'===,fē\ *n* -ES

brachyodont *var of* BRACHYDONT

brachy·oura \,brakē'(y)ürə\ [NL] *syn of* BRACHYURA

brachyoural *or* **brachyouran** *or* **brachyourous** *var of* BRACHYURAL

brachyouran *var of* BRACHYURAN

brachy·pha·lan·gy \,brakēfə'lanjē, -fā'-\ *also* **brachy·pha·lan·gia** \-j(ē)ə\ *n, pl* **brachyphalangies** *also* **brachyphalangias** [NL *brachyphalangia*, fr. *brachy-* + *-phalangia*] **:** BRACHYDACTYLY

brach·y·phyl·lum \,brakə'filəm\ *n, cap* [NL, fr. *brachy-* + *-phyllum*] **:** a genus of fossil coniferous plants found in rocks ranging from Jurassic to Middle Cretaceous and having appressed, scalelike, relatively short and broad leaves

bra·chyp·ter·ism \brə'kiptə,rizəm, brə'-\ *n* -s **:** shortness of wings **:** the state of having short wings

bra·chyp·ter·ous \(')brə¦kiptərəs, brə'k-\ *adj* [Gk *brachypteros*, fr. *brachy-* + *-pteros* (fr. *pteron* wing) — more at FEATHER] **:** SHORT-WINGED **:** having the wings rudimentary or abnormally small — used chiefly of small-winged forms of certain insects

brachy·rhi·nus \,brakə'rīnəs\ *n, cap* [NL, fr. *brachy-* + *-rhinus*] **:** a very large genus of small short-snouted commonly dark-colored parthenogenetic weevils including a number of destructive pests of economic plants — see BLACK VINE WEEVIL, STRAWBERRY ROOT WEEVIL

brachy·rhyn·cha \,brakə'riŋkə\ *n pl, cap* [NL, fr. *brachy-* + *rhyncha* (fr. *rhynchos* snout) — more at RHYNCH-] **:** a superfamily of crabs including most of the Brachygnatha and all having the rostrum reduced or absent

brachy·sclereid \¦brakē+\ *n* -s [*brachy-* + *sclereid*] **:** a more or less isodiametric sclereid typically occurring in pith, cortex, and bark of many stems and in certain fruits (as pear and quince) — called also *stone cell*

brachy·skelic \¦brakə¦skelik\ *also* **brachys·ke·lous** \brə'kiskələs, brə'-\ *adj* [*brachy-* + Gk *skelos* leg + E *-ic* or *-ous* — more at SCEL-] **:** having legs short in proportion to the trunk **:** having a skelic index of 75 to 80

brach·ysm \'bra,kizəm\ *n* -s [blend of *brachy-* and *-ism*] **:** a dwarfing in plants that is characterized by a shortening of the internodes only — **bra·chyt·ic** \brə'kid·ik, brə'-\ *adj*

brach·y·ste·gia \,brakə'stēj(ē)ə\ *n, cap* [NL, fr. *brachy-* + Gk *stegos* roof + NL *-ia* — more at THATCH] **:** a small genus of tropical African trees (family Leguminosae) having compound leaves and small flowers with no calyx and small petals

brachy·syllabic \¦brakə, -kē+\ *adj* [*brachy-* + *syllabic*] **:** of or relating to a short syllable **:** having a short syllable **:** composed of short syllables

bra·chyt·ic \brə'kid·ik, brə'-\ *adj* [irreg. fr. *brachysm* + *-itic*] **:** marked by or relating to brachysm

brachy·ura \,brakē'yürə\ *n pl, cap* [NL, fr. *brachy-* + *-ura*] **:** a tribe of the suborder Reptantia or in some classifications a suborder of Decapoda comprising crustaceans with the abdomen greatly reduced and more or less folded against the ventral surface of the thorax and including the typical crabs — compare ANOMURA, MACRURA

brachy·ural \¦brakē¦yürəl\ *or* **brachy·uran** \-rən\ *or* **brachy·urous** \-rəs\ *also* **brachy·oural** *or* **brachy·ouran** *or* **brachy·ourous** \-ə¦(y)ü-\ *adj* [NL *Brachyura, Brachyoura* + E *-al* or *-an* or *-ous*] **:** of or relating to the Brachyura

brachy·uran \,brakē'yürən\ *also* **brachy·ouran** \-'(y)ü-\ *n* -s **:** a crustacean of the tribe Brachyura

brachy·uran·ic \¦brakēyü¦ranik\ *adj* [*brachy-* + *uran-* + *-ic*] **:** having a short or narrow alveolar arch **:** having a palatal index of 115 or over — **brachy·ura·ny** \-¦yürənē\ *n* -ES

brachy·urus \,brakē'yürəs\ [NL, fr. *brachy-* + *-urus*] *syn of* CACAJAO

[1]**bracing** *n* -s [fr. gerund of [2]*brace*] **:** the act or action of binding, strengthening, or making rigid ⟨the ~ of flood-damaged bridges⟩; *also* **:** material used for such an act or action ⟨beams, logs, and other ~⟩

[2]**bracing** *adj* [fr. pres. part. of [2]*brace*] **:** imparting strength, vigor, or freshness ⟨~ mountain air⟩ — **brac·ing·ly** *adv* — **brac·ing·ness** *n* -ES

[1]**brack** *chiefly Scot past of* BREAK

[2]**brack** \'brak\ *adj* [D *brak* salty fr. MD *brac;* akin to MLG *brak* salty, & perh. to MD *broec* swampy ground, OE *brōc* brook — more at BROOK] **1** *dial* **:** BRACKISH, BRINY ⟨~ water⟩ **2** *or* **brak** \"\ *Africa* **:** ALKALI ⟨~ soil⟩

[3]**brack** \"\ *n* -s **1** *dial* **:** salt water **:** BRINE **2** *or* **brak** \"\ *Africa* **:** alkali esp. in soil

[4]**brack** \"\ *n* -s [alter. of [2]*break*] **1** *archaic* **:** a crack or fissure in a solid body **:** BREAK, BREACH **2** *dial* **:** a flaw esp. in cloth

brack·e·busch·ite \'brakə,bü,shīt, ,==¦=,=\ *n* -s [G *brackebuschit*, fr. Ludwig *Brackebusch* †1906 Ger. mineralogist + G *-it* -ite] **:** a mineral $Pb_4MnFe(VO_4)_4.2H_2O$ consisting of a hydrous vanadate of lead, iron, and manganese

[1]**brack·en** \'brakən\ *n, pl* **bracken** *or* **brackens** [ME *braken*, prob. of Scand origin; akin to OSw *brækne* fern, Norw *burkne*, Icel *burkni;* perh. akin to OE *brecan* to break — more at BREAK] **1 a :** a large coarse fern **b :** the common brake (*Pteridium aquilinum*) and related species of the same genus and of *Pteris* with which it is merged in some classifications **c :** ROYAL FERN **2 :** a growth of brakes (as *Pteridium aquilinum*); *also* **:** an area dominated by such a growth **3 :** BONE BROWN 2

[2]**bracken** *var of* BRECHAN

bracken poisoning *or* **bracken staggers** *n* ['*bracken*] **:** a disease of livestock caused by eating mature bracken and resulting in loss of appetite, diarrhea, weakness, and knuckling of fetlocks and appearing to be a true avitaminosis in that some unknown factor in the bracken renders certain B-complex vitamins unavailable to the animal

[1]**brack·et** \'brakət, *usu* -əd·+V\ *n* -s [earlier *bragget*, fr. MF *braguette* codpiece, dim. of *brague* breeches, fr. OProv *braga*, fr. L *braca* — more at BRACCAE] **1 :** a simple or composite often carved or sculptured overhanging member that projects from a wall, pier, or other structure and is usu. designed to support a vertical load or to strengthen an angle although it sometimes serves merely as a decorative feature only seeming to give support — compare BRACE, CANTILEVER, CONSOLE, CORBEL, CUL-DE-LAMPE, MODILLION, STRUT **2 a** (1) **:** a short crooked ship's timber resembling a knee and used as a support (2) **:** a flat or flanged triangular ship's plate used esp. for connecting frames and deck beams **b :** a piece of formed sheet steel to which the parts of a bicycle frame are fastened and in which the crank axle turns — called also *bottom bracket, crank hanger, main bracket* **3 a :** a short wall shelf (as one with a single support) **b :** a fixture projecting from a wall or column (as for holding a lamp or candle) **c :** the fruiting body of a bracket fungus — called also *conk;* compare POLYPORACEAE **d :** the curved juncture between serif and vertical stem of a type character **4 a :** one of a pair of marks [] used (1) in writing and printing to enclose matter inserted in a direct quotation, matter extraneous or incidental to context, or phonetic symbols or (2) in logic to indicate operands to be grouped and treated as a unit or (3) in mathematics to serve as signs of aggregation — called also *square bracket;* see VINCULUM **b :** one of the pair of marks ⟨⟩ used to enclose a mutilated passage or the expansion of an abbreviation in a text or to enclose quotations or verbal illustrations in a reference work such as a dictionary — called also *angle bracket, broken bracket, pointed bracket* **c :** one of a pair of curves () — called also *parenthesis, round bracket* **d :** BRACE 6b **5 a :** a pair of shots fired to determine the exact distance from gun to target: (1) **:** a pair that falls short of and beyond the target — called also *range bracket* (2) **:** a pair that falls to the right and left of the target — called also *deflection bracket* **b :** the distance often ascertained by instrument between the landings of two shots fired at a distant target and used to correct the aim of the gun **6 :** a section of a continuously numbered or graded series ⟨in the 24 to 55 age ~⟩ ⟨temperatures beyond the 65° to 85° ~⟩; *esp* **:** one of a graded series of income groups ⟨have risen out of the under $2000 class . . . and climbed a ~ or two —F.L. Allen⟩ **7 a :** a pairing of opponents in an elimination tournament **b :** either half of the draw of an elimination tournament ⟨the upper or lower ~⟩ **8 :** a skating figure in which the skater executes from a simple curve a half turn, a cusp, and then another half turn back to the original curve

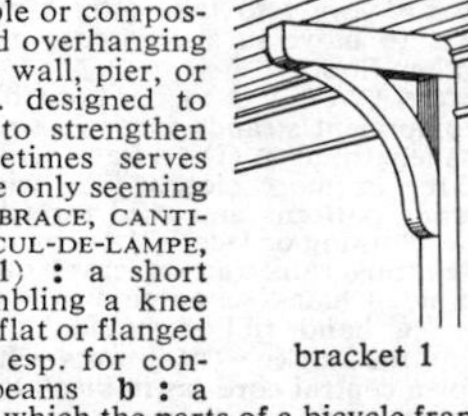

bracket 1

[2]**bracket** \"\ *vt* -ED/-ING/-S **1 a :** to place within or as if within brackets ⟨~ a word⟩ ⟨~ the translation of a quotation in a foreign language⟩ ⟨a face ~*ed* with tousled hair⟩ **b :** to set aside **:** separate out **:** eliminate from consideration ⟨the transcendental view requires nature to be ~*ed* on principle —Marvin Farber⟩ — often used with *off* ⟨the danger of a positivistic approach to . . . history that ~*s* off moral questions —*Times Lit. Supp.*⟩ **2 :** to furnish, fasten, or decorate with brackets ⟨an army trunk ~*ed* to its left running board —E.B.White⟩ ⟨its highly stilted and ~*ed* arcading has distinct Moorish effects —*Amer. Guide Series: Tenn.*⟩ **3 a :** to put into the same class **:** ASSOCIATE ⟨another historical tablet often ~*ed* with the Rosetta stone —Edward Clodd⟩ **b :** CLASSIFY, GROUP ⟨~ together cities of around the same population as if they were alike in all other respects —W.J.Reilly⟩ **4 a :** to treat as a pair **:** deal with simultaneously ⟨Hawaii and Alaska have been ~*ed* together in recent statehood legislation—Ernest Gruening⟩ **b :** to place beside for purposes of comparison **:** COMPARE ⟨teachers at West Point have ~*ed* this retreat with . . . the withdrawal by Napoleon from Moscow —R.L.Neuberger⟩ **5 a :** to obtain a bracket on (as a target) ⟨~ an enemy convoy⟩ **b :** to establish the limits of (as a range of variation or a time interval) ⟨if the guy was murdered in the time you ~ —H.V.Haddock⟩

[3]**bracket** \"\ *adj* [modif. of IrGael *breac*, fr. OIr *brec*] *dial* **:** SPOTTED, SPECKLED

[4]**bracket** \"\ *n* -s [origin unknown] **:** AMERICAN MERGANSER

bracket capital *n* **:** a capital with one or more projecting brackets or corbels to help carry a beam or girder (as in Indian and Syrian architecture and in primitive styles)

bracket clock *n* **:** a clock designed to stand on a shelf or bracket; *esp* **:** a small rectangular clock sometimes with arched top — orig. used of a clock needing space below for weights and pendulum

bracket crab *or* **bracket crane** *n* **:** a hoisting crab placed like a bracket against a wall or post

bracketed *adj, of a serif* **:** curved where it joins the vertical stroke of a letter (as in an old-style *p*)

bracket foot *n* **:** a foot like a bracket found on cabinet furniture mitered at the corner and usu. scrolled on the free sides — see FOOT illustration

bracket fungus *n* **:** a basidiomycete that forms shelflike sporophores (as on tree trunks)

bracketing *n* -s **:** a series or group of brackets; *specif* **:** a framework of wooden ribs (as for supporting a cornice or cove)

brack·et·man \-,man\ *n, pl* **bracketmen :** HANGERMAN

brackets *pl of* BRACKET, *pres 3d sing of* BRACKET

brack·ish \'brakish, -kēsh\ *adj* [[2]*brack* + *-ish*] **1 :** somewhat salt **:** less salt than sea water but undrinkable ⟨the ~ water in the tidal reaches of a river⟩ ⟨a ~ pond⟩ **2 :** UNPALATABLE ⟨coffee was still a harsh ~ draught —Jack Alexander⟩ **:** DISTASTEFUL ⟨a ~ personality⟩

brackish-water crab *n* **:** a crab (*Sesarina roberti*) living in holes along the banks of tidal streams in the West Indies and Central America

brack·mard \'brak,mär(d)\ *n* -s [F *braquemart*, fr. MF, alter. of *bragamas*, prob. fr. MD *breecmes*, fr. *brēken* to break + *mes*, *mets* knife; akin to OE *brecan* to break and to OE *metseax* food knife, OHG *mezzisahs, mezzirahs* knife, MLG *metset, mest*, OS *mezas*, all fr. a WGmc compound whose components are akin respectively to OE *mete* food, meat, and to OE *seax* knife — more at BREAK, MEAT, SAX] **:** a short straight broadsword

bracks *pl of* BRACK

[1]**brac·o·nid** \'brakənəd\ *adj* [NL *Braconidae*] **:** of or relating to the family Braconidae

[2]**braconid** \"\ *n* -s **:** an insect of the family BRACONIDAE

bra·con·i·dae \brə'känə,dē\ *n pl, cap* [NL, fr. *Bracon*, type genus (irreg. fr. Gk *brachys* short) + *-idae* — more at BRIEF] **:** a large family of ichneumon flies some of which are parasitic as larvae on living caterpillars and other insect larvae, others on aphids

bra·con·nière \¦brakən¦ye(ə)r\ *n* -s [F, fr. MF *braconniere*, *bragonniere*, prob. fr. OIt *braconi*, pl., wide breeches worn by halberdiers, aug. of *braca* breeches, fr. L *braca* — more at BRACCAE] **:** a 16th century piece of armor for the thighs consisting of a short skirt of narrow hoop-shaped plates of steel overlapping one another and moving freely

bract \'brakt\ *n* -s [NL *bractea*, fr. L *brattea, bractea* thin metal plate, gold leaf] **1 :** a somewhat modified leaf associated with the reproductive structures of a plant: as **a :** a leaf from the axil of which a flower or floral axis arises **b :** a leaf borne on the floral axis itself (as one subtending the flower or flower cluster) ordinarily smaller than a foliage leaf but occas. large and showy and simulating petals (as in the fever tree and flowering dogwood) — called also *bracteole, bractlet;* see GLUME, INVOLUCRE, SPATHE; compare SCALE **c :** one of the specialized leaves associated with the sexual organs in mosses **d :** a scalelike structure associated with the ovule in the ovulate cone of certain conifers **2 a :** modified medusae of siphonophores having a protective function **:** HYDROPHYLLIUM **b :** a flattened leaflike part of certain crustacean appendages; *specif* **:** the distal exite of the limb of a phyllopod

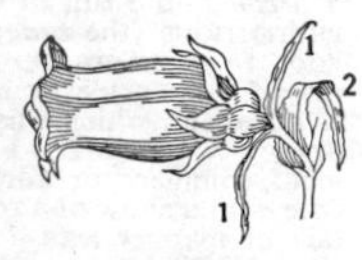

flower showing *1* bracteole, *2* bract

brac·te·al \'braktēəl\ *adj* [NL *bractea* + E *-al*] **:** of, resembling, relating to, or functioning as a bract

[1]**brac·te·ate** \-ēət, -ē,āt\ *n* -s [ML (*nummus*) *bracteatus*, fr. L *nummus* coin + LL *bracteatus* gold-plated, fr. L *bractea*, *brattea* gold plate + *-atus* -ate] **1 :** a thin metal plate usu. of gold or silver chased on one side and often inscribed with runes and found in early Germanic graves and known to have been used for clothing decoration in the Near East about 2000 B.C. **2 :** a very thin coin usu. of silver having a design stamped on one side only and showing through on the reverse and common esp. in Germany in the 12th to 13th centuries

[2]**bracteate** \"\ *adj* [NL *bracteatus*, fr. *bractea* + L *-atus* -ate] **:** furnished with bracts

bract·ed \'braktəd\ *adj* [*bract* + *-ed*] **:** BRACTEATE

bracted bindweed *n* **:** a sprawling herbaceous vine (*Convolvulus spithamaeus*) of eastern No. America with large white flowers subtended by two bracts

bracted plantain *n* **:** a troublesome weed (*Plantago aristata*) of the western U.S. with a prominently bracted spike of flowers

brac·te·o·late \brak'tēələt, -,lāt; 'braktēə,lāt\ *adj* [NL *bracteolatus*, fr. *bracteola* + L *-atus* + *-ate*] **:** furnished with bracteoles

brac·te·ole \'braktē,ōl\ *n* -s [NL *bracteola*, fr. L, thin gold leaf, dim. of *bractea, brattea* gold leaf] **:** a small bract; *esp* **:** one on a floral axis — called also *bractlet;* see BRACT illustration

brac·te·ose \-ē,ōs\ *adj* [NL *bractea* + E *-ose*] **:** having numerous or conspicuous bracts

bract·let \'braktlət\ *n* -s [*bract* + *-let*] **:** BRACTEOLE

bract-scale \'=,=\ *n* **:** an annual erect succulent herb (*Atriplex serenana*) of saline soils in the southeastern U.S. with numerous grayish green sparsely scurfy leaves

[1]**brad** \'brad, 'braa(ə)d\ *n* -s [ME, alter. of *brod* — more at BROD] **1 :** a thin usu. small nail of the same thickness throughout but tapering in width and with a slight projection at the top on one side instead of a head; *sometimes* **:** a small tapering square-bodied finishing nail with a countersunk head **2 :** a slender wire nail with a small deep round head

[2]**brad** \"\ *vt* **bradded; bradded; bradding; brads :** to fasten with brads

bradawl \'=,=\ *n* **:** an awl with chisel edge used to make holes for brads or screws

brad·bury \'brad,berē, *Brit usu* -db(ə)ri\ *n* -s *usu cap* [after Sir John Swanwick *Bradbury* †1950 English treasury official] **:** a British pound note

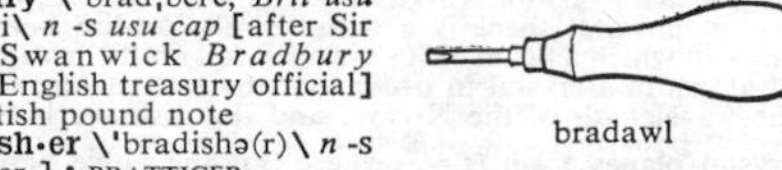

bradawl

brad·dish·er \'bradishə(r)\ *n* -s [by alter.] **:** BRATTICER

bra·den·head \'brādᵊn,hed\ *n* [Glenn T. *Braden* †1923 Am. oilman and inventor + E *head*] **:** a casing head in an oil well having a stuffing box packed (as with rubber) to make a gas-tight connection

brad·ford \'bradfə(r)d\ *adj, usu cap* [fr. *Bradford*, England] **:** of or from the city of Bradford, England **:** of the kind or style prevalent in Bradford

bradford frame \"-\ *n, usu cap B* [after Edward H. *Bradford* †1926 Am. surgeon] **:** a rectangular metal frame fitted with adjustable straps of canvas or webbing and used to support a patient with certain diseases or fractures of the spine, hip, or pelvis

bradford system *n, usu cap B* [fr. *Bradford*, England] **:** a method of preparing and spinning long-staple wool into worsted yarn

brad·le·ian *also* **brad·ley·an** \ˈbradlēən, ⸗ˈ⸗⸗\ *adj, usu cap* [Francis H. *Bradley* †1924 Brit. philosopher + E *-an*] **:** of or relating to Bradley or his objective idealism

brad·ley·ite \ˈbradlē,īt\ *n* -s [Wilmot H. *Bradley* b1899 Am. geologist + E *-ite*] **:** a mineral $Na_3Mg(PO_4)(CO_3)$ consisting of a rare phosphate and carbonate of sodium and magnesium

bradoon *var of* BRIDOON

brad punch *n* **:** a small nail set

brad pusher *n* **:** a tool for grasping and inserting brads by pressure in hard-to-reach places

brad·shaw \ˈbrad(,)shȯ\ *n* -s *usu cap* [short for *Bradshaw's Railway Guide*, a timetable published periodically containing information about all the trains running in the British isles, after George *Bradshaw* †1853 Eng. printer who first issued it in 1839] **:** a comprehensive timetable of British railroad trains

brad·sot \ˈbradsət\ *n* -s [prob. fr. Icel *brāthasōt*, fr. ON, plague, murrain, fr. *brāthr* sudden, hasty, heated + *sōtt* sickness, disease; akin to ON *brāth* tar and to ON *sjūkr* sick — more at BREATH, SICK] **:** BRAXY 1

brady- *comb form* [MF & NL, fr. Gk *bradys*] **1 :** slow ⟨*brady*cardia⟩ **:** dull ⟨*brady*acusia⟩ **2 :** BRACHY- ⟨*brady*dactylia⟩

bra·dy·auxesis \ˌbrādē+\ *n, pl* **bradyauxeses** [NL, fr. *brady-* + *auxesis*] **:** allometric growth characterized by lagging of a part behind the body as a whole in development — compare TACHYAUXESIS — **brady·auxetic** \"+\ *adj* — **brady·auxetically** \"+\ *adv*

bra·dy·car·dia \ˌbradəˈkärdēə\ *n* -s [NL, fr. *brady-* + *-cardia*] **:** a slow heart rate; *esp* **:** an abnormally slow one (as of 50 beats per minute) in man — compare ARRHYTHMIA

bra·dy·genesis \ˌbradə+\ *n* [NL, fr. *brady-* + *-genesis*] *biol* **:** retardation of development by prolonging certain ancestral stages — compare LIPOGENESIS, TACHYGENESIS

bra·dy·pod \ˈbradə,päd\ *also* **brad·y·pode** \-pōd\ *n* -s [NL *Bradypodidae*] **:** an edentate of the family Bradypodidae — **bra·dyp·o·doid** \brəˈdipə,dȯid, brā-\ *adj*

bra·dy·pod·i·dae \ˌbradəˈpädə,dē\ *n pl, cap* [NL, fr. *Bradypod-, Bradypus*, type genus + *-idae*] **:** a family of edentates comprising the true sloths

bra·dy·pus \ˈbradəpəs, -də,pu̇s\ *n, cap* [NL, fr. Gk *bradypous* slow of foot, fr. *brady-* + *pous* foot — more at FOOT] **:** the genus comprising the three-toed sloths

bra·dy·seism \ˈbradē,sīzəm\ *n* -s [*brady-* + *-seism*] **:** a slow quiet upward or downward movement of the earth's crust — **bra·dy·seismal** \ˌbradē+\ *adj* — **bra·dy·seismic** \"+\ *or* **bra·dy·seismical** \"+\ *adj*

bra·dy·tel·ic \ˌbradəˈtelik\ *adj* **:** of or relating to bradytely

bra·dy·tely \ˈbradə,telē\ *n* -ES [*brady-* + *-tely* (irreg. fr. Gk *telos* end, consummation, degree of completion, state of maturity) — more at WHEEL] **:** arrested evolution or evolution at very slow rates outside the rate distribution usual for a given group of plants or animals — compare HOROTELY, TACHYTELY

¹brae \ˈbrā\ *n* -s [ME *bra*, fr. ON *brā* eyelash; akin to OE *brǣw* eyebrow, eyelid, OHG *brāwa* eyelid, eyebrow, OE *bregdan* to move quickly — more at BRAID] **1** *chiefly Scot* **:** HILL; *esp* **:** a hillside along a river **2** *chiefly Scot* **:** the brow of a hill **3** *chiefly Scot* **:** a steep road **4** *chiefly Scot* **:** a mountain or hill district **:** UPLANDS — often used in pl.

²brae \ˈbra, -raa,-rā\ *n, pl* **braees** [Norw *bræ*] **:** GLACIER, ICE CAP — used chiefly in toponyms in Scandinavian areas

bra·ford \ˈbrāfərd, ˈbrīf-\ *n* -s *usu cap* [*Brahman* + *Hereford*] **:** a type of beef cattle developed by crossing Brahman and Hereford; *also* **:** one of these cattle

¹brag \ˈbrag, -aa(ə),-aig\ *adj* **bragger; braggest** [ME] **1** *archaic* **a :** full of spirits **:** LIVELY, LUSTY **b :** BOASTFUL, PRETENTIOUS ⟨the *braggest* of all soldiers⟩ **2 :** superlatively good **:** FIRST-RATE ⟨a ~ dog⟩ — often used of something displayed with pride or self-congratulation ⟨he showed me his ~ cornfield, which was going to fill his crib —H.C.Nixon⟩

²brag \"\ *n* -s [ME] **1 :** a pompous, cocky, or boastful statement, comment, or story **2 a** *obs* **:** ostentatious display **:** POMP ⟨the ~ and show of a royal court⟩ **b :** arrogant or swaggering talk or manner **:** TRUCULENCE, COCKINESS ⟨all his adolescent ~ —A.M.Schlesinger b.1917⟩ ⟨all the ~ and bluster —*Kiplinger Washington Letter*⟩ **3 :** an old card game resembling poker **4 :** BRAGGART

³brag \"\ *vb* **bragged; bragged; bragging; brags** [ME *braggen*] *vi* **1 :** to talk about oneself or things pertaining to oneself in a boastful manner **:** BOAST ⟨mechanics *bragging* about their skill⟩ ⟨his luck had been nothing to ~ about⟩ **2** *obs* **:** SWAGGER, STRUT ~ *vt* **1** *now chiefly Scot* **:** THREATEN, DEFY, CHALLENGE ⟨~ a person to a race⟩ **2 :** to assert boastfully or cockily ⟨*bragging* that his crops were the best in the county⟩ **3** *archaic* **:** boast of **syn** see BOAST

brag·ga·do·cian \ˌbragəˈdōsh(ē)ən, ˌbraig-, -ōsēən,-ōch(ē)ən\ *adj* **:** given to or of the nature of a braggadocio

brag·ga·do·cio \ˌ⸗⸗ˈ⸗shē,ō *also* -(,)shō *or* -sē,ō *sometimes* -,chē,ō *or* -(,)chō *or* -,shə\ *n* -s [after *Braggadocchio*, personification of boasting in *Faerie Queene* by Edmund Spenser †1599 Eng. poet] **1 :** BRAGGART, BOASTER **2 a :** empty boasting **:** BRAGGING ⟨the ~ of dictators⟩ **b :** arrogant pretension **:** COCKINESS ⟨the air of swaggering ~ that all important men are expected to show in fighting —C.W.M.Hart⟩

bragg angle \ˈbrag-\ *n, usu cap B* [after Sir William Henry *Bragg* †1942 and Sir William Lawrence *Bragg* †1971 Eng. physicists] **:** the small angle between an incident X-ray beam and the diffracting planes of a crystal — compare BRAGG'S LAW

¹brag·gart \ˈbragə(r)t, -raag-,-raig- *sometimes* -,gärt *or* -,gät; *usu* -d+V\ *n* -s [³*brag* + *-art*] **:** a loud or arrogant boaster

²braggart \"\ *adj* **1 :** excessively boastful **:** arrogantly pretentious ⟨~ politicians⟩ ⟨he had been loose of tongue and ~ of claims —S.H.Adams⟩ **2 :** of, befitting, or suggestive of an arrant boaster ⟨a large man with a ~ voice⟩ ⟨~ actions⟩ — **brag·gart·ly** *adv*

brag·gart·ism \-d·,izəm, -,tiz-\ *n* -s **:** BOASTFULNESS, SWAGGER

brag·ger \ˈbragə(r), -raag-,-raig-\ *n* -s [ME *braggere*, fr. *braggen* to brag + *-ere* -er] **1 :** one that brags **:** BOASTER **2 :** the jack of clubs or nine of diamonds which in the game of brag were wild cards in forming pairs; *also* **:** the player who made the first bet in the game of brag

brag·get \ˈbragət\ *n* -s [ME *braket, bragot*, fr. MW *bragod*, fr. *brag* malt; akin to MIr *mraich, braich* malt, Gaulish *bracis* grain for making malt, L *marcēre* to wither, droop — more at MARCESCENT] **:** a drink made from ale and fermented honey or from ale sweetened and spiced

brag·ging·ly *adv* **:** in a bragging manner

bragg·ite \ˈbra,gīt\ *n* -s [Sir W.H. & Sir W.L. *Bragg* + E *-ite*] **:** a mineral PtS consisting of platinum sulfide, usu. containing other metals (as palladium and nickel), and occurring in platiniferous rocks

bragg reflection \ˈbrag-, -aa-,-ai-\ *n, usu cap B* [after Sir William H. *Bragg* †1942 and Sir William L. *Bragg* †1971 English physicists] **:** the action of a crystal in reflecting X rays or particle waves (as electrons or neutrons) in a manner analogous to that of a reflection grating upon light incident at a suitable angle — compare BRAGG'S LAW

bragg's law \-gz-\ *n, usu cap B* [after W.H. & W.L. *Bragg*] **:** a law in physics: there is a definite relationship between the angle at which a beam of X rays must fall on the parallel planes of atoms in a crystal in order that there be strong reflection, the wavelength of the X rays, and the distance between the crystal planes **:** $\sin \Theta = \frac{n\lambda}{2d}$ where Θ is the angle between the incident or the reflected beam and the crystal plane, λ is the X-ray wavelength, *d* is the crystal plane separation, and *n* is any integer

brag·gy \ˈbragē, -aag-,-aig-, -gi\ *adj* -ER/-EST [²*brag* + *-y*] **:** BOASTFUL, PRETENTIOUS

brag·less *adj* **:** being without a brag

bra·goz·zo \brəˈgōt(,)sō\ *n, pl* **bragoz·zi** \-t(,)sē\ [It, fr. It dial. (Venice) *bragozo, bargozo*, fr. *braga* trousers, fr. L *braca*; fr. the trouserlike appearance of the nets carried by these boats — more at BRACCAE] **:** a 2-masted trawler common near Venice

brags *pl of* BRAG, *pres 3d sing of* BRAG

¹brah·ma *also* **bra·mah** \ˈbrämə, -ämə,-åmə *also* -amə\ *n* [fr. *Brahmaputra* river, India] **1** *usu cap* **:** an Asian breed of very large domestic fowls having pea combs and feathered legs and occurring in light, dark, and buff-color varieties **2** -s **:** a bird of the Brahma breed

²brahma \"\ *n* -s *usu cap* [by alter.] **:** BRAHMAN 2

brah·ma·cha·ri \ˌbräməˈchärē\ *n* -s [Skt *brahmacārin*, fr. *brahman* prayer + *cārin* one who practices, fr. *carati* he moves, goes, practices — more at WHEEL] *India* **:** CELIBATE; *specif* **:** one in the stage of brahmacharya

brah·ma·char·ya \-ryə\ *n* -s [Skt *brahmacarya*, fr. *brahman* prayer + *carya* conduct, fr. *carati*] *India* **:** the state of celibate student life **:** the initial stage of the Brahmanic ashramas

brah·man *or* **brah·min** \ˈbrämən, -råm-, *in sense 2 often or usu* -rām- *also* -ram-\ *n* -s *usu cap* [Skt *brāhmaṇa*, lit., having to do with prayer, fr. *brahman* prayer] **1** *also* **brahmana** *pl* **brahmana** *or* **brahmanas :** a member of the highest or sacerdotal caste among the Hindus having as chief duty the study and teaching of the Vedas and the performance of religious ceremonies — compare KSHATRIYA, SUDRA, VAISYA **2 a :** any of several breeds of Indian cattle; *specif* **:** a variety or breed of large vigorous heat-resistant and tick-resistant usu. silvery gray cattle evolved in the southern U.S. by interbreeding Indian cattle and now used chiefly for crossbreeding with beef cattle to increase their hardiness and resistance to disease and pests while retaining their beef quality **b :** an animal of this variety or breed — compare ZEBU

brah·ma·na \ˈbrämənə, -råm-\ *n* -s *usu cap* [Skt *brāhmaṇa*] **:** one of a class of Hindu sacred writings composed around the 9th to 6th centuries B.C. and devoted chiefly to the instruction of Brahmins in the performance of Vedic ritual — see VEDA

brah·ma·ni *or* **brah·ma·nee** \-nē,-ni\ *n* -s *usu cap* [Skt *brāhmaṇī*, fr. *brāhmaṇa* — more at BRAHMAN] **:** a woman of the Brahman caste

brah·man·ic \(ˈ)bräˈmanik, -rå-\ *also* **brah·man·i·cal** \-nəkəl\ *adj, usu cap* **:** of or relating to the Brahmans or their doctrines or worship

brah·man·ism \ˈbrämə,nizəm, -råm-\ *n* -s *cap* **:** the religion of the Brahmans and orthodox Hindus; *specif* **:** the later development of the early Vedic religion up to the 12th century A.D.

brah·ma·ny *or* **brah·ma·nee** \-nē,-ni\ *adj, usu cap* **:** of or relating to the Brahmans

brahmany bull *n, usu cap B* **:** the white male zebu sacred to the Hindus

brah·ma·poo·tra \ˌbräməˈpü·trə, -råm- *also* -pyü-\ *n* -s *usu cap* [fr. *Brahmaputra* or *Brahmapootra* river, India] **:** BRAHMA

brah·mi \ˈbrämē, -råmē\ *n* -s *usu cap* [Skt] **:** an ancient alphabet of India of Semitic descent which is found in several varieties and from which descend the later Indian alphabets

brah·min \ˈbrämən, -råm-\ *n* -s *usu cap* **:** an intellectually and socially cultivated and exclusive person ⟨now equalization has come to mean the lowering of the ~ —C.H.Grandgent⟩; *esp* **:** such a person from one of the older New England families — sometimes used disparagingly ⟨a Boston ~⟩ — **brah·min·ic** \(ˈ)bräˈminik, -rå-\ *or* **brah·min·i·cal** \-nəkəl\ *adj, usu cap*

brah·min·ism \ˈbrämə,nizəm, -råm-\ *n* -s *usu cap* **:** the system or practices of or imputed to Brahmins ⟨an ardent devotee of *Brahminism*⟩

brah·mi·ny kite *or* **brah·ma·ny kite** \ˈbräməne-, -råm-\ *n, usu cap B* **:** a common kite (*Haliastur indus*) that is largely chestnut red with white breast and head striped with black, is widely distributed from India to the Solomon islands and the Philippines, and is held sacred by the Hindus

brah·mo \ˈbrä(,)mō\ *n* -s *usu cap* [Bengali *Brahmo (Samāj)* assembly or church of Brahma, the first member of the Hindu trinity] **:** a member of an eclectic Hindu theistic society noted for its pronounced monotheism and vigorous policy of social and political reform

brah·mo·ism \-,izəm\ *n* -s *usu cap* **:** the doctrines or practices of the Brahmos

brahms·ian \ˈbrämzēən, -råm-\ *adj, usu cap* [Johannes *Brahms* †1897 Ger. composer + E *-ian*] **:** of or relating to Brahms or his musical compositions

bra·hui \brəˈhüē\ *n, pl* **brahui** *or* **brahuis** *usu cap* **1 a :** a pastoral people dominant in eastern Baluchistan **b :** a member of such people **2 :** the Dravidian language of the Brahui people

¹braid \ˈbrād\ *vb* -ED/-ING/-S [ME *breyden* to move suddenly, snatch, weave together, fr. OE *bregdan*; akin to OHG *brettan* to draw (a sword), ON *bregtha* to move suddenly, weave together, Gk *phorkon* something white or gray or wrinkled, Skt *bhrāśate* it glitters; basic meaning: to shine] *vt* **1 a :** to form (three or more strands) into a cord or ribbon by repeatedly crossing a left and then a right strand over a central strand and under an opposite strand **b :** to make by braiding ⟨~ a rug⟩ ⟨~ a lanyard⟩ **2 :** to do up (the hair) by interweaving three or more strands together into one or more lengths **3 a :** to place or arrange in a diagonally woven or crisscross pattern ⟨~*ing* bunting around lampposts⟩ ⟨a secondary plot is ~*ed* through the novel⟩ **b :** INTERMINGLE, MIX ⟨~ fact with fiction⟩ **4 :** to ornament esp. with ribbon or braid **:** TRIM ⟨the girls ~*ed* their hair with flowers⟩ ~ *vi* **1** *dial Eng* **:** to take after **:** RESEMBLE — usu. used with *of* **2 :** to move in a crisscross pattern ⟨streams ~*ing* down a valley floor⟩

²braid \"\ *n* -s **1 :** a cord or ribbon having usu. three or more component strands forming a regular diagonal pattern down its length: as **a** (1) **:** a flat or round length of narrow fabric of three or more closely intertwined threads made in various fancy patterns and used for trimming, binding, or outlining (as clothing or lace) (2) **:** a band or cord (as of gold or silver) denoting rank (as on naval uniforms) **b** (1) **:** a length of braided hair ⟨schoolgirls in ~*s* and blue uniforms⟩ (2) **:** a string, band, ribbon, or similar strand binding or intertwined into the hair ⟨a ~ of flowers in her hair⟩ **c :** a woven covering for a central core (as in insulated electrical wire) **d :** a fancy bread made by intertwining lengths of dough **2 :** a coarse grade of wool used chiefly in carpet manufacture **3 :** commissioned military officers; *esp* **:** high-ranking naval officers ⟨differences of opinion between brass and ~ over procurement —Bruce Bliven b.1889⟩ — compare BRASS 5a

³braid \"\ *Scot var of* BROAD

⁴braid \"\ *dial var of* BREAD

braid·ed \ˈbrādəd\ *adj* [ME *breyded*, fr. past. part. of *breyden* to braid] **1 a :** having braids **b :** adorned with braid **c :** ENTWINED; *specif* **:** made by intertwining three or more threads or fabrics **2 :** divided into or following an interlacing network of channels ⟨a ~ river⟩

braided rug *n* **:** a rug made of a braid of three or more strips of cloth sewed or laced into an oval, round, or rectangle

braid·er \-də(r)\ *n* -s **:** one that braids; *specif* **:** a sewing machine attachment for stitching braid in place

braid·ing \-diŋ,-dēŋ\ *n* -s [ME *breyding*, fr. gerund of *breyden* to braid] **:** something made of braided material: as **a :** trimming or braids esp. for clothes or lace **b :** the woven covering for an electric cable or wire

braid wool *n* **:** LUSTER WOOL

braies \ˈbrā\ *n pl* [F, fr. OF, pl. of *braie*, fr. L *braca* — more at BRACCAE] **1 :** BRACCAE **2 :** breeches or trousers worn in medieval times

¹brail \ˈbrāl, *esp bef pause or cons* -āəl\ *n* -s [ME *brayle*, fr. AF *braiel*, fr. OF, girdle, belt, strap, fr. *braies* breeches] **1 :** a rope that is fastened to the leech of a sail and run through a block and by which the sail can be hauled up or hauled in preparatory to furling or in place of furling **2 a :** the feathers at a hawk's rump — usu. used in pl. **b :** a thong of soft leather to restrain a hawk's wing **3 a :** a pipe or rod with many hooks attached that is drawn over a clam bed in harvesting clams **b :** a dip net resembling a small purse seine with which fish are hauled aboard a boat after being gathered in a purse seine or trap; *also* **:** such a dip net full of fish ⟨a ~ of salmon⟩

²brail \"\ *vt* -ED/-ING/-S **1 :** to take in (a sail) by the brails ⟨vessels coming into the wind and ~*ing* up their square sails —Kenneth Roberts⟩ ⟨the spanker was of little use and we . . . ~*ed* it in —C.V.Reilly⟩ **2 :** to restrain (the wings of a hawk) with a brail **3 :** to hoist (fish) by means of a dip net (as from a trap into a ship's hold) ⟨~ sardines aboard⟩

brail·er \-ālə(r)\ *n* -s **:** BRAIL 3b

¹braille \ˈbrāl, *esp bef pause or cons* -āəl\ *n* -s *often cap* [after Louis *Braille* †1852 Fr. teacher of the blind, who invented it] **:** a system of writing for the blind that uses characters made up of raised dots in a 6-dot cell arranged in two vertical columns and that has been adapted for writing various languages and

a b c d e f g h i j
1 2 3 4 5 6 7 8 9 0
k l m n o p q r s t
u v x y z w Capital Sign Numeral Sign

braille alphabet: the first ten letters serve also as numerals and each letter serves also, when standing alone, as a common word

for transcribing music, mathematics, and scientific symbols — see EMBOSS, GRADE, INTERPOINT, SIGN, STEREOTYPER, TRANSCRIBER, WORD-SIGN

²braille \"\ *vt* -ED/-ING/-S *sometimes cap* **:** to transcribe or write in braille characters

braill·er \-ālə(r)\ *n* -s **:** a mechanical device for writing braille; *esp* **:** BRAILLEWRITER

braille slate *or* **braille tablet** *n* **:** SLATE 3d

braillewriter \ˈ⸗,⸗⸗\ *n, often cap* **:** a machine for writing braille that resembles a typewriter in size and action and that has a space bar and six keys, one for each of the six dots of a cell

braill·ist \-āləst\ *n* -s **1 :** an expert in the writing of braille **2 :** one whose work is writing braille

¹brain \ˈbrān\ *n* -s [ME, fr. OE *brægen*; akin to OFris *brein* brain, MLG *bregen* brain, Gk *brechmos* front part of the head] **1 a :** the portion of the vertebrate central nervous system that constitutes the organ of thought and neural coordination, including all the higher nervous centers, receiving impulses from the sense organs, and interpreting and correlating these with stored impressions to formulate the motor impulses that ultimately control all vital activities, that is made up of neurons and their processes organized into layers and nuclei of gray matter and tracts, decussations, and fasciculi of white matter together with various supporting and nutritive structures, and that is enclosed within the skull, being continuous with the spinal cord through the foramen magnum and with the cranial nerves through various other openings — see FOREBRAIN, HINDBRAIN, MIDBRAIN; compare CORTEX, VENTRICLE **b :** a nervous center in invertebrates (as the supraesophageal ganglia of arthropods) corresponding in position and function more or less to the brain of vertebrate animals — compare CEREBRAL GANGLION **2 a** (1) **:** INTELLECT, MIND ⟨it took a queer ~ to think up such a scheme⟩ ⟨successful in reading a man's ~ —Lou Richter⟩ (2) **:** sheer intellect — often used in pl. ⟨he's got ~*s* but no common sense⟩ (3) **:** intellectual endowment **:** INTELLIGENCE — often used in pl. ⟨there's plenty of ~*s* in that family⟩ **b** (1) **:** a supremely bright or intelligent person ⟨he'd been known as a ~ throughout college⟩ (2) **:** the guiding genius or intellectual leader **:** supreme planner — usu. used in pl. ⟨the ~*s* of the Nazi party⟩ ⟨he was the ~*s* of the enterprise⟩ **syn** see MIND — **on the brain :** constantly in mind (as if obsessed) — usu. used with *have* ⟨he had tax reform *on the brain*⟩

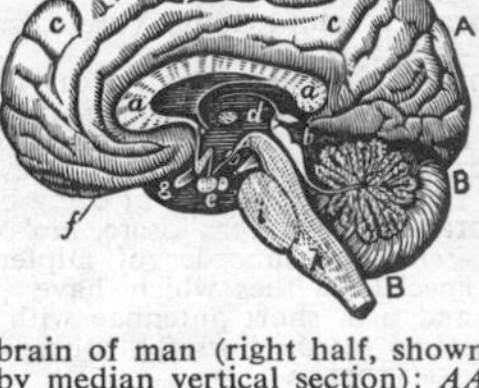

brain of man (right half, shown by median vertical section): *AA* cerebrum; *BB* cerebellum; *aa* corpus callosum; *b* pineal body; *ccc* convolutions; *d* third ventricle; *e* pituitary gland; *f* olfactory lobe; *g* optic nerve; *i* pons; *k* medulla oblongata

²brain \"\ *adj* [ME, fr. ¹*brain*] *archaic Scot* **:** MAD, FURIOUS

³brain \"\ *vt* -ED/-ING/-S [ME *brainen*, fr. ¹*brain*] **1 :** to kill by smashing in the skull ⟨a small flail loaded with lead to ~ the . . . assassins —T.B.Macaulay⟩ **2 :** to bang on the head ⟨~ a person with a book⟩

braincap \ˈ⸗,⸗\ *n* **:** the upper part of the skull

braincase \ˈ⸗,⸗\ *n* **:** the bony or cartilaginous case enclosing the brain — compare CRANIUM

brainchild \ˈ⸗,⸗\ *n* **:** a product of one's creative imagination (as an idea or a work of art) ⟨the festival is the ~ of . . . a Boston magazine publisher —C.M.Barss⟩

brain coral *n* **:** a massive reef-building coral having the surface covered by ridges and furrows — compare MAEANDRA

brained \ˈbrānd\ *adj* [ME *branyd* having a brain, fr. *bran, brain* brain + *-yd, -ed* -ed] **:** having a brain of a specified character ⟨bigger ~ than other animal species —Weston La Barre⟩ — usu. used in combination ⟨muddle*brained*⟩

brain fag *n* **:** mental fatigue

brain fever *n* **:** an inflammation of the brain or its coverings; *specif* **:** EQUINE ENCEPHALOMYELITIS

brain-fever bird *n* [fr. the resemblance of its cry to the words *brain fever*] **:** an Indian hawk cuckoo (*Cuculus varius*) having a loud, shrill, repetitive cry; *also* **:** any of several related birds with monotonous cries

brainge \ˈbrānj\ *var of* BREENGE

brainier *comparative of* BRAINY

brainiest *superlative of* BRAINY

brain·i·ness \ˈbrānēnəs, -nin-\ *n* -ES **:** the quality or state of being brainy

brain·ish \-ānish\ *adj* [¹*brain* + *-ish*] **1** *chiefly Scot* **:** HOT-HEADED, IMPETUOUS **2** *chiefly Scot* **:** mentally unstable **:** DELIRIOUS

brain·less \-nləs\ *adj* [ME, fr. ¹*brain* + *-less*] **1 :** devoid of intellect or intelligence **:** FOOLISH, STUPID ⟨men acting like ~ animals⟩ ⟨the ~ drivers on the highways⟩ **2 :** not demanding understanding or intelligence **:** DULL, STUPEFYING ⟨a ~ task⟩

brainpan \ˈ⸗,⸗\ *n* [ME, fr. ¹*brain* + *pan*] **:** BRAINCASE

brainpower \ˈ⸗,⸗\ *n* **1 a :** intellectual or mental capability ⟨although he was not efficient there were few in his group that had comparable ~⟩ **b :** superior or marked mental ability **:** superior intelligence ⟨~ is no good locked tight behind a handsome brow —*Think*⟩ **2 :** people with developed intellectual or mental ability ⟨mobilizing its ~ for technological warfare⟩

brains *pl of* BRAIN, *pres 3d sing of* BRAIN

brain sand *n* **:** small grains of calcareous matter in the brain (as in the pineal gland and pacchionian bodies) esp. associated with aging

brainsick \ˈ⸗,⸗\ *adj* **1 :** mentally disordered **:** MAD ⟨a ~ criminal⟩ **2 :** arising from mental disorder ⟨~ frenzy⟩ — **brain·sick·ly** *adv*

brain stem *n* **:** the axial part of the brain consisting of all except the cerebellum and cerebral cortex and the white matter immediately connected with them and including the motor and sensory tracts and the nuclei of the cranial nerves **:** SEGMENTAL APPARATUS

brainstone \ˈ⸗,⸗\ *n* or **brainstone coral** *n* **:** BRAIN CORAL

¹brainstorm \ˈ⸗,⸗\ *n* [*brain* + *storm*] **1 :** a violent transient mental derangement **2 :** a sudden inspiration or bright idea **3 :** a harebrained idea **:** a wild or impractical flash of inspiration

²brainstorm \"\ *vi* **:** to practice a conference technique by which a group attempts to find a solution for a specific problem by amassing all the ideas spontaneously contributed by its members

brains trust *n, Brit* **:** BRAIN TRUST; *esp* **:** a panel of experts on a radio program

brainteaser \ˈ⸗,⸗⸗\ *n* **:** something demanding mental effort and acuity for its solution **:** PUZZLE

brain trust *n* **:** expert advisers esp. concerned with planning and strategy and often without official or acknowledged status ⟨a Communist *brain trust* convened . . . to map plans for keeping the strikes from petering out —*Springfield (Mass.) Union*⟩

brain truster *n* **:** a member of a brain trust **:** an unofficial adviser

brain twister *n* **:** BRAINTEASER

brain vesicle *n* **:** CEREBRAL VESICLE

[1]**brainwash** \'ˌ=,=\ *vt* [back-formation fr. *brainwashing*] **1 :** to subject (a person) to brainwashing ⟨denied a previous confession . . . saying that he had been ~*ed* —*Front Page Detective*⟩ ⟨told how he had been *brainwashed* for 527 days in jail —Ed Sullivan⟩ **2 :** to persuade by propaganda ⟨~ the voters⟩

[2]**brainwash** \"\ *n* **1 :** the act of brainwashing ⟨the moral savagery of the ~ —D.H.Gillis⟩ **2 :** an instance of brainwashing ⟨his ~ in prison⟩

brainwashing *n* -s [trans. of Chin *hsi³ nao³*, fr. *hsi³* wash + *nao³* brain] **:** the forcible application of prolonged and intensive indoctrination sometimes including mental torture in an attempt to induce someone to give up basic political, social, or religious beliefs and attitudes and to accept contrasting regimented ideas ⟨life in a highly evolved bureaucratic state where thought control and ~ have dissolved all individual freedom —Laurent LeSage⟩ ⟨~ — the conquest not of a man's body but of his mind and spirit —Gladwin Hill⟩ — compare MENTICIDE

brainwater \'=,==\ *n* **:** HEARTWATER

brain wave *n* **1 :** rhythmic fluctuations of voltage between parts of the brain resulting in the flow of an electric current; *also* **:** the current produced usu. having a pulsation frequency of 10 or more per second **2 :** a flash of inspiration

brainwood \'=,=\ *adj* [ME *brainwode*, fr. [1]*brain* + *wode* mad — more at WOOD] *Scot* **:** FRENZIED

brainwork \'=,=\ *n* **:** deliberate, purposeful, or disciplined mental activity **:** THOUGHT ⟨that fundamental ~ without which no philosopher can get very far —*Times Lit. Supp.*⟩ — **brainworker** *n*

brainy \'brānē, -ni\ *adj* -ER/-EST **1 :** having brains **:** endowed with mental cleverness **:** intellectually active and well developed **:** INTELLIGENT ⟨many men dislike ~ women⟩ **2 :** arising from or showing an alert mentality **:** INGENIOUS ⟨a really ~ suggestion⟩

[1]**braird** \'bra(a)(ə)rd, -a(a)əd\ *n* -s [ME *breirde*, prob. fr. OE *brerd* edge, rim; akin to OE *brord* point, OHG *brort* point, margin, ON *broddr* point, MIr *brot* goad, OSlav *brŭzda* bridle] *Brit* **:** the first shoots or sprouts (of grass or grain) to appear above the ground

[2]**braird** \"\ *vi* -ED/-ING/-S [ME *breirden*, fr. *breirde*, n.] *Brit* **:** to sprout or spring up from the ground **:** GERMINATE

brai·reau *or* **brai·ro** \'bre(ˌ)rō\ *n* -s [modif. of CanF *blaireau*, fr. F, European badger, fr. MF *blarel*, *blareau*, fr. *bler* spotted, of Celt origin; akin to MW *blawr* gray, ScGael *blar* having a white spot; akin to OHG *blāo* blue — more at BLUE] **:** the badger of No. America

[1]**braise** *also* **braize** \'brāz\ *vt* -ED/-ING/-S [F *braiser*, fr. *braise* live coals, fr. OF *brese* — more at BRAZE] **:** to cook (meat or vegetables) slowly in fat and little moisture in a tightly closed pot

[2]**braise** *also* **braize** \"\ *n* -s **:** an item of braised food ⟨squab ~⟩

[3]**braise** *or* **braize** \"\ *n* -s [prob. fr. MLG *brassen*, *bressem* bream — more at BREAM] **:** a European sea bream (*Pagrus pagrus*)

braj bha·sha \brăj'bäshə\ *n*, *usu cap both Bs* [Hindi *braj-bhāṣā*, fr. *Braj*, region round Agra + Skt *bhāṣā* language, fr. *bhāṣate* he takes — more at BELLOW] **:** a dialect of Western Hindi noted for its poetic literature

[1]**brak** *Scot past of* BREAK

[2]**brak** *var of* BRACK

[1]**brake** *archaic past of* BREAK

[2]**brake** \'brāk\ *or* **brake fern** *n* -s [ME, fern, prob. of Scand origin; akin to OSw *brække* fern — more at BRACKEN] **1 :** a fern of the genus *Pteridium* (as *P. aquilinum*) having ternately compound fronds and roots, often growing several feet high, and used for making a beverage, for thatching, and for tanning **2 :** a fern of the genus *Pteris*

[3]**brake** \"\ *vt* -ED/-ING/-S [ME *braken*, fr. MD or MLG, to brake flax, to break on the wheel; akin to MD *breken* to break, OE *brecan* — more at BREAK] **:** to break (flax or hemp) with a brake

[4]**brake** \"\ *n* -s [ME, fr. MLG; akin to OE *brecan* to break] **1 :** a toothed instrument or machine for separating out the fiber of flax or hemp by breaking up the woody parts **2 :** a tool resembling scissors used by basket makers to peel the bark from willow stems **3** *dial* **:** a large heavy harrow **:** DRAG **4 :** a baker's kneading machine **5 :** a machine for bending, flanging, folding, and forming sheet metal — called also *cornice brake*

[5]**brake** \"\ *n* -s [ME] **1** *obs* **:** a bridle with a powerful bit **2 :** the handle of a pump; *esp* **:** one long enough so that a number of men can unite in working the pump **3 a** *also* **break** \"\ (1) **:** a device (as a block or band applied to the rim of a wheel) to arrest the motion of a vehicle, a machine, or other mechanism and usu. employing some form of friction — often used in pl. ⟨to apply the ~*s*⟩; see AIR BRAKE, EMERGENCY BRAKE, FRICTION BRAKE, HYDRAULIC BRAKE, MAGNETIC BRAKE, SERVICE BRAKE, VACUUM BRAKE (2) **:** something designed or used to slow down or stop movement, momentum, or activity ⟨the interest rate acting as a ~ on expenditures⟩ ⟨the government has applied the ~*s* on . . . horse players and other gamblers —Harry Levine⟩ **b :** the end man of a bobsled team who operates the brake

[6]**brake** \"\ *vb* -ED/-ING/-S *vt* **:** to retard or stop by or as if by a brake ⟨~ a car⟩ ⟨impulses being *braked* by inhibition —Fredric Wertham⟩ ~ *vi* **1 :** to operate or manage a brake or brakes: as **a :** to act as a brakeman ⟨retired after 40 years of *braking*⟩ **b :** to manage a winding or hoisting engine for a mine **2 a :** to become checked by a brake ⟨the car *braked* to a stop⟩ **b :** to apply a brake **:** slow up by applying the brake ⟨the driver *braked* around curves⟩

[7]**brake** \"\ *n* -s [ME *-brake*, prob. fr. MLG *brake*; akin to MLG *breken* to break, OE *brecan* — more at BREAK] **:** rough, broken, or marshy land thickly overgrown usu. with one kind of plant ⟨cedar ~*s*⟩ ⟨the thick coastal ~*s* of the Olympia peninsula⟩ — see CANEBRAKE

[8]**brake** \"\ *n* -s [origin unknown] **1** *obs* **:** CAGE, TRAP, SNARE **2 :** an ancient instrument of torture **:** RACK

[9]**brake** *var of* [3]BREAK

brake band *n* **:** the flexible band of a band brake

brake beam *also* **brake bar** *n* **:** a horizontal beam or rod on a wagon or railroad car that operates the brake shoes

brake block *n* **1 :** a device for checking by friction the speed of a rope (as in a hoist) **2 :** the part of a brake that holds the shoe

brake club *n* **:** a stout stick used to increase leverage in setting hand brakes on a railroad car

brake cylinder *n* **:** the cylinder in which the piston of an air or hydraulic brake operates

brake drum *n* **:** a revolving cylinder on the wheel of a vehicle or the revolving part of an engine or machine upon which the brake shoe or brake band presses — see HYDRAULIC BRAKE illustration

brake fluid *n* **:** the liquid used in a hydraulic brake cylinder

brake hanger *n* **:** one of the bars or links suspending a brake beam

brake horsepower *n* **:** the power of an engine or other motor as calculated from the force exerted on a friction brake or absorption dynamometer applied to the flywheel or the shaft

brake hose *n* **:** a flexible tube connecting the brake pipes of adjoining vehicles (as railroad cars)

brake·less *adj* **:** being without a brake

brake lining *n* **:** the facing of brake bands esp. on automobiles; *also* **:** the fabric used for such lining

brakeload \'=,=\ *n* **:** the test load imposed on a prime mover by the brake

brake·man \'brākmən\ *n*, *pl* **brakemen 1 a** (1) **:** a member of a train crew whose duties include operating hand brakes and track switches, inspecting the train for mechanical deficiencies, watching for signals from the engineer and fireman, and on passenger trains assisting the conductor (2) **:** a worker who rides on trains of mine cars to assist in their operation by motor or cable haulage system — called also *dukey rider*, *nipper* **b :** [5]BRAKE 3b **c :** one that inspects, adjusts, and repairs air brakes or hydraulic brakes **2 :** an operator of a power brake for making bends in sheet metal

brake meter *n* **:** a device to measure the decelerating effect of vehicle brakes

brak·en \'brakən\ *dial Brit var of* BRACKEN

brake parachute *n* **:** a deceleration parachute

brake pipe *n* **:** the main pipe of a pressure brake system extending the entire length of the train and connecting the manual and the automatic actuating devices on individual vehicles — called also *train line*; see AIR BRAKE

brak·er \'brākə(r)\ *n* -s [[4]*brake* (kneading machine) + *-er*] **:** a worker who rolls dough for baked goods or macaroni products in a brake — called also *rollerman*

brakes *pl of* BRAKE, *pres 3d sing of* BRAKE

brakes·man \'brāksmən\ *n*, *pl* **brakesmen** *chiefly Brit* **:** BRAKEMAN

brake van *n*, *Brit* **:** a railway car or compartment containing means for operating the brakes

brak·ie *or* **brak·ey** \'brākē, -ki\ *n* -s [by shortening & alter.] *slang* **:** BRAKEMAN 1

braking *pres part of* BRAKE

braky \'brākē, -ki\ *adj* -ER/-EST [[7]*brake* + *-y*] **:** full of brakes **:** abounding with brambles, shrubs, or ferns ⟨in the woods and ~ glens —William Browne⟩

bramah *var of* BRAHMA

bram·ah lock \'bramə-, -ämə-,-ȧmə-\ *n*, *usu cap B* [after Joseph *Bramah* †1814 Eng. engineer, its inventor] **:** a lock in which the tumblers are thin flat notched bars receiving endwise movement from the key instead of the swinging movement of the tumblers of an ordinary lock

bramah press *n*, *usu cap B* [after J.*Bramah*] **:** HYDRAULIC PRESS

bra·man·tesque \ˌbrä,män-ˈtesk, -,mən-; brə,män-\ *adj*, *usu cap* [It *bramantesco*, fr. Donato d'Agnolo *Bramante* †1514 Ital. architect + It *-esco* -esque] **:** of or relating to a Renaissance style of architecture marked by classical forms

bra·ma·pi·the·cus \ˌbrämə'pithəkəs, -'pithȯkəs\ *n*, *cap* [NL, irreg. fr. *Brahma*, first member of the Hindu trinity + NL *-pithecus*] **:** a genus of Lower Pliocene dryopithecine apes from the Siwalik hills of India — compare DRYOPITHECINAE

[1]**bram·ble** \'brambəl, -raam-\ *n* -s [ME *brembel*, fr. OE *brēmel*, *brǣmel*, *brēmbel*; akin to OE *brōm* broom — more at BROOM] **1 :** a plant of the genus *Rubus* or its fruit; *esp*, *Brit* **:** the blackberry bush or its fruit **2 :** a rough prickly shrub or vine

[2]**bramble** \"\ *n* -s **:** TURNOVER

bram·ble·ber·ry \'=-—*see* BERRY\ *n*, *chiefly Brit* **:** BRAMBLE 1

bramblebush \'==,=\ *n* **1 :** BRAMBLE 1 **2 :** a thicket of brambles

bramble finch *n* **:** BRAMBLING

bramble leafhopper *n* **:** a European leafhopper (*Ribautiana tenerrima*) now established on the Pacific coast of No. America where it is very destructive to loganberries and raspberries

bramble rose *n* **:** DOG ROSE

bramble shark *n* **:** a brownish or purplish shark (*Echinorhinus brucus*) that has hard spiny tubercles scattered on the skin and is nearly cosmopolitan in warm seas though rarely numerous

bramble worm *n* [by folk etymology fr. *brandling worm*] **:** BRANDLING

bram·bling \'bram(b)liŋ, -lən\ *n* -s [prob. fr. *bramble* + *-ing*] **:** a brightly colored finch (*Fringilla montifringilla*) that breeds in the northern parts of Europe and Asia and migrates southward in winter and is often kept as a cage bird — called also *bramble finch*

bram·bly \'bramblē, -raam-, -li\ *adj* -ER/-EST **:** like or full of brambles

brame *n* -s [It *brama*, fr. *bramare* to desire ardently, prob. fr. a Gmc word meaning "to roar, bellow" (whence It dial. *bramè* to bellow); akin to OHG *bremen* to buzz, rumble, roar — more at FREMITUS] *obs* **:** PASSION, DESIRE, LONGING

bram·i·dae \'bramə,dē\ *n pl*, *cap* [NL, fr. *Brama*, type genus + *-idae*] **:** a widely distributed family of deep-bodied percoid fishes frequenting open seas — compare POMFRET

bramp·ton stock \'bra|m(p)tən-\ *or* **bromp·ton stock** \'brä|\ *n*, *usu cap B* [fr. *Brompton*, suburb of London, England] **:** any of various biennial garden stocks derived from the common stock (*Matthiola incana*) and grown chiefly for early spring bloom — compare TEN-WEEK STOCK

[1]**bran** \'bran, -aa(ə)n\ *n* -s [ME *bran*, *bren*, fr. OF] **1 a :** the broken coat of the seed of wheat, rye, or other cereal grain separated from the kernel and used esp. for animal feed **b :** a coarsely ground stock feed obtained as a by-product in food canning ⟨pineapple ~⟩ ⟨shrimp ~⟩ **2** *obs* **:** SORT, CLASS **3 :** a light brown to yellowish brown that is lighter than aloma and less strong than pablo

[2]**bran** \"\ *vt* **branned; branned; branning; brans 1 :** to boil in bran drench **2 :** to cleanse (tinned plate) of oil esp. with bran

bran bug *n* **:** CONFUSED FLOUR BEETLE

bran·car·dier \brä^n kärdyā\ *n*, *pl* **brancardiers** \"\ [F, fr. *brancard* stretcher, fr. MF, fr. MF dial. (Normandy), large branch, aug. of *branque* branch, fr. LL *branca*] **:** STRETCHER BEARER

[1]**branch** \'branch, -aa(ə)-,-ai-,-ȧ-\ *n* -ES *often attrib* [ME *braunche*, fr. OF *branche*, fr. LL *branca* paw] **1 :** a stem growing from the trunk or from a limb of a tree; *specif* **:** a shoot or secondary stem growing from the main stem **2 :** something that extends from, enters into, or is an offshoot of a main body or source: as **a** (1) **:** a stream that flows into another usu. larger stream **:** AFFLUENT, TRIBUTARY (2) *South and Midland* **:** CREEK 2 (3) **:** an effluent stream ⟨a delta ~⟩ (4) **:** a reentrant stream **:** BY-CHANNEL, ANABRANCH (5) **:** a fork of a tidal river (as of the Severn river in Maryland) **b :** a side road or way ⟨a logging railroad whose ~*es* spread through thousands of square miles —*Amer. Guide Series: Minn.*⟩ **c** (1) **:** a slender projection (as the tine of an antler or arm of a candelabrum) (2) **:** a rib in Gothic vaulting; *esp* **:** one of the smaller ribs in a complicated vault (3) **:** either side of a horseshoe (4) **:** a pipe joined to and diverging from the barrel of another pipe; *also* **:** a forked pipe connection **d** *archaic* **:** SCION, DESCENDANT **e** (1) *math* **:** one of the portions of a curve (as a hyperbola) (2) **:** either of the two partial series of lines in a spectral band that proceed in opposite directions from the zero line of the band **3 :** a part of a complex body: as **a :** a division of a family descending from a particular ancestor as distinguished from those descending from his relations ⟨the Connecticut ~ of an old Boston family⟩ **b :** an area of knowledge that may be considered or studied apart from related areas ⟨pathology is a ~ of medicine⟩ **c** (1) **:** a section, department, or division of an organization ⟨a ~ of the armed service⟩ ⟨the two ~*es* of Congress⟩ (2) **:** a subordinate or dependent part of a central system or organization ⟨a neighborhood ~ of a city library⟩ ⟨a ~ bank in a suburb⟩ **d** (1) **:** a primary division of the animal kingdom — see PHYLUM (2) *in the classification of languages of the eastern hemisphere* **:** a number of related languages forming a category less inclusive than a family or subfamily ⟨the Germanic ~ of the Indo-European language family⟩ **4 :** a warrant or commission given to a pilot authorizing him to pilot ships in certain waters ⟨a ~ pilot⟩

branch 2c(4): *1* Y branch, *2* double Y branch, *3* Y branch, *4* tee, *5* double tee

[2]**branch** \"\ *vb* -ED/-ING/-ES [ME *braunchen*, fr. *braunche*, n.] *vi* **1 :** to put or hold forth branches **:** RAMIFY ⟨a great elm ~*ing* over the roof⟩ **2 :** to spring off or out (as from a main stem or root) **:** DIVERGE ⟨streets ~*ing* from either side of the highway⟩ — often used with *off* ⟨his mind kept ~*ing off* into the contemplation of silly things —Liam O'Flaherty⟩ **3 :** to become derived **:** be an outgrowth — used with *from* ⟨poetry that ~*ed* from Baudelaire —Douglas Stewart⟩ **4 :** to extend activities **:** enlarge or develop by taking up something different or by adding on something new — usu. used with *out* ⟨car manufacturers ~*ed* out into tank and cannon manufacture⟩ ~ *vt* **1 :** to ornament with designs of branches or foliage ⟨~ velvet⟩ **2 :** to divide up **:** ARRANGE, SECTION ⟨~*ing* his treatment of the problem into three equal parts⟩

syn RAMIFY, DIVARICATE, FORK, FURCATE, BIFURCATE: BRANCH (often used with *off*, *from*, *out*) is applicable to any developing or projecting comparable to the sending out of a branch by a tree or to a split growth comparable to the main fork of a tree trunk ⟨roads *branching* off the main highways⟩ ⟨little streams *branching* from the river⟩ ⟨*branching* out from building houses to selling real estate⟩ ⟨the river *branches* to form the various delta channels⟩ RAMIFY may suggest an intricate dividing or subdividing, sometimes to the extent of interconnecting, permeating, or affecting a whole area ⟨the system of arteries and veins *ramifying* over the whole body⟩ ⟨an inquiry into the nature of the genres and the boundaries of the arts *ramifies* out in every direction —Irving Babbitt⟩ ⟨a *ramifying* network of social relations, with every chance that its force may be multiplied or deflected in the devious process of transmission —Max Lerner & Edwin Mims⟩ DIVARICATE is a technical term indicating splitting into two main branches ⟨elm tree trunks often *divaricate*⟩ FORK indicates a splitting or development at a specific point into what may be likened to tines or branches ⟨the river *forks* forming an island⟩ ⟨the main road *forks* into two smaller roads⟩ FURCATE, now uncommon, and BIFURCATE, explicitly indicating a division into two, are more learned synonyms for FORK ⟨though Islam *bifurcated* into the sects of the Sunnis and the Shi'is as the Christian Church *bifurcated* into the Catholic and Orthodox Churches —A.J. Toynbee⟩ ⟨the inevitable moment when the channel *bifurcated* and a choice had to be made —C.S.Forester⟩

-branch \ˌbraŋk\ *n comb form* -s [NL *-branchia* ones having (such or so many) gills & *-branchus* one having (such or so many) gills (fr. Gk *branchos* gill, irreg. fr. Gk *branchia* gills)] **1 :** one having (such or so many) gills ⟨crypto*branch*⟩ ⟨di*branch*⟩ **2 :** gill ⟨arthro*branch*⟩ **:** organ like a gill ⟨actino*branch*⟩

branch bar *n* **:** a copper strap that connects a main bus bar with a branch circuit in a wiring system

branch bud *n* **:** LEAF BUD

branch circuit *n* **:** the part of an electric wiring system that extends from any set of outlets as far back as the fuse box, supplying and protecting them

branch-climber \'=,==\ *n* **:** a tropical or subtropical woody vine supported in climbing by curling branches rather than tendrils

branched chain *n* **:** an open chain of atoms having one or more side chains (as in isobutane $\begin{smallmatrix}CH_3\\CH_3\end{smallmatrix}{>}CH{-}CH_3$) — opposed to *straight chain*

bran·chel·lion \braŋ'kelyən\ *n*, *cap* [NL, alter. of *Branchiobdellion*, fr. *branchi-* + Gk *bdella* leech + *-ion* (dim. suffix)] **:** a genus of leeches with external gills along the sides of the body that are parasitic on fishes

[1]**branch·er** \'branchə(r), -aa-,-ai-,-ȧ-\ *n* -s [ME *brauncher*, fr. *braunche* branch + *-er*] **:** a young bird (as a fledgling hawk) that has left the nest and taken to the branches

[2]**brancher** \"\ *n* -s [[2]*branch* + *-er*] **:** one that makes artificial flowers or feather designs

branches *pl of* BRANCH, *pres 3d sing of* BRANCH

branch gap *n* **:** a gap that surrounds a branch trace

branch grass *n* **:** CREEK SEDGE

branch herring *n* **:** ALEWIFE 1a

branchi- *or* **branchio-** *comb form* [NL *branchio-*, fr. Gk, fr. *branchia*] **1 :** gills ⟨*branchi*ferous⟩ ⟨*branchio*genous⟩ **2 :** branchial and ⟨*branchio*cardiac⟩

bran·chia \'braŋkēə, -aiŋ-\ *n*, *pl* **branchi·ae** \-ē,ē\ [L *branchia* (sing.) gill, fr. Gk *branchia* gills, pl. of *branchion* gill; akin to Gk *bronchos* trachea — more at CRAW] **:** [3]GILL

[1]**-branchia** \"\ *n pl comb form* [NL, fr. L *branchia*] **:** ones having (such or so many) gills — in taxonomic names in zoology ⟨Crypto*branchia*⟩ ⟨Tetra*branchia*⟩

[2]**-branchia** \"\ *n comb form*, *pl* **-branchi·ae** \-ē,ē\ [NL, fr. L *branchia*] **:** gill ⟨podo*branchia*⟩ **:** organ like a gill ⟨pulmo*branchia*⟩

bran·chi·al \'braŋkēəl, -aiŋ-\ *adj* [*branchi-* + *-al*] **:** of or relating to the gills or to parts of the body derived from the embryonic branchial arches and clefts

branchial arch *n* **:** one of the bony or cartilaginous arches or curved bars extending dorsoventrally and placed one behind the other posterior to the hyoid arch on each side of the pharynx and supporting the gills of fishes and amphibians; *also* **:** a corresponding rudimentary ridge in the embryo of all higher vertebrates

branchial basket *n* **:** the cartilaginous structure supporting the gills in protochordates and lower vertebrates (as ascidians, amphioxi, and cyclostomes)

branchial cleft *n* **:** one of the openings or clefts between the branchial arches in vertebrates that breathe by gills through which water taken in at the mouth passes to the exterior bathing the gills; *also* **:** a rudimentary groove in the neck region of the embryos of air-breathing vertebrates

branchial heart *n* **:** a muscular enlargement of a vein of a cephalopod that contracts and drives the blood into the gills

branchial plume *n* **:** an accessory respiratory organ extending out under the mantle in some gastropods

branchial pouch *n* **:** one of the respiratory cavities in the branchial clefts of cyclostomes and some sharks

branchial sac *n* **:** the dilated pharyngeal part of the alimentary canal in tunicates that has vascular walls pierced with clefts and functions as a gill

bran·chi·a·ta \ˌbraŋkē'ād·ə, -ād·ə\ *n pl*, *cap* [NL, fr. *branchi-* + *-ata*] **:** any of several groups of animals having gills: as **a :** the Crustacea as distinguished from the tracheate arthropods **b :** amphibians and fishes as distinguished from the higher vertebrates

bran·chi·ate \'braŋkēət, -ē,āt\ *adj* [*branchi-* + *-ate*] **:** furnished with gills

bran·chic·o·lous \(ˈ)braŋ'kikələs\ *adj* [*branchi-* + *-colous*] **:** parasitic on gills — used of certain trematode worms

[1]**branchier** *comparative of* BRANCHY

[2]**bran·chier** \brä^n shyā\ *n*, *pl* **branchiers** \-ā(z)\ [LaF, fr. F *branche* branch, fr. OF — more at BRANCH] **:** WOOD DUCK 1

branchiest *superlative of* BRANCHY

bran·chif·er·ous \(ˈ)braŋ'kif(ə)rəs\ *adj* [ISV *branchi-* + *-ferous*] **:** BRANCHIATE

[1]**bran·chi·hy·al** \ˌbraŋkē'hīəl\ *adj* [*branchi-* + *-hyoid* + *-al*] **:** of or relating to the elements or segments composing the branchial arches

[2]**branchihyal** \"\ *n* -s **:** an element or segment of a branchial arch

branching *n* -s [ME *braunching*, fr. gerund of *braunchen* to branch — more at BRANCH] **:** the process of forming a branch — see FALSE BRANCHING, TRUE BRANCHING

branching foxtail *n* **:** WINDMILL GRASS

bran·chi·ob·del·la \ˌbraŋkē,äb'delə, -ēəb-\ *n*, *cap* [NL, fr. *branchi-* + Gk *bdella* leech] **:** a genus (the type of the family Branchiobdellidae) of small annelid worms that live on the gills and surface of crayfishes, have the posterior end modified into an adhesive sucker, and are now usu. considered to form with a few related forms a superfamily of Oligochaeta though formerly regarded as modified leeches

[1]**bran·chi·ob·del·lid** \ˌ==(,)=ˈ=ləd\ *adj* [NL *Branchiobdellidae* family of worms, fr. *Branchiobdella*, type genus + *-idae*] **:** of or relating to the genus *Branchiobdella* or family Branchiobdellidae

[2]**branchiobdellid** \"\ *n* -s **:** a worm of the genus *Branchiobdella*

bran·chio·cardiac \ˌbraŋkē(,)ō+\ *adj* [*branchi-* + *cardiac*] **:** of or relating to the gills and heart

bran·chio·cranium \"+\ *n* [NL, fr. *branchi-* + *cranium*] **:** one of two main divisions of the fish skull constituting the mandibular and hyal regions and the branchial arches — compare NEUROCRANIUM

bran·chi·og·e·nous \ˌbraŋkē'äjənəs\ *adj* [*branchi-* + *-genous*] **:** arising from or formed by the branchial clefts or arches

bran·chi·o·mere \'braŋkēə,mi(ə)r\ *n* -s [*branchi-* + *-mere*] **:** a branchial segment; *esp* **:** one of the metameres indicated by the visceral arches and clefts of the embryo of airbreathing vertebrates — **bran·chi·o·mer·ic** \ˌbraŋkēə'merik\ *adj* — **bran·chi·om·er·ism** \ˌbraŋkē'ämə,rizəm\ *n* -s

bran·chio·pallial \ˌbraŋkē(,)ō+\ *adj* [*branchi-* + *pallial*] **:** of or relating to the gill and mantle of mollusks

bran·chi·op·neus·tic \ˌbraŋkēˌäpˈn(y)üstik,-ēəp-\ *adj* [*branchi-* + Gk *pneustos* having (such) breath + E *-ic* — more at -PNEUSTA] **:** having the spiracles replaced by gills — used of certain immature aquatic insects

¹bran·chi·o·pod \ˈbraŋkēəˌpäd\ *or* **bran·chi·op·o·dan** \ˌbraŋkēˈäpədən\ *or* **bran·chi·op·o·dous** \ˌ≈≈ˈ≈≈dəs\ *adj* [*branchiopod* fr. NL *Branchiopoda; branchiopodan, branchiopodous* fr. NL *Branchiopoda* + E *-an* or *-ous*] **:** of or relating to the Branchiopoda

²branchiopod \ˈ"\ *or* **branchiopodan** \ˈ"\ *n* -s **:** a crustacean of the subclass Branchiopoda or order Branchiopoda

bran·chi·op·o·da \ˌbraŋkēˈäpədə\ *n pl, cap* [NL, fr. *branchi-* + *-poda*] **1 :** a subclass of crustacea comprising primitive aquatic forms typically having an elongated body, a carapace, and many pairs of foliaceous appendages and including the orders Anostraca, Notostraca, Conchostraca, and Cladocera **2** *in some esp former classifications* **a :** an order of Entomostraca including the Cladocera **b :** an order of Phyllopoda excluding the Cladocera **c :** PHYLLOPODA b

bran·chi·o·saur \ˈbraŋkēəˌsȯ(ə)r\ *n* -s [NL *Branchiosaurus*] **:** an amphibian or fossil of Branchiosaurus

bran·chi·o·sau·rus \ˌbraŋkēəˈsȯrəs\ *n, cap* [NL, fr. *branchi-* + *-saurus*] **:** a group of small fossil amphibians like salamanders from the Permian of Europe formerly regarded as constituting a separate order or suborder but now usu. held to be larvae of typical rhachitomous labyrinthodont amphibians — used orig. as a generic name and still commonly as though it were a generic name

¹bran·chi·os·te·gal \ˌbraŋkēˈästəgəl\ *adj* [ISV *branchi-* + *steg-* + *-al*] **:** of or relating to the branchiostegals ⟨the ~ membrane⟩

²branchiostegal \ˈ"\ *or* **branchiostegal ray** *n* -s **:** one of the bony radiating processes of the hyoid arch that support the membranes enclosing the gill chamber in most fishes

bran·chi·o·steg·i·dae \ˌbraŋkēōˈstejəˌdē\ *n pl, cap* [NL, fr. *Branchiostegus*, type genus (fr. *branchi-* + *-stegus*, fr. Gk *stegē* roof, cover) + *-idae* — more at THATCH] **:** a small family of marine percoid fishes (as the blanquillos) having an elongate body, long dorsal and anal fins, and thoracic or subjugular ventral fins

bran·chi·os·te·gite \ˌbraŋkēˈästəˌjīt\ *n* -s [*branchi-* + *stegite*] **:** the extended pleural part of the carapace forming one wall of the gill chamber in crustaceans

bran·chi·os·te·gous \ˌbraŋkēˈästəgəs\ *adj* [prob. fr. F *branchiostège* + E *-ous*] **1 :** BRANCHIOSTEGAL **2 :** having the gills covered

bran·chi·os·to·ma \ˌbraŋkēˈästəmə\ *n, cap* [NL, fr. *branchi-* + *-stoma*] **:** the type genus of Branchiostomidae comprising lancelets with paired gonads and symmetrical metapleura — see AMPHIOXUS

¹bran·chi·os·to·mid \ˌbraŋkēˈästəməd\ *adj* [NL *Branchiostomidae*] **:** of or relating to the family Branchiostomidae

²branchiostomid \ˈ"\ *n* -s **:** a typical lancelet **:** a member of the family Branchiostomidae

bran·chi·o·stom·i·dae \ˌbraŋkēōˈstäməˌdē\ *n pl, cap* [NL, fr. *Branchiostoma*, type genus + *-idae*] **:** the chief and typical family of Cephalochorda containing most of the known recent lancelets

bran·chi·pus \ˈbraŋkəpəs\ *n, cap* [NL, fr. *branchi-* + *-pus*] **:** a genus of European freshwater branchiopod crustaceans (order Anostraca) that resemble the brine shrimp — see EUBRANCHIPUS

bran·chi·reme \-əˌrēm\ *n* -s [*branchi-* + L *remus* oar — more at ROW] **:** a limb of a branchiopod used both for respiration and locomotion

bran·chi·ura \ˌbraŋkēˈ(y)urə\ *n pl, cap* [NL, fr. *branchi-* + *-ura*] **:** an order of Copepoda comprising copepods that have suctorial mouthparts and are parasitic on fish — compare EUCOPEPODA — **bran·chi·uran** \ˌ≈≈ˈ≈rən\ *adj or n* — **bran·chi·urous** \-rəs\ *adj*

branch·less *adj* **:** being without a branch

branch·let \ˈbranchlət, -aan-,-ain-,-ȧn-\ *n* -s **:** a small branch or subdivision of a branch; *esp* **:** a terminal one

-branchs *pl of* -BRANCH

branch trace *n* **:** a trace supplying a branch — compare LEAF TRACE

branch water *n* **1 :** water from a small stream **2 :** plain water ⟨bourbon and *branch water*⟩

branchy \-chē,-chi\ *adj* -ER/-EST [ME *braunchy*, fr. *braunche* branch + *-y* — more at BRANCH] **:** covered or overgrown with branches ⟨a ~ tree trunk⟩

¹brand \ˈbrand, -aa(ə)-\ *n* -s [ME *brand, brond* brand, sword, fr. OE; akin to OHG *brant* brand, ON *brandr* brand, blade of a sword, OE *byrnan, bærnan* to burn — more at BURN] **1 a :** a piece of wood that has been or is burning (as one from a hearth or a burning building) **:** FIREBRAND **b :** something that resembles a burning piece of wood ⟨blinding ~*s* of lightning —P.B.Shelley⟩ **2 a :** a sword blade **b :** SWORD **3 a** (1) **:** a mark of a simple easily recognized pattern made by burning with a hot iron to attest manufacture or quality or to designate ownership (2) **:** a mark made with a stamp or stencil for similar purposes **:** TRADEMARK **b** (1) **:** a mark put on criminals with a hot iron (2) **:** a mark of disgrace **:** STIGMA ⟨a reputation bearing the ~ of criminal negligence⟩ **4 a** (1) **:** a class of goods identified as being the product of a single firm or manufacturer **:** MAKE ⟨stores selling well-known ~*s* of canned foods⟩ (2) **:** PRODUCER, MANUFACTURER ⟨a dozen ~*s* of textile goods competing on the open market⟩ **b :** a characteristic or distinctive kind **:** VARIETY ⟨their ~ of love was a tortured and fretful affection —Evelyn Eaton⟩ **5 :** a tool used to produce a brand (as on cattle, manufactured wares, wine casks) **:** BRANDING IRON **6 :** any rust fungus giving a burnt appearance typically to leaves

brands for cattle: *1* diamond X, *2* box X, *3* circle X, *4* bar X, *5* rocking X, *6* swinging X, *7* tumbling X, *8* walking X, *9* flying X, *10* crazy P, *11* lazy P, *12* reverse P

²brand \ˈ"\ *vt* -ED/-ING/-S [ME *branden, bronden* fr. *brand, brond*, n.] **1 :** to mark with a brand ⟨~ a criminal⟩ ⟨~ wine casks with the vineyard's name⟩; *esp* **:** to place the brand of ownership on (horses or cattle) **2 :** to mark, signal, or expose as being disgraceful or dishonest **:** STIGMATIZE ⟨refusal of such a demand ~*s* one as stingy —Margaret Mead⟩ **3 :** to impress indelibly ⟨history has once again ~*ed* this lesson on the minds of those who choose to see —T.O.Beachcroft⟩

brand·ed \ˈbrandəd, -n(d)ət\ *adj* [ME *brandit, brended* — more at BRINDED] *dial Brit* **:** BRINDLED

branded drum *n* [fr. past part. of ²*brand*] **:** CHANNEL BASS

bran·den·burg \ˈbrandənˌbərg\ *n* -s *usu cap* [modif. (influenced by *Brandenburg*) of F *brandebourg*, fr. *Brandenburg*, region of Prussia, Germany, 17th cent. soldiers of which wore such ornaments on their uniforms] **:** an ornamental braid trimming — usu. used in pl.

¹bran·der \ˈbran(d)ər\ *n* -s [ME *brandire, brandirne*, fr. *branden* to brand + *ire, irne* iron — more at BRAND, IRON] *chiefly Scot* **:** a ribbed open griddle **:** GRIDIRON

²bran·der \ˈbrandə(r), -raan-, *Scot* -an(d)ər\ *vb* **brandered; brandered; brandering** \-n(d)(ə)riŋ\ **branders** *vt* **1** *chiefly Scot* **:** to broil on a brander **2 :** to apply brandering to ~ *vi* **1** *chiefly Scot* **:** to broil meat **2 :** to apply brandering

³brand·er \ˈbrandə(r), -aan-\ *n* -s [²*brand* + *-er*] **:** one that brands; *esp* **:** one that affixes or stamps an identification on a product

bran·der·ing \ˈbrand(ə)riŋ, -aan-\ *n* -s [¹*brander* + *-ing*; fr. the gridironlike appearance of a wall of brandering] **:** furring strips or small blocks used to set plastering lath out from a beam or other solid surface

bran·died \ˈbrandēd, -aan-, -did\ *adj* **:** preserved in brandy ⟨~ peaches⟩

branding chute *n* **:** a narrow enclosed path down which cattle are driven for branding, spraying, or dehorning

branding iron *n* **:** an iron rod with a brand at one end

brand iron *n* [ME *brandire, brandirne* — more at BRANDER] **1** *now chiefly Scot* **:** ¹BRANDER **1 2** *now chiefly Scot* **:** TRIVET

bran·dise \ˈbrandəs\ *n* -s [OE *brandisen*, fr. *brand* burning + *īsen* iron — more at BRAND, IRON] *dial Eng* **:** TRIVET

bran disease *n* **:** a condition resembling rickets occurring in young horses fed excessively on bran and prob. resulting from an unbalanced calcium-phosphorus ratio — called also *bran poisoning*

¹bran·dish \ˈbrandish, -raan-, -dēsh\ *vb* -ED/-ING/-ES [ME *braundisshen*, fr. MF *brandiss-*, stem of *brandir*, fr. OF, fr. *brand* sword, of Gmc origin; akin to OHG *brant* brand — more at BRAND] *vt* **1 :** to shake or wave (a weapon) menacingly ⟨cursed him eloquently . . . and ~*ed* a pistol at him —H.H. Martin⟩ **2 :** to exhibit or expose in an ostentatious, shameless, or aggressive manner ⟨my cherry tree ~*ed* its sparkling blossoms —Adrian Bell⟩ ⟨has . . . not only demonstrated her intellect but ~*ed* it —James Hilton⟩ ~ *vi* **:** FLOURISH, WAVE ⟨swords ~*ed* and banners waved⟩ **syn** see SWING

²brandish \ˈ"\ *n* -ES **:** a flourish esp. with a weapon or whip

brand·less *adj* **:** being without a brand

brand·ling \ˈbran(d)liŋ, -lən\ *n* -s [¹*brand* + *-ling*] **1 :** a small yellowish earthworm (*Eisenia foetida*) with brownish purple rings found in dunghills and used as bait by anglers **2 :** a young salmon **:** PARR

brand-new *also* **bran-new** \ˈbranˈn(y)ü, -raan- *sometimes* -ndˈn-\ *adj* [*brand-new* fr. ¹*brand* + *new*; *bran-new*, alter. of *brand-new*] **:** fresh from the manufacturer **:** conspicuously new and unused ⟨thrust a hand into the . . . pocket and fetched out a *brand-new* pigskin wallet —Frances Crane⟩ ⟨an inventive fellow somewhere who would devise a *brand-new* approach —*New Yorker*⟩

bran·dreth *also* **bran·drith** \ˈbrandrəth\ *n* -s [ME, fr. ON *brandreith* grate, fr. *brandr* fire + *reith* wagon — more at BRAND, ROAD] **:** a wooden framework for support (as a stand for a hayrick)

brands *pl of* BRAND, *pres 3d sing of* BRAND

brand spore *n* **1 :** UREDIOSPORE **2 :** a smut chlamydospore

brandt·ite \ˈbrantˌīt\ *n* -s [Sw or G *brandtit*, fr. Georg *Brandt* †1768 Sw. chemist + Sw or G *-it* -ite] **:** a mineral $Ca_2Mn(AsO_4)_2.2H_2O$ consisting of a hydrous arsenate of calcium and manganese

brandt's cormorant \ˈbran(t)s-\ *n, usu cap B* [after J.F. Von *Brandt* †1879 Ger. zoologist] **:** a large chiefly greenish black cormorant (*Phalacrocorax penicillatus*) of the Pacific coast of No. America

bran duster *n* **:** a machine for separating grain or flour from bran

¹bran·dy \ˈbrandē, -raan-, -di\ *n* -ES [short for *brandywine*] **:** an alcoholic liquor distilled from wine or from the fermented juice of peaches, cherries, apples, or other fruit — compare ARMAGNAC, COGNAC, KIRSCH, QUETSCH, SLIVOVITZ

²brandy \ˈ"\ *vt* -ED/-ING/-ES **1 :** to flavor, blend, or treat with brandy **2 :** to provide or refresh with brandy

³brandy \ˈ"\ *n* -ES [by folk etymology] **:** BARANI

brandy-and-soda \ˌ≈≈≈ˈ≈≈\ *n* **:** a drink of brandy diluted with soda water

brandyball \ˈ≈≈,≈\ *n, Brit* **:** a candy flavored with brandy

brandy-bottle \ˈ≈≈,≈≈\ *n* [so called fr. the shape of the seed vessel] *dial Eng* **:** CANDOCK a

brandy mint *n* **:** PEPPERMINT 1a

brandy snap *n* **:** a gingersnap flavored with brandy

bran·dy·wine \ˈ≈≈,wīn\ *n* [earlier *brandwine*, fr. D *brandewijn* fr. MD *brantwijn*, fr. *brant* (past part. of *bernen* to burn, distill) + *wijn* wine; akin to OE *biernan* to burn and OE *win* wine — more at BURN, WINE] *obs* **:** BRANDY

brang *substand past of* BRING

¹bran·gle \ˈbraŋ(g)əl\ *vi* -ED/-ING/-S [blend of ¹*brawl* and *wrangle*] *now dial Brit* **:** SQUABBLE, WRANGLE

²brangle \ˈ"\ *n* -S *dial Brit* **:** SQUABBLE, SET-TO

¹brank \ˈbraŋk\ *vi* -ED/-ING/-S [ME *branken*] *dial Brit* **:** PRANCE, CAPER

²brank \ˈ"\ *n* -s [origin unknown] **1 a :** an instrument consisting of an iron frame surrounding the head and a sharp metal bit or gag entering the mouth formerly used to punish scolds — called also *scold's bridle;* usu. used in pl. **b branks** *pl, now chiefly Scot* **:** a bridle or halter for horses or cows **2 branks** *pl, Scot* **:** MUMPS

brank·ie *or* **branky** \-kē\ *adj* [¹*brank* + *-ie, -y*] *Scot* **:** GAUDY

brank·ur·sine \braŋˈkərsᵊn\ *n* -s [MF *branque-ursine*, fr. ML *branca ursina*, fr. LL *branca* claw + L *ursina*, fem. of *ursinus* of a bear; fr. the resemblance of the leaves to the claws of a bear — more at URSINE] **:** BEAR'S-BREECH

branle *also* **bransle** \ˈbrä(ä)ⁿl, ˈbrōⁿl\ *or* **brawl** \ˈbrȯl\ *n* -s [MF *branle, bransle*, lit., act of shaking, fr. *branler* to shake, swing, brandish, fr. OF, alter. of *brandir* to brandish — more at BRANDISH] **1 :** one of several couple dances of French origin that were popular in the 16th and 17th centuries, usu. in duple measure, mimetic, accompanied by singing, and danced in groups typically in a circle **2 :** a sideward balance step in a clockwise direction used in branle dances

bran mash *n* **:** a wet mash of bran and hot water

branned *past of* BRAN

bran·ner \ˈbranə(r), -raan-\ *n* -s [²*bran* + *-er*] **1 :** a machine that brans **2 :** the operator of a branning machine

bran·ner·ite \ˈbranəˌrīt\ *n* -s [John C. *Branner* †1922 Am. geologist + E *-ite*] **:** a mineral consisting of a complex uranium titanate with small amounts of rare earths and occurring in black grains and rough prisms

bran-new *var of* BRAND-NEW

bran·ni·gan \ˈbranəgən\ *n* -s [prob. fr. the name *Brannigan*] **1 :** a drinking spree **:** BENDER ⟨go on a ~⟩ **2 :** a difference of opinion **:** CONTROVERSY, SQUABBLE ⟨~ . . . over the location of the schoolhouse —Harry De Lasaux⟩

branning *pres part of* BRAN

bran·ny \ˈbranē, -aan-, -ni\ *adj* -ER/-EST [¹*bran* + *-y*] **:** of, like, or containing bran ⟨the ~ portions of cereal grains⟩

bran poisoning *n* **:** BRAN DISEASE

brans *pl of* BRAN, *pres 3d sing of* BRAN

¹brant \ˈbrant\ *var of* ¹BRENT

²brant \ˈbrant, -aa(ə)-\ *also* **brant goose** \ˈ"-\ *or* **brent** \ˈbrent\ *or* **brent goose** *n, pl* **brant** *or* **brants** [origin unknown] **:** any of several wild geese; *esp* **:** any of several small dark geese of the genus *Branta* that breed in the arctic regions and migrate southward chiefly along the coasts — see WHITE BRANT

bran·ta \ˈbrantə\ *n, cap* [NL, fr. E ²*brant*] **:** a genus of birds (family Anatidae) comprising wild geese with rather elaborately patterned commonly dark plumage, long slender neck, and small weakly serrated bill — see BRANT, CANADA GOOSE; compare ANSER

brant bird *n* [²*brant*] **:** TURNSTONE

brant snipe *n* [²*brant*] **:** RED-BACKED SANDPIPER

bran tub *n, Brit* **:** a tub filled with bran in which presents are concealed

bras *pl of* BRA

bra·sen \ˈbrāzᵊn\ *archaic var of* BRAZEN

bra·se·nia \brəˈsēnēə\ *n, cap* [NL] **:** a monotypic genus of widely distributed aquatic plants (family Nymphaeaceae) with floating oval leaves and small dull-purple flowers — see WATER SHIELD

bra·se·ro \brəˈse(ˌ)rō\ *n* -s [Sp, fr. *brasa* live coals — more at BRAZE] **:** a brick stove built into many Mexican kitchens

¹brash \ˈbrash, -aa(ə)-,-ai-\ *n* -ES [obs. E *brash* to breach a wall, prob. fr. MF *breche* breach — more at BREACH] **1** *dial Brit* **a :** ATTACK, BOUT **b :** a burst of activity **2 a** *chiefly Scot* **:** an attack of illness; *esp* **:** a short severe illness **b :** WATER BRASH **3** *chiefly Scot* **:** a sudden shower **4 :** a mass of fragments or debris: as **a** *or* **brash ice :** small floating fragments of ice esp. near an ice pack or floe **b :** clippings of hedges or prunings of trees

²brash \ˈ"\ *vt* -ED/-ING/-ES **:** to remove the lower branches of (a tree)

³brash \ˈ"\ *adj* -ER/-EST [origin unknown] **1** *of wood* **:** characterized by unusual brittleness and low resistance to shock **:** BRITTLE **2 a :** prone to act in headlong fashion **:** IMPETUOUS ⟨a ~ young cavalry commander⟩ **:** FOOLHARDY ⟨no one was ~ enough to pick a fight with him⟩ **b :** made or done in haste and with little thought or regard for consequences **:** RASH ⟨~ tactics⟩ ⟨meantime you better avoid doing anything ~ —Sinclair Lewis⟩ **3 a :** full of fresh raw vitality **:** EBULLIENT ⟨a ~ and teeming frontier town⟩ **b :** inclined to be uninhibitedly showy or demonstrative **:** BUMPTIOUS ⟨a delightfully ~ comedian⟩ **4 a :** lacking restraint and discernment **:** TACTLESS ⟨he made a ~ speech . . . and told some thunderingly tasteless anecdotes about his wife —*Time*⟩ **b :** shamelessly self-assertive **:** IMPUDENT ⟨an adolescent ~ to the point of arrogance⟩ **c :** lacking refinement, polish, or finesse **:** COARSE ⟨speaking in ~ and raucous accents⟩ **5 a :** piercingly sharp **:** BLATANT ⟨a ~ squeal of brakes⟩ **b :** loudly assertive **:** BLUSTERING ⟨the ~ prophets of political utopias⟩ **6 :** marked by vivid contrast or distinctness of outline **:** BOLD ⟨~ color⟩ **syn** see SHAMELESS

brash·er doubloon \ˈbrashə(r)-\ *n, usu cap B* [after Ephraim *Brasher* or *Brashear*, 18th cent. Am. goldsmith who struck it] **:** a gold coin of the weight of a doubloon struck in New York City in 1787

brash·i·ness \ˈbrashēnəs, -raash-,-raish-, -shin-\ *n* -ES **:** the quality or state of being brashy

brash·ly \-shlē, -li\ *adv* **:** in a brash manner

brash·ness \-shnəs\ *n* -ES **:** the quality or state of being brash

brash oak *n* [³*brash*] **:** a post oak (*Quercus stellata*)

¹brashy \-shē\ *adj* -ER/-EST [³*brash* + *-y*] **:** BRASH ⟨~ timber⟩

²brashy \ˈ"\ *adj* [¹*brash* + *-y*] *Scot* **:** SHOWERY

brasier *var of* BRAZIER

bra·sil \brəˈzil\ *n* -s [MexSp, fr. Sp, brazilwood — more at BRAZIL] **:** LOGWOOD 1b

brasilein *var of* BRAZILEIN

bra·si·let·to \ˌbrazəˈled·(ˌ)ō\ *n* -s [prob. modif. of Sp *brasilete*, fr. *brasil* brazilwood — more at BRAZIL] **:** a tree that yields brazilwood

bra·si·lia *or* **bra·sí·lia** \brəˈzēlyə, -zil-\ *adj, usu cap* [fr. *Brasília*, capital of Brazil] **:** of or from Brasilia, the capital of Brazil **:** of the kind or style prevalent in Brasilia

brasilin *var of* BRAZILIN

¹brass \ˈbras, -aa(ə)-,-ai-,-ȧ-\ *n* -ES [ME *bras*, fr. OE *bræs;* akin to OFris *bress* copper, MLG *bras* metal; all fr. a prehistoric WGmc word perh. borrowed fr. a southwest Asiatic language; akin to the source of Heb & Phoenician *barzel* iron — more at FARRIER] **1 a :** a usu. yellow alloy of copper with zinc or formerly tin and sometimes small amounts of other metals that is malleable and ductile and harder and stronger than copper; *esp* **:** one consisting essentially of 50 to 95 percent copper and 5 to 50 percent zinc — compare BRONZE, COMPOSITION METAL, LATTEN, TOMBAC, WHITE BRASS **b :** an article of brass ⟨finely designed ~*es*⟩ **2 a** *or* **brasses** *pl* **:** the brass musical instruments ⟨the strings and ~ never really got together during the performance⟩ **b** *slang Brit* **:** MONEY; *esp* **:** CASH **c :** a memorial tablet (as of copper and zinc) usu. bearing an inscription and a design or picture and fastened to the floor or against the wall of a church or to a gravestone ⟨a student of late Elizabethan ~*es*⟩ **d :** bright metal fittings and equipment (as on a ship) or metal utensils and ornaments (as in a house) ⟨sailors vigorously polishing the ~⟩ **e :** a lining or step for a bearing (as on a railroad-car axle) usu. in pairs and of brass, bronze, or gunmetal **f :** empty fired cartridge shells **3 :** brazen importunity **:** impudent assurance **:** SHAMELESSNESS ⟨the ~ to borrow large sums of money⟩ **4 :** a moderate yellow that is redder and duller than colonial yellow or quince yellow and redder and deeper than mustard yellow — called also *brazen yellow* **5 a :** commissioned military officers; *esp* **:** high-ranking officers of the army or air force — compare ²BRAID 3, BRASS HAT **b :** the higher levels of civil administration or business management ⟨the top ~ of the industry⟩

²brass \ˈ"\ *adj* [ME *bras*, fr. *bras*, n.] **1 :** consisting or made of brass ⟨a ~ cannon⟩ **2 :** of the color of brass ⟨a ~ sky⟩ **3 a :** loud and resounding **:** RESONANT ⟨rich boozy ~ voices —Mollie Panter-Downes⟩ **b :** made up of or composed for brass instruments ⟨a ~ choir⟩ ⟨a ~ section⟩

³brass \ˈ"\ *n, pl* **brasses** *also* **brass** [F *brasse* length of the arms, fathom, fr. MF *brace* two arms, length of two arms — more at BRACE] **:** a unit of length equal to a fathom

bras·sage \ˈbrasij, brəˈsäzh\ *n* -s [F, act of stirring (as beer mash or fused metal), coining of money, brassage, fr. *brasser* to stir (fr. OF *bracier* to brew, fr. — assumed — VL *braciare*, fr. L *braces*, a kind of spelt, of Celt origin; akin to W *brag* malt) + *-age*] **:** a charge made to an individual under a system of free coinage for the minting of any gold or silver he may bring to the mint and usu. calculated to cover various costs — compare SEIGNIORAGE

brass ankle *n* **1** *usu cap B&A* **:** one of a group of people of mixed white, Indian, and Negro ancestry in So. Carolina — often used disparagingly **2 :** a person sometimes passing as white who is partially Negro — often used disparagingly

bras·sard \brəˈsärd, ˈbraˌs-\ *also* **bras·sart** \-r(t)\ *n* -s [F *brassard*, fr. MF, alter. of *brassal*, fr. OIt *bracciale*, fr. *braccio* arm — more at BRACCIO] **1 :** armor to protect the arm from shoulder to elbow or during the 15th and 16th centuries to protect the entire arm — compare REREBRACE, VAMBRACE **2 :** a cloth band worn around the upper arm usu. to designate its wearer as a member of a special group or service and often bearing some identifying mark

bras·sa·vo·la \ˌbrasəˈvōlə, braˈsavələ\ *n, cap* [NL, after A.M. *Brassavola* †1570 Ital. botanist] **:** a genus of tropical American epiphytic orchids (family Orchidaceae) with thick solitary leaves

brass band *n* **:** a band consisting solely or chiefly of brass and percussion instruments — compare MILITARY BAND

brassbound \ˈ≈ˌ≈\ *adj* **1 :** having trim made of brass or a metal resembling brass or fitted with parts made of brass or a metal resembling brass ⟨a ~ highboy⟩ ⟨a ~ horse pistol⟩ **2 a** (1) **:** tradition-bound and obstinately opinionated ⟨~ naval strategists⟩ (2) **:** UNCOMPROMISING, INFLEXIBLE ⟨a ~ idealist⟩ ⟨~ honesty⟩ **b :** BRAZEN, PRESUMPTUOUS ⟨~ nerve⟩

brass·bound·er \ˈbrasˈbaundə(r)\ *n* [so called fr. the gold binding on the uniform] **:** a boy bound as a cadet or apprentice on a British merchant ship who is given for a premium paid by the parents certain privileges not allowed to the common sailors

brass buttons *n* **:** the golden-yellow flower heads of a So. African composite plant (*Cotula coronopifolia*) naturalized along the coast of California and used as an ornamental

brass check *n* **:** money given somewhat secretly to a journalist for services rendered to or expected by a financial interest

brassed off \ˈbrast-\ *adj, slang Brit* **:** fed up **:** DISGRUNTLED

bras·se·rie \ˌbrasəˈrē\ *n* -s [F, fr. MF, fr. *brasser* to brew + *-erie* -ery — more at BRASSAGE] **:** a restaurant that sells beer and food ⟨breakfast at a little ~ —Frances Alda⟩

brasses *pl of* BRASS

bras·set \ˈbrasət\ *archaic var of* BRASSARD

brass-eye \ˈ≈,≈\ *n* **:** AMERICAN GOLDENEYE

brass hat *n* [so called fr. the gold braid worn on the cap] **1 :** a high-ranking officer in the armed forces **2 :** a person in a high position in civil life

bras·sia \ˈbrasēə\ *n, cap* [NL, fr. William *Brass*, 18th cent. Eng. botanical collector + NL *-ia*] **:** a genus of tropical American epiphytic orchids (family Orchidaceae) with one or two leaves to each pseudobulb and striking axillary racemes of flowers with narrow long-tailed sepals and warty lips — see SPIDER ORCHID

bras·si·ca \ˈbrasəkə\ *n* [NL, fr. L, cabbage] **1** *cap* **:** a large genus of perennial, biennial, or annual herbs (family Cruciferae) that are native to temperate parts of the Old World but now cosmopolitan in cultivation, including the cabbages, cauliflowers, turnips, mustards, and related plants, and are distinguished by the cylindrical pod tipped with a conical beak and containing a single row of seeds **2** -s **:** a plant of the genus *Brassica*

bras·si·ca·ce·ae \ˌbrasəˈkāsēˌē\ *n pl, cap* [NL, fr. *Brassica*, type genus + *-aceae*] *in some classifications* **:** a family coextensive with the Cruciferae

bras·si·ca·ceous \ˌbrasəˈkāshəs\ *adj* [NL *Brassicaceae* + E *-ous*] **:** of or relating to the family Brassicaceae

bras·si·cas·ter·ol \ˌbrasəˈkastəˌrōl, -ōl\ *n* [NL *Brassica* (genus name of *Brassica napus*) + E *sterol*] **:** a crystalline sterol $C_{28}H_{45}OH$ obtained esp. from rapeseed oil; 7,8≈dihydro-ergosterol

bras·sid·ic acid \(ˈ)braˈsidik-\ *n* [ISV *brass-* (fr. L *brassica* cabbage) + *-id* + *-ic*] **:** a white crystalline acid $C_8H_{17}CH{=}CH(CH_2)_{11}COOH$ stereoisomeric with erucic acid and formed from it (as by treatment with nitrous acid)

brass·ie *also* **brassy** *or* **brass·ey** \ˈbrasē, -aas-,-ais-,-ȧs-, -si\ *n, pl* **brass·ies** *also* **brass·eys** [¹*brass* + *-ie, -y, -ey*] **:** a wooden golf club soled with brass or other metal and used esp. for long low shots from a favorable lie on the fairway — see WOOD illustration

bras·siere \brəˈzi(ə)r, -iə *sometimes* ¦brasē¦e(ə)r *or* (ˈ)bras¦ye(ə)r *or* -raas- *or* -eə *or* -azē¦e- *or* -az¦ye-\ *n* -s [fr. obs. E, bodice, fr. obs. F *brassière* (now meaning "a kind of infant's undergarment"), fr. OF *braciere* arm protector — more at BRACER] **:** a woman's close-fitting undergarment having cups for bust support, varying in width from a band to a waist-length bodice, made with or without straps, and often boned or wired for additional support or separation; *also* **:** an adaptation of this garment for sportswear

brass·i·ly \ˈbrasəlē, -aas-,-ais-,-ȧs- -li\ *adv* [¹*brassy* + *-ly*] **:** in a brassy manner

brass·i·ness \-sēnəs, -sin-\ *n* -ES **:** the quality or state of being brassy

brass knuckles *also* **brass knucks** *n pl but sing or pl in constr* **:** a set of four metal finger rings or guards attached to a transverse piece and worn over the front of the doubled fist for use as a weapon

brass pounder *n, slang* **:** a telegraph operator

brass ring *n, slang* **:** a prize or rich opportunity ⟨missed the *brass ring* at the Philadelphia convention —Cabell Phillips⟩

brass tacks *n pl* **:** details of immediate practical importance ⟨this monograph has little to reward the tough-minded reader, in the habit of searching for *brass tacks* —Stanley Newman⟩ —usu. used in the phrase *get down to brass tacks*

brassy \ˈbrasē, -aas-,-ais-,-ȧs-, -si\ *adj* -ER/-EST [¹*brass* + *-y*] **1 a :** BRAZEN **:** coarse and impudent **:** unabashedly loud **:** BOLD ⟨~ confidence⟩ ⟨a big ~ blonde who'd already seen her best years⟩ **b :** piercingly loud **:** SHRILL, STRIDENT ⟨~ advertising⟩ ⟨~ nightclub entertainment⟩ **2** *archaic* **:** of or adorned with brass **3 :** resembling brass in hardness, ductility, or other physical property ⟨a metal with a ~ texture⟩; *esp* **:** of the color of brass **4 a :** resembling the sound of a brass instrument ⟨a ~ cough⟩ ⟨a ~ blare⟩ **b :** OVERBLOWN — used of brass musical instruments

brassy bass *n* **:** YELLOW BASS

brast *archaic past of* BURST

¹**brat** \ˈbrat, ˈbrät, -ȧth\ *n* -s [ME, coarse cloak, fr. OE *bratt*, fr. OIr *brat*; akin to W *brethyn* cloth, Bret *broz* skirt and perh. to Gk *pharos* cloth, Lith *burva*, an article of clothing] **1** *dial Brit* **a :** CLOTHING ⟨dressed in their Sunday ~*s*⟩ **b :** a coarse outer garment **:** CLOAK **2** *dial Brit* **:** a work garment (as an apron or smock) **3** *chiefly Scot* **:** SCUM ⟨~ on the porridge⟩

²**brat** \ˈbrat, *usu* -ad·+V\ *n* -s [perh. fr. ¹*brat*] **1 :** CHILD, OFFSPRING ⟨an army ~ whose father was a colonel⟩ **2 :** an ill-mannered annoying child ⟨like all little girls her age, she could be a ~ —Hamilton Basso⟩

bra·ti·sla·va \ˌbrad·əˈslävə, -rä-\ *adj, usu cap* [fr. *Bratislava*, Czechoslovakia] **:** of or from the city of Bratislava, Czechoslovakia **:** of the kind or style prevalent in Bratislava

brat·ling \ˈbratliŋ\ *n* -s [²*brat* + *-ling*] **:** a little brat

brat·tach *n* -s [ScGael *bratach*, fr. or akin to MIr, fr. *brat* cloak] *archaic Scot* **:** BANNER, FLAG

¹**brat·tice** \ˈbrad·əs, -d·ish\ *n* -s [ME *bretais, bretise, bretasce* parapet, fr. OF *bretesche* wooden tower, parapet, fr. ML *breteschia, britaschia*, prob. fr. (assumed) VL *Brittus* Breton, fr. L *Brito, Britto* Briton, Breton — more at BRITON] **:** an often temporary partition consisting of planks or cloth and used esp. in a mine to control ventilation

²**brattice** \ˈ"\ *vt* -ED/-ING/-s **:** to provide with a brattice — often used with *up*

brat·tic·er \-s(h)ə(r)\ *n* -s **:** one that erects brattices — called also *airman, braddisher, brattice man*

brat·tish \ˈbrad·¦ish, -at¦, ¦ēsh\ *adj* [²*brat* + *-ish*] **:** of, relating to, or suggestive of a brat **:** SPOILED ⟨a ~ kid brother⟩

brat·tish·ing \ˈbrad·əshiŋ\ *n* -s [*brattish* (var. of ¹*brattice*) + *-ing*] **:** a form of openwork cresting of a screen or paneling usu. in a stylized floral form

¹**brat·tle** \ˈbratᵊl\ *n* -s [prob. of imit. origin] **1** *chiefly Scot* **:** a loud clattering noise **2** *chiefly Scot* **:** a sudden forward rush

²**brattle** \ˈ"\ *vi* **brattled; brattled; brattling** \-t(ᵊ)liŋ, -lən\ **brattles** *chiefly Scot* **:** to make a rushing, clattering, or rattling sound ⟨the stream went brattling over the rocks⟩

brat·ty \ˈbrad·ē, -atē, -i\ *adj* -ER/-EST [²*brat* + *-y*] **:** BRATTISH ⟨~ behavior⟩

brat·wurst \ˈbrat,wərst, -wu̇rst; brät,vu̇rst, -vu̇(r)sht\ *n* -s [G, fr. OHG *brātwurst*, fr. *brāt, brāto* meat without waste + *wurst* sausage; akin to OE *brǣd* flesh and to OHG *werran* to confuse — more at BRAWN, WAR] **:** fresh pork sausage for frying

braul \ˈbrau̇(ə)l\ *n* -s [Romanian, fr. F *branle* — more at BRANLE] **:** a lively Romanian round dance related to the French branle

brau·la \ˈbrȯlə, -raülə\ *n* -s [NL *Braula*, genus including the bee louse] **:** BEE LOUSE

bra·una \brăˈünə\ *n* -s [Pg *braúna*] **:** a Brazilian tree (*Melanoxylon brauna*) of the family Leguminosae having fine-grained wood

brau·ne·ria \brȯiˈnirēə, brau̇ˈ-,brȯˈ-\ [NL, fr. J.J.*Bräuner*, 18th cent. Ger. botanist + NL *-ia*] *syn of* ECHINACEA

braun·ite \ˈbrau̇,nīt\ *n* -s [Councilor *Braun*, 19th cent. Ger. treasury official + E *-ite*] **:** a brittle brownish black or steel-gray mineral that consists of manganese silicate and occurs massive and as tetragonal crystals (hardness 6–6.5, sp. gr. 4.75–4.82)

braun·schwei·ger \ˈbrau̇n,shwīgə(r), -shvī, -swī-\ *n* -s *often cap* [G *Braunschweiger* (*wurst*), lit., Brunswick sausage, fr. *Braunschweiger* of Brunswick (fr. *Braunschweig* Brunswick, region and city in Germany) + *wurst* sausage] **:** smoked liver sausage

braun's holly fern \ˈbrau̇nz-\ *n, usu cap B* [after Alexander *Braun* †1877 Ger. botanist] **:** PRICKLY SHIELD FERN

braun tube \ˈbrau̇n-\ *n, usu cap B* [after Karl F. *Braun* †1918 Ger. physicist] **:** a cathode-ray tube with a diaphragm through which a beam of cathode rays can pass and a fluorescent screen on which the beam is received

¹**bra·va** \ˈbrävə, -ävə *also* -avə\ *n* -s *usu cap* [fr. *Brava*, one of the Cape Verde islands] **:** a descendant of immigrants from the Cape Verde islands chiefly of Negro and Portuguese stock resident in Massachusetts esp. on Cape Cod and around New Bedford

²**bra·va** \ˈbrä(,)vä, ˈbrȧ(,)vȧ, ˈ=ˈ=\ *n* -s [It, fem. of *bravo* excellent, courageous — more at BRAVE] **:** BRAVO — used interjectionally in applauding a woman

bra·vade \brəˈväd, -ȧd\ *n* -s [MF] *archaic* **:** BRAVADO

¹**bra·va·do** \brəˈvä(,)dō, -vȧ-\ *n* -ES [MF, OSp & OIt; MF *bravade* & OSp *bravata*, fr. OIt *bravata*, fr. fem. of *bravato*, past part. of *bravare* to threaten, challenge, provoke, show off, fr. *bravo* courageous, wild — more at BRAVE] **1 a :** showy or demonstrative conduct or action often characterized by bluster and swagger ⟨morale is not based on ~ but on deadly competence —*Coast Artillery Jour.*⟩; *also* **:** an instance of such conduct or action ⟨retreating with face-saving ~*es*⟩ **b :** the psychological quality or state conducive to or responsible for perversely capricious, ostentatiously overbearing, or noisy bluffing behavior ⟨to perform idiotic tricks out of sheer ~⟩ **2** *obs* **:** SWAGGERER

²**bravado** \ˈ"\ *vi* -ED/-ING/-ES **:** SWAGGER, BLUSTER ⟨~*ing* ward bosses⟩ **:** put on a show of bravado ⟨the mob ~*ed* a while but never got really violent⟩

bra·vais lattice \ˈbra,vä-; brəˈvä-, braˈ-\ *n, usu cap B* [after Auguste *Bravais* †1863 Fr. physicist] **:** one of the 14 possible arrays of points used esp. in crystallography and repeated periodically in 3-dimensional space so that the arrangement of points about any one of the points is identical in every respect (as in dimension and orientation) to that about any other point of the array — compare SPACE LATTICE

¹**brave** \ˈbrāv\ *adj* -ER/-EST [MF, fr. OIt & OSp *bravo* courageous, wild; OIt *bravo* prob. fr. OProv *brau* wild, fr. L *barbarus* barbarous; OSp *bravo* fr. L *barbarus* — more at BARBAROUS] **1 a :** resolute in facing odds **:** able to meet danger or endure pain or hardship without giving in to fear ⟨a ~ and respected man⟩ **b :** of, arising from, or suggestive of mastery of fear and intelligent use of faculties esp. under duress ⟨a ~ defense⟩ ⟨a ~ gesture⟩ **2 :** making a fine show or display **:** BRIGHT, COLORFUL ⟨girls decked out in ~ new dresses⟩ ⟨~ banners flying over the circus grounds⟩ **3 :** EXCELLENT, SPLENDID ⟨the business folded up despite its ~ start⟩

syn COURAGEOUS, UNAFRAID, FEARLESS, INTREPID, VALIANT, VALOROUS, DAUNTLESS, UNDAUNTED, DOUGHTY, BOLD, AUDACIOUS: BRAVE often indicates lack of fear in alarming or difficult circumstances ⟨the *brave* soldier goes to meet Death, and meets him without a shudder —Anthony Trollope⟩ ⟨he would send an explosion ship into the harbor . . . a *brave* crew would take her in at night, right up against the city, would light the fuses, and try to escape —C.S.Forester⟩ COURAGEOUS implies stout-hearted resolution in contemplating or facing danger ⟨I am afraid . . . because I do not wish to die. But my spirit masters the trembling flesh and the qualms of the mind. I am more than brave. I am *courageous* —Jack London⟩ ⟨a man is *courageous* when he does things which others might fail to do owing to fear —Bertrand Russell⟩ UNAFRAID simply indicates lack of fright or fear ⟨enjoy their homes *unafraid* of violent intrusion —Douglas MacArthur⟩ ⟨a young, daring, and creative people —a people *unafraid* of change —Archibald MacLeish⟩ FEARLESS may indicate lack of fear, or it may be more positive and suggest undismayed resolution ⟨joyous we too launch out on trackless seas *fearless* for unknown shores —Walt Whitman⟩ ⟨he gives always the impression of *fearless* sincerity . . . one always feels that he is ready to say bluntly what every one else is afraid to say —T.S.Eliot⟩ INTREPID suggests either daring in meeting danger or fortitude in enduring it ⟨with the *intrepid* woman who was his wife, and a few natives, he landed there, and set about building a house and clearing the scrub —W.S. Maugham⟩ ⟨the *intrepid* guardians of the place, hourly exposed to death, with famine worn, and suffering under many a perilous wound —William Wordsworth⟩ VALIANT suggests resolute courage and fortitude ⟨this *valiant*, steadfast people [of Yugoslavia], whose history for centuries has been a struggle for life —Sir Winston Churchill⟩ VALOROUS suggests illustrious bravery and sometimes has an archaic or romantic ring ⟨the regiment itself is a proud one, with a *valorous* record —*Infantry Jour.*⟩ DAUNTLESS emphasizes determination, resolution, and fearlessness despite danger or difficulty ⟨the *dauntless* English infantry were receiving and repelling the furious charges — W.M.Thackeray⟩ ⟨nothing appalled her *dauntless* soul — William Beckford⟩ UNDAUNTED indicates continued courage and resolution after danger, hardship, or defeat ⟨he watched them at the points of greatest danger falling under the shots from the scorpions, and others stepping *undaunted* into their places to fall in the same way —J.A.Froude⟩ DOUGHTY combines the implications of *formidable, sturdy*, and BRAVE, but may have an archaic or humorous suggestion ⟨when Fisk reached the head of the stairs leading to the board room, the *doughty* president of the endangered railway knocked him down to the ground floor —C.A. & Mary Beard⟩ ⟨so *doughty* a warrior must break a lance —V.L.Parrington⟩ BOLD may indicate a forward or defiant tendency to thrust oneself into difficult or dangerous situations ⟨it was a *bold* man who dared to walk alone through hundreds of miles of lion-infested country with nothing but a spear in his hand to seek work and adventure —Stuart Cloete⟩ ⟨these fellows who attacked the inn tonight—*bold*, desperate blades, for sure—R.L.Stevenson⟩ ⟨he knew a fool and a tyrant in high places, and was *bold* to call them by their true names —V.L.Parrington⟩ AUDACIOUS implies spirited and sometimes reckless daring ⟨the place where the fiery Ethan Allen first sketched his *audacious* move against Ticonderoga —Budd Schulberg⟩ ⟨hitherto no liberal statesman has been so *audacious* as to . . . lay profane hands on the divine right of nations to seek their own advantage at the cost of the rest —Thorstein Veblen⟩

²**brave** \ˈ"\ *vb* -ED/-ING/-s [prob. fr. MF *braver*, fr. OIt *bravare* — more at BRAVADO] *vt* **1 a** *archaic* **:** CHALLENGE, DEFY **b :** to face (something involving possible unfortunate or disastrous consequences) or endure (as hardship) usu. with self-control and mastery of fear and often with a particular objective in view ⟨men of the merchant marine who *braved* enemy torpedoes —H.S.Truman⟩ ⟨women who . . . for his sake had *braved* all social censure —Oscar Wilde⟩ **2** *obs* **:** to make showy **:** ADORN ~ *vi, archaic* **:** to make a brave show **:** SWAGGER, BLUFF, BOAST **syn** see FACE

³**brave** \ˈ"\ *n* -s [¹*brave*] **1** *archaic* **:** BRAVADO, DEFIANCE, CHALLENGE **2 :** one who is brave **:** WARRIOR ⟨none but the ~ deserves the fair —John Dryden⟩; *specif* **:** a No. American Indian warrior **3** *archaic* **:** BULLY, ASSASSIN

bravehearted \ˈ=ˌ==\ *adj* **:** having a brave heart

brave·ly *adv* **:** in a brave manner: as **a :** COURAGEOUSLY, VALIANTLY ⟨to fight ~ on the side of justice⟩ **b :** FINELY, SHOWILY, GAILY ⟨~ decked houses⟩ **c :** THRIVINGLY, PROSPEROUSLY, WELL ⟨for three years matters went ~ on —O.S. Nock⟩

brave·ness *n* -ES **:** BRAVERY 4

¹**braver** *comparative of* BRAVE

²**brav·er** \ˈbrāvə(r)\ *n* -s [²*brave* + *-er*] **:** one that braves or defies (as danger, hardship, prodigious tasks) ⟨a ~ of rules⟩

brav·ery \ˈbrāv(ə)rē, -ri\ *n* -ES [prob. fr. MF *braverie*, fr. *braver* + *-erie* -ery] **1** *archaic* **:** an act of defiance or bravado **2 a :** clothes of handsome or striking appearance **:** FINERY ⟨crowds wearing their Sunday ~⟩ **b :** something fine, showy, or of good quality **:** a thing to exhibit ⟨tourists visiting all the *braveries* of the city⟩ **3 :** fine or gaudy show **:** DISPLAY ⟨the streets strewed with flowers and full of pageantry, banners, and ~ —John Evelyn⟩ **4 :** the quality or state of being brave ⟨the ~ of troops under fire⟩ **5** *obs, pl also* **bravery :** a fine gentleman **:** BEAU

bravest *superlative of* BRAVE

brave west winds *n pl* **:** the strong westerly to northwesterly winds between the latitudes 40 degrees and 50 degrees in the oceans of the southern hemisphere

brav·ing·ly *adv* **:** in a braving manner

¹**bra·vo** \ˈbrä(,)vō, -rȧ- *sometimes* -ra-\ *n, pl* **bravos** *or* **bravoes** \-vōz\ *also* **bra·vi** \-(,)vē\ [It, fr. *bravo*, adj., wild, courageous — more at BRAVE] **:** VILLAIN, DESPERADO, CUTTHROAT ⟨the Renaissance ~ turned religious fanatic —H.J.Laski⟩; *esp* **:** a hired assassin

²**bravo** \ˈ", =ˈ=\ *n, pl* **bravos** \-vōz\ *also* **bra·vi** \ˈ=(,)vē\ [It, fr. *bravo*, adj., excellent, courageous, wild] **:** a shout of approval or approbation ⟨frenzied ~*s* for the tenor⟩ — often used interjectionally in applauding a performance (as of an artist or speaker); sometimes restricted in use to a man; compare BRAVA

³**bravo** *like* ²BRAVO\ *vt* -ED/-ING/-ES **:** to show approbation or admiration of esp. by shouts of *bravo* ⟨a wildly ~*ing* audience⟩

⁴**bravo** *like* ¹BRAVO\ *usu cap* — a communications code word for the letter *b*

bra·vo·ite \ˈbrä,vō,īt\ *n* -s [José J. *Bravo* †1928 Peruvian mineralogist + E *-ite*] **:** a mineral $(Ni,Fe)S_2$ consisting of a nickel sulfide containing iron related to pyrite

bra·vu·ra \brəˈv(y)u̇rə, -ürə *also* brăˈ- *or* brȧˈ-\ *n* -s *often attrib* [It, lit., bravado, bravery, fr. *bravare* to show off + *-ura* -ure — more at BRAVADO] **1 a :** a florid brilliant virtuoso musical composition ⟨the stunning ~*s* of Verdi⟩ **b :** the virtuosic execution of a musical composition or passage by a performer **2 :** a show of daring or brilliancy ⟨he organized all sorts of ~ stunts, the more senseless or dangerous the better —Charles Ingle⟩ **3 :** an aggressively confident and commanding air ⟨the sinister smiling figure . . . making a ~ exit before the vote —*New Republic*⟩

¹**braw** \ˈbrȯ, ˈbrȧ\ *adj* -ER/-EST [alter. of earlier *brawf* brave, fr. MF *brave* — more at BRAVE] **1** *chiefly Scot* **a** (1) **:** FINE, SPLENDID ⟨a ~ house⟩ ⟨a ~ new gown⟩ (2) **:** PLEASANT, FINE — used esp. of the weather ⟨a ~ night⟩ **b** *of a person* (1) **:** GOOD, NICE ⟨my ~ lad⟩ (2) **:** HANDSOME, ATTRACTIVE ⟨a ~ gallant⟩ (3) **:** well dressed **2** *chiefly Scot* **:** PRETTY ⟨it costs a ~ penny⟩ ⟨a ~ fight⟩

²**braw** \ˈ"\ *adv, Scot* **:** VERY, QUITE ⟨not feeling ~ well⟩

¹**brawl** \ˈbrȯl\ *vb* -ED/-ING/-s [ME *brawlen*; perh. akin to D & LG *brallen* to brag] *vi* **1 :** to quarrel usu. noisily **:** wrangle violently ⟨when statesmen ~*ed* with each other outrageously —*Amer. Guide Series: Texas*⟩ **2 :** to complain loudly **:** raise a clamor ⟨mobs ~*ing* about unfair rationing of food⟩ **3 :** to make a loud confused noise (as of water of a rapid stream running over stones) ⟨the Miami river . . . ~*ed* over 25 feet of rapids in the North Fork —Marjory S. Douglas⟩ ~ *vt* **1** *obs* **:** to call down violently **:** REVILE **2 :** to shout (as orders) in a loud often hoarse voice ⟨sergeants ~*ing* out commands⟩ **3** *archaic* **:** to force or drive by shouting or reviling

²**brawl** \ˈ"\ *n* -s [ME, fr. *brawlen*, v.] **1 a :** a loud, angry, or disorderly quarrel ⟨a ~ between husband and wife that kept the whole neighborhood awake⟩ **b** (1) **:** a rough noisy and often prolonged hand-to-hand fight ⟨a barroom ~⟩ (2) *slang* **:** a social affair **:** DANCE, PARTY; *esp* **:** a drinking party ⟨she always tosses a perfectly savage ~ for all the . . . students —A.O.Myrer⟩ **2 :** a loud tumultuous noise ⟨the spring run became quite a trout brook and its tiny murmur a loud ~ —John Burroughs⟩

syn BROIL, RIOT, FRACAS, MELEE, ROW, RUMPUS, SCRAP: BRAWL indicates a noisy fight or quarrel with racket, recrimination, hurly-burly, and angry blows ⟨a howling *brawl* amongst vicious hoodlums —Jean Stafford⟩ ⟨the settlers in the river towns shivered excitedly at the uproar of the loggers' drunken *brawls*, the shattering of the tavern's glassware —*Amer. Guide Series: Minn.*⟩ BROIL indicates a disordered, confused turmoil, conflict, or fight without clear issues or demarcation between contestants ⟨but village mirth breeds contests, *broils*, and blows —P.B.Shelley⟩ ⟨plunging us in all the *broils* of the European nations —Thomas Jefferson⟩ RIOT may indicate a turbulent tumultuous uproar participated in by a number of persons with violent action breaking civil peace ⟨the draft *riots* in Civil War days⟩ ⟨angered supporters of both teams swarmed out of the stands and the game turned into a *riot*⟩ FRACAS may apply to an excited disturbance or noisy quarrel, with or without blows ⟨cowboys hurt in a gambling *fracas* —Laura Krey⟩ MELEE suggests a swirling unclear series of hand-to-hand conflicts or something similar ⟨in such a *melee*, of course, no chronicler could be very clear, and the more active of the knights are much confused —E.V. Lucas⟩ ⟨in 1934, 8000 lettuce pickers struck; when the police attempted to break up picket lines, the resultant *melee* in which blood was shed made headlines —*Amer. Guide Series: Calif.*⟩ ROW applies to any noisy demonstration or fight; RUMPUS may intensify suggestions of disturbance and commotion; SCRAP indicates a fight, often inconsequential, or a noisy sharp quarrel ⟨a crockery-smashing family *row* —Edward Sackville-West & Desmond Shawe-Taylor⟩ ⟨but the *row* went a good deal deeper than a mere squabble in the children's schoolroom —Alan Moorehead⟩ ⟨such a *rumpus* that everybody in the neighborhood took sides —L.C.Douglas⟩ ⟨a bare-knuckled political *scrap* —*New Republic*⟩

³**brawl** *var of* BRANLE

brawl·er \ˈbrȯlə(r)\ *n* -s [ME, fr. *brawlen* to brawl + *-er*] **:** one that brawls

brawling *adj* **1 :** noisily quarrelsome ⟨~ neighbors⟩ **2 :** extremely noisy and tumultuous ⟨a ~ hurricane⟩ ⟨a ~ torrent⟩ **3 :** violently active **:** vibrant and teeming ⟨a ~ young democracy⟩ — **brawl·ing·ly** *adv*

brawl·some \ˈbrȯlsəm\ *adj* [²*brawl* + *-some*] **:** QUARRELSOME

¹**braw·ly** *also* **braw·lie** \ˈbrȯli, ˈbrȧli\ *adv* [*braw* + *-ly, -lie*] *Scot* **:** very well **:** EXCELLENTLY ⟨he knew the way ~⟩

²**brawly** \ˈbrȯlē, -li\ *adj* -ER/-EST [²*brawl* + *-y*] **1 :** BRAWLING ⟨the soldiers would . . . get drunk and ~ —Meyer Berger⟩ **2 :** characterized by brawls or brawling ⟨hitherto politically ~ Brazil —F.H.Gervasi⟩

¹**brawn** \ˈbrȯn\ *n* -s [ME, fr. MF *braon* fleshy part, muscle, of Gmc origin; akin to OE *brǣd* flesh, OS *brādo* ham, calf of the leg, OHG *brāto* meat without waste, ON *brāth* meat] **1 a :** full strong muscles esp. of the arm or leg **b :** a protuberant muscular part (as on the arm, buttock, or calf) **c** (1) **:** well-developed or powerful-appearing muscles ⟨a youngster with a good build and fine ~⟩ (2) **:** muscular strength ⟨their job — loading and unloading cargo — calls for ~ —*N.Y. Times*⟩ ⟨brains against ~⟩ **d** *obs* **:** thickened or calloused skin **2** *dial Brit* **:** BOAR **3 a** *obs* **:** animal flesh used as food **b** *Brit* **:** flesh of a boar **:** PORK **c :** a product made from chopped, cooked, and molded edible parts of pig's head, feet, legs, and sometimes tongue **4 :** MANPOWER ⟨the West Indian Negro contributed about 60 percent of the ~ required to build the Panama canal —F.J.Haskin⟩

²**brawn** \ˈ"\ *vt* -ED/-ING/-s **1** *obs* **:** to make brawny **2** *Brit* **:** to fatten (a pig) for slaughter

brawned \ˈbrȯnd\ *adj* [¹*brawn* + *-ed*] **:** BRAWNY — **brawnedness** \-nnəs *also* -ndnəs\ *n* -ES

brawn·i·ness \ˈbrȯnēnəs, -nin-\ *n* -ES **:** the quality or state of being brawny

brawny \ˈbrȯnē, -ni\ *adj* -ER/-EST **1 :** having large strong muscles **:** MUSCULAR, STRONG ⟨~ arms and legs⟩ ⟨~ stevedores⟩ ⟨~ girls, wide as they were tall —Truman Capote⟩ **2 :** swollen and hard ⟨a ~ and purple infected foot⟩

braws \ˈbrȯz, ˈbrȧz\ *n pl* [*braw* + *-s*] *chiefly Scot* **:** best clothes

braxy \ˈbraksē\ *n* -ES [origin unknown] **1 :** a malignant edema of sheep that involves gastrointestinal invasion by a spore-forming bacterium (*Clostridium septicum*), produces an enterotoxemia characterized by staggering, convulsions, coma, and death, and is common in Iceland, Scotland, and Norway — compare BLACK DISEASE **2 :** a sheep dead from natural causes, esp. from disease; *also* **:** mutton from such a carcass

¹**bray** \ˈbrā\ *vb* -ED/-ING/-s [ME *brayen*, fr. OF *braire* to cry, make a noise, fr. (assumed) VL *bragere*, of Celt origin; akin to MIr *braigid* he breaks wind, t-air-*brech* crashing noise; akin to L *fragor* crashing noise, *frangere* to break — more at BREAK] *vi* **1** *obs* **:** to cry out (as in pain) **2 a** *of a donkey* **:** to utter a characteristic loud harsh cry **b :** to utter a loud harsh sound resembling or suggesting that made by a donkey ⟨the sea lions ~*ing* and moving in the green sapphire waters —Josephine Johnson⟩ ⟨cannon roared, trumpets ~*ed* —S.E. Morison⟩ ⟨the politicians wept, ranted, and ~*ed*⟩ ~ *vt* **:** to utter, play, or send forth loudly, harshly, or discordantly ⟨a brass band ~*ing* the national anthem⟩ ⟨she ~*ed* out her grievances before the judge⟩

²**bray** \ˈ"\ *n* -s [ME, fr. OF *brait*, fr. *braire*] **1 :** a donkey's characteristic cry **2 :** a loud or discordant noise resembling a donkey's bray ⟨the ~ and roar of traffic⟩

³**bray** \ˈ"\ *vt* -ED/-ING/-s [ME *brayen*, fr. MF *broiier*, fr. OF, of Gmc origin; akin to OHG *brehhan* to break — more at BREAK] **1 a :** to pound, crush, or grind small and fine ⟨~ seeds in a mortar⟩ **b :** to wear down as if by this process ⟨sorrow . . . had ~*ed* her —B.A.Williams⟩ **2 :** to spread thin ⟨~ printing ink⟩

⁴**bray** \ˈ"\ *or* **brey** \ˈ"\ *n* -s **:** a heraldic representation of a brake for braying flax — called also *brake, hemp-brake*

⁵**bray** *var of* ¹BRAE

bray·er \ˈbrāə(r)\ *n* -s [³*bray* + *-er*] **:** one that brays or grinds: as **a** *archaic* **:** a pestle with which ink was brayed before it was dabbed on the printing surface **b :** a printer's hand inking roller

brayer b

bra·yera \brəˈyerə, ˈbrāərə\ *n* -s [fr. NL *Brayera* (genus of trees in some classifications containing *Hagenia abyssinica*) after *Brayer* fl1823 Fr. physician] **:** the dried pistillate flowers of an ornamental Abyssinian tree (*Hagenia abyssinica*) sometimes used as an anthelmintic

bra·yer·in \brəˈyerən, ˈbrāər-\ *n* -s [NL *Brayera* + E *-in*] **:** KOSIN

bray·ton cycle \ˈbrātᵊn-\ *n, usu cap B* [after *Brayton* fl1873 Am. inventor] **:** a thermodynamic cycle composed of two adiabatic and two isobaric changes in alternate order — called also *Joule's cycle*

¹**braze** *vb* -ED/-ING/-s [fr. *brass*, after such pairs as E *glass: glaze*] *obs* **:** to make brazen **:** HARDEN

²**braze** \ˈbrāz\ *vb* -ED/-ING/-s [prob. fr. F *braser*, fr. OF, to burn, fr. *brese* live coals, prob. of non-IE origin; akin to the source of OSp *brasa* live coal, OIt *bragia*] **:** to solder with an alloy (as hard solder or brass) that is relatively infusible as compared with common solder

³**braze** \ˈ"\ *n* -s **:** a brazed joint

¹**bra·zen** \ˈbrāzᵊn\ *adj* [ME *brasen*, fr. OE *bræsen*, fr. *bræs* brass + *-en* — more at BRASS] **1 :** made of brass ⟨priests drinking from ~ cups⟩ **2 :** sounding harsh and loud like resounding brass **:** BRASSY, CLANGOROUS ⟨the horrible ~ voice of the fire bell —Elmer Davis⟩ **3 a** (1) **:** lacking or insensitive to moral principle **:** UNSCRUPULOUS ⟨a ~ criminal⟩ (2) **:** done in the open or in plain sight with or as if with

complete scorn of public opinion, the common good, or ethical principle ⟨~ aggression⟩ ⟨a ~ violation of the rules⟩ **b :** lacking modesty : SHAMELESS ⟨a ~ hussy⟩ **4 a :** unabashedly frank : lacking delicacy or qualifications ⟨a ~ tongue⟩ ⟨~ announcements⟩ **b :** loud and showy : GAUDY ⟨brand new ~ store fronts⟩ **5 a :** of the color of polished brass : as bright or shiny as polished brass ⟨a ~ sky at sunset⟩ **b :** EXTREME, INTENSE ⟨~ heat⟩ **syn** see SHAMELESS

²**brazen** \"\ *vt* **brazened; brazened; brazening** \-z(ᵊ)niŋ\ **brazens :** to face (an accusation or an accuser) with resolution or defiance or impudence : carry off (a situation) boldly and imperturbably — used usu. with *out* or *through* and commonly in the phrase *brazen it out* ⟨would the prisoner ~ it out or break down and confess⟩

brazenface \'==,=\ *n* **:** an impudent or shameless person

bra·zen-faced \'==¦fāst\ *adj* **:** IMPUDENT, SHAMELESS — **bra·zen·fac·ed·ly** \¦==¦fāsədlē, -āstlē, -li\ *adv*

brazen law of wages : IRON LAW OF WAGES

bra·zen·ly *adv* **:** in a brazen manner

bra·zen·ness \'brāzᵊn(n)əs\ *n* -ES **:** the quality or state of being brazen

brazen yellow *n* **:** BRASS 4

braz·er \'brāzə(r)\ *n* -S [²*braze* + *-er*] **:** one that brazes metal parts

¹**bra·zier** *or* **bra·sier** \'brāzhə(r) *also* -zēə- *sometimes* 'brazē-\ *n* -S [ME *brasier*, fr. *bras* brass + *-ier* — more at BRASS] **:** one that works in brass

²**brazier** *or* **brasier** \"\ *n* -S [F *brasier*, fr. OF, fire of hot coals, fr. *brese* live coals — more at BRAZE] **1 :** a pan for holding burning coals **2 :** a cooking utensil in which the food to be cooked is exposed to the source of heat (as live coals or electricity) through a wire grill

brazier

brazier-head rivet *n* [²*brazier*] **:** a light buttonhead rivet with a wide shallow head used esp. on aircraft

bra·ziery \-zh(ə)rē,-zēərē\ *n* -ES [¹*brazier* + *-y*] **:** work done by a brazier

¹**bra·zil** \brə'zil\ *n* -S [ME *brasile*, fr. OSp or OPg *brasil*, fr. *brasa* live coals; fr. the color of the wood — more at BRAZE] **1 :** BRAZILWOOD **2** *or* **brazil red :** a dark reddish orange that is yellower, stronger, and slightly darker than average lacquer red and redder and stronger than ocher red or burnt sienna — called also *roset*

²**brazil** \"\ *adj, usu cap* [fr. *Brazil*, country in So. America] **:** of or from Brazil : of the kind or style prevalent in Brazil

³**braz·il** \'brazəl\ *n* -S [prob. alter. of *brass;* fr. its yellow color] *dial Eng* **:** iron pyrites; *also* **:** coal containing much pyrites

bra·zil·ein *also* **bra·sil·ein** \brə'zilēən\ *n* -S [ISV *brazilin*, *brasilin* + *-ein;* prob. orig. formed as G *brasilein*] **:** a red crystalline dye $C_{16}H_{12}O_5$ — see BRAZILIN

braz·i·lette \¦brazə¦let, ,brazə'led·ē\ *n* -S [prob. fr. Sp *brasilete* brazilwood — more at BRASILETTO] **:** the heartwood of a tropical American brazilwood that yields brazilin

braziletto *var of* BRASILETTO

¹**bra·zil·ian** \brə'zilyən\ *adj, usu cap* [*Brazil*, the country + E *-ian*] **1 :** of, relating to, or characteristic of Brazil **2 :** of, relating to, or characteristic of the people of Brazil **3 :** of, relating to, or constituting the subdivision of the Neotropical biogeographic region that includes tropical So. America

²**brazilian** \"\ *n* -S *cap* **1 :** a native or inhabitant of Brazil **2 :** BRAZILIAN PORTUGUESE

brazilian arrowroot *n, usu cap B* **:** a starch obtained from the bitter cassava and used as a food or industrially as a size, glaze, or laundry starch — compare TAPIOCA

brazilian boxwood *n, usu cap B* **:** a Brazilian tree (*Euxylophora paraensis*) with a lustrous yellowish white wood

brazilian copal *n, usu cap B* **:** copal from the courbaril tree

brazilian cotton *n, usu cap B* **:** KIDNEY COTTON

brazilian duck *n, usu cap B* **:** MUSCOVY DUCK

brazilian emerald *n, usu cap B* **:** a transparent green variety of tourmaline

brazilian guava *n, usu cap B* **:** a So. American tree (*Psidium guineense*) yielding a fruit similar to the true guava

brazilian ipecac *n, usu cap B* **:** IPECAC 2a

bra·zil·ian·ite \brə'zilyə,nīt\ *n* -S [¹*brazilian* + E *-ite;* fr. its discovery in Brazil] **:** a mineral $NaAl_3(PO_4)_2(OH)_4$ consisting of a basic phosphate of sodium and aluminum

brazilian jalap *n, usu cap B* **:** PIPTOSTEGIA ROOT

brazilian mahogany *n, usu cap B* **1 :** either of two Brazilian timber trees (*Plathymenia foliolosa* and *P. reticulata*) of the family Leguminosae with yellowish brown wood **2 :** JEQUITIBA

brazilian morning glory *n, usu cap B* **:** an ornamental Brazilian pink-flowered vine (*Ipomoea setosa*) densely covered with bristly purplish hairs

brazilian pepper tree *n, usu cap B* **:** a Brazilian evergreen resinous tree (*Schinus terebinthifolius*) with dark green leaflets and a bright red fruit

brazilian pine *n, usu cap B* **:** PARANÁ PINE

brazilian portuguese *n, usu cap B&P* **:** the Portuguese language as spoken or written in Brazil

brazilian rhatany *n, usu cap B* **:** PARÁ RHATANY

brazilian rosewood *n, usu cap B* **:** an important Brazilian timber tree (*Dalbergia nigra*) yielding a heavy hard dark-colored wood streaked with black — called also *caviuna wood, jacaranda*

brazilian sapphire *n, usu cap B* **:** a transparent blue variety of tourmaline

brazilian sassafras *n, usu cap B* **:** a So. American tree (*Nectandra puchury*) whose seed is the pichurim bean

brazilian shrimp *n, usu cap B* **:** a large reddish brown shrimp (*Penaeus aztecus*) common in the Gulf of Mexico that is a leading economic species along the gulf coast — called also *brown shrimp, red shrimp*

brazilian spiderflower *or* **brazilian spiderwort** *n, usu cap B* **:** any of certain Brazilian shrubs of the genus *Tibouchina* (as *T. semidecandra*) used in cultivation and having dark green leaves with conspicuous veins and clusters of large purple flowers

brazilian tea *also* **brazil tea** *n, usu cap B* **:** any of several substitutes for tea: as **a :** the dried leaves of a tropical shrub (*Lantana pseudothea*) **b :** the dried leaves of either of two tropical plants (*Stachytarpheta indica* and *S. jamaicensis*) **c :** MATÉ 2,3

brazilian teal *n, usu cap B* **:** a small brightly colored wild duck (*Amazonetta braziliensis* or *Anas brasiliensis*) of So. American tropical forests highly esteemed as a table bird

brazilian walnut *n, usu cap B* **1 :** IMBUIA **2 :** a Brazilian tree (*Cordia goldieana*) yielding a wood similar to black walnut

brazilian yellowwood *n, usu cap B* **:** BRAZILIAN MAHOGANY 1

braz·i·lin *also* **bras·i·lin** \'brazələn, brə'zil-\ *n* -S [F *brésiline*, fr. *brésil* brazilwood (fr. OF *bresil*, prob. fr. OSp *brasil*) + *-ine* — more at BRAZIL] **:** a white or pale yellow phenolic compound $C_{16}H_{14}O_5$ obtained from brazilwoods of the genus *Caesalpinia* and used esp. formerly in dyeing because of its ready oxidation to brazilein

brazil nut *n, usu cap B* [²*brazil*] **1** *also* **brazil-nut tree :** a tall So. American tree (*Bertholletia excelsa*) that bears large globular capsules each containing several closely packed roughly triangular nuts **2 :** any of the brown-shelled white-fleshed nuts borne in the fruit of a brazil nut — called also *cream nut, niggertoe, para nut*

brazil red *n* [¹*brazil*] **:** BRAZIL 2

brazils *pl of* BRAZIL

brazil wax *n, usu cap B* [²*brazil*] **:** CARNAUBA WAX

bra·zil·wood \brə'zil,wu̇d\ *n* [¹*brazil* + *wood*] **1 :** the heavy wood of any of various tropical trees of the genus *Caesalpinia* (as *C. sappan, C. braziliensis*, and *C. crista*) used as red and purple dyewoods and in cabinetwork — see DYE table I (under *Natural Red 24*) **2 :** the wood of a So. American tree (*Haematoxylon brasilletto*) used in the American dye trade

brazing metal *n* [fr. gerund of ²*braze*] **:** the cementing metal used in brazing — compare ²BRAZE, HARD SOLDER, SILVER SOLDER

braz·za·ville \'brazə,vil, -vēl\ *adj, usu cap* [fr. *Brazzaville*, Congo Republic] **:** of or from Brazzaville, Congo Republic : of the kind or style prevalent in Brazzaville

brd *abbr* **1** board **2** braid

brea \'brāə\ *n* -S [AmerSp, fr. Sp, tar, fr. OSp, fr. *brear* to tar, fr. OF *brayer*, fr. ON *bræetha*, fr. *brāth* tar — more at BREATH] **1 a** (1) **:** a tree of the genus *Canarium* (2) **:** the soft resin obtained from it — compare ELEMI a **b :** a resinous thorny tree (*Caesalpinia praecox*) of Chile and Argentina that yields a pale brown gum **2 :** MALTHA

breac·an \'brakən\ [ScGael — more at BRECHAN] *Scot var of* BRECHAN

¹**breach** \'brēch\ *n* -ES [ME *breche*, alter. (influenced by OF *breche* breach, opening made by breaking, fr. OHG *brecha*) of OE *bryce* breach, fracture, breaking; akin to OE *brecan* to break — more at BREAK] **1 a** (1) **:** infraction or violation of a law, obligation, tie, code, or standard ⟨by this ~ of trust they forfeit the power the people had put into their hands —John Locke⟩ (2) **:** unfulfillment or nonfeasance constituting infraction ⟨a ~ of duty⟩ ⟨a ~ of church observances⟩ **b** *archaic* **:** INFRINGEMENT, ENCROACHMENT **c :** the state of being ignored : NONOBSERVANCE, DESUETUDE — used only in the phrase *honored more in the breach than in the observance* **d :** BREACH OF PROMISE **e :** the act of breaking or of aiding another to break into or out of ⟨prison ~⟩ **2 a :** a broken, ruptured, or torn condition : a place showing rupture, split, or fissure ⟨causing a ~ of the skin or bloodshed —G.G.Coulton⟩ ⟨turning over the picture of the ark with too much haste, I unhappily made a ~ in its ingenious fabric —Charles Lamb⟩ **b :** an opening or gap (as in a wall, rampart, or other fortification) made by or as if by battering ⟨once more unto the ~, dear friends, . . . or close the wall up with our English dead —Shak.⟩ ⟨the fatal ~ in the scholastic wholeness —H.O.Taylor⟩ **c :** a position entailing heavy fighting or strenuous exertion : a necessitous situation calling for urgent action ⟨although a thousand fall, there are always some to go into the ~ —R.L. Stevenson⟩ ⟨stepping into the ~ when his leader died⟩ **d :** a way made through a minefield by removing or exploding mines **3 a :** an open break in accustomed friendly or amiable relations : a notable division over an issue : an estranging difference : DISAGREEMENT, QUARREL ⟨a trivial misunderstanding causing a ~ between friends⟩ ⟨a gesture which healed a ~ between the two branches of the family —*Current Biog.*⟩ **b :** an interruption or suspension of something expected to continue : HIATUS ⟨imperil that success by any ~ in the continuity of worship —Compton Mackenzie⟩ ⟨the ~*es* of agrarian routine —F.M.Stenton⟩ **c :** a marked difference : a difference or lack of accord that prevents unity or integration ⟨the traditional ~ between the artist and the Puritan —S.P.Sherman⟩ **4 a :** the action of the breaking of waves or of the sweeping or pounding of breakers **b** *obs* **:** SURF, BREAKERS **c** *obs* **:** CREEK **5 :** the leap of a whale out of water

syn INFRACTION, VIOLATION, TRANSGRESSION, TRESPASS, INFRINGEMENT, CONTRAVENTION: BREACH usually occurs with modifying phrases specifying the thing offended against ⟨a *breach* of faith⟩ ⟨a *breach* of discipline⟩ ⟨a *breach* of the peace⟩ INFRACTION is more often used than BREACH for the breaking of a law or for an action contravening an obligation ⟨an *infraction* of a traffic regulation⟩ ⟨an *infraction* of school rules⟩ ⟨an *infraction* of a citizen's guaranteed rights⟩ VIOLATION adds the notion of overt disregard of law or the rights of others and often suggests the exercise of force ⟨a *violation* of traffic rules⟩ ⟨a *violation* of fundamental principles of good government⟩ ⟨renewed hostilities constitute an unequivocal *violation* of a peace treaty⟩ TRANSGRESSION applies to any act that goes beyond the limits of a law, rule, or order, usu. a moral law or commandment ⟨mistakes of this sort are resisted as any aesthetic *transgression* might be resisted — as being somehow incongruous —Edward Sapir⟩ ⟨what my father made clear to us as the very crux of our *transgressions* was that we had discredited our bringing up —Mary Austin⟩ ⟨a penalty pronounced upon Eve for her *transgression* in the garden of Eden —J.C. Krantz⟩ TRESPASS also implies an overstepping of prescribed ground but suggests encroachment upon another's rights, comfort, or property ⟨visitors had best avoid *trespass* on the lowlands lying west of the Roosevelt mansion —Morris Kaplan⟩ ⟨*trespass* across tribal frontiers is dangerous unless previous relations are friendly and the arrival is frankly announced —C.D.Forde⟩ ⟨the nature and degree of any *trespass* upon academic integrity—W.A.Dorrance⟩ INFRINGEMENT is sometimes interchangeable with INFRACTION ⟨an *infringement* of the law⟩ Often it implies trespass rather than violation and is the usual term in reference to encroachment upon a legally protected right or privilege ⟨an *infringement* of a patent⟩ ⟨an *infringement* upon a citizen's civil rights⟩ CONTRAVENTION implies a going contrary to the law or an act in defiance of what is regarded as right, lawful, or obligatory ⟨acts in direct *contravention* of the provisions of a treaty⟩ ⟨in flagrant *contravention* of commonly accepted academic principles and practices —*Key Reporter*⟩ ⟨so many judgments of common sense in *contravention* to the prevailing theories of our age —Reinhold Niebuhr⟩

syn BREAK, SPLIT, SCHISM, RENT, RUPTURE, RIFT: of these terms BREACH is the most general, carrying no implication of the cause or seriousness of the separation ⟨the widening *breach* between himself and his mother —Thomas Hardy⟩ ⟨flaws in the great structure, which were to widen into *breaches* —John Buchan⟩ BREAK signifies a breach but carries the idea of strain as a cause ⟨a *break* between the formerly friendly countries over the disposition of foreign aid⟩ SPLIT may imply a complete and usually irreparable breach ⟨he became involved in the *split* of the Socialist party into the "broad" and "narrow" factions —*Current Biog.*⟩ ⟨too wide a *split* in the party's ranks to agree on an acceptable candidate⟩ SCHISM implies a clear-cut division of one group, often religious, into two groups, usually opposed, and a consequent discord and dissension between them ⟨their families were on opposite sides of a *schism* that had occurred within the Society of Friends —*Current Biog.*⟩ ⟨to confirm its divisions, and to render apparently irreparable the *schism* in our culture —Hilaire Belloc⟩ ⟨when the *schism* between craft and industrial unionism resulted in the formation of the CIO —*Amer. Guide Series: Tenn.*⟩ RENT implies the literal sense of an opening, as in a fabric, made by tearing, even in its extended meaning suggesting the violence of the action and the jagged result ⟨the violent squabble over the chairmanship caused a very visible *rent* in the generally amicable relations of the club members⟩ ⟨a *rent* in the social fabric —Gilbert Millstein⟩ RUPTURE is like BREACH but carries more clearly the sense of a break in relations between people or groups, sometimes suggesting an actual break not clearly apparent ⟨the *rupture* of diplomatic relations —*N.Y.Times*⟩ ⟨a disagreement between father and son led to a nine-year *rupture* of their relations —*Current Biog.*⟩ ⟨there was no violent *rupture* of relations; the physicians and surgeons must simply have drifted apart again —Harvey Graham⟩ RIFT, carrying the idea of a breach by some natural process as the cracking of the earth, often suggests a small breach likely to get larger ⟨this little *rift* it was that had widened to a now considerable breach —H.G.Wells⟩ ⟨relations between the two groups were harmonious until politics caused a *rift* —*Amer. Guide Series: Texas*⟩

²**breach** \"\ *vb* -ED/-ING/-ES *vt* **1 a :** to make a breach in : smash a gap through : make a hole in by attrition ⟨siege artillery would have been needed to ~ the walls of the city —C.S.Forester⟩ ⟨~*ing* a dam⟩ **b :** to effect an opening in : serve successfully as an entering wedge in ⟨~ the wall of racial segregation⟩ ⟨~*ing* his distant reserve⟩ **c :** to wear or cut an opening in esp. by erosion ⟨where the chalk of the South Downs is ~*ed* by the inlet —L.D.Stamp⟩ **d :** to make a gap through (an enemy minefield) **2 :** BREAK, VIOLATE ⟨the Supreme Court . . . held that our contract had not been impaired but ~*ed* —Hodding Carter⟩ ⟨~*ing* disastrously the whole structure of ideas by which . . . they live and govern —Walter Millis⟩ **~** *vi* **:** to break the water by leaping out ⟨they saw a whale spouting and ~*ing* —Charles Kingsley⟩

breach·er \'brēchə(r)\ *n* -S **:** one that makes or commits a breach

breaches *pl of* BREACH, *pres 3d sing of* BREACH

breach of arrest : the military offense committed by one in arrest of leaving without authority the limits within which he is ordered to remain

breach of contract : failure without legal reason to comply with the terms of a contract

breach of faith : a betrayal of confidence or trust

breach of prison : PRISON BREACH

breach of privilege : a violation of the rights of a privileged assembly

breach of promise : violation of one's plighted word, esp. of a promise to marry

breach of the peace : disorderly conduct that disturbs the public peace

breach of trust : violation by a trustee of the terms of a trust (as by fraudulent appropriation or careless handling of funds)

breachway \'=,=\ *n* **:** a connecting channel

breachy \'brēchē\ *adj* -ER/-EST [²*breach* + *-y*] **1** *now dial* **:** apt to break fences or be wild — used of domestic animals **2** *dial Eng* **:** BRACKISH

¹**bread** \'bred\ *n* -S *often attrib* [ME *breed*, fr. OE *brēad* crumb, bread; akin to OHG *brōt* bread, ON *brauth* bread, OE *brēowan* to brew — more at BREW] **1 a :** a food made of a dough of flour or meal from grain with added liquid, shortening, and a leavening agent, the dough being kneaded, shaped, allowed to rise, and baked **b :** bread made from flours other than those of cereals ⟨potato ~⟩ **c :** a loaf, biscuit, or cake of sweetened bread dough enriched with eggs and fruit ⟨holiday ~⟩ ⟨Easter ~⟩ **2 :** a loaf, roll, or portion of bread ⟨an altar ~⟩ ⟨the ~*s* for the communicants⟩ **3 a :** FOOD ⟨give us this day our daily ~ —Mt 6:11 (AV)⟩ **b :** LIVELIHOOD; *esp* **:** simple necessities without extras ⟨earning his ~ as a laborer⟩ **c** (1) **:** a sustaining element ⟨the price of the ~ of health —Mary B. Spahr⟩ (2) **:** something that is received or accepted in a way felt to resemble accepting or eating food **d** *slang* **:** MONEY **syn** see LIVING —**bread upon the waters :** resources chanced or charitable deeds performed without expectation of return

²**bread** \"\ *vt* -ED/-ING/-S **1 :** to cover with bread crumbs before cooking ⟨a ~*ed* pork chop⟩ **2 :** to provide with a supply of bread

³**bread** \'brēd\ *var of* BREDE

bread and butter *n* **1 :** sliced bread spread with butter **2 a :** ¹BREAD 3b **b :** a sustaining unit or element : source of sustaining income ⟨plainer products being the *bread and butter* of the industry⟩ **3 a :** a toadflax (*Linaria vulgaris*) **b :** a greenbrier (*Smilax rotundifolia*) **syn** see LIVING

bread-and-butter \¦=¦=¦=\ *adj* [*bread and butter*] **1** *now chiefly Brit* **:** ADOLESCENT **:** marked by the weakness, naïveté, or forcelessness of a juvenile : SCHOOLGIRLISH **2 a :** associated or connected with earning a livelihood, making money, or other mundane practical purposes ⟨a practical *bread-and-butter* education⟩ ⟨too busy with the *bread-and-butter* side of life to attend many social functions —A.T.Weaver⟩ **b :** STAPLE, SUSTAINING **:** dependable as a source of income often through being in steady demand ⟨concentrating on *bread-and-butter* products rather than fads⟩ ⟨don't overlook a *bread-and-butter* item that could be boosting your dollar volume —*Circle & Monogram*⟩ **3 :** sent or given by way of thanks for hospitality ⟨a *bread-and-butter* letter to his hostess⟩

bread-and-butter pickle *n* **:** a pickle relish of sliced cucumbers and onions

bread-and-butter plate *n* **:** a plate five to six inches in diameter for individual servings of bread and butter — called also *butter plate*

bread and circuses *n pl* [trans. of L *panis et circenses*] **:** food and entertainment offered by a government (as a dictatorship) to soothe discontent

breadbasket \'=,==\ *n* **1** *slang* **:** STOMACH **2 :** a typically grain-producing agricultural area that provides much of the food needed by other areas ⟨these wide plains are the ~ of the nation⟩

breadboard \'=,=\ *n* **1 :** a board on which dough is kneaded or rolled or bread cut **2 :** a board on which electric or electronic circuit diagrams may be laid out and experimental circuits constructed

bread crumb sponge *n* **:** CRUMB-OF-BREAD SPONGE

bread-crust bomb *n* **:** a volcanic bomb whose surface is disrupted by cracks

bread dance *n* **:** a ritual Amerindian dance performed in supplication for food

bread·en \'bredᵊn\ *adj* [¹*bread* + *-en*] *archaic* **:** made of bread

bread flour *n* **:** a flour from which bread dough with a good quality of gluten can be made

breadfruit \'=,=\ *n* **1 :** a round usu. seedless tropical fruit that varies from 4 to 7 inches in diameter, has a greenish yellow rind and light yellow flesh when ripe, and resembles bread in color and texture when baked **2** *or* **breadfruit tree :** a tall tree (*Artocarpus altilis*) that is prob. native to Malaya but now widespread in the tropics both under cultivation and as an escape, produces breadfruit, has a bark that contains a strong fiber used locally to make cloth, and yields a usable timber and a glutinous material employed in caulking and as a glue or birdlime **3 :** an African tree (*Treculia africana*) that yields numerous seeds used for making meal **4** *Austral* **:** SCREW PINE

breadfruit: branch with fruit and staminate flowers

breadgrain \'=,=\ *n* **:** cereals (as wheat and rye) that yield flour from which bread is made

breading *pres part of* BREAD

bread knife *n* **:** a knife with a long blade that has a serrated or scalloped edge

bread·less \-ləs\ *adj* [ME *bredlees*, fr. *bred, breed* bread + *-lees* -less] **:** being without bread

breadline \'=,=\ *n* **:** a line formed by people waiting to receive food given in charity or issued in relief; *also* **:** the people in such a line

bread mold *n* **:** a mold of the family Mucoraceae (esp. *Rhizopus stolonifer*)

breadnut \'=,=\ *n* **1 :** the nut of a tree (*Brosimum alicastrum*) of Jamaica and Mexico that is roasted and ground into a flour from which bread is made **2 :** a tree (*Brosimum terrabanum*) of British Honduras whose leaves furnish fodder **3 :** a seeded breadfruit

bread riot *n* **:** a riot for food

breadroot \'=,=\ *n* **1 :** the root of a densely hairy plant (*Psoralea esculenta*) of the western U.S. used for food **2 :** the plant that yields breadroot **3 :** CINNAMON FERN

breads *pl of* BREAD, *pres 3d sing of* BREAD

bread sauce *n* **:** a milk-and-butter sauce thickened with bread crumbs

breadstick \'=,=\ *n* **:** a crisp stick-shaped roll often served with soup

breadstuff \'=,=\ *n* **1 :** grain, flour, or other cereal products **2 :** bread of any kind or shape

breadth \'bredth, -etth, *chiefly in substand speech* -eth\ *n* -S [obs. E *brede* breadth (fr. ME, fr. OE *brǣdu*, fr. *brād* broad) + *-th* — more at BROAD] **1 :** distance from side to side : measure taken at right angles to length : WIDTH **2 a** (1) **:** a piece of fabric of full width as manufactured ⟨a ~ of silk⟩ (2) **:** the width in which a fabric is manufactured ⟨lace in 18-inch ~*s*⟩ **b :** a wide expanse ⟨green ~*s* of undulating park —George Eliot⟩ **3 a :** spacious extent : embracing comprehensiveness : WIDENESS, SWEEP, SCOPE ⟨~ of culture, an ease with humanism and Renaissance learning —T.S.Eliot⟩ **b :** freedom from narrow concentration or parochial constraint : LARGENESS, LIBERALITY, GENEROSITY ⟨viewed with dispassionateness and ~ —Ruth Suckow⟩ **4 :** the quality in works of art brought about by elimination of unnecessary detail to produce an impression of largeness and unity ⟨associating colors in large groups to obtain ~⟩ **5 :** DENOTATION 4

breadth·en \'bredthən, -etthən\ *vi* -ED/-ING/-S [*breadth* + *-en*] **:** BROADEN

breadth extreme *n* **:** the width of a ship over the outside of all planking or plating at the widest frame

breadth-height index *n, anthrop* **:** the ratio of the maximum breadth of the head or skull to its maximum height multiplied by 100

breadth·less \-ləs\ *adj* **:** being without breadth

breadth molded *n, pl* **breadths molded :** MOLDED BREADTH

breadth·rid·er \'=,==\ *n* **:** a strengthening timber near the broadest part of a wooden ship

breadth·ways \-ˌwāz\ *or* **breadth·wise** \-ˌwīz\ *adv* (*or adj*) **:** in the direction of the breadth **:** not lengthwise

bread tree *n* **1 :** BREADFRUIT 2 **2 :** WILD MANGO **3 :** BAOBAB

bread wheat *n* **:** any wheat (as club wheat) suitable for making into bread flour

breadwinner \ˈ⸗ˌ⸗⸗\ *n* **1 :** a means (as a tool or a craft) of obtaining a livelihood **:** VOCATION **2 :** a member of a family or household whose wages solely or largely defray its living expenses

breadwinning \ˈ⸗ˌ⸗⸗\ *n* **:** the gaining of a livelihood

[1]**break** \ˈbrāk\ *vb* **broke** \ˈbrōk\ *or archaic* **brake** \ˈbrāk\ *or chiefly Scot* **brack** \ˈbrak\ *or Scot* **brak** \"\ **bro·ken** \ˈbrōkən *sometimes* -kᵊŋ\ *or substand* **broke**; **breaking**; **breaks** [ME *breken*, fr. OE *brecan;* akin to OHG *brehhan* to break, Goth *brikan*, L *frangere* to break, Skt giri*bhraj* breaking forth from mountains] *vt* **1 a :** to split into pieces or smash into parts or fragments typically by a blow or stress and with suddenness or violence **b :** to pull, rend, tear, thrust, or shear apart typically forcefully or roughly and often by accident **c** *now dial Eng* **:** TEAR, RIP ⟨~ cloth⟩ ⟨~ paper⟩ ⟨don't ~ your jacket on the fence⟩ **d :** to snap into pieces **:** FRACTURE ⟨~ a bone⟩ **:** fracture the bone of (a bodily part) ⟨the blow *broke* his arm⟩ **:** suffer fracture of a bone in ⟨he *broke* his leg in the wreck⟩ **:** DISLOCATE ⟨~*ing* his neck⟩ **e :** to fracture the limbs of in torture ⟨a captive *broken* on the wheel⟩; *broadly* **:** MAIM, MUTILATE ⟨the *broken* bodies of the dead soldiers⟩ **f** (1) **:** CUT, RUPTURE ⟨~ the skin⟩ (2) **:** to cut or bruise the skin of (the head) ⟨blacked eyes and *broken* heads were common in such fights⟩ **g :** to cut up **:** tear to pieces **:** CARVE, REND — usu. used with *up* ⟨hunters ~*ing* up the deer⟩ ⟨hounds ~*ing* up a fox⟩ **h :** to cut into and turn over the surface of **:** PLOW ⟨~ the soil⟩ ⟨grasslands have been *broken* and planted to wheat —*Amer. Guide Series: Wash.*⟩ **i :** to rupture the surface of and permit flowing out or effusing ⟨~ an artery⟩ **:** undergo such a rupture of ⟨he *broke* several veins during his seizure⟩ **j** (1) **:** to smash or tear open (2) **:** to lay open and distribute or sort the contents of **:** OPEN (3) **:** to uncover for easy collecting ⟨~*ing* ore⟩ (4) **:** to remove and pry apart caked tobacco from (a hogshead) for inspection as to merchantable quality **2 a :** to violate or transgress by failure to follow, observe, or act in accordance with **:** fail to keep ⟨~*ing* the law⟩ ⟨~*ing* a contract⟩ ⟨~*ing* his promise⟩ ⟨every great novel has *broken* many conventions —Ellen Glasgow⟩ **b :** to invalidate (a will) by action at law **3 a :** to force entry into **:** enter by force or violence **:** open for illegal entry — archaic except in law ⟨accused of attempting to ~ a house⟩ **b :** to burst and usu. to force a way through ⟨~*ing* the barriers in his way⟩ **c :** to make one's escape by force from **:** escape by or as if by severing or bursting barriers that confine ⟨~*ing* jail⟩ **d :** to make or effect by or as if by piercing, cutting, forcing, or pressing through ⟨~*ing* a trail⟩ ⟨~*ing* out a ski area⟩ ⟨~*ing* a hole in the ice⟩ ⟨~*ing* open the snow-clogged roads⟩ ⟨~*ing* the packet open⟩ **e :** PENETRATE, PIERCE **4 a :** to separate or shear by or as if by tearing or rending — often used with *off* ⟨a branch *broken* off the tree⟩ **b :** to make ineffective as a binding force **:** LOOSEN, SUNDER ⟨~*ing* his chains⟩ **:** effect release or escape from ⟨~ a wrestling hold⟩ **c** *cricket* **:** to strike (a wicket) and dislodge one or both bails **d :** to subject to breaking ⟨certain consonant combinations may ~ a preceding vowel⟩ **e :** PICK ⟨~ pineapples⟩ ⟨~ oranges⟩ **f :** to soften the fibers of (a skin) by scraping or pounding **5 a :** to disrupt or split with ensuing dispersal ⟨a quarrel that *broke* the party apart⟩ **:** disrupt the order or compactness of ⟨~*ing* ranks⟩ **b :** to end, close, or destroy by or as if by dispersing — often used with *up* ⟨~ up the counterfeiting ring⟩ ⟨~ up our partnership⟩ **c** *archaic* **:** DISSOLVE, DISBAND **d :** to disrupt by death, divorce, or conflict ⟨children from *broken* homes⟩ — often used with *up* ⟨infidelities that *broke* up their marriage⟩ **e :** to prevent effective operation or performance of by disruptive action ⟨~*ing* up bootlegging operations⟩ ⟨~*ing* up a forward pass play⟩ **f :** to give or receive money units of smaller denomination in exchange for ⟨~*ing* a 10-dollar bill⟩ **6 a :** to defeat utterly and end as an effective force **:** overcome the resistance or strength of **:** SMASH, DEMOLISH, DESTROY ⟨he *broke* the enemy by . . . starvation, attrition, and a slow, deadly scientific envelopment —John Buchan⟩ — sometimes used with *down* **b :** to crush the spirit of **:** sap (one's) will to resist, withstand, or persevere **:** afflict with so much distress that hope, resistance, morale, or self-control is weakened **:** cause (one) to yield — often used with *down* ⟨the brutal method finally *broke* the prisoner so that he confessed⟩ ⟨~ down a prisoner by cross-examination⟩; *sometimes* **:** to agitate and depress — often used with *up* ⟨quite *broken* up by his friend's death⟩ **c :** to make tractable or submissive: as (1) **:** to train (an animal) to adjust to the service or convenience of man ⟨bought a number of horses and *broke* them to saddle⟩ (2) **:** INURE, ACCUSTOM **d :** to exhaust in health, strength, energy, or capacity **:** reduce to weakness or ineptness **:** wear out **:** WEARY — often used with *down* ⟨completely *broken* by his struggle for power⟩ ⟨his heavy duties eventually *broke* him down⟩ **e :** to ruin financially **:** BANKRUPT **:** leave virtually without assets **:** exhaust the funds of ⟨~*ing* his competitors by unfair practices⟩ ⟨~*ing* the bank in the gambling house⟩ **f :** to reduce in rank **:** strip of office or privilege **:** CASHIER, DISMISS ⟨*broken* from sergeant to private⟩ **g :** to shatter (something that is advancing or thrusting) by firm resistance **:** turn aside the force or intensity of ⟨the jetty ~*ing* the waves⟩ ⟨a stand of trees ~*ing* the wind⟩ **h :** to separate the fibers from the woody core of (flax or hemp) after retting esp. by means of fluted rollers preparatory to scutching **i :** to cause failure and discontinuance of (a strike) by measures outside bargaining processes **j :** to better (a score, standard, or record) ⟨golfers trying to ~ 90⟩ ⟨~*ing* the mark for innings pitched⟩ **k :** to win against (an opponent's service) in a racket game **l :** to deprive of all chance or hope of success **:** ruin the standing or prospects of ⟨she could make or ~ the ambitious climber —*Amer. Guide Series: R.I.*⟩ **m :** to demonstrate the falsity or lack of credibility of **:** DISPROVE — often used with *down* ⟨~*ing* an alibi⟩ ⟨~*ing* down a witness⟩ **n :** to cause a sharp reduction of **:** reduce the price of sharply ⟨news that will ~ many oil stocks⟩ **7 a :** to stop, cut short, or bring to an end often suddenly **:** disturb the continuance of **:** HALT, STOP — often used with *off*, sometimes with *up* ⟨the home run that ~*s* the tie⟩ ⟨~*ing* the deadlock by decisive action⟩ ⟨~*ing* off what he was saying⟩ ⟨~*ing* off relations with a hostile country⟩ **b :** to cease the regular continuity of **:** INTERRUPT, SUSPEND ⟨~*ing* their journey⟩ ⟨showers ~*ing* the heat wave⟩ ⟨~*ing* the beam of light⟩ — sometimes used with *up* **c :** to open and thus bring about suspension of operation ⟨~*ing* an electric circuit⟩ **d :** to destroy unity or completeness of ⟨this dinner set is *broken;* two cups are missing⟩ ⟨to have a drink and ~ the quart⟩ **e** (1) **:** to change the appearance of uniformity of **:** bring variety or change into **:** serve to change the impression of regular continuity in ⟨plateau lands *broken* by gullies and ravines⟩ ⟨a level roof *broken* by a dormer⟩ (2) **:** to cause lack of regular continuity in ⟨~*ing* joints in Flemish bond⟩ **f :** to split the surface of ⟨flying fish ~*ing* the water⟩ **g** (1) **:** to cause to discontinue indulgence in a habit — used with *of* ⟨his wife tried to ~ him of swearing⟩ (2) **:** DISCONTINUE — often used with *off* ⟨~*ing* a habit⟩ ⟨~*ing* off smoking⟩ **h :** to stop (a telegraph operator) in order to verify matter sent **i** (1) **:** to continue (a story) on a page later than and usu. not consecutive with the starting page (2) **:** to interrupt the continuity of (type or print or matter in type or print) at the end of a line for continuation in the next line **8 a** *archaic* **:** to reveal or impart a confidence harbored in or at **b :** to make known sometimes with caution and after hesitation **:** TELL, IMPART, REVEAL ⟨~ the news of his death to her⟩ **c :** to utter or crack (a jest) ⟨~ no jests that are sharp and biting —George Washington⟩ **d :** to make public or available for publication; *often* **:** to publicize widely or permit wide publicity of sometimes after a period of withholding ⟨the admiralty office *broke* the news of the loss⟩ **e :** to initiate (a campaign or course of action) often with fanfare and publicity ⟨big companies ~*ing* a sales campaign⟩ **f :** to find an explanation or solution for **:** SOLVE, UNRAVEL ⟨the detective who *broke* the case⟩ **g** (1) **:** to discover the essentials of (a code or cipher system) — often used with *down* (2) **:** to solve (an encrypted message) without full knowledge of the keys (3) **:** DECRYPT ⟨~ a message⟩ **9 a :** to split into smaller units, parts, or processes **:** DIVIDE — usu. used with *up* or *down* ⟨*broken* into countless small bands —R.A.Billington⟩ ⟨the primary colors are *broken* up into thousands of colored bands and lines —Waldemar Kaempffert⟩ **b :** to divide (a musical chord) by sounding the component tones separately (as in an arpeggio) **c :** to separate (a color) in painting into component parts and to lay these side by side on the canvas instead of mixing them on the palette so that the observer's eye recomposes the color — compare DIVISIONISM, POINTILLISM **d :** to bunch (cured tobacco leaves) in the center and tear a string away from a lath preparatory to tying into a hand **e :** to separate (an emulsion) permanently into components ⟨cream is *broken* by churning⟩ **f :** to split (grain) into flour and bran in milling **10 :** to alter the direction or course of **:** bring about such alteration in: as **a :** to impart break to (a cricket ball) in bowling **b :** to make (a pitched or thrown baseball) curve, drop, or rise sharply **11 a :** to open or unfold at a seam, bend, groove, or joint; *sometimes* **:** to fold or bend at a seam or joint **b :** to open the action of (certain firearms) ⟨*broke* the shotgun and loaded both barrels⟩ **c :** to make with joints for folding ⟨an airplane with *broken* wings⟩ **12 :** to alter the tone of (a color) by an admixture of another color or shade ~ *vi* **1 a :** to depart or escape usu. with sudden forceful effort and from restraint or constraint **:** burst free from ties or barriers ⟨~*ing* away from home ties⟩ ⟨~*ing* out of jail⟩ **b :** to come forth or move out or forward usu. forcefully or abruptly as if bursting through restraints or barriers ⟨~ through the crowd⟩ ⟨dogs *broke* out of the trees into the open⟩ **c :** to develop or be formed or uttered with or as if with suddenness and force — often used with *out* or *forth* ⟨a wail *broke* from the child's lips⟩ ⟨laughter *broke* out in the audience⟩ ⟨spots *broke* out on the child's face⟩ ⟨the sunlight *broke* forth in splendor⟩ **d :** to come into being by or as if by bursting forth — often used with *forth* or *out* ⟨as day was ~*ing*⟩ ⟨the buds *broke* forth in red⟩ ⟨trouble *broke* out between the two countries⟩ ⟨fire *broke* out in the old warehouse⟩ ⟨yellow fever *broke* out in the city⟩ **e :** to start an action, assume a role, take on a condition, or give vent to expression with abruptness — usu. used with *out* or *into* ⟨~*ing* into a roar of laughter⟩ ⟨~*ing* out in tears⟩ ⟨~*ing* into revolt⟩ **f :** to emerge from the surface of the water **:** leap up from the water ⟨the fish were ~*ing*⟩ **g** (1) **:** to start usu. abruptly as if overcoming restraint — usu. used with *out* ⟨rioting *broke* out⟩ ⟨rifle fire *broke* out at dawn⟩ ⟨when the war finally *broke*⟩ (2) **:** to come to pass **:** OCCUR **h** (1) **:** to become public or available for publication ⟨the disaster story *broke* at 10 o'clock⟩ (2) **:** to attain to wide publicity **:** become publicly known ⟨when the scandal *broke*⟩ **i :** to become detached or disengaged and usu. displaced by or as if by the rending or severing of bonds ⟨the boat *broke* from its mooring⟩ ⟨deck cargo *broke* loose in the storm⟩; *also* **:** to dissociate (from a group) ⟨splinter factions ~*ing* from the political party⟩ **:** take a different course **:** DEPART — often used with *away* ⟨~*ing* away from his former leader⟩ ⟨~*ing* away from old tradition⟩ **j :** to leave cover **:** dash from cover ⟨when the stag *broke*⟩ **k** (1) **:** to make a sudden dash ⟨infantrymen ~*ing* for cover⟩ ⟨a base runner ~*ing* for home⟩ **:** pick up speed quickly ⟨when a basketball player ~*s* for the basket⟩ (2) **:** to leave a starting mark, gate, or barrier ⟨a horse slow at ~*ing*⟩; *also* **:** to start before the proper signal has been given in a sports event (3) *of a hunting dog* **:** to leave a point and move quickly to retrieve ⟨trained to ~ at gunshot⟩ **l** (1) **:** to separate after a clinch in boxing or a hold in wrestling esp. when so ordered by the referee — often used with *away* (2) **:** to separate as if from such a clinch or hold — often used with *away* **m** *chiefly Midland* **:** to let out **:** come to an end **:** DISMISS ⟨what time does church ~⟩ **2 a :** to come apart or split into pieces typically with sudden violence and with damage or ruin **:** BURST, SHATTER ⟨the cup *broke* when it fell on the floor⟩ **b :** to open with or as if with tearing, splitting, or rupturing ⟨the bag *broke* and the sugar spilled⟩ **c :** to open spontaneously or by pressure from within (as of a boil or a bubble) **d** *of a wave* **:** to curl over and fall apart in surf or foam **:** be shattered and lose driving force **e :** to crack without complete separation into parts ⟨the windshield *broke* but did not shatter⟩ **f** (1) **:** to diminish markedly in force or intensity **:** abate and fade away ⟨when the frost ~*s*⟩ ⟨after an hour of heavy rain the storm *broke*⟩ (2) *dial* **:** to become fair **:** CLEAR ⟨when the weather ~*s*⟩ **g :** to be driven back in retreat **:** be dispersed in disorder **:** give way in disorderly retreat ⟨the volunteer units *broke* when the enemy charged⟩ **h** (1) **:** to fail in health or strength **:** suffer loss of strength, vitality, keenness, or control — often used with *down* ⟨he *broke* down under the strain of his position⟩ (2) **:** to suffer complete or marked loss of resistance, composure, resolution, morale, or command of a situation ⟨the prisoner *broke* under cross-examination and told the whole story⟩ — often used with *down* (3) **:** to become severely affected or crushed by grief, disappointment, or anguish — used of the heart conceived as the seat of emotions or affections ⟨his heart *broke* when his wife died⟩ **i :** to become inoperative or ineffectual because of damage, wear, or strain ⟨the toy *broke*⟩ — often used with *down* ⟨the bus *broke* down on the hill⟩ **j :** to go bankrupt **:** fail in business ⟨the bank *broke* as a result of the run⟩ **k :** to undergo a sudden marked decrease in price or value ⟨rail stocks *broke* sharply yesterday⟩ **l :** to undergo breaking **3** *obs* **:** to speak (with a person concerning some subject) ⟨~ with thee of some affairs —Shak.⟩ **4 a :** to end a relationship, connection, accord, or agreement ⟨*broke* with his leader on this issue⟩ ⟨~ with tradition⟩ — often used with *off* or *up* ⟨her parents *broke* up and got a divorce⟩ ⟨*broke* off with his wife completely⟩ **b :** to effect a departure, termination, interruption, or change from the accustomed — often used with *away* ⟨~*ing* away and living a life of her own⟩ **c :** to release a dancing partner's hands **:** loose hands in dancing **:** separate so that another may cut in **d :** to become unfurled **:** stream out at full length ⟨the royal standard *broke* from the mainmast⟩ **5 a :** to make a sharp change in course **:** deviate from a straight line **b** (1) *of a bowled cricket ball* **:** to change direction on touching the ground ⟨a ball that turns from off to leg ~*s* back; one that turns toward the wicket from either side ~*s* in; one that turns away from the wicket to either side ~*s* away⟩ (2) *of a pitched baseball* **:** to curve, drop, or rise sharply ⟨a fast ball that ~*s* away from a batter⟩ **c :** to change sharply in purport, mood, or attitude ⟨~*ing* to the ridiculous⟩ **d** (1) *of the voice* **:** to alter sharply in tone, pitch, or intensity either momentarily (as under stress of emotion) or permanently ⟨his voice *broke* with excitement⟩ **:** shift from one register to another (as when the voice is changing in adolescence) ⟨the boy's voice *broke* momentarily from its deep new bass to its original high soprano⟩ (2) *of a tone on a wind instrument* **:** to shift abruptly from one register to another **:** fail abruptly in musical quality (as by a sudden uncontrolled harshness or shift in register); *also* **:** to die out **:** FAIL ⟨screamed until his voice *broke* completely⟩ **e** *of a horse* **:** to fail to keep a prescribed gait **f** (1) **:** to be interrupted for continuation in another column or on another page usu. not consecutive ⟨the story ~*s* to page five⟩ — compare JUMP (2) **:** to come to a break ⟨the first two columns ~ nicely⟩ ⟨paragraph three *broke* badly at the ends of the lines⟩ **g :** to move a camera to a new location **h** (1) **:** to announce in a game of rummy that play will end after each player has had one more turn (2) **:** to be first to meld in rummy **i :** to interrupt one's activity or occupation usu. for a brief period ⟨at noon we ~ for lunch⟩ **6 a :** to vary from even continuity or regularity **:** develop notable variation or change **b :** to change abruptly in line or set often with suggestion of opening ⟨her face *broke* into a smile⟩ **c :** to become broken or discontinuous ⟨an electric circuit may ~⟩ **d** (1) *of a fish or whale* **:** to leap wholly or partly out of the water (2) **:** to emerge from the surface of the water ⟨shoals that ~ at low tide⟩ **e :** to make the opening shot of a game or frame of pool or billiards **f :** to exhibit variation (as the flowers from hybrid seedlings or those from plants infected with a virus) **:** SPORT **7 a :** to divide into classes, categories, or types **:** ANALYZE, CLASSIFY — usu. used with *down* or *up* ⟨our cases ~ up into three types⟩ **b :** to fold, bend, lift, or come apart at a seam, groove, or joint ⟨a hospital bed that ~*s*⟩ ⟨a pistol that ~*s*⟩ **c** *of cream* **:** to separate during churning into liquid and fat **d :** to fix a round number for the payoff in pari-mutuel betting and disregard uneven winnings (as pennies) ⟨in some states race tracks ~ to the nearest nickel⟩ **e :** to form branches ⟨a tree bough that ~*s*⟩ **f** (1) **:** to thicken and become cloudy **:** produce a precipitate or suspension of gelatinous matter — used esp. of vegetable oils on being heated (2) *of an emulsion* **:** to separate permanently, usu. into oily and aqueous layers — often distinguished from *cream* **8 :** HAPPEN, DEVELOP ⟨everything *broke* right for him⟩

syn CRACK, BURST, BUST, SNAP, SHATTER, SHIVER: BREAK usu. implies a stress or strain strong enough to cause rupture or fracture in one or many places, or a general disruption, but extends commonly to any depriving (of an object, as a machine) of capacity to work ⟨the dam *broke* and flooded neighboring fields⟩ ⟨*break* a rock with a hammer⟩ ⟨*break* a silence⟩ ⟨the clock is *broken* and does not run⟩ CRACK implies a breaking of something hard, brittle, or hollow, usu. without complete separation of parts ⟨*crack* a plate⟩ ⟨*crack* a mirror⟩ ⟨a *cracked* baseball bat⟩ BURST implies a breaking into pieces, usu. with the scattering of parts or contents, often by the force of internal pressure ⟨the glittering bubble *burst* —G.H.Reed b.1887⟩ ⟨a shell *burst* 50 feet in front and showered the area with shrapnel⟩ BUST is interchangeable with BREAK or BURST in extremely informal conversational English ⟨a *busted* alarm clock —Eric Hodgins⟩ ⟨three *busted* ribs —*Time*⟩ ⟨the doors unhinged, the globes *busted* —Henry Miller⟩ SNAP suggests a quick clean complete break, esp. of something brittle or fragile ⟨the branch *snapped* with the weight of the ice and the force of the wind⟩ ⟨to *snap* a stick in two⟩ SHATTER carries the idea of a totally destructive breaking into pieces esp. forcibly and with a wide scattering of fragments ⟨the force of the explosion *shattered* the windows for ½ mile around⟩ ⟨the burst of fire *shattered* all enemy resistance⟩ SHIVER implies a shattering by forceful sudden clashing or smashing and lays even stronger stress than *shatter* on the scattering of small fragments ⟨one of the men tore the paper plaster off the full-length mirror, . . . hurled his soup bowl at it, *shivering* the glass —R.M.Lovett⟩ ⟨the sound of an explosion *shivered* the quiet —Irwin Shaw⟩

— **break a lance :** to engage in spirited controversy often with quixotic ardor ⟨always ready to *break a lance* in defense of his ideas⟩ — **break and enter :** to gain a passage by force or otherwise and enter into another's dwelling, outbuilding, store, or other building — used with varying legal applications in different jurisdictions; see HOUSEBREAKING; compare BURGLARY — **break bread 1 :** to eat in the company of ⟨refusing to *break bread* with his old enemy⟩ **2 :** to give out bread (as in a Communion service) — **break bulk 1 :** to remove, transfer, or displace part of a load or cargo **:** start to unload **:** unload and distribute all or part of a carload, boatload, or truckload **2** *of a bailee* **:** to treat that which is held by bailment in such a manner as to destroy its entirety in the eyes of the law (as by opening a package and removing part of the contents) — **break camp :** to pack up gear and leave a camp or campsite ⟨the troops *broke camp* early in the morning⟩ — **break cover** *or* **break covert :** to start from a covert or lair ⟨the hunted fox *broke cover*⟩ — **break for color** *or* **break up for color :** to separate (imposed letterpress matter) into parts so that each part may be printed in a different color — **break ground 1 :** to dig open the earth often in excavating for new construction ⟨*breaking ground* for the new arsenal⟩ **2 :** to make new discoveries or introduce new procedures or material **:** PIONEER ⟨this report *breaks* new *ground* in the study of human relations⟩ — **break joints :** to arrange bricks or stone in a wall in such a way that the upright joints of two successive courses are nowhere in line with each other — **break no squares** *obs* **:** to make no difference **:** do no harm — **break one's duck** *of a cricket batsman* **:** to score at least one run — **break one's heart :** to afflict with bitter sorrow, hopeless grief, or despair — **break one's neck :** to strive to the utmost — **break one's wrists :** to turn the wrists as part of the swing of a club or bat (as in baseball) — **break service** *of a mare* **:** to fail to conceive — **break sheer** *of a boat* **:** to turn while at anchor so as to lie obliquely to the anchor and in danger of fouling the cable — **break ship :** to fail to rejoin one's ship after leave ⟨facing court-martial for *breaking ship*⟩ — **break step :** to fail to keep step **:** walk or march out of step — **break the back 1 :** to check, subdue, or overcome the main force **:** leave existent but powerless ⟨to *break the back* of enemy resistance⟩ **2** *of a ship* **:** to break the keel and keelson — **break the ice 1 :** to make a beginning **2 :** to get through the first difficulties in starting a conversation or discussion — **break wind :** to expel gas from the intestine

[2]**break** \"\ *n* -S [ME *breke*, fr. *breken*, v.] **1 a :** an act or action of breaking **:** SHATTERING **:** FRACTURE **b :** a grinding of grain or meal **:** any of the grindings in which flour is separated or extracted from bran **c :** a breaking of flax or hemp; *also* **:** BREAKER 2c(1) **d :** the action of breaking open hogsheads; *also* **:** a sale of tobacco from opened hogsheads **e** (1) **:** a pool shot that touches a ball in the arranged triangle at the beginning of a frame (2) **:** the opening shot in a game of billiards **f :** the act of opening a gap in an electrical circuit **2 a :** a condition produced by breaking or appearing as if so produced **:** GAP, OPENING, APERTURE, BREACH, RENT ⟨through a ~ in the hedge⟩ ⟨a ~ in the pipe⟩ ⟨a ~ in the clouds⟩ **b :** a gap in an otherwise continuous electric circuit **3 :** the action or act of breaking in, out, or forth: as **a :** emergence from darkness **:** LIGHTENING ⟨at ~ of day⟩ **b :** a sometimes forcefully effected escape from confinement ⟨the convicts planned a jail ~⟩ **c :** illegal entry accomplished forcefully ⟨a ~ at the store was thwarted by the police⟩ **d :** an abrupt run (as to reach safety) **:** DASH, RUSH ⟨captives making a ~ for freedom⟩ ⟨the startled deer made a ~ for the thicket⟩ ⟨a base runner making a ~ for home⟩; *esp* **:** a quick offensive thrust toward one's own basket in basketball **e :** the start of a race; *esp* **:** the start of a horse race **f :** the act of separating after a boxing or wrestling clinch often by the referee **g :** the occurrence of a disease in a person or esp. in a domestic animal supposed to be immune to or to have been completely isolated from exposure to that disease **4 :** an interruption in continuity ⟨waiting for a ~ in the bad weather⟩: as **a :** discontinuity in the flow or tone of a composition **:** a notable change of subject matter, attitude, or treatment ⟨a sonnet is often marked by a ~ after the eighth line⟩ **b** (1) **:** an abrupt, significant, or noteworthy change or interruption in a continuous process, trend, course of action, or series of events ⟨a ~ in production for retooling⟩ ⟨army service made a ~ in his career⟩ (2) **:** an interruption from work or duty for rest, relaxation, or recreation ⟨taking a ~ for a cigarette⟩ (3) **:** a planned interruption in a radio or television program ⟨a ~ for the commercial⟩ **c :** a noticeable interruption or change in any continuous surface, level, line, or course: as (1) **:** a marked topographical variation ⟨a plain extending 1000 miles without a ~⟩ **:** a portion of land distinct or divided off from adjacent land **:** a plowed area **:** a strip of land in crop or pasture **:** an irregular rough piece of ground **:** a deep valley, ravine, or gorge; *esp* **:** one that cuts through a ridge or mountain (2) **breaks** *pl* **:** a line of cliffs and associated spurs and small ravines (as at the edge of a mesa or canyon) (3) *chiefly Brit* **:** a portion of pasture or grazing crop to be grazed for a limited period of time ⟨grazing rape in ~*s*⟩ (4) **:** a feature breaking the continuity of a structural line **:** a projection from a surface **:** a change in direction ⟨gates, niches, and other ~*s* in the wall⟩ (5) **:** a part in a ship or deck where a partial deck ends leaving a drop to a deck on a lower level (6) **:** change of direction of flight of a bowled cricket ball after bouncing esp. when caused by spin imparted by the bowler — see LEG-BREAK, OFFBREAK (7) **:** deviation of a pitched baseball from a straight line or from a gravitational curve **d** (1) *mining* **:** DISLOCATION, FAULT (2) **:** an abrupt change of fossil content or lithology at a definite horizon in a chronologic sequence of sedimentary rocks indicative of a disconformity or hiatus ⟨a faunal ~⟩ ⟨a stratigraphic ~⟩; *also* **:** any marked change in lithology in a sedimentary sequence **e :** a disturbing or rippling of the surface of water (as by a fish rising) **f :** an abrupt halt, change of direction, or pivoting separation of partners dancing together **g** (1) **:** interruption of a line (as a crease, fold, or seam) in clothing ⟨trousers with a ~ just above the shoe⟩ **:** change in a line at a seam ⟨the ~ where brim and crown of a hat meet⟩ (2) **:** a wrinkle or series of wrinkles formed in leather at a fold **h :** failure of a horse to maintain the prescribed gait in a harness race **:** change from one pace to another **i** (1) **:** an abrupt change in the quality or pitch of musical tone (2) **:** the shift of a rank to a lower octave in organ mixture stops to avoid impractically small pipes (3) **:** any notable variation in pitch,

intensity, or tone in the voice ⟨speaking passionately, with a ~ in her voice⟩ **j :** a switch of a block of votes (as in a political convention) to create a definite trend — compare STAMPEDE **k :** a noticeable change in quality, character, or nature **:** a departure from a previously followed pattern ⟨a ~ from his customary procedure⟩: (1) **:** any striking departure from the normal color of a flower (as in tulips affected by virus) in which the blooms become variously striped and variegated (2) **:** an interruption of the fibers of a fleece by a zone of inferior quality coinciding with the growth of wool during a period of illness or deficiency of food or water **l** *printing* **:** separation of composed matter at an indicated point **5 :** a rupture in previously friendly relations or firm accord **:** disagreement causing separation **:** an abrupt split or difference with or as if with something previously adhered to or followed ⟨a ~ between the president and the secretary on the matter⟩ ⟨a ~ between the two countries⟩ ⟨a ~ with a tradition previously followed⟩ ⟨a clean ~ with his old associates⟩ **6 a :** a number of chests of tea making up a consignment or shipment **b :** the quantity of hemp prepared in a year **c :** a sequence of successful shots in billiards **:** RUN ⟨a ~ of 20⟩ ⟨a 60 ~⟩ **d :** gelatinous matter that separates in some vegetable oils (as raw linseed oil) on being heated; *also* **:** similar matter that separates on aging — compare FOOT 15 **7 :** a device used in breaking, bending, checking, or changing: as **a :** a tool for bending sheet metal to a required angle ⟨a cornice ~⟩ — compare ⁴BRAKE 5 **b :** a bench on which dough is kneaded **:** a machine used in kneading dough **c :** FLAX BREAKER **d :** the roller or stone mill that grinds the original wheat **e :** FIREBREAK **f :** a commutator in telegraphy **8 :** a place or situation at which a break occurs: **a** (1) **:** the point where one musical register changes to another (as of a voice or of wind instruments) (2) *in compound organ stops* **:** a point where the relative pitch of the pipes changes (3) *in blues or jazz* **:** a short ornamental or rhythmically emphatic passage interpolated between phrases by a performer and filling out the form of a short phrase to periodic length **b :** BRANCH; *esp* **:** one formed after pinching or disbudding — see BOTTOM BREAK **c** (1) **:** BREAK LINE (2) **:** the place where calculation shows that a column or page will end and the continuity of composed matter should be broken (3) **:** the place in a form at which matter that is to be printed in another color is separated from neighboring matter (4) **:** the place at which a word is divided (as at the end of a line) (5) **:** the point in a printed story at which it is continued on another page or column (6) **:** the terminal point of a printed line ⟨headline verbs are seldom split by a line ~⟩ (7) **:** the time at which a news story becomes available for publication **d :** a pause or interruption (as a caesura or diaeresis) within or at the end of a verse or other unit of utterance or composition **e :** a failure to make a strike or a spare on a frame in bowling **f :** a forest fire that escapes immediate control **9 :** a sudden and abrupt decline of prices or values; *broadly* **:** any price decline ⟨the news caused a ~ in rails⟩ **10 :** a rough jet of metal on the shank of a newly cast and unfinished foundry type **11 :** an awkward social blunder; *specif* **:** a gauche, naive, or imprudent comment causing embarrassment **12 :** a stroke of fortune ⟨ascribe his fortune to luck, to getting the ~*s* —J.G.Cozzens⟩; *specif* **:** a favorable or opportune situation or turn arising either through chance or through equitable or kindly consideration or treatment ⟨dwarfs got their best ~ . . . in aircraft factories, inspecting bomber wings from the inside —W.L.Gresham⟩ ⟨a judge often gives a first offender a ~⟩

syn GAP, INTERRUPTION, INTERVAL, INTERIM, HIATUS, LACUNA: BREAK applies to any lapse in continuity of material, course of action, or time ⟨a *break* in the fence⟩ ⟨a *break* in the ice⟩ ⟨the book was written with no *breaks*⟩ ⟨the holiday made a pleasant *break* in the routine⟩ GAP, orig. indicating an opening in a wall, was extended to indicate any means of passage and now may indicate a void, a space unfilled or unfillable ⟨a water *gap*⟩ ⟨a wind *gap*⟩ ⟨a *gap* in the mountain chain⟩ ⟨the *gap* which separates Roman Britain from Anglo-Saxon England has fascinated a long succession of scholars —*Times Lit. Supp.*⟩ INTERRUPTION may apply to breaking of continuity, sometimes disturbing; it may call attention to the action of breaking rather than the result ⟨the time schedule we set up must be tentative, of course, until we find out the *interruptions* — telephone calls, appointments — that are bound to occur —*Better Homes & Gardens*⟩ ⟨the *Newport Mercury*, a publication that has, with one brief *interruption* during the Revolution, come down to the present day —*Amer. Guide Series: R.I.*⟩ INTERVAL may refer to distance in space or period in time between two similar things ⟨along this fertile plain, at *intervals* averaging about seven miles, are thoroughly modern towns —*Amer. Guide Series: Tex.*⟩ ⟨you snatched gladly at such diversions Sunday, for the rest of the day until 2 o'clock was a solemn *interval*, during which all the usual books and plays were interdicted —Mary Austin⟩ INTERIM refers to an interval between specified dates or events ⟨the *interim* between the two wars⟩ ⟨the *interim* between the king's death and the prince's accession⟩ ⟨in a healthy mind there is an *interim* between one duty and another. This prevents them from wearing each other out. These intervals of soothing carelessness, if not unduly prolonged, are very restorative —S.M.Crothers⟩ HIATUS indicates a gap or break, often in regard to something said, composed, or considered ⟨it was believed that a distinct cultural *hiatus* separated the end of the Paleolithic and the beginning of the Neolithic period —R.W. Murray⟩ ⟨it is doubtful if contemporary criticism of fiction, after the critical *hiatus* of the 19th century, has quite found itself again in the classic Aristotelian tradition —R.G. Davis⟩ LACUNA may refer to a blank or gap in or as if in a manuscript ⟨*lacunae* in *Beowulf*⟩ ⟨a difficult man to write a biography of, because there are so many *lacunae* in our factual knowledge of his life —*New Yorker*⟩ **syn** see in addition BREACH, OPPORTUNITY

³break \"\ *also* **brake** \"\ *n* -s [¹*break*] **1 :** a bodiless carriage frame used for breaking in horses **2 :** a four-wheeled straight-bodied horse-drawn pleasure vehicle usu. having a capacity of six or more persons in addition to the driver and footman

⁴break \"\ *var of* BRAKE

¹break·able \ˈbrākəbəl\ *adj* [¹*break* + *-able*] **:** capable of being broken

²breakable \"\ *n* -s **:** an object readily broken ⟨wrap ~*s* well before mailing⟩

break·age \-kij, -kēj\ *n* -s **1 a :** the act or action of breaking **b :** amount or quantity of items broken ⟨~ in the laboratory was excessive⟩ **:** loss caused by breaking **c :** an interruption caused by breakage **:** BREAK **d :** allowance or compensation for things broken **2 :** space left unfilled in stowing the hold of a ship **3 :** odd cents not paid to winning pari-mutuel bettors because exceeding a payoff figure that is calculated at a multiple of 5 or 10

break and entry *var of* BREAKING AND ENTERING

break away *vt* **:** to break and knock or smash down or away ⟨*breaking away* the bars in the windows⟩

¹breakaway \ˈ≈,≈\ *n*, *pl* **breakaways** \-āz\ *also* **breaks·away** \-ksə,wā\ [*break away*] **1 :** an act or instance of breaking away (as from a group, affiliation, standard, or tradition) ⟨a ~ by this discontented faction⟩ ⟨a ~ from classical tradition⟩ **2** *Austral* **a :** a stampede esp. of cattle or sheep **b :** an animal that breaks away from the herd **3 a :** a premature start of one or more contestants in a race; *sometimes* **:** the start of a race or speed trial **b :** the moment when hunting dogs are cast off by the handler **c :** a sudden offensive rush toward an opponent's goal **4 :** a theatrical prop (as a chair) made to shatter harmlessly on slight pressure or impact ⟨belaboring each other with ~*s* in fight scenes⟩ **5** *Austral* **:** an escarpment overlooking a plain or at the edge of a plateau **6 :** a scrummager who does not usu. push but waits in readiness to break away from the scrum immediately after the ball comes out

²breakaway \"\ *adj* **1** *Brit* **:** given to breaking away **:** favoring disaffiliation from a group **:** operating as independent of an original affiliation ⟨a ~ union⟩ ⟨a ~ movement⟩ **2 a :** made as a breakaway **:** constructed to break, shatter, or bend with slight pressure ⟨to slug it out with fists and ~ chairs right up in front of the camera —Gary Cooper⟩ **b :** constructed for very fast dismounting or changing ⟨~ sets cutting time spent between scenes of the play⟩

breakax *or* **breakaxe** \ˈ≈,≈\ *n* **:** any of various hardwoods difficult to chop: as **a :** the wood of a West Indian tree (*Sloanea jamaicensis*) **b :** a quebracho (*Pithecolobium arboreum*)

break back *vi* **1 :** to return usu. abruptly to a former position or state **2** *archit* **:** to return inward from a projection

¹breakback \ˈ≈,≈\ *adj* [¹*break* + *back*, n.] **:** BACKBREAKING, CRUSHING

²breakback \"\ *n* -s [*break back*] **1 :** a return or setting back **2 :** a bowled cricket ball that breaks back toward the wicket from the off

breakbone fever \ˈ≈,≈-\ *n* **:** DENGUE

break–bulk point \ˈ≈,≈-\ *n* **:** a station or point at which all or portions of a truckload, boatload, or carload are unloaded and distributed

break down *vt* **1 a :** to cause to fall or collapse by breaking or shattering **:** batter down **:** DESTROY ⟨*breaking down* the door⟩ **b :** to wear down into a defective or useless condition by attrition **c :** to bring about loss of force or effectiveness of **:** make ineffective **:** IMPAIR, DISPEL ⟨*breaking down* the old legal codes⟩ **2 a :** to separate (as a chemical compound) into simpler substances **:** DECOMPOSE **b :** to take apart esp. for storage or shipment and for later reassembling ⟨a machine that can be *broken down* quickly and transported by plane⟩ **c** (1) **:** to reduce (a log) to a convenient size for sawing in the mill (2) **:** to saw (a log) into cants **3 a :** to tone down **:** QUALIFY ⟨*break down* a color⟩ **b :** to make (rubber) plastic: SOFTEN, MASTICATE **4 :** to stop (a sawmill or machine) because of an accident ~ *vi* **1 a :** to become inoperative through breakage or wear **:** lose ability to operate or function ⟨the old truck *broke down* on the hill⟩ **b :** to become inapplicable or ineffective ⟨the governor fled, royal authority *broke down* —*Amer. Guide Series: N.C.*⟩ ⟨under critical analysis almost all distinctions previously made tended to *break down*⟩ **2 a :** to be susceptible to analysis or subdivision **:** to be readily analyzed ⟨the chronicle *breaks down* into three large parts —Mark Schorer⟩ **b :** to undergo decomposition ⟨the old highly folded rocks have been *breaking down* gradually into soil —L.D. Stamp⟩ **syn** see ANALYZE

¹breakdown \ˈ≈,≈\ *n* -s [*break down*] **1 :** the action or result of breaking down; *esp* **:** a situation in which machinery becomes inoperative through breakage or wear **:** an ending of effective operation ⟨flooding of the mine caused by a ~ of the pumps⟩ **2 a :** a physical, mental, or nervous collapse **:** a sometimes sudden marked loss of health, strength, faculties, or ability to cope ⟨suffering a ~ after years of overwork⟩ **b :** ²BREAK 3g **c :** surrender to agitation or emotion **:** loss of self-control **3 a :** failure of operation **:** disruption checking progress or effectiveness **:** a condition marked by futile ineffectiveness **:** COLLAPSE, DISINTEGRATION ⟨the ~ of the negotiations between the countries⟩ ⟨a ~ of communications with the territories⟩ ⟨a ~ of tribal customs⟩ **b :** failure of insulation; *esp* **:** failure of an insulating material (as air, oil, porcelain, or rubber) to prevent passage of an electric discharge **4 a :** a noisy rapid shuffling dance; *esp* **:** a dance engaged in competitively by groups or pairs in succession **b :** a tune suitable for such a dance **5 :** the part of a drop-forging die that distributes the metal of the work after it leaves the fuller by bending and shaping it in preparation for forging in the roughing die — called also *edger*, *side cut* **6 a :** DECOMPOSITION; *esp* **:** chemical decomposition (as of a complex compound) **b :** softening or plasticization of rubber esp. by mastication **c :** a disorganization of cellular tissue (as of stored apples) resulting in internal discoloration **7 a :** division into categories ⟨a statistical ~ of data⟩ **:** ANALYSIS, CLASSIFICATION; *specif* **:** division (of a job or operation) into several distinct processes or operations **b :** an explanation or account with specific headings or categories ⟨a ~ of the casualties according to various service branches⟩ **:** an itemized account ⟨a budget ~⟩ ⟨a ~ as to sources of revenue⟩ **c :** analysis of a movie script in the interest of economy and convenience in filming **8 :** any amateur wrestling maneuver by which a contestant in advantage position forces his opponent to the mat from a position on his hands and knees or from a bridge position

²breakdown \"\ *adj* **1** *Brit* **:** used or employed to make repairs after a breakdown or wreck ⟨a ~ train speeding to the scene of the accident⟩ **2 :** calculated to lower school-attendance requirements or to impair restrictions on child labor ⟨a ~ bill⟩ **3 :** obtained or resulting from disintegration or decomposition of a substance ⟨salvaging ~ products⟩

breakdown block *n* **:** one of a set of forms or chucks over which a sheet-metal object may be successively spun and at each operation brought nearer the final shape

breakdown voltage *n* **:** the potential difference in volts that when applied across a layer of electrically insulating substance is just sufficient to initiate a disruptive discharge

¹break·er \ˈbrākə(r)\ *n* -s [ME *breker*, fr. *breken* to break + *-er* — more at BREAK] **1 :** one that breaks ⟨a ~ of idols⟩ ⟨a ~ of oaths⟩ ⟨a veteran ~ of horses⟩ **2 :** a device or instrument that breaks: **a :** a machine for breaking up the woody part of flax, hemp, or jute **b :** a plow with a moldboard arrangement facilitating turning over virgin land — see PRAIRIE BREAKER, ROD BREAKER **c** (1) **:** a machine that tears apart clumps of textile fiber as a step toward carding and spinning (2) **:** a papermaking machine similar to a beater but used to break up rags and brush out their threads and to disintegrate old papers for reuse (3) **:** one of a series of perforated projections used in a revolving tumbler or drum for treating skins (4) **:** a machine or plant for breaking rocks or for crushing, sorting, and cleaning anthracite **d** (1) **:** FLESHING KNIFE (2) **:** an implement that breaks curd into pieces in cheese making (3) **:** an implement with long teeth replacing a blade for breaking cake into pieces **e** (1) **:** CIRCUIT BREAKER (2) **:** a mechanically operated commutator (3) **:** a spark-coil interrupter **f :** a strip of open-weave fabric placed above the dome of a tire carcass to provide additional protection at the point of its closest approach to contact with the road **3 a :** a wave breaking into foam against the shore, against a sandbank, or against a rock or reef near the surface **b :** a slight furrow across a road for drainage **4 :** a person whose work consists of breaking: as **a** *Brit* **:** one that breaks up ships or autos into salvage and scrap **b :** the operator of a textile breaker **c :** an operator of a machine that softens hides or skins by pounding them with hammers **d :** SCRAPPER **e :** a quarry worker who splits off blocks of stone by driving wedges into previously made holes or channels — called also *ledgeman* **f :** a power-shear operator who cuts formed angle-iron stock to length

²breaker \"\ *n* -s [by folk etymology fr. Sp *barrica*, fr. F dial. (Gascony) *barrique*] **:** a small water cask esp. for use in a lifeboat

breaker boy *n* [¹*breaker*] **:** a boy employed in a coal breaker usu. to pick slate from coal

breaker card *n* [¹*breaker*] **1 :** the first and coarsest of three cards used in producing wool sliver — compare FINISHER CARD, INTERMEDIATE 5a **2 :** BREAKER 2a

break·er·man \ˈbrākə(r)mən\ *n*, *pl* **breakermen** [¹*breaker* + *man*] **:** one that standardizes the density of cornstarch suspensions that are to be converted into sugar or glucose and pumps the liquid to refinery storage tanks

break even *vi* **:** to emerge from a contest or transaction with balancing gains and losses or other favorable and unfavorable considerations; *esp* **:** to operate a business or enterprise without either loss or profit ⟨the store expects to *break even* next month⟩

break–even \(ˈ)≈ˈ≈≈\ *adj* [*break even*] **:** having equal outgo and return or loss and profit ⟨a *break-even* situation⟩

break–even point *n* **:** the point at which volume of sales or production enables an enterprise to cover related costs and expenses without profit and without loss **:** that volume of trade or degree of activity at which total income equals total expenditures

break facet *n* **:** one of the paired facets on a brilliant-cut gemstone lying next to the girdle

breakfall \ˈ≈,≈\ *n* [¹*break* + *fall*] **:** a potentially injurious fall (as in judo or tumbling) in which the impact is broken by beating an arm or leg against the mat or floor

¹break·fast \ˈbrekfəst\ *n* -s *often attrib* [ME *brekfast*, fr. *breken* to break + *fast* — more at BREAK] **1 :** the first meal of the day **2 :** a meal eaten early in the day in connection with a ceremonial occasion ⟨a wedding ~⟩ ⟨a Communion ~⟩

²breakfast \"\ *vb* -ED/-ING/-S *vi* **:** to eat breakfast ~ *vt* **:** to supply or entertain with breakfast

breakfast bird *n* [so called fr. its typical early-morning call] *Austral* **:** KOOKABURRA

breakfast food *n* **:** a breakfast cereal

break·fast·less \-fəs(t)ləs\ *adj* **:** being without breakfast

breakfast nook *n* **:** a nook often with built-in table and seats for light meals

breakfast plate *n* **:** a plate of china or earthenware from seven to eight inches in diameter

break flour *n* **:** flour obtained from a break in milling; *also* **:** flour made by mingling that obtained from different breaks

breakfront \ˈ≈,≈\ *n* **:** a large cabinet or bookcase in which a center section projects beyond the flanking end sections

breakfront

breakhead \ˈ≈,≈\ *n* **:** the reinforcement of the bow of a ship for breaking through ice

break in *vi* **1 :** to break and enter ⟨thieves *broke in* and stole the money⟩ **2 :** to interrupt in a conversation **:** say something abruptly and forcefully ⟨impatient, he *broke in* with an oath⟩ **3 :** to start in an activity or enterprise ⟨he *broke in* with a minor-league team⟩ ⟨*breaking in* with the company as an office boy⟩ **:** gain entrée; *also* **:** to gain experience or skill in a new role or function ⟨the new men are *breaking in* well⟩ ~ *vt* **1 a :** to accustom to a certain activity or occurrence ⟨a skiing instructor *breaking in* novices⟩; *esp* **:** to initiate (as into a job, office, or sport) by instruction, demonstration, and correction **b :** BREAK, TRAIN ⟨*break in* a green horse⟩ **c :** to overcome the stiffness of (a new article) ⟨*breaking in* the shoes⟩ **:** operate or use to overcome the uncertainties of the new and unfamiliar **:** operate sufficiently to test all parts thoroughly ⟨*breaking in* a new car⟩ **2 :** to break so as to cause to fall inward ⟨the mob *broke in* the door⟩ **3 :** to place (a pictorial illustration) in a space provided in the text

¹break–in \ˈ≈,≈\ *n* -s [*break in*] **1 :** the act or action of breaking in **2 :** a hole in brickwork to receive the end of a timber, a plug, or other member **3 :** a preliminary performance or series of performances serving as a trial run **4 :** ²BREAK 3c

²break–in \"\ *adj* **:** of or relating to a system or arrangement in which an automatic device permits the transmitting radio operator to receive incoming signals in intervals between his own transmitted signals

break·ing \ˈbrākiŋ, -kēŋ\ *n* -s [ME *breking* act of demolishing, fr. gerund of *breken* to break — more at BREAK] **1** [trans. of G *brechung*] **:** change of a simple vowel sound into a diphthong whether through the influence of a nearby sound (as in Old English *weorc* "work" with *eo* from earlier *e* before *r* plus consonant) or regardless of phonetic environment (as in Italian *nuovo* "new" from Latin *novus*) **2 :** ²BREAK 4k(1) **3 :** plowed virgin sod land

breaking and entering *or* **break and entry** *n* **:** the act of forcing a passage into and entering another's dwelling or other building **:** HOUSEBREAKING

breaking cart *n* **:** a long-shafted 2-wheeled cart for breaking horses to single harness

breaking engine *n* **:** BREAKER 2c(2)

breaking joint *n* **:** a place of weakness between the fused second and third segments of the leg in many decapod crustaceans (as lobsters and crabs) where the appendage may be cut off by reflex muscular action — compare AUTOTOMY

breaking length *n* **:** that length of material hung vertically at which it will break through its own weight

breaking load *n* **:** stress or tension steadily applied and just sufficient to break or rupture

breaking piece *n* **:** a short shaft made narrow and relatively weak in order to break if the machine with which it is connected is subjected to excessive strain

breaking plow *n* **:** BREAKER 2b

breaking point *n* **1 :** the degree of tension or stress at which a material breaks **2 :** the point at which a person gives way under difficulty or at which a situation becomes crucial

breaking strength *or* **breaking stress** *n* **:** the greatest stress esp. in tension that a material is capable of withstanding without rupture

break in on *or* **break in upon** *vt* **:** to thrust in on **:** intrude upon with force or exigence **:** INTERRUPT ⟨minor details *breaking in on* his work⟩

break into *vt* **1 :** to proceed or pass into or turn to with or as if with a sudden throwing off of restraint ⟨he *broke into* swearing⟩ ⟨his opponents *broke into* bitter criticism⟩ ⟨the horses *broke into* a gallop⟩ **2 :** to make entry or entrance into **:** overcome resistance or exclusiveness in order to become a part, member, or contributor of ⟨romantic girls trying to *break into* the movies⟩ ⟨*breaking into* elite social circles⟩ **3 :** INTERRUPT ⟨*breaking into* the radio play with an important news bulletin⟩ **4 :** to force (a code or cipher) to yield the first of its secrets after which success in breaking must follow

break iron *n* **1 :** an iron that holds a plane bit in place and directs shavings upward and out of the throat of the plane **2 :** an iron fitting with two insulator pins for dead-ending wires from opposite directions on the same cross arm

break jaw *n* **:** one of the last contacts broken when an electrical switch is opened — called also *arcing contact*

break joint *n* **1 :** a masonry shift joint **2 :** a cartilaginous part of the shank just above the ankle in lambs that ossifies as the animal matures

break·less \-ləs\ *adj* **:** being without a break

break line *n* **:** the last line of a paragraph esp. when not of full length when printed

breakneck \ˈ≈,≈\ *adj* [¹*break* + *neck*] **:** inviting danger esp. of a broken neck: as **a :** very rapid **:** HEADLONG ⟨traveling at ~ speed⟩ **b :** very steep ⟨~ stairs to the attic⟩

break–of–bulk \ˈ≈≈ˈ≈\ *n* **:** the act of unloading, transferring, or distributing part or all of a shipment

break off *vi* **1 :** to stop abruptly **:** leave off **:** interrupt what one is doing or saying ⟨he *broke off* in the middle of a sentence⟩ **2 :** to veer from the course when sailing by the wind because of the wind's drawing ahead

break of forecastle : the extreme end of the forecastle toward the waist

break of poop : the end of the poop toward the waist

break–open \ˈ≈,≈≈\ *adj* [fr. *break open*, v.] **:** characterized by breaking for loading ⟨a *break-open* revolver⟩

break out *vi* **1 a** *of a person or his body* **:** to be affected with a skin eruption ⟨*break out* in spots⟩ esp. with one indicative of the presence of a particular disease ⟨*breaking out* with measles⟩ **b** *of a disease* **:** to manifest itself by skin eruptions **c :** to become covered with ⟨*break out* in a sweat⟩ **2 a :** to break from check or inhibition into displaying or flaunting ⟨to *break out* with a scarlet suit⟩ **:** cast off restraint and express a pent-up emotion or satisfy a desire previously checked **b :** to give vent to sudden forceful or loud utterance or expression ⟨they *broke out* laughing in the middle of the speech⟩ **c :** to become unfurled on being raised ⟨when the flags *break out*⟩ **3 :** to project (as a chimney breast from a wall) ~ *vt* **1 a :** to take from shipboard stowage preparatory to using ⟨a galley helper *breaking out* meat from the locker⟩ ⟨*breaking out* charts in the wheelhouse⟩ **b :** to put into readiness for action or use ⟨the guards *broke out* the machine guns⟩ ⟨time to *break out* life rafts⟩ ⟨*breaking out* tents and preparing to make camp⟩ ⟨*breaking out* a 5-man relief detail⟩ **c :** to unpack, unwrap, or open for consumption **:** to bring out from concealment for eating, drinking, or smoking ⟨*breaking out* champagne to celebrate⟩ **2 a :** to dislodge from the bottom and start pulling up (an anchor) in preparation to sail **b :** to haul up (as a flag) furled and cause to unfurl after reaching the proper height or position ⟨the ensign should never be made up and *broken out;* it should always be hoisted flying⟩; *broadly* **:** FLY **:** display flying and unfurled ⟨patriots *breaking out* the national flags⟩ **c :** DISLODGE; *esp* **:** to start in motion after overcoming inertia or freeing from check or hindrance ⟨*breaking out* the sled from the ice around its runners⟩ **3 :** to draw or paint part of the surface (as of a mechanism) as if broken away in order to reveal normally hidden detail ⟨a *broken-out* section⟩

breakout \ˈ⸗,⸗\ *n* -S [*break out*] **1 :** a violent or forceful breaking from what checks, restrains, circumscribes, or imprisons; *esp* **:** a military attack launched to break through enemy lines **2 :** the process of removing and disconnecting pipes, rods, or casings in well drilling

breakover \ˈ⸗,⸗⸗\ *n* -S [*break over,* v.] **:** the portion of a newspaper or magazine story continued on another page

break pin *n* **:** SHEAR PIN

breakpoint \ˈ⸗,⸗\ *n* **1 :** the point in one method of chlorinating drinking water at which the amount of available chlorine in the water falls to a minimum and after which it increases proportionately with the amount of chlorine being added indicating that most of the undesirable tastes and odors have been removed **2 :** a point (as in a process) at which an interruption can be made

break roll *n* **:** one of several corrugated rollers between which grain is ground into flour

breaks *pl of* BREAK, *pres 3d sing of* BREAK

breaksaway *pl of* BREAKAWAY

breakstone \ˈ⸗,⸗\ *n* [1*break* + *stone*] **1 :** SAXIFRAGE **2 :** any plant growing in stony places (as the parsley piert, the burnet saxifrage, or the pearlwort)

breakthrough \ˈ⸗,⸗\ *n* -S [*break through,* v.] **1 a :** an act or action of breaking through an obstruction, check, or restriction ⟨a ~ to a radically higher and broader conception —Walter Lippmann⟩ **b :** a place at which such an act or action takes place **2 :** a short passage or narrow opening connecting adjacent or parallel mine workings **3 :** the action by water of breaking or wearing a passage **:** the channel made by water in so doing **4 :** an offensive thrust that penetrates and carries beyond a defensive or reinforcing line in warfare **5 :** a sudden marked increase in prices or values above previous levels ⟨the news caused a ~ in steel prices⟩ **6 :** a sensational advance in scientific knowledge in which some baffling major problem is solved ⟨a ~ like atomic fission⟩

break up *vt* **1** *archaic* **:** to enter forcefully **:** break into **:** break and enter **2 :** to disrupt the continuity or flow of ⟨quotations are apt to *break up* a book by making it less easy to read —J.E.Gloag⟩ **3 a :** to bring about the decomposition or destruction of **b :** DISSIPATE, CURE ⟨*break up* a cold⟩ **c :** to bring to an end by settling or disrupting ⟨a home run in the tenth that *broke up* the game⟩ ⟨a fight that *broke up* the meeting⟩ **4 :** to break into pieces in scrapping or salvaging **:** SCRAP ⟨*breaking up* the obsolete warships⟩ **5 :** to check broodiness in (a hen) usu. by isolation or change of diet — compare BROODY COOP ~ *vi* **1 a :** to cease to exist as a unit **:** split into separate components **:** DISBAND, DISPERSE ⟨the party *broke up* at midnight⟩ ⟨his family had *broken up* and scattered⟩ ⟨when school *breaks up* in the spring⟩ **b :** become separated into parts or fragments **:** DISSOLVE ⟨when the ice *breaks up* on the river⟩ **2 a :** to fail physically **b :** to lose morale, composure, or resolution ⟨likely to *break up* under enemy attack⟩ ⟨*broke up* when he heard the joke⟩

breakup \ˈ⸗,⸗\ *n* -S [*break up*] **1 :** a disruption or dissolution into component parts **:** an ending as an effective entity ⟨the ~ of the empire⟩ ⟨the ~ of a political party⟩ ⟨the ~ of a marriage⟩ **2 :** division into smaller units ⟨the ~ of the large estates⟩ **3 :** the breaking, melting, and loosening of ice in streams and harbors in the spring **4 :** DECOMPOSITION, DISINTEGRATION **5 :** an excavation upward to the arch level made in tunneling from bottom drifts to provide a new face

breakup value *n* **:** the value in liquidation esp. of shares of stock of a financial corporation

breakwater \ˈ⸗,⸗⸗\ *n* [1*break* + *water*] **1 :** an offshore structure for breaking the force of waves (as to protect a harbor or beach) **2 :** a steel plate or wood V-shaped structure built on the forward weather deck of a ship or boat to keep the sea off the deck

breakwind \ˈ⸗,⸗\ *n* [1*break* + *wind*] *Brit* **:** SCREEN, WINDBREAK

1bream \ˈbrim (*usual US pronunc*), ˈbrēm *sometimes* ˈbrem\ *n, pl* **bream** *or* **breams** [ME *brem, breme,* fr. MF *breme, bresme, brasme,* fr. OF *braisme, bresme,* of Gmc origin; akin to OHG *brahsima, brahsema* bream, OS *bressemo,* MD & MLG *bressem, brassem* bream, OHG *brettan* to draw a sword — more at BRAID] **1 :** a European freshwater cyprinid fish (*Abramis brama*) of little value as food with a narrow deep body and arched back; *broadly* **:** any of certain related fishes (as the golden shiner of No. America) **2 :** any of various fishes somewhat resembling the European bream in form: as **a :** any fish of the family Sparidae — compare PORGY **b :** any of various freshwater sunfishes of *Lepomis* and related genera; *esp* **:** BLUEGILL **c :** ROSEFISH — compare BLACK BREAM, SEA BREAM

2bream \ˈbrēm\ *vt* -ED/-ING/-S [prob. fr. D *brem* furze, fr. MD *bremme, brimme;* akin to OE *brōm* broom; fr. the use of burning furze in the cleaning — more at BROOM] **:** to clean (a ship's bottom) by means of fire and scraping

breard \ˈbrērd\ *Scot var of* BRAIRD

breas *pl of* BREA

1breast \ˈbrest\ *n* -S *often attrib* [ME *brest, breest,* fr. OE *brēost;* akin to OHG *brust* breast, ON *brjōst,* Goth *brusts* (pl.) breast, OIr *brū* belly, Russ *bryukho*] **1 a :** either of two protuberant milk-producing glandular organs situated on the front of the chest or thorax in the human female and some other mammals and normally functional only during the period of lactation following pregnancy **b :** any discrete mammary gland — compare UDDER **c :** a breast in lactation ⟨giving the infant son the ~⟩; *broadly* **:** a source of nourishment ⟨the university serving as the ~ for this intellectual movement⟩ **d :** either of the paired and normally nonfunctional mammary glands of the human male esp. when excessively enlarged and protuberant (as by reason of accumulated fatty tissue) **2 a :** the fore or ventral part of the body between the neck and the abdomen **:** the front of the chest ⟨a soldier shot in the ~⟩ ⟨a bird with an orange ~⟩; *also* **:** either side of the front of the chest ⟨a wound in the right ~⟩ **b** *obs* **:** the whole upper part of the body **:** THORAX **c :** the breastbone with its attached muscles (as of a calf, lamb, or fowl dressed as meat) **d** *obs* **:** the bodily area containing the lungs; *also* **:** singing voice **3 :** the breast regarded as the seat of emotion, affection, sentiment, thought, or intent **:** BOSOM, HEART ⟨opposing the enemy with dauntless ~⟩ ⟨causing little concern in official ~s⟩ **4 :** something resembling a breast **:** a front, forward, swelling, bulging, or curving part ⟨the ~ of the lake⟩: **a** (1) **:** the portion of a wall between a window and the floor (2) **:** CHIMNEY BREAST 2 (3) **:** the underside of a member (as a handrail, beam, or rafter) (4) **:** a portion of a wall projecting outward (as at a chimney) **b :** the front part of a plow moldboard **c** (1) **:** the face of a tunnel or mine working (2) **:** a room or stall in a coal mine **d** (1) **:** the fore part of the heel of a shoe next to the shank (2) **:** the front face of a shoe heel **e :** the side of the hearth containing the metal notch in a shaft furnace **f :** the first roller of a carding machine **g :** BREAST FAST **h :** the end of a can having a central raised section containing an opening **5** *archaic* **:** the broad even front of a group or body in motion **6 a :** the part of an article of clothing covering the breast ⟨with pockets at the ~⟩ ⟨their ~s were laden with decorations and medals —F.J.Mather⟩ **b :** BREASTPLATE **7 :** the portion of an arrow that touches the bow when in position for shooting

2breast \"\ *vb* -ED/-ING/-S *vt* **1 :** to oppose the breast to **:** FACE, CONFRONT **:** oppose or contend against manfully ⟨~*ing* the waves⟩ ⟨~*ing* the storm of traffic —Adrian Bell⟩ ⟨to dare to ~ an entrenched political machine⟩ **2** *Brit* **:** to climb resolutely **:** ASCEND ⟨the train had ~*ed* the heavy ascent —O.S.Nock⟩ ⟨the ponies ~*ed* the steep shale slopes —Douglas Carruthers⟩ **3 :** to draw abreast of or alongside of **4 :** to haul or bring broadside on ⟨~*ing* the ship against the dock with the winches⟩ **5 :** to thrust the chest against ⟨the sprinter ~*ed* the tape⟩ ~ *vi* **1 :** to press forward with or as if with the breast ⟨ships ~*ing* through the waves⟩ **2 :** to approach esp. in order to accost ⟨a stranger came ~*ing* up to him⟩

breast auger *n* **:** an auger for soft rock or coal that is advanced under pressure from the miner's chest or breast — compare BREAST DRILL

breast backstay *n* **:** a forward backstay set up to sustain an upper mast when the wind is before the beam

breastband \ˈ⸗,⸗\ *n* **1 :** BREAST COLLAR **2 :** a band or rope fastened at both ends to the rigging to support the man who heaves the lead in sounding

breastbeam \ˈ⸗,⸗\ *n* **1 :** a beam where the quarterdeck or forecastle breaks **2 :** the beam or rail over which newly woven cloth passes in a loom on its way to the take-up and cloth roll

breast-beater \ˈ⸗,⸗⸗\ *n* **:** one that engages in breast-beating

breast-beating \ˈ⸗,⸗⸗\ *n* **:** noisy demonstrative protestation (as of grief, anger, or self-recrimination)

breast board *n* **1 :** MOLDBOARD **2 :** a retaining board used at the breast of a mine working to hold back soft ground **3 :** a board at a ship's breastbeam

breastbone \ˈ⸗,⸗\ *n* [ME *brestbon,* fr. OE *brēostbān,* fr. *brēost* breast + *bān* bone — more at BREAST, BONE] **:** the sternum esp. when the parts are largely ossified and fused (as in adult mammals and birds)

breast collar *n* **:** a harness strap extending across the chest in place of a collar—called also *breastband;* see HARNESS illustration

breast cylinder *n* **:** the first large roller serving for initial opening of the stock in carding

breast drill *n* **:** a portable drill with a plate that is pressed by the breast in forcing the drill against the work

breast·ed \ˈbrestəd\ *adj* [ME *brested,* fr. *brest* breast + *-ed*] **:** having a breast **:** having (such) a breast — used chiefly in compounds ⟨broad-*breasted*⟩ ⟨red-*breasted*⟩

breasted arrow *n* **:** an arrow having its greatest diameter at the breast

breast·er \ˈbrestə(r)\ *n* -S [1*breast* + *-er*] **:** one that cuts breasts on shoe heels

breast fast *also* **breast line** *n* **:** a mooring line leading from midship (as to a wharf) at an angle of about 90° from the fore-and-aft line

breast-fed \ˈ⸗,⸗\ *adj* **:** fed from a mother's breast ⟨differences between *breast-fed* and bottle-fed babies⟩

breast-feed \ˈ⸗,⸗\ *vt* **:** to feed (a baby) from a mother's breast rather than from a bottle **:** SUCKLE

breast drill

breast harness *n* **:** the part of a horse's harness worn on or depending from the fore part of the body and including breast collar and hames with straps, traces, or tugs

breast·height \ˈ⸗,⸗\ *n* **:** the height of 4½ feet above ground at which the diameters of standing trees are usu. measured

breast-high scent *n* **:** a scent so strong that dogs course heads up

breast hole *n* **:** a hole in a smelting cupola for raking out cinders

breast·hook \ˈ⸗,⸗\ *n* **:** a V-shaped timber or plate connecting ship timbers or stringers of opposite sides where they run into the stem; *also* **:** a similar connecting piece at the stern — called also *crutch*

1breasting *pres part of* BREAST

2breast·ing \ˈbrestiŋ, -tēŋ\ *n* -S [1*breast* + *-ing*] **1 :** the cutting of a shoe breast to even curve and pitch **2 :** the material covering the breast of a shoe heel — see SHOE illustration **3 :** BREAST STOPING

breasting knife *n* **:** a knife for cutting a clean face on the breast of a heel

breast knee *n* **:** BREASTHOOK

breast·less \-ləs\ *adj* **:** being without a breast

breastmark \ˈ⸗,⸗\ *n* [*abreast* + *mark*] **:** a mark placed abreast of some prominent landmark in surveying

breast milk *n* **:** milk from the human breast

breast molding *n* **:** a molding on the breast of a wall or on a window sill

breast off *vi* **1 :** to moor parallel to but at a distance from a dock **:** install spars between a moored ship and wharf to leave space for lighters in between **2 :** to move back from a dock ⟨a boat *breasting off* to make space⟩

breastpin \ˈ⸗,⸗\ *n* **1 :** a woman's brooch **2 :** TIEPIN

breastplate \ˈ⸗,⸗\ *n* [ME *brestplate,* fr. *brest* breast + *plate*] **1 a :** a metal plate protecting the breast as defensive armor — see ARMOR illustration **b :** SHIELD, DEFENSE **2 :** a vestment worn in ancient times by a Jewish high priest, made of a double piece of rich woven fabric, embroidered, and set with 12 gems bearing the names of the tribes of Israel — see EPHOD illustration **3 :** BREASTSUMMER **4 :** a piece against which the workman presses his breast in operating a breast drill or similar tool **5 :** BREAST STRAP 2 **6 :** a small ornamental metal plate to hold a soldier's shoulder belts at their point of crossing on the breast **7 :** a hard or bony covering of the breast of an animal (as the plastron of a turtle) **8 :** a metal plate for inscriptions on a casket

breastplow \ˈ⸗,⸗\ *n* **:** a plow for cutting turf that is driven by the breast of the workman

breast pump *n* **:** a suction apparatus for milking the breast

breast·rail \ˈ⸗,⸗\ *n* **1 :** the upper rail of a parapet or a balcony **2 :** the railing of a quarterdeck of a ship

breast roll *n* **:** BREASTBEAM 2

breast·rope \ˈ⸗,⸗\ *n* **:** a rope used as a breastband (as around a man making soundings from a ship)

breasts *pl of* BREAST, *pres 3d sing of* BREAST

breast stoping *n* **:** mining in which the ore is broken from a nearly vertical face

breast strap *n* **1 :** a strap attached to the collar and supporting the yoke in team harness **2 :** a band passing around the front of the chest and joining the trace at the saddle and in light and single harness replacing the collar as the point against which the effort of the horse is primarily exerted

breaststroke \ˈ⸗,⸗\ *n* **:** a swimming stroke executed prone and with shoulders parallel to the water's surface by extending the arms in front of the head and sweeping them back simultaneously, palms out, while making a frog kick — compare BUTTERFLY

breaststroke kick *n* **:** the leg action used in swimming the breaststroke in which the feet, moving in a horizontal plane, are drawn toward the hips and then thrust sideward and backward — called also *whip kick*

breast·sum·mer \ˈbres(t),səmə(r), ˈbresəm-\ *n* [1*breast* + *summer* (beam)] **:** a beam, girder, or lintel placed horizontally over an opening (as a window) to support the superstructure

breast tea *n* [so called fr. its use as a pectoral] **:** a tea prepared from cut and bruised althaea, coltsfoot, licorice root, anise, mullein flowers, and orrisroot and formerly used as a household remedy for respiratory disorders

breast wall *n* **:** a wall built to sustain the face of a natural bank of earth — compare RETAINING WALL

breast·weed \ˈ⸗,⸗\ *n* [so called fr. its use in treating mammary inflammation] **:** LIZARD'S-TAIL

breast wheel *n* **:** a waterwheel onto which the water is led at about axle height and which acts partly by impulse and partly by the weight of the descending water in the buckets — compare OVERSHOT WHEEL, UNDERSHOT WHEEL

breastwise \ˈ⸗,⸗\ *adv* [1*breast* + *-wise*] **:** ABREAST

breastwork \ˈ⸗,⸗\ *n* **1 :** an improvised or temporary fortification **2 :** a railing on the quarterdeck and forecastle **3 :** brickwork or masonry making a fireplace breast

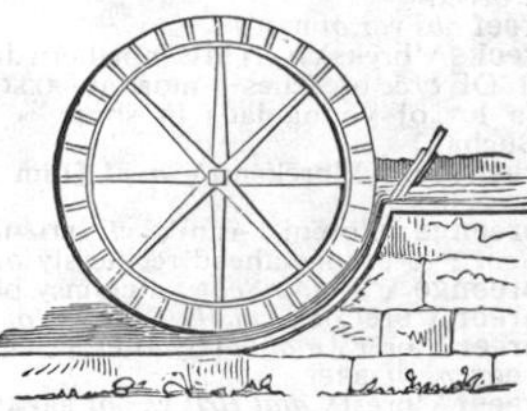

section of breast wheel

breastwork log *n* **:** FENDER SKID

breath \ˈbreth\ *n* -S [ME *breeth, breth,* fr. OE *brǣth;* akin to OHG *brādam* breath, heat, ON *brāth* tar, OE *beorma* yeast — more at BARM] **1 a :** steam, smoke, vapor, or other emanation ⟨the ~ of the fire⟩ ⟨the ~ from the river⟩ **b :** air charged with a certain fragrance, odor, or other suggestion ⟨the ~ of roses in the parlor⟩ ⟨carrying with him the ~ of the grave⟩ **:** EMANATION, SUGGESTION ⟨a ~ of mystery about the proceedings⟩ **2 a :** the faculty or power of breathing freely and naturally ⟨he is near death; his ~ is failing⟩ ⟨recovering his ~ after his mad dash⟩ **b :** the act of breathing **:** a single inhalation or exhalation ⟨fighting to his last ~⟩ ⟨speaking also of his brother in the same ~⟩ **c :** opportunity to breathe **:** time to breathe or recover one's breath **:** time for rest or recovery **:** RESPITE ⟨granting some pause, some ~⟩ **3 :** a slight breeze **:** air in gentle motion ⟨not a breeze — no ~ of air —William Wordsworth⟩ **4 a :** air exhaled from the lungs esp. as made apparent by odor or vapor ⟨his ~ smells bad⟩ ⟨a strong smell of whiskey on his ~⟩ ⟨to see one's ~ on a cold day⟩ **b :** air inhaled and exhaled ⟨to draw ~⟩ ⟨after the ~ has left one's body⟩ **c :** INHALATION **:** amount of gas inhaled ⟨a ~ of nitrous oxide⟩ **5 a :** breath used in speech **:** spoken sound or sounds **:** WHISPER, UTTERANCE ⟨no ~ of objection was heard⟩; *sometimes* **:** a slight utterance, gesture or similar act **b :** moisture condensed from one's breath ⟨to see one's ~ on a pane of glass⟩; *sometimes* **:** a slight stain or tarnish ⟨there had never been a ~ on her reputation —Edith Wharton⟩ **c :** air blown through a musical instrument; *also* **:** the resulting sound ⟨the ~ of the trumpet⟩ **6 :** SPIRIT, ANIMATION, VITALITY, LIFE ⟨many a bard's untimely death lends unto his verses ~ —Edna S.V.Millay⟩ **7 :** expiration of air with the glottis wide open so that there is no audible vibration of the vocal cords (as in the formation of \f\ and \s\ sounds) — compare BREATHED, VOICELESS — **below one's breath** *or* **under one's breath :** in a whisper **:** in an inaudible or barely audible voice — **in one breath** *or* **in the same breath :** practically at once **:** almost simultaneously — **out of breath :** gasping for breath (as after strenuous activity) **:** breathing very rapidly

breath·able *also* **breathe·able** \ˈbrēthəbəl\ *adj* **:** fit for being breathed **:** suitable for normal breathing

breathe \ˈbrēth\ *vb* -ED/-ING/-S [ME *brethen,* fr. *breth, breeth* breath] *vi* **1 a** *obs* **:** to emanate into the air as or as if vapor or steam **b** *obs* **:** to send out an odor or fragrance **:** SMELL **c :** to become perceptible **:** be emanated or suggested **:** be expressed ⟨the spirit of the age as it ~*s* from our novelists —*Times Lit. Supp.*⟩ ⟨a fond complacency *breathed* from both girls —Anne D. Sedgwick⟩ **2 a** (1) **:** to draw air into and expel it out of the lungs **:** inhale and exhale **:** RESPIRE (2) **:** to take in oxygen and give out carbon dioxide through natural processes that resemble or are analogous to breathing ⟨plants *breathing* at night⟩ ⟨a fish cannot ~ out of water⟩ **b :** to inhale and exhale freely without sense or feeling of constriction ⟨an atmosphere of intellectual freedom in which he could ~ —Francis Biddle⟩ **c :** to inhale and exhale audibly ⟨the doctor listened to his *breathing*⟩ **3 a :** to continue in existence **:** LIVE **b :** to continue to have vital force or effect **4 :** to pause and rest (as after strenuous activity) **5 :** to make utterance ⟨in making that plea he will ~ in vain⟩ **:** to be uttered ⟨a whisper *breathing* low⟩ **6 :** to blow softly ⟨a light wind *breathing*⟩ **7 :** to draw in and give out air, gas, or vapor (as of a fuel tank) **:** pass air in and out (as of a cushion) or through (as of leather or other membrane) **8** *of an internal-combustion engine* **:** to use air to support combustion ~ *vt* **1 a :** EXHALE **:** send out by exhaling **:** emit as if in breathing out — often used with *out* ⟨*breathing* out his soul⟩ **b :** to instill by breathing in **:** infuse as if by breathing **:** communicate by breath — often used with *in* or *into* ⟨*breathing* new life into the movement⟩ **2 :** UTTER, EXPRESS: as **a :** to utter vehemently **:** cry out ⟨*breathing* threats about revenge⟩ **b :** to utter softly, quietly, or confidentially **:** WHISPER ⟨*breathing* his advice softly⟩ ⟨don't ~ a word of what he said⟩ **c :** to make manifest **:** EVINCE, SHOW ⟨*breathing* the true spirit of his religion⟩ **3 :** to let breathe **:** give a period of rest from exertion or security from danger to ⟨*breathing* their horses after the hard ride⟩ ⟨a chance for the messenger to ~ himself⟩ **4 a :** to exercise briskly ⟨a chase across the fields to ~ the dogs⟩ **b :** to exercise vigorously and deprive of breath **:** WIND, EXHAUST **5 a :** to draw into and usu. press out of the lungs **:** inhale and exhale ⟨*breathing* fresh air⟩ ⟨*breathing* noxious gases⟩ **b :** to pull in and consume (oxygen) in operation — used esp. of an engine — **breathe a vein :** to open a vein to let blood — **breathe down one's neck :** to threaten or loom threateningly in or as if in pursuit or attack — **breathe easily** *or* **breathe freely :** to enjoy relief from pressure, strain, anxiety, or danger — **breathe one's last :** DIE

breathed \ˈbretht, *in sense 2 sometimes* ˈbrēthd\ *adj* [ME *brethed,* fr. *breth* breath + *-ed*] **1 :** having breath **:** having (such) a breath — used esp. in compounds ⟨a long-*breathed* speaker⟩ **2 :** uttered without voice **:** VOICELESS — by some phoneticians not regarded as applicable to voiceless stops

breathe on *or* **breathe upon** *vt* **:** to taint with scandal **:** TARNISH ⟨when her name was *breathed upon*⟩

breath·er \ˈbrēthə(r)\ *n* -S [*breathe* + *-er*] **1 :** one that utters, speaks, or proclaims ⟨scandal that hurt its ~ more than its subject⟩ **2 :** one that breathes usu. in an indicated way ⟨in his sleep the child was a mouth ~⟩ **3 :** a spell of usu. violent exercise **:** something that occasions violent exercise ⟨climbing the mountain was a real ~⟩ **4 a :** a rest period **:** a break in one's activity for rest and relaxation **:** a brief relaxation of effort ⟨taking a ~ after the heavy work⟩ **b :** a game or match against a weak opponent ⟨opened the season with a ~⟩ **5 :** a small vent in an otherwise airtight enclosure for maintaining equality of pressure within and without (as in oil tanks, transformers, crankcases, instrument cases) **6 :** a device to facilitate breathing esp. under unusual circumstances ⟨a new ~ in the diver's equipment⟩

breathes *pres 3d sing of* BREATHE

breathe to *or* **breathe after** *vt, obs* **:** to long for **:** aspire to

breath group *n* **:** a stretch of utterance between two pauses of sufficient length for an intake of breath to be made at each

breath·i·ness \ˈbrethēnəs, -thin-\ *n* -ES **:** the quality of being breathy ⟨singing with a noticeable ~⟩

breath·ing \ˈbrēthiŋ, -thēŋ\ *n* -S [ME *brething* act of respiration, fr. gerund of *brethen* to breathe] **1 a :** a very brief time ⟨it all happened in a ~⟩ **b :** a pause for taking breath **:** DELAY **2 :** either of the marks ʽ and ʼ used in writing Greek, the former to indicate aspiration, the latter to indicate absence of aspiration — see ROUGH BREATHING, SMOOTH BREATHING **3 :** BREATHER 3 **4 :** the passage of air into or out of an aerostat due to changing volume

breathing capacity *n* **:** VITAL CAPACITY

breath·ing·ly *adv* **:** in a breathing manner

breathing mark *n* **:** a comma or other small mark placed over a score to show a singer or wind-instrument player where to take a breath

breathing space *n* **1 :** an unoccupied space **:** an area set aside for or conducive to rest **2** *or* **breathing spell :** a period of inactivity esp. for rest, recreation, and mustering up strength for subsequent efforts ⟨attacking all along the line and giving the enemy no *breathing space*⟩

breathing valve *n* **:** one of certain folds of membrane that control the direction of the flow of water through the mouth, past the gills, and to the exterior in many fishes

breath·less \ˈbrethləs\ *adj* [ME *brethles,* fr. *breth* breath + *-les* -less] **1 a :** not breathing **:** showing suspension of breath **b :** DEAD **2 a :** out of breath **:** panting or gasping for breath after strenuous activity **b :** leaving one breathless **:** STRENUOUS ⟨the pace was rather ~ —A.H.Vandenberg †1951⟩ **c :** out of breath or holding one's breath because of fear, suspense, intense interest, awe, or other strong emotion ⟨~ at the thought of what I had done —Katherine Mansfield⟩ ⟨~ with a strange, painful, yielding ardor —Morley Callaghan⟩ **d :** bringing about or marked by a holding of breath or a holding of one's breath **:** INTENSE, GRIPPING, DOMINATING ⟨the air was so charged with the ~ tension —Hugh Walpole⟩ ⟨caught up into ~ crisis —John Buchan⟩ **e :** suffering from dyspnea **3 :** marked by complete stillness of the air **:** oppressive and close because of absence of breezes ⟨the summer came, ~ and sultry —W.S.Maugham⟩ ⟨sticky with sirocco moisture under the ~ awning —Norman Douglas⟩ — **breath·less·ly** *adv*

breath·less·ness \-nəs\ *n* -ES **1 :** the state of being out of breath **:** a quality making for a breathless condition **2 :** DYSPNEA

breath of heaven 1 : a small southern African shrub (*Adenandra fragrans*) with small leathery leaves and white or pink flowers that is cultivated in California **2 :** an evergreen shrub (*Diosma ericoides*) with perfumed needlelike foliage

breaths *pl of* BREATH

breathtaker \ˈ⸗,⸗⸗\ *n* **:** one (as an exciting game, a near accident) that is breathtaking

breathtaking \'ˌ=ˌ==\ *adj* **1 :** making one out of breath **:** having shock effects that check breathing ⟨a ~ pain in his side⟩ ⟨a ~ plunge into the icy water⟩ **2 :** commanding intense interest **:** striking with awe and wonder **:** EXCITING, THRILLING ⟨the ~ grandeur of the mountain scenery⟩ ⟨~ in the rapidity and completeness of change —Amy Loveman⟩ ⟨~ beauty⟩ — **breath·tak·ing·ly** *adv*

breathy \'brethē, -thi\ *adj* -ER/-EST [*breath* + *-y*] **1** *of a vocal sound* **:** characterized by or accompanied with the audible passage of unvocalized breath **2** *of a performance on a wind instrument* **:** impaired in purity of tone by the presence of excessive or poorly controlled breath

bre·ba \'brābə, -āvə\ *n* -S [Sp *breva*, alter. of OSp *bebra*, fr. L (*ficus*) *bifera* twice-bearing fig, fr. *ficus* fig + *bifera*, fem. of *bifer* twice-bearing, fr. *bi-* ¹bi- + *-fer* ferous] **:** a fig of the first crop ripening on the old wood

brec·cia \'brech(ē)ə, -esh-\ *n* -S [It] **1 :** a rock consisting of sharp fragments embedded in a fine-grained matrix (as sand or clay) **2 :** an agglomerate deposit of debris in a cave or other site occupied by prehistoric man

brec·cial \-ech(ē)əl, -esh-\ *adj* **:** of or relating to breccia

brec·ciate \'brechē,āt, -e,chāt, -esh-, -e,sh-\ *vt* -ED/-ING/-S **:** to break (a rock or rock formation) into angular fragments **:** form (rock) into a breccia

brecciated *adj* [It *brecciato*, fr. *breccia* + *-ato* -ate] **:** converted into, resembling, or marked by a breccia

brec·ci·a·tion \ˌbrechē'āshən, -esh-\ *n* -S **:** formation of a breccia

brec·cio·la \bre'chōlə, ˌbrechē'ō-, -e'sh-, -esh-\ *n* -S [It, fr. *breccia* + *-ola* -ole] **:** a limestone breccia that is deposited by turbid water and is intraformational in character

brech·am \'brekəm\ *n* -S [ME *berhom, bargham* — more at BARGHAM] *chiefly Scot & Irish* **:** a horse collar

brech·an \'brekən\ *also* **brack·en** \'brakən\ *n* -S [ScGael *breacan*, fr. *breac* spotted, variegated; akin to OIr *brec* spotted, variegated] **:** a plaid of the Scottish Highlands

bre·chi·tes \bre'kīd·ēz, -ī,tēz\ *n, cap* [NL, fr. Gk *brechein* to wet, get wet, to rain + L *-ites* -ite; akin to Russ *morgota* fog, heavy air, Latvian *merguot* to drizzle] **:** a genus of marine bivalve mollusks (suborder Anatinacea) — see WATERING-POT SHELL

¹**breck** \'brek\ *n* -S [ME *brek*, fr. *breken* to break — more at BREAK] *dial Eng* **:** BREACH, GAP

²**breck** \"\ *n* -S [perh. fr. ON *brekka* slope of a hill — more at BRINK] *Brit* **:** a stretch of rough or sandy often undulating ground ⟨scattered trees or the pine hedges which are a feature of the Norfolk ~s —Bruce Campbell⟩; *also* **:** an enclosed portion of such land

breck·an \'brekən\ *chiefly Scot var of* ¹BRACKEN

breck·nock·shire \'brek,näk,shi(ə)r, -ˌnək-, -kshər\ *or* **breck·nock** \-äk,-ək\ *adj, usu cap* [fr. *Brecknockshire* or *Brecknock* county, Wales] **:** of or from the county of Brecknock, Wales **:** of the kind or style prevalent in Brecknock

¹**bred** *past of* ¹BREED

²**bred** \'bred\ *adj* [fr. past part. of *breed*] **1 :** reared or born and reared in (such) a way **:** inculcated with the (specified) traditions — often in compounds ⟨a farm-*bred* youth⟩ ⟨city-*bred* people⟩ **2 :** of (specified) breed — usu. used in compounds ⟨pure*bred*⟩ ⟨cross*bred*⟩ **3** *of a female animal* **:** IMPREGNATED

bred·berg·ite \'bred(ˌ)bər,gīt\ *n* -S [B. G. *Bredberg* 19th cent. American who first described it + E *-ite*] **:** an andradite garnet containing magnesium

brede \'brēd\ *n* -S [alter. of ²*braid*] **1** *archaic* **:** EMBROIDERY **2** *archaic* **:** BRAIDING; *esp* **:** interweaving of colors

bre·di \'brādē\ *n* -ES [Afrik *bredie* (formerly, also a plant of the sorrel family), fr. a native name in Madagascar] *Africa* **:** meat stew containing a vegetable

bred-in-the-bone \ˌ===ˌ=\ *adj* **1 :** very deeply inculcated **:** made an essential of an overall character ⟨his *bred-in-the-bone* honesty⟩ ⟨the *bred-in-the-bone* frugality of the peasantry⟩ **2 :** marked by a quality, trait, or belief that is inveterate, deep, lasting, and genuine ⟨a *bred-in-the-bone* believer in the old religion⟩ ⟨a *bred-in-the-bone* gambler⟩

bred out *adj* **1 :** DEGENERATED **2** *zool* **:** degenerated due to becoming homozygous for latent defective genes by inbreeding

¹**bree** \'brē\ *n* -S [ME *breye, bree* eyelid, eyebrow, fr. OE *brǣw* — more at BRAE] *Scot* **:** EYEBROW, BROW

²**bree** \"\ *n* -S [ME *bre*, prob. alter. of *bri*, fr. OE *brīw, brīg;* akin to OHG *brīo* soup, mush, MD *brī*, OE *brīwan* to cook, MIr *brēo* flame, OE *byrnan* to burn — more at BURN] *now chiefly Scot* **:** liquid in which a substance has been boiled or steeped **:** BROTH, SOUP, GRAVY

¹**breech** *in senses 2-4* 'brēch *also esp in rural areas* 'brich; "*breeches*" (*garment*) *is* 'brichəz *sometimes esp in urban areas* -rēch-, *but* -rēch- *is usual for "breeches buoy"*\ *n* -ES [ME *breech* pair of breeches, fr. OE *brēc* breeches, pl. of *brōc* leg covering; akin to OHG *bruoh* pair of breeches, ON *brōk* leg covering, OE *brecan* to break — more at BREAK] **1 breeches** *pl* **a :** short trousers for covering the hips and thighs that fit snugly around the waist at the top and at the lower edges at or just below the knee — called also *knee breeches;* see RIDING BREECHES **b :** PANTS **2 a :** the hind end of the body **:** BUTTOCKS **b :** BREECHING 3 **3 a :** the part of a cannon or other firearm at the rear of the bore — see CANNON illustration **b :** the bottom of a pulley block **:** the end of a block opposite the swallow **c :** the external angle of a timber knee — compare THROAT **4 a** *or* **breech presentation :** a presentation of the fetus in which the breech is the first part to appear at the uterine cervix **b :** a fetus that is presented breech first

²**breech** *in sense 1* 'brich *also* 'brēch, *in sense 2* 'brēch *also* 'brich\ *vt* -ED/-ING/-ES **1** *archaic & dial* **:** to put breeches on **2** *archaic* **:** to whip on the buttocks

breechblock \'ˌ=ˌ=\ *n* **:** the block in breech-loading firearms that closes the rear of the bore against the force of the charge

breechclout *or* **breechcloth** \'ˌ=ˌ=\ *n* [¹*breech* + *clout* or *cloth*] **:** LOINCLOTH

breech delivery *n* **:** delivery of a fetus with the breech appearing first

breeched \'bricht, 'brēcht — *see* ¹BREECH\ *adj* [¹*breech* + *-ed*] **:** wearing breeches

breeches buoy *see* ¹BREECH\ *n* **:** a canvas seat shaped like a pair of short-legged breeches which is dependent from a circular life buoy suspended from and running upon a hawser and in which a person being rescued is hauled from one ship to another or from ship to shore

1 breeches buoy; *2, 3, 4* tackle for hauling back and forth; *5* supporting block running on the hawser, *6*

breechesflower \'==ˌ=\ *n* **:** DUTCHMAN'S-BREECHES

breeches part *n* **:** a theatrical role that is regularly or frequently played by an actress in male costume

breeches pipe *n* **:** a forked pipe

breech·ing \'brēchiŋ, -chēŋ *also esp in rural areas* 'brich- *or* -chən\ *n* -S [¹*breech* + *-ing*] **1 :** the part of a harness that passes around the breech of a draft animal and enables him to hold back a vehicle — see HARNESS illustration **2** *obs* **:** a whipping on the buttocks **3 :** the short coarse wool on the breech and hind legs of a sheep or goat; *also* **:** the hair on the corresponding parts of a dog **4 :** a rope formerly rove through the cascabel of a cannon used for securing the cannon to the side of a ship **5 :** the breech or breech action of a gun **6 :** a sheet-iron or sheet-steel casing at the end of boilers for conveying the smoke from the flues to the smokestack **7 :** a metal fitting, often containing a valve, that serves to connect two lines of hose or to divide a hose into two legs

breech·less \'brichləs, 'brēch-\ *adj* **:** being without breeches

breechloader \'=ˌ==\ *n* **:** a breech-loading firearm

breech-loading \'=ˌ==\ *adj, of a firearm* **:** receiving the cartridge or projectile at the breech

breech mechanism *n* **:** the mechanism for opening and closing the breech of a breech-loading firearm, esp. of a heavy-caliber gun

breech pin *n* **:** BREECH PLUG

breech plug *n* **1 :** a plug for closing the breech of a gun **:** BREECHBLOCK **2 :** a cascabel plug screwed through the breech to support the inner tube

breech presentation *n* **:** BREECH 4a

¹**breed** \'brēd\ *vb* **bred** \'bred\ **bred; breeding; breeds** [ME *breden*, fr. OE *brēdan;* akin to OHG *bruoten* to brood; denominative fr. the root of OE *brōd* brood — more at BROOD] *vt* **1 :** to produce (offspring) by hatching or gestation **:** give birth to ⟨yet every mother ~s not sons alike —Shak.⟩ **2 a :** BEGET **2 b :** to cause to come into being **:** PRODUCE, ENGENDER ⟨every scholarly discipline ~s its own jargon —*Times Lit. Supp.*⟩ ⟨extended wars always ~ depression —F.A.Bradford⟩ **3 :** to be the native place of ⟨a pond ~s fish⟩ ⟨a northern country ~s stout men⟩ **:** provide conditions conducive to development of ⟨liberty in all its wildness *bred* iron conscience —Van Wyck Brooks⟩ **4 :** to propagate sexually: **a :** to propagate (plants) by artificial pollination **b :** to improve (a stock) by controlled propagation — compare BREEDING 5 **c :** to develop (desired qualities or characteristics) by breeding ⟨chicks with high production *bred* into them —L.E.Card⟩ **5 a :** to develop by tradition or education **:** bring up **:** NURTURE, TRAIN ⟨no care was taken to ~ him a Protestant —Gilbert Burnet⟩ — often used with *in* or *to* ⟨he was *bred* in the tradition of liberalism —Max Whatman⟩ ⟨ships commanded by men who had not been *bred* to the sea⟩ **b :** to inculcate (a quality) by training ⟨good manners were *bred* into them⟩ **6 a :** to mate or mate with **:** INSEMINATE ⟨this cow was *bred* on the 7th, 27th, and 17th, but failed to settle⟩ ⟨a good mature ram may ~ 60 ewes in a season⟩ **b :** IMPREGNATE ⟨cats normally have their kittens 63 days after being *bred*⟩ **7 :** to produce a fissionable element (as plutonium) from a nonfissionable element (as uranium 238) by bombardment with neutrons from a radioactive element so that more fissionable material is produced than is used up ~ *vi* **1 :** to produce offspring by sexual union **:** reproduce its kind ⟨that they may ~ abundantly on the earth —Gen 8:17 (RSV)⟩ ⟨~ true⟩ **:** MULTIPLY **2 :** to be pregnant **3 :** to propagate animals or plants

²**breed** \"\ *n* -S **1 :** a group of animals or plants presumably related by descent from common ancestors and visibly similar in most characters: **a :** a distinctive group of domestic animals differentiated from the wild type under the influence of man and usu. incapable of maintaining its distinctive qualities in nature, being usu. the sum of the progeny of a known and designated foundation stock without admixture of other blood **b :** a similarly distinctive group of plants — compare HORTICULTURAL VARIETY **2 :** a number of persons of the same line of descent or of the same racial stock ⟨twice fifteen thousand hearts of England's ~ —Shak.⟩ **3 :** a group of persons or things distinguished by similar characteristics, interests, or qualities **:** CLASS, KIND, SORT ⟨the undergraduate ~ —J.C.Ransom⟩ ⟨the new ~ of scientific salesmen —*Time*⟩ ⟨horse lovers, a ~ of folk not yet extinct —H.I.Brock⟩ ⟨a new ~ of ship —Carter Henderson⟩ **4** *dial Brit* **:** a litter of young **:** BROOD **5** *chiefly West* **:** the offspring of a white parent and an Indian parent **:** HALF-BREED **6 :** a distinctively delicate taste discernible in some wines **syn** see VARIETY

breed·er \-də(r)\ *n* -S **1 :** one that produces offspring; *specif* **:** an animal or plant kept primarily for propagation **2 a :** one whose work is to breed a specified organism ⟨plant ~⟩ ⟨poultry ~⟩ ⟨rabbit ~⟩ **b :** the owner of a breeding female animal at the time of conception or at the birth of offspring

breeder reactor *also* **breeder** *n* -S **:** a reactor in which the breeding of fissionable material takes place

breeder tulip *also* **breeder** *n* -S **:** any of certain self-colored late-flowering tulips that resemble Darwin tulips but lack the rectangular flower base and are commonly somewhat more somber in coloring

breed·i·ness \-dēnəs\ *n* -ES **:** the distinctive characters or qualities of a breed as evident in an individual animal

breeding *n* -S [ME *breding*, fr. gerund of *breden*] **1 a :** the action or process of bearing or generating **b :** GESTATION, HATCHING, ORIGINATION, DEVELOPMENT **2 :** ANCESTRY **3 :** TRAINING, EDUCATION, BRINGING-UP ⟨she had her ~ at my father's charge —Shak.⟩ **4 a :** training in the proprieties **:** MANNERS ⟨he sometimes seems like a superior interviewer and goes a little beyond good ~ —O.W.Holmes †1935⟩ ⟨his displays of temper show him to be a person of ill ~⟩ **b :** good manners **:** meticulous or habitual observance of the proprieties **5 :** the propagation of plants or animals; *esp* **:** such propagation for the purpose of improving the plants or animals (as by selection after controlled mating or, esp. in plants, hybridization) **6 a :** an instance of mating **:** SERVICE **b :** condition suitable for mating

breeding crate *n* **:** a stall or narrow open-ended enclosure arranged to restrain a cow or sow and to take the weight of a heavy sire during service

breeding ground *n* **1 :** a place to which animals resort for breeding **2 :** a place or set of circumstances considered favorable to the propagation of certain things, ideas, conditions ⟨the district was a *breeding ground* for gangs —Alfred Prowitt⟩

breeding paralysis *n* **:** DOURINE

breeding plumage *n* **:** NUPTIAL PLUMAGE

breeding population *n* **:** a population within which free interbreeding takes place and evolutionary change may appear and be preserved

breeding potential *n* **:** BIOTIC POTENTIAL 1

breeding range *n* **:** the geographic area over which breeding is carried on by individual pairs or breeding populations of a particular kind of animal

breeding territory *n* **:** a part of an animal's home range which is occupied by a family and defended against intruders

breed of cat *or* **breed of cats :** KIND, SORT — often used with *different* ⟨whether controlled inflation is a different *breed of cat* from runaway inflation —Edgar Scott⟩

breed out *vt* **:** to eliminate (a characteristic) in the course of controlled breeding

breeds *pres 3d sing of* BREED, *pl of* BREED

breed smear *or* **breed method** \'brēd-\ *n, usu cap B* [after Robert S. *Breed* †1956 Amer. bacteriologist] **:** a test of the bacteriological purity of milk by direct examination of a film of fat-free milk stained with methylene blue, often used to detect the organism of bovine mastitis

¹**breedy** \-dē\ *adj* -ER/-EST [¹*breed* + *-y*] **:** PROLIFIC

²**breedy** \"\ *adj* -ER/-EST [²*breed* + *-y*] **:** exhibiting esp. in high degree the characteristics or qualities that distinguish a breed

breef *obs var of* BRIEF

breeks \'brēks\ *n pl* [ME (northern dial.) *breke* pair of breeches, fr. OE *brēc* breeches — more at BREECH] *chiefly Scot* **:** BREECHES ⟨a lot of young lads in short ~ and green sarks —John Buchan⟩

bree·kums \'brēkəmz\ *n pl* [dim. of *breeks*] *Scot* **:** short breeches

¹**breenge** \'brēnj, -rānj\ *vi* -ED/-ING/-S [origin unknown] *Scot* **:** to plunge ahead recklessly or impetuously

²**breenge** \"\ *n* -S *Scot* **:** a clumsy plunge or dash

¹**breer** \'brē(ə)r\ *chiefly Scot var of* BRIER

²**breer** \'brēr\ *n or vi* [by alter.] **:** BRAIRD

brees *pl of* BREE

breest \'brēst\ *dial Brit var of* BREAST

breet \'brēt\ *Scot var of* BRUTE

¹**breeze** *or* **breeze fly** \'brēz\ *n* -S [ME *breese, brese*, fr. OE *brēosa, brīosa*] *dial Eng* **:** GADFLY

²**breeze** \'brēz\ *n* -S [MF *brise*, perh. alter. of *bise* — more at BISE] **1 :** a steady light or moderate air current; *esp* **:** one moving either toward or off a seacoast — see LAND BREEZE, SEA BREEZE **2 a :** a light gentle soft-blowing wind ⟨the languid spring ~ rocked the little green bombshells of maple sprays —T.R.Ybarra⟩ ⟨waved in the ~ of an electric fan⟩ **b :** a wind of from 4 to 31 miles an hour — see FRESH BREEZE, GENTLE BREEZE, LIGHT BREEZE, MODERATE BREEZE, STRONG BREEZE; BEAUFORT SCALE table **3 :** DISTURBANCE, QUARREL **4 a :** something easily managed or accomplished **:** CINCH ⟨that test was a ~⟩ **b :** an easy victory **5 :** something likened to a breeze (as in freshness, transience, lightness) ⟨temper the hot winds of romance with the more sensible ~ of historical fact —*Saturday Rev.*⟩ ⟨high-sounding phrases flutter in the ~ of heroic feeling —R.S.Ellery⟩ ⟨a little ~ of applause broke out —Willa Cather⟩ **syn** see WIND — **shoot the breeze** *or* **bat the breeze :** to engage in small talk **:** GOSSIP ⟨we lounged around, drinking and *shooting the breeze*, when all of a sudden the conversation took a serious turn —Frederic Wakeman⟩

³**breeze** \"\ *vb* -ED/-ING/-S *vi* **1** *of the wind* **a :** to blow gently **b :** FRESHEN ⟨it now began *breezing* strongly from seaward —Herman Melville⟩ — often used with *up* ⟨it had been smooth then, but now it was *breezing* up from the southwest —Archie Binns⟩ **2 a :** to move swiftly and airily ⟨the Senator *breezed* in, wearing a light summer suit and a jaunty straw hat —A.M. Schlesinger b. 1917⟩ **b :** to proceed quickly and easily ⟨the pitcher *breezed* to his third victory⟩ — usu. used with *through* ⟨he *breezed* through the report rapidly, remembering little⟩ ⟨so much of the beauty . . . is lost if you just ~ through —Richard Joseph⟩ **c :** to depart in haste ~ *vt* **:** to exercise (a horse) at a brisk gait without urging to great speed

⁴**breeze** \"\ *n* -S [prob. modif. of F *braise* cinders, live coals, fr. OF *brese* — more at BRAZE] **1 a :** residue from the making of coke or charcoal **b :** dust or fine bits of coke or charcoal **c :** coal or coke dust **2 :** furnace ashes **3 :** a construction material (as brick or concrete) made partly of breeze

breeze in *vi* **:** to win easily ⟨he ran for lieutenant governor and *breezed in*⟩

breeze·less \-ləs\ *adj* **:** being without a breeze

breezeway \'ˌ=ˌ=\ *n* [²*breeze* + *way*] **:** a roofed open-air passage or porch connecting two buildings (as a house and garage) or forming a corridor between two halves of a building (as of a cabin) — compare DOGTROT 2

breez·i·ly \'brēzəlē, -li\ *adv* **:** in a breezy manner

breez·i·ness \-zēnəs, -zin-\ *n* -ES **:** a breezy quality or manner

breezy \'brēzē, -zi\ *adj* -ER/-EST [²*breeze* + *-y*] **1 :** swept by breezes ⟨the ~ summit of the tower —Nathaniel Hawthorne⟩ **2 a :** BRISK, ZESTFUL, INFORMAL ⟨a rough and ready, ~, democratic individual —William Land⟩ ⟨delightfully ~ in the telling but serious in its basic intent —Florence Bullock⟩ ⟨a ~ if not chatty descriptive account of his career —Carlos Baker⟩ **b :** AIRY, OFFHAND, BLAND ⟨he talked with a ~ unconcern for her feelings⟩

breg·ma \'bregmə\ *n, pl* **bregma·ta** \-məd·ə\ [NL, fr. LL, front part of the head, fr. Gk; akin to Gk *brechma, brechmos* front part of the head — more at BRAIN] **:** the point of junction of the coronal and sagittal sutures of the skull — see CRANIOMETRY illustration — **breg·mat·ic** \(ˈ)breg'mad·ik\ *adj*

bre·guet hairspring \brə'gā-\ *n, usu cap B* [after Abraham L. *Bréguet* †1823 Fr. horologist] **:** a flat spiral hairspring whose last outer coil is raised and curved back to a point near the center

bre·hon \'brē,hän, bi'rehüv\ *n* -S [IrGael *breitheamh* judge, fr. OIr *brithem*, fr. *breth* act of bearing, judgment; akin to OIr *biru* I bear, OE *beran* to bear — more at BEAR] **:** one of a class of lawyers in ancient Ireland with power to serve as jurist and referee but without power to enforce decisions

brei \'brī\ *n* -S [G, lit., pap, pulp, fr. OHG *brīo* — more at BREE] *physiol* **:** a finely and uniformly divided tissue suspension used esp. in metabolic experimentation

¹**breid** \'brād, -rēd\ *now dial Brit var of* BRAID

²**breid** \'brēd, -red,-rād\ *chiefly Scot var of* BREAD

breist \'brēst\ *chiefly Scot var of* BREAST

breit·haupt·ite \'brīt,haủp,tīt\ *n* -S [G *breithauptit*, fr. J.A.*Breithaupt* †1873 Ger. mineralogist + G *-it* -ite] **:** a copper-colored usu. arborescent mineral NiSb consisting of nickel antimonide

breit·schwantz \'brīt,shfän(t)s, -shvä-\ *n* -ES [G *breitschwanz*, fr. *breit* broad (fr. OHG) + *schwanz* tail, fr. MHG *swanz*, fr. *swanzen* to swing, move back and forth, freq. of *swanken* to move to and fro, fr. *swank* supple, movable, swaying — more at BROAD, SWANK] **:** BROADTAIL 2

bre·lan \brəlän\ *n, pl* **brelans** \-än(z)\ [F, fr. OF *brelenc, berlenc* gaming table, gambling house, of Gmc origin; akin to OHG *bretling* small board, fr. *bret* board + *-ling;* akin to OE & OS *bred* board, OE *bord* — more at BOARD] **1 :** an old French gambling game somewhat like poker **2 :** THREE OF A KIND

brelan car·ré \-län'kärā\ *n, pl* **brelans carré** *or* **brelan carrés** [F, lit., square brelan] **:** FOUR OF A KIND

bre·loque \brə'lōk\ *n* -S [F — more at BERLOQUE] **:** a seal or charm for a watch chain

breme \'brēm, 'brim\ *adj* [ME *breme, brim* fierce, angry, stormy, perh. fr. OE *brēme* famous, glorious, perh. fr. *bi-* be- + a word akin to OS *hrōm* honor, glory, praise, OHG *hruom;* akin to OE *hrēth* glory — more at CADUCEUS] **1** *archaic, of weather* **:** SEVERE, FIERCE **2** *archaic, of a person* **:** KEEN, ALERT, SHARP — **breme·ly** *adv*

bre·men \'bremən, -rām-\ *adj, usu cap* [fr. *Bremen*, Germany] **:** of or from the city of Bremen, Germany **:** of the kind or style prevalent in Bremen

bremen blue *n, often cap 1st B* [prob. trans. of G *bremerblau*] **1 :** a moderate bluish green that is bluer, lighter, and stronger than porcelain green and bluer and paler than sea blue — called also *chemic green, Neuwied blue, Peligot's blue, water blue* **2 :** any of various greenish blue or bluish green pigments consisting essentially of copper hydroxide containing copper carbonate or of basic copper carbonate — compare BLUE VERDITER

bremen green *n, often cap B* [prob. trans. of G *bremergrün*] **1 :** MALACHITE GREEN 3 **2 :** any of various green pigments similar in composition to Bremen blue — compare GREEN VERDITER

bre·mer·ha·ven \'bremə(r),hävən, ¦brāmər¦häfən\ *adj, usu cap* [fr. *Bremerhaven*, Germany] **:** of or from the city of Bremerhaven, Germany **:** of the kind or style prevalent in Bremerhaven

bre·mia \'brēmēə, -rām-\ *n, cap* [NL, fr. J. *Bremi*-Wolf †1857 Swiss naturalist + NL *-ia*] **:** a genus of downy mildew fungi (family Peronosporaceae) including a fungus (*B. lactucae*) that attacks lettuce and related plants

brems·strah·lung \'brem,shträləŋ, -m(p)s(h),sht-\ *n* -S [G, lit., decelerated radiation, fr. *bremse* brake (fr. MHG, clamp, muzzle, fr. MLG *premese*, fr. *pramen* to press) + *strahlung* radiation, fr. *strahlen* to radiate (fr. *strahl* ray, beam, fr. OHG *strāla* arrow, lightning bolt) + *-ung* (fr. OHG *-unga* -ing); akin to MHG *pfrengen* to press and to OE *strǣl* arrow, *strēam* stream — more at PRONG, STREAM] **:** the electromagnetic radiation produced by the sudden retardation of an electrical particle (as an electron or positron) in an intense electric field (as in the atomic nucleus)

brem·sung \'brem,zůŋ\ *n* -S [G, lit., deceleration, fr. *bremsen* to decelerate (fr. *bremse* brake) + *-ung*] **:** the sudden slowing down of a moving charged particle on entering an opposing electric field (as that within or surrounding an atomic nucleus) — compare BREMSSTRAHLUNG

¹**bren** *also* **brenn** \'bren\ *dial Brit var of* BURN

²**bren** \'bren\ *or* **bren gun** *n* -S *usu cap B* [*Brno*, city in Czechoslovakia + *Enfield*, town in England] **:** a light gas-operated air-cooled machine gun that uses .303 caliber ammunition and is fired from the shoulder

¹**brent** \'brent\ *adj* [ME *brent, brant*, fr. OE *brant;* akin to ON *brattr* steep, and prob. to OHG *bor* height, *beran* to bear — more at BEAR] **1** *dial Brit* **:** STEEP, PRECIPITOUS **2** *chiefly Scot* **:** SMOOTH, UNWRINKLED ⟨your bonny brow was ~ —Robert Burns⟩

²**brent** \"\ *or* **brent goose** *var of* BRANT

³**brent** *archaic past of* BURN

bren·ti·dae \'brentə,dē\ *n pl, cap* [NL, fr. *Brentus*, type genus + *-idae*] **:** a family (type genus *Brentus*) of chiefly tropical wood-boring weevils having slender bodies, antennae that are not elbowed, and females with the beak very long and continuing the long axis of the body

brent-new \'bren(t)¦=\ *adj* [by alter.] *chiefly Scot* **:** BRAND-NEW

brer \ˌbrər(·), ˌbrə(r, ˌbrer, ˌbreə, ˌbrə\ *n* -S [by contr.] *chiefly South* **:** BROTHER

brere \'bri(ə)r\ *archaic var of* BRIER

bre·scia \'breshə, -rāshə\ *adj, usu cap* [fr. *Brescia*, Italy] **:** of or from the city of Brescia, Italy **:** of the kind or style prevalent in Brescia

bre·scian \-shən\ *adj, usu cap* [*Brescia*, Italy + E *-an*] **:** of or relating to Brescia, Italy, or its 16th century school of painters ⟨*Brescian* painting⟩

bresh \'bresh\ *dial var of* BRUSH

bres·lau \'bre,slau̇\ *adj, usu cap* [fr. *Breslau,* Germany (now called *Wrocław,* Poland)] **:** WROCLAW

bres·sum·mer \'bresəmə(r)\ *n* -s [by alter.] **:** BREASTSUMMER

brest \'brest\ *adj, usu cap* [fr. *Brest,* France] **:** of or from the city of Brest, France **:** of the kind or style prevalent in Brest

bre·telle \brə'tel\ *n* -s [F, fr. OF *bretele,* carrying strap, of Gmc origin; akin to OHG *brittil* rein — more at BRIDLE] **:** one of a pair of ornamental straps that go from the belt on the front of a dress over the shoulders to the belt in back

bretelles

bre·tes·sé *also* **bret·tes·sé** \ˌbredəˈsā, brəˈte,sā\ *adj* [MF *bretessé, breteschié,* past part. of *breteschier* to furnish with parapets, fr. *bretesche* parapet — more at BRATTICE] *heraldry* **:** embattled on each side with the projections opposite each other

bre·ther \'breth̲ər\ *Scot pl of* BROTHER

brethren *pl of* BROTHER — now used chiefly in formal or solemn address, in referring to the members of a profession, society, or sect, or in the names of certain sects ⟨our scientific ~ have been more blamed for this than we of the humanities —F.N.Robinson⟩ ⟨the obligation to instruct them . . . was shared by his clerical ~ —G.C.Sellery⟩ **:** a member of the Church of the *Brethren*⟩

¹bret·on \'bretᵊn\ *adj, usu cap* [F, fr. ML *Briton-, Brito,* fr. L, Briton — more at BRITON] **1 :** of, relating to, or characteristic of Brittany, a region of France **2 :** of, relating to, or characteristic of the people of Brittany

²breton \"\ *n* -s **1** *cap* **:** a native or inhabitant of Brittany in France — called also *Armorican* **2** *cap* **a :** the Celtic language of the Breton people — see INDO-EUROPEAN LANGUAGES table **b :** the Brythonic division of Celtic **3** *sometimes cap* **:** a woman's hat made on a basic pattern of round crown and wide even brim that is curved upward all around

breton lay *n, usu cap B* **:** a short medieval French narrative poem usu. based upon Celtic legends

bre·tonne sauce \brə'tän-\ *n, often cap B* [F *sauce bretonne,* lit., Breton sauce] **:** a brown sauce containing delicately browned fried red onions

brett \'bret\ *n* -s [by shortening & alter.] **:** BRITSKA

bret·ta·no·my·ces \,bret³nō'mī,sēz\ *n, cap* [NL, fr. Gk *Brettanos, Bretanos* Briton (of Celt origin; akin to W *Brython* Briton) + NL *-myces* — more at BRITON] **:** a genus of molds (family Moniliaceae) that are sometimes included in the genus *Candida,* are active in the secondary fermentation of beers, and are responsible for some cases of beer spoilage

bret·wal·da \'bret,wȯldə, ⸗'⸗⸗\ *n* -s *usu cap* [OE *bretwalda, brytenwealda,* prob. fr. *Bryten* Britain + *-walda, -wealda* (fr. *wealdan* to rule) — more at WIELD] **:** the chief king in Anglo-Saxon England — used as a title in the Old English Chronicle for several kings said to have held supremacy over kingdoms beyond their own

breun·ner·ite \'brȯinə,rīt, 'bru̇n-\ *n* -s [G *breunnerit, breunerit,* fr. Count *Breunner* or *Breuner,* 19th cent. Austrian nobleman + G *-it* -ite] **1 :** a ferruginous dolomite or magnesite **2 :** a mineral consisting of the isomorphous system of magnesium, iron, and manganese carbonate $(Mg,Fe,Mn)CO_3$

brev *abbr* **1** brevet **2** brevier

breve \'brēv, 'brev\ *n* -s [ME — more at BRIEF] **1** *archaic* **:** an authorizing letter: as **a :** a royal mandate **b :** a papal brief **2 a :** a mark ˘ placed over a vowel to indicate that the vowel is short **b :** this mark placed over a syllable or used alone to indicate an unstressed or a short syllable in a metric foot **3 :** an original writ **:** any writ or precept under seal that is issued out of any court **4 a :** a note in mensural notation equivalent in duration to either one half or one third of a long **b :** a note in modern notation equivalent to four half notes

a b

breves: *a* obsolete forms; *b* modern form

breve rest *n* **:** a sign indicating a silence equal in duration to a breve

¹bre·vet \brə'vet, *esp Brit* 'brevət\ *n* -s [ME *brevet, brevette,* fr. MF *brevet,* fr. OF, dim. of *bref, brief* letter — more at BRIEF] **1** *obs* **:** a written official or authoritative message **2 :** an official document from a government granting a privilege, title, or dignity **3 :** a commission giving a military officer higher nominal rank than that for which he receives pay; *specif* **:** such a commission, carrying no right of command, that may be conferred by the president of the U.S. by and with the consent of the Senate upon officers of the Army and Marine Corps for distinguished conduct and public service in presence of the enemy ⟨discharged with the ~ rank of lieutenant colonel⟩ ⟨*Brevet* Major John Doe⟩

²brevet \"\ *vt* **brevetted** *or* **breveted; brevetted** *or* **breveted; brevetting** *or* **breveting; brevets :** to confer rank upon by or as if by brevet

brevi- *comb form* [L, fr. *brevis* — more at BRIEF] **:** short ⟨*brevi*conic⟩ ⟨*brevi*lingual⟩

bre·via·ry \'brēv(y)ərē, -vē,erē, -ri\ *n* -ES [L *breviarium,* fr. *brevi-* + *-arium* -ary] **1 a :** a brief account or summary **:** ABRIDGMENT **b** *obs* **:** EPITOME **2** [ML *breviarium,* fr. L] **a :** an ecclesiastical book containing the daily public or canonical prayers for the canonical hours **b :** the canonical prayers for each day

¹breviate *vt* -ED/-ING/-S [L *breviatus,* past part. of *breviare* to shorten, fr. *brevis* short — more at BRIEF] *obs* **:** ABBREVIATE, ABRIDGE

²bre·vi·ate \'brēvēət\ *n* -s **1 :** COMPENDIUM, SUMMARY, ABSTRACT **2** *obs* **:** a brief note or dispatch; *also* **:** a lawyer's brief

brevi·caudate \ˌbrevə+\ *adj* [*brevi-* + *caudate*] **:** having a short tail

brevi·cip·i·tid \,brevə'sipəd·əd\ *n* -s [NL *Brevicipitidae*] **:** a frog or toad of the family Brevicipitidae

brevi·ci·pit·i·dae \-,sə'pidə,dē\ *n pl, cap* [NL, fr. *Brevicipit-, Breviceps,* type genus (fr. *brevi-* + L *-cipit-, -ceps,* fr. *caput* head) + *-idae* — more at HEAD] **:** a large family of tropical frogs or toads (suborder Diplasiocoela) comprising the narrow-mouthed toads feeding chiefly on termites and usu. lacking maxillary teeth and having ridged palates, large vomers, and the mouth usu. small

brevi·cone \'brevə,kōn\ *n* [*brevi-* + *cone*] **:** a short blunt curved shell characteristic of certain Paleozoic cephalopods; *also* **:** a fossil animal having such a shell — **brevi·con·ic** \ˌbrevə'känik\ *adj*

bre·vier \brə'vi(ə)r, -iə\ *n* -s [prob. fr. D, lit., breviary, fr. ML *breviarium;* fr. the use of this size of type in the printing of breviaries in 16th cent. Holland & Belgium — more at BREVIARY] **:** a size of type between minion and bourgeois, approximately 8 point — compare POINT SYSTEM

brev·i·ger \'brevəjə(r)\ *n* -s [ML, fr. *breve* + L *-ger* -gerous] **:** a friar carrying a license for begging

bre·vil·o·quence \bre'viləkwən(t)s, brə'-\ *n* -s [L *breviloquentia,* fr. *breviloquent-, breviloquens* speaking briefly (fr. *brevi-* + *loquent-, loquens,* pres. part. of *loqui* to speak) + *-ia*] **:** brevity of speaking

bre·vil·o·quent \-nt\ *adj* [L *breviloquent-, breviloquens*] **:** marked by brevity of speech

brev·i·ped \'brevə,ped\ *adj* [*brevi-* + *-ped*] **:** having short legs

¹brevi·ros·trine \ˌbrevə'rästrən, -ä,strīn\ *adj* [*brevi-* + L *rostrum* beak + E *-ine* — more at ROSTRUM] **:** of, relating to, or being any of several extinct Old World Pliocene and Pleistocene mastodons with much-shortened jaws and complex grinding teeth

²brevirostrine \"\ *n* -s **:** a brevirostrine animal

brev·it \'brevət\ *vi* -ED/-ING/-S [origin unknown] **1** *dial Eng* **:** FORAGE, HUNT ⟨the dog is always ~*ing* about⟩ **2** *dial Eng* **:** to pry and prowl around **:** SNOOP ⟨who's ~*ed* through this drawer⟩

²brevit \"\ *n* -s *dial Eng* **:** a snoopy meddlesome person

brev·i·ty \'brevəd·ē, -ətē, -i\ *n* -ES [L *brevitas,* fr. *brevi-* + *-tas* -ty] **1 :** shortness of duration **:** briefness of time ⟨the ~ of human life⟩ **2 :** expression in few words **:** TERSENESS, CONCISENESS ⟨~ is the soul of wit —Shak.⟩ **3 :** a short piece (as of writing, music) ⟨Kipling's work . . . consisted not of a few big books but of an infinite number of significant *brevities* —Katharine F. Gerould⟩

bre·voor·tia \brə'vōrsh(ē)ə\ *n, cap* [NL, prob. fr. J.Carson *Brevoort* †1887 Am. naturalist and ichthyologist + NL *-ia*] **:** a genus of small marine fishes (family Clupeidae) comprising the menhadens

¹brew \'brü\ *vb* -ED/-ING/-S [ME *brewen,* fr. OE *brēowan;* akin to OHG *briuwan* to brew, ON *brugginn* brewed, L *defrutum* new wine boiled down, *fervēre* to boil — more at BURN] *vt* **1 :** to prepare (as beer or ale from malt and hops) by steeping, boiling, and fermentation or by infusion and fermentation **:** convert into a fermented liquor **2 a :** to bring about (something troublesome or woeful) as if by brewing magical potions or spells ⟨~*ing* mischief⟩ **b :** to produce or bring about as if by mixing ingredients **:** CONTRIVE, CONCOCT ⟨aggression that the dictator was ~*ing*⟩ ⟨this air is ~*ed* of hot sun and warm sea water —Wolfgang Langewiesche⟩ **3** *obs* **:** to dilute (liquor) **:** mix (as liquors) **4 :** to prepare (as a drink or other liquid) by infusion esp. in hot water ⟨she is ~*ing* the tea⟩; *broadly* **:** to prepare any drink ~ *vi* **1 :** to brew beer or ale esp. as a business **2 :** to be in a state of preparation ⟨revolutionary . . . ways of getting around are ~*ing* —James Cerruti⟩ **:** be forming ⟨the notion of essence . . . ~*ed* early in Santayana —Justus Buchler⟩ **:** GATHER ⟨a storm ~*s* in the west⟩ **:** IMPEND ⟨trouble is ~*ing*⟩

²brew \"\ *n* -s **1 a :** a beverage formed by brewing **b :** a drink of such beverage (as coffee or tea); *also* **:** a glass of beer ⟨I'll buy you a ~⟩ **2 :** a product of brewing **:** MIXTURE, CONCOCTION, BATCH ⟨a devil's ~ of cynicism, intrigue, and despair —*Time*⟩ ⟨like the ~ of an alchemist —Jean Stafford⟩ — see WITCHES' BREW **3 :** the process of brewing or being brewed ⟨it was a loury evening with rain in ~ —A.N.Whitehead⟩

³brew \"\ *n* -s [ME *brewe,* lit., eyebrow, fr. OE *brū* — more at BROW] *dial Brit* **:** a steep hill or overhanging bank

brew·age \'brüij, -üēj\ *n* -s **:** something brewed or concocted **:** BREW

brew·er \'brüə(r); -ü(ə)r,-üə\ *n* -s [ME, fr. *brewen* + *-er*] **1 :** one that brews; *esp* **:** one that manufactures brewed beverages (as ale or beer) **2 :** a utensil or appliance used in brewing beverages ⟨a coffee ~⟩

brew·er blackbird *or* **brew·er's blackbird** \-r(z)-,-ə(z)-\ *n, usu cap 1st B* [after Thomas M. *Brewer* †1880 Am. ornithologist] **:** a blackbird (*Euphagus cyanocephalus*) widely distributed and common in inhabited areas of western No. America, the male being shining greenish black with a purplish black head, the female largely dark brownish gray

brewers' grains *n pl* **:** the insoluble residue from brewed malt often used as fodder

brewers' grits *n pl* **:** hulled and coarsely crushed grain that is to be treated in a converter before mashing

brewer's mole *n, usu cap B* [after Thomas M. *Brewer*] **:** a hairy-tailed mole (*Parascalops breweri*) of eastern No. America

brewer sparrow *or* **brewer's sparrow** *n, usu cap B* [after Thomas M. *Brewer*] **:** a small sparrow (*Spizella breweri*) of western No. America that is closely related to the chipping sparrow but somewhat smaller and rather more grayish

brewer's pitch *n* **:** a resinous preparation used esp. for coating the inside of beer casks

brewers' rice *n* **:** fragments of broken rice from the milling process that may be used as brewers' grits

brewer's spruce *n, usu cap B* [after William H. *Brewer* †1910 Am. scientist] **:** WEEPING SPRUCE

brewers' yeast *or* **brewer's yeast** *n* **:** a yeast used or suitable for use in brewing; *specif* **:** the dried pulverized cells of a top yeast (*Saccharomyces cerevisiae*) used in medicine and as a dietary supplement as a source of B-complex vitamins and of high-grade protein

brew·ery \'brüərē, -ü(ə)rē, -ri *also* -ür-\ *n* -ES [¹*brew* + *-ery*] **:** a building or plant where beer is manufactured

brewhouse \'⸗,⸗\ *n* [ME *brewhous,* fr. *brewen* to brew + *hous* house] **:** BREWERY

brewing *n* -s [ME, fr. gerund of *brewen*] **1 :** the process of making malt beverages (as beer or ale) by grinding malt into grist, mashing the grist in hot water, boiling the mash, often with the addition of corn or rice, to produce wort, flavoring the wort with hops, fermenting the hopped wort with yeast, and drawing off the fermented wort for storage, packaging, and marketing — compare BOTTOM FERMENTATION, TOP FERMENTATION **2 :** a process of preparation **:** CONCOCTION **3 a :** a quantity brewed **:** BATCH ⟨a new ~ of ale⟩

brewis \'brüz, 'brüəs\ *n* -ES [ME *brewes, browes,* fr. OF *broez,* nom. sing. & accus. pl. of *broet* broth, dim. of *breu* broth, of Gmc origin; akin to OHG *brod* broth — more at BROTH] **1** *dial* **:** broth or pottage; *esp* **:** broth in which beef has been boiled **2** *dial* **:** bread soaked in broth, drippings of roast meat, milk, or water and butter

brewmaster \'⸗,⸗⸗\ *n* **:** one who supervises the brewing process in a brewery

brews *pres 3d sing of* BREW, *pl of* BREW

brew·ster \'brüstə(r)\ *n* -s [ME, female brewer, brewer, fr. *brewen* + *-ster*] *dial Brit* **:** BREWER 1

brew·ster angle \"-\ *or* **brew·ster's angle** \"z-\ *n, usu cap B* [after Sir David *Brewster* †1868 Scot. physicist] **:** POLARIZING ANGLE — compare BREWSTER'S LAW

brewster chair *n, usu cap B* [after William *Brewster* †1644 Am. pioneer] **:** a heavy turned chair with vertical spindles in two tiers in the back and in one or more tiers below the seat in front

brewster green *n, often cap B* [after Sir David *Brewster*] **:** a moderate olive green that is yellower, darker, and slightly stronger than cypress green, greener and duller than holly green (sense 2), and greener and darker than Lincoln green

brew·ster·ite \-ə,rīt\ *n* -s [Sir David *Brewster* + E *-ite*] **:** a mineral consisting of a zeolite containing barium and strontium $(Sr,Ba,Ca)Al_2Si_6O_{16}.5H_2O$ (hardness 5, sp. gr. 2.45)

brewster's booby *n, usu cap 1st B* [after William *Brewster* †1919 Am. ornithologist] **:** a chiefly grayish brown booby (*Sula leucogaster brewsteri*) occurring from the Gulf of California to the Galápagos islands

Brewster chair

brewster's law *n, usu cap B* [after Sir David *Brewster*] **:** a statement in optics: when unpolarized light of given wavelength is incident upon the surface of a transparent substance it experiences maximum plane polarization at the angle of incidence whose tangent is the refractive index of the substance for that wave length — compare POLARIZING ANGLE

¹brey \'brā\ *n* -s [modif. of F *broie,* fr. MF, prob. alter. of *braie* breeches, fr. L *braca* — more at BRACCAE] **:** ¹BARNACLE 1b

²brey \"\ *var of* ⁴BRAY

³brey \"\ *vt* -ED/-ING/-S [Afrik *brei,* fr. MD *bereiden* to prepare, fr. *bereit* ready, fr. *be-* + a word akin to OHG *reiti* ready — more at READY] *Africa* **:** to soften (skins or leather) by working with the hands

brf *abbr* brief

brg *abbr* **1** bearing **2** bridge

¹briar *var of* BRIER

²bri·ar \'brī(ə)r, -īə\ *or* **briar pipe** *n* -s [²*brier, briar* (heath)] **1 :** a tobacco pipe made from the root of any of several brier plants; *esp* **:** a tobacco pipe made from the burl of a brier of southern Europe (*Erica arborea*) **2 :** OAK 3

³briar \"\ *n* -s [perh. fr. ¹*brier, briar;* fr. a comparison of the teeth of a saw to the thorns of a brier] **:** CROSSCUT SAW

briarberry *var of* BRIERBERRY

bri·ard \brē'är(d)\ *n* [F, fr. *Brie,* district in northeastern France + F *-ard*] **1** *usu cap* **:** an old French breed of large strong usu. black dogs that have a long tail and a stiff slightly wavy long coat and that are esp. useful as sheep dogs **2** -s *sometimes cap* **:** a dog of the Briard breed

briarroot *var of* BRIERROOT

briarwood *var of* BRIERWOOD

briary *var of* BRIERY

brib·able *or* **bribe·able** \'brībəbəl\ *adj* **:** capable of being bribed

¹bribe \'brīb\ *vb* -ED/-ING/-S [ME *briben,* fr. MF *briber, brimber* to beg, fr. *bribe, brimbe,* n.] *vt* **1** *obs* **:** ROB, STEAL, PURLOIN, EXTORT **2 a :** to give or promise a bribe to **:** suborn by bribery ⟨*bribed* to vote against a certain candidate⟩ **b :** to induce or influence as if by bribery ⟨~ a cat with a saucer of milk to come indoors⟩ ~ *vi* **:** to give a bribe to a person **:** practice bribery ⟨a man not above *bribing* to gain his end⟩

²bribe \"\ *n* -s [ME, something stolen, fr. MF *bribe, brimbe,* piece of bread given to a beggar, scrap] **1 :** a price, reward, gift, or favor bestowed or promised with a view to pervert the judgment or corrupt the conduct esp. of a person in a position of trust (as a public official) **2 :** something that serves to induce or influence to a given line of conduct ⟨using ~*s* of candy to get a small child to go to bed⟩ ⟨~*s* offered to new readers ranged from cameras to flannel trousers —E.S.Turner⟩

brib·ee \(')brī'bē\ *n* -s **:** one that is bribed ⟨a certain superiority of briber to ~ —Lane Kauffmann⟩

brib·er \'brībə(r)\ *n* -s [ME *bribour* vagrant, scoundrel, thief, fr. MF *bribeur, brimbeur* beggar, scoundrel, fr. *briber, brimber* + *-eur* -or] **1** *obs* **a :** a robber, blackmailer, or extortioner **b :** one that extorts a bribe **c :** something that bribes **:** BRIBE **2 :** one that gives or offers a bribe or that practices bribery

brib·ery \-īb(ə)rē, -ri\ *n* -ES [ME *briberie,* fr. MF *briberie, brimberie* act of begging, fr. *briber, brimber* + *-erie* -ery] **1** *obs* **:** robbery or theft **:** EXTORTION **2 :** the act or practice of giving or taking a bribe **:** the act of influencing the action of another by a bribe ⟨~ and legislative favors were in his opinion legitimate party instruments —Helen C. Boatfield⟩

bri·bri \'brē,brē\ *n, pl* **bribri** *or* **bribris** *usu cap* [Sp, of Amer-Ind origin] **1 a :** a Chibchan people of Panama and Costa Rica **b :** a member of such people **2 :** the language of the Bribri people

bric-a-brac \'brikə,brak *also* -kər- *sometimes* -,bak\ *n* -s [F *bric-à-brac*] **1 :** a miscellaneous collection of often antique articles of virtu **:** miscellaneous objects regarded as decorative or of a sentimental value and usu. collected in one place **:** CURIOS ⟨small china figurines, seashells, ornamental ashtrays, and other such *bric-a-brac* around the parlor⟩ ⟨a baby book—a scrapbook . . . filled with pictures, and sentimental *bric-a-brac* like dried flowers and crayon drawings, and other relics and records of my childhood —Richard Lemon⟩ **2 :** something resembling or suggesting bric-a-brac esp. in extraneous decorative quality ⟨its plot bristles with . . . curses, poisonings, long-lost daughters, and all the other *bric-a-brac* of old-fashioned Italian dramaturgy —Winthrop Sargeant⟩ ⟨sensational journalistic *bric-a-brac* highlighting the seamy side of the nation's greatest industry —*Utilization*⟩

bricht \'brikt\ *Scot var of* BRIGHT

bricht·en \-k(t)ən\ *Scot var of* BRIGHTEN

¹brick \'brik\ *n* -s *see sense 2, often attrib* [ME *bryke,* fr. MF *brique,* fr. MD *bricke;* akin to OE *brecan* to break — more at BREAK] **1 :** a building or paving material that is made by molding clay into blocks while moist and hardening it sometimes in the sun (as was done extensively in ancient times) but usu. today by baking or burning by fire either in a kiln or in clamps and that is ordinarily red in color due to the presence of iron compounds converted by heat into red oxide, a brown or yellow color being obtained by the addition of lime or magnesia to the clay — see SEWER BRICK **2** *pl* **bricks** *or* **brick a :** an individual molded usu. rectangular block of brick with average dimensions in America usu. of 2¼x3¾x8 inches **b :** a block of other material (as concrete, sand and lime, or glass) of similar size and shape **c :** BRICKBAT ⟨a small boy throwing ~*s* at the side of the house⟩ **3 :** a rectangular usu. oblong often compressed mass ⟨a ~ of ice cream⟩ ⟨a ~ of figs⟩ **4** *slang* **:** a good fellow **:** one who is esp. good-hearted or selfless ⟨the women behaved like ~*s* and gave up their usual holiday at this time —O.W.Holmes †1935⟩ **5** *or* **brick red a :** a variable color averaging a moderate reddish brown that is redder, lighter, and stronger than mahogany, oxblood, or rustic brown, paler than Tuscan red, redder and deeper than russet tan, and yellower, lighter, and stronger than roan **b :** a moderate brown that is redder, lighter, and stronger than chestnut brown, bay, coffee, or auburn and deeper and slightly redder than toast brown **6 :** BRICK CHEESE

²brick \"\ *vt* -ED/-ING/-S **1 a :** to fill up or close with brick — used with *up* or *in* ⟨~ up a doorway⟩ ⟨~ in a hole in the sidewalk⟩ **b :** to face, pave, or line with brick ⟨a shed ~*ed* only on the front⟩ — often used with *over* ⟨~ over the front of the house⟩ ⟨~ over the inside of the well⟩ **c :** to make of brick ⟨~*ed* the front of the house —Angus Mowat⟩ **d :** to enclose, buttress, or make firm with brickwork ⟨~ the shaky trunk of the tree⟩ **2 :** to give the appearance of brickwork to (as to plaster by marking it off in brick-shaped areas) ⟨after . . . paint has been applied, guidelines are snapped on regularly over the entire area to be ~*ed* —Herbert Philippi⟩

¹brickbat \'⸗,⸗\ *n* -s [¹*brick* + *bat*] **1 a :** a fragment of a brick **b :** something resembling such a fragment esp. when used as a missile **2 :** an uncomplimentary remark; *esp* **:** an insult or condemnation ⟨it is my purpose in this article to begin with the ~*s* and to end with the bouquets —Angus Wilson⟩ ⟨the religious weeklies and monthlies . . . began to throw ~*s* at him —Van Wyck Brooks⟩

²brickbat \"\ *vt* **brickbatted; brickbatted; brickbatting; brickbats :** to throw a brickbat at ⟨a . . . politician whom he had *brickbatted* —*Time*⟩ ⟨*brickbatting* certain Congressional patriots —*New Yorker*⟩

brick beam *n* **:** a lintel of bricks with iron straps

brick cheese *n* **:** a sweet-curd quick-ripened semisoft mellow and smooth cheese about the size and shape of a brick

brick chisel *n* **1 :** a cold chisel for cutting brick masonry **2 :** a broad-edged chisel used by bricklayers for trimming brick to suitable lengths

brick earth *n* **:** clay used for making bricks

bric·kel·lia \bri'kelēə\ *n, cap* [NL, fr. John *Brickell* *fl*1730 IrAm. physician and naturalist + NL *-ia*] **:** a genus of herbs (family Compositae) of the warmer regions of America having greenish or yellowish white flowers with a pappus of slender bristles

brickfield \'⸗,⸗\ *n, Brit* **:** BRICKYARD

brick·field·er \"+ə(r)\ *n* -s [*brickfield* + *-er;* fr. its having been first applied to dust storms blown up from brickfields near Sydney, Australia] *Austral* **:** DUST STORM

brick hammer *n* **:** BRICKLAYER'S HAMMER

brick·ie \'briki\ *n* -s [by shortening + alter.] *Brit* **:** BRICKLAYER

¹bricking *pres part of* BRICK

²bricking *n* -s [¹*brick* + *-ing*] **:** brickwork or imitation of brickwork

brickkiln \'⸗,⸗\ *n* **1 :** a kiln in which bricks are baked or burned **2 :** a pile of green bricks arched to receive underneath the fuel for burning them

bricklayer \'⸗,⸗(⸗)\ *n* -s [ME *brykeleyer,* fr. *bryke* brick + *leyer* layer — more at BRICK, LAYER] **:** one that constructs buildings, chimneys, or other structures out of brick or building blocks and mortar or that lays brick, blocks, or tile for pavement or sewers or that repairs kilns and fireboxes — called also *brickmason*

bricklayer's hammer *n* **:** a hammer that has a flat face and sharp peen and is used in dressing or breaking brick

brick·le \'brikəl\ *or* **brick·ly** \-k(ə)lē\ *adj* [ME *brekyl, brickyll, brukyl* fragile, weak, brittle, prob. fr. OE *-brucol* (as in *æbrucol* sacrilegious, *onbrucol* rugged, *scipbrucol* causing shipwreck), fr. *brecan* to break — more at BREAK] *dial* **:** BRITTLE

brick·low \'bri(,)klō\ *var of* BRIGALOW

brickmaker \'⸗,⸗⸗\ *n* [ME *brykemaker* one who makes bricks, fr. *bryke* brick + *maker*] **1 :** one that conducts research in processing clays and sets up improved methods of manufacturing and using brick **2 :** a worker who tends a brick-molding machine

brickmaking \'⸗,⸗⸗\ *n* **:** the act or process of making bricks

brickmason \'⸗,⸗⸗\ *n* **:** BRICKLAYER

brick nog *or* **brick nogging** *n* **:** brickwork filled in between the timbers of a wood-framed wall or partition — **brick-nogged** \'⸗,nägd\ *adj*

brick red *n* **:** BRICK 5

bricks *pl of* BRICK, *pres 3d sing of* BRICK

brick set *n* **:** BRICK CHISEL

brick stitch *n* **:** any of several embroidery stitches so spaced and staggered as to resemble laid bricks

brick sugar *n* **:** CUBE SUGAR

brick tea *n* **:** a small brick of tea leaves, stalks, and sometimes dust made in China esp. for export to Tibet, Mongolia, and Siberia — compare TABLET TEA

bricktimber \'⸗,⸗⸗\ *n* **:** MOUNTAIN HOLLY 1

brick trimmer *n* **:** a trimmer arch of brick

brick trowel *n* **:** a flat triangular trowel used in bricklaying for cutting brick and spreading mortar or cement

brick veneer *n* **:** a facing of brick on a wall constructed of a material other than brick
brickwork \ˈ=,=\ *n* **:** construction or a particular piece of construction of bricks and mortar
¹bricky \ˈbrikē, -ki\ *adj, often* -ER/-EST [¹*brick* + -*y*] **1 :** made of bricks **2 :** resembling or suggesting bricks esp. in color
²bricky \-ki\ *var of* BRICKIE
brickyard \ˈ=,=\ *n* **:** a place where bricks are made
bri·cole \briˈkōl\ *n* -S [MF, lit., catapult, fr. ML *bricola*, perh. of Gmc origin; akin to MHG *brechel* breaker, OHG *brehhan* to break — more at BREAK] **1 a :** the rebound of a ball from a wall in court tennis **b :** the side stroke or play by which the ball is driven against the wall in court tennis **2 :** a billiard shot in which the cue ball strikes one of the cushions after contact with the object ball and before hitting the carom ball
brid \ˈbrid\ *now dial var of* BIRD
¹brid·al \ˈbrīdᵊl\ *n* -S [ME *bridale*, fr. OE *brȳdealu*, fr. *brȳd* bride + *ealu* ale — more at BRIDE, ALE] **:** a nuptial festival or ceremony **:** MARRIAGE
²bridal \"\ *adj* [ME *bridale*, fr. *bridale*, n.] **:** of or relating to a bride or a wedding **:** NUPTIAL ⟨a ~ veil⟩ ⟨a ~ procession⟩ ⟨~ preparations⟩ ⟨changed the ~ white for the nun's black habit and white coif —*Springfield (Mass.) Daily News*⟩ — **brid·al·ly** \ᵊl(l)ē\ *adv*
bridal box *or* **bridal chest** *n* **:** HOPE CHEST
brid·ale \ˈbrī,dāl\ *n* -S [ME — more at BRIDAL] **:** a usu. rustic wedding feast **:** BRIDAL
bridal rose *n* **:** CORN MAYWEED 2
brid·al·ty \ˈbrīdᵊltē\ *n* -ES [¹*bridal* + -*ty*] *archaic* **:** BRIDAL
bridal veil *n* **:** a northern African shrub (*Genista monosperma pendula*) of the family Leguminosae with showy sprays of pealike flowers
bridal wreath *n* **1 :** a spirea (*Spiraea prunifolia*) having copious umbels of small white flowers appearing in spring — called also *St.-Peter's-wreath* **2 :** a Chilean shrub (*Francoa ramosa*) of the family Saxifragaceae that resembles a spirea
¹bride \ˈbrīd\ *n* -S [ME, fr. OE *brȳd*; akin to OHG *brūt* bride, ON *brūthr* bride, Goth *brūths* daughter-in-law] **1 :** a woman newly married or about to be married **2 :** a woman taking vows as a member of a Christian religious order ⟨~ of Christ⟩ ⟨the ~s then recited together their pledges of chastity —*Springfield (Mass.) Daily News*⟩
²bride *vi, obs* **:** to appear or act as a bride
³bride \ˈbrīd, ˈbrēd\ *n* -S [F, lit., reins, bridle, fr. OF, rein, prob. fr. MHG *brīdel, britel* rein, fr. OHG *brittil* — more at BRIDLE] **:** a small joining that resembles a bar, consists of one or more threads with or without ornamentation, and is used to connect the various parts of a lace pattern
bridebed \ˈ=,=\ *n* **:** MARRIAGE BED
bridebox \ˈ=,=\ *n* **:** HOPE CHEST
bridecake \ˈ=,=\ *n* **:** WEDDING CAKE
bridechamber \ˈ=,==\ *n, archaic* **:** the room containing the marriage bed
bridecup \ˈ=,=\ *n* **1** *archaic* **:** a spiced drink served a bridal couple on the wedding night **2 :** the specially prepared cup or bowl from which guests drink at a wedding
bride·groom \ˈbrīd,grüm, -rům\ *n* -S [by folk etymology fr. ME *bridegome*, fr. OE *brȳdguma*; akin to OHG *brūtigomo* bridegroom, ON *brūthgumi*; all fr. a prehistoric NGmc-WGmc compound whose first constituent is the word represented by OE *brȳd* bride and whose second constituent is the word represented by OE *guma* man — more at BRIDE, HOMAGE] **:** a man just married or about to be married
bridelace *n, obs* **:** a ribbon of lace for binding sprigs of rosemary used as favors at weddings
bride·less \-ləs\ *adj* **:** being without a bride
bridemaid \ˈ=,=\ *or* **bridemaiden** \ˈ=,==\ *n, archaic* **:** BRIDESMAID
bride·man \ˈbrīdmən\ *n, pl* **bridemen** *archaic* **:** BEST MAN
bride–price \ˈ=,=\ *n* **:** money, property, or services given by or in behalf of a prospective husband to the bride's family esp. among primitive peoples
bride's cake *n* **:** WEDDING CAKE
bride's chest *or* **bride's box** *n* **:** HOPE CHEST
bride service *n* **:** service rendered to the bride's family by the bridegroom as a bride-price or part of a bride-price
brides·maid \ˈbrīdz,mād\ *n* [alter. of earlier *bridemaid*] **:** a usu. young woman who attends the bride during the wedding ceremony often as one of several such attendants — compare MAID OF HONOR, MATRON OF HONOR
brides·man \-mən\ *n, pl* **bridesmen** [alter. of earlier *brideman*] **:** BEST MAN
bridewealth \ˈ=,=\ *n* -S **:** BRIDE-PRICE
brideweed \ˈ=,=\ *n* **:** TOADFLAX
bride·well \ˈbrī,dwel, -,dwəl\ *n* -S *sometimes cap* [fr. *Bridewell*, London house of correction established in the 16th cent.] **:** HOUSE OF CORRECTION, JAIL, PRISON
¹bridge \ˈbrij\ *n* -S [ME *brigge*, fr. OE *brycg*; akin to OHG *brucka* bridge, ON *bryggja* gangplank, *brū* bridge, OSlav *brŭvŭno* beam] **1 a :** a structure erected over a depression or an obstacle to travel (as a river, chasm, roadway, or railroad) carrying a continuous pathway or roadway (as for pedestrians, automobiles, or trains) — see ARCH BRIDGE, BAILEY BRIDGE, CANTILEVER BRIDGE, GIRDER BRIDGE, SLAB BRIDGE, SUSPENSION BRIDGE, TRUSS BRIDGE; FOOTBRIDGE, RAILROAD BRIDGE; BOTTOM-ROAD BRIDGE, DECK BRIDGE, THROUGH BRIDGE; BASCULE BRIDGE, LIFT BRIDGE, SWING BRIDGE, TRANSPORTER BRIDGE, TRAVERSING BRIDGE, VERTICAL LIFT BRIDGE; compare OVERPASS, VIADUCT **b :** a time, place, or means of abstract connection (as in transition or reconciliation) **:** a figurative means of crossing ⟨the soldier as he recrosses the ~ from war to peace —Dixon Wecter⟩ ⟨a gulf too wide to be spanned by the one ~ Australians . . . set any store by — the newspaper —Thomas Wood †1950⟩ **2 a** *obs* **:** PIER, JETTY **b :** a movable landing stage for boats **3 :** something resembling a bridge (as in serving as a support for or a way over something else): as **a :** the upper bony part of the nose; *also* **:** the curved part of a pair of glasses that rests upon this part of the nose **b :** an arch or ridge at right angles to the strings of a musical instrument (as a violin or piano) serving to raise them and transmit their vibrations to the body of the instrument — see VIOLIN illustration **c :** BRIDGING JOIST **d :** a platform elevated above the rail and extending across and over the deck of a ship — compare FORE-AND-AFT BRIDGE **e :** the hand used as a rest for a billiard or pool cue in striking the ball; *also* **:** a notched or crossed piece at the end of a thin wooden rod for use as a cue rest **f :** a plank way or elevator used in ironworking to convey fuel or ore to the mouth of a furnace **g :** the position of a wrestler on his back with his body arched so that he is supported by his head and feet and sometimes elbows **h :** BRIDGE BRACKET **i :** one of the lateral bony plates connecting the carapace and plastron of a turtle shell **j :** the metal separating the ports in a machine valve seat **k :** a timber supported on blocks that rest on another timber and have a narrow space between them through which piles may be driven (as in forepoling a mining excavation) **l :** a framework that spans railroad tracks and supports signals **m** (1) **:** a backstage walk equipped with guardrails, mounting battens, and stanchions for lighting instruments that is adjustable as to height and is generally hung directly behind and parallel to the act drop in a theater — called also *light bridge* (2) **:** the portable or fixed scaffold used in a theater in connection with the paint frame for high scenery — called also *paint bridge* **n :** a plate which is attached to the pillar or baseplate of a watch and in which is mounted the bearing for an arbor, wheel pivot, or balance pivot **o :** a bright band across a sunspot **p :** the platform from which a warship is conned **q** (1) **:** the arch formed by a dancer's body in an extreme backbend (2) **:** the arch formed by the joined raised hands of a couple or a series of couples in a folk dance **4 :** something suggesting a bridge in serving the function of connecting: as **a :** LAND BRIDGE **b** (1) *or* **bridge passage :** the transition from the first subject to the second subject in a sonata or other musical form (2) **:** a color or area of color serving as a transition between two other more dominant or significant colors (3) **:** a passage, section, or scene in a literary or dramatic work serving as a transition between two other more significant passages, sections, or scenes **c :** PONS **d :** a strand of protoplasm extending between two cells **e :** a partial denture held in place by anchorage to adjacent teeth **f :** an atom or group of atoms or a valence bond connecting two different parts of a molecule (as opposite sides of a ring) ⟨the valence ~ in naphthalene⟩ ⟨the carbon ~ in camphor⟩ **g :** an area of physical continuity between two chromatids persisting during the later phases of mitosis and constituting a possible source of somatic genetic change **h :** a conductor extending across from one junction of an electric network to another **i :** a short transitional passage (as of music or sound effects) connecting two parts of a radio or TV program or two programs **5 :** a sliding cover usu. on wheels for the top of a mine shaft **6** *or* **bridge circuit :** an electrical instrument or network for measuring or comparing resistances, inductances, capacitances, or impedances by balancing two opposing voltages through a sensitive current detector whose nil reading indicates the equality of the unknown to a known ratio — see WHEATSTONE BRIDGE **7 :** one of the floor elevators running parallel to the proscenium that are raised and lowered to provide various levels for the stage floor **8 :** two men left on the king row in checkers to prevent the opponent from acquiring kings **9 :** an obstruction lodged part way down a drilled hole (as an oil well)

bridges: *1* simple truss; *2* continuous truss; *3* steel arch; *4* cantilever, *a* suspended span; *5* suspension

²bridge \"\ *vb* -ED/-ING/-S [ME *briggen*, fr. OE *brycgian*, fr. *brycg*, n.] *vt* **1 a :** to make a bridge over **:** span or make a way across with or as if with a bridge ⟨a model railroad . . . I was going to ~ a little creek for it —John Steinbeck⟩ ⟨*bridging* the gaps between the university and the high schools —J.S. Reeves⟩ ⟨a kinship in spirit that could ~ four centuries —Robert Monteith⟩ ⟨ways to ~ the time from supper to bed —John Gould⟩ ⟨a distance greater than the human shout could ~ —Waldemar Kaempffert⟩ ⟨*bridging* the distance in less than two days of actual walking —Farley Mowat⟩ **b :** to provide with a bridge ⟨small *bridged* streams along the route⟩ ⟨the *bridged* human nose —Weston La Barre⟩ **2 :** to make an electrical connection between ⟨~ the two parts of a circuit⟩ **:** SHUNT **~** *vi, of a wrestler* **:** to assume the position called a bridge
³bridge \"\ *vi* -ED/-ING/-S [prob. by folk etymology (the dealer's passing the declaration of trumps to his partner being regarded as a bridging of the table) fr. earlier *biritch*, v. & n., of unknown origin] *of the dealer in bridge-whist* **:** to delegate to one's partner the duty of selecting a suit to be trump or no-trump — used with *it*
⁴bridge \"\ *n* -S [prob. by folk etymology (influence of ³*bridge*) fr. earlier *biritch*] **:** any of various widely differing card games for four players in two partnerships, developed from dummy whist and cayenne, having in common that the hand of the declarer's partner is exposed and played by the declarer who also determines the trump suit or the fact of no-trump play, his adversaries being allowed to double the scoring values and the declarer to redouble them; *esp* **:** CONTRACT BRIDGE — see AUCTION BRIDGE, BRIDGE-WHIST; compare WHIST — **at the bridge :** within one point of winning the game in bridge
bridge·able \ˈbrijəbəl\ *adj* **:** capable of being bridged
bridge bar *n* [¹*bridge*] **:** TIMBER BAR
bridge bird *n* **:** PHOEBE
bridgeboard \ˈ=,=\ *n* **:** a notched board to support the treads and risers of wooden stairs **:** STRING 14a
bridge bracket *n* **:** a small slotted bracket bridging a gap in the end frame of a reeling machine in cotton spinning to facilitate doffing the hanks
bridge circuit *n* **:** BRIDGE 6
bridge coat *n* **:** a long coat of very heavy wool worn by officers on a ship's bridge during cold weather

A, A bridgeboards

bridge coupler *n* **:** a device for engaging and disengaging the interlocking connection between the shore and a movable bridge span
bridge crane *n* **:** a crane in which a beam or bridge carries the hoisting apparatus — see GANTRY CRANE, ROTARY BRIDGE CRANE
bridge deck *n* **:** a partial deck above a superstructure, usu. amidships — see DECK illustration
bridged–T \ˈbrij(d)ˈtē\ *n* **:** a T network with a fourth branch bridging the two series arms of the T from input to output terminal, used to control the ratio of the magnitude of the output to input voltage, their relative phase, or both, such magnitudes or phase relations trips in many cases depending on signal frequency
bridge graft *n* **:** a plant graft made by inserting one or more scions with one end below and the other end above an interruption of the cambium or other weak point in the stock and used esp. to bridge wounds (as from gnawing) or to reinforce weak or defective grafts
bridge guard *n* **:** a guard on a railroad track placed at bridges or gantlet tracks and consisting of two rails gradually drawn in to meet in the center of the track
bridgehead \ˈ=,=\ *n* [trans. of F *tête de pont*] **1 a :** a defensive work covering or commanding the extremity of a bridge nearest the enemy **b :** a locality held by the enemy and garrisoned or fortified to protect a bridge site, ford, or defile on the enemy's side **c :** a position or area around or commanding the end of a bridge ⟨railroad shops were built near the ~ on the north side —*Amer. Guide Series: Ark.*⟩ **2 a :** an advanced position or salient seized in hostile territory and defended as a foothold for further advance **b :** any advanced or initial commanding position (as in politics or commerce) ⟨many ~s have been established along the coast and far up the Amazon to exploit commodities in world demand —Allan Murray⟩ ⟨hold a permanent ~ in No. American markets —Dennis May⟩ ⟨the winning of labor's first international ~ —Carol Riegelman⟩
bridge house *n* **:** a structure amidships above the main deck of a ship the top of which forms a bridge deck
bridge islet *n* **:** an island that becomes a peninsula at low water
bridge lamp *n* [⁴*bridge*] **:** a small floor lamp usu. with an adjustable arm
bridge·less \-ləs\ *adj* **:** being without a bridge
bridge line *n* **:** an intermediate railroad connecting two other railroads to form a through route for traffic
bridge lock *n* **:** a mechanical device to ensure that the rails on a movable bridge are in proper position for trains
bridge·man \ˈbrijmən\ *n, pl* **bridgemen 1 :** one who works on a bridge: as **a :** one who tends the landing bridge where a ferryboat docks and supervises the loading and unloading of the ferry **b :** one who operates the machinery for opening and closing drawbridges or who operates the bridge over which railroad cars are run from wharf to scow **c :** a member of a construction crew that builds bridges with structural steel or iron **2 :** one who works on the loading platform of an icehouse selling ice to wholesale and retail customers
bridgemaster \ˈ=,==\ *n* **1** *Brit* **:** an officer (as of a town corporation) in control of a bridge or a pier **2 :** a man stationed on a ship's bridge to transmit directions to the man at the ship's wheel
bridge of boats : a passageway resting on boats moored abreast across a stretch of water
bridge of sighs *often cap B & S* [fr. *Bridge of Sighs*, a covered bridge in Venice, Italy, that leads from the palace of the Doge to a prison, trans. of It *Ponte dei Sospiri*] **:** BRIDGEWAY 2
bridge passage *n* **:** BRIDGE 4b(1)
bridge pewee *n* [so called fr. its nesting under bridges] **:** PHOEBE
bridge piece *n* **:** a plate, shape, or casting arching over the rudder opening between the sternpost and rudderpost of a ship
bridge plate *n* **:** a gangplank usu. of reinforced steel plate used between a railroad car or truck and a landing platform
bridge·port \ˈbrij,pōrt, -ȯrt, -ōət, -ō(ə)t, *usu* -d·+V\ *adj, usu cap* [fr. *Bridgeport*, Conn.] **:** of or from the city of Bridgeport, Conn. ⟨*Bridgeport* industries⟩ **:** of the kind or style prevalent in Bridgeport
bridge rail *n* **:** a railroad-track rail in the form of an inverted trough

cross section of bridge rail

bridge rectifier *n* **:** a full wave rectifier consisting of four rectifiers connected in the form of a bridge, in which two pairs of rectifying elements are used, each pair being in series and connected to the input in opposite polarity to the other pair, the output being derived from the center points of the two pairs
bridges *pl of* BRIDGE, *pres 3d sing of* BRIDGE
bridge seat *n* **:** the shelf on the face of a bridge abutment that supports the end of the span
bridge stone *n* **1 :** a stone spanning a gutter or sunken area **2 :** stone for building bridges
bridge table *n* [⁴*bridge*] **:** CARD TABLE
bridgetender \ˈ=,==\ *n* **:** one that has charge of a bridge; *esp* **:** one that opens and closes a movable bridge to accommodate both waterway and roadway traffic — called also *bridgeman*
bridge tie *n* **:** a timber resting transversely on railroad bridge stringers for support of the rails
bridge tower *n* **:** a tower on a bridge (as for the support of cables or for defense); *also* **:** a tower serving as a bridgehead
bridge train *n* **:** the personnel and equipment of an army train carrying bridge and pontoon materials
bridgettine *usu cap, var of* BRIGITTINE
bridge wall *n* **:** a low separating wall usu. of firebrick in a furnace; *esp* **:** such a wall in a reverberatory furnace
bridge·ward \ˈbrij,wȯrd\ *n* -S **:** the principal ward of a key
bridgeway \ˈ=,=\ *n* **1 :** a road or walk across a bridge **2 :** an enclosed passageway that is suspended above the level of the first floor and connects two otherwise separate buildings
bridge–whist \ˈ=,=\ *n* [⁴*bridge*] **:** the earliest form of bridge, in which the dealer could name a suit as trump or choose no-trump or require his partner to do so
bridgewing \ˈ=,=\ *n* **:** the end of the bridge of a ship
bridgework \ˈ=,=\ *n* **1 :** the process or trade of bridge building; *also* **:** the structural detail of a bridge **2 :** a dental bridge or dental bridges
bridging *n* -S **1 :** the forming of or causing to assume the form or position of a bridge **2 :** the braces or system of bracing used between floor or other timbers to stiffen them and to distribute the weight — compare CROSS BRIDGING, HERRINGBONE STRUTTING **3 :** the ability of a coating of paint to form a continuous film over a small void or crack
bridging joist *n* **:** a joist resting on the binding joists and supporting the flooring
bridging species *n* **:** a plant species considered to be able to so modify the pathogenicity of a fungus infecting it that the fungus can subsequently infect a plant normally resistant to its attack
¹bri·dle \ˈbrīdᵊl\ *n* -S [ME *bridel*, fr. OE *bridel*, *brigdils*; akin to OHG *brittil* rein, OE *bregdan* to move quickly — more at BRAID] **1 a :** the headgear with which a horse is governed and restrained, consisting of a headstall, a bit, and reins, often with other appurtenances **b :** a strip of metal joining two parts of a machine esp. for limiting or restraining motion **c :** BRANK 1a **2 :** something resembling or suggesting a bridle esp. in shape or in serving as a restraint: as **a :** a length of rope or cable with the ends secured to different parts or sides of an object (as a ship) and with a second rope or cable attached to the bight to which the force for hauling, lifting, or securing is applied **b :** CURB, CHECK, RESTRAINT ⟨how a soldier behaved . . . depended less upon the ~ of the army than upon self-discipline —Dixon Wecter⟩ **c :** FRENUM **d :** a cord tightening or strengthening the sides of a net **e :** a clevis on a plow **f :** the cord or system of cords by which a kite is attached to its string **g :** a device for controlling the speed of logs on a skid road or the speed of logging sleds **h :** a sling of cordage that has its ends attached to the envelope of a captive balloon or airship or to a preceding bridle and to an intermediate point of which a rope or cable is attached **i :** a cloth stay used in tailoring for the neckline of coats and jackets **3** *Brit* **:** TRIMMER 2

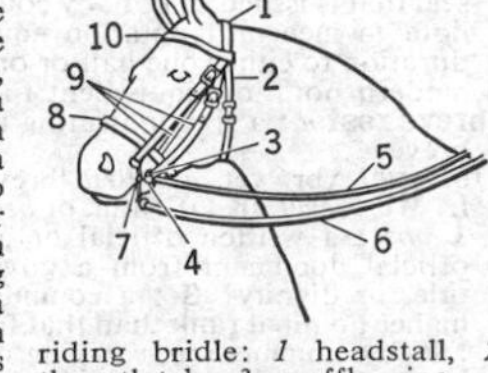

riding bridle: *1* headstall, *2* throatlatch, *3* snaffle ring, *4* snaffle bit, *5* snaffle rein, *6* curb rein, *7* curb bit, *8* noseband, *9* cheek straps, *10* front

²bridle \"\ *vb* **bridled; bridled; bridling** \-d(ᵊ)liŋ\ **bridles** [ME *bridlen*, fr. OE *brīdlian*, fr. *bridel*, n.] *vt* **1 :** to put a bridle upon **:** equip with a bridle ⟨~ a horse⟩ **2 :** to restrain, arrest, govern, or control with or as if with a bridle; *esp* **:** to moderate steadily or guide away from excess or eccentricity ⟨strong in censuring and *bridling* the wicked —H.O.Taylor⟩ **3 :** to carry or move (as the head) like one that bridles **~** *vi* **:** to give evidence of hostility in one's attitude or behavior out of protest, offended pride, scorn, or resentment esp. by holding up the head and drawing in the chin ⟨we ~ when any one of our institutions sets itself up above another —W.L. Sperry⟩ ⟨military commanders who had *bridled* against . . . interference —*Time*⟩ **syn** see RESTRAIN
³bridle \"\ *n* -S **:** the action of one that bridles
bridle cable *n* **:** a cable secured to a bridle (sense 2a)
bridle chain *n* **1 :** one of the safety chains attaching a cage to the hoisting rope in mining **2 :** ROUGH LOCK
bridled minnow *or* **bridled shiner** *n* **:** a small American cyprinid fish (*Notropis bifrenata*) sometimes kept in aquariums
bridled tern *n* **:** a tern (*Sterna anaethetus*) of tropical seas that resembles the sooty tern but is smaller, grayer of body and whiter on the head
bridled titmouse *n* **:** a titmouse (*Parus wollweberi annexus*) having a black crest and black markings resembling a bridle on the throat and ranging from Arizona to Mexico
bridle hand *n* **:** the hand that usu. holds the bridle in riding; *usu* **:** the left hand
bridle head *n* **:** a horse bridle without a bit
bridle joint *n* **:** a joint in carpentry in which the end of one timber deeply recessed fits over another timber with recessed sides
bri·dle·less \-dᵊl(l)əs\ *adj* [ME *brydiless*, fr. *brydil, bridel* + -*less*] **:** being without a bridle
bridle path *or* **bridle trail** *also* **bridle road** *or* **bridle way** *n* **:** a trail passable to or designed primarily for saddle horses or packhorses as distinguished from one for vehicles
bridle port *n* **:** a port formerly in the bow of a ship through which hawsers, bridle cables, and often gun muzzles were passed
bridle rein *n* [ME *bridel reyne*, fr. *bridel* bridle + *reyne* rein] **:** REIN 1
bridle ring *n* **:** a screw hook having the appearance of a pig's tail used for guiding and retaining telephone and signaling wires on buildings or posts
bridle rod *or* **bridle bar** *n* **:** a steel tie bar used to join the ends of two point rails to hold them to gage in the proper position
bridle sling *n* **:** a contrivance of rings, hooks, and chains or ropes serving to attach heavy loads to a crane
bridlewise \ˈ==,=\ *adj* [¹*bridle* + *wise*] *of a horse* **:** responsive to the bridle
bri·doon \brəˈdün\ *or* **bra·doon** \brəˈ-\ *n* -S [F *bridon*, fr. *bride* bridle — more at BRIDE] **1 :** a bit resembling a snaffle

but without cheekpieces used chiefly with a separate curb **2 :** a headstall fitted with a bridoon
brids *pl of* BRID
brie \ˈbrē\ *also* **brie cheese** *n* -s *usu cap B* [F *brie*, fr. *Brie*, district in northeastern France, where it is made] **:** a soft perishable cheese ripened by mold
¹brief \ˈbrēf\ *adj* -ER/-EST [ME *bref, breve*, fr. MF *brief, bref*, fr. L *brevis;* akin to OHG *murg* short, Gk *brachys*, Sogdian *murzak*] **1 a :** not enduring long **:** markedly limited in duration ⟨a ~ interruption⟩ ⟨a ~ speech⟩ ⟨one of the ~*est* republics in human record —Julian Dana⟩ **b :** of limited extent ⟨down across a ~ meadow —E.W.Smith⟩; *esp* **:** SHORT ⟨a ~ paragraph expressing a firm conviction —Margaret E. Hall⟩ ⟨a jacket . . . waist-length in back and ~*er* in front —Lois Long⟩ ⟨consisting of one ~ street⟩ **2 a :** CONCISE, SUCCINCT ⟨a ~ summary of the day's news⟩ ⟨some ~ remarks on the subject⟩ **b :** CURT, ABRUPT **3** *dial, of a communicable illness* **:** extremely common **:** PREVALENT ⟨measles are very ~ here just now⟩
syn BRIEF and SHORT contrast with *long*. BRIEF usu. applies to duration ⟨it was a fleeting visit, all too *brief;* in three short minutes he had seen them all —W.H.Davies⟩ ⟨a mock episode, as *brief* as a dream —L.P.Smith⟩ ⟨fair but mortal youths who paid with their lives for the *brief* rapture of the love of an immortal goddess —J.G.Frazer⟩ It may suggest conciseness or even curtness ⟨their greetings were *brief*. "Hi, kid", Donald said. "Hi, boy", said Will —Wallace Stegner⟩ SHORT, applying to both duration and extent, may be a close synonym for BRIEF ⟨*short* and narrow bound from morn to eventide —W.E. Gladstone⟩ It may imply a sudden abrupt shortening or conclusion ⟨a *short* but exhilarating experience of the power to control lives for good or evil⟩
²brief \ˈbrēf\ *n* -s [ME *bref, breve*, fr. MF *bref, brief*, fr. ML *brevis, breve*, fr. LL, letter, summary, fr. L *brevis* (masc. & fem.), *breve* (neut.), adj., short] **1 :** a formal or official letter or mandate: as **a :** BREVE 3; *esp* **:** BRIEVE **b** *dial Eng* **:** a statement of the causes of a person's poverty used as a petition **:** a begging letter **c :** a papal letter that is less formal than a bull and is signed by the secretary of briefs and sealed with the pope's ring **d** *obs* **:** DISPATCH 2 **e :** a letter patent formerly issued by the English sovereign as head of the established church authorizing a collection to be made in the churches for some specified purpose **2 :** a brief written item or document: as **a :** a short usu. concise article (as in a newspaper) ⟨local ~*s*⟩ **b :** a short version **:** SYNOPSIS, SUMMARY ⟨a ~ of a large scholarly tome⟩ **c** *obs* **:** CATALOG, LIST **d :** an abridgment or concise statement of a client's case made out for the instruction of counsel in a trial at law — called also ¦*trial brief* **e** *obs* **:** MEMORANDUM, INVOICE **f :** ABSTRACT OF TITLE **3 a :** a plan or outline of an argument; *esp* **:** a formal outline with logically related headings that sets forth the main contentions with supporting statements or evidence **b** *or* **brief of argument :** such a plan in behalf of a client that often has considerable detail dealing with the facts or the law and is presented to a trial or appellate court, an administrative or international tribunal, or to a legislative body **c :** a case at law **4** *Scot* **:** SPELL, CHARM **5 :** short snug-fitting pants or underpants that usu. have elastic at the waist and elastic or ribbing at the slant-cut leg openings and are made in a variety of styles for both men and women — usu. used in pl. **syn** see ABRIDGMENT — **hold a brief for :** ADVOCATE, DEFEND ⟨although a workman, he *holds no brief for* an increase in workman's pay⟩ — **in brief** *adv* **:** in a few words **:** CONCISELY, BRIEFLY ⟨he gave the details of the accident *in brief* before discussing its legal aspects⟩ — **make brief of :** to do or perform very quickly ⟨the host *made brief of* the introductions in order to speed the group into the dining room⟩
³brief \"\ *vt* -ED/-ING/-S [¹*brief*] **1 a :** to present in brief or in the form of a brief **:** make a brief, abstract, or abridgment of ⟨entered a solid, old law firm . . . received a salary for ~*ing* up cases —T.W.Duncan⟩ ⟨~ a report⟩ ⟨Miss Sandoz ~*ed* what Cook had said —C.C.Rister⟩ ⟨summarized northeastern Siberian archaeology and has ~*ed* many normally unavailable sources —Wendell Oswalt⟩ **b :** to compose (a written work) in the form of a brief or abstract ⟨a report ~*ed* from the original notes⟩ **2** *Brit* **:** to retain as legal counsel ⟨~ a lawyer⟩ **3 a :** to give final precise and informative instructions to (participants before a mission or action) **b :** to indoctrinate (members of the armed forces) in service standards — compare DEBRIEF **c :** to coach thoroughly in advance, imparting condensed up-to-the-minute information and explicit directions ⟨instructed him in what to say, in other words, ~*ed* him in the current line of propaganda —Evelyn G. Cruickshanks⟩ ⟨thousands of marriages . . . could be kept intact if young couples were properly ~*ed* beforehand on the chief booby traps in married life —*Irish Digest*⟩ **d :** to give usu. essential information to usu. concisely ⟨a visitor can hardly set foot inside the border before someone is ~*ing* him on the general sequence of events —Faubion Bowers⟩
⁴brief *adv* [¹*brief*] *obs* **:** BRIEFLY
brief bag \ˈ⸗,⸗\ *n* [²*brief*] **1** *Brit* **:** the traditional blue or red bag used by barristers to carry their briefs to and from court **2 :** BRIEFCASE; *esp* **:** a briefcase with expanding sides and bottom designed to carry both documents and clothing for an overnight trip
briefcase \ˈ⸗,⸗\ *n* [²*brief* + *case*] **:** a flat flexible case usu. with a handle that is designed to carry legal briefs or other papers
briefing *n* -s [fr. gerund of ³*brief*] **1 :** the action or an instance of briefing **:** the process of being briefed ⟨at the end of each day authorized spokesmen . . . held ~*s* attended by hundreds of newspaper and radio reporters —Clifton Daniel⟩ ⟨at a ~ session, pilots and navigators . . . get data —*N.Y. Times*⟩ **2 :** the instructions or information imparted at a briefing ⟨do what the ~ calls for⟩

briefcase

brief·less \ˈbrēflə̇s\ *adj* [²*brief* + *-less*] *of a lawyer* **:** without clients
brief·ly *adv* [ME *brefly*, fr. *bref* + *-ly*] **1 a :** in a brief way ⟨an attempt has been made to survey ~ the main aspects of this vast . . . subject —W.H.Dowdeswell⟩ **b :** in brief ⟨the procedure adopted consisted ~ of selecting . . . parent trees based on reliability of cropping, yield records, and fruit quality —*Farmer's Weekly (So. Africa)*⟩ **2 :** for a short time ⟨she was ~ associated with the Civil Service Commission —*Current Biog.*⟩
brief·ness *n* -ES [ME *breffnes*, fr. *breff, bref* brief + *nes* -ness — more at BRIEF] **:** the quality or state of being brief
brief of title [²*brief*] **:** ABSTRACT OF TITLE
¹bri·er *or* **bri·ar** \ˈbrī(ə)r\ *n* -s [ME *brere*, fr. OE *brǣr, brēr*] **1 a :** a plant (as members of the genera *Rosa, Rubus*, and *Smilax*) with a woody stem bearing thorns or prickles **b** *Brit* **:** WILD ROSE **2 :** a group or mass of brier bushes **3 :** a thorn or twig of a brier **:** a branch of brier
²brier *or* **briar** \"\ *n* -s [F *bruyère* heath, heather, fr. MF *bruiere*, fr. (assumed) VL *brucaria* heath, fr. LL *brucus* heather, of Celt origin; akin to OIr *froech* heather, W *grug;* akin to Gk *ereikē* heather, Lith *viržis*] **:** a heath (*Erica arborea*) of southern Europe the root of which is used for making pipes — see BRIAR, FRENCH BRIER
bri·er·ber·ry *or* **bri·ar·ber·ry** \ˈbrīə(r)-—*see* BERRY\ *n* [¹*brier, briar* + *berry*] **1 :** the brownish black fruit of a prickly bush (*Rubus cuneifolius*) of the eastern U.S. **2 :** the plant that bears the brierberry
brierroot *or* **briarroot** \ˈ⸗,⸗\ *n* [²*brier, briar* + *root*] **:** the root of various plants (as *Erica arborea* of southern Europe or members of the genera *Rhododendron* and *Smilax* of the U.S.) used in the manufacture of tobacco pipes; *esp* **:** the burl of the brier used in the manufacture of briars
brier rose *n* [¹*brier*] **:** DOG ROSE
brierwood *or* **briarwood** \ˈ⸗,⸗\ *n* [²*brier, briar* + *wood*] **:** the wood of the brierroot
bri·ery *or* **bri·ary** \ˈbrīrē, -ri\ *adj* [¹*brier, briar* + *-y*] **:** full of briers ⟨they were excessively wet vines and ~ —D.L. Sharp⟩
brieve \ˈbrēv\ *n* -s [alter. of ²*brief*] *Scots law* **:** a chancery writ directing trial usu. by jury to be made of certain specified matters
¹brig \ˈbrig\ *n* -s [short for *brigantine*] **1 :** BRIGANTINE **2 :** a 2-masted square-rigged vessel — see HERMAPHRODITE BRIG

brig

²brig \"\ *n* -s [prob. fr. ¹*brig*] **:** a temporary place (as on a ship) for confinement of offenders in the U.S. navy **:** GUARDHOUSE
³brig \"\ *now chiefly Scot var of* BRIDGE
¹bri·gade \brə̇ˈgād\ *n* -s [F, fr. MF, fr. OIt *brigata*, fem. of *brigato*, past part. of *brigare* to fight — more at BRIGAND] **1 a :** a large body of troops **b :** a tactical and administrative unit composed basically of a headquarters and two or more regiments or groups **2 :** a group of people organized for special activity: as **a :** a supply party in the early American fur trade **b :** BUCKET BRIGADE **c :** FIRE BRIGADE **3** *obs* **:** a train of railroad cars
²brigade \"\ *vt* -ED/-ING/-S **:** to form into a brigade **:** unite to form a brigade ⟨this small body of 500 infantry . . . was *brigaded* with the guards —E.H.Collis⟩
brigade major *n* **:** a brigade staff officer in the British army whose duties are similar to those of a regimental executive in the U.S. Army
brig·a·dier \ˌbrigəˈdi(ə)r, -iə\ *n* -s [F, fr. *brigade* + *-ier*] **1 a :** BRIGADIER GENERAL **b :** an officer in the British army assigned to command a brigade **c :** a noncommissioned officer in the French army **2 :** a Salvation Army officer ranking above a senior major and below a lieutenant colonel
brigadier general *n* **:** an army, marine, or air force officer ranking just below a major general and above a colonel
brig·a·dier·ship \ˌ⸗⸗ˈ⸗,ship\ *n* -s **:** the office or the rank of a brigadier
brig·a·low \ˈbrigə,lō\ *n* -s [native name in Australia] *Austral* **:** any of several plants of the genus *Acacia* with hard heavy elastic wood (esp. *A. harpophylla* and *A. doratoxylon*)
brig·and \ˈbrigənd *sometimes* brə̇ˈgand *or* -ˈgaa(ə)nd\ *n* -s [ME *brigaunt*, fr. MF *brigand*, fr. OIt *brigante*, fr. *brigare* to fight, fr. *briga* strife, of Celt origin; akin to OIr *brig* strength, virtue, W *bri* fame, honor] **:** one who lives by plunder usu. as a member of a band **:** BANDIT
brig·and·age \-dij\ *n* -s [F, fr. MF, fr. *brigand* + *-age*] **:** depredation as practiced by brigands **:** PILLAGE
brig·an·dine \ˈbrigən,dēn *sometimes* ¦ēn\ *also* **brig·an·tine** \-ən,tē\ *n* -s [ME *brigandyne, brigantyn*, fr. MF *brigandine*, fr. *brigand* + *-ine*] **:** a late medieval coat of body armor consisting typically of overlapping metal scales or plates sewed within canvas, linen, or leather
brig·and·ish \ˈbrigəndish *sometimes* brə̇ˈgan- *or* -ˈgaan-\ *adj* **:** suggesting or resembling a brigand ⟨two ~ men —Dan Wickenden⟩ ⟨~ tendencies⟩
brig·and·ism \-n,dizəm\ *n* -s **:** BRIGANDAGE
brig·an·tine \ˈbrigən,tēn *sometimes* -tīn\ *n* -s [MF *brigantin*, fr. OIt *brigantino*, fr. *brigante* brigand + *-ino* -ine — more at BRIGAND] **1 a :** a former light swift seagoing vessel esp. of the Mediterranean equipped for both rowing and sailing **b** *obs* **:** any of various light European sailing or rowing vessels **2 a :** a 2-masted square-rigged vessel differing from a brig in not carrying a square mainsail **b :** HERMAPHRODITE BRIG
brig·et·ty \ˈbrigəd·ē, -əte, -i\ *adj* [by alter.] **:** BIGGETY
brigg \ˈbrig\ *now chiefly Scot var of* BRIDGE
briggs logarithm \ˈbrigz-\ *or* **briggs·ian logarithm** \-zēən-\ *n, usu cap B* [after Henry *Briggs* †1631 Eng. mathematician] **:** COMMON LOGARITHM
brig·ham·ite \ˈbrigə,mīt\ *n* -s *usu cap* [*Brigham* Young †1877 Amer. Mormon leader + E *-ite*] **:** a polygamous Mormon
brig·ham tea \ˈbrigəm-\ *n, usu cap B* [after *Brigham* Young; fr. its use in the treatment of gonorrhea, alluding to Mormon polygamy] **:** MORMON TEA
¹bright \ˈbrīt, *usu* -īd·+V\ *adj* -ER/-EST [ME, fr. OE *beorht, byrht, bryht;* akin to OHG *beraht* bright, ON *bjartr*, Goth *bairhts* clear, evident, Skt *bhrājate* it shines] **1 a :** marked by shining or radiating light **:** pervaded by, shedding, or reflecting a relatively great amount of light **:** SHINING, LUMINOUS ⟨a ~ sun⟩ ⟨~ flames⟩ ⟨~ eyes⟩ ⟨some diamonds, very ~ and sparkling —Charles Dickens⟩ **b :** marked by qualities that make conspicuous in a way similar to that of a radiating light: as (1) **:** ringing and clear **:** SHARP — used of sounds or musical tones having a predominance of high overtones ⟨a sharp ~ quality of voice⟩ (2) **:** of high or very high saturation or lightness — used of a color ⟨~ red⟩ **c :** having qualities that make markedly, esp. radiantly, attractive **:** illustrious for qualities that charm or affect the mind pleasurably ⟨~ hours with friends⟩ ⟨~ beauty⟩ ⟨a landscape ~ with flowers⟩ **d :** marked by lightness, cheer, happiness, or qualities inspiring optimism **:** PROMISING, AUSPICIOUS ⟨those ~ mornings when you whistle with a light heart —W.H.Auden⟩ ⟨~ prospects of victory⟩ ⟨his voice sounded so ~ and cheerful, and had such a warm infectious gladness running through it —O.E. Rölvaag⟩ **2** *archaic* **:** ILLUSTRIOUS, GLORIOUS ⟨Troy . . . ~ with fame —Shak.⟩ **3 a :** showing mental quickness, ready understanding or learning, prompt responses, or originality ⟨~ young fellows with a charming literary swagger, they aspired to be wits —V.L.Parrington⟩ **b :** showing lively animation, vivacity, or activity ⟨~ and busy and crowded with tourists —*Amer. Guide Series: Mich.*⟩ ⟨she paused for a ~ wave of her hand —Agnes S. Turnbull⟩ **c :** showing glib quickness or facile resourcefulness without deep intellectuality ⟨~ ideas, some of them showing a superb neglect of practical feasibility —*Countryman*⟩ **4 :** CLEAR, TRANSPARENT ⟨a ~ wine⟩ ⟨~ beer⟩ **5 :** light in color or smooth, clean, or lustrous in any of several ways: as **a** *of lumber* **:** newly sawed or planed and smooth or free from discoloration **b** *of woodwork* **:** scraped and cleaned usu. with sand or canvas but not painted **c** *of coal* **:** shining and banded **:** containing high moisture and sulfur content — compare CLARAIN, VITRAIN **d :** having a high sparkling or glazed finish ⟨~ jewelry⟩ ⟨a ~ leather⟩ **e :** free from dirt and having an attractive luster ⟨~ onions ready for market⟩ **f :** having a natural unbleached color (as in certain market grades of hay or grain) **g** *of yarn* **:** LUSTROUS **h** *of silk* **:** DEGUMMED **i** *of wool or cotton* **:** light colored **:** WHITE **j** *of a Negro* **:** light in complexion ⟨a ~ mulatto⟩ **k** *of wire rope* **:** not galvanized, tinned, or otherwise coated **6 :** FLUE-CURED
syn BRILLIANT, RADIANT, LUMINOUS, LUSTROUS, EFFULGENT, REFULGENT, BEAMING, BEAMY, LAMBENT, LUCENT, INCANDESCENT: BRIGHT indicates emission of or pervasion by a high degree of light ⟨like the *bright* spots that move about the sun —John Keats⟩ ⟨the moon was so *bright* that Smith watered and raked and weeded as if it had been day —C.B.Nordhoff & J.N.Hall⟩ BRILLIANT implies intense, often sparkling brightness ⟨midnight streets are more *brilliant* than noon —*Amer. Guide Series: N.Y. City*⟩ ⟨a luscious prairie . . . *brilliant* with bulb flowers in the springtime —H.J.Mackinder⟩ RADIANT may stress emission of light rays but often it is only a colorful equivalent for *bright* ⟨the sun and moon, then at the prime of their *radiant* power and glory —J.G.Frazer⟩ ⟨the *radiant* mist of the afterglow —Ellen Glasgow⟩ ⟨its beautifully terraced garden *radiant* with bloom —V.G.Heiser⟩ LUMINOUS usu. implies emission of a steady, suffused, glowing light ⟨the château began to make itself strangely visible by some light of its own, as though it were growing *luminous* —Charles Dickens⟩ ⟨the inner surface of the glass is *luminous* of itself, shining with a soft and clear green light —K.K.Darrow⟩ LUSTROUS stresses a tendency to reflect light, esp. in a rich and even way ⟨the *lustrous* salvers in the moonlight gleam —John Keats⟩ ⟨*lustrous* as some huge precious pearl —Henry James †1916⟩ EFFULGENT and REFULGENT indicate resplendent or gleaming brilliance, the latter implying reflectivity ⟨the fiery light of the sinking sun . . . mottled the mountains with *effulgent* spaces —John Tyndall⟩ ⟨the glorious sovereign of day, clothed in light *refulgent*, rolling on his gilded chariot, hastened to revisit the western realms —William Bartram⟩ BEAMING and the poetical BEAMY stress emission of light beams or rays ⟨the rising moon fair *beaming* —Robert Burns⟩ ⟨west and away the wheels of darkness roll, day's *beamy* banner up the east is borne —A.E.Housman⟩ LAMBENT often indicates soft luminosity ⟨another moon new risen . . . of *lambent* flame serene —William Cowper⟩ ⟨kind, quiet, nearsighted eyes, which his round spectacles magnified into *lambent* moons —Margaret Deland⟩ LUCENT, various in its uses and romantic in suggestion, may imply a transfiguring light ⟨she walked below the *lucent* sun —Elinor Wylie⟩ ⟨till every particle glowed clean and new and slowly seemed to turn to *lucent* amber in a world of blue —W.W.Gibson⟩ INCANDESCENT suggests intense, glowing brightness ⟨here gush the sparkles *incandescent* like scattered showers of golden sand —Bayard Taylor⟩ ⟨the air rendered *incandescent* by the vehemence of the impacts of the electrons against its molecules —K.K.Darrow⟩ **syn** see in addition INTELLIGENT
²bright \"\ *adv* -ER/-EST [ME *brighte*, fr. OE *beorhte, byrhte, bryhte*, fr. *beorht, byrht, bryht*, adj.] **:** BRIGHTLY ⟨I say it is the moon that shines so ~ —Shak.⟩ ⟨asked which of the two lamps shone ~*er*⟩
³bright \"\ *n* -s [ME, fr. *bright*, adj.] **1** *obs* **:** BRIGHTNESS, SPLENDOR **2 :** tobacco of a light shade; *specif* **:** flue-cured tobacco **3 :** an artist's brush with short flat square-edged bristles — compare FLAT, ROUND **4 brights** *pl* **:** HIGH BEAM
bright and early *adv* **:** early and with time to spare ⟨starting out *bright and early* on a picnic⟩
bright aqua *n* **:** a variable color averaging light bluish green to greenish blue
bright aqua blue *n* **:** a light greenish blue that is greener and deeper than average aqua blue, bluer and deeper than average aqua, and bluer, lighter, and stronger than average turquoise blue
bright aqua green *n* **:** a variable color averaging a light bluish green that is bluer, lighter, and stronger than robin's-egg blue (sense 2) and stronger and slightly lighter than turquoise (sense 2b)
bright cerulean blue *n* **:** a strong greenish blue that is greener, lighter, and stronger than average cerulean blue (sense 1a), bluer and deeper than grotto, and paler than cobalt blue
bright chartreuse *n* **:** a variable color averaging a brilliant yellow that is yellower, stronger, and slightly darker than average chartreuse (sense 1)
bright chartreuse yellow *n* **:** a variable color averaging a strong greenish yellow that is lighter and stronger than chartreuse yellow — compare BRIGHT CHARTREUSE
bright cherry red *n* **:** a strong to vivid red that is yellower and darker than poinsettia
bright coal *n* **:** a bituminous coal distinguished by its fine banding, higher moisture, nitrogen and sulfur content, and its smaller percentage of ash — compare SPLINT COAL
bright copen blue *n* **:** a variable color averaging a strong blue that is redder and paler than cerulean blue (sense 1b) and redder and lighter than Sèvres
bright coral red *n* **:** a variable color averaging a vivid reddish orange that is redder and lighter than international orange and redder and darker than chrome orange
bright coral rose *n* **:** a moderate reddish orange that is lighter, stronger, and slightly redder than flamingo and redder and slightly paler than crab apple
bright-cut \ˈ⸗;⸗\ *adj* [²*bright*] *of engraving* **:** executed with short sharp strokes of the graver
bright dip *n* **:** an acid bath for cleaning metal before enameling
bright dutch blue *n, often cap D* **:** a variable color averaging strong blue to purplish blue
bright emerald green *n* **:** a variable color averaging a brilliant bluish green that is greener, lighter, and stronger than average bright turquoise green
bright·en \ˈbrīt³n\ *vb* **brightened; brightened; brightening** \-t(³)niŋ\ **brightens** [ME *brightnen*, fr. *bright*, adj.] *vt* **:** to make bright or brighter: as **a :** to cause to shine ⟨~ a tarnished silver mug by polishing⟩ **b :** to make illustrious or more illustrious ⟨~ an already famous name⟩ **c :** to give a brighter hue or luster to ⟨the process of cleaning the oil painting ~*ed* the colors considerably⟩ **d :** to make more cheerful **:** ENLIVEN ⟨his presence ~*ed* up the party⟩ **~** *vi* **:** to become bright or brighter: as **a :** to increase in luminousness ⟨as soon as the moon came out the grove ~*ed* so that one could stroll around without a flashlight⟩ **b :** to become more lively or cheerful ⟨the party began to ~ after the drinks were passed around⟩ **c :** to become more auspicious ⟨business prospects ~*ed* with every year of peace⟩
bright·en·er \-t(³)nə(r)\ *n* -s **1 :** FLUORESCENT BRIGHTENER **2 :** a chemical or mixture of chemicals added to an electroplating bath to increase the brightness of the plate (as nickel plate)
brighter *comparative of* BRIGHT
brightest *superlative of* BRIGHT
bright-eyed \ˈ⸗;⸗\ *adj* **:** having or giving the impression of open and youthful innocence ⟨a *bright-eyed* young lady eating an ice-cream cone⟩
brighteyes \ˈ⸗;⸗\ *n pl but sing in constr* **:** BLUET
bright-field \ˈ⸗;⸗\ *adj* **:** producing or using a strongly lighted background ⟨*bright-field* microscopy⟩ — compare DARK-FIELD
bright fuchsia purple *n* **:** a strong reddish purple that is redder, stronger, and slightly lighter than average fuchsia purple and redder and paler than purple orchid
bright gold *n* **:** a variable color averaging a strong yellow that is deeper than yolk yellow, goldenrod (sense 2b), or light chrome yellow and greener and deeper than gamboge
bright jade green *n* **:** a variable color averaging a strong green that is bluer, lighter, and stronger than mintleaf (sense 1) and bluer, lighter, and less strong than primitive green
bright kelly green *n, often cap K* **:** a variable color averaging a strong yellowish green that is greener and deeper than Cyprus green and greener, lighter, and stronger than emerald (sense 2b)
bright lavender *n* **:** a variable color averaging a moderate purple that is bluer and stronger than average lilac (sense 3a), bluer and paler than heliotrope (sense 4a), and bluer, lighter, and stronger than average amethyst
bright leaf *n* **:** a type of flue-cured burley or Maryland tobacco
bright lemon yellow *n* **:** a variable color averaging a vivid greenish yellow
bright-light district *n* **:** an urban district devoted chiefly to establishments providing entertainment (as cabarets or theaters) usu. advertised by brightly lighted entrances esp. with marquees
bright lime green *n* **:** a vivid yellow green
bright-line spectrum *n* **:** an emission spectrum consisting of bright lines against a dark background
bright·ly *adv* [ME *brightly, brightliche*, fr. OE *beorhtlīce, byrhtlīce, bryhtlīce*, fr. *beorht, byrht, bryht* bright + *-līce* -ly] **1 :** in a bright manner ⟨~ written handbooks —Milton Wilson⟩ ⟨a ~ shining sun⟩ **2 :** to the point of brightness ⟨a ~ polished metal⟩
bright maize *n* **:** a strong orange yellow that is slightly lighter and stronger than Spanish yellow
bright marigold *n* **:** a vivid orange yellow that is yellower and duller than average national school-bus chrome
bright melon yellow *n* **:** a moderate orange yellow that is redder, lighter, and stronger than yellow ocher or deep chrome yellow
bright mint green *n* **:** a brilliant green that is bluer, lighter, and stronger than emerald (sense 2a) and yellower and paler than scarab green
bright navy *n* **:** a variable color averaging a dark blue that is redder and paler than Peking blue or Flemish blue and redder, stronger, and slightly lighter than Japan blue
bright·ness *n* -ES [ME *brightnesse*, fr. OE *beorhtnes, byrhtnes, bryhtnes*, fr. *beorht, byrht, bryht* bright + *-nes* -ness] **1 a :** the quality or state of being bright: as (1) **:** BRILLIANCE, LUSTER (2) **:** SPLENDOR, FAME (3) **:** sharpness of wit **:** ACUTENESS **b :** an instance of such a quality or state **2 a :** the attribute of light-source colors by which the light source appears to emit light varying from a minimum for very dim to a maximum for very bright **b :** LUMINANCE
bright nile green *n, often cap N* **:** a brilliant yellowish green that is greener and paler than average Paris green
bright olive green *n* **:** a variable color averaging a moderate

yellow green that is yellower and deeper than average moss green, average pea green, or apple green (sense 1)

brigh·ton \'brīt°n\ *adj, usu cap* [fr. *Brighton*, England] **:** of or from the county borough of Brighton, England **:** of the kind or style prevalent in Brighton

bright orange *n* **:** a variable color averaging a strong and vivid orange

bright peach *n* **:** a strong yellowish pink that is yellower and deeper than average salmon pink, melon, or peach red

bright peacock blue *n* **:** a brilliant greenish blue

bright periwinkle blue *n* **:** a variable color averaging a light violet that is bluer, stronger, and slightly lighter than wistaria

bright rose *n* **:** a variable color averaging a strong purplish red that is bluer and deeper than madder rose

1**brights** *pl of* BRIGHT

2**brights** \'brīts\ *n pl* **:** BRIGHT COAL

bright's disease \'brīts-\ *n, usu cap B* [after Richard *Bright* †1858 Eng. physician who described kidney diseases in 1827] **:** any of several forms of disease of the kidney attended with albuminuria and edema and destructive changes in the kidney **:** GLOMERULONEPHRITIS

bright shell pink *n* **:** a moderate yellowish pink that is redder, lighter, and stronger than dusty pink, redder than peach pink, and redder and lighter than coral pink

brightsmith \'=,=\ *n* [¹*bright* + *smith*] **:** WHITESMITH

bright stock *n* **:** any of various clear oils (as a heavy lubricating oil) obtained usu. from residues of petroleum distillation by refining (as by removal of wax)

bright teal *n* **:** a moderate bluish green that is bluer and deeper than porcelain green and deeper and very slightly bluer than sea blue

bright teal blue *n* **:** a variable color averaging a moderate greenish blue that is greener than average peacock and greener and deeper than Brittany

bright teal green *n* **:** a moderate bluish green that is bluer and deeper than porcelain green and greener and deeper than sea blue

bright turquoise *n* **:** a variable color averaging a strong bluish green that is bluer and paler than Guinea green and bluer and stronger than average emerald (sense 2c)

bright turquoise blue *n* **:** a variable color averaging a strong greenish blue that is greener and very slightly paler than grotto, greener and paler than cobalt blue, and greener, lighter, and stronger than average cerulean blue (sense 1a)

bright turquoise green *n* **:** a variable color averaging a brilliant bluish green that is bluer and duller than average bright emerald green

brightwork \'=,=\ *n* [¹*bright* + *work*] **1 :** polished or plated metalwork (as on a ship, automobile, or appliance) **2 :** woodwork (as rails and coamings on a ship) that is sanded and varnished but not painted

brig·it·tine *or* **brid·get·tine** \'brijə,tēn\ *n -s usu cap* [after St. *Brigit* or *Bridget* †1373 Swedish nun and mystic, its founder] **:** a member of a religious order founded in Sweden about 1344

brigs *pl of* BRIG

1**brigue** \'brēg\ *vb* -ED/-ING/-S [MF *briguer*, fr. *brigue*, n.] *archaic* **:** PLOT, SCHEME, INTRIGUE

2**brigue** \"\ *n* -s [F, fr. MF, fr. OIt *briga* strife — more at BRIGAND] *archaic* **:** CABAL, INTRIGUE

brill \'bril\ *n, pl* **brill** *or* **brills** [perh. fr. Corn *brȳel*, *brȳthel* mackerel — more at BRIT] **1 :** a European flatfish (*Bothus rhombus*, syn. *Rhombus laevis*) that is related to the turbot and is valued as food **2 :** any of various flatfishes esp. of the family Bothidae **:** TURBOT — see PETRALE SOLE

bril·lan·te \brə'läntē\ *adj* [It, verbal of *brillare* to shine, sparkle — more at BRILLIANT] **:** showy and sparkling in style — used as a direction in music

bril·liance \'brilyən(t)s\ *n* -s **1 :** the state or quality of being brilliant **2 :** performance (as of a musical passage) displaying extraordinary precision and dexterity esp. in achieving speed and clarity; *also* **:** a passage of music calling for such precision and dexterity

bril·lian·cy \-nsē, -si\ *n* -ES **1 :** BRILLIANCE ⟨the ~ of the speech⟩ **2 :** an instance of brilliance ⟨the . . . civilized *brilliancies* of Mendelssohn's Capriccio in B minor —Thomas Heinitz⟩

bril·lian·deer \,brilyən'di(ə)r\ *n* -s [D *briljanteren* to cut facets on diamonds — more at BRILLIANTEER] **:** one who cuts small facets on diamonds

1**bril·liant** \'brilyənt\ *adj* [F *brillant*, pres. part. of *briller* to shine, sparkle, fr. It *brillare*, fr. *brillo* beryl, fr. L *beryllus* beryl — more at BERYL] **1 a :** sparkling with luster **:** very bright **:** GLITTERING ⟨a ~ star⟩ ⟨a ~ light⟩ ⟨his eyes were ~ with pain —Elinor Wylie⟩ ⟨a hot, cloudless, ~ morning —Kenneth Roberts⟩ **b :** markedly rich or conspicuous in quality: as (1) *of color* **:** strong and light ⟨a ~ red⟩ (2) *of a musical tone* **:** bright, clear, and ringing **:** rich in high harmonics **2 a :** STRIKING, ILLUSTRIOUS, DISTINGUISHED ⟨a ~ career⟩ ⟨a series of ~ exploits⟩ ⟨a ~ victory⟩ **b :** distinguished by unusual mental keenness, alertness, originality, or resourcefulness ⟨clever, witty, ~ and sparkling beyond most of her kind —Rudyard Kipling⟩ ⟨a ~ scholar who has made himself a gifted educator —Ordway Tead⟩ ⟨the prosecutor's ~ argument and summation⟩ **3** [by shortening] **:** BRILLIANT-CUT **syn** see BRIGHT, INTELLIGENT

2**brilliant** \"\ *n* -s [F *brillant*, fr. *brillant*, adj.] **1 :** a diamond

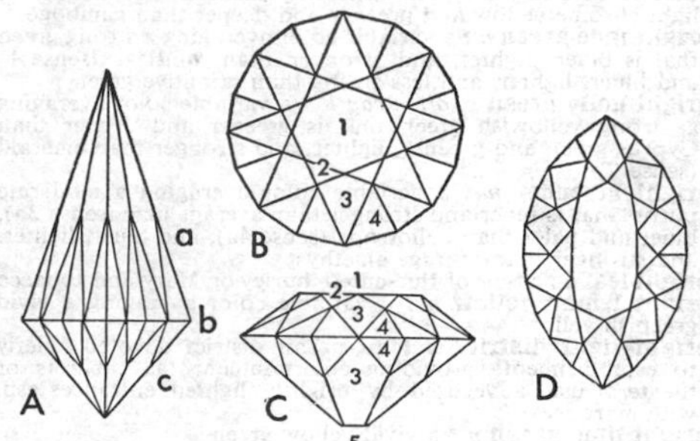

brilliant: *A* briolette; *B*, *C* top and side view of American cut; *D* marquise; *a* bezel, *b* girdle, *c* pavilion; *1* table, *2* star facet, *3* main facet, *4* corner facet, *5* culet

or other gem cut in a particular form with numerous facets so as to have especial brilliancy, ordinarily today cut in two pyramids placed base to base, the upper, usu. with 56 facets, truncated comparatively near its base by the table, the lower, usu. with 24 facets, having only the apex cut off to form the culet around which eight extra facets are sometimes added — compare BEZEL, CROWN, DOUBLE BRILLIANT, GIRDLE, PAVILION, SINGLE BRILLIANT, TABLE, TWENTIETH-CENTURY CUT **2 :** an old size of type (approximately 3½ point) smaller than diamond — compare POINT SYSTEM

brilliant crocein *or* **brilliant croceine** *n, often cap B&C* **:** a bright scarlet acid disazo dye obtained by coupling diazotized *p*-aminoazobenzene with G acid — called also *Croceine Scarlet MOO*; see DYE table I (under *Acid Red 73*)

brilliant-cut \'=,=\ *adj* [²*brilliant*] *of a gem* **:** cut in the form of a brilliant

brilliant cutting *n* [²*brilliant*] **:** a form of decoration made on glass by means of a wheel with which various types of cuts may be made that are subsequently smoothed and polished

brilliant dye *n* **:** any of numerous acid, basic, direct, mordant, or vat dyes or organic pigments — see DYE table I

bril·lian·teer \,brilyən·ti(ə)r\ *vt* -ED/-ING/-S [D *briljanteren*, fr. F *brillanter*, fr. *brillant* brilliant (gem) — more at BRILLIANT] **:** to cut and polish the small usu. triangular facets about the girdle of a brilliant — **bril·lian·teer·er** \-irə(r)\ *n* -s

brilliant green *n, often cap B&G* **:** a basic triphenylmethane dye that is prepared similarly to malachite green from benzaldehyde and diethyl-aniline and that gives yellower shades than malachite green — see DYE table I (under *Basic Green 1*)

bril·lian·tine \'brilyən,tēn, ,==='=\ *n* -s [F *brillantine*, fr. *brillant* brilliant + *-ine* — more at BRILLIANT] **1 :** a usu. colored and perfumed dressing for making hair glossy **2 :** a lightweight lustrous clothing fabric that is similar to alpaca and is woven in plain or fancy weaves usu. with a cotton warp and a mohair or worsted filling

bril·lian·tined \-ēnd\ *adj, of hair* **:** dressed with brilliantine

bril·liant·ly *adv* **:** in a brilliant manner

bril·liant·ness *n* -ES **:** the quality or state of being brilliant

brilliant yellow *n, often cap B&Y* **:** a direct disazo dye derived from stilbene that dyes paper yellow and turns red in alkaline solution — see DYE table I (under *Direct Yellow 4*)

brilliolette *or* **brillolette** *var of* BRIOLETTE

bril·louin zone \,brēyə'wan-\ *n, usu cap B* [after Louis M. *Brillouin* †1948 Fr. physicist] *in solid state theory* **:** one of the limited ranges within which the energy and momentum of an electron in a metallic crystal may vary continuously without any quantum jumps

brills *pl of* BRILL

brill's disease \'brilz-\ *n, usu cap B* [after Nathan E. *Brill* †1925 Am. physician] **:** an acute febrile disease now usu. considered to be a mild recurrence of typhus in an individual who had that disease years before

1**brim** \'brim\ *n* -s [ME *brimme;* akin to MHG *brem* edge, trimming, ON *barmr* brim, and perh. to L *frond-*, *frons* leafy branch, foliage] **1 a** *archaic* **:** the edge or margin of a body of water **b :** the edge or rim esp. of a cup, bowl, or depression resembling a bowl ⟨the ~ of the saucer⟩ ⟨the ~ of the crater⟩ **c :** BRINK, BORDER ⟨on the ~ of unconsciousness⟩ **2 :** the projecting rim of a hat or bonnet **syn** see BORDER

A

A, brim 2

2**brim** \"\ *vb* **brimmed; brimmed; brimming; brims** *vt* **:** to fill to the brim ⟨~ a bowl to good fellowship⟩ ~ *vi* **1 :** to be or become full often to overflowing ⟨a cup *brimming* over onto the table⟩ ⟨children . . . *brimming* over with life and health —F.J.Haskin⟩ ⟨boats . . . ~ with peasants in their folk costumes —Frederic Morton⟩ **2 :** to increase to the point of reaching or overflowing a brim ⟨tears *brimmed* in his eyes⟩ ⟨the sea . . . *brimmed* up to the very lip of the shingle beach —David Garnett⟩

3**brim** \"\ *adj* [ME — more at BREME] *archaic* **:** BREME — **brim·ly** *adv, archaic*

4**brim** \"\ *vi* **brimmed; brimmed; brimming; brims** [ME *brimmen;* akin to MHG *brimmen* to roar, OE *bremman* — more at FREMITUS] *now dial Eng, of swine* **:** to be in heat; *also* **:** COPULATE

5**brim** \"\ *n* -s [perh. fr. ⁴*brim*] *dial Eng* **:** STRUMPET

6**brim** \"\ *dial var of* ¹BREAM

brim·ful *also* **brim·full** \'brim'fu̇l\ *adj* [¹*brim* + *-ful*, *-full*] **:** full to the brim **:** ready to overflow ⟨a child, ~ of curiosity about life and people —Caroline Sherman⟩ ⟨letters ~ of reproach —J.D.Adams⟩ ⟨a mind ~ of information —Elmer Davis⟩ ⟨tasks that filled each day ~ —Bruno Frank⟩ — **brim·ful·ly** \-,fəlē, -,fu̇lē\ *adv* — **brim·ful·ness** \-'fu̇lnəs\ *n* -ES

bri·ming \'brēmən, -rim-, -miŋ\ *n* -s [origin unknown] *dial Eng* **:** phosphorescence of the sea

brim·less \'brimləs\ *adj* **:** being without a brim

brimmed \'brimd\ *adj* [¹*brim* + *-ed*] **:** having a brim ⟨a woman's small ~ hat⟩ — often used in combination ⟨a broad-*brimmed* sombrero⟩

1**brim·mer** \-mə(r)\ *n* -s [²*brim* + *-er*] **:** a cup or glass brimful ⟨feed the flame of their loyalty with copious ~*s* —Sir Walter Scott⟩

2**brimmer** \"\ *n* -s [¹*brim* + *-er*] **1 :** a brimmed hat esp. of straw **2 :** a worker who makes brims for hats or provides hats with brims

brim·ming·ly *adv* [fr. pres. part. of ²*brim* + *-ly*] **:** with a fullness that threatens to overflow ⟨feel ~ happy⟩ ⟨filled the cup ~⟩

brim·my \'brimē\ *adj* -ER/-EST [¹*brim* + *-y*] **:** having a broad brim

brim of the pelvis : the upper boundary of the true pelvis formed by the iliopectineal line, the crests of the pubic bones, and the front margin of the base of the sacrum

1**brim·stone** \'brimz,tōn, -m,st-, *Brit usu & US sometimes* -,tən\ *n* [ME *brinston*, *brimston*, prob. fr. *brinnen*, *birnen* to burn + *ston* stone — more at BURN, STONE] **1 :** SULFUR; *sometimes* **:** native sulfur — used chiefly commercially **2** *or* **brimstone yellow :** SULPHUR YELLOW 2 **3** *archaic* **:** SHREW, VIRAGO **4 :** FIRE AND BRIMSTONE

2**brimstone** \"\ *adj* **:** FIRE-AND-BRIMSTONE ⟨preaching a ~ sermon⟩ ⟨an old-fashioned ~ preacher⟩

3**brimstone** \"\ *also* **brimstone butterfly** *n* **:** a sulphur butterfly; *esp* **:** a rather large yellow and orange European sulphur (*Gonepteryx rhamni*)

brimstone acid *n* **:** sulfuric acid made from brimstone

brim·stony \-nē\ *adj* [ME, fr. *brimston* + *-y*] **:** SULFUROUS 1, 2

brind·ed \'brindəd\ *adj* [ME *brende*, *brended;* prob. akin to OE *brand* brand, fire — more at BRAND] *archaic* **:** BRINDLED

brin·di·si \'brində(,)zē, -rēn-\ *n* -s [It, drinking toast, fr. G (*ich*) *bring dirs*, a toasting formula, lit., I bring it (a glass) to you] **:** a drinking or toasting song

brin·dle \'brind°l\ *n* -s [fr. *brindle*, *brindled*, adj.] **1 :** a brindled color ⟨not white at all . . . but a sort of ~; streaked yellow and gray —Edna Ferber⟩ **2 :** a brindled animal **3 a :** mosaic disease of tobacco **b :** a plant affected with this disease

brin·dled \-d°ld\ *or* **brin·dle** \-d°l\ *adj* [alter. of *brinded*] **:** having dark streaks or spots on a gray or tawny ground esp. with the markings blurred and without sharp margins ⟨eyes that were neither brown nor gray, but a dark ~ mixture of the two —Hamilton Basso⟩ ⟨a ~ dane with black stripes on a brown body⟩

brindled gnu *n* **:** a slaty-blue gnu (*Connochaetes taurinus*) with faint dark transverse bands on neck and withers and dusky blackish mane and tail that is now found in numbers only north of the southern African plains — called also *blue wildebeest*

brindle iron *n* [origin unknown] **:** STIRRUP 2a, 2b

brin·dling \-d(°)liŋ\ *n* -s [*brindle* + *-ing*] **:** the mingling of hairs of more than one color in a single marking **:** a brindled condition or marking

1**brine** \'brīn\ *n* -s [ME, fr. OE *brȳne;* akin to MD *brīne* brine, L *fricare* to rub — more at FRICTION] **1 a :** water saturated or strongly impregnated with common salt **b :** a strong saline solution (as of calcium chloride used in refrigeration) **c :** the water of an ocean, sea, or salt lake **d :** SEA, OCEAN **2** *obs* **:** TEARS

2**brine** \"\ *vt* -ED/-ING/-S **:** to treat (as by steeping or saturating) with brine ⟨*brined* pork⟩ ⟨*brined* hides⟩ — **brin·er** \-nə(r)\ *n* -s

brine fly *n* **:** any of various acalyptrate flies (family Ephydridae) whose larvae live in brine

brine·less \-ləs\ *adj* **:** being without brine

bri·nell hardness \brə'nel-, 'bri,n-\ *n, usu cap B* [after Johann A. *Brinell* †1925 Swedish engineer] **:** the hardness of a metal or alloy measured by a manually operated vertical hydraulic press in which a hard steel or carbide ball of standard size (as 10 millimeters in diameter) is pressed with a standard load (as 3000 kilograms) into the specimen of metal or alloy under test, the resistance to penetration being expressed by a number denoting the applied load in kilograms divided by the spherical area of indentation in square millimeters

brinell number *n, usu cap B* [after J.A.*Brinell*] **:** a number expressing Brinell hardness

brinell test *n, usu cap B* [after J.A.*Brinell*] **:** the test to determine Brinell hardness

brine·man \'brīnmən\ *n, pl* **brinemen 1 :** one that makes brine for preserving foods **2 :** a worker who prepares briny solution for use in electrolytic cells — called also *saltman*

brine pan *n* **:** a pan in which brine is evaporated to form salt

brine pump *n* **:** a ship's pump for circulating the brine in a refrigerating system or for removing the brine from an evaporator shell

brine shrimp *n* **:** any branchiopod crustacean of the genus *Artemia*

bring \'briŋ\ *vb* **brought** \'brȯt, *usu* -ȯd·+V\ *or substand* **brung** \'brəŋ\ *also* **brang** \'braŋ, -aiŋ\ *or* **brought·en** \'brȯt°n\ **brought** *or substand* **brung** *also* **brang** *or* **brought·en; bringing; brings** [ME *bringen* (past *broughte*, past part. *brought*, *ybrought*), fr. OE *bringan* (past *brōhte*, past part. *brōht*, *gebrōht*); akin to OHG *bringan* to bring (past *brāhta*, past part. *brāht*), Goth *bringan* (past *brāhta*), W *hebrwng* to accompany, Toch A *präṅk-* to remove] *vt* **1 a :** to convey, lead, carry, or cause to come along from one place to another, the direction of movement being toward the place from which the action is being regarded ⟨*brought* home a pretty young wife⟩ ⟨*brought* two ponderous lawbooks to the trial⟩ **b :** to cause to be, act, or move in a special way: as (1) **:** ATTRACT ⟨the trial *brought* a crowd to the courtroom⟩ ⟨the turmoil in the street *brought* householders to their windows⟩ (2) **:** PERSUADE, INDUCE ⟨an argument that *brought* many men to his way of thinking⟩ ⟨he may be *brought* to forgive⟩ ⟨we hope to ~ a speaker before you at the next meeting⟩ (3) **:** FORCE, COMPEL ⟨was *brought* sharply to consider his relations to the political state —V.L.Parrington⟩; *esp* **:** to force to go, be, or appear ⟨the new administration *brought* all agencies under a unified control⟩ ⟨the criminal was *brought* before the judge⟩ (4) **:** to handle, act upon, or treat so that the object is in a particular state or condition or acts in a particular way ⟨the helmsman *brought* the boat around and headed for shore⟩ ⟨~ a pot to boil⟩ ⟨the hunter *brought* to bay a lion⟩ ⟨the medicine *brought* the patient around⟩ ⟨the threat *brought* the man to his knees⟩ ⟨the statistics *brought* home the plight of the flood victims⟩ (5) **:** to submit (oneself) ⟨he could not *bring* himself to public confession⟩ **:** overcome the objections in (oneself) ⟨was unable to *bring* himself to do the deed⟩ **c** *now dial* **:** ESCORT, ACCOMPANY ⟨may I ~ you home?⟩ **d** *obs* **:** to carry word or news to **e :** to take or carry along with one ⟨asked for things he needed to ~ to school⟩ ⟨the airplane ~*ing* me from Paris to London⟩ **f :** to carry or bear as an attribute or characteristic ⟨he *brought* to his new life the habits of his old⟩ ⟨the teacher *brought* to his task a fine understanding of children⟩ ⟨~*ing* to the presidency a rich and varied experience⟩ **g :** DELIVER ⟨~ information⟩ ⟨in the absence of the regular minister a visiting preacher *brought* the message⟩ **2 a :** to cause to exist or occur in any of a number of ways: as **a :** to cause to appear esp. as a concomitant **:** PRODUCE ⟨winter will ~ snow and ice⟩ ⟨the war *brought* great changes to these grassy shires —L.D. Stamp⟩ ⟨the photograph *brought* the scene clearly before his eyes⟩ ⟨he always *brought* trouble wherever he went⟩ **b :** to cause to follow as a result **:** result in ⟨doing good generally ~*s* honor⟩ ⟨the drug *brought* immediate relief from pain⟩ ⟨his sudden death *brought* great grief to the community⟩ ⟨his actions are sure to ~ trouble⟩ ⟨the sergeant's bravery under fire *brought* him a medal⟩ **c :** INSTITUTE ⟨~ legal action⟩ ⟨~ a complaint⟩ **d :** ADVANCE, ADDUCE ⟨~ an argument⟩ **3 :** PREFER ⟨~ a charge⟩ **4 :** to lead or cause (something) to be **:** arrive at **:** have experience of (something) — usu. used with *to*, *into*, *up to*, or *out of* ⟨the action *brought* the men into great difficulties⟩ ⟨the pilot *brought* them safely out of danger⟩ ⟨a few steps *brought* us to the front door⟩ ⟨the medicine seemed to ~ the man back to life⟩ ⟨the popularity of the book *brought* it to a fourth printing⟩ ⟨the donation *brought* the fund to over a million dollars⟩ ⟨this history book ~*s* us up to the present day⟩ ⟨his logic ~*s* me to a completely different conclusion than yours⟩ **5 a :** to cause to be apprehended or experienced esp. by the mind or the emotions ⟨~ certain facts to a man's attention⟩ **b :** RECALL ⟨an incident that ~*s* to mind an old friend⟩ ⟨a single verse may ~ a whole poem back⟩ **6** *obs* **:** DERIVE, DEDUCE, TRACE **7 :** to procure in exchange **:** sell for ⟨how much does coal ~ per ton on the open market⟩ ~ *vi, chiefly Midland* **:** YIELD, PRODUCE — **bring abed** *or* **bring to bed :** to be delivered of (a child) ⟨is *brought to bed* of yet another baby —Virginia Woolf⟩ — **bring by the lee :** to turn (a ship) so rapidly to leeward when sailing large as to bring the lee side suddenly to windward and by laying the sails back incur the danger of capsizing — compare ³BROACH — **bring down the house :** to evoke a furor of laughter or applause — **bring home** *of a jockey* **:** to ride (a horse) to victory — **bring home the bacon 1 :** to earn the living for the family **2 :** to win the prize sought **:** secure the desired results — **bring to account 1 :** to bring to book **2 :** to reprimand esp. for negligence or misconduct — **bring to book :** to compel to give an account or make an accounting ⟨after years of dishonest activity the man was finally *brought to book* and jailed⟩ — **bring to light :** to make clear **:** DISCLOSE, REVEAL — **bring to terms :** to compel to agree, assent, or submit **:** force to come to terms — **bring up the rear :** to come last or behind

bring about *vt* **:** to cause to take place **:** EFFECT, ACCOMPLISH ⟨so revolutionary was the change *brought about* by the abolition of slave labor —*Amer. Guide Series: La.*⟩ ⟨*brought about* a settlement of the fight⟩

brin·gal \'briŋ,gȯl, -gäl, ='=; 'briŋ(g)əl\ *var of* BRINJAL

bring down *vt* **1 :** to cause to fall esp. by shooting ⟨*brought down* a deer⟩ **2 :** to carry forward (as a balance in bookkeeping)

bring forth *vt* **1 :** to bear (as fruit or offspring) **:** give birth to **:** PRODUCE ⟨*bring forth* children in pain⟩ ⟨a million and a half . . . acres were *bringing forth* wheat —*Amer. Guide Series: Minn.*⟩ ⟨the Empire style was *brought forth* to glorify . . . Napoleon —*Amer. Fabrics*⟩ ~ *vi* **:** to give birth ⟨the . . . women are not allowed to *bring forth* in the village —J.G.Frazer⟩

bring forward *vt* **1 :** to produce to view **:** INTRODUCE, ADDUCE ⟨*bring forward* some good arguments in one's defense⟩ **2 :** to carry forward

bring in *vt* **1 :** to produce by way of profit or return ⟨each sale *brought in* about five dollars⟩ **2** *obs* **:** to gain an introduction (as to a club) or a place of favor for **3 :** to enable (a man on base) to reach home plate (as by a hit) ⟨his two-bagger *brought in* three men and tied the score⟩ **4 :** to introduce (as a bill in a legislature or a point into a discussion) ⟨members appointed to prepare and *bring in* the bill —T.E.May⟩ **5 :** to report to or lay before a court or other legal body ⟨the jury *brought in* a verdict⟩ ⟨*bring in* a writ of habeas corpus⟩ **6 a :** to cause to produce or be productive (as an oil well) **b :** to win tricks with the long cards of (a suit) in whist or bridge **7 a :** EARN ⟨he *brings in* a good salary each week⟩ **b :** to finish with (as a score) ⟨the golfer *brought in* a 268 for 72 holes of play⟩

bringing *pres part of* BRING

bringing-up \'=='=\ *n* **:** training in childhood **:** REARING ⟨people so unlike her in temperament and *bringing-up* —William Black⟩

bring off *vt* **1 :** to cause to escape **:** RESCUE, SAVE **2 :** to achieve or carry to a successful issue esp. somewhat against expectations ⟨the author has *brought off* a tricky tour de force⟩ ⟨*bring off* a significant success in his field⟩ **3 :** HATCH ⟨*brought off* a brood of young⟩

bring on *vt* **:** to cause to come into action or existence ⟨too much activity by the patient *brings on* a fever⟩ ⟨the small border incidents ultimately *brought on* a full-scale war⟩

bring out *vt* **1 a :** to make apparent or more apparent **:** make markedly noticeable ⟨the incident *brought out* the true graciousness of the lady⟩ ⟨the lecturer *brought out* the significant aspects of the problem⟩ **b :** to develop (as a talent) to the point of effectiveness ⟨the teacher *brought out* whatever writing ability the students had⟩ **2 a :** to present (as a book, play, or invention) to the public (as for patronage or purchase) **:** PUBLISH, PRODUCE, MARKET ⟨*brought out* a practical four-wheeled auto —*Amer. Guide Series: Mich.*⟩ ⟨the author has *brought out* three novels to date⟩ **b :** to introduce socially ⟨just the sort of people who have their uses when one is *bringing out* a girl —Victoria Sackville-West⟩ **3 :** UTTER ⟨I know what I will say, or rather *bring out* nonchalantly, in the course of conversation —O.S.J.Gogarty⟩ ⟨so bored . . . that he can hardly *bring out* a good morning —*Punch*⟩

brings *pres 3d sing of* BRING

bring·sal \'briŋzəl, -iŋsəl\ *or* **brin·sell** \-inzəl, -in(t)səl\ *also* **bring·sal** \-iŋzəl, -iŋsəl\ *n* -s [G *bringsel*, fr. *bringen* to bring, fr. OHG *bringan* — more at BRING] **:** a short stick or other device that is suspended from the collar of a trained dog and that the dog takes in his mouth as a signal to the handler that he has located an objective (as a wounded man)

bring to *vt* **1 :** to check the course of (a boat) **:** cause (a boat) to lie to or come to a standstill ⟨*brought* the ship *to* by dropping the anchor⟩ ⟨*brought* the enemy craft *to* by firing across her bows⟩ **2 a :** BEND ⟨*bring to* a sail⟩ **b :** to take (a cable) around a capstan **3 :** to restore to consciousness ⟨fainted dead away, but was *brought to* by sympathetic bystanders⟩

bring up *vt* **1 :** REAR, EDUCATE ⟨*bring up* one's children in good surroundings⟩ **2 :** to cause to stop suddenly ⟨*brought up* the car with a screeching of brakes⟩ ⟨a new thought *brought* her *up* sharply —Margaret Mitchell⟩ ⟨the remark *brought* me *up* short⟩ **3 :** to bring to attention **:** INTRODUCE ⟨*brought up* the weather⟩ ⟨his remark *brought up* the subject of the last election⟩ **4 :** VOMIT ⟨promptly *brought up* all the water he had drunk, but he felt better, all the same —C.S.Forester⟩ **5 :** to make ready (a letterpress form) ~ *vi* **:** to stop suddenly **:** come to a standstill ⟨the runaway bus careened down the hill and *brought up* against a building⟩

brin·i·ness \ˈbrīnēnəs, -nin-\ *n* -ES **:** the quality or state of being briny

brin·jal *or* **brin·jaul** \ˈbrin,jȯl, -jäl, ≠ˈ≠; ˈbrinjəl\ *n* -S [Pg *bringella, beringela*, fr. Ar *bādhinjān*, fr. Per *bādingān*, prob. fr. Skt *vātiṅgaṇa*] *India & Africa* **:** EGGPLANT

brin·jar·ry \brinˈjärē\ *n* -ES [modif. of Hindi *bājārā*, fr. Skt *vaṇijyā* trade (fr. *vaṇij* merchant) + *-kāraka* one who does; akin to Skt *karoti* he does — more at KARMA] **:** a traveling dealer in grain and salt in India

brink \ˈbriŋk\ *n* -S [ME *brinke*, prob. of Scand origin; akin to ON *brekka* slope, Dan *brink* edge of a precipice; akin to MLG & MD *brink* edge of a field, L *front-, frons* forehead, MIr *braine* front, leader, prow] **1 a :** EDGE, MARGIN, BORDER; *esp* **:** the very edge at the top of a steep place ⟨the ~ of a precipice⟩ **b :** a bank or edge esp. of a river **:** BORDER, BORDER LINE ⟨the ~ of the pond⟩ **:** VERGE **c :** the point of onset ⟨at the ~ of tears⟩ ⟨the ~ of war⟩ ⟨on the ~ of starvation⟩ **2** *now dial Eng* **:** the brim of a hat **syn** see BORDER

brink·man·ship \-mən,ship\ *n* [*brink* + *-manship* (as in *horsemanship*)] **:** the practice of pushing a dangerous situation to the limit of safety before stopping

brin·ser \ˈbrinzə(r), -n(t)sə-\ *n* -S *usu cap* [after Matthias *Brinser* †1855 Am. theologist, founder of the sect] **:** a member of a religious body called United Zion's Children that in 1853 separated from the River Brethren

¹briny \ˈbrīnē, -ni\ *adj* -ER/-EST [*¹brine* + *-y*] **:** of, relating to, or like brine or the sea **:** SALTY ⟨a ~ taste⟩

²briny \"\ *n* -ES *slang* **:** SEA ⟨the pilot descended so fast he disappeared beneath the ~ —Henry La Cossitt⟩

brio \ˈbrē(,)ō\ *n* -S [It, of Celt origin; akin to OIr *brīg* strength, virtue, W *bri* repute, Corn *bry* worth, MBret *bri* regard] **:** VIVACITY, SPIRIT, FIRE ⟨the rector sang with such ~ —Christopher Morley⟩ ⟨driving with the ~ of a Paris taxi-driver —J.M.O'Brien⟩ — see CON BRIO

bri·oche \(ˈ)brē¦ōsh, -ˈō-\ *n* -S [F, fr. MF dial. (Normandy), fr. dial. *brier* to brake flax, to knead, of Gmc origin; akin to OHG *brehhan* to break — more at BREAK] **:** a fancy roll of very light yeast dough rich with eggs and butter baked in muffin tins or cups

bri·o·lette \¦brēə¦let\ *also* **bril·lio·lette** *or* **bril·lo·lette** \-ē(y)ə-\ *n* -S [F *briolette, brillolette*, prob. irreg. dim. of *brillant*, n., brilliant — more at BRILLIANT] **:** a diamond or other gem in the shape of an oval or pear and having its entire surface cut in triangular facets — see BRILLIANT illustration

briony *var of* BRYONY

¹bri·quette *also* **bri·quet** \(ˈ)bri¦ket, *usu* -ed·+V\ *n* -S [F *briquette*, dim. of *brique* brick — more at BRICK] **:** a compact mass often in the shape of a brick formed of usu. finely divided material (as coal dust or sawdust for fuel or metal powders for smelting) by mixing with a binder, by pressure, or both

²briquette \"\ *vt* -ED/-ING/-S **:** to form (as coal dust or metal powders) into briquettes

bris *var of* BERITH

bri·sance \brəˈzän(t)s, brēˈzäⁿs\ *n* -S [F, fr. *brisant*, pres. part. of *briser* to break, fr. OF *brisier*, of Celt origin; akin to OIr *brissim* I break — more at FRICTION] **:** the shattering or crushing effect of an explosive measurable by the crushing of sand or the compression of a metal cylinder and dependent upon the rate of detonation and other factors

bris·bane \ˈbrizbən (*usual Australian pronunc*), -,bān\ *adj*, *usu cap* [fr. *Brisbane*, Queensland, Australia] **:** of or from Brisbane, the capital of Queensland, Australia **:** of the kind or style prevalent in Brisbane

brisbane box *n*, *usu cap 1st B* **:** BRUSH BOX

brisbane lily *n*, *usu cap B* **:** a bulbous plant (*Eurycles sylvestris*) of the family Amaryllidaceae that is native to Australia, Malaysia, and the Philippines and has umbels of white flowers resembling lilies

brisbane quandong *n*, *usu cap B* **:** an Australian tree (*Elaeocarpus grandis*) with hard white timber and edible fruit — called also *blue fig*

bri·sco·la \ˈbrēskō(,)lä\ *n* -S [It] **:** an Italian card game for four players in two partnerships

bri·sé \(ˈ)brē¦zā\ *n* -S [F, fr. *brisé*, past part. of *briser* to break — more at BRISANCE] **:** a movement in ballet in which the feet or legs are clicked together in the air

brise-bise \ˈbrēz,bēz\ *n* [F, lit., windbreaker, fr. *briser* to break + *bise* north wind — more at BISE] **:** a half curtain for the lower part of a window ⟨*brise-bise* curtains in the kitchen⟩

brise-so·leil \¦brēzsō¦lā\ *n* -S [F, fr. *brise* (as in *brise-bise*) + *soleil* sun, fr. (assumed) VL *soliculus*, dim. of L *sol* sun — more at SOLAR] **:** an architectural device (as a projection, louvers, or a screen) to block off unwanted sunlight

bri·sé vo·lé \(,)brē,zāvōˈlā\ *n*, *pl* **brisés volés** \-zāvōˈlā(z)\ [F, lit., flown brisé] **:** a brisé performed with each leg alternately and finished on one foot

¹brisk \ˈbrisk\ *adj* -ER/-EST [prob. modif. of MF *brusque* — more at BRUSQUE] **1 a :** keenly alive and alert **:** LIVELY, VIVACIOUS, SPRIGHTLY ⟨a ~ old lady with no nonsense about her —Jean Stafford⟩ ⟨that ~, managing, lively, imperious woman —W.M.Thackeray⟩ **b** *obs* **:** SPRUCE, SMART **2 :** sharp or keen to the senses: as **a** *of a drink* (1) **:** agreeably lively **:** EFFERVESCENT **:** not flat ⟨a ~ cider⟩ (2) **:** having good flavor **:** pleasingly pungent **:** TANGY ⟨a ~ tea⟩ **b** *of weather conditions* **:** STIMULATING, INVIGORATING, FRESH ⟨~ air⟩ ⟨~ weather⟩ **3 :** sharp in tone or manner ⟨a somewhat ~*er* sort, with more bite and acid in what he says —R.H.Rovere⟩ **4 :** ANIMATED, QUICK, ENERGETIC **:** not slow or sluggish ⟨a ~ walk⟩ ⟨~ trading on a stock exchange⟩ **syn** see AGILE

²brisk \"\ *vb* -ED/-ING/-S *vt* **1** *obs* **:** to make spruce or smart in appearance — often used with *up* **2 a :** to make brisk **:** ENLIVEN, ANIMATE, SHARPEN — now used with *up* ⟨a *brisked*-up voice —Rose Thurburn⟩ ⟨~*ed* up with epigrams —*Time*⟩ **b :** to cause to move in a brisk manner ⟨~*ing* a soft cloth over the silver coffeepot —Russell Thacher⟩ ~ *vi* **:** to become brisk esp. in movement or activity — usu. used with *up* ⟨till the market ~*ed* up —H.L.Davis⟩

brisk·en \ˈbriskən\ *vb* -ED/-ING/-S [*¹brisk* + *-en*] **:** BRISK

bris·ket \ˈbriskət\ *n* -S [ME *brusket*; akin to ON *brjōsk* gristle, MHG *brüsche* bruise, OE *brēost* breast — more at BREAST] **1 a :** the breast of a quadruped animal; *specif* **:** the part of the lower chest of such an animal that includes portions of five ribs and the breastbone — see COW illustration **b :** a cut of meat (as of beef) consisting of the breast muscles and other tissue with bones removed — see BEEF illustration **2** *dial Brit* **:** BREAST, CHEST

brisket disease *n* **:** dropsy of the brisket of cattle in high altitudes caused by dilatation and consequent weakness of the heart

brisk·ly *adv* **:** in a brisk manner ⟨a popular edition that is now selling ~ —Joseph Wechsberg⟩ ⟨walk ~ along⟩ ⟨she got up ~ and tossed down her pen —William DuBois⟩

brisk·ness *n* -ES **:** the quality or state of being brisk

brisky \ˈbriskē\ *adj* -ER/-EST **:** BRISK, LIVELY, ANIMATED

bris·ling \ˈbrizliŋ, -isl-, -lēŋ\ *or* **bris·tling** \-isl-\ *n* -S [Norw *brisling*, modif. (influenced by *brisa* to flash, burn) of LG *bretling*, fr. *bret* broad + *-ling*; akin to ON *bregtha* to move rapidly and to OE *brǣd* broad — more at BRAID, BROAD] **:** a small herring (*Clupea sprattus*) that resembles a sardine and that is cured and tinned esp. in Norway for food

brisque \ˈbrisk, ˈbrēsk\ *n* -S [F] **:** an ace or a ten in certain card games (as bezique) in which the ten ranks between the ace and the king

briss *var of* BERITH

¹bris·tle \ˈbrisəl\ *n* -S [ME *bristil, brustel*, fr. *brust* bristle, fr. OE *byrst*; akin to OHG *burst, borst* bristle, ON *burst* bristle, L *fastigium* top, extremity, Skt *bhṛṣṭi* spike, point] **1 :** a short stiff coarse hair **2 :** something resembling a bristle: as **a :** any of various animal structures similar to hair (as a small fine feather) **b :** the stiff short hair of a plant **c :** the manufactured material used in the face of a hairbrush

²bristle \"\ *vb* **bristled; bristled; bristling** \-s(ə)liŋ, -lēŋ\ **bristles** *vi* **1 :** to rise or stand stiff or erect like bristles ⟨a dragon with fierce eyes and scales *bristling* in defiance —T.B. Costain⟩ ⟨the points of his silvery mustache *bristled* aggressively —D.G.Geraghty⟩ **2 a** *of an animal* **:** to raise the bristles (as in anger) ⟨the dog *bristled* as the stranger approached⟩ **b** *of a person* **:** to assume an aggressive appearance or attitude ⟨I was a little annoyed and *bristled* slightly —A.W. Long⟩ ⟨that sort of antagonism which makes men ~ —Francis Hackett⟩ **3 a :** to become covered with many closely assembled objects thrusting as if aggressively straight upward ⟨the river-bank ~s with factories —*Amer. Guide Series: Pa.*⟩ ⟨a hundred-room house . . . its roof *bristling* with chimneys —*New Yorker*⟩ **b :** to be very noticeably full of a particular kind of thing — usu. used with *with* ⟨his rucksack *bristling* with test tubes —E.E.Shipton⟩ ⟨articles which *bristled* with dark insinuations —Ruth P. Randall⟩ ⟨*bristled* with . . . enthusiasm —J.C.Trewin⟩ ⟨speeches . . . *bristling* with quotations and citations —Van Wyck Brooks⟩ ~ *vt* **1 :** to erect like bristles — sometimes used with *up* ⟨a cock *bristling* up his crest⟩ **2 :** to furnish with bristles **:** attach bristles to **3 :** to make bristly **:** RUFFLE

³bristle \"\ *vb* -ED/-ING/-S [ME *brystyllen*] *dial Brit* **:** to scorch or parch esp. in cooking

bristle-bird \ˈ≠≠,≠\ *n* **:** any of three Australian birds (genus *Dasyornis*) that resemble wrens and have two or three pairs of strong recurved bristles at the angles of the mouth

bristle cell *n* **:** HAIR CELL

bristlecone fir \ˈ≠≠,≠\ *n* **:** SANTA LUCIA FIR

bristlecone pine *n* **:** an upland pine (*Pinus aristata*) of the western U.S. that includes the oldest living things ⟨some *bristlecone pines* are demonstrably over 4500 years old⟩

bris·tled \-səld\ *adj* [ME, fr. *bristil*, *bristle* + *-ed*] **:** emblazoned with bristles on the ridge of the back ⟨a boar rampant argent, tusked, and ~ or⟩

bristle fern *n* **1 :** any fern of the genus *Trichomanes* with coarse pinnatifid fronds — called also *filmy fern* **2 :** HOLLY FERN b

bristle grass *n* [so called fr. the long bristle beneath each spikelet] **:** a grass of the genus *Setaria*

bris·tle·less \-səl(l)əs\ *adj* **:** being without bristles

bristle rat *n* **:** SPINY RAT 1

bristletail \ˈ≠≠,≠\ *n* **1 :** a wingless insect of the orders Thysanura and Entotrophi bearing two or three segmented filaments at the end of the body — compare LEPISMA **2 :** RUDDY DUCK

bristle-thighed curlew \ˈ≠≠,≠-\ *n* **:** a curlew (*Numenius tahitiensis*) with points like bristles on its thigh feathers that breeds in western Alaska and winters chiefly in Polynesia

bristle worm *n* **:** a segmented worm of the class Chaetopoda

bristlewort \ˈ≠≠,≠\ *n* -S **:** a plant of the family Centrolepidaceae

bris·tli·ness \ˈbris(ə)lēnəs, -lin-\ *n* -ES **:** the quality or state of being bristly

¹bristling *pres part of* BRISTLE

²bristling *var of* BRISLING

bris·tly \ˈbris(ə)lē, -li\ *adj* -ER/-EST **1 a :** consisting of or like bristles ⟨a horse with a short ~ mane⟩ ⟨a ~ brown mustache —S.H.Adams⟩ ⟨frowning ~ brows —Lucy M. Montgomery⟩ **b :** thickly set with bristles ⟨a ~ skin⟩ ⟨a ~ shrub⟩ **2 :** tending to bristle easily **:** BELLIGERENT ⟨a man with a ~ temperament⟩ ⟨this aura of ~ independence —*Time*⟩

bristly carrot *n* **:** RATTLESNAKE WEED 2

bristly crowfoot *or* **bristly buttercup** *n* **:** a hairy American buttercup (*Ranunculus pennsylvanicus*) with sharp-beaked fruits

bristly foxtail *n* **:** YELLOW FOXTAIL

bristly greenbrier *n* **:** a greenbrier (*Smilax hispida*) with pliant bristly prickles

bristly ground squirrel *n* **:** an African ground squirrel (*Xerus setosus*) with coarse bristly hair

bristly locust *n* **:** a shrub (*Robinia hispida*) of eastern No. America with bristly stems and large clusters of showy pink flowers — called also *moss locust, rose acacia*

bristly oxtongue *n* **:** a European weed (*Picris echioides*) adventive in eastern No. America with bristly foliage and yellow flowers

bristly sarsaparilla *n* **:** a bristly American herb (*Aralia hispida*) with black fruit and medicinal bark having properties like those of sarsaparilla

¹bris·tol \ˈbristᵊl\ *adj*, *usu cap* [fr. *Bristol*, England] **:** of or from the city of Bristol, England **:** of the kind or style prevalent in Bristol

²bristol \"\ *n* -S **1** *or* **bristol ware** *usu cap B* **:** ceramic ware produced in or about Bristol, England: as **a** *or* **bristol delft** *usu cap B* **:** 17th and 18th century tin-enameled usu. blue and white earthenware **b** *or* **bristol porcelain** *usu cap B* **:** an 18th century soft paste porcelain containing soapstone and indistinguishable from early Worcester porcelain **c** *or* **bristol porcelain** *usu cap B* **:** hard paste porcelain forming a direct continuation of Plymouth porcelain and produced about 1770–1780 **2** *or* **bristol board :** cardboard with a smooth surface suitable for writing or printing, generally of $^6/_{1000}$-inch thickness or more

bristol fashion *adj*, *usu cap B* **:** in good order **:** SHIPSHAPE ⟨spick-and-span, shipshape and *Bristol fashion* —Jack Lusby⟩

bristol glass *n*, *usu cap B* **:** a semiopaque glass of various color tones, notably deep blue, used for decorative glassware and commonly painted with floral designs

bristol glaze *n*, *usu cap B* **:** a lead-free and usu. zinc-containing ceramic glaze used on faïence and stoneware

bri·sure *also* **bri·zure** \brəˈzhü(ə)r\ *n* -S [F *brisure*, lit., break, crack, fr. OF, fr. *brisier* to break — more at BRISANCE] **:** CADENCY MARK **:** DIFFERENCE

brit *or* **britt** \ˈbrit\ *n* -S [modif. of Corn *brȳthel* mackerel, lit., speckled, fr. *brȳth* speckled + *-el* (dim. suffix); akin to W *brith* speckled] **1 a :** the young of the common herring **b :** any of certain small herrings **2 :** the minute marine animals, largely crustaceans (Entomostraca) and pteropods, upon which the right whales feed **3 :** any of the silversides

brit·ain \ˈbritᵊn *also* -itən *or* -id·ən\ *n* -S *usu cap* [alter. (influenced by *Britain* Great Britain) of *Briton*] *obs* **:** BRITON

bri·tan·nia \brəˈtanyə, -nēə\ *n* -S *usu cap* [fr. *Britannia*, poetic name for Great Britain, fr. L] **:** a representation of a female figure usu. seated and with helmet and trident that is symbolic of Great Britain or Great Britain and the dominions

britannia metal *or* **britannia** *n* [fr. *Britannia* Great Britain] **:** a silver-white alloy of tin, antimony, copper, and often also zinc and bismuth that is similar to pewter and was formerly much used for domestic utensils

bri·tan·nian \-yən,-ēən\ *adj*, *usu cap* [*Britannia* Great Britain + E *-an*] **:** BRITISH

¹bri·tan·nic \-nik,-nēk\ *adj*, *usu cap* [L *Britannicus*, fr. *Britannia* + *-icus* -ic] **:** BRITISH ⟨her *Britannic* majesty, Queen Victoria⟩ — **bri·tan·ni·cal·ly** \-nək(ə)lē\ *adv*, *usu cap*

²britannic \"\ *n* -S **:** AMPHIBRACH

bri·tan·ni·cize \-nə,sīz\ *vt* -ED/-ING/-S *often cap* **:** to make British in quality, customs, or behavior

¹britch \ˈbrich\ *n* -ES [by alter.] *dial* **:** ¹BREECH

²britch \"\ *vt* -ED/-ING/-ES [by alter.] *dial* **:** ²BREECH

britch·el \ˈbrichəl\ *adj* [ME *bruchel*, fr. OE *-brycel* (as in *hūsbrycel* burglarious); akin to OE *brecan* to break — more at BREAK] *dial Eng* **:** BRITTLE

britch·en *also* **britch·in** \ˈbrichən\ *n* [by alter.] *dial* **:** BREECHING

britch·es \ˈbrichəz\ *n pl* [alter. of *breeches*] **:** BREECHES, PANTS — **too big for one's britches :** SWELLHEADED, ARROGANT

brith *var of* BERITH

brith·er \ˈbrit͟hə(r), -rēt͟h-\ *n* -S [prob. back-formation fr. dial. *brither*, pl., fr. ME *brether, breither, brither*, pl. of *brother*] *dial* **:** BROTHER

brit·i·cism \ˈbrid·ə,sizəm, -itə-\ *n* -S *usu cap* [*British* + *-icism* (as in *Gallicism*)] **:** a characteristic feature of British English esp. as contrasted with American English (as *waistcoat* contrasted with *vest*, *navvy* with *day laborer*, *to register luggage* with *to check baggage*, *to engage a servant* with *to hire a servant*, *tyre* with *tire*, *kerb* with *curb*)

¹brit·ish \ˈbrid·|ish, -it|, |ēsh\ *adj*, *usu cap* [ME *Bruttische*, *Brytysshe*, fr. OE *Brettisc*, *Bryttisc*, *Brittisc*, of Celt origin; akin to W *Brython* Briton] **1 :** of, relating to, or characteristic of the original inhabitants of Britain **2 a :** of, relating to, or characteristic of Great Britain or its inhabitants **b :** of, relating to, or characteristic of the British Commonwealth **c :** of, relating to, or characteristic of England — **brit·ish·ness** *n* -ES *usu cap*

²british \"\ *n* -ES *cap* **1 a :** the Celtic language of the ancient Britons **b :** BRITISH ENGLISH **2** *pl in constr* **a :** the people native to or naturalized in Great Britain **b :** the primarily British people of the British Commonwealth **c :** the people of the British Commonwealth

british alpine *n*, *usu cap B & sometimes cap A* **:** a goat of a strain that is sometimes considered a separate breed developed in England by interbreeding Swiss Alpine goats with native stock

british an·ti-lew·is·ite \-ˈlüə,sīt\ *n*, *usu cap B* [*¹anti-* + *lewisite*] **:** DIMERCAPROL

british association thread *n*, *usu cap B&A* **:** a screw thread with an angle of 47½° and rounded crests and roots that is used chiefly in Great Britain and other European countries for very small screws

british co·lum·bi·a \¦≠≠kə¦ləmbēə\ *adj*, *usu cap B&C* [fr. *British Columbia*, province of Canada] **:** of or from the province of British Columbia **:** of the kind or style prevalent in British Columbia **:** BRITISH COLUMBIAN

¹british co·lum·bi·an \-ən\ *adj*, *usu cap B&C* **1 :** of, relating to, or characteristic of the province of British Columbia **2 :** of, relating to, or characteristic of the people of British Columbia

²british columbian \"\ *n*, *cap B&C* **:** a native or inhabitant of British Columbia

british dollar *n*, *usu cap B* **:** DOLLAR 2d

british english *n*, *cap B&E* **:** the native language of most inhabitants of England; *esp* **:** a variety of English characteristic of England and clearly distinguishable from those varieties used in the U.S., Australia, and elsewhere — compare AMERICAN ENGLISH, AUSTRAL ENGLISH, AUSTRALIAN ENGLISH

brit·ish·er \ˈbrid·|ishə(r), -it|, |ēsh-\ *n* -S *cap B* **:** BRITON 2

¹british guianese *also* **british guianan** *see* GUIANESE, GUIANAN\ *adj*, *usu cap B&G* [*British Guiana*, former name of Guyana + E *-ese* or *-an*] **:** GUYANESE

²british guianese *also* **british guianan** \"\ *n*, *cap B&G* **:** GUYANESE

british gum *n*, *usu cap B* **:** DEXTRIN; *esp* **:** dextrin produced by heating starch sometimes with small amounts of acid or alkali and used as size for paper and textiles and as an adhesive

¹british honduran *see* HONDURAN\ *adj*, *usu cap B&H* [*British Honduras*, country in Central America + E *-an*] **1 :** of, relating to, or characteristic of British Honduras **2 :** of, relating to, or characteristic of the people of British Honduras

²british honduran \"\ *n*, *cap B&H* **:** a native or inhabitant of British Honduras

brit·ish·ism \|ē,shizəm, |ə,-\ *n* -S *usu cap* **1 :** BRITICISM **2 a :** the distinctive qualities of the people of the British Commonwealth **b :** one of these qualities

brit·ish·ly *adv*, *usu cap* **:** in a British way ⟨a ~ calm bystander⟩

british mold *n*, *usu cap B* **:** a mold of the genus *Brettanomyces*

british oak *n*, *usu cap B* **:** ENGLISH OAK

british thermal unit *n*, *usu cap B* **:** the quantity of heat required to raise the temperature of one avoirdupois pound of water one degree Fahrenheit at or near 39.2°F, its temperature of maximum density, being equal to about 0.252 kilogram calorie — abbr. *Btu*

british warm *n*, *usu cap B* **:** a short double-breasted overcoat worn esp. by British army officers

brito- \¦brid·(,)ō, -i,tō\ *n comb form*, *cap* [prob. fr. L *Brito*] **1 :** of or belonging to the Britons and ⟨*Brito*-Roman⟩ **2 :** British and ⟨*Brito*-Japanese⟩ **3 :** Britain ⟨*Brito*centric⟩

brit·on \ˈbritᵊn *also* -itən *or* -id·ən\ *n* -S *cap* [ME *Breton*, *Bryton*, fr. MF & L; MF *breton*, fr. L *Briton-*, *Brito*, *Britton-*, *Britto*, of Celt origin; akin to W *Brython* Briton] **1 :** a member of one of the peoples inhabiting Britain previous to the Anglo-Saxon invasions, the majority being presumably Cymric Celts intermixed with earlier non-Indo-European-speaking peoples **2 :** a native or subject of Great Britain; *esp* **:** ENGLISHMAN

brits *pl of* BRIT

brits·ka *or* **britz·ska** \ˈbrichkə, -itskə\ *n* -S [G *britschka*, *britzka*, fr. Pol *bryczka*, perh. modif. of G *barutsche*, *birutsche* barouche — more at BAROUCHE] **:** a long open horse-drawn carriage with a folding top over the rear seat and a front seat facing the rear

britt *var of* BRIT

brit·ta·ny \ˈbritᵊnē, -ni\ *or* **brittany blue** *n* -ES *often cap* *Brittany* [fr. *Brittany*, region of northwestern France] **:** a moderate greenish blue that is bluer and paler than average peacock and bluer and slightly paler than larkspur

brittany spaniel *n*, *usu cap B* **:** a rather tall active short-tailed spaniel of a French breed having a smooth or slightly wavy coat of orange and white or liver and white somewhat fringed on chest, forelegs, and thighs that was developed by interbreeding pointers with spaniels of Brittany to produce a competent bird dog with an action suggestive of a setter

¹brit·tle \ˈbrid·ᵊl, -itᵊl\ *adj* [ME *britil*; akin to OE *brēotan* to break, OHG *brōdi* frail, ON *brjōta* to break, Skt *bhrūṇa* embryo] **1 a** (1) **:** easily broken, cracked, or snapped **:** apt to break or snap easily esp. under very slight bending or deformation ⟨~ clay⟩ ⟨~ glass⟩ ⟨as ~ as an eggshell⟩ (2) *of a metal or alloy* **:** having very low malleability or ductility **b :** easily disrupted, overthrown, damaged, or disintegrated **:** FRAIL ⟨a ~ promise⟩ ⟨~ honor —Shak.⟩ ⟨a ~ marriage⟩ **c :** requiring careful handling **:** DIFFICULT ⟨a ~ personality⟩ **d :** SHARP, BRILLIANT, TENSE ⟨the light, ~ tones of an orchestra of xylophones —*Asia & the Americas*⟩ ⟨the ~ staccato of the drums —H.A.Sinclair⟩ ⟨could hardly understand what was said to him, so ~ and sharp was the sound —Pearl Buck⟩ **2 a :** PERISHABLE, MORTAL **b :** TRANSITORY, EVANESCENT **3 :** lacking warmth, depth, or generosity of spirit **:** COLD, CALCULATING ⟨she was harder, more ~, than Effie ever was —Rex Ingamells⟩ ⟨a ~ and selfish woman who calculates her ends coldly and by sheer poise and self-possession usually gets her way —Chad Walsh⟩ ⟨the ~, cynical, beautiful legends of Ovid —Gilbert Highet⟩ — **brit·tle·ly** *or* **brit·tly** \-d·ᵊl(l)ē, -tᵊl-, -)i; -tlē,-tli\ *adv* — **brit·tle·ness** \-id·ᵊlnəs, -itᵊl-\ *n* -ES

²brittle \"\ *n* -S **:** candy made by boiling sugar to the point of caramelization, adding nuts, and cooling in thin sheets

brittle bones *n pl but sing or pl in constr* **:** FRAGILITAS OSSIUM

brittlebush \ˈ≠≠,≠\ *n* **:** a desert plant of the genus *Encelia* (family Compositae) of the southwestern U.S. and adjacent Mexico having brittle stems, small crowded leaves, and yellow flowers and containing a principle toxic to other plants

brittle fern *n* **:** FRAGILE FERN

brittle maidenhair *n* **:** a tropical American fern (*Adiantum tenerum*) with broad pinnae — see FARLEY MAIDENHAIR

brittle mica *n* **:** a mineral of the clintonite group

brittle snake *n* **:** GLASS SNAKE

brittle star *n* **:** OPHIUROID; *esp* **:** a simple-armed ophiuroid (order Ophiurida)

brittle willow *n* **:** CRACK WILLOW

brittlewood \ˈ≠≠,≠\ *n* **:** YELLOW BUCKTHORN

brit·ton·ic \(ˈ)bri¦tänik\ *adj*, *usu cap* [L *Britton-*, *Britto* Briton + E *-ic* — more at BRITON] **:** BRYTHONIC 2

britzska *var of* BRITSKA

¹brix \ˈbriks\ *adj*, *usu cap* [*Brix (scale)*] **:** according to a Brix scale ⟨addition of sugar to the juice to about 50° *Brix*⟩ **:** calibrated in accordance with a Brix scale

²brix \"\ *n* -ES *usu cap* **:** concentration in percent of sugar by weight according to the Brix scale ⟨the *Brix* of a syrup⟩

brix scale *n*, *usu cap B* [after Adolf F. *Brix* †1870, Ger. scientist, its inventor] **:** a hydrometer scale for sugar solutions so graduated that its readings in degrees Brix at a specified temperature represent percentages by weight of sugar in the solution

bri·za \ˈbrīzə\ *n*, *cap* [NL, fr. Gk, rye] **:** a genus of grasses (family Gramineae) native to the Old World and So. America

and distinguished by broad spikelets and cordate lemmas — see QUAKING GRASS
brizure *var of* BRISURE
brizz \ˈbriz\ *vt* -ED/-ING/-ES [ME *brisen, brusen* — more at BRUISE] *chiefly Scot* **:** CRUSH, BRUISE
brl *abbr* barrel
brlp *abbr* burlap
brm *abbr* barometer
brmc *abbr* barometric
brn *abbr* brown
brno \ˈbər(,)nō, -nȯ\ *adj, usu cap* [fr. *Brno*, Czechoslovakia] **:** of or from the city of Brno, Czechoslovakia **:** of the kind or style prevalent in Brno
bro *abbr* **1** bronze **2** brother
¹broach \ˈbrōch\ *n* -ES [ME *broche*, fr. MF, fr. OF, fr. (assumed) VL *brocca*, fr. fem. of L *broccus* projecting (of teeth)] **1** *archaic* **:** a pointed rod usu. of wood or iron used as an awl, bodkin, lance, spear **2 :** any of various pointed or spikelike tools, implements, or parts: as **a :** a spit for roasting meat **b :** the stick from which candlewicks are suspended for dipping **c** *now chiefly Scot* **:** a spindle on which newly spun yarn is wound **d :** a wooden rod sharpened at both ends used by thatchers **e** (1) **:** the pin in a lock that enters the barrel of the key (2) **:** the part of the stem of a key beyond the web or bit made to enter a socket **f :** the steel tooth of the doffer comb of a carding machine **3 :** one of the four semipyramidal slopes marking the transition at the corners of a square tower to the sides of an octagonal spire above — compare BROACH SPIRE **4 :** a point of a young stag's horn resembling a spit **5 :** a cutting tool for removing material from a metal or plastic to shape an outside surface or a hole that has been previously formed (as by casting or drilling) consisting of a bar of suitable length provided on its surface with a series of cutting edges or teeth that increase in size from the entering or starting end, the tool being fed through or past the work by a translational movement along its axis and, because the cutting edges are progressively higher, each succeeding tooth removing additional material **6 :** a fine tapered flexible instrument used in dentistry in removing the dental pulp and in dressing a root canal **7 :** BROOCH
²broach \ˈ"\ *vb* -ED/-ING/-ES [ME *brochen*, fr. MF *brocher*, fr. OF *brochier*, fr. *broche*] *vt* **1** *obs* **:** STAB, PIERCE, PRICK **2** *obs* **:** SPIT **:** fix on a spit **3 a** (1) **:** to pierce (as a cask) in order to draw the contents **:** TAP (2) **:** to open (a vein) to draw blood **b :** to open up or break into (as a mine or stores) **4 :** to shape (a block of stone) roughly by chiseling with a coarse tool **5 :** to shape or enlarge (a hole) with a broach or boring tool **6 :** PRESENT, ANNOUNCE, INTRODUCE ⟨~*ed* a hot lunch program⟩ **:** make known for the first time **:** begin to disclose **:** open up (a subject) for discussion or debate ⟨a suggestion first ~*ed* two years ago⟩ ⟨this is a good time to ~ the subject⟩ **7 :** to drill or cut out (material left between adjacent holes in a row of closely spaced drill holes) in mining and quarrying ~ *vi* **:** to break to the surface from below (as of a whale or a torpedo in the course of a run) **syn** see EXPRESS
³broach \ˈ"\ *vb* -ED/-ING/-ES [perh. fr. *²broach*] *vi* **:** to veer or yaw esp. in a following sea so as to lie beam on to the waves with danger of capsizing or swamping — used chiefly with *to* ⟨strove to keep the tiny boat from ~*ing* to in the heavy seas — G.G.Carter⟩ ~ *vt* **:** to cause (a boat) to swing beam on to the waves
⁴broach \ˈ"\ *n* -ES [*Broach, Bharoch*, city in Bombay state, India] **:** a short-staple cotton grown esp. in Bombay state, India
broached work *n* [*broached* fr. past part. of *²broach*] **:** the finish on a stone that shows a margin around the edge and has the center broached with continuous grooves
broach·er \ˈbrōchə(r)\ *n* -S **:** one that broaches or works with a broach: as **a :** a broaching machine **b :** the operator of a broaching machine **c :** a worker who finishes holes in jewel bearings by use of a broach with diamond dust
broaching machine *n* [*broaching* fr. gerund of *²broach*] **:** a machine tool whose cutting element is a broach
broach post *n* **:** KING POST
broach spire *n* [*¹broach*] **:** an octagonal spire rising from a square tower without an intervening parapet, the four angles of the tower being covered by corner segments of a pyramid seeming to penetrate the spire
broach turner *n* **:** TURNSPIT
¹broad \ˈbrȯd\ *adj* -ER/-EST [ME *brood*, fr. OE *brād*; akin to OHG *breit* broad, ON *breithr*, Goth *braiths*] **1 a :** marked by ample extent from side to side or by relatively large distance between sides or limits **:** not narrow ⟨~ pen strokes⟩ ⟨~ shoulders⟩ ⟨~ streets⟩ ⟨~ fields⟩ **b :** having extension from side to side of a specified dimension ⟨10 feet ~⟩ **2 :** extending far and wide **:** SPACIOUS ⟨the ~ sea⟩ ⟨the ~ western plains⟩ **3 a :** CLEAR, OPEN, FULL ⟨a crime committed in ~ daylight⟩ **b :** PATENT, UNMISTAKABLE, PLAIN ⟨a ~ hint⟩ **4 :** marked by lack of restraint, delicacy, or subtlety: **a** *obs* **:** OUTSPOKEN ⟨from ~ words ... Macduff lives in disgrace —Shak.⟩ **b :** COARSE ⟨a term thought a little too ~ for a radio program⟩ ⟨merry tales and ~ jests⟩ **:** INDELICATE, RISQUÉ ⟨~ burlesque humor⟩ **5 a :** marked by a generous wide-ranging breadth or tolerance **:** not parochial ⟨a man of ~ views and interests⟩ ⟨~ sympathies that knew no barrier of race or creed⟩ **b :** widely applicable **:** not limited or restricted **:** GENERAL ⟨a ~ rule, not to be narrowly construed⟩ ⟨used the word in its ~ sense⟩ **6 a :** relating to or having to do with the main, essential, or general aspects (as of a problem) ⟨scientific knowledge in its ~ outlines —Bertrand Russell⟩ ⟨achieved ~ agreement on the issue, leaving details to be settled by subordinates⟩ **b** *of a library classification* **:** having relatively large subdivisions — compare CLOSE **7** *often cap* **:** marked by Broad Church attitudes or practices **:** LIBERAL **:** not meticulous about niceties of ritual and dogma **8** *of a coin* **:** having a large diameter and small thickness **9** *of a sailing course* **:** with the wind nearly abeam **10 :** of markedly dialectal nature esp. in pronunciation ⟨a ~ North Country accent⟩ **11** *of textiles* **:** woven wide; *esp* **:** woven in widths (as greater than 30 inches) suitable for clothing and decorating uses — compare NARROW **12** *phonetics* **a** *of a vowel* **:** OPEN — used specif. of *a* (alone or as a member of a digraph) pronounced with a vowel sound that has or approaches the quality of the *a* in *father, calm, par* and esp. in a class of words (as *ask, laugh*) in which the pronunciation is \a\ or \aa(ə)\ in most U.S. speech outside of eastern New England **b** *in certain Celtic languages* (1) *of a vowel* **:** BACK (2) *of a consonant* **:** having the allophone that characterizes it when it is pronounced with a back vowel **13 :** characterized by demand and supply for large blocks of securities or by participation by many customers — used of the market for a security or the market as a whole **14 a** *of wool* **:** straight-fibered and nonelastic **:** coarser than usual for the type in question **b** *of bran* **:** consisting of flakes or nearly whole husks **15** *of pronunciation transcription* **a :** PHONEMIC **b :** representing by distinct nondiacritical symbols all qualitatively and phonemically distinct sounds — compare NARROW **16** *of a radio circuit* **:** having a slowly varying response to different frequencies — opposed to *sharp* **17** *of insurance coverage* **:** covering two or more related risks
syn BROAD, DEEP, and WIDE may all refer to horizontal expansion or dimension. BROAD and WIDE are often interchangeable ⟨*broad* and *wide* fields⟩ ⟨to the *broad* ocean and the azure heavens —William Wordsworth⟩ ⟨view the ocean *wide* and bright —William Wordsworth⟩ WIDE is more common than BROAD when units of measurement are mentioned ⟨rugs eight feet *wide*⟩ and when unfilled space between limits is being considered ⟨a *wide* doorway⟩ When no vertical measurement or measurement from a surface downward is likely to be involved, all three words may be used to indicate extent away from the observer ⟨a *wide, broad*, or *deep* flower garden⟩ DEEP is likely to apply to distance extending straight back from a point considered at the front; BROAD and WIDE to lateral distances ⟨that called on Hertha in *deep* forest glades —S.T. Coleridge⟩ ⟨high on a *broad* unfertile tract of forest-skirted down —William Wordsworth⟩ ⟨that we might look into a forest *wide* —John Keats⟩
²broad \ˈ"\ *adv* [ME *broode*, fr. OE *brāde*, fr. *brād* broad — more at ¹BROAD] **:** BROADLY, WIDELY — now used chiefly in phrases ⟨~ awake⟩ ⟨~ off⟩
³broad \ˈ"\ *n* -S [ME *brood*, fr. *brood*, adj. — more at ¹BROAD] **1 :** the broad or flat part of something (as the hand) **2** *Brit* **:** an expansion of a river — often used in pl. ⟨the Norfolk ~*s*⟩ **3 :** BROADPIECE **4 broads** *pl, slang* **:** PLAYING CARDS **5** *slang* **a :** WOMAN **b :** PROSTITUTE **6** [fr. *¹abroad*, taken as containing the indefinite article *a*] *dial* **:** JOURNEY, TRIP ⟨must give up your ~ . . . for I want to have rails right away — *Southern Lit. Messenger*⟩ **7 :** BROADSIDE 6
broad aisle *or* **broad alley** *n* **:** the central aisle of a church
broad arrow *n* [ME *brood arwe*, fr. *brood* broad + *arwe* arrow] **1 :** an arrow with a flat barbed head **2** *heraldry* **:** a pheon that is not engrailed on the inner edge **3** *Brit* **:** an identification mark put on government property including convicts' clothing

broad arrow 3

broadax *or* **broadaxe** \ˈ=,=\ *n* [ME *broodax*, fr. *brood* broad + *ax*] **:** a large ax with a broad blade (as any of various battle-axes or an ax used for hewing timber) — see AX illustration
broad–base terrace *n* **:** a low wide terrace that permits farm machines to pass over it
broad bean *n* **1 :** a large smooth flattened edible seed that is a staple article of food in parts of southern Europe — called also *fava bean, horsebean;* see FAVISM **2 :** a sturdy upright vetch (*Vicia faba*) that is widely cultivated chiefly in the Old World both for the broad beans which it bears in long pods and as fodder
broad–bean weevil *n* **:** a destructive weevil (*Bruchus rufimanus*) that feeds on broad beans and other vetch seeds
broad beech fern *n* **:** a No. American woodland fern (*Dryopteris hexagonoptera*) with finely dissected leaves and straw-colored stipes
broadbill \ˈ=,=\ *n* **1 :** any of several ducks with rather wide flat bills: as **a :** SCAUP DUCK **b :** SHOVELER **2 :** any of certain Old World birds (suborder Eurylaimidae) with a wide short bill, often bright plumage, and sluggish habits **3 :** any of several flycatchers (genus *Myiagra*) of the southwest Pacific **4** *or* **broadbill swordfish :** SWORDFISH 1a
broadbill dipper *n* **:** RUDDY DUCK
broad–billed sandpiper \ˈ=,=-\ *n* **:** a sandpiper (*Limicola falcinellus*) resembling a snipe and breeding in northern parts of the Old World
broad–breasted bronze \ˈ=,==-\ *n, usu cap all 3Bs* **:** a strain of the Bronze turkey notable for the relatively great amount of breast meat and distinguished by vigor, rapid growth, and exceptionally large size
broadbrim \ˈ=,=\ *n* **1 :** a hat with a very wide brim (as that worn by Quakers) **2 :** FRIEND 6
¹broadcast \ˈ=,=\ *adj* [*²broad* + *cast*, fr. past part. of *cast* (to throw)] **1 :** cast or scattered in all directions ⟨seed ~ from the hand in sowing⟩ **:** widely diffused **2 :** made public by means of radio or television ⟨the use of ~ appeals to motorists to keep off the roads⟩
²broadcast \ˈ=,=\ *n* **1 :** a casting or scattering in all directions (as of seed from the hand in sowing) **2 :** the act of making widely known **:** the act of spreading abroad ⟨in this time of . . . excessive ~ of moralities —*Amer. Scholar*⟩; *specif* **:** the act of sending out sound or images by radio or television transmission esp. for general reception ⟨the ~ of court proceedings⟩ **3 :** a single radio or television program ⟨a weekly ~ of world news⟩ ⟨his first appearance in a ~⟩
³broadcast \ˈ"\ *vb* **broadcast** *also* **broadcasted; broadcast** *also* **broadcasted; broadcasting; broadcasts** *vt* **1 :** to scatter or sow (seed) broadcast **2 :** to make widely known **:** disseminate or distribute widely or at random ⟨it's not really a secret but I wouldn't want it ~⟩ **3 :** to send out from a transmitting station (a radio or television program) for an unlimited number of receivers ~ *vi* **:** to send out radio or television signals ⟨~*ing* on a frequency of 600 kilocycles⟩ **:** speak or perform on a broadcast program ⟨he has lectured and ~ on many subjects⟩ **syn** see DECLARE, STREW
⁴broadcast \ˈ"\ *adv* **:** so as to scatter or be scattered in all directions (as of seed) **:** so as to spread widely; *specif* **:** so as to reach by radio or television transmission the greatest possible number of receiving sets
broad·cast·er \-tə(r)\ *n* -S **:** one that broadcasts: **a :** a mechanical device for sowing seed (as of grass or clover) by scattering it broadcast over the ground usu. by centrifugal force **:** a broadcast seeder **b :** an organization or apparatus for broadcasting radio or television programs **c :** a person broadcasting
broadcast spectrum *n* **:** the part of the range of frequencies of electromagnetic waves assigned to broadcasting stations ranging in the U.S. from 550 to 1600 kilocycles per second for AM radio stations
broad church *n, cap B&C* **:** a party or school of theological thought in the Anglican Communion holding liberal views as to doctrine and fellowship and emphasizing a policy of broad inclusiveness, active esp. during the second half of the 19th century under the guidance of such early leaders as Thomas Arnold, Charles Kingsley, A.P.Stanley, and F.W.Robertson
broad churchman *n, usu cap B&C* [*broad church* + *man*] **:** an adherent of the Anglican Broad Church party
broadcloth \ˈ=,=\ *n* [ME *broodcloth*, fr. *brood* broad + *cloth* — more at ¹BROAD] **1 :** any cloth woven on a wide loom as distinguished from a narrow fabric **2 :** a twilled and napped clothing fabric of woolen or worsted with a smooth lustrous face and a close dense texture **3 :** a clothing and decorating fabric usu. of cotton, silk, or rayon made in plain and rib weaves with a soft semigloss finish
broad command pennant *n* **:** a command pennant that is identical with or similar in shape to a broad pennant and is flown by an officer in the U.S. Navy below flag rank who is temporarily in command of a force, squadron, flotilla, or battleship or cruiser division or of a major unit of aircraft — compare BURGEE COMMAND PENNANT
broad·en \ˈbrȯdᵊn\ *vb* **broadened; broadened; broadening** \-d(ᵊ)niŋ\ **broadens** *vi* **:** to grow or become broad or broader ⟨the street ~*s* into an avenue⟩ — sometimes used with *out* ⟨"textile" has ~*ed* out to include many processes besides weaving —Thomas Munro⟩ ~ *vt* **:** to make broader ⟨a mind ~*ed* by travel and education⟩ **:** extend the limits of ⟨~ the basis on which candidates may be accepted⟩
broader *comparative of* BROAD
broadest *superlative of* BROAD
broadfall \ˈ=,=\ *adj, of trousers* **:** having a large flap in front that buttons at the sides and top
broad fold *adj, of paper and paperboard* **:** having the machine direction running the short way of the sheet — compare LONG GRAIN
broad–footed pouched mouse \ˈ=,==-\ *n* **:** any of several Australian pouched mice (genus *Phascogale*) somewhat resembling shrews or tree shrews
broad form *adj, of insurance* **:** covering more property or hazards than the standard form by naming additional specific perils or having fewer restrictions — compare ALL RISK
broad gage *n* **:** any railroad gage that is wider than standard gage
broad–gage *or* **broad–gaged** \ˈ=ˈ=\ *adj* **1 :** having a broad gage **2** *usu* **broad–gauge** *or* **broad–gauged :** of wide scope
broad glass *n* **:** CYLINDER GLASS
broad goods *n pl but sing or pl in constr* **:** cloth woven in standard or wider widths esp. in distinction from ribbons, bands, or trimmings
broad hatchet *n* **:** a hatchet having a short handle and a broad cutting blade with a rectangular hammering face opposite the blade — see HATCHET illustration
broadhead \ˈ=,=\ *n* **1 :** a person with a relatively wide head **:** one who is brachycephalic **2 :** a flat pointed steel arrowhead having sharp edges; *also* **:** an arrow having such a head
broad–headed snake \ˈ=,==-\ *n* **:** an Australian venomous snake (*Hoplocephalus bungaroides*) that is blackish above and marked with a lattice of yellow spots and is related to the tiger snake
broadhorn \ˈ=,=\ *n* [so called fr. the large oar projecting from the roof on each side near the bow] **:** ARK 2b
broad irrigation *n* **:** irrigation with liquid sewage
broad·ish \ˈbrȯdish\ *adj* **:** rather broad ⟨a ~ face⟩ **:** tending toward broadness ⟨~ jokes⟩
broad jump *n* **:** a jump for distance from a standing position or from a running start in track-and-field athletics — **broad jumper** *n*
broad knife *n* **:** a tool like a putty knife but with a larger and broader blade
¹broadleaf \ˈ=,=\ *n* -S **1 a :** a tree (*Terminalia latifolia*) of Jamaica whose wood is used for boards, scantlings, shingles, and staves **b :** PUKA 2 **2** *sometimes cap* **:** any of certain tobaccos having broad drooping leaves (as Connecticut valley cigar tobacco and Maryland cigarette tobacco)
²broadleaf \ˈ"\ *adj* **:** BROAD-LEAVED
broadleaf tree *n* **:** any deciduous tree (as the maple or oak) or any of certain evergreen trees distinguished from trees bearing needlelike leaves (as most conifers) by having relatively broad flat leaves
broadleaf weed *n* **:** any dicotyledonous weedy plant
broad–leaved *or* **broad–leafed** \ˈ=ˈ=\ *adj* **:** having broad or relatively broad leaves ⟨*broad-leaved* weeds⟩
broad–leaved apple *n* **:** either of two Australian trees: **a :** a medium-sized tree (*Angophora subvelutina*) with large leaves that are used as stock feed **b :** a tree (*Careya australis*) of the family Lecythidaceae that has edible fruits and seeds
broad–leaved asarabacca *n* **:** WILD GINGER 2a
broad–leaved dock *n* **:** BITTER DOCK
broad–leaved maple *n* **:** OREGON MAPLE
broad–leaved plantain *n* **1 :** a European plantain (*Plantago major*) naturalized in No. America that has slender flower spikes and broadly oval leaves with leafstalks which are green to the base **2 :** RUGEL'S PLANTAIN
broad ligament *n* **:** either of the two bilaminate lateral ligaments of the uterus passing from the sides of the uterus to the side walls of the pelvis, giving passage between the two layers of each ligament to the uterine tubes, blood vessels, and the epoophoron and paroophoron, and bearing the ovary suspended from the dorsal surface
¹broadloom \ˈ=,=\ *adj, of a rug or carpet* **:** woven on a wide loom; *also* **:** so woven in solid color
²broadloom \ˈ"\ *n* **:** any carpet woven wider than 54 inches, commonly 9 feet or more
broad·ly *adv* **:** in a broad manner: as **a :** WIDELY, EXTENDEDLY **b :** OPENLY, PLAINLY **c** *obs* **:** OUTSPOKENLY **d :** COARSELY, RAUCOUSLY **e :** LIBERALLY, INCLUSIVELY **f :** MAINLY, GENERALLY
broad–minded \ˈ=ˈ==\ *adj* **1 :** receptive to or tolerant of liberal views esp. in religion or politics **2 :** inclined to tolerate, overlook, or condone minor departures from orthodox social or moral behavior — **broad–mind·ed·ly** *adv* — **broad–mind·ed·ness** *n* -ES
broad mite *n* **:** a widely distributed mite (*Hemitarsonemus latus*) that feeds on a number of crop plants causing mottling and stunting of foliage and russeting of fruits
broad·moor patient \ˈbrȯd,mu̇ə-, -mōə-,-mȯ(ə)-\ *n, usu cap B* [*Broadmoor*, asylum for criminal lunatics in Berkshire, England] *Brit* **:** one legally detained as a criminal lunatic
broad·ness *n* -ES [ME *broodnesse*, fr. *brood* broad + *-nesse* -ness — more at ¹BROAD] **:** the quality of being broad ⟨~ of viewpoint⟩ ⟨notorious for the ~ of his humor⟩
broad off *or* **broad on** *prep* **:** on a bearing about 45 degrees from a fore-and-aft line at (the bow or stern) ⟨*broad off* the port bow⟩ ⟨*broad on* the starboard quarter⟩
broad pennant *n* **:** a flag with a gradual taper ending in a broad swallowtail with the ratio of breadth in the hoist to length in the fly conspicuously greater than in the long pennant; *esp* **:** such a flag flown by a commodore in a navy — compare BROAD COMMAND PENNANT, BURGEE COMMAND PENNANT, COMMAND PENNANT
broadpiece \ˈ=,=\ *n* **:** the English 20-shilling piece of hammered gold issued by James I, Charles I, and the Commonwealth — called also UNITE
broads *pl of* BROAD
broad scotch *n, cap S* **:** the dialects of English spoken in the Lowlands of Scotland
broad seal *n* **:** the public seal of a country or state
broad shad *n* **:** a silvery mojarra (*Gerres cinereus*) of Florida and the West Indies
broadshare \ˈ=,=\ *n* **:** a broad flat plowshare used esp. for surface cultivation
broadsheet \ˈ=,=\ *n* **1 :** BROADSIDE **2** *Brit* **:** a small wire-stitched pamphlet
¹broadside \ˈ=,=\ *n* **1 :** the side of a ship above the waterline **2 :** a broad or nearly unbroken surface of an object ⟨couldn't hit the ~ of a barn⟩ **3 a** *archaic* **:** a sizable sheet of paper printed on one side only; *esp* **:** one publicizing a controversy or official proclamation **b :** a sheet printed on one or both sides and folded as for mailing — by some limited in use to a sheet on which the printed text runs from side to side across the folds **c :** printed matter placed broadside **4 :** something printed on a broadside usu. for general sale or distribution; *esp* **:** BROADSIDE BALLAD **5 a :** the whole array of guns on one side of a ship; *also* **:** their simultaneous discharge **b :** a volley esp. of abuse or denunciation **6 :** a large floodlight used to illuminate a film set or television set
²broadside \ˈ"\ *adj* **1 :** directed broadside ⟨a ~ attack⟩ **2 :** placed broadside ⟨a ~ table of figures⟩
³broadside \ˈ"\ *adv* **1 a :** with the broadside turned toward a given object or point **b** *of printed matter* **:** set at right angles to the ordinary text direction ⟨a table printed ~ on two facing pages⟩ **2 :** in one volley **:** all together **3 :** at large **:** at random **:** without selection of a specific target ⟨a sales letter sent out ~ to a number of prospects⟩
⁴broadside \ˈ"\ *vi* -ED/-ING/-S **1 :** to proceed or go broadside **2 :** to discharge broadsides
broadside ballad *n* **:** a descriptive or narrative verse or song mainly of the 16th and 17th centuries, commonly in a simple ballad form, on a popular theme (as the celebration of an event or in praise of or attack upon a public figure), and sung or recited in public places or printed on broadsides for sale in the streets; *also* **:** a song in imitation of this
broadside on \ˈ;=,=;=\ *adv* **:** SIDEWAYS ⟨drifting *broadside on*⟩ **:** with the side or longer dimension foremost
broad sole *n* **:** any of several closely related mostly American flatfishes (family Soleidae)
broad–spectrum \ˈ=ˈ==\ *adj* **:** effective against a large variety of microorganisms ⟨a *broad-spectrum* antibiotic⟩ ⟨*broad-spectrum* insecticides⟩
broad–spoken \ˈ=ˈ==\ *adj* **:** PLAINSPOKEN, OUTSPOKEN
broad stone *n* **:** ASHLAR 1
broadsword \ˈ=,=\ *n* **:** a sword with a broad blade for cutting rather than thrusting — compare BACKSWORD, CLAYMORE
broadtail \ˈ=,=\ *n* **1** *also* **broadtail sheep a :** KARAKUL 1b **b :** FAT-TAILED SHEEP **2 :** the fur or skin of a very young often prematurely born karakul lamb having a flat and wavy appearance resembling moiré silk — compare CARACUL, PERSIAN LAMB **3** *or* **broad–tailed parrot** \ˈ=,=-\ **:** any of several parrots (genus *Platycercus*) chiefly of Australia with full brightly colored tails that they frequently spread and display **:** ROSELLA
broad–tailed hummingbird \ˈ=,=-\ *n* **:** a rather large hummingbird (*Selasphorus platycercus*) of western No. America the male of which resembles the ruby-throated hummingbird but has a metallic reddish purple throat
broad tapeworm *n* **:** the fish tapeworm of man
broad–toothed rat \ˈ=,=-\ *n* **:** a large dark-colored short-tailed rat (genus *Mastacomys*) of southern Australia and Tasmania
broad tuning *n* **:** FLAT TUNING
¹broadway *or* **broadways** \ˈ=,=\ *adv* [*¹broad* + *-way* or *-ways*] **:** BROADWISE
²broadway \ˈ=,=\ *n* [*¹broad* + *way*] **:** a wide road or street **:** HIGHWAY
³broadway \ˈ=,=\ *n* [fr. *Broadway*, street in New York City on or near which are located most of New York's legitimate theaters] **:** the New York commercial theater and amusement world
broad·way·ite \ˈ=,=,īt\ *n* -S *usu cap* [*Broadway*, street in New York City + E *-ite*] **:** an habitué of Broadway **:** one that works in or frequents New York professional theaters
broadwife \ˈ=,=\ *n, pl* **broadwives** [*broad* (fr. *abroad*, prob. after E *alive: live*) + *wife*] **:** a female slave whose husband belonged to another master in the slaveholding states of the U.S.

broad-winged hawk also **broad-wing hawk** \'≠,≠-\ n : a common American hawk (*Buteo platypterus*) that is dark brown above with lower parts white streaked with brown

broadwise \'≠,≠\ adv (or adj) : in the direction of the breadth : with broad side foremost

brob \'bräb\ n -s [perh. alter. of *brod*] : a brad-shaped spike to be driven alongside the end of an abutting timber to prevent its slipping

brob·ding·nag·ian also **brob·dig·nag·ian** \ˌbräbdiŋ'nagēən, -dig'n-, -naig- also -näg- sometimes -də'n-\ adj, usu cap [*Brobdingnag*, imaginary country inhabited by giants in *Gulliver's Travels*, by Jonathan Swift †1745 Eng. satirist + E -*ian*] : characteristic or suggestive of Brobdingnag or its people : marked by tremendous size ⟨the shape of Italy suggests a *Brobdingnagian* boot⟩ syn see HUGE

¹**bro·cade** \brō'kād sometimes attributively '≠,≠\ n -s [Sp *brocado*, fr. Catal *brocat*, fr. It *broccato*, fr. past part. of *broccare* to brocade, spur, fr. *brocco* small nail, projecting tooth, fr. L *broccus* projecting (of teeth)] **1** : a rich oriental silk fabric with raised patterns embroidered in gold and silver threads **2** : a clothing and decorating fabric usu. of silk, rayon, or cotton woven in jacquard construction and characterized by allover formal patterns of slightly raised floral and figure designs that are introduced by additional weft threads

²**brocade** \(')≠'≠\ vt -ED/-ING/-S : to weave patterns into (as a fabric) or to work in (a design) in the manner of a brocade

bro·cad·ed \(')brō'kādəd\ adj **1** : having the weave of a brocade : embellished or embroidered with a raised pattern (as in brocade) **2** : dressed in brocade : richly dressed

bro·card \(')brō'kärd, 'bräkərd, 'brōkərd\ n -s [F, fr. ML *brocardum*, irreg. fr. *Burchardus* Burchard †1025 Ger. bishop who compiled a book of ecclesiastical canons] : an elementary principle or maxim : a short proverbial rule (as in law, ethics, or metaphysics)

bro·ca's aphasia \(')brō'käz-, 'brōkəz-\ n, usu cap B [after Paul *Broca* †1880 Fr. surgeon] : MOTOR APHASIA

broca scale n, usu cap B : a color chart for rating skin color

broca's convolution or **broca's gyrus** or **broca's area** n, usu cap B [prob. trans. of F *circonvolution de Broca*, fr. Paul *Broca*] : CONVOLUTION OF BROCA

broca's point n, usu cap B : the mid-point of the external auditory meatus

broc·a·telle also **broc·a·tel** \ˌbräkə'tel, -rōk-\ n -s [F *brocatelle*, fr. It *broccatello*, dim. of *broccato* brocade] : a stiff formal decorating fabric of brocade construction and design distinguished from brocade by patterns in high relief

broc·co·li or **broc·o·li** \'bräk(ə)lē, -li also -kl-\ n -s [It *broccoli*, pl. of *broccolo* flowering top of a cabbage or turnip, dim. of *brocco* sprout, small nail, projecting tooth — more at BROCADE] **1** : a cauliflower that is larger, hardier, and a better keeper than the common cauliflower — called also *heading broccoli* **2** : a branching cauliflower sometimes considered a separate variety (*Brassica oleracea italica*) that produces a head of functional florets at the end of each main branch which is cut for food while the florets are tight green or purplish buds and is usu. succeeded by smaller heads on secondary branches — called also *sprouting broccoli*

broccoli brown n : a brownish gray that is yellower, lighter, and stronger than taupe, yellower and lighter than chocolate, and lighter and stronger than castor — called also *goat, loam, plover, rabbit*

broccoli rab \-ˌrab\ n, pl **broccoli rabs** [prob. modif. of It *broccoli di rapa* flowering tops of the turnip] : ITALIAN TURNIP

¹**broch** obs var of BROOCH

²**broch** \'bräk, 'brək\ n -s [Sc *broch, bruch*, lit., borough, fr. ME (Sc) *brugh* borough, alter. of ME *burgh* — more at BOROUGH] **1** Scot : a luminous ring around the moon popularly regarded as an omen of bad weather **2** : one of the prehistoric circular stone towers found on the Orkney and Shetland islands and the Scottish mainland and usu. consisting of double walls enclosing small apartments about a central court

broch·an \'bräkən\ n -s [ScGael *brochan* & IrGael *brachān, brochān*] Scot & Irish : porridge or gruel usu. made with oatmeal

bro·chant·ite \brō'shän,tīt\ n -s [A. J. F. M. *Brochant* de Villiers †1840 Fr. geologist + E -*ite*] : a mineral $Cu_4SO_4(OH)_6$ consisting of a basic copper sulfate occurring in emerald-green orthorhombic crystals or massive (hardness 3.5–4, sp.gr. 3.91)

¹**broche** archaic var of BROACH

²**broche** \'brōsh\ n -s [F, pointed tool — more at ¹BROACH] **1** : BROCHETTE 1 **2** : a bobbin or shuttle used in handweaving of tapestry

³**bro·ché** \(')brō'shā\ adj [F, fr. past part. of *brocher* to brocade, sew, fr. MF, to prick — more at ²BROACH] : woven with a raised figure

⁴**broché** \"\ n -s [F, fr. *broché*, adj.] **1** : BROCADE 1 **2** : a fabric (as a shirting or suiting) with a pinstripe or hairline in the warp **3** : a silk or rayon fabric of the brocade type with small designs woven in by swivel shuttles and often combining a plain-woven ground with pile-weave designs

bro·chet de mer \brō'shādə'me(ə)r\ n, pl **brochets de mer** \-shā(z)d-\ [F, lit., sea pike] : a snook (*Centropomus undecimalis*)

bro·chette \brō'shet\ n -s [F, fr. OF *brochete*, fr. *broche* spit, pointed tool + -*ete* -ette — more at ¹BROACH] **1** : a small spit : SKEWER; also : meat broiled on a skewer **2** : a bar pin for medals, ribbons, decorations

broch·i·dod·ro·mous \ˌbräkə'dädrəməs\ also **bro·chid·o·drome** \brō'kidə,drōm\ adj [NL *brochidodromus*, fr. Gk *brochid-, brochis* small noose (dim. of *brochos* noose) + NL -*o-* + -*dromus* -dromous — more at MERMIS] of a leaf nerve : forming loops (as in members of the genera *Aristolochia, Olea, Sapindus*)

bro·cho \'brō(,)kō, -ˌkə\ n -s [Yiddish, *brokhe, brokho*, fr. Heb *bĕrākhāh* blessing] : BERAKAH

brocht Scot var of BROUGHT

bro·chure \(')brō'shu̇(ə)r, -ùə sometimes 'brōshə(r)\ n -s [F, fr. *brocher* to stitch, sew + -*ure*] : PAMPHLET, BOOKLET; also : a treatise or article published in such form

bro·chym·e·na \brō'kimənə\ n, cap [NL, perh. irreg. fr. Gk (Aeol) *brochys* short (akin to Gk *brachys* short) + Gk *hymen-, hymēn* membrane, insect wing — more at ¹BRIEF, HYMEN] : a widely distributed genus of pentatomid bugs that are predators on phytophagous insects

brock \'bräk\ n -s [ME, fr. OE *broc*, of Celt origin; akin to W *broch* badger, OIr *brocc*] **1** : BADGER **2** now dial chiefly Brit : FELLOW — used as a generalized term of abuse

brock·age \'bräkij\ n -s [E dial. *brock* rubbish, refuse, scrap of food, broken piece (fr. ME *broc* break in the skin) + E -*age* — more at BROKE] : an imperfectly minted coin

brock·ed \'bräkit\ adj [earlier Sc *brokit*, prob. alter. of *brukit* streaked with black, fr. ME (Sc) *brukit, brukyd* — more at BROOKED] **1** chiefly Scot, of an animal : striped or spotted with black and white **2** Scot, of a person : streaked with dirt

brock·en specter or **brocken bow** \'bräkən-\ n, usu cap B [fr. *Brocken*, peak in the Harz mountains, Germany; *Brocken specter*, trans. of G *brockengespenst*] : an optical phenomenon sometimes seen from the summit of mountains or from an aircraft when the observer is between the sun and a mass of cloud, the figures of the observer and surrounding objects being seen projected on the cloud much enlarged and often encircled by rainbow colors — compare GLORY 6a (3)

brock·et \'bräkət\ n -s [ME *broket*, prob. modif. of ONF *brocard, brocart* fallow deer a year old, fr. (assumed) ONF *broque* tine of an antler (akin to OF *broche* tine of an antler, pointed tool) + MF -*ard*, -*art* — more at -ARD] **1** : a male red deer two years old — compare PRICKET 2a **2** : any of several small So. American deer that have unbranched horns and are generally regarded as constituting the genus *Mazama*

brock-faced \'≠,≠\ adj : marked with a white streak on the face like a badger

brock·le-face \'bräkəl,fās\ n [obs E dial. *brockle* (alter. of E dial. *brocked*) + E *face*] : an animal having blotches of colored hair on an otherwise white face

brocoli var of BROCCOLI

bro·cot suspension \brə'kō-, 'brō,kō-\ n, usu cap B [after Achille *Brocot* †1878 Fr. horologist] : a clock-pendulum suspension in which the clock can be regulated from the front of the dial

¹**brod** \'bräd\ n -s [ME, brad, goad, fr. ON *broddr* spike, sting; akin to OE *brord* point, OHG *brort* edge, W *brathu* to sting, stab, Russ *brozda* bridle, bit, OE *byrst* bristle — more at BRISTLE] now dial Brit : any of various objects having a pointed end (as a goad, prod, thorn, awl)

²**brod** \"\ vt **brodded; brodded; brodding; brods** [ME *brodden*, fr. *brod*, n.] now dial Brit : GOAD, PROD

brode·glass \'brōd+,-\ n [alter. of BROAD GLASS] : CYLINDER GLASS

bro·de·quin \'brōdəkən, -räd-\ n -s [alter. (influenced by F *brodequin*) of earlier *brodekin, brodkin*, fr. ME *brodkyn*, fr. MF *brodequin*, alter. (influenced by *broder* to embroider) of *brosequin*, of non-IE origin; prob. akin to the source of MF *broissequin*, a sometimes fawn-colored cloth — more at BUSKIN, BROIDER] : BUSKIN; specif : a high shoe once worn by women

bro·der·er \'brōdərə(r)\ n -s usu cap [ME *broderere, brouderere*, fr. *broderen, brouderen* to embroider (modif. of MF *broder, brouder*) + -*ere* -er] : a member of the London City company that represents the guild of embroiderers

bro·de·rie \brō'drē\ n -s [F — more at BROIDERY] : EMBROIDERY; specif : a style of pottery decoration originating at Rouen, France

bro·de·rie an·glaise \-ˌäⁿ'glāz\ n [F, lit., English embroidery] : an embroidery with eyelet and cutwork designs now usu. machine-made and worked in white on white

bro·di·aea \ˌbrōdē'ēə\ n [NL, irreg. fr. J. *Brodie* †1824 Scot. botanist] **1** cap : a genus of western No. American bulbous plants (family Liliaceae) with basal leaves like grass and variously colored flowers **2** -s : a plant of the genus *Brodiaea*

bro·die \'brōdē\ n -s sometimes cap [after Steve *Brodie* fl1886 Am. newsboy who claimed to have jumped off the Brooklyn Bridge] **1** slang : DIVE : suicidal leap ⟨do a ~⟩ **2** slang : FALL, FAILURE : BONER ⟨pull a ~⟩ : FLOP

brod·mann area \'brädmən-\ or **brod·mann's area** \-nz-\ n, usu cap B [after Korbinian *Brodmann* †1918 Ger. anatomist] : one of the several structurally distinguishable and presumably functionally distinct regions into which the cortex of each cerebral hemisphere can be divided

broenner's acid usu cap B, var of BRÖNNER'S ACID

¹**brog** \'bräg\ n -s [ME, perh. alter. of *brod*] now chiefly Scot : a pointed instrument: **a** : AWL **b** : GOAD

²**brog** \"\ vt **brogged; brogged; brogging; brogs** now chiefly Scot : PROD, GOAD

bro·gan \'brōgən also brō'gan or 'brō,gan or -aa(ə)n\ also **brogan shoe** n -s [IrGael *brōgan*, dim. of *brōg* shoe — more at BROGUE] : a heavy shoe; esp : a coarse leather work shoe reaching to the ankle — compare BROGUE 1

brög·ger·ite \'brəgə,rīt\ n -s [Sw *bröggerit*, fr. W. C. *Brögger* †1940 Norw. mineralogist + Sw -*it* -ite] : a thorium-bearing variety of uraninite $(U,Th)O_2$ occurring in octahedral crystals (sp. gr. 9.03)

brogh \'bräk, 'brək\ var of BROCH

¹**brogue** \'brōg\ n -s [origin unknown] Scot : TRICK, PRANK

²**brogue** \"\ n -s [IrGael & ScGael *brōg*, fr. MIr *brōc*, fr. ON *brōk* leg covering — more at BREECH] **1** or **brogue shoe a** : a stout coarse shoe made orig. of half-dressed or untanned leather fastened with thongs and worn formerly in parts of Ireland and in the Scottish Highlands **b** : a heavy shoe often having a hobnailed sole : BROGAN **c** : a stout oxford shoe with ornamental foxing and perforations; esp : one having a wing tip **2 brogues** pl, obs : TROUSERS, LEGGINGS

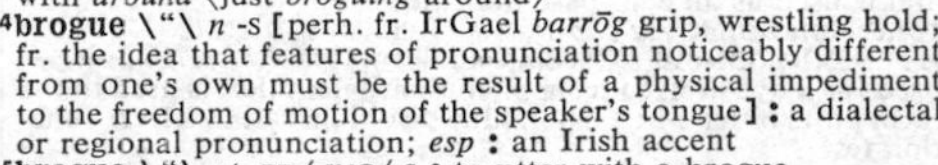

brogue 1c

³**brogue** \"\ vi **brogued; brogued; broguing; brogues** **1** : to walk in brogues **2** chiefly Midland : to go about idly : LOAF — used often with *around* ⟨just *broguing* around⟩

⁴**brogue** \"\ n -s [perh. fr. IrGael *barrōg* grip, wrestling hold; fr. the idea that features of pronunciation noticeably different from one's own must be the result of a physical impediment to the freedom of motion of the speaker's tongue] : a dialectal or regional pronunciation; esp : an Irish accent

⁵**brogue** \"\ vt -ED/-ING/-S : to utter with a brogue

brogued vamp \'brōgd-\ n [²*brogue* + -*ed*] : a vamp having a long usu. perforated tip extension along each side of the shoe

brogue hole \'brōg-\ n [*brogue* (prob. alter. of ¹*brog*) + *hole*] : a vent in a tin can for the escape of steam and air while in an autoclave

brogu·er \'brōgə(r)\ n -s [*brogue* (fr. *brogue hole*) + -*er*] : a solderer of brogue holes

brogu·ery \'brōg(ə)rē\ n -ES [⁴*brogue* + -*ery*] : the use of a dialectal or regional pronunciation; esp : the use of an Irish accent

brogu·ing \'brōgiŋ\ n -s [²*brogue* + -*ing*] : an ornamentation of shoes employing heavy perforations and pinkings

broh var of BRUH

broid obs var of BRAID

broi·der \'bròidə(r)\ vt -ED/-ING/-S [ME *broideren*, modif. (prob. influenced by ME *broiden, broyden*, past part. of *breyden* to weave together) of MF *broder, brouder*, fr. OF *brosder*, of Gmc origin; akin to OE *brord* point, OHG *brort* edge — more at BROD, BRAID] : EMBROIDER ⟨they shall make . . . ~*ed* coat —Exod 28:4 (AV)⟩

broi·der·er \-dərə(r)\ n -s [ME *broiderere* embroiderer, fr. *broideren* + -*ere* -er] archaic : EMBROIDERER

broi·dery \-d(ə)rē\ n -ES [ME *broiderie*, modif. (prob. influenced by ME *broiden, broyden*) of MF *broderie, brouderie*, fr. *broder, brouder* + -*erie* -ery] : EMBROIDERY

broigne \'brȯin\ n -s [OF, of Gmc origin; akin to OHG *brunia, brunna* coat of mail — more at BYRNIE] : a medieval defensive garment consisting of leather or woven fabric on which were sewed metal rings or plates

¹**broil** \'brȯil, esp bef pause or cons -ȯiəl\ vb -ED/-ING/-S [ME *broilen*, fr. MF *bruler* to burn, modif. (perh. resulting from incorrect division of L *amb-ustulare* to roast as *am-bustulare*) of L *ustulare* to scorch, singe, fr. *ustus*, past part. of *urere* to burn — more at EMBER, AMBI-] vt **1** obs : BURN, CHAR **2** : to cook by direct exposure to radiant heat (as on a grill over live coals or beneath a gas flame or electric coil) **3** : to subject to great heat ~ vi : to become subject to the action of heat (as of meat over a fire) : to become greatly heated or made uncomfortable with heat (as of a person in hot sunlight)

²**broil** \"\ n -s **1** : the act or state of broiling : an excessive heat **2** : something broiled (as a broiled steak) : GRILL

³**broil** \"\ vb -ED/-ING/-S [ME *broilen*, fr. MF *brouiller* to mix, confuse, fr. OF *broillier*, fr. *breu* broth — more at BREWIS] vt **1** obs : to mix confusedly : involve in confusion : AGITATE ⟨~*ed* with melancholy —Thomas More⟩ **2** : to entangle in a quarrel or brawl : EMBROIL ~ vi : to engage in a broil : BRAWL, QUARREL

⁴**broil** \"\ n -s : a confused or noisy disturbance : TUMULT; esp : QUARREL syn see BRAWL

broil·er \-ȯilə(r)\ n -s [¹*broil* + -*er*] **1** : one that broils: as **a** : a utensil (as a grill) or an appliance used in broiling **b** : a compartment in a gas or electric stove with heat supplied overhead and a drip pan beneath **c** : a cook who specializes in the broiling of foods **2** : a chicken or other bird fit for broiling; esp : a young chicken weighing up to 2½ pounds dressed **3** : a very hot day **4** : a partly developed mushroom with the cap not fully expanded — compare BUTTON

broil·er·man \-mən\ n, pl **broilermen** : one engaged in raising broilers on a commercial scale

broil·ing·ly adv : in a broiling manner

bro·kage \'brōkij\ n -s [prob. fr. AF *brocage*, fr. (assumed) AF *brocour* broker, after such pairs as MF *pillour, pilleur* pillager: *pillage* — more at BROKER] archaic : BROKERAGE

¹**broke** \'brōk\ n -s [ME *broc* break in the skin, fr. OE *broc* trouble, fragment, fr. *brecan* to break — more at BREAK] **1** archaic : something broken off : a fragment (as of kitchen leavings) **2** obs : a break (as in the skin) : WOUND **3** : paper that becomes unfit for use during any part of its manufacture ⟨wet ~ is from the presses of the paper machine; dry ~ may come from calenders, winders, sorting tables⟩ **4 brokes** pl : SKIRTINGS **5** : a grade of tobacco having damaged leaves

²**broke** \"\ adj [ME, alter. of *broken*] **1** chiefly dial : BROKEN **2** : without money or resources : PENNILESS, BANKRUPT **3 a** of an animal : tamed and trained to a particular function or activity ⟨a halter-*broke* horse⟩ **b** of a person : forced to conform or adapt ⟨the old woman's ~ to my ways now⟩

³**broke** past and substand past part of BREAK

⁴**broke** vi -ED/-ING/-S [prob. back-formation fr. *broker*] obs : NEGOTIATE, TRAFFIC, DEAL

¹**bro·ken** \'brōkən sometimes -kᵊŋ\ adj [ME, fr. OE *brocen*, fr. past part. of *brecan* to break] **1** : violently separated into parts : in a state resulting from breaking : in fragments : SHATTERED ⟨a vase ~ by a fall⟩ ⟨~ bits of glass⟩ **2** : damaged or altered by or as if by breaking: as **a** of body parts : FRACTURED, RUPTURED ⟨a ~ leg⟩; often : having the surface interrupted or flawed (as by a cut or blow) ⟨there'll be more than one ~ head before morning⟩ **b** obs : TORN, RENT — used chiefly of fabrics **c** of land or land surfaces : rough and irregular, interrupted (as by cliffs and ravines), or full of obstacles to passage (as rocks, ledges, or gullies) ⟨a ~ country full of springs and streams⟩ ⟨a long ~ ridge⟩ **d** : violated by transgression : with integrity destroyed ⟨a ~ promise⟩ **e** : made discontinuous or altered in direction (as by bending or refraction) ⟨the ~ antennae of most weevils⟩ ⟨light rays ~ by a prism⟩; sometimes : ZIGZAG ⟨following a ~ course⟩ **f** : INTERRUPTED, DISCONTINUOUS ⟨a ~ sleep⟩ ⟨the ~ pattern of his thoughts⟩ **g** of weather : UNSETTLED; also, of clouds : overspreading much but not all of the sky **h** : disrupted by change ⟨a home ~ by sickness⟩ **i** of a plant or flower : affected with break ⟨a ~ tulip⟩ **j** of cream : separating into large aggregates when shaken due to the action of certain bacteria **k** of an animal's coat : MOLTING **3** : reduced in condition: as **a** : made weak or infirm (as by disease, age, or hardships) **b** : SUBDUED, CRUSHED ⟨a ~ spirit⟩ **c** : ruined financially : BANKRUPT **d** : made submissive : trained for use ⟨a well-*broken* horse⟩ **e** : cashiered or reduced in rank ⟨he was ~ from sergeant to private⟩ : ruined officially or professionally ⟨his career was ~ by the scandal⟩ **f** Scot : declared an outlaw ⟨apprehend all such freebooters and ~ men⟩ **4** : DISCONNECTED : not continuous: as **a** : uttered hesitantly and disjointedly on account of emotion ⟨a few ~ words at parting⟩ **b** : imperfectly spoken or written esp. by a foreigner ⟨~ English⟩ **5 a** archaic : forming or consisting of remnants or leavings esp. when fragmentary ⟨~ beer⟩ ⟨~ meats⟩ **b** : not complete ⟨a ~ line of goods⟩ or completely full ⟨a ~ bale of wool⟩; often : containing fewer than the standard number of sheets or boards but not necessarily of poor quality ⟨as ~ ream⟩ ⟨a ~ bundle⟩ ⟨a ~ carton⟩ **6** of paper : of uneven quality (as when soiled or spotted more than retree) **7 a** of a color : dulled by an admixture of gray : SADDENED; also : produced by blending of primary colors **b** of color effects in painting : produced by laying component color elements side by side on canvas or other surface so that at a distance they appear to blend **c** : consisting of two usu. discrete colors — used chiefly of animal eyes and coats ⟨a ~ red and black coat⟩ **8** of a vowel sound : diphthongized by breaking **9** of a twill weave : having the diagonal lines reversed at regular intervals to produce a zigzag effect — compare HERRINGBONE **10** of a noun plural in Arabic : distinguished from the singular by a difference in vowel sounds

²**broken** \"\ n -s : BROKE 3 — used chiefly in paper mills

broken arch n : a decorative arch (as over a door or in the top of a piece of furniture) with a gap at the apex of the curve that is usu. occupied by some decorative feature

broken ashlar n : ashlar in which the stones are rectangular but of different sizes and shapes

broken-backed \'≠≠'≠\ adj [ME, fr. *broken* + *backed*] : having a broken back: as **a** of a ship : HOGGED, SAGGED : so weakened as to droop at each end **b** of a horse : having bones of the back or loins ankylosed or united by a bony growth

broken-backed line n : a line truncated in the middle — used esp. of many lines in the verse of John Lydgate that have usu. nine syllables and appear to lack an unstressed syllable at the medial break or caesura

broken bank note n : a note issued by a bank, business firm, or other legal body before the issue of an authorized U.S. paper currency in 1861

broken-bone fever \'≠≠,≠-\ n : DENGUE

broken coal n : a size of anthracite coal; also : coal of this size — see ANTHRACITE table

broken consort n : a group of musical instruments of different families ⟨a *broken consort* of viols and flutes⟩

broken-down \'≠≠'≠\ adj : infirm or worn to the point of breaking (as in strength, force, power, health, morals, or structure)

broken field n, football : the area beyond the line of scrimmage where defensive players are rather widely scattered ⟨a good *broken field* runner⟩

broken heart n **1** : a state of extreme grief and depression **2** : rupture of the heart muscle (as after myocardial infarction)

brokenhearted \ˌ≠≠'≠≠\ adj : having the spirits depressed : crushed by grief or despair — **bro·ken·heart·ed·ly** adv — **bro·ken·heart·ed·ness** n -ES

broken-kneed \'≠≠'≠\ adj : characterized by or suffering from broken knees

broken knees n pl : the injured or abnormal knees of a horse that falls frequently while in action

broken line n **1** : a line composed of a series of dashes; often : a guide line painted in dashes on a highway to indicate a stretch on which a driver may lawfully cross the midline of the way (as in passing another vehicle) **2** : a line made up of straight lines that join a number of given points taken in some specified order

broken lot n : a lot of less than 100 shares of stock : ODD LOT

bro·ken·ly adv : in a broken manner; esp : with the voice unsteady from emotion or shock

broken-mouth \'≠≠, in "dentition" sense '≠≠,≠\ n : an old sheep that has become broken-mouthed; also : the faulty dentition of such a sheep

broken-mouthed \'≠≠'≠\ adj : having lost some of the teeth — used chiefly of old sheep

broken music n **1** : music in parts **2** : music by different families of instruments sounding together

bro·ken·ness \'brōkən(n)əs\ n -ES : the quality or state of being broken

broken octave n : SHORT OCTAVE

broken pediment n : a pediment frequent in the baroque style having a gap at the apex (as for a statue or vase)

broken reed n : something or someone that fails when relied on for support or help

broken rhyme n **1** : rhyme in which one of the rhyming elements is divided by the break or by a pause between two words (as in Lord Byron's rhyming ". . . Attic; all . . ." with "mathematical") **2** : rhyme involving division of a word by the break between two lines in order to end a line with a rhyme provided by the first part of the word (as in G. M. Hopkins's dividing *king-/dom* to rhyme *king-* with *wing*)

broken stowage n : stowage of cargo with vacant spaces left in it

broken stripe n : a figure in wood (as veneer) produced when interwoven grain is quarter-cut breaking the strips at irregular intervals — compare RIBBON FIGURE

broken transit n : a transit whose axis forms part of the right-angled telescope tube, the eyepiece remaining stationary at one end of the horizontal axis

broken-up \'≠≠'≠\ adj, of a dog's face : having a projecting jaw, the nose short and set well back, a deep stop, and wrinkles

broken wind n : HEAVES — **broken-winded** \'≠≠'≠≠\ adj

¹**bro·ker** \'brōkə(r)\ n -s [ME *brokour, broker*, fr. (assumed) AF *brocour* (akin to ONF *brokieres* one that sells wine from the tap, AF *brogour* untrustworthy dealer), fr. (assumed) ONF *broquier* to tap (a cask) (akin to OF *brochier* to tap), fr. *broque* tap of a cask (akin to OF *broche* tap of a cask, pointed tool) — more at BROACH] **1** : NEGOTIATOR, INTERMEDIARY ⟨Sir Winston's offers of his good services as ~ between East and West —Max Ascoli⟩: as **a** : a go-between in affairs of love or sex; esp : an agent professionally engaged in the arrangement of marriages — called also *marriage broker* **b** (1) : an agent middleman who for a fee or commission negotiates contracts of purchase and sale (as of real estate, commodities, or securities) between buyers and sellers without himself taking title to that which is the subject of negotiation and usu. without

having physical possession of it — often used with a qualifying attributive ⟨dealings with a produce ~⟩ ⟨wool ~s⟩ ⟨busy stock*brokers*⟩; compare DEALER, STOCKJOBBER (2) : CUSTOMER'S BROKER **c** *archaic* : a person entrusted with the transmission of information : MESSENGER, INTERPRETER **2** : DEALER: as **a** *Brit* : a dealer in secondhand goods; *sometimes* : one that buys and sells the loot of thieves **b** : a dealer who for his own profit negotiates purchases and sales (as of negotiable instruments or commodities) himself taking or holding title to and often physical possession of that which is the subject of negotiation but usu. not altering or processing it — not used technically in fields in which a broker is primarily an agent; compare STOCKJOBBER, PROCESSOR **3** *Brit* : a person licensed to appraise or sell household distrained goods

²**broker** \"\ *vt* **brokered; brokered; brokering** \-k(ə)riŋ\ **brokers** : to function as a broker in respect to ⟨~*ed* a deal⟩

bro·ker·age \'brōk(ə)rij, -krēj\ *n* -S [ME, fr. *brokour, broker* broker + *-age*] **1** : the business of a broker **2** : the fee or commission for transacting business as a broker

bro·ker·ly \-kə(r)lē\ *adv* : in the manner of a broker

brokers' board *n* : a stock exchange open only to member brokers of that exchange

broker's loan *n* **1** : a loan by a bank to a stock-exchange broker secured by negotiable securities **2 brokers' loans** *pl* : the aggregate amount of money loaned to brokers (as in the New York market) at any given time

brokery *n* -ES [¹*broker* + *-y*] **1** *obs* : BROKERAGE 1, AGENCY 3; *sometimes* : shrewd, rascally, or dishonest dealing **2** *obs* : secondhand goods

brokes *pl of* BROKE

¹**brok·ing** \'brōkiŋ, -kēŋ\ *n* -S [fr. gerund of ⁴*broke*] **1** : BROKERAGE 1 **2** *obs* : PAWNBROKING; *sometimes* : tricky or dishonest dealing

²**broking** \"\ *adj* [fr. pres. part. of ⁴*broke*] **1** *obs* : base-dealing : CONTEMPTIBLE, GRASPING **2** : of or relating to brokerage

brol·ga \'brälgə\ *n* -S [native name in Australia] : a pale gray crestless Australian crane (*Grus rubicunda*) that is generally seen in pairs and has a habit of gathering in groups and moving about as if dancing — called also *native companion*

brol·ly \'bräli\ *n* -ES [by shortening & alter. fr. *umbrella*] *Brit* : UMBRELLA; *also, slang* : PARACHUTE

brom- *or* **bromo-** *comb form* [ISV, prob. fr. F *brome* bromine, fr. Gk *brōmos* bad smell] **1** : bromine ⟨*brom*hydrate⟩ ⟨*bromo*prene⟩ **2** *now usu bromo-* : containing bromine in place of hydrogen — in names of organic compounds ⟨*bromo*acetic acid⟩ **3** *now usu bromo-* : containing bromine regarded as replacing hydroxyl or oxygen or as coordinated to a central atom — in names of inorganic acids and salts ⟨*bromo*auric acid⟩ **4** : containing bromine as bromide and sometimes replacing another element or group — in names of minerals and salts occurring as minerals

bromacetone *var of* BROMOACETONE

brom·ar·gy·rite \brō'märjə,rīt\ *n* -S [F, fr. *brom-* + *argyr-* (fr. NL) + *-ite*] : BROMYRITE

¹**bro·mate** \'brō,māt, *usu* -ād·+V\ *n* -S [prob. fr. G *bromat*, fr. *brom-* + *-at* -ate] : a salt of bromic acid

²**bromate** \"\ *vt* -ED/-ING/-S **1** : to treat with a bromate, usu. potassium bromate ⟨*bromated* flour⟩ **2** : BROMINATE — **bro·ma·tion** \brō'māshən\ *n* -S

bro·ma·tium \brō'māsh(ē)əm\ *n, pl* **broma·tia** \-(ē)ə\ [NL, fr. Gk *brōmation* morsel, dim. of *brōmat-, brōma* food, fr. *bibrōskein* to eat, devour — more at VORACIOUS] : one of the swollen globular hyphal tips that develop on certain fungi when grown in their nests by ants and that are used as food by the ants

brombenzyl cyanide *var of* BROMOBENZYL CYANIDE

bromcresol green *var of* BROMOCRESOL GREEN

bromcresol purple *var of* BROMOCRESOL PURPLE

brome·grass \'brōm,=\ *or* **brome** *n, pl* **bromegrasses** *or* **bromes** [NL *Bromus*] : any grass of the genus *Bromus* — see AWNLESS BROMEGRASS

bro·me·lain \'brōmələn, -,lān\ *or* **bro·me·lin** \-lən, brō'mē-\ *n* -S [*bromelain* by alter. (influenced by *papain*) of *bromelin*, fr. NL *Bromelia*, genus name of the pineapple in some classifications + E *-in*] *biochem* : a proteinase obtained from the juice of the pineapple

bro·me·lia \brō'mēlyə, -lēə\ *n* [NL, fr. Olaf *Bromelius* †1705 Swed. botanist + NL *-ia*] **1** *cap* : the type genus of Bromeliaceae comprising tropical American plants with deeply cleft calyx that are often placed in the genus *Ananas* **2** -S : any plant of the genus *Bromelia; broadly* : BROMELIAD

bro·me·li·a·ce·ae \brō,mēlē'āsē,ē\ *n pl, cap* [NL, fr. *Bromelia*, type genus + *-aceae*] : a family of tropical American epiphytic or terrestrial herbs or subshrubs (order Xyridales) that have basal often spiny leaves and flowers in dense spikes, panicles, or heads with large often colored bracts and that include several plants (as the pineapple) of economic importance — **bro·me·li·a·ceous** \brō,mēlē'āshəs\ *adj*

bro·me·li·ad \brō'mēlē,ad\ *also* **bro·mel** \'brōməl\ *n* -S [*bromeliad* fr. NL *Bromelia* + E *-ad; bromel* short for *bromeliad*] : a plant of the family Bromeliaceae

bro·mell·ite \brō'me,līt, 'brämə,l-\ *n* -S [G *bromellit*, fr. Magnus von *Bromell* †1731 Swed. mineralogist + G *-it* -ite] : a mineral consisting of beryllium oxide occurring in white hexagonal crystals

bro·mic \'brōmik\ *adj* [F *bromique*, fr. *brom-* + *-ique* -ic] : of, relating to, or containing bromine — used esp. of compounds in which this element is pentavalent

bromic acid *n* [ISV *bromic* + *acid*] : an unstable strongly oxidizing acid $HBrO_3$ analogous to chloric acid and known only in solution esp. in the form of its salts

¹**bro·mide** \'brō,mīd, *in sense 1 sometimes* -,məd\ *n* -S [ISV *brom-* + *-ide*] **1 a** : a binary compound of bromine and usu. a more electropositive element or a radical, some of these compounds (as potassium bromide) being used as sedatives : a salt or ester of hydrobromic acid **b** : a dose of bromide taken usu. as a sedative **2 a** : a conventional and commonplace or tiresome person : BORE, DULLARD **b** : a commonplace or hackneyed expression, generalization, or notion ⟨greeting card ~s⟩; *also* : a trite artistic or dramatic theme or device

²**bromide** \"\ *vt* -ED/-ING/-S : to treat with a bromide

bromide paper *n* : a sensitized paper coated with an emulsion layer composed chiefly of silver bromide suspended in gelatin — used in photography for enlargements or contact prints

bro·mid·ic \brō'midik\ *adj* **1** : characterized by bromides : TRITE, COMMONPLACE ⟨~ sermons⟩ ⟨a ~ remark⟩ **2** : given to uttering bromides : TIRESOME, UNORIGINAL ⟨a ~ versifier⟩ ⟨~ luncheon speakers⟩—**bro·mid·i·cal·ly** \-dək(ə)lē\ *adv*

bro·mid·i·om \brō'midēəm\ *n* -S [blend of ¹*bromide* and *idiom*] : BROMIDE 2b

bro·mid·ism \'brōmə,dizəm, -ō,mī,d-\ *n* -S [¹*bromide* + *-ism*] : BROMISM

bro·mi·dro·sis \,brōmə'drōsəs\ *also* **brom·hi·dro·sis** \" *sometimes* -mhi'd-\ *n, pl* **bromidro·ses** *or* **bromhidro·ses** \-ō,sēz\ [NL, fr. Gk *brōmos* bad smell + LGk *hidrōsis* perspiration, sweating, fr. Gk *hidroun* to sweat (fr. *hidrōs* sweat) + *-sis* — more at SWEAT] : foul-smelling sweat

bro·min·ate \'brōmə,nāt\ *vt* -ED/-ING/-S [*bromine* + *-ate*] : to treat or cause to combine with bromine or a compound of bromine : introduce bromine into (as an organic compound) — **bro·mi·na·tion** \,brōmə'nāshən\ *n* -S

bro·mine \'brō,mēn, -,mən\ *n* -S [F *brome* bromine + E *-ine* — more at BROM-] : a nonmetallic chiefly univalent and pentavalent element belonging to the halogens that is normally a deep red corrosive toxic liquid giving off an irritating reddish brown vapor of disagreeable odor, that occurs naturally only in combination in minute quantities in sea water and in many salt lakes, brines, and salt deposits from all of which it can be recovered (as by oxidation with chlorine and driving out of the bromine vapor by steam or air), and that is used chiefly in the manufacture of bromine compounds (as ethylene dibromide for antiknock gasoline), dyes, and pharmaceuticals — symbol *Br;* see ELEMENT table

bromine water *n* : a solution of bromine in water; *esp* : the red saturated solution

bro·min·ism \'brōmə,nizəm\ *n* -S [*bromine* + *-ism*] : BROMISM

bro·min·ize \-,nīz\ *vt* -ED/-ING/-S : BROMATE

bro·mism \'brō,mizəm\ *n* -S [ISV *brom-* + *-ism;* prob. orig. formed as F *bromisme*] : the abnormal state produced by overdosage with or prolonged use of bromides

brom·lite \'bräm,līt\ *n* -S [*Bromley* Hill (error for *Brownley Hill*, near Alston, Cumberland, England) + E *-ite*] : a mineral $BaCa(CO_3)_2$ midway between witherite and strontianite — called also *alstonite*

¹**bro·mo** \'brō(,)mō\ *n* -S [*brom-*] : any of certain proprietary effervescent mixtures used as headache remedies, sedatives, and alkalinizing agents; *often* : a dose of such a mixture

²**bromo** \"\ *adj* [*brom-*] : containing bromine — used esp. of organic compounds; compare BROM-

bro·mo- *in pronunciations below*, ¦== = ¦brō(,)mō *or* -,mə\ — see BROM-

bro·mo·acetone \¦==+\ *also* **brom·acetone** \(')brō¦m+,-\ *n* [ISV *brom-* + *acetone*] : a colorless lacrimatory not very stable liquid compound CH_3COCH_2Br made by the action of bromine on acetone

bromo acid *n* [²*bromo* + *acid*] : EOSIN 1a

bro·mo·benzene \¦== *at* BROMO- +\ *n* [ISV *brom-* + *benzene*] : a colorless oily liquid compound C_6H_5Br obtained usu. by bromination of benzene and used chiefly as a solvent and in organic synthesis

bro·mo·benzyl cyanide \¦==+ . . . -\ *also* **brom·benzyl cyanide** \(')brōm+¦ . . . -\ *n* [*brom-* + *benzyl cyanide*] : a light-yellow oily lacrimatory compound $C_6H_5CHBrCN$ having an odor of sour fruit that is made by brominating benzyl cyanide; α-bromo-phenyl-aceto-nitrile

bro·mo·cresol green \¦== *at* BROMO- + . . . -\ *also* **bromcresol green** *n* [ISV *brom-* + *cresol*] : a brominated acid dye of the sulfonephthalein series derived from *meta*-cresol that is obtained as a yellowish crystalline powder and is used as an acid-base indicator

bromocresol purple *also* **bromcresol purple** *n* : a brominated acid dye of the sulfonephthalein series derived from *ortho*-cresol that is obtained as a pinkish crystalline powder and is used as an acid-base indicator

bro·mo·form \'==+,fȯrm\ *n* -S [ISV *brom-* + *-form* (as in *chloroform*)] : a colorless heavy liquid compound $CHBr_3$ that is similar to chloroform in properties and methods of preparation and is used chiefly in separating minerals (as in assaying) and in organic synthesis; tribromo-methane

bro·mo·hy·drin \,==+'hīdrən\ *n* -S [ISV *brom-* + *-hydrin*] : any of various organic compounds that are analogous to the chlorohydrins but that contain bromine in place of chlorine

bro·moil \'brō,mȯi(ə)l\ *n* -S [*brom-* + *oil*] : a print made by the bromoil process

bromoil process *n* : a process of making an oil-pigmented photographic print by bleaching the silver image from a bromide print and applying an oil pigment to it with a special brush or roller so that the pigment sticks only on those parts where the silver has been

bromoil transfer *n* : a photographic print made by transferring under pressure the pigmented image of a bromoil print while still soft to another support

bro·mo·iodide \¦== *at* BROMO- +\ *n* [*brom-* + *-iodide*] : a compound or mixture containing anionic bromine and iodine ⟨silver ~ photographic emulsions⟩

bro·mo·met·ric \¦==+¦me·trik\ *adj* [ISV *bromometry* + *-ic*] : of or relating to bromometry — **bro·mo·met·ri·cal·ly** \-rək(ə)lē\ *adv*

bro·mom·e·try \brō'mämə·trē\ *n* -ES [ISV *brom-* + *-metry*] : quantitative analysis by the use of bromine — compare IODOMETRY

bro·mo·phenol blue \¦== *at* BROMO- + . . . -\ *also* **brom·phenol blue** \(')brōm + . . . -\ *n* [ISV *brom-* + *phenol*] : a dye $C_{19}H_{10}Br_4O_5S$ obtained as pinkish crystals and used as an acid-base indicator; tetrabromo-phenolsulfonephthalein

bromos *pl of* BROMO

bro·mo·thymol blue \¦==+...-\ *or* **brom·thymol blue** \(')brōm+...-\ *n* [ISV *brom-* + *thymol*] : a brominated dye $C_{27}H_{28}Br_2O_5S$ of the sulfonephthalein series derived from thymol that is obtained as a cream to rose colored powder and is used as an acid-base indicator

bromp·ton stock *usu cap B, var of* BRAMPTON STOCK

Brom·sul·phal·ein \¦brōm,səl'falēən, -fāl-\ *trademark* — used for a dye derived from phenolphthalein that is used in the form of its bitter white crystalline disodium salt in a liver function test

bro·mus \'brōməs\ *n, cap* [NL, fr. L *bromos* oats, fr. Gk] : a large genus of grasses (family Gramineae) that are native to temperate regions, comprise the bromegrasses, and have large often drooping spikelets and lemmas usu. awned near the 2-toothed apex

brom·vo·el \'bräm,füəl\ *or* **brom·vo·gel** \-ügəl\ *n* -S [obs. Afrik *bromvogel* (now *bromvoël*), fr. *brom* to grumble + *vogel* bird, fr. MD *vōghel;* akin to MD *brimmen, bremmen* to grumble, growl, OHG *brumman* and to OE *fugol* bird — more at FREMITUS, FOWL] : a southern African hornbill (*Bucorvus leadbeateri*) of large size and more or less terrestrial habits — called also *turkey buzzard*

bro·my·rite \'brōmə,rīt\ *n* -S [*brom-* + Gk argyros silver + E *-ite* — more at ARGENT] : a mineral consisting of native silver bromide AgBr yellow in color — called also *bromargyrite*

bronc \'bräŋk\ *n* -S [by shortening] : BRONCO

bronch- *or* **broncho-** *comb form* [prob. fr. F *bronch-, broncho-* trachea, throat, fr. LL *broncho-*, fr. Gk *bronch-, broncho-*, fr. *bronchos* — more at CRAW] **1** : throat ⟨*broncho*cele⟩ **2** : bronchial ⟨*bronch*itis⟩ ⟨*broncho*phony⟩ **3** : bronchial and ⟨*broncho*pulmonary⟩

bronchi *pl of* BRONCHUS

bronchi- *or* **bronchio-** *comb form* [prob. fr. NL *bronchi-*, fr. LL *bronchium*] : bronchia ⟨*bronchi*ectasis⟩ ⟨*bronchio*crisis⟩

bronchia *pl of* BRONCHIUM

bron·chi·al \'bräŋkēəl, *esp Brit* -ŋkyəl, *substand* -änəkəl *or* -ŋkəl *or* -ŋkəl\ *adj* [prob. fr. NL *bronchialis*, fr. LL *bronchium* + L *-alis* -al] : of, relating to, or associated with the bronchi or their ramifications in the lungs — **bron·chi·al·ly** \-ŋkēəlē, -li\ *adv*

bronchial artery *n* : any branch of the descending aorta or first intercostal artery that accompanies the bronchi

bronchial asthma *n* : asthma resulting from spasmodic contraction of bronchial muscles with constriction of the lumen of the bronchi and accumulation of mucus in the respiratory passages due to psychosomatic, allergic, or other causes

bronchial gland *n* : any of the lymphatic glands situated at the bifurcation of the trachea and along the bronchi

bronchial pneumonia *n* : BRONCHOPNEUMONIA

bronchial tree *n* : the bronchi together with their branches

bronchial tube *n* : a bronchus or any of its branches

bronchial vein *n* : any vein accompanying the bronchi and their branches and emptying into the azygos and superior intercostal veins

bron·chi·ectasis \¦bräŋkē, -äŋkē+\ *also* **bron·chi·ectasia** \"+\ *n, pl* **bronchiectases** *also* **bronchiectasias** [NL, fr. *bronchi-* + *ectasis*] : a chronic inflammatory or degenerative condition of one or more bronchi or bronchioles marked by dilatation and loss of elasticity of the walls — **bron·chi·ec·tat·ic** \+,ek¦tad·ik\ *adj*

bron·chio·gen·ic \¦bräŋkēō¦jenik, -änk-\ *adj* [*bronchi-* + *-genic*] : BRONCHOGENIC

bron·chi·o·lar \¦bräŋkē¦ōlə(r), -änk-; (')brän¦kīəl-, -äŋ¦-\ *adj* [*bronchiole* + *-ar*] : of, relating to, or affecting a bronchiole

bron·chi·ole \'bräŋkē,ōl, -änk-\ *n* -S [NL *bronchiolum*, dim. of LL *bronchium*] : a minute thin-walled branch of a bronchus; *esp* : one that terminates in one or more pulmonary alveoli

bron·chi·ol·itis \,bräŋkē(,)ō'līd·əs, -änk-\ *n* -ES [NL, fr. *bronchiolum* + *-itis*] : inflammation of the bronchioles

bron·chi·o·lus \brän'kīələs, -äŋ'-\ *n, pl* **bronchio·li** \-,lī\ [NL, prob. alter. of *bronchiolum*] : BRONCHIOLE

¹**bron·chit·ic** \(')brän¦kid·ik, -äŋ¦-, it|, |ēk\ *adj* [ISV *bronchit-* (fr. NL *bronchitis*) + *-ic*] : of, relating to, or affected with bronchitis

²**bronchitic** \"\ *n* -S : a bronchitic person

bron·chi·tis \brän'kīd·əs, -äŋ'-, -ītəs\ *n, pl* **bron·chit·i·des** \-kid·ə,dēz, -itə-\ [NL, fr. *bronch-* + *-itis*] : acute or chronic inflammation of the bronchial tubes or any part of them; *also* : any of several diseases of man or animals of which such inflammation is a characteristic feature — see INFECTIOUS BRONCHITIS

bron·chi·um \'bräŋkēəm\ *n, pl* **bron·chia** \-ēə\ [LL, fr. Gk *bronchion*, dim. of *bronchos*] : a branch of a bronchus; *esp* : one joining a primary bronchus to its bronchioles

¹**broncho** *var of* BRONCO

²**bron·cho** \'bräŋ(,)kō\ *n* -S [prob. fr. ¹*broncho*] : OLD ENGLISH BROWN

broncho- *in pronunciations below*, ¦== = ¦bräŋ(,)kō *or* -äŋ(- *or* -,kə\ — see BRONCH-

bron·cho·dilator \¦== *at* BRONCHO- +\ *n* -S [*bronch-* + *dilator*] : any drug that causes relaxation of bronchial muscle resulting in expansion of the air passages of the bronchi — **bron·cho·di·la·to·ry** \"+¦dī¦lād·ərē, -,dəʹl-\ *adj*

bron·cho·gen·ic \¦==+¦jenik\ *adj* [ISV *bronch-* + *-genic*] : relating to or arising in or by way of the air passages of the lungs ⟨~ spread of infection⟩ ⟨~ carcinoma⟩

bron·cho·gram \'==+,gram\ *n* -S [ISV *bronch-* + *-gram*] : a roentgenogram of the bronchial tree after injection of a radiopaque substance

bron·cho·graph·ic \¦==+¦grafik\ *adj* [ISV *bronchography* + *-ic*] : of, relating to, or produced by bronchography — **bron·cho·graph·i·cal·ly** \-fək(ə)lē\ *adv*

bron·chog·ra·phy \brän'kägrəfē, -äŋ'-\ *n* -ES [ISV *bronch-* + *-graphy*] : the roentgenographic visualization of the bronchial tree after injection of a radiopaque substance

bron·choph·o·ny \-äfənē\ *n* -ES [ISV *bronch-* + *-phony;* prob. orig. formed as F *bronchophonie*] : the sound of the voice heard through the stethoscope over a healthy bronchus and over other portions of the chest in cases of consolidation of the lung tissue — compare PECTORILOQUY

bron·cho·pneumonia \¦== *at* BRONCHO- +\ *n* [NL, fr. *bronch-* + *pneumonia*] : pneumonia involving many relatively small areas of the lung adjacent to the smaller bronchi — **bron·cho·pneumonic** \"+\ *adj*

bron·chor·rhea \,==+'rēə\ *n* -S [NL, fr. *bronch-* + *-rrhea*] : the excessive discharge of mucus from the air passages of the lung

¹**bron·cho·scope** \'==+,skōp\ *n* -S [ISV *bronch-* + *-scope*] : a tubular instrument equipped with a small electric lamp which may be passed through the trachea into the large bronchi and through which the bronchi may be inspected or instruments may be passed for the removal of foreign bodies or other purposes — **broncho·scop·ic** \¦== *at* BRONCHO-+¦skäpik\ *adj* — **bron·cho·scop·i·cal·ly** \-pək(ə)lē\ *adv* — **bron·chos·co·pist** \brän'käskəpəst, -äŋ'-\ *n* -S — **bron·chos·co·py** \-pē\ *n* -ES

²**bronchoscope** \"\ *vt* -ED/-ING/-S : to use a bronchoscope on (a patient)

bron·cho·spasm \'== *at* BRONCHO-+,-\ *n* -S [ISV *bronch-* + *spasm*] : constriction of the air passages of the lung by spasmodic contraction of the bronchial muscles (as in asthma) — **bron·cho·spastic** \¦==+¦-\ *adj*

bron·cho·spirometry \¦==+\ *n* -ES [ISV *bronch-* + *spirometry*] : independent measurement of the vital capacity of each lung by means of a spirometer in direct continuity with one of the primary bronchi

bron·cho·stenosis \¦==+\ *n* [NL, fr. *bronch-* + *stenosis*] : stenosis of a bronchus

bron·chus \'bräŋkəs\ *n, pl* **bron·chi** \-än,kī, -äŋ-, -,kē\ [NL, fr. Gk *bronchos* trachea, throat — more at CRAW] : either of the two primary divisions of the trachea that lead respectively into the right and the left lung and that are structurally similar to the trachea; *broadly* : any of the branches of each bronchus that ramify in the substance of the lung, exhibit increasing reduction and ultimate disappearance of cartilage in passing from the largest to the finest branches, and serve to connect the bronchioles with the primary bronchi and form a channel for the distribution of air in the lung

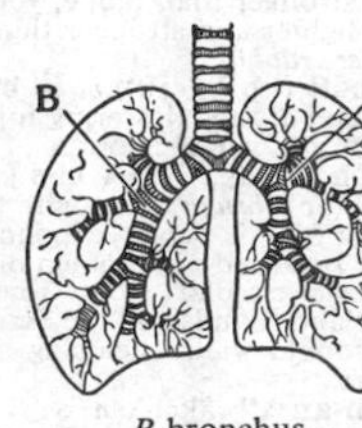

B bronchus

bron·co *also* **bron·cho** \'bräŋ(,)kō, -äŋ(-\ *n* -S [MexSp *bronco*, fr. Sp, rough, wild, fr. (assumed) VL *bruncus* knot in wood (whence It *bronco* stub of a branch, OProv *bronc* projection, roughness)] **1** : an unbroken or imperfectly broken range horse of western No. America; *sometimes* : a vicious or unbreakable horse or one trained to buck — compare CAYUSE **2** : any range horse : MUSTANG

broncobuster \'=(,)=,==\ *n* -S : one that breaks wild horses to the saddle

bronco grass *or* **broncho grass** *n* **1** : a European bromegrass (*Bromus rigidus gussoni*) adventive in Australia and southern Africa **2** *West* : CHEAT 3a

bronc peeler *n, West* : BRONCOBUSTER

broncs *pl of* BRONC

bron·i·cal *or* **bron·i·chal** *or* **bron·i·kal** *dial var of* BRONCHIAL

bronk \'bräŋk\ *n* -S [by shortening & alter.] : BRONCO

brö·ner's acid *or* **broen·ner's acid** \'brenə(r)z-, -rən-,-rōn-\ *n, usu cap B* [prob. fr. the name *Brönner*] : a colorless crystalline naphthylaminesulfonic acid $NH_2C_{10}H_6SO_3H$ used as a dye intermediate; 6-amino-2-naphthalenesulfonic acid

bront- *or* **bronto-** *comb form* [Gk, fr. *brontē;* akin to Gk *bremein* to roar, *bromos* loud noise] : thunder ⟨*bront*ide⟩ ⟨*bronto*meter⟩ — often in generic names esp. of large animals ⟨*Bront*ops⟩ ⟨*Bronto*therium⟩

bron·te·um \brän·'tēəm\ *also* **bron·te·on** \-ēən, -ē,än\ *n* -S [Gk *bronteion*, fr. *brontē* thunder] : a device used in the ancient Greek and Roman theater for making a sound of thunder orig. by means of bronze jars or skins filled with stones

bron·tide \'brän,tīd\ *n* -S [irreg. fr. *bront-*] : a low muffled sound like distant thunder heard in certain seismic regions esp. along seacoasts and over lakes and thought to be caused by feeble earth tremors

bron·to·gram \'bräntə,gram\ *n* -S [*bront-* + *-gram*] : the record made by a brontometer

bron·to·graph \-af\ *n* -S [*bront-* + *-graph*] **1** : BRONTOMETER **2** : BRONTOGRAM

bron·to·lite \-nt°l,īt\ *or* **bron·to·lith** \-°l,ith\ *n* -S [ISV *bront-* + *-lite* or *-lith*] : AEROLITE

bron·tom·e·ter \brän·'tämәd·ə(r)\ *n* [ISV *bront-* + *-meter;* prob. orig. formed as F *brontomètre*] : an instrument for recording the phenomena of thunderstorms (as times of occurrence, frequency, and intensity of the lightning discharges)

bron·to·pho·bia \,bräntə'fōbēə\ *n* [NL, fr. *bront-* + *-phobia*] : abnormal fear of thunder

bron·tops \'brän·,täps\ *n, cap* [NL, fr. *bront-* + *-ops*] : a genus of large extinct perissodactyl Oligocene mammals

bron·to·sau·rus \,bräntə'sȯrəs\ *also* **bron·to·saur** \'bräntə,sȯ(ə)r\ *n* -S [NL *Brontosaurus* (former genus name), fr. *bront-* + *-saurus*] : any of various large quadrupedal and probably herbivorous dinosaurs of the genus *Apatosaurus* — called also *thunder lizard* — **bron·to·sau·ri·an** \,bräntə¦sȯrēən\ *adj*

bron·to·there \'bräntə,thi(ə)r\ *n* -S [NL *Brontotherium*] : any mammal or fossil of the genus *Brontotherium*

bron·to·the·ri·idae \,bräntōthə'rīə,dē\ *n pl, cap* [NL, fr. *Brontotherium*, type genus + *-idae*] : a large family of extinct Eocene and Oligocene mammals (order Perissodactyla) that were widely distributed in the northern hemisphere and included the titanotheres and a number of related animals

bron·to·the·ri·um \-ntə'thirēəm\ *n, cap* [NL, fr. *bront-* + *-therium*] : the type genus of Brontotheriidae comprising large Oligocene ungulate mammals often with horns

bron·to·zo·um \-ntə'zōəm\ *n, cap* [NL, fr. *bront-* + *-zoum* (fr. Gk *zōion* animal) — more at ZOON] : a genus of gigantic dinosaurs known from their 3-toed footprints (some 18 inches long) in the Triassic sandstone of the Connecticut valley

¹**bronx** \'bräŋks\ *adj, usu cap* [fr. the *Bronx*, borough of New York City] : of or from the borough of the Bronx, New York, N.Y. : of the kind or style prevalent in the Bronx

²**bronx** \"\ *or* **bronx cocktail** *n* -ES *usu cap B* : a cocktail made from French and Italian vermouth, gin, and orange juice, well shaken, and served with cracked ice

bronx cheer *n, usu cap B* : RASPBERRY 3

¹**bronze** \'bränz\ *vb* -ED/-ING/-S [F *bronzer*, fr. MF, fr. *bronze*, n.] *vt* **1** : to give the appearance of bronze to (as by coating with bronze powder or exposure to the sun) : give a bronze

color or luster to ⟨casts carefully *bronzed* and polished⟩ ⟨lounging in the sun *bronzing* their backs⟩ **2** *archaic* **:** to make hard or unfeeling **3 :** to form a colored film of one metal or metal compound on the surface of another metal by chemical treatment ~ *vi* **:** to become like bronze esp. in color ⟨children *bronzing* on the beach⟩

2bronze \"\ *n* -s [F, fr. MF, fr. OIt *bronzo*, perh. fr. L *Brundisium* Brindisi, seaport in southeast Italy famed in ancient times for its bronze] **1 a :** an alloy of copper and tin and sometimes small proportions of other elements (as zinc and phosphorus) that is harder and stronger than brass, is used for a variety of industrial items (as wear plates, bushings, springs, clips, fasteners, and chemical hardware) as well as for objects of art and bells, and is prepared from various proportions of the constituent elements according to the purpose for which it is intended **b :** any of certain copper-base alloys containing considerably less tin than other alloying elements or no tin at all **2 a :** a sculpture or artifact cast or wrought in bronze **b :** a bronze coin; *esp* **:** one of the bronze coins of the Roman Empire (as the sestertius, the dupondius, or the as) **3 a :** a moderate yellowish brown that is yellower and darker than antique bronze, Bismarck brown, or cinnamon brown and yellower, darker, and slightly less strong than maple sugar **b :** a substance (as a pigment, powder, or wash) for imparting a bronze or other brilliant metallic surface (as in printing or decorative stenciling) ⟨fire ~⟩ **4** *usu cap* **:** a domestic turkey of a variety distinguished by large size and coppery brown plumage on a background of black and brown

3bronze \"\ *adj* **1 :** made of bronze ⟨a ~ statue⟩ **2 a :** resembling bronze esp. in color **b :** having a rich resonant tone like that of a bronze bell or casting

bronze age *n, usu cap B&A* **:** the period of human culture characterized by the use of bronze tools beginning in Europe about 3500 B.C. and in western Asia and Egypt somewhat earlier — compare IRON AGE, STONE AGE

bronzeback \ˈ=,=\ *also* **bronzeback bass** *n* **:** SMALLMOUTH BLACK BASS

bronze·back·er \"+ə(r)\ *n* -s [*bronze* + *back* + *-er*] **:** LARGEMOUTH BLACK BASS

bronze bells *n pl but sing or pl in constr* **:** a Rocky mountain bulbous herb (*Stenanthium occidentalis*) of the family Liliaceae with narrow leaves and racemose bell-shaped flowers of bronze color

bronze birch borer *n* **:** a slender elongated olive-bronze beetle (*Agrilus anxius*) widely distributed in No. America and having a slender white larva that mines beneath the bark of various birches

bronze blue *n* **1 :** PRUSSIAN BLUE 2 **2 :** an iron-blue pigment; *esp* **:** one having a bronze tone

bronze bream *n* **:** a sparid food and game fish (*Pachymetopon grande*) of southern Africa that is bronzy above and silvery below with faint longitudinal stripes and dark dorsal and pelvic fins; *also* **:** a rare related fish (*P. aeneum*)

bronze brown *n* **:** a brownish gray that is yellower and stronger than taupe, yellower and lighter than chocolate, and slightly yellower and deeper than castor — called also *Asiatic bronze*

bronze copper *n* **:** a large No. American copper butterfly (*Lycaena thoë*)

bronze cross *n* **:** the highest possible award in the Girl Scouts for gallantry given only when the girl candidate has saved a human life at the risk of her own life

bronzed *adj* [fr. past part. of 1*bronze*] **:** of a bronze appearance or color; *esp* **:** tanned by or as if by exposure to the sun

bronzed grackle *n* **:** a grackle of a widely distributed variety (*Quiscalus quiscula versicolor*) of the purple grackle, that is distinguished from the typical variety by the bronzy iridescence of the plumage

bronze diabetes *also* **bronzed diabetes** *n* [so called fr. the characteristic skin color that is one of its symptoms] **:** HEMOCHROMATOSIS

bronze–do·ré \ˌbränzdə¦rā, -ˌdō¦-\ *n, pl* **bronzes–do·rés** \-nz(ˌ)d. . .ā(z)\ [F *bronze doré*] **:** GILT BRONZE

bronze green *n* **:** a grayish olive green that is greener and slightly paler than average ivy green and greener, stronger, and slightly lighter than privet

bronz·en \ˈbränzən\ *adj* [2*bronze* + *-en*] **:** BRONZE

bronze nude *n* **:** OLIVE BROWN

bronze pigeon *n* **:** BRONZEWING

bronze powder *n* **:** any metal (as a copper alloy or aluminum) in fine flake form used as a pigment to give the appearance of a metallic surface

bronz·er \ˈbränzə(r)\ *n* -s **:** one that bronzes, tends a bronzing machine, or applies bronze dust

bronze red *n* **:** PEPPER RED

bronzes *pres 3d sing of* BRONZE, *pl of* BRONZE

bronze·sheen \ˈbränz(h)¦shēn, -än¦sh-\ *n* -s [3*bronze* + *sheen*] **:** a grayish olive that is greener and duller than average olive drab and greener and darker than average covert brown

bronzesmith \ˈ=,=\ *n* **:** an artisan who works bronze into useful artifacts

bronze turkey *n, usu cap B* **:** BRONZE 4

bronzewing \ˈ=,=\ *also* **bronze–winged pigeon** \ˈ=,=-\ *or* **bronzewing pigeon** *n* **:** any of numerous pigeons of the Australian region that are conspicuous for the metallic spots or areas on the wings

bronze–winged duck \ˈ=,=-\ *n* **:** a So. American duck (*Anas specularis*) having a bronzy speculum

bronze yellow *n* **:** a moderate orange to dark orange yellow — called also *nugget, yellow bronze*

bronzing *n* -s [fr. gerund of 1*bronze*] **1 a :** the process of imparting a metallic luster (as to a plaster cast) esp. by coating with a powdered metal **b :** a finely ground metal used in bronzing **2 a :** a bronze coloring or discoloration (as of the skin) **b :** a reddish brown discoloration of plant leaves caused by excessive exposure to sun, deficiency of certain nutrients, or the attack of mites or nematodes **c :** PLUMMING

bronzing fluid *or* **bronzing liquid** *n* **:** a liquid for mixing with metallic powders to make a paint or coating

bronz·ite \ˈbränˌzīt\ *n* -s [G *bronzit*, fr. *bronze* (fr. F) + *-it* -ite — more at BRONZE] **:** a mineral consisting of a ferriferous variety of enstatite often having a luster like that of bronze

bronz·itite \-nzəˌtīt\ *n* -s [*bronzite* + *-ite*] **:** a hypabyssal rock composed essentially of bronzite

bronzy \-nzē\ *adj* -ER/-EST [2*bronze* + *-y*] **:** like or suggestive of bronze esp. in color or metallic luster ⟨a ~ iridescent surface⟩

1broo \ˈbrü\ *n* -s [ME *bro*, prob. fr. MF *breu* — more at BREWIS] *chiefly Scot* **:** the liquid in which food has been cooked **:** BROTH, JUICE

2broo \"\ *n* -s [origin unknown] *chiefly Scot* **:** favorable opinion — usu. used with a negative ⟨I have no ~ of him⟩

3broo \"\ *chiefly Scot var of* BROW

1brooch \ˈbrōch, ˈbrüch\ *n* -ES [ME *broche* brooch, pointed tool — more at BROACH] **1 :** a fastening device often of precious metal and decked with gems and usu. with a clasp or tongue for making it fast (as to a garment) that is now used chiefly for ornament on women's apparel **2** *obs* **:** a jewel or jeweled ornament

2brooch \"\ *vt* -ED/-ING/-ES **:** to adorn or fasten with or as if with a brooch

1brood \ˈbrüd\ *n* -s [ME, fr. OE *brōd;* akin to MHG *bruot* incubation, brood, OE *beorma* yeast — more at BARM] **1 :** the young of animals: as **a :** the young of birds hatched or cared for at one time ⟨as a hen doth gather her ~ under her wings —Lk 13:34 (AV)⟩ **b :** the young from the same dam or the offspring of the same mother esp. if nearly of the same age **:** PROGENY **c :** the eggs and young of various bees **d :** progeny produced at a hatch or as a result of a single breeding period ⟨some insects produce a dozen ~s a year⟩ ⟨the first ~ of black flies always seems to bite hardest⟩ **2** *archaic* **:** a brooding or hatching group **3 :** a group likened to a brood of young esp. in respect to similarity of form or nature ⟨a ~ of meteors⟩, community of origin ⟨the entire ~ of chronicle plays —T.S.Eliot⟩, or shared relation to some other item ⟨the ship that some day will mother her own ~ of modern planes —*N.Y. Times*⟩ ⟨a ~ of crystal cups about the bowl⟩ **4 :** a brood bitch — compare STUD

2brood \"\ *vb* -ED/-ING/-S [ME *broden*, fr. *brod, brood*, n.] *vt* **1 a :** to sit on or incubate (eggs) for the purpose of hatching **b :** to produce as if by incubation **:** HATCH **2 a** *of a bird* **:** to cover (young) with the wings **:** warm and protect with the body **b** *obs* **:** to cherish with care **:** hover over protectingly **3 :** to turn over in the mind **:** think anxiously or moodily upon **:** PONDER ⟨I used to ~ these things on my walk —Christopher Morley⟩ ~ *vi* **1 a** *of a bird* **:** to sit on eggs or cover young with the wings **b :** to sit quietly as if brooding eggs or young ⟨birds of calm sit ~*ing* on the charmed wave —John Milton⟩ **2 :** to hover as if enveloping with wings ⟨the old fort ~*ing* above the valley⟩ **3 a :** to dwell continuously or moodily on a subject — usu. used with *over* or *on* ⟨he ~*ed* over their neglect⟩ **b :** to be in a state of mental gloom and depression **:** to indulge in depressing meditation ⟨nothing relieved his distress, he just sat and ~*ed*⟩

3brood \"\ *adj* [1*brood*] **1** *of a hen* **:** BROODING **:** sitting on eggs **2 a :** kept for breeding ⟨a ~ female⟩ ⟨~ flock⟩ **b :** having or producing young ⟨a ~ sow⟩ **3** *of a plant* **:** infested with insects to an unusual degree ⟨elimination of an occasional ~ tree may cut down insect losses considerably⟩

brood body *n* **:** a gemma (as of a moss or liverwort)

brood bud *n* **1 :** BULBIL **2 :** SOREDIUM

brood capsule *n* **:** one of the secondary scolex-containing cysts that are proliferated from the lining of a hydatid and constitute the infective agent when eaten by a suitable host (as a dog)

brood cell *n* **1 :** GONIDIUM **2 :** a cell in bee comb used for the rearing of a larva

brood chamber *n* **1 :** BROOD POUCH **2** *or* **brood nest** *in a beehive* **:** the part of the comb set aside for brood rearing

brood·er \ˈbrüdə(r)\ *n* -s **1 :** a person or animal that broods **2 a** *also* **brooder house :** a building or enclosed place capable of artificial heating and used for raising chicks and other young fowl without a hen **b :** a heated area or enclosure for keeping young pigs or other animals warm without necessarily separating them from the dam

brooder 2a with section of hover cut away to show oil burner

brooder pneumonia *n* **:** aspergillosis of young birds

brood·i·ness \-dēnə̇s\ *n* -ES [*broody* + *-ness*] **:** the state of a hen ready to brood eggs that is characterized by cessation of laying and by marked changes in behavior and physiology

brooding *adj* [fr. pres. part. of 2*brood*] **1 :** that broods: as **a :** sitting on eggs **b :** given to meditating moodily or sullenly **2** [fr. gerund of 2*brood*] **:** used for breeding or brooding ⟨a ~ pouch⟩ — **brood·ing·ly** *adv*

brood·less \-dlə̇s\ *adj* **:** being without a brood

broodmare \ˈ=,=\ *n* **:** a mare kept for breeding

brood matron *n* **:** a female domestic animal kept for breeding

brood parasitism *n* **:** social parasitism among birds characterized by a bird of one species laying its eggs in the nest of a bird of another species and giving no parental care to the eggs

brood pouch *n* **:** a sac or cavity of the body of an animal where the eggs or embryos are received and undergo a part of their development

broods *pl of* BROOD, *pres 3d sing of* BROOD

broodsac \ˈ=,=\ *n* **:** BROOD POUCH; *sometimes* **:** GEMMULE 3

brood stock *n* **:** a small population of any animal maintained as a source of population replacement or for the establishment of new populations (as of game birds) in suitable habitats

1broody \ˈbrüdē, -di\ *adj* -ER/-EST [1*brood* + *-y*] **1 a** *archaic* **:** tending or seeking to reproduce **:** PROLIFIC **b** *of a hen bird* **:** ready to brood **:** physiologically fit for setting **c** *of a female mammal* **:** suitable for the production of offspring (as by reason of good conformation, vigor, and heredity) ⟨a ~ gilt⟩ **2 :** CONTEMPLATIVE, DEPRESSED, MOODY

2broody \"\ *or* **broody hen** *n* -ES **:** a hen ready to brood — called also *setting hen*

broody coop *n* **:** a small coop designed to break up broodiness of hens by preventing any comfortable settling down

1brook \ˈbrůk\ *vt* -ED/-ING/-S [ME *brouken* to use, enjoy, digest, fr. OE *brūcan;* akin to OHG *brūhhan* to use, Goth *brūkjan* to use, partake of, L *frui* to enjoy] **1 a** *archaic* **:** to possess and enjoy **b** *obs* **:** to merit (a name or epithet); *also* **:** to bear (a name) with credit **2** *obs* **:** to make use of as food **3 :** to put up with **:** ENDURE, BEAR, STOMACH, TOLERATE — now usu. used in negative constructions ⟨they would ~ no interference⟩ ⟨they never would ~ interference⟩

2brook \"\ *n* -s [ME *brook, broke*, fr. OE *brōc;* akin to OHG *bruoh* marshy ground and prob. to OE *brecan* to break — more at BREAK] **1 :** CREEK 2 — in general literary use but used as a common generic term chiefly in England and New England and also in the names of streams in a few northern esp. northeastern states **2 :** BROOK TROUT

3brook \ˈbrük\ *n* -s [Sc *brook, bruik*, fr. *brook, bruik* to soil with soot, make dirty, fr. ME (Sc) *broiken* to make dirty, prob. fr. *brukit, brukyd* streaked with black (taken as a past participle)] *Scot* **:** SOOT

broo·ked \ˈbrükə̇t\ *adj* [ME (Sc) *brukit, brukyd* streaked with black, prob. of Scand origin; akin to Dan *broget* variegated, OSw *brōkoter*] *Scot* **:** streaked with dirt **:** DIRTY

brook feather *n* **:** a Chinese shrub (*Xanthoceras sorbifolia*) of the family Sapindaceae that has showy white racemose flowers that bloom before the leaves expand

brook grass *n* **:** an aquatic perennial grass (*Catabrosa aquatica*) that is widely distributed in the northern hemisphere and sometimes used for pasture, that roots at the lower nodes, and that has overlapping leaf sheaths, soft flat leaves, and a pyramidal inflorescence

1broo·kie \ˈbrükē\ *n* -s [prob. fr. *brooked* + *-ie*] *Scot* **:** a dirty-faced person; *specif* **:** BLACKSMITH

2brookie \"\ *adj, Scot* **:** DIRTY, SOOTY

3brook·ie \ˈbrůkē\ *n* -s [2*brook* + *-ie*] **:** BROOK TROUT

brook·ite \ˈbrůˌkīt\ *n* -s [Henry J. *Brooke* †1857 Eng. mineralogist + E *-ite*] **:** a mineral consisting of titanium dioxide TiO_2 and identical in composition with rutile and octahedrite but occurring in orthorhombic crystals commonly brown and translucent or brown to black and opaque (hardness 5.5–6, sp.gr. 3.87–4.08)

brook lamprey *n* **:** any of numerous usu. small lampreys that live mostly in brooks

brook·less \ˈbrůklə̇s\ *adj* **:** being without a brook

brook·let \ˈbrůklə̇t\ *n* -s **:** a small brook **:** RIVULET, RILL

brook·lime \ˈbrůˌklīm\ *n* -s [by folk etymology fr. earlier *brooklem*, fr. ME *brokelemke*, fr. *broke* brook + *lemke, lemeke* speedwell, fr. OE *hleomoce;* akin to MLG *lōmeke* speedwell — more at 2BROOK] **1 :** any of certain aquatic or semiaquatic plants of the genus *Veronica* (as *V. beccabunga* and *V. americana*) — see WALL INK **2 :** WATERCRESS **3** *Austral* **:** a plant of the genus *Gratiola*

brook lobelia *n* **:** a delicate waterside plant (*Lobelia kalmii*) of eastern No. America with pale blue irregular evanescent flowers

1brook·lyn \ˈbrůklən\ *adj, usu cap* [fr. *Brooklyn*, borough of New York City] **:** of or from the borough of Brooklyn, New York, N.Y. ⟨*Brooklyn* streets⟩ **:** of the kind or style prevalent in Brooklyn

2brooklyn \"\ *n* -s *usu cap, bowling* **:** a hit in which the ball strikes the headpin to the left of center

brook·lyn·ese \ˌbrůkləˈnēz, -ēs, ˌ==ˈ=\ *n, usu cap* **:** the uncultivated speech of greater New York City (including the borough of Brooklyn) and environs among the characteristics of which are the use of \əi\ as the vocalic of words like *bird*, the use of the glottal stop for *tt* in words like *bottle*, and the substitution of \t\ or \d(·)\ for \th\ or \t͟h\ of words like *think, these, brother*

brook·lyn·ite \ˈbrůkləˌnīt\ *n* -s *cap* **:** a native or resident of Brooklyn, N.Y.

brook pimpernel *n* **:** WATER SPEEDWELL

brooks *pl of* BROOK, *pres 3d sing of* BROOK

brookside \ˈ=,=\ *n* [ME *brokeside*, fr. *broke* brook + *side*] **:** the land bordering on a brook

brook tongue *n* **:** either of two water hemlocks: **a :** a European water hemlock (*Cicuta virosa*) **b :** a related American plant (*C. maculata*)

brook trout *n* **:** the common speckled char (*Salvelinus fontinalis*) of eastern No. America highly esteemed as a sport and food fish, widely distributed in cold flowing waters, and introduced in many places outside its natural range — called also *speckled trout, squaretail*

brookweed \ˈ=,=\ *n* **:** either of two small white-flowered herbs (*Samolus valerandi* of Europe and *S. floribundus* of the U.S.) that grow in wet places

brooky \ˈbrůkē\ *adj* -ER/-EST [2*brook* + *-y*] **:** full of brooks

brool \ˈbrül\ *n* -s [prob. fr. G *brüllen* to roar, bellow, fr. MHG *brüelen;* akin to MD *brullen* to roar, bellow, MHG *bral* shout; all from a D-G root of imit. origin] **:** a low roar **:** a deep murmur or humming ⟨list to the ~ of that royal forest voice —Thomas Carlyle⟩

1broom \ˈbrüm, -ům\ *n* -s [ME, fr. OE *brōm;* akin to OHG *brāmo* bramble, MHG *brem* edge — more at BRIM] **1 a :** any of various leguminous shrubs chiefly of the genera *Cytisus* and *Genista* with long slender branches, upright growth, small leaves, and usu. showy yellow flowers **b :** BROOM TREE 1 **c :** HEATHER 1a **2 :** a bundle of firm stiff plant shoots or twigs (as of the tops of broomcorn or of birch spray) or of natural or artificial fibers bound tightly together usu. on a long handle and used for sweeping and brushing — compare 1BRUSH **3 :** the tops of a common broom (*Cytisus scoparius*) formerly used in medicine as a diuretic **4 :** WITCHES'-BROOM **5 :** WOODWAXEN

household brooms

2broom \"\ *vt* -ED/-ING/-S **1 :** to sweep with or as if with a broom; **a :** to cleanse by sweeping ⟨~ off the hearth⟩ **b :** to gather by sweeping ⟨she ~*ed* up the pieces of the broken jar⟩ **c :** to finish (as a surface) by means of a broom ⟨~*ing* the fresh concrete surface gives a pleasing finish⟩ **d :** to apply (as roofing cement or filler in a brick or block pavement) with a broom ⟨carefully ~ the asphalt into the felt⟩ **2 :** to fray or splinter (as a log) at the end by mechanical means ⟨a ~*ed* stick makes a handy stirrer⟩

broom birch *n* **1 :** YELLOW BIRCH **2 :** POPLAR BIRCH

broom brush *n* [so called fr. its use in broommaking] **:** a shrubby American St.-John's-wort (*Hypericum prolificum*) with showy yellow flowers

broom clover *n* **:** INDIGO BROOM

broomcorn \ˈ=,=\ *n* **:** any of several tall cultivated grasses that are derived from a variety of sorghum (*Sorghum vulgare technicum*) and are grown for the stiff-branched elongated panicle which is used for making brooms and brushes

broomcorn millet *n* **:** MILLET 1a

broom crowberry *n* [so called fr. its broomlike appearance] **:** a prostrate shrub (*Corema conradii*) of northeastern No. America resembling the common crowberry but with flowers in terminal heads

broom grass *n* **1 :** BROOM SEDGE 1 **2 :** BROMEGRASS

broom hickory *n* [so called fr. its former use in broommaking] **:** a pignut (*Carya glabra*)

broom·ie *or* **broomy** \ˈbrümē, -ů-\ *n, pl* **broomies** [*broomtail* + *-ie* or *-y*] **:** BROOMTAIL

broom·ing \-miŋ\ *or* **brooming disease** *n* -s [1*broom* + *-ing*] **:** abnormal clustering of branches (as in witches'-broom); *also* **:** an abnormal condition of a plant (as of certain walnuts) leading to such brooming

broom man *n* **:** BRUSHMAN 1c

broom millet *n* **:** BROOMCORN MILLET

broom moss *n* **:** a common moss (*Dicranum scoparium*) with tufts that resemble miniature brushes

broom palm *n* **:** COHUNE PALM

broom pine *n* [so called fr. the broomlike appearance of its leaf cluster] **:** LONGLEAF PINE

broom·rape \-mˌrāp\ *n* [trans. of NL *rapum genistae;* fr. the parasitic growth of one species like a tuber on the roots of broom] **1 :** any of various root-parasitic plants of the family Orobanchaceae (as of the genus *Orobanche*) **2 :** INDIAN PIPE

broomrape family *n* **:** OROBANCHACEAE

broomroot \ˈ=,=\ *n* [so called fr. its former use in brushmaking] **:** a Mexican grass (*Epicampes macroura*) used for forage and papermaking

brooms *pl of* BROOM, *pres 3d sing of* BROOM

broom sage *n* [so called fr. its use in broommaking] **:** RABBIT BRUSH

broom sedge *n* [so called fr. its use in broommaking] **1 :** any of several grasses of the genus *Andropogon* (esp. *A. scoparius, A. virginicus*, and *A. argyraeus*) — called also *broom grass* **2 :** ARROW GRASS 1, 2

broom snakeroot *or* **broom snakeweed** *n* **:** a glabrous and often glutinous low-growing composite shrub (*Gutierrezia sarothrae*) of the southwestern U.S. with narrowly linear leaves and small heads of yellow flowers

broom·stick \ˈ=,=\ *n* -s **:** the long thin handle of a broom

broomstraw \ˈ=,=\ *n* **:** BROOM SEDGE 1

broomtail \ˈ=,=\ *n* [1*broom* + *tail*] **:** a small usu. wild and untrained western range horse of inferior quality — sometimes used specif. of the mare and then contrasted with *fuzztail*

broom top *n* **:** the almost leafless branches of the broom (*Cytisus scoparius*) that contain the alkaloid sparteine; *esp* **:** these tops prepared for pharmaceutical use — used usu. in pl.

broom tree *n* [so called fr. its broomlike appearance] **1 :** a shrub (*Baccharis scoparia*) of Jamaica **2 :** a yellow-flowered prickly shrub (*Genista anglica*) found on the moors of northern Europe and England

broom wattle *n* **:** an Australian shrub or small tree (*Acacia calamifolia*) with showy yellow flowers

broomweed \ˈ=,=\ *n* [so called fr. its use in broommaking] **1 :** an herb (*Scoparia dulcis*) of the family Scrophulariaceae with small whitish flowers that grows in waste places in tropical and subtropical regions — called also *sweet broomweed* **2 :** a tropical American herb (*Corchorus siliquosus*) used for making brooms **3 :** any of several tropical plants of the genera *Sida* and *Triumfetta* used for broommaking **4 :** a shrubby annual plant (*Gutierrezia texana*) of the prairies of the southwestern U.S. with rigid woody branches, glutinous foliage, and yellow flowers

broomwood \ˈ=,=\ *n* **:** a tropical American shrub (*Moluchia tomentosa*) of the family Sterculiaceae that is common in the Bahamas and has papery leaves and bluish purple flowers

broomwort \ˈ=,=\ *n* [so called fr. the parasitic growth of one species on the roots of broom] **1 :** any plant of the family Orobanchaceae **2 :** WATER BETONY

broomy \ˈbrümē, -ů-\ *adj* -ER/-EST [1*broom* + *-y*] **:** abounding in broom

broon \ˈbrün\ *Scot var of* BROWN

broon geor·die \-ˈjȯrdē\ *n, usu cap G* [Sc *broon* + *Geordie*, irreg. dim. of *George* (the name)] *Scot* **:** BROWN GEORGE 1

broos *pl of* BROO

broose \ˈbrüz\ *n* -s [perh. alter. of Sc *brous* violent rush, impact, alter. of ME *brusche* rush — more at BRUSH (encounter)] *chiefly Scot* **:** a race to the bridegroom's house after a country wedding

broo·zled \ˈbrüzəld\ *adj* [*brooz-* (alter. of *bruise*) + *-le* + *-ed*] *Scot* **:** BRUISED, SMASHED

brose \ˈbrōz\ *n* -s [perh. alter. of Sc *bruis* broth, fr. ME *brewes, browes* — more at BREWIS] **:** a chiefly Scottish dish made by pouring some boiling liquid on meal (as oatmeal) and stirring it — usu. used in combination with an attributive indicating the nature of the liquid ⟨water ~⟩ ⟨beef ~⟩

bro·si·mum \ˈbrōsəməm, -räl, ¦zə-\ *n, cap* [NL, fr. Gk *brōsimon*, neut. of *brōsimos* eatable, fr. Gk *bibrōskein* to devour — more at VORACIOUS] **:** a small genus of tropical American trees (family Moraceae) having a milky juice and monoecious flowers and including several of economic importance — see BREADNUT, COW TREE 1, LETTERWOOD

bros·na \ˈbrəsnə\ *n* -s [IrGael, fr. MIr; akin to OE *brȳsan* to bruise — more at BRUISE] *Irish* **:** a bundle of sticks **:** FAGGOT

brosy \ˈbrōzi\ *adj* [*brose* + *-y*] **1** *Scot* **:** fed or smeared with brose **2** *Scot* **:** stout and somewhat bloated in appearance **:** SLUGGISH, TORPID

brotch \ˈbrōch, -räch\ *dial Eng var of* 1BROACH 2d

bröt·chen \ˈbrœtkən\ *n* -s [G, fr. *bröt-* (fr. *brot* bread, fr. OHG *brōt*) + *-chen*, dim. suffix, fr. MHG *-chīn;* akin to MD *-kijn*, dim. suffix — more at BREAD, -KIN] **:** ROLL 2d(1)

broth \'brȯ|th *also* -rä|\ *n, pl* **broths** \ |ths,|(th)z\ [ME, fr. OE; akin to OHG *brod* broth, ON *broth*, L *defrutum* new wine boiled down, OIr *bruth* heat, wrath, L *fervēre* to boil — more at BURN] **1** : liquid in which meat, fish, cereal grains, or vegetables have been cooked : STOCK — compare BOUILLON, CONSOMMÉ **2** : a fluid culture medium **3 a** : something outstanding of its kind as though produced by boiling down to a savory broth — used chiefly in the phrase *a broth of a boy* **b** : something turbulent, disordered, and ebullient like the surface of a boiling stockpot ⟨matters had reached a ~ of discussion —Agnes de Mille⟩

broth·el \'bräthəl, -rȯth-\ *n* -S [ME, fr. *brothen* ruined (past part. of *brethen* to waste away, go to ruin), fr. OE, past part. of *brēothan* to waste away; akin to OHG *brōdi* frail — more at BRITTLE] **1** *obs* : a worthless fellow : a lewd man or woman : PROSTITUTE **2** [influenced in meaning by *bordel*] : an establishment (as a house or apartment) in which prostitutes are domiciled and ply their trade usu. as employees or on a commission basis, the keeping of such an establishment being at common law and usu. by statute a misdemeanor

¹broth·er \'brəthə(r)\ *n, pl* **brothers** \-ə(r)z\ *also* **breth·ren** \'breth(ə)rən *also* -thərn\ [ME, fr. OE *brōthor*; akin to OHG *bruoder* brother, ON *brōthir*, Goth *brothar*, L *frater* brother, Gk *phratēr* member of the same clan, Skt *bhrātṛ* brother] **1 a** : a male human being considered in his relation to another person having the same parents or having one parent in common — see BROTHER-GERMAN, HALF BROTHER; compare UTERINE **b** : a male of any lower animal similarly considered **2 a** (1) : a kinsman by blood (2) : a male member of the same family, clan, or line, in primitive societies being often charged with the same responsibilities as a brother of common parentage **b** : a person regarded as sharing a common national or racial origin with the user of the word — often used without specific consideration of sex ⟨we must help our ~s in the Old Country⟩ **c** : FELLOWMAN ⟨are not all men ~s⟩ **3** *pl often brethren* **a** : CORELIGIONIST; *esp* : a fellow member of a Christian church — often used with a proper noun ⟨*Brother* Jones will pass the collection plate⟩ **b** : a Protestant minister esp. in some evangelical denominations — often used with a proper noun ⟨*Brother* Smith, the Baptist preacher⟩ **4** *pl often brethren* : one related or linked to another by some common tie or interest (as of shared rank, profession, membership in a society, suffering, or labor) **5** : someone or something that closely resembles another in qualities or traits ⟨the ~ qualities of greed and miserliness⟩ **6** *slang* : FELLOW, CHAP, MATE — often used as an informal term of address esp. to a person whose name is unknown ⟨hey, ~, what time is it⟩ **7** *Roman Catholicism* **a** *usu cap* : a member of a congregation of men usu. not in holy orders but commonly engaged in hospital or school work ⟨a Xaverian *Brother*⟩ **b** : a member of a men's religious order who is not preparing for or ready for holy orders ⟨a lay ~⟩

²brother \"\ *vt* **brothered**; **brothered**; **brothering** \-th(ə)riŋ\ **brothers** : to make a brother of : address or treat as a brother; *esp* : to admit to a brotherhood

³brother \"; ¦brə'thər, -'thə\ *interj* — used typically to indicate intensity of feeling about the topic in hand ⟨~ was I ever sick⟩

brother-german \¦==¦==\ *n, pl* **brothers-german** [ME *brother germain*, part trans. of MF *frere germain*, fr. *frere* brother + *germain* having the same parents — more at GERMAN] *civil law* : a brother through both father and mother : a full brother — compare HALF BROTHER

broth·er·hood \'brəthə(r),hu̇d\ *n* -S [ME *brotherhod*, alter. (influenced by *-hod* -hood) of *brotherhede*, alter. (influenced by *-hede* as in *godhede* godhead) of *brotherrede*, fr. OE *brōthorrǣden*, fr. *brōthor* brother + *rǣden* condition — more at KINDRED] **1** : the quality or state of being brothers or a brother : the relation between brothers **2** : brotherly comradeship : FELLOWSHIP, COMPANIONSHIP, ALLIANCE ⟨dwelling with the natives in perfect peace and ~⟩ **3** : an association (as a guild, fraternity, or monastic society) for a particular purpose **4** : any one of several trade unions; *esp* : one among railroad employees **5 a** : the whole body of persons engaged in a business or profession ⟨the medical ~⟩ **b** : a group sharing a common interest or quality ⟨the ~ of wind-swept pines⟩ ⟨the ~ of the handicapped⟩

brother hospitaler of st. john of god \-'jän-\ *usu cap B&H, cap S&J&G* [after *St. John of God* †1550 Span. religious, who founded the institute] : a member of a Roman Catholic religious institute founded in 1540 at Granada, Spain, and devoted esp. to the care of the sick

brother-in-arms \¦===¦=\ *n, pl* **brothers-in-arms** : a close associate; *esp* : a fellow member of a military service

brother-in-law \'brətha(r)ən,lȯ, -thrən-,-thə(r)n-\ *n, pl* **brothers-in-law** \-thə(r)zən-\ [ME *brother in lawe*; prob. fr. the fact that the canon law forbids marriage with one's spouse's sister or brother] **1** : the brother of one's spouse — compare AFFINITY **2** : the husband of one's sister; *broadly* : the husband of one's spouse's sister

brother jon·a·than \,brəthə(r)'jänəthən\ *n, usu cap B&J* [¹*brother* + *Jonathan* (the name); prob. fr. the frequent use of Old Testament given names among the English colonists in America] *chiefly Brit* : a male native or resident of the U.S. — used as a nickname

broth·er·less \'==ləs\ *adj* [ME, fr. *brother* + *less*] : having no brother

broth·er·li·ness \'brəthə(r)lēnəs, -lin-\ *n* -ES : the quality or state of being brotherly

¹broth·er·ly \-lē,-li\ *adj* **1** : of or relating to brothers **2** : such as is natural for or becoming to brothers; *broadly* : AFFECTIONATE, KIND, CHERISHING ⟨~ love⟩

²brotherly \"\ *adv, archaic* : as a brother : AFFECTIONATELY, KINDLY

brother of the christian schools *usu cap B&C&S* **1** : a member of a Roman Catholic religious organization founded by St. Jean Baptiste de la Salle in Reims in 1684 and devoted to teaching — called also *Christian Brother* **2** : a member of a Roman Catholic religious organization founded in Ireland in 1802 and devoted to teaching — called also *Irish Christian Brother*

brothers *pl of* BROTHER, *pres 3d sing of* BROTHER

broths *pl of* BROTH

bro·to·crys·tal \'brōd·ō+,-\ *n* [*broto-* (fr. Gk *brōtos* eatable, verbal fr. *bibrōskein* to devour + *crystal* — more at VORACIOUS] : a crystal occurring in rock and having corroded outlines due to the consolidation of the magma before the crystal was entirely assimilated

¹brot·u·lid \'bräch əlәd\ *n* -S [NL *Brotulidae*] : a fish of the family Brotulidae

²brotulid \"\ *adj* : of or relating to the family Brotulidae

bro·tu·li·dae \brō'tüla,dē, -ō'tyü-\ *n pl, cap* [NL, fr. *Brotula*, type genus (perh. fr. AmerSp *brótula* brotulid fish) + *-idae*] : a family of chiefly deep-sea ophidioid fishes superficially resembling the cods but more nearly related to the blennies

brou·ette \(')brü¦et\ *n* -S [F, fr. OF *brouete*, *broete* 2-wheeled carriage, fr. (assumed) OF *broue*, *broe* 2-wheeled carriage (fr. LL *birota*, fr. fem. of *birotus* 2-wheeled, fr. L *bi-* + LL *-rotus*, fr. L *rota* wheel) + *-ete* -ette — more at ROLL] : a small 2-wheeled vehicle pulled by a man by means of a pair of shafts in front and used for personal transportation in parts of Europe during the 17th and 18th centuries

brough \'bräk, 'brək\ *var of* ²BROCH

brougham \'brü(-ə)m, 'brō(-ə)m\ *n* -S [after Henry Peter *Brougham*, Baron Brougham and Vaux †1868 Scot. jurist] **1** : a light closed carriage with seats inside for two or four and with the forewheels capable of turning sharply **2 a** : a 2-door sedan; *esp* : one electrically driven **b** : a vehicle similar to a limousine but with the driver's seat outside

brougham 1

brougham-landaulet \¦=(=),==¦=, (')=(=)'==,=\ *n* : a brougham in which the top from the rear doors backward is collapsible

brought [ME *broughte* (past), *brought*, *ybrought* (past part.), fr. OE *brōhte* (past), *brōht*, *gebrōht* (past part.); akin to OHG *brāhta* brought (past), *brāht* brought (past part.), Goth *brāhta* (past) — more at BRING] *past of* BRING

broughten [*brought* (past part. of *bring*) + *-en* (as in *forgotten*)] *substand past of* BRING

brou·ha·ha \brü'hä(,)hä, ¦brühä¦hä, -ühə¦-\ *n* -S [F, perh. modif. of Heb *bārūkh habbā'* blessed be he who enters; fr. the frequent use in the synagogue of a passage containing these words, Ps 118:26 (RSV)] **1** : a confused medley of sounds esp. of voices : HUBBUB **2** : publicity, attention, or excitement far beyond the merits or importance of its cause : HULLABALOO, UPROAR, FURORE

brouil·lon \brüyōⁿ\ *n, pl* **brouillons** \-ōⁿ(z)\ [F, fr. MF, fr. *brouiller* to scrawl, fr. OF *brooillier* to mix, confuse — more at BROIL] : a rough draft

brous·so·ne·tia \,brüsə'nēsh(ē)ə\ *n, cap* [NL, fr. P.M.A. *Broussonet* †1807 Fr. naturalist + NL *-ia*] : a genus of Asiatic trees or large shrubs (family Moraceae) with milky juice, sterile flowers in spikes or racemes, and fertile flowers in dense globular heads — see PAPER MULBERRY

¹brow \'brau̇\ *n* -S [ME, fr. OE *brū*; akin to ON *brūn* eyebrow, Gk *ophrys*, Skt *bhrū*] **1 a** : the hair on the ridge over the eye : EYEBROW **b** : the superciliary ridge on which the eyebrow grows **c** : either of the lateral prominences of the forehead **d** : FOREHEAD **2 a** : the projecting upper part or margin of a steep place : the highest margin of a height as viewed in profile ⟨the wind died down after we crossed the ~ of the slope⟩ **b** *dial Eng* : a steep hill or slope **3 a** : the upper face regarded as the seat of expression : the general air of the countenance : MIEN ⟨a proud contemptuous ~⟩ ⟨the grim ~ of tyranny⟩ **b** *obs* : EFFRONTERY, BOLDNESS **4** : intellectual quality or capacity **5** : a curved watershed surmounting a porthole or other opening on a ship

²brow \"\ *vt* -ED/-ING/-S : to be at or form the edge of : BOUND

³brow \'brau̇, -rü\ *var of* ²BROO

⁴brow \'brau̇\ *n* -S [prob. of Scand origin; akin to Dan & Sw *bro* bridge; akin to OE *brycg* bridge — more at BRIDGE] : a gangplank usu. fitted with rollers at the end resting on the wharf to allow for the movement of a ship with the tide

bro·wal·lia \brə'wälēə\ *n* [NL, fr. J. *Browallius* †1755 Swed. theologian and naturalist + NL *-ia*] **1** *cap* : a small genus of tropical American annual plants (family Solanaceae) cultivated for their blue, violet, or white flowers **2** -S : a plant of the genus *Browallia*

brow antler *n* : the first branch of a stag's antler — see ANTLER illustration

browband \'=,=\ *n* : any band designed to cross or cover the forehead; *esp* : the part of a bridle, headstall, or halter that passes from one cheekpiece to the other above the eyes and below the ears

browbeat \'=,=\ *vb* [¹*brow* + *beat*] *vt* : to depress or bear down with haughty stern looks or with arrogant speech : abash or disconcert by impudence or abuse : BULLY ⟨~ witnesses⟩ ~ *vi* : to act in an overbearing manner : BULLY ⟨they fought, bribed, and ~ in order to achieve their goal⟩ **syn** see INTIMIDATE

brow·beat·er \'brau̇,bēd·ə(r), -ētə-\ *n* : one that browbeats

browbound \'=,=\ *adj* [¹*brow* + *bound* (past part of *bind*)] : CROWNED

brow·den \'brau̇dᵊn\ *adj* [ME, fr. OE *brogden*, past part. of *bregdan* to move suddenly, weave together — more at ¹BRAID] *chiefly Scot* : fond of : intently set upon ⟨less ~ still on cash than verse —Allan Ramsay †1758⟩

browed \¦brau̇d\ *adj* [ME, fr. ¹*brow* + *-ed*] : having brows of an indicated character or quality ⟨black-*browed* maidens⟩ ⟨smooth-*browed* and carefree⟩

browis \'brōz, 'brōəs\ *var of* BREWIS

brow·less \'brau̇ləs\ *adj* [¹*brow* + *-less*] **1** : UNABASHED **2** : LACKING EYEBROWS

brow·man \-mən\ *n, pl* **browmen** *mining engin* : one who attaches or detaches tubs from the cable at the brow of an incline

¹brown \'brau̇n\ *adj* -ER/-EST [ME *broun*, fr. OE *brūn*; akin to OHG *brūn* brown, shining, ON *brūnn* brown, Gk *phrynē* toad, Skt *babhru* reddish-brown] **1 a** : DARK, DUSKY **b** : GLOOMY ⟨~ years in boarding houses —Sinclair Lewis⟩ **2** : of the color brown ⟨~ as the oak leaves⟩: as **a** *of a person or a race of men* (1) : having skin of the color brown ⟨little ~ men⟩ (2) : of dark complexion : TANNED **b** *of a kind of animal* : distinguished from related kinds by brown coloration ⟨~ bears⟩ ⟨the gamy ~ trout⟩ **3** : UNBLEACHED — used of linen, cotton cloth, or paper **4** *usu cap* [so called fr. the color of the Storm Troopers' uniform] : NAZI ⟨the madness of *Brown* Bolshevism —*Forum*⟩

²brown \"\ *n* -S [ME *broun*, fr. *broun*, adj.] **1** : one that is brown in color or distinguished by brown coloration: as **a** : a brown-skinned person; *esp* : a comparatively light-skinned black **b** *slang chiefly Brit* : a copper coin **c** : a flock of game birds in flight ⟨aim at one bird; don't blaze into the ~⟩ **d** (1) : BROWN BEAR (2) : BROWN TROUT (3) : BROWN ALGA **2** : any pigment or dye that colors brown **3** : any of a group of colors between red and yellow in hue, of medium to low lightness, and of moderate to low saturation **4** : a coat color in horses not always distinct from dark bay or from black but identifiable by the presence of light brown or tan hair on the muzzle, legs, and usu. the underline

³brown \"\ *vb* -ED/-ING/-S [ME *brounen*, fr. *broun*, adj.] *vi* : to become brown ⟨the roast was ~*ing* in the oven⟩ ~ *vt* **1** : to make brown or dusky: as **a** : to make brown by scorching slightly (as meat or flour) **b** : to give a bright brown color to (as gun barrels) by forming a thin coat of oxide on the surface **c** : to apply the brown coat to (a wall) in plastering **2** : to shoot indiscriminately at (a flock of game birds)

brown alga *n* : an alga of the division Phaeophyta

brown ash *n* **1** : RED ASH 1a **2** : BLACK ASH 1

brownback \'=,=\ *n* : the dowitcher when in brown-backed summer plumage

brown-banded cockroach *or* **brown-banded roach** \'=,==-\ *n* : a small light brown cockroach (*Supella supellectilium*) with two pale crossbands on the wings

brown-banded snake *n* : TIGER SNAKE 1

brown bark spot *n* : a nonparasitic disease of apple and pear trees that produces circular brown spots on the bark

brown bast *n* : a physiological disease of the Para rubber tree characterized by a grayish brown or greenish brown discoloration of the inner bark near the tapping cut and a stoppage in the flow of latex

brown bat *n* : any of various bats somewhat brown in color — see BIG BROWN BAT, LITTLE BROWN BAT

brown bay *n* : CHESTNUT 2b

brown bear *n* : any of several bears predominantly brown in color; *esp* : the common bear (*Ursus arctos*) of Europe

brown bee *n* : BLACK BEE

brown beech *n* : any of several Australian trees; *esp* : NATIVE LAUREL 1

brown bells *n pl but sing or pl in constr* : a fritillary (*Fritillaria parviflora*) of California with brownish purple or greenish flowers

brown bent *or* **brown bent grass** *n* [so called fr. its dark panicles] : DOG BENT

brown-berried cedar *or* **brown-berried juniper** \'=,==-\ *n* : CADE

brown berry \'=¦==\ *n* : a virus disease of the black raspberry characterized by browning, seediness, and drying up of the fruit and by streaking of the foliage — called also *mild streak*

¹brown bess \'=¦bes\ *n, usu cap 2d B* [¹*brown* + *Bess* (nickname of *Elizabeth*); fr. the color of the stock] : the flintlock smoothbore musket with bronzed barrel that was formerly used in the British army

²brown bess *n, usu cap 2d B* [prob. alter. of *brown Beth*] : PRAIRIE WAKE ROBIN

brown beth \'=¦beth\ *n, usu cap 2d B* [prob. fr. ¹*brown* + *beth* (short for *beth root*)] : a trillium with a dusky purplish flower

brown betty *n, usu cap 2d B* [¹*brown* + *Betty* (nickname of *Elizabeth*)] : a betty of sliced or chopped apples, bread crumbs, and spices usu. sweetened with molasses or brown sugar

brown blight *n* : a virus disease of lettuce characterized by spotting and streaking of the leaves, reduction in leaf size, and gradual browning of the leaves from the bases upwards

brown blotch *n* **1** : a disease of the pear possibly caused by the fungus of sooty blotch and characterized by superficial brown spots with indefinite margins on the fruits **2** : a disease of mushrooms caused by a bacterium (*Pseudomonas tolaasi*) and characterized by brown blocthy discoloration

brown body *n* **1** : a body formed in many bryozoans by the degenerating internal organs and believed to have an excretory function **2** : one of numerous flattened or ovoid dark masses in the posterior segments of earthworms resulting from the breakdown of amoebocytes and their included debris

brown bread *n* [ME *broun breed*, fr. *broun* brown + *breed* bread] **1** : any leavened bread darker in color than ordinary wheaten bread: **a** : bread formerly made of native grains (as rye or barley) or maslin often with an admixture of pulses **b** : bread made of whole wheat flour **c** : a dark brown steamed bread made usu. of corn meal, white or whole wheat flours, molasses, soda, and milk or water — called also *Boston brown bread* **2** : SUDAN BROWN

brown brush *n* : BROOM BRUSH

brown bullhead *n* : a dark brown or blackish bullhead (*Ameiurus nebulosus*) that is native to eastern No. America and is an excellent panfish affording considerable sport to anglers

brown canker *n* : a disease of roses caused by a fungus (*Cryptosporella umbrina*) and characterized by lesions that are initially purple, turn white, and finally become buff

brown catechu *n* : CATECHU 1a

brown citrus aphid *n* : a brownish aphid (*Toxoptera citricida*) present in many citrus-growing areas and believed to transmit the tristeza disease of citrus trees

brown coal *n* : LIGNITE; *esp* : loosely consolidated lignite of brownish color and low fuel value

brown coat *n* : the usu. brown coat of plaster that precedes the finishing coat and is often preceded by a scratch coat

brown coati *n* : a largely brown coati (*Nasua narica*) of Mexico and Central America

brown creeper *n* : TREE CREEPER 1a; *esp* : a small No. American tree creeper (*Certhia familiaris americana*) that climbs up the trunks of trees supporting itself by the stiff pointed tail feathers as well as by its feet

brown crowberry *n* : BROOM CROWBERRY

brown dog tick *n* : a widely distributed reddish brown tick (*Rhipicephalus sanguineus*) of the family Ixodidae that occurs on dogs and other mammals and on some birds and that transmits canine babesiasis and possibly other diseases

brown dragon *n* : a jack-in-the-pulpit (*Arisaema atrorubens*)

brown duck *n* **1** : BLACK DUCK **d** **2** : a rather rare New Zealand duck (*Anas chlorotis* or *Elasmonetta chlorotis*) grayish brown above with rufous markings and breast

brown earth *n* : any of a group of intrazonal soils developed in temperate humid regions under deciduous forests from parent material relatively rich in bases and characterized by a dark brown mull horizon that grades through lighter colored soil into parent material — called also *brown forest soil*

brown ebony *n* **1** : WAMARA **2** : GRANADILLA WOOD 4

browned *past of* BROWN

browned-off \'=¦=\ *adj* [*browned* fr. past part. of ³*brown*] *slang* : DISGRUNTLED, DISGUSTED : fed up

browner *comparative of* BROWN

brownest *superlative of* BROWN

brown·ette \(')brau̇¦net\ *n* -S [²*brown* + *-ette*] : a person of intermediate coloring usu. with rather light brown hair, skin fairer than olive, and eyes of blue, gray, or green

brown-eyed su·san \¦=,='süzᵊn\ *n, usu cap S* [*brown-eyed* (fr. ¹*brown* + *eyed*) + *Susan* (as in *black-eyed Susan*)] **1** : any of certain dark-centered coneflowers of the genus *Rudbeckia*: as **a** : a black-eyed Susan (*R. hirta*) **b** : a related Texas herb (*R. bicolor*) **c** : an herb (*R. triloba*) of eastern No. America distinguished by tripartite lower leaves **2** : a blanketflower (*Gaillardia aristata*) of the Rocky mountain area having disk flowers of brownish purple

brown felt blight *n* : a foliage disease of conifers caused by any of several ascomycetous fungi (esp. *Herpotrichia nigra* and *Neopeckia coulteri*) and characterized by a dense cobwebby or felty growth of dark brown to black mycelium on the branches that kills the leaves chiefly by excluding air and light

brown george \-'jȯ(ə)rj\ *n, usu cap G* [¹*brown* + *George* (the name)] **1** *dial Brit* : coarse dark brown bread **2** : a large brown earthenware water vessel

brown hair worm *n* : a small brownish nematode of the genus *Ostertagia* (family Trichostrongylidae) infesting the fourth stomach of sheep

brown hay *n* : hay stacked when partly wilted, turned brown as a result of fermentation, and closely approaching green hay in feeding value

brown-headed nuthatch \'=,==-\ *n* : a nuthatch (*Sitta pusilla*) of the southeastern U.S. that is bluish gray above with the top and back of the head grayish brown

brown heart *n* **1** : ACAPU **2 a** : a physiological disease of stored apples and pears caused by too great a concentration of carbon dioxide and characterized by internal browning **b** : a disease of turnips and related plants caused by a deficiency of boron and characterized by gray or brownish mottling of the outer xylem region of the root

brown hematite *n* : LIMONITE

brown hemp *also* **brown indian hemp** *n* : SUNN

brown hen *n* : GRAY HEN

brown hickory *n* : a pignut (*Carya glabra*)

brown horseshoe bat *n* : an Australian leaf-nosed bat (*Hipposideros bicolor*)

brown hyena *n* : a solitary southern African hyena (*Hyaena brunnea*) often scavenging along the seashore — called also *strand wolf*

brown·ian movement *or* **brownian motion** \'brau̇nēən-\ *n, usu cap B* [after Robert *Brown* †1858 Scot. botanist who discovered it] : the peculiar random movement exhibited by microscopic particles of both organic and inorganic substances when suspended in liquids or gases that is caused by the impact of the molecules of fluid surrounding the particles

brown·ie \'brau̇nē, -ni\ *n* -S [¹*brown* + *-ie*] **1 a** : a good-natured goblin believed to perform helpful services (as threshing, churning, and sweeping) during the night **2 a** : a member of a group of girls between 7½ and 11 years old who are preparing to be Girl Guides **b** : a member of the Girl Scouts in the age group ranging approximately from 7 through 9 years **3 a** *Austral* : a sweet bread made with brown sugar and currants **b** : a small square or rectangle of rich usu. chocolate cake containing nuts **4** : any of various animals somewhat brown in color: as **a** : PECTORAL SANDPIPER **b** : KODIAK BEAR **c** : BROWN TROUT **d** : SMALLMOUTH BLACK BASS **e** : BRAZILIAN SHRIMP **5** *dial* : PENNY, CENT **6** *slang* : a demerit given railroad employees for the infraction of certain rules

brownier *comparative of* BROWNY

browniest *superlative of* BROWNY

¹brown·ing \'brau̇niŋ, -nēŋ\ *n* -S [fr. gerund of ³*brown*] **1** : BROWN COAT **2** : caramelized sugar or browned flour used for coloring and flavoring **3** : any of several abnormalities of plants marked by brownish discoloration of the affected parts: as **a** : a disease of flax caused by a fungus (*Polyspora lini*) and characterized by brownish lesions on and breaking of the stem — called also *stem break* **b** : a boron deficiency disease of cauliflower involving brownish patches in the head **c** : discoloration of cut or injured tissue often resulting from disturbances of respiratory mechanisms (as in cut apples or potatoes) and constituting a serious problem in processing certain fruits and vegetables

²brow·ning \"\ *n* -S *usu cap* [after John M. *Browning* †1926 Am. designer of firearms] : any of several automatic firearms

browning automatic machine rifle *n, usu cap B* : a machine gun identical with the Browning automatic rifle except that the barrel is of the radiator type to facilitate cooling and is provided with a tripod rest

browning automatic rifle *n, usu cap B* : a gas-operated air-cooled portable automatic machine rifle fed from a magazine and mechanically capable of firing 200 to 350 rounds a minute — see RIFLE illustration

browning machine gun *n, usu cap B* : a water-cooled automatic machine gun fed from a web belt, operated by recoil action, and capable of firing more than 500 shots a minute

brown iron ore *n* [trans. of G *brauneisenstein*] : LIMONITE

brown·ish \'braünish, -nēsh\ *adj* : somewhat brown

brown·ism \'braü,nizəm\ *n* -s *usu cap* [Robert *Browne* †1633 Eng. clergyman + E *-ism*] : the views or teachings of Robert Browne who first formulated the principles of Congregationalism and taught that the church is a body of professed believers in Christ united to him and to one another by a covenant, independent of the state, and self-governing by congregations that elect only those officers mentioned in the New Testament

brown·ist \-nəst\ *n* -s *usu cap* : an adherent of Brownism — **brown·is·tic** \(')braü¦nistik\ *adj, usu cap*

brown king snake *n* : a harmless colubrid snake (*Lampropeltis rhombomaculata*) of the southeastern U.S. that preys upon moles

brown knapweed *n* : a perennial knapweed (*Centaurea jacea*) with purplish flowers and involucral bracts entire or irregularly margined but not regularly toothed

brown kurrajong *n* : an Australasian shrub or small tree (*Commersonia platyphylla*) of the family Sterculiaceae with small white flowers in cymes and a capsular bristly fruit

brown leaf rust *n* : a disease of rye caused by a fungus (*Puccinia dispersa*) — compare STEM RUST

brown lemming *n* : a common arctic lemming (*Lemmus trimucronatus*) lacking seasonal variation in pelage

brown·ly *adv* [[1]*brown* + *-ly*] : with brown ⟨~ shadowed⟩ : in a browned condition or manner ⟨a ~ handsome boy⟩

brown madder *n* : CASTILIAN BROWN

brown mahogany *n* : a variable color averaging a dark grayish reddish brown that is lighter, stronger, and slightly yellower than carbuncle and yellower, lighter, and stronger than average burgundy (sense 2a)

brown mallet *also* **brown mallee** *n, Austral* : any of certain shrubs of the genus *Eucalyptus* (esp. *E. astringens*) that are a rich source of tannin

brown malt *n* : malt for brewing kilned at high temperature over a wood fire

brown mica *n* : PHLOGOPITE

brown·mil·ler·ite \'braün,milə,rīt\ *n* -s [G *brownmillerit*, fr. L. T. *Brownmiller* *b*1902 Am. chemist + G *-it* -ite] : a mineral Ca_2AlFeO_5 consisting of an oxide of calcium, iron, and aluminum

brown mite *n* : CLOVER MITE

brown mixture *n* : a dark brown liquid preparation made of fluid extract of licorice root, tartar emetic, camphorated tincture of opium, spirit of ethyl nitrite, glycerol, and water and used as an expectorant

brown mouth *n* : a virus disease of dogs related to and perhaps a phase of distemper

brown mustard *n* **1** : BLACK MUSTARD **2** : INDIAN MUSTARD

brown·ness \-nnəs\ *n* -ES : the quality or state of being brown

brownnose \'=,=\ *vb* [[1]*brown* + *nose*; fr. the implication that servility is tantamount to having one's nose in the anus of the person from whom advancement is sought] *slang* : APPLE-POLISH, TOADY

brown oak *n* : an exceptionally dark reddish brown heartwood occurring in certain English oak trees and highly prized for cabinet and finish work

brown ocher *n* **1** : a limonite that is used as a pigment **2** : OCHER BROWN

brown ore *n* : LIMONITE

brownout \'=,=\ *n* -s [fr. *blackout*, after E *black: brown*] : a curtailment of the use of electric power involving esp. restrictions on the use of lights for advertising or display purposes

brown out *vt* [fr. *black out*, after E *black: brown*] : to be responsible for a brownout in ⟨power shortages *browned out* much of the nation that winter⟩

brown owl *n* : an adult leader of a pack of brownies in the Girl Guide movement

brown oxide *n* : OXIDE BROWN

brown patch *n* : a disease of grasses in golf greens and lawns caused by soil-inhabiting fungi (as *Rhizoctonia solani*) that produce circular brown areas each of which is typically surrounded by a band of grayish black mycelium resembling a smoke ring

brown pelican *n* : an American pelican (*Pelecanus occidentalis*) that is dusky brown above with gray wing coverts and tail, head largely white, neck chestnut brown, and grayish brown underparts, that breeds along the Atlantic coast from So. Carolina to Brazil, and that is represented in the Pacific by several varieties

brown pine *n* **1** : LONGLEAF PINE **2** : a large Australian tree (*Podocarpus elatus*) with straight-grained yellowish wood that turns brown on exposure

brown pod *n* : POD ROT

brown podzolic soil *n* : any of a group of acid zonal soils developed in temperate or cool-temperate humid regions under deciduous or mixed deciduous and coniferous forest and characterized by dark brown humus-mineral soil covered with a thin mat of partly decayed leaves and overlying a brown or yellowish brown B-horizon

brown powder *n* : a gunpowder made by the use of an underburned brown charcoal instead of black charcoal — called also *cocoa powder*

brownprint \'=,=\ *n* : a photographic print like a blueprint but with white lines on brown ground or vice versa

brown rat *n* : the common domestic rat (*Rattus norvegicus*)

brown red *n* : BOLE 3

brown rice *n* : rice removed from the hulls but not polished and retaining most of the bran layers, endosperm, and germ

brown ring *n* : bundle browning in potato tubers caused by freezing or bacterial or fungous infection

brown root disease *n* : a disease of numerous plants (as cacao, coconut, tea, or rubber) throughout the eastern tropics caused by a fungus (*Hymenochaete noxia*) and characterized by defoliation and incrustation of the roots with masses of earth and stones held together by brownish fungal threads

brown root rot *n* **1** : a disease that most frequently affects plants of the pea, potato, and cucumber families, is caused by a fungus (*Thielavia basicola*), and is characterized by brown to blackish discoloration of the roots and stem base accompanied by decay of these parts **2** : a disease of tobacco and other plants comparable to brown root rot of fungus origin and believed to be caused by attack of meadow nematodes

brown rot *n* **1** : any of certain diseases of plants characterized by browning and decay of tissues: as **a** : a disease of stone and pome fruits caused by fungi of the genus *Sclerotinia* and marked by blighting of twigs, blossoms, and leaves and canker of the stems as well as browning **b** *or* **brown rot gummosis** : a destructive disease of citrus fruits caused by a fungus (*Phytophthora citrophthora*) and marked by gummosis of the trunk as well as browning and decay — called also *foot rot* **c** : a destructive disease of potatoes, tomatoes, tobacco, and related plants caused by a bacterium (*Pseudomonas solanacearum*) and marked by browning of the vascular bundles and wilting — called also *ring disease, ring rot, tobacco wilt* **d** : a decay of timber caused by a fungus (*Polyporus sulphureus*) **2** : any organism causing brown rot

brown rust *n* **1** : ORANGE LEAF RUST **2** : BROWN LEAF RUST

browns *pl of* BROWN, *pres 3d sing of* BROWN

brown sauce *n* : a foundation sauce made of stock thickened with flour browned in fat with added seasonings to taste — called also *espagnole*

brown shark *n* **1** : a small brown cat shark (*Apristurus brunneus*) of the Pacific coast of No. America **2** : a common grayish or brownish shark (*Carcharhinus milberti*) widely distributed in the Atlantic ocean **3** : a large gray, brown, or yellowish shark (*Carcharias taurus*) of tropical seas that is chiefly a bottom scavenger alongshore though regarded in southern Africa as the leading man-eater of the area

brownshirt \'=,=\ *n, often cap* [trans. of G *braunhemd*] : a member of the German Sturmabteilung; *broadly* : NAZI

brown shrimp *n* : BRAZILIAN SHRIMP

brownskin \'=,=\ *n* : a Negro with rather light skin coloring

brown snail *n* : a common and now nearly cosmopolitan snail (*Helix aspersa*) having a brown shell with paler zigzag markings and being a serious garden pest in some areas

brown snake *n* **1** : any of several Australian venomous elapid snakes esp. of the genus *Demansia; specif* : a widely distributed brownish or blackish snake (*D. textilis*) **2** : any of a number of small brownish inoffensive colubrid snakes of No. America

brown soft scale *n* : a soft scale (*Coccus hesperidum*) that is a pest esp. on citrus trees

brown soil *n* : any of a zonal group of soils developed in a temperate to cool semiarid climate under short grass, bunch grass, and shrubs and having a brown surface horizon that grades into a layer of carbonate accumulation by way of a layer of lighter-colored soil

brown spot *n* : any of various diseases of plants producing brown discolorations on the leaves; *specif* : a destructive disease of Indian corn caused by a fungus (*Physoderma zeae-maydis*) affecting the leaves and stalks — called also *Physoderma disease*

brown stain *n* : a discoloration of timber caused by oxidation or by accumulation of certain substances during the seasoning process

brown stem rot *n* : a disease of soybeans caused by a fungus (*Cephalosporium gregatum*) and characterized by a marked yellowing followed by browning and withering of the leaves that is due to a brownish internal rot of the stem

brown stock *n* **1** : stock made from beef (as from beef seared to give color) or from a mixture of meats including beef **2** : the unbleached fibers produced by cooking wood by the alkaline processes of papermaking

brownstone \'=,=\ *n* **1 a** : a reddish brown sandstone used for building **b** *also* **brownstone front** : a dwelling faced with brownstone **2** : CHESTNUT 2b — compare BROWN STONE

brown stone \'=¦=\ *n* : COCONUT 4 — compare BROWNSTONE 2

brown stringy rot *n* : a disease of conifers caused by the Indian paint fungus and characterized by rusty-red or brown fibrous stringy streaks in the heartwood

brown study *n* : a mood of serious perplexed absorption or a state of mental abstraction

brown sugar *n* **1** : soft sugar whose crystals are covered by a film of refined dark syrup that imparts color, flavor, and moisture **2** : a moderate yellowish brown that is duller than cinnamon brown and duller and slightly redder than maple sugar or Bismarck brown — called also *Prout's brown*

brown swiss *n, cap B&S* : a breed of large hardy brown dairy cattle originating in Switzerland

brown-tail moth \'=,=-\ *also* **browntail** \'=,=\ *or* **brown-tailed moth** \'=,=-\ *n* : a white-winged moth (*Nygmia phaeorrhoea*) of the family Lymantriidae native to Europe but found in America and chiefly notable for its larva which is covered with long hairs that are irritating or poisonous to the human skin, its nests of silk and leaves, and its feeding on the foliage of various trees

brown thrasher *n* : the common thrasher (*Toxostoma rufum*) of the eastern U.S. that is reddish brown above and streaked below and like the mockingbird to which it is related is a fine singer

brown tick *n* : an African tick (*Rhipicephalus appendiculatus*) that is a common transmitter of east coast fever of cattle

brown tiger *n* : COUGAR

browntop \'=,=\ *n* : any of several grasses of the genus *Agrostis* (esp. *A. tenuis*)

brown towhee *n* : a towhee (*Pipilio fuscus*) that is chiefly dull grayish brown above and is represented by several subspecies in western No. America

brown trout *n* **1** : a common trout (*Salmo trutta*) native to European streams but found in many parts of the world that is dark olive to purplish black above with yellow or brown sides speckled with various colors and pale white, gray, yellow, or pinkish below and that attains a weight in excess of 10 pounds **2** : SMALLMOUTH BLACK BASS

brownweed \'=,=\ *n* : a slender yellow-flowered composite herb (*Bigelowia nudata*) of the southeastern U.S. having disk flowers and resembling a goldenrod in general appearance; *also* : any of several related herbs of the genus *Gutierrezia* of the southwestern U.S.

brown wheat mite *n* : a common mite (*Petrobia latens*) that feeds on growing wheat and other small grains in much of western No. America

browny \'braünē\ *adj* -ER/-EST [[1]*brown* + *-y*] : verging on brown : somewhat brown or browned

browpiece \'=,=\ *n* [[1]*brow* + *piece*] : a heavy upright timber used for underpinning in opening a station for a level in a mine

brow point *n* : BROW ANTLER

browridge \'=,=\ *n* [[1]*brow* + *ridge*] : SUPERCILIARY RIDGE

brows *pl of* BROW, *pres 3d sing of* BROW

[1]**browse** *or* **browze** \'braüz, *esp dial* -aüs\ *n* -s [prob. modif. of MF *brouts*, pl. of *brout* sprout, shoot, fr. OF *brost*, of Gmc origin; akin to OS *brustian* to bud, sprout, OE *brēost* breast — more at BREAST] **1 a** : the tender shoots, twigs, and leaves of trees and shrubs often used as food for cattle and other animals ⟨a good bed of spruce ~⟩ ⟨deer have outmultiplied the available ~⟩ **b** : any plant valued for the production of browse ⟨sagebrush is an important ~⟩ **2** [*browse*, v.] : an act or instance of browsing ⟨cattle out for an evening ~⟩ ⟨at first ~ the book is not impressive⟩

[2]**browse** *or* **browze** \"\ *vb* -ED/-ING/-s [perh. fr. (assumed) MF *brouser* (whence obs. F *brouser*), prob. fr. *brouts*, pl. of *brout* sprout, shoot] *vt* **1 a** : to consume as browse ⟨a donkey *browsing* thistles⟩ **b** : to feed on the browse of ⟨deer *browsed* the hillside⟩ **c** : GRAZE — not used technically **2** : to feed (as cattle) on browse ⟨farmers forced to ~ their stock when hay ran low⟩ **3 a** : to look over casually (as a book) : SKIM ⟨he lazily *browsed* the headlines⟩ **b** : to make (one's way) by browsing ⟨I *browsed* my way through the agony column⟩ ~ *vi* **1 a** : to feed on or as if on browse ⟨fishes that ~ on algae⟩ **b** : GRAZE — not used technically **2 a** : to skim through a book reading at random passages that catch the eye **b** : to look over books (as in a store or library) esp. in order to decide what one wants to buy, borrow, or read **c** : to casually inspect goods offered for sale usu. without prior or serious intention of buying **d** : to make an examination without real knowledge or purpose

browse line *n* : the boundary between upper normal plant growth and lower stripped and eaten-back growth that indicates the height reached in feeding by the larger browsers

brows·er \-zə(r)\ *n* -s : one that browses; *esp* : an animal that habitually feeds by browsing — compare GRAZER

browsing *n* -s [fr. gerund of [2]*browse*] **1** *obs* **a** : BROWSE **b** : a place where there is an abundance of browse **2** : the act of one that browses (as among books or goods or on vegetation)

browsing room *n* : a room or section in a library designed to allow patrons an opportunity to freely examine and browse in a collection of books

browst \'braüst, 'brüst\ *n* -s [prob. back-formation fr. *browster*] **1** *chiefly Scot* : BREWING, BREW **2** *chiefly Scot* : OUTCOME, CONSEQUENCE

brow·ster \-tər\ *chiefly Scot var of* BREWSTER

brow tine *n* : BROW ANTLER

brs *abbr* brass

brt *abbr* brought

bru·ang \'brü,aŋ, =¦=\ *n* -s [Malay *bĕruang*] : SUN BEAR

bru·bru \'brü,brü\ *or* **brubru shrike** *n* -s [native name in Africa] : any of several African shrikes (genus *Nilaus*) widely distributed in dry uplands

bru·cel·la \brü'selə\ *n* [NL, fr. Sir David *Bruce* †1931 Brit. physician and bacteriologist + NL *-ella*] **1** *cap* : the type genus of Brucellaceae comprising nonmotile capsulated bacteria that lack bipolar staining and are pathogenic for man and domestic animals — see BRUCELLOSIS **2** *pl* **brucel·lae** \-e(,)lē\ *or* **brucellas** : a bacterium of the genus *Brucella*

bru·cel·la·ce·ae \,brüsə'lāsē,ē\ *n pl, cap* [NL, fr. *Brucella*, type genus + *-aceae*] : a family of small gram-negative coccoid to rod-shaped eubacteria that are obligate parasites chiefly of warm-blooded vertebrates and that include a number of serious pathogens — see BRUCELLA; compare HEMOPHILUS, PASTEURELLA

bru·cel·lar \brü'selə(r)\ *adj* [NL *Brucella* + E *-ar*] : of, with, or resulting from brucellae : of or relating to the genus *Brucella*

bru·cel·ler·gen *or* **bru·cel·ler·gin** \brü'selə(r)jən\ *n* -s [fr. *Brucellergen*, a trademark] : a nucleoprotein fraction of brucellae used in skin tests to detect the presence of brucella infections

bru·cel·lin \brü'selən\ *n* -s [fr. *Brucellin*, a trademark] : a cell-free polysaccharide-containing culture filtrate of brucellae used in skin tests to detect the presence of brucella infections

bru·cel·lo·sis \,brüsə'lōsəs\ *n, pl* **brucello·ses** \-ō,sēz\ [NL, fr. *Brucella* + *-osis*] : a disease caused by bacteria of the genus *Brucella*: **a** : a disease of man of sudden or insidious onset and long duration characterized by great weakness, extreme exhaustion on slight effort, night sweats, chilliness, remittent fever, and generalized aches and pains and acquired through direct contact with infected animals or animal products or from the consumption of milk, dairy products, or meat from infected animals — called also *Malta fever, undulant fever* **b** : CONTAGIOUS ABORTION

bruce spanworm \'brüs-\ *also* **bruce's spanworm** \'brüsəz-\ *n, usu cap B* [prob. after William S. *Bruce* †1921 Brit. explorer and naturalist] : a spanworm (*Operophtera bruceata*) that feeds in early spring on the foliage of deciduous trees in the northeastern U. S. and southern Canada

[1]**bru·chid** \'brükəd\ *adj* [NL *Bruchidae*] : of or relating to the family Bruchidae

[2]**bruchid** \"\ *n* -s : a beetle of the family Bruchidae

bru·chi·dae \'brükə,dē\ *n pl, cap* [NL, fr. *Bruchus*, type genus + *-idae*] : a family (type genus *Bruchus*) of small beetles most of whose larvae infest the seeds of peas and other legumes

bruch's membrane \'brüḵs-, -ül, ¦ks-\ *n, usu cap B* [after Carl W. L. *Bruch* †1884 Ger. anatomist] : the inner limiting membrane of the retina separating the pigmented layer of the retina from the choroid coat of the eye

bru·chus \'brükəs\ *n* [NL, fr. L, wingless larva of the locust, fr. Gk *broukos, brouchos* locust, wingless larva of the locust] **1** *cap* : the type genus of the family Bruchidae **2** *pl* **bruchus** *or* **bruchuses** : any of the small seed-eating weevils that constitute the genus *Bruchus*

bru·cia \'brüsēə, -üsh(ē)ə\ *n* -s [NL, alter. of *Brucea*] : BRUCINE

bruc·ine \'brü,sēn, -sən\ *n* -s [prob. fr. F, fr. NL *Brucea* (genus name of *Brucea antidysenterica*, a shrub in which it was erroneously considered to be present, after James Bruce †1794 Scot. explorer of Africa) + F *-ine*] : a bitter poisonous crystalline alkaloid $C_{23}H_{26}N_2O_4$ found with strychnine esp. in nux vomica and ignatia and used chiefly in denaturing alcohol; dimethoxy-strychnine

bruc·ite \-,sīt, *usu* -īd.+V\ *n* -s [Archibald *Bruce* †1818 Am. mineralogist + E *-ite*] : a mineral $Mg(OH)_2$ consisting of native magnesium hydroxide occurring in thin pearly folia and in fibrous form (hardness 2.5, sp. gr. 2.38–2.40)

[1]**bruck·le** \'brəkəl, -rük-\ *adj* [ME *brukel* frail, fr. OE *-brucol* — more at BRICKLE] *chiefly Scot* : easily broken or crumbled : BRITTLE

[2]**bruckle** *vt* -ED/-ING/-s [prob. freq. of Sc *brook, bruik* to soil, begrime] *obs* : DIRTY, BEGRIME

brück·ner cycle \'brüknə(r)-, -rik-, -rœk-\ *n, usu cap B* [after Eduard *Brückner* †1927 Ger. meteorologist] : a climatic cycle marked by the recurrence of warm and dry years and cool and rainy years and averaging about 35 years

[1]**brugh** \'brəḵ\ *n* -s [alter. of *borough*] *Scot* : a town or borough

[2]**brugh** \"\ *var of* [2]BROCH

bru·gna·tel·lite \,brünyə'te,līt\ *n* -s [It *brugnatellite*, fr. Luigi *Brugnatelli* †1928 Ital. mineralogist + It *-ite*] : a mineral $Mg_6Fe(OH)_{13}(CO_3).4H_2O$ consisting of a hydrous ultrabasic carbonate of iron and magnesium occurring in flesh-red lamellar masses

bruh \'brü\ *also* **broh** \'brō\ *n* -s [Malay *bĕrok*] **1** : the pig-tailed macaque (*Macaca nemestrina*) of the East Indies **2** : any of various macaques

bruik \'brük, -rœk\ *Scot var of* BROOK

bru·in \'brüən\ *n* -s [D *Bruin* (name of the bear in the beast epic *Reynard the Fox*), fr. MD *Bruun*, fr. *bruun* brown; akin to OE *brūn* brown — more at BROWN] : BEAR — a conventional epithet esp. in tales and familiar use

[1]**bruise** \'brüz\ *vb* -ED/-ING/-s [ME *brusen, brisen*, fr. MF *bruisier* to break, shatter & OE *brȳsan* to bruise, crush; MF *bruisier* of Celt origin; akin to OIr *brūu* I shatter, MW *breu* brittle; OE *brȳsan* akin to OIr *brūu*, MW *breu*, L *frustum* piece, Alb *breshën* hail] *vt* **1 a** *archaic* : to crush or mangle (as by a heavy blow) : DISABLE **b** : BATTER, INDENT ⟨~ armor⟩ **2** : to inflict a bruise on : CONTUSE **3** : to crush or break down (as by a severe blow or by pressure against a hard surface) ⟨be careful not to ~ the tender tobacco leaves⟩ ⟨~ enough berries for a pint of juice⟩ **4** : WOUND, INJURE; *esp* : to inflict psychological hurt on ⟨a human spirit that has been *bruised* by the brutalities of the world —J.C.Powys⟩ ~ *vi* **1** : to inflict a bruise ⟨hailstones are likely to ~⟩ **2** : to bear or show the effects of a bruise : be susceptible to bruising ⟨tomatoes ~ readily unless carefully handled⟩ ⟨she ~s easily⟩

[2]**bruise** \"\ *n* -s [ME *bruse* fr. *brusen*, v.] **1** : an injury esp. produced by a blow or collision that does not break the surface it injures: as **a** : an injury transmitted through unbroken skin to underlying tissue causing rupture of small blood vessels and escape of blood into the tissue with resulting discoloration : CONTUSION **b** : a similar injury to a plant or fruit **2** : an abrasion or scratch on a surface (as of leather or rock) **3** : an injury or hurt (as to the feelings or the pride) **syn** see WOUND

bruis·er \-zə(r)\ *n* -s **1** *slang* : a professional boxer : PUGILIST **2** : a big husky man; *esp* : one somewhat coarse and beefy

bruisewort \'=,=\ *n* [ME *brisewort*, fr. OE *brȳsewyrt*, fr. *brȳsan* to bruise + *wyrt* wort — more at BRUISE, WORT] : any plant supposed to heal bruises: as **a** : DAISY 1a **b** : SOAPWORT **c** : COMFREY 1

bruising *adj* : forceful and compelling esp. in a brutal way : CRUSHING ⟨civilians at home . . . protected from the ~ facts of battle —John Mason Brown⟩

[1]**bruit** \'brüt, *for 2* -üē\ *n* -s [ME *bruit, brute*, fr. MF *bruit*, fr. OF, noise, din, fr. past part. of *bruire* to make a din, to roar, fr. (assumed) VL *brugere*, prob. blend of (assumed) VL *bragere* to yell, bray, make a noise and L *rugire* to roar; akin to OE *rēoc* wild, Goth *inrauhtjan* to become angry, Gk *erygmēlos* bellowing, MIr *rucht* roar, howl, OSlav *ružetŭ* he neighs, and prob. to L *rumor* noise, rumor — more at BRAY, RUMOR] **1** *archaic* **a** : NOISE, CLAMOR, DIN **b** : report or rumor esp. when favorable **2** [F, fr. *bruit* noise, fr. MF] : any of several generally abnormal sounds heard on auscultation

[2]**bruit** \-üt\ *vt* -ED/-ING/-s **1** : to noise abroad : REPORT — often used with *about* **2** : to make celebrated by general mention : PUBLICIZE, TOUT ⟨the much ~*ed* superiority of the male —*Saturday Rev.*⟩

bru·ja \'brü,hä, -,ḵä\ *n* -s [Sp, of non-IE origin; akin to the source of Pg *bruxa* witch, Catal *bruixa*] : WITCH, SORCERESS

bru·jo \-,hō, -,ḵō\ *n* -s [Sp, fr. *bruja*] : SORCERER, WITCH DOCTOR; *esp* : one that works black magic

bru·lé \(')brü¦lā, 'brül(ē)\ *n, pl* **brulé** *or* **brulés** *usu cap* [CanF, fr. F *brûlé*, past part.] : an Indian people constituting a subdivision of the Teton Dakotas

brû·lée *also* **brû·lé** \(')brü¦lā, brüə'lā\ *n* -s [CanF *brûlé*, fr. F, past part. of *brûler* to burn, fr. OF *bruller*, perh. blend of OHG *brennen* + L *ustulare*, fr. *ustus*, past part. of *urere* — more at BURN, EMBER] : a piece of burned-over woodland

brul·yie \'brül(y)ē, -rəl-\ *n* -s [MF *brouillis* quarrel, trouble, disturbance, fr. *brouiller* to mix, confuse — more at BROIL] *Scot & Irish* : DISTURBANCE, ROW, SCUFFLE

bru·mal \'brüməl\ *adj* [L *brumalis*, fr. *bruma* winter + *-alis* -al — more at BRUME] *archaic* : indicative of or occurring in the winter ⟨the bears . . . were sunk in the ~ sleep —Vance Randolph⟩

bru·ma·lia \brü'mālēə, -lyə\ *n pl, cap* [L, fr. neut. pl. of *brumalis*] : a pagan festival held at the winter solstice from which some features of the celebration of Christmas seem to have originated

brum·by \'brəmbē\ *n* -ES [prob. native name in Queensland, Australia] *Austral* : WILD HORSE : OUTLAW

brume \'brüm\ *n* -s [F, mist, winter, fr. MF, fr. OProv *bruma*, fr. L, winter, fr. *brevis* short; fr. the short days — more at BRIEF] : MIST, FOG, VAPOR ⟨the valleys faint with ~ —Christopher Fry⟩

[1]**brum·ma·gem** \'brəməjəm\ *adj* [fr. *Brummagem*, alter. of *Birmingham*, England] **1** *usu cap* : of or belonging to Birmingham, England — sometimes taken to be offensive **2** [fr. the fact that in the 17th cent. notorious counterfeit groats were coined in Birmingham and that in the 19th cent. various cheap and flimsy articles were manufactured there] : spurious esp. in

a cheap and showy way : PHONY, SHAM ⟨a bilious combination of ~ melodrama and synthetic seascapes —John McCarten⟩
²**brummagem** \"\ *n* -s : something cheap or inferior : TINSEL, COUNTERFEIT
brum·my \'brəmi\ *adj* [by shortening & alter.] *chiefly Brit* : BRUMMAGEM
bru·mous \'brüməs\ *adj* [F *brumeux*, fr. *brume* fog — more at BRUME] : FOGGY, MISTY ⟨the ~ October gloaming —John Galsworthy⟩
brum·stone \'brəmztən, -rəm-, -mst\ *dial Brit var of* BRIMSTONE
brunch \'brənch\ *n* -ES [*breakfast* + *lunch*] : a meal served usu. in the late morning : a late breakfast, an early lunch, or a combination of the two
brunch coat *n* : a woman's short housecoat or wraparound dress
brun do·ré \ˌbrəndəˈrā, -ˌdōˈ-\ *n*, *pl* **brun do·rés** *or* **bruns dorés** \-nd . . . āz\ [F, lit., golden brown] : OLIVE WOOD
brune \'brün, 'brēn\ *n* -s [F — more at BRUNET] : BRUNET
bru·nel·lia \brüˈnelēə, -lyə\ *n*, *cap* [NL, fr. G. *Brunelli*, 18th cent. Ital. botanist + NL *-ia*] : a small genus (coextensive with the family Brunelliaceae of the order Ranales) of tropical American trees having unisexual panicled apetalous flowers and follicular fruits
¹**bru·net** *or* **bru·nette** \(ˈ)brüˈnet, *usu* -ed·+V\ *adj* [F *brunet*, masc., & *brunette*, fem, brownish, fr. OF, fr. *brun* brown, fr. ML *brunus*, of Gmc origin; akin to OHG *brūn* brown — more at BROWN] : of or marked by dark or relatively dark pigmentation: **a** *of hair and eyes* : BROWN, BLACK **b** *of skin* : BROWN, OLIVE
²**brunet** *or* **brunette** \"\ *n* -s [F *brunet*, masc., & *brunette*, fem., fr. *brunet*, *brunette*, adj.] : a person with brunet hair or skin or both
brun·fel·sia \brənˈfelzēə\ *n*, *cap* [NL, fr. Otto *Brunfels* †1534 Ger. botanist + NL *-ia*] : a genus of tropical American shrubs (family Solanaceae) that have alternate entire leaves and a fleshy fruit like a berry and that are commonly grown in greenhouses for their flowers
brung *substand past of* BRING
bru·ni·zem \'brünəˌzem\ *n* -s [*bruni-* (fr. ML *brunus* brown) + *-zem* earth (as in *chernozem*)] : a soil of the prairies developed from loess and occurring extensively in Iowa
brun·ne·ous \'brənēəs\ *or* **brun·nes·cent** \(ˈ)brəˈnesᵊnt\ *adj* [irreg. fr. ML *brunus* brown + E *-ous* or *-escent* — more at BRUNET] : dark brown — used chiefly scientifically
brun·ner's gland \'brúnə(r)z-\ *n*, *usu cap B* [after Johann C. *Brunner* †1727 Swiss anatomist] : any of certain compound racemose glands in the submucous layer of the duodenum secreting alkaline mucus and a potent proteolytic enzyme
brun·nich·ia \ˌ(ˌ)brəˈnikēə\ *n*, *cap* [NL, fr. M.T.*Brünnich* †1827 Dan. naturalist + NL *-ia*] : a small genus of herbaceous vines (family Polygonaceae) having climbing tendrils, broad leaves, and inconspicuous racemose flowers — see BUCKWHEAT VINE
brün·nich's murre *also* **brünnich's guillemot** \'briniks-\ *n*, *usu cap B* [after M.T.*Brünnich*] : THICK-BILLED MURRE
brünn race \'brin-, -rœn-\ *n*, *usu cap B* [fr. *Brünn* (now Brno), Czechoslovakia] : an Upper Paleolithic people related to the Cro-Magnons but differing in having shorter stature, narrower face and head, and heavier brow ridges, orig. based on skeletal material found associated with Solutrean artifacts at Brno and Predmost, Czechoslovakia, and subsequently recognized in fossil finds in other parts of Europe, in No. Africa, and in western Asia and as a component in modern man
brunn's membrane \'brünz-\ *n*, *usu cap B* [after Albert von *Brunn* †1895 Ger. anatomist] : the part of the nasal mucous membrane that serves as an organ of smell
bru·no man \'brü(ˌ)nō-\ *n* [*Bruno* (*shovel*), a hand shovel used to move loose ore] : a worker who uses a hand shovel to move loose ore (as to an ore car)
bru·no·nia \brüˈnōnēə, -ōnyə\ *n*, *cap* [NL, irreg. fr. Robert *Brown* †1858 Scot. botanist + NL *-ia*] : a genus (coextensive with the family Brunoniaceae of the order Campanulales) of Australian herbs with radical leaves and a long-stalked globular head of showy blue flowers
bruns·wick \'brənz(ˌ)wik, -ˌwēk\ *adj*, *usu cap* [fr. *Brunswick* (Braunschweig), Germany] : of or from the city of Brunswick, Germany : of the kind or style prevalent in Brunswick
brunswick black *n*, *often cap 1st B* [trans. of G *Braunschweiger schwarz*] : a black varnish usu. similar in composition to black japan
brunswick blue *n*, *often cap 1st B* [trans. of G *Braunschweiger blau*] **1** : a pigment consisting of a mixture of an iron blue with a large amount of barium sulfate **2** : PRUSSIAN BLUE 2
brunswick green *n*, *often cap B* [trans. of G *Braunschweiger grün*] **1 a** : a green pigment consisting of a copper salt (as a basic copper chloride or a basic copper carbonate) — called also *old Brunswick green* **b** : CHROME GREEN 1b **2** : any of three greens: **a** : DEEP BRUNSWICK GREEN **b** : MIDDLE BRUNSWICK GREEN **c** : LIGHT BRUNSWICK GREEN
brunswick stew *n*, *often cap B* [fr. *Brunswick* county, Va., where it originated] **1** : a hunter's stew made with squirrel or rabbit and onion **2** : a stew of two or more meats with vegetables (as game and chicken with corn, okra, and tomatoes)
¹**brunt** \'brənt\ *n* -s [ME] **1** *obs* **a** : a forceful onset : a sudden or violent assault ⟨the garrison withstood the ~ on the castle⟩ **b** : a sudden outburst or effort **2** : the main force, shock, or stress : the impact, strain, or violence calling for greatest resistance ⟨employees in the textile and metal trades exposed to the full ~ of foreign competition —J.A.Hobson⟩ ⟨the ~ of the struggle with the German army fell upon the Russians —Walter Lippmann⟩ **syn** see IMPACT
²**brunt** \'brənt, -rənt\ *dial Brit past of* BURN
¹**brush** \'brəsh\ *n* -ES *often attrib* [ME *brusch*, fr. MF *broce*, fr. OF, perh. of Celt origin; akin to OIr *froech* heather — more at BRIER] **1** : BRUSHWOOD **2 a** : scrub vegetation **b** : land covered with scrub vegetation : BRUSHLAND — often used with *the* ⟨helped work cattle in the Florida ~ —F.B.Gipson⟩ **3** *chiefly Austral* : a dense growth of forest and undergrowth
²**brush** \"\ *vt* -ED/-ING/-ES **1** : to clear (land) of brush and undergrowth ⟨~ the back forty⟩ **2** : to use cut-off branches as supports for (vines and plants) ⟨peas should be ~*ed*⟩

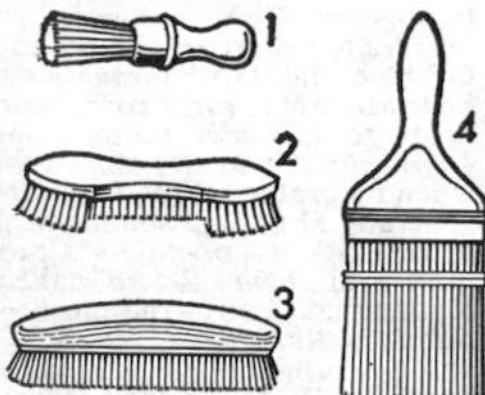

brushes: *1* shaving brush, *2* scrubbing brush, *3* clothes brush, *4* paintbrush

³**brush** \"\ *n* -ES [ME *brusshe*, fr. MF *broisse*, fr. OF *broce* brushwood] **1 a** : a hand-operated or power-driven tool or device composed of bristles set into a back or a handle or attached to a roller and designed or adapted for such uses as sweeping, scrubbing, painting, and smoothing ⟨a floor ~⟩ ⟨a wire ~⟩ **b** : one of a pair of long slender devices of this kind with flexible wire bristles used for making soft rhythmic hissing sounds on a cymbal or snare drum esp. in a dance band **2** : something resembling or suggesting a brush ⟨a thick ~ of wavy hair⟩: as **a** : a heavily haired bushy tail (as that of a fox or squirrel or of certain dogs or cats) ⟨the fox had a handsome red ~⟩ **b** (1) : an herb (*Lepachys columnifera*) of the western U.S. resembling a coneflower (2) : the young strobile or gynoecium of the hop (3) : a tuft of hairs (as on the tip of the wheat kernel) (4) : the inflorescence of the broomcorn **c** : a feather tuft worn on a hat ⟨a cock-green Tyrolean ~ in my hat —Saul Bellow⟩ **3 a** : an electrical conductor commonly in the form of a bundle of copper strips or wire gauze or a block of carbon serving as a means of connection by sliding contact between a stationary and a moving part of an electric circuit (as between line and armature of a generator or a motor) **b** : BRUSH DISCHARGE **4** [⁴*brush*] **a** : an act or instance of brushing ⟨he gave his old suit a quick ~⟩ **b** : a quick light touch : a fleeting momentary contact ⟨she felt the ~ of his coat as he hurried by⟩ **c** (1) : a light stroke with one foot, toe, or heel along the floor in any direction in dancing (2) : a low ballet kick in which the sole of the foot strikes the floor **d** *slang* : a quiet and decisive rejection or dismissal : BRUSH-OFF
⁴**brush** \"\ *vb* -ED/-ING/-ES [ME *brusshen*, fr. *brusshe*, n.] *vt* **1 a** : to apply a brush to or use a brush on ⟨she was ~*ing* her hair⟩ ⟨take the bread from the oven and ~ the loaves with butter⟩ **b** : to apply with a brush ⟨the paint must be ~*ed* carefully onto the porous surface⟩ **2 a** : to remove with a brush or by an act similar to brushing ⟨~ the dust from your shoes⟩ ⟨he . . . ~*ed* the ash from his cigarette —Nevil Shute⟩ **b** : to push or force esp. in the course of physical motion ⟨two men ~*ed* their way through the crowd⟩ ⟨~ obstacles aside⟩ **c** : to dispose of in an offhand way : dismiss or reject summarily or perfunctorily — usu. used with *aside*, *away*, or *off* ⟨impatiently ~*ed* aside the thought —Kathleen Freeman⟩ ⟨~*ed* our thanks away —Thomas Wood †1950⟩ ⟨asked a polite question but was ~*ed off*⟩ **3 a** : to pass lightly over or across : touch gently against in passing ⟨my left hand ~*ed* the wall and found the doorknob —Hartley Howard⟩ **b** : AFFECT, TOUCH ⟨the spirit of compromise which responsibility brings has not ~*ed* him —*Time*⟩ **4** : to beat (fibers) lightly to cause fraying or roughening rather than cutting in papermaking **5** *dial chiefly Eng* : TRIM, CLIP ⟨~*ing* the shrubbery⟩ ~ *vi* **1** : to make the contact or motion or perform the action of brushing something ⟨other stewards and messmen were scouring, scrubbing, ~*ing*, mopping —*Nation's Business*⟩ **2** *of a horse*: to interfere slightly so as to produce abrasion
⁵**brush** \"\ *adj* [³*brush*] : resembling a brush esp. in being bristly or cut relatively short and of even length ⟨a ~ haircut⟩ ⟨a ~ mustache⟩
⁶**brush** \"\ *vb* -ED/-ING/-ES [ME *bruschen* to rush, drive (influenced in meaning by ³ & ⁴ *brush*), fr. MF *brosser* to dash through underbrush, fr. *broce*, *brosse*, *broisse* underbrush] *vi* : to move so lightly or deftly as to be scarcely perceptible : move so as to graze, skim over, or sweep something ⟨~ past people quickly without hitting them carelessly with your umbrella —Agnes M. Miall⟩ ~ *vt* : to force (a horse) to top speed over a short distance
⁷**brush** \"\ *n* -ES [ME *brusche* rush, hostile collision (influenced in meaning by ³ & ⁴ *brush*), fr. *bruschen* to rush, drive] **1 a** : a brief or fleeting encounter; *usu* : one that involves an element of risk or contention ⟨he had several ~*es* with the law⟩ ⟨a ~ with enemy troops⟩ **2** : a usu. short often impromptu race ⟨the horses came even and their riders decided to have a ~⟩
brush·a·bil·i·ty \ˌbrəshəˈbiləd·ē\ *n* -ES : the behavior characteristic of a liquid (as paint) when applied by brush
brush apple *n* [¹*brush*] : BLACK APPLE
brush arbor *n* [¹*brush*] *South & Midland* : an arbor made of brushwood esp. as a place for a camp meeting
brush block *n* [⁶*brush*] : a football maneuver in which an offensive player makes light contact with an opponent and continues downfield for secondary blocking
brush bloodwood *n* [¹*brush*] : BLOODWOOD a(2)
brush border *n* [³*brush*] : a striated border on the cells forming the membrane proper in certain epithelial membranes (as in that of the proximal convoluted tubule of the kidney) that is usu. regarded as associated with absorptive phenomena
brush box *n* [¹*brush*] : an Australian tree (*Tristania conferta*) that has evergreen foliage and is cultivated for shade — called also *Brisbane box*
brush bronzewing *n* [¹*brush*] : a bronzewing (*Phaps elegans*) that is bronze-brown above and largely bluish gray below
brush broom *n* [¹*brush*] *South & Midland* : a broom made of small twiggy branches or corn husks tied together and used for outdoor sweeping ⟨the paths swept with a *brush broom* —Ellen Glasgow⟩
brush burn *n* : an injury of the skin due to intense friction ⟨there were also *brush burns* showing that she had been dragged —M.G.Bishop⟩
brush cherry *n* [¹*brush*] **1** : an Australian timber tree (*Eugenia myrtifolia*) — called also *native myrtle* **2** : the edible fruit of the brush cherry — called also *rose apple* **3** : an Australian shrub (*Trochocarpa laurina*)
brush coating *n* [³*brush*] : a paper-coating process in which the wet coating mixture is smoothed on the surface by means of brushes
brush country *n* : an extensive area of land on which the characteristic plant forms are low shrubby growths — compare CHAPARRAL, THICKET
brush cut *n* [³*brush*] : a very short even haircut often in a flat plane on top so that the hair stands out and suggests a brush
brush dampener *n* [³*brush*] : a machine for spattering water onto paper by means of rotary brushes
brush discharge *n* [³*brush*] : a faintly luminous relatively slow electrical discharge having no spark
¹**brushed** \'brəsht\ *adj* [¹*brush* + *-ed*] : ²BRUSHY
²**brushed** \"\ *adj* [fr. past part. of ⁴*brush*] *of a woven or knitted fabric* : finished with a nap ⟨a ~ rayon bed jacket⟩
¹**brush·er** \'brəshə(r)\ *n* -s [⁴*brush* + *-er*] : one that brushes by hand or by machine esp. as a vocation
²**brusher** \"\ *n* -s [¹*brush* + *-er*] **1** : a worker who cuts and burns small trees and brush **2** : LIMBER **3** : WHITE BISKOP
brushes *pl of* BRUSH, *pres 3d sing of* BRUSH
brush fire *n* [¹*brush*] : a fire involving scrub trees, brush, or other growth that is heavier than grass but not of full tree size
brush-fire \'≠,≠\ *adj* [*brush fire*] *of warfare* : limited in scale or in area ⟨a mobile striking force, always on the ready, to fight *brush-fire* wars —*Newsweek*⟩
brush harrow *n* [¹*brush*] : a crude light harrow made of short tough tree branches (as hawthorn) fastened to one side of a pole and used chiefly to cover seeds
brush hook *n* [¹*brush*] : BUSH HOOK
brushier *comparative of* BRUSHY
brushiest *superlative of* BRUSHY
brushing *n* -s [fr. gerund of ⁴*brush*] : a finishing process for fabrics usu. used to produce a thick nap
brushings *n pl* [fr. gerund of ⁴*brush*] : material removed and collected by brushing
brush·ite \'brəˌshīt\ *n* -s [George J. *Brush* †1912 Am mineralogist + E *-ite*] : a nearly colorless mineral $CaHPO_4 \cdot 2H_2O$ consisting of calcium hydrogen phosphate in slender crystals or massive
brush kangaroo *n* [¹*brush*] : a large wallaby
brushland \'≠,≠\ *n* [¹*brush* + *land*] : an area characterized by scrub growth
brush·less \'brəshləs\ *adj* [³*brush* + *-less*] **1** : lacking a brush **2** : designed for use without a brush ⟨~ shaving cream⟩
brushlike \'≠,≠\ *adj* : resembling a brush
¹**brush·man** \-mən\ *n*, *pl* **brushmen** [³*brush* + *man*] **1** : one who uses a brush esp. as a vocation: as **a** : a worker who assists in cleaning the outside of a building by brushing a previously scoured surface with a chemical cleaner **b** : one who applies coats of finish with a brush **c** : a worker who roughens new concrete pavement with a stiff brush — called also *broom man* **2** : a painter esp. skilled in brushwork
²**brushman** \"\ *n*, *pl* **brushmen** [¹*brush* + *man*] : one who cuts and burns brush
brush mouse *n* [¹*brush*] : a common white-footed mouse (*Peromyscus boylii*) of the western U.S.
brush–off \'≠,≠\ *n* -s [*brush off*, v.] **1** : a quietly curt or disdainful dismissal ⟨she gave him the *brush-off*⟩ **2** : an offensive maneuver used by basketball and lacrosse players to get rid of an opponent by running him into a teammate
brush ore *n* [³*brush*] : an iron ore in stalactitic forms resembling a brush
brushout \'≠,≠\ *n* -s [*brush out*, v.] : a sample application of paint usu. for testing
brush–pen \'≠,≠\ *n* [³*brush*] : a pen with a fibrous point
brushpopper \'≠,≠≠\ *n* -s [¹*brush* + *popper*] *West* : COWBOY; *esp* : one working in brushy country
brush rabbit *n* [¹*brush*] : a small short-legged brownish rabbit (*Sylvilagus bachmani*) found on the Pacific coast
brush scythe *n* [¹*brush*] : BUSH SCYTHE
brushstroke \'≠,≠\ *n* : the configuration given to thick paint (as oil paint) by contact with the bristles of a brush; *also* : the paint left on a surface by a single application of a loaded brush or palette knife
brush–tailed porcupine *or* **brush–tail porcupine** *n* : any of certain Old World porcupines that constitute the genus *Atherurus* and have a tuft of large beaded bristles on the tail
brush–tongued \'≠,≠\ *adj* [³*brush*] : having the tongue papillae long and slender so that the tongue resembles a brush
brush–tongued parrot *n* : LORIKEET
brush–treat \'≠,≠\ *vt* : to apply preservatives to with a brush ⟨*brush-treat* the floorboards⟩
brush turkey *n* [¹*brush*] : MEGAPODE; *esp* : a large megapode (*Alectura lathami*) of the wooded regions of eastern Australia
brush turpentine *n* [¹*brush*] : either of two Australian trees (*Rhodamia trinerva* and *Syncarpia leptopetala*) of the family Myrtaceae used as a source of timber
brush up *vt* **1** : to polish up or improve by eliminating small imperfections ⟨spent their off time in *brushing up* their act⟩ **2** : to refresh one's memory of : renew one's skill in or knowledge of ⟨*brush up* your Shakespeare⟩ ⟨*brushed up* his piano technique⟩ ~ *vi* : to refresh one's memory : renew one's skill or knowledge — used with *on* ⟨*brushing up* on his golf⟩ ⟨*brushing up* on their understanding of the accepted maritime law —F.L.Paxson⟩ ⟨*brush up* on the significant dates before the history exam⟩
brushup \'≠,≠\ *n* -s [*brush up*] **1 a** : review or practice with the intent of refreshing the memory or polishing up a skill ⟨the orchestra needed a good deal of ~ before the performance⟩ ⟨a special ~ course⟩ ⟨a little instructive ~ on English history —Mollie Panter-Downes⟩ **b** : a period of such review or practice ⟨the play had a two-week ~ before opening in New York⟩ **2** : a fixing up of something that has begun to show signs of age or wear or that shows slight imperfections ⟨the painters . . . had been doing some ~ work in the halls —E.D.Radin⟩
brush wheel *n* [³*brush*] **1** : a wheel used formerly to turn another wheel by the friction of bristles fixed in the outer rim **2** : a circular revolving brush used for polishing
brush wolf *n* [¹*brush*] : COYOTE
brushwood \'≠,≠\ *n* [¹*brush* + *wood*] **1** : the wood of small branches esp. when cut or broken **2** : a thicket composed of shrubs and small trees
brushwork \'≠,≠\ *n* [³*brush* + *work*] **1** : work done with a brush (as in painting) **2** : the distinctive and characteristic use of the tools and equipment of an art (as of a brush by a painter or words by a writer) : TECHNIQUE
¹**brushy** \'brəshē, -shi\ *adj* -ER/-EST [³*brush* + *-y*] : resembling a brush; *also* : SHAGGY, ROUGH
²**brushy** \"\ *adj* -ER/-EST [¹*brush* + *-y*] : covered with or abounding in brush or brushwood
brusque *also* **brusk** \'brəsk *sometimes* -rüsk *or* -rü-\ *adj* -ER/-EST [F *brusque*, fr. It *brusco*, fr. ML *bruscus* butcher's-broom, perh. blend of L *ruscus* butcher's-broom and LL *brucus* heather — more at BRIER] : markedly short and abrupt : tending to be brisk, sharp, and often somewhat harsh or lacking gentleness **syn** see BLUFF
brusque·ly *also* **brusk·ly** *adv* : in a brusque manner
brusque·ness *n* -ES : the quality or state of being brusque
brus·que·rie \ˌbrəskəˈrē *sometimes* ˌbrüs- *or* ˌbrüs-\ *n* -s [F, fr. *brusque* + *-erie* -ery] : the quality or state of being brusque
brus·sels \'brəsəlz\ *adj*, *usu cap* [fr. *Brussels*, Belgium] : of or from Brussels, the capital of Belgium : of the kind or style prevalent in Brussels
brussels brown *n*, *often cap 1st B* : NEW BRONZE
brussels carpet *n*, *usu cap B* **1** : a carpet made of variously colored worsted yarns first fixed in a foundation web of strong linen thread and then drawn up in loops to form the pattern — called also *body Brussels*; see WILTON **2** : an inexpensive substitute for Brussels carpet that is made of a single-colored yarn varied in color by dyeing at intervals or of undyed yarn with a printed pattern — called also *tapestry Brussels*
brussels classification *n*, *usu cap B* : UNIVERSAL DECIMAL CLASSIFICATION
brussels griffon *n*, *usu cap B & sometimes cap G* : a shaggy reddish brown wire-haired griffon (sense 1)
brussels lace *n*, *usu cap B* **1** : any of various fine needlepoint or bobbin laces with floral designs made orig. in or near Brussels **2** : a machine-made net of hexagonal mesh
brussels sprout *n*, *often cap B* **1** : any of the edible small green heads resembling diminutive cabbages and borne in the lower axils of the stem of a plant (*Brassica oleracea gemmifera*) closely related to the cabbage and cauliflower **2** : the plant that bears brussels sprouts — usu. used in pl.

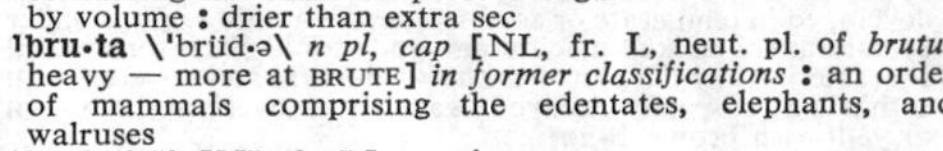

brussels sprouts

brust \'brüst, -rəst\ *dial Brit var of* ¹BURST
brus·tle \'brəsəl, -rüs-\ *dial var of* BRISTLE
¹**brut** \'brüt\ *n* -s *cap* [MW, fr. MF *Brut*, legendary settler of Britain, fr. ML *Brutus*] : any of several medieval chronicles of Britain tracing the history and legend of the country from the exploits of mythical Brutus, descendant of Aeneas
²**brut** \'brüt\ *adj* [F, lit., rough — more at BRUTE] *of champagne* : very dry : usu. containing less than 1.5 percent sugar by volume : drier than extra sec
¹**bru·ta** \'brüd·ə\ *n pl*, *cap* [NL, fr. L, neut. pl. of *brutus* heavy — more at BRUTE] *in former classifications* : an order of mammals comprising the edentates, elephants, and walruses
²**bruta** \"\ [NL, fr. L] *syn of* EDENTATA
bru·tage \brüˈtäzh, brüˈtäzh\ *n* -s [F, fr. *brut* rough + *-age* — more at BRUTE] : BRUTING
bru·tal \'brüd·ᵊl, -ütᵊl\ *adj*, *sometimes* -ER/-EST [ME, fr. MF or ML; MF, fr. ML *brutalis*, fr. *brutus* brute, animal + L *-alis* -al — more at BRUTE] **1** *archaic* : of, belonging to, or typical of beasts or animals as distinguished from man : ANIMAL ⟨the, Serpent . . . to me so friendly grown above the rest of ~ kind —John Milton⟩ **2** : befitting or resembling a brute: as **a** : stemming from or based on crude animal instincts : grossly ruthless ⟨a ~ attack⟩ **b** : devoid of mercy or compassion : cruel and cold-blooded ⟨blunt and occasionally ~, but . . . never niggling and peevish —Cleanth Brooks⟩ **c** : harsh and severe : unpleasant to a degree that is nearly unbearable ⟨another summer of ~ heat⟩ ⟨two ~ winters in a row⟩ **d** : unpleasantly accurate and incisive : undeniable but harsh ⟨the ~ truth⟩ ⟨the ~ facts must be faced and action taken⟩
syn BRUTISH, BESTIAL, FERAL, BEASTLY, BRUTE: BRUTAL stresses sensuality, coarse cruelty, or crude grossness, always without the alleviation of normal human moderation, reticence, sympathy, mercy, or consideration of others ⟨Constance Kent was rather a beauty—a nice girl with an engaging air; yet she cut her little brother's throat in a thoroughly *brutal* manner —W.H. Wright⟩ ⟨*brutal* Ode and St. Dunstan force their rude way into the quiet room, and hurl coarse insults at the sweet-faced queen —J.K.Jerome⟩ BRUTISH stresses either gross sensuality completely unchecked or utter animal stupidity unenlightened by even faint human intelligence ⟨in the mines and factories an indiscriminate sexual intercourse of the most *brutish* kind was the only relief from the tedium and drudgery of the day —Lewis Mumford⟩ ⟨it requires wisdom to liberate ourselves from natural *brutish* stupidity and enslaving passions —M.R. Cohen⟩ BESTIAL usu. indicates either a complete lack of human intelligence and refinement or an utter lustful depravity ⟨they were much impressed with the size and *bestial* ferocity of the niggers whom they had now learned to call "Paythans" —Rudyard Kipling⟩ ⟨he is a thief, a murderer, a defiler, a *bestial*, lecherous dog —Rafael Sabatini⟩ FERAL stresses wild fury and ferocity like a wild beast's ⟨her wrath, savage and *feral*, utterly possessed her. She was like a wild animal, cornered and conscious of defeat —W.H.Wright⟩ BEASTLY may imply beastlike indelicacy, cruelty, or sensuality ⟨some woman, coarse and low and vulgar, some *beastly* creature in whom all the horror of sex is blatant—W.S.Maugham⟩ ⟨systematic mutilation of the body rendered the crime particularly *beastly* —Earl of Birkenhead b. 1907⟩ Often it simply implies irritation or disgust on the speaker's part ⟨she can't eat the soup—no more can I. It's *beastly*. —W.M.Thackeray⟩ BRUTE may connote cruelty or stupidity ⟨the *brute* mentality of the clods who constitute the parish —A.J.Cronin⟩ ⟨murdered, along the coast of Lincolnshire, out of *brute* spite —Charles Kingsley⟩
bru·tal·i·tar·i·an \(ˌ)brüˌtaləˈterēən, *attrib* " *or* (ˈ)brüˈtaləˌt-\ *adj* [*brutality* + *-arian* (as in *humanitarian*; prob. newly coined in the 30s or construed as a blend of *brutal* and *totalitarian*] : advocating or practicing brutality ⟨a ~ regime⟩ — **bru·tal·i·tar·i·an·ism** \(ˌ)brüˌtaləˈterēəˌnizəm\ *n* -s
bru·tal·i·ty \brüˈtaləd·ē, -ətē, -i\ *n* -ES **1** : the quality or state of being brutal ⟨impulse without sensitiveness spells ~ —A.N.

Whitehead⟩ **2 :** a brutal act or course of action ⟨the ~ of war⟩
bru·tal·i·za·tion \ˌbrüd·ᵊlə̇ˈzāshən, -ütᵊl-, -ᵊlˌīˈz-\ *n* -s **:** the act or process of brutalizing **:** the state of being brutalized ⟨the ~ that comes from indifference to the hardships of others —J.R.Ellingston⟩
bru·tal·ize \ˈbrüd·ᵊlˌīz, -ütᵊl-\ *vt* -ED/-ING/-s [*brutal* + *-ize*] **1 a :** to make brutal, unfeeling, or inhuman ⟨perhaps . . . we shall ~ ourselves sufficiently to make regret impossible —E.W. Griffiths⟩ **b :** to alter (as by distorting) so as to lessen or destroy the essential or aesthetic value of **c :** to make less sensitive or humane ⟨the experience of war *brutalized* him somewhat⟩ ⟨in his lower moments *brutalizing* . . . noble legends into farce —O.W.Holmes †1935⟩ **2 :** to treat brutally ⟨man *brutalizing* man on the indifferent earth —I.L.Salomon⟩
bru·tal·ly \ˈbrüd·ᵊlē, -ütᵊlē, -li\ *adv* **:** in a brutal manner **:** to an extent considered brutal
bru·tal·ness \-ᵊlnə̇s\ *n* -ES **:** the quality or state of being brutal
1brute \ˈbrüt, *usu* -üd·+V\ *adj* [ME, fr. MF *brut* rough, brutish, fr. L *brutus* stupid, irrational, lit., heavy; akin to L *gravis* heavy — more at GRIEVE] **1 :** of, relating to, or typical of animals, brutes, or beasts **:** not possessed of human rational powers ⟨the same kind of service for the ~ world that the study of genealogy has rendered to human history —*Encyc. Americana*⟩ **2 :** having neither life nor soul **:** not conscious or animate ⟨as we left the harbor, the North Atlantic, ~ gray, heckled the ship with its strength —Saul Bellow⟩ **3 :** resembling an animal in quality, action, or instinct **:** BRUTAL: as **a :** dull, stupid, and unreasoning **b :** cruel and savage **:** utterly lacking in sensitivity or higher feelings **c :** coarse and grossly sensual ⟨the ~ instinct that prompted the crime⟩ **4 :** purely physical **:** involving no mental exertion or effort ⟨by ~ strength they broke the heavy door⟩ **5 :** not influenced or governed by human intelligence **:** utterly insensible and unaffected by reason **6 :** rough, crude, and unrefined **:** unrelieved and unmodified ⟨the ~ facts with which . . . we have to come to terms —Aldous Huxley⟩ **syn** see BRUTAL
2brute \"\ *n* -s [ML *brutus*, fr. L *brutus*, adj.] **1 a :** an animal other than man of the class of mammals or certain other vertebrates **:** BEAST **b** *chiefly dial* **:** a male bovine animal **:** BULL **2 :** one that is brutal; *esp* **:** a coarse, insensate, unfeeling, crude, or cruel man ⟨he was a drunken loutish ~⟩
3brute \"\ *obs var of* BRUIT
4brute \"\ *vt* -ED/-ING/-s [back-formation fr. *bruting*] **:** to shape (a diamond) by rubbing or grinding with another diamond or a diamond chip
brute·ly *adv* **:** in the manner of a brute
brute·ness *n* -ES **:** the quality or state of being brute
brut·ing \ˈbrüd·iŋ\ *n* -s [modif. (influenced by E *-ing*) of F *brutage* — more at BRUTAGE] **:** the process of bruting a diamond
brut·ish \ˈbrüd·ish, -üt\|, \|ēsh\ *adj* [ME *brutisshe*, fr. 1*brute* + *-isshe* -ish] **1 :** of or relating to animals as opposed to man **:** resembling or typical of a brute or beast ⟨~ form rather than human —John Milton⟩ **2 a :** strongly and grossly sensual **:** utterly without sensitivity or delicacy **b :** marked by very little intelligence or rationality ⟨an insensitive and ~ reaction to any reasonable suggestion⟩ ⟨~ aesthetic apathy —Cyril Connolly⟩ **c :** stupidly cruel ⟨plantations where slavery was . . . ~ —Allan Nevins & H.S.Commager⟩ **syn** see BRUTAL
brut·ish·ly *adv* **:** in a brutish manner
brut·ish·ness *n* -ES **:** the quality or state of being brutish
brut·ter \ˈbrəd·ə(r)\ *n* -s [origin unknown] **1 :** BALLHOOTER **2 :** LIMBER
brux·el·lois \brüesel'wä\ *n, pl* **bruxellois** *cap* [F, fr. *Bruxelles* (Brussels), Belgium] **:** a native or resident of Brussels, Belgium
brux·ism \ˈbrəkˌsizəm\ *n* -s [irreg. (Gk *υ* & *χ* being transliterated respectively as *u* & *x* instead of *y* & *ch*) fr. Gk *brychein* to gnash the teeth + E *-ism*; akin to OIr *brōn* trouble, W *brwyn* stabbing pain, Lith *gráužti* to gnaw, OSlav *grysti*] **:** the habit of unconsciously gritting or grinding the teeth esp. in situations of stress or during sleep
bruxo·mania \ˌbrəksō+\ *n* -s [NL, irreg. fr. Gk *brychein* to gnash the teeth + NL *-o-* + *-mania*] **:** BRUXISM
bru·yère \brüēyeer\ *n* -s [F — more at BRIER] **:** 2BRIER
bry- *or* **bryo-** *comb form* [NL, moss, fr. Gk *bryo-* moss, catkin, fr. *bryon*; perh. akin to OHG *krūt* herb, cabbage — more at SAUERKRAUT] **:** moss ⟨*Bryaceae*⟩ ⟨*bryology*⟩
brya \ˈbrīə\ *n, cap* [NL, fr. L, tamarisk, fr. Gk] **:** a genus of prickly shrubs and small trees (family Leguminosae) of the Caribbean region that yield a very durable hard wood — see GRANADILLA TREE
bry·a·ce·ae \brīˈāsēˌē\ *n pl, cap* [NL, fr. *Bryum*, type genus + *-aceae*] **:** a family of acrocarpous mosses (order Eubryales) having symmetrical often pendent capsules with a double peristome, the inner one being ciliate — compare BRYUM — **bry·a·ceous** \(ˈ)brīˈāshəs\ *adj*
bry·a·les \brīˈā(ˌ)lēz\ *n pl, cap* [NL, fr. *Bryum* + *-ales*] *in some classifications* **:** an order or subclass of Musci comprising the mosses that have the spore case separated from the capsule wall by a hollow cylindrical intercellular space — compare EUBRYALES
bry·an·ite \ˈbrīəˌnīt\ *n* -s *usu cap* [William O'*Bryan* †1868 Eng. preacher + E *-ite*] **:** a member of a Methodist body formerly called Bible Christians founded in England by William O'Bryan in 1815
bry·an·thus \brīˈan(t)thəs\ *n* [NL, fr. *bry-* + *-anthus*] **1** *cap* **:** a genus of Old World prostrate mat-forming evergreen heaths (family Ericaceae) with 4-parted flowers in racemes that was formerly included in *Phyllodoce* **2** *pl* **bryanthuses** \-thəsəz\ *also* **bryan·thi** \-n,thī\ **:** any plant of the genus *Bryanthus* or sometimes of the genus *Phyllodoce*
bryn·za \ˈbrinzə\ *n* -s [Romanian *brînză*] **:** a ewe's-milk cheese made in central Europe and Asia Minor
bry·o·bia mite \(ˈ)brīˈōbēə-\ *n* [NL *Bryobia* genus of mites, fr. *bry-* + *-bia*] **:** CLOVER MITE
bry·o·log·i·cal \ˌbrīəˈläjə̇kəl\ *adj* **:** of or relating to bryology
bry·ol·o·gist \brīˈäləjə̇st\ *n* -s **:** a specialist in bryology
bry·ol·o·gy \-jē\ *n* -ES [ISV *bry-* + *-logy*] **1 a** *obs* **:** the science of mosses **b :** a branch of botany that deals with the bryophytes **2 a :** moss life (as of a region) ⟨the ~ of Wales⟩ **b :** the properties and life phenomena exhibited by a moss or moss type ⟨the ~ of sphagnum⟩
bry·o·nia \brīˈōnēə\ *n* [NL, fr. L, bryony, fr. Gk *bryōnia*, *bryōnē*; akin to *bryon* moss — more at BRY-] **1** *cap* **:** a small genus of perennial Old World herbaceous tendril-bearing vines (family Cucurbitaceae) having large leaves and small dioecious flowers with the staminate borne in racemes — see BRYONY **2** -s **:** the dried root of bryony (*Bryonia alba* or *B. dioica*) used as a cathartic
bry·o·ny *also* **bri·o·ny** \ˈbrīənē, -ni\ *n* -ES [L *bryonia*] **1 :** a plant of the genus *Bryonia* (esp. *B. alba* or *B. dioica*) **2 :** BRYONIA 2
1bryo·phyl·lum \ˌbrīəˈfiləm\ [NL, fr. *bry-* + *-phyllum*] *syn of* KALANCHOE
2bryophyllum \"\ *n* -s [NL, fr. *bry-* + *-phyllum*] **:** a succulent plant (*Kalanchoe pinnata*) with oblong simple or pinnate leaves
bry·oph·y·ta \brīˈäfəd·ə\ *n pl, cap* [NL, fr. *bry-* + *-phyta*] **:** a division of nonflowering plants comprising the mosses and liverworts characterized by rhizoids rather than true roots, by little or no organized vascular tissue, by multicellular archegonia and antheridia in which only some of the cells are sporogenous, and by a clear-cut alternation of generations, the sporophyte being without chlorophyll and remaining attached to and nourished by the gametophyte — see HEPATICAE, MUSCI
bry·o·phyte \ˈbrīəˌfīt\ *n* -s [NL *Bryophyta*] **:** a plant of the Bryophyta — **bry·o·phyt·ic** \ˌ≡≡ˈfid·ik\ *adj*
bry·op·si·da·ce·ae \(ˌ)brīˌäpsəˈdāsēˌē\ *n pl, cap* [NL, fr. *Bryopsid-*, *Bryopsis*, type genus + *-aceae*] **:** a family of marine green algae (order Siphonales) having the characteristics of the genus *Bryopsis*
bry·op·sis \brīˈäpsə̇s\ *n, cap* [NL, fr. *bry-* + *-opsis*] **:** a genus (the type of the family Bryopsidaceae) of marine green algae that occur in warmer seas and have nonseptate filaments forming a rhizomatous prostrate base and an upright pinnately branched portion
bryo·zoa \ˌbrīəˈzōə\ *n pl, cap* [NL, fr. *bry-* + *-zoa*] **1 :** a small phylum of aquatic animals that reproduce by budding, that usu. form branching, flat, or mosslike colonies permanently attached on stones or seaweeds and enclosed by an external cuticle soft and gelatinous or rigid and chitinous or calcareous, and that consist of complex zooids each having an alimentary canal with distinct mouth and anus surrounded by a true coelom and associated with a protrusible lophophore — see AVICULARIUM, VIBRACULUM; BUGULA; ENTOPROCTA, GYMNOLAEMATA, PHYLACTOLAEMATA **2** *in some classifications* **:** a class or other division of Molluscoidea comprising the Bryozoa and the Entoprocta
1bryo·zo·an \ˌbrīəˈzōən\ *or* **bryo·zo·on** \-ō,än\ *adj* [NL *bryozoon*, fr. *bry-* + *-zoon*] **:** of or relating to the Bryozoa
2bryozoan \"\ *or* **bryozoon** \"\ *n, pl* **bryozoans** \-ōənz\ *or* **bryo·zoa** \-ōə\ **1 :** an individual zooid of a bryozoan colony **2 :** an animal of the phylum Bryozoa
bryo·zoologist \ˌbrīə+\ *n* -s [blend of NL *Bryozoa* and E *zoologist*] **:** a specialist on the Bryozoa
bryth·on \ˈbriˌthän\ *n* -s *cap* [W] **1 :** a member of the British branch of Celts **:** BRITON **2 :** a speaker of one of the Brythonic languages — compare GOIDEL
1bry·thon·ic \briˈthänik\ *adj, usu cap* [*Brython* + *-ic*] **1 :** of, relating to, or characteristic of the Brythons **2 :** of, relating to, or characteristic of the division of the Celtic languages that includes Welsh, Cornish, and Breton — compare GOIDELIC
2brythonic \"\ *n* -s *cap* **:** the Brythonic branch of the Celtic languages — see INDO-EUROPEAN LANGUAGES table
bry·um \ˈbrīəm\ *n, cap* [NL, alter. of L *bryon* moss, fr. Gk — more at BRY-] **:** a genus (the type of the family Bryaceae) of mosses containing species distinguished by mostly erect and tufted gametophytes and symmetrical short-necked capsules — compare MNIUM
brz *abbr* bronze
BS *or* **BSc** *abbr or n* -s Bachelor of Science
BS *abbr* **1** balance sheet **2** bill of sale **3** bill of store **4** bishop suffragan **5** bottom settlings **6** British standard
b's *or* **bs** *pl of* B
bsc *abbr* basic
b-scope *n, usu cap B* **:** a radarscope on which signals appear as bright spots that by their vertical or horizontal displacement indicate the angle and range of the target — compare A-SCOPE
bsh *abbr* bushel
b sharp \ˈ≡ˈ≡\ *n, usu cap B* **:** the tone a half step above B and sounding enharmonically the same as C in the tempered scale
bskt *abbr* basket
bsmt *abbr* basement
BSt *abbr* bill of sight
b-stage resin \ˈ≡,≡-\ *n, usu cap B* **:** RESITOL
b star *n, usu cap B* **:** a star of spectral type B — see SPECTRAL TYPE table
b station *n, usu cap B* **:** a radio station aboard a ship
b switchboard *n, usu cap B* **:** a switchboard in a telephone exchange for receiving and completing trunk calls that originate in another exchange
bt *abbr* **1** baronet **2** bent **3** boat **4** bought **5** brevet
BT *abbr* **1** basic training **2** berth terms **3** board of trade
btn *abbr* battalion
btr *abbr* better
BTU *abbr* **1** board of trade unit **2** British thermal unit
btwn *abbr* between
bty *abbr* battery
bu \ˈb(y)ü\ *n, pl* **bu** [Jap] **1 :** an old Japanese rectangular coin orig. made of gold and from 1830 to 1870 of silver; *also* **:** a corresponding unit of value ⟨¼-*bu* and 2-*bu* pieces were issued⟩ **2 :** either of two Japanese units of measure: **a :** a unit of length equal to 0.1 inch **b :** TSUBO
bu *abbr* **1** blue **2** bulletin **3** bureau **4** bushel
bual \ˈbwäl, büˈäl\ *n* -s *usu cap* [Pg *boal*, a kind of wine grape] **:** a rich golden-colored Madeira wine
bu·ang \ˈbüˌäŋ\ *n, pl* **buang** *or* **buangs** *usu cap* **1 :** a Papuan people of the Morobe district, North-East New Guinea **2 :** a member of the Buang people
bu·at \ˈbüət\ *var of* BOUET
bu·a·ze \ˈbwäzē\ *n* -s [Nyanja *bwazi*] **:** an African woody vine (*Securidaca longipedunculata*) of the family Polygalaceae yielding a fiber that resembles flax
1bub \ˈbəb\ *n* -s [perh. short for *bubble*] *archaic* **:** strong malt liquor
2bub \"\ *n* -s [short for 2*bubby*] **:** BROTHER, LAD, BOY — used chiefly as a term of address and with an implication of superiority to the one addressed ⟨come on ~, make it snappy⟩
1bu·ba·line \ˈbyübəˌlīn, -lən\ *adj* [NL *Bubalis* + E *-ine*] **:** like, relating to, or being one of certain large African antelopes of *Alcelaphus* and related genera that were formerly regarded as forming a subfamily (Bubalinae) of Bovidae
2bubaline \"\ *adj* [NL *Bubalus* + E *-ine*] **:** of, like, or relating to *Bubalus* or a related genus
1bu·ba·lis \ˈbyübələ̇s\ [NL, fr. Gk *boubalis*, *boubalos*, an African antelope] *syn of* ALCELAPHUS
2bubalis \"\ *or* **bu·bal** *also* **bu·bale** \ˈbyübəl\ *n, pl* **bubalises** *or* **bubals** *also* **bubales :** the northern hartebeest
bu·ba·lus \ˈbyübələs\ *n, cap* [NL, fr. LGk *boubalos* buffalo, fr. Gk, an African antelope, prob. fr. *bous* head of cattle — more at COW] **:** a genus of Bovidae comprising the nearly hairless mud-wallowing buffaloes of Asia, certain large extinct relatives, and in some classifications the buffaloes of Africa
bubbies *pl of* BUBBY
1bub·ble \ˈbəbəl\ *vb* **bubbled**; **bubbled**; **bubbling** \ˈbəb(ə)liŋ\ **bubbles** [ME *bublen*, *bobelen*, prob. of imit. origin like D *bobbelen* to bubble, MLG *bubbeln*, Lith *bubsėti*] *vi* **1 a :** to form or produce bubbles ⟨soup *bubbling* in the kettle⟩ **b :** to move upward or rise in or as if in bubbles ⟨gases *bubbling* from the mud⟩ — often used with *up* ⟨cool water *bubbling* up from the ground⟩ ⟨these questions ~ up from time to time⟩ **2 :** to flow out or pour out with a gurgling sound suggesting the forming and rising of bubbles ⟨a clear fountain *bubbling* in the shade⟩ **3 :** to suggest bubbling water: **a :** to make gurgling or warbling sounds ⟨a nightingale softly *bubbling* in the shrubbery⟩ ⟨her carefree laughter *bubbled* behind us⟩ **b :** to utter as though giving off bubbles either with sparkle and effervescence ⟨songs that ~ with wit and grace⟩ or with persistent monotonous repetition ⟨they ~ of Marx or Disraeli to their dying day —*Times Lit. Supp.*⟩ **c :** to be or become lively or effervescent (as with joy) **:** bubble over ⟨he looked like a good soldier and *bubbled* with natural joyousness —Alan Sullivan⟩ **d** *Scot* **:** BLUBBER, SNIVEL **e :** to be in agitated movement or activity **:** rise into consciousness usu. unexpectedly **:** CHURN, STIR — used chiefly of intangibles ⟨such contacts soon set his brain to *bubbling* with new ideas⟩ ~ *vt* **1 :** to utter (as words) bubblingly **:** express in bubbles or as if in giving off bubbles ⟨she *bubbled* questions —R.A.W. Hughes⟩ ⟨dozens of birds *bubbling* their joy to the clearing sky⟩ **2 a :** to cause to bubble ⟨~ cocoa and sugar together in a little water —*Better Homes & Gardens*⟩ **b :** BURP **3** *archaic* **:** CHEAT, DECEIVE, DELUDE **4 :** to pass (as gas) through some medium in the form of discrete bubbles
2bubble \"\ *n* -s *often attrib* **1 :** a small globule typically hollow and light: as **a :** a small body of air or gas within a liquid ⟨~*s* rising in champagne⟩ **b :** a thin film of liquid inflated with air or gas ⟨soap ~*s*⟩ **c :** a hollow globule of blown glass (as a small floating bead formerly used for testing the strength of spirits) **d :** a globule (as of air) in a transparent solid ⟨windowpanes marred with ~*s* and wavy patches⟩; *broadly* **:** such globules constituting an imperfection in glass and resulting from the trapping of air or gas during the melting process **e :** the globule of air in the tube of a spirit level; *sometimes* **:** the tube and its contents **f :** BUBBLE SHELL **g** *Scot* **:** mucus from the nose **h :** BUBBLE CANOPY **2 a :** something that lacks firmness, solidity, or reality **:** a false show ⟨a dream of what thou wast . . . a breath, a ~ —Shak.⟩ **b :** a delusive scheme **:** a dishonest speculation ⟨the South sea ~⟩ **3** *archaic* **:** one readily deceived or tricked **:** DUPE, GULL **4 a :** a bubbling as of boiling or flowing water ⟨we'll not be long, the kettle's just at the ~⟩ **b :** a sound like that of bubbling **:** a gurgling or warbling song ⟨the cadenced ~ of certain bird songs⟩
bubble and squeak *n* [so called fr. the sounds made in cooking the dish] **:** a dish consisting of potatoes and cabbage or esp. formerly potatoes, cabbage, and meat fried together
bubble bath *n* **1 :** a liquid or granular perfumed preparation that foams in water **2 :** a bath prepared with bubble bath
bubble bowl *n* **:** a somewhat spherical bowl usu. of clear glass and with a small lipless opening used chiefly for ornamental display (as of floating short-stemmed flowers)
bubble canopy *n* **:** an airplane-cockpit canopy that is usu. transparent, nearly hemispherical, seamless, and without bracing or supports
bubble cap *n* **:** a device (as a metal cup with notches or slots around the edge) that is inverted over a hole in a plate in a bubble tower for effecting contact of vapors rising from the plate below and liquid already on the plate
bubble chamber *n* **:** a chamber in which a superheated liquid is produced so that an ionizing particle passing through the liquid initiates boiling along its path, the strings of bubbles so produced being photographed and indicating the behavior of the ionizing particle
bubble dance *n* **:** a solo dance act performed in or as if in the nude, the dancer using one or more balloons for covering — compare FAN DANCE
bubble disease *n* **:** a disease of mushrooms caused by a fungus (*Mycogone perniciosa*) that grows over infected mushrooms in a white mat causing deformation and sometimes the deposition of brownish drops on the injured surface
bubble fountain *n* **:** a bubbler drinking fountain
bubble glass *n* **:** glass in which bubbles have been induced during manufacture for artistic effect
bubble gum *n* **:** a chewing gum that can be blown into large bubbles
bub·ble·less \ˈbəbəl(l)ə̇s\ *adj* **:** being without bubbles
bub·ble·ment \ˈbəbəlmənt\ *n* -s **:** an effervescent state or condition
bubble nest *n* **:** a collection of bubbles made by certain fishes as a place in which to deposit their eggs
bubble octant *n* **:** an octant using the same principle as a bubble sextant
bubble over *vi* **:** to be so filled with something (as with emotion, an idea, or information) as to be unable to restrain it from escaping as if in bubbles ⟨she came back *bubbling over* with news⟩; *esp* **:** to give vent to emotion in a series of impulses ⟨he frisked around her *bubbling over* with joy —Nathaniel Hawthorne⟩
bub·bler \ˈbəb(ə)lə(r)\ *n* -s **1 :** FRESHWATER DRUM **2 a** (1) **:** DRINKING FOUNTAIN (2) **:** the spout of a drinking fountain **b :** any of several devices in which air or gas is bubbled through liquid
bubble sextant *n* **:** a sextant used esp. in aerial navigation in which the image of the heavenly body being observed is brought to the edge of a bubble instead of to the sea horizon, the bubble appearing in its proper position in the field of view only when the sextant is held so that its zero plane is the observer's horizontal plane
bubble shell *or* **bubble snail** *n* **1 :** any of a number of marine gastropod mollusks (order Opisthobranchia) having the shell comparatively thin and small with the body whorl enveloping the other whorls (as members of the Akeridae or of the genus *Bulla*) — see HAMINOEA **2 :** a freshwater snail of *Physa* or a related genus
bub·blet \ˈbəb(ə)lət\ *n* -s [blend of *bubble* and *-let*] **:** a small bubble
bubble tower *n* **:** a tower in which gas or vapor is bubbled through liquid; *specif* **:** a plate tower (as for fractionating petroleum distillates) in which the plates are provided with bubble caps
bubble tube *n* **:** the glass tube containing the liquid and bubble in a spirit level
bubbling *adj* **:** CHURNING, EFFERVESCENT, EFFUSIVE — **bubbling·ly** *adv*
1bub·bly \ˈbəb(ə)lē, -li\ *adj* -ER/-EST [2*bubble* + *-y*] **1 :** full of bubbles **:** BUBBLING, EFFERVESCENT **2 :** resembling a bubble ⟨buildings with ~ domes⟩
2bubbly \"\ *n* -ES *chiefly Brit* **:** CHAMPAGNE
bub·bly-jock \ˌbəbliˈjäk, ˈbüb-\ *n* -s [1*bubbly* (fr. its cry) + *Jock* (rustic, clown)] *chiefly Scot* **:** a male turkey
1bub·by \ˈbəbē *also* ˈbübē\ *n* -ES [perh. imit. of the noise made by a sucking infant] **:** BREAST — now often considered vulgar
2bub·by \ˈbəbē\ *n* -ES [prob. baby talk alter. of 1*brother*] **:** little boy **:** BROTHER — used chiefly as a familiar or affectionate term of address
bubbybush \ˈ≡≡,≡\ *or* **bubby-blossom** \ˈ≡≡,≡≡\ *also* **bubby** *or* **bubby-flower** *or* **bubby-shrub** *n* [1*bubby*; prob. fr. the red flowers compared to human nipples] **:** CAROLINA ALLSPICE
bu·be \ˈbüˌbā\ *or* **bu·bi** \-(ˌ)bē\ *n, pl* **bube** *or* **bubes** *or* **bubi** *or* **bubis** *usu cap* **1 a :** a Bantu-speaking people of the island of Fernando Po, West Africa **b :** a member of such people **2 :** a Bantu language of the Bube people
bu·binga \büˈbiŋ(g)ə\ *n* -s [Bantu] **1 :** any of several large leguminous trees of tropical West Africa (esp. *Didelotia africana* and members of the genera *Copaifera* and *Brachystegia*) **2 :** the wood of a bubinga; *esp* **:** the hard heavy heartwood of a bubinga that is similar in appearance to rosewood and is used for veneers — called also *African rosewood*
1bu·bo \ˈb(y)ü(ˌ)bō\ *n* -ES [ML, fr. Gk *boubōn* groin, gland, bubo] **1 :** an inflammatory swelling of a lymph gland esp. in the groin that is due to the absorption of infective material (as in gonorrhea, syphilis, or the plague) **2 :** LYMPHOGRANULOMA
2bubo \"\ *n, cap* [NL, fr. L, horned owl; akin to Gk *byas*, *byza* owl, Arm *bu*, *buēč*, Per *bum*] **:** a nearly cosmopolitan genus of large horned owls including the eagle owls — see GREAT HORNED OWL
bu·bon·ic \(ˈ)b(y)üˈbänik, -nēk\ *adj* [ML *bubon-*, *bubo* + E *-ic*] **:** of or attended with buboes
bubonic plague *n* **:** plague in which the formation of buboes is a prominent feature — compare PNEUMONIC PLAGUE
bu·bon·i·dae \b(y)üˈbänəˌdē\ [NL, fr. *Bubon-*, *Bubo*, type genus + *-idae*] *syn of* STRIGIDAE — used in place of Strigidae as usu. restricted when Strigidae replaces Tytonidae
bu·bon·o·cele \-nəˌsēl\ *n* -s [Gk *boubōnokēlē*, fr. *boubōn* groin + *-o-* + *-kēlē* -cele] **:** an inguinal hernia; *esp* **:** a hernia in which the hernial pouch descends only as far as the groin and forms a swelling there like a bubo
bubs *pl of* BUB
bubu *var of* BOO-BOO
bu·buk·le \ˈb(y)üˌbəkəl\ *n* -s [blend of 1*bubo* and *carbuncle*] *archaic* **:** a large red blemish or pimple — **bu·buk·led** \-kəld\ *adj, archaic*
bucan *var of* BUCCAN
bu·ca·re \ˈbükəˌrā, -ˌrē, büˈkärē\ *n* -s [Sp *búcare*, *bucare*] **:** a spiny Peruvian tree (*Erythrina poeppigiana*) widely planted for shading coffee and cacao plantations in the West Indies
bucayo *var of* BUKAYO
1buc·ca \ˈbəkə\ *n* -s [L — more at POCK] **:** CHEEK; *specif* **:** the part of the insect head wall adjoining and sometimes including the mouth
2bucca \"\ *n* -s [Corn, hobgoblin, scarecrow; akin to W *bwgan* bogey] *dial Eng* **:** SCARECROW
buc·cal \ˈbəkəl\ *adj* [L *bucca* cheek + E *-al*] **1** *of an oral structure* **:** directed toward the cheek ⟨the ~ aspect of the gum⟩ **2 :** of, relating to, or involving the cheeks ⟨a large ~ ganglion⟩ **3 :** of, relating to, involving, or lying within the mouth **:** ORAL ⟨~ organs⟩ ⟨a strong ~ capsule⟩
buccal gland *n* **1 :** any of the small racemose mucous glands in the mucous membrane lining the cheeks **2 :** any of the lymphatic glands situated near the buccinator muscle
buc·cal·ly \-kəl(l)ē\ *adv* **:** toward the cheek
buccal mass *n* **:** the mouthparts in mollusks other than bivalves and the muscles by which they are operated and with which they generally form a more or less compact mass
1buc·can \(ˌ)bəˈkan, ˈbəkən\ *or* **bu·can** *or* **bou·can** \(ˈ)büˈkan, -kän\ *vt* -ED/-ING/-s [MF *boucaner*, fr. *boucan*] **:** to expose (meat) in strips to fire and smoke upon a buccan
2buccan \"\ *or* **bucan** *or* **boucan** \"\ *n* -s [MF *boucan*, of Tupian origin; akin to Tupi *mukém* buccan] **1 :** a wooden frame or grid for roasting, smoking, or drying meat over fire **2 :** buccaned meat
1buc·ca·neer \ˌbəkəˈni(ə)r, -iə\ *n* -s [F *boucanier* French woodsman of the 17th century in the West Indies, pirate, fr. *boucaner* to buccan; fr. their typical manner of conserving meat] **1 :** a person who dries and smokes flesh or fish after the manner of the Indians — orig. used of the French settlers in Haiti who hunted wild cattle and swine **2 :** one of the freebooters preying upon Spanish ships and settlements esp. in the West Indies in the 17th century; *broadly* **:** PIRATE **3 a :** a dark reddish orange that is deeper and slightly redder than

average lacquer red, redder, stronger, and slightly darker than ocher red, and redder and deeper than burnt sienna **4 :** an unscrupulous adventurer esp. in politics or business ⟨railroad ~s —Owen Lattimore⟩ ⟨financial ~s —John Dos Passos⟩

2buccaneer \"\ *vi* ED/-ING/-S **:** to act or live as a buccaneer

buc·che·ro \'bükə,rō\ *n* -S [It, fr. Sp *búcaro* clay vase, prob. fr. Pg — more at BOCCARO] **:** an ancient unglazed and unpainted gray, red, or black pottery often ornamented with designs in relief that is found in Tuscany, Italy

buc·ci·na \'bəksənə\ *also* **buc·cin** \-sən\ *n, pl* **bucci·nae** \-,nē\ *also* **buccins** [L *buccina, bucina,* fr. *bu-* (fr. *bov-, bos* head of cattle) + *-cina* (fr. *canere* to sing, play) — more at COW, CHANT] **:** a Roman military trumpet shaped like the letter C

buc·ci·na·tor \'bəksə,nād·ə(r)\ *n* -S [NL, fr. L *bucinator, buccinator* trumpeter, fr. *bucinatus, buccinatus* (past part. of *bucinare, buccinare* to sound the trumpet, fr. *bucina, buccina* trumpet) + *-or*] **:** a thin broad muscle forming the wall of the cheek and serving to compress the cheek against the teeth and to retract the angle of the mouth — **buc·ci·na·to·ry** \-,nə-,tōrē,-,nād·ərē\ *adj*

buc·cin·i·dae \,bək'sinə,dē\ *n pl, cap* [NL, fr. *Buccinum,* type genus + *-idae*] **:** a family of marine gastropod mollusks (suborder Stenoglossa) — see WHELK

buc·ci·num \'bəksənəm\ *n, cap* [NL, fr. L *buccinum, bucinum* trumpet, a shellfish, fr. *buccina, bucina* trumpet] **:** a genus (the type of the family Buccinidae) of marine gastropod mollusks comprising the typical whelks

bucco *var of* BUCHU

bucco- *comb form* [prob. fr. NL, fr. L *bucca* cheek — more at POCK] **:** buccal and ⟨*bucco*gingival⟩ ⟨*bucco*lingual⟩

buc·con·i·dae \(,)bə'känə,dē\ *n pl, cap* [NL, fr. *Buccon-, Bucco,* type genus (fr. L, babbler, blockhead, fr. *bucca* cheek, mouth) + *-idae* — more at POCK] **:** a family of large-headed insectivorous tropical American birds (order Piciformes) having long heavy bills and comprising the puffbirds

buccra *var of* BUCKRA

buc·cu·la \'bəkyələ\ *n, pl* **buccu·lae** \-,lē, -,lī\ [NL, fr. L, small cheek, dim. of *bucca* cheek] **:** one of the elevated plates or ridges beneath the head on either side of the rostrum of insects of the order Heteroptera

buc·cu·la·trix \,bəkyə'lā·triks\ *n, cap* [NL, fr. L *buccula* + *-trix*] **:** a genus of small moths (family Lyonetiidae) having larvae that feed in or on leaves and spin fusiform ribbed cocoons — see APPLE BUCCULATRIX

bu·cel·las \b(y)ü'seləs\ *n* -ES *usu cap* [Pg, fr. *Bucellas,* village near Lisbon, Portugal, where it is made] **:** a Portuguese white wine

bu·ceph·a·la \byü'sefələ\ *n, cap* [NL, fr. Gk *boukephalē,* fem. of *boukephalos* bullheaded, fr. *bous* bull, ox, head of cattle + *kephalē* head — more at COW, CEPHALIC] **:** a genus of ducks consisting of the goldeneyes and the buffleheads

bu·ce·phal·i·dae \,byüsə'falə,dē\ *n pl, cap* [NL, fr. *Bucephalus,* type genus + *-idae*] **:** a family of atypical digenetic trematodes that parasitize the intestines of various fishes and that have the mouth in the middle of the ventral surface, a saccular intestine, a single anterior sucker, and a posterior genital pore

1bu·ceph·a·lus \byü'sefələs\ *n, pl* **bucephaluses** \-ləsəz\ *or* **bucepha·li** \-,lī\ [after *Bucephalus,* horse of Alexander the Great †323B.C. king of Macedon, fr. L, fr. Gk *Boukephalos*] *archaic* **:** a riding horse esp. if spirited and mettlesome — often used ironically

2bucephalus \"\ *n, cap* [NL, fr. Gk *boukephalos* bullheaded — more at BUCEPHALA] **:** a genus of small digenetic trematodes having the mouth near the center of the ventral surface and the intestine saclike and not bifurcated and comprising intestinal parasites of carnivorous fishes

bu·ce·ros \'byüsə,räs\ *n, cap* [NL, fr. Gk *boukerōs* with horns like those of cattle, fr. *bous* head of cattle + *keras* horn — more at HORN] **:** the type genus of a family (Bucerotidae) comprising a number of typical hornbills — see BUCEROTES

bu·ce·ro·tes \,byüsə'rōd·(,)ēz\ *n pl, cap* [NL, fr. pl. of *Buceros-, Buceros*] **:** a suborder (coextensive with the family Bucerotidae) of Coraciiformes comprising the hornbills

bu·cha·rest \'bükə,rest, ,==='= *also* -byü-\ *adj, usu cap* [fr. *Bucharest,* capital of Romania] **:** of or from Bucharest, the capital of Romania **:** of the kind or style prevalent in Bucharest

buch·ite \'bü,kīt\ *n* -S [G *buchit,* fr. Baron Christian L. von *Buch* †1853 Ger. mineralogist + G *-it* -ite] **:** a vitreous metamorphic rock produced by the contact action of basalt or by friction metamorphism

bu·chloë \'byüklə,wē\ *n, cap* [NL, fr. Gk *bous* head of cattle + *chloē* young grass; akin to Gk *chloos* light green — more at COW, GLOW] **:** a genus of perennial stoloniferous grasses (family Gramineae) having pistillate and staminate spikelets borne on the same or separate plants, the pistillate in sessile capitate clusters and the staminate in elongated one-sided racemes — see BUFFALO GRASS

buch·man·ism \'bükmə,nizəm, 'bək-\ *n* -S *cap* [Frank N.D. *Buchman* †1961 Am. evangelist, its founder + E *-ism*] **:** OXFORD GROUP MOVEMENT

buch·man·ite \-,nīt\ *n* -S *usu cap* [F. *Buchman* + E *-ite*] **:** a member of the Oxford Group movement **:** a follower of the religious reformer Frank Buchman or his teachings

buch·nera \'bəknərə, 'bük-\ *n, cap* [NL, after J.G.*Buchner,* 18th cent. Ger. botanist] **:** a genus of herbs (family Scrophulariaceae) chiefly of warm regions with mostly opposite leaves and showy white or bluish purple flowers in bracted spikes — see BLUEHEARTS

büch·ner funnel \'büknə(r), 'bɪɛkn-\ *n, usu cap B* [after Ernst *Büchner fl*1888 Ger. chemist, its inventor] **:** a cylindrical often porcelain filtering funnel that has a perforated plate on which the filter paper is placed and that is used usu. with a vacuum

bu·chu \'b(y)ü(,)k(y)ü\ *also* **buc·co** \'bə(,)kō\ *or* **bucku** \'bə(,)k(y)ü\ *n* -S [Zulu *bucu*] **1 :** the dried leaves of certain plants of the genera *Barosma* and *Diosma* that are used as a diuretic and diaphoretic: as **a :** those of either of two short-leafed plants (*B. setulina* and *B. crenulata*) — called also *short buchu* **b :** those of a long-leafed plant (*B. serratifolia*) — called also *long buchu* **2 :** a plant of the genera *Barosma* and *Diosma*

buchu camphor *n* **:** DIOSPHENOL

1buck \'bək\ *n* -S *see senses 1&3, often attrib* [ME *buck, bucke,* fr. OE *buc, bucca* he-goat, stag; akin to OHG *boc* he-goat, ON *bukkr,* MIr *bocc* he-goat, Arm *buc* lamb] **1** *or pl* **buck :** a male animal: **a :** a male deer or antelope — not usu. used of the male elk or moose or technically of the male red deer; compare BULL, STAG **b :** a male of any of several other four-footed mammals (as the goat, sheep, hare, rabbit, guinea pig, or rat); *specif* **:** RAM **c :** a male of some game fishes (as the salmon or shad) **2 :** a male human being **:** MAN: **a :** a dashing fellow **b :** a male Indian or Negro — often used disparagingly **3** *or pl* **buck :** ANTELOPE — often used in combination ⟨bush*buck*⟩ ⟨spring*buck*⟩ **4 a** [by shortening] **:** BUCKSKIN; *often* **:** an article (as a shoe) made of buckskin **b** *archaic* **:** a deerskin regarded as a unit of exchange in early dealings with American Indians **c :** DOLLAR 4a **5** [short for *sawbuck*] **:** SAWHORSE **6 a :** a supporting rack or frame: as (1) **:** a heavy square framework used in the glazing of leather (2) **:** a rack for plate glass (3) **:** a frame on which a clay model is built up (4) **:** a large jig used esp. in aircraft assembly operations **b :** a rough doorframe placed in a wall or partition during construction and used as a support to which the finished frame is made fast **c :** the padded usu. horizontal part of a pressing machine on which clothes are placed for pressing — compare SHOE **d :** a short thick leather-covered block for gymnastic vaulting usu. without pommels and adjustable for height — **go to buck** *of female rabbits and hares* **:** COPULATE

2buck \"\ *vb* -ED/-ING/-S [*1buck,* influenced in some meanings by *butt,* v.] *vi* **1** *of a horse or mule* **:** to spring with a quick plunging leap arching the back and descending with the forelegs rigid and the head held as low as possible **2 :** to meet head on as if in butting: **a :** to charge an obstruction under power ⟨the plows . . . ~*ed* day and half the night to keep the roads open —Helen Rich⟩ **b :** to act, move, or stand firm in opposition ⟨East Bay legislators ~*ed* in vain —*Fortnight*⟩ — often used with *against* ⟨salmon ~*ing* against the stiff current⟩ ⟨you're the one who has ~*ed* against your churchmen —Zane Grey⟩ **c :** to oppose one electric potential or field to another so that there is counteraction or neutralization **3 a :** to move or react jerkily or erratically ⟨the vehicles ~*ed* in and out of the obstructions —Darrell Berrigan⟩ ⟨the way those early outboard motors would ~ and die on you —*Newsweek*⟩ **b :** to refuse to submit or agree **:** BALK; *sometimes* **:** to become resentful **4 :** to strive diligently for advancement or reward sometimes without regard to ethical behavior or the rights or interests of others — usu. used with *for* ⟨~*ing* for sergeant's stripes⟩ ~ *vt* **1 :** to throw or dislodge (as a rider) by bucking ⟨the pinto sunfished and ~*ed* Charley over the paddock fence⟩ — often used with *off* ⟨leaned all his weight on it as the pressure of the water tried to ~ him off the hose —C.D.Lewis⟩ **2 a** *archaic* **:** 1BUTT **b :** to move in opposition to ⟨was ~*ing* sleet and snow all the way⟩ **c :** to act in opposition to **:** fight against **:** OPPOSE, RESIST ⟨there's no point in ~*ing* a well-established trend⟩; *sometimes* **:** to compete with ⟨the show occupied one of the toughest spots of the week . . . ~*ing* the fantastically popular Charlie McCarthy at the same hour —Charles Jackson⟩ **d :** to play or gamble against ⟨~*ing* the odds⟩ **e :** to hold a tool against (a rivet) in order to resist the force of hammering — often used with *up* ⟨the man who ~*s* up the rivets has a hot difficult job⟩ **f :** to carry, move, or load (heavy or troublesome objects) esp. with mechanical equipment **3 :** to charge into (the opponents' line in football) **4 :** to buck up — usu. used in passive ⟨Jumbo was greatly ~*ed* over it —*Time*⟩ **5 :** to restrain (a person) by tying the wrists together, passing the arms over the bent knees, and putting a stick across the arms and through the angle formed by the knees; *usu* **:** to punish (as a soldier) by so restraining **6 :** to pass esp. from one person to another **:** hand on ⟨it was easier to ~ the heavy sacks down the line than to carry them one by one⟩ ⟨the Post Office department ~*ed* the question on to Postmaster Pafford —*Time*⟩ — **buck the board :** to work as an employee of a railroad on the extra board or roster for part-time employment — **buck the tiger :** to play against the faro bank

3buck \"\ *n* -S **:** the act or an instance of bucking ⟨he gave easily to the first excited ~*s* of his pony —Rudyard Kipling⟩; *esp* **:** a charge by the ball carrier into the opposing line in football

4buck *adj* [prob. fr. *1buck* (man)] *slang* **:** being of the lowest grade within the military category to which one belongs ⟨a ~ private⟩ ⟨a ~ general⟩

5buck \"\ *vt* -ED/-ING/-S [prob. fr. *1buck* (sawhorse)] **1 :** to saw (felled trees) into logs or small pieces (as with a bucksaw) **2 :** BRING, CARRY ⟨~ water⟩ **3 :** to split (a stick of timber) into two crossties

6buck \'bək, 'bük\ *vt* -ED/-ING/-S [ME *bouken;* akin to MHG *büchen* to wash with lye, OHG *buohha* beech tree — more at BEECH] **1** *dial chiefly Brit* **:** to soak, steep, or boil in lye or suds **2** *dial chiefly Brit* **:** to wash (clothes) in lye or suds or by beating on stones in running water

7buck \"\ *n* -S **1** *dial chiefly Brit* **:** lye or suds in which cloth or yarn is soaked or boiled in bleaching or in which clothes are washed **2** *dial chiefly Brit* **:** the cloth or clothes soaked or washed in buck **:** WASH ⟨a jolly brown wench, a-washing of her ~ —Thomas D'Urfey⟩

8buck \'bək\ *vt* -ED/-ING/-S [D *beuken* (fr. MD *bōken, böken*) or LG *böken* to strike, fr. MLG *bōken;* akin to MHG *bocken, pochen* to strike, beat — more at POKE] **:** to break up **:** PULVERIZE ⟨~ ore samples⟩

9buck \"\ *n* -S [origin unknown] *Brit* **:** a basket for catching eels; *sometimes* **:** a frame supporting a group of such baskets

10buck \"\ *n* -S [short for earlier *buckhorn knife*] **1 :** an object formerly used in poker to mark the next player to deal or to deal a jackpot, the winner of each jackpot placing the buck in front of him; *esp* **:** a buckhorn-handled knife used for this purpose — see PASS **2 :** a token used as a mark or reminder in a gambling game (as one used to designate a player's point in a dice game) **3 :** a small object (as a silver token) used to mark the place of the officer who is to be served first in a naval wardroom

11buck \"\ *var of* BUKH

12buck \"\ *adv* [origin unknown] *South & Midland* **:** STARK, COMPLETELY — usu. used in the phrase *buck naked*

buck ague *also* **buck ager** \-'āgə(r)\ *n* [*1buck*] **:** BUCK FEVER

buck–and–wing \'==='=\ *n* **:** a solo tap dance with sharp foot accents, springs, leg flings, and heel clicks that was adapted to the stage from a blend of Negro and Irish clog dancing

buck arm *n* **:** a crossarm placed parallel to line wires usu. to afford a takeoff for a branch circuit

buck·a·roo *or* **buck·e·roo** \'bəkə,rü, ,=='=\ *n* -S [by folk etymology fr. Sp *vaquero,* fr. *vaca* cow, fr. L *vacca* — more at VACCINE] **1 :** COWBOY 3a **2 :** BRONCOBUSTER

buckass \'=,=\ *adj* [*4buck* + *ass* (buttocks)] *slang* **:** LOW-DOWN ⟨a ~ private who does just what he's told —James Jones⟩

buck basket *n* [*7buck* (clothes) + *basket*] **:** CLOTHES BASKET ⟨conveyed me into a *buck basket* —Shak.⟩

buckbean \'=,=\ *n* [trans. of D *boksboon*] **:** a plant (*Menyanthes trifoliata*) that grows in bogs in Europe and America and has racemes of white or purplish flowers and trifoliolate intensely bitter leaves — called also *bogbean, bog myrtle, marsh trefoil*

buckbean family *n* **:** MENYANTHACEAE

buck·ber·ry \'bək-— *see* BERRY\ *n* [*1buck* + *berry*] **1 :** a huckleberry (*Gaylussacia ursina*) of the southern U.S. having black insipid fruit eaten by deer **2 :** a deerberry (*Vaccinium stamineum*)

buck·board \"+,-\ *n* [obs. E *buck* body of a wagon + *board*] **:** a 4-wheeled driving vehicle having an elastic platform fastened without springs directly to the rear axle and the bolster of the front axle usu. with a seat above it often mounted on springs

buckboard

buckbrush \'=,=\ *n* [*1buck* + *brush*] **:** any of various shrubby No. American plants that furnish browse for sheep, deer, and other animals: as **a :** either of two plants of the genus *Ceanothus* (*C. velutinus* and *C. sanguineus*) **b :** BUTTONBUSH **c :** a low much-branched shrub (*Purshia tridentata*) of the Rocky mountain region **d :** a shrub (*Cornus femina*) of eastern No. America with white flowers and fruit **e :** BUCKBUSH 1

buckbush \'=,=\ *n* [*1buck*] **1 a :** WOLFBERRY 1 **b :** CORALBERRY 1 **2 :** BUCKBRUSH d

1bucked \'bəkt\ *adj* [fr. past part. of *2buck*] **:** PLEASED, ENCOURAGED **:** bucked up

2bucked \"\ *adj* [*1buck* + *-ed*] *of teeth* **:** somewhat protuberant

bucked shin *n* [fr. past part. of *2buck*] **:** stiffness of the leg of a horse due to muscular strain

1buck·een \,bə'kēn\ *n* -S [*1buck* + *-een*] *chiefly Irish* **:** a rather shabby young dandy ⟨after college he lived for some years the life of a ~ —W.M.Thackeray⟩

2buckeen \"\ *n* -S [D *bokkin,* fem. of *bok* male Indian (trans. of E *buck*), buck, fr. MD *boc;* akin to OHG *boc* he-goat — more at BUCK] *in Guiana* **:** an Indian woman

1buck·er \'bəkə(r)\ *n* -S [*2buck* + *-er*] **:** one that bucks: as **a :** a bucking horse ⟨rodeo owners, who search all over the country for good ~*s* —Mary Elting⟩ **b :** a workman who cuts felled trees into shorter lengths — called also *crosscutter* **c :** a person who carries or moves something (as water or wood); *esp* **:** a workman who uses mechanical equipment to handle material (as bales) and load it **d :** one that bucks rivets — called also *bucker-up, dollyman* **e :** a miner that shovels coal down a chute or into a bin or mine car **f :** one that saws logs in making a fireguard **g :** one that lifts bales of hay onto a wagon or truck **h :** one that loads filled vegetable or fruit sacks in the field **i :** one that cuts staves for kegs **j :** a football player who bucks the line of scrimmage

2bucker \"\ *n* -S [*8buck* + *-er*] **:** one that bucks ore samples; *also* **:** a broad-headed hammer used in bucking ore

buckeroo *var of* BUCKAROO

bucker-up \'==,=, ,=='=\ *n, pl* **buckers-up** *or* **bucker-ups** **1 :** 1BUCKER d ⟨the *bucker-up,* who holds the red-hot rivet in place with a combination of iron bars and brute strength —*San Francisco Chronicle*⟩ **2 :** BUCKING BAR

1buck·et \'bəkət, *usu* -əd·+V\ *n* -S [ME, fr. AF *buket,* fr. OE *būc* pitcher, belly; akin to OHG *būh* belly, ON *būkr* trunk of the body, Latvian *buga* hornless cow, Skt *bhūri* abundant — more at BOAST] **1 a :** a typically round and wooden vessel for drawing up water from a well **b :** any comparable vessel (as of wood, metal, or plastic) for catching, holding, or carrying liquids or solids **:** PAIL — often used in combination with a term suggesting the function ⟨ice ~⟩ ⟨fire ~⟩ ⟨lunch ~⟩ **2 a :** a vessel (as a tub or scoop) for hoisting and conveying material (as coal, ore, grain, gravel, mud, or concrete) **b :** the dipper or scoop at the end of the arm of a bucket dredge **c :** one of the receptacles on the rim of a water wheel into which the water rushes causing the wheel to revolve **d :** a float or paddle of a waterwheel or of a boat's side wheel or stern wheel **e :** one of the containers of an endless-belt type of conveyor **f :** one of the vanes of a turbine rotor upon which the force of the steam or gas is exerted to cause rotation **g :** a frame covered with canvas that is sometimes used as a signal for boats **3 :** the quantity that a bucket contains; *often* **:** a very or unexpectedly large quantity ⟨the rain came down in ~*s*⟩ ⟨I could drink a ~ right now⟩ **4 :** a leather socket for holding a whip, lance, or carbine **5 :** a curved surface designed to deflect flowing water gradually and to prevent shock and erosion (as between the overflow face and apron of a dam) **6** *slang* **:** a means of conveyance (as an automobile); *esp* **:** a slow old ship — usu. used disparagingly **7** *slang* **:** JAIL, PRISON **8 :** a part of a basketball court keyhole bounded by the free-throw lane and the free-throw line — **in the bucket** *baseball* **:** drawn back from the plate ⟨left foot *in the bucket* so that he is half facing the pitcher —*Time*⟩ **:** with the foot nearest the pitcher drawn back from the plate ⟨batting *in the bucket*⟩ **:** so that one foot is in such a position ⟨step *in the bucket* while batting⟩

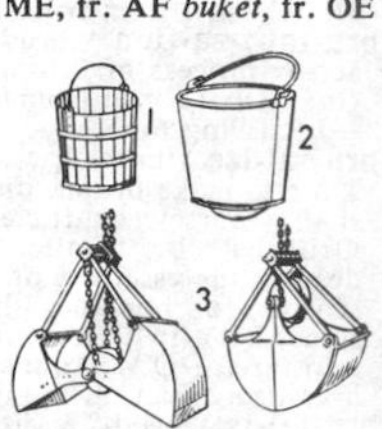

buckets: *1* wooden bucket, *2* fire bucket, *3* clamshell automatic bucket for excavating, open and closed

2bucket \"\ *vb* -ED/-ING/-S *vt* **1 :** to draw or lift in or as if in buckets ⟨~*ing* water from the well⟩ — often used with *out* or *up* ⟨you can ~ out the slops before dark⟩ **2** *Brit* **a :** to ride (a horse) hard **b :** to drive (as a car) hurriedly or roughly ⟨~*ed* his car down the drive and pulled up . . . with a savage jerk —Ngaio Marsh⟩ **3 :** to deal with (an order to buy or sell stocks) in or as if in a bucket shop ~ *vi* **1 :** to drive or progress rapidly **:** HUSTLE, HURRY ⟨the scow was ~*ing* through the heavy seas —Joyce Cary⟩ ⟨they ~*ed* into their household chores⟩ **2 :** to do a bucket-shop business **3 a :** to move haphazardly without a well-defined objective or without restraint ⟨you can't let such a valuable horse ~ about the pasture at his own good pleasure⟩ ⟨hordes of people go ~*ing* all over the shop —G.F.T.Ryall⟩ ⟨jaunty ladies who ~ around foreign parts —*New Yorker*⟩ **b :** to move roughly or jerkily ⟨the jeep ~*ed* over the rocky road⟩ ⟨as we jolted, jerked, ~*ed* along —Nancy Hale⟩

bucket brigade *n* **1 :** a chain of persons acting to suppress a fire by passing buckets of water from hand to hand **2 :** any chain (as of persons) acting to meet an emergency

bucket conveyor *n* **:** CONVEYER 2a(6)

bucket dredge *or* **bucket dredger** *n* **:** a dredge that excavates and raises material either by a series of closely connected scoops or buckets or with a single bucket operated by a boom

bucket elevator *n* **:** an endless-chain elevator having buckets

buck·et·er \'bəkəd·ər\ *or* **buck·e·teer** \,bəkə'ti(ə)r\ *n* -S **:** a broker who conducts a bucket shop **:** one that buckets orders

buck·et·ful \'bəkət,fu̇l\ *n, pl* **bucketfuls** \-lz\ *or* **bucketsful** \-t,sfu̇l\ **:** 1BUCKET 3

bucketing *n* -S **1 :** the operation of a bucket shop **2 :** the practice of a broker who buckets orders or takes the other side of customers' trades

bucketline \'==,=\ *n* **:** the train of buckets in a bucket conveyor, bucket elevator, or similar device

bucket loader *n* **1 :** a mobile bucket conveyor for loading loose materials into trucks or railway cars **2 :** a tractor with a bucket mounted on the front used for digging and truck loading

bucket pump *n* **1 :** a vertical-piston usu. duplex pump whose valves are in the piston or pistons **2 :** CHAIN PUMP **3 :** a hand-operated force pump commonly used for spraying with liquids contained in a bucket

buckets *adv* [fr. pl. of *1bucket*] **:** in great quantity — used with an intransitive verb ⟨it's raining ~⟩

bucket seat *n* **:** a low separate seat that is designed for one person and that has a rounded back, is often hinged for tipping or folding forward, and is used chiefly in autos and planes

bucket shop *n* [fr. *bucket shop* "low gin mill where alcoholic beverages were dispensed in small amounts in buckets"; fr. the small speculations that originally took place there] **1 :** a dishonest brokerage house operating in securities or commodities that does not execute orders placed on margin by customers, anticipating a profit from market fluctuations adverse to the customer's interests **2 :** a gambling establishment in which wagers are made in the form of orders or options at current prices for securities or commodities without real intention to purchase or deliver, losses or gains being computed on the basis of changes in market quotations

bucket trap *n* **:** a contrivance to let air and condensed water out of steam pipes and radiators with but little escape of steam

bucket wheel *n* **:** a wheel having buckets attached to its rim or to a rope or chain passing over it (as for raising water)

1buckeye \'=,=\ *n* -S [*1buck* + *eye*] **1** [so called fr. the appearance of the seed] **a :** any No. American shrub or tree of the genus *Aesculus; esp* **:** OHIO BUCKEYE **b :** the large nutlike seed of one of these plants — called also *horse chestnut* **c :** a shrub or small tree (*Ungnadia speciosa*) of the southwestern U.S. and Mexico having pink flowers resembling those of the buckeyes and reputedly poisonous seeds — called also *Mexican buckeye* **2** *usu cap* **:** OHIOAN — used as a nickname **3 :** BUGEYE **4 :** a No. and So. American nymphalid butterfly of the genus *Precis* (*P. lavinia*) having dark brown wings, each with 2-ringed eyespots and larvae that feed on plantain, snapdragon, and related plants **5 :** a small cigar-manufacturing unit often operated in a private home

2buckeye \"\ *adj* **:** showing unsophisticated lack of taste ⟨~ advertisements⟩ ⟨~ paintings⟩

buckeyed \"+d\ *adj* [*1buckeye* + *-ed*] **:** poisoned by buckeye (sense 1a) or one of its products (as seeds or honey)

buckeye rot *n* [*1buck* + *eye;* fr. the resemblance of the rotten spot to a buck's eye] **:** a fungous rot of tomato fruit caused by a phycomycete (*Phytophthora parasitica*) that causes a gray-green or brown discoloration usu. with darker zonate bands at the blossom end of the fruit

buck·ey-wrack \'bəkē+,-\ *n* [alter. of Sc *boxie-wrack,* fr. Sc *boxie* (dim of *box*) + *wrack;* fr. the form of its air capsules] **:** BLADDER WRACK

buck fever *n* [*1buck*] **1 :** the nervous excitement of an inexperienced hunter at the sight of game **2 :** extreme tension or nervousness accompanying initial or unexpected exposure to some new situation or responsibility that requires positive action — compare STAGE FRIGHT

buck hook *n* [*3buck*] *West* **:** a blunt upcurved projection on the frame of a spur that is thrust into the cinch to hold a rider on a bucking horse

buckhorn \'=,=\ *n* [ME, fr. *buck* + *horn*] **1 :** the horn of a buck: *often* **:** the substance of such a horn ⟨knives with ~ handles⟩ **2 :** DEERHORN 2 **3 a :** CINNAMON FERN **b** *also* **buckhorn plantain :** any of several plantains having leaves that suggest a buck's horn in shape; *esp* **:** the common ribgrass (*Plantago lanceolata*)

buckhorn brake *or* **buckhorn fern** *n* **:** ROYAL FERN

buckhorn sight *also* **buckhorn** *n* **:** a rear sight with a deep curved notch used on some rifles

buckhound \'=,=\ *n* [*1buck* + *hound*] **:** a dog used for coursing deer

1buck·ie \'bəkē\ *n* -S [perh. modif. of L *buccinum, bucinum,* a shellfish used in dyeing purple, fr. *bucina, buccina* trumpet, shell used as a trumpet — more at BUCCINA] *chiefly Scot* **:** a spiral-shelled marine gastropod or its shell; *esp* **:** RED WHELK

2buckie \"\ *n* -s [perh. modif. of L *buccinum*] *Scot* **:** a perverse intractable person

3buckie \"\ *n* -s [origin unknown] *NewEng* **:** ALEWIFE 1a; *esp* **:** an alewife smoked for food

buckier *comparative of* BUCKY

buckiest *superlative of* BUCKY

bucking *n* -s [ME *bouking*, fr. gerund of *bouken* to buck — more at BUCK] **1** *obs* **:** liquid used in bucking clothes or fabric **2** *archaic* **:** a quantity of clothes or fabric bucked at one time

bucking bar *n* [fr. pres. part. of ²*buck*] **:** a steel block serving to back up a rivet while it is being headed and clinched

bucking board *or* **bucking plate** *n* [fr. pres. part. of ⁸*buck*] **:** a flat plate usu. of chilled steel upon which ore is pulverized with a hand-operated bucking hammer

bucking hammer *or* **bucking iron** *n* [fr. pres. part. of ⁸*buck*] **:** a heavy iron instrument shaped like a pestle with a wooden handle attached hammer fashion and operated by hand on a bucking board

buck·ing·ham·shire \'bəkiŋəm,shi(ə)r, *US also* -ŋ,ham-\ *or* **buckingham** *adj, usu cap* [fr. *Buckinghamshire* or *Buckingham* county, England] **:** of or from the county of Buckingham, England **:** of the kind or style prevalent in Buckingham

bucking plate *var of* BUCKPLATE

bucking roll *n* [fr. pres. part. of ²*buck*] **:** a usu. leather pad that is fastened on either side of the pommel of a saddle to help a rider hold his seat on a bucking horse

bucking transformer *n* [fr. pres. part. of ²*buck*] **:** a transformer connected to oppose partly or wholly the voltage from a second transformer

buck·ish \'bəkish\ *adj* [¹*buck* + *-ish*] **1 :** DANDIFIED, FOPPISH **2 :** lively and vigorous; *also* **:** IMPETUOUS — **buck·ish·ly** *adv*

buck·ism \'bə,kizəm\ *n* -s [¹*buck* + *-ism*] *archaic* **:** DANDYISM

buckjump \'ˌ=\ *vb* [²*buck* + *jump*] **1** *of a horse or other equine* **:** BUCK **2 :** to leap or leap on like a bucking horse

buckjumper \"+ə(r)\ *n* **:** a bucking horse

buck knee *n* [³*buck*] **:** a knee (as of a horse) inclining inwards — usu. used in pl. — **buck-kneed** \'ˌ=\ *adj*

buck lateral *n* [³*buck*] **:** a football play in which the back who receives the pass from center either (1) bucks into the line with the ball after faking a hand-off to a teammate who in turn fakes a pitchout or (2) fakes a buck into the line after giving the ball to a teammate who in turn may lateral the ball, hand it off, keep it and run with it, or drop back and pass

buck law *n* [¹*buck*] **:** a game law or regulation that limits the hunter to taking only male deer

1buck·le \'bəkəl\ *n* -s [ME *bocle*, fr. MF *bocle, boucle* boss of a shield, buckle, fr. L *buccula* small cheek, dim. of *bucca* cheek — more at POCK] **1 :** a fastening for two loose ends (as of a belt or strap) attached to one and holding the other by a catch **2 :** an ornamental device that suggests a buckle in form but often does not act as a fastening and that is used esp. on women's garments and shoes **3** *archaic* **a :** a curl esp. when crisp **b :** the state of being in curl **4 :** one of the thin openwork plates of lead sometimes shaped like buckles that are exposed to the action of carbon dioxide in the manufacture of white lead **5** *or* **buckle joint :** CLAMP CONNECTION

2buckle \"\ *vb* **buckled; buckled; buckling** \-k(ə)liŋ, -lēŋ\ **buckles** [ME *boclen*, fr. MF *boucler*, fr. *boucle*] *vt* **1 a :** to fasten or make fast with a buckle — often used with *on* ⟨he *buckled* on his spurs⟩ **b :** to fasten the buckle of ⟨be sure to ~ your belt⟩ **2 :** to prepare (as oneself) for action **:** apply intensively and with vigor ⟨Redworth *buckled* himself to the task —George Meredith⟩ **3** *chiefly Scot* **:** MARRY **4 :** to cause to bend, give way, or crumple ⟨changing stresses *buckled* the land surface into a series of ridges that now form the main coastal range⟩ ⟨*buckled* the car fender⟩ **5 :** to make (hair) curly **:** CRIMP ~ *vi* **1 a :** to equip oneself or make ready for a contest or undertaking by or as if by buckling on armor **b :** to apply oneself ardently or with vigor **:** STRIVE — often used with *down* ⟨he'll finish if he ~s down to the job⟩ ⟨they were advised to ~ down⟩ **2** *obs* **:** to join in combat **:** CONTEND, GRAPPLE — often used with *with* **3** *chiefly Scot* **:** MARRY **4 :** to close or become confined with a buckle ⟨this dress won't ~⟩ **5 :** to bend, heave, warp, or kink usu. under the influence of some external agency ⟨the pavement *buckled* in the heat⟩ ⟨his knees *buckled* with exhaustion⟩ — often used with *up* ⟨the floor *buckled* up under the weight of so many people⟩ **6 :** to become altered or distorted usu. permanently by buckling ⟨the panels did not ~ under pressure⟩; *broadly* **:** to fall to pieces or into a heap **:** CRUMBLE, CRUMPLE, COLLAPSE ⟨the balloon *buckled* together⟩ ⟨the *buckling* imperialisms of western Europe —C.W. de Kiewiet⟩ — often used with *up* **7 a :** to give way **:** YIELD — usu. used with *under* ⟨less devout creatures . . . would have *buckled* under this severe test of faith —Paul Willen⟩ **b** *now dial Eng* **:** to be or become subservient **:** CRINGE

3buckle \"\ *n* -s **1 :** a product of buckling **:** BEND, WARP, FOLD, KINK: as **a :** a small fold in land **b :** one of the wrinkles that develop at the top edge of the leaves of a book near the backbone margin during folding **c :** a depression or flaw on the surface of a casting caused by fault or failure of the mold (as from inadequate venting) **2 :** a machine for folding printed sheets of paper

buckle chain *n* **:** SWIVEL CHAIN

buckled *adj* **:** BENT, CRINKLED, WARPED, WAVY

buck·le·less \'bəkəl(l)əs\ *adj* **:** being without a buckle

buckle plate *or* **buckled plate** *n* **:** a slightly arched steel plate used as a floor plate to give rigidity

1buck·ler \'bəklə(r)\ *n* -s [ME *bocler*, fr. OF, shield with a boss, fr. *bocle* boss — more at BUCKLE] **1 a :** a small shield generally round and held by a handle at arm's length and used not to cover the body but to stop or parry blows **b :** a shield of varying shape and size usu. worn on the left arm to protect the front of the body **2 :** something or someone that shields and protects **3 :** a crab whose shell is sufficiently firm to give only slightly under the fingers **4 :** a cover of wood or metal made to fit a hawsehole or other opening on a ship **5 :** the anterior shield of the shell of a trilobite **6 :** one of the large bony external plates found on many ganoid fishes

2buckler \"\ *vt* -ED/-ING/-S **:** to shield or defend with or as if with a buckler

buckler fern *n* **:** SHIELD FERN

buckler mustard *n* **:** a plant of the genus *Biscutella* (family Cruciferae) with yellow flowers like those of mustard and pods with open valves that resemble bucklers

buck·leya \'bəklēə, ˌ='==\ *n, cap* [NL, after Samuel B. *Buckley* †1883 Am. naturalist] **:** a small genus of Asiatic and American partly parasitic shrubs (family Santalaceae) with opposite leaves, small greenish flowers, and an oily nutlike drupe

1buck·ling \'bək(ə)liŋ, -lēŋ\ *n* -s [fr. gerund of ²*buckle*] **:** an act or instance of bending or of being distorted by bending or crumpling; *specif* **:** failure (as of a column) when subjected to a compressive stress in excess of its elastic limit

2buck·ling \'bəkliŋ, -lēŋ\ *n* -s [¹*buck* + *-ling*] **:** a male goat between one and two years of age

buck moth *n* [so called fr. its prevalence in the deer season] **:** a large autumn-flying saturniid moth (*Hemileuca maia*) of the eastern U.S. with smoky translucent wings crossed by a white band and a spiny larva that feeds on oak foliage

bucko \'bə(ˌ)kō\ *n* -ES [¹*buck* + *-o*] **1 :** one who is domineering and bullying — used esp. of officers on sailing ships who maintained control of their crews by free resort to physical violence **2** *chiefly Irish* **:** young fellow **:** LAD, CHAP — often used as a term of address ⟨and as for you, my ~⟩

buck passer *n* [¹⁰*buck*] **:** a person that habitually evades responsibility — **buck-passing** \'ˌ=\ *n*

buckplate \'ˌ=\ *or* **bucking plate** *n* [⁸*buck* + *plate*] **:** BUCKING BOARD

buckpot \'ˌ=\ *n* [¹*buck* (Indian) + *pot*] **:** a clay cooking pot of British Guiana

buck·ra *also* **buc·cra** \'bəkrə\ *n* -s [Ibibio and Efik *mbakara*, lit., master] **1** *chiefly South* **:** a white man or a person of predominantly white as opposed to Negro blood — used chiefly by Negroes and often disparagingly **2** *chiefly South* **:** BOSS, MASTER

buck rake *n* [²*buck* (to charge against, push)] **:** a wide horse-drawn or tractor-mounted long-toothed rake for gathering hay from a windrow and carrying it — called also *go-devil, hay sweep*

1buck·ram \'bəkrəm\ *n* -s [ME *bukeram, bokeram*, fr. OF *boquerant, bouquerant*, fr. OProv *bocaran*, fr. *Bokhara, Bukhara*, city of central Asia (now in Uzbekistan, U.S.S.R.) whence it was imported] **1** *archaic* **:** a fabric of fine linen or cotton formerly used for church vestments and wearing apparel **2 a :** a stiff-finished heavily-sized fabric of cotton or linen used for interlinings in garments and stiffening in millinery and in bookbinding **b :** a similar fabric made by plying together with glue two or more layers of open-weave cotton cloth **3** *archaic* **:** stiffness of manner or reaction **:** precise formality **:** RIGIDITY; *also* **:** a precise or starchy person **4 :** BUCKLER 3

2buckram \"\ *adj* **:** suggesting buckram esp. in stiffness, formality, and rigidity ⟨in translation the flow of his prose took on a ~ quality⟩ ⟨a ~ pretense prevented the world from piercing to his hollowness —G.D.Brown⟩

3buckram \"\ *vt* -ED/-ING/-S **1 :** to strengthen with or as if with buckram **2** *archaic* **:** to make pretentious **:** give a false appearance of strength, worth, or beauty to

bucks *pl of* BUCK, *pres 3d sing of* BUCK

buck sail *n* [part modif., part trans. of Afrik *bokseil*, fr. *bok* beam of a wagon + *seil* sail, sailcloth — more at BUCKWAGON] *Africa* **:** CANVAS, TARPAULIN; *esp* **:** one used to cover a buckwagon

bucksaw \'ˌ=\ *n* [¹*buck* (sawhorse) + *saw*] **:** a saw set in a usu. H-shaped frame that is used for sawing wood on a sawbuck

buck scraper *n* [²*buck* (to charge against, push)] **:** a modified drag scraper having two runners to lift the scoop from the ground when filled

buck's extension \'bəks-\ *n, usu cap B* [after Gurdon *Buck* †1877 Am. surgeon] **:** an apparatus for extension of a fractured limb by the application of a weight controlled by a rope and pulley; *also* **:** the traction so applied

bucksaw

buck's-eye \'ˌ=\ *n, pl* **buck's-eyes** [¹*buck*] *archaic* **:** BUCKEYE 1a

buck·shee \'ˌbək'shē\ *n* -s [Hindi *bakhśiś*, fr. Per *bakhshīsh* — more at BAKSHEESH] *Brit* **:** GRATUITY, WINDFALL; *esp* **:** extra rations — used chiefly in military circles

buck's horn *n* [¹*buck*] **1** *also* **buck's horn plantain :** BUCKHORN 3b **2 :** SWINE CRESS **3 :** BRASS BUTTONS

buckshot \'ˌ=\ *n, pl* **buckshot** *or* **buckshots** [¹*buck* + *shot*] **1 :** a coarse lead shot manufactured in sizes ranging from a quarter to a third of an inch in diameter and used in shotgun shells for hunting and police purposes **2 a** *also* **buckshot soil** *or* **buckshot land :** a soil that contains or that on drying breaks into pellets resembling buckshot (as certain heavy clays of the Mississippi delta area and some sandy alluviums of Australia) **b :** one of the pellets of such soil

buckskin \'ˌ=\ *n, often attrib* [ME, fr. ¹*buck* + *skin*] **1 a :** the skin of a buck **b :** a soft pliable usu. suede-finished leather made from deer or elk skins and used chiefly for gloves and shoe uppers **c :** any leather resembling buckskin (as certain goat and sheepskin leathers) — not used technically in the leather trade **2 a buckskins** *pl* **:** a garment of buckskin; *esp* **:** buckskin breeches **b** *archaic* **:** a person dressed in buckskin garments; *often* **:** a backwoodsman or countrified person of the earlier periods of American settlement **3** *chiefly West & Southwest* **:** a horse of a light yellowish dun color and usu. with a dark stripe down the back and dark mane and tail **4 a :** a heavy thick cotton fabric with a smooth face, napped back, and satin weave used for outerwear **b :** a durable woolen cloth for outerwear made in satin weave and napped and sheared for a smooth face **5 a :** a leathery scurfy condition of the skin of grapefruit and sometimes of sweet oranges caused by attacks of the citrus rust mite **b :** a virus disease of cherry, peach, and other stone fruit characterized by small pointed fruits that remain green and underdeveloped and shrivel prior to ripening, the affected cherry trees having also a lusterless leathery-skinned pale fruit **6 :** a log with bark removed or lost

buck-skinned \"+d\ *adj* **:** dressed in buckskin

buck slip *n* [prob. fr. ¹⁰*buck*] **:** a routing slip used esp. in military offices to indicate the persons to whom the attached material is to go and usu. the kind of action to be taken with such material

buckstay \'ˌ=\ *also* **buckstave** \'ˌ=\ *n* -s [¹*buck* (steel support) + *stay* or *stave*] **:** either of two connected girders used one on each side of the masonry structure of a furnace or flue to take the thrust of an arch; *also* **:** any girder similarly used as a stay

A B C A
A BUCKSTAY
B. TIE ROD
C TURNBUCKLE

bucktail \'ˌ=\ *n* [¹*buck* + *tail*] **1** [so called fr. the fact that members wore deer tails in their hats on certain occasions] *archaic* **:** a member of the Tammany political society during the period from about 1817–26; *also* **:** an opponent of Governor DeWitt Clinton of New York State of about the same period **2 a :** an artificial angler's fly made of hairs from the tail of a deer or a similar material **b :** a fishing lure used in saltwater angling with a similar dressing and a weighted head — see LURE illustration

buckthorn \'ˌ=\ *n* [trans. of It *spino cervino* & NL *cervi spina*] **1 :** a shrub or tree of the genus *Rhamnus* sometimes having thorny branches and often containing purgative principles in bark or sap and producing fruits sometimes used as a source of yellow and green dyes or pigments — see CASCARA BUCKTHORN **2 :** a shrub or tree of the genus *Bumelia* — usu. used in combination; see SOUTHERN BUCKTHORN **3 :** a prickly shrub (*Ceanothus seriedatus*) of the California chaparral

buckthorn aphid *n* **:** an aphid (*Aphis nasturtii*) common in eastern No. America and a destructive pest of potatoes in some areas

buckthorn berries *n pl* **:** the dried unripe berries of various buckthorns a powder or extract of which is used to dye mordanted wool and cotton — called also *yellow berries*

buckthorn brown *n* **:** a strong yellowish brown that is stronger, slightly yellower, and darker than centennial brown and yellower, less strong, and slightly lighter than orange rust — called also *chamoline, sumac*

buckthorn family *n* **:** RHAMNACEAE

buckthorn fencing *n* **:** fencing of a steel band or ribbon with sawtooth barbs

buckthorn weed *also* **buckthorn** *n* **:** FIDDLE-NECK 2

bucktooth \'ˌ=\ *n, pl* **buckteeth** [¹*buck*] **:** a large projecting front tooth — **buck-toothed** \'ˌ=\ *adj*

bucku *var of* **buchu**

buck up *vb* [²*buck*] *vi* **:** to become encouraged or cheerful **:** brace up ~ *vt* **1 :** IMPROVE, SMARTEN **2 :** to cheer up **:** give a lift to **:** raise the morale of ⟨mountain air *bucked* her *up*⟩

buck·wagon \'bək+,-\ *n* [part modif., part trans. of Afrik *bokwa*, fr. *bok* beam of a wagon, stand, tripod, male goat (fr. MD *boc* male goat) + *wa* wagon; akin to OHG *boc* male goat — more at BUCK] **:** a large strong wagon with the frame projecting over the wheels that is used in southern Africa for hauling loads

buckwash \'ˌ=\ *vt* [⁶*buck* + *wash*] *archaic* **:** BUCK

buckwheat \'ˌ=\ *n, often attrib* [part modif., part trans. of D *boekweit*, fr. MD *boecweit* (akin to MLG *bōkwēte*), fr. *boec-* (akin to OHG *buohha* beech tree) + *weit* wheat; fr. the similarity of the seeds to beechnuts — more at BEECH] **1 :** an herb of the genus *Fagopyrum*, characterized by alternate hastate or cordate leaves and clusters of pink-tinged white dimorphous flowers rich in nectar; *esp* **:** either of two species (*F. esculentum* and *F. tataricum*) long cultivated as cereal plants — see COMMON BUCKWHEAT, TARTARIAN BUCKWHEAT **2 :** the triangular seed of buckwheat containing somewhat less protein than wheat and used as animal feed or cracked or ground for flour or cereal for human consumption **3 :** WILD BUCKWHEAT 2

buckwheat cake *n* **:** a griddlecake that is made with buckwheat flour

buckwheat coal *also* **buckwheat** *n* **:** anthracite coal in any one of five small sizes — see ANTHRACITE table

buck·wheat·er \-ēd·ə(r), -ētə-\ *n* -s *slang* **:** a novice at lumbering

buckwheat family *n* **:** POLYGONACEAE

buckwheat honey *n* **:** a dark strongly flavored honey produced from buckwheat esp. in parts of the northeastern U.S.

buckwheat note *n* **:** SHAPE NOTE

buckwheat tree *n* **:** TITI 1a

buckwheat vine *n* **:** a high-climbing woody vine (*Brunnichia cirrhosa*) with ovate leaves cordate or truncate at the base, the lower flower spikes solitary and axillary and the upper ones in a loose panicle

bucky \'bəkē\ *adj* -ER/-EST [¹*buck* + *-y*] **:** like a buck or like that of a buck; *esp* **:** exhibiting characteristics of an entire male ⟨some discount is usual on ~ lambs⟩

bu·co·li·ast \byü'kōlē,ast, -ˌəst\ *n* -s [Gk *boukoliastēs*, fr. *boukoliazesthai* to sing or write pastorals, fr. *boukolos* cowherd] *obs* **:** a pastoral poet

1bu·col·ic \(')byü'kälik\ *also* **bu·col·i·cal** \-ləkəl\ *adj* [L *bucolicus*, fr. Gk *boukolikos*, fr. *boukolos* cowherd (fr. *bous* head of cattle + *-kolos*; akin to L *colere* to cultivate) + *-ikos* -ic, -ical — more at COW, WHEEL] **1 :** of or relating to shepherds or herdsmen **:** PASTORAL ⟨~ poetry⟩ **2 a :** relating to or typical of rural life **:** RUSTIC ⟨a pleasant ~ scene⟩ **b :** countrified and unsophisticated or unaffected **:** natural and without artful elaboration ⟨his calm ~ writings⟩ — **bu·col·i·cal·ly** \-lək(ə)lē\ *also* **bu·col·ic·ly** \-ləklē\ *adv*

2bucolic \"\ *n* -s [L *bucolicum*, fr. neut. of *bucolicus*] **1 :** a pastoral poem **:** ECLOGUE, IDYL — usu. used in pl. ⟨the *Bucolics* of Theocritus⟩; compare GEORGIC **2 :** a bucolic person or condition; *sometimes* **:** RUSTIC, BUMPKIN

bucolic caesura *or* **bucolic diaeresis** *n* **:** a diaeresis after the fourth foot in a dactylic hexameter esp. common in pastoral poetry

bu·cor·vus \byü'kȯrvəs\ *n, cap* [NL, fr. *bu-* (fr. *Buceros*) + *Corvus*] **:** a genus of African birds (family Bucerotidae) consisting of the ground hornbills — compare BUCEROS

bu·cra·ni·um \byü'krānēəm\ *also* **bu·crane** \(')byü'krān\ *n, pl* **bucra·nia** \byü'krānēə\ *also* **bucranes** [L, fr. Gk *boukranion* ox head, fr. *bous* ox, head of cattle + *kranion* skull — more at COW, CRANIUM] **:** a sculptured ornament (as on a Roman Ionic or Corinthian frieze) composed of an ox skull adorned with ribbons or garlands

bucranium

1bud \'bəd\ *n* -s [ME *budde*; akin to OE *budda* beetle, D *bot* bud, MLG *buddich* swollen, OHG *būtil* bag, MHG *butzen* to swell, Icel *budda* purse, Skt *bhūri* abundant — more at BOAST] **1 :** a small lateral or terminal protuberance on the stem of a plant consisting of an undeveloped shoot made up of rudimentary foliage leaves or floral leaves or both overarching a growing point and often protected by specialized bud scales or by a coating of resin or hairs or by both — see FLOWER BUD, LEAF BUD, MIXED BUD **2 :** something not yet mature or attained to full growth and development: as **a :** an incompletely opened flower ⟨the ~s are getting full of color⟩ — often used in combination ⟨one red rosebud⟩ **b** *dial Eng* **:** a yearling calf **c :** a young girl just entering social life **d :** CHILD, YOUTH — compare ³BUD **e :** an outgrowth from the body of an organism that differentiates into a new individual **:** GEMMA; *also* **:** a primordium having potentialities for growth and development into a definitive structure ⟨an embryonic limb ~⟩ ⟨a horn ~⟩ **f :** an initial phase of development ⟨raised havoc with the first ~s of a contemporary and a functional architecture in Dixie —M.W.Fishwick⟩ **3 :** state of budding **:** INCIPIENCE — used esp. in the phrase *in the bud* ⟨the plot was nipped in the ~⟩ **4 :** something likened to or suggestive of a bud esp. in shape: as **a :** an anatomical structure resembling a bud (as a tactile corpuscle); *esp* **:** NIPPLE **b :** a small somewhat conical morsel of sweet chocolate

2bud \"\ *vb* **budded; budded; budding; buds** [ME *budden*, fr. *budde*, n.] *vi* **1** *of a plant or its parts* **a :** to set buds ⟨the plant will not ~ well without heavy fertilizing⟩ **b :** to commence growth from buds **:** break dormancy ⟨spring is here, all the trees are *budding*⟩ — often used with *out* ⟨the leaves have *budded* out almost overnight⟩ **2 a :** to be like a bud in youth and freshness or in the unfolding of growth and promise **b :** to develop like a plant part through the unfolding of a bud ⟨new antlers ~ during the summer⟩ **c :** to arise like a bud from some precursor — often used with *off* ⟨a number of sects have *budded* off from the early churches of the Reformation⟩ **3 :** to reproduce asexually; *specif* **:** to produce a new cell (as in yeasts) by pinching off a small part of the parent cell **4 :** to perform the operation of budding a plant **5** *of a bird* **:** to feed on buds ~ *vt* **1 :** to produce or develop (as leaves) from buds ⟨some honeysuckles ~ their leaves very early in the spring⟩ — often used with *off* or *out* ⟨some zoophytes ~ off young at regular intervals⟩ **2 :** to cause (as a plant) to bud — often used with *out* ⟨warm weather will ~ out trees⟩ **3 :** to insert a bud from a plant of one kind into an opening in the bark of (a plant of another kind) usu. in order to propagate a desired variety — compare GRAFT *vt* **1 4 :** to produce (as young) by gemmation — often used with *out*

3bud \"\ *n* [short for ²*buddy*] **:** BROTHER, BUDDY — often used in informal address ⟨say ~, have you got the right time⟩

bu·da·pest \'büdə,pest *also* 'bùd- *or* 'byüd- *or* ˌ='= *or* -esht *sometimes* -esh\ *adj, usu cap* [fr. *Budapest*, Hungary] **:** of or from Budapest, the capital of Hungary **:** of the kind or style prevalent in Budapest

budbreak \'ˌ=\ *n* **:** initiation of growth from a bud ⟨~ may be delayed after pruning in hot dry weather⟩

bud brush *n* [so called fr. its clusters of leaves and flowers that resemble buds] **:** a half-shrubby perennial (*Artemisia spinescens*) valuable as sheep forage in the western U.S.

bud cutting *n* **:** a plant cutting containing a single bud

bud·da *also* **bud·dah** \'bədə\ *n* -s [native name in Australia] **:** a hoary Australian forage shrub (*Pholidia mitchelli* or *Eremophila mitchelli*) of the family Myoporaceae with alternate leaves, 2-lipped corolla, and globular drupaceous fruits

bud·der \'bədə(r)\ *n* -s **:** one that buds; *esp* **:** a person who inserts buds in plant stocks

bud·dha \'büdə, 'bù-\ *n* -s [Skt *buddha* awakened, enlightened, fr. *bodhati* he awakes, understands — more at BID] **1** *usu cap* **:** a person who has attained Buddhahood **2** [after Gautama *Buddha* †*ab* 483 B.C. Indian philosopher who founded Buddhism] **:** a representation of the philosopher Gautama Buddha

buddha-field \'ˌ=\ *n, usu cap B* **:** a paradisiacal sphere beyond the conditions of historical existence and under the beneficent control of a Buddha

buddha 2

bud·dha·hood \-,hùd\ *n* -s *usu cap* **:** a state of enlightenment or religious salvation characterized negatively as release from the earthly fetters of suffering, sorrow, and illusion and positively as the state of perfect spiritual fulfillment

buddha-nature \'ˌ=\ *n, usu cap B* **:** the essence of and potency to attain Buddhahood

buddha's-hand \'ˌ=\ *n, pl* **buddha's-hands** *usu cap B* **:** a citron (*Citrus medica* var. *sarcodactylis*) that is cultivated in eastern Asia as an ornamental and for its very fragrant fruit which is split into several usu. pulpless sections

bud·dhi \'büdē, 'bù-\ *n* -s [Skt, lit., understanding, fr. *bodhati* he awakes, understands — more at BUDDHA] **:** the faculty of intuitive discernment or direct spiritual awareness in the beliefs of Hinduism and Buddhism

bud·dhism \-,dizəm\ *n* -s [Gautama *Buddha* + E *-ism*] **1** *usu cap* **:** the teaching ascribed to Gautama Buddha holding that suffering is inherent in life and that one can escape it into nirvana by mental and moral self-purification — see EIGHTFOLD PATH, FOUR NOBLE TRUTHS **2** *cap* **:** a religion of eastern and central Asia growing out of the teaching of Gautama Buddha and comprising widely differing sects — see HINAYANA, MAHAYANA

1bud·dhist \-ˌdəst\ *n* -s *usu cap* [Gautama *Buddha* + E *-ist*] **:** an adherent of Buddhism

2buddhist \"\ *or* **bud·dhis·tic** \(ˈ)ₑ;distik\ *also* **bud·dhis·ti·cal** \-tәkәl\ *adj, usu cap* **:** of or relating to Buddha or Buddhism — **bud·dhis·ti·cal·ly** \-tәk(ә)lē\ *adv, usu cap*

bud·dho·log·i·cal \ˌbüdəˈläjəkəl, ˈbu̇-, -dᵊlˈä-\ *adj, usu cap* **:** of, relating to, or contained in Buddhology

bud·dhol·o·gy \büˈdäləjē, bu̇-\ *n* -ES *usu cap* [Gautama *Buddha* + E *-ology* (as in *theology*)] **:** the theology of the deified Buddha

budding *adj* [fr. pres. part. of *2bud*] **:** beginning to make one's way or to come into notice ⟨a ~ diplomat⟩

budding yeast *n* **:** a yeast that buds off daughter cells smaller than the parent cell — compare FISSION YEAST

1bud·dle \ˈbu̇dᵊl, ˈbüd-,ˈbәd-\ *n* -s [origin unknown] *dial Eng* **:** CORN MARIGOLD

2bud·dle \ˈbәdᵊl, ˈbu̇d-\ *n* -s [origin unknown] **:** an apparatus (as an inclined trough or platform) on which crushed ore is concentrated by running water which washes out the lighter and less valuable portions

3buddle \"\ *vt* -ED/-ING/-S **:** to wash (ore) on a buddle

bud·dle·ia \ˈbәdlēә, ₑˈₑₑ\ *n* [NL, fr. Adam *Buddle* †1715 Eng. botanist + NL *-ia*] **1** *cap* **:** a genus of showy shrubs or trees (family Loganiaceae) of warm regions with opposite leaves and terminal clusters of yellow or violet flowers **2** *also* **bud·dle·ja** \"\ -s **:** a plant of the genus *Buddleia*

bud·dler \ˈbәd(ᵊ)lә(r), ˈbu̇d-\ *also* **bud·dle·man** \-dᵊlmәn\ *n, pl* **buddlers** *also* **buddlemen :** one that buddles

1bud·dy \ˈbәdē, -di\ *adj* -ER/-EST [*1bud* + *-y*] **:** full or suggestive of buds

2buddy \"\ *also* **bud·die** \"\ *n, pl* **buddies** [prob. baby talk alter. of *1brother*] **1 :** little boy — used chiefly in address **2 a :** COMPANION, PARTNER; *esp* **:** fellow soldier **b :** an intimate friend **c :** one of two persons paired off in the buddy system **3 :** FELLOW — used in informal address ⟨hey, ~, when's the next bus leave⟩

3buddy \"\ *vi* -ED/-ING/-ES **:** to become friendly — often used with *up* ⟨he *buddied* up with the other corporal⟩

buddy-buddy \ₑₑ;ₑₑ\ *adj* [redupl. of *2buddy*] *slang* **:** closely associated **:** INTIMATE

buddy sap *n* [*1buddy*] **:** a late run of sugar-maple sap gathered after the buds have begun to swell and usu. producing syrup of poor quality

buddy system *n* [*2buddy*] **:** an arrangement (as for military activity or engagement in hazardous sports) in which two individuals are paired for mutual assistance or protection

1budge \ˈbәj\ *n* -s [ME *bugee, bogey,* fr. AF *bogee*] **:** a fur formerly prepared from lambskin dressed with the wool outward

2budge \"\ *vb* -ED/-ING/-S [MF *bouger,* fr. OF *bougier,* fr. (assumed) VL *bullicare,* fr. L *bullire* to boil — more at BOIL] *vi* **:** MOVE, SHIFT; *esp* **:** to give way **:** YIELD — usu. used with an expressed or implied negative ⟨the mule refused to ~⟩ ~ *vt* **:** to start or cause to move ⟨the door was stuck fast, I couldn't ~ it⟩; *often* **:** to move (someone) to make a new decision **:** cause (a person) to change his mind ⟨once he decided to stay no one could ~ him⟩

3budge \"\ *adj* [origin unknown] *archaic* **:** austere or stiff in manner **:** POMPOUS, SOLEMN

4budge *n* -s [origin unknown] *obs slang* **:** THIEF

5budge \ˈbәj\ *n* [origin unknown] *slang* **:** intoxicating liquor

bud·ger·ee \ˈbәjәrē\ *adj* [native name in Australia] *Austral* **:** GOOD, FINE, PRETTY

bud·ger·i·gar \ˈbәjәrēˌgär, -gȧ(r\ *also* **bud·ger·ee·gah** *or* **bud·ger·y·gah** \-gä,-gȧ\ *n* -s [native name in Australia] **:** a small Australian parrot (*Melopsittacus undulatus*) that is usu. light green with black and yellow markings in the wild but that under domestication has been bred in many colors and has become a favored cage and show bird — called also *grass parrakeet, lovebird, shell parrakeet*

bud·ger·ow \ˈbәj(ә)ˌrō\ *n* -s [Hindi *bajrā*] **:** a large cumbrous barge without a keel used on the Ganges river

1bud·get \ˈbәjәt, *usu* -әd-+V; *chiefly dial* ˈbu̇j-\ *n* -s [ME *bowgette,* fr. MF *bougette,* dim. of *bouge* leather bag, fr. L *bulga,* fr. Gaulish; akin to MIr *bolg* bag, OE *bælg* bag, skin — more at BELLY] **1 a** *now dial* **:** a usu. leather pouch or wallet; *often* **:** a pack to be carried on the back **b** *archaic* **:** a leather or skin bottle — compare WATER BOUGET **c :** PACKAGE, BUNDLE, COLLECTION — now dial. except of written or printed matter ⟨grandma made me up a snack in a ~⟩ ⟨a neatly stacked ~ of letters⟩ **2 :** STOCK, SUPPLY, QUANTITY ⟨building up her ~ of complaints⟩ ⟨he was a ~ of foibles and contradictions⟩; *sometimes* **:** a quantity (as of energy or water) involved in, available for, or assignable to a particular situation ⟨the A-bomb . . . yields its ~ of energy . . . in a fraction of a second —*Scientific American Reader*⟩ **3 a :** a statement of the financial position of a sovereign body (as of a nation) for a definite period of time based on detailed estimates of planned or expected expenditures during the period and proposals for financing them — used orig. of such a statement presented annually by the chancellor of the exchequer to the British House of Commons **b :** a plan for the coordination of resources (as of money or manpower) and expenditures ⟨a good family ~ keeps something in reserve for emergencies⟩; *esp* **:** such a plan covering a definite period of time **c :** the amount of money available, required, or assigned to a particular purpose in or as if in a budget ⟨a minimum weekly ~ for a family of five⟩ ⟨trying to operate efficiently on a ~ of less than $3000⟩

2budget \"\ *vb* -ED/-ING/-S *vt* **1 a :** to put or allow for in a budget ⟨funds ~*ed* by the administration for navigation⟩ ⟨I doubt that we can ~ a new car this year⟩ **b :** to put on a budget ⟨~*ed* shoppers⟩ **2a :** to plan expenditures for (as an enterprise) in a budget ⟨the new municipal hospital became a major undertaking and over a million was ~*ed* for it⟩ **b :** to plan or provide for the use of in detail ⟨in the present tight labor market manpower must be ~*ed* carefully⟩ ⟨the wise man ~*s* his time⟩ ~ *vi* **:** to formulate or draw up a budget — usu. used with *for* ⟨in case you're ~*ing* for an auto trip —Richard Joseph⟩ ⟨he actually ~*ed* for a trifling £1,000,000 —*Melbourne (Australia) Herald*⟩

3budget \"\ *adj* **:** suitable for one using or adhering to a budget esp. in cheapness ⟨several attractive ~ dresses⟩ ⟨~ cuts of meat usu. require slow cooking⟩

bud·get·ary \ˈbәjәˌterē, -ri\ *adj* **1 :** of, relating to, involved in, or provided for a budget ⟨~ plans⟩ ⟨~ accounts⟩ ⟨~ expenditures⟩ **2 :** involving or exercised through a budget ⟨~ control of production⟩ ⟨~ questions in the assembly⟩

bud·ge·teer \ˌbәjәˈti(ә)r, -iә\ *or* **bud·get·er** \ˈbәjәd·ә(r), -әtә-\ *n* -s **:** a person who prepares or uses a budget

bud·gie \ˈbәjē\ *n* -s [by alter. and shortening] **:** BUDGERIGAR

bud grafting *n* **:** the grafting of a plant by budding

bud gum *n* **:** the sticky exudation covering a plant bud

bud·less \ˈbәdlәs\ *adj* **:** being without a bud

bud·let \ˈbәdlәt\ *n* -s **:** a young, small, or secondary bud ⟨some yeasts form several ~*s* on their primary buds before breaking up⟩

bud·ling \-liŋ\ *n* -s **:** the shoot that develops from the scion bud in bud grafting

bud·mash \ˈbәdˌmäsh\ *n* -ES [Per *badma'āsh* immoral, fr. *bad* bad (fr. MPer *vat*) + *ma'āsh* living, life, fr. Ar] *India* **:** a bad character **:** a worthless person

bud mite *n* **:** any of a number of minute phytophagous mites that attack the young buds of plants and commonly cause failure of normal development of infested buds

bud moth *n* **:** any of certain moths which in the larval state are destructive to buds of fruit trees; *esp* **:** EYE-SPOTTED BUD MOTH

bud mutation *n* **:** bud variation resulting from local genetic alteration and producing a permanent modification that usu. can be perpetuated by grafting ⟨the navel orange is a notable product of *bud mutation*⟩

bu·dong monkey \ˈb(y)üˌdȯŋ-\ *n* [prob. native name in Ceylon] **:** PURPLE-FACED LANGUR

bu·dor·cas \byüˈdȯrkәs\ *n, cap* [NL, fr. Gk *bous* head of cattle + *dorkas* gazelle — more at COW, DORCAS GAZELLE] **:** a genus of heavy-coated Asiatic bovines comprising the takins

bud rot *n* **:** a plant disease or symptom of disease involving decay of the buds: as **a :** COCONUT BUD ROT **b :** a disease of carnations caused by an imperfect fungus (*Sporotrichum poae*) that is carried by mites and produces a rotting of the petals while yet in the bud

buds *pl of* BUD, *pres 3d sing of* BUD

bud sage *also* **bud sagebrush** *n* **:** BUD BRUSH

bud scale *or* **bud sheath** *n* **:** one of the leaves resembling scales that form the external covering of a plant bud and are often densely coated with hair, gum, or resin

bud sport *n* **:** a product of bud mutation or bud variation ⟨a red-flowered branch on a white-flowering plant is a typical *bud sport*⟩ — compare BUD VARIETY

bud stick *n* **:** a shoot usu. of the current year's growth which is cut from a tree and from which buds are removed for budding

budtime \ˈₑ,ₑ\ *n* **:** the season of budding **:** SPRING

bu·du·kha \bәˈdükә\ *n, pl* **budukha** *or* **budukhas** *usu cap* [Russ *Budukhi, Budugi*] **1 :** a Lezghian people dwelling in the Caucasus **2 :** a member of the Budukha people

bu·du·ma \bәˈdümә\ *n, pl* **buduma** *or* **budumas** *usu cap* **1 :** a Negroid people dwelling on the shores and islands of Lake Chad **2 :** a member of the Buduma people

bud variation *n* **1 :** marked deviation from the normal in the development of a plant shoot from a bud — see BUD MUTATION **2 :** a product of bud variation **:** a shoot or clone originating from a single bud unlike other buds of the parent plant — see BUD SPORT, BUD VARIETY

bud variety *n* **:** a strain or variety of plant originating by bud variation **:** a clonal bud variation — compare BUD SPORT

budwood \ˈₑ,ₑ\ *n* **:** wood consisting of strong young shoots bearing buds suitable for use in budding

budworm \ˈₑ,ₑ\ *n* **:** a larval moth that feeds on the buds of plants — see BLACK-HEADED BUDWORM, SPRUCE BUDWORM

bue·nos ai·res \ˌbwānәˈs|a(ә)rēz, |er-,|īr-, -riz *also* ˈbōn- *or* -rәs *sometimes* ˈbwen- *or* -nōˈz| *or* |är- *or* |ȧr- *or* |ar- *or* |a(ә)rz *or* |e(ә)rz *or* |a(ә)әz *or* |eәz\ *adj, usu cap B&A* [fr. *Buenos Aires,* Argentina] **:** of or from Buenos Aires, the capital of Argentina **:** of the kind or style prevalent in Buenos Aires

buen re·ti·ro \ˌbwānrәˈtē(ˌ)rō, ˌbwen-\ *n* [Sp, lit., good retreat] **1 :** a resting place or retreat **2** *usu cap B&R* [fr. *Buen Retiro,* near Madrid, Spain, where it was manufactured] **:** a soft-paste porcelain produced during the latter half of the 18th century in the private manufactory of the king of Spain

buer·ger's disease \ˈbәrgәrz-, ˈbu̇r-\ *n, usu cap B* [after Leo *Buerger* †1943 Am. physician] **:** THROMBOANGIITIS OBLITERANS

buetsch·li·ite *also* **bütsch·li·ite** \ˈbüchlēˌīt\ *n* -s [Otto *Bütschli* (*Buetschli*) †1920 Ger. zoologist + E *-ite*] **:** a mineral $K_6Ca_2(CO_3)_5.6H_2O$ consisting of hydrous carbonate of potassium and calcium

1buett·ne·ri·a·ce·ae \(ˌ)byütˌnirēˈāsēˌē\ *n* [NL, fr. *Buettneria,* type genus (fr. David S. A. *Buettner* †1768 Ger. botanist + NL *-ia*) + *-aceae*] *syn of* STERCULIACEAE

2buettneriaceae \"\ [NL, fr. *Buettneria,* type genus + *-aceae*] *syn of* CALYCANTHACEAE

bu·fa·gin \ˈbyüfәjәn\ *n* -s [ISV *bufag-* (fr. NL *Bufo agua* agua toad) + *-in*] **:** a crystalline toxic steroid genin $C_{24}H_{34}O_5$ obtained from the poisonous secretion of a skin gland on the back of the neck of the agua toad and like digitalis in biological action; *also* **:** any of several similar genins from secretions of other toads — see BUFOTOXIN

1buff \ˈbәf\ *n* -s [ME *buffe,* fr. MF, of imit. origin] *now chiefly dial* **:** BUFFET, BLOW ⟨a ~ on the head⟩

2buff \"\ *vt* -ED/-ING/-S *chiefly Scot* **:** STRIKE, BEAT

3buff \"\ *adv, archaic* **:** FIRMLY, STURDILY — used in the phrase *to stand buff*

4buff \"\ *n* -s [MF *buffle,* fr. OIt *bufalo* — more at BUFFALO] **1 :** a buffalo or other wild ox **2 a :** BUFF LEATHER **b :** a garment made of buff leather; *esp* **:** a buff leather uniform or military garment **3 :** the bare skin **4 a :** a moderate orange yellow **b :** a light to moderate yellow **5** [*6buff*] **:** any of various devices employed in buffing: as **a :** BUFF STICK **b :** a device (as a stick or block) having a soft absorbent surface (as of cloth or velvet) by which polishing material is applied (as to the fingernails) **c :** BUFFING WHEEL **6 :** a country cattlehide weighing 45 to 60 pounds untrimmed **7 a** [so called fr. the buff overcoats worn by volunteer firemen in New York City ab1820] **:** an enthusiast about going to fires **b :** FAN, ENTHUSIAST, DEVOTEE ⟨theater ~*s* of all sorts⟩ ⟨twelve-year-old history ~*s* should have a fine time with this big volume —Katharine T. Kinkead⟩

5buff \"\ *adj* **1 :** made of or like buff leather **2 :** of the color buff

6buff \"\ *vt* -ED/-ING/-S **1 :** to polish with a buff; *broadly* **:** POLISH, SHINE ⟨shoes freshly ~*ed*⟩ ⟨~*ing* her nails on her sleeve⟩ **2 :** to give a buff or velvety surface to (leather) **3 :** to color or stain buff (as willow rods)

7buff \"\ *n* -s [origin unknown] *Scot* **:** silly talk **:** NONSENSE

8buff \"\ *vi* -ED/-ING/-S [back-formation fr. *3buffer*] **:** to act as a buffer in preventing contact or deadening the shock of contact

buf·fa \ˈbüfә, -(ˌ)fä\ *n, pl* **buf·fe** \-(ˌ)fā\ [It, fem. of *buffo* — more at BUFFO] **1 :** a woman singer of comic roles in opera **2 :** OPERA BUFFA

buff·a·bil·i·ty \ˌbәfәˈbilәd·ē\ *n* -ES **:** the capability of being polished by buffing

buff·able \ˈbәfәbәl\ *adj* [*6buff* + *-able*] **:** capable of being buffed

1buf·fa·lo \ˈbәfәˌlō *also* -f(ˌ)lō\ *n, pl* **buffalo** *or* **buffaloes** *also* **buffalos** [It *bufalo* & Sp *búfalo,* fr. LL *bufalus,* alter. of L *bubalus* buffalo, African gazelle, fr. Gk *boubalos* African gazelle, irreg. fr. *bous* ox, cow — more at COW] **1 :** any of several wild oxen: as **a :** the water buffalo (*Bubalus bubalis*) orig. from India but now domesticated, developed into several breeds, and used as draft and milch animals in most of the warmer countries of Asia and adjacent islands, being larger and less docile than the common ox and fond of marshy places and rivers **b :** CAPE BUFFALO **c :** a member of the genus *Bison; esp* **:** a large shaggy-maned No. American wild ox (*B. bison*) having short horns and heavy forequarters with a large muscular hump formed by the withers and prolonged spinal processes of the ribs — called also *bison* **d :** ANOA **2 :** something derived from the American buffalo: **a :** a coverlet or rug of buffalo skin **b :** a horn (as for powder) made from the horn of a buffalo **3 :** BUFFALO FISH **4 :** a large heavily armored and armed amphibious military vehicle **5 :** a tapₑ dance step suggestive of a buffalo's pawing

2buffalo \"\ *vt* -ED/-ING/-ES **:** BAMBOOZLE, BEWILDER, OVERAWE, BAFFLE ⟨he tried to ~ me at first meeting but I soon caught on to his tricks⟩

3buffalo \"\ *adj, usu cap* [fr. *Buffalo,* N.Y.] **:** of or from the city of Buffalo, N.Y. ⟨*Buffalo* factories⟩ **:** of the kind or style prevalent in Buffalo

buffalo bean *or* **buffalo apple** *n* **1** [so called fr. its location in buffalo country] **:** GROUND PLUM **2 :** any of certain African climbing legumes (genus *Stizolobium*) having a velvety seed pod and hairs which cause intolerable itching when they come in contact with the skin

buffalo berry *n* [so called fr. its location in buffalo country] **1** *or* **buffalo bush :** either of two shrubs (*Shepherdia argentea* and *S. canadensis*) of the western U.S. having silvery foliage — called also *bullberry, rabbitberry* **2 :** the edible scarlet berry of the buffalo berry

buffalo bug *or* **buffalo carpet beetle** *n* [so called fr. its appearance] **:** CARPET BEETLE

buffalo bunchgrass *n* [so called fr. its location in buffalo country] **:** a densely tufted perennial fescue (*Festuca scabrella*) of western No. America with usu. scabrous culms and narrow or involute leaf blades

buffalo bur *n* [so called fr. its being frequently entangled in the hair of buffalo] **:** a No. American nightshade (*Solanum rostratum*) with prickly foliage and racemose yellow flowers

buffalo chips *n pl* **:** dry dung of buffalo or of livestock esp. when used as fuel

buffalo cholera *or* **buffalo disease** *n* **:** BARBONE

buffalo cloth *n* [so called fr. its shaggy appearance] **:** a woolen fabric with a shaggy pile

buffalo clover *n* [so called fr. its location in buffalo country] **1 :** either of two clovers (*Trifolium reflexum* and *T. stoloniferum*) of the western U.S. **2 :** BLUEBONNET 3b

buffalo cod *n* **:** LINGCOD

buffalo currant *n* [so called fr. its location in buffalo country] **1 :** an ornamental hardy currant (*Ribes odoratum*) of the western U.S. with fragrant yellow flowers and black fruit **2 :** GOLDEN CURRANT 1

buffalo dance *n* **:** a ritual group dance of No. American Indians imitative of the buffalo for cure, for success in the hunt, or as part of the sun-dance ceremony

buffalofish *n* **:** any of several large suckers (family Catostomidae) mostly found in the Mississippi valley, some being important food fishes: as **a :** BIGMOUTH BUFFALO **b :** BLACK BUFFALO 1 **c :** SMALLMOUTH BUFFALO

buffalo fly *n* **:** a small gray biting muscid fly (*Siphona exigua*) widespread in Indo-Malaysia and Australia where it is a major pest of water buffalo and other domestic animals

buffalo gnat *n* **1 :** BLACKFLY a **2 :** HORN FLY

buffalo gourd *n* [so called fr. its location in buffalo country] **:** CALABAZILLA

buffalo grass *n* **1 :** either of two No. American grasses: **a :** a low-growing dioecious grass (*Buchloë dactyloides*) very common on former feeding grounds of the American buffalo and sometimes used to establish permanent sod in droughty areas **b :** GRAMA **2** *Austral* **:** SAINT AUGUSTINE GRASS **3 :** any of several African grasses; *esp* **:** a hairy guinea grass (*Panicum maximum* var. *hirsutissimum*)

buffalo gun *n* **:** a large-caliber rifle used primarily in hunting the American buffalo

buffalo hump *n* **:** fat pads localized on the back of the neck that produce a resemblance to the hump of a bison and constitute one of the clinical features of Cushing's disease

buffalo indian *n, usu cap B&I* **:** PLAINS INDIAN

buffalo leather *n* **:** leather produced from the hides of Old World buffalo (as the water buffalo)

buffalo moth *n* [so called fr. its appearance] **:** the larva of the carpet beetle

buf·fa·lo·nian \ˌbәfәˈlōnēәn, -nyәn\ *n* -s *cap* [blend of *Buffalo,* N. Y. and E *-onian* (as in *Oxonian*)] **:** a native or resident of Buffalo, N.Y.

buffalo nut *n* **1 :** the oily drupaceous fruit of rabbitwood — called also *elk nut, oil nut* **2 :** RABBITWOOD

buffalo pea *n* [so called fr. its location in buffalo country] **1 :** GROUND PLUM **2 :** AMERICAN VETCH

buffalo robe *n* **:** the hide of an American buffalo dressed with the hair on, commonly trimmed to rectangular shape, lined on the skin side with fabric, and used as a carriage robe, rug, or article of bedding

buffalo rye *n* [so called fr. its growing in buffalo country] **:** LYME GRASS

buffalos *pl of* BUFFALO

buffalo soldier *n* **:** a Negro soldier serving in the western U.S. after the Civil War

buffalo thorn *n* **:** a low tree (*Acacia latronum*) of western India that is shaped like an umbrella and covered with long straight spines borne in pairs and connected at the base

buffalo tree *n* **:** RABBITWOOD

buffalo treehopper *n* [so called fr. its horned prothorax] **:** a bright green treehopper (*Stictocephala bubalus*) that has two lateral horns on the prothorax, is common throughout the U.S., and damages fruit and other trees by laying its eggs in the bark of the twigs

buffalo wallow *n* **:** a shallow undrained depression occurring on the Great Plains, often containing water in wet seasons, and generally thought to have been produced or deepened by the rolling and wallowing of herds of buffalo in mud and dust

buffalo weaver *n* [so called fr. the massive and rough appearance of its nest] **:** any of several gregarious African weavers constituting a subfamily of Ploceidae and being distinguished from other weavers by their bulky untidy nests that are placed on rather than suspended from branches

buffalo weed *n* **:** GREAT RAGWEED

buffalo wolf *n* [so called fr. its former abundance in the buffalo country] **:** the gray wolf of central and western U.S.

buff-backed heron \ˈₑ,ₑ-\ *n* **:** CATTLE EGRET

buff·bar \ˈbәfˌbär\ *n, usu cap* [*buff* Orpington + *barred* Rocks] **:** a breed of buff or golden autosexing fowls developed by interbreeding barred Rocks and buff Orpingtons

buff-bare \ˈₑ;ₑ\ *adj* [*4buff*] **:** completely unclothed **:** stark naked

buff-breasted sandpiper \ˈₑ,ₑₑ-\ *n* **:** a small stocky sandpiper (*Tryngites subruficollis*) having uniformly buff underparts and yellowish legs, breeding on the northwest coast of No. America, wintering in Argentina, and migrating chiefly by the central flyway or to the east coast of Canada and over the Atlantic

buffcoat \ˈₑ,ₑ\ *n* [*4buff* + *coat*] **1 a :** a coat of buff leather; *specif* **:** a close short-sleeved military coat worn for defense in the 17th century **b** *archaic* **:** SOLDIER **2 :** BUFFY COAT

buffe *pl of* BUFFA

buffed *adj* [*6buff* + *-ed*] **:** SMOOTH, POLISHED

buf·fel grass \ˈbәfәl-\ *n* [part trans. of Afrik *buffelgras,* fr. *buffel* buffalo (fr. MD, fr. MF *buffle*) + *gras* grass — more at BUFF] **:** an erect tussock-forming perennial bur grass (*Pennisetum cenchroides*) used esp. in Australia and southern Africa for pasture and forage

buffelhead *var of* BUFFLEHEAD

1buff·er \ˈbәfә(r)\ *n* -s [obs. E *buff* to bark (of imit. origin) + *-er*] *archaic slang* **:** DOG 1

2buf·fer \"\ *n* -s [origin unknown] **1** *slang* **:** FELLOW, GUY; *esp* **:** DUFFER — often used with *old* **2** *slang Brit* **:** a chief boatswain's mate

3buff·er \"\ *n* -s *often attrib* [*2buff* + *-er*] **1 :** any of various devices, apparatus, or pieces of material designed primarily to reduce shock due to contact: as **a :** an apparatus on the end of a railway car to close the space between adjoining cars and to absorb shocks incident to car coupling and movement **b** *Brit* **:** a bumper-type shock absorber usu. installed in pairs on the ends of railway cars in Europe **2 :** a means or device used as a cushion against the shock of fluctuations in business or financial activity **3 :** something that serves to separate two items: as **a :** BUFFER STATE **b :** a person who shields another esp. from trivial and annoying routine matters that would interfere with more important activities **c :** an electronic device (as a circuit) used to isolate two radio circuits to avoid undesired reactions between them **d :** an animal that by serving as food for predators cuts down the predation losses of another animal (as a game bird) more desired in a community **e :** a member of a complex of multiple factors that tends to modify the expression of a major gene and reduce the variability of its response to environment **f :** a temporary storage unit (as in a computer); *esp* **:** one that accepts information at one rate and delivers it at another **4 a :** a substance or mixture of substances (as acid salts of weak acids or amphoteric substances) that in solution is capable of neutralizing within limits both acids and bases and thus acts to maintain the original hydrogen-ion concentration of the solution, various of such substances playing fundamental roles in natural processes (as bicarbonates and proteins in biological fluids or clay and organic matter in soils) **b :** BUFFER SOLUTION

4buff·er \"\ *vt* -ED/-ING/-S **1 :** to modify the effect of **:** lessen the impact of **:** CUSHION ⟨the canopy likewise ~*s* the burning sun —*Newsweek*⟩ **2 :** to treat (as an acid solution) with a buffer

5buff·er \"\ *n* -s [*6buff* + *-er*] **1 :** a worker who buffs a particular thing or material (as shoes or leather) or who uses a particular buffing device (as a buffing wheel) **2 :** any of various devices used in buffing: as **a :** BUFFING WHEEL **b :** a horseshoer's tool with a chisel blade to remove heads of nails and a point or prod to drive the nails out **c :** a padded device for polishing fingernails

buffer solution *n* [*3buffer*] **:** a solution that usu. contains on the one hand either a weak acid (as carbonic acid) together with one of the salts of this acid or at least one acid salt of a weak acid or on the other hand a weak base (as ammonia) together with one of the salts of the base and that by its resistance to changes in hydrogen-ion concentration on the addition of acid or base is useful in many chemical, biological, and technical processes

buffer state *n* [*3buffer*] **:** a small neutral state lying between two or more larger potentially rival powers and serving as a military barrier and a means of preventing friction between such powers

buffer stock *n* **:** a stock of a basic commodity (as tin) acquired (as by a cartel) in a period of low or unstable prices and distributed in a period of high prices to stabilize the market

buffer stop *n* [³*buffer*] *Brit* **:** a bumping post placed at the end of a track in train sheds or at stations as an emergency stop for incoming trains and locomotives

buffer strip *n* [³*buffer*] **:** a grassed strip between strips of cropland subject to erosion

¹**buf·fet** \ˈbəfət, *usu* -əd·+V\ *n* -s [ME, fr. MF, fr. OF, dim. of *buffe* blow — more at BUFF] **1 :** a blow with the hand **:** SLAP, CUFF **2 a :** a blow from any source ⟨recurrent ~*s* of fate⟩ **b :** something that affects like a blow (as the violence of wind or water) **c :** the shaking and vibrating of an airplane when forced to a speed greater than that for which it was designed — see BUFFETING

²**buffet** \"\ *vb* -ED/-ING/-S [ME *buffeten*, fr. OF *buffeter*, fr. *buffet*] *vt* **1 :** to strike with or as if with the hand **:** CUFF, SLAP **2 a :** to strike repeatedly **:** POMMEL, BATTER ⟨the wind ~*ed* him as he climbed the slope⟩ **b :** to contend against **:** strive with ⟨~*ing* the billows⟩ **3 :** to drive, force, or move by or as if by repeated blows — often used with *about* ⟨he was ~*ed* about by his somber thoughts⟩ ⟨~*ed* about by one failure after another⟩ ~ *vi* **1 :** STRIVE, CONTEND, STRUGGLE **2 a :** to progress or make one's way esp. under conditions of stress or difficulty or by or as if by physical struggle ⟨the . . . child as he ~*s* back and forth between mother with lovers and father with . . . mistresses —James Kelly⟩ ⟨the milk train ~*ing* along through the valley⟩ **b** *of an airplane* **:** to undergo or become subjected to buffeting **syn** see BEAT

³**buf·fet** \ˌbəˈfā, (ˈ)bü¦fā, bəˈfā *sometimes* (ˈ)bu̇¦fā; *Brit usu* ˈbu̇(ˌ)fā *for sense 3b and often* ˈbəfit *for senses 1 & 2; sense 4 is* ˈbəfi(t)\ *n* -s [F] **1 :** a sideboard often without a mirror **2 :** a cupboard or set of shelves either movable or fixed to a wall for the display of tableware **3 a :** a counter for refreshments **b** *chiefly Brit* **:** a restaurant operated in conjunction with some other enterprise and primarily as a public convenience (as in a railway station or theater); *specif* **:** BUFFET CAR **c :** a meal at which persons help themselves to food set out on a buffet or a table and eat while standing or sitting but not at a formally arranged table ⟨a ~ luncheon⟩ **4** *usu* **buffet stool** *chiefly Scot* **:** FOOTSTOOL, HASSOCK

buffet car *n* [³*buffet*] *chiefly Brit* **:** a railway passenger car having facilities for preparing and serving light meals or snacks usu. in combination with other facilities (as for sleeping or lounging); *also* **:** DINING CAR

buf·fet·ing \ˈbəfəd·|iŋ, -ət|, |ēŋ\ *n* -s [fr. gerund of ²*buffet*] **:** repeated alteration of the aerodynamic forces acting on any part of an airplane in flight due to unsteady air flow that originates in a disturbance set up by some other part of the airplane; *often* **:** irregular oscillation of the airplane or its parts resulting from such buffeting

buffi *pl of* BUFFO

buffier *comparative of* BUFFY

buffiest *superlative of* BUFFY

¹**buffing** *n* -s [fr. gerund of ⁶*buff*] **1 a :** the action of a buffer **b :** the process by which something (as leather) is buffed **2 :** material removed by a buffing machine — usu. used in pl.

²**buffing** *n* -s [⁴*buff* + *-ing*] **:** a thin sheet of leather split from a hide and commonly used for bookbinding

buffing head *n* **:** a frame supporting a spindle with means for revolving it and attaching a buffing wheel

buffing wheel *n* **:** a wheel (as a bob) covered with buff leather, muslin, felt, bristle brushes, or comparable material and used in polishing

buff jerkin *n* [⁴*buff* & ⁵*buff*] **:** a buff-leather jacket formerly worn by soldiers under the corselet; *sometimes* **:** a buff-colored jacket or waistcoat

buf·fle \ˈbəfəl\ *n* -s [MF — more at BUFF] *archaic* **:** BUFFALO

buff leather *n* [⁴*buff*] **:** a strong supple oil-tanned leather usu. rather light in color and with a velvety surface that is now produced chiefly from cattle hides

buffle duck *n* [*bufflehead*] **:** BUFFLEHEAD

bufflehead \ˈ⸗,⸗\ *n* **1** *now dial* **:** BLOCKHEAD, FOOL **2** *also* **buf·fel·head** \"\ **:** a small No. American diving duck (*Bucephala albeola*) that in general resembles the goldeneye but is distinguished by the lobed hind toe and by the very densely feathered head of the male with a white patch behind the eye — called also *butterball, spirit duck*

bufflehead

buffle-headed \¦⸗¦⸗⸗\ *adj, now chiefly dial* **:** STUPID, FOOLISH

buf·fle·horn \ˈbəfəl‚hȯrn\ *n* [trans. of Afrik *buffelhoring*] **:** a small African tree (*Burchellia capensis*) of the family Rubiaceae that has very hard tough wood and scarlet flowers

buf·fler \ˈbəflə(r)\ *n* -s [by alter.] *dial* **:** BUFFALO

buff nor stye *n* [⁷*buff* + *stye*, origin unknown] *Scot* **:** head nor tail **:** one thing or another ⟨couldn't make *buff nor stye* of his letter⟩

¹**buf·fo** \ˈbü(ˌ)fō\ *n, pl* **buffos** \-ōz\ *also* **buf·fi** \-fē\ [It, fr. *buffone* buffoon — more at BUFFOON] **:** CLOWN, BUFFOON; *specif* **:** a male singer of comic roles in opera

²**buffo** \"\ *adj* **1 a :** of, relating to, or suitable for an operatic buffo ⟨a fine ~ aria⟩ **b :** adapted to or competent in buffo singing ⟨a noted ~ tenor⟩ **2 :** COMIC, FARCICAL ⟨a ~ character⟩

¹**buf·foon** \ˌbəˈfün, ˌbəˈf-\ *n* -s *often attrib* [MF *bouffon*, fr. OIt *buffone*, fr. ML *bufon-, bufo*, fr. L, toad — more at BUFO] **1 a :** a man professionally engaged in entertaining others by tricks, gestures, or comic pantomime **:** JESTER, MERRY-ANDREW, CLOWN; *broadly* **:** COMEDIAN **b :** a person who strives for comical effects **2 :** a gross and clownish person; *esp* **:** one ill-educated or stupid — **buf·foon·ish** \-nish, -nēsh\ *adj*

²**buffoon** \"\ *vb* -ED/-ING/-S *vt* **:** to treat with buffoonery **:** RIDICULE, BURLESQUE ~ *vi* **:** to play the buffoon **:** behave like a buffoon

buf·foon·ery \(ˌ)bəˈfün(ə)rē, -ri\ *n* -ES [F *bouffonnerie*, fr. *bouffon* + *-erie* -ery] **:** the practices of a buffoon; *esp* **:** coarse loutish behavior

buffs *pl of* BUFF, *pres 3d sing of* BUFF

buff stick *n* [⁶*buff*] **:** a strip of wood covered with buff leather or chamois and used in polishing

buff stop *n* [⁹*buff*] **:** a partially damping or muffling device on a harpsichord or piano

buff-tip \ˈ⸗,⸗\ *or* **buff-tipped moth** \ˈ⸗,⸗-\ *n* [⁵*buff*] **:** a European moth (*Phalera bucephala*) having violet-gray forewings with creamy tips and caterpillars that feed on the leaves of elm, beech, birch, oak, and fruit trees

buff top *n* [⁶*buff*] **:** a style of cut of certain gemstones in which the top is cut cabochon and the bottom is step-cut

buff·y \ˈbəfē\ *adj, often* -ER/-EST [⁴*buff* + *-y*] **1 :** of the color buff **2** *slang* **:** INTOXICATED

buffy coat *n* **:** the superficial layer of yellowish or buff coagulated plasma from which the red corpuscles have settled out in slowly coagulated blood

bu·fo \ˈb(y)ü(ˌ)fō\ *n* [NL, fr. L, toad; perh. akin to OS *quappa* tadpole, MLG *quappe*, Dan *kvabbe* burbot, OPruss *gabawo* toad, OSlav *žaba* frog] **1** *cap* **:** a large genus (the type of the family Bufonidae) of toads that contains the common toads of America and Europe and the agua toad and is represented on all the continents except Australia **2** -s **:** any toad of the genus *Bufo*

bu·fo·gen·in \ˌbyüfəˈjenən, byü¦fäjənən\ *n* [NL *Bufo* + E *-genin*] **:** BUFAGIN

bu·fo·nid \ˈbyüfənəd, -ˌnid\ *n* -s [NL *Bufonidae*] **:** a toad of the family Bufonidae

bu·fon·i·dae \byü¦fänəˌdē\ *n pl, cap* [NL, fr. *Bufon-, Bufo*, type genus + *-idae*] **:** a large family of toads (suborder Procoela) including all the typical toads that are distinguished by an incompletely fused shoulder girdle and dilated or cylindrical transverse sacral processes

bu·fo·nite \ˈbyüfəˌnīt\ *n* -s [L *bufon-, bufo* toad + E *-ite*] **:** a fossil consisting of the petrified teeth and palatal bones of pycnodont fishes — see TOADSTONE

bu·fo·tal·in \ˌbyüfəˈtalən, -tāl-\ *n* -s [ISV *bufo-* (fr. NL *Bufo*, genus name of *Bufo vulgaris*) + *digitalin*] **:** a crystalline bufagin $C_{26}H_{36}O_6$ obtained esp. from the poisonous secretion of skin glands of the common European toad (*Bufo vulgaris*)

bu·fo·ten·ine \ˌbyüfəˈteˌnēn, -ˌnən\ *n* -s [ISV *bufo-* (fr. NL *Bufo*) + *-ten-* (origin unknown) + *-ine*] **:** a crystalline toxic alkaloid $C_{12}H_{16}N_2O$ derived from indole that is obtained from poisonous secretions of toads and is like epinephrine in biological action

bu·fo·tox·in \ˌbyüfəˈtäksən\ *n* [ISV *bufo-* (fr. NL *Bufo*, genus name of *Bufo vulgaris*) + *toxin*] **:** a crystalline toxic steroid $C_{40}H_{60}N_4O_{10}$ obtained from the poisonous secretion of skin glands of the common European toad (*Bufo vulgaris*) that is like digitalis in biological action and that yields bufotalin and suberyl-arginine on hydrolysis; *also* **:** any of several similar steroids from the secretions of other toads that yield a bufagin and suberylarginine on hydrolysis

¹**bug** \ˈbəg\ *n* -s [ME *bugge* scarecrow; akin to G dial. *bögge* piece of dried nasal mucus, hobgoblin, Norw dial. *bugge* important man — more at BOAST] *obs* **:** BOGEY, BUGBEAR

²**bug** \"\ *n* -s [origin unknown] **1 a :** an insect or other creeping or crawling invertebrate (as a spider or small crustacean) — not used technically **b :** any of certain insects commonly considered esp. obnoxious: as (1) **:** BEDBUG (2) **:** COCKROACH (3) **:** HEAD LOUSE **c :** an insect of the order Hemiptera; *esp* **:** a member of the suborder Heteroptera **2 :** an unexpected defect, fault, flaw, or imperfection (as in a plan, a mechanism, or a piece of legislation) — used esp. of such items as are regarded as capable of alteration or ready improvement ⟨there are still some ~*s* to iron out but the new motor will do the job⟩; compare JOKER **3 a :** a disease-producing germ or other microorganism **b :** a disease caused by such bugs ⟨probably caused by a ~ . . . as yet unknown —Horace Sutton⟩; *esp* **:** any of various respiratory conditions of virus origin (as influenza or grippe) ⟨stricken with a virus ~⟩ **4 a :** FAD, CRAZE, HOBBY ⟨bitten by the miniature-golf ~⟩ ⟨got the trailer ~ on a vacation trip⟩ **b :** enthusiasm, concern, or deep interest esp. in respect to some particular matter or objective ⟨I have rather a ~ about learning in class —Jean Nison⟩ **c :** a person notably concerned with, enthusiastic about, or efficient at a specified interest or activity ⟨he's a ~ on proper training of young shooters⟩ ⟨she was a ~ at languages —*Newsweek*⟩ ⟨a perfect ~ for detail⟩ **d :** HOBBYIST ⟨camera ~*s*⟩ ⟨ski ~*s*⟩ **e :** a crazy person; *esp* **:** FIREBUG **5 a** *archaic* **:** a vain or self-important person **b :** a person of prominence or high social standing ⟨we'll have all the ~*s* to lunch⟩ — see BIG BUG **6** *poker* **:** the joker when considered wild only for the purpose of filling straights or flushes or of acting as an ace **7 a :** an alarm system (as a burglar alarm) **b :** a concealed microphone **c :** a device for wiretapping **d :** a high-speed telegrapher's key that makes repeated dots or dashes automatically and saves motion of the operator's hand **8** [so called fr. its designation by an asterisk on race programs] **:** the weight allowance given apprentice jockeys **9** *slang* **:** NUMBERS GAME **10 :** a light usu. two-seater stripped-down automobile **11 :** a fishing plug felt to resemble a large insect

³**bug** \"\ *vb* **bugged; bugged; bugging; bugs** *vt* **1 :** to rid (as plants) of insects ⟨we'll have to ~ the potatoes again next week⟩ **2 :** BOTHER, ANNOY, IRRITATE; *sometimes* **:** to drive (a person) crazy **3 a :** to equip with a burglar alarm **b :** to plant a concealed microphone in **:** WIRETAP ⟨~ a meeting⟩ ~ *vi* **:** to hunt for or collect bugs

⁴**bug** \"\ *also* **bug light** *n* -s [prob. fr. (*lightning*) *bug*] **1 :** a small channel or harbor light with intermittent flash **2 :** FLASHLIGHT b

⁵**bug** \ˈbəg, ˈbu̇g\ *adj* [perh. of Scand origin; akin to Norw *bugge* important man] *dial Eng* **:** CONCEITED, STUCK-UP

⁶**bug** \ˈbəg\ *vb* **bugged; bugged; bugging; bugs** [prob. alter. (influenced by ¹*bug*) of *bulge*] *vi, of the eyes* **:** PROTRUDE, BULGE — often used with *out* ~ *vt* **:** BULGE, PROTRUDE ⟨his eyes were *bugged* with horror⟩

bug·a·boo \ˈbəgəˌbü *sometimes* ˈbu̇g-\ *n* -s [alter. of earlier *buggybow*] **1 :** an imaginary object of fright **:** BUGBEAR, BOGEY ⟨they scurried home, seeing goblins and ~*s* in every shadow⟩ **2 :** a source of concern ⟨the ~ of inbreeding — W.L.McAtee⟩; *esp* **:** something that causes fear or distress often out of proportion to its actual importance in a situation ⟨the old ~ of insufficient purchasing power . . . is real enough to warrant deep study and careful planning—Nathan Robertson⟩

bu·ga·ku \büˈgä(ˌ)kü\ *n* -s *usu cap* [Jap, lit., dancing, music] **:** a stately classical Japanese dance orig. introduced from China

bu·gala \büˈgalə\ *n* -s [Ar *baqlah*] **:** a large dhow used chiefly in the Red sea

bu·gan \ˈbu̇gən, ˈbüg-,ˈbəg-\ *n* -s [W *bwgan* hobgoblin, fr. MW, perh. fr. ME *bugge* — more at BUG] *dial Eng* **:** HOBGOBLIN, GHOST

bu·gara \büˈgarə\ *n* -s [origin unknown] **:** RAINBOW PERCH

bugbane \ˈ⸗,⸗\ *n* **1 :** a plant of the genus *Cimicifuga*; *esp* **:** a perennial herb (*C. racemosa*) with flowers reputed to be distasteful to insects — called also *snakeroot* **2 :** AMERICAN HELLEBORE

bug·bear \ˈbəgˌba(a)(ə)r, -ˌbe(ə)r, -ˌba(a)ə, -ˌbeə\ *n* -s [¹*bug* (goblin) + *bear*] **1 :** an imaginary goblin or specter used to excite needless fear (as in children) **2 a :** an object or source of dread or abhorrence ⟨the French tendency to make a ~ of Germany is exactly what the Russians want —*New Yorker*⟩ **b :** PROBLEM; *esp* **:** a continuing source of irritation or annoyance ⟨their biggest ~ has been the cross-filing system that California adopted a generation ago —Gladwin Hill⟩

bugbite \ˈ⸗,⸗\ *n* **:** a bite or sting by an insect

bug boy *n* [¹*bug* (weight allowance)] *slang* **:** an apprentice jockey

bug dust *n* **:** fine coal produced in mining with a cutting machine

bug-eater \ˈ⸗,⸗⸗\ *n, usu cap B* [fr. *bug-eater*, a species of goatsucker common in Nebraska] **:** NEBRASKAN — a nickname

bugeye \ˈ⸗,⸗\ *n* **:** a small shallow-draft flat-bottomed boat with a centerboard and two raked masts carrying jib and triangular sails that is largely used by oystermen and others in Chesapeake Bay

bug-eyed \ˈ⸗¦⸗\ *adj* **:** having the eyes bulging (as with astonishment)

bugfish \ˈ⸗,⸗\ *n* [so called fr. a parasite that often adheres to the roof of its mouth] **:** MENHADEN

bugged *past of* BUG

¹**bug·ger** \ˈbu̇gə(r), ˈbəg-\ *or* **boog·er** \ˈbu̇g-\ *n* -s [ME *bougre* heretic, sodomite, fr. MF, fr. ML *Bugarus, Bulgarus*, lit., Bulgarian; fr. the adherence of the Bulgarians to the Eastern Church considered heretical] **1 :** one that commits buggery **2 a :** a worthless person **:** GUY, FELLOW — a generalized term of abuse **b :** ROGUE, RASCAL, SCAMP — often used affectionately esp. of children and animals

²**bugger** \"\ *vb* -ED/-ING/-S *vt* **1 :** to commit buggery with — usu. considered vulgar **2** *slang* **:** DAMN, BLAST, DARN ⟨I'll be ~*ed*⟩ **3** *slang* **:** to wear out **:** EXHAUST ⟨we had tramped for hours and were completely ~*ed*⟩ ~ *vi, slang Brit* **:** to go away **:** LEAVE, SCRAM — usu. used with *off*

³**bugger** *var of* BOOGER

bug·ger·man \ˈbu̇gə(r)ˌman, -maa(ə)n *sometimes* ˈbəg- *or* ˈbüg-\ *var of* BOOGEYMAN

bugger up *vt* [²*bugger*] **:** to mix up **:** put into disorder **:** CONFUSE

bug·gery \ˈbu̇gərē, ˈbəg-, -ri\ *n* -ES [ME *bugerie*, fr. MF *bougrerie* heresy, sodomy, fr. *bougre* bugger + *-erie* -ery — more at BUGGER] **:** unnatural sexual intercourse **:** SODOMY

bug·gi·ness \ˈbəgēnəs, -gin-\ *n* -ES **:** the quality or state of being buggy

bugging *pres part of* BUG

¹**bug·gy** \ˈbəgē, -gi\ *adj* -ER/-EST [¹*bug* + *-y*] **1 a :** infested with bugs **b :** of, relating to, or suggestive of bugs ⟨a ~ odor⟩ **2** *slang* **a :** lacking restraint or good judgment **:** SILLY, BATTY ⟨she's ~ about horses⟩ **b :** INSANE, DEMENTED

²**buggy** \"\ *n* -ES [origin unknown] **1 :** a light one-horse carriage made with two wheels in England and with four wheels in the U.S. **2 :** a small wagon or truck used for short transportations of heavy materials (as coal in a mine or ingots in a steel mill); *specif* **:** a 2-wheeled cart used for transporting freshly mixed concrete short distances on construction jobs **3** *slang* **:** CABOOSE; *sometimes* **:** OBSERVATION CAR **4 :** any of various vehicles: as **a** *slang* **:** AUTOMOBILE **b :** BABY CARRIAGE **c :** MARSH BUGGY

American buggy

³**buggy** \"\ *adj* -ER/-EST [⁵*bug* + *-y*] *of the eyes* **:** BULGING

buggy cultivator *n* [²*buggy*] **:** a sulky cultivator

bug·gy·man \ˈbəgēmən, -gim-, -ˌman\ *n, pl* **buggymen** [²*buggy* + *man*] **:** a worker who handles a barrow or buggy for the transportation of bulk material (as coal, ore, concrete, or slag)

buggy plow *n* [²*buggy*] **:** a sulky plow

bughead \ˈ⸗,⸗\ *n* [so called fr. a parasite that adheres to the roof of its mouth] **:** MENHADEN

¹**bughouse** \ˈ⸗,⸗\ *n* [¹*bug* (crazy person) + *house*] *slang* **:** an insane asylum

²**bughouse** \ˈ⸗,⸗\ *adj, slang* **:** mentally deranged **:** INSANE, CRAZY

bught *Scot var of* BOUGHT

bu·gi \ˈbügē\ *or* **bu·gis** \-gəs\ *n, pl* **bugi** *or* **bugis** *usu cap* [Malay *Bugis*] **:** BUGINESE

bu·gia \ˈb(y)üj(ē)ə\ *n* -s [NL, fr. ML *candela Bugiae, candela de Bugia* candle from Bougie, seaport town in northeastern Algeria from which they were exported, trans. of MF *chandelle de Bougie*] **:** a low candlestick with a short handle

bu·gi·nese \¦bügə¦nēz, -ēs\ *n, pl* **buginese** *or* **bugineses** *usu cap* [D *Boeginees*, fr. Malay *Bugis*] **1 a :** an Indonesian people of the southern part of Celebes island, Indonesia **b :** a member of such people **2 :** the language of the Buginese people

bug juice *n, slang* **:** inferior whiskey or other strong liquor

bu·gin·vil·laea *or* **bu·gin·vil·lea** *syn of* BOUGAINVILLAEA

¹**bu·gle** \ˈbyügəl\ *n* -s [ME, fr. OF, fr. LL *bugula*] **:** a plant of the genus *Ajuga*; *esp* **:** a low European annual (*A. reptans*) with spikes of blue flowers that is now naturalized in parts of the U. S.

²**bugle** \"\ *n* -s [ME, fr. OF, fr. L *buculus, boculus* young steer, dim. of *bos* head of cattle — more at COW] **1** *obs* **:** a wild ox; *esp* **:** BUFFALO **2 :** a signal horn; *esp* **:** one made of an animal's horn **3 a :** a brass instrument with a cupped mouthpiece like the trumpet but having a shorter and more conical tube and now chiefly for military and parade use ⟨drum and ~ corps⟩ **b :** one of a family of valved brass instruments of sizes grading from flügelhorns to tubas now chiefly used in brass bands — compare EUPHONIUM, SAXHORN

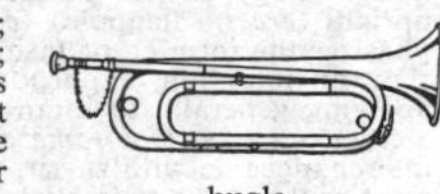

bugle

³**bu·gle** \"\ *vb* **bugled; bugled; bugling** \-g(ə)liŋ\ **bugles** *vt* **:** to sound or summon by or as if by a bugle call ~ *vi* **1 :** to sound a bugle **2** *of bull elks or certain other large deer* **:** to utter a prolonged cry that suggests the sound of a bugle and is the characteristic rutting call

⁴**bugle** \"\ *adj, of a hunting dog* **:** having a strong deep melodious bay

⁵**bugle** \"\ *or* **bugle bead** *n* -s [perh. fr. ²*bugle*; fr. its resemblance to a trumpet] **:** a small cylindrical bead of glass or plastic used for trimming esp. on women's clothing

⁶**bugle** \"\ *adj* **1 :** like a bugle; *esp* **:** jet-black like most early glass bugles **2 :** trimmed or fashioned with bugles ⟨a band of dainty ~ work about the neckline⟩

bugle horn *n* [²*bugle*] **:** BUGLE 2

bu·gler \ˈbyüglə(r)\ *n* -s [²*bugle* + *-er*] **:** a person who plays on or signals with a bugle

bu·glet \ˈbyüglət\ *n* -s [²*bugle* + *-et*] **:** a small bugle

bugleweed \ˈ⸗⸗,⸗\ *n* **1** *also* **buglewort :** a mint of the genus *Lycopus*; *esp* **:** a mildly narcotic and astringent herb (*L. virginicus*) **2 :** INDIGO BROOM **3 :** BUGLE

bug light *var of* ³BUG

bu·gloss \ˈbyüˌgläs, -lȯs\ *n* -ES [MF *buglosse*, fr. L *buglossa*, irreg. fr. Gk *bouglōssos, bouglōsson*, fr. *bous* head of cattle + *-glōssos, -glōsson* (fr. *glōssa* tongue) — more at COW, GLOSS] **1 :** a plant of the genus *Anchusa* (esp. *A. officinalis*) sometimes cultivated for its delicate usu. blue flowers — called also *alkanet* **2 :** GERMAN MADWORT **3 :** a European hawkweed (*Picris echioides*) with yellow flowers that is now naturalized in the eastern U.S. **4 :** a very bristly annual European herb (*Lycopsis arvensis*) naturalized in eastern No. America

bugloss cowslip *n* **:** LUNGWORT 2 a

bug·ol·o·gist \ˌbəˈgäləjəst\ *n* -s **:** ENTOMOLOGIST — not used technically

bug·ol·o·gy \-jē\ *n* -ES [¹*bug* + *-ology* (as in *entomology*)] **:** ENTOMOLOGY — not used technically

bugong moth *var of* BOGONG MOTH

bug out \ˈbəg-\ *vi* [prob. short for ²*bugger*] **:** to retreat during a military action; *esp* **:** to flee in panic or without orders

bugout \ˈ⸗,⸗\ *n* -s [*bug out*] **:** an act or instance of bugging out; *also* **:** DESERTER

bu·gre \ˈbügrə\ *n* -s [Pg, fr. F *bougre* bugger — more at BUGGER] **:** a Brazilian Indian — usu. taken to be offensive

¹**bugs** *pl of* BUG, *pres 3d sing of* BUG

²**bugs** \ˈbəgz\ *adj* [fr. pl. of ¹*bug* (craze)] *slang* **:** CRAZY — used in the predicate ⟨the man was totally ~ and thought he was Napoleon⟩

bugseed *or* **bugweed** \ˈ⸗,⸗\ *n* **:** an herb of the genus *Corispermum* of the family Chenopodiaceae: *esp* **:** a fleshy annual (*C. hyssopifolium*) with flat oval seeds that is a common weed in north temperate regions

bu·gu·la \ˈbyügyələ\ *n, cap* [NL, fr. LL, bugle (plant)] **:** a common and widespread genus (the type of the family Bugulidae) of marine shallow-water branching bryozoans that sometimes cause fouling of ships

bug word *also* **bug's word** *n* [¹*bug*] **1** *obs* **:** a word to terrify **2** *obs* **:** threatening language — usu. used in pl.

bu·hid \büˈ(h)ēd\ *also* **bu·id** \-ˈēd\ *or* **bu·kid** \-ˈkēd\ *n, pl* **buhid** *or* **buhids** *usu cap* [Buhid *Buhid, Buid, Bukid*] **1 :** a predominantly pagan people inhabiting southern Mindoro, Philippines **2 :** a member of the Buhid people

buhl *var of* BOULLE

buhl and counter *n* **:** decorative work in which a material is divided into two parts by sawing out a pattern and each part is made complete again by inlay

buhr \ˈbər\ *n* -s [by shortening] **:** BUHRSTONE 2; *also* **:** one of the projections resembling teeth on such a stone

buhrmill \ˈ⸗,⸗\ *n* **:** a mill that uses buhrstones for grinding grain

buhrstone *also* **burrstone** *or* **burstone** \ˈ⸗,⸗\ *n* [*buhrstone*, alter. of *burrstone, burstone*, prob. fr. *burr, bur* + *stone*] **1 :** a siliceous rock used as a material for millstones **2 :** a millstone cut from buhrstone

buik \ˈbyük, ˈbu̇ek\ *Scot var of* BOOK

¹**build** \ˈbild\ *vb* **built** \-lt\ *or archaic* **builded** \-ldəd\ **built** *or archaic* **builded; building; builds** [ME *bilden*, fr. OE *byldan*, denominative fr. the root of *bold* house; akin to ON *bōl* abode, farm, OE *būan* to dwell — more at BOWER] *vt* **1 a :** to construct for a dwelling ⟨birds ~*ing* their nests⟩ ⟨they *built* a snug little cottage beside the stream⟩ **b :** to form by ordering and uniting materials by gradual means into a composite whole — used esp. with reference to comparatively large or massive structures ⟨they *built* churches and roads and power lines⟩ ⟨he is making a model of the boat his father *built*⟩ **2 :** to cause to be constructed **:** be responsible for the building of ⟨some contractors ~ hundreds of houses every year⟩; *esp* **:** to be the source of the money for building ⟨sugar and cotton *built* the gracious plantation houses⟩ **3 :** to fashion or develop according to a systematic plan, by a

definite process, or on a particular base ⟨~*ing* security for the future⟩ ⟨an argument *built* on solid facts⟩: as **a :** to give form **:** CREATE — used passively and of human or other living bodies ⟨a horse *built* for speed⟩ **b :** to give an inherent tendency **:** orient fundamentally — usu. used passively ⟨he was *built* to fight for what he believed in⟩ ⟨I'm not *built* that way⟩ **c :** MAKE, CONSTRUCT, FORM: as (1) **:** to arrange the combustibles for and usu. to light (a fire) (2) **:** TAILOR ⟨vest pockets are cut and *built* much in the same way —Clarence Poulin⟩ (3) **:** to cook up (a dish) ⟨Grandma will ~ one of her famous fruitcakes⟩ (4) *dial* **:** ROLL ⟨~ a cigarette⟩ (5) **:** to produce (a work of art or literature) ⟨~*ing* a new book⟩ esp. as an elaboration or exposition of a particular basis or theme ⟨a recurring phrase . . . upon which this whole book seems to be *built* —Richard Sullivan⟩ (6) **:** to make the blank parts of (a wax mold) higher by adding molten wax to ensure that the corresponding areas of the finished electrotype will be well below the face — often used with *up* **d :** ENLARGE, INCREASE ⟨~ an inventory⟩; *esp* **:** to improve the status of **:** ENHANCE, EXALT ⟨~ a candidate⟩ — usu. used with *up* ⟨his scholarly interpretation *built* up the role⟩ **e :** to bring into being **:** develop through deliberate effort ⟨beginning to ~ some understanding . . . of health practices among these people —Roger Angell⟩ ⟨~*ing* a society without extremes of poverty and wealth —Maurice Cranston⟩ **f** (1) *casino* **:** to put together (a numerical combination of cards) to be taken in by a card of that value (2) *in word games* **:** to form (a word) by assembling letters **4 a :** to employ so as to produce a structure ⟨they *built* the stones into sturdy fences⟩ **b :** to use as material from which to form or formulate something ⟨you could ~ these arguments into a whole new philosophy⟩ **5 :** to improve the cleansing action of (as soap) by the addition of a builder **~** *vi* **1 :** to perform the act, exercise the art, or practice the business of building ⟨you can trust his work, he's been ~*ing* for 30 years⟩ **2 :** to be in the course of construction — usu. used as a present participle ⟨ships ~*ing* in the docks⟩ ⟨the road turned west and *built* slowly across Dakota —R.A.Billington⟩ **3 :** to reach or progress towards a peak (as of intensity or interest) ⟨the wind began to ~ and the sleet to blow about⟩ ⟨a good boxing card ~*s* from the first minute of the first bout⟩

syn BUILD, CONSTRUCT, ERECT, FRAME, RAISE, REAR: these all have in common the sense of to form a structure or something comparable to a structure. BUILD stresses the fitting together of parts or materials to form the thing desired ⟨*build* a cathedral⟩ ⟨*build* a nest⟩ ⟨*build* a road⟩ ⟨*build* a city⟩ CONSTRUCT, very close in meaning to BUILD, usu. lays stress upon the problem, or intricacy of the process, of fitting the parts together often implying more skill and intelligence than BUILD ⟨*construct* a railroad⟩ ⟨*construct* a plan⟩ ⟨*construct* a poem⟩ ERECT, true to its etymology, carries the idea of putting up something that is upright ⟨*erect* a flagpole⟩ ⟨*erect* a building⟩ FRAME usu. emphasizes the forming or fashioning to suit a preconceived design, an intention, a purpose, or certain unavoidable facts, applying generally to intangibles ⟨*frame* an answer⟩ ⟨*frame* a financial report⟩ ⟨*frame* a constitution⟩ RAISE and REAR, interchangeable with ERECT, usu. apply to things that are upright or that have or imply height ⟨*raise* a wall⟩ ⟨*raise* a building of several stories⟩ ⟨*rear* a tower⟩ ⟨*rear* a complex philosophical and metaphysical construction⟩

— **build a fire under :** to stimulate (someone or something) to vigorous action — **build around :** to fashion, construct, or develop (a whole) in orientation to some constituent factor ⟨usually a sponsor buys a show *built around* a star —Arthur Godfrey⟩ ⟨their lives are *built around* their house and garden⟩ — **build into :** to make an integral part of something ⟨quality is *built into* our product⟩ — **build on 1 :** to use as a foundation ⟨Scott has renewed the literature of his people by *building on* this ancient balladry —Van Wyck Brooks⟩ **2 :** to rely upon ⟨he did not *build on* these promises —J.D.Beresford⟩

²build \"\ *n* -s **1 a :** form or mode of structure (as of a ship) **:** MAKE **b :** the bodily conformation of a person or lower animal **:** PHYSIQUE, MAKEUP ⟨a man of heavy ~⟩ ⟨a horse of good ~⟩ **c :** the structural arrangement of a landmass (as an island) or country ⟨the ~ of the country . . . explains the sites of . . . the towns —J.M.Mogey⟩ **d** *of a coating* **:** capacity to form a relatively substantial continuous film ⟨some of the resins have excellent ~⟩ **2 :** a combination (as of playing cards) formed by building **3 :** a vertical joint in masonry **4 :** a mounting state of intensity or of steady progress toward a climax ⟨the author . . . neglected to give the continuous ~ that the more complex literary situation demands —Virgil Thomson⟩ ⟨a good actor instinctively gives ~ to an important scene⟩ **syn** see PHYSIQUE

build·able \-ləbəl\ *adj* **:** suitable for building; *esp* **:** capable of being built or built from without excessive outlay (as of money, time, or materials) ⟨designs for attractive ~ benches⟩

builded *archaic past of* BUILD

build·er \-ldə(r)\ *n* -s [ME *bilder*, fr. *bilden* + *-er*] **1 :** one that builds: as **a :** a worker (as a carpenter, shipwright, or mason) whose occupation is to build **b :** a person who supervises and usu. has a financial interest in building operations and the arts and trades involved in their progress — compare CONTRACTOR **c :** a person or organization that creates something (as a business or a railroad); *esp* **:** one that is a pioneer organizer or developer (as of a country) ⟨the empire ~*s*⟩ **2 :** a substance (as a sodium polyphosphate or sodium carbonate) added to soaps or synthetic detergents or used with them to increase their cleansing action (as by softening hard water or controlling the hydrogen-ion concentration of the bath) **3 :** a man in backgammon that can be moved without leaving a blot **4** *or* **builder motion :** the mechanism in a textile mill that distributes yarn or roving onto a bobbin, spool, or other holder to form a package **5 :** a worker who builds up (as wax molds for electrotype plates) or assembles (as tires or parts of tires)

builders' hardware *n* **:** articles of hardware (as hinges, locks, catches, sash lifts) that are used in the construction of buildings

builder's iron *n* **:** BUILDING IRON

builder's jack *n* **1 a :** a bracket that rests on a windowsill and projects outside for a worker to stand or sit upon in repairing a window **b :** a bracket fastened to a wall to support a scaffold **2 :** a jack (as a jackscrew) used by builders

builder's knot *n* **:** CLOVE HITCH

builder's risk insurance *n* **:** insurance on an increasing-value basis against loss by fire and related hazards covering buildings or ships in course of construction

build·er-up·per \ˈbildə(r)ˈəpə(r)\ *n* **:** one that builds up ⟨an occasional change is a great *builder-upper* of morale⟩

build in *vt* **1 :** to enclose or fill in by building ⟨the open fields are now entirely *built in*⟩ **2 :** to construct (as furniture) as an integral part of something ⟨I want the carpenter to *build in* chests, cabinets, everything⟩ ⟨our children will get a sort of *built-in* balance wheel —Sidonie M. Gruenberg⟩

build·ing \ˈbildiŋ, -dēŋ\ *n* -s [ME *bilding*, fr. gerund of *bilden* to build] **1 :** a thing built: **a :** a constructed edifice designed to stand more or less permanently, covering a space of land, usu. covered by a roof and more or less completely enclosed by walls, and serving as a dwelling, storehouse, factory, shelter for animals, or other useful structure — distinguished from structures not designed for occupancy (as fences or monuments) and from structures not intended for use in one place (as boats or trailers) even though subject to occupancy **b :** a portion of a house occupied as a separate dwelling **:** APARTMENT, TENEMENT — used only in some legal statutes **2 :** the act or practice of making, erecting, or establishing; *specif* **:** the art or business of assembling materials into a structure — sometimes distinguished from *architecture* and *construction* as involving relatively simple artistic and engineering problems **3** *archaic* **:** a flock of rooks **:** ROOKERY

building and loan association *n* **:** SAVINGS AND LOAN ASSOCIATION

building block *n* **1 :** BLOCK 1d, 1f (7), 1i **2 :** a unit of construction or composition ⟨*building blocks* of nucleic acids⟩

building carpenter *n* **:** a person in charge of a stage building crew that prepares scenery for theatrical productions

building code *n* **:** a collection of regulations adopted by a city to govern the construction of buildings

building drain *n* **:** HOUSE DRAIN

building iron *n* **:** a tool with which wax is melted and applied in building an electrotype mold

building lease *n* **:** a lease of land for a long term of years in consideration of the payment of rent and of a covenant of the lessee to erect or alter a building or other improvement thereon — called also *ground lease*

build·ing·less \-ləs\ *adj* **:** being without a building

building line *n* **:** a line usu. set with respect to the frontage of a plot of land which is fixed by statute or by deed or contract and beyond which the owner of the land may not build

building lot *n* **:** a surveyed and bounded plot of land that is set aside for a building — compare SUBDIVISION

building paper *n* **:** paper used for insulation (as in walls, roofs, and between floors)

building sewer *n* **:** HOUSE SEWER

building slip *or* **building berth** *n* **:** the inclined structure on which a vessel is built

building superintendent *n* **:** one who is responsible for the cleaning and maintenance of a building and its equipment — called also *custodian*

building trades *n pl* **:** trades (as carpentry, bricklaying, plumbing) that are essential to and chiefly practiced in connection with building construction

building trap *n* **:** HOUSE TRAP

build on *vt* **:** to add (a new part) to an existent structure ⟨we plan to *build on* a porch⟩

builds *pres 3d sing of* BUILD, *pl of* BUILD

build up *vt* **1 a :** to construct or erect gradually, little by little, piece by piece, or layer by layer **b :** to construct (a whole, as a wheel) of separate parts **2 a :** to obstruct or close by building ⟨they *built up* the door between the two houses⟩ **b :** to obstruct or fill with buildings ⟨the fields where we played are all *built up* now⟩ **3 :** to develop, increase, or improve esp. by successive increments ⟨he *built up* his business by good service and attention to detail⟩ ⟨anyone can *build up* his constitution by heeding a few simple rules⟩: as **a :** to add fuel to and freshen (a fire) **b :** to enhance the prominence of ⟨she had a talent for *building up* minor roles⟩; *esp* **:** to give favorable publicity to ⟨they *built* him *up* with a series of articles and broadcasts⟩ **c :** to increase the voltage or current of (an electric generator or circuit) **d :** to stimulate or arouse the interest or emotions of (as a team) esp. with a particular aim in view ⟨the coach *built* the team *up* to a fighting pitch⟩ **~** *vi* **:** to increase esp. by successive increments — used chiefly of pressure

buildup \ˈ=,=\ *n* [*build up*] **1 :** the act of building up **2 :** something produced by building up: **a :** a quantity (as of pressure or water) so produced **b :** a marked or excessive increase in a natural population usu. resulting from progressively altered ecological relations **c :** something intended to enhance the popularity or prestige of an individual, product, or organization; *esp* **:** excessively favorable publicity designed to sway public opinion often without regard to the merits of the case ⟨his last boss gave him a good ~ but he was not up to our job⟩

¹built *adj* [fr. past part. of ¹*build*] **1 :** FORMED, SHAPED, CONSTRUCTED, MADE — usu. used with a qualifying word ⟨a Clyde-*built* vessel⟩ ⟨a well-*built* house⟩ **2 :** composed of pieces or parts joined systematically **:** BUILT-UP; *esp* **:** LAMINATED **3 :** formed as to physique or bodily contours ⟨delicately ~ and slender —*Current Biog.*⟩; *esp* **:** well or attractively formed ⟨that movie star is really ~⟩

²built *n* -s [irreg. fr. ¹*build*] **:** SHAPE, BUILD

¹built-in \ˈ=ˈ=\ *adj* **1 :** forming an integral part of a structure ⟨a *built-in* range finder⟩; *esp, of furnishings* **:** constructed as or in a recess in a wall ⟨I want *built-in* bookcases next to the fireplace⟩ **2 :** present by reason of the nature or makeup of some other relevant matter **:** INHERENT, CONSTITUTIONAL ⟨the *built-in* safeguards that our constitution provides against tyranny⟩ ⟨release of the atom's *built-in* energy —Stuart Chase⟩

²built-in \"\ *n* -s [¹*built-in*] **:** a piece of built-in furniture

built-up \ˈ=ˈ=\ *adj* **1 :** made of several sections or layers fastened together ⟨a *built-up* girder⟩ ⟨*built-up* roofing⟩ **2** *of a land area* **:** having many buildings **:** covered with buildings **3 :** THICKENED, ENLARGED ⟨a *built-up* heel of a shoe⟩ **:** piled higher by gradual accumulation ⟨*built-up* slag⟩ ⟨*built-up* land where the old town dump was⟩; *often* **:** filled in **:** WIDENED ⟨a *built-up* neckline on her dress⟩

built-up fraction *n* **:** PIECE FRACTION

built-up gun *n* **:** a gun whose parts are formed separately and then so united as to utilize to the best advantage the elastic qualities of the metals

built-up mast *n* **:** a mast made of several pieces bound together

buird \ˈbü(ə)rd\ *Scot var of* BOARD

buird·ly \ˈbœr(d)li, ˈbür-\ *adj* [prob. alter. of ¹*burly*] *Scot* **:** stalwart and husky **:** well built ⟨a ~ lad for twelve⟩

buis·son \bwēˈsōⁿ, *F* bwʸēsōⁿ\ *n* -s [F, lit., bush, of Gmc origin; akin to OHG *busc* bush — more at BUSH] **:** a fruit tree with a very short stem and a closely pruned head

bu·ka \ˈb(y)ükə\ *n* -s [prob. modif. of Zulu *bucu*] **:** BUCHU

bu·kaua \bü'kaùə\ *n, pl* **bukaua** *or* **bukauas** *usu cap* **1 a :** a people inhabiting the Huon gulf region of Morobe, North-East New Guinea **b :** a member of such people **2 :** the Austronesian language of the Bukaua people

bu·ka·yo *also* **bu·ca·yo** \bü'kī(,)ō\ *n* -s [Tag *bukayò*] **:** a Philippine sweetmeat of grated coconut fried in brown sugar

bu·ke·yef \bü'kā(y)əf\ *n pl, usu cap* [Russ *Bukeyevskoi* (pl.)] **:** a subdivision of the Kazak living between the Ural and the Volga rivers

bukh \ˈbük\ *vi* [Hindi *bak*] *India* **:** PRATE, TALK

bukhara *often cap, var of* BOKHARA

¹bu·kha·ran \bü'kärən, -karən\ *or* **bo·kha·ran** \bō'-\ *adj, usu cap* [*Bukhara* or *Bokhara*, city and state in Russian central Asia + E *-an*] **1 :** of, relating to, or characteristic of Bukhara in central Asia **2 :** of, relating to, or characteristic of the people of Bukhara

²bukharan \"\ *or* **bokharan** \"\ *n* -s *cap* **:** a native or resident of Bukhara

bukid *usu cap, var of* BUHID

bu·kid·non \bü'kid,nän\ *n, pl* **bukidnon** *or* **bukidnons** *usu cap* [Bisayan *Bukidnon* hill people, fr. *búkid* mountain + *-non* people] **1 a :** a predominantly pagan people inhabiting central northern Mindanao, Philippines **b :** a member of such people **2 :** an Austronesian language of the Bukidnon people — called also *Binokid*

buksha *var of* BUQSHA

buk·sheesh *or* **buk·shish** \ˈbək,shēsh, ,=ˈ=\ *var of* BAKSHEESH

buk·shi \ˈbəkˈshē\ *n* -s [Per *bakhshī*, lit., giver, fr. *bakhshīdan* to give — more at BAKSHEESH] *India* **:** a military paymaster

bul \ˈbül\ *n* -s *usu cap* [Heb *būl*, fr. Canaanite] **:** the 8th month of the ancient Hebrew calendar, corresponding to Heshvan

¹bulb \ˈbəlb, ˈbəùb\ *n* -s [L *bulbus* onion, bulb, fr. Gk *bolbos* bulbous plant; akin to Arm *bołk* radish and perh. to Skt *balbaja* yard grass (*Eleusine indica*)] **1 a :** a mass of overlapping membranous or fleshy leaves on a short stem base enclosing one or more buds that may develop under suitable conditions into new plants and constituting the resting stage of many plants (as lily, onion, hyacinth, tulip) — distinguished from *corm, rhizome, tuber* **2 a :** a fleshy tuber, corm, or other plant structure resembling a bulb in appearance ⟨a dahlia ~⟩ ⟨a crocus ~⟩ — not used technically **b** *Brit* **:** a fleshy bulbous root ⟨beet and turnip ~*s*⟩ **3 :** a plant having or developing from a bulb ⟨spring-flowering ~*s*⟩ **4 :** a protuberance resembling a plant bulb: as **a :** a rounded dilatation or expansion of something cylindrical ⟨the ~ of a thermometer⟩; *esp* **:** a rounded or pear-shaped enlargement on a small base ⟨the ~ of an eyedropper⟩ **b :** the thickened edge characteristic of certain construction elements (as a bulb angle or bulb bar) **c :** a rounded or pear-shaped glass envelope enclosing the light source of an incandescent or other electric lamp; *broadly* **:** such an envelope together with the light source it encloses ⟨a fluorescent ~⟩ — see INCANDESCENT LAMP illustration **5 :** a rounded part: as **a :** a rounded enlargement of one end of a part ⟨the ~ of the urethra⟩ — see END BULB, OLFACTORY BULB **b :** MEDULLA OBLONGATA; *broadly* **:** the rhombencephalon exclusive of the cerebellum **c :** the upper portion of the heel of a horse's hoof **d :** a thick-walled muscular enlargement of the pharynx of certain nematode worms **e :** the modified tarsal tip of a male spider that contains the coiled seminal receptacle, is often highly complex, and constitutes a character of taxonomic importance **6** [so called fr. the pneumatic bulb sometimes used to control the shutter] **:** a camera setting that indicates that the shutter can be opened by pressing on the release and closed by ending the pressure and that is used in making short time exposures and flashlight exposures — abbr. *B.*

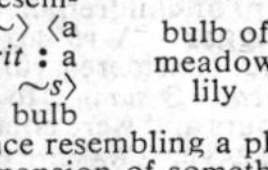

bulb of meadow lily

²bulb \"\ *vi* -ED/-ING/-S **1 :** to assume a bulbous form **:** SWELL **2** *of a plant* **:** to produce bulbs ⟨the onions ~*ed* poorly in this cold wet season⟩

bulb- *or* **bulbo-** *comb form* [MF & L; MF *bulb-*, fr. L, fr. *bulbus*] **1 :** bulb ⟨*bulb*ar⟩ ⟨*Bulbo*codium⟩ **2 :** bulbar and — esp. in terms referring to the medulla oblongata or to the bulb of the penis or urethra ⟨*bulbo*spinal⟩ ⟨*bulbo*rectal⟩

bul·ba·ceous \ˌbəlˈbāshəs\ *adj* [L *bulbaceus*, fr. *bulbus* + *-aceus* -aceous] **:** producing or growing from bulbs

bulb angle *n* **:** an angle iron with one edge thickened out into a bulbous rib

bul·bar \ˈbəlbə(r), -l,bär, -l,bȧ(r\ *adj* [¹*bulb* + *-ar*] **:** of or relating to a bulb; *specif* **:** involving the medulla oblongata

bulbar paralysis *n* **:** destruction of nerve centers of the medulla oblongata and paralysis of the parts innervated from the medulla with interruption of their functions (as swallowing or speech), usu. encountered as a symptom of pseudorabies in cattle or of botulism in fowls

bulb bar *n* **:** a rolled bar of iron or steel that is thickened along one edge so as to have a cross section bulbous at that edge

bulbed \ˈbəlbd\ *adj* **1 :** shaped like a bulb **:** BULBOUS **2 :** having a bulb

bulb eelworm *or* **bulb nematode** *n* **:** a plant-parasitic nematode (*Ditylenchus dipsaci*) of the family Tylenchidae that infests bulbs and leaves of numerous plants and is esp. destructive to narcissus

bulberry *var of* BULLBERRY

bulb fly *n* **1 :** NARCISSUS BULB FLY 1 **2 :** LESSER BULB FLY

bulbi *pl of* BULBUS

bul·bil \ˈbəlbəl, -l,bil\ *or* **bul·bel** \-lbəl, -l,bel\ *n* -s [F *bulbille*, dim. of *bulbe* bulb, fr. L *bulbus* — more at BULB] **1 a :** a small or secondary plant bulb; *esp* **:** one produced on the aerial part of the plant and capable when separated of producing a new plant — called also *brood bud bulblet*, **b :** an underground node of algae of the genus *Chara* **2 :** any of the small resting few-celled masses produced in great numbers by certain fungi

bulb·less \ˈbəlbləs\ *adj* **:** being without a bulb

bulb·let \ˈbəlblət\ *n* **1 :** BULBIL 1a **2 :** CORMEL

bulblet fern *n* **:** a No. American bladder fern (*Cystopteris bulbifera*) often bearing bulbils on the rachis near the base of the pinnae

bulb mite *n* **:** a cosmopolitan mite (*Rhizoglyphus echinopus* or related species) that burrows in lily and other bulbs

bul·bo·cap·nine \ˌbəlbōˈkap,nēn, -pnən\ *n* [ISV *bulbocapn-* (fr. NL *Bulbocapnos*, in some esp. former classifications a genus of herbs now included in the genus *Corydalis*, from a species of which it was extracted, fr. *bulb-* + Gk *kapnos* smoke) + *-ine* — more at COVET] **:** a crystalline alkaloid $C_{19}H_{19}NO_4$ that induces catalepsy and that is obtained from the roots of plants of the genus *Corydalis* and from squirrel corn

bul·bo·cav·er·no·sus \ˌbəl(,)bō,kavə(r)ˈnōsəs\ *n, pl* **bulbocavernosi** \-ō,sī, -ō,sē\ [NL, fr. *bulb-* + L *cavernosus* hollow — more at CAVERNOUS] **:** a muscle in the male surrounding and compressing the bulb of the penis and the bulbar portion of the urethra and in the female divided into lateral halves that extend from immediately behind the clitoris along either side of the vagina to the central tendon of the perineum and serve to compress the vagina — called also in the female *sphincter vaginae*

bul·bo·cav·er·nous \-ˈkavə(r)nəs\ *adj* [NL *bulbocavernosus*] **:** of, relating to, or located near the bulb of the penis

bulbocavernous gland *n* **:** COWPER'S GLAND

bul·bo·chae·te \ˌbəlbōˈkēd-ē\ *n, cap* [NL, fr. *bulb-* + Gk *chaitē* flowing hair — more at CHAET-] **:** a genus of freshwater green algae (family Oedogoniaceae) having much-branched filaments with each cell bearing a long hair with a bulbous base

bul·bo·co·di·um \ˌbəlbəˈkōdēəm\ *n* [NL, fr. *bulb-* + Gk *kōidion* small sheepskin, fleece, dim. of *kōas* sheepskin] **1** *cap* **:** a monotypic genus of bulbous herbs (family Melanthaceae) native to the Mediterranean region and having purple flowers that resemble crocuses **2** -s **:** any plant of the genus *Bulbocodium*

bulb of percussion *archeol* **:** a cone-shaped bulge on a fractured surface of flint that is made by a blow applied at an angle

bulb of the penis : the proximal expanded part of the corpus cavernosum of the male urethra

bul·bose \ˈbəl,bōs\ *adj* [L *bulbosus* — more at BULBOUS] **:** BULBOUS

bul·bo·urethral \ˈbəl(,)bō+\ *adj* [*bulb-* + *urethral*] **:** of or relating to the bulb of the penis and the urethra

bulbourethral gland *n* **:** COWPER'S GLAND

bul·bous \ˈbəlbəs\ *adj* [MF & L; MF *bulbeux*, fr. L *bulbosus*, fr. *bulbus* bulb + *-osus* -ose — more at BULB] **1 :** like or being a plant bulb ⟨a thick ~ root⟩ ⟨~ and tuberous structures⟩ **2 a :** bearing or producing bulbs **b :** growing from a bulb ⟨~ plants⟩ **3 :** resembling or suggesting a bulb esp. in roundness or in the gross enlargement of a part ⟨thick ~ fingers⟩ ⟨an oak table mounted on a ~ pedestal⟩

bulbous begonia *n* **:** a tuberous begonia with a tuber resembling a bulb

bulbous bluegrass *n* **:** an erect tufted perennial grass (*Poa bulbosa*) used in the U.S. for pasture, lawns, and golf courses

bulbous bow *n* **:** a form of entrance in high-speed ships designed for the avoidance of wavemaking at high speeds, the stem being sharp at and below the waterline but expanding into a pear-shaped form as it nears the keel, the displacement necessary at this section of the hull thus being transferred in part to the vicinity of the keel where it becomes subject to the laws governing a totally submerged body

bulbous buttercup *or* **bulbous crowfoot** *n* **:** a common European herb (*Ranunculus bulbosus*) having a bulbous base and naturalized in No. America

bulbous fumitory *n* **:** MOSCHATEL

bulbous iris *n* **:** any of certain irises having a rootstock formed like a bulb

bul·bous·ly *adv* **:** in a bulbous manner

bulb plate *n* **:** a structural metal plate reinforced by a thickening on one edge

bulbs *pl of* BULB, *pres 3d sing of* BULB

bulb scale *n* **:** one of the leaves of a bulb (as of the lily)

bulb-tee \ˈ=,=\ *adj, of a T bar or beam* **:** having the web thickened into a bulbous rib at its edge

bul·bul \ˈbu̇l,bu̇l\ *n* -s [Per, fr. Ar] **1 a :** a Persian songbird frequently mentioned in poetry that is prob. a nightingale (*Luscinia golzii*) **b :** any of a group of gregarious arboreal passerine birds (family Pycnonotidae) of Asia and Africa that feed on fruits, berries, and insects — see CHLOROPSIS, GREEN BULBUL **2 :** a maker or singer of sweet songs

bul·bus \ˈbəlbəs\ *n, pl* **bul·bi** \-l,bī, -l,bē\ [NL, fr. L, bulb of a plant — more at BULB] **:** BULB 5

bulbus ar·te·ri·o·sus \-(,)är,tirēˈōsəs\ *also* **bulbus aor·tae** \-āˈȯr,tē\ *n* [NL *bulbus arteriosus*, lit., arterial bulb & *bulbus aortae*, lit., bulb of the aorta] **:** the dilated part of the aorta just in front of the heart from which the aortic arches arise in vertebrate embryos and in the adult of many lower vertebrates

bule \ˈb(y)ül\ *var of* ²BOOL

¹bul·gar \ˈbəl,gär, ˈbu̇l-, -gȧ(r\ *n* -s *cap* [ML *Bulgarus*] **1 a :** a people native to or inhabiting Bulgaria **b :** a member of such people **2 :** the Slavic language of the Bulgar people

²bulgar \"\ *n* -s [fr. *Bolgar*, *Bolghar*, former kingdom on the Volga river around Kazan] **:** a Russian leather orig. from Bolgar

bul·gar·ia \ˌbəlˈga(a)rēə, (ˈ)bu̇l-, -ger-,-gär-\ *adj, usu cap* [fr. *Bulgaria*, country in southeastern Europe] **:** of or from Bulgaria **:** of the kind or style prevalent in Bulgaria **:** BULGARIAN

¹bul·gar·i·an \-ēən\ *n* -s *cap* [*Bulgaria* + E *-an*] **1 :** one of the people of modern Bulgaria speaking a southern Slavic language and orig. being Finno-Ugrians living along the Volga **2 :** the language of the Bulgarians written in a modified Russian alphabet

²**bulgarian** \"\ *adj, usu cap* **:** of or relating to Bulgaria, the Bulgarians, the language of the Bulgarians, or the Bulgarian Orthodox church autonomously governed by a synod with an exarch as head and now in full communion with all Eastern Orthodox churches

bulgarian milk *n, usu cap B* **:** a fermented milk; *esp* **:** YOGURT

bul·gar·ic \-ˌgarik *also* -ger-\ *adj, usu cap* [*Bulgar* + *-ic*] **:** BULGARIAN

bul·ga·rize \ˈbəlgəˌrīz, ˈbu̇l-\ *vt* -ED/-ING/-S *often cap* [*Bulgar* + *-ize*] **:** to bring under Bulgar domination or influence

¹**bulge** \ˈbəlj, ˈbu̇lj\ *vb* -ED/-ING/-S [prob. alter. of ²*bilge*] *vt* **1** *archaic* **:** to stave in (as a ship's bottom) **2 :** to cause to bulge ~ *vi* **1** *archaic, of a ship* **:** BILGE **2 a :** to jut out **:** SWELL **b** *of a structure under pressure* **:** to bend outward ⟨the wall buckled and *bulged*⟩ **c :** to become protuberant ⟨his eyes will ~ when he sees what we've brought him⟩ **3 :** to enter hastily, clumsily, or unexpectedly — usu. used with *in* or *into* ⟨he *bulged* into the road ahead of me⟩ **4** *of a fish* **:** to cause bulges of the overlying water while feeding (as in pursuing insect nymphs and larvae) **5 :** to become filled to overflowing — used with *with* ⟨notebook *bulged* with ideas⟩ ⟨a big new market *bulging* with sales potential —*Printers' Ink*⟩ **syn** PROTUBERATE, JUT, STICK OUT, PROTRUDE, PROJECT, OVERHANG, BEETLE: BULGE and the now uncommon PROTUBERATE may suggest a swelling out, sometimes abnormally, through defect, imperfection, or unwholesome condition ⟨above her boots . . . the calves *bulged* . . . out —Arnold Bennett⟩ ⟨cans so imperfectly sealed that their contents ferment and *bulge* the can noticeably —Emily Holt⟩ ⟨houses that *bulged* with the tumors and warts of the ornamental architecture of the jigsaw period —W.A.White⟩ JUT and STICK OUT may indicate the fact of position, situation, or arrangement whereby something extends out from a surface ⟨a window that *jutted* out and looked up the narrow street —Willa Cather⟩ ⟨a tiny platform that *jutted* out over the side of the carrier —J.A. Michener⟩ ⟨a square block of stone that *jutted* from the floor —Liam O'Flaherty⟩ PROTRUDE may suggest an unexpected or unusual thrusting out ⟨the jacket slipped to the ground and from the inner pocket he saw the white tops of three envelopes *protruding* —Victor Canning⟩ ⟨Bill March was carried out, a naked white foot *protruding* from beneath the white sheet —Robert Tallant⟩ PROJECT may apply to a throwing or pressing forward or outward or to something comparable to the results of such an action ⟨the young man *projected* from the side of the car like the figurehead of a ship —Ernest Hemingway⟩ ⟨a long spit of land covered with pine trees *projecting* out from the shore —Frank Gibney⟩ ⟨Sullivan was always obliged to think far ahead of its progress. He must *project* himself hours ahead, a thousand miles beyond the horizon —E.K.Gann⟩ OVERHANG and BEETLE imply a jutting out over a support, the latter sometimes suggesting ominousness or precariousness ⟨the booths where goods were exposed to sale projected far into the streets and were *overhung* by the upper stories —T.B.Macaulay⟩ ⟨the limestone bluff rolls closer to the water's edge, *overhanging* the road with cedar —*Amer. Guide Series: Mich.*⟩ ⟨a small dark courtyard above which *beetled* the walls of the castle —John Buchan⟩ ⟨he half arose from his chair and *beetled* over her. His face was full of the surreptitious joy of having trapped her —Augusta Walker⟩

²**bulge** \"\ *n* -S [prob. alter. of ¹*bilge*] **1 :** BILGE 1, 2 **2** [prob. fr. ¹*bulge*] **:** a swelling or protuberant part: as **a :** an outward bend produced by pressure ⟨a ~ in the wall⟩ **b :** a landmass projecting beyond the general contour of the body of which it is a part ⟨the ~ of Brazil⟩ **c :** a part of a military front that is advanced beyond the general line of the front **:** SALIENT **d :** the rounded fill of a well-packed container of fresh produce **3 :** ADVANTAGE, UPPER HAND — often used in the phrase *get the bulge on* **4 :** an upward trend or movement esp. when relatively abrupt, limited in extent, and transitory in nature ⟨the usual seasonal ~ in inventories⟩: as **a :** a rippling of the surface of water; *esp* **:** one caused by the movement of feeding fish below the surface **b :** a rise in prices **c :** an increase in numbers ⟨using schools in the summer could help provide essential space for the growing ~ in the youth population —W.H.Gaumnitz⟩; *esp* **:** one associated with a particular social phenomenon

bulge hoop *n* **:** the hoop nearest the middle of a cask

bulg·er \-jə(r)\ *n* -S **:** one that bulges; *specif* **:** a wooden golf club with a convex face

bulg·i·ly \-jəlē, -li\ *adv* **:** in a bulgy manner

bul·gur \(ˈ)bu̇lˈgu̇(ə)r\ *n* -S [Turk] **:** parched crushed wheat as prepared and used as a dietary staple in Turkey and adjacent regions

bulgy \ˈbəljē, ˈbu̇l-, -ji\ *adj* -ER/-EST **:** BULGED, BULGING; *esp* **:** PROTUBERANT

-bu·lia \ˈbyülēə\ *also* **-bou·lia** \ˈbü-\ *n comb form* -S [NL *-bulia*, fr. Gk *-boulia*, fr. *boulē* will; prob. akin to Gk *ballein* to throw — more at DEVIL] **:** condition of having (such) will ⟨hyperbulia⟩

-bu·lic \ˈbyülik\ *also* **-bou·lic** \ˈbü-\ *adj comb form* [ISV, fr. NL *-bulia* + ISV *-ic*] **:** of, relating to, or characterized by a (specified) state of the will

bu·lim·ia \byüˈlimēə\ *also* **bou·lim·ia** \bü-\ *n* -S [NL, fr. Gk *boulimia* great hunger, fr. *bous* head of cattle + *limos* hunger, famine + *-ia* — more at COW, LESS] **:** an abnormal and constant craving for food

bu·lim·i·dae \byüˈliməˌdē\ *n pl, cap* [NL, fr. *Bulimus*, type genus + *-idae*] **:** a family of operculate snails (order Pectinibranchia) that includes numerous intermediate hosts of medically and economically important flukes

bu·li·moid \ˈbyüləˌmȯid\ *adj* [NL *Bulimus* + E *-oid*] **:** resembling the land snails of the family Bulimulidae esp. in having ovate somewhat elongate shells with an ovate aperture

bu·li·mu·li·dae \ˌbyüləˈmyüləˌdē\ *n pl, cap* [NL, fr. *Bulimulus*, type genus (dim. of *Bulimus*) + *-idae*] **:** a family of land snails many of which are large and beautifully colored — see BULIMOID

bu·li·mus \byüˈlīməs\ *n, cap* [NL, prob. fr. L, great hunger, fr. Gk *boulimos*, fr. *bous* head of cattle + *limos* hunger — more at COW, LESS] **1 :** a genus of small freshwater snails that is the type of the family Bulimidae and includes a species (*B. fuchsianus*) that is the chief intermediate host of the Chinese liver fluke **2** *in former classifications* **:** a genus of land snails somewhat equivalent to the family Bulimulidae

bu·li·my \ˈbyüləmē\ *n* -ES [alter. of ME *bolisme*, *bolismus*, fr. MF & ML; MF *bolisme*, fr. ML *bolismus*, alter. of L *bulimus* — more at BULIMUS] **:** an insatiable appetite; *esp* **:** BULIMIA

¹**bu·li·nus** \byüˈlīnəs\ *n, cap* [NL, perh. irreg. fr. L *bulla* bubble + *-inus* -ine — more at POLL (head)] **:** a genus (the type of the family Bulinidae) of small sinistral freshwater pulmonate snails including a number that are intermediate hosts of flukes of domestic animals

²**bulinus** \"\ *n, cap* [NL, alter. of *Bulimus*] *in some classifications* **:** a genus coextensive with *Bulimus* — used chiefly in medical literature

¹**bulk** \ˈbəlk, ˈbu̇lk, ˈbəu̇k\ *n* -S [ME *bulke*, fr. ON *bulki* cargo; prob. akin to OE *blāwan* to blow — more at BLOW] **1 a** *obs* **:** HEAP, PILE **b :** one of the long stacks in which salted fish are layered for curing **c :** a large pile of tobacco arranged for fermentation **d** *archaic* (1) **:** the cargo of a ship (2) **:** the whole quantity of a commodity **2 a :** spatial dimension **:** MAGNITUDE, VOLUME; *esp* **:** great extent ⟨his industry was proven by the ~ of his accomplishment⟩ **b** *archaic* **:** POWER, MIGHT **c :** thickness of paper: (1) **:** thickness of a book exclusive of its cover (2) thickness of a specified number of sheets of paper or board (as of leaves in a book) (3) **:** thickness of a sheet of paper or board in relation to its weight ⟨of two sheets of equal weight the thicker is said to be of higher ~⟩ **d :** MASS 1c(1) **e :** material (as fibrous residues of food) that forms a mass in the intestine and is usu. felt to promote intestinal motility **3 a :** the body of a man or lower animal whether living or dead; *esp* **:** TRUNK — now usu. used of human bodies and with an implication of largeness or corpulence ⟨he hauled his black-clad ~ out of the armchair —Herman Wouk⟩ **b :** an organized structure **:** BODY; *esp* **:** one considered primarily as a mass of material substance ⟨the dark ~s of stalled cars —Raymond Chandler⟩ ⟨the giant ~ of Mt. Katahdin — Jackson Rivers⟩ **c :** a large mass **4 a :** the main or greater part ⟨the ~ of his work was finished before supper⟩ ⟨the ~ of our property is in bonds⟩ **b :** MAJORITY ⟨the ~ of the citizens agreed⟩ — often used with adjectives of magnitude ⟨the great ~ of the population⟩ — **in bulk :** in a mass **:** not divided into parts or packaged in separate units ⟨unmilled grains are shipped *in bulk*⟩

²**bulk** \"\ *vb* -ED/-ING/-S *vt* **1 a :** to cause to swell or bulge **:** STUFF — often used with *out* ⟨a dozen petticoats ~*ing* out her figure⟩ **b :** to add bulk to ⟨any inert innocuous material can be used to ~ the trace-element mixture⟩ **2 :** to gather into a mass ⟨she ~*ed* up her hair with one hand as she reached for the shears with the other⟩: as **a :** to pile (fish or tobacco) in bulks — often used with *down* **b :** to mix (as tea of different lots or grades) in order to secure a uniform product **c :** to assemble (as funds) in aggregates ⟨baggage is often ~*ed* for the determination of charges⟩ **3 :** to have a bulk of **:** amount to ⟨the Hoover Dam ~*s* about 4,400,000 cubic yards — Joseph Bryan⟩ ~ *vi* **1 :** SWELL, EXPAND — often used with *up* ⟨the loaf ~*ed* up and browned nicely⟩ **2 a :** to have bulk **:** present a bulky appearance **:** LOOM ⟨a dark mass that ~*s* on the horizon⟩ **b :** to be weighty, significant, or impressive ⟨the factor that ~*s* largest in the present discussion⟩ **c** *of sheets of paper or board* **:** to reach a certain thickness ⟨the pages of your book ~ 400 to the inch⟩ **3 a :** to form into a cohesive mass ⟨esparto paper pulp ~*s* well⟩ **b** *of sewage sludge* **:** to form into masses that will not concentrate normally

³**bulk** \"\ *adj* **1 :** in bulk ⟨~ cement⟩ ⟨~ cargoes⟩ **2 :** dealing with or involving materials in bulk ⟨a ~ buyer⟩ ⟨the ~ window at the post office⟩

⁴**bulk** \"\ *n* -S [perh. fr. ON *bālkr* partition; akin to ON *bjalki* beam — more at BALK] *archaic* **:** a small structure projecting from a building (as a shop or booth) — compare BULKHEAD

bulked \ˈbəlkt, ˈbu̇l-\ *adj* [ME, fr. *bulke* + *-ed*] **1 :** having bulk — usu. used in combination ⟨big-*bulked* rugged frame⟩ **2 :** handled in bulk ⟨~ wheat⟩

¹**bulker** *n* -S [perh. fr. ⁴*bulk* + *-er*] **1** *obs* **:** a pickpocket's helper **2** *archaic* **:** STRUMPET, PROSTITUTE

²**bulk·er** \ˈbəlkə(r), ˈbu̇l-\ *n* -S [²*bulk* + *-er*] **:** one that bulks; *esp* **:** a worker who bulks tobacco

bulk eraser *n* **:** a device for erasing previous recordings on an entire reel of magnetic tape

¹**bulk·head** \ˈbəlˌked, ˈbu̇l-, -lkˌhed\ *n* -S [⁴*bulk* + *head*] **1 :** an upright partition separating compartments; *esp* **:** such a partition separating compartments on a ship **2 :** a stone, wood, or concrete structure or partition designed to resist pressure or to shut off water, fire, or gas; *esp* **:** the retaining wall along a waterfront **3 a** *chiefly NewEng* **:** a projecting framework with a sloping door giving access to a cellar stairway or a shaft **b :** PENTHOUSE 2a

bulkhead 3a

²**bulkhead** \"\ *vt* **:** to enclose, separate, or support with bulkheads — used with *off* ⟨~ off part of the hold and make twenty bunks for the crew —Ken Leuty⟩

bulkhead deck *n* **:** the uppermost continuous deck of a ship to which all main transverse watertight bulkheads are carried

bulk·head·ed \-edəd\ *adj* **:** equipped with bulkheads or partitioned off by a bulkhead

bulkhead line *n* **:** a line marking the limit to which piers or wharves may project along a waterfront

bulk·i·ly \-lkəlē, -li\ *adv* **:** in a bulky manner

bulk·i·ness \-kēnəs, -kin-\ *n* -ES **:** the quality or state of having bulk or being bulky

bulking power *n* **:** the relative capacity of a textile fiber to build up a bulk of material ⟨wool has high *bulking power*⟩

bulking value *n* **:** the relative capacity of a pigment or other ingredient to add volume to a paint

bulk-line system *n* **:** a system of fixing prices sufficiently high to cover the costs of marginal producers so as to stimulate production

bulk mail *n* **:** second-class, third-class, or fourth-class mail consisting of identical pieces mailed under permit in quantity and paid for as one lot

bulk modulus *n* **:** the ratio of the intensity of stress to the volume strain produced by stress — used of an elastic medium subjected to volume compression

bulk-pile \ˈ=,=\ *vt* **:** to pile (as seasoned lumber) closely esp. without cross strips

bulk process *n* **:** CHARMAT PROCESS

bulks *pl of* BULK, *pres 3d sing of* BULK

bulk-sales law *n* **:** a statute regulating the sale of stocks of goods in bulk where creditors may be prejudiced

bulky \ˈbəlkē, ˈbu̇l-, -ki\ *adj* -ER/-EST **1 a :** having bulk; *esp* **:** large of its kind ⟨a ~ volume⟩ **b :** STOUT, CORPULENT — used of the human body **2 :** occupying overmuch space **:** CLUMSY, UNWIELDY ⟨a ~ ill-packed load⟩; *esp* **:** having great bulk in proportion to weight ⟨a pound of feathers is *bulkier* than a pound of lead⟩ **3** *of explosives* **:** having considerable bulk in proportion to disruptive power **syn** see MASSIVE

bulk yarn *n* **:** synthetic staple-fiber yarn containing a proportion of stretched fiber that will contract and crimp during wet finishing, used in knitted and woven fabrics for a full well-covered appearance

bulky color *n* **:** any partly or wholly transparent color perceived as filling a space in three dimensions — compare FILM COLOR

¹**bull** \ˈbu̇l\ *n* -S [ME *bule*, fr. OE *bula*; akin to OE *bulluc* young bull, MLG *bulle* bull, ON *boli* bull, OE *blāwan* to blow — more at BLOW] **1 a :** a sexually mature uncastrated male of any wild or domesticated animal of the genus *Bos* **b :** a male esp. when sexually mature of any of various other large mammals (as of the elephant, moose, elk, whale, or seal) **c :** any of certain other large male animals (as a male terrapin or alligator) **2 a :** one who operates on a stock, commodity, or produce exchange in expectation of a rise in the price of securities or commodities or in order to effect such a rise — compare BEAR **b :** a person with an optimistic attitude as to the course of events, esp. as to business **3 :** one that resembles or is likened to a bull (as in size, strength, or loud roaring): as **a :** a large powerful often somewhat stolid and clumsy person **b :** an elephant whether male or female — used chiefly of elephants semidomesticated in circuses and zoos **c** *or* **bull of the woods :** FOREMAN, STRAW BOSS, SUPERVISOR — used esp. of a working foreman in a lumber camp **d :** an ox or steer esp. when used for draft **4** *slang Brit* **:** a crown piece **5** [by shortening] **a :** BULL'S-EYE 5 **b :** BULLDOG **6** *slang* **:** POLICEMAN, DETECTIVE

²**bull** \"\ *adj* [ME *bule*, fr. *bule*, n.] **1 :** MALE ⟨a ~ calf⟩ **2 a :** of or relating to a bull ⟨tough ~ beef⟩ **b :** like or like that of a bull ⟨a strong ~ back⟩ **3 a :** large of its kind ⟨a ~ ladle⟩ ⟨a ~ lathe⟩ **b :** COARSE, HARSH ⟨a ~ screen⟩ ⟨a heavy ~ voice⟩ **4 a** *of markets* **:** RISING; *esp* **:** marked by the activities of bulls **b :** acting as a bull in the markets ⟨a ~ body of speculators⟩

³**bull** \"\ *vb* -ED/-ING/-S [ME *bulen*, fr. *bule*, n.] *vi* **1** *of a cow or heifer* **:** to be in heat **:** take the bull **2 a :** to behave like a bull; *esp* **:** to press on or advance vigorously **b :** to advance in price — used esp. of stocks and speculative commodities or of markets dealing in these ~ *vt* **1** *of a bull* **:** to serve (a cow or heifer) **2 :** to try to raise the market price of (as stocks or bonds); *sometimes* **:** to try to raise prices in (a market) **3 a :** to enforce or bring into existence against opposition — usu. used with *through* ⟨they had decided to ~ through a demand for outright repeal —Helen Fuller⟩ **b :** to act on with or as if with the physical violence of a bull ⟨he ~*ed* his opponent all over the ring⟩ — **bull one's way :** to move forward against opposition by or as if by the exertion of physical violence **:** PUSH, SHOVE ⟨he *bulled his way* homeward through the storm⟩

⁴**bull** \"\ *n* -S [ME *bulle*, fr. ML *bulla*, fr. L *bulla* bubble, amulet — more at POLL (head)] **1 :** BULLA 2 **2 :** a papal letter distinguished from other apostolic letters by being sealed with a bulla or with a red-ink imprint of the device on the bulla, by being written on parchment and in the third person, by opening with the pope's name and the formula "Bishop, servant of the servants of God", and by significance of subject matter **3 :** an edict (as of the Holy Roman Empire) or other formal and supposedly authoritative statement ⟨~s issued by certain groups of professional educators —H.J.Fuller⟩

⁵**bull** \"\ *n* -S [perh. fr. obs. *bull* to make fun of, mock, prob. fr. MF *bouler* to deceive, cheat, roll, fr. *boule* ball — more at BOWL] **1** *obs* **:** an absurd jest **2 a :** a grotesque blunder in language (as in "his brother and sister are much alike, esp. his sister"); *esp* **:** IRISH BULL **b :** a serious error **:** a bad or sometimes ludicrous blunder **3** *slang* **a :** trivial and commonly boastful and inaccurate talk ⟨sat there shooting the ~⟩ **b :** something regarded as undesirable, superfluous, or incorrect ⟨that's ~, I'll tell you the whole story⟩ ⟨this business of sending flowers and things like that is the ~ —Jerome Weidman⟩ **syn** see ERROR

⁶**bull** \"\ *vb* -ED/-ING/-S *vi* **1** *slang* **:** to talk bull **:** BLOW **2 :** to act blunderingly; *sometimes* **:** BALK ~ *vt, slang* **:** to fool or bemuse esp. by fast talking and bull

⁷**bull** \"\ *n* -S [origin unknown] **:** a weak drink made by pouring water into an emptied spirit cask or rinsing out a sugar bag

⁸**bull** \"\ *or* **bull board** *n* -S [origin unknown] **:** a game that resembles quoits and is often played on shipboard

bull *abbr* bulletin

bul·la \ˈbu̇lə\ *n, pl* **bul·lae** \-ˌlē, -ˌlī, *esp in sense 2* -ˌlā\ [L, bubble, boss, amulet — more at POLL (head)] **1 :** a small case of leather or of metal usu. lenticular in shape, designed to contain amulets, and suspended by a cord around the neck by ancient Romans; *broadly* **:** a rounded ornament used as a pendant, boss, knob, or stud in Roman costume or architecture **2** [ML, fr. L] **:** a seal appended to a document; *esp* **:** the round usu. lead seal attached to the papal bulls that has on one side a representation of St. Peter and St. Paul and on the other the name of the pope who uses it **3** [NL, fr. L] **:** a hollow thin-walled rounded bony prominence (as that situated beneath the opening of the ear of many mammals) **4** [NL, fr. L] **:** a large vesicle or an elevation of the cuticle usu. containing serum **:** a large blister — compare BLEB **5** [NL, fr. L] **:** a transparent or weakly chitinized spot in the wing vein of certain insects

bul·lace \ˈbu̇ləs\ *n* -S [ME *bolace*, fr. MF *beloce*, fr. ML *bolluca*, *bulluga*] **1 :** a small wild or half-domesticated European plum (*Prunus domestica insititia*) related to the damson and having small ovoid fruit in clusters **2 :** BALATA 2 **3** *or* **bullace grape :** MUSCADINE

bul·la·ma·cow *or* **bul·la·ma·cau** \ˈbu̇ləməˈkau̇\ *n* -S [Pidgin English, prob. modif. of E *bull* + *cow*] **1** *Pacific Islands* **:** tinned beef **:** canned meat **2** *Pacific Islands* **:** cattle in general

bul·lar·i·um \bu̇ˈla(a)rēəm\ *or* **bul·la·ry** \ˈbu̇lərē\ *n, pl* **bullar·ia** \-a(a)rēə\ *or* **bullaries** [ML *bullarium*, fr. *bulla* seal, papal bull + L *-arium* -ary] **:** a collection of papal bulls

bul·late \ˈbu̇ˌlāt\ *or* **bul·lat·ed** \-ˌād·əd\ *adj* [NL *bulla* + E *-ate*, *-ated*] **1 :** appearing as if blistered **:** PUCKERED ⟨a ~ leaf⟩ — compare RUGOSE **2 :** like or having a bulla ⟨a ~ tympanic bone⟩

bullbaiting \ˈ=,==\ *n* -S **:** the former practice of baiting bulls with dogs

bull band *also* **bull banding** *n* -S *Midland* **:** CHARIVARI

bullbat \ˈ=,=\ *n* -S [so called fr. their roaring sound in flight] **:** NIGHTHAWK 1a; *esp, South* **:** a nighthawk (*Chordeiles minor*)

bull bay *n* **:** EVERGREEN MAGNOLIA

bull·beg·gar \ˈbu̇lˌbegə(r)\ *n* [perh. blend of obs. E *bullbear* (alter. of *bugbear*) + *beggar*, by folk etymology fr. *boggard*, *boggart*] *dial Brit* **:** GOBLIN, BUGBEAR

bull·ber·ry \ˈbu̇l- —*see* BERRY\ *also* **bul·ber·ry** \"\ *n* [¹*bull* + *berry*] **:** BUFFALO BERRY

bull birch *n, NewZeal* **:** BEECH 4

bull bit *n* **:** a single-edged rock-drilling bit

bull block *n* **1 :** a perforated block or die through which wire is drawn to reduce its size **2 :** a large wide-throated pulley block used in yarding logs

bullboat \ˈ=,=\ *n* [so called fr. its construction of bull or buffalo skins] **:** a shallow-draft skin boat shaped like a tub and formerly used (as by Indians) in the Great Plains area

bullbrier \ˈ=,==\ *n* **:** any of several American plants of the genus *Smilax* with large farinaceous rootstocks formerly used as food by the Indians — compare GREENBRIER

bull bucker *n, slang* **:** the man in charge of the fallers and buckers in a lumber camp

bull cane *n* **:** a thick vigorous grape cane that usu. bears inferior fruit

bull chain *n* **1 :** a heavy chain to which are attached short chains having each a hook on one end and dogs on the other that is used for drawing logs **2 :** JACK CHAIN 2

bull cook *n* [so called fr. his job of caring for oxen once used in logging camps] **:** a handyman in a camp (as of loggers); *esp* **:** one who does caretaking chores and acts as cook's helper

bull ditcher *n* **:** a large heavy plow that has a double moldboard and is used in ditching

¹**bulldog** \ˈ=,=\ *n* [¹*bull* + *dog*] **1 :** a compact muscular short-haired dog of a breed developed in England and used orig. in bull baiting but now usu. kept as a domestic pet, being noted equally for its vigor and sagacity and for its equable disposition, having the forelegs set widely apart and the lower jaw longer than the upper so that its grip is very powerful against resistance, and being usu. white, brindle, or a combination of brindle and white — see BOSTON TERRIER, FRENCH BULLDOG **2 :** a pistol or a revolver; *esp* **:** one of large caliber and short barrel **3 :** a proctor's attendant at Oxford and Cambridge **4 a :** BULLDOG ANT **b** *or* **bulldog fly :** HORSEFLY **5 :** a refractory material used as a furnace lining that is obtained by calcining mill cinder **6 :** any of several devices designed to obtain a firm and steady grip **7** *or* **bulldog pipe :** a tobacco pipe with a square shank and squat bowl, the latter having two grooves cut around its widest circumference **8 :** BULLDOG EDITION

²**bulldog** \"\ *adj* **1 :** of, relating to, or characteristic of a bulldog ⟨the mechanism of the ~ jaw⟩ **2 a :** like or suggestive of a bulldog (as in courage or stubbornness) **b :** having a powerful grip ⟨~ clips⟩ ⟨a ~ wrench⟩ **c :** having an excessively or abnormally undershot jaw ⟨~ bats⟩ **d** *of cattle* **:** affected with a destructive mutation of which such a jaw is a characteristic

³**bulldog** \"\ *vt* **1 :** to behave like a bulldog toward esp. in attacking with fierceness and vigor or in proceeding with methodical deliberation **2** *West* **:** to throw (a steer) by seizing the horns and twisting the neck

bulldog ant *n* **:** any of the large pugnacious fiercely biting Australian ants of the genus *Myrmecia*

bulldog bat *n* **:** MASTIFF BAT

bulldog edition *n* **:** the earliest edition of a morning or Sunday newspaper usu. appearing the evening before

bull·dog·ged \ˈbu̇lˌdȯgəd *sometimes* -dăg-\ *adj* [blend of ¹*bulldog* and *dogged*] **:** stubbornly tenacious — **bull·dog·ged·ness** *n* -ES

bull·dog·ger \-gə(r)\ *n* [³*bulldog* + *-er*] **1** *West* **:** one that bulldogs cattle **2 :** ROUGHER

bull·dog·gish \-gish\ *adj* **:** BULLDOG; *esp* **:** BULLDOGGED

bull·dog·gy \-gē\ *adj* **:** BULLDOGGED

bulldog spear *n* [so called fr. its grasping ability] **:** a fishing tool for recovering well pipe or casings

bulldog toe *n* **:** a high bulging box toe

bull donkey *n* [*donkey* (engine)] **:** a large donkey engine fitted with drum and cable for hauling logs

bull·doze \ˈbu̇lˌdōz\ *vb* -ED/-ING/-S [perh. fr. ¹*bull* + alter. of *dose*] *vt* **1 :** to coerce, restrain, or intimidate esp. by overt or implicit threats (as of violence) **:** BULLY **2 :** to break (boulders of rock or ore) by secondary blasting (as by mudcapping or blockholing) **3 :** to move, clear, gouge out, or level off by pushing with a bulldozer **4 :** BULLDOG 2 **5 :** to force (as one's way) or push out of the way (as obstructions) as if by using a bulldozer ~ *vi* **1 :** to operate a bulldozer **2 :** to engage in bulldozing **:** BULLY **syn** see INTIMIDATE

shoe with a bulldog toe

bull·doz·er \-zə(r)\ *n* -s **1 :** one that bulldozes: as **a :** BULLY, INTIMIDATOR **b :** PISTOL, REVOLVER **c :** an operator of a machine for bulldozing **2 :** an upsetting machine (as a forging or bending press) in which the ram slides in a horizontal path and is actuated by a pair of powerful cranks and connecting rods **3 :** a tractor-driven machine having a broad blunt horizontal blade or ram for clearing land, road building, or comparable activities; *also* **:** the blade or ram of such a machine

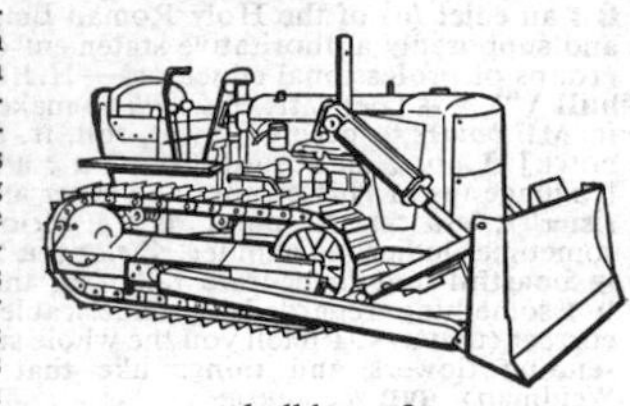
bulldozer 3

bull driver *n* **:** a driver of cattle **:** an ox driver **:** DROVER
bulldust \'⸗,⸗\ *n, Austral* **:** coarse dust or silt
bull earing *n* **:** an earing fixed to the yard instead of to the sail — see SAIL illustration
bulled \'bu̇ld\ *adj* [¹*bull* + *-ed*] **:** THICKENED, STRENGTHENED — used esp. of the neck
¹**bul·len** \'bu̇lən\ *or* **bullen nail** *n* -s [alter. of earlier *bullion⸗nail*, fr. *bullion* (boss on harness) + *nail*] **:** a nail with a round head and short shank, tinned and lacquered
²**bullen** \"\ *n* -s [origin unknown] **:** a device for catching large turtles consisting essentially of a metal ring that settles over the turtle and an attached net in which it becomes entangled
¹**bul·ler** \'bələr, 'bu̇l-,'bu̇l-\ *vi* -ED/-ING/-S [ME *bulleren* to bubble, boil, prob. of Scand origin; akin to Icel *bulla* to boil, Sw *bullra* to make a noise — more at BULLER (to roar)] *Scot* **:** BOIL, SEETHE
²**buller** \"\ *n* -s [ME, bubble, fr. *bulleren*, v.] *Scot* **:** WHIRLPOOL
³**buller** \"\ *vi* -ED/-ING/-S [prob. of Scand origin; akin to Sw *bullra* to make a noise, Dan *buldra*, OE *bellan* to roar — more at BELLOW] *Scot* **:** ROAR, BELLOW
⁴**bull·er** \'bu̇lə(r)\ *n* -s [³*bull* + *-er*] **:** a cow or heifer constantly in heat **:** a bovine nymphomaniac
⁵**bull·er** \"\ *n* -s [*bulldog* + *-er*] **:** BULLDOG
¹**bul·let** \'bu̇lət, *usu* -əd·+V\ *n* -s [MF *boulette* small ball, small missile & *boulet* cannonball, missile, diminutives of *boule* ball — more at BOWL] **1** *archaic* **a :** CANNONBALL **b :** a small round mass **c :** a missile for a sling **2 :** a missile (as of lead, steel, or lead with a steel casing) that is round or elongated and designed to be fired from a rifle, musket, or pistol; *broadly* **:** CARTRIDGE 1a **3 :** something suggesting or likened to a bullet esp. in form or vigor of action: as **a** *slang* **:** an ace of a deck of cards **b :** a hollow hemispherical iron shell filled with pitch and used to hold small objects during metalcraft tooling **c :** a large solid dot so placed in printed matter as to call attention to a particular passage **d :** a conical part or structure; *esp* **:** an electric lamp enclosed in a cone-shaped metal case that is usu. supported by a flexible shaft **e :** something (as a neutron) that can be bombarded against an atomic nucleus to induce fission

revolver cartridge showing *S* shell, *B* bullet

²**bullet** \"\ *adj* **:** relating to or resembling a bullet (as in form, in speed of action, or in producing a single impact)
³**bullet** \"\ *vi* -ED/-ING/-S **:** to move fast ⟨the car ~*ed* toward him⟩
bullet bolt *n* **:** a bolt contracted or extended by the turning of a knob or handle — compare SPRING BOLT
bullet catch *also* **bullet latch** *n* **:** a catch having a bullet bolt
bullet hawk *n* **:** ACCIPITER 2
bullethead \'⸗⸗,⸗\ *n* **1 :** a head that is round or shaped like a bullet **2 :** a pigheaded person — **bullet-headed** \¦⸗⸗¦⸗⸗\ *adj*
¹**bul·le·tin** \'bu̇lət°n, -ətən, -əd·ən\ *n* -s [F, fr. It *bullettino*, dim. of *bulla* papal edict, fr. ML, papal edict, document, seal — more at BILL (document)] **:** a brief or condensed public notice or announcement usu. concerning a matter of marked current interest and issuing from a source that might reasonably be considered authoritative: as **a :** a brief statement from an official source concerning the current status of a source of prolonged interest (as of a war or the health of a sovereign) **b :** an announcement of future plans; *esp* **:** a college or university catalog **c :** a brief monograph; *esp* **:** one issued by a public agency to provide popular information on a subject ⟨the state college issued several ~*s* on local plants⟩ **d :** a brief statement of news considered to be of outstanding importance or interest and made public at the earliest possible moment (as by last-minute insertion on the front page of a newspaper or by interruption of a radio program) — compare FLASH
²**bulletin** \"\ *vt* -ED/-ING/-S **:** to make public by means of or in the form of a bulletin
bulletin board *n* **:** a board on which bulletins or other notices are posted
bul·le·tin·ize \-°n,īz, -ə,nīz\ *vt* -ED/-ING/-S **:** to approach or notify by means of a bulletin ⟨we will ~ the whole membership⟩
bullet jacket *n* **:** the outer metal casing of a bullet
bul·let·less \'bu̇lətləs\ *adj* **:** being without a bullet
bullet money *n* **:** an old Siamese money in the form of bullet⸗shaped lumps of gold and silver that was valued in divisions and multiples of the tical
¹**bulletproof** \'⸗⸗¦⸗\ *adj* **1 :** impenetrable to bullets ⟨~ glass⟩ **2 :** not subject to correction, alteration, or modification ⟨a ~ argument⟩
²**bulletproof** \"\ *vt* -ED/-ING/-S [¹*bulletproof*] **:** to make impenetrable to bullets ⟨~ a car⟩
bullet trap *n* **:** a backstop for small-arms firing that acts as a target frame and that serves to deflect and arrest bullets safely by means of its heavy steel sides
bul·let tree \'bu̇lət-\ *n* [by folk etymology fr. AmerSp *balata* — more at BALATA] **1 :** a bully tree (esp. *Manilkara bidentata*) **2 :** a tree (*Terminalia buceras*) of Central America and the West Indies with brownish gray very close-grained wood
bulletwood \'⸗⸗,⸗\ *n* **1 :** the wood of a bully tree **2 :** a bully tree (*Manilkara bidentata*)
bul·lety \'bu̇ləd·ē\ *adj* **:** like a bullet in shape or hardness
bull-eye \'⸗¦⸗\ *n* **:** an eye (as of a pigeon) having both iris and pupil dark in color
bull fiddle *n* **:** CONTRABASS — **bull fiddler** *n*
bullfight \'⸗,⸗\ *n* -s **:** a Spanish, Portuguese, and Latin⸗American spectacle in which a bull is ceremonially fought and usu. killed in an arena by a matador assisted by picadors and banderilleros — called also *corrida*
bullfighter \'⸗,⸗⸗\ *n* **:** one that fights bulls; *esp* **:** TORERO
bullfighting \'⸗,⸗⸗\ *n* **:** the activity of a bullfight; *also* **:** the custom of presenting bullfights
¹**bullfinch** \'⸗,⸗\ *n* [prob. so called fr. the thick neck] **1 :** a finch of the genus *Pyrrhula; esp* **:** a European finch (*P. pyrrhula*) that is often kept as a cage bird and taught to whistle various airs, the male having rose-red underparts, blue-gray back, black cap, chin, tail, and wings, and white rump, the female being chiefly pinkish brown below, grayish brown above **2 :** any of several other finches that resemble the European bullfinch (as a pyrrhuloxia or grosbeak)
²**bullfinch** \"\ *n* [fr. earlier *bullfinch* (*fence*)] **:** a hedge too high for a mounted hunter to leap
bull·fist *or* **bull·fice** \'bu̇l,fīs(t)\ *n* -s [*bullfist* fr. ¹*bull* + *fist* flatus, fr. ME; *bullfice* alter. of *bullfist* — more at FEIST] **:** GIANT PUFFBALL
bullfoot *var of* BULL'S-FOOT
bullfrog \'⸗,⸗\ *n* [so called fr. its size and its bull-like croak] **:** FROG; *esp* **:** any of numerous large heavy-bodied deep⸗voiced frogs chiefly of the genus *Rana* (esp. *R. catesbeiana*)
bull gang *n* [*bullwork*] **:** a crew of unskilled laborers
bull gear *n* **:** a bull wheel having gear teeth
bull·gine \'bu̇l,jīn\ *n* -s [¹*bull* + *engine*] *dial* **:** ENGINE — used specif. of steam locomotives
bull grape \'bu̇l+,-\ *n* [*bullace grape*] **:** MUSCADINE
bull grass *n* **1 :** SOFT CHEAT **2 :** PRAIRIE CORDGRASS
bull-grip \'⸗,⸗\ *n* **:** any of several prickly plants of the genus *Smilax* (esp. *S. rotundifolia*)

bull grunter *n* **:** a silvery dark-dotted marine percoid fish (*Pomadasys multimaculatus*) of the east coast of southern Africa highly regarded for food and sport
bull gun *n* **:** a heavy-barreled target rifle
bullhead \'⸗,⸗\ *n* **1 :** any of numerous large-headed fishes: as **a :** any of several scorpaenid fishes: as (1) **:** MILLER'S-THUMB 1 (2) **:** FATHER-LASHER (3) **:** SEA POACHER (4) **:** SCULPIN **b :** any of several catfishes (genus *Ameiurus*) abundant in fresh waters of No. America **c :** a marine sciaenid food fish (*Laumus fasciatus*) of the southern U.S. **d :** a small primitive brown shark (*Heterodontus japonicus*) of Australasia **2 :** a stupid person; *esp* **:** one stupidly headstrong and stubborn **3 a :** BLACK⸗BELLIED PLOVER **b :** GOLDEN PLOVER **c :** AMERICAN GOLDEN-EYE **4 :** a deformed or atrophied flower; *esp* **:** one that is abnormally double **5 :** a head (as of a rivet or a rail) of approximately bulbous section; *also* **:** a bullheaded rail **6 :** a caltrop (*Tribulus terrestris*) of the southwestern U.S. **7** *also* **bullhead clam :** a freshwater mussel (*Plethobasis cyphus*) of the upper Mississippi drainage with a nacreous shell used for making buttons
bullheaded \'⸗¦⸗⸗\ *adj* [*bull* + *headed*] **1 :** having a massive head suggesting that of a bull **2 :** stupidly stubborn **:** HEADSTRONG, OBSTINATE **3 a :** having a bullhead **b** *of railway rails* **:** being double-headed with one bulbous end larger than the other, the small end being designed to fit in a chair **syn** see OBSTINATE
bull·head·ed·ly *adv* **:** in a bullheaded manner **:** OBSTINATELY
bull·head·ed·ness *n* -ES **:** OBSTINACY
bull header *n* **:** a header brick laid on its edge; *also* **:** a brick having one of its corners rounded, laid with one of its ends exposed, and serving as the sill under and beyond a window frame, as a quoin, or as a part of the masonry around a doorway
bullhead lily *n* [¹*bull* + *head*] **:** SPATTERDOCK
bullhead shark *n* [¹*bull* + *head*] **:** a shark of the family Heterodontidae — see HETERODONTUS
bullhoof \'⸗,⸗\ *n, Jamaica* **:** a West Indian passionflower (*Passiflora murucuja*) with leaves like a cloven hoof
bullhorn \'⸗,⸗\ *n* **:** a loudspeaker esp. on naval vessels
bull-horn acacia *n* [so called fr. the shape of the thorns] **:** any of several hollow-thorned trees of the genus *Acacia; esp* **:** a large-thorned chiefly Central American tree (*A. cornigera*) the thorns of which are inhabited by ants
bul·li·dae \'bu̇lə,dē\ *n pl, cap* [NL, fr. *Bulla*, type genus (fr. L, bubble) + *-idae* — more at POLL (head)] **:** a family of gastropod mollusks (order Opisthobranchia) including a number of typical bubble shells
bullied *past of* BULLY
bullier *comparative of* BULLY
bullies *pl of* BULLY, *pres 3d sing of* BULLY
bulliest *superlative of* BULLY
bul·li·form \'bu̇lə,fȯrm\ *adj* [L *bulla* bubble + E *-iform*] **:** shaped like a bubble **:** BULLATE — used chiefly of plant structures
bulliform cell *n* **:** one of the large thin-walled apparently empty cells that occur in the epidermis of many grass leaves and that by their turgor changes cause rolling and unrolling of the leaves thus regulating water loss — called also *hygroscopic cell, motor cell*
bullimong *n* -s [ME *bulimong, bolymong*, prob. fr. *bule* bull + *imong* mixture, fr. OE *gemong, gemang* mixture, mingling, crowd — more at BULL, AMONG] *dial Eng* **:** a mixture of various grains and forage plants sown together
bull in a china shop : a person notably clumsy or ill-adapted to the situation in which he finds himself
bull index *n* **:** a measure of the relative ability of a dairy bull to transmit desirable qualities to his daughters obtained by comparing the productivity of a certain number of daughters with that of their dams
bulling *n* -s [fr. gerund of ³*bull*] **:** the dislodging of rock by exploding blasting charges in fissures
bulling bar *n* **:** a bar used to ram clay into cracks before blasting
bulling heifer *n* [fr. pres. part. of ³*bull*] *Brit* **:** a heifer unbred but of an age for breeding usu. from 15 months to the first service
bul·lion \'bu̇lyən\ *n* -s [ME *bullioun* gold or silver as metal measurable by weight, fr. AF *bullion* mint, prob. fr. MF *bouillir, boillir* to boil — more at BOIL] **1 a :** gold or silver considered merely as so much metal without regard to any value imparted to it by its form ⟨the ~ contained in a silver dollar⟩; *specif* **:** uncoined gold or silver in the shape of bars, ingots, or comparable masses **b :** metal in the mass ⟨lead ~⟩ **2** *obs* **:** a place where precious metals are tested, minted, or exchanged **3** *obs* **:** an ornamental metal boss used on harness, jewelry, or other objects **4 a :** lace of gold or silver threads used esp. formerly in church vestments, robes of state, or other formal costumes **b :** cord with a core usu. of wire or cotton covered with textile or metal threads of gold, silver, or other color and used esp. to form braids or twisted fringes (as for military insignia or ornamentation); *also* **:** braid or fringe so made **5 :** BULL'S-EYE 4a
bullion balance *n* **:** a sensitive beam balance of heavy construction that is used for weighing bullion and specie
bul·lioned \-nd\ *adj* **:** trimmed or finished with bullion
bul·lion·ism \-,nizəm\ *n* -s **:** the principles and practices advocated by a bullionist
bul·lion·ist \-nəst\ *n* -s **1 :** an advocate of a metallic medium of exchange **2 :** a believer in the prohibition of the export of specie and in the regulation of trade so as to insure an import of bullion preferably after each transaction — used esp. in ref. to early mercantilist doctrine **3 :** one who holds that a premium on bullion is indicative of bank-note depreciation — used esp. in ref. to the English currency controversies of the early 19th century
bul·lion·less \-yənləs\ *adj* **:** being without bullion
bullion point *n* **1 :** GOLD EXPORT POINT **2 :** GOLD IMPORT POINT
bullion stitch *or* **bullion knot** *n* **:** a decorative stitch similar to the French knot forming very short bars
bull·ish \'bu̇lish, -lēsh\ *adj* **1 :** of, relating to, or suggestive of a bull; *esp* **:** obstinate as a bull **2 a :** inclined to bull the market ⟨speculators are feeling ~⟩ **b :** characterized by a trend toward rising prices ⟨a ~ market⟩ **c :** looking toward a rise in prices ⟨a ~ report⟩ ⟨~ commitments for the new year⟩ **d :** marked by hopefulness for the future **:** OPTIMISTIC — **bull·ish·ly** *adv*
bul·li soil \'bu̇,lī-\ *also* **bulli** *n* -s *usu cap B* [fr. *Bulli*, town in New South Wales, Australia, whence it comes] **:** a black soil used as a topdressing to produce a hard surface (as of a cricket pitch)
bull kelp *n* **:** any of certain large brown Pacific seaweeds (division Phaeophyta) esp. of the large genus *Nereocystis*
bull mastiff *n* [*bulldog* + *mastiff*] **:** a large powerful dog of an English breed developed from crossings of the bulldog and mastiff that is brindled or fawn with black mask and is used esp. in South Africa as a watch or guard dog
bull moose \'⸗'⸗\ *also* **bull moos·er** \"+ə(r)\ *n, usu cap B&M* [*bull moose*, the emblem of the Progressive party formed in 1912 by Theodore Roosevelt †1919 Am. president] **:** a follower of Theodore Roosevelt in the U.S. presidential campaign of 1912
bullneck *in senses 1 & 3* '⸗,⸗, *in sense 2* '⸗¦⸗\ *n* **1 :** leather made from the neck hide of a bull **2** *usu* **bull neck a :** a thick short powerful neck **b :** a swelling of the neck in severe diphtheria filling and distending the space beneath the jaw from ear to ear **3 :** any of several American wild ducks: as **a :** CANVASBACK **b :** RUDDY DUCK **c :** RING-NECKED DUCK
bullnecked \'⸗¦⸗\ *adj* **:** having a bull neck
bull nettle *n* **1 :** HORSE NETTLE **2 :** SPURGE NETTLE
bullnose *in sense 3* '⸗,⸗, *in other senses* '⸗,⸗\ *n* **1** *or* **bullnosed plane :** a small plane with the iron set near the fore end of the stock **2 :** BULL'S-NOSE **3 :** a necrobacillosis arising in facial wounds of swine and characterized by swelling of the face, nose, and mouth and sloughing of the tissues **4** *slang* **:** the front drawbar of a locomotive

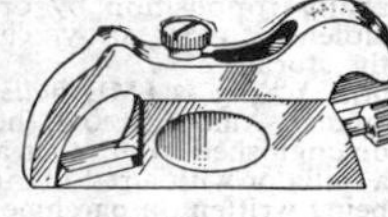
bullnose 1

bullnose pepper *n* **:** SWEET PEPPER

bullnose tool *n* **:** a tool that is shaped like a roundnose tool but has a wider and stronger point and that is used for taking heavy roughing cuts (as on a lathe or planer)
bullnut \'⸗,⸗\ *n* **:** MOCKERNUT
bull oak *n* [prob. by folk etymology fr. *beloh*] **:** any of several Australian trees of the genus *Casuarina* (esp. *C. equisetifolia, C. glauca*, and *C. luehmanni*)
¹**bull·ock** \'bu̇lək\ *n* -s [ME *bullok*, fr. OE *bulluc* — more at BULL] **1 :** a young bull **2 :** a castrated bull **:** OX, STEER, STAG **3 :** a domestic bovine **:** COW, ZEBU
²**bullock** \"\ *vb* -ED/-ING/-S *vt* [prob. influenced in meaning by ³*bully*] *dial Brit* **:** BULLY ~ *vi, Austral* **:** to work hard; *esp* **:** to do heavy manual labor
bullock block *n* **:** a large iron-strapped gin block fitted under the topmast crosstrees to take the topsail tyes
bull·ock·ing \-kiŋ\ *adj* [¹*bullock* + *-ing*] **1** *Austral* **:** resembling a bullock in size or strength ⟨a big ~ fellow⟩ **2** *Austral, of work* **:** HARD, ARDUOUS
bul·lock·ite \'bu̇lə,kīt\ *n* -s *cap* [Jeremiah *Bullock*, 19th cent. Am. leader of the sect + E *-ite*] **:** one of three Freewill Baptist groups
bul·lock oriole \'bu̇lək-\ *or* **bul·lock's oriole** \-ks-\ *n, usu cap B* [after William *Bullock* fl1827 Eng. naturalist] **:** a common black and yellow oriole (*Icterus bullockii*) of western No. America
bullock's-heart *also* **bullock heart** \'⸗⸗,⸗\ *n* [so called fr. its size and appearance] **:** a light green to yellow slightly bristly and somewhat acid tropical fruit that turns brown when fully ripe, is closely related to the soursop and sweetsop, and is produced on a small tree (*Annona reticulata*) native to tropical America but widely cultivated
bul·lock's lungwort \'bu̇ləks-\ *n* **1 :** MULLEIN **2 :** LUNGWORT 2a
¹**bull·ocky** \'bu̇ləkē\ *n* -ES *Austral* **:** a bullock-team driver
²**bullocky** \"\ *adj* **1** *Austral* **:** relating to or concerned with the driving or management of cattle ⟨~ lore⟩ **2 :** like that of a bullock ⟨thick ~ shoulders⟩
bull of the bog [so called fr. its booming cry] **:** the common bittern (*Botaurus stellaris*) of Europe
bull of the woods : ¹BULL 3c
bul·lous \'bu̇ləs\ *also* **bul·lose** \-,lōs\ *adj* [NL *bulla* + E *-ous* or *-ose*] **:** resembling or characterized by bullae **:** VESICULAR ⟨a ~ lesion⟩
bullpates \'⸗,⸗\ *n pl but sing in constr* [¹*bull* + *pates*, pl. of *pate*] **:** TUFTED HAIR GRASS 2
bull peep *n* **1 :** WHITE-RUMPED SANDPIPER **2 :** SANDERLING
bullpen \'⸗,⸗\ *n* [¹*bull* + *pen*] **1 a** *archaic* **:** an enclosure (as of logs) used as a temporary place of confinement **b :** a prison, guardhouse, or other place of confinement; *esp* **:** a large detention cell (as in a police station or courthouse) where prisoners are held until brought into court **2 :** a place on a baseball field where relief pitchers warm up during a game; *sometimes* **:** the relief pitchers ⟨got good support from the ~⟩ **3 :** any of certain places in which a number of people congregate for a common purpose: as **a :** DORMITORY, BUNKHOUSE **b :** a business office that is not divided into individual compartments **c :** a place designed for the comfort and relaxation of employees; *esp* **:** a designated smoking area in a plant where smoking is not generally permitted
bull pine *n* **1 :** PONDEROSA PINE **2 :** any of several pines (as the Digger pine, loblolly, pond pine, Jeffrey pine, and limber pine)
bull-point *also* **bull-prick** \'⸗,⸗\ *n* **:** a pointed steel bar usu. driven with a sledge for making drill holes in soft rock
bull·pout \'bu̇l,pau̇t\ *n, pl* **bullpout** *also* **bullpouts** [*bull*head + *pout*] **:** the brown bullhead or a related catfish
bull pump *n* **:** a direct single-acting pumping engine with the steam cylinder placed above the pump, the return stroke being effected by gravity
bullpup \'⸗¦⸗\ *n* -s **:** a rifle whose barrel is bedded well back on the stock so that the end of the receiver is very close to the heel of the butt
bull quartz *n* **:** BASTARD QUARTZ
bull rattle *n* **1 :** BLADDER CAMPION **2 :** WHITE CAMPION a
bull redfish *n* **:** CHANNEL BASS
bullring \'⸗,⸗\ *n* **1 a :** an arena for bullfights **b :** a ring passed through the septal cartilage of the nose of a bull and used in directing and controlling him **2 :** a T-section ring usu. shrunk on a piston, the ring acting as a carrier and distance ring to support and separate two split piston rings
bull riveter *n* **:** a large stationary riveter operated by a ram
bull-roarer \'⸗¦⸗⸗\ *n* **:** a slat of wood tied to the end of a thong and making an intermittent roaring sound when whirled that is used esp. by Australian aborigines in religious rites or among western peoples as a children's toy
bull rope *n* [*bull* (*wheel*)] **:** a strong fiber or wire rope: **a :** a rope working through a bull's-eye; *esp* **:** one used in securing a light yard or mast **b :** the rope that drives a bull wheel
bull runner *n* [*bull* (*ladle*)] **:** a foundry worker who pours molten metal from a bull ladle into molds
bullrush *var of* BULRUSH
bulls *pl of* BULL, *pres 3d sing of* BULL
bull screen *n* **:** a coarse screen for separating knots and unground material from freshly ground wood pulp
bull session *n* [⁵*bull*] **:** an informal discursive group discussion ⟨evening *bull sessions* where the talk moved roughly from women to football and back again —Millard Lampell⟩
bull set *n* **:** a small hammer for breaking stone often used with a sledge hammer
bull's-eye \'⸗,⸗\ *n, pl* **bull's-eyes 1 a :** a small circular or oval wooden block without sheaves having a groove around it and a hole through it **b :** a round usu. margined spot or opening **2 :** a small thick disk of glass inserted (as in a deck, roof, floor) to let in light — compare DEADLIGHT **3 :** a very hard globular candy **4 a :** a lump left on glass by the end of the blowpipe — see CROWN GLASS **b :** a raised circular design on glass **c :** a white glass marble with a dark center **5 a :** the center of a target; *also* **:** something regarded as central or crucial **b :** a shot that hits the bull's-eye; *broadly* **:** anything that precisely attains a desired end **6 a :** a simple lens of large numerical aperture for concentrating rays of light **b :** a lantern with a bull's-eye lens **:** DARK LANTERN — see LANTERN illustration **7 :** a circular or oval opening (as in a wall) for air or light **8 :** DAISY 2 **9** *usu* **bullseye :** a reddish small-scaled Australian food fish (*Priacanthus macracanthus*)

b bull's-eye 5a

bull's-eye rot *n* **:** a disease of apples characterized by spots resembling eyes on the fruit and caused by either of two fungi (*Neofabraea malicorticis* and *Gloeosporium perennans*)
bull's-eye window *n* **:** a circular window or a window filling a bull's-eye
bull's feather *n, obs* **:** HORN 4b
bull's-foot *or* **bullfoot** \"\ *n, pl* **bull's-foots** *or* **bullsfoots :** COLTSFOOT a
¹**bullshit** \'⸗,⸗\ *n* [¹*bull* + *shit*] **:** NONSENSE; *esp* **:** foolish insolent talk — usu. considered vulgar
²**bullshit** \"\ *vi* **:** to talk bullshit — usu. considered vulgar
bull's-horn thorn *n* **:** BULL-HORN ACACIA
bull's mouth *n* **:** a large handsome helmet shell (*Cypraecassis rufa*) that is reddish brown externally with a brilliant orange⸗red lining and is common throughout the Indo-Pacific area
bull snake *n* **:** any of several large harmless colubrid snakes widely distributed in No. America, feeding chiefly on rodents, and constituting a genus *Pituophis* — called also *gopher snake, pine snake*
bull's noon *n, dial Eng* **:** MIDNIGHT
bull's-nose \'⸗,⸗\ *n, pl* **bull's-noses** *archit* **:** an external angle when obtuse or rounded
bull stag *n* **:** a bull castrated when full-grown
bull stick *n* [*bull* (*wheel*)] **:** a lever used in lieu of a bull wheel to swing a derrick into position to pick up its load
bull stretcher *n* **:** a stretcher brick laid on edge; *also* **:** a brick with one corner rounded and laid with the face exposed (as in a quoin)
bullsucker \'⸗,⸗⸗\ **:** any of several West Indian cacti of the genus *Opuntia* with prickly flat joints
bulls·wool \'⸗,⸗\ *n, Austral* **:** STRINGYBARK 1, 2

bull team *n* : OXTEAM

bullterrier \ˈ=ˌ==\ *n* [*bull*dog + *terrier*] : a short-haired terrier of a breed originated in England by crossing the bulldog with terriers to develop a dog of speed, hardihood, and powerful bite for use in dog fights, dogs of this breed having great courage and strength but being built on the trim lines of a terrier

bull thistle *n* **1** : a European thistle (*Cirsium lanceolatum*) with rather large heads and prickly leaves that is extensively naturalized as a weed in the U.S. **2** : HORSE NETTLE

bull tongue *n* : a shovel or wide tooth attached to a cultivator or plow to stir the soil, kill weeds, or mark furrows; *also* : an instrument fitted with such an attachment

bull train *n* : a train of ox-drawn wagons that was used esp. for haulage in western U.S. before establishment of the railroads

bull trout *n* **1** *Brit* : SEA TROUT; *esp* : a large old sea trout **2** : DOLLY VARDEN 2

bull-voiced \ˈ=ˌ=\ *adj* : having a loud deep voice

bullweed \ˈ=ˌ=\ *n* [ME *bulwed*, prob. fr. *bule* bull + *wed* weed] : KNAPWEED

¹bullwhack \ˈbu̇l,(h)wak\ *n* [back-formation fr. *bullwhacker*] *chiefly West* : a long heavy whip with short handle used esp. when driving teams of four or more animals

²bullwhack \"\ *vb* [back-formation fr. *bullwhacker*] *vt*, *chiefly West* : to drive (as an ox team) using a whip rather than a goad ~ *vi*, *chiefly West* : to drive a team (as of oxen) using a whip rather than a goad

bullwhacker \ˈ=ˌ==\ *n* [¹*bull* + *whacker*] **1** *chiefly West* : a driver of an ox wagon or other heavy freight wagon esp. in the early settlement of the West **2** *chiefly West* : BULLWHACK

bull wheel *n* **1** : the main driving wheel or gear of a machine, usu. the largest and strongest wheel in the train of mechanism, in some machines (as a shaper) transmitting the power received by the machine to the various mechanisms, in others (as a tractor) delivering to the driving wheels the power transmitted to it from the motor **2** : a drum on which a rope is wound for hauling or lifting (as logs or well-boring tools) **3** : a wheel attached to the boom of a derrick at the base and used to swing the boom about a vertical axis

bullwhip \ˈ=ˌ=\ *n* [¹*bull* + *whip*] : a rawhide whip with plaited lash 15 to 25 feet long

bullwork \ˈ=ˌ=\ *n* : hard manual labor

¹bul·ly \ˈbu̇lē, -li\ *n* -ES [prob. modif. of D *boel* lover, fr. MD *boele*, fr. MHG *buole*, prob. alter. (baby talk) of *bruoder* brother — more at BROTHER] **1** *archaic* **a** : SWEETHEART, DARLING — used of either sex **b** : a good fellow : a fine chap **2 a** *archaic* : a man of outstanding physical powers **b** : a blustering fellow more insolent than courageous : one given to hectoring, browbeating, and threatening; *esp* : one habitually threatening, harsh, or cruel to others weaker or smaller than himself **c** : the protector of a prostitute : PIMP, PANDER **3 a** : a hired ruffian : BRAVO **b** *dial Brit* : a fellow workman : MATE **c** : KEELBOATMAN **d** : the boss of a logging camp **4 a** : any of several blenniold fishes **b** : any of several gobies

²bully \"\ *adj*, *sometimes* -ER/-EST **1** *of a person* : JOVIAL, DASHING, GALLANT — used esp. in *bully boy*, a term of familiar address **2** : of the best quality : EXCELLENT, FIRST-RATE ⟨what a ~ car⟩ ⟨that's a ~ idea⟩ **3** : like, characteristic of, or in the manner of a bully ⟨don't try your ~ tricks around here⟩

³bully \"\ *vb* -ED/-ING/-ES *vt* : to intimidate by an overbearing swaggering demeanor or by threats : act the part of a bully toward : DOMINEER ~ *vi* : to act as a bully : BLUSTER **syn** see INTIMIDATE

⁴bully \"\ *interj* [²*bully*] — used to express satisfaction, congratulation, or pleasure

⁵bully \"\ *adv* [²*bully*] : VERY, EXTREMELY, OUTSTANDINGLY ⟨a ~ good dinner⟩

⁶bully \"\ *or* **bully beef** *n* -ES [prob. modif. of F (*bœuf*) *bouilli* boiled beef, fr. *bouilli*, past part. of *bouillir* to boil — more at BOIL] : pickled or canned usu. corned beef

⁷bully \"\ *n* -ES [origin unknown] : a procedure of putting the ball in play in field hockey in which two opposing players face one another and alternately strike the ground and the opponent's stick three times after which the ball may be played

⁸bully \"\ *vb* -ED/-ING/-ES *vt* : to put (a field hockey ball) in play with a bully ~ *vi* : to put a field hockey ball in play with a bully

bullyboy \ˈ=ˌ=\ *n* [¹*bully* + *boy*] : a swaggering overbearing tough; *esp* : one associated with or acting as an agent of a political faction

bullyhuff \ˈbu̇lē,həf\ *n* [¹*bully* + *huff*] *archaic* : a bragging bully

bullying *adj* : OVERBEARING, BLUSTERING — **bul·ly·ing·ly** *adv*

bul·ly·ism \ˈbu̇lē,izəm\ *n* -S : bullying behavior or practice

bully-off \ˈ=ˌ=\ *n* -S [⁸*bully*] *Brit* : ⁷BULLY

bul·ly·rag \ˈbu̇lē,rag\ *or* **bal·ly·rag** \ˈbal-\ *vt* [modif. of earlier *balarag*] **1** : to intimidate by bullying : BULLDOZE **2** : to abuse, scold, harass, or vex with teasing or complaining words; *broadly* : BADGER, BAIT, TORMENT

bullyrook *also* **bullyrock** \ˈ=ˌ=\ *n* [*bullrook* fr. ¹*bully* + *rook* (cheat, simpleton); *bullyrook* by folk etymology fr. *bullyrook*] *archaic* : BULLY 1b, 3a

bul·ly tree \ˈbu̇lē-\ *or* **bul·let tree** \-lət-\ *n* [by folk etymology fr. AmerSp *balata* — more at BALATA] : any of several hard-wooded tropical American trees of the family Sapotaceae; *esp* : a large tree (*Manilkara bidentata*) of the West Indies and northern So. America that yields balata gum and a heavy red timber — called also *balata*, *beefwood*

bul·oke \ˈbu̇,lōk\ *n* -S [by alter.] : BELAH 1

bul·rush *also* **bull·rush** \ˈbu̇l,rəsh\ *n* [ME *bulrysche*, *bolroysche*, perh. fr. *bule* bull + *rysche*, *roysche*, *rusche* rush — more at BULL, RUSH] **1** : any of several large rushes growing in wet land or water: as **a** : a sedge of the genus *Scirpus* (esp. *S. lacustris*) **b** *Brit* : either of two cattails (*Typha latifolia* and *T. angustifolia*) **c** : a common American rush (*Juncus effusus*) **2** *in the Old Testament* : PAPYRUS — **bul·rushy** \-shē\ *adj*

bulrush millet *n* : PEARL MILLET; *esp* : a type widely grown in Africa and the Orient and commonly referred to a distinct species (*Pennisetum typhoideum*)

buls *pl of* BUL

bulse \ˈbəls\ *n* -S [Pg *bolsa*, lit., purse, fr. ML *bursa* — more at PURSE] : a purse or bag in which to carry or measure valuables (as diamonds or gold dust); *broadly* : a parcel of jewels

bult \ˈbəlt\ *n* -S [Afrik, fr. MD; akin to OE *bold* house — more at BUILD] *Africa* : a rocky outcropping : ridge of land : HILLOCK

bult·fon·tein·ite \ˌbəlt(ˌ)fän·ˈtā,nīt, -ˌfən\ *n* -S *usu cap* [*Bultfontein*, village in Cape Province, Union of So. Africa + E *-ite*] : a mineral $Ca_2SiO_2(OH,F)_2$ consisting of calcium silicate with hydroxyl or fluoride that is found at Bultfontein, So. Africa

bulti *var of* BOLTI

bul·to \ˈbu̇l(ˌ)tō, ˈbül-\ *n* -S [Sp, image, bulk, form, body, statue, fr. L *vultus*, *voltus* countenance, expression, shape; perh. akin to Goth *wulthus* glory, W *gweled* to see] **1** : an image of a saint carved in wood and polychromed made in the southwestern U.S. and Latin America in the 18th and 19th centuries **2** : a bundle esp. of fibers for rope making

bul·tow \ˈbu̇l(ˌ)tō\ *n* -S [origin unknown] : LONGLINE; *esp* : SETLINE

bu·lu \ˈbü(ˌ)lü\ *n*, *pl* **bulu** *or* **bulus** *usu cap* **1** : a Bantu language of the southern Cameroons **2** : a people of the southern Cameroons who speak the Bulu language **3** : a member of the Bulu people

¹bul·wark \ˈbu̇l,wə(r)k; ˈbu̇l,wərk, -,wōk, -,wəik; ˈbu̇l,wȯrk, -ō(ə)k; ˈbu̇l,wärk, -wäk; *also* ˈbəl,wə(r)k *or* ˈbəl,wərk *or* ˈbəl,wōk *or* ˈbəl,wəik\ *n* -S [ME *bulwerke*, fr. MD, fr. MHG *bolwerc*, fr. *bole* plank + *werc* work, fr. OHG; akin to ON *bolr* tree-trunk — more at BOLE, WORK] **1 a** : a solid wall-like structure raised for defense usu. not too high for the defenders to fire over : RAMPART, PARAPET **b** : BREAKWATER, SEAWALL **2** : something that offers strong support or protection in danger : a powerful means of defense : an imposing safeguard ⟨a strong representative government is a ~ of liberty⟩ **3** : the side of a ship above the upper deck — usu. used in pl.; see SHIP illustration

²bulwark \"\ *vt* -ED/-ING/-S [ME *bulwerken*, fr. *bulwerke*, n.] : to fortify, secure, or reinforce with or as if with a bulwark : PROTECT ⟨ability to ~ a moral choice —Margaret Mead⟩ ⟨trying to ~ the country against internal disorder⟩

bulwark plating *n* : the light plating that projects above the hull plating of a ship and serves as a bulwark

bul·wer's petrel \ˈbu̇lwə(r)z-\ *n*, *usu cap B* [after James *Bulwer* †1879 Brit. clergyman and fellow of the Linnaean society] : a small sooty black petrel (*Bulweria bulwerii*) with a gray chin and pinkish feet

¹bum \ˈbəm\ *n* -S [ME *bom*] *chiefly Brit* : BUTTOCKS — often considered vulgar

²bum \ˈbəm, ˈbu̇m\ *vi* **bummed; bummed; bumming; bums** [ME *bumben*, of imit. origin] *dial chiefly Brit* : to make a droning or murmuring sound : HUM ⟨hear the bagpipes ~⟩

³bum \ˈbəm\ *n* -S *chiefly Scot* : a constant humming noise : DIN ⟨the ~ and bustle of the street⟩

⁴bum \ˈbəm\ *vt* **bummed; bummed; bumming; bums** [prob. imit.] : BEAT, POUND

⁵bum \ˈbəm\ *n* -S [by shortening] : BUMBAILIFF

⁶bum \ˈbəm\ *vb* **bummed; bummed; bumming; bums** [prob. back-formation fr. *bummer*] *vi* : to go around in the manner of a bum: **a** : LOAF ⟨he had been *bumming* around the house all day⟩ **b** : to wander esp. like a tramp ⟨he had *bummed* through the far West⟩ ~ *vt* : MOOCH, CADGE ⟨he tried to ~ a ride home⟩ ⟨she was always *bumming* cigarettes⟩

⁷bum \ˈbəm\ *n* -S [prob. short for *bummer*] **1 a** : LOAFER, VAGRANT; *esp* : one who drinks heavily ⟨a ~ from down on skid row⟩ **b** : a lazy indolent person; *esp* : one inclined to sponge off others and avoid work — often a generalized expression of disparagement ⟨Mickey . . . dwells in a black-and-white world where a guy is either your pal or probably a ~ —Hal Boyle⟩ **c** : HOBO, TRAMP ⟨hallelujah, I'm a ~⟩ **d** : one who travels around pursuing a particular activity and working only enough to keep going — usu. used with a qualifying noun ⟨the fruit ~s followed the peach harvest north from Georgia⟩: as (1) : a nonprofessional so enthusiastic about a sport that he lives on what he can earn in temporary jobs or on what he can sponge and devotes most of his time to the sport ⟨tennis ~s trying to keep their amateur status⟩ (2) : a person so enthusiastic about a sport that he devotes most of his leisure to it ⟨a train loaded with ski ~s off for a weekend⟩ **2** : an empty mail sack **3** : a lamb whose mother has died or deserted it **syn** see VAGABOND

⁸bum \ˈbəm\ *adj* **1** : of poor quality or nature : not good : INVALID, INFERIOR ⟨a ~ check⟩ **2 a** : not in working order or condition **b** *of a part of the body* : permanently or frequently stiff, sore, lame, or otherwise disabling ⟨a ~ knee from an old football injury⟩

⁹bum \ˈbəm\ *n* -S [prob. fr. ⁶*bum*] : a drinking spree : BENDER ⟨a terrific 2-day ~⟩ — **on the bum** *adv* (*or adj*) **1** : footloose and wandering around the country in the manner of a tramp : in the manner or role of a vagrant ⟨he would go back *on the bum* awhile and try some other city —James Jones⟩ ⟨travel across country *on the bum*⟩ **2** : SPONGING, CADGING ⟨when his money ran out he always came to me *on the bum*⟩ **3** : in poor order or condition ⟨my wrists are a bit *on the bum* —Sinclair Lewis⟩ : in a state of depression ⟨the old days in the States before everything went *on the bum* there —Ernest Hemingway⟩

bum·bai·liff \ˌbəmˈbāləf\ *n* -S [¹*bum* + *bailiff*; fr. his close pursuit of debtors] *Brit* : BAILIFF — usu. used contemptuously ⟨a confounded, pettifogging ~ —W.M.Thackeray⟩

bum ball *n* [by alter.] : BUMP BALL

bumbalo *var of* BUMMALO

bumbass \ˈ=ˌ=\ *n* -ES [prob. fr. ³*bum* + *bass* (musical instrument)] **1** : BLADDER-AND-STRING **2** : ¹DRONE 3a

bumbast *obs var of* BOMBAST

bumbaste \ˌ=ˈ=\ *vt* -ED/-ING/-S [¹*bum* + *baste*] *dial Eng* : to beat on the buttocks : THRASH

bum·baze \ˌbəmˈbāz\ *vt* -ED/-ING/-S [perh. alter. of Sc *baze* to dismay, fr. ME *baisen*, *baishen* to dismay, be dismayed, fr. MF *baissier* to lower, abase, fr. (assumed) VL *bassiare* to lower — more at ABASE] *chiefly Scot* : BEWILDER, PERPLEX

bumbee \ˈ=ˌ=\ *n* -S [²*bum* + *bee*] *chiefly Scot* : BUMBLEBEE

bum·ber·shoot \ˈbəmbə(r),shüt\ *n* -S [*bumber-* (alter. of *umbr-* in *umbrella*) + *-shoot* (alter. of *-chute* in *parachute*)] *slang* : UMBRELLA ⟨a bowler and ~ to go with his tidy, official face —*Time*⟩

¹bum·ble \ˈbəmbəl\ *vi* **bumbled; bumbled; bumbling** \-mb(ə)liŋ\ **bumbles** [ME *bomblen* to boom, of imit. origin] **1** : to make a humming sound : BUZZ ⟨the June bugs *bumbled* foolishly against the window screens —Jean Stafford⟩ **2** : to make a low hollow sound : RUMBLE ⟨we *bumbled* across the trestle into the city —Grace H. Flandrau⟩

²bumble \"\ *vb* **bumbled; bumbled; bumbling** \-mb(ə)liŋ\ **bumbles** [prob. alter. (influenced by ¹*bumble*) of *bungle*] *vi* **1** : BUNGLE, BLUNDER ⟨someone *bumbled* and the advantage was lost⟩; *specif* : to speak ineptly, stuttering and faltering ⟨he *bumbled* through his speech⟩ **2** : to move or proceed unsteadily : STUMBLE ⟨*bumbling* along absent-mindedly on rope-soled shoes —Sybille Bedford⟩ ~*vt* : BUNGLE

³bumble \"\ *n* -S **1 a** : JUMBLE, SNARL **b** : BUNGLE, BOTCH **2** *chiefly Scot* : BUNGLER, BLUNDERER

⁴bum·ble \ˈbəm(b)əl, ˈbu̇m-\ *n* -S [short for *bumblebee*] **1** *dial Eng* : BUMBLEBEE **2** *chiefly Scot* : IDLER, LOAFER **3** [¹*bumble*] *dial Eng* : BITTERN

⁵bum·ble \ˈbu̇məl\ *n* -S [origin unknown] *dial Eng* : BULRUSH

⁶bum·ble \ˈbəmbəl\ *n* -S [after *Bumble*, a parish beadle in the novel *Oliver Twist* (1837-9) by Charles Dickens †1870 Eng. novelist] *Brit* : a pompous self-important minor official; *esp* : BEADLE

bum·ble·bee \ˈbəmbəl,bē\ *n* [¹*bumble* + *bee*] : any of numerous large robust hairy social bees of the genus *Bombus* that form small annual colonies and like the honeybees store up honey in their underground nests, often using for this purpose the cells vacated by the young

bumblebee buzzer *or* **bumblebee coot** *n* : RUDDY DUCK

bumblebee hawkmoth *n* : a day-flying clearwing hawkmoth (*Hemaris diffinis* or related species) of the U.S., Europe, and Asia having the body largely yellow and resembling a bumblebee when in flight

bumblebee root *n* : PURPLE TRILLIUM

bum·ble·dom \ˈbəmbəldəm\ *n* -S *often cap* [*Bumble*, a parish beadle in *Oliver Twist* + E *-dom*] : the actions and mannerisms of pompous but inefficient government officials ⟨a strain of mild obstinacy exquisitely calculated to infuriate the self-important ~ of that time —G.M.Trevelyan⟩

bumble flower beetle *n* [prob. fr. ⁴*bumble*] : a hairy yellowish brown black-marked beetle (*Euphoria inda*) that may sometimes become a pest by feeding on corn ears and certain fruits

bumblefoot \ˈ=ˌ=\ *n* [³*bumble*] **1** *dial Eng* : a misshapen foot; *specif* : CLUBFOOT **2** : a disease of poultry characterized by a swelling on the ball of the foot with or without abscess formation

bum·ble·kite \ˈbu̇məl,kīt\ *n* -S [¹*bumble* + *kyte*; fr. a belief that blackberries cause flatulence] *dial Eng* : BLACKBERRY

bum·ble·pup·py \ˈbəmbəl,pəpē\ *n* [²*bumble* + *puppy*] **1** : the old game of nineholes **2** : whist played poorly or without regard for rules

¹bum·bler \ˈbəm(b)(ə)lə(r), ˈbu̇m-\ *n* -S [¹*bumble* + *-er*] *dial* : BUMBLEBEE

²bum·bler \ˈbəmb(ə)lə(r)\ *n* -S [²*bumble* + *-er*] : one that bumbles : BLUNDERER, BUNGLER

¹bumbling *n* -S [fr. gerund of ²*bumble*] : stupid and awkward blundering ⟨a story of military fatuity, of pompous ~, of reckless waste of lives —J.H.Powers⟩

²bumbling *adj* [fr. pres. part. of ²*bumble*] **1 a** : blundering and awkward : likely to make foolish mistakes ⟨a kindly, ~ ne'er-do-well who had lately lost his job —Dixon Wecter⟩ **b** : ineffective as a speaker (as because of faltering and stuttering) ⟨animated and splendidly communicative one evening and ~ the next —R.H.Rovere⟩ **2** : marked by conspicuous blundering, inefficiency, ineffectiveness, and lack of organization ⟨the ~ policies of the administration led to its downfall⟩

¹bum·bo \ˈbəm(ˌ)bō\ *also* **bom·bo** \ˈbäm-\ *n* -S [perh. fr. It (baby-talk) *bombo* drink, of imit. origin] : an alcoholic drink usu. made with rum or gin, sugar, water, and sometimes spices

²bumbo \"\ *n* -S [of West African origin; prob. akin to Mende *bogbo*, a tree whose fruit is used for vegetable sauce] : a West African leguminous tree (*Daniella thurifer*) that is the chief West African source of copal and has a soft pleasant-scented and damp-resistant wood

bum·boat \ˈbəm+,-\ *n* [prob. fr. LG *bumboot*, fr. *bum*, *bōm* tree + *boot* boat, fr. ME; akin to OHG *boum* tree — more at BEAM, BOAT] : a boat that brings provisions and commodities for sale to larger ships in port or offshore ⟨I bought a bunch of the tiny Azores bananas from a ~ under the side —F.M Ford⟩ ⟨Nelson's raiders had their ~ women who used to swarm aboard by rope's end and anchor chains —H.W.Baldwin⟩

bum·clock \ˈbəm,kläk\ *n* -S [²*bum* + *clock* (beetle)] *Scot* : DORBEETLE

bu·me·lia \byüˈmēlēə\ *n* [NL, fr. L, ash, fr. Gk *boumelia*] **1** *cap* : a genus of tough spiny American trees and shrubs (family Sapotaceae) that bear edible berries **2** -S : any plant of the genus *Bumelia*

bumf \ˈbəm(p)f\ *n* -S [short for *bumfodder*, fr. ¹*bum* + *fodder*] **1** *slang Brit* : TOILET PAPER **2** *slang Brit* : documents and official papers — usu. used disparagingly

bumfeg *vt* **bumfegged; bumfegged; bumfegging; bumfegs** [¹*bum* + obs. *feague*, *fegue* to beat, prob. fr. D *vegen*, lit., to sweep, fr. MD *vēghen*; akin to OS *fegon* to sweep, MHG *vegen* to sweep, clean, OE *fæger* beautiful — more at FAIR] *obs* : THRASH

bumfreezer \ˈ=ˌ==\ *n* [¹*bum*] *Brit* : a boy's short jacket; *esp* : ETON JACKET

bum·fuz·zle \ˌbəmˈfəzəl\ *vt* -ED/-ING/-S [prob. alter. of E dial. *dumfoozle*, prob. alter. of E *dumfound*] *chiefly dial* : CONFUSE, PERPLEX, FLUSTER

bum·icky \ˈbəməkē\ *n* -S [origin unknown] : a mixture of cement and powdered stone used for filling crevices in building stones

bumkin *var of* BUMPKIN

bum·ma·lo *or* **bum·ma·low** *or* **bum·me·lo** \ˈbəmə,lō\ *also* **bum·ba·lo** \-mbə-\ *n* -S [prob. modif. of Marathi *bombīlā*, oblique case form of *bombīl*] : BOMBAY DUCK

bummed *past of* BUM

¹bum·mel *or* **bum·mle** \ˈbəməl\ *vi* -ED/-ING/-S [by alter.] *chiefly Scot* : ¹BUMBLE

²bummel *or* **bummle** \"\ *n* -S [by alter.] *chiefly Scot* : ⁴BUMBLE 1, 2

³bum·mel \ˈbəməl\ *vi* **bummeled** *or* **bummelled; bummeled** *or* **bummelled; bummeling** *or* **bummelling; bummels** [G *bummeln* to loaf] : to go or wander around at a leisurely pace : STROLL, SAUNTER

bum·mer \ˈbəmə(r)\ *n* -S [prob. modif. of G *bummler* loafer, tramp, fr. *bummeln* to loaf, dangle] **1** : one that bums; *specif* : one that subsists by cadging **2** : PLUNDERER, MARAUDER — used esp. of looting soldiers during the Civil War **3** : a low 2-wheeled logging truck or tracked cart for skidding logs **4** : the workman in charge of the conveyors in a mine or quarry

bumming *pres part of* BUM

bum·mler \ˈbəm(ə)lər\ *n* -S [¹*bummel* + *-er*] *chiefly Scot* : one that bumbles: **a** : BUMBLEBEE **b** : BUNGLER, BLUNDERER

¹bump \ˈbəmp\ *vb* -ED/-ING/-S [imit.] *vt* **1 a** : to strike or knock typically with a degree of force or violence and making a thudding impact and usu. with a degree of injury or damage ⟨he ~*ed* his head on the low ceiling⟩ **b** *chiefly Brit* : SMASH **c** *chiefly Brit* : NIP **2** : to meet with or come up against forcibly (as an obstruction, buffer, or guard rail) ⟨the front fender was crushed as it ~*ed* the stone wall⟩ **3 a** : to displace, dislodge, or move from a position by bumping : knock out of place ⟨the passenger was ~*ed* out of his seat by the impact⟩ **b** : to oust (another) from a job or position and fill it oneself usu. by virtue of seniority rights ⟨he was ~*ed* from his job as a switchman by an older railroader⟩ **c** : to deprive (another) of travel accommodations esp. on an airplane by virtue of higher priority or rank or greater need ⟨he was ~*ed* at the airport to make room for a top-ranking army officer⟩ **d** : to demote in rank usu. suddenly : BUST ⟨he was ~*ed* from colonel to major⟩ **e** : to oust or dismiss from membership ⟨a move to ~ the senator from the committee⟩ **4 a** : to approach or attain to in a manner suggesting irregular jolting and forceful progress ⟨prices began ~*ing* officially approved limits⟩ **b** : to increase or raise with suddenness or force — usu. used with *up* ⟨demand has ~*ed* up prices⟩ **5 a** : to apply pressure to (sheet or plate metal) so as to make or remove a concavity or convexity **b** : to raise a low area of (a printing plate) esp. by hammering on the back or by interlaying — often used with *up* ~ *vi* **1** : to strike or knock against something with a forceful thud or jolt — often used with *into* or *against* ⟨the car ~*ed* into the light pole⟩ **2** : to travel or proceed in or as if in a series of bumps — often followed by an adverb or a preposition ⟨~*ed* over the dirt road⟩ ⟨the jeep turned and ~*ed* back onto the highway —Donald Stokes⟩ **3** : to encounter usu. forcibly or somewhat unpleasantly something that is an obstacle, hindrance, or threat — usu. used with *into* or *against* ⟨expected to ~ against serious opposition —Ned Russell⟩ **4** : to boil suddenly and sometimes with explosive violence (as of water covered with a layer of oil and rapidly heated) **5** *of a bowled cricket ball* : to rise to an unusual height after pitching **6** : to thrust the hips forward with a quick, convulsive, or suggestive motion in or as if in a burlesque striptease ⟨the strippers still ~ and grind in the clubs, although with modifications —*Time*⟩

syn CLASH, COLLIDE, CONFLICT: BUMP indicates forceful knocking or running against, typically with thudding impact ⟨the ferry *bumped* into the mooring post⟩ ⟨he *bumped* his foot on the stove⟩ It may suggest encountering an obstacle or difficulty ⟨the builder *bumped* up against the problem of shoring up the wall⟩ CLASH may suggest hitting, knocking, or dashing together or against with sharp force and jangling metallic din ⟨the swords *clashed*⟩ ⟨where ignorant armies *clash* by night —Matthew Arnold⟩ or sharp, although sometimes short-lived, variance, incompatibility, or opposition ⟨Cavour and Victor Emmanuel *clashed* sharply, and on these occasions it was usu. the King who won —*Times Lit. Supp.*⟩ ⟨when the new demands of our changing economic life *clash* with the old dogmas —M.R.Cohen⟩ COLLIDE suggests a more or less direct running together or against with a certain force or shock ⟨the tanker sank after it *collided* with the freighter⟩ It also indicates a forceful direct disagreement or opposition ⟨an English East India Company was using the Portuguese route around Africa and *colliding* with the Portuguese in India —Stringfellow Barr⟩ CONFLICT, archaic in senses involving physical contact, indicates variance, incompatibility, or opposition ⟨*conflicting* testimony by two witnesses⟩ ⟨to stand up amid *conflicting* interests —William Wordsworth⟩

— **bump into** : to encounter or meet with esp. by chance ⟨just happened to *bump into* him at the meeting⟩

²bump \"\ *n* -S **1 a** : a somewhat forceful, sudden, thudding, or jolting blow or impact : the action, the effect, or the noise of such a blow ⟨the freight cars came together with a ~⟩ ⟨the ~ of a chestnut falling —Sylvia Stallings⟩ ⟨a ~ that still hurts⟩: as (1) : a jolt experienced in an airplane in flight that is caused by local ascending or descending air currents (2) : a sudden shock or rock concussion sometimes accompanying rock subsidence in and around mines **b** : displacement to a lower position : DEMOTION ⟨a ~ to the bottom of his class⟩ **2** : a relatively abrupt convexity or protuberance on a surface: as **a** : a swelling of tissue usu. resulting from a bump ⟨a week later she still had a bad ~ on her forehead⟩ **b** : a protuberance on the body: as (1) : BREAST ⟨a young girl beginning to mature and show ~s⟩ (2) : a cranial protuberance associated in phrenology with one of various faculties or personal qualities **c** (1) : a sudden rise in a road surface likely to jolt a passing vehicle (2) : any marked unevenness in a road surface likely to cause such a jolt ⟨an old pavement now full of ~s and holes⟩ **d** : a hill or other bulky rounded protuberance typically somewhat isolated geographically ⟨the lone ~ of hill that stands on the Jersey flats —Horace Sutton⟩ **3 a** : an obstruction giving sudden check or pause ⟨help people over the ~s of defeat —L.C.May⟩; *also* : the abrupt perception of an obstruction or difficulty ⟨Mrs. Miniver remembered with a ~, felt dismayed —Jan Struther⟩ **b** : OBSTACLE, DIFFICULTY ⟨the ~s he encountered on his way to success⟩ **4** : natural endowment : FACULTY, QUALITY ⟨has need of a big ~ of irreverence —John Raymond⟩ ⟨possessing a ~ of skepticism and a bent toward rationality —C.J.Rolo⟩ ⟨children with big ~s of curiosity⟩ **5** : an action of thrusting the hips forward with a quick suggestive motion typically in a burlesque striptease act — compare GRIND **syn** see IMPACT

bump ball *n* **:** a ball hit (as by a batsman in cricket) so that it strikes the ground and then rises ⟨a fielder caught a *bump ball* and mistakenly thought he had caught the batsman out⟩

1bump·er \ˈbəmpə(r)\ *n* -s [prob. fr. 1*bump* (in obs. sense, to bulge, be protuberant) + *-er*] **1 :** a cup or glass filled to the brim or till the liquor runs over esp. in drinking a toast **2 :** something unusually large **3 :** a fish (*Chloroscombrus chrysurus*) of the family Carangidae of the southern U.S. and West Indies

2bumper \"\ *vb* -ED/-ING/-S *vt* **1 :** to fill to the brim (as a wineglass) and empty by drinking **2 :** to toast with a bumper ~ *vi* **:** to drink bumpers of wine or other alcoholic beverages

3bumper \"\ *adj* **1 :** unusually large ⟨a ~ crop of wheat⟩ **2 :** very good, fine, or successful ⟨going to be a ~ winter on TV — probably the best ever —*Glasgow Sunday Post*⟩

4bumper \"\ *n* -s [1*bump* + *-er*] **1 :** one that bumps or operates a machine or device that bumps: as **a :** a bumping-die press operator **b :** one who backs up a riveting dolly with another hammer **c :** one who molds handmade bricks **d :** one that hammers sheet metal into shape by hand or machine: (1) **:** one who removes dents from automobile bodies and fenders or from sheet-metal parts of airplanes — called also *dingman* (2) **:** one who straightens damaged ship plates by a heating and cooling process **e :** an engraver's assistant in the making of textile printing rolls **f :** a bowled ball in cricket that bumps **g** *chiefly Brit* **:** a smashing machine in bookbinding; *also* **:** the operator of such a machine **h** (1) **:** a hand canceler for canceling stamps on second, third, and fourth-class mail; *also* **:** a hand canceler for use on registered mail (2) **:** a cancellation mark made by such a canceler **i :** a worker who bumps broomcorn fibers up and down on a table to even them prior to measuring and cutting **2 :** a device or attachment (as on a vehicle) for absorbing shock and lessening or preventing damage in collision or impact with another object: as **a :** a metal bar or metal bars attached to either end of an automobile or other powered transportation vehicle to prevent damage to the body **b :** a buffer (as a log or a bundle of rope) suspended down the side of a ship or boat or suspended or floating alongside a landing or docking place **c** *also* **bumper beam :** a timber or casting across the frame ends of a railroad engine, tender, or car **d :** BUMPING POST **e :** a usu. rubber-tipped doorstop attached to a wall behind a door to keep the door from hitting the wall **f :** a protective cornerpiece (as on a suitcase) made of metal, leather, or other durable material **g :** a rubber or plastic guard running around the base portion of a vacuum cleaner as a protection to furniture **h :** a protective pad designed to fit around the inside of a baby's crib **3 :** a flat metallic disk in or on the pavement that is used in some traffic signaling systems and that may be run over without being injured and without damaging the vehicle **4 :** a woman's hat with a narrow brim fashioned like a tube or padded roll; *also* **:** an imitation of this style **5** *Austral* **:** a cigarette butt

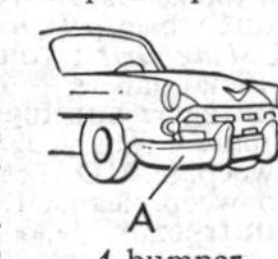

A bumper

5bumper \"\ *adj* **:** having a curved armless end or ends — used of an upholstered divan or unit of one ⟨a ~ sofa⟩ ⟨sofas fitted with ~ units⟩

bumper guard *n* **:** either of two vertical shoes attached to the bumper of an automobile to prevent the locking of bumpers with other cars and to facilitate pushing

bumper jack *n* **:** a jack designed to lift an automobile by its bumper

1bump·e·ty *or* **bump·i·ty** \ˈbəmpəd·ē, -pətē, -i\ *or* **bumpety-bump** *or* **bumpity-bump** \¦==¦==\ *adv* [*bumpety* & *bumpity* irreg. fr. 1*bump; bumpety-bump* & *bumpity-bump* redupl. of 1*bump*] **:** in a bumping, thudding, or jolting way ⟨he felt his heart go ~⟩

2bumpety *or* **bumpity** \"\ *adj* [irreg. fr. *bumpy*] **:** JOLTING, BUMPY ⟨a ~ ride in a wagon over rough roads⟩

bumpety-bump *or* **bumpity-bump** *see* 1BUMPETY\ *or* **bumpety-bumpety** *or* **bumpity-bumpity** \¦===¦===\ *n* [redupl. of 2*bump*] **:** an uneven jolting, thudding, or beating ⟨the *bumpety-bump* of the wagon over the cobblestones⟩ ⟨the nervous *bumpety-bumpety* of his heart⟩

bumph \ˈbəm(p)f\ *var of* BUMF

bump·i·ly \ˈbəmpəlē, -li\ *adv* **:** in a bumpy manner

bump·i·ness \-pēnəs, -pin-\ *n* -ES **:** the quality or state of being bumpy

bumping *pres part of* BUMP

bumping conveyor *or* **bumping trough** *n* **:** a suspended chute or trough along which broken ore or coal is conveyed by a longitudinal reciprocating action that terminates on the forward stroke with a bump

bumping die *n* **:** a die designed to form sheet-metal tubing

bumping hammer *n* **:** a usu. power-driven hammer with two broad flat faces on a narrow head used in bumping sheet metal

bumping post *n* **:** a post placed as a buffer at the end of a spur of railroad track

bumping race *n* **:** a rowing race in certain English universities in which the boats start at a fixed distance behind one another and each boat endeavors to overtake and bump the boat ahead of it so as to take its place in the following race if successful

bumping table *n* **:** a vibrating table upon which heavy minerals in a stream of water are separated from the lighter particles

bump joint *n* **:** a pipe-and-flange joint in which the end of the pipe or tubing is driven into a recess in the flange

1bump·kin \ˈbəm(p)kən\ *n* -s [perh. fr. Flem *bommekijn* small cask, fr. MD, fr. *bomme* cask + *-kijn* -kin] **:** a typically awkward blockish and utterly unsophisticated rustic ⟨they gawked up at the tall buildings like ~s⟩ **syn** see BOOR

2bump·kin *or* **bum·kin** \ˈbəm(p)kən\ *also* **boom·kin** \ˈbümk-\ *n* -s [prob. fr. Flem *boomken* little tree, fr. *boom* tree (fr. MD) + *-ken*, dim. suffix, fr. MD *-kijn;* akin to OHG *boum* tree — more at BEAM, -KIN] **:** a projecting boom: as **a :** one projecting from each bow of a ship to haul the foretack to — called also *tack bumpkin* **b :** one from each quarter for the main-brace blocks — called also *brace bumpkin;* see SHIP illustration **c :** a small outrigger over the stern of a ship to extend the mizzen

bump·kin·ly \ˈbəm(p)kənlē\ *adj* [1*bumpkin* + *-ly*] **:** like or suggesting a bumpkin

bump off *vt* [1*bump* + *off*] *slang* **:** KILL; *esp* **:** to murder with crude and brutal violence ⟨two hoodlums were *bumped off* by a rival gang⟩

bump-off \ˈ=,=\ *n* [*bump off*] *slang* **:** MURDER

bump·ol·o·gist \,bəmˈpäləjəst\ *n* -s [*bumpology* + *-ist*] **:** PHRENOLOGIST — usu. used disparagingly

bump·ol·o·gy \-jē\ *n* -ES [2*bump* + *-o-* + *-logy*] **:** PHRENOLOGY — usu. used disparagingly

bump·om·e·ter \,bəmˈpäməd·ə(r)\ *also* **bump meter** \ˈbəmp-,mēd·ə(r)\ *n* [*bumpometer* fr. 2*bump* + *-o-* + *-meter; bump meter* fr. 2*bump* + *meter* (measurer)] **:** a device that indicates irregularities in a pavement or roadbed

bumps *pl of* BUMP, *pres 3d sing of* BUMP

bump supper *n, Brit* **:** a usu. riotous celebration by a college making a certain number of bumps or retaining its first-place position in a bumping race

bump·tious \ˈbəm(p)shəs\ *adj* [1*bump* + *-tious* (as in *fractious*)] **:** presumptuously, obtusely, and often noisily self-assertive **:** somewhat arrogantly self-confident **:** OBTRUSIVE ⟨the least ~ and aggressive and the one least given to self-serving publicity —R.H.Rovere⟩ ⟨every ~ adventurer and fluent charlatan —G.B.Shaw⟩ ⟨the police keep crowds from becoming ~ —L.C.Stevens⟩ ⟨our ~, prodigal days are nearly ended —Russell Lord⟩ — **bump·tious·ly** *adv* — **bump·tious·ness** *n* -ES

bumpy \ˈbəmpē, -pi\ *adj* -ER/-EST [2*bump* + *-y*] **1 a :** having or covered with bumps ⟨a ~ road⟩ **:** NUBBY ⟨a ~ book cover⟩ **:** exhibiting protuberances ⟨a ~ face⟩ **b :** PROTUBERANT ⟨~ muscles⟩ **2 a :** causing or giving bumps or jolts ⟨a ~ ride⟩ ⟨the plane ran into ~ air⟩ **b :** rhythmically choppy **:** somewhat unpleasantly irregular ⟨an especially ~ kind of short-winded prose —S.E.Fitzgerald⟩ **c :** full of difficulties ⟨an unusually ~ life for a man of reflection —P.R.Levin⟩

bumpy ash *n* **:** BUNJI-BUNJI

bum rap *n* [8*bum*] *slang* **:** a false charge or conviction of crime esp. resulting in a prison term **:** FRAME-UP ⟨a bookie who has done five years . . . on a *bum rap* and is once more on the loose —John McCarten⟩

bums *pl of* BUM, *pres 3d sing of* BUM

bum's rush *n* [7*bum*] *slang* **1 :** forcible eviction or dismissal ⟨they gave him the *bum's rush*⟩ **2 :** any compulsion applied against one's will or before one can consider the significance or consequences of an action

bum steer *n* [8*bum*] *slang* **:** an instance of false or misleading information or directions esp. when purposely so ⟨a man who got himself a *bum steer* . . . and was attempting to brazen it out rather than admit his error —R.H.Rovere⟩

bumtrap *n* [1*bum*] *slang* **:** BAILIFF

bum·wood \ˈbəm+,-\ *n* [prob. fr. 8*bum*] **:** POISONWOOD 1

1bun \ˈbən, ˈbu̇n\ *n* -s [ME *bune, bunne*, fr. OE *bune* reed; akin to ON *buna* jet of water, clumsy leg] *dial Eng* **:** a hollow stem or stalk **:** STUBBLE

2bun \ˈbən\ *chiefly Scot var of* BOUND

3bun \ˈbən\ *n* -s [ME *bunne*, prob. fr. (assumed) MF *bugne* (whence F dial. *bugne* pancake), fr. MF *bugne* bump on the head, prob. of non-IE origin; akin to the source of Catal *bony* bump on the head] **1 a :** any of a variety of sweet or plain breads that are leavened with yeast or baking powder and shaped in a variety of forms **b :** a usu. round or oblong roll **2 :** a knot or coil of hair (as at the nape of the neck) used in dressing women's long hair

4bun \ˈbən, ˈbu̇n\ *n* -s [ScGael, root, stump, bottom; akin to MIr *bun* bottom, W *bôn* trunk, stump] **1** *chiefly dial* **:** the hind part or tail esp. of a squirrel or rabbit **2** *chiefly dial* **a :** SQUIRREL **b :** RABBIT

5bun \ˈbən\ *n* -s [perh. alter. of E dial. (chiefly Sc) *bung, bungie* intoxicated] *slang* **:** a drunken condition **:** JAG ⟨arrive at a party with a ~ on⟩

Bu·na \ˈb(y)ünə\ *trademark* — used for synthetic rubber and rubberlike materials

bunce \ˈbən(t)s\ *n* -s [origin unknown] *slang Brit* **:** unexpected gain **:** GRAVY, BONUS; *also* **:** unexpected luck

1bunch \ˈbənch\ *n* -ES [ME *bunche;* perh. akin to D *bonk* bone, mass (as of flesh), cluster (of fruits), OHG *bungo* tuber, ON *bunki* cargo, *bunga* hump, Gk *pachys* thick — more at PACHY-] **1 :** PROTUBERANCE, HUMP, SWELLING **2 a :** AGGREGATE, CLUSTER, TUFT ⟨a ~ of odds and ends out of the attic⟩ ⟨a ~ of grapes⟩ ⟨pull up a ~ of grass⟩; *esp* **:** an aggregate of things of the same kind existing as a natural group or considered together ⟨a ~ of cattle⟩ ⟨a ~ of liberals⟩ **b :** a group of friends bound together by intimate social or cultural ties ⟨he was the handiest with tools in our ~ —John O'Hara⟩ **3 :** a small irregular ore body **4 :** the filler and binder of a cigar without the wrapper **5 a :** a proposal in various card games that the current deal be called off for a new deal **b :** an alternative name for any game in which this proposal is permitted; *esp* **:** such a form of auction pitch

2bunch \"\ *vb* -ED/-ING/-ES [ME *bunchen*, fr. *bunche* protuberance] *vi* **1 :** to swell into a protuberance **:** PROTRUDE — usu. used with *out* ⟨his shoulder and arm muscles ~*ed* out with the effort of lifting⟩ **2 :** to gather into clusters, tufts, or groups — often used with *up* **3 :** to throw in playing cards for a new deal in a card game **:** assemble the cards for shuffling and dealing — compare 1BUNCH 5 ~ *vt* **1 :** to form into a bunch: as **a :** to group together **:** ASSEMBLE ⟨~*ing* cattle preparatory to shipment⟩ ⟨more than 2000 saloons that were ~*ed* at the southern end of Manhattan —John Lardner⟩ **b :** to make into a cluster or tuft ⟨onions sent to West Indian ports were always strung or ~*ed* —*Amer. Guide Series: Conn.*⟩ **c :** to fill out **:** make protuberant ⟨a raised chair that was ~*ed* out with cushions —V.S.Pritchett⟩ **d :** to form or pull or squeeze into a small compact unit ⟨I wish you wouldn't ~ the paper so —A.J.Cronin⟩ ⟨all his fingers ~*ed* together on his chest —Richard Llewellyn⟩ **e :** to make into a usu. compact pile — usu. used with *up* ⟨~*ing* up haycocks and pitching them into wagons —Christopher Rand⟩ **2 :** to assemble (railroad cars) for loading or unloading in excess of the number ordered or of the number which can be handled at one time with available loading and unloading facilities

3bunch \", ˈbu̇n-\ *vt* -ED/-ING/-ES [ME *bunchen*, perh. of imit. origin] *dial Brit* **:** to strike esp. with the foot **:** KICK

bunch bean *n* **:** KIDNEY BEAN

bunch·ber·ry \ˈbənch-—*see* BERRY\ *n* **1 :** DWARF CORNEL **2 :** the fruit of the stone bramble

bunch·er \ˈbənchə(r)\ *n* -s [2*bunch* + *-er*] **:** one that bunches: as **a :** one who makes bunches (sense 4) by rolling filler tobacco in binder leaves — called also *binder* **b :** the velocity-modulating element that effects the electron bunching in a klystron — compare CATCHER 4, RHUMBATRON

bunch evergreen *n* **:** any of several club mosses of erect bushy habit (esp. *Lycopodium obscurum*)

bunchflower \ˈ=,=\ *n* **:** a plant of the genus *Melanthium; esp* **:** a tall summer-blooming herb (*M. virginicum*) of the eastern and southern U.S. bearing a panicle of small greenish flowers

bunchflower family *n* **:** MELANTHACEAE

bunch grape *n* **:** SUMMER GRAPE

bunchgrass \ˈ=,=\ *n* **:** any of several grasses chiefly of the western U.S. which grow in tufts (as *Sporobolus airoides, Elymus condensatus, Andropogon scoparius, Oryzopsis hymenoides* and various grasses of the genus *Stipa*)

bunch·i·ly \ˈbənchəlē\ *adv* **:** in a bunchy manner ⟨knee-length coat, cocoon-shaped through the middle and wrapping ~ —Lois Long⟩

bunching *n* -s [fr. gerund of 2*bunch*] **:** the velocity modulation of an orig. steady electron beam in a klystron in such a way that the electrons travel in uniformly spaced concentrations or bunches

bunch light *n* **1 :** an open-faced metal hood in which a group of low-wattage lamps is used **2 :** a single light-source unit

bunch oyster *n* **:** COON OYSTER

bunch peanut *n* **:** a peanut having upright bushy growth with the pods clustered about the base — compare RUNNER PEANUT

bunch pink *n* **:** SWEET WILLIAM

bunch plum *n* **:** DWARF CORNEL

bunchy \ˈbənchē, -chi\ *adj* -ER/-EST [1*bunch* + *-y*] **1 a :** protruding or swelling out in a bunch or in bunches **:** showing protuberances ⟨women in ~ cotton dresses —Nadine Gordimer⟩ ⟨a round ~ face —Mary Carter Roberts⟩ **b :** growing in bunches **:** resembling a bunch **:** marked by tufts ⟨the scanty and ~ nature of the grass cover —G.R.Stewart⟩ **2** *of a mine or a vein* **:** yielding irregularly: here rich, there poor ⟨a ~ vein of silver⟩

bunchy top *n* **:** any of various plant diseases esp. caused by viruses which produce shortening of the internodes and crowding of the twigs and leaves at the shoot apex ⟨banana *bunchy top*⟩

1bun·co *or* **bun·ko** \ˈbəŋ(,)kō\ *n* -s [perh. alter. of Sp *banca* bench, banking business, bank in gambling (or, a card game), fr. It, bank, bench — more at 4BANK] **1 :** swindling by misrepresentation (as in a confidence game) **2 :** any of various games (as card games) in which the person who proposes the game expects to win by virtue of an opponent's ignorance, lack of skill, or naiveté

2bunco *or* **bunko** \"\ *vt* -ED/-ING/-S **:** to swindle by a bunco game or scheme **:** cheat or victimize in any similar way ⟨knew when he was being ~*ed* but there was not much he could do —H.A.Sinclair⟩

buncombe *var of* BUNKUM

bunco steerer *or* **bunko steerer** *n* **:** a confidence man **:** SWINDLER

1bund \ˈbən(d)\ *dial Brit var of* BOUND

2bund \ˈbənd\ *n* -s [Hindi *band*, fr. Per; akin to Skt *bandha* fetter — more at 1BAND] **1 :** an embankment used esp. in India to control the flow of water (as on a river or on irrigated land) **2 :** an embanked thoroughfare along a river or the sea esp. in the Far East

3bund \"\ *vt* -ED/-ING/-S *Far East* **:** to construct a bund (as for the control of flowing water) **:** EMBANK

4bund \ˈbu̇nd, ˈbənd, ˈbu̇nt\ *n* -s *often cap* [G, fr. MHG *bunt;* akin to MD *bont* league, MLG *bunt*, OS *gibund* bundle, OE *byndel* — more at BUNDLE] **:** FEDERATION, LEAGUE, CONFEDERACY, ASSOCIATION; *esp* **:** a politically oriented association of people

bun·da-bun·da \ˈbəndə,bəndə\ *var of* BANDY-BANDY

bun·de·li \ˈbündə(,)lē\ *n* -s *cap* [Hindi *bundelī*] **:** the dialect of Western Hindi spoken in Bundelkhand

bunder *var of* BANDAR

bun·der boat \ˈbəndə(r)-\ *n* [Hindi *bandar* harbor, landing-place, fr. Per] **:** a coastal and harbor boat in the Far East

bun·des·rat \ˈbu̇ndəs,rät, *G* -ˈrāːt\ *n* -s *usu cap* [G, fr. *bundes* (gen. of *bund* federation) + *rat* council, advice, fr. OHG *rāt* advice; akin to *rātan* to advise — more at READ] **:** a federal council esp. having legislative or executive functions: as **a :** the upper house of the German and Austrian parliaments composed of members selected by the state governments **b :** the chief executive authority of Switzerland consisting of members elected by the Federal Assembly

bun·des·staat \-dəs(h),shtät, *G* -ˈtāːt\ *n* -s *usu cap* [G, fr. *bundes* (gen. of *bund*) + *staat* state, fr. MHG *stat* condition, fr. L *status* condition, position — more at STATE] **:** a federated state **:** FEDERATION 2a — contrasted with *Staatenbund*

bun·des·tag \-də,stäk, *G* -ˈtāːk\ *n* -s *usu cap* [G, fr. *bundes* (gen. of *bund* federation) + *-tag* (fr. MHG, prob. fr. *tagen* to hold court, to hold a meeting, fr. *tag-, tac* day, fr. OHG *tag*) — more at DAY] **:** an assembly of representatives of a bund (as the assembly of the German Confederacy of 1815 or the lower house of parliament of the Federal Republic of Germany)

bundies *pl of* BUNDY

bund·ist \ˈbu̇ndəst, ˈbən-\ *n* -s *often cap* [4*bund* + *-ist*] **:** a member of a bund; *esp* **:** a member of a pro-Nazi bund

1bun·dle \ˈbəndᵊl\ *n* -s [ME *bundel*, fr. MD *bundel, bondel;* akin to OE *byndel* bundle, OHG *gibuntili* bundle, *bintan* to tie — more at BIND] **1 a :** a number of things fastened together into a mass or bunch convenient for handling or conveyance ⟨a ~ of sticks⟩ ⟨a ~ of shirts⟩ **b :** PACKAGE; *often* **:** a loose package esp. wrapped in paper **:** PARCEL, ROLL ⟨make up soiled clothes into a ~⟩ ⟨a ~ of groceries⟩ **c :** a number or group of things considered as a unit **:** LOT, COLLECTION ⟨a large ~ of mistakes⟩ ⟨a ~ of contradictions⟩ ⟨a ~ of energies⟩ **d :** a group of isoglosses running close together in the same general direction whether coinciding, diverging, converging, or crossing each other — called also *fascicle* **2 :** the amount contained in a bundle esp. as fixed for a certain commodity and sometimes used as a unit of quantity: as **a :** a board measure unit equalling 50 pounds that is used in papermaking **b :** a shipping unit of about 125 pounds that is used in papermaking **3 :** a small band or group of mostly parallel fibers (as of nerves or muscles) **:** FASCICULUS, TRACT **4 :** VASCULAR BUNDLE **5** *slang* **:** a sizable sum of money ⟨left a fortune of half a million bucks — quite a ~ for that day —Pete Martin⟩

2bundle \"\ *vb* **bundled; bundled; bundling** \-nd(ᵊ)liŋ, ÷nliŋ\ **bundles** *vt* **1 a :** to tie or bind in a bundle **:** assemble in a bundle **b :** to make into a roughly rounded loose unit ⟨he *bundled* the coat into a human outline⟩ **c :** to compress (book sections) in groups after the folding operation in bookbinding **2 :** to hustle or hurry unceremoniously often by shoving or throwing ⟨*bundled* the children off to school⟩ ⟨he *bundled* his possessions into an empty carriage —David Garnett⟩ ~ *vi* **1 a :** to prepare for departure **b :** to set off or go in a hurry or without ceremony **:** HURRY ⟨a group of servants came *bundling* from the kitchen —Charlotte Brontë⟩ **2 :** to practice bundling

bundle boy *n* **:** a boy employed by a store or market to carry articles purchased to a wrapping counter or a shipping room or sometimes outside to the purchaser's automobile

bundle branch *n, anat* **:** either of the parts of the atrioventricular bundle passing respectively to the right and left ventricles

bundle branch block *n* **:** heart block due to a lesion in one of the bundle branches

bundle browning *n* **:** a symptom of disease consisting of browning or necrosis of the vascular bundles in stems or tubers (as of the potato)

bundle burial *n* **:** the burial of the dead with arms and legs flexed; *also* **:** a secondary burial in a bundle of the bones only

bundle of his \-ˈhis\ *usu cap H* [trans. of G *hissches bündel*, after Wilhelm *His* †1934 Ger. anatomist] **:** ATRIOVENTRICULAR BUNDLE

bundle pillar *n* **:** a clustered column or pillar

bun·dler \ˈbənd(ᵊ)lə(r), ÷nlə-\ *n* -s **:** one that bundles; *esp* **:** one whose vocation is to bundle material or products for ease of handling

bundle sheath *n* **:** a compact layer of commonly parenchymatous cells forming a sheath around a vascular bundle

bundle up *vb* **:** to dress warmly or cumbrously ⟨the man *bundled up* in a sweater and heavy coat⟩ ⟨the woman *bundled up* her children in heavy jackets and woollen underwear⟩

bundle work *n* **:** commercial laundry work done by the bundle instead of by the piece

bundling *n* -s [fr. gerund of 2*bundle*] **:** the custom of unmarried couples' occupying the same bed without undressing, practiced chiefly in earlier days esp. during courtship in some British and American communities

bun·do·bust \ˈbəndə,bəst\ *n* -s [Hindi *band-o-bast*, lit., tying and binding, fr. Per] *India* **:** arrangement or settlement of details

bundocks *var of* BOONDOCKS

bund·weed \ˈbən,(d)wēd, ˈbu̇n-\ *n* [alter. of earlier *bunweed*, fr. ME *bunwed*, perh. fr. *bune* hollow stalk + *wed, weed* weed — more at 1BUN, WEED] *dial Eng* **:** any of various weedy plants (as the knapweed, ragwort, scabious, or cow parsnip)

1bun·dy \ˈbəndē\ *n* -ES [origin unknown] **:** a small often crooked Australian tree (*Eucalyptus elaeophora*) with pendulous branches

2bundy \"\ *n* -ES [prob. fr. *Bundy*, alter. of *Bundaberg*, seaport town in Queensland, Australia] *Austral* **:** TIME CLOCK

bune·most \ˈbün,mōst, ˈbēn-, -,məst\ *adj* [E dial. *bunemost, boonmost*, fr. E dial. *boon* above (short for E dial. *aboon*) + E *-most* — more at ABOON] *dial Brit* **:** UPPERMOST, HIGHEST

bun-fight \ˈ=,=\ *n* [3*bun*] *slang Brit* **:** TEA PARTY

bun foot *n* [3*bun*] **:** a slightly flattened ball foot on a piece of furniture

1bung \ˈbəŋ\ *n* -s [ME *bunge*, fr. MD *bonghe*, alter. of *bonne*, fr. LL *puncta* puncture, fr. L, fem. of *punctus*, past part. of *pungere* to prick — more at POINT] **1 :** the stopper in the bunghole of a cask; *also* **:** BUNGHOLE **2 a :** ANUS — used esp. of a domestic or game animal **b :** the cecum of a slaughter animal; *also* **:** a sausage casing made from this **3 :** a stack of ceramic ware in a sagger; *also* **:** a stack of filled saggers in a kiln

2bung \"\ *vt* -ED/-ING/-S **1 a :** to stop (as a bunghole) with a bung **:** close (as a cask); *also* **:** to enclose (as in a cask) — usu. used with *up* **b** *slang* **:** FILL, PLUG ⟨by the time the furniture was unloaded and moved in, the house was ~*ed* up to the attic⟩ **2** *slang* **:** THROW, HEAVE, TOSS ⟨~*ing* rocks through a neighbor's window⟩ ⟨in a position to ~ a spanner into the works —P.G.Wodehouse⟩ **3** *slang* **:** to bung up

3bung *n* -s [origin unknown] *obs slang* **:** PURSE; *also* **:** PICKPOCKET

4bung \ˈbəŋ\ *adj* [prob. fr. a native word in Australia] *Austral* **:** out of commission: **a :** DEAD **b :** BANKRUPT — usu. used in the phrase *go bung*

bun·ga \ˈbəŋgə\ *n* -s *usu cap* [Xhosa *i-Bunga*, fr. *bunga, bungana* to meet in council] **:** a native council in the Transkeian Territories, Union of So. Africa, having limited power to consider and act upon native interests generally

bun·ga·loid \ˈbəŋgə,lȯid\ *adj* [*bungalow* + *-oid*] **:** resembling or suggesting a bungalow ⟨when the prairie house was a pink ~ rash on the great open spaces —*Times Lit. Supp.*⟩ **:** characterized by constructions resembling bungalows ⟨depressed by the uglier and drearier parts of the town, or alarmed by its ~ outskirts —William Plomer⟩ — usu. used disparagingly

bun·ga·low \ˈbəŋgə,lō\ *n* -s [Hindi *baṅglā*, lit., (house) in the Bengal style] **1 :** a lightly built low-sweeping single-story house or cottage of the Far East (as in India) that is usu. thatched or tiled and surrounded by a veranda **2 a :** a quite solidly constructed house for permanent residence that is usu. one but sometimes one and a half stories high and that preserves the low sweeping lines and wide veranda, usu. on the front only, of the bungalow **b :** a cottage intended chiefly for summer occupancy

bun·ga·rum \,bəŋˈgärəm\ *n* -s [modif. of Telugu *baṅgāru*] **:** one of several venomous snakes of the genus *Bungarus; esp* **:** KRAIT

bun·ga·rus \-rəs\ *n, cap* [NL, fr. Telugu *baṅgāru*, fr. *baṅgāramu* gold, fr. Skt *bhṛṅgāra*] **:** a genus of exceedingly venomous Asiatic snakes including the krait and related to the cobra but with shorter fangs and without a dilatable hood

bun·gee \ˌbən¦jē\ *n* -s [origin unknown] **:** an auxiliary spring device esp. on the movable controls of an airplane designed to make the movement of the controls easier and to limit their motion; *also* **:** an elasticized cord used as a fastening or shock-absorbing device esp. for planes on the deck of a carrier

bun·ger·some \ˈbəŋgə(r)səm\ *adj* [*bunger-* (prob. alter. of *bungle*) + *-some*] *dial* **:** AWKWARD, CLUMSY

bung–eyed \ˈbəŋˌīd\ *adj* [perh. fr. 4*bung*] **:** having an eye swollen; *also* **:** BUG-EYED

bung–full \ˈ=¦=\ *adj* [1*bung* + *full*] **:** very or completely full **:** CHOCK-FULL ⟨an auto *bung-full* of children⟩ ⟨zealots who are *bung-full* of schemes —A.J.Nock⟩

bung head *n* [perh. fr. 1*bung*] **:** a tapered square head on a bolt or screw

bunghole \ˈ=ˌ=\ *n* [1*bung*] **:** an opening usu. in the bilge of a cask for filling it with or emptying it of liquids — see BARREL illustration

1**bun·gle** \ˈbəŋgəl\ *vb* **bungled; bungled; bungling** \-g(ə)liŋ\ **bungles** [perh. of Scand origin; akin to Sw dial. *bangla* to work ineffectually, Icel *banga* to hammer — more at BANG] *vi* **:** to act or work in a clumsy and awkward manner ⟨officials said and did stupid things and inexperience led to *bungling* —*Saturday Rev.*⟩ **~** *vt* **:** to do, make, perform, or handle clumsily or badly **:** MISHANDLE, BOTCH ⟨the job of cleaning up the slums was *bungled* badly by incompetent and venal administrators⟩

2**bungle** \"\ *n* -s **:** a clumsy or inadequate performance **:** BOTCH, BLUNDER ⟨a bureaucratic ~⟩

bun·gler \-g(ə)lə(r)\ *n* -s **:** a clumsy and awkward workman ⟨could not think with calmness of the possibility of appearing in the light of a ~ and an incompetent —J.C.Kirkpatrick⟩ ⟨muddleheaded ~*s* —C.W.M.Hart⟩

bun·gle·some \-gəlsəm\ *adj* **:** bungling or tending to lead to bungling ⟨a tedious and ~ enterprise⟩ ⟨carrying a load of ~ paraphernalia with him⟩

1**bungling** *adj* [fr. pres. part. of 1*bungle*] **:** UNSKILLFUL, AWKWARD, CLUMSY ⟨a ~ workman⟩ ⟨~ diplomacy —Stuart Portner⟩ — **bun·gling·ly** *adv*

2**bungling** *n* -s [fr. gerund of 1*bungle*] **:** unskillful or clumsy handling, acting, or performing **:** MISHANDLING ⟨a piece of ~ due to hot heads —H.J.Laski⟩

bun·go \ˈbəŋ(ˌ)gō\ *also* **bon·go** \ˈbäŋ-\ *n* -s [Sp *bongo*] **:** a large canoe or dugout of the southwestern U.S. and parts of Central and So. America

1**bungs** *pl of* BUNG, *pres 3d sing of* BUNG

2**bungs** \bəŋz\ *n pl but sing in constr* [prob. fr. pl. of 1*bung*] **1** *slang* **:** a ship's cooper **2** *slang* **:** a dock worker who repairs boxes and cases

bung starter *n* **:** a wooden mallet used for loosening the bung of a cask

bung·town \ˈbəŋˌtau̇n\ *n* -s [prob. fr. *Bungtown* (now Barneysville), Rehoboth, Massachusetts, where it was manufactured] **:** a copper token resembling an English halfpenny that circulated in the U.S. in the 18th and 19th centuries

bung up *vt* [2*bung*] **1** *slang* **:** BRUISE, BATTER, LACERATE ⟨his eyes and face were all *bunged up* from the fistfight⟩ **2 :** to damage or dent considerably ⟨an automobile body pretty *bunged up* from an accident⟩

bungy *n* -s [Hindi *bhaṅgī* — more at BHANGI] **:** BHANGI

bu·ni·na·wa *or* **bu·ni·na·hua** \ˌbünəˈnäwə\ *n, pl* **buninawa** *or* **buninawas** *or* **buninahua** *or* **buninahuas** *usu cap* [native name] **1 :** a people that constitute a branch of the Cashibo **2 :** a member of the Buninawa people

bun·ion \ˈbənyən\ *n* -s [prob. irreg. fr. *bunny* (swelling)] **1 :** an enlargement of the first joint of the great toe resulting from excessive growth of bone at the joint margin associated with a bursal sac filled with fluid **2 :** the egg mass on a berried female blue crab

bun·ji–bun·ji \ˌbənjē¦bənjē\ *n* -s [native name in Australia] **:** an Australian tree (*Flindersia schottiana*) closely related to the flindosa and having bark that contains a poison

1**bunk** \ˈbəŋk\ *n* -s [perh. fr. Ar, an odoriferous root] **1 :** CHICORY **2 :** POISON HEMLOCK

2**bunk** \"\ *n* -s [prob. short for *bunker*] **1 a :** a built-in frame that usu. has low sides and a canvas, mesh, or spring bottom and that serves as a bed or sleeping place (as on a ship or in a camp) and often is one of a series in tiers **b :** a sleeping place **:** BED **2 a :** a heavy timber or crossbeam on a logging sled or car on which the logs rest **b :** a log car or log truck **3 :** a long usu. wood or concrete trough or manger for feeding cattle — called also *feed bunk*

3**bunk** \"\ *vb* -ED/-ING/-S *vi* **1 :** to occupy a bunk or bed ⟨~ in the attic⟩ **:** share a bed ⟨having no hotel room, he ~*ed* with a friend for the night⟩ **2 :** to stay the night **:** occupy sleeping quarters **:** put up ⟨~ at a neighbor's house for a couple of days⟩ **~** *vt* **1 :** to place (logs) on bunks **2 :** to provide with a bunk, bed, or sleeping quarters ⟨I don't know where the exec means to ~ you so we can't move you into a stateroom just yet —Wirt Williams⟩

4**bunk** \"\ *vi* -ED/-ING/-S [perh. fr. 3*bunk* (in the phrase *to bunk across* to go across by ship)] *slang Brit* **:** to go away esp. as an escape **:** LEAVE, SCRAM ⟨suddenly got frightened and ~*ed* —Margery Allingham⟩

5**bunk** \"\ *n* -s *slang chiefly Brit* **:** a hurried departure usu. in escaping something — used in the phrase *do a bunk* ⟨the pranksters did a ~ before the police arrived⟩

6**bunk** \"\ *n* -s [short for *bunkum*] *slang* **:** BUNKUM, NONSENSE

7**bunk** \"\ *vt* -ED/-ING/-S *slang* **:** FOOL, DECEIVE, MISLEAD ⟨on both sides of the Senate aisle there are men . . . who will go down to defeat before they will try to ~ the people —Blair Moody⟩

8**bunk** \"\ *vi* -ED/-ING/-S [prob. alter. of 1*bump*] **:** BUMP, RUN ⟨~ into a post⟩ ⟨~ into a friend on the street⟩

bunk bed *n* **:** a bed for two people with one sleeping place above the other in the manner of tiered bunks

bunk car *n* [2*bunk*] **:** CAMP CAR

1**bun·ker** \ˈbəŋkə(r)\ *n* -s [alter. of earlier Sc *bonker*, perh. alter. of E *banker* covering for a bench — more at BANKER] **1 a** *Scot* **:** a chest or box often used as a window seat **b :** a large bin or other storage place: as (1) **:** a large compartment on shipboard for storing the ship's coal or oil (2) **:** metal containers in a refrigerator railroad car for ice or other refrigerants (3) **:** a coal bin in a locomotive terminal; *also* **:** a coal receptacle at the rear of a tank engine **c :** a fortification chamber mostly below ground level built of reinforced concrete or similar material and usu. provided with embrasures; *also* **:** a dugout that is reinforced (as with logs or bags of sand) and usu. has firing slits **2 a** *chiefly Scot* **:** a small sand hole or pit **b :** a sand trap or embankment with soil exposed constituting a hazard on a golf course **c :** OBSTACLE, DIFFICULTY

bunk bed

2**bunker** \"\ *vb* **bunkered; bunkered; bunkering** \-k(ə)riŋ\ **bunkers** *vi* **:** to fill a ship's bunker with coal or oil **~** *vt* **1 :** to put (as oil or coal) into a bunker ⟨the flattop . . . will ~ oil to refuel its protective screen of ships —*Newsweek*⟩ **2 a :** to hit (a golf ball) into a bunker **b :** to stop the advance or progress of; *also* **:** to entangle in difficulties **3 :** to provide or protect with bunkers ⟨a well-*bunkered* golf course⟩ ⟨the ~*ed* Japanese position —*Infantry Jour.*⟩

3**bunker** \"\ *n* -s [by shortening] **:** MOSSBUNKER

bun·ker·age \ˈbəŋk(ə)rij\ *n* -s **1 :** the filling of a bunker (as of a ship) with oil or coal ⟨~ service⟩ **2 :** the facilities for the storing of oil or coal ⟨an oil ~ that consisted of two huge tanks⟩

bunker charge *n* **:** the charge for loading coal or oil into a ship's bunker

bunker coal *n* **:** coal on a collier for its own use

bunker fuel *or* **bunker oil** *n* **:** any of various fuel oils used esp. on ships

bunker suit *or* **bunker clothes** *n* [3*bunk* + *-er*] **:** fire fighters' apparel that consists of trousers or overalls tucked into a pair of boots and is designed for dressing quickly when answering an alarm

bunk fatigue *n, slang* **:** sleeping or resting in bed esp. during the daytime

bunkhouse \ˈ=ˌ=\ *n* **:** a rough simple building providing sleeping quarters usu. with bunks (as for workers on construction projects or for logging crews, ranch hands, or harvest crews)

bunk·ie \ˈbəŋkē\ *n* -s [2*bunk* + *-ie*] **:** BUNKMATE

bunk in *vi* [3*bunk*] **:** stay in one's bed or bunk ⟨don't think you can *bunk in* late —L.M.Uris⟩

bunkload \ˈ=ˌ=\ *n* [2*bunk*] **:** a load of logs not over one log in depth

bunkmate \ˈ=ˌ=\ *n* **:** a person occupying the same sleeping quarters as oneself or as another esp. in one of the armed services; *esp* **:** such a person occupying the next bunk or bed

bunko *var of* BUNCO

bunko steerer *var of* BUNCO STEERER

bunks *pl of* BUNK, *pres 3d sing of* BUNK

1**bun·kum** *or* **bun·combe** \ˈbəŋkəm\ *n* -s [*Buncombe* County, N.C.; fr. a remark made by Felix Walker *fl*1820, U.S. representative from the Congressional district including this county, who explained a seemingly irrelevant speech in Congress by saying that he was speaking to Buncombe] **:** insincere public talk or action **:** NONSENSE, CLAPTRAP, FOOLISHNESS

2**bunkum** \"\ *adj* [perh. fr. CanF *le buncum sa* (F *il est bon comme ça*; it is good as it is] **1** *dial* **:** of outstanding quality **:** very fine ⟨these are ~ apples⟩ **2** *dial* **:** in good health **:** well and strong ⟨I don't feel so ~⟩

bun·nia \ˈbənyə\ *n* -s [Hindi *baniyā* — more at BANYAN] **:** BANYAN 1a

bun·ning \ˈbəniŋ\ *n* -s [origin unknown] **:** a timber shelf or platform in a mine working on which stones and other waste material are deposited

1**bun·ny** \ˈbəni, ˈbu̇ni\ *n* -ES [ME *bony*, prob. fr MF *bugne* bump on the head — more at BUN] *dial Eng* **:** SWELLING; *specif* **:** a swelling on an animal's joint

2**bun·ny** \ˈbənē, -ni\ *n* -ES [4*bun* + *-y*] **1** *also* **bunny rabbit :** RABBIT; *esp* **:** a young rabbit — often used as a pet name **2 :** BISMARCK BROWN

bunny cat *n* [2*bunny*] **1 :** ABYSSINIAN CAT **2 :** a bobtail cat

bunny hop *n* **:** a short leap in figure skating often to gain speed that is made by hopping from a forward edge to the toe point of the free foot and stepping off immediately onto the forward edge of the take-off foot

bunny hug *n* [2*bunny*] **:** an American ballroom dance in ragtime rhythm in which the couple hold each other closely and which was esp. popular at the early part of this century

bun ochra *n* -s [1*bun* + *ochra* (alter. of *okra*)] *India* **:** the bast fiber of the Caesar weed

1**bu·no·dont** \ˈbyünəˌdänt\ *adj* [NL *Bunodonta*] **:** having tubercles on the crown of the molar teeth — opposed to *lophodont*

2**bunodont** \"\ *n* -s [NL *Bunodonta*] **:** one of the Bunodonta

bu·no·don·ta \ˌbyünəˈdäntə\ *n pl, cap* [NL, fr. *bun-* (fr. Gk *bounos* mound, hill) + *-odonta*; fr. the tuberculated molar teeth] *in some classifications* **:** a division of the Artiodactyla including the hogs and hippopotami

bu·no·loph·o·dont \ˌbyünəˈläfəˌdänt\ *adj* [*bun-* (fr. Gk *bounos*) — *-o-* + *loph-* + *-odont*] **1** *of teeth* **:** having the outer cusps blunt cones and the inner cusps modified to form transverse ridges (as in the tapirs) **2** *of an animal* **:** having bunolophodont teeth

1**bu·no·mas·to·dont** \-ˈmastəˌdänt\ *adj* [NL *Bunomastodontidae*] **:** of or relating to the Bunomastodontidae

2**bunomastodont** \"\ *n* -s [NL *Bunomastodontidae*] **:** one of the Bunomastodontidae

bu·no·mas·to·don·ti·dae \ˌ=ˌ==ˈdäntəˌdē\ *n pl, cap* [NL, fr. *bun-* (fr. Gk *bounos*) + *-o-* + *mast-* + *-odont-*, *-odon* + *-idae*] *in former classifications* **:** a family of extinct mastodons with trefoils or conelets of enamel in the valleys between the main crests of the molars that is now considered invalid because it is based on no type and is replaced in modern taxonomy by the family Gomphotheriidae

bu·no·se·le·no·dont \ˌbyünōsə¦lēnəˌdänt\ *adj* [ISV *bun-* (fr. Gk *bounos*) + *-o-* + *selen-* + *-odont*] **1** *of teeth* **:** having inner cusps that are blunt cones and outer ones modified into longitudinal crescents (as in the extinct titanotheres) **2** *of an animal* **:** having bunoselenodont teeth

bu·nos·to·mum \byüˈnästəməm\ *n, cap* [NL, fr. *bun-* (fr. Gk *bounos*) + *-o-* + *-stomum*] **:** a genus of nematode worms including the hookworms of sheep and cattle

buns *pl of* BUN

bun·sen burner \ˈbən(t)sən-*sometimes* ˈbünzən- *or* ˈbu̇n(t)sən-\ *n, usu cap 1st B* [after Robert Wilhelm *Bunsen* †1899 Ger. chemist who invented it] **:** a burner used esp. in the laboratory that consists typically of a straight tube four or five inches long with a gas orifice and holes near the bottom for admission of air, the mixture of gas and air formed burning at the top with a feebly luminous but intensely hot flame

Bunsen burner: *1* gas inlet, *2* barrel, *3* air inlet, *4* movable collar

bun·sen·ite \-əˌnīt\ *n* -s [Robert Wilhelm *Bunsen* + E *-ite*] **:** a mineral NiO consisting of nickel monoxide occurring in green octahedrons

bun·sen–kirch·hoff law \-ən'kirˌkȯf-, -rk-, ˌhȯf-\ *n, usu cap B&K* [after Robert Wilhelm *Bunsen* and Gustav Robert *Kirchhoff* †1887 Ger. physicist, its formulators] **:** a statement in spectroscopy: each chemical element has an emission spectrum of bright lines and an absorption spectrum of dark lines which are characteristic of the element

1**bunt** \ˈbənt\ *n* -s [perh. fr. LG *bunt* bundle, fr. MLG; akin to OE *byndel* bundle — more at BUNDLE] **1 :** the middle part of a square sail; *also* **:** the part of a furled square sail which is gathered up in a bunchy roll at the center of the yard **2 :** the central or bagging portion of a fishing net; *also* **:** something resembling this

2**bunt** \"\ *n* -s [origin unknown] **:** a destructive kernel smut of wheat caused by either of two fungi (*Tilletia caries* or *T. foetida*) and characterized by replacement of the normal grains with considerably smaller greasy masses of fishy smelling smut spores — called also *stinking smut*

3**bunt** \", ˈbu̇nt\ *n* -s [prob. alter. of 4*bun*] *dial Brit* **:** a rabbit tail

4**bunt** \ˈbənt\ *vb* -ED/-ING/-S [alter. of *butt* (to strike)] *vt* **1 a :** to strike or push with the horns or head; BUTT ⟨the goat ~*ed* the small boy so that he sat down with a jolt⟩ **b :** to strike or push (a railroad car) without coupling to the striking car or locomotive **2 :** to block or push (the ball) in a game of baseball within the infield by meeting with a loosely held bat and no swing **~** *vi* **:** to bunt something ⟨the team coach instructed the next batter to ~⟩ ⟨a goat very good at ~*ing*⟩

5**bunt** \"\ *n* -s **1 :** a push or shove esp. with the head **2 :** the act of bunting in a baseball game; *also* **:** a bunted ball — see DRAG BUNT

6**bunt** \"\ *n* -s [origin unknown] **:** a prehistoric stone arrowhead or spearhead having a blunt straight or curved tip

bun·tal \bu̇nˈtäl, ˈbəntᵊl\ *n* -s [Tag *buntál* talipot palm fiber, hat made of talipot palm fiber] **:** a very fine white Philippine fiber obtained from the stalks of unopened leaves of the talipot palm and used in making hats

bunt·ed \ˈbəntəd\ *adj* [2*bunt* + *-ed*] **:** affected with bunt ⟨~ wheat⟩

bun·ter \ˈbu̇ntə(r), ˈbən-\ *adj, usu cap* [G *bunter (sandstein)* mottled sandstone] **:** of or relating to the lowest division of the European Triassic — see GEOLOGIC TIME table

bunt·er dog \ˈbəntə(r)-\ *also* **bunter** *n* -s [*bunter* (fr. 4*bunt* + *-er*) + *dog* (holding device)] **:** a gripping device for a planing machine consisting of a piece having a hook end to engage in the T slot of the table and a setscrew

1**bun·ting** \ˈbəntiŋ, -tēŋ\ *n* -s [ME *buntynge*] **1 :** any of various stout-billed birds of *Emberiza* and related genera usu. included in the finch family (Fringillidae) and distinguished from typical finches by their more angular gape and often by a bony knob on the palate — see INDIGO BUNTING, REED BUNTING **2 a :** COWBIRD **b :** BOBOLINK

2**bunting** \"\ *n* -s [perh. fr. gerund of E dial. *bunt* to sift (meal), fr. ME *bonten*] **1 a :** a lightweight loosely woven fabric of plain weave used chiefly for flags and festive decorations and draperies **b :** FLAGS **2 :** festive decorations made of bunting or sometimes of paper; *esp* **:** such decorations in the colors of the national flag or the national coat of arms for patriotic occasions

3**bunting** \"\ *n* -s [*bunting* (term of endearment in the nursery rhyme "Bye, baby bunting"), perh. alter. of 2*bunny*] **1 :** a thickly napped fabric of natural or synthetic fiber used esp. for infant wear **2 :** an outdoor garment for infants consisting of a large envelope with attached hood

bunting 2

bunting crow \"-\ *n* [part modif. (influenced by E 1*bunting*), part trans. of D *bonte kraai*, lit., pied crow] **:** HOODED CROW 1

bunting iron \"-\ *n* [by folk etymology (influence of *bunting*, gerund of 4*bunt*) fr. *punty iron* punty, fr. *punty* + *iron*] **1 :** BLOWPIPE 4 **2 :** a flat piece of metal against which molten glass is bunted to stop its elongation in the forming period

bunt·line \ˈbəntˌlīn, -ˌlən\ *n* [1*bunt* + *line*] **:** one of the ropes attached to the foot of a square sail to haul the sail up to the yard for furling — see SAIL illustration

buntline cloth *n* **:** a strengthening piece of canvas on the forward part of a square sail from foot to bellyband where the strain and chafe of the buntlines is greatest

buntline hitch *n* **:** a knot consisting of two half hitches used to secure the buntlines to the foot of a square sail

bun·ton \ˈbəntᵊn\ *or* **bun·ting** \", -tən, -tiŋ\ *n* -s [E dial. *bunting* piece of squared timber] **:** DIVIDER 3

bunts *pl of* BUNT, *pres 3d sing of* BUNT

1**bun·ty** \ˈbəntē\ *n* -ES [E dial. *bunty* tailless fowl, perh. fr. 1*bunt* + *-y*] **:** RING-NECKED DUCK

2**bunty** \"\ *adj* -ER/-EST **:** short and stout **:** STUMPY ⟨the little ~ streetcars on the long, single track —Booth Tarkington⟩

bu·ñu·e·lo \ˌbünyəˈwā(ˌ)lō\ *n* -s [Sp; akin to Catal *bunyol* buñuelo, *bony* bump on the head — more at BUN] **:** a flat semisweet cake made mainly of eggs, flour, and milk fried in deep fat and usu. served with sugar and cinnamon or cane syrup

bun·ya bun·ya \ˌbənyə¦bənyə\ *or* **bunya** *or* **bunya pine** *n* -s [Australian *bunya bunya*, *bunya*, perh. fr. *bunya* shade] **:** an Australian coniferous tree (*Araucaria bidwillii*) bearing seeds about two inches long which have the flavor of roasted chestnuts when ripe and are a staple food of the aborigines among whom the tree is hereditary property and is protected by law

bun·yan·esque \ˌbənyə¦nesk\ *adj, usu cap* [John *Bunyan* †1688 Eng. preacher and writer + E *-esque*] **1 :** resembling or suggesting the allegorical writings of John Bunyan (as *Pilgrim's Progress*) ⟨*Bunyanesque* names like Sir Adroit and Cunning and The Dragon Evasive⟩ **2** [Paul *Bunyan*, legendary giant lumberjack associated with Canada and the northern and northwestern U.S.] **:** of or befitting the tales of Paul Bunyan ⟨such *Bunyanesque* characters as Babe the Blue Ox and Big Joe the Cook⟩; *esp* **:** of fantastically large size ⟨if all of a year's consumption were brewed in a *Bunyanesque* retort and decanted into the Niagara river —*Time*⟩

bun·yip \ˈbənˌyip\ *n* -s [native name in Australia] **1** *Austral* **:** a legendary wild animal usu. described as a monstrous swamp-dwelling man-eater **2** *Austral* **:** IMPOSTOR, PHONY

buon fres·co \bwȯnˈfre(ˌ)skō\ *n* [It, lit., good fresco] **:** FRESCO 1a(1)

1**buoy** \ˈbüi, ˈbu̇i, ˈbȯi — ˈbȯi *is usual in pronunc of "life buoy"*\ *n* -s [ME *boye*, fr. (assumed) MF *boie* (whence MF & F *bouée* buoy), of Gmc origin; akin to OHG *bouhhan* sign — more at BEACON] **1 :** 1FLOAT 4; *esp* **:** an object floating in a body of water and moored to the bottom to mark a channel or to point out the position of something beneath the water (as an anchor, rock, or shoal) **2 :** LIFE BUOY

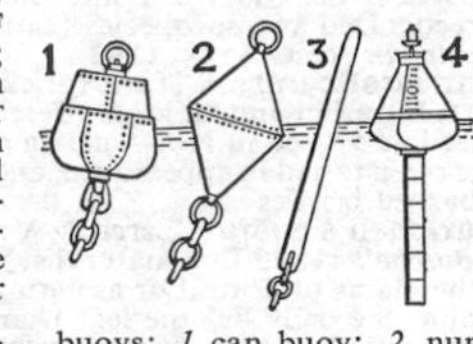

buoys: *1* can buoy; *2* nun buoy; *3* spar buoy; *4* whistling buoy

2**buoy** \"\ *vb* -ED/-ING/-S [in sense *vt* 1, fr. 1*buoy*; in other senses, prob. fr. Sp *boyar* to float, fr. *boya* buoy, fr. (assumed) MF *boie*] *vt* **1 :** to provide with or mark by a buoy ⟨~ an anchor⟩ ⟨~ a channel⟩ **2 a :** to keep afloat on a liquid **:** keep from sinking — usu. used with *up* ⟨the raft was ~*ed* up by airtight oil drums⟩; *also* **:** to keep floating in the air — usu. used with *up* ⟨for a moment the falling leaf was ~*ed* up by a rising air current⟩ **b :** SUPPORT, SUSTAIN — usu. used with *up* ⟨with a patience ~*ed* only by the stimulus of a great idea —Waldemar Kaempffert⟩ ⟨~*ed* up during the trying period by high hopes of recovery⟩ ⟨an economy ~*ed* by the dramatic postwar growth of industry —*Time*⟩ **3 a** *archaic* **:** RAISE, LIFT — usu. used with *up* **b :** to raise the spirits of **:** make happier (as after a period of emotional depression) — usu. used with *up* ⟨the waltz ~*ed* her up —Scott Fitzgerald⟩ **~** *vi* **1** *obs* **:** to swell up **:** flood up — usu. used with *up* **2 :** to come to the surface of a liquid ⟨bound and thrown into the water . . . they ~*ed* up like a cork —*Amer. Guide Series: Conn.*⟩

buoy·age \ˈbüi-ij, ˈbu̇(i)ij, ˈbȯi-ij\ *n* -s **1 a :** BUOYS **b :** a system of buoys (as for marking a channel) **2 :** the fee for the use of a buoy for mooring a boat

buoy·an·cy \ˈbȯiənsē, ˈbüyən-, ˈbüiən-, ˈbȯiyən-, ˈbu̇in-\ *also* **buoy·ance** \-n(t)s\ *n, pl* **buoyancies** *or* **buoyances** [*buoyancy* fr. *buoyant* + *-cy*; *buoyance* fr. *buoyancy*, after such pairs as E *elegancy*: *elegance*] **1 a :** the property of floating on the surface of a liquid or in a fluid **:** the tendency of a body to float or to rise when submerged in a fluid being dependent upon the excess of the specific gravity of the fluid over that of the body **b :** the property of a fluid by which it exerts an upward force on a body placed in it; *specif* **:** the upward force exerted on a lighter-than-air craft due to the air which it displaces **2 a :** resilience of spirit **:** the ability to emerge from or to elude depression **:** LIGHTHEARTEDNESS, SPRIGHTLINESS **:** the ability to recover quickly from discouragement **b :** generating or resulting in such lightheartedness or recovery ⟨a novel of great ~ and optimism⟩ **3 :** LIGHTNESS, SPRINGINESS ⟨walking with amazing ~ considering his increasing age⟩ **4 :** the property (as of prices or business activity) of maintaining a satisfactorily high level ⟨the future of the fund depends on the ~ of national wealth —*Meet New Zealand*⟩ ⟨~ of bank deposits —*Economist*⟩

buoyancy tank *n* **:** an airtight tank fitted into the stern or bow of a small boat (as a lifeboat) to keep it afloat if it fills with water or capsizes

buoy·ant \-nt\ *adj* [prob. fr. Sp *boyante*, fr. pres. part. of *boyar*] **1 :** having the quality or property of buoyancy ⟨iron is ~ in mercury⟩ ⟨held up by the ~ water⟩ ⟨floating in midair in the ~ gas⟩ ⟨a person cheerful of face and ~ of spirits⟩ ⟨a ~ stock market⟩ ⟨walking with a ~ step⟩ **2 :** light and floating ⟨a wonderfully delicate and ~ evening gown⟩ **syn** see ELASTIC

buoyant force *n* **:** the upward force exerted by any fluid upon a body placed in it — compare ARCHIMEDES' PRINCIPLE

buoy·ant·ly *adv* **:** in a buoyant manner ⟨go at a hard task cheerfully and ~⟩

buoy·ant·ness *n* -ES **:** the quality or state of being buoyant

buph·thal·mic \(ˈ)b(y)üfˈthalmik, ¦bəf-\ *adj* [ISV *buphthalm-* (fr. NL *buphthalmos*) + *-ic*] **:** of, relating to, or affected with buphthalmos

buph·thal·mos \b(y)üfˈthalməs, ˌbəf-, -ˌmäs\ *also* **buph·thal·mia** \-ˌmēə\ *n, pl* **buphthalmos·es** \-ˌməsəz, -ˌmäsəz\ *also* **buphthalmi·as** \-ˌmēəz\ [*buphthalmos* fr. NL, fr. Gk *bo-* (fr. *bous* cow, ox) + *ophthalmos* eye; *buphthalmia* fr. NL, fr. *buphthalm-* (fr. *buphthalmos*) + *-ia* — more at COW, OPHTHALMIA] **:** marked enlargement of the eye usu. congenital and attended by symptoms of glaucoma

buph·thal·mum \-lməm\ *n, cap* [NL, fr. Gk *bouphthalmon* oxeye (flower), fr. *bo-* (fr. *bous*) + *-ophthalmon* (fr. *ophthalmos*)] **:** a genus of Eurasian perennial herbs (family Compositae) sometimes cultivated in gardens for their bright yellow-rayed flower heads — see OXEYE

bu·pleu·rum \byüˈplu̇rəm\ *n, cap* [NL, fr. L *bupleuron* hare's-ear (*Bupleurum rotundifolium*), alter. of Gk *boupleuros*, fr. *bou-* (fr. *bous*) + *-pleuros* (fr. *pleura* rib) — more at PLEURISY] **:** a genus of widely distributed herbs (family Umbelliferae) having simple often stem-clasping leaves and greenish yellow flowers

bu·plev·er \-ˈplevə(r)\ n -s [F *buplèvre* hare's-ear, fr. L *bupleuron*] **:** a plant of the genus *Bupleurum*

¹bu·pres·tid \-ˈprestəd\ adj [NL *Buprestidae*] **:** of or relating to the Buprestidae

²buprestid \"\ n -s [NL *Buprestidae*] **:** a beetle of the family Buprestidae

bu·pres·ti·dae \-tə,dē\ n pl, cap [NL, fr. *Buprestis*, type genus + *-idae*] **:** a large family of beetles having rather short serrate antennae, an elongate form usu. sharply tapering behind, and an exceedingly hard thick integument often of brilliant metallic colors and producing larvae that are fleshy legless grubs that usu. bore in wood and are often destructive to trees

bu·pres·tis \-təs\ n, cap [NL, fr. L, poisonous beetle causing cattle that ate it in the grass to swell up and die, fr. Gk *bouprēstis*, fr. *bou-* (fr. *bous*) + *-prēstis* (fr. *prēthein* to blow up) — more at FROTH] **:** the type genus of the family Buprestidae

buq·sha or **buk·sha** \ˈbəkshə\ or **bog·sha** \ˈbägshə\ n -s [Ar *buqsha*] **1 :** a unit of value of the Yemen Arab Republic equal to 1/40 rial — see MONEY table **2 :** a coin representing one buqsha

bur var of BURR

bur abbr **1** bureau **2** buried

bu·ran \büˈrän\ n -s [Russ, of Turkic origin; akin to Turk & Kazan Tatar *buran*, Kirghiz *boran*] **:** a northeasterly wind of gale force in Russia and central Asia usu. identified with sandstorms in summer and blizzards in winter; *also* **:** a sandstorm or blizzard of this kind — compare PURGA

burbark \ˈ⸗,⸗\ n -s [*burr* (prickly envelope) + *bark*] **1 :** the bark of certain tropical shrubs of the genus *Triumfetta* (esp. *T. rhomboidea* and *T. semitriloba*) that yield a fiberlike jute **2 :** a plant that yields burbark

Bur·ber·ry \ˈbərbərē, -,berē\ trademark — used for various usu. wool fabrics used esp. for coats for outdoor wear

¹bur·ble \ˈbər|bəl, ˈbə̄|, ˈbəi|\ vb **burbled; burbled; burbling** \|b(ə)liŋ\ **burbles** [ME *burblen*, prob. of imit. origin] vi **1 :** to make a bubbling sound **:** GURGLE ⟨brooks . . . that ~ past our own home windows —Gladys B.Stern⟩ **2 :** to talk incessantly and usu. with enthusiasm **:** PRATTLE ⟨passengers who ~ on about how small . . . the world has become —Richard Thruelsen⟩ **3 :** to separate from the surface of an airfoil and break up into eddies **:** become turbulent ~ vt **1** *Scot* **:** CONFUSE, MUDDLE **2 :** to utter with unrestrained enthusiasm **:** GUSH

²burble \"\ n -s [ME *burble* bubble, fr. *burblen*, v.] **1** *Scot* **:** DISORDER, TROUBLE **2 :** a bubbling noise; *esp* **:** burbling talk **3 :** the breaking up into eddies of the streamline flow of air about a body (as an airplane wing)

burble point n **:** the angle of attack of an airfoil at which the first signs of burble appear

bur·bler \|b(ə)lə(r)\ n -s **:** one that burbles

bur·bly \|b(ə)lē\ adj, sometimes -ER/-EST [ME, fr. *burble* bubble + -y] **:** BURBLING, BUBBLING ⟨a novel, told in ~, panting tones —*New Yorker*⟩

bur·bot \ˈbərbət\ n, pl **burbot** *also* **burbots** [ME *borbot*, fr. MF *bourbotte, bourbete*, fr. *bourbeter* to burrow in the mud, fr. OF, fr. *bourbe* mud, prob. of Celt origin; akin to MIr *berbaim* I boil, W *berwi* to boil, Gaulish *Borvo*, deity associated with medicinal springs; akin to L *fervēre* to boil — more at BURN] **:** a freshwater fish (*Lota lota*) that is related to the cod, has two small barbels on the nose and a larger one on the chin, and is usu. held to exist in distinct forms in the northern parts of the Old World and the New, that of the latter being recognized as a subspecies (*Lota lota maculosa*) — called also *eelpout*; see LAWYER, LING

bur bristlegrass n [*burr* (prickly envelope) + *bristle grass*] **:** a Eurasian annual grass (*Setaria verticillata*) that is naturalized as a weed in No. America esp. in the northeastern states, is often tufted in appearance, and has spikelets with backward-barbed bristles

bur·chell's zebra \ˈbərchəlz-\ n, usu cap B [after William J. *Burchell* †1863 Eng. naturalist] **:** a zebra (*Equus burchelli*) of the plains of central or eastern Africa with stripes continuing onto the belly but the legs nearly or wholly unstriped — see CHAPMAN'S ZEBRA, GRANT'S ZEBRA

bur chervil n **:** WILD CHERVIL 1

bur clover or **burr clover** n **:** any of several clovers of the genus *Medicago* (esp. *M. denticulata*) having prickly seed pods

bur cucumber n **1 :** a herbaceous vine (*Sicyos angulatus*) of the U.S. naturalized in Europe **2 :** GHERKIN 1

¹burd \ˈbərd\ n -s [ME *bird, byrd, burde*, perh. alter. of OE *brȳd* bride — more at BRIDE] *chiefly Scot* **:** a young woman

²burd \"\ *Scot var of* BIRD

burd-alane \ˈbərdə¦lān\ adj [prob. fr. Sc *burd, bird* bird + *alane* alone — more at ALANE] *Scot* **:** all alone **:** SOLITARY

bur·de·kin duck \ˈbərdəkən-\ n, usu cap B [*Burdekin* river, Queensland, Australia] **:** a white-headed sheldrake (*Tadorna radjah*) of tropical Australia and islands to the north

burdekin plum n, usu cap B **1 :** an Australian tree (*Pleiogynium solandri*) of the family Anacardiaceae **2 :** the edible red fruit of the Burdekin plum

burdekin vine n, usu cap B **:** an Australian vine (*Vitis opaca*) bearing large edible tubers

¹bur·den \ˈbərdᵊn, ˈbə̄d-, ˈbəid-\ n -s [ME *burden, burthen*, fr. OE *byrthen*; akin to OS *burthinnia* burden, OHG *burdī*, ON *byrthr*, Goth *baurthei*; derivatives fr. the root of OE *beran* to carry — more at BEAR] **1 a :** something that is carried **:** LOAD ⟨a donkey hidden under his ~ of firewood⟩ ⟨a ~ of dust carried by the wind⟩ ⟨images carry the ~ of the poem's effect⟩ **b** *obs* **:** a child in the womb **c :** something that is borne as a duty, obligation, or responsibility often with labor or difficulty ⟨the ~ of empire⟩ ⟨executive ~s⟩ ⟨tax ~s⟩ **d :** the aggregate load of instruments supplied with current by an instrument transformer in proration usu. downward from the actual load in the circuit being metered **2 :** something that weighs down, oppresses, or causes worry ⟨she came with little but her ~ of fear⟩ **:** ENCUMBRANCE ⟨to have the ~ of a foreign tongue removed was . . . an inexpressible relief —William Black⟩ **3 :** LADING — usu. used in the phrases *beast of burden, ship of burden* **4** *dial* **:** something the soil brings forth **:** CROP, PRODUCE **5 :** the capacity of a ship for carrying cargo ⟨a ship of a hundred tons ~⟩ **6** *Scots law* **:** an obligation, restriction, or encumbrance upon a person or property **7 :** the proportion of ore and flux in relation to the coke or other fuel in the charge of an iron blast furnace **8 :** the part of the cost of manufacturing that does not contribute directly to production **:** OVERHEAD; *specif* **:** all manufacturing costs other than direct labor and materials **9 a :** OVERBURDEN 2 **b** (1) **:** the resistance that an explosive charge must overcome in breaking the rock adjacent to a drill hole in mining (2) **:** the material that must be moved by the blast **10 :** the degree of infestation of an animal body esp. with parasitic worms

²burden \"\ vt **burdened; burdened; burdening** \-d(ᵊ)niŋ\ **burdens 1 :** to load with or as if with something heavy, grievous, unwieldy, difficult, or unmanageable ⟨the numerous pretty things . . . which ~ the tables —Herbert Spencer⟩ ⟨~*ed* his men with endless labors⟩ **2 :** to trouble, vex, or afflict with nonmaterial burdens ⟨I will not ~ you with a lengthy account⟩ **:** CHARGE ⟨~*ing* his conscience with a grave moral responsibility⟩ **3** *archaic* **:** BLAME, CHARGE **4 :** to regulate the ratio of ore and flux to fuel in charging an iron blast furnace

syn ENCUMBER, CUMBER, WEIGH, WEIGHT, LOAD, LADE, SADDLE, CHARGE, TAX: BURDEN stresses the fact of bearing a heavy or grievous weight, often figuratively, sometimes literally ⟨men *burdened* with such intellectual tasks as theirs —H.O.Taylor⟩ ENCUMBER is likely to suggest cumbersome and unwieldy burdens making progress difficult, literally or figuratively ⟨*unencumbered* with luggage they would soon overtake the coach —Charles Dickens⟩ ⟨the overheavy richness and *encumbered* gait of the Asiatic style —Matthew Arnold⟩ CUMBER suggests what is unwieldy, bulky, and cluttering but is less likely to stress motion than ENCUMBER ⟨beyond the power of Rome, *cumbered* already with so many duties —John Buchan⟩ ⟨the whole Palace had been burnt in 1698, and its roofless walls still *cumbered* the river bank —G.M.Trevelyan⟩ Usu. figurative, WEIGH in such phrases as *weigh on one* or *weigh one down* suggests the depressing effect of some burden carried over a long period ⟨the tyranny at Bulaire *weighed* so heavily on the countryside —T.B.Costain⟩ ⟨for nearly a century the Dutch problem had *weighed* on Spain —Stringfellow Barr⟩ WEIGHT now often suggests a tendency to inclination, bias, slanting, often through a contrived arrangement ⟨there is no doubt that the new magazine will be heavily *weighted* on the American side —Crane Brinton⟩ ⟨those who fear that such planning councils . . . will be nothing but a further addition to an already *weighted* bureaucracy are in error —Norman Thomas⟩ LOAD is likely to suggest a full or more than adequate supply ⟨her hands . . . *loaded* with rings —Victoria Sackville-West⟩ and may suggest a packing with significance or perhaps the slanting associated with WEIGHT ⟨the discoverers of a new theory . . . may have *loaded* a useful notion with more than it can bear —B.N.Cardozo⟩ ⟨his absolutism *loaded* legality in his favor —Francis Hackett⟩ LADE, more common in the past participle *laden* than in other uses, is occas. used in situations involving burdens or grief ⟨with rue my heart is *laden* —A.E.Housman⟩ SADDLE may suggest an inescapable oppressive burden or responsibility lasting over a long period ⟨the reason being that . . . the abbeys were *saddled* with multitudes of statutory masses —G.G.Coulton⟩ ⟨the indemnity for the Opium War . . . *saddled* the Chinese government with an international debt —Owen & Eleanor Lattimore⟩ CHARGE in this series may refer to either heavy responsibilities or packed or loaded significances ⟨I *charge* myself with him; let him remain with me —Charles Dickens⟩ ⟨all the perennial, elemental processes of nature . . . were *charged* for psalmist and prophet with spiritual significance —J.L.Lowes⟩ TAX indicates continuing heavy demands ⟨the labor of calculating and recording would have *taxed* energy beyond endurance —Edward Clodd⟩

³burden \"\ n -s [by folk etymology (influence of ¹*burden*) fr. *bourdon*] **1** *archaic* **:** a bass or accompanying part **:** DRONE ⟨I would sing my song without a ~; thou bringest me out of tune —Shak.⟩ **2 :** the verse repeated in a song or the return of the theme at the end of each stanza **:** CHORUS, REFRAIN **3 :** a recurring or emphasized idea or theme **:** central topic **:** GIST ⟨the ~ of the argument⟩ ⟨words of praise are fraught with that desire to hear lost laughter which is the ~ of every century's lament —Agnes Repplier⟩

burdened adj [fr. past part. of ²*burden*] **:** responsible by the nautical rules of the road to keep clear of another ship ⟨a sailboat on the port tack is ~⟩ — contrasted with *privileged*

bur·den·less \-dᵊnləs\ adj **:** being without a burden

bur·den·man \-mən, -,man\ n, pl **burdenmen** [¹*burden* + *man*] **:** CRANE FOLLOWER

burden of proof [trans. of L *onus probandi*] **:** the duty of proving a disputed presumption, assertion, or charge ⟨the *burden of proof* is upon the critic⟩; *specif* **:** the duty of proving a particular position in a court of law under penalty against the party on whom the duty is imposed

burdenous adj, obs **:** BURDENSOME

burdens pl of BURDEN, *pres 3d sing of* BURDEN

bur·den's grass \ˈbərdᵊnz-, ˈbə̄d-, ˈbəid-\ n, usu cap B [prob. fr. the name *Burden*] **:** REDTOP 1

bur·den·some \-ᵊnsəm\ adj **:** difficult or distressing to carry or to bear **:** OPPRESSIVE ⟨a ~ load⟩ ⟨a ~ responsibility⟩ **syn** see ONEROUS

bur·den·some·ly adv **:** in a burdensome manner

bur·den·some·ness n -ES **:** the quality or state of being burdensome

burd·ie \ˈbərdē\ n -s [¹*burd* + *-ie*] *Scot* **:** GIRL, WOMAN ⟨the bonnie ~s —Robert Burns⟩

burdock \ˈ⸗,⸗\ n -s [*burr* (prickly envelope) + *dock*] **1 :** any plant of the genus *Arctium* **2 :** COCKLEBUR 1

burds pl of BURD

¹bure \ˈbu̇r\ *Scot var of* BORE

²bu·re \ˈbü(,)rā\ n -s [Fijian] **:** a large house or temple in the Fiji islands

³bure \ˈbyu̇(ə)r, ˈbu̇ər\ n -s [F, coarse woolen cloth] **:** a moderate yellowish brown that is redder, lighter, and stronger than Bismarck brown, bronze, or maple sugar and lighter, stronger, and slightly redder than cinnamon brown

bu·reau \ˈbyu̇(,)rō, ˈbyü- *also esp when no pause follows* -,rə\ n, pl **bureaus** *also* **bureaux** [F, office, desk, cloth covering for desks or tables, coarse woolen cloth, fr. OF *burel* coarse woolen cloth, fr. (assumed) OF *bure* coarse woolen cloth (whence MF *bure*), fr. (assumed) VL *bura*, alter. of LL *burra* shaggy cloth, prob. of non-IE origin; akin to the source of Gk *berberion* shabby garment] **1 a** *Brit* **:** a writing desk; *esp* **:** one having drawers and a slant top — called also *writing bureau* **b :** a low chest of drawers with a mirror for use in a bedroom — compare CHIFFONIER, DRESSER **2 a :** a specialized administrative unit ⟨the university testing ~⟩; *esp* **:** a subdivision of an executive department of a government ⟨the Internal Revenue *Bureau* of the Department of the Treasury⟩ **b :** a usu. commercial agency that serves as a clearinghouse or intermediary for exchanging information, making contacts, or coordinating cooperative activities ⟨credit ~⟩ ⟨speakers' ~⟩ **c :** a branch of a newspaper, newsmagazine, or wire service in an important news center ⟨the Washington ~ of the Associated Press⟩ **3 :** an executive committee or small directing body: as **a :** the small body of officers in each chamber of the French parliament that controls proceedings in its chamber **b** [Russ *byuro*, fr. F *bureau*] **:** the policy-forming committee of the Communist party of the U.S.S.R. **4** or **bureau print** usu cap B **:** a postage stamp precanceled by the U.S. Bureau of Engraving and Printing

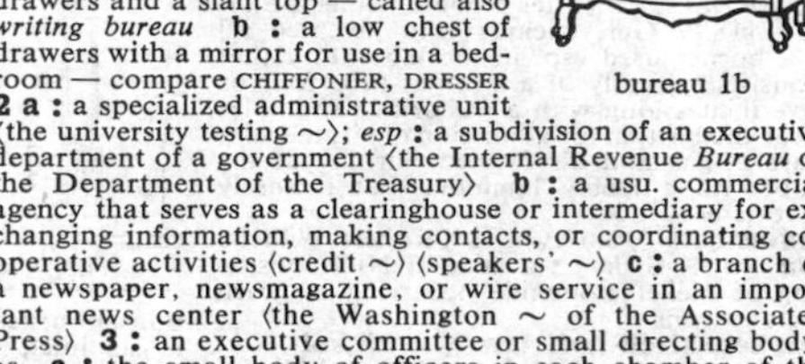

bureau 1b

bu·reauc·ra·cy \byu̇ˈräkrəsē, byu̇ˈ-, byəˈ- *sometimes* ÷bəˈ- or -rōk-\ n -ES [F *bureaucratie*, fr. *bureau* + *-cratie* -cracy] **1 a** (1) **:** the whole body of nonelective government officials ⟨criticized the growth of the ~⟩ (2) **:** a particular group of government officials ⟨Uncle Sam's vast overseas ~ —Carter Henderson⟩ **b :** the administrative policy-making group in any large organization ⟨a cleavage between the ~ and the working membership of the unions⟩ **2 :** systematic administration characterized by specialization of functions, objective qualifications for office, action according to fixed rules, and a hierarchy of authority **3 a :** a system of administration marked by constant striving for increased functions and power, by lack of initiative and flexibility, by indifference to human needs or public opinion, and by a tendency to defer decisions to superiors or to impede action with red tape ⟨inveighed against the evils of ~⟩ **b :** the body of officials that gives effect to such a system ⟨caught in the meshes of a timid and heartless ~⟩

bu·reau·crat \ˈbyu̇rə,krat, ˈbyü-, -rō,-, *usu* -ad·+V\ n -s [F *bureaucrate*, fr. *bureau* + *-crate* -crat] **:** an official of a bureau or a member of a bureaucracy; *esp* **:** a government official confirmed in a narrow rigid formal routine or established with great authority in his own department

bu·reau·crat·ic \¦⸗⸗¦krad·|ik, -at|, |ēk\ adj [F *bureaucratique*, fr. *bureau* + *-cratique* -cratic] **:** of, relating to, or resembling a bureaucrat or a bureaucracy — **bu·reau·crat·i·cal·ly** \|ək(ə)lē, |ēk-, -li\ adv

bu·reau·crat·ism \¦⸗⸗ *as at* BUREAUCRAT + ,krad·,izəm *or* -a,ti-; ⸗ˈ⸗ *as at* BUREAUCRACY + ,krə,tizəm\ n -s **:** a bureaucratic system **:** BUREAUCRACY

bu·reauc·ra·ti·za·tion \byu̇,räkrəd·əˈzāshən, byu̇,-, byə,-, -krə,tīˈz- *sometimes* ÷bə,- *or* -,rōk-\ n -s **:** the action or result of bureaucratizing ⟨~ of economic life and the growth of the octopus state —David Dubinsky⟩

bu·reauc·ra·tize \⸗ˈ⸗rə,tīz\ vt -ED/-ING/-S [F *bureaucratiser*, fr. *bureaucratie* bureaucracy + *-iser* -ize] **:** to make bureaucratic **:** subject to bureaucracy

bureau print n, usu cap B **:** BUREAU 4

bur·el \ˈbərəl\ var of BORREL

bu·re·lage \¦bu̇rə¦läzh\ n -s [F, fr. *burèle, burelle* barrulet (back-formation fr. *burelé* barruly) + *-age*] **:** a fine network or allover pattern of lines or dots printed on the face or back of stamp paper as a protection against fraudulent changes — compare MOIRÉ

bu·re·lé \¦bu̇rə¦lā\ adj [F, lit., barruly, fr. OF] **:** having a burelage ⟨~ paper⟩ ⟨~ pattern⟩

bur·el·ly or **bu·re·ly** \ˈb(y)u̇rəlē\ *also* **bu·ru·lée** \-r(y)ə,lā\ or **bu·ru·ly** \-r(y)əlē\ adj [OF *burelé*, fr. *burel* coarse woolen cloth — more at BUREAU] **:** BARRULY

bures pl of BURE

bu·rette \byüˈret\ n -s [F, fr. MF, cruet esp. for sacramental wine, alter. of *buirette* cruet, fr. *buire* pitcher (perh. fr. OF, alter. of *buie*, of Gmc origin and akin to OE *būc* pitcher, belly) + *-ette* — more at BUCKET] **1** *or* **bu·ret :** a laboratory apparatus consisting typically of a graduated glass tube with a small aperture and stopcock and used for delivering measured quantities of liquid or for measuring the liquid or gas received or discharged **2 :** a cruet esp. for sacramental wine

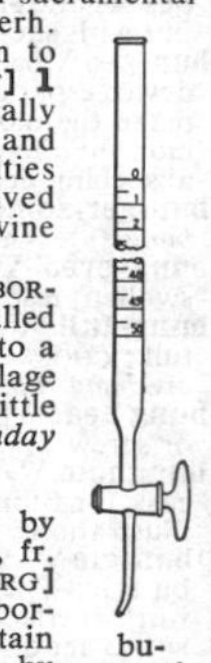
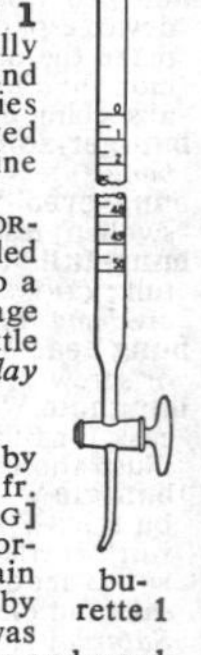
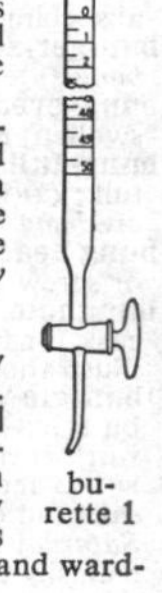
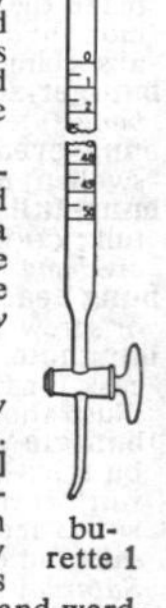

burette 1

burfish var of BURRFISH

burg \ˈbərg\ n -s [OE *burg, burh* — more at BOROUGH] **1 :** an ancient or medieval fortress or walled town **2 a :** CITY, TOWN ⟨mushroomed . . . into a booming ~ of 36,000 —*Newsweek*⟩ **b :** a village typically unimportant and out of the way ⟨little mountain ~s not down on the map —*Boston Sunday Herald*⟩

burg abbr **1** burgess **2** burgomaster

bur·gage \ˈbərgij\ n -s [ME, property held by burgage tenure, fr. MF *bourgage*, lit., burgage, fr. OF, *bourg, borc* town + *-age* — more at BOURG] **1 :** a tenure by which real property in English boroughs was held of the king or other lord for a certain yearly rent — compare SOCAGE **2 :** a tenure by which real property in Scottish royal burghs was held directly of the king for the service of watching and warding

bur·gall \ˈbər,gōl\ n -s [origin unknown] **:** CUNNER b

bur·ga·mot \ˈbərgə,mät, -,mət, *usu* -d·+V\ *var of* BERGAMOT

bur·gao *also* **bur·gau** \bərˈgau̇\ *or* **bur·go** \-gō\ n -s [AmerSp & F & Pg; AmerSp *burgao* & F *burgau*, fr. Pg *burgó, burgão*, fr. Tupi *perigoá*] **:** a common top shell (*Livona pica*) of the West Indies whose flesh is esteemed as food and whose shell is used in making buttons and ornamental novelties

bur·gee \,bərˈjē, ˈ⸗,⸗\ *also* **bou·gee** \büˈjē, ˈ⸗,⸗\ n -s [perh. fr. F dial. (Jersey) *bourgeais* shipowner, fr. MF *borjois, borgeis* shipowner, master of the house, freeman of a borough, fr. OF, master of the house, freeman of a borough] **1 :** a swallow-tailed flag used esp. by ships for signals and house flags **2 :** the usu. triangular identifying flag of a yacht club flown by the boats of members

burgee command pennant n **:** a personal command pennant flown by U.S. Naval vessels to denote an officer below flag rank commanding a division of warships or a major subdivision of an aircraft wing — compare BROAD COMMAND PENNANT

burgees

¹bur·geon *or* **bour·geon** \ˈbərjən, ˈbə̄j-, ˈbəij-\ n -s [ME *burjon, burjoun* bud, fr. OF *burjon*, fr. (assumed) VL *burrion-, burrio*, fr. LL *burra* shaggy cloth; prob. fr. the downiness of some buds — more at BUREAU] **:** BUD, SPROUT

²burgeon *or* **bourgeon** \"\ vi -ED/-ING/-S [ME *burjonen, burjounen*, fr. *burjon, burjoun*, n.] **:** to grow or begin to grow like a plant **:** DEVELOP ⟨hope that the festival will ~ slowly but steadily —*N.Y.Times*⟩: as **a :** to be full to the point of bursting **:** SWELL ⟨the great ~*ing* of a full barn —Meridel Le Sueur⟩ **b :** to spring up suddenly **:** SPROUT ⟨only stick a root or a seed in the ground for some lush green thing to ~ . . . like magic —Marcia Davenport⟩ **c :** to expand rapidly and widely **:** FLOURISH ⟨the love of the narrative and the hero ~*ed* in the drum songs —Jeremy Ingalls⟩ ⟨tiny events which ~ into national alarums —Herman Wouk⟩ **d :** to burst into bloom **:** BLOSSOM ⟨when the flame trees and jacaranda are ~*ing* —Alan Carmichael⟩

burg·er \ˈbərgər; ˈbə̄gə(r, ˈbəig-\ n -s [*-burger*] **1 :** a flat cake of ground or chopped meat or meat substitute fried or grilled and served between slices of bread **2 :** a sandwich containing a burger; *esp* **:** HAMBURGER

-burg·er \,⸗⸗\ n comb form -s [*hamburger*] **1 a :** patty of a (specified) kind of food usu. meat or a meat substitute ⟨porkburger⟩ ⟨nutburger⟩ **b :** sandwich made of such a patty ⟨porkburger⟩ **2 :** sandwich with a filling consisting of a hamburger patty topped with a (specified) food ⟨cheeseburger⟩

bur·gess \ˈbərjəs, ˈbə̄j-, ˈbəij-\ n -ES [ME *burgeis*, fr. OF *borjois, borgeis*, fr. *borc* town, fr. L *burgus* fortified place] **1 :** a citizen of a British borough ⟨the plaintiff was a ~ of Aylesbury and as such entitled to vote for two Members of Parliament —T.E.May⟩ **2 :** a magistrate or member of the governing body of a town or borough; *specif* **:** the chief executive officer of a borough in Pennsylvania **3 a :** a member of the British Parliament formerly representing a borough, corporate town, or university **b :** a representative in the popular branch of the legislatures of colonial Maryland and Virginia.

burgh *like* BOROUGH\ n -s [ME — more at BOROUGH] **1** *archaic* **:** BOROUGH **2 :** CITY, TOWN; *specif* **:** an incorporated town in Scotland possessing a charter and having local jurisdiction of certain services — see PARLIAMENTARY BURGH, POLICE BURGH

burgh·al \ˈbərgəl\ adj **:** of or relating to a burgh or municipal corporation **:** URBAN

burgh·er \ˈbərgər; ˈbə̄gə(r, ˈbəig-\ n -s [G *bürger* & D *burger*; G *bürger* fr. MHG *burgære, burger* freeman of a borough, fr. OHG *burgāri* inhabitant of a town or city, fr. *burg* fortified place, city; D *burger* fr. MD *burgher* freeman of a borough, fr. MHG *burgære, burger*] **1 a :** a resident of a town **:** TOWNSMAN **b :** a member of the middle class **:** a prosperous solid citizen ⟨shock the Boston ~s out of their staid decorum —Van Wyck Brooks⟩ **2** *usu cap* **:** a member of the party in the Scottish Secession Church that held it permissible for members to take an oath requiring acceptance of the authorized religion of the realm **3 a** *usu cap* **:** a Ceylonese of mixed blood; *specif* **:** one of Dutch descent **b** [Afrik *burger*, fr. D] **:** a citizen of the former Dutch republics of So. Africa

bur·gher·hood \-,hu̇d\ n -s **:** the status or condition of a burgher

bur gherkin n [*burr* (prickly envelope) + *gherkin*] **:** GHERKIN 1

bur·gher·ly adj **:** of or relating to a prosperous solid citizen

burgh·master \ˈbə·rə+,-\ n [by folk etymology (influence of *burgh*) fr. earlier *bargh-master* — more at BARMASTER] *Brit* **:** BARMASTER

¹bur·glar \ˈbərglər; ˈbə̄glə(r, ˈbəig-\ n -s [AF *burgler*, fr. ML *burglator, burgulator*, prob. alter. of *burgator*, fr. *burgatus*, past part. of *burgare* to commit burglary, fr. L *burgus* fortified place, of Gmc origin; akin to OHG *burg* fortified place — more at BOROUGH] **:** one who commits burglary

²burglar \"\ vb -ED/-ING/-S *Brit* **:** BURGLARIZE

burglar alarm n **:** a device for automatically giving an alarm in case of burglary

bur·glar·i·ous \,bərˈgla(a)rēəs\ adj [*burglary* + *-ous*] **1 :** of, involving, or resembling burglary ⟨a ~ entry⟩ ⟨no adequate notification was given to the Indians of this ~ measure —H.L.Ickes⟩ **2 :** of or suitable for the use of a burglar ⟨~ tools⟩ — **bur·glar·i·ous·ly** adv

bur·glar·ize \ˈbərglə,rīz, ˈbə̄g-, ˈbəig-\ vb -ED/-ING/-S vt **:** to break into and steal from ~ vi **:** to commit burglary **syn** see ROB

burglarproof \¦⸗⸗¦⸗\ adj **:** proof against burglars or burglary ⟨a ~ safe⟩

bur·glary \ˈbərglərē, ˈbə̄g-, ˈbəig-, -ri\ n -ES [AF *burglarie*, fr. *burgler* + *-ie* -y] **:** the act of breaking into a building illegally esp. with intent to steal; *specif* **:** the act of breaking into and entering the dwelling house of another at night with felonious intent — see THEFT; compare HOUSEBREAKING

burglary insurance n **:** insurance against loss or damage resulting from or following the unlawful breaking and entering of designated premises or places of safekeeping

bur·gle \ˈbərgəl\ vb **burgled; burgled; burgling** \-g(ə)liŋ\ **burgles** [back-formation fr. *burglar*] **:** BURGLARIZE

burgo var of BURGAO

bur·go·master \ˈbərgə, ˈbə̄gə, ˈbəigə+\ *also* **bur·gher·master** \R -gə(r), -R -gə+\ n -s [part modif., part trans. of D *burgemeester*, fr. *burg* town (fr. MD *burch*) + *meester* master; akin to OHG *burg* fortified place, town, city] **1 :** the chief magistrate of a town in some European countries **:** MAYOR **2 :** GLAUCOUS GULL

bur·go·net \ˈbərgənət, ¦⸗⸗¦net\ n -s [modif. of MF *bourguig-*

notte, fr. *bourguignon* Burgundian, fr. *Bourgogne* Burgundy; fr. its use by Burgundian soldiers] : either of two 16th century helmets: **a** : a light helmet resembling a morion but having cheekpieces and sometimes a nosepiece **b** : a visored helmet resembling an armet

bur·goo \'bər,gü, (,)bər'gü\ *n* -s [origin unknown] **1** : oatmeal gruel **2** : hardtack and molasses cooked together **3 a** : a savory highly seasoned stew or thick soup containing several kinds of meat and vegetables orig. served at political rallies, barbecues, picnics, and community occasions **b** : a picnic at which burgoo is served

bur grass *n* [*burr* (prickly envelope) + *grass*] : a grass of the genus *Cenchrus*

bur·grave \'bər,grāv\ *n* -s *often cap* [modif. of G *burggraf*, fr. MHG *burcgrāve*, fr. *burc* fortress, town (fr. OHG *burg* fortified place) + *grāve* count, fr. OHG *grāvo*, *grāvio* count, overseer; akin to OFris *grēva* overseer, MD *grave, greve*, MLG *grēve*, and perh. to Goth *gagrefts* decree] **1** : the military governor of a German city in the 12th and 13th centuries **2** : a noble ruling by hereditary right a German castle or town and its adjacent lands — compare LANDGRAVE, MARGRAVE

burgs *pl of* BURG

¹bur·gun·di·an \bə(r)'gəndēən, ,bər'-, bə̄'-, bəi'-\ *n* -s *usu cap* [*Burgundy* + E *-an*, n. suffix] **1** : a member of a Germanic people that entered Gaul early in the 5th century A.D. and established the kingdom of Burgundy **2** : a native or inhabitant of the prerevolutionary French province of Burgundy — called also *Bourguignon*

²burgundian \bə(r)'g-, ¦bər¦g-, (')bə̄¦g-, (')bəi¦g-\ *adj, usu cap* [*Burgundy* + E *-an*, adj. suffix] : of or relating to Burgundy or the Burgundians

bur·gun·dy \'bərgəndē, 'bə̄g-, 'bəig-\ *n* -ES [*Burgundy*, region in east central France] **1** *usu cap* **a** : any of the red or white table wines from vineyards in the departments of Côte d'Or, Yonne, and Saône-et-Loire, France, usu. possessing stronger flavor and heavier body than Bordeaux wines **b** : a table wine that resembles the red Burgundy of France but is produced elsewhere and that is usu. darker red and heavier-bodied than claret (sense 1b) though sometimes made from the same grapes **2** *often cap* **a** : a variable color averaging a dark grayish reddish brown that is redder and slightly stronger than carbuncle and redder and duller than average brown mahogany **b** : a blackish purple that is redder and less strong than average eggplant

burgundy mixture *n, usu cap B* : a fungicide similar to Bordeaux mixture but containing sodium carbonate instead of lime

burgundy pitch *n, usu cap B* [trans. of F *poix de Bourgogne*] **1** : a yellowish brown or reddish brown hard viscous resin obtained as an exudation from the Norway spruce and used esp. formerly in medicinal plasters **2** : resin from any of various pines or firs sometimes mixed with other substances (as turpentine)

burgundy violet *n, often cap B* : MANGANESE VIOLET

burhead \'=,=\ *n* [*burr* (prickly envelope) + *head*] **1** : CLEAVERS **2** : a plant of the genus *Echinodorus*

burh·el \'bərəl\ *var of* BHARAL

bu·rhin·i·dae \byü'rinə,dē\ *n pl, cap* [NL, fr. *Burhinus*, type genus + *-idae*] : a family (coextensive with the superfamily Burhenoidea of the Charadrii) of large long-legged wading birds that resemble the plovers and comprise the stone curlews

bu·rhi·nus \byü'rīnəs\ *n, cap* [NL, fr. Gk *bou-* (fr. *bous* cow, ox) + NL *-rhinus*; fr. an incorrect illustration showing a broad bill — more at COW] : the type genus of Burhinidae including a number of typical stone curlews — see THICK-KNEE

bu·ri \bü'rē, 'bürē\ *n* -s [Tag *buri*] **1** : TALIPOT PALM **2** : BUNTAL

buri·al \'berēəl\ *n* -s *often attrib* [ME *berial*, alter. (influenced by *-al*, n. suffix) of *beriel, buryel*, back-formation fr. *beriels, buryels* tomb (taken as a plural), fr. OE *byrgels*; akin to OS *burgisli* tomb; derivative fr. the root of OE *byrgan* to bury — more at BURY] **1** : a place of interment : GRAVE, TOMB ⟨artifacts occurring in ~s were few —G.W.Hewes⟩ **2 a** (1) : the act or ceremony of burying ⟨the ~ took place yesterday⟩ (2) : the process of being buried ⟨~ of the deposits by sediment⟩ **b** : the act or process of irrevocably dismissing, abandoning, or putting away : LOSS, ABANDONMENT ⟨the ~ of dangerous illusions —*N.Y.Times*⟩ **3** : an interred human body or its remains — see PRIMARY BURIAL, SECONDARY BURIAL

burial case *n* : CASKET 3

burial ground *n* : a piece of land used for burying the dead : CEMETERY

burial mound *n* : a mound erected over the dead; *esp* : one constructed by the Indian Mound Builders of No. America

buriat *usu cap, var of* BURYAT

bu·ri·dan's ass \'byürədᵊnz-, -dənz-\ *n, usu cap B* [after Jean Buridan †ab1358 Fr. philosopher, who is reputed to have posed the problem] : a hypothetical dilemma in which a person is postulated as presented with two equally attractive and attainable alternatives and therefore loses freedom of choice

buried *past of* BURY

buried hill *n* : an elevation on an ancient land surface now concealed by younger sedimentary rocks

buried suture *n* : a surgical stitch not appearing above the skin

buried valley *n* : a depression in an ancient land surface now concealed by younger deposits

bur·i·er \'berēə(r)\ *n* -s [ME *buryere*, fr. OE *byrgere*, fr. *byrgan* + *-ere* -er] : one that buries

buries *pres 3d sing of* BURY, *pl of* BURY

bu·rin \'byürən, 'bərən\ *n* -s [F, perh. fr. Catal *buri*, perh. of Celt origin; akin to MIr *bern, berna* gap, chasm; akin to OE *borian* to bore — more at BORE] **1** : an engraver's tool having a tempered steel shaft ground obliquely to a sharp point at one end and inserted into a handle at the other — called also *graver* **2** : a flint tool with a point like that of a chisel found chiefly in upper Paleolithic sites of western Europe and in Mesolithic sites of Siberia

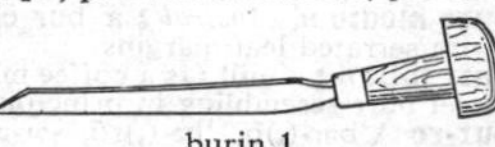
burin 1

bu·rin·ist \-nəst\ *n* -s : ENGRAVER

bu·ri·on \'byürēən, bür'yōn\ *n* -s [MexSp *burrión*, perh. alter. of Sp *gorrión* sparrow] *Southwest* : HOUSE FINCH

buri palm *n* : TALIPOT PALM

buri straw *n* : BUNTAL

bu·ri·ti *or* **bu·ri·ty** \¦bürə¦tē\ *n, pl* **buritis** *or* **burities** [Pg *buriti* — more at MURITI PALM] : MURITI PALM

¹bur·ka \'bürkə\ *n* -s [Russ, prob. fr. *buryĭ* dark brown (of a horse), prob. of Turkic origin; akin to Turk *bur* red like a fox; the Turkic word prob. fr. Per *bōr* reddish brown; akin to Skt *babhru* reddish brown — more at BROWN] : a coarse cloak worn esp. in Russia

²bur·ka *or* **bur·kha** *or* **bour·kha** \"\ *n* -s [Hindi *burqa'*, fr. Ar *burqu'*] : a loose enveloping garment with usu. veiled eyeholes that is worn in public by Muslim women esp. of India and Pakistan

burke \'bərk\ *vt* -ED/-ING/-s [after William *Burke* †1829 Ir. criminal, executed for this crime] **1** : to murder by suffocation or strangulation in order to obtain a body to be sold for dissection **2 a** : to suppress quietly or indirectly : hush up ⟨she had never believed such a thing as the *burking* of the enquiry into the raid possible —H.W.Nevinson⟩ **b** : to set aside without consideration or decision : BYPASS, AVOID ⟨~ the issue⟩

burk·ean \'bərkēən\ *adj, usu cap* [Edmund *Burke* †1797 Brit. statesman + E *-an*] : of, relating to, or resembling Edmund Burke or his political philosophy

burke·ite \'bər,kīt\ *n* -s [William Edmund *Burke* b1880 Am. chemical engineer + E *-ite*] : a mineral $Na_6(CO_3)(SO_4)_2$ consisting of a carbonate-sulfate of sodium

bur·kun·daz \¦bərkən¦däz\ *n* -ES [Hindi *barqandāz*, fr. Per, fr. *barq* lightning (fr. Ar) + *andāz* thrower] : an armed guard or policeman of 18th and 19th century India

burk·wood viburnum \'bər,kwüd-\ *n, usu cap B* [after Albert *Burkwood* b1890 and Arthur *Burkwood* b1888 Brit. nurserymen] : a nearly evergreen shrub (*Viburnum burkwoodii*) having leaves with shiny upper and gray tomentose lower surface and heads of pink-flushed flowers

¹burl \'bərl, 'bə̄l, 'bəil, *esp bef pause or cons* 'bər·əl\ *n* -s [ME *burle*, fr. (assumed) MF *bourle* tuft of wool (fr. OF *burle*), fr. (assumed) VL *burrula*, dim. of LL *burra* shaggy cloth — more at BUREAU] **1** : a knot or lump in thread or cloth **2 a** : a hard woody growth often of a flattened hemispherical form that occurs on the trunks or branches of trees usu. in association with adventitious buds and is used to make bowls and veneers **b** : veneer made from such burls **c** : a mottled figure in the grain produced by cutting through such burls

²burl \"\ *vt* -ED/-ING/-s [ME *burlen*, fr. *burle*, n.] : to finish (cloth) by inspecting and repairing usu. by hand any imperfections (as loose threads and knots)

³burl \"\ *n* -s [prob. alter. (influenced by *birl*) of *whirl* (in the expression *give it a whirl*)] *Austral* : ATTEMPT, TRY ⟨give it a ~⟩

bur·la \'bürlə, -(,)lä\ *n, pl* **bur·le** \-(,)lā\ *or* **burlas** [It, joke] **1** : a musical composition or movement of a humorous or playful and often boisterous character **2** : an interpolated comic episode in the commedia dell' arte usu. involving a practical joke — compare LAZZO

bur·la·de·ro \,bürlə'de(,)rō\ *n* -s [Sp, fr. *burlar* to deceive, make fun of, fr. *burla* joke] : a wooden shield set parallel to and a little distance out from the barrera behind which bullfighters can take shelter if pursued ⟨safe behind a ~ . . . he found that his fever to fight bulls had all drained away —Tom Lea⟩

¹bur·lap \'bər,lap, 'bə̄,-, 'bəi,-\ *n* -s [alter. of earlier *borelap*, perh. fr. ²*bore* (of a cannon) + *lap* (rag)] **1** : a coarse heavy plain-woven fabric usu. of jute or hemp used for bagging and wrapping and in furniture and linoleum manufacture — called also *gunny, hessian* **2** : a material resembling burlap but of lighter weight used in interior decoration and for clothing

²burlap \"\ *vt* **burlapped; burlapped; burlapping; burlaps** : to wrap in or cover with burlap ⟨a balled and *burlapped* evergreen⟩

bur·lap·per \-pə(r)\ *n* -s : one that puts burlap coverings on cloth for shipment

burlaw *var of* BYRLAW

bur·le·cue *or* **bur·ley·cue** \'bərlē,kyü, 'bə̄l-, 'bəil-\ *n* -s [by alter.] : ²BURLESQUE 3

burled \'bər(ə)ld, 'bə̄ld, 'bəild\ *adj* [¹*burl* + *-ed*] : having a burl figure ⟨a humidor of ~ walnut⟩

burl·er \'bərlər; 'bə̄lə(r, 'bəil-\ *n* -s [²*burl* + *-er*] **1** : one that removes loose threads, knots, and other imperfections from cloth **2** : one that inspects rugs before the finishing process, mends dropped stitches on the back, and pulls matching yarn into spots where tufts are missing or shearing is uneven

bur·les·ca \bür'leskə, ,bər-\ *n* -s [It, fem. of *burlesco*] : BURLA 1

¹bur·lesque \bər¦lesk, (')bə̄¦l-, (')bəi¦l-, ,bə(r)'l-\ *adj* [F, fr. It *burlesco*, fr. *burla* joke, fr. Sp, prob. modif. of LL *burra* trifle, bit of nonsense, perh. fr. *burra* shaggy cloth — more at BUREAU] **1** *archaic* : DROLL, JOCULAR, ODD **2** : marked by an effect of comic or grotesque imitation or exaggeration usu. with the intent of mocking or making ridiculous : derisively imitative ⟨a ~ account of the adventures of a knight errant⟩ ⟨a ~ version of the heroic epic⟩ ⟨a favorite bulldog, whose . . . great corpulence gave it a ~ resemblance to its master —Sir Walter Scott⟩ **3** : of, relating to, or having the characteristics of burlesque entertainment ⟨a ~ house⟩ ⟨~ jokes⟩ ⟨jolt the chorus regulars out of their usual sloppy, tawdry, ~ style —Flora Lewis⟩ — **bur·lesque·ly** *adv*

²burlesque \" — '=,= *is esp freq for sense 3*\ *n* -s **1 a** : literary composition or dramatic representation that ridicules something, usu. the serious and dignified (as Samuel Butler's *Hudibras*) but sometimes the trivial and commonplace (as Alexander Pope's *Rape of the Lock*) by means of grotesque exaggeration or comic imitation ⟨the literature of ~⟩ **b** : a work (as a play or novel) of this kind ⟨a first-class ~ in response . . . to Scott's "Ivanhoe" —Harvey Breit⟩ **2** : a grotesque likeness or exaggerated imitation : CARICATURE ⟨he has become a perversion of its ideals and a ~ of his own earlier hopes —J.W.Aldridge⟩ **3** *also* **bur·lesk** \"\ : theatrical entertainment of a broadly humorous often earthy character consisting of comic skits, striptease acts, and songs and dances performed by soloists or a chorus **syn** see CARICATURE

³burlesque \"\ *vb* -ED/-ING/-s *vt* : to make ridiculous by burlesque : make the subject of a burlesque : MOCK ⟨each of the three dancers *burlesqued* his own style —John Martin⟩ ⟨the act that ~s a magician sawing a person in half —Henry La Cossitt⟩ ~ *vi* : to employ burlesque **syn** see COPY

bur·lesqu·er \-kə(r)\ *n* -s : one that burlesques; *specif* : an actor in burlesque

burlet *n* -s [ME, fr. MF *bourrelet*, fr. OF *borrelet*, fr. *borrel, bourel* cushion (dim. of *borre, bourre* padding, fr. LL *burra* shaggy cloth) + *-et* — more at BUREAU] : a padded roll of cloth formerly used for decoration on a child's cap or a woman's headdress

bur·let·ta \bür'led·ə, ,bər-\ *n* -s [It, dim. of *burla* joke] : a usu. entirely musical comic opera popular in England in the latter half of the 18th century

¹bur·ley \'bərlē, 'bə̄l-, 'bəil-, -li\ *n* -s *often cap* [prob. fr. the name *Burley*] : a thin-bodied air-cured tobacco varying in color from buff to chocolate, high in content of alkaloids and nitrogenous constituents, grown mainly in Kentucky and neighboring states, and used in cigarettes and to a lesser extent in plugs and smoking mixtures

²burley \"\ *or* **bur·ly** \"\ *n, pl* **burleys** *or* **burlies** [by shortening & alter.] : BURLESQUE

bur·li·ly \-lə̇lē, -li\ *adv* : in a burly manner

bur·li·ness \-lēnəs, -lin-\ *n* -ES : the quality or state of being burly

burling *pres part of* BURL

burls *pl of* BURL, *pres 3d sing of* BURL

¹bur·ly \'bərlē, 'bə̄l-, 'bəil-, -li\ *adj, usu* -ER/-EST [ME *burly, borlich*; prob. akin to OE *borlīce* extremely, excellently, OHG *burlīh* lofty; derivative fr. the root of OE *beran* to carry — more at BEAR] **1** : strongly built : STOUT, STURDY ⟨~ 205-pound . . . blocking quarterback —Eddie Beachler⟩ ⟨his ~ ship slashed through 4-foot-thick ice —R.E.Byrd⟩ **2** : heartily frank or direct esp. in manner : ROUGH-AND-READY, BLUFF, FORTHRIGHT ⟨an evocative story less ~ than the real thing but entertaining —E.A.Weeks⟩

²burly \"\ *n* -ES *slang* : one of burly frame; *specif* : TRAMP

bur·ma \'bərmə, 'bə̄mə, 'bəimə\ *adj, usu cap* [fr. *Burma*, country in southeast Asia] : of or from Burma : of the kind or style prevalent in Burma : BURMESE

burma mahogany *n, usu cap B* : the hard heavy wood of a Burmese tree (*Pentace burmanica*) of the family Tiliaceae — called also *thitka*

¹bur·man \-mən\ *also* **bir·man** \"\ *n* -s *cap* [*Burma* (formerly also *Birma*) + E *-an*] : BURMESE; *specif* : a member of the Mongolian ethnic group in Burma

²burman *also* **birman** \"\ *adj, usu cap* : of or relating to Burma or the Burmans : BURMESE

bur·man·nia \(,)bər'manēə\ *n, cap* [NL, fr. Johannes *Burmann* †1779 Du. botanist + NL *-ia*] : a genus (the type of the family Burmanniaceae) of slender herbs native to warm regions and having leaves resembling scales and flowers with a 3-angled or 3-winged perianth

bur·man·ni·a·ce·ae \(,)bər,manē'āsē,ē\ *n pl, cap* [NL, fr. *Burmannia*, type genus + *-aceae*] : a family (order Orchidales) of chiefly tropical herbs having the leaves basal or arranged like bracts along the flower stalk and small flowers — **bur·man·ni·a·ceous** \-āshəs\ *adj*

burma padauk *n, usu cap B* **1** : a tree (*Pterocarpus macrocarpus*) of India and Burma that yields a wood resembling mahogany **2** : the wood of the Burma padauk

bur marigold *or* **burr marigold** *n* [*burr* (prickly envelope) + *marigold*] : any plant of the genus *Bidens* — called also *beggar-ticks*

¹bur·mese \¦bər¦mēz, (')bə̄¦m-, (')bəi¦m-, -ēs *sometimes* ,bər'm-\ *adj, usu cap* [*Burma* + E *-ese*] : of or relating to Burma or the Burmese

²burmese \"\ *n, pl* **burmese** **1** *cap* : a native or inhabitant of Burma **2** *cap* : the language of the Burmans **3** *usu cap* : a late 19th century American opaque glassware of graduated color shading from yellow to pink **4** *usu cap* : BURMESE CAT

burmese cat *n, usu cap B* **1** : a breed of cat resembling the Siamese but of solid and darker color and with orange rather than blue eyes **2** : a cat of the Burmese breed

burmese lacquer *n, usu cap B* : a thick grayish liquid from the black-varnish tree (*Melanorrhoea usitata*) used as a varnish

burmese rosewood *n, usu cap B* : BURMA PADAUK

burmese ruby *n, often cap B* : PEONY 2

bur·mite \'bər,mīt\ *n* -s [*Burma*, its locality + E *-ite*] : a dark brown variety of amber found in Upper Burma

bur·mo-chinese \¦bər(,)mō +\ *adj, cap B&C* [*Burmo-* (fr. *Burma*) + *Chinese*] : of, relating to, or being the subregion of the Oriental biogeographic region that includes southeast Asia east of the Indian subregion except the Malay peninsula

¹burn \'bərn, 'bə̄n\ *n* -s [ME *burn, bourne* — more at BOURN] **1** *Brit* : STREAM, BROOK, RIVULET **2** *chiefly Scot* : WATER; *esp* : water used in brewing

²burn \'bərn, 'bə̄n, 'bəin\ *vb* **burned** \-nd\ *or* **burnt** \-nt\ *or archaic* **brent** *or dial Brit* **brunt**; **burned** *or* **burnt** *or archaic* **brent** *or dial Brit* **brunt**; **burning**; **burns** [ME *birnen, brinnen, brennen, barnen*, fr. OE *byrnan* (intransitive), *bærnan* (transitive); akin to OHG *brinnan* to burn (intransitive), *brennen* to burn (transitive), ON *brenna, brinna* (intransitive), *brenna* (transitive), Goth *brinnan* (intransitive), *-brannjan* (transitive), L *fervēre* to boil, Gk *porphyrein* to surge, Skt *bhurati* he quivers] *vi* **1 a** (1) *of fire* : to consume fuel and give off light, heat, and gases ⟨a small fire ~s on the hearth⟩ (2) *of a light source* : to give off light ⟨headlights ~ing bright⟩ **b** *of fuel* : to be on fire : undergo combustion ⟨even green ash ~s well⟩ **c** : to contain a fire — used of stoves, furnaces, or other devices in which fire is customarily shielded ⟨the stove is ~ing brightly⟩ **2 a** : to be hot as if on fire ⟨the sand ~ing under the torrid sun⟩ **b** : to become excited by a specified emotion or feeling ⟨~ing with curiosity⟩: as (1) : to yearn ardently ⟨he ~ed to tell the story⟩ ⟨~ing to get out into the country⟩ (2) : to become excited sexually ⟨better to marry than to ~ —1 Cor 7:9 (AV)⟩ — often used with *for* (3) : to be or become very angry or utterly disgusted ⟨when I heard what he had done I really ~*ed*⟩ — usu. used with *up* ⟨they ~*ed* up for fair over his statement⟩ **3 a** : to appear as if on fire : glow brightly ⟨windows that ~ in the setting sun⟩ ⟨zinnias ~ing along the fence⟩ **b** : to produce a sensation of heat ⟨the blood ~*ed* in her cheeks⟩ **c** : to produce or undergo discomfort suggestive of the pain accompanying a burn ⟨iodine ~s so⟩ ⟨the old scar throbbed and ~*ed*⟩; *sometimes* : STING, TINGLE ⟨our ears are ~ing with the cold⟩ ⟨my arm ~*ed* where her softness had passed —Herbert Gold⟩ **4 a** : to become altered by the action of fire or heat ⟨coal ~ing in the stove⟩; *esp* : to become charred, scorched, seared, or consumed by excessive heat ⟨the potatoes ~*ed* to a crisp⟩ **b** : to become affected as if by fire: as (1) *of the skin* : to become reddened or irritated by or as if by exposure to sun or wind (2) *of herbage* : to become desiccated or withered (3) *of crop plants* : to wither or discolor as a result of chemical damage due to excessive or improper use of fertilizers or sprays and dusts (4) *of a rubber compound* : SCORCH **5 a** : to die by fire esp. through execution by burning **b** : to die in the electric chair **c** : to become damned **6** : to force or make a way by or as if by burning — used with *into* ⟨her words ~*ed* into his memory⟩ **7** : to be hot in search of an answer or object **8** *of a chemical element* : to undergo fission or fusion ⟨uranium ~s by absorption of neutrons⟩ ⟨hydrogen ~s to form helium⟩ ~ *vt* **1 a** *of fire* : to consume as fuel in burning — often used with adverbs or phrases of degree or direction ⟨their house was ~*ed* down last Saturday⟩ ⟨if lightning strikes, the haystack will be ~*ed* up in no time⟩ **b** : to cause to undergo combustion ⟨~ iron in oxygen⟩ **c** : to employ as a source of light or heat ⟨we shall ~ oil this year⟩ ⟨this hotel ~s gas for all cooking and heating⟩ **d** *of fires or firing devices* : to require or use as fuel ⟨this stove ~s coal or wood⟩ ⟨the new system ~s cheap heavy oils⟩ **2** : to produce by the action of fire or heat ⟨you'll ~ a hole in your sleeve⟩ ⟨supplementing their income by ~ing charcoal for the smelters⟩ **3 a** : to subject to the action of or cause to be consumed by fire ⟨we ~*ed* up all the rubbish⟩ ⟨pile and ~ the brush as you go⟩: as (1) : to execute by burning ⟨heretics ~*ed* by the church⟩; *broadly, slang* : ELECTROCUTE (2) : to make an offering of (as incense) by burning (3) : to mark (as a criminal) by branding (4) *slang* : DAMN ⟨well, I'll be ~*ed*⟩ **b** : to injure by fire or heat : alter a property of by undue exposure to fire or heat : SCORCH, SCALD, BLISTER, SEAR, SINGE, CHAR ⟨~ steel in the forging⟩ ⟨grass ~*ed* brown by the sun⟩ ⟨the cook ~*ed* the roast⟩ ⟨look out, you'll ~ your fingers⟩ **c** (1) : to produce a comparable effect upon by an agent other than fire or heat (as by certain radiations, chemicals, or friction) ⟨the sun ~*ed* his shoulders badly⟩ ⟨overfertilization may ~ the plants⟩ ⟨his face chapped and ~*ed* by the wind⟩ (2) *of a rubber compound* : SCORCH **d** : to subject to the action of fire or heat for some economic purpose (as for the alteration or elimination of undesired qualities); *specif* : to transform by the action of controlled fire or heat ⟨~ clay to bricks⟩ ⟨~ wood into charcoal⟩ — compare CALCINE **4 a** *obs* : to inflame with emotion or passion **b** *slang* : IRRITATE, ANNOY ⟨the constant bickering ~*ed* her⟩ — usu. used with *up* ⟨he ~s me up⟩ **c** *slang* : CHEAT, BEFOOL, DO ⟨he surely *burnt* me over that deal⟩ **5 a** : to wear out : DIMINISH, EXHAUST ⟨his anger is ~ing him up⟩ **b** : WASTE, SQUANDER, DISSIPATE — usu. used as an infinitive ⟨money to ~⟩ **c** : to traverse or cause to traverse at high speed — usu. used with *up* ⟨~ up the road⟩ ⟨~*ed* up the international cables —Cameron Hawley⟩ **6 a** : to touch or move (a piece) in a manner forbidden by the rules of a game **b** : to expose and then turn (a playing card) face up on the bottom of the pack **c** : to throw (as a baseball) very hard ⟨he ~*ed* a fast one over the plate⟩ **7** : to join (pieces of metal) by flowing molten metal through or over the joint to be fused until adjacent surfaces soften and unite with the added metal — often used with *in, on,* or *together*; compare LEAD-BURN **8** : to cause (a plating) to become dark or rough because of change in physical or chemical character usu. by exposure to excessive current **9** : to cause (a chemical element) to burn

syn CHAR, SEAR, SCORCH, SINGE: BURN is a general term usable in any situation in which fire or heat has had a positive destructive effect and consequently interchangeable with any of the following except SINGE in some of its uses. CHAR indicates a burning that reduces to carbon or to cinder ⟨only a few *charred* planks remaining after the conflagration⟩ ⟨a third-degree burn occurs when the flesh is *charred*⟩ SEAR typically indicates burning through quick exposure to high heat, with resulting cauterizing, closing of tissues, deadening, branding, or unforgettably impressing ⟨*searing* the tissues with an electric needle⟩ ⟨the roast was first *seared*, then cooked slowly⟩ ⟨the *searing* effect of the first atomic bombs⟩ SCORCH indicates superficial burning of exposed surface or area, burning which changes color or texture without consuming ⟨the paint on the garage was *scorched* by the bonfire⟩ ⟨the potatoes at the bottom *scorched* when the pan went dry⟩ SINGE implies quick passing over or otherwise exposing to a flame with extremely superficial burning, often with burning only of an integument like hair or feathers ⟨some of the coats on the rack were *singed*⟩ ⟨his hair was *singed* when the gas flared up⟩ ⟨to *singe* a chicken before cooking it⟩

— **burn a hole in one's pocket** *of money* : to get itself spent quickly — **burn daylight** *archaic* : to make a light before it is dark; *also* : to waste time or energy — **burn one's bridges** *also* **burn one's boats** : to cut off all means of retreat — **burn one's ears** *slang* : to rebuke strongly : call down : BLISTER — **burn one's fingers** : to get into unexpected trouble, embarrassment, or distress (as by interfering in the affairs of others or by an injudicious or rash venture) — **burn the books** : to act as a suppressive force esp. by withholding knowledge that would affect the actions of others — **burn the candle at both ends** : to be unreasonably prodigal with one's material or physical resources — **burn the midnight oil** : to work or study far into the night — **burn the water** : to spear salmon by torchlight — **burn the wind** : to go speedily; *also* : dissipate rapidly

³burn \"\ *n* -s **1** : an injury, damage, or effect produced by burning (as with fire): **a** : bodily injury resulting from exposure to heat, caustics, electricity, or certain radiations, marked by varying degrees of skin destruction and hyperemia often with the formation of watery blisters and in severe cases by charring of the tissues, and classified according to the extent and degree of the injury as first degree, second degree, or third degree **b** (1) : BRAND 3a(1) (2) : BRANDING IRON **c** : a burned area ⟨a ~ on the table top⟩; *esp* : an area denuded of vegetation by burning produced deliberately (as in land-clearing) or by chance ⟨poplars coming in on an old ~⟩ **d** : an abrasion (as of the skin) having the appearance of a burn ⟨friction ~s⟩ ⟨cold ~⟩ ⟨a floor marred by rubber ~⟩ **e** : a burning sensation or appearance ⟨the ~ of iodine on a cut⟩ ⟨the ruddy ~ of her hair⟩ **2 a** : the process, operation, or result of burning ⟨bricks properly baked have a good ~⟩ **b** : an instance of burning; *specif* : burning of vegetation from the surface of land ⟨the rate of deterioration after a severe ~ was about the same for spruce, balsam, and jackpine —*Biol. Abstracts*⟩ **3** : the capacity of ignited tobacco to continue burning without producing a flame **4** : a worn place on a railroad rail caused by the friction of spinning engine drivers **5** *slang* : ANGER; *esp* : increasing fury — used chiefly in the phrase *slow burn*

burn·able \-nəbəl\ *adj or n* : COMBUSTIBLE

burn away *vi* : to dissipate as though consumed by fire ⟨the haze has *burned away*⟩ ~ *vt* : to eliminate by or as if by burning ⟨his style *burns away* overlocalized fact —*Saturday Rev.*⟩

burn·beat \'bərn,bēt, -,bāt\ *vt* [²*burn* + *beat* (turf)] : to pare off and burn the sod or turf from in order to improve (sour or soggy land) for cultivation

burn blue *n* : a pale blue to purplish blue

burned *past of* BURN

burned-out *or* **burnt-out** \'=;=\ *adj* [fr. past part. of *burn out*] **1** : debilitated or excessively worn by excessive consumption of energy or physical resources **2** *of a negative or a print* : overexposed so that detail is lacking in the highlights

burned-over *also* **burnt-over** \'=;=,=\ *adj, of land* : freed of vegetation by fire

burn·er \'bərnər; 'bə̄nə(r, 'bəin-\ *n* -s [ME *brennere*, fr. *brennen* to burn + *-ere* -er — more at BURN] **1** : one that burns: **a** : a person whose occupation involves burning or the use of heat in the preparation or production of some desired product: as (1) : a worker in charge of a kiln in which brick or tile is burned — called also *baker* (2) *also* **burner man** : a worker who burns a mineral substance (as lime, ground stone, or filter clay) to alter its properties in some desired manner (3) : a worker who cuts metals with a flame-cutting torch **b** : a device for burning some particular material: as (1) : the part of a lamp, gas stove, or other fluid-burning device where the flame is produced; *broadly* : a device for consuming fluid fuel including accessories concerned with such matters as firing, fuel distribution, and vaporization and being typically a compact unit attached to or incorporated in a boiler, stove, furnace, or engine (2) : INCINERATOR (3) : a blowtorch or other device used for softening old paint to facilitate its removal (4) : an ornamental vessel usu. of clay, porcelain, or metal in which incense is burned **2** : a furnace for burning sulfur or a sulfide ore (as pyrite) to produce sulfur dioxide and other gases (as for making sulfuric acid or sulfite pulp)

burner man *n* : a worker who burns or heats something: as **a** : one that burns up sawmill waste **b** : one in charge of the mobile kettle in which asphalt paving material is kept soft by an oil flame — called also *kettleman* **c** : BURNER 1a(2)

bur·net \,bər'net, ,bər'net, 'bərnət\ *n* -s [ME, fr. OF *burnete*, *brunete*, fr. *brun* brown — more at BRUNET] **1** : black or brown woolen fabric used for clothing from the 13th to the 16th century **2 a** : BURNET SAXIFRAGE **b** : any plant of the genus *Sanguisorba*: as (1) : a New World herb (*S. canadensis*) (2) : SALAD BURNET **3** : BURNET MOTH

burnet bloodwort *n* : SALAD BURNET

burnet moth *n* : any of numerous moths of the family Zygaenidae; *esp* : a diurnal European moth (*Zygaena filipendula*) with crimson spots on the wings

burnet rose *n* : SCOTCH ROSE

burnet saxifrage *n* : a European herb (*Pimpinella saxifraga*) with pinnate leaves and white flowers and an aromatic root

bur·nett·ize \(,)bər'ned·,īz, (')bərnə̇,tīz\ *vt* -ED/-ING/-S [Sir William *Burnett* †1861 Scot. physician, inventor of the process + E *-ize*] : to impregnate (as wood or fabrics) with zinc chloride solution under pressure to prevent decay

burnett salmon \,bər'net, ,bər'net, 'bərnət\ *n, usu cap B* [*Burnett* river, Queensland, Australia] : BARRAMUNDA a

bur·ne·win \'bərnə̇,win\ *var of* BURN-THE-WIND

burn·ie \'bərnē\ *n* -s [¹*burn* + *-ie*] *Scot* : a little stream

burnier *comparative of* BURNY

burniest *superlative of* BURNY

burn in *vt* **1** : to heat (a metal photoengraving plate) after development of the printed image until the enamel carbonizes and becomes acid-resisting **2** : to increase the density of (certain areas of a photographic print) during enlarging by giving extra exposure — compare DODGE

¹**burning** *adj* [ME *brenninge*, fr. pres. part. of *brennen* to burn] **1 a** : on fire : ALIGHT, AFLAME, IGNITED ⟨the house is ~⟩ **b** : excessively hot : FIERY, ARDENT, SHINING, GLOWING ⟨under a ~ sun⟩ ⟨a ~ and dedicated spirit drove her⟩ **2 a** : affecting with or as if with heat : HEATING ⟨a ~ fever⟩ **b** : INFLAMING, EXCITING ⟨a ~ enthusiasm⟩; *also* : INTENSE ⟨~ wrath⟩ **c** : of fundamental and immediate import : URGENT ⟨a ~ need⟩ ⟨the ~ issue of the day⟩ **d** *of sensations* : like that produced by a burn ⟨a ~ sensation on the tongue⟩ **3** : prominently in view : GLARING, SHOCKING — used esp. of unpleasing states or conditions ⟨a ~ shame⟩ ⟨a ~ disgrace to his family⟩

²**burning** *n* -s [ME *brenninge*, fr. gerund of *brennen*] **1 a** : a consuming or being consumed by fire or heat **b** : the state or sensation of being on fire, as if on fire, or excessively heated **2** : subjection to the action of heat or of an agent that burns : COMBUSTION: as **a** : the calcining esp. of limestone or ore **b** : the heating of ores without access to air preparatory to smelting **c** : a firing of ceramic materials (as for maturing, glazing, fixing colors) **d** : the sterilizing of soil for tobacco beds by burning piles of brush and wood on the area **3** : the effect produced on something by subjection to the action of heat or of an agent that burns: as **a** : the cutting or wearing caused by friction (as from blown sand); *esp* : the roughening or discoloration of material from heat produced in machining or abrasive finishing **b** : vulcanization by heat **c** : a withered brownish appearance of foliage (as in hopperburn or tipburn) **4** *obs* : an inflammatory disease; *esp* : a venereal disease

burning bush *n* [so called fr. the bush in Exod 3:2 that was on fire but was not consumed] : any of several plants: as **a** : ²WAHOO a **b** : FRAXINELLA **c** : ARTILLERY PLANT **d** : SUMMER CYPRESS

burning ghat *n* : the space in a ghat (as at the head) where the Hindus cremate their dead

burning glass *n* : a positive lens for producing intense heat by converging the sun's rays approximately to the principal focus of the lens the point of convergence being a very small image of the sun

burning index *n* : a number which is determined from the moisture content of a forest, wind speed, and other factors that affect burning conditions and from which ease of ignition and behavior of a forest fire may be estimated

burn·ing·ly *adv* [ME *brenningly*, fr. *brenning*, *brenninge* burning + *-ly* — more at BURNING] : in a burning manner : with heat : ARDENTLY

burning mountain *n* : VOLCANO

burning nettle *n* **1** : SMALL NETTLE **2** : ROMAN NETTLE

burning oil *n* : an oil used for burning; *specif* : KEROSENE

burning point *n* : FIRE POINT

burning time *n* : the time during which the propellant charge of a rocket engine is fully consumed

burning torch *n* : a gas torch with an intensely hot oxidizing flame that is used for cutting metal by burning

burning-wood \'==,=\ *n* : LEATHERWOOD 1b

¹**bur·nish** \'bərnish, 'bə̄n-, 'bəin-, -nēsh, *esp in pres part* -nəsh\ *vb* -ED/-ING/-ES [ME *burnischen*, fr. MF *bruniss-*, stem of *brunir* to make brown, burnish, fr. OF, fr. *brun* brown, shining, fr. ML *brunus*, of Gmc origin; akin to OHG *brūn* brown, shining — more at BROWN] *vt* **1** : to make shiny or lustrous : POLISH; *specif* : to polish by friction with something hard and smooth ⟨~ metal⟩ ⟨*burnished* leather⟩ **2** *of a deer* : to rub (as the head) so as to remove the dead velvet and polish the antlers **3** : to rub with a burnisher: as **a** : to fix with a burnisher ⟨~ a glass into a metal rim⟩ **b** : to make an area of (a halftone printing plate) darker by rubbing down the dots and thus enlarging them ~ *vi* : to take a polish : become lustrous under burnishing

²**burnish** \"\ *n* -ES : a polished surface : superficial luster; *also* : POLISH 4

burnished *adj* [ME *burnisched*, fr. past part. of *burnischen*] : having a surface like that produced by burnishing : LUSTROUS ⟨the ~ light of the evening sun —F. Tennyson Jesse⟩

burnished gold *n* : a dark orange yellow to strong yellowish brown — called also *pinchbeck brown*

burnished straw *n* : a light brown that is yellower and deeper than blush, deeper and yellower than alesan, and redder and deeper than cork

bur·nish·er \-shə(r)\ *n* -s **1** : a worker employed in burnishing ⟨a shoe ~⟩ **2** : a tool, variously shaped, with a hard smooth rounded end or surface (as of steel, ivory, or agate) used in smoothing, polishing, turning an edge, or other manipulation by rubbing

burnishing die *n* : one of a set of cutting dies whose matrix is a little smaller at the bottom than at the cutting edge so that the edge of the work forced through the die becomes burnished

burn off *vb* [²*burn* + *off*] *vt* **1** : to clear up : break away : DISSIPATE — used of weather phenomena (as fog, dew, clouds) that are regarded as adverse and particularly subject to the sun's warmth and often with *it* as an indefinite nominative ⟨it will *burn off* before noon⟩ **2 a** : to remove (as debris on a surface) by burning ⟨I want to *burn off* the rest of the brush this fall⟩ **b** : to free (a piece of land) of unwanted vegetation or plant residues ⟨we'll *burn off* the north field the next time it rains⟩ ~ *vi, of the sun* : to cause watery vapor (as clouds or fog) to dissipate

burn-off \'=,=\ *n* -s [*burn off*] : an act or process of removing unwanted material (as old paint or superfluous metal) by burning; *sometimes* : material so removed

bur·nous *or* **bur·noose** \(,)bər'nüs, '=,=\ *n, pl* **burnouses** *or* **burnooses** [F *burnous*, fr. Ar *burnus*, fr. Gk *birros* cloak with a hood, fr. (assumed) L *birrus* (whence LL *birrus*) — more at BIRETTA] **1** : a long loose flowing hooded cloak of wool woven in one piece and worn by Arabs and Moors **2** : an outer garment for women based on the design of the burnous

burnous 1

burn out *vb* [²*burn* + *out*] *vt* **1** : to destroy or obliterate by fire or heat ⟨we found that we had *burned out* a bearing⟩ **2** : to drive out or destroy the property of by fire — usu. passive ⟨we were *burnt out* just before Christmas⟩ ⟨the store was completely *burnt out*⟩ **3 a** : to cause to fail, wear out, or become exhausted by making excessive demands on energy, strength, or resources ⟨he will *burn* himself *out* unless he gets more sleep⟩ **b** : to spoil the condition of (livestock) esp. for breeding by too rich feeding or overfeeding ~ *vi* **1** : to cease to be in a condition to perform a normal function by reason of usu. prolonged exposure to fire or heat ⟨the bulb in the kitchen light just *burned out*⟩ ⟨the grate in the furnace is nearly *burned out*⟩ **2** : to fail, wear out, or become exhausted by reason of excessive demands on energy, strength, or resources ⟨at this rate you'll *burn out* before you're 30⟩ ⟨the best soil *burns out* under constant heavy cropping⟩

burnout \'=,=\ *n* -s [*burn out*] **1** : a fire that consumes all the flammable contents (as of a building); *broadly* : a large and destructive fire **2** : a breakdown of an electrical circuit caused by fusion or combustion (as of a conducting element or insulation) resulting from abnormal increase in temperature **3** : an area of soil from which the organic material has been removed by fire or other agency leaving usu. a distinct depression of unfertile mineral soil **4** : the moment at which a jet or rocket motor exhausts its fuel

burn-out *var of* BURNT-OUT

burnover \'=;==\ *n* -s [*burn over*, v., fr. ²*burn* + *over*] : an imperfectly burned brick that requires reburning

burns *pl of* BURN, *pres 3d sing of* BURN

¹**burns·ian** \'bərnzēən\ *adj, usu cap* [Robert *Burns* †1796 Scot. poet + E *-ian*] : of, relating to, or like the poet Robert Burns or his writings

²**burnsian** \"\ *n* -s *usu cap* : a devotee of the poet Burns

burnside \'=,=\ *n* [ME, fr. ¹*burn* + *side*] *Brit* : BROOKSIDE

burn·sides \'bərn,sīdz, 'bə̄n-,'bəin-\ *n pl* [after Ambrose E. *Burnside* †1881 Am. general, who wore them] : SIDE WHISKERS; *esp* : full muttonchop whiskers

burns meter *or* **burns stanza** \'bərnz-, 'bə̄nz-, 'bəinz-\ *n, cap B* : a stanza often used by Robert Burns and other Scottish poets consisting of six lines rhyming *aaabab* of which the fourth and sixth are regularly iambic dimeters and the others iambic tetrameters

burnt *adj* [fr. past part. of ²*burn*] : consumed or altered by or as if by fire or heat: as **a** *of iron or steel* : rendered crumbly and unfit for welding or otherwise damaged by excessive heat **b** *of colors* : giving a somewhat dull appearance as though scorched ⟨~ carnelian⟩ **c** *of gems* : altered in color by heating

burnt almond *n* **1** : roasted sweet almond — usu. used in pl. **2** : COCONUT BROWN

burnt alum *n* : alum that has been dried at 200° C and powdered, being a caustic used to remove dead tissues — called also *dried alum*

burnt brass *n, obs* : COPPER SULFATE

burnt carmine *or* **burnt crimson lake** *or* **burnt lake** *n* : a moderate to deep red that is slightly bluer than cadmium purple — called also *old red, purple lake*

burn-the-wind \'==,=\ *n, chiefly Scot* : BLACKSMITH

burnt iron *n* : iron that has been subjected in the Bessemer or the open-hearth process to excessive oxidation following the removal of impurities

burnt italian earth *or* **burnt italian ocher** *n, often cap I* : BURNT SIENNA 2

burnt lime *n* : LIME 2a

burnt ocher *n* **1** : a brown-red pigment made by calcining yellow ocher **2** : a moderate reddish orange that is yellower and duller than crab apple and yellower and darker than flamingo — called also *light red*

burnt offering *or* **burnt sacrifice** *n* : a sacrifice offered to a deity and burned typically on or at an altar

burnt orange *n* : a moderate reddish orange that is yellower and duller than crab apple, yellower and darker than flamingo, yellower than burnt ocher, and deeper than average persimmon (sense 3a)

¹**burnt-out** *var of* BURNED-OUT

²**burnt-out** \'=;=\ *or* **burn-out** \'=,=\ *adj* [*burnt-out* fr. past part. of *burn out*; *burn-out* fr. *burn out*] **1** *of machine-made laces* : made by embroidering on a sheer foundation cloth that is later destroyed by chemicals **2** *of fabrics with two different yarns* : having patterns formed by the destruction of one yarn by chemicals

burnt-over *var of* BURNED-OVER

burnt roman ocher *n, often cap R* : OCHER ORANGE

burnt rose *n* : POMPEII

burnt russet *n* : WALLFLOWER 4

burnt sienna *n* **1** : a yellowish red to reddish brown pigment made by calcining raw sienna and used esp. in stains and glazes and as an artist's color **2** : a dark reddish orange that is yellower and less strong than average lacquer and yellower and slightly lighter than ocher red — called also *burnt Italian earth*

burnt terre verte *n* : VANDYKE BROWN

burnt umber *n* **1** : a dark brown pigment made by calcining raw umber and used esp. in stains and paints and as an artist's color **2** : a moderate brown that is yellower, lighter, and stronger than bay or tobacco, yellower and deeper than toast brown, redder, lighter, and stronger than coffee, and stronger and slightly redder than chestnut brown — called also *manganese velvet brown, umber, velvet brown*

burntweed \'=,=\ *n* [so called fr. its growing in burned-over areas] **1** : FIREWEED b **2** : HART'S-TONGUE 1

burnt work *n* : PYROGRAPHY

burnup \'=,=\ *n* -s [fr. *burn up*, v.] **1** : the amount of fuel destroyed (as in a nuclear reactor) ⟨uranium ~⟩ ⟨a fuel ~ of five percent —Richard Stephenson⟩ **2** : the heating and vaporization of a rocket or satellite due to air resistance

burnut \'=,=\ *n* -s [*burr* (prickly envelope) + *nut*; fr. its spiny fruit] : any plant of the genus *Tribulus*

burnwood \'=,=\ *n* : LEATHERWOOD 1b

burny \'bərnē\ *adj* -ER/-EST [²*burn* + *-y*] : inclined to burn ⟨a ~ liqueur⟩ : suggestive of burning ⟨a ~ odor⟩

¹**bu·ro** *like* BUREAU, *or* =ˈrō\ *n* -s [Russ *byuro*, fr. F *bureau* — more at BUREAU] : BUREAU 3b

²**bu·ro** \'bü(,)rō\ *n* -s [Tag] : a Philippine dish of fish prepared with boiled rice, salt, and spicy seasonings

bur oak *or* **burr oak** *n* : a useful and ornamental oak (*Quercus macrocarpa*) of central and eastern No. America with ovoid acorns enclosed in very large fringed cups and tough close-grained durable wood — called also *mossy-cup oak*

bu·row's solution \'bü(,)rōz-\ *n, usu cap B* [after Karl A. *Burow* †1874 Ger. surgeon] : a solution of aluminum acetate used as an antiseptic and astringent

¹**burp** \'bərp, 'bə̄p, 'bəip\ *n* -s [imit.] : BELCH

²**burp** \"\ *vb* -ED/-ING/-S *vi* : BELCH ~ *vt* : to help (a baby) expel gas from the stomach esp. by patting or rubbing the back

bur parsley *n* : a spreading hairy Old World annual herb (*Anthriscus neglecta*) that is closely related to wild chervil

burp gun *n* : MACHINE PISTOL

bur·qa \'bu̇rkə\ *n* -s [Hindi *burqa'* — more at BURKA] : BURKA

¹**burr** \'bər, +V 'bər-; 'bə̄, +V 'bər- *also* 'bə̄r\ *n* -s [ME *burre*; akin to OSw *borre* bur, OE *byrst* bristle — more at BRISTLE] **1** *usu* **bur a** : any rough or prickly envelope of a fruit whether a pericarp, a persistent calyx, or an involucre: as (1) : the husk of a chestnut (2) : the hull of a mature cotton boll (3) : the cone of a hop plant at the time of flowering **b** : any weed that bears burs **c** : plant debris in raw wool **2 a** : something that resembles a bur (as in sticking or clinging) ⟨a ~ in the throat⟩ **b** : HANGER-ON ⟨hang off thou cat, thou ~ —Shak.⟩ **3** [ME *burwhe* circle, perh. alter. of *burgh* borough — more at BOROUGH] **a** *obs* : a broad iron ring on a tilting lance fixed just below the grip to prevent slipping of the hand **b** : a small washer put on the end of a rivet before swaging it down **c** : a disk or cylinder of metal punched from a sheet **d** : NUT 3 **4** : the external part of the ear; *esp* : the irregular inner part of the pinna of the ear (as of a dog) **5** : the circular boss at the base of an antler or horn **6 a** : any rounded knot or excrescence on a tree : BURL **b** : lumber or veneer cut from such a burr **7** : a thin ridge or area of roughness produced in cutting or shaping metal (as in drilling, turning, or blanking): as **a** : the fin left on a casting at the mold junctions; *also* : a thin protrusion of excess metal on a newly cast slug or piece of type **b** : edges of metal raised above the face of an engraved plate by the graving tool **8 a** : a trilled uvular *r* as used by some speakers of English esp. in northern England and in Scotland **b** : a tongue-point trill that is the usual Scottish *r* **c** : a pronunciation regarded as odd and uncouth **9 a** *usu* **bur** : a small rotary cutting tool often with fluted edges arranged spirally that is used on a powered apparatus (as a dental drill) **b** : a small circular saw **c** *or* **burr chisel** : a chisel with three cutting edges that is used to clear the burrs from machine-cut corners **d** : a wheel with projections for forming loops between needles in a circular knitting machine **10** : a rough humming sound : WHIR, BIRR

²**burr** \"\ *vb* -ED/-ING/-S *vi* **1** : to speak with a burr **2** : to make a whirring sound ~ *vt* **1** : to pronounce with a burr ⟨~*ed* his *r's*⟩ **2 a** : to form into a projecting edge **b** : to remove burrs from (a hole or sharp edge)

³**burr** \"\ *also* **bur** \"\ *n* -s [perh. fr. ¹*burr*; fr. its roughness] **1** : BUHRSTONE **2** : a knob or boss of siliceous rock in softer formations **3** : WHETSTONE **4** : ¹CLINKER 2a, 2b

⁴**burr** \"\ *also* **bur** \"\ *n* -s [Hindi *bar*, fr. Prakrit *vaṭa*, fr. Skt *vṛta* covered, surrounded, fr. *vṛṇoti* he covers, surrounds — more at WEIR] *India* : BANYAN 2

bur·ra \'bə(,)rä\ *adj* [Hindi *baṛā*, fr. Skt *vṛddha*, fr. *vardhate* he increases — more at ORTH-] *India* : GREAT — used chiefly in phrases as a title of respect and specif. to designate a father or elder brother or a chief officer ⟨~ sahib⟩

bur·rage \'bərij\ *n* -s [ME *borage* — more at BORAGE] *archaic* : BORAGE

burr-ragweed \'=;=,=\ *n* [¹*burr* + *ragweed*] : FRANSERIA 2

burr artichoke *n* : ARTICHOKE 1

bur·ra·wang \'bərə,waŋ\ *n* -s [prob. after Mt. *Burrawang*, New South Wales, Australia] : an Australian plant of the genus *Macrozamia* (esp. *M. spiralis*)

burr clover *var of* BUR CLOVER

burred \'bərd, 'bə̄d\ *adj* [¹*burr* + *-ed*] **1** : rough and prickly ⟨a ~ edge of metal⟩ **2** : enclosed in a bur ⟨~ fruits⟩

bur reed *n* : any plant of the genus *Sparganium* having elongated linear leaves and globose fruits resembling burs

bur-reed family *n* : SPARGANIACEAE

burr·er \'bərə(r) *also* 'bə̄rə(r\ *n* -s : a worker who removes burr or burrs from textile fibers or metal objects

burrfish *also* **burfish** \'=,=\ *n* : a spiny globefish : PORCUPINE FISH

burrhel *var of* BHARAL

burrier *comparative of* BURRY

bur·ri·er's oak \'bərēə(r)z-\ *n, usu cap B* [prob. fr. the name *Burrier*] : BARTRAM OAK

burriest *superlative of* BURRY

burring *n* -s [fr. gerund of ²*burr*] : the mechanical removal of burs from wool during processing

burrio *n* -ES [MF *bourreau*, prob. fr. *bourrer* to mistreat, beat — more at BOURRÉE] *obs Scot* : EXECUTIONER

bur·ri·to \bə'rēd·(,)ō\ *n* -s [AmerSp, fr. Sp, little donkey, dim. of *burro*] : any of several small grunts of tropical American waters

burrknot \'=;=\ *n* : a rough excrescence often present on the trunk or roots of certain trees and characteristic of some varieties that was formerly thought to be a form of crown gall but is now believed to be nonpathogenic

burrlike \'=,=\ *adj* : like a burr (as in being prickly)

burr marigold *var of* BUR MARIGOLD

burr medic *n, Austral* : a bur clover (*Medicago denticulata*) with serrated leaf margins

burr mill *n* : a mill (as a coffee mill) that grinds by means of a steel burr resembling in principle the old-fashioned millstone

bur·ro \'bər·(,)ō, 'bə·(,)rō, -ər·ə,-ə·rə *also* 'bu̇(,)rō *or* -ürə, *often* -r·əw *or* -·rəw+V\ *n* -s [Sp, irreg. fr. *borrico* donkey, fr. LL *burricus* small horse] : DONKEY; *esp* : a small donkey used as a pack animal or that is feral in the southwestern U. S. and adjacent Mexico

burr oak *var of* BUR OAK

burro-back \'==,=\ *adv* : on the back of a burro

burrobrush \'==,=\ *n* : a spreading-branched composite shrub (*Hymenoclea monogyra*) with filiform leaves and numerous small unisexual flower heads in mixed panicles that is common on rangeland in the western U. S. — called also *arrowwood*

burrobush \'==,=\ *n* [*burro* + *bush*; fr. its use as food by donkeys] : BUR SAGE

burro deer *n* : MULE DEER

burro grass *n* : a tufted grass (*Scleropogon brevifolius*) of semiarid plains and open valleys of the southwestern U. S. with wiry stolons, leaves that are flat and crowded at the base, and spikelets with long twisted awns

¹**burrough** *obs var of* BOROUGH

²**burrough** *obs var of* BURROW

¹**bur·row** \'bər·(,)ō, 'bə·(,)rō, -ər·ə,-ə·rə, *often* -ər·əw *or* -ə·rəw +V\ *n* -s [ME *borugh*, *borow*, perh. fr. *borugh* borough — more at BOROUGH] **1** : a hole in the ground made by certain animals (as rabbits) for shelter and habitation **2** : PASSAGE, GALLERY; *esp* : one formed in or under the skin by the wandering of a parasite (as the mite of scabies or a foreign hookworm) **3** : a miserable dwelling : HOVEL, HOLE

²**burrow** \"\ *vb* -ED/-ING/-S *vt* **1** *archaic* : to hide (as oneself) in or as if in a burrow — usu. passive **2** : to produce like a burrow : construct by digging and tunneling ⟨~*ed* a dwelling in the side of the hill⟩ ⟨he can ~ passages underneath a river bed —F.M.Godfrey⟩ **3** : to pass or extend like a burrow ⟨the tunnel ~*ed* its way under the mountain⟩ **4** : to make a motion suggestive of burrowing with : SNUGGLE, NESTLE ⟨she ~s her grubby hand into mine⟩ ~ *vi* **1** : to conceal oneself in or lodge in a mean abode — used chiefly of persons **2 a** *of an animal* : to dig a burrow ⟨rats ~*ing* in the wall⟩ **b** : TUNNEL, DELVE, DIG ⟨he ~*ed* into his records⟩ ⟨~*ing* through the mass of reports⟩ **3 a** *of an animal* : to progress through the earth by means of digging movements ⟨many worms ~ freely in the surface soil⟩ **b** : to form and move along a tunnel in a specified direction ⟨they ~*ed* under the wall⟩ **c** : to enter into as though through a hidden burrow ⟨Communists ~*ing* into the labor unions⟩ **4** : to make a motion suggestive of burrowing : SNUGGLE, NESTLE ⟨~*ed* against his back for warmth⟩

³burrow \"\ *n* -s [ME *borough, borgh,* prob. alter. of *bergh* barrow — more at BARROW] *archaic* **:** BARROW, HILLOCK

burro·weed \'ˌ=ˌ=\ *n* [*burro* + *weed*] **1 :** a weed (*Suaeda moquini*) of the family Chenopodiaceae growing on alkaline lands in the southwestern U.S. **2 :** IODINE BUSH **3 :** BUR SAGE **4 :** any of several rayless goldenrods

bur·row·er \'bər·əwə(r), 'bə·rəw-; 'bər·ōə(r), 'bə·rō-\ *n* -s **:** one that burrows; *specif* **:** an animal that makes a hole underground and lives in it

burrower bug *also* **burrowing bug** *n* **:** any of numerous largely subterranean usu. dark-colored small bugs constituting the family Cydnidae and resembling beetles

burrowing anemone *n* **:** any of various sea anemones that burrow in muddy or sandy sea bottoms

burrowing nematode *n* **:** a soil nematode (*Radopholus similis*) attacking the roots of sugarcane in Hawaii

burrowing owl *n* **:** a small chiefly terrestrial owl (*Speotyto cunicularia*) of western No. America, Florida, and So. America living in burrows (as those abandoned by prairie dogs)

burrowing shrimp *n* **:** GHOST SHRIMP

bur·row-town *also* **bur·rows-town** \'bə·rə(z),tün\ *n* [*burrows-town* fr. ME *borwtown,* fr. *borw, borugh* borough (fr. OE *burg, burh* fortress) + *town; burrows-town* fr. ME (northern dial.) *borowstown,* prob. fr. *borows* (gen. of *borow* borough, fr. OE *burg, burh*) + *town* — more at BOROUGH] *Scot* **:** BOROUGH

burrs *pl of* BURR, *pres 3d sing of* BURR

burrstone *var of* BUHRSTONE

bur·ry \'bər·|ē, |i *also* 'bə̄r|\ *adj* -ER/-EST [ME, fr. *burre* + *-y* — more at BURR] **1 :** abounding in or containing burs ⟨~ wool⟩ **2 :** like a bur **:** PRICKLY **3** *of speech* **:** characterized by a burr

¹bur·sa \'bərsə\ *n, pl* **bursas** \-səz\ *or* **bur·sae** \-ˌsē, -ˌsī\ [NL, fr. ML *bursa* bag, purse — more at PURSE] **1 :** a pouch-shaped bodily cavity **:** SAC: as **a :** any of the small serous sacs enclosing viscid fluid and being interposed between moving parts (as tendons and bony prominences) where they lessen friction effects **b :** BURSA COPULATRIX **2 :** a residence hall for students at a medieval university

²bur·sa \(')bu̇r¦sä, 'bu̇rsə\ *adj, usu cap* [fr. *Bursa,* Turkey] **:** of or from the city of Bursa, Turkey **:** of the kind or style prevalent in Bursa

bursa cop·u·la·trix \-ˌkäpyə'lā·triks\ *n* [NL, fr. *bursa* + *copulatrix* of copulation, fr. LL, she that unites, fem. of *copulator* he that unites, fr. L *copulatus,* past part. of *copulare* to bind, join, unite — more at COPULATE] **1 :** a pouch receiving spermatozoa during copulation (as in certain insects) **2 :** a thin fan or bell-shaped expansion of the cuticle of the tail of many male nematode worms that functions as a clasper during copulation

bur sage *n* [¹*burr* + *sage*] **:** a plant of the genus *Franseria; esp* **:** a low spiny shrub (*F. dumosa*) having the leaves densely covered with whitish hairs and being widely distributed in desert regions of the southwestern U.S. and adjacent Mexico

bur·sal \'bərsəl\ *adj* [NL *bursa* + E *-al*] **:** of, relating to, or affecting a bursa

bursa of fa·bri·cius \-fə'brish(ē)əs\ *usu cap F* [trans. of NL *bursa Fabricii,* fr. *bursa* + *Fabricii,* gen. of *Fabricius* (Hieronymous *Fabricius* of Aquapendente †1619 Ital. anatomist)] **:** a blind glandular sac that opens into the cloaca of birds and functions in immunoglobulin production

bur·sar \'bərsər, -ˌsär; 'bəsə(r, 'bəis-, -ˌsä(r\ *n* -s [ML *bursarius,* fr. *bursa* purse + L *-arius* -ary, n. suffix] **1 :** an administrative officer (as of a monastery or college) in charge of funds **:** TREASURER, PURSER; *sometimes* **:** an officer or other agent supervising material as distinguished from intellectual or spiritual matters **2** *chiefly Scot* **:** a student receiving a scholarship **3 :** a student living in a bursa

bur·sar·i·al \(')bər¦sa(a)rēəl\ *adj* [ML *bursarius* + E *-al*] **:** of or relating to a bursar or bursary

bur·sar·ship *pronunc at* BURSAR+ˌship\ *n* -s **:** BURSARY 2

bur·sa·ry \'bərsərē, 'bəs-, 'bəis-\ *n* -ES [ML *bursaria,* fr. *bursa* + L *-aria* -ary, n. suffix] **1 :** the treasury of a college or monastery **2 :** a sum of varying amount granted to a needy student at a British college or university

bur·sate \'bərˌsāt\ *adj* [NL *bursa* + E *-ate*] **:** having a bursa ⟨a ~ worm⟩

bur·sa·ti *also* **bur·sat·tee** \bə(r)'säd·ē\ *n* -s [Hindi *barsātī* of the rainy season, fr. *barsāt* the rainy season, fr. Skt *varṣārātri,* fr. *varsati* it rains; akin to Gk *arrhēn* male — more at ARRHENATHERUM] **1 :** East Indian cutaneous habronemiasis of the horse esp. prevalent in the rainy season **2** *India* **:** a waterproof cloak or coat

burse \'bərs\ *n* -s [MF *bourse,* fr. ML *bursa* bag, purse — more at PURSE] **1** *obs* **:** EXCHANGE, BOURSE **2 a :** PURSE **b** *obs* **:** a covering resembling a purse (as a vesicle, pod, or hull) **c :** a square pocket or case used in some Christian liturgies to carry the communion cloth

burse 2c

burseed \'ˌ=ˌ=\ *n* **:** STICKSEED

bur·sera \'bərsərə\ *n, cap* [NL, after Joachim *Burser* †1649 Ger. botanist] **:** the type genus of Burseraceae comprising a number of tropical and subtropical American shrubs and trees that have flowers with three to five petals and fleshy capsular fruit and including some that are valuable sources of timber and resins

bur·ser·a·ce·ae \ˌbərsə'rāsē,ē\ *n pl, cap* [NL, fr. *Bursera,* type genus + *-aceae*] **:** a family of resinous or aromatic chiefly tropical shrubs or trees (order Geraniales) with alternate pinnately compound leaves, small greenish usu. panicled flowers, and drupaceous fruit — see BURSERA, ELEMI — **bur·ser·a·ceous** \ˌbərsə¦rāshəs\ *adj*

bur·si·cle \'bərsə̇kəl\ *n* -s [NL *bursicula,* dim. of ML *bursa* bag, purse — more at PURSE] *bot* **:** a pursed or pouched receptacle

bur·sic·u·late \ˌbər¦sikyələt\ *adj* [NL *bursicula* + E *-ate*] **:** shaped like a small pouch or purse

bur·si·form \'bərsəˌfȯrm\ *adj* [ML *bursa* bag, purse + E *-iform* — more at PURSE] **:** shaped like a pouch

bur·si·tis \ˌbər'sīd·ə̇s, bə̄-, bəi'-, ˌbə(r)'-, -ītə̇s\ *n* -ES [NL, fr. *bursa* + *-itis*] **:** inflammation of a bursa; *esp* **:** a painful inflammation involving bursae of the shoulder or elbow

¹burst \'bərst, 'bə̄st, 'bəist\ *vb* **burst** \"\ *also* **bursted** \-təd\ *or archaic* **brast** \'brast\ **burst** *also* **bursted** *or archaic* **brast; bursting; bursts** [ME *bersten, bresten,* fr. OE *berstan;* akin to OHG *brestan* to burst, ON *bresta* to burst, MIr *brosc* noise, and perh. to Lith *braškėti* to make a cracking noise] *vi* **1 :** to break or fail by breaking when subjected to tension ⟨the rope ~ in two as they pulled⟩; *specif* **:** to splinter on impact — used esp. of manual weapons (as swords or lances) **2 a** *of a boil or similar lesion* **:** to rupture and discharge its contents ⟨the pain will ease when the abscess ~s⟩ **b :** to break to pieces esp. from pressure from within **:** EXPLODE ⟨the shell ~ overhead⟩ ⟨if you eat any more you will ~⟩; *broadly* **:** to give way suddenly, explosively, or unexpectedly ⟨the dam ~ under the pressure of flood waters⟩ ⟨he was ready to ~ with disgust⟩ **3 a :** to pass from one place to another esp. with great vigor against obstacles or on release from some restraint ⟨he ~ into the room⟩ ⟨~*ing* free from the clinging mud⟩ ⟨the water ~ through the break in the dam⟩ **b :** to appear or disappear suddenly or unexpectedly — usu. used with words expressing direction (as *forth, out, away, into, through*) ⟨the sun ~ through⟩ ⟨the valley ~ into view⟩ **c :** to make or undergo an abrupt change: as (1) **:** to pass from a less to a more vigorous, ardent, or glowing state ⟨the smoldering logs ~ into flame⟩ ⟨the whole slope will ~ into bloom in another month⟩ (2) **:** to come into bloom **:** OPEN, UNFOLD ⟨buds are ~*ing* on all the trees⟩ **4 a :** to give or receive sudden or unexpected release or expression (as of a cry previously repressed) ⟨he let his fear ~ out in a babble of meaningless chatter⟩ ⟨they ~ out laughing at the sight of us⟩ **b :** to make an abrupt beginning **:** LAUNCH, PLUNGE — usu. used with *into* and esp. of expressions of emotion ⟨he ~ into song⟩ ⟨~*ing* into a furious rage⟩ ⟨he ~ into print without adequate preparation⟩ **5 a :** to be full to the point of breaking open or overflowing ⟨barns ~*ing* with grain⟩ ⟨streams ~*ing* after the late thaw⟩ **b :** to be at the point of giving way to suppressed emotion ⟨he was like to ~ with fury⟩ **6 :** to make a play in forty-one pool that scores more than 41 points ~ *vt* **1 a** *obs* **:** BREAK, SHATTER **b :** to break, rend, or shatter by or as if by violent action or by strain or pressure esp. from within ⟨a blow that nearly ~ his skull⟩ ⟨the ever-increasing number of children who are constantly ~*ing* the walls of outmoded buildings —*Saturday Rev.*⟩ **2 a :** to force open (as a door) or open (as a way) by sudden or vigorous action ⟨he ~ his way through the underbrush⟩ ⟨open up or we'll ~ the door⟩ **b :** to produce (as an opening) by an act or through the effect of bursting ⟨~ a hole through the wall⟩ **3 :** to cause to burst ⟨this warm weather will ~ the buds in a hurry⟩ **syn** see BREAK — **burst at the seams** *also* **burst one's seams :** to be very full or crowded; *esp* **:** to be larger, fuller, or more crowded than could reasonably have been anticipated

²burst \"\ *n* -s **1 a :** a sudden intense outbreak (as of sound or light) ⟨a ~ of flames coming through the roof⟩ ⟨one great ~ of thunder⟩; *esp* **:** a vehement outburst (as of emotion) ⟨a ~ of furious rage⟩ **b :** EXPLOSION, ERUPTION ⟨a ~ of violence⟩; *esp* **:** the explosion of a projectile ⟨the devastating effect of ground ~s⟩ **c :** a brief, intense, or violent effort or exertion ⟨reaching 102 miles per hour in one sustained ~ —A.W. Baum⟩ **:** SPURT ⟨put on a final ~ of speed and crossed the line first⟩; *sometimes* **:** a hard fast ride on horseback **d :** a series of shots fired from an automatic weapon by one pressure of the trigger; *also* **:** the period covered by such a series ⟨a 10-second ~⟩ **2 a :** an act of bursting ⟨beech buds were near the ~ —George Meredith⟩ **b :** a sudden and often unexpected breaking forth, expressing, or manifesting ⟨in a ~ of confidence he told me⟩ ⟨a wild ~ of sobbing⟩ **3 :** a result of bursting: **a :** a flaw or break (as in a water pipe) produced by bursting **b :** a visible puff accompanying the blast of an antiaircraft shell **c :** an intense ionization caused by cosmic rays or by particles resulting from spallation and seen in a cloud chamber or photographic emulsion as a figure resembling a bursting artillery shell **d :** a sudden increase in signal strength of radio waves being received by ionospheric reflection that is believed to be caused by a disturbance of the ionosphere meteors **4 :** a sudden unfolding to view **:** an expanse made visible ⟨a fine ~ of country —Jane Austen⟩ **5 :** a play in the game of forty-one pool that scores more than 41 points and requires the player to begin again with no points **6** *chiefly Brit* **:** SPREE, BLOWOUT

³burst \"\ *also* **bursted** \"\ *adj* **:** that has broken esp. by reason of tension or stress ⟨a ~ bubble⟩ ⟨~ seams⟩

burst·en \-tən\ *adj* [ME, fr. past part. of *bersten* to burst — more at BURST] *archaic* **:** ³BURST

burst·er \-tə(r)\ *n* -s **:** one that bursts: as **a :** a workman who breaks up stone with a light hammer **b :** an explosive charge used to break open and scatter the contents of chemical shells, bombs, and mines **c :** a heavy southerly gale accompanied by a sharp fall in temperature that occurs chiefly along the east coast of Australia **d :** an abnormally double flower (as of the carnation) in which the calyx splits or fragments

bursting charge *n* **:** a charge of explosive designed to burst a projectile

bursting heart *n* [so called fr. its dehiscent red capsules] **:** ²WAHOO

bursting point *n* **:** the point at which emotional control esp. of oneself is lost

bursting strength *n* **:** the capacity of a material (as a paper or textile) or object (as a metal pipe) to maintain its continuity when subjected to pressure; *broadly* **:** the pressure often expressed in pounds per square inch required to rupture such a material or object under rigidly controlled conditions

burstone *var of* BUHRSTONE

burstwort \'ˌ=ˌ=\ *n* [²*burst* + *wort;* fr. the belief that it cured ruptures] **:** RUPTUREWORT

bur·su·la \'bərsələ\ *n, pl* **bursu·lae** \-ˌlē, -ˌlī\ [NL, dim. of *bursa*] **:** a small anatomical bursa

bur·then \'bərthən\ *var of* BURDEN

bur·then·some \-səm\ *archaic var of* BURDENSOME

¹bur·ton \'bərtᵊn\ *n* -s [origin unknown] **1 :** any of several arrangements of hoisting tackle; *usu* **:** one with a single and a double block **2 :** stowage (as of casks) athwartships in the hold of a ship

²burton \"\ *n* -s [fr. *Burton* on Trent, county borough, Staffordshire, England, the locality of the water orig. used] **:** a strong dark ale

burton-ail \"+ˌāl\ *n, usu cap B* [prob. after Glenn W. *Burton* b1910 Am. agronomist] *in N. H.* **:** cobalt deficiency disease of cattle and sheep **:** PINE

bur·ton·ing \'bərt(ᵊ)niŋ\ *n* -s [¹*burton* + *-ing*] **:** a system of handling a ship's cargo by means of a sling rigging between two derricks or masts

bur·ton·ize \'bərtᵊnˌīz\ *vt* -ED/-ING/-S *often cap* [*Burton* on Trent, England, + *-ize*] **:** to harden (water used in brewing) by adding gypsum or certain salts esp. for the purpose of approximating the flavor of burton

1 2 3

1 Spanish burton, single; *2* Spanish burton, double; *3* top burton

burulée *or* **buruly** *var of* BURELLY

bu·run·di \bu̇'ründē, bə-,bü-, -'rün-,-'rən-\ *adj, usu cap* [fr. *Burundi,* country in east central Africa] **:** of or from the country of Burundi **:** of the kind or style prevalent in Burundi

bu·run·di·an \-dēən\ *n* -s *cap* [*Burundi,* Africa + E *-an*] **:** a native or inhabitant of Burundi — **burundian** *adj, usu cap*

burunduki *var of* BARONDUKI

bu·ru·shas·ki \ˌbu̇rə'shäskē\ *n* -s *usu cap* **:** a language of unknown affinity spoken in northwestern Kashmir, India

bu·rut *or* **bou·rout** \bə'rüt\ *n* -s *usu cap* **:** KARA KIRGHIZ

burweed \'ˌ=ˌ=\ *n* **:** any of certain plants having the fruit enclosed in a bur: as **a :** COCKLEBUR **b :** BURDOCK **c :** any of certain plants of the genera *Galium, Triumfetta,* or *Amsinckia*

burweed marsh elder *n* **:** a tall annual marsh elder (*Iva xanthifolia*) that is common in moist rich soil in central No. America, causes contact dermatitis in many people, and produces much pollen that is a major cause of hay fever where the plant occurs — called also *false ragweed*

¹bury \'berē, -ri\ *vb* -ED/-ING/-ES [ME *berien, burien,* fr. OE *byrgan;* akin to OE *beorgan* to preserve, defend, *borgian* to borrow, OHG *bergan* to shelter, hide, ON *bjarga* to save, Goth *bairgan* to keep, save, Russ *berech'* to look after, save] *vt* **1 a :** to dispose of (a corpse) by depositing in the earth, a grave, or a tomb, by consigning to the water, or by cremation ⟨they *buried* the victims where they fell⟩ ⟨he was *buried* at sea⟩; *esp* **:** to inter with appropriate funeral ceremonies ⟨they *buried* him with full military honors⟩ **b :** to perform the burial rites of ⟨the priest that *buried* my father⟩ **c :** to lose by death ⟨she has *buried* three husbands⟩ **d :** to be or become responsible for the burial costs of ⟨he left nothing, the town had to ~ him⟩ **2 :** to cover esp. with earth ⟨like a dog ~*ing* his bone⟩: as **a :** to dispose of by covering out of sight in the earth ⟨a wise camper *buries* his garbage every day⟩ — used esp. when the object dealt with is regarded as permanently abandoned **b :** to conceal by or as if by covering with earth ⟨~*ing* treasures in the sand⟩ **c :** to cover from view ⟨she *buried* her face in her hands⟩ **3 :** to put irrevocably or completely out of sight or mind: as **a :** to consign to oblivion **:** have done with **:** give up ⟨finally ~*ing* their differences⟩ **b :** to conceal in obscurity **:** remove from the world of action or affairs (as by remoteness) ⟨*buried* his family in the country⟩ ⟨*buried* herself in the cloister⟩; *often* **:** to render negligible by depriving of proper prominence ⟨*buried* the retraction among the classified ads⟩ **c :** SUBMERGE, ENGROSS — usu. used with *in* ⟨had necessarily *buried* himself in his books⟩ ⟨*buried* in grief and despair⟩ **d** *in card games* **:** to put (one or more cards) permanently or temporarily out of play (as by placing an exposed card in or under the dealer's pack or by covering a card in certain solitaire games) ~ *vi* **:** to become buried; *specif* **:** to thrust the bow of a ship under water **syn** see CONCEAL — **bury the hatchet :** to settle a disagreement **:** make peace

²bury \"\ *n* -ES **1 :** a dugout or pit in the earth in which potatoes or other vegetables are protected against freezing; *often* **:** a heap or quantity of produce stored in a bury **:** CLAMP **2 :** the depth at which something is buried beneath a surface ⟨in milder regions a ~ of two feet will protect the pipes⟩

³bury \'bəri\ *n* -ES [alter. of ¹*burrow*] *dial Brit* **:** ¹BURROW 1

bur·yat *also* **bur·iat** \(')bu̇r¦yät, ¦bu̇rē¦ät\ *n, pl* **buryat** *or* **buryats** *also* **buriat** *or* **buriats** *usu cap* [Russ *buryat,* fr. Mongolian *burijad*] **1 a :** a Mongol people of eastern Siberia **b :** a member of such people **2 :** the language of the Buryat people

¹burying *n* -s [ME *berying, burying,* fr. gerund of *berien, burien* to bury — more at BURY] **:** a funeral and interment ⟨the country preacher who took charge of the ~s⟩

²burying *adj* [fr. pres. part. of ¹*bury*] **:** used for or concerned with burying **:** BURIAL ⟨a ~ lot⟩ ⟨~ places near small towns⟩

burying beetle *n* **:** any of various carrion beetles of *Necrophorus, Silpha,* and related genera that bury small dead animals by digging away the earth beneath them for the purpose of feeding their larvae on the fly maggots that develop in such carcasses

burying ground *n* **:** a plot of land set aside for burying the dead

¹bus \'bəs\ *n, pl* **bus·es** *or* **bus·ses** \-səz\ *often attrib* [short for *omnibus*] **1 a :** a large motor-driven vehicle designed to carry passengers usu. according to a schedule along a fixed route but sometimes under charter for a special trip (as by a social group or an athletic team) ⟨sightseeing ~⟩ ⟨~ station⟩ ⟨the ~ is usually on time⟩ **b :** any vehicle either publicly owned or privately owned and operated for compensation used for transporting children to or from school **c :** any of various conveyances resembling a bus (as in carrying passengers or traveling a fixed route according to a schedule) ⟨up the Grand Canal by water —Nigel Balchin⟩ ⟨a horse ~⟩ ⟨a milk ~⟩ **d** *slang* **:** AUTOMOBILE ⟨not a bad old ~ —A.J.Cronin⟩ **e :** a hand-pushed usu. 4-wheeled vehicle used typically for carrying dishes in a restaurant **2 :** BUSBOY **3** *or* **bus bar :** an assembly of conductors usu. bare but supported on insulators for collecting electric currents from sources and distributing them to outgoing feeders

²bus \"\ *vb* **bused** *or* **bussed** \'bəst\ **bused** *or* **bussed** \"\ **busing** *or* **bussing** \'bəsiŋ\ **buses** *or* **busses** \'bəsəz\ *vi* **1 :** to travel by bus **2 :** to work as a busboy or bus girl ⟨made extra money *bussing* at a nearby restaurant⟩ ~ *vt* **:** to move or transport by bus ⟨~ children to school⟩

³bus \'bəs\ *var of* BAS

bus *abbr* business

busaun *obs var of* POSAUNE

bus·boy \'bəsˌbȯi\ *n* **:** a boy or man who cleans up restaurant tables for reuse, removes dirty dishes, keeps ready a supply of needed items (as dishes, silver, napkins), and helps clean up the place **:** a waiter's assistant ⟨he has been all through the mill, from counterman in a hash house to ~ to banquet waiter —Dwight Macdonald⟩

bus·by \'bəzbē\ *n* -ES [prob. fr. the name *Busby*] **1 :** a large bushy wig **2 a :** a military full-dress hat made of fur with a bag usu. of cloth and of the color of the facings of the regiment hanging from the top on the right **b :** the bearskin worn by British guardsmen — not used technically

busby 2a

buscarle *n* -s [alter. of OE *butsecarl,* fr. (assumed) ON *būzukarl,* fr. ON *būza* buss (ship) + *karl* man — more at BUSS, CARL] *archaic* **:** MARINER

bus driver *n* **:** one that drives a bus

bus duct *n* **:** an electric conduit prefabricated in sections and containing heavy conductors for transmission of large currents at relatively low voltage

bus girl *n* **:** a girl or woman whose duties are those of a busboy

¹bush \'bu̇sh\ *n* -ES *often attrib* [ME *bush, busk, bosk;* akin to MD *busch, bosch* bush, forest, OHG *busc,* OSw *buske* bush] **1 a :** SHRUB; *esp* **:** a low densely branched shrub suggesting a single plant ⟨a blueberry ~⟩ **b :** a close thicket of shrubs ⟨~*es* suitable for a hedge⟩ **c** *dial Eng* **:** THORN **2 a** (1) **:** common uncultivated usu. undesirable bushes ⟨a field overgrown with ~⟩ (2) **:** the mixed plant growth typical of an uncleared or uncultivated area esp. when other than grass or trees ⟨part of the land once cultivated has been abandoned, to the sea, to flood waters, or to ~ —W.A.Lewis⟩ (3) **:** FOREST, WOODS, JUNGLE ⟨in the dense ~ . . . creepers of many kinds and of every size, from huge cables to thin cords, loop from tree to tree, pushing up to the sunlight and knotting the undergrowth into impenetrable thickets —C.D.Forde⟩ **b :** a large uncleared or uncultivated area usu. scrub-covered or heavily forested **:** WILDERNESS ⟨all this property . . . was ~ where last year nothing thrived but zebra and impala, wildebeest and bad snakes —Basil Davidson⟩ **c :** a usu. vast sparsely settled area **:** BACKCOUNTRY ⟨~ doctor⟩ ⟨~ flying⟩ ⟨~ airline⟩ — usu. used with *the* when not attributive ⟨in the lonely ~ —Henry Lawson⟩ ⟨boys from the ~ —Esther Warner⟩; *specif* **:** any of certain vast and sparsely settled geographical areas esp. in New Zealand, Australia, Africa, and Canada **3 a** (1) *archaic* **:** a bunch or branch of ivy formerly hung outside a tavern to indicate wine for sale (2) *obs* **:** TAVERN **b :** ADVERTISING — used esp. with *need* ⟨good wine needs no ~ —Shak.⟩ ⟨good essays need no ~ —*Yale Review*⟩ **4 :** something resembling or felt to resemble a bush ⟨the ermine ~ of feathers that formed the crest —W.H.St. John Hope⟩ ⟨~*es* of black smoke —Barrett McGurn⟩ ⟨a ~ of hair —Roger Senhouse⟩ **5 :** SUGAR BUSH **6** [by shortening] **:** BUSH LEAGUE — usu. used in pl. ⟨finally decided to ship him back to the ~*es* —*Scholastic Coach*⟩

²bush \"\ *vb* -ED/-ING/-ES *vt* **1 :** to support (as a plant) with bushes ⟨the birch he said I could have to ~ my peas —Robert Frost⟩ **2 :** to mark (as a route) with bushes ⟨a logging road across the river was ~*ed* when the ice was safe⟩ **3 :** to protect (land or game) from net poachers by placing obstacles (as bushes) to prevent effective use of a net ~ *vi* **:** to extend like a bush **:** have the appearance of a bush ⟨his eyebrows ~*ed* together⟩ ⟨he looked about 30 but surprising gray hair ~*ed* out of his fore-and-aft cap —Richard Llewellyn⟩ — **bush it** *Austral* **:** to live in the bush

³bush \"\ *adj* **:** having a low-growing compact bushy habit — used esp. of cultivated beans ⟨~ snap beans⟩

⁴bush \"\ *n* -ES [D *bus* bushing, box, fr. MD *busse* box, fr. LL *buxis* — more at BOX] **1 :** BUSHING **2 :** a threaded socket flush with a surface of a camera or projector for attachment to a tripod

⁵bush \"\ *vt* -ED/-ING/-ES **:** to furnish with a bushing

⁶bush \"\ *vt* -ED/-ING/-ES [by shortening] **:** BUSHHAMMER

bush baby *n* **:** any of several small African lemurs of the genus *Galago*

bush basil *n* **:** a small cultivated annual herb (*Ocimum minimum*) with nearly entire leaves

bush·beat \'bu̇sh,bēt, *usu* -ēd·+V\ *vi* [back-formation fr. *bushbeater*] **:** to beat the bushes

bush·beat·er \"+ə(r)\ *n* [¹*bush* + *beater*] **:** one that beats the bushes; *esp* **:** a scout esp. for promising young actors or ballplayers

bushberry \'bu̇sh- —*see* BERRY\ *n* **:** any of various berries or fruits resembling berries borne on bushes (as raspberries, gooseberries, currants)

bushboy \'ˌ=ˌ=\ *n* **:** BUSHMAN

bushbuck \'ˌ=ˌ=\ *n, pl* **bushbuck** *or* **bushbucks** [trans. of Afrik *bosbok*] **:** a small southern African harnessed antelope (*Tragelaphus scriptus* syn. *Strepsiceros scriptus*) having spirally twisted horns and frequenting forests — called also *boschbok*

bush canary *n* **:** a small New Zealand bird (*Mohua ochrocephala*) having a yellow head and breast

bush cat *n* **1 a :** SERVAL **b :** any of various small Asiatic and African cats **2 :** an Asiatic civet cat

bush cinquefoil *n* **:** a much-branched shrub (*Potentilla fruticosa*) with compound leaves and yellow flowers common through the north temperate zone often as a weed

bush clover *n* **:** any of certain usu. shrubby lespedezas (as bicolor lespedeza)

bush cow *n* **1 :** the short-horned buffalo of West Africa which is sometimes regarded as a separate species (*Syncerus nanus*) **2 :** TAPIR

bushcraft \ˈ=,=\ *n* **:** the skill gained by or necessary for living in bush country
bush disease *n* **:** ¹PINE 3
bush doe *n* **:** the female of the bushbuck
bush dog *n* **1 :** a small wild dog (*Speothos venadictus* syn. *Icticyon venaticus*) of northern So. America **2 :** POTTO
bushed \ˈbu̇sht\ *adj* [¹*bush* + *-ed*] **1 :** covered with or as if with a bushy growth ⟨we had to land the boat on a steep, densely ~ bank⟩ **2** *chiefly Austral* **a :** lost in the bush ⟨he said it would be dangerous for me to go up without him; I was bound to get ~ and he was too busy to be bothered having to waste a day hunting for me —F.S.Anthony⟩ **b :** AMAZED, BEWILDERED ⟨adapting his language to my ~ comprehension —Henry Lawson⟩ **3 :** TIRED, EXHAUSTED ⟨I heard a noise, and yells, but I was too ~ to worry —Christopher Morley⟩
¹**bush·el** \ˈbu̇shəl\ *n* -s [ME *busshel, boyschel*, fr. OF *boissel*, fr. (assumed) OF *boisse* one sixth of a bushel (whence MF *boisse*), of Celt origin; akin to MIr *boss, bass* palm of the hand] **1 :** any of various units of capacity: as **a :** a unit of dry capacity used in the U.S. equal to 2150.42 cubic inches **:** WINCHESTER BUSHEL **b :** a British unit of dry and liquid capacity equal to 8 imperial gallons or 2219.36 cubic inches — see MEASURE table **2 a :** a container used as a bushel measure ⟨nor do men light a lamp and put it under a ~, but on a stand —Mt 5:15 (RSV)⟩ **b :** something that conceals by or as if by covering ⟨razzle-dazzle journalism continued to be a *Times* specialty, albeit one well hidden under the ~ of its solemn thoroughness —*Newsweek*⟩ **3 :** a large quantity **:** LOTS, LOADS ⟨~*s* of fun⟩ ⟨didn't do anything wrong, except tell a ~ of cockeyed lies —Calder Willingham⟩ ⟨~*s* of love letters —G.B.Shaw⟩ ⟨pamphlets mailed out by the ~⟩
²**bushel** \"\ *vt* **busheled** *also* **bushelled; busheled** *also* **bushelled; busheling** *also* **bushelling** \-sh(ə)liŋ\ **bushels 1 :** to hide under or as if under a bushel ⟨don't ~ your light in the city⟩ ⟨~*ed* information⟩ **2** [so called fr. the fact that scrap iron was formerly sold by the bushel] **:** to heat (scrap iron) to a welding temperature esp. in a reverberatory furnace
³**bushel** *vb* **busheled** *also* **bushelled; busheled** *also* **bushelled; busheling** *also* **bushelling** \-sh(ə)liŋ\ **bushels** [prob. fr. G *bosseln* to do poor work, to do odd jobs, to patch, fr. MHG *bōzeln* to beat, freq. of *bōzen*, fr. OHG *bōzan* — more at BEAT] *vt* **:** ALTER, FINISH, REPAIR ⟨~*s* men's suits⟩ ~ *vi* **:** to alter, finish, or repair garments and esp. men's suits
bush·el·age \ˈbu̇shəlij\ *n* -s [¹*bushel* + *-age*] **:** amount in bushels
bush·el·er \-sh(ə)lə(r)\ *n* -s [prob. fr. G *bossler*, fr. *bosseln* + *-er*] **:** one that bushels
bush·el·ful \-shəl,fu̇l\ *n, pl* **bushelfuls** \-,fu̇lz\ *also* **bushelsful** \-shəlz,fu̇l\ **:** as much as a bushel will hold
bush·el·man \-shəlmən\ *n, pl* **bushelmen** [³*bushel* + *man*] **:** BUSHELER
bush·er \ˈbu̇shə(r)\ *n* -s [¹*bush* + *-er*] **1 :** SWAMPER **2 :** BUSH LEAGUER ⟨who gave you a ticket to get into the game, ~⟩
bushes *pl of* BUSH, *pres 3d sing of* BUSH
bushfelling \ˈ=,==\ *n* -s *Austral* **:** the cutting of timber in bush country
bushfighter \ˈ=,==\ *n* **:** one that engages in bushfighting
bushfighting \ˈ=,==\ *n* **1 :** warfare in or as if in the bush **:** hard fighting that involves a resourceful dodging, hiding, or moving warily and surreptitiously among trees, rocks, and undergrowth **2 :** a hard skirmishing between resourceful opponents
bush fly *n* **:** any of several small flies related to the housefly that are often extremely abundant in pastoral parts of Australia and that swarm over cattle and other animals
bush forest *n* **:** CHAPARRAL
bush fowl *n* **:** MEGAPODE
bush fruit *n* **1 :** a small fruit growing on a woody bush (as the currant and gooseberry) **2 :** a plant producing bush fruit — compare CANE FRUIT
bush goat *n* [trans. of Afrik *bosbok*] **:** BUSHBUCK
bush grape *n* **1 :** SAND GRAPE **2 :** a shrubby wild grape (*Vitis acerifolia*) of the southern U.S. having leaves permanently pilose beneath and fruit with persistent heavy bloom
bushgrass \ˈ=,=\ *n* **:** a stout erect perennial Eurasian grass (*Calamagrostis epigejos*) having spikelets with a profusion of basal silky hairs longer than the lemmas
¹**bush-hammer** \ˈbu̇sh+,-\ *n* [modif. of G *bosshammer*, fr. obs. G *bossen* to beat (fr. OHG *bōzan*) + G *hammer*, fr. OHG *hamar* — more at BEAT, HAMMER] **:** a hammer with a serrated face for dressing stone and concrete
²**bushhammer** \"\ *vt* **:** to dress (stone or concrete) with a bushhammer

bushhammer

bush harrow *n* **:** BRUSH HARROW
bush-harrow \ˈ=,(,)=\ *vb* [*bush harrow*] **:** to till with a brush harrow
bush hawk *n* **:** a small falcon (*Falco novaeseelandiae*) of New Zealand that resembles the kestrel
bush honeysuckle *n* **1 :** a plant of the genus *Diervilla; esp* **:** a shrub (*D. lonicera*) of the northeastern U.S. having opposite leaves and fragrant yellow flowers **2 :** any of several shrubby honeysuckles of the genus *Lonicera* (esp. *L. tatarica*)
bush hook *n* **:** a short stout hooked blade fitted to an ax handle and used for cutting bushes — called also *bush scythe*

bush hook

bush huckleberry *n* **:** a low shrub (*Gaylussacia dumosa*) of eastern No. America with rather watery and tasteless black fruit
bu·shi·do \ˈbushi,dō, ˈbüsh-, *Japanese approximately* ˈbu̇sh-ˈdō\ *n* -s *usu cap* [Jap *bushidō*, fr. *bushi* warrior (fr. *bu* military + *shi* man) + *dō* doctrine] **:** a traditional specif. feudal-military Japanese code of behavior emphasizing loyalty, benevolence, bravery, self-control, and the valuing of honor above life
bushier *comparative of* BUSHY
bushies *pl of* BUSHY
bushiest *superlative of* BUSHY
bush·i·ly \ˈbu̇shəlē, -li\ *adv* **:** in a bushy manner
bush·i·ness \ˈbu̇shēnəs, -shin-\ *n* -ES **:** the quality or state of being bushy
bush·ing \ˈbu̇shiŋ, -shēŋ\ *n* -s [fr. gerund of ⁴*bush*] **1 :** a usu. removable lining or sleeve of metal or other material that is inserted or screwed into an opening (as of a mechanical part) to limit its size, resist wear or erosion, or serve as a guide **2 :** an insulating sleeve inserted in an opening in a metal plate or case (as of a microphone or electric clock) to protect a through conductor from abrasion and possible short circuit **3 :** an internally and externally threaded plug for connecting a pipe or fitting with another of different size
bush jacket *n* **:** a long cotton jacket like a shirt with four patch pockets, self belt, and sometimes collar worn esp. in rough country
bushland \ˈ=,=\ *n* **:** BUSH 2b
bush lark *n* **:** any of several larks (genus *Mirafra*) of the Old World frequenting bushy and wooded places
bush lawyer *n* **1 :** NEW ZEALAND BRAMBLE **2** *Austral* **:** a person pretending to have considerable legal knowledge
bush league *n* **:** a minor league esp. in baseball **:** a sports league of low classification or poor quality ⟨a good catcher but not a great one, he was tricky and tough enough to move up through the *bush leagues* into the big time —*Time*⟩
bush-league *adj* [*bush league*] **:** belonging to an inferior class or group of its kind **:** MINOR, MEDIOCRE ⟨a *bush-league* demagogue⟩ ⟨a *bush-league* college⟩ **:** INADEQUATE ⟨a *bush-league* carrier and three 4-stack destroyers too old for anything else —Wirt Williams⟩
bush leagu·er \ˈbu̇sh¦lēgə(r)\ *n* **1 :** someone in a bush league; *esp* **:** a player in such a league **2 :** an incompetent performer or small-time operator ⟨in the business world he was regarded as a *bush leaguer*⟩ — called also *busher*
bush lespedeza *n* **:** BUSH CLOVER
bush·less \ˈbu̇shləs\ *adj* **:** being without a bush
bush·man \ˈbu̇shmən\ *n, pl* **bushmen** [modif. (influenced by ¹*bush*) of obs. Afrik *boschjesman*, fr. *boschjes* (gen. of obs. *boschje*, dim. of *bosch* forest — now *bos*) + *man*, fr. MD; akin to OHG *man* person, man — more at BOSCHBOK, MAN] **1** *usu cap* **:** one of a race of nomadic hunters of southern Africa now chiefly confined to the Kalahari desert that are of short stature and have leathery yellow skin, a flat triangular face, often excessive development of fat on the buttocks esp. of females, and low cranial capacity **2** *usu cap* **:** a Khoisan language of the Bushmen **3** [¹*bush* + *man*] *chiefly Austral* **a :** one that lives in the bush **b :** one skilled in bushcraft **c :** FARMER, RUBE, HICK
bushman grass *n* **:** any of a number of southern African grasses; *specif* **:** a perennial forage grass (*Stipa dregeana*) of the arid veld
bush·man·oid \-,nȯid\ *adj, usu cap* **:** resembling the Bushman people or their artifacts
bushmanship \-mən,ship\ *n* -s **:** BUSHCRAFT
bushman's poison *n, pl* **bushman's poisons :** ORDEAL TREE 3
bush maple *n* **1 :** MOUNTAIN MAPLE **2 :** STRIPED MAPLE
bush marrow *n* **:** a squash with a bushy habit
bushmaster \ˈ=,==\ *n* **:** the largest of the New World pit vipers (*Lachesis mutus*) sometimes reaching a length of 12 feet, producing immense quantities of venom, and being widely distributed in tropical American forests and of notably irritable aggressive disposition
bush meeting *n* **:** a religious gathering held in a woods — compare CAMP MEETING
bush metal *n* [³*bush*] **:** an alloy that is similar in composition to gun metal and used for bushings
bush monkey *n* **:** a logger who piles tanbark into ricks
bush monkeyflower *n* **:** a low shrubby plant (*Mimulus longiflorus*) of California with evergreen viscid foliage and showy light yellow to salmon flowers
bush morning-glory *n* **:** MAN-OF-THE-EARTH
bush negro *n, usu cap B&N* [trans. of D *bosneger*] **:** one of a people of African ancestry descended from runaway slaves and inhabiting the interior of the Guianas in So. America
bush nut *n* **1 :** MACADAMIA 2a **2 :** MACADAMIA NUT
bush oak *n* **:** a scrub oak (*Quercus ilicifolia*)
bu·shon·go \bü'shäŋ(,)gō\ *n, pl* **bushongo** *or* **bushongos** *usu cap* **:** ²KUBA
bush out *vt* **:** to clear or make (as a path or road) through bush country
bush parole *n, slang* **:** escape from prison
bush pea *n* **:** a plant of the genus *Thermopsis*
bush pepper *n* **:** BIRD PEPPER
bushpig \ˈ=,=\ *n* [trans. of Afrik *bosvark*] **:** an African wild swine (*Koiropotamus koiropotamus* or *Potamochoerus koiropotamus*) having a reddish coat that turns gray with age, white cheek patches, and a white erectile crest
bush pilot *n* **:** an airplane pilot who flies over uninhabited country (as in Canada or Alaska) esp. off regular commercial lanes ⟨a frontier still penetrated only by river barge, dog team, tractor train, and *bush pilot* — W.C.Gilman⟩
bush poppy *n* **:** a California evergreen shrub (*Dendromecon rigida*) of the family Papaveraceae with yellowish green foliage often cultivated for its long-stalked golden-yellow flowers
bush pumpkin *or* **bush squash** *n* **:** any of various cultivated pumpkins derived from the variety *Cucurbita pepo melopepo* and having the internodes of the plant axis greatly shortened so that the whole plant forms a compact bushy growth with no tendency to vine
bushranger \ˈ=,==\ *n* **1 :** FRONTIERSMAN, WOODSMAN **2** *Austral* **:** an outlaw living in the bush
bush rat *n* **1 :** WOOD RAT **2 :** YUNGAS **3 :** DEGU
bush robin *n* **:** any of several small Oriental birds related to the American robin but resembling the European robin
bushrope \ˈ=,=\ *n* **:** LIANA
bush scythe *n* **:** any of several implements: **a :** a scythe that has a short thick heavy blade and a stout handle and is used for cutting brush and bushes **b :** BUSH HOOK **c :** BILLHOOK
bush shirt *n* **:** BUSH JACKET
bush shrike *n* **:** any of various African thicket-dwelling shrikes
bush sickness *n* [so called fr. its occurrence in the New Zealand bushland] **:** cobalt deficiency disease of cattle and sheep **:** PINE
bush soul *n, among some primitive peoples* **:** a man's second soul believed to inhabit a wild animal of the bush
bush swamp *n* **:** a plant association found in wet places, dominated by shrubs or low trees, and common in Europe and the southeastern U.S.
bush-tailed opossum \ˈ=,=-\ *n* **:** a common Australian marsupial (*Trichosurus vulpecula*) with thick woolly grizzled fur
bush tamarind *n* **:** an African tree (*Machaerium schomburgkii*) that is the source of tigerwood
bush tea *n* **1 :** a southern African plant (*Cyclopia subternata*) of the family Leguminosae **2 :** the leaves of the bush-tea plant used as a beverage
bush telegraph *n* **1 :** a means whereby the natives of a jungle or bush rapidly spread news from person to person **2** *chiefly Austral* **:** an informal but well-organized system of word-of-mouth communication transmitting plans and movements of the police **:** GRAPEVINE **3 :** unofficial information **:** RUMOR
bush tick *n* **:** a tick (*Haemaphysalis bispinosa*) common on cattle in Australia
bushtit \ˈ=,=\ *n* -s **:** any of several titmice (genus *Psaltriparus*) of the Pacific coast from British Columbia to Lower California and inland and southward to Wyoming, Texas, and Guatemala usu. considered varieties of a single species (*P. minimus*)
bush trefoil *n* **:** TICK TREFOIL
bush up *vi, chiefly South and Midland* **:** HIDE
bush·veld \ˈbu̇sh,felt\ *n* -s *sometimes cap* [modif. of obs. Afrik *boschveld* — more at BOSCHVELD] **:** southern African veld characterized by abundant shrubby and often thorny vegetation (as of acacias and aloes)
bush vetch *n* **:** a European purple-flowered vetch (*Vicia sepium*) with slender stems that occurs as a weed in hedgerows
bush·wa *or* **bush·wah** \ˈbu̇sh(,)wä, -wȯ\ *n* -s [prob. euphemism for *bullshit*] **:** BUNKUM, HOOEY ⟨there it was again: the ~, the sloganeering, being poured out to him with no regard for the truth —David Driscoll⟩
bush warbler *n* **:** any of various chiefly tropical warblers (family Sylviidae) of open or brushy country
bush·whack *also* **bush·wack** \ˈbu̇sh,(h)wak\ *vb* -ED/-ING/-S [back-formation fr. *bushwhacker, bushwacker*] *vi* **1 a :** to clear a path through thick woods esp. by chopping down bushes and low branches **b :** to propel a boat by pulling on bushes along the bank **2 a :** to make repeated emphatic gestures while speaking specif. in a manner felt to resemble the chopping of bushes **b :** to make a speech accompanied by such gestures **3 a :** to hide out in the woods **b :** to travel through thick woods (as in making a thorough search) **4 :** to fight as a bushwhacker ~ *vt* **1 :** to propel (a boat) by pulling on bushes along the bank **2 :** to fight or attack as a bushwhacker **:** AMBUSH
bush·whack·er *also* **bush·wack·er** \-kə(r)\ *also* **bushwhack** \-k\ *n* -s [*bushwhacker* fr. ¹*bush* + *whacker; bushwacker & bushwack*, alter. of *bushwhacker*] **:** one that bushwhacks: as **a :** a person who clears away the bush (as in preparing land for grazing); *also* **:** an implement for this **b :** one that lives in or frequents the woods **:** WOODSMAN **c :** a Confederate soldier who engaged in guerrilla warfare in the Civil War **d :** one that fires from ambush **:** SNIPER **e :** a deserter or draft dodger who became an outlaw esp. during and after the Civil War **f :** BUSHFIGHTER, RAIDER, GUERRILLA **g :** OUTLAW, BANDIT
bush willow *n* **:** any of a number of southern African trees of the genus *Combretum:* as **a :** a small deciduous tree (*Combretum apiculatum*) 15 to 20 feet high that is a common constituent of the Transvaal bushveld **b :** a small tree (*Combretum erythrophyllum*) bearing 4-winged fruits and usu. growing on the banks of streams
bushwood *n* **:** BRUSHWOOD, UNDERGROWTH; *specif* **:** a woodland in which shrubs predominate
¹**bushy** \ˈbu̇shē, -shi\ *adj* -ER/-EST [ME, fr. ¹*bush* + *-y*] **1 :** full of or overgrown with bushes ⟨~ country⟩ ⟨a ~ garden⟩ **2 :** resembling a bush; *esp* **:** thick and spreading ⟨~ eyebrows⟩ ⟨a ~ tail⟩
²**bushy** \"\ *n* -ES [by shortening & alter.] **:** BUSHMAN 3
bushy aster *n* **:** a stiff perennial herb (*Aster dumosus*) of the eastern U.S. having small linear leaves and numerous tiny white flower heads
bushy gerardia *n* **:** a conspicuous yellow-flowered perennial herb (*Aureolaria pedicularia*) of the family Scrophulariaceae of eastern No. America with divided sticky foliage
bushy stunt *n* **:** a virus disease of tomato causing yellowing and purpling of the foliage, necrotic lesions, and a dwarfed much-branched growth habit
bushy-tailed rat \ˈ==,=-\ *n* **:** CLOUD RAT
busied *past of* BUSY
busier *comparative of* BUSY
busies *pres 3d sing of* BUSY
busiest *superlative of* BUSY
busi·ly \ˈbiz(ə)lē, -li\ *adv* [ME *bisily*, fr. *bisy* busy + *-ly* — more at BUSY] **:** in a busy manner **:** INDUSTRIOUSLY, ACTIVELY, BRISKLY ⟨his tongue wagged ~ —Dorothy Sayers⟩ **:** INTENTLY ⟨studying ~⟩
bu·sine \bü'zēn\ *or* **bo·zine** \bō'z-\ *n* -s [ME *bosyne*, fr. MF *buisine, busine, bosine*, fr. L *bucina* — more at BUCCINA] **:** a medieval straight trumpet
busi·ness \ˈbiznəs, -nəz, *rapid or substand* ˈbidnə- *or* ˈbinə-; *sometimes* ÷ ˈbizˈnə-\ *n* -ES *often attrib* [ME *bisinesse*, fr. *bisy* busy + *-nesse* -ness] **1 a** (1) *archaic* **:** purposeful activity **:** activity directed toward some end ⟨the greatest master of parliamentary tactics and political ~ in his generation —Walter Bagehot⟩ (2) **:** an activity engaged in as normal, logical, or inevitable and usu. extending over a considerable period of time **:** ROLE, FUNCTION ⟨formal study is the primary ~ of a college student⟩ ⟨how the human mind went about its ~ of learning —H.A.Overstreet⟩ (3) **:** an activity engaged in toward an immediate specific end and usu. extending over a limited period of time **:** TASK, CHORE, MISSION, ASSIGNMENT ⟨what is your ~ here at this hour⟩ ⟨a mob of a thousand people may lynch a Negro on the slightest provocation and apparently enjoy the dirty ~ —C.C.Furnas⟩ ⟨this knife will do the ~⟩ **b** (1) **:** a usu. commercial or mercantile activity customarily engaged in as a means of livelihood and typically involving some independence of judgment and power of decision ⟨the ~ of a printer being generally thought a poor one —Benjamin Franklin⟩ and sometimes contrasted with the arts ⟨but in a sick world it is not literature, it becomes simply the writing ~ —Francis Hackett⟩ or professions ⟨there was none . . . who did more to raise it from the dull routine of a ~ to something approaching a profession —R.R.Rowe⟩ or sport ⟨hunting and fishing were favorite pastimes but the abundance of game and its use as food made these amusements less sport than ~ or slaughter —*Amer. Guide Series: N.C.*⟩ or other activity considered less practical, serious, respectable, or mundane ⟨he changed the processing and marketing of petroleum from a gamble to a ~ —Marquis James⟩ ⟨the way therefore to avoid public comment is to avoid the speech of affection and to use that of ~ —R.M.Weaver⟩ **:** OCCUPATION, POSITION, TRADE, LINE (2) **:** a commercial or industrial enterprise ⟨he's in ~ for himself⟩ ⟨he sold out his ~⟩; *collectively* **:** such enterprises ⟨the city is a ~ center⟩ ⟨~ does not act as a unit⟩ (3) **:** a place where such an enterprise is carried on ⟨the explosion broke windows in ~*es* several blocks away⟩ (4) **:** transactions, dealings, or intercourse of any nature ⟨they were far away from the Zidonians and had no ~ with any man —Judg 18:7 (AV)⟩ but now esp. economic (as buying and selling) ⟨~ as usual⟩ ⟨you can't do ~ with that heel⟩ ⟨the company did more ~ than ever⟩; *esp* **:** PATRONAGE ⟨how's ~⟩ ⟨I'll take my ~ somewhere else⟩ (5) **:** the procedures and techniques of such enterprises ⟨a strong ~ sense⟩ ⟨he supervised the manufacturing while his brother handled the ~⟩ **c :** serious activity that requires time and effort and usu. the avoidance of distracting influences ⟨she got down to ~ and finished all of the letters in less than an hour⟩ **:** JOB, DUTY, WORK ⟨~ before pleasure⟩ ⟨she means ~⟩ **d :** a particular field of endeavor ⟨the best comedian in the ~⟩ ⟨that jockey really knows his ~⟩ **2 a :** AFFAIR, MATTER ⟨the ~ of people being able to feed themselves is fundamentally . . . a local matter —S.A.Cain⟩ ⟨I'm sick of this stupid ~⟩ **b :** a difficult or complicated matter **:** PROJECT ⟨getting her down the mountain next day was a ~ —*Time*⟩ **3 :** something that is so put together as to be not easily classified or felt not worth classification: **a :** CONCOCTION, CREATION ⟨one of the slinky printed cotton dresses here, a halter neck ~ —*New Yorker*⟩ **b :** DEVICE, GADGET ⟨assistant laundressing is another merry game. Instead of a washboard they use a patent ~ —Sinclair Lewis⟩ **4 a :** a movement or action (as sitting down, lighting a cigarette, or winding a clock) by an actor intended esp. to establish atmosphere, reveal character, or explain a situation ⟨stage ~ is often written into the script by the playwright . . . but just as often it is introduced by the director —F.H.O'Hara & Marguerite Bro⟩ **b :** all such movements and acting esp. in the performance of one dramatic work or the portrayal of one dramatic role ⟨generally speaking the composer and original producer have conferred during the first rehearsals of a new opera and the stage ~ has therefore become a tradition . . . altered by successive producers and artists —Warwick Braithwaite⟩ **5 a :** something felt to be one's particular concern or responsibility ⟨none of your ~⟩ ⟨told him to mind his own ~⟩ **b :** something felt to be one's right — usu. used in the negative ⟨you had no ~ hitting her⟩ **6 :** everything possible (as all-out effort) applied toward a desired end or enough of something (as trickery) to bring it about **:** WORKS: as **a :** all that one is capable of **:** utmost effort ⟨I wish you'd give it the old ~ today. One of the big shots is coming through —Mary J. Ward⟩ **b :** HARM, INJURY, DAMAGE, ABUSE; *esp* **:** something that disables or destroys ⟨that quarterback really got the ~. They carried him off on a stretcher⟩ **c :** a setback or rebuke usu. deserved **:** COMEUPPANCE ⟨he thought he was the hero of the outfit until the sarge gave him the ~⟩ **d :** a good tongue-lashing **:** a hard time ⟨a witness has given him the ~ such as I've never heard a senator take before —F.C.Othman⟩ **e :** DOUBLE CROSS ⟨he's been giving his partner the ~ for years⟩ **f :** a bowel movement **syn** see WORK
business agent *n* **:** one that handles business affairs for another; *esp* **:** a paid official of a union local who administers union business with its members and with the employer
business car *n* **:** a private railroad car usu. equipped with office and living accommodations for the use of railway officials while traveling
business card *n* **:** a card that bears information (as the name, address, type of business) about a business or business representative
business cycle *n* **:** a recurring succession of business conditions loosely divisible into periods of prosperity, crisis, liquidation, depression, and recovery
business double *n* **:** a double in bridge made with the purpose of increasing penalties
business education *n* **:** education designed for use in business: **a :** training in subjects (as business administration, finance) useful in developing general business knowledge **b :** training in subjects (as accounting, shorthand) useful in developing commercially useful skills
business end *n* **:** the end at, from, or through which a thing's function is fulfilled ⟨the *business end* of the broom⟩
business english *n, cap E* **1 :** English as used in business; *specif* **:** the study and practice of composition with emphasis on correctness, propriety, spelling, punctuation, and the forms of business correspondence **2 :** English as taught in non-English-speaking countries in courses that emphasize its commercial rather than its cultural importance and that are normally designed to produce conversational fluency within a limited vocabulary
business income *n* **:** the income of a business from current production as sometimes distinguished from incidental or extraneous income (as from the investments of a manufacturer)
business interruption insurance *n* **:** insurance against loss of net profits and continuing fixed charges during a period of total or partial suspension of business activity because of damage to described premises from specified perils
business life insurance *n* **1 :** insurance on the life of a member of a partnership or upon an officer or stockholder in a corporation payable so as to finance purchase by surviving owners of the insured's interest at his death **2 :** insurance on the life of a sole proprietor payable so as to finance the purchase of the business by an outside interest at the owner's

death **3 :** insurance on the life of a key employee for the benefit of a business concern

businesslike \ˈ⸗⸗,⸗\ *adj* **:** characterized by or exhibiting qualities felt to be common or advantageous in business: as **a :** EFFICIENT, PRACTICAL, SYSTEMATIC ‹a ~ administration› ‹she went about her housework in a ~ way› **b :** SERIOUS, PURPOSEFUL ‹a ~ rain› ‹got off and went to her waiting father with a firm ~ air —Sherwood Anderson› **c :** competent but lacking in enthusiasm, imagination, or emotion ‹always the skillful pianist, attending to the music in a ~ manner, frequently turning a phrase with spirit but never showing any great identification with the musical style —*N.Y.Times*›

business machine *n* **:** a machine (as a computer or tabulator) designed esp. to facilitate clerical operations common in business or industrial firms

busi·ness·man \ˈ⸗⸗,man, -,maa(ə)n *sometimes* -,mən\ *n, pl* **businessmen :** a man who transacts business; *esp* **:** a business executive

business paper *n* **:** COMMERCIAL PAPER

business pass *n* **:** a pass in bridge to avoid interfering with a partner's double

business reply card *n* **:** a postcard for enclosure with a mailed communication bearing indicia stating that postage for its use in making reply will be paid by the one requesting the reply; *also* **:** a double postcard

business reply envelope *n* **:** an envelope bearing indicia like those on a business reply card

business suit *n* **:** a man's suit for business wear consisting of matching coat and trousers and sometimes a vest of the same material

business trust *n* **:** MASSACHUSETTS TRUST

business unionism *n* **:** the theory and practice of trade unionism esp. associated with Samuel Gompers that is directed toward the attainment of practical limited material advantages (as better wages, hours, and working conditions) through collective bargaining within the framework of capitalism rather than toward the achievement of extensive social changes or reforms

busi·ness·wom·an \ˈ⸗⸗,wu̇mən\ *n, pl* **businesswom·en** \-,wimən\ **:** a woman active in business

¹busing *pres part of* BUS

²bus·ing \ˈbəsiŋ\ *n* -S [¹*bus* + -*ing*] **:** an assembly of bus bars

¹busk \ˈbəsk, ˈbu̇sk\ *n* -S [ME — more at BUSH] *dial Brit* **:** ¹BUSH 1

²busk \ˈ"\ *vb* -ED/-ING/-S [ME *busken*, fr. ON *būask* to prepare oneself, get ready, fr. *būa* to prepare, make ready, dwell + -*sk* oneself, fr. *sik* (accus.) oneself — more at BOWER, SUICIDE] *vt* **1** *dial Brit* **:** to make ready **:** PREPARE ‹they're ~*ing* the *Covenant* for sea —R.L.Stevenson› **2** *dial Brit* **:** to dress up **:** ADORN ‹cowslips ~ the brae› **3** *dial Brit* **:** to dress (flies) on hooks for fishing ~ *vi, dial Brit* **:** to make oneself ready esp. hastily **:** hurry up

³busk \ˈbəsk\ *n* -S [MF *busc*, prob. fr. OIt *busco* stick, mote, of Gmc origin; akin to MHG *büsch* cudgel — more at BEASTINGS] **:** a thin rigid strip (as of metal, whalebone, or wood) inserted in the front of a bodice or corset for stiffening and support used from the 16th to the 19th centuries

⁴busk \ˈ"\ *n* -S [Creek *púskita* fast, fasting] **:** a Creek Indian festival of first-fruits and purification that was celebrated when the first green corn was edible and that marked the beginning of the new year

⁵busk \ˈ"\ *vi* -ED/-ING/-S [origin unknown] *Brit* **:** to entertain esp. by singing or reciting on the street or in a pub

busk·er \ˈbəskə(r)\ *n* -S [⁵*busk* + -*er*] **:** one who busks; *esp* **:** an itinerant entertainer ‹as a ~ along the Bowery and then as a singing waiter —*Nation*›

bus·kin \ˈbəskən\ *n* -S [perh. modif. of Sp *borcegui* (OSp also *borzeguina*), of non-IE origin; prob. akin to the source of MF *broisseguin*, a sometimes fawn-colored cloth, ML *brucequinus* buskin] **1 :** a strong thick-soled laced foot covering with a legging reaching halfway or more to the knee **2 a :** COTHURNUS **b :** TRAGEDY ‹they witnessed 10 new plays in 12 days, which is plenty of sock and a lot of ~ —*Newsweek*›; *esp* **:** tragedy felt to resemble that of the ancient Greek drama in style or spirit — compare SOCK 3b **3 :** a woman's low-cut house shoe in leather or fabric having a piece of elastic goring at the instep **4 buskins** *pl* **:** gold-threaded silk stockings worn by a Roman Catholic bishop at a pontifical mass

bus·kined \-nd\ *adj* **:** of, relating to, or befitting tragedy; *esp* **:** in the manner of tragic drama

busky \ˈbəskē\ *adj* [¹*busk* + -*y*] *obs* **:** BOSKY

bus line *n* **1 :** TRAIN LINE 1 **2 a :** a route over which a bus regularly travels **b :** a company operating such buses

busload \ˈ⸗,⸗\ *n* **:** a load that fills a bus ‹a ~ of school children› **:** bus capacity

bus·man \ˈbəsmən, -,sman, -,smaa(ə)n\ *n, pl* **busmen** *chiefly Brit* **:** an operator of a bus

busman's holiday *n* **:** a holiday spent in following or observing the practice of one's usual occupation

bus-mile \ˈ⸗,⸗\ *n* **:** a statistical unit denoting one mile traveled by one bus — compare CAR-MILE, TON-MILE

bus rod *n* **:** BUS BAR

¹buss \ˈbəs\ *n* -ES [ME *busse*, fr. MF, fr. ON *būza*, fr. ML *bucia*] **:** a rugged square-sailed boat formerly used esp. in herring fishery

²buss *n* -ES [prob. of imit. origin like G *buss* kiss, Sw *puss* kiss, MIr *bus*, *pus* lip, Lith *bučiuoti* to kiss] **:** KISS

³buss \ˈ"\ *vt* -ED/-ING/-ES **:** KISS ‹we ~ our wantons but our wives we kiss —Robert Herrick †1674› ‹when the tumult stilled, the doctor had ~*ed* his wife heartily —A.J.Cronin›

⁴buss \ˈ"\ *n* -ES [ME (northern dial.) *bus*, alter. of *busk* — more at BUSH] *chiefly Scot* **:** ¹BUSH

⁵buss \ˈ"\ *vt* -ED/-ING/-ES [by alter.] *chiefly Scot* **:** ²BUSK

bussed *past of* BUS *or of* BUSS

busses *pl of* BUS *or of* BUSS, *pres 3d sing of* BUS *or of* BUSS

bussing *pres part of* BUS *or of* BUSS

bus·sock \ˈbu̇|sək, ˈbəl, |zək\ *n* -S [origin unknown] *dial Eng* **:** DONKEY

bus stop *n* **:** a point (as a street corner) on a bus route at which buses stop and which is often marked by an overhead sign

bus·su \bəˈsü\ *n* -S [Pg *bussú*, fr. Tupi *ubu-ussu*, fr. *ubu* leaf + *ussu* big] **:** a low palm (*Manicaria saccifera*) of Central and So. American tidal swamps having enormous undivided oblong leaves often used in thatching, spathes like sacs, and a very large fruit — see TROOLIE

bussy \ˈbəsē\ *n* -ES [²*buss* + -*y*] *dial* **:** SWEETHEART

¹bust \ˈbəst\ *n* -S [F *buste*, fr. It *busto*, fr. L *bustum* tomb, crematory, prob. short for *ambustum*, neut. of *ambustus*, past part. of L *amburere* to burn up, consume, fr. *ambi-* on both sides, around + *urere* to burn — more at AMBI-, EMBER] **1 a :** a sculptured representation of the upper part of the human figure including the head and neck and usu. part of the shoulders and breast **b :** a pictorial representation (as in a painting or on a coin) of this part of the human figure **2 a :** the upper portion of the human torso between neck and waist; *esp* **:** the breasts of a woman **b :** a measure around the female body marking the maximum projection of the breasts ‹a 36-inch ~› **c :** the part of a woman's garment covering the bust

bust 1a

²bust \ˈ"\ *vb* **busted** *also* **bust; busted** *also* **bust; busting; busts** [alter. of *burst*] *vt* **1 :** HIT, PUNCH, SLUG ‹he and his instructor had an overpowering compulsion to ~ each other in the snoot —H.H.Martin› **2 a :** to break open ‹going to ~ you wide open —Erle Stanley Gardner› or break up ‹helped ~ trusts —*Newsweek*›; *specif* **:** FRACTURE ‹~ his arm trying —Helen Eustis› **b :** to break financially ‹the game of cheaters, which has ~*ed* more men than blackjack —Arthur Mayse› **c :** DEMOTE ‹~*ed* them to the bottom of the seniority list —*Time*›; *specif* **:** to reduce in military grade or rank ‹he went over the hill and got ~*ed* —Mack Morriss› **d** (1) **:** TAME ‹~ a horse› (2) **:** to throw (as a steer) by roping the legs **3 :** to burst esp. by too much or too sudden swelling or growth ‹this westernmost province . . . is beginning to ~ its industrial britches —*Wall Street Jour.*› ~ *vi* **1 :** to burst esp. from too much or too sudden swelling or growth ‹laughing fit to ~› ‹the book winds up with hell ~*ing* loose —Marshall Sprague› **2 :** to break down completely while making an all-out effort ‹engineers . . . busy making sure that the world shall be convenient if they ~ doing it —E.B.White› **3 :** to fail financially **:** go broke ‹they threw their sudden money around and ~*ed* —Noel Houston› **4 a :** to fail to complete a straight or a flush in poker usu. by one card **b :** to lose at cards by exceeding a limit (as the count of 21 in blackjack) **syn** see BREAK

³bust \ˈ"\ *n* -S **1** *slang* **:** PUNCH, SOCK ‹a good ~ on the nose —J.T.Farrell› **2 a :** FAILURE ‹we think he's going to be either a genius or a ~ —Josephine Pinckney› **b :** a very weak hand in cards **3 a :** BENDER, BINGE, SPREE ‹he could get more action in El Paso or Juarez when he went on a ~ —Ross Santee› **b :** a drinking bout ‹a beer ~› **4 :** a reduction in military grade **5 a :** a sudden break and sharp decline in business activity, prices, and employment **b :** a severe recession or a depression ‹boom and ~›

⁴bust \ˈ"\ *or* **bust·ed** \-təd\ *adj* [*bust*, alter. of *busted*; *busted* fr. past part. of ²*bust*] **:** BANKRUPT, BROKE ‹her father, before he went ~, had owned a drygoods store —Saul Bellow› ‹to play roulette side by side with a *busted* . . . duke —David Dodge›

bu·sta·men·te furnace \,büstəˈmentē-\ *n* [after Juan Alonso de *Bustamante*, 18th cent. Span. metallurgist] **:** a shaft furnace for roasting quicksilver ores that has aludels for condensing the vapors — called also *aludel furnace*

bu·sta·mite \ˈbüstə,mīt\ *n* -S [Anastasio *Bustamente* †1853 Mexican general + E -*ite*] **:** a mineral $CaMnSi_2O_6$ consisting of a calcium manganese pyroxene

bus·tard \ˈbəstə(r)d\ *n* -S [ME *bustarde*, modif. (perh. influenced by MF *oustarde* bustard, fr. L *avis tarda*) of MF *bistarde*, fr. OIt *bistarda*, fr. L *avis tarda*, lit., slow bird, fr. *avis* bird + *tarda* fem. of *tardus* slow — more at AVIARY] **:** any of a family (Otididae) of large chiefly terrestrial game birds of the Old World and Australia that are related both to the cranes and plovers and that frequent grassy steppes and cultivated areas, being somewhat slow and stately on the ground but capable of powerful swift flight when alarmed — see GREAT BUSTARD, KORHAAN, PLAIN TURKEY

bustard quail *n* **:** BUTTON QUAIL

bus·tee *or* **bus·ti** \ˈbə,stē\ *n* -S [Hindi *bastī*, fr. *basnā* to dwell, fr. Skt *vasati* he dwells — more at WAS] **1** *India* **:** a small village **2** *India* **:** a group of poor huts **:** SLUM

bust·er \ˈbəstə(r)\ *n* -S [²*bust* + -*er*] **1 a :** a person who is extraordinary (as in size, energy, or ability) **:** an esp. male child who is healthy and full of life ‹a tough little ~, square-chinned and full of fight —John & Ward Hawkins› **b** *often cap* **:** FELLOW — usu. used as a noun of address ‹they shoot deserters, ~ —Martin Dibner› **2 :** one that breaks or breaks up ‹tank ~›: as **a :** PLOW — compare LISTER **b** [short for *broncobuster*] **:** one that breaks horses ‹sometimes a contract ~ goes from ranch to ranch breaking horses at so much a head —S.E.Fletcher› **3** *Austral* **:** a sudden violent wind often coming from the south — called also *southerly buster* **4 :** a crab or other decapod after the shell has split but before it is shed — compare SHEDDER 2a **5** *slang* **:** a bad fall ‹he took a ~ that jarred the ground —F.B.Gipson›

buster brown \ˈ⸗⸗ˈbrau̇n\ *adj, usu cap both Bs* [after *Buster Brown*, boy comic strip character pictured with wide-brimmed sailor hat, Lord Fauntleroy suit, and pageboy haircut, created by Richard F. Outcault †1928 Am. artist] **:** resembling or suggestive of Buster Brown (as in style of clothing or haircut) ‹he felt the pinch and chafe of the *Buster Brown* collar as he turned to watch the minister —Charles Jackson›

busthead \ˈ⸗,⸗\ *n* [²*bust* + *head*] **1** *dial* **:** MOONSHINE 3 **2** *dial* **:** HEADACHE

bustian *n* -S [ME *busteyne*] *obs* **:** a cotton fabric formerly used in clothing (as vestments, waistcoats)

bus·tic \ˈbəstik\ *n* -S [origin unknown] **:** a tree (*Dipholis salicifolia*) of the family Sapotaceae of southern Florida and the West Indies with hard wood, shining lanceolate leaves, and white flowers

busting *pres part of* BUST

¹bus·tle \ˈbəsəl\ *vb* **bustled; bustled; bustling** \ˈbəs(ə)liŋ\ **bustles** [prob. alter. of obs. *buskle* to prepare, bustle about, freq. of ²*busk*] *vi* **1 a :** to move energetically and often with apparent purpose but usu. noisily or inefficiently ‹she never ~*s* but she is constantly busy —*Time*› **b :** HURRY, HUSTLE ‹the head waiter *bustled* up, full of apologies —Ian Bevan› **2** *obs* **:** STRUGGLE, CONTEND **3 :** TEEM, CRAWL ‹all the river landings *bustled* with colorful activity —*Amer. Guide Series: Minn.*› ~ *vt* **:** to cause to bustle **:** HURRY, HUSTLE

²bustle \ˈ"\ *n* -S **1 :** a stir or commotion of bustling **:** noisy or energetic activity ‹the hustle and ~ of the city› **2** *archaic* **:** STRUGGLE, SCUFFLE **syn** see STIR

³bustle \ˈ"\ *n* -S [origin unknown] **:** a framework (as of metal, whalebone, crinoline) or a padded cushion that expands and supports the fullness and drapery of the back of a woman's skirt in some former fashions; *also* **:** a recurrent fashion adapted from this

bustle

bus·tled \ˈbəsəld\ *adj* [³*bustle* + -*ed*] **:** wearing a bustle

bustle pipe *n* [¹*bustle*] **:** the outside pipe that supplies the blast to the tuyeres in a blast furnace

bus·tler \ˈbəs(ə)lə(r)\ *n* -S **:** one that bustles **:** HUSTLER

bustling *adj* **:** making a bustle **:** given to or full of bustle ‹he had the ~ ways of an amateur nurse —Stephen Crane› — **bus·tling·ly** *adv*

bus·to \ˈbə(,)stō, ˈbü(-\ *n, pl* **bustos** *or* **bustoes** [It — more at BUST] *archaic* **:** ¹BUST 1a

bust out *vi* **:** to fail to attain in a school or training program the minimum grades required for continuing **:** flunk out ~ *vt* **1** *dial* **:** to plough out **2 :** to drop (as from a school or training program) usu. because of failure to maintain minimum grades or other standards **:** flunk out ‹sooner or later he must be *busted out* —A.Q.Maisel›

bust-out man \ˈ⸗ˈ⸗-\ *n* **:** one skilled at switching crooked dice in and out of a game

bust peg *n* [¹*bust*] **:** a post fixed to a flat base and used as a support for the clay or wax a bust is modeled from

bustrophedon *or* **bustropheidon** *var of* BOUSTROPHEDON

busts *pl of* BUST, *pres 3d sing of* BUST

bust-up \ˈ⸗,⸗\ *n* -S [*bust up*, v.] **1 :** a breaking up or apart ‹the *bust-up* of camp› ‹the *bust-up* of their marriage› **2 :** a big party or celebration ‹there'll be an awful crowd — a regular *bust-up* —Norman Douglas›

busty \ˈbəstē, -ti\ *adj, usu* -ER/-EST [¹*bust* + -*y*] **:** having a large bust ‹a ~ actress›

bus·way \ˈ⸗,⸗\ *n* **:** BUS DUCT

¹busy \ˈbizē, -zi\ *adj* -ER/-EST [ME *bisy*, fr. OE *bisig*; akin to MD & MLG *besich* busy] **1 :** engaged in something requiring time or attention **:** not idle or at leisure **:** OCCUPIED, ENGAGED ‹keeping the American front ~ while Howe and his other divisions were moving —F.V.W.Mason› **2 :** full of business activity **:** ACTIVE, BUSTLING ‹a ~ seaport› ‹the snow and ice melted . . . and Mount Vernon was soon ~ with its old hospitality —H.E.Scudder› **3 :** foolishly or intrudingly active **:** OFFICIOUS, MEDDLING ‹a ~, fussy sort of man much concerned with regulating everything —A.M.Young› **4** *of a telephone line* **:** being used **5 :** full of distracting details — used esp. of an artistic design ‹a ~ floral wallpaper› ‹small patterns can look annoyingly ~ in a large room›

syn INDUSTRIOUS, DILIGENT, ASSIDUOUS, SEDULOUS: BUSY, the most general of these words, mainly stresses activity as opposed to idleness ‹always *busy*, making it a point never to suspend for one moment his occupation —John Burroughs› ‹the merchants of Charleston and Portsmouth, Norfolk and Boston with their *busy* offices full of bustling clerks —Allan Nevins & H. S. Commager› The word may connote purposive activity ‹this man of action wanted to get *busy* on the proposition without loss of time —Upton Sinclair› INDUSTRIOUS may suggest habitual or continual earnest enterprise ‹a vigorous and *industrious* girl, who, single-handed, kept the farm in a sort of order —Dorothy Sayers› DILIGENT may stress care, constancy, attentiveness, and thoroughness ‹when we came to start, the Yankee's boots were missing, and after a *diligent* search were not to be found —Herman Melville› ‹the young investigator becomes a *diligent* student of literature and laboriously examines the relevant passages —Havelock Ellis› ASSIDUOUS suggests constant, unremitting effort ‹he inherited the strict and severe piety of his father; he was *assiduous* in his attendance on religious services whether by night or day —J.R.Green› ‹even the most *assiduous* critic can scarcely hope to keep abreast of the growing flood of translated books —*Times Lit. Supp.*› SEDULOUS connotes careful painstaking attentiveness ‹too prolonged and heated and discursive to interest any but the most *sedulous* reader —H.G.Wells› ‹this man who, after weeks of *sedulous* and disheartening analysis, eventually ferreted out the source —W.H.Wright›

²busy \ˈ"\ *vb* -ED/-ING/-ES [ME *bisien*, fr. OE *bisgian*, fr. *bisig*, adj.] *vt* **:** to make busy ‹the faithful servant *busied* himself about the room —Winston Churchill› **:** ENGAGE, OCCUPY ‹I have need to ~ my heart with quietude —Rupert Brooke› ~ *vi* **:** to get or keep busy ‹I *busied* about and I made him two good-sized sandwiches —Edwin Corle›

¹busybody \ˈ⸗⸗,⸗⸗\ *n* [¹*busy* + *body*] **1 :** one who concerns himself with affairs not his own **:** SNOOPER, MEDDLER **2 :** a device consisting typically of three mirrors mounted in a metal frame usu. attached to the side of an upper window and used to enable a person indoors to see places not ordinarily within his view ‹with her ~ she could see both doors from her favorite chair›

²busybody \ˈ"\ *vi* -ED/-ING/-ES **:** to behave like a busybody — usu. used in the form *busybodying* ‹~*ing* about —Nathaniel Burt› — **busy·body·ism** \-,izəm\ *n* -S

bu·sy·con \byüˈsī,kän\ *n, cap* [NL, fr. Gk *bousykon*, a large fig, fr. *bous* head of cattle + *sykon* fig] **:** a genus of large marine snails of the family Buccinidae — see WINKLE

busy·ness \ˈbizēnəs, -zin-\ *n* -ES [¹*busy* + -*ness*] **:** the quality or state of being busy ‹his presence caused a marked increase in ~ on the staff —J.G.Cozzens›; *often* **:** the condition or appearance of busily engaging in some trivial, unproductive, or meaningless labor or activity ‹sterile ~ . . . has crept into the colleges and universities —Robert Ulich› ‹his main object in life was to combine an elaborate obstructionist policy with an appearance of intense ~ and affability —J.B.D.Cotter› ‹ceremonial and vacuous ~ —Mary McCarthy›

busywork \ˈ⸗⸗,⸗\ *n* **:** work that usu. appears productive or of intrinsic value but actually only keeps one occupied ‹freshmen know perfectly well that most of the writing assigned to them is pedagogical ~ —Mary P. Keeley›

¹but \(ˈ)bət, *usu* -əd·+V\ *conj* [ME, conj. & prep., fr. OE *būtan*, *būte*, conj. & prep., without, except, outside; akin to OS *būtan*, *biūtan* without, except, OHG *būzan*, *biūzan*; all fr. a prehistoric WGmc compound whose first and second constituents respectively are the preposition represented by OE *be*, *bī* by and the adverb represented by OE *ūtan* outside, from outside, OHG *ūzana*, *ūzan*, ON *ūtan*, Goth *ūtana*; derivative fr. the root of OE *ūt* out — more at BY, OUT] **1 a :** except for the fact — used to introduce a dependent clause ‹he would have protested ~ that he was afraid› **b :** THAT — sometimes used more or less tautologically with *that*; used after negatives ‹there is no doubt ~ he was killed in the wreck› ‹he did not question ~ that he would win› ‹it is 10 to 1 ~ the challenger will lose› **c :** without the concomitant that ‹it never rains ~ it pours› ‹you cannot look into the index ~ you will find the word› **d :** if not **:** UNLESS ‹may I die ~ she is right› **:** if it were not true that ‹~ my noble Moor is true of mind . . . it were enough to put him to ill thinking —Shak.› **e :** that . . . not ‹there was never a new plan ~ someone objected to it› ‹he was not so stupid ~ he could drive a hard bargain› ‹it was impossible ~ he should notice it› ‹a pity ~ he knew more about him› **f** (1) *archaic* **:** WHEN, BEFORE **:** at the time that (2) *now substand* **:** THAN — used after *no sooner* ‹no sooner started ~ it stopped again› **2 a :** on the contrary **:** on the other hand **:** in opposition **:** NOTWITHSTANDING — used to connect coordinate elements ‹not peace ~ a sword› ‹not Smith ~ Smyth› ‹not with haste ~ with caution› ‹he was called ~ he did not answer› **b :** despite that fact ‹he was commonly thought to be wealthy ~ he had no money› — sometimes used at the beginning of a separate sentence ‹the rebels' cause looked hopeless. *But* they received help from the provinces› and sometimes interpreted as an adverb when so used **c :** EXCEPT **:** with the exception of — used before a word often taken to be the subject of a clause ‹whence all ~ he had fled —Felicia D. Hemans› ‹none ~ the brave deserves the fair —John Dryden› **d** — used with little meaning as a formal connective ‹all men are mortal ~ he is a man› **e** — used in connection with interjectional expressions to express a degree of restraining, countering, or modifying ‹heavens, ~ it rains› — **but and** *archaic Scot* **:** and also **:** in addition — **but what 1 :** but that ‹not . . . such an opprobrious nickname *but what* kings have been so nicknamed —E.C.Smith› **2 :** that . . . not — used to indicate possibility or uncertainty ‹I don't know *but what* I will go›

²but \ˈ"\ *prep* [ME, conj. & prep.] **1** *Scot* **a :** WITHOUT, LACKING ‹touch not the cat ~ a glove —*Motto of the Mackintoshes*› **b :** to or into the outer room of **:** OUTSIDE ‹go ~ the house› **2 :** EXCEPT: **a :** EXCLUDING, BARRING **:** with the exception of ‹there was no one left ~ me —R.L.Stevenson› ‹wanting nothing ~ a little time› ‹what could he do ~ protest› — see ¹BUT 2c **b :** other than **:** otherwise than **:** anything else than ‹this letter is nothing ~ an insult› ‹who could fill the position ~ this man› ‹how would he look ~ haggard› ‹nothing would please him ~ that we go along›

³but \ˈ"\ *adv* [ME, fr. *but*, conj. & prep.] **1 :** ONLY: **a** (1) **:** no other or no more than indicated ‹he is ~ a child› (2) **:** more than ‹I never heard of ~ one man that survived such an experience› — often considered substand. **b :** without alternative **:** with no other choice ‹we could ~ listen to his plea› **c :** no longer ago than ‹it happened ~ yesterday› ‹he was here ~ five minutes ago› **d :** MERELY ‹the presence of ~ a little poisonous gas› **2** *Scot* **:** to or into the outer room or kitchen of a house **:** OUTSIDE, WITHOUT — opposed to *ben* **3 :** to the contrary — usu. used with *that* beginning a following clause ‹who knows ~ that he may succeed› **4 :** DEFINITELY, POSITIVELY, STRONGLY, THOROUGHLY **:** to a degree precluding doubt or reservation ‹get there ~ fast›

⁴but \ˈ"\ *pron* [¹*but*] **:** that not **:** who not ‹nobody ~ has his fault —Shak.› ‹nothing indeed ever entered that little country ~ came out rejuvenated and clarified —Norman Douglas›

⁵but \ˈ"\ *adj* [³*but*] *Scot* **:** in the outer room or kitchen of a house **:** OUTER

⁶but \ˈ"\ *n* -S *Scot* **:** the outer apartment of a house; *esp* **:** the kitchen of a but-and-ben

⁷but *var of* BUTT

but- *or* **buto-** *comb form* [ISV, fr. *butyric*] **:** containing a group of four carbon atoms ‹*butene*› ‹*butanone*› ‹*butopyronoxyl*›

bu·ta-bu·ta \ˈbüd·ə,büd·ə\ *n* -S [Malay] **:** a tree (*Excoecaria agallocha*) of the family Euphorbiaceae that is native along the coastal regions in southern Asia and has a poisonous milky juice and flowers in axillary spikes

bu·ta·caine \ˈbyüd·ə,kān, ,⸗⸗ˈ⸗\ *n* -S [*butane* + -*caine* (as in *cocaine*)] **:** a local anesthetic $NH_2C_6H_4COO(CH_2)_3NH(C_4H_9)_2$ that is an ester of *para*-aminobenzoic acid and is applied in the form of its white crystalline sulfate to mucous membranes

bu·ta·di·ene \,byüd·əˈdī,ēn, ,⸗⸗ˈ⸗⸗\ *n* -S [ISV *butane* + *di-* + -*ene*] **:** a flammable gaseous diolefin $CH_2{=}CHCH{=}CH_2$ very reactive and polymerizing readily that is made by several processes (as by catalytic dehydrogenation of normal butane or normal butylenes at high temperatures) and is used chiefly in making synthetic rubbers (as GR-S and nitrile rubbers) — called also *bivinyl*, *1,3-butadiene*, *divinyl*

bu·tal·de·hyde \byüˈtaldə,hīd\ *n* -S [by alter.] **:** BUTYRALDEHYDE

bu·ta·nal \ˈbyüd·ə,nal, -üt°n,al\ *n* -S [*butane* + -*al*] **:** normal butyraldehyde

but and ben \,bət°nˈben\ *adv* [Sc ³*but* (out) + *ben* (in)] *Scot* **1 :** back and forth **:** in and out; *specif* **:** from one part of a house to the other **2 :** on opposite sides or at opposite ends of (a house, a corridor) ‹we lived *but and ben* with them›

but-and-ben \ˈ"\ *n, Scot* **:** a 2-roomed cottage

bu·tane \ˈbyü,tān, ⸗ˈ⸗\ *n* -S [ISV *but-* + -*ane*] **:** either of two isomeric flammable easily liquefiable gaseous paraffin hydrocarbons C_4H_{10} obtained usu. from petroleum or natural gas and occurring in gasoline and in liquefied petroleum gas: **a :** the normal compound $CH_3CH_2CH_2CH_3$ used chiefly in making butadiene and as a fuel gas — called also *n-butane*, *normal butane* **b :** ISOBUTANE

bu·tane·di·ol \ˈbyü(ˌ)tān(ˌ)dīˌōl, -ˌōl\ *n* -s [*butane* + *-diol*] **:** any of four isomeric glycols $C_4H_8(OH)_2$: as **a :** a hygroscopic liquid $CH_3CHOHCH_2CH_2OH$ made usu. by hydrogenation of aldol and used chiefly as a humectant and plasticizer — called also *1,3-butanediol, 1,3-butylene glycol* **b :** a viscous liquid $CH_2OHCH_2CH_2CH_2OH$ made from acetylene, formaldehyde, and hydrogen and used chiefly in making polyurethane resins — called also *1,4-butanediol, 1,4-butylene glycol, tetramethylene glycol* **c :** a hygroscopic viscous liquid or crystalline solid $CH_3CHOHCHOHCH_3$ known in four optically different forms, obtained usu. by fermentation (as of grains or molasses), and used chiefly in organic synthesis — called also *2,3-butanediol, 2,3-butylene glycol*

bu·ta·no·ic acid \ˌbyüd·əˌnōik-\ *n* [*butane* + *-o-* + *-ic*] **:** BUTYRIC ACID a — used in the system of nomenclature adopted by the International Union of Pure and Applied Chemistry

bu·ta·nol \ˈbyüd·əˌnōl, -nōl; -üt°nˌōl, -nˌōl\ *n* -s [ISV *butane* + *-ol*] **:** either of the two butyl alcohols derived from normal butane and distinguished as 1-butanol and 2-butanol; *esp* **:** BUTYL ALCOHOL a

bu·tan·o·lide \byüˈtanəˌlīd, -ləd\ *n* -s [ISV *butanol* + *-ide*] **:** BUTYROLACTONE

bu·ta·none \ˈbyüd·əˌnōn, -üt°nˌōn\ *n* -s [ISV *butane* + *-one*; prob. orig. formed in F] **:** METHYL ETHYL KETONE

¹butch \ˈbüch, ˈbəch\ *vt* -ED/-ING/-ES [back-formation from ¹*butcher*] **1** *dial* **:** BUTCHER, SLAUGHTER **2** *dial* **:** to make a clumsy job of **:** BOTCH

²butch \ˈbüch\ *n* -ES [perh. fr. *Butch*, a nickname for boys, esp. tough boys; fr. the close-cropped appearance of some stereotype ruffians] **:** a close haircut **:** CREW CUT

¹butch·er \ˈbu̇chə(r), *dial sporadically* ˈbüch- *also* ˈbəch-\ *n* -s [ME *bocher*, fr. OF *bochier, bouchier*, fr. *bouc* he-goat, prob. of Celt origin; akin to MIr *bocc* he-goat, W *bwch* — more at BUCK] **1 :** one who slaughters animals or dresses the flesh of animals, fish, or poultry for market; *also* **:** a dealer in meat **2 :** one that kills ruthlessly or brutally or bloodily ⟨oh pardon me . . . that I am meek and gentle with these ~s —Shak.⟩ **3 :** an unskillful or careless workman **:** BOTCHER **4 :** a hog suitable for slaughter for general table purposes usu. as distinguished from light porkers and from very heavy hogs chiefly fit for the sausage trade **5 :** a vendor esp. on trains or in theaters ⟨candy ~⟩

²butcher \"\ *vt* **butchered; butchered; butchering** \-ch(ə)riŋ\ **butchers 1 :** to slaughter and dress for market ⟨~ hogs⟩ **2 :** to kill in a bloody barbarous, or cruel manner **3 :** BOTCH ⟨~ a text⟩ ⟨~ a musical composition⟩

³butcher \"\ *adj* [²*butcher*] *of animals* **:** suitable for butchering

butcher-bird \ˈ==ˌ=\ *n* [so called fr. their habit of impaling their prey on thorns] **:** any of various shrikes: as **a :** a member of the genus *Lanius* (esp. the common European species *L. excubitor* and in America the northern shrike *L. borealis*) **b :** any of several pied birds (genus *Cracticus*) widely distributed in Australia

butcher-bird

butch·er·er \-ch(ə)rə(r)\ *n* -s **:** one that butchers

butcher knife *n* **:** a heavy-duty knife usu. 6 to 8 inches long having a broad rigid blade that curves slightly at the tip

butch·er·less \-chə(r)ləs\ *adj* **:** being without a butcher

butcher linen *also* **butcher's linen** *also* **butcher rayon** *n* **:** a strong heavy linen of plain weave used orig. for butchers' aprons; *also* **:** a similar fabric for clothing made of rayon staple or cotton with a finish like linen

butch·er·ly \-chə(r)lē, -li\ *adj* **:** like a butcher: as **a :** without compunction **:** SAVAGE, BLOODY **b :** CLUMSY, UNSKILLFUL ⟨~ mob⟩

butcher paper *n* **:** a strong wrapping paper resistant to the penetration of blood and meat fluids

butcher's-broom \ˈ==ˌ=\ *n, pl* **butcher's-brooms :** a European leafless plant (*Ruscus aculeatus*) that bears stiff-pointed cladophylls and is often cultivated for its twigs which are used for ornament and for whisk brooms

butch·ery \-ch(ə)rē, -ri\ *n* -ES [ME *bocherie*, fr. MF *bocherie, boucherie*, fr. *bochier, bouchier* butcher + *-ie* -y — more at BUTCHER] **1** *now chiefly Brit* **:** a place where slaughtered meat is cut up **:** SLAUGHTERHOUSE **2 :** the process or business of preparing meat for sale **3 :** violent, cruel, or bloody slaughter **:** MASSACRE, CARNAGE **4 :** BOTCH, BUNGLE

bu·tea \ˈbyüd·ēə\ *n, cap* [NL, after John Stuart, 3d earl of *Bute* †1792 Scot. statesman and scholar] **:** a genus of East Indian trees or shrubs (family Leguminosae) having 3-flowered racemes and a downy bracted calyx — see DHAK

butea gum *n, often cap B* **:** the dried juice of the dhak tree obtained as reddish or dark translucent masses and used as an astringent — called also *Bengal kino*

bu·te·in \ˈbyüd·ēən\ *n* -s [ISV *bute-* (fr. NL *Butea*, genus name of *Butea frondosa*) + *-in*] **:** a yellow crystalline coloring matter $C_{15}H_{12}O_5$ derived from chalcone that is obtained esp. from the flowers of the dhak tree

bu·tene \ˈbyüˌdēn, -ü(ˌ)tēn\ *n* -s [ISV *but-* + *-ene*] **:** BUTYLENE 1a, 1b

bu·te·nyl \ˈbyüt°nəl\ *n* -s [ISV *butene* + *-yl*] **:** any of three univalent radicals C_4H_7 derived from the two butenes by removal of one hydrogen atom — see CROTYL

bu·teo \ˈbyüd·ēō\ *n* [NL, fr. L, a falcon or hawk — more at BUZZARD] **1** *cap* **:** a genus of hawks that have broad rounded wings and fan-shaped tails and that soar and wheel high in the air **2** -s **:** a hawk of the genus *Buteo* (as the rough-legged hawks and red-shouldered hawks); *also* **:** a hawk resembling a member of this genus in appearance or habits of flight

¹bu·te·o·nine \ˈbyüd·ēəˌnīn, -ˌnən; byüˈtē-\ *adj* [NL *Buteon-, Buteo* + E *-ine*] **:** of or relating to the genus *Buteo* or to the short-winged hawks — compare ACCIPITRINE, CATHARTINE

²buteonine \"\ *n* -s **:** BUTEO 2

bute·shire \ˈbyütshi(ə)r\ *or* **bute** \ˈbyüt\ *adj, usu cap* [fr. *Buteshire* or *Bute* county, Scotland] **:** of or from the county of Bute, Scotland **:** of the kind or style prevalent in Bute

bu·thi·dae \ˈbyüthəˌdē\ *n pl, cap* [NL, fr. *Buthus*, type genus + *-idae*] **:** a widely distributed family of scorpions having a large triangular sternum with the sides strongly convergent anteriorly

bu·thus \ˈbyüthəs\ *n, cap* [NL] **:** the type genus of Buthidae containing a number of dangerous scorpions of warm regions of the Old World

bu·tine \ˈbyüˌtīn\ *archaic var of* BUTYNE

but·ler \ˈbətlə(r)\ *n* -s [ME *buteler, boteler*, fr. OF *bouteillier* bottle bearer, fr. *bouteille* bottle — more at BOTTLE] **1 :** a manservant having charge of the wines and liquors **2 :** an officer of a royal household who was orig. the supplier of wines **3 :** the chief servant of a household who has charge of other employees, receives guests, performs personal services as requested, and serves or directs the serving of meals **4 :** a receptacle used for collecting, carrying, holding, or serving esp. food or drinks ⟨silent ~⟩

but·ler·age \-lərij\ *n* -s [ME *botelerage*, fr. *boteler, buteler* + *-age*] **1 :** a former duty on wine imported into England payable to the king's butler — compare PRISAGE **2 :** the part of a household's management under a butler's charge

butler finish *n* [so called fr. the fact that silver polishing is a traditional task of butlers] **:** a satin finish produced on silver by first buffing bright and then dulling to simulate the appearance of old silver

but·ler·ite \ˈbətləˌrīt\ *n* -s *usu cap* [Dean G. M. *Butler* b1881 Am. geologist and mineralogist + E *-ite*] **:** a mineral $Fe(SO_4)(OH).2H_2O$ consisting of hydrous basic sulfate of iron

butler's pantry *n* **:** a pantry for the use of a butler **:** a service room between kitchen and dining room

butler's tray *n* **1 :** an oval wooden tray whose four sides are hinged to fold out flat when set down **2 :** a tray with attached and usu. folding legs

but·lery \ˈbətlərē, -ri\ *n* -ES [ME *botelerie*, fr. OF *bouteillerie* wine cellar, fr. *bouteille* bottle + *-erie* -ery — more at BOTTLE] **:** BUTTERY

bu·to·ma·ce·ae \ˌbyüd·əˈmāsēˌē\ *n pl, cap* [NL, fr. *Butomus*, type genus + *-aceae*] **:** a small family of monocotyledonous water or marsh herbs (order Najadales) distinguished chiefly by the many ovules and the dehiscent carpels of the fruit — compare WATER POPPY — **bu·to·ma·ceous** \ˌ==ˈmāshəs\ *adj*

bu·to·mus \ˈbyüd·əməs\ *n, cap* [NL, fr. Gk *boutomos, boutomon* sedge] **:** a genus (the type of the family Butomaceae) of bog herbs having leaves ensiform and 3-angled at the base and flowers in umbels

bu·to·py·ro·nox·yl \ˌbyüd·əˌpīrəˈnäksəl\ *n* -s [*but-* + *pyrone* + *oxyl*] **:** a yellow to reddish brown liquid $C_{12}H_{18}O_4$ used as an insect repellent

bu·tox·ide \byüˈtäkˌsīd, -ˌsəd\ *n* -s [*but-* + *oxide*] **:** a binary compound of butoxyl; *esp* **:** a base formed from a butyl alcohol by replacement of the hydroxyl hydrogen ⟨sodium ~⟩

bu·toxy \byüˈtäksē\ *adj* [*butoxy-*] **:** of, relating to, or containing butoxyl

butoxy- *comb form* [ISV, fr. *butoxyl*] **:** containing butoxyl

bu·tox·yl \byüˈtäksəl\ *n* -s [blend of *butyl* and *oxy-*] **:** a univalent radical C_4H_9O— composed of butyl united with oxygen; *esp* **:** the radical corresponding to normal butyl

buts *pl of* BUT

bütschliite *var of* BUETSCHLIITE

butsudan \ˈbu̇tsəˌdän\ *n, pl* **butsudan** *or* **butsudans** [Jap, fr. *butsu* Buddha + *dan* platform, altar] **:** a small household Buddhist altar shelf found in many Japanese homes and bearing typically the image of the principal family deity and ancestral name tablets

¹butt \ˈbət, *usu* -əd·+V\ *vb* -ED/-ING/-S [ME *butten*, fr. OF *boter, bouter*, of Gmc origin; akin to OHG *bōzan* to beat — more at BEAT] *vi* **1 :** to thrust or push headforemost **:** strike with the head or horns ⟨~*ing* and kicking⟩ ⟨~*ing* against the fence⟩ **2** *of gears* **:** to mesh improperly so that only the tips of the teeth touch ~ *vt* **:** to strike or shove with the head or horns ⟨~*ed* his opponent heavily in the ribs⟩ **:** drive by striking or pushing with the head ⟨~*ed* him through the gate and out of the yard⟩

²butt \"\ *n* -s **:** a blow or thrust with the head or horns **:** an act of butting

³butt \"\ *or* **but** \"\ *n* -s [ME *butte*, fr. MD *but, butte* or MLG *but;* akin to MD *bot* blunt, LG *butt*, ON *būtr* log, OHG *bōzan* to beat — more at BEAT] **:** FLOUNDER, FLATFISH; *esp* **:** HALIBUT

⁴butt \"\ *n* -s [ME *but, butte*, partly fr. MF *but* goal, target, of Gmc origin (akin to ON *būtr* log); partly prob. fr. MF *bute* mound of earth serving as backstop for a target, fr. *but* target] **1 a :** a mound, bank, or other backstop for catching arrows shot at a target **b :** TARGET **c :** a mound or bank that catches rifle bullets or other projectiles (as for protecting men operating targets on a target range) **d butts** *pl* **:** RANGE 5a(3) **e :** a stand concealed by a parapet or thicket or sunk in the ground and used for shooting birds **2 a** *obs* **:** LIMIT, BOUND, GOAL **b** *archaic* **:** the object of one's efforts **:** END, AIM **3 a :** a person at whom ridicule or jokes are directed **:** LAUGHINGSTOCK ⟨a favorite ~ of the village wits⟩ **b :** an object of criticism, abuse, contempt, or swindling **:** VICTIM, MARK ⟨the ~ of a propaganda attack⟩ ⟨cardsharpers and their ~*s*⟩

⁵butt \"\ *vb* -ED/-ING/-S [partly fr. ⁴*butt*, partly fr. ⁶*butt*] *vi* **:** to meet or adjoin at the end **:** ABUT — used with *on* ⟨the crofts are usually long and narrow, one end ~*ing* on the fields —M.W.Beresford⟩ or *against* ⟨the plate ~*s* against the end stop secured on the front end of the planer —J.M.Walter⟩ ~ *vt* **1** *obs* **:** to lay out the limits of **:** BOUND **2 a :** to place (as a beam) end to end with another **:** set (two pieces) together with the ends meeting but not overlapping **b :** to trim or otherwise cause to meet or be joined along the edges (as strips of wallpaper) **3 a :** to place end to end (as two type slugs to make a longer line than can be cast in one piece) **b :** to fit corner to corner (as border rules to make a box) **c :** to position (two printing plates) so close together that the printing surfaces meet **4 :** to trim or square off the end of (as a log or a shoulder of meat) **5 a :** to strike (a fish) by depressing the butt of the rod so as to obtain a sudden tension of the line **b :** to set (as a ladder) on the bottom end **6 :** to reduce (as a cigarette) to a butt by stubbing or stamping ⟨hastily ~*ed* their cigarettes and came to attention⟩

⁶butt \"\ *n* -s [ME *but, butte*, prob. of native origin and akin to OE *buttuc* end, piece of land, ME *buttok* buttock, LG *butt* blunt — more at BUTT (fish)] **1 a** *slang* **:** BUTTOCKS **b** (1) **:** the large end of a beef loin (2) **:** the body end of a pork shoulder **c :** the thicker or handle end of a tool or weapon ⟨the ~ of a spear⟩ ⟨the ~ of a whip⟩ ⟨the ~ of an arrow⟩ **d** (1) **:** the end of a rifle stock that is placed against the shoulder when fired **:** the end of a rifle opposite the muzzle (2) **:** the bottom of the grip of a pistol **e :** the base section of a fishing rod upon which the reel is mounted **f :** the end of a connecting rod or similar link in a machine, enlarged and squared off (as for the attachment of an adjacent link) **g** *of the hand* **:** the heel or part nearest the wrist **h :** BUTT HINGE **2 a :** the end of a plant from which the roots spring (as the base of a tree trunk) **:** the big end of a log; *also* **:** the end of a stalk or twig opposite to the flowering end ⟨the ~ of a cornstalk⟩ ⟨asparagus ~*s*⟩ **b :** the thick end of a plank, plate, bar, board, or shingle **c :** the heavy or bottom end of a ladder **d** (1) **:** a fitting that serves as a coupling at the end of a line of hose (2) **:** the end of a hose **3 a :** a tree stump; *specif* **:** a walnut stump **b :** an unused or unburned end (as of a candle or a cigarette or cigar) **c** *slang* **:** CIGARETTE **d** *slang* **:** a remaining part ⟨two more years and a ~ of a prison term⟩ **e** *obs* **:** a strip of plowed land shortened by abutting against some object (as a river, a highway, or a neighboring furlong) **:** SELION **4 a :** the part of a hide or skin corresponding to the animal's back and sides after trimming off shoulders and belly, containing the thickest and stoutest leather, and used for harness, belting, soles of shoes — see HIDE illustration **b :** the thickest part of a leaf spring where the leaves have not been thinned by tapering or drawing **5 :** a place where a stratum of rock to be quarried is cut off by other rock **6 :** the posterior end of the dubbing of an artificial fly — see FLY illustration

⁷butt \"\ *n* -s [ME, fr. MF *botte*, fr. OProv *bota*, fr. LL *buttis*, perh. of non-IE origin; akin to the source of Gk *pytinē*, a kind of wine bottle, Gk dial. (Tarentum) *bytinē* chamber pot] **1 :** a large cask esp. for wine, beer, or water or formerly for salmon and shrimps **2 :** any of various units of liquid capacity: as **a :** a measure equal to 108 imperial gallons (2 hogsheads of 54 gallons each) **b :** a Spanish unit for wine equal to 140 U. S. gallons or 116.57 imperial gallons

⁸butt \"\ *n* -s [ME *but, butt* ridge of ground between two furrows, fr. ML *butta, butta*, perh. fr. LL *buttis* cask] *now dial* **:** a small piece of ground separated or set out in any way from the surrounding land

butt block *n* [⁶*butt*] **:** a block of hardwood to which the ends of adjoining planks of a ship's frames are fastened

butt chain *n* [⁶*butt*] **:** a chain to attach the end of a trace to a singletree in a harness

butt chisel *n* [⁶*butt*] **:** a short woodworking chisel suitable for fitting hinges or strike plates

butt cut *n* [⁶*butt*] **1 :** the log next above the stump — called also *butt log* **2 :** tanbark taken from the lower part of a tree before felling it for subsequent further peeling

butte \ˈbyüt, *usu* -üd·+V\ *n* -s [F, knoll, hillock, fr. MF *bute* mound of earth serving as backstop for a target — more at BUTT (mound)] **:** an isolated hill or small mountain with steep or precipitous sides and a top variously flat, rounded, or pointed that may be a residual mass isolated by erosion (as at Butte, Montana), a volcanic cone (as East Butte, Idaho), or an exposed volcanic neck (as Ship Rock, New Mexico) and that usu. has a smaller summit area than a mesa

butted *past of* BUTT

butt end *n* [⁶*butt*] **1 :** the thicker or handle end **2 :** an unused or remaining portion **:** FAG END

¹but·ter \ˈbəd·ə(r), ˈbətə-\ *n* -s [ME, fr. OE *butere;* akin to OFris & OHG *butera* butter; all fr. a prehistoric WGmc word borrowed fr. L *butyrum* butter, fr. Gk *boutyron*, fr. *bou-* (fr. *bous* cow) + *-tyron* (fr. *tyros* cheese); akin to Av *tūiri-* whey and perh. to L *tumēre* to swell — more at COW, THUMB] **1 :** an important food consisting of a solid emulsion mainly of fat globules, air bubbles, and water droplets made to coalesce by churning the cream obtained from milk and used esp. as a spread on bread and in cooking **2 :** a substance resembling butter esp. in consistency: as **a :** an inorganic chloride — not now used technically ⟨~ of zinc⟩ **b :** any of various fatty oils remaining nearly solid at ordinary temperatures ⟨vegetable ~*s*⟩ **c :** a smooth food spread made from fruit, nuts, or other food ⟨anchovy ~⟩ ⟨apple ~⟩ **d :** dairy butter mixed with a savory food or food product ⟨parsley ~⟩ ⟨garlic ~⟩ **3 :** BUTTER DISH **4 :** FLATTERY, CAJOLERY

²butter \"\ *vt* **buttered; buttered; buttering** \ˈbəd·əriŋ, ˈbət(ə)riŋ\ **butters** [ME *butteren*, fr. OE *buterian* to butter, fr. *butere*, n.] **1 :** to cover or spread with butter **2 :** to beguile or cover with lavish or fulsome flattery or praise — usu. used with *up* **3 :** to spread the surface of (as a brick or tile) with a plastic material (as mortar) before setting in place

butter-and-egg man \ˌbəd·ə(r)ˈneg-, -ə(r)nˈdeg-\ *n, slang* **:** a free spender or wealthy investor **:** a naive prosperous businessman

butter-and-eggs \ˌbəd·ə(r)ˈnegz, -ə(r)nˈdegz\ *n pl but sing or pl in constr* **:** any of several plants having flowers of two shades of yellow: as **a :** TOADFLAX **b :** OWL'S CLOVER

butterball \ˈ==ˌ=\ *n* **1 :** a fat chubby person **2 :** any of certain ducks: as **a :** BUFFLEHEAD **b :** RUDDY DUCK

butter basket *n* **:** GLOBEFLOWER

butter bean *n* **1 :** WAX BEAN **2 :** LIMA BEAN: as **a** *chiefly South & Midland* **:** a large dried lima bean **b :** SIEVA BEAN **3 :** a green shell bean; *also* **:** a shell bean as opposed to snap bean

butterbill \ˈ==ˌ=\ *n* **:** AMERICAN SCOTER

butterboat \ˈ==ˌ=\ *n* **:** a small gravy boat

butterboat-bill *or* **butterboat-billed coot** \ˈ==ˌ=ˌ=-\ *n* **:** SURF SCOTER

butterbread \ˈ==ˌ=\ *n* [trans. of PaG *budderbrot* & G *butterbrot*] *dial* **:** a piece of bread and butter ⟨hey ma, can I have a ~⟩

but·ter·bump \ˈbətə(r)ˌbəmp\ *n, dial Eng* **:** the common European bittern (*Botaurus stellaris*)

but·ter·bur \ˈbəd·ərˌbər\ *n* -s **:** any of certain composite plants of the genus *Petasites* (esp. *P. hybridus*) with broad leaves and purplish rayless flowers

butterbush \ˈ==ˌ=\ *n* **:** a plant of the genus *Pittosporum; esp* **:** POISONBERRY TREE

butter cake *n* **:** a cake made with shortening as distinguished from sponge cake — see GOLD CAKE, WHITE CAKE

butter chip *n* **:** an individual dish for butter

butter clam *n* **:** either of two species (*Saxidomus nuttallii* or *S. giganteus*) of large delicately flavored clams (family Veneridae) of the Pacific coast of No. America

butter color *n* **:** a yellow dye (as annatto) used to impart the desired color to butter and butter substitutes

buttercream \ˈ==ˌ=\ *n* **1 :** fondant to which butter is added before creaming **2 :** a cake filling or frosting made by creaming butter, cream, and powdered sugar to which a desired flavoring may be added

buttercup \ˈ==ˌ=\ *n* [so called fr. its yellow cup-shaped flowers] **1 :** a plant of the genus *Ranunculus* (esp. *R. acris* and *R. bulbosus*) with bright yellow flowers — called also *butterflower, goldcup, kingcup;* see TALL BUTTERCUP **2 :** a variable color averaging a vivid yellow that is redder and deeper than dandelion (sense 3b) or goldenrod (sense 2a) — compare BUTTERCUP YELLOW **3 a** *usu cap* **:** a breed of medium-sized fowls of Italian origin distinguished by a comb with a cup-shaped blade **b** *sometimes cap* **:** a bird of this breed, the male being orange-red with black tail, the female golden buff spangled with buff

buttercup family *n* **:** RANUNCULACEAE

buttercup primrose *n* **:** an Asiatic primrose (*Primula floribunda*) grown in greenhouses for its golden yellow bloom

buttercup squash *n* **:** a turban squash with flesh resembling sweet potato in flavor

buttercup yellow *n* **1 :** a grayish yellow that is paler and slightly redder than chamois and redder, lighter, and stronger than old ivory — compare BUTTERCUP 2 **2 :** ZINC YELLOW

butter dish *n* **:** a usu. round or rectangular dish often with a drainer and a cover for holding butter at table

butter dock *n* **1 :** BUTTERBUR **2 :** CURLED DOCK **3 :** BITTER DOCK

butter duck *n* **:** any of several American ducks: as **a :** RUDDY DUCK **b :** BUFFLEHEAD **c :** SHOVELER

buttered *past of* BUTTER

buttered joint *n* **:** a thin masonry joint made by applying the mortar to one end and on the four edges of the bottom of the brick before it is laid

butterfat \ˈ==ˌ=\ *n* **:** the natural fat of milk and the chief component of butter that consists essentially of a mixture of glycerides derived from lower fatty acids (as butyric acid) as well as from higher fatty acids and has a melting range low enough that the fat becomes liquid in the mouth, the amount of fat in dairy products serving as one of the main criteria of their quality

butterfingered \ˈ==ˌ==\ *adj* **:** apt to let things fall or slip through the fingers **:** CLUMSY, CARELESS

butterfingers \ˈ==ˌ==\ *n pl but sing in constr* **:** a butterfingered person

butterfish \ˈ==ˌ=\ *n* **:** any of numerous fishes esp. of the family Stromateidae and the suborder Percoidea that have a distinctly slippery mucus coating: as **a :** a small, deep-bodied marine food fish (*Poronotus triacanthus*) of the east coast of the U.S. **b :** GUNNEL **c :** CONEY 5a **d** *Austral* **:** MULLOWAY

butterflower \ˈ==ˌ==\ *n* **:** BUTTERCUP 1

¹but·ter·fly \ˈbəd·ə(r)ˌflī, -ətə-\ *n* [ME *butterflie*, fr. OE *buterflēoge*, fr. *butere* butter + *flēoge* fly, perh. fr. the belief that butterflies or witches in the shape of butterflies stole milk and butter — more at BUTTER, FLY] **1 :** any of certain slender-bodied diurnal insects forming the division Rhopalocera of the order Lepidoptera that have very large broad wings which are often strikingly colored and patterned and are usu. held vertically over the back or expanded when at rest and slender usu. somewhat club-shaped antennae sometimes hooked near the ends — distinguished from *moth* **2 a :** a person who dresses gaudily or extravagantly **b :** a person chiefly occupied with the pursuit of pleasure ⟨a social ~⟩ **3 :** something resembling a butterfly in shape or motion: as **a :** BUTTERFLY VALVE **b :** an auxiliary support like a cross attached to a sculptor's armature **c :** a roof distinguished by a pitch that rises to the eaves leaving a valley **d** *slang* **:** a usu. weighted note thrown from a moving train **e :** a gauze-covered frame for diffusing light in motion-picture photography **f :** a marking in butterfly shape on an animal **g** (1) *also* **butterfly breaststroke :** a swimming stroke not now used in competition that is executed in a prone position with both arms extended and moving simultaneously in a circular motion and being out of the water during the recovery half of the cycle, the kick consisting of one breaststroke kick to each arm cycle (2) *also* **butterfly dolphin :** a competitive swimming stroke with this same arm motion but with a kick consisting of a simultaneous up-and-down action of the feet, two kicks being executed to each complete arm cycle — called also *dolphin, dolphin butterfly, dolphin fishtail* **4 butterflies** *pl* **:** a feeling of hollowness or queasiness esp. caused by emotional or nervous tension or anxious anticipation ⟨the paratrooper got *butterflies* in his stomach before the jump⟩ **5 :** a rope spinning stunt in which a loop is spun vertically and moved in front of the body from left to right without interruption

²butterfly \"\ *adj* **:** resembling a butterfly: **a :** cut or shaped to resemble the outlines of a butterfly ⟨~ collar⟩ **b** *in cookery* **:** resembling a butterfly in form by being partially split and spread apart ⟨a ~ steak⟩ ⟨~ fillet⟩ **c** *of a dog's nose* **:** PARTI-COLORED

³butterfly \"\ *vt* -ED/-ING/-ES **:** to split almost entirely and spread apart in such a way as to resemble the spread wings of a butterfly ⟨a *butterflied* steak⟩

butterfly banners *n pl* **:** DUTCHMAN'S-BREECHES

butterfly bat *n* [so called fr. its fluttery flight] **:** any of several small delicate African bats (genus *Glauconycteris*) with translucent pearly or amber-bronze wings

butterfly bomb *n* **:** a small antipersonnel bomb fitted with two folding wings that flutter and arm the fuze as the bomb falls

butterfly bush *n* [so called fr. its flowers that attract butterflies] **:** a shrub of the genus *Buddleia*

butterfly chair *n* [so called fr. the resemblance of the cloth

sling to the outspread wings of a butterfly] **:** a lounging chair consisting of a cloth sling supported by a frame of metal tubing or bars
butterfly clam *or* **butterfly mussel** *n* **:** a freshwater mussel (*Plagiola securis*) found in the Ohio and Illinois rivers and reported to produce pearls of fine quality
butterfly cod *n* [so called fr. the winglike fins] **:** a percoid fish (*Pterois volitans*) of tropical coral reefs having vertical scarlet stripes on a creamy ground and the dorsal and pectoral fins greatly enlarged and shaped like a fan
butterfly crab *n* [so called fr. the resemblance of its shell to the outspread wings of a butterfly] **:** a small shallow-water crab (*Cryptolithodes typicus*) of the Pacific coast of No. America
butterfly dam *n* [so called fr. its opening like the wings of a butterfly] **:** a movable steel dam pivoted at top and bottom and opened and closed by a rack-and-pinion mechanism and electric motor
butterfly damper *n* **:** BUTTERFLY VALVE 2
butterfly dolphin *n* **:** ¹BUTTERFLY 3g(2)
butterfly fish *n* **1 :** any of various fishes having variegated colors, broad expanded fins, or both: as **a :** OCELLATED BLENNY **b :** FLYING GURNARD **c :** a flying fish (*Exocoetus volitans*) of the Atlantic **d :** any of numerous small brilliantly colored carnivorous spiny-finned fishes of tropical seas that constitute the family Chaetodontidae and have narrow deep bodies and fins partly covered with scales **e :** a small brown fish (*Pantodon buchholzi*) of the streams of western Africa that has elongate lacy pectoral fins suggestive of wings and is often kept in the tropical aquarium **f :** BUTTERFLY COD **2 :** CHITON 2
butterfly flower *n* **:** a flower of the genus *Schizanthus*
butterfly hinge *n* **:** a decorative hinge that has the appearance of a butterfly when the leaves are spread flat
butterfly knot *n* **:** a knot used by mountain climbers to form a middle loop in the climbing rope — called also *lineman's loop knot*
butterfly lily *n* **1 :** a plant of the genus *Hedychium* often cultivated for the white, yellow, or red irregular flowers **2 :** MARIPOSA LILY
butterfly net *n* **:** a conical net for catching insects that is made of light cheesecloth or muslin and held open by a metal ring attached at the end of a wooden handle
butterfly nut *n* **:** WING NUT
butterfly orchid *also* **butterfly orchis** *n* **1 :** either of two European terrestrial orchids of the genus *Platanthera* (*P. bifolia* and *P. chlorantha*) **2 :** a Mexican epiphytic orchid (*Epidendrum venosum*) often cultivated **3 :** BUTTERFLY PLANT **4 :** an orchid of the genus *Gymnadenia*
butterfly pea *n* **:** any of several large-flowered wild peas of the closely related genera *Clitoria* and *Centrosema:* as **a :** a common twining vine (*Clitoria mariana*) of the southeastern and central U.S. with pale blue 2-inch flowers having very large standards **b :** a weakly twining to prostrate vine (*Centrosema virginianum*) occurring from New Jersey to tropical eastern No. America and sometimes cultivated for its purple and white flowers
butterfly plant *n* **1 :** ONCIDIUM 2 **2 :** an East Indian orchid (*Phalaenopsis amabilis*) having spikes of white-and-yellow flowers
butterfly ray *n* [so called fr. the winglike shape of the pectoral fins] **:** any of several short-tailed broad-finned sting rays
butterfly shell *n* **:** a shell suggestive of a butterfly: as **a :** BRACHIOPOD **b :** one of the plates of a chiton
butterfly table *n* **:** a usu. small drop-leaf table with splayed legs, oval top, and leaves supported by brackets shaped like a butterfly's wings

butterfly table

butterfly tulip *n* **:** MARIPOSA LILY
butterfly valve *n* [so called fr. the winglike clappers] **1 :** a double clack valve (as in a lift-pump piston) consisting of two semicircular clappers hinged to a cross rib **2 :** a damper or throttle valve in a pipe consisting of a disk turning on a diametral axis
butterfly weed *n* **1 :** an orange-flowered showy milkweed (*Asclepias tuberosa*) of eastern No. America — called also *pleurisy root* **2 :** a prairie plant (*Gaura coccinea*) of western No. America with irregular scarlet flowers
butterfly window *n* [so called fr. its winglike shape and manner of opening] **:** a small usu. 3-cornered portion of the front window of an automobile that is independently hinged on a vertical axis
butterhead \ˈ==,=\ *or* **butterheading** \ˈ==,==\ *adj, of lettuce* **:** forming a substantial but soft head of delicate-flavored tender leaves that tend to bleach at the heart to a clear yellow
butterier *comparative of* BUTTERY
butteries *pl of* BUTTERY
butteriest *superlative of* BUTTERY
but·ter·i·ness \ˈbədərēnəs, -ətər-, -ri-\ *n* -ES **:** the quality or state of being buttery
buttering *pres part of* BUTTER
but·ter·is \ˈbədərəs, -ət(ə)rəs\ *n* -ES [alter. of ME *buttyr,* fr. MF *boutoir,* fr. *bouter* to thrust, strike — more at BUTT (thrust)] **:** a steel instrument for paring the hoofs of horses

butteris

butter knife *n* **1 :** a usu. silver knife for cutting butter from a butter dish **2 :** BUTTER SPREADER
butter leaves *n pl* [so called fr. their use in packing butter] **1 :** GARDEN ORACH **2 :** BEET **3 :** ALPINE DOCK
but·ter·less \ˈbədələs, ˈbət|, -*R* |əl- *or* |ᵊl-\ *adj* **:** being without butter
but·ter·man \ˈbədə(r),man, -ətə-, -,maa(ə)n, -,mən\ *n, pl* **buttermen :** one whose chief work is making, selling, or dealing in butter
buttermilk \ˈ==,=\ *n* **1 :** the fluid remaining after the solids in cream have coalesced into butter in the churning process **2 :** cultured milk made by the addition of certain organisms to sweet milk
butter muslin *n* [so called fr. its use in butter making] *Brit* **:** CHEESECLOTH
butternose \ˈ==,=\ *n* **:** AMERICAN SCOTER
butternut \ˈ==,=\ *n* [so called fr. the oil in the nut] **1 a :** the sweet-flavored edible nut of an American tree (*Juglans cinerea*) that is distinguished from the black walnut by being ellipsoid and pointed **b :** the tree that bears butternuts — called also *white walnut;* see TREE illustration **2 :** SOUARI NUT **3 a** (1) **:** coarse homespun cloth or jean of a brown color dyed with an extract from the butternut tree (2) **butternuts** *pl* **:** an outer garment (as trousers or overalls) made of this cloth **b** *slang* **:** a soldier or partisan of the Confederacy during the Civil War
butternut squash *n* [so called fr. its color] **:** a smooth somewhat bottle-shaped straight-necked winter squash that is buff to yellow in color and has fine textured orange to yellow flesh
butter of antimony [trans. of NL *butyrum antimonii;* fr. its softness] **:** ANTIMONY CHLORIDE a
butter of tin [prob. trans. of NL *butyrum stanni;* fr. its softness] **:** stannic chloride or its pentahydrate
butter oil *n* **:** butterfat melted and clarified (as for use in making process butter) — compare GHEE
butter paper *n* **:** greaseproof paper that is used for wrapping butter or lard
butter pat *n* **:** a piece of butter formed into a ball or other ornamental shape for table use or an individual square cut from a quarter-pound stick of commercial butter
butter pear *n* **:** AVOCADO
butter plate *n* **1 :** BUTTER DISH **2 :** BREAD-AND-BUTTER PLATE
butter print *n* **1 :** a piece of carved wood used to mark molds of butter; *also* **:** the impress made by it **2 :** INDIAN MALLOW 1
butt·er-rigged \ˈbədə(r)ˌrigd, -ətə-\ *adj* [⁵butt + -er; fr. the topgallant yard's being butted against the topsail yard when the sails are furled] *of a topsail schooner* **:** having the topgallant yard hoist with halyards rather than fixed by lifts
butter-rose \ˈ==,=\ *n* **:** BUTTERCUP

butters *pl of* BUTTER, *pres 3d sing of* BUTTER
butter sauce *n* **:** a sauce made of butter, water or broth, and seasonings, thickened with flour, and used also as a basis for the making of other sauces (as caper sauce or shrimp sauce) by the addition of special ingredients
butterscotch \ˈ==ˌ=\ *n, often attrib* [prob. fr. ¹butter + Scotch] **1 :** a hard candy made by boiling together brown sugar, corn syrup, and water **2 :** the flavor of brown sugar and butter cooked together **3 a :** a dark orange yellow that is yellower, stronger, and slightly lighter than average topaz and duller than average amber (sense 3b) **b :** a moderate brown to yellowish brown
butter spreader *n* **:** a small knife with rounded blade used for buttering bread at table

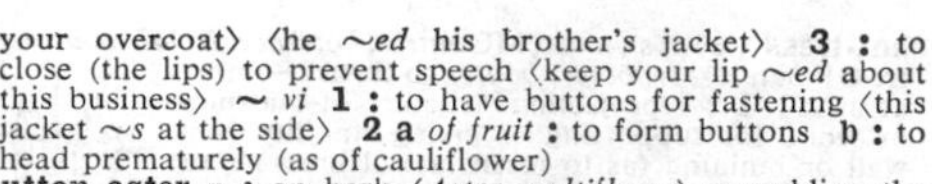
butter spreader

butter tree *n* **:** any of various trees the seeds of which yield a substance similar to butter: as **a :** SHEA TREE **b :** a Himalayan tree (*Madhuca butyracea*) related to the illupi tree **c :** a tropical African tree (*Combretum butyrosum*)
butterweed \ˈ==,=\ *n* **:** any of several plants having yellow flowers or smooth soft foliage: as **a :** HORSEWEED 1 **b :** INDIAN MALLOW 1 **c :** an American wild lettuce (*Lactuca canadensis*) **d :** any of several plants of the genus *Senecio; esp* **:** an American ragwort (*Senecio glabellus*) **e :** FIREWEED a
butter weight *n* **1 :** a pound weight once used for butter equal to 18 or more ounces **2** *obs* **:** OVERWEIGHT **:** good measure
butterwort \ˈ==,=\ *n* [so called fr. the mucilage secreted by the leaves] **:** a plant of the genus *Pinguicula*
¹**but·tery** \ˈbədərē, -ət(ə)rē, -ri\ *n* -ES [ME *boterie,* fr. MF, alter. of *bouteillerie* — more at BUTLERY] **1 :** a storeroom for liquors **2 a** *now dial* **:** PANTRY, LARDER **b :** a room where ale, wine, and other provisions are kept for sale to students (as in an English college)
²**buttery** \ˈ"\ *adj, sometimes* -ER/-EST [ME, fr. ¹butter + -y] **1 a :** having the qualities, consistency, or appearance of butter **b :** containing or spread with butter **2 :** FLATTERING, WHEEDLING
buttery bar *n* [¹buttery] **:** a serving bar on a buttery hatch
butter yellow *n* **1 :** OIL YELLOW 1b **2 :** a brilliant yellow that is greener and paler than lemon chrome — called also *jasmine yellow;* compare JASMINE
buttery hatch *n* [¹buttery] **:** a half door between a buttery and the hall
buttes *pl of* BUTTE
butt gauge *n* [⁶butt] **:** a gauge usu. with three independent cutters used chiefly for marking the outlines of mortises for door butts or strike plates
butt·gen·bach·ite \ˈbətgən,ba,kīt, ˈbüt-\ *n* -S [F, fr. Henri J. F. *Buttgenbach* b1874 Belg. mineralogist + F *-ite*] **:** a mineral composed of a hydrous copper nitrate with chlorine occurring in mattes of light-blue acicular crystals
butt-headed \ˈ=ˌ==\ *adj* [⁶butt] *dial, of an animal* **:** without horns **:** MULEY
butt hinge *n* [⁶butt] **:** a hinge applied on and usu. mortised flush into the edge of a door and the face of the casing against which this edge of the door butts when closed
butties *pl of* BUTTY
butt in *vi* [¹butt] **1 :** to thrust oneself upon others **:** INTRUDE, INTERFERE, MEDDLE ⟨*butting in* on other people's private affairs⟩
butt-in \ˈ=,=\ *n* -S [*butt in*] **1 :** one who butts in **2** *Brit* **:** the first bid in contract bridge made by a member of the side that did not open the bidding **:** OVERCALL
butt·ing \ˈbəd·iŋ, -ətiŋ\ *n* -S [fr. gerund of ⁵butt] **:** ABUTTAL, BOUNDARY
butt·in·sky \bəd·ˈinskē\ *n* -ES [*butt in* + *-sky* (last element in many Slavic names)] *slang* **:** one given to butting in **:** a troublesome meddler **:** PEST

butt hinges: *1* loose-pin butt, *2* fast-pin butt, *3* double-acting spring butt

butt joint *n* [⁶butt] **:** a joint made by fastening the parts together end-to-end and in wood usu. perpendicular to the grain or edge-to-edge without overlap and often strengthened (as with a strap)
butt knuckle *n* [²butt] **:** a projection shaped like a knuckle usu. of metal and designed to receive pressure (as from a window pole)
but·tle \ˈbəd·ᵊl, -ətᵊl\ *vi* **buttled; buttled; buttling** \-əd·ᵊliŋ, -ət(ᵊ)liŋ\ **buttles** [back-formation fr. *butler*] *substand* **:** to serve or act as butler
butt log *n* [⁶butt] **:** BUTT CUT 1
¹**but·tock** \ˈbəd·ək, -ətək\ *n* -S [ME *buttok* — more at BUTT (end)] **1 a** (1) **:** either of the two rounded prominences separated by a median cleft that form the lower part of the back in man and consist largely of the gluteus muscles (2) **:** the lower part of the back made up of these prominences **:** SEAT — usu. used in pl. **b buttocks** *pl* **:** the corresponding part of a quadruped **:** RUMP **2 a :** the convex aftermost part of a ship above the water line **:** COUNTER — usu. used in pl. **b** *or* **buttock line :** a line of intersection of a longitudinal vertical plane with the hull of a ship or the body or float of an aircraft **3** *chiefly Brit* **:** a maneuver in which a wrestler gets his opponent across his back and throws him over his head
²**buttock** \ˈ"\ *vt* -ED/-ING/-S **:** to throw with a buttock ⟨~*ed* his opponent onto the mat⟩
¹**but·ton** \ˈbətᵊn\ *n* -S *often attrib* [ME *boton,* fr. MF *boton, bouton,* fr. OF, fr. *boter, bouter* to strike, thrust — more at BUTT (to thrust)] **1 a :** a disk, ball, or device of other shape having holes or a shank by which it is sewn or secured to an article (as of clothing or upholstery) and that is used as a fastener by passing it through a buttonhole or loop or as a trimming and is made of glass, shell, bone, wood, leather, or cloth ⟨on Fortune's Cap, we are not the very *Button* —Shak.⟩ **b :** an ornament or badge of similar shape often of metal with a stamped design or of plastic with a slogan imprinted on the face **c :** a thing of slight value ⟨not worth a ~⟩ **d :** a unit of one inch used in determining length of gloves and measured from base of thumb towards wrist ⟨a 12-*button* glove reaches nearly to the elbow⟩ **e buttons** *pl but sing in constr* [so called fr. the buttons on his livery] *now chiefly Brit* **:** PAGE, BELLBOY **2 :** any of various parts or growths of plants resembling buttons: as **a :** BUD **b :** the fruit of a rose or the flower head of one of the Compositae ⟨a ~ chrysanthemum⟩ **c :** a small round seed vessel **d :** an immature whole mushroom; *esp* **:** one just before expansion of the pileus **e :** an abnormally small fruit **f :** an onion bulb or a garlic clove **3 :** a small knob or piece resembling a button in shape: as **a :** an incipient or stunted growth of horn (as in the calf or stag) — see SCUR **b buttons** *pl,* dung esp. of a sheep **c :** the terminal segment of a rattlesnake's rattle **d :** a uterine cotyledon **e :** a small mass or globule of metal remaining after fusion (as at the bottom of a crucible or cupel) **4** *West* **:** YOUNGSTER, BOY **5 :** a device suggestive of a button: as **a :** an oblong or elongated piece of wood or metal turning on a nail, pin, or screw (as to fasten a door or window) **b :** a leather washer for a nail or screw **c :** PUSH BUTTON **d :** the knob in the end block to which the tailpiece of a stringed instrument (as a violin) is anchored **e :** a marker in the pavement indicating a proper pivoting point for traffic or one of a set marking vehicle or pedestrian lanes **f :** a leather ring running along the reins of a bridle for tightening or loosening it **g :** a guard on the tip of a fencing foil **h :** one of the push buttons on a musical instrument (as an accordion) **i :** the earpiece of a hearing aid **6** *slang* **:** the point of the chin esp. as the target for a knockout blow ⟨the next punch landed square on the ~⟩ **7 :** a small white spot on the throat or chest of a solid-colored cat **8 buttons** *pl, slang* **:** WITS ⟨hasn't got all his ~*s*⟩ **— on the button :** on the dot **:** PRECISELY
²**button** \ˈ"\ *vb* **buttoned; buttoned; buttoning** \ˈbət(ᵊ)niŋ\ **buttons** [ME *botonen,* fr. MF *botoner,* fr. OF, fr. *boton,* n., button] *vt* **1 :** to furnish or decorate with buttons **2 a :** to pass (a button) through a buttonhole or loop **b :** to fasten, secure, or close with a button — often used with *up* ⟨~ up your overcoat⟩ ⟨he ~*ed* his brother's jacket⟩ **3 :** to close (the lips) to prevent speech ⟨keep your lip ~*ed* about this business⟩ ~ *vi* **1 :** to have buttons for fastening ⟨this jacket ~*s* at the side⟩ **2 a** *of fruit* **:** to form buttons **b :** to head prematurely (as of cauliflower)
button aster *n* **:** an herb (*Aster multiflorus*) resembling the bushy aster but having smaller flowers and spiny-tipped involucral bracts
buttonball \ˈ==ˌ=\ *n* **1 :** *also* **buttonball tree** *chiefly North* **:** SYCAMORE 3a **2 :** BUTTONBUSH
buttonboard \ˈ==ˌ=\ *n* [so called fr. its use in making button-molds] **:** a hard stiff paperboard
buttonbur \ˈ==,=\ *n* -S **:** COCKLEBUR
buttonbush \ˈ==,=\ *n* **:** a No. American shrub (*Cephalanthus occidentalis*) with globular flower heads
button cactus *n* **:** a small cactus (*Epithelantha micromeris*) of Texas and adjacent Mexico shaped like a globe and having flattish tubercles, white spines, and edible fruits
button chrysanthemum *n* **:** a garden chrysanthemum with numerous small heads in profuse clusters
button clover *n* **:** an annual European forage plant (*Medicago orbicularis*) introduced into the U.S. that has sharply toothed leaflets and greenish yellow flowers
button day *n, chiefly Austral* **:** TAG DAY
button-down \ˈ==ˌ=\ *adj* [*button down,* v.] **:** fastened down with buttons ⟨a *button-down* collar on a man's shirt⟩
button ear *n* **:** a dog's ear which falls forward and completely hides the inside — called also *drop ear* — **button-eared** \ˈ==ˌ=\ *adj*
buttoned *adj* **1 :** furnished with or decorated with buttons — usu. used in combination with adjective or noun ⟨pearl-*buttoned*⟩ **2 :** closed or secured with or as if with buttons
but·ton·er \ˈbət(ᵊ)nə(r)\ *n* -S **1 :** one that buttons; *specif* **:** BUTTONHOOK **2 a :** one who sews on buttons **b :** a worker who buttons articles (as shoes or shirts) prior to packaging
button flower *n* **:** a tropical tree or shrub of the genus *Gomphia* (family Ochnaceae)
button grass *n* **1 :** TALL OAT GRASS **2 :** any of several Australian grasses: **a :** a crab grass (*Digitaria sanguinalis*) **b :** any of several grasses (genus *Dactyloctenium*) that are used to some extent for hay and pasture
¹**buttonhead** \ˈ==ˌ=\ *adj, of a bolt, rivet, or screw* **:** having a head with a spherical exposed surface and plane shoulder, the height of the head being usu. less than a hemisphere
²**buttonhead** \ˈ"\ *n* **:** a buttonhead bolt, screw, or rivet — see RIVET illustration
buttonhold \ˈ==,=\ *vt* [back-formation fr. *buttonholder* one who buttonholes a person, fr. ¹button + holder] *archaic* **:** ³BUTTONHOLE
¹**buttonhole** \ˈ==,=\ *n* **1 :** a bound or stitched slit or a loop through which a button is passed **2** *chiefly Brit* **:** BOUTONNIERE **3 :** HART'S-TONGUE 1
²**buttonhole** \ˈ"\ *vt* **:** to furnish with buttonholes or to work with buttonhole stitch
³**buttonhole** \ˈ"\ *vt* [alter. of *buttonhold*] **:** to hold by or as if by the buttonhole in order to detain in conversation ⟨be *buttonholed* by a bore —Virginia Woolf⟩ ⟨peddlers of gossip who ~ each other —Carl Sandburg⟩ ⟨ready to ~ members as they leave an executive session and to find out what has just happened —F.L.Mott⟩ **:** catch the attention of ⟨a voice from our radio *buttonholed* us —E.B.White⟩
buttonholer \ˈ==,==\ *n* **1 :** one that makes buttonholes by hand or machine **2 :** a sewing-machine attachment for making buttonholes
buttonhole stitch *n* **:** an embroidery stitch made by drawing the needle and thread from the upper through the lower edge of the design and out over the lower thread of a preceding stitch held in place with a thumb, the stitches being repeated to form a firm line of closely spaced loops at the lower edge of the design

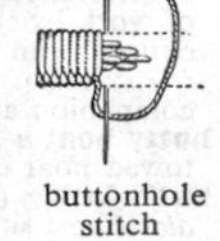
buttonhole stitch

buttonhook \ˈ==,=\ *n* **1 :** a hook for drawing small buttons through buttonholes **2 :** a forward-pass play in football in which the intended receiver runs straight toward a defensive back, then stops and pivots or doubles back toward the passer
buttoning *n* -S **1 :** a closing with two or more buttons **2 :** a decorative method of fastening padded upholstery
button lac *n* **:** lac formed into cakes shaped like buttons by melting and solidifying
but·ton·less \-tᵊnləs\ *adj* **:** being without a button
button mangrove *n* **:** BUTTON TREE 1
buttonmold *also* **buttonmould** \ˈ==,=\ *n* **:** a disk (as of wood or metal) to be made into a button by covering with cloth
button-on \ˈ==ˌ=\ *adj* [fr. *button on,* v.] **:** attached with buttons ⟨a child's *button-on* waist⟩
button onion *n* **:** an onion picked before it has reached full size and used esp. for pickling or as a garnish
button pearl *var of* BOUTON PEARL
button pink *n* **:** a much-branched pink having flowers in clusters of two to four surrounded by bracts and being considered as a hybrid between the sweet william and the China pink or as a distinct species (*Dianthus latifolius*)
button quail *n* **:** any of various small terrestrial birds that resemble quails, are widely distributed in the Old World, and constitute a family (Turnicidae) of the order Gruiformes distinguished by the absence of a hind toe — called also *bustard quail, hemipode*
buttons *pl of* BUTTON, *pres 3d sing of* BUTTON
button sage *n* **:** BLACK SAGE 3
button-seal \ˈ==,=\ *n* **:** a stamp seal of the Near East (including Egypt) that is flat and resembles a button
button sedge *n* **:** a sedge of the genus *Kyllinga* (family Cyperaceae)
button shell *n* **:** any of several somewhat flattened gastropod mollusks: as **a :** a large Australian top shell (*Trochus niloticus*) **b :** the marine pulmonate snail (*Gadinia reticulata*) of the California coast that resembles a limpet
button shoe *n* **:** a shoe fastened with buttons
button snakeroot *n* **1 :** a plant of the genus *Liatris* **2 :** any of several plants of the genus *Eryngium; esp* **:** a coarse prickly plant (*E. aquaticum*) of the southern U.S. with compact umbels and aromatic roots
button snakeweed *n* **:** a very spiny plant (*Eryngium leavenworthii*) of the central U.S. with palmately divided leaves and heads of flowers resembling thistles
button spider *n* [prob. trans. of Afrik *knopiespinnekop*] **:** either of two venomous spiders (*Latrodectus indistinctus* and *L. geometricus*) of southern Africa closely related to the American black widow and resembling it in appearance and habits
button stick *n* **:** a strip of metal or wood slotted in such a way that it will pass over a row of buttons (as on a military tunic) allowing each button to appear through a slit so that the buttons may be polished without soiling the cloth
button strike *n* **:** a strike called by a union to compel members to pay dues and to prevent employment of workers without union buttons
button test *n* **:** a test of the fusibility of enamel frits made by heating button-shaped masses
button thistle *n* **:** BULL THISTLE 1
button tree *n* **1 :** a shrub or tree of the genus *Conocarpus* having hard tough fruits like buttons **2 :** SYCAMORE 3a
button up *vt* **1 :** to close tightly and securely ⟨a tank *buttoned up* and ready for action⟩ **2 :** to carry to completion (as an order or assignment) **3 :** to bring to complete and final decision or irrevocable settlement ~ *vi* **:** to become mum
buttonweed \ˈ==,=\ *n* **1 :** a small troublesome weed (*Diodia teres*) with linear leaves and small flowers and fruits resembling buttons **2 :** any of several plants of the genus *Spermacoce* (family Rubiaceae) of similar appearance to buttonweed **3 :** INDIAN MALLOW 1 **4 :** KNAPWEED **5 :** CLUSTERED BLUET
button willow *n* **:** BUTTONBUSH
buttonwood \ˈ==,=\ *n* **1** *chiefly North* **:** SYCAMORE 3a **2 :** BUTTONTREE 1 **3 :** WHITE MANGROVE 1 **4 :** BUTTONBUSH
buttonwood shrub *n* **:** BUTTONBUSH
but·tony \ˈbət(ᵊ)nē, -ni\ *adj* **1 :** ornamented with many buttons **2 :** like a button ⟨~ eyes⟩
butt plate *n* [⁶butt] **:** the usu. metal plate on the butt end of a gunstock

[1]**but·tress** \'bətrəs\ *n* -ES [ME *butres, boterace,* fr. MF *bouterez,* fr. OF *boterez,* fr. *boter, bouter* to thrust — more at BUTT] **1 :** a projecting structure of masonry or wood for supporting or giving stability to a wall or building (as to resist lateral pressure or strain acting at a particular point in one direction) but sometimes serving chiefly for ornament **2 :** any of various things that resemble a buttress in appearance: **a :** COUNTERFORT **b :** a projecting part of a mountain or hill **c :** a horny protuberance on a horse's hoof at the heel where the wall bends inward and forward **d :** the broadened basal portion of a tree trunk or a thickened vertical part of it **3 :** something that supports, strengthens, or helps to defend ⟨a ~ of the cause of peace⟩ **4 :** an abutment built from a river bank to prevent logs in a drive from injuring the bank or jamming

buttress 1

[2]**buttress** \"\ *vt* -ED/-ING/-ES **1 :** to furnish or support with a buttress ⟨~*ing* the bridge piers⟩ **:** shore up **:** PROP, SUSTAIN ⟨the present river system ~*ed* now with . . . good levees —A.W. Baum⟩ **2 :** SUPPORT, SUSTAIN, STRENGTHEN ⟨arguments ~*ed* by solid facts⟩ ⟨measures to ~ the national economy against the stresses of war⟩ **syn** see SUPPORT

[3]**buttress** \"\ *adj, of a saw blade* **:** having widely separated teeth with one edge perpendicular and the other oblique to the direction of motion

but·tress·less \-ləs\ *adj* **:** being without a buttress

buttress pier *n* **1 :** a pier serving wholly or in part as a buttress **2 :** the part of a buttress above the point of thrust **3 :** the pier receiving the thrust of a flying buttress

buttress root *n* **:** an adventitious root serving as an added support to a tree (as in the banyan and ceiba) — compare KNEE

buttress thread *n* **:** a screw thread in which the driving face is made perpendicular to the axis of the screw (as in a square thread) while the back face makes an angle with the axis (as in a V thread) in order to combine efficiency in the transmission of power with strength

buttress tower *n* **:** a tower at either side of an archway (as for defense of a gate wall)

butt rot *n* [[6]*butt*] **:** a fungous decay of the basal portion of a tree trunk generally involving primarily the heartwood and caused by polypores (as species of *Fomes*)

butts *pres 3d sing of* BUTT, *pl of* BUTT

butts and bounds *n pl* [[4]*butt*] **:** abuttals and boundaries of a property — compare METES AND BOUNDS

butt saw *or* **butting saw** *n* [[6]*butt*] **:** a circular or band saw for crosscutting logs or lumber **:** CUTOFF SAW

butt seam *n* [[6]*butt*] **:** a seam in a shoe affixing edges that are brought together edge to edge with a zigzag or straight stitch

butt shaft *n* [[4]*butt*] **:** a target arrow

butt sling *n* [[7]*butt*] **:** a sling for suspending casks consisting of a rope looped round one end by means of an eye and round the other end with two half hitches

buttstock \'⸗,⸗\ *n* [[6]*butt* + *stock*] **:** the stock of a firearm in the rear of the breech mechanism — compare TIPSTOCK

butt strap *n* [[6]*butt*] **:** a strap or plate covering a butt joint and secured to both pieces

butt-strap \'⸗,⸗\ *vt* [*butt strap*] **:** to fasten by butt straps

butt veneer *n* [[6]*butt*] **:** veneer cut from roots of trees (as walnut) to show a curly figure resulting from intertwined fibers

butt weld *n* [[6]*butt*] **:** a butt joint made by welding

butt-weld \'⸗,⸗\ *vt* [[6]*butt*] **:** to unite by a butt weld — **butt welding** *n*

buttwood \'⸗,⸗\ *n* [[6]*butt* + *wood*] **:** STUMP WOOD

but·ty \'bəd·ē, -ət|ē, |i\ *n* -ES [origin unknown] **1** *dial Brit* **:** a fellow workman **:** CHUM, PARTNER **2** *also* **buttyman** \-man\ *pl* **buttymen :** a worker or middleman who takes an allotment of work by contract at so much per ton of coal or ore for execution as an individual or foreman of a gang ⟨~ collier⟩ ⟨~ system⟩ **3** [prob. fr. [4]*butt* + *-y*] **:** an archer's shooting companion at the butts

butty boat *n* **:** a boat or barge towed by another boat; *esp* **:** a towed boat used in cruising on canals and rivers in England

butty lark *n* [so called fr. the cuckoo's laying eggs in its nest] *dial Eng* **:** MEADOW PIPIT

bu·tyl \'byüd·ᵊl, -üt ᵊl, -ü,til\ *n* -S [ISV *but-* + *-yl*] **:** any of four isomeric alkyl radicals C_4H_9 derived from butane and isobutane: **a :** the normal radical $CH_3CH_2CH_2CH_2$— — called also *n-butyl* **b :** the secondary radical $CH_3CH_2CH(CH_3)$— — called also *sec-butyl* **c :** the tertiary radical $(CH_3)_3C$— — called also *tert-butyl* **d :** ISOBUTYL

Butyl \"\ *trademark* — used for any of a class of synthetic rubbers that are made by polymerizing isobutylene with a small proportion usu. of isoprene at a low temperature (as −140°F) with aluminum chloride as catalyst, that are characterized by low permeability to gases and good resistance to oxygen, ozone, and many chemicals, and that are used esp. in inner tubes for tires

butyl acetate *n* **:** a colorless liquid ester $CH_3COOC_4H_9$ of acetic acid that has a fruity odor and is used as a solvent esp. in cellulose nitrate lacquers — called also *n-butyl acetate, normal butyl acetate*

butyl alcohol *n* **:** any of four flammable liquid alcohols C_4H_9OH derived from the butanes and used chiefly in organic synthesis and as solvents often in the form of their esters: **a :** the normal alcohol $CH_3CH_2CH_2CH_2OH$ made by bacterial fermentation of molasses or grain or synthetically (as by dehydration and reduction of aldol); 1-butanol — called also *n-butyl alcoho* **b :** the secondary alcohol $CH_3CH_2CH(OH)CH_3$ known in three optically different forms and made by hydration of 1-butene; 2-butanol — called also *sec-butyl alcohol* **c :** the tertiary alcohol $(CH_3)_3COH$ made by hydration of isobutylene; 2-methyl-2-propanol — called also *tert-butyl alcohol, trimethylcarbinol* **d :** ISOBUTYL ALCOHOL

butyl aldehyde *n* **:** BUTYRALDEHYDE

bu·tyl·amine \¦byüd·ᵊl¦a,mēn, -üt ᵊl-, -l¦amən\ *n* -S [ISV *butyl* + *amine*] **1 :** any of four flammable liquid bases $C_4H_9NH_2$; *esp* **:** the normal amine $CH_3CH_2CH_2CH_2NH_2$ used chiefly in organic synthesis **2 :** any amine in which butyl is attached to the nitrogen atom

butyl aminobenzoate *n* **:** a white odorless crystalline ester $C_{11}H_{15}NO_2$ used as a local anesthetic; *n*-butyl *para*-aminobenzoate

[1]**bu·tyl·ate** \'byüd·ᵊl,āt, -üt ᵊl-, -lət, *usu* -d· +V\ *n* -S [*butyl* + *-ate*] **:** BUTOXIDE

[2]**butylate** \-lāt, *usu* -d·+V\ *vt* -ED/-ING/-S **:** to introduce the butyl group into (a compound) — **bu·tyl·a·tion** \,byüd·ᵊl-'āshən\ *n* -S

butyl chloral hydrate *n* **:** a bitter crystalline compound $CH_3CHClCCl_2CH(OH)_2$ obtained as a by-product in the manufacture of chloral hydrate and used similarly

bu·tyl·ene \'byüd·ᵊl,ēn, -üt ᵊl-\ *n* -S [ISV *butyl* + *-ene*] **1 :** any of three isomeric flammable easily liquefiable gaseous hydrocarbons C_4H_8 of the ethylene series obtained usu. by the cracking of petroleum and converted into gasoline by polymerization: **a :** the normal compound $CH_2{=}CHCH_2CH_3$ used in making butadiene — called also *alpha-butylene, 1-butene* **b :** the normal symmetrical compound $CH_3CH{=}CHCH_3$ occurring in cis and trans forms used in making butadiene — called also *beta-butylene, 2-butene* **c :** ISOBUTYLENE **2 :** any of four isomeric alkylene radicals C_4H_8 (as tetramethylene) derived from normal butane

butylene glycol *n* **:** BUTANEDIOL

butyl phthalate *n* **:** a butyl ester of phthalic acid; *usu* **:** DIBUTYL PHTHALATE

Bu·tyn \'byüt ᵊn, -ü,tin\ *trademark* — used for butacaine

bu·tyne \'byü,tīn\ *n* -S [ISV *but-* + *-yne, -ine*] **:** either of two isomeric hydrocarbons C_4H_6 of the acetylene series: **a :** an easily condensable gas $CH{\equiv}CCH_2CH_3$ — called also *1-butyne, ethylacetylene* **b :** a volatile liquid $CH_3C{\equiv}CCH_3$ of strong odor — called also *2-butyne, dimethylacetylene*

butyr- *or* **butyro-** *comb form* [ISV, fr. *butyric*] **:** butyric **:** related to butyric acid or butyraldehyde ⟨*butyr*aldol⟩ ⟨*butyro*nitrile⟩

bu·tyr·a·ceous \¦byüd·ə¦rāshəs\ *adj* [L *butyrum* butter + E *-aceous*] **:** having the qualities of butter **:** resembling butter; *also* **:** yielding or containing a substance like butter

bu·tyr·al \'byüd·ə,ral, -rəl\ *n* -S [*butyr-* + *-al*] **:** an acetal of butyraldehyde ⟨~ resins⟩

bu·tyr·aldehyde \¦byüd·ər +\ *n* -S [ISV *butyr-* + *aldehyde*] **:** either of the two aldehydes C_3H_7CHO corresponding to the two butyric acids; *esp* **:** normal butyric aldehyde $CH_3CH_2CH_2CHO$ obtained as a pungent flammable liquid by partial hydrogenation of crotonaldehyde or by dehydrogenation of normal butyl alcohol and used chiefly in making polyvinyl butyral resins for safety glass and condensation products (as with aniline) for rubber accelerators

bu·tyr·ate \'byüd·ə,rāt\ *n* -S [*butyr-* + *-ate*] **1 :** a salt or ester of butyric acid **2 :** CELLULOSE ACETATE BUTYRATE

[1]**bu·tyr·ic** \(')byü¦tirik\ *adj* [F *butyrique,* fr. L *butyrum* butter + F *-ique* -ic — more at BUTTER] **:** relating to or producing butyric acid ⟨~ fermentation⟩

[2]**butyric** \"\ *n* -S **:** a microorganism that engages in butyric fermentation

butyric acid *n* **:** either of two isomeric fatty acids C_3H_7COOH **: a :** the normal acid $CH_3CH_2CH_2COOH$ found esp. in butter in the form of glycerides and in rancid butter as the free acid, obtained as a colorless liquid of unpleasant odor usu. by oxidation of normal butyl alcohol or butyraldehyde or by fermentation (as of molasses), and used chiefly in making esters (as simple esters for use as flavoring materials or esters of cellulose for use as plastics) — called also *butanoic acid, n-butyric acid* **b :** ISOBUTYRIC ACID

butyric fermentation *n* **:** fermentation occurring in putrefaction and apparently in the digestion of herbivorous mammals in which butyric acid is produced by certain chiefly anaerobic bacteria acting upon various organic substances (as lactic acid or butter)

bu·tyr·in \'byüd·ərən\ *n* -S [alter. (influenced by L *butyrum* butter) of earlier *butirine,* fr. F, fr. *butir-* butyr- (irreg. fr. L *butyrum*) + *-ine*] **:** any of the three liquid glycerides of butyric acid; *esp* **:** TRIBUTYRIN

bu·tyr·in·ase \-nās, -nāz\ *n* -S [*butyrin* + *-ase*] **:** an enzyme occurring esp. in blood serum and capable of hydrolyzing any butyrin

bu·tyr·o·lactone \¦byüd·ə(,)rō, -ə,rə +\ *n* -S [*butyr-* + *lactone*] **:** a mobile liquid lactone $C_4H_6O_2$ made usu. by dehydrogenation of 1,4-butanediol and used chiefly as a solvent for resins (as polymers of acrylonitrile) — called also *butanolide*

bu·tyr·om·e·ter \,byüd·ə'rämad·ə(r)\ *n* -S [ISV *butyr-* + *-meter*] **:** an instrument for determining the amount of butterfat in dairy products (as milk) — **bu·tyr·o·met·ric** \¦byüd·ə(,)rō¦me·trik, -rə¦m-\ *adj*

bu·tyr·one \'byüd·ə,rōn\ *n* -S [ISV *butyr-* + *-one*] **:** a liquid ketone $(C_3H_7)_2CO$ obtained by heating calcium butyrate and used as a solvent — called also *dipropyl ketone*

bu·tyr·ous \-rəs\ *adj* [L *butyrum* butter + E *-ous* — more at BUTTER] **:** BUTYRACEOUS

bu·tyr·yl \'byüd·ərəl\ *n* -S [ISV *butyr-* + *-yl*] **:** the radical $CH_3CH_2CH_2CO$— of normal butyric acid

bu·vette \bü'vet, bü'v-\ *n* -S [F, fr. MF *beuvette, buvette,* fr. *beuv-, buv-* (stem of *beivre* to drink) + *-ette* — more at BEVERAGE] **:** TAPROOM, BAR, TAVERN

buwayhid *also* **buwaihid** *usu cap, var of* BUYID

bux·a·ce·ae \bək'sāsē,ē\ *n pl, cap* [NL, fr. *Buxus,* type genus + *-aceae*] **:** a small family of widely distributed shrubs, trees, or sometimes herbs (order Sapindales) having evergreen foliage and flowers with no corolla and a 3-loculed ovary — **bux·a·ceous** \(')bək¦sāshəs\ *adj*

bux·bau·mia \,bəks'bōmēə\ *n, cap* [NL, after J. C. *Buxbaum* †1730 Ger. botanist + NL *-ia*] **:** a genus of mosses (order Buxbaumiales) having a capsule which is placed obliquely on the erect stalk and resembles a small bug

bux·bau·mi·a·les \,bəks,bōmē'ā(,)lēz\ *n pl, cap* [NL, fr. *Buxbaumia* + *-ales*] **:** a small order of minute atypical mosses often isolated in a distinct subclass of Musci and characterized by a reduced gametophore consisting of a few leaves which die shortly after fertilization leaving an asymmetrical capsule

bux·om \'bəksəm\ *adj, sometimes* -ER/-EST [ME *buxom, buhsum, buxsum,* fr. (assumed) OE *būhsum,* fr. OE *būgan* to bend, bow + *-sum* -some — more at BOW] **1** *archaic* **:** marked by obedience **:** TRACTABLE, COMPLIANT ⟨are disposed to be ~ and obedient to the customs and laws of the republic —George Borrow⟩ **2** *obs* **:** physically flexible **:** PLIANT, UNRESISTING ⟨wing silently the ~ air —John Milton⟩ **3** *archaic* **:** full of gaiety **:** BLITHE, LIVELY ⟨how jovial it is and ~ —Andrew Marvell⟩ **4 a :** vigorously or healthily plump **:** sturdily formed ⟨a ~ warm friendly woman —Burl Ives⟩ **b :** FULL-BOSOMED ⟨~ blondes⟩ — **bux·om·ly** *adv*

bux·om·ness *n* -ES [ME *buxomnesse, buhsumnesse* obedience, submissiveness, fr. *buxom, buhsum* + *-nesse* -ness] **:** the quality or state of being buxom

bux·us \'bəksəs\ *n, cap* [NL, fr. L, box (shrub) — more at BOX] **:** a genus (the type of the family Buxaceae) of evergreen shrubs and small trees having opposite entire leaves and capsular fruit

[1]**buy** \'bī\ *vb* **bought** \'bȯt, *usu* -ȯd· +V\ **bought; buying; buys** [ME *byen* (past *boughte,* past part. *bought, ybought*), fr. OE *bycgan* (past *bohte,* past part. *boht, geboht*); akin to OS *buggean* to buy (past part. *giboht*), Goth *bugjan* (past *bauhta,* past part. *-bauhts*), and perh. to OHG *biogan* to bend — more at BOW] *vt* **1 :** to get possession or ownership of by giving or agreeing to give money in exchange **:** PURCHASE — opposed to *sell* **2 :** to obtain at a price of sacrifice ⟨~*ing* peace at the sacrifice of sovereignty⟩ ⟨fame is dearly *bought* at the cost of honor⟩ **3 :** to pay the price for so as to free **:** redeem esp. by a ransom — used chiefly in a theological sense ⟨He that *bought* us with his blood⟩ **4 :** to gain the support or obedience of by an inducement **:** BRIBE, HIRE ⟨~ a public official⟩ — often used with *over* ⟨whether they would go to jail or ~ over the jury when the Act began to operate —H.J.Laski⟩ **5 :** to be the purchasing equivalent of ⟨$2000 will ~ this land⟩ ⟨the dollar ~*s* less than it used to⟩ **6 :** to obtain for cash or other consideration the rights to the services of **:** to take over the contract of ⟨if a baseball club cannot get players in trades it must ~ them⟩ **7** *card games* **:** to obtain (a specified card or cards) by drawing or from a widow **8** *slang* **:** BELIEVE ⟨I won't ~ any part of that explanation⟩ **:** ACCEPT, APPROVE ⟨whether Britain . . . would ~ that compromise . . . remained to be seen —*Time*⟩ ~ *vi* **:** to perform the act of buying something ⟨the ~*ing* public⟩ ⟨the advantages of catalog ~*ing*⟩ — **buy it** *also* **buy a packet** *slang Brit* **:** to get killed **:** DIE — **buy on a scale :** to buy usu. on a falling market at intervals in order to average the costs more advantageously than would be possible with a purchase made at the beginning at a single price

[2]**buy** \"\ *n* -S **1 :** an act of buying **:** PURCHASE ⟨make a ~ of wheat⟩ **2 :** a thing bought or to be bought **:** something of value at a favorable price; *esp* **:** BARGAIN ⟨this stock is a good ~ at the current asking price⟩

buy boat *n* **:** a boat operated to buy the catch (as of shellfish) from fishing boats at sea and bring it in to market

buy·er \'bī(ə)r\ *n* -S [ME *byer,* fr. *byen* to buy + *-er* — more at BUY] **1 :** PURCHASER ⟨let the ~ beware⟩; *specif* **:** PURCHASING AGENT **2 :** one that has charge of the selection, purchasing, pricing, and display of the goods of a department of a retail store ⟨hat ~⟩ **3 :** BUY BOAT

buyers' market *n* **:** a market in which goods are plentiful, buyers have a wide range of choice, and prices tend toward costs — contrasted with *sellers' market*

buyer's option *n* **:** an option allowed to one who contracts to buy stocks at a certain future date and at a certain price to demand instead the delivery of the stock (giving one day's notice) at any previous time at the market price

bu·yid \'büyəd\ *or* **bu·way·hid** *also* **bu·wai·hid** \'büwā,hid\ *n, pl* **buyids** \'büyədz\ *or* **bu·yides** \", -,yīdz\ *or* **buwayhids** \'büwā,hidz\ *or* **buway·hides** \-,hīdz\ *usu cap* [Abu Shaja *Buya* or *Buwayha fl* A.D. 932 founder of the dynasty + E *-id*] **:** a member of a Persian Shi'ite dynasty that arose in A.D. 932 and extended its authority into Baghdad and reduced the caliphs to puppets before being overthrown by the Seljuk sultans in 1055

buy in *vt* **1 :** to buy a number or quantity of (as stock in a fund or partnership) **2 :** to buy (undelivered securities or commodities) according to the rules of the exchange by claiming against the original seller the difference in price and expense of broker's commissions **3 :** to buy for oneself (what one has offered to sell at auction) ~ *vi* **1 :** to buy a place in a stock company or regiment **2 :** to cover a commodity or security contract previously sold short

buying option *n* **:** [2]CALL 3d

buying power *n* **:** PURCHASING POWER

buy into *vt* **:** to obtain a place, footing, or interest in by purchase

bu·yo \'büyō\ *n* -S [Sp, fr. Bisayan *buyò*] *Philippines* **:** a masticatory consisting of betel leaf, the areca nut, lime, and often tobacco — compare [5]PAN

buy off *vt* **1 :** to induce to refrain (as from prosecution) by a payment or other consideration ⟨the police were *bought off* with several well-placed gifts⟩ **2 :** to free (as from military service) by payment

buy out *vt* **1 :** to purchase the share or interest of (as in a partnership) ⟨in spite of the disagreement he would neither *buy out* his partner nor sell out to him⟩ **2 :** to purchase the entire stock in trade and the goodwill of (a business) or the entire holdings in real estate of (a group) **3 :** to buy off

buys *pres 3d sing of* BUY, *pl of* BUY

buys bal·lot's law \'bīsbə'läts-, 'bȯis-\ *n, usu cap both Bs* [after C.H.D. *Buys Ballot* †1890 Dutch meteorologist] **:** a law in meteorology: when the observer has his back to the wind the lower barometric pressure is to his left in the northern hemisphere and to his right in the southern hemisphere owing to rotation of the earth

buy up *vt* **1 :** to buy freely or extensively ⟨*buying up* land right and left⟩ **2 :** to buy the entire available stocks of ⟨the government *bought up* the whole domestic rubber crop⟩

bu·zain \bü'zān, bə'z-, -zan\ *n* -S [prob. modif. of G *posaune* — more at POSAUNE] **:** POSAUNE 2

[1]**buzz** \'bəz\ *vb* -ED/-ING/-ES [ME *bussen,* of imit. origin] *vi* **1 :** to make a steady rasping low-pitched sound like that made by a flying insect ⟨flies darted and ~*ed* above the sorry nags —Kenneth Roberts⟩ **2** *archaic* **:** to speak in a muttering or half-whispering way esp. so as to irritate or incite one ⟨disturbers of our peace ~ in the people's ears —Shak.⟩ **3 :** to make a confused sibilant noise of many people talking at once ⟨the village ~*ed* with excitement at the news⟩ **4 a :** to move about like or with the sound of flying insects ⟨delegates ~*ing* about in a convention⟩ **b :** to go quickly **:** DART, WHIZ — often used with *off* ⟨~*ing* off to New York for a weekend⟩ **c :** to act in an ineffectually busy or agitated manner ⟨the forest seemed a vast hive of men ~*ing* about in frantic circles —Stephen Crane⟩ **d :** to move or travel with the steady rapidity of a motor ⟨~*ing* along superhighways⟩ **5 :** to make a signal with a buzzer ⟨~*ed* for his secretary⟩ ~ *vt* **1 a :** to tell with an air of suppressed excitement, secrecy, or urgency **:** to spread as gossip or rumor ⟨I will ~ abroad such prophecies —Shak.⟩ **b :** to express with buzzing ⟨the committee ~*ed* its indignation⟩ **2 a :** to cause to buzz ⟨a fly ~*ed* its wings⟩ **b :** to summon or signal by buzzing ⟨~*ed* the control room to make his report⟩ **c** *slang* **:** to call on the telephone ⟨I'll ~ you in the morning⟩ **3** *dial chiefly Eng* **:** to throw violently **:** FLING **4** *dial Eng* **:** to drink to the last drop **:** finish the contents of ⟨get some more port whilst I ~ this bottle —W.M. Thackeray⟩ **5 :** to cut with a buzz saw **6 :** to dive and fly low and fast over ⟨two U.S. Air Force planes ~*ed* the crowd to add glory to the ceremony —T.H.White b.1915⟩ **7 :** to ask questions of **:** INTERVIEW

[2]**buzz** \"\ *n* -ES **1 :** the insistent rasping sound characteristic of flying insects **:** a sound produced by very fast irregular pulsations **:** a sibilant hum ⟨the angry ~ of a bluebottle fly⟩ **2 :** a noisy vibration or very rapid flutter esp. of a poorly functioning mechanical part ⟨a badly tracking phonograph needle will make a ~⟩ ⟨a ~ developing in the ailerons of a plane at high speed⟩ **3 a :** a confused sibilant murmuring of many voices esp. in suppressed excitement ⟨a ~ went through the crowded courtroom⟩ **b :** a sound of busy activity **:** STIR **:** continuous bustle **4 :** RUMOR, GOSSIP, NEWS **5** *phonetics* **a :** the friction that characterizes the utterance of a fricative consonant; *also* **:** the combined sound of friction and of vocal-cord vibration that characterizes a voiced fricative **b :** a fricative esp. when voiced; *specif* **:** \z\ — compare HISS **6** *slang* **:** a call on the telephone ⟨I'll give you a ~ some time tomorrow⟩ **7 :** a game in which players quickly count round in turn, a player whose turn comes at a number containing 7 or at a multiple of 7 being required to say "buzz" instead of the number **8** *or* **buzz step :** a square-dance step in which one foot is kept firmly on the floor and the other is used for a series of pushes to effect the in-place pivot used in swinging one's partner **9** *slang* **:** a reaction from alcohol or narcotics ⟨had a good ~ on⟩; *also* **:** pleasurable excitement ⟨the kids will love this toy and adults will get a ~ out of it too⟩

[3]**buzz** \"\ *n* -ES [perh. alter. of *burrs,* pl. of [1]*burr*] **1** *dial Eng* **:** the bur of a plant **2 :** a bushy fishing fly

[1]**buzzard** \'bəzə(r)d\ *n* -S [ME *busard,* fr. OF *busard, buisard,* alter. (influenced by OF *-ard*) of *buison* buzzard, fr. L *buteon-, buteo;* prob. akin to L *bubo* horned owl — more at BUBO] **1** *chiefly Brit* **:** BUTEO 2; *esp* **:** the common European short-winged hawk (*Buteo buteo*) that is rich dark brown above and mottled with white on the underparts **2 :** any of various birds of prey: as **a :** TURKEY BUZZARD **b :** HONEY BUZZARD **c :** CONDOR **3 :** a person exhibiting rapacity or disgusting habits — used often as a generalized expression of disapproval ⟨the old ~ won't sell his land⟩ ⟨a cranky old ~⟩ **4 :** a golf score of two strokes over par on a hole

[2]**buzzard** \"\ *n* -S [[1]*buzz* + *-ard*] *dial Eng* **:** a buzzing insect (as a cockchafer or dorbeetle)

buzzard cult *n, often cap B&C* [so called fr. the symbol of the eagle on artifacts of its members] **:** SOUTHERN CULT

buzzard curlew *n* **:** LONG-BILLED CURLEW

buzzard eagle *n* **:** any of several buteos somewhat resembling eagles: **a :** a member of a genus (*Butastur*) of Africa and eastern Asia **b :** one of a So. American genus (*Geranoaetus*)

buzzard hawk *n* **:** BUTEO 2

buzzard's–berry \'⸗⸗'⸗⸗\ *n, pl* **buzzard's–berries :** BEARBERRY C

buzz bomb *n* **:** ROBOT BOMB

buzzed *adj, slang* **:** somewhat drunk

buzz·er \'bəzə(r)\ *n* -S **1 :** one that buzzes: as **a :** the interrupter of an induction coil **b :** an electric signal device producing a buzzing sound **c :** a miniature spark generator of which the principal element is a small vibrator actuated by an electromagnet **2** *Brit* **:** a textile burrer **3** *slang* **:** a detective's or policeman's badge

buzzes *pres 3d sing of* BUZZ, *pl of* BUZZ

buzzing *pres part of* BUZZ

buzz·ing·ly *adv* **:** in a buzzing manner

buzz planer *n* **:** a wood-planing machine consisting of a revolving horizontal cutter projecting slightly above a slit in the surface of a flat table

buzz saw *n* **:** CIRCULAR SAW

buzz stick *n* **:** a wooden rod fitted with two metal prongs like forks and used for testing suspension insulators on a high-tension transmission line

buzz–track \'⸗,⸗\ *n* **:** a motion-picture film that contains a special sound track and is used for testing alignment of the optical system in a reproducer

buzz wig *n* [perh. fr. [3]*buzz*] **:** a large bushy wig

buzz-wig \'bə,zwig\ *n* [*buzz wig*] **:** a person wearing a buzz wig; *specif* **:** BIGWIG

buzzy \'bəzē, -zi\ *adj* -ER/-EST **1 :** making a buzz **:** filled with a buzz **2 :** GOSSIPY, TALKATIVE

BV *abbr* **1** [LL *Beata Virgo*] Blessed Virgin **2** book value

B.V.D. \,bē,vē'dē\ *trademark* — used for underwear

BVM *abbr* [LL *Beata Virgo Maria*] Blessed Virgin Mary

bvt *abbr* brevet; brevetted

BW *abbr* **1** bacteriological warfare; biological warfare **2** black and white **3** board of works **4** bonded warehouse **5** bread and water

bwa·na \'bwänə\ *n* -S [Swahili, fr. Ar *abūna* our father] *Africa* **:** MASTER, BOSS

bwd *abbr* backward

BWD *abbr* bacillary white diarrhea

BWG *abbr* Birmingham wire gauge

bx *abbr* box

bxd *abbr* boxed

[1]**by** \¦bī *also esp bef cons* bə\ *prep* [ME, prep. & adv., fr. OE *be, bī,* prep., & *bī,* adv., by, near; akin to OHG *bī* by, near, Goth *bi* by, about, at, L *ambi-, amb-* on both sides, around, Gk *amphi* around, Skt *abhi* to, toward] **1 a :** in proximity to **:** in the immediate neighborhood of — used of place or position: (1) **:** at the side or edge of **:** NEAR ⟨the tree ~ the fence⟩ ⟨a

cottage ~ the sea⟩ ⟨sat ~ him on the train⟩ (2) **:** close to or on (one's person) **:** within easy reach of **:** ABOUT ⟨kept the rabbit's foot ~ him day and night⟩ **b :** in the general region of ⟨they commonly commanded both ~ sea and land —John & William Langhorne⟩ **2 a :** ALONG, OVER, THROUGH ⟨the family drove to the farm ~ the old highway⟩ ⟨came from the garden ~ a path⟩ ⟨entered the house ~ the back door⟩: (1) **:** along the surface or through the medium of ⟨went to Europe ~ water and returned ~ air⟩ (2) **:** in passing along ⟨was cozened ~ the way and lost all my money —Shak.⟩ **b** (1) *now dial* **:** at or to the home of ⟨am going ~ Grandma for a week⟩ (2) **:** at or into (as another's house) on passing ⟨he came ~ the house for a few minutes yesterday⟩ **c :** in the direction of **:** TOWARD — used esp. of points of the compass ⟨sailed north ~ east⟩ **d :** into the presence of **:** close to ⟨we are not to stay together but to come ~ him where he stands —Shak.⟩ **e :** into the vicinity of and beyond **:** PAST ⟨drove rapidly ~ the church⟩ ⟨went ~ him without saying a word⟩ **3 a :** during the course of **:** within the period of ⟨worked ~ day and studied ~ night⟩ **b** *archaic* **:** for a specified period of time — used esp. in the phrase *by the space of* ⟨~ the space of three years I ceased not to warn everyone —Acts 20:31 (AV)⟩ **c :** not later than (a specified time) **:** at or before ⟨expected to arrive ~ two o'clock⟩ ⟨ought to be here ~ now⟩ **d** *dial Eng* **:** AFTER ⟨seventeen minutes ~ noon⟩ **4 a :** through the means or instrumentality of ⟨put to death ~ the sword⟩ ⟨a town taken ~ force⟩ **b :** through the direct agency of ⟨put to death ~ the executioner⟩ ⟨ordered ~ the captain to stand guard⟩ ⟨a poem written ~ Keats⟩ **c :** through the medium of (an indirect or subordinate agent) ⟨represented ~ his deputy⟩ ⟨votes ~ proxy⟩ **d :** through the work or operation of (as natural agencies) ⟨changes wrought ~ time⟩ ⟨eaten away ~ corrosion⟩ ⟨came to the right house ~ luck⟩ **e** (1) **:** born or begot of ⟨had two sons ~ his first wife⟩ ⟨children ~ her second husband⟩ (2) *in animal breeding* **:** sired by **f :** in consequence of **:** as a result of **:** THROUGH ⟨blunders of foreign policy ~ which Austria declined . . . from a great and stable power to a satellite —Hugh Seton-Watson⟩ **g** — used as a function word to indicate something that forms an accompanying setting or condition ⟨ate ~ candlelight⟩ or that constitutes a manner ⟨began ~ criticizing the style of the poem⟩ often with an added sense of means ⟨the case went ~ default⟩ **5 :** with the witness or sanction of **:** in the presence of — used esp. in oaths ⟨~ heaven I'll know thy thoughts —Shak.⟩ ⟨swear ~ all that is holy⟩ **6 a :** in conformity or harmony with (as a standard of action) ⟨judged them ~ our customs⟩ ⟨he plays ~ the rules⟩ **b :** according to — used esp. with verbs of calling and naming ⟨call him ~ whatever name you choose⟩ **c :** according to (as a unit of measurement) ⟨sold beef ~ the pound⟩ ⟨works ~ the hour⟩ ⟨workers paid ~ the piece⟩ **7 a :** on behalf of — used esp. to indicate direction of effort ⟨did his duty ~ his country⟩ ⟨did his best ~ his family⟩ **b :** on the basis of (as a distinction or classification) **:** in the matter of **:** with respect to ⟨a Kansan ~ birth⟩ ⟨a lawyer ~ profession⟩ **8 a :** in or to the amount or extent of — used in expressions involving comparison to indicate an amount or degree of excess or increase or of deficiency or decrease esp. in space, time, quantity, or weight ⟨won the race ~ two yards⟩ ⟨missed the train ~ five minutes⟩ ⟨carried his ward ~ 80 votes⟩ ⟨lighter ~ six pounds⟩ ⟨better ~ far⟩ **b** *now chiefly Scot* **:** in comparison with **:** BESIDE ⟨was but as a fly ~ an eagle —Shak.⟩ **9** — used as a function word to indicate a succession of units or groups of the same class ⟨they left the party two ~ two⟩ ⟨the snow fell flake ~ flake⟩ ⟨count ~ 5s to 100⟩ ⟨he succeeded little ~ little⟩ **10 a** *chiefly Scot* **:** in addition to **:** over and above **:** BESIDES ⟨few folks ken o' this place . . . there's just twa living ~ myself —Sir Walter Scott⟩ **b** *now chiefly Scot* **:** outside the range or sphere of **:** BEYOND — often used in combination with an adjective or adverb ⟨my father was a man of *by*-ordinary mildness —Margaret Oliphant⟩ **11 a** *now chiefly Scot* **:** contrary to **:** DESPITE ⟨I could not deny him but was forced ~ myself to give —Samuel Pepys⟩ **b** *obs* **:** AGAINST ⟨for I know nothing ~ myself —1 Cor 4:4 (AV)⟩ **12 a** — used as a function word in multiplication to connect multiplicand and multiplier ⟨multiply 15 ~ 12⟩ **b** — used as a function word to indicate two or more dimensions in measurements ⟨a room 20 feet ~ 12⟩; compare 4X **13 :** in the opinion of **:** from the point of view of ⟨it's O.K. ~ me⟩ — **by oneself 1 :** apart from others **:** ALONE ⟨we left them *by themselves* for a few hours⟩ **2 :** through the agency of oneself **:** without help **:** INDEPENDENTLY ⟨the boy finished the job *by himself*⟩ **3** *chiefly Scot* **:** out of one's mind — **by the bye** *or* **by the by** *adv* **:** INCIDENTALLY ⟨*by the by* have you seen my father —Anthony Trollope⟩

2by \ˈbī\ *adv* [ME, prep. & adv.] **1 a :** near at hand **:** in the immediate neighborhood ⟨they live close ~⟩ — often used in combination with a noun ⟨others of the . . . *by*-sitters put various questions —Nathaniel Hawthorne⟩ **b :** at or to another's home ⟨he stopped ~ for a few minutes yesterday⟩ **2 :** to and beyond a point near at hand **:** PAST ⟨the parade had gone ~ when I reached the corner⟩ — often used in combination with a noun ⟨each window has blinds to prevent the *by*-passers from looking in —Robert Southey⟩ **3 a :** off to one side **:** ASIDE, AWAY ⟨put her sewing ~ when he came in⟩ **b :** in reserve for future use **:** in store ⟨had laid enough ~ for his old age⟩ **4** *archaic* **:** over and above **:** BESIDES **5 :** in the past ⟨in days gone ~⟩

3by \"\ *or* **bye** \"\ *adj* [ME *by*, fr. *by*, adv.] **1 :** aside esp. in position or direction **:** out of the way **:** off the beaten track ⟨the mule preferred the high road to the ~ one —Robert Southey⟩ ⟨nothing can be more ~ and unfrequented —Samuel Richardson⟩ — often used in combination with a noun ⟨would slip into the next shop or *by*-passage to avoid them —John Dryden⟩ **2 :** aside esp. in purpose or importance **:** INCIDENTAL, SECONDARY ⟨the ~ effect may be unfavorable —William Paley⟩ ⟨too serious a work to be undertaken in a ~ way —John Ruskin⟩ — often used in combination with a noun ⟨the *by*-productions of a busy man —J.R.Lowell⟩ **3** *chiefly Scot* **:** done with **:** PAST, OVER

4by *or* **bye** \"\ *n, pl* **byes :** something of secondary importance **:** a side issue — now used chiefly in the phrase *by the by*

5by \"\ *vi* **byed; byed; bying; bys** \ˈbīz\ [prob. fr. *by*, adv.] **:** PASS 12a(1)

6by \"\ *n, pl* **bys** \ˈbīz\ [prob. fr. *by*, adv.] **:** a pass in certain card games (as bridge)

7by *or* **bye** [by shortening] **:** GOOD-BYE — used interjectionally often with *now* ⟨~ now⟩

by–alley \ˈ=,==\ *n* **:** a side alley

by–altar \ˈ=,==\ *n* **:** a side altar **:** a secondary altar

by and by \ˌbīən(d)ˈbī, (ˈ)bīn(d)ˈbī, (ˈ)bīmˈbī, ˌbīəmˈbī, ˌbəmˈbī\ *adv* [2by] **1** *obs* **:** at once **:** IMMEDIATELY ⟨the end is not *by and by* —Lk 21:9 (AV)⟩ **2 :** in a little while **:** before long **:** SOON ⟨*by and by* he discovered that the black night had changed to gray —Zane Grey⟩

by–and–by \"\ *n* [*by and by*] **:** a future time or occasion ⟨in the sweet *by-and-by* we shall meet on that beautiful shore —S.F.Bennett⟩

by and large \ˌbīən(d)ˈ=\ *adv* [2by] **1 :** alternately close-hauled and free — used of sailing a ship ⟨they soon found out one another's rate of sailing *by and large* —*Fraser's Mag.*⟩ **2 :** on the whole **:** in general ⟨*by and large* he gave us a lot of trouble —Mary R. Rinehart⟩

by–bidder \ˈ=,==\ *n* **:** one who bids at an auction in behalf of the auctioneer or owner in order to run up the price

byb·lis \ˈbibləs\ *n, cap* [NL, fr. L *Byblis*, a nymph, fr. Gk] **:** a small genus of low Australian shrubs with a superficial resemblance to the sundews that in some classifications is isolated in a monotypic family but is more commonly included in Droseraceae

by–blow \ˈ=,=\ *n* **1 :** an indirect or incidental blow ⟨pass these incidents off as *by-blows* and as being of no real consequence —*Springfield (Mass.) Daily News*⟩ **2 :** an illegitimate child **:** BASTARD ⟨they were obviously gentlemen and, it is hinted, *by-blows* of some nobleman —C.R.Anderson⟩

by–by *var of* BYE-BYE

by–channel \ˈ=,==\ *n* **:** a stream at one side of the main stream

by–child \ˈ=,=\ *n, dial Eng* **:** an illegitimate child

by·cok·et \(ˈ)bīˈkäkət\ *or* **aba·cot** \ˈabəˌkät\ *also* **abo·cock·et** \ˌabəˈkäkət\ *n* -s [ME *bycoket*, fr. ME, fr. MF *bicoquet; abacot, abococket* alter. of *a bycoket*, fr. 2a + *bycoket*] **:** a hat with a high crown and a wide brim turned up in back and coming to a point like a beak in front worn esp. in the 15th century

by–corner \ˈ=,==\ *n* **:** an out-of-the-way corner

by–day \ˈ=,=\ *n* **:** an off day

byd·goszcz \ˈbid,gȯsh(ch)\ *adj, usu cap* [fr. *Bydgoszcz*, Poland] **:** of or from the city of Bydgoszcz, Poland **:** of the kind or style prevalent in Bydgoszcz

by dint of *prep* **:** through the force or power of ⟨he succeeded *by dint of* hard work⟩

by–drinking \ˈ=,==\ *n, archaic* **:** a drinking between meals

1bye *var of* BY

2bye \ˈbī\ *interj* [ME *by*, of unknown origin] — used to lull a child ⟨~ baby bunting⟩

3bye \"\ *n* -s [alter. of 2by] **1 :** a run made on a bowled ball that passes without touching or being touched by the batsman in cricket — compare LEG BYE, WIDE **2 :** the position of a participant in a tournament who has no opponent after pairs are drawn and advances to the next round without playing ⟨drew a first-round ~ in the tennis tournament⟩

4bye \"\ *n* -s [by shortening & alter.] **:** BY-WATER

1bye–bye *or* **by–by** \(ˈ)bīˈbī\ *interj* [baby-talk redupl. of *goodbye*] — used to express farewell

2bye–bye *or* **by–by** \"\ *adv* **:** out esp. for a walk or ride — used with the verb *go* ⟨if he wants to go *bye-bye* the baby may pat his head to indicate his desire for a hat —A.L.Gesell & Frances Ilg⟩

3bye–bye *or* **by–by** \"\ *n* [redupl. of 2bye] **:** BED, SLEEP ⟨lie down . . . and go to *bye-bye* —Rudyard Kipling⟩

4bye–bye *or* **by–by** \"\ *adv* **:** to bed or sleep — used with the verb *go* ⟨I'll run in and read for just a second . . . and then perhaps I'll go *bye-bye* —Sinclair Lewis⟩

by–effect \ˈ==,=\ *n* **:** an additional effect **:** an unintended effect

bye hole *n* [1bye] **:** a small opening in the side of a glass furnace for withdrawing samples of molten glass, heating the punty, or reheating small articles

by–election *also* **bye–election** \ˈ==,==\ *n* **:** a special election held between regular elections in order to fill a vacancy

byelorussian *cap, var of* BELORUSSIAN

bye·man \ˈbīmən\ *n, pl* **byemen** [1bye + *man*] **:** a worker underground in a mine

by–end \ˈ=,=\ *n* **1 :** a subordinate end; *esp* **:** a selfish motive ⟨they are all for *by-ends*, the whole clan of them —R.L. Stevenson⟩ **2 :** FRAGMENT, SNATCH ⟨*by-ends* of old rhymes —J.B.Cabell⟩

by·er·ite \ˈbī(ə),rīt\ *n* -s [William N. Byers †1903 Am. surveyor and pioneer + E *-ite*] **:** bituminous coal resembling albertite

byes *pl of* BY *or of* BYE

by–fellow \ˈ=,==\ *n* **:** a fellow of one of the colleges of Cambridge University holding a secondary often nominal fellowship — **by–fellowship** \ˈ=,==,=\ *n*

by–form \ˈ=,=\ *n* **:** a parallel and sometimes less important form ⟨certain expressions have slurred and shortened *by-forms* in which the phonetic pattern is lost —Leonard Bloomfield⟩

bygane \(ˈ)bīˌgān\ *chiefly Scot var of* BYGONE

by·go·ing \ˈbīˌgōiŋ\ *n* **:** the action of passing by — **in the bygoing :** in passing **:** INCIDENTALLY

1by·gone \ˈbīˌgȯn\ *adj* [ME (Sc dial.) *bygane*, fr. 2by + *gane*, var. of *gon*, past part. of *gon* to go — more at GO] **1 :** that is past **:** gone by **:** FORMER ⟨the music of a ~ day⟩ **2 a :** of or relating to the past **:** OUTMODED ⟨current fashions . . . are revivals of ~ styles —P.M.Gregory⟩ **b :** no longer living **:** DEAD, EXTINCT ⟨circles of burned and broken stone remain as evidence of its popularity with ~ tribes —*Amer. Guide Series: Mich.*⟩ ⟨~ species of animals —Weston LaBarre⟩

2bygone \"\ *n* -s **1 :** something that is past; *esp* **:** a past grievance — usu. used in pl. ⟨a gesture to show that ~*s* are ~*s* —William Walton⟩ ⟨let ~*s* be ~*s*⟩ **2 :** one that belongs to the past ⟨to them he is a ~ —*Bookman*⟩ ⟨a museum in search of ~*s* —H.V.Morton⟩

by–hour \ˈ=,=\ *n* **:** a leisure hour

bying *pres part of* BY

by–interest \ˈbī+,-\ *n* **:** an additional esp. private interest

by–job \ˈ=,=\ *n* **:** an odd job

byke *chiefly Scot var of* 1BIKE 1

by–lane \ˈ=,=\ *n* **:** a side lane

bylaw *or* **byelaw** \ˈ=,=\ *n* [ME *bilage, bilawe*, prob. fr. (assumed) ON *bȳlǫg*, fr. ON *bȳr* town (fr. *būa* to live) + *lǫg* law — more at BE, LAW] **1 a :** the local law esp. of a vill or manor **b :** an ordinance made by a court leet or court baron **2 :** a law, ordinance, or regulation made by a public or private corporation or an association or unincorporated society for the regulation of its own local or internal affairs and its dealings with others or for the government of its members **3** [influenced in meaning by 2by] **:** a secondary or subordinate law

by·law·man \ˈbī,lȯmən\ *n, pl* **bylawmen** [by folk etymology] **:** BYRLAWMAN

by–lead \ˈbī,lēd\ *n* **:** BY-WASH

by·li·na \bəˈlēnə\ *n, pl* **byli·ny** \-nē\ *or* **bylinas** \-nəz\ [Russ, fr. *bylina* what has been, fr. *byl* was, past of *bit'* to be; akin to Skt *bhavati* he is — more at BE] **:** a Russian folk epic or ballad

1by–line \ˈ=,=\ *n* **1 :** a secondary line **:** SIDELINE **2 a :** a line at the head of a newspaper or magazine article giving the writer's name **b :** something resembling such a by-line ⟨his calm "This is London" was one of the war's most famous *by-lines* —*Newsweek*⟩

2by–line \"\ *vt* **:** to write under a by-line ⟨has *by-lined* numerous magazine pieces —*Publishers' Weekly*⟩

byliner \ˈ=,==\ *n* -s **:** a journalist who writes under a by-line

by means of *prep* **:** through the agency or instrumentality of

bymeby *var of* BIMEBY

by–motive \ˈ=,==\ *n* **:** a hidden motive

byname \ˈ=,=\ *n* [ME, fr. 2by + *name*] **1 :** a secondary name (as a cognomen or surname) **2 :** NICKNAME

by·on \ˈbī,än, -īən\ *n* -s [prob. native name in Burma] **:** a clayey gem-bearing earth of Burma

1byous \ˈbīəs\ *adj* [2by + *-ous*] *Scot* **:** EXTRAORDINARY

2byous \"\ *adv, Scot* **:** EXTREMELY, MARKEDLY

byp *abbr* bypass

1bypass \ˈ=,=\ *n* [2by + *pass*] **1 :** a passage to one side; *esp* **:** a passage providing an alternative deflected route (as a road to carry traffic around a congested district or a channel to deflect flood water) **2 a :** an auxiliary passage (as a channel or pipe) through which a fluid passes around a particular place or part and returns to the main passage **:** a passage forming a secondary outlet for a fluid **b :** a path for shunting part or all of an electric current around one or more elements of a circuit

2bypass \(ˈ)=ˈ=\ *vt* **1 :** to make a circuit or detour around ⟨the new highway ~*es* the city⟩ **:** avoid by means of a bypass ⟨we ~*ed* most congested areas on our trip⟩ **2 :** to make (as a fluid or gas) follow a bypass ⟨incoming air was ~*ed* through the intercoolers in the intake air line⟩ **3 :** to neglect or ignore usu. intentionally ⟨critics have tended to ~ this side of his work —L.A.G.Strong⟩ ⟨these problems cannot be ~*ed* —Walter Terry⟩ **:** get around **:** EVADE ⟨men seek to ~ the law —H.J. Laski⟩ **4 :** to go around and beyond (an enemy) without attempting to attack

bypass condenser *n* **:** a capacitor providing a path for alternating current around some part of a circuit through which the current cannot so readily pass

bypasser \"+ə(r)\ *n* **:** PASSERBY

bypass valve *n* **:** a valve placed to control the flow of fluid through a bypass

bypast \(ˈ)=ˈ=\ *adj* [ME (Sc dial.), fr. 2by + *past*] **:** BYGONE

bypath \ˈ=,=\ *n* [ME, fr. 2by + *path*] **:** BYWAY

by–place \ˈ=,=\ *n* **:** an out-of-the-way place **:** an odd corner

by–play \ˈ=,=\ *n* **:** action engaged in on the side while the main action proceeds ⟨one bit of ~ unnoticed by the seconds —Joseph Conrad⟩; *specif* **:** incidental stage business

by–plot \ˈ=,=\ *n* **:** a subordinate plot (as in a play)

by–product \ˈ=,==\ *n* **1 :** a secondary or additional product **:** something produced (as in manufacturing) in addition to the principal product ⟨glycerol is principally obtained as a *by-product* of soap manufacture —P.O.Powers⟩ **2 :** a secondary and sometimes unexpected or unintended result of an action or process ⟨pleasure is a very important *by-product* of education —Agnes Repplier⟩

by–product coke *n* **:** coke made in a by-product oven, usu. obtained in various sizes, and when made by high-temperature carbonization having great structural strength and being esp. suitable for use in blast furnaces and cupola furnaces

by–product oven *n* **:** a coke oven consisting typically of rows of long narrow coking chambers that alternate with flues in which fuel gas is burned, used esp. for high-temperature and medium-temperature carbonization of coal, and having provision for recovery of volatile products (as gas, ammonia, light oils, and tar)

byre \ˈbī(ə)r, ˈbīə\ *n* -s [ME, fr. OE *bȳre*; akin to OE *būr* cottage, dwelling — more at BOWER] *chiefly Brit* **:** a stable for cows

by–reaction \ˈ==,==\ *n* **:** an accompanying reaction (as in a chemical process)

byre·man \ˈbī(ə)rmən, ˈbīəm-\ *n, pl* **byremen** *chiefly Brit* **:** COWMAN

byre·woman \ˈbī(ə)r, ˈbīə+,-\ *n, pl* **byrewomen** *chiefly Brit* **:** a woman that tends cows

byr·lady \(ˌ)bī(ə)r, ˌbīə+\ *interj* [contr. of *by our Lady*] — a mild oath

byrlakin *interj* [contr. of *by our Ladykin*] *obs* — a mild oath

byr·law \ˈbir,lȯ, ˈbiə,lȯ\ *or* **bur·law** \ˈbər,lȯ, ˈbə,lȯ\ *n* -s [ME *birelage, birlawe*, perh. fr. (assumed) ON *bȳjar lǫg*, fr. ON *bȳjar* (gen. of *bȳr* town) + *lǫg* law — more at BYLAW] **:** the local custom or law of a vill, township, or rural district in the north of England or in Scotland that governs disputes relating esp. to boundaries, dates of plowing, and use of common land; *also* **:** a particular custom or law established by common consent of the landholders of such a district

byr·law·man \ˈbir,lȯmən, ˈbiə,l-\ *n, pl* **byrlawmen** [ME, fr. *birlawe* + *man*] **:** a local officer appointed at a court leet in northern England or in Scotland to perform such duties as framing byrlaws and administering petty justice

byr·nie \ˈbərnē\ *n* -s [ME *brinie*, fr. ON *brynja*; akin to OE *byrne* coat of mail, OHG *brunia, brunna*, Goth *brunjo*, and prob. to OIr *bruinne* breast] **:** a coat of mail **:** HAUBERK

byroad \ˈ=,=\ *n* **:** a road that is little traveled ⟨wander along the ~*s* . . . soaking up atmosphere from the out-of-the-way hamlets —Richard Joseph⟩; *specif* **:** SIDE ROAD ⟨to the right a ~ suddenly branched off —George Bellairs⟩

by·ron·ic \(ˈ)bīˈränik\ *adj, usu cap* [George N. Gordon, Lord *Byron* †1824 Eng. poet + E *-ic*] **:** of, relating to, or having the characteristics of the poet Byron or his writings ⟨with despair and *Byronic* misanthropy —W.M.Thackeray⟩ ⟨his attitude, his smile were *Byronic*, at once world-weary and contemptuous —Aldous Huxley⟩ — **by·ron·i·cal·ly** \-nək(ə)lē, -li\ *adv, usu cap*

by·ron·ics \bīˈräniks\ *n pl, usu cap* **:** Byronic behavior or utterances ⟨was not to be taken in by any *Byronics* —*Times Lit. Supp.*⟩

by·ron·ism \ˈbīrə,nizəm\ *n* -s *usu cap* [Lord *Byron* + E *-ism*] **:** the characteristics of the poet Byron or his writings ⟨he's got a streak of his father's *Byronism* —John Galsworthy⟩

by–room \ˈ=,=\ *n* **:** a side or private room

byrrus *var of* BIRRUS

byr·son·i·ma \bərˈsänəmə\ *n, cap* [NL, irreg. fr. Gk *byrseuein* to tan + *onēmōn* useful] **:** a large genus of tropical American trees or shrubs (family Malpighiaceae) having entire leaves, yellow flowers, and fleshy edible fruits — see NANCE

bys *pres 3d sing of* BY, *pl of* BY

by–sitter \ˈ=,==\ *n* **:** one sitting nearby **:** ONLOOKER

bys·ma·lith \ˈbizmə,lith\ *n* -s [Gk *bysma* plug + E *-lith*] **:** a modified laccolith in which the roof has been lifted in part by peripheral faulting

bys·sa·ceous \bəˈsāshəs\ *adj* [NL *byssus* + E *-aceous*] **:** like a byssus

bys·sal \ˈbisəl\ *adj* [NL *byssus* + E *-al*] **:** of or relating to a byssus ⟨the ~ gland⟩

bys·sif·er·ous \bəˈsif(ə)rəs\ *adj* [NL *byssus* + E *-i-* + *-ferous*] **:** having a byssus

bys·sine \ˈbisən\ *adj* [L *byssinus*, fr. Gk *byssinos*, fr. *byssos* byssus + *-inos* -ine] **:** made of byssus

bys·si·no·sis \ˌbisəˈnōsəs\ *n, pl* **byssino·ses** \-ˌsēz\ [NL, fr. LL *byssinum* linen garment (fr. neut. of L *byssinus*) + NL *-osis*] **:** a chronic industrial disease associated with the inhalation of cotton dust over a long period of time and characterized by chronic bronchitis sometimes complicated by emphysema or asthma — called also *mill fever*

bys·soid \ˈbi,sȯid\ *adj* [NL & L *byssus* + E *-oid*] **1 :** BYSSACEOUS **2 :** COTTONY 1

bys·so·lite \ˈbisə,līt\ *n* -s [F, fr. Gk *byssos* flax, linen + F *-lite* — more at BYSSUS] **:** a mineral consisting of an olive-green fibrous amphibole

bys·sus \ˈbisəs\ *n, pl* **byssuses** \-səz\ *or* **bys·si** \-,sī, -,sē\ [L *byssus*, fr. Gk *byssos* flax, linen, of Sem origin; akin to Heb *būṣ* linen cloth] **1 :** a fine cloth of ancient times believed to have been made of linen, cotton, or silk **2** [NL, fr. L] **:** a tuft of long tough filaments secreted by a gland in a groove of the foot of certain bivalve mollusks (as those of the genera *Pinna* and *Mytilus*), issuing from between the valves, and serving as the means whereby the mollusk attaches itself to rocks or other foreign bodies

by–stake \ˈ=,=\ *n* **:** a rod serving as an upright framing rod in a basket — see BASKET illustration

bystander \ˈ=,==\ *n* -s **:** one present but not taking part **:** a chance spectator ⟨there are no ~*s* in modern warfare —A.M. Sullivan⟩

bystreet \ˈ=,=\ *n* **:** a street off a main thoroughfare **:** a side street ⟨the wanderer passed into a ~ comparatively deserted —E.A.Poe⟩

by–stroke \ˈ=,=\ *n* **:** a subtle and indirect action as a means to an end

bys·trom·ite \ˈbistrə,mīt\ *n* -s [prob. fr. the name *Byström* + E *-ite*] **:** a mineral $MgSb_2O_6$ consisting of a magnesium antimony oxide

by–talk \ˈ=,=\ *n* **:** SMALL TALK

by–term \ˈ=,=\ *n* **:** a term at Cambridge University that is not the usual one for entering or for taking a degree

by the way *adv* **1 :** along or near the side of the road **2 :** in the course of a journey **3 :** by way of incident or digression **:** in passing **:** INCIDENTALLY

1by–the–way \ˈ=ˈ=\ *adj* [*by the way*] **:** CASUAL, OFFHAND ⟨asked in a *by-the-way* fashion about his army service —J.N. Hall⟩

2by–the–way \"\ *n* -s [*by the way*] **:** an incidental remark **:** a casual comment

by–thing \ˈ=,=\ *n* **:** a thing of little importance

by·thin·ia \bəˈthinēə\ [NL, irreg. fr. *Bithynia*, ancient province of Asia Minor, fr. L, fr. Gk] *syn of* BULIMUS

by–time \ˈ=,=\ *n* **:** a leisure interval

by·tom \ˈbi,tȯm\ *adj, usu cap* [fr. Bytom, Poland] **:** of or from the city of Bytom, Poland **:** of the kind or style prevalent in Bytom

by·town·ite \ˈbī(,)tau̇,nīt, =ˈ=,=\ *n* -s [*Bytown* (now Ottawa), Canada + E *-ite*] **:** a plagioclase feldspar consisting of 10 to 30 percent albite and 90 to 70 percent anorthite

by–track \ˈ=,=\ *n* **:** a little-used track

by–trail \ˈ=,=\ *n* **:** a side trail

by virtue of *prep* **:** by reason of **:** as a result of ⟨they survive through adaptive change and by *virtue* of their natural boundaries —A.L.Locke⟩

bywalk \ˈ=,=\ *n* **:** a secluded or private walk **:** BYWAY

by–wash \ˈ=,=\ *n* **:** a spillway or weir made to permit the escape of surplus water (as from a dam or reservoir)

by–water \ˈ=,==\ *n* **:** a diamond of yellowish tint

byway \ˈ=,=\ *n* [ME, fr. 2by + *way*] **1 :** a secluded, roundabout, or little traveled road **:** SIDE ROAD ⟨along the stretch of sandy creek-road and thence by the rough ill-tended county ~ to the main road —Elizabeth M. Roberts⟩ — contrasted with *highway* **2 :** a secondary or little known aspect or field ⟨has explored with great skill this ~ in the development of political theory —Gordon Wright⟩

by·wo·ner \ˈbī,vōnə(r), ˈbā,v-\ *n* -s [Afrik, fr. *by* with, at (fr. MD *bī*) + *woner* dweller (fr. *woon* to dwell — fr. MD *wōnen* — + *-er*); akin to OHG *bī* with, at, and to OHG *wonēn* to dwell — more at BY, WONT] *southern Africa* **:** a laborer or farmer working another person's land: **a :** SQUATTER **b :** SHARECROPPER

byword \ˈ=,=\ *n* [ME, fr. OE *bīword*, fr. *bī* by + *word* — more at BY, WORD] **1 :** a proverbial saying **:** PROVERB ⟨the old ~ of necessity being the mother of invention —A.L.Kroeber⟩ **2 a :** one that is proverbial as a type of specified characteristics ⟨John Henry has become a ~ with them, a synonym for superstrength and superendurance —G.B.Johnson⟩ ⟨the mountain view from its spacious glassed-in porches is a White Mountain ~ —E.W.Smith⟩ **b :** an object of scorn or derision ⟨we ourselves shall become a reproach and ~ down to future ages —Benjamin Franklin⟩ **3 :** EPITHET; *esp* **:** a scornful epithet **4 :** a word or phrase frequently used by a particular person **:** a favorite expression ⟨we called him "the Deacon" because of his favorite ~ "Praise be" —H.A.Chippendale⟩

bywork \ˈ=ˌ=\ *n* **:** work done on the side **:** work done in intervals of leisure ⟨won popular fame . . . by a piece of ~ —*Times Lit. Supp.*⟩

by-your-leave \ˈ==ˈ=\ *n* **:** a request for permission ⟨look over one's correspondence without so much as a *by-your-leave* —Frances Towers⟩

byzant *var of* BEZANT

[1]**by·zan·tian** \bəˈzansh(ē)ən, -zantēən, -tyən\ *n* -S *usu cap* [*Byzantium*, ancient city on the site of İstanbul, Turkey + E *-an*] **:** BYZANTINE

[2]**byzantian** \"\ *adj, usu cap* **:** BYZANTINE ⟨*Byzantian* civilization⟩

[1]**byz·an·tine** \ˈbizənˈtēn *also* -ˈtīn *sometimes* ˈbīz-; ˈbizəntən; bəˈzan,tēn, -zaan,-, *also* -,tīn, -tən *sometimes* bīˈz-\ *n* -S [LL *Byzantinus* native of Byzantium, fr. *Byzantium* + L *-inus* -ine] **1 :** BEZANT **2** *usu cap* **:** a native or inhabitant of the ancient city of Byzantium

[2]**byzantine** \"\ *adj, usu cap* [LL *Byzantinus*, adj. & n.] **1 a :** of, relating to, or characteristic of the ancient city of Byzantium **b :** of, relating to, or characteristic of the Eastern Roman Empire **2 a :** of, relating to, or having the characteristics of a style of architecture developed in the Byzantine Empire esp. in the 5th and 6th centuries and having as its central structural feature the dome carried on pendentives over a square and as its chief decorative feature the incrustation of walls, vault faces, and spandrels with marble veneering and with richly colored mosaic on grounds of gold **b :** of, relating to, or having the characteristics of a school of painting that originated in the Byzantine Empire, was influential until the 14th century throughout western Europe esp. in Italy, and survived until recent times esp. in Bulgaria and Russia and that was characterized by formality of design, by absence of shadow and of the appearance of relief, and by the free use of gilding in the background **3 :** of or relating to the Eastern Orthodox Church ⟨*Byzantine* monks⟩ ⟨the *Byzantine* rite⟩ **4 :** of, relating to, or marked by Byzantinism

byzantine speedwell *n, usu cap B* **:** a Eurasian annual herb (*Veronica persica*) having long-stalked blue flowers and being widely distributed as a weed

by·zan·tin·esque \bəˌzantəˈnesk\ *adj, usu cap* **:** in the Byzantine style

by·zan·tin·ism \bəˈzantə,nizəm\ *n* -S *usu cap* **1 :** the political principles, social patterns, manner, style, and spirit characteristic of Byzantine life esp. when manifested in architecture, art, or literature **2 :** the doctrine or system of state supremacy in ecclesiastical affairs — compare CAESAROPAPISM, ERASTIANISM

by·zan·ti·nist \-tənəst\ *n* -S *usu cap* **:** a student of Byzantine culture

by·zan·tin·ize \-tə,nīz\ *vt* -ED/-ING/-S *often cap* **:** to make Byzantine

by·zen *also* **bi·zen** \ˈbīzən, ˈbēz-\ *n* -S [ME *bysen* example, disgraceful spectacle, fr. OE *bisen*, *bysen* example; akin to ON *bȳsn* marvel, Goth an*abusns* command, OE *bēodan* to command — more at BID] *dial Eng* **:** a disgraceful spectacle or example

¹c \ˈsē\ *n, pl* **c's** *or* **cs** \ˈsēz\ *often cap, often attrib* **1 a :** the third letter of the English alphabet **b :** an instance of this letter printed, written, or otherwise represented **c :** a speech counterpart of orthographic *c* (as hard *c* in *cat* or soft *c* in *cell*) **2 a :** one hundred — see NUMBER table **b** *slang* **:** a sum of $100 **3 a :** the keynote of C major or C minor **b :** the tone C **4 :** a printer's type, a stamp, or some other instrument for reproducing the letter *c* **5 :** someone or something arbitrarily or conveniently designated *c* esp. as the third in order or class ⟨A deeded land to B and *C* together⟩ **6 a :** a grade assigned by a teacher or examiner rating a student's work as fair, average, or mediocre in quality ⟨pass Latin with a *C*⟩ **b :** one graded or rated with a C ⟨a *C* student⟩ ⟨the movie was a *C*⟩ ⟨your quiz papers are all *C's*⟩ **7 :** something having the shape of the letter C

²c *abbr, often cap* **1** calm **2** calorie **3** Canadian **4** canceled **5** candle **6** canon **7** capacitance; capacity **8** cape **9** captain **10** caput **11** carat **12** cargo **13** case **14** castle **15** catcher **16** cathode **17** Catholic **18** caught **19** cause **20** Celsius **21** cent **22** cental **23** centavo **24** center **25** centi- **26** centigrade **27** centime **28** centimeter **29** centum **30** century **31** chairman **32** chancellor; chancery **33** chapter **34** chief **35** child **36** church **37** circa; circiter; circum **38** circuit **39** circumference **40** clearance **41** clockwise **42** cloudy **43** cobalt **44** cocaine **45** codex **46** coefficient **47** cognate **48** cold **49** college **50** color **51** colt **52** combat **53** commander **54** common meter **55** common time **56** companion **57** condemned **58** conductor **59** confessor **60** confidential **61** congius **62** congregation **63** congress **64** conservative **65** constable **66** consul **67** contact **68** continental **69** contra **70** contraction **71** contralto **72** copper **73** copy **74** copyright **75** cord **76** cordoba **77** corps **78** correct **79** cost **80** coulomb **81** count **82** coupon **83** court **84** cousin **85** created **86** crowned **87** cubic **88** cum **89** cup **90** currency **91** current **92** cycle **93** cylinder

³c *symbol* **1** 4/4 time — used after the clef sign on a musical staff **2** *cap* carbon **3** copyright — often enclosed in a circle **4 a** cipher — used as a subscript ⟨$F_p = T_c$ means that the plaintext letter F has the cipher substitute T⟩ **b** *cap* the numerical value of a cipher letter when the cipher component is serially numbered from 0 to 25 ⟨P+K=C is the Vigenère keying method⟩ **5** *cap* consonant

ca *abbr* **1** cable **2** candle **3** case **4** cathode **5** centare **6** circa

CA *abbr* **1** capital account **2** chartered accountant **3** chief accountant **4** chronological age **5** claim agent **6** coast artillery **7** cold air **8** [It *coll'arco*] with the bow **9** commercial agent **10** controller of accounts **11** [F *cor anglais*] English horn **12** cost accountant **13** council accepted **14** court of appeal **15** credit account **16** crown agent **17** current account

Ca *symbol* calcium

ca' \ˈkȯ, ˈkä\ *Scot var of* CALL

caaba *usu cap, var of* KAABA

caa·ing whale *also* **ca'·ing whale** \ˈkȯiŋ, ˈkä·iŋ, ˈkä-\ *n* [*caaing, ca'ing,* gerund of *ca'* to call, drive (whales into shallow water)] **:** a blackfish (*Globicephala melaena*) of the north Atlantic — called also *pilot whale*

caam \ˈkäm, -äm\ *n* -s [D *kam,* lit., comb, fr. MD *cam;* akin to OE *camb* comb — more at COMB] **:** the heddles of a loom

caa·ma \ˈkämə\ *n* -s [of African origin; akin to Vai *ka¹ma³* elephant] **1** *also* **ca·ma fox** \ˈkä-\ **:** a southern African fox (*Vulpes chama*) **2 :** CAPE HARTEBEEST

caam·ing \ˈkämiŋ, -ˈä-\ *n* -s [*caam* + *-ing*] **:** the setting of the reed in weaving by the proper placing of the threads of the warp

caa·pi \ˈkäpē\ *n* -s [Pg, fr. Tupi] **1 :** a vine (*Bannisteria caapi*) of the family Malpighiaceae of northwestern So. America **2 :** the rhizome and roots of the caapi vine used in preparing a stimulating native beverage

caa·tin·ga \kä'tiŋgə, kə-\ *n* -s [Pg, modif. of Tupi *caá-tinga* white forest, fr. *caá* forest + *tinga* white] **:** stunted rather sparse forest that is leafless in the dry season and is widespread in certain areas of small rainfall in northeastern Brazil

¹cab *or* **kab** \ˈkab, -äb\ *n* -s [Heb *qabh*] **:** an ancient Hebrew unit of capacity equal to about two quarts

²cab \ˈkäb\ *vt* **cabbed; cabbed; cabbing; cabs** [short for *cabbage* (steal)] *slang Scot* **:** PURLOIN

³cab \ˈkab, -aa(ə)b\ *n* -s [short for *cabriolet*] **1 :** a horse-drawn carriage: as **a :** CABRIOLET **b :** a similar light closed carriage (as a hansom) **c :** any carriage for hire whether closed or open and drawn by one or two horses **:** a hackney carriage **2** [by shortening] **:** TAXICAB **3** [short for *cabin*] **a :** the part of a locomotive that houses the engineer, fireman, and operating controls **b :** a shelter for operator and controls of a power-driven vehicle, tractor, or hoisting apparatus: as (1) **:** an enclosed compartment on a motor truck or trailer truck having a windshield at the front and a seat for the driver (2) **:** a suspended control compartment for the operator of a traveling crane or monorail tractor (3) **:** the car or cage of an elevator **c :** CABIN 4d

⁴cab \"\ *vi* **cabbed; cabbed; cabbing; cabs :** to travel in a cab

⁵cab \"\ *n* -s [perh. alter. of *gob* (lump)] *dial* **:** something sticky or dirty

⁶cab \"\ *n* -s [by shortening] **:** CABOCHON

cab *abbr* **1** cabin **2** cabinet **3** cable

ca·ba \kə'bä\ *n* -s [F *cabas,* fr. OProv, prob. fr. (assumed) VL *capacium,* fr. L *capere* to take, contain — more at HEAVE] **:** a woman's workbasket or handbag

¹ca·bal \kə'bal, -ˈä- *also* -ˈa·\ *n* -s [F *cabale,* fr. ML *cabala, cabbala,* fr. Heb *qabbālāh* received or traditional lore, fr. *qābal* to receive] **1** *obs* **:** CABALA 2a **2 a :** a number of persons secretly united and using devious and undercover means to bring about an overturn or usurpation esp. in public affairs or to undermine and cause the downfall of a person in a position of authority **b :** the artifices and intrigues of such a group **c :** a coterie in artistic circles **syn** see PLOT

²cabal \"\ *vi* **caballed; caballed; caballing; cabals :** to unite in or form a cabal

cab·a·la *or* **cab·ba·lah** *or* **kab·a·la** *or* **kab·ba·la** *or* **kab·ba·lah** *also* **qab·ba·la** *or* **qab·ba·lah** \ˈkabələ; kə'bälə, -ˈä-\ *n* -s *often cap* [ML — more at CABAL] **1 :** a system of occult theosophy or mystical interpretation of the Scriptures orig. developed orally among Jewish rabbis in the Geonic period and transmitted to certain medieval Christians, holding such tenets as creation through emanation, supremacy of man's spirit over his desires, Messianic restoration of the world to a perfect state, and laying stress on hidden senses in the Scriptures and occult means of interpretation even to foretelling events by these methods **2 a :** a traditional, esoteric, occult, or secret matter **b :** esoteric doctrine or mysterious art ⟨of the several ~s the most prominent are the mystic and the psychoanalytic, while the Marxist method . . . itself at times threatens to expand to the nebulousness of a ~ —Charles Neider⟩

cab·a·las·sou \ˌkabə'la(ˌ)sü\ *n* -s [perh. alter. of *cabassou*] **:** GIANT ARMADILLO

cab·a·let·ta \ˌkabə'led·ə, -ˈäb-\ *n* -s [It, prob. alter. of *coboletta* stanza, dim. of *cobola* stanza, couplet, fr. OProv *cobla* couplet, fr. L *copula* bond — more at COUPLE] **1 :** an operatic song or a short melodious instrumental composition in a simple popular style characterized by uniform rhythm in the accompaniment **2 :** the lively bravura conclusion of an aria or duet

cabalic *adj, often cap* [*cabala* + *-ic*] *obs* **:** learned in cabala

cab·a·lism \ˈkabə,lizəm\ *n* -s [*cabala* + *-ism*] **1** *often cap* **:** esoteric doctrine or interpretation according to the Jewish cabala **2 :** adherence to some traditional theological interpretation or tenets ⟨the "key verse" and "key word" theory is a form of ~ based on a fundamental misconception of the nature of the Biblical material —J.C.Swaim⟩

¹cab·a·list \ˈkabələst\ *n* -s [ML *cabbalista,* fr. *cabbala, cabala* + L *-ista* -ist] **1** *often cap* **:** a student, interpreter, or devotee of the Jewish cabala **2 :** one skilled in esoteric or mysterious art

²cabalist *n* -s [prob. fr. F *cabaliste,* fr. *cabale* cabal + *-iste* -ist — more at CABAL] *obs* **:** an adherent to a cabal

cab·a·lis·tic \ˌkabə¦listik, -ēk\ *adj* **1** *sometimes cap* **:** belonging, relating, or according to the Jewish cabala ⟨a ~ explanation of an Old Testament text⟩ ⟨~ asceticism⟩ **2 :** having an occult, mystical, or esoteric meaning **:** MAGIC, MYSTERIOUS ⟨a few ~ words from our guide —Herman Melville⟩ ⟨the potency of certain ~ signs over the lintel⟩ ⟨by describing with the hands certain ~ patterns on the air and uttering at the same time the proper Sanskrit formulas it was believed that goblins and demons . . . could be exorcised —J.B.Noss⟩ — **cab·a·lis·ti·cal·ly** \-tək(ə)lē, -ēk-, -li\ *adv*

ca·ba·lla·da \ˌkavə'yädə, -abə-, -ē'y-\ *n* -s [Sp, fr. *caballo* horse (fr. L *caballus*) + *-ada* -ade — more at CAVALCADE] *West* **:** REMUDA

ca·bal·ler \kə'balə(r) *also* -ˈä- *or* -ˈa-\ *n* -s [²*cabal* + *-er*] **:** one that cabals or intrigues

ca·bal·le·ro \ˌkabə'le(ə)(ˌ)rō, -ə'ye-, *Cast* kȧbȧ'lʸārō\ *n* -s [Sp, knight, horseman, fr. LL *caballarius* groom, hostler — more at CAVALIER] **1 :** KNIGHT, CAVALIER **2** *chiefly Southwest* **:** HORSEMAN

cab·al·line \ˈkabə,līn, -ˌən\ *adj* [ME *caballin,* fr. L *caballinus,* lit., of a horse, fr. *caballus* horse, nag + *-inus* -ine; fr. the ancient belief that the Muses' spring Hippocrene came from a hoofprint of the winged horse Pegasus — more at CAVALCADE] *of a fountain* **:** imparting poetic inspiration

caballine aloes *n pl but sing or pl in constr* **:** impure aloes formerly used in veterinary practice

ca·ba·lli·to \ˌkabə'yē(ˌ)tō\ *n* -s [AmerSp. short for *caballito del mar,* lit., little sea horse, fr. *caballito* (dim. of *caballo* horse) + *del mar* of the sea] **:** a small fishing boat made of reeds and used off the coast of Peru

ca·ba·llo \kə'bī(ˌ)ō\ *n* -s [Sp, fr. L *caballus* nag] *Southwest* **:** HORSE

cabals *pres 3d sing of* CABAL, *pl of* CABAL

caban *var of* CAVAN

ca·bana \kə'ban(y)ə\ *n* -s [Sp *cabaña,* fr. ML *capanna*] **1 :** a tentlike often portable shelter with a projecting canopy over an open side facing a beach or swimming pool **2 :** a lightweight cabinlike structure with living facilities providing recreation quarters

ca·bane \kə'ban, -ˈän\ *n* -s [F, lit., cabin — more at CABIN] **1 :** a framework supporting the wings of an airplane at the fuselage **2 :** the system of trussing for supporting overhang in an airplane wing

¹cab·a·ret \ˌkabə¦rā\ *n* -s [F, fr. ONF, prob. irreg. fr. LL *camera* chamber — more at CHAMBER] **1** *archaic* **:** a shop having wines and liquors for sale **2 :** a porcelain coffee, tea, or chocolate service of 18th century manufacture with tray decorated with painted figures **3 :** a restaurant serving liquor and providing entertainment, usu. singing or dancing **4 :** the floor show at a cabaret

²cabaret \"\ *vi* -ED/-ING/-S **:** to attend or frequent a cabaret

cab·a·rine red MB \ˈkabə,rēn-\ *n, usu cap C&R* [origin unknown] **:** an organic pigment — see DYE table I (under *Pigment Red 55*)

cabas *pl of* CABA

ca·ba·sa \kə'bäsə\ *n* -s [AmerSp, fr. Pg *cabaça,* lit., gourd, fr. OPg *calabaço;* akin to Sp *calabaza* gourd, Catal *carbassa*] **:** a percussion instrument made of a hollow gourd enclosed in a net of threaded beads for use in a Cuban band

cab·as·set \ˌkabə¦set\ *n* -s [F, dim. of *cabas* — more at CABA] **:** a morion of small size

ca·bas·sou \kə'ba(ˌ)sü, ¦kabə¦sü\ *n* -s [F, prob. fr. Galibi *capaçou*] **:** TATOUAY

ca·bas·so·us \kə'basəwəs, ˌkabə'sōəs\ *n, cap* [NL, fr. F *cabassou*] **:** a genus of short-tailed armadillos with the third front claw very large and falcate that includes only the tatouay

cabazone *var of* CABEZON

¹cab·bage \ˈkabij, -ēj\ *n* -s *often attrib* [ME *caboche,* fr. ONF, head, perh. fr. *boche* swelling, bump; akin to OF *boce* bump — more at BOSS] **1 :** a leafy garden plant (*Brassica oleracea capitata*) derived from a wild European plant (*B. oleracea*) and distinguished by a short stem upon which is crowded a mass of leaves usu. green but in some varieties red or purplish forming a dense globular head that is used as a vegetable **2 :** a terminal bud of certain palm trees that resembles a head of cabbage and is eaten as a vegetable **3 :** CABBAGE PALMETTO ⟨~ woods⟩ **4** *slang* **:** paper money or bank notes

²cabbage \"\ *vt* -ED/-ING/-S **:** to compress (loose sheet-metal scrap) into a form convenient for handling and remelting

³cabbage \"\ *n* -s [perh. by folk etymology fr. MF *cabas* cheating, theft, lit., basket — more at CABA] *Brit* **:** cloth remaining after the cutting out of a garment and traditionally said to be appropriated by the tailor as a perquisite

⁴cabbage \"\ *vb* -ED/-ING/-S *vt* **:** to take surreptitiously **:** STEAL, FILCH ⟨they also cabbaged our bats, balls, and gloves —H.L. Mencken⟩ ~ *vi* **:** to take something surreptitiously — sometimes used with *onto*

cabbage aphid *also* **cabbage aphis** *n* **:** a widely distributed and destructive grayish green plant louse (*Brevicoryne brassicae*) that lives on cabbage leaves and other cruciferous plants

cabbage bark *or* **cabbage–bark tree** *n* [*cabbage* (*palm*) + *bark*] **:** an angelim (*Andira inermis*) widely distributed in tropical America and western Africa having a shaggy unpleasant-smelling toxic bark that has been used together with the seeds as a purgative, vermifuge, and narcotic and yielding a hard strong durable wood variable in color and susceptible of a fine polish — called also *cabbage tree*

cabbage butterfly *n* **:** any of several largely white butterflies (family Pieridae) the green larvae of which are cabbageworms: as **a :** a small cosmopolitan form (*Pieris rapae*) — called also *small white* **b :** a larger Old World form (*P. brassicae*) — called also *large white* **c :** a common No. American form (*P. protodice*) — called also *southern cabbage butterfly*

cabbage curculio *n* **:** a small weevil (*Ceutorhynchus rapae*) that feeds within the stems and on the leaves of cabbage and other cruciferous plants

cabbage family *n* **:** CRUCIFERAE

cabbage fly *n* **:** the adult cabbage maggot

cabbage green \ˈ==,=\ *n* **:** a greenish gray that is bluer and deeper than hathi gray and slightly bluer and less strong than artemisia green

cabbage gum *n* [prob. so called fr. the fleshy leaves] **:** any of certain Australian gum trees (esp. *Eucalyptus pauciflora* and *E. virgata*) with very soft wood and thick leaves

cabbagehead \ˈ==,=\ *n* **1 :** the compact head formed by the leaves of a cabbage **2 :** a thick-witted person **3 :** an abnormal growth in rutabagas caused by the larvae of a gall midge (*Contarinia nasturtii*) feeding in the basal part of the stalks

cabbage-leaf miner *n* **:** a small fly (*Phytomyza rufipes*) whose maggot is injurious to cabbages and related plants

cabbage lettuce *n* **:** HEAD LETTUCE

cabbage looper *n* **:** a pale green white-striped measuring worm (*Trichoplusia ni*) that is the larva of a moth of the family Noctuidae and that feeds on the leaves of cabbage and other cruciferous plants

cabbage maggot *n* **:** a small white maggot (*Hylemya brassicae*) that feeds in the roots and stems of cabbage and other cruciferous plants and becomes as an adult a grayish fly resembling a small housefly

cabbage moth *n* **:** DIAMONDBACK MOTH

cabbage palm *n* **1 :** a palm whose terminal bud is eaten like cabbage as a vegetable: as **a :** CABBAGE PALMETTO **b :** a tall West Indian palm (*Roystonea oleracea*) **c :** CABBAGE TREE 1a **2 :** ASSAI PALM **3 :** a palm of the genus *Areca*

cabbage palmetto *n* **:** a fan palm of the genus *Sabal* (*S. palmetto*) that is native to the southern U.S. near the coast and to the Bahamas

cabbage–root fly *n* **:** the adult of the cabbage maggot; *broadly* **:** any stage of this pest

cabbage rose *n* **:** a fragrant garden rose (*Rosa centifolia*) with upright branches and large full white or pink flowers

cabbages *pl of* CABBAGE, *pres 3d sing of* CABBAGE

cabbage seedpod weevil *n* **:** a small grayish black weevil (*Ceutorhynchus assimilis*) related to the cabbage curculio but smaller and feeding on and destroying the developing seeds of cabbage and other cruciferous plants

cabbage snake *n* **:** a nematode worm of the family Mermithidae

cabbage tree *n* **1 :** any of several palms having an edible terminal bud: **a :** an Australian palm of the genus *Livistona* (esp. *L. australis*) **b** *NewZeal* **:** TI 1 **c :** CABBAGE PALMETTO **2 :** any of certain trees resembling in some respect a cabbage palm: as **a :** CABBAGE BARK **b :** any of several African araliaceous trees (genus *Cussonia*) with soft spongy wood and sparse angular branches that terminate in tufted foliage or in a spike-like inflorescence

cabbage–tree hat *n* **:** an Australian broad-brimmed hat plaited from the fibrous leaves of the cabbage tree

cabbage webworm *n* **:** a widely distributed webworm (*Hellula undalis*) native to southern Europe or Asia that injures cabbages and other vegetables in the Gulf states

cabbage white \ˈ==,=\ *n* **:** CABBAGE BUTTERFLY

cabbage wilt *n* **:** CABBAGE YELLOWS

cabbagewood \ˈ==,=\ *n* [*cabbage* (*tree*) + *wood*] **1 :** ACAPU 1b **2 :** CEIBA 2a **3 :** PRIVET 1a(1)

cabbageworm \ˈ==,=\ *n* **:** any of numerous insect larvae that feed on cabbages: **a :** the green larva of the cabbage butterflies that is a destructive pest eating the leaves of cabbages and related plants and being toxic to animals that consume the infested foliage — see IMPORTED CABBAGEWORM **b :** the larva of the cabbage moth **c :** CUTWORM

cabbage yellows \ˈ==,==\ *n pl but sing in constr* **:** a destructive disease of cabbage caused by a fungus (*Fusarium conglutinans*) and characterized by yellowing and dwarfing

cabbaging *pres part of* CABBAGE

cabbaging press *n* **:** a packing press for cabbaging loose sheet-metal scrap

cab·bagy \ˈkabəjē, -i\ *adj* **1 :** having the odor, taste, or color of cabbage **2 :** like or suggestive of a cabbage

cabbala *or* **cabbalah** *var of* CABALA

cabbed *past of* CAB

cab·ber \ˈkabə(r), -aab-\ *n* -s [³*cab* + *-er*] **:** CAB HORSE

cabbing *pres part of* CAB

cab·by *or* **cab·bie** \ˈkabē, -aabē, -i\ *n, pl* **cabbies** [³*cab* + *-y*] **:** CABDRIVER

cabdriver \ˈ=,==\ *n* **:** a driver of a taxicab or a horse-drawn cab

ca·be·car \kə'bā,kär\ *n, pl* **cabecar** *or* **cabecars** *usu cap* [Sp *cabécar,* of AmerInd origin] **1 a :** a Chibchan people of eastern Costa Rica **b :** a member of such people **2 :** the language of the Cabecar people

ca·be·ce·ra \ˌkabə'serə\ *n* -s [Sp, fr. *cabeza* head — more at CABEZON] **:** the chief city of a province or district in a Spanish-speaking country

ca·be·cu·do \ˌkabə'sü(ˌ)dō\ *n* -s [Pg *cabeçudo,* fr. *cabeçudo* big-headed, fr. *cabeça* head, fr. (assumed) VL *capitia* — more at CABEZON] **:** OURICURY

cabeiri *usu cap, var of* CABIRI

ca·ber \ˈkäbə(r), -ˈäb-,-ˈab-\ *n* -s [ScGael *cabar*] **1** *Scot* **:** RAFTER **2 :** a young tree trunk used in a Scottish sport in which it is raised vertically in the hands and tossed across a line

ca·ber·net \ˌkabə(r)¦nā\ *n* -s *usu cap* [F] **:** a dry red California table wine like claret with medium body and fruity flavor

ca·bes·tro \kə'be(ˌ)strō; -bre(ˌ)stō, -ˌtə\ *n* -s [AmerSp, fr. Sp, halter, fr. L *capistrum,* fr. *capere* to take — more at HEAVE] *Southwest* **:** a rope of hair used esp. as a lasso or tether

cab·ette \(ˈ)ka¦bet\ *n* -s **:** a woman who drives a taxicab

ca·be·za \kə'bäzə\ *n* -s [Sp] **1** *Southwest* **:** the head of a person or animal **2 :** a headman of a Philippine group of families

cab·e·zon *or* **cab·e·zone** \ˈkabə,zōn, ˌ==ˈ=\ *n* -s [Sp *cabezón,* aug. of *cabeza* head, fr. (assumed) VL *capitia,* fr. L *capit-, caput* — more at HEAD] **1** *also* **cab·a·zone a :** a large green-fleshed edible sculpin (*Scorpaenichthys marmoratus*) of the Pacific coast of No. America **b :** a smaller related fish (*Leptocottus armatus*) of southern California **2 :** a croaker (*Larimus breviceps*) of the West Indies and southwest Atlantic ocean having a short thick head and a nearly vertical mouth

cab horse *n* **1 :** a horse used for drawing a cab **2 :** a horse of moderate weight and size with ability to draw a fair load at a moderate speed

ca·bil·do \kə'bil(ˌ)dō\ *n* -s [Sp, fr. ML *capitulum,* fr. L, small head — more at CHAPTER] **1** *chiefly Southwest* **:** the chapter house of a cathedral or collegiate church **2 :** a town council or a town hall in a country formerly a Spanish colony

¹cab·in \ˈkabən\ *n* -s [ME *cabane,* fr. MF, fr. OProv *cabana,* fr. ML *capanna*] **1** *obs* **a :** a prison or convent cell **b :** an individual study cubicle **2 a :** a small room on a ship providing private accommodations for one or a few persons — see CABIN CLASS **b :** a compartment below deck for passengers or crew on a small boat **c :** a closed airplane compartment for cargo, crew, or passengers **3** *obs* **:** a temporary shelter (as one made of boughs or a soldier's tent) or a structure of stakes with withes woven between them and a roof of thatch **4 :** a small one-story low-roofed dwelling usu. of plain construction: as **a :** a 4-sided dwelling of logs built as a home by early settlers of No. America or by mountain folk **b :** a similar structure serving as the home of the family of a servant or plantation hand in the South **c :** a dwelling used during a vacation esp. for hunting and fishing **d :** a small typically one-room house suitable for overnight lodging for tourists: *also* **:** a unit in a block of apartments belonging to a motel ⟨10 ~s in each building⟩ **5 a :** an interlocking or block station on a railroad **b** *chiefly Brit* **:** ³CAB 3a **c** *Brit* **:** ³CAB 3b(1) **d** *Brit* **:** ³CAB 3b(2) **e :** a passenger cage of an aerial tram **f :** a glassed-in shelter on top of a lookout tower **g :** the part of a passenger trailer used for living quarters **6** *obs* **a :** COT, LITTER **b :** BENCH **7** *obs* **:** a cabinet advisory to a sovereign **8 :** a shelved container

cabin 4

²cabin \"\ *vb* -ED/-ING/-S *vi* **:** to live or lodge in a cabin or within narrow confines ~ *vt* **:** to lodge or confine in a cabin or within a narrow space or limits

cabin boy *n* **:** a boy acting as servant to the officers and cabin passengers of a ship

cabin car *n* **:** CABOOSE

cabin class *n* **:** a class of accommodations on a passenger ship superior to tourist class and inferior to first class

cabin court *n* **:** MOTEL

cabin cruiser *n* **:** CRUISER 3

ca·bin·da \kə'bində\ *n, pl* **cabinda** *or* **cabindas** *usu cap* [Pg] **1 :** a Bantu people north of the lower Congo skilled in boat-building **2 :** a member of the Cabinda people

cab·in·eer \ˌkabə¦ni(ə)r\ *n* -s **:** one that occupies a cabin

¹cab·i·net \ˈkab(ə)nət\ *n* -s *often attrib* [MF, dim. of ONF *cabine* gambling house, gambling booth] **1 :** a box for storing chiefly small articles usu. closed by a hinged or sliding door, fitted with shelves or drawers, and suitably finished as an item of home, office, or laboratory furniture: **a :** an upright case or cupboardlike repository for utensils, materials, or documents conveniently accessible for use ⟨a bathroom wall ~ for medicines, bandages, and toilet articles⟩ ⟨cards alphabetically arranged in rows of file ~s⟩ ⟨installation of a ~ sink in the kitchen⟩ **b :** a similar repository for specimens of a biological, mineralogical, numismatic, antiquarian, or curio collection usu. ordered for display; *also* **:** a collection of specimens regarded independently of the repository ⟨original owner of the ~ that was the basis of a classical work in the field⟩ **c :** an enclosed framework for printers' cases or material **d :** an upright case housing a radio or television receiver **:** CONSOLE **e :** a box having a tight-closing door and containing an ovenlike chamber in which a desired temperature, humidity, and circulation of air may be maintained for humidification, sterilization, or evaporation or for incubation of biological samples **f :** a small box containing both writing paper and envelopes **g :** a cupboardlike compartment usu. of steel with a swinging door used to house an electric panelboard **2 a** [prob. influenced by *cabin*] *archaic* **:** a small room providing seclusion (as for study or reading) **b :** a room for the safekeeping and exhibition of treasured art works or art objects; *specif* **:** a small exhibition room in a museum **c :** a small enclosed space or stall for a person performing some action ⟨a shower ~ installed in the bathroom⟩ **3** *obs* **a :** a bower in a garden **b :** a retreat or shelter **4 a** *archaic* (1) **:** the private room serving as council chamber of the chief councilors or ministers of a sovereign, in England orig. of the members of the privy council (2) **:** the consultations and actions of these councilors **b** *often cap* **:** a body of advisers of a sovereign or head of a state: (1) **:** an executive or policy-making body consisting of a prime minister and the ministers in charge of the principal departments of government whose members take the leadership of all legislation and are by custom responsible for it to parliament ⟨a constitutional monarchy with a ~ system⟩ ⟨the ~ consists of about twenty members appointed nominally by the governor-general but really by the prime minister —F.A.Magruder⟩ — compare MINISTRY 7a (2) **:** an advisory council of a president composed of the heads of the executive departments of the government whose members have been appointed by the president and who are responsible only to him ⟨the ~ of the president of the U.S.⟩ ⟨at present the civil service commissioner, the director of the budget, and the chief U.S. delegate to the U.N. are also de facto ~ members —Ernest Maass⟩ (3) **:** a similar advisory council of a national chief executive (as a chancellor) (4) **:** a similar advisory council of a governor of a state or a mayor in the U.S. **c** *Brit* **:** a meeting of a cabinet **d** *Brit* **:** GOVERNMENT 8c (1) **5 :** the advisory or executive council of an organization (as religious, fraternal, academic)

²**cabinet** \"\ *adj* **1 :** suitable by reason of small size for a private compartment or by reason of attractiveness and antique character or perfection as a specimen for preservation and display in a cabinet ⟨~ painting is a defunct art —Herbert Read⟩ ⟨porcelain ~ plates with figural centers⟩ **2 :** belonging to a governmental cabinet ⟨~ ministers⟩ ⟨the new post carries ~ rank⟩ **3 a :** used or adapted for cabinetmaking ⟨mahogany, walnut, and other fine ~ woods⟩ **b :** done, made, or used by a cabinetmaker

³**cab·i·net** \'kab(ə)nət, -bə,net\ *vt* **cabineted** *or* **cabinetted; cabineted** *or* **cabinetted; cabineting** *or* **cabinetting; cabinets 1** *archaic* **:** to put in a cabinet **2** *archaic* **:** to lock up **:** SHUT

cabinet ball *n* **:** a game played on a volleyball court by two teams usu. of nine players each using a small medicine ball and scoring points by errors in either catching or throwing

cabinet beetle *n* **:** DERMESTID

cabinet bench *n* **:** a steel cabinet with doors or drawers and a flat top that is used as a workbench

cabinet cherry *n* **:** BLACK CHERRY 2

cabinet council *n, archaic* **:** the English cabinet; *also* **:** a session of it

cab·i·ne·teer \¦kab(ə)nə¦ti(ə)r\ *n* -s *slang* **:** a member of a government cabinet

cabinet file *n* [so called fr. its use in cabinetmaking] **:** a thin woodworking file with coarse teeth that is flat on one side and convex on the other

cabinet finish *n* **:** interior building finish in hardwoods framed, paneled, molded, and varnished or polished like cabinetwork as distinguished from that in softwoods nailed together and usu. painted

cabinet government *n* **:** a government in which the real executive power rests with a cabinet of ministers who are individually and collectively responsible to the legislature

cabinetmaker \'=(=)=,==\ *n* [¹*cabinet* (furniture) + *maker*] **:** a skilled woodworker who cuts, shapes, and assembles high-grade articles of furniture calling for fine finish (as decorative cabinets, desks, and chairs, store fixtures, office equipment)

cabinetmaking \'=(=)=,==\ *n* -s **:** the occupation or art of the cabinetmaker

cabinet organ *n* [so called fr. its shape] **:** a reed organ having pedal-operated bellows and mounted in a case about the size and shape of an upright piano

ca·bi·net par·ti·cu·lier \kȧbēnāpȧrtēkü̅lyā\ *n, pl* **cabinets particuliers** \-nāp...lyā\ [F] **:** a small private room for guests in a restaurant

cabinet photograph *n* **:** a photograph in a mount about four by six inches

cabinet piano *n* **:** a small upright piano

cabinet projection *n* **:** an oblique projection in mechanical drawing in which dimensions parallel to the third axis of the object are shortened one half to overcome apparent distortion

cabinet pudding *n* **:** a pudding of bread or cake, candied or dried fruit, milk, and eggs often molded and usu. served hot with a tart sauce

cab·i·net·ry \'kab(ə)nətrē, -i\ *n* -ES **1 :** CABINETMAKING **2 :** CABINETWORK

cabinets *pl of* CABINET, *pres 3d sing of* CABINET

cabinet saw *n* **:** a short broad-bladed saw with parallel edges, one sharpened for ripping and the other for crosscutting

cabinet scraper *n* **:** a scraper with the blade clamped in a single-handled or double-handled frame for smoothing wood

cabinet system *n* **:** CABINET GOVERNMENT

cab·in·ette \¦kabə¦net\ *n* -s **:** a small cabin

cabinet trim *n* **:** CABINET FINISH

cabinet ware *n* **:** CABINETWORK

cabinet wine *n* [trans. of G *kabinettwein*] **1 :** a bottled German Rhine wine usu. representing the vintner's choice of his best wine **2 :** any wine of excellent quality

cabinetwork \'=(=)=,=\ *n* **:** finished woodwork made by a cabinetmaker — compare MILLWORK 2

cabinetworn \'=(=)=,=\ *adj* **:** slightly worn from frequent removal from dealers' cabinets for display to customers ⟨a ~ coin⟩

cabin fever *n* **:** extreme irritability and combativeness resulting from the boredom of living in a remote region alone or with only a few companions

cabin hook *n* **:** a small hook and eye for use on cabinet doors

cabin house *n* **:** the part of a cabin that projects above deck (as on a small yacht)

cabining *pres part of* CABIN

cabin passenger *n* **1** *obs* **:** a passenger on a ship privileged to dine or lounge in the captain's cabin **2 :** a passenger on a ship who pays for and is allotted the use of a cabin or part of a cabin, the minimum allotted space for each such passenger being fixed by law

cabins *pl of* CABIN, *pres 3d sing of* CABIN

cabin supercharger *n* **:** a supercharger used to pressurize a cabin of an airplane

ca·bio \kə'bī(,)ō, -īə\ [Bisayan *kabayo*, fr. Sp *caballo* horse, fr. L *caballus* — more at CAVALCADE] *var of* COBIA

ca·bi·ri *or* **ca·bei·ri** \kə'bīrē, -bī,rī\ *n pl, usu cap* [L *Cabiri, Cabeiri*, fr. Gk *Kabiroi, Kabeiroi*] **:** a group of ancient Greek deities of Phrygian prob. chthonic origin whose mysteries of Samothrace were second in prestige only to the Eleusinian mysteries

¹**ca·ble** \'kābəl\ *n* -s *often attrib* [ME, fr. ONF, fr. ML *capulum* lasso, fr. L *capere* to take — more at HEAVE] **1 a :** a strong rope; *esp* **:** a rope 10 or more inches in circumference **b :** a cable-laid rope **c :** a wire rope or metal chain of great strength used esp. for hauling, for securing a ship to an anchor, or for supporting the rods and roadway of a suspension bridge **d :** a wire or wire rope by means of which force is exerted to control or operate a mechanism ⟨ailerons operated by control ~*s*⟩ **2 :** CABLE LENGTH **3 a :** a ropelike usu. stranded assembly of electrical conductors or of groups of two or more conductors insulated from each other but laid up together usu. by being twisted around a central core, the whole usu. heavily insulated by outside wrappings; *specif* **:** a submarine cable — see TELEGRAPH CABLE **b** [by shortening] **:** CABLEGRAM **c :** CABLE TRANSFER **4 a :** something resembling or fashioned like a cable ⟨creepers of many kinds and of every size, from huge ~*s* to thin cords, loop from tree to tree —C.D. Forde⟩ ⟨a ~ motif⟩ **b :** a convex molding that occupies a flute of a column or pilaster usu. in the lower part of the shaft **c** *also* **cable stitch :** a knitting stitch that produces a pattern resembling the twist of a 2-ply cable ⟨a ~ on a sweater⟩

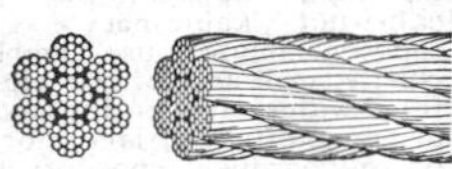

cross section and view of suspension-bridge cable showing arrangement of strands

²**cable** \"\ *vb* **cabled; cabled; cabling** \'kāb(ə)liŋ\ **cables** *vt* **1 :** to fasten with or as if with a cable **2 :** to ornament with something resembling a cable **3 :** to telegraph by a submarine cable **4** *archit* **:** to fill (flutes) with cables **5 :** to make into a cable or into a form resembling a cable; *specif* **:** to twist together (two or more strands, plied yarns, or threads) ~ *vi* **1 :** to communicate by a submarine cable ⟨~ for immediate delivery of goods⟩ **2 :** to make a cable stitch

cable address *n* **:** the address for a cable message esp. when condensed into a code word

cable bend *n* **1 :** a small rope used for lashing the end of a cable into a loop for securing an anchor **2 :** the clinch by which an anchor is secured to its cable

cable buoy *n* **:** a float used to support a submarine cable (as over a rocky bottom)

cable car *n* **:** a car used on a cable railway or overhead cableway

cable chain *n* **:** a heavy chain having links with a crossbar across the inside of each link usu. used as a ship's cable **:** CHAIN CABLE

cable desk *n* **:** a department or section of a newspaper or news bureau where overseas news esp. as received by cable is edited

cable driller *n* **:** a supervisor of the setup and operation of a cable-drilling rig for drilling oil and gas wells

cable drilling *n* **:** ROPE DRILLING

cable engineer *n* **:** an engineer who plans and directs the laying and repair of undersea cable lines

ca·ble·gram \'kābəl,gram, -aa(ə)m\ *n* -s [¹*cable* + *-gram*] **:** a message sent by a submarine telegraph cable

cable grip *n* **:** the grip of a cable car

cablehead \'==,=\ *n* -s **:** a terminal for cable or radio circuits to and from foreign countries

cable holder *or* **cable lifter** *n* **:** WILDCAT 4

cable-laid \'==¦=\ *adj* **:** composed of three ropes laid together left-handed with each containing three strands twisted together ⟨*cable-laid* rope⟩

cable length *n* **:** a maritime unit of length based on the length of a ship's cable and variously reckoned as equal to 100 fathoms, 1/10 of the nautical mile of 6080 ft., or 120 fathoms

ca·ble·less \'kābəlləs\ *adj* **:** being without a cable

ca·ble·man \-lmən, -,man, -,maa(ə)n\ *n, pl* **cable·men** \-lmən, -,men\ **1 :** a worker who installs and repairs conduit systems transmitting electric power **2 :** a worker who lays out cables used in electrical prospecting for petroleum-bearing formations **3 :** a worker who installs aerial and underground cables used for communication and signaling **4 :** a worker who installs engine-control equipment in airplane fuselages and wings

cable net *n* **:** coarse-meshed cotton net used for curtains

cable paper *n* **:** a strong paper used as insulation around electric cables

ca·bler \'kāblə(r)\ *n* **:** one that cables

cable railway *n* **:** a railway on which the cars grip and are moved by an endless cable that is sometimes laid underground and that is driven by a stationary engine — see FUNICULAR RAILWAY

cable rate *n* **:** the charge per unit of currency for a cable transfer

cable release *n* **:** a flexible wire moving within a sheath and used to trip a camera shutter — called also *antinous release*

cable rope *n* **:** CABLE 1

cables *pl of* CABLE, *pres 3d sing of* CABLE

ca·blese \¦kābə¦lēz, -ēs\ *n* -s [¹*cable* + *-ese*] **:** the language of a cablegram or language resembling that of a cablegram characterized by the omission of connectives and by the use of special combinations, abbreviations, and code symbols ⟨in my memorandum book wrote a reminder in ~, "Uplook kids" —W.L.White⟩

cable ship *n* **:** a ship fitted for laying and repairing submarine cables

cable's length *n, pl* **cables' lengths :** CABLE LENGTH

cable stitch *n* **:** CABLE 4c

cable stopper *n* **:** a device to hold an anchor cable so as to prevent the anchor from running out or to relieve the strain at the inboard end

cable system *n* **1 :** a system of propelling cars, plows, or other working units from a stationary source by means of cable, esp. endless cable and accessory tackle **2 :** ROPE DRILLING

ca·blet \'kāblət\ *n* -s [¹*cable* + *-et*] **:** a small cable; *specif* **:** a cable-laid rope less than 10 inches in circumference

cable tank *n* **:** a large cylindrical watertight iron tank used for storing or testing telegraph cable

cable tier \-,ti(ə)r, -iə\ *n* **:** the part of a ship where cables and spare rigging are stowed **:** CHAIN LOCKER

cable tool *n* **:** a tool of the set used in rope drilling

cable transfer *n* **:** the transfer of credit between persons or firms in different countries by means of cable, radio, or transoceanic telephone

cable vault *n* **:** a manhole giving access to underground electrical cables and their connections

cableway \'==,=\ *n* **:** a transporting system typically consisting of a cable suspended between elevated supports so as to constitute a track along which carriers can be pulled

cable wheel *n* **:** a drum of a windlass or capstan on which cable is wound **:** WILDCAT

cabling *n* -s **1 :** CABLE 1 **2 :** a cable or cables used in decoration ⟨~ running down the front of a knitted sweater⟩ ⟨~ on the lower part of a pilaster⟩

cab·man \'ka(a)bmən\ *n, pl* **cabmen :** CABDRIVER

cabnt *abbr* cabinet

cabob *var of* KABOB

cab·o·ceer \¦kabə¦si(ə)r, -bō-, -iə\ *n* -s [Pg *cabeceira*, fr. *cabeça* head, fr. (assumed) VL *capitia* — more at CABEZON] **:** a West African native chief

caboched *var of* CABOSHED

¹**cab·o·chon** \'kabə,shän\ *n* -s [MF, aug. of ONF *caboche* head — more at CABBAGE] **1 :** an uncut gem somewhat polished **2 a :** a gem or bead cut in convex form, highly polished, but not faceted — see CUT illustration **b :** this style of cutting gems or other ornaments

²**cabochon** \"\ *adv* **:** in cabochon ⟨a stone cut ~⟩

ca·bo·clo \kə'bō(,)klü, -'ō-\ *n* -s [Pg, fr. Tupi *caboco, caboculo, caboclo*] **1 a :** an acculturated pure-blooded Brazilian Indian **b :** a Brazilian of mixed Indian and white blood — compare MAMELUCO **2 :** a So. American rural half-breed

ca·bom·ba \kə'bämbə\ *n, cap* [NL, fr. Sp *cabomba*, a So. American aquatic plant] **:** a small genus of American aquatic plants (family Nymphaeaceae) comprising the water shield and having minute white or yellow flowers and submerged dissected leaves as well as peltate floating ones

ca·bom·ba·ce·ae \,ka,bäm'bāsē,ē\ *n pl, cap* [NL, fr. *Cabomba*, type genus + *-aceae*] *in some classifications* **:** a small family of aquatic plants comprising those members of the family Nymphaeaceae that constitute the genera *Cabomba* and *Brasenia* and have flowers with three or four persistent sepals and petals and distinct coriaceous carpels

ca·boo·dle \kə'büd³l\ *n* -s [prob. fr. *ca-* (alter. or earlier spelling of *ker-*) + *boodle*] *slang* **:** COLLECTION, LOT — often used with *whole* ⟨sell the whole ~⟩; compare BOODLE 1, ¹KIT 3

ca·book \kə'bu̇k\ *n* -s [prob. modif. of Pg *cavouco* quarry, irreg. fr. *cavo* hollow, concave, fr. L *cavus* — more at CAVE] **:** laterite as used as building material in Ceylon

¹**ca·boose** \kə'büs\ *n* -s [prob. fr. D *kabuis, kombuis*, fr. MLG *kabūse*] **1** *also* **cam·boose** \kam'b-\ **a :** a deckhouse where cooking is done **:** a ship's galley **b :** an open-air cooking oven **2** *dial* **:** HUT **3 :** a freight-train car usu. attached to the rear of a train mainly for the use of trainmen in the performance of their duties although sometimes used to transport passengers, esp. livestock caretakers

²**caboose** \"\ *n* -s [by contraction] *slang* **:** CALABOOSE

ca·boshed \kə'bäsht\ *also* **ca·bossed** \-äst\ *or* **ca·boched** \-äsht\ *adj* [fr. past part. of obs. *caboche* to behead (a deer) close behind the horns, fr. ME *cabochen*, fr. ONF *caboche* head — more at CABBAGE] *heraldry* **:** borne affronté without the neck showing — used of an animal's head

ca·bot \kə'bō\ *n* -s [F dial.] **:** a unit of capacity in the Channel islands (Jersey) equal to ½ bushel

cab·o·tage \'kabə,täzh, -ázh, -,tij\ *n* -s [F, fr. *caboter* to sail along the coast (prob. fr. Sp *cabo* cape, promontory, fr. L *caput* head) + F *-age* — more at HEAD] **1 :** trade or transport in coastal waters or between two points within a country esp. by other than domestic carriers **2 a :** the right to engage in cabotage **b :** restriction of the right of cabotage to domestic carriers

cab·o·ti·nage \¦kabə̇tə̇¦näzh\ *n, pl* **caboti·nages** \"\ [F, fr. *cabotin* strolling actor, charlatan (fr. Cabotin, 17th cent. Fr. actor) + *-age*] **:** behavior befitting a second-rate actor **:** obvious playing to the audience **:** THEATRICALITY

cab·ot's ring \'kabəts-\ *or* **cab·ot ring** \-ət·'r-\ *n, usu cap C* [after Richard C. *Cabot* †1939 physician] **:** a ringlike body present in many immature red blood cells that stains with nuclear dyes and may represent remains of the nuclear membrane

cabot's tern *n, usu cap C* [prob. fr. the name *Cabot*] **:** SANDWICH TERN

ca·bou·ca \kə'bükə\ *n* -s [AmerF] **:** LAZY CRAB

cab-over \'=,==\ *or* **cab-over-engine** \¦=,==¦==\ *n* -s **:** an automotive vehicle with a cab at the front end over the engine

ca·bra·lea \kə'brälēə, -'ā-\ *n, cap* [NL, fr. Pedro A. *Cabral* †*ab*1526 Portuguese navigator] **:** a genus of trees of southern tropical America (family Meliaceae) noted chiefly for their wood which resembles cedar but is firmer and stronger and which is used for construction, joinery, furniture, and sculpture

cab rank *n* **1** *Brit* **:** a row of cabs at a cabstand **2** *Brit* **:** TAXI STAND

ca·bree *also* **ca·bri** *or* **ca·brie** *or* **ca·brit** \kə'brē, 'kabrē\ *or* **ca·bret** \'kabrē\ *n* -s [LaF *cabri*, fr. F, kid, fr. OProv *cabrit*, fr. LL *capritus*, fr. L *capr-, caper* goat — more at CAPRIOLE] **:** PRONGHORN

ca·bret·ta \kə'bred·ə\ *n* -s [modif. (influenced by It *-etta*, fem. dim. suffix) of Pg and Sp *cabra* goat] **:** leather tanned from hair sheepskins and used for gloves, garments, and shoe uppers

ca·bre·u·va \,kabrē'üvə\ *n* -s [Pg *cabriúva*, fr. Tupi *cabreúva, cabureiba*] **:** either of two timber trees (*Myrocarpus frondosus* and *M. fastigiatus*) of the family Leguminosae of southern Brazil and Argentina whose wood is brownish, strong, and hard, takes a high polish, and yields a balsam

ca·bri·lla \kə'brē(y)ə, -rilə\ *n* -s [Sp, fr. dim. of *cabra* goat, fr. L *capra* she-goat, fem. of L *caper* he-goat] **:** any of various sea basses of the Mediterranean, the coast of California, and the warmer parts of the western Atlantic **:** as **a :** RED HIND 1 **b :** ROCK BASS

cab·ri·ole \'kabrē,ōl\, (*esp sense 2*) kȧbrēōl\ *n* -s [F, leap, caper; fr. its resemblance to the foreleg of a capering animal] **1 :** a form of furniture leg frequent in Queen Anne and Chippendale furniture that curves outward from the structure which it supports and then descends in a tapering reverse curve terminating in an ornamental foot **2 :** a ballet leap in which one leg is extended in mid-air and the other struck against it

cabrioles 1: *A* early 18th century; *B* mid-18th century; *C* early Georgian; *D* second half of 18th century

cab·ri·o·let \¦kabrēə¦lā\ *n* -s [F, dim. of *cabriole*, *capriole* leap, caper; fr. its skipping lightness — more at CAPRIOLE] **1 :** a light 2-wheeled one-horse carriage with a single seat, a folding leather hood, a large rigid apron, gracefully upward-curving shafts, and usu. a rear platform between the C springs for a groom **2 :** an automobile resembling a coupe in appearance and capacity but with a folding top **:** a convertible coupe

ca·bri·to \kə'brē,tō\ *n* -s [Sp, dim. of *cabro* male goat, fr. L *capr-, caper* — more at CAPRIOLE] *southwest* **:** the flesh of a young kid roasted or stewed

cabs *pl of* CAB, *pres 3d sing of* CAB

cab signal *n* **:** a visual signal in the cab of a locomotive used in conjunction with interlocking signals and in conjunction with or in lieu of block signals to provide continuous data for the engineman on conditions affecting train or engine movement

cabstand \'=,=\ *n* **:** a place where cabs may stand awaiting hire

cab system \'kab-, 'kaa(ə)b-\ *n* [command bids + approach bids + Baron *system*] **:** a system of bidding at contract bridge popular in England

ca·bu·ya *also* **ca·bu·ja** *or* **ca·bu·lla** \kə'büyə\ *n* -s [Sp, fr. Taino] **1 :** any of several hard fibers (as sisal, cajun, or Mauritius hemp) **2 :** a plant yielding cabuya — see GIANT CABUYA

cac- *or* **caco-** *comb form* [NL, fr. Gk *kak-, kako-*, fr. *kakos* bad — more at CACK] **1 :** bad ⟨*cac*onym⟩ **:** incorrect ⟨*caco*epy⟩ **:** unpleasant ⟨*caco*phonous⟩ **2 :** diseased ⟨*caco*chylia⟩

cac·a·fue·go \,kakə'fyü(,)gō, -fwā(-\ *also* **cac·a·fu·go** \-fyü(-\ *n* -s [Sp *Cacafuego*, name of a ship captured in 1579 by Sir Francis Drake, fr. L *cacare* to void as excrement + Sp *fuego* fire, fr. L *focus* hearth — more at CACK, FOCUS] *obs* **:** a swaggering braggart or boaster

ca·ca·jao \¦kakə¦jaü, ,kakə'jā(,)ō\ *n, cap* [NL, fr. Pg *cacajão*, fr. Tupi *cacajao*] **:** the genus consisting of the ouakaris

ca·ca·lia \kə'kālyə, -lēə\ *n* [NL, fr. L, a plant, fr. Gk *kakalia, kakkalia*] **1** *cap* **:** a genus of tall smooth herbs (family Compositae) with alternate often petioled leaves and large heads in flat corymbs — see MESADENIA **2** -s **:** any plant of the genus *Emilia*

¹**ca' can·ny** \'kȯ'kanē, 'kä'-, 'kȧ'-, -i\ *vi* [*ca'* + *canny*] **1** *Scot* **:** to proceed cautiously **:** go slow **2** *Brit* **:** to work slowly in order to prolong work

²**ca' canny** \"\ *n, Brit* **:** a deliberate slackening by workmen in the rate of work or quantity produced **:** SLOWDOWN

ca·cao \kə'kaü, -'kä(,)ō, -'kā(,)ō\ *n* -s [Sp, fr. Nahuatl *cacahuatl* cacao beans] **1** *or* **cacao bean** *or* **cocoa bean :** the dried and usu. partly fermented seed of the cacao tree used chiefly in the preparation of cocoa, chocolate, and cocoa butter **2 :** any of several trees of the genus *Theobroma*; *esp* **:** a tree (*T. cacao*) native to So. America and now extensively cultivated (as in the West Indies, Mexico, Central America) that bears on the trunk or the old branches flowers with a pink calyx and yellowish corolla succeeded by fleshy yellow pods six or more inches long and three or four inches in diameter containing numerous seeds — called also *chocolate tree* **3 :** ANTIQUE BRONZE

cacao brown *n* **:** a strong brown that is paler and slightly yellower than rust, rust brown, or average russet and very slightly paler and redder than gold brown

cacao butter *var of* COCOA BUTTER

cacao moth *n* **:** TOBACCO MOTH

cacao nib *or* **cocoa nib** *n* **:** a piece of a cacao bean that has been roasted, dried, dehusked, and degermed — usu. used in pl.

cacao thrips *n* **:** RED-BANDED THRIPS

ca·ca·tua \,kakə'tüə, -ə'työə\ [NL, fr. D or Malay; D *kakatoe*, fr. Malay *kakatua* — more at COCKATOO] *syn of* KAKATOE

ca·cax·te \kə'käste\ *n* -s [AmerSp *cacaxtle, cacaxte*, fr. Nahuatl *cacaxtli* small ladder for carrying things on the back] **:** a square wooden packing frame or crate that has four legs and a net cover and is carried on the back esp. by Guatemalan Indians with the help of a tumpline

cac·cia \'kä(,)chə\ *n, pl* **cac·ce** \-(,)chā\ *or* **caccias** \-(,)chäz\ [It, lit., hunt, chase, fr. *cacciare* to chase, fr. (assumed) VL *captiare* — more at CATCH] **:** a part song in canon form portraying the hunt or village scenes and usu. employing such sounds as the cries of beggars and vendors and the barks of dogs

cac·cia·to·re \,kächə'tōrē\ *also* **cac·cia·to·ra** \-rə\ *or* **cac·cia·to·ri** \-rē\ *adj* [It *cacciatore*, lit., hunter, fr. *cacciato* (past part. of *cacciare*) + *-ore* -or] **:** simmered or stewed with herbs and other seasonings ⟨chicken ~⟩

-ca·ce \kə,sē\ *n comb form* -s [Gk *kakē* badness, fr. *kakos* bad — more at CACK] **:** diseased or vitiated condition of a (specified) bodily part ⟨arthro*cace*⟩ ⟨carpo*cace*⟩

cacha *n* -s [Bengali *kaṣāy* or Marathi *kāṣāy*, fr. Skt *kaṣāya* yellowish red, brownish red] *obs* **:** AUBURN

cach·a·lot \'kashə,lät, -'aa-,-'ai-, -,lō\ *n* -s [F, fr. F dial. (Bayonne, 17th century) *cachalut*] **:** SPERM WHALE

ca·char \'kä,chär\ *n* -s *usu cap* [fr. *Cachar*, district in India where it is produced] **:** any of several teas of India

ca·cha·ri \'kächərē, kə'chärē\ *n, pl* **cachari** *or* **cacharis** *usu cap* **:** BODO

ca·cha·za \kə'chäsə, -äsə\ *n* -s [Sp] **:** PRESS CAKE a

¹**cache** \'kash, -aa-,-ai-\ *n* -s [F, hiding place, fr. *cacher* to hide, fr. (assumed) VL *coacticare* to press together, fr. L *coactare* to compel, fr. *coactus*, past part. of *cogere* to drive together, compel — more at COGENT] **1 a :** a hiding place; *esp* **:** one used by settlers, explorers, or campers for concealing and preserving provisions or implements **b :** a secure place of storage **2 a :** something that is hidden or stored in a cache **b :** a group of artifacts occurring alone or with a burial **3 a :** the hibernation place of a group of insects (as a hole in the ground) **b :** the mass of insects hibernating in such a place

²**cache** \"\ *vt* -ED/ -ING/ -s **:** to place in a cache **:** place or store in safety or concealment ⟨~ camp supplies by a lake⟩ ⟨coins *cached* in a teapot⟩ **syn** see CONCEAL

ca·chec·tic \ka'kektik, kə-\ *adj* [F *cachectique,* fr. L *cachecticus,* fr. Gk *kachektikos,* fr. *kak-* cac- + *hektikos* habitual, constitutional, fr. *hekt-* (stem of *echein* to have) + *-ikos* -ic — more at SCHEME] **1 :** relating to cachexia **2 :** having the symptoms of cachexia; *esp* **:** thin or emaciated of body

cache–peigne \'kash,pān\ *n* -s [F, lit., comb hider, fr. *cacher* to hide + *peigne* comb, fr. L *pecten* — more at CACHE, PECTINATE] **:** trimming on the back part of a woman's hat either placed under the brim or attached to the edge

cache·pot \'kash,pät, -,pō\ *n* -s [F, lit., pot hider, fr. *cacher* to hide + *pot,* fr. (assumed) VL *pottus* — more at POT] **:** an ornamental receptacle to hold and usu. to conceal a flowerpot

cache–sexe \-¦seks\ *n* -s [F, lit., sex hider, fr. *cacher* to hide + *sexe* sex, fr. L *sexus* — more at SEX] **:** a small garment (as a loincloth) worn to cover the genitals

¹ca·chet \(')ka¦shā\ *n* -s [MF, fr. *cacher* to press, hide] **1 a :** a seal or stamp that is used esp. as a mark of official approval **b :** an indication or sign of approval usu. carrying with it great prestige ⟨the president placed his ~ upon the project⟩ **2 a :** a characteristic feature or quality conferring prestige or distinction or inspiring respect ⟨regarded the possession of . . . land as a ~ of respectability —G.W.Johnson⟩ **b :** high status **:** PRESTIGE ⟨being a guard gave you a certain ~ —*New Yorker*⟩ ⟨few read them but those who do acquire ~ —Bernard De Voto⟩ **3 :** two circles of wafer sheet sealed together with powdered medicine between them to form a dose that can be easily swallowed after being dipped in water — called also *wafer capsule* **4 a :** a picture, design, or inscription stamped or printed on an envelope to commemorate some postal or philatelic event **b :** a pictorial or slogan advertisement on a piece of mail as part of a postal meter impression — called also *postmark ad* **c :** a motto or slogan included in a postal cancellation on a piece of mail

²cachet \"\ *vt* -ED/-ING/-S **:** to put a cachet on ⟨a ~*ed* envelope⟩

ca·chex·ia \ka'keksēə, kə-\ *also* **ca·chexy** \'ka,keksē; ka'keksē, kə-\ *n, pl* **cachexias** *also* **cachexies** [LL *cachexia,* fr. Gk *kachexia* bad condition of body, fr. *kak-* cac- + *-hexia* (fr. *hexis* possession, condition, fr. *echein* to have) — more at SCHEME] **1 :** a general physical wasting and malnutrition caused by a chronic disease (as tuberculosis or cancer) **2** *usu cachexy* **:** a chronic debased condition esp. of mind or outlook

ca·chi·mi·lla \,kächə'mē(y)ə, -,a-\ *also* **ca·cha·ni·lla** \-'nē(y)ə\ *n* -s [MexSp] **:** a shrub (*Pluchea sericea*) of the family Compositae of southwestern U.S. and adjacent Mexico whose slender tough stems are used to make arrows, birdcages, and baskets

cachina *var of* KACHINA

cach·in·nate \'kakə,nāt\ *vi* -ED/-ING/-S [L *cachinnatus,* past part. of *cachinnare;* prob. of imit. origin like OE *ceahhetan* to laugh loudly, OHG *kachazzen,* Gk *kachazein* to laugh loudly, Skt *kakhati* he laughs] **:** to laugh usu. loudly or convulsively ⟨*cachinnated* till his sides must have ached —John Burroughs⟩ — **cach·in·na·tion** \,kakə'nāshən\ *n* -s

cach·o·long \'kashə,lȯŋ\ *n* -s [F, prob. fr. a native name in Kalmuck, U.S.S.R.] **:** an opaque bluish white or pale yellow variety of opal containing a little alumina

ca·chou \ka'shü, kə-; 'ka,shü, -'aa-, -'ai-\ *n* -s [F, fr. Pg *cachu,* fr. Malayalam *kāccu*] **1 :** CATECHU **2 :** an aromatic pill or pastille made of licorice, various aromatics, and gum and used to sweeten the breath **3 :** CACHOU DE LAVAL **4 :** AUBURN

ca·chou de la·val \-dələ'val\ *n, usu cap C&L* [F, fr. *Laval,* city in France, place of its first manufacture] **:** a direct dark brown dye for cotton obtained as the first sulfur dye by heating organic materials (as sawdust or bran) with sulfur and sodium sulfide — see DYE table I (under *Sulfur Brown 1*)

ca·chua \kə'chüə, 'kächə,wä\ *also* **ka·shua** \kə'shüə, 'käsh(,)wä\ *or* **ka·swa** \'kä(,)swä\ *n* -s [AmerSp *cachúa*] **1 a :** a Peruvian dance in rapid unsyncopated 2/4 time **2 :** the music for a cachua

ca·chu·cha \kə'chüchə\ *also* **ca·chu·ca** \-ükə\ *n* -s [Sp, small boat, cap, cachucha, prob. fr. *cacho* shard, piece, prob. fr. (assumed) VL *cacculus* pot, alter. of L *caccabus,* fr. Gk *kakkabos,* of Sem origin; akin to Assyr *kukubu* vessel] **:** a gay Andalusian solo dance in triple time done with castanets

ca·ci·cus \kə'sēkəs\ *n, cap* [NL, fr. AmerSp *cacique*] **:** a genus of tropical American orioles (family Icteridae) — see CACIQUE 2

ca·cio·ca·val·lo \¦kächōkə'vä(,)lō\ *or* **caciocavallo cheese** *n* -s [It *caciocavallo,* lit., horse cheese, fr. *cacio* cheese (fr. L *caseus*) + *cavallo* horse, fr. L *caballus* nag — more at CHEESE, CAVALCADE] **:** a cheese originating in southern Italy and made from matted curd worked in hot water or whey and often molded into the shape of an Indian club or tenpin

ca·cique \kə'sēk\ *or* **ca·zique** \-'z-\ *n* -s [Sp *cacique,* of Arawakan origin; akin to Taino *cacique* chief, Arawak *kassequa*] **1 a :** a native Indian chief in areas dominated primarily by a Spanish culture, esp. the West Indies and Central and So. America **b :** a local political boss in Spain and Latin America **2** [AmerSp, fr. Sp] **:** any of numerous tropical American orioles, some black in plumage, others conspicuously colored, of *Cacicus* or related genera, having the base of the bill expanded into a frontal shield **3** [PhilSp, fr. Sp] **:** a powerful landowner in the Philippines, usu. Spanish or of Spanish descent

ca·ciqu·ism \-ē,kizəm\ *n* -s [Sp *caciquismo,* fr. *cacique* + *-ismo* -ism] **:** domination by caciques ⟨economic and administrative ~ —C.A.Buss⟩

ca·ci·quis·mo \,käsē'kēz(,)mō\ *n* -s [Sp] **:** CACIQUISM

¹cack \'kak, -ā-\ *vi* -ED/-ING/-S [ME *cakken,* fr. L *cacare;* akin to Gk *kakkan* to void excrement, MIr *cacc* dung, and perh. to Gk *kakos* bad] **1** *dial* **:** to discharge excrement **2** *dial* **:** VOMIT

²cack \"\ *n* -s *dial* **:** DUNG, MUCK

³cack \'kak\ *n* -s [origin unknown] **:** a baby's heelless shoe with a soft leather sole

¹cack·le \'kakəl\ *vi* **cackled; cackled; cackling** \'kak(ə)liŋ\ **cackles** [ME *cakelen,* of imit. origin] **1 :** to make the sharp broken noise or cry characteristic of or resembling that of a goose or of a hen after laying **2 :** to laugh with a broken somewhat harsh noise suggestive of a hen's cackle **3 :** to converse in a silly noisy way **:** CHATTER

²cackle \"\ *n* -s **1 :** the action or noise of cackling ⟨a hen's ~⟩ ⟨there should be no ~ of voices at your elbow —R.L.Stevenson⟩ **2 :** idle chatter **:** pointless conversation ⟨the constant ~ at a club meeting⟩

cack·ler \'kak(ə)lə(r)\ *n* -s **:** one that cackles; *specif* **:** BABBLER 2

cackling goose *n* **:** a goose of a western variety (*Branta canadensis minima*) of the Canada goose resembling but much smaller than the white-cheeked goose

caco- —see CAC-

caco·chy·my \'kakō,kīmē\ *n* -ES [NL *cacochymia,* fr. Gk *kakochymia,* fr. *kak-* cac- + *-chymia* (fr. *chymos* juice, fr. *chein* to pour) — more at FOUND] *obs* **:** an unhealthy condition of the humors of the body, esp. of the blood

caco·de·mon *also* **caco·dae·mon** \¦kakə¦dēmən\ *n* -s [Gk *kakodaimōn,* fr. *kak-* cac- + *daimōn* demon — more at DEMON] **:** an evil spirit **:** DEVIL, DEMON — opposed to *eudaemon* — **caco·de·mon·ic** *also* **caco·dae·mon·ic** \¦kakədē¦mänik\ *adj*

caco·de·mo·nia \,kakədē'mōnēə\ *or* **caco·de·mo·no·ma·nia** \-,dēmənō'mānēə\ *n* -s [*cacodemonia* fr. NL, fr. Gk *kakodaimonia* possession by an evil spirit, fr. *kakodaimon-, kakodaimōn; cacodemonomania* fr. NL, fr. Gk *kakodaimon-, kakodaimōn* + NL *-o-* + *mania*] **:** insanity in which the patient has the delusion of being possessed by an evil spirit

caco·doxy \'kakə,däksē\ *n* -ES [LGk *kakodoxia* heretical opinion, fr. Gk *kak-* cac- + *-doxia* (fr. *doxa* opinion, fr. *dokein* to seem) — more at DECENT] **:** perverse teachings **:** HETERODOXY

cac·o·dyl \'kakə,dil\ *n* -s [ISV *cacod-* (fr. Gk *kakōdēs* ill-smelling, fr. *kak-* cac- + *-ōdēs,* akin to *ozein* to smell) + *-yl;* orig. formed as G *kakodyl* — more at ODOR] **1 :** an arsenical radical $As(CH_3)_2$ whose compounds are noted for their vile smell and poisonous properties **2 :** a colorless poisonous liquid compound $As_2(CH_3)_4$ consisting of two cacodyl radicals and having an offensive odor

cac·o·dyl·ate \,kakə'di,lāt\ *n* -s [ISV *cacodylic* + *-ate*] **:** a salt of cacodylic acid

cac·o·dyl·ic acid \¦kakə¦dilik-\ *n* [part trans. of G *kakodylsäure,* fr. *kakodyl* + *säure* acid] **:** a crystalline deliquescent compound $(CH_3)_2AsOOH$ obtained by oxidizing cacodyl oxide and used in medicine in the form of its salts; dimethyl-arsinic acid — compare SODIUM CACODYLATE

cacodyl oxide *n* [ISV *cacodyl* + *oxide;* orig. formed as G *kakodyloxyd*] **:** a heavy oily liquid $(AsC_2H_6)_2O$ that has a repulsive odor and is obtained by distilling arsenic trioxide with potassium acetate

caco·epy \'kakə,wepē; ka'kōəpē, kə-\ *n* -ES [*cac-* + *-epy* (as in *orthoepy*)] **:** bad pronunciation — opposed to *orthoepy*

cac·o·ë·thes \,kakə'wē(,)thēz\ *n* [L, fr. Gk *kakoēthes* wickedness, fr. neut. of *kakoēthēs* malignant, fr. *kak-* cac- + *-ēthēs* (fr. *ēthos* custom) — more at ETHICAL] **:** a habitual and uncontrollable desire **:** MANIA, ITCH

cacoëthes scri·ben·di \-skrə'bendē, -,dī\ *n* [L] **:** an uncontrollable urge to write ⟨his book tempts us to encourage him in a senile *cacoëthes scribendi — Spectator*⟩

caco·gen·e·sis \,kakə'jenəsəs\ *n* [NL, fr. *cac-* + *genesis*] **1 :** inability to produce hybrids that are both viable and fertile **2 :** racial deterioration esp. when due to the retention of inferior breeding stock

caco·gen·ic \¦kakə¦jenik\ *adj* [*cac-* + *-genic* (as in *eugenic*)] **1 :** DYSGENIC **2 :** of or relating to cacogenesis

caco·gen·ics \,==¦=iks\ *n pl but usu sing in constr* [*cac-* + *-genics* (as in *eugenics*)] **1 :** DYSGENICS **2 :** CACOGENESIS 2

ca·cog·ra·phy \ka'kägrəfē, kə-\ *n* -ES [*cac-* + *-graphy*] **1 :** bad handwriting — opposed to *calligraphy* **2 :** bad spelling — opposed to *orthography*

ca·col·o·gy \ka'käləjē, kə-\ *n* -ES [prob. fr. F *cacologie,* fr. *cac-* + *-logie* -logy] **:** bad diction or pronunciation

ca·co·mis·tle \'kakə,misəl\ *also* **cac·o·mixl** *or* **cac·o·mix·le** \-i(k)səl\ *n* -s [MexSp *cacomistle, cacomixtle,* fr. Nahuatl *tlacomiztli,* fr. *tlaco* half + *miztli* mountain lion] **1 :** a slender carnivorous mammal (*Bassariscus astutus*) of the southwestern U. S. and Mexico related to the raccoons but distinguished by the long bushy black-and-white ringed tail — called also *civet cat, ringtail* **2 :** the fur or pelt of the cacomistle

cac·onym \'kakə,nim\ *n* -s [*cac-* + *-onym*] **:** a taxonomic name that is objectionable for linguistic reasons — **cac·onym·ic** \¦kakə¦nimik\ *adj*

ca·coon \ka'kün, kə-\ *n* -s [perh. of African origin; akin to Twi *kankua,* a tree and its fruit] **1** *West Indies* **:** SNUFFBOX BEAN **2 :** a tropical American plant (*Fevillea cordifolia*) of the family Cucurbitaceae with seeds which have cathartic qualities

caco·phon·ic \¦kakə¦fänik\ *adj* [*cacophony* + *-ic*] **:** CACOPHONOUS — **caco·phon·i·cal·ly** \-nək(ə)lē\ *adv*

ca·coph·o·nist \ka'käfənəst, kə-\ *n* -s [*cacophony* + *-ist*] **:** a composer of cacophonous or atonal music — usu. used disparagingly

ca·coph·o·nous \-ənəs\ *adj* [Gk *kakophōnos,* fr. *kak-* cac- + *-phōnos* (fr. *phōnē* sound); akin to Gk *phanai* to say — more at BAN] **:** marked by cacophony **:** harsh-sounding ⟨as ~ as a henyard —John McCarten⟩ ⟨whose writing is . . . uniformly ~ —Brand Blanshard⟩ ⟨a ~ melody⟩ ⟨ ~ laughter⟩ — **ca·coph·o·nous·ly** *adv*

ca·coph·o·ny \-ənē, -i\ *n* -ES [F & NL; F *cacophonie* & NL *cacophonia,* fr. Gk *kakophōnia,* fr. *kak-* cac- + *-phōnia* -phony] **1 :** harsh or discordant sound **:** DISSONANCE ⟨marshes sent forth the multitudinous ~ of song and croak and trill and call and scream —D.C.Peattie⟩; *specif* **:** harshness in the sound of words or phrases ⟨the subtle blending of vowels and consonants so as to avoid even the suspicion of ~ —Irving Babbitt⟩ —opposed to *euphony* **2 :** an instance of cacophony ⟨wooden wheels screeching a ~ —*Amer. Guide Series: Minn.*⟩

ca·coth·e·line \kə'käthə,lēn, ka-, -lən\ *n* -s [ISV *cacothel-* (fr. LGk *kakothelēs* malevolent, fr. Gk *kak-* cac- + *-thelēs,* fr. *thelein* to wish, will) + *-ine;* orig. formed as F *cacothéline* — more at MONOTHELETE] **:** a poisonous base $C_{21}H_{21}N_3O_7$ obtained as the orange-yellow crystalline nitrate by heating brucine with nitric acid

ca·cox·e·nite \kə'käksə,nīt, ka-\ *also* **ca·cox·ene** \kə'käk,sēn, ka-\ *n* -s [G *kakoxen* cacoxenite (fr. *kak-* cac- + *-xen* -xene) + E *-ite*] **:** a mineral $Fe_4(PO_4)_3(OH)_3.12H_2O$ consisting of a hydrous iron phosphate occurring in yellow or brownish radiated tufts

cac·ta·ce·ae \kak'tāsē,ē\ *n pl, cap* [NL, fr. *Cactus,* type genus + *-aceae*] **:** a family of plants (order Opuntiales) that are nearly all American and common in desert areas and characterized chiefly by fleshy stems and branches on which the foliage leaves are much reduced or early deciduous being usu. replaced by spines, scales, or hairs borne in areoles — see CACTUS 1 — **cac·ta·ceous** \(')kak¦tāshəs\ *adj*

cac·ta·les \kak'tā(,)lēz\ *n pl, cap* [NL, fr. *Cactus,* type genus + *-ales*] *syn of* OPUNTIALES

cac·to·blas·tis \,kaktə'blastəs\ *n* [NL, fr. *cactus* + *-o-* + *-blastis* -blast] **1** *cap* **:** a genus of small moths (family Phycitidae) native to So. America including the cactus moth (*C. cactorum*) which has been introduced into Australia to control prickly-pear infestation **2** *pl* **cactoblas·tes** \-,tēz\ **:** CACTUS MOTH

cac·tus \'kaktəs\ *n* [NL, fr. L, cardoon, fr. Gk *kaktos*] **1** *cap, in some classifications* **:** a genus of globose spiny plants (family Cactaceae) now referred to several other genera (as *Melocactus* and *Coryphantha*) **2** *pl* **cac·ti** \-,tī, -(,)tē\ *or* **cactuses** \-,təsəz\ **:** any plant of the family Cactaceae — see CARNEGIEA, ECHINOCACTUS, MESCAL, OPUNTIA

cactus alkaloid *n* **:** ANHALONIUM ALKALOID

cactus coral *n* **:** any of various corals (family Mussidae) related to the brain corals but distinguished by well-developed walls between the polyp grooves

cactus dahlia : any of various dahlias having flower heads with the rays revolute wholly or in part and resembling the flowers of cacti of the genus *Cereus*

cactus fig *n* **:** INDIAN FIG 2

cactus moth *n* **:** a moth having a larva that feeds on cactus; *specif* **:** a small whitish or yellowish moth (*Cactoblastis cactorum*) with dusky markings the larva of which is an orange-red gregarious borer that invades and consumes prickly pear — see CACTOBLASTIS

cactus mouse *n* **:** a white-footed mouse (*Peromyscus eremicus*) of desert areas of southwestern No. America

cactus woodpecker *n* **:** a small desert woodpecker (*Dryobates scalaris cactophilus*) of the southwestern U. S. with the back barred black and white

cactus wren *n* **:** a large harsh-voiced wren (*Heleodytes brunneicapillus*) occurring in several varieties or subspecies in southwestern No. America

ca·cu·mi·nal \ka'kyümənᵊl, kə-\ *adj* [ISV *cacumin-* (fr. L *cacumin-, cacumen* top, point) + *-al*] **:** RETROFLEX

¹cad \'kad, -aa(ə)d\ *n* -s [short for ¹*caddie*] **1** *dial Eng* **:** an assistant who does tasks which call for no special talent **:** HELPER ⟨a bricklayer's ~⟩ **2** *obs* **:** an omnibus conductor **3** *Brit* **:** a town boy or townsman as distinguished from a student at a local school **4 :** a person without gentlemanly instincts **:** one that deliberately and callously violates the code of decent responsible behavior esp. in relations with women

²cad \'kad, -ā-\ *n* -s [by shortening] *dial Eng* **:** CADDISWORM

cad *abbr* **1** cadenza **2** cadet

cad·a·lene \'kadᵊl,ēn\ *n* -s [*cadinene* + naphth*alene*] **:** a colorless liquid hydrocarbon $C_{15}H_{18}$ obtained by dehydrogenating cadinene and other sesquiterpenes; 4-isopropyl-1,-6-dimethyl-naphthalene

ca·dang–ca·dang \'kä,däŋ'kä,däŋ\ *n* -s [Iloko *kadang-kadang* stilts; fr. the appearance of the palm affected by the disease] **:** an infectious chlorotic disease of the coconut palm particularly destructive in the Philippines and characterized by yellow-bronzing esp. of the older lower leaves

ca·das·tral \kə'dastrəl\ *adj* [F, fr. *cadastre* + *-al*] **1 :** of or relating to the records of a cadastre **:** concerned with assembling or keeping the records necessary to a cadastre **2** *of a map or survey* **:** showing or recording property boundaries, subdivision lines, buildings, and other details — **ca·das·tral·ly** \-rəlē\ *adv*

ca·das·tre \kə'dastə(r)\ *n* -s [F, fr. It *catastro,* alter. of OIt (Venetian dial.) *catastico,* fr. LGk *katastichon* notebook, fr. Gk *kata-* cata- + *stichos* line — more at DISTICH] **:** an official register of the quantity, value, and ownership of real estate used in apportioning taxes

ca·dav·er \kə'davə(r) *also* -äv- *or* -āv- *or* -av-\ *n* -s [L, fr. *cadere* to fall — more at CHANCE] **1 :** a dead human or animal body usu. intended for dissection **:** CORPSE — compare CARCASS **2 a :** a sculptured representation of a human corpse usu. emaciated or in a state of partial decomposition made as part of a funerary monument

ca·dav·er·ic \kə'dav(ə)rik\ *adj* [F *cadavérique,* fr. *cadavre* cadaver + *-ique* -ic] **:** of or relating to a cadaver ⟨~ rigidity⟩ — compare CADAVEROUS

ca·dav·er·ine \kə'davə,rēn, -v(ə)rən\ *n* -s [ISV *cadaver* + *-ine;* orig. formed as G *kadaverin*] **:** a syrupy nontoxic ptomaine $H_2N(CH_2)_5NH_2$ formed esp. in putrefaction of flesh—called also *pentamethylenediamine*

ca·dav·er·ous \kə'dav(ə)rəs\ *adj* [F or L; F *cadavéreux,* fr. L *cadaverosus,* fr. *cadaver* + *-osus* -ous] **1 a :** of or relating to a corpse ⟨a peculiar, fetid, ~ odor —W.H.Lowe⟩ **b :** suggestive of corpses or tombs ⟨in that ~ library —Ngaio Marsh⟩ **2 a** *of a complexion* **:** like that of a corpse **:** PALLID, LIVID ⟨the deputy's face looked ~ in the light of the green-shaded table lamp —C.D.Lewis⟩ **b :** GAUNT, EMACIATED — **ca·dav·er·ous·ly** *adv*

cad·bait \'kad,bāt, -'ā-\ *n* [alter. of *codbait*] *dial Eng* **:** CADDISWORM

¹cad·die *or* **cad·dy** *or* **cad·ie** \'kadē, -i\ *n, pl* **caddies** *or* **cadies** [F *cadet* — more at CADET] **1** *Scot* **:** a military cadet **2** *Scot* **:** one that waits about for odd jobs; *specif* **:** an 18th century Edinburgh commissionaire **3** *Scot* **:** young fellow **:** LAD **4 a :** one that assists a golf player esp. by carrying his clubs around the course during play **b :** CADDIE CART **c :** any small cartlike device for conveying things inconvenient to carry by hand

²caddie *or* **caddy** \"\ *vi* **caddied; caddied; caddying; caddies :** to serve as a caddie

caddie cart *n* **:** a long-handled 2-wheeled cart (as for carrying upright a golf bag and clubs on a golf course)

caddies *pl of* CADDY

¹cad·dis *or* **cad·dice** \'kadəs, -'ā-\ *n, pl* **caddises** *or* **caddices** [ME *cadas,* prob. fr. MF *cadaz, cadarce,* fr. OProv *cadarz,* perh. fr. Gk *akathartos* unclean, fr. *a-* ²a- + *-kathartos* cleansed (fr. *kathairein* to cleanse) — more at CATHARTIC] **1** *dial Brit* **a :** FLOSS, COTTON WOOL, LINT **b :** shreds esp. of cloth **2 :** worsted yarn **:** CREWEL; *specif* **:** a worsted ribbon or binding often used for garters **3** [MF *cadis,* fr. OProv] **a :** a heavy woolen twill used by the clergy in France **b :** a cheap sergelike woolen used in Scotland

²cad·dis *or* **cad·dice** \'kadəs\ *n, pl* **caddises** *or* **caddices** [by shortening] **:** CADDISWORM

caddis fly *n* [²*caddis*] **:** any of numerous insects constituting the order Trichoptera or sometimes included among the Neuroptera, having four membranous wings more or less densely hairy, vestigial mouth parts, and slender many-jointed antennae — see CADDISWORM

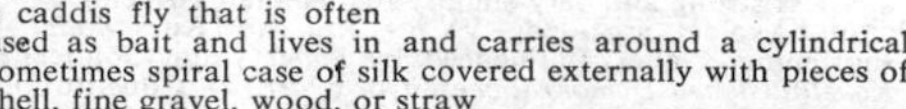

caddis fly

cad·dish \'kadish, -aad-, -ēsh\ *adj* **:** like a cad **:** ILL-BRED — **cad·dish·ness** *n*

cad·dis·worm \'kadə-,swərm, -wōm\ *n* [prob. alter. of obs. *cadworm,* alter. of *codworm*] **:** the wormlike aquatic larva of a caddis fly that is often used as bait and lives in and carries around a cylindrical sometimes spiral case of silk covered externally with pieces of shell, fine gravel, wood, or straw

¹cad·dle \'kadᵊl\ *vb* -ED/-ING/-S [perh. alter. of *caudle*] *vt, dial* **:** CONFUSE, ANNOY, TEASE ~ *vi, dial* **:** PUTTER, LOAF, GOSSIP

²caddle \"\ *n* -s **1** *dial* **:** confused mess **:** CONFUSION **2** *dial* **:** WORRY, TROUBLE, FUSS

¹cad·do \'ka(,)dō\ *n, pl* **caddo** *or* **caddos** *usu cap* [prob. modif. of Caddo *Kädohädächo* (name of a leading tribe in the confederacy), lit., real chiefs] **1 :** a group of Indian peoples of Arkansas, No. and So. Dakota, Kansas, Nebraska, Louisiana, Oklahoma, and Texas, comprising the Hasinai, Kadohadacho, and Natchitoches confederacies and the Adai, Arikara, Eyeish, Kichai, Pawnee, Wichita, and other tribes **2 :** a member of the Caddo group of peoples

²caddo \"\ *or* **cad·do·an** \'kadəwən\ *adj, usu cap* **:** of or relating to an ancient culture of the lower Mississippi valley characterized by pottery having decoration engraved on the polished surface after firing

cad·do·an \'kadəwən\ *n* -s *usu cap* **:** a language family comprising the Caddo languages

¹cad·dow \'ka(,)dō\ *n* -s [ME *cadaw, cadowe,* prob. fr. (northern dial.) *ca* chough + *daw, dawe* jackdaw — more at KAE, DAW] *now dial Eng* **:** JACKDAW

²caddow \"\ *n* -s [perh. alter. of ¹*caddis*] *dial* **:** a coarse woolen quilt or covering

¹caddy *var of* CADDIE

²cad·dy \'kadē, -i\ *n* -ES [modif. of Malay *kati*] **1 a :** a small box, can, or chest esp. to keep tea in **b :** a paper, wood, or metal case used to package or display (as cookies or plugs of tobacco) **2 :** any container or device for storing or holding frequently used things (as clothes or tools) when they are not in use

³caddy *var of* KADY

caddying *pres part of* CADDIE

¹cade \'kād\ *n* -s [ME, fr. L *cadus* jar, bottle, fr. Gk *kados,* of Sem origin; akin to Heb *kadh* water jar] **:** BARREL, CASK, KEG; *esp* **:** a small barrel for 500 herrings or 1000 sprats

²cade \"\ *n* -s [ME *cad* pet lamb] *dial* **:** a pet animal; *esp* **:** a pet lamb

³cade \"\ *adj* **1** *of an animal* **:** left by the mother and reared by hand **:** PET ⟨a ~ lamb⟩ **2 :** PETTED, INDULGED

⁴cade \"\ *n* -s [MF, fr. OProv, fr. ML *catanus*] **:** a European juniper (*Juniperus oxycedrus*) with angled branchlets, awl-shaped needles in alternate whorls of three, and a reddish brown berry

-cade \¦kād\ *n comb form* -s [¹*cavalcade*] **:** procession ⟨motor*cade*⟩ **:** spectacle ⟨aqua*cade*⟩

cadee *obs var of* CADET

ca·delle \kə'del\ *n* -s [F, fr. Prov *cadello,* fr. L *catella,* fem. of *catellus* little dog, whelp; akin to MHG *hatele* goat, ON *hathna* young she-goat, L *catulus* young of an animal, Russ *kotit' sya* to bear young] **:** the larva or adult of a small cosmopolitan black beetle (*Tenebroides mauritanicus*) destructive to stored grain and sometimes preying on other insects — compare GRAIN BEETLE

¹ca·dence \'kādᵊn(t)s\ *n* -s [ME, fr. OIt *cadenza,* fr. *cadere* to fall (fr. L) + *enza* -ence; in senses other than 1, prob. mostly fr. MF or F *cadence,* fr. OIt *cadenza* — more at CHANCE] **1 a :** a rhythmic sequence or flow of sounds in language; *specif* **:** a particular rhythmic sequence distinctive of an individual author or literary composition ⟨the grand ~ of his poetry⟩ **b :** the beat, time, measure, or sequence of any rhythmical motion or activity (as marching, dancing, rowing) **c :** a sequence of motions, colors, or events ⟨the ~ of glittering ripple and moving leaf—Richard Jefferies⟩ ⟨slower ~ of life—*Irish Digest*⟩ **2 a :** a falling inflection of the voice (as in reading or speaking (as at the end of a sentence) **b :** a concluding and usu. falling strain; *specif* **:** a musical chord sequence moving to a harmonic close or point of rest and giving a sense of partial or total harmonic completion **3 a :** the modulated and rhythmic recurrence of any sound, esp. the sounds of nature (as of waves or wind) **b :** the general or a characteristic rhythmic modulation of the voice ⟨the ~ of the countryman's speech⟩ **4 :** the characteristic unit of the harmonic structure of tonal music consisting of a musical progression from harmonic stability to suspension and back to stability **5 a :** the rising or falling order of strong, long, or stressed syllables and weak, short, or unstressed syllables ⟨ris-

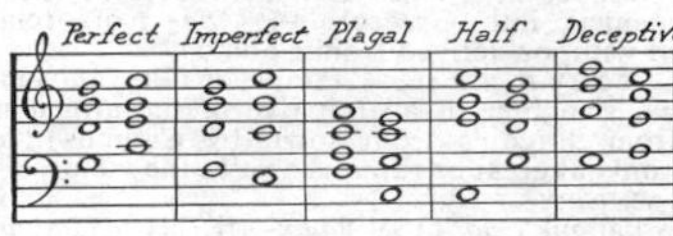

cadence 2b

ing ~⟩ ⟨iambic ~⟩ — compare ARSIS, IONIC, METER **b :** an unmetrical or irregular arrangement of stressed and unstressed syllables in prose or free verse based on natural stress groups **syn** see RHYTHM

²**cadence** \"\ *vt* -ED/-ING/-S **:** to put into cadence or rhythm

ca·denced \ˈkād³n(t)st\ *adj* **:** marked by cadence: RHYTHMICAL ⟨the ~ crunch of GI shoes on cinder —Alan Surgal⟩ ⟨in verse or ~ prose —John Gassner⟩

ca·den·cy \ˈkād³nsē, -i\ *n* -ES **1 :** CADENCE **2 a** (1) **:** the status of being a younger son or brother or of belonging to a younger branch of a family (2) **:** the status of being one (as an heir apparent or a cadet) whose proper coat of arms is a differenced version of that to which the head of the family is entitled **b :** the status of being a younger branch of a family

cadency mark *n* **:** an addition to a coat of arms to mark the position of the bearer with respect to a present or former head of the family — called also *mark of cadency*; compare DIFFERENCE; ANNULET, CRESCENT, CROSS MOLINE, DOUBLE QUATREFOIL, FLEUR-DE-LIS, LABEL, MARTLET, MULLET, ROSE; BORDURE

ca·dent \ˈkād³nt\ *adj* [L *cadent-, cadens,* pres. part. of *cadere* to fall — more at CHANCE] **1** *archaic* **:** FALLING **2 :** having rhythmic fall

ca·den·tial \kāˈdenchəl\ *adj* [fr. ¹*cadence,* after such pairs as E *essence: essential*] **:** of or relating to a cadence, esp. a concluding cadence

ca·den·za \kəˈdenzə\ *n* -S [It — more at CADENCE] **1 a :** a parenthetic flourish in the course of an aria or other solo piece commonly just before the final or other important cadence **b :** a technically brilliant sometimes improvised solo passage toward the close of a concerto in which the main themes of the preceding movement are given further development **2 :** an episodic departure from the main theme of a larger musical work

cade oil *n* [⁴*cade*] **:** a dark thick oily liquid that has a tar odor and is obtained by destructive distillation of the wood of the cade and used locally in skin diseases — called also *juniper-tar oil*

cades *pl of* CADE

-cades *pl of* -CADE

¹**ca·det** \kəˈdet, *usu* -ded·+V, *West Point slang* ˈkā,d-\ *n* -S *often attrib* [F, fr. F dial. (Gascon) *capdet* chief, captain, fr. LL *capitellum* small head, dim. of L *capit-, caput* head — more at HEAD] **1 a :** a younger brother or son **b :** the youngest son **c :** a younger branch of a family ⟨a ~ of a royal line⟩ **d :** a member of such a younger branch **2 a :** a gentleman who enlisted in a military regiment for the purpose of acquiring military skill and eventually a commission **b :** one in training for military or naval service as a commissioned officer in the armed forces; *specif* **:** a pupil in a national military school **c :** a trainee working to gain a merchant-marine license (as for third mate) **d :** a member of the armed forces assigned as a student in a special-service school to train for a commission ⟨an aviation ~⟩ **e :** a student in a private military academy **f :** one undergoing training for officership in the Salvation Army **3 a :** a junior in a business or occupation who is engaged principally in learning ⟨entered the civil service as a ~⟩ ⟨a ~ teacher⟩ **b** *Austral* **:** an apprentice on a sheep or cattle farm **4** *slang* **:** PIMP **5 :** a grayish blue that is redder and paler than electric, redder and duller than copenhagen, and less strong and very slightly redder than Gobelin

²**ca·det** \kəˈdet, *usu* -ded·+V\ *n* -S *usu cap* [Russ *Kadet,* by shortening & alter. (influenced by *kadet* young soldier) fr. *Konstitutsionno-Demokraticheskaya (Partiya)* Constitutional Democratic Party] **:** a member of the former Constitutional Democratic party of Russia

cadet blue *n* **1 :** a variable color averaging a grayish blue that is redder and paler than electric, greener and slightly paler than copenhagen, and redder, lighter, and stronger than Gobelin **2 :** a moderate blue that is redder and duller than average copen and redder and deeper than azurite blue or Dresden blue

cadet cloth *n* **:** a heavy firm bluish gray woolen fabric often used for uniforms in military schools

cadet gray *n* **:** a variable color averaging a pale blue that is redder and duller than average powder blue, redder, less strong, and slightly darker than Sistine, and redder and deeper than old blue

ca·det·ship \-,ship\ *n* -S **:** the position, rank, or commission of a cadet

¹**cadge** \ˈkaj, -aa(ə)j\ *vb* -ED/-ING/-S [back-formation fr. *cadger*] *vt* **1** *dial Brit* **:** CARRY ⟨~ a burden⟩ **2 :** to get by begging esp. habitually or as a means of livelihood **:** SPONGE ⟨*cadging* dimes from passers-by⟩ ⟨~ a meal from a chance acquaintance⟩ ~ *vi* **:** to cadge food or money **:** SPONGE ⟨no men loitering around the hotels from whom he could ~ —J.A. Lee⟩ ⟨you have *cadged* on me for your keep —F.M.Ford⟩ ⟨a footsore tramp *cadging* for a meal⟩

²**cadge** \"\ *n* -S [prob. alter. of *cage*] **:** a wooden frame on which live hawks are carried

cadg·er \ˈkajə(r), -aaj-\ *n* -S [ME *cadgear,* fr. *caggen, cagen* to tie + *-ear, -er* -er; perh. fr. the hitching of the horse used for transporting wares] **1** *chiefly Scot* **:** CARRIER; *esp* **:** a dealer who takes dairy produce to the towns and town wares to the country **2** *chiefly Scot* **:** an itinerant huckster or street seller **3 :** one that cadges ⟨a most celebrated ~ of drinks —Allan Temko⟩ **4** [²*cadge* + *-er*] **:** one that carries hawks on a cadge

cadg·i·ly \-jəlē, -i\ *adv, dial* **:** in a cadgy manner

cadgy \ˈkajē, -aaj-, -i\ *adj* [origin unknown] **1** *chiefly Scot* **:** CHEERFUL, MERRY **2** *dial* **:** sexually excited **:** in rut **:** AMOROUS

cadi *var of* QADI

cadie *var of* CADDIE

cad·i·nene \ˈkad³n,ēn\ *n* -S [ISV *cadin-* (fr. NL *cadinus* of cade, fr. F *cade* + L *-inus* -ine) + *-ene* — more at CADE] **:** an oily hydrocarbon $C_{15}H_{24}$ of the sesquiterpene class found as the chief constituent in cade oil and in many essential oils

cá·diz *or* **ca·diz** *also* **ca·diz** \kəˈdiz *also* kāˈdiz *or* kāˈdiz *or* -ˈdēz *or* ˈkādəz *or* ˈkādəz *or* ˈkadəz; *Sp* ˈkāthēth *or* -ēs\ *adj, usu cap* [fr. *Cádiz,* Spain] **:** of or from the city of Cádiz, Spain **:** of the kind or style prevalent in Cádiz

cadj·an *also* **ca·jan** \ˈkajən, ,jän\ *or* **ca·jang** \-,jäŋ\ *n* -S [Malay *kajan*] **1 :** interwoven coco-palm leaves for thatching **2 :** a strip of fan-palm leaf (as of the talipot) used as writing material; *also* **:** a document written on a palm leaf

cad·me·an *or* **cad·mae·an** \(ˈ)kadˈmēən, ˈkad,m-\ *adj, usu cap* [L *Cadmeus* (fr. Gk. *Kadmeios,* fr. *Kadmos* Cadmus, mythical founder of Thebes and introducer of the alphabet from Phoenicia into Greece) +E *-an*] **:** of, relating to, associated with, or derived from Cadmus

cadmean victory *n, usu cap C* [trans. of Gk *Kadmeia nikē;* fr. the mutual slaughter of all but five of the armed men who sprang from dragon's teeth sown by Cadmus] **:** a victory obtained only at great or ruinous cost to the victor — compare PYRRHIC VICTORY

cad·mic \ˈkadmik\ *adj* [ISV *cadm-* (fr. NL *cadmium*) + *-ic;* orig. formed as F *cadmique*] **:** of, relating to, or derived from cadmium

cad·mif·er·ous \(ˈ)kadˈmif(ə)rəs\ *adj* [ISV *cadmi-* (fr. NL *cadmium*) + *-ferous*] **:** containing cadmium

cad·mi·um \ˈkadmēəm\ *n* -S [NL, fr. L *cadmia* calamine (fr. Gk *kadmeia,* fr. fem. of *Kadmeios* Cadmean) + NL *-ium;* fr. the occurrence of its ores together with calamine] **:** a tin-white malleable ductile toxic bivalent metallic element capable of a high polish and emitting a crackling sound when bent, occurring in greenockite and also in small amounts in ores of zinc from which it is separated as a by-product, and used chiefly in the protective electroplating of iron and steel and in the manufacture of bearing metals — symbol *Cd;* see ELEMENT table

cadmium blende *n* **:** GREENOCKITE

cadmium carmine *n* **:** GOYA

cadmium cell *n* **:** a Weston cell

cadmium green *n* **:** a strong green that is bluer and paler than primitive green and bluer, lighter, and stronger than mintleaf —called also *Empire*

cadmium lamp *n* **:** a vapor lamp in which the fluorescence of cadmium vapor produces red light whose wavelength taken as 6438.4696 international angstroms is used as a standard of length

cadmium lemon *n* **:** a brilliant to vivid greenish yellow — called also *Mutrie yellow*

cadmium lithopone *n* **:** a pigment analogous to lithopone consisting essentially of cadmium yellow or cadmium red and containing barium sulfate — called also *cadmopone*

cadmium ocher *n* **:** GREENOCKITE

cadmium orange *n* **1 :** an orange-hued cadmium-yellow pigment **2 :** a strong orange that is yellower, lighter, and stronger than pumpkin, redder, stronger, and slightly darker than cadmium yellow, and yellower, lighter, and stronger than mandarin orange — called also *marigold*

cadmium purple *n* **:** a moderate to deep red that is slightly yellower than burnt carmine

cadmium red *n* **1 :** a pigment consisting of a mixture of cadmium sulfide, cadmium selenide, and often barium sulfate and varying in hue from light red to maroon **2 :** FRENCH VERMILION

cadmium sulfate *n* **:** a colorless salt $CdSO_4$ ordinarily crystallizing with 2⅔ molecules of water

cadmium sulfide *n* **:** a compound CdS occurring naturally as greenockite and obtained as a bright-yellow precipitate by the action of hydrogen sulfide on solutions of cadmium salts — see CADMIUM YELLOW

cadmium vermilion *n* **:** BLOOD RED

cadmium yellow *n* **1 :** a pigment consisting of cadmium sulfide and barium sulfate with or without zinc sulfide and varying in hue from lemon yellow to orange — called also in its orange hues *cadmium orange* **2 :** a strong orange that is yellower and paler than pumpkin, yellower, less strong, and slightly lighter than cadmium orange, and yellower and paler than mandarin orange — called also *aurora yellow, daffodil yellow, nasturtium yellow, orient yellow, radiant yellow*

cad·mo·pone \ˈkadmə,pōn\ *n* -S [NL *cadmium* + *-o-* + *-pone* (as in *lithopone*)] **:** CADMIUM LITHOPONE

cad·re \ˈkadrē *also* -ˈä- *or* -ˈā- *or* -(,)drā *or* -,drə; *Brit often* ˈkādrᵊ *or* -də\ *n* -S [F, fr. It *quadro,* fr. L *quadrum* square — more at QUARREL] **1 :** FRAME, FRAMEWORK **:** SCHEME **:** skeletal organization ⟨the current specialisms and ~s of our university curricula —H.M.McLuhan⟩ **2 a :** a nucleus or core group esp. of trained personnel or active members of an organization who are capable of assuming leadership or of training and indoctrinating others ⟨a highly skilled ~ of technicians and workers —*Economist*⟩ ⟨only a ~ of maintenance men worked here in the winter —T.W.Duncan⟩ ⟨the permanent ~ of the Indian Civil Service —H.N.Brailsford⟩: as (1) **:** a group of key officers and enlisted men assigned to a new unit as a nucleus for its formation, administration, and training (2) [prob. fr. Russ *kadr,* fr. F *cadre*] **:** a cell of indoctrinated leaders active in promoting the interests of a revolutionary party ⟨a ~ of dedicated men ready to initiate any violence the party demanded⟩ **b** [prob. fr. Russ *kadr,* fr. F *cadre*] **:** a member of a cadre, esp. a political cadre ⟨do not want a conflict . . . before their own ~s are already —*New Republic*⟩

cad·re·man \-mən,-,man,-,maa(ə)n\ *n, pl* **cadremen :** a member of a military cadre

cads *pl of* CAD

ca·du·ca·ry \kəˈd(y)ükərē\ *or* **ca·du·ci·ary** \-üs(h)ē,erē, -üshərē\ *adj* [L *caducarius,* fr. *caducus* caducous + *-arius* -ary] **:** relating to or transferred by escheat, lapse, or forfeiture

ca·du·ce·an \kəˈd(y)üsēən, -üshən\ *adj* [*caduceus* + *-an*] **:** of or relating to a caduceus

ca·du·ce·us \kəˈd(y)üs(h)ēəs\ *n, pl* **ca·du·cei** \-s(h)ē,ī\ [L *caduceus, caduceum,* modif. of Gk (Dor) *karykeion* (Attic *kērykeion*) herald's staff, fr. *karyx* (Attic *kēryx*) herald; akin to OE *hrēth* glory, OHG *hruod-,* ON *hrōthr* praise, Goth *hrotheigs* triumphant, Skt *carkṛti* praise] **1 :** the symbolic staff of a herald; *specif* **:** a conventionalized representation of a staff with two snakes curled around it and with two wings at the top **2 :** an insignia consisting of or bearing a caduceus: as **a :** one of the symbols of a physician — compare STAFF OF AESCULAPIUS **b :** the emblem of a medical corps or department of the armed services (as of the U.S. Army)

caduceus 1

ca·du·ci·ary \kəˈd(y)üs(h)ē,erē, -üshərē\ *n* -ES [modif. (influenced by E *fiduciary*) of L *caducarius* — more at CADUCARY] **:** a caducary estate or subject of property

ca·du·ci·branch \kəˈd(y)üsə,braŋk\ *adj* [NL *Caducibranchiata*] **:** of or relating to the Caducibranchiata

ca·du·ci·bran·chi·a·ta \kə¦d(y)üsə,braŋkēˈäd·ə, -ˈād·ə\ *n pl, cap* [NL, fr. *caduci-* (fr. L *caducus* falling) + L *branchiae* gills + NL *-ata;* akin to Gk *bronchos* throat — more at CRAW] **1** *in former classifications* **:** a division of tailed amphibians whose gills are lost in adult life **2 :** THALIACEA

ca·du·ci·bran·chi·ate \¦⸗⸗⸗ˈbraŋkēət, -ē,āt\ *adj* [NL *Caducibranchiata*] **:** CADUCIBRANCH

ca·du·ci·corn \kəˈd(y)üsə,kȯrn\ *adj* [*caduci-* (fr. L *caducus* falling) + *-corn*] **:** having deciduous horns ⟨~ deer⟩

ca·du·ci·ty \kəˈd(y)üsəd·ē\ *n* -ES [F *caducité,* fr. *caduc* falling, decrepit (fr. L *caducus*) + F *-ité* -ity] **1 :** PERISHABLENESS, TRANSITORINESS **2 a :** feebleness from age **:** SENILITY **b :** old age ⟨the housebound old man...in his peaceable ~ —Christopher Morley⟩ **3 :** LAPSE ⟨the ~ of a legacy⟩ ⟨the ~ of a treaty may also be declared when...the causes which originated it have disappeared —*Havana Convention on Treaties*⟩

ca·du·cous \kəˈd(y)ükəs\ *adj* [L *caducus* falling, inclined to fall, fr. *cadere* to fall — more at CHANCE] **1 :** falling off easily or before the usual time — used esp. of floral organs and opposed to *persistent* ⟨the ~ calyx of a poppy⟩; compare DECIDUOUS, FUGACIOUS **2** *law* **:** subject to caducity **:** LAPSED

ca·du·veo \,kädüˈvā(,)ō\ *n* -S *usu cap* [Sp or Pg, of AmerInd origin] **:** GUAICURU

cad·wal·a·der·ite \kadˈwäləd·ə,rīt\ *n* -S [Charles B.M. *Cadwalader* b1885 Am. mineralogist + E *-ite*] **:** a mineral $Al(OH)_2Cl{\cdot}4H_2O$ consisting of a hydrous basic aluminum chloride

cady *var of* KADY

cae- *or* **caeci-** *or* **caeco-** — see CEC-

caecal *var of* CECAL

cae·ci·dae \ˈsēsə,dē, -ēkə-\ *n pl, cap* [NL, fr. *Caecum,* type genus (fr. L, neut. of *caecus* blind) + *-idae* — more at CAECUM] **:** a family of minute marine gastropod mollusks (order Pectinibranchia) having the shells initially spiral but ultimately cylindrical and comprising the blind shells

¹**cae·cil·i·an** *or* **coe·cil·i·an** \sēˈsilyən, sə-, -ˈsēl-, -lēən\ *adj* [NL *Caecilia* + E *-an*] **:** of or relating to the Caeciliidae

²**caecilian** *or* **coecilian** \"\ *n* -S **:** an amphibian of the family Caeciliidae

cae·ci·li·idae \,sēsəˈlīə,dē\ *n pl, cap* [NL, fr. *Caecilia,* type genus (fr. L *caecilia,* a lizard, fr. *caecus* blind) + *-idae;* fr. the small eyes — more at CAECUM] **:** a family (type genus *Caecilia*) of small slender wormlike burrowing amphibians that is coextensive with the order Gymnophiona

caecum *var of* CECUM

caed·mo·nian \(ˈ)kadˈmōnēən\ *also* **caed·mon·ic** \-mänik\ *adj, usu cap* [*Caedmon fl* A.D.670 English Christian poet + E *-an* or *-ic*] **:** of or relating to the poet Caedmon

¹**caen-** *or* **caeno-** — see ¹CEN-

²**caen-** *or* **caeno-** — see COEN-

cae·nag·nath·i·for·mes \,sē,nag,nathəˈfȯr,mēz, ¦kī,n-\ *n pl, cap* [NL, fr. ¹*caen-* + *agnath-* (fr. *a-* ²a- + Gk *gnathos* jaw) + *-iformes* — more at GNATH-] **:** an order of Canadian Cretaceous birds (Neognathae) known from a single immense jaw and believed to be related to the ostriches though in some respects the jaw resembles that of a toothless dinosaur

caenobium *var of* COENOBIUM

caenogenesis *var of* CENOGENESIS

cae·no·les·tes \,sēnəˈle(,)stēz, ,kīn-\ *n, cap* [NL, fr. ¹*caen-* + Gk *lēistēs* robber; akin to L *lucrum* gain — more at LUCRE] **:** a genus (the type of the family Caenolestidae) of small carnivorous diprotodont marsupials comprising the opossum rats

¹**cae·no·les·tid** \¦⸗⸗ˈlestəd\ *adj* [NL *Caenolestidae*] **:** of or relating to the Caenolestidae

²**caenolestid** \"\ *n* -S **:** a member of the Caenolestidae

cae·no·les·ti·dae \,⸗⸗ˈlestə,dē\ *n pl, cap* [NL, fr. *Caenolestes,* type genus + *-idae*] **:** a family of diprotodont marsupials that includes all recent diprotodonts occurring outside the Australian region and many extinct related forms — see CAENOLESTES

cae·no·les·toi·dea \,⸗nə(,)leˈstȯidēə\ *n pl, cap* [NL, fr. *Caenolestes,* type genus + *-oidea*] **:** a superfamily of diprotodont marsupials comprising the opossum rats and extinct related forms

cae·no·pi·the·cus \,sēnōpəˈthēkəs, ,kīn-, -ōˈpithikəs\ *n, cap* [NL, fr. ¹*caen-* + *-pithecus*] **:** a genus of primates (family Adapidae) of the Eocene of Switzerland in some respects intermediate between tarsioids and the higher primates

cae·no·sty·lic \¦⸗nə¦stīlik\ *adj* [¹*caen-* + *-stylic*] **:** having the first two visceral arches without gills but attached to the cranium and serving in taking food — used of sharks, chimaeras, and amphibians — **cae·no·sty·ly** \ˈ⸗⸗,stīlē\ *n* -ES

caenozoic *usu cap, var of* CENOZOIC

caenozoology *var of* CENOZOOLOGY

caen stone \ˈkäⁿ-, ˈkān-\ *n, usu cap C* [*Caen,* city in Normandy, France, near which it is found] **1 :** a yellowish limestone marked with a rippled figure **2 :** FREESTONE 3

cae·o·ma \sēˈōmə, kī-\ *n* [NL, irreg. fr. Gk *kaiein* to burn; fr. its fiery red color — more at CAUSTIC] **1** *cap* **:** a form genus of rust fungi that produce an aecium having no peridium **2** -S **:** an aecium without a peridium

caer·nar·von·shire \kärˈnärvən,shi(ə)r, kə(r)ˈnärv-, -,shər\ *or* **caernarvon** *adj, usu cap* [fr. *Caernarvonshire* or county of *Caernarvon,* Wales] **:** of or from the county of Caernarvon, Wales **:** of the kind or style prevalent in Caernarvon

caerulean *var of* CERULEAN

caes·al·pin·ia \,se,zalˈpinēə, ,sē-\ *n, cap* [NL, fr. Andrea Cesalpino (Andreas *Caesalpinus*) †1603 Ital. botanist + NL *-ia*] **:** a genus of usu. small spiny tropical trees (family Leguminosae) having evenly bipinnate leaves and small whitish-green, yellow, or reddish flowers in showy racemes — see BRAZILWOOD

caes·al·pin·i·a·ce·ae \-,pinēˈāsē,ē\ *n pl, cap* [NL, fr. *Caesalpinia,* type genus + *-aceae*] *in some classifications* **:** a large family of chiefly tropical shrubs and trees having a regular or slightly irregular corolla, the petals imbricated in the bud, and the fruit a legume, important genera being *Caesalpinia, Cassia, Bauhinia, Tamarindus,* and *Copaifera* — **caes·al·pin·i·a·ceous** \-ˈāshəs\ *adj*

cae·sar \ˈsēzə(r)\ *n* -S [after Gaius Julius *Caesar* †44 B.C. Roman general and statesman] **1** *often cap* **:** a Roman emperor succeeding Augustus Caesar **2 a** *often cap* **:** a powerful ruler **:** EMPEROR **:** AUTOCRAT, DICTATOR ⟨there were ~s before Caesar —H.D.Scott⟩ ⟨no tyrant of history, neither khan nor ~ nor czar —*Time*⟩ **b** *usu cap* [so called fr. the reference in Mt 22:21 (RSV)] **:** the civil power **:** a temporal ruler ⟨a dual loyalty — a loyalty to *Caesar* and a loyalty to God —J.H. Hallowell⟩ **3 :** TOMTATE

¹**cae·sar·e·an** *or* **cae·sar·i·an** \sēˈza(a)rēən, -zer-,-zär-\ *adj, usu cap* [L *caesareus, caesarianus,* fr. *Caesar*] **:** of or relating to Julius or Augustus Caesar or to one of the Caesars who succeeded Augustus Caesar as Roman emperor

²**caesarean** *or* **caesarian** *often cap, var of* CESAREAN

cae·sar·ism \ˈsēzə,rizəm\ *n* -S *usu cap* **:** imperial authority or system **:** political absolutism **:** DICTATORSHIP ⟨he feared the coming of *Caesarism* and of military autocracy —Ernest Barker⟩

cae·sar·ist \-,rəst\ *n* -S *usu cap* **:** an advocate of or adherent to Caesarism

cae·sa·ro·pa·pism \¦sēzə(,)rōˈpā,pizəm\ *n* -S *often cap* [*caesar* + *-o-* + LL *papa* pope + E *-ism* — more at POPE] **1 :** exercise of supreme authority over ecclesiastical matters by a secular ruler **2 :** government in which the church is subordinate to the state or a secular ruler — compare BYZANTINISM, ERASTIANISM

caesar's agaric *or* **caesar's mushroom** *n, usu cap C* [after Gaius Julius *Caesar* — more at CAESAR] **:** ROYAL AGARIC

caesar substitution *also* **caesar shift** *n, usu cap C, cryptography* **:** the replacement of each letter in a text by the one at a certain constant distance in the alphabet, esp. a normal alphabet — compare JULIUS CAESAR CIPHER

caesar weed *n, usu cap C* **:** a tropical shrub (*Urena lobata*) valued for its strong bast fiber

cae·si·ous \ˈsēzēəs, ˈkī-\ *adj* [L *caesius;* prob. akin to L *caelum* sky — more at CELESTIAL] **:** having a blue color very low in chroma

caesium *var of* CESIUM

cae·spi·tose *also* **ces·pi·tose** \ˈsespə,tōs\ *adj* [NL *caespitosus,* fr. L *caespit-, caespes* turf + *-osus* -ose] **:** arranged or combined in a thick mat or clumps **:** TUFTED: as **a :** having low stems forming a dense turf or sod **b :** growing in clusters ⟨the ~ spore fruits of some fungi⟩

caestus *var of* CESTUS

cae·su·ra *also* **ce·su·ra** \səˈz(h)ürə, sə̇, |ü- *also* |zˈy|\ *n, pl* **caesuras** \-rəz\ *or* **caesu·rae** \-(,)rē\ [L, cutting off, fr. *caedere* to cut — more at CONCISE] **1** *in Greek and Latin prosody* **a :** a break in the flow of sound in a verse caused by the ending of a word within a foot (arma vi|rumque ca|no|| Tro|jae qui| primus ab|oris) — symbol ||; usu. distinguished from *diaeresis;* see HEPHTHEMIMERAL CAESURA, PENTHEMIMERAL CAESURA, TRITHEMIMERAL CAESURA **b** *obs* **:** a lengthening of the last syllable of a word by the break in the verse **c :** DIAERESIS — see BUCOLIC CAESURA **2** *in modern prosody* **:** a break in the flow of sound in a line of verse occasioned usu. by a rhetorical pause and occurring usu. at about the middle of the verse (of man's | first dis|obe|dience || and | the fruit) — see EPIC CAESURA, FEMININE CAESURA, MASCULINE CAESURA **3 :** STOP, BREAK, INTERRUPTION ⟨the ~ between vol. I and vol. II —Erich Dinkler⟩ ⟨it was a ~, a pause between the last classes and the afternoon exercises —Nathaniel Burt⟩ ⟨the trenchant ~ which occurs between the apprehension of data and the judgment —Mary W. Hess⟩ **4 :** a pause marking a rhythmic point of division in a melody

cae·su·ral \-rəl\ *adj* **:** of or relating to a caesura

caeteris paribus *var of* CETERIS PARIBUS

CAF *abbr, often not cap* **1** clerical, administrative, and fiscal **2** cost and freight **3** cost, assurance, and freight

ca·fard \kăfär\ *n* -S [F, lit., cockroach, fr. MF, cockroach, hypocrite, modif. of Ar *kāfir* infidel — more at KAFFIR] **:** severe depression or apathy — used esp. of white men in the tropics

ca·fé *also* **ca·fe** \(ˈ)ka¦fā, kəˈfā\ *n* -S *often attrib* [F *café,* fr. Turk *kahve* — more at COFFEE] **1 a :** a room for coffee and light refreshments **:** COFFEEHOUSE ⟨they went into the ~ for a cup or two of something hot —Richard Llewellyn⟩ **b :** COFFEE **2 a :** RESTAURANT ⟨enjoy your dinner in a hotel dining room or ~ —Helen E.Stiles⟩ ⟨the dining room was not yet open, but he knew that there were several all-night ~s near the station —Hamilton Basso⟩ ⟨glass windows of a . . . ~ full of sugary cakes —Barbara Beecher⟩ **b :** an open-air eating place often partly on the sidewalk ⟨sat at the table in front of the big ~ —R.H.Newman⟩ ⟨a ~ with tables in the street . . . surrounded by a shallow fence of dark-green creeper —William Sansom⟩ **3 :** BARROOM, SALOON ⟨speakeasies, some of which have survived as legitimate saloons, nightclubs, or ~s —D.W.Maurer⟩ **4 :** CABARET, NIGHTCLUB

ca·fé au kirsch \¦ka,fā(,)ōˈki(ə)rsh\ *n, pl* **cafés au kirsch** \¦ka,fā(,)zō-\ [F, coffee with kirschwasser] **:** a drink consisting of black coffee, kirschwasser, white of egg, and sugar shaken with cracked ice and strained before serving

ca·fé au lait \¦ka,fā(,)ōˈlā\ *n, pl* **cafés au lait** \¦ka,fā(,)zō-\ [F, coffee with milk] **1 :** coffee with esp. hot milk in about equal portions **2 :** the color of coffee with milk **:** ALESAN

ca·fé brû·lot \¦ka,fā,brüˈlō\ *n, pl* **café brûlots** \-lōz\ [AmerF (La.), lit., burned-brandy coffee] **:** a drink prepared with black coffee, cognac that is ignited and allowed to burn briefly, sweetening, and flavoring (as lemon peel, cloves, cinnamon, vanilla)

ca·fe car \kaˈfā-, kə-\ *n* **:** a railroad passenger car having a kitchen, usu. in the center, and one end equipped to serve meals or beverages, the other end being fitted for other uses (as coach, lounge, parlor, smoking room)

ca·fé chan·tant \kăfāshäⁿtäⁿ\ *n, pl* **café chantants** *or* **cafés chantants** \"\ [F, lit., singing café] **:** a café where singers or musicians entertain the patrons **:** CABARET

ca·fé con·cert \kăfākōⁿseer\ *n, pl* **café concerts** \"\ [F, lit., concert café] **:** a café offering a program of light music

ca·fé crème \¦ka,fāˈkrem\ *n, pl* **café crèmes** \-mz\ [F, coffee with cream] **:** SUEDE 3

ca·fe curtain \ka'fā-, kə-\ *n* **:** a plain straight-hanging curtain usu. hung in pairs on a pole by loops or rings and used to cover the lower part of a window or door

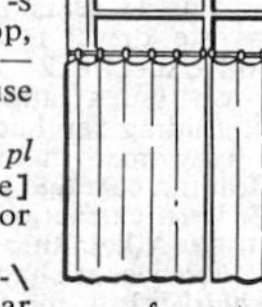

cafe curtains

ca·fe·neh *or* **ca·fe·net** \'kafə,nā\ *n* -s [Turk *kahvane, kahvehane* coffee shop, café, fr. *kahve* coffee + *hane* house — more at COFFEE] **:** a Turkish coffeehouse or inn

ca·fé noir \'ka,fān(ə)'wär, -ár\ *n, pl* **cafés noirs** \"\ [F, black coffee] **1 :** black coffee **:** coffee without milk or cream; *also* **:** DEMITASSE **2 :** MUSK 4

ca·fé society \'ka,fā- *also* ka'fā *or* kə-\ *n* **:** society of persons who are regular patrons of fashionable cafés

ca·fe·tal \,kafə'täl\ *n, pl* **cafeta·les** \-ä(,)lās\ [Sp, fr. *café* coffee, fr. F & It; F, fr. It *caffè* — more at COFFEE] **:** a Spanish-American coffee plantation

caf·e·te·ria \,kafə'tirēə, -ēr-\ *n* -s *often attrib* [AmerSp *cafetería* retail coffee store, fr. Sp *café* coffee] **1 :** a self-service restaurant or lunchroom **2 :** a feeding regime for domestic animals in which varied foodstuffs are kept before them at all times **:** FREE-CHOICE FEEDING **3 :** something so arranged and presented that one can freely make his own choice of individual items ⟨an educational ~⟩ ⟨a ~ questionnaire⟩

cafeteria car *n* **:** a railroad passenger car having facilities for preparing and serving food or beverages cafeteria style

caf·e·to·ri·um \,kafə'tōrēəm\ *n* -s [blend of *cafeteria* and *auditorium*] **:** a large room (as in a school building) designed for use both as a cafeteria and an auditorium

caff \'kaf, 'käf\ *n* -s [ME, fr. OE *ceaf* — more at CHAFF] *dial Brit* **:** ¹CHAFF

caf·fa \'kafə\ *n* -s [Ar dial. *kaffa, kaffiyah* (literary Ar *kūfīyah*), fr. al-*Kufah* Al Kufa, town in Iraq where it was made] **1 :** a rich silk cloth with printed or woven designs popular in the 16th century **2 :** a painted cotton cloth formerly made in India

caf·fè \kä'fā\ *n* -s [It — more at COFFEE] **:** CAFÉ

caf·fe·ate \'kafē,āt\ *n* -s [ISV *caffeic* + *-ate;* prob. orig. formed as F *caféate*] **:** a salt or ester of caffeic acid

caf·fe·ic acid \(')ka¦fēik-, -fē-ēk-\ *n* [*caffeic* ISV *caffe-* (fr. F *café* coffee) + *-ic*] **:** a yellow crystalline acid $C_6H_3(OH)_2$-CH=CHCOOH obtained by hydrolysis of chlorogenic acid; 3,4-dihydroxy-cinnamic acid

caf·feine \(')ka¦fēn *also* 'kafēən\ *also* **caf·fei·na** \ka'fēnə; ,kafē'ēnə, -'ī-\ *n* -s [G *kaffein* (now usu. *koffein*, after NL *coffea*), fr. *kaffee* coffee (fr. F *café*) + *-in* -ine — more at CAFÉ] **:** a feebly basic bitter crystalline compound $C_8H_{10}N_4O_2$ that occurs in coffee, tea, maté, guarana, and kola nuts, is synthesized by methylation of theobromine, and acts as a stimulant of the central nervous system and as a diuretic; 1,3,7-trimethyl-xanthine

caffeine citrate *n* **:** CITRATED CAFFEINE

caf·fein·ic \(')ka¦fēnik, ¦kafē¦inik\ *adj* **:** of or containing caffeine

caf·fe·ol \'kafē,ōl, -ōl\ *also* **caf·fe·one** \-ē,ōn\ *n* -s [G *kaffeol*, fr. *kaffee* coffee + *-ol*] **:** a fragrant oil produced by roasting coffee

caffer *or* **caffre** *usu cap, var of* KAFFIR

caf·fe·tan·nin \¦kafə¦tanən, -fē-\ *or* **caf·fe·tan·nic acid** \-anik-\ *n* -s [*caffetannin* fr. *caffeic* + *tannin; caffetannic* fr. *caffetannin* + *-ic*] **:** a crystalline substance obtained from coffee berries and other plant products and consisting chiefly of chlorogenic acid

caf·fle \'kafəl\ *vi* -ED/-ING/-s [alter. of ¹*cavil*] *dial Eng* **:** WRANGLE, ARGUE

caffre cat *or* **caffer cat** *usu cap 1st C, var of* KAFFIR CAT

ca·fi·la \'kafələ, 'kä-\ *n* -s [Ar *qāfilah*] **:** a company of travelers esp. in Arabia, Iran, or the Indian subcontinent

caf·tan \'kaftən, -,tan, kaf'tan\ *n* -s [Russ *kaftan*, fr. Turk, fr. Per *qaftān*] **:** an ankle-length coatlike garment, usu. of cotton or silk, often striped, with very long sleeves and a sash fastening, common throughout the Levant

ca·fu·so \kə'fü(,)zō\ *n* -s [Pg, perh. of African origin; akin to Hausa *ka³fur³chi¹* heathenism, *,ka³fu¹ri²* heathen] *in Brazil* **:** ZAMBO

¹**cag** \'kag, -aa(ə)-,-ai-\ *dial var of* KEG 1

²**cag** \"\ *vt* **cagged; cagged; cagging; cags** [origin unknown] *dial Eng* **:** OFFEND, INSULT

cá·ga·ba \'kägəbə\ *n, pl* **cágaba** *or* **cágabas** *usu cap* [Sp, of AmerInd origin] **1 a :** a Chibcha people of northern Colombia **b :** a member of such people **2 :** the language of the Cágaba people

ca·ga·yan \,kägə¦yän, -gē¦än\ *n, pl* **cagayan** *or* **cagayans** *usu cap* [Sp *cagayán*, fr. Río Grande del *Cagayán*, river in northern Luzon, Philippines, on the banks of which they reside] **:** IBANAG

¹**cage** \'kāj\ *n* -s [ME, fr. OF, fr. L *cavea* cavity, cage, fr. *cavus* hollow — more at CAVE] **1 :** a box or enclosure having some openwork (as of wires or bars) esp. for confining or carrying birds or animals **2 a :** a barred cell for confining prisoners **b :** a strongly fenced area for prisoners of war **3 :** a framework serving as support ⟨the ~ of a staircase⟩ ⟨the steel ~ of a skyscraper⟩ ⟨the ~ of a field gun⟩ **4 :** a small enclosing or sheltering structure designed (as by the use of openwork, glass, or windows) to admit air or light or to allow visibility or accessibility from outside ⟨bank teller's ~⟩: as **a :** the car of an elevator **b :** a chapel or chantry in a church formed by partitioning off a section with a screen of open tracery **5 :** a drum on which the rope is wound in a hoisting whim **6 :** an enclosing or containing screen or strainer: as **a :** a wirework strainer on an intake pipe **b :** a wire shield enclosing electrical apparatus **c :** a revolving drum of wire netting for shaking dust out of furs or cotton **7 a :** a frame to limit the motion of a loose part (as of a ball valve) **b :** the frame for holding bearings in place around a shaft journal — see ROLLER BEARING illustration **8 :** CADGE **9 a :** a movable screen placed behind home plate to stop baseballs during batting practice **b :** a goal structure consisting of goalposts or a goal frame with a net attached (as in ice hockey) **c :** a basketball basket **10 :** a large building with unobstructed area for practicing outdoor sports and often adapted for indoor events — compare FIELD HOUSE

²**cage** \"\ *vt* -ED/-ING/-s **1 :** to place in a cage **:** confine, shut in, keep in or as if in a cage **:** enclose in or with a strong structure to prevent escape ⟨~ circus animals⟩ ⟨*caged* birds⟩ **2 :** to put (as a puck) into a cage and score a goal **3 :** to inactivate (a gyroscopic instrument) esp. in an airplane (as by means of a control knob) **syn** see ENCLOSE

cage antenna *n* **:** an antenna whose conductor consists of parallel wires stretched between two hoops and arranged as elements of the curved surface of a cylinder

cage bird *n* **:** a bird adaptable to being kept in a cage

cage construction *n* **:** SKELETON CONSTRUCTION

caged *adj* **1 :** confined in or as if in a cage **2 :** like a cage or prison ⟨the ~ cloister —Shak.⟩

cage·ful \'kāj,fu̇l\ *n* -s **:** the number held in a cage

cage·less \-jləs\ *adj* **:** being without a cage

cage·ling \'kājliŋ, -ēŋ\ *n* -s [*cage* + *-ling*] **:** a caged bird

cage·man \'kājmən, -,man, -,aa(ə)n\ *n, pl* **cagemen 1 :** CAGER 1a **2 :** HOISTMAN **3 :** a basketball player

cage mast *n* **:** BASKET MAST

cag·er \'kājə(r)\ *n* -s [¹*cage* + *-er*] **1 a :** a workman who loads and unloads cages and gives hoisting signals — called also *cageman, cage tender, onsetter, skip tender* **b :** a mechanical apparatus for pushing cars on or off a cage **2 :** a basketball player

cage tender *n* **:** CAGER 1a

cagework \'ₛ,ₛ\ *n* **:** OPENWORK

¹**ca·gey** *also* **ca·gy** \'kājē, -i\ *adj* **cagier; cagiest** [origin unknown] **1 :** reluctant to act or speak in a direct or open manner **:** hesitant about committing oneself ⟨the speaker was ~ about giving a ruling —B.A.Young⟩ **2 :** wary of being taken advantage of or deceived ⟨a ~ buyer⟩ **:** SHREWD ⟨a ~ lawyer⟩ **:** FORESIGHTED — **ca·gey·ness** *or* **ca·gi·ness** *n* -ES

²**cagey** \"\ *dial var of* CADGY

cagged *past of* CAG

cagging *pres part of* CAG

ca·gi·ly \'kājəlē, -i\ *adv* **:** in a cagey manner

ca·glia·ri \'kälyərē\ *adj, usu cap* [fr. *Cagliari*, Sardinia, Italy] **:** of or from the city of Cagliari, Sardinia, Italy **:** of the style or kind prevalent in Cagliari

cag·mag \'kag,mag\ *n* -s [origin unknown] **1** *dial Eng* **:** inferior meat **2** *dial Eng* **:** something inferior

ca·gou·lard \¦kagü¦lär\ *n, pl* **cagoulards** \-är(z)\ *usu cap* [F, fr. *cagoule* hood, cowl (fr. LL *cuculla* monk's cowl) + *-ard* — more at COWL] **:** a member of a secret reactionary revolutionary French organization suppressed in 1937-38

cags *pl of* CAG, *pres 3d sing of* CAG

ca·hens·ly·ism \kə'henzlē,izəm, -n(t)sl-\ *n* -s *usu cap* [Peter P. *Cahensly fl* 1891 Ger. parliamentarian who proposed the plan + E *-ism*] **:** a movement to divide the foreign-born Roman Catholic population of the U.S. for ecclesiastical purposes according to European nationalities and to appoint bishops and priests of the same national origin and language as the majority of the members of a diocese or parish

ca·hier \ka'yā, kä-,kä-\ *n* -s [F, signature (section of a bound book), written statement presented to the sovereign by a representative body of the state, fr. L *quaterni* four each, by fours — more at QUIRE] **1 :** a report or memorial embodying resolutions or instructions concerning policy esp. of a parliamentary body; *specif* **:** one of the memorials prepared by the French States-General before the revolution of 1789 **2 :** a number of sheets of paper put together for binding or bound loosely together to form a notebook or pamphlet

ca·hin·ca root \kə'hiŋkə-\ *also* **ca·in·ca root** \kə'i-\ *n* [Pg *cahinca, cainca*, fr. Tupi] **1 :** the root of a tropical American shrub (*Chiococca alba*) used medicinally as a purgative and diuretic **2 :** the root of a So. American shrub (*Chiococca anguifuga*) used as an antidote for snake poison

ca·hin·nio \kə'hinē,ō\ *n, pl* **cahinnio** *or* **cahinnios** *usu cap* [Caddo] **1 :** a Caddoan people of the Kadohadacho confederacy **2 :** a member of the Cahinnio people

ca·hi·ta \kə'hēd·ə\ *n, pl* **cahita** *or* **cahitas** *usu cap* [Sp, prob. fr. *Cahita*, lit., nothing] **1 a :** a Taracahitian people of southwestern Sonora and northwestern Sinaloa, Mexico, the only survivors being the Mayo and Yaqui **b :** a member of such people **2 :** the language of the Cahita people

cahn·ite \'kä,nīt\ *n* -s [Lazard *Cahn* †1940 Am. mineral collector who first recognized it + E *-ite*] **:** a mineral $Ca_2B(OH)_4$-(AsO_4) consisting of hydrous calcium boroarsenate occurring in white sphenoidal crystals

ca·hoot \kə'hüt\ *n* -s [perh. fr. F *cahute* hut, cabin, modif. (prob. influenced by *cabane* hut, cabin) of *hutte* — more at CABIN, HUT] **1 :** PARTNERSHIP — usu. pl. ⟨in ~s with the devil⟩ ⟨go into ~s with someone⟩ **2 :** COLLUSION, CONNIVANCE **:** secret agreement — usu. pl. ⟨officials in ~s with the underworld⟩

ca·hot \kä(h)ō\ *n* -s [F] *chiefly Canad* **:** THANK-YOU-MA'AM

ca·houn palm \kə'hün-\ *n* [by alter.] **:** COHUNE

ca·how *or* **co·how** *or* **co·howe** \kə'hau̇\ *n* -s [imit.] **:** a brown-and-white earth-burrowing nocturnal edible petrel (*Pterodroma cahow*) formerly abundant in Bermuda but now nearly extinct

ca·hua·pa·na \,käwə'pänə\ *n, pl* **cahuapana** *or* **cahuapanas** *usu cap* [Sp *cahuapana, caguapana*, of AmerInd origin] **1 a :** a people of northern Peru **b :** a member of such people **2 :** the language of the Cahuapana people constituting with Chébero the Cahuapana language family

ca·hui·lla \kə'wēə\ *n, pl* **cahuilla** *or* **cahuillas** *usu cap* [Sp, of AmerInd origin] **1 a :** a Shoshonean people of southeastern California **b :** a member of such people **2 :** the language of the Cahuilla people

cai·a·ra·ra \,kīə'rärə\ *n* -s [Pg, fr. Tupi & Guarani, fr. *caí* monkey + *arára* macaw] **:** a large-headed arboreal monkey (*Cebus gracilis*) of the Amazon valley

ca·id *or* **qa·id** \kä'ēth, 'kīth\ *n* -s [Sp *caíd, caid*, fr. Ar *qā'id*] **1 :** ALCAIDE **2 a :** a Muslim local administrator, judge, and tax collector in Algeria, Morocco, and Tunisia **b :** a chief esp. of the Berber tribal communities of the Atlas region

cail·ce·dra \kīl'sēdrə, -'e-\ *n* -s [origin unknown] **:** an African mahogany (*Khaya senegalensis*)

cai·lin \(')kä¦lēn\ *Irish var of* COLLEEN

cail·leach *also* **cail·liach** \'käl,yək, 'käl,(y)əḵ\ *n* -s [ScGael & IrGael *cailleach*, fr. OIr *caillech* nun, fr. *caille* veil, fr. L *pallium* cloak — more at PALL] *Irish & Scot* **:** an old woman **:** CRONE, HAG

cai·man \kā'man, kī-, -maa(ə)n, 'ₛ,ₛ; 'kāmən\ *n* [Sp *caimán* caiman, alligator, prob. fr. 16th cent. Carib *caymán*] **1** *or* **cay·man** \"\ -s **:** any of several Central and So. American crocodilians fundamentally similar to alligators but differing in ventral armor and often superficially resembling crocodiles — called also *jacare;* see SPECTACLED CAIMAN **2** *cap* [NL, fr. Sp *caimán*] **:** a genus of crocodilians comprising most of the caimans

cai·mi·ti·llo \,kīmə'tē(,)(y)ō\ *n* -s [Sp, dim. of *caimito*] **:** a tropical American timber tree (*Chrysophyllum oliviforme*) with dark hard heavy wood — called also *satinleaf*

cai·mi·to \kī'mēd·(,)ō, -ē,tō\ *n* -s [Sp, fr. Taino *caymito*] **:** STAR APPLE

¹**cain** \'kān\ *n* -s *usu cap* [after *Cain*, the eldest son of Adam and the first murderer, described in Gen 4, fr. Heb *Qayin*] **:** TROUBLE, DISTURBANCE, UPROAR — used chiefly in the phrase *raise Cain* ⟨the children were raising *Cain* upstairs⟩ ⟨if I'm late again the boss will raise *Cain*⟩

²**cain** \"\ *n* -s [ME *cane*, fr. ScGael *cāin* rent; akin to MIr *cāin* law, prob. fr. LL *canon* decree, tribute, fr. L, model — more at CANON] *Scot* **:** animals or produce of the land paid as a rent in kind

cainca root *var of* CAHINCA ROOT

cain–colored \'kān,-\ *adj, usu cap 1st C* [after *Cain*, son of Adam; fr. the supposed red color of Cain's hair] **:** reddish yellow

-caine \¦kān\ *n comb form* -s [G *-kain*, fr. *kokain* cocaine] **:** synthetic alkaloid anesthetic ⟨dibu*caine*⟩ ⟨pro*caine*⟩

cain·gang \'kīn,gaŋ\ *n, pl* **caingang** *or* **caingangs** *usu cap* [Pg, of AmerInd origin] **1 a :** the non-Guarani-Indian peoples of southern Brazil comprising a number of distinct but related groups **b :** a member of any such people **2 a :** a language of any Caingang people **b :** a language family of the Ge stock comprising the several Caingang languages

caingin *or* **caiñgin** [Sp, fr. Tag *kaingin*] *var of* KAINGIN

cain·gi·ne·ro *also* **caiñ·gi·ne·ro** \,kīŋə'ne(,)rō\ *n* -s [Sp, fr. *caingin* + *-ero* -er] *Philippines* **:** one that makes and cultivates a kaingin

cain·gua \'kīŋ,gwä\ *n, pl* **caingua** *or* **cainguas** *usu cap* [Sp, fr. a native name, lit., inhabitants of the forest] **:** CAYUA

ca'ing whale *var of* CAAING WHALE

cain·ite \'kā,nīt\ *n* -s *usu cap* [*Cain*, son of Adam + E *-ite* — more at CAIN] **1 :** a descendant of Cain, one of the sons of Adam **2** [LL *Cainita*, fr. *Cain* + L *-ita* -ite] **:** a member of a gnostic sect that regarded the Old Testament as an account of the work of a demiurge and a distortion of the true nature of such men as Cain, whom they honored

cain·it·ic \(')kā¦nid·ik\ *adj, usu cap* **:** of or relating to the Cainites

cainozoic *usu cap, var of* CENOZOIC

cains *pl of* CAIN

cai·po·to·ra·de \,kīpətə'rädē\ *n, usu cap* [Sp *caipatorade, caipotade*, of AmerInd origin] **:** a dialect of the Zamuco people

¹**ca·ique** \kä'ēk, kī'ēk, 'kīk\ *n* -s [alter. (influenced by F *caïque*, fr. Turk *kayık*) of earlier *caik*, fr. Turk *kayık*] **1 :** a light skiff used on the Bosporus **2 :** a Levantine sailing vessel

²**ca·i·que** \kä'ē(,)kä, kī'-, -ēkə\ *n, pl* **ca·i·ques** \-āz, -əz\ *or* **ca·i·que·nes** \,kä-ē'kā(,)nās, kī'k-\ [Sp *or* Pg] **:** any of various small stocky often brightly colored parrots native to northeastern So. America

ca·ique·jee \kä'ēk(,)jē, kī'ē-, 'kīk-(\ *n* -s [alter. (influenced by *caique*) of earlier *caikjee*, fr. Turk *kayıkçı* boatman, fr. *kayık* boat + *-çı* (occupational suffix)] **:** a rower of a caique

¹**caird** \'kärd\ *Scot var of* CARD

²**caird** \"\ *n* -s [ScGael *ceard* tinker; akin to OIr *cerd* smith, poet, W *cerdd* music, Gk *kerdos* profit, and perh. to OE *horsc* wise, OHG *horsk* quick, ON *horskr* wise] **1** *Scot* **:** a traveling tinker **2** *Scot* **:** TRAMP, VAGRANT, GYPSY

¹**cai·rene** \'kī,rēn, ₛ'ₛ\ *adj, usu cap* [*Cairo*, Egypt + E *-ene* (as in *Nazarene*)] **:** of or relating to Cairo, Egypt

²**cairene** \"\ *n* -s *cap* **:** a native or resident of Cairo, esp. Cairo, Egypt

cairn \'ka(a)(ə)rn, 'ke(ə)rn\ *also* **carn** \'kärn\ *n* -s [ME *carne*, fr. ScGael *carn;* akin to OIr & W *carn* cairn and perh. to OE *heard* hard — more at HARD] **:** a rounded or pyramidal heap of stones made as a monument or memorial or as a landmark or trail marker for explorers, surveyors, or hikers — **cairned** \-nd\ *adj*

cairn·gorm \-,gȯrm\ *or* **cairngorm stone** *n* -s [fr. *Cairngorm*, mountain in Scotland, its locality] **:** a yellow or smoky-brown variety of crystalline quartz — called also *smoky quartz*

cairn's ash *or* **cairn's hickory** \'ka(a)(ə)rnz-, 'ke(ə)rnz-\ *n, usu cap C* [prob. fr. *Cairns*, seaport in Queensland, Australia] **:** QUEENSLAND HICKORY

cairn terrier *n* [so called fr. its use in hunting among cairns] **:** a small compactly built hard-coated terrier of a breed originating in Scotland

cai·ro \'kī(,)rō\ *adj, usu cap* [fr. *Cairo*, Egypt] **:** of or from Cairo, the capital of Egypt **:** of the kind or style prevalent in Cairo **:** CAIRENE

cais·son \'kā,sän, -,sᵊn, *Brit often* kə'sün\ *n* -s [F, aug. of *caisse* box, fr. OProv *caisa*, fr. L *capsa* small box — more at CASE (box)] **1 a :** a chest packed with explosives so that it can be laid in the way of an enemy and exploded on his approach **b :** a chest to hold ammunition **c :** a 2-wheeled vehicle for artillery ammunition attachable to a horse-drawn limber for marching **2 a :** a watertight chamber used in construction work under water (as in a harbor or river) or as a foundation — see BOX CAISSON, OPEN CAISSON, PNEUMATIC CAISSON; compare COFFERDAM **b :** a large cistern used to float forward materials of construction during the work of extending a canal over lower ground **c :** a float for raising a sunken vessel **:** CAMEL **d :** a hollow floating box or a boat used as a floodgate for a dock or basin **3 :** COFFER 4a

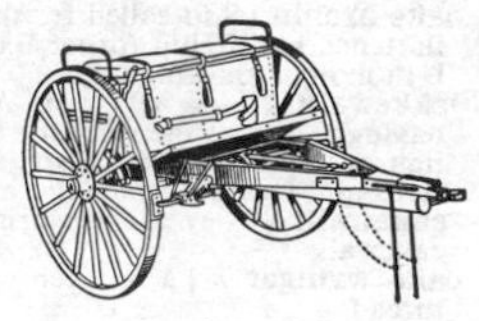

caisson 1c

caisson crib *n* **:** a platform of heavy timbers on which rests the caisson used in construction of an underwater pier or foundation

caisson disease *n* **:** a sickness induced by too rapid decrease in air pressure after a stay in compressed atmosphere (as in a caisson, diving bell, or tunnel) and caused by nitrogen bubbles forming in blood and tissues — called also *bends, chokes, staggers;* see AEROEMBOLISM

caith·ness \'kāth,nes\ *adj, usu cap* [fr. county of *Caithness*, Scotland] **:** of or from the county of Caithness, Scotland **:** of the kind or style prevalent in Caithness

¹**cai·tiff** \'kād·əf, -ātəf\ *adj* [ME *caitif*, fr. ONF, captive, miserable, vile, fr. L *captivus* captive — more at CAPTIVE] **1** *obs* **:** CAPTIVE **2 :** BASE **:** wicked and mean **:** COWARDLY, DESPICABLE

²**caitiff** \"\ *n* -s [ME *caitif*, fr. *caitif*, adj.] **1** *obs* **a :** CAPTIVE, PRISONER **b :** a wretched or unfortunate man **2 :** a base despicable person **:** a mean and wicked man

cai·xi·nha \kī'shēnyə\ *n* -s [Pg, fr. dim. of *caixa* box, fr. L *capsa* — more at CASE (box)] **:** a box rattle used in Brazilian dance orchestras

¹**cajan** *or* **cajang** *var of* CADJAN

²**cajan** *cap, var of* CAJUN

³**ca·jan** \'kājən, -,jän\ [NL] *syn of* CAJANUS

ca·ja·nus \kə'jānəs, -än-\ *n, cap* [NL, prob. fr. *Cajan*, fr. Malay *kachang* bean, pea] **:** a genus of woody herbs of the family Leguminosae including solely the pigeon pea

caj·e·put \'kajəpət, -,pu̇t\ *n* -s [Malay *kayu puteh*, fr. *kayu* wood, tree + *puteh* white] **1** *or* **caj·a·put** *or* **caj·u·put** \'kajə-\ **:** an East Indian tree (*Melaleuca leucadendron*) that yields a pungent oil — called also *paperbark* **2 :** CALIFORNIA LAUREL

caj·e·put·ene *or* **caj·u·put·ene** \-,pə,tēn\ *n* -s [ISV *cajeput* or *cajuput* (*Melaleuca leucadendron*) + *-ene*] **:** DIPENTENE

cajeput oil *or* **cajuput oil** *n* **:** a pungent essential oil obtained from cajeput and certain other plants of the genus *Melaleuca* and used chiefly as a local application in skin disease and as a stimulating expectorant

caj·e·put·ol *or* **caj·u·put·ol** \-,pə,tōl, -ōl\ *n* -s [*cajeput* or *cajuput* (*Melaleuca leucadendron*) + *-ol*] **:** CINEOLE

ca·ji \kə'hē, kä-\ *n* -s [AmerSp *cají*] **:** SCHOOLMASTER 3

ca·jole \kə'jōl\ *vt* -ED/-ING/-s [F *cajoler* to chatter like a jay, cajole, prob. blend of MF *gaioler* to chatter like a jay in a cage (fr. ONF *gaiole* birdcage, fr. LL *caveola*, dim. of L *cavea* cage) and MF *cage* — more at CAGE] **1 a :** to persuade with deliberate flattery esp. in the face of reasonable objection or reluctance **:** COAX ⟨lulled into . . . repose or *cajoled* into specious reconciliation —Havelock Ellis⟩ **b :** to obtain (an object or a favor) from someone by cajoling **:** WHEEDLE ⟨~ an autograph from him —H.T.Moore⟩ **2 :** to deceive with soothing words or false promises ⟨*cajoled* himself with thoughts of escape —Robertson Davies⟩

ca·jole·ment \-mənt\ *n* -s **:** CAJOLERY **:** a means of cajoling

ca·jol·ery \-l(ə)rē, -i\ *n* -ES [F *cajolerie*, fr. *cajoler* + *-ie* -y] **:** the act or practice of cajoling **:** use of delusive enticements

ca·jol·ing·ly *adv* **:** in a cajoling manner

ca·jón \kə'hōn\ *n, pl* **cajo·nes** \-ō(,)nās, -ōnēz\ [AmerSp, fr. Sp, big box, aug. of *caja* box, fr. L *capsa* — more at CASE] **1** *Southwest* **:** a narrow gorge with vertical sides **:** BOX CANYON **2** [Sp] **:** a Spanish and Spanish-American method of construction in which walls are made of mud rammed into a narrow boxlike frame and allowed to harden

¹**ca·jun** *also* **ca·jan** *or* **ca·jin** \'kājən\ *n* -s *usu cap* [alter. of *Acadian* (native of Acadia)] **1 :** ACADIAN 2 — sometimes taken to be offensive **2** *usu cajan* **:** one of a people of mixed white, Indian, and Negro ancestry in southwest Alabama and adjoining sections of Mississippi

²**ca·jun** \kə'hün\ *n* -s [AmerSp *cajún, cajum*, fr. Maya] **:** a West Indian fiber plant (*Furcraea cubensis*)

cajuput *var of* CAJEPUT

cajuputene *var of* CAJEPUTENE

cajuputol *var of* CAJEPUTOL

cak·chi·quel *also* **cak·chi·kel** \¦käkchə¦kel\ *n, pl* **cakchiquel** *or* **cakchiquels** *usu cap* [Sp *cakchiquel, cachiquel*, of AmerInd origin] **1 a :** an Indian people of south central Guatemala **b :** a member of such people **2 :** a Mayan language of the Cakchiquel people

¹**cake** \'kāk\ *n* -s [ME, fr. ON *kaka;* akin to OE *cœcil* small cake, OHG *kuocho* cake, and prob. to Lith *guoge* cabbage-head, head] **1 a :** any of a variety of breads usu. small in size and typically round and flat in shape: as (1) **:** a flat mass of dough, sometimes unleavened, shaped round or oval by hand, and baked with a crust on both sides (2) *Scot* **:** a thin hard-baked bread of oatmeal (3) **:** a thin flat bread (as a griddlecake) made from batter fried on a griddle or other utensil (4) **:** biscuit dough enriched with shortening and eggs and baked and served hot with fruit or meat (as shortcake) **b :** any of a variety of fancy sweetened breads: as (1) **:** a loaf baked in a variety of forms and sizes, made from a sweet dough or batter of flour and other ingredients, and often coated with an icing (2) **:** a usu. small mass of firm dough variously shaped, leavened with yeast or baking powder, and cooked in deep fat (as a friedcake) **c :** a flattened usu. round mass of food (as potato, hashed meat, fish) baked or fried **2 a :** a block of compacted or congealed matter ⟨a ~ of soap⟩ ⟨an ice ~⟩ **b :** a hard or brittle layer or deposit **:** CRUST ⟨the ~ formed in a pipe⟩ **c :** a hollow cylinder of yarn produced by the spinning process for viscose rayon **3 :** OIL CAKE, FILTER CAKE

²**cake** \"\ *vb* -ED/-ING/-s *vt* **:** to cover (a surface) with a crust **:** ENCRUST ⟨his jacket was *caked* with dust⟩ **:** fill (a space) with a packed mass ⟨*caked* fingernails⟩ **~** *vi* **1 :** to form or harden into a mass ⟨coral is formed by the *caking* of minute shells into stone⟩ — see CAKED BREAST **2 :** to fuse (as of coal) into a pasty mass when heated

cakebread \'ₛ,ₛ\ *n, now dial Brit* **:** bread made in cakes or of a quality like cake

cake cooler *n* **:** a wire-mesh rack on which cakes or cookies are placed to cool

caked breast *n* **:** a localized hardening in one or more segments of a lactating breast caused by accumulation of blood in dilated veins and milk in obstructed ducts — compare BLUE BAG, BOVINE MASTITIS

caked udder *n* **:** BOVINE MASTITIS
cake–eater \ˈ-ˌ--\ *n, slang* **:** an effeminate party-going dandy
cake flour *n* **:** flour ground from soft wheat to a highly refined texture
cake former *n* **:** an operator of a machine for wrapping crushed and steam-cooked cottonseed kernels and shaping into cloth-wrapped cakes prior to the expression of oil
cake makeup *n* **:** a tinted cosmetic base usu. in semimoist cake form used as a foundation for face powder
cake mill *n* **:** a machine for crushing stock-feed cake
cake puller *n* **:** a worker who pulls pressed cottonseed cakes from the press and trucks them to a cake stripper — called also *knocker*
cakes and ale *n* **:** the good things of life **:** PLEASURE, ENJOYMENT ⟨dost thou think because thou art virtuous, there shall be no more *cakes and ale* —Shak.⟩
cake stripper *n* **:** one that feeds cottonseed cakes after expression of the oil into a machine that strips off the press cloth
cake urchin *n* [so called fr. the disklike shape] **:** a strongly flattened sea urchin (order Exocycloida): as **a :** SAND DOLLAR **b :** KEYHOLE URCHIN
¹**cakewalk** \ˈ-ˌ-\ *n* **1 :** an American Negro entertainment having a cake as the prize for the most accomplished steps and figures in walking **2 :** a stage dance developed from walking steps and figures; *typically* **:** a high prance with backward tilt
²**cakewalk** \"\ *vi* **:** to perform, dance, or walk in or as if in a cakewalk
cake wringer *n* **:** a worker who centrifuges cakes of rayon thread
cak·ey *or* **caky** \ˈkākē, -i\ *adj* **cakier; cakiest :** having or tending to form crusts or lumps ⟨~ face powder⟩
cak·i·le \ˈkakəˌlē\ *n, cap* [NL, fr. Ar *qāqulla*] **:** a small genus of annual succulent herbs (family Cruciferae) found along sandy shores of No. America and Europe and having opposite fleshy leaves — see SEA ROCKET
caking *pres part of* CAKE
cakra *var of* CHAKRA
cal \ˈkal\ *n* -s [prob. fr. OCorn *cal* cunning, sly, fr. L *callidus*; fr. its presence in tin ore, considered by the miners an impish intrusion of a worthless substance — more at CALLIDITY] *Cornwall* **:** WOLFRAMITE
cal *abbr* **1** calando **2** calendar **3** calends **4** caliber; calibrate **5** calorie
¹**ca·la** \kəˈlä\ *n* -s [of African origin; akin to Vai *ko¹lo³* uncooked rice, Bambara *kala* stalk of a cereal] **:** a Creole fried cake made mainly of rice
²**cala** \ˈkalə\ *or* **cali** \ˈkalē\ *n* -s [short for *California ham*] **:** PICNIC HAM
ca·la·ba \kəˈläbə\ *n* -s [Sp, of Cariban origin; akin to Galibi *calaba, carapa* oil, Calinago *kalapa*] **:** SANTA MARIA TREE
cal·a·bar bean \ˈkaləˌbär-, -bə-\ *n, usu cap C* [fr. *Calabar*, Nigeria] **:** the dark brown highly poisonous seed of a tropical African woody vine (*Physostigma venenosum*) of the family Leguminosae serving as a source of physostigmine and as an ordeal bean in native witchcraft trials
calabar potto *n, usu cap C* **:** ANGWANTIBO
calabar swelling *n, usu cap C* **:** a transient subcutaneous swelling marking the migratory course of the adult filarial eye worm through the tissues — compare LOAIASIS
¹**cal·a·bash** \ˈkaləˌbash, -ˌaa(ə)-,-ˌai-\ *n* -ES *often attrib* [F & Sp; F *calebasse* gourd, fr. Sp *calabaza*, perh. fr. Ar *qar'ah yābisah* dry gourd, fr. *qar'ah* gourd + *yābisah* dry] **1 :** GOURD; *esp* **:** the common bottle gourd **2 a** *or* **calabash tree :** a tropical American tree (*Crescentia cujete*) **b :** the hard globose fruit of the calabash **3 a :** a utensil (as a dipper, bottle, kettle) made from the shell of a calabash **b :** a noise-making device made from the calabash gourd **4 :** BAOBAB **5 :** MEDAL BRONZE **6 :** a usu. curved-stemmed tobacco pipe made from the calabash gourd
²**calabash** \"\ *adj* [perh. so called fr. the fact that close friends ate from the same calabash] *Hawaii* **:** related by ties of affection rather than blood
calabash curare *n* **:** curare obtained from a So. American woody vine (*Strychnos toxifera*)
calabash nutmeg *n* **1 :** the fruit of a tropical shrub (*Monodora myristica*) of the family Annonaceae about the size of an orange and containing many aromatic seeds that are used like nutmegs **2 :** the shrub that bears calabash nutmegs
ca·la·ba·za \ˌkaləˈbäzə, -sə\ *n* -s [Sp, gourd] **:** CALABASH
cal·a·ba·zi·lla \ˌkaləbəˈzē(y)ə\ *or* **cal·a·ba·ci·lla** \-ˈsē-\ *n* -s [MexSp *calabacilla*, fr. Sp, squirting cucumber, dim. of *calabaza*] *Southwest* **:** PRAIRIE GOURD
cal·a·ber *or* **cal·a·bar** \ˈkaləbə(r)\ *n* -s [ME *calabre*, fr. MF, fr. *Calabria*, region in Italy] **1 :** a deep-brown Calabrian squirrel fur **2 :** the gray fur of a Siberian squirrel
cal·a·boose \ˈkaləˌbüs\ *n* -s [modif. of Sp *calabozo* dungeon] *dial* **:** JAIL; *esp* **:** the local jail
cal·a·bo·zo \ˌkaləˈbō(ˌ)zō, -ōzə\ *or* **cal·a·bo·za** \-ōzə\ *n* -s [Sp] *Southwest* **:** JAIL
cal·a·bra·sel·la \ˌkaləbrəˈzelə, -ˈs-\ *n* -s [It *calabresella*, fr. *calabrese* Calabrian, fr. *Calabria* + *-ese*] **:** an Italian card game for three players played with a 40-card pack
cal·a·bre·se \ˌkaləˈbrāzē, -sē\ *n* -s [It, Calabrian] **:** a broccoli (*Brassica oleracea italica*) having a greenish terminal head and similar lateral heads that develop after the terminal one is cut
¹**ca·la·bri·an** \kəˈlābrēən, -ˈä-\ *also* **cal·a·brese** \ˌkaləˈbrēz, -ēs\ *adj, usu cap* [*Calabrian* fr. *Calabria*, region in Italy + E *-an*; *Calabrese* fr. It *Calabrese*, fr. *Calabria* + It *-ese*] **:** of or relating to Calabria, Italy
²**calabrian** \"\ *also* **calabrese** \"\ *n, pl* **calabrians** *also* **calabrese** *cap* **:** a native or inhabitant of Calabria, Italy
calabrian manna *n* -s *usu cap C* **:** MANNA 2
cal·a·bur tree \ˈkaləˌbu(ə)r-, -(ˌ)bər-\ *n* [NL *calabura*] **:** a tropical American shrub or small tree (*Muntingia calabura*) of the family Elaeocarpaceae whose bark yields a silky fiber used in cordage and whose wood is valuable for staves — called also *capulin, Jamaica cherry, silkwood*
ca·la·di·um \kəˈlādēəm\ *n* [NL, fr. Malay *kĕladi*, any of a number of aroids including taro] **1** *cap* **:** a small genus of tropical American plants (family Araceae) with variously colored usu. peltate arrow-shaped leaves and a boat-shaped spathe **2** -s **:** any plant of the genus *Caladium* (as *C. bicolor* often cultivated as a pot plant for its foliage)
calaite *n* -s [F *calaïte* (now usu. *callaïte*), fr. L *callais* (fr. Gk *kalais, kallais*) + F *-ite*] *obs* **:** TURQUOISE
cal·a·lu \ˌkaləˈlü\ *n* -s [AmerSp *calalú*] **:** a tropical American plant (*Xanthosoma hastifolium*) whose leaf is used as a vegetable in the West Indies
calam- *or* **calami-** *or* **calamo-** *comb form* [NL, fr. Gk *kalam-, kalamo-*, fr. *kalamos* reed — more at HAULM] **:** reed **:** reedlike ⟨*Calam*agrostis⟩ ⟨*Calamo*dendron⟩
cal·a·ma·gros·tis \ˌkaləməˈgrästəs\ *n, cap* [NL, fr. *calam-* + L *agrostis* couch grass, fr. Gk *agrōstis* dog's-tooth grass, perh. fr. *agros* field — more at ACRE] **:** a genus of tall mostly perennial grasses having single-flowered spikelets, the lemmas entire, and the rachillae usu. extending beyond the palea into a hairy bristle or stalk — see BLUEJOINT 1
cal·a·man·co *also* **cal·i·man·co** \ˌkaləˈmaŋ(ˌ)kō\ *n* -ES *often attrib* [perh. modif. of Sp *calamaco*, modif. of LL *calamaucus* felt cap, skullcap] **1 :** a glossy woolen fabric of satin weave with striped or checkered designs manufactured from the 16th to the 19th centuries **2 :** a garment made of calamanco
cal·a·man·der \ˈkaləˌmandə(r), ˌ--ˈ--\ *or* **calamander wood** *n* -s [prob. fr. D *kalamander-* (in *kalamanderhout* calamander wood), perh. modif. of *Coromandel* (in *Coromandel Coast*, southeast India)] **:** the wood of any of several East Indian trees of the genus *Diospyros* (esp. *D. quaesita*) colored a mottled hazel brown striped with black and used in furniture manufacturing
cal·a·mar·i·a·ce·ae \ˌkaləˌmerēˈāsēˌē\ *n pl, cap* [NL, fr. L *calamarius* of a writing reed (fr. *calamus* reed, fr. Gk *kalamos*) + NL *-aceae* — more at HAULM] **:** a family of Paleozoic horsetaillike pteridophytes having *Calamites* as its principal genus and being variously considered as belonging to the order Equisetales or in some classifications as coextensive with a separate order — **cal·a·mar·i·a·ceous** \ˌ--ˌ--ˈāshəs\ *adj* — **cal·a·mar·i·an** \ˌ--ˈmerēən\ *n* -s
cal·a·mary \ˈkaləˌmerē\ *or* **cal·a·mar** \-ˌmär\ *n, pl* **calamaries** *or* **calamars** [ML *calamarium* pen case] **:** SQUID; *esp* **:** GIANT SQUID
cal·am·bac \ˈkaləmˌbak\ *or* **cal·am·bour** \-ˌbu̇(ə)r\ *n* -s [F, fr. Pg *calambac, calambuco*, fr. Malay *kĕlĕmbak, kĕlambak*] **:** AGALLOCH
calami *pl of* CALAMUS
calami- — see CALAM-
cal·a·mine \ˈkaləˌmīn, -mən\ *n* -s *often attrib* [F, fr. ML *calamina*, alter. of L *cadmia*, Gk *kadmeia*, lit., Cadmean (earth), Theban (earth)] **1** *obs* **a** *Brit* **:** SMITHSONITE **b :** HEMIMORPHITE **c :** HYDROZINCITE **2 :** an alloy of zinc, lead, and tin formerly used for coating iron to prevent oxidation **3 :** a pink powder consisting of a mixture of zinc oxide with a small amount of ferric oxide used in lotions, liniments, and ointments in skin treatment
calamine blue *n* **:** a light greenish blue that is greener, lighter, and stronger than average robin's-egg blue (sense 1), bluer and deeper than average aqua, and bluer and lighter than average turquoise blue
cal·a·mint \ˈkaləˌmint\ *or* **calamint balm** *n* -s [alter. (influenced by E *mint* [plant] and by LL *calaminthe*, fr. Gk *kalaminthē*) of ME *calament*, fr. OF, fr. ML *calamentum*, modif. of Gk *kalaminthē*] **:** a mint of the genus *Satureja* (esp. *S. calamintha*) — called also *basil thyme*
cal·a·mis·trum \ˌkaləˈmistrəm\ *n, pl* **calamis·tra** \-rə\ [L, curling iron, irreg. fr. Gk *kalamis*, fr. *kalamos* reed — more at HAULM] **:** a spinose comb on the hind metatarsi of a cribellate spider that aids in organizing silk spun from the cribellum
cal·a·mi·ta·ce·ae \ˌkaləˌmīˈtāsēˌē, -ˌməˈt-\ *n pl, cap* [NL, fr. *Calamites*, type genus + *-aceae*] **:** a family of fossil plants coextensive with Calamariaceae — used by strict adherents to the International Rules of Botanical Nomenclature
cal·a·mite \ˈkaləˌmīt\ *n* -s [NL *Calamites*] **:** any fossil of the genus *Calamites* or related genera — **cal·a·mit·ean** \ˌkaləˈmīd·ēən, -mīˈtē-\ *adj*
cal·a·mi·tes \ˌkaləˈmīd·(ˌ)ēz\ *n, cap* [NL, fr. LGk *kalamitēs* reedlike, fr. Gk, of a reed, fr. *kalamos* reed] **:** a genus of Paleozoic fossil plants (family Calamariaceae) having large grooved and jointed stems bearing verticillate branches at the nodes
cal·a·mi·toid \ˌkaləˈmīˌtȯid\ *adj* [NL *Calamites* + E *-oid*] **:** resembling a calamite
ca·lam·i·tous \kəˈlamәd·əs, -ətəs\ *adj* [MF *calamiteux*, fr. L *calamitosus*, fr. *calamitas* calamity + *-osus* -ous] **1 :** marked by distress, affliction, or disaster **:** **a :** constituting or causing calamity **:** bringing distress ⟨the ~ disregard of mine-safety regulations⟩ **b :** concerned with or relating to disaster ⟨this ~ catalog of serious problems —J.J.McCloy⟩ **2** *obs* **:** involved personally in calamity ⟨thou hast seen me happy and ~ —Samuel Johnson⟩ — **ca·lam·i·tous·ly** *adv*
ca·lam·i·ty \-əd·ē, -ətē, -i\ *n* -ES [MF *calamité*, fr. L *calamitat-, calamitas*; akin to L *incolumis* unharmed, Gk *kolobos* docked — more at HALT (lame)] **1 :** a state of deep distress or misery connected with major misfortune or loss ⟨life is neither a pleasure nor a ~ —Agnes Repplier⟩ **2 :** an extraordinarily grave event marked by great loss and lasting distress and affliction ⟨*calamities* of nature such as flood and drought — *Notes & Queries on Anthropology*⟩ **syn** see DISASTER
calamity howler *n* **:** one that makes dismal predictions of impending disaster
calamo- — see CALAM-
cal·a·mo·den·dron \ˌkaləmōˈdendrən\ *n, cap* [NL, fr. *calam-* + *-dendron*] **:** a form genus of fossil plants based on remains of stems only
cal·a·mon·din \ˌkaləˈməndən\ *n* -s [Tag *kalamunding*] **1 :** a small spiny citrus tree (*Citrus mitis*) native to the Philippines **2 :** the small very acid loose-skinned fruit of the calamondin
cal·a·moph·y·ton \ˌkaləˈmäfəˌtän\ *n, cap* [NL, fr. *calam-* + Gk *phyton* plant — more at PHYT-] **:** a genus (the type of the family Calamophytaceae) of sphenopsid plants from the Middle Devonian of Germany that have bifurcated leaves and naked pendulous sporangia and are the earliest indubitable sphenopsids
cal·a·mos·ta·chys \ˌkaləˈmästəkəs\ *n, cap* [NL, fr. *calam-* + Gk *stachys* ear of grain; akin to OE *stingan* to sting — more at STING] **:** a genus of Carboniferous fossil plants (family Calamariaceae) with cone-shaped fructifications and peltate sporophylls
cal·a·mus \ˈkaləməs\ *n* [L, fr. Gk *kalamos* — more at HAULM] **1** *pl* **cala·mi** \-ˌmī, -ē\ **a** *obs* **:** REED, CANE **b :** a reed pen ⟨a manuscript that was written with a ~⟩ **2** *pl* **calami :** SWEET FLAG **3** *pl* **calami :** the aromatic peeled and dried rhizome of the calamus used as a carminative and tonic **4** *cap* [NL, fr. L] **:** a genus of tropical Asian tufted pinnate-leaved palms whose hooked petioles enable them to climb over tall trees and from whose light tough stems rattan canes are made with one species (*C. rotang*) being used for Malacca canes **5** *pl* **calami :** the barrel of a feather **:** QUILL
calamus oil *n* **:** a yellow aromatic carcinogenic essential oil obtained from the underground parts of the sweet flag and used as a perfume and formerly as a flavor
ca·lan·do \käˈlän(ˌ)dō\ *adj* (*or adv*) [It, fr. L *calandum*, gerund of *calare* to slacken, let down, fr. Gk *chalan*; perh. akin to Skt *jahāti* he leaves, abandons — more at GO] **:** diminishing in rapidity and loudness **:** dying away — used as a direction in music
ca·lan·dra \kəˈlandrə\ *n, cap* [NL, fr. F *calandre* weevil] *in some classifications* **:** a genus of weevils (family Curculionidae) equivalent to *Calendra* or to *Sitophilus* of other classifications and sometimes made the type of a separate family
calandra lark \"-\ *also* **ca·lan·der** \kəˈlandə(r)\ *n* -s [MF *calandre*, fr. OProv *calandra*, fr. LGk *kalandros*, prob. fr. Gk *charadrios*, a bird — more at CHARADRIUS] **:** a large European lark (*Melanocorypha calandra*) noted for its ability to mimic the songs of other birds and sometimes kept as a cage bird
¹**ca·lan·dria** \kəˈlandrēə\ *n* -s [Sp, lit., calandra lark] **:** a heating element of an evaporator; *esp* **:** a part of a vacuum evaporating system in which the liquid to be concentrated rises through tubes surrounded by steam and descends through a central well
²**calandria** \"\ *n* -s [AmerSp, fr. Sp, calandra lark, fr. (assumed) VL, modif. of LGk *kalandros*] **:** a black-headed So. American mockingbird (*Mimus modulator* or *M. orpheus*) often kept as a cage bird
cal·an·drin·ia \ˌkalənˈdrinēə\ *n, cap* [NL, after Jean Louis *Calandrini* †1758 Swiss botanist] **:** a large genus of mostly So. American and Australian succulent herbs of the family Portulacaceae that have basal or alternate leaves and purplish ephemeral flowers in bracted racemes or panicles — see ROCK PURSLANE
calangall *var of* GALINGALE
¹**cal·a·nid** \ˈkalənəd, -(ˌ)nid\ *adj* [NL *Calanidae*, fr. *Calanus*, type genus + *-idae*] **:** of or relating to the genus *Calanus* or the family Calanidae
²**calanid** \"\ *n* -s **:** a calanid copepod
ca·lanque \kəˈläŋk\ *n* -s [F, fr. Prov *calanco, calanca*] **:** a cove or inlet esp. on the Mediterranean coast of France
calantas [Sp *calantás*, fr. Tag *kalantas*] *var of* KALANTAS
ca·lan·the \kəˈlan(t)thē\ *n* [NL, fr. *cal-* + Gk *anthē* blossom; akin to Gk *anthos* flower — more at ANTHOLOGY] **1** *cap* **:** a large and widely distributed genus of terrestrial showy orchids having white, rose-colored, or yellow flowers and broad leaves folded lengthwise **2** -s **:** any plant of the genus *Calanthe*
cal·a·nus \ˈkalənəs\ *n, cap* [NL, after *Calanus* (Kalanos) †*ab* 325 B.C. Indian Brahman] **:** a genus (the type of the family Calanidae) of reddish marine copepods widely distributed in northern seas where they are a major food for herring, mackerel, and whales
ca·lao \kəˈlau̇\ *n* -s [Sp, fr. Tag *kalaw*] **:** a very large Philippine hornbill (*Buceros hydrocorax*) with a large red bill and casque, rufous head and neck, dull black breast, brown back and wings, and a white tail often stained yellowish buff — called also *rufous hornbill*
calapooya *or* **calapuya** *usu cap, var of* KALAPOOIA
ca·lap·pa \kəˈlapə\ *n, cap* [NL] **:** a genus (the type of the family Calappidae) of brachyuran crustaceans of tropical seas that includes a number of typical box crabs
calas *pl of* CALA
ca·la·scio·ne \ˌkaləˈshōnē\ *n* -s [It, prob. fr. (assumed) VL *calassium* basket, irreg. fr. Gk *kalathos*] **:** a guitar with two or three strings used esp. in southern Italy
ca·lash \kəˈlash, -ˈaa(ə)-,-ˈai-\ *n* -ES [F *calèche*, fr. G *kalesche*, fr. Czech *kolesa* wheels, carriage; akin to OSlav *kolo* wheel, Gk *kyklos* — more at WHEEL] **1 a :** a light carriage with small wheels, inside seats for four passengers, a separate driver's seat, and a folding top **b :** CALÈCHE 2 **2 a :** a large hood made on an arrangement of hoops to permit folding far back on the head and worn by women in the late 18th century **b :** a folding carriage top **3 :** a seaman of Far Eastern extraction

calash 2a

cal·a·thea \ˌkaləˈthēə\ *n* [NL, irreg. fr. L *calathus* basket shaped like a flower, fr. Gk *kalathos*] **1** *cap* **:** a genus of chiefly tropical American herbs (family Marantaceae) having showily marked basal leaves and small flowers in clusters on short stems and used as foliage plants **2** -s **:** any plant of the genus *Calathea*
cal·a·thos \ˈkaləˌthäs, -thəs\ *or* **cal·a·thus** \-thəs\ *n, pl* **cala·thi** \-ˌthī, -ē\ [L & Gk; L *calathus*, fr. Gk *kalathos*; perh. akin to Gk *klōthein* to spin] **:** a flared fruit basket borne on the head as a symbol in Greek and Egyptian art of fruitfulness
calavance *var of* GARAVANCE
cal·a·ver·as warbler \ˌkaləˈverəs-\ *n, usu cap C* **:** the Pacific coast subspecies (*Vermivora ruficapilla ridgwayi*) of the Nashville warbler
cal·a·ver·ite \ˌkaləˈveˌrīt\ *n* -s [*Calaveras* county, California, its locality + E *-ite*] **:** a yellowish mineral having a metallic luster and consisting of gold telluride and variable minor amounts of silver (hardness 2.5, sp. gr. 8.35)
calc *abbr* calculate
calc- *or* **calci-** *or* **calco-** *comb form* [L *calc-, calx* lime — more at CHALK] **:** calcium **:** calcium salts ⟨*calc*ite⟩ ⟨*calci*meter⟩ ⟨*calco*spherite⟩
cal·ca·ne·al \(ˈ)kalˈkānēəl\ *also* **cal·ca·ne·an** \-ēən\ *adj* [LL *calcaneus* heel + E *-al* or *-an*] **1 :** relating to the heel **2 :** relating to the calcaneus
calcaneo- *comb form* [calcaneum] **:** calcaneal and ⟨*calcaneo*astragalar⟩ ⟨*calcaneo*cuboid⟩
cal·ca·neo·cu·boid ligament \kalˈkānē(ˌ)ōˈkyüˌbȯid-\ *n* **:** either of two ligaments of the tarsus connecting the calcaneus and the cuboid
cal·ca·ne·um \kalˈkānēəm\ *n, pl* **calca·nea** \-nēə\ [L, heel, fr. *calc-, calx* — more at CALK] **1 :** CALCANEUS **2 :** a process of the back upper part of the tarsometatarsal bone of birds prob. not homologous to the calcaneum of mammals
cal·ca·ne·us \kalˈkānēəs\ *n, pl* **calca·nei** \-nēˌī\ [LL, heel, alter. of L *calcaneum*] **:** one of the bones of the tarsus which in man forms the great bone of the heel homologous to the fibulare of certain lower vertebrates
¹**cal·car** \ˈkalˌkär\ *n, pl* **calcar·ia** \kalˈka(a)rēə\ [L, spur, fr. *calc-, calx* heel] **:** a spur or spurlike prominence: as **a :** a clawlike process on the leg or wing of a bird that is not the termination of a digit **b :** a process of the calcaneum of a bat helping to support the web between the leg and tail — see BAT illustration **c :** a spur at the end of the tibia of an insect **d :** PREHALLUX
²**calcar** \"\ *n* -s [It *calcara*, fr. LL *calcaria* limekiln, fr. L *calc-, calx* lime — more at CHALK] **:** an oven or reverberatory furnace used in early glassmaking processes for calcination of the batch into frit
cal·ca·rate \ˈkalkəˌrāt\ *also* **cal·ca·rat·ed** \-ˌrād·əd\ *adj* [¹*calcar* + *-ate* or *-ate* + *-ed*] *bot* **:** SPURRED
calcar avis \-ˈāvəs, -ˈä-\ *n, pl* **calcaria avi·um** \-vēəm\ [NL, lit., bird's spur] **:** a curved ridge on the medial wall of the posterior horn of each lateral ventricle of the brain opposite the calcarine fissure
cal·car·ea \kalˈka(a)rēə\ *n pl, cap* [NL, alter. of L *calcaria*, neut. pl. of *calcarius* of lime] *in some classifications* **:** CALCISPONGIAE
cal·ca·re·nite \ˌkalkəˈrēˌnīt\ *n* -s [*calc-* + L *arena* sand + E *-ite* — more at ARENA] **1 :** a detrital carbonate rock formed of particles of sand-grain size **2 :** a consolidated lime sand
calcareo- *comb form* [calcareous] **:** calcareous ⟨*calcareo*corneous⟩ ⟨*calcareo*sulfurous⟩
cal·car·e·ous *also* **cal·car·i·ous** \kalˈka(a)rēəs, -ker-, -kār-\ *adj* [*calcareous* alter. (influenced by *-eous*) of *calcarious*, fr. L *calcarius* of lime, fr. *calc-, calx* lime + *-arius* -ary — more at CHALK] **1 a :** like calcite or calcium carbonate esp. in hardness **b :** consisting of or containing calcium carbonate **c :** containing calcium or any calcium compound **d :** relating to rocks containing calcium carbonate **2 :** growing on limestone or in soil impregnated with lime ⟨a ~ plant⟩ — **cal·car·e·ous·ly** *adv* — **cal·car·e·ous·ness** *n* -ES
calcareous sinter *n* **:** TRAVERTINE
calcareous spar *n* **:** CALCITE
calcaria *pl of* CALCAR, CALCARIUM
cal·ca·rine \ˈkalkəˌrīn\ *adj* [L *calcar* spur + E *-ine* — more at CALCAR] **1 :** shaped like a spur **2 :** belonging to or situated near the calcar avis
calcarine fissure *n* **:** a fissure in the mesial surface of the occipital lobe of the cerebrum
cal·car·i·um \kalˈka(a)rēəm\ *n, pl* **calcar·ia** \-rēə\ [NL, fr. ¹*calcar* + *-ium*] **:** ¹CALCAR
calced \ˈkalst\ *adj* [back-formation fr. *discalced*] **:** SHOD — used of religious who wear shoes; compare DISCALCED
calcedony *var of* CHALCEDONY
cal·ce·i·form \ˈkalsēəˌfȯrm, kalˈsē-\ *adj* [*calcei-* (fr. L *calceus* shoe) + *-form*] **:** shaped like a slipper ⟨the ~ lip in the flowers of certain orchids⟩
cal·ce·o·lar·ia \ˌkalsēəˈla(a)rēə\ *n* [NL, fr. L *calceolus* small shoe (dim. of *calceus* shoe, fr. *calc-, calx* heel) + NL *-aria* — more at CALK] **1** *cap* **:** a large genus of tropical American plants (family Scrophulariaceae) with highly irregular 2-parted showy flowers having a small upper lip and a large inflated slipper-shaped lower lip **2** -s **:** any garden plant of the genus *Calceolaria* — called also *slipperwort*
cal·ce·o·late \ˈkalsēəˌlāt\ *adj* [L *calceolus* + E *-ate*] **:** CALCEIFORM — **cal·ce·o·late·ly** *adv*
calces *pl of* CALX
cal·ce·us \ˈkalsēəs\ *n, pl* **cal·cei** \-sēˌī, -sēˌē\ [L *calceus, calcius*] **:** an ancient Roman ankle-length shoe usu. of leather
cal·cha·qui \ˌkälchəˈkē\ *n, pl* **calchaqui** *or* **calchaquis** *usu cap* [Sp *calchaqui*, fr. *Calchaqui* valley in Argentina] **1 a :** an ancient Indian people of northwest Argentina and northern Chile — called also *Diaguita* **b :** a member of such people **2 :** the language of the Calchaqui of unknown affinity
cal·cha·qui·an \-ən\ *adj, usu cap* **:** of or relating to an American Indian language family formerly occupying a large area in northwest Argentina and including the language of the Calchaqui
calci- — see CALC-
cal·cic \ˈkalsik\ *adj* [ISV *calc-* + *-ic*] **:** derived from or containing calcium or lime **:** rich in calcium
cal·ci·coat·er \ˈkalsəˌkōd·ə(r)\ *n* -s **:** a flat paint that is usu. made with lime-treated oils and that gives a uniform appearance when applied to porous surfaces
cal·ci·cole \ˈkalsəˌkōl\ *n* -s [fr. *calcicole*, adj.] **:** a plant that grows solely or predominantly in an alkaline medium rich in calcareous matter (as a limestone soil) — called also *calciphile*; compare CALCIFUGE
cal·cic·o·lous \(ˈ)kalˈsikələs\ *or* **calcicole** *adj* [*calcicolous* fr. F *calcicole* + E *-ous*; *calcicole*, fr. F, fr. *calci-* + *-cole* -colous] **:** growing or living in an alkaline medium rich in calcareous matter
cal·ci·co·sis \ˌkalsəˈkōsəs\ *n, pl* **calcico·ses** \-ˌsēz\ [NL, fr. *calc-* + *-cosis* (as in *silicosis*)] **:** a lung disease caused by inhalation of limestone dust; *sometimes* **:** pneumonoconiosis so caused
cal·cif·er·ol \kalˈsifəˌrōl, -ōl\ *n* -s [*calciferous* + *ergosterol*] **:** VITAMIN D_2
cal·cif·er·ous \(ˈ)kalˈsif(ə)rəs\ *adj* [*calc-* + *-ferous*] **1 :** bearing, producing, or containing calcium, calcium carbonate, or calcite **2** *cap* [so called fr. its calciferous sandstone] *geol* **:** of or relating to a subdivision of the Ordovician in New York and elsewhere
calciferous gland *n* **:** one of a series of glands that open into the esophagus of various oligochaete worms, that secrete

calcium carbonate, and that are believed to assist in adjusting the pH of the food material

cal·cif·ic \(')kal¦sifik\ *adj* [*calcify* + *-ic*] **:** involving or caused by calcification

cal·ci·fi·ca·tion \,kalsəfə'kāshən\ *n* -s [fr. *calcify*, after such pairs as E *ossify: ossification*] **1 :** impregnation with calcareous matter: as **a :** deposition of calcium salts within the matrix of cartilage often as the preliminary step in the formation of bone — compare OSSIFICATION **b :** abnormal deposition of calcium salts within tissue ⟨~ of a tuberculosis focus in the lung⟩ **c :** accumulation or deposition of calcium and magnesium carbonates at a level in the soil profile approximating the depth to which most of the water percolates **2 :** a calcified structure or part ⟨the lung X rays clearly showed the ~⟩

[1]**cal·ci·fuge** \'kalsə,fyüj\ *or* **cal·cif·u·gous** \(')kal¦sifyəgəs\ *adj* [*calcifuge* fr. F, fr. *calc-* + *-fuge* (fr. L *fugere* to flee); *calcifugous* fr. F *calcifuge* + E *-ous* — more at FUGITIVE] **:** growing or living in an acid medium that is poor in calcareous matter

[2]**calcifuge** \"\ *n* -s **:** a plant that grows solely or predominantly in an acid medium that is poor in calcareous matter ⟨heathers are well-known ~*s*⟩ — compare CALCICOLE

cal·ci·fy \'kalsə,fī\ *vb* -ED/-ING/-ES [*calc-* + *-fy*] *vt* **1 :** to make calcareous by deposit or secretion of calcium salts **2 :** to make inflexible or unchangeable **:** FIX ⟨~ the state of things as they are — *Fortune*⟩ ~ *vi* **1 :** to become calcareous **2 :** to become inflexible and changeless **:** become fixed **:** HARDEN

cal·ci·lu·tite *or* **cal·ci·lu·tyte** \,kalsə'lü,tīt\ *n* -s [*calc-* + L *lutum* mud + E *-ite* or *-yte* — more at POLLUTE] **:** a consolidated lime mud

cal·cim·e·ter \kal'simәd·ə(r)\ *n* -s [ISV *calc-* + *-meter*] **:** an instrument for liberating and measuring carbon dioxide (as in limestone or soil) and for estimating the amount of lime in soils

[1]**cal·ci·mine** *or* **kal·so·mine** \'kalsə,mīn\ *n* -s *often attrib* [*calcimine*, alter. (influenced by *calc-*) of *kalsomine; kalsomine*, origin unknown] **:** a typically white but sometimes tinted wash made by mixing clear glue, whiting or zinc white, and water and used mainly on plastered surfaces

[2]**calcimine** *or* **kalsomine** \"\ *vt* -ED/-ING/-S **:** to paint or wash with calcimine

cal·ci·min·er \-nə(r)\ *n* -s **:** one that calcimines ceilings or walls

cal·ci·nate \'kalsə,nāt\ *vt* -ED/-ING/-S [back-formation fr. *calcination*] **:** CALCINE

cal·ci·na·tion \,kalsə'nāshən\ *n* -s [ME *calcinacioun*, fr. MF *calcination*, fr. *calciner* + *-ation*] **:** the action or process of calcining **:** state of being calcined

[1]**cal·cine** \(')kal¦sīn\ *vb* -ED/-ING/-S [ME *calcenen, calcynen*, fr. MF *calciner*, fr. L *calc-, calx* lime — more at CHALK] *vt* **:** to heat (as inorganic materials) to a high temperature but without fusing in order to effect useful physical and chemical changes: as **a :** to convert to a powder or to a friable state by heating **b :** to heat in order to drive off volatile matter (as carbon dioxide from limestone, ores, or concentrates, or chemically combined water from clay) and thus usu. to disintegrate (as bones) — compare BURN *vt* 3d **c :** to heat under oxidizing conditions (as for producing metal oxides) — compare ROAST *vt* 2 ~ *vi* **:** to undergo calcination

[2]**cal·cine** \'kal,sīn\ *n* -s **:** a product (as a metal oxide) of calcination or roasting

calcined gypsum *n* **:** gypsum partially dehydrated by heat; *specif* **:** PLASTER OF PARIS

cal·cin·er \(')kal¦sīnə(r)\ *n* -s **:** one that calcines: as **a :** BURNER 1a(2) **b :** a furnace or kiln that calcines (as for converting coal to coke or sodium bicarbonate to soda ash)

cal·ci·no \kal'chē(,)nō, käl-\ *n* -s [It, fr. L *calc-, calx* lime — more at CHALK] **:** a disease of silkworms and other larval moths caused by a fungus (*Beauveria bassiana* or a related species) and marked by a mummified chalky appearance of the larva after death

cal·ci·no·sis \,kalsə'nōsəs\ *n, pl* **calcino·ses** \-ō,sēz\ [NL, fr. *calc-* + connective *-n-* + *-osis*] **:** the abnormal deposition of calcium salts in the skin, subcutaneous tissues, or other parts of the body

calcio- *comb form* [*calcium*] **:** calcium — used chiefly in names of minerals ⟨*calcio*biotite⟩

cal·cio·fer·rite \¦kalsē(,)ō'fe,rīt\ *n* -s [ISV *calcio-* + L *ferrum* iron + ISV *-ite*; orig. formed as G *kalkoferrit* — more at FARRIER] **:** a mineral consisting of a hydrous calcium iron phosphate occurring in yellow to green nodular masses

cal·cio·vol·borth·ite \¦kalsē(,)ō'vōl,bȯr,thīt, -väl-\ *n* -s [ISV *calcio-* + *volborthite*; orig. formed as G *kalkvolborthit*] **:** a mineral $CuCa(VO_4)(OH)$ consisting of a basic vanadate of calcium and copper

cal·cip·e·tal \(')kal¦sipəd·ᵊl\ *adj* [*calci-* + *-petal*] **:** CALCICOLOUS

[1]**cal·ci·phile** \'kalsə,fīl\ *or* **cal·ci·phil·ic** \¦kalsə¦filik\ *also* **cal·ciph·i·lous** \(')kal¦sifələs\ *adj* [*calci-* + *-phile, -philic, -philous*] **:** CALCICOLOUS

[2]**calciphile** \"\ *n* -s **:** CALCICOLE

cal·ci·phobe \'kalsə,fōb\ *n* -s [fr. *calciphobe*, adj.] **:** CALCIFUGE

cal·ci·pho·bic \¦kalsə¦fōbik\ *or* **cal·ci·phobe** \'kalsə,fōb\ *also* **cal·ciph·o·bous** \(')kal¦sifəbəs\ *adj* [*calci-* + *-phobic, -phobe, -phobous*] **:** CALCIFUGE

cal·ci·sponge \'kalsə,spənj\ *n* -s [NL *Calcispongiae*] **:** one of the Calcispongiae

cal·ci·spon·gi·ae \,kalsə'spənjē,ē, -'ä-\ *n pl, cap* [NL, fr. *calci-* + *-spongiae*] **:** a class of Porifera comprising marine sponges with a skeleton of calcareous spicules commonly divided into orders Asconosa and Syconosa on the basis of the complexity of the canal system

cal·cite \'kal,sīt\ *n* -s [ISV *calc-* + *-ite*; orig. formed as G *kalzit*] **:** a mineral consisting of calcium carbonate crystallized in hexagonal form, cleaving readily into rhombohedrons, and including besides common limestone chalk, marble, dogtooth spar, Iceland spar, stalactites, and stalagmites (hardness 3, sp. gr. of crystals 2.71) — distinguished from *aragonite* — **cal·cit·ic** \(')kal¦sid·ik\ *adj*

cal·ci·trate \'kalsə-,trāt\ *vb* -ED/-ING/-S [L *calcitratus*, past part. of *calcitrare* to kick, fr. *calc-, calx* heel — more at CALK] *archaic* **:** KICK — **cal·ci·tra·tion** \,kalsə'trāshən\ *n* -s

cal·ci·um \'kalsēəm\ *n* -s *often attrib* [NL, fr. L *calc-, calx* lime + NL *-ium* — more at CHALK] **1 :** a silver-white rather soft bivalent metallic element of the alkaline-earth group that quickly tarnishes in air and when heated burns with a brilliant light, used chiefly in alloys and in various metallurgical processes, often as a scavenger, and never occurring native but very common in combination in certain minerals and rocks, esp. as a carbonate (as in limestone), sulfate, or phosphate, in practically all natural waters, and in most animals and plants as an essential constituent — symbol *Ca;* see ELEMENT table **2 a :** a very strong white light source given by lime heated to incandescence in an oxyhydrogen flame — compare LIMELIGHT **b :** the flame of acetylene gas generated by reaction of calcium carbide with water

calcium aluminate *n* **:** any of various compounds of lime and alumina (as monocalcium aluminate $CaO.Al_2O_3$ and tricalcium aluminate $3CaO.Al_2O_3$) important as constituents of hydraulic cements

calcium arsenate *n* **:** an arsenate of calcium as the normal tricalcium arsenate $Ca_3(AsO_4)_2$ or a basic salt $3Ca_3(AsO_4)_2.Ca(OH)_2$]; *esp* **:** a commercial mixture obtained as a white powder usu. by heating arsenic pentoxide and calcium hydroxide in water and used as an insecticide esp. in the form of a dust

calcium bisulfite *n* **:** acid calcium sulfite $Ca(HSO_3)_2$ obtained as a yellowish solution usu. containing free sulfur dioxide by reaction of sulfur dioxide with limestone in the presence of water or with calcium hydroxide and used in the sulfite process for making wood pulp and as a disinfectant and antichlor — called also *bisulfite of lime, calcium hydrogen sulfite*

calcium carbide *n* **:** a crystalline compound CaC_2 that is colorless when pure but usu. varying from dark gray to brown made commercially by heating lime and carbon together in an electric furnace and used for the generation of acetylene and for making calcium cyanamide

calcium carbonate *n* **:** a salt $CaCO_3$ found in nature as calcite (as in limestone, chalk, and marble) and aragonite and in plant ashes, in bones, and in many shells, obtained also as a white precipitate by passing carbon dioxide into a suspension of calcium hydroxide in water, and used chiefly as a pigment, pigment extender, and filler, in dentifrices and pharmaceuticals esp. as an antacid, and in making lime and portland cement — compare CHALK 1, LIMESTONE, [2]WHITING 2

calcium chloride *n* **:** a deliquescent salt $CaCl_2$ obtained chiefly as a by-product in making soda ash and other chemicals, appearing in its anhydrous state as a white porous solid used as a drying and dehumidifying agent and in a more or less hydrated state as a solid, as colorless flakes, or in water solution used for controlling dust and ice on roads, for freezeproofing, in freezing mixtures and refrigeration brine, and with concrete as an accelerator or aid in curing

calcium cloud *n* **:** a patch of ionized calcium vapor in the sun's atmosphere

calcium cyanamide *also* **calcium cyanamid** *n* **:** a compound $CaCN_2$ obtained in impure cokelike form by passing dry nitrogen over calcium carbide at about 1100° C and used chiefly as a fertilizer, as a weed killer, in the defoliation of crops (as cotton), and as a source of other nitrogen compounds — called also *lime nitrogen, nitrolim*

calcium cyanide *n* **:** a compound $Ca(CN)_2$ that gives off hydrogen cyanide on exposure to air, is made usu. in impure black or gray flakes, powder, or cast blocks by heating crude calcium cyanamide in the presence of salt in an electric furnace, and is used chiefly as an insecticide and rodenticide and in making hydrogen cyanide and ferrocyanides — called also *black cyanide*

calcium fluoride *n* **:** a salt CaF_2 that is colorless when pure and is found in nature chiefly as the mineral fluorite

calcium gluconate *n* **:** a white crystalline or granular powdery salt $[HOCH_2(CHOH)_4COO]_2Ca.H_2O$ used in medicine as a source of calcium

calcium hydrate *n* **:** HYDRATED LIME — used chiefly commercially

calcium hydride *n* **:** a saltlike compound CaH_2 that is white and crystalline when pure but is usu. obtained in gray to grayish brown lumps and that is used chiefly as a reducing agent in the preparation of powdered metals, as a portable source of hydrogen, and as a drying agent — called also *hydrolith*

calcium hydrogen sulfite *n* **:** CALCIUM BISULFITE

calcium hydroxide *n* **:** a strong alkali $Ca(OH)_2$ commonly sold as a white powder or in water solution — see HYDRATED LIME, LIMEWATER

calcium hypochlorite *n* **:** any hypochlorite of calcium: as **a :** the normal anhydrous salt $Ca(ClO)_2$ that is white and relatively stable when pure **b :** a commercial product usu. containing 70 to 75 percent available chlorine and used as a bleaching agent, disinfectant, bactericide, and deodorant — called also *high-test hypochlorite*

calcium iodobehenate *n* **:** a white or yellowish-white powder $(C_{21}H_{42}ICOO)_2Ca$ used in medicine in place of inorganic iodides

calcium lactate *n* **:** a white almost tasteless crystalline salt $(CH_3CHOHCOO)_2Ca.5H_2O$ made by the action of lactic acid on calcium carbonate and used chiefly in medicine as a source of calcium and in foods (as in baking powder)

calcium levulinate *n* **:** a white powdery salt $(CH_3COCH_2CH_2COO)_2Ca.2H_2O$ used in medicine as a source of calcium

calcium light *n* **:** LIMELIGHT 1a, 1b

calcium nitrate *n* **:** a colorless crystalline deliquescent salt $Ca(NO_3)_2$ occurring often in natural waters and soil and as the mineral nitrocalcite, made by reaction of nitric acid or nitrogen oxides with lime or calcium carbonate, and used as a fertilizer

calcium oxalate *n* **:** a colorless crystalline salt $CaC_2O_4.H_2O$ noted for its insolubility, normally deposited in many plant cells, and in animals sometimes excreted in urine or retained in the form of urinary calculi

calcium oxide *n* **:** a caustic solid CaO that is white when pure and that is the chief constituent of lime

calcium pantothenate *n* **:** a white powdery salt $(C_9H_{16}NO_5)_2Ca$ made synthetically and used as a source of pantothenic acid for animals

calcium phosphate *n* **1 :** an orthophosphate of calcium: as **a :** one of the three simple orthophosphates, white or colorless when pure, usu. prepared by reaction of phosphoric acid or phosphorus pentoxide with lime, hydrated lime, or limestone: (1) **:** the primary phosphate $CaH_4(PO_4)_2$ or its monohydrate $CaH_4(PO_4)_2.H_2O$ used in the form of superphosphate as a fertilizer and in pure form as an acid ingredient in baking powder, prepared flours, and bakery products — called also *calcium dihydrogen phosphate, monobasic calcium phosphate, monocalcium phosphate* (2) **:** the secondary phosphate $CaHPO_4$ or its dihydrate $CaHPO_4.2H_2O$ found in nature as monetite or brushite respectively and used as a mineral supplement in pharmaceutical preparations and animal feeds and as a polishing agent in tooth powders and pastes — called also *calcium hydrogen phosphate, dibasic calcium phosphate, dicalcium phosphate* (3) **:** the tertiary phosphate $Ca_3(PO_4)_2$ found in nature as whitlockite and made by fusion of phosphorus pentoxide and lime or by fusion and defluorination of phosphate rock or phosphate sand for use as a fertilizer — called also *tribasic calcium phosphate, tricalcium phosphate* **b** (1) **:** a naturally occurring apatite (2) **:** an industrial product consisting essentially of hydroxylapatite usu. prepared by adding phosphoric acid to a lime slurry and used chiefly in ceramics, in making enamels and milk glass, as a noncaking agent esp. in salt and sugar, and as a source of calcium and phosphorus in pharmaceutical preparations — called also *tertiary calcium phosphate, tribasic calcium phosphate, tricalcium phosphate* **2 :** a phosphate of calcium (as calcium metaphosphate, calcium pyrophosphate) other than an orthophosphate

calcium-phosphorus ratio *n* **:** the proportional relation existing between calcium and phosphorus in the form of phosphate in body fluids and bone that in man is normally about 2.2 to 1

calcium resinate *n* **:** a yellowish-white powder or lumpy solid obtained by treating rosin with hydrated lime and used chiefly in varnishes, paints, and printing inks and in core oils and binders for foundry cores — called also *limed rosin*

calciums *pl of* CALCIUM

calcium silicate *n* **:** any of several silicates of calcium: as **a :** tricalcium silicate Ca_3SiO_5 found as an essential constituent of portland cement **b :** dicalcium silicate Ca_2SiO_4 also found as an essential constituent of portland cement **c :** calcium metasilicate $CaSiO_3$ found in nature as wollastonite

calcium stearate *n* **:** a white powder consisting essentially of calcium salts of stearic acid and palmitic acid and used chiefly in waterproofing, in paints (as flat-finish coatings), and in printing inks

calcium sulfate *n* **:** a white salt $CaSO_4$ known best in the hydrated forms gypsum and plaster of paris but also found as the anhydrous mineral anhydrite, obtained as a by-product in chemical processes, and used in its anhydrous form chiefly in Keene's cement, in composite pigments, as a filler (as in paper), and as a drying agent

calcium sulfite *n* **:** either of the two sulfites of calcium: **a :** the normal salt $CaSO_3$ prepared as a white powder and used as a disinfectant, preservative, and antichlor **b :** CALCIUM BISULFITE

calcium tungstate *n* **:** a white crystalline salt $CaWO_4$ found in nature as scheelite and used chiefly in screens for radiography, in luminous paint, and in fluorescent lamps

cal·cla·cite \'kalklə,sīt\ *n* -s [ISV *cal*cium + *Cl* (symbol for *chlorine*) + *acetate* + *-ite*; orig. formed in F] **:** calcium chloride acetate $CaCl(C_2H_3O_2).5H_2O$ found as an efflorescence on museum specimens (as of calcareous rocks and fossils)

calco- — see CALC-

cal·co·sphe·rite *or* **cal·co·sphae·rite** \,kal(,)kō'sfi,rīt\ *n* -s [ISV *calc-* + *spher-* or *sphaer-* + *-ite*; prob. orig. formed as F *calcosphérite*] **:** a granular or laminated deposit of calcium salts in the fat body or Malpighian tubules of certain insects

cal·crete \'kal,krēt\ *n* -s [*calcium* + *-crete* (as in *concrete*, n.)] **:** a limestone formed by the cementation of soil, sand, gravel, shells, by calcium carbonate deposited by evaporation, or by the escape of carbon dioxide from vadose water **:** CALICHE

calc-sin·ter \'kalk¦sintə(r)\ *n* -s [G *kalksinter*, fr. *kalk* lime (fr. OHG) + *sinter* — more at CHALK, SINTER] **:** calcareous sinter **:** TRAVERTINE

calc-spar \-,spär, -â(r\ *n* -s [part trans. of Sw *kalkspat*, fr. *kalk* lime (fr. OSw *kalker*, fr. MLG *kalk*) + *spat* spar — more at CHALK] **:** CALCITE

calc-tu·fa \'kalk¦tüfə\ *or* **calc-tuff** \-,təf, -üf\ *n* -s [G *kalk* + E *tufa* or *tuff*] **:** calcareous tufa — compare TRAVERTINE, TUFA

cal·cu·la·bil·i·ty \,kalkyələ'biləd·ē\ *n* -ES **:** the quality of being calculable

cal·cu·la·ble \'kalkyələbəl\ *adj* [*calculate* + *-able*] **1 :** capable of being calculated **:** ascertainable by calculation **2 :** that may be counted on or depended on **:** DEPENDABLE, PREDICTABLE ⟨a systematic man, as ~ as the stars⟩ — **cal·cu·la·ble·ness** *n* -ES — **cal·cu·la·bly** *adv*

cal·cu·late \'kalkyə,lāt, 'kaůk-, *usu* -ād·+V; *chiefly dial* 'kalk(ə),lā- *or* 'kaůk(- *or* 'ka(l),lā-\ *vb* -ED/-ING/-S [L *calculatus*, past part. of *calculare*, fr. *calculus* pebble, small stone used in reckoning, dim. of *calc-, calx* stone used in gaming, limestone, lime — more at CHALK] *vt* **1 a :** to ascertain or determine by mathematical processes esp. of some intricacy ⟨~ atomic weights⟩ **b :** to reckon by exercise of practical judgment rather than by strict mathematical process **:** ESTIMATE **c :** to solve the significance of **:** probe the meaning of **:** figure out **:** INTERPRET ⟨trying to ~ his expression —Hugh MacLennan⟩ **2 :** to plan the nature of beforehand **:** think out **:** FRAME **3 :** to design, prepare, or adapt by forethought or careful plan **:** fit or prepare by appropriate means — used chiefly as past part. with complementary infinitive ⟨*calculated* to succeed⟩ **4** *chiefly North* **a :** to judge to be true or probable on the basis of evidence at hand **:** SUPPOSE, BELIEVE, THINK **b :** INTEND, PURPOSE, PLAN ~ *vi* **1 a :** to make a calculation **:** form an estimate **b :** to make a judgment about the future **:** forecast consequences **2 :** COUNT, RELY — used with *on* or *upon* ⟨my uncle was *calculating* on the thing as concluded —Charles Lever⟩

syn COMPUTE, RECKON, ESTIMATE: CALCULATE is usu. preferred in ref. to more complex, difficult, and lengthy mathematical processes executed with precision and care ⟨*calculate* the velocity of light⟩ ⟨in 1920 it was *calculated* that in the twenty years . . . Gulf coast hurricanes caused $105,642,000 damage —A.F.Harlow⟩ COMPUTE is often used for simpler mathematical processes, esp. arithmetical ones, and with less abstruse and problematical questions ⟨*compute* interest due⟩ ⟨*compute* time in hours or days⟩ ⟨one half the children born, it is *computed*, die before the age of manhood —Adam Smith⟩ RECKON, an informal and familiar term, usu. suggests the simplest arithmetical processes ⟨*reckon* up a small grocery bill⟩ ⟨eighteen pence a day may be *reckoned* the common price of labor in London and its neighborhood —Adam Smith⟩ ESTIMATE may suggest the degree of complexity of any of the foregoing, but is likely to be used in situations in which data or figures are incomplete, guessed at, or unverified, and with processes perhaps simplified, to attain usable but tentative and approximate results ⟨experts now *estimate* the Easter island gaunt stone faces to be less than 800 years old —R.W.Murray⟩ Often it is used in connection with computing in advance, before the acquisition of sure data ⟨*estimate* next year's rainfall⟩

calculated *adj* **1 a :** worked out by calculation **:** computed mathematically ⟨~ tables⟩ **b :** ascertained or estimated by calculation ⟨the ~ velocity of a bullet⟩ **c :** engaged in, undertaken, or displayed after reckoning or estimating the statistical probability of success or failure — see CALCULATED RISK **2 :** planned or contrived so as to accomplish a purpose or achieve an effect **:** thought out in advance **:** deliberately planned ⟨his ways are not ~; he considers himself as honest as noonday —G.W.Brace⟩ ⟨that political justice is attainable only by a nicely ~ system of checks and balances —V.L.Parrington⟩ **3 :** brought about or brought into existence as a consequence of deliberate intent and planning **4 :** LIKELY — used with complementary infinitive ⟨a circumstance ~ to excite strong suspicion —W.E.Gladstone⟩ ⟨not ~ to be soft on such a subject —A.H.Vandenberg †1951⟩ **5 :** SUITED, FITTED, ADAPTED ⟨of such a nature as — used with complementary infinitive ⟨she was perfectly ~ to convince the sisters that times had worsened —Arnold Bennett⟩ — **cal·cu·lat·ed·ly** *adv*

calculated risk *n* **1 :** a hazard or chance of failure whose degree of probability has been reckoned or estimated before some undertaking is entered upon **2 :** an undertaking or the actual or possible product of an undertaking whose chance of failure has been previously estimated

calculating *adj* **1 :** performing calculations **2 a :** marked by the performance of calculation or by prudent and deliberate analysis ⟨examining his hurts with a ~ eye —Jack London⟩ **b :** marked by coldhearted calculation as to what will most promote self-interest **:** SCHEMING ⟨to Kate, ~ and cold, the most important thing was power —Ruth Randall⟩ **syn** see CAUTIOUS

cal·cu·lat·ing·ly \'===,===, ,=='===\ *adv* **:** in a calculating manner

calculating machine *n* **:** a machine for performing arithmetical operations (as multiplication) that are usu. more complex than can be done on an adding machine — called also *calculator;* compare COMPUTER

calculating punch *n* **:** a calculating machine into which problems or data are fed on punched cards and which presents its output in the form of similarly punched cards — compare PUNCH CARD

cal·cu·la·tion \,kalkyə'lāshən, ,kaůk-\ *n* -s [ME *calculacioun*, fr. LL *calculation-, calculatio*, fr. L *calculatus* (past part. of *calculare* to calculate) + *-ion-, -io* -ion] **1 a :** the action or process of calculating **b :** an instance of such action **:** an act of calculating **c :** the result of an act of calculating **:** a conclusion reached by reckoning or estimation sometimes accompanied by a verbal or written statement of the steps by which the conclusion has been reached **2 a :** deliberate prudent studied care in analyzing, planning, or contriving **b :** cold heartless planning to promote self-interest ⟨by every effort of subterfuge and ~ —Hilaire Belloc⟩

cal·cu·la·tion·al \¦==¦=shən°l, -shnəl\ *adj* **:** CALCULATORY

cal·cu·la·tive \'==,lād·iv, -ātiv, -ēv\ *adj* **1 :** of or relating to calculation **2 :** involving calculation **3 :** given to calculation

cal·cu·la·tor \-,lād·ə(r), -ātə-\ *n* -s [ME, fr. L, fr. *calculatus* + *-or*] **1 :** one that calculates: as **a :** CALCULATING MACHINE **b :** a person who operates a calculating machine esp. in checking figures in financial or statistical papers **c :** a computing clerk and supervisor of a mutuel department who calculates the amounts due to patrons holding parimutuel tickets on the leading horses in each race **2 :** a set or book of tables for facilitating computations **:** READY RECKONER

cal·cu·la·to·ry \-lə,tōrē, -,ȯ-\ *adj* [LL *calculatorius*, fr. L *calculatus* + *-orius* -ory] **:** of or relating to calculation ⟨how the Maya carried out their ~ operations —A.L.Kroeber⟩

cal·cu·li·form \-lə,fȯrm\ *adj* [ISV *calcul-* (fr. L *calculus* pebble) + *-iform*] **:** shaped like a pebble

cal·cu·lo·sis \,kalkyə'lōsəs\ *n, pl* **calculo·ses** \-ō,sēz\ [NL, fr. *calculus* + *-osis*] *med* **:** the formation of or the condition of having a calculus or calculi

cal·cu·lous \'kalkyələs, 'kaůk-\ *adj* [F or L; F *calculeux*, fr. L *calculosus*, fr. *calculus* pebble + *-osus* -ous] **1 :** caused or characterized by the presence of a calculus **2 :** affected with gravel or stone

cal·cu·lus \'kalkyələs, 'kaůk-\ *n, pl* **calcu·li** \-,lī, -ē\ *also* **calcu·lus·es** \-ləsəz\ [L, pebble, stone in the bladder or kidneys, stone used in calculating, act of calculating — more at CALCULATE] **1 a :** a solid concretion usu. composed of mineral salts, formed around organic material, and found mainly in hollow organs, ducts, passages, and cysts ⟨renal *calculi*⟩ ⟨a small ~ was eliminated from the bladder⟩ — see GALLSTONE, RENAL CALCULUS, URINARY CALCULUS **b :** a concretion on teeth **:** TARTAR **2** *archaic* **:** CALCULATION, COMPUTATION **3 :** a method or process of reasoning by computation of symbols: as **a :** a branch of mathematics (as the infinitesimal calculus) involving calculation **b :** any one of the commonly distinguished divisions of symbolic logic **4** *pl* **calculuses :** a book or treatise on infinitesimal calculus

calculus of classes : ALGEBRA OF CLASSES

calculus of enlargement : a method in the calculus of finite differences of finding analytical expansions by means of *E* and other operators, where $Ef(x) = f(x + 1)$

calculus of finite differences : a branch of mathematics that interprets variation as a succession of small increments but permits those increments to be finite instead of infinitesimally small

calculus of individuals : a branch of symbolic logic designed to avoid the terminological platonism inherent in an algebra of classes by recourse to the notion of individuals esp. in their relationships of overlapping, discreteness, and being a part

calculus of relations *or* **calculus of relatives :** ALGEBRA OF RELATIONS

calculus of variations : a branch of infinitesimal calculus whose fundamental notion is the variation of a curve and whose problem is to find the form of curve that will make a definite integral of a given function along the curve have a stationary value, the curve playing the role of the independent variable in ordinary differential calculus

¹cal·cut·ta \(')kal¦kəd·ə, -ətə\ *adj, usu cap* [fr. *Calcutta,* India] **:** of or from the city of Calcutta, India **:** of the kind or style prevalent in Calcutta

²calcutta \"\ *n* -s **1** [short for *Calcutta cane*] **:** a fishing rod made from a single piece of bamboo cane **2** *or* **calcutta pool** *usu cap C* [fr. the *Calcutta* sweepstakes, famous auction pool held in Calcutta, India] **:** a form of auction pool in which each contestant esp. in golf and bridge tournaments is sold at a fixed price but at a handicap established by bidding in an auction

calcutta hemp *n, usu cap C* [fr. *Calcutta,* India] **:** JUTE

cal·de·ra \kal'derə, -dirə\ *n* -s [Sp, lit., caldron, fr. LL *caldaria*] **:** a crater whose diameter is many times that of the volcanic vent because of the collapse or subsidence of the central part of a volcano or because of explosions of extraordinary violence

cal·dron *also* **caul·dron** \'kȯldrən\ *n* -s [ME, alter. (influenced by L *caldus, calidus*) of *cauderon,* fr. ONF, dim. of *caudiere,* fr. LL *caldaria,* fr. L, warm bath, fr. fem. of *caldarius* suitable for warming, fr. *caldus, calidus* warm, fr. *calēre* to be warm — more at LEE] **1 :** a large kettle or boiler **2 :** something resembling a boiling caldron or its contents (as in being a mixture of elements or forces in a state of unrest or upheaval) ⟨from this witches' ~ of politics, race, language . . . arose fierce . . . hatred —A.L.Guerard⟩ **3 :** MOROCCO RED

ca·le·an \¦kalē¦än\ *n* -s [Per *qalyān*] **:** a Persian water pipe

ca·leb·ite \'kāləˌbīt\ *n* -s *usu cap* [*Caleb fl ab* 1200 B.C. Israelite who participated in the conquest of Canaan + E *-ite*] **:** a member of a clan that traces its descent to the biblical Caleb and was once a part of the tribe of Judah

ca·lèche *or* **ca·leche** \kə'lesh\ *n* -s [F *calèche* — more at CALASH] **1 :** CALASH 1a **2 :** a 2-wheeled horse-drawn vehicle with or without a folding top and with a driver's seat on the splashboard that is used in Quebec, Canada **3 :** CALASH 2a

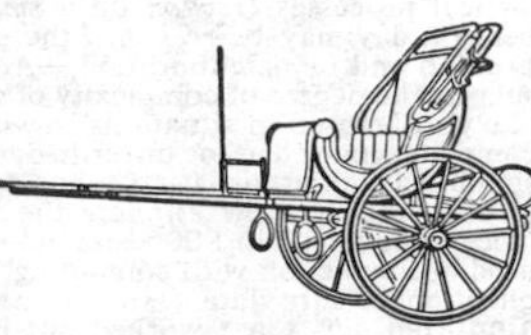
calèche 2

¹cal·e·do·ni·an \¦kalə¦dōnēən, -nyən\ *adj, usu cap* [NL *Caledonia* Scotland (fr. L, province of ancient Britain) + E *-an*] **1 :** of or relating to Scotland **:** SCOTTISH, SCOTS, SCOTCH **2 :** of or relating to mountain-making movements of the European Paleozoic era — see GEOLOGIC TIME table

²caledonian \"\ *n* -s **1** *cap* **:** a native or inhabitant of Scotland **:** SCOTSMAN **2 caledonians** *pl but sing in constr, usu cap* **:** a square dance for eight resembling the quadrille

caledonian brown *n, usu cap C* **1 :** a permanent natural pigment that consists chiefly of hydrated oxides of manganese and iron and is ruddy brown when raw but nearly black when burnt **2 :** GYPSY 4

cal·e·do·nite \ˌkalə'dōˌnīt\ *n* -s [F *calédonite,* fr. L *Caledonia* Scotland, its locality + F *-ite*] **:** a mineral $Cu_2Pb_5(SO_4)_3(CO_3)(HO)_6$ consisting of basic copper lead sulfate occurring in minute green crystals

cal·e·don jade green \'kaləˌdän-, -əd°n-\ *n, usu cap C, often cap J&G* [*caledon,* prob. modif. of NL *Caledonia*] **:** VAT JADE GREEN

¹cal·e·fa·cient \¦kalə¦fāshənt\ *adj* [L *calefacient-, calefaciens,* pres. part. of *calefacere* to warm — more at CHAFE] **:** making warm **:** HEATING

²calefacient \"\ *n* -s **:** a calefacient remedy

cal·e·fac·tion \¦kalə¦fakshən\ *n* -s [ML *calefaction-, calefactio,* fr. L *calefactus* (past part. of *calefacere*) + *-ion-, -io* -ion] **1 :** WARMING **2 :** the state of being warmed

¹cal·e·fac·to·ry \¦kalə¦fakt(ə)rē\ *n* -ES [ML *calefactorium,* fr. LL, neut. of *calefactorius*] **:** a monastery room warmed and used as a sitting room

²calefactory \"\ *adj* [LL *calefactorius,* fr. L *calefactus* + *-orius* -ory] **:** making hot **:** producing or communicating heat

cal·e·fy \'kaləˌfī\ *vb* -ED/-ING/-ES [ML *calejicare, calificare* to heat, fr. L *calēre* to be warm — more at LEE] *vt* **:** to make warm ~ *vi* **:** to become warm

ca·lem·bour \¦kaləm¦bu̇(ə)r\ *n* -s [F] **:** PUN

calenda *var of* CALINDA

¹cal·en·dar \'kaləndə(r)\ *n* -s [ME *calender,* fr. AF or ML; AF *calender,* fr. ML *kalendarium,* fr. L, moneylender's account book, fr. *kalendae* calends — more at CALENDS] **1 :** a system by which the beginning, length, and divisions of the civil year are fixed and by which days and longer divisions of time (as weeks, months, and years) are arranged in a definite order — see GREGORIAN CALENDAR, JULIAN CALENDAR; MONTH table, YEAR table **2 a :** a tabular register of days according to a system usu. covering one year, referring the days of each month to the days of the week, often giving also important astronomical data, and sometimes indicating the dates of ecclesiastic festivals, holidays, and other events connected with particular days **b :** ALMANAC; *esp* **:** one giving agricultural information (as dates most suitable for planting a particular crop) **3** *obs* **:** an example to be followed **:** MODEL **4 :** an orderly list of persons, things, or events: as **a :** a chronological register of documents with a brief summary of the contents of each, made to serve as an index to the documents of a period **b :** a list of cases to be tried in court or of prisoners to be tried with the time and reason for their commitment **c :** a list of bills, resolutions, or other items in the order in which they are reported out of committee for consideration by a legislative assembly **d :** a list of events or activities giving dates and details of planned events ⟨the college ~ begins with Freshman Week⟩; *also* **:** a list of events or the series of events scheduled for a particular period or time ⟨many new offerings of corporate securities on the ~ this week⟩ ⟨parades, parties, concerts, dances make up a full ~ for the weekend⟩ **e :** the whole range of possible variations in any type or category ⟨wanted for murder . . . and almost every other crime in the ~ —James Thurber⟩ **5** *Brit* **:** a university catalog

²calendar \"\ *vt* **calendared; calendared; calendaring** \-d(ə)riŋ\ **calendars 1 :** to enter (as a name or event) in a calendar or list **2 :** to enter an analysis or summary of (as a book or document) in a catalog or index **3 :** to assign a date to ⟨~*ed* predictions⟩

calendar art *n* **:** pictures of widely popular appeal displayed on wall calendars distributed esp. as advertisements ⟨have no more vitality or originality than *calendar art* —Elizabeth Hardwick⟩

calendar clock *n* **:** a clock that shows the days of the week and month, phases of the moon, and sometimes other phenomena in addition to hours, minutes, and seconds

calendar day *n* **:** a civil day **:** the time from midnight to midnight

cal·en·dar·i·al \¦ˌ=¦da(a)rēəl\ *adj* [¹*calendar* + *-ial*] **:** CALENDRICAL

cal·en·dar·ic \¦ˌ=¦darik\ *adj* [¹*calendar* + *-ic*] **:** CALENDRICAL

cal·en·dar·ist \'kaləndərəst\ *n* -s **:** one devoted to the study or making of calendars

calendar month *n* **1 :** one of the months as named in the calendar **2 :** the period from a day of one month to the corresponding day of the next month if such exists or if not to the last day of the next month (as from Jan. 3 to Feb. 3 or from Jan. 31 to Feb. 29)

calendar quarter *n* **:** one of the four periods of three months each of a calendar year

calendar round *n* **:** a period of fifty-two 365-day years after which the combinations of day names, day numbers, and month positions repeat in the Maya or Aztec calendars

calendar stone *n* **:** a stone with an inscription elucidating an ancient time-reckoning system ⟨the Aztec *calendar stone,* 12 feet in diameter, is preserved at Mexico City⟩

calendar watch *n* **:** a watch that shows the days of the week and month and sometimes other phenomena as well as hours, minutes, and seconds

calendar wednesday *n, usu cap C&W* **:** the Wednesday of each week that committees of the U.S. House of Representatives may bring unprivileged bills before that house

calendar week *n* **:** a week beginning with Sunday and ending with Saturday

calendar year *n* **1 :** a period of a year beginning and ending with the dates which are conventionally accepted as marking the beginning and end of a numbered year (as Jan. 1 and Dec. 31 in the Gregorian calendar) **2 :** a period of time equal in length to that of the year in the calendar conventionally in use (as in the Gregorian calendar 365 days or when a Feb. 29 is included 366 days)

¹cal·en·der \'kaləndə(r)\ *archaic var of* CALENDAR

²calender \"\ *vt* **calendered; calendered; calendering** \-d(ə)riŋ\ **calenders** [MF *calandrer,* fr. *calandre*] **:** to press (as cloth, rubber, paper) between rollers or plates in order to make smooth and glossy or glazed or to thin into sheets — see SUPERCALENDER, ²WATER 5c

³calender \"\ *n* -s [F *calandre* machine for calendering, modif. of Gk *kylindros* cylinder — more at CYLINDER] **1** *archaic* **:** CALENDERER **2 :** a machine for calendering cloth, rubber, or paper by passing it between rollers or plates — see FRICTION CALENDER, SUPERCALENDER **3 :** a machine for giving tubular knitted fabric the desired width by applying steam and stretching

⁴calender \"\ *n* -s [Per *qalandar,* fr. Ar, fr. Per *kalandar* uncouth man, perh. fr. *kaland* pickax, shovel] **:** one of a Sufic order of wandering mendicant dervishes

cal·en·der·er \-dərə(r)\ *n* -s [ME *calenderar,* fr. MF *calendrer* to calender + ME *-ar* (var. of *-er*)] **:** one that calenders

calender man *n* **:** CALENDERER; *also* **:** a worker who processes plastics or rubber sheets or fabrics in rolling or embossing machines

ca·len·dra \kə'lendrə\ *n, cap* [NL, modif. of F *calandre* weevil] **:** a genus of weevils (family Curculionidae) including a number of pests (as the maize billbug) of Indian corn and other field crops

ca·len·dri·cal \kə'lendrəkəl, ka-\ *also* **ca·len·dric** \-rik\ *adj* [*calendr-* (alter. of *calendar*) + *-ical* or *-ic*] **1 :** of, relating to, characteristic of, or used in a calendar **2 a :** serving to measure time in calendar units or to record the calendar time or sequence of events ⟨~ inscriptions⟩ ⟨~ systems⟩ **:** serving the purposes of chronologizing **b :** having to do with or relating to the measuring and recording of calendar units of time or recording the calendar time or sequence of events ⟨solstice is a time of ~ importance⟩ **3 :** occurring on special days as marked in a calendar ⟨~ festivals⟩

cal·en·dry \'kaləndrē\ *n* -ES [³*calender* + *-ry*] **:** a place for calendering

cal·ends *or* **kal·ends** \'kalən(d)z\ *n pl but sometimes sing in constr* [ME *kalendes,* fr. L *kalendae;* akin to L *calare* to call, proclaim — more at LOW] **:** the first day of the ancient Roman month from which days were counted backward to the ides — compare NONES; see GREEK CALENDS

ca·len·du·la \kə'lenjələ\ *n* [NL, fr. ML, fr. L *calendae, kalendae* calends + *-ula;* perh. fr. its use in folk medicine against menstrual disorders] **1** *cap* **:** a small genus of herbs (family Compositae) native to temperate regions and having alternate simple oblong to oblong-ovate leaves and large heads of yellow-rayed flowers with a naked receptacle and incurved achenes — see POT MARIGOLD **2** -s **:** any plant of the genus *Calendula* **3 :** the dried florets of plants of the genus *Calendula* (esp. *C. officinalis*) sometimes used as a mild aromatic and diaphoretic

ca·len·du·lin \-lən\ *n* -s [ISV *calendul-* (fr. NL *Calendula*) + *-in;* orig. formed as G *kalendulin*] **:** a yellowish pigment found in the pot marigold

cal·en·ture \'kalənˌchu̇(ə)r\ *n* -s [earlier *calentura,* fr. Sp, fever, fr. *calentar* to heat, fr. L *calent-, calens,* pres. part. of *calēre* to be warm — more at LEE] **1 a :** a fever formerly supposed to affect sailors in the tropics causing them to imagine the sea a green field and to leap into it **b :** any fever supposedly caused by heat **2 :** PASSION, ARDOR, ZEAL

ca·le·sa \kə'lāsə\ *n* -s [Sp, fr. F *calèche* — more at CALASH] **:** a small 2-wheeled calash used in the Philippines

ca·le·sin \¦kalə¦sēn\ *n* -s [Sp, dim. of *calesa*] **:** a small one-horse hooded chaise or gig having a seat behind for the driver and used in the Philippines

ca·ley pea \'kālē-\ *n, usu cap C* [prob. fr. the name *Caley*] **:** SINGLETARY PEA

¹calf \'kaf, -aa(ə)-,-ai-,-á-,-ä-\ *n, pl* **calves** \|vz\ *also* **calfs** \|fs\ *often attrib* [ME, fr. OE *cealf;* akin to OHG *kalb* calf, ON *kālfr,* Goth *kalbo,* ON *kalfi* calf of the leg, Gaulish *galba* fat man, L *galla* gall on a tree — more at GALL (excrescence)] **1 :** the young of the domestic cow or of certain other larger members of the Bovidae **2 :** the young of the domestic cow when past the vealer stage but not yet mature enough to be considered a beef **3 :** the young of the elephant, rhinoceros, hippopotamus, moose, whale, or various other large animals **4** *pl calfs* **a :** the fur or skin of the young of the domestic cow **b :** leather made of the skin of the calf; *esp* **:** a fine light-colored bookbinder's leather made from the skin of a calf **5 :** an awkward or silly boy or youth **6 :** a small mass of ice set free from a coast glacier or from an iceberg or floe — **in calf :** PREGNANT — used of a cow

²calf \"\ *n, pl* **calves** [ME, fr. ON *kalfi*] **:** the fleshy hinder part of the leg below the knee

calfbound \'=ˌ=\ *adj, of a book* **:** bound in calfskin

calf diphtheria *n* **:** necrobacillosis of the mouth and pharynx of calves and young cattle commonly passing into pneumonia or generalized septicemia and terminating in death

calf·hood \-ˌfu̇d,-fˌhu̇d\ *n* -s **:** the state or time of being a calf ⟨~ vaccination⟩ ⟨~ disease⟩

calf·kill \'=ˌkil\ *n* -s **1 :** any of several plants whose foliage is poisonous to cattle: as **a :** MOUNTAIN LAUREL **b :** SHEEP LAUREL **c :** an evergreen shrub (*Leucothoë catesbaei*) of the southeastern U.S. cultivated for ornament **2 :** VELVET GRASS

calf knee *n* **:** BUCK KNEE—**calf–kneed** \'=¦=\ *adj*

calf·less \-fləs\ *adj* **:** being without a calf

calf love *n* **:** transitory affection felt by a boy or a girl for one of the opposite sex ⟨the ambiguous ardors of *calf love* —H.M.Kallen⟩ — called also *puppy love*

calf rope *n, dial*—a cry of surrender ⟨they punched him until he hollered *calf rope*⟩

calf's–foot jelly \-vz,-,-f,s-\ *n* **:** jelly made from gelatin obtained by boiling calves' feet

calf·skin \'=ˌ=\ *n* -s **:** leather made of the skin of a calf

calf's–mouth \-vz,-,-f,s-\ *n, pl* **calf's–mouths :** SNAPDRAGON 1 a

calf's–tongue molding \-vz,-,-f,s-\ *n, archit* **:** a molding bearing in relief a series of tonguelike members

calf ward *n, Scot* **:** a small enclosure for calves

calf wheel *n* [so called fr. its resemblance to a bull wheel] **:** a drum for raising and lowering heavy strings of well casing

calfy \-fē\ *adj* **:** in calf

cal·ga·ry \'kalgərē, -ri\ *adj, usu cap* [fr. *Calgary,* Alberta, Canada] **:** of or from the city of Calgary, Alberta **:** of the kind or style prevalent in Calgary

Cal·gon \'kal,gän\ *trademark* — used for a sodium phosphate glass that approximates a sodium metaphosphate in composition and is used chiefly in water softening, in detergents, in tanning leather, and in deflocculating suspensions

¹ca·li \'kälē\ *adj, usu cap* [fr. *Cali,* Colombia] **:** of or from the city of Cali, Colombia **:** of the kind or style prevalent in Cali

²cali *var of* CALA

cali- — see CALLI-

¹ca·lia·na \kal'yänə\ *n, pl* **caliana** *or* **calianas** *usu cap* [Sp, of AmerInd origin] **1 a :** an Indian people of Venezuela **b :** a member of such people **2 :** the language of the Caliana people constituting a language family

²ca·lia·ná \¦kalyə¦nä\ *n, pl* **calianá** *or* **calianás** *usu cap* [Pg, of AmerInd origin] **1 a :** a Tupi-Guaranian people of northeastern Brazil **b :** a member of such people **2 :** the language of the Calianá people

cal·i·ban \'kaləˌban *also* -ˌbən\ *n* -s *usu cap* [after *Caliban,* a brutal and deformed slave in Shakespeare's *Tempest*] **:** a person or thing that is or is felt to be slavish, brutal, monstrous, or deformed

calibash *obs var of* CALIPASH

cal·i·ber *or* **cal·i·bre** \'kaləbə(r), *Brit also* kə'lēb-\ *n* -s [MF *calibre,* fr. OIt *calibro,* fr. Ar *qālib* shoemaker's last, prob. fr. Gk *kalapous,* fr. *kalon* wood (fr. *kaiein* to burn) + *pous* foot — more at CAUSTIC, FOOT] **1 a :** the bore diameter of the barrel of a weapon (as a firearm) measured in rifled arms from land to land — compare LAND DIAMETER **b :** the diameter of the projectile fired from such a weapon **c :** the land-to-land diameter of the bore of a piece of ordnance used as a unit of measurement for stating the length of the tube of the piece — now used only of naval and coastal defense guns ⟨a 3″/50 gun is 3″ in bore and 50 ~*s* or 150″ long⟩ **2 :** the diameter of a round or cylindrical body; *esp* **:** the internal diameter of a tube or hollow cylinder **3** *obs* **:** degree of importance or station in society **:** RANK **4 a :** degree in personal qualities (as mental capacity or breadth of knowledge) or moral qualities ⟨a man of high intellectual ~⟩ **b :** degree of excellence or importance **:** QUALITY ⟨the ~ of instruction⟩ **5 :** the model number given to a watch movement by the factory **syn** see QUALITY

caliber compass *n* **:** CALIPERS

caliber rule *n, obs* **:** a gunmaker's calipers

cal·i·bo·gus *also* **cal·li·bo·gus** \ˌkalə'bōgəs\ *n* -ES [origin unknown] **:** a drink consisting of rum, spruce beer, and molasses

cal·i·brate \'kaləˌbrāt, *usu* -ād·+V\ *vt* -ED/-ING/-S [*caliber* + *-ate*] **1 a** *obs* **:** to ascertain the caliber of (as a thermometer tube) **b :** to determine or mark the capacity or the graduations of or to rectify the graduations of (as a graduated measuring instrument) **c :** to standardize (as a measuring instrument) by determining the deviation from standard esp. so as to ascertain the proper correction factors **2 :** to determine by actual firing the corrections in range or elevation settings required to make (a piece of artillery) fire uniformly with a standard or reference piece

calibrated airspeed *n* **:** the reading (of an airspeed indicator) corrected for instrumental and installation errors

cal·i·bra·tion \ˌkalə'brāshən\ *n* -s **1 :** the act or process of calibrating **:** state of being calibrated **2 :** a set of graduations marked to indicate values — usu. used in pl. ⟨pressure ~*s* on steam gauges⟩

cal·i·bra·tor *or* **cal·i·brat·er** \'kaləˌbrād·ə(r), -ātə-\ *n* -s **:** one that calibrates: as **a :** an instrument for measuring the caliber of any passage **b :** an instrument that measures variable quantities or elements (as frequency or capacity) in electronic equipment

calibre *var of* CALIBER

caliceal *var of* CALYCEAL

calices *pl of* CALIX

ca·li·che \kə'lēchē\ *n* -s [AmerSp, fr. Sp, pebble in a brick, flake of lime, fr. *cal* lime, fr. L *calx* — more at CHALK] **1 :** the nitrate-bearing gravel or rock of the sodium nitrate deposits of Chile and Peru **2 :** a crust or succession of crusts of calcium carbonate that forms within or on top of the stony soil of arid or semiarid regions

ca·lic·i·form \kə'lisəˌfȯrm\ *adj* [ISV *calic-* (fr. L *calic-, calix* cup) + *-iform* — more at CHALICE] **:** shaped like a calyx or bell; *specif* **:** of or relating to a type of pottery of the late neolithic and early bronze age found in France, Spain, England, and central Europe

cal·i·cle \'kaləkəl\ *n* -s [L *caliculus,* dim. of *calic-, calix* cup] **:** CALYCULUS

¹cal·i·co \'kaləˌkō, -lē-\ *n, pl* **calicoes** *or* **calicos** [fr. *Calicut,* city in India from which it was first imported] **1 a** *obs* **:** cotton cloth usu. figured imported from India **b :** any of various cotton stuffs of European make **c** *Brit* **:** a plain white cotton fabric that is heavier than muslin **d :** any of various cheap cotton fabrics with figured patterns **2 :** any of several plant diseases usu. of virus origin characterized by leaf variegation: as **a :** the mosaic disease of tobacco; *also* **:** a plant affected with this disease **b :** a virus disease of the potato **c :** a virus disease of celery **3 :** a blotched or spotted animal: as **a :** a horse with calico markings **:** PIEBALD **b :** BLACK CRAPPIE **c :** a goldfish of any fancy breed having thin transparent scales and a pigmented skin showing spots and blotches **4** *slang* **:** GIRL, WOMAN

²calico \"\ *adj* **1 :** made of calico **2 :** resembling calico in appearance **:** MULTICOLORED; *specif* **:** marked with well-defined patches of color (as on a tortoiseshell cat)

calico ash *n* [²*calico*] **:** lumber from a white ash (*Fraxinus americana*) esp. from the southern U.S.

calico bass *n* [²*calico*] **1 :** BLACK CRAPPIE **2 :** KELP BASS

calico bean *n* [²*calico*] **1 :** KIDNEY BEAN **2 :** SIEVA BEAN

calico bird *n* [²*calico*] **:** TURNSTONE

calico bush *n* [²*calico*] **:** MOUNTAIN LAUREL

calico corn *n* [²*calico*] **:** Indian corn having red, yellow, and brownish red striping and mottling of the kernels

calico crab *n* [²*calico*] **1 :** LADY CRAB **2 :** a shallow-water crab (*Hepatus epheliticus*) brilliantly spotted with red and occurring along the coast from Maryland to Cuba and Texas

cal·i·coed \-ˌkōd\ *adj* **:** dressed in calico

calico flower *n* [²*calico*] **1 :** MOUNTAIN LAUREL **2 :** a Brazilian vine (*Aristolochia elegans*) often cultivated for its brown-purple beautifully veined flowers somewhat resembling a bent pitcher in shape **3 :** FIVE-SPOT

calico marble *n* [²*calico*] **:** a brecciated limestone conglomerate found in Maryland and used as a decorative stone

calico plover *or* **calico snipe** *n* [²*calico*] **:** TURNSTONE

calico printing *n* [¹*calico*] **:** the process of making fast-color designs on cotton fabrics, esp. calico

calico salmon *n* [²*calico;* fr. its variegated color in summer] **:** DOG SALMON

calico scale *n* [²*calico*] **:** a scale (*Lecanium cerasorum*) that is brown mottled with yellow and attacks various fruit and ornamental trees in California

calico tree *n* [²*calico*] **:** MOUNTAIN LAUREL

calico wood *n* [²*calico*] **1 :** the wood of the silver bell **2 :** SILVER BELL

calicular *var of* CALYCULAR

caliculate *var of* CALYCULATE

cal·i·cut \'kaləkət\ *adj, usu cap* [fr. *Calicut,* India] **:** of or from the city of Calicut, India **:** of the kind or style prevalent in Calicut

cal·id \'kaləd\ *adj* [L *calidus* — more at CALDRON] *archaic* **:** WARM, HOT, BURNING

cal·i·duct \'kaləˌdəkt\ *n* -s [L *calidus* hot + E *-duct* (as in *aqueduct, ventiduct*)] **:** a duct to convey hot air, hot water, or steam for heating

calif *var of* CALIPH

califate *var of* CALIPHATE

cal·i·for·nia \¦kalə¦fȯrnyə, -ō(ə)n-, -nēə\ *adj, usu cap* [fr. *California,* state in the western U.S., fr. Sp, prob. fr. the name of an island in the romance *Las Sergas de Esplandian* (1510), by García Ordóñez de Montalvo, 15th cent. Span. writer] **:** of or from the state of California **:** of the kind or style prevalent in California **:** CALIFORNIAN ⟨*California* weather⟩

california barberry *n, usu cap C* **:** OREGON GRAPE

california bayberry *n, usu cap C* **:** a Pacific coast shrub or small tree (*Myrica californica*) with waxy resinous fruit

california bay tree *n, usu cap C* **:** CALIFORNIA LAUREL

california bearberry *n, usu cap C* **:** CALIFORNIA COFFEE 2

california blackberry *n, usu cap C* **:** an evergreen prostrate or semierect shrub (*Rubus vitifolius*) with oblong black fruit

california black oak *n, usu cap C* **:** a Pacific coast deciduous tree (*Quercus kelloggii*) with deeply parted bristle-tipped leaves

california black walnut *n, usu cap C* **:** a medium-sized tree (*Juglans californica*) with somewhat aromatic compound leaves and channeled or smooth edible nuts

california blight *n, usu cap C* **:** a fungous disease of peaches,

apricots, plums, and cherries caused by an imperfect fungus (*Coryneum carpophilum*) and producing shot holes, pustular spots on the leaf and fruit, cankers, and bud and twig blight
california bluebell *n, usu cap C* **:** a desert herb (*Phacelia minor*) of the western U.S. having blue or purple tubular flowers in one-sided clusters
california bluegrass *n, usu cap C* **:** MUTTON GRASS
california box elder *n, usu cap C* **:** a Pacific coast maple that is a variety (*Acer negundo* var. *californicum*) of the box elder having fruits that are crimson when young and white when mature
california brown pelican *n, usu cap C* **:** a Pacific coast pelican that is a variety (*Pelecanus occidentalis californicus*) of the brown pelican and has a creamy head and bright red gular pouch
california buckeye *n, usu cap C* **:** a shrub or small tree (*Aesculus californica*) with palmately compound leaves and fragrant white or rose-colored flowers
california buckthorn *n, usu cap C* **:** CALIFORNIA COFFEE 2
california bulrush *n, usu cap C* **:** a tall marsh sedge (*Scirpus californicus*) with 3-sided or nearly round almost leafless stems used for packing and as thatch for haystacks
california bur clover *n, usu cap 1st C* **:** an aggressive adventive clover (*Medicago hispida*) from Europe now widespread in southwestern U.S. and distinguished esp. by the double row of hooked spines on the spiral ridges of the seed pod
california buttercup *n, usu cap C* **:** a common herb (*Ranunculus californicus*) of moist foothills and canyons with twice-divided leaves and large showy yellow flowers
california calycanth *n, usu cap 1st C* **:** SPICEBUSH 2
california clapper rail *n, usu cap 1st C* **:** a large short-tailed clapper rail (*Rallus obsoletus*) of the Pacific coast of No. America from Puget Sound to Lower California
california coffee *n, usu cap 1st C* **1 :** CASCARA BUCKTHORN **2 :** a buckthorn (*Rhamnus californica*) with alternate but scattered dark green leaves, small greenish flowers, and reddish black berries
california color *n, usu cap 1st C* **:** a moderate brown that is yellower, lighter, and stronger than auburn, bay, or chestnut brown and redder, lighter, and stronger than coffee
california condor *n, usu cap 1st C* **:** a very large nearly extinct No. American vulture (*Gymnogyps californianus*) related to the condor of So. America and sometimes larger though of lighter build, chiefly dull black with some white and with a bare head and neck

California condor

california coneflower *n, usu cap 1st C* **:** a stiff hairy perennial herb (*Rudbeckia californica*) of the Pacific coast with coarse hispid foliage and long-stalked heads of yellow flowers
california cress *n, usu cap 1st C* **:** a hedge mustard (*Sisymbrium officinale*)
california dandelion *n, usu cap C* **:** CAT'S-EAR 1
california day lily *n, usu cap C* **:** DESERT LILY
california everlasting *n, usu cap C* **:** a stout biennial weedy plant (*Gnaphalium decurrens californicum*) with white woolly foliage that becomes green in age
california fan palm *n, usu cap C* **:** WASHINGTON PALM
california feverbush *n, usu cap C* **:** BEAR BRUSH
california flying fish *n, usu cap C* **:** a large flying fish (*Cypselurus californicus*) of the open seas off the coast of southern California and adjacent Mexico
california fuchsia *n, usu cap C* **:** a plant of the genus *Zauschneria* (esp. *Z. californica*) with brilliant scarlet flowers
california geranium *n, usu cap C* **:** a Mexican groundsel (*Senecio petasitis*) having leaves like those of a garden geranium and a much-branched cluster of yellow flower heads
california golden bells *n pl but sing or pl in constr, usu cap C* **:** CALIFORNIA YELLOW BELLS
california greasewood *n, usu cap C* **:** IODINE BUSH
california green *n, usu cap C* **:** a dark grayish yellow that is greener, less strong, and slightly darker than honey or yellowstone and redder and less strong than olivesheen
california ground squirrel *n, usu cap C* **:** a grizzled brown-and-gray burrowing squirrel (*Citellus beecheyi*) widely distributed in California and important as a vector of endemic plague and as a destructive pest on cultivated land
california gull *n, usu cap C* **:** a large gull (*Larus californicus*) resembling the herring gull in color and breeding in the plains region of the western U.S. where it is important as a consumer of noxious insects
california halibut *n, usu cap C* **:** a large greenish brown or grayish brown flatfish (*Paralichthys maculosus*) of the southern Californian and Mexican coasts important as a food fish and sport fish
california harebell *n, usu cap C* **:** a slender herb (*Campanula prenanthoides*) of the Pacific coast having a much-branched leafy stem and showy racemes of blue flowers with narrow corolla segments and long exserted style
california hazel *n, usu cap C* **:** a Pacific coast hazel that is a variety (*Corylus cornuta californica*) of the beaked hazel having velvety foliage and finely fringed nut beaks
california holly *n, usu cap C* **:** TOYON
california indigo bush *n, usu cap C* **:** MOCK LOCUST
california jack *n, usu cap C&J* **:** a two-handed card game that is a variety of high-low jack in which the winner of each trick draws first from the top of the stock which is kept face up
california jay *n, usu cap C* **:** a crestless jay (*Aphelocoma californica*) of the Pacific coast with blue to brownish gray above and white underneath
california job case *n, usu cap 1st C* **:** a job case widely used in the U.S. and typically having capitals on the right

California job case showing typical lay of type

california juniper *n, usu cap C* **:** a dense much-branched shrub or sometimes an erect tree (*Juniperus californica*) with ashy-gray shredding bark and reddish or brownish sweet berries covered with a dense whitish bloom
california laurel *n, usu cap C* **:** a Pacific coast tree (*Umbellularia californica*) of the laurel family having hard tough wood, very aromatic evergreen foliage, and small umbellate flowers succeeded by fleshy drupes resembling olives — called also *California bay tree, mountain laurel, Oregon myrtle, pepperwood, sassafras laurel, spice tree*
california lilac *n, usu cap C* **:** BLUEBLOSSOM
california lion *n, usu cap C* **1 :** an extinct very large lionlike cat (*Felis atrox*) of California **2 :** COUGAR
california live oak *n, usu cap C* **:** COAST LIVE OAK
california maidenhair *n, usu cap C* **:** a delicate California fern (*Adiantum emarginatum*) resembling the common maidenhair but having broadly fan-shaped pinnules
california maybush *n, usu cap C* **:** TOYON
california mountain holly *n, usu cap C* **:** REDBERRY 2c
california mussel *n, usu cap C* **:** an edible mussel (*Mytilus californianus*) sometimes responsible for mussel poisoning

¹cal·i·for·ni·an \ˌkalə¦fȯrnyən, -ō(ə)n-, -nēən\ *adj, usu cap* **1 :** of, relating to, or characteristic of the state of California **2 :** of, relating to, or characteristic of Californians
²californian \"\ *n* **1** -s *cap* **:** a native or resident of California **2** *usu cap* **:** a breed of domestic rabbits that is white with black points and developed by intercrossing large commercial breeds with the Himalayan
california newt *n, usu cap C* **:** GIANT NEWT
california nutmeg *n, usu cap C* **:** a California evergreen tree (*Torreya californica*) having a fleshy fruit resembling a nutmeg but with a strong turpentine flavor
california oakworm *n, usu cap C* **:** the larva of a small brownish California moth (*Phryganidia californica*) that feeds on the leaves of and frequently defoliates various oaks
california onyx *n, usu cap C* **:** an amber-and-brown variety of aragonite
california orange *n, usu cap C* **:** an orange grown in California; *specif* **:** NAVEL ORANGE
california pepper tree *n, usu cap C* **:** PEPPER TREE 1
california pitcher plant *n, usu cap C* **:** a marsh or bog herb (*Darlingtonia californica*) of the family Sarraceniaceae having leaves formed into a curved hood, the circular orifice at one side of the hood being covered by a 2-forked appendage
california pocket mouse *n, usu cap C* **:** a small mouselike rodent (*Perognathus californicus*) related to the ground squirrel
california pompano *n, usu cap C* **:** a Pacific coast butterfish (*Palometa simillima*) highly esteemed as a food
california poppy *n, usu cap C* **1 :** a yellow-flowered plant of the genus *Eschscholtzia* (esp. *E. californica*) widely cultivated in varieties ranging in color from creamy yellow to dark red and often bicolored **2 :** WESTERN POPPY **3 :** CREAMCUPS 1
california poppy tree *n, usu cap C* **:** BUSH POPPY
california privet *n, usu cap C* **:** a Japanese privet (*Ligustrum ovalifolium*) used for hedges and having deciduous or half-evergreen foliage
california process *n, usu cap C* **:** a process of shoe construction in which the upper and the sock lining are stitched together, a platform cover is stitched to the upper, the platform is pressed into place, and the sole attached by cementing or vulcanizing — compare SLIP-LASTED
california quail *n, usu cap C* **:** a quail (*Lophortyx californica*) having an erectile black crest, the back brownish gray, the throat black bordered by white, the breast bluish, and the belly and flanks marked with black, white, and chestnut; *esp* **:** a member of the typical subspecies (*L. c. californica*) inhabiting the humid coast region of Oregon and California — compare VALLEY QUAIL
california red fir *n, usu cap C* **:** the largest of the native American true firs (*Abies magnifica*) having 4-angled leaves and purplish brown cones 6 to 9 inches long
california red scale *n, usu cap C* **:** a common California armored scale (*Aonidiella aurantii*) that is a major pest of citrus in California and that resembles but is somewhat larger than the San Jose scale and has a transparent covering shield so that the red or yellow body shows through
california rose *n, usu cap C* [prob. so called fr. a belief that it came from California] **:** an Asiatic bindweed (*Convolvulus japonicus*) naturalized in the eastern U.S. and having pink much-doubled sterile flowers
california rosebay *n, usu cap C* **:** a usu. pink-flowered rhododendron (*Rhododendron macrophyllum*) of the Pacific coast
california sage *or* **california sagebrush** *n, usu cap C* **:** a low ashy-gray California shrub (*Artemisia californica*) having finely divided leaves and long loose racemes of yellowish flowers
california sardine *n, usu cap C* **:** a sardine (*Sardinops caerulea*) of the Pacific coast — called also *pilchard*
california sassafras *n, usu cap C* **:** CALIFORNIA LAUREL
california scrub oak *n, usu cap C* **:** a low evergreen shrub (*Quercus dumosa*) of the California chaparral valuable for its resistance to and recovery from fire and intense drought
california sea trout *n, usu cap C* **:** a common greenling (*Hexagrammos decagrammus*) of the Pacific coast that is brownish or grayish in color, the males often being tinged with blue or copper and having sky-blue spots about the head
california skullcap *n, usu cap C* **:** a slightly hairy herb (*Scutellaria californica*) with oval leaves and yellowish white flowers
california slippery elm *n, usu cap C* **:** FLANNELBUSH
california soaproot *n, usu cap C* **:** SOAPPLANT a
california strawberry shrub *also* **california sweetshrub** *n, usu cap C* **:** SPICEBUSH 2
california sycamore *n, usu cap C* **:** a tall tree (*Platanus racemosa*) having deciduous bark, large alternate palmately lobed leaves, and ball-like clusters of greenish flowers without petals or sepals
california tea *n, usu cap C* **:** an erect herb (*Psoralea physodes*) that has greenish purple flowers and whose herbage can be dried and used as tea
california thistle *n, usu cap C* [prob. so called fr. a belief that it came from California] **:** CANADA THISTLE
california thrasher *n, usu cap C* **:** the common thrasher (*Toxostoma redivivum*) of California that is brown above and unstriped buffy below
california tokay *n, usu cap C&T* **:** TOKAY 2
california towhee *n, usu cap C* **:** a chiefly dull-brown towhee (*Pipilo fuscus crissalis*)
california tree poppy *n, usu cap C* **:** MATILIJA POPPY
california vetch *n, usu cap C* **:** a very slender almost prostrate herb (*Vicia exigua*) with compound leaves and long-stalked clusters of white or purplish flowers
california vine disease *n, usu cap C* **:** PIERCE'S DISEASE
california vulture *n, usu cap C* **:** CALIFORNIA CONDOR
california white oak *n, usu cap C* **:** a tall graceful tree (*Quercus lobata*) native to California and much planted as a shade tree having deep-lobed leaves dark green above and whitish beneath and nearly sessile long-conical acorns — called also *roble, valley oak, valley white oak*
california white pine *n, usu cap C* **:** PONDEROSA PINE
california wild grape *n, usu cap C* **:** a woody vine (*Vitis californica*) that climbs on and often smothers trees and that has a fragrant dense white bloom and purple fruit
california wild rose *n, usu cap C* **:** a prickly shrub (*Rosa californica*) of the Pacific coast with pink flowers in leafy-bracted clusters
california wine *n, usu cap C* **:** a complex of wines produced in California, some resembling in varying degree Old World Burgundy, Chablis, Chianti, claret, Marsala, muscatel, port, Riesling, sauterne, sherry, and vermouth and others having distinctive characteristics not duplicated elsewhere but made from the grapes of an imported vine (*Vinis vinifera*)
california woodpecker *n, usu cap C* **:** a common woodpecker (*Melanerpes formicivora bairdi*) of the Pacific states noted for its habit of storing acorns in little holes which it digs in the bark of trees
california yellow bells *n pl but sing or pl in constr, usu cap C* **:** a California annual plant (*Emmenanthe penduliflora*) of the family Hydrophyllaceae with pendulous yellow flowers — called also *whispering bells*
california yellowtail *n, usu cap C* **:** a yellowtail (*Seriola dorsalis*) of the California coast and southward that reaches a length of three feet and is an esteemed sport fish
california yew *n, usu cap C* **:** PACIFIC YEW
cal·i·for·nio \ˌkalə'fȯrn(ˌ)yō, -ō(ə)n-, -nē,ō\ *n* -s *cap* [Sp, fr. *California*] **1 :** CALIFORNIAN 1 **2 :** one of the original Spanish colonists of California or their descendants
cal·i·for·nite \-ˌnīt\ *n* -s [*California*, its locality + E *-ite*] **:** a compact variety of idocrase of an olive-green or grass-green color closely resembling jade
cal·i·for·ni·um \-ˌnēəm, -nyəm\ *n* -s [NL, fr. *California* + NL *-ium*] **:** a radioactive element discovered by bombarding curium 242 with alpha particles — symbol *Cf;* see ELEMENT table
cal·i·ga \'kaləgə\ *n, pl* **cali·gae** \-lə,gī, -ə,jē\ [L] **1 :** a heavy-soled Roman military shoe or sandal worn by all ranks up to and including centurions **2** [ML, fr. L] **:** a stocking worn by bishops — compare BUSKIN 4
ca·lig·i·nous \kə'lijənəs\ *adj* [MF or L; MF *caligineux*, fr. L *caliginosus*, fr. *caligin-, caligo* darkness + *-osus* -ous; akin to L *columba* dove — more at COLUMBINE] **:** MISTY, DARK, OBSCURE
ca·li·go \kə'lē(ˌ)gō, -'ī-\ *n* [NL, fr. L, darkness, dimness of sight] **1** *cap* **:** a genus of very large butterflies of tropical America that are related to the morphos and satyrs and have wings richly but somberly colored above and with eyespots and intricate lines below **2** *pl* **caligos** *or* **caligoes :** a butterfly of the genus *Caligo*
caligraphy *var of* CALLIGRAPHY
calimanco *var of* CALAMANCO
ca·lim·er·is \kə'limərəs\ *n, cap* [NL, fr. *cali-* + Gk *meris* part; akin to L *merēre* to deserve — more at MERIT] **:** a small genus of Asiatic herbs (family Compositae) resembling the genus *Aster* but differing in having the bracts of the involucre scarious-margined
cal·i·myr·na fig \ˌkalə¦mərnə-, -mōnə-\ *n, usu cap C* [fr. *Calimyrna*, a trademark] **:** the Smyrna fig when grown in California
ca·lin \kȧlaⁿ\ *n* -s [F, fr. Pg *calaim*, fr. Ar *qala'ī*] **:** an alloy apparently of lead and tin of which the Chinese make tea canisters and other utensils
ca·li·na·go \ˌkalə'nä(ˌ)gō\ *n* -s *usu cap* [Sp, fr. Carib *karinako*, lit., brave men, fr. *kari-* (fr. *ka* sky, spirit) + *-na* group + *-ko* (group pl.)] **1 :** a Carib of the Lesser Antilles **2 :** ISLAND CARIB
ca·lin·da \kə'lində\ *or* **ca·len·da** \-'e-\ *n* -s [AmerSp] **:** a Negro ceremonial dance of the West Indies and formerly of the U.S.
ca·line \'kā,lēn\ *n* -s [origin unknown] **:** the complex of hormones or hormonelike factors not including auxin that are involved in the formation of roots, stems, and leaves
cal·i·nut \'kalē,nət\ *n* -s [of African origin; akin to Mende *kale* seed, stone of a fruit, Bambara, a kind of plant] **:** the flattened brown circular seed of a tropical African woody vine (*Physostigma cylindrosperma*)
cal·i·pash \'kalə,pash, -ˌaa(ə)-,-ai-, ˌ==¦=\ *n* -ES [origin unknown] **:** the fatty gelatinous dull-greenish substance found under the upper shell of a turtle and esteemed as a delicacy
cal·i·pee \'kalə,pē, ˌ==¦=\ *n* -s [origin unknown] **:** the fatty gelatinous light-yellow substance found immediately over the lower shell of a turtle and esteemed as a delicacy
¹cal·i·per *or* **cal·li·per** \'kaləpə(r)\ *n* -s [alter. of *caliber*] **1 a :** a measuring instrument having two legs or jaws that can be adjusted to determine thickness, diameter, caliber, and distance between surfaces — usu. used in pl. and often with *pair* ⟨a pair of ~*s*⟩; see HERMAPHRODITE CALIPER, INSIDE CALIPER, MICROMETER CALIPER, ODD-LEG CALIPER, OUTSIDE CALIPER, VERNIER CALIPER **b :** an instrument consisting of a graduated beam and at right angles to it a fixed arm and a movable arm which slides along the beam to measure the diameter of logs and trees **c :** a watchmaker's tool with adjustable female center points for holding a wheel while it is being trued **d :** CALIPER SPLINT **2 :** thickness esp. of paper, paperboard, or a tree — compare POINT 16e

calipers: *1* outside, *2* inside

²caliper *or* **calliper** \"\ *vt* **calipered** *or* **callipered; calipered** *or* **callipered; calipering** *or* **callipering** \-p(ə)riŋ\ **calipers** *or* **callipers :** to measure by or as if by calipers
³caliper *var of* CALIBER
caliper compass *n* **:** a divider or a hermaphrodite caliper
caliper gauge *n* **1 :** a gauge of fixed size for calipering **2 :** VERNIER CALIPER
caliper rule *n* **:** a rulelike scale with one fixed and one adjustable jaw
caliper splint *n* **:** a support for the leg consisting of two metal rods extending between a foot plate and a padded thigh band and worn so that the weight is borne mainly by the hipbone
caliper square *n* **:** a caliper consisting of jaws placed at right angles to a graduated beam, one or both jaws being adjustable
ca·liph *or* **ca·lif** \'kāləf *also* -'a-\ *n* -s [ME *caliphe, califfe*, fr. MF *calife*, fr. Ar *khalīfah* successor, fr. *khalafa* to succeed] **1 :** a successor of Muhammad as temporal and spiritual head of the community and religious faith of Islam — used primarily in historical reference following Turkey's abolition of the caliphate on March 23, 1924 **2 :** a Muslim political leader claiming rightful succession to the caliphate
ca·liph·al \-əl\ *adj* **:** of or relating to a caliph
ca·liph·ate *also* **ca·lif·ate** \-ˌfāt,-ˌfət, -ə·d-+V\ *n* -s [F *califat*, fr. ML *caliphatus*, fr. *calipha* caliph (fr. Ar *khalīfah*) + *-atus* -ate] **:** the office, term, or dominion of a caliph
ca·lip·pus \kə'lipəs\ *n, cap* [NL, irreg. fr. *cali-* + *-hippus*] **:** a genus of dwarf horses of the Pliocene of No. America prob. not directly ancestral to modern horses
ca·lir·oa \kə'lirəwə\ *n, cap* [NL, alter. of L *Callirrhoe*, a water nymph — more at CALLIRRHOË] **:** a genus of sawflies (family Tenthredinidae) including the pear slugs
cal·i·saya bark \ˌkalə¦sīə-\ *n* [Sp *calisaya*, perh. fr. *Calisaya*, 17th cent. Indian who revealed the properties of quinine to the Spaniards] **:** cinchona bark obtained from either of two cinchonas (*Cinchona calisaya* and *C. ledgeriana*) or from a hybrid of either of these with other cinchonas — called also *yellow cinchona*
cal·is·then·ic \ˌkaləs¦thenik, -ēk\ *also* **cal·is·then·i·cal** \-ə̇kəl, -ēk-\ *adj* [*cali-* + Gk *sthenos* strength + E *-ic* or *-ical* — more at ASTHEN-] **:** of or relating to calisthenics ⟨well-planned ~ periods —*Athletic Jour.*⟩
cal·is·then·ics \ˌ==¦=niks, -ēks\ *n pl but sometimes sing in constr* [*cali-* + Gk *sthenos* strength + E *-ics*] **1 :** systematic exercises performed usu. in rhythm and often in a group without apparatus or with light hand apparatus to improve the strength, suppleness, balance, and health of the body **2** *usu sing in constr* **:** the art or practice of calisthenics
cal·is·the·ni·um \ˌ==¦thēnēəm, -en-\ *n* -s [*calisthenics* + *-ium* (as in gymnasium)] **:** a gymnasium for calisthenics
calithump *var of* CALLITHUMP
cal·i·ver \'kaləvə(r)\ *n* -s [modif. of MF *calibre* caliber] **:** an early handgun like a harquebus
ca·lix \'kāliks, -ēks *also* -'a-\ *n, pl* **cali·ces** \-lə,sēz\ [L — more at CHALICE] **:** CUP; *esp* **:** an ecclesiastical chalice
¹ca·lix·tin \kə'likstən\ *or* **ca·lix·tine** \", -ˌtēn,-ˌtīn\ *n* -s *usu cap* [F *calixtin*, fr. ML *calixtinus*, fr. L *calix* cup] **:** a member of a Hussite body that maintained that the laity should receive the cup as well as the bread in the Eucharist
²calixtin \"\ *or* **calixtine** \"\ *n* -s *usu cap* [Georg *Calixt* (Latinized as Georgius Calixtus) †1656 Ger. theologian + E *-in* or *-ine*] **:** a follower of Georgius Calixtus — compare SYNCRETISM 1
¹calk *var of* CAULK
²calk *or* **caulk** \'kȯk\ *n* -s [prob. back-formation fr. *calkin* (taken as a pl. or a verbal n.), fr. ME *kakun*, fr. MD or ONF; MD *calcoen* horse's hoof, fr. ONF *calcain* heel, fr. L *calcaneum*, fr. *calc-, calx;* akin to Lith *kulnis* heel, Skt *kaṭi* hip, Gk *kōlon* limb, OHG *scelah* squinting, crooked — more at CYLINDER] **1 :** a tapered wedge or cone-shaped piece of iron or steel projecting downward on the shoe of a draft animal to prevent slipping — called also *calkin* **2 :** a pointed metal piece or a device with sharp points worn on the sole of a shoe or boot to prevent slipping

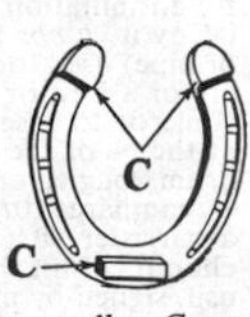
calks, *C*

³calk *or* **caulk** \"\ *vt* -ED/-ING/-S **1 :** to furnish with calks to prevent slipping ⟨~ the shoes of a horse⟩ **2 :** to wound with a calk ⟨the lame horse had ~*ed* himself⟩
¹calker *var of* CAULKER
²calk·er \'kȯkər\ *Scot var of* ²CALK 1
cal·kin *also* **caul·ken** \'kȯkən, 'kalk-\ *n* -s [ME *kakun* — more at CALK] **:** ²CALK 1
calking *var of* CAULKING
calking roll *n* [*calking*, fr. pres. part. of ³*calk*] **:** ³BOOT 3b
¹call \'kȯl\ *vb* -ED/-ING/-S [ME *callen*, prob. fr. ON *kalla;* akin to OE hilde*calla* battle herald, OHG *kallōn* to talk loudly, MIr *gall* swan, OSlav *glasŭ* voice] *vi* **1 a :** to speak in a loud distinct voice so as to be heard at a distance esp. in

order to attract the attention of, summon, or make a request of another : CRY, SHOUT ⟨~ for help⟩ **b :** to make a request, appeal, or demand ⟨~ upon all nations to keep the peace⟩ ⟨he ~*ed* for an investigation of the facts⟩ **c** *of an animal* **:** to utter a characteristic note or cry ⟨the thrush ~*s*⟩ **d :** to communicate with or try to get into communication with a person by telephone — often used with *up* **e** *card games* (1) **:** to make a demand (as by requesting or signaling for a particular card or suit to be played) (2) *bridge* **:** to make a declaration (sense 4) (3) *poker* **:** to make one's total bet equal to that of the last preceding bettor **f :** to give the calls for a square dance — often used with *off* **2** *Scot* **:** to become driven **:** DRIVE — usu. used in the form *ca';* compare CA' CANNY **3 :** to make a brief stop or visit at a place ⟨~ to pay your respects⟩ ⟨only one ship a year ~*s* at the island⟩ — often used with *on* ⟨a salesman ~*ing* on his customers⟩ **~** *vt* **1 a** (1) **:** to utter in a loud distinct voice **:** SHOUT, CRY — often used with *out* ⟨~ out a number⟩ (2) **:** to announce or read out loudly or authoritatively ⟨~ the roll⟩ ⟨~ a halt⟩ — often used with *off* ⟨~ off a row of figures⟩ **b** (1) **:** to command or request (as by an utterance) to come or be present ⟨I can ~ spirits from the vasty deep —Shak.⟩ **:** SUMMON ⟨~*ed* to testify in court⟩ ⟨~ off the dogs⟩ (2) **:** to cause to come **:** BRING ⟨~ a new principle into operation⟩ ⟨~ to mind the words of his brother⟩ **c** (1) **:** to summon to a particular activity, employment, or office ⟨~*ed* to the presidency of the university⟩ ⟨~*ed* to active duty in the army⟩ (2) **:** to move or impel (as by divine influence) to a particular condition or activity ⟨America is ~*ed* to greatness —A.E.Stevenson b.1900⟩ (3) **:** to summon (a Jewish male) to read a benediction or a set portion of the Torah before the congregation at public worship in the synagogue **d :** to invite or command (a group) to meet **:** CONVOKE ⟨~ a meeting⟩ **e :** to rouse from sleep or summon to get up by a call **f :** to give the order for **:** bring into action ⟨~ a case in court⟩ ⟨~ a strike⟩ **g** (1) *bridge* **:** to make a demand for (a particular card or suit to be played) (2) *poker* **:** to make one's total bet equal to (the preceding bet) or equal to the bet of (the preceding bettor) (3) **:** to challenge (a person) to make good on a statement ⟨if he is not telling the truth someone should ~ him⟩ (4) **:** to charge with or censure for an offense — often used with *on* ⟨they ~*ed* him on his sloppy dress⟩ **h :** to decoy (game) by imitating the characteristic cry **i :** to halt (a baseball game or other public event) because of unsuitable conditions (as rain or darkness) **j :** to rule on the status of (as a played ball or a player's action) ⟨~ a tennis serve out⟩ ⟨~ a base runner safe⟩ **k :** to give the calls for (a square dance or a square-dance figure) — often used with *off* **l** (1) **:** to communicate with or try to get in communication with (a person) by telephone — sometimes used with *up* ⟨~ me up tomorrow⟩ (2) **:** to deliver (a message) by telephone (3) **:** to make a signal to (an addressee as by transmitting his call sign) to indicate the desire to transmit a message — often used with *up* ⟨~ up the flagship⟩; compare CQ **m :** to suspend (playing time) ⟨time was ~*ed* while the field was cleared⟩ **n** *cricket* (1) **:** to inform (one's fellow batsman) that it is safe to run (2) **:** to inform (a bowler) that a delivery is unfair — used of an umpire **o** (1) **:** to demand payment of esp. by formal notice ⟨directors ~*ed* an assessment of 10 percent⟩ (2) **:** to demand presentation of (an issue of bonds) for redemption and payment ⟨the bonds could be ~*ed* 10 years after issue⟩ **2 a :** to speak of or address by a specified name ⟨they ~ her Kitty⟩ **:** give a name to **:** NAME ⟨forces . . . which Empedocles ~*s* love and hate —Arnold Toynbee⟩ **b** (1) **:** to give a descriptive name to ⟨the actual price at which any commodity is commonly sold is ~*ed* its market price —Adam Smith⟩ **:** regard as or characterize as of a certain kind **:** describe as **:** CONSIDER ⟨you don't ~ this keeping what belongs to you —Lillian Hellman⟩ ⟨a world where nothing can be ~*ed* unknowable —W.R.Inge⟩ (2) **:** ESTIMATE **:** reckon to be ⟨how far would you ~ it to town⟩ **:** consider for purposes of an estimate or for convenience ⟨99 cents, ~ it an even dollar⟩ **c** *dial Eng* **:** SCOLD, REVILE **d** *dial* **:** to announce or publish as an official notice of intention ⟨when our names have been ~*ed* in church we can be married⟩ **e** *South & Midland* **:** MENTION, SPEAK ⟨~*ed* the loved name⟩ ⟨carefully refrained from ~*ing* his name —Ellen Glasgow⟩ **f :** to describe correctly in advance of or without knowledge of the event ⟨he ~*ed* the upward trend of the market in February⟩ **:** name or describe in advance **:** PREDICT, GUESS ⟨~ the toss of a coin wrongly⟩ **3** *chiefly Scot, usu* **ca'** \'kȯ\ **a :** DRIVE ⟨~ an animal to market⟩ **b :** to drive into place **:** KNOCK, HAMMER **c :** PROPEL, RUN ⟨~ some machinery⟩ **:** USE ⟨~ an instrument⟩ **4 :** to pay a brief visit to ⟨I'll ~ you at your house —Shak.⟩ — **call a spade a spade :** to give a thing its plain name even if considered offensive **:** speak plainly or bluntly without elaboration or euphemism — **call cousin :** to claim relationship ⟨*call cousin* with the mayor⟩ — **call for 1 :** to call (as at one's house) to get ⟨I'll *call for* you at 8 o'clock⟩ **2 :** to require as necessary or appropriate ⟨lifting the box *called for* all her strength⟩ **:** make necessary ⟨more business *calls for* more judges —S.D.Bailey⟩ **3 :** to give an order for **:** DIRECT ⟨legislation *calling for* the establishment of two new schools⟩ **:** provide for ⟨the design *calls for* three windows⟩ — **call in question** *or* **call in doubt 1 :** to cast doubt upon **:** challenge the soundness of **:** IMPUGN ⟨standards of value which are never *called in question* —F.R.Leavis⟩ **2** *obs* **:** to make inquiry into — **call it a day :** to stop at least for the present whatever one has been doing — **call it quits 1 :** call it a day **2 :** to cease efforts (as of both parties of a rivalry, strife, or competition) ⟨neither side having a clear advantage, they decided to *call it quits*⟩ — **call names :** to address or speak of a person or thing with contemptuous or offensive names — **call on :** to call upon — **call one's bluff :** to challenge and expose an empty pretense or threat — **call one's shot :** to declare from a knowledge of the alignment of sights at the instant of firing a rifle or pistol the spot which a bullet should strike on the target; *also* **:** to predict in any game or sport the result of a shot — **call the shots :** call the tune — **call the tune :** to be in charge or control **:** MANAGE **:** determine policy or procedure ⟨the secretary *called the tune* all through the meeting⟩ — **call the turn 1** *in faro* **:** to name the order in which the last three cards in the dealing box will appear on the last turn of the deal **2 :** CALL *vt* 2f **3 :** call the tune — **call to account :** to hold responsible **:** REPRIMAND ⟨*called to account* for violation of the rules⟩ — **call to order :** to request to come to order: as **a :** to open (a meeting) for business **b :** to warn or restrain (a person transgressing the rules of debate) — **call to the bar :** to admit as a barrister — **call to the colors :** to summon for active military duty — **call upon :** REQUIRE, OBLIGE ⟨may be *called upon* to do several jobs⟩ **:** make a demand upon **:** depend on ⟨universities are *called upon* to produce trained men⟩ — **call within the bar :** to appoint as king's or queen's counsel

[2]call \"\ *n* -s [ME, fr. *callen*, v.] **1 a :** a loud vocal utterance (as in addressing or summoning) **:** SHOUT. CRY ⟨a ~ for help⟩ **b :** an imitation of the cry of a bird or other animal made to decoy it **c** *obs* **:** a decoy bird **d :** an instrument (as a whistle or pipe) used for calling ⟨a boatswain's ~⟩ ⟨a duck ~⟩ **e :** the cry of a bird or other animal **2 a :** a request or command to come or to assemble **:** SUMMONS, INVITATION ⟨the council met at the ~ of the president⟩ **b :** a summons or signal esp. on a drum, bugle, or pipe ⟨bugle ~*s* were heard in the distance⟩ — compare HUNT'S-UP, REVEILLE **c :** admission to the bar as a barrister **d** (1) **:** an invitation to become the minister of a church; *also* **:** the official written form of such an invitation usu. signed by members of the congregation (2) **:** an invitation to accept a professional appointment ⟨he accepted a ~ to the state university⟩ **e** (1) **:** a divine vocation or prompting to a special service or duty (2) **:** a strong inner prompting to undertake a particular course of action or to enter a particular type of vocation **f :** a summons, invitation, or appeal to undertake a particular course of action ⟨a ~ for the restoration of spiritual values⟩ **g :** a summoning (as by a posted notice) of actors to rehearsal or members of a film unit to a rehearsal or a take ⟨the ~ is for 11 o'clock⟩; *also* **:** REHEARSAL **h :** a signal summoning firemen and apparatus into action ⟨a fire ~⟩ ⟨a drill ~⟩; *also* **:** the response of men and equipment to such a call **i :** the attraction or appeal of a particular activity, condition, or place ⟨islanders feel strongly the ~ of the sea⟩ **j :** an announcement issued by the national committee of a political party concerning a nominating convention to be held, its date and place, and the rules governing the choosing and apportionment of delegates to it **k :** CALL OF NATURE **l :** an order specifying the number of men to be inducted into the armed services during a specified period ⟨the November ~ is for 10,000 men⟩ **m :** an order left at a hotel desk setting a specified hour for being wakened ⟨leave a ~ for 7:30⟩ **3 a :** DEMAND, REQUIREMENT ⟨maintaining order makes the greatest ~ on his energies⟩ **:** CLAIM ⟨the aircraft industry continues to have first ~ on aluminum production —*Americana Annual*⟩ **b :** NECESSITY, OBLIGATION, OCCASION, JUSTIFICATION ⟨there is no ~ for the federal government to apologize for the views of a private citizen —J.L.Teller⟩ **c :** a demand for payment of money: as (1) **:** a notice by the U.S. Treasury to depository banks to transfer a part of its deposit balance to the Federal Reserve bank (2) **:** a notice to a stockholder or subscriber to pay an assessment or an installment of subscription to capital **d :** an option to buy a certain amount of stock, grain, or other commodity at a fixed price at or within a certain time — compare [2]PUT 3 **e :** an instance of asking for something **:** REQUEST ⟨the library has many ~*s* for Christmas stories⟩ **4** *obs* **:** CALLING 4 **5 :** a roll call (as to discover absentees or to take the ayes and noes) ⟨the speaker ordered a ~ of the house⟩ **6 :** a short usu. formal visit ⟨pay a ~ on a neighbor⟩ **:** a brief stop in passing (as to conduct business or make a delivery) ⟨a salesman making his ~*s*⟩ **7 :** the name or thing called or indicated by calling ⟨his ~ was heads; mine was tails⟩ **8 :** the act or an instance of calling in a card game **9 :** a reference in a land survey or grant to an object, a measurement, or other descriptive detail requiring a corresponding physical detail on the land **10 :** the act or an instance of calling on the telephone **11 a :** CALL SIGN **b :** a signal (as a letter or combination of letters) sent by a caller to inform an addressee that the caller has a message to transmit to him — compare CQ **12 :** the solo or recitative part of a folk song or rhyme; *esp* **:** the stanza answered by the refrain ⟨the standard West African song pattern of ~ and response, by a leader and chorus —Roger Angell⟩ **13 :** the score at any given time while a tennis game is in progress ⟨what's the ~, please⟩ **14 :** a direction or a succession of directions for the next movement or figure of a square dance chanted or rhythmically called to the dancers by a caller **15 :** a decision or ruling made by an official of a sports contest — **at call** *or* **on call 1 :** available for use **:** at the service of ⟨thousands of men *at* his *call*⟩ **:** ready to respond to a summons or command ⟨a doctor *on call* at any hour⟩ **2 :** subject to demand for payment or return without previous notice ⟨money lent *at call*⟩ ⟨cotton bought *on call*⟩ — compare CALL LOAN — **have the call :** to be in the leading position or in greatest demand — **within call :** within hearing or reach of a summons **:** subject to summons

cal·la \'kalə\ *n* [NL, modif. of Gk *kallaia* rooster's wattles, perh. fr. *kallos* beauty — more at CALLI-] **1** *cap* **:** a genus of bog herbs (family Araceae) with ovate cordate leaves and a spreading spathe with white upper surface and a short cylindrical spadix — see WATER ARUM **2** -s **a** *or* **calla lily :** a familiar house plant or greenhouse plant (*Zantedeschia aethiopica*) with a flowerlike inflorescence consisting of a pure white showy spathe and yellow spadix **b :** any of various plants resembling but not necessarily related to the calla — see BLACK CALLA, GOLDEN CALLA, PINK CALLA

call·a·ble \'kȯləbəl\ *adj* **:** capable of being called **:** liable to be called; *specif* **:** subject to a demand for presentation for payment before maturity ⟨a ~ bond⟩

calla green *n* **:** a moderate yellow green that is greener and deeper than average moss green, yellower and darker than average pea green, yellower and duller than apple green (sense 1), and greener and darker than box green

cal·la·ïs \'kalēəs\ *n, pl* **cal·la·ï·des** \kə'lāə,dēz\ [L, fr. Gk *kalaïs, kallaïs*] **:** an ancient green stone, prob. turquoise

calla lily begonia *n* **:** a wax begonia the youngest leaves of which are white and somewhat resemble the calla lily flower

cal·lant \'kälən(t)\ *or* **cal·lan** \-ən\ *n* -s [D or ONF; D *kalant* customer, fellow, fr. ONF *calland* customer, fr. L *calent-, calens*, pres. part of *calēre* to be warm — more at LEE] *chiefly Scot* **:** BOY, LAD, FELLOW

cal'·late \'ka(l),lāt\ *vt* [by contraction] *dial* **:** CALCULATE 4

callathump *var of* CALLITHUMP

call–back \'=,=\ *n* -s **1 :** a return call on a customer to transact unfinished business or give repair or maintenance service on goods sold **2 a :** a recall of an employee to work after a lay-off **b :** a summons back to work after regular working hours

call–back pay *n* **:** guaranteed minimum payment to a worker called back for work after completing his regular shift and leaving the plant

call bell *n* **:** a bell used to summon an attendant or give an alarm or notice

call bird *n* **:** a bird used to lure others **:** a decoy bird

call–board *n* **:** BULLETIN BOARD: as **a :** a backstage bulletin board on which rehearsal calls and notices to the company are posted **b :** a board on which train times and the assignments of train crews are posted

call box *n* **1 :** a post-office box from which the renter can get his mail only by calling for it at a delivery window **2** *Brit* **:** a public telephone booth **3 :** a street telephone for police communications or for reporting fires

callboy \'=,=\ *n* **1 a :** a page who gives periodic warning calls before curtain time and individual warnings to actors when time for their appearance on stage is approaching **b :** a page who notifies sleeping railroad train-crew members in time for duty — called also *caller* **2 :** a hotel employee who pages guests and delivers messages

call button *n* **:** a push button to operate a call bell or other summoning device

call card *n* **:** CALL SLIP

call change *n* **:** a change rung on bells according to the directions of the conductor or according to written instructions

call down *vt* **1 :** to cause or entreat to descend **:** bring or draw down **:** INVOKE ⟨*call down* a blessing on the crops⟩ ⟨*call down* upon himself the displeasure of the village⟩ **2 :** to reprimand or scold for an offense ⟨she *called* me *down* for coming in late⟩

call–down \'=,=\ *n* -s **:** REPRIMAND

call duck *n* **:** a breed of very small domestic ducks consisting of a gray variety like the mallard and a pure white variety, both often used by hunters as decoys

called *past of* CALL

called strike *n* **:** a pitched ball not swung at by a baseball batter but ruled by the umpire to have passed through the strike zone

call·ee \(')kȯ;lē\ *n* -s [[1]*call* + *-ee*] **:** one that is called

ca·lle·jón \kälʸe'kōn\ *n, pl* **calle·jo·nes** \-kōnās\ [Sp, lit., narrow lane, narrow pass, aug. of *calleja* small street, lane, dim. of *calle* street, fr. L *callis* path] **:** the narrow passageway between the shoulder-high barrier around a bullring and the wall of the grandstand

[1]cal·ler \'kälər\ *adj* [ME *callour*, prob. alter. of *calvur*] **1** *Scot* **:** FRESH ⟨~ fish⟩ ⟨~ herrings⟩ **2** *Scot* **:** COOL, REFRESHING ⟨blessed by the ~ upland air —R.P. Kennedy⟩

[2]call·er \'kȯlə(r)\ *n* -s **:** one that calls: as **a :** one that makes the calls for a square dance **b :** one that announces train departures and arrivals in a railroad waiting room **c :** CALLBOY **d :** an announcer of winning numbers in a gambling establishment — called also *floorman*

cal·let \'kalət\ *n* -s [perh. fr. MF *caillette* frivolous person, after *Caillette fl* 1500 Fr. court fool] **1** *now Scot* **:** TRULL, PROSTITUTE **2** *now dial Eng* **:** SCOLD, SHREW

call–fire \'=,=\ *n* **:** naval artillery support supplied to ground troops as called for

call forth *vt* **:** to bring into being or action **:** ELICIT ⟨these events *call forth* great emotions⟩

call game *n* **:** a game of pocket billiards in which a player before shooting calls the ball he intends to make and the pocket in which he intends to drop it

call girl *n* **:** a prostitute who may be called by telephone to visit male customers

call house *n* **:** a house or apartment where call girls may be procured

calli *pl of* CALLUS

calli- *or* **callo-** *or* **cali-** *or* **calo-** *comb form* [*calli-* fr. L, fr. Gk *kalli-*, fr. *kallos* beauty; akin to Gk *kalos* beautiful, Skt *kalya* healthy; *calo-* fr. ML, fr. Gk *kalo-*, fr. *kalos; callo- & cali-* fr. blending of other forms] **:** beautiful ⟨*calli*graph⟩ ⟨*Callo*rynchus⟩ ⟨*Cali*meris⟩ **:** white ⟨*calo*mel⟩ **:** beauty ⟨*Calli*phora⟩

cal·li·a·nas·sa \,kalēə'nasə\ *n, cap* [NL, fr. *calli-* + Gk *anassa* queen, fem. of *anax* lord] **:** a genus (the type of the family Callianassidae) of marine burrowing crustaceans (order Decapoda) having the chelipeds very unequal in size — **cal·li·a·nas·sid** \;===;nasəd\ *adj or n*

cal·li·an·dra \,kalē'andrə\ *n, cap* [NL, fr. *calli-* + *-andra*] **:** a genus of tropical pinnate-leaved trees and shrubs (family Leguminosae) with clustered flowers having conspicuous stamens

callibogus *var of* CALIBOGUS

cal·li·car·pa \,kalə'kärpə\ *n, cap* [NL, fr. *calli-* + *-carpa* (fem. of *-carpus* -carpous)] **:** a genus of widely distributed shrubs and trees (family Verbenaceae) with small 4-parted flowers some of which are cultivated for their attractive red or purple berrylike fruit — see FRENCH MULBERRY

cal·li·ce·bus \,kalə'sēbəs\ *n, cap* [NL, fr. *calli-* + Gk *kēbos*, a long-tailed monkey — more at CEBUS] **:** a genus of So. American monkeys containing the titis

cal·lich·thy·idae \,ka,lik'thīə,dē\ *n pl, cap* [NL, fr. *Callichthys*, type genus (fr. Gk *kallichthys*, a sea fish, fr. *kalli-* calli + *ichthys* fish) + *-idae* — more at ICHTHUS] **:** a family of So. American armored catfishes (type genus *Callichthys*) including several species sometimes kept in the tropical aquarium

cal·lid·i·ty \ka'lidəd·ē, kə-\ *n* -ES [L *calliditas*, fr. *callidus* crafty, shrewd (fr. *callēre* to have a thick skin, be witty, experienced) + *-itas* -ity; akin to L *callum* thick skin — more at CALLOUS] **:** CRAFTINESS, CUNNING, SHREWDNESS

cal·lier quotient \'kal,yā-\ *n, cap C* [after A. *Callier fl* 1909 Fr. photography expert] **:** the ratio of specular density to diffuse density — called also *Q factor*

cal·li·gram \'kalə,gram *n* -s [*calli-* + *-gram*] **:** a design in which the letters of a word (as a name) are rearranged so as to form a decorative pattern or figure (as for a seal) — compare MONOGRAM

cal·lig·ra·pha \kə'ligrəfə, ka-\ *n* -s [NL, genus of beetles, fr. *calli-* + *-grapha* (fr. Gk *graphein* to write) — more at CARVE] **:** a beetle of a genus (*Calligrapha*) of brightly marked foliage-eating beetles — see ELM CALLIGRAPHA

cal·lig·ra·pher \-fə(r)\ *n* -s [*calligraphy* + *-er*] **1 :** one that writes a beautiful, ornamental, or stylized hand **:** a handwriting artist **2 :** one that writes **:** PENMAN ⟨a fair ~⟩ **3 :** a professional copyist or engrosser

cal·li·graph·ic \;kalə;grafik\ *adj* [MGk *kalligraphikos*, fr. Gk *kalligraphos* calligrapher + *-ikos* -ic] **1 :** of or relating to calligraphy: as **a** *of writing or hand-lettering* **:** elaborate or ornamental in style **b** *of a document* **:** written by hand esp. in an elaborate or ornamental style **2 a :** consisting of or ornamented with lines resembling the flourishes of ornate or decorated handwriting or hand-lettering ⟨~ scrolls⟩ ⟨a ~ figure⟩ **b :** printed, engraved, or otherwise produced in a style imitative of ornamental handwriting, hand-lettering, or freehand drawing ⟨a printed ~ title⟩ ⟨engraved ~ ornament⟩ **c :** bearing writing or a representation of writing that is regarded as being in itself a source of aesthetic pleasure — used esp. of works of art displaying Chinese characters or one of the ornamental types of Arabic script **3 :** drawn, painted, or formed in the manner of calligraphy (sense 3) ⟨a wiry arabesque of swift ~ line —Eric Newton⟩ — **cal·li·graph·i·cal·ly** \-ək(ə)lē\ *adv*

cal·lig·ra·phist \kə'ligrəfəst, ka-\ *n* -s **:** CALLIGRAPHER

cal·lig·ra·phy *also* **ca·lig·ra·phy** \-əfē, -i\ *n* -ES [F or Gk; F *calligraphie*, fr. Gk *kalligraphia*, fr. *kalli-* calli- + *-graphia* -graphy] **1 a :** fair or elegant writing or penmanship — opposed to *cacography* **b :** the art or profession of producing fair or elegant writing **2 :** HANDWRITING, PENMANSHIP **3 :** ornamental line in drawing or painting; *esp* **:** drawn or painted line having the variety, flexibility, expressiveness, and characteristic feeling of rapid execution of brilliant penmanship

cal·li·mi·co \,kalə'mē(,)kō\ *n* [NL, fr. *calli-* + Pg & Sp *mico*, a kind of marmoset — more at MICO] **1** *cap* **:** a genus of small marmosetlike monkeys of the Amazon basin related to the spider monkeys and howlers but usu. considered to constitute a separate subfamily of Cebidae **2** -s **:** any monkey of the genus *Callimico*

cal·lim·o·mid \kə'limə,mid\ *adj* [NL *Callimomidae*] **:** of or relating to the Callimomidae

cal·li·mom·i·dae \,kalə'mämə,dē\ *n pl, cap* [NL, fr. *Callimome*, type genus (irreg. fr. Gk *kallimos* beautiful, fr. *kallos* beauty) + *-idae* — more at CALLI-] **:** a large family (type genus *Callimome*) of minute brilliantly iridescent parasitic or seed-infesting chalcidoid wasps

call in *vt* **1 :** to order to return or to be returned: as **a :** to withdraw from an advanced position ⟨*call in* a battalion's outposts⟩ **b :** to withdraw from circulation ⟨*call in* bank notes and issue new ones⟩ **c :** CALL *vt* 1o (2) **2 :** to summon to one's aid or for consultation ⟨*call in* a mediator to settle the dispute⟩

cal·li·nec·tes \,kalə'nek(,)tēz\ *n, cap* [NL, fr. *calli-* + *-nectes*] **:** a genus of swimming crabs (family Portunidae) comprising the New World blue crabs

call·ing \'kȯliŋ, -ēŋ\ *n* -s [ME, fr. gerund of *callen* to call] **1** *obs* **:** NAME, APPELLATION **2 :** a strong inner impulse toward a particular course of action or duty ⟨a conflict between outer pressure and inner ~ —Siegfried Kracauer⟩; *specif* **:** such an impulse accompanied by conviction of divine influence **3** *obs* **:** station or position in life **:** RANK ⟨let every man abide in the same ~ wherein he was called —1 Cor 7:20 (AV)⟩ **4 :** the activity in which one customarily engages as a vocation or profession ⟨when literature and journalism were not yet distinct ~*s* —A.B.Faust⟩ **5 :** the characteristic cry of the female cat during heat; *also* **:** the period of heat **syn** see WORK

calling card *n* **:** VISITING CARD

calling crab *n* [so called fr. the apparently beckoning position of its larger claw] **:** FIDDLER CRAB

calling hare *n* [so called fr. its cry] **:** PIKA

call–in pay \'=,=-\ *n* **1 :** REPORTING PAY **2 :** payment of not less than an agreed amount to a worker called in for work at a time other than that of his regular shift ⟨four hours' *call-in pay*⟩

cal·li·o·nym·i·dae \,kalēō'nimə,dē\ *n pl, cap* [NL, fr. *Callionymus*, type genus (fr. Gk *kalliōnymos* stargazer, fr. *kalli-* calli- + *-ōnymos*, fr. *onyma, onoma* name) + *-idae* — more at NAME] **:** a family of percomorph fishes widely distributed in shallow seas and comprising the dragonets

cal·li·o·pe \kə'līə(,)pē, ÷'kalē,ōp\ *n* -s [fr. *Calliope*, chief of the Muses, fr. L, fr. Gk *Kalliopē*] **1 :** a musical instrument consisting of a series of crude steam or air whistles used on riverboats and in circuses and carnivals **2** *also* **calliope hummingbird** [NL, fr. L *Calliope*] **:** a tiny hummingbird (*Stellula calliope*) of California and adjacent regions that is golden-green above and white below and marked with reddish brown and lavender **3** *slang* **:** a steam locomotive

cal·li·o·pe·an \kə;līə;pēən, ÷;kalē;ōp-\ *adj* **:** resembling the sound of a calliope **:** loud and piercing

cal·li·op·sis \,kalē'äpsəs\ *n* [NL, fr. *calli-* + *-opsis*] **1** *cap, in some classifications* **:** a genus of plants comprising chiefly the annual members of the genus *Coreopsis* **2** *pl* **calliopsis :** COREOPSIS 2; *esp* **:** a cultivated annual plant of the genus *Coreopsis*

callipash *var of* CALIPASH

calliper *var of* CALIPER

cal·liph·o·ra \kə'lif(ə)rə\ *n, cap* [NL, fr. *calli-* + *-phora*] **:** a genus (the type of the family Calliphoridae) of large bluebottle flies — see BLOWFLY — **cal·liph·o·rine** \-fə,rīn\ *adj*

[1]cal·liph·o·rid \-fərəd\ *adj* **:** of or relating to the family Calliphoridae

[2]calliphorid \"\ *n* -s [NL *Calliphoridae*] **:** a fly of the family Calliphoridae **:** BLOWFLY

cal·li·phor·i·dae \,kalə'fȯrə,dē\ *n pl, cap* [NL, fr. *Calliphora*, type genus + *-idae*] **:** a family of large usu. hairy metallic blue or green calyptrate flies comprising the blowflies and a few related forms with parasitic larvae — compare BLUEBOTTLE

cal·li·pyg·i·an \;kalə;pij(ē)ən\ *also* **cal·li·py·gous** \-pīgəs\ *adj* [*callipygian* fr. Gk *kallipygos* callipygian (fr. *kalli-* calli- + *-pygos*, fr. *pygē* buttocks) + E *-ian; callipygous* fr. Gk *kallipygos* — more at FOG] **:** having shapely buttocks

cal·lir·rhoë \kə'lirə,wē\ *n* [NL, fr. L *Callirrhoe*, a water nymph, daughter of the river Achelous and wife of Alcmeon, fr. Gk *Kallirrhoē*] **1** *cap* **:** a small genus of No. American herbs (family Malvaceae) having usu. red or purple flowers, truncate petals, and beaked carpels **2** *-s* **:** any plant of the genus *Callirrhoë*, several species of which are cultivated — called also *poppy mallow*

cal·li·sau·rus \ˌkaləˈsȯrəs\ *n, cap* [NL, fr. *calli-* + *-saurus*] **:** a small genus of lizards (family Iguanidae) having stripes around the tail, seven species occurring in the southwestern U.S. — see GRIDIRON-TAILED LIZARD

cal·lis·te green \kəˈlistē-\ *n* [prob. fr. Gk *kallistē*, fem. superl. of *kalos* beautiful — more at CALLI-] **:** a moderate to strong yellow green

cal·li·ste·mon \ˌkaləˈstēmən\ *n, cap* [NL, fr. *calli-* + Gk *stēmōn* warp, thread — more at STAMEN] **:** a genus of Australian trees and shrubs of the family Myrtaceae having brushlike spikes of showy flowers — see BOTTLEBRUSH

cal·lis·te·phus \kəˈlistəfəs\ *n, cap* [NL, fr. *calli-* + Gk *stephos* crown, fr. *stephein* to encircle, bewreath] **:** a genus of erect Asiatic herbs (family Compositae) having ovate alternate leaves of which the upper become narrow and spatulate, leafy reflexed outer involucral bracts, and showy solitary flower heads that are two to five inches across — see CHINA ASTER

cal·li·thric·id \ˌkaləˈthrisəd\ *n* -s [NL *callithricidae*] **:** a monkey of the family Callithricidae

cal·li·thric·i·dae \-səˌdē\ *n pl, cap* [NL, alter. of *Callitrichidae*] **:** a family of So. American monkeys comprising the marmosets and the tamarins

[1]**cal·li·thrix** \ˈkaləˌthriks\ *n, cap* [NL, fr. L, an ape, fr. Gk *kallithrix* beautiful-haired, fr. *kalli-* calli- + *thrix* hair] **:** a genus consisting of the true marmosets

[2]**callithrix** \"\ [NL, fr. L, an ape] *syn of* CALLICEBUS — a prior name invalid as a homonym of [1]*Callithrix*

cal·li·thump *or* **cal·la·thump** *also* **cal·i·thump** \ˈkaləˌthəmp\ *n* -s [back-formation fr. *callithumpian, callathumpian, calithumpian*, adj., alter. of E dial. (Dorsetshire & Devonshire) *gallithumpian* disturber of order at elections in 18th century, perh. fr. *galli-* (alter. of *gallows*) + *thump* + *-ian*] **1 :** a noisy boisterous parade **2** *chiefly NewEng* **:** SHIVAREE — **cal·li·thump·i·an** \ˌ==ˈ=pēən\ *adj*

callithumpian duck *n, dial* **:** OLD-SQUAW

cal·li·tri·cha·ceous \kəˌlitrəˈkāshəs, ˌkalə-\ *adj* [NL *Callitriche* + E *-aceous*] **:** of or relating to the genus *Callitriche*

cal·lit·ri·che \kəˈli·trəˌkē\ *n, cap* [NL, modif. of LGk *kallitrichos* beautiful-haired, fr. Gk *kalli-* calli- + LGk *-trichos*, fr. Gk *trich-, thrix* hair — more at TRICHINA] **:** a genus (the type of the family Callitrichaceae of the order Geraniales) comprising widely distributed aquatic herbs having opposite linear leaves and minute monoecious flowers — see WATER STARWORT

cal·li·trich·i·dae \ˌkaləˈtrikəˌdē\ *or* **cal·li·tric·i·dae** \-risə-\ [NL, fr. *Callitrich-* or *Callitric-*, *Callithrix*, type genus + *-idae*] *syn of* CALLITHRICIDAE

cal·li·tris \ˈkalə·trəs\ *n, cap* [NL, irreg. fr. *calli-*] **:** a genus of African and Australasian evergreen trees (family Pinaceae) with small scalelike leaves — see SANDARAC TREE

cal·li·tro·ga \ˌkaləˈtrōgə\ *n, cap* [NL, fr. *calli-* + *-troga* (fr. Gk *trōgein* to gnaw) — more at TERSE] **:** a genus of No. American blowflies (family Calliphoridae) having larvae that are screwworms and including two serious pests of domestic animals, the common screwworm (*C. hominivorax*) and the secondary screwworm (*C. macellaria*)

call letters *n pl* **:** CALL SIGN

call loan *n* **:** a loan payable on demand of either party and usu. secured by stock or bond collateral and used chiefly by stock-exchange brokers to finance margin purchases

call man *n* **:** a man subject to call; *specif* **:** a part-time fireman available for emergency call at an hourly wage

call market *n* **:** the market for call loans

call money *n* **:** money loaned or ready to be loaned on call

call note *n* **:** a note used by a bird or other animal to call another (as its mate or young)

call number *or* **call mark** *n* **:** a combination of characters assigned to a library book to indicate its place on the shelf relative to other books — compare PRESSMARK

callo- — see CALLI-

call off *vt* **1 :** to draw away **:** DIVERT ⟨her attention was *called off* by a new arrival⟩ **2 :** to give up (an undertaking or planned activity) **:** CANCEL ⟨*call off* a baseball game⟩ ⟨*call* the trip *off*⟩

call office *n, Brit* **:** PAY STATION

call of nature : the need to expel body wastes

cal·lop \ˈkaləp\ *n* -s [native name in Australia] **:** an edible serranid fish (*Plectroplites ambiguus*) of inland waters of Australia — called also *golden perch*

cal·lo·phis \ˈkaləfəs\ *n, cap* [NL, fr. *callo-* + *-ophis*] **:** a genus comprising the Indian coral snakes

cal·lo·rhi·nus \ˌkaləˈrīnəs\ *n, cap* [NL, fr. *callo-* + *-rhinus*] **:** a genus consisting of the No. Pacific fur seals

cal·lo·ryn·chus \ˌkaləˈriŋkəs\ *n, cap* [NL, fr. *callo-* + *-rynchus* (alter. of *-rhynchus*)] **:** a genus (coextensive with the family Callorynchidae) of chimaeralike fishes comprising the elephant fishes, found in south temperate seas, and having the snout elongated and provided with a pendent tactile organ

cal·lo·sal \(ˈ)kaˈlōsəl, kəˈl-\ *adj* [NL *callosum* + E *-al*] **:** of, relating to, or adjoining the corpus callosum

callosal convolution *n* **:** a convolution of the mesial surface of the cerebrum curving around the corpus callosum from which it is separated by a callosal fissure

cal·lo·sci·u·rus \ˌkalōˌsīˈ(y)ürəs\ *n, cap* [NL, fr. *callo-* + *Sciurus*] **:** a genus of squirrels of southeastern Asia comprising the red-bellied squirrels

[1]**cal·lose** \ˈkaˌlōs\ *adj* [ISV *call-* (fr. L *callum* hard skin) + *-ose*; orig. formed in F — more at CALLOUS] **:** having protuberant hardened spots ⟨~ leaves⟩

[2]**callose** \"\ *n* -s [L *callosus* callous] **:** a carbohydrate component of cell walls that is readily stained by aniline blue and is found esp. on sieve plates where it forms the callus

cal·los·i·ty \kaˈläsəd·ē, kə-, -ətē, -i\ *n* -ES [MF *callosité*, fr. L *callositas*, fr. *callosus* + *-itas* -ity] **1 :** the condition or quality of being callous: as **a :** abnormal hardness and thickness (as of the skin) **b :** lack of feeling or capacity for emotion **2 :** a hard or thickened area or protuberance esp. on the skin or on the bark of a plant **:** CALLUS

cal·lo·so·bru·chus \kəˌlōsōˈbrükəs\ *n, cap* [NL, fr. L *callosus* hard-skinned + LL *bruchus* a kind of locust, fr. Gk *bronchos, brokos* locust; perh. akin to Russ *brukat'* to kick out with the hind legs, Slovenian *brkniti, brkati* to kick, to propel with the fingers, Lith *briankšt, brūkšt* a cry made during throwing] **:** a small genus of weevils (family Bruchidae) closely related to the bean weevil and including the cowpea weevil

callosum *n, pl* **callosa** [NL, fr. L, neut. of *callosus*] **:** CORPUS CALLOSUM

[1]**cal·lous** \ˈkaləs\ *adj* [MF *calleux*, fr. L *callosus*, fr. *callum, callus* callous skin; akin to Skt *kiṇa* callosity, OIr *calath* hard] **1 :** hardened and thickened ⟨~ skin on the heel⟩ ⟨~ plant bark⟩ **:** having calluses ⟨with labouring ~ hands —William Congreve⟩ **2 a :** hardened in sensibility **:** feeling no emotion ⟨piety . . . is made ~ and inactive by kneeling too much —W. S.Landor⟩ **b :** feeling no sympathy for others **:** without regard for the feelings or welfare of others **:** indifferent to the suffering of others ⟨a ~ disregard for human rights —W.O. Douglas⟩ — **cal·lous·ly** *adv* — **cal·lous·ness** *n* -ES

[2]**callous** \"\ *vt* -ED/-ING/-ES **:** to make callous

[3]**callous** *var of* CALLUS

cal·loused \ˈkaləst\ *adj* **:** having calluses **:** CALLOUS

call out *vt* **1 :** to summon or order into action ⟨*call out* troops to control rioting⟩ **:** call forth ⟨danger *called out* the best in him⟩ **2 :** to challenge to fight a duel **3 :** to order to go on strike ⟨*call out* the steelworkers⟩

call–over \ˈ=ˌ==\ *n* -s *Brit* **:** a meeting of bookmakers at which a list of entries in a coming race is read, odds are offered, and bets are made

[1]**cal·low** \ˈka(ˌ)lō, -lə; -ləw,-lō+V\ *adj, sometimes* -ER/-EST [ME *calu, calewe* bald, fr. OE *calu*; akin to OHG *kalo* bald, OSlav *golŭ* naked] **1 a** *of a bird* **:** lacking feathers **:** UNFLEDGED **b :** characteristic of or indicating immaturity ⟨the ~ down began to clothe my chin —John Dryden⟩ **2 :** marked by lack of adult sophistication, experience, perception, or judgment ⟨a troop of newly arrived students, very young, pink and ~, followed nervously . . . at the director's heels —Aldous Huxley⟩ **3 a** *dial Eng, of land* **:** BARE **b** *Irish* **:** LOW-LYING **:** MARSHY — used esp. of a meadow **syn** see RUDE

[2]**callow** \"\ *n* -s **1** *Irish* **:** a low-lying or marshy meadow **2** *dial Eng* **:** the layer of soil above the subsoil **:** the top or rubble bed of a quarry **3 :** a freshly transformed insect not yet fully colored

cal·low·ness \-ōnəs, -ən-\ *n* -ES **:** the quality or state of being callow

call pay *n* **:** payment made to a worker who reports upon schedule but finds no work for him to do

call price *n* **:** the price required by the terms of a bond to be paid if the bond is called before maturity

call rate *n* **:** the interest rate charged on call loans

calls *pres 3d sing of* CALL, *pl of* CALL

call sheet \ˈ=,=\ *n* **:** a summons to a film actor or technician to report for a take often specifying costume or properties

call sign *n* **:** the combination of identifying letters or letters and numbers assigned to an operator, office, activity, or station for use in communication (as in the address of a message sent by radio)

call slip *n* **:** a form filled out by a library patron for a book that he wishes to see or borrow — called also *call card*

call to quarters : a bugle call usu. shortly before taps that summons soldiers to their quarters

call to worship : the opening sentences or prayer often including a congregational response in a worship service

cal·lu·na \kəˈl(y)ünə\ *n, cap* [NL, irreg. fr. Gk *kallynein* to beautify, sweep clean, fr. *kallos* beauty; fr. its use in making brooms — more at CALLI-] **:** a genus of low shrubs (family Ericaceae) included by some in the genus *Erica* but distinguished by opposite leaves and sepals which are much longer than the petals — see HEATHER

call up *vt* **1 :** to bring to mind or recollection **:** RECALL, EVOKE ⟨the music *calls up* other times and emotions⟩ **2 :** to summon before an authority or tribunal ⟨*called up* by the investigating committee⟩ **3 :** to summon together or collect (as for a united effort) ⟨*call up* all his forces for the attack⟩ **4 :** to summon for active military duty **:** DRAFT **5 :** to bring forward for consideration or action ⟨*call up* a bill for senate approval⟩

call–up \ˈ=,=\ *n* -s **:** an order to report for military service; *also* **:** DRAFT 13c

call–up–a–storm \ˌ=(ˌ)==ˈ=\ *n, NewEng* **:** COMMON LOON

[1]**cal·lus** *or* **cal·lous** \ˈkaləs\ *n, pl* **callus·es** \-ləsəz\ *or* **callous·es** *also* **cal·li** \-ˌlī\ [*callus* fr. L; *callous*, alter. (influenced by *callous*, adj.) of *callus* — more at CALLOUS (adj.)] **1 a** *usu callous* **:** a thickening of the horny layer of the epidermis as a result of friction or pressure **:** CALLOSITY 1a **b** *usu callous* **:** an area of skin so thickened **:** CALLOSITY 2 **c :** the soft parenchymatous tissue from which new roots form in cuttings and which develops from the phloem or cortex or more frequently from the cambium itself over any cut or wounded surface of a stem or root, the outer cells usu. becoming suberized or covered by a periderm **d :** a thickened area or protuberance on the surface of a plant **:** CALLOSITY; *specif* **:** the hard often hairy swelling from which the lemma and palea arise in grasses **e :** a growth of shelly material within or about the umbilicus of a gastropod shell **f :** a cuticular swelling on the body of an insect; *esp* **:** one serving as a point of articulation for a wing **2 :** a substance that is exuded around the ends of a broken bone and that by conversion into true bone bridges the gap and restores the continuity of the bone **3** *usu callous* **:** a protective condition of mental or emotional insensitivity ⟨beneath my defensive ~ of belligerence, I was filled with feelings of guilt —*Harper's*⟩ **4** *bot* **:** an accumulation of callose formed first as cylinders around the protoplasmic strands passing through the sieve plate and developing toward the end of the functional period of the sieve tube as a cushion or pad on each surface of the sieve plate

[2]**callus** \"\ *vb* -ED/-ING/-ES *vi* **:** to form callus ~ *vt* **:** to cause callus to form on (as a cutting)

callused *adj* [[1]*callus* + *-ed*] **:** having calluses **:** covered with callus

[1]**calm** \ˈkä(l)m, ˈkȧ| *also* |lm; *sporadic & old-fash* ˈkam\ *n* -s [ME *calme*, fr. MF *calme*, fr. OIt *calma*, fr. LL *cauma* heat, fr. Gk *kauma* burning heat, heat of the day, fr. *kaiein* to burn — more at CAUSTIC] **1 a :** a period or condition of freedom from storms, high winds, or rough activity **:** STILLNESS, QUIETUDE ⟨gradual sinks the breeze into a perfect ~ —James Thomson †1748⟩ **b :** complete lack of wind ⟨a sailing ship motionless in the ~⟩ **c :** complete absence of wind or presence of wind having a speed no greater than one mile per hour — see BEAUFORT SCALE table **2 :** a state or condition of repose and freedom from turmoil, disturbance, or marked activity or from agitation, tension, or vexation ⟨the bustle subsides and relative ~ is resumed —*Amer. Guide Series: N.C.*⟩ ⟨the majesty of artistic contemplation, looking in sacred ~ upon all this world . . . itself unmoved —Josiah Royce⟩

[2]**calm** \"\ *adj, usu* -ER/-EST [ME *calme*, fr. *calme*, n.] **1 :** marked by calm **:** STILL ⟨the weather is without rough motion, storminess, or agitated activity ⟨the sea was ~, save for a heavy but smooth ground swell —Jack London⟩ **2 :** marked by quiet unruffled freedom from agitation, passion, excitement, hurry, or disturbance ⟨we men are all in a fever of excitement, except Harker, who is ~ —Bram Stoker⟩ ⟨be rational . . . consider, and make a cool, ~ choice —T.L.Peacock⟩ **3 a :** COOL, DELIBERATE, ASSURED ⟨a ~ liar⟩ **b :** SELF-ASSURED, BRAZEN **:** unmoved by any delicate or lofty feeling ⟨a ~ scoundrel⟩

syn TRANQUIL, SERENE, PLACID, PEACEFUL, HALCYON: CALM suggests simple quietude, sometimes quietude in the face of disaster ⟨when winds that move not its *calm* surface sweep the azure sea —P.B.Shelley⟩ ⟨the senate, surprised but *calm* and energetic as usual, hushed up the news of these many defeats —H. W. Van Loon⟩ TRANQUIL may suggest a somewhat deeper, more settled or composed quietude with less notion of previous agitation dispelled ⟨on the balmy zephyrs *tranquil* rest the silver clouds —John Keats⟩ ⟨with footsteps quiet and slow at a *tranquil* pace —Elinor Wylie⟩ ⟨all unhappiness, all discontent, seemed banished, giving way to a *tranquil* content —Charles Nordhoff & J.N.Hall⟩ ⟨a *tranquil* trust in God amid tortures and death too horrible to be related —J.L.Motley⟩ SERENE suggests sheer and utter peace, lofty, happy, and quite unruffled ⟨gliding o'er ocean, smooth, *serene*, and even —P.B.Shelley⟩ ⟨the large fair face . . . was neither clouded nor ravaged, but finely *serene* —Henry James †1916⟩ ⟨his [Washington's] unflagging patriotism, his calm wisdom, his *serene* moral courage, because in the gloomiest hours he never lost his dignity, poise, or decision —Allan Nevins & H.S. Commager⟩ It is occasionally used in situations involving an enervating absence of challenge ⟨his marriage had relapsed into the *serene* monotony that so often wears the aspect of happiness —Ellen Glasgow⟩ PLACID may stress utter lack of agitation more strongly than the positive fact of peace and composure ⟨the *placid* gleam of sunset after storm —Alfred Tennyson⟩ ⟨a plump and *placid* figure...[she] received the invasion with competent tranquillity —Dorothy Sayers⟩ In derogation it may imply stupidity ⟨no teasing worried Una; she was as *placid* as a young cow —Rose Macaulay⟩ PEACEFUL, which has less suggestion than the others in this group, stresses the fact of undisturbed repose unlikely to change ⟨now sleeping in those *peaceful* groves —William Wordsworth⟩ ⟨I am grown *peaceful* as old age tonight —Robert Browning⟩ HALCYON suggests magic or golden stillness ⟨the brightest hour of unborn spring...the *halcyon* morn —P.B.Shelley⟩ ⟨change into such *halcyon* days the winter of the world, that the birds . . . may have their nests in peace —John Ruskin⟩

[3]**calm** \"\ *vb* -ED/-ING/-S [ME *calmen*, prob. fr. *calme*, adj.] *vi* **:** to become calm **:** to become quiet and calm after storm or agitation — usu. used with *down* ⟨the tempest ~*ed*⟩ ⟨the madman ~*ed* down⟩ ~ *vt* **1 :** to make calm **:** still, abate, or reduce the force or activity of ⟨~ the tempest —John Dryden⟩ **2 :** to make peaceful **:** induce quietude and repose in in place of agitation, passion, or excitement — often used with *down* ⟨~ feelings excited by civil war —T.M.Whitfield⟩ ⟨~ him down; get him to be reasonable —S.H.Adams⟩ **3** *obs* **:** BECALM

syn COMPOSE, QUIET, QUIETEN, STILL, LULL, SOOTHE, SETTLE, TRANQUILIZE are here treated only as they relate to persons and their feelings and moods. CALM may indicate return to inner quietude aided by judgment, fortitude, or faith ⟨Christian faith *calmed* in his soul the fear of change and death —William Wordsworth⟩ ⟨her also I with gentle dreams have *calmed* —John Milton⟩ COMPOSE, often reflexive, may heighten suggestions of conscious effort, resolution, and fortitude ⟨my child, if ever you were brave and serviceable in your life . . . you will *compose* yourself now —Charles Dickens⟩ ⟨a most *composed* invincible man, in difficulty and distress knowing no discouragement —Thomas Carlyle⟩ QUIET and QUIETEN may connote a temporary external calmness in speech or demeanor rather than lasting inner calm ⟨the most unreasonable of Franklin's impulses had now been *quieted* by this most reasonable of marriages —Carl Van Doren⟩ These words are likely to be used in indicating the effect of actions of persons in authority on others ⟨threats to the physical well-being of the unborn baby can *quieten* a noisy and uncooperative patient in labour —*Lancet*⟩ STILL, now somewhat literary or poetic, stresses the fact of cessation of agitation ⟨flattened, silenced, *stilled* —Virginia Woolf⟩ ⟨a voice *stilled* by death⟩ It may suggest more peremptory action than others in this list, connoting a return to quietude induced by power, authority, or awe ⟨the debate was *stilled* by the crash of guns⟩ ⟨it was Mary who *stilled* the hideous bawling of Peter —H.G.Wells⟩ LULL is the only word in this group that does not imply noticeable previous agitation or excitation. It connotes the somnolence of *lullaby*, to which it is related ⟨Aiken has *lulled* the reader with a seductive music and has transported him into the dreamworld of Freudian fantasy —F.O.Matthiessen⟩ It often suggests sleepy relaxation into repose, complacence, unawareness, or apathy when one should be vigilant ⟨we must not let a year or two of prosperity *lull* us into a false feeling of security —H.S.Truman⟩ SOOTHE suggests bland, gentle mitigation, assuagement, or solace ⟨it [the weather] cool'd their fever'd sleep, and *soothed* them into slumbers full and deep —John Keats⟩ ⟨when they [babies] wake screaming and find none to *soothe* them —Charles Lamb⟩ SETTLE stresses the subsiding of swirling agitation ⟨I'll read a bit before supper to *settle* my mind —Agnes S. Turnbull⟩ ⟨if I can't *settle* my brains, your next news of me will be that I am locked up —Mary W. Montagu⟩ TRANQUILIZE, more than the others in this group, stresses the depth of peace achieved ⟨when contemplation . . . sends deep into the soul its *tranquilizing* power —William Wordsworth⟩

[4]**calm** \ˈkäm\ *n* -s [origin unknown] *now chiefly Scot* **:** a mold or frame esp. as used for casting metal

[5]**calm** \ˈkäm\ *var of* CAME

calm·ant \ˈkä(l)mənt, -ä(l)m-, -alm-\ *n* -s [F, fr. *calmer* to calm, fr. *calme* calm] **:** CALMATIVE

calm·a·tive \-məd·iv\ *n or adj* [[3]*calm* + *-ative* (as in *sedative*)] **:** SEDATIVE

cal·ma·to \kälˈmäˌtō\ *adj (or adv)* [It, past part. of *calmare* to calm, fr. *calma* calm] **:** TRANQUIL, CALM — used as a direction in music

cal·me·cac \ˈkälmäˌkäk\ *n* -s [Sp, fr. Nahuatl] **:** an Aztec school that prepared the sons of nobles in the duties of priests and chiefs — distinguished from *telpuchcalli*

calm·ing·ly *adv* **:** in a calming manner

calm·ly *adv* **:** in a calm manner **:** with calm

calm·ness *n* -ES **:** the quality or state of being calm

calms *pres 3d sing of* CALM, *pl of* CALM

calmuck *var of* KALMUCK

calmy *adj, usu* -ER/-EST [[1]*calm* + *-y*] *archaic* **:** CALM

ca·ló \käˈlō\ *n* [Sp, fr. Romany, gypsy] **:** a language spoken by Spanish gypsies and widely influencing the argots of the Spanish-speaking underworld and of bullfighting

calo- — see CALLI-

cal·o·car·pum \ˌkaləˈkärpəm\ *n, cap* [NL, fr. *calo-* + *-carpum* (irreg. fr. Gk *karpos* fruit) — more at HARVEST] **:** a genus of tropical American trees (family Sapotaceae) having obovate to oblanceolate leaves clustered towards the branch ends, nearly sessile white flowers with densely imbricated sepals and filamentous staminodia, and a berrylike fruit — see MARMALADE TREE

cal·o·chor·tus \ˌkaləˈkȯrd·əs\ *n, cap* [NL, fr. *calo-* + Gk *chortos* fodder, grass, farmyard — more at YARD] **:** a large genus of western No. American leafy-stemmed herbs (family Liliaceae) having flowers with three sepals and three petals

ca·lom·ba \kəˈlämbə\ *n* -s [native name in New South Wales, Australia] **:** an Australian annual cloverlike plant (*Trigonella suavissima*) with yellow flowers and fragrant foliage valued as forage

calombo *var of* CALUMBA

cal·o·mel \ˈkaləməl, -ˌmel\ *n* -s [prob. fr. (assumed) NL *calomelas*, fr. *calo-* + Gk *melas* black — more at MULLET] **:** a white tasteless salt Hg_2Cl_2 found in nature as a sectile tetragonal mineral (hardness 1.5, sp. gr. 7.15), obtained as a heavy powder by precipitation from solution or by sublimation of a mixture of mercury and chlorine, and used as a cathartic, fungicide, and insecticide — called also *mercurous chloride*

calomel electrode *n* **:** a reference electrode consisting of mercury, calomel, and potassium chloride solution

cal·o·mor·phic \ˌkaləˈmȯrfik\ *adj* [*calo-* (fr. *calcium*, influenced by *halo-*) + *-morphic*] **:** of or relating to intrazonal soils characterized by a high content of available calcium in the parent material — compare HALOMORPHIC, HYDROMORPHIC

cal·o·neu·ro·dea \ˌkalōn(y)üˈrōdēə\ *n pl, cap* [NL, fr. *calo-* + *neur-* + *-odea* (alter. of *-oidea*)] **:** a small order of neopterous insects with two similar pairs of wings and with legs adapted for running that appeared in the Upper Pennsylvanian and became extinct after the Permian — **cal·o·neu·ro·de·an** \-dēən\ *n* -s

ca·lon–sé·gur \kälōⁿsāgœr\ *n* -s *usu cap C&S* [F, fr. the Château *Calon-Ségur*, Gironde dept., France, where it is produced] **:** a dry red table wine from Bordeaux, France, made from the Médoc grape

cal·o·nyc·ti·on \ˌkaləˈniktēˌän\ *n, cap* [NL, fr. *calo-* + Gk *nyktion*, neut. of *nyktios* of the night, fr. *nykt-, nyx* night — more at NIGHT] **:** a small genus of tropical American vines (family Convolvulaceae) having a salverform corolla with a long cylindrical tube and with a pointed capsular fruit — see MOONFLOWER

ca·lool \kəˈlül\ *n* -s [native name in New South Wales] **:** an Australian kurrajong (*Sterculia quadrifida*)

caloosa *cap, var of* CALUSA

cal·o·phyl·lum \ˌkaləˈfiləm\ *n, cap* [NL, fr. *calo-* + *-phyllum*] **:** a genus of tropical trees (family Guttiferae) having thick shiny feather-veined leaves, clustered white flowers, aromatic resinous juice, and oily seeds — see SANTA MARIA TREE, TACAMAHAC

cal·o·po·gon \ˌkaləˈpōˌgän\ *n, cap* [NL, fr. *calo-* + *-pogon*] **:** a small genus of American bulbous orchids having grasslike leaves and spikelike racemes of pink bearded flowers — see GRASS PINK

cal·o·res·cence \ˌkaləˈresᵊn(t)s\ *n* -s [L *calor* heat + E *-escence*] **:** the incandescence of a body produced by the incidence upon it of infrared rays which are thus converted indirectly into radiant energy of shorter wavelength — **cal·o·res·cent** \-ᵊnt\ *adj*

calori- *comb form* [L, fr. *calor*] **:** heat ⟨*calori*meter⟩

[1]**ca·lor·ic** \kəˈlȯrik, -ˈlä-, ˈkalər-, -ēk\ *n* -s [F *calorique*, fr. L *calor* heat (fr. *calēre* to be warm) + F *-ique* -ic — more at LEE] **1 :** a supposed fluid form of matter to which the phenomena of heat and combustion were ascribed according to an obsolete concept of heat **2** *archaic* **:** HEAT

[2]**caloric** \"\ *adj* **1 :** of or relating to heat **2 :** of or relating to calories ⟨comparison of foods on a ~ basis⟩ — **ca·lor·i·cal·ly** \-ə·k(ə)lē, -ēk-, -li\ *adv*

caloric engine *n* **:** HOT-AIR ENGINE

cal·o·ric·i·ty \ˌkaləˈrisəd·ē\ *n* -ES [F *caloricité*, fr. L *calor* heat + F *-icité* (fr. L *-icus* -ic + F *-ité* -ity)] **:** physiological ability to develop and maintain bodily heat

caloric punsch *or* **caloric punch** *n* **:** SWEDISH PUNSCH

cal·o·rie *also* **cal·o·ry** \ˈkal(ə)rē, -i\ *n, pl* **calories** [F *calorie*, fr. L *calor* heat + F *-ie* -y — more at CALORIC] **:** any of several thermal units: **a :** the amount of heat required at a pressure of one atmosphere to raise the temperature of one gram of water one degree centigrade esp. from 15° to 16° — abbr. *cal;* called also *gram calorie, small calorie* **b** cap (1) **:** the amount of heat required to raise the temperature of one kilogram of water one degree centigrade **:** 1000 gram calories or 3.968 Btu — abbr. *Cal;* called also *kilogram calorie, large calorie* (2) **:** a unit expressing a heat-producing or energy-producing value in food that when oxidized in the body is capable of releasing one large calorie of energy (3) **:** an amount of food (as in a diet) having an energy-producing value of one large calorie **c :** 1/100 of the amount of heat required to raise the temperature of one gram of water from 0° to 100° C — called also *mean calorie*

ca·lor·i·fa·cient \kə¦lórə¦fāshənt, -är-, ¦kalərə̇-\ *adj* [*calori-* + *-facient*] **:** heat-producing — usu. used of foods

cal·o·rif·ic \¦kalə¦rifik\ *adj* [F or L; F *calorifique*, fr. L *calorificus*, fr. *calori-* + *-ficus* -fic] **:** of or relating to heat or to calories **:** productive of heat ⟨the ~ properties of various fuels⟩

calorific value *or* **calorific power** *n* **:** the heat produced by the combustion of a unit weight of a fuel

calorific wool *n* **:** CAPSICUM WOOL

ca·lor·i·fi·er \kə'lórə,fī(ə)r, -'är-\ *n* -S [L *calor* heat + E *-ify* + *-er* — more at CALORIC] **:** an apparatus for heating a fluid (as water) by circulating it past usu. steam-filled heating coils

ca·lor·i·gen·ic \kə¦lórə¦jenik, -är-, ¦kalərə̇-\ *adj* [*calori-* + *-genic*] **:** generating heat or energy ⟨the ~ action of carbohydrates⟩

cal·o·rim·e·ter \,kalə'rimәd·ә(r)\ *n* -S [ISV *calori-* + *-meter;* orig. formed as F *calorimètre*] **:** any of several apparatuses for measuring quantities of absorbed or evolved heat or for determining specific heats by means of (1) the change in temperature of a solid (as copper or silver), (2) the heat of combustion (as of coal) in a chamber consisting of a strong steel shell, (3) the continuous flow through a heat exchanger of a fluid whose specific heat is being measured, (4) the melting of a known mass of ice, (5) the condensation of a known mass of steam, (6) the change in temperature of a known mass of water or other liquid — called also respectively (1) *aneroid calorimeter*, (2) *bomb calorimeter*, (3) *flow calorimeter*, (4) *ice calorimeter*, (5) *steam calorimeter*, (6) *water calorimeter;* see RESPIRATION CALORIMETER

cal·o·ri·met·ric \¦kalərə̇¦me·trik; kə¦lórə¦-, -är-\ *or* **cal·o·ri·met·ri·cal** \-ə̇kəl\ *adj* [*calorimetry* + *-ic* or *-ical*] **:** of or relating to calorimetry — **cal·o·ri·met·ri·cal·ly** \-ə̇k(ə)lē\ *adv*

cal·o·rim·e·try \,kalə'rimə·trē\ *n* -ES [F *calorimétrie*, fr. *calori-* + *-métrie* -metry] **:** measurement of quantities of heat

ca·lo·ris \kə'lórə̇s\ *n, pl* **caloris·es** \-rəsə̇z\ [irreg. fr. L *calor* heat — more at CALORIC] **:** SUMMER SORES

cal·o·rist \'kalərə̇st\ *n* -S [*calori-* + *-ist*] **:** one that holds to the caloric theory of heat

ca·lor·i·za·tor *or* **ca·lor·i·sa·tor** \kə'lórə,zād·ə(r), -'är-, -,sā-\ *n* -S [fr. (assumed) *calorize* to heat (fr. L *calor* heat + E *-ize*) + *-ator*] **:** an apparatus used in beet-sugar factories to heat juice in order to aid the diffusion of sugar

cal·o·rize \'kalə,rīz\ *vt* -ED/-ING/-S [L *calor* + E *-ize*] **:** to treat by a process for coating metal (as iron or steel) with aluminum in which the metal is heated in a reducing atmosphere in a closed retort with a mixture containing finely divided aluminum that alloys with the metal to a depth dependent on the length of the treatment — compare SHERARDIZE

calory *var of* CALORIE

cal·o·so·ma \,kalə'sōmə\ *n* [NL, fr. *calo-* + *-soma*] **1** *cap* **:** a genus of large predaceous ground beetles (family Carabidae) that are green, black, or bronze in color and that feed on injurious caterpillars **2** -S **:** any beetle of the genus *Calosoma*

ca·lot \kə'lät\ *n* -S [modif. of F *calotte*] **:** a close-fitting cap without visor or brim; *also* **:** a woman's or child's cap of this basic design

calotermes *syn of* KALOTERMES

calotermitid *var of* KALOTERMITID

calotermitidae *syn of* KALOTERMITIDAE

cal·o·thrix \'kalə,thriks\ *n, cap* [NL, fr. *calo-* + *-thrix*] **:** a genus of blue-green algae (family Rivulariaceae) with free nonmucilaginous simple or falsely branched filaments

ca·lot·ro·pis \kə'lä·trəpə̇s\ *n, cap* [NL, fr. *calo-* + Gk *tropis* keel; akin to Gk *trepein* to turn — more at TROPE] **:** a genus of Asiatic or African shrubs or trees (family Asclepiadaceae) having bell-shaped flowers with showy keel-shaped hoods and used as fiber plants — see MUDAR

ca·lotte \kə'lät\ *n* -S [F] **1 a :** CALOT, SKULLCAP **b :** ZUCCHETTO **2 a :** an ice cap or a large glacier not confined to a single valley **b :** a snow-capped summit or dome **3 a :** CALVA **b** *zool* **:** a cap or a part likened to a cap **4 a :** a caplike architectural construction; *esp* **:** the interior of a small cupola or a cup-shaped vault

cal·o·type \'kalə,tīp\ *n* -S [*calo-* + *type*] **1 :** an early photographic-negative process in which paper is sensitized with silver iodide, brushed over with a solution of silver nitrate and acetic and gallic acids, and after exposure developed in a gallic acid-silver nitrate solution **2 :** a positive print made from a calotype negative — **cal·o·typ·ic** \¦ₑₑ¦tipik\ *adj* — **cal·o·typ·ist** \'ₑₑ,tīpə̇st\ *n* -S

ca·loy·er \kə'lòiə(r), -òyə-, 'ka,l-; 'kalәyә-\ *n* -S [It & F; F *caloyer*, fr. obs. It *caloiero*, fr. MGk *kalogēros* venerable, lit., having a beautiful old age, fr. *kalo-* calo- + *-gēros* (fr. Gk *gēras* old age) — more at CORN] **:** a monk of the Eastern Church

cal·pac *or* **cal·pack** \'kal,pak, ₑ'ₑ\ *n* -S [Turk *kalpak*] **:** a high-crowned cap usu. of sheepskin or felt that is worn in Turkey, Iran, and neighboring countries

cal·pul·li \kal'pülē\ *also* **cal·pol·li** \-'ō-\ *or* **cal·pul** \'kal,pül\ *n, pl* **cal·pul·li** \-ülē\ *also* **cal·pul·lec** \-ü(,)lek\ [Nahuatl *calpulli*, lit., big house, aug. of *calli* house] **:** a clan or ward constituting the fundamental unit of Aztec society

calque \'kalk, -ä-\ *n* -S [F, lit., copy, fr. *calquer* to trace, fr. It *calcare* to trace, trample, fr. L, to trample — more at CAULK] **1 :** a linguistic borrowing that consists of the imitation in one language of some part of the peculiar range of meaning of a particular word in another language ⟨English *foot* meaning a metrical unit is a ~ from Latin *pes*⟩ **2 :** LOAN TRANSLATION

cal·tha \'kalthə\ *n, cap* [NL, fr. L, pot marigold] **:** a small genus of marsh or aquatic herbs (family Ranunculaceae) growing in arctic and temperate regions and having rounded and cordate or reniform leaves and apetalous flowers with yellow, white, or pink showy sepals — see MARSH MARIGOLD

cal·throps \'kalthrəps, -'ō-\ *n pl but usu sing in constr* [var. of *caltrop*] **:** a tetraxon sponge spicule in which the rays are equal or nearly equal in length

cal·trap \'kal·trəp, -'ō-\ *or* **galtrap** *n* -S [var. of *caltrop*] **:** a heraldic representation of a military caltrop

cal·trop \'kal·trəp, -'ō-\ *also* **cal·throp** \-thrəp\ *n* -S [ME *calketrappe*, a plant, fr. OE *coltetræppe*, *calcatrippe*, fr. ML *calcatrippa*, prob. fr. (assumed) *calcitrappa*, fr. *calci-* (fr. L *calc-*, *calx* heel) + *trappa* trap, of Gmc origin; akin to OE *træppe* trap — more at CALK, TRAP] **1 :** any of several plants having stout spines on the fruit or flower heads: as **a :** STAR THISTLE **b :** a plant of either of two genera (*Tribulus* and *Kallstroemia*) of the family Zygophyllaceae **c :** WATER CHESTNUT **2 a :** a device with four metal points so arranged that when any three are on the ground the fourth projects upward as a hazard to the hoofs of horses or to pneumatic tires — see CALTRAP **b :** a calk on a horseshoe

caltrop 2a

ca·lum·ba *also* **co·lum·ba** *or* **co·lom·ba** \kə'ləmbə\ *or* **colom·bo** *or* **co·lum·bo** *or* **ca·lom·bo** \kə'ləm(,)bō\ *n* -S [perh. of African origin, akin to Hausa *ka'lu'mbo²*, a small tree] **:** the root of an African plant (*Jatrorrhiza palmata*) of the family Menispermaceae that contains the bitter principle columbin and is used as a tonic

cal·u·met \'kalyə,met, ₑₑ'ₑ, 'ₑₑ,mət\ *n* -S *often attrib* [AmerF, fr. F dial., straw, fr. LL *calamellus* little reed, dim. of L *calamus* reed — more at CALAMUS] **:** a highly ornamented ceremonial pipe of the No. American Indians that was smoked at sacrifices and other magical or religious rites and on state occasions

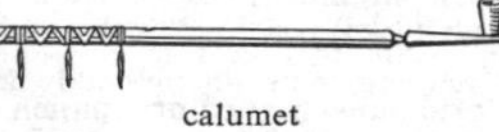

calumet

calumet dance *n* **1 :** a ritual dance with a plumed calumet originated by Indians of the Great Plains as an invocation by pipe and later combined with mimicry of the eagle **2** *among the Iroquois* **:** EAGLE DANCE

ca·lum·ni·ate \kə'ləmnē,āt, *usu* -ād·+V\ *vt* -ED/-ING/-S [L *calumniatus*, past part. of *calumniari*, fr. *calumnia* calumny] **1 :** to utter false statements, charges, or imputations in order to impair the public reputation of ⟨it provides an always welcome opportunity to ~ the masses —R.W.Brown b.1925⟩ **2 :** to injure or impair the public reputation of by calumny ⟨trying to ~ the leaders of the opposition⟩ ⟨gallantly defended the sage . . . against those who sought to ~ his memory —A.L. Sachar⟩ **syn** see MALIGN

ca·lum·ni·a·tion \kə,ləmnē'āshən\ *n* -S [LL *calumniation-*, *calumniatio*, fr. L *calumniatus* + *-ion-*, *-io* -ion] **1 :** the act of calumniating **:** SLANDERING ⟨the constant ~ engaged in by the courtiers⟩ **2 :** a slanderous report **:** CALUMNY

ca·lum·ni·a·tor \kə'ləmnē,ād·ə(r), -ātə-\ *n* -S [MF or L; MF *calomniateur*, fr. L *calumniator*, fr. *calumniatus* + *-or*] **:** one that calumniates

ca·lum·ni·ous \-nēəs\ *adj* [MF or LL; MF *calomnieux*, fr. LL *calumniosus* full of trickery, fr. L *calumnia* trickery, calumny + *-osus* -ous] **:** given to calumny ⟨~ backbiting rivals⟩ **:** constituting or marked by calumny ⟨hurt by ~ reports⟩ **:** SLANDEROUS

ca·lum·ni·ous·ly *adv* **:** in a calumnious manner

calumnize *vt* -ED/-ING/-S [*calumny* + *-ize*] *obs* **:** CALUMNIATE

cal·um·ny \'kal(y)əmnē, -i\ *n* -ES [MF & L; MF *calomnie*, fr. L *calumnia*, fr. *calvi* to deceive; akin to OE *hōl* calumny, OHG *huolen* to deceive, ON *hōl* flattery, Goth *holon* to accuse falsely, Gk *kēlein* to beguile] **1 :** the act of uttering false charges or misrepresentations maliciously calculated to damage another's reputation ⟨a circle of false friends spending their time in *calumnies*⟩ **2 :** a false charge or misrepresentation intended to blacken one's reputation **:** SLANDER ⟨this publication was felt to be a ~ on the innocence of the nursery —Ernest Jones⟩ ⟨there are always such *calumnies* about rebels —H.F.West⟩ **syn** see DETRACTION

calumpang *var of* KALUMPANG

calumpit *var of* KALUMPIT

ca·lu·sa *also* **ca·loo·sa** \kə'lüsə\ *n, pl* **calusa** *or* **calusas** *usu cap* [perh. modif. of Sp *Carlos* (Charles V †1558 Holy Roman emperor)] **1 :** a people of southern Florida of uncertain, perhaps Muskogean, relationship **2 :** a member of the Calusa people

ca·lu·sar \kə,lü'shär\ *n, pl* **calusa·ri** \-ärē\ *sometimes cap* [Romanian *calușar*, fr. *caluș* hobbyhorse] **:** a Romanian hobbyhorse dance done by members of a sworn brotherhood in wild steps and fierce mock combat

cal·u·tron \'kalyə,trän\ *n* -S [*Cal*ifornia *U*niversity + E *-tron*] **:** an electromagnetic apparatus for separating isotopes according to their masses on the principle of the mass spectrograph

cal·va \'kalvə\ *n, pl* **calvas** \-vəz\ *or* **cal·vae** \-,vē, -,ī\ [NL, fr. L, scalp without hair — more at CALVARIUM] **:** the upper part of the human cranium — compare CALVARIUM

cal·va·dos \¦kalvə¦dōs, -ōs, -äs\ *n* -ES *often cap* [F, fr. *Calvados* dept., Normandy, France, where it originated] **:** a dry fruity brown brandy distilled esp. from apples grown in Auge and Bessin in the department of Calvados

cal·vaire \kal'va(a)(ə)r\ *n* -S [F, fr. LL *Calvaria*] **:** CALVARY

cal·var·ia \kal'va(a)rēə\ *n* -S [L, skull] **:** CALVARIUM

cal·var·i·al \-ēəl\ *adj* [NL *calvarium* + E *-al*] **:** of or relating to the calvarium

cal·var·i·um \-ēəm\ *n, pl* **calvar·ia** \-ēə\ [NL, alter of L *calvaria* skull, fr. fem. of *calvarius* (assumed) fr. *calva* scalp without hair, fr. fem. of *calvus* bald; akin to Skt *atikulva* completely bald] **:** an incomplete skull: **a :** a skull lacking the lower jaw **b :** a skull lacking the lower jaw and facial portion **c :** CALVA

cal·va·ry \'kalv(ə)rē, -i\ *n* -ES *sometimes cap* [fr. *Calvary*, the hill near the ancient city of Jerusalem where Jesus was crucified, fr. ME *Calvarie*, fr. OE, fr. LL *Calvaria* (fr. L, skull), trans. of Gk *kranion*, trans. of Aram *gūlgaltā*] **1 :** a cross with the figure of the crucified Christ typically flanked by two other crosses with figures of thieves and set out of doors as a shrine **2 :** experience of intense suffering **:** TRIAL, ORDEAL ⟨penury and financial dependency constituted a veritable ~ for Michelangelo —*Publ's Mod. Lang. Assoc. of Amer.*⟩

calvary clover *n, usu cap 1st C* **:** a prickly-fruited medic (*Medicago echinus*) of the Mediterranean region

calvary cross *n, usu cap 1st C* **:** a Latin cross set upon three steps or upon a mount — called also *cross Calvary*, *cross of Calvary*

Calvary cross

cal·va·tia \kal'vāsh(ē)ə\ *n, cap* [NL, irreg. fr. L *calvus* bald] **:** a genus of fungi (family Lycoperdaceae) including the giant puffball (*C. gigantea*) that have outer casings whose upper parts break at maturity into angular pieces to expose the spores

¹calve \'kav, 'kaf, -aa(ə)-,-ai-,-å-,-ä-\ *vb* -ED/-ING/-S [ME *calven*, fr. OE *cealfian*, fr. *cealf* calf — more at CALF] *vi* **1 a :** to give birth to a calf — sometimes used with *down* **b :** to bear young **:** produce offspring **2** *of an ice mass* **:** to separate or break so that a part becomes detached ~ *vt* **1 :** to produce by birth **2 :** *of an ice mass* **:** to let break off and become detached ⟨the glacier *calved* a large iceberg⟩

²calve \'kåv, -ō-\ *vi* -ED/-ING/-S [prob. fr. Flem *inkalven* to cave in, fr. *in* + *kalven* to bear a calf, to calve (said of a glacier); akin to OE *cealfian*] *dial Eng, of an earth or rock mass* **:** to fall esp. from undermining **:** CAVE — used with *in*

calved *adj* [fr. past part. of ¹*calve*] **:** having produced a calf — often used with *down* ⟨a *calved*-down heifer⟩

calv·er \'kavə(r), -afə-, -aa-,-ai-,-å-,-ä-\ *n* -S [¹*calve* + *-er*] **:** a pregnant cow

calves *pl of* CALF, *pres 3d sing of* CALVE

cal·vin·ism \'kalvə̇,nizəm\ *n* -S *cap* [John *Calvin* (Jean Chauvin or Caulvin) †1564 Fr. theologian + E *-ism*] **:** the theological system or distinguishing tenets of the Christian reformer John Calvin and his followers; *esp* **:** the theological doctrines that emphasize the sovereignty of God in the bestowal of grace and that specif. include election or predestination, limited atonement, total depravity, irresistibility of grace, and the perseverance of saints — compare ARMINIANISM

¹cal·vin·ist \-_nə̇st\ *n* -S *usu cap* **:** a follower of John Calvin **:** an adherent of Calvinism

²calvinist \"\ *or* **cal·vin·is·tic** \¦ₑₑ¦nistik, -ēk\ *also* **calvin·is·ti·cal** \-ə̇kəl, -ēk-\ *adj, usu cap* **:** of, relating to, or characteristic of Calvinism or Calvinists — **cal·vin·is·ti·cal·ly** \-ə̇k(ə)lē, -ēk-, -li\ *adv, usu cap*

calvinistic baptist *n, usu cap C&B* **1 :** PARTICULAR BAPTIST **2 :** a Baptist holding Calvinistic doctrinal views

calvinistic methodist *n, usu cap C&M* **:** a member of a British religious body following the Calvinistic opinion of George Whitefield and antedating the Arminian form of Methodism

cal·vin·ize \'kalvə̇,nīz\ *vb* -ED/-ING/-S *often cap* [John *Calvin* + E *-ize* — more at CALVINISM] *vi* **:** to follow Calvinism ~ *vt* **:** to convert to Calvinism **:** imbue with Calvinism

cal·vi·ti·es \kal'vishē,ēz, -ishēz\ *n, pl* **calvities** [L, baldness, fr. *calvus* bald — more at CALVARIUM] **:** BALDNESS

¹calx \'kalks\ *n, pl* **calxes** \-ksə̇z\ *or* **cal·ces** \-l,sēz\ [ME *cals* powder produced by calcining a mineral, fr. L *calx* lime — more at CHALK] **:** the friable residue (as a metal oxide) left when a mineral or metal has been subjected to calcination or roasting **:** CALCINE

²calx \"\ *n, pl* **cal·ces** \-l,sēz\ [L — more at CALK] **:** HEEL

calyc- *or* **calyco-** *comb form* [NL, fr. Gk *kalyk-*, *kalyko-*, fr. *kalyk-*, *kalyx* — more at CHALICE] **:** calyx ⟨*calyc*oid⟩ ⟨*Calyco*phora⟩

cal·y·canth \'kalə̇,kan(t)th\ *n* -S [NL *Calycanthus*] **:** a plant of the genus *Calycanthus*

cal·y·can·tha·ce·ae \,kalə̇(,)kan'thāsē,ē\ *n pl, cap* [NL, fr. *Calycanthus*, type genus + *-aceae*] **:** a family of shrubs (order Ranales) of the eastern U. S. and eastern Asia having opposite simple leaves, aromatic bark, and large solitary flowers — see CALYCANTHUS — **cal·y·can·tha·ceous** \¦ₑₑ(,)ₑ¦thāshəs\ *adj*

cal·y·can·the·my \,ₑₑ'kan(t)thəmē\ *n* -ES [*calyc-* + Gk *anthemon* flower + E *-y* — more at ANTHEMION] **:** abnormal development of calyx parts into petals or petallike structures

cal·y·can·thine \-'kan,thēn, -an(t)thən\ *n* -S [NL *Calycanthus* + E *-ine*] **:** a bitter and poisonous crystalline alkaloid $C_{22}H_{26}N_4$ that is obtained from seeds of plants of the genus *Calycanthus*

cal·y·can·thus \-n(t)thəs\ *n* [NL, fr. *calyc-* + *-anthus*] **1** *cap* **:** a small genus (the type of the family Calycanthaceae) of American shrubs having aromatic bark, opposite entire leaves, and purple or red flowers — see CAROLINA ALLSPICE **2** -ES **:** CAROLINA ALLSPICE

ca·ly·cate \'kālə̇,kāt, -'a-, -,kə̇t\ *adj* [NL *calycatus*, fr. *calyc-* + *-atus* -ate] *bot* **:** having a calyx

ca·ly·ce·al *or* **cal·i·ce·al** \¦kalə¦sēəl, ¦kā-\ *also* **ca·ly·cal** \'kālə̇kəl, -'a-\ *adj* [*calyc-* + *-eal* or *-al*] **:** of or relating to a calyx

cal·y·ce·ra·ce·ae \,kaləsə'rāsē,ē\ *n pl, cap* [NL, fr. *Calycera*, type genus (irreg. fr. *calyc-* + Gk *keras* horn) + *-aceae* — more at CEREBRAL] **:** a family of So. American herbs or subshrubs (order Campanulales) having flowers in heads like the composites but differing in the variable number of perianth lobes and the more or less distinct anthers — **cal·y·ce·ra·ceous** \¦ₑₑₑ¦rāshəs\ *adj*

calyces *pl of* CALYX

calyci- *comb form* [L *calyc-*, *calyx*] **:** calyx ⟨*calyci*ferous⟩ ⟨*calyci*floral⟩

ca·ly·cine \'kālə,sīn, -'a-\ *also* **ca·lyc·i·nal** \kə'lisᵊnəl\ *adj* [*calycine* fr. *calyc-* + *-ine; calycinal* fr. *calycine* + *-al*] **:** relating to or resembling a calyx

ca·ly·cle *sense 1* 'kalə̇kəl *or* -'a-, *sense 2* -'a-\ *n* -S [modif. of F *calicule*, fr. L *calyculus* small flower bud, calyx, dim. of *calyc-*, *calyx* — more at CALYX] **1 :** EPICALYX **2** [alter. of *calicle*] **:** CALYCULUS

ca·ly·cled \-kəld\ *adj* **:** having a calycle **:** CALYCULATE

calyco- — see CALYC-

ca·ly·coid \'kālə,kȯid, -'a-\ *also* **ca·ly·coi·de·ous** \¦ₑₑ¦ₑdēəs\ *adj* [*calyc-* + *-oid*] **:** like a calyx in form, color, or appearance

ca·ly·coph·o·ra \,kālə'käfərə, -al-\ *n pl, cap* [NL, fr. *calyc-* + *-phora*] **:** a suborder of Siphonophora containing forms having a long stem with the zooids arranged along it and one or more swimming bells but no air sac near its upper end — **ca·ly·coph·o·ran** \¦ₑₑ¦ₑₑrən\ *adj or n* — **ca·ly·co·phore** \'ₑlәkə,fō(ə)r\ *n* -S

ca·ly·coph·o·rae \,ₑ ₑ'käfə,rē\ *syn of* CALYCOPHORA

ca·ly·co·phyl·lum \,ₑlәkō'filəm\ *n, cap* [NL, fr. *calyc-* + *-phyllum*] **:** a genus of tropical American trees (family Rubiaceae) of medium to large size characterized by smooth shiny reddish or brown shredding bark — see DAGAME

ca·ly·co·zoa \-kə'zōə\ [NL, fr. *calyc-* + *-zoa*] *syn of* STAUROMEDUSAE

ca·ly·co·zo·an \¦ₑₑₑ¦zōən\ *adj or n* [NL *Calycozoa* + E *-an*] **:** STAUROMEDUSAN — **ca·ly·co·zo·ic** \-ōik\ *adj*

ca·lyc·u·lar *also* **ca·lic·u·lar** \kə'likyələ(r)\ *adj* [*calycular* fr. L *calyculus* small flower bud + E *-ar; calicular* fr. F *calicule* calycle + E *-ar* — more at CALYCLE] **:** of the nature of or relating to a calycle or calyculus

ca·lyc·u·late *also* **ca·lic·u·late** \-,lāt, -lə̇t\ *adj* [*calyculate* fr. L *calyculus* + E *-ate; caliculate* fr. F *calicule* + E *-ate*] **1 :** having a calycle **2 :** having the surfaces pitted

ca·lyc·u·lus \-ləs\ *n, pl* **calycu·li** \-,lī, -ē\ [NL, modif. (influenced by E *calycle* and L *calyculus* small flower bud, calyx) of E *calicle*, fr. L *caliculus* small cup, dim. of *calic-*, *calix* cup — more at CHALICE] **:** a small cup-shaped structure (as a taste bud, an optic cup, or a cavity of a coral containing a polyp)

cal·y·don·i·an \¦kalə̇¦dōnēən, -ōnyən\ *adj, usu cap* [*Calydon*, ancient city of Aetolia, Greece (fr. L, fr. Gk *Kalydōn*) + E *-ian*] **:** of or relating to Calydon

ca·lym·e·ne \kə'limə(,)nē\ *n, cap* [NL, modif. of Gk *kekalymmenē*, fem. of *kekalymmenos*, perf. pass. part. of *kalyptein* to cover, conceal — more at HELL] **:** a genus of trilobites of the Ordovician, Silurian, and Devonian periods

ca·lym·ma \kə'limə\ *n* -S [NL, fr. Gk *kalymma* covering, fr. *kalyptein*] **:** the matrix of a chromosome

ca·lym·ma·to·bacterium \kə¦limәd·ō+\ *n, cap* [NL, fr. Gk *kalymmat-*, *kalymma* covering + NL *-o-* + *Bacterium*] **:** a genus of pleomorphic nonmotile bacterial rods (family Brucellaceae) that includes solely the causative organism of human granuloma inguinale — see DONOVAN BODY

¹ca·lyp·so \kə'lip(,)sō\ *n* [NL, prob. fr. L *Calypso*, island nymph who detained Odysseus 7 years on his journey home from Troy, fr. Gk *Kalypsō*] **1** *cap* **:** a genus of delicate bulbous bog herbs (family Orchidaceae) of northern Europe and No. America **2** -S **:** any plant of the genus *Calypso* or its single flower which is white variegated with purple, pink, and yellow

²calypso \"\ *n* -S *sometimes cap* [prob. after *Calypso*, island nymph] **:** a balladlike improvisation in African rhythm usu. satirizing current events first composed and sung in competition in the British West Indies

¹ca·lyp·so·ni·an \kə,lip'sōnēən, ¦ka(,)lip¦s-\ *n* -S *sometimes cap* [²*calypso* + connective *-n-* + *-ian*] **:** a composer and singer of calypso songs

²calypsonian \"\ *adj* **:** of, relating to, or characteristic of calypso music

ca·lyp·ter \kə'liptə(r), 'kaləp-\ *n, pl* **ca·lyp·ters** \-ə(r)z\ *or* **ca·lyp·te·res** \,kaləp'ti(ə)(,)rēz\ [NL, fr. Gk *kalyptēr* sheath, fr. *kalyptein* to cover, conceal — more at HELL] **1 :** the alula of a two-winged fly esp. when large enough to cover the halter **2 :** CALYPTRA

ca·lyp·te·rae \kə'liptə,rē\ *syn of* CALYPTRATAE

ca·lyp·to·blas·tea \kə,liptō'blastēə\ [NL, fr. Gk *kalyptos* covered (fr. *kalyptein*) + *blastos* shoot, bud + NL *-ea* (neut. pl. of L *-eus*) — more at -EAE] *syn of* LEPTOMEDUSAE

ca·lyp·to·blas·tic \¦ₑ¦ₑₑ¦tik\ *adj* [Gk *kalyptos* + E *-blastic*] **1 :** having the gonophores in a gonotheca — used of hydroids of the order Leptomedusae **2** *also* **ca·lyp·to·blas·te·an** \-tēən\ **:** LEPTOMEDUSAN

ca·lyp·to·pis \kə'liptəpə̇s\ *or* **cal·yp·top·sis** \,kaləp'täpsə̇s\ *n, pl* **calypto·pes** \-,pēz\ *or* **calyptop·ses** \-(,)sēz\ [NL, fr. Gk *kalyptos* + NL *-opis* or *-opsis*] **:** a modified zoea larva typical of euphausiid crustaceans

ca·lyp·to·rhyn·chus \kə,liptə'riŋkəs\ *n, cap* [NL, fr. Gk *kalyptos* + NL *-rhynchus*] **:** a genus of chiefly black Australian insectivorous cockatoos

ca·lyp·tra \kə'liptrə\ *n* -S [NL, fr. Gk *kalyptra* veil, fr. *kalyptein*] **1 :** the archegonium of a liverwort or moss when distended and modified by the growth of the enclosed sporophyte; *esp* **:** such an archegonium when forming a thin membranous hood over the capsule of a moss **2 :** a caplike covering of a flower or fruit (as the calyx of plants of the genus *Eschscholtzia*) **3 :** ROOT CAP

cal·yp·trae·i·dae \,kaləp'trēə,dē\ *n pl, cap* [NL, fr. *Calyptraea*, type genus (irreg. fr. Gk *kalyptra*) + *-idae*] **:** a family (order Pectinibranchia) of limpetlike marine gastropod mollusks having a curved internal lamina in the shell — see CUP-AND-SAUCER LIMPET

cal·yp·tran·thes \,kaləp'tran(,)thēz\ *n, cap* [NL, fr. *calyptra* + *-anthes*] **:** a large genus of tropical American aromatic shrubs or trees of the family Myrtaceae with evergreen leathery leaves and small flowers in which the top of the calyx falls away like a calyptra — see WHITE STOPPER

cal·yp·tra·ta \,kaləp'trād·ə, -'ä-\ [alter. (influenced by NL *-ata*) of NL *Calyptratae*] *syn of* CALYPTRATAE

cal·yp·tra·tae \-ād·,ē, -äd·-\ *n pl, cap* [NL, fr. *calyptr-* (fr. *calypter*) + *-atae* (fem. pl. of *-atus* -ate)] **:** a group of dipterous flies (suborder Schizophora) including in recent classifications the Muscidae and related families distinguished by the large calypters

¹ca·lyp·trate \kə'lip,trāt, -,trə̇t, 'kaləp,trāt\ *adj* [NL *calyptra* + E *-ate*] **1** *bot* **:** having a calyptra **2 a** [²*calyptrate*] **:** of or relating to the Calyptratae **b** [NL *calyptr-* (fr. *calypter*) + E *-ate*] **:** furnished with calypters

²calyptrate \"\ *n* -S [NL *Calyptratae*] **:** one of the Calyptratae

calyptri- *or* **calyptro-** *comb form* [NL *calyptra*] **:** calyptra **:** hood **:** cap ⟨*calyptri*form⟩ ⟨*calyptro*gen⟩

ca·lyp·tro·gen \kə'liptrəjən, -,jen\ *n* -S [ISV *calyptro-* + *-gen*] **:** the layer of cells from which the rootcap originates

cal·yp·trog·y·ne \,kaləp'träjə(,)nē\ *n, cap* [NL, fr. *Calyptro-* + Gk *gynē* woman — more at QUEEN] **:** a small genus of almost stemless tropical American palms with pinnate almost stalkless leaves and small flowers half hidden by the spadix

ca·lys·so·zoa \kə,lisə'zōə\ [NL *calysso-* (prob. alter. of *calyc-*) + *-zoa*] *syn of* ENTOPROCTA

cal·y·ste·gia \,kalə'stējə̇ə\ *n, cap* [NL, irreg. fr. *calyx* + Gk *stegē* roof (fr. *stegein* to cover) + NL *-ia* — more at THATCH] **:** a small genus of twining or prostrate perennial herbs closely related to and by some included in *Convolvulus* but distinguished by the large bracts below the calyx

ca·lyx \ˈkāliks, -ēks *also* ˈka-\ *n, pl* **calyx·es** \-ksə̇z\ *or* **caly·ces** \-lə,sēz\ [L, fr. Gk *kalyx* — more at CHALICE] **1 :** the outer set of floral leaves making up the external part of the flower and consisting of separate or fused sepals that are usu. green and foliaceous but often colored like the corolla — see COROLLA, PERIANTH **2 :** a cuplike division of the pelvis of the kidney surrounding one or more of the renal papillae **3 :** any of various more or less cup-shaped zoological structures (as the body or the test of a crinoid or the calyculus of a coral)

calyx, *C*

calyx spray *n* **:** a pesticidal spray applied to fruit trees (as apple and pear) just after the petals fall but before the calyx closes — called also *petal fall spray, shuck spray*

calyx tooth *n* **:** a tip of a calyx lobe or division

calyx tube *n* **1 :** the lower tubular or cup-shaped portion of a gamosepalous calyx **2 :** HYPANTHIUM

cal·zo·ne·ras *or* **cal·zo·ne·ros** \,kalzəˈnerəs\ *n pl* [MexSp *calzoneras*, fr. Sp *calzón* pants, fr. *calza* stocking, fr. ML *calcea*, fr. L *calceus* shoe] *Southwest* **:** trousers buttoned at the sides and usu. slit at the bottom

¹**cam** *dial Brit past of* COME

²**cam** \ˈkam\ *adv* [prob. fr. W, crooked] *dial* **:** CROOKEDLY, AWRY, ASKEW

³**cam** \"\ *adj* [prob. fr. W; akin to OIr *camm* crooked — more at CHANGE] *dial* **:** CROOKED, TWISTED, PERVERSE

⁴**cam** \ˈkam, -aa(ə)m\ *n* -S [perh. fr. F *came*, fr. G *kamm*, lit., comb, fr. OHG *kamb* — more at COMB] **1 :** a rotating or sliding piece of machinery (as a wheel or a projection on a wheel) that imparts motion to a roller moving against its edge or to a pin free to move in a groove on its face or that receives motion from such a roller or pin **2 :** a curved wedge movable about an axis and used for forcing or clamping two pieces together

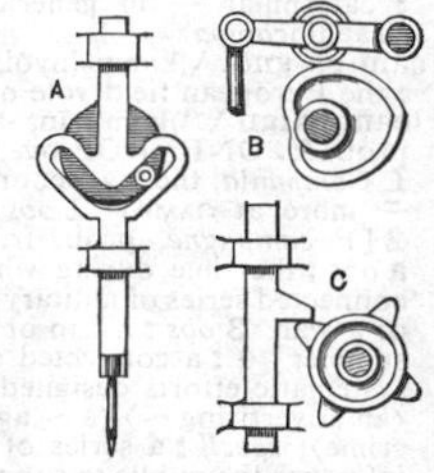

needlebar cam, *A;* heart cam, *B;* cam wheel, *C*

⁵**cam** \"\ *vt* **cammed; cammed; camming; cams 1 :** to move or control the movement of with a cam **2 :** to shape into a cam (as by grooving) — often used with *out*

cam *abbr* camouflage

cam·a·ca *also* **cam·a·ka** \ˈkaməkə\ *n* -S [ME, fr. MF *camocas* or ML *camoca*, fr. Ar & Per *kamkha, kimkha*] **:** a medieval fabric prob. of silk and camel's hair used for draperies and garments

ca·ma·chi·le \,kāməˈchilē\ *n* -S [AmerSp *camachile, cuamóchil, guamúchil*, fr. Nahuatl *cuauh-mochitl*] **:** a common tropical American tree (*Pithecolobium dulce*) yielding good timber, a yellow dye, a mucilaginous gum, and a widely used edible fruit — called also *huamuchil;* see MANILA TAMARIND

cam·a·du·la seed \¦kamə¦düla-\ *n* [origin unknown] **:** the seed of the adlay

cama fox *var of* CAAMA

ca·ma·gon \ˈkamə,gän\ *n* -S [Sp *camagón*, fr. Tag *kamagóng*] **1 :** a timber tree (*Diospyros discolor*) of the Philippines that yields an edible fruit **2 :** the wood of the camagon noted for its dark color

ca·ma·güey *or* **ca·ma·guey** \¦kamə¦gwā\ *adj, usu cap* [fr. *Camagüey*, Cuba] **:** of or from the city of Camagüey, Cuba **:** of the kind or style prevalent in Camagüey

ca·ma·ïeu \kämäyœ\ *n, pl* **camaïeux** \-yœ\ [MF; akin to It *cammeo* — more at CAMEO] **1** *obs* **:** CAMEO **2 :** MONOCHROME 1

ca·mail \kəˈmāl\ *n* -S [F, fr. OProv *capmalh*, perh. fr. *cap* head (fr. L *caput*) + *malha* mesh, ring of mail, fr. L *macula* spot, mesh — more at HEAD, MAIL] **:** a hood or neck guard of chain mail usu. hanging from the basinet

ca·mal·do·lese \kə¦maldə¦lēz, -ēs\ *n, pl* **camaldolese** *usu cap* [It, fr. *Camaldoli*, monastery in So. Italy where the order was founded + It *-ese*] **:** a member of a barefooted order of hermit Benedictines founded in 1012 by St. Romuald

ca·ma·lig \kəˈmälig\ *n* -S [Tag *kamalig*] **1** *Philippines* **:** STOREHOUSE **2** *Philippines* **:** HUT

¹**ca·ma·lo·te** \,kaməˈlōd·ē\ *n* -S [AmerSp] **:** WATER LILY

²**camalote** \"\ *n* -S [AmerSp, perh. alter. of Sp *camelote* camlet, fr. MF *camelot* — more at CAMLET] **:** any of several coarse grasses of tropical America (esp. *Echinochloa crus-galli, Gynerium sagittatum*, and *Hymenachne amplexicaulis*)

ca·man \kəˈmän\ *n* -S [IrGael *camán*, fr. OIr *camm* crooked — more at CHANGE] *Irish & Scot* **:** CAMMOCK

cam·a·nay \¦kamə¦nī\ *n* -S [AmerSp] **:** BLUE-FOOTED BOOBY

ca·man·cha·ca \,kamənˈchäkə\ *n* -S [AmerSp] **:** a thick fog on the coasts of Peru and Chile

ca·man·si *or* **ka·man·si** \kəˈmän(t)sē\ *n* -S [Sp, fr. Tag *kamansi*] *Philippines* **:** BREADFRUIT 1

cam·a·ra \ˈkamərə, ¦kamə¦rä\ *n* -S [Pg *camará*, fr. Tupi] **1 :** the hard and durable wood of the tonka-bean tree and other plants of the genus *Dipteryx* **2 :** the camara nutmeg tree **3 :** a tropical American shrub (*Lantana camara*) having showy yellow-orange tubular flowers

ca·ma·ra·de·rie \,kam(ə)ˈradərē, -ām-; ,käm(ə)ˈräd-, ,kam(ə)ˈräd-, -am-; *also* ,=(=)=ˈ=\ *n* -S [F, fr. *camarade* comrade + *-erie* -ery — more at COMRADE] **:** the spirit of friendly familiarity and goodwill that exists between comrades **:** GOOD-FELLOWSHIP ⟨a greater spirit of tolerance and ~ among the drivers —Priscilla Hughes⟩ ⟨a great deal of affection on both sides, but little ~ —A.C.Benson⟩

camara nutmeg *n* [perh. fr. Pg *camará*] **:** the fruit of a tree (*Licaria camara*) of the family Lauraceae of Guiana somewhat resembling the nutmeg

cam·a·ra·sau·rus \¦kamərə¦sȯrəs\ *n, cap* [NL, fr. Gk *kamara* vaulted chamber + NL *-saurus* — more at CHAMBER] **:** a genus of American Jurassic dinosaurs (order Sauropoda) with the orbits and nares large and situated high on the head suggesting adaptation to an amphibious mode of life

cam·a·ril·la \,kaməˈrilə, -rē(y)ə\ *n* -S [Sp, lit., small room, dim. of *cámara* room, fr. LL *camara, camera* — more at CHAMBER] **:** a group of unofficial often secret and usu. scheming advisers esp. of one in power (as a king or premier) **:** CABAL, CLIQUE ⟨a vivid picture of the sycophantic timeservers who constituted the Kaiser's court ~ —L.P.Lochner⟩

cam·as \ˈkaməs\ *also* **cam·ash** \-mish\ *or* **cam·ass** \-məs\ *or* **quam·ash** \ˈkwämish\ *n* -ES [Chinook Jargon *kamass*, fr. Nootka *chamas* sweet] **1 :** an American plant of the genus *Camassia* (esp. *C. quamash*) of the western U.S. **2 :** a plant of the genus *Zigadenus* — see DEATH CAMAS

camas rat *n* **:** a large dark pocket gopher (*Thomomys bulbivorus*) of the northwestern U.S. that feeds on the camas

ca·mas·sia \kəˈmasēə\ *n, cap* [NL, fr. E *camass* + NL *-ia*] **:** a genus of scapose herbs (family Liliaceae) mostly of western No. America having edible bulbs, basal linear leaves, and racemes of blue, purple, or white flowers — see CAMAS

ca·ma·ta \kəˈmäd·ə\ *n* -S [origin unknown] **:** the almost unripe acorns and cups of the valonia oak gathered from the ground, dried, and used for tanning — compare CAMATINA

cam·a·ti·na \,kaməˈtēnə\ *n* -S [*camata* + *-ina* (It dim. suffix)] **:** the unripe acorns and cups of the valonia oak picked from the tree, dried, and used for tanning — compare CAMATA

ca·mau·ro \kəˈmau̇(,)rō\ *n* -S [It, prob. fr. ML *camaurum*] **:** a red velvet cap bordered with ermine formerly used by popes

cam·bar \ˈkam,bär\ *n, usu cap* [*Campine* + *barred* Rock] **:** a breed of autosexing domestic fowls with the male chicks pale gray striped with brown and the females much darker that was developed in England from crosses of barred rocks and golden Campines

cam·ba·rus \ˈkambərəs\ *n, cap* [NL, alter. (influenced by LL *gambarus*, alter. of L *cammarus*) of L *cammarus* sea crab, lobster, fr. Gk *kammaros;* akin to ON *humarr* lobster, Skt *kamaṭha* tortoise, and prob. to L *camur* curved — more at CHAMBER] **:** a genus of crayfishes (family Astacidae) lacking pleurobranchiae, having a specialized sperm receptacle, and including the common large crayfishes of eastern No. America some of which (esp. *C. limosus*) are used as food

cam·baye \(ˈ)kam¦bā\ *n* -S [earlier *cambaya*, prob. fr. Pg. *cambaia*, fr. *Cambaia* (Cambay) India] **:** a coarse cotton cloth made in India

¹**cam·ber** \ˈkambə(r), -aam-\ *vb* -ED/-ING/-S [F *cambrer*, fr. MF *cambre* curved] *vi* **:** to bend or curve upward toward the middle ~ *vt* **:** to cut, bend, or fashion to a slight convex curve **:** arch slightly ⟨above and athwartships ran a narrow platform, heavily ~*ed* and naked to the weather —Thomas Wood †1950⟩

²**camber** \"\ *n* -S [obs. *camber*, adj., curved, fr. obs. F *cambre*, fr. L *camur* — more at CHAMBER] **1 a :** a slight convexity, arching, or curvature (as of a beam, a deck, or a road) **b :** the greatest perpendicular distance in a semielliptical spring from an imaginary line drawn through the centers of the spring eyes to the top of the master leaf or to the bottom of the short plate **c :** the convexity or rise of the curve of an airfoil from its chord **:** the ratio of the maximum departure of this curve from the chord to the length of the chord **2 :** a setting of the front wheels of an automotive vehicle closer together at the bottom than at the top ⟨excessive ~ prevents the tire from having correct contact with the road —Joseph Heitner⟩ **3 :** a superficial geological structure induced during erosion, the strata dipping downward from hilltops toward adjacent valleys

camber angle *n* **1 :** the angle between two joined plane surfaces with a camber at the joining point or edge **2 :** the angle between the center line of the front wheel of an automotive vehicle and the vertical

camber arch *n* **:** an arch having a straight horizontal extrados and a slightly arched intrados

camber beam *n* **:** a beam that cambers

camber-keeled \ˈ= =¦=\ *adj, of a ship* **:** having the keel cambered but not actually hogged

camber piece *or* **camber slip** *n* **:** a piece or frame of wood cambered for use as a center in building camber arches

cam·ber·well beauty \ˈkambə(r),wel-, -,wəl-\ *n, usu cap C* [fr. *Camberwell*, formerly parish of Surrey, England, now metropolitan borough of London] **:** MOURNING CLOAK

cam·bi·al \ˈkambēəl\ *adj* [NL *cambium* + E *-al*] **:** of, relating to, or functioning as cambium

cam·bia·ta \,kambēˈäd·ə\ *n* -S [It, fem. of *cambiato*, past part. of *cambiare* to change, fr. L, to exchange — more at CHANGE] **:** a nonharmonic note of a melody reached by a skip of a third and resolved by a step

cam·bi·form \ˈkambə,fȯrm\ *adj* [ISV *cambi-* (fr. NL *cambium*) + *-form;* prob. orig. formed as G *kambiform*] **:** of the form or character of cambium or cambium cells

cam·bio \ˈkambē,ō\ *n* -S [It, fr. *cambiare* to exchange, fr. L — more at CHANGE] **:** a money exchange esp. in a Latin country

cam·bism \ˈkam,bizəm\ *n* -S [fr. *cambist*, after such pairs as E *journalist : journalism*] **:** the theory and practice of exchange in commerce

cam·bist \-bə̇st\ *n* -S [F *cambiste*, fr. It *cambista*, fr. *cambio* + *-ista* -ist] **1 :** one who deals in bills of exchange or who is skilled in the science and practice of exchange **2 :** a table or manual giving the exchange values of moneys, weights, and measures of various countries

cam·bist·ry \-trē\ *n* -ES [*cambist* + *-ry*] **:** the science of exchange esp. in its international aspects

cam·bi·um \ˈkambēəm\ *n, pl* **cambiums** \-ēəmz\ *or* **cam·bia** \-ēə\ [NL, fr. ML, exchange, fr. L *cambiare* to exchange — more at CHANGE] **:** a formative layer one cell thick occurring between the xylem and phloem of most vascular plants, being persistently capable of giving rise to new cells, often for many years in woody plants, and being responsible for secondary growth — compare MERISTEM, PHELLOGEN

camblet *var of* CAMLET

cam·bo·dia \(ˈ)kam¦bōdēə\ *adj, usu cap* [fr. *Cambodia*, Indochina] **:** of or from Cambodia **:** of the kind or style prevalent in Cambodia **:** CAMBODIAN

¹**cam·bo·di·an** \(ˈ)kam¦bōdēən\ *adj, usu cap* [*Cambodia*, Indochina + E *-an*] **:** of or relating to the independent state of Cambodia resulting from the breakup of French Indochina after World War II and situated in the lower Mekong river valley

²**cambodian** \"\ *n* -S *cap* **1 :** a native or resident of Cambodia **2 :** the language of the Cambodians, which is of Mon-Khmer origin

¹**camboge** *var of* GAMBOGE

²**cam·bo·gé** \¦kambō¦zhā\ *n* -S [origin unknown] **:** pierced concrete block used to make brise-soleils in Latin-American architecture ⟨achieve ventilation and decoration at the same time by the skillful insertion of ~ —*House Beautiful*⟩

cam·bo·gia \kamˈbōjə\ *n* -S [NL, alter. of *cambugia, cambugium* — more at GAMBOGE] **:** GAMBOGE 1

camboose *var of* CABOOSE

cam·brel \ˈkam(b)rəl\ *dial Eng var of* GAMBREL 1, 2

¹**cam·bri·an** \ˈkambrēən, -ˈā-\ *adj, usu cap* [*Cambria* Wales (fr. ML *Cambria, Cumbria*, perh. fr. — assumed — OW *combrog* fellow countryman, Welshman) + E *-an* — more at CYMRY] **1 :** of or relating to Cambria **:** WELSH **2** *or* **cambric** \-brik, -ēk\ **:** of or relating to the earliest geologic period of the Paleozoic era and the lowest system of Paleozoic rocks whose formations (as conglomerates, sandstones, shales, and limestones) indicating conditions of shallow sea water, a far from uniform climate, and a period of great duration show scarcely recognizable plant fossils but record every great animal type except the vertebrate, trilobites being one of the most characteristic groups — see GEOLOGIC TIME table

²**cambrian** \"\ *n* -S **1** *cap* **:** a native or resident of Cambria **:** WELSHMAN **2** *usu cap* **:** the Cambrian period or system of rocks

¹**cam·bric** \ˈkāmbrik, -ēk\ *n* -S [alter. of earlier *cameryk*, fr. obs. Flem *Kameryk* Cambrai, city of France (formerly of Flanders), where it was first made] **1 :** a fine thin closely woven plain white linen fabric **2 :** a cotton fabric that resembles cambric, is usu. white or piece-dyed, and is made with a glossy or glazed finish for clothing and with various finishes for industrial uses

²**cam·bric** \ˈkambrik, -ām-, -ēk\ *usu cap, var of* CAMBRIAN

cambric grass \-ām-\ *n* [prob. so called fr. the use of its fibers in making cloth] **:** RAMIE

cambric tea \-ām-\ *n* [so called fr. its being thin and white] **:** a hot drink made of water, milk, sugar, and often a very small portion of tea that is usu. given to children as a tea substitute

cam·bridge \ˈkāmbrij, -rēj\ *adj, usu cap* [fr. the place name *Cambridge*] **1** [fr. *Cambridge*, England] **:** of or from the municipal borough of Cambridge, England **:** of the kind or style prevalent in Cambridge, England **:** CANTABRIGIAN **2** [fr. *Cambridge* University, England] **:** of, relating to, or characteristic of Cambridge University **3** [fr. *Cambridge*, Mass.] **:** of or from the city of Cambridge, Mass. ⟨a *Cambridge* street⟩ **:** of the kind or style prevalent in Cambridge, Mass.

cambridge blue *n, often cap C* [fr. *Cambridge*, England, seat of Cambridge University] **:** ETON BLUE

cambridge platonist *n, usu cap C&P* [fr. *Cambridge* University, England, a center of the movement] **:** one of a group of 17th century Christian philosophers who united in opposition to empiricism and Hobbesian mechanism and who sought to reconcile science and religion within a Neoplatonic framework

cambridge red *n, often cap C* **:** a grayish to moderate red that is bluer and lighter than dianthus

cam·bridge·shire \-,shi(ə)r,-,shiə,-,shə(r)\ *or* **cambridge** *adj, usu cap* [fr. *Cambridgeshire* or the county of *Cambridge*, England] **:** of or from the county of Cambridge, England **:** of the kind or style prevalent in the county of Cambridge

cam·bril \ˈkam(b)rəl\ *dial Eng var of* GAMBREL 1, 2

cam·den \ˈkamdən, -aam-\ *adj, usu cap* [fr. *Camden*, N.J.] **:** of or from the city of Camden, N.J. ⟨*Camden* schools⟩ **:** of the kind or style prevalent in Camden

¹**came** *past of* COME

²**came** \ˈkām\ *also* **calm** \ˈkām\ *n* -S [origin unknown] **:** a slender grooved rod of cast lead used to hold together panes of glass in a window esp. with latticework or stained glass

cam·eist \ˈkamēə̇st\ *n* -S [*cameo* + *-ist*] **1 :** a maker of cameos **2 :** a collector or connoisseur of cameos

cam·el \ˈkaməl\ *n* -S [ME *camel* (fr. OE & ONF) & *chamel*, fr. OF; all fr. L *camelus*, fr. Gk *kamēlos*, of Sem. origin; akin to Heb & Phoenician *gāmāl* camel, Ar *jamal*] **1 a :** either of two large ruminant mammals used as draft and saddle animals in desert regions esp. of Africa and Asia and peculiarly adapted to desert life in their ability to live on tough thorny plants, in their capacity to conserve water in the body, and in their highly modified feet with broad thick calloused soles and small hoofs situated at the end of the toes: (1) **:** the Arabian camel (*Camelus dromedarius*) with a single large hump on the back **:** DROMEDARY (2) **:** the Bactrian camel (*C. bactrianus*) with two humps **b :** any member of the family Camelidae **2 :** a watertight structure (as a large box or cylinder) used esp. to lift submerged ships by being sunk, attached to the object to be raised, and then pumped free of water **3 a :** a variable color averaging a light yellowish brown that is slightly redder and very slightly less strong than khaki, yellower and less strong than cinnamon, and yellower and duller than walnut brown **b :** a brownish gray that is lighter than average chocolate, redder, lighter, and stronger than taupe (sense 1) or castor, and redder than mouse gray **4 :** a wooden float used as a fender esp. to fend ships off piers

Bactrian camel

¹**camelback** \ˈ= =,=\ *n* **1 :** the back of a camel ⟨crossed the desert on ~⟩ **2 :** a back (as of a dog) that is slightly curved upward **:** ROACH BACK — opposed to *swayback* **3** *or* **camelback locomotive :** a steam locomotive with the cab astride the boiler **4** *or* **camelback house :** a house one story high at the front and two stories high in the rear **5** [so called fr. the shape of one kind of retread made with it] **:** an uncured compound of rubber made chiefly of reclaimed or synthetic rubber and used for retreading or recapping pneumatic tires

²**camelback** \"\ *adj* **:** having a back slightly curved upward — opposed to *swaybacked*

³**camelback** \"\ *adv* **:** on camelback

camel bird *n* **:** OSTRICH

camel cricket *n* **:** CAVE CRICKET

cam·el·eer \¦kamə¦li(ə)r, -iə\ *or* **cam·el·teer** \-məlˈti-\ *n* -S [*cameleer* fr. *camel* + *-eer; camelteer* alter. (influenced by *muleteer*) of *cameleer*] **:** a driver and tender of a camel

cameleon *var of* CHAMELEON

camel grass *or* **camel hay** *n* [so called fr. its serving as feed for camels] **:** any sweet-scented Asiatic grass of the genus *Cymbopogon* (esp. *C. schoenanthus*)

camel hair *var of* CAMEL'S HAIR

camelia *var of* CAMELLIA

ca·mel·i·dae \kəˈmelə,dē\ *n pl, cap* [NL, fr. *Camelus*, type genus + *-idae*] **:** a small family of ruminant mammals (order Artiodactyla) comprising camels, llamas, and extinct related forms all having long limbs with two toes and fused but distally divergent metapodials, a 3-chambered stomach, and oval red blood cells

cam·e·li·na \,kaməˈlīnə, -lē-; kəˈmelənə\ *n, cap* [NL, fr. ML *camelina, chamaelinum*, alter. of L *chamaemelinus* of chamomile, fr. *chamaemelon* chamomile — more at CHAMOMILE] **:** a small genus of Old World herbs (family Cruciferae) distinguished by their ovoid flaxlike seed pods — see FALSE FLAX, GOLD OF PLEASURE, SMALL-SEEDED FALSE FLAX

cam·e·line \ˈkamə,lēn, -m(ə)lən\ *n* -S [ME *camelyn*, fr. MF *camelin*, fr. ML *camelinum*, fr. L, neut. of *camelinus* of a camel, fr. *camelus* camel — more at CAMEL] **1 :** a twilled camel's-hair fabric **2 :** a garment made of cameline

cam·e·line oil \ˈkamə,līn-, -ēn-\ *n* **:** a pungent yellow semidrying oil obtained from the seeds of gold of pleasure — called also *dodder oil, German sesame oil*

camelion *obs var of* CHAMELEON

¹**ca·mel·lia** \kəˈmēlyə, -lēə *also* -el-\ *n* [NL, fr. Georg Josef Kamel (Georgius Josephus *Camellus*) †1706 Moravian Jesuit missionary + NL *-ia*] **1** *cap* **:** a genus of tropical Asiatic evergreen shrubs or small trees (family Theaceae) having alternate elliptic short-petioled leaves and solitary usu. reddish or white flowers with stamens that are connate at the base **2** *also* **ca·me·lia** \-ēl-\ *n* -S **:** any of several shrubs or trees of the genus *Camellia; esp* **:** an ornamental greenhouse shrub (*C. japonica*) with glossy evergreen leaves and showy roselike flowers **3** -S **:** a moderate to strong red that is bluer and lighter than blood red

²**camellia** \"\ [NL] *syn of* THEA

ca·mel·li·a·ce·ae \=,=lēˈāsē,ē\ [NL, fr. *Camellia*, type genus + *-aceae*] *syn of* THEACEAE

cam·el·oid \ˈkamə,lȯid\ *adj* [*camel* + *-oid*] **:** like a camel

cam·el·o·pard \kəˈmelə,pärd, -pȧd *also* ˈkamə(,)lō,p-\ *n* -S [ML *camelopardus*, alter. of L *camelopardalis*, fr. Gk *kamēlopardalis*, fr. *kamēlos* camel + *pardalis* leopard — more at PARD] **:** GIRAFFE

ca·mel·o·par·da·lis \kə,meləˈpärdᵊləs, ,kamə(,)lōˈ-\ [NL, fr. L] *syn of* GIRAFFA

cam·el·ry \ˈkaməlrē\ *n* -ES [*camel* + *-ry* (as in *cavalry*)] **:** troops mounted on camels ⟨a column of ~ moved in from the north —*Time*⟩

camel's hair *n* **1** *also* **camel hair a :** the hair of a camel **b :** a substitute for camel's hair (as hair from the tail of a squirrel) **2** *also* **camel hair :** cloth made of camel's hair or a mixture of camel's hair and wool usu. light tan and soft and silky to the touch **3 :** the color deer

camel's hay *n* **:** CAMEL GRASS

camel spin *n* **:** an arabesque spin executed by a skater with back humped instead of arched

camelteer *var of* CAMELEER

camel thorn *also* **camel's thorn** *n* [so called fr. the use of its seed as feed for camels] **1 a :** a low spiny shrub (*Alhagi camelorum*) of the Arabian desert that yields manna **b :** a related shrub (*A. maurorum*) **2 :** an East Indian spiny shrub (*Zizyphus nummularius*) used as fodder for sheep and goats **3 :** any of several southern African acacias; *esp* **:** a browse plant (*Acacia giraffae*) of the veld

ca·me·lus \kəˈmēləs\ *n, cap* [NL, fr. L, camel] **:** a genus comprising the true camels and a number of extinct related animals

cam·em·bert *or* **camembert cheese** \ˈkaməm,be(ə)r, -,a(ə)(ə)r, -,eə, -,a(ə)ə, ,=ˈ=¦=\ *n* -S *usu cap 1st C* [F *camembert*, fr. *Camembert*, town in Normandy, France, where it was first made] **:** a soft unpressed cheese having a characteristic odor and flavor produced by the presence of a blue mold (*Penicillium camemberti*) and usu. covered with a feltlike rind inside which the cheese softens progressively toward the center

cam engine *n* [⁴*cam*] **:** an engine in which the reciprocating motion of the piston is converted into rotary motion by means of a cam and roller instead of the more usual crank

¹**cam·eo** \ˈkamē,ō\ *n* -S *often attrib* [It *cammeo, cameo;* akin to MF *camaïeu*, ML *camahutus, camaeus*] **1 a :** a gem carved in relief; *esp* **:** a small piece of sculpture on a stone (as onyx or sardonyx) or on a shell having layers of different colors, the figure being cut in relief in one layer and another serving as background — compare INTAGLIO **b :** a small medallion usu. simulating stone or shell with a profiled head in relief **2 :** a carving or sculpture made in the manner of a cameo **3 :** any of several colors varying in hue from purplish red to bluish green, in chroma from low to moderate, and in lightness from medium to very high — see CAMEO BLUE, CAMEO BROWN, CAMEO GREEN, CAMEO PINK, CAMEO YELLOW **4 :** a usu. brief literary or dramatic piece that brings into delicate or sharp relief the character of a person, place, or event ⟨his ~*s* and short commentaries on men and manners —R.T.Dunlop⟩

²**cameo** \"\ *vt* -ED/-ING/-S **1 :** to make into or as if into a cameo ⟨polished basalt ~*ed* upon malachite —Amy Lowell⟩

2 : to treat in cameo form ⟨the North American College . . . has never been properly ~*ed* for history —J.P.Boland⟩
cameo blue *n* **:** a light to very light bluish green
cameo brown *n* **:** a grayish red to light reddish brown
cameo glass *n* **:** glass consisting of layers of different colors and cut after the manner of a cameo
cam·eo·graph \'kamē(,)ō,graf\ *n* -s [blend of *cameo* & *photograph*] **:** an image in relief produced largely mechanically from photographs
cam·e·og·ra·phy \,kamē'ägrəfē\ *n* -ES [blend of *cameo* & *photography*] **:** the art or process of producing cameographs
cameo green *n* **:** a pale green to light yellowish green — called also *hazy blue, mist blue*
cameo paper *n* **:** a clay-coated paper having an ivory tint and a dull finish used by artists for making pencil drawings
cameo pink *n* **:** a grayish purplish pink that is redder and deeper than average orchid mist and bluer and stronger than dawn pink
cameo shell *also* **cameo conch** *n* **:** a large gastropod shell used for cameos: as **a :** QUEEN CONCH **b :** a large king conch
cameo ware *n* **1 :** a fine ware decorated with relief figures on a different-colored ground (as Wedgwood ware) **2 :** a highly glazed shell-tinted ware usu. pink shading into white
cameo yellow *n* **:** a pale yellow that is greener, stronger, and slightly darker than ivory and deeper and slightly greener than cream
cam·era \'kam(ə)rə, 'kaamrə\ *n* -s *often attrib* [LL, chamber, room — more at CHAMBER] **1** *pl also* **camer·ae** \'kamə,rē, -ī\ **:** a chamber, room, or small hall: as **a :** a room having a vaulted or domical ceiling **b :** a judge's chamber **2 :** the treasury department of the papal curia **3 a** [NL, by shortening] **:** CAMERA OBSCURA **b :** a lightproof box fitted with a lens through the aperture of which the image of an object is recorded on a light-sensitive material **c :** the part of a television transmitting apparatus in which the image to be televised is formed for conversion into electrical impulses — **in camera 1 :** in the judge's chamber ⟨the trial was held *in camera*⟩ **2 :** in private **:** PRIVATELY, SECRETLY — **on camera :** before a live televising camera ⟨at the studio for rehearsals by 5 and *on camera* from 7 to 10 —*Newsweek*⟩

camera 3b: *1* lens, *2* bellows, *3* plateholder, *4* tripod

camera-eye \'==,=\ *n* **1 :** the capacity for reporting that is as detailed and detached as a photograph ⟨does not pretend that his is the impartial *camera-eye* —Robert Graves⟩ **2 :** observation or reporting that is detached and photographic in detail ⟨*camera-eye* reportage —Angus Wilson⟩
cam·er·al \'kam(ə)rəl, 'kaamrəl\ *adj* [G *kameral-*, fr. ML *cameralis*, fr. *camera* treasury (fr. L, arched roof) + L *-alis* -al — more at CHAMBER] **1 :** of or relating to a legislative or judicial chamber **2 :** CAMERALISTIC ⟨the ~ sciences⟩
cam·er·a·lism \-ə,lizəm\ *n* -s [*cameral* + *-ism*] **:** the theories and practices of the cameralists
cam·er·a·list \-ələst\ *n* -s [G *kameralist*, fr. NL *cameralista*, fr. ML *cameralis* + L *-ista* -ist] **1 :** a public administrative servant of continental rulers of the 17th and 18th centuries who was a mercantilist and advocated economic policies tending to strengthen the position of the ruler **2 :** an economist who strongly emphasizes political factors in recommending economic policy
cam·er·a·lis·tic \'=(=)=¦listik\ *adj* [G *kameralistisch*, fr. *kameralist* + *-isch* -ic] **1 :** of or relating to public finance **2 :** of or relating to cameralism
cam·er·a·lis·tics \-ks\ *n pl but usu sing in constr* [G *kameralistik*, fr. *kameralist* + *-ik* -ics] **:** the science of public finance
camera lu·ci·da \¦=(=)=¦lüsədə\ *n, pl* **camera lucidas** [NL, lit., light chamber] **:** an instrument that by means of a prism of a peculiar form or an arrangement of mirrors and often a microscope causes a virtual image of an external object to appear as if projected upon a plane surface (as of paper or canvas) so that an outline may be traced
cam·era·man \'=(=)=,man, -,mən, -,maa(ə)n\ *n, pl* **cameramen 1 :** one that operates a camera: as **a :** a news photographer **b :** an operator of a motion-picture or television camera — compare CINEMATOGRAPHER **2 :** one who sells photographic equipment
camera ob·scu·ra \¦=(=)=,əbz'kyůrə, -(,)äb-, -b'sk-\ *n, pl* **camera obscuras** [NL, lit., dark chamber] **:** a darkened box or boxlike enclosure having an aperture usu. provided with a lens through which light from external objects enters to form an image of the objects on the opposite surface used esp. for making exact drawings or for taking photographs
camera rehearsal *n* **:** a dress rehearsal of a television show
camera script *n* **:** a cue sheet indicating the various camera positions to be used in a telecast
cam·er·a·ta \,kamə'rād-ə, -'ä-\ *n pl, cap* [NL, fr. L, neut. pl. of *cameratus*, past part. of *camerare* to arch, fr. *camera* arched roof — more at CHAMBER] **:** the largest order of crinoids including all Paleozoic species that have the lower brachial plates included in the cup and the mouth and food grooves closed
¹cam·er·ate \'kamə,rāt, -(ə)rət\ *adj* [NL *cameratus*, fr. LL *camera* chamber + L *-atus* -ate] **1** *or* **cam·er·at·ed** \-mə,rād·əd\ **:** divided into chambers ⟨a ~ shell⟩ ⟨a ~ eye⟩ **2** [NL *Camerata*] **:** of or relating to the Camerata
²camerate \"\ *n* -s **:** one of the Camerata
cam·er·a·tion \,kamə'rāshən\ *n* -s [¹*camerate* + *-ion*] **:** division into chambers
camera tube *n* **:** the television vacuum tube that by means of scanning converts the image into electrical impulses
cam·er·i·na \,kamə'rīnə, -'ē-\ [NL, fr. LL *camera* chamber, room + NL *-ina* — more at CHAMBER] *syn of* NUMMULITES
cam·er·in·i·dae \,kamə'rinə,dē\ [NL, fr. *Camerina*, type genus + *-idae*] *syn of* NUMMULITIDAE
cam·er·ist \'kam(ə)rəst\ *n* -s **:** PHOTOGRAPHER
cam·er·len·go \,kamə(r)'leŋ(,)gō\ *also* **cam·er·lin·go** \-'i-\ *n* -s *often cap* [It *camarlingo*, *camerlingo*, of Gmc origin; akin to OHG *chamarling* chamberlain — more at CHAMBERLAIN] **:** the cardinal who heads the Apostolic Camera and administers papal affairs when there is no pope
¹cam·er·o·ni·an \,kamə'rōnyən, -nēən\ *n* -s *usu cap* [Richard *Cameron* †1680 Scottish religious leader + E *-ian*] **:** one that holds the ecclesiastical and political doctrines of Richard Cameron and his followers who refused to recognize any civil government that did not explicitly admit that it derived its power from Jesus Christ, who were called Scottish Covenanters after 1680, and who later formed the Reformed Presbytery that in time became the Reformed Presbyterian Church
²cameronian \¦==¦=(=)=\ *adj, usu cap* **1 :** of or relating to Richard Cameron or the Cameronians
¹cam·er·oon \¦kamə¦rün\ *or* **cam·er·oons** \-nz\ *n, pl* **cameroons** [perh. fr. *Cameroon, Cameroons*, W. Africa] **:** a dice game played with five dice in which the object is to make certain combinations in several casts
²cameroon *adj, usu cap* **1** *or* **cameroons** \-ünz\ [fr. *Cameroon, Cameroons*, W. Africa] **:** of or from the Cameroons region **:** of the kind or style prevalent in the Cameroons **2** *or* **cam·er·oun** \-ün\ [fr. *Cameroon, Cameroun*, republic in W. Africa] **:** of or from the Republic of Cameroon **:** of the kind or style prevalent in Cameroon
cam·er·oon·ian *or* **cam·er·oun·ian** \¦kamə¦rünēən\ *n*-s *cap* [*Cameroon, Cameroun*, republic in W. Africa + E *-ian*] **:** a native or inhabitant of the Republic of Cameroon or the Cameroons region — **cameroonian** *or* **camerounian** *adj, usu cap*
cam·er·o·stome \'kam(ə)rə,stōm\ *n* -s [NL *camerostoma*, fr. *camero-* (fr. LL *camera* chamber) + *-stoma* — more at CHAMBER] **:** the anterior marginal depression of the body wall of a tick in which its capitulum lies
cam follower *n* [⁴*cam*] **:** the peg or roller which follows the curvature of a cam and to which the motion of the cam is thereby directly communicated
camias *var of* KAMIAS
cam·i·knick·ers \'kamē,nikə(r)z\ *n pl* [*camisole* + *knickers*] *Brit* **:** a woman's one-piece undergarment similar to a chemise but usu. shorter and more fitted
ca·mi·no re·al \kə¦mē(,)nōrā'äl\ *n, pl* **caminos re·a·les** \-nō(s)rā'ä(,)läs\ *or* **camino reals** \-'älz\ [Sp, highway, lit., royal road] **:** a main highway; *esp* **:** a highway orig. existing during the period of Spanish rule in the Southwest, Mexico, and Central America ⟨wagons will not travel along that *camino real* beyond Vao Colorao —Oliver La Farge⟩
ca·mion \kämyōⁿ\ *n* -s [F] **1 :** a low wagon **:** DRAY **2 :** MOTORTRUCK, BUS
ca·mi·o·nette \¦kamyə¦net, -mēə-\ *n* -s [F *camion* cart, wagon + *-ette*] **:** a small truck or bus
camis *or* **camus** *n* -ES [prob. modif. of Sp *camisa*] *obs* **:** a light loose robe
ca·mi·sa \kə'mēsə\ *n* -s [Sp, fr. LL *camisia* — more at CHEMISE] **1 :** a shirt or undershirt for men or women **2 :** a woman's embroidered blouse with loose sleeves
cam·i·sa·do \,kamə'sā(,)dō, -'z-, -'ä-\ *also* **cam·i·sade** \-'ād, -'äd\ *n* -s [*camisado* prob. fr. obs. Sp *camisada*, fr. *camisa* shirt; *camisade* prob. fr. MF, prob. fr. OSp *camisada*] *archaic* **:** an attack by night ⟨on march all night, intending a night attack or ~ —Thomas Carlyle⟩
cam·i·sard \¦kamə¦zärd, *Fr* kåmēzåår\ *n* -s *usu cap* [F, fr. F dial. *camiso* shirt (fr. LL *camisia*) + F *-ard*; fr. the peasants' smocks that the Camisards wore] **:** one of the French Protestant insurgents of the Cévennes who early in the 18th century rebelled against Louis XIV on account of the persecutions that followed the revocation of the Edict of Nantes
ca·mise \kə'mēz, -ēs\ *n* -s [Ar *gamīṣ*, fr. LL *camisia* — more at CHEMISE] **:** a light loose long-sleeved shirt, gown, or tunic sometimes worn as an undergarment
cam·i·sole \'kamə,sōl\ *n* -s [F, prob. fr. OProv *camisolla*, fr. *camisa* shirt, fr. LL *camisia*] **1 :** a jacket or jersey with sleeves formerly worn by men **2 :** a short negligee jacket for women **3 a :** an underwaist usu. with straight top and shoulder straps and often elaborately trimmed and worn orig. to cover a corset but now esp. with sheer clothing to camouflage underwear **b :** a woman's blouse without sleeves but often with shoulder straps and a low neckline **4 :** a long-sleeved straitjacket
¹cam·let \'kamlət\ *also* **cam·blet** \-m(b)l-\ *n* -s *often attrib* [ME *cameloit*, fr. MF *camelot*, fr. Ar *ḥamlat* woolen plush] **1 a :** a medieval Asiatic fabric of camel's hair or Angora wool **b :** a European imitation of this fabric of silk and wool **c :** a fine lustrous woolen of plain weave usu. dyed bright red **2 :** a garment made of camlet
²camlet *vt* -ED/ -ING/ -s *obs* **:** to mark with wavy lines like those of watered cloth
cam·le·teen *also* **cam·le·tine** \¦kamlə¦tēn\ *n* -s [prob. fr. ¹*camlet* + *-een*] **:** a worsted cloth in imitation of camlet
¹cammed \'kamd\ *adj* [alter. (influenced by *-ed*) of ³*cam*] **1** *dial Eng* **:** CROOKED, AWRY **2** *dial Eng* **:** ILL-TEMPERED
²cammed *past of* CAM
camming *pres part of* CAM
cam·mock \'kamək\ *n* -s [ME *cambok*, fr. ML *cambuca*, of Celt origin; akin to W *camog* bent stick, ScGael] *camag* curl, crook, OIr *camm* crooked — more at CHANGE] **1** *Scot* **:** a curved or crooked stick; *esp* **:** a field-hockey stick **2** *Scot* **:** FIELD HOCKEY
ca·mog \kə'mōg\ *n* -s [IrGael, fr. *cam* crooked, fr. OIr *camm*] *Irish* **:** a stick similar to a cammock
ca·mo·gie \kə'mōgē\ *n* -s [*camog* + *-ie*] **:** a team sport similar to hurling played with camogs by women in Ireland
camomile *var of* CHAMOMILE
ca·moo·di *also* **ca·moo·die** *or* **ca·mou·die** \kə'müdē\ *n* -s [Arawak *kamudu*] **:** any large tropical American constricting snake ⟨some huge ~, able to crush my bones like brittle twigs in its constricting coils —W.H.Hudson †1922⟩
ca·mor·ra \kə'mòrə, -'ä-\ *n* -s [It] **:** a group of persons united for dishonest or dishonorable ends ⟨the ~ of Welsh and Scotch political scoundrels —H.L.Mencken⟩
ca·mor·ris·ta \,kä,mò'rēstə, ,mə-\ *also* **ca·mor·rist** \kə'mòrəst, -'ä-\ *n, pl* **camorris·ti** \-əstē\ *also* **camorrists** \-ə(t)s\ [It *camorrista*, fr. *camorra* + *-ista* -ist] **1 :** a member of a camorra **2** *often cap* **:** a member of an Italian secret organization engaged esp. in extortion ⟨like a true *Camorrista* he never lost an opportunity of showing that he could do what he pleased with everybody —Norman Douglas⟩
ca·mo·te \kə'mōd·ē\ *n* -s [AmerSp, fr. Nahuatl *camotli* yam] **:** SWEET POTATO
camote de ra·ton \-dərə'tōn\ *n* [MexSp *camote de ratón*, lit., mouse yam] **:** an herb (*Hoffmanseggia densiflora*) of the family Leguminosae found in alkaline areas of the desert of southern U. S. having orange-red flowers and glandular-dotted chiefly basal tufted leaves with several pairs of leaflets
¹cam·ou·flage \'kamə,flä|zh, -,ä| *also* -äm- *or* -åm- *or* |j\ *n* -s *often attrib* [F, fr. *camoufler* to disguise (modif. of It *camuffare*) + F *-age*] **1 a :** the disguising of an installation, vehicle, gun position, or ship with paint, garnished nets, or foliage to reduce its visibility or conceal its actual nature or location from the enemy **b :** the disguise so applied or utilized ⟨battleship-gray paint is an effective ~ on a cloudy day⟩ **2 a :** concealment by means of disguise ⟨a totally different means of ~ is used by the spider crab —W.H.Dowdeswell⟩ **b :** a disguise, behavior, or expedient adopted or designed to deceive or hide ⟨behind this undistinguished ~ of "everyman" resides a subtle and confusing individuality —C.L.Sulzberger⟩
²camouflage \"\ *vb* -ED/-ING/-s *vt* **:** to conceal or disguise by camouflage ⟨guns that had been *camouflaged* with green saplings —Edmund Wilson⟩ ⟨his carriage flanked by detectives thinly *camouflaged* in tall hats and frock coats —J.J.Horgan⟩ ⟨they wanted to prevent and correct their mistakes, not ~ them —Milton Silverman⟩ ~ *vi* **:** to practice camouflage ⟨you can ~ all you want to —Sinclair Lewis⟩
camouflage discipline *n* **:** discipline (as enforcement of the proper methods of movement within, into, and out of a camouflaged area) necessary to maintain a military camouflage
ca·mou·flet \¦kamə¦flā\ *n* -s [F, lit., smoke blown into a sleeper's face from lighted paper] **1 :** a mine so charged and placed that its detonation will destroy enemy mining tunnels **2 a :** an underground or subsurface explosion of a bomb or shell that leaves a sealed pocket of smoke and gas **b :** a pocket formed in this way
ca·mou·fleur \¦kamə¦flər, +V -ər·\ *n* -s [F, fr. *camoufler* to disguise + *-eur* -or] **:** a person employed in camouflaging or skilled in the techniques of camouflage
¹camp \'kamp, -aa(ə)-,-ai-\ *n* -s *often attrib* [MF, prob. fr. ONF or OProv, fr. L *campus* plain, field; akin to OHG *hamf* crippled, Goth *hamfs* maimed, Gk *kampē* bend, turning, Lith *kampas* corner, region; basic meaning: bend; hence, concavity, depression] **1 :** a place of temporary shelter, lodging, or residence often at a distance from urban areas or the tents, cabins, or other buildings used for such shelter, lodging, or residence: **a :** the ground on which tents or buildings are erected for shelter or usu. temporary residence (as for troops, prisoners, or vacationers) **b :** the group of tents, cabins, or buildings either temporary or permanent in construction or location erected on such ground ⟨an army ~⟩ ⟨fishing ~*s* are located all along the river⟩ **c :** a town usu. new and often temporary sprung up esp. in an isolated lumbering or mining region ⟨the well-known gold ~*s* of Canada —A.M.Bateman⟩ **d** *Austral* **:** a place of rest, lodging, or assembly; *specif* **:** a place where cattle or other livestock are rounded up **e** (1) **:** a place provided with tents or cabins usu. in mountain or lake areas designed for rest or recreation esp. for children during the summer ⟨the boys went to ~ every July⟩ (2) **:** the institution of going or sending children to such a camp ⟨~ during the summer gets children away from the hot cities⟩ **2 a :** a company or body of persons (as soldiers) encamped or moving in a group **b** (1) **:** a group or body of persons acting unanimously; *esp* **:** a group engaged in promoting or defending a given theory or doctrine ⟨testified that the world was divided into two ~*s*, the exploiting capitalists and the proletariat —Eleanor Davis & Valentine Ughet⟩ (2) **:** an ideological position usu. strongly defended ⟨had unexpectedly gone over to the rival ~⟩ **3 a :** the scene of military service ⟨the soldier's conduct was all right for ~ but was not acceptable in polite society⟩ **b :** MILITARY SERVICE **:** life in the military service ⟨the recreations of ~ and court⟩ **4** *Austral* **:** a camping expedition (as for hunting) **5 :** a lodge or local chapter of a society or league ⟨addressed the veteran ~*s* throughout the state⟩ **6** *southern Africa* **:** a large field usu. used for pasture ⟨the farm was divided into a dozen ~*s*⟩ **7 :** a shack used for permanent habitation **8 :** a military post that is not a permanent installation
²camp \"\ *vb* -ED/-ING/-s [MF *camper*, fr. *camp*, n.] *vi* **1 a :** to pitch or occupy a camp ⟨he had ~*ed* under a tree . . . and slept until dawn —Irwin Shaw⟩ ⟨you drive down the hill . . . where Rochambeau's army ~*ed* —Gladys Taber⟩ **b :** to live usu. temporarily in a camp or outdoors esp. for recreation — often used with *out* ⟨it had been a cold time of year to ~ out —H.L.Davis⟩ **2 a :** to take up one's quarters **:** LODGE ⟨it was in a modest little flat . . . that he now ~*ed* whenever the claims of scholarship brought him to town —Aldous Huxley⟩ **b :** to occupy quarters that are unsuitable or temporarily uncomfortable ⟨the whole family ~*ed* on the first floor of the unfinished house⟩ **3 a :** to take up one's position **:** settle down ⟨they ~*ed* around the room, talking idly among themselves and waiting —Maeve Brennan⟩ **b :** to settle down to or as if to a siege or pursuit ⟨reporters ~*ed* upon his doorstep day and night —H.L.Mencken⟩ ⟨they ~*ed* on his trail for 20 miles⟩ **4** *Austral* **:** SLEEP, NAP, REST ~ *vt* **1 a :** to put or station in a camp **:** establish a camp for ⟨all his host ~*ed* themselves in Willingham field —Charles Kingsley⟩ **b :** to provide with temporary shelter or accommodations ⟨it was necessary to ~ the refugees on the wall —Nora Waln⟩ **2** *Southern Africa* **:** to divide into camps ⟨the farm is fenced and ~*ed*⟩
cam·pa \'kämpə\ *n, pl* **campa** *or* **campas** *usu cap* [Sp, prob. of AmerInd origin] **1 a :** an Arawakan people of the upper valley of the Ucayali river in eastern Peru **b :** a member of such people **2 :** the language of the Campa people
-cam·pa \'kampə, -'aa-,-'ai-\ *n comb form* [NL, fr Gk *kampē*; prob. akin to Gk *kampē* bend, turning — more at CAMP] **:** caterpillar — in generic names of insects ⟨Lasio*campa*⟩ ⟨Taenio*campa*⟩
cam·pa·gnol \¦kampə¦nyōl, -ōl\ *n* -s [F, fr. *campagne* plain] **:** the European field vole or a related species
¹cam·paign \(')kam¦pān, -aam-\ *n* -s *often attrib* [F *campagne*, prob. fr. ONF or OProv, fr. LL *campania* level country, fr. L *Campania*, the level country about Naples, fr. *campus* field — more at CAMP] **1** *obs* **:** a tract of open country **:** PLAIN **2** [F *campagne*, prob. fr. It *campagna*, fr. LL *campania*] **a** *obs* **:** the time during which an army is in the field **b :** a connected series of military operations forming a distinct phase of a war **3** *obs* **:** a trip or excursion into the country esp. in summer **4 :** a connected series of determined operations or systematic efforts designed to bring about a particular result ⟨an advertising ~⟩ ⟨a ~ against tuberculosis⟩ ⟨a ~ to combat crime⟩; *specif* **:** a series of operations or efforts designed to influence the public to support a particular political candidate, ticket, or measure ⟨a presidential ~⟩ ⟨the manager of the governor's ~⟩ **5 :** a period of activity usu. continuous and often competitive esp. in any seasonal occupation or industry ⟨the football team ended its ~ with an unexpected defeat⟩ **6 a :** the working life of a blast-furnace lining **b :** the working life of a melting unit in glass manufacturing
²campaign \"\ *vb* -ED/-ING/-s *vi* **:** to go on, engage in, or conduct a campaign ⟨they ~*ed* vigorously against the zoning laws⟩ ~ *vt* **:** to race (a horse) in a series of major races ⟨was at that time ~*ing* a big steeplechase stable —A.H.Higginson⟩
cam·paign·er \-ə(r)\ *n* -s **1 :** one that goes on, engages in, or conducts a campaign ⟨an effective ~ for slum clearance⟩ **2 :** one that has taken part in many campaigns; *esp* **:** a veteran in any field or vocation who takes pleasure in his activities ⟨that stout, battle-scarred old ~ —Frank Yerby⟩
campaign hat *n* **:** a broad-brimmed felt hat having a high crown with four dents worn by U. S. Army and Marine Corps personnel
campaign ribbon *n* **:** a narrow ribbon-covered bar or strip of ribbon whose distinctive coloring indicates a military campaign in which the wearer has taken part
campaign wig *n* **:** a wig worn for traveling in the late 17th and early 18th centuries having a twisted lock on each side and curls about the forehead
cam·pa·na \kam'panə, -'ä-,-'ā-\ *n* -s *often attrib* [LL, bell, fr. L, fem. of *campanus* Campanian, fr. *Campania*, the level country about Naples; fr. the use of Campanian metal in making bells] **:** BELL, GUTTA — usu. used of shape in decoration
cam·pa·na·rio \,kampə'närē,ō\ *n* -s [Sp, fr. *campana* bell (fr. LL) + *-ario* (fr. L *-arius* -ary)] **:** CAMPANILE
cam·pa·ne·ro \,kampə'ne(,)rō\ *n* -s [Sp, lit., bellman, fr. *campana* bell + *-ero* -er] **:** the bellbird of So. America
campania *n* -s [LL] *obs* **:** CAMPAIGN
cam·pan·i·form \(')kam¦panə,fòrm\ *adj* [LL *campana* + E *-iform*] **:** shaped like a bell
cam·pa·ni·le \,kampə'nēlē, -aam-,-äm-\ *n, pl* **campaniles** \-lēz\ *or* **campani·li** \-lē\ [It, fr. *campana* bell, fr. LL] **:** a bell tower usu. freestanding — compare BELFRY
cam·pa·nil·la \,kampə'nilə, -nē(y)ə\ *n* -s [Sp, lit., small bell, dim. of *campana* bell, fr. LL] **1 :** FLORIPONDIO **2 :** a West Indian morning glory (*Ipomoea triloba*) with showy white or pink flowers **3** *Philippines* **:** a plant of the genus *Allamanda* (esp. *A. cathartica*)
cam·pa·nist \'kampənəst\ *n* -s [LL *campana* bell + E *-ist*] **:** CAMPANOLOGIST, CARILLONNEUR — **cam·pa·nis·tic** \¦==¦nistik\ *adj*
cam·pa·no·log·i·cal \¦kampənō¦läjəkəl, -m,pan³l¦ä-\ *adj* [*campanology* + *-ical*] **:** of or relating to campanology
cam·pa·nol·o·gist \,kampə'näləjəst\ *n* -s [*campanology* + *-ist*] **:** one that practices or is skilled in campanology
cam·pa·nol·o·gy \-jē\ *n* -ES [NL *campanologia*, fr. LL *campana* + NL *-o-* + *-logia* -logy] **1 :** the science of making bells **2 :** the art of bell ringing — compare CARILLON, CHANGE RINGING

campanile

cam·pan·u·la \kam'panyələ\ *n, cap* [NL, dim. of LL *campana*] **:** a large genus (the type of the family Campanulaceae) of widely distributed herbs with a regular bell-shaped corolla, separate anthers, and laterally dehiscent capsule — see BELLFLOWER, CANTERBURY BELL
campanula blue *n* [NL *Campanula*] **:** a light purplish blue that is redder and deeper than lupine and bluer and slightly darker than average periwinkle
cam·pan·u·la·ce·ae \(,)kam,panyə'lāsē,ē\ *n pl, cap* [NL, fr. *Campanula*, type genus + *-aceae*] **:** a large family of dicotyledonous plants (order Campanulales) including herbs, shrubs, trees, and some climbers and having an acrid mostly milky juice, alternate leaves, and rather showy usu. regular flowers — **cam·pan·u·la·ceous** \¦=,==¦lāshəs, =,==¦==\ *adj*
cam·pan·u·la·les \(,)kam,panyə'lā(,)lēz\ *n pl, cap* [NL, fr. *Campanula* + *-ales*] **:** an order comprising dicotyledonous plants with a tubular 5-lobed corolla and five stamens with the anthers connivent and often partly or wholly united and including the Campanulaceae, Lobeliaceae, Cucurbitaceae, Goodeniaceae, Stylidiaceae, Calyceraceae, and Compositae
cam·pan·u·lar·i·ae \(,)kam,panyə'la(a)rē,ē\ *n pl, cap* [NL, pl. of *Campanularia*, genus of polyps, fr. *campanula* bell-shaped part (dim. of LL *campana* bell) + *-aria*] *in some classifications* **:** a division of Hydroida comprising forms in which each polyp is able to retract into a bell-shaped hydrotheca — used as more or less exactly equivalent to Leptomedusae
¹cam·pan·u·lar·i·an \¦=,==¦rēən, =,==¦===\ *adj* [NL *Campanulariae* + E *-an*] **:** of or relating to the Campanulariae
²campanularian \"\ *n* -s **:** a campanularian hydroid
cam·pan·u·la·ri·i·dae \(,)kam,panyələ'rīə,dē\ *n pl, cap* [NL, fr. *Campanularia*, type genus + *-idae*] **:** a large family of marine hydrozoan polyps (suborder Leptomedusae) having globular manubria and comprising forms with free medusae (as those of the genus *Obelia*) and others with the medusae replaced by sessile gonophores (as in the type genus *Campanularia*)
cam·pan·u·la·tae \(,)kam,panyə'lād·(,)ē, -'ā-\ *n pl, cap* [NL, fr. *Campanula* + L *-atae* (fem. pl. of *-atus* -ate)] *syn of* CAMPANULALES
cam·pan·u·late \(')kam¦panyələt, -,lāt\ *or* **cam·pan·u·lat·ed**

\-,lad·əd\ *also* **cam·pan·u·lar** \-lə(r)\ *or* **cam·pan·u·lous** \-ləs\ *adj* [NL *campanula* bell-shaped part (dim. of LL *campana* bell) + E *-ate* or *-ate* + *-ed* or *-ar* or *-ous* — more at CAMPANA] **:** shaped like a bell

campanula violet *or* **campanula purple** *n* [NL *Campanula*] **:** a grayish reddish purple that is redder and duller than heather (sense 2 a) and paler than livid purple

campas *pl of* CAMPA

camp bed *n* **:** a small portable bed **:** COT

camp·bell·ism \'kam(b)ə,lizəm, -ambə-\ *n* -s *usu cap* [Alexander *Campbell* + *-ism*] **:** the doctrines or practices of the Campbellites

¹camp·bell·ite \-,līt\ *n* -s *usu cap, often attrib* [Alexander *Campbell* †1866 Am. theologist, the founder + E *-ite*] **1 :** a follower of Alexander Campbell who founded the denomination called the Disciples of Christ — often taken to be offensive **2** [so called fr. its supposed similarity, as a fish that does not keep well when out of water, to a member of the Disciples of Christ, who emphasize the saving power of baptism by immersion] *Midland* **:** WHITE CRAPPIE

²campbellite \"\ *n* -s *usu cap* [John McLeod *Campbell* †1872 Scotch theologian + E *-ite*] **:** a follower of John McLeod Campbell who was ejected from the Church of Scotland because of his views on the atonement

camp car *n* **:** a car equipped for feeding and housing construction and maintenance employees of a railroad — called also *bunk car, outfit car*

camp ceiling *n* [alter. (influenced by *camp*) of earlier *cant ceiling*, fr. *cant* + *ceiling*] **:** a ceiling common in top stories and attics that consists of a plane horizontal central surface joined at two sides by inclined surfaces which meet the side walls

camp chair *n* **:** a light folding chair

camp circle *n* **:** a circle or a series of concentric circles of tepees arranged by the Plains Indians in a definite order in accordance with their tribal custom

camp cot *n* **:** a light portable folding cot

campcraft \'ˌ,ˌ\ *n* -s **:** skill and practice in the activities that relate to camping

cam·pea·chy hat \(')kam¦pēchē-\ *n, sometimes cap C* [fr. *Campeche*, city & state in Mexico] **:** a broad-brimmed hat formerly worn in the southern U.S. in hot weather

campeachy wood *n* [fr. *Campeche*, Mexico] **:** LOGWOOD

camped *past of* CAMP

cam·pe·phag·i·dae \,kampə'fajə,dē\ *n pl, cap* [NL, fr. *Campephaga*, type genus (fr. Gk *kampē* caterpillar + NL *-phaga*) + *-idae* — more at -CAMPA] **:** the family of passerine birds consisting of the cuckoo shrikes — **cam·peph·a·gine** \(')kam-¦pefə,jīn\ *adj*

cam·peph·i·lus \kam'pefələs\ *n, cap* [NL, fr. Gk *kampē* caterpillar + NL *-philus*] **:** a genus of birds (family Picidae) including some of the largest woodpeckers (as the ivory-billed woodpecker, the imperial woodpecker, and related tropical American species)

camp·er \-pə(r)\ *n* -s **1 a :** one that lives temporarily in a tent or lodge or outdoors without shelter esp. for recreation **b :** one that occupies a lodge, cabin, or summer residence in a vacation area only during the summer season or part of it **c :** one that attends a summer camp esp. for boys or girls **d :** one that lives in a work camp and participates in an outdoor work program **2 :** one that attends or participates in a camp meeting

cam·per·down elm \'kampə(r),daun-\ *n, usu cap C* [prob. fr. *Camperdown*, seat of the earls of Camperdown, Dundee, Scotland] **:** an elm (*Ulmus glabra camperdownii*) derived from the wych elm and having long drooping branches

cam·per·nelle jonquil *also* **campernelle** \¦kampə(r)¦nel\ *n* -s *often cap C* [prob. fr. the name *Campernelle*] **:** a bulbous plant (*Narcissus odorus*) similar to the common jonquil but having a crown at least half as long as the perianth segments

camp·er·ship \'ˌˌ,ship\ *n* -s [*camper* (fr. ²*camp* + *-er*) + *-ship* (as in *scholarship*)] **:** a grant to a boy or girl to aid him in attending a summer camp

cam·pe·si·no \,kampə'sē(,)nō\ *n* -s [Sp, fr. *campo* country, field, fr. L *campus* field — more at CAMP] **:** a native of a Latin-American rural area; *esp* **:** a Latin-American Indian farmer or farm laborer

cam·pes·tral \(')kam¦pestrəl\ *adj* [L *campestr-, campester* of the fields (fr. *campus* field) + E *-al*] **:** of or relating to fields or open country **:** RURAL ⟨living in secluded ~ concentration in his country house —Janet Flanner⟩

camp fever *n* **:** TYPHUS

campfight \'ˌ,ˌ\ *n* -s [prob. trans. of ML *pugna campi*] **:** trial by fighting; *esp* **:** the decision of a case by duel

campfire \'ˌ,ˌ\ *n* -s **1 :** a fire usu. built outdoors (as in a camp or on a picnic) for cooking, heat, or illumination; *esp* **:** such a fire designed to serve as the focal point of a social gathering ⟨his conduct was the one topic of discussion around ~*s* —W.E. Woodward⟩ **2 :** a social gathering of the members of a lodge or local chapter of a society or league ⟨cheery ~*s* in the hall of George H. Thomas post —Meredith Nicholson⟩

camp fire girl *n* [fr. *Camp Fire Girls*, Inc., founded in 1912] **:** a member of a national organization for girls from 7 to 18 years old that conducts activities combining recreation with the development of responsible citizenship and the acquisition of various skills; *specif* **:** such a member aged 10 to 14

camp follower *n* **1 :** a civilian that follows or takes up lodging near a military unit for the purpose of attending or exploiting military personnel; *specif* **:** PROSTITUTE ⟨she behaved more like a *camp follower* than a land girl —Ralph Hammond-Innes⟩ **2 :** one that is a disciple or follower (as of a group or theory) but is not of the main body of members or adherents; *esp* **:** one that follows with little understanding or for the purpose of personal gain ⟨a new dogmatism spread by the *camp followers* of science —N.E.Nelson⟩ ⟨and then those *camp followers* of the arts, those delicious Bohemians —Aldous Huxley⟩

campground \'ˌ,ˌ\ *n* -s **:** the area or place (as a field or grove) used for a camp, for camping, or for a camp meeting

camph- *or* **campho-** *comb form* [NL *camphora*] **:** camphor ⟨*camph*ene⟩ ⟨*campho*carboxylic⟩

cam·phane \'kam,fān\ *n* -s [*camph-* + *-ane*] **:** BORNANE

cam·pha·nyl \'kam(p)fə,nil, -ēl\ *n* -s [*camphane* + *-yl*] **:** BORNYL

cam·phene \'kam,fēn, ˌ'ˌ\ *n* -s [ISV *camph-* + *-ene*] **:** any of several terpenes related to camphor; *specif* **:** a colorless crystalline terpene $C_{10}H_{16}$ found in three optically different forms in several essential oils, made synthetically from pinene as a step in synthesizing camphor, and used in making insecticides (as toxaphene); 3,3-dimethyl-2-methylene-norbornane

cam·phine *or* **cam·phene** \'kam,fēn, ˌ'ˌ\ *n* -s [ISV *camph-* + *-ine* or *-ene*] **:** oil of turpentine or a mixture of oil of turpentine and alcohol used as an illuminant

¹cam·phire \'kam,fī(ə)r\ *now dial var of* CAMPHOR

²camphire \"\ *n* -s [ME *camphire, caumfre* camphor — more at CAMPHOR] **:** HENNA ⟨a cluster of ~ —Song of Sol 1:14 (AV)⟩

campho- — see CAMPH-

cam·phoid \'kam,fȯid\ *n* -s [*camph-* + *-oid*] **:** a solution of pyroxylin in an alcoholic solution of camphor used as a substitute for collodion

cam·phol \'kam,fōl, -ōl\ *n* -s [ISV *camph-* + *-ol;* orig. formed in F] **:** BORNEOL

cam·pho·lide \'kam(p)fə,līd\ *n* -s [ISV *camphol* + *-ide*] **:** either of two crystalline isomeric lactones $C_{10}H_{16}O_2$ distinguished as α and β and made indirectly from camphoric acid

cam·pho·lyt·ic acid \¦kam(p)fə¦lid·ik-\ *n* [*camph-* + electro*lytic;* fr. the acid's having been first obtained by electrolysis] **:** either of two unsaturated acids $C_8H_{13}COOH$ distinguished as α and β and made indirectly from camphoric acid

cam·phor \'kam(p)fə(r)\ *n* -s [alter. (influenced by ML & NL *camphora*) of ME *caumfre*, fr. AF, fr. ML *camphora*, fr. Ar *kāfūr*, fr. Malay *kāpūr*, prob. of Austroasiatic origin (whence Skt *karpūra* camphor); akin to Khmer *kāpōr* camphor] **1 :** a tough gumlike crystalline terpenoid ketone $C_{10}H_{16}O$ existing in three optically different forms all of which have the same qualities of volatility, fragrance, and taste; 2-keto-bornane: (1) the dextrorotatory form obtained esp. from the wood and bark of the camphor tree and used chiefly as a carminative and stimulant in medicine, as a plasticizer in cellulose nitrate plastics (as celluloid and photographic films), and as an insect repellent; (2) the levorotatory form found in some essential oils (as that of feverfew); and (3) the inactive form found in the oil of an Asiatic chrysanthemum or made synthetically from certain terpenes and their derivatives (as α-pinene, camphene, isoborneol) and used similarly to dextrorotatory camphor — called also respectively (1) *d-camphor, dextro-camphor, Formosa camphor, gum camphor, Japan camphor, laurel camphor* (2) *l-camphor, levo-camphor, matricaria camphor* (3) *dl-camphor, racemic camphor*, and, when synthetized, *synthetic camphor* **2 :** any of several compounds similar in properties to camphor (as certain terpene alcohols and ketones): **a :** dextrorotatory borneol **b :** levorotatory menthol

cam·pho·ra·ceous \¦ˌfə¦rāshəs\ *adj* [*camphor* + *-aceous*] **:** being or having the properties of camphor ⟨~ odor⟩

¹cam·phor·ate \'ˌfə,rāt, *usu* -ād· + V\ *vt* -ED/ -ING/ -S [*camphor* + *-ate*] **:** to treat or impregnate with camphor

²camphorate \", -,rə-\ *n* -s [ISV *camphor*ic + *-ate*] **:** a salt or ester of camphoric acid

camphorated oil *n* **:** a solution of about 20 percent camphor in cottonseed oil used as a counterirritant — called also *camphor liniment*

cam·phor·ene \-fə,rēn\ *n* -s [ISV *camphor* + *-ene*] **:** a liquid diterpene $C_{20}H_{32}$ derived from cyclohexene and obtained from camphor oil

cam·phor·ic \(')kam¦fȯrik, -aam-, -är-, -ēk\ *adj* [ISV *camphor* + *-ic*] **:** of, relating to, derived from, or containing camphor

camphoric acid *n* **:** a white crystalline acid $C_5H_5(CH_3)_3(COOH)_2$ existing in three optically different forms, esp. the dextrorotatory form obtained by the oxidation of dextrorotatory camphor and used in pharmaceuticals; *cis*-1,2,2-trimethyl-1,3-cyclopentane-dicarboxylic acid

camphor ice *n* **:** a cerate made chiefly of camphor, white wax, spermaceti, and castor oil

cam·phor·ize \'kam(p)fə,rīz, -aam-\ *vt* -ED/ -ING/ -S **:** CAMPHORATE

camphor liniment *n* **:** CAMPHORATED OIL

camphor oil *n* **:** an essential oil obtained by distilling the wood and other parts of the camphor tree; *esp* **:** that portion of the oil left after removing part or all of the camphor usu. separated into safrole and various fractions of oils often distinguished by color (as white or red) or volatility (as light or heavy) and used as a solvent, flavoring agent, and technical perfume (as in soap)

cam·phor·one \'kam(p)fə,rōn, -aam-\ *n* -s [ISV *camphor* + *-one*] **:** a liquid ketone $C_9H_{14}O$ obtained by distilling calcium camphorate; 2-isopropylidene-5-methyl-cyclopentanone

cam·phor·on·ic acid \¦ˌˌ¦ränik-\ *n* [ISV *camphor* + *-one* (fr. Gk *-ōnē*, suffix denoting a female descendant) + *-ic*] **:** a crystalline tribasic acid $C_6H_{11}(COOH)_3$ obtained by the oxidation of camphor or camphoric acid

cam·phor·o·yl \kam'fȯrə,wil, -aam-, -ēl\ *n* -s [*camphoric* + *-oyl* (as in *benzoyl*)] **:** the bivalent radical $C_8H_{14}(CO)_2$ of camphoric acid

camphor scale *n* **:** a scale (*Pseudaonidia duplex*) native to eastern Asia but now established in the southern U. S. where it is sometimes destructive to citrus and various ornamental plants

cam·phor·sul·fon·ic acid \¦kam(p)fə(r),səl¦fänik-, -aam-, 'ˌ ˌ'ˌ,ˌ ˌ-\ *n* **:** a white crystalline acid $C_{10}H_{15}OSO_3H$ made by reaction of camphor with sulfuric acid and acetic anhydride and used esp. in the form of salts as a stimulant (as in heart failure, shock, or some types of poisoning) — called also *beta-camphorsulfonic acid*

camphor tree *or* **camphor laurel** *n* **:** a large evergreen tree (*Cinnamomum camphora*) prob. native to China but now grown in most warm countries which has lax smooth branches and shining triple-nerved lanceolate leaves and from which camphor is collected by steaming the chips and subliming the product so obtained

camphor water *n* **:** a saturated solution of camphor in distilled water

camphor weed *n* **:** any of several aromatic herbs: as **a :** BLUE CURLS **b :** a ragweed (*Ambrosia bidentata*) of the prairie region of the U. S., with hairy stiff stems, sessile leaves, and 4-angled spiny fruits

camphorwood \'ˌˌ,ˌ\ *n* **1 a :** the wood of the camphor tree **b :** the wood of the tree that produces Borneo camphor **2 :** any of several Australian cypress pines; *esp* **:** DARK PINE

cam·phor·yl \'kam(p)fə,ril, -aam-, -ēl\ *n* -s [ISV *camphor* + *-yl*] **1 :** any of six univalent radicals $C_{10}H_{15}O$ of which camphor is the hydride **2 :** CAMPHOROYL

camp hospital *n* **:** STATION HOSPITAL

campi *pl of* CAMPUS

cam·pi·da·nese \,kämpədə'näsē, -äzē\ *n* -s *usu cap* [It, fr. *Campidano*, lowland in southeast Sardinia + It *-ese*] **:** the dialect of southern Sardinia

cam·pi·gnian \(')kam¦pēnyən\ *adj, usu cap* [*Campigny*, town in No. France + E *-ian*] **:** of or relating to a late Mesolithic or early Neolithic culture characterized by coarse pottery, hewn stones, milling stones, and some indication of plant raising and domestic animals

campilan *var of* KAMPILAN

cam·pim·e·ter \kam'pimәd·ə(r)\ *n* -s [ISV *campi-* (fr. L *campus* field) + *-meter* — more at CAMP] **:** an instrument for testing indirect or peripheral visual perception of form and color

cam·pi·nas \kam'pēnəs\ *adj, usu cap* [fr. *Campinas*, Brazil] **:** of or from the city of Campinas, Brazil **:** of the kind or style prevalent in Campinas

cam·pine \(')kam¦pēn, -äm-\ *n, usu cap* [fr. *Campine*, district in northern Belgium, where it was developed] **:** a European breed of gold-colored or silver-colored domestic fowls that resemble the Hamburgs but that have a single comb

camping *pres part of* CAMP

cam·pi·ni engine \(')kam¦pēnē-\ *n, usu cap C* [after *Campini*, 20th cent. Ital. airplane engine designer] **:** an aircraft propulsion system consisting of a reciprocating-engine-driven compressor, a burner, and an exhaust nozzle from which the stream of air passing through the compressor is ejected to the rear with increased momentum

cam·pi·on \'kampēən\ *n* -s [prob. fr. obs. *campion* champion, fr. ME, fr. ONF, fr. ML *campion-, campio* — more at CHAMPION] **1 :** a plant of the genus *Lychnis* **2 :** any of several species of *Silene*: as **a :** ALPINE CAMPION **b :** BLADDER CAMPION

cam·ple \'kampəl\ *vi* -ED/ -ING/ -S [freq. of obs. *camp* to wrangle, fight, fr. ME *campen* to fight, fr. OE *campian*, fr. *camp* war, combat; akin to OHG *kamph* combat, ON *kapp* war, contest, energy; all fr. a prehistoric NGmc-WGmc word borrowed fr. L *campus* field, battlefield — more at CAMP] *dial Eng* **:** to speak angrily or sharply **:** SCOLD, WRANGLE

camp·man \'ˌmən, -,man, -,maa(ə)n\ *n, pl* **campmen :** a building-maintenance man in a logging camp

campmaster \'ˌ,ˌˌ\ *n* [trans. of MF *maistre de camp*] **:** a 16th century or 17th century military officer corresponding to a colonel

camp meat *n, North* **:** illegal venison ⟨they had one legal buck on the fender and the trunk full of *camp meat*⟩

camp meeting *n* **:** a meeting conducted usu. by an evangelical denomination in the open air (as in a field or grove) or in a tent and attended by families who bring provisions and often stay more than one day to hear preaching and exhortation and to participate in worship services

cam·po \'kam(,)pō, -'ä-\ *n* -s [AmerSp (Argentina), fr. Sp, field, countryside, fr. L *campus* plain, field — more at CAMP] **:** a grassland plain in So. America having scattered perennial herbs and in some places stunted trees **:** SAVANNA — compare LLANO, PAMPA, PRAIRIE

cam·po·dea \kam'pōdēə\ *n, cap* [NL, fr. Gk *kampē* caterpillar + NL *-odea* (modif. of Gk *-ōdēs* -ode) — more at -CAMPA] **:** a genus of wingless elongated insects (order Entotrophi) lacking eyes, having the abdomen ending in two long filaments, and regarded as illustrating a generalized form from which many insects are descended — **cam·po·de·id** \-ēəd\ *n or adj* — **cam·po·de·oid** \-ē,ȯid\ *adj*

cam·po·de·i·form \-ēə,fȯrm\ *adj* [NL *Campodea* + E *-iform*] **:** having the shape of a bristletail of the genus *Campodea* — used esp. of larvae of some beetles and other higher insects

campong *var of* KAMPONG

cam·po·no·tus \,kampə'nōd·əs\ *n, cap* [NL, fr. *campo-* (fr. Gk *kampē* bend) + *-notus* — more at CAMP] **:** a genus of ants represented by many species throughout the world — see CARPENTER ANT, SUGAR ANT

cam·poo·dy \kam'püdē\ *n* -ES [Paiute, fr. Sp *campo* camp, field, fr. L *campus* field] *Southwest* **:** an Indian village

camp·o·ree \¦kampə¦rē, -aam-\ *n* -s [¹*camp* + jamb*oree*] **:** a gathering of boy scouts or girl scouts esp. from a given geographic area, usu. in a camp, for purposes of contests or exhibitions in scoutcraft or campcraft — compare JAMBOREE

cam·po san·to \¦kam(,)pō'san(,)tō, -äm(,)pō'sän-\ *n, pl* **campos santos** \-pōs...tōs\ *or* **cam·pi san·ti** \¦kämpē'säntē\ [It & Sp, lit., holy field] *chiefly Southwest* **:** burial ground **:** CEMETERY

camp-out \'ˌ,ˌ\ *n* -s [²*camp* + *out*] **:** an occasion on which a group camps out

cam press *n* [⁴*cam*] **:** a punch press in which power is applied to the ram by means of a cam

camp robber *n* **:** CANADA JAY

camps *pl of* CAMP, *pres 3d sing of* CAMP

camp·shed \'kamp,shed\ *or* **camp·shot** \-ät\ *n* -s [by folk etymology fr. earlier *camp shede, campshide*, prob. fr. ¹*camp* + obs. *shede, shide* strip of wood, plank, fr. ME *schide*, fr. OE *scīd*; akin to OHG *skīt* strip of wood, board, ON *skīth* strip of wood, snowshoe, OE *scēadan, scādan* to divide, separate — more at SHED] *Brit* **:** a facing of piles and planking usu. along the bank of a river used to protect or keep up the side of a bank

camp·sis \'kam(p)səs\ *n, cap* [NL, fr. Gk *kampsis* bending; fr. the curved stamens; akin to Gk *kampē* bend, turn — more at CAMP] **:** a genus of deciduous woody vines (formerly included in *Bignonia* or *Tecoma*) climbing by aerial roots and having opposite odd-pinnate toothed leaves and large orange or scarlet flowers in showy clusters

campsite \'ˌ,ˌ\ *n* [*camp* + *site*] **:** a place suitable for or used as the site of a camp

campstool \'ˌ,ˌ\ *n* **:** a small portable folding backless stool

camp stove *n* **:** a small portable stove for cooking or heating used esp. by campers or picnickers

campto- *comb form* [NL, fr. Gk *kamptos* flexible; akin to Gk *kampē* bend — more at CAMP] **:** bent **:** curved ⟨*campto*drome⟩ ⟨*Campto*sorus⟩

camp·to·cor·mia \,kam(p)tə'kȯrmēə\ *n* -s [NL, fr. *campto-* + *-cormia* (fr. Gk *kormos* tree trunk + NL *-ia*) — more at CORMUS] **:** an hysterical condition marked by forward bending of the trunk and sometimes accompanied by lumbar pain

campstool

camp·to·drome \'kam(p)tə,drōm\ *adj* [prob. fr. NL *camptodromus*, fr. *campto-* + *-dromus* -dromous] **:** having a bent course — used of a form of leaf venation in which the secondary veins curve forward before reaching the margin of the leaf and anastomose in arches

camp·ton·ite \'kam(p)tə,nīt\ *n* -s [G *camptonit*, fr. *Campton (Falls)*, N.H., its locality + G *-it* -ite] **:** a dark porphyritic lamprophyric rock occurring in dikes

camp·to·saur \'kam(p)tə,sȯ(ə)r\ *n* -s [NL *Camptosaurus*] **:** any dinosaur of the genus *Camptosaurus*

camp·to·sau·rus \¦ˌˌ'sȯrəs\ *n, cap* [NL, fr. *campto-* + *-saurus*] **:** a genus of small unspecialized bipedal duck-billed dinosaurs (order Ornithischia) widely distributed in Upper Jurassic and Early Cretaceous formations of Europe and No. America

camp·to·so·rus \-'sōrəs, -ȯr-\ *n, cap* [NL, fr. *campto-* + *-sorus*] **:** a genus of ferns (family Polypodiaceae) having lanceolate fronds that root at the tips — see WALKING FERN

¹cam·pus \'kampəs, -'aa-,-'ai-\ *n, pl* **campuses** \-pəsəz\ *also* **cam·pi** \-,pī, -ē\ *often attrib* [L, plain, field — more at CAMP] **1 a :** the grounds and buildings of a university, college, or school ⟨visitors crowded the ~ on graduation day⟩ **b :** a particular part of such grounds and buildings; *esp* **:** the open grassy area in the center or in a central part of the grounds of a university, college, or school ⟨he left the library and walked out on the ~⟩ **c :** a geographically separate part of a university ⟨the new laboratory lies between the east and west ~*es*⟩ **d :** a college, school, or division of a university that is complete in itself in having its own faculty and physical facilities but that is linked to the university by a common president and policy-making body ⟨the University of California has a number of ~*es*⟩ **2 :** a university, college, or school that is an educational, social, or spiritual entity **:** the academic world ⟨these critics have exerted considerable influence on the American ~⟩ **3 :** any grounds that resemble a campus ⟨the Maine camp has a ~ that includes the adjacent mainland —R.M. Hodesh⟩

²campus \"\ *vt* -ED/-ING/-ES **:** to punish by confinement to a university, college, or school campus or dormitory usu. after a certain hour in the evening ⟨a student ~*ed* for a month⟩

cam·pyl·o·drome \kam'pilə,drōm, 'kampə(,)lō,-\ *adj* [Gk *kampylo-* (fr. *kampylos* bent, curved) + E *-drome;* akin to Gk *kampē* bend — more at CAMP] **:** ACRODROME

cam·py·lot·ro·pous \¦kampə¦lä·trəpəs\ *also* **cam·py·lot·ro·pal** \-pəl\ *adj* [ISV *campylo-* (fr. Gk *kampylo-*) + *-tropous* or *-tropal;* orig. formed as F *campylotrope*] *bot* **:** having the ovule curved so that the micropyle is located near the base — compare AMPHITROPOUS, ANATROPOUS, ORTHOTROPOUS

cams *pl of* CAM, *pres 3d sing of* CAM

camshaft \'ˌ,ˌ\ *n* -s [⁴*cam* + *shaft*] **:** a shaft to which a cam is fastened or of which a cam forms an integral part

cam·stea·ry *or* **cam·stee·ry** \käm'stārē, -'ē-\ *adj* [perh. fr. Sc & E dial. ³*cam* + Sc *steery* busy, fr. *steer* (var. of E *stir*) + E *-y*] *Scot* **:** PERVERSE, STUBBORN, REFRACTORY, WILLFUL

cam·stone \'kämz,tōn, -m,st-\ *or* **cam·stane** \-ān\ *n* -s [Sc *cam* pipeclay (fr. ME *calm* limestone) + E *stone* or Sc *stane*, var. of E *stone*] **1** *Scot* **:** a limestone containing much clay **2** *Scot* **:** pipe clay used to whiten hearths or doorsteps

cam switch *n* [⁴*cam*] **:** a switch actuated by a cam

camuning *var of* KAMUNING

¹cam·us \'kaməs\ *adj* [ME *camuse*, fr. MF *camus*] **1** *of the nose* **:** short and flat or concave **2 :** having a camus nose **:** PUG-NOSED

²camus *var of* CAMIS

cam wheel *n* **:** [⁴*cam*] a wheel set or shaped so that it acts as a cam — see CAM illustration

cam·wood \'kam,wu̇d\ *n* -s [Temne *k'am* camwood + E *wood*] **1 :** the hard red wood of an African tree (*Baphia nitida*) used as a dyewood **2 :** BARWOOD

¹can \,kan, (¦)kan; *esp after a stressed vowel* ,kᵊŋ; *esp in NewEng* (¦) ke(ə)n; *esp dial* (¦) kin\ *vb, past* **could** \,kəd, (¦) ku̇d\ *or archaic 2d sing* **couldst** \,kətst; (¦) ku̇dzt, -ůdst, -ůtst\ (with *thou*) *pres sing & pl* **can** *or archaic 2d sing* **canst** \,kənzt, (¦) kan-, -n(t)st\ (with *thou*) [ME, know, know how, am able (1st & 3d sing. pres. indic. of *cunnen*, past *coude, couthe*), fr. OE *can, con* (infin. *cunnan*, past *cūthe*); akin to OHG *kan* know, am able (infin. *kunnan*), ON *kann* (infin. *kunna*), Goth *kann* know (infin. *kunnan*), OE *cnāwan* to know — more at KNOW] *vt* **1** *obs* **:** KNOW, UNDERSTAND ⟨most of the inhabitants ~ no word of Cornish —Richard Carew⟩ **2 :** to be able to do, make, or accomplish ⟨the will of Him who all things ~ —John Milton⟩ **~** *vi, archaic* **:** to have knowledge or skill — used with following *of* ⟨thou *canst* well of woodcraft —Sir Walter Scott⟩ **~** *verbal auxiliary* **1 a :** know how to **:** have the skill to ⟨he ~ read⟩ ⟨she ~ play the piano⟩ **b :** be physically or mentally able to ⟨he ~ lift 200 pounds⟩ ⟨I ~ tell red from green⟩ **c :** may perhaps **:** may possibly ⟨do you think he ~ still be living⟩ ⟨it *could* be true⟩ **d :** have the necessary courage or resolution to ⟨he ~ accept defeat without complaining⟩ **e :** be permitted by conscience or feeling to ⟨~ hardly blame him⟩ ⟨I ~ forgive anything but that⟩ **f :** be made possible or probable by circumstances to ⟨he ~ hardly have meant that⟩ ⟨I *could* cry for shame⟩ **g :** be inherently able or designed to ⟨everything that money ~ buy⟩ ⟨this car ~ hold five persons⟩ **h :** be logically or axiologically able to ⟨2 + 2 ~ also be written 3 + 1⟩ ⟨we ~ reasonably conclude from this that such is the case⟩ **i :** be enabled by law, agreement, or custom to **:** have a right to ⟨only the House ~ originate financial measures⟩ **j :** have permission to — used interchangeably with *may* ⟨you ~ go now if you like⟩; see COULD **2** *dial* **:** to be able to — used as infinitive ⟨I may ~ go⟩ ⟨he'll ~ tell us —Alexander Wardrop⟩

2can \'kan, -aa(ə)n\ *n* -s [ME *canne,* fr. OE; akin to OHG *channa,* ON *kanna;* all perh. fr. a prehistoric NGmc-WGmc word borrowed from LL *canna,* a vessel, fr. L, reed; fr. the long thin spout of certain ancient vessels — more at CANE] **1 :** a receptacle (as for holding liquids) usu. cylindrical in shape: **a :** a vessel for holding or carrying water, wine, beer, or other liquids ⟨I have brought thee in this ~ fresh water from the brook —William Wordsworth⟩; *specif* **:** a drinking vessel ⟨in his hand did bear a boozing ~ —Edmund Spenser⟩ — compare CANNIKIN **b :** a cylindrical metal receptacle usu. with an open top, often with a removable cover, and sometimes with a spout or side handles (as for holding milk, oil, coffee, tobacco, ashes, or garbage) **c :** a single-trip tinplate container in which perishable foods or other products are hermetically sealed for preservation until use — called also *tin* **d :** a glass or earthenware jar with an airtight cover used for packing or preserving fruit or vegetables in the home ⟨we put up a dozen ~*s* of tomatoes last fall⟩ **e :** a small usu. cylindrical container made of paper or paper compound — compare COMPOSITE CAN, FIBER CAN **2 a :** a steam-heated hollow metal cylinder over which cloth is passed to be dried **b :** a hollow cylindrical combustion chamber of an airplane engine **c :** an air cleaner for a carburetor **3** *slang* **:** JAIL **4 :** TOILET 5 — not often in formal use **5** *slang* **:** BUTTOCKS, SEAT **6 :** DEPTH CHARGE **7 :** DESTROYER 2 — **in the can** *of a motion picture* **:** filmed, edited, and ready for release

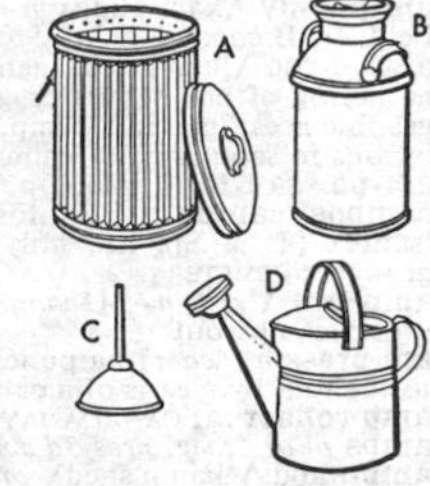

can 1b : ash can, *A;* milk can, *B;* oilcan, *C;* sprinkling can, *D*

3can \'kan, -aa(ə)n\ *vt* **canned; canned; canning; cans** **1 a :** to put up in a can; *esp* **:** to preserve by sealing in airtight cans or jars **b :** to hit (a golf ball) into the cup **:** HOLE **2** *slang* **:** to expel esp. from school **:** discharge esp. from employment ⟨they *canned* him within a month of his arrival⟩ **3** *slang* **:** to put a stop or end to **:** refrain from ⟨~ the chatter⟩ **4 a :** to enclose completely (as a pump or motor) in a housing **b :** to seal hermetically (as an oil tank or a package enclosed in metal foil) **5 :** to record (as a singing voice) on discs or tape ⟨he wouldn't let me ~ his voice —J.A.Lomax⟩ ⟨laughter *canned* for comedy programs⟩

4can \(ˈ)kan\ *verbal auxiliary* [ME, alter. of *gan,* past of *ginnen* to begin — more at GIN] *obs* **:** DID ⟨with gentle words he ~ her fairly greet —Edmund Spenser⟩

5can *obs var of* KHAN

6can \'kan, -aa(ə)n\ *n* -s [by shortening] **:** CANVASBACK DUCK

can *abbr* **1** canceled; cancellation **2** canon **3** canto **4** cantoris

ca·naan \'kānən\ *n* -s *usu cap* [LL *Chanaan* Canaan, the part of Palestine west of the Jordan, considered by the ancient Israelites as a land promised to them by God, fr. Gk *Chanaan, Kanaan,* fr. Heb *Kĕna'an*] **1 :** a promised land **:** place of rest, reward, or fulfillment **2 :** the region beyond death **:** HEAVEN

1ca·naan·ite \'kānə,nīt\ *n* -s *usu cap* [Gk *Kananitēs,* fr. *Kanaan, Chanaan* + *-itēs* -ite] **1** *in the Bible* **a :** a member of a pre-Israelite people of Palestine which dwelt in the lowlands of Canaan — distinguished from *Amorite* **b :** any pre-Israelite inhabitant of Palestine **:** AMORITE 1b **2 a :** a member of a Semitic people which settled in Palestine and Syria subsequent to the Amorites, dwelt in various independent cities each of which had its separate Baal cult, and were ultimately absorbed by the Israelites and Aramaeans **b :** the Semitic language spoken by this people, closely allied to Phoenician, and known principally from glosses in the Tell el-'Amarna letters of approximately 1400 B.C. **3 :** the various languages of the Canaanitic subgroup of the Semitic subfamily sometimes regarded as constituting merely dialects of a single language

2canaanite \"\ *adj, usu cap* **:** of or relating to Canaan, any of the peoples known as Canaanites, or the Canaanite language

3canaanite \"\ *n* -s *usu cap* [Gk *Kananitēs*] **:** CANANAEAN

1ca·naan·it·ic \'kānə'nid·ik\ *adj, usu cap* **1 :** 2CANAANITE **2 :** constituting or belonging to a subdivision of the Northwest Semitic languages that includes Canaanite, Phoenician, Hebrew, and various allied languages

2canaanitic \"\ *n* -s *usu cap* **:** the Canaanitic subdivision of languages

ca·naan·it·ish \'=,nīd·ish\ *adj, usu cap* **:** 1CANAANITIC

ca·na bra·va \,känyə'brävə\ *n* [Sp *caña brava* wild cane] **:** either of two tall grasses of tropical America: **a :** a bamboo (*Bambusa vulgaris*) **b :** UVA GRASS

ca·na·cuas \kə'näkwəs\ *n pl but sing or pl in constr* [MexSp, pl. of *canacua*] **:** a wedding dance of Tarascan Indian girls wearing crowns of flowers

1can·a·da \'kanədə\ *adj, usu cap* [fr. dominion of *Canada,* country in No. America] **:** of or from the dominion of Canada **:** of the kind or style prevalent in Canada **:** CANADIAN ⟨*Canada* wheat⟩

2canada \"\ *n, usu cap, var of* CANADA GOOSE

3ca·ña·da \kən'yädə, -adə\ *n* -s [Sp, fr. *caña* cane, long hollow object, fr. L *canna* — more at CANE] **1** *chiefly West* **a :** a small canyon **:** GLEN **b :** an open valley **2** *chiefly West* **:** a small stream of fresh water **:** CREEK

canada anemone *n, usu cap C* **:** a common woodland herb (*Anemone canadensis*) with palmately parted leaves and flowers having waxy white sepals and no petals

canada balsam *n, usu cap C* **:** an oleoresin exuded by the balsam fir as a viscous yellowish to greenish liquid, solidifying to a transparent mass, and used as a transparent cement esp. in microscopy for mounting specimens and in optical instruments — called also *Canada turpentine*

canada birch *n, usu cap C* **:** SWEET BIRCH

canada blueberry *n, usu cap C* **:** a low shrub (*Vaccinium myrtilloides*) of northeastern No. America having hairy foliage, white flowers, and sweet bluish black fruit

canada bluegrass *n, usu cap C* **:** WIRE GRASS a

canada buffalo berry *n, usu cap C* **:** a buffalo berry (*Shepherdia canadensis*)

canada field pea *n, usu cap C* **:** FIELD PEA

canada fleabane *n, usu cap C* **:** HORSEWEED 1

canada ginger *n, usu cap C* **:** WILD GINGER 2a

canada goose *also* **canada** *n, pl* **canada geese** *also* **canadas**

Canada goose

usu cap C **:** the common wild goose (*Branta canadensis*) of No. America that is chiefly gray and brownish with black head and neck and a white patch from the sides of the head under the throat and represented by several varieties differing chiefly in size and details of coloring — see CACKLING GOOSE, HUTCHINS'S GOOSE, WHITE-CHEEKED GOOSE

canada hare *n, usu cap C* **:** the varying hare of No. America

canada hemp *n, usu cap C* **:** INDIAN HEMP 1

canada jay *n, usu cap C* **:** a jay (*Perisoreus canadensis*) having gray and sooty plumage and no crest, widely distributed in northern and western No. America, ranging southward in the Rocky mountains, and noted for its boldness in stealing provisions from hunters' camps — called also *camp robber, moosebird, whisky jack;* see ROCKY MOUNTAIN JAY

canada lily *n, usu cap C* **:** MEADOW LILY

canada lyme grass *n, usu cap C* **:** a wild rye (*Elymus canadensis*)

canada lynx *n, usu cap C* **:** CANADIAN LYNX

canada mayflower *n, usu cap C* **:** FALSE LILY OF THE VALLEY

canada mint *n, usu cap C* **:** a common wild American mint (*Mentha canadensis*) that has whorled flowers in the upper axils

canada moonseed *n, usu cap C* **:** a woody vine (*Menispermum canadense*) of eastern No. America with large oval leaves, small white flowers, and black fruits

canada pea *n, usu cap C* **:** TUFTED VETCH

canada pitch *n, usu cap C* **:** the resinous exudation of the hemlock spruce — called also *hemlock pitch*

canada plum *n, usu cap C* **:** a native plum (*Prunus nigra*) of northeastern No. America with oblong orange-red fruit

canada porcupine *n, usu cap C* **:** the porcupine (*Erethizon dorsatus*) of northeastern No. America being about two feet long with barbed spines largely concealed in the coarse fur, feeding chiefly on bark and leaves, and sometimes causing considerable damage to isolated buildings which it gnaws for the salt and grease accumulated in their substance

canada rockrose *n, usu cap C* **:** FROSTWEED a

canada root *n, usu cap C* [prob. so called fr. a belief that it is esp. prevalent in Canada] **:** BUTTERFLY WEED

canada snakeroot *n, usu cap C* **:** WILD GINGER 2a

canada sweet gale *n, usu cap C* **:** SWEET FERN 2

canada tea *n, usu cap C* [so called fr. the use of its leaves as a substitute for tea] **:** WINTERGREEN 2a

canada thistle *n, usu cap C* **:** a European thistle (*Cirsium arvense*) naturalized in the U.S. and Canada where it is a pernicious weed

canada turpentine *n, usu cap C* **:** CANADA BALSAM

canada violet *n, usu cap C* **:** a leafy-stemmed No. American perennial herb (*Viola canadensis*) with heart-shaped pointed leaves and white flowers streaked with violet

canada warbler *n, usu cap C* **:** a common warbler (*Wilsonia canadensis*) of northern No. America that is blue-gray above and yellow below and has a necklace of black streaks below the throat

canada wild rye *n, usu cap C* **:** a wild rye (*Elymus canadensis*)

canada wormwood *n, usu cap C* **:** an aromatic weedy herb (*Artemisia canadensis*) with divided leaves and a terminal raceme of greenish flower heads found chiefly in Canada

canada yew *n, usu cap C* **:** GROUND HEMLOCK

ca·na de am·bar \,känyəthā'äm,bär\ *n* [Sp *caña de ámbar,* lit., amber cane] **:** a butterfly lily (*Hedychium coronarium*)

can·a·der \'kanədə(r)\ *n* -s [*Canada* + *-er*] *Brit* **:** CANOE

1ca·na·di·an \kə'nādēən *also* -dyən\ *adj, usu cap* [F *canadien,* fr. *Canada* + F *-ien* -ian] **1 :** of, relating to, or characteristic of the dominion of Canada **2 :** of, relating to, or characteristic of the people of Canada **3 :** relating to or being a biogeographic zone extending across No. America including parts of Canada, the northern tier of states of the U.S., and certain mountain slopes and summits farther south and comprising the southern part of the coniferous forest region between the Hudsonian and Transition zones — compare BOREAL **4 :** of or relating to the earliest major subdivision of the Ordovician period in America — see GEOLOGIC TIME table

2canadian \"\ *n* -s *cap* **:** a native or inhabitant of Canada

canadian bacon *n, usu cap C* **:** bacon cut from the loin of a pig

canadian burnet *n, usu cap C* **:** a common herb (*Sanguisorba canadensis*) of eastern No. America

canadian football *n, usu cap C* **:** a game resembling American football played between two 12-man teams on a field 110 x 65 yards

canadian-french *adj, usu cap C&F* **:** FRENCH-CANADIAN

canadian french *n, cap C&F* **:** the language of the French Canadians

canadian goldenrod *n, usu cap C* **:** a large goldenrod (*Solidago canadensis*) of eastern No. America with 3-nerved leaves and large flower clusters

canadian goose *n, usu cap C* **:** CANADA GOOSE

canadian hemlock *n, usu cap C* **:** EASTERN HEMLOCK

canadian hemp *n, usu cap C* **:** INDIAN HEMP 1

canadian holly *n, usu cap C* **:** MOUNTAIN HOLLY 1

ca·na·di·an·ism \-,nizəm\ *n* -s *usu cap* **1 :** a quality distinctive of Canadians **2 :** allegiance to or pride in Canada **3 :** a characteristic feature of English as used in Canada

ca·na·di·an·ize \-,nīz\ *vt* -ED/-ING/-S *see -ize in Explan Notes, often cap* **:** to make Canadian **:** assimilate to a pattern of life and interests distinctive of Canadians

canadian lynx *n, usu cap C* **:** a No. American lynx (*Lynx canadensis*) that is distinguished from the bobcat by larger size, longer ear tufts, heavier looser coat, large padded paws, and wholly black tail tip and that is now largely restricted to Canada though formerly widely distributed in forested eastern and central U.S. — called also *Canada lynx*

canadian moonseed *n, usu cap C* **1 :** CANADA MOONSEED **2 :** YELLOW PARILLA 2

canadian pondweed *n, usu cap C* **:** WATERWEED a

canadian red pine *n, usu cap C* **:** RED PINE 1

canadian rig *n, usu cap C* **:** an oil-well rig with slender wooden poles joined end to end instead of a cable or rope

canadian small reed *n, usu cap C* **:** BLUEJOINT 1

canadian warbler *n, usu cap C* **:** CANADA WARBLER

canadian waterleaf *n, usu cap C* **:** a woodland perennial herb (*Hydrophyllum canadense*) with purplish white flowers

can·a·dine \'kanə,dēn, -dən\ *n* -s [ISV *canad-* (fr. NL *canadensis,* specific epithet of the goldenseal, *Hydrastis canadensis,* fr. *Canada,* country in No. America) + *-ine*] **:** a crystalline alkaloid $C_{20}H_{21}NO_4$ found in the root of the goldenseal

can·a·dol \'kanə,dōl, -ōl\ *n* -s [G *kanadol,* fr. *Kanada* Canada + G *-ol* (fr. L *oleum* oil); fr. its having been obtained by fractional distillation of Canadian petroleum — more at OIL] **:** a light ligroin

ca·na dul·ce \,känyə'dülsē\ *n* [MexSp *caña dulce,* fr. Sp, sugar cane] **:** the seeds of the cana dulce tree (*Licania arborea*) of Mexico that yield an oil used for illumination and in soapmaking

ca·na es·pi·na \'känyəe'spēnə\ *n* [Sp *caña espina,* lit., spiny cane] **:** a valuable bamboo (*Bambusa spinosa*) of tropical Asia grown in the Philippines and used in building

ca·na·fis·tu·la \,känyə'fis(h)chələ\ *also* **ca·na·fis·to·la** \-stələ\ *n* -s [Sp *cañafístula,* fr. *caña* cane (fr. L *canna*) + *-fístula* prob. fr. obs. *casiafístula,* fr. ML *cassia fistula*] — more at CANE, CASSIA FISTULA] **1 a :** DRUMSTICK TREE **b :** CASSIA FISTULA **2 :** a tropical American tree (*Cassia grandis*) related to the drumstick tree — called also *horse cassia*

ca·nai·gre \kə'nīgrē\ *n* -s [MexSp] **:** a large dock (*Rumex hymenosepalus*) of the southwestern U.S. and northern Mexico having a root rich in tannin

ca·naille \kə'nī, -'nā(ə)l\ *n* [F, fr. It *canaglia,* fr. *cane* dog, fr. L *canis* — more at HOUND] **1** *sing or pl in constr* **:** MOB, RABBLE, RIFFRAFF ⟨the shoeblacks and linkboys and all the idling ~ of Dublin —Malachy Hynes⟩ **2** -S **:** a member of the canaille

can·a·jong \'kanə,jōŋ, -äŋ\ *n* -s [perh. fr. Tasmanian] *Austral* **:** BEACH APPLE

canakin *var of* CANNIKIN

1ca·nal \kə'nal\ *n* -s [ME, fr. L *canalis* pipe, channel, fr. *canna* reed — more at CANE] **1** *obs* **:** a pipe esp. for conveying liquids **2 a :** CHANNEL, WATERCOURSE; *esp* **:** STRAIT **b** *obs* **:** a long narrow ornamental pond **3 a :** a tubular passage or channel either in bone (as the haversian canals) or formed by soft tissues (as the alimentary canal or inguinal canal) **:** DUCT **b :** a groove which prolongs the shell aperture and in which the siphon of certain snails rests **4 :** an artificial waterway designed for navigation or for draining or irrigating land ⟨the Panama ~⟩ **5** *obs* **:** a means of communication **6 :** a groove or channel in an architectural member; *specif* **:** the recess or drip in the undersurface of a corona **7 :** a narrow arm of the sea usu. extending far inland and approximately uniform in width ⟨Lynn ~⟩ **8** [It *canale* channel, fr. L *canalis*] **:** any of various faint narrow markings on the planet Mars

2canal \"\ *vt* **canalled** *or* **canaled; canalled** *or* **canaled; canalling** *or* **canaling; canals** **1 :** to construct a canal through or across **:** provide with canals **2 :** CANALIZE ⟨they can ~ the natural forces —Elizabeth Bowen⟩

3ca·nal \kə'näl\ *n, pl* **ca·na·les** \-ä(,)lās\ [Sp, fr. L *canalis*] *Southwest* **:** WATERSPOUT, EAVES TROUGH

canalboat \=ˈ=,=\ *n* **:** a boat for use on a canal; *esp* **:** a long narrow boat having a bluff nearly vertical bow and stern that give it large freight capacity

canal-built \=ˈ=,=\ *adj* **:** built for canal navigation

canal cell *n* [trans. of G *kanalzelle*] *bot* **:** one of the single row of cells constituting the axial row within the neck of an archegonium — compare NECK CELL

can·a·lete \,kanᵊl'ed·ē\ *also* **can·a·let·ta** \-ed·ə\ *n* -s [AmerSp *canalete*] **:** PRINCEWOOD 1

can·a·lic·u·lar \'kanᵊl'ikyələ(r)\ *adj* [NL *canalicularis,* fr. L *canaliculus* + *-aris* -ar] **:** relating to, like, or provided with a canaliculus

can·a·lic·u·late \-lət,-,lāt\ *also* **can·a·lic·u·lat·ed** \-,lād·əd\ *adj* [L *canaliculatus* channeled, fr. *canaliculus* + *-atus* -ate] **:** grooved or channeled longitudinally ⟨the ~ leafstalk of certain palms⟩

can·a·lic·u·la·tion \,kanᵊl,ikyə'lāshən\ *also* **can·a·lic·u·li·za·tion** \-yələ'zāshən, -,lī'z-\ *n* -s **:** the formation of canaliculi

can·a·lic·u·lus \,kanᵊl'ikyələs\ *n, pl* **canaliculi** \-,lī, -ē\ [L, dim. of *canalis* channel — more at CANAL] **:** a minute canal in a bodily structure: as **a :** one of the hairlike channels ramifying an haversian system in bone and linking the lacunae with one another and with the haversian canal **b :** one of the narrow spaces between cells in the cell cords that make up a liver lobule

can·a·lif·er·ous \'kanᵊl'if(ə)rəs\ *adj* [1*canal* + *-iferous*] **:** having canals or canaliculi

can·a·line \'kanᵊl,ēn, -,ən\ *n* -s [irreg. fr. NL *Canavalia* + E *-ine*] **:** a crystalline amino acid $NH_2OCH_2CH_2CH(NH_2)COOH$ obtained from canavanine by enzymatic hydrolysis

ca·na·lis \kə'naləs, -'ä-\ *n, pl* **ca·na·les** \-a(,)lēz, -ä(,)lās\ [L — more at CANAL] **1** *anat* **:** CANAL **2 :** the slightly convex or concave area between the fillets of an Ionic volute

can·a·li·za·tion \,kanᵊlə'zāshən, -l,ī'z-\ *n* -s [F *canalisation,* fr. *canaliser* + *-ation*] **1 :** the act of canalizing: **a :** the construction or formation of canals **b :** the providing of a channel or an outlet **c :** the direction into a channel or groove **2 a :** a system of canals or conduits conveying or distributing gas, electricity, water, or steam **b :** the conveyance or distribution esp. of gas or water **3 a :** surgical formation of holes or canals for drainage without tubes **b :** natural formation of new channels in tissue (as formation of new blood vessels through a blood clot) **c :** establishment by repeated passage of nerve impulses of new pathways in the central nervous system

can·a·lize \'kanᵊl,īz\ *vb* -ED/-ING/-S *see -ize in Explan Notes* [F *canaliser,* fr. *canal* (fr. L *canalis*) + *-iser* -ize] *vt* **1 a :** to provide with canals **:** build a canal through or across **b :** to make into or like a canal; *specif* **:** to make navigable or improve the navigation of by constructing canals **2 :** to provide with an outlet or a channel of expression **:** facilitate the discharge of (as an emotion) ⟨rituals both arouse and ~ emotion⟩ **3 :** to direct into certain channels ⟨*canalizing* such energies as he had towards the business of ruling —Hilaire Belloc⟩ **4 :** to drain (a wound) by forming channels without the use of tubes ~ *vi* **1 :** to flow in or into a channel **2 :** to develop new channels (as new capillaries in a blood clot)

ca·nal·ler *also* **ca·nal·er** \kə'nalə(r)\ *n* -s [*canal* + *-er*] **1 :** one that works on canal transportation esp. on a canal or a canalboat **2 :** CANALBOAT

canalling *n* -s **1 :** canal construction or work **2 :** travel or commerce by canal **:** canal traffic

canal of schlemm \-'shlem\ *usu cap S* [trans. of G *schlemmscher kanal,* after Friedrich *Schlemm* †1858 Ger. anatomist] **:** SCHLEMM'S CANAL

canal ray *n* [trans. of G *kanalstrahl;* fr. the openings in the cathode through which the ions pass] **:** POSITIVE RAY

canals *pl of* CANAL, *pres 3d sing of* CANAL

canal system *n* **:** a system of passages connecting various cavities of the animal body (as in corals and sponges)

ca·na·nae·an *or* **ca·na·ne·an** \,kānə'nēən, -,a-\ *n* -s *usu cap* [LL *Cananaeus* (fr. Gk *Kananaios,* fr. Aram *qan'ānā* zealot) + E *-an*] **:** a member of a Jewish sect that bitterly opposed the Roman domination of Palestine **:** ZEALOT 1

ca·nan·ga \kə'naŋgə\ [NL, fr. Malay *kĕnanga,* a tree of the genus *Canangium*] *syn of* CANANGIUM

cananga oil *n* **:** a yellow essential oil obtained from the flowers of the ilang-ilang tree and characterized by a less fragrant odor than ilang-ilang oil

ca·nan·gi·um \kə'nanjēəm\ *n, cap* [NL, fr. Malay *kĕnanga* + NL *-ium*] **:** a small genus of Malayan trees (family Annonaceae) distinguished by the simple alternate leaves and linear sepals and petals and including the ilang-ilang tree

ca·nao *also* **kan·yaw** \kən'yaů\ *n* -s [Sp *cañao,* fr. Iloko *kanyaw* sacred or ritual sanction] **:** a pagan religious feast in the mountain regions of the Philippines

ca·na·pé \'kanəpē, -,pā *also* ,kanə'pā\ *n* -s [F, lit., sofa, fr. ML *canapeum, canopeum* mosquito net; fr. the conception that the bread is a seat for the delicacy — more at CANOPY] **1 :** an appetizer consisting of a piece of bread or toast or a cracker topped with savory food (as cheese or caviar) — compare HORS D'OEUVRE **2 :** SOFA ⟨a Louis XV ~⟩

ca·na·pi·na \,kanə'pēnə\ *n* -s [AmerSp, fr. It *canapino* hempen, fr. *canapa* hemp, fr. LL *canapis, cannapis,* fr. L *canabis, cannabis,* prob. fr. Gk *kannabis* — more at HEMP] **:** the fine silky strong fiber of the Indian mallow

ca·nard *senses 1 & 3* kə'närd, ka-, -nȧd; *sense 2* kȧnȧr\ *n, pl* **canards** *senses 1 & 3* -dz; *sense 2* -ȧr\ [F, duck, fr. OF *quanart* drake, fr. *caner* to cackle (of imit. origin) + *-art* -ard; in sense 1, F, fr. the expression MF *vendre des canards à moitié* to cheat, deceive, lit., to half-sell ducks] **1 a :** a false or unfounded report or story; *esp* **:** a fabricated report (as by a newspaper) **b :** a groundless rumor or belief **2** *cookery* **:** DUCK 1b **3 :** an airplane having the horizontal stabilizing and control surfaces in front of the main supporting surfaces

canarese *usu cap, var of* KANARESE

canari *var of* KANARI

1ca·nar·i·an \kə'nerēən, -'a(a)-,-'ä-\ *also* **ca·nar·i·ote** \-rē-,ōt, -,ət\ *adj, usu cap* [*Canary* Islands + E *-an* or *-ote*] **:** of or relating to the Canary Islands

2canarian \"\ *n* -s *cap* **:** a native or inhabitant of the Canary Islands; *esp* **:** one of the ancient Guanches

ca·nar·i·um \-rēəm\ *n, cap* [NL, fr. Malay *kĕnari* Java almond + NL *-ium*] **:** a large genus of tropical Asiatic and African trees (family Burseraceae) having compound leaves, panicled flowers, and triangular drupaceous often edible fruits and yielding balsamic resins — see BLACK DAMMAR, ELEMI, JAVA ALMOND

1ca·nary \kə'nerē, -'eə-,-'a(a)(ə)-,-'ä-, -ri\ *n* -ES *often attrib* [in sense 1, fr. MF *canarie, canaries,* fr. OSp *canario,* fr. *Islas Canarias* Canary Islands, group in the Atlantic ocean southwest of Spain, fr. LL *Canariae insulae,* lit., dog islands; in other senses, fr. *Canary* Islands, *Canaries,* fr. Sp *Islas Canarias*] **1 :** a lively court dance of the 16th century **2 a :** a Canary Islands usu. sweet wine similar to Madeira and once popular in England **3** *or* **canary bird a :** a small finch (*Serinus canarius*) that is native to the Canary Islands, that is greenish with brown streaks above and yellowish below with many variations in size, form, and color, and that is now extensively bred as a cage bird and singer — see CHOPPER, 2ROLLER 2 **b :** any of various small birds of different countries most of which are largely yellow in color (as some American warblers of the genus *Dendroica,* some of the African weaverbirds, and the American goldfinch) **4** *slang* **a** (1) **:** SOPRANO; *esp* **:** a coloratura singer (2) **:** a woman singer with a dance band **b :** INFORMER, SQUEALER **5** *or* **canary yellow** [so called fr. the color of the canary bird] **a :** a light to moderate greenish yellow **b :** a moderate yellow **6 :** a diamond of a pale yellow color **7** *or* **canary bird a :** a device for detecting gases in mines **b :** GAS MASK

2canary \"\ *vi* -ED/-ING/-ES *obs* **:** to dance nimbly (as in the canary dance)

canary banana *n, usu cap C* [fr. *Canary* Islands] **:** DWARF BANANA

canary bellflower *n, usu cap C* [fr. *Canary* Islands] **:** a tall Canary Islands herb (*Canarina campanula*) of the family Campanulaceae with yellow flowers

canarybird flower *n* **1** *also* **canarybird vine :** a climbing plant (*Tropaeolum peregrinum*) with canary-colored flowers **2 :** BIRD PLANT

canary broom *n, usu cap C* [fr. *Canary* Islands] **:** a much-branched yellow-flowered shrub (*Cytisus canariensis*) native to the Canary Islands — called also *genista*

canary cedar *n, usu cap 1st C* [fr. *Canary* Islands] **:** an evergreen tree (*Juniperus cedrus*) that has pendulous branches, bluish foliage, and orange-brown fruit and is endemic in the Canary Islands

canary creeper *n* **:** CANARYBIRD FLOWER 1

canary fly *n* **:** the Australian apple leafhopper

canary glass *n* [so called fr. its color] **:** glass colored with oxide of uranium

canary grass *n* [fr. *Canary* Islands] **1 :** a Canary Islands grass (*Phalaris canariensis*) the seeds of which are used as food for cage birds **2 :** a plant of the genus *Lepidium* of which the pods are sometimes fed to tame birds

canary island bellflower *n, usu cap C&I* **:** CANARY BELLFLOWER

canary island date palm *n, usu cap C&I* **:** a date palm (*Phoenix canariensis*) indigenous in the Canary Islands, larger and more graceful than the common date palm, and often used for ornament

canary island juniper *n, usu cap C&I* **:** CANARY CEDAR

canary island pine *n, usu cap C&I* **:** CANARY PINE

canary ivy *n, usu cap C* [fr. *Canary* Islands] **:** ALGERIAN IVY

canary pine *n, usu cap C* [fr. *Canary* Islands] **:** a tall evergreen tree (*Pinus canariensis*) of the Canary Islands with reddish bark, long drooping needles, and ovoid cones — called also *blue pine*

canary pox *n* **:** a virus disease of canaries closely related to fowl pox

canary seed *n* [fr. *Canary* Islands] **1 :** seed of the canary grass used as food for cage birds — compare BIRDSEED **2 :** seed of the common plantain (*Plantago major*)

canary stone *n* [so called fr. its color] **:** a yellow species of carnelian

canary vine *n* [so called fr. the color of the flowers of *Tropaeolum peregrinum*] **1 :** CANARYBIRD FLOWER 1 **2 :** CLIMBING FUMITORY

canary wood *n* [fr. *Canary* Islands] **1 :** the wood of various trees: as **a :** that of either of two laurels (*Persea indica* and *P. canariensis*) of Madeira and the Canary Islands **b :** that of the Indian mulberry **c :** that of an Australian tree (*Eucalyptus hemiphloia*) **d :** that of Leichhardt's pine **2** *Brit* **:** the wood of a tulip tree

canary yellow *n* **:** CANARY 5

ca·nas·ta \kə'nastə, -'ä-, -'aa-, -'å-\ *n* -s [Sp, lit., basket, prob. back-formation fr. *canastillo* wicker tray, fr. LL *canistellum*, dim. of L *canistrum* basket — more at CANISTER] **1 :** a card game that is a form of rummy played usu. as a 2-hand or as a 4-hand partnership game using two full decks plus four jokers, all jokers and deuces being wild, red threes having special scoring value, and black threes having special value in play, the object being to meld groups but not sequences of cards esp. of seven or more of the same rank which earn large bonuses — called also *basket rummy;* compare BOLIVIA, SAMBA **2 :** a combination of at least seven cards of the same rank melded in the game of canasta and related games

ca·nas·ter \kə'nastə(r)\ *n* -s [D *kanaster*, prob. fr. Sp *canastro* basket, prob. fr. Gk *kanastron;* fr. its being shipped from South America in baskets — more at CANISTER] **:** a smoking tobacco made of the dried leaves coarsely broken

can·a·val·ia \,kanə'valyə, -'ä-, -'ā-\ *n, cap* [NL] **:** a small genus of tropical twining herbs (family Leguminosae) having long tough pods with large seeds that are sometimes used for food but more often to adulterate coffee — see JACK BEAN

ca·na·va·lin \,══'══lən, kə'navələn\ *n* -s [NL *Canavalia* + E *-in*] **:** a globulin found in the jack bean

can·a·van·ine \,kanə'va,nēn, -'ä-, -'a-; kə'navə,n-\ *n* -s [ISV *canavan-* (irreg. fr. NL *Canavalia*) + *-ine*] **:** an amino acid $NH_2C(:NH)NHOCH_2CH_2CH(NH_2)COOH$ occurring in the jack bean

ca·nawl·er \kə'nȯlə(r)\ *substand var of* CANALLER

can·ber·ra \'kan,berə, -bərə\ *adj, usu cap* [fr. *Canberra*, Australia] **:** of or from Canberra, the capital of Australia **:** of the kind or style prevalent in Canberra

can buoy *n* **:** a truncated buoy having a flat top — see BUOY illustration

can·can \'kan,kan, 'kaan,kaa(ə)n\ *n* -s *often attrib* [F, prob. fr. (baby talk) *cancan* duck, of imit. origin or alter. of *canard;* fr. the resemblance of some of the movements to those of a duck — more at CANARD] **:** a woman's dance of French origin characterized by high kicking usu. while holding up the front of a full ruffled skirt

¹can·cel \'kan(t)səl, -'aa-, -'ai-\ *vb* **canceled** *or* **cancelled**; **canceled** *or* **cancelled**; **canceling** *or* **cancelling** \-s(ə)liŋ\ **cancels** [ME *cancellen*, fr. MF *canceller*, fr. LL *cancellare*, fr. L, to make like a lattice, fr. *cancelli* lattice, dim. of *cancer* lattice, alter. of *carcer* prison] *vt* **1 a :** to mark or strike out for omission or deletion typically with lines crossed latticewise over the passage in question or by a line through the symbols involved ⟨~ an offensive passage⟩ ⟨a section ~*ed* as unimportant⟩ **b** (1) **:** OMIT ⟨~ matter set in type and not yet printed⟩ ⟨~ sheets printed but not yet bound⟩ (2) **:** to remove (a leaf) from a book (3) **:** to remove (a blank leaf) from a printed sheet before binding **2 :** to remove from significance or effectiveness: as **a :** to destroy the force, effectiveness, or validity of **:** REVOKE, ANNUL, INVALIDATE ⟨~ an order⟩ ⟨~*ing* a magazine subscription⟩ **b :** to bring to nothingness **:** DESTROY, RUIN ⟨~*ing* more material and labor with the same weight of explosives —Harland Manchester⟩ **c :** to remove from need for consideration **:** reduce or vitiate to the point of insignificance ⟨was slavery so deep an evil that it ~*ed* all other political rights and interests —Herbert Agar⟩ **d :** to match or nullify in force or effect **:** COUNTERBALANCE, NEUTRALIZE, OFFSET — often used with *out* ⟨his irritability ~*ed* out his natural kindness —Osbert Sitwell⟩ **e :** to cease from planning or expecting **:** call off usu. without expectation of conducting or performing at a later time **:** DROP, RELINQUISH ⟨~ a trip⟩ ⟨a football game ~*ed* because of heavy snow⟩ **3 a :** to remove (a common divisor) esp. from numerator and denominator **b :** to remove (equivalents) on opposite sides of an equation or account **c :** BALANCE ⟨~ an equivalent of opposite sign⟩ — often used with *out* **4 :** to counteract the effect of (a previous sharp or flat) by inserting in musical notation a natural sign **5 a :** to deface (a postage or revenue stamp) esp. with a set of parallel lines, a postmark, or a series of cuts or slits to invalidate for reuse **b :** to deface the stamps on (a piece of mail) **~** *vi* **1 :** to neutralize each other's strength or effect **:** become counterbalanced or offset — often used with *out* ⟨the various pressure groups to a large degree ~*ed out* —J.B.Conant⟩ **2 :** to admit of being dropped together as equal or equivalent ⟨the x's on each side of the equation ~⟩ **syn** see ERASE — **cancel to order :** to cancel (a stamp) as an indication of sale to a collector rather than passage through the mails

²cancel \"\ *n* -s **1 :** CANCELLATION **:** the act of annulling or rescinding ⟨an order quickly followed by a ~⟩ **2 a :** a written part or passage suppressed or deleted **b :** a passage or page from which something has been suppressed and to which new matter has been added in its place **:** the leaf containing matter so replaced — called also *cancelland* **c :** a new leaf, sheet, or pasted-in slip substituted for or emending matter already printed as part of a book — called also *cancellans* **d :** blank pages removed from a printed sheet before binding **3 :** a canceling direction in music **:** NATURAL **4 :** a postal cancellation **5 :** a punch for canceling tickets — usu. used in pl. and often with *pair* ⟨a pair of ~*s*⟩

can·cel·able *or* **can·cel·lable** \-sələbəl\ *adj* **:** that can be canceled

canceled *adj* [fr. past part. of *cancel*] **:** represented or cast with a slant line across the face ⟨a ~ arabic numeral⟩

can·ce·leer *or* **can·ce·lier** \,kan(t)sə'li(ə)r\ *n* -s [ONF *canceler* to waver, totter, fr. LL *cancellare* to cross the legs, fr. L, to make like a lattice — more at CANCEL] **:** the turn of a hawk in flight made before seizing or after missing the prey

can·cel·er *or* **can·cel·ler** \'kan(t)s(ə)lə(r), -'aa-, -'ai-\ *n* -s **:** one that cancels; *esp* **:** a machine for canceling postage stamps

can·cel·land \,kan(t)sə'land\ *or* **can·cel·lan·dum** \,══'══dəm\ *n, pl* **cancellands** \-n(d)z\ *or* **cancellan·da** \-ndə\ [LL *cancellandum*, neut. of *cancellandus*, gerundive of *cancellare* to strike or cross out — more at CANCEL] **:** ²CANCEL 2b

can·cel·lans \══'══lanz\ *n, pl* **cancellans·es** \-nzəz\ *or* **cancellan·tia** \,══'══nchēə\ [LL, pres. part. of *cancellare*] **:** ²CANCEL 2c

can·cel·la·re·sca cor·si·va \(,)kän,chelə'reskə(,)kȯr'sēvə\ *also* **cancellaresca** *n* [*cancellaresca corsiva*, modif. of It *cancelleresca corsiva* cursive cancelleresca; *cancellaresca*, modif. of It *cancelleresca*, prob. short for *lettera cancelleresca* chancellery handwriting, fr. *lettera* handwriting + *cancelleresca*, fem. of *cancelleresco* of a chancellery, fr. *cancelleria* chancellery (fr. F *chancellerie*) + *-esco* -esque — more at CHANCELLERY] **:** a style of cursive manuscript handwriting that had its origin at the Vatican in the 15th century

can·cel·lar·ia \,kan(t)sə'la(a)rēə\ *n, cap* [NL, fr. L *cancelli* bars, lattice + NL *-aria* — more at CANCEL] **:** the type genus of Cancellariidae comprising the nutmeg shells that are nearly cosmopolitan in warm seas

can·cel·la·ri·idae \(,)kan,selə'rīə,dē\ *n pl, cap* [NL, fr. *Cancellaria*, type genus + *-idae*] **:** a family of herbivorous marine snails (order Pectinibranchia) having nonoperculate oval shells strongly sculptured with axial ribs and spiral ridges forming a latticelike pattern — see CANCELLARIA

can·cel·late \kan'selət, 'kan(t)sə,lāt\ *or* **can·cel·lat·ed** \-ləd·əd, -,lād·əd\ *adj* [L *cancellatus*, past part. of *cancellare* to make like a lattice — more at CANCEL] **1 :** marked with numerous crossing lines or ridges **:** RETICULATE ⟨~ leaves⟩ **2 :** divided into small spaces by laminae **:** CANCELLOUS

can·cel·la·tion *also* **can·cel·ation** \,kan(t)sə'lāshən, -,aa-, -,ai-\ *n* -s [*cancel* + *-ation*] **1 a :** the act of canceling, of deleting, or of nullifying or invalidating ⟨the ~ of the faulty passage⟩ ⟨~ of the town ordinance⟩ **b** (1) **:** the calling off of an arrangement (as for travel) (2) **:** the accommodation released ⟨was lucky to get a late ~ for the trip to Chicago⟩ **2 :** the result of canceling: as **a :** the set of marks on a piece of mail made in the process of canceling the stamp **b :** the marks applied to the stamp itself as distinct from the postmark **3 :** the termination by the insured or the insurer or both of insurance in accordance with the specified terms of a policy

cancelled *past of* CANCEL

can·cel·li \kan'se,lī, -(,)lē, *in sense 1 also* kän'chelē\ *n pl* [L, lattice — more at CANCEL] **1 :** screens or rails typically of latticework or stone grating used to enclose or separate a part of a church; *specif* **:** the partitions between the nave of a church and the altar or choir — compare CHANCEL **2** [NL, fr. L] **a :** the intersecting osseous plates and bars of which cancellous bone is composed **b :** the interstices between such plates and bars

cancelling *pres part of* CANCEL

can·cel·lous \kan'seləs, 'kan(t)sələs\ *adj* [NL *cancelli* + E *-ous*] **:** having a spongy or porous structure **:** made up of intersecting plates and bars that form small cavities or cells —used of the bony tissue near the ends of long bones and elsewhere where both rigidity and lightness are essential

can·cel·lus \kan'seləs\ *sing of* CANCELLI

cancels *pres 3d sing of* CANCEL, *pl of* CANCEL

can·cer \'kan(t)sə(r), -'aa-, -'ai-\ *n* [ME, Cancer (sign of the zodiac), fr. L, crab, cancer; akin to Gk *karkinos* crab, cancer, Skt *karkaṭa* crab, *karkara* hard — more at HARD] **1** -s *usu cap* **:** the 4th sign of the zodiac — see SIGN table **2** -s **a :** a mass of tissue cells possessed of potentially unlimited growth that serves no useful function in the body, robs the host of nutrients necessary for survival, expands locally by invasion and systemically by transmission of cells along lymphatic and blood pathways, and unless recognized early and removed kills the host and that is usu. considered due to a combination of carcinogens and predisposing factors (as heredity, age, trauma, or chronic irritation), cancer itself never being directly inherited though a predisposition to certain forms may be heritable — compare CARCINOMA, SARCOMA; NEOPLASM, TUMOR; METASTASIS **b :** an abnormal condition characterized by the presence of a cancer or cancers **3** -s **:** an often malignant source of spreading and corroding destructive evil ⟨a man who offends in this way should be removed at once as a ~ in the body politic —Robert Graves⟩ **4** -s **a :** an enlarged tumorlike growth (as that typical of crown gall) **b :** a disease characterized by such growths **5** *cap* [NL, fr. L] **:** a genus of crabs almost cosmopolitan in distribution both in deep water and alongshore containing important edible crabs and common shore crabs (as the Dungeness crab, the rock crabs, and the Jonah crab) and being the type of the family Cancridae

can·cer·ate \-ə,rāt, *usu* -ād·+V\ *vi* -ED/-ING/-S [LL *canceratus* cancerous, fr. L *cancer* + *-atus* -ate] **:** to become cancerous **:** develop into a cancer

cancer eye *n* **:** a malignant epithelioma originating in the mucous membranes of the eye of cattle, common in regions of intense sunlight, chiefly affecting animals with white or light-colored skin about the eyes, and ultimately destroying the eye and adjacent bony structures and metastasizing widely

can·cer·i·ci·dal \══rə'sīd³l\ *or* **can·cer·o·ci·dal** \-rō;-\ *adj* [*cancer* + *-i-* or *-o-* + *-cidal*] **:** destructive of cancer cells

can·cer·ism \'══,rizəm\ *n* -s [ISV *cancer* + *-ism*] **:** a hypothetical tendency to develop cancer

can·cer·i·za·tion \,══rə'zāshən, -,rī'z-\ *n* -s [ISV *cancer* + *-ize* + *-ation*] **:** transformation into cancer or from a normal to a cancerous state ⟨~ of a wart⟩ ⟨epithelial ~⟩

cancer jalap *n* [perh. so called fr. a belief in folk medicine that it was effective against cancer] **:** POKEBERRY

can·cer·o·gen·ic \══rō'jenik\ *or* **can·cer·i·gen·ic** \-rə-\ *adj* [*cancer* + *-o-* or *-i-* + *-genic*] **:** CARCINOGENIC

can·cer·ol·o·gist \══'räləjəst\ *n* -s [*cancerology* + *-ist*] **:** a cancer specialist

can·cer·ol·o·gy \-əjē\ *n* -ES [*cancer* + *-o-* + *-logy*] **:** the study of cancer

can·cer·o·lyt·ic \══rō'lid·ik\ *adj* [*cancer* + *-o-* + *-lytic*] **:** CARCINOLYTIC

can·cer·ous \'kan(t)s(ə)rəs, -'aa-, -'ai-\ *adj* [*cancer* + *-ous*] **1 :** affected with cancer ⟨a ~ lung⟩ ⟨a leprous or ~ man —J.G.Frazer⟩ **2 :** of or relating to cancer **:** constituting a cancer ⟨a ~ indication⟩ ⟨a ~ tumor⟩ **3 :** like a cancer ⟨the months of spreading ~ distrust —Jean Stafford⟩ ⟨if we consider only the sordid aspects of urban life the American city of the period seems a ~ growth —A.M.Schlesinger b. 1888⟩ — **can·cer·ous·ly** *adv*

can·cer·pho·bia \,kan(t)sə(r)'fōbēə\ *or* **can·cer·o·pho·bia** \══(t)sərō'f-\ *n* -s [NL, fr. L *cancer* + *-phobia*] **:** an abnormal dread of cancer

cancerroot \'══,══\ *n* [*cancer* + *root;* prob. fr. its use in folk medicine as a cancer remedy] **:** any of several root parasites of the family Orobanchaceae (as the squawroot)

cancers *pl of* CANCER

cancer virus *n* **:** TUMOR VIRUS

cancerweed \'══,══\ *n* [so called fr. its use in folk medicine as a cancer remedy] **1 :** a rattlesnake root (*Prenanthes alba*) of which the root has bitter tonic properties **2 :** a sage (*Salvia lyrata*) of the eastern U. S.

can·cer·wort \'══,wərt, -,ȯ-\ *n* -s [perh. so called fr. a belief in folk medicine that it was effective against cancer] **:** either of two European plants (*Kickxia spuria* and *K. elatine*) of the family Scrophulariaceae

canch \'kanch\ *n* -ES [origin unknown] **1** *dial Eng* **:** a sloping slice removed from the roof or floor of a mine roadway to adjust the gradient between adjacent workings **2** *dial Eng* **:** a small stack or pile **:** a small quantity

can·cha \'känchə\ *n* -s [Sp, fr. Quechua] **1** *Southwest* **:** an enclosed yard; *esp* **:** a yard used for cockfights or games **2 :** a jai alai court

can·cha·la·gua \,känchə'lägwə\ *n* -s [Sp, alter. of *cachanlaguen*, modif. of Araucan *cachanlahuen*, fr. *cachan* pain in the side + *lahuen* medicinal herb] **:** a bitter tonic herb of the genus *Centaurium* (esp. *C. chilensis* of Chile and *C. venustum* of California)

can·cion *also* **can·ción** *AmerSp* kän'syōn, *Cast* -n'thyōn\ *n, pl* **cancio·nes** \-yōnās\ [Sp, *canción*, fr. L *cantion-, cantio* song — more at CANZONE] **:** SONG; *esp* **:** a popular song of Spain or Spanish America

can·cio·ne·ro \,känchō'ne(,)rō\ *or* **can·cio·nei·ro** \", -'ā-\ *n* -s [*cancionero* fr. Sp, fr. *canción* + *-ero* -ary; *cancioneiro* fr. Pg, fr. Sp *cancionero*] **:** a Spanish or Portuguese collection of songs and poems usu. by several authors

cancln *abbr* cancellation

¹can·crid \'kaŋkrəd\ *adj* **:** of or relating to the Cancridae

²cancrid \"\ *n* -s [NL *Cancridae*] **:** a crab of the family Cancridae

can·cri·dae \'kaŋkrə,dē\ *n pl, cap* [NL, fr. *Cancri-, Cancer*, type genus + *-idae*] **:** a large family of crabs (tribe Brachyura) that are nearly cosmopolitan in distribution and include many of the best-known edible crabs — see CANCER 5

can·cri·nite \-,nīt\ *n* -s [G *cancrinit*, fr. Count Georg *Cancrin* †1845 Russian statesman + G *-it* -ite] **:** a mineral $(Na_2,Ca)_4(AlSiO_4)_6CO_3.nH_2O$ consisting of an aluminosilicate and carbonate of sodium and calcium occurring in igneous rocks usu. as transparent to translucent masses of various colors (hardness 5–6, sp. gr. 2.42–2.5)

can·criv·o·rous \(')kan'krivərəs, -aŋ;-\ *adj* [NL *cancrivorus*, fr. *cancr-, cancer* crab + *-i-* + *-vorus* -vorous — more at CANCER] **:** feeding on crustaceans

can·cri·zans \'kaŋkrə,zanz, -ank-\ *adj* [ML, pres. part. of *cancrizare* to go backwards, fr. L *cancr-, cancer* crab + LL *-izare* -ize] *music* **:** having the theme or subject repeated backwards note for note ⟨a ~ canon⟩ ⟨a 12-tone composition that is ~⟩ — compare CRAB FORM

¹can·croid \'kaŋ,krȯid, -an,-\ *adj* [L *cancr-, cancer* crab + E *-oid* — more at CANCER] **1 :** resembling a crab ⟨a ~ spider⟩ **2** [F *cancroïde*, fr. L *cancr-, cancer* crab, cancer + F *-oïde* -oid] **:** like a cancer ⟨a ~ tumor⟩

²cancroid \"\ *n* -s [F *cancroïde*, fr. L *cancr-, cancer* + F *-oïde* -oid] **:** a skin cancer of low or moderate malignancy

can·crum oris \,kaŋkrə'mōrəs, -ȯr-,-är-\ *n, pl* **can·cra oris** \-rə'ō-, -'ȯ-,-'ä-\ [NL, lit., canker of the mouth] **:** NOMA

cand \'kand\ *n* -s [prob. modif. of Corn *can* brightness, whiteness, fluorite; prob. akin to L *candidus* white, bright — more at CANDID] **:** FLUORITE

can·da·reen *also* **can·da·rin** \,kandə'rēn\ *n* -s [Malay *kĕndĕri*, fr. Tamil *kunri* Indian licorice (*Abrus precatorius*); fr. the use of its berries as weights] **1 :** a Chinese unit of weight equivalent to $^1/_{100}$ tael **2 a :** a Chinese unit of value equivalent to $^1/_{100}$ tael of silver

C and D *abbr* collection and delivery

can·de·la \kan'dēlə, -'ā-\ *n* -s [L, candle] **:** CANDLE 4b

can·de·la·bra \,kandə'läbrə, -aan-, -ab-,-äb-,-āb-\ *n* -s [L, pl. (taken as sing.) of *candelabrum*] **:** CANDELABRUM ⟨four silver ~*s* holding great waxen torches — Sir Walter Scott⟩ ⟨a solid-brass ~⟩

can·de·la·brum \-brəm\ *n, pl* **candela·bra** \-brə\ *also* **candelabrums** \-brəmz\ [L, fr. *candela* candle — more at CANDLE] **1 a :** a large candlestick or a lamp usu. ornamented and having several arms or branches ⟨taking a ~ with no less than six tapers in it —Hervey Allen⟩ ⟨oil for the eight-branched ~ —Maurice Samuel⟩ ⟨on the left . . . we found two fine *candelabra* —Arthur Milton⟩ — compare CHANDELIER **b :** a usu. ornate and often heavy and large standard supporting a candlestick or lamp **2 a :** a small decorated modified column or columnlike rib of molded profile **b :** a design of which such a candelabrum forms the center

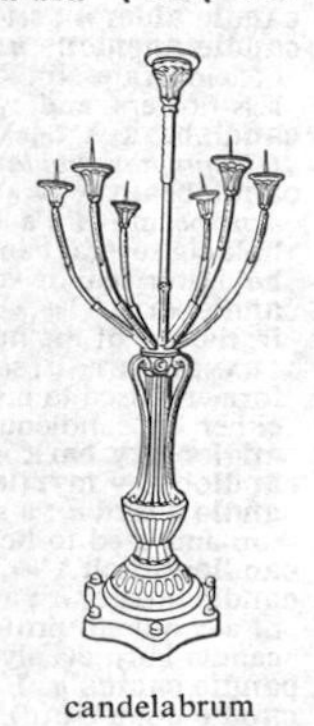

candelabrum

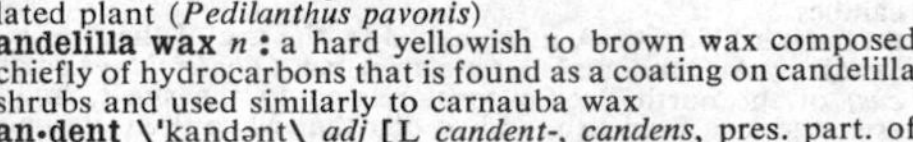

candelabrum tree *n* **:** a tropical African shrub or tree (*Pandanus candelabrum*) with a huge spreading head of foliage — called also *chandelier tree*

can·de·li·lla \,kandə'lē(y)ə, *attrib* ══ ══\ *n* -s [AmerSp, fr. Sp, little candle, dim. of *candela* candle, fr. L — more at CANDLE] **1 :** a wax-coated shrub (*Euphorbia antisyphilitica*) of northern Mexico and southwestern U. S. **2 a :** any of several Mexican euphorbias **b :** a related plant (*Pedilanthus pavonis*)

candelilla wax *n* **:** a hard yellowish to brown wax composed chiefly of hydrocarbons that is found as a coating on candelilla shrubs and used similarly to carnauba wax

can·dent \'kandənt\ *adj* [L *candent-, candens*, pres. part. of *candēre* to shine — more at CANDID] **:** white or glowing usu. from great heat

can·des·cence \kan'des³n(t)s\ *n* -s **:** a candescent state or condition **:** dazzling clear whiteness ⟨the ~ of the full moon⟩

can·des·cent \(')kan'des³nt\ *adj* [L *candescent-, candescens*, pres. part. of *candescere*, incho. of *candēre* to shine] **:** glowing or dazzling often from great heat ⟨a ~ meteorite⟩

C and F *abbr* cost and freight

C and I *abbr* cost and insurance

can·di·ci·din \,kandə'sīd³n\ *n* -s [NL *Candida* + E *-cide* + *-in*] **:** an antibiotic elaborated by a streptomyces and active against certain molds of the genus *Candida*

¹can·did \'kandəd *also* -'aa-\ *adj, sometimes* -ER/-EST [F & L; F *candide*, fr. L *candidus* white, bright, fr. *candēre* to shine, be white; akin to LGk *kandaros* ember, Skt *candra* shining, moon] **1 :** WHITE ⟨a welding blast of ~ flame —E.C.Stedman⟩ **2 :** free from bias, prejudice, or malice **:** marked by concern for truth and justice **:** fairly disposed **:** DISINTERESTED, FAIR, JUST ⟨in the back of his ~ mind he knew that . . . the charges against him were true —Irwin Edman⟩ **3** *archaic* **:** free from stain **:** CLEAR, PURE **4 a :** marked by honest sincere expression **:** uttered or given out as fair and unbiased **:** free from expedient reservation and modification ⟨to tell you my private and ~ opinion . . . I think he's a man from the other camp —James Joyce⟩ **b :** indicating or suggesting sincere honesty and absence of deception and duplicity ⟨his ~ eyes took on an expression of genuine sympathy —Archibald Marshall⟩ **c :** performed, expressed, or acknowledged without concealment or reservation ⟨her eyes burning with a ~ excitement —Edith Wharton⟩ **d :** disposed to criticize severely **:** BLUNT, FORTHRIGHT ⟨as a leader . . . I have never lacked ~ critics in my own ranks —Clement Attlee⟩ **5 :** relating to photography or other presentation or recording of subjects acting naturally, informally, or spontaneously without being posed, rehearsed, or inhibited ⟨a ~ picture⟩ ⟨a ~ microphone interview⟩ — see CANDID CAMERA **syn** see FRANK

²candid \"\ *n* -s [by shortening] **:** a candid photograph

can·di·da \'kandədə\ *n, cap* [NL, fr. L, fem. sing. of *candidus* white, bright] **:** a genus of parasitic yeastlike imperfect fungi (order Moniliales) producing small amounts of mycelium — see MONILIA, THRUSH

can·di·da·cy \'kan(d)ədəsē, -aandə-, -i\ *n* -ES [fr. ¹*candidate*, after such pairs as E *magistrate: magistracy*] **:** the quality or state of being a candidate **:** standing as a candidate

¹can·di·date \'kan(d)ə,dāt, -aandə-; *esp freq in S* -dət; *rapid also* -n,dāt, -ndət; *usu* -ād·,-əd·+V\ *n* -s [L *candidatus*, fr. *candidatus* clothed in white, fr. *candidus* white + *-atus* -ate; fr. the white toga worn by candidates for office in ancient Rome — more at CANDID] **1 :** one that presents himself or is presented by others often formally or officially as suitable for and aspiring to an office, position, membership, right, or honor — usu. used with *for* ⟨a ~ for governor⟩ ⟨a ~ for the board of directors⟩ ⟨~*s* for admission to the club⟩ **2 :** one that is likely or worthy to gain a post, position, or distinction or to come to a certain place, end, or fate **:** CHOICE ⟨I am not ambitious of ridicule — not absolutely a ~ for disgrace —Edmund Burke⟩ ⟨a ~ for the penitentiary⟩ ⟨this play is a ~ for the prize⟩ **3 :** a student taking a course of study leading to a degree; *esp* **:** one in the process of meeting final requirements ⟨a ~ for the Ph.D⟩

²candidate \"\ *vi* -ED/-ING/-S **:** to be a candidate ⟨intends to ~ for the new position⟩; *esp* **:** to preach on invitation in a church preparing to call a minister

³candidate *adj* [L *candidatus*] *obs* **:** dressed in white

can·di·da·ture \-,də,chü(ə)r, -üə *also* -dəchə(r) *or* ,dāchə(r)\ *n* -s [F, fr. *candidat* (fr. L *candidatus*) + *-ure*] *chiefly Brit* **:** CANDIDACY

candid camera *n* **1 :** a usu. small camera equipped with a fast lens and used for taking informal photographs of unposed subjects often without their knowledge **2 :** a miniature camera

can·di·di·a·sis \,kandə'dīəsəs\ *n, pl* **candidia·ses** \-,sēz\

[NL, fr. *Candida* + *-iasis*] **:** infection with or disease caused by a fungus of the genus *Candida* — compare MONILIASIS, THRUSH

can·did·ly *adv* **:** in a candid manner

can·did·ness *n* -ES **:** the quality or state of being candid

candied *adj* [fr. past part. of *candy*] **1 :** encrusted or coated with sugar or with a sugarlike or candylike substance ‹~ fruits› **2 :** cooked esp. by baking with sugar or syrup until translucent ‹~ sweet potatoes›

candies *pl of* CANDY, *pres 3d sing of* CANDY

[1]**can·di·ote** \'kandē,ōt, -ēət\ *or* **can·di·ot** \-ēət,-ē,ät\ *adj, usu cap* [F *candiote*, fr. *candiote*, n.] **:** of or relating to Candia **:** CRETAN

[2]**candiote** \"\ *or* **candiot** \"\ *n* -S *cap* [prob. fr. F *candiote*, fr. *Candie* Candia (Crete, island south of the mainland of Greece) + F *-ote*] **:** a native or inhabitant of the island of Crete **:** CRETAN

can·di·ru \,kandə;rü\ *n* -S [Pg *candirú*, fr. Tupi *candirú*, *candérú*] **:** a minute bloodsucking catfish (*Vandellia cirrhosa*, family Pygidiidae) of the Amazon that commonly parasitizes the gill chambers of freshwater fishes but may enter orifices of human or other animal bodies from which it is dislodged only with great difficulty due to the erectile spines on its gill covers

can·dite \'kan,dīt\ *n* -S [*Candy* (now *Kandy*), Ceylon + E *-ite*] **:** a blue spinel

C and LC *abbr* capitals and lower case

[1]**can·dle** \'kand°l, -'aa-\ *n* -S *often attrib* [ME *candel*, fr. OE, fr. L *candela*, fr. *candēre* to shine — more at CANDID] **1 a :** a long slender cylindrical mass typically of tallow or wax containing a wick of loosely twisted linen or cotton threads made by dipping or by casting in a metal mold and burned to give light **2 :** something that gives light; *specif* **:** a heavenly body ‹he that can count the ~s of the sky —Richard Linche› **3 :** a medicated candle or pastille used for fumigation **4 a :** an international unit of luminous intensity equal to the luminous intensity of five square millimeters of platinum at its solidification point of 1773.5°C — called also *international candle* **b :** a similar unit equal to one sixtieth of the luminous intensity of one square centimeter of a blackbody surface at the solidification point of platinum **:** a unit about 98.1 percent of a candle (sense 4 a) — called also *candela*, *new candle* **5 :** FILTER 1b **6 :** a device for emitting thick colored smoke for various military purposes — **by the candle :** with a time limit determined by the burning of a candle

[2]**candle** \"\ *vt* **candled; candled; candling** \-d(ə)liŋ\ **candles :** to examine by holding between the eye and a light; *esp* **:** to test (eggs) in this way for staleness, blood clots, fertility, and growth

candle alder *n* **:** SMOOTH ALDER

candle anemone *n* **:** a silky-haired herb (*Anemone cylindrica*) of temperate No. America having divided leaves, white petalless flowers, and cylindrical silky fruits

candlebark \'==,=\ *or* **candlebark gum** *n* **:** a ribbon gum (*Eucalyptus rubida*)

candlebeam \'==,=\ *n* [ME *candelbem*, fr. *candel* candle + *bem* beam] **1 :** a hanging wooden or metal lighting fixture holding several candles **2 :** a horizontal beam or rail used to hold liturgical or votive candles in old churches

candleberry \'==,==\ *n* **1** *also* **candleberry tree a** [so called fr. the use of the nuts as candles by natives in the So. Pacific] **:** CANDLENUT **b** [so called fr. the wax obtained from its berries, formerly used to make candles] **:** WAX MYRTLE **2 :** the fruit of either the candlenut or the wax myrtle

candleberry bark *n* **:** BAYBERRY BARK

candleberry myrtle *n* **:** WAX MYRTLE

candle board *n* **:** a small shelf or ledge usu. fitted below a table top and used to hold a candlestick

candlebranch \'==,=\ *n* **:** CHANDELIER

candle burner *n* **:** a protective metal tip placed on the wick end of a candle to protect the flame against drafts and to help the candle burn evenly and cleanly

candle cactus *n* **1 :** CANDLEWOOD 1a **2 :** CANE CACTUS

candle coal \-n(d)°l-\ *var of* CANNEL COAL

candle dance *n* **:** a dance that requires manipulation of lighted candles

candlefish \'=d°l,fish\ *n* [so called fr. the use of the fish as a candle by Am. Indians] **1 :** a marine fish (*Thaleichthys pacificus*) of the north Pacific coast related to the smelt, highly esteemed as a food fish, and so oily that when dried its body may be equipped with a wick and used as a candle — called also *eulachon* **2 :** SABLEFISH **3** *southern Africa* **:** HALFBEAK

candle fly *n* **:** LANTERN FLY

candle–foot \'==;=\ *n, pl* **candle–feet :** FOOTCANDLE

candle hour *n* **:** a unit of light or luminous energy equal to the total luminous energy emitted in one hour by a source having a luminous intensity of one candle

candle larkspur *n* **:** any of several perennial hybrid larkspurs having tall spikelike racemes of showy flowers and usu. assigned to *Delphinium elatum* but sometimes grouped under the name *D. cultorum*

candlelight \'= =,=\ *n, often attrib* [ME *candel-liht*, fr. OE *candel-lēoht*, fr. *candel* candle + *lēoht* light] **1 a :** the light of a candle or candles ‹sat by ~ in his study meditating on the eight years that had passed —C.G.Bowers› **b :** any soft artificial light **2** *also* **candlelighting :** the time for lighting up **:** TWILIGHT, DUSK ‹meet in the courthouse Saturday evening at early ~ —Carl Sandburg›

candlelighter \'= = =\ *n* [*candle* + *lighter*] **:** an ecclesiastical implement made with a long handle surmounted by a wick on one side and a bell-like candlesnuffer on the other and used for the ceremonial lighting and extinguishing of candles

candlelighter

candlemaker \'= =,= =\ *n* **:** one that performs one or more of the operations in making candles

can·dle·mas \'kand°lməs, -'aa- *also* -,mas \ *n*, *pl* **candlemases** *usu cap, often attrib* [ME *candelmasse*, fr. OE *candelmæsse*, fr. *candel* candle + *mæsse* mass, feast; fr. the candles blessed and carried in procession in celebration of the feast — more at MASS] **1 a :** the church feast celebrated on February 2 in commemoration of the presentation of Christ in the temple **b :** this feast commemorating additionally in the Roman Catholic Church the purification of the Virgin Mary **c :** this feast commemorating additionally in the Eastern Orthodox Church the meeting with Simeon and Anna **2** *or* **candlemas day** *usu cap C & D* **:** GROUNDHOG DAY

candlemas term *n, usu cap C* **:** the second of the three terms of the academic year in Scottish universities

candle–meter \'= =;= =\ *n* **:** LUX

candlenut \'==,=\ *n* **1 :** the oily seed of a tropical tree used locally to make candles and commercially as a source of oil — see CANDLENUT OIL **2 :** a large tree (*Aleurites moluccana*) that is probably native to southeast Asia but is now widely distributed in tropical regions, produces candlenuts, and is closely related to the tung — called also *varnish tree*

candlenut oil *n* **:** a drying oil obtained from candlenut seeds and used in paints and soap — called also *kekune oil*, *kukui oil*, *lumbang oil*

candlepin \'= =,=\ *n* **1 :** a slender nearly cylindrical bowling pin tapering toward top and bottom **2 candlepins** *pl but sing in constr* **:** a bowling game using candlepins and differing from tenpins in that a smaller ball is used, three balls per frame are bowled, and fallen pins are left on the alley

candle plant *n* **1 :** a southern African succulent plant (*Kleinia articulata*) with white flowers **2 :** MULLEIN 1

candlepower *n* **:** luminous intensity (as of an electric lamp) expressed in candles ‹a flare which produced 800,000 ~ for six minutes —Stanley Frank› — see CANDLE 4

candler \-d(ə)lə(r)\ *n* -S **:** one that candles

candle rent *n, obs* **:** rent derived from houses and consequently liable to diminution through loss or deterioration

candles *pl of* CANDLE, *pres 3d sing of* CANDLE

candle snuff *n* **:** a burnt wick of a candle

candlesnuffer \'= =,= =\ *n* **1 :** an instrument for snuffing candles **2 :** an attendant in charge of the candles (as formerly in a theater)

candlestand \'= =,=\ *n* **1 :** an iron tripod fitted with candlesticks **2 :** a small wooden stand or table

candlestand

candlestick \'= =,=\ *n* [ME *candlestikke*, fr. OE *candelsticca*, fr. *candel* candle + *sticca* stick — more at STICK] **:** a plain or ornate utensil with a spike or socket for holding a candle

candlestick lily *n* [prob. so called fr. its erect flower clusters] **:** a Siberian herb (*Lilium dauricum*) with terminal clusters of spotted red flowers

candlestick tulip *n* **:** LADY TULIP

candle tree *n* **1 :** WAX MYRTLE **2 :** a tree (*Parmentiera cerifera*) of Panama having a long yellow candlelike pod **3 :** a catalpa (*Catalpa bignonioides*) that has a long slender pod

candlewaster *n, obs* **:** one that consumes candles by late study

candlewick \'= =,=\ *n* **1 :** the wick of a candle **2 :** CATTAIL **3** [so called fr. the downy leaves and stalks, formerly used for making candlewicks] **:** MULLEIN **4** *or* **can·dle·wick·ing** \-iŋ\ **a :** a soft cotton yarn of loosely twisted threads used for embroidery **b :** embroidery made with this yarn usu. in tufts or French knots and often on unbleached muslin in making bedspreads

candlewood \'= =,=\ *n* [so called fr. its use for illumination] **1 :** any of several trees or shrubs chiefly of resinous character: as **a :** a plant of the genus *Fouquieria*; *esp* **:** OCOTILLO 1 **b :** a torchwood (*Amyris balsamifera*) **c :** a So. American tree (*Diporidium guianense*) **d :** a So. American shrub (*Panax capitatum*) **e :** a West Indian tree (*Dacryodes excelsa*) of the family Burseraceae yielding a fine lustrous brown wood **2 :** slivers and fine pieces of resinous wood burned for light

candlewood pine *n* **:** OCOTE

candling *pres part of* CANDLE

can·dock \'kan,däk\ *n* -S [[3]*can* + *dock* (plant); fr. its docklike leaves and flagon-shaped capsules] **:** any of several water lilies: as **a :** a yellow-flowered European water lily (*Nuphar luteum*) **b :** the common white-flowered European water lily (*Nymphaea alba*) **c :** SPATTERDOCK 1 **d :** WATER CHINQUAPIN

[1]**can·dol·lea** \kan'dälēə, -'ō-\ [NL, fr. Augustin Pyrame de *Candolle* †1841 Swiss botanist + L *-a* (fem. nom. sing. adj. ending)] *syn of* STYLIDIUM

[2]**candollea** *n* -S [NL] **:** a plant of the genus *Stylidium*

can·dol·le·a·ce·ae \(,)=,=ē'āsē,ē\ [NL, fr. *Candollea*, type genus + *-aceae*] *syn of* STYLIDIACEAE

can·dol·le·a·ceous \;=,= =;āshəs, =,= =;ā-\ *adj* [NL *Candolleaceae* + E *-ous*] **:** of, relating to, or like the Stylidiaceae

can·dom·blé \,kan,dōm'blā\ *n* -S [Pg] **:** a Brazilian Negro matriarchal fetish cult combining African, Indian, and Roman Catholic elements; *specif* **:** the ceremony or dance connected with this cult

can·dor \'kandə(r), -'aa- *also* -,dȯr *or* -,dō(ə)\ *n* -S *see -or in Explan Notes* [F & L; F *candeur*, fr. L *candor*, fr. *candēre* to shine, be white — more at CANDID] **1 a :** WHITENESS, BRILLIANCE ‹the sun poured with a more golden ~ —Christopher Morley› **b** *obs* **:** unstained purity and innocence ‹a young prince of valor and ~› **2 :** disposition to open-mindedness **:** freedom from bias, prejudice, and malice **:** FAIRNESS, IMPARTIALITY ‹a heavy accusation . . . from a gentleman of your talents, liberality, and ~ —Noah Webster› **3** *archaic* **:** KINDLINESS ‹~ in pardoning errors› **4 :** unreserved, honest, or sincere expression **:** FRANKNESS, CANDIDNESS ‹the ~ with which he acknowledged a weakness in his own case —Aldous Huxley› ‹~ and courtesy, the desire to please and perfect openness, are mutually inimical —W.C.Brownell›

cands *pl of* CAND

C and SC *abbr* capital and small capitals

[1]**can·dy** \'kandē, -'aa-, -di *also* -'ai-\ *n* -ES *often attrib* [short for *sugar candy*, fr. ME *sugre candy*, part trans. of MF *sucre candi*, part trans. of OIt *zucchero candi*, fr. *zucchero* sugar + Ar *qandī* candied, fr. *qand* cane sugar, prob. of Dravidian origin (whence Skt *khaṇḍaka* candy); akin to Tamil *kaṇṭu* candy, *kaṭṭu* to harden, condense] **1 a :** crystallized sugar formed by boiling down sugar syrup **b :** a confection of crystallized sugar **c :** the density at which boiling syrup will form candy ‹boil to a ~› **2 a :** a food made of a sugar paste or syrup often enriched and varied with coloring and flavoring (as chocolate) and filling (as fruits or nuts) and shaped into various attractive forms **b :** a piece of this food **3 :** a doughy bee food of sugar and honey **:** boiled sugar prepared as food for bees

[2]**candy** \"\ *vb* -ED/ -ING/ -ES [perh. fr. It *candire*, back-formation fr. *candito* (in *zucchero candito*), alter. of *candi* (in *zucchero candi*)] *vt* **1 :** to encrust in or coat with sugar often by cooking down in a heavy syrup ‹~ fruits› **:** saturate with syrup **:** coat with sugar by rolling or pressing ‹~ dates› **2 :** to make seem pleasant and attractive **:** SUGAR, SWEETEN ‹~*ing* up the duke's reputation› **3 :** to crystallize into sugar, candy, or a candylike substance ‹excessive boiling *candies* jelly› ~ *vi* **:** to become coated or encrusted with sugar crystals **:** become crystallized into sugar

[3]**candy** \"\ *n* -ES [Marathi *khaṇḍī* & Tamil-Malayalam *kaṇṭi*, prob. fr Skt *khaṇḍa* piece, portion, prob. of Proto-Munda origin, akin to Santali *gunda* pieces, small parts] **:** any of various units of weight used in India, Burma, and Ceylon usu. equal to between 500 and 600 pounds

candy grass *n* [so called fr. its sweet secretion] **:** MOLASSES GRASS

candy kitchen *n* **:** an establishment for making and selling candy at retail

candymaker \'= =,= =\ *n* **:** one that makes candy **:** CONFECTIONER

candy pink *n* **:** a deep yellowish pink that is yellower and paler than tigerlily

candy pull *n also* **candy pulling :** a party at which taffy or molasses candy is made

can·dys \'kandəs\ *n* -ES [Gk *kandys*] **:** a long loose wide-sleeved woolen outer gown worn by the Medes and Persians

candy stripe *n* [so called fr. the similarity of the design to that of some stick candy] **:** a design consisting usu. of bright-colored stripes of one color against a plain background esp. in textiles ‹his shirts . . . were silk with *candy stripes* —Joseph Mitchell› — **can·dy–striped** \'= =;strīpt\ *adj*

can·dy·tuft \'= =,təft\ *n* [obs. *Candy* (now *Candia*) Crete, Greek island + E *tuft*] **:** a cultivated plant of the genus *Iberis* (as the perennial *I. sempervirens* and the annuals *I. amara* and *I. umbellata*)

candyweed \'= =,=\ *n* [[1]*candy* + *weed*] **:** ORANGE MILKWORT

[1]**cane** \'kān\ *n, pl* **canes** *or* **cane** *often attrib* [ME, fr. MF, fr. OProv *cana*, fr. L *canna*, fr. Gk *kanna*, of Sem origin; akin to Ar *qanāh* hollow stick, reed, Heb *qāneh*, Assyr *qanū*] **1 :** a hollow or pithy jointed stem that is usu. slender and more or less flexible **2** *obs* **:** PIPE, TUBE; *esp* **:** a slender glass tube **3 a :** a slender jointed stem used as a walking stick **b :** a short staff used as an aid in walking **:** WALKING STICK **c :** a rod or stick used for flogging **4 :** a slender rod or cylinder (as of solid glass or sulfur) **5 a :** RATTAN; *esp* **:** split rattan used in chair seats and wicker articles **b (1) :** the stem of any one of various bamboolike grasses esp. of the genus *Arundinaria* (2)**:** any plant of this genus **c (1) :** SUGARCANE (2)**:** the stems of sugarcane **d :** SORGHUM; *esp* **:** SORGO **6 :** one of the stems of certain plants; *esp* **:** a shoot directly from the base (as in the raspberry, grape, or rose) **7 :** a warp in handweaving

[2]**cane** \"\ *vt* -ED/ -ING/ -S **1 :** to punish by whacking or beating with a cane ‹he sat in a professor's chair and *caned* sophomores for blowing spitballs —H.L.Mencken› **2 :** to weave or furnish with cane (as seats or backs of chairs)

[3]**cane** \"\ *n* -S [origin unknown] *Brit* **:** WEASEL; *esp* **:** a small female weasel

cane apple \'kā,napəl\ *n* [modif. of IrGael *caithne* strawberry tree + E *apple*] **:** a strawberry tree (*Arbutus unedo*)

cane ash *n* [[1]*cane* + *ash* (tree); perh. fr. its use in making walking sticks] **:** WHITE ASH 1a

cane blight *n* **:** a disease affecting the canes of various bush fruits (as currants, where it is caused by the fungus *Botryosphaeria ribis*, and raspberries, where it is caused by the fungus *Leptosphaeria coniothyrium*)

cane borer *n* **:** any of various insects having larvae that bore into the pith and destroy the stalks of certain plants — see RASPBERRY CANE BORER, SUGARCANE BORER

cane·brake *also* **cane·break** \'kān,brāk\ *n* -S [[1]*cane* + *brake* or *break* (thicket)] **:** a thicket of canes; *esp* **:** a dense growth of the giant cane

canebrake rattler *or* **canebrake rattlesnake** *n* **:** a rattlesnake that is a southern variety (*Crotalus horridus atricaudatus*) of the American timber rattlesnake

cane cactus *n* **:** any of several cylindrical-stemmed cacti of the genus *Opuntia*

cane chair *n* **:** a chair having cane in the seat or back

canecutter \'=,= =\ *n, South* **:** SWAMP RABBIT

cane–cutter's cramp *n* **:** HEAT CRAMPS

cane fruit *n* **:** a fruit (as the blackberry) growing on canes

cane grass *n* **:** any of several grasses; *esp* **:** an Australian grass (*Glyceria ramigera*) having wax-coated stems and used for thatching and making chair seats

cane killer *n* **:** an annual plant (*Melasma melampyroides*, family Scrophulariaceae) that is parasitic on sugar-cane roots

cane knife *n* **:** a heavy wide-bladed hooked knife used for cutting sugarcane

canel *var of* CANNEL

ca·nel·la \kə'nelə\ *n* [ML, dim. of L *canna* reed; fr. the shape of the rolls of prepared bark — more at CANE] **1** *also* **canela** -S **:** CINNAMON **2** *cap* [NL, fr. ML, cinnamon] **:** a monotypic genus of trees (order Parietales) having alternate simple entire leathery gland-dotted leaves and flowers with three sepals and producing a berry **3** *or* **canella al·ba** \-'albə *also* -'ō-\ *or* **canella bark** *also* **ca·ne·lo** \-'ne(,)lō, -'ā-\ -S [*canella* fr. NL *canella*; *canella alba* fr. NL *Canella alba*, syn. of *Canella winterana*; *canelo* fr. AmerSp, fr. Sp, cinnamon tree, fr. *canela* cinnamon, fr. ML *canella*] **:** the highly aromatic orange-colored inner bark of a tree (*Canella alba* or *C. winterana*) used as a condiment and in medicine as a tonic — called also *white cinnamon* **4** *also* **ca·nela** \-'nelə, -'ā-\ *or* **canelo** -S [*canella* fr. NL *canella*; *canela* fr. AmerSp, fr. Sp, cinnamon; *canelo*, fr. AmerSp, fr. Sp, cinnamon tree] **:** any of various trees of the family Lauraceae

[1]**ca·ne·lo** \kə'ne(,)lō, -'ā-\ *n, pl* **canelo** *or* **canelos** *usu cap* [Sp, of American Indian origin] **1 :** a Quechua-speaking Indian people of central Ecuador **2 :** a member of the Canelo people

[2]**canelo** *var of* CANELLA

can·e·phore \'kanə,fō(ə)r, -ȯ(ə)r\ *also* **can·e·phor** \-ȯ(ə)r\ *or* **ca·neph·o·ra** \kə'nefərə\ *or* **ca·neph·o·ros** \=' =rəs, -,räs\ *or* **ca·neph·o·rus** \=' =rəs\ *n, pl* **can·e·phores** \' = =,=\ *also* **ca·neph·o·rae** \=' = =,rē, -,rī\ *or* **ca·neph·o·ri** \=' = =,rī, -,rē\ [L *canephoros*, *canephora*, fr. Gk *kanēphoros*, fr. *kaneon* reed basket (fr. *kanna* reed) + *-phoros* -phorous — more at CANE] **1 :** a maiden bearing a basket on her head in an early Greek religious festival **2 :** a caryatid supporting a basket-like member that serves as a capital

ca·ne·pin \'kanəpən, *F* kȧnpaⁿ\ *n, pl* **canepins** \-pənz, -paⁿ\ [F] **:** a fine leather made from the skins of kids, lambs, and chamois

can·er \'kānə(r)\ *n* -S **:** one that weaves cane seats and backs of chairs

cane rat *n* [so called fr. its feeding on sugarcane] **1 :** a large ratlike African rodent (*Thryonomys swinderianus* or related species) that is related to the porcupine — called also *ground pig* **2 :** HUTIA

cane rust *n* **1 :** any of several diseases of the stems of blackberries and raspberries (as orange rust) **2 :** a disease of roses caused by a rust (*Earlea speciosa*)

canes *pl of* CANE, *pres 3d sing of* CANE

ca·nes·cent \kə'nes°nt\ *adj* [L *canescent-*, *canescens*, pres. part. of *canescere*, incho. of *canēre* to be gray, be white, fr. *canus* white, hoary — more at HARE] **1 :** growing white, whitish, or hoary ‹the ~ moon› **2** *bot* **:** having a fine grayish white pubescence **:** HOARY, GLAUCOUS

cane sugar *n* **:** sucrose from sugar cane

cane trash *n* **:** refuse of sugar cane **:** BAGASSE

caneware \'=,=\ *n* -S [so called fr. its color] **:** a buff or yellowish stoneware developed by Wedgwood

canework \'=,=\ *n* -S **:** interwoven split cane used for the seats and backs of chairs

can·field \'kan,fēld\ *n* -S *usu cap* [after Richard A. *Canfield* †1914 Am. gambling-house proprietor] **1 :** KLONDIKE 2 **2 :** a form of solitaire in which the player deals a reserve pile of 13 cards, lays out 4 face-up cards as a tableau, and turns up the remaining cards one or three at a time, the object being to build additional piles of each suit in ascending sequence

can·field·ite \'kan,fēl,dīt\ *n* -S [F.A. *Canfield* †1926 Am. mining engineer, + E *-ite*] **:** a mineral Ag_8SnS_6 consisting of silver thiostannate isomorphous with the germanium mineral argyrodite that occurs in black metallic octahedrons (sp.gr. 6.28)

can frame *n* **:** a machine used in spinning for forming the rove and delivering it into cans

can·ful \'kan,fu̇l\ *n, pl* **can·fuls** *also* **cans·ful :** the quantity a can holds

can·gia \'kanj(ē)ə\ *n* -S [It & Ar; It *cangia*, fr. Ar *qanjah*] **:** a long light sailboat used on the Nile

can·gle \'kāŋəl\ *vi* -ED/ -ING/ -S [perh. alter. of *jangle*] *chiefly Scot* **:** WRANGLE

[1]**cangue** *also* **cang** \'kaŋ, -'ai-\ *n* -S [F *cangue*, fr. Pg *canga* yoke, perh. of Celt origin; akin to OIr *camm* crooked — more at CHANGE] **:** a wooden collar three or four feet square used in Oriental countries for confining the neck and sometimes also the hands for punishment

cangue

[2]**cangue** \"\ *vt* -ED/ -ING/ -S **:** to compel to wear a cangue

can hook *n* [prob. fr. [2]*can* "barrel"] **:** a device that consists of a short rope or jointed bar with flat hooks at each end and that is used for hoisting casks or barrels by the ends of the staves

ca·ni·cha·na \,kānē'chänə\ *n, pl* **canichana** *or* **canichanas** *usu cap* [Sp, of American Indian origin] **1 :** an Indian people of northern Bolivia **2 :** a member of the Canichana people

ca·nic·o·la fever \kə'nikələ-\ *n* [NL *canicola* (specific epithet of *Leptospira canicola*), fr. L *canis* dog + NL *-cola* inhabitant (fem. of *-colus* -colous) — more at HOUND, -COLOUS] **:** an acute febrile disease in man and dogs characterized by gastroenteritis and mild jaundice and caused by a spirochete (*Leptospira canicola*) — compare STUTTGART DISEASE

ca·nic·u·lar \kə'nikyələ(r)\ *adj* [ME, fr. LL *canicularis*, fr. *canicula* Sirius, lit., small bitch, dim. of *canis* dog — more at HOUND] **1 :** immediately preceding and following the heliacal rising of the Dog Star ‹the days ~ —Edith Sitwell› **2 :** of or relating to the dog days ‹the ~ heat of the Deep South›

can·i·cule \'kanə,kyül\ *n* -S [F, dog days, Sirius, fr. L *canicula* Sirius] **:** DOG DAYS ‹the ~ of 1825›

can·id \'kanəd, -'ā-\ *n* -S [NL *Canidae*] **:** a member of the family Canidae

can·i·dae \'kanə,dē\ *n pl, cap* [NL, fr. *Canis*, type genus + *-idae*] **:** a cosmopolitan family comprising digitigrade carnivorous mammals (superfamily Arctoidea) that in many respects resemble members of the Felidae but that have in general longer coarser fur, comparatively long limbs with strong nonretractile claws, head rounded to elongated with well-developed often somewhat pointed muzzle and jaws, ears erect or drooping, and eyes with rounded pupils and that are commonly more diurnal and social in habits, often hunting in packs, running down rather than stalking their prey and taking it with their jaws rather than claws, and including the dogs, wolves, jackals, foxes, and extinct related animals

canier *comparative of* CANY

caniest *superlative of* CANY

canikin *var of* CANNIKIN

[1]**ca·nine** \'kā,nīn *also* -'a-\ *adj* [L *caninus*, fr. *canis* dog + *-inus* -ine — more at HOUND] **1 :** of or relating to dogs or to the family Canidae ‹the most graceful of the ~ race› **2 :** resembling that of a dog ‹she had followed him with a kind of ~ devotion through his senior year —Robert Carson›

[2]**canine** \"\ *n* -S **1** *also* **canine tooth :** a conical pointed tooth: **a :** such a tooth situated between the lateral incisor

and the first premolar on each side of each jaw in man and many mammals — see DENTITION illustration **b** : one of the conical teeth in the front part of the jaw in some fishes **2 a** : DOG **b** : a member of the family Canidae

canine chorea *n* : chorea in dogs that is believed to be caused by a virus

canine eminence *n* : a prominence on the surface of the superior maxillary bone caused by the socket of the canine tooth

canine fossa *n* : a depression external to and somewhat above the canine eminence

canine hysteria *n* : an epileptic condition of dogs usu. considered due to toxic elements in the food in which the affected dog may suddenly run or bark senselessly, hide without cause, or undergo spasms or convulsions — called also *fright disease, running fits*

canine letter *n* : DOG'S LETTER

canine madness *n* : RABIES

canine muscle *n* : CANINUS

canine typhus *n* : CANICOLA FEVER

caning *pres part of* CANE

ca·ni·ni·form \(ˈ)kā¦nīnə,fȯrm, -¦nin-, kəˈn-\ *adj* [²*canine* (tooth) + *-iform*] : having the form of a typical canine tooth

ca·nin·i·ty \kāˈninəd·ē, kə-\ *n* -ES [*canine* + *-ity*] **1** : canine quality or nature ⟨only now did Nip emerge into his full ~ —Israel Zangwill⟩ **2** : the canine race ⟨a lover of ~⟩

ca·ni·nus \kāˈnīnəs, kə-\ *n, pl* **cani·ni**\-ī,nī\ [NL, fr. L, adj., canine] : a muscle that elevates the corner of the mouth

can·ions \ˈkanyənz\ *n pl* [Sp *cañones*, pl. of *cañón*, lit., tube, pipe, fr. *caña* reed, fr. L *canna* — more at CANE] : close-fitting usu. ornamental kneepieces joining the upper and lower parts of the leg covering and worn by men esp. in Elizabethan and Jacobean England

ca·nis \ˈkānəs, -ˈa-,-ˈä-\ *n, cap* [NL, fr. L, dog — more at HOUND] : the chief and type genus of the dog family including the domestic dogs, the wolves and jackals, and sometimes in older classifications the foxes

can·is·tel \,kanə¦stel\ *n* -S [AmerSp *canistel, canisté*] : the ovoid orange-yellow mealy sweet fruit of a tropical tree (*Pouteria campechiana* var. *nervosa*) of Florida and the West Indies — called also *eggfruit*

¹can·is·ter *also* **can·nis·ter** \ˈkanəstə(r)\ *n* -S [L *canistrum* basket, fr. Gk *kanastron*, fr. *kanna* reed — more at CANE] **1** *archaic* : a small basket for holding bread, fruit, or flowers **2 a** : a cylindrical or rectangular container usu. of lightweight metal, plastic, or laminated pasteboard used for holding a dry product (as tea, crackers, flour, matches) **b** : any of various cylindrical metal receptacles usu. with a removable close-fitting top **3 a** : encased shot for close-range artillery fire consisting of a large number of balls in a light cylindrical case fitting the gun's bore and bursting by the force of the firing charge **b** : a metal drum or cylindrical barrel ⟨~*s* of TNT dropped by a destroyer⟩ **4** : a light perforated metal box that contains material to adsorb, filter, or detoxify poisons and irritants in the air and is used with gas masks — see GAS MASK illustration

canisters 2a

²canister \"\ *vt* -ED/-ING/-S : to place or enclose in a canister

ca·ni·ti·es \kəˈnishē,ēz, -ishēz\ *n, pl* **canities** \"\ [L, fr. *canus* white, hoary — more at HARE] : grayness or whiteness of the hair

can·i·tist \ˈkanətəst\ *n* -S [*canities* + *-ist*] : one who dyes or tints hair esp. in a beauty shop

¹can·ker \ˈkaŋkə(r), -ˈai-\ *n* -S [ME *canker, cancre*, fr. ONF *cancre* & OE *cancer*, fr. L *cancer* crab, cancer — more at CANCER] **1 a** *obs* : a spreading sore that corrupts and eats away body tissues : GANGRENE **b** : CANKER SORE **2** *archaic* : a caterpillar destructive of buds and leaves of plants **3** *now dial* **a** : RUST **b** : VERDIGRIS 3 **4 a** : an area of necrotic tissue in a woody stem or sometimes other plant organ caused by various agents (as fungi, bacteria, or toxic substances) and marked by shrinkage, cracking, and sloughing of tissue that leave an open wound surrounded by zones of callus often girdling and killing the affected stem **b** : POWDERY SCAB **c** : POTATO WART **5** : a center and source of spreading corruption, debasement, or enfeeblement ⟨the metropolis was the ~ of a continent and the wickedest city since Gomorrah —Herbert Asbury⟩ **6** *now dial* : DOG ROSE **7 a** : an obstinate chronic inflammation of the ear in dogs, cats, or rabbits; *esp* : a localized form of mange **b** : a chronic and progressive inflammation of the deep horn-producing tissues of the frog and sole of the hoofs of horses resulting in softening and destruction of the horny layers **c** : FOWL POX **d** : pigeon trichomoniasis

²canker \"\ *vb* **cankered; cankered; cankering** \-k(ə)riŋ\ **cankers** *vt* **1** *obs* : to infect with a spreading sore **2** *now dial* : to corrode with rust **3** : to corrupt with a malignancy of mind or spirit ⟨God help that country, ~*ed* deep by doubt —Archibald MacLeish⟩ ⟨~*ed* by a persecution complex⟩ ~ *vi* **1** *obs* : to become rusty **2** : to become infested with canker ⟨blighted stems often ~⟩ **3** : to undergo corruption and disintegration

cankerberry \ˈ==,==\ *n* **1** : the fruit of the dog rose **2 a** : the red berry of a West Indian soft prickly herb (*Solanum bahamense*) **b** : the West Indian herb bearing the cankerberry

cankered *adj* **1 a** : affected with canker **b** : eaten by a cankerworm **2** : debased by slow moral corruption **3** : cantankerous from deep-seated bitterness : malicious from ill temper : CRABBED, SPITEFUL — **can·kered·ly** \-kə(r)dlē\ *adv* — **can·kered·ness** *n* -ES

canker lettuce *n* [prob. so called fr. a belief that it cures canker] : FALSE WINTERGREEN

can·ker·ous \ˈkaŋk(ə)rəs, -ˈai-\ *adj* **1 a** *obs* : having the effect of a spreading sore **b** : eating into and corrupting the flesh **2** : that spreads corruption of mind or spirit ⟨his firmness of mind soon relapsed into a ~ intolerance —Maurice Cranston⟩ **3** : affected with or caused by canker ⟨a ~ stem disease⟩

cankerroot \ˈ==,=\ *n* [so called fr. the use of the roots in folk medicine as a cure for canker] : any of several plants with astringent roots: as **a** : SEA LAVENDER 1 **b** : GOLDTHREAD 1

canker rose *n* **1** : DOG ROSE **2** : CORN POPPY

cankers *pl of* CANKER, *pres 3d sing of* CANKER

canker sore *n* : any of various oral lesions (as a cold sore) that begin as one or more vesicles, rupture, and form ulcers

canker stain *n* : a disease of plane trees caused by a fungus (*Endoconidiophora fimbriata platani*) and marked by bluish black or reddish brown discoloration which forms a radial pattern beneath elongate blackened cankers on the trunk and less frequently on the branches

cankerweed \ˈ==,=\ *n* **1** : TANSY RAGWORT **2** : RATTLESNAKE ROOT a

cankerworm \ˈ==,=\ *n* : any of various insect larvae that injure plants esp. by feeding on buds and foliage — see FALL CANKERWORM, SPRING CANKERWORM

can·ker·wort \ˈ==,wərt, -,ȯ-\ *n* : DANDELION 1

can·kery \ˈkaŋk(ə)rē, -ˈai-\ *adj* **1** : affected with canker ⟨a ~ root⟩ **2** *dial* : RUSTY **3** *Scot* : CRABBED, ILL-NATURED

cann \ˈkan, -aa(ə)n\ *n* -S [ME — more at CAN (vessel)] : a drinking cup; *esp* : a bulbous mug

¹can·na \ˈkanə\ *n* [NL, fr. L, reed — more at CANE] **1** *cap* : a genus (coextensive with the family Cannaceae of the order Musales) of tropical perennial herbs having simple stems, large alternate broad entire leaves, and a terminal spike or spikelike cluster of very irregular flowers with the four staminodia forming the enlarged and colored portion — see ACHIRA, INDIAN SHOT **2** -S : a plant of the genus *Canna*; *esp* : any of a number of hybrids cultivated as ornamentals **3** -S : ANTIQUE RED

²can·na \ˈkänə\ *dial Brit var of* CANNOT

can·nab·ic \kəˈnabik, ka'-\ *adj* [L *cannabis* + E *-ic*] : of, relating to, or derived from hemp

can·na·bi·di·ol \,kanəbəˈdī,ōl, -,ōl\ *n* -S [NL *Cannabis* (genus name of *Cannabis sativa*) + E *-diol*] : a crystalline diphenol $C_{21}H_{28}(OH)_2$ that is obtained from the resin of the hemp plant and is physiologically inactive but is rearranged by acids into tetrahydro-cannabinol which has a high marijuana activity

can·na·bin \ˈkanəbən\ *n* -S [L *cannabis* + E *-in*] : a greenish black resin that is extracted from the dried leaves and flowering tops of the pistillate hemp plants and contains the physiologically active principles of cannabis — compare CHARAS

can·na·bi·nol \ˈkanəbə,nōl, kəˈnab-, -ōl\ *n* -S [*cannabin* + *-ol*] : a crystalline phenol $C_{21}H_{25}O(OH)$ that is obtained from the resin of the hemp plant and is physiologically inactive

can·na·bis \ˈkanəbəs\ *n* [NL, fr. L, hemp, fr. Gk *kannabis* — more at HEMP] **1** *cap* : a genus of tall rough annual herbs (family Moraceae) having erect stems, leaves with three to seven elongate leaflets, and pistillate flowers in spikes along the leafy stems — see HEMP **2** -ES : the dried flowering spikes of the pistillate plants of the hemp — compare GANJA, HASHISH, MARIJUANA

cannabis in·di·ca \-bəˈsindikə\ *n, pl* **cannabes indicae** \-,bēˈzində,sē, -,bāˈsində,kī\ [NL, Indian hemp] : a variety of cannabis (sense 2) obtained in India — used esp. in pharmacy

can·na·bism \ˈkanə,bizəm\ *n* -S [*Cannabis* + *-ism*] **1** : habituation to the use of cannabis **2** : chronic poisoning from excessive smoking or chewing of cannabis

can·na·ble \ˈkanəbəl, -ˈaa-\ *adj* : suitable for canning

can·na·ceous \(ˈ)ka¦nāshəs\ *adj* [NL *Cannaceae*, monotypic family containing the genus *Canna* (fr. *Canna* + *-aceae*) + E *-ous*] : of or relating to the genus *Canna*

cannach *n* -S [ScGael *canach*; akin to MIr *canach* sedge] *Scot* : COTTON GRASS

canna–down \ˈ==,=\ *n* -S [so called fr. the soft bristles of the perianth] : either of two sedges (*Eriophorum vaginatum* and *E. callitrix*) of temperate regions

canned *adj* **1** : sealed in cans usu. after sterilization and esp. for commerce ⟨~ peaches⟩ **2** : transcribed (as on a phonograph record or magnetic tape) for reproduction esp. over a radio or television system ⟨his major points were that live TV had spontaneity and topicality that ~ shows did not have —F.N. Karmatz⟩ **3 a** : prepared in identical form for wide or repeated use : SYNDICATED ⟨~ editorials for country newspapers⟩ **b** : having a stereotyped cast : HACKNEYED, CUT-AND-DRIED ⟨the salesman's ~ phrases⟩ **4** *slang* : DRUNK

Canned Heat *trademark* — used for a solid fuel furnished in small containers

¹cannel *or* **canel** *n* -S [ME *canel*, fr. OF *canele*, fr. ML *canella* — more at CANELLA] *obs* : CINNAMON

²cannel *n* -S [ME *canel* channel, gutter, fr. ONF *canel* channel, fr. L *canalis* — more at CANAL] *obs* : a gutter in a road

³cannel *var of* CANNEL COAL

cannel bone *n* [ME *canel-bon*, fr. *canel* neck, channel + *bon* bone] *obs* : CLAVICLE

can·nel coal *also* **cannel** \ˈkanᵊl\ *or* **candle coal** \ˈka(a)n-(d)ᵊl-\ *n* -S [prob. fr. E dial. *cannel* candle, fr. ME *candel* — more at CANDLE] : a bituminous coal of fine texture and little luster containing much volatile matter and burning with a bright flame

can·nel·lat·ed *or* **can·ne·lat·ed** \ˈkanᵊl,ād·əd\ *adj* [modif. (influenced by E *-ated*, as in past participles of verbs in *-ate*) of F *cannelé*, fr. *cannelé*, past part. of *canneler* to flute, fr. MF, irreg. fr. *cannelature*] : FLUTED

can·nel·oid \ˈkanᵊl,ȯid\ *adj* [*cannel* + *-oid*] : resembling cannel coal

can·ne·lon \ˈkanᵊl,än\ *n* -S [prob. fr. It *cannellone* tubular noodle for soup, aug. of *cannello* segment of a stalk of cane, small tube, fr. *canna* cane, reed, fr. L — more at CANE] **1** : a hollow roll or cone of baked puff paste usu. stuffed with a savory filling as an appetizer or with cream as a dessert **2** : a roll of highly seasoned minced meat baked or fried

can·nel·lo·ni \,kanᵊlˈōnē\ *n pl* [It, pl. of *cannellone*] : tubes esp. of pasta filled with a savory stuffing (as of meat)

can·ne·lure \ˈkanᵊl,(y)u̇(ə)r\ *or* **chan·ne·lure** \ˈcha-\ *n* -S [F *cannelure*, alter. of MF *cannelature*, fr. OIt *cannellatura*, prob. fr. *cannella* small tube, cinnamon, fr. ML *canella* — more at CANELLA] **1** : a groove running lengthwise on the surface of a cylinder or column **2 a** : a groove around the cylinder of an elongated bullet for small arms to contain a lubricant **b** : a groove around a bullet into which the edge of the cartridge case is crimped **c** : a groove around the rotating band of a gun projectile to lessen the resistance offered to the rifling **d** : a groove around the base of a cartridge where the extractor takes hold

can·ner \ˈkanə(r), -ˈaa-\ *n* -S **1** : one engaged in or making a business of canning food **2** : an animal (as a steer) whose meat is fit only for canned products **3** : a vessel for holding cans or jars of food in the process of canning; *specif* : PRESSURE COOKER

can·nery \ˈkan(ə)rē, -ˈaa-, -i\ *n* -ES : a factory or other place for the canning of foods

can·nery·man \-,man,-,mən,-,maa(ə)n\ *n, pl* **cannerymen** : a worker in or owner of a cannery

can·ne·tille \,kanə¦tē(l), *F* kantēy\ *n* -S [F, fr. It *cannutiglia, canutiglia*, fr. Sp *cañutillo*, lit., small tube, dim. of *cañuto* tube, pipe, fr. Ar dial. (Spain) *qannūt*, fr. (assumed) VL *cannutus*, fr. L *canna* cane — more at CANE] : a fine gold or silver thread twisted spirally that is used in embroidery and often made into lace for vestments or into military braid

can·ni·bal \ˈkanəbəl\ *n* -S *often attrib* [NL *Canibalis* Carib, fr. Sp *canibal, caribal*, fr. 15th cent. Arawakan *caniba, carib* (forms recorded by Columbus in Cuba and Haiti respectively), of Cariban origin; akin to Carib *calina, calinago, galibi* Caribs, lit., strong men, brave men] **1** : a human being that eats human flesh — called also *anthropophagite* **2** : an animal that devours its own kind **3** : one that cannibalizes machines for replacement parts

can·ni·bal·ic \¦==¦balik\ *adj* **1** : rapaciously savage : CRUEL, SANGUINARY **2** : like that of a cannibal **3** : marked by barbarity traditionally suggestive of cannibals

can·ni·bal·ism \ˈkanəbə,lizəm\ *n* -S **1** : the eating of human flesh by a human being seldom done for nutritional purposes but among cannibals done in conjunction with religious or sacramental rites and usu. including the eating of certain organs believed to be the seat of desired virtues or powers — compare ENDOCANNIBALISM **2 a** : the eating of the flesh or the eggs of any animal by its own kind **b** : the eating of human flesh by a lower animal **3** : the pecking and tearing of the live flesh of its own members in a domestic poultry flock — compare PECK ORDER **4** : the act or practice of weakening or destroying a competitor or rival ⟨threatened only from time to time by the incursions of political or economic ~ —Paul Schrecker⟩ **5** : CANNIBALIZATION **6** : oral sadism

can·ni·bal·is·tic \,kanəbə¦listik, -ēk\ *adj* **1** : addicted or inclined to cannibalism among humans or animals ⟨an inherent ~ tendency in poultry⟩ **2 a** : analogous with or suggestive of the voracity of cannibalism ⟨~ impulses attendant on teething⟩ ⟨a mother's ~ fixation on a son⟩ **b** : derived from or akin to cannibalism ⟨the ~ principle of an acquisitive society⟩ **3** : given to or exhibiting cannibalism among associates in civilized society ⟨a school of ~ novelists⟩ ⟨a view of business as ~⟩ ⟨a chronic and ~ appetite for personalities —Aldous Huxley⟩ **4** : performed or involved in the process of cannibalization **5** : orally sadistic

can·ni·bal·is·ti·cal·ly \-tək(ə)lē, -tēk-, -i\ *adv* : in a cannibalistic manner : toward, in, or through the practice of cannibalism

can·ni·bal·i·ty \,kanəˈbaləd·ē\ *n* -ES : CANNIBALISM; *esp* : ANTHROPOPHAGY

can·ni·bal·i·za·tion \,kanəbələˈzāshən, -,līˈz-\ *n* -S : the action of cannibalizing an operating unit or enterprise

can·ni·bal·ize \ˈkanəbə,līz\ *vb* -ED/-ING/-S *see -ize in Explan Notes*, *vt* **1** : to eat the flesh of (a live animal) **2 a** : to dismantle (as a new or usable airplane, vehicle, or other machine) for parts to be used as replacements in other machines of the same make **b** : to strip (a disabled or outmoded machine) of salvageable parts for repair or for assembling into a serviceable machine **c** : to deprive or strip (a combat group) of manpower or equipment for building up the striking power of another group **3** : to deprive or strip of integral parts or essential tools, equipment, or personnel for rehabilitating or strengthening another facility or enterprise of the same kind ⟨war plants *cannibalized* by peacetime buyers⟩ ~ *vi* **1** : to practice cannibalism **2** : to cannibalize one operating unit or enterprise for building up another of the same kind

can·ni·bal·ly \-bəlē\ *adv* : according to the nature or practice of a cannibal

cannier *comparative of* CANNY

canniest *superlative of* CANNY

can·ni·kin *also* **can·a·kin** *or* **can·i·kin** \ˈkanəkən, -ˈaa-, -nēk-\ *n* -S [prob. fr. obs. D *kanneken*, fr. MD *canneken*, dim. of *canne* can (akin to OE *canne*) + *-ken* -kin — more at CAN (vessel)] **1** : a small can or drinking vessel **2** *NewEng* : a wooden bucket

can·ni·ly \ˈkanᵊlē, -i\ *adv* [*canny* + *-ly*] : in a canny manner: as **a** : KNOWINGLY, SHREWDLY **b** : CAREFULLY, CAUTIOUSLY

can·ni·ness \ˈkanēnəs, -nin-\ *n* -ES [*canny* + *-ness*] : a canny propensity or trait: as **a** : PRUDENCE, WARINESS **b** : CLEVERNESS, SHREWDNESS **c** : FORESIGHTEDNESS, SAGACITY

canning *n* -S [fr. gerund of ⁴*can*] : a method of food preservation in which packed cans or jars are subjected to temperatures high enough to sterilize the containers and their contents — compare COLD-PACK METHOD, HOT-PACK METHOD

cannister *var of* CANISTER

can·niz·za·ro reaction \,kanə¦zä(,)rō-, -nət¦sä-\ *n, usu cap C* [after Stanislao *Cannizzaro* †1910 Ital. chemist] : a reaction of aldehydes with caustic alkali in which one molecule of aldehyde is reduced to the corresponding alcohol and another molecule is oxidized to the salt of the corresponding acid

¹can·non \ˈkanən\ *n, pl* **cannons** *or* **cannon** [MF *canon*, fr. It *cannone*, lit., large tube, aug. of *canna* reed, tube, fr. L, reed — more at CANE] **1** *pl usu cannon* **a** : a weapon consisting of a metal tube now usu. steel and either cast in one piece or built up from a series of forgings, supported by a carriage or mount, and used for firing projectiles — compare GUN **b** : a heavy-caliber automatic aircraft gun firing explosive shells **2 a** *also* **cannon bit** : a smooth round horse bit **b** : the straight portion of the mouthpiece of certain bits **3** *or* **can·on** : the projecting part of a bell by which it is hung : EAR **4** *also* **cannon curl** : a cylindrical curl of hair worn in a horizontal position **5** *Brit* **a** *also* **canon** : a carom in billiards and bagatelle **b** : bagatelle played with only three balls and sometimes without cups **c** : a rebound after colliding : CAROM **6** *Brit* : a hollow spindle or shaft containing another spindle having an independent motion **7** : the part of the leg where the cannon bone is situated : SHANK — see HORSE illustration **8** *slang* **a** : PICKPOCKET **b** : PISTOL, REVOLVER **9** : a blackish green that is yellower and deeper than ultramarine green

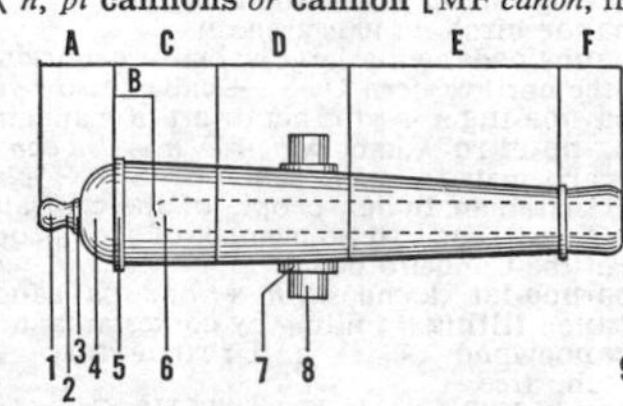

cannon (muzzle-loading): *A* sometimes called cascabel; *B* breech; *C* first reinforce; *D* second reinforce; *E* chase; *F* swell of muzzle; *1* knob; *2* neck; *3* fillet; *4* base of breech; *5* base ring; *6* chamber; *6-9* bore; *7* rimbase; *8* trunnion; *9* face of the piece

²cannon \"\ *vb* -ED/-ING/-S [prob. fr. MF *canonner*, fr. *canon*] *vi* **1** : to discharge cannon **2 a** *Brit* : to carom in billiards **b** *chiefly Brit* : to bump violently so as to rebound : rebound after colliding ~ *vt* **1** : CANNONADE **2** *Brit* **a** : to cause to rebound by violent collision **b** : to carom into

¹can·non·ade \,kanə¦nād\ *n* -S [MF *canonnade* cannon shot, modif. of It *cannonata*, fr. *cannone* cannon + *-ata* -ade] **1** : a firing of artillery in considerable quantity for an appreciable length of time **2 a** : a loud noise like a cannonade of artillery **b** : a noisy bombardment (as of questions)

²cannonade \"\ *vb* -ED/-ING/-S *vt* **1** : to attack with artillery : batter with artillery fire ~ *vi* **1** : to deliver artillery fire **2** : to make a noise like that of artillery fire **3** : ²CANNON 2b

¹cannonball \ˈ==,=\ *n* **1 a** : a round solid missile made for firing from a cannon **b** : a missile of any solid or hollow shape made for cannon **2 a** : a jump into the water made with the arms holding the knees tight against the chest **b** : a hard tennis service with a virtually flat trajectory **3** : a fast train; *esp* : EXPRESS TRAIN

²cannonball \"\ *vi* -ED/-ING/-S : to travel with a speed like that of a cannonball

cannonball tree *n* **1** : a So. American tree (*Couroupita guianensis*) of the family Lecythidaceae bearing a large globose fruit with a hard woody rind **2** : an East Indian tree (*Xylocarpus granatum*) of the family Meliaceae bearing a hard woody fruit and yielding a hard useful wood

cannon bit *n* : CANNON 2a

cannon bone *n* [F *canon*, lit., cannon — more at CANNON] : a bone in hoofed mammals that supports the leg from the knee or hock joint to the fetlock; *esp* : the enlarged metacarpal or metatarsal of the third digit in the horse — compare METACARPUS

cannon cracker *n* : a large firecracker

cannon curl *n* : CANNON 4

can·non·eer *also* **can·non·ier** \,kanə¦ni(ə)r, -iə\ *n* -S [MF *canonnier*, fr. *canon* cannon + *-ier* -eer — more at CANNON] : an artilleryman assigned to the care and use of a gun

cannon fodder *n* [trans. of G *kanonenfutter*] : soldiers who are subject to the risk of being wounded or killed by artillery fire

can·non·ism \ˈkanə,nizəm\ *n* -S *usu cap* [Joseph G. *Cannon* †1926 Am. politician + E *-ism*] : concentration of the means of control over the procedure and business of the U.S. House of Representatives in the hands of its speaker

cannon metal *n* : GUNMETAL

cannon pinion *n* : a small steel tube having at the lower end teeth that mesh with the teeth of the minute wheel of a timepiece and at the upper end the minute hand which is mounted on the arbor of the center wheel friction-tight so as to allow hand-setting

can·non·ry \ˈkanənrē, -i\ *n* -ES **1** : CANNONADING **2** : ARTILLERY

cannons *pl of* CANNON, *pres 3d sing of* CANNON

cannon–shot \ˈ==,=\ *n* : the range of a cannon

cannon stove *n* : a cast-iron stove resembling a cannon set up on its breech

can·not \ˈka(,)nät, kəˈnät, kaˈnät, ˈkanət, ˈka(n)ˈnät, *usu* -d·+V\ [ME, fr. ¹*can* + *not*] : can not — **cannot but 1** : to be inescapably constrained to (as out of a sense of fitness or rightness) : be left with no alternative than to ⟨an obsequiousness one *cannot but* feel aversion to⟩ **2** : to be bound to : be sure to : MUST ⟨his personality *cannot but* come through in his letters⟩ **3** : to be unable to do otherwise than to ⟨the outsider *cannot but* be struck by the frequent reluctance of the learned world to recognize important discoveries —Edmund Wilson⟩ — compare ²BUT 2b

can·nu·la *also* **can·u·la** \ˈkanyələ\ *n, pl* **cannulas** \-ləz\ *or* **cannu·lae** \-,lē\ [NL, fr. L *cannula* small reed, dim. of *canna* reed — more at CANE] : a small tube made for insertion into a body cavity (as for drainage) or into a duct or vessel and sometimes fitted with a trocar during the act of insertion

can·nu·lar \-lə(r)\ *adj* [NL *cannula* + E *-ar*] : having the form of a cannula : TUBULAR

can·nu·late \-,lāt\ *vt* -ED/-ING/-S [*cannula* + *-ate*] : to insert a cannula into

can·nu·la·tion \,kanyəˈlāshən\ *n* -S : the act or process of cannulating

can·nu·lize \ˈkanyə,līz\ *vt* -ED/-ING/-S [NL *cannula* + E *-ize*] : CANNULATE

¹can·ny \ˈkanē, -i\ *adj* -ER/-EST [¹*can* + *-y*] **1 a** : FORESIGHTED, KNOWING, WISE **b** : CAUTIOUS, PRUDENT, WARY **c** : CLEVER, CUNNING, SLY **d** : FRUGAL, THRIFTY **e** : shrewd in worldly affairs : watchful for self-interest : SHARP-WITTED **2** *Scot* **a** : FORTUNATE, LUCKY **b** : free from weird qualities or unnatural powers : safe to deal with — used in a negative constr. **c** : wise in supernatural affairs : having occult powers **3 a** *Scot* : CAREFUL, GENTLE, STEADY **b** *Scot* : COMFORTABLE, COZY, QUIET, SNUG **c** *dial Brit* : agreeable to the eye or perception : PLEASANT, WORTHY — used as a general term of approbation **d** *Scot* : considerable esp. in extent, number, or amount

²canny \"\ *adv, Scot* : in a canny manner: as **a** : CAREFULLY, CAUTIOUSLY **b** : GENTLY, QUIETLY — compare CA' CANNY

canny moment *n, archaic Scot* : the moment of childbirth

ca·noa \kəˈnōə\ *n* -S [Pg, canoe, fr. Sp] : a sloop-rigged fishing boat common in the Amazon delta

[1]**ca·noe** \kə'nü\ *n* -s *often attrib* [alter. (prob. influenced by MF *canoue*, MF & F *canoe*, fr. Sp *canoa*) of earlier *canoa*, *canow*, fr. Sp *canoa*, fr. Sp, fr. 15th cent. Arawakan *canoa* (form recorded by Columbus), of Cariban origin; akin to Galibi *canaoua*, Chayma & Cumanagoto *canagua*, *canahua*, Carib & Macusi *canaoa*] **1 :** a long and narrow boat that is sharp at both ends, has curved sides, is usu. built of lightweight materials (as bark, hide, canvas, light wood, or light metal), and is usu. propelled by hand-driven paddles although sometimes mounting a sail or sails **2 :** a synchronized swimming stunt executed with arched back, head and heels above water, and hands at hip level propelling the body forward by sculling

canoe

[2]**canoe** \"\ *vb* **canoed; canoed; canoeing; canoes** *vi* **1 :** to paddle a canoe **:** manage a canoe **2 :** to go or travel in a canoe ⟨~ across the lake⟩ ~ *vt* **:** to transport in a canoe ⟨munitions being *canoed* across the river⟩

canoe birch *n* **:** PAPER BIRCH

canoe cedar *n* **:** a large valuable arborvitae (*Thuja plicata*) of the northwestern U. S. — called also *red cedar*

ca·noe·ing *n* -s **:** the act or art of managing a canoe

ca·no·ei·ro \,kanə'wā(,)rō\ *n* -s *usu cap, often attrib* [Pg, lit., canoeman, fr. *canoa* canoe (fr. Sp) + *-eiro* -er] **1 a :** a Tupi-Guaranian Indian people of the central part of the state of Goiaz, Brazil **b :** a member of such people **2 :** the language of the Canoeiro people

ca·noe·ist \kə'nüəst\ *n* -s **:** one that canoes

canoe tilting *n* **:** tilting by contestants in canoes

canoewood \-ˌ-\ *n* **1 :** TULIP TREE **2 :** the wood of the tulip tree

can·oid \'ka,nȯid, -'ā-\ *adj* [NL *Canoidea*] **:** of or relating to the Arctoidea

ca·noi·dea \kə'nȯidēə\ [NL, fr. *Canis* + *-oidea*] *syn of* ARCTOIDEA

[1]**can·on** \'kanən\ *n* -s *often cap* [ME *canoun*, *canon*, fr. OE & OF *canon*, fr. LL, fr. L, model, standard, fr. Gk *kanōn* rod, measuring line, standard; akin to Gk *kanna* reed — more at CANE] **1 :** a decree, decision, regulation, code, or constitution made by ecclesiastical authority; *specif* **:** a law or rule of doctrine or discipline enacted by a council and confirmed by highest ecclesiastical authority **2** [ME, prob. fr. OF, fr. LL] **a :** a fundamental and relatively unchangeable part of the Roman Catholic mass containing the fixed rule according to which the sacrifice of the mass is to be offered; *specif* **:** the part of the mass beginning after the sanctus with the prayer "Te igitur" and ending just before the paternoster or with the consumption of the eucharistic elements **b :** a book containing the canon and ordinary used at pontifical mass **3** [ME, fr. LL] **a :** a collection or authoritative list of books accepted as holy scripture: as (1) **:** books forming the accepted Hebrew list of the Holy Scriptures collected under the divisions of the Law, the Prophets, and the Writings accepted by Protestant Christians as the original and definitive canon of the Old Testament but supplemented by Roman Catholics with additional books drawn from the Septuagint (2) **:** books forming the Christian New Testament (3) **:** books forming the Old and New Testaments and constituting the Christian Bible **b :** an accepted or sanctioned list of books ⟨established in the ~ of literature⟩ **c :** the authentic works of a writer ⟨the Chaucer ~⟩ **4** *archaic* **:** a general mathematical rule, formula, or table **5 a :** a basic general principle or rule commonly accepted as true, valid, and fundamental ⟨I accept Plato's well-known ~ that only the perfectly real can be perfectly known —W.R.Inge⟩ **b :** a norm, criterion, model, or standard for evaluating, judging, testing, or criticizing ⟨Novalis . . . set up the fairy tale as the ~ of art —Irving Babbitt⟩ **c :** a body of principles, rules, standards, or norms (as in the normative sciences) ⟨according to newspaper ~ . . . a big story calls for a lot of copy —A.J. Liebling⟩ **d** [G *kanon*, fr. L *canon* or Gk *kanōn*] *in Kant* **:** the totality of fundamental a priori principles for the correct use of our capacities for knowledge **e** *in Mill* **:** any one of the five methods for induction — compare INDIRECT METHOD OF DIFFERENCE, METHOD OF AGREEMENT, METHOD OF CONCOMITANT VARIATIONS, METHOD OF DIFFERENCE, METHOD OF RESIDUES **6** [LGk *kanōn*, fr. Gk] **:** a contrapuntal musical composition in two or more voice parts in which the melody is imitated exactly and completely by the successively entering voices though not always at the same pitch and which either ends with a coda or begins over again — see CIRCULAR CANON; compare CATCH 5, ROUND **7** [LL] **a :** a fixed annual or customary payment or tribute (as to the church) **:** QUITRENT **b :** the annual rent payable under a Roman emphyteusis **8** [F; prob. fr. having been used in printing the canon of the mass] **:** a type of either about 44 point or about 48 point which is the largest size having a specific name **9** [ML, list, fr. LL, catalog of saints, fr. Gk *kanōn* table (as of dates)] **a :** a list (as of clergy, deaconesses, or those receiving charity) in the early church **b :** a catalog of recognized saints **10 :** a liturgical sequence of the Eastern Orthodox Church consisting normally of nine odes each comprising several troparia sung as an integral part of matins and also at certain other offices (as at compline during the first week of Lent) ⟨the *Canon* of the Holy Fathers⟩ ⟨the Great *Canon* of St. Andrew of Crete⟩ **11 :** a dance in which certain dancers follow the patterns previously set by others who then change to new patterns **syn** see LAW

Aa

canon type

[2]**canon** \"\ *n* -s [ME *canoun*, fr. AF *canunie*, fr. LL *canonicus* one living under a rule, fr. L *canonicus* according to rule, fr. Gk *kanonikos*, fr. *kanon-*, *kanōn* rod, rule + *-ikos* -ic — more at [1]CANON] **1 :** one of the clergy of a medieval cathedral or large church living as a community under a rule **2 :** a clergyman belonging to the chapter or the staff of a cathedral or collegiate church — compare HONORARY CANON, MINOR CANON **3 :** CANON REGULAR 2

[3]**canon** *var of* CANNON

[4]**ca·non** \kə'nōn\ *var of* CANUN

[5]**ca·ñon** \'kanyən\ *var of* CANYON

canon cancrizans *n* **:** CRAB CANON

can·on·ess \'kanənəs\ *n* -ES [[2]*canon* + *-ess*] **1 :** a woman living with others in a community or college under a rule but not under a perpetual vow **2 :** a woman holding a canonry in a conventual chapter

[1]**ca·non·ic** \kə'nänik, -ēk\ *adj* [LL *canonicus* one living under a rule — more at CANON (clergyman)] **1 :** CANONICAL ⟨~ rights⟩ **2 :** of, relating to, or resembling a musical canon ⟨tonal balance is important in all ~ writing —Walter Piston⟩

[2]**canonic** \"\ *n* -s [LL *canonicus* belonging to the canon of Scripture, fr. L, according to rule — more at CANON (clergyman)] **1 :** a system of philosophical or logical canons; *esp* **:** Epicurean logic **2 :** a person in canonical orders

ca·non·i·cal \-əkəl, -ēk-\ *adj* [[1]*canonic* + *-al*] **1 a :** of, relating to, established by, or conforming to a canon **b :** of or relating to canon law **2 :** like or conforming to a general rule **:** accorded wide acceptance **:** SANCTIONED, ORTHODOX, AUTHORITATIVE ⟨the ~ code of the party⟩ ⟨the drinking of cocktails was as ~ a rite as the mixing —Sinclair Lewis⟩ **3 :** belonging to or accepted as forming a canon ⟨a ~ book⟩ ⟨~ scriptures⟩ **4 :** of or relating to a clergyman (as a canon) or to an ecclesiastical chapter ⟨a ~ house⟩ **5 :** relating to various of the simplest and most significant forms or schemata to which general equations, statements, or expressions may be reduced without loss of generality **:** STANDARD, BASIC ⟨the ~ equations of dynamics⟩ — compare NORMAL FORM — **ca·non·i·cal·ly** \-k(ə)lē, -i\ *adv*

canonical age *n* **:** the age at which an individual may in accordance with the canons of a particular church become liable to certain obligations (as fasting) or eligible for certain privileges (as ordination)

canonical hour *n* **1 :** any of certain stated times of the day appointed by various churches for the offices of prayer and devotion — see COMPLINE, LAUD, MATINS, NONE, PRIME, SEXT, TIERCE, VESPER **2 :** any of the hours of the period from 8 a.m. to 3 p.m. before and after which marriage cannot be legally performed in any parish church in England **3 :** an appropriate or climactic hour or time

canonical purgation *n* [trans. of ML *purgatio canonica*; fr. its use in the ecclesiastical courts] **:** purgation by means of oath helpers — compare COMPURGATION, VULGAR PURGATION

ca·non·i·cals \-kəlz\ *n pl* **:** the vestments prescribed by canon to be worn by an officiating clergyman of certain churches

canonical sin *n* **:** a sin (as idolatry, murder, adultery, heresy) for which excommunication or public penance was decreed by the canons of the early church

ca·non·i·cate \kə'nänəkət, -ēk-, -,kāt\ *n* -s [ML *canonicatus*, fr. *canonicus* canon (fr. LL, one living under a rule) + *-atus* -ate] **:** the office of a canon **:** CANONRY

can·on·ic·i·ty \,kanə'nisəd·ē, -ətē, -i\ *n* -ES [F *canonicité*, fr. *canonique* canonical, authoritative (fr. LL *canonicus*, fr. L, according to rule) + *-ité* -ity — more at CANON (clergyman)] **1 :** the status or character of belonging within the biblical canon **2 :** canonical acceptability, authority, or genuineness

ca·non·ics \kə'näniks, -ēks\ *n pl but usu sing in constr* **:** a division of theology that deals with the origin, history, or authority of the biblical canon

can·on·ist \'kanənəst\ *n* -s [MF *canoniste*, fr. *canon* (fr. LL) + *-iste* -ist — more at CANON (rule)] **:** one skilled in canon law

can·on·is·tic \¦kanə¦nistik, -ēk\ *adj* **1 :** pertinent to or characteristic of a canonist **2 :** relating to canon law

can·on·i·za·tion \,kanənə'zāshən, -,nīz-\ *n* -s [ME *canonizacioun*, fr. ML *canonization-*, *canonizatio*, fr. *canonizatus* (past part. of *canonizare* to canonize) + L *-ion-*, *-io* -ion] **:** the act of canonizing or the state of being canonized; *specif* **:** the final process or decree by which the name of a deceased person is placed in the catalog of saints and commended to perpetual veneration and invocation

can·on·ize \'kanə,nīz\ *vt* -ED/ -ING/ -S [ME *canonizen*, fr. ML *canonizare*, fr. LL *canon* — more at CANON (rule)] **1 :** to declare (a deceased person) a saint **:** put in the catalog of saints **:** SAINT — compare BEATIFY **2 :** to include in a canon esp. of Scripture **:** make canonical **3 :** to sanction or ratify by or as if by ecclesiastical authority **4** *archaic* **:** to make into a god or into something divine **:** APOTHEOSIZE **5 :** to regard as sanctioned, rightly and securely established, or sacrosanct ⟨*canonized* as dean of drama critics⟩ ⟨his mother had *canonized* all his timidities as common sense —Scott Fitzgerald⟩

canon law *n* [alter. of ME *lawe canoun*, prob. trans. of MF *droit canonel*] **1 :** a body of ecclesiastical law for the government of a Christian church; *esp* **:** a codified body of rules and regulations as distinguished from other noncodified forms of church law **2 :** a body of religious law governing the conduct of members of a particular faith ⟨the *canon law* of Islam⟩

canon lawyer *n* **:** CANONIST

ca·non oak \'kanyən-\ *n* **:** CANYON LIVE OAK

can·on regular \'kanən-\ *n, pl* **canons regular 1 :** one of the clergy of a cathedral organized as a monastic community under a rule **2 :** a priest of the Roman Catholic Church belonging to an order or congregation bound by the vows of religion, living in community under usu. the Augustinian rule, and formerly monastic but in modern times being largely engaged in parish, educational, or hospital work

can·on·ry \'kanənrē, -i\ *n* -ES [[2]*canon* + *-ry*] **1 :** the prebend or office of a canon or canoness **2 :** a body of canons

canons *pl of* CANON

ca·noo·dle \kə'nüd[ə]l\ *vb* **canoodled; canoodled; canoodling** \-d(ə)liŋ\ **canoodles** [perh. fr. E dial. *canoodle*, n., donkey, fool, silly lovemaker, perh. alter. of *noodle* (blockhead)] *vi* **:** PET, CARESS, FONDLE ⟨the best way of dealing with lovers . . . found *canoodling* in church doors —Bruce Marshall⟩ ~ *vt* **:** to persuade by or as if by caresses

can opener *n* **:** a device for opening cans

ca·no·pic \kə'nōpik, -äp-\ *adj, usu cap* [L *canopicus*, fr. *Canopus*, city in ancient Egypt (fr. Gk *Kanōbos*, *Kanōpos*) + L *-icus* -ic] **:** of or relating to Canopus

canopic jar *or* **canopic vase** *n, often cap C* **:** a jar in which the ancient Egyptians preserved the viscera of a deceased person usu. for burial with the mummy

[1]**can·o·py** \'kanəpē, -i\ *n* -ES [ME *canope*, *canape*, fr. ML *canopeum*, *canapeum* mosquito net, fr. L *conopeum*, *conopium*, fr. Gk *kōnōpion*, fr. *kōnōps* mosquito, gnat] **1 :** a covering usu. for shelter or protection ⟨from midships aft she was covered with a vast ~ of solid construction —C. S. Forester⟩: **a :** a covering usu. of cloth suspended from the four high posts of a bed **b :** a covering typically of cloth carried on poles above an exalted personage or sacred object **:** BALDACHIN **c :** SKY ⟨the wild blue ~ above⟩ **d :** a temporary or permanent cover providing shelter and decoration (as over a door or window) **e :** a formation of branches affording a cover of foliage ⟨the fabulous avenue . . . covered with a ~ of chestnut trees —Horace Sutton⟩; *specif* **:** the uppermost spreading branchy layer of a forest — see UNDERSTORY **f :** an awning or marquee often stretching from doorway to curb or covering a section of grandstand **2 a :** the rooflike construction above the stage of an Elizabethan theater **b :** a curtained recess at the back of such a stage **3 :** an ornamental rooflike structure that provides or suggests shelter and that projects from a wall or is supported by columns **4 :** a metal covering used to enclose wiring where an electric fixture protrudes (as from a ceiling) **5 a :** the transparent enclosure over an airplane cockpit **b :** the lifting or supporting surface of a parachute

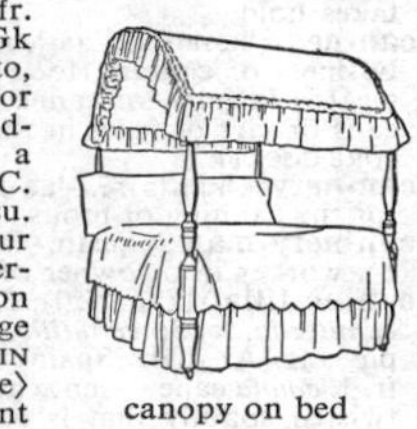
canopy on bed

[2]**canopy** \"\ *vt* -ED/ -ING/ -ES **:** to cover with or as if with a canopy ⟨the streets were quiet as churches and *canopied* by stately trees —Hugh MacLennan⟩

canopy stringer *n* **:** one of a pair of workers who thread shroud lines through holes down the panel seams of a parachute canopy to connect with the harness

canopy switch *n* **:** a small compact electric switch installed in the canopy of a ceiling fixture for direct control of the light at the fixture and usu. operated by a cord or chain

ca·no·rous \kə'nōrəs, -'ó-; 'kanər-\ *adj* [L *canorus*, fr. *canor* melody, fr. *canere* to sing — more at CHANT] **:** marked by or suggestive of melody or song, often full loud swelling song ⟨the ~ noise of the revelers⟩ — **ca·no·rous·ly** *adv*

ca·nos·sa \kə'näsə, -'ó-\ *n* -s *usu cap* [fr. *Canossa*, village in northern Italy where Emperor Henry IV made humble submission to Pope Gregory VII in 1077] **:** a place or occasion of submission, humiliation, or penance — often used with *go to* ⟨he went to his *Canossa* when he reversed his policy⟩

can·o·tier \¦kanə¦tyā\ *n* -s [F, sailor, sailor's hat, fr. MF, sailor, fr. *canot* small boat, alter. of *canoe*, *canoa* canoe — more at CANOE] **:** SAILOR 4

cans *pl of* CAN, *pres 3d sing of* CAN

cansful *pl of* CANFUL

can·so \'kan,sō\ *also* **can·zo** \-,zō\ *n* -s [Prov, fr. L *cantion-*, *cantio* song — more at CANZONE] **:** a troubadour's love song usu. in stanza form

canst *archaic pres 2d sing of* CAN

canstick *n* [by contr.] *obs* **:** CANDLESTICK

[1]**cant** \'kant\ *adj* [ME, prob. fr. (assumed) MLG *kant* (whence LG *kant*)] *dial Eng* **:** LIVELY, VIGOROUS, CHEERFUL

[2]**cant** \'kant, -aa(ə)-, -ai-\ *n* -s [ME, prob. fr. MD or ONF; MD, edge, fr. ONF, fr. L *cantus*, *canthus* iron ring round a carriage wheel, perh. of Celt origin; akin to W *cant* rim, Bret *cant* circle; akin to Gk *kanthos* corner of the eye, Russ *kut* corner] **1** *obs* **:** CORNER, NOOK, NICHE **2 :** an outer or external angle (as of a building) **3 a :** a frame joined obliquely to the keel of a ship **b :** a segment forming a sidepiece in the head of a cask **4** [prob. modif. of D *kanthout*, fr. *kant* edge + *hout* wood; akin to OE *holt* wood — more at HOLT] **:** a log slabbed on one or more sides **5 a :** a sudden thrust producing a bias **b :** the bias so given ⟨to give a beam a ~⟩ **6 :** an oblique or slanting surface (as of a polygon, a buttress, or a bank) **7 :** an inclination from a horizontal, vertical, or other given line **:** SLOPE, BEVEL, TILT ⟨the ~ of a gun barrel⟩ ⟨~ of a helm⟩

[3]**cant** \"\ *vb* -ED/ -ING/ -S *vt* **1 :** to give a cant or oblique edge to **:** cut off an angle from (as the head of a bolt) **:** BEVEL — often used with *off* ⟨~ off a corner⟩ **2 :** to slab (a log) thereby producing cants **3 :** to set at an angle **:** tip or tilt up or over **:** SLOPE, SLANT, INCLINE ⟨~ a cask⟩ ⟨~ a ship⟩ **4 :** to turn completely **:** turn upside down — often used with *over* ⟨~ over a net⟩ **5 :** to turn or throw off or out by tilting or rotating ⟨~ a rifle⟩ **6** *chiefly Brit* **:** to give a sudden turn or new direction to **:** pitch esp. by an unexpected lurch **:** throw with a sudden jerk **:** TOSS ⟨~ round a piece of timber⟩ ~ *vi* **1 :** to pitch to one side **:** LEAN, TILT ⟨the ~*ing* deck of a destroyer⟩ **:** TURN — often used with *over* ⟨the ship ~*ed* over⟩ **2 :** to have a sloping position **:** SLANT, SLOPE ⟨a ~*ing* yardarm⟩ **3** *of a ship* **:** to move into or assume a position oblique to a defined direction or course **:** change direction or swing from a position — sometimes used with *round* or *across*

[4]**cant** \"\ *adj* **1 :** having canted corners or sides ⟨a ~ molding⟩ **2 :** inclined from a perpendicular or other given straight line **:** SLOPING, SLANTING, CANTING, CANTED ⟨a ~ buttress⟩

[5]**cant** \"\ *vb* -ED/ -ING/ -S [prob. fr. ONF *canter* to tell, say, lit., to sing, chant, fr. L *cantare* to sing — more at CHANT] *vi* **1 :** to speak in a whining voice or an affected singsong tone **:** BEG ⟨bade me ~ and whine in some other place —Samuel Johnson⟩ **2 :** to use or speak in cant (as that of thieves or gypsies) or technical terms **3** *dial Eng* **:** TALK, GOSSIP **4 :** to talk with an affectation of piety **:** use religious or solemn language insincerely to gain a reputation for goodness or piety **:** practice hypocrisy ⟨~ about brotherly love⟩ ⟨let them jabber and ~ —Rose Macaulay⟩ ~ *vt* **1 :** to speak or utter as cant or in a manner suggestive of cant esp. of a particular subject, school, or specialty **2** *dial Eng* **:** WHEEDLE, INDULGE

[6]**cant** \"\ *n* -s *often attrib* **1 :** affected singsong speech ⟨a beggar's ~⟩ **2 a :** ARGOT **1 b** *obs* **:** the phraseology peculiar to a religious class or sect **c :** [1]JARGON 3a **3 a** *obs* **:** a set form of words **b :** a set or stock phrase **:** SLANG ⟨a ~ phrase⟩ **4 :** the expression or repetition of conventional, trite, or unconsidered ideas, opinions, or sentiments; *esp* **:** the insincere use of pious phraseology **5** *obs* **:** a user of religious cant **:** HYPOCRITE **6** *chiefly Scot* **:** GOSSIP **syn** see DIALECT

[7]**cant** \'kant\ *n* -s [modif. of MF *encant*, *inquant*, fr. ML *incantum*, *inquantus*, fr. *in quantum* for how much, fr. L *in* + *quantum*, accus. neut. of *quantus* how much — more at IN, QUANTITY] **1** *chiefly Irish* **:** AUCTION **2** *civil law* **:** a mode of partitioning property held in common by sale at auction

[8]**cant** \"\ *vt* -ED/ -ING/ -S *chiefly Irish* **:** to sell by auction

can't \'kant, -aa(ə)-, -ai-; *esp S* -ā-; *esp NewEng & Brit* -ȧ-, -ä-; *sporadically* -e-\ [by contr.] **:** can not

can·tab \'kan·,tab\ *n* -s *usu cap* [by shortening] **:** CANTABRIGIAN

can·ta·bank \'kantə,baŋk\ *n* -s [modif. of It *cantambanco*, *cantimbanco*, fr. *cantare* to sing (fr. L) + *in* on, in (fr. L) + *banco* bench, fr. a Gmc word akin to E *bench* — more at CHANT, [1]IN] **:** a singer from benches or platforms **:** a ballad singer

[1]**can·ta·bi·le** \kän·'täbə,lā, kan·'ta-, kän·'tá-, kən·'t-, -¦lē\ *adj (or adv)* [It, fr. LL *cantabilis* worthy to be sung, fr. L *cantare* to sing] **:** in a singing manner **:** MELODIOUS, FLOWING ⟨a smooth ~ tone⟩ — often used as a direction in music

[2]**cantabile** *n* -s **1 :** cantabile style — used esp. of instrumental music in distinction from recitative or parlando or from the marked rhythm of dance music **2 :** a piece or passage in cantabile style ⟨Schumann's passionate and pleading ~*s* —Abram Chasins⟩

[1]**can·ta·brig·i·an** \,kantə'brij(ē)ən\ *n* -s *cap* [ML *Cantabrigia* Cambridge + E *-an*] **1 a :** a native or resident of Cambridge, England **b :** a student or graduate of Cambridge University **2 a :** a native or resident of Cambridge, Mass. **b :** a student or graduate of Harvard University

[2]**cantabrigian** \¦-ˌ-(ə)-\ *adj, usu cap* **1 :** of, relating to, or characteristic of Cambridge, England, or its university **2 :** of, relating to, or characteristic of Cambridge, Mass. or Harvard University

can·tal \kä'n'täl\ *n* -s *often cap* [F, fr. *Cantal*, department in France where it is made] **:** a hard Cheddar-type cheese made in the south of France

can·ta·la \kan·'tälə\ *n* -s [origin unknown] **:** a hard fiber produced from the leaves of an agave (*Agave cantala*) grown esp. in the Philippines and used for coarse twines (as binder twine) — called also *Cebu maguey*, *maguey*, *manila maguey*

can·ta·loupe *also* **can·ta·loup** *or* **can·ta·lope** *or* **can·te·lope** \'kant[ə]l,ōp, -'aa-, -tə,lōp *also* -üp\ *n* -s [fr. *Cantalupo*, former papal villa near Rome, Italy, where it was first grown in Europe] **1 :** a muskmelon (*Cucumis melo cantalupensis*) grown chiefly in Europe and having a hard ridged or warty rind and reddish orange flesh that is eaten raw as a fruit **2 :** any of several muskmelons resembling the cantaloupe; *broadly* **:** MUSKMELON

can·tan·do \kän·'tän(,)dō\ *adj (or adv)* [It, fr. L *cantandum*, gerund of *cantare* to sing — more at CHANT] **:** CANTABILE — used as a direction in music

can·tan·ker·ous \(')kan·¦ta(i)ŋk(ə)rəs, -aan·¦taŋ-, kən·'t-\ *adj* [perh. irreg. (influence of *cankerous*, *rancorous*) fr. obs. *conteck*, *contack* contention (fr. ME *contek*, *contak*, fr. AF *contek*) + *-ous*] **1** *of a person* **:** marked by ill humor, irritability, and determination to disagree ⟨a ~ and venomous-tongued old lady —Dorothy Sayers⟩ **2** *of an animal or thing* **:** difficult and irritating to deal with or use ⟨a ~ burro⟩ ⟨a ~ pump⟩ **syn** see CONTRARY

can·tan·ker·ous·ly *adv* **:** in a cantankerous manner

can·tan·ker·ous·ness *n* -ES **:** the quality or state of being cantankerous

can·tar *var of* KANTAR

can·ta·rist \'kantərəst\ *n* -s [ML *cantarista*, fr. *cantaria* chantry (fr. L *cantare* to sing) + L *-ista* -ist] **:** a chantry priest

can·ta·ta \kən·'täd·ə, -ä|, ka(a)-,kä-,kȧ-, |tə\ *n* -s [It, fr. *cantare* to sing, fr. L — more at CHANT] **1 :** a narrative poem set to recitative or alternate recitative and melody for a single voice accompanied by one or more instruments **2 :** a sacred or secular choral composition comprising choruses, solos, recitatives, and interludes, usu. accompanied by organ, piano, or orchestra, and arranged in a somewhat dramatic manner but not intended to be acted

can·ta·to·ry \'kantə,tōrē\ *adj* [L *cantatus* + E *-ory*] **:** of or relating to a singer, singing, or esp. chanting

can·ta·trice \,käntə'trēchē; ¦kä'n'tə¦trēs, -änt-\ *n, pl* **cantatrices** \-trēchēz,-trēs(əz)\ *or* **canta·tri·ci** \,käntə'trēchē\ [It & F; F, fr. It, fr. LL *cantatric-*, *cantatrix*, fem. of L *cantator* singer, fr. *cantatus* (past part. of *cantare*) + *-or*] **:** a woman singer; *esp* **:** an opera singer

cant block *n* [[2]*cant*] **:** either block of a cant purchase

cantboard \'-ˌ-\ *n* [[2]*cant* + *board*] **1 :** a board that slopes (as one placed to shed or divert water) **2 :** a board showing the curved outline of a carriage body

cant body *n* [[2]*cant*] **:** a part of the body of a ship in which the frames run obliquely to the keel to form the bow or stern — compare SQUARE BODY

cant dog *n* [[2]*cant*] **:** PEAVEY

canted *adj* [fr. past part. of [3]*cant*] **:** placed at or given a cant **:** ANGLED, SLANTED

can·teen \(')kan·¦tēn, -kaa-\ *n* -s [F *cantine* bottle case, canteen (the shop), fr. It *cantina* wine cellar, fr. *canto* corner, fr. L *cantus* iron ring round a carriage wheel — more at CANT (angle)] **1 a :** a sutler's shop connected with a military post for supplying to enlisted men extra provisions, tobacco, or liquors **b :** POST EXCHANGE — formerly used as the official designation **c** *chiefly Brit* **:** a restaurant or refreshment bar provided by an industrial or commercial concern for employees (as in an office building) **d :** a place of refreshment and recreation maintained by civilians for servicemen **e :** a temporary or mobile restaurant ⟨~*s* were set up in the flooded areas⟩ **2 a :** a partitioned chest or box for holding cutlery **b :** a soldier's mess kit **3 :** a flask typically cloth-jacketed for carrying water or other liquids (as by soldiers or campers)

can·te hon·do *or* **can·te jon·do** \¦käntā'kȯndō, -¦ä-, -'hō-\ *n* [Sp, lit., deep song] **:** FLAMENCO

cantelope *var of* CANTALOUPE

[1]**cant·er** \'kantə(r), -'aa-,-'ai-\ *n* -s [[5]*cant* + *-er*] **:** one that cants **:** one that uses cant: as **a :** BEGGAR, VAGABOND **b :** one that uses professional or religious cant — used esp. in the 17th century as a nickname for a Puritan ⟨the days when he was a ~ and a rebel —T.B.Macaulay⟩

[2]**can·ter** \"\ *vb* **cantered; cantered; cantering** \-ntəriŋ, -n·triŋ\ **canters** [prob. short for obs. *canterbury* to canter,

fr. *canterbury*, n.] *vi* **1 :** to move at or as if at a canter (as of a horse) **:** LOPE **2 :** to ride or go on a cantering horse (as of a rider) ~ *vt* **:** to cause to go at a canter **:** make canter

³**can·ter** \"\ *n* -s **1 a :** a 3-beat gait resembling but smoother and slower than the gallop **b :** a ride at such a gait **:** a brisk ride or other progression **2 :** a waltz step in which the same foot leads at each repetition

⁴**cant·er** \"\ *n* -s [³*cant* + *-er*] **:** an overhead log-turning device in a sawmill that is used in making cants

can·ter·bu·ri·an \ˌkantə(r)ˈbyürēən, ˌkaan-\ *adj, usu cap* [*Canterbury*, city in England + E *-an*] **:** of, relating to, or characteristic of Canterbury, esp. its archbishopric

¹**can·ter·bury** *R* ˈkantə(r),berē, -ˈaa-, -i, *-R* -tə,b-\ *adj, usu cap* [fr. *Canterbury*, city in England] **1 :** of or from the city of Canterbury, England **:** of the kind or style prevalent in Canterbury **:** CANTERBURIAN **2 :** of or from the provincial district of Canterbury, New Zealand **:** of the kind or style prevalent in Canterbury provincial district

²**canterbury** \"\ *n* -ES **1** *usu cap* [fr. the supposed gait of horses ridden by pilgrims to the shrine of Thomas à Becket in Canterbury] *archaic* **:** a moderate and easy gait like a gallop **:** ³CANTER **2** *often cap* **:** a stand with divisions for music, magazines, or loose papers

canterbury bell *n, usu cap C* [fr. *Canterbury*, city in England; prob. fr. the resemblance of the flowers to the small bells on the horses of pilgrims going to Canterbury] **1 :** any of several plants of the genus *Campanula* (esp. *C. medium*, *C. trachelium*, and *C. glomerata*) having blue, pink, or white bell-shaped flowers **2 :** CUCKOOFLOWER 1

canterbury palm *n, usu cap C* [fr. *Canterbury*, provincial district of New Zealand] **:** UMBRELLA PALM 1

canterbury tale *or* **canterbury story** *n, usu cap C* [fr. *The Canterbury Tales*, literary work by Geoffrey Chaucer †1400 Eng. poet, consisting mostly of narrative poems which he puts into the mouths of persons on a pilgrimage to Canterbury] **1 :** a cock-and-bull story **:** YARN, FABLE ⟨a *Canterbury tale* of a leg and an eye and heaven knows what —George Colman †1794⟩ **2 :** a long tedious tale ⟨it grows into a long *Canterbury tale* of two hours —Richard Steele⟩

cant file *n* [²*cant*] **:** a fine-toothed file that is isosceles-triangular in cross section, tapered to a point, and used for sharpening saw teeth

cant frame *n* [*cant (body)*] **:** the frame of the cant body of a ship

canth- *or* **cantho-** *comb form* [NL, fr. *canthus*] **:** canthus **:** canthal ⟨*canth*itis⟩ ⟨*cantho*lysis⟩

can·thal \ˈkan(t)thəl\ *adj* [NL *canthus* + E *-al*] **:** belonging to a canthus

can·tha·rel·lus \ˌkan(t)thəˈreləs\ *n, cap* [NL, dim. of L *cantharus* drinking vessel — more at CANTHARUS] **:** a genus of fungi (family Agaricaceae) distinguished from other white-spored agarics by the low ridgelike and sometimes forked gills of the pileus and including the chanterelle

¹**can·thar·i·dae** \kanˈtharə,dē\ [NL, fr. *Cantharis*, type genus + *-idae*] *syn of* MELOIDAE

²**cantharidae** \"\ *n pl, cap* [NL, fr. *Cantharis*, type genus + *-idae*] **:** a family of nonluminescent elongated soft-bodied beetles (as the soldier beetles) related to and in some classifications including the Lampyridae

can·thar·i·dal \-rədᵊl\ *adj* [*cantharides* + *-al*] **:** relating to or containing cantharides ⟨a ~ plaster⟩

can·thar·i·date \-rə,dāt\ *vt* -ED/-ING/-S [*cantharides* + *-ate*] **:** to treat or impregnate with cantharides

cantharides *pl of* CANTHARIS

cantharides cerate *n* **:** BLISTERING CERATE

can·tha·rid·i·an *or* **can·tha·rid·e·an** \ˌkan(t)thəˈridēən, ˌkaan-\ *adj* [*cantharides* + *-ian* or *-ean* (var. of *-ian*)] **:** composed of or containing cantharides

can·thar·i·din \kanˈtharədᵊn, kaan-, -dən\ *n* -s [F *cantharidine*, fr. L *cantharid-, cantharis* + F *-ine* -in] **:** a bitter crystalline compound $C_{10}H_{12}O_4$ constituting the active vesicating principle of cantharides

can·thar·i·dism \-,dizəm\ *n* -s [*cantharides* + *-ism*] **:** poisoning due to misuse of cantharides

can·thar·i·dize \-,dīz\ *vt* -ED/-ING/-S [*cantharides* + *-ize*] **:** to treat with cantharides

¹**can·tha·ris** \ˈkan(t)thərəs, ˈkaan-\ *n* [alter. (influenced by L *cantharis*) of ME *cantharide*, fr. L *cantharid-, cantharis*, fr. Gk *kantharis*] **1** *pl* **can·thar·i·des** \kanˈtharə,dēz, kaan- *also* -ˈe-\ **:** SPANISH FLY 1 **2 cantharides** *pl but sing or pl in constr* **:** a preparation of dried beetles (as Spanish flies) used as a counterirritant and formerly as an aphrodisiac but being toxic when taken internally — called also *Spanish fly* **3** *cap* [NL, fr. L] **:** the type genus of Cantharidae

²**cantharis** \"\ [NL, fr. L] *syn of* LYTTA

can·tha·rus \ˈkan(t)thərəs\ *or* **kan·tha·ros** \-,räs\ *n, pl* **can·tha·ri** \-,rī, -ē\ *or* **kan·tha·roi** \-ȯi\ [L & Gk; L *cantharus*, fr. Gk *kantharos*] **1 :** a deep cup of ancient Greece with a high stem and loop-shaped handles continuing the curve of the bottom of the body and rising above the brim **2 :** a stoup for holy water

cantho- — see CANTH-

cant hook *n* [²*cant*] **:** a wooden lever resembling a peavey but having a blunt end often with a toe ring and lip instead of a sharp spike

cant hook

can·thus \ˈkan(t)thəs\ *n, pl* **can·thi** \-n,thī, -ē\ [LL, fr. Gk *kanthos* — more at CANT (angle)] **:** either of the angles formed by the meeting of the upper and lower eyelids **:** one of the corners of the eye

canthus ros·tra·lis \-räˈstrāləs, -ˈä-,-ˈā-\ *n, pl* **canthi rostrales** \-(,)lēz\ [NL, lit., rostral canthus] **:** the more or less angular ridge from the anterior border of the eye to the nostril in reptiles and amphibians

can·ti·cle \ˈkantəkəl, -ˈaa-, -ēk-\ *n* -s [ME, fr. L *canticulum* little song, dim. of *canticum* song, fr. *cantus*, past part. of *canere* to sing — more at CHANT] **:** SONG, POEM, HYMN; *specif* **:** one of the biblical hymns or songs of praise (as the Benedicite, the Magnificat, and the Nunc Dimittis) used in church services

can·ti·co \ˈkantə,kō\ *n* -s [modif. of Del *kántka* to dance] **1 :** a ceremonial dance of the Algonquian Indians of the Atlantic seaboard **2 :** a lively social gathering **:** a dancing party **:** DANCE

can·ti·ga \kanˈtēgə\ *n* -s [Sp & Pg; Sp, prob. fr. Pg, prob. of Celt origin; akin to OIr *canim* I sing; akin to L *canere* to sing — more at CHANT] **:** a Portuguese or Spanish folk song usu. having love or religion as its theme

can·til \kanˈtēl, kä-\ *n, pl* **canti·les** \-ē(,)lās\ [AmerSp] **:** a dark-colored Mexican moccasin snake (*Agkistrodon bilineatus*) having a pair of white or yellow lines on each side of the head and the body markings outlined in white

can·ti·le·na \ˌkantᵊlˈānə, -ˈē-\ *n* -s [It, fr. L, song, fr. *cantus*] **1 :** a brief simple melody often repeated (as in a lullaby or folk song) **2 :** sustained melody **:** CANTABILE

¹**can·ti·le·ver** \ˈkantᵊl,ēvə(r), -ˈaa-, -tə,lē- *also* -,e-\ *n* -s *often attrib* [perh. fr. ²*cant* + *-i-* + *lever*] **:** a projecting beam or member supported at only one end (as by being built into a wall or a pier): as **a :** a bracketlike member supporting a balcony or a cornice — compare BRACKET **b :** either of the two beams or trusses that project from piers toward each other and that when joined directly or by a suspended connecting member form a span of a cantilever bridge

cantilever a

²**cantilever** \"\ *vt* -ED/-ING/-S **:** to build or project as a cantilever

cantilever arch *n* **:** an archlike spanning structure made by corbeling opposed surfaces **:** a corbel arch

cantilever bridge *n* **1 :** a bridge whose span consists of two cantilever trusses that project toward each other and that are usu. joined by a suspended connecting member — see BRIDGE illustration **2 :** a dental bridge having one end attached to a natural tooth and the other resting unattached in a tooth depression

cantilever spring *n* **:** a flat spring supported at one end and fastened to its load at the center and the other end; *specif* **:** a leaf spring so used in the rear suspension of an automobile

cantilever truss *n* **:** a horizontal truss supported at the middle and sustaining a load at one end or both ends (as in a cantilever bridge)

can·til·late \ˈkantᵊl,āt\ *vt* -ED/-ING/-S [L *cantillatus*, past part. of *cantillare* to sing low, hum, fr. *cantare* to sing — more at CHANT] **:** to recite with musical usu. improvised tones (as in synagogues and highly liturgical churches) **:** CHANT, INTONE

can·til·la·tion \ˌ==ˈāshən\ *n* -s [L *cantillatus* + E *-ion*] **:** liturgical chanting **:** INTONATION

cant·i·ly \ˈkantəli, -ˈä-\ *adv* [*canty* + *-ly*] *Scot* **:** CHEERFULLY

can·ti·na \kan·ˈtēnə\ *n* -s [AmerSp, fr. Sp, lunch box, canteen (the shop), wine cellar, fr. It, wine cellar — more at CANTEEN] *Southwest* **1 :** a pouch or bag at the pommel of a saddle ⟨put the mail into his ~s and rode off⟩ **2** [AmerSp, fr. Sp, canteen (the shop)] **:** a small barroom **:** SALOON

cant·ing \ˈkantiŋ, -ˈaa-, -ˈai-, -ēŋ\ *adj* [fr. pres. part. of ⁵*cant*] **1 :** affectedly pious **:** HYPOCRITICAL ⟨a ~ moralist⟩ **2 :** ALLUSIVE; *esp* **:** alluding in the manner of a rebus to the name of the bearer or owner — used of heraldic bearings, figures on bookplates, and other emblems ⟨the three castles of the Castletons are ~ bearings⟩

canting quoin *or* **canting coin** *n* [fr. pres. part. of ³*cant*] **:** a triangular block for steadying stowed casks in a ship

can·ti·no \kanˈtē(,)nō, kä-\ *n* -s [It, fr. *canto* song — more at CANTO] **:** ²CHANTERELLE

cantion *n* -s [L *cantion-, cantio* — more at CANZONE] *obs* **:** SONG

¹**can·tle** \ˈkantᵊl, -ˈaa-,-ˈai-\ *n* -s [ME *cantel*, fr. ONF, dim. of *cant* edge, corner — more at CANT (angle)] **1 :** a segment or slice cut off or out from something (as from a piece of land or a cheese) **:** PART, PORTION ⟨cutting off . . . a solid ~ of high land from the rest of Yorkshire —Richard Blackmore⟩ **2 :** the upwardly projecting rear part of a saddle — compare POMMEL; see STOCK SADDLE illustration **3** *Scot* **:** the crown of the head

²**can·tle** *vt* -ED/-ING/-S *obs* **:** to divide into cantles **:** PORTION

cant·let \ˈkantlət\ *n* -s [¹*cantle* + *-et*] **:** a small cantle **:** PIECE, FRAGMENT ⟨a ~ of cold custard pudding —Charlotte Brontë⟩

cantline *var of* CONTLINE

cant·ly \ˈkantlē, -ˈaa-,-ˈai-, -i\ *adv* [⁶*cant* + *-ly*] **:** in canting terms **:** SLANGILY

cant molding *n* [²*cant*] **:** a beveled molding

can·to \ˈkan(,)tō, -ˈä-,-ˈaa-,-ˈá-\ *n* -s [It, fr. L *cantus* song — more at CHANT] **1 :** one of the major divisions of a long poem **2 :** the melody in choral or instrumental music **3** *slang* **:** one of the divisions of a sports contest (as an inning of baseball)

can·to fer·mo \ˌkän(,)tōˈfer(,)mō\ *n* [It, lit., firm song, trans. of ML *cantus firmus*] **:** CANTUS FIRMUS

¹**can·ton** \ˈkantᵊn, -ˈaa-, -ntən; ˈka(a)n·ˌtän, (ˈ)=ˈ=\ *n* -s [MF, fr. OProv, fr. *cant* edge, fr. L *cantus, canthus* iron ring round a carriage wheel — more at CANT (angle)] **1** *obs* **:** DIVISION, PART, SECTION; *esp* **:** CORNER **2** [MF, fr. It *cantone*, fr. *canto* corner, fr. L *cantus, canthus*] **a :** a small territorial division of a country **b :** a district or local governing unit: as (1) **:** one of the states of the Swiss confederation (2) **:** a division of a French arrondissement **3 a :** the area in the upper inner corner of a flag; *specif* **:** a rectangular division occupying the upper inner corner of a flag, usu. comprising one fourth or less of its surface, and usu. containing the national or other device — compare UNION 4 **b :** any one of the four quarters of the surface of a flag **4 a** (1) **:** a rectangular division of a heraldic field usu. placed in the dexter chief (2) **:** the dexter chief region of a heraldic field **b :** any one of the spaces left in the four corners of a heraldic field by a cross; *specif* **:** the dexter chief canton

canton 4a(1)

²**can·ton** *vb* -ED/-ING/-S *vt* **1** \"\ **:** to divide into parts **:** PORTION; *specif* **:** to divide into cantons or districts — often used with *out* **2** \ˈ(ˌ)ka(a)n·ˌtōn, -tän, kən·ˈt- *also* ˈka(a)ntᵊn *or* -ntən; *Brit usu, US sometimes* (ˈ)ka(a)n·ˌtün *or* kən-ˈt-\ [F *cantonner*, fr. *canton* part of a country] **:** to allot quarters to (as to a body of troops) **:** QUARTER ~ *vi* *pronounced like vt 2*\ *of troops* **:** to take up quarters

³**can·ton** \ˈkan·ˌtän, -ˈaa-, =ˈ=\ *adj, usu cap* [fr. *Canton*, city in S.E. China] **:** of or from the city of Canton, China **:** of the kind or style prevalent in Canton **:** CANTONESE

⁴**can·ton** \ˈkantᵊn, -ˈaa-, -tən\ *adj, usu cap* [fr. *Canton*, city in Ohio] **:** of or from the city of Canton, Ohio ⟨a *Canton* product⟩ **:** of the kind or style prevalent in Canton

⁵**canton** *like* ³CANTON\ *n* -s *often cap* [prob. fr. *Canton*, city in S.E. China] **:** HOLLAND BLUE

can·ton·al \ˈka(a)ntᵊnᵊl, -tən-, (ˈ)ka(a)n·ˌtän-\ *adj* [F, fr. *canton* + *-al*] **:** of or relating to a canton — **can·ton·al·ism** \-,lizəm\ *n* -s

canton crepe \ˈka(a)n·ˌtän-\ *n, often cap 1st C* [fr. *Canton*, China] **:** a soft thick dress crepe made of silk or rayon in plain weave with fine crosswise ribs

cantoned *adj* [fr. past part. of ²*canton*] **1** *of a heraldic cross* **:** having a charge in each of the four cantons or angular spaces between the branches ⟨a cross ~ with four martlets⟩ **2 :** having the angles or exterior corners provided or decorated with projecting members (as moldings or small columns) ⟨a ~ pier⟩

¹**can·ton·ese** \ˌka(a)ntᵊnˈēz, -ntəˈn-, -ēs\ *adj, usu cap* [*Canton*, China + E *-ese*] **:** of or relating to Canton, China, its inhabitants, or their dialect

²**cantonese** \"\ *n, pl* **cantonese** *cap* **1 :** a native or inhabitant of Canton, China **2 :** the dialect of Chinese spoken in and around Canton

canton flannel \ˈka(a)n·ˌtän-\ *n, often cap C* [fr. *Canton*, China] **:** FLANNEL 1b (2)

canton ginger \"–\ *n, usu cap C* [fr. *Canton*, China] **:** a fine grade of crystallized or preserved ginger

can·ton·i·za·tion \ˌka(a)ntᵊnəˈzāshən, (ˌ)ka(a)n·ˌtän-\ *n* -s **:** the process of cantonizing

can·ton·ize \ˈka(a)ntᵊn,īz\ *vt* -ED/-ING/-S [¹*canton* + *-ize*] **:** CANTON 1

can·ton·ment \kan·ˈtōnmənt, kaan-·,kən-·, -tän- *also* ˈka(a)ntᵊn- *or* -ntən- *or* -n·,tän-; *Brit usu, US sometimes* ka(a)n·ˈtün- *or* kən-·\ *n* -s [F *cantonnement*, fr. *cantonner* to canton (troops) — more at CANTON] **1 :** the quartering of troops **2 a :** a group of more or less temporary structures for housing troops ⟨all hands now set to work to prepare a winter ~ —Washington Irving⟩ **b** *India* **:** a permanent military station

cantons *pl of* CANTON, *pres 3d sing of* CANTON

can·ton's phosphorus \ˈka(a)ntᵊnz-, -ntənz-\ *n, usu cap C* [after John *Canton* †1772 Eng. physicist, its discoverer] **:** phosphorescent calcium sulfide CaS

canton ware \ˈka(a)n·ˌtän-, (ˈ)=ˈ=-\ *n, usu cap C* [fr. *Canton*, China, whence it was imported] **:** ceramic ware exported from China esp. during the 18th and 19th centuries mostly by way of Canton and including blue-and-white and enameled porcelain and various ornamented stonewares

can·tor \ˈkantə(r), -ˈaa-,-ˈai-\ *n* -s [L, singer, fr. *cantus* (past part. of *canere* to sing) + *-or* — more at CHANT] **1 :** a choir leader **:** PRECENTOR ⟨the ~ of the church intones the Te Deum —H.H.Milman⟩ **2 :** a synagogue official who sings or chants liturgical music and leads the congregation in prayer — called also *hazan*

can·tor·ate \-ərət,-ə,rāt\ *n* -s **1 :** the office or tenure of office of a cantor **2 :** the body of cantors

can·to·ria \ˌkantəˈrēə\ *n, pl* **cantori·as** \-ˈrēəz\ *or* **canto·rie** \-ˈrē,ā\ [It, fr. *cantore* singer (fr. L *cantor*) + *-ia* -y] **:** a balcony for singers; *specif* **:** the choir gallery in an Italian church

can·to·ri·al \(ˈ)kan·ˌtōrēəl, -ˌȯ-\ *or* **can·tor·al** \ˈka(a)ntərəl, -ˈai- *also* **can·tor·ous** \ˈ==rəs\ *adj* [*cantor* + *-ial* or *-al* or *-ous*] **1 :** of or being the ecclesiastical north side of the choir of a cathedral or church — contrasted with *decanal* **2:** of or relating to a cantor ⟨a ~ position⟩

can·to·ris \(ˈ)kan·ˌtōrəs, -aan-, -ȯr-\ *adj* [L, gen. of *cantor*] **:** CANTORIAL

cantos *pl of* CANTO

cant purchase *n* [²*cant*] **:** a powerful tackle used to cant a whale in the operation of flensing

can·tred \ˈkan·,tred\ *or* **can·tref** \-ev\ *n* -s [ME *cantrede*, *candrede* fr. ML *cantredus, candredus*, modif. (prob. influenced by ML *hundredus* hundred, division of an English county) of MW *cantref*, fr. *cant* hundred + *tref* home, town; akin to L *centum* hundred and to OE *thorp* village] **:** an obsolete Welsh territorial unit composed of a hundred trefs **:** HUNDRED

can·trip *also* **can·trap** *or* **can·traip** \ˈkän·trəp\ *n* -s *often attrib* [prob. alter. of *caltrop*] *chiefly Scot* **:** SPELL **:** a witch's trick **:** a mischievous or extravagant act

cants *pl of* CANT, *pres 3d sing of* CANT

cant·saw file \ˈ=,=-\ *n* [²*cant* + *saw*] **:** a file similar to the cant file but slightly thicker and not tapered

cant spar *n* [prob. fr. *cant* "frame joined obliquely to the keel" — more at ²CANT] **:** a small pole suitable for a small mast, yard, or boom

cant strip *n* [²*cant*] **1 :** a beveled strip placed in the angle between a roof and a wall against which the roof abuts so as to avoid a sharp bend in the roofing material **2 :** a strip used under the lower edge of the lowest row of tiles on a roof to give this row the same slope as the rows above it

cant timber *n* [²*cant*] **:** a timber of a cant frame of a ship

can·tua \kan·ˈtüə\ *n, cap* [NL, fr. Sp *cantú* cantuta, fr. Quechua *ccantu*] **:** a genus of shrubs or small trees (family Polemoniaceae) having crowded, simple, short-stalked or sessile leaves, flowers in close terminal clusters, and a corolla with a slender tube much exceeding the calyx — see CANTUTA

can·tus \ˈkantəs, -ˈaa-\ *n, pl* **cantus** [L, song — more at CHANT] **1 :** CANTUS FIRMUS **2 :** the principal melody or voice

cantus fir·mus \-ˈfirməs, -ˈfər-\ *n* [ML, lit., fixed song] **1 :** the plainchant or simple Gregorian melody that was orig. sung in unison and prescribed as to form and use by ecclesiastical tradition **2 :** a melodic theme or subject; *esp* **:** one for contrapuntal treatment

cantus ge·mel·lus \-jəˈmeləs, -gə-\ *n* [ML, lit., twin song] **:** GYMEL

cantus men·su·ra·bi·lis \-,men(t)səˈräbələs, -nchə-, -ab-\ *n* [ML, lit., measurable song] **:** MEASURED MUSIC 2

cantus pla·nus \-ˈplänəs, -ˈā-\ *n* [ML, lit., plain song] **:** CANTUS FIRMUS 1

can·tu·ta \kan·ˈtüd·ə\ *also* **can·tut** \-üt\ *n* -s [Sp, *cantuta*, var. of *cantú* — more at CANTUA] **:** a shrub or small tree (*Cantua buxifolia*) used as an ornamental in the southwestern U. S. and having a showy yellow-striped pink or red flower — called also *Inca magic flower*

cant window *n* [²*cant*] **:** a projecting window with angles — sometimes distinguished from *bow window*

canty \ˈkanti, -ˈä-\ *adj* [¹*cant* + *-y*] *dial Brit* **:** CHEERFUL, SPRIGHTLY, LIVELY

ca·nuck \kəˈnək\ *n* -s *cap, often attrib* [prob. alter. of ²*Canadian*] **1 :** CANADIAN **2** *chiefly Canad* **:** FRENCH CANADIAN **3 :** CANADIAN FRENCH — usu. used disparagingly

canula *var of* CANNULA

ca·nun \käˈnün\ *or* **ca·non** \-ˈnōn\ *n* -s [Turk & Ar; Turk *kānun*, fr. Ar *qānūn*, fr. Gk *kanōn* monochord, measuring line, standard — more at CANON] **:** ZITHER

can·u·ti·llo \ˌkan(y)əˈtē(,)ō\ *n* -s [MexSp, fr. Sp *canutillo*, *cañutillo* little tube, dim. of *canuto, cañuto* tube, pipe, section of cane, fr. Ar dial. (Spain) *qannūt*, fr. (assumed) VL *cannutus* of cane, fr. L *canna* cane — more at CANE] **:** MORMON TEA

¹**can·vas** *also* **can·vass** \ˈkanvəs, -ˈaa-\ *n* -ES *often attrib* [ME *canevas*, fr. ONF, fr. (assumed) VL *cannabaceus* hempen, fr. L *cannabis* hemp, fr. Gk *kannabis* — more at HEMP] **1 :** a firm closely woven cloth of plain weave made in various weights usu. of linen, hemp, or cotton and used esp. for clothing, sails, tarpaulins, and awnings — compare ⁴DUCK **2 :** a set of sails **:** SAIL ⟨sailing under full ~⟩ ⟨under light ~⟩ **3 :** a piece of canvas used for a particular purpose: as **a :** a covering over the end of a racing boat to keep out water **b :** APRON 4a **4 :** a tent or a group of tents: **a :** CIRCUS, CARNIVAL ⟨the lure of the ~⟩ **b :** a military or camping tent ⟨sleeping under ~⟩ **5 a** (1) **:** a cloth surface prepared to receive an oil painting (2) **:** the painting on such a surface **b :** the background, setting, or scope of an historical or fictional account or narrative ⟨the crowded ~ of history⟩ **c :** PICTURE 9a **6 :** a stiff material with coarse even meshes woven usu. of hard-twisted yarns in a plain weave often with drawable threads for tapestry and embroidery **7 :** a linen or hair-and-wool canvas with a soft or sized finish used as an interlining or foundation to give body to some part of a garment, esp. a coat front **8 :** the floor of a boxing or wrestling ring — **on the canvas :** knocked down **:** close to defeat

²**canvas** \"\ *vt* **canvased** *or* **canvassed; canvased** *or* **canvassed; canvasing** *or* **canvassing; canvases** *or* **canvasses** **:** to cover, line, or furnish with canvas ⟨the door had been nailed up and ~*ed* over —Charles Dickens⟩

³**canvas** *var of* CANVASS

can·vas·back \ˈ=,=\ *also* **canvasback duck** *n* [so called fr. its color] **:** a No. American wild duck (*Aythya valisineria*) formerly abundant in Chesapeake Bay and somewhat resembling the redhead in plumage but differing in the longer deeper bill and in the duller reddish brown head of the male which has the back finely vermiculated with gray and white

canvas board *n* **1 :** a board having a textured surface often stamped or molded in imitation of canvas to receive an artist's painting **2 :** CANVAS PANEL

can·vas·man \-,man, -mən, -,maa(ə)n\ *n, pl* **canvasmen** **1 :** a circus employee who assists in the pitching and taking down of tents **2 :** BRATTICER

canvas panel *n* **:** a surface composed of canvas mounted on stiff board and prepared to receive an artist's painting

¹**can·vass** *also* **can·vas** \ˈkanvəs, -ˈaa-\ *vb* -ED/-ING/-ES [¹*canvas*] *vt* **1** *obs* **:** to toss in or as if in a canvas sheet by way of sport or punishment ⟨I'll ~ thee between a pair of sheets —Shak.⟩ **2 a** *obs* **:** to knock about **:** BEAT, TROUNCE **b** *archaic* **:** to lash with criticism or invective **:** CASTIGATE ⟨the ribald style in which Martin Marprelate ~*ed* the bishops —E.K.Chambers⟩ **3 a :** to examine in detail **:** subject to scrutiny or investigation; *specif* **:** to examine (votes) officially for authenticity **b :** DISCUSS, DEBATE ⟨~*ed* all the items on the agenda⟩ **4** *archaic* **:** to strive after (as approval) ⟨kings sometimes ~*ed* that title for themselves —Oliver Goldsmith⟩ **5 a :** to go through (a district) or go to (persons) to solicit orders, subscriptions, or advertising **b :** to cover (a district) or go to (persons) to solicit political support or to try to ascertain the probable vote before an election ⟨the candidate is ~*ing* the farm belt this week⟩ **c :** to determine the opinions or sentiments of (as the members of a club or the staff of an institution) esp. by informal questioning **:** POLL ⟨the faculty was ~*ed* on its preferences in teaching schedules⟩ **6** *chiefly Brit* **a :** to put forward (as a plan or an idea) **b :** SPREAD, CIRCULATE ⟨~*ing* rumors⟩ ~ *vi* **1 :** DEBATE, DISCUSS **2 a :** to seek orders, contributions, support, subscriptions, or advertising **:** SOLICIT ⟨~ for a newspaper⟩ ⟨~ in behalf of a charity⟩ **b :** to solicit votes or seek political support in an election campaign ⟨~ for a seat in Parliament⟩

²**canvass** \"\ *n* -ES **1 a :** a detailed examination esp. by means of discussion or debate **:** full discussion ⟨learned ~*es* of the deep points of divinity —Joseph Hall⟩ **b :** a scrutiny esp. of votes ⟨a ~ of the election returns⟩ **2 :** the act or action of canvassing ⟨a house-to-house ~⟩: as **a :** the personal solicitation of votes **b :** a survey to ascertain the probable vote before an election

³**canvass** *var of* CANVAS

can·vass·er \-sə(r)\ *n* -s **:** one that canvasses: as **a :** one that takes or counts votes **b :** a solicitor esp. for funds or subscriptions **:** a campaign worker **c :** a door-to-door salesman

canvas shoe *n* **:** a light shoe with a canvas upper and a rubber, leather, or fiber sole **:** TENNIS SHOE

canvas work *n* **:** embroidery worked usu. in cross-stitch or tent stitch on canvas or by the aid of canvas — compare PETIT POINT

cany \ˈkānē\ *adj, sometimes* -ER/-EST [¹*cane* + *-y*] **1 :** made of cane **2 :** abounding in canes **3 :** characterized by canebrakes

¹**can·yon** *also* **ca·ñon** \ˈkanyən\ *n* -s [AmerSp *cañón*, prob. alter. of obs. Sp *callón*, aug. of *calle* street, fr. L *callis* footpath; akin to Czech *klanec* mountain pass] **1 a :** a deep narrow valley with precipitous sides characteristic of regions where downward cutting of the streams greatly exceeds weathering **:** GORGE **b :** a long deep steep-sided depression in the ocean floor typically on the continental shelf and opening out in a deep basin — called also *submarine canyon;* compare DEEP, TRENCH, TROUGH **c :** a city street bordered on both sides by lofty buildings ⟨the ~*s* of the financial district⟩ **2 :** PLUM VIOLET

[2]canyon *also* **cañon** \"\ *vb* -ED/-ING/-S *vt* : to make a canyon in : pierce with canyons ~ *vi* : to enter or flow into a canyon (as of a stream) : narrow into a canyon (as of a valley)

canyon gooseberry *n* **1** : the globose bristly fruit of a low shrub (*Ribes menziesii*) of the western U. S. **2** : the shrub yielding the canyon gooseberry

canyon grape *n* : a grape (*Vitis arizonica*) of Texas and Arizona yielding inferior black fruit

canyon live oak *or* **canyon oak** *n* : a California evergreen oak (*Quercus chrysolepis*) with oblong leathery often spiny-edged leaves covered on the under side with a yellow tomentum — called also *iron oak, maul oak*

canyon mouse *n* : a white-footed mouse (*Peromyscus crinitus*) widely distributed in rocky areas of the western U. S.

can·yon·side \'==,=\ *n* : the steeply sloping side of a canyon

canyon wren *n* : a common wren (*Catherpes mexicanus*) having a white breast and rusty belly and occurring in several local races in the southwestern U. S.

canzo *var of* CANSO

canzon *n* -S [It *canzone*] *archaic* : SONG

can·zo·ne \kan'zōnē, känt'sō(,)nā\ *also* **can·zo·na** \-ōnə\ *n, pl* **canzo·ne** \-ō(,)nā\ *also* **canzonas** \-ōnəz\ *or* **canzo·ni** \-ō(,)nē\ *or* **canzones** \-ōnēz, -ō(,)nāz\ [It, fr. L *cantion-, cantio* song, fr. *cantus* (past part. of *canere* to sing) + *-ion-, -io* -ion — more at CHANT] **1 a** : a medieval Italian or Provençal lyric poem in stanzaic form **b** : an elaborately constructed ode suited to musical setting **2 a** : the melody of a canzone **b** : a setting of a canzone in polyphonic style resembling that of the madrigal **c** : an instrumental composition in similar style

can·zo·net \,kanzə'net\ *also* **can·zo·net·ta** \,kanzə'ned·ə\ *n, pl* **canzonets** \-ets\ *also* **canzonettas** \-ed·əz\ *or* **canzo·net·te** \-ed·ē\ [It *canzonetta*, dim. of *canzone*] **1** : a short canzone : a part-song resembling but less elaborate than a madrigal **2** : a light and graceful song

CAO *abbr* chief administrative officer

ca·o·ba \kä'ōbə\ *n* -S [Sp, fr. Taino *caoban*] **1** : MAHOGANY 3a **2** : QUIRA

cao dai \(')kaủ'dī\ *n, pl* **cao dai** *cap C&D* [Vietnamese] : CAODAISM

cao·da·ism \(')kaủ'dī,izəm\ *n* -S *cap* [Vietnamese *Cao Dai*, lit., great palace + E *-ism*] : an Indo-Chinese religion originating in Cochin China in 1926, consisting of an amalgamation of elements from Buddhism, Taoism, Confucianism, Christianity, and spiritualism, and having its clergy headed by a pope who as the direct representative of its supreme deity exercises both spiritual and temporal power

cao·da·ist \-īəst\ *n* -S *usu cap* : an adherent of Caodaism

caoine \'kēn\ *n* -S [IrGael] *Irish* : [5]KEEN

caou·tchouc \(')kaủ'chük, -ük, kə'ch-, *F* kaüchü\ *n* -S [F, fr. obs. Sp *cauchuc* (now *caucho*), fr. Quechua *cauchu, caucho, cauchuc*] : [1]RUBBER 2a

caoutchouc tree *n* : PARA RUBBER

[1]cap \'kap\ *n* -S *often attrib* [ME *cappe*, fr. OE *cæppe*, fr. LL *cappa* head covering, cloak, perh. irreg. fr. L *caput* head — more at HEAD] **1** : a covering for the head typically fairly tight-fitting, brimless, and relatively simple: as **a** : one with a full crown and a ruffled edge gathered on or held by a ribbon band and worn formerly by women **b** : one of fabric, yarn, rubber, or leather, without brim, with or without visor, chin strap, or earflaps, and with a crown ranging from shallow to deep and from soft to stiff **c** : HELMET, HEADPIECE **d** : a man's or boy's cap typically with a visor of some stiffness **e** : one without a brim, fitting close to the crown of the head, made usu. of fabric, often elaborately trimmed, and worn by women **2** : something that covers naturally : a natural cover or top: as **a** : an overlying rock layer or stratum usu. hard to penetrate: as (1) : an impervious layer immediately over the oil-producing or gas-producing formation in an oil pool (2) : dense usu. limestone or anhydrite rock immediately above the salt in a salt dome (3) *or* **cap rock** : a bed of resistant rock, boulders, or gravel at the summit of a mesa, hill, or cliff **b** (1) : PILEUS (2) : CALYPTRA **c** : KNEECAP, PATELLA **d** : WHITECAP **e** : POLAR CAP, ICE CAP **f** (1) : the whole top of a bird's head from the base of the bill to the nape of the neck (2) : a patch of distinctively colored feathers on the head of many birds **g** : the wax covering for the individual cell made by bees in sealing up honey or pupae in the comb **h** *Northeast* : CORNHUSK **3** : something that serves as a cover or protection esp. for a tip, knob, or end : something designed to cover and to protect, preserve, or close (as over a camera lens, fountain pen, automobile hub, or narrow-mouthed bottle): **a** : the separate piece of leather commonly attached to the vamp at the toe of a shoe as a covering — called also *tip* **b** : a fitting for closing the end of a tube (as a water pipe or electric conduit); *esp* : an internally threaded cup-shaped part that screws on **c** : a covering of tarred canvas for the end of a rope **d** : a readily removable protective cover or plate over a lock (as on a door) or latch **e** : the part of an electrical attachment plug or cord connector to which a flexible conductor is attached **f** : a paper covering placed over the gold edges of fine books until they are bound **g** : a sheet-steel cone placed over the end of a log to facilitate its being skidded esp. by steam power **h** : a layer of new rubber fused onto the worn surface of a pneumatic tire **i** : a blunt nose that is fitted onto an armor-piercing projectile (as a shell) **4** *archaic* : a respectful doffing of one's cap ⟨he that will give a ~ and make a leg in thanks —Thomas Fuller⟩ **5** : a cap as a token or symbol: as **a** : a cardinal's biretta **b** : a cap worn by students and officers of schools, colleges, and universities typically tight-fitting and having a flat projecting square top with a tassel — see MORTARBOARD **c** *Brit* (1) : a cap awarded to an athlete (as a soccer player) in recognition of membership on a national or other representative team ⟨he gained his county ~⟩ (2) : a player awarded a cap ⟨a new ~ was brought in to replace the halfback⟩ **d** : a white cap worn by graduate nurses or by student nurses after a probationary period **6** : an overlaying or covering structure : something that is placed or constructed above ⟨the galleried ~ of the old water tower is sometimes open to visitors⟩: **a** : the uppermost of any assemblage of architectural parts esp. of a column, door, or molding (as a capital, lintel, cornice, or coping) **b** (1) : a horizontal support typically of heavy timber for the roof of a mine working (2) : the narrowing of an ore vein by contraction at its upper part **c** : CAPSHEAF **7** : a device for joining together masts or spars consisting either of a thick wood block with two large holes or of a metal collar — see SHIP illustration **8 a** : a paper or metal container holding an explosive charge : such a device used to detonate another charge **b** : a firearm primer **c** : a minute explosive charge sealed between the layers of a paper strip for use in a toy gun **d** : a BB or CB cap **9** : a blue tip on a safety-lamp flame that shows the presence of firedamp **10** *Brit* : the collection taken at a fox hunt esp. from nonsubscribers — **cap in hand** : RESPECTFULLY, SUBMISSIVELY, OBSEQUIOUSLY

caps 3, *A*

[2]cap \"\ *vb* **capped; capped; capping; caps** [ME *cappen*, fr. *cappe*, n.] *vt* **1** : to provide with a cap : put a cap on : cover, protect, or close with or as if with a cap : cover the top or end of ⟨Corinthian columns *capped* by Grecian spans of Bedford limestone —*Amer. Guide Series: Texas*⟩: as **a** : to give a cap to as a symbol of honor or rank: (1) *Scot* : to confer a university degree on (2) : to invest (a student nurse) with a cap as an indication of completion of a probationary period of study **b** : to cover (a diseased or exposed part of a tooth) with a protective substance (as a paste) **c** : to seal off (an oil or gas well) by clamping a cap over the end of a casing **d** : to seal (a cell of a honeycomb) with wax **e** (1) : to put a cap on the nipple of (a percussion lock) (2) : to seat a cap or primer in the recess in the base of (a cartridge case) **2** *archaic* : to salute by tipping one's cap to ⟨you would not ~ the pope's commissioner —Alfred Tennyson⟩ **3** *dial* : SURPRISE, PUZZLE, PERPLEX **4** : to form a cap over : CROWN, COVER, OVERLAY ⟨limestone ledges a few feet in thickness ~ the hills —*Amer. Guide Series: La.*⟩ ⟨the mountains were *capped* with mist —John Buchan⟩ **5 a** : to follow with something more noticeable or more significant : proffer as better or more extreme : OUTDO, SURPASS, EXCEL ⟨*capped* the comment with a remark still more immodest —Dorothy Sayers⟩ **b** : to provide with a high point, zenith, or acme : CLIMAX ⟨suppose he ~s his studies by marrying one of the doctor's daughters —William Black⟩ ⟨St. Thomas ~s his ethical system with a doctrine of salvation —Frank Thilly⟩ **c** : to reply to in order with an appropriate answer or quotation according to set rules (as calling for a verse beginning with the initial or final letter of what has been previously offered) ⟨I'll ~ verses with him —John Dryden⟩ ⟨a group of farmers *capping* alliterative sentences with one another —F.M.Stenton⟩ **6** : to take the cap off or away from ⟨~ a bottle⟩ ⟨~ a comb of honey⟩ ~ *vi* : to take off one's cap in respectful salute ⟨they ~ when they pass the dean⟩ — **cap the climax** : to exceed a plausible climax : pass the limits of what might be expected

[3]cap *vt* **capped; capped; capping; caps** [prob. fr. ONF *caper* to seize, prob. fr. *cape* cloak with hood, fr. LL *cappa* head covering, cloak — more at CAP (head covering)] *obs* : ARREST, SEIZE

[4]cap \'kap\ *n* -S [alter. of earlier Sc *cop*, fr. ME, cup, bowl, fr. OE *copp* cup; akin to OHG *kopf* cup, ON *koppr*; all fr. a prehistoric NGmc-WGmc word borrowed fr. LL *cuppa* — more at CUP] *Scot* : a shallow wooden bowl often with two handles

[5]cap \'kap\ *n* -S *often attrib* [by shortening] : a capital letter ⟨the names of places written in ~s⟩

[6]cap \"\ *vt* **capped; capped; capping; caps** [by shortening] : CAPITALIZE

[7]cap \"\ *n* -S [by shortening] : a handicap race

[8]cap \"\ *n* -S [by shortening] : a capsule esp. of heroin

cap *abbr* **1** capacity **2** \'kap\ capital **3** capitulum **4** captain **5** caput

ca·pa \'käpə\ *n* -S [Sp, fr. LL *cappa* hooded cloak — more at CAP (head covering)] **1 a** : a circular mantle or cloak **b** : a bullfighter's cape **2** [AmerSp, fr. Sp, cloak] : a fine grade of Cuban tobacco used largely for wrappers

ca·pa·bil·i·ty \,kāpə'biləd·ē, -ətē, -i\ *n* -ES [LL *capabilis* + E *-ity*] **1** : the quality or state of being capable physically, intellectually, morally, or legally : CAPACITY, ABILITY ⟨participating in sports according to their *capabilities*⟩ ⟨developed the *capabilities* that made him a nationally known mining engineer⟩ **2** : a feature or faculty capable of development or likely to improve : a latent usu. valuable characteristic : POTENTIALITY ⟨there were great *capabilities* in the scenery —T.L.Peacock⟩ **3** : the quality or state of being susceptible to action or treatment as indicated ⟨the ~ of a metal to be fused⟩

ca·pa·ble \'kāpəbəl, *rapid* -pb-\ *adj, sometimes* -ER/-EST [MF or LL; MF *capable*, fr. LL *capabilis*, irreg. fr. L *capere* to take, contain — more at HEAVE] **1** *archaic* **a** : able to take in, contain, receive, or accommodate ⟨a room ~ of 20 people⟩ ⟨a harbor ~ of the largest ships⟩ **b** : able to perceive or comprehend ⟨an ear ~ of faint sounds⟩ ⟨when he became ~ of ordinary occurrences she detailed all —James Stephens⟩ **2** : constituted, situated, or characterized as susceptible or open to being affected — used postpositively with following *of* ⟨such as we, not ~ of death or pain —John Milton⟩ ⟨an order ~ of execution⟩ ⟨a passage ~ of misinterpretation⟩ ⟨a formal doctrine ~ of being expressed in a few catchwords —Lewis Mumford⟩ **3** *obs* : INCLUSIVE, COMPREHENSIVE ⟨a ~ and wide revenge —Shak.⟩ **4** : having sufficient power, prowess, intelligence, resources, strength, or other needed attributes to perform or accomplish — usu. used postpositively with *of* followed by a gerund or actional noun ⟨a highly intelligent man, ~ of close application of mind —Charles Dickens⟩ ⟨children are not ~ of looking after their own interests —Bertrand Russell⟩ ⟨ships ~ of facing the heavy seas —J.A.Froude⟩ **5** : marked by or possessed of a predisposition to : having characteristics or personality traits conducive to or admitting of — used postpositively with *of* ⟨all who are ~ of absorption in an inward passion —Bertrand Russell⟩ ⟨this woman is ~ of murder by violence —Robert Graves⟩ ⟨a grace and dexterity of which no common maid is ~ —Lafcadio Hearn⟩ **6** : possessed of or marked by general efficiency and ability and by adequate resourcefulness, skill, and reliability ⟨~ pilots⟩ ⟨the ~ direction of the play⟩ ⟨the ~ fashioning fingers of the artist —W.S.Maugham⟩ ⟨still composed, still ~, still mistress of herself and any emergency —Ellen Glasgow⟩ **7** *obs* : having legal qualification or right to own, enjoy, or perform ⟨of my land. . . to make thee ~ —Shak.⟩ **syn** see ABLE

ca·pa·ble·ness \-bəlnəs\ *n* -ES : CAPABILITY

ca·pa·bly \-blē, -i\ *adv* : in a capable manner

ca·pa·cious \kə'pāshəs\ *adj* [L *capac-, capax* capacious (fr. *capere* to take, contain) + E *-ious* — more at HEAVE] **1** *obs* : having size or scope enough to contain — used with *of* or an infinitive ⟨a jar ~ of six gallons⟩ **2 a** : able to contain a great deal : affording much space : LARGE, COPIOUS ⟨his ~ pockets contained a pruning knife and twine —John Buchan⟩ ⟨a colonial fireplace ~ enough to roast an ox —*Amer. Guide Series: Pa.*⟩ **b** : not narrow or constricted : marked by ample scope : INCLUSIVE ⟨the rule did not tie men of quick and ~ minds —R.W.Southern⟩ **3** *archaic* : fitted or disposed to receive or entertain ⟨a mind ~ of such interests⟩ **syn** see AMPLE

ca·pa·cious·ly \-slē, -i\ *adv* : in a capacious manner

ca·pa·cious·ness \-snəs\ *n* -ES : the quality or state of being capacious

ca·pac·i·tance \kə'pasətən(t)s, -əd·ən-\ *n* -S [[1]*capacity* + *-ance*] **1** : the property of an electric nonconductor that permits the storage of energy as a result of electric displacement when opposite surfaces of the nonconductor are maintained at a difference of potential (as in a capacitor), its measure being the ratio of the charge on either surface to the potential difference between the surfaces and its value for a capacitor being the sum of the combined values of its several dielectric plates — called also *capacity* **2** : a part of a circuit or network that possesses capacitance

ca·pac·i·tate \kə'pasə,tāt\ *vt* -ED/-ING/-S [[1]*capacity* + *-ate*] : to make capable : QUALIFY ⟨by this instruction we may be *capacitated* to observe those errors —John Dryden⟩

ca·pac·i·ta·tion \kə,pasə'tāshən\ *n* -S : the act of capacitating : QUALIFICATION

ca·pac·i·tive \kə'pasəd·iv\ *also* **ca·pac·i·ta·tive** \-sə,tād·iv\ *adj* [*capacitive* fr. [1]*capacity* + *-ive*; *capacitative* fr. *capacitate* + *-ive*] : of or relating to capacitance — **ca·pac·i·tive·ly** *adv*

capacitive coupling *n* : a coupling in which the two circuits have a common capacitor

capacitive reactance *n* : reactance due to the presence of capacitance in an alternating-current circuit

ca·pac·i·tiv·i·ty \kə,pasə'tivəd·ē\ *n* -ES : DIELECTRIC CONSTANT

ca·pac·i·tor \kə'pasəd·ə(r), -ətə-\ *n* -S [[1]*capacity* + *-or*] : a device giving large capacitance or desired values of capacitance usu. consisting of conducting plates or foils separated by thin layers of dielectric (as air, paraffin paper, or mica), the plates on opposite sides of the dielectric layers being oppositely charged by a source of voltage and the electrical energy of the charged system being stored in the polarized dielectric with the capacitance proportional to the area and dielectric constant of the dielectric layer and inversely proportional to its thickness — called also *condenser*

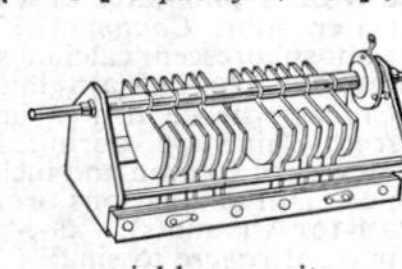
variable capacitor

capacitor motor *n* : a single-phase alternating-current motor having a main winding that receives energy directly from the power line and a second usu. auxiliary winding that receives energy through a capacitor, the currents in the two windings differing in phase and producing torque

[1]ca·pac·i·ty \kə'pasəd·ē, -s(ə)tē, -'aa-, -i\ *n* -ES [ME *capacite*, fr. MF *capacité*, fr. L *capacitat-, capacitas*, fr. *capac-, capax* capacious, capable + *-itat-, -itas* -ity — more at CAPACIOUS] **1 a** : the power or ability to hold, receive, or accommodate ⟨had our great palace the ~ to camp this host, we all would sup together —Shak.⟩ **b** *obs* : an empty space : a hollowed-out area : CAVITY **c** : a containing space : a measure of content for gas, liquid, or solid : the amount held : the measured ability to contain : VOLUME ⟨a tank with a ~ of 20 gallons⟩ ⟨the air ~ of a normal lung⟩ ⟨one modern cement elevator has a storage ~ of 114,000 barrels —*Amer. Guide Series: Minn.*⟩ **d** : the ability to absorb ⟨the ~ of warm air for moisture⟩ **e** : the ability to accommodate people : the size or number of accommodations : the condition of maximum service with all accommodations used ⟨an auditorium with a seating ~ of 5000⟩ ⟨taxing the *capacities* of nearby hospitals⟩ ⟨the stadium was filled to ~⟩ **f** : the ability to store, process, treat, manufacture, or produce : an instrumentality or facility for production : maximum processing, production, or output ⟨a flood of war orders that strained the ~ of factories long idle —Oscar Handlin⟩ ⟨the largest spruce mill in the world, with a ~ of 400,000 board feet every eight hours —*Amer. Guide Series: Oregon*⟩ ⟨steel mills operating at ~⟩ ⟨a generating ~ measured in kilovolt amperes⟩ **g** : the ability to yield and to sustain ⟨ranchers considering the carrying ~ of the range lands⟩ **h** (1) : CAPACITANCE (2) : the quantity of electricity that a battery can deliver under specified conditions **i** : the ability of a stream to transport detritus as measured by the quantity carried past a point in a certain time — compare COMPETENCE **j** : potentiality for production or use : maximum potentiality : facilities for production or service **2** : legal qualification, competency, power, or fitness **3 a** : ABILITY, CALIBER, STATURE **b** : mental power, capability, and acumen blended to enable one to grasp ideas, to analyze and judge, and to cope with problems : maximum potential mental ability ⟨inexpressibly ordinary, yet giving an impression of ~ —G.K.Chesterton⟩ ⟨not a philosophical treatise but a work intended for the ~ of the popular mind —S.F.Mason⟩ **c** : blended power, strength, and ability ⟨encourage physical activity to the limit of the child's ~ —Morris Fishbein⟩ ⟨the *capacities* of present-day rockets —*Time*⟩ **d** : capability or faculty for executing, considering, appreciating, or experiencing — used with *for* or an infinitive ⟨with all her ~ for violence, Lola possessed also a strong ~ for affection —Margaret Mead⟩ ⟨a ~ for delicate discrimination —J.L.Lowes⟩ ⟨the ~ of American idealism to survive a major disillusionment —Archibald MacLeish⟩ **4 a** *archaic* : a situation enabling or making capable ⟨a ship in a ~ to begin the battle⟩ **b** : a position, character, or role either duly assigned or assumed without sanction ⟨in his ~ as legal adviser⟩ ⟨served the government in several *capacities*⟩ — **at capacity** : in service or production with all facilities utilized : at maximum production

[2]capacity \"\ *adj* : attaining to or equaling maximum capacity ⟨a ~ crowd⟩ ⟨~ production of electricity⟩

capacity coupling *n* : CAPACITIVE COUPLING

capacity factor *n* : the ratio of the average load carried by a power station or system for a given period to the rated capacity of the station or system for the same period — compare LOAD FACTOR

cap-and-ball *adj* : having a lock that utilizes a percussion cap to fire a separately loaded charge

cap and bells *n, pl* **caps and bells** **1** : a cap with bells attached worn by a court fool or professional jester **2** : a fool's bauble : MAROTTE

cap and gown *n, pl* **caps and gowns** : the cap and gown that together constitute academic costume

capape *obs var of* CAP-A-PIE

cap-a-pie *or* **cap-à-pie** \,kapə'pē\ *adv* [MF (*de*) *cap a pé* from head to foot, fr. OProv *de cap a pe*] : from head to foot : at all points ⟨he was armed *cap-a-pie* —W.H.Prescott⟩

ca·pa pri·eto \kə'pä,prē'ād·(,)ō\ *n, pl* **capa prietos** [AmerSp *capá prieto*, lit., black capá (tree of the genus *Cordia*)] : SPANISH ELM

[1]ca·par·i·son \kə'parəsən, -əzən *also* -'e-\ *n* -S [MF *caparaçon*, fr. OSp *caparazón*] **1 a** : an ornamental covering for a horse **b** : decorative trappings and harness **2** : rich clothing : ADORNMENT, DECORATION

[2]caparison \"\ *vt* -ED/-ING/-S **1** : to cover with a caparison : deck out with ornamental trappings **2** : to dress richly : ADORN ⟨the trees stood majestically ~*ed*, with their innumerable leaves gilt —Virginia Woolf⟩

caparison 1a, 13th century

capas *pl of* CAPA

ca·pa·taz \,kapə'taz\ *also* **ca·pa·tas** \-ās\ *n, pl* **capata·ces** \,kapə'tä,sās\ [Sp *capataz*, irreg. fr. L *caput* head — more at HEAD] : BOSS, FOREMAN, OVERSEER ⟨behaved very well under their ~ —Joseph Conrad⟩

cap board *n* : paperboard used in circular stoppers of bottles

cap bolt *n* : TAP BOLT

capcase *n* -S [perh. fr. [1]*cap* + *case*] **1** *obs* : a small traveling case or bag **2** *obs* : CHEST 1

cap cloud *n* : a small cloud surmounting a mountain peak

[1]cape \'kāp\ *n* -S *often attrib* [ME *cap*, fr. MF, fr. OProv, fr. L *caput* head — more at HEAD] **1** : a point or extension of land jutting out into water either as a peninsula ⟨*Cape* Cod⟩ or as a projecting point ⟨*Cape* Hatteras⟩ — compare HEADLAND, PROMONTORY **2** *usu cap* [fr. *Cape* of Good Hope] **a** : a product of the Cape of Good Hope Province or of another part of So. Africa ⟨a *Cape* diamond⟩ **b** : leather produced from a So. African hair sheepskin; *broadly* : a sheepskin or lambskin glove or garment leather with natural grain retained — compare CAPESKIN **c** : a triangular postage stamp issued by the Cape of Good Hope Colony from 1853 to 1864

[2]cape \"\ *n* -S [prob. fr. Sp *capa* cloak, fr. LL *cappa* head covering, cloak — more at CAP (head covering)] **1 a** : a sleeveless outer garment of fabric or fur that fits closely at the neck, hangs loosely from the shoulders, and is made in all lengths **b** : an attached collarlike part of a garment **2** : the short feathers covering the shoulders of a fowl below the hackle — see COCK illustration **3** : the pelt from the head, neck, and forepart of the shoulders of an animal esp. for mounting as a trophy **4** : a red cloak used by a bullfighter or capeador to attract a bull and direct its charge

[3]cape \"\ *vt* -ED/-ING/-S [trans. of Sp *capear*] : to attract and direct the charge of (a bull) by flourishing a cape

ca·pe·ador \kāpāä'thór\ *n, pl* **capeadors** \-thórz\ *or* **capeado·res** \-thōrās\ [Sp, fr. *capear* to play tricks on the bull with one's cloak, fr. *capa* cloak — more at CAPE] : a bullfighter's aide who uses a capa to distract or excite the bull

cape aloe *n, usu cap C* [fr. *Cape* of Good Hope, Union of South Africa] : a much-branched southern African plant (*Aloe ferox*) with reddish prickly succulent leaves

cape anteater *n, usu cap C* [fr. *Cape* of Good Hope] : AARDVARK

cape armadillo *n, usu cap C* [fr. *Cape* of Good Hope] : the scaly anteater (*Manis temminckii*) of southern Africa that like the true armadillo rolls into a ball when alarmed — compare PANGOLIN

cape ash *n, usu cap C* [fr. *Cape* of Good Hope] **1** : a southern African tree (*Ekebergia capensis*) of the family Meliaceae **2** : the tough wood of the Cape ash

cape asparagus *n, usu cap C* [fr. *Cape* of Good Hope] : LATTICE PLANT

cape baboon *n, usu cap C* [fr. *Cape* of Good Hope] : CHACMA

cape beech *n, usu cap C* [fr. *Cape* of Good Hope] **1** : a southern African hardwood tree (*Myrsine melanophleos*) **2** : the wood of the Cape beech

cape bladder senna *n, usu cap C* [fr. *Cape* of Good Hope] : a scarlet-flowered southern African shrub (*Sutherlandia frutescens*) cultivated in California

cape bonnet *n* [[2]*cape*] : a bonnet with a projecting front edge and a deep ruffle on the bottom

cape box *or* **cape boxwood** *n, usu cap C* [fr. *Cape* of Good Hope] : a southern African timber tree (*Buxus macowani*)

cape buffalo *n, usu cap C* [fr. *Cape* of Good Hope] : a large powerful often very savage buffalo (*Syncerus caffer*) of southern Africa having the horns joined at the bases to form a heavy frontal casque

cape bulb *n, usu cap C* [fr. *Cape* of Good Hope] : any of various bulbs or bulbous plants from southern Africa esp. of the genus *Ixia* or *Sparaxis* — compare DUTCH BULB

cape cart *n, usu cap 1st C* [fr. *Cape* of Good Hope] *Africa* **:** a 2-wheeled vehicle usu. seating four, drawn by two horses, and having a bowed canvas or leather hood

cape cat *n, usu cap 1st C* [*Cape* Cod, Mass., where it originated + E *catboat*] **:** a catboat for fishing and pleasure sailing

cape chestnut *n, usu cap 1st C* [fr. *Cape* of Good Hope] **:** an ornamental southern African evergreen tree (*Calodendrum capense*) of the family Rutaceae having large panicles of white or flesh-colored flowers

cape chincherinchee *n, usu cap 1st C* [fr. *Cape* of Good Hope] **:** CHINCHERINCHEE

cape chisel *n* [perh. fr. ¹*cape*] **:** a cold chisel that has a long taper on the top and bottom of the cutting end and a narrow edge and is used for cutting keyways and similar flat grooves

cape chisel

cape cobra *n, usu cap 1st C* [fr. *Cape* of Good Hope] **:** an aggressive partly arboreal cobra (*Naja nivea*) of southern Africa that is extremely variable in coloring, being predominantly yellow, reddish, brown, or black — called also *yellow cobra*

cape cod cottage \(ˈ)kāp¦käd-\ *also* **cape cod** \ˈ=ˌ=\ *n, usu cap 1st & 2d Cs* [fr. *Cape Cod*, Mass.; fr. the frequent occurrence there of this type of house] **:** a compact rectangular dwelling of one or one-and-a-half stories usu. with a central chimney and a steep gable roof and with the main entrance on one of the long sides

cape cod lighter *n, usu cap both Cs* **:** a lump of porous material fixed upon a handle and soaked with kerosene for use in lighting fires

cape cod turkey *n, usu cap both Cs* **:** CODFISH

cape colored *n, pl* **cape colored** *or* **cape coloreds** *usu cap both Cs* [fr. *Cape* of Good Hope] **:** a native or inhabitant of So. Africa of mixed European and African or Malayan descent

cape cotton *n, usu cap 1st C* [fr. *Cape* of Good Hope] **:** a shrub (*Gomphocarpus fruticosus*) native to Africa but now found elsewhere often as a troublesome weed

cape cowslip *n, usu cap 1st C* [fr. *Cape* of Good Hope] **:** a southern African bulb or plant of the genus *Lachenalia* bearing bell-shaped flowers

cape crawfish *or* **cape crayfish** *n, usu cap 1st C* [fr. *Cape* of Good Hope] **:** the common spiny lobster (*Jasus lalandii*) of the coast of southern Africa valued as food and shipped canned or frozen to the U. S. — see ROCK LOBSTER

cape dagga *n, usu cap C* [fr. *Cape* of Good Hope] **:** DAGGA

cape diamond *n, usu cap C* [fr. *Cape* of Good Hope] **:** a diamond of yellowish tinge

cape doctor *n* [fr. *Cape* of Good Hope; fr. the belief that it carries germs out to sea] *Africa* **:** a strong southeast wind

cape dutch *n, cap C & D* [fr. *Cape* of Good Hope] **:** AFRIKAANS

cape ebony *n, usu cap C* [fr. *Cape* of Good Hope] **1 :** an African timber tree (*Euclea pseudebenus*) **2 :** the valuable hard wood of the Cape ebony

cape elk *n, usu cap C* [fr. *Cape* of Good Hope] **:** ELAND

cape fennel *n, usu cap C* [fr. *Cape* of Good Hope] **:** a southern African herb (*Foeniculum capense*) having a thick aromatic edible root

cape foot *n, usu cap C* [fr. *Cape* of Good Hope] **:** a unit of measure of the Union of So. Africa equal to 1.033 English feet

cape forget-me-not *n, usu cap C* [fr. *Cape* of Good Hope] **:** either of two southern African anchusas (*Anchusa capensis* and *A. riparia*)

cape fox *n, usu cap C* [fr. *Cape* of Good Hope] **:** CAAMA 1

cape fuchsia *n, usu cap C* [fr. *Cape* of Good Hope] **:** a southern African shrub (*Phygelius capensis*) of the family Scrophulariaceae often cultivated for its tubular scarlet flowers like those of a fuchsia

cape fur seal *n, usu cap C* [fr. *Cape* of Good Hope] **:** CAPE SEAL

cape gooseberry *n, usu cap C* [fr. *Cape* of Good Hope; fr. its extensive cultivation in So. Africa] **:** any of several groundcherries (esp. *Physalis peruviana*) bearing edible acid berries

cape grape *n, usu cap C* [fr. *Cape* Cod, Mass., where it was developed] **:** a tuberous-rooted grapelike vine (*Cissus capensis*) having very long forked tendrils and red-black glossy fruit in short clusters and used esp. in southwestern U. S. as an ornamental

cape gum *n, usu cap C* [fr. *Cape* of Good Hope] **1 a :** a gum arabic obtained from various southern African acacias (esp. *Acacia horrida* and *A. giraffae*) — see KARROO BUSH **2 a :** a tree yielding Cape gum

cape hare *n, usu cap C* [fr. *Cape* of Good Hope] **:** a large swift long-legged hare (*Lepus capensis*) that resembles the American cottontail rabbit and is widely distributed in arid southern African grasslands

cape hartebeest *n, usu cap C* [fr. *Cape* of Good Hope] **:** a large reddish hartebeest (*Alcelaphus caama*) with black-marked face, limbs, and tail and white underparts

cape hen *n, usu cap C* [fr. *Cape* of Good Hope] **:** any of several sea birds of southern seas; *esp:* a large white-chinned petrel (*Procellaria aequinoctialis*)

cape holly *n, usu cap C* [fr. *Cape* of Good Hope] **:** a southern African timber tree (*Elaeodendron croceum*)

cape honeysuckle *n, usu cap C* [fr. *Cape* of Good Hope] **:** a southern African evergreen woody vine (*Tecomaria capensis*) of the family Bignoniaceae with orange-red flowers in dense terminal clusters

cape horn·er \kāˈpȯrnər, kāpˈhȯ-\ *n, usu cap C&H* [*Cape Horn*, southern extremity of So. America + E *-er*] **:** a ship that voyages around Cape Horn

cape hunting dog *n, usu cap C* [fr. *Cape* of Good Hope] **:** AFRICAN HUNTING DOG

cape hyacinth *n, usu cap C* [fr. *Cape* of Good Hope] **:** SUMMER HYACINTH

cape hyrax *n, usu cap C* [fr. *Cape* of Good Hope] **:** DASSIE 1

cape ivy *n, usu cap C* [fr. *Cape* of Good Hope] **:** GERMAN IVY

cape jasmine *or* **cape jessamine** *n, usu cap C* [fr. *Cape* of Good Hope; fr. its having been found in So. Africa] **:** an Asiatic shrub (*Gardenia jasminoides*) long cultivated for its fragrant white flowers

cape jumping hare *n, usu cap C* [fr. *Cape* of Good Hope] **:** JUMPING HARE

cape lancewood *n, usu cap C* [fr. *Cape* of Good Hope] **:** ASSEGAI 2

cape·let \ˈkāplət\ *n* -s [²*cape* + *-let*] **:** a small cape usu. covering the shoulders

cape lily *n, usu cap C* [fr. *Cape* of Good Hope] **:** a southern African bulbous herb (*Crinum longifolium*) with showy pinkish red flowers

cap·e·lin *also* **cap·e·lan** \ˈkap(ə)lən\ *or* **cap·lin** \-plən\ *or* **cap·ling** \-pliŋ, -lən\ *n* -s [CanF *capelan*, fr. F, codfish, fr. OProv *capelan*, *cappellan* chaplain, codfish, fr. ML *cappellanus* chaplain — more at CHAPLAIN] **:** a small salmonoid marine fish (*Mallotus villosus*) related to and resembling the smelts that is very abundant off Greenland, Iceland, Newfoundland, and Alaska and is used as food and as bait for the cod

cap·e·line \ˈkapəˌlēn, -ˌlən\ *n* -s [ME *capleyne*, fr. MF *capeline*, fr. OProv *capelina*, fr. *capa* cloak, fr. LL *cappa* head covering, cloak — more at CAP] **1 :** a small skullcap of steel or iron worn by foot soldiers in medieval times **2** [F, fr. MF] **:** a cap-shaped or hood-shaped bandage for the head, the shoulder, or the stump of an amputated limb **3** [F, woman's hat, woman's hood, fr. MF] **:** a woman's hat with a small crown and a wide soft brim

cape lion *n, usu cap C* [fr. *Cape* of Good Hope] **:** a large black-maned lion formerly abundant in southern Africa but extinct since about 1850

ca·pel·la \kəˈpelə\ *n, cap* [NL, fr. L, she-goat, star in the constellation Auriga, dim. of *caper* goat — more at CAPRIOLE] **:** a genus of birds (family Scolopacidae) comprising the snipes

capelle *often cap, var of* KAPELLE

cape lobster *n, usu cap C* [fr. *Cape* of Good Hope] **1 :** CAPE CRAWFISH **2 :** a small lobster (*Homarus capensis*) from the Cape of Good Hope

cape marigold *n, usu cap C* [fr. *Cape* of Good Hope] **:** a daisylike plant of the genus *Dimorphotheca* often cultivated for ornament

cape may goody \(ˈ)kāp¦mā-\ *n, usu cap C&M* [*Cape May*, New Jersey, near which it is found + E *goody* (fish)] **:** ¹SPOT 7

cape may warbler *n, usu cap C&M* [fr. *Cape May* county, New Jersey, where it was first identified] **:** an American warbler (*Dendroica tigrina*) that is olive green with dark streaks above and yellow with black streaks on the underparts

cape merchant *n* [prob. fr. It *capo* leader, lit., head, or MF *cap* (fr. OProv), fr. L *caput* head — more at HEAD] **1** *obs* **:** SUPERCARGO 1 **2** *obs* **:** the head merchant in a trading post

cape mole rat *n, usu cap C* [fr. *Cape* of Good Hope] **:** MOLE RAT c

cape otter *n, usu cap C* [fr. *Cape* of Good Hope] **:** a large clawless otter (*Aonyx capensis*) of southern Africa

cape periwinkle *n, usu cap C* [fr. *Cape* of Good Hope] **:** PERIWINKLE 1c

cape pigeon *n, usu cap C* [fr. *Cape* Horn, southern extremity of So. America] **:** a pigeon-sized black-and-white petrel (*Daption capense*) of southern seas breeding chiefly in southern So. America

cape polecat *n, usu cap C* [fr. *Cape* of Good Hope] **:** MUISHOND

cape pondweed *n, usu cap C* [fr. *Cape* of Good Hope] **:** a southern African aquatic plant (*Aponogeton distachyus*) with long-petioled floating leaves and emersed fragrant flower spikes — called also *water hawthorn*

cape primrose *n, usu cap C* [fr. *Cape* of Good Hope] **:** an herb of the genus *Streptocarpus* cultivated for its primroselike flowers

¹ca·per \ˈkāpə(r)\ *n* -s *often attrib* [back-formation fr. earlier *capers*, taken as a plural, fr. ME *caperis*, *capres*, fr. L *capparis*, fr. Gk *kapparis*] **1 :** a plant of the genus *Capparis*; *esp* **:** a low prickly shrub (*C. spinosa*) of the Mediterranean region cultivated in Europe for its buds — see CAPPARIS **2 capers** *pl* **:** the greenish flower buds and young berries of the caper plant pickled and used as a condiment in sauces and dressings **3 :** a marsh marigold (*Caltha palustris*)

²caper \"\ *vi* **capered**; **capered**; **capering** \-p(ə)riŋ\ **capers** [prob. by shortening & alter. fr. *capriole*] **:** to leap about, prance, or cavort in a gay frolicsome way **:** prance, frisk, or gambol playfully or wildly ⟨lambs ~*ing* in the meadow⟩ ⟨~*ing* like a witch doctor among African natives —Geoffrey Household⟩

³caper \"\ *n* -s [prob. by shortening & alter. fr. *capriole*] **1 a :** a gay unrestrained bounding leap **:** SKIP, JUMP ⟨the skip of the lamb and the ~ of the kid —Douglas Kennedy⟩ **b :** a leaping or cavorting dance motion ⟨the couples jigging in from opposite corners, performing ~*s* and shuffles —H.L.Davis⟩ **2 a :** a capricious or madcap escapade **:** PRANK, ANTIC ⟨lead in all kinds of pranks and ~*s* —W.A.White⟩ **b :** PERFORMANCE, ACTIVITY, PURSUIT **3** *slang* **:** an illegal or questionable escapade **:** criminal action **:** CRIME ⟨an elegant piece of jewel robbery called a ~ in the jungle patois —Robert Hatch⟩ **4 :** three quick jumps in morris dancing followed by a leap with one leg forward and the other back

⁴caper *n* -s [D *kaper*, fr. *kapen* to privateer, fr. *kaap* privateering, prob. fr. Fris, fr. OFris *kāp* trade; akin to OHG *kouf* trade — more at CHEAP] **1** *archaic* **:** PRIVATEER **2** *archaic* **:** PIRATE

⁵ca·per \ˈkāpər, -ˈä-\ *n* -s [ScGael *ceapaire*, prob. fr. *ceap* shoemaker's last, clog on an animal's foot, pair of stocks, akin to MIr *cepp* block, fr. L *cippus* stake, post — more at CEPE] *chiefly Scot* **:** a piece of buttered bread usu. with cheese on it

caper berry *n* [¹*caper*] **:** the small berrylike fruit of the caper

caperbush \ˈ=ˌ=ˌ=\ *n* **:** ¹CAPER 1

cap·er·cail·lie \ˌkapə(r)ˈkāl(y)ē, ˌkāp-\ *or* **cap·er·cail·zie** \-ālzē\ *n* -s [modif. of ScGael *capalcoille*, lit., horse of the woods, fr. *capall* mare, horse (akin to OIr *capall* horse, fr. L *caballus*) + *coille* forest; akin to MIr *caill* forest, Gk *klados* branch — more at CAVALCADE, GLADIATOR] **:** a large true grouse (*Tetrao urogallus*) found in many wooded areas of Europe and Asia and in parts of Britain to which it has been reintroduced after being exterminated and where it feeds on fruits and small invertebrates and esp. in winter on pine shoots which give the flesh a strong flavor, the dark-gray and black male being the size of a wild turkey and the mottled female much smaller — called also *cock of the wood*

caper family *n* [¹*caper*] **:** CAPPARIDACEAE

ca·per·ing·ly *adv* **:** in a capering manner

ca·per·na·ite \kəˈpərnēˌīt\ *n* -s *usu cap* [*Capernaum*, city in ancient Palestine + E *-ite*] **1 :** a native or inhabitant of Capernaum **2 :** one who believes in transubstantiation; *specif* **:** one who interprets literally Jesus' discourse at Capernaum on the bread of life (Jn 6:26–58) — usu. used disparagingly

cap·er·noi·ted \¦kapər¦nȯitəd\ *adj* [perh. fr. *capernaite* (believer in transubstantiation) + *-ed*] **1** *Scot* **:** PEEVISH **2** *Scot* **:** MUDDLEHEADED, TIPSY

cap·er·noi·tie \-tē\ *n* -s [origin unknown] *Scot* **:** HEAD, NODDLE

cape robin *n, usu cap C* [fr. *Cape* of Good Hope] **:** a southern African songbird (*Caffrornis caffra*) of the family Turdidae that is dusky brown above fading to brownish red on the tail with an orange throat patch and pale or whitish underparts and that is common in settled areas where it feeds on insects and berries

cape rock lobster *n, usu cap C* [fr. *Cape* of Good Hope] **:** CAPE CRAWFISH

capers *pl of* CAPER, *pres 3d sing of* CAPER

caper spurge *n* [¹*caper*] **:** a poisonous European spurge (*Euphorbia lathyrus*) that is adventive in America and has seeds that yield a purgative oil — called also *mole plant*

caper tree *n* [¹*caper*] **:** the common cultivated caper (*Capparis spinosa*); *also* **:** a related shrub (*C. cynophallophora*) of Florida and the West Indies

cape ruby *n, usu cap C* [fr. *Cape* of Good Hope] **:** a ruby-colored garnet **:** PYROPE

ca·per·wort \ˈkāpərˌwərt, -ˌȯ-\ *n* -s [¹*caper* + *wort*] **:** a plant of the family Capparidaceae

capes \ˈkāps\ *n pl* [perh. fr. pl. of ²*cape*] **1** *dial Brit* **:** ears of grain broken off in threshing **2** *dial Brit* **:** grain that threshing has not removed the husks from

cape salmon *n, usu cap C* [fr. *Cape* of Good Hope] **1 :** GEELBEC 2 **2** *Africa* **:** TENPOUNDER 1

cape seal *or* **cape sea lion** *n, usu cap C* [fr. *Cape* of Good Hope] **:** a fur seal (*Arctocephalus pusillus*) inhabiting islands off the coast of southern Africa

capeskin \ˈ=ˌ=\ *n, often attrib* [*Cape* of Good Hope + E *skin*] **1 :** a hair sheepskin from southern Africa **2 :** glove or garment leather made from capeskin

cape sparrow *n, usu cap C* [fr. *Cape* of Good Hope] **:** a very dark southern African sparrow (*Passer melanurus*) common in settled areas

cape spiny lobster *n, usu cap C* [fr. *Cape* of Good Hope] **:** CAPE CRAWFISH

cape·stane \ˈkāpˌstān\ *Scot var of* COPESTONE

cape teal *or* **cape widgeon** *n, usu cap C* [fr. *Cape* of Good Hope] **:** a small rather drably colored duck (*Nolonetta capensis*) of southern and eastern Africa

¹ca·pe·tian \kəˈpēshən, kā-\ *adj, usu cap* [F *capétien*, fr. Hugh (Hugues) *Capet* †996 Fr. king, founder of the dynasty + F *-ien* -ian] **:** of or relating to the French dynasty founded in 987 and with its collateral branches reigning until 1848 except during the years 1795–1814

²capetian \"\ *n* -s *usu cap* **:** a member of the Capetian dynasty; *esp* **:** a Capetian king

cape·to·ni·an \kāpˈtōnēən\ *n* -s *cap* [irreg. (influence of such words as *Newtonian*, *Bostonian*) fr. *Cape Town*, Union of So. Africa + E *-ian*] **:** a native or inhabitant of Cape Town, Union of So. Africa

cape town \ˈkāpˌtau̇n\ *adj, usu cap C&T* [fr. *Cape Town*, city in the Union of So. Africa] **:** of or from Cape Town, the legislative capital Union of So. Africa **:** of the kind or style prevalent in Cape Town

ca·pette \(ˈ)kā¦pet\ *n* -s [*capon* + *-ette*] **:** CAPONETTE

cape tulip *n, usu cap C* [fr. *Cape* of Good Hope] **1 :** BLOOD LILY **2 :** a plant of the genus *Homeria*

capeweed \ˈ=ˌ=\ *n, often cap* [*Cape* Verde islands, Portuguese colony off West Africa + E *weed*] **1 :** an archil lichen (*Roccella tinctoria*) abundant in the Cape Verde islands **2** [*Cape* of Good Hope + E *weed*] **:** a low-growing yellow-flowered composite herb (*Cryptostemma calendulacea*) that is native to southern Africa but introduced into Australia and New Zealand where it is usu. considered a troublesome weed **3** [*Cape* of Good Hope + E *weed*] **:** CAT'S-EAR

cape wine *n, usu cap C* [fr. *Cape* of Good Hope] **:** wine made in the Cape Province region of So. Africa

cape wolf snake *n, usu cap C* [fr. *Cape* of Good Hope] **:** a small wolf snake (*Lycophidion capense*) of tropical and southern Africa

capework \ˈ=ˌ=\ *n* [²*cape* + *work*] **:** the art of the bullfighter in working a bull with the cape

cape yellowwood *n, usu cap C* [fr. *Cape* of Good Hope] **:** SOUTH AFRICAN YELLOWWOOD

cap-flash \ˈ=ˌ=\ *vt* [¹*cap* + *flash*] **:** to construct with one flashing superimposed on another to protect against leakage of water

cap flashing *n* [¹*cap* + *flashing*] **:** COUNTERFLASHING

cap·ful \ˈkapˌfu̇l\ *n* -s **:** a light puff ⟨a ~ of wind⟩

cap gun *n* [¹*cap* (explosive)] **:** CAP PISTOL

caph *var of* KAPH

ca·phar·na·um \kəˈfärnēəm\ *n* -s [F, fr. *Capharnaum*, Aram form of *Capernaum*, ancient city of Palestine; fr. the crowd before the house where Jesus preached (Mk 2:2)] **:** a confused jumble **:** a place marked by a disorderly accumulation of objects

caph·to·rim \ˈkaftəˌrim\ *or* **caph·to·rims** \-mz\ *n pl, cap* [Heb *Kaphtōrīm* (pl.), fr. *Kaphtōr* Caphtor, biblical name of the land of origin of the Philistines] **:** the people of biblical Caphtor, prob. present-day Crete

ca·pi·as \ˈkāpēəs\ *n* -ES [ME, fr. L, you should seize, 2d pers. sing. pres. subj. of *capere* to take, seize — more at HEAVE] **:** a legal writ or process commanding the officer to arrest the person named in it

capibara *var of* CAPYBARA

cap·il·la·ceous \¦kapə¦lāshəs\ *adj* [L *capillaceus*, fr. *capillus* hair + *-aceus* -aceous] **1 :** having filaments ⟨a ~ leaf⟩ **2 :** like a hair

cap·il·laire \¦kapə¦la(a)(ə)r\ *n* -s [F, fr. LL (*herba*) *capillaris*, fr. L *capillaris* of hair, fr. *capillus* hair + *-aris* -ary] **1 :** MAIDENHAIR **2 :** CREEPING SNOWBERRY **3 :** a syrup prepared from the maidenhair **4 :** a syrup flavored with orange flowers

ca·pi·lla ma·yor \kä¦pē(l)yəˌmīˈō(ə)r\ *n* [Sp, lit., larger chapel] **:** a main chapel or chancel in churches of Spanish architecture

cap·il·lar·ec·ta·sia \ˌkapəˌlarekˈtāzh(e)ə, -lär-\ *n* -s [NL, fr. L *capillaris* capillary + NL *ectasia*] **:** TELANGIECTASIA

cap·il·lar·ia \ˌkapəˈla(a)rēə\ *n* [NL, fr. L *capillus* hair + NL *-aria*] **1** *cap* **:** a genus of slender white nematode worms (family Trichuridae) that includes serious pathogens of the alimentary tract of fowls and certain tissue and organ parasites of mammals one of which (*C. hepatica*) is common in rodents and occas. invades the human liver sometimes with fatal results **2** -s **:** a worm of the genus *Capillaria* — **cap·il·lar·id** \-rəd, kəˈpilərəd\ *n* -s

ca·pil·la·ri·a·sis \kəˌpiləˈrīəsəs\ *also* **cap·il·lar·i·o·sis** \ˌkapəˌlerēˈōsəs, -la(a)r-\ *n, pl* **capillaria·ses** \-əˌsēz\ *also* **capillario·ses** \-ōsēz\ **:** infestation with or disease caused by nematode worms of the genus *Capillaria*

cap·il·lar·i·ty \ˌkapəˈlarədˌē, -ətē, -i, *also* -ˈe-\ *n* -ES [F *capillarité*, fr. *capillaire* capillary (fr. L *capillaris* of hair) + *-ité* -ity] **1 :** the quality or state of being capillary **2 :** the action by which the surface of a liquid where it is in contact with a solid is elevated or depressed depending upon the relative attraction of the molecules of the liquid for each other and for those of the solid and being esp. observable in capillary tubes where it determines the elevation or depression of the liquid above or below the level of the liquid in which the tube is dipped — compare SURFACE TENSION

cap·il·la·rized \ˈkapələˌrīzd, kəˈpilə-\ *adj* [²*capillary* + *-ize* + *-ed*] **:** infiltrated with or divided into capillaries

cap·il·lar·o·scope \ˌkapəˈlarəˌskōp, -ˈe-\ *n* -s [ISV *capillary* + *-o-* + *-scope*; orig. formed as G *kapillaroskop*] **:** a microscope that permits visual examination of the living capillaries in nail beds, skin, and conjunctiva

cap·il·la·ros·co·py \ˌkapələˈräskəpē\ *also* **cap·il·lar·i·os·co·py** \-ˌlerēˈäskəpē, -ˌla(a)r-\ *n* -ES [ISV *capillar-* (fr. *capillary*) or *capillary* + *-o-* + *-scopy*; orig. formed as G *kapillaroskopie*] **:** diagnostic examination of capillaries, esp. of the nail beds, with a microscope

¹cap·il·lary \ˈkapəˌlerē, -ri, *Brit usu* kəˈpiləri\ *adj* [F or L; F *capillaire*, fr. L *capillaris*, fr. *capillus* hair + *-aris* -ary] **1 :** belonging or relating to hair ⟨~ growth⟩ **2 :** resembling a hair **:** FINE, MINUTE, SLENDER; *esp* **:** having a very small or thin bore usu. permitting capillarity ⟨a ~ tube⟩ **3 :** involving or held by capillary action ⟨~ water⟩ **:** resulting from surface tension in the soil ⟨~ capacity is a measure of the ability of a soil to hold water in the surface layers against the action of gravity⟩ **4 a :** showing or suggesting an arrangement of capillaries ⟨a ~ network⟩ **b :** relating to capillarity or to an apparatus employing it ⟨~ action⟩

²capillary \"\ *n* -ES **:** a minute thin-walled vessel of the body; *esp* **:** any of the smallest constituent vessels of the blood-vascular system connecting arterioles with venules so as to form networks practically throughout the body, averaging ½ millimeter in length and at their widest being not many times the diameter of a blood corpuscle, and being walled by a single layer of endothelial cells that permits ready exchange of nutrients and metabolic wastes between the tissues and the circulating blood — see ROUGET CELL

capillary analysis *n* **:** analysis by chromatography (as paper chromatography)

capillary attraction *n* **:** the force of adhesion between a solid and a liquid in capillarity

capillary bed *n* **:** the whole system of capillaries of a body, part, or organ

capillary chemistry *n* **:** a branch of physical chemistry that is concerned with phenomena in very small pores sometimes including adsorption, absorption, catalysis, and colloid chemistry

capillary electrometer *n* **:** an electrometer for measuring small electric potential differences based upon change of surface tension between mercury and an electrolytic solution in a capillary tube with change of potential difference between the liquids

capillary potential *n* **1 :** the work done in bringing a unit mass of liquid from a level liquid surface to any point within a capillary region **2 :** the driving force that causes moisture to move in soil by capillarity

capillary pyrites *n* **:** MILLERITE

capillary water *n* **:** water that remains in the soil after gravitational water is drained out, that is subject to the laws of capillary movement, and that is in the form of a film around the soil grains

ca·pil·li·cul·ture \kəˈpiləˌkəlchə(r)\ *n* -s [ISV *capilli-* (fr. L *capillus* hair) + *culture*; prob. orig. formed in F] **:** treatment to cure or prevent baldness

ca·pil·li·form \kəˈpiləˌfȯrm\ *adj* [ISV *capilli-* (fr. L *capillus* hair) + *-form*] **:** having the form of a hair **:** like a hair

cap·il·li·tial \¦kapə¦lishəl\ *adj* [NL *capillitium* + E *-al*] **:** of or belonging to a capillitium

cap·il·li·ti·um \ˌkapəˈlishēəm\ *n, pl* **capilli·tia** \-ēə\ [NL, fr. L, hair (collectively), fr. *capillus*] **:** an assemblage or network of simple or branched noncellular strands formed of waste materials cast off in elongate vacuoles during cleavage of the spores in the sporangium of many slime molds and within the fruiting body of certain gasteromycetes

ca·pil·lus \kəˈpiləs\ *n, pl* **capil·li** \-iˌlī, -(ˌ)lē\ [NL, fr. L] **1 :** a hair esp. of the head **2** [NL, fr. L] **:** the bore of a capillary tube

cap·i·lo·tade \¦kapəlō¦täd, ke¦pilə¦t-\ *n* -s [F *capilotade*, *capirotade*, fr. Sp *capirotada* sauce containing herbs, eggs, and garlic, fr. *capirote* hood, fr. *capa* cloak — more at CAPE] **:** a stew often of several minced meats

ca·pim gor·du·ra \kä¦pim(ˌ)gȯrˈdu̇(ə)rə\ *n* [Pg, lit., fatness grass] **:** a hardy forage grass (*Melinis minutiflora*) much used in Brazil for fattening cattle and introduced into the southern U.S.

caping *pres part of* CAPE

cap iron *n* [¹*cap*] **:** a stiffening plate fastened to the upper side of the cutter of a carpenter's plane

capita *pl of* CAPUT

¹cap·i·taine \¦kapə¦tān\ *n* -s [F, lit., captain — more at CAPTAIN] **1 :** NILE PERCH **2 :** an African fish (*Lates microlepis*) closely related to the Nile perch

²capitaine *var of* CAPITAN

1cap·i·tal \ˈkapəd·ᵊl, -p(ə)tᵊl\ *adj* [ME, fr. L *capitalis*, fr. *capit-, caput* head — more at HEAD] **1** *obs* **:** of or relating to the head ⟨his ~ bruise —John Milton⟩ **2 a** *archaic* **:** DEADLY, FATAL ⟨an inexorable ~ enemy⟩ ⟨a plague ~ to many⟩ **b :** punishable by death **:** involving execution ⟨a ~ crime⟩ ⟨a ~ verdict⟩ ⟨put to death a ~ offender —John Milton⟩ **c :** involving or punishable by loss of legal personality **d :** most serious **:** fatally detrimental **:** EGREGIOUS ⟨a ~ error⟩ ⟨the ~ folly of cutting herself off from her family —Arnold Bennett⟩ **3 a** *obs* **:** standing at the beginning of a page, passage, or line ⟨the illumination of the ~ words in the manuscript⟩ **b** *of a letter* **:** comparatively large, clear, or elegant in form and in print like the majuscule letters of ancient inscriptions and consequently regarded as esp. fit for use in initial position **:** of or conforming to the series A, B, C, etc. rather than a, b, c, etc. **4 a** *archaic* **:** having authority or preeminence **:** most important **:** CHIEF ⟨the ~ lords of the realm⟩ — used of a person **b :** above comparable matters in importance, significance, worth, or influence **:** PROMINENT, PREDOMINANT, MAJOR, MAIN ⟨whatever is ~ and essential in Christianity should be clearly and strenuously affirmed —Isaac Taylor⟩ ⟨the ~ importance of criticism in the work of creation itself —T.S.Eliot⟩ **5** *of a city* **:** most important; *specif* **:** being the seat of government ⟨London is the ~ city of England⟩ **6** [*2capital*] **a :** consisting of, serving as, or intended as capital **b :** accruing to or from capital **c :** carried on or conducted by means of capital **d :** of or having to do with capital **7 :** highly meritorious **:** most enjoyable **:** EXCELLENT, FIRST-RATE ⟨a ~ essay, still diverting after three quarters of a century —H.L.Mencken⟩ ⟨~ dinners they give at those crack hotels —George Meredith⟩ **syn** see CHIEF — **with a capital :** EMPHATICALLY, CERTAINLY — used with a following relevant capital letter ⟨not an accident but murder *with a capital* M⟩

2capital \ˈ"\ *n* -s [F or It; F, fr. It *capitale*, fr. *capitale*, adj., principal, fr. L *capitalis*] **1 a** *or* **capital goods** *or* **capital account :** a stock of accumulated goods esp. at a specified time and in contrast to income received during a specified period **b :** the value of these accumulated goods **c** *or* **capital goods :** accumulated goods devoted to the production of other goods **:** facilities or goods utilized as factors of production ⟨~ is not money but means of production —Bertrand Russell⟩ ⟨the employer who could set ~ and land and labor to work —G.B.Shaw⟩ **d :** any accumulated factors of production capable of being owned ⟨working ~ in the form of plow beasts, heavy plows, and slaves —F.M.Stenton⟩ **e :** the proprietary claim in a business **f :** the principal of a loan as contrasted with interest **g :** NET ASSETS **:** excess of assets over liabilities **h :** CAPITAL STOCK **i :** accumulated possessions calculated to bring in income ⟨a thousand acres of haying land meant a ~ as reliable as government bonds —Margaret Deland⟩ **j :** accumulated assets, resources, sources of strength, or advantages utilized to aid in accomplishing an end or furthering a pursuit ⟨the accumulated scientific and mathematical ~ on which our technology flourishes —W.F.Albright⟩ **k :** available money ⟨walking into Hollisburg on a ~ of twenty cents —Elmer Davis⟩ **l :** persons holding capital **:** investors, potential or actual ⟨troubled international conditions have made ~ reluctant to invest heavily —*Amer. Guide Series: Ark.*⟩ **m :** asset, gain, or profit through utilization of an adventitious characteristic or development ⟨to make poetic ~ out of the suffering of others —C.D.Lewis⟩ ⟨a keen and wary ruler who made ~ of his weakness —Agnes Repplier⟩ **2** [*1capital*] **a :** a capital letter; *esp* **:** an initial capital letter **b :** a letter belonging to a style of alphabet modeled upon and departing in form relatively little from the style customarily used in inscriptions — see ROMAN CAPITAL, RUSTIC CAPITAL, SQUARE CAPITALS; compare CURSIVE, HALF UNCIAL, MINUSCULE, UNCIAL **3** [*1capital*] **a :** the chief city of a country or region ⟨Scranton . . . ~ of the anthracite basin —*Amer. Guide Series: Pa.*⟩ **b :** a city serving as a seat for the government of a larger area or as a seat of a government branch (as of sovereign, legislature, or administration) ⟨Washington is the ~ of the U. S.⟩ **c :** a city preeminent or dominant in some special activity — used with a specifying attributive ⟨had once been considered the world's diamond ~⟩ ⟨Paris reigned as the fashion ~ of the world⟩ ⟨San Antonio, a veritable cattle ~ —*Amer. Guide Series: Texas*⟩

3capital \ˈ"\ *n* -s [ME *capitale*, by folk etymology (influence of *1capital*) fr. ONF *capitel*, fr. LL *capitellum* small head, top of column, dim. of L *capit-, caput* head — more at HEAD] **1 :** the head or uppermost member of a column or pilaster crowning the shaft and taking the weight of the entablature — see COLUMN illustration **2 :** the head or cap esp. of a chimney or a crucible

capitals 1: *1* Doric, *2* Ionic, *3* Corinthian

capital account *n* **1 a :** an account representing ownership in a business: as (1) **:** a proprietor's account (2) **:** a partner's account **b :** any corporation account classified as part of net worth: as (1) **:** a capital stock account (2) **:** a surplus account **c :** *2*CAPITAL 1 a **2 :** a capital assets account

capital assets *n pl* **:** long-term assets either tangible or intangible (as land, buildings, patents, or franchises); *specif* **:** any assets so designated by statute or governmental regulation (as the U.S. Internal Revenue Code) — contrasted with *current assets*

capital budget *n* **:** a financial statement of estimated capital expenditures for a period of time usu. including proposed methods for financing

capital coefficient *n* **:** the ratio of the value of capital to the value of output

capital expenditure *n* **:** an expenditure for long-term additions or betterments properly chargeable to a capital assets account

capital gain *n* **:** the excess over market or book value at purchase or other acquisition realizable or realized from the sale of a capital asset; *specif* **:** a gain so designated by statute or governmental regulation (as the U.S. Internal Revenue Code) — compare LONG-TERM, SHORT-TERM

capital goods *n pl* **:** *2*CAPITAL 1a, 1c

capital grant *n* **:** a contribution usu. by a government to an independent governmental body or authority to cover part of the cost of the latter's facilities (as federal grants for highways or public housing) — compare GRANT-IN-AID

capital investment *n* **:** the amount of money invested or required to be invested in an enterprise or undertaking

cap·i·tal·ism \ˈ=(=)=ˌlizəm, *Brit also* kəˈpitᵊl,i-\ *n* -s [*2capital* (wealth) + *-ism*] **:** an economic system characterized by private or corporation ownership of capital goods, by investments that are determined by private decision rather than by state control, and by prices, production, and the distribution of goods that are determined mainly in a free market — compare INDUSTRIALISM, LIBERALISM, SOCIALISM

capital issue *n* **:** stocks or bonds issued by a corporation or government

1cap·i·tal·ist \ˈ=(=)=ləst, *Brit also* kəˈpitᵊl-\ *n* -s [F, D, or G; F *capitaliste* fr. D or G; D *kapitalist*, fr. G, fr. *kapital* capital + *-ist*] **:** a person who has capital esp. invested or to be invested in business ⟨spare money is called capital; its owner is called a ~ —G.B.Shaw⟩; *broadly* **:** a person of wealth **:** PLUTOCRAT

2capitalist \ˈ"\ *adj* **1 :** owning capital ⟨the ~ class⟩ **2 a :** practicing capitalism **:** adhering to or defending capitalism ⟨~ nations⟩ **b :** marked by capitalism ⟨the modern ~ period of history from 1815 to 1914 —Norman Thomas⟩

cap·i·tal·is·tic \ˌ=(=)=ˈlistik, -ēk, *Brit also* kəˌpitᵊlˈi-\ *adj* [*1capitalist* + *-ic*] **1 :** existing or accomplished under capitalism ⟨~ production⟩ **:** typical of or according with capitalism ⟨~ methods and incentives⟩ **2 :** practicing, favoring, or furthering capitalism ⟨~ nations⟩ ⟨~ propaganda⟩ — **cap·i·tal·is·ti·cal·ly** \-ək(ə)lē, -ək-, -li\ *adv*

cap·i·tal·i·za·tion \ˌkapəd·ᵊlə̇ˈzāshən, -p(ə)tᵊl-, -lˌīˈz-, *Brit also* kəˌpitᵊl-\ *n* -s [F *capitalisation*, fr. *capitaliser* + *-ation*] **1 a :** the act or process of capitalizing **b :** a sum resulting from a process of capitalizing **c :** the total liabilities of a business including both ownership capital and borrowed capital **d :** the total par value or the stated value of issues of no par value of the authorized capital of a company — called also *capital stock* **e :** the bonds and capital stock of a company **f :** the act or process of recording capital expenditures **2** [*capitalize* + *-ation*] **:** the use of a capital letter in writing or printing ⟨the ~ of proper nouns⟩

cap·i·tal·ize *also* **cap·i·tal·ise** \ˈkapəd·ᵊlˌīz, -p(ə)tᵊl-, *Brit also* kəˈpitᵊl-\ *vb* -ED/-ING/-S [F *capitaliser*, fr. *capital* + *-iser* -ize] *vt* **1 a** [*2capital* (letter) + *-ize*] **:** to write or print with an initial capital letter ⟨days of the week are usu. *capitalized*⟩ **b :** to write or print in capital letters ⟨abbreviations like B.A. and M.D. are usu. *capitalized*⟩ **2 :** to convert into capital **:** arrange for use in acquiring capital ⟨~ the company's reserve funds⟩ **3 :** to profit by **:** utilize gainfully **:** turn to one's advantage ⟨the producer and his designer assistant ~ the curiosity and vanity of their customers —Edward Sapir⟩ **4 a :** to compute, appraise, or estimate the present value of (an income extended over a period of time) ⟨*capitalized* earnings⟩ **b :** to convert (a periodic payment) into an equivalent capital sum ⟨*capitalized* annuity⟩ **5 a :** to charge (an expenditure) to a capital assets account **b :** to fix or determine the amount of capital stock to be authorized or issued by (a company) **6 :** to supply capital for **:** arrange available capital for the operation of ⟨some troubles in *capitalizing* the new venture⟩ ~ *vi* **:** to gain by opportune use of the adventitious **:** PROFIT — used with *on* or *upon* ⟨Lee hoped to ~ on his victory by pressing a further invasion —Horace Sutton⟩ ⟨unscrupulous industrialists and politicians, ever ready to ~ on baseless popular superstitions —M.F.A.Montagu⟩

capital justiciar *n* **:** JUSTICIAR 2

capital levy *n* **:** a levy on personal or industrial capital in addition to income tax and other taxes **:** a general property tax

capital liability *n* **1 :** the capital stock of a company representing the ownership interest for which the company is answerable to its stockholders even though a debtor and creditor relationship does not exist **2 :** a fixed liability (as a bond or mortgage) representing borrowed capital

capital loss *n* **:** the excess of book value or cost over the amount realized from the sale of a capital asset; *specif* **:** a loss so designated by statute or governmental regulation (as the U. S. Internal Revenue Code)

cap·i·tal·ly \ˈkapəd·ᵊlē, -p(ə)tᵊlē, -li\ *adv* **1 :** with a procedure or in a manner involving or likely to involve the death sentence ⟨punish ~⟩ ⟨try ~⟩ **2 :** in a capital manner ⟨she talks ~⟩

cap·i·tal·ness \-ᵊlnə̇s\ *n* -ES **:** the quality or state of being capital

capital punishment *n* **:** the death penalty for crime

capitals *pl of* CAPITAL

capital ship *n* **:** a warship of the first rank in size and armament **:** a major surface ship (as a battleship, cruiser, aircraft carrier)

capital sin *n* **:** DEADLY SIN

capital stock *n* **1** *or* **capital :** the outstanding shares of a joint-stock company considered as an aggregate ⟨the control of a majority of the *capital stock*⟩ **2 :** CAPITALIZATION 1d **3 :** the ownership element of a corporation divided into shares and represented by certificates

capital sum *n* **:** the amount specified for maximum injury or damage in an insurance policy

capital surplus *n* **:** the portion of the surplus of a business arising from sources other than earnings **:** all surplus other than earned surplus usu. including amounts received from sale or exchange of capital stock in excess of par or stated value, profits on resale of treasury stock, donations to capital by stockholders or others, or increment arising from revaluation of fixed or other assets

cap·i·tan \ˌkapəˈtan, -ān\ *or* **cap·i·taine** \-ān\ *n* -s [*capitan* fr. AmerSp *capitán*, fr. Sp, captain, fr. (assumed) VL *capitanus*; *capitaine* prob. fr. AmerFr, fr. AmerSp *capitán*] **:** HOGFISH 1 a

ca·pi·ta·nia \ˌkapətəˈnēə\ *n* -s [Pg, fr. Sp *capitania* captaincy, company of soldiers, military district, fr. *capitán* + *-ia* -ia] **:** a territorial division in colonial Brazil **:** PROVINCE

ca·pi·ta·no \ˌkapəˈtä(ˌ)nō\ *n, pl* **capita·ni** \-ä(ˌ)nē\ *or* **capitanos** [It, lit., captain, fr. (assumed) VL *capitanus* foremost, chief, fr. L *capit-, caput* head] **:** a vainglorious and cowardly soldier esp. appearing as a stock character in the commedia dell' arte

cap·i·tate \ˈkapəˌtāt\ *adj* [L *capitatus* headed, fr. *capit-, caput* head + *-atus* -ate — more at HEAD] **1** *also* **cap·i·tat·ed** \-ād·əd\ *bot* **:** forming a head ⟨~ inflorescence⟩ ⟨~ flowers⟩ **2** *biol* **:** abruptly enlarged and globose ⟨a ~ stigma⟩ ⟨a ~ antenna⟩ — see ANTENNA illustration

cap·i·ta·tim \ˌkapəˈtād·əm, -ˈta-\ *adj* [NL, fr. L *capit-, caput* head + NL *-atim* (as in ML *verbatim*)] **:** levied or granted at so much per head ⟨a ~ tax⟩

cap·i·ta·tion \ˌkapəˈtāshən\ *n* -s *often attrib* [LL *capitation-, capitatio* poll tax, fr. L *capit-, caput* head + *-ation-, -atio* -ation] **1 a :** a direct uniform tax imposed upon each head or person **:** POLL TAX **b :** the amount of tax so levied **2 :** a uniform payment payable on a per capita basis: as **a :** an annual fee paid a doctor or medical group for each patient enrolled under a health plan **b :** a payment by a subordinate body (as a local union) of a prescribed amount per member to a parent body

capitation grant *n* **:** a grant of a definite sum per person

cap·i·ta·tum \ˌkapəˈtād·əm, -ˈä-\ *n, pl* **capita·ta** \-d·ə\ [NL, fr. L, neut. of *capitatus* headed — more at CAPITATE] **:** the largest bone of the wrist articulating with the third metacarpal

cap·i·tel·late \ˌkapəˈtelət, -ˌlāt\ *adj* [NL *capitellum* + E *-ate*] **1** *bot* **:** having a very small knoblike termination **2** *bot* **:** collected into small capitula

1cap·i·tel·lid \ˌkapəˈteləd\ *n* -s [NL *Capitellidae*] **:** a capitellid worm

2capitellid \ˈ"\ *adj* **:** of or relating to the Capitellidae

cap·i·tel·li·dae \ˌkapəˈteləˌdē\ *n pl, cap* [NL, fr. *Capitella*, type genus (alter. of LL *capitellum* small head) + *-idae*] **:** a widely distributed family of polychaete worms that resemble the terrestrial oligochaetes in the simplicity of their structure

cap·i·tel·lum \ˌkapəˈteləm\ *n, pl* **capitel·la** \-lə\ [NL, fr. LL, small head, dim. of L *capit-, caput* head — more at HEAD] **1 :** a knoblike protuberance esp. at the end of a bone ⟨the ~ of the humerus⟩ **2 :** CAPITULUM

ca·pi·tis de·mi·nu·tio \ˈkapəd·ə̇s,deməˈn(y)üshēˌō, ˈkä . . .-ˌdāməˈnüd·ēˌō\ *n, pl* **capitis deminuti·o·nes** \-ˌn(y)üshēˈō(ˌ)nēz, -ˌnüd·ēˈō(ˌ)nās\ [L, lit., diminution of life] *Roman law* **:** impairment of legal status or civil capacity before the strict law through loss of freedom, citizenship, or family membership

cap·i·to \ˈkapəˌtō\ *n, cap* [NL, fr. L, large-headed one, fr. *capit-, caput* head] **:** the type genus of Capitonidae comprising most of the So. American and Central American barbets

cap·i·tol \ˈkapəd·ᵊl, -p(ə)tᵊl\ *n* -s *often attrib* [L *Capitolium* temple of Jupiter at Rome on the Capitoline hill] **:** the building in which a legislative body meets **:** STATEHOUSE ⟨many state ~s have gilded domes⟩ ⟨the national *Capitol* in Washington⟩

cap·i·to·line \ˈkapəd·ᵊlˌīn, -ətᵊl-, *Brit usu* kaˈpitəˌlīn\ *adj, usu cap* [L *capitolinus*, fr. *Capitolium* + *-inus* -ine] **:** belonging or relating to the smallest of the seven hills of Rome, to the ancient temple on it, or to the gods worshiped there

cap·i·ton·i·dae \ˌkapəˈtänəˌdē\ *n pl, cap* [NL, fr. *Capiton-, Capito*, type genus + *-idae*] **:** a family of stocky chiefly tropical arboreal birds (order Piciformes) with large stout bills swollen at the base and usu. with brilliantly colored plumage including a number of New and Old World barbets and sometimes esp. formerly the honey guides

cap·i·toph·o·rus \ˌkapəˈtäfərəs\ *n, cap* [NL, fr. L *capit-, caput* head + *-o-* + NL *-phorus* — more at HEAD] **:** a genus of aphids including the widespread currant aphid (*C. ribis*) and the strawberry aphid (*C. fragaefolii*)

capitula *pl of* CAPITULUM

ca·pit·u·lant \kəˈpichələnt\ *n* -s [F, pres. part. of *capituler* to capitulate, fr. ML *capitulare* to distinguish by heads or chapters — more at CAPITULATE] **:** one that capitulates

1ca·pit·u·lar \-lər, -ˌlär\ *adj* [ML *capitularis*, fr. *capitulum* ecclesiastical chapter, meeting place of canons — more at CHAPTER] **1 :** of or relating to an ecclesiastical chapter **:** CAPITULARY ⟨~ estates⟩ **2** [NL *capitulum* + E *-ar*] **:** of or relating to a capitulum

2capitular \ˈ"\ *n* -s **1 :** CAPITULARY 1 **2** [ML *capitulare*, lit., document divided into sections] **:** a law or canon of a chapter or council **3 :** a member of a chapter

1ca·pit·u·lary \-ˌlerē\ *n* -ES [ML *capitulare*, lit., document divided into sections, fr. LL *capitulum* section, chapter, fr. L, small head — more at CHAPTER] **1 a :** a civil or ecclesiastical ordinance esp. of the Frankish kings **b :** a collection of ordinances — usu. used in pl. **2 :** a member of a chapter, esp. an ecclesiastical chapter **:** CAPITULAR **3** [ML *capitularium*, fr. LL *capitulum* section, chapter] **:** a book containing an index of first and last words of portions of the Bible read in the liturgy of the Roman Catholic Church

2capitulary \ˈ"\ *adj* [ML *capitularis* — more at CAPITULAR] **:** belonging or relating to a chapter, esp. an ecclesiastical or masonic chapter **:** CAPITULAR

1ca·pit·u·late \kəˈpichəˌlāt, *usu* -ād· + V\ *vb* -ED/-ING/-S [ML *capitulatus*, past part. of *capitulare* to distinguish by heads or chapters, fr. LL *capitulum* section, chapter, fr. L, small head] *vi* **1** *archaic* **a :** to arrange for bargaining and parleying **:** TREAT, NEGOTIATE ⟨magistrates . . . *capitulated* with the . . . agricultural rioters —Robert Southey⟩ **b :** to assent to terms arranged or proposed **:** AGREE ⟨two gentlemen ~ to fight on horseback —William Segar⟩ **2 a :** to surrender often according to terms agreed on **:** YIELD ⟨the Continentals, outnumbered, fled to Forty Fort, which *capitulated* on July 4 —F.E. Ross⟩ **b :** to cease withholding, resisting, or contending **:** ACQUIESCE ⟨I always tip for special services rendered but I will not ~ before sheer impertinence —Joseph Wechsberg⟩ ~ *vt, archaic* **:** to arrange in or as if in chapters **:** draw up under or as if under heads or articles ⟨sadly the wise youth *capitulated* Berry's words —George Meredith⟩ **syn** see YIELD

2ca·pit·u·late \-ˌlət,-ˌlāt\ *adj* [NL *capitulatus*, fr. L, having a small head, fr. *capitulum* small head + *-atus* -ate — more at CAPITULUM] **:** CAPITELLATE

ca·pit·u·la·tion \ˌ=,==ˈlāshən\ *n* -s [MF, fr. *capituler* to capitulate (fr. ML *capitulare*) + *-ation* -ation] **1 :** a listing of the main headings of a subject **:** ENUMERATION **2 a :** a set of terms or articles constituting an agreement (as a treaty or convention) between governments **b :** an agreement with specified stipulations (as the granting of special privileges and rights of extraterritoriality) exacted by one government of another **c :** one of the articles or terms of such an agreement **3 a :** the act or agreement of one that surrenders to an enemy upon stipulated terms ⟨the ~ of the defenders of the besieged town⟩ **b :** the instrument setting forth the terms of such an agreement **4 :** a giving way **:** a ceasing to resist **:** YIELDING ⟨~ to jealousy —Marcia Davenport⟩

ca·pit·u·la·tor \=ˈ==ˌlād·ə(r), -ātə-\ *n* -s [*1capitulate* + *-or*] **:** one that capitulates

ca·pit·u·la·to·ry \=ˈ==lə,tōrē, -ȯrē, -i\ *adj* [*1capitulate* + *-ory*] **:** of, relating to, or established by capitulation **:** EXTRATERRITORIAL ⟨the claims of U.S. ~ rights —*Current History*⟩

ca·pit·u·li·form \-lə̇ˌfȯrm\ *adj* [ISV *capituli-* (fr. NL *capitulum*) + *-form*; prob. orig. formed as F *capituliforme*] **:** resembling a capitulum

ca·pit·u·lum \kəˈpichələm\ *n, pl* **capitu·la** \-lə\ [LL, fr. L, small head, dim. of *capit-, caput* head — more at HEAD] **1 :** a passage or reading from the Bible **2** [NL, fr L] **:** a rounded usu. terminal protuberance of a part: as **a :** the knob at the end of a bone or cartilage **b :** the enlarged tip of the proboscis of a fly **c :** the enlarged end of a halter of a fly **d :** the end of a capitate antenna **e :** the beak of a tick composed of the mouthparts and palpi **f :** the body of a barnacle as distinguished from the peduncle **3** [NL, fr. L] **a :** one of the rounded cells borne upon the manubrium in the antheridium of plants of the family Characeae **b :** a simple racemose inflorescence in which the primary axis is shortened and dilated forming a rounded or flattened cluster of sessile flowers (as in the buttonbush and in all composite plants) — called also *head*

capitulum of the buttonbush

capivara *var of* CAPYBARA

ca·pi·vi \kəˈpēvē, -ˈpī-\ *n* -s [modif. of Sp & Pg *copaiba* — more at COPAIBA] **:** COPAIBA 1

caple *n* -s [ME *capel, capul*, prob. of Celt origin; akin to OIr *capall* horse, ScGael, mare, horse, fr. L *caballus* nag — more at CAVALCADE] *archaic* **:** HORSE

cap·less \ˈkapləs\ *adj* **:** being without a cap

caplin *or* **capling** *var of* CAPELIN

caplock \ˈ=,=\ *n* -s **:** a muzzle-loader fired by a percussion cap

cap·mint \ˈkap,mint\ *n* -s [prob. alter. of *catmint*] **:** CALAMINT

-cap·nea \ˈkapnēə\ *n comb form, pl* **-capni·as** \-nēəz\ *or* **-capni·ae** \-nēˌē\ [NL, fr. Gk *kapnos* smoke + NL *-ia*; akin to L *cupere* to desire — more at COVET] **:** carbon dioxide in the blood ⟨hyper*capnia*⟩ ⟨hypo*capnia*⟩

cap·no·di·a·ce·ae \(ˌ)kapˌnōdēˈāsēˌē\ *n pl, cap* [NL, fr. *Capnodium*, type genus + *-aceae*] **:** a family of ascomycetous fungi that includes most of the sooty molds, is usu. placed in the order Dothideales but sometimes in Perisporiales, and is characterized by dark-colored mycelium and a dark massive brittle stroma

cap·no·di·um \kapˈnōdēəm\ *n, cap* [NL, fr. Gk *kapnōdēs* smoky, dark (fr. *kapnos* smoke) + NL *-ium* — more at COVET] **:** a genus of sooty molds that is the type of the family Capnodiaceae and includes some fungi that attack economic plants (as citrus, coffee, and olive)

cap nut *n* **:** BOX NUT

ca·po \ˈkä(ˌ)pō\ *n* [by shortening] **:** CAPOTASTO

capoc *var of* KAPOK

ca·po·col·lo \ˌkapəˈkōlə, - äp-, -ȯl-, -(ˌ)lō\ *n, pl* **capocol·li** \-(ˌ)lē\ *or* **capocollos** [It, fr. *capo* head of an animal (fr. L *caput* head) + *collo* neck, fr. L *collum* — more at HEAD, COLLAR] **:** a cured and smoked pork product cased like a sausage

ca·po di mon·te \ˌkä(ˌ)pōdēˈmäntē\ *n, usu cap C&M* **:** an 18th century soft paste porcelain produced at Capodimonte, Italy, under patronage of the King of Naples

cap of liberty : LIBERTY CAP

cap of maintenance *also* **cap of dignity** *or* **cap of estate 1 :** a cap formerly worn as a symbol of office or high rank and still used as the cap of state borne before the British sovereign on certain ceremonial occasions and in modified form as the lining of British royal crowns and peers' coronets **2 :** the fur hat worn by the city sword-bearer or borne before the mayor on ceremonial occasions in several cities in England and Ireland **3 :** a heraldic cap showing a fur lining turned up about the bottom and split at the back sometimes borne as a charge and often used instead of a wreath to support the crest — called also *chapeau*

cap of maintenance 3

capolin *var of* CAPULIN

ca·po·mo \kəˈpō(ˌ)mō\ *n* -s [MexSp] **:** a breadnut tree (*Brosimum alicastrum*) whose fruits and leaves are fed to cattle

1ca·pon \ˈkāˌpän *also* -ˌpən\ *n* -s [ME, fr. OE *capūn*, prob. fr. ONF *capon*, fr. L *capon-, capo*; akin to Gk *koptein* to smite, cut off, *skaptein* to dig, Lith *skopti* to hollow out with a knife, Russ *shchepat'* to split, OSlav *kopati* to dig, *skopiti* to castrate] **1 :** a castrated male chicken — compare POULARDE **2 :** a castrated male rabbit

2capon \ˈ"\ *vt* -ED/-ING/-S **:** CASTRATE, CAPONIZE

ca·pon·ette *also* **ca·pon·et** \ˌkāpəˈnet\ *n* -s [*capon* + *-ette* or *-et*] **:** a chemically castrated fowl **:** a capon produced by use of diethylstilbestrol

ca·pon·i·za·tion \ˌkāpənə̇ˈzāshən, -ˌnīˈz-\ *n* -s **:** castration esp. of a fowl

ca·pon·ize \ˈkāpəˌnīz\ *vt* -ED/-ING/-S [*capon* + *-ize*] **:** CASTRATE — compare POULARDIZE

ca·pon·iz·er \-zə(r)\ *n* -s **:** one that caponizes

capon's-feather \ˈ=(ˌ)=ˌ==\ *or* **capon's-tail** \ˈ=(ˌ)=ˌ=\ *n, pl* **capon's-feathers** *or* **capon's-tails :** the common columbine (*Aquilegia vulgaris*)

capon's-grass \ˈ=(ˌ)=ˌ=\ *or* **capon's-tail grass** \ˈ=(ˌ)=ˌ=ˌ=\ *n, pl* **capon's-grasses** *or* **capon's-tail grasses :** RATTAIL FESCUE

ca·poor cutch·ery \kəˈpu̇(ə)rˈkəchərē\ *n* [Hindi *kapūr-kacarī*, fr. *kapūr* camphor (fr. Skt *karpūra*) + *kacarī* (*Hedychium spicatum*) — more at CAMPHOR] **:** the dried root of an East Indian plant (*Hedychium spicatum*)

¹cap·o·ral \ˈkap(ə)rəl *also* ¦kapəˈral *or* -ȧl\ *n* -S [F, lit., corporal — more at CORPORAL] **:** a coarse tobacco

²cap·o·ral \¦kapəˈral, -ȧl\ *n* -S [Sp, foreman, fr. It *caporale* corporal — more at CORPORAL] *Southwest* **:** a foreman or assistant manager on a stock ranch

¹ca·pot \kəˈpät, -ˈpō\ *n* -S [F, adj., not having made a trick at piquet, fr. *capot* hooded cloak] **:** the winning of all the tricks in piquet and other games

²ca·pot \kəˈpō\ *n* -S [F, hooded cloak, fr. MF *cape* cloak, fr. LL *cappa* head covering, cloak — more at CAP] **1 :** CAPOTE **2 :** an old large worthless bud or fruit of the caper

ca·po·ta·sto \ˌkäpōˈtä(ˌ)stō\ *n, pl* **capotastos** \-(ˌ)stōz\ *or* **ca·pi·ta·sti** \ˌkäpēˈtä(ˌ)stē\ [It, lit., chief key, fr. *capo* head, chief (fr. L *caput* head) + *tasto* key of a musical instrument, fr. *tastare* to feel, touch, fr. (assumed) VL *tastare* — more at HEAD, TASTE] **:** a bar or movable nut attached to the fingerboard of a guitar or other fretted instrument to uniformly raise the pitch of all the strings

ca·pote \kəˈpōt\ *n* -S [F, fr. *cape* cloak, fr. MF] **1 a :** a usu. long and hooded cloak or overcoat of rough cloth worn esp. by travelers and soldiers **b :** a Levantine long cloak of coarse fur **c :** a rain cape made of vegetable fibers **d :** a long mantle worn by women **e :** a bullfighter's cape **2 :** a small Victorian bonnet with tie strings and varied trimmings

cap·pa \ˈkäpə, -ˈa-\ *n, pl* **cap·pae** \ˈkä(ˌ)pā, ˈka(ˌ)pē\ *or* **cappas** [LL — more at CAP] **:** a cape esp. as part of ecclesiastical or academic garb

¹cap·pa·do·ci·an \ˌkapəˈdōsh(ē)ən\ *adj, usu cap* [*Cappadocia*, ancient country in extreme eastern Asia Minor + E *-an*] **:** of or relating to Cappadocia, its people, or their language

²cappadocian \¦==¦=(=)=\ *n* -S *cap* **1 :** a native or inhabitant of Cappadocia **2 :** the ancient language of the Cappadocians

cap·pagh brown *or* **cap·pah brown** \ˈkapə-\ *n, usu cap C* [fr. *Cappagh*, near Cork, Ireland, its locality] **1 :** a natural pigment consisting chiefly of hydrated oxides of manganese and iron and having a hue of reddish brown that heating makes richer **2 :** RUSSIAN CALF

cap·pa ma·gna \¦käpəˈmänyə\ *n* [ML, lit., large cope] **:** a flowing long-trained ceremonial vestment with ermine or silk hood worn by cardinals, bishops, and a few other prelates

cap·pa·ri·da·ce·ae \ˌkapərəˈdāsēˌē, kəˌpar-\ *n pl, cap* [NL, irreg. fr. *Capparis*, type genus + *-aceae*] **:** a family of herbs, shrubs, and trees (order Rhoeadales) distinguished from the related Cruciferae by a one-celled capsule — **cap·pa·ri·da·ceous** \¦===¦dāshəs, =¦==-\ *adj*

cap·pa·ris \ˈkapərəs\ *n, cap* [NL, fr. L, caper, fr. Gk *kapparis*] **:** a genus (the type of the family Capparidaceae) of shrubs or small trees widely distributed in warm regions, sometimes climbing by stipular thorns, and having simple leaves and showy flowers with four sepals, four petals, and numerous stamens — see ¹CAPER

capped *adj* [fr. past part. of ²*cap* "to cause to swell"] **:** affected with a bursal swelling tending to become a hard fibrous mass resulting from pressure or repeated injury — used chiefly of leg affections of horses ⟨~ hock⟩ ⟨~ knee⟩ ⟨~ elbow⟩

capped dice *n pl* **:** crooked dice covered on one or more sides with resilient faces

capped macaque *n* **:** BONNET MONKEY

capped pawn *n* **:** a chess handicap in which a player undertakes to give checkmate with a specified pawn

cap·pe·len·ite \ˈkap(ə)ləˌnīt\ *n* -S [G or Sw *cappelenit*, fr. D. Cappelen *fl* 1885 Norwegian scientist + G or Sw *-it* -ite] **:** a rare yttrium-barium borosilicate in greenish brown hexagonal crystals

cap·pel·let·ti \ˌkapəˈled·ē\ *n pl* [It, pl. of *cappelletto*, dim. of *cappello* hat, fr. ML *cappellus, capellus* cap, dim. of LL *cappa* head covering, cloak — more at CAP] **:** small cases of dough usu. filled with meat or cheese — compare RAVIOLI

cap·per \ˈkapə(r)\ *n* -S [ME, fr. *cappe* cap + *-er*] **1 :** a maker or seller of caps **2 :** one that caps: as **a :** an operator or a machine that applies the closure or cap to bottles, jars, cans, or tubes **b :** one that presses a paper disk into the top of a paper cup **3 :** a device for applying a percussion cap **4 a :** one that bids up prices artificially at auctions **b :** a lure, decoy, or steerer esp. in some illicit or questionable activity **:** SHILL **5 :** a worker who withdraws cylinders of curved window glass from the blowing machine and cuts them into desired lengths — called also *corker, sealer* **6 :** a worker who impregnates log piling at the butt end with preserving chemicals

cap·pie \ˈkapi\ *n* -S [⁴*cap* + *-ie*] *Scot* **:** a small wooden drinking vessel

capping *n* -S **1 :** something that caps: as **a :** rock overlying the mineral body of a mine **b :** a fore-and-aft finishing piece at the frame heads in an open boat **2 :** the architectural member that serves as a cap **3 :** the wax that covers honey or cells in a comb **4 :** the action of one that caps

capping plane *n* **:** a plane for working the upper surface of staircase rails

cap pistol *n* [¹*cap* (explosive)] **:** a toy pistol that fires caps

cap plate *n* **:** HEADPLATE

cap·po \kəˈpō\ *n* -S [modif. of F *capote*] **:** CAPOTE 1a

cap·py \ˈkapē\ *adj, often* -ER/-EST **1 :** like a cap ⟨a ~ hairdo⟩ **2** *of dairy products* **:** having a tallow taste because of butterfat oxidation

ca·pra \ˈkaprə\ *n, cap* [NL, fr. L, she-goat, fem. of *caper* goat — more at CAPRIOLE] **:** a genus of ruminant mammals (family Bovidae) consisting of the goats, the ibex, and related animals

cap·ral·de·hyde \kaˈpraldəˌhīd\ *n* -S [*capric* + *aldehyde*] **:** DECANAL

cap·rate \ˈkaˌprāt\ *n* -S [ISV *capric* + *-ate*; orig. formed in F] **:** a salt or ester of capric acid

ca·prel·la \kəˈprelə\ *n, cap* [NL, dim. of L *capra* — more at CAPRA] **:** a genus of small amphipod crustaceans that are found chiefly on seaweeds and that have a grotesque form suggestive of the praying mantis

ca·pre·o·line \kəˈprēəˌlīn, ˈkapr-\ *adj* [NL *Capreolus* + E *-ine*] **:** of or belonging to the genus *Capreolus*

ca·pre·o·lus \kəˈprēələs\ *n, cap* [NL, fr. L, wild goat — more at CAPRIOLE] **:** a genus consisting of the roe deer

ca·pret·to \kəˈpred·(ˌ)ō\ *n, pl* **caprettos** \-ōz\ *or* **capret·ti** \-(ˌ)ē\ [It, kid, dim. of *capra* goat, fr. L, she-goat, fem. of *capr-, caper* goat, male goat] **:** the meat of a kid

ca·pri \kaˈprē, kə-; ˈkä(ˌ)prē, -ˈa-\ *n* -S *often cap* [fr. *Capri*, island in the Bay of Naples] **1 :** a pale dry wine made orig. on the island of Capri and now also on the island of Ischia and in the vicinity of Naples **2 :** a strong greenish blue that is bluer and deeper than grotto, greener and duller than cobalt, and greener and deeper than average cerulean blue (sense 1a)

capri- *comb form* [L, fr. *capr-, caper*] **:** goat ⟨*Capri*corn⟩

capri blue *n, often cap C* [fr. *Capri*, island in the Bay of Naples, Italy; prob. fr. the famous blue grotto on the island] **1 :** a vivid blue that is greener and slightly less strong than Ch'ing and greener and duller than Cleopatra or ultramarine — compare CAPRI 2 **2 :** a blue oxazine dye

cap·ric \ˈkaprik\ *adj* [*capri-* + *-ic*] **:** of or relating to a goat

capric acid *n* [ISV *capri-* + *-ic*; fr. its goatlike odor; orig. formed as F *caprique*] **:** a low-melting crystalline fatty acid $CH_3(CH_2)_8COOH$ occurring in fats and oils often along with caproic acid — called also *decanoic acid*

capric aldehyde *n* **:** DECANAL

ca·pric·ciet·to \ˌkaprəˈched·(ˌ)ō, -ȧp-, kəˌprēchēˈed-\ *n, pl* **capricciettos** \-ōz\ *or* **capric·ciet·ti** \-(ˌ)ē\ [It *capriccetto*, dim. of *capriccio*] **:** a short musical capriccio

ca·pric·cio \kəˈprē(ˌ)chō, -ˈi-, -chēˌō\ *n, pl* **capriccios** \-ōz\ *also* **ca·pric·ci** \-(ˌ)ē\ [It] **1 :** a sudden apparently unmotivated turn of mind **:** FANCY, WHIMSY ⟨notwithstanding his excellences . . . Lamb could be guilty of ~ —John Mason Brown⟩ **2 :** a sudden sportive motion or action **:** CAPER, PRANK ⟨magnificent were thy ~*s* on this globe of earth —Charles Lamb⟩ **3 a :** a composition or adornment (as in sculpture) showing unrestrained fancy ⟨a neobaroque monument covered with decorative forms which . . . are intended as ~*s* —J.T.Soby⟩ **b :** an instrumental piece in free form usu. lively in tempo and brilliant in style — called also *caprice*

ca·pric·ci·o·so \kəˌprēchēˈō(ˌ)sō, -ich-\ *adj* [It, fr. *capriccio* + *-oso* -ous] **:** free and impulsive — used chiefly as a direction in music

ca·price \kəˈprēs *also* ka-\ *n* -S [F, fr. It *capriccio* caprice, shiver, fr. *capo* head (fr. L *caput*) + *riccio* hedgehog, fr. L *ericius*; basic meaning: head with hair standing on end, hence, horror, shivering, then (after It *capra* goat), whim — more at HEAD, URCHIN] **1 a :** a sudden impulsive apparently unmotivated change of mind **:** WHIM, FANCY ⟨a gang of unruly children whose ~*s* may be tolerated —Kenneth Tynan⟩ ⟨she sang a verse of it, merely out of ~ —William Black⟩ **b :** any sudden change or series of changes or vicissitudes hard to predict or explain ⟨the large and small ~*s* of the weather —C.C. Furnas⟩ ⟨between unchanging custom and the legitimate ~ of custom which is fashion —Edward Sapir⟩ **2 :** a disposition to change one's mind suddenly, impulsively, or without apparent motive **:** WHIMSICALITY ⟨his owners worked him sorely and with the ~ of Indians alternately . . . tortured him and treated him as one of themselves —Bernard DeVoto⟩ **3 a :** a fanciful work of art **b :** CAPRICCIO 3b

ca·pri·cious \kəˈprishəs, -ēsh- *also* ka-\ *adj* [It *capriccioso*] **1 :** marked or guided by caprice **:** given to changes of interest or attitude according to whims or passing fancies **:** not guided by steady judgment, intent, or purpose ⟨he judged her to be ~ and easily wearied of the pleasure of the moment —Edith Wharton⟩ ⟨the editing of these papers is so ~ and so wholly without any consistent and discriminating standards —C.P. Aiken⟩ **2 :** lacking a standard or norm **:** marked by variation or irregularity **:** lacking predictable pattern or law **:** CHANGEABLE, ERRATIC, WHIMSICAL ⟨the revenue of government from the taxes was not regular but ~ and exceptional —Hilaire Belloc⟩ ⟨the demand for fur felt provided a steadier, less ~ market —D.G.Creighton⟩ **syn** see INCONSTANT

ca·pri·cious·ly \-lē, -i\ *adv* **:** in a capricious manner

ca·pri·cious·ness \-snəs\ *n* -ES **:** the quality or state of being capricious

cap·ri·corn \ˈkaprəˌkȯrn, -rēˌk-, -ȯ(ə)n\ *n* -S *usu cap* [ME *capricorne*, a southern zodiacal constellation, fr. L *capricornus* (trans. of Gk *aigokerōs*, lit., goat-horned), fr. *capri-* + *-cornus* (fr. *cornu* horn) — more at HORN] **:** the 10th sign of the zodiac — see SIGN table; ZODIAC illustration

capricorn beetle *n* [earlier *capricorn*, prob. fr. (assumed) NL *capricornus*, fr. L; fr. the hornlike antennae] **:** any of various beetles of the family Cerambycidae

cap·ri·cor·nis \¦==¦=nəs\ *n, cap* [NL, fr. *capri-* + *-cornis* (irreg. fr. *cornu* horn) — more at HORN] **:** the genus (family Bovidae) consisting of the serow

¹cap·rid \ˈkaprəd\ *adj* **:** of or relating to Capridae or goats

²caprid \"\ *n* -S [NL *Capridae*] **:** one of the Capridae; *esp* **:** GOAT

cap·ri·dae \ˈkaprəˌdē\ *n pl, cap* [NL, fr. *Capra*, type genus + *-idae*] *in former classifications* **:** a family of Artiodactyla comprising the sheep, goats, and related forms now usu. included in Bovidae

cap·ri·fi·cate \ˈkaprəfəˌkāt, kəˈprif-\ *vt* -ED/-ING/-S [back-formation fr. *caprification*] **:** to subject to caprification

cap·ri·fi·ca·tion \ˌkaprəfəˈkāshən\ *n* -S [L *caprification-, caprificatio*, fr. *caprificatus*, past part. of *caprificare* to ripen figs by caprification, fr. *caprificus* wild fig, fr. *capri-* + *ficus* fig — more at FIG] **:** a horticultural operation in which flowering branches of the caprifig are hung in fig trees so as to facilitate pollination by the fig wasp which carries pollen from the flower of the caprifig to that of the edible fig

cap·ri·fig \ˈkaprəˌfig\ *n* -S [ME *caprifige*, part trans. of L *caprificus*] **1 :** a wild fig (*Ficus carica sylvestris*) of southern Europe and Asia Minor used in most fig-raising countries for pollination of the edible fig — see CAPRIFICATION **2 :** the fruit of the caprifig

caprifoil *or* **caprifole** *n* -S [modif. of ML *caprifolium*] *obs* **:** HONEYSUCKLE

cap·ri·fo·li·a·ce·ae \ˌkaprəˌfōlēˈāsēˌē\ *n pl, cap* [NL, fr. *Caprifolium*, type genus + *-aceae*] **:** a large family of plants (order Rubiales) characterized by opposite usu. exstipulate leaves and flowers with calyx tube adnate to the ovary

cap·ri·fo·li·um \-ˈfōlēəm\ *n* [NL, fr. ML, honeysuckle, fr. L *capri-* + *folium* leaf — more at BLADE] **1** *cap, in some esp former classifications* **:** a genus of plants that is the type of the family Caprifoliaceae but is now usu. considered a subgenus of *Lonicera* **2** -S **:** a plant of the family Caprifoliaceae (as a honeysuckle)

cap·ri·fy \ˈkaprəˌfī\ *vt* -ED/-ING/-ES [ME *caprifien*, fr. L *caprificare* — more at CAPRIFICATION] **1 :** to induce the formation of fig fruits in (a tree) by caprification **2 :** to induce the development of parthenocarpic fig fruits in (a tree) by the use of chemical growth regulators

cap·ri·mul·gid \ˌkaprəˈməljəd, -lg-\ *n* -S [NL *Caprimulgidae*] **:** one of the Caprimulgidae **:** GOATSUCKER

cap·ri·mul·gi·dae \-əˌdē\ *n pl, cap* [NL, fr. *Caprimulgus*, type genus (fr. L, milker of goats, goatsucker, fr. *capri-* + *-mulgus*, fr. *mulgēre* to milk) + *-idae* — more at MILK] **:** a family of birds with a deeply cleft broad bill comprising the goatsuckers and constituting with the frogmouths a suborder of the order Caprimulgiformes

cap·ri·mul·gi·for·mes \ˌ==¦==əˈfȯrˌmēz\ *n pl, cap* [NL, fr. *Caprimulgus*, type genus + *-iformes*] **:** an order of long-winged nonpasserine birds comprising the goatsuckers, frogmouths, and oilbirds — see CAPRIMULGIDAE

cap·rin \ˈkaprən\ *n* -S [ISV *capric* + *-in*; prob. orig. formed as F *caprine*] **:** glycerol tri-caprate

cap·rine \ˈkaˌprīn\ *adj* [L *caprinus*, fr. *capr-, caper* + *-inus* -ine] **1 :** being a goat **:** belonging to a group typified by the goat ⟨a ~ creature⟩ ⟨~ antelopes⟩ **2 :** like or suggestive of a goat **:** like that of a goat ⟨a ~ voice⟩ **3 :** developing or thriving in a goat ⟨a ~ strain of virus⟩

ca·prin·ic \kəˈprinik, (ˈ)ka¦p-\ *adj* [prob. fr. G *kaprin-* (prob. modif., influenced by L *caprinus* caprine, of F *caprique* capric) + E *-ic*] **:** CAPRIC

¹cap·ri·ole \ˈkaprēˌōl\ *vi* -ED/-ING/-S [prob. fr. It *capriolare*, fr. *capriola*] **:** to perform a capriole

²capriole \"\ *n* -S [MF or OIt; MF *capriole*, fr. OIt *capriola*, fr. *capriolo* roebuck, fr. L *capreolus* roebuck, wild goat, fr. *capr-, caper* goat; akin to OE *hæfer* goat, ON *hafr*, Gk *kapros* wild boar] **1** *dancing* **a :** CAPER **b :** CABRIOLE **2** *of a trained horse* **:** a vertical leap with a backward kick of the hind legs at the height of the leap

ca·pri·ote \ˈkaprēˌōt, ˈkä-, -ēət\ *n* -S *cap* [*Capri*, island in the Bay of Naples, Italy + E *-ote*] **:** a native or inhabitant of Capri

cap·ro·al·de·hyde \¦ka(ˌ)prōˈaldəˌhīd\ *n* -S [*caproic* (in *caproic acid*) + *aldehyde*] **:** HEXANAL

cap·ro·ate \ˈkaprəˌwāt\ *n* -S [*caproic* + *-oate*] **:** a salt or ester of caproic acid

cap rock *n* **:** ¹CAP 2a(3)

ca·pro·ic acid \kəˈprōik-, (ˈ)ka¦p-\ *n* [ISV *capr-* (fr. L *capr-, caper* goat) + *-oic*; orig. formed as F *caproïque* — more at CAPRIOLE] **:** a liquid fatty acid $CH_3(CH_2)_4COOH$ that is found in the form of its glycerol ester in fats and oils (as butter and coconut oil) or made synthetically and used in synthesizing pharmaceuticals and flavors — called also *hexanoic acid*

cap·ro·in \ˈkaprəwən\ *n* -S [ISV *caproic* + *-in*] **:** glyceryl caproate

cap·ro·lac·tam \ˌkaprōˈlakˌtam, ¦==ˌlakˈtam\ *n* -S [ISV *caproic* + *lactam*] **:** a white crystalline cyclic amide $C_6H_{11}NO$ that yields epsilon-amino-caproic acid on hydrolysis and is used chiefly in making one type of nylon — called also *epsilon-caprolactam*

cap·ro·yl \ˈkaprəˌwil, -ēl\ *n* -S [ISV *caproic* + *-yl*] **:** the radical $C_5H_{11}CO$— of caproic acid — called also *hexanoyl*

cap·ryl \ˈkaprəl\ *n* -S [ISV *capric* + *-yl*] **1 :** the radical $C_9H_{19}CO$— of capric acid — called also *decanoyl* **2 :** the univalent radical $CH_3(CH_2)_5CH(CH_3)$— derived from 2-octanol; 1-methyl-heptyl

cap·ryl·al·de·hyde \ˌkaprəˈlaldəˌhīd\ *n* -S [ISV *capryl* + *aldehyde*] **:** OCTANAL

cap·ry·late \ˈkaprəˌlāt\ *n* -S [ISV *caprylic* + *-ate*] **:** a salt or ester of caprylic acid

ca·pryl·ic \kəˈprilik, (ˈ)ka¦p-\ *adj* [ISV *capryl* + *-ic*] **1 :** relating to caprylic acid **2** [*capri-* + *-yl* + *-ic*] *of an odor* **:** suggesting an animal body in rank pungency

caprylic acid *n* **:** a liquid fatty acid $CH_3(CH_2)_6COOH$ having a rancid odor and occurring in fats and oils often along with caproic acid — called also *octanoic acid*

cap·ry·lin \ˈkaprələn, -(ˌ)lin; kəˈprilən, ka-\ *n* -S [ISV *caprylic* + *-in*] **:** glycerol caproate

cap·ry·lyl \ˈkaprəˌlil; kəˈprilәl, ka-\ *n* -S [ISV *capryl* + *-yl*] **:** the radical $C_7H_{15}CO$— of caprylic acid—called also *octanoyl*

caps *pl of* CAP, *pres 3d sing of* CAP

caps *abbr* capsule

cap·sa·i·cin \kapˈsāəsən\ *n* -S [alter. (perh. influenced by L *capsa* box) of *capsicine* "an extract from cayenne pepper", fr. NL *Capsicum* + E *-in*] **:** a colorless crystalline phenolic amide $C_9H_{17}CONHCH_2C_6H_3(OCH_3)OH$ that is a powerful irritant and the pungent principle of cayenne pepper

cap·san·thin \kapˈsan(t)thən\ *n* -S [ISV *caps-* (fr. NL *Capsicum*) + *anth-* + *-in*] **:** a carmine red crystalline carotenoid pigment $C_{40}H_{58}O_3$ found in paprika

cap screw *n* **:** TAP BOLT

cap scuttle *n* **:** a ship scuttle having a cap set closely over coamings into a rabbet

cap·sel·la \kapˈselə\ *n, cap* [NL, fr. L *capsa* box, case + NL *-ella* — more at CASE] **:** a genus of widely distributed weeds of the family Cruciferae with basal tufted leaves, small white racemose flowers, and notched markedly flattened pods—see SHEPHERD'S PURSE

capsheaf \ˈ=ˌ=\ *n, pl* **capsheaves** **1 :** the top sheaf of a shock or stack of grain **2 :** the crowning point **:** most extreme instance **:** dominant element **:** CLIMAX, ACME ⟨insulting his benefactor was the ~ of folly⟩

capshore \ˈ=ˌ=\ *n* -S [*cap* + *shore*] **:** a support under the fore part of the cap of a lower mast

cap·si·an \ˈkapsēən\ *adj, usu cap* [F *capsien*, fr. *Capsa* (L name for Gafsa, town & oasis in W. cen. Tunisia, near where prehistoric remains were found) + F *-ien* -ian] **:** of or relating to a paleolithic culture of northern Africa and southern Europe characterized by microlithic stone implements in geometric forms and rock paintings of hunting scenes, the early period being regarded as contemporaneous with the Aurignacian and the later with the Solutrean-Magdalenian

cap·si·cum \ˈkapsəkəm\ *n* [NL, prob. fr. L *capsa* box + *-icum* (neut. sing. of *-icus* -ic) — more at CASE] **1** *cap* **:** a genus of chiefly tropical perennial shrubby plants (family Solanaceae) that are widely grown as annuals for their fruits which under cultivation occur as many-seeded berries with a thickened usu. fleshy integument and vary greatly in size, shape, color, and pungency — see BIRD PEPPER, CAYENNE PEPPER, HOT PEPPER, SWEET PEPPER **2** -S **:** any plant of the genus *Capsicum* **3** -S **:** the dried-ripe fruit of any of certain plants of the genus *Capsicum* (esp. *C. frutescens*) containing capsaicin and used as a gastric and intestinal stimulant and as a rubefacient

capsicum wool *n* **:** cotton impregnated with oleoresin of capsicum — called also *calorific wool*

cap·sid \ˈkapsəd\ *n* -S [NL *Capsidae*] **:** any of several small to moderate-sized delicate-bodied active bugs constituting a family (Miridae) and including certain destructive pests of cultivated plants some of which are important vectors of plant diseases as well as predaceous forms that are important in the biological control of insect pests

cap·si·dae \ˈkapsəˌdē\ *n pl*, [NL, fr. *Capsus*, type genus (irreg. fr. Gk *kapsis* gulping, fr. *kaptein* to gulp down) + *-idae* — more at HEAVE] *syn of* MIRIDAE

cap·size \ˈkapˌsīz, =ˈ=\ *vb* -ED/-ING/-S [origin unknown] *vt* **1 :** to turn over; *specif* **:** to cause to keel over or upset from a safe or accustomed level position to one involving danger or loss ⟨~ a canoe⟩ **2 :** COLLAPSE ~ *vi* **1 :** to turn over **:** become overturned **:** UPSET ⟨the ship *capsized* in the storm⟩ **2 :** to fold down **:** COLLAPSE **syn** see OVERTURN

cap sleeve *n* **:** a sleeve cut in one piece with the bodice and usu. covering only the cap of the shoulder

cap spinning *n* **:** a method of spinning by means of a cap on the spindle used in the production of Bradford-spun worsted

cap·stan \ˈkapstən\ *n* -S *often attrib* [ME] **1 :** a machine for moving or raising heavy weights (as in warping a ship or hoisting an anchor) by winding cable (as a chain or hawser) around a vertical spindle-mounted drum which is rotated manually by bars fitted into sockets in the drumhead or driven by steam or electric power, pawls at the foot of the drum permitting rotation in one direction only — compare WINCH 2, WINDLASS **2 :** a flangeless pulley used to control the motion of magnetic tape through a recorder

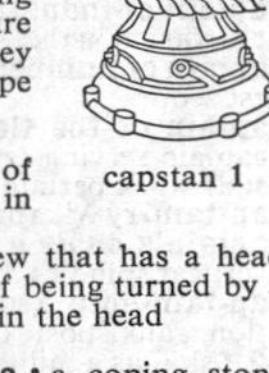
capstan 1

capstan lathe *n* **:** TURRET LATHE

capstan nut *n* **:** a nut resembling the head of a capstan and operated by a bar inserted in one of several holes about its periphery

capstan screw *or* **capstan bolt** *n* **:** a screw that has a head resembling a capstan and that is capable of being turned by a bar inserted in one of several radial holes in the head

capstern *or* **capstorm** *obs var of* CAPSTAN

capstone \ˈ=ˌ=\ *n* -S [¹*cap* + *stone*] **1 a :** a coping stone **:** COPING **b :** the horizontal topmost stone of a dolmen **2 :** the crowning point **:** most important element **:** decisive factor **:** CLIMAX, ACME ⟨a system of primary and secondary schools . . . with the university the ~ —*Amer. Guide Series: Va.*⟩

cap strip *n* **:** a continuous strip of material on the outer edge of an airplane wing rib for adding strength and providing increased area for the attachment of wing-covering material

capsul- *or* **capsuli-** *or* **capsulo-** *comb form* [NL, fr. *capsula*] **:** capsule ⟨*capsul*itis⟩ ⟨*capsuli*form⟩ ⟨*capsulo*lenticular⟩

cap·su·la \ˈkapsələ\ *n, pl* **capsu·lae** \-ˌlē, -ˌī\ [NL, fr. L, small box — more at CAPSULE] **:** CAPSULE

cap·su·lar \ˈkapsələ(r) *also* -syə-\ *adj* [NL *capsularis*, fr. *capsula* capsule + *-aris* -ar] **1 :** of, relating to, or like a capsule **2 :** CAPSULATE

capsular ligament *n* **:** a ligamentous sac surrounding the articular cavity of a freely movable joint and attached to the bones thus completely enclosing the joint

capsulary *adj* [NL *capsularius*, fr. *capsula* + *-arius* -ary] *obs* **:** CAPSULAR

cap·su·late \ˈkapsəˌlāt, -lət *also* -syə-\ *or* **cap·su·lat·ed** \-ˌlād·əd\ *adj* [*capsulate* fr. NL *capsulatus*, fr. *capsula* + L *-atus* -ate; *capsulated* fr. NL *capsulatus* + E *-ed*] **:** enclosed in a capsule

cap·su·la·tion \ˌ==ˈlāshən\ *n* -S [¹*capsule* + *-ation*] **:** enclosure in a capsule **:** ENCAPSULATION

¹cap·sule \ˈkapsəl, -(ˌ)sül *also* -ps(ˌ)yül *or* -psyəl\ *n* -S [F, fr. L *capsula* small box, dim. of *capsa* chest, case — more at CASE] **1 a :** a membrane or saclike structure enclosing a part or organ ⟨the ~ of the kidney⟩ ⟨an insect egg ~⟩ **b :** either of two layers or laminae of white matter in the cerebrum: (1) **:** a layer that consists largely of fibers passing to and from the cerebral cortex and that lies internal to the lenticular nucleus — called also *internal capsule* (2) **:** one that lies between the lenticular nucleus and the claustrum — called also *external capsule* **2 :** a closed container bearing spores or seeds: **a** *in seed plants* **:** a dry dehiscent usu. many-seeded fruit composed of two or more carpels and releasing its seed at maturity through pores or by breaking into valves — compare POD; see FRUIT illustration **b :** the spore sac of the sporogonium of a moss — called also *theca, pyxidium* **3 a** *obs* **:** an earthenware saucer for roasting or melting samples of ores **:** SCORIFIER **b :** a small shallow cup or boat (as of porcelain, platinum, or glass) used in chemical manipulation to hold a substance being heated **4 a :** a gelatin shell enclosing medicine **b :** any similar gelatin container **5 :** a metal seal over the cork of a bottle **6** *biol* **:** a viscous or gelatinous often polysaccharide envelope surrounding certain microscopic organisms (as the pneumococcus or many plantlike flagellates) **7 a :** an extremely brief condensation **:** OUTLINE, SURVEY ⟨~*s* of information too small to contain extended discussion —William Bridgwater⟩ **b :** a small quantity or amount **:** a little dose ⟨~*s* of history given to students⟩ **8 :** a compact usu. detachable receptacle ⟨watches operating on energy ~*s*⟩ **9 :** a small pressurized compartment for an aviator or astronaut for high-altitude flight, space flight, or emergency escape

capsules 2: *1* datura, *2* poppy, *3* gentian

²capsule \"\ *vt* -ED/-ING/-S **1 :** to equip with or enclose in a capsule ⟨a *capsuled* bottle of wine⟩ **2 :** to condense into or formulate in a very brief compact form ⟨*capsuled* the news⟩

³**capsule** \"\ *adj* **1 :** extremely brief and condensed ⟨a ~ biography⟩ ⟨~ coverage of the news⟩ **2 :** small and very compactly arranged and equipped ⟨a ~ submarine⟩

cap·sul·ec·to·my \ˌkapsəˈlektəmē *also* -syə-\ *n* -ES [ISV *capsul-* + *-ectomy*] **:** excision of a capsule (as of a joint, kidney, or lens)

capsule of bow·man \-ˈbōmən\ *usu cap B* **:** BOWMAN'S CAPSULE

capsule of glis·son \-ˈglisᵊn\ *usu cap G* **:** GLISSON'S CAPSULE

capsule of te·non \-təˈnōⁿ\ *usu cap T* **:** TENON'S CAPSULE

capsuli- — see CAPSUL-

cap·sul·ize \ˈkapsəˌlīz *also* -syə-\ *vt* -ED/ -ING/ -S **:** CAPSULE ⟨a *capsulized* account of the news⟩

capsulo- — see CAPSUL-

cap·su·min \ˈkapsəmən\ *n* -S [ISV *capsum-* (irreg. fr. NL *Capsicum*) + *-in*; orig. formed as G *kapsumin*] **:** a red crystalline carotenoid pigment in a Guinea pepper (*Capsicum annuum*)

¹**cap·tain** \ˈkaptən, *rapid or before a name sometimes* -pᵊm\ *n* -S [ME *capitane, captein*, fr. MF *capitaine, capitain*, fr. LL *capitaneus* foremost, chief, fr. L *capit-, caput* head — more at HEAD] **1 :** a person having authority over and responsibility for a group or unit **:** CHIEF, LEADER: as **a :** the commander of a body of troops or of a military establishment (as a fortress) **b :** an officer entrusted with a command under a sovereign or general **c :** a ranking naval or maritime officer: (1) **:** an officer in charge of a warship (2) **:** an officer in charge of any ship and responsible for its navigation and for direction of its operations regardless of official rank — often used as a courtesy title (3) **:** a senior naval officer ranking just below a rear admiral or commodore and above a commander **d :** an army, marine, or air-force officer ranking below a major and above a first lieutenant **e :** a distinguished or highly skilled military leader **f** *chiefly Eng* **:** a mine superintendent or manager **g** *obs* **:** an Indian chief **h** *chiefly Eng* **:** a leader of a student group **:** HEAD BOY **i :** a leader in charge of the personnel of a train, caravan, or airplane: as (1) **:** a railroad conductor in charge of a freight or passenger train (2) **:** a pilot of a plane in flight; *esp* **:** a pilot of an air-force plane **j :** a leader of a side or team in a sports contest or similar activity **k :** a fire or police department officer usu. ranking between a chief and a lieutenant **l :** a party officer charged with organizing voters in a ward, precinct, or electoral district **m** (1) **:** a restaurant functionary in charge of waiters **:** HEADWAITER (2) **:** a hotel functionary in charge of bellboys — called also *bell captain* **n** *chiefly South* **:** BOSS — sometimes used as a generalized term of respect **o :** a Salvation Army officer ranking above a first lieutenant and below a senior captain **p :** the player in chouette who plays against the man in the box — abbr. *capt.* **2 :** a dominant figure **:** a person of importance and influence ⟨~*s* of commerce⟩

²**captain** *adj, obs* **:** CHIEF, HEAD

³**cap·tain** \ˈkaptən\ *vt* -ED/-ING/-S **:** to be captain of **:** fill the role of captain of **:** LEAD

captain ball *n* **:** a game similar to basketball played on an area marked with six circles by teams of seven or more players who try to pass the ball to the player stationed in the end circle

cap·tain·cy \ˈkaptənsē, -i\ *n* -ES **1 :** a captain's post, rank, or commission ⟨promoted to a ~⟩ **2 :** the caliber of a captain's actions **:** CAPTAINSHIP ⟨neither diplomatic statesmanship nor military ~⟩ **3 :** an administrative district under a captain

captaincy general *n, pl* **captaincies general :** the office, power, territory, or jurisdiction of a captain general

cap·tain·ess \ˈkaptənəs\ *n, pl* **captainesses** \-nəsəz, -ˌnes-\ [ME *captenesse*, fr. *captein* captain + *-esse* -ess] **:** a female captain

captain general *n, pl* **captains general** *or* **captain generals 1 :** the commander in chief of an army **2 :** the commander in chief of the militia of a colony or state **3 :** the military governor of a colony, esp. a Spanish colony

cap·tain-gen·er·al·cy \ˌ≈≈(≈)≈sē\ *n* **:** CAPTAINCY GENERAL

cap·tain·ly *adv* **:** in the manner of a captain

captain of fortune : ADVENTURER

captain of industry : the head of a great industrial enterprise **:** ENTREPRENEUR

captain of numbers : the archery contestant making the highest score

captain of the fleet : a British naval officer of the rank of captain serving on the staff of a flag officer and in charge of staff work pertaining to maintenance of material

cap·tain·ry \ˈkaptənrē\ *n* -ES **:** CAPTAINCY

captain's chair *n* **:** an armchair with a low curved back with vertical spindles and a saddle seat

cap·tain·ship \-tənˌship\ *n* -S **1 :** condition, rank, post, or authority of a captain **2 :** skill as a military leader **3 :** CAPTAINCY 3

captain's mast *n* **:** a disciplinary proceeding at which the commanding officer of a naval vessel hears and disposes of cases against members of his command charged with an offense — called also *mast*

captain's chair

captain's walk *n* **:** WIDOW'S WALK

cap·ta·tion \kapˈtāshən\ *n* -S [L *captation-, captatio*, fr. *captatus* (past part. of *captare* to chase, strive to seize) + *-ion-, -io* -ion — more at CATCH] **1 :** an attempt to achieve or acquire something (as favor or applause) esp. artfully ⟨the candidate's obvious ~⟩ **2 :** the making of an ad captandum appeal

¹**cap·tion** \ˈkapshən\ *n* -S [ME *capcioun*, fr. L *caption-, captio*, fr. *captus*, past part. of *capere* to take — more at HEAVE] **1 a** *archaic* **:** act of taking or seizing **:** SEIZURE **b** *chiefly Scots law* **:** arrest by legal process **2 :** CAVIL, QUIBBLE ⟨a mere ~ unworthy of answer⟩ **3 :** the part of a legal instrument (as a commission, indictment, or deposition) that shows where, when, and by what authority it was taken, found, or executed **4** [influenced in meaning by L *caput* head] **a :** the heading or title of an article, story, document, chapter, or other composition or of a page or section **b :** the explanatory comment or designation accompanying a pictorial illustration usu. as an underline or overline **c :** a motion-picture subtitle

²**caption** \"\ *vt* **captioned; captioned; captioning** \-sh(ə)niŋ\ **captions :** to furnish with a caption **:** ENTITLE

caption code *n* **:** a code book in which phrases are listed under their important words rather than alphabetized by their first words

cap·tious \ˈkapshəs\ *adj* [ME *capcious*, fr. MF or L; MF *captieux*, fr. L *captiosus*, fr. *captio* act of taking, deception, fallacious argument + *-osus* -ous] **1 :** calculated to confuse, entrap, or entangle in argument **:** likely to perplex or discomfit ⟨a ~ question demanding a careful answer⟩ **2 :** marked by an inclination to stress faults and raise often trivial objections **:** perversely hard to please esp. because overstrict or capricious ⟨it is perhaps ~ when one is given so much, to wish for more —Bergen Evans⟩ ⟨never willfully unjust, but . . . too often ~ in his justice, fond of legal chicanery —J.R.Green⟩ **syn** see CRITICAL

cap·tious·ly \-lē, -i\ *adv* **:** in a captious manner

¹**cap·ti·vate** \ˈkaptəˌvāt, *usu* -ād· + V\ *vt* -ED/-ING/-S [LL *captivatus*, past part. of *captivare*, fr. L *captivus* captive] **1** *archaic* **:** take or hold as prisoner or prize **:** SEIZE, CAPTURE ⟨our prize, *captivated* from the British in a fair fight —P.L. Ford⟩ **2 :** to influence and dominate by some special charm, art, or trait and with an irresistible appeal precluding considered reservation ⟨every charm of person and address that can ~ a woman —Jane Austen⟩ ⟨*captivated* the delegates with his patriotic speech⟩ **syn** see ATTRACT

²**captivate** *adj* [LL *captivatus*] *obs* **:** CAPTIVATED

captivating *adj* **:** CHARMING, WINNING **:** showing ability to captivate ⟨a prose ~ in its music⟩ — **cap·ti·vat·ing·ly** *adv*

cap·ti·va·tion \ˌkaptəˈvāshən\ *n* -S [LL *captivation-, captivatio*, fr. *captivatus* + L *-ion-, -io* -ion] **1 :** act of captivating **2 :** state of being captivated

cap·ti·va·tor \ˈ≈≈ˌvād·ə(r)\ *n* -S **:** one that captivates

¹**cap·tive** \ˈkaptiv, -ēv\ *n* -S [ME, fr. L *captivus*, fr. *captivus*, adj.] **1 :** one captured **:** PRISONER **:** one taken and held usu. in confinement and esp. by an enemy in war **2 :** one captivated, dominated, or controlled ⟨a ~ to love⟩ ⟨the politician seemed a ~ of hidden interests⟩

²**captive** \"\ *adj* [ME, fr. L *captivus*, fr. *captus* (past part. of *capere* to take, seize) + *-ivus* -ive — more at HEAVE] **1 a :** taken and held as prisoner esp. by an enemy in war ⟨~ knights⟩ **b :** CONFINED **:** kept within bounds **:** CAGED ⟨a ~ bird⟩ **:** fenced in ⟨~ herds⟩ **c :** checked from free activity or course ⟨a ~ balloon riding on its cable⟩ ⟨~ waters impounded by the dam⟩ **2 :** indicative of or relative to a captive **:** making captive ⟨~ hours⟩ ⟨~ chains⟩ **3 :** CAPTIVATED, CHARMED, ENCHANTED ⟨her woman's heart ~ to his blandishments⟩ ⟨writing that holds the mind ~⟩ **4 a :** owned or controlled by another concern and operated according to its needs or demands rather than for an open market ⟨a ~ coal mine⟩ ⟨~ railroads⟩ **b :** dominated by a state, government, or philosophy alien to one's own often despite ostensible autonomy ⟨~ states on the boundaries of the empire⟩ **:** controlled by others despite semblance of independence ⟨a ~ candidate⟩ **5 :** in a situation making departure or inattention difficult **:** obliged to stay within hearing of a speech or demonstration ⟨a ~ audience⟩

³**captive** \"\ *vt* -ED/-ING/-S [ME *captiven*, fr. LL *captivare*, fr. L *captivus*] **1** *archaic* **:** CAPTURE **2** *archaic* **:** CAPTIVATE

captive bolt *n* **:** a gunlike instrument used in slaughtering animals that projects an attached plunger from the barrel

cap·tiv·i·ty \kapˈtivəd·ē, -atē, -i\ *n* -ES [ME *captivite*, fr. MF *captivité*, fr. L *captivitas*, fr. *captivus* captive + *-itas* -ity] **1 a :** state or condition of being held captive esp. in war **:** subjection to a captor ⟨troops remaining in ~ years after the war⟩ **b :** state of being kept caged or fenced in ⟨some birds thrive in ~⟩ **2 :** domination by or subjection to another **:** oppressive control by another ⟨the ~ of science and invention by business —W.H.Hamilton⟩ **3** *archaic* **:** a group of captives ⟨they delivered up the whole ~ to Edom —Amos 1:9 (AV)⟩

cap·tor \ˈkaptə(r), -ˌtȯ(r), -ˌtȯ(ə)\ *n* -S [LL, catcher of animals, fr. L *captus* + *-or*] **:** one that has captured a person or thing

cap·to·rhi·no·morph \ˌkaptəˈrīnəˌmȯ(ə)rf\ *n* -S *sometimes cap* [NL *Captorhinomorpha*] **:** one of the Captorhinomorpha

cap·to·rhi·no·mor·pha \ˌ≈≈≈≈ˈmȯrfə\ *n pl, cap* [NL, fr. *Captorhinus*, type genus + *-o-* + *-morpha*] **:** a suborder of Cotylosauria comprising reptiles of the Carboniferous and Lower Permian which are sometimes held to be generalized forms ancestral to most later reptiles and to mammals and birds though possessing distinctly specialized dentition

cap·tress \ˈkaptrəs\ *n* -ES [*captor* + *-ess*] **:** a female captor

¹**cap·ture** \ˈkapchə(r), -psh-\ *n* -S [MF, fr. L *captura*, fr. *captus* (past part. of *capere* to take, seize) + *-ura* -ure — more at HEAVE] **1 a :** the act of catching and holding by force, show of strength, stratagem, or guile often despite attempt to resist or to escape ⟨the ~ of the town by the enemy⟩ ⟨the ~ of an escaped convict⟩ ⟨snares, traps, gins, and pitfalls for the ~ of men by women —G.B.Shaw⟩ **b :** the act of winning, seizing, gaining control, or coming to dominate ⟨the ~ of the party by extremists⟩ ⟨the ~ of one's fancy by a piece of music⟩ **2 :** one that has been seized or taken; *esp* **:** a prize ship **3 :** the natural diversion of one stream into the channel of another — called also *stream piracy* **4 :** the act of moving so as to take one of an opponent's chessmen or one or more of his checkers **5 :** the coalescence of an atomic nucleus with an elementary particle (as a neutron or electron) that may result in an emission (as of gamma rays) from the nucleus or in fission of the nucleus

²**capture** \"\ *vb* **captured; captured; capturing** \-pchəriŋ -psh(ə)r-\ **captures** *vt* **1 :** to take, seize, or catch esp. as captive or prize by force, surprise, stratagem, craft, or skill: as **a :** to subdue into surrender and loss of independence ⟨*captured* prisoners⟩ **b :** to seize and occupy ⟨the king's forces *captured* the city⟩ **c :** to get control or secure domination of **:** take over ⟨making plans to enter the highest finance and to ~ the banking of the country —Hilaire Belloc⟩ **d :** to circumscribe, hold, or preserve in or as if in some pattern, medium, record, or other relatively permanent form ⟨at any such moment as a photograph might ~ —C.E.Montague⟩ **e :** to influence as though captive **:** captivate and hold the interest of ⟨*captured* their imagination⟩ **2 :** to take (as a piece in chess or a trick in cards) according to rules of a game **3** *of a stream* **:** to divert (another stream) into its own channel usu. by a process of erosion — compare BEHEAD 2 **4 :** to bring about the capture of (an elementary particle) ⟨the uranium 238 nucleus may ~ a slow-moving neutron to form uranium 239⟩ — see ¹CAPTURE 5 ~ *vi* **:** to take an opponent's checker or chessman from the board **syn** see CATCH

cap·u·an \ˈkapyəwən\ *adj, usu cap* [*Capua* ancient city of Italy known for its luxury (fr. L) + E *-an*] **:** of, relating to, or having the characteristics of Capua; *esp* **:** LUXURIOUS ⟨found the *Capuan* comforts he expected in Virginia —Henry Adams⟩

ca·puche \kəˈpüch, -üsh\ *n* -S [It *cappuccio*, fr. *cappa* cloak, fr. LL, head covering, cloak — more at CAP] **:** HOOD; *esp* **:** the cowl of a Capuchin friar

cap·u·chin \ˈkapyə|shən, kəˈp(y)ü|, |ch-\ *n* -S *often attrib* [MF *capuchin, capucin*, fr. OIt *cappuccino*, fr. *cappuccio* hood + *-ino* -ine] **1** *usu cap* **:** a Franciscan friar of the austere branch established in 1526 by Matteo di Bassi in Italy **2** *also* **cap·u·chine** \", ˈkapyəˌshēn, -ˌch-\ **:** a hooded cloak for women that resembles the habit of a Capuchin friar **3** [so called fr. the hoodlike appearance of the hair at the back of the head] **a :** a long-tailed So. American monkey (*Cebus capucinus*) having the forehead naked and wrinkled with the hair on the crown reflexed and resembling a friar's cowl **b :** a monkey of the genus *Cebus* **4** [so called fr. the hoodlike tuft of feathers on the head and neck] **:** a variety of the domestic pigeon

capuchin cross *n, usu cap 1st C* [prob. so called fr. its resemblance to a pilgrim's staff, an important tenet of the Capuchin order being that men are but pilgrims and strangers on earth] **:** a cross pommée

ca·pu·chin·ess \kəˈp(y)üshənəs, -üch-\ *n* -ES *usu cap* **:** a member of an austere order of Franciscan nuns under Capuchin rule

cap·u·cine \ˈkapyəˌsēn\ *n* -S [F, nasturtium, fr. *capucin* Capuchin; fr. the resemblance of the flower to a hood] **:** QUINCE YELLOW

capucine buff *n* **:** a pale orange yellow that is slightly yellower, lighter, and stronger than sunset and redder and stronger than freestone

capucine lake *n* **:** a moderate reddish orange that is yellower and lighter than flamingo and yellower and paler than crab apple

capucine madder *n* **:** a moderate orange that is yellower and slightly less strong than honeydew and less strong and slightly lighter than Persian orange

capucine orange *n* **:** a moderate orange that is yellower and slightly lighter and stronger than honeydew and yellower and paler than Persian orange

capucine red *n* **:** a vivid yellowish pink to strong reddish orange that is very slightly yellower than Chinese orange

capucine yellow *n* **:** a moderate orange that is yellower, stronger, and slightly lighter than honeydew and yellower and lighter than Persian orange

capul *var of* CAPLE

ca·pu·lin \ˌkäpəˈlēn\ *also* **ca·pu·li** \-lē\ *or* **ca·po·lin** \-pəˈlēn\ *n* -S [AmerSp *capulin, capuli*, fr. Nahuatl *capulin*] **1 :** a Mexican tree (*Prunus capuli*) that is sometimes considered to be a form of black cherry (*P. serotina*) and that yields a sap used in native remedies and has edible cherries of which the kernels of the pits furnish a flour **2 :** a tropical American tree (*Trema micrantha*) the bark of which yields a strong fiber **3 :** a ground cherry (*Physalis pubescens*) **4 :** a Mexican timber tree (*Condalia obovata*) whose hard wood furnishes a blue dye **5 :** CALABUR TREE

ca·put \ˈkäˌpu̇t, -ˌpət; ˈkapət, -ˈā-\ *n, pl* **ca·pi·ta** \ˈkäpəˌtä, ˈkapəd·ə\ [L, head — more at HEAD] **1 :** a knoblike protuberance (as of a bone or muscle) **2 :** a university council **3** *Roman law* **:** legal status or civil capacity embracing the status of being a free man, a Roman citizen, and a member of a Roman family

caput mor·tu·um \-ˈmȯrchəwəm\ *n, pl* **capita mor·tua** \-wə\ [NL, lit., dead head] **1** *alchemy* **:** the residuum after distillation or sublimation **2 :** DROSS **:** worthless residue **3** *or* **caput mortuum vi·tri·o·li** \-ˌvi·trēˈōˌlē, -ī\ **:** a red iron-oxide pigment made by calcining iron sulfate

caput suc·ce·da·ne·um \-ˌsəksəˈdānēəm\ *n, pl* **capita succeda·nea** \-nēə\ [NL, lit., substituted head] **:** a swelling formed upon the presenting part of the fetus during labor

capy *abbr* capacity

cap·y·bara *also* **cap·i·bara** \ˌkapəˈbarə, -ärə\ *or* **cap·i·vara** \-ˈv-\ *n* -S [Pg *capibara*, fr. Tupi] **:** an edible So. American rodent (*Hydrochoerus capybara*) that reaches in maturity over four feet in length and is the largest rodent in existence, is largely aquatic in habit having partly webbed feet, has no tail, has coarse fur, and somewhat resembles the guinea pig to which it is related

capybara

ca·que·tio \ˌkäkəˈtē(ˌ)ō\ *n, pl* **caquetio** *or* **caquetí·os** *usu cap* [Sp *caquetio, caquetío*, of AmerInd origin] **1 a :** an extinct Arawakan people of the coast of Venezuela **b :** a member of this people **2 :** the language of the Caquetio people

¹**car** \ˈkär, ˈkȧ(r\ *n* -S [ME *carre*, fr. AF, fr. L *carra*, pl. of *carrum*, alter. of *carrus*, of Celt origin; akin to OIr & MW *carr* vehicle, Bret *karr* — more at CURRENT] **1 :** a vehicle moving on wheels: **a** *archaic* **:** CARRIAGE, CART, WAGON **b :** a chariot of war or of triumph **:** a vehicle of splendor, dignity, or solemnity **c :** a vehicle adapted to the rails of a railroad or street railway and used for carrying passengers and mail, baggage, freight, or other things — in British usage usu. applied only to city tramways not railroads; compare CARRIAGE, COACH, TRUCK, VAN, WAGON **d :** AUTOMOBILE; *esp* **:** a private passenger automobile as distinguished from a bus or truck **2 :** the cage of an elevator **3 :** the portion of an airship or balloon that is intended to carry the power plant, personnel, cargo, or equipment **4** [by folk etymology fr. *corf*] **:** a large live-box for keeping fish or lobsters alive

²**car** \ˈkär\ *adj* [ScGael *cearr*] **1** *chiefly Scot* **:** LEFT-HANDED **2** *chiefly Scot* **a :** AWKWARD **b :** WRONG, SINISTER, PERVERSE

car *abbr* **1** carat **2** cargo

¹**ca·ra** \ˈkärə\ *n, pl* **cara** *or* **caras** *usu cap* [Sp, of AmerInd origin] **1 a :** an ancient Indian people possibly Barbacoan people of northern Ecuador conquered by the Incas in the 15th century **b :** a member of this people **2 :** the language of the Cara people

²**ca·rá** \kəˈrä\ *n* -S [Pg] **:** CUSH-CUSH

car·ab \ˈkarəb\ *or* **carab beetle** *n* -S [F, L, or Gk; F *carabe*, fr. L *carabus*, fr. Gk *karabos* — more at CARAVEL] **:** a beetle of the family Carabidae

car·a·bao \ˌkarəˈbau̇, ˌkä-\ *n, pl* **carabao** *or* **carabaos** [PhilSp, fr. Eastern Bisayan (Samar-Leyte) *karabáw*] **1** *chiefly Philippines* **:** BUFFALO 1a **2** *also* **carabao mango :** a highly prized and widely planted Philippine variety of the mango

car·a·been \ˈkarəˌbēn\ *n* -S [native name in New South Wales] **:** an Australian tree (*Sloanea woollsii*)

car·a·bid \ˈkarəbəd, kəˈrabəd\ *n* -S [NL *Carabidae*] **:** a beetle of the family Carabidae **:** GROUND BEETLE

ca·rab·i·dae \kəˈrabəˌdē\ *n pl, cap* [NL, fr. *Carabus*, type genus + *-idae*] **:** a large family of beetles comprising the ground beetles which are usu. shining black or metallic in color, have long antennae and 5-jointed tarsi, are mostly of active, predaceous, and largely terrestrial habits, and destroy many injurious insects — compare BOMBARDIER BEETLE — **ca·rab·i·dan** \kəˈrabəᵈn\ *adj or n* — **car·a·bid·e·ous** \ˌkarəˈbidēəs\ *adj*

car·a·bin \ˈkarəbən\ *n* -S [MF — more at CARBINE] *archaic* **:** CARABINEER

car·a·bi·neer *or* **car·a·bi·nier** \ˌkarəbəˈni(ə)r\ *or* **car·bi·neer** \ˌkärbəˈni(ə)r, ˌkȧb-\ *n* -S [F *carabinier*, fr. *carabine* carbine + *-ier* -eer — more at CARBINE] **:** a soldier armed with a carbine

car·a·bi·ner *or* **kar·a·bi·ner** \ˌkarəˈbēnə(r)\ *n* -S [G *karabiner*, short for *karabinerhaken* carbine hook, fr. *karabiner* carbine (modif. of F *carabine*) + *haken* hook; fr. its original use to fasten carbines to bandoleers — more at CARBINE] **:** an oblong ring that snaps to the eye or link of a piton to hold a freely running rope

ca·ra·bi·ne·ro \ˌkarəbəˈne(ˌ)rō\ *n* -S [Sp, fr. *carabina* carbine (fr. F *carabine*) + *-ero* -er] **1 :** a member of a Spanish national police force serving esp. as frontier guards **2 :** a customs or coast guard officer in the Philippines

ca·ra·bi·nie·re \ˌkarəbəˈnyerē, -e(ˌ)rā\ *n, pl* **carabinie·ri** \-ērē\ [It, fr. F *carabinier*] **:** a member of the Italian national police

car·a·boid \ˈkarəˌbȯid\ *adj* [NL *Caraboidea*] **1 :** of or relating to the Caraboidea **2** *of a beetle larva* **:** active and predacious with well-developed thoracic legs and considerable chitinization

car·a·boi·dea \ˌkarəˈbȯidēə\ *n pl, cap* [NL, fr. *Carabus*, type genus + *-oidea*] **:** a superfamily coextensive with the suborder Adephaga comprising beetles that have the eyes entire and the antennae slender and elongated

car·a·bus \ˈkarəbəs\ *n* [NL, fr. Gk *karabos* horned beetle — more at CARAVEL] **1** *cap* **:** a genus (the type of the family Carabidae) of large ground beetles **2** -ES **:** an insect of the genus *Carabus*

car·a·cal \ˈkarəˌkal, ˌ≈≈ˈ≈\ *n* -S [F, fr. Sp, fr. Turk *karakulak*, lit., black-ear, fr. *kara* black + *kulak* ear] **1 :** a cat (*Felis*, or *Caracal*, or *Lynx, caracal*) of Africa and parts of Asia that is somewhat larger than a fox and has reddish brown fur, black ears, and long lynxlike ear tufts **2 :** the fur or pelt of the caracal

car·a·cara \ˌkarəˈkarə, -əkəˈrä\ *n* -S [Sp *caracara* & Pg *caracará*, fr. Tupi *caracará*, of imit. origin] **:** any of certain large mostly So. American hawks of vulturelike habits having rather long legs and able to run well on the ground — see AUDUBON'S CARACARA

ca·ra·cas \kəˈrakəs, -ˈäk-\ *adj, usu cap* [fr. *Caracas*, city in Venezuela] **:** of or from Caracas, the capital of Venezuela **:** of the kind or style prevalent in Caracas

car accounting *n* **:** the record of the movement of cars from one railroad system to another and of the debits and credits thereby created

carack *or* **carac** *var of* CARRACK

car·a·co \ˈkarəˌkō\ *n* -S [F, perh. fr. Turk *kerrake* alpaca coat] **:** a woman's short coat or jacket usu. about waist length

¹**car·a·cole** \ˈkarəˌkōl\ *n* -S [F, fr. Sp *caracol* snail, spiral stair, caracole (of a horse), perh. modif. of L *conchylium* shellfish — more at COCKLE] **1 :** a staircase in a spiral form **2 a :** a half turn either to the right or the left executed by a mounted horse **b :** a turning, wheeling, prancing, or capering movement ⟨his dog . . . came around the corner . . . with a ~ —Paul Horgan⟩

²**caracole** \"\ *vb* **caracoled** *also* **caracolled; caracoled** *also* **caracolled; caracoling** *also* **caracolling; caracoles** [F *caracoler*, fr. *caracole*] *vi* **1 :** to perform a caracole or move in caracoles **2 :** to ride a caracoling horse ~ *vt* **:** to cause to caracole

car·a·co·li \ˌkarəkōˈlē\ *n* -S [AmerSp *caracolí*, of Cariban origin; akin to Oyana *caracouli* silver, Carib *calluculi* trinkets, gold] **:** ESPAVÉ

car·a·co·lite \ˌkarəˈkōˌlīt\ *n* -S [G *caracolit*, fr. *Caracoles*, town in Chile, its locality + G *-it* -ite] **:** a rare mineral occurring as a colorless crystalline incrustation and consisting of lead sulfate together with chlorine and sodium

car·a·core \ˈkarəˌkō(ə)r\ *also* **car·a·co·ra** \ˌ≈≈ˈkōrə\ *or* **car·a·coa** \ˌ≈≈ˈkōə\ *n* -S [F, fr. Malay *kurakura*] **:** a proa used by Moro peoples

¹**caract** *n* -S [ME *carecte, caracte*, fr. MF, fr. L *character* mark, sign — more at CHARACTER] *obs* **:** MARK, SIGN, CHARACTER

²**caract** *obs var of* CARAT

caracul *var of* KARAKUL

²**car·a·cul** \ˈkarəkəl *also* -er-\ *n* -S **:** the pelt of a karakul lamb after the curl begins to loosen — compare BROADTAIL, PERSIAN LAMB

caracul cloth *n* **:** a heavy fabric woven in imitation of caracul

ca·rafe \kəˈraf, -aa(ə)f,-aif,-äf\ *n* -S [F, fr. It *caraffa*, fr. Ar *gharrāfah*, fr. *gharafa* to dip up water] **:** a bottle usu. made of glass with a narrow neck and spherical body and used to hold water or beverages ⟨a ~ on the desk⟩

car·a·ga·na \ˌkarəˈgānə,-anə,-änə\ *n* [NL, of Turkic origin; akin to Kirghiz *karaghan* Siberian pea tree] **1** *cap* **:** a large genus of Asiatic shrubs or small trees (family Leguminosae) having even-pinnate leaves with small leaflets and solitary or clustered mostly yellow flowers and bearing seeds in a linear pod — see CHINESE PEA TREE, SIBERIAN PEA TREE **2** -s : any plant of the genus *Caragana* shrubby members of which are extensively used in dry parts of the central U. S. for hedges and in shelter belts

carageen *var of* CARRAGEEN

¹car·a·gua·ta \ˌkarəgwə'tä\ *n* -s [AmerSp *caraguatá*, fr. Pg, fr. Tupi *caragoatá, caraquatá*, lit., which scratches those walking] **1** : a plant (*Bromelia argentina*) of Argentina and Paraguay with leaves that yield a long silky fiber **2** : the fiber yielded by the caraguata

²caraguata \"", ˌkarə'gwädə\ [NL, fr. Sp or Pg *caraguatá*] *syn of* GUZMANIA

car·a·ibe \ˌkarə'ēb, kə'rīb\ *n* -s [prob. fr. F *caraïbe* Carib, modif. of Sp *caribe* — more at CARIB] : BROWN SUGAR 2

¹ca·rai·pi *or* **ca·rai·pe** \kə'rīpē\ *n* -s [Pg *caraipe*] : POTTERY TREE

²ca·rai·pi \ˌkarə'pē\ *or* **ca·rai·pe** \-'pā\ *n* -s [Pg *caraipé*, fr. Tupi] : any of several Brazilian timber trees of the genus *Caraipa* (family Guttiferae) yielding a strong hard valuable wood

ca·ra·já \ˌkarə'hä\ *also* **ca·ra·ya** \-'yä\ *n, pl* **carajá** *or* **carajás** *also* **caraya** *or* **carayas** *usu cap* [Sp & Pg, fr. *Carajá*, lit., great people] **1** a : a people or group of peoples of eastern Brazil **b** : a member of such people **2** : the language of the Carajá people constituting a language family

car·a·ju·ra \ˌkarə'zhu̇rə\ *also* **car·a·ju·ru** \-zhə'rü\ *or* **ca·ra·ja·ra** \-'zhärə\ *n* -s [Pg *carajura, carajurú*, fr. Tupi *carajurú*, perh. of Cariban origin; akin to Galibi *caraerú, cariarú*] **1** : a Brazilian plant (*Bignonia chica*) that is the source of a red dye **2** : the red pigment extracted from the leaves of the carajura — called also *chica*

car·am·bo·la \ˌkarəm'bōlə\ *n* -s [Pg, fr. Marathi *karambal*] **1** : an East Indian tree (*Averrhoa carambola*) widely cultivated in the tropics **2** : the green to yellow usu. somewhat acid fruit of the carambola that is much used in Chinese cookery

¹car·am·bole \'karəm,bōl\ *n* -s [Sp *carambola*, lit., carambola (the fruit), fr. Pg] **1** *obs* : CAROM **2** *obs* : a shot in billiards in which the cue ball strikes more than one cushion before completing a carom

²carambole \"\ *vi* -ED/-ING/-S : CAROM

¹car·a·mel \'karəməl, 'kerə-, ÷'kärməl, ÷'kȧm- *also* 'karə,mel *or* 'kerə- *or* ÷kär'mel *or* ÷kȧ'm-\ *n* -s [F, fr. Sp *caramelo*, fr. Pg, icicle, caramel, fr. LL *calamellus* small reed — more at SHAWM] **1** : an amorphous brittle brown and somewhat bitter substance obtained as a porous mass by heating sugar to about 170–180° C that is usu. made commercially by heating dextrose with a small amount of ammonia or ammonium salts and used as a coloring agent (as in carbonated beverages, bakery products, confections, and liquors) **2** a : a firm chewy usu. caramel-flavored candy often containing fruits and nuts and typically cut in small blocks **b** : a piece of this candy **3** : a brownish orange to light brown that is lighter than sorrel or tawny and redder and lighter than raw sienna

²caramel \"\ *vb* -ED/-ING/-S : CARAMELIZE

caramel brown *n* : a moderate to dark brown

car·a·mel·iza·tion \ˌkarəmələ'zāshən, -er-, -,mel-, -,məˌlī'z-; ÷ˌkärmələ'zāshən, ÷ˌkȧm-, -əˌlī'z-\ *n* -s : the process of caramelizing

car·a·mel·ize \'karəmə,līz, ÷'kärm-,÷'kȧm- *also* 'kerəm-\ *vb* -ED/-ING/-S [¹*caramel* + *-ize*] *vt* **1** : to change (sugar or the sugar content of a food) into caramel **2** : to change (as a carbohydrate) to a brown caramellike color ~ *vi* : to change to caramel or a caramellike substance or color

car·a·mel·like \-əməl,līk\ *adj* : resembling caramel

car·a·mous·sal \ˌkarəmə'sal\ *n* -s [Turk *karamürsel, karamusal*, perh. fr. *kara* black + *mürsel* envoy, apostle] : a high-pooped Turkish or Moorish merchant ship esp. of the 17th century

ca·ran·cha \kə'ranchə, -än-\ *or* **ca·ran·cho** \-(,)chō\ *n* -s [AmerSp *carancho*, fr. Quechua *caranchi*] : any of several So. American caracaras (esp. *Polyborus plancus*)

ca·ran·dá \ˌkarən'dä\ *n* -s [AmerSp, of Guaranian origin; akin to Guarani *caranday*] **1** : a tropical palm (*Copernicia australis*) that yields a wax similar to carnauba **2** : CARNAUBA

ca·ran·das \kə'randəs\ [NL, fr. Malayalam *karanta*] *syn of* CARISSA

ca·ran·day \ˌkarən'dī\ *n* -s [AmerSp, fr. Guarani] : CARNAUBA

¹ca·ran·gid \kə'ranjəd\ *adj* [NL *Carangidae*] : of or relating to the Carangidae

²carangid \"\ *n* -s : a fish of the family Carangidae

ca·ran·gi·dae \-jə,dē\ *n pl, cap* [NL, fr. *Carang-, Caranx*, type genus + *-idae*] : a large family of marine percoid fishes containing the pompanos, amberfishes, cavallas, and a number of other narrow-bodied food fishes with widely forked tail chiefly of warm seas

¹ca·ran·gin \-jən\ *adj* [²*carangin*] : of or relating to the genus *Caranx*

²carangin \"\ *n* -s [NL *Carang-, Caranx* + E *-in*] : a fish of the genus *Caranx*

¹ca·ran·goid \kə'raŋ,gȯid\ *adj* [prob. fr. NL *Carang-, Caranx* + E *-oid*] : like or belonging to the Carangidae

²carangoid \"\ *n* -s : CARANGID

ca·ran·gus \kə'raŋgəs\ [NL, fr. F *carangue* shad, horse mackerel — more at CARANX] *syn of* CARANX

ca·ran·na \kə'ranə\ *or* **caranna gum** *also* **ca·ra·na** \"", -anyə\ *or* **ca·rau·na** \-rȯnə\ *n* -s [Sp *caraña*, prob. fr. a native name in Venezuela] : a dark resinous medicinal gum obtained from any of several So. American trees (*esp. Protium carana, P. altissimum*, and *Pachylobus hexandrus*)

ca·ranx \'ka,raŋks, 'kā,-\ *n* [NL, fr. F *carangue* shad, horse mackerel, fr. Sp *caranga, carangue*] **1** *cap* : the type genus of Carangidae — see CAVALLA **2** *pl* **caranx** : any fish of the genus *Caranx*

ca·rapa \kə'rapə\ *n* [NL, fr. Galibi *carapa, krapa*, lit., oil] **1** *cap* : a small genus of tropical trees (family Meliaceae) having abruptly pinnate leaves and flowers with four or five petals and monadelphous stamens **2** *also* **ca·rap** \kə'rap\ *or* **crab** \'krab\ -s [*carap*, short for *carapa*; *crab*, by folk etymology fr. *carapa*] : any tree of the genus *Carapa* ⟨*carap* wood⟩ ⟨*crab* nut⟩ — see CRABWOOD

car·a·pace \'karə,pās\ *n* -s [F, fr. Sp *carapacho*] **1** a : a bony or chitinous case or shield covering the back or part of the back of an animal (as the upper shell of a turtle, the shell of an armadillo, or the shell of a crab) **b** : the entire shell of a turtle comprising the carapace and the plastron **2** a : a hard superficial crust ⟨the ~ of a lava flow⟩ **b** : any hard protective outer covering; *specif* : a manner, attitude, or state of mind (as indifference or hostility) serving to protect or isolate from external influence ⟨their ~ of incuriosity —William Sansom⟩

car·a·pa·cial \ˌkarə'pāshəl\ *adj* : of or relating to a carapace

carapato *var of* CARRAPATO

car·a·pax \'karə,paks\ *n* -ES [by alter.] : CARAPACE 1a

ca·rap·i·dae \kə'rapə,dē\ *n pl, cap* [NL, fr. *Carapus*, type genus + *-idae*] : a small family of percomorph fishes related to the brotulids and comprising the pearl fishes — see CARAPUS

ca·rap nut \kə'rap-\ *n* : the seed of the carapa (esp. of *Carapa procera* and *C. guianensis*) yielding a bitter oil or fat that is used as a protective against vermin and insects

car·a·pus \'karəpəs\ *n, cap* [NL, fr. Pg *carapó*] : a genus (the type of the family Carapidae) of small slender fishes living as inquilines in the alimentary canal of large holothurians or between the valves of large bivalve mollusks — see PEARLFISH 1

ca·ra·que·ño \ˌkarə'kān(,)yō\ *n* -s *cap* [Sp, fr. *Caracas*, Venezuela + Sp *-eño* (suffix denoting an inhabitant)] : a man or boy of Caracas; *broadly* : a native or inhabitant of Caracas

ca·rara \kə'rarə, -'ä-\ [NL] *syn of* CORONOPUS

¹caras *pl of* CARA

²carás *pl of* CARÁ

ca·ra spo·sa \ˌkärä'spōzä\ *n* [It] : a dear wife

¹carat *var of* KARAT

²car·at \'karət *also* -er-\ *n* -s [prob. fr. ML *carratus*, fr. Ar *qīrāṭ* bean or pea pod, weight of four grains, carat, fr. Gk *keration* carob bean, small weight, carat, lit., small horn, dim. of *kerat-, keras* horn — more at HORN] **1** : any of various units of weight for precious stones (as diamonds and pearls): as **a** : a unit equal to 205.3 milligrams used in the U.S. before 1913 **b** : an international unit equal to 200 milligrams that had already been adopted in most European countries and in Japan when it was made standard in the U.S. in 1913 — abbr. *c*; called also *international carat, metric carat* **2** *obs* : WORTH, VALUE, ESTIMATE ⟨of too good ~ to be left so without a guard —Ben Jonson⟩

ca·ra·te \kə'räd·ē\ *n* -s [Sp] : a disease endemic in tropical America that is characterized by the presence of white, brown, blue, red, or violet spots on the skin and caused by a spirochete (*Treponema carateum*)

carat grain *n* : a unit of weight equal to ¼ carat used esp. for pearls — called also *pearl grain*

carauna *var of* CARAVANCE

ca·raun·da \kə'rau̇ndə, -,dä\ *n* -s [Hindi *karaṅdā*, fr. Skt *karamardaka*] : an East Indian evergreen shrub or small tree (*Carissa carandas*) having a somewhat acid fruit that is pickled green or eaten ripe

¹car·a·van \'karə,van, -aa(ə)n *also* -er- *or* -vən; *Brit often* ˌ==='van\ *n* -s [It *caravana, carovana*, fr. Per *kārwān*] **1** a : a company of travelers, pilgrims, or merchants on a long journey through desert or hostile regions : a train of pack animals **b** : a group of vehicles proceeding or traveling together in a file ⟨a ~ of buses⟩ **2** *obs* a : a Russian or Turkish fleet esp. of merchant ships with convoy **b** : a sea campaign against the Muslims obligatory upon each member of the Knights of Malta **3** : a covered vehicle : VAN: as **a** : a covered wagon or motortruck equipped as traveling living quarters or office **b** *Brit* : TRAILER 4e

²caravan \"\ *vb* **caravaned** *or* **caravanned**; **caravaned** *or* **caravanned**; **caravaning** *or* **caravanning**; **caravans** *vt* : to convey in a caravan ~ *vi* : to travel in a caravan

caravance *var of* GARAVANCE

car·a·van·sa·ry \ˌkarə'van(t)sərē\ *or* **car·a·van·se·rai** \-sə,rī\ *n, pl* **caravansaries** *or* **caravanserais** *or* **caravanserai** [modif. of Per *kārwānsarāī*, fr. *kārwān* caravan + *sarāī* palace, large house, inn; akin to Av *thrāya-* to protect] **1** : an inn in eastern countries where caravans rest at night that is commonly a large bare building surrounding a court ⟨stopped for food and shelter at an unpromising ~ situated on a small oasis —L.C.Douglas⟩ **2** : HOTEL, INN ⟨a ~ for cosmopolitans with more money than sense —Frank Clune⟩

car·a·vel \'karə,vel, -vəl\ *n* -s [MF *caravelle, carvelle*, fr. OPg *caravela*, dim. of *cávavo*, a ship, fr. LL *carabus* coraclelike boat, fr. L, a sea crab, fr. Gk *karabos*, a sea crab, a horned beetle; prob. akin to Gk *karis*, a sea crab — more at -CARIS] : any of several sailing vessels: as **a** : a small vessel of the 15th and 16th centuries with broad bows, high narrow poop, three or four masts, and usu. lateen sails on the two or three aftermasts ⟨the ~s of Columbus⟩ **b** : a Portuguese vessel of 100 to 150 tons burden **c** : a small fishing boat used on the French coast **d** : a Turkish man-of-war

caravel, 15th century

car·a·way *also* **car·ra·way** \'karə,wā *also* -er-\ *n* -s [ME *caraway, carway, carwy*, prob. fr. ML *carvi*, fr. Ar *karawyā*, fr. Gk *karon*] **1** : a biennial usu. white-flowered herb (*Carum carvi*) **2** *or* **caraway seed** : the aromatic pungent-tasting fruit of the caraway used in cookery and confectionery, in the manufacture of certain beverages, and as a source of an oil **3** *obs* : a cake or sweetmeat containing caraway seeds

caraway oil *n* : an essential oil obtained from caraway seeds and used in pharmaceuticals and as a flavoring agent in foods and liqueurs

caraya *cap, var of* CARAJÁ

carb \'kärb, -ȧb\ *n* -s [by shortening] *slang* : CARBURETOR

carb- *or* **carbo-** *comb form* [F, fr. *carbone* — more at CARBON] : carbon : carbonic : carbonyl : carboxyl ⟨*carbo*diimide⟩ ⟨*carbo*hydrazide⟩ ⟨*carbo*hydrate⟩

car·ba·chol \'kärbə,kōl, -ōl\ *n* -s [*carbamoyl-choline*] : a synthetic drug $C_6H_{15}ClN_2O_2$ used as a cholinergic agent in the treatment of urinary retention and abdominal distention and topically in glaucoma : carbamoyl-choline chloride

carb·ac·i·dom·e·ter \(ˌ)kär,basə'dämədˌər\ *n* -s [ISV *carbonic* + *acid* + *-o-* + *-meter*; orig formed as G *karbazidometer*] : an instrument for determining the percentage of carbon dioxide in the air

carb·alk·oxy \ˌkär,bal'käksē\ *adj* [*carbalkoxy-*, fr. *carbalkoxyl*] : relating to or containing carbalkoxyl

carb·alk·ox·yl \ˌ=,='==səl\ *n* -s [*carb-* + *alkoxyl*] : a radical —COOR consisting of carbonyl combined with alkoxyl

car·ba·mate \'kärbə,māt, kär'ba,māt\ *n* -s [ISV *carbamic* + *-ate*] : a salt or ester of carbamic acid — see URETHANE

car·bam·ic acid \(')kär'bamik-\ *n* [ISV *carb-* + *amide* + *-ic*] : an acid NH_2COOH known in the form of its salts (as ammonium carbamate) and esters (as urethan) : the half amide of carbonic acid

car·bam·ide \kär'ba,mīd, -məd; 'kärbə,m-\ *n* -s [ISV *carb-* + *amide*] : UREA

carb·am·i·do- \kär'bamə,dō, ˌkärbə'mē(,)dō\ *comb form* [*carbamide*] : UREIDO- ⟨5-*carbamido*hydantoin⟩

carb·am·i·no \kär'bamə,nō, ˌkärbə'mē(,)nō\ *adj* [ISV *carb-* + *amino-*; orig. formed as G *karbamino-*] : relating to any carbamic acid derivative formed by reaction of carbon dioxide with an amino acid or a protein (as hemoglobin)

car·bam·o·yl \kär'bamə,wil, -ēl\ *or* **car·ba·myl** \'kärbə,mil, -ēl\ *n* -s [*carbamoyl* fr. *carbamic* (in *carbamic acid*) + *-o-* + *-yl*; *carbamyl* fr. *carbamic* + *-yl*] : the radical NH_2CO— of carbamic acid

car·ba·nil \'kärbə,nil\ *n* -s [ISV *carb-* + *anil*] : PHENYL ISOCYANATE

car·ba·nil·ate \ˌkärbə'ni,lāt, -lət; kär'ban°l,āt, -ət\ *n* -s [*carbanilic* (in *carbanilic acid*) + *-ate*] : a salt or ester of carbanilic acid

car·ba·nil·ic acid \ˌkärbə'nilik-\ *n* [ISV *carbanil* + *-ic*] : an acid $C_6H_5NHCOOH$ known in the form of its salts and esters — called also *phenylcarbamic acid*

car·ba·nil·ide \ˌkärbə'ni,līd, -ləd, kär'ban°l,īd, -əd\ *n* -s [ISV *carb-* + *anilide*] : a silky crystalline compound $(C_6H_5NH)_2CO$ obtained by heating aniline with urea and in other ways — called also *symmetrical diphenyl-urea*

carb·an·i·on \kär'ban,īən *also* -ī,än\ *n* -s [*carb-* + *anion*] : an organic ion carrying a negative charge at a carbon location (as methyl carbanion or butenyl carbanion) — compare CARBONIUM

carbarn \'=,=\ *n* -s [¹*car* + *barn*] : a building that houses the cars of a street railway or the buses of a bus system

car·bar·sone \kär'bär,sōn\ *n* -s [*carbanilic* + *-arsone* (fr. *arsonic*)] : a white powder $NH_2CONHC_6H_4AsO_3H_2$ used in treating amebic dysentery; *p*-ureido-benzene-arsonic acid

car·ba·sus \'kärbəsəs\ *n* -ES [L, fine linen; prob. akin to Gk *karpasos* fine flax, Skt *karpāsa* cotton] *archaic* : surgical gauze : LINT

car·baz·ic acid \(')kär'bazik-\ *n* [*carb-* + *az-* + *-ic*] : an acid $NH_2NHCOOH$ known chiefly in the form of its esters and derivatives (as amino-carbamic acid, hydrazine-carboxylic acid)

car·ba·zide \'kärbə,zīd, kär'ba-, -zəd\ *n* -s [ISV *carb-* + *az-* + *-ide*] **1** : CARBOHYDRAZIDE **2** : a crystalline explosive compound $CO(N_3)_2$ made by the action of nitrous acid on carbohydrazide : the azide of carbonic acid

car·ba·zole \'kärbə,zōl, kär'ba-\ *n* -s [ISV *carb-* + *az-* + *-ole*] : a white crystalline feebly basic cyclic compound $C_{12}H_9N$ occurring in crude anthracene and constituting the parent of a number of dyes — called also *diphenylenimine*

carbazole blue R *n, usu cap C&B* : a vat dye — see DYE table I (under *Vat Blue 43*)

carb·azot·ic acid \ˌkärbə'zäd·ik-, -zōl\ *n* [*carb-* + *azotic*] : PICRIC ACID

car·been \'kär,bēn\ *n* -s [native name in Australia] : an Australian eucalypt (*Eucalyptus tessellaris*) yielding a white crystalline kino

car·bene \'kär,bēn\ *n* -s [*carb-* + *-ene*] : one of the components of bitumen soluble in carbon disulfide but insoluble in carbon tetrachloride — usu. used in pl.; compare ASPHALTENE

car·be·ni·um \kär'bēnēəm\ *n* -s [NL, by alter.] : CARBONIUM

carb·eth·oxy \ˌkär,be'thäksē\ *adj* [*carbethoxy-*] : relating to or containing carbethoxyl

carbethoxy- \"\ *comb form* [ISV, fr. *carbethoxyl*] : containing carbethoxyl ⟨*carbethoxy*alanine⟩

carb·eth·ox·yl \ˌ=,='==səl\ *n* -s [blend of *carboxyl* and *ethyl*] : the radical —$COOC_2H_5$ consisting of the ethyl ester of carboxyl — called also *ethoxycarbonyl*

carb·eth·ox·yl·a·tion \ˌ=,=,==sə'lāshən\ *n* -s [*carbethoxyl* + *-ation*] : the introduction of carbethoxyl into an organic compound

carb·he·mo·glo·bin \'kärb'h-\ *or* **car·bo·he·mo·glo·bin** \'kär(,)bō'h-\ *n* -s [ISV *carb-* + *hemoglobin*] : a compound of hemoglobin with carbon dioxide

car·bide \'kär,bīd, 'kȧ,b-\ *n* -s [ISV *carb-* + *-ide*] : a binary compound of carbon with a more electropositive element: as **a** : CALCIUM CARBIDE **b** : a very hard material made by cementing together with a binder or by means of powder metallurgy a mixture of powdered carbides of heavy metals (as tungsten and titanium) and used in metal-cutting tools — called also *cemented carbide*

car·bi·mide \'kärbə,mīd, kär'bi-; kär'bimәd\ *n* -s [ISV *carb-* + *imide*] : ISOCYANIC ACID

car·bin·a·mine \kär'binə,mēn\ *n* -s [ISV *carbin-* (fr. obs. G *karbin* methyl) + *amine* — more at CARBINOL] : METHYLAMINE — used in the names of derivatives; *also* : any amine derived from methylamine

car·bine \'kär,bēn, 'kȧ,b-, -īn *also* -bən\ *n* -s [F *carabine* carbine, carabineer, fr. MF *carabin* harquebusier, carabineer, prob. alter. of *escarrabin, scarrabin* preparer of plague corpses for burial, prob. alter. of *scarabée* dung beetle — more at SCARAB] **1** a : a short-barreled shoulder firearm used by cavalry **b** : any short-barreled lightweight rifle **2** : a light automatic or semiautomatic military rifle using ammunition of relatively low power and often issued to troops that are not primarily riflemen

carbineer *var of* CARABINEER

car·bi·nette \ˌkärbə'net\ *n* -s [origin unknown] : KINGFISH 1a (2)

car·bi·nol \'kärbə,nōl, -ōl\ *n* -s [ISV *carbin-* (fr. obs. G *karbin* methyl, fr. *karb-* carb- + *-in*) + *-ol*; orig. formed as G *karbinol*] **1** : METHANOL — used esp. in the names of alcohols derived from methanol ⟨phenyl-acetyl-*carbinol*⟩ **2** : an alcohol derived from methanol

car·bi·nyl \'kärbə,nil\ *n* -s [prob. fr. obs. G *karbin* + E *-yl*] **1** : METHYL — used esp. in the names of derivatives of methyl ⟨triphenyl-*carbinyl*⟩ **2** : the univalent radical corresponding to any carbinol ⟨a ~ chloride⟩

car bit *n* [so called fr. its being originally used in car building] : a long auger bit for use in boring deep holes

Car·bi·tol \'kärbə,tȯl, -ōl\ *trademark* — used for a high-boiling ether-alcohol used esp. as an organic solvent

car·bo \'kär,bō\ *n* -s [L, charcoal, ember — more at CARBON] : CHARCOAL

carbo- — see CARB-

carbo a·ni·ma·lis \-,anə'malәs, -äl-, -āl-\ *n* [NL, lit., animal charcoal] : charcoal prepared from bone : BONE BLACK, IVORY BLACK

car·bo·ben·zoxy \ˌkär(,)bō,ben'zäksē\ *or* **car·bo·ben·zy·loxy** \'==benzə'läksē\ *adj* [*carbobenzoxy-* or *carbobenzyloxy-*] : relating to or containing the radical —$COOCH_2C_6H_5$ ⟨~ synthesis of peptides⟩

carbobenzoxy- \"\ *or* **carbobenzyloxy-** \"\ *comb form* [ISV, fr. *carb-* + *benzoxy-* or *benzyloxy-*] : containing the univalent radical —$COOCH_2C_6H_5$ composed of a benzyloxy radical united with carbonyl ⟨*carbobenzyloxy*glycine⟩

car·bo·cer \'kärbə(,)sər\ *n* -s [*carb-* + NL *cerium*] : a mineral consisting of a carbonaceous, ocherous, or pitchy substance containing rare-earth elements

car·bo·cy·a·nine \ˌkär(,)bō'sīə,nēn, -nən\ *or* **carbocyanine dye** *n* -s [ISV *carb-* + *cyanine*; orig. formed as G *karbozyanin*] : any of a class of cyanine dyes in whose structure the two heterocyclic rings are joined by a three-carbon chain (as =CH—CH=CH—); *specif* : any such dye containing two quinoline rings — called also *trimethine*

car·bo·cy·clic \ˌkärbō'sīklik, -si-\ *adj* [ISV *carb-* + *cyclic*] : relating to or characterized by a ring composed of carbon atoms — used esp. of organic compounds classed as alicyclic or aromatic

car·bo·di·i·mide \ˌkär(,)bō'dīə,mīd, -ō,dī'i,m-, -məd\ *n* -s [ISV *carb-* + *di-* + *imide*; prob. orig. formed in F] : a tautomeric form of cyanamide NH=C=NH known in the form of its derivatives

Car·bo·frax \'kärbō,fraks\ *trademark* — used for an acid-resisting refractory cement

carbohemoglobin *var of* CARBHEMOGLOBIN

car·bo·hy·drase \ˌkärbō'hī,drās\ *n* -s [ISV *carbohydrate* + *-ase*] : any of a group of enzymes (as invertase or an amylase) that hydrolyze disaccharides and more complex carbohydrates

car·bo·hy·drate \ˌkärbō'hī,drāt, -bə-, -drət\ *n* -s [*carb-* + *hydrate*; fr. the former classification of such compounds as hydrates of carbon] : any of a group of neutral compounds composed of carbon, hydrogen, and oxygen including the sugars, starches, dextrans, glycogens, celluloses, and pentosans some of which are formed by all green plants and used immediately for growth or stored for future use and which as a whole constitute a major class of animal foods characterized chemically as hydroxy aldehydes, hydroxy ketones, or compounds hydrolyzing to hydroxy aldehydes or ketones and classified into monosaccharides, disaccharides, trisaccharides, and polysaccharides on the basis of the number of aldehyde or ketone groups present in one molecule

car·bo·hy·drat·u·ria \ˌ=='=,drə·'yu̇rēə, -,drāt-; ˌ=,=,drə-'t(y)u̇rēə\ *n* -s [NL, fr. ISV *carbohydrate* + NL *-uria*] : GLYCOSURIA

car·bo·hy·dra·zide \ˌkärbō'hīdrə,zīd, -zəd\ *n* -s [ISV *carb-* + *hydrazide*; orig. formed as G *karbohydrazid*] : a crystalline compound $CO(NHNH_2)_2$: the hydrazide of carbonic acid

carbol- *comb form* [ISV *carb-* + L *oleum* oil; orig. formed as G *karbol-* — more at OIL] : carbolic acid ⟨*carbol*uria⟩ ⟨*carbol*xylol⟩ ⟨*carbol*ate⟩

¹car·bo·late \'kärbə,lāt\ *n* -s [*carbol-* + *-ate*] : a salt of carbolic acid : PHENOXIDE 1

²carbolate \"\ *vt* -ED/-ING/-S : PHENOLATE

car·bol·fuch·sin \ˌkär,bäl'fyüksən, -bōl- *also* -'fyüshən *or* -'füksən\ *n* -s [*carbol-* + *fuchsin*] : a mixture of aqueous solution of phenol and alcoholic solution of fuchsine used as a stain in microscopy esp. in staining bacteria

carbolfuchsin paint *n* : a solution containing boric acid, phenol, resorcinol, and fuchsine in acetone, alcohol, and water and applied externally in the treatment of fungous infections of the skin — called also *Castellani's paint*

car·bol·ic acid \(')kär'bälik-, kȧ'b-, -ēk\ *also* **carbolic** *n* -s [ISV *carb-* + L *oleum* oil + ISV *-ic*] : PHENOL 1 — not used technically

carbolic oil *n* : a fraction obtained in coal-tar distillation that contains chiefly tar acids and sometimes naphthalene — called also *middle oil*

car·bo lig·ni \ˌkär(,)bō'lig(,)nē, -g,nī\ *n* [NL, lit., charcoal of wood] : charcoal prepared from soft wood and used as an adsorbent

Car·bo·lin·e·um \ˌkärbə'linēəm\ *trademark* — used for a heavy oily substance distilled from an anthracene-oil or creosote-oil fraction of coal tar and used as a wood preservative, disinfectant, or insecticide

car·bo·lize \'kärbə,līz\ *vt* -ED/-ING/-S [*carbol-* + *-ize*] : PHENOLATE

Car·bo·loy \'kärbə,lȯi\ *trademark* — used for a hard metallic substance that consists essentially of a cemented carbide of tungsten with cobalt or nickel as a binder, is produced by powder metallurgy, and is used in metal-cutting tools

car·bom·e·ter \kär'bämədˌər\ *n* -s [ISV *carb-* + *-meter*] : an instrument for measuring the carbon content of steel

car·bo·meth·oxy \ˌkär(,)bōmə'thäksē\ *adj* [*carbomethoxy-*] : relating to or containing carbomethoxyl

carbomethoxy- \"\ *comb form* [ISV, fr. *carbomethoxyl*] : containing carbomethoxyl ⟨*carbomethoxy*glycine⟩

car·bo·meth·ox·yl \ˌ=(,)=='=səl\ *n* -s [blend of *carboxyl* and *methyl*] : the radical —$COOCH_3$ consisting of the methyl ester of carboxyl — called also *methoxycarbonyl*

car·bo·my·cin \ˌ=='mīsᵊn\ *n* -s [*carb-* + *-mycin*] : a colorless crystalline basic antibiotic $C_{42}H_{67}NO_{16}$ produced by an actinomycete (*Streptomyces halstedii*) and active esp. in inhibiting the growth of gram-positive bacteria

¹car·bon \'kärbən, 'kȧb- *also* -,bän; *rapid sometimes* -bᵊm\ *n* -s *often attrib* [F *carbone*, fr. L *carbon-, carbo* ember, charcoal — more at HEARTH] **1 :** a nonmetallic chiefly tetravalent element occurring native (as in the diamond and graphite) and forming a constituent of coal, petroleum, and asphalt, of limestone and other carbonates, and of all organic compounds and also obtained artificially in varying degrees of purity esp. as carbon black, lampblack, activated carbon, charcoal, and coke and used in these and other forms (as baked carbon and resin-impregnated impervious carbon and graphite) chiefly as a pigment, adsorbent, fuel, electrode material, structural material, and reducing agent (as for metal oxides) — symbol *C*; see ELEMENT table; CARBON FOURTEEN, CARBON THIRTEEN **2 a :** a sheet of carbon paper **b :** CARBON COPY **3 a :** a carbon rod used in an arc lamp **b :** a plate or piece of carbon used as one of the elements in a voltaic cell **4 :** ³CARBONADO **5 :** CARBON TRANSFER

²carbon \"\ *vt* -ED/-ING/-S **1 :** to deposit carbon upon (as a cylinder or spark plug) **2 :** to make a carbon copy of (as a letter)

car·bo·na \kär'bōnə\ *n* -s [prob. irreg. fr. ¹*carbon*; fr. the frequently black color of the ore] *Brit* **:** an irregular deposit of tin ore consisting of many reticulating veinlets **:** STOCKWORK

car·bo·na·ceous \¦kärbə¦nāshəs, ¦kȧb-\ *adj* [¹*carbon* + *-aceous*] **1 :** rich in carbon **:** COALY ⟨~ sandstone⟩ **2 :** relating to, containing, or composed of carbon **3** *bot* **:** CARBONOUS

¹car·bo·na·do \,kärbə'nā(,)dō\ *n, pl* **carbonados** *or* **carbonadoes** [obs. *carbonado*, n., scored and broiled piece of meat, fr. Sp *carbonada*, fr. *carbón* charcoal, coal, cinder] *archaic* **:** a broiled or grilled piece of meat scored before cooking

²carbonado \"\ *vt* -ED/-ING/-S **1** *archaic* **:** to make a carbonado of **2** *archaic* **:** to cut, hack, or slash esp. with a sword

³carbonado \"\ *n* -s [Pg, lit., carbonated, fr. *carbone* carbon, fr. F — more at CARBON] **:** an impure opaque dark-colored and fine-grained aggregate of diamond particles held together in a matrix composed mainly of diamond that is valuable for its superior toughness resulting from the fine-grained structure and absence of planes of cleavage — called also *black diamond, carbon diamond*

carbon arc *n* **1 :** an arc lamp having carbon electrodes **2 :** an arc between carbon electrodes or between a carbon electrode and another material (as the parent metal in welding by carbon arc)

car·bo·na·ri \,kärbə'närē\ *n pl, usu cap* [It, pl. of *Carbonaro*, fr. It dial. *carbonaro* charcoal burner or seller, fr. L *carbonarius* charcoal burner, fr. *carbon-, carbo* charcoal, ember + *-arius* -ary — more at HEARTH] **:** the members of a secret political association organized in the early 19th century in Italy to establish a republic

carbon assimilation *n* **:** PHOTOSYNTHESIS

car·bon·a·ta·tion \,kärbənə'tāshən\ *n* -s [ISV ¹*carbonate* + *-ation*] **:** CARBONATION

¹car·bon·ate \'kärbə,nāt, 'kȧb-, -,nət, *usu* -d.+V\ *n* -s [F, fr. *carbone* carbon + *-ate*] **1 :** a salt or ester of carbonic acid **2 :** an ore containing a large proportion of lead carbonate

²car·bon·ate \-,nāt, *usu* -ād·+V\ *vt* -ED/-ING/-S [¹*carbon* + *-ate*] **1** *obs* **:** to burn to carbon **:** CARBONIZE **2 :** to convert into a carbonate **3 a :** to impregnate with carbon dioxide; *specif* **:** to impregnate (a beverage) with carbon dioxide to infuse with freshness and sparkle **b :** to make lively, pungent, or sparkling ⟨*carbonated* prose⟩

³car·bon·ate \-,nət\ *adj* [¹*carbonate*] **1 :** of or relating to a carbonate **2 :** composed of one or more members of the calcite, dolomite, and aragonite groups of minerals

carbonate-apatite *n* **:** apatite containing a considerable amount of carbonate: as **a :** apatite in which the calcium phosphate carbonate predominates over other components **b :** calcium phosphate carbonate of uncertain formula prob. $Ca_{10}(PO_4)_6(CO_3)(H_2O)$ — called also *dahllite*

carbonated water *n* **:** SODA WATER 2a

carbonated wine *n* **:** artificially carbonated wine — distinguished from *sparkling wine*

carbonate of lime **:** CALCIUM CARBONATE

carbonate of potash **:** POTASSIUM CARBONATE

carbonate of soda **:** SODIUM CARBONATE

car·bon·a·tion \,kärbə'nāshən, ,kȧb-\ *n* -s [ISV ²*carbonate* + *-ion*] **:** the process of carbonating

car·bon·a·tite \kär'bänə,tīt\ *n* -s [¹*carbonate* + *-ite*] **:** a carbonate rock of intrusive origin

car·bon·at·i·za·tion \,kärbə,nād·ə'zāshən\ *n* -s [²*carbonate* + *-ization*] **:** conversion into a carbonate

car·bon·a·tor \'kärbə,nād·ər\ *n* -s [²*carbonate* + *-or*] **:** one that carbonates

carbon bisulfide *n* **:** CARBON DISULFIDE — used chiefly commercially

carbon black *n* **:** any of various colloidal black substances consisting wholly or principally of carbon obtained usu. as soot by partial combustion of hydrocarbons and used chiefly as reinforcing agents in automobile tires, as extremely black pigments of high hiding power in paint, printing ink, and carbon paper, and in electric resistors; *esp* **:** FURNACE BLACK — see CHANNEL BLACK, THERMAL BLACK; compare BONE BLACK, LAMPBLACK, VEGETABLE BLACK

carbon copy *n* **1 :** a copy made by use of carbon paper **2 :** an exact duplicate **:** REPLICA

carbon cycle *n* **1 :** a cycle of thermonuclear reactions that involves the synthesis of four hydrogen atoms into a helium atom with the release of nuclear energy and is held to be the source of most of the energy radiated by the sun and stars **2 :** the cycle of carbon in living beings consisting of the uptake and fixing of carbon dioxide by photosynthesis, its consumption in carbohydrate, protein, and fat by animals and plants lacking photosynthesis (as in plant tissues eaten or organic matter absorbed), and its return to the inorganic state through respiratory processes and the decay of plant and animal bodies

carbon diamond *n* **:** ³CARBONADO

carbon dichloride *n* **:** TETRACHLOROETHYLENE

carbon dioxide *n* **:** a heavy colorless gas CO_2 that does not support combustion, that dissolves in water to form carbonic acid, that is formed esp. by the action of acids on carbonates, by the fermentation of liquors, and by the combustion and decomposition of organic substances (as in animal respiration, in the decay of animal and vegetable matter, and in the explosion of firedamp in mines), that is absorbed from the air by plants in the first step in photosynthesis, and that is used in the gaseous and liquefied forms chiefly in the carbonation of beverages, in fire fighting, in therapeutical work, in mining operations, in the chemical industry, and as a source of power (as in spray painting and inflating life rafts) and in the solidified form as dry ice — called also *carbonic acid gas*; see AFTERDAMP, BLACKDAMP

carbon disulfide *n* **:** a colorless flammable poisonous liquid CS_2 of high refractive power made usu. by reaction of sulfur vapor with charcoal or hydrocarbons at high temperature and used chiefly in the manufacture of viscose rayon, cellophane, xanthates, carbon tetrachloride, and rubber accelerators, as a solvent esp. for rubber, and as a fumigant for rodents and insects

carboned *past of* CARBON

carbon flame *n* **:** the white flame produced by burning carbon

carbon 14 *n* **:** a heavy radioactive isotope of carbon having the mass number 14 that is formed by the action of cosmic rays on nitrogen in the atmosphere and made artificially by bombardment of nitrogen compounds with neutrons and is valuable in tracer studies in chemistry and biology and in dating archaeological and geological materials — symbol C^{14} or ^{14}C; called also *radiocarbon*

carboni- *comb form* [L *carbon-, carbo* ember, charcoal — more at CARBON] **:** coal ⟨*carboniferous*⟩ ⟨*carbonigenous*⟩

car·bon·ic \(')kär¦bänik, -¦ȧb-, -ēk\ *adj* [F *carbonique*, fr. *carbone* carbon + *-ique* -ic — more at CARBON] **1 :** of, relating to, or derived from carbon, carbonic acid, or carbon dioxide **2** *usu cap* **:** CARBONIFEROUS 2

carbonic acid *n* **:** a weak dibasic acid H_2CO_3 known only in solution, decomposing readily into water and carbon dioxide, and reacting with bases to form carbonates

carbonic acid gas *n* **:** CARBON DIOXIDE

carbonic anhydrase *n* **:** a zinc-containing enzyme occurring in living tissues (as red blood cells) that accelerates in either direction the reversible hydration of carbon dioxide to carbonic acid and thereby aids carbon-dioxide transport from the tissues and its release from the blood in the lungs

carbonic anhydride *n* **:** CARBON DIOXIDE

carbonic oxide *n* **:** CARBON MONOXIDE

¹car·bon·if·er·ous \¦kärbə¦nif(ə)rəs, ¦kȧb-\ *adj* [*carboni-* + *-ferous*] **1 :** producing or containing carbon or coal **2** *usu cap* **a :** of or relating to the period of the Paleozoic geologic era between the Devonian and the Permian — see GEOLOGIC TIME table **b :** of or relating to the system of rocks formed in the Carboniferous period

²car·bon·if·er·ous \,==¦=(=)=\ *n* -ES *usu cap* **:** the Carboniferous period or system of rocks

car·bon·i·fi·ca·tion \(,)kär,bänəfə'kāshən\ *n* -s [*carboni-* + *-fication*] **:** conversion of vegetable matter to coal

car·bon·i·mide \kär'bänə,mīd, ,kärbə'ni,m-, -,məd\ *n* -s [ISV ¹*carbon* + *imide*] **:** ISOCYANIC ACID

carboning *pres part of* CARBON

car·bon·ite \'kärbə,nīt\ *n* -s [ISV ¹*carbon* + *-ite*; orig. formed as G *karbonit*] **1 :** a blasting explosive varying greatly in formula but containing among its ingredients a carbonaceous substance (as oak bark), a nitrate, and now usu. nitroglycerin **2** [¹*carbon* + *-ite*] **:** a natural coke usu. resulting from contact of coal deposits with igneous rock intrusions

¹car·bon·i·tride \,kärbō'nī-,trīd, -,trəd\ *n* -s [*carb-* + *nitride*] **:** a compound with carbon and nitrogen

²carbonitride \"\ *vt* -ED/-ING/-S **:** to treat (an iron alloy) by heating in a gaseous atmosphere of such composition that carbon and nitrogen are absorbed and then cooling in such a way as to produce case hardening

car·bo·ni·trile \-'nī·trəl; -,trēl, -īl\ *n* -s [*carb-* + *nitrile*] **:** NITRILE

car·bo·ni·um \kär'bōnēəm\ *n* -s [*carb-* + *-onium*] **:** an organic ion (as triphenylmethyl carbonium) carrying a positive charge at a carbon location owing to an electron deficiency — compare CARBANION

car·bon·i·za·tion \,kärbənə'zāshən, ,kȧb-, -,nī'z-\ *n* -s [F *carbonisation*, fr. *carbone* carbon + *-isation* -ization — more at CARBON] **:** the process of carbonizing; *esp* **:** destructive distillation (as of coal, lignite, or peat)

car·bon·ize \'kärbə,nīz, 'kȧb-\ *vb* -ED/-ING/-S [F *carboniser*, prob. back-formation fr. *carbonisation*] *vt* **1 :** to convert into carbon or a residue of carbon (as by the action of heat or some corrosive agent) **2 :** CARBURIZE 1 **3 :** to remove (vegetable matter) from wool fleece or fabric by chemically reducing the burrs, cotton, and other vegetable impurities to dust **4 :** to apply carbon black to (as the back of a printed form) in preparation for making a carbon copy ~ *vi* **:** to become carbonized **:** CHAR

car·bon·iz·er \-zə(r)\ *n* -s **:** one that carbonizes: as **a :** a worker who carbonizes wool fabrics **b :** one that fills retorts

carbon knock *n* **:** preignition with resultant knocking in an internal-combustion engine caused by the overheating of an accumulation of carbon in the combustion chambers

carbon lamp *n* **1 :** an incandescent lamp with a carbon filament **2 :** an arc lamp with the arc formed between carbon points esp. for therapeutic use

car·bon·less \-bənləs\ *adj* **:** being without carbon

carbon microphone *n* **:** a microphone whose operation depends on the alteration of the electrical resistance of carbon contacts

carbon monoxide *n* **:** a colorless odorless very toxic gas CO that burns to carbon dioxide with a blue flame, that is formed as a product of the incomplete combustion of carbon (as in water gas and producer gas, in the exhaust gases from internal-combustion engines, and in the gases from the detonation of explosives), and that is used chiefly in the synthesis of carbonyls (as nickel carbonyl in the refining of nickel), phosgene, and many organic compounds (as hydrocarbons for fuels, methanol and higher alcohols, aldehydes, and formates) — see CARBONYLHEMOGLOBIN

carbon-nitrogen cycle *n* **:** CARBON CYCLE 1

carbon oil *n, Midland* **:** KEROSINE

car·bon·ous \'kärbənəs, 'kȧb-\ *adj* [¹*carbon* + *-ous*] **1 :** derived from, containing, or resembling carbon **2 :** brittle and dark or almost black in color

carbon oxide *n* **:** any of the three oxides of carbon: **a :** CARBON DIOXIDE **b :** CARBON MONOXIDE **c :** CARBON SUBOXIDE

carbon oxychloride *n* **:** PHOSGENE

carbon paper *n* **1 :** a thin paper having a waxy pigmented coating on the face and used in making duplicate copies by being placed face down between two sheets of paper so that the pressure of writing or typing on the top sheet causes a transfer of the pigment to the bottom sheet **2 :** gelatin-coated paper used in the carbon process

carbon pencil *n* **:** a small stick of carbon or charcoal containing a small amount of niter that on being lighted is used for cracking glass

carbon process *n* **:** a photographic printing process in which a sheet of paper coated with bichromated gelatin mixed with a pigment is exposed under the negative and transferred to a support, the image then being developed by washing away the unexposed gelatin

carbons *pl of* CARBON, *pres 3d sing of* CARBON

carbon silicide *n* **:** SILICON CARBIDE

carbon spot *n* **:** a black spot in the body of a diamond

carbon steel *n* **:** steel that derives its physical properties (as strength and hardness) chiefly from the presence of carbon, other alloying elements (as manganese, silicon, and phosphorus) being present only in unimportant amounts — contrasted with *alloy steel*

carbon suboxide *n* **:** a gas having an extremely unpleasant odor and having the structure of a ketene O=C=C=C=O prepared by pyrolysis of biacetyl-tartaric anhydride or by dehydration of malonic acid

carbon sulfochloride *n* **:** THIOPHOSGENE

carbon tetrachloride *n* **:** a colorless mobile nonflammable toxic liquid CCl_4 with a chloroformlike odor made usu. by chlorination of carbon disulfide or hydrocarbons and used chiefly as a solvent (as in dry cleaning), in extinguishing small fires, and in medicine as an anthelmintic

carbon 13 *n* **:** a heavy isotope of carbon having the mass number 13, constituting about $^1/_{70}$ of natural carbon, and used in tracer studies in chemistry and biology — symbol C^{13} or ^{13}C

carbon tissue *n* **:** CARBON PAPER 2

carbon transfer *n* **:** a photographic print made by the carbon process

car·bon·yl \'kärbə,nil, -ēl\ *n* -s [ISV ¹*carbon* + *-yl*] **1 :** the bivalent radical CO occurring in aldehydes, ketones, carboxylic acids, esters, acid halides, and amides **2 :** a compound of the carbonyl radical with a metal (as chromium *carbonyl*) — **car·bon·yl·ic** \¦kärbə¦nilik\ *adj*

car·bon·y·late \kär'bänᵊl,āt\ *vt* -ED/-ING/-S [*carbonyl* + *-ate*] **:** to introduce the carbonyl group into (an organic compound) — **car·bon·yl·a·tion** \(,)kär,bänᵊl'āshən\ *n* -s

carbonyl chloride *n* **:** PHOSGENE

car·bon·yl·he·mo·glo·bin \'kärbə,nil¦h-, -ēl-\ *n* -s [*carbonyl* + *hemoglobin*] **:** a very stable pinkish red combination of hemoglobin and carbon monoxide formed in the blood when carbon monoxide is inhaled with resulting loss of ability of the blood to combine with oxygen — called also *carbon monoxide hemoglobin, carboxyhemoglobin*

car·bo·ra \kär'bōrə\ *n* -s [native name in Australia] **1** *Austral* **:** KOALA **2** *Austral* **:** a wood-boring worm that eats into timber in tidal rivers

Car·bo·run·dum \,kärbə'rəndəm, ,kȧb-\ *trademark* — used for various abrasives

carbos *pl of* CARBO

car·bo·ther·mic \¦kärbō¦thərmik\ *also* **car·bo·ther·mal** \-məl\ *adj* [*carb-* + *thermic* or *thermal*] **:** relating to a process for producing magnesium by reduction of magnesia with carbon at high temperatures

Car·bo·wax \'kärbō,waks\ *trademark* — used for any of a series of liquid and solid polyethylene glycols

carboxy- *or* **carbox-** *comb form* [ISV, fr. *carboxyl*] **:** carboxyl ⟨*carboxamide*⟩ ⟨*carboxyphenyl*⟩

car·boxy·he·mo·glo·bin \(')kär¦bäksē¦h-\ *n* -s [ISV *carboxy-* + *hemoglobin*] **:** CARBONYLHEMOGLOBIN

car·box·yl \(')kär¦bäksəl\ *n* -s [ISV *carb-* + *ox-* + *-yl*] **:** the univalent radical —COOH characteristic of the largest class of organic acids including formic, acetic, and benzoic acids

car·box·yl·ase \kär'bäksə,lās\ *n* -s [ISV *carboxyl* + *-ase*] **:** an enzyme of either of two groups that catalyze decarboxylation or carboxylation: **a :** any enzyme that accelerates the removal of carbon dioxide from a carboxyl group esp. in alpha-keto acids; *specif* **:** an enzyme first recognized in yeast that converts pyruvic acid to acetaldehyde and carbon dioxide in living cells and in alcoholic fermentation — see COCARBOXYLASE **b :** any enzyme that accelerates the addition of carbon dioxide to form a carboxyl group (as in the conversion of pyruvic acid to oxalacetic acid) — usu. distinguished from *decarboxylase*

¹car·box·yl·ate \-,lāt,-lət\ *n* -s [*carboxyl* + *-ate*] **:** a salt, ester, or acylal of a carboxylic acid

²car·box·yl·ate \-,lāt\ *vt* -ED/-ING/-S [*carboxyl* + *-ate*] **:** to introduce carboxyl or carbon dioxide into (a compound) with formation of a carboxylic acid — **car·box·yl·a·tion** \(,)kär,bäksə'lāshən\ *n* -s

car·box·yl·ic \¦kär,bäk¦silik\ *adj* [*carboxyl* + *-ic*] **:** of, relating to, or containing carboxyl

carboxylic acid *n* **:** an organic acid (as acetic acid, benzoic acid, phthalic acid) characterized by the presence of one or more carboxyl groups

car·box·y·meth·yl cellulose \(,)kär,bäksē¦methəl-\ *n* [*carboxymethyl*, the univalent radical $HOOCCH_2$—, fr. *carboxyl* + *methyl*] **:** an acid ether derivative of cellulose best known in the form of its sodium salt — see SODIUM CARBOXYMETHYL CELLULOSE

car·box·y·pep·ti·dase \-'peptə,dās\ *n* -s [ISV *carboxy-* + *peptidase*; orig. formed as G *karboxypeptidase*] **:** an enzyme (as obtained in crystalline form from the pancreas) that hydrolyzes peptides and esp. polypeptides by splitting off the amino acids containing free carboxyl groups

car·boy \'kär,bȯi, -ȧ,b-\ *n* -s [Per *qarāba*, fr. Ar (Iraq) *qarrābah* demijohn, carboy] **:** a cylindrical container of about 5 to 15 gallons capacity for corrosive or pure liquids (as strong acids or drinking water) made of glass, plastic, or metal with a neck and sometimes a pouring tip and cushioned in a wooden box, wicker basket, or special drum — compare DEMIJOHN

carboy

car·bro \'kär,brō\ *or* **carbro process** *n* -s [blend of *carb-* and *bro-* (in *bromide*)] **:** a photographic process of making either a carbon transfer or color print from a developed silver image by soaking in a bichromate bleach solution a gelatin-coated tissue containing either carbon particles or color pigments and then placing the tissue in contact with a wet silver-bromide print, after which the unhardened parts of the gelatin are washed away leaving a carbon image that is then transferred to another support

car·bro·mal \kär'brōməl\ *n* -s **:** a white crystalline compound $(C_2H_5)_2CBrCONHCONH_2$ used as a sedative and hypnotic; (2-bromo-2-ethyl-butyryl)-urea

carbs *pl of* CARB

car·bun·cle \'kär,bəŋkəl, 'kȧ,b-\ *n* -s [ME, fr. MF, fr. L *carbunculus* small coal, dark red precious stone, tumor, dim. of *carbon-, carbo* ember — more at CARBON] **1 a** *obs* **:** any of several red precious stones (as the ruby) **b :** the garnet cut cabochon **c :** ESCARBUNCLE **2 a :** a painful local inflammation of the skin and deeper tissues esp. of the back of the neck and trunk characterized by hardness, formation of openings for the discharge of pus from multiple pockets, breakdown of the surface skin and sloughing of dead tissue, usu. accompanied by fever **b** *obs* **:** a pimple or red spot (as on the face) believed to be due to intemperance **3 :** a dark grayish reddish brown that is duller and slightly redder than average brown mahogany and yellower and slightly less strong than average Burgundy (sense 2a) — called also *London brown*

car·bun·cled \-əld\ *adj* **1 :** set with carbuncles **2 :** affected with a carbuncle

car·bun·cu·lar \(')kär¦bəŋkyələr, -ȧ¦b-, -lə\ *adj* [L *carbunculus* + E *-ar*] **:** related to or resembling a carbuncle **:** afflicted with a carbuncle **:** RED, INFLAMED

car·bun·cu·lo·sis \(,)kär,bəŋkyə'lōsəs\ *n, pl* **carbunculo·ses** \-ō,sēz\ [NL, fr. L *carbunculus* + NL *-osis*] **:** a condition marked by the formation of many carbuncles simultaneously or in rapid succession

car·bun·gi \kär'bənjē\ *n* -s [native name in Australia] **:** a narrow-leaved cattail (*Typha angustifolia*) of Australia — see MURRAY DOWN

car·bu·ran \'kärbyə,ran\ *n* -s [Russ *karburan*, fr. *karb-* carb- + *uran* uranium, fr. G, fr. *Uranus* (the planet) — more at URANIUM] **:** a pitchlike hydrocarbon containing uranium

car·bu·rant \'kärb(y)ərənt\ *n* -s [prob. fr. F, fr. *carburant* containing a hydrocarbon, fr. *carbure* carbide (fr. *carb-* + *-ure* binary chemical compound) + *-ant* — more at -URET] **:** a substance (as oil gas) used to carburet a gas (as water gas)

car·bu·rate \'kärb(y)ə,rāt, 'kȧb-\ *vt* -ED/-ING/-S [back-formation fr. *carburation*] **:** CARBURET

car·bu·ra·tion \,==rāshən\ *n* -s [F, fr. *carbure* + *-ation*] **:** CARBURETION

car·bu·ra·tor \'==,rād·ə(r), -ātə-\ *n* -s **:** CARBURETOR

¹car·bu·ret \'kärbyə,ret, 'kȧb-\ *n* -s [*carb-* + *-uret*] *archaic* **:** CARBIDE

²car·bu·ret \-byə,ret; *with reference to gasoline engines, usu* -b(y)ə,rāt *by nonchemists; usu* -d.+V\ *vt* **carbureted** *also* **carburetted; carbureted** *also* **carburetted; carbureting** *also* **carburetting; carburets** **1 :** to combine chemically with carbon **2 :** to enrich (a gas) by mixing with volatile carbon compounds (as hydrocarbons) — see CARBURETED WATER GAS

car·bu·ret·ant \-etᵊnt, -āt-\ *n* -s **:** CARBURANT

carbureted hydrogen *n, archaic* **:** any of several gaseous compounds of carbon and hydrogen (as methane)

carbureted water gas *n* **:** water gas enriched by mixing with hydrocarbon gases (as oil gas) of high fuel value

car·bu·re·tion \,=b(y)ə'rāshən *also* -esh-\ *n* -s [alter. (influenced by *carburetor*) of *carburation*] **:** the act or process of carbureting; *specif* **:** the process of mixing usu. in a carburetor the vapor of a flammable hydrocarbon (as gasoline) with air to form an explosive mixture esp. for use in vapor-type internal-combustion engines

car·bu·ret·or *also* **car·bu·ret·er** *or chiefly Brit* **car·bu·ret·ter** *or* **car·bu·ret·tor** \'kärb(y)ə,rād·ər, 'kȧb(y)ə,rād·ə, -ātə(r), *Brit usu & US rarely* -re-\ *n* -s [²*carburet* + *-or*] **1 :** an apparatus for supplying an internal-combustion engine with vaporized fuel mixed with air in an explosive mixture commonly by means of an atomizer discharging the fuel into an air stream produced by the suction of the engine pistons **2 :** the part of an apparatus for manufacturing carbureted water gas in which the enriching oil is vaporized and cracked

diagram of an early type (Maybach) carburetor: gasoline inlet pipe, *A*; mixing chamber, *B*; spray nozzle or jet, *C*; float, *D*; gasoline adjusting screw, *E*; main air inlet, *F*; float needle valve, *G*

car·bu·ri·za·tion \,kärbyərə'zāshən, ,kȧb-, -,rī'z-\ *n* -s **:** the process of carburizing

car·bu·rize \'kärbyə,rīz, 'kȧb-\ *vt* -ED/-ING/-S [¹*carburet* + *-ize*] **1 :** to combine or impregnate (a metal) with carbon; *specif* **:** to introduce carbon into (a solid ferrous alloy) by heating the metal in contact with a solid, liquid, or gaseous carbonaceous material to a sufficiently high temperature and holding at that temperature — see CASE HARDEN 1; compare CEMENTATION 2 a **2 :** ²CARBURET 2

car·bu·riz·er \-zə(r)\ *n* -s **1 :** one that carburizes **2 :** a substance used as a source of carbon in carburizing

car·byl \'kärbəl, -(,)bil\ *n* -s [ISV *carb-* + *-yl*] **:** a carbon atom acting as a bivalent radical

car·byl·a·mine \,kär,bilə'mēn, =='==,=\ *n* -s [ISV *carb-* + *-yl* + *amine*; orig. formed in F] **:** ISOCYANIDE ⟨phenyl*carbylamine* C_6H_5NC⟩

car·byl·ox·ime \ˌkärbə'läkˌsēm, -ˌsəm\ *n* -s [*carbyl* + *oxime*] : FULMINIC ACID
carbyl sulfate *n* : ETHIONIC ANHYDRIDE
car·ca·jou \'kärkəˌjü, -ˌzhü\ *n* -s [CanF, fr. Algonquian Montagnais *karkajou* wolverine — more at QUICKHATCH] : WOLVERINE
car·ca·net \'kärkənət, -ˌnet\ *also* **car·can** \-kən\ *n* -s [*carcanet* fr. MF *carcan* + E *-et*; *carcan* fr. MF, iron collar for criminals, ornamental collar or necklace, fr. ML *carcannum* collar for criminals] *archaic* : an ornamental gold or jeweled chain, necklace, collar, or headband
car card *n* **1** : a small cardboard placard for advertising or other display esp. in or on streetcars and buses **2** : cardboard coated on one side only
car·case \'käkəs\ *Brit var of* CARCASS
¹car·cass \'kärkəs, 'kȧk-\ *n* -ES [MF *carcasse*, alter. of OF *carcois*, perh. fr. *carquois*, *carquais* quiver, alter. of *tarquais*, fr. ML *tarcasius*, fr. Ar *tarkāsh*, fr. Per *tīrkash*, fr. *tīr* arrow (fr. OPer *tigra* pointed) + *-kash* bearing (fr. *kashidan* to pull, draw, fr. Av *karsh-*); akin to Gk *stizein* to tattoo and to Skt *karṣati* he pulls, draws — more at STICK] **1 a** : a dead body of a human being or an animal : CORPSE **b** *of a slaughtered animal* : the trunk after the hide, head, feet, edible organs, and offal have been removed : the dressed body **2** : the living, material, or physical body **3 a** : the decaying or corroding remains (as the framework or skeleton) of a structure ⟨~*es* of old cars lay rusting among the trees —Calvin Kentfield⟩ **b** : a thing from which vitality, soul, or essence is gone : SHELL, HUSK ⟨the mere ~ of nobility —William Shenstone⟩ **4** : the framework about which or upon which a structure is built: as **a** : the shell of a building **b** : an uncovered, undecorated, or unfinished framework (as of a piece of furniture) **c(1)** : the foundation structure of a pneumatic tire consisting of several superimposed layers of cord fabric insulated in rubber **(2)** : a worn rubber tire still capable of useful service when recapped **d** : the cover or the cover and bladder of an inflated or inflatable ball **5** : a hollow case or shell filled with combustibles and thrown from a mortar or howitzer and formerly used to set fire to buildings, ships, or fortifications
²carcass \"\ *vt* -ED/-ING/-ES : to erect the framework of (a structure)
car·cass·less \-ləs\ *adj* : being without a carcass
car·ca·vel·los *also* **car·ca·ve·los** \ˌkärkə'veləs\ *n, usu cap* [Pg *carcavelos*, fr. *Carcavelos*, village near Lisbon, Portugal] : a sweet Portuguese wine usu. white
car·ce·ag \'kärsēˌag\ *n* -s [Romanian] : babesiasis of the sheep
car·cel \'kärsəl\ *n* -s [Sp *cárcel*, fr. L *carcer*] *Southwest* : JAIL, PRISON
car·cer \'kärˌke(ə)r, -rsər\ *n, pl* **carce·res** \'kärkəˌrās, -rsəˌrēz\ [L, lit., prison] : one of the stalls at the starting point of the racecourse of a Roman circus
car·cha·rhin·i·dae \ˌkärkə'rinəˌdē\ *n pl, cap* [NL, fr. *Carcharhinus*, type genus + *-idae*] : a large cosmopolitan family comprising sharks with no spines in the dorsal fin and with the last gill opening above the pectoral fin and including the dangerous tiger shark and the economically important soupfin shark
car·cha·rhi·nus \-'rīnəs\ *n, cap* [NL, fr. Gk *karcharos* sawlike + NL *-rhinus*] : the type genus of Carcharhinidae
car·char·i·as \kär'ka(a)rēəs\ *n, cap* [NL, fr. Gk *karcharias*, a shark, fr. *karcharos* sawlike, jagged; akin to Skt *khara* harsh, rough] **1** : the type and sole recent genus of Carchariidae that comprises the common sand sharks **2** *in some classifications* : a genus of sharks variously limited; *esp* : one coextensive with the genus *Carcharhinus*
car·cha·ri·idae \ˌkärkə'rīəˌdē\ *n pl, cap* [NL, fr. *Carcharias*, type genus + *-idae*] : a family of sharks that has existed at least since Lower Cretaceous times and as now understood contains *Carcharias* and various extinct genera but formerly included many other genera (as *Galeorhinus* and *Mustelus*) and in some classifications was coextensive with Carcharhinidae
car·cha·ri·nus \-īnəs\ *syn of* CARCHARHINUS
car·char·o·don \kär'karəˌdän\ *n, cap* [NL, fr. Gk *karcharodōn*] : a genus of sharks (family Lamnidae) comprising the man-eater and a number of extinct related forms having carcharodont teeth
car·char·o·dont \-ˌdänt\ *adj* [Gk *karcharodont-*, *karcharodōn* having jagged teeth, fr. *karcharos* jagged + *odont-*, *odōn* tooth — more at TOOTH] : of, belonging to, or resembling the man-eater shark; *esp* : having teeth of sharp triangular flattened form with finely serrate edges like those of this shark
car checker *n* **1** : one that reports and records the identifying numbers on cars in a freight yard **2** : a worker who inspects new automobiles before delivery to customers
carcin- *or* **carcino-** *comb form* [Gk. *karkin-*, *karkino-*, fr. *karkinos* — more at CANCER] **1** : crab ⟨*carcinology*⟩ **2** : tumor ⟨*carcinogenic*⟩ : cancer ⟨*carcinemia*⟩ ⟨*carcinosarcoma*⟩
car·cin·i·des \kär'sinəˌdēz\ *n, cap* [NL, fr. *Carcinus* + *-ides* (pl. of *-is* -id)] *syn of* CARCINUS
car·ci·noe·ci·um \ˌkärsə'nēs(h)ēəm\ *n, pl* **carcinoe·cia** \-s(h)ēə\ [NL, fr. *carcin-* + *-oecium* (fr. Gk *oikion* house, nest, dim. of *oikos* house) — more at VICINITY] : a colony of zoanthidean anemones (genus *Epizoanthus*) enclosing a hermit crab after dissolving the shell in which the crab lodged
car·cin·o·gen \kär'sinəjən, 'kärs°nəˌjen\ *n* -s [*carcin-* + *-gen*] : a substance or agent producing or inciting cancerous growth — compare LEUKEMOGEN
car·ci·no·gen·e·sis \ˌkärs°n(ˌ)ō'jenəsəs\ *n* [NL, fr. *carcin-* + L *genesis*] : the production of cancer
car·ci·no·gen·ic \ˌ==(ˌ)=ˌ'jenik\ *adj* [*carcin-* + *-genic*] : producing or tending to produce cancer ⟨the ~ action of certain chemicals —*Jour. Amer. Med. Assoc.*⟩ — **car·ci·no·ge·nic·i·ty** \ˌ==(ˌ)=jə'nisəd-ē\ *n* -ES
car·ci·noid \'kärs°nˌȯid\ *n* -s *often attrib* [*carcin-* + *-oid*] : a usu. gastrointestinal and sometimes malignant tumor typically associated with excessive serotonin production
car·ci·no·log·i·cal \ˌkärs°nō'läjəkəl\ *adj* : of or relating to carcinology
car·ci·nol·o·gist \ˌkärs°n'äləjəst\ *n* -s : a specialist in carcinology
car·ci·nol·o·gy \-jē\ *n* -ES [ISV *carcin-* + *-logy*; prob. orig. formed as F *carcinologie*] : a branch of zoology that treats of the Crustacea
car·ci·no·lyt·ic \ˌkärs°nō'lid-ik\ *adj* [ISV *carcin-* + *-lytic*; prob. orig. formed as G *karzinolytisch*] : destructive of cancer cells
car·ci·no·ma \ˌkärs°n'ōmə, ˌkȧs-\ *n, pl* **carcinomas** \-ōməz\ *or* **carcinoma·ta** \-ōməd-ə, -ətə\ [L, fr. Gk *karkinōma* cancer, fr. *karkinos*] : a malignant tumor consisting of epithelial cells lying within the connective tissue framework of an organ or other structure of a human or an animal body — compare CANCER, SARCOMA
carcinoma in situ *n* [NL] : carcinoma in the stage of development when the cancer cells are still within their site of origin (as the mouth or uterine cervix)
car·ci·no·ma·toid \ˌ=='ämə,tȯid, -ōm-\ *adj* [L *carcinomat-*, *carcinoma* + E *-oid*] : resembling a carcinoma
car·ci·no·ma·to·sis \-ˌōmə'tōsəs\ *n, pl* **carcinomato·ses** \-ōˌsēz\ [NL, fr. L *carcinomat-*, *carcinoma* + NL *-osis*] : a condition in which carcinomas are developing simultaneously in many parts of the body as a result of dissemination from a primary source
car·ci·nom·a·tous \ˌ==ˌ'ämədəs, -ōm-, -ətəs\ *adj* [L *carcinomat-*, *carcinoma* + E *-ous*] : being of or relating to carcinoma ⟨a ~ lesion⟩
car·ci·no·mor·phic \ˌ==ō'mȯrfik\ *adj* [*carcin-* + *-morphic*] : resembling a crab
car·ci·no·ne·mer·tes \ˌ===nə'mərd-ēz\ *n, cap* [NL, fr. *carcin-* + *Nemertes*, genus of worms, fr. Gk *Nēmertēs* daughter of Nereus] : a genus of nemertine worms (order Hoplonemertea) with rudimentary proboscis and a single stylet that are parasitic on the gills and eggs of crabs
car·ci·no·sar·co·ma \'kärs°n(ˌ)ōˌsär'kōmə\ *n, pl* **carcinosarcomas** \-ōməz\ *or* **carcinosarcoma·ta** \-ōməd-ə\ [NL, fr. *carcin-* + *sarcoma*] : a malignant tumor combining elements of carcinoma and sarcoma
car·ci·no·sis \ˌkärs°n'ōsəs\ *n, pl* **carcino·ses** \-ōˌsēz\ [NL, fr. *carcin-* + *-osis*] : dissemination of carcinomatous growths in the body : CARCINOMATOSIS
car·ci·nus \'kärs°nəs\ [NL, fr. Gk *karkinos* crab — more at CANCER] : a genus of swimming crabs (family Portunidae) including only the common edible green crab (*C. maenas*)
car·coon \(')kär'kün\ *n* -s [Marathi *kārkūn*, fr. Per *kārkun* manager, fr. *kār* work, business + *-kun* doer] *India* : CLERK
car cooper *n* : one that makes minor repairs to the bodies of freight cars to prepare them for hauling of such bulk commodities as grain
¹card \'kärd, 'kȧd\ *vt* -ED/-ING/-S [ME *carden*, fr. MF *carder*, fr. *carde*] **1** : to cleanse, disentangle, and collect together (as animal or vegetable fibers) by the use of a card preparatory to spinning, the process being used to prepare fibers of relatively short length — compare COMB *vt* 1b **2** *obs* : to stir together and mix as if by combing together with a card **3** : to torture by drawing a wool card or similar instrument over the bare back or other part of the body
²card \"\ *n* -s [ME *carde*, fr. MF, fr. LL *cardus* thistle, fr. L *carduus* — more at CHARD] **1** : an implement (as a wire brush) for raising a nap on cloth **2 a** : a hand instrument for cleaning, disentangling, and ordering animal or vegetable fibers preparatory to spinning usu. consisting of bent wire teeth set closely in rows in a thick piece of leather fastened to a back **b** : CARDING MACHINE
³card \"\ *n* -s [ME *carde*, modif. of MF *carte*, prob. fr. OIt *carta*, lit., leaf of paper, fr. L *charta* leaf of papyrus, fr. Gk *chartēs*] **1 a** : PLAYING CARD **b** : a playing card considered in terms of its rank, value, or function ⟨a high ~⟩ ⟨a trump ~⟩; *esp* : a relatively high or valuable card ⟨they had all the ~*s*⟩ ⟨I didn't hold a ~⟩ **2 cards** *pl but sometimes sing in constr* **a** : a game played with cards : card playing ⟨lose a fortune at ~*s*⟩ **b** : the winning of a majority of the cards in certain games (as casino) ⟨give three points for ~*s*⟩ **c** : playing cards used for fortunetelling or to reveal what is destined to be ⟨read the ~*s* correctly⟩ — used esp. with *in* or *on* ⟨it is not in the ~*s* for him to win the election⟩ **3** : something compared to a valuable playing card in one's hand : an act, fact, force, or means advantageous to the attainment of an object ⟨hold strong ~*s* in the negotiations⟩ **4** : an amusing person : one given to freakish, clownish, or uninhibited behavior : an amateur comedian : WAG **5 a** *obs* : CHART ⟨a ~ of the sea⟩ **b** : COMPASS CARD **6 a** : a flat stiff piece of paper or thin paperboard suitable for writing or printing, typically small and rectangular, and carrying (1) a communication for transmission by mail (as a postcard), (2) an invitation or announcement ⟨wedding ~⟩ ⟨graduation ~⟩, (3) a person's or firm's name or name and address (as a visiting card), (4) a certification of membership, reference, or credential (as in a labor union or political party), (5) a record (as a unit in a system of filing or sorting) ⟨the information was punched on ~*s*⟩ **b** : a piece of paper or thin paperboard having any of a variety of shapes and formats and bearing a greeting or a message of sentiment, sympathy, or congratulation ⟨birthday ~⟩ **c** : PROGRAM; *esp* : a sports program ⟨racing ~⟩ ⟨boxing ~⟩ **d** : a tally sheet (as for a player's golf score) : SCORECARD **e** (1) : a wine list (2) : MENU **f** : STORE CARD **g** : a number of articles attached to a piece of stiff paper or bound together in a flat sheet to be sold as a unit ⟨a ~ of buttons⟩ **h** : CARDBOARD **7** : a published note (as in a newspaper) containing a brief statement, request, or advertisement **8** : any of the perforated boards or plates in a dobby or a jacquard loom for operating the successive combinations of wires that move the warp threads **9** *slang* : a single portion of a narcotic drug
⁴card \"\ *vb* -ED/-ING/-S *vi, archaic* : to play cards — sometimes used with *it* ⟨~ it all night —Henry Fielding⟩ ~ *vt* **1** : to place or fasten on or by means of a card ⟨his name was ~*ed* upon three staterooms —E.A.Poe⟩ **2** : to provide with a card : attach a card to **3** : to enter or list on a card **4** *sports* : SCORE; *specif* : to record (a score) upon a scorecard ⟨golfers who ~*ed* 80 on an 18-hole course⟩ **5** : SCHEDULE ⟨~ a train⟩ **6** : ⁵SLIP 2
card *abbr, usu cap* cardinal
car·dam·i·ne \kär'damə(ˌ)nē\ *n* [NL, fr. Gk *kardaminē* water cress, fr. *kardamon* garden peppergrass] **1** *cap* : a large genus of mostly perennial glabrous herbs (family Cruciferae) growing in temperate regions and having flat pods and wingless seeds **2** -s : a plant of the genus *Cardamine*
car·da·mom \'kärdəməm *also* -ˌmäm\ *also* **car·da·mum** \-məm\ *or* **car·da·mon** \-mən *also* -ˌmän\ *n* -s [L *cardamomum*, fr. Gk *kardamōmon*, blend of *kardamon* garden peppergrass & *amōmon*, an Indian spice plant] **1 a** : the aromatic capsular fruit of an East Indian herb (*Elettaria cardamomum*) the seeds of which are used as a condiment and in medicine as an adjuvant to other aromatics and stomachics **b** : a similar fruit of certain related plants (as members of the genus *Amomum*) that are sometimes used as adulterants **2** : a plant that produces cardamoms
cardamom oil *n* : a colorless or pale-yellow essential oil with a camphoraceous odor and pungent taste distilled from cardamom seeds and used in pharmaceutical preparations and as a flavoring for foods
car·dan \'kärˌdan\ *or* **cardan joint** *n* -s *usu cap C* [after Jerome *Cardan* (Geronimo Cardano) †1576 Ital. mathematician, its inventor] : a universal joint that transmits motion unchanged
car·da·nol \'kärd°nˌȯl, -ōl\ *n* -s [*card-* (fr. NL *Anacardium*, genus name of *Anacardium occidentale*) + *-an* + *-ol*] : a nonvesicant oily liquid that is composed chiefly of monohydroxy phenols, obtained from cashew nutshell liquid or anacardic acid, and used esp. in making phenolic resins
cardan shaft *n, usu cap C* [after Jerome *Cardan*, its inventor] **1** : a shaft that has a universal joint at one or both ends enabling it to rotate freely when in varying angular relation to another shaft or shafts to which it is joined **2** : a shaft (as on a motor vehicle) that transmits power
car·dan suspension \'kärˌdan-\ *or* **car·dan·ic suspension** \(')kär'danik-\ *n, usu cap C* [after Jerome *Cardan*] : a support in which an instrument (as a chronometer) is hung on gimbals
¹cardboard \'=ˌ=\ *n* -s [³*card* + *board*] : a stiff moderately thick paperboard sometimes coated and of a quality suitable for signs or printed matter — compare ¹BOARD 6a
²cardboard \"\ *adj* **1** : made of or as if of cardboard : FLAT : TWO-DIMENSIONAL ⟨~ Spanish ironwork —Cyril Connolly⟩ **2** : UNREAL, UNLIFELIKE : STIFF : STEREOTYPED ⟨the detective story is partial to ~ characters and notoriously fatal to any real emotion —J.P.Bishop⟩
card catalog *n* [³*card*] : a catalog (as of books) the entries in which are on cards
card clothier *also* **card clother** \-ˌklōth̲ə(r)\ *n* [²*card*] : one that removes and replaces the card clothing of carding machines
card clothing \-ˌklōth̲iŋ\ *n* [²*card*] : material consisting of leather or cloth in which teeth are set that is used esp. for covering the cylinders of carding machines
card cutter *n* [³*card*] : one that perforates a card in a pattern to be woven in a jacquard loom
car·de·cu \'kärdəˌkyü\ *n* -s [F *quart d'écu* quarter of an ecu] : an old French silver coin equal to ¼ ecu that was first issued by Henry III
¹carded *adj* [fr. past part. of ¹*card*] : prepared by the action of a card or carding machine ⟨~ wool⟩
²carded *adj* [fr. past part. of ⁴*card*] **1** : entered on a card : PROGRAMMED **2** : mounted on a card
carded silk *n* [¹*carded*] : waste silk or silk from imperfect cocoons carded for making into spun silk
carded yarn *n* [¹*carded*] : yarn of any fiber spun from carded stock — compare COMBED YARN
car·del \'kärˌdel, -ˌd°l\ *n* -s [D *kardeel*, prob. modif. of MF *quartel*, *cartel*, dim. of *quart* fourth — more at QUART] : a cask used by Dutch whalers
card·er \'kärdər, 'kȧdə\ *n* -s [ME, fr. *carden* to card (comb) + *-er*] : one that cards: as **a** : CARDING MACHINE **b** : one that attaches articles (as jewelry, needles, hairpins) to cards for display or sale
card field *n* [³*card*] : a particular group of columns, rows, or punching positions in a punched card
card grinder *n* [²*card*] : a textile worker who cleans and sharpens the wire teeth of a carding or napping machine
cardholder \'=ˌ==\ *n* [³*card* + *holder*] **1** : one whose membership in a union or political party is attested by a membership card **2** : a person who has a card issued by a library entitling him to borrow books **3** : one of two metal ears in front of the line scale on a typewriter that when raised to a vertical position help to hold cards or envelopes in place during typing
cardhouse \'=ˌ=\ *or* **cardcastle** \'=ˌ==\ *n* -s *often attrib* [³*card* + *house* or *castle*] : a structure or situation felt to resemble a construction built of playing cards in being insubstantial, unsound, or in constant danger of collapse ⟨a ~ plan that collapsed at the first test⟩ — called also *house of cards*
cardi- *or* **cardia-** *or* **cardio-** *comb form* [Gk. *kardi-*, *kardio-*, fr. *kardia* — more at HEART] **1** : heart : cardiac ⟨*cardiagra*⟩ ⟨*cardio*aortic⟩ ⟨*cardio*ptosis⟩ ⟨*cardio*puncture⟩ **2** : heart action ⟨*cardia*gram⟩
car·dia \'kärdēə, 'kȧd-\ *n, pl* **cardi·ae** \-dēˌē\ *or* **cardias** \-dēəz\ [NL, fr. Gk *kardia* heart, upper orifice of the stomach] **1 a** : the opening of the esophagus into the stomach **b** : the part of the stomach adjoining this opening **2** : the enlarged anterior portion of the ventriculus of some insects (as sucking insects that lack a proventriculus)
-cardia \"\ *n comb form* -s [NL, fr. Gk. *kardia*] **1** : heart action or location (of a specified type) ⟨dextro*cardia*⟩ ⟨tachy*cardia*⟩ **2 a** : animal or animals having a (specified) type of heart ⟨Diplo*cardia*⟩ ⟨Lepto*cardia*⟩ **b** : heart-shaped animal — esp. in generic names of mollusks
¹car·di·ac \'kärdēˌak, 'kȧd-\ *adj* [L *cardiacus*, fr. Gk *kardiakos*, fr. *kardia* heart] **1 a** : of, relating to, or acting on the heart : situated near the heart — see CARDIAC MUSCLE **b** : of or relating to the cardia or sometimes to the whole stomach except the narrow part near the pyloric end **2** : of or relating to heart disease ⟨~ patient⟩ ⟨~ clinic⟩
²cardiac \"\ *n* -s : a person with heart disease
cardiac arrest *n* : temporary or permanent cessation of the heartbeat
cardiac asthma *n* : asthma due to heart disease (as heart failure) that occurs in paroxysms usu. at night and is characterized by difficult wheezing respiration, pallor, and anxiety — called also *paroxysmal dyspnea*
cardiac cycle *n* : the complete sequence of events in the heart from the beginning of one beat to the beginning of the following beat : a complete heartbeat including systole and diastole
car·di·a·cea \ˌkärdē'āsh(ē)ə\ *n pl, cap* [NL, fr. *Cardium*, type genus + *-acea*] : a suborder of Eulamellibranchia comprising the cockles and related mollusks — **car·di·a·cean** \ˌ==ˌ'āshən\ *adj or n*
cardiac failure *n* : HEART FAILURE
cardiac gland *n* : any of the branched tubular mucus-secreting glands of the cardia of the stomach; *also* : one of the similar glands of the esophagus
cardiac impulse *n* : the wave of cardiac excitation passing from the sinoatrial node to the atrioventricular node and along the atrioventricular bundle and initiating the cardiac cycle; *broadly* : HEARTBEAT
cardiac jelly *n* : a layer of resilient jellylike material lying between the cardiac endothelium and the epimyocardium in the early development of the vertebrate heart
cardiac muscle *n* : the principal muscle tissue of the vertebrate heart made up of striated fibers that appear to be separated from each other under the electron microscope but that function in long-term rhythmic contraction as if in protoplasmic continuity
cardiac nerve *n* : any of the nerves connecting the cervical ganglia of the sympathetic system with the cardiac plexus
cardiac neurosis *n* : a condition marked by shortness of breath, fatigue, rapid pulse, and heart palpitation sometimes with extra beats that occurs chiefly with exertion and is not due to physical disease of the heart — called also *effort syndrome*, *irritable heart*, *neurocirculatory asthenia*, *soldier's heart*
cardiac orifice *n* : CARDIA 1 a
cardiac plexus *n* : a plexus of nerves derived from the sympathetic and vagus and supplying the heart and neighboring structures
cardiac sphincter *n* : the somewhat thickened muscular ring surrounding the opening between esophagus and stomach
cardiac tamponade *n* : mechanical compression of the heart by large amounts of fluid or blood within the pericardial space that limits the normal range of motion and function of the heart
cardiac vein *n* : any of the veins returning the blood from the tissues of the heart that open into the right auricle either directly or through the coronary sinus
car·di·al·gia \ˌkärdē'alj(ē)ə\ *n* -s [NL, fr. Gk *kardialgia*, fr. *kardia* heart + *-algia* — more at HEART] **1** : HEARTBURN **2** : pain in the heart
car·di·a·zol \kär'dīəˌzōl, -ōl, 'kärdēə-\ *also* **car·di·a·zole** \-ōl\ *n* -s [fr. *Cardiazol*, a trademark] : PENTYLENETETRAZOL
car·di·ec·to·my \ˌkärdē'ektəmē\ *n* -ES [ISV *cardi-* (fr. NL *cardia*) + *-ectomy*] : excision of the cardiac portion of the stomach
car·diff \'kärdəf\ *adj, usu cap* [fr. *Cardiff*, county borough in Wales] : of or from the county borough of Cardiff, Wales : of the kind or style prevalent in Cardiff
car·di·form \'kärdəˌfȯrm\ *adj* [²*card* + *-iform*] : arranged like a series of combs or wool cards (as the teeth of certain fishes)
¹car·di·gan \'kärdəgən, 'kȧd-, -ēg-\ *n* -s *often attrib* [after James Thomas Brudenell, 7th Earl of *Cardigan* †1868 Eng. soldier] : a sweater or jacket that opens the full length of the center front and usu. has a round or V-shaped collarless neck

cardigan

²cardigan \"\ *n* -s *usu cap* [fr. *Cardigan*, county in Wales] : a Welsh Corgi of a variety characterized by rounded ears, slightly bowed forelegs, and long tail
car·di·gan·shire \-ˌshi(ə)r, -iə, -shə(r)\ *or* **cardigan** *adj, usu cap* [fr. *Cardiganshire*, or the county of *Cardigan*, Wales] : of or from the county of Cardigan, Wales : of the kind or style prevalent in Cardigan
car·di·i·dae \kär'dīəˌdē\ *n pl, cap* [NL, fr. *Cardium*, type genus + *-idae*] : a family of marine bivalve mollusks (order Eulamellibranchia) that have an equivalve ribbed shell with prominent umbones, a large foot adapted for creeping over sandy bottoms, and much-folded gills and that include the true cockles
¹car·di·nal \'kärd(°)nəl, 'kȧd-\ *adj* [ME, fr. OF, fr. LL *cardinalis*, fr. L, of a hinge, fr. *cardin-*, *cardo* hinge + *-alis* -al; akin to OE *hratian* to rush, hasten, MHG *scherzen* to leap for joy, jest, ON *hrata* to stagger, fall, Gk *kradan* to shake, brandish, *kordylē* bump, swelling, *skairein* to gambol, Skt *kūrdati* he leaps; basic meaning: to spring, turn] **1** : of basic importance : central, basic, or critical to any system, construction, organization, or framework of thought ⟨might ask for the return of the German colonies, but this was evidently not ~ —Sir Winston Churchill⟩ ⟨the ~ element in the plan was speed⟩ : of principal importance : CHIEF, PRIMARY ⟨progress had been elevated into a ~ doctrine of the educated classes —Lewis Mumford⟩ ⟨a ~ symptom in diagnosis⟩ **2 a** : of or relating to the hinge of a bivalve shell **b** : of or relating to the cardo of an insect **3** : of a cardinal red color **syn** see ESSENTIAL
²cardinal \"\ *n* -s [ME, fr. ML *cardinalis*, fr. LL *cardinalis*, adj., principal] **1** : a high ecclesiastical official taking precedence over every other dignitary of the Roman Catholic Church below papal rank who is appointed by the pope to assist him as a member of the college of cardinals **2** : CARDINAL NUMBER — usu. used in pl. **3** : a woman's short hooded cloak orig. of scarlet cloth **4** [so called fr. the color of a cardinal's robes] *or* **cardinal red** : a variable color averaging a vivid red that is yellower and duller than madder crimson or carmine, bluer and duller than scarlet or Castilian red, and duller than apple red **5** [so called fr. its red color, compared with that of a cardinal's robes] *also* **cardinal bird** : any of several American songbirds (genus *Richmondena*) of the family Fringillidae of the southern and middle U.S., the male being bright red with a black face, pointed crest, and loud song and the female being much duller in color — see ARIZONA CARDINAL
cardinal archbishop *n* [trans. of ML *cardinalis archiepiscopus*] : a cardinal who governs an archdiocese — not used as a canonical title

car·di·nal·ate \-əlȧt, -ˌlāt\ *n* -s [F *cardinalat*, fr. ML *cardinalatus*, fr. *cardinalis* + L *-atus* -ate] **1 :** the office, rank, or dignity of a cardinal **2 :** CARDINALS

cardinal bishop *n* [trans. of ML *episcopus cardinalis*] **:** a member of the first order of cardinals holding until 1932 one of the suburbicarian sees of Rome

cardinal climber *n* [²*cardinal*] **:** an annual vine (*Quamoclit sloteri*) resembling the cypress vine

cardinal deacon *n* [trans. of ML *diaconus cardinalis*] **:** a member of the third order of cardinals who is also titular chief officer of a Roman deaconry

cardinal dean *n* [trans. of ML *diaconus cardinalis*] **:** the senior cardinal bishop of the college of cardinals at Rome

cardinal fish *n* [²*cardinal;* fr. its color, compared with that of a cardinal's robes] **:** a fish of the genus *Apogon* or family Apogonidae related to the family Percidae and commonly red; *esp* **:** the common European cardinal fish (*Apogon imberbis*)

cardinal flower *n* [²*cardinal*] **1 :** the brilliant red flower of a No. American herb (*Lobelia cardinalis*) **2 :** the plant bearing the cardinal flower

car·di·nal·i·tial \ˌkärd(ᵊ)nə¦lishəl\ *also* **car·di·nal·i·tian** \-shən\ *adj* [irreg. fr. It *cardinalizio* cardinalitial (fr. *cardinale* cardinal, fr. ML *cardinalis*) + E *-al* or *-an* — more at CARDINAL] **:** of or relating to a cardinal

car·di·nal·ly \ˈ=d(ᵊ)nəlē, -i\ *adv* **:** in a cardinal manner or degree **:** PREEMINENTLY

cardinal number *or* **cardinal numeral** *n* [¹*cardinal*] **1 a :** a primary number used in simple counting **:** a number (as one, two, three) answering the question "how many?" — distinguished from *ordinal number;* see NUMBER table

cardinal point *n* [¹*cardinal*] **1 a :** one of the four principal points of the compass north, south, east, and west **b** *in magical ritual* **:** one of the four principal directional points of the compass or one of the additional points zenith, nadir, and center **2** *of a lens or lens system* **:** one of the two principal foci, the two principal points, or the two nodal points — called also *Gauss point*

cardinal points of the ecliptic : the two equinoctial and the two solstitial points

cardinal priest *n* [trans. of ML *presbyter cardinalis*] **:** a member of the second order of cardinals orig. but now only titularly in charge of a parish church at Rome

cardinal process *n* [¹*cardinal*] **:** a projection in the shells of many brachiopods at the posterior edge of the dorsal valve to which the muscles that open the shell are attached — see BRACHIOPOD illustration

cardinal red *n* **:** CARDINAL 4

cardinals *pl of* CARDINAL

cardinal sauce *n* [²*cardinal;* fr. its color, compared with that of a cardinal's robes] **:** a white sauce variously flavored and colored red

cardinal's hat *n* [²*cardinal*] **:** a red hat with low crown and broad brim symbolic of the dignity of a cardinal — called also *red hat*

car·di·nal·ship \-ˌship\ *n* -s [²*cardinal* + *-ship*] **:** CARDINALATE

cardinal sign *n* [¹*cardinal*] **:** one of the four zodiacal signs Aries, Cancer, Libra, and Capricorn corresponding to cardinal points of the ecliptic

cardinal tooth *n* [¹*cardinal*] **:** a tooth of the hinge of a bivalve mollusk's shell situated just under the umbo and often relatively large — compare LATERAL TOOTH

coat of arms showing cardinal's hat

cardinal vein *also* **cardinal sinus** *n* [¹*cardinal*] **:** any of four longitudinal veins of the vertebrate embryo running anteriorly and posteriorly along each side of the vertebral column with the pair on each side meeting at and discharging blood to the heart through the corresponding duct of Cuvier

cardinal virtue *n* [¹*cardinal*] **:** one of a group of preeminent virtues: as **a** *among the ancients and in scholasticism* **:** one of the natural virtues prudence, justice, temperance, or fortitude **b :** one of seven virtues including in addition to the natural virtues the three theological virtues faith, hope, and charity

cardinal vowel *n* [¹*cardinal*] **:** one of a series of 16 invariable vowel sounds set up as a standard for describing the quality of the vowels of any language or speaker

cardinal wind *n* [¹*cardinal*] **:** one of the winds that blow from the cardinal points of the compass

card index *n* [³*card*] **:** an index having the entries on cards

card–in·dex \ˈ=ˌ=ˌ=\ *vt* **1 :** to list in a card index **:** CATALOG **2 :** to analyze or categorize elaborately and systematically

cardines [L] *pl of* CARDO

carding *n* -s [fr. gerund of ¹*card*] **1 :** a roll of wool or other fiber from a carding machine **2** [by shortening] **:** CARDING MACHINE

carding engine *n, Brit* **:** CARDING MACHINE

carding leather *n* **:** a cattlehide leather produced for use on cards of textile machinery

carding machine *n* **:** a machine for carding wool, cotton, or other fiber consisting of cylinders having intermeshing wire teeth and revolving at different speeds or in opposite directions — compare BREAKER 2c(1), COMBING MACHINE

carding wool *n* **:** CLOTHING WOOL 1

cardio- *in words below,* ¦=== = ¦kärdēō *or* ¦kȧd- *or* -ēə, ¦==(ˌ)= = " *or* -ēˌō, ˌ==ˈ= = ˌkärdēˈä *or* ˌkȧd-\ — see CARDI-

car·dio·blast \ˈ===ˌblast\ *n* -s [*cardi-* + *-blast*] *of an insect* **:** any of certain early embryonic cells occurring segmentally in pairs from which the heart develops

car·dio·car·pon \ˌ===ˈkärˌpän\ *also* **car·dio·car·pum** \-ˌpəm\ *n* -s [NL, fr. *cardi-* + *-carpon, -carpum* (fr. Gk *karpos* fruit) — more at HARVEST] **:** any of certain nutlike fruits or seeds of plants of the fossil genus *Cordaites*

car·dio·gen·ic plate \¦===¦jenik-\ *n* [*cardiogenic* fr. *cardi-* + *-genic*] **:** an area of splanchnic mesoderm anterior to the head process of the early mammalian embryo that subsequently gives rise to the heart

car·dio·gram \ˈ===ˌgram, -aa(ə)m\ *n* -s [ISV *cardi-* + *-gram*] **:** the curve or tracing made by a cardiograph

car·dio·graph \-ˌgraf, -aa(ə)f, -aˌf\ *n* -s [ISV *cardi-* + *-graph;* orig. formed as F *cardiographe*] **:** an instrument that registers graphically the heart's movements — **car·di·og·ra·pher** \ˌ==ˈ=grəfə(r)\ *n* -s — **car·dio·graph·ic** \¦===¦grafik, -ēk\ *adj* — **car·di·og·ra·phy** \ˌ==ˈ=grəfē, -i\ *n* -ES [ISV *cardiograph* + *-y*] **:** the use of the cardiograph **:** examination by cardiograph

¹**car·di·oid** \ˈkärdēˌȯid\ *n* -s [*cardi-* + *-oid*] **:** a heart-shaped closed curve traced by a point on the circumference of a circle as it rolls completely around an equal fixed circle and forms an epicycloid of one cusp and one loop, the polar equation with cusp as pole being $r = a\ (1 - \cos\theta)$, where a is the diameter of either circle

²**cardioid** \"\ *adj* **:** connected with or relating to a cardioid

cardioid: *ABP* fixed circle; *PCD* first position of rolling circle; *P* tracing point; *PM* diameter through *P;* P_1, P_2, P_3, P_4 various positions of *P;* P_1M_1, P_2M_2, P_3M_3, P_4M_4 various positions of *PM*

cardioid condenser *n* **:** a substage condenser that may be used with a microscope to give illumination approximating that obtained with the ultramicroscope

cardioid microphone *n* **:** a microphone having approximately uniform response over 180 degrees in front and minimum response in back, a polar curve representing its directional response being a cardioid

car·dio·in·hib·i·to·ry \¦==(ˌ)=-\ *adj* [*cardi-* + *inhibitory*] **:** interfering with or slowing the normal sequence of events in the cardiac cycle ⟨the ~ center of the medulla⟩

car·dio·lip·in \ˌ===ˈlipən\ *n* -s [*cardi-* + *lip-* + *-in*] **:** a phosphatide obtained esp. from beef heart and used in antigens for diagnostic blood tests for syphilis

car·dio·log·ic \¦===¦läjik\ *adj* [ISV *cardiology* + *-ic*] **:** relating to the study of the heart — **car·dio·log·i·cal** \-ə̇kəl\ *adj*

car·di·ol·o·gist \ˌ==ˈ=ləjəst\ *n* -s **:** a specialist in cardiology

car·di·ol·o·gy \-jē, -i\ *n* -ES [ISV *cardi-* + *-logy*] **:** the study of the heart and its action and of the diagnosis and therapy of its diseases

car·di·om·e·ter \ˌ==ˈ=məd·ə(r)\ *n* -s [*cardi-* + *-meter*] **:** an instrument used in measuring the force of the heart's action — **car·dio·met·ric** \¦===¦me·trik\ *adj* — **car·di·om·e·try** \ˌ==ˈ=mə·trē\ *n* -ES

car·dio·path \ˈ===ˌpath\ *n* -s [back-formation fr. *cardiopathy*] **:** a person having heart disease

car·di·op·a·thy \ˌ==ˈ=pəthē\ *n* -ES [prob. fr. NL *cardiopathia,* fr. *cardi-* + *-pathia*] **:** a disease of the heart

car·dio·pho·bia \ˌ===ˈfōbēə\ *n* -s [NL, fr. *cardi-* + *phobia*] **:** abnormal fear of heart disease

car·dio·pul·mo·nary machine \¦==(ˌ)=-\ *n* [ISV *cardi-* + *pulmonary*] **:** HEART-LUNG MACHINE

car·dio·res·pi·ra·to·ry \¦==(ˌ)=-\ *adj* [*cardi-* + *respiratory*] **:** relating to the heart and lungs and their functions

car·di·or·rha·phy \ˌ==ˈȯrəfē\ *n* -ES [ISV *cardi-* + *-rrhaphy*] **:** a surgical operation of suturing the heart muscle (as in the repair of a stab wound)

car·dio·scope \ˈ===ˌskōp\ *n* -s [*cardi-* + *-scope*] **1 :** an instrument that permits direct visual inspection of the interior of the heart **2 :** an instrument that permits continuous electrocardiographic observation of the heart's action during an operation **3 :** an instrument equipped with a screen on which tracings of the heart's action and sounds can be demonstrated

car·dio·spasm \ˈ===ˌspazəm\ *n* -s [ISV *cardi-* + *spasm*] **:** failure of the cardiac sphincter to relax during swallowing with resultant esophageal obstruction — compare ACHALASIA — **car·dio·spas·tic** \¦===¦spastik\ *adj*

car·dio·sper·mum \ˌ===ˈspərməm\ *n, cap* [NL, fr. *cardi-* + *-spermum* (neut. of *-spermus* -spermous)] **:** a large genus of tropical American herbaceous vines (family Sapindaceae) having alternate biternate leaves, coarsely serrate leaflets, small white flowers, and an inflated capsular fruit — see BALLOON VINE

car·dio·ta·chom·e·ter \¦==(ˌ)=-\ *n* -s [*cardi-* + *tachometer*] **:** a device for prolonged graphic recording of the heartbeat

car·di·ot·o·my \ˌ==ˈ=d·əmē\ *n* -ES [ISV *cardi-* + *-tomy*] **1 :** surgical incision of the heart **2 :** surgical incision of the cardia of the stomach

¹**car·dio·ton·ic** \¦===¦tänik\ *adj* [ISV *cardi-* + *-tonic*] **:** tending to increase the tonus of heart muscle

²**cardiotonic** \"\ *n* -s **:** a cardiotonic substance

car·dio·vas·cu·lar \¦==(ˌ)=-\ *adj* [ISV *cardi-* + *vascular*] **:** of, relating to, or involving the heart and blood vessels ⟨~ disease⟩ ⟨~ system⟩

car distributor *n* **1 :** one that directs the distribution of railroad cars and equipment to points where they are required for loading or other use **2 :** MOTOR BOSS

car·di·ta \kärˈdīd·ə, -ē-\ *n* [NL, fr. Gk *kardia* heart + L *-ita* -ite] **1** *cap* **:** a genus (the type of the family Carditidae) of marine lamellibranch mollusks resembling the cockles but lacking siphons and having a short foot **2** -s **:** any mollusk of the genus *Cardita*

car·dite \ˈkärˌdīt\ *n* -s [F, fr. NL *Cardita*] **:** CARDITA 2

car·di·tis \kärˈdīd·ə̇s\ *n* -ES [NL, fr. *cardi-* + *-itis*] **:** inflammation of the heart muscle **:** MYOCARDITIS — see ENDOCARDITIS, PERICARDITIS

car·di·um \ˈkärdēəm, ˈkȧd-\ *n, cap* [NL, fr. Gk *kardia* heart + NL *-ium;* fr. its shape] **:** the type genus of Cardiidae including a number of cockles esteemed as food

-car·di·um \"\ *n comb form, pl* **-car·dia** \-ēə\ [NL, fr. Gk *-kardion,* fr. *kardia* — more at HEART] **:** heart ⟨endo*cardium*⟩ ⟨meso*cardium*⟩

cardium clay *n, cap 1st C* **:** a Pleistocene glacial clay of northern Europe characterized by fossil shells of the genus *Cardium*

car·do \ˈkärˌdō\ *n, pl* **car·di·nes** \-dᵊnˌēz, -ˌās\ [L, hinge — more at CARDINAL] **:** a basal or proximal part (as the basal joint of the insect maxilla or the hinge of a bivalve shell)

¹**cardon** *var of* CARDOON

²**car·don** \ˈkärˌdän, =ˈ=\ *n* -s [AmerSp *cardón,* fr. Sp, teasel, fr. LL *cardon-, cardo* thistle] **1** *also* **car·do·na** \kärˈdōnə\ **:** any of several large columnar cacti esp. of the genus *Cereus* that have a woody skeleton sometimes used for lumber (as in furniture making), may attain a height of 60 feet, and often form forestlike stands from Lower California to Chile and in Venezuela **2 :** any of several cactuslike plants of the genus *Euphorbia* of Central America and the West Indies

car·don·ci·llo \ˌkärdᵊnˈsē(ˌ)yō\ *n* -s [MexSp, fr. Sp, milk thistle (*Silybum marianum*), dim. of *cardón* teasel] **:** a cactus (*Wilcoxia papillosa*) of tropical America used for food and fuel

car·doon \(ˈ)kärˈdün, -kȧˈd-\ *or* **car·don** \-ōn\ *n* -s [F *cardon,* fr. LL *cardon-, cardo* thistle, fr. *cardus,* fr. L *carduus* thistle, artichoke — more at CHARD] **:** a large thistlelike plant (*Cynara cardunculus*) related to the artichoke, the blanched leaves and stalks and the thick main roots being used as food

card page *also* **card plate** *n* [³*card*] **:** a page in a book on which are listed other works by the same author or publisher

cardplayer \ˈ=ˌ==\ *n* [³*card* + *player*] **:** one that plays cards

card punch *n* [³*card*] **:** a machine or hand tool that punches coded information onto cards — compare PUNCH CARD

cardroom \ˈ=ˌ=\ *n* -s **1 :** a room in which gambling with playing cards is carried on **2 :** a room equipped for pastime card playing ⟨a game of bridge in the ~ of the club —Raymond Paton⟩ **3 :** a room equipped for cloth carding

cards *pl of* CARD, *pres 3d sing of* CARD

cards and spades *n pl* **:** a liberal handicap ⟨could give him *cards and spades* and still beat him at his own game⟩

card setter *n* [²*card*] **:** a machine for setting the wire teeth in making card clothing

cardsharper \ˈ=ˌ==\ *or* **cardsharp** \ˈ=ˌ=\ *n* -s [³*card* + *sharper* (cheat) *or sharp*] **:** one that consistently seeks to win at card games by cheating

card strip *n* [²*card*] **:** cotton waste consisting of cleanings from a carding machine

card stripper *n* [²*card*] **:** one that cleans accumulated fiber from the teeth of a carding or doffing drum

card table *n* [³*card*] **:** a table for playing cards: **a :** a table with folding top that can be placed against a wall like a console when not in use **b :** a square table with folding legs

card teasel *n* [²*card;* fr. its use in dressing cloth] **:** WILD TEASEL

card tender *n* [²*card*] **:** a worker who feeds lap into one or more textile or asbestos carding machines and removes slivers — called also *winder*

card thistle *n* [²*card;* fr. its use in dressing cloth] **:** TEASEL

car·du·a·ce·ae \ˌkärjəˈwāsēˌē\ *n pl, cap* [NL, fr. *Carduus,* type genus + *-aceae*] *in some classifications* **:** a family of plants comprising all the composites (as thistles and asters) that have syngenesious stamens and flower heads containing tubular flowers or both tubular and ligulate flowers but not ligulate flowers alone — **car·du·a·ceous** \¦==¦wāshəs\ *adj*

car·du·e·line \ˌkärjəˈwēlən\ *adj* [NL *Carduelis* + E *-ine*] **:** of or relating to the genus *Carduelis*

car·du·e·lis \-ləs\ *n, cap* [NL, fr. L, goldfinch, fr. *carduus* thistle] **:** the genus of birds (family Fringillidae) containing the European goldfinch and often the siskins, redpolls and linnets, and related birds — compare SPINUS

car·du·us \ˈkärjəwəs\ *n, cap* [NL, fr. L, thistle — more at CHARD] **:** a genus of annual or perennial prickly thistles (family Compositae) having the bristles of the pappus not plumose and being native to the Old World — compare CIRSIUM; see MUSK THISTLE

card voting *n* [³*card*] **:** a system of voting (as in some European trade unions) by which one vote is cast by a person bearing a card that specifies the number of voters he represents

¹**care** \ˈke(ə)r, ˈkeə, ˈka(a)(ə)r, ˈka(a)ə\ *n* -s [ME, fr. OE *caru, cearu;* akin to OHG *kara* lament, Goth *kara* care, L *garrire* to chatter, talk, Gk *gērys* voice, Ossetic *zar* song] **1 :** suffering of mind **:** GRIEF, SORROW ⟨a *care*-marked face⟩ **2 a :** a burdened or disquieted state of blended preoccupation, uncertainty, apprehension or fear, and consideration of expedients ⟨oppressed by sickness, grief, or ~ —William Wordsworth⟩ **b :** a cause for such state **3 :** serious attention; *esp* **:** attention accompanied by caution, pains, wariness, personal interest, or responsibility ⟨his gentlemen conduct me with all ~ to some securest lodging —John Keats⟩ **4 :** regard coming from desire or esteem **:** INCLINATION, WISH — usu. used with *of* or *for* ⟨a ~ for the common good⟩ **5 :** CHARGE, SUPERVISION, MANAGEMENT **:** responsibility for or attention to safety and well-being ⟨under a doctor's ~⟩ ⟨the ~ of all the churches —2 Cor 11:28 (AV)⟩ **:** CUSTODY **:** temporary charge — used esp. in the phrase *care of* or *in care of* on mail sent to a person through another person or other agency ⟨I addressed him ~ of general delivery⟩; abbr. *c/o* **6 :** a person or thing that is an object of attention, anxiety, or solicitude ⟨the flower garden was her special ~⟩

syn SOLICITUDE, CONCERN, WORRY, ANXIETY: CARE designates a troubled, preoccupied, or oppressed mental condition induced by responsibilities and duties or by doubts and apprehensions ⟨the king . . . most sovereign slave of *care* —H.D.Thoreau⟩ ⟨she was free . . . to go where she liked and do what she liked. She had no responsibilities, no *cares* —Arnold Bennett⟩ SOLICITUDE designates an apprehensive or thoughtful protectiveness, attentiveness, or regard for well-being or success, usu. another's ⟨with motherly *solicitude,* he insisted that Tom get to his feet —Sherwood Anderson⟩ ⟨no amount of parental *solicitude* can give a boy or girl the same advantages at home as are to be enjoyed in a good school—Bertrand Russell⟩ CONCERN, the antonym of *indifference,* means primarily an interest in one's well-being or safety but is likely to suggest apprehension or doubt about difficulties, dangers, or failures ⟨but your friends, Señora, would feel less *concern* for your safety if you kept them [valuables] further from your person —Mary Austin⟩ ⟨she really did feel *concern* for her fellow creatures, for the rural poor upon whom it was not the custom of Church or State to waste sympathy or help —Agnes Repplier⟩ WORRY suggests troubled fretting about adverse developments from uncertain conditions ⟨thought that now all the *worries* were over . . . a most soothing certitude —Joseph Conrad⟩ ⟨alternating *worry* with quiet qualms —Robert Browning⟩ ANXIETY adds a strong suggestion of dread and distress in the expectation of an evil issue or outcome ⟨I shut my eyes, but *anxiety* forced me to open them again . . . we were not twenty yards from the rocks —Frederick Marryat⟩ ⟨when the child told her first lie her foster-mother was nearly sick with dismay and *anxiety* —Margaret Deland⟩

²**care** \"\ *vb* -ED/-ING/-S [ME *caren,* fr. OE *carian,* fr. *caru, cearu,* n.] *vi* **1 a :** to feel trouble or anxiety ⟨*cared* for his safety⟩ **b :** to feel interest, concern, or solicitude ⟨~ about freedom⟩ ⟨did not much ~ about her children's hunger⟩ **:** feel resentment or irritation ⟨the child doesn't ~ if his toy is taken away⟩ **:** consider as a matter of relevance or interest or as having a bearing on the issue or event ⟨I do not ~ about what you believe; I am certain I am right⟩ — usu. used with a negative and with *for* or *about* **2 a :** to give care (as to the safety, well-being, or maintenance of a charge) **:** provide for or attend to needs or perform necessary personal services (as for a patient or a child) ⟨~ for the sick⟩ **:** give proper use and maintenance ⟨know how to ~ properly for a car⟩ — used with *for* **b :** to afford accommodation ⟨parking space to ~ for all the cars that come⟩ **3 a :** to have a liking, fondness, or taste ⟨never *cared* for a human creature before —Margaret Deland⟩ ⟨doesn't ~ for ice cream⟩ **:** have regard or respect ⟨I *cared* for what he had to say —Edna S.V.Millay⟩ **b :** to have an inclination, wish, or disposition — usu. used with a complementary infinitive ⟨few men *cared* to contradict him⟩ or with *for* ⟨would you ~ for some apples⟩ **~** *vt* **1** *dial* **:** to take care of **2 a :** to be concerned about ⟨nobody ~*s* what I do⟩ **b :** to be concerned to the extent of ⟨~ a damn⟩ **3 :** to long for **:** WISH ⟨if you ~ to go⟩ — **not care :** to be willing **:** have no objection **:** be pleased — usu. used in response to an invitation ⟨I *don't care* if I do, thanks⟩

¹**ca·reen** \kəˈrēn\ *n* -s [MF *carène* keel, fr. OIt *carena,* fr. L *carina* keel, nutshell; akin to Gk *karyon* nut, Skt *karkara* hard — more at HARD] *archaic* **:** the act or process of careening **:** the state of being careened — used chiefly in the phrase *on the careen*

²**careen** \"\ *vb* -ED/-ING/-S *vt* **1 a :** to cause (a boat) to lean over on one side (as on a beach) making the other side accessible for repairs below the waterline **b :** to clean, calk, or repair (a boat in this position) **2 :** to cause to heel over ⟨high waves ~*ed* the ship⟩ **~** *vi* **1 a :** to perform the operation of careening a boat **b :** to clean, calk, or repair a boat in a careened position ⟨orders were to ~ and refit⟩ **c :** to undergo this process ⟨the ship is ~*ing* at that port⟩ **2 :** to heel over (as of a ship under a breeze) **3 :** to sway from side to side **:** LURCH ⟨the taxi ~*ed* west toward the main avenue⟩

ca·reen·age \-ij\ *n* -s [F *carénage,* fr. *caréner* to careen (fr. *carène* keel) + *-age*] **1 :** the expense of careening **2** *also* **ca·re·nage** \kəˈrēnij\ **:** a harbor suitable for careening

¹**ca·reer** \kəˈri(ə)r, -iə\ *n* -s *often attrib* [MF *carrière,* fr. OProv *carriera* street, fr. ML *carraria* road for vehicles, fr. L *carrus* wheeled vehicle — more at CAR] **1 a :** COURSE, PASSAGE ⟨the sun's ~ across the sky⟩ ⟨the ~ of armed steeds —P.B.Shelley⟩ **b :** SPEED **:** full speed or exercise of activity — used esp. in the phrase *in full career* or *in the full career* ⟨he was now in the full ~ of conquest —T.B.Macaulay⟩ **2 a** *of a horse* **:** a short gallop or run at full or great speed — used esp. in the phrase *to pass career* or *to pass a career* **b :** CHARGE **:** an encounter esp. in a tournament **c :** the way or route over which one passes **3 :** a course of continued progress (as in the life of a person or nation) **:** a field for or pursuit of consecutive progressive achievement esp. in public, professional, or business life ⟨Washington's ~ as a soldier⟩ ⟨~*s* open to educated men⟩ **4 :** a profession for which one undergoes special training and which is undertaken as a permanent calling ⟨a ~ diplomat⟩ ⟨ambassadorships were . . . treated as ~ posts —*Wall Street Jour.*⟩ **:** an occupation or profession engaged in as a lifework ⟨~ girl⟩

²**career** \"\ *vb* -ED/-ING/-S *vi* **1 a :** to make a short gallop **:** CHARGE **b :** to turn to one side and another in running **:** PRANCE, CARACOLE **2 a :** to go, drive, or run at top speed esp. in a headlong or reckless manner ⟨sightseers had gathered in clumps to watch the cars ~*ing* homeward —James Joyce⟩ ⟨mobs ~*ing* through the streets —Kenneth Roberts⟩ **b :** to go or run rapidly with veering or sidelong rocking **~** *vt* **:** to cause (as a horse) to career **syn** see RUN

ca·reer·ing·ly *adv* **:** in a careering manner

ca·reer·ism \kəˈri(ə)ˌrizəm\ *n* -s **:** the policy or practice of advancing one's career (as in the arts and professions) often at the cost of professional or personal integrity **:** career building as a deliberate aim

ca·reer·ist \-rəst\ *n* -s **:** one that engages in careerism

careers master *n, Brit* **:** vocational adviser

carefree \ˈ=ˌ=\ *adj* **:** free from care: as **a :** having no worries **:** HAPPY, LIGHT-HEARTED ⟨the ~ joys of childhood⟩ **b :** IRRESPONSIBLE, INCAUTIOUS **:** neglectful of consequences ⟨~ with his money⟩ — **care·free·ness** \ˈ=ˌ=nəs\ *n* -ES

care·ful \ˈ=fəl, *-R also* ˈkaf-\ *adj, sometimes* **carefuller** \-f(ə)lə(r)\ *sometimes* **carefullest** \-f(ə)ləst\ [ME, fr. OE *carful, cearful,* fr. *caru, cearu* care + *ful* or *full* full — more at CARE, FULL] **1** *archaic* **a :** full of care **:** SOLICITOUS, TROUBLED ⟨be ~ for nothing —Phil 4:6(AV)⟩ **b :** filling with care or solicitude **:** causing or exposing to concern, anxiety, or trouble ⟨by Him that raised me to this ~ height —Shak.⟩ **2 :** exercising thoughtful supervision or making solicitous provision **:** taking good care — usu. used with *for* or *of* ⟨~ of a child's welfare⟩ **3 :** marked by care: as **a :** marked by attentive concern and solicitude ⟨a sad accident! He will need very ~ watching —Bram Stoker⟩ **b :** marked by wary caution or prudence ⟨be very ~ of the moving blades⟩ ⟨the perpetual fear which prompts ~ stepping —Herbert Spencer⟩ **c :** marked by painstaking effort to avoid errors or omissions ⟨a ~, sober, and accurate description of the events⟩ ⟨~ of detail, laborious, methodical —J.R.Green⟩ — often used with *of* or with an infinitive ⟨~ of money⟩ ⟨~ to adjust the machine⟩

syn METICULOUS, PUNCTILIOUS, SCRUPULOUS, PUNCTUAL: CAREFUL indicates a varying blend of attentiveness and caution ⟨Oh, I intend being very *careful* —Jack London⟩ ⟨have given the matter very *careful* attention —J.P.Marquand⟩ ⟨a *careful* search conducted by three young ladies and the postmaster in question —Dorothy Sayers⟩ METICULOUS describes extreme attentiveness to detail or timorous caution about minutiae ⟨the *meticulous* care with which the operation in Sicily was planned has paid dividends. For our casualties . . . have been low —F.D.Roosevelt⟩ ⟨McKinley . . . was too polite, too *meticulous* in his observation of the formalities of the political Sanhedrin —W.A.White⟩ PUNCTILIOUS describes extreme attention to fine points ⟨lecture scripts, every one of them marked with *punctilious* care for emphasis, accent, and pause —A.T.Quiller-Couch⟩ ⟨the *punctilious* honor of the Spanish gentleman —George Santayana⟩ SCRUPULOUS describes painstaking attention to the proper and fitting, the fair and ethical, or the exact and true ⟨it's simply that I owe my city the most *scrupulous* performance of duty in safeguarding it from disease —Sinclair Lewis⟩ ⟨more zealous about the triumph of their righteous cause than *scrupulous* about the justice of their arguments —M.R.Cohen⟩ Once a synonym of PUNCTILIOUS, PUNCTUAL now stresses fidelity to agreed-on times, as for appointments or payments ⟨I made Mr. Middleditch *punctual* before he died, though when he married me he was known far and wide as a man who could not be up to time —Compton Mackenzie⟩

care·ful·ly \-f(ə)lē, -i\ *adv* [ME, fr. OE *carfullīce*, fr. *carful* + *-līce* -ly] **:** in a careful manner **:** with care **:** with attention to precision or to details **:** CAUTIOUSLY

care·ful·ness \ˈ⸗fəlnəs\ *n* -ES [ME, fr. OE *carfulnes*, fr. *carful* + *-nes* -ness] **:** the quality of being careful **:** close or steady attention (as to a task) **:** CAUTION, HEED, FORESIGHT

¹care·less \ˈ⸗ləs, -R *also* ˈkal-\ *adj* [ME *carelees*, fr. OE *carlēas*, fr. *caru* care + *-lēas* -less] **1 a :** free from care, anxiety, or responsibility ⟨~ infancy⟩ **b :** having no concern or interest **:** UNCONCERNED, UNMINDFUL ⟨raise all kinds of hope, ~ of the disillusionment that will certainly follow —Granville Hicks⟩ **2 :** not taking ordinary or proper care **:** NEGLECTFUL, HEEDLESS, INATTENTIVE, REGARDLESS ⟨my brother was too ~ of his charge —Shak.⟩ ⟨~ of hardship⟩ **3 :** not receiving or exhibiting care: **a** *obs* **:** not attended to or cared for **b :** done, made, or caused without attention to rule or system **:** UNSTUDIED, SPONTANEOUS ⟨her ~ refinement of manner —G.B. Shaw⟩ **c :** done, said, or written without due care **:** NEGLIGENT, HEEDLESS, SLOVENLY ⟨writing that is ~ and full of errors⟩ — **care·less·ly** *adv* — **care·less·ness** *n* -ES

²careless \"\ *also* **careless weed** *n* -ES [*careless* (uncared for)] **1 :** any of several herbs of the genus *Amaranthus* (esp. *A. palmeri*) **2 :** BURWEED MARSH ELDER

carelian *usu cap, var of* KARELIAN

carenage *var of* CAREENAGE

car·ene \ˈka,rēn\ *n* -S [*Carum* (genus name of the caraway *Carum carvi*) + *-ene* — more at CARUM] **:** either of two liquid bicyclic terpenes $C_{10}H_{16}$ found esp. in some turpentine oils and pine oils and in the oil of an East Indian grass (*Cymbopogon iwarancusa*) and distinguished as 3-(or Δ^3-)carene and 4-(or Δ^4-)carene

cares *pl of* CARE, *pres 3d sing of* CARE

¹ca·ress \kəˈres\ *n* -ES [F *caresse*, fr. It *carezza*, fr. *caro* dear, fr. L *carus* — more at CHARITY] **1 :** an act or expression of kindness or affection **:** ENDEARMENT ⟨he exerted himself to win by indulgence and ~*es* the hearts of all who were under his command —T.B.Macaulay⟩ **2 a :** a light stroking, rubbing, or patting **b :** KISS

²caress \"\ *vt* -ED/-ING/-ES [F *caresser*, fr. It *carezzare*, fr. *carezza* caress] **1 :** to treat with tokens of fondness, affection, or kindness **:** CHERISH ⟨the regiment was fed and ~*ed* at station after station —Stephen Crane⟩ **2 a :** to touch or stroke in a loving or endearing manner **:** FONDLE, EMBRACE, PET ⟨left hand . . . ~*es* the boy's face —Henry Adams⟩ **b :** to touch or affect as if with a caress ⟨echoes that ~ the ear⟩

caressing *adj* **:** touching with or as if with a caress ⟨the doctor's voice, soothing, ~, infinitely consoling —Ellen Glasgow⟩ — **ca·ress·ing·ly** *adv*

ca·ress·ive \kəˈresiv\ *adj* **1 :** like a caress **:** CARESSING ⟨diminutives have a ~ character⟩ **2 :** given to caresses ⟨childishly ~⟩ — **ca·ress·ive·ly** *adv*

¹car·et \ˈkarət *also* -ˈaa-, -ˈaə-, -ˈe(ə)-, -ˈā-\ *n* -S [L, there is lacking, 3d pers. sing. pres. indic. of *carēre* to lack, be without — more at CASTE] **:** a mark made on written or printed matter to indicate the place where something is inserted or is to be inserted **:** an inverted v placed below the line or in the margin

²caret \"\ *vt* **careted** *or* **caretted**; **careted** *or* **caretted**; **careting** *or* **caretting**; **carets :** to indicate with a caret the place at which to insert (new matter) — usu. used with *in* or *into* ⟨~*ed* the revision into the manuscript⟩

caretaker \ˈ⸗,⸗⸗\ *n* -S **1 :** one that is placed usu. as occupant in charge of the upkeep, repairs, and protection of the house, estate, or farm of an owner who may be absent **2 :** one fulfilling the functions of office on a temporary or provisional basis ⟨a ~ government⟩

caretaking \ˈ⸗,⸗⸗\ *n* -S [*caretaker* + *-ing*] **:** the act or occupation of serving as a caretaker

ca·ret·ta \kəˈredə\ *n, cap* [NL, fr. F *caret* hawksbill turtle, fr. Sp *carey*, fr. Taino] **:** a genus of marine turtles (family Chelonidae) comprising all the loggerhead turtles or in some classifications solely the common loggerhead (*C. caretta*)

ca·ret·to·che·lyd·i·dae \kə¦red·(,)ōkəˈlidə,dē\ *n pl, cap* [NL, fr. *Carettochelyd-*, *Carettochelys*, type genus (fr. *caretta* + *-o-* + Gk *chelys* tortoise) + *-idae* — more at CHELYS] **:** a family of pleurodiran freshwater turtles including a New Guinea turtle (*Carettochelys insculpta*)

careworn \ˈ⸗,⸗\ *adj* **:** showing the effect of grief or anxiety ⟨a ~ face⟩

car·ex \ˈka(a),reks\ *n* [NL, fr. L, sedge; perh. akin to L *carrere* to card — more at CHARD] **1** *cap* **:** a genus of perennial grasslike herbs (family Cyperaceae) of very wide distribution and distinguished by having the seedlike achenes enclosed in a sac in the axil of a bract — see SEDGE **2** *pl* **car·i·ces** \ˈkarə,sēz\ **:** any plant of the genus *Carex*

ca·rey \kəˈrā\ *n* -S [AmerSp, fr. Sp, fr. Taino] **1 :** HAWKSBILL TURTLE **2 :** the tortoiseshell obtained from the hawksbill turtle

carf \ˈkärf\ *dial var of* KERF

carfare \ˈ⸗,⸗\ *n* -S **:** fare for carrying a passenger on a streetcar or railroad

car·fax \ˈkär,faks, -ȧ,f-\ *n* -ES [ME *carfouk*, *carfuks*, modif. of AF *quarrefourc*, fr. LL *quadrifurcum*] *Brit* **:** a place where four or more roads meet — used chiefly in place names

car ferry *n* **:** a ferry of special design for the transportation of railroad cars by water

car float *n* **:** a barge equipped with tracks on which railroad cars are moved in harbors and inland waterways

carfour *n* -S [MF *carrefour*, fr. LL *quadrifurcum*, neut. of *quadrifurcus* having four forks, fr. L *quadr-* + *-furcus* (fr. *furca* fork) — more at FORK] *obs* **:** CARFAX

¹car·fuf·fle \kärˈfəfəl, kər-\ *vt* -ED/-ING/-S [Sc *car-* (fr. ScGael *car* turn, twist) + *fuffle*, v.] *Scot* **:** DISORDER, DISARRANGE, RUFFLE

²carfuffle \"\ *n* -S *Scot* **:** RUFFLE, AGITATION, DISORDER, FLURRY

car·ga \ˈkärgə\ *n* -S [Sp, lit., load] **:** a unit of weight usu. of a value about equal to 300 lbs. used in Mexico and certain other Spanish-American countries

car·ga·dor \,kärgəˈdȯ(ə)r\ *n, pl* **cargado·res** \,⸗⸗ˈdōrēz, -ōr-\ [AmerSp, fr. Sp, loader, fr. *cargar* to load] **1 :** PORTER **2 :** STEVEDORE

cargason *or* **cargazon** *n* -S [Sp *cargazón*, aug. of *cargo*] *obs* **:** CARGO

car·go \ˈkär(,)gō, ˈkȧ(,)-\ *n, pl* **cargoes** *or* **cargos** [Sp *cargo*, *carga* load, burden, charge, fr. *cargar* to load, fr. LL *carricare* — more at CHARGE] **:** the lading or freight of a ship, airplane, or vehicle **:** the goods, merchandise, or whatever is conveyed **:** LOAD, FREIGHT — usu. used of goods only and not of live animals or persons

cargo cult *n, often cap both Cs* **:** a religiopolitical movement among natives of various So. Pacific islands characterized by the messianic expectation of the return of their ancestors in ships or planes carrying cargoes of the products of modern civilization that will suffice for all native needs, render work unnecessary, and free natives from white control

cargo liner *n* **1 :** a ship that carries general cargo and usu. follows a fixed schedule **2 :** a transport plane that carries freight

cargo mill *n* **:** a sawmill with dockage facilities for direct loading on ships

car·hop \ˈkär,häp, ˈkȧ,h-\ *n* -S [¹*car* + *-hop* (as in *bellhop*)] **:** a waiter at a drive-in who serves customers in their cars

car·i·ama \,karēˈamə\ *n* [NL, fr. Pg, seriema, modif. of Tupi *çariama* — more at SERIEMA] **1** *cap* **:** a genus of long-legged So. American birds (order Gruiformes) having as sole recent representative the Brazilian cariama **2** -S **:** a bird (*Cariama cristata*) of southern Brazil or a closely related bird (*Chunga burmeisteri*) of northern Argentina, both being large long-legged birds with short wings and limited powers of flight that feed on berries, insects, and to some extent snakes and lizards and that are usu. regarded as related to the cranes and bustards though formerly sometimes included with the birds of prey — called also *seriema*; see CHUNGA, CRESTED CARIAMA

¹car·i·an \ˈka(a)rēən, -er-, -ar-\ *n* -S *usu cap* [*Caria*, ancient division of SW Asia Minor (fr. L, fr. Gk *Karia*) + E *-an*] **1 :** a native or inhabitant of ancient Caria, a division of southwest Asia Minor **2 :** the ancient language of the Carians

²carian \"\ *adj, usu cap* **1 a :** of, relating to, or characteristic of Caria **b :** of, relating to, or characteristic of the people of Caria **2 :** of, relating to, or characteristic of the language of the Carians

car·ib \ˈkarəb\ *n, pl* **carib** *or* **caribs** *usu cap* [NL *Caribes* (pl.), fr. Sp *caribe*, fr. 15th cent. Arawakan *carib* (form recorded by Columbus in Haiti) — more at CANNIBAL] **1 a :** an Indian people of northern Brazil, the Guianas, Venezuela, Colombia, the Lesser Antilles, and the Caribbean coast of Honduras, Guatemala, and British Honduras **b :** a member of such people **2 :** the language of the Caribs

car·ib·al \ˈkarəbəl\ *adj, usu cap* [prob. fr. Sp *caribal* — more at CANNIBAL] **:** of or relating to the Caribs

cari·ban \ˈkarəbən, -,ban; kəˈrēb-\ *n* -S *usu cap* [Sp *caribán*, fr. *caribe* Carib] **1 a :** a group of Amerindian peoples of northern So. America, the Lesser Antilles, and the Caribbean coast of Honduras, Guatemala, and British Honduras **b :** a member of any such peoples **2 :** the language family comprising the languages of the Cariban peoples

¹carib·be·an \¦karə¦bēən *also* ¦ker- *or* kəˈribēə-\ *adj, usu cap* [NL *Caribaeus*, *Caribbaeus* (fr. *Caribes*) + E *-an*] **1 :** of, relating to, or characteristic of the Caribs **2 a :** of, relating to, or characteristic of the eastern and southern West Indies **b :** of, relating to, or characteristic of the Caribbean sea, which lies between the West Indies and Central America

²caribbean \"\ *n, pl* **caribbean** *or* **caribbeans** *usu cap* **:** CARIB 1

caribbean pine *n, usu cap C* **:** a timber tree (*Pinus caribaea*) of Florida, the Bahamas, and Cuba, having two or three very long leaves in each fascicle and cones with thick-edged scales tipped with slightly recurved prickles

car·ib·bee *or* **car·i·bee** \ˈkarə(,)bē\ *n, pl* **caribbee** *or* **caribbees** *or* **caribee** *or* **caribees** *usu cap* [Sp or Pg *caribe*] **:** CARIB 1

ca·ri·be \kəˈrēbē, -(,)bā\ *n* -S [AmerSp, fr. Sp, cannibal, Carib — more at CARIB] **:** any of several So. American freshwater fishes of the genus *Serrasalmus* (family Characidae) remarkable for their voracity, in spite of their small size often attacking and inflicting dangerous wounds upon men and large animals — called also *piranha*

carib grass *n, usu cap C* **:** a native West Indian grass (*Eriochloa polystachya*) grown in Florida and Texas for forage and resembling Para grass but finer-stemmed and leafier

car·i·bou \ˈkarə,bü *also* -ˈe-\ *n, pl* **caribou** *or* **caribous** [CanF, of Algonquian origin; akin to Micmac *khalibu* caribou, lit., pawer, scratcher, Quinnipiac *maccarib*] **:** any of several large deer (genus *Rangifer*) of northern No. America that are related to the Old World reindeer and have large palmate antlers in both sexes, broad flat hooves, a heavy double coat, and short ears and tail—see BARREN GROUND CARIBOU, WOODLAND CARIBOU

caribou eskimo *n, usu cap C&E* [so called fr. the fact that they live chiefly from caribou] **:** an Eskimo of the Barren Grounds of northern Canada

caribou moss *n* **:** REINDEER MOSS

caric- *or* **carico-** *comb form* [NL *Caric-*, *Carex*] **:** carex **:** sedges ⟨*caricetum*⟩ ⟨*caricology*⟩

car·i·ca \ˈkarəkə\ *n, cap* [NL, fr. L, a dried fig, fr. fem. of *caricus* Carian, fr. Gk *karikos*, fr. *Karia*, ancient division of Asia Minor + Gk *-ikos* -ic] **:** a genus (the type of the family Caricaceae) of chiefly tropical American trees — see PAPAYA

car·i·ca·ce·ae \,karəˈkāsē,ē\ *n pl, cap* [NL, fr. *Carica*, type genus + *-aceae*] **:** a family of trees (order Parietales) native to tropical and subtropical America and Africa having milky juice, a rarely branched trunk, and large palmately lobed leaves and including the papaya and a few related plants — **car·i·ca·ceous** \¦⸗⸗¦kāshəs\ *adj*

car·i·ca·tur·a·ble \¦karəkə¦chu̇rəbəl\ *adj* **:** suitable for caricature **:** having features easily caricatured

car·i·ca·tur·al \-ˈu̇(ə)rəl\ *adj* **:** like or having the characteristics of caricature

¹car·i·ca·ture \ˈkarəkə,chu̇(ə)r, -u̇ə, -rēk- *also* ˈker- *or* -,t(y)u̇- *or* -kəchə(r)\ *n* -S [earlier *caricatura*, fr. It, affectation, caricature, lit., a loading, fr. *caricare* to load, fr. LL *carricare* — more at CHARGE] **1 a :** exaggeration by means of deliberate simplification and often ludicrous distortion of parts or characteristics ⟨the art of ~⟩ **b :** an instance of such caricature ⟨in her rambling and her idleness she might only be a ~ of herself, but in her silence and sadness she was the very reverse of all that she had been before —Jane Austen⟩ **2 :** a representation esp. in literature or art that has the qualities of caricature ⟨a series of satirical ~*s* of the faculty of a progressive college for women —Orville Prescott⟩ **3 :** a distortion so gross as to seem like caricature ⟨the kangaroo court a ~ of justice⟩

syn BURLESQUE, PARODY, TRAVESTY all indicate kinds of grotesque and exaggerated imitation. CARICATURE suggests ludicrous distortion of a peculiar feature ⟨*caricature* is a very special kind of portraiture, permitting extravagance and enunciating the awkward and uncomplimentary —*Christian Science Monitor*⟩ ⟨his *caricature* of the "gentleman" . . . is a biting sarcasm of the respectable, gentle, and polite bourgeois —*Commonweal*⟩ BURLESQUE is likely to imply humor sought or attained in imitation of the dignified, heavy, or grand ⟨ridiculing follies with a *burlesque* as riotous as that in *The Innocents Abroad* —Carl Van Doren⟩ ⟨he whipped off his old slouch hat with an air of gallantry which reminded Dorinda of the *burlesque* of some royal cavalier —Ellen Glasgow⟩ PARODY, like CARICATURE, involves the heightening of a peculiar feature and, like BURLESQUE, is likely to aim at humor. It may differ from the first in attempting less obvious and pictorial and more sustained and subtle imitation, from the second in aiming at a quieter, less boisterous effect ⟨Dryden's method here is something very near to *parody*; he applies vocabulary, images, and ceremony which arouse epic associations of grandeur —T.S.Eliot⟩ ⟨played in the manner of a *parody*, an intention which . . . cannot possibly be recognized by any hearer who has not previously been warned of it —Eric Blom⟩ TRAVESTY is perhaps the strongest word in the group. It may apply to any palpably extravagant imitation designed to mock and consistently sustained, esp. in stylistic matters ⟨in producing *Androcles and the Lion* his motion picture executor has already managed to make a public *travesty* of his work —*New Republic*⟩ All these terms may be used in reference to a situation that contains grotesque distortion ⟨a *caricature* of the truth⟩ ⟨a *burlesque* on religious observations⟩ ⟨a *parody* of justice⟩ ⟨a *travesty* on decent marriage⟩

²caricature \"\ *vt* -ED/-ING/-S **:** to make or draw a caricature of **:** represent in caricature ⟨he could draw an ill face or ~ a good one —George Lyttelton⟩

caricature plant *n* [so called fr. the yellowish leaf blotches, often suggesting a human profile] **:** an East Indian ornamental foliage plant (*Graptophyllum pictum*) of the family Acanthaceae

car·i·ca·tur·ist \¦⸗⸗⸗¦chu̇(ə)rəst *also* -¦t(y)u̇-\ *n* -S **:** one that makes caricatures

carices *pl of* CAREX

carico- — see CARIC-

car·id \ˈkarəd\ *n* -S [NL *Carides*] **:** a crustacean of the tribe Carides

ca·ri·da \¦kəˈrīdə, ˈkarədə\ *or* **ca·rid·ea** \kəˈridēə\ *syn of* CARIDES

ca·rid·e·an \kəˈridēən\ *adj* **:** of or relating to the Carides ⟨~ prawn⟩

car·i·deer \ˈkarə,di(ə)r\ *n, pl* **carideer** [*caribou* + *reindeer*] **:** a hybrid between the caribou and the reindeer

ca·ri·des \kəˈrī(,)dēz, ˈkarə,dēz\ *n pl, cap* [NL, fr. L, pl. of *carid-*, *caris*] **:** a tribe of decapod crustaceans (suborder Natantia) containing most shrimps, prawns, and related forms in which the lateral plates of the second abdominal segment overlap those of the first — **car·i·doid** \ˈkarə,dȯid\ *adj or n*

car·ies \ˈka(ə)rēz, -e(ə)r-,-aa-,-är-, -riz *also* -rē,ēz\ *n, pl* **caries** [L, decay; akin to Gk *kēr* death, Skt *śṛṇāti* he breaks, crushes] **:** the decay of animal tissues: **a :** ulceration and destruction of bone ⟨~ of the spine⟩ **b :** tooth decay; *specif* **:** the pathological process of localized destruction of tooth tissue by microorganisms

car·i·gnane \¦karə¦nyan, -än, ˈkarəgən\ *n* -S *usu cap* [F, fr. *Carignan*, town near Bordeaux, France] **:** a French red wine produced from a grape grown primarily in the departments of Hérault and Pyrénées-Orientales

car·i·jo·na \,karəˈhōnə\ *n, pl* **carijona** *or* **carijonas** *usu cap* [Sp, fr. Carib *carihona* people] **1 a :** a Cariban people of southeastern Colombia **b :** a member of such people **2 :** the language of the Carijona people

car·il·lon \ˈkarə,län *also* -er- *or* -ələn *or* -rə,yän *or* kȧrēyōⁿ *or* (*esp Brit*) kəˈrilyən\ *n* -S [F, alter. of OF *quarregnon*, fr. LL *quaternion-*, *quaternio* set of four; prob. fr. its consisting in early times of four bells — more at QUATERNION] **1 a :** a set of fixed bells pitched in chromatic series of at least two octaves and sounded by hammers controlled by a keyboard, each bell being tuned to harmonize with the others — compare CHIME **b :** a mixture stop in a pipe organ imitating a carillon **c :** an instrument imitating a carillon by electronically amplifying the sounds made by striking small variously shaped metallic bodies — called also *electronic carillon* **2 a :** a composition for the carillon **b :** a composition suggesting the sound of bells **3 :** BELL TOWER, CAMPANILE

car·il·lon·ic \¦karə¦länik\ *adj* **:** of, produced by, or imitating a carillon

car·il·lon·is·tic \¦karə(,)lä¦nistik, -lə¦- *also* kə¦rilyə¦n-\ *adj* **:** having the characteristics of, suitable for, or produced by a carillon

car·il·lon·neur *also* **car·il·lo·neur** \¦karə(,)lä¦nər, -ələ¦- *also* ¦karē(,)yä¦- *or* kə¦rilyə¦-\ *n* -S [F *carillonneur*, fr. *carillon* + *-eur* -er] **:** a carillon player — called also *bellmaster*

ca·ri·na \kəˈrīnə, -ˈē-\ *n, pl* **carinas** \-nəz\ *or* **cari·nae** \-ˈrī,nē -ˈrē,nī\ [NL, fr. L, keel — more at CAREEN] **:** any of various keel-shaped anatomical structures, ridges, or processes: as **a :** a ridge on the lower surface of the fornix of the brain — called also *carina fornicis* **b :** the ventral distal part of the vagina — called also *carina urethralis*, *carina vaginae* **c :** the part of a papilionaceous flower that encloses the stamens and pistil and consists of two commonly united petals **d :** the median ridge on the breastbone of most birds **:** KEEL **e :** a thickened ridge on the median dorsal plate of a barnacle **f :** any of several reinforcing ridges on the exoskeleton of an insect

carina c: carina and calyx of bristly locust (standard and wings removed)

ca·ri·nal \kəˈrīnᵊl, -ˈē-, ˈkarən-\ *adj* [NL *carina* + E *-al*] **:** relating to or resembling a carina

carinal canal *n* **:** LACUNA 2c (2)

car·i·nar·ia \,karəˈna(a)rēə\ *n, cap* [NL, fr. L *carina* + NL *-aria*; fr. the shape of the shell] **:** a genus of oceanic heteropod mollusks having a thin glassy bonnet-shaped shell covering only the nucleus and gills

car·i·na·tae \,karəˈnād·,ē, -ād-\ *n pl, cap* [NL, fr. *carina* + L *-atae* (fem. pl. of *-atus* -ate)] *in old classifications* **:** a division of Aves including all the Neognathae together with the tinamous or with these and the penguins

¹car·i·nate \ˈkarə,nāt, -,nət\ *also* **car·i·nat·ed** \-,nād·əd\ *adj* [L *carinatus*, fr. *carina* keel + *-atus* -ate] **:** shaped like the keel or prow of a ship **:** KEELED, RIDGED ⟨a ~ sepal⟩ ⟨a ~ scale⟩ — compare RATITE

²carinate \"\ *n* -S [NL *Carinatae*] **:** a bird with a keeled breastbone **:** one of the Carinatae

carinate fold *n* **:** a closely compressed almost isoclinal anticline or syncline

car·i·na·tion \,karəˈnāshən\ *n* -S **1 :** the quality or state of being carinate **2 :** a carinate formation

caring *pres part of* CARE

ca·rin·i·a·na \kə,rinēˈänə, -ˈa-, -ˈā-\ *n, cap* [NL, irreg. fr. L *carina* keel — more at CAREEN] **:** a genus of tropical So. American timber trees (family Lecythidaceae) having small flowers, the lid of the fruit joined with the woody column, and seeds with one long lateral wing — see COLOMBIAN MAHOGANY, JEQUITIBA

ca·rin·i·form \kəˈrinə,fȯ(ə)rm\ *adj* [NL *carina* + E *-iform*] **:** having the form of a carina

ca·rin·thi·an \kəˈrin(t)thēən\ *adj, usu cap* [*Carinthia*, province in Austria + E *-an*] **:** of or relating to the Austrian province of Carinthia

ca·rin·u·la \kəˈrinyələ\ *or* **car·i·nule** \ˈkarə,n(y)ül\ *n* -S [NL *carinula*, dim. of *carina*] **:** a small carina — **ca·rin·u·late** \kəˈrinyə,lāt, -lət\ *adj*

cario- *comb form* [*caries*] **:** caries ⟨*cariogenic*⟩ ⟨*cariostatic*⟩

car·i·o·ca \,karēˈōkə *also* -er-\ *n* -S [Pg, fr. Tupi, fr. *cari* white + *oca* house] **1** *usu cap* **:** a native or resident of Rio de Janeiro **2 a :** the samba adapted to ballroom dancing **b :** the music for such a dance

car·i·o·gen·ic \¦ka(a)rēō¦jenik\ *adj* [*cario-* + *-genic*] **:** conducive to the development of caries

car·i·ole *or* **car·ri·ole** \ˈkarē,ōl\ *n* -S [F *carriole*, fr. OProv *carriola* small two-wheeled carriage, dim. of *carri* chariot, fr. (assumed) VL *carrium*, fr. L *carrus* vehicle — more at CAR] **1 :** a light four-wheel open or covered one-horse carriage **2 :** a light covered cart **3 :** a dog-drawn toboggan

car·i·ous \ˈka(a)rēəs, -ˈer-, -ˈär-\ *adj* [L *cariosus*, fr. *caries* decay + *-osus* -ous — more at CARIES] **1 :** relating to or affected with caries ⟨a ~ tooth⟩ **2 :** ROTTING, DECAYING ⟨~ timbers⟩

car·i·pu·na \,karəˈpünə\ *n, pl* **caripuna** *or* **caripunas** *usu cap* [prob. fr. Carib *karipona*, fr. *kari-* (fr. *ka* sky, spirit) + *-po* at + *-na* group] **1 a :** a Panoan people of Brazil and Bolivia **b :** a member of such people **2 :** the language of the Caripuna people

car·i·ri \¦karə¦rē\ *n, pl* **cariri** *or* **cariris** *usu cap* [Pg, of AmerInd origin] **1 a :** an Indian people of eastern Brazil **b :** a member of such people **2 :** the language of the Cariri people

-car·is \ˈka(ə)rəs, -e(ə)r-, -aar-, -är-\ *n comb form* [NL, fr. L *caris*, a kind of sea crab, fr. Gk *karis*; perh. akin to Gk *kara* head — more at CEREBRAL] **:** shrimp **:** prawn — in generic names of crustacea ⟨*Echinocaris*⟩

ca·ris·sa \kəˈrisə\ *n* [NL] **1** *cap* **:** a large genus of spiny shrubs (family Apocynaceae) found in tropical Africa, Asia, and Australia **2** -S **:** any plant of the genus *Carissa* **3** *also* **carissa plum** -S **:** the plumlike fruit of a plant of the genus *Carissa* — see NATAL PLUM

car·i·tas \ˈkarə,tas, ˈkärə,täs\ *n* [LL — more at CHARITY] **:** CHARITY 1

car·i·ta·tive \ˈkarə,tād·iv, -ətətiv\ *adj* [ML *caritativus*, fr. LL *caritat-*, *caritas* + L *-ivus* -ive] **:** charitable in nature or tendency ⟨the ~ principle of Christianity⟩

car·i·tive \ˈkarəd·iv\ *adj* [L *caritus* (past part. of *carēre* to be without) + E *-ive* — more at CASTE] **:** ABESSIVE

ca·ri·us method \ˈkärēəs-, -a(a)r-\ *n, usu cap C* [after G. Ludwig *Carius* †1875 Ger. chemist] **:** a method for determining halogens, sulfur, and phosphorus in organic compounds by heating them in sealed glass tubes with fuming nitric acid in a special furnace, the glass tubes being enclosed in iron tubes to avoid danger from explosion

¹cark \ˈkärk\ *vb* -ED/-ING/-S [ME *carken*, lit., to load, burden, fr. ONF *carquier*, fr. LL *carricare* — more at CHARGE] *vt* **:** to burden with care or anxiety **:** VEX, WORRY, TROUBLE ⟨fate had not smiled on him . . . he was beset by ~*ing* troubles and anxieties —Max Beerbohm⟩ ~ *vi* **1 :** to be anxious or troubled **:** FRET ⟨a covetous man . . . ~*ing* about his bags —Isaac Barrow⟩ **2 :** to labor anxiously ⟨why for sluggards ~ and moil? —Charles Kingsley⟩

²cark \"\ *n* -s [ME, lit., load, burden, fr. ONF *carque*, fr. *carquier*, v.] **1 :** something that burdens the spirit **:** TROUBLE ⟨its artless advocacy of freedom from ~ and care —*Harper's*⟩ **2 :** a troubled state of mind **:** DISTRESS ⟨by ~ and care deranged —Robert Browning⟩

car knocker *n* **:** one that taps or knocks the wheels of a railroad car to check their soundness **:** one that checks the running gear of a train **:** a car inspector **:** a car repairman

¹carl *or* **carle** \ˈkärl, -rəl\ *n* -s [ME, fr. OE *-carl*, fr. ON *karl* man, man of the common people; akin to OE *ceorl* man, man of the common people — more at CHURL] **1 :** a man of the common people **:** WORKER, FARMER, CRAFTSMAN **2** *now dial* **:** a base or lowbred fellow **:** CHURL, BOOR — used as a term of contempt **3** *now Scot* **:** a niggardly man **:** PINCHPENNY **4** *chiefly Scot* **:** FELLOW, LAD

²carl *vi* -ED/-ING/-S [prob. fr. ¹*carl*] *obs* **:** to behave churlishly **:** SNARL

carlacue *var of* CURLICUE

car·let \ˈkärlət\ *n* -s [F *carrelet*, dim. of OF *carrel*, *quarrel* square-headed arrow for an arbalest — more at QUARREL] **:** a 3-square single-cut file used by combmakers

carl·ie \ˈkärli\ *n* -s [¹*carl* + *-ie*] *Scot* **:** a man of small stature

¹car·lin \ˈkärlən\ *or* **car·line** \", -ˌlēn\ *or* **car·li·no** \kärˈlē(ˌ)nō\ *n, pl* **carlins** *or* **carlines** \-nz\ *or* **carli·ni** \-(ˌ)nē\ [It *carlino*, after Charles (*Carlo*) of Anjou] **1 a :** a small silver coin of the kingdom of the Two Sicilies first struck in the 13th century **b :** any of several old Italian coins **2 :** a unit of value equivalent to a carlin

²carlin *var of* CARLING

car·li·na \kärˈlīnə, -ēnə\ *n* [NL, fr. ML, carline thistle, prob. fr. OIt — more at CARLINE THISTLE] **1** *cap* **:** a genus of herbs (family Compositae) of the Mediterranean region differing from the true thistles in having the outer involucral scales leaflike and spiny-toothed and the inner ones colored, raylike, and longer than the flowers **2** *pl* **carli·nae** \-ī(ˌ)nē, -ēˌnī\ **:** a plant of the genus *Carlina*

¹car·line *or* **car·lin** \ˈkärlən\ *n* -s [ME *kerling*, fr. ON, fr. *karl* man — more at CARL] *chiefly Scot* **:** WOMAN; *esp* **:** an old woman — often used contemptuously or disparagingly (as of a witch)

²carline *var of* CARLING

car line *n* **:** a street railway line

car·line thistle \ˈkärlən-, -ˌlīn-\ *n* [MF *carline*, fr. OIt *carlina*, prob. irreg. fr. *cardo* thistle, fr. LL *cardus*, fr. L *carduus* — more at CHARD] **:** a plant of the genus *Carlina* (esp. *C. acaulis* or *C. vulgaris*)

¹car·ling \ˈkärliŋ, -lən\ *also* **car·lin** *or* **car·line** \-lən\ *n* -s [F *carlingue*, fr. ONF *calingue*, fr. ON *kerling*, lit., old woman — more at CARLINE] **:** a fore-and-aft member supporting a deck of a ship or framing a deck opening where the beams have been cut — usu. used in pl.

²carling *pres part of* CARL

car·lings *or* **car·lins** \ˈkärlənz\ *n pl* [*Care* (*Sunday*), the fifth Sunday in Lent, when they were traditionally eaten in the north of England + *-ling*] *dial Eng* **:** parched peas

carlino *var of* CARLIN

carl·ish \ˈkärlish\ *adj* [ME, fr. ¹*carl* + *-ish*] **:** CHURLISH

car·lisle \(ˈ)kärˈlīl, -ˈä,l-, kə(r)ˈl-, -ˈīəl\ *n* -s *usu cap* [short for *Carlisle hook*, prob. fr. the name *Carlisle*] **:** a fishhook of short-curved pattern — see FISHHOOK illustration

carlisle table *n, usu cap C* [fr. *Carlisle*, England, where the statistics were gathered] **:** a mortality table for the years 1779–87

car·lism \ˈkärˌlizəm\ *n* -s *usu cap* [Sp *carlismo*, fr. Don *Carlos* María Isidro de Borbón †1855 pretender to the throne of Spain + Sp *-ismo* -ism] **:** adherence to Don Carlos of Spain or his successors or to Carlist principles, plans, or claims

car·list \ˈkärləst\ *n* -s *usu cap* [Sp *carlista*, fr. Don *Carlos* + *-ista* -ist] **:** a supporter of Don Carlos or his successors whose claims to the Spanish throne were annulled by repeal of the Salic law of succession in 1829

carload \ˈ=,=\ *n* **1 :** a load that fills a car, esp. a freight car **2 :** the minimum number of tons required for shipping at carload rates — abbr. *CL*

carloading \ˈ=,==\ *n* -s **:** the amount of freight loaded into freight cars during a specified period — usu. used in pl. ⟨~s increased during October⟩

carload rate *n* **:** a rate per hundred pounds or per ton for large shipments lower than that quoted for less-than-carload lots of the same class

¹carlot *n* -s [dim. of ¹*carl*] *obs* **:** CHURL, BOOR

²carlot \ˈ=,=\ *n* -s [¹*car* + *lot*] **:** a shipment of freight of the minimum amount required to secure the carload rate

car·lo·vin·gi·an \ˌkärləˈvinj(ē)ən, -äl-, -lə-\ *adj, usu cap* [F *carlovingien*, prob. blend of obs. F *carlien* Carolingian (irreg. fr. ML *Carolus* Charles) and F *mérovingien* Merovingian] **:** CAROLINGIAN

car·low \ˈkär(ˌ)lō\ *adj, usu cap* [fr. *Carlow*, county in Ireland] **:** of or from County Carlow, Ireland **:** of the kind or style prevalent in County Carlow

car·lo·witz \ˈkärləˌwits\ *n* -ES *usu cap* [G *karlowitzer*, fr. *Karlowitz* (now *Karlovci Sremski*), town in Yugoslavia where it is made] **:** a strong sweet red wine

¹carls \ˈkär(ə)lz\ *n pl* [by shortening] *dial Eng* **:** CARLINGS

²carls *pl of* CARL, *pres 3d sing of* CARL

carl·ton table \ˈkärltᵊn-, -tən-\ *n, usu cap C* [fr. *Carlton* House, onetime London residence of the prince of Wales, for which it was designed] **:** a writing table with compartments and drawers on the top

car·lu·do·vi·ca \ˌkärˌlüdəˈvēkə, -īkə\ *n, cap* [NL, after Charles IV (*Carolus*) †1819 king of Spain, and María Luisa (*Ludovica*) †1819 his queen] **:** a genus of tropical American erect or climbing palmlike plants (family Cyclanthaceae) differing from the palms in having tetramerous flowers and many-seeded fruit — see JIPIJAPA

¹car·lyl·e·an *also* **car·lyl·i·an** *or* **car·lyle·i·an** \(ˈ)kärˈlīlēən, -äˈl-, kə(r)ˈl-, -īlyən\ *adj, usu cap* [Thomas *Carlyle* + E *-an* or *-ian*] **:** of, relating to, or resembling Thomas Carlyle or his writings — compare CARLYLISM

²carlylean *also* **carlylian** *or* **carlyleian** \"\ *n* -s *usu cap* **:** a student of Thomas Carlyle or a follower of his beliefs

car·lyl·ese \(ˌ)kärˌlīˈlēz, -äˌl-, -ēs, kärˈlīˌl-, käˈl-; kə(r)ˌlīˈl-\ *n, usu cap* [Thomas *Carlyle* + E *-ese*] **:** Carlylean use of language — often used of style imitative of Carlyle's literary excesses

car·lyl·ism \(ˈ)kärˈlīˌlizəm, -äˈl-, kə(r)ˈl-\ *n* -s *usu cap* [Thomas *Carlyle* †1881 Scot. essayist and historian + E *-ism*] **1 :** the characteristic teachings, ideas, or opinions of Thomas Carlyle who arraigned modern society and emphasized the need for strong leaders **2 :** the literary style or a literary mannerism characteristic of Thomas Carlyle whose writings are marked by long and irregular sentence constructions, neologisms, and Germanisms

car·ma·gnole \ˌkärmənˈyōl\ *n* -s [F, fr. F dial. (Dauphiné) *carmagnola* jacket worn by peasants on festive occasions, fr. *Carmagnola*, town in northwestern Italy where the jacket presumably originated] **1 :** a lively song popular at the time of the first French Revolution **2 :** a street dance in a meandering course to the tune of the carmagnole

carm·al·um \kärˈmaləm\ *n* -s [*carminic* + *alum*] **:** a stain composed of carminic acid, alum, and water for use in microscopy

car·man \ˈkärmən, ˈkäm-\ *n, pl* **carmen 1 :** one who drives or conveys goods in a car or cart **:** CARTER **2 :** a motorman or conductor on an electric railway **3 :** a worker who handles or guides the handling of materials conveyed in cars (as in a mine, mill, or factory) **4 :** a skilled workman who performs one or more operations in the building, repairing, dismantling, maintaining, and inspection of railroad cars at a station, shop, or yard

car·ma·ni·an \kärˈmānēən, -nyən\ *n* -s *usu cap* [L *Carmanus* Carmanian (fr. Gk *Karmanos*) + E *-ian*] **:** a member of an ancient people that prob. lived north of the Persian gulf

car·mar·then·shire \kärˈmärthənˌshi(ə)r, -ˌshər\ *or* **car·marthen** *adj, usu cap* [fr. *Carmarthenshire*, or the county of *Carmarthen*, Wales] **:** of or from the county of Carmarthen, Wales **:** of the kind or style prevalent in Carmarthen

carmathian *usu cap, var of* QARMATIAN

car·mel·ite \ˈkärməˌlīt, ˈkäm-, *usu* -īd· + V\ *n* -s *usu cap, often attrib* [ME, fr. ML *carmelita*, fr. *Carmel* (*Mons*) Mount Carmel, Palestine, where the order was founded + L *-ita* -ite] **:** a member of the Roman Catholic mendicant Order of Our Lady of Mount Carmel founded in the 12th century **:** WHITE FRIAR

car·men \ˈkärmən\ *n, pl* **carmi·na** \-mənə\ [L, fr. *canere* to sing — more at CHANT] **:** SONG, POEM, INCANTATION

car·met·ta \kärˈmed·ə\ *n* -s [¹*carmine* + It *-etta* (dim. suffix)] **:** vermilion or a color resembling it

car-mile \ˈ=,=\ *n* **:** a statistical unit denoting one mile traveled by one railroad car and used in comparing freight earnings or costs — compare BUS-MILE

car mileage *n* **1 :** car-miles used as a basis by which a railroad reimburses another railroad or private car owner for the use of a car **2 :** the amount paid for the use of a car on a mileage basis — compare PER DIEM

¹car·mi·na·tive \kärˈminəd·iv, ˈkärməˌnād-\ *adj* [F *carminatif*, fr. L *carminatus* (past part. of *carminare* to card, fr. *carrere* to card) + F *-if* -ive — more at CHARD] **:** expelling gas from the alimentary canal **:** relieving colic, griping, or flatulence

²carminative \"\ *n* -s **:** a carminative agent

¹car·mine \ˈkärmən, ˈkäm-, -ˌmīn *also* -ˌmēn\ *n* -s [F *carmin*, fr. ML *carminium*, irreg. fr. Ar *qirmiz* kermes + L *minium* — more at CRIMSON, MINIUM] **1 a :** a vivid red lake consisting essentially of an aluminum salt of carminic acid made from cochineal usu. by treatment with water and alum and used as a biological stain and as coloring in foods, drugs, and cosmetics — see DYE table I (under *Natural Red 4*) **b :** any of certain other coloring matters (as indigo carmine) **2** *or* **carmine lake :** a vivid red that is bluer and darker than apple red, bluer and duller than pimento or Castilian red, bluer and less strong than madder crimson, and bluer and darker than scarlet — called also *animal rouge, lake, Munich lake, Roman lake, Venetian lake, Vienna lake*

²carmine \"\ *vt* -ED/-ING/-S **:** to make carmine in color **:** add or apply carmine to

car·mi·nette \ˌkärməˈnet\ *n* -s [¹*carmine* + *-ette*] **:** CARMETTA

car·min·ic \(ˈ)kärˈminik\ *adj* [ISV *carmine* + *-ic*] **:** relating to or derived from carmine

carminic acid *n* [ISV *carminic* + *acid*] **:** a red crystalline anthraquinone dye $C_{22}H_{20}O_{13}$ best known as the essential coloring matter of cochineal and used chiefly as a biological stain

car·min·ite \ˈkärməˌnīt\ *n* -s [*carmine* + *-ite*] **:** a mineral $PbFe_2(AsO_4)_2(OH)_2$ consisting of a carmine arsenate of lead and iron

car·moi·sin \ˌkärm,wäˈzēn, (ˈ)kärˈmȯizᵊn\ *n* -s [prob. fr. G *karmoisin* carmine, alter. (influenced by F *cramoisi* crimson) of *karmesin*, fr. obs. It *carmesino*, modif. of Ar *qirmizī* kermes-colored, fr. *qirmiz* kermes — more at CRIMSON] **:** AZO RUBINE

car movement *n* **:** the total number of miles traveled by cars on a given railroad system during a given period expressed in car-miles

carn *var of* CAIRN

car·na·cian \(ˈ)kärˈnāshən\ *adj, usu cap* [*Carnac*, town in Brittany, France, the locality of its type station + E *-ian*] **:** of or relating to a late period in neolithic culture characterized by many-chambered dolmens

car·nage \ˈkärnij, ˈkän-, -nēj\ *n* -s [MF, fr. ML *carnaticum* tribute consisting of animals or meat, fr. L *carn-*, *caro*] **1 :** the flesh of slain animals or men **:** a heap of dead bodies ⟨a multitude of dogs came to feast on the ~ —T.B.Macaulay⟩ **2 :** great destruction of life (as in battle) **:** great bloodshed **:** SLAUGHTER, BUTCHERY, MASSACRE ⟨appeals to put a stop to the ~ of war⟩

car·nal \ˈkärnᵊl, ˈkän-\ *adj* [ME, fr. ONF or LL; ONF, fr. LL *carnalis* (trans. of Gk *sarkikos*), fr. L *carn-*, *caro* flesh; akin to Gk *keirein* to cut — more at SHEAR] **1 a :** BODILY, CORPOREAL ⟨armed against ghostly as well as ~ attack —Bram Stoker⟩ ⟨~ interment⟩ **b :** consanguineous and bodily in relationship ⟨the ~ mother of Christ⟩ **c** *obs* **:** BLOODTHIRSTY **2 a :** marked by sexuality that is often frank, crude, and unrelieved by higher emotions ⟨~ infatuation —T.S.Eliot⟩ **b :** relating to or given to crude bodily pleasures ⟨gluttony and other ~ traits⟩ **3 :** UNSPIRITUAL**: a :** TEMPORAL ⟨the superiority of the spiritual and eternal over the ~ —H.O.Taylor⟩ **b :** WORLDLY ⟨should abstain from singing vain and ~ ballads —Charles Kingsley⟩ **c :** FLESHY, SENSUAL ⟨with red and bloated cheeks and ~ eyes —Nathaniel Hawthorne⟩

syn FLESHLY, SENSUAL, ANIMAL: CARNAL, once equivalent to *bodily* or *physical*, now refers almost exclusively to sexual or other sensual actions or interests ⟨Barbara Villiers . . . is the most unpleasant of Charles II's mistresses . . . he was besotted by her purely *carnal* attractions —*Times Lit. Supp.*⟩ FLESHLY is close to CARNAL in meaning but less severe and sometimes a little apologetic in suggestion ⟨punishments were set for the *fleshly* sins of monks and nuns and clergy —H.O.Taylor⟩ SENSUAL may simply indicate gratification of any bodily desire or pleasure ⟨his feet and hands were always cold and there was for him an almost *sensual* satisfaction to be had from . . . letting the hot sun beat down on him —Sherwood Anderson⟩ Usu. it indicates concentration on bodily satisfaction and absence of anything intellectual or spiritual ⟨it ceases to be sensuous and becomes *sensual*. This isolation of sense is not characteristic of esthetic objects but of such things as narcotics, sexual orgasms, and gambling —John Dewey⟩ Often it implies gross sexuality ⟨a coarse heavy face, loose-featured, red, and *sensual* —Thomas Wolfe⟩ ANIMAL, often without derogation, simply indicates bodily or sentient characteristics common to both man and animal or traits resembling those found in animals rather than man ⟨the state in his view is not merely a convenient machinery that raises a man above his *animal* wants —G. L. Dickinson⟩ ⟨he taught the boy boxing . . . and superintended the direction of his *animal* vigor —George Meredith⟩

carnal abuse *n* **:** genital contact between a male and a female minor with or without penetration and with or without the consent of the female; *broadly* **:** rape esp. of a female child

car·nal·ist \-nᵊləst\ *n* -s **:** one given to sensual esp. sexual pleasures

car·nal·i·ty \kärˈnaləd·ē, käˈn-, -ətē, -i\ *n* -ES [ME *carnalite*, fr. LL *carnalitas*, fr. L *carnalis* carnal + *-itas* -ity] **1 :** the quality or state of being flesh ⟨matter is not intrinsically corrupt, and ~ is not a sin in Hebrew thought —O.J.Baab⟩ **2 :** fleshly lust or its indulgence **:** SENSUALITY **3 :** indulgence of the senses **:** WORLDLINESS ⟨he looked upon my . . . fight for flesh-colored silk stockings as a form of incomprehensible feminine ~ —Hannah Smith⟩ **4 :** a carnal act; *specif* **:** SEXUAL INTERCOURSE ⟨dancing has often been denounced as disposing to ~⟩

car·nal·ize \ˈkärnᵊlˌīz, ˈkän-\ *vt* -ED/-ING/-S **:** to make carnal **:** SENSUALIZE

carnal knowledge *n* **:** SEXUAL INTERCOURSE — usu. used of acts involving a female child, the precise legal interpretation varying with different jurisdictions

car·nall·ite \ˈkärnᵊlˌīt\ *n* -s [G *carnallit*, fr. Rudolf von *Carnall* †1874 Ger. mining engineer + G *-it* -ite] **:** a mineral $KMgCl_3.6H_2O$ consisting of a hydrous potassium-magnesium chloride occurring commonly as white or reddish deliquescent masses and useful as a source of potassium

car·nal·ly \-nᵊlē, -i\ *adv* **:** in a carnal manner

car·nal·ness \-nᵊlnəs\ *n* -ES **:** CARNALITY

car·nap·tious \(ˈ)kärˈnapshəs, kərˈn-\ *adj* [perh. fr. *ker-* + *knap* (to bite) + connective *-t-* + *-ious*] *dial chiefly Brit* **:** bad-tempered

car·nar·ia \kärˈna(a)rēə\ *n pl, cap* [NL, fr. L *carn-*, *caro* flesh + NL *-aria*] *in old classifications* **:** an order of mammals including the Carnivora, Insectivora, Chiroptera, and carnivorous marsupials

¹car·nas·si·al \(ˈ)kärˈnasēəl\ *adj* [modif. (influenced by *-al*) of F *carnassier* carnivorous, fr. (assumed) OProv *carnassier* (whence Prov *carnassié*), fr. *carnasso* meat in plenty, fr. *carn* flesh, fr. L *carn-*, *caro*] **:** of, relating to, or being teeth of a carnivorous mammal that are larger and longer than adjacent teeth and adapted for cutting rather than tearing **:** SECTORIAL ⟨the last premolars of the upper jaw and first true molars of the lower constitute the ~ teeth of most carnivores⟩

²carnassial \"\ *n* -s **:** a carnassial tooth

car·nate \ˈkärˌnāt, -nət\ *adj* [by shortening] **:** INCARNATE

car·na·tion \kärˈnāshən, käˈn-, *attrib* (ˈ)=ˈ==\ *n* -s [MF, color or complexion of a person, fr. OIt *carnagione*, fr. *carne* flesh, fr. L *carn-*, *caro* — more at CARNAL] **1 a :** the variable color of human flesh averaging the color seed pearl **b :** CARNATION RED **2 :** any of the numerous cultivated usu. double-flowered varieties of the clove pink (*Dianthus caryophyllus*) orig. flesh-colored but now found in many color variations — compare ²BIZARRE, ²FLAKE 3, PICOTEE, PINK **3 :** PRIDE OF BARBADOS

carnation 2

car·na·tioned \(ˈ)=ˈ=shənd\ *adj* **:** made red or ruddy ⟨her cheeks ~ by the wind —Thomas Hardy⟩

carnation red *n* **:** a moderate red that is bluer and paler than cerise, claret (sense 3a), average strawberry (sense 2a), Turkey red, or Harvard crimson (sense 1)

carnation rose *n* **:** a strong pink that is bluer and less strong than coral (sense 3c), bluer and stronger than rose d'Althaea, and bluer, lighter, and stronger than sea pink

carnation rust *n* **:** a disease of carnations caused by a rust fungus (*Uromyces caryophyllinus*) characterized by discoloration and spotting of the leaves and the production of chocolate-brown powdery spore masses

car·nau·ba \kärˈnȯbə, ˌkärnəˈübə *also* kärˈnübə *or* -ˈnaübə\ *n* -s [Pg] **1 :** a fan palm (*Copernicia cerifera*) of Brazil that has an edible root and is the source of a useful leaf fiber and a brittle yellowish wax **2 :** CARNAUBA WAX

carnauba wax *n* **:** a yellowish to dark-brownish gray hard brittle high-melting wax obtained from the surface of leaves of the carnauba palm and used chiefly in polishes (as for floors, furniture, and shoes), in coatings for paper (as carbon paper), in phonograph records, and in pharmaceutical and cosmetic preparations

car·nau·bic acid \(ˈ)=ˈ=bik-, ˌ==ˈübik-\ *n* [ISV *carnaubic* (fr. *carnauba* + *-ic*) + *acid*; orig. formed as G *karnaubasäure*] **:** a crystalline fatty acid that is found as esters and esp. in carnauba wax and wool fat and that may be a mixture of acids

car·neau \(ˈ)kärˈnō\ *n, pl* **car·neaux** \-ō(z)\ *also* **carneaus** \-ōz\ *usu cap* [F] **:** a pigeon of a popular stocky close-feathered utility breed producing large squabs freely, the preferred colors being reddish and white

car·ne·giea \ˌkärˈnegēə\ *n, cap* [NL, fr. Andrew *Carnegie* †1919 Am. industrialist and humanitarian] **:** a monotypic genus of cacti consisting of the saguaro

car·ne·gie·ite \ˈkärnəgēˌīt, kärˈneg-\ *n* -s [Andrew *Carnegie* + E *-ite*; fr. the fact that it was synthesized at the Carnegie Institution of Washington, D.C., founded by Andrew Carnegie] **:** an artificial mineral $NaAlSiO_4$ consisting of sodium aluminum silicate and related to feldspar

car·ne·gie unit \ˈkärnəgē-, -ān- *also* (ˈ)kärˈnegē- *or* -äˈn- *or* kə(r)ˈn-\ *n, usu cap C* [so called fr. the fact that it was first defined by the Carnegie Foundation for the Advancement of Teaching, founded by Andrew Carnegie] **:** the credit given for the successful completion of a year's study of one subject in a secondary school — called also *unit*

car·ne·lian \kärˈnēlyən, käˈn-\ *n* -s [alter. (prob. influenced by L *carn-*, *caro* flesh) of *cornelian*; fr. its flesh-red color] **1 :** a chalcedony that has a clear deep red, flesh red, or reddish white color, that polishes well, and that being hard and tough is much used for seals **2 :** COPPER 5a

carnelian red *n* **:** a moderate reddish orange that is yellower and lighter than flamingo and yellower and paler than crab apple

car·ne·ol *or* **car·ne·ole** \ˈkärnēˌȯl, -ōl\ *n* -s [prob. fr. ML *carneolus*, prob. fr. LL *carneus*, fr. *carn-*, *caro* flesh — more at CARNAL] **:** CARNELIAN 1

car·net \(ˈ)kärˈnā\ *n* -s [F, lit., notebook, fr. MF *quernet*, fr. L *quaterni* group of four — more at QUIRE] **1 a :** a card issued to an aviator by the Fédération Aéronautique Internationale and designed to eliminate the necessity for his having a passport **b :** an international credit card for aviation fuel **2 :** a customs pass permitting an automobile free passage across national boundaries

¹car·ney *or* **car·ny** \ˈkärnē\ *vb* **carneyed** *or* **carnied**; **carneyed** *or* **carnied**; **carneying** *or* **carnying**; **carneys** *or* **carnies** [origin unknown] *Brit* **:** CAJOLE, WHEEDLE

²carney *var of* CARNY

carnie *var of* CARNY

car·ni·fex \ˈkärnəˌfeks\ *n, pl* **carnifexes** \-ksəz\ *or* **car·nif·i·ces** \kärˈnifəˌsēz, -əˌkās\ [L, fr. *carni-* (fr. *carn-*, *caro* flesh) + *-fex* (fr. *facere* to make) — more at CARNAL, DO] **:** EXECUTIONER; *specif* **:** the public executioner in ancient Rome

car·ni·fi·ca·tion \ˌkärnəfəˈkāshən\ *n* -s [*carnify* + *-fication*] **1 :** the process by which lung tissue becomes converted into fibrous tissue as a result of unresolved pneumonia **2 :** the conversion of bread into flesh through transubstantiation

car·ni·fi·cial \ˌkärnəˈfishəl\ *adj* [L *carnific-*, *carnifex* + E *-ial*] **:** of or relating to an executioner or a butcher ⟨a ~ knife⟩

car·ni·fy \ˈkärnəˌfī\ *vb* -ED/-ING/-ES [*carni-* (fr. L *carn-*, *caro* flesh) + *-fy* — more at CARNAL] *vt* **:** to make or turn into flesh ~ *vi* **:** to undergo carnification

car·ni·o·lan \ˌkärnēˈōlən, (ˈ)kärˈnyō-\ *adj, usu cap* [*Carniola*, region in Yugoslavia + E *-an*] **:** of or relating to the former Austro-Hungarian crownland of Carniola or its later subdivisions

carniolan bee *n, usu cap C* [*Carniola*, region in southern Europe northeast of the head of the Adriatic sea + E *-an*] **:** a honeybee of a race characterized by grayish color, quiet disposition, and high honey production with minimal production of propolis and marked by a strong tendency to swarm

car·ni·tine \ˈkärnəˌtēn\ *n* -s [ISV *carn-* (fr. G *karnin*, basic substance isolated fr. meat extract) + *-ite*, + *-ine*; orig. formed as G *karnitin*] **:** a white betaine $(CH_3)_3N^+CH_2CH(OH)CH_2COO^-$ that is found esp. in muscle tissue and is an essential food factor for certain insect larvae (as the mealworm) — called also *vitamin B_T*

car·ni·val \ˈkärnəvəl, ˈkän-\ *n* -s *often attrib* [It *carnevale*, *carnovale*, alter. of OIt *carnelevare*, lit., removal of meat, fr. *carne* flesh (fr. L *carn-*, *caro*) + *levare* to raise, take away, fr. L — more at CARNAL, LEVER] **1 :** the season or festival of merrymaking and revelry before Lent observed esp. by Roman Catholics and orig. extending from the feast of the Epiphany to Ash Wednesday but now usu. confined to a few days just before Lent **:** SHROVETIDE — compare MARDI GRAS **2 a :** any merrymaking, feasting, or masquerading ⟨in a ~ mood⟩ **b :** a time of exuberance or of riotous excesses ⟨the ~ of spring⟩ **3 a :** a traveling enterprise consisting of such amusements as sideshows, games of chance, Ferris wheels, merry-go-rounds, and shooting galleries **:** CIRCUS **b :** an organized program of entertainment or exhibition **:** FESTIVAL ⟨a winter ~⟩ ⟨a book ~⟩

car·ni·val·esque \ˌ===ˈesk\ *adj* [It *carnivalesco*, fr. *carnivale* + *-esco* -esque] **:** like or suggestive of a carnival ⟨Venice . . . is like a museum with ~ overtones —Truman Capote⟩

car·niv·o·ra \kärˈniv(ə)rə\ *n pl* [NL, fr. L, neut. pl. of *carnivorus* carnivorous — more at CARNIVOROUS] **1** *cap* **:** an order of eutherian mammals that are believed to have arisen from generalized insectivores during the Paleocene and are mostly carnivorous in habit having teeth adapted for flesh eating, a simple stomach and short intestine, feet with four or more usu. clawed toes, a well-developed brain, clavicles wanting or vestigial, and a zonary deciduate placenta — compare CREODONTA, FISSIPEDA, PINNIPEDIA **2 :** carnivorous animals; *esp* **:** members of the Carnivora

car·ni·vore \ˈkärnəˌvō(ə)r, ˈkän-, -vȯ(ə)r, -vōə, -vȯ(ə)\ *n* -s [NL *Carnivora*] **1 a :** a flesh-eating animal; *esp* **:** one of the Carnivora **2** [F, fr. *carnivore* carnivorous, fr. L *carnivorus*] **:** an insectivorous plant

car·nivo·ri \kärˈnivəˌrī, -ˌrē\ *syn of* CARNIVORA

car·nivo·rism \kärˈnivəˌrizəm, ˈkarnəˌvōrˌiz-\ *n* -s [*carnivorous* + *-ism*] **:** the consuming or digesting of insects by plants

car·ni·vor·i·ty \ˌkärnəˈvȯrəd·ē\ *n* -ES [ISV *carnivorous* + *-ity*] **:** the quality or state of being carnivorous

car·niv·o·rous \(ˈ)kärˈniv(ə)rəs, -äˈn-\ *adj* [L *carnivorus*, fr. *carni-* (fr. *carn-*, *caro* flesh) + *-vorus* -vorous — more at CARNAL] **1** *of an animal* **:** eating flesh ⟨the dog is a typical ~ mammal⟩ **:** subsisting or feeding on animal tissues ⟨many larval insects are ~⟩ **:** ZOOPHAGOUS ⟨the ~ hunting spiders⟩ — compare HERBIVOROUS, OMNIVOROUS **2** *of a plant* **:** subsisting on nutrients obtained from the breakdown of animal protoplasm — compare PHYTOPHAGOUS **3 :** of or relating to the Carnivora **4** *anthrop* **:** having a slender body build and a short small intestine — opposed to *herbivorous* and nearly equivalent to *ectomorphic* — **car·niv·o·rous·ly** *adv* — **car·niv·o·rous·ness** *n* -ES — **car·niv·o·ry** \ˈ=ˌvərē\ *n* -ES

car·no·sau·ria \ˌkärnəˈsȯrēə\ *n pl, cap* [NL, fr. L *carn-, caro* flesh + NL *-o-* + *-sauria*] **:** a group of moderate to large-sized carnivorous saurischian dinosaurs that had recurved daggerlike teeth and were widely distributed in the Upper Triassic and Jurassic — compare ALLOSAURUS, CERATODUS

car·nose \ˈkärˌnōs\ *adj* [L *carnosus*, fr. *carn-, caro* + *-osus* -ose] **1 :** like or relating to flesh **:** FLESHY **2 :** of a fleshy consistence — used of succulent parts of plants

car·no·sine \ˈkärnəˌsēn, -sən\ *n* -S [ISV *carnos-* (fr. L *carnosus* fleshy) + *-ine;* orig. formed as G *karnosin*] **:** a colorless crystalline dipeptide $C_9H_{14}N_4O_3$ occurring in the muscles of most mammals; *β*-alanyl-histidine

car·not cycle \(ˈ)kärˈnō-\ *or* **car·not's cycle** \-ōz-\ *n, usu cap 1st C* [trans. of F *cycle de Carnot*, after N.L.S. *Carnot* †1832 Fr. physicist] **:** an ideal heat-engine cycle in which the working substance goes through the four successive operations of isothermal expansion to a desired point, adiabatic expansion to a desired point, isothermal compression, and adiabatic compression back to its initial state

carnot engine *n, usu cap C* **:** an ideal reversible heat engine esp. as postulated in the statement of Carnot's principle of engine efficiency

car·no·tite \ˈkärnəˌtīt\ *n* -S [F, fr. M. A. *Carnot* †1920 Fr. inspector general of mines + F *-ite*] **:** a mineral $K_2(UO_2)_2(VO_4)_2.3H_2O$ consisting of a hydrous strongly radioactive vanadate of uranium and potassium that occurs as a powder or in loosely coherent masses of a canary-yellow color at various points in western Colorado and is a source of radium and uranium

car·not's law \(ˈ)kärˈnōz-\ *n, usu cap C* [after N.L.S. *Carnot* †1832, Fr. physicist] **:** a statement in physics: the specific heat of a gas at constant pressure minus the specific heat at constant volume multiplied by the mechanical equivalent of heat equals the gas constant for the gas in question

carnot's theorem *or* **carnot's principle** *n, usu cap C* [trans. of F *principe de Carnot*, after N.L.S. *Carnot*, its formulator] **:** a principle in thermodynamics: an engine working in a reversible cycle is at least as efficient as any other engine working between the same limits of temperature, the efficiency of such an engine being a function of the two limiting temperatures and not dependent on the mechanical design or the working substance of the engine

¹carny *var of* CARNEY

²car·ny *or* **car·ney** *or* **car·nie** \ˈkärnē\ *n, pl* **carnies** *or* **carneys** *often attrib* [short for *carnival*] **1 :** CARNIVAL 3a **2 :** one who works with a carnival

ca·roa \ˌkarəˈwä\ *n* -S [Pg *caroá*, fr. Tupi] **1 :** a Brazilian plant (*Neoglaziovia variegata*) related to the pinguin **2 :** the silky resistant leaf fiber of the caroa plant used esp. locally in making cordage, coarse cloth, and paper

car·ob \ˈkarəb\ *n* -S [MF *carobe, caroube*, fr. ML *carrubium*, fr. Ar *kharrūbah*] **1** *also* **carob bean a** *or* **carob tree : a** leguminous tree (*Ceratonia siliqua*) of the Mediterranean region having evergreen pinnate leaves and apetalous flowers in small red racemes **b :** one of the long pods of this tree containing a sweetish pulp, having small seeds that were formerly employed as standards of weight, and used as food for humans and livestock — called also *algarroba, locust bean, locust pod, St.-John's-bread* **2** [alter. of *caroba*] **:** any of several So. American timber trees of the genus *Jacaranda*

ca·ro·ba \kəˈrōbə\ *n* -S [Pg, caroba tree, fr. Tupi *caa-roba*] **1 :** the leaflets of any of certain trees of the family Bignoniaceae (esp. *Jacaranda procera* and *Cybistax antisyphilitica*) used in Brazil as a remedy for syphilis **2 :** CAROB 2

carob brown *n* **:** RUSSIAN CALF

carob flour *n* **:** a powder extracted from the fruit of the carob tree and used in the pharmaceutical, textile, and food industries as a thickener, stabilizer, and sizing agent — called also *locust bean gum powder*

carob gum *n* **:** a gummy substance made from carob flour

ca·roche \kəˈrōch, -ōsh\ *n* -S [MF *carroche*, fr. OIt *carroccio*, aug. of *carro* vehicle, fr. L *carrus* — more at CAR] **:** a luxurious or stately carriage for persons

¹car·ol \ˈkarəl *also* -er-\ *n* -S [ME *carole*, fr. OF, modif. of LL *choraula* choral song, fr. L, one that accompanies a chorus on a reed instrument, alter. of *choraules*, fr. Gk *choraulēs*, fr. *choraulein* to accompany a chorus on a reed instrument, fr. *choros* chorus + *aulein* to play a reed instrument, fr. *aulos* reed instrument like an oboe — more at CHORUS, ALVEOLUS] **1** *or* **car·ole** \ˈ"\ **:** an old round dance with singing by couples associated orig. with May-day celebrations of western Europe **2 :** a song of joy, exultation, or mirth ⟨I float this ~ with joy —Walt Whitman⟩ ⟨the ~ of a bird —Lord Byron⟩ **3 a :** a song of praise or devotion **:** a popular song or ballad of religious joy ⟨a Christmas ~⟩ ⟨an Easter ~⟩ ⟨sing your ~ of high praise —John Keble⟩ **b :** the music of such a song

²carol \ˈ"\ *vb* **caroled** *or* **carolled; caroled** *or* **carolled; caroling** *or* **carolling; carols** [ME *carolen*, fr. OF *caroler*, fr. *carole*, n.] *vi* **1 :** to sing esp. in a joyful manner ⟨he used to ~ cheerfully in the morning, locked in the single bathroom —H.S. Canby⟩ ⟨a wren on a tree stump ~*ed* clear —John Masefield⟩ **2 :** to sing carols; *specif* **:** to go about outdoors in a group singing Christmas carols on Christmas Eve ⟨gone ~*ing*⟩ ~ *vt* **1 :** to praise in or as if in song ⟨the shepherds . . . ~ her goodness loud in rustic lays —John Milton⟩ ⟨the union's star salesman . . . has been ~*ing* its glories for many a year —*Newsweek*⟩ **2 :** to sing esp. in a cheerful manner ⟨the robin . . . ~*s* from the treetops his loud, hearty strain —John Burroughs⟩ ⟨they ~*ed* nothing but love ditties —J.D.Hart⟩

carolean *var of* CAROLINE

car·ol·er *or* **car·ol·ler** \ˈkarələ(r) *also* -er-\ *n* -S **:** one that carols

caroli *pl of* CAROLUS

car·o·lin \ˌkarəˈlēn\ *n, pl* **carolins** \-nz\ *or* **caroli·ner** \ˌ==ˈlēnə(r)\ [Sw *karolin*, fr. NL *carolinus* of Charles, fr. ML *Carolus* Charles (after Charles XI †1697, Charles XII †1718 & Charles XIV †1844, kings of Sweden) + L *-inus* -ine] **1 :** any of several coins issued under Swedish kings named Charles **2** *or* **kar·o·lin** \ˌkarəˈlēn\ [G *karolin*, fr. NL *carolinus*, fr. ML *Carolus* (after Charles Albert †1745 prince of Bavaria) + L *-inus* -ine] **a** (1) **:** an old gold coin of Bavaria first struck in the 18th century (2) **:** any of several similar coins of southern German states, esp. Württemberg **b :** a unit of value equivalent to a German carolin ⟨half-*carolin* and ¼-*carolin* coins⟩ **3** [modif. of It *carlino*] **:** ¹CARLIN

car·o·li·na \ˌkarəˈlīnə *also* ˌker-; *chiefly in substand speech* kə(r)ˈlī-\ *adj, usu cap* [fr. *Carolina*, English colony from which No. & So. Carolina were formed — more at CAROLINIAN] **:** of or from the state of No. Carolina or the state of So. Carolina **:** of the kind or style prevalent in No. Carolina or So. Carolina **:** CAROLINIAN

carolina allspice *n, usu cap C* **:** a shrub of the genus *Calycanthus* — called also *strawberry shrub*

carolina anemone *n, usu cap C* **:** a prairie herb (*Anemone caroliniana*) with a solitary showy purplish white flower found in the central and southern U.S.

carolina ash *n, usu cap C* **:** a water ash (*Fraxinus caroliniana*)

carolina bay *n, usu cap C* **:** any of various shallow often oval depressions in the coastal plain of the southeastern U.S. ranging from a few hundred feet to several miles long and being usu. marshy and rich in humus, heavily forested, and covered with a pure stand of trees (as cypress, bay, or black gum) different from the dominant tree (as pine) of surrounding areas

carolina bean *n, usu cap C* **:** SIEVA BEAN

carolina beechdrops *n pl but often sing in constr, usu cap C* **:** a rare purple or purplish brown American herb (*Monotropsis odorata*) with pink flowers

carolina box tortoise *n, usu cap C* **:** the common box tortoise (*Terrapene carolina*)

carolina buckthorn *n, usu cap C* **1 :** YELLOW BUCKTHORN **2 :** SOUTHERN BUCKTHORN

carolina chickadee *n, usu cap C* **:** a chickadee (*Penthestes carolinensis carolinensis*) of the southeastern U.S. resembling but smaller than the black-capped chickadee

carolina duck *n, usu cap C* **:** WOOD DUCK 1

carolina grasshopper *or* **carolina locust** *n, usu cap C* **:** a large dark-colored grasshopper (*Dissosteira carolina*) common throughout the U.S. that has the edge of the wing bordered with bright yellow

carolina hemlock *n, usu cap C* **:** a hemlock (*Tsuga caroliniana*) of the southeastern U.S. having wide spreading leaves and widely divergent cone scales

carolina horsenettle *n, usu cap C* **:** HORSENETTLE

carolina ipecac *n, usu cap C* **:** IPECAC SPURGE

carolina jessamine *or* **carolina jasmine** *n, usu cap C* **:** YELLOW JESSAMINE 2

carolina junco *n, usu cap C* **:** a slaty-gray junco (*Junco hyemalis carolinensis*) of the higher Allegheny mountains

carolina moonseed *n, usu cap C* **:** a woody vine (*Cocculus carolinus*) of the southern U.S. resembling the common moonseed (*Menispermum canadense*) but having red fruits

carolina parakeet *or* **carolina paroquet** *n, usu cap C* **:** an extinct parrakeet (*Conuropsis carolinensis*) having a long tail and mostly green plumage but with yellow head, red face, and blue and yellow on the wings and being the only parrot whose range extended far into the U.S.

Carolina parakeet

carolina pink *n, usu cap C* **1 :** a wild pink (*Silene caroliniana*) **2 :** PINKROOT a

carolina pompano *n, usu cap C* **:** a pompano (*Trachynotus carolinus*)

carolina poplar *n, usu cap C* **1 a :** a common cottonwood (*Populus deltoides*) **b :** a hybrid resulting from crosses involving this species and also two other poplars (*P. nigra italica* and *P. canadensis amoena*) **2 :** BALSAM POPLAR

carolina rail *n, usu cap C* **:** SORA

carolina rhododendron *n, usu cap C* **:** an evergreen shrub (*Rhododendron carolinianum*) of the southeastern U.S. cultivated for its showy pale rose-purple flowers

carolina rose *n, usu cap C* **:** SWAMP ROSE

carolina tea *n, usu cap C* **:** a yaupon (*Ilex vomitoria*)

carolina vanilla *n, usu cap C* **:** WILD VANILLA

carolina water shield *n, usu cap C* **:** FANWORT

carolina whiting *n, usu cap C* **:** KING WHITING

carolina wild woodbine *n, usu cap C* **:** YELLOW JESSAMINE 2

carolina wren *n, usu cap C* **:** a large wren (*Thryothorus ludovicianus*) familiar as a loud songster

¹car·o·line \ˈkarəˌlīn, -lən *also* -er-\ *or* **car·o·le·an** \ˌ==ˈlēən\ *adj, usu cap* [*caroline* fr. NL *carolinus*, fr. ML *Carolus* Charles + L *-inus* -ine; *carolean* alter. (influenced by *jacobean*) of *caroline*] **:** of or relating to Charles — used esp. with ref. to Charles I and Charles II of England or their times

²caroline \ˈ"\ *or* **caroline hat** *n* -S *chiefly Irish* **:** STOVEPIPE HAT

caroline minuscule *n, usu cap C* [¹*caroline*] **:** the Carolingian script

caroling *pres part of* CAROL

¹car·o·lin·gi·an \ˌkarəˈlinj(ē)ən *also* -er-\ *adj, usu cap* [F *carolingien*, fr. ML *karolingi* French people (prob. fr. assumed OHG *karling, kerling* Frenchman — whence MHG *kerlinc* — fr. *Karl* Charles + OHG *-ing*) + F *-ien* -ian] **1 :** of or relating to a Frankish family that was founded about A.D. 613 and including among its members the rulers of France from 751 to 987, of Germany from 752 to 911, and of Italy from 774 to 961 **2 :** being a script developed in France in the 8th century and combining characteristics of cursive and half uncial

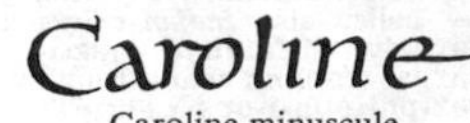

Caroline minuscule

²carolingian \ˈ"\ *n* -S *usu cap* **:** a member of the Carolingian dynasty

¹car·o·lin·ian \ˌkarəˈlinyən, -nēən *also* -er- *or* -lē-; *chiefly substand* kə(r)ˈl-\ *adj, usu cap* [*Carolina*, English colony from which No. and So. Carolina were formed, after Charles I (*Carolus*) †1649 king of England + E *-ian*] **1 :** of, relating to, or characteristic of the state of No. Carolina or of So. Carolina or of both **2 :** of, relating to, or characteristic of the people of No. Carolina or of So. Carolina or of both **3 :** of, relating to, or being the part of the Upper Austral life zone that lies east of the 100th meridian, has a northern mean daily temperature of 71.6°F during the 6 hottest weeks and a similar southern mean daily temperature of 78.8°F, extends from southern New England to Georgia, and forms the humid division of the Upper Austral zone **4 :** [¹*caroline* + *-ian*] **:** CAROLINGIAN 1 **5** [¹*caroline* + *-ian*] **:** CAROLINE

²carolinian \ˈ"\ *n* -S *cap* **:** a native or resident of No. Carolina or So. Carolina

³carolinian \ˈ"\ *n* -S *cap* [*Caroline* (*islands*), archipelago in west Pacific + E *-ian*] **1 :** a native or inhabitant of the Caroline islands **2 :** any or all of the closely related Micronesian languages spoken by the native inhabitants of the Caroline islands

carolins *pl of* CAROLIN

carolled *past of* CAROL

caroller *var of* CAROLER

carolling *pres part of* CAROL

carols *pl of* CAROL, *pres 3d sing of* CAROL

car·o·lus \ˈkarələs\ *n, pl* **caroluses** \-ləsəz\ *or* **caro·li** \-ˌlī, -ˌlē\ [NL, Charles, fr. ML] **:** any of various coins issued under monarchs called Charles: as **a :** an English gold coin of the reign of Charles I orig. worth 20 shillings **b** *or* **carolus dollar** *usu cap C* **:** a Spanish-American peso or piece of eight issued by Charles III (1759-88) and Charles IV (1788-1808) of Spain

car·o·lyt·ic *or* **car·o·lit·ic** \ˌkarəˈlid·ik\ *adj* [modif. of F *corollitique*, fr. *corolle* corolla (fr. L *corolla*) + *-itique* -itic] *of a column* **:** having a foliated shaft

¹car·om \ˈkarəm *also* -er-\ *n* -S [by shortening & alter. fr. ¹*carambole*] **1 :** a shot in billiards in which the cue ball strikes each of two object balls **2 :** a rebounding esp. at an angle **:** a glancing off **3** [fr. *Carroms*, a trademark] **a carroms** *pl but sing in constr* **:** a game played by two or four persons with round wooden counters on a large square board having corner pockets **b :** a counter used in caroms

²carom *also* **carrom** \ˈ"\ *vb* -ED/-ING/-S *vi* **1 :** to make a carom **2 :** to strike and rebound **:** GLANCE **:** rebound or glance after striking ⟨his drive hit a tree and ~*ed* off into a roadway —*Time*⟩ **3 :** to proceed by or as if by caroms ⟨she tried to ~ from my corner of the room to the bar —Henry Miller⟩ ~ *vt* **:** to make (an object) bounce off something ⟨place an object ball on the table and try to ~ the cue ball from it —Willie Hoppe⟩

carom ball *n* **:** the second ball hit by the cue ball in making a carom in billiards

carom billiards *n pl but usu sing in constr* **:** any of several games of billiards played with a cue and three balls on a pocketless table, points being scored by a player's causing the cue ball to carom from one object ball to another — compare BALKLINE, POOL, STRAIGHT RAIL, THREE-CUSHION BILLIARDS

ca·ro·ny bark \kəˈrōnē-\ *n, usu cap C* [fr. *Caroni*, river in Venezuela, where it is found] **:** ANGOSTURA BARK

caroome *n* -S [perh. irreg. fr. ¹*car*] **:** a license to keep a cart granted by the lord mayor of London

ca·ro's acid \ˈkä(ˌ)rōˈz-\ *n, usu cap C* [trans. of G *Caro'sche säure*, after Heinrich *Caro* †1910 Ger. chemist] **:** PERMONOSULFURIC ACID

car·o·sel·la \ˌkarəˈselə, -ˈz-\ *n* -S [It] **:** a fennel (*Foeniculum vulgare peperitum*) grown for its edible young stems which are used in salads — called also *Italian fennel*

carot *var of* CAROTTE

car·o·tene \ˈkarəˌtēn *also* -er-\ *also* **car·o·tin** \-ət°n, -tən\ *or* **car·ro·tene** *or* **car·ro·tin** *n* -S [ISV *carot-* (fr. LL *carota* carrot) + *-ene* or *-in;* prob. orig. formed as G *karotin* — more at CARROT] **:** any of several orange or red crystalline pigments of the class of carotenoid hydrocarbons commonly occurring in the chromoplasts of plants and in the fatty tissues of plant-eating animals: as **a :** a mixture of three such pigments $C_{40}H_{56}$ convertible in the animal body to vitamin A, obtained esp. from various plant sources (as carrots and alfalfa), and used as a precursor of vitamin A and as a color for foods **b :** any of the three pigments $C_{40}H_{56}$ convertible in the animal body to vitamin A, characterized chemically by one or two unsaturated rings terminating a long aliphatic polyene chain, and distinguished according to the number and nature of these rings as *α-, β-*, and *γ-carotene; specif* **:** the dark-red *β*-carotene that is the most widely distributed carotenoid and the principal pigment of carrots, that is also made synthetically, and that is the most active provitamin A since its molecule contains two rings of the type present in the vitamin A molecule

car·o·ten·emia *or* **car·o·ten·aemia** *also* **car·o·tin·emia** \ˌ==təˈnēmēə, -t°nˈē-\ *n* -S [NL, fr. ISV *carotin* + NL *-emia* or *-aemia*] **:** the presence in the circulating blood of carotene which may cause a yellowing of the skin resembling jaundice

¹ca·rot·enoid *also* **ca·rot·i·noid** \kəˈrät°nˌȯid\ *n* -S [*carotene, carotin* + *-oid*] **:** any of several highly unsaturated pigments (as carotenes and xanthophylls) most of which are yellow, orange, or red and many of which occur widely in plants, esp. in all green tissues, and in animals, being characterized chemically by a long aliphatic polyene chain composed of isoprene units — compare LIPOCHROME

²carotenoid *also* **carotinoid** \ˈ"\ *adj* **:** relating to or consisting of a carotenoid

ca·rot·enol \kəˈrät°nˌȯl, -ōl\ *n* -S [*carotene* + *-ol*] **:** a hydroxy derivative of a carotene **:** a carotenoid alcohol — compare XANTHOPHYLL

¹ca·rot·id \kəˈräd·əd, -ätəd\ *adj* [F or Gk; F *carotide*, fr. Gk *karōtides* carotid arteries, fr. *karos* heavy sleep, back-formation fr. *karoun* to stupefy; fr. the belief that pressure on these arteries causes stupor; akin to Gk *kara* head — more at CEREBRAL] **:** belonging to or situated near a carotid artery

²carotid \ˈ"\ *or* **carotid artery** *n* -S **:** either of the two main arteries that supply blood to the head, the left in man arising from the arch of the aorta, the right by bifurcation of the innominate artery, each passing along the corresponding anterolateral aspect of the neck and dividing opposite the upper border of the thyroid cartilage into an external branch supplying the face, tongue, and external parts of the head and an internal branch supplying the brain, eye, and other internal parts of the head

ca·rot·id·al \-əd°l\ *or* **car·o·ti·de·an** \kəˌräd·əˈdēən, -ätə-, ˌkarəˈtid-\ *adj* [ISV *carotid* + *-al* or *-ean*] **:** CAROTID

carotid body *or* **carotid gland** *n* **:** a small body of highly vascular chromaffin tissue adjoining the carotid sinus and serving as a chemoreceptor sensitive to changes of the oxygen tension in blood and mediating reflex changes in respiratory activities

carotid canal *n* **:** the canal by which the internal carotid artery enters the skull

carotid plexus *n* **:** a network of nerves of the sympathetic system surrounding the internal carotid artery

carotid sinus *n* **:** the slight enlargement of the common carotid artery at the point where it divides into external and internal carotid arteries, being richly supplied with sensory nerve endings and playing a major part in the mechanism regulating heart rate and blood pressure

carotin *var of* CAROTENE

carotinemia *var of* CAROTENEMIA

carotinoid *var of* CAROTENOID

car·o·tol \ˈkarəˌtȯl, -ōl\ *n* -S [LL *carota* + E *-ol*] **:** a liquid sesquiterpenoid alcohol $C_{15}H_{25}OH$ found in the essential oil of carrots

ca·rotte *also* **ca·rot** \kəˈrät\ *n* -S [F, *carotte*, lit., carrot — more at CARROT] **:** a cylindrical roll of tobacco

ca·rou·bi·er \kəˈrübēˌā\ *n* -S [F, carob tree, fr. *caroube* — more at CAROB] **:** RUSSIAN CALF

¹ca·rous·al \kəˈrauzəl\ *n* -S [by folk etymology (influence of ²*carouse*)] **:** CARROUSEL 1

²carousal \ˈ"\ *n* -S [²*carouse* + *-al*] **:** CAROUSE 2 ⟨the spirit of continual carnival and ~ —Carleton Beals⟩

¹ca·rouse \kəˈrauz\ *n* -S [MF *carrousse, carroux*, fr. *carous, carroux*, adv., all out (in *boire carous* to empty the cup), modif. of G *garaus* (in *garaus trinken* to empty the cup), fr. *gar* quite, entirely (fr. OHG *garo*, fr. *garo*, adj., ready, complete) + *aus* out (fr. OHG *ūz*) — more at YARE, OUT] **1** *archaic* **:** a large draft of liquor **:** a cupful drunk up **:** TOAST ⟨drank a deep ~ to the queen's health —John Milton⟩ **2 :** a drinking bout **:** a drunken revel ⟨drowning care in a perpetual ~ —R.L.Stevenson⟩

²carouse \ˈ"\ *vb* -ED/-ING/-S *vi* **1 :** to drink deeply or freely and repeatedly (as in compliment) ⟨he had been aboard *carousing* to his mates —Shak.⟩ **2 :** to take part in a carouse ⟨the sailors went ashore to ~⟩ ~ *vt, obs* **:** to drink up **:** QUAFF

carousel *var of* CARROUSEL

ca·rous·er \kəˈrauzə(r)\ *n* -S **:** one that carouses **:** REVELER

ca·rous·ing·ly *adv* **:** in a carousing manner

¹carp \ˈkärp, ˈkȧp\ *vb* -ED/-ING/-S [ME *carpen*, of Scand origin; akin to Icel *karpa* to dispute, wrangle, ON *karp* arrogance, boasting; akin to OFris *kerp* dispute, ON *korpr* raven] *vi* **:** to find fault ill-naturedly, complain querulously, or cavil sharply ⟨perhaps it would be wise not to ~ or criticize —W.S.Gilbert⟩ — often used with *at* ⟨ancient critics were never at a loss for something to ~ at —E.S.McCartney⟩ ~ *vt* **:** to complain esp. in a censorious or peevish manner ⟨lest anyone ~ that such conditions are too ancient to mean anything —Eugene Burr⟩

²carp \ˈ"\ *n, pl* **carp** *or* **carps** [ME *carpe*, fr. MF, fr. LL *carpa*, prob. of Gmc origin; akin to MD *carpe* carp, MLG *karpe*, OHG *karpfo*, ON *karfi*] **1 a :** a soft-finned freshwater fish (*Cyprinus carpio*) that inhabits ponds and sluggish streams feeding chiefly on vegetable matter, attaining a large size, and sometimes living to a great age and that is indigenous to Asia but was early introduced into Europe where it is extensively reared in artificial ponds and esteemed as food and later into America where it has escaped into natural waters and in many areas has become a pest destroying the growth of water plants and crowding out more valued fishes — see LEATHER CARP, MIRROR CARP **b :** any of a number of other fishes of the family Cyprinidae — see CRUCIAN CARP **2 :** any of several somewhat carplike fishes that do not belong to the family Cyprinidae (as the carpsucker and the European sea bream)

carp *abbr* carpenter

¹carp- *or* **carpo-** *comb form* [F & NL, fr. Gk *karp-, karpo-*, fr. *karpos* fruit — more at HARVEST] **:** fruit ⟨*Carpoidea, carpology*⟩

²carp- *or* **carpo-** *comb form* [NL, fr. Gk *karp-, karpo-*, fr. *karpos* wrist — more at WHARF] **:** carpus ⟨*carpitis*⟩ **:** carpus and ⟨*carpometacarpus*⟩ **:** carpal and ⟨*carpopedal*⟩

-carp \ˌkärp, ˌkȧp\ *also* **-car·pi·um** \ˈkärpēəm, -ȧp-\ *n comb form, pl* **-carps** \-ps\ *also* **-car·pia** \-pēə\ [NL *-carpium*, fr. Gk *-karpion*, fr. *karpos* fruit] **1 :** part of a fruit ⟨*pericarp*⟩ **:** fruit ⟨*schizocarp*⟩ ⟨*amphicarpium*⟩ **2** [NL *-carpus*, fr. Gk *-karpos* -carpous, fr. *karpos*] **:** plant having fruit (in a specified place) ⟨*acrocarp*⟩ ⟨*pleurocarp*⟩

car·pa·ine \ˈkärpəˌēn\ *n* -S [ISV *carpa-* (irreg. fr. NL *Carica papaya*, species name of the papaya, fr. *Carica* + *papaya*, fr. Sp) + *-ine;* orig. formed as D *carpain* — more at CARICA, PAPAYA] **:** a crystalline alkaloid $C_{14}H_{25}NO_2$ obtained esp. from the leaves, fruit, and seeds of the papaya

¹car·pal \ˈkärpəl, -ȧp-\ *adj* [NL *carpalis*, fr. ²*carp-* + L *-alis* -al] **:** relating to the carpus

²carpal \ˈ"\ *n* -S **:** a carpal element

car·pa·le \kärˈpā(ˌ)lē\ *n, pl* **carpa·lia** \-ālēə\ [NL, neut. of *carpalis* carpal] **:** a carpal bone; *esp* **:** one of the distal series articulating with the metacarpals

car park *n, chiefly Brit* **:** an area set apart for the parking of motor vehicles **:** PARKING LOT

¹car·pa·thi·an \(ˈ)kärˈpāthēən *also* -th-\ *adj, usu cap* [prob. fr. G *Karpathen* Carpathian mts. (fr. L *Carpatus*, fr. Gk *Karpatos*) + E *-ian*] **:** situated in or relating to the Carpathian mountains of central Europe

²carpathian \ˈ"\ *adj, usu cap* [*Carpathus* (now usu. *Karpathos*) Greek island between Rhodes & Crete (fr. L, fr. Gk *Karpathos*) + E *-ian*] **:** of or relating to the island of Karpathos

car·pa·tho-rus·sian \kärˌpā(ˌ)thōˈrəshən *also* -th-\ *n, cap C & R* [*Carpatho-Russia*, former name of Carpathian Ruthenia (fr. *Carpathian* mts. + *-o-* + *Russia*) + E *-an*] **:** RUTHENIAN

carp dropsy *n* [²*carp*] **:** a bacterial disease of carps and suckers marked by intense inflammation of the fins, belly, and body cavity

car·pe di·em \ˌkärpēˈdēˌem, -(ˌ)pā-; ˌkärpēˈdī-\ *n, pl* **carpe diems** [L, enjoy the day!] **:** the enjoyment of the pleasures of the moment without concern for the future

car·pel \'kärpəl, 'kȧp- *also* -,pel\ *n* -s [F & NL; F *carpelle* & NL *carpellum*, fr. NL ¹*carp-* + F *-elle* & NL *-ellum* -el] **:** one of the structures in a seed plant comprising the innermost whorl of a flower, functioning as megasporophylls, and collectively constituting the gynoecium — compare PISTIL

flower with some parts removed showing: *1* petal, *2* stamen, *3* carpel, *4* sepal

car·pel·lary \-,pə,lerē, -i\ *adj* [NL *carpellum* + E *-ary*] **:** belonging to, forming, or containing carpels

car·pel·late \-,pə,lāt, -,lət\ *adj* [NL *carpellum* + E *-ate*] **:** having carpels

car·pen·tar·i·an \,kärpən¦terēən\ *n* -s *cap* [Gulf of *Carpentaria*, Australia + E *-an*] **:** a member of an ethnic group native to north and central Australia — compare MURRAYIAN

¹**car·pen·ter** \'kärpəntə(r), 'kȧp-, -pᵊmt-\ *n* -s [ME, fr. ONF *carpentier*, fr. L *carpentarius* carriage maker, fr. *carpentarius* of a carriage, fr. *carpentum* carriage, wagon, of Celt origin; akin to Gaulish place name *Carbantia*] **1 :** a workman who builds with wood: **a :** a workman who shapes and assembles structural woodwork esp. in the construction of buildings, stage settings, ships, tunnels, and mines **b :** a workman who cuts, fits, and installs floors, windows, doors, baseboards, cabinets, and other trim work — called also *finish carpenter* **c :** one who works at a bench in an industrial establishment making and assembling wood sections of boxes or furniture according to blueprints — called also *bench carpenter* **2 a :** a petty officer on merchant ships who attends to repairs not made by engineers **b :** a warrant officer in the U.S. Navy whose chief shipboard duties are hull maintenance and damage control

²**carpenter** \"\ *vb* **carpentered; carpentered; carpentering** \-pəntəriŋ, -n·triŋ, -pᵊmt(ə)riŋ\ **carpenters** *vi* **:** to do carpentry **:** follow the trade of a carpenter ⟨he ~*ed* in his youth, then graduated to heavy construction work —John Kobler⟩ ~ *vt* **1 :** to make by or as if by carpentry ⟨a doctor ~*ed* a splint for the broken arm —Frederick Way⟩ **2 :** to put together often in a mechanical manner ⟨I've ~*ed* dozens of scripts but this is cabinetmaking —Clemence Dane⟩ **:** CONSTRUCT ⟨is well ~*ed*, easily written, and well calculated to shorten a train ride —*Time*⟩

carpenter ant *n* **:** an ant (as American members of the genus *Camponotus*) that gnaws galleries in wood esp. when dead or partially decayed and constructs its nest in them

carpenter bee *n* **:** any of various large solitary bees (family Xylocopidae) that gnaw long galleries in sound timber — see GREAT CARPENTER BEE

carpenter bird *n* **:** CALIFORNIA WOODPECKER

carpenter frog *n* **:** a frog (*Rana virgatipes*) of the southeastern U.S. having a loud hammerlike call and large vocal sacs that when fully inflated resemble air bladders

carpenter grass *or* **carpenter's grass** *n* [so called fr. its supposed power to cure wounds inflicted by carpenter tools] **:** a yarrow (*Achillea millefolium*)

car·pen·te·ria \,kärpən'tirēə\ *n, cap* [NL, fr. William M. *Carpenter* †1848 Am. physician + NL *-ia*] **:** a genus of California evergreen shrubs (family Saxifragaceae) comprising a single species (*C. californica*) having opposite leaves and showy fragrant white flowers in few-flowered terminal clusters

carpentering *n* -s [fr. gerund of ²*carpenter*] **:** the act, occupation, or work of a carpenter **:** CARPENTRY

carpenter moth *n* **:** the adult of the carpenterworm or a related moth (family Cossidae) — called also *goat moth*

carpenter's clamp *n* **:** a bar with adjustable jaws that can be spread to hold cabinets, doors, and similar large pieces

carpenter's level *n* **1 :** PLUMB LEVEL **2 :** a straight bar (as of aluminum or wood) with a small spirit level embedded in it

carpenter's scene *or* **carpenter scene** *n* **:** a scene played on the forepart of the stage to give the stage carpenters opportunity to construct a scene behind the backdrop

carpenter's square *n* **1 :** a usu. steel square used by carpenters **2 :** either of two plants of the genus *Scrophularia:* **a :** the common figwort (*S. nodosa*) of Europe **b :** a related American species (*S. marylandica*)

carpenter weed *also* **carpenter's herb** *n* [so called fr. its supposed power to heal wounds inflicted by carpenter tools] **:** SELF-HEAL

carpenter's square 1

car·pen·ter·worm \'ˌˌˌ,ˌ\ *n* [so called fr. its wood boring] **:** the wood-boring larva of the American goat moth (*Prionoxystus robiniae*) that bores large galleries in living trees and is esp. destructive to oaks and locusts

car·pen·try \'kärpəntrē, 'kȧp-, -pᵊmt-, -i\ *n* -ES [ME *carpentrie*, fr. ONF *carpenterie*, fr. *carpentier* carpenter] **1 :** the art or trade of a carpenter; *specif* **:** the art of shaping and assembling structural woodwork (as in constructing buildings) **2 :** timberwork constructed by a carpenter; *specif* **:** an assemblage of pieces of timber connected by being framed together (as in a roof) **3 :** the form or manner of putting together the parts (as of a literary or musical composition) **:** STRUCTURE, ARRANGEMENT ⟨as neat a piece of interlocking dramatic ~ as can be imagined —Peter Forster⟩

carp·er \'kärpər, 'kȧp- *n* -s [ME, fr. *carpen* to carp, talk + *-er*] **:** one that carps; *esp* **:** a perverse faultfinder ⟨vast and general discontent . . . not only among professional ~*s* —Joel Carmichael⟩

¹**car·pet** \'kärpət, 'kȧp-, *usu* -əd· + V\ *n* -s *often attrib* [ME *carpete*, fr. MF *carpite*, fr. OIt *carpita*, fr. *carpire* to pluck, modif. of L *carpere* — more at HARVEST] **1 :** a heavy woven or felted fabric usu. made of wool: **a :** a floor covering made in breadths to be sewed together and tacked to the floor — see ORIENTAL RUG; compare RUG **b** *obs* **:** a thick wrought fabric used for covering tables or beds; *specif* **:** an altar covering **c** *archaic* **:** a luxurious floor covering found esp. in boudoirs — now used only attributively to convey the notion of effeminacy ⟨a ~ poet⟩; see CARPET KNIGHT **2 a :** a surface resembling or suggesting a carpet (as in smoothness or softness) ⟨the grassy ~ of this plain —Shak.⟩ **b :** the surface of a cricket field ⟨a ~ drive⟩ **3 a :** a thin skin of boards laid as a wearing surface on a floor **b** *chiefly Brit* **:** a thin layer of resurfacing material (as asphalt) covering a previously paved roadway — **on the carpet** *adv* (*or adj*) **1 :** under consideration or deliberation ⟨he nodded and asked was there something fresh *on the carpet* —F.W.Crofts⟩ **2 :** before an authority for censure or reproof ⟨called a salesman *on the carpet* and reprimanded him for not reaching his quota —W.J. Reilly⟩

²**carpet** \"\ *vt* -ED/-ING/-s **1 a :** to furnish with a carpet **:** spread with carpets ⟨the floors were ~*ed* —Al Spiers⟩ **b :** to cover as if with a carpet ⟨flowers ~ the streets —Claudia Cassidy⟩ **2** *chiefly Brit* **:** to take to task **:** REPRIMAND ⟨if the chap's a casualty and anything happens, we might be ~*ed* —Richard Llewellyn⟩

¹**carpetbag** \'ˌˌ,ˌ\ *n* [so called fr. its having been originally made of carpet] **1 :** a traveling bag often made in the style of the Boston bag and esp. common in the U.S. in the 19th century **2 :** any traveling bag

²**carpetbag** \"\ *adj* **:** following the practices of carpetbaggers **:** of or characteristic of carpetbaggers ⟨~ adventurers⟩ ⟨a ~ government⟩

³**carpetbag** \"\ *vi* **1 :** to travel with little luggage **2 :** to act in the manner characteristic of carpetbaggers ~ *vt* **:** to infest or oppress with carpetbaggers

car·pet·bag·ger \-ə(r)\ *n* -s [¹*carpetbag* + *-er*] **1 :** one that travels with a carpetbag or has all of his property with him in a carpetbag: **a :** a promoter of wildcat banks or stocks in the western U.S. in the 19th century **b :** a Northerner in the South after the American Civil War esp. seeking private gain under the reconstruction governments **2 :** STRANGER, OUTSIDER, TRANSIENT; *esp* **:** a nonresident who meddles in politics — **car·pet·bag·gery** \-(ə)rē, -i\ *n* -ES

car·pet·bag·gism *or* **car·pet·bag·ism** \-,gizəm\ *n* -s **:** carpetbag practices

carpet bedding *n* **:** a patterned arrangement of low or clipped herbaceous and usu. varicolored foliage plants — distinguished from *design bedding*

carpet beetle *n* **:** any of several small beetles having larvae that feed in and damage materials of animal origin (as woolen carpets): as **a :** a small black, red, and white dermestid beetle (*Anthrenus scrophulariae*) having such habits — called also *buffalo carpet beetle* **b :** a related solid-black beetle (*Attagenus piceus*) — called also *black carpet beetle*

carpet bomb *vt* **:** to drop bombs on (an area) so as to cover as if by a carpet ⟨and *carpet bombed* the . . . front with 400 tons —*Newsweek*⟩ — see AREA BOMBING

carpet cut *n* **:** a long narrow slot near the front of a stage into which the edge of a stage carpet is dropped and made secure

carpet dance *n* **:** a dance on the carpet instead of on a prepared floor **:** an informal dance

carpeted *past of* CARPET

carpet grass *n* [so called fr. the carpetlike smoothness of its turf] **1 :** a tropical American pasture grass (*Axonopus affinis*) having broad leaves and flat prostrate stems and being useful for lawns in mild climates and also as a sand binder — called also *Louisiana grass* **2 :** SMUT GRASS

carpeting *n* -s **:** material for carpets; *also* **:** CARPETS

carpet knight *n* [so called fr. the carpet's having been a symbol of luxury and effeminacy] **:** a knight who has spent his time in ease and luxury **:** a man devoted to idleness and pleasure

car·pet·less \-pətləs\ *adj* **:** being without a carpet

carpetmonger \'ˌˌ,ˌˌ\ *n* -s *obs* **:** a frequenter of boudoirs **:** GALLANT ⟨a whole bookful of these quondam ~*s* —Shak.⟩

carpet moth *n* **:** a moth (*Trichophaga tapetzella*) of the family Tineidae whose larva feeds on carpets and woolen goods

carpet pink *n* **:** MOSS CAMPION

carpet rod *n* **:** STAIR ROD

carpets *pl of* CARPET, *pres 3d sing of* CARPET

carpet shark *n* **:** a shark (*Orectolobus barbatus*) of the western Pacific having a flattened body and mottled skin; *also* **:** any related species

carpet shell *n* **:** any of several marine clams (family Veneridae); *esp* **:** the common hard clam (*Protothaca*, or *Paphia, staminea*) of the Pacific coast of the U.S.

carpet slipper *n* [so called fr. its having been originally made of carpet] **:** HOUSE SLIPPER

carpet snake *n* [perh. so called fr. its variegated coloring] **1 :** a rather large Australian constricting snake (*Python variegatus* or *spilotes*) chiefly pale brown with a mottled pattern — see DIAMOND SNAKE **2** *in Tasmania* **:** a pale form of the tiger snake **3 :** a common Indian wolf snake (*Lycodon aulicus*)

carpet strip *n* **:** the molding used between the baseboard and the floor; *also* **:** a piece attached to the floor under a door

carpet sweeper *n* **:** one that sweeps carpets; *specif* **:** a long-handled implement with a revolving brush pushed along on and rotated by wheels on a containing box

carpet tack *n* **:** a short wire tack having a flat disk-shaped head that is used esp. to nail down carpets

carpet viper *n* [perh. so called fr. its variegated coloring] **:** SAW-SCALED VIPER

carpetweed \'ˌˌ,ˌ\ *n* [so called fr. its matted appearance] **:** a prostrate annual weed (*Mollugo verticillata*) of No. America — called also *Indian chickweed;* see AIZOACEAE

carpetweed family *n* **:** AIZOACEAE

carpet wool *n* **:** coarse rough wool of a low grade

car·phi·oph·i·ops \,kärfē'äfē,äps\ [NL, fr. Gk *karphos* dry stalk, stick + NL *ophis* + *ops*] *syn of* CARPHOPHIS

car·pho·lite \'kärfə,līt\ *n* -s [G *karpholith*, fr. Gk *karphos* dry stalk + G *-lith* -lite] **:** a fibrous mineral $MnAl_2Si_2O_6(OH)_4$ consisting of a hydrous aluminum manganese silicate and occurring in straw-yellow tufts (sp. gr. 2.93)

car·phol·o·gy \kär'fäləjē\ *also* **car·pho·lo·gia** \,kärfə'lōj(ē)ə\ *n, pl* **carphologies** *also* **carphologi·as** [NL *carphologia*, fr. LL, twitching of blankets, picking of straws from mud walls, fr. Gk *karphologia*, fr. *karphos* dry stalk, stick + *-logia* gathering — more at -LOGY] **:** an aimless semiconscious plucking at the bedclothes observed in conditions of exhaustion or stupor or in high fevers

car·pho·phis \'kärfəfəs, -(,)fis, kär'fäfəs\ *n, cap* [NL, fr. Gk *karphos* dry stalk, stick + NL *-ophis* — more at HARP] **:** a monotypic genus of small No. American colubrid snakes that are brownish black to glossy black above and pinkish below, have narrow flat heads, and feed chiefly on earthworms — see WORM SNAKE

car·pho·sid·er·ite \,kärfō'sidə,rīt\ *n* -s [G *karphosiderit*, fr. Gk *karphos* dry stalk + *sidēros* iron + G *-it* -ite] **:** a mineral consisting of a basic hydrous iron sulfate occurring in yellow masses and crusts

carpi *pl of* CARPUS

-carpia *pl of* -CARPIUM

-carpic *adj comb form* [prob. fr. NL *-carpicus*, fr. Gk *karpos* fruit + L *-icus* -ic] **:** -CARPOUS ⟨eucarpic⟩

-carpies *pl of* -CARPY

car pincher *n* **:** a mine worker who by means of a pinch bar moves railroad cars under or away from loading chutes (as at a tipple) — called also *spotter*

car·pin·cho *also* **car·pin·choe** \kär'pin(,)chō, 'kärpən,-\ *n* -s [AmerSp *carpincho*, prob. fr. Tupi *caapim* grass + *suú* to bite, eat] **1 :** CAPYBARA **2 a :** the hide of the capybara **b :** a fine soft-grained leather prepared from this hide and resembling pigskin

carping *adj* [ME, fr. pres. part. of *carpen* to carp — more at CARP] **:** likely to carp **:** characterized by frequent ill-natured, querulous, or disgruntled faultfinding ⟨Eliza's nagging and ~ attack —Thomas Wolfe⟩ **syn** see CRITICAL

carp·ing·ly \-lē, -i\ *adv* **:** in a carping manner

car·pi·nus \kär'pīnəs, -ēn-\ *n, cap* [NL, fr. L, hornbeam; akin to Lith *skirpstus* copper beech and prob. to Gk *karpos* fruit — more at HARVEST] **:** a genus of small trees (family Corylaceae) of the northern hemisphere having smooth fluted beechlike bark, straight-veined leaves, fruit that is a nut in the axil of a leaflike lobed bract, and very hard strong wood

car·pi·o·des \kär'pīə,dēz\ *n, cap* [NL, fr. *carpio* (specific epithet of the carp *Cyprinus carpio*, fr. ISV *carp*) + *-odes*] **:** the genus comprising the carpsuckers

car·pi·tis \kär'pīd·əs\ *n* -ES [NL, fr. ²*carp-* + *-itis*] **:** arthritis of the carpal joint in domestic animals

-carpium — see -CARP

carp louse *n* [²*carp* + *louse*] **:** any of the members of the copepod genus *Argulus* (order Branchiura) all of which are parasites on the skin or gills of fish — see FISH LOUSE

carpo- *below* ¦ˌˌ = ¦kärpə *or* -äp- *or* -pō, ˌ'ˌ = kär'pä *or* kȧ'pä\ — see CARP-

car·po·cap·sa \,ˌ'kapsə\ *n, cap* [NL, fr. ¹*carp-* + *-capsa* (modif. of Gk *kapsis* act of gulping down, fr. *kaptein* to gulp down) — more at CAPSIDAE] **:** a genus of moths (family Tortricidae) including the codling moth

car·po·ceph·a·lum \,ˌˌ'sefələm\ *n, pl* **carpocepha·la** \-lə\ [NL, fr. ¹*carp-* + *cephal-* + *-um*] **:** the sporogonial receptacle in certain liverworts (as members of the genus *Marchantia*)

car·po·cra·tian \,kärpə'krāshən\ *n* -s *usu cap* [ML *Carpocratianus*, fr. Gk *Karpokratianos*, fr. *Karpokratēs* Carpocrates, 2d cent. A.D. Alexandrian Gnostic + *-ianos* -ian] **:** a follower of Carpocrates who taught that men can attain to a higher degree of illumination than that of Jesus — compare GNOSTICISM

car·pod·a·cus \ˌ'ˌdəkəs\ *n, cap* [NL, fr. ¹*carp-* + Gk *dakos* biting animal, fr. *daknein* to bite — more at TONGS] **:** a genus of finches including the purple finch and house finch

car·pod·e·tus \ˌ'ˌdəd·əs\ *n, cap* [NL, fr. ¹*carp-* + *-detus* (irreg. fr. Gk *dein* to bind); fr. the fact that the fruit is surrounded by the calyx — more at DIADEM] **:** a genus of shrubs or trees (family Escalloniaceae) with marbled leaves, small fragrant flowers in broad axillary cymes, and black berrylike fruit — see WHITE MAPAU

car·pog·e·nous \ˌ'ˌjənəs\ *or* **car·po·gen·ic** \¦ˌˌ¦jenik\ *adj* [¹*carp-* + *-genous* or *-genic*] **:** producing fruit — used of those cells of the procarp forming the carpogonium of red algae

car·po·gone \'ˌˌ,gōn\ *n* -s [by alter.] **:** CARPOGONIUM

car·po·go·ni·al \¦ˌˌ¦gōnēəl\ *adj* [NL *carpogonium* + E *-al*] **:** of or relating to a carpogonium

car·po·go·ni·um \,ˌˌ'gōnēəm\ *n, pl* **carpogo·nia** \-ēə\ [NL, fr. ¹*carp-* + *-gonium*] **1 a :** the flask-shaped egg-bearing portion of the female reproductive branch in some thallophytes (as the red algae) in which fertilization occurs and which usu. terminates in an elongate receptive trichogyne **b :** PROCARP **2 :** ASCOGONIUM

car·poi·dea \kär'pȯidēə\ *n pl, cap* [NL, fr. ¹*carp-* + *-oidea*] **:** a small class (formerly an order of Cystoidea) of widely distributed Paleozoic echinoderms having a movable tail or stalk, a bilaterally compressed body, and no evident traces of radial symmetry

car·po·lite \'ˌˌ,līt\ *or* **car·po·lith** \-,lith\ *n* -s [prob. fr. NL *carpolithus*, fr. ¹*carp-* + *-lithus* -lite] **:** a fossil fruit, nut, or seed

car·pol·o·gy \ˌ'ˌləjē\ *n* -ES [ISV ¹*carp-* + *-logy*] **:** a branch of plant morphology dealing with the structure of fruit and seeds

¹**car·po·meta·car·pal** \'ˌˌ¦med·ə,kärpəl\ *adj* [²*carp-* + *metacarpal*] **:** relating to a carpus and metacarpus or to the carpometacarpus of birds

²**carpometacarpal** \'ˌˌˌˌ,ˌˌ\ *n* -s [NL *carpometacarpus* + E *-al*] **:** a carpometacarpal bone

car·po·met·a·car·pus \'ˌˌˌˌ,ˌpəs\ *n, pl* **carpometacar·pi** \'ˌˌ,ˌˌ'ˌ,pī\ [NL, fr. ²*carp-* + *metacarpus*] **:** the fused distal carpal and metacarpal bones of birds or the portion of the wing supported by these bones

car pool *n* **:** a joint arrangement by a group of private automobile owners or drivers in which each in turn drives his own car and takes the other passengers; *also* **:** the group entering into such an arrangement

car·po·ped·al spasm \¦ˌˌ¦pedᵊl-, -ēd-\ *n* [ISV *carpopedal* (fr. ²*carp-* + *pedal*) + *spasm*] **:** a spasmodic contraction of the muscles of the hands and feet or esp. of the wrists and ankles in disorders such as alkalosis and tetany

car·poph·a·gous \(')kär'päfəgəs\ *adj* [Gk *karpophagos*, fr. *karp-* ¹carp- + *-phagos* -phagous] **:** feeding on fruits

car·po·phore \'ˌˌ,fō(ə)r\ *n* -s [prob. fr. NL *carpophorum*, fr. ¹*carp-* + *-phorum* -phore] **1 a :** the stalk of a fruiting body in fungi **b :** the entire fruiting body (as in many mushrooms) **2 :** a slender often forked prolongation of a receptacle or pistil or both which develops as the fruit ripens and from which the ripened carpels are suspended (as in members of the genus *Geranium* and in the Umbelliferae)

car·po·phyll *also* **car·po·phyl** \'ˌˌ,fil\ *n* -s [prob. fr. NL *carpophyllum*, fr. ¹*carp-* + *-phyllum* -phyll] **:** CARPEL

car·po·phyte \'ˌˌ,fīt\ *n* -s [¹*carp-* + *-phyte*] **1 :** a thallophyte that forms a sporocarp after fertilization (as the red seaweeds and the ascomycetous fungi) **2 :** PHANEROGAM

car·pop·o·dite \kär'päpə,dīt\ *n* -s [*carp-* + Gk *pod-, pous* foot + E *-ite* — more at FOOT] **:** CARPUS 2 — **car·pop·o·dit·ic** \¦kär,päpə¦did·ik, kär¦p-\ *adj*

carport \'ˌ,ˌ\ *n* **:** an open-sided roofed automobile shelter that is usu. formed by extension of the roof from the side of a building

car·po·sperm \'ˌˌ,spərm\ *n* -s [¹*carp-* + *sperm*] **:** the egg of a red alga or of any alga after fertilization

car·po·spo·ran·gi·al \¦ˌˌspə¦ranjēəl\ *adj* [NL *carposporangium* + E *-al*] **:** of or relating to a carposporangium

car·po·spo·ran·gi·um \,ˌˌˌ'ˌjēəm\ *n, pl* **carposporan·gia** \-jēə\ [NL, fr. ¹*carp-* + *sporangium*] **:** one of the sporangia forming the cystocarp in the red algae and containing carpospores

car·po·spore \'ˌˌ,spō(ə)r\ *n* -s [¹*carp-* + *spore*] **:** a diploid spore of a red alga that is produced terminally by a gonimoblast that germinates to produce the diploid tetrasporic plant — compare TETRASPORE

car·po·spor·ic \¦ˌˌ¦spōrik\ *also* **car·pos·po·rous** \ˌ'ˌspərəs\ *adj* **1 :** of, relating to, or resembling a carpospore **2 :** having carpospores

car·po·stome \'ˌˌ,stōm\ *n* -s [¹*carp-* + *-stome*] **:** the opening in the red algae through which a cystocarp discharges its spores

-car·pous \¦kärpəs, ¦kȧp-\ *adj comb form* [NL *-carpus*, fr. Gk *-karpos*, fr. *karpos* fruit — more at HARVEST] **:** fruited **:** having (such) fruit or (so many) fruits ⟨syncarpous⟩ ⟨monocarpous⟩ — **-car·py** \,kärpē, ,kȧp-, -i\ *n comb form* -ES

car·po·xe·nia \,ˌˌ'zēnēə, -nyə\ *n* -s [NL, fr. ¹*carp-* + *xenia*] **:** the direct effect of pollen on the carpel tissue — compare METAXENIA, XENIA

carps *pl of* CARP, *pres 3d sing of* CARP

-carps *pl of* -CARP

carpsucker \'ˌ,ˌˌ\ *n* [²*carp* + *sucker*] **:** any of several No. American suckers of the family Catostomidae and the genus *Carpiodes* (as *C. carpio*) — compare BUFFALO FISH

car puller *n* **:** a vehicle or mechanical device for moving a freight car short distances

car·pus \'kärpəs, 'kȧp-\ *n, pl* **car·pi** \-,pī,-,pē\ [NL, fr. Gk *karpos* wrist — more at WHARF] **1 a :** the wrist or the part of the forelimb between the antebrachium and the metacarpus **b :** the group of bones supporting the wrist comprising in man a proximal row which contains the navicular, lunatum, triquetrum, and pisiform that articulate with the radius and a distal row which contains the trapezium, trapezoid, capitatum, and hamatum that articulate with the metacarpals, the number being modified in many specialized forelimbs (as those of birds) by disappearance or fusion of certain of the bony elements or by addition of a bone between the two rows — compare CENTRALE **2 :** the fifth segment from the base of a generalized appendage of a crustacean (as one of the walking legs of a lobster)

-car·pus \¦kärpəs, -ȧp-\ *n comb form* [NL, fr. Gk *-karpos* -carpous] **:** plant having (such) fruit — in generic names ⟨Corynocarpus⟩ ⟨Thysanocarpus⟩

carr \'kär\ *n* -s [ME *ker*, of Scand origin; akin to ON *kjarr* underbrush, Sw *kärr* marsh — more at CHARE] **1** *Brit* **:** FEN, MARSH **2** *Brit* **:** an alder grove

carr *abbr* **1** carriage **2** carrier

car·rack *also* **car·ack** *or* **car·ac** \'karək\ *n* -s [ME *carryk, carrake*, fr. MF *caraque*, fr. OSp *carraca*, fr. Ar *qarāqīr*, pl. of *qurqūr* merchant vessel] **:** a large Mediterranean merchant ship sometimes fitted for fighting **:** GALLEON

car·ra·geen *or* **car·ra·gheen** *also* **car·a·geen** \'karə,gēn, ,ˌˌ'ˌ\ *n* -s [fr. *Carragheen*, near Waterford, Ireland] **1 :** a dark purple branching cartilaginous seaweed (*Chondrus crispus*) found on the coasts of northern Europe and North America — compare IRISH MOSS **2 :** CARRAGEENIN

car·ra·gee·nin *or* **car·ra·ghee·nin** \,ˌˌ'ˌnən\ *n* -s [*carrageen* or *carragheen* + *-in*] **:** a colloidal extractive of carrageen and other red algae (as *Gigartina mammillosa*) composed of a mixture of sodium, potassium, calcium, and magnesium salts of an acid sulfate of a galactose-containing polysaccharide and used chiefly as a suspending agent in foods, pharmaceuticals, cosmetics, and industrial liquids, as a clarifying agent for beverages, and in controlling crystal growth in frozen confections — called also *Irish moss extractive*

car·ra·pa·to *or* **car·a·pa·to** \,karə'päd·(,)ü, -(,)ō\ *n* -s [Pg] **:** any of several So. American ticks (genus *Amblyomma*) including pests of man and domestic animals, some being implicated as disease vectors

car·ra·ra marble *also* **carrara** \kə'rärə, -'a-\ *n, usu cap C* [fr. *Carrara* (now part of Apuania), Italy, where it is found] **:** a white statuary marble — **car·ra·ran** \-rən\ *adj, usu cap*

carraway *var of* CARAWAY

car·re·four \¦karə¦fü(ə)r\ *n* -s [MF — more at CARFOUR] **1 :** CROSSROADS ⟨he was not much on maps and drove too fast to read the signs at ~*s* —A.J.Liebling⟩ **2 :** SQUARE, PLAZA ⟨the farmers . . . preferred the open ~ for their transactions —Thomas Hardy⟩

car·rel *also* **car·rell** \'karəl *also* -er-\ *n* -s [alter. of ME *carole* round dance, carol, ring — more at CAROL] **:** a small enclosure or alcove designed for individual study or reading in the stack room of a library — called also *cubicle, stall*

car·rel–da·kin solution \kə'rel/'dākən-, 'karəl- *also* 'kerəl-\ *n, usu cap C&D* **:** Dakin's solution in which sodium bicarbonate replaces the boric acid

carrel–dakin treatment *n, usu cap C&D* [after Alexis *Carrel* †1944 Fr. surgeon and biologist, and Henry Drysdale *Dakin* †1952 Eng. chemist] **:** an antiseptic treatment of wounds in World War I consisting of regular intermittent irrigation through surgically placed rubber tubes to obviate infection in contaminated wounds and to hasten asepsis in suppurating wounds — compare CARREL-DAKIN SOLUTION, DAKIN'S SOLUTION

car·re·ta \kə'red·ə\ *n* -s [Sp, fr. *carro* cart, fr. L *carrus* wheeled vehicle — more at CAR] *Southwest* **:** a two-wheeled cart

car·riage \'karij, -ēj *also* -er-\ *n* -s *often attrib* [ME *cariage*, fr. ONF, fr. *carier* to transport in a vehicle — more at CARRY]

1 : the act of carrying **:** TRANSPORT, CONVEYANCE ⟨the ~ of weapons inside the . . . town —P.A.Rollins⟩ ⟨impassable to any other ~ but a mule —Tobias Smollett⟩ **2 a** *archaic* **:** moral or social behavior **:** DEPORTMENT ⟨her very prudent ~ —Lord Byron⟩ **b :** manner of bearing the body **:** POSTURE ⟨that slender unrigid erectness and the fine ~ of head —Willa Cather⟩ **3** *archaic* **:** the act or manner of conducting measures or projects **:** MANAGEMENT, EXECUTION, ADMINISTRATION ⟨the passage and whole ~ of this action —Shak.⟩ **4 :** the price or expense of carrying **5** *obs* **:** something that is carried **:** BURDEN, LOAD, BAGGAGE **6** *obs* **:** IMPORT, SENSE ⟨missed the whole ~ of the former chapter⟩ **7 :** means of conveyance **:** VEHICLE: **a** *obs* **:** any means of carrying or conveying (as a litter, wheelbarrow, or barge) **b :** a wheeled vehicle for people; *esp* **:** a horse-drawn vehicle designed for private use and for comfort or elegance **c** *Brit* **:** a railway passenger coach **8 :** a wheeled support carrying a burden ⟨a gun ~⟩ ⟨a log ~ in a sawmill⟩ **9 :** a movable part of a machine for supporting or carrying some other movable object or part ⟨the ~ on a lathe⟩ ⟨a typewriter ~⟩ **10 a :** a frame in or on which something is carried or supported **b :** the wheeled supporting framework of a carriage or other vehicle **:** RUNNING GEAR **11** *obs* **:** a hanger for a sword **12 :** the timber or iron joist supporting a wooden staircase **13 :** CHAIR 5a

car·riage·a·ble \-jəbəl\ *adj* **1 :** PORTABLE **2 :** passable by carriages

carriage band *n* **:** DRAWBAND

carriage bolt *n* **:** a square-necked threaded bolt with a snaphead

carriage boot *n* **1 :** a fur-trimmed boot for winter wear made usu. of fabric with a fur or felt lining **2 :** ³BOOT 5a

carriage bow *n* **:** a shooting bow made in jointed sections for convenience in carrying

carriage bolt

carriage dog *n* **:** COACH DOG

carriage folk *n pl* **:** people wealthy enough to keep carriages

carriage forward *adv, Brit* **:** with charges to be paid on delivery **:** COLLECT ⟨the parcels were sent *carriage forward*⟩

carriage guard *n* **:** CRAMP IRON 2

carriage horse *n* **:** a horse esp. adapted for carriage use by appearance and stylish action

carriage piece *n* **:** ROUGHSTRING

carriage porch *n* [prob. intended as trans. of F *porte-cochère*] **:** a roofed structure that extends from the entrance of a building over an adjacent driveway and that shelters callers as they get in or out of their vehicles

carriage rail *n* **:** a track along which the carriage of a typewriter moves by means of ball or roller bearings

carriage return *n* **:** LINE SPACE LEVER

carriage rod *n* **:** a round rod along which the carriage of a typewriter moves

carriage starter *n* **:** one that directs the flow of vehicles taking on passengers at the curbside — compare DOORMAN

carriage trade *n* **1 :** trade from the well-to-do or the wealthy **2 :** people of wealth and social position **:** upper-class people ⟨a sophisticated, elegantly equipped shop for the *carriage trade* —Welden Reynolds⟩

carriageway \'==,=\ *n, Brit* **:** a roadway used by vehicular traffic **:** HIGHWAY ⟨walk on the right of the ~ —*English Highway Code*⟩; *specif* **:** LANE 3c ⟨these roads are 150 feet wide with two 22-foot ~*s* —S.P.B.Mais⟩

car·rick bend \'karik-\ *n* [*carrick* prob. fr. obs. E *carrick* carrack, fr. ME *carryk* — more at CARRACK] **:** a knot used to join the ends of two large ropes or hawsers

carrick bitts *n pl* **:** heavy upright pieces of timber supporting each end of the windlass of a ship

carrick bend

car·rick·ma·cross \'karikmə,krȯs\ *or* **carrickmacross lace** *n, usu cap C* [fr. *Carrickmacross*, Ireland, where it is made] **:** a guipure or appliqué lace of Irish origin usu. having floral or foliage designs

carried *adj* [fr. past part. of *carry*] *dial Brit* **:** RAPT, ABSTRACTED, LIGHT-HEADED, VAIN

car·ri·er \'karēə(r) *also* 'ker-\ *n* -s [ME *cariere*, fr. *carien* to carry + *-ere* -er] **1 :** one that carries **:** BEARER, MESSENGER ⟨the air is but . . . a ~ of the sounds —Francis Bacon⟩ **2 a :** an individual, partnership, corporation, or any organization engaged in transporting passengers or goods for hire by land, water, or air; *specif* **:** COMMON CARRIER **b :** a transportation line holding a government contract for carrying mail between post offices **c :** a postal employee who delivers or collects mail ⟨a rural ~⟩ **d :** a worker who transfers materials, equipment, or products from one part of an establishment to another — called also *distributor* **e :** one that delivers newspapers to subscribers on a specified route — called also *newsboy* **3 :** CARRIER PIGEON **4 :** a device for holding something while it is carried: as **a :** a conduit or drain for conveying liquids or gases **b :** a receptacle made of wood, metal, or paperboard used to ship small containers (as baskets for fruits and vegetables) — compare CRATE **c :** a frame or a box attached to a vehicle (as a bicycle or automobile) for carrying objects securely or conveniently **d :** a device or machine part that carries or drives another part: as (1) **:** CONVEYER 2a (2) **:** DOG 3d **e** *railroading* (1) **:** a grooved roller that works in a stand and that supports and permits the longitudinal movement of a signal pipeline (2) **:** a device for supporting and guiding a wire line used in signaling **5 a :** a boat that takes the catch from a fishing fleet to market **b :** AIRCRAFT CARRIER **6** *usu cap* **a :** an Athapaskan people of south-central British Columbia **b :** a member of such people **7** *usu cap* **:** the language of the Carrier people **8 a :** a person, animal, or plant that harbors and disseminates the specific microorganism or other agent causing an infectious disease from which it has recovered or to which it is immune and that may therefore become a spreader of a disease ⟨~ of typhoid fever⟩ ⟨~ of plant viruses⟩ — compare RESERVOIR, VECTOR **b :** an individual possessing a specified gene and capable of transmitting it to offspring but not of showing its typical expression; *esp* **:** one that is heterozygous for a recessive factor **9 :** a usu. inactive substance used in association with an active substance esp. for aiding in the application of the active substance: as **a :** a support for a catalyst **b :** an insoluble substance used in the preparation of certain pigments as a base upon which to precipitate the coloring matter **c :** a dyeing assistant that penetrates the textile fibers and aids diffusion and absorption of the dye **d :** a chemical element (as a stable isotope) or a compound associated with a radioactive element (as for giving a ponderable quantity for use in reactions) **e :** a vehicle serving esp. as a diluent (as for an insecticide or a drug) **10 a :** a substance (as a catalyst) by whose agency some element or group is transferred from one compound to another ⟨iron is a ~ of oxygen⟩ **b :** a fertilizer or fertilizer component considered as a source of a plant nutrient ⟨ammonium nitrate is a nitrogen ~⟩ **11 :** CARRIER'S STAMP **12 a :** a spool or bobbin holder in a braiding machine **b :** a yarn feeder in a machine knitting full-fashioned hosiery **13** *or* **carrier current** *or* **carrier wave :** an electric wave or alternating current whose modulations are used as signals in radio, television, telephonic, or telegraphic transmission **14 :** an organization acting as an underwriter or insurer

carrier pigeon *n* **1 :** a pigeon used to carry messages; *specif* **:** one of a fancy chiefly English breed of pigeons of large size having long wings and body, much bare skin about the eyes, and a greatly developed carunculated cere **2 :** HOMING PIGEON

carrier shell *n* **:** the carrier snail or its shell

carrier's lien *n* **:** a common-law lien for freight conferring the right to retain the property only until the claim is paid

carrier snail *n* **:** a marine snail of the genus *Xenophora*

carrier's option *n* **:** the option allowed to a carrier of fixing freight charges on the basis of either the weight of the goods or the space occupied

carrier's stamp *n* **:** a stamp issued in the U.S. from 1842 to 1861 by a government or private carrier or by a postmaster to pay for delivery of mail from post office to addressee, government service being limited to carriage between post offices — compare POSTMASTER'S STAMP

carrier suppression *n* **:** a method of signal transmission in which the power associated essentially with the carrier frequency is not transmitted

carries *pres 3d sing of* CARRY, *pl of* CARRY

carriole *var of* CARIOLE

car·ri·on \'karēən *also* -er-\ *n* -s *often attrib* [ME *carion, caroine*, fr. AF *caroine*, fr. (assumed) VL *caronia*, irreg. fr. L *carn-, caro* flesh — more at CARNAL] **1** *obs* **:** a dead body **:** CARCASS, CORPSE ⟨croaking like so many ravens about a ~ —Charles Johnstone⟩ **2 :** the dead and putrefying flesh of an animal **:** flesh that is unfit for food ⟨we killed a tiger and a wolf; but God be thanked, we were not so reduced as to eat ~ —Daniel Defoe⟩ **3 a :** a scavenging animal ⟨enemy dead were left to rot or be eaten by ~⟩ **b :** a worthless or noxious animal **:** VERMIN **4 :** something that is corrupt, vile, or rotten ⟨Roman fashionable society hated Caesar, and any ~ was welcome to them which would taint his reputation —J.A.Froude⟩

carrion beetle *n* **:** any of numerous beetles of the genera *Necrophorus* and *Silpha* (family Silphidae) that feed chiefly on dead animals though a few (as *S. bituberosa*) attack economic plants — see SPINACH CARRION BEETLE

carrion buzzard *n* **:** an American vulture of the family Cathartidae

carrion crow *n* **:** the common European black crow (*Corvus corone*)

carrion flower *n* **1 :** an American catbrier (*Smilax herbacea*) whose flowers smell like carrion **2 :** a plant of the genus *Stapelia*

carrion fly *n* **:** a fly that lays its eggs in decaying flesh; *specif* **:** a widespread and destructive blowfly (*Phormia terrae-novae*)

carrion fungus *n* **:** STINKHORN

carrion hawk *n* **:** CARACARA

carrion poisoning *n, Austral* **:** botulism of sheep

car·ri·on's disease \'karē¦ōnz-\ *n, usu cap C* [after Daniel A. *Carrión* †ab1886 Peruvian medical student, who voluntarily contracted the disease and died from it] **:** BARTONELLOSIS

car·ritch \'karich, -ij\ *n* -ES [back-formation fr. *carritches*, taken as pl., alter. of ¹*catechise*] *Scot* **:** CATECHISM — often used in pl. but sing. in constr.

car·ri·witch·et \,karə'wichət, '==,==\ *or* **car·witch·et** \kär-'w-, '=,==\ *n* -s [origin unknown] **:** a hoaxing or riddling question

car·ri·zo \kə'rē(,)zō, -(,)sō\ *n* -s [Sp, irreg. fr. L *caric-, carex* reed grass, sedge — more at CAREX] **:** a reed grass of the genus *Phragmites*

car·roc·cio \kə'rō(,)chō, -ōchē,ō\ *n, pl* **carroc·ci** \-ō(,)chē\ [It — more at CAROCHE] **:** a large wheeled vehicle bearing a standard and used in medieval times esp. by Italian free cities to serve as a rallying point for an army in battle

car·roll·ite \'karə,līt\ *n* -s [*Carroll* co., Maryland, its locality + E *-ite*] **:** a mineral $CuCo_2S_4$ consisting of a light steel-gray copper cobalt sulfide

carrom *var of* CAROM

car·ro·ma·ta \,karə'mäd·ə\ *n* -s [PhilSp, alter. of Sp *carromato* horse-drawn covered cart, fr. It *carromatto* low 4-wheeled cart without sides, fr. *carro* cart, vehicle, (fr. L *carrus*) + *matto* mad, crazy, fr. L *mattus* stupid, drunk — more at CAR, MAT] *Philippines* **:** a light 2-wheeled boxlike passenger vehicle usu. drawn by a single native pony

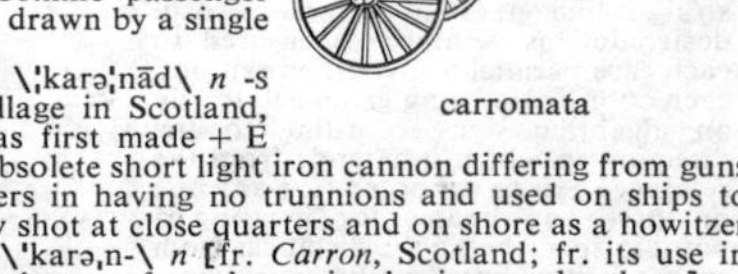

carromata

car·ron·ade \¦karə¦nād\ *n* -s [*Carron*, village in Scotland, where it was first made + E *-ade*] **:** an obsolete short light iron cannon differing from guns and howitzers in having no trunnions and used on ships to throw heavy shot at close quarters and on shore as a howitzer

car·ron oil \'karə,n-\ *n* [fr. *Carron*, Scotland; fr. its use in treating the burns of workmen in the ironworks there] **:** a lotion of equal parts of linseed oil and limewater formerly applied to burns and scalds — called also *lime liniment*

car·ros·se·rie \kärōsrē\ *n, pl* **carrosseries** \-rē(z)\ [F, fr. *carrosse* carriage (fr. It *carrozza*, fr. *carro* cart, vehicle, fr. L *carrus*) + *-erie* -ery — more at CAR] **:** the carriage body of an automobile — compare CHASSIS

¹car·rot \'karət *also* -er, *usu* -əd·+V\ *n* -s [MF *carotte*, fr. LL *carota*, modif. of Gk *karōton*; prob. akin to Gk *kara* head — more at CEREBRAL] **1 a :** a biennial plant (*Daucus carota*) having a yellow or orange-red tapering root that is used as a vegetable **b :** the root of this plant **2 :** something felt to resemble a carrot in shape or color: **a :** a spindle-shaped bundle of rolled and twisted tobacco leaves **b :** a red-haired person **3 :** a chemical agent used in producing hatter's felt from fur **4** [so called fr. the traditional method of urging a donkey on by holding a carrot in front of him] **:** a promised often illusory reward or advantage used esp. as a political enticement ⟨failed to offer the community either the ~ of private enterprise or the stick of compulsion —D.B.Copland⟩

²carrot \"\ *vt* -ED/-ING/-S [so called fr. the color of fur so treated] **:** to treat (fur) with a chemical agent (as a solution of mercuric nitrate) to improve the felting property — **car·rot·er** \-əd·ə(r)\ *n* -s

carrot aphid *n* **:** an aphid (*Cavariella aegopodii*) of Australia and Tasmania that is highly destructive to carrots, parsnips, and celery

carrot beetle *n* **:** a large reddish or dark brown beetle (*Ligyrus gibbosus*) of the family Scarabaeidae that in the adult stage injures carrots by attacking the roots

carrotene *or* **carrotin** *var of* CAROTENE

carrot family *n* **:** UMBELLIFERAE

carrot oil *or* **carrot-seed oil** *n* **:** either of two oils obtained from seeds of the carrot: **a :** a light-yellow essential oil having a spicy odor and used in liqueurs, flavors, and perfumes **b :** a golden yellow fatty oil that is rich in vitamin A and that is used in coloring butter and margarine

carrot red *n* **1 :** the color of the carrot **:** a moderate to strong orange that is lighter than Mars yellow and redder and darker than zinc orange or sunburst **2 :** a moderate reddish orange that is yellower and duller than crab apple or flamingo

carrot rust fly *also* **carrot fly** *n* **:** a small two-winged fly (*Psila rosae*) whose larva burrows in the roots of the carrot

carrot soft rot *n* **:** a soft rot of carrots caused by a bacterium (*Erwinia carotovora*)

carrottop \'==,=\ *n, slang* **:** a red-haired person

carrotweed \'==,=\ *n* [so called fr. the resemblance of the leaves to those of the carrot] **:** a ragweed (*Ambrosia elatior*)

carrotwood \'==,=\ *n* [so called fr. the color of the fruit] **:** a wood derived from an Australian tree (*Blighia anacardioides*) of the family Sapindaceae having compound leaves and white flowers in axillary racemes

car·roty \-əd·ē, -ətē, -i\ *adj, sometimes* -ER/-EST **1 :** resembling carrots in color ⟨~ hair⟩ **2 :** having hair the color of carrots

car·rou·sel *or* **car·ou·sel** \,karə'sel, '==,=\ *also* -er- *or* -zel\ *n* -s [F *carrousel*, fr. It *carosello* tourney in which the contestants threw balls of clay at each other, prob. fr. It dial. (Neapolitan) *carusello* ball of clay, fr. *caruso* shorn head, boy] **1 a :** a tournament in which troops of horsemen execute various evolutions **b :** a riding exhibition performed to music in dancelike patterns by a group on horseback **2 a :** MERRY-GO-ROUND **b :** a conveyer (as for assembly-line work) on which objects are placed and carried around a complete circuit on a horizontal plane

carrow *n* -s [IrGael *cearrbhach*; akin to ScGael *cearrach* gambler, dexterous] *Irish* **:** an itinerant gambler

carr-price reaction \'kär'prīs-\ *n, usu cap C&P* [fr. the names *Carr & Price*] **:** a reaction of antimony trichloride and vitamin A in chloroform solution that gives a blue color and is used for the identification and assay of vitamin A

¹car·ry \'karē, -i *also* -er-\ *vb* -ED/-ING/-ES [ME *carien*, fr. ONF *carier* to transport in a vehicle, fr. *car* vehicle, fr. L *carrus* — more at CAR] *vt* **1 :** to move while supporting (as in a vehicle or in one's hands or arms) **:** move an appreciable distance without dragging **:** sustain as a burden or load and bring along to another place ⟨gas, oil, water, and food [are] available at desert hamlets, but extra supplies should be *carried* —*Amer. Guide Series: Calif.*⟩ ⟨her legs refused to ~ her further —Ellen Glasgow⟩ **2 :** CONVEY ⟨~ the news⟩ ⟨~ a message⟩ **:** TAKE ⟨*carried* his complaint to the president⟩ **3** *chiefly dial* **:** CONDUCT, ESCORT, LEAD, GUIDE ⟨he *carried* her to the party⟩ ⟨~ the cow through the gate⟩ **4 :** to lead along or influence by mental or emotional appeal **:** MOVE, SWAY ⟨~ an audience with one⟩ **5 :** to get possession or control of (as in a contest or by effort or force) **:** WIN, CAPTURE ⟨~ a town by storm⟩ ⟨~ off the prize⟩ **6 :** to transfer from one place (as a book or column) to another ⟨~ an account to the ledger⟩ ⟨~ a number in adding⟩ **7 :** CHANNEL, CONDUCT **:** contain and direct the course of ⟨the canal *carries* the water⟩ ⟨the drain *carries* sewage⟩ **8 a :** to hold, wear, or have upon one's person ⟨he *carries* a watch⟩ **b :** to be burdened or ladened with **:** bear upon or within one ⟨~ an unborn child⟩ **9 :** to hold or contain without apparent effort or discomposure ⟨he knows how to ~ his liquor⟩ **10 :** to have as a mark, attribute, or property ⟨~ a scar⟩ **:** IMPLY, INVOLVE ⟨the crime *carried* a heavy penalty⟩ **11 :** to hold (the body or some part of it) as if well-supported ⟨he *carries* his head high⟩ **12 :** to behave (oneself) in a specified manner **:** DEMEAN ⟨~ himself proudly⟩ **13 :** to sustain the weight or burden of **:** BEAR ⟨pillars ~ an arch⟩ **14 :** to bear as a crop **:** SUPPORT, MAINTAIN ⟨~ livestock⟩ — usu. used of land **15 a :** to sing with reasonable correctness of pitch ⟨he can ~ a tune⟩ **b :** SING, PLAY ⟨only two men to ~ the violins⟩ ⟨he *carried* the tenor⟩ **16 a :** to keep in stock **:** maintain on hand for sale ⟨a department store *carries* hardware⟩ **b :** to have or maintain on a list or record ⟨~ a person on a payroll⟩ **17 :** to maintain and cause to continue through financial support or personal effort ⟨he has *carried* the magazine single-handedly⟩ **18 :** to extend, prolong, or continue in space, time, or degree ⟨~ the chimney through the roof⟩ ⟨~ the war into Africa⟩ ⟨~ a principle too far⟩ **19 a :** to gain victory for (a principle or a candidate); *esp* **:** to secure the adoption or passage of (a motion or bill) **b :** to succeed in (an election) **:** win a majority of votes in (as a legislative body or a state) ⟨the bill *carried* the Senate⟩ **20** *archaic* **:** MANAGE, CONDUCT, PROSECUTE **21 :** PUBLISH ⟨newspapers ~ weather reports⟩ **:** BROADCAST ⟨the committee's proceedings were *carried* on a network⟩ **22 a :** to bear the charges (as interest or insurance) of holding or having (as stocks or merchandise) from one time to another ⟨a packing house *carries* meat for future export⟩ **b** (1) **:** to keep on one's books as a debtor **:** await payment by ⟨a merchant *carries* a customer⟩ (2) **:** to keep on one's books as a debt ⟨~ an account⟩ **c :** to hold (issues of new securities) in anticipation of a rise in price **23** *hunting* **a :** to keep and follow ⟨the dog could not ~ the scent⟩ **b :** SUPPORT ⟨this land will ~ a scent⟩ **24 :** to hold (the staff of a color or a guidon) at the carry **25 :** to hoist and maintain (a sail) in use ⟨the ship *carried* too much sail⟩ **26 :** to cover (a distance) or pass (an object) at a single stroke in golf ⟨his drive *carried* the bunker⟩ **27 a :** to propel and control (a puck) along the playing surface with a hockey stick **:** DRIBBLE **b** *basketball* **:** ²PALM c **28 a** *of a student* **:** to be enrolled in (as a course) ⟨~ both French and Spanish this semester⟩ **b** *of a teacher* **:** TEACH ⟨~ a class⟩ ⟨no instructor will be asked to ~ more than three sections of freshman English⟩ **29 a :** to allow (an opponent) to make a good showing by lessening one's opposition **b :** to perform with sufficient ability to make up for the poor performance of (a partner or teammate) ~ *vi* **1 :** to act as a bearer **:** convey something — often used in the phrase *fetch and carry* **2 a :** to reach or penetrate to a distance **:** sustain flight ⟨voices ~ well over water⟩ ⟨a golf drive will not ~ against the wind⟩ **b :** to project itself to a distance with full effect — usu. used of a work of art **c :** to convey itself to a reader or audience **:** get across — usu. used of a literary or dramatic work **3 :** to undergo or admit of carriage in a specified way ⟨a load that *carries* easily⟩ **4** *of a horse* **:** to hold head and neck properly esp. when in action **5** *hunting* **a** (1) *of a running animal* **:** to collect mud on the feet ⟨a hare *carries* on wet plowland⟩ (2) *of soft ground* **:** to stick to the feet of a running animal **b** *of a hunting dog* **:** to keep and follow the scent **6** *falconry* **:** to fly away with the quarry **7** *of a goalkeeper* **:** to take more than the legal number of steps while in possession of the soccer ball **8 :** to win adoption (as in a legislative body) ⟨the motion *carried* by a vote of 71 to 25⟩

syn BEAR, CONVEY, TRANSPORT, TRANSMIT: CARRY indicates moving to a location some distance away while supporting or maintaining off the ground. Orig. indicating movement by car or cart, it is a natural word to use in ref. to cargoes and loads on trucks, wagons, planes, ships, or even beasts of burden. It has spread widely from its original meaning and may be substituted in most situations for the following words. BEAR in this sense may more strongly suggest maintaining or holding aloft the weight involved, more incidentally the fact of its being moved. It may also suggest some special kind of carrying or carriage, for instance, one attended by ceremony ⟨over his head was *borne* a rich canopy —Samuel Johnson⟩ ⟨two boats were lowered; one . . . *bore* the captain —B.N.Cardozo⟩ CONVEY may be used of passage or carriage in which the nature of the sustaining and moving agency is less significant, noteworthy, definite, or individual ⟨irrigation water *conveyed* from rivers⟩ ⟨he looked white and tired and listless, even his bristling hair and mustache *conveyed* his depression —H.G.Wells⟩ TRANSPORT refers to carriage in bulk or number over an appreciable distance and, typically, by a customary or usual carrier agency ⟨how many merchants and carriers . . . must have been employed in *transporting* the materials from some of those workmen to others who often live in a very distant part of the country —Adam Smith⟩ TRANSPORT is also used to signify the carrying of persons into very distant or strange spheres, esp. by unusual instrumentalities ⟨the astrophysicist with the aid of his spectroscope *transports* himself through millions of miles to worlds incredibly terrifying and beautiful —Waldemar Kaempffert⟩ TRANSMIT is sometimes used as a synonym for *send* or *ship* in reference to tangible things ⟨*transmit* baggage⟩ but it is now much more commonly used in reference to agencies that impart or communicate more intangible items ⟨the typewriter has become the direct means of *transmitting* even poetry to the page —T.S.Eliot⟩ ⟨such a youth has come into an inheritance of illusions as important and perhaps as valuable as anything else which his ancestors have *transmitted* to him —J.W.Krutch⟩

— **carry a torch** *or* **carry the torch 1 :** CRUSADE **2 :** to be in love esp. without success or return **:** cherish a longing or a devotion ⟨she still *carries a torch* for him even though their engagement is broken⟩ — **carry one's bat** *of a cricket batsman* **:** to be not out at the close of play or of one's side's innings — **carry the ball :** to perform or assume the chief role **:** bear the major portion of work or responsibility — **carry the banner :** to be destitute

²carry \"\ *n* -ES **1 :** a vehicle, receptacle, or contrivance used for carrying; *specif, dial Brit* **:** a 2-wheeled barrow **2 :** the range of a gun or projectile or of a struck or thrown ball **:** carrying power **3** *chiefly Scot* **a :** the drift of the clouds **b :** CLOUDS, SKY **4 a :** the act or method of carrying ⟨fireman's ~⟩ ⟨one-hand ~⟩ **b :** a portage esp. between two bodies of navigable water **5 :** the position assumed by a color bearer or guidon bearer with color staff or guidon in position for marching **6 :** ⁴RUSH 4 **7 :** the holding of securities with borrowed money esp. to secure a higher rate of return than the interest paid for the money borrowed

car·ry·all \'karē,ȯl *also* -er-\ *n* -s [by folk etymology fr. F *carriole* — more at CARIOLE] **1 a :** a light covered carriage having four wheels and seats for four or more persons and usu. drawn by one horse **b :** a passenger automobile having a closed body and two facing seats along the sides **2** [¹*carry* + *all*] **:** a capacious bag or case **3 :** a carrier with a scraperlike self-loading device drawn by a tractor, pushed by a bulldozer, or self-propelled and used esp. for hauling earth and crushed rock

carry away *vt* **1 :** to cause the death of **:** carry off **2 :** to break off **:** DEMOLISH ⟨the gale *carried away* the foremast⟩ **3 :** to drive or draw out of the control of reason and judgment (as by passion, flattery, or charm) ⟨the girl was *carried away* by her pity —Winston Churchill⟩ ~ *vi* **1 :** to break off (as of a mast) **:** become swept away ⟨the bridge *carried away*⟩ **2 :** to lose rigging ⟨the ship *carried away* in the storm⟩

carry back *vt* **:** to deduct (a loss or an unused credit) from taxable income of a prior period ⟨*carry back* an unused excess-profits-tax credit⟩

carry-back \'==,=\ *n* -s **:** a loss sustained or a portion of a credit not used in a given period that may be deducted from taxable income of a prior period ⟨showed operating losses in 1946 despite heavy tax *carry-backs* allowed by the government —*Newsweek*⟩

carry bag *n* **:** a deep bag made typically of heavy paper, having handles, and used for carrying small purchases
carry forward *vt* **1 :** to transfer (an amount) to the succeeding column, page, or book relating to the same account **2 :** to carry over (sense 2)
carry–forward \ˈ==,==\ *n* -s **1 :** CARRY-OVER **2** *Brit* **:** the accumulated undivided profits of a corporation after provision has been made for reserves and dividends
carrying *pres part of* CARRY
carrying capacity *n* **:** the population (as of one species of animal) that a given area (as of water or pasture) will support without undergoing deterioration ⟨when deer herds are allowed to exceed the *carrying capacity*, permanent damage to woodland results⟩ ⟨a *carrying capacity* of one sheep per acre⟩ — compare BIOTIC POTENTIAL 1
carrying charge *n* **1 :** expense incident to the continued ownership or use of property (as taxes on real estate); *specif* **:** a charge made for carrying a debtor (as interest charged on a margin account with a broker) **2 :** a charge added to the price of merchandise sold on the installment plan
carrying–on \ˈ===ˈ=\ *n, pl* **carryings–on :** foolish, excited, or improper behavior; *also* **:** an instance of such behavior ⟨scandalous *carryings-on*⟩
carrying place *n* **:** PORTAGE 4b
carrying trade *n* **:** trade or commerce consisting in transporting goods (as from one country to another)
carrying value *n* **:** BOOK VALUE
carry–log \ˈ==,=\ *n* [¹*carry* + *log*] **:** a high-wheeled cart for hauling logs suspended from the axle
carry off *vt* **1 :** to cause the death of ⟨the plague *carried off* thousands⟩ **2 :** to perform easily or successfully **3 :** to make acceptable ⟨her charm *carried off* her husband's fiery temper⟩ **4 :** to brave out **:** face out
carry on *vt* **:** CONDUCT, MANAGE ⟨*carry on* the new enterprise⟩ ~ *vi* **1 :** to behave in a foolish, excited, or improper manner: as **a :** to frolic noisily or destructively **b :** to rage in anger or in grief **c :** to act indiscreetly or immorally **2 :** to continue one's course or activity; *esp* **:** to persevere unfalteringly in spite of hindrance or discouragement **3 :** to carry sail up to or beyond the limits of prudence **:** spread the utmost extent of canvas possible
carry out *vt* **1 :** to put into execution **2 :** to bring to a successful issue **3 :** to continue to an end or stopping point
carry over *vt* **1 a :** to hold over (as goods) for another season **b :** to transfer (an amount) to the succeeding column, page, or book relating to the same account **c** *on the London stock exchange* **:** to carry (a customer) until the next settlement **:** extend (the date of settlement for stock) until the end of the next account — compare CONTANGO **2 :** to deduct (a loss or an unused credit) from taxable income of a subsequent period ~ *vi* **:** to persist from one stage to another or from one sphere of activity to another
carry–over \ˈ==,==\ *n* -s **1 :** the act or process of carrying over **2 :** something that is carried over
carrytale \ˈ==,=\ *n* **:** GOSSIP, TALEBEARER
carry through *vt* **:** to carry out ~ *vi* **1 :** to bring to completion or carry out a task or obligation ⟨they *carried through* on the agreement⟩ **2 :** PERSIST, SURVIVE ⟨feelings that *carry through* to the present⟩
cars *pl of* CAR
carse \ˈkärs\ *n* -s [ME *cars, kerss*, perh. fr. *kerres*, pl. of *ker* carr] *Scot* **:** low fertile land usu. along a river
car service *n* **1 :** the work performed by a railroad car **2 :** the supply of cars and subsidiary equipment by one railroad carrier to another or to a shipper
carshop \ˈ=,=\ *n* **:** a group of workshops for the construction, maintenance, and repair of railroad equipment (as rolling stock) — usu. used in pl.
carshuni *usu cap, var of* KARSHUNI
carsick \ˈ=,=\ *adj* **:** affected with car sickness
car sickness *n* **:** motion sickness experienced when riding in vehicles, esp. automobiles
car·son city \ˌkärsᵊnˈ==\ *adj, usu cap both Cs* [fr. *Carson City*, city in Nevada] **:** of or from Carson City, the capital of Nevada ⟨a *Carson City* street⟩ **:** of the kind or style prevalent in Carson City
car·stone \ˈkär,stōn\ *n* [by folk etymology fr. *quernstone*] **:** a firmly cemented ferruginous sandstone found in the British isles; *esp* **:** one of Cretaceous age used as a building stone
¹**cart** \ˈkärt, ˈkȧt, *usu* -d·+V\ *n* -s [ME *carte, cart*, prob. fr. ON *kartr*; akin to OE *cræt* cart, OHG *kranz* wreath, Lith *grandis* hoop, OE *cradol* cradle — more at CRADLE] **1** *obs* **:** CHARIOT **2 :** a heavy 2-wheeled vehicle without springs used for the ordinary purposes of farming or for transporting freight — compare WAGON **3 :** any lightweight 2-wheeled vehicle drawn by a horse, pony, or dog: as **a :** a light vehicle for delivery (as by bakers or butchers) **b :** an open 2-wheeled pleasure carriage **c :** SULKY **4 :** any small wheeled vehicle (as for groceries, golf clubs, or tea service) — **cart before the horse :** two things in illogical, improper, or unnatural order ⟨his emphasis on method at the expense of content puts the *cart before the horse*⟩ — **in the cart** *adv (or adj), slang Brit* **:** in an embarrassing position (as from deception or defeat)

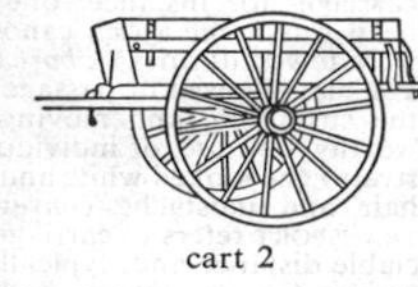
cart 2

²**cart** \"\ *vb* -ED/-ING/-S [ME *carten*, fr. *cart*, n.] *vt* **1 :** to carry or convey in or as if in a cart ⟨buses to ~ the kids to and from school —L.S.Gannett⟩; *specif, archaic* **:** to carry publicly in or drag behind a cart as a punishment ⟨suspected, tried, condemned, and ~*ed* in a day —George Crabbe⟩ **2 :** to take or drag (a person) away without ceremony or by force — usu. used with *off* ⟨they ~*ed* him off to jail⟩ ~ *vi* **:** to drive a cart esp. in transporting freight **:** follow the business of a carter
cart·age \ˈkärd·ij, ˈkȧ|, |tij, -ēj\ *n* -s [ME, fr. *cart* or *carten* + *-age*] **1 :** the act of carrying by cart or truck usu. within a city **:** HAULING **2 :** the rate charged for carting or hauling
car·ta·ge·na \ˌkärd·əˈjēnə, -ˈgänə, -ˈhänə\ *adj, usu cap* [fr. *Cartagena*, city in Spain] **1 :** of or from the city of Cartagena, Spain **:** of the kind or style prevalent in Cartagena, Spain **2 :** of or from the city of Cartagena, Colombia **:** of the kind or style prevalent in Cartagena, Colombia
cartagena bark *n, usu cap C* [fr. *Cartagena*, seaport in Colombia] **:** a cinchona bark derived from a Colombian tree (*Cinchona lancifolia*)
cartagena ipecac *n, usu cap C* [fr. *Cartagena*, seaport in Colombia where it is exported] **:** ipecac derived from a Brazilian tree (*Cephaelis acuminata*) — called also *Panama ipecac*
cart–driver \ˈ=,==\ *n* **:** a widely distributed active yellowish burrowing shore crab (*Ocypode gaudichaudii*) of the western coast of Central and So. America
carte *n* -s [ME, charter, playing card, fr. MF — more at CARD] **1** \ˈkärt, -e-\ *Scot* **a :** PLAYING CARD **b :** a game of cards — usu. used in pl. **2** *obs* **:** CHART, MAP ⟨the distance . . . when measured on the ~ does not exceed 90 miles —Tobias Smollett⟩
carte blanche \ˈkärtˈbläⁿsh, ˈkȧt-, -änch\ *n, pl* **cartes blanches** \-t...sh(əz), -ch(əz)\ [F] **1 :** a blank document signed in advance by one party to an agreement and given to the other with permission to fill in what conditions he pleases **2 :** full discretionary power **:** unlimited delegated authority ⟨the architect was given *carte blanche* to build, landscape, and furnish the house⟩ **3 :** a hand of cards (as in piquet) containing no king, queen, or jack but having special value
carted *adj, of a deer* **:** brought to the scene of the hunt and released in order to be tracked down but not killed
carte d'en·trée \ˈkärt,däⁿˈtrā, ˈkȧt-, -dän-\ *n, pl* **cartes d'entrée** \"\ [F] **:** card of admission **:** TICKET
carte de vi·site \ˌ=dəviˈzēt, -vē-\ *n, pl* **cartes de visite** \"\ [F] **1 :** VISITING CARD **2 :** a close-trimmed portrait photograph approximately 2¼x3¾ in. intended as a substitute for a visiting card
carte du jour \-dəˈzhü(ə)r, -üə\ *n, pl* **cartes du jour** \"\ [F, lit., the day's menu] **:** MENU
car·tel \(ˈ)kärˈtel, -ȧˈt-\ *n* -s [MF, fr. OIt *cartello* letter of defiance, placard, fr. *carta* card, leaf of paper — more at CARD] **1 :** a letter of defiance or challenge (as to single combat) **2 a :** a written agreement between belligerent nations esp. for the treatment and exchange of prisoners and the regulation of nonbelligerent relations **b :** an exchange of prisoners **c :** CARTEL SHIP **3 :** a card or paper bearing writing or printing ⟨he ordered a ~ with some Greek verses —Horace Walpole⟩ **4** [G *kartell*, lit., written agreement between opposing belligerents, fr. F *cartel*, lit., letter of defiance] **:** a voluntary often international combination of independent private enterprises supplying like commodities or services that agree to limit their competitive activities (as by allocating customers or markets, regulating quantity or quality of output, pooling returns or profits, fixing prices or terms of sale, exchanging techniques, trademarks, or patents, or by other methods of controlling production, price, or distribution) **5** [G & F; G *kartell*, fr. F *cartel*] **:** a combination of or an agreement between political groups for common action — compare BLOC
cartel clock \ˈ=,=ˈ=\ *n* [F *cartel* decorative scrollwork, dial case of a clock, framed hanging clock, fr. It *cartella* frieze or slab with space for an inscription, leaflet, ticket, dim. of *carta*] **:** a hanging wall clock of French origin usu. of gilt bronze and asymmetrical in design
carte–let·tre \kärtəletr(ᵊ), -et(rə)\ *n, pl* **carte–lettres** \-trᵊ, -t(rə)\ [F, fr. *carte* card + *lettre* letter — more at CARD, LETTER] **:** LETTERCARD
car·tel·ism \kärˈte,lizəm, kȧˈ-\ *n* -s **:** the practice of forming cartels **:** CARTELIZATION
¹**car·tel·ist** \-ləst\ *n* -s **:** one that belongs to or favors a cartel
²**cartelist** \"\ *or* **car·tel·is·tic** \ˌkärd·ᵊlˈistik, ˌkȧd-, ˌ=,teˈli-\ *adj* **:** relating to, favoring, or characterized by cartelization
car·tel·i·za·tion *or* **car·tel·li·za·tion** \(ˌ)kär,teləˈzāshən, (ˌ)kȧ,-; ˌ=d·ᵊləˈzāshən, -ˌīˈz-\ *n* -s **:** organization into cartels ⟨~ of the chemical industry⟩
car·tel·ize \kärˈte,līz, kȧˈ-, ˈ=d·ᵊl,īz\ *vb* -ED/-ING/-S *vt* **:** to form into a cartel **:** bring under the control of a cartel ~ *vi* **:** to form a cartel
cartel ship *n* **:** a ship commissioned in time of war to sail under a safe-conduct for the exchange of prisoners or conveyance of proposals between belligerents
cart·er \ˈkär|d·ə(r), ˈkȧ|, |tə-\ *n* -s [ME, fr. ¹*cart* + *-er*] **:** one that drives a cart or a truck **:** one engaged in vehicle transport **:** TEAMSTER
car·ter grass \"-\ *n, usu cap C* [prob. fr. the name *Carter*] **:** NAPIER GRASS
carterly *adj, obs* **:** resembling a carter **:** BOORISH
carter process *n, usu cap C* [after Levi *Carter* fl1885 Am. industrial chemist] **:** a process for making white lead by treating powdered lead in water suspension with acetic acid and carbon dioxide
cartes *pl of* CARTE
¹**car·te·sian** \(ˈ)kärˈtēzhən, -ȧˈt-\ *adj, usu cap* [NL *cartesianus*, fr. *Cartesius* (René Descartes) †1650 Fr. scientist and philosopher + *-anus* -an] **:** of or relating to Descartes, his writings, theories, or methods — see CARTESIANISM
²**cartesian** \"\ *n* -s *usu cap* **:** a follower of Descartes **:** an adherent of Cartesian philosophy
cartesian coordinate *n, usu cap 1st C* **1 :** either of two coordinates for locating a point on a plane being the distances of the point from each of two infinite intersecting straight-line axes of reference usu. designated as X and Y measured in each case parallel to the other axis and each coordinate being given arbitrarily an algebraic sign according to the direction in which it extends from the reference axis to the point **2 :** any one of three coordinates for locating a point in space being the distances from each of three intersecting coordinate planes measured in each case parallel to that one of three straight-line axes that is the intersection of the other two planes — compare RECTANGULAR COORDINATE

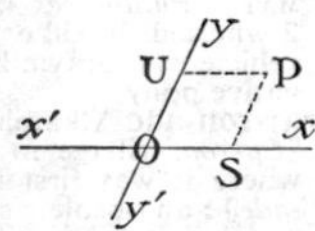

Cartesian coordinates in a plane: P point in a plane; x′,x and y′,y straight-line axes intersecting at O; UP,SP Cartesian coordinates

cartesian diver *n, usu cap C* **:** a small hollow glass figure placed in a vessel of water that has an elastic cover so arranged that by an increase of pressure the water can be forced into the figure producing the effects of suspension, sinking, and floating as the pressure varies
cartesian equation *n, usu cap C* **:** an equation of a curve or surface in which the variables are the Cartesian coordinates of a point on the curve or surface
car·te·sian·ism \=ˈ==,nizəm\ *n, usu cap* [¹*Cartesian* + *-ism*] **:** the philosophy of René Descartes and his followers deriving its chief significance from its reaction to scholastic subtleties, its utilization of radical doubt and of the postulate of cogito as its starting point, its proclamation of mathematical certitude as an ideal in metaphysical demonstration, and its dualistic distinction between thought and extension or mind and matter
¹**car·tha·gin·i·an** \ˌkärthəˈjinēən, -ȧth-, -nyən\ *adj, usu cap* [L *Carthagin-, Carthago* Carthage, ancient city of northern Africa + E *-ian*] **1 :** of, relating to, or characteristic of Carthage **2 :** of, relating to, or characteristic of the people of Carthage
²**carthaginian** \"\ *n* -s *usu cap* **:** a native or inhabitant of Carthage
carthaginian peace *n, usu cap C* **:** a treaty of peace so severe that it means the virtual destruction of the defeated contestant
car·tha·min \ˈkärthəmən\ *also* **car·thame** \-,thäm\ *or* **car·tham·ic acid** \(ˈ)kärˈthamik-\ *n* -s [*carthamin*, ISV *cartham-* (fr. NL *Carthamus tinctorius*, species name of the safflower) + *-in*; *carthame* fr. F, fr. NL *Carthamus*; *carthamic* fr. NL *Carthamus* + E *-ic*] **:** a red crystalline glucoside $C_{21}H_{22}O_{11}$ constituting the coloring matter of the safflower
car·tha·mus \ˈkärthəməs\ *n, cap* [NL, fr. Ar (colloq.) *qarṭam* safflower] **:** a genus of Eurasian herbs (family Compositae) resembling the members of the genus *Centaurea* but distinguished by their spiny leaves and spreading outer involucral scales — see SAFFLOWER
carthamus red *or* **carthamus rose** *n, often cap C* **:** a vivid red that is yellower, lighter, and slightly stronger than apple red, yellower, lighter, and stronger than carmine, and lighter, stronger, and slightly bluer than scarlet — called also *artillery, leaf red, Lincoln red, Portuguese red, rose Carthame, rouge vegetal, safflor, safflower red, vegetable red, vegetable rouge*
cart horse *n* **:** a large strong horse bred or used for drawing heavy loads
¹**car·thu·sian** \kärˈth(y)üzhən, kȧˈ-\ *n* -s *usu cap* [modif. (perh. influenced by *charterhouse* or ME *charthous* Carthusian) of ML *cartusiensis*, irreg. fr. OF *Chartrouse, Chartrose* (now *Grande Chartreuse*), mother house of the Carthusian order, mountainous region near Grenoble in southeast France where that house was founded] **:** a member of an austere religious order founded by St. Bruno in 1084
²**carthusian** \(ˈ)=ˈ==\ *adj, usu cap* **:** of or relating to the Carthusians
cartier *comparative of* CARTY
cartiest *superlative of* CARTY
car·ti·lage \ˈkär|d·ᵊlij, -ȧ|,|tᵊl-;|tlij,|tlēj\ *n* -s [L *cartilago*; akin to L *cratis* wickerwork — more at HURDLE] **1 :** a translucent elastic tissue that composes most of the skeleton of the embryos and very young of vertebrates and is for the most part converted into bone in the higher forms but remains through life the chief constituent of the skeleton of primitive forms (as the sturgeons and elasmobranchs) **:** GRISTLE — see CHONDRIN, ELASTIC CARTILAGE, FIBROCARTILAGE, HYALINE CARTILAGE **2 :** a part or structure composed of cartilage (as a piece of a cartilaginous skeleton or an articular cartilage)
cartilage bone *n* **:** a bone formed by ossification of cartilage — distinguished from *membrane bone*
cartilage glottis *n* **:** WHISPER GLOTTIS
cartilage of ja·cob·son \-ˈjākəbsən, -əps-\ *usu cap J* **:** JACOBSON'S CARTILAGE
cartilage of san·to·ri·ni \-,santəˈrēnē\ *usu cap S* [after G.D. *Santorini* †ab1737 Ital. physician and anatomist] **:** CORNICULATE CARTILAGE
cartilage of wris·berg \-ˈriz,bərg, *G* -ˈvris,berk\ *usu cap W* [trans. of G *Wrisberger knorpel*, after Heinrich A. *Wrisberg* †1808 Ger. anatomist] **:** a cuneiform cartilage
cartilage pit *n* **:** one of the concave or spoon-shaped depressions in the valves of mollusks of the class Lamellibranchia fitted to receive the ligament
car·ti·la·gin·e·ous \ˌkärd·ᵊləˈjinēəs, -nyəs\ *adj* [L *cartilagineus*, fr. *cartilagin-, cartilago* cartilage + *-eus* -eous] **:** CARTILAGINOUS
car·ti·lag·i·noid \ˌkärd·ᵊlˈajə,nȯid\ *adj* [L *cartilagin-, cartilago* + E *-oid*] **:** resembling cartilage
car·ti·lag·i·nous \ˌkär|d·ᵊlˈajənəs, -ȧ|, |tᵊl-\ *adj* [MF *cartilagineux*, fr. L *cartilaginosus*, fr. *cartilagin-, cartilago* cartilage + *-osus* -ous] **:** composed of or relating to cartilage **:** firm and tough like cartilage **:** GRISTLY
cartilaginous fish *n* **:** any of the fishes having the skeleton wholly or largely composed of cartilage **:** one of the Cyclostomi or Chondrichthyes
carting *pres part of* CART
cart ladder *or* **cart leather** *n* [¹*cart* + *ladder* or *leather*, E dial. var. of *ladder*] **:** a framework attached to a cart to increase its carrying capacity
cartload \ˈ=ˌ=\ *n* **1 :** as much as will fill or load a cart; *sometimes* **:** an indefinitely large amount ⟨collected by the ~⟩ **2 :** one third of a cubic yard (as of dirt)
cart·man \-mən\ *n, pl* **cartmen :** CARTER, TEAMSTER
car toad *n, slang* **:** a railroad-car repairman
car·to·bib·li·og·ra·phy \ˌkärd·ō-\ *n* -ES [*carto-* (as in *cartography*) + *bibliography*] **:** a history or description of printed maps
car·to·gram \ˈkärd·ə,gram\ *n* -s [F *cartogramme*, fr. *carto-* + *-gramme* -gram] **:** a map showing geographically diagrammatic statistics of various kinds usu. by the use of shades, curves, or dots
car·to·graph \-,graf\ *n* -s [back-formation fr. *cartographer* and *cartography*] **:** MAP, CHART; *specif* **:** an illustrated map
car·tog·ra·pher \kärˈtägrəfər, kȧˈt-, -fə\ *n* -s [*cartography* + *-er*] **:** one that makes maps
car·to·graph·ic \ˌkär|d·əˈgrafik, -ȧ|, |tə-, -ēk\ *or* **car·to·graph·i·cal** \-ǝkǝl, -ēk-\ *adj* [F *cartographique*, fr. *cartographie* + *-ique* -ic, -ical] **:** of or relating to cartography
cartographic unit *n* **:** rock that is represented on a geologic map by a single color or pattern
car·tog·ra·phy \kärˈtägrəfē, kȧˈt-, -i\ *n* -ES [F *cartographie*, fr. *carto-* (fr. *carte* map, card) + *-graphie* -graphy — more at CARD] **:** the science or art of making maps
car·to·man·cy \ˈkärd·ə,man(t)sē\ *n* -ES [F *cartomancie*, fr. *carto-* (fr. *carte* card) + *-mancie* -mancy] **:** fortune-telling by means of playing cards
¹**car·ton** \ˈkärtᵊn, ˈkȧt-\ *n* -s [F, fr. It *cartone* pasteboard] **1 a :** a cardboard box or container; *esp* **:** a relatively small container that when filled with merchandise is enclosed in a larger and stronger container for shipping **b :** cardboard or a piece of cardboard suitable for making cartons **2 :** a material like pasteboard or papier-mâché made by insects (as certain wasps or termites) of chewed vegetable matter often mixed with soil for use in building their nests
²**carton** \"\ *vb* **cartoned; cartoned; cartoning** \-t(ᵊ)niŋ\ **cartons** *vt* **:** to pack or enclose in a carton ~ *vi* **:** to shape cartons from cardboard sheets ⟨a ~*ing* machine⟩
car·ton·er \ˈkärt(ᵊ)nər, -ȧt-, -nə\ *n* -s **:** one that cartons; *specif* **:** a machine that opens a folding carton, inserts a packaged product, and closes the carton ends
car·ton·nage \ˌkärtᵊnˈäzh\ *n* -s [F, fr. *carton* pasteboard + *-age*] **:** the material of which many Egyptian mummy cases are made consisting of linen or papyrus glued together in many thicknesses and usu. coated with stucco; *also* **:** a mummy case made of such material
car·ton pierre \ˈkär,tōⁿ ˈpye(ə)r, -ⁿ pēˈe-\ *n* [F *carton-pierre*, lit., stone pasteboard, fr. *carton* pasteboard + *pierre* stone, fr. L *petra*, fr. Gk, rock] **:** a papier-mâché made to imitate stone or bronze and usu. used for statuary and architectural ornaments
¹**car·toon** \(ˈ)kärˈtün, -ȧˈt-\ *n* -s [It *cartone* pasteboard, cartoon, aug. of *carta* card — more at CARD] **1 :** a preparatory design, drawing, or painting (as for a fresco, painting, mosaic, or tapestry); *esp* **:** a drawing in full size usu. on paper which is traced or copied on a surface to be used for a final work ⟨tapestry weaves that closely follow the modeling in the ~⟩ **2 a :** a drawing that is often symbolic and usu. intended as humor, caricature, or satire and comment on public and usu. political matters ⟨a political ~⟩ **b :** COMIC 3a **3 :** ANIMATED CARTOON
²**cartoon** \"\ *vb* -ED/-ING/-S *vt* **1 :** to make a cartoon or preparatory sketch of **2 :** to make simple outline drawings of **3 :** to caricature pictorially ~ *vi* **:** to make a cartoon
car·toon·ery \=ˈ=n(ə)rē, -i\ *n* -ES **:** the art or practice of cartooning
car·toon·ist \=ˈ=nəst\ *n* -s **:** one who draws cartoons
cartoon set *n* **:** a television studio set with a background consisting of a large line drawing
cartop \ˈ=,=\ *adj* **:** suitable in size and weight for carrying on top of an automobile ⟨~ canoe⟩
car·touche *or* **car·touch** \(ˈ)kärˈtüsh, -ȧˈt-\ *n, pl* **cartouches** [F, fr. It *cartoccio*, fr. *carta* card, paper — more at CARD] **1 :** a gun cartridge having a paperboard case **2 a** *obs* **:** a scroll-shaped architectural ornament or member sometimes used for inscriptions **:** MODILLION **b :** an ornamental enframement (as for an inscription, a monogram, a map title, or a coat of arms) often in a baroque or rococo style **c :** an ornately framed ornamental tablet often bearing a design or an inscription **3 :** an oval shield sometimes used for the display of heraldic bearings (as of women or of ecclesiastics) **4 :** an oval or oblong figure (as on ancient Egyptian monuments) enclosing a sovereign's name **5 :** a contour (as of a table top) based on the superimposition of an oval and a rectangle **6 :** a moderate brown that is yellower, lighter, and stronger than auburn, lighter, stronger, and slightly redder than chestnut brown, and redder, lighter, and stronger than coffee — called also *Durango, mesa*

cartouche 3

cartouse *obs var of* CARTOUCHE
cart path *n, North* **:** a narrow unimproved road **:** LANE
car·tridge \ˈkär·trij, ˈkȧ-, -ēj, *chiefly dial & old-fash* ˈka-\ *n* -s *often attrib* [alter. of earlier *cartage*, modif. of MF *cartouche*] **1 a :** a tube of metal, paper, or a combination of both containing a complete charge for a firearm and in modern ammunition usu. containing a cap or other initiating device — compare FIXED AMMUNITION **b :** a case containing an explosive charge for blasting **2 :** a usu. replaceable or refillable case containing loose material and designed to permit ready insertion into a larger mechanism, apparatus, or installation **:** CAPSULE ⟨a filter ~⟩ ⟨a ~ of compressed gas⟩ **3 :** a pointed metal cylinder attachment to a mole plow which is pulled through the soil at the drain depth and forms the drainage passage **4 :** a roll of light-protected film ready to be inserted in a camera for exposure **5 a :** a small removable case in a pickup on a phonograph containing the needle and the mechanism for translating stylus motion into an electrical voltage **b :** a small case containing a reel of magnetic tape or wire, a take-up reel, and suitable guides that allows use of tape or wire without the necessity of threading through heads and guides

1 3 2 3
cartridge for shotgun cut away to show: *1* powder, *2* shot, *3* wad

cartridge bag *n* **:** a cloth bag for holding a cannon charge
cartridge belt *n* **:** a belt having loops or pockets that is usu. worn around the waist and used to carry ammunition (as cartridges for small arms) and other equipment (as a canteen)
cartridge box *n* **:** a usu. leather case attached to a belt or strap and used to carry cartridges
cartridge brass *n* **:** a wrought brass containing usu. about 70 percent copper and 30 percent zinc and having sufficient ductility and other properties to stand the severe mechanical treatment necessary in making cartridge cases
cartridge buff *n* **:** SEED PEARL 2
cartridge fuse *n* **:** an electric fuse in which the link is enclosed in a cartridge
cartridge heater *n* **:** an electric heating coil enclosed in a metal case shaped like a cartridge

cartridge paper *n* **1 :** a strong durable paper used for making cartridges **2 :** a strong hard paper sometimes with a rough finish suitable for printing by offset lithography **3 :** a cheap drawing paper

cartridge pleat *n* **:** one of a series of small rounded standaway folds of cloth so stitched to a foundation cloth as to resemble the webbing for cartridges on a cartridge belt and used decoratively (as on clothes or curtains)

cartridge starter *n* **:** a starter for gasoline engines that consists of a cartridge containing an explosive which on being electrically detonated forces the piston forward and starts the engine — called also *combustion starter*

cart rope *n* [ME, rope for a cart, fr. ¹*cart* + *rope*] **:** rope strong enough for drawing a heavy load

carts *pl of* CART, *pres 3d sing of* CART

cart–track plant *n* **:** BROAD-LEAVED PLANTAIN 1

car·tu·lary \ˈkärchə,lerē\ *n* -ES [ML *cartularium, chartularium,* fr. L *chartula* little paper + *-arium* -ary — more at CHARTER] **:** a collection or register of charters; *esp* **:** a book containing duplicates of the charters and title deeds relating to an estate (as a monastery)

car–tunnel kiln *n* **:** CONTINUOUS KILN

cartway \ˈ≠,≠\ *n* [ME *cart-way,* fr. *cart* + *way*] **:** a road for carts **:** a rough unimproved road

¹**cartwheel** \ˈ≠,≠\ *n* [ME, fr. ¹*cart* + *wheel*] **1 :** the wheel of a cart **2 :** a large coin: as **a :** a silver dollar **b :** CROWN 8a **c :** one of the penny and twopenny copper coins issued in England in 1797 **3 a :** a rolling or spinning motion suggesting that of a turning wheel; *specif* **:** a lateral handspring with arms and legs extended ⟨they stood on their heads and turned ~s down the garden path —Evelyn R. Sickels⟩ **b :** a figure performed in baton twirling in which the baton describes a circle alternately on each side of the body **4 :** a shallow-crowned hat with a wide stiff brim

²**cartwheel** \ˈ"\ *vi* -ED/-ING/-S **:** to move like a turning wheel; *specif* **:** to turn cartwheels

cart whip *n* **:** a heavy short-handled horsewhip

cartwhip \ˈ≠,≠\ *vt* **:** to flog with a cart whip

cart·wright \ˈkärt-,rīt\ *n* -S [ME, fr. ¹*cart* + *wright*] **:** one that makes carts

carty \ˈkärd·ē\ *adj* -ER/-EST **:** resembling a cart horse

carucage *n* -S [ML *carrucagium,* fr. *carruca* plow, fr. L, coach, of Celt origin; akin to OIr *carr* vehicle — more at CAR] *Old Eng law* **:** a tax on every plow or plowland

carucate *n* -S [ME, fr. ML *carrucata,* fr. *carruca* plow] **:** any of various old English units of land area that in the counties of Suffolk, Norfolk, York, Lincoln, Derby, Nottingham, and Leicester corresponded to the hide; *esp* **:** a unit equal to 120 acres

car·um \ˈka(a)rəm\ *n, cap* [NL, fr. Gk *karon* caraway — more at CARAWAY] **:** a large genus of biennial aromatic herbs (family Umbelliferae) having fusiform or tuberous roots, pinnate leaves, and white or yellow flowers in compound umbels having few or no bracts — see CARAWAY

car·un·cle \ˈka,rəŋkəl, kəˈr-\ *n* -S [modif. of obs. F *caruncule,* fr. L *caruncula* little piece of flesh, dim. of *caro* flesh — more at CARNAL] **1 a :** a naked fleshy outgrowth (as a bird's wattle or comb or as on certain caterpillars) **b :** COTYLEDON 1 **2 :** an outgrowth on a seed developed by proliferation of integumentary tissue adjacent to the micropyle **3 :** a small fleshy growth; *specif* **:** a reddish growth situated at the urethral meatus in women causing pain and bleeding

ca·run·cu·la \kəˈrəŋkyələ, ka-\ *n, pl* **caruncu·lae** \-,lē, -ī\ [L] **:** CARUNCLE

ca·run·cu·lar \kəˈrəŋkyələ(r), ka-\ *also* **ca·run·cu·lous** \-ləs\ *adj* [L *caruncula* + E *-ar* or *-ous*] **1 :** like a caruncle **2 :** CARUNCULATE

ca·run·cu·late \-ət, -,lāt\ *also* **ca·run·cu·lat·ed** \-,lād·əd\ *adj* [prob. fr. NL *carunculatus,* fr. L *caruncula* + NL *-atus* -ate] **:** having a caruncle

car·va·crol \ˈkärvə,krōl, -ōl\ *n* -S [ISV *carv-* (fr. NL *carvi,* specific epithet of the caraway *Carum carvi,* fr. ML *carvi* caraway) + L *acr-, acer* sharp + ISV *-ol* — more at CARAWAY, EDGE] **:** a liquid phenol $CH_3C_6H_3(C_3H_7)OH$ found in the essential oils of various plants of the mint family (as origanum and thyme) and used as an antiseptic; 2-methyl-5-isopropylphenol

car·va·cryl \-,kril\ *n* -S [*carvacrol* + *-yl*] **:** the univalent radical $C_{10}H_{13}$ of which carvacrol is the hydroxide

carve \ˈkärv, -äv\ *vb* -ED/-ING/-S [ME *kerven,* fr. OE *ceorfan;* akin to MHG *kerben* to notch, Gk *graphein* to scratch, write] *vt* **1 :** to cut (as with knife or chisel) with deliberate care or practiced precision ⟨*carved* fretwork⟩ **2 :** to cut or hew out ⟨~ a path⟩ **:** make or get by or as if by cutting — often used with *out* ⟨~ out a fortune⟩ **3 :** to cut into pieces or slices (as meat at table) **:** divide or cut off for distribution or apportionment **4 :** to cut up (as a county into districts) **:** SUBDIVIDE ~ *vi* **1 :** to cut up **:** cut up and serve ⟨~ for all the guests⟩ **2 :** to practice the trade of a sculptor or engraver

syn see CUT

carved rug *n* **:** a rug having a pattern produced by cutting the pile to different levels

car·vel \ˈkärvəl, -,vel\ *n* -S [ME *carvile,* fr. MF *carvelle* — more at CARAVEL] **:** CARAVEL a

carvel–built \ˈ≠(,)≠,≠\ *adj* [prob. fr. D *karveel* caravel (in compounds such as *karveelwerk* carvel-built construction), fr. MF *carvelle*] *of a ship* **:** built with the planks meeting flush at the seams instead of overlapping — compare CLINKER-BUILT

carvel joint *n* **:** a flush joint of the planks of a ship

carvel–planked \ˈ≠(,)≠,≠\ *adj* **:** CARVEL-BUILT

carv·en \ˈkärvən, -äv-\ *adj* [alter. of ME *corven,* past part. of *kerven* to carve] **:** wrought or ornamented by carving **:** CARVED

car·vene \ˈkär,vēn\ *n* -S [prob. fr. F *carvène,* fr. *carvi* caraway (fr. Ar *karawyā*) + *-ène* -ene — more at CARAWAY] **:** dextrorotatory limonene

carv·er \ˈkärvər, ˈkàvə\ *n* -S [ME *kerver,* fr. *kerven* to carve + *-er* — more at CARVE] **:** one that carves or produces by carving: as **a :** one that carves meat at table **b :** one that carves designs or figures on or in wood, stone, or metal **c :** CROPPER c **d** (1) **:** a knife for carving or slicing meat (2) **:** either one of a knife and fork set ⟨a pair of ~s⟩

car·ver chair \ˈ"-\ *n, usu cap 1st C* [after John Carver †1621 first governor of Plymouth Colony; fr. a specimen belonging to him] **:** a heavy turned chair having three vertical and three horizontal spindles in the back

Carver chair

car·ves·trene \kärˈve,strēn, ˈkärvə,s-\ *n* -S [blend of ISV *carvol* carvone (fr. ML *carvi* caraway + *-ol*) and *sylvestrene;* orig. formed as G *karvestren* — more at CARAWAY] **:** inactive sylvestrene

carving *n* -S [ME *kerving,* fr. gerund of *kerven* to carve — more at CARVE] **1 :** the act or art of one who carves **2 :** carved work **:** decorative sculpture **:** a design or figure made by carving

carving set *n* **:** a table set comprised of a carving knife, two-tined fork with finger guard, and usu. a sharpening steel — called also *roast set*

car·vol \ˈkär,vōl, -ōl\ *n* -S [ISV *carv-* (fr. ML *carvi* caraway) + *-ol*] **:** CARVONE

car·vo·men·thene \,kärvōˈmen,thēn\ *n* -S [ISV *carvone* + *menthene*] **:** a colorless oily hydrocarbon $C_{10}H_{18}$; 1-*p*-menthene

car·vo·men·thol \-,thōl, -ōl\ *n* -S [*carvo-* (fr. ML *carvi* caraway) + *menthol*] **:** an oily terpenoid alcohol $C_{10}H_{19}OH$ made synthetically (as by reducing carvomenthone)

car·vo·men·thone \-,thōn\ *n* -S [*carvo-* + *menthone*] **:** a colorless oily terpenoid ketone $C_{10}H_{18}O$ occurring with carvotanacetone in some essential oils

car·vone \ˈkär,vōn\ *n* -S [prob. fr. G *karvon,* fr. ML *carvi* caraway + G *-on* -one — more at CARAWAY] **:** an oily liquid terpenoid ketone $C_{10}H_{14}O$ having a characteristic odor of caraway, found in many essential oils (as caraway, dill, or spearmint), and used as a flavoring agent and perfume

car·vo·ta·nac·e·tone \ˈkär(,)vōtəˈnasə,tōn\ *n* -S [*carvo* + *tanacetone*] **:** an oily terpenoid ketone $C_{10}H_{16}O$ found in the essential oils of some plants of the genus *Blumea*

car wash *n* **:** an establishment equipped to wash automobiles

car whacker *n, slang* **:** CAR KNOCKER

carwitchet *var of* CARRIWITCHET

cary \ˈka(a)rē\ *n* -S *usu cap* [fr. *Cary,* Ill.] **:** a substage of the Wisconsin glacial stage; *also* **:** its drift

cary- *or* **caryo-** — see KARY-

car·ya \ˈka(a)rēə\ *n, cap* [NL, fr. Gk *karya* nut tree, fr. *karyon* nut — more at CAREEN] **:** a genus of No. American hardwood trees (family Juglandaceae) with the husk of the fruit dehiscent and the nuts angular — see BITTERNUT, HICKORY, PECAN, PIGNUT; compare JUGLANS

car·y·at·ic \,karēˈad·ik\ *adj* [*caryatid* + *-ic*] **:** of, relating to, or using a caryatid ⟨~ order⟩

car·y·at·id \,karēˈad·əd, ˈkarēə,tid, kəˈrīətəd\ *n, pl* **caryatids** \-ədz,-idz\ *or* **caryat·i·des** \,karēˈad·ə,dēz\ [L *Caryatides,* pl., fr. Gk *Karyatides,* lit., priestesses of Artemis at Caryae (Gk *Karyai*) in Laconia] **:** a draped female figure supporting an entablature in the place of a column or pilaster — compare ATLAS

caryatid from a Greek temple

car·y·at·id·al \,karēˈad·ədᵊl\ *or* **car·y·at·i·de·an** \,≠≠,≠≠ˈdēən; ¦karēə¦tid-, kə¦rīə¦t-\ *or* **car·y·a·tid·ic** \¦karēə¦tidik, kə¦rīə¦-\ *adj* [*caryatid* + *-al* or *-ean* or *-ic*] **:** of or resembling a caryatid

car·y·i·nite \ˈkarēə,nīt, kəˈrīə,-\ *n* -S [ISV *caryin-* (fr. Gk *karyinos* nut-brown, fr. *karyon* nut) + *-ite* — more at CAREEN] **:** a mineral $(Ca\text{-}PbNa)_5(Mn,Mg)_4(AsO_4)_5$ consisting of a rare calcium manganese arsenate containing other elements

cary·o·car \kəˈrīə,kär, ˈkarēō,-\ *n, cap* [NL, fr. *cary-* + Gk *kar* head; fr. the size of the fruit; akin to Gk *kara* head — more at CEREBRAL] **:** a genus (the type of the family Caryocaraceae) of So. American trees having strong fine-grained wood useful for furniture and shipbuilding and bearing edible seeds — see SOUARI NUT

car·y·o·ca·ra·ce·ae \¦karē(,)ōkəˈrāsē,ē\ *n pl, cap* [NL, fr. *Caryocar,* type genus + *-aceae*] **:** a family of tropical So. American trees (order Parietales) differing from Theaceae in having coherent petals and separate styles — **car·y·o·ca·ra·ceous** \-kə¦rāshəs\ *adj*

car·y·o·my·ia \,karēōˈmī(y)ə\ *n, cap* [NL, fr. *cary-* + *-myia*] **:** a genus of gallflies (family Cecidomyiidae) including the hickory midges

car·y·oph·a·na·les \,karē,äfəˈnā(,)lēz\ *n pl, cap* [NL, fr. *Caryophanon* + *-ales*] **:** a small order of filamentous bacteria that occur in water, decaying organic matter, and the alimentary canal and have in general the characteristics of members of the genus *Caryophanon*

car·y·oph·a·non \,karēˈäfə,nän\ *n, cap* [NL, fr. *cary-* + Gk *phanon,* neut. of *phanos* bright, fr. *phaos* light — more at FANCY] **:** a genus (coextensive with the family Caryophanaceae) of large filamentous or bacillary bacteria of oral mucous membranes and the alimentary tract of various mammals that are closely related to the chlamydobacteria though usu. placed in a separate order and are distinguished by well-defined nuclei comparable to isolated chromosomes, peritrichous or no flagella, and absence of spores

car·y·o·phyl·la·ce·ae \¦karē(,)ōfəˈlāsē,ē\ *n pl, cap* [NL, fr. ²*Caryophyllus,* type genus + *-aceae*] **:** a large widely distributed family of herbs or occas. subshrubs (order Caryophyllales) usu. with stems swollen at the nodes and opposite linear leaves and with symmetrical pentamerous or tetramerous flowers that have distinct stamens as numerous or twice as numerous as the sepals

car·y·o·phyl·la·ceous \-¦lāshəs\ *adj* [NL *Caryophyllaceae* + E *-ous*] **1 :** of or relating to the Caryophyllaceae **2 :** having long-clawed petals enclosed in a tubular calyx

car·y·o·phyl·lae·i·dae \-ˈlēə,dē\ *n pl, cap* [NL, fr. *Caryophyllaeus,* type genus (alter. of *Caryophyllus,* fr. *cary-* + *-phyllus* -phyllous) + *-idae*] **:** a family that contains monozootic tapeworms infesting the intestine of fishes and that is placed in the Pseudophyllidea or with related forms in a separate order

car·y·o·phyl·la·les \-ˈlā(,)lēz\ *n pl, cap* [NL, fr. ²*Caryophyllus,* type genus + *-ales*] **:** an order of dicotyledonous herbs and shrubs distinguished by a superior unilocular ovary and a generally coiled or curved embryo, important member families being the Chenopodiaceae, Amaranthaceae, and Caryophyllaceae

car·y·o·phyl·lene \,≠≠≠ˈfi,lēn\ *n* -S [ISV *caryophyll-* (fr. NL ²*Caryophyllus*) + *-ene*] **:** a liquid sesquiterpene $C_{15}H_{24}$ obtained from various essential oils (as clove oil) as a mixture of stereoisomers distinguished as α-, β-, and γ-caryophyllene — compare HUMULENE

car·y·o·phyl·lid \-ˈfiləd\ *adj* [NL *Caryophyllidae,* family of worms, fr. *Caryophyllus,* type genus + *-idae* — more at CARYOPHYLLAEIDAE] **:** of or relating to the family Caryophyllaeidae

car·y·o·phyl·lin \-ˈfilən\ *n* -S [ISV *caryophyll-* + *-in*] **:** OLEANOLIC ACID

¹**car·y·o·phyl·lus** \-ˈfiləs\ [NL, modif. of Gk *karyophyllon* clove — more at GILLYFLOWER] *syn of* JAMBOS

²**caryophyllus** \ˈ"\ [NL, modif. of Gk *karyophyllon*] *syn of* DIANTHUS

car·y·op·sis \,karēˈäpsəs\ *n, pl* **caryop·ses** \-p,sēz\ *or* **caryop·si·des** \-psə,dēz\ [NL, fr. *cary-* + *-opsis*] **:** a small one-seeded dry indehiscent fruit with a thin membranous pericarp adhering so closely to the seed that fruit and seed are incorporated in one body forming a single grain (as in wheat, barley, Indian corn, and other grasses) — see FRUIT illustration

car·y·op·ter·is \-ˈäptərəs\ *n* [NL, fr. *cary-* + *-pteris* (irreg. fr. Gk *pteron* wing); fr. the wings on the carpels — more at FEATHER] **1** *cap* **:** a genus of Asiatic shrubs (family Verbenaceae) with a 5-lobed corolla, four exserted stamens, and a fruit of 4-winged nutlets — see ³BLUEBEARD **2** *pl* **caryop·terides** \-¦äptərə,dēz\ **:** any plant of the genus *Caryopteris*

car·y·o·ta \,karēˈōd·ə\ *n, cap* [NL, fr. L *caryota* nut-shaped date, modif. of Gk *karyōtis* date, fr. *karyon* nut — more at CAREEN] **:** a small genus of East Indian palms having bipinnate leaves with wedge-shaped divisions and including several species that are cultivated — see FISHTAIL PALM, JAGGERY PALM; compare KITTUL

cas *abbr* **1** casing **2** castle **3** casualty

ca·sa \ˈkäsə, -ˈsa-, -ˈä-\ *n* -S [Sp & It, fr. L, hut, cabin; prob. akin to L *catena* chain — more at CHAIN] *Southwest* **:** DWELLING HOUSE

ca·sa·ba *or* **cas·sa·ba** \kəˈsäbə, -ˈä-\ *also* **casaba melon** *or* **cassaba melon** *n* -S [fr. *Kasaba* (now Turgutlu), Turkey, whence it was introduced] **:** any of several long-keeping winter melons having a yellow rind and sweet flesh

ca·sa·be \kəˈsäbē\ *n* -S [Sp] **:** ¹BUMPER 3

ca·sa·blan·ca \¦kasə¦blaŋkə, ¦kazə-, -läŋ-; ¦käsə¦bläŋ-, ¦käzə-\ *adj, usu cap* [fr. *Casablanca,* city in Morocco] **:** of or from Casablanca **:** of the kind or style prevalent in Casablanca

ca·sa·gha pine \kəˈsägə-\ *n* [modif. of Singhalese *kasagaha,* fr. Skt *kaśā* whip + *gaccha* tree] **:** a beefwood (*Casuarina equisetifolia*)

ca·sa·le process \kəˈsälē-\ *n, usu cap C* [after Luigi Casale †*ab*1937 Ital. chemist] **:** a method of synthesizing ammonia similar in principle to the Haber process

cas·al·ty \ˈkazəltē, -as-\ *adj* [alter. of *casualty*] **1** *dial Eng* **:** susceptible to chance or accident **:** UNCERTAIN, UNRELIABLE **2** *dial Eng* **:** INSECURE, SHAKY, INFIRM

ca·sa·no·va \,kazəˈnōvə, -asə-\ *n* -S *usu cap* [after Giovanni Jacopo *Casanova* †1798 Ital. adventurer] **:** LOVER; *esp* **:** a man who is a promiscuous and unscrupulous lover

ca·saque \kəˈzak\ *n* -S [F, fr. MF, cassock — more at CASSOCK] **:** a kind of woman's blouse

ca·sa·sia \kəˈsāzh(ē)ə, -ˈa-\ *n, cap* [NL, fr. Luis de las Casas y Arargorri †1800 Span. soldier + NL *-ia*] **:** a small genus of tropical American shrubs or trees (family Rubiaceae) having opposite leathery leaves and white or yellow flowers with a salverform corolla

casava *var of* CASSAVA

cas·bah *or* **kas·bah** *also* **kas·ba** \ˈkaz,bä, -äz-, -àz- -,bə,-,bä\ *n* -S *usu cap* [F, fr. Ar dial. (No. Africa) *qaṣbah, qaṣabah*] **1 :** a No. African castle or fortress **2 :** the native section of a No. African city surrounding the castle or fortress; *specif* **:** a section containing nightclubs and houses of prostitution

cas·ca·bel \ˈkaskə,bel\ *n* -S [Sp, lit., small spherical bell like a sleigh bell, fr. OProv *cascavel,* fr. ML *cascabellus,* dim. of *cascabus* cooking pot, alter. of L *caccabus,* fr. Gk *kakkabos, kakkabē,* of Sem origin; akin to Assyr *kukubu* vessel] **1 :** a knoblike projection, sometimes in the form of a loop, behind the breech of a muzzle-loading cannon; *also* **:** all the rear part of the cannon behind the base ring — see CANNON illustration **2 :** a vicious So. and Central American rattlesnake (*Crotalus durissus terrificus*) that has a powerful neurotoxic venom and is the only rattlesnake of eastern So. America **3 :** a small hollow perforated spherical bell enclosing a loose pellet which causes it to jingle when moved — called also *jingle bell*

¹**cas·cade** \(ˈ)kaˈskād\ *n* -S [F, fr. It *cascata,* fr. *cascare* to fall, fr. (assumed) VL *casicare,* fr. L *casus,* past part. of *cadere* to fall — more at CHANCE] **1 :** a fall of water over steeply slanting rocks (as in a river or brook); *esp* **:** a small fall or one of a series **2 a :** something arranged, formed, or piled up in a series of steps or ranks ⟨the ~s of the Deville glacier⟩ **b :** SERIES 8 **c :** a fall of material (as lace) that is so arranged in folds at the upper edge that the lower edge hangs in a zigzag line and that is used esp. in clothing and draperies **d :** a succession of stages (as in a process or in the arrangement of the parts of an apparatus) in which each stage derives from or acts, sometimes cumulatively, upon the product or output of the preceding ⟨relays in ~⟩ ⟨a ~ amplifier⟩ ⟨a distillation column with a ~ with each plate representing a stage —Richard Stephenson⟩ **e :** a series of equally spaced and similarly oriented airfoils or hydrofoils that direct the flow of a fluid (as the stator blades direct the flow of air in a compressor) **3 a :** something falling or rushing forth in quantity ⟨a ~ of sound so great that you cannot hear a word anyone says —Douglas Brown⟩ **b :** an arrangement of flowers fastened together so that an extended part or strip trails down from the main body

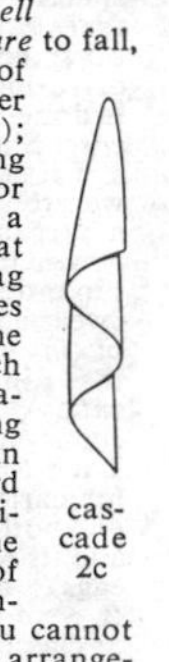

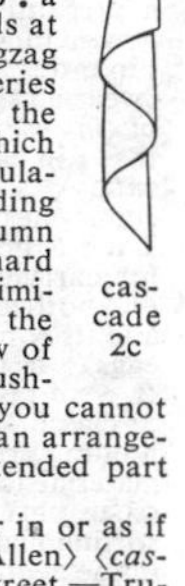

cascade 2c

²**cascade** \ˈ"\ *vb* -ED/-ING/-S *vi* **1 :** to fall or pour in or as if in a cascade ⟨the price *cascaded* to 140 —F.L.Allen⟩ ⟨*cascaded* down a flight of steps and spilled into the street —Truman Capote⟩ **2** *dial* **:** VOMIT ~ *vt* **1 :** to cause to fall like a cascade **2** *also* **cascade–connect :** to connect in cascade (as an electric circuit) **3 :** to carry out (as a manufacturing process) in a number of stages

cascade amplification *n* **:** multistage amplification **:** the use of two or more electron tubes each amplifying the output of the preceding

cascade fir *n, usu cap C* [fr. *Cascade* range, Washington, Oregon, and northern California] **:** AMABILIS FIR

cascade shower *n* **:** a cosmic-ray shower in which a high-energy electron produces one or more photons that convert into electrons and positrons, these secondary electrons producing the same effect as the primary, the shower thus building up until the level of energy becomes so low that photon emission and pair production cannot occur

cascade transformer *n* **:** a high-voltage source consisting of a limited number of step-up transformers with their secondaries in series, the primary of each after the first being supplied from a pair of taps on the secondary of the preceding

cas·ca·di·an \(ˈ)ka¦skādēən\ *adj, usu cap* [*Cascadian* (revolution, a group of earth movements that uplifted the mountain ranges of the Pacific coast of No. America, fr. *Cascadia,* hypothetical land mass along western border of No. America (fr. *Cascade* Range) + E *-an*] **:** of or relating to mountain-making movements in the Cenozoic era — see GEOLOGIC TIME table

cascading glacier *n* **:** a glacier that because of its steep and uneven bed is much broken by crevasses and suggestive in appearance of a cascading stream

cas·ca·do \kaˈskä(,)dō, -ˈā-\ *n* -S [Sp, cracked, broken, fr. past part. of *cascar* to crack, break — more at CASCARA] **:** a verminous crustated dermatitis of cattle caused by a nematode (*Stephanofilaria dedoesi*) and occurring esp. in Indonesia but reported also in the U. S.

cas·ca·du·ra \,kaskəˈdürə\ *n* -S [AmerSp, fr. Sp, breaking, fr. *cascado* + *-ura* -ure] **:** an armored catfish of the family Callichthyidae

cas·ca·lo·te \,kaskəˈlōd·ē\ *n* -S [MexSp *cascalote, nacascolote* divi-divi, fr. Nahuatl *nacazcolotl,* lit., twisted ear, fr. *nacaztli* ear + *colotl* twisted] **1 :** any of several tropical American trees that yield extracts rich in tannin: **a :** a West Indian tree (*Croton cascarilla*) **b :** a Mexican tree (*Caesalpinia cacalaco*); *also* **:** the closely related divi-divi **2 :** HUISACHE

cas·cara \kaˈskarə *also* -ˈe- *or* -ˈä- *or* ˈkaskərə\ *n* -S [Sp *cáscara* bark, fr. *cascar* to crack, break, fr. (assumed) VL *quassicare* to shake, break, fr. L *quassare* — more at QUASH] **1 :** CASCARA BUCKTHORN **2 :** CASCARA SAGRADA

cascara amar·ga \-əˈmärgə\ *n* [AmerSp *cáscara amarga,* lit., bitter bark] **:** the dried bark of a tropical American tree (*Picramnia antidesma*) formerly used in treatment of syphilis and skin diseases — called also *Honduras bark*

cascara buckthorn *n* **:** a buckthorn (*Rhamnus purshiana*) of the Pacific coast of the U.S. yielding cascara sagrada — called also *bearberry, bearwood, coffeeberry*

cascara sa·gra·da \-səˈgrädə\ *n* [AmerSp *cáscara sagrada,* lit., sacred bark] **:** the dried bark of cascara buckthorn used as a mild laxative — called also *chittam bark*

cas·ca·ril·la \,kaskəˈrilə, -ˈrēə\ *n* -S *or* **cascarilla bark** *n* -S [Sp, dim. of *cáscara* bark] **1 :** the aromatic bark of a West Indian shrub (*Croton eluteria*) used for making incense and as a tonic — called also *eleuthera bark, sweetwood bark* **2 :** the shrub that yields cascarilla bark

cascarilla oil *n* **:** a pale-yellow essential oil with a spicy odor obtained from cascarilla bark and used in perfumes

cas·ca·ron \,kaskəˈrōn\ *n, pl* **cascaro·nes** \-ōnez\ [AmerSp *cascarón,* fr. Sp, eggshell, aug. of *cáscara* bark] *Southwest* **:** an eggshell filled with confetti and thrown by revelers and dancers at balls or carnivals

cas·ca·vel \ˈkaskə,vel\ *n* -S [AmerSp *cascabel,* fr. Sp, small spherical bell — more at CASCABEL] **:** CASCABEL 2

cas·co \ˈka(,)skō\ *n* -S [Sp, potsherd, ship's hull — more at CASK] **:** a long almost rectangular barge or lighter sometimes with sails used in the Philippines

¹**case** \ˈkās\ *n* -S [ME *cas,* fr. OF, fr. L *casus* fall, event, chance, fr. *casus,* past part. of *cadere* to fall — more at CHANCE] **1 a :** a special set of circumstances or conditions **:** a peculiar situation or series of developments; *esp* **:** the circumstances and situation of a particular person, thing, or action ⟨the lost not a single life in any ~ where the men were under his personal control —W.J.Ghent⟩ **b :** a set of circumstances constituting a problem **:** a matter for consideration or decision: as (1) **:** a circumstance or situation (as a crime) requiring investigation or action by the police or other agency (2) **:** one that is the object of investigation, consideration, or attention ⟨the man is a relief ~⟩ **2 a :** the state of being or of affairs **:** the condition with respect to welfare or success ⟨the critic of fiction is in no worse ~ than the critic of verse —C.H.Rickword⟩; *specif* **:** the condition of body or mind ⟨cows, red of hide and in good ~ —Llewelyn Powys⟩ **b :** a condition of readiness **:** a suitable state of mind ⟨I am in ~ to justle a constable —Shak.⟩ **c :** the order (sense 2d) of leaf tobacco **3** [ME *cas,* fr. MF, fr. L *casus,* trans. of Gk *ptōsis,* lit., fall; fr. the idea that cases other than the nominative are like deviations fr. a perpendicular line — more at PTOSIS] *of a noun, adjective, or pronoun* **a :** an inflectional form indicating the sense relation (as that of subject, object, possessor, thing possessed) to another word in the sentence **b :** a sense relation to another word in the context of a kind that may be but is not necessarily indicated by a particular inflectional form ⟨the subject of a verb is in the nominative ~⟩ **c :** the characteristic of having inflectional forms indicating the sense relation to another word or words in the context ⟨a Latin noun has gender, number, and ~⟩ **4 :** what actually exists or happens **:** the existing situation **:** FACT — used with *the* ⟨advance was slower than had ever been the ~ before⟩ **5 a** (1) **:** the matters of fact or conditions involved in a suit **:** a suit or action in law or equity **:** CAUSE (2) **:** the printed

report of the decision of a case at law **b** (1) **:** the body of evidence tending to support a conclusion or judgment ⟨the ~ for an industrialized Oxford lies in its ideal geographical position —S.P.B.Mais⟩ (2) **:** a statement of the evidence or arguments relevant to a proposition **:** ARGUMENT; *esp* **:** an apparently valid or convincing argument ⟨make a ~ for the privately endowed college⟩ **6 a :** an instance of disease or injury ⟨10 ~*s* of pneumonia⟩; *also* **:** a patient under treatment **b :** an instance or example of a particular type ⟨Napoleon is the supreme ~ of reason in the novel —E.K.Brown⟩ ⟨a ~ of a sacred marriage was reported —J.G.Frazer⟩ **c :** a person who is peculiar or extraordinary in some way **:** CHARACTER ⟨the rustlers were hard ~*s*⟩ **7 :** ²CRUSH 6 **8** *mapping* **:** the position of the plane of projection relative to a point on the sphere ⟨polar ~⟩ ⟨oblique ~⟩ ⟨equational ~⟩ **syn** see INSTANCE — **in any case :** without regard to or in spite of other considerations ⟨a scandal which, *in any case*, would drive him out of public life —S.H.Adams⟩ **:** whatever else is done or is the case ⟨you could not have caught her *in any case*. She sailed two days ago —Pearl Buck⟩ — **¹in case** *conj* **1 :** if it should happen that **:** supposing that **:** IF ⟨*in case* we are surprised, keep by me —Washington Irving⟩ **2 :** as a precaution against the event that ⟨people still carry guns *in case* they need them —*N. Y. Herald Tribune*⟩ — **²in case** *adv* **:** in order to provide against any chance event or circumstance ⟨wear a raincoat just *in case*⟩ — **in case of** *prep* **:** in the event of ⟨*in case of* trouble, yell⟩ — **in case that** *conj* **:** in the event that **:** in case

²case \"\ *n* -s *often attrib* [ME *cas*, fr. ONF *casse*, fr. L *capsa* chest, case, fr. *capere* to take, hold — more at HEAVE] **1 a :** a box or receptacle to contain or hold something (as for carrying, shipping, or safekeeping) ⟨a silver cigarette ~⟩ ⟨12 bottles in a ~⟩ ⟨a display ~ in a meat market⟩ **b :** a box and its contents **:** the quantity contained in a box ⟨three ~*s* of eggs⟩ **c :** SET ⟨a ~ of instruments⟩; *specif* **:** PAIR, BRACE ⟨a ~ of pistols⟩ **d :** a compartmented box or rack for sorting or classification: as (1) **:** a shallow tray divided into boxes for holding printing type; *also* **:** any similar container for auxiliary material (as leads, slugs, or accents) — see JOB CASE, LOWER CASE, UPPER CASE (2) **:** a rack used in the postal service for sorting mail **e** (1) **:** the fourth card of any denomination left in the dealing box in faro ⟨~ card⟩ (2) **:** the remaining card of a denomination or suit of which the other cards have been played or dealt ⟨a ~ king⟩ **2 a :** an outer protective covering, sheath, or housing ⟨a watch*case*⟩ ⟨a pillow*case*⟩ ⟨seed*case*⟩ **b** *obs* **:** the skin, hide, or pelt of an animal **c :** CASE SHOT **d :** the carcass of a building or of a piece of furniture **e** (1) **:** a book cover that is made complete before it is affixed to a book (2) **:** SLIPCASE **f :** a large triangular cavity in the upper anterior part of the head of a sperm whale formed by the transverse crest of the skull and the lateral crests of the maxillary bones; *also* **:** the fluid mixture of spermaceti and oil that it contains **g :** the hardened surface layer of case-hardened iron or steel ⟨a ~ of 0.040 inch⟩ **h :** the metal or paper and metal tube into which the components of a round of ammunition are loaded — compare CARTRIDGE 1a **3 :** the enclosing frame in which a door or window is set **:** CASING **4** *slang* **:** DOLLAR ⟨a 5-*case* note⟩ **5 :** a form in plaster made from a block mold and used for making the working molds in ceramics **6 :** a flat metal plate having on one side a layer of wax that when impressed forms a mold for an electrotype — **down to cases :** to the point **:** to the actual matter concerned ⟨get right *down to cases* without any preliminaries⟩

³case \"\ *vt* -ED/-ING/-S **1 a :** to enclose or put in a case or casing **:** cover or protect with or as if with a case **:** ENCASE ⟨the man who, *cased* in steel, had passed whole days and nights in the saddle —W.H.Prescott⟩ **b** *building* **:** to cover with a facing of different material usu. of a better grade ⟨~ a brick wall with stone⟩ **c :** to apply an overlay of glass to — compare CASING 1b **d :** to affix (a book) in a case by adhering the pastedowns to the inside of the covers — usu. used with *in;* compare BIND **e :** to lay (new type) **f :** to sort (mail) into a case **2 :** to strip the skin from specif. by making a single slit along the hind legs from heel to heel rather than along the belly **3 :** to line (a shaft or well) with supporting material (as metal pipe) **4 :** to order (tobacco leaf) **5** *slang* **a :** to inspect or study esp. with a view to the commission of a crime ⟨the bank was carefully *cased* before the robbery⟩ **b :** to inspect or examine closely **:** CANVASS **6 :** to cover the compost in (a mushroom bed) with a thin layer of soil to induce fruiting after the mycelium from the spawn has penetrated the bed **7 :** to keep track of (cards played)

case- *or* **caseo-** *comb form* [casein] **:** casein ⟨case*ase*⟩ ⟨*caseolysis*⟩

cas·e·ar·ia \ˌkasēˈa(a)rēə, ˌkā-\ *n, cap* [NL, fr. Johannes *Casearius* †1678 Dutch clergyman + NL *-ia*] **:** a large genus of cosmopolitan tropical trees (family Flacourtiaceae) having alternate toothed leaves, apetalous flowers, and capsular fruits and including some plants of which the leaves and bark are medicinal and others of which the fruit is used as a fish poison

¹ca·se·ate \ˈkāsēˌāt\ *vi* -ED/-ING/-S [L *case*us cheese + E *-ate* — more at CHEESE] *med* **:** to become cheesy **:** undergo caseation

²caseate \"\ *n* -s [*case-* + *-ate*] **:** CASEINATE

ca·se·a·tion \ˌkāsēˈāshən\ *n* -s [²caseate + *-ion*] **:** necrosis with conversion of damaged tissue into a soft cheeselike substance occurring particularly in the lesions of tuberculosis

case bay *n* [²case] **:** a bay or division of a roof or floor, except a tail bay, comprising two principals with the joists or purlins between them

casebearer \ˈ=ˌ==\ *n* **:** any of various insect larvae; *specif* **:** a moth larva that forms a protective case of silk or of fragments of leaves or other substances and is often a serious pest of cultivated plants — see CIGAR CASEBEARER, PISTOL CASEBEARER

case binding *n* [²case] **:** a process of bookbinding in which the book is fastened into a case

casebook \ˈ=ˌ=\ *n* [¹case + book] **:** a book containing records of cases illustrative of general principles or typifying significant situations that is used for reference and instruction (as in law, medicine, sociology, or psychiatry)

case bottle *n* [²case] **:** a bottle fitting into a case, sometimes with others

case-bound \ˈ=ˌ=\ *adj* [²case] **:** produced by case binding

casebox \ˈ=ˌ=\ *n* [³case + box] **:** a frame resembling an abacus with miniature cards at the end of each rod for marking the denomination of the cards as they are withdrawn from the dealing box in faro

case count *n* [²case] **:** a count of items to the case irrespective of quality — used in the buying of ungraded eggs

cased frame *n* **:** BOX FRAME

cased glass *also* **case glass** *n* **:** glass consisting of two or more fused layers of different colors often decorated by cutting so that the inner layers show through

case goods *n pl* [²case] **1** *also* **case furniture a :** furniture (as buffets, bureaus, bookcases, or vanities) that serves principally to provide interior space for storage (as by drawers or shelves) **b :** dining-room and bedroom furniture sold as sets **2 :** any of a number of products (as whiskey or canned milk) often sold by the case

case gun *n* [²case] **:** a gun of a caliber greater than one inch using ammunition with the powder charge in a metallic case — formerly called *rapid-fire gun*

case harden *vb* [²case (covering) + harden] *vt* **1 :** to harden (a ferrous alloy) so that the surface layer is made considerably harder than the interior (as by carburizing and quenching, cyaniding, carbonitriding, or nitriding) **2 :** to make callous or insensible **3 a :** to harden superficially, producing a hard, durable, or inflexible surface; *specif* **:** to affect (lumber) with case hardening **b :** to temper (glass) ~ *vi* **:** to become affected by the process of case hardening

case-hardened \ˈ=ˌ==\ *adj* **:** not easily moved or affected **:** INSENSIBLE, CALLOUS ⟨people are more *case-hardened* to sensation —E.D.Canham⟩ **:** set in a pattern of thought or behavior **:** resistant to change ⟨boys and girls are not yet *case-hardened* —*Canadian Forum*⟩

case hardening *n* **1 :** a condition in lumber in which too rapid drying and setting of the surface results in the shrinkage being inhibited by the still moist interior, the subsequent drying and shrinking of which sets up opposing stresses in the wood **2 :** the hardening and darkening of the surface of certain foods caused by too rapid evaporation during dehydration

case history *n* [¹case] **1 :** a record of an individual's personal and family history and environment for use in analyzing his case or as an instructive illustration of a type ⟨a *case history* of the patient⟩ **2 :** a genetic description of a single concrete case esp. as illustrative of a type ⟨the study is a *case history* of the . . . bogging down of a great reform movement —R.L. Strout⟩ **3 :** the history of a case ⟨trace the *case history* of a storm —Jerome Namias⟩ **4 :** a typical example **:** a significant illustration **:** TYPE ⟨a *case history* in corrupt municipal government —M.D.Hirsch⟩

ca·sein \kāˈsēn, ˈkāˌsēn, ˈkāsēən\ *n* -s *often attrib* [prob. fr. F *caséine*, fr. L *caseus* cheese + F *-ine* -in — more at CHEESE] **:** any of various phosphoproteins characteristic of the milk of mammals: as **a :** the phosphoprotein occurring as a colloidal suspension in milk — called also *caseinogen* **b :** the phosphoprotein that is precipitated as a cream-colored to light yellow curd from milk (as skim milk from a cow) by heating with an acid (as sulfuric acid) or by the action of lactic acid formed in the milk by souring and that is used chiefly in coating paper, in making cold-water and emulsion paints, adhesives, and synthetic fibers, and as an emulsifying and stabilizing agent — called also *acid casein* **c :** the phosphoprotein produced when milk is curdled by rennet and precipitated as a calcium compound in the form of a cream-colored curd that constitutes the principal protein of cheese and is used also in making casein plastics — called also *paracasein, rennet casein*

ca·sein·ate \kāˈsēˌnāt, ˈkāsēə,n-\ *n* -s [casein + *-ate*] **:** a compound of casein with a metal ⟨calcium ~⟩

casein glue *n* **:** a water-resistant adhesive made from casein and usu. hydrated lime and mixed with cold water for use esp. in making plywood and furniture

ca·sein·o·gen \kāˈsēnəjən, ˌkāsēˈin-\ *n* -s [ISV *casein* + *-o-* + *-gen*] **:** CASEIN a

casein paint *n* **:** a paint having as its vehicle an alkaline solution of casein

casein plastic *n* **:** any of certain tough hard hornlike substances obtained from powdered casein, usu. rennet casein, with water as the usual plasticizer, hardened after molding by the action of formaldehyde or some other agent, and used chiefly in making buttons and buckles

casekeeper \ˈ=ˌ==\ *n* [²case + keeper] **1 :** CASEBOX **2 :** the person in charge of the casebox

case knife *n* [²case] **1 :** a knife carried or kept in a sheath and formerly often used at table **2 :** a table knife; *esp* **:** one with a wooden handle

case law *n* [¹case] **:** law established by legal precedent or by judicial decision in particular cases **:** judge-made law

case·less \ˈkāsləs\ *adj* **:** being without a case

case liner *n* [²case] **:** a moisture-resistant and oil-resistant paper bag or other covering used to line a shipping case

case load *n* [¹case + load] **:** the number of cases handled in a particular period (as by a court, welfare agency, or clinic)

cas·el·ty *var of* CASALTY

case made *n* [¹case] **:** a statutory mode of procedure, often briefer than at common law, for making an appeal to a higher court and often including matters which do not appear in the record at common law and sometimes presenting only certain points of law sought to be reviewed **:** a case reserved for consideration of an appellate court in the manner provided for by statute

casemaker \ˈ=ˌ==\ *n* **1 :** one that makes cases; *specif* **:** a worker or machine that makes cases for books **2 :** one that assembles and pastes pieces of leather for later sewing to make articles such as pocketbooks

casemaking clothes moth \ˈ=ˌ==-\ *n* **:** a common clothes moth (*Tinea pellionella*) having a larva that makes and lives in a tube of its food material fastened with silk which it spins

case·mate \ˈkāˌsmāt, *usu* -ād+V\ *n* -s [MF, fr. OIt *casamatta*, prob. fr. *casa* house + *matta*, fem. of *matto* mad, crazy, fr. L *mattus* stupid, drunk — more at CASA, MAT] **1 :** a fortified usu. masonry position or chamber in which cannon or other guns may be placed to fire through embrasures **2 :** an armored enclosure for a gun on a warship and with an embrasure for firing through

case·mat·ed \-ād·əd\ *adj* **:** furnished with, protected by, or built like a casemate

case·ment \ˈkāsmənt, *older Brit* -āzm-\ *n* -s [ME, prob. modif. of ONF *encassement* frame, fr. *encasser* to enchase, frame, fr. *casse* case — more at CASE (box)] **1 :** a hollow molding similar to a cavetto or scotia **2 a :** a window sash that opens on hinges fastened to the upright side of the frame **b** *or* **casement window :** a window with such a sash or sashes **c :** WINDOW **d :** CASEMENT CLOTH

casement 2b

casement cloth *n* **:** a plain or figured fabric in a sheer weave used for window draperies

case·ment·ed \-məntəd, -ˌmen-\ *adj* **:** having a casement

case method *n* [¹case] **1 :** CASE SYSTEM **2 :** a method of instruction used esp. in colleges and universities that presents for observation and analysis actual recorded or current instances of the problem under study and often calls upon the student to render practical help

case moth *n* [caseworm] *Austral* **:** any of several moths having larvae that are caseworms

caseo- — see CASE-

case of first impression [¹case] **:** a case presenting a novel question of law for which no controlling precedent can be found

case oil *n* [²case] **:** kerosene contained in 5-gallon tin cans packed by twos in wooden cases

ca·se·o·lyt·ic \ˌkāsēōˈlid·ik\ *adj* [*case-* + *-lytic*] **:** capable of breaking down casein; *broadly* **:** PROTEOLYTIC ⟨~ bacteria⟩

case on appeal [¹case] **:** the statement which an appellant lays before the court for the prosecution of his appeal as the presentation of the facts on which the appeal is based

ca·se·ous \ˈkāsēəs\ *adj* [L *case*us cheese + E *-ous* — more at CHEESE] **:** characterized by caseation

caseous lymphadenitis *n* **:** a chronic infectious disease of sheep and goats characterized by caseation of the lymph glands and occas. of parts of the lungs, liver, spleen, and kidneys that is caused by a bacterium (*Corynebacterium pseudotuberculosis*) — called also *pseudotuberculosis*

case-phrase \ˈ=ˌ=\ *n* [¹case] **:** a prepositional phrase indicating sense relations of a kind that may also be indicated by a case form (as *head of a cow* compared with *cow's* head)

case piece *n* [²case] **:** a piece of case goods

cas·er \ˈkāsə(r)\ *n* -s [² and ³case + *-er*] **1 :** one that cases or that makes, packs, or works with cases or casings **2 :** a pottery worker who makes block, case, and working molds of plaster of paris — called also *blocker* **3 :** one that applies casing to tobacco leaves or lump tobacco **4 :** a shoe-factory worker who selects and bundles paired soles from stock according to orders from the lasting and bottoming departments

case reserved *n* [¹case] **:** a statement of facts and of the points of law arising thereon drawn up by counsel and certified by the trial judge as the basis for argument and determination before the full bench

ca·sern *or* **ca·serne** \kəˈzərn, -ze(ə)rn\ *n* -s [F *caserne*, fr. MF, small room for the night watch, fr. OProv *cazerna* group of four persons, modif. of L *quaterni* four each — more at QUATERNARY] **:** a military barracks in a garrison town

cases *pl of* CASE, *pres 3d sing of* CASE

case shot \ˈkās(h),shät\ *n* [²case] **:** an artillery projectile consisting of a number of balls or metal fragments enclosed in a case — see CANISTER 3

case spring *n* [²case] **:** one of two springs controlling the hinged cover of a hunting watch, a lock spring that keeps it closed and a lift spring that causes it to open when the lock spring is released by pressure on the crown

case stated *n* [¹case] **:** an agreed statement of facts made for presentation to a court in order to obtain a decision of law upon the facts stated

case study *n* [¹case] **1 :** an intensive analysis of an individual unit (as a person, social group, institution, community, or culture) stressing developmental factors in relation to environment ⟨the *case study* of a juvenile delinquent⟩ ⟨a *case study* of capitalism⟩ **2 :** CASE HISTORY; *specif* **:** a detailed analysis of the personal and social history of an individual pupil used esp. in student counseling

case study method *n* **:** a method of research used esp. in sociology by which accumulated case histories are analyzed with a view toward formulating general principles

case system *n* [¹case] **:** a system of teaching law in which the instruction is chiefly on the basis of leading or selected cases as primary authorities instead of from textbooks

caseweed \ˈ=ˌ=\ *n* [²case + weed] **:** SHEPHERD'S PURSE

casewood \ˈ=ˌ=\ *n* [²case + wood] **:** wood for making case furniture

¹casework \ˈ=ˌ=\ *n* [²case + work] **1** *bookbinding* **:** the making of cases **2** *printing* **:** HAND COMPOSITION

²casework \"\ *n* [¹case + work] **:** social work involving direct consideration of the problems, needs, and adjustments of the individual case (as a person or family)

caseworker \ˈ=ˌ==\ *n* [¹case + worker] **:** a worker (as in a social welfare agency) who investigates, diagnoses, and often assists in individual cases (as of persons or families in need of financial or psychiatric aid)

caseworm \ˈ=ˌ=\ *n* [²case + worm] **:** an insect larva (as a caddisworm or a casebearer) that makes a case for its body

¹cash \ˈkash, -aa(ə)-,-ai-\ *n* -ES *often attrib* [modif. of MF or OIt; MF *casse* money box, fr. OIt *cassa* box, money box, fr. L *capsa* chest, case — more at CASE] **1** *obs* **:** a money box or chest **:** TILL **2 a :** ready money (as coin, specie, paper money, an instrument, token, or anything else being used as a medium of exchange) ⟨a check made payable to "cash" will be paid in ~ to the bearer⟩; *broadly* **:** bank deposits and certain readily negotiable paper (as checks, drafts, notes, bearer bonds, coupons) **b :** money or its equivalent paid immediately or promptly after purchasing ⟨sell goods for ~⟩ ⟨a ~ sale⟩ **3** *obs* **:** an amount of money **:** SUM ⟨keep a large ~ on hand⟩ — **cash on the nail** *or* **cash on the barrelhead :** CASH 2b ⟨my price is 10 dollars *cash on the nail*⟩

²cash \"\ *n, pl* **cash** [Pg *caixa*, fr. Tamil *kācu*, a small copper coin, fr. Skt *karṣa*, a weight of gold or silver; akin to OPer *karsha-*, a weight] **1 :** any of various coins of small value in China and southern India: as **a :** any of several usu. copper coins formerly issued in the Madras States of British India, in French India, and Danish Tranquebar **b :** a Chinese coin usu. of copper alloy that is about the size of a U.S. quarter, has a square hole in the center, and was formerly issued by both the central and provincial governments **2 :** a unit of value equivalent to one cash coin

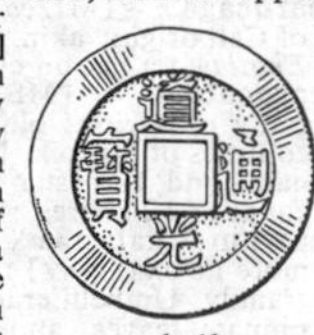

cash 1b

³cash \"\ *vt* -ED/-ING/-ES [¹cash] **1 :** to pay or obtain cash for (as a check or bond) **:** exchange for money ⟨the store will ~ your check⟩ ⟨~ your check at the bank⟩ **2 :** to lead and win a bridge trick with (a card that is the highest remaining card of its suit) — **cash in one's chips :** DIE

⁴cash \"\ *adj* [¹cash] **:** to be delivered and paid for within a specified period ⟨~ grain⟩

cash *abbr* cashier

cash account *n* **1 :** an account in which money transactions are recorded **2** *Scot* **:** bank credit

¹cash-and-carry \ˈ==ˈ==\ *adj* **:** sold for cash and without delivery service

²cash-and-carry \"\ *n* [¹cash-and-carry] **:** selling or the policy of selling cash-and-carry

cash assets *n pl* **:** assets consisting of cash and items readily convertible to cash (as marketable securities or life insurance)

¹cashaw *var of* CUSHAW

²ca·shaw \kəˈshȯ\ *n* -s [of African origin; akin to Yoruba *ka²shā²*, a running plant, Bobangi *nkasa*, a tree] *Jamaica* **:** MESQUITE 1a

cash basis *n* **:** a method of keeping accounts that includes as income only what has been received in cash and as expenses only those paid in cash — compare ACCRUAL BASIS

cashbook \ˈ=ˌ=\ *n* **:** a book of original entry in which record is kept of all cash receipts and disbursements **:** a cash journal

cashbox \ˈ=ˌ=\ *n* **:** a box or other receptacle for keeping cash — see BOX illustration

cashboy \ˈ=ˌ=\ *n* **1 :** a store messenger given the job of carrying customers' money from the salesperson to a cashier and bringing back change **2 :** a general helper and errand boy at the exchange desk of a retail store

cash budget *n* **:** a projection of the future receipts and expenditures of a business

cash carrier *n* **:** a device (as a pneumatic tube) for conveying cash to and from a cashier

cash contract *n* **:** a sale on a stock exchange requiring cash settlement by a certain time on the day the contract is made

cash credit *n, in Scottish banking* **:** credit given to a depositor for an overdraft allowed by agreement up to a specified sum

cash crop *n* **:** a crop produced or gathered primarily for the market and readily salable (as cotton, tobacco, or vegetables)

cash customer *n* **:** a customer that pays cash for purchases

cash discount *n* **:** a discount granted in consideration of immediate payment or payment within a prescribed time

cash·el \ˈkashəl\ *n* -s [IrGael *caiseal*, fr. MIr *caisel* castle, fr. L *castellum* — more at CASTLE] **:** the ancient circular wall found in Scotland and Ireland enclosing a group of ecclesiastical buildings

cash·ew \ˈka(ˌ)shü, -ˈaa-,-ˈai-; kəˈshü\ *n* -s [Pg *cajú, acajú*, fr. Tupi *acajú*] **1 :** a tropical American tree (*Anacardium occidentale*) naturalized in all warm countries and important chiefly for its nut but yielding also a gum **2 a :** CASHEW NUT **b :** CASHEW APPLE

cashew apple *n* **:** the pear-shaped edible receptacle on which the cashew nut is borne

cashew family *n* **:** ANACARDIACEAE

cashew lake *n* **:** AUBURN

cashew nut *n* **1 :** the kidney-shaped fruit of the cashew borne at the apex of a fleshy receptacle and rendered edible by expelling the caustic oil from the shell by roasting **2 :** SEDGE 3

cashew nutshell liquid *n* **:** a phenolic oily liquid obtained from the double shell of the cashew nut and used chiefly in making phenolic resins notable for their flexibility and alkali resistance

cashgirl \ˈ=ˌ=\ *n* **:** a girl having the duties of a cashboy

ca·shi·bo \kəˈshē(ˌ)bō\ *n, pl* **cashibo** *or* **cashibos** *usu cap* [Sp, perh. fr. Pano, lit., vampire (orig. an insult)] **1 a :** a Panoan people of eastern Peru **b :** a member of such people **2 :** the language of the Cashibo people

¹ca·shier \(ˈ)kaˈshi(ə)r, -kaa-,-kai-, -iə\ *vt* -ED/-ING/-S [modif. of D *casseren*, fr. MF *casser* to discharge, annul — more at QUASH] **1 :** to dismiss from service; *esp* **:** to dismiss summarily, ignominiously, and formally from a military or state position ⟨a court-martial sentenced him to two years' hard labor and ordered him ~*ed* —*Time*⟩ **2 :** to discard or reject **:** do away with ⟨~ the literal express sense of the words —Robert South⟩ **syn** see DISMISS

²cash·ier \"\ *n* -s [modif. of D or MF; D *kassier*, fr. MF *cassier*, fr. *casse* merchandise box, money box — more at CASH] **:** one that has charge of money: as **a :** one of the higher officers in a bank or trust company responsible for moneys received (as for discounts, interest, dividends) and for moneys expended (as for operating expenses, letters of credit); *sometimes* **:** the chief executive officer of a bank charged with the management of its property and business in the ordinary way **b :** an officer usu. of the treasurer's department of a company who has responsibility for receipt, disbursement, and cash on hand **c :** a clerical worker in any business who handles and keeps records of cash transactions, receipts, and disbursements **d :** one that handles customer payments for goods or services rendered, either at the time (as one that takes money at a ticket window) or for bills previously rendered (as one that receives payments on credit accounts)

cashier's check *n* **:** a check drawn by a bank upon its own funds and signed by the cashier

cash in *vt* : to convert into cash ⟨*cashed in* all his bonds⟩ ~ *vi* **1 a** : to cash in one's chips in a gambling game (as poker) : retire from a gambling game **b** : to settle accounts and withdraw from a business arrangement; *also* : to withdraw from any involvement **2** : to obtain monetary profit or other advantage ⟨the rise in the market will enable investors to *cash in*⟩ — often used with *on* ⟨politicians *cashed in* on the people's apathy⟩ **3** : DIE

cash letter *n* : a deposit slip or list mailed by the transit department of a bank to a correspondent bank together with items to be credited immediately upon receipt

cash·mere *or* **kash·mir** \ˈkazh,mi(ə)r, -aizh-, -iə; -ash-, -aa-,-ai-\ *n* -s [fr. *Cashmere, Kashmir,* region in the northern part of the Indian subcontinent] **1 a** : fine soft light wool from the undercoat of the Kashmir goat of the Himalayan regions **b** : a fine yarn made of this wool alone or in a blend and used for sweaters and overcoatings **2 a** : a fine soft twilled fabric handloomed orig. from the underwool of Kashmir goats but imitated now on jacquard looms and used esp. for shawls with brilliant coloring and embroidery **b** : a soft lightweight clothing fabric of twill weave usu. of wool but often of other fibers or blends of fibers

cashmere goat *n, usu cap C* [fr. *Cashmere,* region] : KASHMIR GOAT

cashmere stag *n, usu cap C* [fr. *Cashmere,* region] : a deer (*Cervus cashmirianus*) of the northern Indian subcontinent that is similar to but larger than the red deer

cash·mer·ette \¦==ˈret\ *n* -s [*cashmere* + *-ette*] : a clothing fabric of cotton or of wool and silk made with a soft and glossy surface to imitate cashmere

cashmiri *usu cap, var of* KASHMIRI

cash money *n, South & Midland* : money in cash

cash nexus *n* : an agglomerate of impersonal monetary factors specif. considered as the basis for human relations

cash on delivery *adj (or adv)* : collect on delivery — abbr. *COD*

cash refund annuity *n* : a refund annuity payable in cash to a beneficiary upon the annuitant's death

cash register *n* : a business machine that records the amount of money received (as in running daily sales), that usu. has a money drawer, that exhibits the amount of each sale, and that often performs related operations (as totaling receipts, counting particular operations, certifying sales slips, or punching coded data on tape for later recording in ledgers or analysis sheets)

cash tenant *n* : a tenant who pays a money rent for a farm — compare SHARE-TENANT

cash value *n* : the amount available to the owner of a life insurance policy upon termination before maturity, being the reserve held by the company against the policy less the surrender charge if any

casimire *var of* CASSIMERE

cas·i·mi·roa \,kazəməˈrōə, -ˈmirəwə\ *n, cap* [NL, fr. *Casimiro* Gómez Ortega †1810 Span. botanist] : a small genus of tropical American evergreen trees and shrubs (family Rutaceae) having alternate digitately compound leaves and small greenish yellow flowers

casinet *var of* CASSINETTE

cas·ing \ˈkāsiŋ, -ēŋ\ *n* -s [fr. gerund of ³*case*] **1** : something that encases : material for encasing : a case esp. for ornament, protection, or support: as **a** : an enclosing frame; *specif* : the wide molding used around door and window openings **b** : a thin layer of glass fused upon glass of a different kind or color **c** : a metal pipe used to case a well **d** : TIRE 2c **e** : a skinlike case for processed meat (as sausage) usu. made of the cleaned intestines of cattle, hogs, or sheep or of cellulose **f** : ²CASE 2e(1) **g** : the layer of soil with which a mushroom bed is cased **2** : the layer of rock enclosing a vein, usu. modified by contact with the intruded ore **3** : an opening or pocket between two parallel lines of stitching through at least two layers of cloth into which something (as a rod, string, or bone) may be inserted for supporting, gathering, or stiffening and which is used esp. in curtains and clothing **4** : a solution of flavoring materials in either water or alcohol that is applied to cigarette blends, chewing plugs, and smoking mixtures during manufacture

casing dog *also* **casing spear** *n* : a tool for removing sections of casing from a drilled or bored well

casinghead \ˈ==,=\ *n* : a fitting at the top of the casing of an oil or gas well to allow pumping, cleaning, and the separation of gas from oil

casinghead gas *n* : natural gas rich in hydrocarbon vapors that is taken without processing from an oil well

casinghead gasoline *n* : NATURAL GASOLINE

casing nail *n* : a wire nail that has a small slightly flared head and is used for finish work

casing shoe *n* : a cylinder or ring of hard steel with a cutting edge attached to the bottom of a string of well casing

ca·si·no \kəˈsē(,)nō\ *n* -s [It, fr. *casa* house — more at CASA] **1** : a building or room used for social meetings and public amusements (as dancing); *specif* : a building or room for gambling **2 a** : a small usu. decoratively designed Italian country house **b** : SUMMERHOUSE **3** *also* **cas·si·no** : a card game played by two or more persons in which each player wins cards by matching or combining cards exposed on the table with cards from his hand — see BIG CASINO, LITTLE CASINO; ROYAL CASINO, SPADE CASINO

casino pink *n* : MADDER ROSE

ca·si·ta \kəˈsēd·ə\ *n* -s [Sp, dim. of *casa* house — more at CASA] : a small house

¹**cask** \ˈkask, -aa(ə)-,-ai-,-ȧ-\ *n* -s [Sp *casco* potsherd, skull, helmet, cask, fr. *cascar* to crack, break — more at CASCARA] **1** : any barrel-shaped vessel made of staves, headings, and hoops usu. closely fitted together so as to hold liquids — see BUTT, HOGSHEAD, KEG, PIPE, TUN **2 a** *archaic* : CASKET **b** *obs* : CASE, SHELL **3** : a cask and its contents ⟨a ~ of wine⟩; *also* : the quantity contained in a cask

²**cask** \"\ *vt* -ED/-ING/-S : to put or store in a cask

¹**cas·ket** \-kəskət, -ˈaa-,-ˈai-,-ˈȧ-, *usu* -əd·+V\ *n* -s [ME, modif. of MF *cassette* — more at CASSETTE] **1** : a small usu. ornamental chest or box (as for jewels or other valuables) **2** : something regarded as a repository ⟨the individual is only the ~ of the continuing race —J.S.Huxley⟩ **3** : a usu. ornamented and lined rectangular box or chest for a corpse to be buried in — compare COFFIN

²**casket** \"\ *vt* -ED/-ING/-S : to put into or enclose in a casket

cask shell *n* : TUN SHELL

cas·par·i·an dot \(ˈ)kaˈspa(a)rēən-, (ˈ)käˈspär-\ *n, usu cap C* : the Casparian strip viewed in cross section

casparian strip *n, usu cap C* [Robert *Caspary* †1887 Ger. botanist + E *-an*] : a secondary thickening in many endodermal cells in the form of a continuous band or strip on the radial and transverse walls — compare ENDODERMIS

cas·pi·an \ˈkaspēən, -ˈaa-\ *adj, usu cap* [L *caspius* (fr. Gk *kaspios*) + E *-an*] : of, relating to, or characteristic of the Caspian sea

caspian languages *n pl, usu cap C* : a group of Iranian languages or dialects spoken chiefly in the Caspian provinces of Persia but distinct from Persian and including Tat, Talishi, Gilaki, Mazanderani, and Samnani

caspian tern *n, usu cap C* : a large scarlet-billed tern (*Sterna caspia* or *Hydropygne caspia*) widely distributed in the northern hemisphere with one subspecies occurring in much of northern No. America

casque \ˈkask, -aa(ə)-,-ai-,-ȧ-\ *n* -s [alter. (influenced by F *casque,* fr. Sp *casco*) of *cask*] **1** : a piece of armor for the head : a helmet or military headpiece of any kind **2** : a helmet-shaped hat or headdress **3** : a process or structure suggestive of a helmet: as **a** : the process of the bill of a hornbill **b** : the frontal shield of a coot or gallinule **c** : the covering of bony plates enclosing the head of certain extinct fishes

light casque, 15th cent.

casqued \-skt\ *adj* : provided with a casque : wearing a casque

cas·quet \ˈkaskət, -ˈaa-,-ˈai-,-ˈȧ-\ *n* -s [F or Sp; F, fr. Sp *casquete,* fr. *casco* helmet] : CASQUE; *also* : a light open headpiece

cas·que·tel \¦==ˈtel\ *n* -s [*casquet* + *-el*] : a light open helmet without beaver or visor

cas·quette \(ˈ)=ˈket\ *n* -s [F, dim. of *casque* helmet — more at CASQUE] : a cap with visor

cass *vt* -ED/-ING/-ES [ME *cassen,* fr. MF *casser* — more at QUASH] **1** *Scots law, obs* : to render useless or void : QUASH, ANNUL **2** *obs* : DISCHARGE, CASHIER

cassaba *var of* CASABA

cas·sa·ba·nana \¦kasəbəˈnanə\ *n* -s [origin unknown] : a tropical vine (*Sicana odorifera*) of the family Cucurbitaceae that is often cultivated for its ornamental slender fruit similar to the vegetable marrow — called also *curuba, musk cucumber*

cas·san·dra \kəˈsandrə, -ˈaan-\ *n* -s *usu cap* [after *Cassandra,* daughter of King Priam of Troy, renowned as a prophetess of evil, fr. L, fr. Gk *Kassandra*] **1** : one who prophesies misfortune or disaster **2** [NL, fr. L] : LEATHERLEAF 1

cas·san·dran \-rən\ *or* **cas·san·dri·an** \-rēən\ *adj, usu cap* [*Cassandra* + E *-an* or *-ian*] : prophetic of misfortune

cas·sa·pan·ca \,kasəˈpaŋkə\ *n* -s [It *cassapanca, cassabanca,* fr. *cassa* box (fr. L *capsa*) + *panca, banca* bench — more at CASE, BANK] : a cassone with wooden back and arms added to form a settee

cas·sa·reep \ˈkasə,rēp\ *n* -s [alter. of earlier *casserepo,* of Cariban origin; akin to Galibi *kaseripu,* Akawai *cassiripo*] : a flavoring agent orig. made in the West Indies by boiling the juice of the bitter cassava to a thick syrup

cassate *vt* -ED/-ING/-S [LL *cassatus,* past part. of *cassare*] *obs* : CASS

¹**cas·sa·tion** \kaˈsāshən, kə-\ *n* -s [ME *cassacioun,* fr. MF *cassation,* fr. *casser* to annul + *-ation* — more at QUASH] : the act of annulling, canceling, or quashing : ABROGATION ⟨a general ~ of their constitutions —J.L.Motley⟩ — see COURT OF CASSATION

²**cassation** \"\ *n* -s [G *kassation,* fr. G dial. (orig. students' slang) *kassation, gassation* serenade, fr. *kassaten, gassaten* (in the phrase *kassaten gehen, gassaten gehen, gassatim gehen* to roam the streets at night serenading ladies or looking for love affairs or fights), fr. G *gasse* street, fr. OHG *gazza* — more at GATE] : an 18th century instrumental composition in several short movements that is similar in style to the serenade and often performed outdoors

cas·sa·va *also* **ca·sa·va** \kəˈsävə, -ˈä-\ *n* -s [Sp *cazabe* cassava bread, fr. Taino *caçábi*] **1** : any of several plants of the genus *Manihot* having fleshy rootstocks yielding a nutritious starch and cultivated throughout the tropics where it provides a staple food — called also *manioc, tapioca plant;* see BITTER CASSAVA, CASSAREEP, CASSIRI, SWEET CASSAVA **2** : the rootstock of the cassava plant used in making tapioca, cassava bread, and starch

casse \ˈkas\ *n* -s [F, lit., breakage, fr. *casser* to break — more at QUASH] : a disorder that sometimes occurs in wine usu. due to the formation of colloidal complexes of metals resulting from the use of metallic utensils

cas·se·grain·i·an telescope \¦kasə¦grānēən-\ *n, usu cap C* [N. *Cassegrain* 17th cent. Fr. physician who invented it in 1672 + E *-ian*] : a reflecting telescope that has a paraboloidal primary mirror and hyperboloidal secondary mirror, is equivalent in its optical effects to a telephoto lens, and usu. has the light brought to a focus through a perforation in the center of the primary mirror

cassel *usu cap, var of* KASSEL

cas·sel brown *or* **cas·sel earth** \ˈkasəl-, -ˈä-\ *n, often cap C* [fr. *Cassel* (*Kassel*), Germany] : VANDYKE BROWN

cassel green *n, often cap C* : MANGANESE GREEN

cas·sel·mann's green \ˈkasəlmənz-, -ˈä-\ *n, usu cap C* [prob. trans. of G *Casselmanns grün,* after *Casselmann fl* 1890 Ger. chemist, its discoverer] : a basic copper sulfate used as a pigment

cas·sel yellow \ˈkasəl-, -ˈä-\ *n, often cap C* **1** : an oxychloride of lead approximately $PbCl_2.7PbO$ used as a pigment — called also *mineral yellow, Turner's yellow* **2** : LEMON YELLOW 1b

cas·se·na \kəˈsēnə\ *n* -s [earlier *casseena,* fr. Timucua] : a yaupon (*Ilex vomitoria*)

¹**cas·se·role** \ˈkasə,rōl, ˈkaas- *also* ˈkaz-\ *n* -s [F, saucepan, fr. MF, irreg. fr. *casse* ladle, dripping pan, fr. OProv *cassa* ladle, saucepan, fr. ML *cattia* dipper, modif. of Gk *kyathion* small ladle, dim. of *kyathos* ladle — more at CYATHUS] **1** : a deep round usu. porcelain dish with a handle used for heating substances in the laboratory **2** : a vessel of earthenware, glass, or metal usu. having a cover and a handle or a separable holder of metal and in which food may be baked and served **3** : a dish cooked and served in a casserole **4** : RUSTIC BROWN

casserole 1

²**casserole** \"\ *vt* -ED/-ING/-S : to cook in a casserole

casses *pres 3d sing of* CASS

cas·sette \kəˈset, ka-\ *n* -s [F, fr. MF, dim. of ONF *casse* box, case — more at CASE] **1** : CASKET **2** : SAGGER 1a **3** : a lighttight magazine for holding sensitized film or plates for use in a camera; *specif* : one for holding the intensifying screens and film in X-ray photography

cas·sia \ˈkashə, -ˈaa-,-ˈai- *also, esp in sense 2,* -sēə\ *n* [ME, fr. OE, fr. L *casia, cassia,* fr. Gk *kasia, kassia,* of Sem origin; akin to Heb *qĕṣīʽāh* cassia] **1** -s : any of the coarser varieties of cinnamon bark — see CHINESE CINNAMON **2** *cap* [NL, fr. L, cassia bark] : a genus of herbs, shrubs, and trees (family Leguminosae) that are native to warm regions and have even-pinnate leaves sometimes much reduced and nearly regular flowers with calyx teeth equal and usu. longer than the corolla — see RINGWORM BUSH, SENNA **3** -s : CASSIA FISTULA

cassia bark *n* : CHINESE CINNAMON

cassia bud *n* : the dried flower bud of any of several plants of the genus *Cinnamomum* (esp. *C. cassia*)

cas·si·a·ce·ae \,kasēˈāsē,ē\ [NL, fr. *Cassia,* type genus + *-aceae*] *syn of* CAESALPINIACEAE

cassia fis·tu·la \-ˈfis(h)chələ\ *n* [ME, fr. ML, lit., fistulous (spongy) cassia] : the dried pods of the drumstick tree the sweet pulp of which is a mild laxative — called also *purging cassia*

cassia flask *n* : a small volumetric flask with a long graduated neck used in pharmacy for determining cinnamaldehyde in cassia bark and other forms of cinnamon

cassia lig·nea \-ˈlignēə\ *n, pl* **cassia ligne·as** [ME, fr. ML lit., ligneous (woody) cassia] : Chinese cinnamon in thick flat pieces taken from wild trees

cassia oil *n* : a yellowish or brownish essential oil that contains chiefly cinnamaldehyde, is obtained from the leaves and young twigs of Chinese cinnamon (*Cinnamomum cassia*), and is used chiefly as a flavor and in medicine — called also *Chinese cinnamon oil, cinnamon oil*

cassia pulp *n* : the sweet pulp of cassia fistula

cas·sic acid \ˈkasik-\ *n* [NL *Cassia* (genus name of *Cassia reticulata*) + E *-ic*] : RHEIN

cas·sid·e·ous \kəˈsidēəs, ka-\ *adj* [L *cassid-, cassis* helmet + E *-eous*] *bot* : shaped like a helmet

cas·sid·i·dae \kəˈsidə,dē, ka-\ *n pl, cap* [NL, fr. *Cassid-, Cassis,* type genus + *-idae*] : a family of usu. large marine gastropod mollusks (order Pectinibranchia) having thick heavy shells of which many are used for making cameos — see HELMET SHELL

¹**cas·sie** \ˈkāzē, ˈkasē\ *n* -s [Orkney Islands Norse *kassi;* akin to Icel *kassi, kass* box, creel, ON *kjarr* underbrush — more at CHARE] *Scot* : a basket made of twisted straw

²**cas·sie** \ˈkasē\ *n* -s [F, fr. Prov *cacio,* short for *acacio* acacia, fr. L *acacia* — more at ACACIA] : HUISACHE

cas·sie paper \ˈkasē-\ *n* [part modif., part trans. of F *papier cassé,* lit., broken paper, fr. *papier* paper + *cassé,* past part. of *casser* to break — more at QUASH] : the top and bottom sheets of packaged paper when damaged (as in transportation) — compare RETREE

cas·si·mere *also* **cas·i·mire** \ˈkazə,mi(ə)r, -asə-,-aasə-\ *n* -s [fr. *Cassimere* (now usu. *Kashmir*), region in northern part of the Indian subcontinent] : a smooth twilled suiting fabric usu. made of wool; *also* : any of various fancy woolen clothing fabrics

cas·si·na *or* **cas·si·ne** \kəˈsēnə\ *n* -s [*cassina* fr. Timucua *cassiné; cassine* fr. MF *casiné,* fr. Timucua] : a yaupon (*Ilex vomitoria*)

cas·si·nese \¦kasᵊn¦ēz, -ēs\ *adj, usu cap* [It, fr. Monte *Cassino,* Italy, site of the monastery from which the Benedictine rule spread + It *-ese*] **1** : of or relating to a congregation of Benedictine monasteries organized in the 15th century to promote the primitive observance of the Benedictine rule **2** : of or relating to the American Cassinese congregation established in 1855 and including a majority of the Benedictine abbeys in the U. S.

cas·si·nette *also* **cas·i·net** \¦kasᵊn¦et\ *n* -s [perh. irreg. fr. *cassimere*] : a lightweight twilled trousering usu. with cotton warp and wool filling

cas·sin finch \ˈkasᵊn-, -sin-\ *n, usu cap C* [after John *Cassin* †1869 Am. ornithologist] : a large finch (*Carpodacus cassinii*) of the Rocky mountain region the male being rosy red with dusky-brown shoulders, wings, and tail and the female drab and sparrowlike

cassing *pres part of* CASS

cassino *var of* CASINO

cas·sin's auklet \ˈkasᵊnz-, -sinz-\ *n, usu cap C* [after John *Cassin*] : a very small chubby auklet (*Ptychoramphus aleuticus*) common along the Pacific coast of No. America

cassin's kingbird *n, usu cap C* : a kingbird (*Tyrannus vociferans*) of southwestern No. America that is largely gray with a sulfur-yellow abdomen and has in the male an orange-red tuft of feathers on the crown

cas·sio·ber·ry \ˈkashə,berē\ *n* -ES [*cassina* + *-o-* + *berry*] **1** : a yaupon (*Ilex vomitoria*); *also* : its fruit **2** : a shrub (*Viburnum obovatum*) of the southern U.S.; *also* : its fruit **3** : a winterberry (*Ilex laevigata*); *also* : its fruit

cas·si·o·pe \kaˈsīə(,)pē\ *n, cap* [NL, fr. L *Cassiope, Cassiopea,* mythical queen of Ethiopia and mother of Andromeda, fr. Gk *Kassiopē, Kassiopeia, Kassiepeia*] : a genus of low tufted shrubs of the family Ericaceae with mosslike foliage and nodding white or pink flowers found in the colder parts of the north temperate zone

cas·si·o·pe·ian \¦kasēə¦pē(y)ən\ *adj, usu cap* [*Cassiopeia,* a northern constellation between Andromeda and Cepheus (fr. L *Cassiopeia, Cassiepeia,* fr. Gk *Kassiopeia, Kassiepeia*) + E *-an*] : of or relating to the constellation Cassiopeia

cas·si·ri \¦kasə¦rē\ *n* -s [Carib *cassiri,* of Tupian origin; akin to Tupi *cassiri, caxiri* cassiri] : a drink resembling beer made by allowing cassava juice to ferment

¹**cas·sis** \ˈkasəs\ *n, cap* [NL, fr. L, helmet — more at HOOD] : a genus (the type of the family Cassididae) of mollusks comprising forms (as the cameo shell) with the body whorl very large and the shell more or less globular

²**cas·sis** \kaˈsēs\ *n* -ES [F, fr. L *cassia* — more at CASSIA] **1** : a black currant (*Ribes nigrum*) of Europe **2** : a syrupy liquor of low alcoholic strength made from black currants and used chiefly as a flavoring and sweetening agent with vermouth, water, or spirits — see VERMOUTH CASSIS

cassite *usu cap, var of* KASSITE

cas·sit·er·ite \kəˈsid·ə,rīt\ *n* -s [F *cassitérite,* fr. Gk *kassiteros* tin + F *-ite*] : a brown or black mineral that consists of tin dioxide SnO_2, is the chief source of metallic tin, and occurs in tetragonal crystals of brilliant adamantine luster and also in massive forms sometimes (1) compact with concentric fibrous structure resembling wood and sometimes (2) in rolled or pebbly fragments (hardness 6–7, sp. gr. 6.8–7.1) — called also respectively (1) *wood tin* (2) *stream tin*

cassius purple *n, usu cap C* : PURPLE OF CASSIUS

cas·sock \ˈkasək, -ˈaa-\ *n* -s [MF *casaque,* fr. Per *kazhāghand* padded jacket, fr. *kazh, kaj* raw silk + *āghand* stuffed] **1** : a long loose coat or gown formerly worn by men and women; *specif* : a long coat formerly worn by soldiers **2 a** : a long close-fitting garment reaching to the feet that is worn by the clergy of certain churches often during divine service under a surplice or vestments and by choristers under a surplice or cotta and by vergers as an outer garment **b** : a shorter light double-breasted coat or jacket usu. of black silk that is worn under the Geneva gown **c** : an apronlike garment worn under vestments at outdoor ceremonies esp. by Anglican clergymen — called also *skirt cassock* **3 a** : the clerical or priestly office **b** : CLERGYMAN, PRIEST

cas·so·lette \¦kasə¦let\ *n* -s [F, fr. MF, fr. OProv *casoleta* small saucepan, dim. of *casola* saucepan, fr. *cassa* ladle, saucepan — more at CASSEROLE] **1** : a vessel often with a perforated cover in which perfumes may be kept or burned **2** : a small casserole in which an individual portion of food is cooked and served

cas·son \ˈkasᵊn, -zᵊn\ *n* -s [earlier *casen,* prob. of Scand origin; akin to ON *kǫs* heap, Dan *kokase* cow dung; akin to ON *kasta* to throw — more at CAST] *dial Eng* : dried dung of cattle used for fuel — usu. used in pl.

cas·so·ne \kəˈsōnē, -,nā\ *n, pl* **casso·ni** \-(,)nē\ [It, aug. of *cassa* box — more at CASH] : a large Italian chest having a hinged lid and often decorated with carving or painting

cas·soon \kəˈsün\ *n* -s [It *cassone* — more at CAISSON] **1** : CAISSON 1 **2** : COFFER 5a

cas·sou·let \¦kasə¦lā\ *n* -s [F, fr. F dial., lit., stone dish (where this food is prepared), dim. of *cassolo* bowl, dim. of *casso* ladle; akin to OProv *cassa* ladle — more at CASSEROLE] : a casserole of beans baked with herbs and pork sausage and sometimes other meats

cas·so·wary \ˈkasə,werē\ *n* -ES [Malay *kĕsuari*] : any of several large ratite birds of New Guinea, Australia, the Aru islands, and Ceram closely related to the emu and constituting a genus and family of the order Casuariiformes and having the claw of the inner toe elongated, a horny casque on the head, wattles on the neck, slender hairlike feathers of dark color with the aftershaft as large as the main portion, and wing quills reduced to a few stout barbless shafts

cassubian *cap, var of* KASHUBIAN

cas·sy·tha \kəˈsīthə, -thə\ *n, cap* [NL, modif. of LGk *kasytas* dodder, of Sem origin; akin to Syr *kĕsūthā,* Aram *kĕsūthā*] : a genus of widely distributed tropical climbing parasites (family Lauraceae) which form masses of leafless threadlike stems on branches of trees and shrubs — see DODDER LAUREL

¹**cast** \ˈkast, -aa(ə)-,-ai-,-ȧ-\ *vb* **cast; cast; casting; casts** [ME *casten,* fr. ON *kasta;* akin to ON *kǫs* heap and perh. to L *gerere* to bear, wear, cherish] *vt* **1 a** (1) : to cause to move by throwing : send forth by throwing : impel with force : THROW ⟨~ dice⟩ ⟨~ myself on my grass bed —W.H.Hudson †1922⟩ (2) : to throw out (a bait) by means of a fishing rod ⟨~ a plug into the surf⟩ : throw out (a net) : fish (an area) by casting **b** (1) : DIRECT ⟨~ a glance⟩ ⟨~ her mind back in an effort to remember⟩ (2) : to put forth ⟨the fire ~s a warm glow⟩ : project or send forth esp. in a particular direction ⟨his words ~ new light on the problem⟩ : (3) to place or propel as if by throwing ⟨~ another burden on the reader⟩ ⟨~ doubt upon their reliability⟩ ⟨the player ~ a spell on the audience⟩ (4) *obs* : to cause to enter or begin a state or activity (5) : to deposit (a ballot) formally or officially : give (a vote) **c** (1) : to throw off or away (as something lost, outworn, or no longer wanted) : get rid of : DISCARD ⟨the horse ~ a shoe⟩ — often used with *off, away, aside* ⟨~ off all restraint⟩ (2) *now dial Brit* : VOMIT (3) : to reject or dismiss as unfit or disqualified : CASHIER, CULL ⟨the state cannot with safety ~ him —Shak.⟩ — now used chiefly of farm animals ⟨ewes were ~ for age at five years⟩ (4) *Brit* : to bring forth, bear, or drop prematurely : SLINK *vt* 1 ⟨an infected cow may ~ its calf at the sixth month⟩ (5) : SHED, MOLT ⟨~ feathers⟩ ⟨~ leaves⟩ (6) *of honeybees* : to throw off (a swarm) (7) : to bring forth : BEAR, YIELD **d** (1) : to throw to the ground : overthrow esp. in wrestling : throw (an animal) down ⟨the cow was ~ and her legs tied⟩ (2) : to defeat in a lawsuit (3) *archaic* : CONVICT, CONDEMN ⟨she was ~ to be hanged —Francis Jeffrey⟩ **e** *now dial Brit* : to dig or shovel up (as earth or sod) ⟨they were ~*ing* the peats⟩; *also* : to form by digging or throwing up earth ⟨~ a ditch⟩ ⟨~ a mound⟩ **2 a** (1) : to perform arithmetical operations on : compute or reckon (as accounts) : ADD ⟨~ the page of entries in an account book⟩ — often used with *up* ⟨~ up a row of figures⟩ (2) : to calculate by means of astrology ⟨~ a person's horoscope⟩ (3) *archaic* : to examine (urine) to diagnose disease (4) *printing* : to cast off **b** (1) : CONTRIVE, DEVISE, PLAN ⟨~ a cheap way how they may be all destroyed —Francis Beaumont & John Fletcher⟩ (2) *archaic* : DECIDE, INTEND ⟨we ~ to dine there⟩ (3) *now dial Brit* : to meditate on : CONSIDER, PONDER ⟨~ no more doubts —Christopher Marlowe⟩ — now often used with *over* **3 a** : to dispose or arrange into parts or into a suitable order : DEVISE ⟨I shall ~ what I have to say under two principal heads —*Tatler*⟩ **b** : to arrange or dispose (as ele-

ments or details in a painting) ⟨~ the draperies in a graceful arrangement⟩ **c** : to assign (as a part in a play) to an actor ⟨~ the leading part⟩ : assign the parts of (a dramatic production) to actors ⟨~ the play⟩ : assign to a role or part ⟨~ him as Othello⟩ ⟨the president and Congress have been ~ for opposite parts —W.E.Binkley⟩ **4 a** (1) : to give a particular shape to (a substance) by pouring in liquid or plastic form into a mold and letting or causing to harden without pressure ⟨~ steel⟩ : form by this process ⟨~ machine parts⟩ ⟨~ concrete pillars⟩ ⟨toys ~ from plastic⟩ (2) : to make a stereotype, electrotype, or other printing plate from (letterpress matter) : PLATE : make (as type, slugs, rules, stereotypes) by forcing hot metal into a matrix or mold **b** : to give form to : ARRANGE ⟨the book is ~ in the form of an autobiography⟩ : establish or create in a particular form ⟨those who were *~ing* the new Protestant state of England and Scotland —Padraic Colum⟩ : EXPRESS, FORMULATE ⟨*~ing* of morality in terms of economic gain —Abraham Edel⟩ **5** : TURN ⟨~ the scale slightly⟩ : DECIDE ⟨~ the balance between the outward advantages and disadvantages —J.H.Newman⟩ **6** : to make into a knot or stitch ⟨~ a square knot⟩ ⟨~ a stitch⟩ **7** : TWIST, WARP ⟨a beam ~ by age⟩ **8** : to cause (a dog or a pack) to make a cast : put (a dog) on the scent **~** *vi* **1 a** : to throw or project something; *specif* : to throw out a lure or bait with a fishing rod **b** *now dial Brit* : VOMIT **c** *dial Eng* : to bear fruit : YIELD ⟨the wheat *~s* well⟩ **2 a** : to perform addition ⟨~ and balance at a desk —Alfred Tennyson⟩ **b** *obs* : ESTIMATE, CONJECTURE ⟨~ beyond ourselves in our opinions —Shak.⟩ **3** : WARP ⟨lumber *~s*⟩ **4** : to make a cast — used of hunting dogs or trackers **5** *of a boat* : to turn the bow from the wind so as to bring it on the desired side (as when getting under way from a mooring) : VEER **6 a** : to undergo the process of shaping in a mold : take form in a mold ⟨overheated metal may ~ badly⟩ **b** *printing* : to produce a cast ⟨the safety device will not permit a loose line of matrices to ~⟩ **syn** see DISCARD, THROW — **cast anchor** : to let drop an anchor to keep a ship at rest : ANCHOR — **cast in one's teeth** : to reproach or reproach with ⟨*cast* his cowardice *in his teeth*⟩ — **cast loose** : to untie or unfasten (as a boat) : UNLASH — **cast lots** : to draw or use lots to determine a matter by chance — **cast one's lot with** *or* **cast in one's lot with** : to associate oneself with for good or ill : share the fortunes of ⟨leaving home he *cast in his lot with* the trappers⟩ : take the side of : align oneself with ⟨*cast his lot with* the Republicans⟩ — **cast out nines** : to check the results obtained in multiplication, division, addition, and subtraction of integral numbers by a series of divisions by the factor 9 and comparison of the remainders obtained, the operation in multiplication being as follows: (1) divide each factor by 9, (2) divide the products of the remainders obtained by 9, (3) divide the number being checked by 9, the result being prob. correct if the remainders in operations (2) and (3) are equal — **cast the lead** : to make a sounding with the lead — **cast the withers** *of cattle* : to evert the uterus after calving due to failure of normal contraction

[2]**cast** \"\ *n* -S [ME, fr. *casten* to cast] **1** : an act or the action or process of casting **2 a** : an act of casting a throw (as of a missile) **b** : something that happens as a result of chance : a stroke of fortune : CHANCE, FATE, VENTURE ⟨his future depended on this ~⟩ **c** : a throw of dice ⟨a seven on the first ~⟩; *also* : the number of spots showing or counted in a single throw of dice ⟨a ~ of seven⟩ **d** (1) : a throw of a line (as a fishing line or lariat) or net (as a fishing net or butterfly net) (2) : a place for casting : a fishing place ⟨a good ~ near the bridge⟩ **3 a** : the form in which a thing is constructed ⟨forcing argument to the ~ of rhyme —Karl Shapiro⟩ **b** (1) : the set of actors assigned parts in a dramatic production (2) : a descriptive list of these parts (3) : the set of characters in a narrative **c** : the arrangement or disposition of draperies in a painting **4** : the distance to which a thing can be thrown; *specif* : the distance a bow can shoot **5 a** : a turning of the eye in a particular direction : GLANCE, LOOK; *also* : EXPRESSION ⟨this freakish, elfish ~ came into the child's eye —Nathaniel Hawthorne⟩ **b** : a twist or turn to one side; *specif* : a slight strabismus **6** : something that is thrown or the quantity thrown: as **a** : the number (as a couple) of hawks released by a falconer at one time **b** : the number (as of herrings, crabs, or oysters) that can be thrown into a vessel at one time by hand : WARP **c** *Brit* : a length of silkworm gut or nylon used to connect a fish lure or fly to the line : LEADER **d** : the quantity of metal cast at a single operation **7 a** : something that is formed by casting in a mold or form: as (1) : a reproduction or copy (as of a work of art) in metal or plaster : CASTING (2) : a fossil reproduction of the external details of a natural object produced by infiltration of a mold of the object by water-borne minerals (as lime salts) — compare PETRIFACTION **b** : an impression taken from an object by covering its surface with a liquid or plastic substance that when hardened retains form and detail of the original and can serve as a mold for reproduction **c** : a rigid dressing usu. made from gauze or crinoline impregnated with plaster of paris or other material used for immobilizing a diseased, deformed, or broken part **8** : a forecast or conjecture concerning future events or conditions ⟨to make a long ~ ahead⟩ **9** : the quality of elastic resilience in a bow that determines its ability to propel an arrow ⟨improving the ~ of a bow⟩ **10** *archaic* : a specimen intended to show the quality of the whole : EXAMPLE ⟨showing us a ~ of his logic⟩ — used esp. in the phrase *a cast of one's office* **11 a** : an overspread of a color or modification of the appearance of a substance by a trace of some added hue : SHADE ⟨the rock itself had a deep purplish ~ —Willa Cather⟩ ⟨gray with a greenish ~⟩ **b** : a trace of a particular quality : TINGE, SUGGESTION ⟨had a small ~ of the coxcomb —Laurence Sterne⟩ ⟨a ~ of bitterness in his words —Walter O'Meara⟩ **12 a** : a ride on one's way in a vehicle : LIFT ⟨a wagoner gave him a ~ as far as the town⟩ **b** *Scot* : HELP, ASSISTANCE ⟨if we had the ~ of a cart to bring it —Sir Walter Scott⟩ **13 a** : physical form or character : SHAPE, APPEARANCE ⟨the delicate ~ of his features⟩ **b** : characteristic quality ⟨Russia, the culture of which has as definite a ~ as that of France —Edward Sapir⟩ : NATURE, CHARACTER, BENT ⟨his mental habits . . . were always of a Quakerish ~ —H.S.Canby⟩ : TYPE, KIND ⟨Madison, Washington, and others of that ~ —J.C.Miller⟩ **c** : BENT, COMPLEXION ⟨~ of mind⟩ ⟨a mind of scientific ~⟩ **14** : something that is thrown out or off, shed, or ejected: as **a** *of honeybees* : an afterswarm, esp. the first **b** : the excrement of an earthworm **c** : PELLET 1e **d** : a mass of plastic matter formed by effusion in cavities of certain usu. diseased organs and subsequently discharged from the body — see RENAL CAST **e** : the skin of an insect **15** : the right to shoot first in an archery match given to the winner of the last shot — used with *the* **16** : the ranging over the field in search of a trail by a dog, hunting pack, or tracker ⟨the setter made a wide ~⟩

[3]**cast** *adj* [ME, fr. L *castus* — more at CASTE] *obs* : CHASTE

[4]**cast** *obs var of* CASTE

[5]**cast** \ˈkast, -aa(ə)-,-ai,-á-\ *adj* [fr. past part. of [1]*cast*] *of an animal* : down or on its back and unable to get up

cast·a·ble \-əbəl\ *n* -S : a refractory material that has a bonding agent added and can be mixed with water and poured in a mold to set

cast about *vt* : to lay plans concerning : CONSIDER, CONTRIVE ⟨*cast about* how he was to go⟩ ~ *vi* **1 a** : to turn one's course **b** *of a ship* : to go about **2** : to seek here and there : look around : SEARCH ⟨*cast about* for means of amusement —Rudyard Kipling⟩ ⟨*casting about* for something he is likely to be able to do for a living —G.N.Shuster⟩

[1]**cas·ta·lia** \kaˈstālyə, -lēə\ *or* **cas·ta·lie** \ˈkastəlē\ *n* -S *usu cap* [fr. *Castalia*, spring on Parnassus sacred to the Muses, fr. L, fr. Gk *Kastalia*] : a source of poetic inspiration

[2]**castalia** \"\ [NL, fr. *Castalia* (spring)] *syn of* NYMPHAEA

cas·ta·li·an \(ˈ)kaˈstālyən, -lēən\ *adj, usu cap* [*Castalia* + E *-an*] : of or relating to the Castalia

cas·ta·na \kaˈstan(y)ə\ *n* -S [Pg *castanha*, lit., chestnut, fr. L *castanea*] **1 a** : BRAZIL NUT **b** : the Brazil-nut tree **2** [AmerSp *castaña*, fr. Sp, chestnut, fr. L *castanea*] *Puerto Rico* : BREADFRUIT

cas·ta·nea \kaˈstānēə\ *n, cap* [NL, fr. L, chestnut — more at CHESTNUT] : a small genus of rough-barked trees or shrubs (family Fagaceae) native to temperate regions and characterized by having four bud scales on each bud, unlobed leaves, and staminate flowers in stiff cylindrical catkins, the fruit ripening in one season and being a single nut or group of two or three nuts within a 2- to 4-valved scaly prickly involucre — see CHESTNUT; compare QUERCUS

cas·ta·ne·an *or* **cas·ta·ni·an** \(ˈ)kaˈstānēən\ *adj* [NL *Castanea* + E *-an*] : of or belonging to the genus *Castanea*

cas·ta·ne·ous \-nēəs\ *adj* [L *castanea* + E *-ous*] : of the color chestnut

cas·ta·net \ˌkastəˈnet, -aas-, -ais-, *usu* -ned.+V\ *n* -S [modif. of Sp *castañeta* fr. *castaña* chestnut, fr. L *castanea*] : a rhythm instrument used esp. by dancers that consists of two small shells of ivory, hard wood, or plastic which are fastened together to hang from the thumb by a double loop and are clicked together by the other fingers — usu. used in pl.

castanets

cas·ta·nop·sis \ˌkastəˈnäpsə̇s\ *n, cap* [NL, fr. *Castanea* + *-opsis*] : a small genus of trees (family Fagaceae) that contains one or two species in the Pacific coastal U.S. and a number in Asia and is closely related to *Castanea* but whose members are distinguished by having numerous bud scales on each bud, persistent leaves, a 3-celled ovary, and a fruit consisting of a nut that ripens at the end of the second season — see CHINQUAPIN

cas·ta·no·sper·mum \ˌkastənōˈspərməm\ *n, cap* [NL, fr. *castano-* (fr. *Castanea*) + *-spermum*] : a genus of Australian trees (family Leguminosae) having pinnate leaves, orange-yellow flowers, and chestnutlike seeds borne in large thick almost woody pods — see BEAN TREE a

cast around *vi* : cast about (sense 2)

cast away *vt* **1** : to waste wantonly : SQUANDER ⟨*cast* his life *away*⟩ **2** : WRECK ⟨*cast away* a ship⟩ : throw upon the shore as a survivor of a shipwreck ⟨a man *cast away* on a desert island⟩

[1]**castaway** \ˈ==,=\ *adj* [fr. past part. of *cast away*] **1** : cast off as of no value : thrown away : REJECTED **2 a** : cast adrift or cast ashore as a survivor of a shipwreck **b** : thrown out or left without friends or resources : OUTCAST

[2]**castaway** \"\ *n* -S **1** : one who has been cast away, cast off, or rejected ⟨*~s* from God —E.F.Burr⟩ **2** *archaic* : a disqualified person ⟨I keep under my body, and bring it into subjection: lest that by any means, when I have preached to others, I myself should be a ~ —1 Cor 9:27 AV⟩ **3** : one cast away at sea : a shipwrecked person **4** : one cast out by society : OUTCAST

cast back *vt, obs* : to drag back : IMPEDE **~** *vi* : to go back, search back, or refer back (as in history or in the memory) ⟨he *casts back* to the fiction of his own region for a helpful analogy —Katharine F. Gerould⟩

cast behind *vt, archaic* : to leave behind : OUTRUN

cast coating *n* [[2]*cast*] : a process for making paper with a fine glossy surface in which the coating of the paper while still soft is pressed against a highly polished heated cylinder until dry

[1]**cast down** *vt* : to bring down (as from high position) : ABASE, DESTROY, DEMOLISH ⟨the proud will be *cast down*⟩

[2]**cast down** *adj* : DOWNCAST

caste \ˈkast, -aa(ə)-,-ai-,-á-\ *n* -S *often attrib* [in sense 1, fr. Sp *casta* race, breed, lineage, fr. *casta*, fem. of *casto* chaste, fr. L *castus*; in other senses, fr. Pg *casta*, lit., race, breed, lineage, fr. *casta*, fem. of *casto* chaste, fr. L *castus* pure, chaste; akin to L *carēre* to be without, Gk *keazein* to split, Skt *śasati* he cuts to pieces; basic meaning: to cut] **1** *obs* : a race, stock, or breed of men or animals **2** : one of the hereditary classes into which the society of India is divided in accordance with a system fundamental in Hinduism, reaching back into distant antiquity, and dictating to every orthodox Hindu the rules and restrictions of all social intercourse and of which each has a name of its own and special customs that restrict the occupation of its members and their intercourse with the members of other castes — see BRAHMAN, KSHATRIYA, SUDRA, VAISYA, VARNA **3 a** : a division or class of society comprised of persons within a separate and exclusive order based variously upon differences of wealth, inherited rank or privilege, profession, occupation ⟨the tinkers then formed an hereditary ~ —T.B.Macaulay⟩ ⟨his sturdy brown legs were tattooed in blue to the thighs, indicating his high ~ —Robert Trumbull⟩; *broadly* : CLASS **b** : the position conferred by caste standing : PRESTIGE, FACE — used esp. in the phrase *lose caste* ⟨art and religion have lost ~ —F.L.Baumer⟩ **4** : a system of social stratification more rigid than a class and characterized by hereditary status, endogamy, and social barriers rigidly sanctioned by custom, law, or religion **5** : a form of polymorphic social insects (as ants, bees, and termites) that carries out a particular function in the colony ⟨worker ~⟩ ⟨soldier ~⟩

caste·less \-ləs\ *adj* **1** : not divided into rigid social classes ⟨there is no leisure class in that ~ country⟩ **2** *India* : outside the caste system and thus having no place or status in society ⟨the foreigner was a ~ person⟩

cas·te·let *or* **cas·tel·let** \ˌkas(t)əˈlet\ *n* -S [ME, fr. ONF, dim. of *castel* — more at CASTLE] : a small castle

cas·tel·lan \ˈkastələn, -ˌlan, kaˈstelən\ *n* -S [alter. (influenced by L *castellanus*) of ME *castelleyn*, fr. ONF *castelain*, fr. L *castellanus* occupant of a castle, fr. *castellanus*, adj., of a castle, fr. *castellum* castle — more at CASTLE] : a governor or warden of a castle or fort

cas·tel·la·ni's paint \ˌkastəˈlänēz-\ *n, usu cap C* [after Aldo *Castellani* b1875 Ital. physician & bacteriologist] : CARBOL-FUCHSIN PAINT

cas·te·lla·no \ˌkastəˈl(y)ä(ˌ)nō\ *n* -S [Sp, lit., *Castilian* — more at CASTILIAN] **1** : an ancient Spanish gold coin bearing the Castilian arms; *esp* : one weighing ¹⁄₅₀ of a mark **2** : an ancient Spanish unit of weight equivalent to ¹⁄₅₀ of a mark

cas·tel·lany \ˈkastəˌlanē, -ˌlā-,-lə-, kaˈstelənē\ *n* -ES [ML *castellania*, fr. *castellanus* castellan (fr. L, occupant of a castle) + L *-ia* -y] : the office or jurisdiction of a castellan : the extent of land and jurisdiction appertaining to a castle

cas·tel·lar \(ˈ)kaˈstelə(r), ˈkastəl-\ *adj* [L *castellum* castle + E *-ar*] : belonging to or suggestive of a castle ⟨mansions of a ~ style⟩

cas·tel·late \ˈkastəˌlāt, *usu* -ād.+V\ *vb* -ED/-ING/-S [back-formation fr. *castellated*] *vt* : to build like a castle : build or furnish with battlements **~** *vi* : to take the form of a castle ⟨*castellating* clouds⟩

cas·tel·lat·ed \-ād.əd\ *adj* [ML *castellatus* (past part. of *castellare* to fortify, fr. L *castellum* castle) + E *-ed*] **1** : built or formed like a castle : having battlements or parts resembling battlements ⟨~ country houses⟩ ⟨~ cliffs⟩: as **a** : having a design or decoration resembling a line of battlements ⟨a ~ cornice⟩ ⟨a ~ band of velvet⟩ **b** *of clouds* : of the type altocumulus castellatus **2** : CASTLED 1 **3** : lodged in a castle : securely established in a position of strength ⟨~ power and wealth —*No. Amer. Rev.*⟩

castellated nut *n* : a nut with radial grooves in its upper face to receive a split pin passed through a hole in the bolt to prevent the nut from turning

cas·tel·la·tion \ˌkastəˈlāshən\ *n* -S [ML *castellation-*, *castellatio*, fr. *castellatus* + *-ion-*, *-io* -ion] **1** : the act of castellating **2** : a castellated structure **3 a** : BATTLEMENT **b** : a groove or recess in a castellated structure (as a nut) ⟨a cotter pin passing through the ~ and the hole in the bolt⟩

cas·tel·la·tus \ˌ==ˈlād.əs, -ˈä-\ *adj* [ML] *of a cloud formation* : shaped like a turret or a row of turrets — see ALTOCUMULUS CASTELLATUS

caste mark *n* **1** : a mark or symbol that is worn on the forehead esp. in India and denotes the wearer's caste **2** : a distinguishing characteristic or trait that identifies a member of a particular class or group ⟨the *caste mark* of the intellectual⟩

[1]**cast·er** \ˈkastə(r), -ˈaa-,-ˈai-,-ˈá-\ *n* -S [ME, fr. *casten* to cast + *-er*] **1 a** : one that casts: as (1) : a worker who shapes (as in a mold) molten metal, semiliquid clay, or other plastic material into finished products or bodies to be finished esp. in founding, jewelry making, brickmaking, tilemaking, or the making of hat blocks — compare MOLDER, POURER (2) : a machine that casts type **b** *also* **caster plate** : a plate (as an electrotype) used as a master printing surface for the molding of other plates — called also *master, pattern plate*; compare WORKER **2** *also* **cas·tor** \-tə(r)\ **a** : a cruet, sifter, or other small container for condiments used at the table **b** : a stand for holding a set of casters **3** *also* **castor** [[1]*cast* (turn) + *-er*, *-or*] : a wheel or set of wheels mounted in a frame free to swivel about an axis perpendicular to the axis of the wheel or set and used for supporting furniture, trucks, and various portable machines or inverted on the upper ends of posts for handling plate and sheet metal in rolling mills **4** : the slight usu. backward tilt of the upper end of the knuckle pin of an automotive vehicle employed as a means of giving directional stability to the front wheels

caster 3

[2]**caster** *also* **castor** \"\ *vb* -ED/-ING/-S [[1]*caster* (wheel)] *vt* **1** : to mount (as an airplane wheel) so as to permit to swivel freely ⟨*~ed* nosewheel⟩ **2** : to equip (as table legs) with casters **~** *vi* : to swivel freely ⟨*~ing* and steerable nosewheel —*Flying*⟩

castering landing gear *n* : an airplane landing gear having means to permit castering of the wheels about substantially vertical axes during crosswind landings

cast·er·less \-ləs\ *adj* : lacking casters

castes *pl of* CASTE

cas·ti·gate \ˈkastəˌgāt, -aas-, *usu* -ād.+V\ *vt* -ED/-ING/-S [L *castigatus*, past part. of *castigare* to correct, punish — more at CHASTEN] **1 a** : to punish or subdue by punishment ⟨~ thy pride —Shak.⟩ **b** : to reprove for error or criticize with drastic severity ⟨those poems in which he *~s* man's general inhumanity and lack of sincerity —J.G.Southworth⟩ ⟨not even the ablest critic can ~ an artless generation into repentance and creative vigor —A.J.Barnouw⟩ **2** : to correct or revise (a literary text) **3** *obs* : to tone down or subdue in intensity or boldness **syn** see PUNISH

cas·ti·ga·tion \ˌ==ˈgāshən\ *n* -S [ME *castigacioun*, fr. L *castigation-*, *castigatio*, fr. *castigatus* + *-ion-*, *-io* -ion] **1 a** : severe punishment : CHASTISEMENT **b** : severe reproof or criticism **2** : revision or correction (of a literary text)

cas·ti·ga·tor \ˈ==ˌgād.ə(r), -ātə-\ *n* -S [L, fr. *castigatus* + *-or*] : one that castigates

[1]**cas·ti·ga·to·ry** \-ˌgəˌtōrē\ *adj* [L *castigatorius*, fr. *castigatus* + *-orius* -ory] : of or concerned with castigation : PUNITIVE

[2]**castigatory** *n* -ES *obs* : an instrument for castigation; *specif* : CUCKING STOOL

cas·ti·glia·no's theorem \ˌkästᵊlˈyä(ˌ)nōz-, ˌkas-\ *n, usu cap C* [after Carlo Alberto *Castigliano* †1884 Ital. engineer] : a theorem in structural mechanics: when an external force is applied at any point of a structure composed of rigidly connected elastic members the resulting internal work throughout the structure is equal to the product of the force by the displacement of the point of application in the direction of the force and the derivative of the internal work with respect to either factor thereof is equal to the other factor

cas·tile *or* **castile soap** \(ˈ)kaˈstēl, -kaa-,-kai-\ *n* -S *often cap C* [fr. *Castile*, region of Spain where it was orig. made] **1** : a fine hard bland soap usu. white or cream-colored but sometimes marbled or green that is made from olive oil and sodium hydroxide — called also *olive-oil castile soap* **2** : any of various hard soaps (as a white neutral toilet soap) made partly from olive oil together with other fats or oils (as coconut oil) or wholly from other fats and oils

[1]**castilian** *n* -S [modif. of L *castellanus* — more at CASTELLAN] *obs* : one of the garrison of a castle

[2]**cas·til·ian** \kaˈstilyən *also* kə-\ *n* -S *cap* [modif. of Sp *castellano*, fr. *castellano*, adj., Castilian, fr. L *castellanus* of a castle, fr. *castellum* castle — more at CASTLE] **1** : a native or inhabitant of the central Spanish provinces of Old and New Castile or of the former kingdom of Castile; *broadly* : SPANIARD **2 a** : the dialect of Castile **b** : the official and literary language of Spain based on this dialect : standard Spanish

[3]**castilian** \(ˈ)kaˈstilyən *also* kəˈs-\ *adj, usu cap* [modif. of Sp *castellano*] **1** : of, relating to, or characteristic of the Spanish province of Castile or its inhabitants : native to Castile; *broadly* : SPANISH **2** : of, relating to, or characteristic of the standard Spanish language

castilian brown *n, usu cap C* : a moderate reddish brown that is yellower than roan and redder and slightly lighter and stronger than mahogany — called also *brown madder, Columbian red, madder brown, old cedar, Tanagra*

cas·til·ian·ism \=ˈ==,nizəm\ *n* -S *usu cap* [modif. of Sp *castellanismo*, fr. *castellano* + *-ismo* -ism] : a characteristic feature of the Castilian dialect or of Castilian Spanish occurring in another language or dialect

castilian red *n, usu cap C* : a vivid red that is lighter, slightly yellower, and stronger than apple red, yellower, lighter, and stronger than carmine, yellower and lighter than madder crimson, bluer and lighter than pimento, and bluer, lighter, and stronger than scarlet — called also *cochineal, Dutch scarlet, fire scarlet, goblin scarlet*

cas·til·la \kaˈstilə, -tē(y)ə\ [NL, after Juan *Castillo* y López] *syn of* CASTILLOA

cas·til·le·ja *also* **cas·til·le·ia** \ˌkastəˈlē(y)ə\ *n, cap* [NL, irreg. (influence of Sp *-eja*, dim. suffix) fr. Juan *Castillo* y López] : a large genus of root-parasitic herbs (family Scrophulariaceae) abundant in western No. America and characterized by irregular hooded flowers in dense spikes usu. with brightly colored bracts — see INDIAN PAINTBRUSH

cas·til·loa \ˌkastəˈlōə, kaˈstilәwə\ *n, cap* [NL, fr. Juan *Castillo* y López †1793 Span. botanist] : a genus of tropical American trees (family Moraceae) of which some yield caucho and all are characterized by the development of long slender deciduous twigs which bear large showy usu. densely hairy leaves

casting *n* -S [ME, fr. gerund of *casten* to cast] **1** : the act of one that casts: as **a** : the act or process of making casts or impressions or of shaping in a mold (as in making pottery or forming metal objects by pouring molten metal into a mold) **b** : the throwing of a fishing line by means of a rod and reel — see BAIT CASTING, FLY CASTING, SURF CASTING **c** : the assignment of parts and duties to actors or performers ⟨insight into the workings of an opera house, its ~, its repertory and its general management —Harriett Johnson⟩ **2** : something that is cast in a mold; *specif* : an object (as of metal, plaster or glass) so cast **3** : something that is cast out or off (as skin, feathers, or excrement): as **a** : WORMCAST **b** : PELLET 1e

casting bottle *n* : a bottle for sprinkling perfumes

casting box *n* : the matrix-holding receptacle into which hot metal is poured in casting a stereotype

casting director *n* : one that supervises the casting of plays, operas, or other dramatic performances

casting glass *n, obs* : CASTING BOTTLE

casting man *n* **1** : one who backs electrotype shells **2** : one who casts stereotypes **3** : a stock clerk who issues castings and other mechanical equipment used in textile-machine repair

casting net *var of* CAST NET

casting sheet *n* : a list containing descriptions of the types of actors needed for a particular play or other dramatic work

casting slip *n, pottery* : a slurry of clay and additives mixed to a creamy consistency in water with deflocculating agents and ready to pour into a plaster mold

casting table *or* **casting plate** *n* : a table with raised edges and polished metal surface used as a mold for casting plate glass

casting vote *or* **casting voice** *n* [fr. pres. part. of [1]*cast* (decide)] : a deciding vote cast by a presiding officer or judge to break a tie or sometimes to create a tie

casting wax *n* : any clean free-flowing wax out of which the pattern or matrix for a casting (as of a metal) is made

cast iron *n* [fr. past part. of [1]*cast*] : a commercial alloy of iron, carbon, and silicon cast in a mold, being hard, brittle, nonmalleable, and incapable of being hammer-welded but more easily fusible than steel, containing usu. 2.0 to 4.5 percent carbon and 1 to 4 percent silicon, and having a melting point of 1200 to 1250°C and a weight per cubic foot of 425 to 475 pounds (sp. gr. 7.0–7.6)

cast-iron \ˈ=ˈ=\ *adj* **1** : made of cast iron **2** : resembling cast iron: as **a** : capable of withstanding great hardship or strain ⟨a *cast-iron* stomach⟩ **b** : not admitting change, adaptation, or exception : RIGID, STRICT ⟨a man of *cast-iron* will⟩

cast-iron front \ˈ=ˌ=ˈ=\ *n* : a type of usu. commercial architecture employing large window areas and columns and spandrels of cast iron

cast-iron plant \ˈ=ˈ=,=\ *n* [so called fr. its hardiness] : a commonly cultivated foliage plant (*Aspidistra elatior*)

1cas·tle \ˈkasəl, -ˈaa-,-ˈai-,-ˈȧ-\ *n* -s [ME *castel,* fr. OE, fr. ONF & LL; ONF *castel* castle and LL *castellum* village, fr. L *castellum* castle, dim. of *castrum* fortified place; akin to L *castrare* to castrate — more at CASTRATE] **1 a :** a large fortified building or set of buildings (as of a prince or nobleman) built orig. in medieval times as a single donjon often surrounded by inferior buildings (as stables), a palisaded enclosure, and a moat and later often having more elaborate accessory buildings (as a great hall and a chapel), courtyards, surrounding defensive walls, and a drawbridge over the moat **b :** a large dwelling that has served as a fortress **c :** a large dwelling that has replaced a fortress **d :** a large building; *esp* **:** a massive or imposing house or mansion **2 :** a retreat or stronghold safe against intrusion or invasion ⟨a man's house is his ~⟩ **3 :** a raised structure on the deck of an early sailing ship or galley **4 :** 3ROOK **5** [trans. of D *kasteel* castle, stronghold] **:** a fortified place or village of an Indian tribe in the northeastern U.S. **6 :** a heraldic representation of a castle or of a portion of an embattled wall often having a gateway and crowned with usu. three towers **7 :** CASTLE IN THE AIR — usu. used in pl.

castle (Viollet-le-Duc's restoration of the Louvre in Paris before 1527) showing: *1* fortified approach; *2* moat; *3* drawbridge; *4* tower flanking main entrance; *5* donjon, or keep, encircled by fosse; *6* angle tower for defense of outer wall; *7* chapel

2castle \"\ *vb* **castled; castled; castling** \-s(ə)liŋ\ **castles** *vt* **1** *obs* **:** to enclose (as a water conduit) in stone walls **2 :** to establish in a secure position in or as if in a castle ⟨*castled* up in his mountain retreat⟩ **3** *chess* **:** to move (the king) in castling ~ *vi* **:** to move the king two squares toward a rook and then, in the same move, the rook to the square next past the king; *also, of the king* **:** to be moved in this way — usu. designated in notation by 0-0 (king's side) or 0-0-0 (queen's side)

castle–builder \ˈ==,==\ *n* **:** one that builds castles in the air or forms visionary schemes

castle–building \ˈ==,==\ *n* **:** building castles in the air **:** DAYDREAMING

castled *adj* **1 :** having a castle ⟨a ~ village⟩ **:** supporting a castle ⟨a ~ height⟩ **2 :** CASTELLATED

castle earth *n* [alter. of *cassel earth*] **:** CASSEL BROWN

castle–guard \ˈ==,=\ *n* **1 :** a feudal knight service of the tenant to defend the lord's castle; *also* **:** the tenure of such service **2 :** a tax or charge now mostly fallen into desuetude that was orig. imposed in lieu of castle-guard

castle in the air *also* **castle in spain** *usu cap S* **:** a visionary project **:** DAYDREAM

castle nut *n* [so called fr. the resemblance of its grooves to the crenels of a battlement] **:** CASTELLATED NUT

cas·tle·ry \-səlrē\ *n* -ES [*castle* + *-ry*] **:** a territory subject to a feudal castle and organized for its maintenance and defense

castles *pl of* CASTLE, *pres 3d sing of* CASTLE

cas·tlet \ˈkaslət, ˌkasəˌlet\ *n* -s [alter. (influenced by *castle*) of *castelet*] **:** a small castle

castle walk *n, usu cap C* [after Vernon Blythe *Castle* †1918 Eng. dancer who originated it] **:** a ballroom dance consisting basically of a straight forward walk with reach and lift, one step to each musical beat

cas·tle·ward \ˈ==,wȯ(ə)rd\ *n* **:** CASTLE-GUARD

1castling *pres part of* CASTLE

2cast·ling \ˈkastliŋ, -slən\ *n* -s [*cast* (past part. of 1*cast*) + *-ling*] **1** *now dial Eng* **:** an offspring brought forth prematurely **:** ABORTION **2** *obs* **:** CAST 14a

cast·ner cell \ˈkastnə(r)-\ *n, usu cap 1st C* [after H.Y.*Castner* †1899 Am. chemist] **1 :** a rocking cell with a layer of mercury on the bottom for making sodium hydroxide and chlorine by electrolysis of sodium chloride solution **2 :** a cell for making metallic sodium and hydrogen by electrolysis of fused sodium hydroxide

cast net *also* **casting net** *n* **:** a circular or conical weighted net designed to be cast mouth downward by hand and withdrawn by lines attached to its margin — compare DIP NET, SETNET

ca·stock \ˈkȧ,stȯk, -stək\ *n* -s [alter. of ME *calstok,* fr. ME *cal* kale + *stok* stock, stem — more at KALE, STOCK] *chiefly Scot* **:** a cabbage stalk

cast off *vt* **1 :** LOOSE, SLIP ⟨*cast off* a hunting dog⟩ **2 :** UNFASTEN, UNHITCH ⟨*cast off* a boat⟩ **:** let go **:** UNTIE ⟨*cast off* a line⟩ **:** loose from a mooring **3 :** to bind off **4 :** to measure (copy or set type) to determine the amount of printed matter that will be made or the space that will be occupied when set or reset in a particular face, size, and measure ~ *vi* **1 :** to unfasten or untie a boat or a line **2 :** to turn from one's partner in a country or square dance and pass around the outside of the set and back

cast–off \ˈ=,=\ *adj* [*cast off,* past part. of *cast off*] **:** thrown away or aside **:** worn out **:** DISCARDED ⟨wearing his brother's *cast-off* clothing⟩

cast·off \"\ *n* -s **1 :** a person or thing that has been cast off ⟨dressed in his older brother's ~*s*⟩ **2 :** the lateral offset of the stock of a shotgun that enables the shooter's eye to be brought in line with the sights **3 :** an estimate of typographical space made by casting off

cast on *vt* **:** to place (stitches) on a knitting needle for beginning or enlarging knitted work

1cas·tor \ˈkastə(r), -ˈaa-,-ˈai-,-ˈȧ-\ *n* [ME, fr. L, fr. Gk *kastōr,* fr. *Kastōr* Castor, one of the Dioscuri (the other being L *Pollux,* Gk *Polydeukēs*), twin heroes or demigods of Greek mythology] **1 a** -s **:** BEAVER 1 **b** *cap* [NL, fr. L] **:** the type genus of Castoridae comprising the beavers **2** -s **:** a creamy orange-brown substance with strong penetrating odor and bitter taste that consists of the dried perineal glands of the beaver and their secretion or an extract of this and is used by perfumers as a fixative and by professional trappers to scent bait — called also *castoreum* **3** -s **a :** a beaver or other hat made often of fur in imitation of a beaver **b :** the skin of a beaver **c :** a glove leather with a soft finish made by grinding off or suede-finishing the grain surface of goatskins or certain sheepskins **4** -s **:** a brownish gray that is yellower and slightly lighter than taupe, yellower and paler than chocolate, and duller and slightly yellower than mouse gray **5** -s **:** MADE-BEAVER

2castor \"\ *var of* CASTER

3castor \"\ *var of* CASTORITE

4castor \"\ *n* -s [origin unknown] **:** CHESTNUT 5

5castor \"\ *n* -s [by shortening] **:** CASTOR-OIL PLANT

castor bean *also* **castor–oil bean** *n* [*castor (oil)* + *bean*] **1 :** the seed of the castor-oil plant from which castor oil is extracted — see RICIN **2 :** CASTOR-OIL PLANT

castor–bean tick *n* **:** a widely distributed tick (*Ixodes ricinus*) that resembles the castor-bean seed in color and shape, lives on various mammals, and is a vector of piroplasmosis and certain virus diseases of domestic animals

cas·tor·ette \ˌkastəˈret\ *n* -s [1*castor* (beaver) + *-ette*] **:** rabbit fur sheared and dyed to simulate beaver

cas·to·re·um \kaˈstōrēəm\ *n* -s [ME *castorium,* fr. L *castoreum,* fr. *castor* beaver — more at CASTOR] **:** 1CASTOR 2

castor gray *n* [prob. fr. 1*castor*] **:** a dark greenish gray that is bluer and paler than sagebrush green and yellower and slightly less strong than muscovite

cas·tor·i·dae \kaˈstȯrəˌdē\ *n pl, cap* [NL, fr. *Castor,* type genus + *-idae*] **:** a family of rather large heavy-skulled sciuromorph rodents comprising the beavers and extinct related forms

cas·tor·ite \ˈkastəˌrīt, -ˈaa-,-ˈai-,-ˈȧ-\ *or* **cas·tor** \-tə(r)\ *n* -s [*castorite* fr. G *kastor* (fr. *Kastor* mythological personage, fr. L *Castor*) + E *-ite; castor* fr. G *kastor;* fr. its appearance with pollucite (previously called *pollux*)] **:** a mineral consisting of a variety of petalite occurring in transparent crystal

cas·to·roi·des \ˌkastəˈrȯi(ˌ)dēz\ *n, cap* [NL, fr. *Castor* + *-oides* -oid] **:** a genus of extinct giant beavers of the Pleistocene of the eastern and southern U.S.

castor oil *n* [1*castor* + *oil;* prob. fr. a supposed connection with the substance castor] **:** a colorless to amber or greenish viscous nondrying fatty oil expressed or extracted from castor beans and used chiefly as a cathartic and usu. after processing as a lubricant and drying oil — called also *ricinus oil;* see TURKEY-RED OIL

castor–oil plant *n* **:** a tropical African and Asiatic herb (*Ricinus communis*) naturalized in all tropical countries and growing as an annual in temperate regions, having large palmate bronze-green leaves, small apetalous flowers, and spiny capsules containing beanlike mottled seeds that yield castor oil and are poisonous because of the presence of ricin — called also *palma Christi;* see CASTOR BEAN

castor pomace *or* **castor cake** *n* [*castor (bean)*] **:** a pomace produced by the extraction of oil from castor beans and used as a fertilizer and soil conditioner

castors *pl of* CASTOR

castor seed *n* **:** CASTOR BEAN

castor sugar *n* [2*castor*] *chiefly Brit* **:** finely granulated or powdered white sugar that can be shaken through the perforated top of a caster

castor ware *n, usu cap C* [fr. *Castor,* Peterborough, England, where it was found] **:** an ancient Roman pottery having ornaments and animal forms laid in white slip on a dark ground

castory *n* -ES [ME, castoreum, modif. of L *castoreum*] *obs* **:** a reddish brown coloring material from castoreum

cast out *vt* **:** to drive out **:** BANISH, EXPEL ~ *vi, chiefly Scot* **:** to fall out **:** QUARREL ⟨he *cast out* with his brother⟩

castra *pl of* CASTRUM

cas·tra·me·ta·tion \ˌkastrəməˈtāshən\ *n* -s [F, fr. ML *castrametation-, castrametatio,* fr. L *castra metatus* (past part. of *castra metari* to pitch a camp, fr. *castra* camp — pl. of *castrum* fortified place — + *metari* to measure out) + *-ion-, -io* -ion; akin to L *munire* to fortify — more at CASTLE, MUNITION] **:** the making or laying out of a military camp

1cas·trate \ˈkaˌstrāt, -ˈaa-, *esp Brit* =ˈ=; *usu* -ād.+V\ *vt* -ED/-ING/-S [L *castratus,* past part. of *castrare;* akin to Skt *śasati* he cuts to pieces — more at CASTE] **1 a :** to deprive of the testes **:** EMASCULATE, GELD **b :** to deprive of the ovaries **:** SPAY **2 a :** to deprive of vigor or vitality ⟨intelligence is *castrated* —John Dewey⟩ **:** weaken by removal of the most effective or forceful elements **:** ⟨the bill was *castrated* by removal of the enforcement provisions⟩ **b :** to render impotent esp. by psychological means **3 :** to delete a part of (a text) so as to render innocuous; *esp* **:** EXPURGATE ⟨~ a text⟩ **4 :** to remove the stamens from (a flower)

2castrate \ˈ=,=\ *adj* [L *castratus*] **:** of a castrate **:** CASTRATED

3castrate \ˈ=,=\ *n* -s [L *castratus,* past part.] **:** a castrated individual

cas·trat·er *or* **cas·tra·tor** \ˈ=,=d.ə(r),-tə(r), =ˈ==\ *n* -s **:** one that castrates

cas·tra·tion \kaˈstrāshən, kaaˈ-\ *n* -s [ME *castracioun,* fr. L *castration-, castratio,* fr. *castratus* + *-ion-, -io* -ion] **1 a :** the removal of testes or ovaries **:** GELDING, SPAYING **b :** inhibition of the function or development of the gonads (1) by inadequate nutrition in worker bees, (2) by the action of certain parasites, or (3) by the use of synthetic hormones in domestic animals — called also respectively (1) *alimentary castration,* (2) *parasitic castration,* (3) *chemical castration* **2 :** a depriving of vigor **:** WEAKENING ⟨mass persecution of most eminent scientists, a ~ of science —A.G.Mazour⟩ **3 :** the deletion of a part of (a text) esp. for purposes of expurgation; *also* **:** a part deleted **4 :** the removal of the stamens of a flower

castration complex *n* **:** a child's fear or delusion of genital injury at the hands of the parent of the same sex as punishment for unconscious guilt over oedipal strivings; *broadly* **:** the often unconscious fear or feeling of bodily injury or loss of power at the hands of authority

cas·tra·tive \ˈkaˌstrād.iv, ˈkaa-, =ˈ==\ *adj* [*castrate* + *-ive*] **:** of, relating to, or tending to produce castration

cas·tra·to \kaˈsträd.(ˌ)ō\ *n, pl* **castra·ti** \-d.(ˌ)ē\ [It, fr. L *castratus*] **:** a singer castrated in boyhood to preserve the soprano or contralto range of his voice

cas·tren·sian \(ˈ)kasˌtrenchən\ *adj* [L *castrensis* (fr. *castra* camp — pl. of *castrum* fortified place — + *-ensis* -ese) + E *-an*] **:** of or relating to a camp

cas·trum \ˈkastrəm\ *n, pl* **cas·tra** \-rə\ [L — more at CASTLE] **1 :** an old Roman fortress **2** *castra pl* **:** a Roman encampment

casts *pres 3d sing of* CAST, *pl of* CAST

cast shadow *n* **:** a shadow cast by an object or figure in a painting or other picture

cast stone *n* [fr. past part. of 1*cast* (mold)] **:** a concrete building block with a face formed to resemble natural stone

cast up *vt* **1 :** to bring up or say by way of reproach ⟨*casting up* to her that she had failed⟩ **2 a :** to measure (set type) usu. in ems pica in order to determine the cost or charge to be made **b :** to lay out (tabular matter) before setting in type **3 :** to add up (figures) in making an accounting ~ *vi, chiefly Scot* **:** to turn up esp. unexpectedly

cast ware *n* [fr. past part. of 1*cast*] **:** ceramic ware formed by pouring slip into a mold (as of plaster of paris) that absorbs water and causes a layer of clay body to form on the mold wall and then removing the excess slip

cast–weld \ˈ=,=\ *vt* [2*cast*] **:** to join (parts) by placing together in a mold and pouring molten metal between or around

1ca·su·al \ˈkazhəwəl *also* -zhəl\ *adj* [ME *casuel, casual,* fr. MF & LL; MF *casuel,* fr. LL *casualis,* fr. L *casus* fall, chance — more at CASE] **1 a :** subject to or produced as a result of chance ⟨where ~ fire had wasted woods —John Milton⟩ **:** without design **:** not resulting from plan ⟨not merely ~ but a part of one great plan⟩ **b :** occurring, appearing, or singled out by chance or without calculated intent ⟨seek help from ~ passers-by⟩ **:** without specific motivation, special interest, or constant purpose ⟨an unusual ability to interest ~ students —John Gillin⟩ ⟨most comment, whether ~ or deliberate —Felix Frankfurter⟩ **c :** without foresight, plan, or method **:** not considered **:** HAPHAZARD ⟨information collected by ~ methods and in their spare time⟩ **2 a :** occurring, encountered, acting, or performed without regularity or at random **:** OCCASIONAL ⟨~ kindnesses⟩ ⟨exhausted firemen were getting ~ soup and sleep on the floors —Christopher Morley⟩ **b** *Brit* (1) **:** of the class of poor persons receiving occasional relief as distinguished from those receiving regular relief or being permanent inmates of workhouses ⟨the ~ poor⟩ (2) **:** of or for those poor persons or vagrants who are not residents of the place where they receive public aid or work — see CASUAL WARD **c** *of a workman* **:** having no steady employment but engaged for irregular periods esp. at an hourly or daily rate and at jobs requiring little training **3** *obs* **:** subject to accident **:** UNCERTAIN, PRECARIOUS ⟨the body is frail and ~⟩ **4 a :** feeling or showing little concern or interest **:** not giving close attention **:** INDIFFERENT, NONCHALANT ⟨tried to look ~ . . . but it was the handsomest house he had ever entered —Sinclair Lewis⟩ **b** (1) **:** without ceremony or formality **:** UNSTUDIED, INFORMAL ⟨referring to dear friends by their Christian names in a ~ and familiar way —Havelock Ellis⟩ **:** free from constraint **:** not showing effort or strain **:** NATURAL, EASY ⟨a difficult feat performed with ~ mastery⟩ (2) **:** suited by simplicity, comfort, and informality of design for everyday wear or use or for any occasion other than formal ⟨a ~ coat for town or country wear⟩ **c :** of little interest, concern, or importance **:** without significance **:** UNIMPORTANT ⟨subjects homely, slight, and ~ —E.J.Banfield⟩ **syn** see ACCIDENTAL, RANDOM

2casual \"\ *n* -s **1 a :** a casual or migratory worker **b** *Brit* **:** VAGRANT; *esp* **:** one who receives relief in a casual ward **2 :** an officer or enlisted man who is awaiting assignment or who is awaiting transportation to his unit **3 :** an article of dress for casual wear **4 :** an essay written in a familiar often humorous style

casual ejector *n, Eng law* **:** a fictitious person alleged to have ousted the lessee of the plaintiff in the old action of ejectment, the real defendant being substituted for him after notice

ca·su·al·ism \-,lizəm\ *n* -s [*casual* + *-ism*] **1 :** a condition of things in which chance rules **2 :** the theory that all things exist or are controlled by chance — compare TYCHISM

casuality *n* -ES [alter. (prob. influenced by MF *casualité* or ML *casualitas*) of *casualty*] *obs* **:** CASUALTY 1, 2, 3

ca·su·al·ly \ˈkazhəlē, -zhəwəlē, -i\ *adv* **:** in a casual manner

ca·su·al·ness \-lnəs\ *n* -ES **:** the quality or state of being casual

1ca·su·al·ty \ˈkazhəltē, -i *also* -zhəwəl-\ *n* -ES [ME *casuelte,* fr. *casuel* casual + *-te* -ty] **1** *archaic* **:** CHANCE, FORTUNE ⟨losses that befall them by mere ~ —Walter Raleigh⟩ **2 a :** an unfortunate occurrence **:** MISCHANCE ⟨yielding to the *casualties* of trade —H.S.Canby⟩ **b :** serious or fatal accident **:** DISASTER ⟨*casualties* at sea during the storm⟩ ⟨losses from fire, storm, or other ~ —J.S.Seidman⟩ **3** [trans. of ML *casualitas*] **a :** a casual charge or payment **b** *Scots law* **:** a payment demandable by a superior from his tenant upon the happening of various uncertain events as distinguished for example from a payment at a certain time (as rent) **4 :** a person lost to a command through death, wounds, injury, sickness, internment, capture, or through being missing in action ⟨*casualties* were heavy⟩ **5 a :** injury or death from accident **b :** one injured or killed (as by an accident) ⟨the dog was a traffic ~⟩ **6 :** a person or thing that has failed, been injured, lost, or destroyed as a result of uncontrollable circumstance or of some action **:** VICTIM ⟨the ex-senator was a ~ of the last election⟩ ⟨the factory was a ~ of the recession⟩

2ca·su·al·ty \ˈkazəltē, -asə-\ *var of* CASALTY

casualty insurance *n* **:** insurance against loss from accident (as automobile, burglary, liability, accident and health, and workmen's compensation insurance and corporate suretyship) consisting in the U.S. of all forms of insurance written commercially except life insurance and the forms of property insurance written by fire and marine companies

casual ward *n* [2*casual*] *Brit* **:** a ward in which vagrants seeking temporary public relief are detained for brief specified periods

casual water *n* [1*casual*] **:** a temporary accumulation of water not forming a regular hazard of a golf course

ca·su·ari·for·mes \ˌkazhə,wa(a)rēəˈfȯr,mēz\ *n pl, cap* [NL, fr. *Casuarius,* type genus + *-iformes*] **:** an order of large ostrichlike birds (superorder Neognathae) comprising the cassowaries and the emus

ca·su·a·ri·na \ˌkazhə(wə)ˈrēnə\ *n* [NL, fr. Malay (*pohon*) *kĕsuari* cassowary tree (fr. *pohon* tree + *kĕsuari* cassowary) + NL *-ina* (fem. of L *-inus* -ine); fr. the resemblance of its twigs to the cassowary's feathers] **1** *cap* **:** a genus (coextensive with the family Casuarinaceae and order Casuarinales) of dicotyledonous trees and shrubs now widely naturalized and used for hedge and ornamental work in southern No. America and the West Indies and characterized by jointed horsetaillike stems with whorls of scalelike leaves, some species yielding heavy hard wood — see BEEFWOOD, SHE-OAK **2** -s **:** a tree of the genus *Casuarina*

ca·su·ar·i·na·les \ˌkazhə,warəˈnā(ˌ)lēz\ *n pl, cap* [NL, fr. *Casuarina* + *-ales*] **:** an order of chiefly Australian woody plants comprising the casuarinas

ca·su·ar·i·us \ˌkazhəˈwa(a)rēəs\ *n, cap* [NL, fr. Malay *kĕsuari*] **:** a genus (the type and sole representative of the family Casuariidae) of ratite birds comprising the cassowaries

casubian *cap, var of* KASHUBIAN

ca·su·ist \ˈkazhəwəst\ *n* -s [prob. fr. Sp *casuista,* fr. L *casus* fall, chance, case + Sp *-ista* -ist — more at CASE] **:** one skilled in or given to casuistry

ca·su·is·tic \ˌkazhəˈwistik, -ēk\ *adj* [L *casus* + E *-istic*] **:** of or based upon actual cases or case histories

ca·su·is·ti·cal \-tȯkəl, -tēk-\ *or* **ca·su·is·tic** \-tik,-tēk\ *adj* [*casuist* + *-ical, -ic*] **:** using or marked by casuistry ⟨~ argument⟩ — **ca·su·is·ti·cal·ly** \-k(ə)lē, -i\ *adv*

ca·su·ist·ry \ˈkazhəwəstrē, -i\ *n* -ES [*casuist* + *-ry*] **1 a :** the study of or the doctrine that deals with cases of conscience **b :** the reasoning about or resolution of questions of right or wrong in conduct through the application of religious or secular ethical principles and rules **2 :** sophistical, equivocal, or specious reasoning **:** false application of principles specif. in regard to law or morals ⟨no ingenious ~ will convince us that this loss is really a victory⟩

ca·su·la \ˈkäsü,lä\ *n* -s [LL & ML, prob. fr. L, little hut, dim. of *casa* hut, cabin — more at CASA] **:** CHASUBLE

ca·sus bel·li \ˌkäsəsˈbe,lē, ˌkāsəsˈbe,lī\ *n, pl* **casus belli** \"\ [NL, occasion of war] **1 :** an event, circumstance, or action that justifies the making of war (as interference with the exercise of a nation's rights or injury to a nation's vital interest or national honor) **2 :** a cause or occasion for war or other strife **:** an excuse for declaring war ⟨greeting an oil embargo as a *casus belli* —John Gunther⟩

casus foe·de·ris \-ˈfōidərəs -ˈfed-,-ˈfēd-\ *n, pl* **casus foederis** \"\ [NL, case of the treaty] **:** a case or event covered by the provisions or stipulations of a treaty or compact ⟨the *casus foederis* had arisen. When Italy attacked Ethiopia . . . no one could doubt . . . that . . . it had been in breach of the clearest obligations of the Covenant —Robert Cecil †1958⟩

casus for·tu·i·tus \-(ˌ)fȯrˈtüəd.əs, -ˈtyü-\ *n, pl* **casus fortui·ti** \-üə,tē, -ī\ [NL, fortuitous event] **:** an accident or chance **:** an inevitable accident — compare ACT OF GOD

casus omis·sus \-ōˈmisəs\ *n, pl* **casus omis·si** \-,sē, -ī\ [NL] **:** a case omitted or not provided for (as by a statute) and therefore governed by the common law

cas·well·ite \ˈkazwə,līt\ *n* -s [John H. *Caswell,* 19th cent. Am. mineralogist + E *-ite*] **:** a mineral from Franklin, N.J., consisting of an altered biotite

1cat \ˈkat, *usu* -ad.+V\ *n* -s *often attrib* [ME *cat, catte,* fr. OE *catt, catte;* akin to OFris *katte,* OHG *kazza,* ON *köttr* cat; all fr. a prehistoric NGmc-WGmc word prob. borrowed fr. LL *cattus, catta,* perh. of Hamitic origin; akin to Berber *kaddiska* cat, Nubian *kadīs*] **1 a :** a long-domesticated carnivorous mammal that is usu. regarded as a distinct species (*Felis catus* syn. *F. domestica*) though probably ultimately derived by selection from among the hybrid progeny of several small Old World wildcats (as the Kaffir cat and the European wildcat), that occurs in several varieties distinguished chiefly by length of coat, body form, and presence or absence of tail, and that makes a pet valuable in controlling rodents and other small vermin but tends to revert to a feral state if not housed and cared for — see ABYSSINIAN CAT, ANGORA CAT, MANX CAT, PERSIAN CAT, SIAMESE CAT **b :** a member of the family Felidae (as a lion, leopard, jaguar, or wildcat) **c :** an animal that in appearance or behavior resembles any member of the family Felidae — usu. used with a qualifying term (bear ~) ⟨toddy ~⟩ ⟨polecat⟩ ⟨native ~⟩ **d :** the fur or pelt of the domestic cat **2 :** a malicious woman; *esp* **:** one given to making catty remarks about other women **3 :** a low movable defensive structure used in medieval warfare as a means of approaching fortifications **4 a :** the tapered peg used in tipcat **b** [by shortening] **:** TIPCAT **5 :** a strong tackle used to hoist an anchor to the cathead of a ship **6 a :** a seagoing ship with a narrow stern, projecting quarters, and deep waist formerly used in England in the coal and timber trade **b :** an old-fashioned 3-masted Deal lugger **c** [by shortening] **:** CATBOAT **d :** CATAMARAN **7** [by shortening] **:** CAT-O'-NINE-TAILS **8** [by shortening] **:** CATFISH — usu. used with a qualifying term ⟨channel ~⟩ ⟨blue ~⟩ ⟨mud ~⟩ **9 :** a double tripod that rests on three of its legs however it is set down and is usu. used as a stand near or over an open fireplace **10 :** ONE OLD CAT **11** *slang* **a :** SKAT **b :** 3KITTY 2c **12 :** the part of the first coat of plaster going between laths **13 a :** BIG CAT **b :** LITTLE CAT **14** *slang* **a :** a player or a devotee of hot jazz **:** HEPCAT **b :** GUY, PERSON, CHARACTER ⟨some young Indian ~ asked me to go drinking with him —Jack Kerouac⟩ **15 :** the heraldic representation of a European wildcat or a domestic cat

2cat \"\ *vb* **catted; catted; catting; cats** *vt* **1 :** to bring (the anchor) up to a ship's cathead **2 :** to flog with a cat-o'-nine-tails ~ *vi* **1** *Brit* **:** VOMIT **2 :** to search for a sexual mate — usu. used in the phrase *go catting;* usu. considered vulgar

3cat *var of* KAT

cat *abbr* **1** catalog **2** catalyst **3** cataplasm **4** catechism

Cat \"\ *trademark* — used for a Caterpillar tractor

cata– *or* **cat–** *or* **cath–** *prefix* [Gk *kata-, kat-, kath-,* fr. *kata* down; akin to OW *cant* with, along, Hitt *katta* under, with,

L *com-* with, together — more at CO-] **1 :** down ⟨*cation*⟩ ⟨*catabiotic*⟩ **2 :** against ⟨*catabaptist*⟩

cata·bap·tist \¦kad·ə¦⸗⸗\ *n* -s [prob. fr. NL *catabaptista*, fr. LGk *katabaptistēs*, fr. Gk *kata-* cata- + *baptistēs* baptizer — more at BAPTIST] **:** one who opposes baptism

catabasis *var of* KATABASIS

cata·bi·o·sis \ˌkad·ə,bīˈōsəs, -ˌbēˈ-\ *n, pl* **catabio·ses** \-ō,sēz\ [NL, fr. *cata-* + *biosis*] **:** the degenerative biological changes accompanying cellular senescence

cata·bi·ot·ic \ˌkad·ə,bī¦äd·ik, -ˌbē-\ *adj* [*cata-* + *biotic*] **:** of, relating to, or exhibiting catabiosis

cat·a·bol·ic \-¦bälik, -ēk\ *adj* [Gk *katabolē* + E *-ic*] **:** relating to or characterized by catabolism

ca·tab·o·lism *or* **ka·tab·o·lism** \kəˈtabə,lizəm\ *n* -s [Gk *katabolē* throwing down (fr. *kataballein* to throw down, fr. *kata-* cata- + *ballein* to throw) + E *-ism* — more at DEVIL] **:** destructive metabolism involving release of energy and resulting in true excretion products although certain new substances may be formed in metabolic processes that are mainly catabolic — opposed to *anabolism*

ca·tab·o·lite \-,līt\ *n* -s [*catabolism* + *-ite*] **:** a substance (as nectar) produced in catabolism; *esp* **:** a waste product so produced

ca·tab·o·lize \-,līz\ *vb* -ED/-ING/-S [fr. *catabolism*, after E *metabolism: metabolize*] *vt* **:** to subject to catabolism; *specif* **:** OXIDIZE ~ *vi* **:** to undergo catabolism

cata·caus·tic \¦kad·ə¦kȯstik\ *adj* [*cata-* + *caustic*] **:** relating to a caustic curve or caustic surface formed by reflection — compare DIACAUSTIC

cat·a·chre·sis \ˌ⸗⸗ˈkrēsəs\ *n, pl* **catachre·ses** \-ē,sēz\ [L, fr. Gk *katachrēsis* misuse, fr. *katachrēsthai* to use up, misuse, fr. *kata-* cata- + *chrēsthai* to use — more at CHRESTOMATHY] **:** the misuse of words: as **a :** the use of the wrong word for the context **b :** the use of a forced figure of speech, esp. one that involves or seems to involve strong paradox (as *blind mouths*)

cat·a·chres·tic \¦⸗⸗¦krestik, *esp Brit* -ēs-\ *or* **cat·a·chres·ti·cal** \-əkəl\ *adj* [Gk *katachrēstikos*, fr. *katachrēsthai* + *-ikos* -ic] **:** constituting, characterized by, or given to catachresis — **cat·a·chres·ti·cal·ly** \-ək(ə)lē\ *adv*

catachromasis *var of* KATACHROMASIS

cat·a·cla·sis \ˌkad·əˈklāsəs; kəˈtakləsəs, kaˈ-\ *n, pl* **catacla·ses** \-,sēz\ [NL, fr. Gk *kataklasis*, fr. *kata-* cata- + *klasis* breaking — more at -CLASIA] **:** the crushing or fracturing of rocks and minerals during metamorphism — compare BRECCIA, CRUSH BRECCIA

cat·a·clasm \ˈkad·ə,klazəm\ *n* -s [irreg. (after Gk *klasma* fragment, fr. *klan* to break) fr. Gk *kataklan* to break down, fr. *kata-* cata- + *klan* to break — more at GLADIATOR] **:** a breaking down **:** DISRUPTION — **cat·a·clas·mic** \¦⸗⸗¦klazmik\ *adj*

cata·clas·tic \¦⸗⸗¦klastik\ *adj* [prob. modif. of Norw *kataklastisk*, fr. Gk. *kataklastos* broken down (fr. *kataklan*) + Norw *-isk* -ish] **1 :** of, relating to, or caused by cataclasis ⟨a pronounced ~ texture⟩ **2 :** having the granular fragmental texture induced in rocks by mechanical crushing ⟨~ structures⟩

cata·cli·nal \¦⸗⸗¦klīnᵊl\ *adj* [*cata-* + *-clinal*] **:** descending in the same direction as that of the dip of the geological strata ⟨a ~ valley⟩ ⟨a ~ river⟩ — opposed to *anaclinal*

cat·a·clysm \ˈkad·ə,klizəm, -atə-\ *n* -s [F *cataclysme*, fr. L *cataclysmos*, fr. Gk *kataklysmos*, fr. *katakluzein* to inundate, fr. *kata-* cata- + *klyzein* to wash — more at CLYSTER] **1 :** a surging flood of water **:** DELUGE **2 :** a violent geologic change involving sudden and extensive alterations of the earth's surface **:** CATASTROPHE **3 :** a momentous and violent event or series of events marked by overwhelming upheaval and demolition (as of a political or social order) ⟨if all future world organization were rent asunder and if new ~s . . . destroyed all that is left —Sir Winston Churchill⟩ **syn** see DISASTER

cat·a·clys·mic \¦⸗⸗¦klizmik, -ēk\ *or* **cat·a·clys·mal** \-məl\ *adj* **:** of, relating to, or having the characteristics of a cataclysm ⟨a ~ nuclear war⟩ — **cat·a·clys·mi·cal·ly** \-ək(ə)lē, -ēk-, -li\ *adv*

cat·a·clys·mist \ˈ⸗⸗,⸗məst, ,⸗⸗ˈ⸗⸗\ *n* -s **:** CATASTROPHIST

cat·a·comb \ˈkad·ə,kōm, -atə-, *Brit also* -üm\ *n* -s [MF *catacombe*, prob. fr. OIt *catacomba*, fr. LL *catacumbae*, pl., prob. alter. of (assumed) VL *cata tumbas* near the tombs, fr. *cata* near, by (fr. Gk *kata* down, against, opposite) + *tumbas*, accus. pl. of *tumba* tomb — more at CATA-, TOMB] **1 :** a subterranean cemetery consisting of galleries or passages with side recesses for tombs — usu. used in pl. ⟨the ~s at Rome⟩ **2 :** a place like a catacomb: as **a :** a subterranean passageway or vault or a group of such passageways or vaults used esp. for storing the bones of the dead ⟨the underground stone quarries which form the ~s of Paris⟩ **b :** a complex set of interrelated passageways or rooms ⟨the sulphurous ~s of Liverpool Street Station in London —Fred Majdalany⟩

catacorner *or* **cata-cornered** *var of* CATERCORNER

cata·di·op·tric \¦kad·ə,dī¦äptrik\ *also* **cata·di·op·tri·cal** \-trəkəl\ *adj* [*cata-* + *dioptric* or *dioptrical*] **:** belonging to, produced by, or involving both the reflection and the refraction of light ⟨~ prisms⟩

cata·drom·ic \¦⸗⸗¦drämik\ *adj* [NL *catadromus* + E *-ic*] *bot* **:** having the lowest interior segment of a pinna nearer the rachis than the lowest superior one

ca·tad·ro·mous \kəˈtadrəməs, kaˈ-\ *adj* [prob. fr. NL *catadromus*, fr. *cata-* + *-dromus* -dromous] **1 :** living in fresh water and going to the sea to spawn ⟨the eel is ~⟩ — compare ANADROMOUS **2 :** CATADROMIC

catadupe *n* -s [L *Catadupa* (pl.), first cataract of the Nile, near Aswân, Egypt, fr. Gk *Katadoupoi* (pl.)] *obs* **:** CATARACT, WATERFALL

cat·a·falque \ˈkad·ə,falk, ˈkatə-, -fȯ(l)k\ *also* **cat·a·fal·co** \ˌ⸗⸗ˈfal(,)kō\ *n, pl* **catafalques** *also* **catafalcoes** [It *catafalco*, fr. (assumed) VL *catafalicum* scaffold, irreg. fr. *cata-* + L *fala* siege tower] **1 :** an ornamental sometimes very elaborate structure used in many churches in solemn funerals for the lying in state of the body **2 :** a pall-covered coffin-shaped structure used at requiem masses celebrated after burial **3 :** HEARSE

catafalque 2

cata·gen·e·sis \ˌkad·əˈjenəsəs\ *n, pl* **catagene·ses** \-,sēz\ [NL, fr. *cata-* + *genesis*] **:** regressive evolution

cata·ge·net·ic \¦kad·əjə¦ned·ik\ *adj* [fr. NL *catagenesis*, after E *genesis: genetic*] **:** of or relating to catagenesis

cat·a·hou·la hog dog \¦kad·ə¦hülə-\ *n, usu cap C* [fr. *Catahoula*, parish in Louisiana] **:** a large vigorous speckled houndlike dog of the southern U.S. used in hunting and in herding wild hogs

cataian *n* -s *usu cap* [ML *Cataya* Cathay + E *-an* — more at CATHAY] **1** *obs* **:** a native of Cathay **2** [so called fr. the reputation for thievery given to the Chinese by early travelers] *obs* **:** SHARPER, SCOUNDREL

¹cat·a·lan \ˈkad·ᵊlən, -atᵊl-; -l,an, -,aa(ə)n, ,⸗⸗ˈ⸗\ *n, cap* [Sp *catalán*] **1 :** a native or inhabitant of Catalonia, an eastern region of Spain **2 a :** the Romance language of Catalonia, Valencia, and the Balearic islands **b :** a speaker of this language

²catalan \"\ *adj, usu cap* [Sp *catalán*] **1 a :** of, relating to, or characteristic of Catalonia **b :** of, relating to, or characteristic of the Catalans **2 :** of, relating to, or characteristic of the Catalan language

catalan ass *n, usu cap C* **:** CATALONIAN ASS

catalan forge *or* **catalan furnace** *n, usu cap C* **:** a bloomery that produces wrought iron from ore and that has a siliceous bottom lined with charcoal and a tuyere inclining downwards, the front being piled with ore and the back with charcoal and the whole covered with fine mixed ore and charcoal dust moistened with water

cat·a·lan·ist \-nəst\ *n* -s *usu cap* [Sp *catalanista*, fr. *catalán* + *-ista* -ist] **:** one who favors regional autonomy for Catalonia

cat·a·lase \ˈkad·ᵊl,ās\ *n* -s [*catalysis* + *-ase*] **:** a red crystalline enzyme widely distributed in plant and animal cells (as red blood cells) and consisting of a protein complex with hematin groups that catalyzes the decomposition of hydrogen peroxide into water and oxygen and the oxidation by hydrogen peroxide of alcohols to aldehydes and is held to function in tissues as an oxidative catalyst — compare PEROXIDASE — **cat·a·lat·ic** \¦⸗⸗¦ad·ik\ *adj*

¹cat·a·lec·tic \¦kad·ᵊl¦ektik\ *adj* [LL *catalecticus*, fr. Gk *katalēktikos* incomplete, fr. *katalēgein* to leave off, fr. *kata-* cata- + *lēgein* to leave off, stop — more at SLACK] **:** lacking a syllable at the end or terminating in an imperfect foot

²catalectic \"\ *n* -s **:** a catalectic line of verse

cat·a·lep·sy \ˈkad·ᵊl,epsē, -atᵊl-, -si\ *n* -ES [alter. (influenced by ML, LL, and/or Gk) of earlier *catalency*, modif. of ME *cathalempsia*, modif. of ML *catalepsia*, modif. of LL *catalepsis*, fr. Gk *katalēpsis*, lit., act of seizing, fr. *katalambanein* to seize, fr. *kata-* cata- + *lambanein* to take, seize; akin to OE *læccan* to seize — more at LATCH] **1 :** a condition of suspended animation and loss of voluntary motion associated with hysteria and schizophrenia in man and with organic nervous disease in animals and characterized by a trancelike state of consciousness and a posture in which the limbs hold any position they are placed in **2 :** CATAPLEXY

¹cat·a·lep·tic \¦⸗⸗¦eptik, -ēk\ *adj* [LL *catalepticus*, fr. Gk *katalēptikos* able to check, fr. *katalambanein*] **:** of, having the characteristics of, or affected with catalepsy ⟨a ~ state⟩ ⟨a ~ person⟩ — **cat·a·lep·ti·cal·ly** \-ək(ə)lē, -ēk-, -li\ *adv*

²cataleptic \"\ *n* -s **:** one affected with catalepsy

cat·a·lep·ti·form \¦⸗⸗¦eptə,fȯrm\ *adj* [*cataleptic* + *-form*] **:** CATALEPTOID

cat·a·lep·toid \¦⸗⸗¦ep,tȯid\ *adj* [*cataleptic* + *-oid*] **:** resembling catalepsy

cat·a·lex·is \ˌkad·ᵊlˈeksəs\ *n, pl* **catalexes** \-,sēz\ [NL, fr. Gk *katalēxis* close of a rhetorical period, fr. *katalēgein* to leave off — more at CATALECTIC] **:** omission or incompleteness in the last foot of a line or other unit in metrical verse **:** terminal truncation

Cat·a·lin \ˈkad·ᵊlən\ *trademark* — used for a thermosetting plastic made of a cast phenol-formaldehyde resin and marked by high compressive strength and ready machinability

cat·a·li·na \ˌkad·ᵊlˈēnə, -atᵊl-\ *n* -s [fr. Santa *Catalina* Island, Calif.] **:** a synchronized swimming stunt executed from a back-floating position in which one leg is raised and held vertically while the body rolls over and submerges, the legs being brought together before submersion is complete

catalina cherry \¦⸗⸗¦⸗⸗-\ *n, usu cap 1st C* **:** an evergreen shrub or tree (*Prunus lyonii*) found on islands off the coast of California

catalina ironwood *n, usu cap C* **:** a tree (*Lyonothamnus floribundus*) of the family Rosaceae found on the islands off southern California and having thin brown shredding bark and opposite long-stalked leaves some of which are simply toothed and others irregularly compound

cat·a·li·neta \ˌkad·ᵊlaˈned·ə\ *n* -s [AmerSp, dim. of Sp *Catalina* Catherine (fem. prop. name), modif. of ML *Katharina*, by folk etymology (influence of Gk *katharos* pure) fr. *Katerina*, modif. of LGk *Aikaterinē*] **1 :** any of several angelfishes (esp. *Holacanthus tricolor*) **2 :** PORKFISH

cat·a·li·nite \ˌkad·ᵊlˈē,nīt\ *n* -s [Santa *Catalina* Island, Calif., its locality + E *-ite*] **:** an agate beach pebble used as a gem

cat·al·lac·tics \ˌkad·ᵊlˈaktiks\ *n pl but sing in constr* [Gk *katallakt-* (fr. *katallassein* to exchange, fr. *kata-* cata- + *allassein* to change, fr. *allos* other) + E *-ics* — more at ELSE] **:** political economy as the science of exchanges

catalo *var of* CATTALO

¹cat·a·log *or* **cat·a·logue** \ˈkad·ᵊl,ȯg, -atᵊl-, -äg\ *n* -s [ME *cateloge*, fr. MF *catalogue*, fr. LL *catalogus*, fr. Gk *katalogos* list, fr. *katalegein* to list, enumerate, fr. *kata-* cata- + *legein* to gather, speak — more at LEGEND] **1 a :** a detailed enumeration **:** LIST, REGISTER ⟨the narrative is broken by a ~ of kings⟩ ⟨it does not pretend to be a ~ of past achievements —Mortimer Graves⟩ **b :** a group of similar or related things often standing or succeeding in order **:** SERIES ⟨began to recapitulate items in the ~ of his escapades —H.G.Wells⟩ ⟨gave little support to the long-believed ~ of disorderly and brutal private crimes —F.L.Paxson⟩ **2 a :** a complete enumeration of items (as of books for sale or courses of instruction in a college) arranged systematically in a pamphlet or a book often alphabetically and with descriptive details (as of price or content) accompanying each item — see CARD CATALOG **b :** a pamphlet or book that contains such a list often with other related matter ⟨a mail-order ~⟩ ⟨a ~ of secondhand books⟩ ⟨a college ~⟩ ⟨a museum ~⟩ **c :** the material in such a list (as the works of a composer or author) ⟨his ~ of more than 300 numbers in active use today includes overtures, operatic selections, solos —*Baton*⟩ **3 :** the price quoted for a particular article in a stamp or coin catalog ⟨that stamp sold under ~⟩ ⟨this coin has a high ~⟩

²catalog *or* **catalogue** \"\ *vb* **cataloged** *or* **catalogued**; **cataloged** *or* **catalogued**; **catalog·ing** *or* **catalogu·ing**; **catalogs** *or* **catalogues** *vt* **1 :** to make a catalog of ⟨~ a collection of books⟩ ⟨~ items for sale at auction⟩ **2 :** to enter the name of or appropriate information about in a catalog; *esp* **:** to describe the physical format of and classify (books or other library material) ~ *vi* **1 :** to make or work on a catalog **2 :** to become listed in a stamp or coin catalog at a specified price ⟨this stamp ~s at two dollars⟩

cat·a·log·er *or* **cat·a·logu·er** \-gə(r)\ *n* -s **:** one that catalogs; *esp* **:** a person engaged in cataloging material for a library

cat·a·lo·gia \ˌkad·ᵊlˈōj(ē)ə\ *n* -s [NL, fr. *cata-* + *-logia*] **:** VERBIGERATION

cat·a·log·ic \¦kad·ᵊl¦äjik, -ēk\ *adj* **:** having the characteristics of or belonging to a catalog ⟨much of the volume is, in spite of the lightness of touch, ~ —*Times Lit. Supp.*⟩

cataloging *or* **cataloguing** *n* -s **:** the science or the profession of classifying books or other library material and making out appropriate entries for library catalogs

cat·a·log·ize *or* **cat·a·logu·ize** \ˈ⸗⸗,ō,gīz, -,ä,-\ *vt* -ED/-ING/-S *archaic* **:** CATALOG

catalog paper *n* **:** a lightweight paper of good printing quality suitable for use in mail-order catalogs or telephone directories

catalogue rai·son·né \-ˌrāzᵊnˈā, -ez-\ *n, pl* **catalogues raisonnés** \-g(z)ˌr...nˈā\ [F, lit., reasoned catalog] **:** a systematic catalog with critical or descriptive notes; *esp* **:** a critical bibliography arranged according to subject

cat·a·lo·ni·an \¦kad·ᵊl¦ōnēən, ¦katᵊl-, -nyən\ *adj or n, usu cap* [*Catalonia*, region of Spain + E *-an*] **:** CATALAN

catalonian ass *n, usu cap C* **:** an ass of a Spanish breed noted for its style, quality, and black or brown color with light or mealy points — called also *Catalan ass*

catalonian jasmine *n, usu cap C* **:** SPANISH JASMINE 1

ca·tal·pa \kəˈtalpə *also* -ȯl-\ *n* [NL, fr. E, fr. Creek *kutuhlpa*, lit., head with wings; fr. the shape of its flowers] **1** *cap* **:** a small genus of American and Asiatic trees (family Bignoniaceae) having broad cordate leaves, large white or mottled flowers in terminal panicles, and long terete pods — see HARDY CATALPA, INDIAN BEAN **2** -s [Creek *kutuhlpa*] **:** a tree of the genus *Catalpa*

catalpa sphinx *n* **:** a large American hawk moth (*Ceratomia catalpae*) having a larva that feeds on leaves of the catalpa and in some areas is highly regarded as fish bait

catalpa worm *n* **:** the green and black larva of the catalpa sphinx

cat·a·lu·fa \ˌkad·ᵊlˈüfə\ *n* -s [AmerSp, fr. Sp, variegated material used in making carpets, fr. OIt *cataluffa*, a cloth made in Venice] **:** any of various brightly colored carnivorous marine percoid fishes (family Priacanthidae) of tropical seas; *esp* **:** a fish (*Priacanthus arenatus*) of the western Atlantic and West Indies

ca·tal·y·sis \kəˈtaləsəs\ *n, pl* **cataly·ses** \-ə,sēz\ [Gk *katalysis*, fr. *katalyein* to dissolve, fr. *kata-* cata- + *lyein* to loosen, release — more at LOSE] **1 :** the change in the rate of a chemical reaction brought about by often small amounts of a substance that is unchanged chemically at the end of the reaction; *specif* **:** acceleration of a reaction (as the oxidation of sulfur dioxide to sulfur trioxide in the presence of platinized asbestos) — compare AUTOCATALYSIS, CONTACT CATALYSIS, NEGATIVE CATALYSIS **2 :** an action or reaction between two or more persons or forces provoked or precipitated by a separate agent or force, esp. by one that is essentially unaltered by the reaction ⟨a representative list of questions . . . valuable for the ~ of class discussions —B.S.Meyer & D.B.Anderson⟩ ⟨George Washington wrote friends of the powerful ~ that "Common Sense" was working —Eric Goldman⟩

cat·a·lyst \ˈkad·ᵊləst, -atᵊl-\ *n* -s [fr. *catalysis*, prob. after E *analysis: analyst*] **1 :** a substance that brings about catalysis and that may or may not actually take part chemically in the reaction; *broadly* **:** any substance (as an enzyme) that initiates a reaction and enables it to take place under milder conditions (as at a lower temperature) than in the absence of the catalyst — compare BIOCATALYST **2 :** an agent that provokes or precipitates catalysis ⟨the housing program is intended to become the ~ of the new French economy —Edmond Taylor⟩ ⟨the major ~ in his writing life has been the Mississippi countryside —C.H.Baker⟩ ⟨he was rumored to be the ~ in a native uprising —H.W.Wind⟩

cat·a·lyte \-,īt\ *n* -s [prob. back-formation fr. *catalytic*] **:** CATALYST

¹cat·a·lyt·ic \¦⸗⸗¦id·ik, -itik, -ēk\ *adj* [Gk *katalytikos*, fr. *katalysis* + *-ikos* -ic] **:** causing, involving, or relating to catalysis ⟨a ~ agent⟩ ⟨a ~ reaction⟩ ⟨a ~ function⟩ ⟨a ~ personality⟩ — **catalytically** *adv*

²catalytic \"\ *n* -s **:** CATALYST ⟨duty is sometimes still offered as a ~ —Irwin Edman⟩

catalytic cracker *n* **:** the unit in a petroleum refinery in which catalytic cracking is carried out — called also *cat cracker*

catalytic cracking *n* **:** cracking of petroleum oils (as gas oils or diesel oils) esp. for the production of high-octane gasoline in the presence of a catalyst (as clay) in various forms (as pellets or beads either stationary in a fixed bed or moving through the oil or as a fine powder fluidized by a stream of air or hydrocarbon vapors) — distinguished from *thermal cracking*

cat·a·lyze \ˈ⸗⸗,īz\ *vt* -ED/-ING/-S [prob. fr. F *catalyser*, fr. *catalyse* catalysis, fr. E *catalysis*] **1 :** to bring about the catalysis of (a chemical reaction); *specif* **:** to speed up (a chemical reaction) **2 :** to produce (a substance) by means of chemical catalysis **3 :** to bring about **:** PROVOKE, PRECIPITATE, INSPIRE ⟨religious faith which alone ~s important sacred art —Janet Flanner⟩ ⟨his vigorous efforts to ~ us into activity —Harrison Brown⟩ **4 :** to transform or alter significantly by catalysis ⟨innovations in basic chemical theory that have *catalyzed* the field and its technology —*Newsweek*⟩ ⟨take over the proletarian formula, revolution and all, and ~ it into one of the epics of the twentieth century —Leo Gurko⟩

cat·a·lyz·er \-zə(r)\ *n* -s **:** CATALYST

cat·a·ma·ran \¦kad·əmə¦ran, -atə-, -raa(ə)n\ *n* -s [modif. of Tamil *kaṭṭumaram*, fr. *kaṭṭu* to tie + *maram* tree, timber] **1 :** a raft or float consisting of two or more logs or pieces of wood lashed together, propelled by paddles or sails, and used esp. as a surfboat on the coasts of India, the East Indies, the West Indies, and So. America **2 :** a boat with twin hulls or planing surfaces side by side; *esp* **:** a fast pleasure boat having two hulls joined by a framework that supports the mast or motor **3 :** an early 19th century fire raft **4 :** a raft with windlass and grapple used in logging **5 :** a raft that consists of a rectangular platform attached to two parallel cylindrical floats and is used in lifesaving or for work alongside a ship **6 :** an ill-natured quarrelsome person; *esp* **:** a faultfinding woman

cat·a·me·nia \ˌkad·əˈmēnēə, -nyə\ *n pl but sing or pl in constr* [NL, fr. Gk *katamēnia*, neut. pl. of *katamēnios* monthly, fr. *kata-* cata- + *mēn* month — more at MOON] **:** MENSES — **cat·a·me·ni·al** \¦⸗⸗¦nēəl, -nyəl\ *adj*

cat·a·mite \ˈkad·ə,mīt, ˈkatə-, *usu* -īd·+V\ *n* -s [L *catamitus*, fr. *Catamitus* Ganymede, cupbearer of the gods, fr. Etruscan *Catmite*, fr. Gk *Ganymēdēs*] **:** a boy kept for purposes of sexual perversion

cat·am·ne·sis \ˌkad,amˈnēsəs\ *n, pl* **catamne·ses** \-ē,sēz\ [NL, fr. *cata-* + *-mnesis* memory (as in *anamnesis*)] **:** the follow-up medical history of a patient — compare ANAMNESIS — **cat·am·nes·tic** \¦⸗,⸗¦nestik\ *adj*

catamorphism *var of* KATAMORPHISM

cat·a·mount \ˈkad·ə,maůnt\ *n* -s [short for *cat-a-mountain*] **:** any of various wild animals of the cat family: as **a :** COUGAR **b :** LYNX

cat-a-mountain \¦kad·ə¦⸗⸗\ *n, pl* **cat-a-mountains** *or* **cats-a-mountain** [alter. of ME *cat of the mountaine*] **:** any of various wild animals of the cat family: as **a :** the European wildcat **b :** LEOPARD

ca·tan *or* **cat·tan** \kəˈtän\ *n* -s [Sp *catán*, fr. Jap *katana*] **:** a Japanese sword resembling a broad cutlass

cat·a·nan·che \ˌkad·əˈnaŋ(,)kē\ *n* [NL, modif. of L *catanance*, plant used in love potions, fr. Gk *katanankē*, lit., means of compulsion, fr. *kata-* cata- + *anankē* force, compulsion — more at ANANKE] **1** *cap* **:** a genus of Mediterranean herbs (family Compositae) having linear or lanceolate leaves crowded toward the base of the stem and ligulate blue or yellow flowers in long-stalked heads **2** -s **:** a plant of the genus *Catananche*

cat and clay *n* [Sc *cat* wisp of straw, perh. fr. E *cat*] **:** straw and clay worked together to form a building or chinking material

cat-and-dog \¦⸗⸗¦⸗\ *adj* **1 :** resembling or having the character of the proverbial antagonism of dogs and cats: **a :** QUARRELSOME, INHARMONIOUS ⟨they led a *cat-and-dog* life together —Ellen Glasgow⟩ **b** *of a fight* **:** malicious and incessant ⟨the *cat-and-dog* fight among the early wire companies —F.L.Mott⟩ **2 :** being or consisting of cheap or questionable securities **:** highly speculative ⟨*cat-and-dog* stocks are swinging through sensational gyrations — rising 100 percent in ten days, then collapsing —Sylvia F. Porter⟩

cat-and-mouse \¦⸗⸗¦⸗\ *adj* **1 :** consisting of constant torment prior to destruction or defeat ⟨the *cat-and-mouse* technique of handling an opponent⟩ **2 :** consisting of constant pursuit, near captures, and repeated escapes ⟨a . . . *cat-and-mouse* kind of thriller with the hunter and the hunted occasionally switching roles —Martin Levin⟩ **3 :** consisting of watchful waiting for the best opportunity to attack or strike an opponent ⟨a *cat-and-mouse* mood⟩

cat and mouse *or* **cat and rat** \¦⸗⸗¦⸗\ *n* **:** a children's game in which players in a circle raise their joined hands to let one player in and out of the circle and lower them to bar a second player who chases the first

ca·ta·nia \kəˈtänyə, -tän-\ *adj, usu cap* [fr. *Catania*, city in Italy] **:** of or from the city of Catania, Italy **:** of the kind or style prevalent in Catania

cat·a·pan \ˈkad·ə,pan\ *n* -s [ML *catapanus*, *catipanus*, fr. MGk *katapanos*, modif. of OIt *capitano* leader, commander, fr. (assumed) VL *capitanus* foremost, chief, fr. L *capit-*, *caput* head — more at HEAD] **:** the governor of Calabria and Apulia under the Byzantine emperors

cata·pha·sia \ˌkad·əˈfāzh(ē)ə\ *n* -s [NL, fr. *cata-* + *-phasia*] **:** VERBIGERATION

cata·pho·re·sis \ˌkad·əfəˈrēsəs\ *n, pl* **cataphore·ses** \-ē,sēz\ [NL, fr. *cata-* + *-phoresis*] **:** ELECTROPHORESIS — **cata·pho·ret·ic** \¦⸗⸗⸗¦red·ik\ *adj* — **cata·pho·ret·i·cal·ly** \-ək(ə)lē\ *adv*

cata·phor·ic \¦kad·ə¦fȯrik\ *adj* [Gk *kataphorein* to carry down, wash downstream (fr. *kata-* cata- + *phorein* to carry, freq. of *pherein*) + E *-ic*] **:** of or relating to cataphoresis

cat·a·phract \ˈkad·ə,frakt\ *n* -s [L *cataphractes*, fr. Gk *kataphraktēs*, fr. *kataphraktos* covered, armored, fr. *kataphrassein* to protect, fortify, fr. *kata-* cata- + *phrassein* to enclose — more at FARCE] **1 :** a suit of armor for the whole body **:** COAT OF MAIL **2** [L *cataphractus*, lit., armored, fr. Gk *kataphraktos*] **:** a soldier wearing a cataphract

cat·a·phrac·ta \ˌ⸗⸗ˈ⸗tə\ *n, pl, cap* [NL, fr. L, neut. pl. of *cataphractus* armored] *in former classifications* **:** a division of reptiles including the crocodilians, chelonians, and some others

cat·a·phrac·ti \ˌ⸗⸗ˈ⸗,tī, -,tē\ [NL, fr. L, pl. of *cataphractus*] *syn of* SCLEROPAREI

cata·phre·nia \ˌ⸗⸗ˈfrēnēə\ *n* -s [NL, fr. *cata-* + *-phrenia*] **:** a dementia from which the sufferer usu. recovers — **cata·phren·ic** \¦⸗⸗¦frenik\ *adj*

cata·phyll \ˈkad·ə,fil\ *n* -s [*cata-* + *-phyll*; intended as trans. of G *niederblatt*, lit., lower leaf] **:** a rudimentary scalelike leaf (as a bud scale) that precedes the foliage leaves of a plant — compare HYPSOPHYLL — **cata·phyl·la·ry** \¦⸗⸗¦filərē\ *adj*

cata·pla·sia \ˌkad·əˈplāzh(ē)ə\ *n* -s [NL, fr. *cata-* + *-plasia*] **:** regressive biological change in cells or tissues **:** reversion to more primitive character — **cata·plas·tic** \¦⸗⸗¦plastik\ *adj*

cat·a·plasm \ˈkad·ə,plazəm\ *n* -s [MF *cataplasme*, fr. L *cataplasma*, fr. Gk *kataplasma*, fr. *kataplassein* to plaster over

fr. *kata-* cata- + *plassein* to form, mold — more at PLASTIC] : POULTICE
cataplasm of kaolin : a paste made of purified clay, glycerin, boric acid, thymol, methyl salicylate, and oil of peppermint and used like a poultice
cat·a·plec·tic \ˌkad·əˈplektik\ *adj* [fr. *cataplexy*, after such pairs as E *apoplexy: apoplectic*] : of, relating to, or affected with cataplexy
cat·a·plei·ite \ˌkad·əˈplīˌīt\ *n* -s [G *katapleiit*, fr. Gk *kata* in the region of, down + *pleiōn* more + G *-it* -ite; fr. its occurrence together with other rare minerals — more at CATA-, PLEONASM] : a rare mineral ($(Na_2,Ca)ZrSi_3O_9.2H_2O$) consisting of hydrous silicate of sodium, calcium, and zirconium occurring in thin tabular yellow or yellowish brown crystals (hardness 6, sp. gr. 2.8)
cat·a·plexy \ˈkad·əˌpleksē\ *n* -ES [G *kataplexie*, modif. of Gk *kataplēxis* fixation (of the eyes), fr. *kataplēssein* to strike down, terrify, fr. *kata-* cata- + *plēssein* to strike — more at PLAINT] : sudden loss of muscle power in animals and man following a strong emotional stimulus (as fright, anger, or shock) characterized by clear consciousness but loss of muscular control and in animals sometimes associated with narcolepsy
¹**cat·a·pult** \ˈkad·əˌpəlt, -atə-, -ůlt\ *n* -s [MF or L; MF *catapulte*, fr. L *catapulta*, modif. of Gk *katapaltēs*, *katapeltēs*, fr. *kata-* cata- + *-paltēs*, *-peltēs* (fr. *pallein* to hurl) — more at POLEMIC] 1 : an ancient military device used for hurling heavy missiles (as stones) or for hurling other missiles (as spears, arrows) with extreme force; *esp* : ONAGER 2 2 *Brit* : SLINGSHOT 3 a : any of various mechanical devices utilizing the recoil of a spring (as for hurling grenades or bombs) b : a device for launching an airplane at flying speed (as from an aircraft carrier) usu. consisting of a carriage accelerated on a track by the explosion of powder, by hydraulic pressure, or by steam pressure

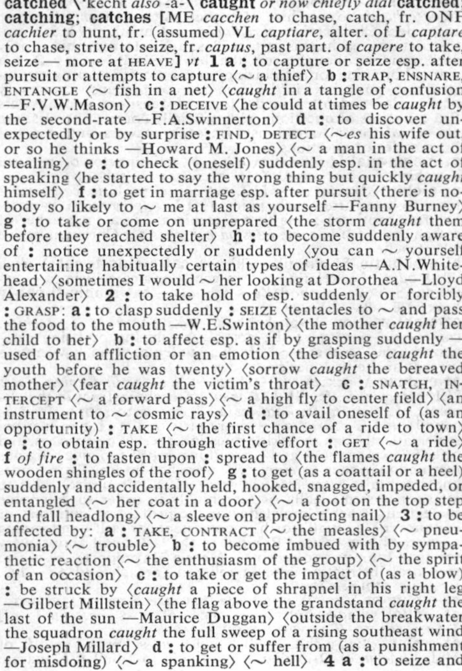
catapult 1

²**catapult** \"\ *vb* -ED/-ING/-s *vt* 1 : to throw, drive, discharge, move, or launch by or as if by means of a catapult ⟨he is . . . ~*ed* some fifteen to twenty feet before his flight is stayed —Henry LaCossitt⟩ ⟨factors which ~*ed* him into absolute power —Andrew Gyorgy⟩ ⟨the question ~*s* us at once into . . . highly technical controversy —Bernard Brodie⟩ 2 *Brit* : to shoot or shoot at with a slingshot ⟨might be stealing shell eggs somewhere or ~*ing* farmers, shepherds, or sheep —Rose Macaulay⟩ ~ *vi* 1 : to become catapulted ⟨the plane ~*ed* from the carrier deck⟩ ⟨the flier ~*ed* from the cockpit of the damaged plane⟩ 2 : to move with a suddenness or force as if propelled by a catapult ⟨the stream ~*ing* down from the gray, cold boulders —Curtis Zahn⟩ ⟨the turmoil which ~*ed* through him —Marcia Davenport⟩
¹**cat·a·ract** \ˈkad·əˌrakt, -atə-\ *n* -s [ME *cataracte* floodgate, fr. L *cataracta*, *catarractes* waterfall, portcullis, floodgate, fr. Gk *kataraktēs*, *katarrhaktēs*, lit., sheer, abrupt, fr. *katarassein* to dash down, fr. *kata-* cata- + *arassein* to strike, smash] 1 *obs* : FLOODGATE — used in pl. ⟨the rain descended for forty days, the ~*s* . . . of heaven being opened —John Milton⟩ 2 [MF or ML; MF *cataracte*, fr. ML *cataracta*; perh. fr. its likeness to a portcullis in constituting an obstruction] : a clouding of the lens of the eye or of its capsule varying in degree from slight to complete opacity and obstructing the passage of light 3 [L *cataracta*, *catarractes* waterfall] a *obs* : WATERSPOUT b : WATERFALL; *esp* : a great fall of water over a precipice — compare CASCADE 1 c : steep rapids in a large river ⟨the ~*s* of the Nile⟩ d : an overwhelming downpour or rush : FLOOD ⟨~*s* of rain poured down —C.S.Forester⟩ ⟨his ~ of eloquence —Herman Wouk⟩ — **cat·a·ract·al** \ˌ≈ˈ≈tᵊl\ *adj*
²**cataract** \"\ *vb* -ED/-ING/-s *vt* : to cause to fall like a cataract ⟨the . . . rotor ~*s* water over the top of the case —*Flow Quarterly*⟩ ~ *vi* : to fall like a cataract ⟨rain ~*ing* down the windowpanes⟩
cataract bird *n*, *Austral* : ROCK WARBLER
cat·a·ract·ous \ˌ≈ˈ≈təs\ *adj* : of, relating to, or affected with an eye cataract
catarhina *syn of* CATARRHINA
catarhine *var of* CATARRHINE
cata·rhi·ni \ˌkad·əˈrīˌnī\ *n pl*, *syn of* CATARRHINA
ca·tar·ia \kəˈta(a)rēə\ *n* -s [NL (specific epithet of the catnip *Nepeta cataria*), fr. LL *cattus*, *catus* cat + NL *-aria* (fr. L, fem. of *-arius* -ary) — more at CAT] : CATNIP
cat·a·ri·nite \ˌkad·əˈrēˌnīt\ *n* -s [F, fr. Santa *Catarina*, state of Brazil, its locality + F *-ite*] : a class of iron meteorites remarkable for high percentage of nickel
ca·tarrh \kəˈtär, -tä(r\ *n* -s [MF or LL; MF *catarrhe*, fr. LL *catarrhus*, fr. Gk *katarrhous*, *katarrhoos*, fr. *katarrhein* to flow down, fr. *kata-* cata- + *rhein* to flow — more at STREAM] 1 : inflammation of a mucous membrane in man or animals characterized by congestion and secretion of mucus ⟨gastrointestinal ~ of the horse⟩; *specif* : such inflammation when chronically affecting the human nose and air passages 2 : COMMON COLD — not used technically — **ca·tarrh·al** \kəˈtärəl, -är-\ *adj* — **ca·tarrh·al·ly** \-əlē, -li\ *adv*
catarrhal fever *n* : any of several diseases of livestock (as influenza of the horse, pasteurellosis of sheep and cattle, or bluetongue and carceag of sheep) marked by edema of the respiratory tract and adjacent tissues
catarrhal jaundice *n* : INFECTIOUS HEPATITIS
catarrhal pneumonia *n* : BRONCHOPNEUMONIA
cat·ar·rhi·na \ˌkad·əˈrīnə\ *n pl*, *cap* [NL, fr. Gk *katarrhina*, neut. pl. of *katarrhin* hooknosed, fr. *kata-* cata- + *rhin-*, *rhis* nose — more at RHIN-] *in many classifications* : a division of Anthropoidea comprising the Old World monkeys, higher apes, and man, all having the nostrils close together and directed downward, 32 teeth, often cheek pouches and ischial callosities, and the tail if present never prehensile — **cat·ar·rhin·i·an** \ˌ≈ˈrinēən\ *adj*
¹**cat·ar·rhine** *also* **cat·a·rhine** \ˈkad·əˌrīn\ *adj* : of or relating to the Catarrhina
²**catarrhine** *also* **catarhine** \"\ *n* -s [NL *Catarrhina*] : a monkey of the division Catarrhina
cat·ar·rhi·ni \ˌ≈ˈrīˌnī\ *syn of* CATARRHINA
ca·tarrh·ous \kəˈtärəs, -är-\ *adj* [F *catarrheux*, fr. *catarrhe* + *-eux* -ous] *archaic* : CATARRHAL
cat·a·sar·ka \ˌkad·əˈsärkə\ *n* -s [MGk *katasarka*, fr. Gk *kata sarka* next to the skin, fr. *kata* next to, down + *sarka*, accus. of *sarx* flesh — more at CATA-, SARCASM] : the second of three altar cloths in the Eastern Church
cata·se·tum \ˌkad·əˈsēd·əm\ *n*, *cap* [NL, fr. *cata-* + L *seta*, *saeta* bristle + NL *-um*; fr. the appendages of the column — more at SINEW] : a genus of tropical American orchids having globose expanded flowers in racemes and the column provided with a sensitive appendage that when touched releases the pollen suddenly from the stamens — see JUMPING ORCHID
ca·tas·ta·sis \kəˈtastəsəs\ *n*, *pl* **catasta·ses** \-əˌsēz\ [Gk *katastasis* settlement, establishment, fr. *kathistanai* to set in order, fr. *kata-* cata- + *histanai* to set, place — more at STAND] 1 : the dramatic complication immediately preceding the climax of a play 2 : the climax of a play — compare CATASTROPHE, EPITASIS, PROTASIS
cata·state \ˈkad·əˌstāt\ *n* -s [*catabolism* + *-state*] : CATABOLITE — **cata·stat·ic** \ˌ≈ˈstad·ik\ *adj*
ca·tas·tro·phe \kəˈtastrə(ˌ)fē, -aas-, -ais-\ *n* -s [Gk *katastrophē*, fr. *katastrephein* to overturn, fr. *kata-* cata- + *strephein* to turn — more at STROPHE] 1 a : the final action that completes the unraveling of the plot in a play, esp. a tragedy : DENOUEMENT ⟨pat he comes like the ~ of the old comedy —Shak.⟩ ⟨the need for some element of reconciliation in a tragic ~ —A.C.Bradley⟩ b : a similar action in a novel or story ⟨the novel's ~ did not occur until the closing scene⟩ 2 : a momentous tragic usu. sudden event marked by effects ranging from extreme misfortune to utter overthrow or ruin : DISASTER ⟨the ~ of war⟩ ⟨what ~ had overwhelmed them —Willa Cather⟩ 3 *Scot* : broken pieces (as of china) — usu. used in pl. 4 : a violent and sudden change in a feature of the earth — compare CATASTROPHISM 1 5 : utter failure : FIASCO ⟨monuments, most of them artistic ~*s* —Robert O'Brien⟩ 6 : death (as from an inexplicable cause) before, during, or after an operation **syn** see DISASTER
cat·a·stroph·ic \ˌkad·əˈsträfik, -atə-, -ēk *also* -ōf-\ *also* **cat·a·stroph·i·cal** \-äfəkəl, -ēk-\ *or* **ca·tas·tro·phal** \kəˈtastrəfəl\ *adj* 1 : of, relating to, resembling, or resulting in catastrophe ⟨a time of ~ history —Herbert Agar⟩ ⟨he has ~ energy —H.M.Robinson⟩ ⟨a ~ depression —T.W.Arnold⟩ ⟨lawsuits are rare and ~ experiences —B.N.Cardozo⟩ 2 *of an illness* : financially ruinous — **cat·a·stroph·i·cal·ly** \ˌkad·əˈsträfək(ə)lē, -atə-, -ēk-, -li *also* -ōf-\ *adv*
ca·tas·tro·phism \kəˈtastrəˌfizəm\ *n* -s 1 a : the doctrine that changes in the earth's crust have in the past been brought about suddenly by physical forces operating in ways that cannot be observed today — compare UNIFORMITARIANISM b : a similar doctrine concerning the changes in the earth's fauna and flora 2 : the theory that the millennium or a particular historical condition will be ushered in by a catastrophic event
ca·tas·tro·phist \-ˌfəst\ *n* -s : a believer in the doctrine or theory of catastrophism — called also *cataclysmist*
catathermometer *var of* KATATHERMOMETER
cata·thy·mic crisis \ˌkad·əˈthīmik-\ *n* [*cata-* + Gk *thymos* spirit + E *-ic* — more at FUME] : an unexpected explosive outburst of impulsive often destructive behavior understandable only in terms of unconscious motivation
cata·to·nia \ˌkad·əˈtōnēə\ *also* **cata·to·ny** \ˈ≈≈ˌtōnē, kəˈtatᵊnē\ *n*, *pl* **catatonias** *also* **catatonies** [NL, fr. G *katatonie*, fr. *kata-* cata- + *-tonie* -tonia] 1 : CATALEPSY 2 : CATATONIC SCHIZOPHRENIA
¹**cata·ton·ic** \ˌkad·əˈtänik\ *adj* [NL *catatonia* + E *-ic*] : of, relating to, or marked by catatonia
²**catatonic** \"\ *n* -s : a catatonic person
catatonic schizophrenia *n* : schizophrenia characterized by negativism, mutism, catalepsy, and an underlying thinking disorder and often accompanied by hallucinations and delusions of omnipotence and occas. by a state of violence
cat·a·wam·pous·ly \ˌkad·əˈwämpəslē -ad·ē- *also* -ôm-\ *adv*, *dial* : FIERCELY, EAGERLY
¹**cat·a·wam·pus** \ˌ≈≈ˈ≈pəs\ *n* -ES [prob. alter. of *catamount*] *dial* : an imaginary fierce wild animal : BOGEY
²**catawampus** *also* **cat·a·wam·pous** \ˌ≈≈ˈ≈pəs\ *adj* [prob. by folk etymology fr. *catercorner*] 1 *dial* : FIERCE, SAVAGE, DESTRUCTIVE 2 *dial* : ASKEW, AWRY, CATER-CORNERED
ca·taw·ba \kəˈtȯbə\ *n* -s *see sense 1* [Choctaw *Katápa*, lit., separated] 1 *or pl* **catawba** *usu cap* a : a Siouan people of No. Carolina and So. Carolina b : a member of such people 2 *usu cap* : the language of the Catawba people 3 [fr. *Catawba* river, No. & So. Carolina] *usu cap* : a white wine usu. dry and either still or sparkling produced from a native American grape grown extensively in Ohio and New York 4 *often cap* a : a very dark to blackish red b *of textiles* : a dark purplish red that is bluer and paler than dahlia purple and bluer and duller than pansy purple
catawba rhododendron *n* : a pink-flowered rhododendron (*Rhododendron catawbiense*) of the southern Allegheny mountains
catawba tree *n* [by folk etymology fr. *catalpa*] : either of two American catalpas (*Catalpa bignonioides* and *C. speciosa*)
cat back *n* [*cat (block)*] : a lanyard sometimes fastened to the hook of a cat block to aid in hooking the ring of the anchor
cat bear *n* : PANDA
catberry \ˈ≈ˌ≈≈\ *n* : MOUNTAIN HOLLY
catbird \ˈ≈ˌ≈\ *n* [so called fr. the fact that one of its calls resembles that of a cat] 1 : an American songbird (*Dumetella carolinensis*) dark gray in color with black cap and reddish under tail coverts related to the mockingbird but having a weaker and less varied song 2 *Austral* a : any of several birds (genus *Ailuroedus*) closely related to the bowerbirds but building no bowers and having a mewing catlike call b : APOSTLE BIRD
catbird grape *n* : MISSOURI GRAPE
catbird seat *n* : a position of great prominence or advantage ⟨sitting in the *catbird seat*⟩
catbite fever *n* [so called fr. the cat's being a carrier of the disease] : RAT-BITE FEVER
cat block *n* [²*cat*] : a heavy iron-strapped block with a large hook used in catting an anchor
catboat \ˈ≈ˌ≈\ *n* : a sailboat having a cat rig and usu. a centerboard and being of light draft and broad beam
catbrier \ˈ≈ˌ≈≈\ *n* [¹*cat* + *brier*; fr. its prickles] : any of several plants of the genus *Smilax* (esp. *S. rotundifolia*)
cat-built \ˈ≈ˌ≈\ *adj* : built like a catboat
cat burglar *n* : a burglar who enters by way of upper-story windows or skylights — called also *cat man*
¹**catcall** \ˈ≈ˌ≈\ *n* 1 a : a small instrument for producing a sound like the cry of a cat formerly used esp. in theaters to express disapproval or contempt b : the sound made by this instrument c : a similar sound made by the human voice 2 : a loud or raucous cry expressing disapproval (as at a political gathering)

catboat

²**catcall** \"\ *vt* : to deride or assail with catcalls : express disapproval of by catcalls ~ *vi* : to sound catcalls (as at a theater) ⟨the audience booed and ~*ed*⟩
¹**catch** \ˈkach, -e-\ *vb* **caught** \ˈkȯt\ *or now chiefly dial* **catched** \ˈkecht *also* -a-\ **caught** *or now chiefly dial* **catched**; **catching**; **catches** [ME *cacchen* to chase, catch, fr. ONF *cachier* to hunt, fr. (assumed) VL *captiare*, alter. of L *captare* to chase, strive to seize, fr. *captus*, past part. of *capere* to take, seize — more at HEAVE] *vt* 1 a : to capture or seize esp. after pursuit or attempts to capture ⟨~ a thief⟩ b : TRAP, ENSNARE, ENTANGLE ⟨~ fish in a net⟩ ⟨*caught* in a tangle of confusion —F.V.W.Mason⟩ c : DECEIVE ⟨he could at times be *caught* by the second-rate —F.A.Swinnerton⟩ d : to discover unexpectedly or by surprise : FIND, DETECT ⟨~*es* his wife out, or so he thinks —Howard M. Jones⟩ ⟨~ a man in the act of stealing⟩ e : to check (oneself) suddenly esp. in the act of speaking ⟨he started to say the wrong thing but quickly *caught* himself⟩ f : to get in marriage esp. after pursuit ⟨there is nobody so likely to ~ me at last as yourself —Fanny Burney⟩ g : to take or come on unprepared ⟨the storm *caught* them before they reached shelter⟩ h : to become suddenly aware of : notice unexpectedly or suddenly ⟨you can ~ yourself entertaining habitually certain types of ideas —A.N.Whitehead⟩ ⟨sometimes I would ~ her looking at Dorothea —Lloyd Alexander⟩ 2 : to take hold of esp. suddenly or forcibly : GRASP: a : to clasp suddenly : SEIZE ⟨tentacles to ~ and pass the food to the mouth —W.E.Swinton⟩ ⟨the mother *caught* her child to her⟩ b : to affect esp. as if by grasping suddenly — used of an affliction or an emotion ⟨the disease *caught* the youth before he was twenty⟩ ⟨sorrow *caught* the bereaved mother⟩ ⟨fear *caught* the victim's throat⟩ c : SNATCH, INTERCEPT ⟨~ a forward pass⟩ ⟨~ a high fly to center field⟩ ⟨an instrument to ~ cosmic rays⟩ d : to avail oneself of (as an opportunity) : TAKE ⟨~ the first chance of a ride to town⟩ e : to obtain esp. through active effort : GET ⟨~ a ride⟩ f *of fire* : to fasten upon : spread to ⟨the flames *caught* the wooden shingles of the roof⟩ g : to get (as a coattail or a heel) suddenly and accidentally held, hooked, snagged, impeded, or entangled ⟨~ her coat in a door⟩ ⟨~ a sleeve on a projecting nail⟩ ⟨~ a foot on the top step and fall headlong⟩ 3 : to be affected by: a : TAKE, CONTRACT ⟨~ the measles⟩ ⟨~ pneumonia⟩ ⟨~ trouble⟩ b : to become imbued with by sympathetic reaction ⟨~ the enthusiasm of the group⟩ ⟨~ the spirit of an occasion⟩ c : to take or get the impact of (as a blow) : be struck by ⟨*caught* a piece of shrapnel in his right leg —Gilbert Millstein⟩ ⟨the flag above the grandstand *caught* the last of the sun —Maurice Duggan⟩ ⟨outside the breakwater the squadron *caught* the full sweep of a rising southeast wind —Joseph Millard⟩ d : to get or suffer from (as a punishment for misdoing) ⟨~ a spanking⟩ ⟨~ hell⟩ 4 a : to seize and hold; *esp* : to take in and retain ⟨a barrel to ~ rain water⟩ b : to grip or hold against one's will; *esp* : to make immovable or vulnerable by placing between equally undesirable alternatives ⟨the branches *caught* the deer's antlers⟩ ⟨a ship *caught* between fire from shore batteries and sea attack⟩ c : to cause to be seized and held : FASTEN ⟨~ down a loose edge of a dress⟩ ⟨~ back a curtain⟩ 5 : to take or get usu. momentarily, quickly, or for a brief intervening period ⟨~ a glimpse of a friend⟩ ⟨~ a nap⟩ ⟨catching a cup of coffee between trains⟩ 6 a *obs* : GAIN, ATTAIN ⟨torment myself to ~ the English crown —Shak.⟩ b : to come up with : OVERTAKE ⟨~ the man before he had a chance to go a mile⟩ c : to meet and get aboard (as a train or plane) : get to in time ⟨~ a plane⟩ ⟨~ the last bus home⟩ d : to be in time for ⟨~ an early show with minutes to spare⟩ 7 : to attract and hold : ARREST ⟨the idea of cooperation did not ~ general attention —W.C.Allee⟩ ⟨one of the guests who *caught* his fancy —Abram Kardiner⟩ 8 a : STRIKE ⟨his fist shot out and *caught* the small man directly on the mouth —Sherwood Anderson⟩ b : to make contact with ⟨a searchlight . . . *caught* and held them in its glare —Nevil Shute⟩ ⟨her high notes ~ the microphone —Edward Sackville-West & Desmond Shawe-Taylor⟩ 9 a : to grasp or apprehend with the senses or the mind ⟨his ears open to ~ all the night noises —W.F.Davis⟩ ⟨from their pages we ~ something of the philosophy of the men and women —C.R. Woodward⟩ b : to apprehend and fix by artistic means ⟨~ a person's likeness⟩ ⟨the writer ~*s* the atmosphere of the 17th century court⟩ 10 a : to catch out in cricket b : to serve as catcher for in baseball ⟨*caught* both ends of the doubleheader⟩ ⟨*caught* the lefthander⟩ 11 : to deal with in some fitting fashion (as by picking, tapping, or slaughtering) ⟨the cowslips are good *caught* early —Meridel Le Sueur⟩ ⟨the pig had been *caught* early before it lost flesh —Pearl Buck⟩ ⟨they *caught* the maple trees too early in the season⟩ 12 : to see or listen to (as a play or sports event) ⟨~ the first part of the evening's performance⟩ ~ *vi* 1 *of fire* : to take hold ⟨the flame *caught* in the chimney⟩ 2 : to grasp by a hasty motion or make a hasty motion to grasp or as if to grasp — used with *at* ⟨~ at someone's coat as he passes⟩ ⟨~ at the first opportunity that comes up⟩ 3 a : to become held or impeded esp. by entanglement or an obstruction ⟨the kite *caught* in the tree branches⟩ ⟨the boy's foot *caught* on the edge of the step⟩ b *of the breath* : to become involuntarily drawn in in a quick gasp ⟨make your breath ~ with suspense —Bernard De Voto⟩ 4 : to take and retain hold ⟨the hook does not ~⟩ 5 *of a sail or sailing boat* : to catch the wind 6 a : to catch fire b *of a gasoline engine* : to begin to function by the regular igniting and exploding of gasoline vapor in the cylinders 7 *dial*, *of water* : to freeze slightly — usu. used with *over* 8 *of a domestic mammal* : CONCEIVE 9 *of a plant* : to sprout and become established ⟨the clover *caught* well at the first sowing⟩ 10 : to play the position of catcher on a baseball team 11 *slang* : to catch on (sense 2) 12 : to begin to burn and stick to the pan ⟨the water boiled away and the potatoes *caught*⟩
syn CAPTURE, TRAP, ENTRAP, SNARE, ENSNARE, BAG: all these words indicate taking or seizing and their ramifications. They are likely to connote the hunter's craft or strength in taking or seizing. CATCH is a general term and in its first senses may often substitute for any of the other words on this list ⟨the hunters *caught* the fox⟩ ⟨the police *caught* the killer⟩ ⟨it may have seemed to Augustus an easy way of filling his treasury and it *caught* the imagination of the Roman poets —John Buchan⟩ CAPTURE is narrower in range than CATCH in often implying somewhat greater magnitude or importance of the thing caught, longer duration of the capture, and less necessary constriction or confinement during that period ⟨he *captured* 27 prizes in the *Comet* —R.G.Albion⟩ ⟨the business of the major parties is to *capture* control of the government —H.S.Commager⟩ ⟨no artist can set out to *capture* charm —A.C.Benson⟩ TRAP suggests craft or guile on the pursuer's part or unwariness on the quarry's. It stresses the existence of an adverse situation from which escape is unlikely, but may leave open the possibility, while CAPTURE indicates finality of seizure ⟨*trap* wild animals⟩ ⟨the Texans *trapped* in the Alamo⟩ ⟨his reliance on feeling . . . frequently *trapped* him into absurdities —F.B. Millett⟩ The verb SNARE differs from the verb TRAP as the noun SNARE from the noun TRAP. SNARE may suggest entanglement as in a net in contrast to the clamping stricture of TRAP ⟨folks who are still *snared* in the toils of mortal compulsions —R.P.Warren⟩ ENSNARE and ENTRAP are interchangeable with SNARE and TRAP most of the time but may occasionally suggest greater subtlety of contrivance and more entanglement and complexity in the victim's situation ⟨as if he would clear away some entanglement which had *entrapped* his thought —Louis Bromfield⟩ ⟨sympathetic to the regime that *ensnared* them in its monstrous net —*Saturday Rev.*⟩ BAG implies what is implicit in a hunter's putting game in his bag, that is, unquestioned success in seizing a difficult quarry by a hunter's arts ⟨Victor Weybright, of the American branch, *bagged* the British rights to John Hersey's *Hiroshima* while other English publishers were asleep —Bennett Cerf⟩
— **catch a crab** 1 : to fail to raise the oar clear of the water on the recovery 2 : to miss the water completely when making a stroke with an oar — **catch fire** 1 : to become ignited ⟨the barn roof is thought to have *caught fire* from flying sparks from a passing locomotive⟩ 2 : to become fired with enthusiasm ⟨the poet *caught fire* from the philosopher's talk⟩ 3 : to increase greatly in scope, interest, or effectiveness ⟨the movie really *catches fire* —*Time*⟩ ⟨his imagination *caught fire* —Dorothy C. Fisher⟩ — **catch it** *slang* : to get a scolding or a punishment — **catch one's breath** 1 : to take in a short involuntary gasp of air ⟨make you *catch your breath* in excitement —H.J.Laski⟩ 2 : to rest long enough to restore normal breathing ⟨they let the horses *catch their breath* at the top of the long hill⟩ — **catch the wind** : to fill with wind (as of a sail)
²**catch** \"\ *n* -ES [ME *cacche*, fr. *cacchen*, v.] 1 : something that is caught; *esp* : the total quantity caught at one time ⟨the ~ of valuable native fur —F.S.Cohen⟩ ⟨a good ~ of fish⟩ 2 : the act, action, or fact of catching: a : the act of catching fish b : a momentary audible impeding (as of the breath or voice) ⟨a sudden ~ in the speaker's voice⟩ c : the act of catching the ball esp. before it touches the ground ⟨a good running ~⟩ d : a game for two or more people in which a ball is thrown and caught e : the initial force and application of an oar or a swimmer's hand to the water 3 a : something that checks or holds immovable b : a device (as a rod, bar, or hook) for temporarily holding immovable an otherwise moving or movable part or mechanism: as (1) : a latch esp. on a door, window, or trunk (2) : the fastening mechanism on a brooch, decorative pin, or belt 4 : one that is worth catching or acquiring ⟨another important ~ of the patrol was a submarine⟩; *esp* : one particularly desirable as a husband or wife ⟨he was an excellent ~⟩ 5 : a round for three or more unaccompanied voices written out as one continuous melody with each succeeding singer taking up a part in turn; *specif* : a ludicrous or coarse round 6 : FRAGMENT, SNATCH ⟨young men . . . sing ~*es* of a traditional Genoese melody as they mend their sails —J.V.Taberner⟩ 7 : an unsuspected or trickily concealed consideration or difficulty designed esp. to take advantage of the unwary ⟨there must be a ~ in it somewhere⟩ 8 : the germination of a field crop esp. to such an extent that replanting is unnecessary — compare ²STAND 12 9 : GLOTTAL STOP
³**catch** \"\ *adj* [¹*catch*] : CATCHY ⟨a ~ question⟩
cat chain *n* [²*cat*] : a small chain that reeves through a block at the cathead or at a davit head and is used with the ground chain to cat an anchor in ships with ram bows
catchall \ˈ≈ˌ≈\ *n* -s : something designed or serving to catch, hold, account for, or include a variety of odds and ends ⟨the third room . . . was a ~ for harness and tools and implements —Margaret I. Ross⟩ ⟨the docks act as a ~ for the overflow from other trades and for the failures and misfits from all walks of life —E.P.Hohman⟩ ⟨a ~ statute is one which covers a multitude of sins —R.V.Sherwin⟩
¹**catch-as-catch-can** \ˌ≈≈ˈ≈ˌ≈\ *n* -s : a style of wrestling in which all holds are permitted except those that may be barred by mutual consent and in which a fall is gained by the contestant who pins his opponent's shoulders to the ground
²**catch-as-catch-can** \"\ *adj* : utilizing or exploiting any

available means or method : UNPLANNED, UNSYSTEMATIC ⟨a *catch-as-catch-can* existence begging and running errands —*Time*⟩

catch basin *n* **1 :** a cistern located at the point where a street gutter discharges into a sewer and designed to catch and retain matter that would not pass readily through the sewer **2 :** a reservoir or well into which surface water may drain off

catch boom *n* **:** a boom used in logging to prevent logs from floating downstream

catch colt *n* **:** WOODS COLT

catch crop *n* **:** a crop grown between two crops in ordinary sequence, between the rows of a main crop, or as a substitute for a staple crop that has failed — compare COVER CROP — **catch cropping** *n*

catchcry \ˈ=,=\ *n* **:** a distinctive word or expression (as a catchword or slogan) serving to attract attention or rally support

catch dog *n, dial* **:** a large dog used for catching and holding something (as livestock)

catched *now chiefly dial past of* CATCH

catch·er \ˈkachə(r), -ech-\ *n* -s [ME *caccher*, fr. *cacchen* to catch + *-er*] **1 :** one that catches: as **a :** the baseball or softball player stationed behind home plate to catch pitched balls and to defend the plate and the area around it **b :** a member of a flying-trapeze act who hanging head down from a trapeze catches the flier **c** *or* **catcher arm :** a movable metal arm on railway post-office cars used to pick up mail pouches from trackside cranes while the train is in motion **2 a :** a worker in the tobacco, woodworking, or paper-goods industry who removes materials or products from the delivery end of conveyors or machines **b :** a laundry worker who removes flatwork from an ironing machine **c :** a basketry worker who keeps the splitting machine free of rattan, reeds, dust, and fiber particles **3 :** a small boat accompanying a whaling boat and specif. intended for the pursuit and catching of sighted whales **4 :** the element in a klystron that resonates to the beam of bunched electrons and then generates the oscillator output — compare BUNCHER, BUNCHING, RHUMBATRON

catcher-off \ˈ=,=ˈ=\ *n, pl* **catchers-off :** one that catches laces as they come through the cutting machine, cuts them to even lengths by hand, and bundles them

catcher pouch *n* **:** a mail sack used in transferring mail to and from small stations and moving trains

catches *pres 3d sing of* CATCH, *pl of* CATCH

catchfly \ˈ=,=\ *n* **:** any of various plants having on the stems or inflorescence a viscid secretion to which small insects adhere; *esp* **:** any of various members of the genera *Lychnis* and *Silene*

catchfly grass *n* **:** a marsh grass (*Leersia lenticularis*) of the southern U. S.

catchier *comparative of* CATCHY

catchiest *superlative of* CATCHY

catch·ing \ˈkachiŋ, -ech-\ *adj* [ME *cacching*, fr. pres. part. of *cacchen* to catch] **1 :** INFECTIOUS, CONTAGIOUS ⟨colds are ~⟩ ⟨her laughter was the most ~ I ever heard —W.S.Maugham⟩ **2 :** CAPTIVATING, ALLURING, CATCHY ⟨she had such a ~ way with her⟩ ⟨their rhyme . . . is abundant and ~ —H.O.Taylor⟩ — **catch·ing·ly** *adv*

catching bargain *n* **:** an entrapping or overreaching bargain; *specif* **:** one made with an heir expectant for the purchase of his expectancy at an inadequate price

catch-letter \ˈ=,==\ *n* **:** a faint letter written in the margin of a manuscript as a guide for the rubricator in filling in the required initial

catchlight \ˈ=,=\ *n* -s **:** a small spot of light reflected from a shiny surface (as from an eye in portraiture or from metal or glass in photography)

catch line *n* **1 a :** a line containing a catchword **b :** a short line (as of less important words in a title or display advertisement) between lines that are longer and sometimes larger **c :** an identification line (as on a printer's proof or a manuscript) **2 :** a phrase or sentence designed to catch attention esp. in an advertisement or as a heading or title of a story, article, or newspaper item **3 :** a line in a theatrical production expected to cause a laugh and often repeated as a gag

catch·man \-,man, -,mən\ *n, pl* **catchmen :** one who sorts floating logs according to owner's mark by deflecting them with a pike pole

catch·ment \ˈkachmənt, -ech-\ *n* -s **1 :** the act or action of catching water ⟨water conservation and ~ —W.B.Fisher⟩ **2 a :** something that catches water ⟨a separate house . . . set in a waste as sheer as a rain ~ —Jean Stafford⟩ **b :** CATCHMENT AREA **3 :** the amount of water that is caught

catchment area *or* **catchment basin** *n* **:** the entire area from which drainage is received by a body of water (as a reservoir, lake, or river) **:** WATERSHED

catch on *vi* **1 :** to seize hold **:** attach oneself ⟨the swimmer *caught on* to the back of the boat⟩ **2 :** UNDERSTAND, LEARN, TUMBLE ⟨the police *caught on* to what he was doing⟩ ⟨you can *catch on* to the job in two or three days⟩ **3 :** to become popular ⟨this movement has already *caught on* in other states —Bernard Smith⟩ **4 :** to get a job ⟨he finally *caught on* as a cook for an outfit in New Mexico —Ross Santee⟩

cat-chop \ˈ=,=\ *n* [¹*cat* + *chop* (jaw)] **:** a fig marigold (*Mesembryanthemum felinum*) having pointed teeth on the leaf margins

catch out *vt* **1 :** to put out (a cricket player) by catching a batted ball before it touches the ground **2 :** to detect in error or wrongdoing ⟨he watched carefully in the hope of *catching* one of the dishonest employees *out*⟩

¹**catchpenny** \ˈ=,==\ *adj* [¹*catch* + *penny*] **1 :** designed esp. to make a ready appeal to the ignorant or unwary through sensationalism or cheapness ⟨for his countless miscellaneous pieces any ~ subject would do —Douglas Bush⟩ **2 :** aiming at making even the smallest sum of money quickly by almost any expedient ⟨caused the fly-by-night ~ boomers to move out, taking their quick money with them —*Amer. Guide Series: Texas*⟩ **3 :** popular but ill-considered and superficial ⟨clever ~ critical objections —J.C.Powys⟩

²**catchpenny** \"\ *n* -ES **:** something that is catchpenny ⟨you know already by the title that it is no more than a ~ —Washington Irving⟩

catchphrase \ˈ=,=\ *n* **:** a phrase that is or has become a catchword ⟨are apt to take fiction for reality, to fool ourselves and others with ~s and make-believe —Wilhelm Roepke⟩

catch·pole *or* **catch·poll** \ˈkach,pōl, -ech-\ *n* -ES [ME *cacchepol*, fr. OE *cæcepol*, fr. (assumed) ONF *cachepol*, lit., chicken chaser, fr. *cachier* to hunt, chase + *poul*, *pol* rooster, fr. L *pullus* young animal, young fowl — more at CATCH, PULLET] **1 :** a sheriff's deputy; *esp* **:** one who makes arrests for debt **2 :** DEPUTY, REPRESENTATIVE ⟨hires out to other private citizens to go about as a sort of ~ on Sunday —W.J.Gaynor⟩

catch ring *n* **:** a wooden hoop that holds the staves of a slack barrel in place after the head hoop is removed

catch-rope \ˈ=,=\ *n* **:** LARIAT

catch-roper \ˈ=,rōpə(r)\ *n* **:** LASSOER

catch-roping \ˈ=,rōpiŋ\ *n* **:** lassoing esp. as a rodeo event

catch stitch *n* **1 :** KETTLE STITCH **2 :** a large cross-stitch of uneven proportions used esp. on bulky materials for finishing and hemming — called also *catstitch*

catch-stitch \ˈ=ˈ=\ *vt* [*catch stitch*] **:** to sew with a catch stitch

catch the ten *n* **:** a card game in which the chief object is to catch the ten of trumps — called also *Scotch whist*

catch title *n* **1 :** a distinguishing abbreviation of or a short substitute for a full title used esp. in book lists and catalogs **2 :** the often abbreviated titles of the first and last entries or articles appearing on the spine of any volume of a multivolume set **3 :** a faintly written title in the margin of a manuscript page intended as a guide for the rubricator

catch up *vt* **1 a :** to pick or lift up often abruptly ⟨a thief *caught* the purse *up* and ran⟩ **b :** ENSNARE, ENTANGLE ⟨*caught up* in the trivia of everyday things —Honor Tracy⟩ **c :** to involve often against the will ⟨the firms have been *caught up* in a revolution —Percy Winner⟩ **d :** ENTHRALL ⟨*caught up* in the ecstasy of *Vanity Fair* —Bernard De Voto⟩ **2 :** to adopt or take over (as an expression) ⟨*catch up* all the new fads and slang terms⟩ **3 :** to interrupt (a speaker) usu. to question or criticize what is being said ⟨you *catch* me *up* so very short —Charles Dickens⟩ **4** *Brit* **:** OVERTAKE ⟨*catch* a friend *up* before he gets out of sight⟩ **5 :** to provide with the latest information ⟨*catch* me *up* on what's happening at the office⟩ ~ *vi* **1 a :** to travel fast enough to join company ⟨*catch up* with an advance battalion⟩ **b :** to bring about arrest for illicit activity — used with *with* ⟨the police *caught up* with the thieves⟩ **c :** to have the expected ill effect or result — used with *with* ⟨his evil ways *caught up* with him at last and he died a poverty-stricken and miserable man⟩ **2** *West* **:** to prepare horses, mules, or oxen for travel ⟨we were told to *catch up* and begin the march at daybreak⟩ **3 a :** to bring something to an end or to a final state — used with *on* ⟨*catch up on* your bookkeeping⟩ **b :** to acquire belated information ⟨*catch up* on what's happening in the news⟩

catchup *var of* CATSUP

catch-up \ˈka,chəp, ˈke,-\ *n* -s [*catch up*] **1 :** an activity or move intended to catch up to a theoretical norm (as a level of production or supply) esp. following a period of curtailment of such activity ⟨postwar *catch-up* in construction work was rapid⟩ **2 :** the fact of catching up to a theoretical norm esp. in industrial production ⟨the *catch-up* in quantity —*Wall Street Jour.*⟩

catchwater \ˈ=,==\ *or* **catchwater drain** *n* **:** a ditch to catch water on sloping land designed to divert the flow or to irrigate the soil — called also *catchwork*

catchweed \ˈ=,=\ *n* [so called fr. the hooked bristles covering the stem] **:** a rough-stemmed plant of the genus *Galium*

¹**catchweight** \ˈ=,=\ *n* [¹*catch* + *weight*] **:** the weight of a contestant in a sports event as he happens or chooses to be instead of as fixed by an agreement or by rule ⟨many interesting bouts at ~s —John Lardner⟩

²**catchweight** \"\ *adv* **:** without restriction or artificial handicap as to the weight of contestants in a sports event ⟨to fight ~⟩

catchword \ˈ=,=\ *n* **1 :** an identifying or distinguishing word: as **a :** a word standing under the right-hand side of the last line of text on a book page that repeats the first word of text on the following page — called also *direction word* **b :** either one of the pair of terms placed to right and left of the head of a page of an alphabetical reference work (as a dictionary) indicating the alphabetically first and last entries or articles on the page — called also *guide word* **2 a :** a usu. sloganlike and telling word or expression caught up and repeated so that it becomes representative of a political party or belief, a school of thought, or a point of view ⟨worlds of contemporary controversy with their ~s, their insensitive condemnations, and their callow proofs —*Times Lit. Supp.*⟩ **b :** a word or phrase distinctive of a subject, scheme of thought, or point of view used esp. for effect by one having only superficial acquaintance with the subject or scheme of thought ⟨the freeing of mankind from labels and ~s —*Times Lit. Supp.*⟩ **c :** a catchy word or phrase devised esp. for advertising purposes

catchword entry *or* **catchword title** *n* **1 :** a title entry (as of a book) in a catalog, list, or index beginning with a significant or an easily remembered word in the title (“Architecture, A history of” is a *catchword entry*) **2 :** the method of entry in a catalog, list, or index that uses catchword entries

catchwork \ˈ=,=\ *n* **:** CATCHWATER

catchy \ˈkachē, -ech-, -chi\ *adj* -ER/-EST **1 a :** having the power or tending to catch the interest or attention ⟨a ~ idea⟩ ⟨a ~ title⟩ **b :** easily retained in the memory ⟨a ~ melody⟩ **2** *of a question* **:** tending to mislead the unwary **:** TRICKY ⟨the examiner asked several purposely ~ questions⟩ **3 :** FITFUL, IRREGULAR ⟨a ~ wind⟩ ⟨~ breathing⟩ **4** *dial* **:** CAPTIOUS

catclaw *var of* CAT'S-CLAW

catclaw acacia *n* **:** a cat's-claw (*Acacia greggii*)

cat-clover \ˈ=,==\ *n* **:** a bird's-foot trefoil (*Lotus corniculatus*)

cat cracker \ˈkat,==\ *n* [by shortening] **:** CATALYTIC CRACKER

cat davit *n* [*cathead*] **:** the forward bow davit of a ship for hoisting the stock end of the anchor — compare FISH DAVIT

cat distemper *n* **:** PANLEUCOPENIA

cate \ˈkāt\ *n* -s [ME, short for *acate*, fr. ONF *acat* purchase, fr. *acater* to buy, fr. (assumed) VL *accaptare* to buy, procure, by folk etymology (influence of L *captare* to chase) fr. L *acceptare* to accept — more at ACCEPT] **1 a** *obs* **:** an article of food bought as distinguished from that prepared at home — usu. used in pl. **b** *archaic* **:** an article of food **:** VIAND — usu. used in pl. **2 :** a dainty or choice food **:** DELICACY

cat·e·che·sis \,kad·əˈkēsəs, -atə-\ *n, pl* **cateche·ses** \-ē,sēz\ [LL, fr. Gk *katēchēsis* instruction, fr. *katēchein* to teach — more at CATECHIZE] **1 :** oral instruction of catechumens **:** CATECHIZING **2 :** a discourse marked by catechesis; *esp* **:** a formal discourse sometimes committed to writing ⟨the *catecheses* of St. Cyril of Jerusalem⟩

cat·e·chet·i·cal \ˌ==ˈked·əkəl, -et|, |ēk-\ *also* **cat·e·chet·ic** \-ik,-ēk\ *adj* [*catechetical* fr. NL *catecheticus* fr. LL *catechesis*, after such pairs as LL *haeresis* heresy: LL *haereticus* heretical) + E *-al; catechetic* fr. NL *catecheticus*] **1 :** of, relating to, or associated with catechesis or catechetics **2 :** of, relating to, or conforming to a church catechism **3 :** using questions and answers ⟨the ~ method of Socrates⟩; *esp* **:** using set questions and answers (as in a church catechism) — **cat·e·chet·i·cal·ly** \-ək(ə)lē, -ēk-, -li\ *adv*

catechetical school *n* **:** any of certain early Christian schools (as at Alexandria and at Antioch) in which both sacred and secular studies were pursued

cat·e·chet·ics \ˌ==ˈ=iks, -ēks\ *n pl but usu sing in constr* [G *katechetik*, fr. NL *catechetica*, fem. sing. or neut. pl. of *catecheticus*] **:** practical theology dealing with catechesis

cat·e·chin \ˈkad·əchən, -əsh-, -ək-\ *n* -s [G *katechin*, fr. *katechu* catechu (fr. E) + *-in* — more at CATECHU] **:** a white crystalline phenol-alcohol $C_{15}H_{14}O_6$ related chemically to the flavones and found as the dextrorotatory form in catechu — called also *catechol* **2 :** PYROCATECHOL

¹**cat·e·chise** *or* **cat·e·chis** \ˈkäd·ə,jiz, -,chis\ *n, pl* **catechis·es** \-,jizəz,-,chisəz\ [*catechise*, modif. of F *catéchèse*, fr. MF, fr. LL *catechesis*; *catechis*, prob. short for *catechism*] *now dial* **:** CATECHISM

²**cat·e·chise** \ˈkad·ə,kīz, -atə-\ *var of* CATECHIZE

cat·e·chism \ˈkad·ə,kizəm, -atə-\ *n* -s [LL *catechismus*, prob. fr. *catechizare* to catechize, after such pairs as LL *christianizare* to profess Christianity: *christianismus* Christianity] **1 :** oral instruction ⟨teaches his history class and interrupts his ~ only with random thoughts on the boys —W.P.Jones⟩ **2 :** a manual or guide for catechizing (as for moral and religious instruction) sometimes in the form of a comprehensive summary of doctrine and often in the form of questions and answers **3 a :** a series of questions with officially correct answers; *esp* **:** a set of formal questions with such answers put as a test **b :** a series of questions

cat·e·chis·mal \ˌ==ˈkizməl\ *adj* **:** of, relating to, or using a catechism ⟨~ responses⟩ ⟨a ~ exercise⟩ ⟨~ schools⟩

cat·e·chist \ˈ=əkəst\ *n* -s [LL *catechista*, prob. fr. *catechizare* to catechize, after such pairs as LL *baptizare* to baptize: *baptista* baptizer] **:** one that catechizes: as **a :** a teacher of catechumens **b** *in some mission churches* **:** a Christian native who teaches

cat·e·chis·tic \ˌ=əˈkistik, -ēk\ *or* **cat·e·chis·ti·cal** \-əkəl, -ēk-\ *adj* **:** of or relating to a catechist or a catechism ⟨a ~ examination⟩ ⟨a ~ school⟩ ⟨a ~ method⟩ — **cat·e·chis·ti·cal·ly** \-ək(ə)lē, -ēk-, -li\ *adv*

cat·e·chi·za·tion \,=əkəˈzāshən, -ə,kīˈz-\ *n* -s [*catechize, catechise* + *-ation*] **:** the act of catechizing or being catechized ⟨the teacher's ~ of the students⟩ ⟨the lawyer was present at the prisoner's ~⟩

cat·e·chize \ˈ=ə,kīz\ *vb* -ED/-ING/-S *see -ize in Explan Notes* [LL *catechizare*, fr. Gk *katēchein* to teach, instruct in the elements of religion (fr. *kata-* cata- + *ēchein* to sound, fr. *ēchē* sound) + LL *-izare* -ize — more at ECHO] *vt* **1 :** to instruct systematically esp. by asking questions, receiving answers, and offering explanations and corrections; *specif* **:** to give religious instruction in such a manner ⟨he preached informally in homes and hospitals, *catechized* children —K.S.Latourette⟩ **2 :** to question systematically or searchingly in order to determine the extent of one's knowledge or the probity of opinions or conduct or to call forth inconsistent or self-condemning answers ⟨he *catechized* Randall to the last detail about every toy that John was to receive —Marcia Davenport⟩ ~ *vi* **:** to give oral instruction esp. in religion ⟨preach and ~ —J.C. Brauer⟩ **syn** see ASK

cat·e·chiz·er \-zə(r)\ *n* -s **:** one that catechizes **:** CATECHIST

cat·e·chol \ˈkad·ə,chōl, -ə,sh-, -ə,k-, -ōl\ *n* -s [*catechu* + *-ol*] **1 :** CATECHIN **2 :** PYROCATECHOL

cat·e·chu \ˈkad·ə,chü, -,shü, -,kyü\ *n* -s [prob. modif. of Malay *kachu*, of Dravidian origin; akin to Tamil & Kanarese *kācu*, Malayalam *kāccu*] **1 :** any of various dry, earthy, or resinous astringent substances obtained by extraction and evaporation from the wood, leaves, or fruits of various tropical Asiatic plants: as **a :** an extract of the heartwood of an East Indian acacia that is used for dyeing, tanning, preserving fish nets and sails, and formerly in medicine — called also *black catechu* **b :** GAMBIER — see DYE table I (under *Natural Brown 3*) **c :** ¹CUTCH 2 **2 :** an East Indian spiny tree (*Acacia catechu*) that has twice-pinnate leaves, yellow flowers, and flat pods and is the source of catechu **3 :** a variable color averaging auburn — called also *cutch*

cat·e·chu·men \ˌkad·əˈkyümən, -atə-\ *n* -s [alter. (influenced by LL *catechumenus*) of ME *cathecumyn*, fr. MF *cathecumine*, fr. LL *catechumenus*, fr. Gk *katēchoumenos*, pres. pass. part. of *katēchein* to teach, instruct in the elements of religion — more at CATECHIZE] **1 :** one receiving instruction in doctrines, discipline, and morals preliminary to admission among the faithful of the early church **2 :** one receiving rudimentary instruction in the doctrines of Christianity **:** NEOPHYTE

cat·e·chu·men·al \-nᵊl\ *or* **cat·e·chu·men·i·cal** \-(,)kyü¦menəkəl\ *adj* **:** of or relating to a catechumen — **cat·e·chu·men·i·cal·ly** \-(,)kyü¦menək(ə)lē\ *adv*

cat·e·chu·men·ate \,==ˈkyümə,nāt, -,nət\ *n* -s **1 a :** the status of a catechumen **b :** the duration of this status **2 :** the body of catechumens **3 :** the institution by which catechumens are prepared for church membership through a course of religious instruction

cat·e·chu·tan·nic acid \ˈkad·ə,chü¦tanik-, -ə,shü-, -ə,kyü-\ *n* [prob. part trans. of G *katechugerbsäure*, fr. *katechu* catechu + *gerbsäure* tannic acid] **:** the tannin of catechu obtained as a reddish brown amorphous powder

cat·e·go·rem \ˈkad·əgə,rem, kəˈtegərəm\ *n* -s [Gk *katēgorēma* predicate] **:** a categorematic expression

cat·e·gor·e·mat·ic \ˌkad·ə,gōrəˈmad·ik\ *adj* [F *catégorématique*, fr. Gk *katēgorēmat-*, *katēgorēma* predicate (fr. *katēgorein* to predicate) + F *-ique* -ic — more at CATEGORY] **:** capable of standing alone as the subject or predicate of a logical proposition **:** expressing a complete substantive meaning ⟨*man* is a ~ word⟩ — opposed to *syncategorematic*

cat·e·go·ri·al \ˌkad·əˈgōrēəl\ *adj* [*category* + *-al*] **:** of, dealing with, or involving a category **:** A PRIORI ⟨a ~ system⟩ — **cat·e·go·ri·al·ly** \-ēəlē\ *adv*

¹**cat·e·gor·i·cal** \ˌkad·əˈgōrəkəl, -atə-, -är-,-ōr-, -ēk-\ *also* **cat·e·gor·ic** \-rik, -ēk\ *adj* [*categorical* fr. LL *categoricus* (fr. Gk *katēgorikos*, fr. *katēgoria* category) + E *-al; categoric* fr. LL *categoricus*] **1 a :** ABSOLUTE, UNQUALIFIED — distinguished from *conditional* and *hypothetical* **b :** marked by clear certain positive statement or effect without qualifying, reserving, temporizing, or obscuring ⟨asked for a ~ answer —Allan Nevins & H.S.Commager⟩ ⟨a ~ no⟩ **2 :** CATEGORIAL **syn** see EXPLICIT

²**categorical** \"\ *n* -s **:** a categorical proposition or judgment

categorical imperative *n* [trans. of G *kategorischer imperativ*] **:** a moral obligation or command that is unconditionally and universally binding — contrasted with *hypothetical imperative*

cat·e·gor·i·cal·ly \-ək(ə)lē, -ēk-, -li\ *adv* **:** in a categorical way: **a :** without qualification or reservation **:** ABSOLUTELY **b :** DIRECTLY, EXPLICITLY **c :** CATEGORIALLY

categorical proposition *n* **:** a proposition having the verbal form of direct assertion or denial

categorical syllogism *n* **:** a syllogism with all the propositions categorical

cat·e·go·rist \ˈ==,gōrəst\ *n* -s [*category* + *-ist*] **:** one that categorizes

cat·e·go·ri·za·tion \ˌ=əgərəˈzāshən, -,rīˈz-; -ə,gōrəˈz-, -ōr-\ *n* -s **:** the act of categorizing or the state of being categorized **:** CLASSIFICATION

cat·e·go·rize \ˈ=əgə,rīz; -ə,gōr,īz, -,gō,rīz\ *vt* -ED/-ING/-S [*category* + *-ize*] **:** to put into a category or class **:** CLASSIFY

cat·e·go·ry \ˈkad·ə,gōrē, -atə-, -ōr-, -ri\ *n* -ES [LL *categoria*, fr. Gk *katēgoria*, fr. *katēgorein* to accuse, affirm, predicate, fr. *kata-* cata- + *-agorein* to speak publicly, fr. *agora* assembly — more at GREGARIOUS] **1 :** one of the most abstract and universal terms, concepts, or notions: **a** *in Aristotle* (1) **:** one of the major forms of predication (2) **:** one of the most ultimate modes of being (as substance, quantity, quality, relation, place, time, position, possession, action, affection) **b** *in Kant* **:** one of the pure a priori forms of the understanding ⟨the ~ of quantity (unity, plurality, universality)⟩ ⟨the ~ of quality (relation, negation, limitation)⟩ ⟨the ~ of relation (substantiality, causality, reciprocity)⟩ ⟨the ~ of modality (possibility, actuality, necessity)⟩ **c** *in post-Kantian philosophy* **:** any major fundamental conception or general class of concepts ⟨*categories* — that is, controlling conceptions of inquiry —John Dewey⟩ **2 :** a class, group, or classification of any kind: as **a :** one of several groupings of related soils in the international classification developed by the U.S. Department of Agriculture **b :** a division of the dependent population whose needs are attended to by specific government measures ⟨the aged, the blind, dependent children are in separate relief *categories*⟩ **3 categories** *n pl but sing in constr* **:** a game in which the players decide on a keyword and a list of categories (as cities, animals, tools) and then try within a time limit to fill in under each letter of the keyword a name beginning with that letter to fit each category — called also *guggenheim* **syn** see CLASS

cat·elec·tro·ton·ic \ˌkad·əˌlektrəˈtänik, -dᵊl,e-\ *adj* [NL *catelectrotonus* + E *-ic*] **:** of, relating to, or caused by catelectrotonus

cat·elec·trot·o·nus \,==,=ˈträtᵊnəs\ *n* [NL, fr. *cata-* + *electrotonus*] **:** the local depolarization and increased irritability of a nerve in the region of the negative electrode or cathode; *also* **:** the passage of a current of electricity through it — compare ANELECTROTONUS

ca·te·na \kəˈtēnə, -tā-\ *n, pl* **cate·nae** \-ē(,)nē, -ā,nī\ *or* **cate·nas** \-nəz\ [ML & L; ML, extract from patristic writings, fr. L, chain — more at CHAIN] **1 :** a connected series of related things ⟨a ~ of passages which indicates a kind of amoral determinist attitude —S.G.F.Brandon⟩: as **a :** a series of extracts from patristic writings serving to expound some portion of scripture **b :** a group of closely associated soils within a given geographic zone or region that originated from the same or similar parent material but that developed differing characteristics of the solum because of local variations in relief or drainage **2 a :** a bast fiber found in any of several Mexican trees of the genus *Heliocarpus* **b** [NL, fr. L] **:** a tree of the genus *Heliocarpus* in which catena is found

cat·e·nar·in \ˌkad·əˈna(a)rən\ *n* -s [ISV *catenar-* (fr. NL *catenarium* — specific epithet of *Helminthosporium catenarium* —, fr. L, neut of *catenarius*) + *-in*; orig. formed as G *katenarin*] **:** a red pigment $C_{15}H_{10}O_6$ produced as a metabolic product of certain fungi (as *Helminthosporium catenarium*); 1,4,5,7-tetrahydroxy-2-methyl-anthraquinone

¹**cat·e·nary** \ˈkad·ə,nerē, -atə,ne-,-atᵊn,e-, -ri, *esp Brit* kəˈtēnər-\ *n* -ES [NL *catenaria*, fr. L, fem. of *catenarius*, fr. *catena* + *-arius* -ary] **1 :** the curve assumed by a perfectly flexible inextensible cord of uniform density and cross

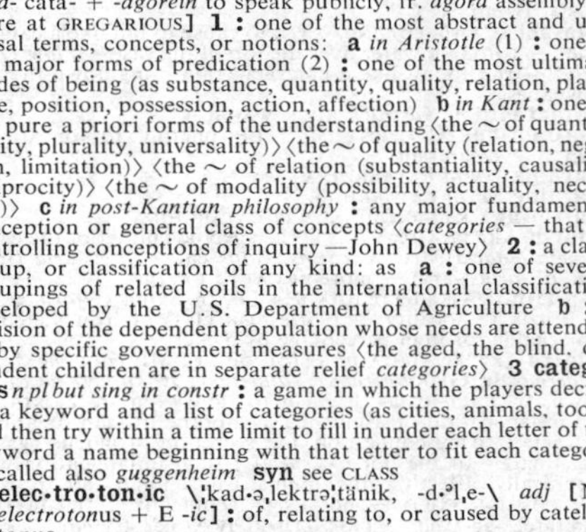

catenary

section hanging freely from two fixed points **2 :** something having or being in the form of a catenary or a series of catenaries: as **a :** a cable suspended between two points (as in a suspension bridge) **b :** a length of cordage secured to or in a piece of fabric in the form of such a curve

2catenary \"\ *adj* [L *catenarius*] **1 :** being or belonging to a catena **2 :** like or belonging to a catenary

1cat·e·nate \'kad·ə,nāt, -atə-, -tᵊn,āt\ *vt* -ED/-ING/-S [L *catenatus*, past part. of *catenare*, fr. *catena* chain — more at CHAIN] **:** to connect in a series of links or ties **:** form into a catena **:** LINK

2catenate \"\ *adj* [L *catenatus*] **:** CATENULATE

cat·e·na·tion \,₌ə'nāshən, ,₌ᵊn'ā-\ *n* -S [1*catenate* + *-ion*] **:** connection, arrangement, or succession in a regular or connected series (as in a chain): as **a :** formation in meiosis by chromosomes that have undergone reciprocal translocation, of rings or chains due to the tendency of the homologous portions of chromatin to attain synapsis **b :** linkage between atoms of the same chemical element (as carbon or silicon) — compare CONCATENATION

1catenoid \'₌ə,nȯid, '₌ᵊn,ȯid\ *n* -S [L *catena* + E *-oid*] **:** the surface described by the rotation of a catenary about its axis

2catenoid \"\ *adj* [L *catena* + E *-oid*] **:** chain-shaped **:** FILIFORM — used esp. of the colonies of certain protozoans

ca·ten·u·late \kə'tenyələt, -,lāt\ *adj* [ISV *catenula* (fr. LL, little chain, dim. of L *catena* chain) + *-ate*] **:** having a chainlike form ⟨~ bacterial cell colonies⟩ ⟨the ~ color marks or indentations on butterflies' wings⟩

1cater *n* -S [ME *catour*, short for *acatour*, fr. AF, fr. *acater* to buy — more at CATE] *obs* **:** a buyer of provisions often for a large household

2ca·ter \'kād·ə(r), -ātə-\ *vb* **catered; catered; catering** \-əriŋ *also* 'kā·triŋ\ **caters** *vi* **1 :** to provide a supply of usu. prepared food **:** act as caterer ⟨~ for a large banquet⟩ ⟨~ to local parties and entertainments⟩ **2 a :** to supply what is required or desired ⟨carry a good supply of charts so as to ~ for such emergencies —Peter Heaton⟩ ⟨too many movies, novels, and comic books ~ to an appetite for violence —J.P.Sisk⟩ **b :** to act with special consideration ⟨~ to a very sick boy⟩ ~ *vt* **:** to provide prepared food and service for ⟨the full-course dinner will be ~*ed* by a local firm⟩

3ca·ter \'kād·ə(r), -id·-,-ad·-\ *vb* -ED/-ING/-S [obs. *cater*, n., four-spot of cards or dice, fr. ME, fr. MF *quatre* four, fr. L *quattuor* — more at FOUR] *vt, dial* **:** to place, move, or cut across diagonally ~ *vi, dial* **:** to move or cut diagonally

cat·er·an \'kad·ərən, 'ka·trən\ *n* -S [alter. of ME *ketharan*, prob. fr. ScGael *ceathairneach* freebooter, robber; akin to MIr *cethern* band of soldiers — more at KERN] **1 :** a military irregular of the Scottish Highlands **2 :** MARAUDER, BRIGAND

cat·er·cor·nered *or* **cat·er·cor·ner** *or* **cata·cor·nered** *or* **cata·cor·ner** *or* **cat·ty·cor·nered** *or* **cat·ty·cor·ner** *or* **kit·ty·cor·nered** *or* **kit·ty·cor·ner** \'kad·|ē|-, -id·|,-at|,-it|, |i- *also* |ə-\ *adv (or adj)* [*catercorner, cater-cornered* fr. obs. *cater* four-spot + *corner, cornered; catty-corner, catty-cornered* & *kitty-corner, kitty-cornered* by folk etymology fr. *catercorner, cater-cornered*] **:** in a diagonal or oblique position or on a diagonal or oblique line ⟨situated *catercorner* to each other on opposite sides of Bradford Island —*Time*⟩ ⟨the ship had come down *catercorner* across two roofs —*Reader's Digest*⟩ ⟨walking *cater-cornered* through the field —A.J. Liebling⟩ ⟨sailing *catty-cornered* across the bay —Louisa W. Peat⟩ ⟨the house stood *catercorner* across the square⟩ ⟨told the movers to place the divan *catercorner* at the end of the long room⟩

ca·ter-cous·in \'kād·ə(r)¦-\ *n* [perh. fr. 1*cater*] **:** an intimate friend

ca·ter·er \'kād·ərə(r), -ātə-\ *n* -S [prob. fr. 2*cater* + *-er*] **:** one that caters: as **a :** one whose business is to arrange for and supervise all the details as to food and service for any social affair (as at a club or private house) **b :** a worker in a hotel or restaurant who solicits, promotes, and arranges for social functions to be held there

ca·ter·ess \'kād·ərəs, -ātər-,-ā·tr-\ *n* -ES [*caterer* + *-ess*] **:** a female caterer

cat·er·pil·lar *R* 'kad·ə(r),pilər, *-R* 'kad·ə,pilə; -atə-\ *n* -S *often attrib* [ME *catyrpel*, modif. of ONF *catepelose*, lit., hairy cat, fr. *cate* female cat (fr. LL *catta*) + *pelose, pelouse*, fem. of *pelous* hairy, fr. L *pilosus*, fr. *pilus* hair — more at CAT, PILE] **1 a :** the elongated wormlike larva of a butterfly or moth that has strong biting jaws, short antennae, three pairs of true legs, several pairs of abdominal prolegs armed with hooks, and often a somewhat complete coat of fine bristles or coarse shining hairs and that is almost exclusively vegetarian, feeding on leaves, fruit, or other succulent parts of plants — called also *worm* esp. in combination (as *armyworm, cutworm*, or *silkworm*) **b :** any of various other insect larvae (as those of sawflies or scorpion flies) that resemble true caterpillars **2** *archaic* **:** a rapacious person preying on the community **3 :** a machine (as an army tank) traveling on two endless belts consisting of series of flat treads with one belt on each side of the machine and the belts kept in motion by toothed driving wheels so that the machine moves forward or backward with the revolution of the belts **4 :** an amusement-park device consisting of a series of connected cars equipped with an enclosing canopy and running on a circular undulating track

Caterpillar \"\ *trademark* — used for a tractor made for use on rough or soft ground and moved on two endless metal belts

caterpillar-eater \'₌₌,₌₌,₌₌\ *n* **:** TRILLER

caterpillar fungus *n* **:** a fungus of the genus *Cordyceps*

caterpillar hunter *n* **:** any of various beetles of the family Carabidae that feed largely upon caterpillars

caterpillar tread *n* **:** the endless chain belt on which a caterpillar-type vehicle runs

ca·ters *or* **qua·ters** \'kād·ə(r)z, -ad·-\ *n pl but usu sing in constr* [prob. fr. F *quatre* four — more at CATER] **:** a system of ringing changes on nine bells in which four pairs of bells interchange at each permutation

1cat·er·waul \'kad·ə(r),wȯl, -atə-\ *vi* -ED/-ING/-S [alter. (influenced by *wawl*) of earlier *caterwawe*, fr. ME *caterwawen, caterwrawen*, perh. fr. (assumed) MD *katerwrauwen*, fr. MD *cāter* tomcat (akin to OE *catt* cat) + *wrauwen* to wail, of imit. origin — more at CAT] **1 a** *of a cat* **:** to make a harsh cry at rutting time — compare CALLING 5 **b :** to cry as cats do in rutting time **:** make a harsh offensive noise ⟨the continuous ~*ing* of the . . . street bands —H.A.Sinclair⟩ **c :** to quarrel noisily like cats ⟨government can . . . degenerate into a ~*ing* of hatred and venom —*New Republic*⟩ **2 :** to be lecherous **:** go in lecherous pursuit of women

2caterwaul \"\ *n* -S **1 :** the cry of cats at rutting time **:** CATERWAULING ⟨the ~ of an alley-cat —Marcia Davenport⟩ **2 :** a sound resembling a caterwaul ⟨the Great Eastern sailed in a mass ~ from the banks —James Dugan⟩

cates *pl of* CATE

Cates·baea \kāts'bēə, '₌₌₌\ *n, cap* [NL, fr. Mark Catesby (*Catesbaeus*) †1749 Eng. naturalist and traveler] **:** a genus of West Indian spiny shrubs or trees (family Rubiaceae) having small crowded leaves and solitary white flowers

cat-eyed \'₌,₌\ *adj* **1 :** having eyes like a cat **2 :** able to see in the dark

catface \'₌,₌\ *n* **:** a partially healed scar on a tree or log

cat·fac·ing \'kat,fāsiŋ\ *also* **cat·face** \-,ās\ *n* **:** a disfigurement or malformation of fruit suggesting a cat's face in appearance (as that caused in peaches by punctures of various sucking insects or in tomatoes by unsatisfactory water balance in the plant)

catfall \'₌,₌\ *n* [1*cat* (tackle) + *fall* (rope, chain)] **:** a rope or chain used in hoisting an anchor to a cathead

cat family *n* **:** FELIDAE

cat fever *n* [short for *catarrhal fever*] **:** a respiratory infection accompanied by fever

catfight \'₌,₌\ *n* **:** a bitter and usu. intensely personal dispute ⟨there'll be questions from the floor and a general ~ —Helen Howe⟩

catfish \'₌,₌\ *n* [so called fr. the catlike appearance of the head] **:** any of the numerous fishes comprising the suborder Siluroidea of the order Ostariophysi, being mostly stout-bodied, large-headed, and voracious with long tactile barbels, some being marine but most inhabiting lakes and streams esp. in the tropics, generally lurking close to the bottom, often attaining a large size, and some being important food fishes though their flesh is not of the finest quality — see ARMORED CATFISH, BULLHEAD, ELECTRIC CATFISH, NAKED CATFISH, SEA CATFISH

catfit \'₌,₌\ *n* **:** CONNIPTION

cat flea *n* **:** a common flea (*Ctenocephalides felis*) that breeds chiefly on cats, dogs, and rats and is often a pest where these animals are harbored

catfoot \'₌,₌\ *n* -S [prob. so called fr. the shape of the leaves] **:** a biennial cudweed (*Gnaphalium obtusifolium*) with linear lanceolate leaves that are decurrent as wings down the stem

cat foot *n* **:** a short round compact foot like a cat's ⟨a hound with a good *cat foot* —A.J.Liebling⟩

cat-foot \'₌,₌\ *vi* **:** to move in a manner suggesting a cat (as stealthily or silently) ⟨the butler came *cat-footing* back along the hall —Raymond Chandler⟩

cat·foot·ed \'₌¦₌₌\ *adj* **1 :** having cat feet ⟨~ dogs⟩ **2 :** soft-footed like a cat **:** stealthy or noiseless in walking

cat grape *n* [short for *catbird grape*] **:** MISSOURI GRAPE

cat·gut \'₌,gət *also* -,gət\ *n* -S [1*cat* + *gut*] **1 :** a tough cord that is made from the intestines of certain animals (as sheep) and that is used for strings of musical instruments, for sports rackets, or for sutures in closing wounds — called also *gut* **2 :** a heavy linen or cotton fabric that has an open plain weave and is used for stiffening in clothes and for embroidery **3 a :** an almost prostrate herb (*Tephrosia virginiana*) of eastern No. America with yellowish purple flowers — called also *goat's rue, wild sweet pea* **b :** the strong wiry root of this herb which is the only known significant No. American native source of rotenone

cath- — see CATA-

cath *abbr* **1** cathedral **2** cathode

catha \'kathə\ *n, cap* [NL, fr. Ar *qāt* kat] **:** a genus of African evergreen shrubs (family Celastraceae) characterized by thick leaves, small white flowers in axillary cymes, and seed with a white aril at the base

cat·hair \'kat,ha(ə)(ə)r\ *n, dial* **:** BOIL, SORE

cat ham *n* **:** a thin flat thigh

cat-hammed \'₌,₌\ *adj* **:** having cat hams with an incurving of the rear line of the thigh — used of cattle or horses

cath·ar \'ka,thär\ *n, pl* **cath·a·ri** \-,thə,rī, -ē\ *or* **cath·ars** \-,thärz\ *usu cap* [LL *catharus*, fr. LGk *katharos*, fr. Gk, adj., pure] **:** a member of any of various widely distributed sects found in medieval Europe; *specif* **:** a member of a sect that interpreted Christianity from a dualistic Manichaean point of view and that practiced rigorous asceticism

catharine wheel *var of* CATHERINE WHEEL

cath·a·rism \'kathə,rizəm, -a,thä,r-\ *n* -S *usu cap* **:** the doctrines and practices of the Cathari

cath·a·rist \-,rəst\ *n* -S *usu cap* [LL & ML *Catharista*, fr. *Cathar* + *-ista* -ist] **:** CATHAR

cath·a·ris·tic \¦₌(,)₌¦ristik\ *adj, usu cap* **:** of or relating to the Cathari or their doctrines and practices

ca·thar·sis \kə'thärsəs, -thås-\ *n, pl* **cathar·ses** \-,sēz\ [NL, fr. Gk *katharsis*, fr. *kathairein* to clean, purify, fr. *katharos* pure] **1 :** PURGATION 1 **2 a :** the purification or purgation of the emotions (as pity and fear) primarily through art ⟨leaves the spectator "as empty, as changed, and as sad" as any other tragic ~ —Carlos Baker⟩ — used by Aristotle in his description of the effect of tragedy **b :** any purification or purgation that brings about a spiritual renewal or a satisfying release from tension ⟨these drawings served as a ~, relieving him of his burden of terrible memories, at the same time releasing hidden creative forces —Eva Michaelis-Stern⟩ **3 a :** the process of bringing repressed ideas and feelings into consciousness esp. by the technique of free association as employed in psychoanalysis, drugs or hypnosis sometimes being used as adjuvants — compare HYPNOTHERAPY, NARCOANALYSIS **b :** ABREACTION

ca·thar·tae \kə'thär,d·ē\ *n pl, cap* [NL, fr. *Cathartes*] **:** the suborder of Falconiformes comprising the New World vultures and related extinct birds — see CATHARTIDAE

ca·thar·tes \-d·(,)ēz\ *n, cap* [NL, fr. Gk *kathartēs* cleanser, fr. *kathairein* to clean] **:** the type genus of Cathartidae comprising the New World turkey vultures and related extinct birds

1ca·thar·tic \kə'thär|d·ik, -thå|, |tik, -ēk\ *also* **ca·thar·ti·cal** \-ə̇kəl, -ēk-\ *adj* [LL or Gk; LL *catharticus*, fr. Gk *kathartikos*, fr. (assumed) Gk *kathartos* (verbal of Gk *kathairein*) + Gk *-ikos* -ic, -ical] **:** of, relating to, or having the effect of catharsis **:** CLEANSING, PURIFYING ⟨argument as to how Aristotle thought the ~ process worked —Hunter Mead⟩ ⟨cold, ~ rain —R.P.Warren⟩; *specif* **:** cleansing the bowels — **ca·thar·ti·cal·ly** \-ə̇k(ə)lē, -ēk-, -lī\ *adv*

2cathartic \"\ *n* -S [LL or Gk; LL *catharticum*, fr. Gk *kathartikon*, fr. neut. of *kathartikos*] **:** a cathartic medicine **:** PURGATIVE

ca·thar·tid \kə'thärd·əd\ *n* -S [NL *Cathartidae*] **:** NEW WORLD VULTURE

ca·thar·ti·dae \kə'thärd·ə,dē\ *n pl, cap* [NL, fr. *Cathartes*, type genus + *-idae*] **:** a family of American carnivorous birds constituting with a few extinct related forms the suborder Cathartae of Falconiformes and comprising the New World vultures (as the condor, turkey buzzard, or king vulture), all differing from the Old World vultures in many points of structure (as in having pervious nostrils, no ceca, and no syringeal muscles) but resembling them in general appearance and habits and like them feeding chiefly on carrion

1ca·thar·tine \kə'thärd·,īn, 'kathər,tīn\ *adj* [NL *Cathartes* + E *-ine*] **:** of or relating to the genus *Cathartes* or to the typical vultures ⟨the distinctive features of the ~ head⟩ — compare ACCIPITRINE, BUTEONINE

2cathartine \"\ *n* -S **:** a bird of the genus *Cathartes; broadly* **:** a vulture or vulturelike member of the family Cathartidae

cat-haul \'₌,₌\ *vt* **:** to punish by forcibly dragging a cat along the bare back ⟨*cat-haul* a slave for a misdemeanor⟩

ca·thay \kə'thā, ka'-\ *n, often cap* [*Cathay* China, fr. ML *Cataya, Kitai*, of Turkic origin; akin to Kazan Tatar *Kytai* China, Old Turk *Qytan* Khitan] **:** FRENCH YELLOW

ca·thay·an \-āən\ *adj, usu cap* [*Cathay* + E *-an*] **:** of or relating to the Tatar race in northern China in the 10th and 11th centuries; *broadly* **:** CHINESE

1cathead \'₌,₌\ *n* [1*cat* (tackle) + *head*] **1 :** a projecting piece of timber or iron near the bow of a ship to which the anchor is hoisted and secured **2** *dial Eng* **:** a nodule of ironstone **3 :** a sleeve clamped around a noncylindrical piece of lathework to make suitable contact with the steady rest **4 :** a winch forming part of the drawworks of an oil-well rig

2cathead \"\ *vt* **:** CAT ⟨~ an anchor⟩

cathead line *n* **:** CATLINE

ca·thect \kə'thekt, ka-\ *vt* -ED/-ING/-S [back-formation fr. *cathectic*] **:** to invest with libidinal energy

ca·thec·tic \kə'thektik, (')ka¦th-\ *adj* [fr. NL *cathexis*, after Gk *kathexis* holding: *kathektikos* capable of holding; intended as trans. of G *besetzt*, lit., occupied] **:** of or relating to cathexis **:** libidinally invested

ca·thec·tion \kə'thekshən, ka-\ *n* -S **:** CATHEXIS

ca·the·dra \kə'thēdrə *also* 'kathədrə *or* kə'thādrə *or* kə'thedrə *or* 'kätä,drä\ *n* -S [L, chair — more at CHAIR] **:** the official throne of a bishop in the principal church of his diocese

1ca·the·dral \kə'thēdrəl\ *adj* [ME, fr. ML *cathedralis*, fr. L *cathedra* + *-alis* -al] **1 :** of, relating to, or containing a cathedra **:** of, relating to, or being a bishop's church ⟨a ~ church⟩ **2 :** emanating from the chair of office or authority (as of a bishop) **:** OFFICIAL, AUTHORITATIVE ⟨a ~ pronouncement⟩ **3 :** fit for or suggestive of a cathedral ⟨great elms forming ~ arches above its roads —Phyllis Duganne⟩

2cathedral \"\ *n* -S [LL *cathedralis*, prob. short for (assumed) *ecclesia cathedralis* cathedral church] **1 a :** a church that contains a cathedra and that is officially the principal church of a diocese ⟨the *Cathedral* of St. John the Divine in New York⟩ **b :** a church that was once a bishop's church **c :** any of various large or important nonepiscopal churches **2 a :** something that resembles or suggests a cathedral esp. in its proportions or architectural features ⟨a Broadway cinema ~⟩ ⟨that red-brick secular ~, Memorial Hall —A.N. Whitehead⟩ ⟨elms that turn those streets into great ~*s* in summer —Maxwell Mays⟩ **b :** the chapter house of a Scottish rite consistory **3 :** PLUM PURPLE

cathedral bells *n pl, often cap C* **:** a plant of the genus *Cobaea; specif* **:** an herb (*C. scandens*) — called also *cup-and-saucer vine*

cathedral ceiling *n* **:** a ceiling left open to expose the underside of a peaked roof

cathedral chimes *n pl* **:** bell-metal tubes of different lengths hung vertically and played by striking the upper ends with a mallet, the tones produced closely resembling distant church bells

cathedral glass *n* **:** translucent sheet glass made by casting and rolling but without polishing

cathedras *pl of* CATHEDRA

cath·e·drat·ic \¦kathə¦drad·ik\ *adj* [ML *cathedraticus*, fr. *cathedraticum*] **:** of or relating to an episcopal see; *specif* **:** AUTHORITATIVE

cath·e·drat·i·cum \,₌₌'₌₌kəm\ *n, pl* **cathedrati·ca** \-kə\ [ML, fr. L *cathedra* + *-aticum* -age] **:** an annual sum paid by a Roman Catholic parish for the support of the bishop

ca·thep·sin \kə'thepsən, ka-\ *n* -S [Gk *kathepsein* to boil down, digest (fr. *kata-* cata- + *hepsein* to boil) + E *-in*; akin to Arm *epem* I boil] **:** any of a class of proteases present in most animal tissues (as in kidney, liver, and spleen) that aid in autolysis in certain diseased conditions and after death — **ca·thep·tic** \-tik\ *adj*

cath·er·ine wheel \'kath(ə)rən-\ *n, often cap C* [after St. *Catherine* of Alexandria †*ab* 307 Christian martyr; fr. the attempt made to torture her on a spiked wheel] **1 a** *also* **cathar·ine wheel :** a wheel with spikes projecting from the rim **b :** a representation of such a wheel used esp. in heraldry **2 :** WHEEL WINDOW **3 :** PINWHEEL 2b **4 :** CARTWHEEL 2a

catherine wheel 1b

cath·e·ter \'kathəd·ə(r), -ətə-, *rap.* -thtə-\ *n* -S [LL, fr. Gk *kathetēr*, fr. *kathienai* to send down, fr. *kata-* cata- + *hienai* to send — more at JET] **:** any of various tubular medical devices designed for insertion into canals, vessels, passageways, or body cavities so as to permit injection or withdrawal of fluids or substances or to maintain the openness of a passageway

catheter fever *n* **:** fever ascribed to the passage of a urethral catheter and associated with infection of the bladder

cath·e·ter·i·za·tion \,₌(₌)₌rə'zāshən, -,rī'z-\ *n* -S **:** the use or insertion of a catheter (as into the bladder, the trachea, or the heart)

cath·e·ter·ize \'₌(₌)₌,rīz\ *vt* -ED/-ING/-S [*catheter* + *-ize*] **:** to introduce a catheter into

catheterized *adj* **:** obtained by catheterization ⟨~ urine specimens —*Science*⟩

cath·e·tom·e·ter \,kathə'tämәd·ə(r)\ *n* -S [ISV *catheto-* (fr. Gk *kathetos* vertical height, perpendicular line, fr. *kathetos* let down, fr. *kathienai*) + *-meter*] **:** an instrument for accurate measurement of small differences in height (as of columns of mercury or other fluids) consisting of a telescopic leveling apparatus that slides up or down a perpendicular standard with a finely graduated scale — **cath·e·to·met·ric** \¦kathəd·ə¦me·trik\ *adj*

ca·thex·is \kə'theksə̇s, ka-\ *n, pl* **cathex·es** \-k,sēz\ [NL, fr. Gk *kathexis* holding, fr. *katechein* to hold fast, occupy, fr. *kata-* cata- + *echein* to have, hold; intended as trans. of G *besetzung*, lit., act of occupying — more at SCHEME] **1 :** the investment of libidinal energy in a person, object, idea, or activity **2 :** libidinal energy that is either invested or being invested

cathisma *var of* KATHISMA

cath·ode \'ka,thōd\ *n* -S [Gk *kathodos* way down, descent, fr. *kata-* cata- + *hodos* way; fr. the belief that the electric current passes from east to west — more at CEDE] **1 :** the electrode at which electrons enter a device from the external circuit — opposed to *anode* **2 a :** the negative terminal of an electrolytic cell **b :** the positive terminal of a primary cell or of a storage battery that is delivering current **c :** the electron-emitting electrode (as a tungsten filament or an oxide-coated metal) of an electron tube

cathode current *n* **:** the current consisting of the total emission of electrons from the cathode of a vacuum tube expressed usu. in milliamperes

cathode dark space *n* **:** CROOKES DARK SPACE

cathode follower *n* **:** an electronic amplifier circuit in which the input is applied between the grid and the remote end of the cathode circuit and the output taken between the cathode and ground, producing an unusually low output impedance

cathode glow *n* **:** a thin layer of luminosity immediately surrounding the cathode in a Crookes tube

cathode ray *n* [part trans. of G *kathodenstrahl*, fr. *kathode* cathode + *strahl* ray] **1 :** one of the high-speed electrons (as a thermion) projected in a stream from the heated cathode of a vacuum tube under the propulsion of a strong electric field **2 :** a stream of cathode-ray electrons

cathode-ray oscillograph *n* **:** an oscillograph in which the moving element is a vibrating beam of cathode rays — compare OSCILLOSCOPE

cathode-ray oscilloscope *n* **:** OSCILLOSCOPE

cathode-ray tube *n* **:** a vacuum tube in which cathode rays usu. in the form of a slender beam are projected upon a fluorescent screen that serves as an anticathode where the rays produce a luminous spot

cathode spot *n* **1 :** a small area of the anticathode of an X-ray tube upon which the cathode rays are focused and from which proceed the X rays **2 :** a small area on the mercury cathode of a mercury-arc rectifier where the arc strikes it and liberates electrons

cath·od·ic \(')ka¦thädik, -ōd-, kə'thä-\ *adj* **1 a :** of, at, or relating to a cathode ⟨~ deposition of metals⟩ — opposed to *anodic* **b** *of a chemical element* **:** tending to form a cathode in an electrochemical cell in relation to another element, often hydrogen ⟨copper is ~ to zinc⟩ **2** *or* **kathodic :** turned away — used of that half of a leaf which is turned away from the course of the genetic spiral; compare ANODIC — **cath·od·i·cal·ly** \-ə̇k(ə)lē\ *adv*

cathodic protection *n* **:** the control of the electrolytic corrosion of an underground or underwater metallic structure (as a pipeline) by the application of an electric current in such a way that the structure is made to act as the cathode instead of anode of an electrolytic cell

cath·o·do·flu·o·res·cence \'kathə,dō-\ *n* -S [*cathode* + *-o-* + *fluorescence*] **:** fluorescence due to exposure to cathode rays

cath·o·do·lu·mi·nes·cence \'kathə,dō-\ *n* -S [*cathode* + *-o-* + *luminescence*] **:** luminescence produced when a substance is bombarded with cathode rays — **cath·o·do·lu·mi·nes·cent** \¦₌₌,₌,₌¦₌₌¦₌₌\ *adj*

cathole \'₌,₌\ *n* **1 :** a small opening (as in a door) for a cat to go through **2 :** any small opening that allows passage

1cath·o·lic \'kath(ə)lik, -ēk, *esp Brit also* 'kȧ-\ *n* -S *usu cap* [ME *catholike*, fr. MF *catholique*, fr. *catholique*, adj.] **1 :** a person who belongs to the universal Christian church **2 :** a member of a Catholic church: as **a :** a member of the Roman Catholic Church **b :** a member of an Eastern Orthodox church ⟨a Greek *Catholic*⟩ **c :** a member of an Anglican or Episcopal church ⟨an Anglo-*Catholic*⟩ **d :** a member of an Old Catholic church **e :** a member of a national Catholic church ⟨Polish National *Catholics*⟩

2catholic \"\ *adj* [MF & LL; MF *catholique*, fr. LL *catholicus*, fr. Gk *katholikos* universal, general, fr. *katholou* in general, fr. *kata* down, concerning + *holou*, gen. neut. of *holos* whole — more at CATA-, SAFE] **1** [prob. fr. Gk *katholikos*] **:** WIDESPREAD: **a** *obs* **:** universally prevalent ⟨a ~ legal system⟩ **b** *obs* **:** universally applicable ⟨a ~ remedy⟩ **2** [prob. fr. Gk *katholikos*] **:** general, universal, or inclusive in human affairs: **a :** affecting people generally **:** concerning or influencing all or much of mankind **b :** comprehensive or very broad in sympathies, understanding, appreciation, or interest **:** not narrow, isolative, provincial, or partisan ⟨a much more ~ appreciation of different styles and points of view than the 18th century allowed —Edmund Wilson⟩ **3** *usu cap* **a :** of, relating to, or being the church universal ⟨a truly *Catholic*, ecumenical church⟩ **b :** of, relating to, or being the ancient undivided Christian church **c :** of, relating to, or being a body of Christians belonging to any of various churches claiming historical continuity from the ancient undivided Christian Church — see [1]CATHOLIC 2 **4** *usu cap* **:** of, relating to, or constituting one of a number of usu. clericalist political parties arising in the late 19th and early 20th centuries principally in continental European countries and characterized by basic principles drawn chiefly from the social and economic teachings of the Roman Catholic Church ⟨European countries with solidly organized *Catholic* parties are Switzerland, Belgium . . . and Austria —C.J.Friedrich⟩ ⟨selection of a *Catholic* chancellor⟩ **syn** see UNIVERSAL

ca·thol·i·cal·ly \kə'thälək(ə)lē\ *or* **cath·o·lic·ly** \-ləklē, -kli\ *adv* **:** in a catholic manner

catholic apostolic *adj, usu cap C&A* **:** of or relating to the body of premillenarian Christians founded about 1832 on the teachings of those they regard as inspired prophets that call their religious body the Catholic Apostolic Church, that observe a highly ritualistic and symbolic form of worship, that have an elaborate hierarchy of apostles and prophets, that emphasize the existence in modern times of the miraculous and prophetic element in early Christianity, and that are commonly known as Irvingites

ca·thol·i·cate \kə'thälə,kāt, -lәkәt\ *n* -s [ML *catholicatus*, fr. *catholicus* catholicos + *-atus* -ate] **:** the see of a catholicos

catholic creditor *n, Scots law* **:** a creditor whose debt is a lien or charge on two or more items of the debtor's property

catholic existentialism *n, usu cap C* **:** CHRISTIAN EXISTENTIALISM 1

catholic frog *n, usu cap C* **:** a toad (*Notaden bennetti*) of eastern Australia with a mark like a cross on its back

ca·thol·i·cism \kə'thälə,sizəm, ka'-\ *n* -s *usu cap* [prob. fr. F *catholicisme*, fr. *catholique* catholic + *-isme* -ism] **1 :** the faith, practice, or system of the Catholic church **:** adherence to the Catholic church ⟨by *Catholicism* is meant that traditional faith expressed in the days of "the undivided Church" —W.N. Pittenger⟩ ⟨Greek, Roman, and Anglican *Catholicism*⟩ **2 :** the faith, practice, or system of a Catholic church, specif. the Roman Catholic Church **:** CATHOLICITY 1a **3 :** a peculiarity or characteristic of a Catholic **4 :** a political philosophy derived chiefly from the doctrines of the Roman Catholic Church and constituting the primary basis of the principles and policies of Catholic political parties ⟨*Catholicism* inclines toward socialism on many economic questions⟩

cath·o·lic·i·ty \,kathə'lisəd·ē, -ətē, -i\ *n* -ES [prob. fr. F *catholicité*, fr. *catholique* + *-ité* -ity] **1** *usu cap* **a :** the character of belonging to or being in conformity with a Catholic church, esp. the Roman Catholic Church **b :** CATHOLICISM 1 **2** [[1]*catholic* + *-ity*] **a :** liberality esp. of sentiments or views ⟨∼ of viewpoint —W.V.O'Connor⟩ **b :** UNIVERSALITY ⟨any church . . . which lays prophetic claim to ∼ —W.L.Sperry⟩ **c :** comprehensively wide range **:** INCLUSIVENESS ⟨better to err on the side of ∼ than of exclusiveness —C.D.Lewis⟩ ⟨the ∼ of subjects represented by the press's trade list —*Current Biog.*⟩

ca·thol·i·ci·za·tion \kə,thäləsə'zāshən, -,sī'z-\ *n* -s *usu cap* **:** the process or the result of becoming Catholic

ca·thol·i·cize \kə'thälə,sīz\ *vb* -ED/-ING/-S *often cap* [[2]*catholic* + *-ize*] *vt* **:** to make Catholic; *specif* **:** ROMANIZE ∼ *vi* **:** to become Catholic; *specif* **:** ROMANIZE

cath·o·lic·ness \-liknəs, -lēk-\ *n* -ES **:** CATHOLICITY

ca·thol·i·con \kə'thälə,kän\ *n* -s [F or ML; F, fr. ML, fr. Gk *katholikon*, neut. of *katholikos* universal — more at CATHOLIC] **:** CURE-ALL, PANACEA ⟨less inclined to look upon this technique as the ∼ it appeared to represent —T.M.Pryor⟩

ca·thol·i·cos \kə'thäləkəs, -ə,käs\ *also* **ca·thol·i·cus** \-əkəs\ *n, pl* **catholi·cos·es** \-əkəsəz,-ə,käsəz\ *or* **catholi·coi** \-ə-,koi\ *also* **catholi·ci** \-ə,sī,-ə,kē\ *often cap* [LGk *katholikos*, fr. Gk *katholikos*, adj. — more at CATHOLIC] **:** any of the heads of certain independent Eastern churches (as the Armenian Church) ⟨manuscripts written for the ∼ Nerses the Gracious⟩ — used only in the non-Greek churches orig. as an honorary title given certain exarchs or primates ranking below a patriarch but above a metropolitan

catholics *pl of* CATHOLIC

cath·o·lyte \'kathə,līt\ *n* -s [ISV *catho*de + electr*olyte*] **:** the portion of the electrolyte in the immediate vicinity of the cathode in an electrolytic cell — opposed to *anolyte*

cat hook *n* **:** a hook attached to a ship's cat block

cat·hop \'kat,häp\ *n* -s **:** the situation in faro in which two of the three cards left in the dealing box for the last turn are of the same denomination

cathouse \'⸗,⸗\ *n* **:** BROTHEL 2

ca'·thro *or* **ca'·throw** \'kȯ,thrō, 'kä-, -rü\ *n* -s [Sc *ca'thro'*, v., to work hard, lit., drive through, fr. *ca'* + *thro'*] *Scot* **:** DISTURBANCE, COMMOTION

cat ice *n* **:** thin often milky ice from under which the water has receded **:** SHELL ICE

[1]**cat·i·li·nar·i·an** \,kad·ᵊl;nerēən\ *adj, usu cap* [L *Catilinarius* Catilinarian (fr. Lucius Sergius *Catilina* (Catiline) †62 B.C. Roman politician) + E *-an*] **:** of, relating to, or like Catiline, who conspired against the government; *specif* **:** CONSPIRATORIAL ⟨a *Catilinarian* existence⟩

[2]**catilinarian** \"\ *n* -s *usu cap* **:** CONSPIRATOR; *specif* **:** a participant in Catiline's conspiracy ⟨Cicero had written to Pompey about the suppression of the *Catilinarians* —J.H.Taylor⟩

ca·tin·ga *var of* CAATINGA

cat·ion \'kad·,īən *also* -,ī,än *or* 'ka,tī-\ *n* -s [Gk *kation*, neut. of *katiōn*, pres. part. of *katienai* to go down, fr. *kata-* cata- + *ienai* to go — more at ISSUE] **1 :** a positively charged ion (as a hydrogen, calcium, or ammonium ion) — opposed to *anion* **2 a :** the ion in an electrolyzed solution that migrates to the cathode and is there discharged and liberated or deposited **b :** a positive gaseous ion

cation-active \'⸗,⸗(,)⸗;⸗⸗\ *adj* **:** CATIONIC 2

cation exchange *n* **:** ion exchange in which one cation (as sodium or hydrogen) is substituted for one or more other cations (as calcium and magnesium in hard water) — called also *base exchange*

cation exchanger *n* **:** a cation-exchange agent that can exchange its cation with the cation or cations of a solution passed through it and that consists of an insoluble saltlike or acidic substance: as **a :** a natural or synthetic zeolite **b :** a sulfonated coal **c :** a synthetic organic resin containing sulfonic or carboxylic acid groups

cat·ion·ic \¦kad·,ī¦änik, -a,tī-, -ēk\ *adj* **1 :** relating to or consisting of cations **2** *of a chemical compound* **:** characterized by an active cation, esp. by a surface-active cation (as a large hydrophobic organic group) ⟨∼ germicide⟩ ⟨∼ surface-active agent⟩ — **cat·ion·i·cal·ly** \-ək(ə)lē, -ēk-, -li\ *adv*

cationic detergent *n* **:** any of a class of synthetic detergents usu. consisting essentially of a quaternary ammonium salt (as cetyl-trimethyl-ammonium chloride $[C_{16}H_{33}N(CH_3)_3]^+Cl^-$) with 12 to 24 carbon atoms in the cation and valuable as a wetting and emulsifying agent in acid or neutral solutions or as a germicide or fungicide — called also *invert soap*

cat·ion·oid \(')⸗;⸗,nȯid\ *adj* [*cation* + *-oid*] **:** ELECTROPHILIC

cat·ion·o·trop·ic \'⸗,⸗,änə-¦träpik\ *adj* [*cationotropy* + *-ic*] **:** of or relating to cationotropy

cat·ion·ot·ro·py \¦⸗,⸗'nä-trəpē\ *n* -ES [*cation* + *-o-* + *-tropy*] **:** tautomerism involving migration of a cation, the best-known type being prototropy — compare *anionotropy*

ca·ti·vo \kə'tē(,)vō, -,vȯ\ *also* **cau·ti·vo** \kaů'-\ *n* -s [modif. of AmerSp *cativa*, fr. Sp, fem. of *cativo* captive, miserable, fr. L *captivus* captive — more at CAPTIVE] **:** a large tree (*Prioria copaifera*) of the family Leguminosae of Panama

ca·tjang \'kä,chäŋ\ *or* **catjang pea** *n* -s [D *katjang*, fr. Malay & Sundanese *kachang* bean, pea] **:** PIGEON PEA

cat·kin \'katkən\ *n* -s [trans. of obs. D *katteken* catkin, kitten; fr. its resemblance to a cat's tail] **:** an ament esp. long and densely crowded with bracts — **cat·kin·ate** \-ə,nāt\ *adj*

cat·la \'kätlə, -,lä\ *n* -s [Bengali *kātlā*] **:** either of two very large cyprinid fishes extensively used as food in southeast Asia: **a :** an Indian fish (*Catla catla*) often cultivated in ponds and attaining a length of six feet **b :** a fish (*C. siamensis*) that is most common in Thailand and that may exceed nine feet in length

catlap \'⸗,⸗\ *n* -s [prob. fr. *cat* + *lap* (something lapped up)] *chiefly Scot* **:** weak drink fit only for a cat to lap

catlike \'⸗,⸗\ *adj* **:** resembling, suggestive of, or having the characteristics of a cat **:** STEALTHY, NOISELESS

catline \'⸗,⸗\ *n* [[1]*cat* (tackle) + *line*] **:** a heavy line used for general hoisting in oil-well drilling — called also *cathead line*

cat·ling \'katliŋ\ *n* -s [[1]*cat* + *-ling*] **1 :** a small cat **:** KITTEN **2 :** a catgut string for a musical instrument **3 :** the smallest string on a stringed instrument (as a lute) **4** *also* **cat·lin** \-lən\ **:** a long double-edged sharp-pointed knife used in amputations to divide tissues between close-lying bones

cat·lin·ite \'katlə,nīt\ *n* -s [George *Catlin* †1872 Am. artist + E *-ite*] **:** a red indurated clay from the upper Missouri region used by Indians for tobacco pipes **:** PIPESTONE

cat·lin mark \'katlən-\ *n, usu cap C* [fr. *Catlin*, name of a family in which this fenestration is typical] **:** bilateral fenestration of the parietal bones of the skull occurring as a congenital anomaly that was orig. known from primitive human skulls and thought to be the result of trephining

cat louse *n* **:** a biting louse (*Felicola subrostratus*) of the family Trichodectidae common on cats esp. in warm regions

cat·mal·i·son \'kat,maləsən, -əzən\ *n* -s [[1]*cat* + *malison;* prob. fr. the fact that the cat cannot get in] *dial Eng* **:** a cupboard in or near the ceiling

cat man *n* **1 :** the member of a circus staff responsible for the care and training of lions, tigers, and other large members of the cat family **2 :** CAT SKINNER **3 :** CAT BURGLAR

catmint \'⸗,⸗\ *n* [alter. of ME *cattesminte*, fr. *cattes* (gen. of [1]*cat*) + *minte* mint — more at MINT] **:** CATNIP

[1]**catnap** \'⸗,⸗\ *n* **:** a very short light nap ⟨didn't go to bed for two days and nights but caught ∼*s* at my desk —Ralph Ellison⟩

[2]**catnap** \"\ *vi* [[1]*catnap*] **:** to take a catnap **:** DOZE

cat·nip \'kat,nip\ *also* **cat·nep** \-,nep, -,nəp\ *n* -s [[1]*cat* + *nip*] **:** a strong-scented herb (*Nepeta cataria*) that has whorls of small dull-white purple-dotted flowers in a terminal spike, was often used in the past as a domestic remedy, and is much relished by cats — called also *catmint*

cato- *prefix* [Gk *katō-*, fr. *katō* downwards, fr. *kata* down — more at CATA-] **:** down **:** lower ⟨*catogene*⟩ ⟨*Catostomus*⟩

ca·toc·a·la \kə'täkələ; ,kad·ə'kälə, -'kalə\ *n* [NL, fr. *cato-* + *-cala* (irreg. fr. Gk *kalos* beautiful); fr. the red or yellow hind wings — more at CALLI-] **1** *cap* **:** a widely distributed genus of large moths (family Noctuidae) having the fore wings dull and the hind wings larger and brightly colored **2** *also* **ca·toc·a·lid** \-ləd\ -s **:** a moth of the genus *Catocala* **:** UNDERWING 2

ca·toc·tin \kə'täktən\ *n* -s [fr. *Catoctin* Mountain, Maryland & Virginia] **:** a residual hill or ridge that rises above a peneplain and preserves on its summit a remnant of an older peneplain

cat·o·met·o·pa \,kad·ə'med·əpə\ *n pl, cap* [NL, fr. *cato-* + L *metopa* metope — more at METOPE] *in former classifications* **:** a division of crabs comprising the grapsoid members of Brachyrhyncha — **cat·o·met·ope** \-'med-,ōp, -e,tōp\ *n* -s

ca·to·nian \kä'tōnēən, -nyən\ *or* **ca·ton·ic** \kä'tänik\ *adj, usu cap* [*catonian* fr. L *catonianus*, fr. *Caton-*, *Cato* (Marcus Porcius *Cato* †149 B.C. Roman statesman, or Marcus Porcius *Cato* †46 B.C. Roman Stoic philosopher, both celebrated for austerity) + E *-ian* -ian; *catonic* fr. L *Caton-*, *Cato* + E *-ic*] **:** AUSTERE, HARSH

cat-o'-nine-tails \,kad·ə'nīn,tālz, ,kat³nī-, ,katə'nī-\ *n, pl* **cat-o'-nine-tails** [so called fr. a comparison of its blows to the scratches of a cat] **1 :** a whip made of usu. nine knotted lines or cords fastened to a handle and used for flogging **2 :** CATTAIL

cat-o'-nine-tails

ca·top·tric \kə'täptrik\ *also* **ca·top·tri·cal** \-əkəl\ *adj* [*catoptric* fr. Gk *katoptrikos*, fr. *katoptron* mirror (fr. *katopsesthai* to be going to observe — fr. *kata-* cata- + *opsesthai* to be going to see — + *-tron*) + *-ikos* -ic; *catoptrical* fr. Gk *katoptrikos* + E *-al* — more at OPTIC] **:** of or relating to a mirror or reflected light **:** produced by or based on reflection — **ca·top·tri·cal·ly** \-ək(ə)lē\ *adv*

ca·top·trite *or* **ka·top·trite** \kə'täp,trīt, 'kad·əp,-\ *n* -s [Sw *katoptrit*, fr. Gk *katoptron* + Sw *-it* -ite; fr. its mirrorlike cleavage surfaces] **:** a mineral consisting of a silico-antimonate of manganese, aluminum, magnesium, and iron occurring in metallic black monoclinic crystals

ca·top·tro·man·cy \kə,täptrə,man(t)sē\ *n* -ES [prob. fr. F *catoptromancie*, fr. Gk *katoptron* mirror + F *-mancie* -mancy] **:** divination by a mirror or by crystal gazing

cat·o·rama \,kad·ə'ramə, -ämə\ *n, cap* [NL, fr. *cato-* + Gk *horama* that which is visible, fr. *horan* to see] **:** a genus of deathwatch beetles (family Anobiidae) including some that are pests of stored grain

ca·tos·to·mid \kə'tästəməd\ *n* -s [NL *Catostomidae*] **:** a fish of the family Catostomidae **:** SUCKER

cat·o·stom·i·dae \,kad·ə'stämə,dē\ *n pl, cap* [NL, fr. *Catostomus*, type genus + *-idae*] **:** a family of freshwater fishes (order Ostariophysi) consisting of the suckers and being closely related to and sometimes included in the Cyprinidae — **ca·tos·to·moid** \kə'tästə,mȯid\ *adj or n*

ca·tos·to·mus \kə'tästəməs\ *n, cap* [NL, fr. *cato-* + *-stomus*] **:** a large genus (the type of the family Catostomidae) of suckers

ca·touse \kə'taůs, -aůz\ *n* -s [origin unknown] *North* **:** UPROAR, COMMOTION

cat owl *n* **:** an owl having ear tufts (as the great horned owl, long-eared owl, or screech owl)

cat pea *n* **:** TUFTED VETCH

catpiece \'⸗,⸗\ *n* **:** a stick with holes at regular intervals into which uprights fastened in floating booms are fitted so as to regulate the width of a logging sluiceway entrance

cat pine *n* **:** WHITE SPRUCE 1a

cat plague *n* **:** PANLEUCOPENIA

cat rig *n* **:** a rig consisting of a single mast placed far forward and carrying a single large sail extended by a long boom

cat-rigged \'⸗;⸗\ *adj* **:** having a cat rig

cats *pl of* CAT, *pres 3d sing of* CAT

[1]**cats and dogs** *adv* **:** in great quantities **:** very hard — used with an intransitive verb, esp. *rain* ⟨it was raining *cats and dogs*⟩

[2]**cats and dogs** *n pl* **1** *slang* **:** speculative securities of dubious standing or little value **2** *slang* **:** ODDS AND ENDS; *esp* **:** miscellaneous merchandise usu. sold at or below cost

cat schooner *n* **:** a cat-rigged 2-masted boat formerly used for inshore fishing

cat's-claw *or* **catclaw** \'⸗,⸗\ *n, pl* **cat's-claws** *or* **catclaws** **1 a :** a climbing shrub (*Doxantha unguis-cati*) with hooked tendrils **b :** an erect shrub (*Pithecolobium unguis-cati*) with curved pointed pods and black shining seeds **2 :** any of several prickly shrubs (as *Acacia greggii* or *Mimosa biuncifera*)

cat's cradle *n* **1 :** a game in which an endless string looped in a cradlelike pattern on the fingers of one person's hands is transferred to the hands of another in such a way as to form a different symmetrical figure at each transfer — compare STRING FIGURE **2 a :** any of the figures formed with string in the game of cat's cradle **b :** something resembling one of these figures esp. in intricacy ⟨trees . . . latticed and knitted and strung together by a *cat's cradle* of lianas and creepers —Nadine Gordimer⟩

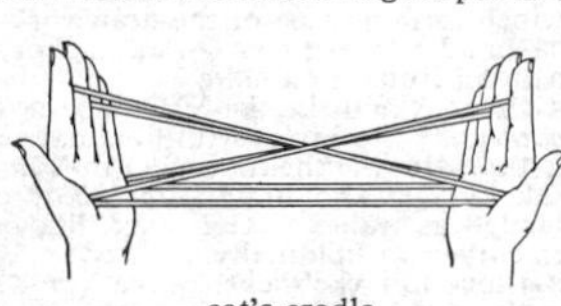

cat's cradle

cat's-cradle \'⸗,⸗⸗\ *n, pl* **cat's-cradles** **:** RIBGRASS

cat scratch disease *n* **:** an illness that is characterized by chilliness, slight fever, and swelling of the lymph glands and is assumed to be caused by a virus infection starting in a scratch or other skin lesion

cat's-ear \'⸗,⸗\ *n, pl* **cat's-ears** **1 :** a European weed (*Hypochaeris radicata*) now widely naturalized in No. America that has yellow flower heads and leaves resembling a cat's ear — called also *California dandelion, capeweed, gosmore* **2 :** any of various plants with soft hairy blossoms or leaves (as the cudweed or the hawkweed) **3** *West* **:** a plant of the genus *Calochortus*

Catseye \'⸗,⸗\ *trademark* — used for a small reflector placed to reflect beams from automobile headlights

cat's-eye \"\ *n, pl* **cat's-eyes** **:** any of various things resembling the eye of a cat: as **a :** any of various gems (as a chrysoberyl or a chalcedony) usu. cut cabochon exhibiting opalescent reflections from within **b :** a child's marble (as an agate) light in color (as yellow) or with eyelike concentric circles **c :** the operculum of various turban shells of the Pacific islands and adjoining seas that is externally convex with a lustrous brightly colored central area surrounded by zones of white, ivory, and brown and is sometimes used for ornamentation

cat's-foot \'⸗,⸗\ *n, pl* **cat's-feet** **1 :** GROUND IVY **2 :** any of several plants of the genus *Antennaria* (esp. *A. neodioica*)

cat shark *n* **1 :** any of several small mottled sharks comprising the galeoid family Scyliorhinidae **2 :** LEOPARD SHARK **3 :** any of several small sharks (genus *Parascyllium*) related to and resembling the carpet sharks

catskin \'⸗,⸗\ *n* **1 :** the skin of a cat esp. when used for fur clothing **2** *archaic slang* **:** an inferior silk hat

cat skinner *n* **:** an operator of a Caterpillar tractor — called also *cat man*

catslide \'⸗,⸗\ *n* [[1]*cat* + *slide* (inclined plane)] **:** a side of a roof that slopes very low and often nearly to the ground (as in a saltbox house)

cat sloop *n* **:** a catboat on which a bowsprit may be rigged in order to carry a jib

cat snake *n* [so called fr. its manner of stalking lizards] **1 :** a back-fanged terrestrial snake (*Tarbophis fallax*) of southern Europe and Syria **2 :** a member of the genus *Boiga* which includes various green-eyed nocturnal arboreal Old World back-fanged snakes

catso *n* -s [It *cazzo*, lit., penis, perh. modif. of ML *cattia* dipper — more at CASSEROLE] *obs* **:** BLACKGUARD, RASCAL

cat's-paw \'⸗,⸗\ *n, pl* **cat's-paws** **1 :** a light air that ruffles the surface of the water in irregular patches during a calm **2** [so called fr. the fable of the monkey that used a cat's paw to draw roasting chestnuts from the fire] **:** one used by another to accomplish his purposes **:** DUPE, TOOL ⟨had no intention of becoming a *cat's-paw* for either belligerent —F.L. Paxson⟩ **3 :** a hitch in the bight of a rope so made as to form two eyes into which a tackle may be hooked **4 :** CAT'S-FOOT

cat's-paw 3

cat spruce *n* **:** WHITE SPRUCE 1a

cat's purr *n* **:** a vibratory murmur heard on auscultation or a vibratory fremitus felt on palpation in some cases of valvular disease of the heart

cat squirrel *n* **1 :** a reddish-coated fox squirrel found in the eastern part of its range **2 :** the common European squirrel **3 :** CACOMISTLE **4 :** GRAY SQUIRREL

[1]**cat's-tail** \'⸗,⸗\ *also* **cat's-tail grass** *n, pl* **cats'-tails** [ME *cattestail*, a kind of plant, prob. mullein, fr. *cattes* (gen. of [1]*cat*) + *tail*] **:** any of several grasses of the genus *Phleum; esp* **:** TIMOTHY

[2]**cat's-tail** *var of* CATTAIL

catstep \'⸗,⸗\ *n* -s **:** one of a succession of small terracelike forms created on a steep hillside by the slumping of the soil — usu. used in pl.

catstick \'⸗,⸗\ *n* [[1]*cat* (pointed stick) + *stick*] **:** a stick or club used as a bat in tipcat or trapball

cat·stitch \'kat,stich\ *n* [by alter.] **:** CATCH STITCH

cat·sup *or* **catch·up** *or* **ketch·up** *or* **kat·sup** \'kechəp, 'kachəp *also* 'katsəp\ *n* -s [*catsup, catchup, katsup* by folk etymology fr. *ketchup; ketchup* fr. Malay *kĕchap* spiced fish sauce] **1 :** a seasoned sauce of puree consistency the principal ingredient of which is usu. tomatoes but sometimes another foodstuff (as mushrooms or walnuts) **2** *usu catchup* **:** a moderate red that is yellower and slightly lighter than cerise, yellower than claret (sense 3 a), yellower and very slightly lighter than average strawberry (sense 2 a), and yellower and lighter than Turkey red

cat swamper *n* **:** one that clears logging trails for tractors

cat's whisker *var of* CAT WHISKER

cattail \'⸗,⸗\ *n* [alter. of *cat's-tail*] **1** *or* **cat's-tail** *or* **cattail flag :** a plant of the genus *Typha; esp* **:** a tall marsh plant (*T. latifolia*) with long flat leaves used for making mats and chair seats — called also *reed mace* **2 :** MUSK 4

cattail family *n* **:** TYPHACEAE

cattail fungus *n* **:** an ascomycetous fungus (*Epichloe typhina*) of the family Hypocreaceae forming cylindrical whitish or gray stromata around the stems of certain grasses and often affecting development of the inflorescence — see CHOKE 5

cattail millet *n* **1 :** FOXTAIL MILLET **2 :** PEARL MILLET

cattail (*Typha latifolia*)

cat·ta·lo \'kad·ᵊl,ō\ *n, pl* **cattaloes** *or* **cattalos** *also* **cattalo** [*cattle* + *buffalo*] **:** a hybrid between the American buffalo and domestic cattle that is hardier than the latter

cattan *var of* CATAN

cat tapeworm *n* **:** a common tapeworm (*Taenia taeniaeformis* or *T. crassicollis*) of cats who ingest the cysticercus from various rodents in whose livers this larva forms conspicuous tumors

[1]**catted** *past of* CAT

[2]**cat·ted** \'kad·əd\ *adj* [cat (plaster) + *-ed*] **:** built up or bonded with clay or cat and clay ⟨a ∼ chimney⟩

cat·tery \'kad·ərē\ *n* -ES **:** a place for the breeding, raising, or care of cats

cat thyme *n* **:** a low-growing germander (*Teucrium marum*) formerly used in cosmetics that has tiny hairy or woolly leaves and reddish purple flowers and is attractive to cats — called also *marum*

cattier *comparative of* CATTY

cat·tier·ite \kə'ti,rīt\ *n* -s [fr. *Cattier*, railroad workshops in Leopoldville province, Congo + E *-ite*] **:** a mineral CoS_2 consisting of cobalt sulfide and belonging to the pyrite group

catties *pl of* CATTY

cattiest *superlative of* CATTY

cat·ti·ly \'kad·ᵊlē, -at|, |əlē, -li\ *adv* **:** in a catty manner

cat·ti·ness \'kad·ēnəs, -atē-\ *n* -ES **:** the quality or state of being catty

catting *pres part of* CAT

cat·tish \'kad·ish, -ati-, -ēsh\ *adj* **1 :** like a cat **:** like that of a cat **:** FELINE ⟨he had a ∼ secrecy and serenity —Esther Forbes⟩ **2 :** SPITEFUL, CATTY — **cat·tish·ly** *adv*

cat·tle \'kad·ᵊl, 'katᵊl\ *n, pl* **cattle** *usu pl in constr, often attrib* [ME *catel*, fr. ONF, personal property, fr. ML *capitale*, fr. L, neut. of *capitalis* of the head — more at CAPITAL] **1 a :** live domesticated quadrupeds (as sheep, horses, swine) held as property or raised for some use; *specif* **:** bovine animals (as cows, bulls, steers) kept on a farm or ranch **b :** domesticated or feral animals of the genus *Bos* comprising the many breeds of the common ox that have arisen either from the urus with some admixture of zebu blood by crossbreeding and selection among strains or according to some authorities from the Celtic ox (*B. longifrons*) — see BEEF BREED, DAIRY BREED, DUAL-PURPOSE BREED **2 :** human beings especially en masse — usu. used derogatorily

cattlebush \'⸗⸗,⸗\ *n* **:** an Australian tree (*Atalaya hemiglauca*) of the family Sapindaceae that is often used for fodder in droughts

cattle cake *n, chiefly Brit* **:** a concentrated ration for cattle processed in the form of blocks or cakes

cattle egret *n* [so called fr. its habit of feeding on insects on or in the vicinity of cattle] **:** a small white buff-backed egret (*Bubulcus ibis*) native to Africa, southern Europe, and southwestern Asia but now occurring also in northern So. America and intermittently in the eastern U. S.

cattle farcy *n* **:** FARCY 2

cattle fever *n* **1 :** TEXAS FEVER **2 :** bovine pasteurellosis

cattle fly *n* **:** HORN FLY

cattle grid *n, Brit* **:** CATTLE GUARD

cattle grub *n* **1 :** the maggot of a warble fly **2 :** the adult warble fly

cattle guard *n* **1 :** a device consisting of a shallow ditch across which ties or rails are laid far enough apart to prevent livestock from crossing that is often used instead of a gate at a fence opening ⟨where the *cattle guard* barred the entrance to horses, he dismounted —Oliver La Farge⟩ **2 :** an opening in a fence where a cattle guard has been laid

cattlehide \'⸗⸗,⸗\ *n* **:** leather made from the hides of mature bovines — contrasted with *calfskin, kip*

cat·tle·less \'==ləs\ *adj* **:** being without cattle

cattle louse *n* **:** a louse infesting cattle — see CATTLE RED LOUSE, LONG-NOSED CATTLE LOUSE, SHORT-NOSED CATTLE LOUSE

cat·tle·man \'==mən, -,man, -,aa(ə)n\ *n, pl* **cattlemen** **1 :** one who tends cattle **2 :** a rancher who raises beef cattle on the open range

cattle pass *n* **:** a passageway for livestock; *esp* **:** one under a highway or railroad

cattle plague *n* [trans. of G *rinderpest*] **:** RINDERPEST

cattle red louse *or* **cattle biting louse** *n* **:** the common red louse of the genus *Trichodectes* (*T. bovis* syn. *Bovicola bovis*) that infests domestic cattle and feeds chiefly on the hair

cattle tick *n* **:** a tick (*Boophilus annulatus*) infesting cattle in the warmer parts of the U.S. and in tropical America and transmitting the parasite that causes Texas fever; *broadly* **:** any of several other ticks attacking cattle esp. in Australia

cattle-tick fever *n* **:** TEXAS FEVER

cat·tleya \'katlēə, ='==; kat'lāə\ *n* [NL, fr. William *Cattley* †1832 Eng. patron of botany] **1** *cap* **:** a genus of tropical American epiphytic orchids the flowers of which are among the showiest known and are characterized by a hood-shaped 3-lobed lip enclosing the column **2** -s **:** a plant of the genus *Cattleya* **3** -s **:** a moderate purple that is redder and paler than heliotrope (sense 4a), bluer and paler than average amethyst, and paler and slightly bluer than manganese violet

cattleya fly *n* **:** a small black chalcid fly (*Eurytoma orchidearum*) the larvae of which live in and damage and deform the shoots of orchids — called also *orchid fly*

cattle yard \'==,=\ *n* **1 :** a barnyard used by cattle **2 :** STOCKYARD

cat·tley guava \'katlē-\ *n* [after William *Cattley*] **:** STRAWBERRY GUAVA

cat train *n* [¹*cat* (caterpillar) + train] **:** a train of large connected sleds drawn by a tractor and used for transportation in arctic areas

cat twist *n* **:** a tumbling and trampolining stunt consisting of a full or partial twisting of the shoulders and hips in the air with the body usu. in pike position

¹**cat·ty** *also* **kati** \'kad·ē, -atē, -i\ *n* -ES [Malay *kati*] **:** any of various units of weight used in China and southeast Asia varying around 1⅓ pounds or 600 grams; *also* **:** a Chinese unit according to a standard set up in 1929 equal to 1.1023 pounds or 500 grams

²**cat·ty** \"\ *adj, usu* -ER/-EST [¹*cat* + *-y*] **1 :** having characteristics resembling those of a cat ⟨writes of its problems with a ~ aloofness charmingly disguised as sympathy —Lewis Mumford⟩: as **a :** STEALTHY ⟨a noiseless ~ walk⟩ **b :** AGILE ⟨three of the *cattiest* men who ever rode a log —S.H.Holbrook⟩ **c :** slyly spiteful ⟨a ~ remark⟩ **d :** given to malicious gossip ⟨a ~ woman⟩ **2 :** of, relating to, or like a cat ⟨a ~ smell in the house⟩

catty-corner *or* **catty-cornered** *var of* CATERCORNER

cat typhoid *n* **:** PANLEUCOPENIA

cat·ty·wam·pus *var of* CATAWAMPUS

ca·tul·li·an \kə'tələn\ *adj, usu cap* [L *catullianus*, fr. Gaius Valerius *Catullus* †54 B.C. Roman poet + L *-ianus* -ian] **:** of, relating to, or like Catullus or his lyric poems, which are marked by facility of language, perfection of form, and intensely personal subject matter

cat wagon \'=,==\ *n* [¹*cat* (caterpillar) + *wagon*] **:** a truck trailer on caterpillar treads used esp. on soft ground

catwalk \'=,=\ *n* **:** a narrow walkway affording passage over or around areas not otherwise traversable or giving access to places otherwise inaccessible: as **a :** a raised gangway that runs the length of a tanker and gives passage forward and aft when the upper deck is awash **b :** a high narrow steel platform over the engine room or stokehold of a ship **c :** a narrow footway along the keel of a rigid airship **d :** a walkway along the roof of a railway freight car **e :** a narrow footway along a bridge

cat whisker *or* **cat's whisker** *n* **:** a fine wire making contact with the crystal in the crystal detector or mixer of certain types of radio or electronic circuits

cat willow *n* **:** FALSE INDIGO 1a

cat·wort \'kat·,wərt, -ȯrt\ *n* [ME, fr. *cat, catte* + *wort*] **:** CATNIP

cat yawl *n* **:** a yawl without headsails and with the mainmast set forward

catydid *var of* KATYDID

catzerie *n* -s [prob. fr. *catso* + *-ery*] *obs* **:** KNAVERY

cau·been \(')kȯ¦bēn\ *n* -s [IrGael *cáibín*, dim. of *cába* cape, prob. fr. ML *capa* cope — more at COPE] *Irish* **:** a man's hat

¹**cau·ca·sian** \(')kȯ¦kāzhən *also* -azh- *or* -aizh-\ *adj, usu cap* [*Caucasus* or *Caucasia*, region between the Black & Caspian seas (fr. L *Caucasus*, fr. Gk *Kaukasos*) + E *-ian* or *-an*] **1 :** of or relating to the Caucasus or its inhabitants **2 :** CAUCASIC 2 **3 :** of or relating to the Caucasian race

²**caucasian** \"\ *n* -s **1** *cap* **:** a member of one of various native peoples of the Caucasus (as the Abkhas, Georgians, Mingrelians, Circassians, Kartvelians, Chechens, and Lezghians) most of whom are racially white but linguistically isolated **2** *cap* **a :** a member of the white race of mankind as opposed by classification according to physical features (as skin color, hair form, or body and skeletal characteristics) but without regard to language or culture to members of the Negroid, Mongoloid, or other putative races of mankind **b :** a member of the white race as defined by law (as in California or So. Africa); *specif* **:** a descendant of European, No. African, or southwest Asian immigrants **c** *chiefly Southwest* **:** a person of white race or European descent as opposed to those of other ethnic affiliation or descent (as certain Mexicans, Indians, Negroes, Orientals) **:** ANGLO **3** *usu cap* **:** a rug of any of the types woven in the Caucasus mountains and the adjacent plains to the north and south

caucasian walnut *n, usu cap C* **:** a tall often forked tree (*Pterocarya fraxinifolia*) native to the Caucasus and distinguished from other walnuts by its 2-winged fruit

cau·cas·ic \(')kȯ¦kasik, -zik\ *adj, usu cap* [*Caucasus* + E *-ic*] **1 :** CAUCASIAN, CAUCASOID **2 :** of or relating to the languages of the Caucasus region that are not Indo-European or Altaic

¹**cau·ca·soid** \'kȯkə,sȯid\ *adj, usu cap* [*Caucasian* + *-oid*] **:** of, resembling, or related to the Caucasian race

²**caucasoid** \"\ *n* -s *cap* **:** CAUCASIAN 2a

cauch \'kōch\ *n* -ES [modif. of Corn *caugh* dung; akin to MIr *cacc* dung — more at CACK] *dial Eng* **:** MESS

cau·che·ro \kaù'che(,)rō\ *n* -s [AmerSp, fr. Sp *caucho* + *-ero* -er] **:** one who gathers rubber sap

cau·chi·llo \kaù'chē(,)(y)ō\ *n* -s [AmerSp] **:** a tropical American timber tree (*Lecythis ollaria*) yielding a valuable reddish brown wood and bearing fruits with seeds resembling Brazil nuts — see CREAM NUT

cau·cho \'kaù(,)chō, -)shü\ *n* -s [Sp — more at CAOUTCHOUC] **:** RUBBER; *specif* **:** the wild rubber obtained from a Brazilian tree (*Castilloa ulei*) or from a Central American tree (*C. elastica*) — see CASTILLOA

¹**cau·cus** \'kȯkəs *also* -'ä-\ *n* -ES *often attrib* [earlier *corcas*, prob. of Algonquian origin; akin to *caucauasu* elder, counselor (in some Algonquian language of Virginia), Abnaki *kakesoman* to encourage, arouse, Natick *kogkahtimau* he gives advice to] **1 a :** a conference of party or organization leaders (as legislators) to decide on policies, plans, appointees, and candidates **b :** a local or regional meeting of party members to choose candidates or delegates **c** *chiefly West* **:** an open meeting to nominate township candidates **2 :** a system of party organization by representative committees that determine and implement policies

²**caucus** \"\ *vi* -ED/-ING/-ES **:** to hold a caucus **:** meet in a caucus

caud- *or* **caudi-** *or* **caudo-** *comb form* [L *cauda*] **:** tail ⟨*caud*ad⟩ ⟨*caudi*form⟩ **:** caudal and ⟨*caudo*dorsal⟩

cau·da \'kaùdə, 'kȯdə\ *n, pl* **cau·dae** \'kaù,dī, 'kȯ,dē\ [L, tail — more at COWARD] **1 :** a taillike appendage **:** TAIL **2 :** TAIL 16, CODA

cau·dad \'kȯ,dad\ *adv* [*caud-* + *-ad*] *anat* **:** toward the tail or posterior end — opposed to *cephalad*

cauda equi·na \'kaùdəe'kwēnə, 'kȯdəē'kwīnə\ *n, pl* **cau·dae equi·nae** \'kaù,dīe'kwē,nī, 'kȯ,dēə'kwī,nē\ [NL, fr. L, horse's tail] **:** the roots of the upper sacral nerves which are of great length because the spinal cord does not extend beyond the first lumbar vertebra and which form a bundle of filaments within the spinal canal

cau·da he·li·cis \'kaùdə'heləkəs, 'kȯdə'heləsəs\ *n, pl* **cau·dae helicis** \'kaù,dī-, 'kȯ,dē-\ [NL, lit., tail of the helix] **:** the lower posterior part of the helix of the external ear

¹**cau·dal** \'kȯdᵊl\ *adj* [NL *caudalis*, fr. L *cauda* tail + *-alis* -al — more at COWARD] **1 :** constituting, belonging to, or relating to a tail ⟨~ appendage⟩ ⟨~ veins⟩ **2 :** situated in or directed toward the hind part of the body or the part from which the tail arises **:** POSTERIOR ⟨a ~ nerve⟩ ⟨the ~ end of the body⟩ — **cau·dal·ly** \-dᵊlē, -li\ *adv*

²**caudal** \"\ *n* -s **:** a caudal part (as a fin or scale)

caudal anesthesia *or* **caudal analgesia** *n* **:** loss of pain sensation below the umbilicus produced by injection of an anesthetic into the caudal portion of the spinal canal

caudal artery *n* **:** the portion of the dorsal aorta of a vertebrate that passes into the tail

caudal fin *n* **:** the terminal fin of a fish — called also *tail fin*; see FISH illustration

caudal peduncle *n* **:** the narrow region of the body of a fish immediately in front of the caudal fin

caudal vesicle *n* **:** the posterior part of certain larval tapeworms into which the scolex and neck may be retracted — compare CYSTICERCOID

cau·da·ta \kȯ'dād·ə, kaù'däd·ə\ *n pl, cap* [NL, fr. ML, neut. pl. of *caudatus* caudate] **:** an order of Amphibia containing the salamanders, newts, congo snakes, and related forms and having long bodies, long tails retained through life, short weak limbs, and feebly ossified crania

¹**cau·date** \'kȯ,dāt, *usu* -ād·+V\ *also* **cau·dat·ed** \-ād·əd\ *adj* [It & NL; It *caudato*, fr. ML (& NL) *caudatus*, fr. L *cauda* tail + *-atus* -ate — more at COWARD] **:** having a tail or a taillike appendage or termination **:** TAILED — **cau·da·tion** \kȯ'dāshən\ *n* -s

²**caudate** \"\ *n* -s [NL *Caudata*] **:** one of the Caudata **:** a tailed amphibian

caudate lobe *n* **:** a lobe of the liver bounded on the right by the inferior vena cava, on the left by the fissure of the ductus venosus, and connected with the right lobe by a narrow prolongation

caudate nucleus *or* **caudate** *n* **:** a mass of gray matter in the corpus striatum of the brain forming part of the floor of the lateral ventricle and separated from the lenticular nucleus by the internal capsule

cau·da·to·len·tic·u·lar \kȯ¦dād·(,)ō,len¦tikyələ(r)\ *adj* [¹*Caudate* + *-o-* + *lenticular*] **:** relating to the caudate and lenticular nuclei of the corpus striatum

cau·dex \'kȯ,deks\ *n, pl* **caudi·ces** \-,də,sēz\ *or* **caudex·es** \-,deksəz\ [L — more at CODE] **:** the main axis including both stem and root of a plant: **a :** the stem of a palm or tree fern covered with persistent leaf bases or marked with their scars **b :** the woody base of a perennial plant

caudi- — see CAUD-

cau·di·cle \'kȯdəkəl\ *n* -s [prob. fr. NL *caudicula*, dim. of L *cauda* tail — more at COWARD] **:** the slender stalklike appendage of the pollen masses in orchids

cau·di·form \'kȯdə,fȯrm\ *adj* [*caud-* + *-form*] **:** having the shape of a tail

cau·di·llis·mo \,kaùt͟hē(l)'yēz(,)mō\ *n* -s [Sp, fr. *caudillo* + *-ismo* -ism] **:** the doctrine or practice of a caudillo **:** DICTATORSHIP

cau·di·llo \kaù't͟hē(l)(,)yō\ *n* -s [Sp, fr. LL *capitellum* small head — more at CADET] **:** a military leader (as in a Latin-American country) usu. of guerrilla or irregular forces loyal to him personally; *specif* **:** a political boss with his own military following

¹**cau·dle** \'kȯdᵊl\ *n* -s [ME *caudel*, fr. ONF, fr. *caud-, caut* warm, fr. L *caldus, calidus* warm — more at CALDRON] **:** a drink made usu. of warm ale or wine mixed with bread or gruel, eggs, sugar, and spices and often taken medicinally

²**caudle** \"\ *vt* **caudled; caudled; caudling** \-d(ᵊ)liŋ\ **caudles** **:** to serve a caudle to

caudle cup *n* **:** a small 2-handled cup having a bulbous body, contracted neck, and usu. a top, made typically of silver, and esp. popular in the late 17th century

caudle of hempseed *obs* **:** a hangman's rope

caudo- — see CAUD-

cauff \'kȯf\ *Scot var of* CHAFF

caugh·na·wa·ga \,kägnə'wägə\ *n* -s *cap* [Mohawk *Gahnawa'ge*, lit., at the rapids] **:** a native or inhabitant of Caughnawaga, a settlement founded by the French near Montreal, Canada, for Mohawk converts to Christianity

¹**caught** *past of* CATCH

²**caught** *past part of* CATCH — **caught dead :** publicly known even though dead and impervious to criticism **:** DISCOVERED, FOUND ⟨I wouldn't be *caught dead* wearing that shirt⟩ — **caught short 1 :** taken unawares **:** found ill-prepared, inadequately equipped, or poorly supplied ⟨he was *caught short* by the blunt question⟩ **2 :** inopportunely seized with a need to relieve oneself

³**caught** *adj* [²*caught*] **:** PREGNANT — often used in the phrase *get caught*

¹**cauk** \'kȯk, -åk-\ *n* -s [ME (northern dial.) *calke*, fr. OE (northern dial.) *calc* (in other dialects *cealc*) — more at CHALK] *dial Brit* **:** CHALK, LIMESTONE

²**cauk** \"\ *vt* -ED/-ING/-S *Scot* **:** CHALK

³**cauk** \"\ *dial Brit var of* ¹CAWK

⁴**cauk** \'käk, -ók-\ *vt* -ED/-ING/-S [prob. alter. of *cock* (to cog)] **:** to secure by a tenon

¹**caul** \'kȯl\ *n* -s [ME *calle*, fr. MF *cale*, perh. back-formation fr. *calotte* skullcap] **1 :** a covering network: **a** *archaic* **:** a woman's netted close-fitting cap **b** *obs* **:** a net used to enwrap **c** *obs* **:** a net foundation for a wig **d :** the network at the back of a woman's cap **2 :** an enclosing or investing membrane: **a :** GREATER OMENTUM **b :** the inner fetal membrane of higher vertebrates esp. when unruptured or covering the head at birth **:** AMNION

²**caul** \"\ *n* -s [F *cale* chock, shim, modif. of G *keil* wedge, fr. OHG *kīl*; akin to OE *cīth* sprout, *cīnan* to gape, crack, OHG *kīmo* sprout, *kīnan* to sprout, ON *kīll* inlet, Goth *keinan* to germinate, sprout, Lith *žydėti* to bloom] **:** a usu. heated sheet of metal or other material used to equalize pressure in making plywood and in shaping veneer to a surface

³**caul** \"\ *var of* CAWL

caul- *or* **cauli-** *or* **caulo-** *comb form* [*cauli-* fr. L *caulis*; *caul-, caulo-* fr. NL, fr. Gk. *kaul-, kaulo-*, fr. *kaulos* — more at HOLE] **:** stem **:** stalk ⟨*caul*ome⟩ ⟨*cauli*flory⟩

¹**cauld** \'kål(d), -ō-\ *chiefly Scot var of* COLD

²**cauld** \"\ *n* -s [origin unknown] *chiefly Scot* **:** WEIR

cauld·rife \'kål(d)rif, -ōl-, -,(d)rīf\ *adj* [¹*cauld* + *rife*] **1** *Scot* **a :** COLD, CHILLING **b :** susceptible to cold **2** *Scot, of a person* **:** COLD, CHEERLESS

caul·dron \'kȯldrən\ *var of* CALDRON

cauldron subsidence *n* **:** the sinking of part of the roof of a magma chamber usu. involving downward movement along circumferential faults

cau·ler·pa \kȯ'lərpə\ *n, cap* [NL, fr. *caul-* + *-erpa* (fr. Gk *herpein* to creep) — more at SERPENT] **:** a genus (coextensive with the family Caulerpaceae) of green algae of the order Siphonales occurring on tropical sea bottoms, having a thallus composed of a single coenocyte differentiated into a long creeping stemlike portion that forms rhizoids below and variously shaped foliose expansions above, and reproducing asexually by detached vegetative shoots — **cau·ler·pa·ceous** \¦kȯ(,)lər¦pāshəs\ *adj*

cau·les·cent \(')kȯ¦lesᵊnt\ *adj* [ISV *caul-* + *-escent*; orig. formed in F] *bot* **:** having a stem evident above ground — opposed to *acaulescent*

caul fat *n* [¹*caul*] **:** fat from the visceral cavity of a slaughtered animal

cauli- — see CAUL-

cau·li·cle \'kȯləkəl\ *n* -s [L *cauliculus*, dim. of *caulis* stem, stalk — more at COLE] **:** a rudimentary stem; *specif* **:** the stem of an embryo or young seedling

cau·li·cole \'kȯlə,kōl\ *also* **cau·li·co·lo** \kaù'lēkə,lō\ *n, pl* **cau·li·coles** \-,kōlz\ *or* **cau·li·co·li** \-,kə,lē\ [F & It; F *caulicole*, fr. It *caulicolo*, fr. L *cauliculus*, lit., little stalk, dim. of *caulis* stalk — more at HOLE] **:** one of the eight stalks rising out of the leafage in a Corinthian capital and ending in leaves that support the volutes

cau·lic·o·lous \(')kȯ¦likələs\ *adj* [ISV *caul-* + *-colous*; prob. orig. formed as F *caulicole*] **:** growing on the stems of other plants ⟨many fungi are ~⟩

cau·li·cule \'kȯlə,kyül\ *n* -s [L *cauliculus*] **:** CAULICLE

cau·li·flo·rous \¦kȯlə¦flōrəs\ *adj* [ISV *caul-* + *-florous*] **:** producing flowers from the main stem or older branches ⟨the redbud, chocolate tree, and many tropical trees are ~⟩ — **cau·li·flo·ry** \'==,rē\ *n* -ES

¹**cau·li·flow·er** \'kȯlə, 'käl-, -lē *also* 'kəl-+,-\ *n* -s *often attrib* [alter. (influenced by L *caulis* cabbage and E *flower*) of earlier *coleflorie*, modif. of It *caoli fiori*, pl. of *cavolfiore*, lit., cabbage flower, fr. *cavolo* cabbage (fr. LL *caulus*, alter. of L *caulis*) + *fiore* flower, fr. L *flor-, flos* — more at COLE, FLOWER] **1 :** a garden plant (*Brassica oleracea botrytis*) that is closely related to the cabbage and is grown for its edible head of greatly modified and compacted white or purplish undeveloped flowers — see BROCCOLI **2 :** the flower cluster of the cauliflower used as a vegetable **3 :** something resembling a cauliflower; *esp* **:** a cloud shaped like a cauliflower cluster

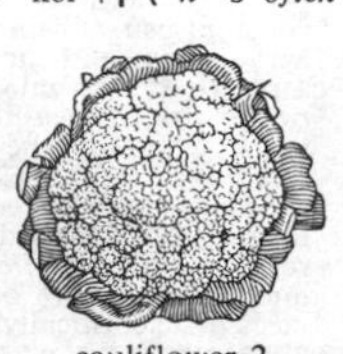
cauliflower 2

²**cauliflower** \"\ *vt* -ED/-ING/-S **:** to disfigure (an ear) esp. by repeated blows in boxing

cauliflower disease *n* **1 :** an eelworm disease of the strawberry characterized by clustered, malformed, and puckered leaves **2 :** a disease of the strawberry and other plants caused by a bacterium (*Corynebacterium fascians*)

cauliflower ear *n* **:** an ear deformed from injury (as by repeated blows in boxing) and excessive growth of reparative tissue

cauliflower growth *n* **:** a wartlike growth of tissue that is usu. a condyloma but sometimes a stage of cancer and resembles a cauliflower

cau·line \'kȯ,līn\ *adj* [prob. fr. NL *caulinus*, fr. L *caulis* stem + *-inus* -ine] *bot* **:** belonging to or growing on a stem; *specif* **:** growing on the upper portion of a stem — contrasted with *radical*

cauline bundle *n* **:** a vascular bundle remaining within a stem and having no connection with leaves — compare COMMON BUNDLE

¹**caulk** *or* **calk** \'kȯk\ *vb* -ED/-ING/-S [ME *caulken, calken*, fr. ONF *cauquer* to trample, fr. L *calcare*, fr. *calc-, calx* heel — more at CALK] *vt* **1 a :** to stop up and make watertight the seams of (a boat or ship) by driving in tarred oakum or cotton twist or wicking and filling up with a waterproofing compound **b :** to stop up and make tight against leakage (as the seams of a boat, the cracks in a window frame, or the joints of a pipe) by forcing in a sealing substance **c :** to tighten (a joint formed by overlapping or abutting metal plates) by driving the edge of one plate into closer contact with the surface of the other or by driving the edges of abutting plates together **2 :** to shape (the insole of a shoe) closely to the surface contours of the sole of the foot **~** *vi, slang* **:** to take a nap **:** SLEEP — used with *off*

²**caulk** *or* **calk** \"\ *n* -s [origin unknown] *slang* **:** a short sleep **:** NAP

³**caulk** *var of* CALK

caulk·en *var of* CALKIN

caulk·er *or* **calk·er** \'kȯkə(r)\ *n* -s [ME *calker*, fr. *calken* + *-er*] **1 :** a worker who forces sealing matter into seams or joints with a caulking tool to make them watertight **2 :** a tool for caulking; *specif* **:** a caulking iron operated by compressed air **3** *slang* **:** a drink of liquor **:** DRAM

caulking *or* **calking** *n* -s [ME *calking*, fr. gerund of *calken*] **1 :** the action of one that caulks **2 :** the material used to caulk

caulking iron *also* **caulking chisel** *or* **caulking tool** *n* **:** a chisellike tool used for caulking seams or joints; *specif* **:** a chisellike tool with a concave edge for receiving a caulking yarn and driving it into a seam

caulking mallet *n* **:** a wooden mallet with a very long head used for driving a caulking iron

caulk weld *n* **:** a weld that seals a joint

caulk-weld \'=¦=\ *vt* **:** to unite by a caulk weld

caulo- — see CAUL-

cau·lo·bac·ter \'kȯlō,baktə(r)\ *n, cap* [NL, fr. *caul-* + *-bacter*] **:** a genus (the type of the family Caulobacteraceae) of gram-negative aquatic bacteria that are motile by polar flagella when young but later fixed to the substrate by a stalk and that multiply by transverse binary fission — **cau·lo·bac·te·ri·um** \¦==,='tirēəm\ *n*

cau·lo·bac·te·ra·ce·ae \¦==,=,tirə'āsē,ē\ *n pl, cap* [NL, fr. *Caulobacter*, type genus + *-aceae*] **:** a family of nonfilamentous fresh-water aquatic bacteria that form stalks or zoogleal masses of ferric hydroxide or gum and that are now usu. placed in the order Pseudomonadales though they are sometimes esp. in former classifications included in Enbacteriales or isolated in a separate order — see CAULOBACTER, CAULOBACTERALES

cau·lo·bac·te·ra·les \¦==,=tə'rā(,)lēz\ *n pl, cap* [NL, fr. *Caulobacter* + *-ales*] *in some classifications* **:** an order of bacteria coextensive with the family Caulobacteraceae

cau·lo·bac·te·ri·a·les \¦==,=,tirē'ā(,)lēz\ [NL, fr. *Caulobacter* + *-i-* + *-ales*] *syn of* CAULOBACTERALES

cau·lo·ca·line \,==kā,lēn\ *n* -s [*caul-* + *caline*] **:** a hormone or hormonelike factor distinct from auxin that is held to play a role in the formation of plant stems — compare RHIZOCALINE

cau·lo·car·pic \¦==¦kärpik\ *also* **cau·lo·car·pous** \-pəs\ *adj* [ISV *caul-* + *-carpic* or *-carpous*] **:** having stems that bear flowers and fruit year after year

cau·loid \'kȯ,lȯid\ *adj* [*caul-* + *-oid*] **:** resembling a stem

cauloid theory *n* **:** a theory of the origin of the sporophyte of vascular plants that proposes that the plant body has been differentiated from a primeval axis or stem — compare PROTOCORM THEORY

cau·lo·lat·i·lus \,=='lad·ᵊləs\ *n, cap* [NL, fr. *caul-* + *latilus*, fr. L *latus* broad] **:** a genus of percoid fishes (family Branchiostegidae) including the ocean whitefish and other important food fishes — compare BLANQUILLO

cau·lome \'kȯ,lōm\ *n* -s [ISV *caul-* + *-ome*; prob. orig. formed as G *kaulom*] **:** a stem structure or stem axis of a plant — **cau·lo·mic** \(')kȯ¦lōmik, -äm-\ *adj*

cau·lo·phyl·line \,=='fi,lēn, -lən\ *n* -s [NL *Caulophyllum* + E *-ine*] **:** a crystalline alkaloid $C_{12}H_{16}N_2O$ found in the root of the blue cohosh; methyl-cytisine

cau·lo·phyl·lum \,=='=ləm\ *n, cap* [NL, fr. *caul-* + *-phyllum*] **:** a genus of herbs (family Berberidaceae) of eastern Asia and the eastern U.S. having a single sessile triternate basal leaf and a raceme of yellowish flowers succeeded by blue berries — see BLUE COHOSH

cau·lop·ter·is \kȯ'läptərəs\ *n* [NL, fr. *caul-* + *-pteris*] **1** *cap* **:** a genus of fossil tree ferns (family Marattiaceae) **2** *pl* **caulopter·es** \-,rēz\ **:** any fossil trunk of certain tree ferns

caulp *n* -s [ME *cawp*, prob. modif. of ScGael *colpach* heifer] **:** a fee or gift formerly given to the head of a Scottish clan for his maintenance and protection or exacted by him out of one's estate after death

cauls *pl of* CAUL

caup \'käp, -ó-\ *var of* ⁴CAP

cauponate *vt* -ED/-ING/-S [L *cauponatus*, past part. of *cauponari*, fr. *caupon-, caupo* huckster, innkeeper + *-atus* -ate — more at CHEAP] *obs* **:** to traffic in **:** HAWK

cau·qui \'kaù(,)kē\ *n, pl* **cauqui** *or* **cauquis** *usu cap* [Sp, of AmerInd origin] **1 a :** an Indian people of central Peru **b :** a member of such people **2 :** the language of the Cauqui

caure \'kär, -ó-\ *n pl* [alter. of (assumed) ME *calver*, fr. OE *calfur, cealfru*, pl. of *cealf* calf] *Scot* **:** CALVES

cauri *var of* CHOWRIE

cau·sa \'kaùsə, -,zä,-,sä,-,zə; 'kȯzə\ *n, pl* **cau·sae** \'kaù,sī, -,zī; 'kȯ,zē\ [L — more at CAUSE] **:** CAUSE — used in various Latin phrases

caus·a·ble \'kȯzəbəl\ *adj* **:** capable of being caused

¹**caus·al** \'kȯzəl\ *adj* [LL *causalis*, fr. L *causa* + *-alis* -al — more at CAUSE] **1 :** expressing or indicating cause **:** CAUSATIVE ⟨a ~ conjunction⟩ **2 :** of, relating to, or dealing with a cause ⟨the ~ part of the exposition⟩ **3 a :** constituting or acting as a cause ⟨whether any one of the factors is so predominant

that it is the ~ force —John Dewey⟩ **b :** containing or involving cause or a cause **:** marked by cause and effect ⟨the relationship . . . was not one of ~ antecedence so much as one of analogous growth —H.O.Taylor⟩ **c :** arising from a cause **:** ensuing according to cause ⟨a ~ development⟩ — **caus·al·ly** \-əlē, -li\ *adv*

²causal \"\ *n* -s **:** a causal word or form

cau·sal·gia \kȯ'zalj(ē)ə, -'sa-\ *n* -s [NL, fr. Gk *kausos* fever + NL *-algia*; akin to Gk *kaiein* to burn — more at CAUSTIC] **:** a constant usu. burning pain resulting from injury to a peripheral nerve — **cau·sal·gic** \(')⸗;⸗⸗\ *adj*

cau·sal·i·ty \kȯ'zalәd·ē, -әtē, -i\ *n* -ES [F *causalité*, fr. MF, fr. *causal* (fr. LL *causalis*) + *-ité* -ity] **1 :** a causal quality or agency ⟨the ~ of the divine mind —William Whewell⟩ **2 :** the relation of cause and effect or between certain regularly correlated events or phenomena: as **a :** a necessary connection or intrinsic bond embedded in the very nature of things **b :** the regular sequence of events that the mind connects from habit, innate disposition, or experience or that it correlates on the basis of scientifically elaborated theories

causal necessity *n* **:** NECESSITY 1d(2)

cau·sa·tion \kȯ'zāshәn\ *n* -s [ML *causation-, causatio*, fr. *causatus* (past part. of *causare* to cause, fr. L *causa*) + L *-ion-, -io* -ion] **1 a :** the act or process of causing ⟨scientific ~ means that nothing happens arbitrarily but always as the result of a definite chain of causes —H.P.Becker⟩ **b :** the act or agency by which an effect is produced ⟨in a complex situation ~ is likely to be multiple —W.O.Aydelotte⟩ **2 :** the relation of cause and effect **:** CAUSALITY ⟨the law of ~ . . . is but the familiar truth that invariability of succession is found by observation to obtain between every fact in nature and some other fact which has preceded it —J.S.Mill⟩

cau·sa·tion·al \-shәn°l, -shnәl\ *adj* **:** of or relating to causes, causation, or the doctrine of causation

cau·sa·tion·ism \-shә,nizәm\ *n* -s **:** the principle or law of universal causation

cau·sa·tion·ist \-sh(ә)nәst\ *n* -s **:** a believer in causationism

¹caus·a·tive \'kȯzәd·iv, -әtiv\ *adj* [ME, fr. LL *causativus*, fr. L *causa* + *-atus* -ate + *-ivus* -ive] **1 :** effective or operating as a cause or agent **:** CAUSING ⟨poverty as a ~ factor in crime⟩ **2** *of a linguistic form or set of linguistic forms* **:** expressing cause ⟨~ case⟩ ⟨~ mood⟩; *specif* **:** indicating that the subject of a verb causes an act to be performed or a condition to come into being ⟨the ~ verb *fell*, meaning "cause to fall"⟩ ⟨the ~ suffix *-en* in *darken*, meaning "cause to be dark"⟩ — **caus·a·tive·ly** *adv* — **caus·a·tiv·i·ty** \,kȯzә'tivәd·ē, -әtē, -i\ *n* -ES

²causative \"\ *n* -s **:** a causative word or form

cau·sa·tum \kaủ'zäd·әm, kȯ'zād·-\ *n, pl* **causa·ta** \-d·ә\ [ML, neut. of *causatus*, past part. of *causare* to cause — more at CAUSATION] **:** something that is caused **:** EFFECT

¹cause \'kȯz\ *n* -s [ME, fr. OF, fr. L *causa*; perh. akin to L *cudere* to beat — more at HEW] **1 a :** a person, thing, fact, or condition that brings about an effect or that produces or calls forth a resultant action or state ⟨it should be obvious that it is the conditions producing the end effects which must be regarded as the efficient ~*s* of them —M.F.A.Montagu⟩ ⟨trying to find the ~ of the accident⟩ **b :** a reason or motive for an action or condition ⟨a ~ for celebrating⟩ ⟨~ for regret⟩ **c :** a good or adequate reason **:** a sufficient activating factor ⟨an employee discharged for ~⟩ **2 a** (1) **:** a ground of legal action (2) **:** a legal process (as a suit or action in court) by which a party endeavors to obtain his claim or what he regards as his right **:** CASE **b :** the presupposition or underlying fact of a transaction in civil law **3 a :** something that occasions or effects a result **:** the necessary antecedent of an effect **:** something that determines any motion or change or produces a phenomenon — see EFFICIENT CAUSE, FINAL CAUSE, FORMAL CAUSE, MATERIAL CAUSE; FIRST CAUSE; IMMANENT CAUSE, TRANSIENT CAUSE; OCCASIONAL CAUSE **b :** an event or set of events that on the basis of scientific methods and laws has been established as the invariant antecedent or concomitant necessary for the occurrence of another event or set of events — compare REGULARITY THEORY **4 :** a charge or accusation brought against one ⟨what was thy ~? adultery? —Shak.⟩ **5 a** *now dial* **:** a matter occupying one's attention **:** CONCERN, AFFAIR, PURSUIT ⟨now to our French ~*s* —Shak.⟩ **b** *obs* **:** INTENT, PURPOSE, END — see FINAL CAUSE **6 :** a principle or movement supported militantly or zealously **:** a belief advocated or upheld ⟨God befriend us, as our ~ is just —Shak.⟩ ⟨the insurgents' ~⟩ ⟨he served the ~ of truth less devotedly than the ~ of party —V.L.Parrington⟩ **7** *obs* **:** DISEASE

syn REASON, DETERMINANT, OCCASION, ANTECEDENT: CAUSE indicates a condition or circumstance or combination of conditions and circumstances that effectively and inevitably calls forth an issue, effect, or result or that materially aids in that calling forth ⟨there was more in it than a struggle for wages. The unrest in the towns had deeper *causes* —G.M.Trevelyan⟩ REASON is often interchangeable with CAUSE, but it may add to CAUSE notions of that which explains, clarifies, or justifies or that which suggests a conditioning by human action, consideration, or thought ⟨they admire the rich and titled for the good *reason* that the rich and titled are themselves —Aldous Huxley⟩ ⟨the *reason* why the distinguished chairman of the committee feels that the conference report should not be debated —*Congressional Record*⟩ DETERMINANT indicates that factor which determines or shapes the nature of an outcome, issue, or result rather than indicating that which calls it forth or causes it ⟨so habituated have most persons become to believing . . . that moral forces are the ultimate *determinants* of the rise and fall of all human societies —John Dewey⟩ ⟨asserts that the final *determinant* of the lawyer's thought and activity is now the maxim of the best fee —R.D.Mack⟩ OCCASION refers to a time or situation at which underlying causes may be manifested or activated or, loosely, to an immediate or ostensible factor ⟨in 1837 Baxley became the *occasion*, if not the cause, of the temporary disruption of the University of Maryland Medical School —C.R.Bardeen⟩ ⟨there exists, not as the *occasion* of this war but as the cause of a series of wars in which we are engaged, a desire, shared by all peoples, to redefine the concepts of freedom and order —*Times Lit. Supp.*⟩ ANTECEDENT refers to that which has preceded or gone before or which may or may not be a cause or determinant of something following ⟨it is certainly true that these twelfth-century windows break the French tradition. They had no *antecedent* and no fit succession —Henry Adams⟩ ⟨the *antecedents* of emperor worship lay far back in history —John Buchan⟩

²cause \"\ *vt* -ED/-ING/-S [ME *causen*, prob. fr. *cause*, n.] **1 :** to serve as cause or occasion of **:** bring into existence **:** MAKE ⟨careless driving ~*s* accidents⟩ ⟨trying to find what *caused* the fire⟩ ⟨~ the water to flow into the new channel⟩ **2 :** to effect by command, authority, or force ⟨the president *caused* the ambassador to protest⟩

'cause \(')kȯz, (;)kәz\ *conj* [by shortening] **:** BECAUSE

cause cé·lè·bre \¦kȯzsā'lebr(ᵊ), ¦kōz-, -eb(rә)\ *n, pl* **causes célèbres** \-br(ᵊ),-b(rәz)\ [F] **1 :** a celebrated legal case **:** a case whose revelations excite widespread interest **2 :** a notorious incident or episode **:** a situation attracting much attention ⟨the paper made the controversy a *cause célèbre* —S.H. Adams⟩

cause·less \'kȯzlәs\ *adj* **1 :** having no cause or no apparent cause **:** FORTUITOUS **:** inexplicable by natural causes ⟨a ~ miracle⟩ **2 :** having no justifying reason or motive ⟨a senseless, ~ murder⟩ ⟨~ war that never had an aim —William Morris⟩ — **cause·less·ly** *adv*

cause list *n* **:** a legal calendar

cause of action : the ground on which the plaintiff's case is based

caus·er \'kȯzә(r)\ *n* -s **:** one that causes ⟨a ~ of disease⟩

cau·se·rie \,kōz(ә)'rē, 'kōzә,rē\ *n* -s [F, fr. *causer* to chat, fr. L *causari* to plead, discuss, debate, fr. *causa* cause — more at CAUSE] **1 :** an informal light conversation **:** CHAT **2 :** a short familiar composition in informal style ⟨~*s* and light sketches⟩

cau·seur \kō'zәr\ *n* -s [F, fr. *causer* + *-eur* -or] **:** a fluent and often witty talker or conversationalist

cau·seuse \kō'zә(r)z, -zǣz\ *n* -s [F, fr. lit., talkative woman, fem. of *causeur*] **:** a small sofa for two persons **:** TÊTE-À-TÊTE

¹cause·way \'kȯz,wā\ *n* [alter. of ME *cauciwey*, fr. *cauci*, *cause* causey + *wey* way — more at WAY] **1 :** a way of access or raised road typically across marshland or water ⟨for access to the mainland they depended on a ~, flooded at high tide —F.M.Stenton⟩ **2 :** CAUSEY; *esp* **:** a paved or corduroy highway ⟨the Roman ~*s* of early Britain⟩

²causeway \"\ *vt* -ED/-ING/-S **1 :** to pave with cobblestones or pebbles ⟨the ~*ed* streets of the village⟩ **2 :** to provide with a causeway **:** make a causeway through or over ⟨a ~*ed* swamp⟩

¹cau·sey \'kȯzē, *dial Brit also* -ōs| *or* |ā *or* |ә\ *n* -s [ME *cauci*, *cause*, fr. ONF *caucie, cauciée*, fr. ML *calciata* paved highway, fr. *calciata*, fem. of *calciatus* paved with limestone, fr. L *calc-, calx* limestone, lime + *-atus* -ate — more at CHALK] **1** *obs* **:** a mound retaining water **:** an earth dam **2 :** a raised way of access (as a road or sidewalk) typically across wet land or water **:** CAUSEWAY **3 a** *dial* **:** a paved way (as a street or sidewalk) **b** *dial Brit* **:** an area (as part of a farmyard) paved with cobblestones **4** *obs* **:** HIGHWAY; *esp* **:** a highway of or like those of ancient Roman construction in Britain

²causey \"\ *vt* -ED/-ING/-S *dial* **:** to pave esp. with stones or logs

causing *pres part of* CAUSE

causse \'kōs\ *n* -s [F, fr. Prov, fr. (assumed) VL *calcinus* of limestone, fr. L *calc-, calx* + *-inus* -ine] **:** a small limestone plateau deeply pitted with sinkholes common in south-central France

¹caus·tic \'kȯstik, -ēk\ *adj* [L *causticus*, fr. Gk *kaustikos*, fr. *kaustos* (verbal of *kaiein* to burn) + *-ikos* -ic; akin to Lith *kulė* smut of plants] **1 :** capable of destroying the texture of anything or eating away its substance by chemical action **:** CORROSIVE: as **a :** capable of destroying animal or other organic tissue ⟨silver nitrate and sulfuric acid are ~ agents⟩ **b :** strongly alkaline ⟨~ liquors⟩ ⟨~ lyes⟩ **2 :** marked by or indicative of tart sharpness; *specif* **:** characterized by incisive wit ⟨a ~ reply⟩ ⟨a bitter, ~, and backbiting humor —Sir Walter Scott⟩ ⟨a ~ and disillusioned satirist, trenchant, arrogant —J.L.Lowes⟩ — **caus·ti·cal·ly** \-tәk(ә)lē, -ēk-, -li\ *or* **caus·tic·ly** \-klē, -kli\ *adv* — **caus·tic·ness** \-tiknәs, -tēk-\ *n* -ES

²caustic \"\ *n* -s **1 :** a caustic agent: as **a :** a substance or means that can burn, corrode, or destroy animal or other organic tissue by chemical action **:** ESCHAROTIC **b :** CAUSTIC ALKALI **2 a :** CAUSTIC CURVE **b :** CAUSTIC SURFACE

caustic alcohol *n* **:** SODIUM ETHOXIDE

caustic alkali *n* **:** a strong corrosive alkali; *esp* **:** a hydroxide of an alkali metal (as caustic soda or caustic potash)

caustic ammonia *n* **:** ammonia esp. in water solution

caustic baryta *n* **:** BARIUM HYDROXIDE — used esp. commercially

caustic creeper *n* [so called fr. the caustic quality of fresh latex] **:** an Australian euphorbia (*Euphorbia drummondii*) — called also *milk plant*

caustic curve *n* **:** a plane section through the cusp of a caustic surface that is visible on a plane surface where light has been reflected from a smooth concave surface (as the inside of a metal ring)

caus·tic·i·ty \kȯ'stisәd·ē, -әtē, -i\ *n* -ES [F *causticité*, fr. L *causticus* + F *-ité* -ity] **1 :** the quality or state of being caustic **:** CORROSIVENESS ⟨the ~ of potash⟩ **2 :** dry tart sharpness esp. of biting wit ⟨the ~ of his retort⟩

caus·ti·ci·za·tion \,kȯstәsә'zāshәn, -,sī'z-\ *n* -s **:** the process of causticizing

caus·ti·cize \'kȯstә,sīz\ *vt* -ED/-ING/-S [*caustic* + *-ize*] **1 :** to make caustic; *esp* **:** to convert (alkaline carbonate) into a hydroxide by the use of lime **2 :** to treat (textiles) with caustic alkali — compare MERCERIZE

caus·ti·ciz·er \-zә(r)\ *n* -s **1 :** a chemical worker who makes caustic soda by controlling chemical reactions of soda ash and milk of lime in a dissolving tank and a reactor **2 :** one who makes caustic liquor for digesting wood chips into pulp by mixing and heating lime, soda ash, and water in a wooden vat

caustic lime *n* **:** LIME 2a

caustic man *or* **caustic mixer** *n* [²*caustic*] **:** a worker who mixes caustic-soda solution for use in cloth-finishing or yarn-finishing processes

caustic potash *n* **:** POTASSIUM HYDROXIDE — used esp. commercially

caustic soda *n* **:** SODIUM HYDROXIDE — used esp. commercially

caustic surface *n* **:** the cusped surface of maximum brightness that is sometimes observed when light is reflected or refracted by a curved mirror or interface and is geometrically the envelope of the system of reflected or refracted rays

caustic vine *or* **caustic plant** *n* **:** an Australian vine (*Sarcostemma australe*) of the family Asclepiadaceae that is poisonous to cattle

cau·sus \'kȯzәs, -ōsәs\ *n, cap* [NL, fr. Gk *kausos* fever, heat, fr. *kaiein* to burn — more at CAUSTIC] **:** a genus of nocturnal venomous African snakes (family Viperidae) comprising the night adders

cautel *n* -s [ME, fr. MF *cautele*, fr. L *cautela* caution, precaution, fr. *cautus*, past part. of *cavēre* to be on one's guard — more at SHOW] **1** *obs* **a :** TRICK **b :** TRICKERY ⟨no soil nor ~ doth besmirch the virtue of his will —Shak.⟩ **2** *obs* **a :** CAUTION **b :** PRECAUTION

cautelous *adj* [ME, fr. MF *cauteleux, cautileus*, fr. *cautele* + *-eux, -eus* -ous] **1** *archaic* **:** CRAFTY, CUNNING **2** *archaic* **:** CAUTIOUS, WARY — **cautelously** *adv, archaic*

cau·ter \'kȯd·ә(r)\ *n* -s [earlier *cautere*, fr. MF *cautère*, fr. L *cauterium* — more at CAUTERY] **:** an iron for cauterizing **:** CAUTERY

¹cau·ter·ant \'kȯd·әrәnt\ *n* -s [*cauter-* + *-ant*] **:** a cauterizing substance

²cauterant \"\ *adj* **:** CAUTERIZING

cau·ter·i·za·tion \,kȯd·әrә'zāshәn, -ōtәr-, -,rī'z-\ *n* -s [MF *cautérisation*, fr. *cautériser* + *-ation*] **1 :** the act of searing abnormal or injured tissue by a cautery **2 :** the effect of cauterization

cau·ter·ize \'kȯd·ә,rīz, -ōtә-\ *vt* -ED/-ING/-S [MF *cautériser*, fr. LL *cauterizare* to brand, fr. L *cauterium* + LL *-izare* -ize] **1 :** to burn or sear with a cautery or caustic ⟨~ a wound⟩ **2** *obs* **:** BRAND **3 :** to make insensible **:** DEADEN

cau·tery \-әrē, -ri\ *n* -ES [L *cauterium* cautery, branding iron, fr. Gk *kautērion* branding iron, fr. *kaiein* to burn — more at CAUSTIC] **1 :** a burning or searing (as of abnormal or injured tissue) with a hot iron or caustic **2 :** the hot iron, caustic, or other agent used to burn, sear, or destroy tissue

cau·tio \'kȯshē,ō, 'kaủd·ē,ō\ *n, pl* **cauti·o·nes** \-shē'ō,nēz, -d·ē'ō,nās\ [L] *Roman, Scots, & civil law* **:** an oral or written agreement to indemnify **:** GUARANTY: **a :** a written assurance given as evidence of the receipt of money or as an acknowledgment of the making of a promise or of an existing state of affairs **b :** an agreement by one furnishing security, a pledge, or a mortgage **c :** an agreement often imposed by a judge or magistrate whereby one guarantees to protect another from loss or harm caused by the guarantor or a third person for whom the guarantor is responsible or whereby one guarantees payment or performance of an obligation of another

¹cau·tion \'kȯshәn\ *n* -s [ME *caucioun*, fr. OF *caution*, fr. L *caution-, cautio*, fr. *cautus* (past part. of *cavēre* to be on one's guard) + *-ion-, -io* -ion — more at SHOW] **1 a :** security for the performance of an obligation (as bail, a guarantee, or a pledge) **b :** the person giving such security **:** SURETY — called also *cautionary* **2** *obs* **:** a contingent provision **:** RESERVATION, SAVING CLAUSE ⟨with the ~ that the procedure be found legal⟩ **3 :** a warning or admonishment esp. in counseling vigilance, due attention or consideration, safety, or reservation ⟨the first ~ which we shall do well to bear in mind is that religion is not always true or good —W.R.Inge⟩ **4 :** the action of taking heed **:** PRECAUTION ⟨a surgeon taking the ~ of sterilizing his equipment⟩ **5 :** heedful prudent forethought to minimize risk or danger **:** provident care about the results of an action or course **:** careful avoidance of undue risk **:** reserve in acceptance ⟨my dear Percy's wonderful ~ . . . a thing that no mere reckless woman can hope to emulate —Rose Macaulay⟩ ⟨a difficult climb, safe but requiring ~ —*Amer. Guide Series: Calif.*⟩ **6 :** a preparatory warning of a maneuver or direction given prior to a decisive command (as *forward* preceding the command *march*) **7 a :** one that arouses alarm or astonishment or commands attention or interest **:** an extreme or grotesque example ⟨a fun-loving life of the party, a real ~⟩ **b :** an incident or example that startles and may serve as a check, admonition, or incentive ⟨the way he drove was a ~⟩

²caution \"\ *vt* **cautioned**; **cautioned**; **cautioning** \-sh(ә)niŋ\ **cautions :** to advise caution to **:** admonish or put on guard typically against danger, carelessness, imprudence, or excess ⟨we . . . while experience ~*s* us in vain, grasp seeming happiness and find it pain —William Cowper⟩ **syn** see WARN

¹cau·tion·ary \'kȯshә,nerē, -ri\ *adj* **1 :** of, relating to, or constituting a cautio or a caution **2** *archaic* **:** characterized by caution **:** CAUTIOUS, WARY **3 :** having the characteristics of, serving as, or offering a caution **:** ADMONITORY ⟨a warmly human story rather than the usual mere ~ tale intended to warn us —J.W.Krutch⟩

²cautionary \"\ *n* -ES **:** SECURITY, SURETY, CAUTION

cau·tion·er \'kȯsh(ә)nә(r)\ *n* -s [¹*caution* + *-er*] **:** SURETY, GUARANTOR

cautiones *pl of* CAUTIO

caution money *n* **:** money deposited by a student on entering a British university typically as security for possible damages (as to laboratory equipment)

cau·tion·ry \'kȯshәnrē\ *n* -ES [*caution* + *-ry*] **:** SURETYSHIP

cau·tious \'kȯshәs\ *adj* [¹*caution* + *-ous*] **:** marked by caution, by careful prudence in reducing risk or danger, and by reluctance to proceed or advance rashly ⟨~ in all his movements, always acting as if surrounded by invisible spies—W.H. Hudson †1922⟩ ⟨too ~ and too conservative to seek any revolutionary end —V.L.Parrington⟩

syn CIRCUMSPECT, WARY, CHARY, CALCULATING: CAUTIOUS may suggest limited objectives, prudence and forethought in proceeding, and fear of failure, danger, or harm ⟨meek, humble, timid persons . . . , who are *cautious*, prudent, and submissive, leave things very much as they find them —A.C. Benson⟩ ⟨we were *cautious* in keeping to windward of them, their sense of smell and hearing being . . . extremely acute —Herman Melville⟩ ⟨*cautious*, deliberate, methodical, he was in no danger, she felt, of plunging precipitately into marriage —Ellen Glasgow⟩ Without connoting fear, as CAUTIOUS does, CIRCUMSPECT stresses prudence, discretion, vigilance, and consideration of consequences ⟨the packages were examined by the police and found to contain bombs . . . for the next few days people in high station were very *circumspect* about undoing brown paper packages —F.L.Allen⟩ ⟨they do not live very happy lives, for they even more than the others are restricted in their movements, and they must live the most *circumspect* of lives —John Steinbeck⟩ WARY implies suspicious alertness to danger, difficulty, or loss, and cunning in escaping or evading it ⟨a *wary* old rabbit stealing out at dawn with quivering nose and oscillating ears —Kenneth Roberts⟩ ⟨we must always be *wary* of those who with sounding brass and tinkling cymbal preach the 'ism' of appeasement —F.D. Roosevelt⟩ ⟨girls like her . . . , wild and lost and lonely, full of distrust, letting him approach with a *wary* look in their eyes as if they would dash away before he could touch them —Katherine A. Porter⟩ CHARY stresses hesitancy, reserve, and discretion in proceeding ⟨the high priests were *chary* of adding tumult to tumult, and they did not dare to take action against Reb Jacob —Maurice Samuel⟩ ⟨contempt for the chattering fool runs through the *Edda*. Let a man be *chary* of speech —H.O.Taylor⟩ ⟨my business experience has taught me to be *chary* of committing anything of a confidential nature to any more concrete medium than speech —William Faulkner⟩ CALCULATING stresses very deliberate and careful planning ⟨Aunt Ella, ostensibly meek, confused, helpless, and self-effacing, has actually a steel core of *calculating* purposiveness and a genius for devious expedients; under the appearance of tender sisterly devotion she fights by methods of sly sabotage a lifelong duel —Wilson Follett⟩ Sometimes this word connotes not care and caution but a cold-blooded objectivity approaching disdain of and even cruelty to others ⟨that selfish and *calculating* principle has taken . . . the form of a national and racial egoism that has turned a continent into a shambles —J.L.Lowes⟩

cau·tious·ly *adv* **:** in a cautious manner

cau·tious·ness *n* -ES **:** the quality or state of being cautious

cautivo *var of* CATIVO

cav *abbr* **1** cavalier **2** cavalry **3** caveat **4** cavity

¹ca·va \'kävә, 'kā-,'kà-\ *n, pl* **ca·vae** \'kä,vē, 'kā-, -,vī; 'kā,vē\ **:** VENA CAVA — **ca·val** \-vәl\ *adj*

²cava *var of* KAVA

³cava *pl of* CAVUM

¹cav·al·cade \¦kavәl¦kād\ *n* -s [MF, ride on horseback, fr. OIt *cavalcata*, fr. *cavalcare* to go on horseback, fr. LL *caballicare*, fr. L *caballus* horse, nag; akin to Gk dial. (Black sea) *kaballeion* horse-drawn vehicle, OSlav *kobyla* horse; all perh. of eastern European origin; akin to the source of Finn *hepo* horse] **1 a :** a procession of riders or carriages **:** a company in procession **b :** a train, procession, or sequence of vehicles or ships **2 :** a dramatic sequence or pageant **:** PROCESSION, SERIES ⟨the ~ of years⟩ ⟨the ~ of scientific research⟩

²cavalcade \"\ *vi* -ED/-ING/-S **:** to take part in a cavalcade ⟨horsemen *cavalcading* along⟩

¹cav·a·lier \¦kavә¦li(ә)r, -iә\ *n* -s [MF, fr. OIt *cavaliere*, fr. OProv *cavalier*, fr. LL *caballarius* groom, hostler, fr. L *caballus* + *-arius* -ary] **1 :** a raised fortified structure usu. rising from the middle of a bastion but sometimes erected by besiegers and designed to command the enemy's works **2 :** a gentleman trained in arms and manege **:** a gallant courtly soldier **3 :** a mounted soldier of rank, often colorful and with romantic appeal **:** KNIGHT **4** *usu cap* **a :** an adherent of Charles I of England as contrasted with a supporter of parliament **:** ROYALIST **b :** a Southerner of the plantation-owning class; *specif* **:** VIRGINIAN **5 :** a lady's escort or dancing partner **:** GALLANT

²cavalier \"\ *vi* -ED/-ING/-S **1 :** to play the cavalier **2 :** to act in a cavalier manner

³cavalier \"\ *adj* **1 :** insouciant and debonair **2 :** marked by lofty disregard of others' interests, rights, or feelings **:** high-handed and arrogant or supercilious **:** given to airy dismissal of things worthy of attention ⟨~ in his methods, too lordly over appointments and forgotten promises —F.Tennyson Jesse⟩ ⟨~ ignoring of his arguments⟩ **3 a** *usu cap* **:** of or relating to the party of Charles I of England **:** ROYALIST ⟨an old *Cavalier* family⟩ **b :** marked by colorful self-confident affluence **:** ARISTOCRATIC ⟨older middle-class Virginia . . . being superseded by a ~ Virginia —V.L.Parrington⟩ **c** *usu cap* **:** of, relating to, or resembling the work of the English Cavalier poets of the mid-17th century **:** valuing courtliness, urbanity, and polish **d :** imitative of the flaring ornamental dress of the Cavaliers ⟨a ~ cuff⟩ — **cav·a·lier·ness** *n* -ES

ca·va·lie·re \,kavәl'yerē\ *n, pl* **cavalieres** \-ēz\ *or* **cava·lie·ri** \-rē\ [It] **1 :** CAVALIER **2 :** CAVALIER SERVENTE

cav·a·lier·ism \,kavә'lirizәm\ *n* -s *often cap* **:** the practice or principles of cavaliers, esp. of the 17th century Cavaliers

cav·a·lier·ly \;⸗⸗¦li(ә)rlē, -iәl-, -li\ *adv* **:** in a cavalier manner

ca·va·lier ser·vant \kåvålyåserväⁿ, ¦kavә,li(ә)r'sәrvәnt\ *n* [trans. of It *cavalier servente*] **:** CAVALIER SERVENTE

ca·va·lier ser·ven·te \¦kävәl¦ye(ә)rsәr'ventē, ¦kav-\ *or* **ca·va·lie·re servente** \-¦yerē-sәr-\ *n, pl* **cavalie·ri serven·ti** \-¦yerē...ntē\ [It, lit., serving cavalier] **:** LOVER, GALLANT

ca·va·lier seul \kåvålyäsœl\ *n, pl* **cavaliers seuls** [F, lit., gentleman alone] **:** a quadrille figure performed in turn by each man of two opposite couples while the other man and the women face him

ca·val·la \kә'valә, -'vīә\ *n, pl* **cavalla** *or* **cavallas** [Sp *caballa*, a fish, fr. LL, mare, fem. of L *caballus* horse — more at CAVALCADE] **1 :** CERO **2** *also* **ca·val·ly** -ES **:** any of various fishes of *Caranx* or other closely related genera — compare CREVALLE

cavalla (*Caranx hippos*)

ca·val·let·ti \,kavә'led·ē\ *n* -s [It *cavalletti*, pl. of *cavalletto*, lit., little horse, dim. of *cavallo* horse, fr. L *caballus*] **:** a series of timber jumps that are adjustable in height for schooling horses

cavallo *var of* CABALLO

cav·al·ry \'kavəlrē, -ri\ *n* -ES *often attrib* [It *cavalleria* cavalry, chivalry, fr. *cavaliere* cavalier + *-ia* -y — more at CAVALIER] **1 a** *obs* : HORSEMANSHIP ⟨the art of ~⟩ **b** *obs* : KNIGHTHOOD ⟨the ~ of the court⟩ **c** : HORSEMEN ⟨a thousand ~ in flight⟩ **2 a** (1) : the component of an army that maneuvers and fights on horseback (2) : a similar component that maneuvers on horseback but fights on foot **b** : the component of an army mounted on horseback or moving in motor vehicles and having combat missions (as reconnaissance and counterreconnaissance) that require great mobility **3** : DEEP CHROME YELLOW

cavalry bone *n* : RIDER'S BONE

cav·al·ry·man \-mən, -ˌman, -ˌmaa(ə)n\ *n, pl* **cavalrymen** : a cavalry soldier

cavalry twill *n* : a sturdy suiting usu. woolen or worsted but sometimes cotton or rayon, woven of tightly twisted yarns in a steep double twill, and similar to elastique but with a coarser raised cord effect

¹**ca·van** \kə'vän\ *or* **ca·ban** \-'b-\ *n, pl* **cavans** \-änz\ *or* **ca·va·nes** *or* **caba·nes** \-ä,nās\ [PhilSp *caván, cabán,* fr. Tag *kabán,* lit., trunk, coffer] : a Philippine unit of dry measure equal to 2.13 bushels

²**cav·an** \'kavən\ *adj, usu cap* [fr. *Cavan,* county in Ireland] : of or from County Cavan, Ireland : of the kind or style prevalent in County Cavan

ca·va·qui·nho \ˌkavə'kē(ˌ)nyü\ *n* -S [Pg, dim. of *cavaco* piece of wood, fr. *cavar* to dig out, hollow out, fr. L *cavare* to hollow out] : a Brazilian stringed musical instrument somewhat smaller than a ukulele

cav·a·scope \'kavə,skōp\ *n* -S [*cava-* (fr. L *cavus* hollow) + *-scope*] : an instrument for illuminating bodily cavities (as the throat)

ca·vate \'kā,vāt\ *adj* [L *cavatus,* past part. of *cavare* to hollow out] : cut in soft rock : EXCAVATED ⟨~ cliff dwelling⟩

cav·a·ti·na \ˌkavə'tēnə, ˌkä-\ *n* -S [It, fr. *cavata* production of sound, fr. *cavare* to extract, dig out, fr. L, to hollow out, fr. *cavus* hollow] **1** : an operatic solo that is simpler and briefer than an aria **2** : a sustained melody

cav·a·yard \'kavə,yärd\ *or* **cavy·yard** \-vē,y-\ *n* -S [modif. of Sp *caballada,* fr. *caballo* horse (fr. L *caballus*) + *-ada* -ade — more at CAVALCADE] *West* : REMUDA

¹**cave** \'kāv\ *n* -S *often attrib* [ME, fr. OF, fr. L *cava,* fr. *cavus* hollow; akin to OE *hyse* young man, ON *hūnn* bear cub, Gk *koilos* hollow, *kyein* to be pregnant, Skt *śvayati* he swells, *śāva* young of an animal; basic meaning: hollow, swelling] **1** : a hollowed-out chamber in the earth or in the side of a cliff or hill : CAVERN; *esp* : a natural underground chamber (as one produced in limestone by running water) with an opening to the surface **2 a** : an underground chamber or recess for storage or safety; *esp* : an outdoor cellar dug or natural ⟨if she had bacon in the ~ —Willa Cather⟩ **b** : a cached supply ⟨selling the ~s of wine⟩ **3** *Brit* **a** : the act of secession from a political party **b** : a group of persons seceding from a political party — compare ADULLAMITE **4** : a tunnel under a glass furnace used for raking the fire, removing ashes, or regulating heat **5** : a heavily shielded enclosure for radioactive experiments controlled and observed from outside

²**cave** \"\ *vb* -ED/-ING/-S [prob. fr. MF *caver,* fr. L *cavare*] *vt* : to form a cave in or under : HOLLOW, UNDERMINE ⟨the waters *caving* the banks⟩ ~ *vi* : to explore caves

³**cave** \"\ *vt* -ED/-ING/-S [ME (northern dial.) *caven,* fr. *caf* chaff (in other dialects *chaf, chef*) — more at CHAFF] *now dial* : to separate (as grain) from chaff

⁴**cave** \"\ *vb* -ED/-ING/-S [perh. fr. ON *kafa* to dive — more at BAPTIZE] *vi* **1** *dial Brit* : OVERTURN **2** *Midland* : to be noisily and demonstratively angry ~ *vt* **1** *dial Brit* : to tilt over **2** *dial Brit* : to give a toss to (the head) **3** *dial Brit* : PLUNGE

⁵**cave** \"\ *vb* -ED/-ING/-S [prob. alter. (influenced by ²*cave*) of *calve*] *vi* **1** : to fall in or down esp. from being undermined — usu. used with *in* ⟨the road *caved* in above the old mine⟩ **2** : to collapse esp. from exhaustion — usu. used with *in* ⟨the challenger *caved* in during the seventh round⟩ **3** : to cease to resist : become forceless or disorganized : admit defeat or culpability : SUBMIT — usu. used with *in* ⟨the defenders *caved* in and surrendered⟩ ~ *vt* **1** : to cause to fall or collapse — usu. used with *in* ⟨the floodwaters *caved* in the retaining wall⟩ **2** : to smash in or down — usu. used with *in* ⟨a car with its fenders *caved* in⟩

⁶**cave** \"\ *n* -S [⁵*cave*] : the action of caving in or being caved in

⁷**cave** *adj* [ME & L; MF, fr. L *cavus* hollow] *obs* : CONCAVE, HOLLOW

ca·vea \'kāvēə, 'kä-\ *n, pl* **cave·ae** \'kāvē,ē, 'kävē,ī\ [L — more at CAGE] : the tiered semicircular seating space of an ancient theater

caveare *obs var of* CAVIAR

cave art *n* : the art of Paleolithic man represented by drawings and paintings on the walls of caves esp. in Europe

¹**ca·ve·at** \'kāvē,at, 'kävē,ät, -ēət, *often* -d·+V\ *n* -S [L, let him beware, 3d pers. sing. pres. subj. of *cavēre* to be on one's guard — more at SHOW] **1** : CAUTION: **a** : a warning enjoining one from certain acts or practices ⟨a ~ against unfair practices⟩ **b** : a cautionary explanation to prevent misinterpretation ⟨to enter a ~ about the sense in which a word is used⟩ **2** : a legal notice given by an interested party to some officer not to do a certain act until the party is heard in opposition ⟨a ~ entered in a probate court to stop the proving of a will⟩

²**caveat** \"\ *vi* ED/-ING/-S : to enter a caveat

ca·ve·a·tee \ˌ==ə¦tē\ *n* -S [²*caveat* + *-ee*] : one against whose interest a caveat is entered or filed

caveat emp·tor \ˌ==-'em(p)tər, -ˌäd--, -əd--, -ˌtō(ə)r\ *n* [NL, let the buyer beware] : a warning principle in trading: the purchaser should be alert to see that he gets the quality and the quantity he is paying for

ca·ve·at·or \'==,ad·ər, -ˌäd·ər, ¦==¦tō(ə)r\ *n* -S [²*caveat* + *-or*] : one that enters or files a caveat

cave bat *n* : any of various cave-dwelling bats; *esp* : a member of a No. American genus (*Antrozous*)

cave bear *n* : a very large extinct bear (*Ursus spelaeus*) known from remains in caves in Europe and England and believed to be contemporaneous with Paleolithic man

cave beetle *n* : any of various cave-inhabiting beetles without eyes or with degenerate eyes

cave cricket *n* : any of several wingless cricketlike grasshoppers (family Stenopelmatidae) found in caves or other dark moist places — compare STONE CRICKET

caved *past of* CAVE

cave dweller *n* **1** : one that dwells in a cave; *esp* : a prehistoric man whose remains and utensils have been discovered in ancient caves **2** : a city dweller

cave earth *n* : the residual accumulation of insoluble materials on the floor of a cave, many of such deposits being covered with a layer of stalagmite and some of them containing remains of extinct animals

cave fish *n* : any of various fishes found in cave waters having usu. vestigial and functionless eyes — compare BLINDFISH

cave hunter *n* : a caveman subsisting by hunting rather than by agriculture

cave hyena *n* : an extinct hyena whose remains are found abundantly in British caves and now usu. regarded as a large variety of the living African spotted hyena

cave-in \'=,=\ *n* -S **1** : the action of caving in : ⁶CAVE **2** : a place where earth has caved in

¹**cav·el** \'kavəl, -ev-, -āv-\ *n* -S [ME, fr. MD *kavele;* akin to ON *kefli* stick of wood — more at KEVEL] *dial Brit* : a lot determined by a cast

²**cavel** \"\ *vt* **cavelled; cavelled; cavelling** \-v(ə)liŋ, -lən\ **cavels** *dial Brit* : to allot or apportion according to lots cast ⟨the working positions *cavelled* by the miners⟩

³**cavel** *n* -S [ME *kevell,* perh. fr. ON *kefli* stick of wood] *obs* : a mean fellow

⁴**cavel** *var of* KEVEL

cave lion *n* : a lion known from remains found in European and English caves and believed to be an extinct variety of the existing lion

cave locust *n* : WETA

cave·man *in senses 1 & 2* 'kāv,man *or* -aa(ə)n, *in senses 3 & 4* " *or* -,mən\ *n, pl* **cavemen** **1** : a cave dweller esp. of the Stone Age — compare PALEOLITHIC MAN **2** : a man who acts with rough violent directness **3** *Brit* : one who clears the cave of a furnace **4** : an explorer of caves : SPELEOLOGIST

cav·en·dish \'kavən(ˌ)dish\ *n* -ES [prob. fr. the name *Cavendish*] : leaf tobacco softened, sweetened, and pressed into plugs or cakes

cavendish banana *n, usu cap C* : DWARF BANANA

cavendish experiment *n, usu cap C* [after Henry *Cavendish* †1810 Eng. chemist and physicist who first performed it] : measurement of gravitation constant by a sensitive torsion balance

cave of adul·lam \-ə'dələm\ *usu C&A* [fr. *Adullam,* biblical cave where David fled to escape Achish, king of Gath, & where he was joined by other discontented people (1 Sam 22:1-2)] : a group of seceders from a particular political or intellectual position

cave onyx *n* : a fine-grained banded calcite aragonite found in caves

cave pearl *n* : a small smooth round concretion of carbonate of lime found in limestone caves

cav·er \'kāvə(r)\ *n* -S : one that studies or explores caves

¹**cav·ern** \'kavə(r)n\ *n* -S *often attrib* [ME *caverne,* fr. MF, fr. L *caverna,* fr. *cavus* hollow — more at CAVE] **1** : an underground chamber often large or indefinite in extent : CAVE ⟨~s attracting tourist trade⟩ ⟨Carlsbad *Caverns*⟩ **2** : a large dark recess ⟨his eye sockets were dark ~s —Kenneth Roberts⟩ ⟨the ~s of his memory —Earl Birney⟩ **3** : a cavity (as in the lung) caused by disease

²**cavern** \"\ *vt* -ED/-ING/-S **1** : to place or enclose in or as if in a cavern **2** : to form a cavern of : hollow out — used with *out*

ca·ver·ni·cole \ka'vərnə,kōl, kə'-, 'kavərnə,-\ *n* -S [F, fr. *cavernicole,* adj., fr. *caverne* cavern + *-i-* + *-cole* -colous] : a cavernicolous animal

cav·er·nic·o·lous \¦kavər¦nikələs\ *adj* [*cavern* + *-i-* + *-colous*] : inhabiting caverns ⟨a ~ fauna⟩

cav·er·no·ma \ˌkavə(r)'nōmə\ *n, pl* **cavernomas** \-məz\ *or* **cavernoma·ta** \-məd·ə\ [NL, fr. L *caverna* cavern + NL *-oma*] : a vascular tumor or angioma containing hollow spaces

cav·er·nos·to·my \-'nästəmē\ *n* -ES [L *caverna* cavern, cavity + E *-o-* + *-stomy*] : incision and drainage of a tuberculous cavity

cav·ern·ous \'kavə(r)nəs\ *adj* [ME, fr. L *cavernosus,* fr. *caverna* + *-osus* -ous] **1 a** : having many caverns ⟨a ~ limestone area⟩ **b** : having many cavities or interstices ⟨a ~ substance⟩ **c** : productive of caverns ⟨~ weathering⟩ **2 a** : constituting or suggesting a cavern : deep, vast, and commodious ⟨the chilly ~ chambers, hollowed out of carboniferous limestone —*Amer. Guide Series: Calif.*⟩ ⟨a ~ cellar⟩ ⟨a ~ mind⟩ **b** : of or relating to a cavern ⟨ill-smelling ~ waters⟩ **3** *of animal tissue* : composed of vascular sinuses intercalated between afferent arteries and efferent veins and capable of becoming dilated with blood to bring about the erection of a body part — **cav·ern·ous·ly** *adv*

cavernous body *n* [trans. of NL *corpus cavernosum*] : CORPUS CAVERNOSUM

cavernous plexus *n* : a nerve plexus of the sympathetic system lying below and internal to the carotid artery at each side of the sella turcica

cavernous respiration *n* : a peculiar blowing respiratory sound heard over abnormal lung cavities

cavernous sinus *n* : either of a pair of large venous sinuses situated in a groove at the side of the body of the sphenoid bone in the cranial cavity and opening behind into the petrosal sinuses

ca·ver·nu·lous \ka'vərnyələs, kə-\ *adj* [L *cavernula* (dim. of *caverna* cavern) + E *-ous*] : full of little cavities

caves *pl of* CAVE, *pres 3d sing of* CAVE

cav·es·son *or* **cav·e·son** \'kavəsən\ *n* -S [modif. of It *cavezzone* halter with noseband, aug. of *cavezza* halter, irreg. fr. L *capitium* opening in tunic for head to go through, fr. *capit-, caput* head — more at HEAD] **1** : a noseband made of metal or other stiff material well padded and used on horses esp. during breeding or training **2** : a halter or bridle with a cavesson

ca·vet·to \kə'ved·(ˌ)ō\ *n, pl* **cavet·ti** \-d·ē\ *or* **cavettos** \-d·(ˌ)ōz\ [It, fr. *cavo* hollow, fr. L *cavus* — more at CAVE] : a concave molding having a curve that roughly approximates a quarter circle — see MOLDING illustration

cavi *pl of* CAVUS

ca·via \'kāvēə\ *n, cap* [NL, modif. of obs. Pg *çaviá* (now *saviá*), fr. Tupi *sawiya* rat] : the type genus of Caviidae consisting of the guinea pigs and a few related forms

cav·i·ar *or* **cav·i·are** \'kavē,är, -ˌa(r *also* -äv- *or* -āv- *or* ,==¦=\ *n* -S [alter. (prob. influenced by F *caviar*) of earlier *caviari, cavery,* fr. OIt *caviari,* pl. of *caviaro* caviar, fr. Turk *havyar*] **1** : processed salted roe of the sturgeon and certain other large fish prepared as an appetizer **2** : a choice product or production too delicate or lofty for mass appreciation ⟨this play will be ~ to the general public⟩ **3** [so called fr. the resemblance of the blotch to caviar] : a passage canceled by a censor

cav·i·ary \'kavē,erē\ *n* -ES [¹*cavy* + *-ary* (as in *aviary*)] : a place for keeping or raising cavies

cav·i·corn \'kavə,kȯrn\ *adj* [NL *Cavicornia*] : having hollow horns ⟨~ members of the family Bovidae⟩

cav·i·cor·nia \ˌ==¦=nēə, -nyə\ [NL, fr. *cavi-* (fr. L *cavus* hollow) + *-cornia* (fr. L, neut. pl. of *-cornis* -corn)] — more at CAVE] *syn of* BOVOIDEA

ca·vie *also* **cavey** \'kāvē\ *n* -S [obs. D or obs. Flem *kavie,* fr. MD *cavie;* akin to OS & OHG *kevia* cage; all fr. a prehistoric D-LG-HG word borrowed fr. L *cavea* cage — more at CAGE] *Scot* : a coop or cage for hens

cavies *pl of* CAVY

ca·vi·i·dae \kā'vīə,dē, kə-\ *n pl, cap* [NL, fr. *Cavia,* type genus + *-idae*] : a family of more or less tailless rodents having but three toes on each hind foot — see CAVY

¹**cav·il** \'kavəl, *Brit often* -vil\ *vb* **caviled** *or* **cavilled; caviled** *or* **cavilled; caviling** *or* **cavilling** \-v(ə)liŋ, -vil-\ **cavils** [L *cavillari* to jest, mock, cavil, fr. *cavilla* raillery, sophistry; prob. akin to L *calvi* to deceive — more at CALUMNY] *vi* : to raise captious and frivolous objection : object or criticize adversely for trivial reasons — usu. used with *at, about,* or *with* ⟨mere captiousness . . . that ~s at a whetstone because it's not a sword blade —J.L.Lowes⟩ ~ *vt* : to raise picayune objections to : cavil at ⟨~ the conditions of the agreement⟩

²**cavil** \"\ *n* -S **1** : a captious frivolous picayune objection : QUIBBLE ⟨accept without ~ whatever he was told —Samuel Butler †1902⟩ **2** : tendency to cavil : susceptibility to cavils ⟨the general standard of the judicature is above reproach or ~ —Ernest Barker⟩

cav·il·er *or* **cav·il·ler** \-ələ(r), -il-\ *n* -S : one that cavils

caviling *or* **cavilling** *adj* : disposed to cavil : inclined to find fault and raise picayune ill-grounded objections ⟨~ pettifoggers and quibbling pleaders —Edmund Burke⟩ **syn** see CRITICAL

cav·il·ing·ly *adv* : in a caviling manner

cav·il·ing·ness *n* -ES : the quality or state of being caviling

cav·il·la·tion \ˌkavə'lāshən, -vi'-\ *n* -S [ME *cavillacioun,* fr. MF *cavillation,* fr. L *cavillation-, cavillatio,* fr. *cavillatus,* (past part. of *cavillari* to cavil) + *-ion-, -io* -ion] **1** *archaic* : CAVIL ⟨sophistical ~⟩ **2** *archaic* : the raising of cavils

cav·il·lous \'==ləs\ *adj* : given to cavil : CAVILING

ca·vi·na \kə'vēnyə\ *n, pl* **cavina** *or* **cavinas** *usu cap* [Sp *caviña,* of AmerInd origin] **1 a** : a Tacanan people of northwest Bolivia and adjacent Brazil **b** : a member of such people **2** : the language of the Cavina people

cav·ing \'kāviŋ, -vēŋ\ *n* -S **1** : a falling or hollowing in **2** : the exploring of caves

cav·ings \-ŋz, -vənz\ *n pl* [fr. gerund of *cave* (to separate from chaff)] *dial Brit* : chaff and refuse esp. of threshed grain

cav·i·tar·i·ly \¦kavə¦terəlē\ *adv* : in a cavitary manner

cav·i·tary \'kavə,terē\ *adj* [*cavity* + *-ary*] : characterized by cavitation

cav·i·tate \-,tāt\ *vi* -ED/-ING/-S [back-formation fr. *cavitation*] **1** : to form a partial vacuum by cavitation **2** : to form a cavity (as in cavitation)

cav·i·ta·tion \ˌ==¦tāshən\ *n* -S [*cavity* + *-ation*] **1 a** : the formation of partial vacuums in a liquid esp. as a result of the passage through it of a swiftly moving solid body (as a propeller blade) or of high-frequency sound waves **b** : the pitting and wearing away of solid surfaces (as metal or concrete) as a result of the collapse of these vacuums **2** : the formation of one or more cavities in an organ or tissue (as in the brain, lung, spinal cord, or teeth) esp. as a result of disease **3** : a cavity formed by cavitation

ca·vi·te·no \ˌkavə'ten(ˌ)yō, -ān-\ *n* -S *cap* [PhilSp *caviteño,* fr. *Cavite,* province & city of SW Luzon, Philippines] : a Spanish-based pidgin language spoken around Cavite, Philippines

cav·i·tied \'kavəd·ēd, -vət¦ēd, ¦id\ *adj* : having cavities

cav·i·to·ma \ˌkavə'tōmə\ *n* -S [NL, fr. L *cavitas* + NL *-oma*] : a series of changes in cotton fiber involving loss of strength and resulting from the activities of microorganisms — **cav·i·to·mic** \¦==¦tōmik, -äm-\ *adj*

cav·i·ty \'kavəd·ē, -ətē, -i\ *n* -ES [MF *cavité,* fr. LL *cavitas* hollowness, fr. L *cavus* hollow + *-itas* -ity — more at CAVE] : a three-dimensional discontinuity in the substance of a mass or body : a space within a mass ⟨a water-filled ~ in limestone⟩; *also* : a space hollowed out (as by decay) ⟨teeth full of *cavities*⟩ ⟨an old ~ excavated by a woodpecker —John Burroughs⟩

cavity oscillator *n* : an ultrahigh-frequency oscillator whose frequency is controlled by means of a cavity resonator

cavity resonator *n* : an electronic device consisting of a space usu. enclosed by metallic walls within which resonant electromagnetic fields may be excited and extracted for use in microwave systems

cavity wall *n* : a usu. masonry wall built in two thicknesses separated by an air space that provides thermal insulation

cav·i·u·na wood \¦kavē¦ünə-, kə'vyü-\ *n* [Pg *cabiuna,* prob. fr. Tupi *caa- biuna*] : BRAZILIAN ROSEWOOD

ca·vo-re·lie·vo *or* **ca·vo-ri·lie·vo** \¦kä(ˌ)vōrē'lē(ˌ)vō, ¦kā-, ¦kä-; ¦kä(ˌ)vōrēl'yä-, ¦kä-, -ye-\ *n, pl* **cavo-relievos** \-vōz\ *or* **ca·vi-ri·lie·vi** \¦kä(ˌ)vērēl'yä(ˌ)vē, ¦kā-, -ye-\ [It *cavo rilievo*] : SUNK RELIEF

ca·vort \kə'vȯ(ə)rt, -ȯ(ə)t\ *vi* -ED/-ING/-S [perh. alter. of *curvet*] **1** : to bound, prance, or frisk about ⟨the forest ponies kicking up their heels and ~*ing* . . . in sheer delight of living —S.P.B.Mais⟩ **2** : to engage in any agile frisky extravagant showy behavior ⟨lads . . . ~*ed* with the buxom lassies in the reel and barn dance —A.D. Graeff⟩

CAVU *abbr* ceiling and visibility unlimited

ca·vum \'kävəm, 'kā-\ *n, pl* **ca·va** \-və\ [L, cavity, fr. neut. of *cavus* hollow — more at CAVE] : RECESS, HOLLOW: as **a** : the lower part of the concha of the ear adjoining the origin of the helix **b** : the nasal cavity

cav·vy *or* **cavy** \'kavē\ *n* -ES [short for *cavayard*] *West* : REMUDA

ca·vy \'kāvē\ *n* -ES [NL *Cavia*] **1** : any of several short-tailed rough-haired So. American rodents constituting the family Caviidae; *specif* : GUINEA PIG **2** : any of several rodents (as the paca and agouti) related to the Caviidae

cavyyard *var of* CAVAYARD

¹**caw** \'kȯ\ *Scot var of* CALL

²**caw** \"\ *vi* -ED/-ING/-S [imit.] : to utter a harsh raucous cry; *typically, of a crow, raven, or rook* : to utter its natural call ⟨the crows ~ above the wood —John Burroughs⟩

³**caw** \"\ *n* -S : a harsh raucous throaty outcry; *typically* : the natural call of the crow, raven, or rook

⁴**caw** \"\ *var of* ²COE

ca·wa·hib \'käwə,hēb\ *n, pl* **cawahib** *or* **cawahibs** *usu cap* [Cawahib, perh. fr. *kab, kāwa* wasp] **1 a** : a Tupian people including the Cawahib proper and the Parintintin of the Tapajoz river area in northern Brazil **b** : a member of such people **2** : the language of the Cawahib people

caw·die \'kädē\ *Scot var of* CADDIE

¹**cawk** \'kōk\ *n* -S [ME *calke* chalk, limestone — more at CAUK] **1** : an opaque compact variety of barite **2** : BARITE

²**cawk** \"\ *vi* -ED/-ING/-S [ME *cauken,* fr. ONF *cauquer,* fr. L *calcare* to tread] *of hawks* : MATE

cawky \'kōkē\ *adj* -ER/-EST : containing cawk : like cawk

cawl \'kȯl\ *n* -S [OE *cawl, ceawl* basket, fr. ML *cavellum,* fr. L *cavus* hollow — more at CAVE] *dial Brit* : a wooden basket with handholes instead of handles used esp. in Cornwall to carry fish

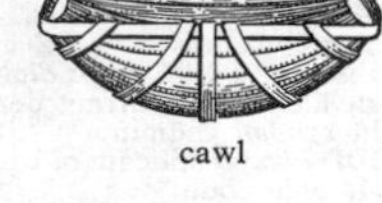

cawl

cawn·pore \'kȯn,pō(ə)r, ¦=¦=\ *or* **kan·pur** \'kän,pů(ə)r, ¦=¦=\ *adj, usu cap* [fr. *Cawnpore,* city in India] : of or from the city of Cawnpore, India : of the kind or style prevalent in Cawnpore

caw·quaw \'kȯ,kwȯ\ *n* -S [Cree *kaakwa*] : CANADA PORCUPINE

cax·on \'kaksən\ *n* -S [perh. fr. the name *Caxon*] : WIG; *esp* : a much-worn wig

cax·to·nian \(ˈ)kak¦stōnēən, -nyən\ *adj, usu cap* [William *Caxton* †1491 Eng. printer & translator + E *-ian*] : of or relating to William Caxton or his work

¹**cay** \'kē (*usual in W Indies*), 'kā\ *n* -S [Sp *cayo* — more at KEY] : a small low island or emergent reef of sand or coral : ISLET, KEY — used esp. in the West Indies

²**cay** \'kī\ *n* -S [AmerSp *cay, caí,* fr. Guarani *caí,* lit., bashful; fr. its habit of hiding its face in its hands] : a monkey of the genus *Cebus* : CAPUCHIN

ca·ya·bi \¦kīyə¦bē, ¦kīə¦-\ *n, pl* **cayabi** *or* **cayabis** *usu cap* [Pg, of AmerInd origin] **1 a** : a Tupian people of the Tapajoz river area in northern Brazil **b** : a member of such people **2** : the language of the Cayabi people

cayak *var of* KAYAK

ca·ya·pa \kə'yäpə, kī'äpə\ *n, pl* **cayapa** *or* **cayapas** *usu cap* [Sp, of AmerInd origin] **1 a** : a Barbacoan people of the province of Esmeraldas in northwestern Ecuador **b** : a member of such people **2** : the language of the Cayapa people

ca·ya·po \¦käyə¦pō, ¦kīə¦-\ *n, pl* **cayapo** *or* **cayapos** *usu cap* [Pg *Cayapó,* of AmerInd origin] **1 a** : a Gesan people of the state of Mato Grosso in Brazil **b** : a member of such people **2** : the language of the Cayapo people

¹**cay·enne** \(ˈ)kī¦en, -kā- *also* (ˈ)kī¦an\ *n* -S *sometimes cap* **1** : CAYENNE PEPPER **2** : a small reddish marine surface-swimming copepod that is a food of whales and certain fishes

²**cayenne** \"\ *also* **cayenne whist** *n* -S [fr. *Cayenne,* city and island in French Guiana] : a card game in which the dealer may designate the trump suit; *also* : the turned-up card that affects the scoring values in this game

cayenne cherry *n, usu cap 1st C* : SURINAM CHERRY 2

cayenne linaloe oil *n, usu cap C* : BOIS DE ROSE OIL

cayenne pepper *n, sometimes cap C* [alter. (influenced by *Cayenne,* city and island in French Guiana) of earlier *cayan, chian, kayan,* modif. of Tupi *kyinha, quiynha*] **1** : a very hot and pungent powder made by drying and grinding the whole fruits or the seeds of several hot peppers (as the long pepper) **2** : HOT PEPPER 2; *often* : any of several cultivated peppers derived from one variety (*Capsicum frutescens longum*) and characterized by very long twisted pungent red fruits **3** : the fruit of a cayenne pepper

cayman *var of* CAIMAN

cay·o·mi·to \ˌkīə'mēd·(ˌ)ō\ *var of* CAIMITO

cay·to·nia \kā'tōnēə, -nyə\ *n, cap* [NL, fr. *Cayton,* England + NL *-ia*] : a genus (the type of the family Caytoniaceae and the order Caytoniales) of fossil gymnospermous plants of the Mesozoic era having seeds enclosed in a carpellike case that suggests their ancestry to the angiosperms

ca·yuá \¦käyə¦wä, ¦kīə¦-\ *n, pl* **cayuá** *or* **cayuás** *usu cap* [Sp *cayuá* & Pg *caiuá,* of AmerInd origin] **1 a** : a non-Christian Guarani people of southwestern Brazil and northern Paraguay **b** : a member of such people **2** : the language of the Cayuá people

ca·yu·co \kä'yü(ˌ)kō, kī'(y)ü-\ *or* **ca·yu·ca** \-kə\ *n* -S [AmerSp] : a small native fishing dugout of Central and So. America

ca·yu·ga \kē'ügə, 'kyü-; kā'(y)ü-, kī'(y)ü-, *attrib* (ˈ)=¦==\ *n, pl* **cayuga** *or* **cayugas** *usu cap* [prob. modif. of Mohawk *Kweñiógwě'* (place name), lit., place where locusts were taken out] **1 a** : an Iroquois people of New York state **b** : a member of such people **2** : the language of the Cayuga people

cayuga duck *n, usu cap C* : an American breed of ducks resembling but slightly smaller than the Pekin ducks and having greenish black plumage

ca·yu·gan \-ügən\ *adj, usu cap* [*Cayuga* lake, N. Y. + E *-an*] : of or relating to the uppermost major division of the American Silurian — see GEOLOGIC TIME table

cay·use \'kī,(y)üs, ¦=¦=\ *n, pl* **cayuse** *or* **cayuses** **1** *usu cap* **a** : a Waiilatpuan people of Washington and Oregon **b** : a member of such people **2** : the language of the Cayuse people **3** *pl cayuses, West* : a native range horse; *esp* : INDIAN PONY — compare BRONCO, MUSTANG

ca·yu·va·va \ˌkīyəˈvävə, ˌkīəˈ-\ *also* **ca·yu·ba·ba** \-ˈbäbə\ *n, pl* **cayuvava** *or* **cayuvavas** *also* **cayubaba** *or* **cayubabas** *usu cap* [Sp, of AmerInd origin] **1 a :** a people of northern Bolivia **b :** a member of such people **2 :** the language of the Cayuvava people

ca·yu·va·van \-vən\ *also* **ca·yu·ba·ban** \-bən\ *n* -s *usu cap* **:** a language family of northern Bolivia comprising only the Cayuvava

ca·za \kəˈzä\ *n* -s [Turk *kaza* district, judgment, sentence, fr. Ar *qaḍā'* decision, judging, fr. *qaḍā* to decide, judge] **:** a subdivision of a Turkish vilayet

caz·can \(ˈ)käˌskän\ *n, pl* **cazcan** *or* **cazcans** *usu cap* [Sp *cazcán*, fr. Nahuatl] **1 :** a Nahuatlan people of southern Zacatecas and northern Jalisco, Mexico **2 :** a member of the Cazcan people

cazique *var of* CACIQUE

cb *abbr* centibar

Cb *abbr* cumulonimbus

CB *abbr* **1** cashbook **2** [It *col basso*] with the bass **3** confined to barracks **4** construction battalion **5** contrabass **6** currency bond

Cb *symbol* columbium

cbal *abbr* counterbalance

c battery *n, usu cap C* **:** a battery used to maintain the potential of a grid-controlled electron tube at a desired value, constant except for signals superposed upon it

CBC *abbr* contraband control

cb cap *n, usu cap 1st C & B* **:** a .22-caliber rimfire cartridge similar to a BB cap but with a larger bullet

CBD *abbr* cash before delivery

c-bias \ˈ=ˌ==\ *n, usu cap C* **:** the voltage applied to the control grid of a vacuum tube to make it negative with respect to the cathode

cbn *abbr* carbine

CBR *abbr* chemical, bacteriological, and radiological

cbt *abbr* cabinet

cby *abbr* carboy

cc *abbr* **1** centuries **2** chapters **3** copies **4** cubic centimeter

CC *abbr* **1** carbon copy **2** cash credit **3** cashier's check **4** chamber of commerce **5** chess club **6** chief clerk **7** circuit court **8** city council **9** civil commotion **10** combat command **11** common carrier **12** common council **13** company commander **14** confined to camp **15** connecting carrier **16** continuation clause **17** contra credit **18** council of churches **19** counterclockwise **20** country club **21** county council **22** county court **23** cricket club **24** crown colony **25** cubic contents **26** current cost **27** cycling club

CCA *abbr* circuit court of appeals

cckw *abbr* counterclockwise

c-clamp \ˈ=ˌ=\ *n, cap 1st C* **:** a C-shaped general-purpose clamp that clamps between the open ends of the C by means of a long flat-ended screw that threads through one end and presses the clamped material against the other

c clef *n, usu cap 1st C* **:** a movable clef indicating middle C by its placement on one of the five lines of the staff — see ALTO CLEF, SOPRANO CLEF, TENOR CLEF; CLEF illustration; compare F CLEF, G CLEF

C-clamp

CCP *abbr* court of common pleas

CCS *abbr* **1** casualty clearing station **2** combined chiefs of staff

ccw *abbr* counterclockwise

cd *abbr* **1** candela **2** canned **3** card **4** cataloged **5** command **6** commissioned **7** condemned **8** cord **9** could

CD *abbr* **1** carried down **2** cash discount **3** certificate of deposit **4** chief of division **5** civil defense **6** coast defense **7** [It *colla destra*] with the right hand **8** commercial dock **9** completely denatured **10** confidential document **11** congressional district **12** consular declaration **13** contagious disease **14** [F *corps diplomatique*] diplomatic corps **15** cum dividend **16** current density

Cd *symbol* cadmium

CDD *abbr* certificate of disability for discharge

cde *abbr* code

cdg *abbr* commanding

cdl *abbr* cardinal

cdr *abbr* commander

cdre *abbr* commodore

CDS *abbr* cash on delivery service

cdt *abbr* commandant

ce *var of* CEE

CE *abbr or n* -s civil engineer

CE *abbr* **1** *often not cap* caveat emptor **2** Christian Era **3** Common Era **4** counterespionage **5** customs and excise

Ce *symbol* cerium

ce·a·no·thus \ˌsēəˈnōthəs\ *n, cap* [NL, fr. Gk *keanōthos*, a thistle] **:** a large genus of American vines, shrubs, and small trees (family Rhamnaceae) distinguished by having the calyx disk adherent to the ovary which develops into a dry fruit that splits into three carpels — see NEW JERSEY TEA

ce·a·rá rubber \ˌsāəˈrä-, ˌsēə-\ *n, usu cap C* [fr. *Ceará*, state in Brazil] **:** wild rubber obtained from any of certain So. American trees of the genus *Manihot* (esp. *M. glaziovii*)

[1]**cease** \ˈsēs *sometimes* ˈsez\ *vb* -ED/-ING/-S [ME *cesen, cessen*, fr. OF *cesser*, fr. L *cessare* to delay, be idle, fr. *cessus*, past part. of *cedere* to withdraw — more at CEDE] *vt* **1 :** to leave off **:** bring to an end **:** DISCONTINUE, TERMINATE ⟨his efforts had no . . . chance of success, and he had made up his mind to ~ them —Arnold Bennett⟩ ⟨the resort hotel *ceased* to function after the fire⟩ **2** *obs* **:** to put a stop to **:** HALT ⟨he *ceased* her fears⟩ ⟨~ the rioters' noise⟩ ~ *vi* **1 a :** to come to an end **:** break off or taper off to a stop ⟨these demonstrations *ceased* as suddenly as they had broken out —Charles Dickens⟩ ⟨the squealing which became slower and fainter and at last *ceased* —Jean Stafford⟩ **b :** to give over or bring to an end an activity or action **:** DISCONTINUE ⟨rock for hours before the fire without *ceasing*⟩ — often used with *from* ⟨the admonition that men ~ from their wickedness —*Amer.Scholar*⟩ **2** *obs* **:** to die out **:** become extinct ⟨the poor will never ~ out of the land —Deut 15:11 (RSV)⟩ **syn** see STOP

[2]**cease** \ˈ"\ *n* -s [ME *ces*, fr. MF *ces, cesse*, fr. *cesser*, v.] **:** CESSATION — usu. used with *without* ⟨I kept an eye upon her without ~ —R.L.Stevenson⟩

cease and desist order *n* **:** an order by an administrative agency to refrain from a method of competition or a labor practice found by the agency to be unfair

cease-fire \ˈ=ˈ=\ *n* -s **1 :** a military order to cease firing **2 :** a suspension of active hostilities ⟨the armistice, which was never more than an imperfect *cease-fire* —A.J.Liebling⟩

cease·less \-ləs\ *adj* **:** continuing without pause, check, or interruption **:** CONSTANT, CONTINUAL ⟨paying ~ attention to the lecturer⟩ ⟨the ~ tinny tumult of the jukebox —John McNulty⟩ ⟨a ~ stream of newspaper articles —J.F.Golay⟩ — **cease·less·ly** *adv* — **cease·less·ness** *n* -ES

cebadilla *var of* SABADILLA

ceb·a·tha \ˈsebəthə\ [NL, fr. Ar *kebath*, a plant] *syn of* COCCULUS

ce·bell \səˈbel\ *n* -s [origin unknown] **:** an old English dance similar to the gavotte

ce·bid \ˈsēbəd, ˈseb-\ *n* -s [NL *Cebidae*] **:** a monkey of the family Cebidae

ceb·i·dae \ˈsebəˌdē\ *n pl, cap* [NL, fr. *Cebus*, type genus + *-idae*] **:** a family of platyrrhine monkeys comprising all the New World monkeys except the marmosets and tamarins, having one more pair of molar teeth in each jaw than the marmosets and usu. a long prehensile tail, and constituting with the marmosets a superfamily that includes all the New World monkeys — compare PLATYRRHINA — **ce·boid** \ˈsēˌbȯid\ *adj*

ce·bil \səˈbēl\ *n* -s [AmerSp] **:** the So. American tree that yields angico gum

ce·bol·lite \(ˈ)sēˈbȯi,(y)īt, ˈsebəˌlīt\ *n* -s [*Cebolla* Creek, Gunnison county, Colo. + E *-ite*] **:** a mineral $H_2Ca_4Al_2Si_3O_{16}$ consisting of hydrous calcium aluminum silicate occurring in greenish to white fibrous aggregates (hardness 5, sp. gr. 3)

ce·bu \sāˈbü, sə-\ *adj, usu cap* [fr. *Cebu*, Philippines] **:** of or from the city of Cebu, Philippines **:** of the kind or style prevalent in Cebu

ce·bu·an \-üən\ *also* **ce·bua·no** \sābˈwä(ˌ)nō\ *n, pl* **cebuan** *or* **cebuans** *usu cap* [Sp *cebuano*, fr. *Cebú*, island & province of the Philippines + Sp *-ano* -an] **1 a :** a Bisayan people inhabiting Cebu **b :** a member of such people **2 :** the Austronesian language of the Cebuans — called also *Sugbuhanon*

ce·bu hemp *n, usu cap C* [fr. *Cebu*, island in the Philippines] **:** ABACA

cebu maguey *n, usu cap C* **:** CANTALA

ce·bus \ˈsēbəs\ *n, cap* [NL, fr. Gk *kēbos, kēpos* long-tailed monkey, prob. fr. Egypt *gif*, an East African ape] **:** a genus (the type of the family Cebidae) that comprises medium-sized monkeys with well-developed thumbs and fully haired prehensile tails — see CAPUCHIN

cec- *or* **ceci-** *or* **ceco-** *or* **caec-** *or* **caeci-** *or* **caeco-** *comb form* [NL, fr. *cecum*] **:** cecum ⟨*cecectomy*⟩ ⟨*ceciform*⟩ ⟨*cecitis*⟩ ⟨*cecocolic*⟩

ceca *pl of* CECUM

ce·cal *or* **cae·cal** \ˈsēkəl\ *adj* [NL *caecum* + E *-al*] **:** of or like a cecum — **ce·cal·ly** *or* **cae·cal·ly** \-əlē\ *adv*

cecal coccidiosis *n* **:** a destructive infectious disease of the domestic fowl caused by a protozoan (*Eimeria tenella*) that develops in the cecal tissue producing acute hemorrhagic diarrhea frequently fatal in young birds

cecal fluke *n* **:** a digenetic trematode (*Postharmostomum gallinum*) infesting the ceca of chickens and causing severe hemorrhages

cecal worm *n* **:** a worm parasitizing the cecum; *specif* **:** a nematode worm (*Heterakis gallinae*) of gallinaceous birds that serves as an intermediate host and transmitter of the blackhead organism

cecchine *obs var of* CHEQUEEN

ce·cec·to·mized \sēˈsektəˌmīzd\ *adj* **:** surgically deprived of the cecum

ce·cec·to·my \-ˌmē\ *n* -ES [*cec-* + *-ectomy*] **:** excision of all or part of the cecum

čech *usu cap, var of* CZECH

ce·cid·i·ol·o·gy \səˌsidēˈäləjē\ *n* -ES [NL *cecidium* + E *-o-* + *-logy*] **:** a branch of biology that treats of the galls produced on plants by insects, mites, and fungi

ce·cid·i·um \səˈsidēəm, sēˈ-\ *n, pl* **cecid·ia** \-ēə\ [NL, fr. Gk *kēkidion*, dim. of *kēkid-, kēkis* anything gushing out, dye, oak gall; akin to OE *hengest* stallion, OHG *hengist*, ON *hestr*, W *caseg* mare, Lith *šokti* to leap, dance] **:** GALL; *esp* **:** one caused by insects or mites — used esp. in combinations ⟨*acarocecidium*⟩ ⟨*zoocecidium*⟩

cec·i·dog·e·nous \ˌsesəˈdäjənəs\ *adj* [Gk *kēkid-, kēkis* + E *-o-* + *-genous*] **:** producing galls on plants ⟨~ insects⟩

cec·i·dol·o·gy \ˌ==ˈdäləjē\ *n* -ES [by alter.] **:** CECIDIOLOGY

cec·i·do·my·ia \ˌsesədōˈmī(y)ə\ *n* [NL, fr. Gk *kēkid-, kēkis* oak gall + NL *-o-* + *-myia*] **1** *cap* **:** a very large genus (the type of the family Cecidomyiidae) of gall-forming midges **2** -s **:** a midge of the genus *Cecidomyia; broadly* **:** GALL MIDGE

cec·i·do·my·id \-ī(y)əd\ *var of* CECIDOMYIID

cec·i·do·my·iid \-ī(y)əd\ *n* -s [NL *Cecidomyiidae*] **:** an insect of the genus *Cecidomyia* or family Cecidomyiidae **:** GALL MIDGE

cec·i·do·my·i·i·dae \ˌsesə(ˌ)dōməˈīəˌdē, -ˈmīə-\ *n pl, cap* [NL, fr. *Cecidomyia*, type genus + *-idae*] **:** a family of small mosquitolike nematocerous flies comprising the gall midges

ce·cil \ˈsēsəl\ *n* -s *usu cap* [fr. *Cecil* county, Maryland, its locality] **:** a series of reddish soils derived from material weathered from metamorphic and igneous rocks and found chiefly in the southern and central parts of the Piedmont plateau region of the U. S.

ce·ci·tis \sēˈsīdəs\ *n* -ES [NL, fr. *cec-* + *-itis*] **:** inflammation of the cecum

ce·ci·ty \ˈsesəd·ē\ *n* -ES [MF *cécité*, fr. L *caecitat-, caecitas*, fr. *caecus* blind + *-itat-, -itas* -ity — more at CECUM] **:** BLINDNESS

ce·cos·to·my \sēˈkästəmē\ *n* -ES [*cec-* + *-stomy*] **:** the surgical formation of an opening into the cecum to serve as an artificial anus

ce·cot·o·my \sēˈkäd·əmē\ *n* -ES [*cec-* + *-tomy*] **:** incision of the cecum

ce·cro·pia \səˈkrōpēə, sēˈ-\ *n, cap* [NL, fr. L, fem. of *Cecropius* Athenian, Attic, fr. Gk *Kekropios*, fr. *Kekrop-, Kekrops*, mythical first king of Athens] **:** a large genus of tropical American trees (family Moraceae) that have stems hollow between the nodes and peltate deeply lobed rough leaves usu. whitish beneath and clustered at the ends of the branches and that yield a bast fiber used for cordage, a bark used in tanning, and caoutchouc from their milky juice — see TRUMPETWOOD

cecropia moth \"-\ *also* **cecropia** *n* -s *sometimes cap C* [NL *cecropia* (specific epithet of *Samia cecropia*), fr. L *Cecropia*, fem. of *Cecropius*, adj.] **:** a large silkworm moth (*Hyalophora cecropia*) that is the largest moth native to the eastern U. S., that is represented by related species in the West, and that has larvae which feed on and are sometimes serious defoliators of many forest and fruit trees

ce·cum *or* **cae·cum** *also* **coe·cum** \ˈsēkəm\ *n, pl* **ce·ca** *or* **cae·ca** *also* **coe·ca** \-kə\ [NL, fr. L *intestinum caecum*, fr. *intestinum* intestine + *caecum*, neut. of *caecus* blind; akin to Goth *haihs* one-eyed, OIr *caech*, one-eyed, Skt *kekara* squint-eyed] **:** a cavity open at one end (as the blind end of a duct); *esp* **:** the blind pouch in which the large intestine begins and into which the ileum opens from one side — called also *blind gut*; see DIGESTION illustration

ce·dar \ˈsēdə(r)\ *n* -s *often attrib* [ME *cedre*, fr. OF, fr. L *cedrus*, fr. Gk *kedros* cedar, juniper; akin to Lith *kadagys* juniper, and perh. to OSlav *kaditi* to fumigate, Skt *kadru* tawny] **1 a :** CEDAR OF LEBANON; *broadly* **:** a tree of the genus *Cedrus* (as a deodar) — called also *true cedar* **b :** any of numerous coniferous trees chiefly of temperate or subtropical regions that are felt to resemble the true cedars esp. in the fragrance and durability of their wood: as (1) **:** a tree of the genus *Juniperus; esp* **:** RED CEDAR (2) **:** a tree of the genus *Chamaecyparis; esp* **:** SOUTHERN WHITE CEDAR (3) **:** a tree of the genus *Thuja* (as western red cedar) (4) **:** a tree of the genus *Libocedrus* (as incense cedar or kaikawaka) **c :** any of various chiefly tropical trees of the family Meliaceae having typically a reddish aromatic wood: as (1) **:** a tree of the genus *Cedrela* (as Spanish cedar or toon) (2) **:** MAHOGANY 3a, 3b **d :** any of several tropical American trees of the genera *Tabebuia* and *Tecoma; esp* **:** a medium-sized West Indian tree (*Tabebuia pallida*) with compound leaves and showy pink or white flowers **e** *Austral* **:** SILKY ASH **2 a :** CEDARWOOD **b :** any of various woods that are felt to resemble cedarwood esp. in fragrance, durability, or color — not used technically without a qualifying term **3 :** a variable color averaging a grayish red that is yellower and duller than bois de rose or appleblossom, yellower and less strong than blush rose, and duller than Pompeian red

cedar apple *also* **cedar ball** *n* **:** a hard brown more or less spherical excrescence on cedar trees of the genus *Juniperus* formed by various rusts (genus *Gymnosporangium*) during their telial stage — compare APPLE RUST

cedar-apple rust *n* **:** APPLE RUST

cedarbird \ˈ==ˌ=\ *n* **:** CEDAR WAXWING

cedar camphor *n* **:** CEDROL

cedar elm *n* **:** an elm (*Ulmus crassifolia*) of the southern U. S. and Mexico having spreading pendulous corky branches and yielding valuable timber

cedar green *n* **:** a moderate olive green that is lighter, stronger, and slightly yellower than forest green (sense 2), yellower, lighter, and stronger than cypress, and stronger and slightly greener and lighter than Lincoln green

cedarleaf oil \ˈ==ˌ=-\ *n* **:** THUJA OIL

cedar mahogany *n* **:** MAHOGANY 1b(2)

cedar man *n* **:** one who grades cedar poles according to size, length, and specified standards

cedar moss *n* **:** a hornwort (*Ceratophyllum demersum*) found as a submerged aquatic plant throughout No. America and grown in aquariums for its feathery foliage and as an aerator

ce·darn \ˈsēdə(r)n\ *adj* [*cedar* + *-n* (fr. *-en*)] *archaic* **:** made or suggestive of cedar ⟨carved ~ doors—Alfred Tennyson⟩

cedar nut *n* **:** the seed of the Swiss pine (*Pinus cembra*) — called also *cembra nut*

cedar of atlas *usu cap A* **:** ATLAS CEDAR

cedar of goa \-ˈgōə\ *cap G* [prob. trans. of Pg *cedro de Goa*, fr. *Goa*, Portuguese possession in India; prob. fr. a belief that it was introduced into Portugal from there] **:** MEXICAN CYPRESS

cedar of leb·a·non \-ˈlebənən\ *cap L* [fr. *Lebanon*, mountain range in the Republic of Lebanon; trans. of LL *cedrus Libani*, trans. of Heb *arzē hallĕbhānōn* (Ps 29: 5), *arzē lĕbhānōn* (Ps 104: 16)] **:** an evergreen tree (*Cedrus libani*) having short fascicled leaves and erect cones and attaining a great age and height

cedar pencil *n, dial* **:** an unpainted pencil

cedar rose *n* **:** a grayish red that is bluer and paler than bois de rose, yellower, lighter, and stronger than blush rose, and bluer and slightly paler than Pompeian red

cedar rust *n* **:** APPLE RUST

cedar waxwing *n* [prob. so called fr. its feeding on the berries of the red cedar (*Juniperus virginiana*)] **:** a waxwing (*Bombycilla cedrorun*) that is widely distributed over temperate No. America — see WAXWING

cedarwood \ˈ==ˌ=\ *n* **:** the wood of various cedars, esp. of a red cedar (*Juniperus virginiana*), used as a source of cedarwood oil and because it repels insects for lining wardrobes and closets

cedarwood oil *n* **:** a colorless to yellow essential oil obtained from the heartwood of various cedars (as red cedar) and used in soaps and perfumes and with immersion lenses in microscopy

cede \ˈsēd\ *vb* -ED/-ING/-S [F or L; F *céder*, fr. L *cedere* to go, proceed, withdraw, yield; prob. akin to L *cis* on this side and to Gk *hodos* way, journey, OSlav *chodŭ* gait, Skt *āsad* to arrive at, L *sedēre* to sit — more at HE, SIT] *vt* **1 :** to give up, give over, grant, or concede typically by treaty or negotiated pact ⟨the territory *ceded* by France, under the name of Louisiana —R.B.Taney⟩ **2 :** ASSIGN, TRANSFER ⟨~ his stock holdings to his children⟩ **3 :** to transfer by reinsurance (all or part of one's liability as insurer under an insurance policy) to some other insurer ~ *vi* **:** to give way **:** yield precedence — used with *to* **syn** see RELINQUISH

ce·dent \ˈsēdᵊnt\ *n* [L *cedent-, cedens*, pres. part. of *cedere* to yield] **1** *also* **ce·dens** -ES \ˈsēˌdenz\ **:** an assignor of a debt or claim **2** *Scots law* **:** an assignor of property or claims by a deed of conveyance

ced·er \ˈsēdə(r)\ *n* -s **:** one that cedes

ce·dil·la \səˈdilə, sēˈ-\ *n* -s [Sp, the obs. letter *ç* (actually a medieval form of the letter *z*), cedilla, fr. dim. of *ceda, zeda* the letter *z*, fr. LL *zeta* — more at ZED] **:** a mark or diacritic ¸ placed under a letter or symbol to indicate a sound different from that which the unmodified character bears in certain or all situations (as under *c* in French and in Portuguese before *a, o*, or *u* to indicate a pronunciation\s\ rather than \k\)

ced·or \ˈsēdə(r)\ *n* -s [*cede* + *-or*] **:** CEDENT 1

ce·drat *or* **ce·drate** \ˈsēdrət\ *also* **ce·dra** \-rə\ *n* -s [F *cédrat*, fr. It *cedrato*, fr. *cedro* citron, fr. L *citrus* — more at CITRON] **:** CITRON

ce·dre \ˈsēdə(r), ˈsedrᵊ, ˈsedrə\ *n* -s [F *cèdre* cedar — more at CEDAR] **:** CEDAR GREEN

ce·dre·la \səˈdrēlə\ *n, cap* [NL, modif. of Sp *cedrelo*, dim. of *cedro* cedar, fr. L *cedrus* — more at CEDAR] **:** a small genus of large tropical American timber trees (family Meliaceae) that are characterized by bipinnate leaves and flowers with a 5-celled ovary which produces winged seeds and that yield ornamental wood used for furniture — see SPANISH CEDAR

ce·drene \ˈsēˌdrēn\ *n* -s [ISV *cedr-* (fr. L *cedrus* cedar) + *-ene*] **:** a sesquiterpene $C_{15}H_{24}$ occurring in cedarwood oil and oils of other conifers

ced·ri·ret \ˌsed(r)əˈret\ *n* -s [G *zedriret*, fr. L *cedrium* cedar oil (fr. Gk *kedrion*, fr. *kedros* cedar) + *rete* net; fr. the netlike pattern of the crystals on a filter — more at CEDAR, RETINA] **:** CERULIGNONE

ce·dro \ˈse(ˌ)drō, ˈsā-\ *n* -s [Sp & Pg, lit., cedar, fr. L *cedrus* — more at CEDAR] **:** any of several reddish cedarlike woods (as of Spanish cedar and other species of *Cedrela*)

ce·drol \ˈsēˌdrōl, -ōl\ *n* -s [ISV *cedr-* (fr. L *cedrus*) + *-ol*] **:** a colorless crystalline sesquiterpenoid alcohol $C_{15}H_{25}OH$ found in cedarwood oil and oils of other conifers and used in perfumes

ce·dron \səˈdrōn\ *n* -s [AmerSp *cedrón*, fr. Sp *cedro* cedar, fr. L *cedrus*] **1 :** a tropical American tree (*Simaba cedron*) **2 :** the fruit of the cedron

ce·drus \ˈsēdrəs\ *n, cap* [NL, fr. L, cedar — more at CEDAR] **:** a small genus of Old World evergreen trees (family Pinaceae) having erect cones and leaves clustered as in the larches but persistent

ce·du·la \ˈsāthəˌlä, ˈthāth-\ *n* -s [Sp *cédula*, fr. LL *schedula* — more at SCHEDULE] **1 :** any of various official documents or certificates in Spain, Latin America, or the Philippines: as **a :** a permit or order issued by the government **b :** a personal registration tax certificate in the Philippines **c :** any of certain securities issued by some of the So. and Central American governments or banks **2 :** a Philippine personal registration tax

cee *also* **ce** \ˈsē\ *n* -s **1 :** the letter *c* **2 :** something having the shape of the letter C

cee spring *n* **:** C SPRING

cei·ba \ˈsābə\ *n* [NL, fr. Sp, prob. of Arawakan origin; akin to Taino *ceyba*] **1** *cap* **:** a large genus of tropical American trees (family Bombacaceae) with palmately compound leaves and showy bell-shaped flowers **2** -s [Sp *ceiba*] **a** *or* **ceiba tree :** a massive tree (*Ceiba pentandra*) widely cultivated in the tropics having a trunk of large size with buttresslike ridges and bearing large pods filled with seeds invested with a silky floss that yields in the cultivated state the fiber kapok — called also *Bombay ceiba, God tree, silk-cotton tree* **b :** KAPOK

cei·bo \ˈsā(ˌ)bō\ *n* -s [AmerSp, ceibo, ceiba tree, fr. Sp. *ceiba*] **1 :** a So. American shrub or small tree (*Erythrina crista-galli*) with crimson and scarlet flowers **2 :** KAPOK

ceil \ˈsēl, -ēəl\ *vt* -ED/-ING/-S [ME *celen, cylen*, prob. fr. (assumed) MF *celer* (OF *celé*, *cielé* provided with an ornate ceiling), fr. L *caelare* to carve, engrave, fr. *caelum* chisel, graver, fr. *caedere* to cut, hew — more at CONCISE] **1 a** *obs* **:** to overlay (as a wall) with a covering (as of thin boards or plaster) **b :** to line the bottom and sides of (a wooden ship) with planking **2 a :** LINE ⟨~ a roof⟩ **b :** to furnish with a ceiling

ceiled \ˈsēld, -ē(ə)ld\ *adj* [ME *cyled*, fr. past part. of *cylen, celen* to ceil] **1 :** having a ceiling **2 :** finished with wainscot

cei·lidh *also* **cei·lidhe** \ˈkālē\ *n* -s [IrGael *céilidhe* & ScGael *cèilidh*, fr. MIr *célide*, fr. OIr *céle*, *céile* companion, husband; akin to L *civis* citizen — more at CEMETERY] **1** *Irish & Scot* **:** a friendly call **:** VISIT **2** *Irish & Scot* **:** an evening entertainment usu. with storytelling and singing or dancing

ceil·ing \ˈsēliŋ, -ēŋ\ *n* -s *often attrib* [ME *celing*, fr. *celen* to ceil + *-ing* — more at CEIL] **1 a** *obs* **:** woodwork lining the roof or walls of a room **:** WAINSCOTING **b** *obs* **:** a wall hanging or tapestry **c :** the overhead inside lining of a room **:** the underside of the floor above **d :** planking that lines the inside and bottom of a wooden ship or that covers the inner bottom of a steel ship — see SHIP illustration **e :** material used to ceil a wall or roof of a room; *esp* **:** narrow beaded matchboards used for wainscoting **f :** an uppermost surface of a cavity or chamber **2 :** something thought of as an overhanging shelter or lofty canopy ⟨above the gulls was a ~ of terns —Llewellyn Howland⟩ ⟨an incredible ~ of stars —M.P. O'Connor⟩ **3 a :** the height above the ground from which prominent objects on the ground can be seen and identified **b :** the height above the ground of the base of the lowest layer of clouds when over half of the sky is obscured **4 a :** ABSOLUTE CEILING **b :** SERVICE CEILING **5 :** the maximum height to which a projectile rises upon being fired from a gun **6** *or* **ceiling frame :** a canvas-covered frame suspended horizontally over a theater set to close it off on top **7 a :** an upper limit imposed by an authoritative ruling above which a particular quantity or rate is not to be allowed to rise ⟨a ~ on prices, wages, rents, profits, new construction⟩ ⟨asking Congress to raise the debt ~⟩ ⟨a 4-million manpower ~ on the armed forces⟩ **b :** an uppermost limit determined by conditions and circumstances of a particular situation ⟨the speed ~ of a helicopter⟩ **c :** a top level determined by economic factors ⟨today's stock market averages broke through all previous ~s⟩ **d :** any deliberately prescribed limit on increase in amount or quantity **e :** a barrier against potential rise in status or prestige **f :** an upper limit of ability or capability ⟨a low ~ of tolerance⟩

ceiling climbing *n, slang* **:** playing high notes for display of virtuosity in jazz improvization
ceil·inged \'sēlind, -ēnd\ *adj* **:** provided with a ceiling ⟨the studio was high-*ceilinged* —Winifred Bambrick⟩ ⟨the large, beam-*ceilinged* living room —John McDowell⟩
ceiling floor *n* **:** the framework of a room receiving a ceiling framed separately from the floor of the story above
ceiling hook *n* **:** a wood screw with head formed of a loop left open at its base to serve as a down-hanging hook
ceiling joist *n* **:** one of a series of small joists supporting the lath and plaster of a ceiling
ceiling note *n* **:** a note of spectacularly high pitch (as made by a jazz trumpet)
ceiling plate *n, in the theater* **:** a metal plate with ring attached that is bolted to a ceiling frame for use in fastening or flying it
ceiling unlimited *n* **:** a cloudless or nearly cloudless sky **:** a sky less than half obscured by clouds at levels lower than an arbitrary fixed altitude
ceil·om·e·ter \sē'lämәd·ә(r), sә'-\ *n* -s [*ceiling* + *-o-* + *-meter*] **:** a photoelectric instrument for determining the height of the cloud ceiling above the earth by indicating the angular elevation of a spot of light formed where a strong modulated beam of light meets the cloud so that the height may be computed automatically by triangulation
cein·ture \saⁿ(n)'tyü(ә)r, 'sanchәr, *F* saⁿtüeer\ *n* -s [F, fr. L *cinctura* — more at CINCTURE] **1 :** a girdle or belt for the waist **2 a :** a connected series of fortifications around a city **b :** a railroad encircling a city
ce·ja \'sā,hä, 'sāә\ *n* -s [Sp, lit., eyebrow, fr. L *cilia*, pl. of *cilium*] *Southwest* **:** a jutting edge along the top of a mesa or upland plain
cel *or* **cell** \'sel\ *n* -s [short for *celluloid*] **:** one of the transparent sheets of celluloid on which objects or sections of objects are drawn or painted in the making of animated cartoons for motion pictures and television
cel *abbr, usu cap* Celsius
cel- — see COEL-
cel·a·don \'selә,dän, -,dᵊn\ *or* **cé·la·don** \sälädōⁿ\ *n* -s [F *céladon*, fr. *Céladon*, Astrée's lover in Honoré d'Urfé's romance *L'Astrée* (1610)] **1 :** a grayish yellow green that is paler and slightly yellower than average sage green, yellower and lighter than palmetto, and greener and lighter than mermaid **2 :** a reduction-fired iron-containing ceramic glaze originated in China that ranges from putty colored or greenish brown or gray to true green or bluish green and is used esp. in the Orient on various stonewares and porcelains; *also* **:** an article or ware with a celadon glaze **3 :** a monochrome glaze
celadon gray *n* **:** a pale green that is yellower and very slightly lighter and stronger than bayberry gray and yellower and duller than spray green
celadon green *or* **sel·a·don green** *n* [*celadon* fr. F *céladon; seladon* fr. G] **:** a variable color averaging a grayish yellow green that is yellower and paler than average sage green, greener and stronger than mermaid, yellower, lighter, and stronger than palmetto, and yellower and deeper than celadon
cel·a·don·ite \'seladᵊn,īt\ *n* -s [prob. fr. G *seladonit*, fr. *seladon* celadon green (fr. F. *céladon*) + *-it* -ite] **:** a soft green earthy mineral consisting of silicate of iron, magnesium, and potassium
celadon tint *n* **:** a very pale green that is yellower and paler than tourmaline, yellower and duller than emerald tint, and yellower and slightly less strong than microcline green
cel·an·dine \'selәn,dīn *also* -,dēn\ *n* -s [ME *salendyne*, *celidoine*, fr. MF *celidoine*, fr. L *chelidonia*, fr. fem. of *chelidonius* of the swallow, fr. Gk *chelidonios*, fr. *chelidon-*, *chelidōn* swallow; akin to OE *giellan* to yell — more at YELL] **1 :** a perennial herb (*Chelidonium majus*) of the family Papaveraceae with a branched woody stock and bright yellow flowers — called also *swallowwort* **2 :** LESSER CELANDINE **3 :** a variable No. American jewelweed (*Impatiens capensis*) sometimes cultivated as an ornament in Europe
celandine green *n* **:** a pale to grayish green
celandine poppy *n* **:** a yellow-flowered herb (*Stylophorum diphyllum*) of the family Papaveraceae of the eastern U.S. resembling the celandine but with flowers having a long style and a hirsute capsule
cel·as·tra·ce·ae \,selәs'trāsē,ē\ *n pl, cap* [NL, fr. *Celastrus*, type genus + *-aceae*] **:** a family of trees, shrubs, and woody vines (order Sapindales) having simple leaves, small regular flowers, and usu. brightly colored fruit with arillate seeds
cel·as·tra·ceous \;=;=shәs\ *adj* [NL *Celastraceae* + E *-ous*] **:** belonging to the Celastraceae
ce·las·trus \sә'lastrәs\ *n, cap* [NL, fr. Gk *kēlastros* holly] **:** a genus (the type of the family Celastraceae) of woody vines and erect shrubs native chiefly to Asia and Australia and having alternate deciduous leaves, flowers in panicles or racemes, and fruit a 3-valved orange or yellow capsule — see BITTERSWEET
ce·la·tion \sә'lāshәn, sē-\ *n* -s [L *celatus* (past part. of *celare* to conceal) + E *-ion* — more at HELL] **:** CONCEALMENT; *esp* **:** concealment of pregnancy or childbirth
cel·a·ture \'selә,chü(ә)r\ *n* -s [ME, fr. L *caelatura*, fr. *caelatus* (past part. of *caelare* to engrave) + *-ura* -ure; — more at CEIL] **:** embossed work or figures **:** EMBOSSING
¹-cele \,sēl\ *n comb form* -s [MF, fr. L, fr. Gk *kēlē* tumor; akin to OE *hēala* hydrocele, hernia, OHG *hōla* hernia, ON *haull*, OSlav *kyla*] **:** tumor **:** hernia ⟨*cystocele*⟩ ⟨*gastrocele*⟩
²-cele \"\ — see -COELE
ce·leb \sә'leb\ *n* -s [by shortening] *slang* **:** CELEBRITY 3
cel·e·be·sian \;selә;bēzhәn\ *adj, usu cap* [*Celebes*, island in the Malay archipelago + E *-ian*] **:** of, relating to, or characteristic of Celebes
cel·e·brant \'selәbrәnt\ *n* -s [F & L; F *célébrant*, fr. L *celebrant-*, *celebrans*, pres. part. of *celebrare*] **1 :** one who celebrates a public religious rite; *esp* **:** the officiating priest in the celebration of the Eucharist or mass as distinguished from his assistants **2 a :** one who takes part in ceremonious or convivial festivities celebrating a special occasion **b :** one who participates in any noisy party (as one at which there is a good deal of drinking) **3 :** one who sedulously exalts or extols a particular theme esp. in literary or art form ⟨a ~ of city life⟩
¹celebrate *adj* [ME *celebrat*, fr. L *celebratus*] *obs* **:** CELEBRATED
²cel·e·brate \-,brāt, *usu* -ād·+V\ *vb* -ED/-ING/-S [L *celebratus*, past part. of *celebrare* to frequent, celebrate, fr. *celebr-*, *celeber* much frequented, famous; akin to L *celer* swift — more at CELERITY] *vt* **1 :** to perform (a sacrament or solemn ceremony) publicly and with appropriate rites **:** SOLEMNIZE ⟨~ the mass⟩ ⟨~ a marriage⟩ **2 a :** to honor (as a holy day or feast day) by conducting or engaging in religious, commemorative, or other solemn ceremonies or by refraining from ordinary business **b :** to demonstrate grateful and happy satisfaction in (as an anniversary or event) by engaging in festivities, indulgence, merrymaking, or other similar deviation from accustomed routine ⟨as though he had had a drink or two — which indeed he might have had in reality, to ~ the occasion —Joseph Conrad⟩ **3 :** to proclaim or broadcast for the attention of a wide public ⟨that bloody nationalism which *celebrated* itself on so large a scale in 1914-1918 —Francis Hackett⟩ **4 a :** to portray with a high valuation and usu. in enhanced or poetic form or in exalted interpretation in a way to contribute to public awareness, edification, or enjoyment **:** hold up or play up for public acclaim or homage **:** EXTOL, GLORIFY ⟨verses *celebrating* the personal idiosyncrasy of the Yankee farmer⟩ ⟨American fiction had regularly *celebrated* the American village as the natural home of the pleasant virtues —Carl Van Doren⟩ **b :** to commemorate in appreciative interpretation for posterity esp. in some literary or art form ⟨his birthplace, *celebrated* by him in his early poetry —Padraic Colum⟩ ⟨the sort of beauty that is *celebrated* by the heroic male sculptures in the fountains of Rome —Tennessee Williams⟩ ~ *vi* **1 :** to observe a holiday, perform a religious ceremony, or take part in a festival ⟨in an Eastern liturgy several priests may ~ together⟩ ⟨in the Western mass, the priests ~ in the Latin fashion⟩ **2 a :** to observe the occasion of an achievement, reunion, anniversary, or other notable occasion with gaiety **b :** to engage in hilarious festivities usu. including drinking **syn** see KEEP
celebrated *adj* **:** widely or commonly known and often referred to because of some memorable quality or association **:** NOTED ⟨a ~ physician⟩ ⟨~ for its marble quarries⟩ ⟨one of the most ~ cases in the annals of crime⟩ — **cel·e·brat·ed·ness** *n* -ES
cel·e·brat·er \-,brād·ә(r), -ātә-\ *n* -s *archaic var of* CELEBRATOR
cel·e·bra·tion \,selә'brāshәn\ *n* -s [MF & L; MF *célébration* fr. L *celebration-*, *celebratio*, fr. *celebratus*, past part. of *celebrare* + *-ion-*, *-io* -ion] **1 :** the act or process of celebrating ⟨the ~ of a wedding anniversary⟩ ⟨a rowdy Saturday night ~⟩ ⟨moving ~ of an intricately human marriage —Robert Phelps⟩; *specif* **:** the performance of a public religious ceremony or of a sacred rite ⟨the ~ of the Eucharist⟩ **2** *obs* **:** RENOWN
cel·e·bra·tive \'selә,brād·iv, -,brәd··\ *adj* **:** designed or set apart for celebrating
cel·e·bra·tor \-,brād·ә(r), -ātә-\ *n* -s [L, fr. *celebratus* + *-or*] **:** one that celebrates
cel·e·bra·to·ry \'selәbrә,tōrē\ *adj* **:** used or intended for use in celebrating a solemn or festive occasion
cel·e·bret \'selә,bret\ *n* -s [L, let him celebrate, 3d sing. pres. subj. of *celebrare* to celebrate — more at CELEBRATE] **:** a letter from a Roman Catholic bishop or religious superior testifying that the bearer is a priest and asking that he be permitted to say mass in dioceses other than his own
ce·leb·ri·ous \sә'lebrēәs\ *adj* [L *celebr-*, *celeber* + E *-ious*] **1** *obs* **:** THRONGED **2 :** FESTIVE **3 :** FAMOUS
ce·leb·ri·ty \sә'lebrәd-ē, -әtē, -i\ *n* -ES [MF & L; MF *célébrité*, fr. L *celebritat-*, *celebritas*, fr. *celebr-*, *celeber* famous + *-itat-*, *-itas* -ity — more at CELEBRATE] **1** *obs* **:** a solemn celebration **2 :** the state of being celebrated, acclaimed, or widely known on account of specific accomplishments ⟨that was in the spring of 1820, and the season of ~ was often quite as short then as it is today —H.V.Gregory⟩ ⟨made a sensational debut as a pianist at the age of six . . . but by adolescence, her ~ was finished —Roul Tunley⟩ **3 :** a celebrated or widely known person **:** one popularly honored for some signal achievement ⟨he found himself a ~, sought after by civic leaders and journalists —R.A. Cordell⟩ **syn** see FAME
celebrous *adj* [L *celebr-*, *celeber* + E *-ous*] *obs* **:** CELEBRATED
celenteron *var of* COELENTERON
cel·er·i·ac \sә'lerē,ak, -ir-\ *n* -s [irreg. fr. *celery*] **:** a celery of a variety (*Apium graveolens rapaceum*) grown for its thickened turniplike edible root — called also *celery root, knob celery, root celery, turnip-rooted celery*
ce·ler·i·tous \sә'lerәd-әs\ *adj* [*celerity* + *-ous*] **:** swift-moving
ce·ler·i·ty \-әd-ē, -әtē, -i\ *n* -ES [ME *celerite*, fr. MF *célérité*, fr. L *celeritat-*, *celeritas*, fr. *celer* swift + *-itat-*, *-itas* -ity; akin to Goth *haldan* to feed, tend (animals), Gk *kellein* to beach (a ship), Skt *kalayati* he drives] **:** rapidity of motion or action: **a :** PROMPTNESS, ALACRITY ⟨disposing of the parsnip wine with a ~ which might have been due to eagerness —Dorothy Sayers⟩ **b :** SWIFTNESS, SPEED ⟨reptiles swim with great ~⟩
cel·ery \'sel(ә)rē, -ri\ *n* -ES [prob. fr. It dial. (Lombardy) *seleri*, pl. of *selero*, modif. of LL *selinon*, fr. Gk] **1 :** a European herbaceous plant (*Apium graveolens*); *specif* **:** one of a cultivated variety (*A. graveolens dulce*) the leafstalks of which are eaten raw or cooked **2** *also* **celery grass :** TAPE GRASS
celery blight *n* **:** early blight, late blight, or bacterial blight of celery or a combination of these
celery cabbage *n* **:** CHINESE CABBAGE
celery calico *n* **:** a virus disease of celery and certain other plants (as delphinium) characterized by conspicuous green and yellow, orange, or amber mottling usu. on the older leaves
celery family *n* **:** UMBELLIFERAE
celery fly *n* **1 :** a small brown-winged green-eyed European fly (*Trypeta*, or *Acidia*, *heraclei*) whose larvae are leaf miners in celery, parsnips, and uncultivated related plants **2 :** an Australian agromyzid fly whose larvae mine celery stalks
celery leaf ti·er \-,tī(ә)r\ *n* **:** a small pale reddish brown European moth (*Udea rubigalis*) of the family Pyralididae that is widespread in No. America and whose yellowish green larvae are a major pest on the leaves of celery and greenhouse crops
celery-leaved buttercup \-,lēvd-\ *n* **:** CURSED CROWFOOT
celery mosaic *n* **:** a mosaic disease of celery producing stiff bushy growth
celery pine *n* **:** CELERY-TOPPED PINE
celery root *n* **:** CELERIAC
celery salt *n* **:** a mixture of ground celery seed and salt
celery seed *n* **:** minute seedlike fruits of a widely cultivated celery plant (*Apium graveolens*) that are dried for use as a condiment
celery-seed oil *or* **celery oil** *n* **:** a colorless or yellowish essential oil with a celery odor and taste obtained from celery seeds and used chiefly as a flavoring agent
celery-topped pine \-,täpt-\ *or* **celery top pine** *n* **:** an Australasian coniferous tree of the genus *Phyllocladus* (esp. *P. rhomboidalis* and *P. trichomanoides*) of the family Taxaceae cultivated for the graceful heads of celerylike foliage composed of rhombic phyllodes borne in the axils of scaly leaves
celery yellows *n pl but sing in constr* **:** a disease of celery caused by a fungus of the genus *Fusarium* and characterized by yellowing and stunting
-celes *pl of* -CELE
ce·les·ta \sә'lestә, *or* chә'- *as if from It*\ *n* -s [F *célesta*, irreg. fr. *céleste*] **:** a keyboard instrument having an action like that of a piano with hammers that strike steel plates suspended above wooden resonance boxes, producing a tone similar to that of a glockenspiel, and having a range of four octaves sounding an octave higher than the notes indicate

celesta

ce·leste \sә'lest\ *n* -s [F *céleste*, lit., heavenly, fr. L *caelestis*] **1 :** a grayish blue to pale purplish blue **2 a :** VOIX CÉLESTE **b :** a pedal that mutes the strings of a piano by interposing a muffling strip between the hammers and the strings **3 :** CELESTA
¹ce·les·tial \sә'les(h)chәl *sometimes* -estēәl\ *adj* [ME, fr. MF, fr. L *caelestis* celestial (fr. *caelum* sky, heaven, atmosphere, temperature) + MF *-al* — more at -HOOD] **1 a :** of or relating to heaven ⟨~ hosts⟩ ⟨the gods of the ~ regions⟩ **b :** felt to resemble or as if proceeding from something divine ⟨a ~ brightness . . . on her face —H.W.Longfellow⟩ **2 :** of or relating to the sky; *specif* **:** representing the visible bodies in the sky ⟨a ~ map⟩ ⟨a ~ globe⟩ **3 a :** ETHEREAL, OTHERWORLDLY ⟨the ~ quiet of an autumn snow⟩ **b :** OLYMPIAN, SUPREME ⟨the ~ impudence of the boy —Leonard Bacon⟩ **4 :** of the color celestial **5** [fr. *Celestial* Empire, old name for China, trans. of Chin *T'ien¹ Ch'ao²*] *usu cap* **:** of or relating to a native of China, the Chinese, or the Chinese nation — **ce·les·tial·ly** \-әlē, -li\ *adv* — **ce·les·tial·ness** *n* -ES
²celestial \"\ *n* -s **1 :** a heavenly or mythical being ⟨the ~s instructed the Indian maid to summon her people to council⟩ **2** *usu cap* **:** a native of China **3** *or* **celestial blue :** SKY BLUE
celestial blue *n* **:** a pale iron-blue pigment usu. containing a large amount of barium sulfate — compare CELESTIAL 3
celestial body *n* **:** an aggregation of matter in the universe that constitutes a unit (as a planet, nebula) for astronomical study
celestial coordinate *n* **:** a member of any system of coordinates used for locating a point on the celestial sphere — compare ECLIPTIC COORDINATE, EQUATOR SYSTEM OF COORDINATE, GALACTIC COORDINATE, HORIZON COORDINATE
celestial crown *n* **:** a heraldic crown having rays like an antique crown but with a star at the end of each ray
celestial equator *n* **:** the great circle on the celestial sphere midway between the celestial poles
celestial glory *n* **:** the highest of the three Mormon degrees or kingdoms of glory attainable in heaven — compare TELESTIAL GLORY, TERRESTIAL GLORY

celestial crown

celestial hierarchy *n* **:** a hierarchy of angels based upon interpretations of various scriptural references and ranked from those nearest to God into nine orders (as seraphim, cherubim, thrones; dominions, virtues, powers; principalities, archangels, angels)
celestial horizon *n* **:** the great circle on the celestial sphere midway between the zenith and the nadir
ce·les·tial·ize \-,līz\ *vt* -ED/-ING/-S **:** to make divine or spiritual in quality or appearance **:** ETHEREALIZE ⟨the *celestialized* figure of a saint⟩ ⟨a face *celestialized* with joy⟩
celestial latitude *n* **:** latitude in the ecliptic system of celestial coordinates
celestial lily *n* **:** a plant of the genus *Nemastylis*
celestial longitude *n* **:** longitude in the ecliptic system of coordinates measured eastward from the March equinox
celestial marriage *n* **:** marriage for eternity solemnized in a Mormon temple
celestial mechanics *n pl but sing or pl in constr* **:** the application of the methods of analytic mechanics to the determination of the motions of the celestial bodies under the action of gravitation — called also *gravitational astronomy*
celestial meridian *n* **:** a great circle of the celestial sphere passing through the celestial poles and the zenith
celestial navigation *n* **:** navigation in which the observed positions of celestial bodies at exact instants of time are employed by a navigator to determine his position
celestial pole *n* **:** one of the two points on the celestial sphere around which the diurnal rotation of the stars appears to take place — compare NORTH POLE, SOUTH POLE
celestial sphere *n* **:** an imaginary sphere of infinite radius against which the celestial bodies appear to be projected and of which the apparent dome of the visible sky forms half
celestial teacher *n, usu cap C&T* [trans. of Chin (Pek) *T'ien¹ Shih¹*] **:** HEAVENLY PRECEPTOR
celestial telescope *n* **:** a variety of telescope goldfish in which the eye pupils are directed upward
celestical *adj* [L *caelestis* + E *-ical* — more at CELESTIAL] *obs* **:** CELESTIAL
celestify *vt* -ED/-ING/-ES [*celestial* + *-ify*] *obs* **:** to make like heaven
¹cel·es·ti·na \,selә'stēnә, ,che-\ *n* -s [It, fem. of *celestino* heavenly, fr. *celeste*, fr. L *caelestis* — more at CELESTIAL] **:** a 4-foot organ stop of flute quality
²cel·es·ti·na \"\ *n* -s [prob. irreg. fr. L *caelestis* heavenly] **:** a largely experimental keyboard musical instrument producing sustained tones by means of a usu. rosined-silk wheel that is made to rub against a tuned string or bar during the depression of each key
¹cel·es·tine *or* **coel·es·tine** \'selә,stēn, -īn; sә'lestәn\ *n* -s [G *zölestin* — more at CELESTITE] **:** CELESTITE
²ce·les·tine \;selә;stēn\ *adj* [F *célestine* (in *à la célestine* in the Celestine manner) Celestine ("of an order of monks"), after Pope Celestine (F *Célestine*) V (Pietro di Murrone or Morone) †1296, its founder] *of food* **:** garnished with finely shredded pancakes — usu. used postpositively ⟨consommé ~⟩
cel·es·tite \'selә,stīt, sә'le,-\ *n* -s [G *zölestin* (fr. L *caelestis* celestial + G *-in* -ine) + E *-ite*; fr. its blue color] **:** a mineral $SrSO_4$ consisting of native strontium sulfate commonly white and occas. of a delicate blue color and occurring in orthorhombic crystals and in compact massive and fibrous forms
celi- — see COELI-
¹celiac *var of* COELIAC
²ce·li·ac \'sēlē,ak\ *adj* [*celiac* (*disease*)] **:** belonging to or prescribed for celiac disease ⟨the ~ syndrome⟩ ⟨a ~ diet⟩
celiac disease *n* [¹*celiac*] **:** a chronic nutritional disturbance in young children that is characterized by defective digestion and utilization of fats and by abdominal distention, diarrhea, and fatty stools
cel·i·ba·cy \'selәbәsē, -si\ *n* -ES [L *caelibatus* celibacy + E *-cy*] **1 :** the state of not having a spouse **:** single life ⟨~ can usu. be tolerated as a state favorable to education —*New Statesman & Nation*⟩ **2 a :** abstention from sexual intercourse **b :** CHASTITY; *specif* **:** the obligation (as of certain priests) not to marry
cel·i·ba·tar·i·an \;selәbә;ta(a)rēәn\ *adj* [¹*celibate* + *-arian*] **:** favoring or marked by celibacy
¹cel·i·bate \'selәbәt\ *n* -s [L *caelibatus*, fr. *caelib-*, *caelebs* unmarried + *-atus* -ate; akin to Skt *kevala* alone and to Skt *liban* to live — more at LIVE] **1 :** CELIBACY ⟨the ~ of priests⟩ **2** [²*celibate*] **:** one who lives a single life (as a bachelor)
²celibate \"\ *adj* [L *caelib-*, *caelebs* + E *-ate*] **:** of or relating to celibacy
celio- — see COELI-
ce·li·ot·o·my \,sēlē'ädәmē\ *n* -ES [ISV *celio-* + *-tomy*] **:** surgical incision of the abdomen
ce·lite \'sē,līt\ *n* -s [ISV *ce-* (fr. *c*) + *-lite*; fr. its being considered as third in a group including also alite and belite] **:** a constituent of portland-cement clinker now identified as brownmillerite
Celite \"\ *trademark* — used for any of a series of diatomaceous silica and perlite products including filter material and fillers
¹cell \'sel\ *n* -s [ME *celle*, fr. OF, fr. L *cella*; akin to L *celare* to hide — more at HELL] **1 :** a small religious house dependent on and at some distance from a monastery or convent **2 a :** a dwelling of one room occupied by a solitary person (as a hermit) **b :** a single room usu. housing only one person within a building having numerous similar rooms (as in a convent or in a prison) **c :** a small abode or enclosure (as the den of a wild animal) **d :** GRAVE ⟨each in his narrow ~ for ever laid —Thomas Gray⟩ **3 :** a compartment, hollow receptacle, or compartmentlike demarcation: as **a :** one of the compartments of a honeycomb **b :** a ring-shaped enclosure in which an object is secured for observation under a microscope **c :** the entire structure of the wings and wing trussing in an airplane on one side of the fuselage or between fuselages or nacelles when there is more than one **d :** a bag containing aerostatic gas in a balloon or airship **4 a** (1) **:** the bounding walls of a cell (sense 5) that has lost its living content — used esp. of cavities in cork before the discovery of the protoplast (2) **:** a calyculus enclosing a zooid in hydroids and corals **b :** a membranous area bounded by veins in the wing of an insect **c** (1) **:** one of the cavities or compartments into which a compound ovary is partitioned or the whole interior of a monocarpellary ovary (2) **:** THECA 1b **5 :** a small usu. microscopic mass of protoplasm bounded externally by a semipermeable membrane, usu. including one or more nuclei and various nonliving products of its activities (as ergastic granules or rigid external walls), and being capable alone or interacting with other cells of performing all the fundamental functions of life **:** the least structural aggregate of living matter capable of functioning as an independent unit **:** a protoplast with its derivative structures **6 :** a cup, jar, or other vessel or a division of a compound vessel containing electrodes and an electrolyte either for generating electric currents by chemical action or for use in electrolysis — see PRIMARY CELL, SECONDARY CELL, STANDARD CELL, STORAGE CELL **7 a :** CELLA **b :** a space between ribs in a vaulted roof **c :** a compartment of a frame or truss **d :** an air space introduced into a piece of building material (as a cement block or hollow tile) for thermal insulation **8 a :** a unit of a statistical array comprising a group of individuals and formed by the intersection of a column and a row **b :** a set in n-dimensional euclidean space homeomorphic to the closed or open set in space of the same number of dimensions that is analogous to the set of points included in a closed or open circle or sphere in two or three dimensions ⟨a circle is a ~ with respect to its interior⟩ **9 :** a small group dedicated to the study and development of a social, religious, or political program; *esp* **:** the smallest organizational unit of a proscribed or clandestine political party often located within and made up of employees of a particular business, industry, or school **10 :** the oblong ar-

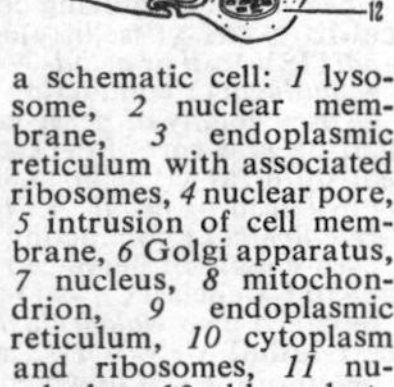

a schematic cell: *1* lysosome, *2* nuclear membrane, *3* endoplasmic reticulum with associated ribosomes, *4* nuclear pore, *5* intrusion of cell membrane, *6* Golgi apparatus, *7* nucleus, *8* mitochondrion, *9* endoplasmic reticulum, *10* cytoplasm and ribosomes, *11* nucleolus, *12* chloroplast

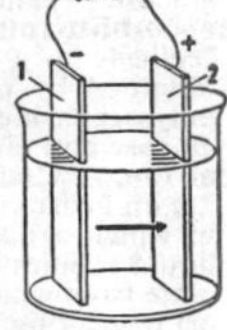

cell 6: *1* negative pole (zinc plate); *2* positive pole (carbon plate)

rangement of braille dots in two vertical rows of three high and two wide which in various combinations represent letters, figures, punctuation marks, and other characters **11 :** any portion of the atmosphere from a few cubic feet to many thousands of cubic miles in volume that moves or behaves as a unit despite varying conditions of temperature, humidity, and air movement inside of it and that takes part in a systematic circulation **12 :** a single unit in a device for converting radiant energy into electrical energy or for varying the intensity of an electric current in accordance with radiation

²**cell** \"\ *vb* -ED/-ING/-S *vi* **:** to live in a cell ⟨the anchorite ~*ed* underground⟩ ⟨the embezzler ~*ed* with two other prisoners⟩ ~ *vt, of bees* **:** to store (honey) in a comb

³**cell** *var of* CEL

cell- *or* **cello-** *comb form* [¹cellulose] **:** cellulose ⟨*Cell*falcicula⟩ ⟨*cello*biose⟩

cel·la \'selə\ *n, pl* **cel·lae** \-,lē\ [L — more at CELL] **:** the frequently hidden inner part of a Greek or Roman temple that housed the image of the deity; *also* **:** the corresponding part of a modern building of similar design — called also *naos*

¹**cel·lar** \'selə(r)\ *n* -S [ME *celer*, fr. AF, fr. L *cellarium*, fr. *cella* small room, storeroom — more at CELL] **1 a** *archaic* **:** an above-ground storeroom for foodstuff or produce (as a pantry or granary) **b :** a room or set of rooms below the ground often used for storage and for protecting the building above from ground dampness and sometimes not possessing a finished interior — sometimes distinguished from *basement* **c :** an underground room (as one partitioned off in a basement or one dug in the earth and often roofed over with sod) used to store provisions (as vegetables) or as a refuge — see CYCLONE CELLAR **d :** the bottommost stage or rank ⟨their spirits were in the ~⟩; *esp* **:** the lowest place in the standings of an athletic league or conference **2 :** a stock of wine ⟨a ~ depleted by festivities⟩ **3** *obs* **:** a case esp. for holding bottles

²**cellar** \"\ *vt* -ED/-ING/-S **:** to put into a cellar (as for storage)

³**cellar** \"\ *n* -S [by shortening] **:** SALTCELLAR

cel·lar·age \'selərij\ *n* -S **1 a :** CELLAR 1 b **b :** a storage cellar or connected group of storage cellars **2 :** charge for storage in a cellar or storehouse **3 :** a region resembling cellarage as in its relative position or in what it comprises ⟨comment lifted out of the ~ at the foot of various pages and spread over the upper levels of print —V.L.O.Chittick⟩ ⟨had driven that down into the ~ of his mind, and had almost forgotten it —Robertson Davies⟩

cellar club *n* **:** a social club made up of young men in a poor urban area

cel·lar·er \'selərə(r)\ *n* -S [ME *celerer*, fr. OF *celerer, celerier*, fr. LL *cellariarius*, fr. L *cellarium* storeroom] **:** an official (as in a monastery) in charge of procuring, storing, and distributing provisions

cel·lar·ess \-ərəs\ *n* -ES [*cellarer* + *-ess*] **:** a member of a religious community of women who is officially in charge of the procuring, storing, and distributing of provisions

cel·lar·ette *also* **cel·lar·et** \,selə'ret\ *n* -S [¹*cellar* + *-ette, -et*] **:** a case or sideboard designed to hold a few bottles of wine or liquor

cellar hole *n* **:** an excavation intended for a cellar or the exposed cellar area where a house has once stood

cel·lar·less \'selə(r)ləs\ *adj* **:** having no cellar ⟨~ houses⟩

cel·lar·man \-mən\ *n, pl* **cellarmen 1 :** a stock clerk in a hotel or restaurant who handles the alcoholic-beverage supply **2 :** one who clarifies wine before it is filtered

cellar pipe *n* **:** a fire-fighting device consisting of a hose nozzle at the end of a tube designed to be inserted into a burning area (as a cellar or ship's hold) and so controlled from without that it can direct a spray toward any area within

cellarway \'≈,≈\ *n* **:** a way leading through or into a cellar or cellars

cellblock \'≈,≈\ *n* **:** a group of cells constituting a subdivision of a prison

cell-blockade phenomenon *n* **:** INTERFERENCE PHENOMENON

cell body *n* **:** a living cell proper exclusive of its processes

cell bridge *n* **:** PLASMODESMA

cell count *n* **:** a count of cells esp. of a body fluid (as blood) in a standard volume (as a cubic millimeter)

cell division *n* **:** the process by which cells multiply involving both nuclear and cytoplasmic division — see AMITOSIS, MITOSIS; compare MEIOSIS

-celled \,seld\ *adj comb form* **:** having (such or so many) cells ⟨nerve-*celled*⟩ ⟨single-*celled* organisms⟩

cel·le·por·i·dae \,selə'pȯrə,dē\ *n pl, cap* [NL, fr. *Cellepora*, type genus (irreg. fr. L *cella* cell + NL *-pora*) + *-idae*] **:** a family of bryozoans resembling coral, having tubular calcareous zooecia with terminal openings, and forming erect or encrusting colonies

cell·fal·cic·u·la \,sel,fal'sikyələ\ *n, cap* [NL, fr. *cell-* + LL *falcicula* small sickle, dim. of L *falc-, falx* sickle — more at FALCHION] **:** a genus of motile gram-negative monotrichous soil bacteria (family Spirillaceae) that oxidize cellulose to oxycellulose and thus cause disintegration of vegetable fiber, appearing as short rods with pointed ends and containing metachromatic granules — compare CELLVIBRIO

cell house *n* **:** a prison building having a number of separate cells each ordinarily designed for one occupant

cel·lif·er·ous \(')se¦lif(ə)rəs\ *adj* [¹*cell* + *-i-* + *-ferous*] **:** bearing or producing cells

cel·lif·u·gal \(')se¦lif(y)əgəl\ *or* **cel·lu·lif·u·gal** \¦selyə¦li-\ *adj* [ISV ¹*cell* or *cellul-* + *-i-* + *-fugal*; prob. orig. formed as G *zellulifugal*] **:** conducting or conducted away from a cell body — used chiefly of nerve-cell processes and nerve impulses

celling *pres part of* CELL

cel·lip·e·tal \(')se¦lipəd·əl\ *or* **cel·lu·lip·e·tal** \¦selyə¦li-\ *adj* [ISV ¹*cell* or *cellul-* + *-i-* + *-petal*; prob. orig. formed as G *zellulipetal*] **:** conducting or conducted toward a cell body — used chiefly of nerve-cell processes and nerve impulses

cel·list \'cheləst\ *n* -S [¹*cello* + *-ist*] **:** one that plays the cello — called also *violoncellist*

cell–lethal \'≈¦≈\ *n* -S **:** a chromosome deficiency that induces death of the cell in which it occurs

cell lineage *n* **:** the developmental history of a cell from the first cleavage division until its ultimate fate is determined

cell membrane *n* **1 :** PLASMA MEMBRANE **2 :** CELL WALL

¹**cel·lo** \'che(,)lō\ *n, pl* **cellos** \-ōz\ *also* **cel·li** \-(,)lē\ [short for *violoncello*] **:** the bass member of the violin family tuned an octave below the viola and played from a sitting position with the instrument held almost vertically on the floor — compare CONTRABASS

²**cel·lo** \'se(,)lō\ *adj* [short for *cellophane*] **1 :** made of cellophane ⟨a ~ bag⟩ **2 :** wrapped in cellophane ⟨a dozen carrots, ~⟩

cello

cello- — see CELL-

cel·lo·bi·ose \,selō'bī,ōs\ *n* -S [ISV *cell-* + *biose*; orig. formed as G *zellobiose*] **:** a white crystalline faintly sweet-tasting sugar $C_{12}H_{22}O_{11}$ of the disaccharide class obtained by partial hydrolysis of cellulose; 4-β-glucosyl≈glucose — called also *cellose*

cel·lo·bi·u·ron·ic acid \¦selō,bīyə¦ränik-\ *n* [*cell-* + *bi-* + *uronic*] **:** an aldobiuronic acid obtained by partial hydrolysis of a specific polysaccharide of pneumococci and yielding glucose and glucuronic acid on hydrolysis

cel·lo·cut \'selō,kət, -lə,-\ *n* -S [²*cello* + *cut*] **1 :** an artist's print made from a plastic plate in which a design determined by the use of liquid plastics has been cut in relief; *also* **:** the plate from which such a print is made **2 :** the art of making and printing from cellocuts

cel·lo·dex·trin \,selə'dekstrən\ *n* [*cell-* + *dextrin*] **:** a polysaccharide obtained by partial hydrolysis of cellulose

cell of clau·di·us \-'klaudēəs, -ōd-\ *usu cap 2d C* [after Friedrich Matthias *Claudius* †1869 Austrian anatomist] **:** one of the low cuboidal cells covering the outermost part of the basilar membrane of the organ of Corti

cell of cor·ti \-'kȯrd·ē\ *usu cap 2d C* [after Alfonso *Corti* †1876 Ital. anatomist] **:** a hair cell in the organ of Corti

cell of dei·ters \-'dīd·ə(r)z, -)s\ *usu cap D* [after Otto Friedrich Karl *Deiters* †1863 Ger. anatomist] **:** one of the slender cells that end in rigid filaments terminated by platelike structures and that are placed among and support and separate the outer hair cells of the organ of Corti

cell of golgi *usu cap G* **:** GOLGI CELL

cell of leydig *usu cap L* **:** LEYDIG CELL

cell of purkinje *usu cap P* **:** PURKINJE CELL

cell of schwann *usu cap S* **:** SCHWANN CELL

cell of sertoli *usu cap S* **:** SERTOLI CELL

cel·loi·din \(')se¦lȯidᵊn\ *n* -S [ISV *cell-* + *-oid* + *-in*; prob. orig. formed as G *zelloidin*] **:** a purified form of pyroxylin obtained from collodion by precipitation and used chiefly in microscopy for embedding

cel·lo·phane \'selə,fān\ *n* -S [ISV *cell-* + *-phane* (as in *diaphane*); orig. formed in F] **:** a transparent sheet or tube of regenerated cellulose highly impermeable to dry gases, grease, and bacteria made by extruding alkaline viscose solution through a narrow straight or circular die into an acid bath, usu. moisture-proofed by thin coatings and sometimes dyed, and used chiefly as wrappers or bags for packaging food and merchandise, window envelopes, or bags for dialysis

cel·lose \'se,lōs\ *n* -S [ISV *cell-* + *-ose*; orig. formed as G *zellose*] **:** CELLOBIOSE

Cel·lo·solve \'selə,sälv\ *trademark* — used for a colorless mobile liquid ether-alcohol used chiefly as a solvent (as for lacquers and varnishes) and component of hydraulic fluids

cell plasm *n* **:** CYTOPLASM

cell plate *n* **:** a disk formed in the phragmoplast of a dividing plant cell, marking the beginning of separation into two daughter cells, developing gradually from the center toward the parent cell, and eventually forming the true middle lamella of the wall between the daughter cells

cells *pl of* CELL, *pres 3d sing of* CELL

cell sap *n* **1 :** the liquid content of the vacuole of a plant cell consisting of an aqueous solution of organic acids and their salts as well as pigments, proteins, tannins, emulsified fats, and other complex compounds chiefly in the colloidal state **2 :** the more fluid part of protoplasm **:** KARYOLYMPH, HYALOPLASM

cell theory *n* **:** either of two theories in biology: (1) the cell is the fundamental unit of living matter, and (2) the organism is a mosaic of autonomous cells, its properties being the sum of those of the constituent cells

Cel·lu·cot·ton \'selyə,kätᵊn\ *trademark* — used for a soft absorbent creped cellulose used in surgical dressings

¹**cellul-** *or* **celluli-** *or* **cellulo-** *comb form* [NL, fr. *cellula*] **1 :** plant or animal cell ⟨*celluli*cidal⟩ ⟨*cellulo*toxic⟩ **2 :** cellular and ⟨*cellulo*fibrous⟩

²**cellul-** *or* **cellulo-** *also* **cellu-** *comb form* [¹cellulose] **:** cellulose ⟨*cellu*loid, *cellulo*lytic⟩

cel·lu·la \'selyələ\ *n, pl* **cellu·lae** \-,lē\ [NL, fr. L, small storeroom] **:** a small cell **:** CELLULE

cel·lu·lar \-lə(r)\ *adj* [NL *cellularis*, fr. *cellula* living cell, fr. L, small storeroom, dim. of *cella* small room — more at CELL] **1 :** characterized by, consisting of, or dealing with cells ⟨~ structure⟩ ⟨~ physiology⟩ **2 a :** containing cavities **:** POROUS ⟨~ rubber⟩ **b** *of igneous rock* **:** having a porous texture produced by the expansion of gases within the fluid lava ⟨~ basalt⟩ **3 :** consisting of or employing separate semi-independent sections or units ⟨a ~ plan of defense⟩ ⟨the ~ structure of medieval society⟩; *specif* **:** using or marked by the use of cell-like rooms or living quarters ⟨~ confinement⟩ — **cel·lu·lar·ly** *adv*

cellular cryptogam *or* **cellular plant** *n* **:** a cryptogamous plant possessing little or no vascular tissue (as algae, fungi, lichens, and mosses) — compare VASCULAR CRYPTOGAM

cellular glass *n* **:** a lightweight glass of spongelike appearance widely used as a heat and sound insulator

cel·lu·lar·i·ty \,selyə'larəd·ē\ *n* -ES **:** the quality or state of being cellular

cellular kite *n* **:** BOX KITE

cellular tissue *n* **1 :** areolar connective tissue **2** *bot* **:** tissue entirely parenchymatous

cel·lu·lase \'selyə,lās\ *n* -S [ISV ²*cellul-* + *-ase*] **:** any of a group of enzymes that are found in various fungi, bacteria, insects, and lower animals and that hydrolyze cellulose

cel·lu·late \-ˌāt\ *vt* -ED/-ING/-S [¹*cellul-* + *-ate*] **:** to provide with cells ⟨glass *cellulated* in manufacture⟩

cel·lu·la·tion \,selyə'lāshən\ *n* -S **:** division into cells; *esp* **:** division of a syncytium into cells

cel·lule \'sel(,)yül\ *n* -S [F or L; F, monk's cell, fr. L *cellula* small storeroom — more at CELLULAR] **1** *archaic* **:** a small receptacle (as a pigeonhole) **2 :** a minute cavity **:** INTERSTICE, CELL

celluli- — see CELLUL-

cellulifugal *var of* CELLIFUGAL

cel·lu·lin \'selyələn\ *n* -S [²*cellul-* + *-in*] **:** a celluloselike carbohydrate chiefly of animal origin but found also in certain fungi (as Leptomitales)

cellulipetal *var of* CELLIPETAL

cel·lu·li·tis \,selyə'līd·əs\ *n* -ES [NL, fr. ¹*cellul-* + *-itis*] **:** diffuse and usu. subcutaneous or intrapelvic spreading inflammation of connective tissue

cellulo- — see CELLUL-

¹**cel·lu·loid** \'selyə,lȯid *also* -elə,l- *or* ,≈≈'\ *n* -S [fr. *Celluloid*, a trademark] **1 :** a tough highly flammable but not usu. explosive synthetic thermoplastic composed essentially of cellulose nitrate and a plasticizer (as camphor) and used in the manufacture of toilet articles (as combs and brushes), novelties, and photographic films **2 :** motion-picture film ⟨the story was on ~ in a year⟩; *also* **:** MOTION PICTURES ⟨repeated for ~ her stage role —*Springfield (Mass.) Union*⟩ ⟨movie buffs with their insatiable appetite for ~ —John Simon⟩

²**celluloid** \"\ *adj* **:** of or relating to the motion pictures **:** CINEMATIC

cel·lu·lo·lyt·ic \¦selyəlō¦lid·ik\ *adj* [²*cellul-* + *-lytic*] **:** having the capacity to hydrolyze cellulose — used of certain bacteria and protozoans

cel·lu·lo·mo·nas \,selyə'lämənəs, -,nas\ *n, cap* [NL, fr. ²*cellul-* + *-monas*] **:** a genus of short peritrichous gram-negative rod-shaped soil-inhabiting bacteria (family Corynebacteriaceae) that digest cellulose

cel·lu·los·an \¦selyə¦lōsᵊn, ¦selyə,lō¦san\ *n* -S [¹*cellulose* + *-an*] **:** any of several carbohydrates (as xylan and mannan) that occur in close association with cellulose in cell walls (as in wood) and are sometimes classed as hemicelluloses

¹**cel·lu·lose** \'selyə,lōs\ *n* -S [F, fr. *cellule* living cell (fr. NL *cellula*) + *-ose* — more at CELLULAR] **1 :** any of several fibrous substances constituting the chief part of the cell walls of plants and of many fibrous products (as paper, cotton, linen) — see HEMICELLULOSE, LIGNIN, MICELLE **2 a :** a complex polymeric carbohydrate $(C_6H_{10}O_5)_x$ having the same percentage composition as starch and also yielding only glucose on complete hydrolysis by acid but consisting of a long chain of beta-glucosidic residues linked through the 1,4-positions **b :** the portion of a cellulosic material that does not dissolve in a 17.5 to 18 percent sodium hydroxide solution and constitutes the most abundant form of cellulose — called also *alpha cellulose* **c :** the portion of a cellulosic material that dissolves in an alkaline solution and is precipitated on acidification — called also *beta cellulose* **d :** the portion of a cellulosic material that dissolves in an alkaline solution and is not precipitated on acidification — called also *gamma cellulose* **e :** the white fibers obtained from vegetable matter (as wood or cotton linters) by purification (as by treatment with acid sulfite or dilute alkali) that usu. consist chiefly of alpha cellulose and are used esp. in making regenerated cellulose products (as rayon and cellophane) and cellulose derivatives (as cellulose esters and cellulose ethers) — called also *chemical cellulose*

²**cellulose** \"\ *vt* -ED/-ING/-S **:** to coat or treat with some cellulose preparation (as with cellulose acetate)

³**cellulose** \"\ *adj* **:** containing or made from cellulose or a derivative of cellulose ⟨~ plastic⟩ ⟨~ sponge⟩ ⟨~ tape⟩

cellulose acetate *n* **:** any of several esters that are obtained by the partial or complete acetylation of cellulose (as cotton linters or wood) usu. with acetic anhydride, acetic acid, and concentrated sulfuric acid, that are soluble in acetone, thermoplastic, and less flammable than cellulose nitrates, and that are used chiefly in making acetate fibers and tough plastics (as films, molded articles, and foamed insulation) — called also *acetate*

cellulose acetate butyrate *n* **:** any of several mixed esters that are formed by acylation of cellulose with a mixture of acetic and butyric acids and anhydrides and an acid catalyst, that are thermoplastic like cellulose acetates but have a wider range of solubility and are more moisture-resistant, and that are used in molded and extruded plastics and in lacquers

cellulose acetate propionate *n* **:** any of several mixed esters of cellulose and acetic and propionic acids that are similar to cellulose acetate butyrates in method of manufacture, properties, and uses

cellulose ester *n* **:** an ester of cellulose (as cellulose nitrate or cellulose acetate) with an inorganic or organic acid

cellulose ether *n* **:** an ether (as ethyl cellulose or sodium carboxymethyl cellulose) made usu. by etherification of alkali cellulose

cel·lu·lose·like \'selyə,lō,slīk\ *adj* **:** resembling cellulose

cellulose nitrate *n* **1 :** any of several esters that are obtained as white fibrous flammable solids by the nitration of cellulose (as cotton linters or wood) usu. with a mixture of nitric and sulfuric acids — called also *nitrocellulose* **2 a :** a low-nitrated plastics grade of cellulose nitrate containing less than 12.5% nitrogen that is soluble in a variety of organic solvents (as mixtures of ether and alcohol) and is used chiefly in making photographic films, lacquers and other coatings (as for automobiles, furniture, and fabrics simulating leather), tough thermoplastic materials, and adhesives — see PYROXYLIN **b :** a high-nitrated ballistics grade of cellulose nitrate containing 12.5 to 13.5 percent nitrogen that is insoluble in most organic solvents and is used in explosives — see GUNCOTTON, SMOKELESS POWDER

cellulose propionate *n* **:** any of several esters made by the action of propionic anhydride on cellulose and used as thermoplastics for making tough molded products (as frames for eyeglasses and goggles, pens, and flashlight housings)

cellulose xanthate *n* **:** any of several colorless esters obtained usu. as alkali salts in the form of orange-colored crumbs by xanthation of alkali cellulose with carbon disulfide as a step in the manufacture of viscose

¹**cel·lu·los·ic** \¦selyə¦lōsik\ *adj* **:** of, containing, or made from cellulose ⟨~ fibers⟩

²**cellulosic** \"\ *n* -S [¹*cellulosic*] **:** a substance (as a plastic or fiber) made from cellulose or a derivative of cellulose

cell·vib·rio \(')sel'vibrē,ō\ *n, cap* [NL, fr. cell- + *Vibrio*] **:** a genus of long slender slightly curved monotrichous motile rod-shaped bacteria (family Spirillaceae) with rounded ends that oxidize cellulose to oxycellulose and cause disintegration of vegetable fiber — compare CELLFALCICULA

cell wall *n* **1 :** the somewhat rigid permeable wall typical of plant cells (as the cellulose or celluloselike layers secreted by the cytoplasm in most plants) at first thin and delicate but modified in extent, thickness, and chemical nature as it develops and matures — compare CUTINIZATION, LIGNIFY, PRIMARY WALL **2 :** a membrane bounding an animal cell; *usu* **:** PLASMA MEMBRANE

celo- — see COEL-

celom *var of* COELOM

ce·lo·nav·i·ga·tion \'sē(,)lō-, 'se-\ *n* [*ce*lestial + *-o-* (as in *geonavigation*) + *navigation*] **:** CELESTIAL NAVIGATION

ce·lo·sia \sē'lōzh(ē)ə\ *n, cap* [NL, irreg. fr. Gk *kēleos* burning or LGk *kēlos* dry; akin to Gk *kaiein* to burn — more at CAUSTIC] **:** a large genus of tropical annual herbs (family Amaranthaceae) having alternate leaves and showy flowers in spikes which in cultivated forms are often fasciated and form compact often feathery clusters — see COCKSCOMB 2b

cels *pl of* CEL

cel·sia \'selsēə, -lsh(ē)ə\ *n, cap* [NL, fr. Olaf *Celsius* †1756 Swed. botanist + NL *-ia*] **:** a genus of mostly European herbs of the family Scrophulariaceae with large yellow flowers resembling snapdragons — see CRETAN BEAR'S-TAIL, CRETAN MULLEIN

cel·si·an \'selsē,an\ *n* -S [prob. fr. Anders *Celsius* + E *-an*] **:** a mineral $BaAl_2Si_2O_8$ that consists of a barium feldspar and is isomorphous with orthoclase

celsitude *n* -S [prob. fr. L *celsitudo* loftiness, fr. *celsus* high, lofty — more at HILL] *archaic* **:** HEIGHT, ALTITUDE, EXALTATION

cel·si·us \'selsēəs, -lshəs\ *adj, usu cap* [after Anders *Celsius* †1744 Swed. astronomer who invented the centigrade scale] **:** relating to, conforming to, or having the international thermometric scale on which the interval between the two standard points, the triple point and the boiling point of water, is divided into 99.99 degrees, 0.01° representing the triple point and 100.00° the boiling point; *also* **:** CENTIGRADE ⟨a ~ thermometer⟩ ⟨10° ~⟩ — abbr. *C*

¹**celt** \'selt, 'ke-\ *also* **kelt** \'ke-\ *n* -S *cap* [F *Celte*, sing. of *Celtes*, fr. L *Celtae*] **1 a :** a member of a division of the early Indo-European peoples in Iron-Age and pre-Roman Europe distributed from the British Isles and Spain to Asia Minor and in part absorbed into the Roman Empire as Britons, Gauls, Boii, Galatians, or Celtiberians **b :** a descendant of these people who has somewhere in his background a native knowledge of a Celtic language **2 :** a modern Gael, Highland Scot, Irishman, Welshman, Cornishman, or Breton

²**celt** \'selt\ *n* -S [LL *celtis* chisel] **:** a prehistoric implement shaped like a chisel or ax head made of polished stone in neolithic times and later of metal

¹**celt·ibe·ri·an** \¦seltə¦birēən, ¦ke-, -l,tī¦-\ *adj, usu cap* [L *Celtiberia* (fr. *Celtiberi* Celtiberians, fr. *Celtae* Celts + *Iberi* Iberians) + E *-an*] **1 :** of, relating to, or characteristic of Celtiberia, a mountainous district of ancient Spain **2 :** of, relating to, or characteristic of the people of Celtiberia

²**celtiberian** \"\ *n* -S *cap* **:** one of the Celts of Iberian intermixture that inhabited ancient Celtiberia

¹**celt·ic** \'seltik, 'ke-, -ēk\ *or* **kelt·ic** \'ke-\ *adj, usu cap* [L *Celticus*, fr. *Celtae* Celts + L *-icus* -ic] **1 :** of or relating to the Celts, their language, civilization, or abode **2 :** of or relating to certain ancient strains of European domestic animals — see CELTIC HORSE, CELTIC OX

²**celtic** \"\ *or* **keltic** \"\ *n* -S *cap* **:** a group of languages closely akin to the Italic and now largely confined to Brittany, Wales, western Ireland, the Scottish Highlands, and the Isle of Man usu. subdivided into Brythonic and Goidelic, and possessed of a copious medieval prose and verse literature — see INDO≈EUROPEAN LANGUAGES table

celtic cross *n, usu cap 1st C* **:** a cross having essentially the form of a Latin cross with a ring about the intersection of the crossbar and upright shaft; *also* **:** something having the form of such a cross (as a monument, badge, emblem)

Celtic cross

celtic fringe *n, usu cap C* **:** the portion of the population of the British Isles which is of Celtic origin or the native land of such people

celtic horse *or* **celtic pony** *n, usu cap C* **:** a small shaggy large-headed horse of northwestern Europe and Iceland of which the Shetland pony is an improved breed

celt·i·cism \-tə,sizəm\ *n* -S *usu cap* **:** a Celtic custom, expression, or idiom ⟨the *Celticisms* within modern English⟩

celt·i·cist \-,səst\ *n* -S *usu cap* **:** a specialist in Celtic languages or cultures

cel·tic·i·ty \(,)sel'tisəd·ē, -sətē, -i\ *n* -ES *usu cap* **:** the quality or state of being Celtic

celt·i·cize \-,sīz\ *vt* -ED/-ING/-S *sometimes cap* **:** to make Celtic in language practices, culture, or customs

celtic ox *n, usu cap C* [so called fr. its occurrence in Alpine regions where Celts lived in early historical times] **:** a small prehistoric European ox (*Bos longifrons*) having a high forehead and short horns and considered by some to be the ancestor or an ancestor of domestic cattle

cel·tis \'seltəs\ *n, cap* [NL, fr. L, an African lotus] **:** a large genus of widely distributed trees and shrubs (family Ulmaceae) characterized by a berrylike fruit and leaves predominantly 3≈veined at the base — see HACKBERRY

celt·ist \'seltəst, 'ke-\ *n* -S *usu cap* [F *celtiste*, fr. F *Celte* Celt + *-iste* -ist] **:** CELTICIST

cel·ti·um \'selshēəm, -ltēəm\ *n* -S [NL, fr. L *Celtae* Celts + NL *-ium*] **:** HAFNIUM

celts *pl of* CELT

cel·tuce \'seltəs\ *n* -S [*cel*ery + *let*tuce] **:** a celerylike vegetable that is derived from lettuce and has edible stalks and leaves that combine the flavors of celery and lettuce

cem *abbr* 1 cement 2 cemetery

cem·bal d'a·mo·re \ˈchem,bäldəˈmōrē, ˈchäm-\ *n, pl* **cemba·li d'amore** \-,bə(,)lēdə-\ [It, lit., clavichord of love] **:** a clavichord with double-length strings

cem·ba·list \ˈchembələst, -äm-\ *n* -s [*cembalo* + *-ist*] **1 :** a player on the harpsichord **2 :** a player of any keyboard instrument in an orchestra

cem·ba·lo \-,lō\ *n, pl* **cemba·li** \-(,)lē\ *or* **cembalos** [It, clavichord, tambourine, fr. L *cymbalum* cymbal — more at CYMBAL] **1 :** DULCIMER 1 **2** [short for *clavicembalo*] **:** HARPSICHORD **3 :** the manual as distinguished from the pedal part of early organ music **4 :** the continuo part of a concerto

cembalon *var of* CIMBALOM

cem·bra nut \ˈsembrə-\ *n* **:** CEDAR NUT

cembra pine \"-\ *or* **cem·bran pine** \-brən-\ *n* [*cembra* fr. NL (specific epithet of the Swiss pine *Pinus cembra*), modif. of G dial. *zember, zimber* timber, fr. OHG *zimbar* wood; *cembran* fr. NL *cembra* + E *-an* — more at TIMBER] **:** SWISS PINE

[1]**ce·ment** \sə̇ˈment, sēˈ- *sometimes* ˈsē,m-\ *n* -s [ME *sement, siment*, fr. OF *ciment*, fr. L *caementum* rough unhewn stone, marble chips used in making mortar, fr. *caedere* to cut, hew — more at CONCISE] **1 a :** a powder made from alumina, silica, lime, iron oxide, and magnesia burned together in a kiln and finely pulverized which when mixed with water to form a plastic mass hardens by chemical combination and by gelation and crystallization and is used as an ingredient of mortar and concrete; *esp* **:** PORTLAND CEMENT — see ALUMINA CEMENT, NATURAL CEMENT **b :** a substance (as concrete or mortar) of which cement is a major ingredient **2 :** a binding element or agency: as **a :** any fabricated substance to make objects adhere to each other (as asphalt, glue, gypsum, lime, paste, or plaster) **b :** any of various secretions chiefly produced by special glands of invertebrates that harden rapidly when exposed to air or water and are used to fasten objects together (as an animal to its substrate, sand grains into the wall of a test, or nits to hairs) **c :** a notion or feeling serving to unite firmly **:** any agency making for lasting union ⟨the States, on their part, lacking the ~ of national feeling —Percival Spear⟩ **3 :** CEMENTUM **4 :** a plastic composition usu. made of zinc, copper, or silica for filling dental cavities **5 :** the fine-grained groundmass or glass of a porphyry **:** residual uncrystallized material

[2]**cement** \"\ *vb* -ED/-ING/-S [ME *simenten*, fr. *siment*, n.] *vt* **1 :** to join, unite, or cause to adhere by or as if by means of a cement ⟨layers ~*ed* together with glue⟩ **2 a :** to bind together, unite firmly, unify **:** exert a marked cohesive influence on ⟨~ scattered groups from all the northern states into a national party —*Amer. Guide Series: Pa.*⟩ **b :** to stop or end disruptive tendencies and ensure the continuation of (as an association or friendship) **:** establish firmly ⟨in ~*ing* a more stable Pan-American union —R.W.Murray⟩ **3 :** to overlay with concrete ⟨~ a cellar floor⟩ **4 :** to subject to cementation ⟨~*ed* steel⟩ ~ *vi* **:** to become cemented **:** unite firmly or solidify as if into cement **:** COHERE, STICK ⟨the snow . . . compacting and ~*ing* until the streams are spanned —John Muir †1914⟩

[3]**cement** \"\ *adj* [[1]*cement*] **1 :** of or relating to cement **2 :** obtained by cementation ⟨~ steel⟩ ⟨~ copper⟩

ce·ment·al \sə̇ˈmentᵊl, (ˈ)sē¦m-\ *adj* **:** of or relating to cement

ce·men·ta·tion \,sē,menˈtāshən\ *n* -s **1 :** the act or process of cementing **:** the state of being cemented ⟨~ of sand into stone⟩ **2 a :** a process that consists in surrounding a solid body with the powder of other substances and heating the whole to a degree not sufficient to cause fusion, the physical properties of the body being changed by chemical combination with the powder ⟨iron becomes steel by ~ with charcoal⟩ ⟨green glass becomes porcelain by ~ with sand⟩ **b :** the process of obtaining a metal from a solution of one of its compounds by precipitation with another metal (as the obtaining of copper from a solution of copper sulfate by means of metallic iron)

ce·ment·a·to·ry \sə̇ˈmentə,tōrē, sēˈ-\ *adj* [[2]*cement* + *-atory* (as in *separatory*)] **:** cementing firmly **:** tending to unify

cement block *n* **:** CONCRETE BLOCK

cement clinker *n* **:** the glassy clinkerlike product of fusing together clay and limestone as the first stage in the manufacture of portland cement

cement disease *n* **:** pneumonia in young pigs kept on cold damp concrete floors

cemented shoe *or* **cement shoe** *n* **:** a shoe in which the outsole, upper, and insole are cemented together instead of being sewed

ce·ment·er \-ə(r)\ *n* -s **1 :** one that cements or makes cement **2 a :** GLUER **b :** a shipworker who applies cement on ships' bottoms, in crevices, or in any joints to make them watertight **c :** CEMENT FINISHER **d :** one who directs and assists workers in cementing the space between the sidewalls and steel casings of an oil or gas well to provide protection and control for underground operations **e :** a vulcanizer of breaks and holes in pneumatic tires — called also *patcher* **f :** a repairer of broken concrete structural parts and equipment — called also *cement mason*

cement finisher *n* **:** one that makes a cement surface of specified texture by using hand tools (as trowels)

cement gland *n* **:** a gland that secretes an adhesive substance (as those in the foot of many rotifers that produce secretions to anchor the animals to the substrate or as those associated with the female reproductive system of many insects)

cement gravel *n* **:** gravel consolidated by clay, calcium carbonate, silica, or some other binding material

ce·ment·i·cle \sə̇ˈmentə̇kəl, sē-\ *n* -s [NL *cementum* + E *-icle* (as in *clavicle*)] **:** a calcified body formed in the periodontal membrane of a tooth

ce·ment·i·fi·ca·tion \ˌ=,=fəˈkāshən\ *n* -s [[1]*cement* + *-i-* + *-fication*] **:** the process by which cementum of a tooth is formed

ce·men·tin \=ˈ=tᵊn\ *n* -s [[1]*cement* + *-in*] **:** intercellular material uniting the borders of squamous endothelial cells

ce·ment·ite \=ˈ=,tīt\ *n* -s [[1]*cement* + *-ite*] **:** a hard brittle iron carbide Fe_3C occurring in steel, cast iron, and nearly all iron-carbon alloys

ce·men·ti·tious \ˌsē,menˈtishəs\ *adj* [[1]*cement* + *-itious*] **:** having the properties of cement **:** like or relevant to cement ⟨the adhesion of ~ materials⟩

ce·ment·less *pronunc at* [1]CEMENT + ləs\ *adj* **:** lacking cement **:** bonded without cement

cement mixer *n* **1 :** one that produces a thin rubber cement by mixing latex or raw rubber with a solvent **2 :** one that produces slurry for cement by mixing clay or shale with powdered limestone and water — called also *boxman* **3 :** CONCRETE MIXER

cement mortar *n* **:** mortar of portland cement and sand sometimes with a little lime to make it more plastic

ce·ment·o·blast \sə̇ˈmentə,blast, sē- -ntō,-\ *n* -s [NL *cementum* + E *-o-* + *-blast*] **:** one of the specialized osteoblasts of the dental sac that produce cementum

ce·ment·o·gen·e·sis \=,==ˈjenəsə̇s\ *n, pl* **cementogene·ses** \-ə,sēz\ [NL, fr. *cementum* + *-o-* + L *genesis*] **:** formation or development of the cementum of a tooth

ce·men·to·ma \,sē,menˈtōmə\ *n, pl* **cementomas** \-ōməz\ *or* **cementoma·ta** \-ōməd·ə\ [NL, fr. *cementum* + *-oma*] **:** a tumor resembling cementum in structure

cement organ *n* **:** ADHESIVE ORGAN

cement plaster *n* **1 :** a gypsum plaster with certain impurities present or added in the calcining process mixed with sand or wood fiber and water to form a mortar for plastering interior surfaces — called also *hard wall plaster, patent plaster* **2 a :** a mortar consisting of portland cement, sand, and water used for plastering interior surfaces of a building **b :** STUCCO

cement rock *or* **cement stone** *n* **:** a clayey limestone having approximately the ratio of alumina, lime, and silica in cement

cement rod *n* **:** the rod to one end of which a gem is cemented while being cut **:** DOP STICK

cements *pl of* CEMENT, *pres 3d sing of* CEMENT

cement stucco *n* **:** STUCCO

cement substance *n* **1 :** the intercellular substance in certain tissues (as endothelium) **2 :** the substance binding together the enamel rods in the teeth

cement-temper \=ˈ=¦==\ *vt* **:** to mix (a lime plaster) with portland cement to improve its strength and durability

ce·men·tum \sə̇ˈmentəm, sē-\ *n, pl* **cemen·ta** \-tə\ [NL, fr. L *caementum* rough stone — more at CEMENT] **:** the specialized external bony layer enclosing the dentin of the part of a tooth normally within the gum — see TOOTH illustration

cem·e·te·ri·al \¦semə¦tirēəl\ *adj* [*cemetery* + *-ial*] **:** of or belonging to a cemetery or burial

cem·e·tery \ˈsemə,terē, -ri\ *n* -ES [ME *cimitery*, fr. MF *cimitere, cimetière*, fr. LL *cimiterium, coemeterium*, fr. Gk *koimētērion* sleeping chamber, burial place, fr. *koiman* to put to sleep; akin to L *cunae* cradle, Gk *keisthai* to lie, Skt *śete* he lies, sleeps] **:** an area for burial or entombment: **a :** a Roman catacomb **b :** a consecrated churchyard **c :** any burial ground, typically a large one **:** GRAVEYARD

CEMF *abbr* counter electromotive force

[1]**cen-** *or* **ceno-** see COEN-

[2]**cen-** *or* **ceno-** *or* **caen-** *or* **caeno-** *comb form* [Gk *kain-, kaino-*, fr. *kainos* new — more at RECENT] **1 :** recent ⟨*cenozoic*⟩ **2 :** novel ⟨*cenogenesis*⟩

[1]**cé·na·cle** \sānäkl(ᵊ), -k(lə)\ *n, pl* **cénacles** \"\ [F, lit., room where Christ and his apostles had the Last Supper, fr. LL *cenaculum*, fr. L, dining room, fr. *cena* dinner; akin to Gk *keirein* to cut — more at SHEAR] **:** a philosophical, literary, or artistic group **:** COTERIE

[2]**cen·a·cle** \ˈsenəkəl\ *n* -s [fr. *The Society of Our Lady of the Cenacle*, congregation of nuns founded in France in 1826 to direct retreats for women] **:** a retreat house; *esp* **:** one under the direction of the Society of Our Lady of the Cenacle

cen·chrus \ˈseŋkrəs\ *n, cap* [NL, fr. Gk *kenchros* millet; prob. akin to L *frendere* to grind — more at GRIND] **:** a genus of grasses having spikelets enclosed in ovoid spiny involucres that form burs, the plants providing good forage before the bur develops

cendal *var of* SENDAL

cen·dre \ˈsä(ä)ⁿdr(ᵊ), -d(rə)\ *n, pl* **cendres** \"\ [F, lit., ash, fr. L *cinis* — more at INCINERATE] **:** AZURITE BLUE

-cene \,sēn\ *adj comb form* [Gk *kainos* new — more at RECENT] **:** recent — in names of geologic periods ⟨*eocene*⟩; compare CENOZOIC

cenesthesia *var of* COENESTHESIA

ce·ni·zo \sə'nē(,)zō, -sō\ *n* -s [AmerSp, fr. Sp, white goosefoot, prob. fr. *ceniza* ashes, fr. (assumed) VL *cinisia*, irreg. fr. L *cinis* — more at INCINERATE] **1** *Southwest* **:** SHAD SCALE **2** *West Indies* **:** any of a variety of shrubs and herbs with silver-gray foliage

cenobe *var of* COENOBE

ce·no·bi·an \sə̇ˈnōbēən, sē-\ *adj* [*cenoby* + *-an*] **:** relating to a cenoby **:** MONKISH, MONASTIC

cenobiar *var of* COENOBIAR

ce·no·bite *or* **coe·no·bite** \ˈsenə,bīt, *usu* -īd·+V; *Brit usu* -sēn-\ *n* -s [LL *coenobita*, fr. *coenobium* cenoby + *-ita* -ite] **:** a member of a religious group living in common — opposed to *hermit*

ce·no·bit·ic \¦==¦bid·ik\ *or* **cen·o·bit·i·cal** \-d·ə̇kəl\ *or* **coe·no·bit·ic** \¦==¦bid·ik\ *or* **coe·no·bit·i·cal** \-d·ə̇kəl\ *adj* [*cenobitic, coenobitic*, fr. F *cénobitique* fr. MF, fr. *cénobite* + *-ique* -ic; *cenobitical, coenobitical*, fr. F *cénobitique* + E *-al*] **:** of or relating to cenobites or cenobitism — **cen·o·bit·i·cal·ly** \-d·ə̇k(ə)lē\ *adv*

cen·o·bit·ism \ˈ==,bīd·,izəm\ *n* -s [*cenobite* + *-ism*] **:** the state, system, or practices of cenobites

cenobium *var of* COENOBIUM

cen·o·by *or* **coen·o·by** \ˈsenəbē, *Brit usu* ˈsēn-\ *n* -ES [ME *cenobie*, fr. LL *coenobium*, fr. LGk *koinobion*, fr. Gk, neut. of *koinobios* living in community, fr. *koin-* coen- + *bios* life — more at QUICK] **:** a conventual establishment or religious community

ce·no·genesis *or* **coe·no·genesis** *also* **cae·no·genesis** \¦sēnə, ¦senə +\ *n* [G *zänogenesis*, fr. *zän-* [2]cen- + L *genesis* birth — more at GENESIS] **:** introduction during development of adaptive characters or structures that are absent from the earlier phylogeny of a strain (as addition of the placenta to the common vertebrate pattern in mammalian evolution) — opposed to *palingenesis*

ce·no·genetic *or* **coe·no·genetic** *also* **cae·no·genetic** \"+\ *adj* [G *zänogenetisch*, fr. *zäno-* [2]cen- + *genetisch* genetic] **:** of or relating to cenogenesis — **ce·no·genetically** *or* **coe·no·genetically** *also* **cae·no·genetically** \"+\ *adv*

ce·nog·o·nous *or* **coe·nog·o·nous** \sēˈnägənəs\ *adj* [[1]*cen-* + *-gonous* (fr. Gk *gonos* generation); akin to Gk *genea* race, family — more at KIN] **:** oviparous at one season of the year and ovoviviparous at another —used esp. of certain aphids

cen·o·ma·nian \¦senə¦mānēən, -nyən\ *adj, usu cap* [F *cénomanien*, fr. ML *Cenomania* Le Mans, city in northwestern France, fr. L *Cenomani*, a Celtic tribe of northern Italy] **:** of or relating to the division of the European Upper Cretaceous between the Albian and the Turonian — see GEOLOGIC TIME table

cen·o·site \ˈsenə,sīt\ *n* -s [modif. (influenced by E [2]*cen-*) of Sw *kainosit*, fr. Gk *kainos* new + Sw *-it* -ite — more at RECENT] **:** a yellowish brown mineral composed of hydrous silicate and carbonate of calcium and rare earths

ce·no·species *or* **coenospecies** \¦sēnə, ¦senə +\ *n* [*coen-* + *species*] **1 :** the sum of the possible expressions of a complex genotype **2 :** a group of biological units (as varieties, subspecies, and ecospecies) that is capable by reason of closely related genotypes of essentially free gene interchange between units, is rarely capable of such interchange with units not part of the group, and is typically more or less equivalent to the taxonomic subgenus or superspecies in scope

cen·o·taph \ˈsenə,taf, -taa(ə)f,-taif,-táf\ *n* -s [F *cénotaphe*, fr. L *cenotaphium*, fr. Gk *kenotaphion*, fr. *keno-* (fr. *kenos* empty) + *-taphion* (fr. *taphos* funeral rites, tomb); akin to Arm *sin* empty — more at EPITAPH] **:** a tomb or a monument erected in honor of a person whose body is elsewhere ⟨his remains were removed . . . and a ~ was placed at the original grave —*Amer. Guide Series: N.C.*⟩

ce·no·te \sə̇ˈnōd·ē\ *n* -s [Sp, fr. Maya *tzonot*] **:** a deep sinkhole esp. in Central America and the Yucatán peninsula formed by the collapse of strata overlying solution cavities in limestone and having a pool at the bottom fed by the water table; *esp* **:** such a natural well into which sacrificial offerings were thrown in Mayan ceremonies

[1]**ce·no·zo·ic** *or* **cae·no·zo·ic** \¦sēnə¦zōik, ¦sen-\ *also* **cai·no·zo·ic** *or* **kai·no·zo·ic** \¦kīnə-, ¦kanə-\ *adj, usu cap* [[2]*cen-* + *-zoic*] **:** of or relating to a grand division of geological history including the entire interval from the beginning of the Tertiary period to the present time marked by a rapid evolution of mammals and birds and of grasses, shrubs, and higher flowering plants and by little change in the invertebrates — see GEOLOGIC TIME table

[2]**cenozoic** *or* **caenozoic** \"\ *also* **cainozoic** *or* **kainozoic** \"\ *n* -s *usu cap* **:** the Cenozoic era or system of rocks

ce·no·zoology *also* **cae·no·zoology** \¦sēnə, ¦senə +\ *n* -ES [[2]*cen-* + *zoology*] **:** the zoology of existing animals disregarding those extinct

cens \ˈsäⁿs\ *n, pl* **cens** [F, fr. LL *census* land tax, fr. L, valuation of property for the purpose of imposing taxes — more at CENSUS] *French & Canadian law* **:** a payment or service reserved to an owner of an estate as a recognition of his title

[1]**cense** \ˈsen(t)s\ *vt* -ED/-ING/-S [ME *censen*, prob. short for *encensen* to incense — more at INCENSE] **:** to perfume (as in a religious ritual by swinging a censer of burning incense) ⟨*censing* the area around the altar⟩

[2]**cense** *n* -s [MF, irreg. fr. L *census*] **1** *obs* **:** CENSUS **2** *obs* **:** RANK, RATING

[3]**cense** *vt* -ED/-ING/-S [obs. F *censer*, fr. L *censēre* — more at CENSOR] *obs* **:** ESTIMATE, ASSESS

cen·ser \ˈsen(t)sə(r)\ *n* -s [ME *censer, senser*, fr. OF *censier, senser*, short for *encensier*, fr. ML *incensarium*, fr. LL *incensum* incense — more at INCENSE] **:** a vessel for burning incense; *esp* **:** a covered incense burner swung on chains in a religious ritual **:** THURIBLE

censer

cen·si·taire \säⁿsēteer\ *n, pl* **censitaires** \-r(z)\ [F, irreg. fr. *cens* — more at CENS] **1 a :** one who paid a quitrent to his feudal lord **b :** one who paid the dues required to qualify as an elector in certain jurisdictions **2** *Canad* **:** one who renders cens

cen·sive \säⁿsēv\ *adj* [F *censif*, fr. *cens*] **:** relating to or held by cens

cen·so \ˈsen(t)sō, -n,sō\ *n* -s [Sp, fr. LL *census* land tax — more at CENS] *Spanish law* **:** ANNUITY; *esp* **:** GROUND RENT

[1]**cen·sor** \ˈsen(t)sə(r)\ *n* -s [L, fr. *censēre* to assess, tax; akin to Skt *śaṁsati* he recites, praises] **1 :** one of two magistrates of early Rome who acted as census takers, assessors, and inspectors of morals and conduct **2 :** a supervisor or inspector esp. of conduct and morals: **a :** an official empowered to examine written or printed matter (as manuscripts of books or plays) in order to forbid publication, circulation, or representation if it contains anything objectionable **b :** one having authority to guide and supervise students in English colleges and universities **c :** one of a council, since abolished, in some states of the U.S. (as Vermont and Pennsylvania) responsible for ensuring constitutional government and for inquiring into the conduct of state officials **d :** an officer or official charged with scrutinizing communications to intercept, suppress, or delete material harmful to his country's or organization's interests **e :** one who lacking official sanction but acting ostensibly in society's interests scrutinizes communications, compositions, and entertainments to discover anything immoral, profane, seditious, heretical, or otherwise offensive **3** *archaic* **:** CRITIC; *esp* **:** a faultfinding or severe critic ⟨moderating both eulogists and ~s⟩ **4** [G *zensur* censorship, fr. L *censura* — more at CENSURE] **:** the agency which represses or veils unacceptable notions before they reach the level of consciousness

[2]**censor** \"\ *vt* **censored**; **censored**; **censoring** \-n(t)s(ə)riŋ\ **censors :** to subject to a censor's examination; *often* **:** to alter, delete, or ban completely after examination ⟨~ out risqué passages⟩ ⟨slanted news officially ~*ed*⟩

cen·sor·a·ble \-n(t)s(ə)rəbəl\ *adj* **:** subject to being censored; *specif* **:** likely to be expunged or objected to by a censor ⟨~ dialogue⟩

cen·sor·ate \-n(t)s(ə)rə̇t, -n(t)sə,rāt\ *n* -s [[1]*censor* + *-ate*] **:** a body of censors **:** a department for censoring

censored *adj* **:** subjected to a censor's actions: **a :** deleted or suppressed **b :** approved as acceptable after scrutiny

cen·so·ri·al \(ˈ)sen¦sōrēəl, -ȯr-\ *adj* [F, fr. L *censorius* of a censor (fr. *censor*) + F *-al*] **:** belonging or relating to a censor **:** exercising a censor's function

cen·so·ri·an \-ēən\ *adj* [[1]*censor* + *-ian*] **:** CENSORIAL

cen·so·ri·ous \(ˈ)sen¦sōrēəs, -ȯr-\ *adj* [L *censorius* of a censor, fr. *censor* — more at CENSOR] **:** marked by or given to censure or an inclination to discover and severely condemn esp. social, moral, or artistic errors ⟨one who thus berated pope and clergy might be ~ of princes —H.O.Taylor⟩ ⟨even the most ~ could find nothing to complain of —Samuel Butler †1902⟩ **syn** see CRITICAL

cen·so·ri·ous·ly *adv* **:** in a censorious manner

cen·so·ri·ous·ness *n* -ES **:** the quality or state of being censorious

cen·sor·ship \ˈsen(t)sə(r),ship\ *n* -s **1 :** the institution, system, or practice of censoring **:** the actions or practices of censors or censorates; *esp* **:** censorial control exercised repressively ⟨~ that has . . . permitted a very limited dispersion of facts —Philip Wylie⟩ **2 :** the office, power, or term of a Roman censor ⟨during the ~ of Claudius⟩ **3 :** the process of excluding from consciousness those ideas and feelings that would be intolerable in other than symbolic form

censos *pl of* CENSO

cen·su·al \ˈsen(t)shəwəl, -nchəw-\ *adj* [LL *censualis*, fr. L *census* — more at CENSUS] **:** relating to a census **:** containing or constituting a census roll

cen·sur·a·ble \ˈsench(ə)rəbəl\ *adj* **:** deserving or open to censure **:** BLAMABLE, REPREHENSIBLE

[1]**cen·sure** \ˈsenchə(r) *sometimes* -n,shu̇(ə)r *or* -u̇ə, *chiefly substand* -n(t)sə(r)\ *n* -s [L *censura*, fr. *censēre* to assess — more at CENSOR] **1 :** a judgment involving condemnation: **a :** spiritual chastisement by an ecclesiastical agency ⟨acts receiving public ~ of the church⟩ **b :** sentence of punishment by civil or military authority ⟨awaiting the ~ of the ruling council⟩ **2 :** CENSORSHIP **3** *archaic* **:** OPINION, JUDGMENT ⟨will you go to give your ~s in this weighty business —Shak.⟩ **4 :** adverse judgment **:** the act of blaming, finding fault with, or condemning sternly ⟨heads turning all along the block in discreet ~ of his unsabbatical behavior —Mary Austin⟩ **5 :** critical recension **6 :** expression of official disapproval ⟨army letters of ~⟩; *often* **:** a resolution by a legislative body expressing disapproval of a government official

[2]**censure** \"\ *vb* **censured**; **censured**; **censuring** \-nch(ə)riŋ, *chiefly substand* -n(t)s(ə)riŋ\ **censures** *vt* **1** *obs* **:** ESTIMATE, JUDGE **:** to form or pronounce an opinion on **2 a :** to find fault with and criticize adversely as blameworthy esp. with stern judgment **:** disapprove of or dispraise ⟨appraisements imply censures and it is not one writer's business to ~ others —F.M.Ford⟩ **b :** to express official censure of ⟨a resolution on the floor to ~ the senator⟩ **3** *obs* **:** to condemn with judicial sentence ~ *vi, obs* **:** JUDGE — used with *of* or *on* **syn** see CRITICIZE

cen·sur·er \ˈsench(ə)rə(r), *chiefly substand* -n(t)s(ə)rə(r)\ *n* -s **:** one that censures

cen·sure·less *pronunc at* [1]CENSURE + ləs\ *adj* **:** free from censure

[1]**cen·sus** \ˈsen(t)səs\ *n* -ES *often attrib* [L, fr. *censēre* to assess, tax — more at CENSOR] **1** *archaic* **:** POLL TAX **2 :** a count of the, esp. male, population and a property evaluation held every fifth year in early Rome **3 :** an official enumeration of the population of a country, city, or other administrative district generally including vital statistics and other classified information relating to the social and economic conditions ⟨~ returns⟩ ⟨~ bureau⟩ **4 :** a count, list, or tally typically concerning items not easy to count and conducted with care and thoroughness ⟨a ~ of manufacturing establishments⟩ ⟨a ~ of deer in a game refuge⟩ ⟨a ~ of extant copies of a first edition⟩ **5** *civil law* **:** a ground rent or rent charge

[2]**census** \"\ *vt* -ED/-ING/-ES **:** to take a census of **:** count in a census ⟨~ the game birds of an area⟩

census taker *n* **:** one who goes from house to house to obtain data for a census

census tract *n* **:** an administrative district used in collating census data

cent \ˈsent\ *n* -s [MF, hundred, fr. L *centum* — more at HUNDRED] **1 a :** a unit of value equal to 1/100 part of some basic monetary unit (as in the U.S. and Canada 1/100 dollar, in Sri Lanka 1/100 rupee, in British East Africa 1/100 shilling, in the Netherlands 1/100 guilder, in Indonesia 1/100 rupiah) — see MONEY table **b :** a coin or token, often of copper or some copper alloy, representing one cent **c :** a note representing one cent; *specif* **:** a Hong Kong note representing 1/100 Hong Kong dollar **d :** a coin similar to a cent (as to the U.S. or Canadian cent) but not equal to 1/100 unit of value (as in the British West Indies a halfpenny) **e :** a smallest unit of money **:** a petty sum of money **:** MITE ⟨didn't make a ~ on the deal⟩ ⟨haven't got a ~⟩ **2 :** an old card game similar to piquet — called also *sant* **3 :** the interval between two pure tones whose frequency ratio is the 1200th root of 2 or the 100th root of the tempered semitone interval — **cent per cent 1 :** a hundred for every hundred **2 :** without exception

cent *abbr* **1** cental **2** center; central **3** centiare **4** centigrade **5** centime **6** centum **7** century

cen·tage \ˈsentij\ *n* -s [*cent* + *-age*] **:** PERCENTAGE

cen·tal \ˈsentᵊl\ *n* -s [L *centum* hundred + E *-al* (as in *quintal*)] *chiefly Brit* **:** SHORT HUNDREDWEIGHT

cen·tare \ˈsen,ta(a)(ə)r, -tär\ *or* **cen·ti·are** \ˈsentē,a(a)(ə)r, ˈsän-, -tē,är, ˌ==ˈ=, F säⁿtyäär\ *n* -s [F *centiare*, fr. *centi-* + *are*] **:** a metric unit of area equal to 1/100 of an are **:** SQUARE METER — see METRIC SYSTEM table

cen·tas \ˈsen,täs\ *n, pl* **cen·tai** \-tī\ [Lith, fr. E *cent*] **:** a Lithuanian unit of value equivalent to 1/100 of a litas; *also* **:** a coin representing this value

centaur \ˈsen,tȯ(ə)r, -tär, -tȯ(ə), -tå(r\ *n* -s [ME *Centaur, Centaurus*, fr. L *Centaurus*, fr. Gk *Kentauros*] **:** one of an ancient mythical Greek race dwelling in the mountains of Thessaly and imagined as men with the bodies of horses and half-bestial natures

cen·tau·rea \sen·ˈtȯrēə\ *n, cap* [NL, fr. ML, centaury (*Chlora perfoliata* or *Centaurium umbellatum*) — more at CENTAURY] **:** a large genus of plants (family Compositae) including the cornflower and the knapweed native chiefly to the Old World but now widely cultivated and characterized by flower heads composed entirely of tubular florets, the outer ones often sterile and enlarged so as to simulate ray florets

cen·tau·ri·um \sen'tȯrēəm\ *n, cap* [NL, fr. L *centaureum, centaurion* centaury — more at CENTAURY] **:** a genus of low-growing herbs (family Gentianaceae) distinguished by flowers with exserted spirally twisted anthers

cen·tau·ro·mach·ia \(ˌ)sen,tȯrō'makēə\ *n* -s [Gk *kentauromachia*, fr. *Kentauros* Centaur + *-machia* (fr. *machē* battle)] **:** a battle in which centaurs take part

cen·tau·ry \'sen,tȯrē, -ärē\ *n* -ES [ME *centaure*, fr. MF *centaurée*, fr. ML *centaurea*, fr. L *centaureum* & LL *centauria*, fr. Gk *kentaureion, kentauriē*, fr. *Kentauros* centaur; fr. the belief that its medicinal properties were discovered by the centaur Chiron] **1 :** a plant of the genus *Centaurium; esp* **:** an Old World herb (*Centaurium umbellatum*) formerly used as a tonic **2 :** AMERICAN CENTAURY **3 :** any of several plants of the genus *Centaurea; esp* **:** KNAPWEED

[1]**cen·ta·vo** \sen'tä(ˌ)vō\ *n* -s [Sp, lit., hundredth part, fr. L *centum* hundred — more at HUNDRED] *in the monetary systems of some Spanish-American countries* **:** CENT: **a :** a unit equal to 1/100 peso (as in Bolivia, Colombia, Cuba, Dominican Republic, Mexico, Philippines), 1/100 sucre (Ecuador), 1/100 colon (El Salvador), 1/100 quetzal (Guatemala), 1/100 lempira (Honduras), 1/100 cordoba (Nicaragua), or 1/100 sol (Peru) — see MONEY table **b :** a coin representing one centavo

[2]**cen·ta·vo** \sen'tä(ˌ)vü, -vō\ *n* -s [Pg, fr. Sp] **1 :** a Portuguese or Brazilian cent: **a :** a unit equal to 1/100 escudo (Portugal) or 1/100 cruzeiro (Brazil) — see MONEY table **b :** a Portuguese coin representing one centavo **2 :** a unit equal to 1/100 dobra (Sao Tome and Principe), 1/100 metical (Mozambique), or 1/100 peso (Guinea-Bissau) — see MONEY table

[1]**cen·te·nar·i·an** \ˌsent°n'erēən, -ntə'ne-, -a(a)r-,-är-\ *adj* [L *centenarius* + E *-an*] **1 :** marked by 100 years **:** 100 years old or older **2 :** of or pertinent to a centenary

[2]**centenarian** \"\ *n* -s **:** one that is 100 years old or older

cen·te·nar·i·an·ism \-ˌnizəm\ *n* -s **:** the state of being a centenarian

[1]**cen·ten·a·ry** \sen'tenərē, -ri; 'sent°n,er-, -ntə,ne-; *Brit often* sen'tēn-\ *n* -ES [LL *centenarium, centenarius*, fr. L *centenarius*, adj.] **1** *obs* **:** a weight of 100 pounds **2 :** a period, space, or age of 100 years **:** CENTURY **3 :** a commemoration or celebration of an event that occurred 100 years before **:** CENTENNIAL **4 :** the governor of a county hundred

[2]**centenary** \"\ *adj* [L *centenarius* of a hundred, fr. *centeni* one hundred each, fr. *centum* hundred — more at HUNDRED] **1 :** being 100 years later **:** marking a duration of 100 years **:** lasting 100 years **:** measured by hundred-year spans **:** CENTENNIAL ⟨a ~ celebration⟩ ⟨a ~ practice⟩ **2 :** belonging or relating to a county hundred

cen·te·nier \ˌsent°n'i(ə)r, -iə\ *n* -s [ME *centener*, fr. (assumed) OF *centenier* (whence MF *centenier*), fr. LL *centenarius*, fr. L *centenarius* of a hundred] **:** a police officer in the island of Jersey

[1]**cen·ten·nial** \(')sen'teneəl, sən't-, -nyəl\ *adj* [L *centum* hundred + E *-ennial* (as in *biennial*)] **1 :** of or relating to a period of 100 years or its completion **:** completing 100 years **2 :** relating to or associated with the commemoration of an event that happened 100 years before ⟨a ~ exhibition⟩ **3 :** lasting or aged 100 years ⟨~ pines⟩ — **cen·ten·nial·ly** \-əlē, -əli\ *adv*

[2]**centennial** \"\ *n* -s **1 :** a 100th anniversary or its celebration ⟨the ~ of the U.S. in 1876⟩ **2 :** a dice game in which two players throw three dice to get singly or in combination sequences from 1 to 12 and then 12 to 1

centennial brown *n* **:** a strong yellowish brown less strong and slightly redder and lighter than buckthorn brown and yellower and paler than orange rust — called also *pygmalion*

[1]**cen·ter** \'sentə(r)\ *n* -s *see -er in Explan Notes, often attrib* [ME *centre*, fr. MF, fr. L *centrum*, fr. Gk *kentron* sharp point, stationary point of a drawing compass, center of a circle, fr. *kentein* to prick, goad; akin to OHG *hantag* pointed, ON *hannarr* skillful, Goth *handugs* wise, Latvian *sīts* hunting spear] **1 a :** the point around which a circle or sphere is described **:** the point equidistant from all points on a circumference; *broadly* **:** MIDDLE **:** the point at an average distance from the exterior angles, points, or lines of a figure or body **b** *archaic* **:** the middle point of the earth **2 a :** a point around which things revolve; *often* **:** a focal point for attraction, concentration, or activity **:** a point, area, person, or thing that is most important or pivotal in relation to an indicated activity, interest, or condition ⟨St. Thomas and his God placed man in the ~ of the universe and made the sun and stars for his uses —Henry Adams⟩: **a :** PIVOT, AXIS **:** cardinal point ⟨the ~ from which the spokes branch out⟩ **b :** a point, area, person, or thing upon which attention, feeling, or action converges **:** FOCUS ⟨the old school was the ~ of our lives somehow: dances, socials, Sunday services, political meetings —E.A. McCourt⟩ ⟨the . . . Abilene region . . . has been the ~ of considerable controversy —R.W.Murray⟩ **c :** a place, area, person, group, or concentration marked significantly or dominatingly by an indicated activity, pursuit, interest, or appeal ⟨a railroad ~⟩ ⟨a tobacco ~⟩ ⟨a ~ for textile research⟩ ⟨the landing . . . is usually the ~ of much activity, because of the constant ferrying —*Amer. Guide Series: R.I.*⟩ ⟨the Emperor Napoleon was the real ~ of French sympathy for the South —A.L.Churchill⟩ **d :** a source or point of origin for an influence, force, process, action, or effect **:** HEART **:** a vital or stimulating factor ⟨intensive propaganda from the ~ —Alex Comfort⟩ **e :** a group of nerve cells having a common function ⟨the respiratory ~⟩ ⟨the visual or motor ~⟩ **f :** a region showing concentration of population **:** a large city ⟨do not produce here or import . . . from any other provincial ~ such perfect musical tailoring —Virgil Thomson⟩ **g :** a group of activities of the military each under its own commander but all having closely related functions and an overall commander ⟨medical ~⟩ ⟨separation ~⟩ **h :** a concentration of requisite facilities for an activity, pursuit, or interest along with various likely adjunct conveniences ⟨shopping ~⟩ ⟨medical ~⟩ ⟨amusement ~⟩ **i :** the ultimate head of an endocentric construction **3 :** middle part in contrast to sides, boundaries, outskirts, circumference, or peripheral features **:** middle area **:** MIDST ⟨the crown or arching ~ of the road —Thomas De Quincey⟩ ⟨at the ~ of the battle⟩ **:** a person or persons stationed or acting at or near the middle **:** a thing placed at the middle **:** a shot or stroke toward the middle: **a :** CORE, NUCLEUS **:** material constituting a middle part ⟨chocolates with hard ~s⟩ **b :** the middle element laterally of a military formation **c** *sometimes cap* **:** legislators and other political figures holding moderate views esp. between those of conservatives and liberals; *esp* **:** legislators holding moderate views and occupying seats in the middle of a chamber between the right and the left **d** *sometimes cap* **:** a position marked by moderation of political, economic, social, or religious views; *also* **:** adherents of moderate views **e :** the middle part of a theater stage **:** the most prominent part **f :** a part of a ballet practice floor away from the bar ⟨ballet exercises are easier done at the bar than in the ~⟩ **4 :** [1]CENTERING **5 a :** a player position in the middle of a playing surface or of a line of player positions: (1) **:** the position in the line in football between the guards, the lineman in this position having the extra duty of handing or passing the ball to a back to start each of his team's downs (2) **:** the position in basketball in the center circle at the start of play, the player of this position engaging in the center jump (3) **:** the position in hockey and lacrosse in the mid-area facing circle, the player of this position engaging in the initial face-off (4) **:** CENTER THREE-QUARTER **b :** the player of this position **6 a :** a pass of a puck or ball in hockey or lacrosse from either side to or toward the middle of the playing surface **b :** the handing or passing of a football by the center from his position in the line of scrimmage to one of the backs ⟨his bad ~ sailed over the fullback's head⟩ **c :** the starting point of a skating figure **7 a :** one of two tapered metal rods that support work in a lathe or grinding machine and about or with which the work revolves **b :** a conical recess in the end of work (as a shaft) for receiving such a center

syn MIDDLE, MIDST, FOCUS, NUCLEUS, HEART, CORE, HUB: in the meaning of that around which a circumference or periphery exists and in the metaphorical extensions of this, these words are often interchangeable and are often used together ⟨the very *center* and *focus* of literary education —F.N.Robinson⟩ ⟨the true *center* of the book is its *core* of irony —Dayton Kohler⟩ ⟨making that Sunday school what it ought to have been . . . the *heart* and *focus* of the parochial life —Compton Mackenzie⟩ In its geometrical sense CENTER suggests more exactness than MIDDLE. The latter word may be used for considerations of time ⟨in the *middle* (but not the *center*) of the night⟩ or of a sequence ⟨the *middle* of a series⟩ CENTER differs further from MIDDLE in being able to suggest capacity for acting, influencing, effecting. Contrast "he was the *center* of the conflict" and "he was in the *middle* of the conflict". MIDST suggests location well within a perimeter or situation of being surrounded or beset by matters important, demanding, or threatening ⟨the small democratic island in the *midst* of the European sea of dictatorship —*Books Abroad*⟩ ⟨we were in the *midst* of the foam, which boiled around us —Frederick Marryat⟩ FOCUS may suggest a center to which lines converge or on which forces act ⟨gold — the *focus* of desire —Bernard De Voto⟩ ⟨the *focus* of religious life was the church building —H.S.Bennett⟩ NUCLEUS suggests a center likely to grow, increase, undergo accretion, acquire surrounding or additional matter, force, or numbers ⟨not primarily boarding schools but rather day schools with a *nucleus* of boarders —J.B.Conant⟩ ⟨these two institutions have provided our Army and our Navy with the *nucleus* of their corps of officers —C.T.Lanham⟩ HEART indicates a center which either gives an essential nature to the whole or serves as a vital, positive, or motivating part ⟨sense knowledge cannot therefore be genuine knowledge, for it does not . . . get at the *heart* of reality —Frank Thilly⟩ ⟨the industrial northeast, widening westward, became the ruling region, the economic *heart;* the plantation South and the agrarian West became colonies —Roger Burlingame⟩ CORE may add to the ideas of NUCLEUS and HEART the idea of resistant firmness in which reliability may be placed and imply that peripheral matters are unimportant and adventitious ⟨the *core* of the *nucleus* upon which all the other civilized democracies of Europe . . . can one day rally —Sir Winston Churchill⟩ ⟨the *core* of the book, to wit, the allegory —J.L.Lowes⟩ HUB may contrast with FOCUS and suggest a center whence lines or influences radiate out, a center on which matters peripheral may depend ⟨the *hub* of roads fanning out to the four points of the compass —*N.Y. Times*⟩ ⟨some activities . . . are relatively isolated; other activities such as those at Pearl Harbor are grouped together to form a vast naval *hub* —*All Hands*⟩

[2]**center** \"\ *vb* **centered**; **centered**; **centering** \-ntəriŋ, -n·triŋ\ **centers** *see -er in Explan Notes, vt* **1 a :** to place or fix at a center or central area or position ⟨~ a typewriter carriage⟩ ⟨~ a picture on a wall⟩ ⟨the shaft is ~*ed* in a city square —*Amer. Guide Series: Minn.*⟩ **b :** to place near a center **:** cluster near a focal point ⟨a hamlet that was ~*ed* around the church⟩ **2 :** to gather to or around a center, fixed point, or pivot **:** draw together within a limit **:** COLLECT, CONCENTRATE, FOCUS ⟨a story to tell, ~*ed* around the political development of a great state —J.T.Adams⟩ ⟨everything had prepared the Boston mind to ~ its thoughts on history —Van Wyck Brooks⟩ ⟨all work on the plantation was ~*ed* on raising foodstuffs —A.W.Long⟩ ⟨more scholarship than is usual was ~*ed* around the main problems⟩ **3 :** to constitute a center of or for **:** serve as center or centerpiece for **:** occupy or adorn the center of **:** give, form, or shape a center for ⟨the business square, neat and compact, ~*s* the village —*Amer. Guide Series: Vt.*⟩ ⟨a bowl of white flowers ~*ed* the table⟩ **4 a :** to rig up between centers (as in a lathe) **b :** to form a recess or indentation in (work) for the reception of a center (as in a lathe) **5 a :** to adjust (lenses, mirrors, or other elements in an optical system) so that the axes coincide **b :** to grind the periphery of (a lens or mirror) to make optical center coincide with geometrical center **6 a :** to pass (a ball or a puck) from either side to or toward the middle of the playing area **b :** to play center on (a team) **c :** to hand or pass (a football) backward between one's legs from a position on the ground at the line of scrimmage to a back to begin a down **7 a :** to perforate (a stamp) so that all four margins are of equal width **b :** to place (a stamp) in relation to the perforations ⟨a stamp may be ~*ed* to the right or left⟩ ⟨a stamp well ~*ed*⟩ ~ *vi* **1** *obs* **:** to rest on something as a cardinal point **2 a :** to have a center **:** cluster or be concentrated **:** pivot or revolve **:** FOCUS — used with *in, at, on, upon, about,* or *around* ⟨the community ~*s* around a small circular park — *Amer. Guide Series: Ark.*⟩ ⟨the tribal organization ~*ed* in the chief⟩ **b :** to be primarily concerned **:** have a dominant theme or climax — used with *in, at, on, about,* or *around* ⟨another trilogy . . . would have ~*ed* in the battle of Gettysburg —Carl Van Doren⟩ ⟨discussions ~*ing* successively about such subjects as the weather, the house, the farm —M.L. Hanley⟩

[3]**center** \"\ *adj, see -er in Explan Notes* **:** CENTRAL **:** constituting a center **:** occupying or occurring at a center **:** MIDDLE ⟨a ~ table⟩ ⟨a ~ panel⟩ ⟨a ~ seat in a theater⟩ ⟨the ~ aisle⟩

center back *n* **:** the volleyball or water polo player stationed in the middle of the back line — see VOLLEYBALL illustration

center bet *n* **:** a crapshooter's bet placed in the center of the playing surface for fading

center bit *n* **:** a bit with a sharp conical or threaded center spur for guiding it, a scorer for marking the circumference of the hole, and a lip for cutting away the wood inside the circumference

centerboard \'==,=\ *n* -s [[1]*center* + *board*] **1** *in a shallow-draft sailing vessel* **:** a device (as a broad board or slab of wood or metal pivoted at its forward lower corner) in a casing or trunk amidships so that it may be raised either in shallow water or when the vessel is beached or lowered to increase the area of lateral resistance and prevent leeway when the vessel is working to windward or sailing wind abeam — called also *drop keel, sliding keel* **2** *also* **center boarder** [short for *centerboard boat*] **:** a boat with a centerboard

section of boat showing *1* trunk, *2* centerboard

center circle *n* **:** the circle marked at the center of a playing surface (as in basketball, hockey, lacrosse, or soccer) where a center jump, face-off, or kickoff takes place

center down *vi* **1 :** to achieve steadiness, sobriety, and concentration **:** amend habits of flighty irresponsibility **2** *in Quaker worship* **:** to turn one's attention in reverent silence toward the religious meaning of life

center draw *n* **:** the face-off in lacrosse at the center circle following a score or beginning a quarter

center drill *n* **:** a small twist drill used to make centers in a piece of work about to be turned

cen·tered \'sentə(r)d\ *adj* **1 :** having a center; *specif* **:** having a center of curvature ⟨the ~ arc of a circle⟩ ⟨a *3-centered* arch⟩ or center of figure ⟨a ~ crystal⟩ **2 :** placed in the center: **a :** having equal bordering areas ⟨an *off-centered* postage stamp⟩ **b** *of periods, points, or dots* **:** at hyphen level and placed equidistant from characters to left and right

cen·ter·er \'sentərə(r)\ *n* -s **:** one that works with a centering apparatus

center field *n* **1 :** the sector of the outfield beyond second base and between right field and left field in baseball or softball **2 :** the player position for defending this area

center fielder *n* **:** the baseball or softball player stationed in center field — see BASEBALL illustration

center-fire *also* **central-fire** \'==,=\ *adj* **1** *of a cartridge* **:** fired by the striking of a hammer or firing pin upon a cap or primer at the center of the base — distinguished from *rimfire* **2 :** designed for or adapted to the use of center-fire cartridges ⟨a *center-fire* rifle⟩

center forward *n* **:** the player position in the middle of the attacking line in soccer, field hockey, volleyball, or water polo; *also* **:** the player who plays this position — see VOLLEYBALL illustration

center gauge *n* **:** a gauge for testing angles (as of lathe centers, screw threads, or the points of cutting tools) or for testing the setting of a thread-cutting tool with reference to work under way

center halfback *n* **:** the player position in the center of the middle line in soccer, speedball, or field hockey; *also* **:** the player who plays this position

center ice *n* **:** the zone between the blue lines in hockey

[1]**centering** *n* -s [[1] and [2]*center* + *-ing*] **:** a usu. timber falsework used to support the parts of a masonry arch during construction

[2]**centering** *adj* [fr. pres. part. of [2]*center*] *of a diphthong or triphthong* **:** concluded with the tongue in the position for the central vowel \ə\ (as \'iə\, one pronunciation of *ear*)

centering machine *n* **:** a machine like a small speed lathe used esp. to drill and countersink work to be turned on lathe centers

centering: *1* bearers, *2* bearing strips, *3* stiffening pieces, *4* braces, *5* wedges

center jam *n* **:** STREAM JAM

center jump *n* **:** a jump ball by the centers in basketball

cen·ter·less grinder \'sentə(r)ləs-\ *n* **:** a grinder for production of cylindrical work in which centers are replaced by a work-supporting member and two abrasive wheels one of which grinds work while the other regulates the speed of its rotation — **centerless grinding** *n*

center line *n* **1 :** a straight or curved line that continuously bisects a plane figure (as a building plan, a machine-work layout, or the surface of a paved highway or playing field) **2 :** AXIS 1

cen·ter·man \-tə(r)mən, -ˌman\ *n, pl* **centermen :** a worker who uses plumb bobs to locate the center line of underground mine openings and marks them so that the openings (as entries, rooms, and haulageways) can be driven in a straight line

cen·ter·most \-tə(r)ˌmōst, *esp Brit also* -ˌməst\ *adj* [[3]*center* + *-most*] **:** MIDDLEMOST, MIDMOST

center of action : any of several large oval areas where the average seasonal or annual barometric pressure is distinctly low or high

center of area : the point of a plane figure that would coincide with the center of mass of a thin uniform distribution of matter over the area of the figure — compare CENTER OF FIGURE

center of buoyancy *or* **center of displacement :** the center of mass of the fluid displaced by a floating or submerged body (as a ship, submarine, or balloon)

center of curvature : the center of the osculating circle at a given point of a curve

center of effort : the point on a sail at which application of the whole propelling force of the wind would produce an effect identical with that produced by its distribution over the whole sail

center of figure : the center of area of a plane figure or the center of volume of a 3-dimensional figure

center of flotation : the center of gravity of the water plane of a vessel

center of gravity [prob. trans. of F *centre de gravité*, trans. of Gk *kentron bareos*] **1 :** CENTER OF MASS **2 :** the single point in a body (as a homogeneous sphere) toward which every particle of matter external to the body is gravitationally attracted **3 :** the point or area of greatest concentration, significance, or interest **:** a predominating or controlling situation **:** FOCAL POINT ⟨a shifting of the industrial *center of gravity* is taking place —Lewis Mumford⟩

center of inversion : the point *O* from which the distances of two points *P* and *P′* which correspond to one another in an inversion are measured, the inversion being characterized by the fact that the product *OP·OP′* is constant

center of mass *or* **center of inertia :** the point that represents the mean position of the matter in a body

center-of-mass system *n* **:** a system of polar coordinates used in describing processes involving moving swarms of particles (as cosmic-ray bursts) with the moving common center of mass as origin and the path of that center as polar axis

center of origin : an area in which extensive and often rapid speciation has taken place within a natural group

center of oscillation : a point in a pendulum at which if the mass were concentrated the period would be unchanged — compare CENTER OF SUSPENSION

center of ossification : a point within a developing bone at which ossification begins within the preexistent cartilaginous matrix

center of percussion : the point in a body free to move about a fixed axis at which the body may be squarely struck without jarring the axis

center of pressure **1** *of an airfoil section* **:** the point in the chord (prolonged if necessary) that is at the intersection of the chord and the line of action of the resultant air force **2 :** the point of a surface exposed to external pressure (as of a fluid) at which a single force must be applied to equal or counterbalance the pressure forces acting on the whole surface

center of projection : PROJECTION AREA

center of similitude : a point in which concur all lines joining corresponding points in two similar figures similarly or oppositely placed and which divides all such lines in a fixed ratio that is direct or inverse according as the division is outside of or between the points

center of suspension : the point about which a pendulum oscillates — compare CENTER OF OSCILLATION

center of symmetry **1 :** a point within a crystal with respect to which similar planes and edges are symmetrical in opposite pairs **2 :** the property exhibited by some crystals whereby every direction (as AB) through the crystal is alike in both senses (AB and BA) with respect to all characteristics

center of volume : the point of a 3-dimensional figure that would coincide with the center of mass of a homogeneous material body having the same boundaries — compare CENTER OF FIGURE

centerpiece \'==,=\ *n* [[3]*center* + *piece*] **:** an object occupying a central or most conspicuous position; *specif* **:** an adornment in the center of a table ⟨a bowl of roses for a ~⟩

centerplate \'==,=\ *n* **:** a metal centerboard

center punch *n* **:** a machinist's hand punch consisting of a short steel bar with a hardened conical point at one end used for marking the centers of holes to be drilled

centerpuncher \'==,==\ *n* **:** one that punches indentations in metal to indicate where holes are to be drilled or punched

center rest *n* **:** STEADY REST

centers *pl of* CENTER, *pres 3d sing of* CENTER

center-sawed \'=='=\ *adj* **:** QUARTERSAWED

cen·ter·scope \'sentə(r),skōp\ *n* -s **:** a device to magnify layout lines for accurate placing of center-punch marks for drilling

center seal *n* **:** a compound hydraulic valve used in gas manufacturing for regulating the passage of the gas through a set of purifiers so as to cut out each in turn for renewal of the lime

center-second \'=='==\ *n* **:** SWEEP-SECOND

center spread *n* **:** a unit of printed matter usu. without columnar division and largely pictorial on the two center facing pages of typical magazine format — compare DOUBLE TRUCK

center square *n* **:** a combination of straightedge and sliding square used for finding the center of a circle

center staff *n* **:** the arbor upon which are mounted the minute hand and cannon pinion of a timepiece

center strap *n* **:** a band on the center of a tennis net that anchors to the ground to keep the net secure at the right height

center tester *n* **:** CENTER GAUGE

center three-quarter *n* **:** a rugby three-quarter positioned next to a wing three-quarter; *also* **:** the position of such a player

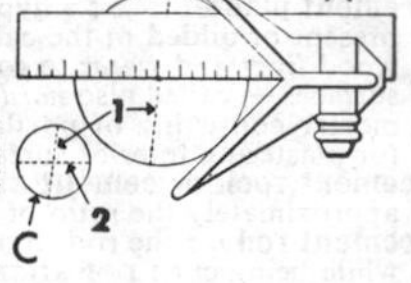

A center square with circle *B* in position for ruling the diameter, two such rulings (*1* and *2*) giving its center as in *C*

cen·ter·velic \ˌsentə(r)+\ *n* -s [*center* + *velic*] **:** CENTER OF EFFORT

center wheel *n* **:** the first wheel in the going train of a timepiece driving the wheels leading to the escapement and having a pinion post on which the minute hand is carried

cen·tes·i·mal \(')sen'tesəməl\ *adj* [L *centesimus* hundredth (fr. *centum* hundred) + E *-al* — more at HUNDRED] **1 :** marked by division into hundredths ⟨a ~ or centigrade thermometer⟩ **2 :** relating to marking in hundredths or to devices using it

cen·tes·i·mate \-ˈ==,māt\ *vt* -ED/-ING/-S [LL *centesimatus*, past part. of *centesimare*, fr. L *centesimus* hundredth + *-atus* -ate] **:** to punish or execute every hundredth man of ⟨the legion was *centesimated* on account of mutinous tendencies⟩

[1]**cen·te·si·mo** \chen·ˈteza,mō\ *n, pl* **centesi·mi** \-(,)mē\ [It *centesimo*, lit., hundredth, fr. L *centesimus*] **:** an Italian cent: **a :** a unit of value equal to 1/100 lira — see MONEY table **b :** a coin representing one centesimo

[2]**cen·te·si·mo** \sen·ˈtesə,mō\ *n* -S [Sp *centésimo*, fr. L *centesimus*] **1 :** a unit of value equal to 1/100 balboa (Panama) or 1/100 peso (Uruguay) — see MONEY table **2 :** a coin representing one centesimo

cen·te·sis \sen·ˈtēsəs\ *n, pl* **cente·ses** \-ē,sēz\ [NL, fr. Gk *kentēsis* act of pricking, fr. *kentein* to prick — more at CENTER] **:** surgical puncture (as of a tumor or membrane) — usu. used in compounds ⟨para*centesis*⟩ ⟨thora*centesis*⟩

cen·te·tes \sen·ˈtēd·,ēz\ [NL, fr. LGk *kentētēs* piercer, fr. Gk *kentein* to prick; fr. the spines on the back — more at CENTER] *syn of* TENREC

cen·tet·i·dae \-ted·ə,dē\ [NL, fr. *Centetes*, type genus + *-idae*] *syn of* TENRECIDAE

cent·ge·ner \ˈsentjənə(r)\ *n* -S [L *centum* hundred + *gener-, genus* birth, race — more at KIN] **1 :** a large number of plants or animals having a common parentage; *esp* **:** 100 plants (as of wheat) derived from a single parent and so planted (as in plots or rows) that the value of the breed may be determined **2 :** a device for planting 100 seeds equally spaced and at a uniform depth

centi- *comb form* [F & L; F, hundredth, fr. L, hundred, fr. *centum* hundred — more at HUNDRED] **1 :** hundred ⟨*centi*pede⟩ **2 :** hundredth part ⟨*centi*meter⟩ ⟨*centi*normal⟩ — chiefly in terms belonging to the metric system

centiare *var of* CENTARE

cen·ti·bar \ˈsentə,bär\ *n* -S [ISV *centi-* + *bar*; orig. formed as G *zentibar*] **:** a unit of atmospheric pressure equal to 1/100 bar — abbr. *cb*

cen·ti·day \-,dā\ *n* -S [*centi-* + *day*] **:** a period of 14 minutes 24 seconds used esp. in the study of plant growth

[1]**cen·ti·grade** \ˈsentə,grād *also* ˈsän-\ *adj* [F, fr. *centi-* + *grade* degree, grade — more at GRADE] **:** relating to, conforming to, or having a thermometric scale on which the interval between two standard points, the freezing point and the boiling point of water, is divided into 100 degrees, 0° representing the freezing point and 100° the boiling point ⟨10° ~⟩ ⟨a ~ instrument⟩ — abbr. *C*; compare CELSIUS

[2]**centigrade** \"\ *n* -S **1 :** a centigrade thermometer **2 :** a centigrade scale

cen·ti·gram \-,gram, -aa(ə)m\ *n* -S [F *centigramme*, fr. *centi-* + *gramme* gram — more at GRAM] **:** a unit of mass and weight equal to 1/100 gram — see METRIC SYSTEM table

cen·tile \ˈsen·,tīl\ *n* -S [L *centum* hundred + E *-ile* — more at HUNDRED] **:** PERCENTILE

cen·ti·liter \ˈsentə, ˈsän- +,-\ *n* -S [F *centilitre*, fr. *centi-* + *litre* liter — more at LITER] **:** a unit of liquid capacity equal to 1/100 liter — see METRIC SYSTEM table

cen·til·lion \sen·ˈtilyən\ *n* -S *often attrib* [L *centum* hundred + E *-illion* (as in *million*)] — see NUMBER table

cen·time \ˈsän·,tēm, ˈsen-, =ˈ=\ *n* -S [F, fr. *cent* hundred, fr. L *centum* — more at HUNDRED] **1 :** a monetary unit equivalent to 1/100 Algerian dinar, 1/100 Moroccan dirham, 1/100 franc, or 1/100 gourde — see MONEY table **2 :** a coin representing one centime

cen·ti·meter \ˈsentə *also* ˈsän-+,-\ *n* -S [F *centimètre*, fr. *centi-* + *mètre* meter — more at METER] **:** a unit of length equal to 1/100 meter — see METRIC SYSTEM table

centimeter dyne *n* **:** ERG

centimeter-gram-second *adj* **:** of, relating to, or being a system of units based upon the centimeter as the unit of length, the gram as the unit of mass, and the mean solar second as the unit of time — abbr. *cgs*

cen·ti·mo \ˈsentə,mō\ *n* -S [Sp *céntimo*, modif. of F *centime*] **1 :** a unit of value equal to 1/100 bolivar, 1/100 Costa Rican colon, 1/100 ekuele, 1/100 guarani, or 1/100 peseta — see MONEY table **2 :** a coin representing one centimo

cen·ti·molar \ˌsentə *also* ˌsän- +\ *adj* [*centi-* + *molar*] **:** 1/100 molar

cen·ti·normal \ˌsentə, -tē +\ *adj* [*centi-* + *normal*] *of a chemical solution* **:** having 1/100 of normal strength

cen·ti·pede \ˈsentə,pēd\ *n* -S [L *centipeda*, fr. *centi-* + *-peda* (fr. *ped-, pes* foot)—more at FOOT] **1 :** any of various flattened elongated arthropods constituting the class Chilopoda, having a single posterior genital aperture and the body divided into a number of segments each bearing one pair of legs of which the foremost pair is modified into poison fangs, and being active, predaceous, and chiefly nocturnal animals useful as destroyers of noxious insects — compare MILLIPEDE **2 :** a rope with short crosspieces that runs the length of a jib boom and is used in stowing jibs in port

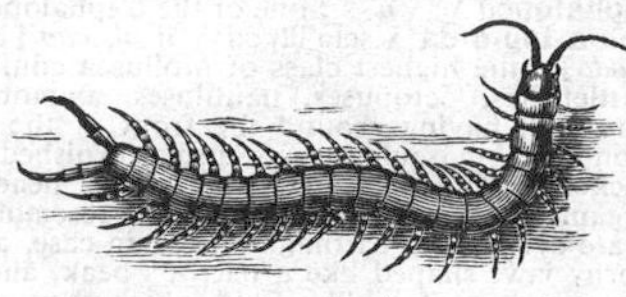

centipede

centipede grass *n* [prob. so called fr. the appearance of the creeping stolons] **:** a grass (*Eremochloa ophiuroides*) introduced into the southern U.S. from China esp. for lawn use

centipede plant *n* **:** an erect shrub (*Homalocladium platycladum*) of the islands of the Pacific with flat ribbonlike jointed stems and with leaves only on the young branches — called also *ribbon bush, tapeworm plant*

cen·ti·poise \ˈsentə,pȯiz\ *n* -S [*centi-* + *poise*] **:** a unit of viscosity equal to 1/100 poise

cen·ti·stoke \ˈsentə,stōk, -tē,-\ *n* -S [*centi-* + *stoke*] **:** a unit of kinematic viscosity equal to 1/100 stoke

cent·ner \ˈsentnə(r) *also* ˈtse- *with reference to Germany*\ *n* -S [prob. fr. LG; akin to MD *centenaer*, OHG *centenāri*; all fr. a prehistoric D-LG-HG word borrowed fr. L *centenarius* of a hundred — more at CENTENARY] **:** any of various units of weight: as **a :** a unit used in Germany and Scandinavia usu. equal to 110.23 pounds **b :** a unit used in the U.S.S.R. equal to 220.46 pounds — see METRIC CENTNER

cen·to \ˈsen·,tō, -ntō\ *n, pl* **cento·nes** \sen·ˈtō(,)nēz\ *or* **centoes** *or* **centos** \ˈsen·,tōz, -ntōz\ [L; akin to OHG *hadara* rag, Skt *kanthā* patched garment] **1** *obs* **:** a garment of patches **2 :** an often poetic patchwork composition of parts from other works

cen·to·ni·cal \(ˈ)sen·ˌtänəkəl\ *adj* [L *centon-, cento* + E *-ical*] **:** of, like, or constituting a cento

cen·to·nism \ˈsentə,nizəm\ *also* **cen·to·ni·za·tion** \ˌsentənəˈzāshən\ *n* -S [L *centon-, cento* + -E *-ism* or *-ization*] **:** the act or practice of composing centos

centr- *or* **centro-** *comb form* [Gk *kentr-, kentro-*, fr. *kentron* center, sharp point] **1 :** center ⟨*centr*oid⟩ **:** central and ⟨*centro*dorsal⟩ **2 :** spiny ⟨*centr*archid⟩ ⟨*centro*sema⟩

centra *pl of* CENTRUM

[1]**cen·trad** \ˈsen·,trad\ *adv* (*or adj*) [*centr-* + *-ad*] **:** toward the center (as of the body) ⟨~ to the epidermis⟩

[2]**centrad** \"\ *n* -S [*cent-* (fr. *centi-*) + *rad*ian] **:** a unit of angular measure equal to 1/100 of a radian or about 0.57 degrees

[1]**cen·tral** \ˈsen·trəl\ *adj, sometimes* -ER/-EST [L *centralis*, fr. *centrum* center — more at CENTER] **1 :** containing or constituting a center **:** relevant or pertinent to a center ⟨the sun having a ~ place in the solar system⟩ ⟨the ~ areas⟩ **2 :** belonging to the center as most important part **:** BASIC, ESSENTIAL, PRINCIPAL, DOMINANT **:** not peripheral or incidental **:** cardinally related ⟨these efforts have been marginal and not ~ —Max Lerner⟩ ⟨ethical values ~ to the democratic way of life —Sidney Hook⟩ ⟨the ~ virtues . . . courage, honor, faithfulness, veracity, justice —Walter Lippmann⟩ ⟨a notion ~ to his beliefs⟩ **3 a :** situated at, in, or near the center **:** occupying a center **:** proceeding from a center ⟨the ~ block of the city⟩ ⟨the ~ part of the state⟩ **b :** placed at a center and accessible from all outlying points without undue or disproportionate difficulty ⟨a new theater in a ~ location⟩ **4 a :** centrally placed and superseding or eliminating separate scattered units ⟨~ heating⟩ ⟨~ offices⟩ **b :** controlling or directing local or branch activities **:** constituting a governing or administrative center ⟨decided by the ~ committee⟩ **5 :** holding to a middle course or position between extremes **:** MODERATE, CENTER **6 a :** of or concerning the centrum of a vertebra **b :** of, relating to, or indicating the part of the nervous system comprising the brain and spinal cord — distinguished from *peripheral* **7** *of a vowel* **:** articulated at a point in the oral passage between front and back

[2]**central** \"\ *n* -S **1** *sometimes cap* **a :** a telephone exchange **b :** a telephone operator — now usu. called *operator* ⟨ask ~ to cancel the call⟩ **2 :** CENTRALE **3 :** a central office or bureau usu. controlling or dominating others ⟨~ ran the various branches⟩ **4** *usu cap* **:** a branch of the Niger-Congo language family including Bantu, Ekoi, Ibibio, and Tiv

[3]**cen·tral** \sen·ˈträl\ *n, pl* **centrals** \-lz\ *or* **centra·les** \-ä(,)lās\ [AmerSp, fr. Sp *central*, adj., fr. L *centralis*] *in Spanish America & the Philippines* **:** a mill for making raw sugar out of cane

central african *n, cap C & A* **:** a native or inhabitant of the Central African Republic — **central african** *adj, usu cap C & A*

central algonquian *n, usu cap C&A* **:** a subdivision of the Algonquian language stock including Cree, Ojibwa, Fox, Menomini, Potawatomi, Illinois, and Shawnee

[1]**central american** \ˌ===ˌ===\ *adj, usu cap C&A* [*Central America* + E *-an*] **1 :** of or relating to Central America **2 :** of, relating to, or being the subregion of the Nearctic region that includes tropical America north of Panama

[2]**central american** \"\ *n, cap C&A* **:** a native or inhabitant of Central America

central american cedar *n, usu cap 1st C&A* **:** SPANISH CEDAR

central apparatus *n* **:** the centrosome or centrosomes including usu. a surrounding area of differentiated cytoplasm — called also *cytocentrum*; compare MICROCENTRUM

central bank *n* **:** a bank that deals mainly with other banks and the government and assumes broad responsibilities in the interests of the national economy apart from the earning of profits (as by regulating the volume, character, and cost of outstanding bank credit)

central basin *adj, usu cap C&B* [prob. so called fr. sites in the Illinois river valley in central Illinois] **:** of or relating to a phase of Woodland culture preceding and related to Hopewell and characterized by small habitation sites, flexed burials, and incised and stamped grit-tempered pottery

central body *n* **1 :** CENTROSOME 1 **2 :** the colorless inner portion of the protoplasm in the cells of blue-green algae and of certain bacteria that is assumed by some to be a primitive nucleus lacking nucleoli and nuclear membrane — called also *centroplasm*; compare CHROMATOPLASM

central canal *n* **:** a minute canal running through the gray matter of the whole length of the spinal cord and continuous anteriorly with the ventricles of the brain

central cell *n* **1 :** CHIEF CELL 1 **2 :** the cell in the venter of the archegonium whose division produces the egg and usu. also the ventral canal cell (as in cycads)

central convolution *n* **:** any of the gyri bordering the central sulcus in the brain

central cylinder *n* **:** STELE

cen·tra·le \sen·ˈträ(,)lē, -al(,)ē, -ä(,)lē\ *n, pl* **centra·lia** \-ˈlēə\ [NL, fr. L, neut. of *centralis* central] **:** a bone in the carpus or tarsus situated between the proximal and distal rows of bones, in man that of the carpus usu. fusing with the navicular and that of the tarsus being replaced by the navicular

central eclipse *n* **1 :** a solar eclipse at the point when the centers of the sun and moon are in line with the observer **2 :** a lunar eclipse in which the moon passes through the center of the earth's shadow

cen·tra·les \sen·ˈträ(,)lēz\ *n pl, cap* [NL, fr. L *centrum* center + NL *-ales*] **:** an order of diatoms having cylindrical disklike or even-angular cells always lacking a raphe or pseudoraphe and having radial markings and often spines — compare PENNALES

central-fire *var of* CENTER-FIRE

central force *n* **:** a force of attraction toward or of repulsion from a fixed or moving definite point

cen·tral·id \ˈsen·trəlèd, -,lid\ *n* -S *usu cap* [*central* + *-id*] **:** an early American Indian of a physical type characterized by broad high-vaulted head and relatively broad face and found primarily in southwestern U.S. and the northern Mississippi valley — compare PACIFID, SYLVID

cen·tral·ism \ˈsen·trə,lizəm\ *n* -S **:** CENTRALIZATION **:** disposition to centralize **:** a system marked by centralization esp. in government

[1]**cen·tral·ist** \-ˌləst\ *n* -S [Sp *centralista*, fr. *central* (fr. L *centralis*) + *-ista* -ist, fr. L — more at CENTRAL] **:** an advocate of centralization esp. in government

[2]**centralist** \"\ *adj* **:** advocating centralization — **cen·tral·is·tic** \ˌ==ˈlistik, -tēk\ *adj*

cen·tral·ite \-,līt\ *n* -S [fr. *Centralite*, a trademark] **:** a dialkyl derivative of carbanilide (as diethyl-diphenyl-urea) used as a stabilizer for smokeless powder

cen·tral·i·ty \sen·ˈtraləd·ē, -ətē, -i\ *n* -ES **:** the quality or state of being central **:** tendency to remain in or at the center

cen·tral·i·za·tion \ˌsen·trələˈzāshən, -,līˈz-\ *n* -S [F *centralisation*, fr. *centraliser* + *-ation*] **1 :** the act or process of centralizing **:** the state of being centralized **2 a :** concentration of the powers and agencies of government in the central or national organization **b :** concentration of authority and power in the hands of a few ⟨he believed in strong ~ — the concentration of power in a few hands, the strict regimentation —H.L. Mencken⟩

cen·tral·ize \ˈsen·trə,līz\ *vb* -ED/ -ING/ -S *see -ize in Explan Notes* [F *centraliser*, fr. *central* + *-iser* -ize] *vi* **:** to form a center **:** to cluster around a center ⟨a tendency of the whirling particles to ~⟩ ~ *vt* **1 :** to serve as center for **:** draw to a central point **:** gather about a center ⟨the post office *centralizing* the town⟩ **2 :** to concentrate by placing power and authority in a center or central organization ⟨I urge upon the Congress the desirability of *centralizing* these functions in a single agency —H.S.Truman⟩

cen·tral·iz·er \-zə(r)\ *n* -S **1 :** an advocate or agent of centralization **2 :** one that centralizes

cen·tral·la·site \sen·ˈtralə,sīt\ *n* -S [*centr-* + Gk *allassein* to change + E *-ite*] **:** a mineral composed of a hydrous silicate of calcium, probably $Ca_4Si_7O_{18}.5H_2O$

central lobe *n* **:** ISLAND OF REIL

cen·tral·ly \ˈsen·trəlē, -li\ *adv* [[3]*central* + *-ly*] **:** in a central position **:** at, near, or toward a center **:** according to a central role or function

central nervous system *n* **:** the part of the nervous system which in vertebrates consists of brain and spinal cord, to which sensory impulses are transmitted and from which motor impulses pass out, and which supervises and coordinates the activity of the entire nervous system — compare AUTONOMIC NERVOUS SYSTEM

cen·tral·ness *n* -ES **:** CENTRALITY

central quadric *n* **:** a second-degree surface possessing a center about which there is a symmetrical figure (as an ellipsoid, 1-sheeted or 2-sheeted hyperboloid, or cone)

central reserve city *n* **:** a major financial center in which banks are usu. subject to higher legal reserve requirements than those in other cities — compare COUNTRY BANK, RESERVE CITY

centrals *pl of* CENTRAL

central school *n* **:** CONSOLIDATED SCHOOL

central staging *n* **:** ARENA THEATER

central station *n* **1 :** a central electric-power-generating plant **2 :** a communications center esp. on a warship

central sudanic *n, cap C&S* **:** a branch of the Chari-Nile language family including Bagirmi, Efe, Lendu, Lugbara, Moru, Madi, and Mangbetu that is spoken in northeastern Zaire, northern Uganda, southern Republic of Sudan, and westward toward Lake Chad

central sulcus *n* **:** the sulcus separating the frontal lobe of the cerebral cortex from the parietal — called also *fissure of Rolando*

central symmetry *n, math* **:** symmetry with respect to a point

central tendency *n* **:** the degree of clustering of the values of a statistical distribution that is usu. measured by the arithmetic mean, mode, or median

central time *or* **central standard time** *n, often cap C* **:** the time of the 6th time zone west of Greenwich that is based on the 90th meridian, is used in east central Canada, central U.S., Mexico, and Central America, and is one hour slower than eastern time — abbr. *CT, CST*

cen·tranth \ˈsen·,tran(t)th\ *n* -S [NL *Centranthus* (genus name), fr. *centr-* + *-anthus*] **:** a plant of a genus (*Centranthus*) of the family Valerianaceae; *esp* **:** RED VALERIAN

cen·trar·chid \sen·ˈträrkəd, -äk-, -,kid\ *n* -S [NL *Centrarchidae*] **:** a fish of the family Centrarchidae

cen·trar·chi·dae \-ˌkə,dē\ *n pl, cap* [NL, fr. *centrarchus*, type genus (fr. Gk *kentron* sharp point + *archos* rectum) + *-idae* — more at CENTER] **:** a family of No. American carnivorous percoid freshwater fishes containing the sunfishes, crappies, black basses, and others valuable as food and game — **cen·trar·choid** \-ˌkȯid\ *adj or n*

cen·tra·tion \sen·ˈtrāshən\ *n* -S [*centr-* + *-ation*] **:** the act of centering

cen·trax·o·nia \ˌsen·trakˈsōnēə\ *n pl, cap* [NL, fr. *centr-* + *axonia*] *biol* **:** organisms having a median axis regarded as a group — **cen·trax·o·ni·al** \ˌ=ˌ=ˌ=nēəl\ *adj*

cen·tre \ˈsentə(r)\ *chiefly Brit var of* CENTER

cen·trech·i·noi·da \(,)sen·,trekəˈnȯidə\ *n pl, cap* [NL, fr. *Centrechinus* + *-oida*] **:** a large order of sea urchins having peristomial gills, sphaeridia, and an apically located anus — compare CIDAROIDA, EXOCYCLOIDA

cen·tre·chi·nus \ˌsen·trēˈkīnəs\ *n, cap* [NL, fr. *centr-* + *Echinus*] **:** a widely distributed genus of tropical reef-dwelling black sea urchins having slender poisonous spines

cen·tred \ˈsentə(r)d\ *chiefly Brit var of* CENTERED

cen·tre·man \-tə(r)(,)m-\ *n, pl* **centremen** *Brit* **:** CENTER 5b

centri- *comb form* [NL, fr. L CENTRUM] **:** center ⟨*centri*fugal⟩ ⟨*centri*ole⟩

cen·tric \ˈsen·trik, -rēk\ *adj* [Gk *kentrikos* of the center, fr. *kentron* center, sharp point] **1 :** located in or at a center **:** CENTRAL ⟨a ~ point⟩ **2 a :** having a center **:** having parts grouped around or directed to a center ⟨a ~ activity⟩ **b :** tending to cluster around a center **:** marked by concentration on something as of central importance ⟨~ ideas⟩ **3 :** of or relating to a nerve center **4 a** *of leaves* **:** CYLINDRICAL, TERETE **b :** of or concerning the order Centrales **c** *of a diatom* **:** having the surface markings radially arranged (as in members of the order Centrales) **5** [trans. of G *zentrisch*] *of a rock* **:** having a texture (as oolitic, ocellar) in which the constituents are grouped about a center **6 :** possessing or relating to a centromere **7** *of dental occlusion* **:** involving spatial relationships such that all teeth of both jaws meet in a normal manner and forces exerted by the lower on the upper jaw are perfectly distributed in the dental arch

-cen·tric \ˌsen·trik, -rēk\ *adj comb form* [ME *-sentrik* (in *consentrik* concentric), fr. ML *-centricus* (in *concentricus* concentric, *eccentricus* eccentric) — more at ECCENTRIC] **:** having (such) a center or (such or so many) centers ⟨hetero*centric*⟩ ⟨homo*centric*⟩ ⟨poly*centric*⟩ **:** having (something specified) as its center ⟨anthropo*centric*⟩ ⟨helio*centric*⟩

cen·tri·cae \ˈsen·trə,sē\ *n pl, cap* [NL, fem. pl. of *centricus* centric, fr. Gk *kentrikos*] *in some classifications* **:** a group of diatoms equivalent to the order Centrales

cen·tri·cal \ˈsen·trəkəl\ *adj* **:** CENTRAL, CENTRIC ⟨in the ~ part of town⟩ — **cen·tri·cal·ly** \-rək(ə)lē\ *adv*

cen·tric·i·ty \sen·ˈtrisəd·ē, -ətē, -i\ *n* -ES [*centric* + *-ity* (as in *eccentricity*)] **:** the quality or state of being centric ⟨the ~ of the family in Western values⟩

centries *pl of* CENTRY

[1]**cen·trif·u·gal** \(ˈ)sen·ˈtrifyəgəl, -fəˌg-, -fēˌg-, ˌk-, *Brit also* ˌsen·trəˈfyüg-\ *adj* [NL *centrifugus* (fr. *centri-* + *-fugus*, fr. L *fugere* to flee) + E *-al* — more at FUGITIVE] **1 :** moving, proceeding, or acting in a direction away from a center or axis — opposed to *centripetal* ⟨~acceleration of a body⟩ **2 a :** using or acting by centrifugal force ⟨a ~ compressor⟩ **b :** separated or freed from (as liquid) by centrifugal force ⟨~ flotation of solids from liquids⟩ **3 a :** developing and expanding successively outward and downward from the center or summit — used of the flowers of an inflorescence **b :** having the radicle turned toward the sides of the fruit **4 :** passing outward (as from a nerve center to a muscle or gland) **:** EFFERENT **5 :** tending away from centralization **:** SEPARATIST ⟨must soon discover that a system ~ in tendency and decentralizing in spirit, unless closely restrained, was certain to lead them far from the Canaan of their hopes —V.L.Parrington⟩

[2]**centrifugal** \"\ *n* -S **1 a :** CENTRIFUGAL MACHINE **b :** a drum in such a machine **2 :** CENTRIFUGAL SUGAR — often used in pl.

centrifugal blower *n* **:** a blower that operates on the principle of a centrifugal pump

centrifugal casting *n* **:** the casting of metal in a rapidly revolving mold — used esp. of the casting of pipe in which a rotating tube serves as mold

centrifugal clutch *n* **:** an automatic friction clutch in which contact between driving and driven parts is established and maintained through centrifugal force commonly against the action of springs that break the contact when the driving part slows down

centrifugal compressor *n* **:** an air or gas compressor utilizing a centrifugal pump

centrifugal field *n* **:** a space in which centrifugal forces may be detected (as in a rotating centrifuge or in a vehicle rounding a curve)

centrifugal force *n* **:** the force that a material particle moving along a curve exerts on the body constraining the motion and that is directed outwardly along the radius of the curve **:** the reaction to the centripetal force ⟨a stone whirled about on the end of a string exerts *centrifugal force* on the string⟩ — compare CENTRIPETAL FORCE

centrifugal governor *n* **:** a governor (sense 4a) operated by centrifugal force

cen·trif·u·gal·i·za·tion \(,)=,===ləˈzāshən, -,līˈz-\ *n* -S **:** the process of being centrifugal or otherwise submitted to centrifugal force

cen·trif·u·gal·ize \-ˈ===,līz\ *vt* -ED/-ING/-S [[1]*centrifugal* + *-ize*] **:** CENTRIFUGE

cen·trif·u·gal·ly \-ˈ==gəlē, -li\ *adv* **:** in a centrifugal manner or direction **:** by or as if by centrifugal force

centrifugal machine *n* **:** a machine (as a blower, compressor, fan, filter, or separator) acting by centrifugal force

centrifugal pump *n* **:** a pump having vanes that rotate in a casing and whirl the fluid around so that it acquires sufficient momentum to discharge from the extremities into a volute casing which surrounds the impeller and in which the fluid is conducted to the discharge pipe

centrifugal separator *n* **:** a machine that separates two mixed substances of different density (as cream and milk or oil and sludge) by centrifugal force

centrifugal sugar *n* **:** sugar freed from liquid by a centrifugal machine

[1]**cen·trif·u·gate** \sen·ˈtrif(y)ə,gāt, *usu* -ād·+V\ *vt* -ED/-ING/-S [[1]*centrifugal* + *-ate*] **:** to drive out centrifugally **:** CENTRIFUGE

[2]**cen·trif·u·gate** \-ˌgət, -,gāt, *usu* -d·+V\ *n* -S **:** the denser material separated by centrifugal action

cen·trif·u·ga·tion \(,)sen·,trif(y)əˈgāshən\ *n* -S **:** the process of centrifuging

[1]**cen·tri·fuge** \ˈsen·trə,fyüj *also* ˈsän-\ *n* -S [F, fr. *centrifuge* centrifugal, fr. NL *centrifugus* — more at CENTRIFUGAL] **1 :** a machine for whirling fluids rapidly to separate substances of different densities by centrifugal force (as cream from milk, sediment from oil) **2 :** a centrifugal machine that produces artificial gravity

[2]**centrifuge** \"\ *vt* -ED/-ING/-S **:** to subject to centrifugal action; *esp* **:** to whirl in a centrifuge

cen·trif·u·gence \sen·ˈtrif(y)əjən(t)s, -əgən(t)s; ˌsen·trəˈfyüjə-\ *n* -S [NL *centrifugus* + E *-ence*] **:** centrifugal force, tendency, or action

cen·tring \ˈsentəriŋ, -n·triŋ\ *chiefly Brit var of* CENTERING

cen·tri·ole \ˈsen·trē,ōl\ *n* -S [ISV *centri-* + *-ole*; orig. formed as G *zentriol*] **1 :** a minute body forming the center of a centrosome **2 :** CENTRAL APPARATUS **3 :** CENTROSOME

cen·trip·e·tal \(')sen·¦tripəd·əl, -pət·əl, *esp Brit also* ¦sen·trə-¦pēt-\ *adj* [NL *centripetus* (fr. *centri-* + *-petus*, fr. L *petere* to go toward, seek) + E *-al* — more at FEATHER] **1** : moving, proceeding, or acting in a direction toward a center or axis ⟨~ acceleration of a body⟩ — opposed to *centrifugal* **2 a** : developing and expanding successively upward and inward toward the summit or center — used of the flowers of an inflorescence **b** : having the radicle turned toward the axis of the fruit — used of an embryo **3** : passing inward (as from a sense organ to the brain or spinal cord) : AFFERENT **4** : tending toward centralization : UNIFYING, INTEGRATIVE ⟨one of the chief ~ factors in the empire, a power which automatically held the parts together —John Buchan⟩

centripetal force *n* : the force that constrains a material particle to follow a curved path and that acts inwardly toward the center of curvature of the path causing centripetal acceleration (as a railroad train is prevented from leaving the track on a curve by the force exerted on the flanges of the outer wheels by the outer rail) — compare CENTRIFUGAL FORCE

cen·trip·e·tal·ism \-,lizəm\ *n* -s : the tendency to centralize

cen·trip·e·tal·ly \-əlē,-əli\ *adv* : in a centripetal manner or direction : by or as if by centripetal force

cen·tris·ci·dae \sen'trisə,dē\ *n pl, cap* [NL, fr. *Centriscus*, type genus + *-idae*] : a family (order Solenichthyes) of tropical marine fishes comprising the shrimpfishes

1cen·tris·cus \sen'triskəs\ *n, cap* [NL, fr. Gk *kentriskos*, a fish] : the type genus of Centriscidae

2centriscus \"\ [NL, fr. Gk *kentriskos*, a fish] *syn of* MACRORHAMPHOSUS

cen·trist \'sen·trəst\ *n* -s [*centr-* + *-ist*] **1** *often cap* : a member of a center party : one who holds views between those of the left and the right **2** : one who holds moderate views between extremes : MODERATE

cen·tro \'sen·(,)trō\ *n* -s [modif. of NL *Centrosema*] : a twining perennial (*Centrosema pubescens*) used as a forage and pasture plant esp. in Australia

cen·tro- *in pronunciations below*, ¦=(,)= = ¦sen·(,)trō *or* -,trə\ — see CENTR-

cen·tro·ac·i·nar \¦=(,)=¦asənər, -,när\ *or* **cen·tro·ac·i·nose** \-,nōs\ *adj* [*centr-* + *acinus* + *-ar* or *-ose*] : relating to or being certain specialized cells in the central part of glandular acini (as in the pancreas) of some animals

cen·tro·bar·ic \-¦barik\ *adj* [LGk *kentrobarikos*, fr. Gk *kentron bareos* center of gravity (fr. *kentron* center + *bareos*, gen. of *baros* weight) + Gk *-ikos* -ic — more at GRIEVE] **1** : relating to the center of gravity or to the process of finding it **2** : having a center of gravity

cen·tro·blepharoplast \¦=(,)=+\ *n* -s [ISV *centrosome* + *blepharoplast*] : a body that combines the function of basal granule and centrosome in certain flagellates

cen·tro·clinal \-¦klīn·əl\ *adj* [*centr-* + *-clinal*] *of geologic strata* : dipping toward a common point or center — opposed to *quaquaversal*

cen·tro·des·mose \-¦dez,mōs\ *n* -s [modif. of NL *centrodesmus*] : a fibril connecting the intranuclear centrioles during mitosis esp. in certain protozoans — compare PARADESMOSE

cen·tro·des·mus \-zməs\ *n* -ES [NL, fr. *centr-* + Gk *desmos* bond, band — more at DIADEM] : CENTRODESMOSE

cen·tro·dorsal \¦=(,)=+\ *adj* [*centr-* + *dorsal*] : central and dorsal ⟨the ~ median aboral plate of certain crinoids⟩ — **cen·tro·dorsally** \¦=(,)=+\ *adv*

cen·tro·gen·ic \-¦jenik\ *adj* [*centr-* + *-genic*] : originating in the central nervous system ⟨~ factors in the control of respiration⟩

cen·troid \'sen,trȯid\ *n* -s [*centr-* + *-oid*] **1 a** : CENTER OF MASS **b** : CENTER OF FIGURE **2** *prosody* : the central peak or crest of intensity of utterance in a stress-group : the nuclear syllabic in a word or stress-group : a primary or quasi-primary stress

cen·troi·dal \(')sen·¦trȯid·əl\ *adj* : of or relating to a centroid; *esp* : passing through the centroid

cen·tro·lec·i·thal \¦sen·(,)trō¦lesəthəl\ *adj* [*centr-* + Gk *lekithos* yolk of an egg + E *-al*] *of arthropod eggs* : having the yolk massed centrally and surrounded by a thin layer of clear cytoplasm

cen·tro·lep·i·da·ce·ae \-,lepə'dāsē,ē\ *n pl, cap* [NL, fr. *Centrolepid-, Centrolepis*, type genus (fr. Gk *kentron* sharp point + NL *-lepis*) + *-aceae* — more at CENTER] : a small family (order Xyridales) of plants resembling sedges or mosses, occurring in the southern hemisphere (as in Australia) and comprising the bristleworts — **cen·tro·lep·i·da·ceous** \-¦dāshəs\ *adj*

cen·tro·line·ad \-'linē,ad, -ēəd\ *n* -s [irreg. fr. *centr-* + L *linea* line — more at LINE] : a long ruler that has two adjustable arms fastened to one end of it by wing nuts and is used for drawing convergents toward inaccessible vanishing points in perspective

cen·tro·mere \'sen·trə,mi(ə)r\ *n* -s [ISV *centr-* + *-mere*; orig. formed as G *zentromer*] : a specialized portion of a chromosome to which a spindle fiber apparently attaches in mitosis — **cen·tro·mer·ic** \¦=(,)=¦mirik, -mer-\ *adj*

cen·tro·plasm \¦=(,)=,plazəm\ *n* -s [ISV *centr-* + *-plasm*] **1** : the protoplasm of the central apparatus **2** : CENTRAL BODY

cen·tro·plast \'=(,)=,plast\ *n* -s [*centr-* + *-plast*] : CENTRIOLE

cen·tro·pom·i·dae \-¦pämə,dē\ *n pl, cap* [NL, fr. *Centropomus*, type genus (fr. Gk *kentron* sharp point + *pōma* lid) + *-idae* — more at POMACENTRIDAE] : a family of percoid fishes (type genus *Centropomus*) comprising the snooks

centros *pl of* CENTRO

cen·tro·se·ma \¦=(,)=¦sēmə\ *n, cap* [NL, fr. Gk *kentron* spur, sharp point + *sēma* sign — more at SEMANTICS] : a genus of chiefly tropical American vines (family Leguminosae) having trifoliate leaves and large lilac or white flowers and including the butterfly pea

cen·tro·some \'sen·trə,sōm\ *n* -s [G *zentrosom* (trans. of F *corpuscule central*), fr. *zentr-* centr- + *-som* -some] **1** : a minute protoplasmic body found in the cytoplasm, less often in the nucleus, of many animal and some plant cells that takes an important part in mitosis, being regarded by many as the center of the dynamic activity manifested in that process, and that comprises one or two centrioles surrounded by a centrosphere and when active in mitosis by an aster — called also *central body*; compare MITOSIS **2** : CENTRIOLE **3** : CENTROSPHERE — **cen·tro·so·mic** \¦=¦sōmik, -äm-, -ēk\ *adj*

cen·tro·sper·mae \,sen·(,)trō'spər,mē\ [NL, fr. *centr-* + *-spermae*] *syn of* CARYOPHYLLALES

cen·tro·sphere \'=(,)=+\ *n* -s [ISV *centr-* + *sphere*; orig. formed as G *zentrosphäre*] **1 a** : the differentiated layer of cytoplasm surrounding the centriole within the centrosome **b** : CENTRAL APPARATUS **2** : the central part of the earth composed of very dense material and having a radius of about 2200 miles

cen·tro·symmetric \¦=(,)=+\ *or* **cen·tro·symmetrical** \¦=(,)=+\ *adj* **1** : symmetric with respect to a center : radially symmetric **2** : having no polar direction

cen·tro·symmetry \¦=(,)=+\ *n* -ES [*centr-* + *symmetry*] : the quality or state of being centrosymmetric

cen·tro·tus \sen·'trōd·əs\ *n, cap* [NL, fr. Gk *kentrōtos* spiky, fr. *kentron* sharp point — more at CENTER] : a common genus of treehoppers (family Membracidae) comprising many bizarrely shaped forms

cen·trum \'sen·trəm\ *n, pl* **centrums** \-rəmz\ *or* **cen·tra** \-rə\ [L — more at CENTER] **1** : the body of a vertebra **2 a** : the central air space in hollow-stemmed plants esp. of the horsetails (genus *Equisetum*) **b** *in fungi* : the tissue within the hard rind of many perithecia including the asci — called also *core* **3** : CENTROSOME **4** : the point, line, or place within the earth from which an earthquake wave is propagated

cen·tru·roi·des \,sen·trə'roi(,)dēz\ *n, cap* [NL, prob. fr. *Centrurus*, genus of arachnids (fr. *centr-* + *-urus*) + *-oides* -oid] : a genus of scorpions containing the only forms dangerously virulent to man that occur in the U.S.

1centry *n* -ES [alter. of *center*] **1** *obs* : CENTER **2** *archaic* : CENTERING

2centry *obs var of* SENTRY

cents *pl of* CENT

1cen·tum \'sentəm\ *n* -s [L — more at HUNDRED] : HUNDRED — sometimes used instead of *cent* in phrases ⟨per ~⟩

2cen·tum \'kentəm, -n,tům\ *adj* [L, hundred; fr. the fact that the initial sound of L *centum* (pronounced approximately \'ken,tům\) represents an IE palatal stop — more at HUNDRED] : belonging to or constituting that part of the Indo-European language family in which the palatal stops did not in prehistoric times become palatal or alveolar fricatives — opposed to *satem*

cen·tum·vir \sen·'təmvər, ken·'tům,vi(ə)r\ *n, pl* **cen·tum·vi·ri** \-əmvə,rī, -ůmvə,rē\ [L, *centumviri*, pl. fr. *centum viri* hundred men, fr. *centum* hundred + *viri*, pl. of. *vir* man — more at VIRILE] : one of orig. about 100 judges or jurors of a Roman court for civil suits

1cen·tu·ple \'sen·,t(y)üpəl, ='==; 'sentəp-\ *adj* [F, fr. LL *centuplus*, fr. L *centum* hundred + *-plus* multiplied by — more at HUNDRED, DOUBLE] : HUNDREDFOLD

2centuple \"\ *vt* **centupled; centupled; centupling** \-p(ə)liŋ\

centuples : CENTUPLICATE

cen·tu·pli·cate \sen·'t(y)üplə,kāt\ *vt* -ED/-ING/-S [L *centuplicatus*, past part. of *centuplicare*, fr. *centuplic-, centuplex* hundredfold, fr. *centum* hundred + *-plex* (as in *duplex*)] : to make 100 times as much or as many : CENTUPLE

cen·tu·ri·al \(')sen·¦t(y)ůrēəl\ *adj* [L *centurialis*, fr. *centuria* century + *-alis* -al] : relating to 100 years : marking or beginning a century ⟨the ~ years 1600 and 1700⟩

cen·tu·ri·ate \=¦==ət, -,āt\ *adj* [L *centuriatus*, past part. of *centuriare* to divide into hundreds, fr. *centuria* group of one hundred — more at CENTURY] **1** : of or relating to centuries or hundreds ⟨~ assemblies⟩ **2** : divided into centuries or hundreds ⟨~ lands⟩

cen·tu·ri·a·tion \(,)=,==¦āshən\ *n* -s [L *centuriation-, centuriatio*, fr. *centuriatus* + *-ion-, -io* -ion] : division into hundreds

cen·tu·ri·a·tor \='==,ād·ə(r)\ *n* -s [NL, fr. L *centuriatus* (past part. of *centuriare* to divide into hundreds) + *-or*] : a historian who distinguishes time by centuries

cen·tu·ried \'sench(ə)rēd, -id\ *adj* : having lasted for a century or centuries ⟨a ~ castle⟩ ⟨~ traditions which gave stability to peasant life⟩

cen·tu·ri·on \sen·'t(y)ůrēən, -ür-\ *n* -s [ME *centurioun*, *centurio*, fr. L & MF; MF *centurion*, fr. L *centurion-, centurio*, fr. *centuria*] **1** : an officer commanding a Roman century **2** : an officer commanding a hundred men

1cen·tu·ry \'sench(ə)rē, -ri\ *n* -ES *often attrib* [L *centuria*, irreg. fr. *centum* hundred — more at HUNDRED] **1 a** : a subdivision of the Roman legion **b** : a unit of 100 men **2 a** (1) : a group, sequence, or series of 100 like things ⟨a ~ of sonnets⟩ (2) : a score of 100 or more runs by one batsman in one inning of a cricket match (3) : a work of 100 units (4) : a division into hundreds **b** : 100 pounds sterling or a hundred-pound note **c** : $100 or a hundred-dollar bill **3** : a Roman voting unit constituted according to property qualifications **4** : a period of 100 years ⟨did a detailed study of the way people lived two *centuries* ago⟩; *specif* : one of the 100-year divisions of the Christian era or of the preceding period ⟨the 19th ~⟩ ⟨the fourth ~ B.C.⟩ **5** : a race over a distance of 100 units (as yards or miles)

2century \"\ *adj* : CENTENNIAL

century plant *n* [so called fr. its reaching maturity and flowering only after many years] : any plant of the genus *Agave*; *esp* : the commonly cultivated Mexican plant (*A. americana*) having fleshy leaves in a massive rosette, maturing and flowering only once in many years, then dying, and being perpetuated by suckers at its base

ceorl \'chā,ȯr(ə)l\ *n* -s [OE — more at CHURL] : a freeman of the lowest rank in Anglo-Saxon England

cep \(')sep\ *prep* [by shortening] *chiefly dial* : EXCEPT

cepe \'sēp, 'sep\ *also* **cep** \'sep\ *n* -s [F *cèpe*, fr. F dial. (Gascon) *cep* tree trunk, mushroom, cepe, fr. L *cippus* stake, post; akin to Alb *thep* sharp rock, Skt *śepa* tail, penis, and prob. to OHG *sciba* disk — more at SHEAVE] : an edible mushroom of the genus *Boletus* (esp. *B. edulis*)

ce·pha·eline \se'fāə,lēn, -,lən\ *n* -s [ISV *cephael-* (fr. NL *Cephaelis*, genus name of ipecac + *-ine*] : a colorless crystalline alkaloid $C_{28}H_{38}N_2O_4$ extracted from ipecac root

cepha·elis \,sefə'ēləs, -fā'ē-\ *n, cap* [NL, irreg. fr. *cephal-* + Gk *eilein* to compress; perh. akin to L *vulgus* common people — more at VULGAR] : a large genus of tropical shrubs and trees (family Rubiaceae) with small tubular flowers crowded into dense bracteate heads — see IPECAC

cephal- *or* **cephalo-** *comb form* [L, fr. Gk *kephal-, kephalo-*, fr. *kephalē* head — more at CEPHALIC] **1** : head ⟨*cephal*itis⟩ ⟨*cephalo*meter⟩ **2** : cephalic and ⟨*cephalo*facial⟩

cephala *pl of* CEPHALON

-cephala *pl of* -CEPHALUS

1ceph·a·lad \'sefə,lad\ *adv* [*cephal-* + *-ad*] : toward the head or anterior end of the body — opposed to *caudad*

2cephalad \"\ *adj* : located cephalad

ceph·a·lal·gia \,sefə'lalj(ē)ə\ *n* -s [L, fr. Gk *kephalalgia*, fr. *kephal-* cephal- + *-algia*] : HEADACHE

ceph·a·las·pid \-'laspəd\ *n* -s [NL *Cephalaspid-, Cephalaspis*]

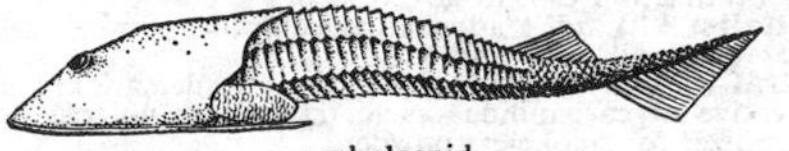

cephalaspid

: any ostracoderm of the genus *Cephalaspis*, family Cephalaspidae, or class Cephalaspida

ceph·a·las·pi·da \-pədə\ *n pl, cap* [NL, fr. *Cephalaspis* + *-ida*] : a class or lesser division of primitive extinct vertebrates including *Cephalaspis* and a few related genera of Devonian ostracoderms

ceph·a·las·pis \-pəs\ *n, cap* [NL, fr. *cephal-* + *-aspis*] : a genus (the type of the family Cephalaspidae) of Devonian ostracoderms having the head covered by a flattened shield rounded in front and prolonged into posteriorly directed lateral points and the eyes close together in the middle of the head shield — see CEPHALASPIDA

ceph·a·late \'sefələt, -,lāt, *usu* -d.+V\ *or* **ceph·a·lat·ed** \-,lād·əd\ *adj* [*cephal-* + *-ate*] *zool* : having a head or an enlargement suggesting a head

ceph·a·leu·ros \,sefə'lürəs\ *n, cap* [NL, fr. *cephal-* + Gk *eurōs* mold, mustiness; perh. akin to L *operire* to cover — more at WEIR] : a genus of epiphytic and parasitic green algae (family Trentepohliaceae) that includes the causative organism of red rust

-cephali *pl of* -CEPHALUS

ce·phal·ic \sə'falik, -lēk *also* se-, *Brit often* k-\ *adj* [MF *céphalique*, fr. L *cephalicus*, fr. Gk *kephalikos*, fr. *kephalē* head + *-ikos* -ic; akin to OHG *gebal* skull, *gibil* housetop, gable, ON *gafl* gable, Goth *gibla* pinnacle, Toch A *śpāl-* head] **1** : of or relating to the head; *esp* : directed toward or situated on or in or near the head **2** : CEREBRAL 3a — **ce·phal·i·cal·ly** \-lək(ə)lē, -ēk-, -li\ *adv*

-cephalic \¦=¦==\ *adj comb form* [NL *-cephalus*, F *-céphale*, E *-cephalous* + E *-ic*] : -headed : having (such) a head or (so many) heads ⟨brachy*cephalic*⟩ ⟨disco*cephalic*⟩ ⟨bi*cephalic*⟩ — **-ceph·a·lism** \¦sefə,lizəm\ *n comb form* -s — **-ceph·a·ly** \-fəlē, -li\ *n comb form* -ES

cephalic index *n* : the ratio multiplied by 100 of the maximum breadth of the head to its maximum length — compare CRANIAL INDEX; see BRACHYCEPHALIC, DOLICHOCEPHALIC, MESATICEPHALIC

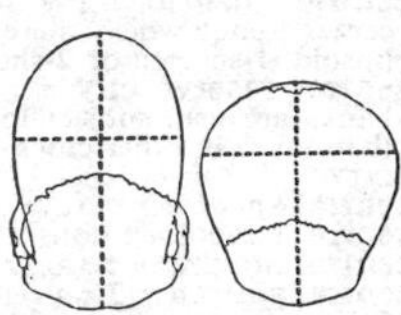

cephalic index: dotted lines in the brachycephalic (right) and dolichocephalic (left) skulls above indicate measurements taken

cephalic module *n* : an anthropological measure of absolute head size obtained by averaging the length, breadth, and auricular height of the head

cephalic vein *n* [prob. trans. of MF *veine céphalique* — prob. fr. a former practice of opening it to relieve ailments of the head] : any of certain superficial veins of the arm; *specif* : a large vein of the upper arm lying along the outer edge of the biceps muscle and emptying into the axillary vein

1ceph·a·lin \'sefələn\ *n* -s [NL *Cephalina*] : a gregarine trophozoite complete with epimerite and usu. attached to the cells of the host — compare SPORADIN

2cephalin \"\ *n* -s [ISV *cephal-* + *-in*; orig. formed as G *kephalin*] : any of various acidic phosphatides that are similar to lecithins but contain ethanolamine, serine, or inositol instead of choline, occur esp. in the nervous tissue of the brain, and have marked thromboplastic activity

ceph·a·li·na \,sefə'līnə, -lē-\ *n pl, cap* [NL, fr. *cephal-* + *-ina*] : a tribe of gregarines comprising forms with septate trophozoites that do not undergo schizogony and are inhabitants of the alimentary tract of arthropods and other invertebrates — **ceph·a·line** \'sefə,līn, -ēn\ *adj*

ceph·a·li·za·tion \,sefələ'zāshən, -,lī'z-\ *n* -s [*cephal-* + *-ize* + *-ation*] **1** : specialization of the anterior part of the animal body resulting in localization and concentration of sensory and neural organs in an anterior head **2** : the tendency to cephalization as a factor in evolution

ceph·a·lo- \ *in pronunciations below*, ¦==(,)= = ¦sefə(,)lō *or* -ələ\ — see CEPHAL-

ceph·a·lob \'sefə,lōb, -äb\ *n* -s [modif. of NL *Cephalobidae*] : a member of the family Cephalobidae

ceph·a·lo·bi·dae \,sefə'lōbə,dē\ *n pl, cap* [NL, fr. *Cephalobus*, type genus (prob. irreg. fr. *cephal-* + *-lobus*) + *-idae*] : a family of rhabditoid nematode worms that are saprophagous or associated with the roots of plants — compare VINEGAR EEL — **ceph·a·lo·boid** \¦==¦=,bȯid\ *adj*

ceph·a·lo·cereus \,==(,)=+\ *n, cap* [NL, fr. *cephal-* + *Cereus*] : a large genus of tropical American cacti (family Cactaceae) having usu. columnar erect stems topped with white wool, no leaves, and showy nocturnal flowers and including the old-man cactus

ceph·a·lo·chord \'==(,)=,kȯrd\ *n* -s [NL *Cephalochorda*] : one of the Cephalochorda : LANCELET

ceph·a·lo·chor·da \,==(,)='kȯrdə\ *n pl, cap* [NL, fr. *cephal-* + *-chorda* (neut. pl. of *-chordus* having such a chorda, fr. *chorda*)] : a subphylum or other division of Chordata consisting of the lancelets in which the notochord extends to the anterior as well as the posterior end of the body — **ceph·a·lo·chor·dal** \¦==(,)=¦=d·əl\ *adj*

ceph·a·lo·chor·da·ta \-,kȯr'däd·ə, -'ād·ə\ [NL, fr. *cephal-* + *chorda* + *-ata*] *syn of* CEPHALOCHORDA

ceph·a·lo·dis·cus \,==(,)='diskəs\ *n, cap* [NL, fr. *cephal-* + *-discus*] : a genus of colonial Pterobranchia with the zooids inhabiting a common gelatinous tube or test

ceph·a·lo·di·um \,sefə'lōdēəm\ *n, pl* **ceph·a·lo·dia** \-ēə\ [NL, fr. Gk *kephalōdēs* like a head (fr. *kephal-* cephal- + *-ōdēs* -ode) + NL *-ium*] : an irregular internal or external gall-like growth in lichens that differs from an isidium in having an algal component other than that natural to the lichen

ceph·a·loid \'sefə,lȯid\ *adj* [*cephal-* + *-oid*] : CAPITATE

ceph·a·lom·e·ter \,sefə'lämad·ə(r)\ *n* -s [ISV *cephal-* + *meter*; prob. orig. formed as F *céphalomètre*] : an instrument for measuring the living head

ceph·a·lo·met·ric \¦==¦me·trik, -ēk\ *adj* [ISV *cephal-* + *-metric*; prob. orig. formed as F *céphalométrique*] : of or relating to cephalometry

ceph·a·lom·e·try \,sefə'lämə·trē, -i\ *n* -ES [ISV *cephal-* + *-metry*; prob. orig. formed as F *céphalométrie*] : the science of measuring the head esp. for determining the dimensions and proportions characteristic of a particular race, sex, or somatotype or for determining the relation of a fetal head to the maternal pelvic outlet — distinguished from *craniometry*

ceph·a·lon \'sefə,län, -ələn\ *n, pl* **cepha·la** \-ələ\ [NL, irreg. fr. Gk *kephalē* head — more at CEPHALIC] **1** : HEAD 1 **2** : the anterior shield of a trilobite

ceph·a·lo·pelvic disproportion \,==(,)=+...-\ *n* [*cephal-* + *pelvic*] : a condition in which the maternal pelvis is small in relation to the size of the fetal head

ce·phal·o·phine \sə'falə,fīn\ *adj* [NL *Cephalophus* + E *-ine*] : of or relating to the duikers

ceph·a·lo·pho·lis \,==(,)='fōləs\ *n, cap* [NL, fr. *cephal-* + *Pholis*, genus of fishes, fr. Gk *phōlis*, a sea fish that hides in mud; akin to Gk *phōleos* den and perh. to OE *būan* to dwell — more at BOWER] : a genus of groupers (family Serranidae) including the coney (*C. fulvus*) and other food fish

ce·phal·o·phus \sə'faləfəs\ *n, cap* [NL, irreg. fr. *cephal-* + Gk *lophos* crest] : a genus of small alert African antelopes comprising the typical duikers some of which are no larger than hares

1ceph·a·lo·pod \'sefələ,päd\ *adj* [NL *Cephalopoda*] : of or belonging to the Cephalopoda

2cephalopod \"\ *n* -s : one of the Cephalopoda

ceph·a·lop·o·da \,sefə'läpədə\ *n pl, cap* [NL, fr. *cephal-* + *-poda*] : the highest class of Mollusca containing the squids, cuttlefishes, octopuses, nautiluses, ammonites, and related forms all having around the front of the head a group of elongated muscular arms usu. furnished with prehensile suckers or hooks, a highly developed head with large well-organized eyes showing remarkable resemblance to the vertebrate eye, usu. a cartilaginous brain case, a pair of powerful horny jaws shaped like a parrot's beak, and in most existing forms a bag of inklike fluid which they can eject from the siphon, the higher forms (as the cuttlefishes and squids) being able to swim rapidly by ejecting a jet of water from the tubular siphon beneath the head — **ceph·a·lop·o·dan** \¦==¦=d·ən\ *adj or n* — **ceph·a·lo·pod·ic** \¦==(,)lō¦pädik\ *adj*

ceph·a·lop·ter·us \,sefə'läptərəs\ *n, cap* [NL, fr. *cephal-* + *-pterus*] : a genus of birds of the family Cotingidae including the umbrella bird and its related forms that are remarkable for their development of crests and wattles

ceph·a·lo·spo·ri·um \,==(,)='spōrēəm\ *n, cap* [NL, fr. *cephal-* + *-sporium*] : a form genus of imperfect fungi with conidia held together by a slimy secretion in more or less spherical heads at the ends of the fertile branches

ceph·a·lo·thecium \,==(,)=+\ [NL, fr. *cephal-* + *thecium*] *syn of* TRICHOTHECIUM

ceph·a·lo·thorax \¦==(,)=+'-\ *n* [ISV *cephal-* + *thorax*; prob. orig. formed as F *céphalothorax*] : the united head and thorax of arachnids and higher crustaceans

ceph·a·lo·tus \,sefə'lōd·əs\ *n, cap* [NL, fr. Gk *kephalōtos* headed, fr. *kephalē* head — more at CEPHALIC] : a monotypic genus (coextensive with the family Cephalotaceae of the order Rosales) of Australian perennial herbaceous marsh plants having some leaves modified to saclike pitchers with lids and thickened rims and comprising the Australian pitcher plant

-ceph·a·lous \¦sefələs\ *adj comb form* [Gk *-kephalos*, fr. *kephalē* — more at CEPHALIC] : -CEPHALIC

-ceph·a·lus \"\ *n comb form* [NL, fr. Gk *-kephalos*] **1** *pl* **-cephali** : cephalic abnormality (of a specified type) ⟨micro*cephalus*⟩ ⟨hydro*cephalus*⟩ **2** *pl* **-cepha·li** \-,lī\ *or* **-cepha·la** \-,lə\ : organism having a (specified) type of head ⟨Ichthyo*cephali*⟩ ⟨Phenero*cephala*⟩

-cephaly — see -CEPHALIC

ceph·a·ran·thine \,sefə'ran,thīn, -,thən\ *n* -s [*cepharanth-* (fr. NL *cepharantha*, specific epithet of *Stephania cepharantha*) + *-ine*] : an alkaloid $C_{37}H_{38}N_2O_6$ obtained from the tuberous roots of a Formosan plant (*Stephania cepharantha*) and used experimentally in the treatment of tuberculosis

ce·phe·id \'sēfēəd *also* 'sef-\ *or* **cepheid variable** *n* -s *usu cap C* [ISV *cephe-* (fr. L *Cepheus*, a northern constellation, fr. *Cepheus*, mythical king of Ethiopia and father of Andromeda, fr. Gk *Kēpheus*) + *-id*] : one of a class of pulsating stars whose intrinsic light variations are very regular, occurring in periods up to two months

ce·phe·no·my·ia \sə,fēnə'mī(y)ə, ,sefənō'-\ *n* [NL, fr. Gk *kēphēn* + NL *-o-* + *-myia*] **1** *cap* : a genus of large gray-brown beelike botflies (family Oestridae) chiefly attacking the nostrils and pharyngeal cavity of members of the deer family and being among the fastest moving living things, reputedly attaining speeds in excess of 800 miles per hour **2** -s : any insect of the genus *Cephenomyia*

ce·phus \'sēfəs\ *n, cap* [NL, irreg. fr. Gk *kēphēn* drone bee] : a genus (the type of the family Cephidae) of small sawflies having larvae that bore in the stems of plants and including serious pests esp. of cereal grasses — see WHEAT STEM SAWFLY

ce·pol·i·dae \sə'pälə,dē, -pōl-\ *n pl, cap* [NL, fr. *Cepola*, type genus + *-idae*] : a family of elongated marine percoid fishes having the dorsal and anal fins elongated and confluent at the end of the pointed tail — see RIBBONFISH 1b

cer- or **cero-** comb form [Gk kēr-, kēro-, fr. kēros — more at CEREUS] : wax ⟨cerophilous⟩ ⟨cerotype⟩

-cera \sərə\ n comb form, pl **-cera** [NL, fr. Gk keras horn — more at CEREBRAL] : horned one : horned ones — in taxonomic names in zoology ⟨Acrocera⟩ ⟨Cladocera⟩ ⟨Nematocera⟩

ce·ra al·ba \¦sirə'albə\ n [NL] : bleached beeswax

ce·ra·ceous \sə'rāshəs\ adj [L cera wax + E -aceous — more at CEREUS] : like wax : WAXY

ce·ra fla·va \¦sirə'flävə, -āvə\ n [NL] : yellow unbleached beeswax

ce·ram·al \sə'raməl\ n -s [¹ceramic + alloy] : CERMET

¹ce·ram·by·cid \sə'rambəsəd, -(,)sid\ adj [NL Cerambycidae] : of or relating to the Cerambycidae

²cerambycid \"\ n -s [NL Cerambycidae] : a beetle of the family Cerambycidae

cer·am·byc·i·dae \,ser,am'bisə,dē, -rəm-\ n pl, cap [NL, fr. Cerambyc-, Cerambyx, type genus (fr. Gk kerambyx, a horned beetle, fr. keras horn) + -idae] : a large family of beetles comprising the long-horned beetles, including large oblong or somewhat cylindrical beetles with antennae often longer than the body, and having larvae that usu. bore in the roots or wood of trees or shrubs with some (as the locust borer and twig pruner) doing great damage — **ce·ram·by·coid** \sə'rambə,kȯid\ n or adj

ce·ram·i·a·ce·ae \sə,ramē'āsē,ē, -rām-\ n pl, cap [NL, fr. Ceramium, type genus + -aceae] : a family of delicate filamentous red algae (order Ceramiales) branched dichotomously or unilaterally pinnate and found in nearly all seas — see FAVELLA — **ce·ram·i·a·ceous** \=¦==¦āshəs\ adj

ce·ram·i·a·les \sə,ramē'ā(,)lēz, -rām-\ n pl, cap [NL, fr. Ceramium + -ales] : an order of red algae characterized by having the auxiliary cell formed after fertilization — compare CERAMIACEAE, RHODYMENIALES

¹ce·ram·ic \sə'ramik, -mēk\ adj [Gk keramikos, fr. keramos potter's clay, pottery] **1** : of or relating to the art of fashioning clay into useful or ornamental objects and hardening them by firing at high temperatures **2 a** : of or relating to the manufacture of any product (as earthenware, porcelain, tile, brick, glass, vitreous enamels, cement, plaster refractories) made essentially from a nonmetallic mineral by firing at high temperatures — in Brit. use not usu. extended to include glassmaking **b** : of, relating to, or consisting of such a product

²ceramic \"\ n -s [prob. fr. F céramique, fr. céramique ceramic, fr. Gk keramikos] **1 ceramics** pl but usu sing in constr **a** : the art or process of making useful or ornamental articles from clay by shaping and then firing at high temperatures **b** : the industry concerned with making any ceramic product : the technology of ceramic manufacturing and processing **2** : a product of ceramic art or manufacture **3** : AZURITE BLUE

ceramic aggregate n **1** : an ornamental portland-cement concrete containing ceramic products in the form of lumps or fragments and usu. coloring ingredients **2** : concrete containing bloated clay to reduce weight

ceramic bond n : mechanical strength in a body developed by heating earthy materials and thus producing glass or effective crystallization; esp : a bond used in abrasive wheels and shapes

ceramic engineering n : a branch of engineering dealing with the treatment of earthy nonmetallic minerals by fire or heat and the design and operation of plant and equipment for ceramic production

ceramic glaze n : a mixture of powdered materials that often includes a premelted glass made into a slip and applied to a ceramic body by spraying or dipping and capable of fusing to a glassy coating when dried and fired

ce·ram·i·cite \sə'ramə,sīt\ n -s : a porcelainlike pyrometamorphic rock consisting of basic plagioclase and cordierite with accessory hypersthene and a groundmass of glass

ceramic mosaic n : mosaic formed by setting small glazed or unglazed tiles in cement

ce·ram·ist \sə'ramәst also 'serəm-\ or **ce·ram·i·cist** \sə'raməsəst\ n -s [F céramiste, fr. céramique, n. + -iste -ist] : one who engages in ceramic arts, manufacturing, or technology

ce·ram·i·um \sə'ramēəm, -rām-\ n, cap [NL, fr. Gk keramion earthen vessel, fr. keramos potter's clay, pottery] : a genus (the type of the family Ceramiaceae) of delicate red algae comprising the rosetangles

cer·a·mog·ra·phy \,serə'mägrəfē\ n -ES [ISV ¹ceramic + -o- + -graphy] : the description or study of ceramics

ce·rar·gy·rite \sə'rärjə,rīt\ n -s [F kérargyre cerargyrite (fr. Gk keras horn + argyros silver), trans. of Sw hornsilver + E -ite — more at CEREBRAL, ARGENT] **1** : a white to pale-yellow or gray mineral consisting of silver chloride AgCl and darkening on exposure to light **2** : a group of isomorphous silver halides that includes mainly cerargyrite, bromyrite, and embolite

cer·as \'serəs, 'k-\ n, pl **cera·ta** \-rəd·ə\ [NL, fr. Gk keras horn] : one of the often brightly colored and branching integumentary papillae that serve as gills and occur on the backs of nudibranchs and certain related mollusks

-cer·as \sərəs\ n comb form [NL, fr. Gk keras] : horned one — in generic names of plants and animals ⟨Cyrtoceras⟩ ⟨Dinoceras⟩

¹ce·ras·tes \sə'ras(,)tēz\ n, pl **cerastes** [ME, fr. L, fr. Gk kerastēs cerastes, horned, fr. keras horn — more at HORN] : HORNED VIPER

²cerastes \"\ [NL, fr. L] syn of ASPIS

ce·ras·ti·um \sə'raschēəm, -stē-\ n, cap [NL, fr. Gk kerastēs horned + NL -ium] : a large genus of low herbs (family Caryophyllaceae) containing the mouse-ear chickweed and the field chickweed and having small white flowers with bifid petals and cylindrical often curved capsules

cer·a·sus \'serəsəs\ n, cap [NL, fr. L, cherry tree — more at CHERRY] in some classifications : a genus of shrubs or trees comprising the cherries and now included in the genus Prunus

cerat- or **cerato-** also **kerat-** or **kerato-** comb form [NL, fr. Gk kerat-, kerato-, fr. keras horn] **1** : horn : horny ⟨Ceratodus⟩ **2** usu kerat- or kerato- : cornea ⟨keratitis⟩

¹ce·rate \'sir,āt, -,ət, usu -d·+V\ n -s [L ceratum wax salve, fr. cera wax + -atum -ate — more at CEREUS] : an unctuous preparation for external application consisting essentially of wax (sometimes resin or spermaceti) mixed with oil, lard, and medicinal ingredients and having a melting point above body temperature

²cerate \"\ n -s [cerium + -ate] : a compound having an anion containing cerium in the tetravalent state

ce·rat·ed \-ād·əd\ adj [L ceratus, past part. of cerare to wax, fr. cera wax] : covered with wax

cer·a·ti·i·dae \,serə'tīə,dē\ n pl, cap [NL, fr. Ceratias, type genus (fr. Gk keratias horned, fr. kerat-, keras horn) + -idae — more at HORN] : a family of deep-sea fishes (order Pediculati) comprising the black sea devils and related to the anglers but black in color and often having luminous organs, the males in several species being diminutive and carried in the gill cavity or attached to the body or head of the female

ceratin var of KERATIN

¹cer·a·ti·oid \,serə¦tī,ȯid\ adj [NL Ceratioidea] **1** : resembling the Ceratiidae **2** : of or relating to the Ceratioidea

²ceratioid \"\ n -s [NL Ceratioidea] : a ceratioid fish

cer·a·ti·oi·dea \-,tī'ȯidēə\ n pl, cap [NL, fr. Ceratias (fr. Gk keratias horned) + -oidea] : a suborder of Pediculati comprising oceanic anglers that lack pelvic fins and usu. have a luminous tip on the illicium

cer·a·tite \'serə,tīt\ n -s [NL Ceratites] : a fossil of the genus Ceratites

cer·a·ti·tes \,serə'tīd·ēz\ n, cap [NL, fr. cerat- + -ites -ite] : a genus (the type of the large family Ceratitidae) of Triassic ammonites having the septa with simple rounded saddles and finely denticulated lobes — **cer·a·tit·ic** \¦serə¦tid·ik\ adj — **cer·a·ti·toid** \,serə'tī,tȯid\ adj or n

cer·a·ti·tis \,serə'tīd·əs\ n, cap [NL, fr. Gk keratitis horned, fr. kerat-, keras horn] : a genus of acalyptrate flies (family Trypetidae) including the Mediterranean fruit fly

ce·ra·ti·um \sə'rāshēəm\ n, cap [NL, fr. Gk keration, dim. of kerat-, keras horn] : a genus of marine and freshwater flagellates (order Dinoflagellata) certain species of which form an important part of the plankton of northern seas

¹cer·a·to·branchial \¦serə(,)tō+¦-\ adj [ISV cerat- + branchial] : belonging to the segment next below the epibranchial in a branchial arch

²ceratobranchial \"\ n -s : a ceratobranchial bone or cartilage

cer·a·to·con·junc·ti·vi·tis var of KERATOCONJUNCTIVITIS

cer·a·to·cricoid \¦serə(,)tō+¦-\ adj [cerat- + cricoid] : belonging to or associated with the inferior horn of the thyroid and the cricoid cartilages

ce·rat·o·dus \sə'rad·ədəs\ n [NL, fr. cerat- + -odus] **1** cap : a

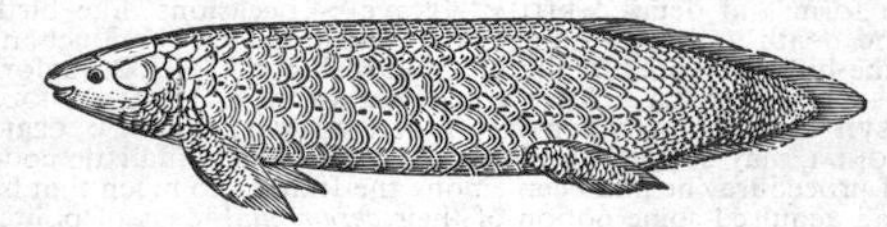

a fish of the genus Ceratodus

genus (the type of the family Ceratodontidae) comprising dipnoan fishes that have archipterygial pectoral and pelvic fins and dental plates with radiating ridges, being orig. based on and now usu. restricted to fossil forms from the Mesozoic but in some esp. former classifications including the surviving Australian lungfish — see BARRAMUNDA **2** -ES : any fish or fossil of Ceratodus or a closely related genus

¹cer·a·to·glos·sal \¦serə(,)tō¦gläsəl, -ȯs-\ adj [NL ceratoglossus + E -al] : belonging or relating to the cornua of the hyoid bone and the tongue

²ceratoglossal \"\ n -s : the ceratoglossus muscle

cer·a·to·glos·sus \-səs\ n, pl **ceratoglos·si** \-,sī, -(,)sē\ [NL, fr. cerat- + -glossus (fr. Gk glōssa tongue) — more at GLOSS] : the part of the hyoglossus muscle attached to the greater cornu of the hyoid

cer·a·to·hy·al \¦serə(,)tō¦hīəl\ or **cer·a·to·hy·oid** \-ī,ȯid\ n -s [ceratohyal ISV cerat- + hyoid + -al; ceratohyoid fr. cerat- + hyoid] : a horn or cartilage lying below the epihyal and forming a segment of the hyoid arch, in man being the small horn of the hyoid

cer·a·to·mandibular \¦serə(,)tō+\ adj [cerat- + mandibular] : belonging to the horns of the hyoid and the mandible

cer·a·to·mor·pha \,serətō'mȯrfə\ n pl, cap [NL, fr. cerat- + -morpha] in some classifications : a suborder of perissodactylous mammals comprising tapirs, rhinoceroses, and extinct related forms

cer·a·to·phyl·la·ce·ae \,serə(,)tōfə'lāsē,ē\ n pl, cap [NL, fr. Ceratophyllum + -aceae] : a family of aquatic plants that is coextensive with the genus Ceratophyllum and is usu. included in the order Ranales

cer·a·to·phyl·lum \-'filəm\ n, cap [NL, fr. cerat- + -phyllum] : a cosmopolitan genus of rootless thin-stemmed aquatic herbs that occur in quiet freshwaters and that have flowers with a sepaloid perianth and a single carpel — see CERATOPHYLLACEAE, HORNWORT

cer·a·to·phyl·lus \-ləs\ n, cap [NL, prob. irreg. fr. cerat- + Gk phyllon leaf — more at PHYLL-] : a genus of fleas formerly coextensive with the family Dolichopsyllidae but now restricted to certain parasites of birds — see EUROPEAN CHICKEN FLEA, WESTERN CHICKEN FLEA

cer·a·to·po·gon \,serətō'pō,gän\ n, cap [NL, fr. cerat- + -pogon] : the type genus of the family Ceratopogonidae

¹cer·a·to·po·go·nid \¦==¦pōgənəd\ adj [NL Ceratopogonidae] : of or relating to the Ceratopogonidae

²ceratopogonid \"\ n -s [NL Ceratopogonidae] : one of the Ceratopogonidae

cer·a·to·po·gon·i·dae \,serə(,)tōpə'gänə,dē\ n pl, cap [NL, fr. Ceratopogon + -idae] : a large family of tiny long-legged nematocerous two-winged flies that have piercing mouthparts, that comprise the biting midges which attack man, various other mammals, and birds, and that include various vectors of filarial worms

cer·a·tops \'serə,täps\ n, cap [NL, fr. cerat- + -ops] : the type genus of the family Ceratopsidae

cer·a·top·sia \,serə'täpsēə\ n pl, cap [NL, fr. Ceratops + -ia] : a group of large dinosaurs, usu. made a suborder of the order Ornithischia, known chiefly from the Upper Cretaceous of No. America and Mongolia, and comprising animals of robust build that walked on all four feet and had an enormously developed skull, long horns, and a sharp horny beak — see TRICERATOPS — **cer·a·top·si·an** \¦==¦sēən\ adj or n

¹cer·a·top·sid \¦==¦==\ adj [NL Ceratopsidae] : of or relating to the Ceratopsidae

²ceratopsid \"\ n -s [NL Ceratopsidae] : a dinosaur or fossil of the family Ceratopsidae

cer·a·top·si·dae \,serə'täpsə,dē\ n pl, cap [NL, fr. Ceratops, type genus + -idae] : a large family of American dinosaurs (suborder Ceratopsia) that includes Triceratops

cer·a·top·te·ris \,serə'täptərəs\ n, cap [NL, fr. cerat- + -pteris] : a genus of aquatic ferns (family Parkeriaceae) having leaves in rosettes, the sterile floating or emergent, the fertile more erect and with margins revolute over the sporangia

¹cer·a·to·rhine \'serətə,rīn\ n -s [NL Ceratorhinus (proposed genus name), fr. cerat- + -rhinus] : any of a group of 2-horned rhinoceroses having well-developed lower canine teeth (as the Sumatran rhinoceros)

²ceratorhine \"\ adj : belonging to or like a ceratorhine

cer·a·to·sa \,serə'tōsə, -ōzə\ [NL, fr. neut. pl. of (assumed) ceratosus keratose] syn of KERATOSA

cer·a·to·sau·rus \¦serətō¦sȯrəs\ n, cap [NL, fr. cerat- + -saurus] : a genus of American Jurassic carnivorous dinosaurs nearly 20 feet long that had a bony horn core on the united nasal bones

ceratose var of KERATOSE

cer·a·to·spon·gi·ae \,serətō'spənjē,ē, -pän-\ [NL, fr. cerat- + -spongiae] syn of KERATOSA

cer·a·to·spon·gi·da \-jədə\ [NL, fr. cerat- + Spongida] syn of KERATOSA

cer·a·tos·to·ma·ta·ce·ae \,serə,tästəmə'tāsē,ē, ¦serə(,)tō-,stōmə-\ n pl, cap [NL, fr. Ceratostomat-, Ceratostoma, type genus (fr. cerat- + -stoma) + -aceae] : a family of fungi (order Sphaeriales) characterized by carbonous perithecia with long necks

cer·a·tos·to·mel·la \,serə,tästə'melə, ¦serə(,)tōstə-\ n, cap [NL, fr. Ceratostoma + -ella] : a genus of fungi (family Ceratostomataceae) forming continuous hyaline spores — see BLUE ROT, DUTCH ELM DISEASE

cer·a·to·the·ca \,serətō'thēkə\ n, pl **ceratothe·cae** \-ē,sē\ [NL, fr. cerat- + theca] : the part of the integument of an insect pupa that covers the antenna — **cer·a·to·the·cal** \¦==¦kəl\ adj

cer·a·to·za·mia \,serətō'zāmēə\ n, cap [NL, fr. cerat- + Zamia] : a small genus of Woody Mexican cycads (family Cycadaceae) having short scaly woody trunks, fernlike foliage, and woody cones

ceraun- or **cerauno-** comb form [Gk keraun-, kerauno-, fr. keraunos thunderbolt; akin to Gk kēr death — more at CARIES] : thunder ⟨ceraunograph⟩ ⟨ceraunophone⟩

ce·rau·no·gram \sə'rȯnə,gram\ n -s [ceraun- + -gram] : the record obtained by a ceraunograph

ce·rau·no·graph \-,graf\ n -s [ceraun- + -graph] : an instrument for recording chronologically by pen the occurrence of thunder and lightning

cer·be·re·an \sə(r)'birēən, ,sər'-, sə̄-; ¦sərbə¦rēən, ¦səb-\ adj, usu cap [L cerbereus of Cerberus (fr. Cerberus) + E -an] : of, relating to, or like Cerberus

cer·ber·us \'sərb(ə)rəs, 'səb-\ n, pl **cerberuses** \-rəsəz\ or **cer·beri** \-bə,rī\ [L Cerberus, three-headed dog guarding the entrance to Hades, fr. Gk Kerberos; akin to Skt śabara, śabala spotted (used as name of one of the two dogs of Yama, god of the dead)] **1** sometimes cap : WATCHDOG, GATEKEEPER, CUSTODIAN **2** [NL, fr. L] cap : a genus of East Indian water snakes (family Homalopsidae) related to and sometimes including Hurria

cerc- or **cerco-** comb form [NL, fr. Gk kerk-, kerko-, fr. kerkos tail] : tail : tailed ⟨cercaria⟩ ⟨cercopod⟩

cerc·aër·tus \,sərkē'ərd·əs\ n, cap [NL, fr. cerc- + -aertus (fr. Gk aertan, aertazein to lift up)] : a genus of marsupials consisting of the dormouse opossums

cer·cal \'sərkəl, -ək-\ adj [cerc- + -al] : of or relating to a tail

-cer·cal \¦sərkəl, -ək-\ adj comb form [F -cerque (fr. Gk kerkos tail) + E -al] : tailed ⟨homocercal⟩ ⟨isocercal⟩

cer·car·ia \(,)sər'ka(a)rēə\ n, pl **cercari·ae** \-rē,ē\ [NL, fr. cerc- + -aria] : a tadpole-shaped larval trematode worm produced in the molluscan host by a redia and later freed into water to encyst as a metacercaria or to actively penetrate a suitable definitive host — **cer·car·i·al** \-ēəl\ adj — **cer·car·i·an** \-ēən\ adj or n — **cer·car·i·form** \-kərə,fȯrm\ adj

cercaria of Fasciola: 1 oral sucker, 2 pharynx, 3 intestine, 4 spherules in nephridia, 5 acetabulum, 6 nephridium in tail

cer·car·i·ae·um \(,)sər,karē'ēəm\ n, pl **cercari·aea** \-ē'ēə\ [NL, irreg. fr. cercaria] : a tailless cercaria usu. remaining in the snail host until eaten by the proper definitive host

cercarial dermatitis n : an itching inflammation caused by infestation of the skin by cercariae and usu. acquired when wading or swimming in infested waters

cercelée var of SARCELLY

cerci pl of CERCUS

cer·cis \'sərsəs\ n, cap [NL, fr. Gk kerkis Judas tree, weaver's shuttle, perh. fr. kerkos tail; fr. the movement of its leaves] : a small genus of widely distributed shrubs or low trees (family Leguminosae) having irregular pink to reddish flowers borne on the old wood — see JUDAS TREE, REDBUD

cer·cle \'serkl(ᵊ), -k(lə)\ n, pl **cercles** \"\ [F — more at CIRCLE] : a French administrative district; esp : an administrative subdivision in a French colony

cerco- — see CERC-

cer·co·ce·bus \,sərkō'sēbəs\ n, cap [NL, fr. cerc- + Gk kēbos, a long-tailed monkey — more at CEBUS] : a genus of long-tailed monkeys of western Africa comprising the mangabeys and having prominent ischial callosities and white upper eyelids

cer·col·a·bes \(,)sər'kälə,bēz\ [NL, fr. cerc- + -labes (irreg. fr. Gk lambanein to take, seize); akin to OE læccan to seize — more at LATCH] syn of COENDOU

cer·com·o·nas \(,)sər'kämənəs\ n, cap [NL, fr. cerc- + -monas] : a genus of commensal or coprophilous flagellated protozoans (order Protomonadina) having two anterior flagella, one of which is trailing

¹cer·co·pid \'sərkəpəd, -,pid\ adj [NL Cercopidae] : of or relating to the Cercopidae

²cercopid \"\ n -s : one of the Cercopidae : FROGHOPPER

cer·cop·i·dae \(,)sər'käpə,dē\ n pl, cap [NL, fr. Cercopis, type genus (prob. modif. of Gk kerkōpē long-tailed cicada, alter. of kerkōps, a long-tailed ape & Kerkōps, one of a pair of malicious brothers captured by Heracles, fr. kerk- cerc- + ōps eye, face) + -idae — more at OPTIC] : a family of insects (suborder Homoptera) including the froghoppers that suck the juices of plants and live in a mass of froth which they secrete

cer·co·pith \'sərkə,pith\ n -s [modif. of NL Cercopithecidae] : a monkey of the family Cercopithecidae

cer·co·pi·the·ci·dae \¦sərkōpə'thēsə,dē, -ēkə-\ n pl, cap [NL, fr. Cercopithecus, type genus + -idae] : an anthropoid family that includes all the Old World monkeys except the anthropoid apes and is coextensive with a superfamily (Cercopithecoidea) — compare CATARRHINA — **cer·co·pith·e·coid** \-¦pithə,kȯid, -,pə¦thē,k-\ adj or n

cer·co·pi·the·cus \,==,pə'thēkəs, -'pithəkəs\ n, cap [NL, fr. L, a long-tailed ape, fr. Gk kerkopithēkos, fr. kerk- cerc- + pithēkos ape — more at BEBUNG] : a genus (the type of the family Cercopithecidae) of slender long-tailed African monkeys comprising the guenons and related forms and having cheek pouches and ischial callosities

cer·co·pod \'sərkə,päd\ n -s [cerc- + -pod] : CERCUS

cer·cos·po·ra \(,)sər'käspərə\ n, cap [NL, fr. cerc- + -spora] : a form genus of imperfect fungi (family Dematiaceae) that are leaf parasites with long slender multiseptate spores

cercospora leaf spot n, usu cap C : any of several leaf spots caused by fungi of the genus Cercospora (as sigatoka, beet leaf spot, and early blight of celery) — compare GRAY MOLD

cer·cos·po·rel·la \(,)sər,käspə'relə\ n, cap [NL, fr. Cercospora + -ella] : a form genus of imperfect fungi (family Moniliaceae) distinguished from the genus Cercospora and from other members of the family Dematiaceae mainly by the lack of pigment in the conidiophores and spores — see FROSTY MILDEW

cer·cos·po·ri·o·sis \(,)sər,käspərē'ōsəs\ n, pl **cercosporioses** \-ō,sēz\ [NL, fr. Cercospora + -i- + -osis] : a disease of plants caused by fungi of the genus Cercospora

cer·cus \'sərkəs, 'ker-\ n, pl **cer·ci** \'sər,sī, 'ker,kē\ [NL, fr. Gk kerkos tail] : either of a pair of simple or segmented appendages believed to be sensory in function situated at the posterior end of many insects and certain other arthropods

-cer·cy \,sər|sē, ,səs|, -kē, -i\ n comb form -ES [ISV -cercal + -y; prob. orig. formed as F -cerquie] : tail formation (of a specified type) ⟨diphycercy⟩

¹cere \'si(ə)r\ vt -ED/-ING/-S [ME ceren, seren, fr. MF cirer, fr. L cerare, fr. cera wax — more at CEREUS] **1** obs : to smear or cover with or as if with wax **2** : to wrap in or as if in a cerecloth

²cere \"\ n -s [ME sere, fr. MF cire, cere, fr. ML cera, fr. L, wax] : a protuberance or tumid area at the base of the bill of a bird; specif : a soft swollen mass through which the nostrils open at the base of the upper mandible and which occurs esp. in birds of prey and parrots and in the latter is often feathered

ce·rea flex·i·bil·i·tas \¦sirēə,fleksə'bilə,tas\ n [NL, lit., waxen flexibility] : the capacity to maintain bodily parts (as the limbs) in whatever position they have been placed (as in catalepsy)

¹ce·re·al \'sirēəl, 'sēr-\ adj [F or L; F céréale, fr. L cerealis of Ceres, of agriculture, of grain, fr. Ceres, goddess of grain; akin to L crescere to grow — more at CRESCENT] : relating to grain or to the plants that produce it : made of grain ⟨a ~ beverage⟩

²cereal \"\ n -s **1** : a plant (as a grass) yielding farinaceous seeds suitable for food (as wheat, maize, rice); also : the seeds or grain so produced either in their original state or commercially prepared **2** : a prepared foodstuff of grain (as oatmeal or cornflakes) used esp. as a breakfast food

ce·re·a·lian \¦==¦ālyən, -lēən\ also **ce·re·al·ic** \-¦alik\ adj [²cereal + -ian or -ic] : of or relating to cereals

ce·re·al·ist \'==ələst\ n -s [²cereal + -ist] : a specialist in the study of cereals

cer·e·bel \'serə,bel\ n -s [ML cerebellum] : CEREBELLUM

cerebell- or **cerebelli-** or **cerebello-** comb form [cerebellum] **1** : cerebellum ⟨cerebellitis⟩ **2** : cerebellar : cerebellar and ⟨cerebellocortex⟩ ⟨cerebellospinal⟩

cer·e·bel·lar \¦serə¦belə(r)\ adj [cerebellum + -ar] : of or relating to the cerebellum

cerebellar artery n : any of several branches of the basilar and vertebral arteries that supply the cerebellum

cerebellar peduncle n : any of three large bands of nerve fibers that join each hemisphere of the cerebellum with the parts of the brain below and in front

cer·e·bel·lo·ru·bral \¦serə¦belō¦rübrəl\ adj [cerebell- + L rubr-, ruber red + E -al — more at RED] : of or relating to the cerebellum and red nucleus

cer·e·bel·lum \,serə'beləm\ n, pl **cerebellums** \-ləmz\ or **cerebel·la** \-lə\ [ML, fr. L, small brain, dim. of cerebrum brain] : a large dorsally projecting part of the brain that is concerned esp. with the coordination of muscles and the maintenance of equilibrium, that is situated anterior to and above the medulla which it partly overlaps, that consists in man of two lateral lobes and a median lobe connected with the other parts of the brain by three pairs of peduncles, of which the superior connects it with the cerebrum, the middle with the pons, and the inferior with the medulla, and that has a surface exhibiting transverse sulci of varying depth consisting of gray matter and an interior consisting chiefly of white matter which branches into the laminae formed by the sulci in such a way that an anteroposterior section has a treelike appearance — see ARBORVITAE, BRAIN illustration

cerebr- or **cerebri-** or **cerebro-** comb form [cerebrum] **1** : brain : cerebrum ⟨cerebroid⟩ ⟨cerebriform⟩ ⟨cerebroscope⟩ **2** : cerebral and ⟨cerebrospinal⟩

cerebra pl of CEREBRUM

¹ce·re·bral \sə'rēbrəl, 'serəb-\ adj [F cérébral, fr. L cerebrum brain + F -al; akin to OHG hirni brain, ON hjarni, Gk kara head, *keras* horn, Skt *śiras* head — more at HORN] **1 a :** of or relating to the brain or the intellect **b :** of, relating to, or being the cerebrum or the hemispheres of the brain **2 a :** appealing to intellectual and critical rather than emotional appreciation **:** demanding thought for perception of subtleties ⟨~ music⟩ ⟨~ drama⟩ **b :** characterized by the usu. subtle use of the mind **:** primarily intellectual in nature ⟨a ~ poet⟩ **3** [trans. of Skt *mūrdhanya*, lit., of the head] **a :** articulated with or involving the participation of the tongue tip curled up and back until its under surface touches the hard palate — used esp. of various consonants in Asiatic-Indian languages **b :** RETROFLEX **syn** see MENTAL

²**cerebral** \"\ *n* -s **1 :** a cerebral speech sound **2 :** a cerebral anatomical element (as an artery)

cerebral accident *n* **:** a sudden damaging occurrence (as of hemorrhage) within the cerebrum — compare APOPLEXY

cerebral apophysis *n* **:** PINEAL BODY

cerebral aqueduct *n* **:** AQUEDUCT OF SYLVIUS

cerebral artery *n* **:** any of the arteries supplying the cerebral cortex, the anterior and middle arising from the internal carotid and the posterior bifurcating from the basilar

cerebral cortex *n* **:** the superficial layer of gray matter overlying the cerebral hemispheres and functioning chiefly in coordination of higher nervous activity

cerebral dominance *n* **:** dominance in development and functioning of one of the cerebral hemispheres

cerebral fossa *n* **:** CRANIAL FOSSA

cerebral ganglion *n* **:** one of a pair of ganglia situated in the head or anterior part of the body in many invertebrates in front of or dorsal to the esophagus; *also* **:** a median ganglion formed by the fusion of such a pair

cerebral hemisphere *n* **:** either of the two lateral halves of the cerebrum

cerebral hemorrhage *n* **:** the bleeding into the tissue of the brain, esp. of the cerebrum, from a ruptured blood vessel — compare APOPLEXY

cere·bral·ism \sə'rēbrə,lizəm, 'serəb-\ *n* -s [*cerebral* + *-ism*] **1 :** the theory that consciousness is merely a function or product of the brain **2 :** a tendency to emphasize or to place undue stress upon cerebral, intellectual, or abstract ideas

cere·bral·ly \-brəlē, -li\ *adv* **:** in a cerebral manner

cerebral palsy *n* **:** a disability that results from direct or indirect damage to the motor centers of the brain before or during birth and is outwardly manifested according to the degree and area of injury by muscular incoordination (as in walking) and speech disturbances — compare SPASTIC PARALYSIS

cerebral peduncle *n* **:** either of two large bundles of nerve fibers passing from the pons forward and outward to form the main connection between the cerebral hemispheres and the spinal cord

cerebral thrombosis *n* **:** the formation within a cerebral artery of a blood clot preventing the circulation of blood in the blocked area of brain tissue

cerebral vesicle *n* **:** one of the divisions or dilatations into which the developing brain of vertebrates is marked off by incomplete transverse constrictions

cer·e·brate \'serə,brāt\ *vi* -ED/-ING/-S [back-formation fr. *cerebration*] **:** to use the mind **:** THINK ⟨legal helpers should do their *cerebrating* in their offices —Clarence Woodbury⟩

cer·e·bra·tion \,serə'brāshən\ *n* -s [*cerebr-* + *-ation*] **:** the act or the product of cerebrating **:** mental activity **:** THOUGHT

cer·e·brat·u·lus \,serə'brachələs\ *n, cap* [NL, irreg. fr. L *cerebrum* brain; prob. fr. the resemblance of its coils to the convolutions of the brain — more at CEREBRAL] **:** a genus of marine burrowing nemertine worms usu. of flattened form and often many feet long

cerebri- — see CEREBR-

ce·re·bric \sə'rēbrik, -eb-, -ēk, 'serəbrik\ *adj* [ISV *cerebr-* + *-ic*] **:** of, relating to, or derived from the brain or cerebrum

ce·re·bri·form \sə'rēbrə,fȯrm, -eb-, 'serəb-\ *adj* [ISV *cerebr-* + *-iform;* orig. formed as F *cérébriforme*] **:** like the brain in form or structure **:** CONVOLUTED

cer·e·brip·e·tal \,serə'bripəd·ᵊl\ *adj* [*cerebr-* + *-petal*] *of nerve fibers or impulses* **:** AFFERENT

cere·bro- *in pronunciations below,* ≠≠≠ = sə¦rēbrō *or* -brə *or* ¦serə(,)brō\ — see CEREBR-

cere·bro·ganglion \≠≠≠ *at* CEREBRO- +\ *n, pl* **cerebroganglia** [*cerebr-* + *ganglion*] **:** the cerebral ganglion of invertebrates — **cere·bro·ganglionic** \"+\ *adj*

cer·e·broid \'serə,brȯid\ *adj* [ISV *cerebr-* + *-oid*] **:** resembling or analogous to the cerebrum or brain

cer·e·bron·ic acid \¦serə¦bränik-\ *n* [ISV *cerebron*, a substance derived from brain tissue (fr. *cerebr-* + *-on*) + *-ic*] **:** a hydroxy fatty acid obtained from phrenosin by hydrolysis — called also *phrenosinic acid*

cere·bro·pedal \≠≠≠ *at* CEREBRO- +\ *adj* [*cerebr-* + *pedal*] **:** relating to or connecting the cerebral ganglion and pedal ganglia in mollusks

cer·e·brose \'serə,brōs *also* -ōz\ *n* -s [*cerebr-* + *-ose*] **:** GALACTOSE

cer·e·bro·side \'serəbrō,sīd\ *n* -s [*cerebrose* + *-ide*] **:** any of a group of white waxlike basic glycolipides found esp. in the brain and other nerve tissue that on hydrolysis yield sphingosine, a fatty acid, and a sugar (as galactose)

cere·bro·spinal \≠≠≠ *at* CEREBRO- +\ *adj* [*cerebr-* + *spinal*] **:** of or relating to the brain and spinal cord

cerebrospinal axis *n* **:** a primary bodily axis consisting of the brain and spinal cord **:** CENTRAL NERVOUS SYSTEM

cerebrospinal fluid *n* **:** a liquid comparable to serum but containing less dissolved material and in health no floating cells that is secreted from the blood into the lateral ventricles of the brain by the choroid plexus, circulates through the ventricles to the spaces between the meninges about the brain and spinal cord, and is resorbed into the blood through the subarachnoid sinuses, serving chiefly to maintain uniform pressure within the brain and spinal cord but also assisting in the metabolic exchanges

cerebrospinal meningitis *or* **cerebrospinal fever** *n* **:** inflammation of the membranes enveloping the brain and spinal cord in man or animals; *specif* **:** an infectious epidemic febrile disease caused by the meningococcus, producing severe headaches, vomiting, muscular spasm esp. of the neck, and delirium, often marked by a skin eruption of petechial or purpuric spots, and often ending fatally

cerebrospinal nervous system *n* **:** the portion of the nervous system in vertebrates comprising the brain, cranial nerves, spinal cord, and the spinal nerves concerned with transmission of impulses from sense organs to the voluntary muscles — compare AUTONOMIC NERVOUS SYSTEM

cere·bro·to·nia \"+'tōnēə\ *n* -s [NL, fr. *cerebr-* + *-tonia*] **:** a pattern of temperament typical of the ectomorphic individual marked by predominance of intellectual over social or physical factors and by exhibition of sensitivity, introversion, and shyness

¹**cere·bro·ton·ic** \"+¦tänik\ *adj* [NL *cerebrotonia* + E *-ic*] **:** exhibiting cerebrotonia

²**cerebrotonic** \"\ *n* -s **:** a cerebrotonic person **:** ECTOMORPH

cere·bro·vascular \≠≠≠ *at* CEREBRO- +\ *adj* [*cerebr-* + *vascular*] **:** of or involving the cerebrum and the blood vessels supplying it ⟨~ accident⟩ ⟨~ disease⟩

cere·bro·visceral \"+\ *adj* [*cerebr-* + *visceral*] **:** belonging to or connecting cerebral and visceral ganglia in mollusks

cere·brum \sə'rēbrəm, 'serəb-\ *n, pl* **cerebrums** \-rəmz\ *or* **cere·bra** \-rə\ [L, brain — more at CEREBRAL] **1 a :** BRAIN 1a — now used chiefly figuratively or affectedly **b :** an enlarged anterior or upper part of the brain: (1) **:** all the brain anterior to the isthmus **:** the forebrain and midbrain with their derivatives (2) **:** FOREBRAIN 1b (3) **:** the two cerebral hemispheres — see BRAIN illustration **2 :** the chief cephalic ganglion of an invertebrate **:** SUPRA-ESOPHAGEAL GANGLION

¹**cere·cloth** \'si(ə)r+,-\ *n* -s [alter. of earlier *cered cloth*, fr. *cered* (past part. of *cere*) + *cloth*] **1 :** cloth or a cloth smeared or impregnated with melted wax or with gummy or glutinous matter and formerly used esp. as a waterproof or protective material for wrapping a dead body or as a plaster in medicine **2 :** a covering for an altar table that is placed under the altar cloths

²**cerecloth** \"\ *vt* -ED/-ING/-S *obs* **:** to cover with a cerecloth

cered *past of* CERE

Ce·re·lose \'sirə,lōs *also* -ōz\ *trademark* — used for dextrose

cere·ment \'serəmənt, 'si(ə)rm-\ *n* -s [*cere* + *-ment*] **:** a usu. waxed winding-sheet — usu. used in pl. ⟨the corpses of royal children . . . wrapped up in ~s of gold —J.C.Powys⟩

¹**cer·e·mo·nial** \¦serə¦mōnēəl, -nyəl\ *adj* [ME *ceremonial*, fr. MF, fr. LL *caerimonialis*, fr. L *caerimonia* ceremony + *-alis* -al] **1 :** marked by, involved in, or belonging to a ceremony **:** marked by careful, full, and often elaborate attention to form and detail **:** RITUAL ⟨grave ~ occasions, like birth and death and the assumption of manhood —John Buchan⟩ ⟨the highly colored ~ life of the Greek court —H.O.Taylor⟩ ⟨~ paraphernalia⟩ **2** *obs* **:** observant of forms **:** CEREMONIOUS

syn CEREMONIOUS, FORMAL, CONVENTIONAL, SOLEMN: CEREMONIAL may suggest an elaborate, prescribed, ritualistic code of procedure ⟨he had been among the Indians so much that he had acquired some notion of their *ceremonial* ideas of politeness, which demand a decent interval of light conversation before any important announcement is made —C.B.Nordhoff & J.N.Hall⟩ CEREMONIOUS also suggests elaborate procedures, perhaps punctilious and dignified ⟨the gay throngs of the people moved . . . outside the huge many-moated castle of the Shogun . . . but had no lot in the *ceremonious* existence within them —Laurence Binyon⟩ CEREMONIOUS is more likely than CEREMONIAL to refer to people ⟨the Zuñi are a *ceremonious* people . . . their interest is centered upon their rich and complex *ceremonial* life —Ruth Benedict⟩ FORMAL indicates accordance with a set procedure and may suggest stiffness, restraint, or old-fashioned custom ⟨his air was grave and stately, and his manners were very *formal* —Jane Austen⟩ ⟨"I kiss your hand, Miss", said Mr. Lorry, with the manners of an earlier date, as he made his *formal* bow again —Charles Dickens⟩ CONVENTIONAL indicates accord with general custom or usage ⟨when she herself had been seriously sick or in danger they uttered a *conventional* word of sympathy at the news, and forgot all about it immediately —Thomas Hardy⟩ ⟨your *conventional* morality is stronger than you. You are the slave to the opinions which have credence among the people you have known and have read about —Jack London⟩ CONVENTIONAL may suggest stodgy lack of originality ⟨I discovered . . . that the right people were often the most tiresome and the most *conventional* —A.C.Benson⟩ SOLEMN, in this sense now applicable mostly to religious, legalistic, or state procedures, stresses attention to all forms and details ⟨a *solemn* rite⟩

²**ceremonial** \"\ *n* -s [ME *cerimonial*, fr. *cerimonial*, adj.] **1 :** a system of formal rules and ceremonies enjoined by law, protocol, or custom for observance in religious worship, social affairs, or courtly procedure **2 :** a ceremonial usage or formality **:** a standardized rite, ceremony, or ritual ⟨the magic and religious ~s of primitive cultures⟩ **syn** see FORM

cer·e·mo·nial·ism \,serə'mōnēə,lizəm, -nyə,l-\ *n* -s **1 :** observance of or adherence to ceremonies esp. of religion **2 :** the addiction to or particular fondness for ceremonies

cer·e·mo·nial·ist \-ləst\ *n* -s **:** one who favors an emphasis on ceremonial forms esp. in religious affairs **:** RITUALIST

ceremonial law *n* **:** law prescribing the ceremonies of religion (as those of the Jewish religion contained in the Old Testament)

cer·e·mo·nial·ly \¦serə¦mōnēəlē, -nyəlē, -li\ *adv* **1 :** in a ceremonial manner **2 :** in regard to ceremonial law

cer·e·mo·nial·ness \,≠≠'mōnēəlnəs, -nyəl-\ *n* -ES **:** the quality or state of being ceremonial

ceremonial tea *n* [so called fr. its use in chanoyu] **:** a Japanese green tea cured by steaming, drying, and powdering selected shade-grown leaves and used in chanoyu

cer·e·mo·ni·ar·i·us \,serə,mōnē'a(a)rēəs\ *n, pl* **ceremoniar·ii** \-rē,ī\ [NL, fr. L *caerimonia* sacred rite + *-arius* -ary] **:** MASTER OF CEREMONIES b

cer·e·mo·nious \¦serə¦mōnēəs, -nyəs\ *adj* [MF *cérimonieux*, *cérémonieux*, fr. *cérimonie*, *cérémonie* + *-eux* -ous] **1 :** CEREMONIAL **2 :** devoted to forms and ceremony **:** punctilious about ceremony and formal procedure ⟨~ courtiers⟩ ⟨it was evidently to be a ~ occasion, for . . . he found his dress clothes put out for him —Compton Mackenzie⟩ **3 :** in accord with esp. stiff or formal usage or prescribed procedures ⟨the mere ~ salutation attending his entrance —Jane Austen⟩ ⟨that kind of ~ devotion punctually observed by a gentleman of the old school —Washington Irving⟩ **4 :** marked by ceremony, esp. by full, elaborate, and often showy observance of prescribed forms ⟨a ~ procession⟩ ⟨his ~ diction wore the aspect of pomposity —Sir Winston Churchill⟩ **syn** see CEREMONIAL

cer·e·mo·nious·ly *adv* **:** in a ceremonious manner

cer·e·mo·nious·ness *n* -ES **:** the quality or state of being ceremonious

cer·e·mo·ny \'serə,mōnē, -ni, *Brit usu & US sometimes* -əmən-\ *n* -ES [ME *cerimonie*, *ceremonie*, fr. MF *cérimonie*, *cérémonie*, fr. L *caerimonia*, perh. of Etruscan origin; akin to *Caere*, Etruscan city near Rome] **1 :** a formal act or series of acts typically conducted elaborately, solemnly, and as prescribed by the ritual or protocol of religious, state, courtly, social, or tribal procedure ⟨after the death of a king, a solemn ~ of purification was performed by a princess —J.G Frazer⟩ ⟨the marriage ~⟩ ⟨a religious ~⟩ ⟨the new republic was formally proclaimed with elaborate *ceremonies* —*Collier's Yr. Bk.*⟩ **2 a :** a conventional act or gesture of politeness or etiquette esp. when done elaborately ⟨the ~ of introductions completed, the party resumed⟩ **b :** an action performed with formality but lacking deep significance, force, or effect ⟨the drift towards conformity revealed itself . . . in the emphasis upon gestures and *ceremonies* of loyalty —H.S.Commager⟩ **c :** a commonplace routine action performed with elaboration, pomp, or punctiliousness ⟨the weekly ~ of giving out the wages to the help⟩ **3 a** *obs* **:** a symbol or device used in an elaborate ritual procedure **b :** pomp or display associated with such a procedure **c** *obs* **:** PORTENT, OMEN **4 a :** prescribed procedures **:** USAGES, OBSERVANCES ⟨the ~ attending the inauguration⟩ **b :** accordance with or observance of an established code of civility or politeness ⟨the door of Major Post's small office . . . opened without ~ and a young flight officer strode in —J.G.Cozzens⟩ **c :** a special occasion or function (as a parade, review, or escort) performed according to prescribed regulations **syn** see FORM

ce·ren·kov radiation *or* **che·ren·kov radiation** \chə'reŋkəf, chər'ye-\ *n, usu cap C* [after P.A.*Cherenkov* b. 1904 Russ. physicist, its discoverer] **:** polarized light produced by charged particles (as electrons) traversing pure solids or liquids at a speed greater than that of light in the same medium

cereous *adj* [L *cereus*, fr. *cera* wax] *obs* **:** like wax **:** WAXEN

¹**ceres** *pl of* CERE, *pres 3d sing of* CERE

²**ce·res** \'sir(,)ēz, 'sē(,)rēz\ *n* -ES *often cap* [L *Ceres*, goddess of grain] **:** a moderate orange that is slightly yellower and paler than honeydew and redder and paler than Persian orange

cer·e·sin \'serəsən\ *also* **cer·e·sine** \'serə,sēn, -,sən\ *n* -s [ISV *ceres-* (irreg. fr. L *cera* wax) + *-in, -ine*] **:** a white or yellow hard brittle wax made by purifying ozokerite and used as a substitute for beeswax; *also* **:** a petroleum wax (as paraffin wax) having similar physical properties

ce·re·us \'sirēəs\ *n, cap* [NL, fr. L, wax candle, fr. *cera* wax, prob. fr. Gk *kēros*; akin to Lith *korys* honeycomb] **:** a genus of cacti of the western U.S. and tropical America including mostly erect and columnar much-branched forms with spiny ribs and large elongated nocturnal flowers usu. borne singly along the ribs — compare NIGHT-BLOOMING CEREUS, SAGUARO

ce·re·za \sə'rāzə, -āsə, -re-\ *n* -s [AmerSp, fr. Sp, cherry, fr. LL *ceresia* — more at CHERRY] **1** *in tropical America* **a :** any of several plants having fruits resembling cherries (as *Malpighia glabra, M. coccigera,* and various species of *Cordia*) **b :** the fruit of these plants **2** *in Mexico* **:** CAPULIN 1

ce·ria \'sirēə\ *n* -s [NL, fr. *cerium* + *-a*] **:** the cerium oxide CeO_2

ce·ri·an·thar·ia \,sirē,an'tha(a)rēə\ *n pl, cap* [NL, fr. *Cerianthus*, type genus (fr. Gk *kērion* honeycomb — fr. *kēros* wax — + NL *-anthus*) + *-aria* — more at CEREUS] *in some classifications* **:** an order of Anthozoa coextensive with Cerianthidae and usu. included in Actiniaria — **ce·ri·an·thar·i·an** \¦≠≠¦≠'rēən\ *adj or n*

ce·ri·an·thid \,sirē'an(t)thəd\ *n* -s [NL *Cerianthidae*] **:** any actinian of the family Cerianthidae

ce·ri·an·thi·dae \-thə,dē\ *n pl, cap* [NL, fr. *Cerianthus*, type genus + *-idae*] **:** a family of elongated tube-building Actiniaria comprising the vestlets and related forms

ce·ri·an·thid·ea \,sirē,an'thidēə\ [NL, fr. *Cerianthus* + *-idea*] *syn of* CERIANTHARIA

ce·ric \'sirik, 'ser-\ *adj* [ISV *cer-* (fr. NL *cerium*) + *-ic*] **:** of, relating to, or containing cerium in the tetravalent state

ceric oxide *n* **:** the cerium oxide CeO_2

ce·ride \'sir,īd, -,əd\ *also* **ce·rid** \-əd\ *n* -s [*cer-* + *-ide, -id*] **:** any of the simple lipides that are esters of higher monohydroxy alcohols and fatty acids esp. of higher molecular weight — compare WAX

ce·ri·llo \sə'rē(,)(y)ō\ *n* -s [AmerSp, hog gum (*Symphonia globulifera*), princewood (*Exostema caribaeum*), cogwood, zapatero, wax taper, match, alter. of Sp *cerilla* wax taper, fr. *cera* wax, fr. L — more at CEREUS] **1 :** ZAPATERO 2 **2 :** PRINCEWOOD 2

ceri·man \¦serə¦man, -ān\ *n* -s [AmerSp *cerimán*] **:** a plant of the genus *Monstera; esp* **:** a tropical American vine (*M. deliciosa*) with hanging cordlike roots

ce·rin \'sirən\ *n* -s [ISV *cer-* + *-in;* orig. formed in G] **1 :** a crystalline triterpenoid $C_{30}H_{50}O_2$ that is extracted from cork **2 :** CEROTIC ACID

ce·rine \'sir,ēn, -,ən\ *n* -s [ISV *cer-* (fr. NL *cerium*) + *-ine*] **1 :** ALLANITE **2 :** CERITE 1

cering *pres part of* CERE

ce·rin·the \sə'rin(t)thē\ *n, cap* [NL, fr. L *cerinthe, cerintha* honeywort, fr. Gk *kērinthē*, prob. fr. *kērinthos* beebread, perh. fr. *kēros* wax — more at CEREUS] **:** a genus of Eurasian herbs of the borage family with alternate leaves and yellow flowers — see HONEYWORT 1

¹**ce·rin·thi·an** \-ēən\ *adj, usu cap* [*Cerinthus*, 1st cent. A.D. Syrian heresiarch + E *-ian*] **:** relating to Cerinthus or his doctrine of adoptionist Christology

²**cerinthian** \"\ *n* -s *usu cap* **:** a follower of Cerinthus

ce·ri·om·e·try \,sirē'ämə·trē\ *or* **ce·rim·e·try** \sə'rim-\ *n* -ES [NL *cerium* + E *-ometry* (fr. *-o-* + *-metry*) or *-metry*] **:** volumetric chemical analysis by the use of a ceric compound [as ceric sulfate $Ce(SO_4)_2$]

ce·ri·on \'sirē,än\ *n* [NL, fr. Gk *kērion* honeycomb, fr. *kēros* wax] **1** *cap* **:** a genus (family Cerionidae) of pupa-shaped land snails that are confined to the West Indies and the southern tip of Florida **2** -s **:** any mollusk of the genus *Cerion* **:** PUPA SHELL

cerion

ce·ri·on·i·dae \,sirē'änə,dē\ *n pl, cap* [NL, fr. *Cerion*, type genus + *-idae*] **:** a family (order Pulmonata) of land snails coextensive with the genus *Cerion*

ce·ri·ops \'sirē,äps\ *n* -ES [NL, perh. fr. Gk *kērion* honeycomb + *ōps* eye, face — more at OPTIC] **:** an East Indian mangrove (*Ceriops tagal*) that is the source esp. in the Philippines of a valuable tanning extract

ceriph *var of* SERIF

ce·rise \sə'rēs *also* -ēz\ *n* -s [F, lit., cherry, fr. LL *ceresia* — more at CHERRY] **:** a moderate red that is slightly darker than claret (sense 3a), slightly lighter than Harvard crimson (sense 1), very slightly bluer and duller than average strawberry (sense 2a), and bluer and very slightly lighter than Turkey red

ce·rite \'sir,īt\ *n* -s [Sw *cerit*, fr. NL *Ceres*, an asteroid + Sw *-it* -ite] **1 :** a mineral consisting of a hydrous silicate of cerium and allied metals occurring generally in brownish masses (hardness 5.5, sp. gr. 4.86) **2** [Sw *cerin* allanite (fr. *cerium* + *-in* -ine) + E *-ite*] **:** ALLANITE

cer·i·thid·ea \,serə'thidēə\ *n, cap* [NL, prob. irreg. fr. *Cerithium*] **:** a genus of brackish-water snails (family Cerithiidae) having a long usu. dark brown or blackish spiral shell, common on tidal mud flats, and including intermediate hosts of the intestinal fluke (*Heterophyes heterophyes*)

cer·i·thi·idae \,serə'thīə,dē\ *n pl, cap* [NL, fr. *Cerithium*, type genus + *-idae*] **:** a family of slender elongated spirally coiled gastropod mollusks (order Pectinibranchia) comprising the horn shells of fresh and brackish waters — **ce·rith·i·oid** \sə'rithē,ȯid\ *adj*

cerithium \sə'rithēəm\ *n, cap* [NL, modif. of Gk *keration*, dim. of *kerat-, keras* horn — more at HORN] **:** the type genus of Cerithiidae

ce·ri·um \'sirēəm\ *n* -s [NL, fr. *Ceres*, an asteroid (fr. L *Ceres*, goddess of grain) + *-ium* — more at CEREAL] **:** the most abundant element of the rare-earth group that occurs combined in monazite, cerite, and other rare-earth minerals, that resembles iron in color and luster but is soft and malleable and ductile, and that emits sparks when scratched with steel and forms pyrophoric iron alloys used as flints (as for lighters) — symbol *Ce;* see ELEMENT table

cerium metal *n* **:** any of a group of rare-earth metals separable as a group from other metals occurring with them and in addition to cerium including lanthanum, praseodymium, neodymium, promethium, samarium, and sometimes europium

cerium oxalate *n* **1 :** a yellowish white crystalline salt $Ce_2(C_2O_4)_3.9H_2O$ **2 :** a mixture of the oxalates of cerium metals prepared as a white or pinkish powder and formerly used to allay gastric irritation

cerium oxide *n* **:** an oxide of cerium; *esp* **:** the dioxide CeO_2 obtained as a colorless to yellow heavy powder usu. by igniting a cerium compound (as the oxalate) and used as a polishing agent and esp. in the hydrated form as a decolorizer for glass

cer·met \'sər,met\ *n* -s [¹*ceramic* + *metal*] **:** a strong alloy of a heat-resistant compound (as titanium carbide) and a metal (as nickel) used esp. for turbine blades and other objects made by powder metallurgy — called also *ceramal*

cern \'sərn\ *vi* -ED/-ING/-S [L *cernere*, lit., to sift — more at CERTAIN] *Roman law* **:** to resolve to enter upon an inheritance; *also* **:** to make known the determination formally

cer·ni·ture \'sərnə,chu̇(ə)r\ *n* -s [L *cernitus* (past part. of cernere) + E *-ure*] *Roman & civil law* **:** a formal acceptance of an inheritance

cer·nu·ous \'sərnyəwəs\ *adj* [L *cernuus* with the face turned toward the earth; akin to L *cerebrum* brain — more at CEREBRAL] *of a plant* **:** inclining or nodding **:** PENDULOUS, DROOPING

ce·ro \'ser(,)ō\ *n, pl* **cero** *or* **ceros** [modif. of Sp *sierra* saw, sawfish, cero — more at SIERRA] **:** either of two large mackerel-like food and sport fishes (*Scomberomorus cavalla* and *S. regalis*) of the warmer parts of the western Atlantic ocean — called also *cavalla, kingfish, pintado*

cero- — see CER-

ce·ro·graph \'sirə,graf\ *n* -s [back-formation fr. *cerography*] **:** a writing or engraving on wax

ce·rog·ra·phy \sə'rägrəfē\ *n* -ES [Gk *kērographia*, fr. *kēr-* cer- + *-graphia* -graphy] **:** the art of making characters or designs in or with wax

ce·roid \'si,rȯid\ *n* -s [*cer-* + *-oid*] **:** a yellow to brown pigment found esp. in the liver in cirrhosis and brought about by various experimental diets

cero·lite \'sirə,līt, 'ser-\ *n* -s [G *kerolith*, fr. *ker-* cer- + *-lith* -lite] **:** a hydrous magnesium silicate like serpentine occurring in yellow or greenish waxlike masses

ce·ro·ma \sə'rōmə\ *n* -s [NL, fr. L, cerate, fr. Gk *kērōma*, fr. *kēros* wax — more at CEREUS] **:** the cere of a bird

ce·ro·man·cy \'sirə,man(t)sē, 'ser-\ *n* -ES [prob. fr. F *céromancie*, fr. *cér-* cer- + *-mancie* -mancy] **:** divination from figures formed by melted wax in water

ceroon *var of* SEROON

cero·plastic \¦sirō, ¦serō+\ *adj* [Gk *kēroplastikos*, fr. *kēr-* cer- + *plastikos* plastic] **1 :** relating to the art of modeling in wax **2 :** modeled in wax

cero·plastics \"+\ *n pl* [Gk *kēroplastikē*, fr. fem. of *kēroplastikos*] **1** *sing in constr* **:** the art of modeling in wax **2** *sometimes sing in constr* **:** WAXWORKS

ce·ro·tate \'sirə,tāt, 'ser-\ *n* -s [ISV *cerotic* + *-ate*] **:** a salt or ester of cerotic acid

ce·ro·tic acid \sə'rōd·ik, -räd-\ *n* [L *cerotum*, a pomade, fr. Gk *kērōton* (fr. *keros* wax) + E *-ic*] **:** a solid fatty acid $C_{25}H_{51}COOH$ occurring usu. as an ester in most waxes (as Chinese wax, beeswax, montan wax) and some fats

ce·rous \'sirəs\ *adj* [ISV *cer-* (fr. NL *cerium*) + *-ous*] **:** of or relating to or containing cerium in the trivalent state

ce·rox·y·lon \sə'räksə,län, -lən\ *n, cap* [NL, fr. Gk *kēr-* cer- + *-xylon*] **:** a small genus of tall So. American palms — see WAX PALM

cer·ris \'serəs\ *n, pl* **cerris** [NL, alter. of L *cerrus*] **:** the European Turkey oak

cer·ro green \'ser(,)ō-\ *n* [perh. fr. Sp *cerro* hill, fr. L *cirrus* curl, ringlet, tuft of hair on an animal — more at CIRRUS] **:** a moderate yellow green that is greener and deeper than average moss green and yellower and deeper than average pea green or apple green (sense 1)

cert \ˈsərt, ˈsə̄t\ *n* -S [short for *certainty*] *slang Brit* **:** a sure thing **:** CERTAINTY

cert *abbr* **1** certificate; certified **2** certiorari

¹**cer·tain** \ˈsərtᵊn, ˈsə̄t-, ˈsəit- *sometimes* -tə̇n\ *adj, sometimes* **certainer** \-t(ᵊ)nə(r)\ *sometimes* **certainest** \-t(ᵊ)nə̇st\ [ME *certain, certein,* fr. OF *certain,* fr. (assumed) VL *certanus,* fr. L *certus* determined, fixed, certain, fr. *cernere* to sift, discern, understand, decide; akin to OE *hriddel* sieve, OHG *rītera* sieve, *hreini* clean, pure, ON *hreinn,* Goth *hrains,* Gk *krinein* to separate, decide, Lith *krijas* hoop around a sieve, Gk *keirein* to cut — more at SHEAR] **1 a :** FIXED, SETTLED, STATED ⟨guaranteed a ~ percentage of the profit⟩ ⟨where an agency such as a board of education has by law been granted ~ powers —M.R.Cohen⟩ ⟨fair play means ~ definite things —Margaret Mead⟩ —sometimes used as a postpositive modifier ⟨a rent ~ in money —Adam Smith⟩ **b :** EXACT, PRECISE ⟨I could not find the ~ reasons for thinking the modern society was destitute of its normal humanity —J.C.Ransom⟩ **c** *of a statement* **:** proved to be either logically or factually correct **:** thoroughly confirmed **:** believed without reservation or doubt **2 a :** PARTICULAR **:** of a character difficult or unwise to specify —used to distinguish a person or thing not otherwise distinguished or not distinguishable in more precise terms ⟨he telephoned a ~ Mr. Smith⟩ ⟨~ people would like him to speak⟩ ⟨the comfortable-looking houses . . . along the tree-lined streets give it a ~ charm —*Amer. Guide Series: Md.*⟩ **b :** small but tangible **3 :** SURE, DEPENDABLE: **a :** entirely reliable ⟨no ~ early likeness of him survives —Carl Van Doren⟩ ⟨a ~ remedy for the disease⟩ **b :** not to be doubted as a fact **:** INDISPUTABLE ⟨it is ~ that we exist⟩ **4 a :** INEVITABLE ⟨the ~ advance of age and decay⟩ **b :** incapable of failing **:** DESTINED —used with a following infinitive ⟨he is ~ to see her⟩ ⟨he is ~ to be a success⟩ **5 a :** given to or marked by complete assurance and conviction, lack of doubt, reservation, suspicion, or wavering through or as if through infallible knowledge or perception **b :** firm and assured as though practiced **:** without hesitation, wavering, or diffidence ⟨I am sure that he was candid . . . I am ~ that he had no guile —W.A.White⟩ **6** *obs* **:** STEADFAST **syn** see SURE —**of a certain age :** past youth but yet not old ⟨a lady *of a certain age* —Crabb Robinson⟩

²**certain** \"\ *n* -S [ME *certain, certein,* fr. *certain, certein,* adj.] **:** CERTAINTY, CERTITUDE—**for certain** *adv* **:** ASSUREDLY **:** as a certainty ⟨never knew *for certain* how it happened —*Time*⟩

³**certain** \"\ *adv* [ME *certain, certein,* fr. *certain, certein,* adj.] *now dial* **:** CERTAINLY

⁴**certain** \"\ *pron, pl in constr* [¹*certain*] **:** certain ones ⟨~ of my generation —W.B.Yeats⟩

cer·tain·ly *adv* [ME, fr. ¹*certain* + *-ly*] **1 :** in a manner that is certain **:** with certainty **:** without fail **:** INFALLIBLY **:** with assurance **2 :** without doubt **:** UNQUESTIONABLY ⟨~ innocent⟩

cer·tain·ness \-n(n)ə̇s\ *n* -ES **:** CERTAINTY

cer·tain·ty \-ntē, -i\ *n* -ES [ME *certeinte,* fr. AF *certeinté,* fr. *certein, certain* + *-té* -ty] **1 :** something that is certain **2 :** the quality or state of being certain—**for a certainty** *also* **of a certainty** *or* **to a certainty :** CERTAINLY, ASSUREDLY **:** beyond doubt

cer·ta·tion \(ˌ)sərˈtāshən\ *n* -S [L *certation-, certatio* contest, fr. *certatus,* past part. of *certare* to fight, contend, settle something by a contest, fr. *certus* certain—more at CERTAIN] **:** competition between male elements of different genotype for opportunity to fertilize available female elements esp. as manifested by differential growth of pollen tubes

certes \ˈsərd·ēz, -r(ˌ)tēz, ˈsərts\ *adv* [ME, fr. OF, fr. *cert* certain, fr. L *certus*—more at CERTAIN] *archaic* **:** CERTAINLY **:** in truth

cer·thia \ˈsərthēə\ *n, cap* [NL, alter. of *certhius* tree creeper, fr. Gk *kerthios*] **:** a genus (the type of the family Certhiidae) of small songbirds with a slender more or less decurved bill and stiff pointed tail feathers serving as props in climbing trees — see CREEPER 4

cer·thi·i·dae \(ˌ)sərˈthīə̇ˌdē\ *n pl, cap* [NL, fr. *Certhia,* type genus + *-idae*] **:** a family (suborder Passeres) of small Old World and New World birds including the typical creepers

cer·tie \ˈsertī\ *n* -S [prob. back-formation fr. *certes,* taken as a plural] *chiefly Scot* **:** FAITH, TROTH — usu. used in exclamation

cer·ti·fi·a·ble \ˈsər|d·əˌfīəbəl, ˈsə̄|, ˈsəi|, |tə-, ˌ≈≈ˈ≈≈≈\ *adj* **1 :** capable of being certified **2 a :** fit to be certified as insane ⟨the very real increase in the number of ~ defectives —*Times Lit. Supp.*⟩ **b :** befitting an insane person ⟨a ~ urge to torture⟩ — **cer·ti·fi·a·bly** \-blē, -bli\ *adv*

¹**cer·tif·i·cate** \sə(r)ˈtifə̇kə̇t, ˌsərˈt-, ˌsə̄ˈt-, ˌsəiˈt-, -fēk-, *usu* -kəd· + V\ *n* -S [ME *certificat,* fr. MF, fr. ML *certificatum,* fr. LL, neut. of *certificatus,* past part. of *certificare* to certify — more at CERTIFY] **1 :** a document containing a certified and usu. official statement **:** a signed, written, or printed testimony to the truth of something (as a personal claim) ⟨he must present a ~ that he has never been arrested —Ernest Hemingway⟩; *esp* **:** a document issued by a school, a state agency, or a professional organization certifying that one has satisfactorily completed a course of studies, has passed a qualifying examination, or has attained professional standing in a given field and may officially practice or hold a position in that field ⟨a teacher's ~⟩ **2 :** something resembling or serving the same end as a certificate **:** CERTIFICATION ⟨a mood which she could surely take as a ~ that all was well —Rebecca West⟩ ⟨describes a pilgrimage thither as a ~ of patriotism —A.M.Young⟩ **3 :** a document evidencing ownership or debt ⟨stock ~⟩ ⟨~ of deposit⟩ **4 :** a document issued by a qualified officer of an organization asserting that a person is a member in good standing, holds a given rank or office, or has attained a specified honor; *also* **:** a blank form for such a document **5 :** a contract issued in place of an insurance policy by an insurer to one insured as evidence of membership in an insurance or pension plan

²**cer·tif·i·cate** \-fəˌkāt, *usu* -ād· + V\ *vt* -ED/-ING/-S **:** to testify to, furnish with, authorize, or license by a certificate; *esp* **:** to certify by means of a certificate showing adequate training or competence to practice a particular trade or profession ⟨the *certificated* airlines —*Air Transportation*⟩ ⟨a *certificated* parachute technician —C.A.Zweng⟩ ⟨~ a physician⟩

certificated stock *n* **:** a quantity of a commodity available in a warehouse and certified by a commodity exchange as deliverable on future contracts — usu. used in pl.

certificate of age : an official certificate permitting the employment of a minor

certificate of convenience and necessity : a certificate from a public board or commission required by federal or state statute before engaging in certain public undertakings or services to protect existing franchises against injurious competition

certificate of deposit 1 : a receipt issued by a bank for an interest-bearing time deposit coming due at a specified future date **2 :** a negotiable receipt issued by a trust company for bonds or stocks deposited under a recapitalization or reorganization or other plan or agreement

certificate of incorporation : an instrument authorized by existing law and regulation and serving as evidence of the creation of a corporation — compare CHARTER

certificate of indebtedness : a short-term negotiable promissory note issued by a government or a corporation as evidence of a floating indebtedness

certificate of mailing : a certificate issued by a post office on special request and for a small fee attesting the nature, destination, and date of mailing of a particular piece of mail

certificate of necessity : a document issued by a certifying government agency under authority of which the internal revenue service allows deductions from taxable income for accelerated amortization of all or a part of the cost of emergency facilities

certificate of participation 1 : a certificate issued by some forms of investment trust evidencing a proportionate equitable interest of the holder in securities held by the issuing concern **2 :** a certificate of membership in a pension plan issued by the trustee who holds the policies as issued by the insuring company

certificate of public convenience and necessity : CERTIFICATE OF CONVENIENCE AND NECESSITY

cer·ti·fi·ca·tion \(*certifying*)ˌsər|d·əfə̇ˈkāshən, ˌsə̄|, ˌsəi|, |tə-; (*certificating*) sə(r)ˌtifə̇ˈk-, ˌsərˌt-, ˌsə̄ˌt-, ˌsəiˌt-\ *n* -S [ME *certificacioun,* fr. MF or ML; MF *certification,* fr. ML *certification-, certificatio,* fr. LL *certificatus,* past part. of *certificare* to certify + *-ion-, -io* -ion —more at CERTIFY] **1 :** the act of certifying or certificating or the state of being certified or certificated **2 :** a certified statement **:** CERTIFICATE **3** *Scots law* **:** a notice certifying to a party to a suit the consequences of his default in the matters specified as required of him **4 :** a guarantee of the genuineness of the signature on a check by an authorized bank official **5 :** an authorization of a labor union by an appropriate public agency to act as a bargaining agent for all employees in a bargaining unit

cer·tif·i·ca·to·ry \(ˌ)sərˈtifə̇kəˌtōrē, *Brit sometimes* -ˌkātəri\ *adj* [ML *certificatorius,* fr. LL *certificatus* + L *-orius* -ory] **:** serving to certify **:** constituting or of the nature of a certificate

certified *adj* **:** endorsed authoritatively **:** guaranteed or attested as to quality, qualifications, fitness, or validity

certified check *n* **:** a check certified to be good by the bank upon which it is drawn by the signature of usu. the cashier or paying teller with the word *certified* or *accepted* across the face of the check

certified mail *n* **:** first class mail for which proof of delivery is secured but no indemnity value is claimed — compare REGISTERED MAIL

certified milk *n* **:** pasteurized or unpasteurized milk produced in dairies which operate under the rules and regulations of an authorized medical milk commission

certified public accountant *n* **:** an accountant usu. in professional public practice who has met the requirements of a state law and has been granted a state certificate — abbr. *C.P.A.;* compare CHARTERED ACCOUNTANT

certified seed *n* **:** seed of good quality and established identity verified by an official agency after inspection

certified transfer *n* **:** MARKED TRANSFER

cer·ti·fi·er \ˈsər|d·əˌfī(ə)r, ˈsə̄|,ˈsəi|, |tə-, -īə\ *n* -S **:** one that certifies

cer·ti·fy \-ˌfī\ *vb* -ED/ -ING/ -ES [ME *certifien,* fr. MF *certifier,* fr. LL *certificare,* fr. *certi-* (fr. L *certus* certain) + L *-ficare* -fy — more at CERTAIN] *vt* **1 :** to attest esp. authoritatively or formally: **a :** CONFIRM ⟨cards ~*ing* me as a member of the . . . Civil Defense Corps —Wilder Hobson⟩ ⟨she is not permitted aboard a plane unless a doctor *certifies* the trip is necessary —Henry La Cossitt⟩ ⟨*certifies* his dramatic talent as the assassin in a nerve-thrumming piece —*Newsweek*⟩ **b :** to present in formal communication, esp. in a document under hand or seal ⟨the judges shall ~ their opinion to the chancellor —William Blackstone⟩ **c :** to confirm or attest often by a document under hand or seal as being true, meeting a standard, or being as represented ⟨the director . . . has *certified* about 140 acres as meeting the conditions presented in the statute —H.S.Truman⟩ ⟨they could ~ on their honor that their extract contained no salicylic acid —V.G.Heiser⟩ ⟨a *certified* copy of the record⟩ ⟨a *certified* agent of the law⟩ **d :** to attest officially to (a person's) insanity ⟨a *certified* mental case⟩ ⟨*certified* defectives⟩ **2 :** to inform with certainty **:** ASSURE ⟨it does not, of course, ~ us of the truth of any event in the past or future —W.R.Inge⟩ **3 :** to guarantee (a personal check) as to signature and amount by so indicating on its face — see CERTIFIED CHECK **4 a :** to designate as having met the requirements for pursuing a certain kind of study or work ⟨~ a student for college⟩ **b :** CERTIFICATE, LICENSE ⟨~ a teacher⟩ ⟨~ a physician⟩ ~ *vi* **:** to attest by a certificate ⟨five year program leading to examination by the American Board which *certifies* in that specialty —*Bull. of Meharry Med. Coll.*⟩ **syn** see APPROVE

cer·tio·ra·ri \ˌsərsh(ē)əˈrerē, -ˈrerˌī,-ˈrärē\ *n* -S [ME, fr. L, to be informed, be shown, pass. infin. of *certiorare* to inform, fr. *certior* more certain, compar. of *certus* certain; fr. the use of the word *certiorari* in the Latin form of the writ — more at CERTAIN] **:** a writ issuing out of a superior court to call up the records of an inferior court or a body acting in a quasi-judicial capacity (as commissioners and assessors of taxes) in order that the party may have more sure and speedy justice or that errors and irregularities may be corrected

certiorate *vt* -ED/-ING/-S [L *certioratus,* past part. of *certiorare*] *archaic* **:** CERTIFY, APPRISE, ASSURE

cer·ti·tude \ˈsər|d·əˌtüd, ˈsə̄|,ˈsəi|, |tə-, -əˌtyüd\ *n* -S [ME, fr. LL *certitudo,* fr. L *certus* certain — more at CERTAIN] **1 :** the state of being certain of the truth or rightness of something **:** freedom from doubt **:** CONFIDENCE ⟨~ is not the test of certainty —O.W.Holmes †1935⟩ **2 :** accuracy, precision, or unfailingness of act or event ⟨the objective moral ~*s* have dissolved —Walter Lippmann⟩ ⟨demonstrate the absolute ~ of its conclusions —J.W.Krutch⟩

cer·to·si·na \ˌcherd·əˈsēnə\ *n* -S [It *certosino* Carthusian, fr. *certosa*] **:** a Renaissance Italian style of elaborate inlay of bone, ivory, light-colored wood, metal, or other material in stylized designs against a dark background

certs *pl of* CERT

cer·ty \ˈsertī\ *var of* CERTIE

¹**ce·ru·lean** *also* **cae·ru·lean** \sə̇ˈrülēən, sē-, -lyən\ *adj* [L *caeruleus* dark blue (prob. fr. *caelum* sky) + E *-an* — more at CELESTIAL] **1 :** somewhat resembling the blue of the sky **2 :** of the color sky blue

²**cerulean** \"\ *n* -S **:** the color of the sky on a bright cloudless day **:** deep blue or azure

cerulean blue *n* **1 a :** a variable color averaging a strong greenish blue that is bluer and duller than grotto or cobalt blue and bluer and lighter than indigo carmine **b :** a strong blue that is greener and stronger than Sèvres and greener, lighter, and stronger than Victoria blue — called also *coelin* **2 :** a stable light greenish blue pigment consisting essentially of oxides of cobalt and tin and used as an artist's color

cerulean warbler *n* **:** an eastern U. S. wood warbler (*Dendroica cerulea*) mostly blue above and white below that migrates to northern So. America in winter

cerulein *var of* COERULEIN

ce·ru·le·ite \sə̇ˈrülēˌīt\ *n* -S [F *céruléite,* fr. *cérulé* cerulean (fr. L *caeruleus*) + *-ite*] **:** a mineral $CuAl_4(AsO_4)_2(OH)_2.4H_2O$ consisting of a hydrous copper aluminum arsenate occurring in turquoise-blue microcrystalline masses (sp. gr. 2.80)

ce·ru·le·um \-lēəm\ *n* -S [L *caeruleum,* fr. neut. of *caeruleus*] **:** CERULEAN BLUE 2

ce·ru·lig·nol *also* **coe·ru·lig·nol** \ˌsē(ˌ)rü|ligˌnōl, -ōl\ *n* -S [*ceru-* (fr. L *caeruleus*) + L *lignum* wood + E *-ol;* prob. fr. the color which its alcoholic solution gives with barium hydroxide — more at LIGNEOUS] **:** a colorless oily phenol $C_{10}H_{14}O_2$ of burning taste obtained from wood-tar oils

ce·ru·lig·none *also* **coe·ru·lig·none** \-|ˌnōn\ *n* -S [ISV *ceru-* (fr. L *caeruleus*) + L *lignum* + ISV *quinone;* orig. formed as G *zörulignon*] **:** a dark blue crystalline quinone $C_{16}H_{16}O_6$ obtained from beechwood tar

ce·ru·men \sə̇ˈrümən, sēˈ-\ *n* -S [NL, irreg. fr. L *cera* wax — more at CEREUS] **1 :** the yellow waxlike secretion from the glands of the external ear — called also *earwax* **2 :** a mixture of wax, resin, and sometimes earth that is used in place of pure wax in the building activities of stingless bees

ce·ru·mi·nous \-mənəs\ *also* **ce·ru·mi·nal** \-nᵊl\ *adj* [NL *cerumin-, cerumen* + E *-ous, -al*] **:** relating to or secreting cerumen

ceruminous gland *n* **:** one of the modified sweat glands of the ear that produce earwax

-ce·rus \sərəs\ *n comb form* [NL, fr. Gk *-kerōs,* fr. *keras* horn — more at HORN] **:** horned one — in generic names of insects ⟨*Tetracerus*⟩

ce·ruse \sə̇ˈrüs, ˈsirˌüs, -üz\ *n* -S [ME, fr. MF *céruse,* fr. L *cerussa,* perh. fr. (assumed) Gk *kērōessa* waxen, fr. *kēros* wax — more at CEREUS] **1 :** white lead used as a pigment **2 :** a cosmetic containing white lead

ce·rus·site \sə̇ˈrəsˌīt\ *also* **ce·ru·site** \-rüˌsīt, -üˌz-\ *n* -S [G *zerussit,* fr. L *cerussa* + G *-it* -ite] **:** native lead carbonate $PbCO_3$ occurring in colorless white or yellowish transparent crystals and also massive

cer·van·tite \sə(r)ˈvanˌtīt\ *n* -S [*Cervantes,* town in northwestern Spain, its supposed locality + E *-ite*] **:** a mineral $Sb^{III}Sb^{V}O_4$ composed of an antimony oxide occurring in yellow or white crystals and also massive

cer·ve·lat \ˈsərvəˌlat; -ˌlä, ˈservəˌlä\ *n* -S [obs. F *cervelat* (now *cervelas*) — more at SAVELOY] **1** *also* **cer·ve·las** \ˈsərvəˌlä, ˈser-\ -ES **:** sausage of several regional kinds made of varying proportions of pork and beef with added fat and spices, stuffed into casings, and smoked **2** *also* **cer·va·let** \ˈsərvəˌlā, ˈser-\ **:** RACKETT

cer·ve·lière \ˌservəl|ye(ə)r\ *n* -S [F, fr. *cervelle* brain, irreg. fr. L *cerebellum* small brain — more at CEREBELLUM] **:** a close-fitting steel cap sometimes worn under a hood of mail or a helmet in medieval and later armor

cervi- *comb form* [F & NL, fr. L *cervus* — more at HART] **:** deer ⟨*Cervi*capra⟩

cervic- *or* **cervici-** *or* **cervico-** *comb form* [L *cervic-, cervix* neck] **:** neck ⟨*cervic*odynia⟩ **:** cervix of an organ ⟨*cervic*ectomy⟩ **:** cervical and ⟨*cervico*facial⟩

¹**cer·vi·cal** \ˈsərvə̇kəl, ˈsə̄v-,ˈsəiv-, -vēk- *esp Brit also* ˌsərˈvīk- *or* sə̄ˈv-\ *adj* [prob. fr. NL *cervicalis,* fr. L *cervic-, cervix* neck + *-alis* -al — more at CERVIX] **:** of or relating to a neck or cervix or to a part like a neck

²**cervical** \"\ *n* -S **:** a cervical vertebra, nerve, or artery

cervical canal *n* **:** the passage through the cervix uteri

cer·vi·cale \ˌsərvəˈkal(ˌ)ē, -ā(ˌ)lē, -ä(ˌ)lē\ *n* -S [NL, fr. neut. of *cervicalis*] **:** the tip of the dorsal spine of the seventh cervical vertebra

cervical flexure *n* **:** a ventral bend in the neural tube of the vertebrate embryo marking the point of transition from brain to spinal cord

cervical ganglion *n* **:** one of the sympathetic ganglia of the neck, being in man usu. three in number on each side

cervical nerve *n* **:** one of the spinal nerves of the cervical region, being eight on each side in man and most mammals

cervical plexus *n* **:** a plexus formed by the anterior divisions of the four upper cervical nerves

cervical plug *n* **:** a mass of tenacious secretion by glands of the uterine cervix present during pregnancy and tending to close the uterine orifice

cervical rib *n* **:** a supernumerary rib sometimes found in the neck above the usual first rib

cer·vi·cap·ra \ˌsərvəˈkaprə\ [NL, fr. *cervi-* + L *capra* she-goat, fr. *capr-, caper* goat — more at CAPRIOLE] *syn of* REDUNCA

cer·vi·cap·rine \-pˌrīn\ *adj* [NL *Cervicapra* + E *-ine*] **:** of or relating to the reedbucks

cer·vi·ci·tis \ˌsərvəˈsīd·ə̇s\ *n* -ES [NL, fr. *cervic-* + *-itis*] **:** inflammation of the cervix uteri

cer·vi·co·facial nerve \ˌsərvə(ˌ)kō+-\ *n* **:** a branch of the facial nerve supplying the lower part of the face and upper part of the neck

cer·vi·corn \ˈsərvəˌkȯrn\ *adj* [ISV *cervi-* + *-corn;* prob. orig. formed as F *cervicorne*] **1 :** branching like antlers **2 :** bearing antlers

cer·vi·cum \ˈsərvə̇kəm\ *n* -S [NL, irreg. fr. *cervic-*] **:** the flexible intersegmental region joining the insect head and thorax

cer·vid \ˈsərvə̇d\ *n* -S [NL *Cervidae*] **:** one of the Cervidae **:** DEER, MOOSE, ELK

cer·vi·dae \-vəˌdē\ *n pl, cap* [NL, fr. *Cervus,* type genus + *-idae*] **:** a large family of ruminant mammals (order Artiodactyla) that are distinguished from the related Bovidae by possession of solid deciduous antlers and that include deer, elk, moose, and related forms — compare ANTLER — **cer·void** \-ˌvȯid\ *adj or n*

cer·vine \-ˌvīn\ *adj* [L *cervinus* of a deer, fr. *cervus* + *-inus* -ine] **:** belonging to or resembling deer

cer·vix \ˈsərviks, ˈsə̄v-, ˈsəiv-, -vēks\ *n, pl* **cer·vi·ces** \-vəˌsēz; ˌsərˈvī(ˌ)s-, sə̄ˈvī-,səiˈvī-\ *or* **cervixes** [L, neck; prob. akin to L *cerebrum* brain and to L *vincire* to bind, tie — more at CEREBRAL, VETCH] **1 :** NECK; *esp* **:** the back part of the neck **2 :** a constricted portion of an organ or part: as **a** *also* **cervix ute·ri** \-ˈyüd·əˌrī\ **:** the narrow lower or outer end of the uterus **b** *also* **cervix cor·nu** \-ˈkȯr,n(y)ü\ **:** the constricted cementoenamel junction on a tooth

cer·voi·dea \(ˌ)sərˈvȯidēə\ *n pl, cap* [NL, fr. *Cervus* + *-oidea*] **:** a superfamily of ruminants coextensive with the family Cervidae

cer·vu·lus \ˈsərvyələs\ [NL, dim. of *Cervus*] *syn of* MUNTIACUS

cer·vus \ˈsərvəs\ *n, cap* [NL, fr. L, stag, deer — more at HART] **:** a genus (the type of the family Cervidae) formerly including all the deers but now limited to the larger forms (as the red deer and elk)

ce·ryl alcohol \ˈsirəl-\ *n* [ISV *cer-* + *-yl*] **:** a white crystalline alcohol $C_{26}H_{53}OH$ occurring as an ester in waxes (as Chinese wax and beeswax)

ces *pl of* CE

¹**ce·sar·e·an** *or* **ce·sar·i·an** *also* **cae·sar·e·an** *or* **cae·sar·i·an** \sə̇ˈza(a)rēən, sə̇-, -zer-, -zär-\ *adj, often cap* [alter. of earlier *caesarean*] **:** having to do with abdominal delivery

²**cesarean** *or* **cesarian** *also* **caesarean** *or* **caesarian** \"\ *n* -S *often cap* [by shortening & alter. fr. earlier *caesarean section,* prob. trans. of ML *sectio caesaria;* fr. the belief that Julius Caesar was so brought into the world] **:** a surgical operation through the walls of the abdomen and uterus for the purpose of delivering the young of a human or animal

ce·sar·e·vich \sə̇ˈzarəˌvich, -zär-\ *n* -ES *often cap* [Russ *tsesarevich,* fr. *tsesar'* emperor (fr. L *caesar*) + *-evich* (patronymic suffix) — more at CZAR] **1 :** the eldest son of the czar **2 :** the heir to the Russian throne — compare CZAREVITCH

ce·sa·ro·lite \ˌchäzəˈrōˌlīt\ *n* -S [F, fr. G.R.P.*Cesaro* †1939 Italian-Belgian mineralogist + F *-lite*] **:** a mineral $H_2PbMn_3O_8$ occurring in spongy steel-gray masses and supposed to be a hydrous lead manganate (hardness 4.5, sp. gr. 5.3)

ce·si·um *also* **cae·si·um** \ˈsēzēəm *sometimes* ˈsēzhē- *or* ˈsēsē- *or* ˈkīsē-\ *n* -S [NL, fr. L *caesius* bluish gray + NL *-ium;* fr. two blue lines in its spectrum — more at CAESIOUS] **:** a silver-white soft ductile metallic element of the alkali metal group that is the most electropositive element known, found usu. with rubidium and lithium (as in pollucite), and used esp. in the form of its compounds and alloys in electron tubes and photoelectric cells — symbol *Cs;* see ELEMENT table

cespitose *var of* CAESPITOSE

¹**cess** \ˈses\ *vt* -ED/-ING/-ES [ME *cessen, sessen,* short for *assessen* — more at ASSESS] *Brit* **:** TAX

²**cess** \"\ *n* -ES **1 :** ASSESSMENT, LEVY, TAX: **a** *now dial Brit* **:** a local tax **b** *Scot* **:** the land tax **c** *India* **:** a tax esp. upon a commodity or for a special purpose ⟨a tea ~⟩ ⟨a road ~⟩ ⟨an education ~⟩ **2 :** an exaction of provisions at a fixed price for the supply of the household and soldiers of the lord lieutenant of Ireland; *broadly* **:** a military exaction or imposition — **out of all cess** *obs* **:** beyond measure **:** in the extreme

³**cess** \"\ *n* -ES [prob. short for *success*] *chiefly Irish* **:** LUCK — used chiefly in the phrase *bad cess to* ⟨wish bad ~ to all his enemies⟩

ces·sa·tion \seˈsāshən, səˈ-\ *n* -S [ME *cessacioun,* fr. MF *cessation,* fr. L *cessation-, cessatio* delay, idleness, fr. *cessatus,* past part. of *cessare* to delay, be idle + *-ion-, -io* -ion — more at CEASE] **1 :** a temporary or final ceasing or discontinuance (as of action) **:** STOP ⟨the ~ of hostilities⟩ ⟨the ~ of relief activities⟩ ⟨the ~ of pain⟩ **2** *obs* **:** INACTIVITY, IDLENESS

ces·sa·tive \ˈsesəd·iv *also* seˈsād· *or* ˈseˌsād·\ *adj* [L *cessatus* + E *-ive*] *of a verb form* **:** expressing cessation

ces·ser \ˈsesə(r)\ *n* -S [MF, fr. *cesser,* v. — more at CEASE] *law* **:** CEASING: **a :** a neglect of a tenant to perform due services or make payment for two years **b :** a ceasing of liability **c** *obs* **:** a ceasing to hold office

ces·sio \ˈses(h)ēˌō\ *n* -S [L] *civil law* **:** act of ceding **:** CESSION; *specif* **:** CESSIO BONORUM

cessio bo·no·rum \-bəˈnōrəm\ *n* [L, lit., cession of goods] *Roman & civil law* **:** a voluntary assignment by a debtor of all his property to his creditors by which he escapes the more painful penalties of insolvency (as liability to arrest and imprisonment) but is not generally discharged from liability for the debts **:** VOLUNTARY BANKRUPTCY

cessio in ju·re \-inˈjürē, -ˈyü-\ *n* [NL, cession in law] **:** IN JURE CESSIO

ces·sion \ˈseshən\ *n* -S [ME, fr. MF, fr. L *cession-, cessio,* fr. *cessus,* past part. of *cedere* to withdraw, yield + *-ion-, -io* -ion — more at CEDE] **1 :** a yielding (as of property or territory or rights) to another **:** act of ceding **:** CONCESSION ⟨no territorial ~*s* in the west were envisaged —Vera M. Dean⟩ ⟨his ~ to her of every right of judgment in the home —Mary Austin⟩ **2** *obs* **:** a yielding to physical or moral force, persuasion, or temptation **:** COMPLIANCE ⟨they shall prevail by ~, by sweetness and counsel —Jeremy Taylor⟩ **3** *civil law* **:** an assignment to another of the rights of a creditor or of ownership of a right of action or a claim **4** *ecclesiastical law* **:** the vacating of a benefice by becoming a bishop or by accepting another without proper dispensation **5** *international law* **:** a transfer usu. evidenced by a treaty of sovereignty over territory by one sovereign state to another apparently willing to accept it

ces·sio·naire \ˌseshəˈna(a)(ə)r\ *n* -s [F *cessionnaire*, fr. *cession*] *civil law* **:** CESSIONARY

ces·sio·nar·i·us \ˌ-ˈna(a)rēəs\ *n, pl* **cessionar·ii** \-ēˌī\ [ML, fr. LL, adj., ceding, fr. L *cession-, cessio* + *-arius* -ary] *Roman law* **:** CESSIONARY

ces·sion·ary \ˈseshəˌnerē\ *n* -ES [ML *cessionarius*] *civil & Scots law* **:** an assignee or grantee of property, a claim, or a debt under a deed of conveyance

ces·sion·ee \ˌseshəˈnē\ *n* -s [*cession* + *-ee*] *Scots law* **:** CESSIONARY

cess·pit \ˈsesˌpit\ *n* -s [*cesspool* + *pit*] **1 :** a pit for the disposal of sewage and other refuse **2 :** something resembling or suggesting a cesspit ⟨a ~ of vice⟩

cess·pool \-ˌpül\ *n* -s [by folk etymology fr. earlier *cesperalle*, alter. of *suspiral* vent, pipe leading to a conduit, cesspool, fr. ME, fr. MF *souspirail* air hole, ventilator, fr. *soupirer, souspirer* to sigh, breathe, fr. L *suspirare* — more at SUSPIRE] **1 :** an underground catch basin that is used where there is no sewer and into which household sewage or other liquid waste is drained to permit leaching of the liquid into the soil **2 :** SINK 2

cest \ˈsest\ *n* -s [MF *ceste*, fr. L *cestus* — more at CESTUS] *archaic* **:** [1]CESTUS

ces·ta \ˈsestə\ *n* -s [Sp, lit., basket, fr. L *cista* — more at CHEST] **:** a narrow curved wicker basket used to catch and propel the ball in jai alai

cesti *pl of* CESTUS

ces·ti·da \ˈsestədə\ *n pl, cap* [NL, fr. *Cestus* + *-ida*] **:** a small order of ctenophores (class Tentaculata) comprising a single family (Cestidae) characterized by a greatly flattened and elongated body

[1]**ces·to·da** \seˈstōdə\ [NL, alter. (influenced by NL *-odes*) of *Cestoidea*] *syn of* [1]CESTOIDEA

[2]**cestoda** \"\ *n pl, cap* [NL, alter. of *Cestoidea*] **:** the subclass of Cestoidea comprising the tapeworms — **ces·to·dan** \(ˈ)seˈstōdᵊn\ *adj* — **ces·tode** \ˈsesˌtōd\ *adj or n* — **ces·toid** \-ˌtȯid\ *adj or n*

ces·to·dar·ia \ˌsestəˈda(a)rēə\ *n pl, cap* [NL, fr. [1]*Cestoda* + *-aria*] **:** a subclass of Cestoidea comprising intestinal parasites of primitive fishes that differ from the tapeworms in possession of a 10-hooked embryo and in the lack of strobilation — **ces·to·dar·i·an** \ˌ==ˈ=rēən\ *adj or n*

ce·sto·des \seˈstō(ˌ)dēz\ [NL, fr. *Cestus* + *-odes*] *syn of* [2]CESTODA

ces·to·di·a·sis \ˌsestəˈdīəsəs\ *n, pl* **cestodia·ses** \-əˌsēz\ [NL, fr. *Cestoda* + *-iasis*] **:** infestation with tapeworms

[1]**ces·toi·dea** \seˈstȯidēə\ *n pl, cap* [NL, fr. *Cestus* + *-oidea* — more at CESTUS] **:** a class of Platyhelminthes comprising dorsoventrally flattened nonciliated parasitic flatworms typically consisting of a differentiated scolex and a chain of proglottides each including a complete more-or-less mature set of reproductive organs — see [2]CESTODA, CESTODARIA — **ces·toi·de·an** \(ˈ)sesˈtȯidēən\ *adj or n*

[2]**cestoidea** \"\ [NL, fr. *Cestus* + *-oidea*] *syn of* CESTIDA

ceston *n* -s [modif. (prob. influenced by Gk *-on*, neut. ending) of L *cestus* — more at CESTUS, -ON] *obs* **:** [1]CESTUS

ces·tra·ci·on \seˈstrāshēˌän\ *n*, cap [NL, fr. Gk *kestra* a kind of fish, hammer + *kiōn* pillar, uvula, division of the nostrils; akin to Arm *siun* pillar] *syn of* HETERODONTUS

[1]**ces·tra·ci·ont** \-nt\ *adj* [NL *Cestraciontidae*] **:** of or relating to the genus *Heterodontus*

[2]**cestraciont** \"\ *n* -s **:** a shark of the genus *Heterodontus*

ces·tra·ci·on·tes \(ˌ)sesˌtrāshēˈänˌtēz\ *n pl, cap* [NL, pl. of *Cestraciont-, Cestracion*, type genus] *in some classifications* **:** an order of primitive sharks

ces·tra·ci·on·ti·dae \-ntəˌdē\ [NL, fr. *Cestraciont-, Cestracion*, type genus + *-idae*] *syn of* HETERODONTIDAE

[1]**ces·tri·an** \ˈsestrēən\ *adj, usu cap* [OE *Cester, Ceaster* Chester + E *-ian*] **1 :** of, relating to, or characteristic of Chester or Cheshire, England **2 :** of, relating to, or characteristic of the people of Chester or Cheshire

[2]**cestrian** \"\ *n* -s *cap* **:** a native or resident of Chester or Cheshire, England

ces·trum \ˈsestrəm\ *n, cap* [NL, fr. Gk *kestron* betony] **:** a large genus of fragrant tropical American shrubs (family Solanaceae) having red, yellow, or white fragrant clustered tubular flowers — see DAY JESSAMINE, NIGHT JASMINE

ces·tui \ˈsed·ē, ˈsestwē\ *n* -s [MF, fr. OF, dat. of *cist* that one, fr. VL *ecce iste*, fr. L *ecce* behold + *iste* this, that; L *ecce* akin to Gk *ekeinos* that one, OSlav *jedinŭ* one, Skt *asau* that one, and to L *cis* on this side; L *iste* akin to L *is* he and to Gk *to* (neut.) the — more at HE, ITERATE, THAT] **:** BENEFICIARY

cestui que trust \-(ˌ)kēˈtrəst, -ˌkwe-ˈ-\ *n, pl* **cestuis que trust** *or* **cestuis que trustent** \-ˈtrəst\ [AF, lit., he for whom (the) trust (is held)] **:** a person who has the equitable and beneficial interest in property the legal interest in which is vested in a trustee

cestui que use \-ˈyüz\ *n, pl* **cestuis que use** [AF, lit., he for whose use (something is held)] **:** a person for whose use land or other property is legally held by another

cestui que vie \-ˈvē\ *n, pl* **cestuis que vie** [AF, lit., he for whose lifetime (something is held)] **1 :** the person whose life measures the duration of an estate **2 :** the person on whose life an insurance policy is written

ces·tum \ˈsestəm\ *n, cap* [NL, alter. of L *cestus* girdle] **:** a genus of ctenophores (order Cestida) including the Venus's-girdle

[1]**ces·tus** \ˈsestəs\ *n, pl* **ces·ti** \-ˌtī\ [L, girdle, belt, fr. Gk *kestos*, fr. *kestos* stitched, embroidered; akin to Gk *kentron* point — more at CENTER] **:** a woman's belt; *esp* **:** a symbolic one worn by a bride

[2]**ces·tus** \"\ [NL, fr. L] *syn of* CESTUM

[3]**ces·tus** \"\ *also* **caes·tus** \", ˈkīs-\ *n, pl* **cestus** *or* **caestus** [L *caestus*, fr. *caedere* to strike — more at CONCISE] **:** a boxer's hand covering in ancient Rome made of leather bands and often loaded with lead or iron

cestus

cestuy *obs var of* CESTUI

cesura *var of* CAESURA

cesure *n* -s [MF *césure*, fr. L *caesura*] *obs* **:** CAESURA

cet- *or* **ceto-** *comb form* [F *cét-, céto-*, NL *cet-, ceto-*, fr. L *cetus* — more at CETE] **:** whale ⟨*cetyl*⟩ ⟨*cetotolite*⟩ ⟨*Cetorhinus*⟩

ce·ta·cea \sēˈtāshēə\ *n pl, cap* [NL, fr. neut. pl. of *cetaceus* cetaceous] **:** an order of completely aquatic mostly marine eutherian mammals consisting of the whales, dolphins, porpoises, and related forms, all having a very large head, a tapering body like a fish and nearly devoid of hair, forelimbs like paddles, no hind limbs, a tail ending in a broad horizontal fin, a large brain, a complex stomach of four or more chambers, and two mammae posterior in position

[1]**ce·ta·cean** \-shən\ *adj* [NL *Cetacea* + E *-an*] **:** of or relating to the Cetacea

[2]**cetacean** \"\ *n* -s **:** an animal of the order Cetacea

ce·ta·ceous \-shəs\ *adj* [NL *cetaceus*, fr. *cet-* + L *-aceus* -aceous] **:** CETACEAN

ce·ta·ce·um \-s(h)ēəm\ *n* -s [NL, fr. neut. of *cetaceus* cetaceous] **:** SPERMACETI

ce·tane \ˈsēˌtān\ *n* -s [*cet-* + *-ane*; fr. its belonging to the cetyl series] **:** a colorless oily hydrocarbon $C_{16}H_{34}$ found in petroleum; normal hexadecane

cetane number *or* **cetane rating** *n* **:** a measure of the ignition value of a diesel fuel oil **:** the percentage by volume of cetane in a mixture of cetane and 1-methylnaphthalene that gives the same ignition lag as the oil being tested

[1]**cete** \ˈsēt\ *n* -s [L *cetus*] **:** WHALE

[2]**ce·te** \ˈsēˌtē\ [NL, fr. L (pl. of *cetus* whale), fr. Gk *kētē* (pl. of *kētos* sea monster, whale)] *syn of* CETACEA

[3]**cete** \ˈsēt\ *n* -s [perh. fr. L *coetus* coming together, assembly, fr. *coitus*, past part. of *coire* to come together, fr. *co-* + *ire* to go — more at ISSUE] *of badgers* **:** GROUP, COMPANY

ce·tene \ˈsēˌtēn\ *n* -s [ISV *cet-* + *-ene*; orig. formed as F *cétène*; fr. its being derived from spermaceti] **:** an oily hydrocarbon $C_{16}H_{32}$ of the ethylene series obtained by dehydrating cetyl alcohol — called also *1-hexadecene*

cet·er·ach \ˈsed·əˌrak\ *n* [ML *ceterah*, fr. Ar *shītaraj*, fr. Per *shitarakh*] **1** -s **:** SCALE FERN **2** *cap* [NL, fr. ML *ceterah*] **:** a small genus of mainly Old World ferns (family Polypodiaceae) typified by the scale fern

ce·te·ris pa·ri·bus *also* **cae·te·ris pa·ri·bus** *or* **coe·te·ris pa·ri·bus** \ˌkād·ərəsˈsparəbəs, ˌse-, ˌchā-, -əˌrēs-, -ˌbüs\ *adv* [NL, other things being equal] **:** if all other relevant things (as factors or elements) correspond or remain unaltered ⟨staple-growing states are, *ceteris paribus*, more favorable to slave labor than manufacturing states —Joseph Dorfman⟩

ce·tin \ˈsētᵊn\ *n* -s [ISV *cet-* + *-in*; orig. formed as F *cétine*] **:** a crystalline fat $C_{32}H_{64}O_2$ constituting the chief component of spermaceti **:** cetyl palmitate

ce·ti·o·sau·rus \ˌsēd·ē(ˌ)ōˈsȯrəs, ˌsēshē-\ *n, cap* [NL, fr. Gk *kēteios* of sea monsters, monstrous (fr. *kētos* sea monster, whale) + NL *-saurus*] **:** a genus of primitive generalized sauropod dinosaurs found in the Jurassic of England

cet·ole·ic acid \ˌsēd·+...-\ *n* [*cet-* + *oleic*] **:** a crystalline unsaturated fatty acid $C_{21}H_{41}COOH$ occurring in the form of esters in many fish oils (as those from sharks' livers)

ce·tol·o·gy \sēˈtäləjē\ *n* -ES [ISV *cet-* + *-logy*] **:** a branch of zoology dealing with the whales

ce·to·mi·mid \ˌsēd·əˈmīməd\ *n* -s [NL *Cetomimidae*] **:** a fish of the family Cetomimidae

ce·to·mim·i·dae \-ˈmiməˌdē\ *n pl, cap* [NL, fr. *Cetomimus*, type genus (fr. *cet-* + *-mimus*) + *-idae*] **:** a family of small feeble degenerate deep-sea fishes (order Iniomi) resembling whales in shape and in having smooth black skin

ce·to·mor·pha \-ˈmȯrfə\ *n pl, cap* [NL, fr. *cet-* + *-morpha*] **:** a formerly recognized subdivision of Mammalia consisting of the Sirenia and Cetacea — **ce·to·mor·phic** \ˌ==ˈ=fik\ *adj*

ce·to·ni·an \səˈtōnēən, -nyən\ *adj* [NL *Cetonia* + E *-an*] **:** of or relating to the Cetoniidae

ce·to·ni·i·dae \ˌsēd·əˈnīəˌdē\ *n pl, cap* [NL, fr. *Cetonia*, type genus (irreg. fr. Gk *kētos* sea monster) + *-idae*] **:** a family of rather large brightly colored diurnal beetles comprising the sap chafers, having the mandibles thin and feeble and the mouth parts adapted to soft or liquid food, and being closely related to and often included as a subfamily of the Scarabaeidae — see GOLIATH BEETLE

ce·to·rhi·nus \-ˈrīnəs\ *n, cap* [NL, fr. *cet-* + *-rhinus*] **:** a genus that includes the basking shark as its only living species and is commonly placed in the family Lamnidae or sometimes made the type of a separate family (Cetorhinidae)

ce·to·there \ˈsēd·əˌthi(ə)r\ *n* -s [NL *Cetotherium*] **:** one of the Cetotheriidae — **ce·to·the·re·an** \ˌ==ˈthirēən\ *adj*

ce·to·the·ri·i·dae \ˌsēd·ōthəˈrīəˌdē\ *n pl, cap* [NL, fr. *Cetotherium*, type genus (fr. *cet-* + *-therium*) + *-idae*] **:** a family of extinct whalebone whales

cet·oto·lite \sēˈtōd·ᵊlˌīt\ *n* -s [*cet-* + *otolite* "ear bone"] **:** a fossil bone of a whale; *usu* **:** one of the often detached and well-preserved tympanic or petrosal bones

ce·trar·ia \səˈtra(a)rēə\ *n, cap* [NL, fr. L *caetra, cetra* short Spanish shield + NL *-aria*; fr. the shape of the apothecia] **:** a genus of foliose lichens (family Parmeliaceae) chiefly of northern latitudes — see ICELAND MOSS — **ce·trar·ic** \-ˈtrarik\ *adj*

cetraric acid *n* [ISV *cetrar-* (fr. NL *Cetraria*) + *-ic*] **:** a bitter crystalline acid that is obtained from lichens (esp. *Cetraria islandica*)

ce·tyl \ˈsēd·ᵊl *also* ˈse-\ *n* -s [ISV *cet-* + *-yl*; fr. the occurrence of some of its compounds in spermaceti] **:** a univalent radical $C_{16}H_{33}$ compounds of which occur in waxes (as beeswax, spermaceti) **:** normal hexadecyl

cetyl alcohol *n* **:** a waxy crystalline solid alcohol $C_{16}H_{33}OH$ found in the form of palmitate in spermaceti and used in pharmaceutical and cosmetic preparations (as creams and lotions) and in making detergents — called also *1-hexadecanol*

ce·tyl·pyridinium chloride \"+...-\ *n* [*cetyl* + *pyridinium*] **:** a white powder consisting of a quaternary ammonium salt $C_{21}H_{38}ClN.H_2O$ and used as a cationic detergent and antiseptic

ceu·to·rhyn·chus \ˌsüd·əˈriŋkəs\ *n, cap* [NL, fr. *ceuto-* (irreg. fr. Gk *keuthein* to hide) + *-rhynchus* — more at HIDE] **:** a large nearly cosmopolitan genus of weevils (family Curculionidae) including a number of forms very destructive to cruciferous plants

cev·a·dil·la \ˌsevəˈdilə, -dē(y)ə\ *n* -s [Sp *cebadilla* — more at SABADILLA] **:** SABADILLA

cev·a·dine \ˈsevəˌdēn, -ˌdən\ *n* -s [*cevadilla* + *-ine*] **:** a poisonous crystalline alkaloid $C_{32}H_{49}NO_9$ found in sabadilla seeds and green hellebore — called also *crystalline veratrine*

ce·va's theorem \ˈchāvəz-, -ev-\ *n, usu cap C* [after Giovanni *Ceva* †ab 1734 Ital. mathematician, its formulator] **:** a theorem in geometry: if three lines from a point *O* to the vertices *A*, *B*, and *C* of a triangle meet the opposite sides in *A′*, *B′*, and *C′* respectively then $AB'.BC'.CA'+AC'.BA'.CB' = 0$ and conversely if this relation holds the three lines *AA′*, *BB′*, *CC′* meet in a point

ce·vi·an \ˈchāvēən, -ev-\ *n* -s *often cap* [Giovanni *Ceva* + E *-ian*] **:** a straight line drawn through a vertex of a triangle or of a tetrahedron and intersecting the opposite side or face

ce·vi·che *var of* SEVICHE

cev·ine \ˈsevˌēn, ˈsēˌvēn\ *n* -s [ISV *cevadine*] **:** a crystalline alkaloid $C_{27}H_{43}NO_8$ found in sabadilla seeds and formed from cevadine by hydrolysis

ce·vi·tam·ic acid \ˌsēˌvīˈtamik-\ *n* [*ce-* (fr. *c*) + *vitamin* + *-ic*] **:** ASCORBIC ACID

cewa *usu cap, var of* CHEWA

cey·lon \səˈlän, sē-,sā-\ *adj, usu cap* [fr. *Ceylon*, island south of India] **:** of or from Ceylon **:** of the kind or style prevalent in Ceylon **:** CEYLONESE

ceylon bowstring hemp *n, usu cap C* **:** a bowstring hemp (*Sansevieria zeylanica*)

ceylon cinnamon *n, usu cap 1st C* **:** the bark of a Ceylonese tree (*Cinnamomum zeylanicum*)

ceylon cinnamon oil *n, usu cap 1st C* **:** CINNAMON-BARK OIL

ceylon creeper *n, usu cap 1st C* **:** IVY-ARUM

[1]**cey·lon·ese** \ˌsāləˈnēz, ˌsē-, -ēs; ˌsēˌläˈn-, ˌsā-; səˌläˈn-, sē-,sā-\ *adj, usu cap* [*Ceylon* + E *-ese*] **1 :** of, relating to, or characteristic of Ceylon **2 :** of, relating to, or characteristic of the people of Ceylon

[2]**ceylonese** \"\ *n, pl* **ceylonese** *cap* **:** a native or inhabitant of Ceylon; *esp* **:** SINHALESE

ceylon gooseberry *n, usu cap C* **:** KETEMBILLA

cey·lon·ite *also* **cey·lan·ite** \səˈläˌnīt, sē-,sā-\ *n* -s [earlier *ceylanite*, fr. F, fr. *Ceylan* Ceylon, its locality + F *-ite*] **:** a dark-colored spinel — called also *pleonaste*

ceylon lily *n, usu cap C* **:** a large tropical Asiatic and African bulbous herb (*Crinum zeylanicum*) of the amaryllis family having white flowers striped with red

ceylon moss *n, usu cap C* **:** an East Indian red alga (*Gracilaria lichenoides*) that is one of the chief sources of agar

ceylon oak *n, usu cap C* **:** KUSAM

ceylon pearl oyster *n, usu cap C* **:** a small pearl oyster (*Pinctada vulgaris*) widely distributed in the Indian ocean

ceylon tea *n, usu cap C* **:** a pekoe tea produced in Ceylon

ceylon tea tree *n, usu cap C* **:** a tropical Asiatic tree (*Elaeodendron glaucum*) of the family Celastraceae having leaves like those of the tea plant

ceys·sa·tite \ˈsāsəˌtīt\ *n* -s [F, fr. *Ceyssat*, France, its locality + F *-ite*] **:** RANDANNITE

cf *abbr* **1** calf **2** *pronounced like* COMPARE *also* (ˈ)sēˈef *sometimes* kənˈfər *or* -fə\ [L *confer*, imp. of *conferre* to compare — more at CONFER] compare

CF *abbr* **1** cannot find **2** [ML *cantus firmus*] plain chant **3** carried forward **4** center field **5** center forward **6** *often not cap* centrifugal force **7** corresponding fellow **8** cost and freight

Cf *symbol* californium

CFH *abbr, often not cap* cubic feet per hour

CFI *abbr, sometimes not cap* cost, freight, and insurance

c fiber *n, usu cap C* **:** an unmyelinated nerve fiber esp. of the autonomic system

c flat \ˈ=ˈ=\ *n, usu cap C* **1 :** the keynote of C-flat major **2 :** the tone a half step below C

c–flat major \ˈ=,=ˈ==\ *n, usu cap C* **:** the major musical key having a signature of seven flats

CFM *abbr, often not cap* cubic feet per minute

CFO *abbr* canceling former order

CFS *abbr, often not cap* cubic feet per second

cg *abbr* centigram

CG *abbr* **1** captain general **2** *sometimes not cap* center of gravity **3** coast guard **4** combat group **5** commanding general **6** commissary general **7** complete games **8** comptroller general **9** consul general

CGA *abbr* **1** certified general accountant **2** cargo's proportion of general average

cge *abbr* carriage

cgm *abbr* centigram

cgo *abbr* **1** cargo **2** contango

CGS *abbr* **1** *usu not cap* centimeter-gram-second **2** chief of general staff

ch *abbr* **1** chain **2** chairman **3** chaldron **4** *usu cap C* champion **5** chancellor; chancery **6** chaplain **7** chapter **8** check **9** checkered **10** chervonets **11** chest **12** chestnut **13** chief **14** child **15** choice **16** choir organ **17** choke **18** chromogenic **19** church

CH *abbr* **1** case-hardened **2** central heating **3** clearing house **4** compass heading **5** courthouse **6** customhouse

chaac *or* **chac** \ˈchäk\ *n* -s *sometimes cap* [Sp *chaac, chac*, fr. Maya] **:** one of the Mayan gods of rain and fertility — usu. used in pl.

cha·ba·ka·no \ˌchäbəˈkä(ˌ)nō\ *n, usu cap* [PhilSp *chabacano*, fr. Sp, insipid, tasteless, crude, awkward] **:** a Spanish-based pidgin language spoken in and around Zamboanga, Philippines

chab·a·zite *or* **chab·a·site** \ˈkabəˌzīt\ *n* -s [G *chabasit*, fr. F *chabasie* (fr. LGk *chabazios*, MS var. of *chalazios* precious stone resembling a hailstone, fr. Gk *chalazios* of hail, fr. *chalaza* hailstone) + G *-it* -ite — more at CHALAZA] **:** a zeolite $CaAl_2Si_4O_{12}.6H_2O$ consisting of a hydrous silicate of calcium and aluminum that occurs in glassy rhombohedral crystals, varies in color from white to yellow or red, and is used in some water softeners (hardness 4–5, sp. gr. 2.08–2.16)

chaber *n, pl* **chaberim** *var of* HAVER

cha·ber·tia \shəˈberd·ēə, -bər-\ *n, cap* [NL, fr. Philibert *Chabert* †1814 Fr. veterinary + NL *-ia*] **:** a genus of nematode worms (family Strongylidae) infesting the colon of sheep and other ruminants and causing a bloody diarrhea

cha·blis \ˈsha(ˌ)blē, shäˈblē\ *n, pl* **chablis** \-lēz\ *usu cap* [F, fr. *Chablis*, France, where it is made] **1 :** a dry white Burgundy table wine of a straw-gold to pale amber color produced in the department of Yonne, France **2 :** a wine resembling Chablis and retailed under the name Chablis usu. with the addition of its geographical designation ⟨California *Chablis*⟩

cha·bu·tra *or* **cha·boo·tra** \chəˈbü·trə, -ü-,trä\ *n* -s [Hindi *cabūtrā*] *India* **:** a raised platform **:** TERRACE, DAIS

cha·ca·te \chəˈkäd·ē\ *n* -s [MexSp, fr. Nahuatl *chacatl*] **:** a small shrub (*Krameria grayi*) of Mexico and the southwestern U.S. the bark of which furnishes a brownish red dye

[1]**chace** *var of* CHASE

[2]**chace** \ˈchās\ *n, pl* **chaces** \-ās(əz)\ [MF *chace, chasse*, lit., chase — more at CHASE] **:** a 14th century French part-song in the form of a canon at the unison

[1]**cha-cha** \ˈshä,shä\ *n* -s *usu cap 1st C & often cap 2d C* [origin unknown] **:** one of a group of poor whites of French ancestry in the Virgin islands

[2]**cha-cha** \ˈchä,chä\ *also* **cha-cha-cha** \ˈchä,chäˈchä\ *n* -s [AmerSp (Cuba) *cha-cha-cha*] **:** a fast rhythmic ballroom dance of Latin-American origin with a basic pattern of three steps and a shuffle

cha·cha·la·ca \ˌchächəˈläkə\ *n* -s [Sp, fr. Nahuatl, twittering of a bird, of imit. origin] **:** any of several large chiefly arboreal guans of *Ortalis* and related genera that somewhat resemble wild turkeys but are longer legged and have a well-developed feathered crest, that are native to Central America and Mexico with one variety (*O. vetula macalli*) extending into southern Texas, and that are highly regarded as game birds

chachamim *or* **chachomim** *pl of* CHOCHEM

cha·cha·poya \ˌchächəˈpȯiə\ *n, pl* **chachapoya** *or* **chachapoyas** *usu cap* [Sp, of AmerInd origin] **1 :** an unusually light-skinned Indian people of the Chinchaisuyu group **2 :** a member of the Chachapoya people

chack \ˈchak\ *n* -s [Sc *chack* to snap with the teeth, bite, of imit. origin] *chiefly Scot* **:** a bite or small portion of food **:** SNACK

chack·le \ˈchakəl\ *vi* -ED/-ING/-S [prob. blend of [1]*chatter* and [1]*cackle*] *dial Eng* **:** CACKLE, RATTLE

chac·ma \ˈchakmə\ *n* -s [Hottentot] **:** a large brownish black baboon (*Papio comatus*) of southern Africa often a serious pest of cultivated crops

chac·mool *or* **chac·mol** \ˈchäkˌmōl\ *n* -s *usu cap* [Maya *Chac*, a god + *mool* paw] **:** a reclining figure with flexed knees found in the prehistoric remains of Mexico and Central America, esp. in Yucatan

cha·co·bo \chäˈkō(ˌ)bō\ *n, pl* **chacobo** *or* **chacobos** *usu cap* [Sp, of AmerInd origin] **1 a :** a Panoan people of northern Bolivia **b :** a member of such people **2 :** the language of the Chacobo people

cha·conne *also* **cha·con** \shäˈkȯn, sha-,shə-,shä-, -än,-on,-ōn\ *or* **cha·co·na** \chäˈkōnə\ *n* -s [F & Sp; F *chaconne*, fr. Sp *chacona*, prob. of imit. origin; fr. the sound of castanets used in the dance] **:** an old orig. Spanish dance in moderate three-quarter measure resembling the slower passacaglia; *also* **:** a musical composition with stress on the second beat and consisting typically of continuous variations based on a repeated succession of chords

cha·cra \ˈchäkrə\ *n* -s [AmerSp, fr. Quechua *chakhra*] *in So. America* **:** a small farm or ranch

[1]**chad** \chəd, (ˈ)chad\ [alter. of ME *ich hadde*] *dial Eng* **:** I had

[2]**chad** \ˈchad, -aa(ə)d\ *n* -s [prob. alter. of *shad*] **:** a young European sea bream

[3]**chad** \"\ *n* -s [perh. fr. Sc, gravel] **:** small pieces of paper or cardboard produced in punching paper tape or punch cards; *also* **:** a piece of chad

[4]**chad** \"\ *n* -s *usu cap* **:** a branch of the Afro-Asiatic language family comprising a large number of languages of northern Nigeria and Cameroons — see AFRO-ASIATIC LANGUAGES table

[5]**chad** \"\ *adj, usu cap* [fr. *Chad*, republic formerly part of French Equatorial Africa] **:** of or relating to Chad **:** of the kind or style prevalent in Chad

chadarim *pl of* CHEDER

chad·ian \ˈchadēən\ *n* -s *cap* [*Chad*, country in central Africa + E *-ian*] **:** a native or inhabitant of Chad — **chadian** *adj, usu cap*

chadlock *var of* CHARLOCK

cha·dor *or* **cha·dar** *or* **chud·dar** *or* **chud·der** *also* **chad·dar** \ˈchədə(r)\ *n* -s [Hindi *caddar*, fr. Per *chaddar*] **:** a large cloth used as a combination head covering, veil, and shawl usu. by women among Muslim and Hindu peoples esp. in India and Iran

chae·nac·tis \kēˈnaktəs\ *n, cap* [NL, fr. Gk *chainein* to gape + *aktis* ray; akin to L *hiare* to gape — more at YAWN, ACTIN-] **:** a genus of herbs (family Compositae) found in the western U.S. and characterized by entire or pinnately lobed leaves and long peduncled heads of white or yellow flowers

chae·no·me·les \ˌkēnəˈmē(ˌ)lēz\ *n, cap* [NL, fr. *chaeno-* (fr. Gk *chainein*) + *-meles* (irreg. fr. Gk *mēlon* apple, fruit) — more at MALUS] **:** a genus of Asiatic shrubs (family Rosaceae) comprising the flowering quinces and having alternate serrate leaves, 5-petaled flowers, and many seeds in each cell of the ovary — see JAPANESE QUINCE

chae·ro·pus \ˈkirəpəs\ *n, cap* [NL, fr. *chaer-* (irreg. fr. Gk *choiros* pig) + *-pus*; fr. the resemblance of the forefeet to those of a pig; akin to L *horrēre* to bristle — more at HORROR] **:** a genus of marsupial mammals consisting of the pig-footed bandicoots

chaet- *or* **chaeto-** *comb form* [NL, fr. Gk *chaitē*] **:** bristle **:** hair ⟨*Chaetodon*⟩ ⟨*chaetophorous*⟩

chae·ta \ˈkēd·ə\ *n, pl* **chae·tae** \-ēˌtē, -ēd·(ˌ)ē\ [NL, fr. Gk *chaitē* long flowing hair; akin to MIr *gaiset* bristle, Av *gaēsa* curly hair] **:** SPINE, BRISTLE, SETA

-chae·ta \ˈkēd·ə, -ētə\ *n comb form* [NL, fr. Gk *-chaitēs* -haired, fr. *chaitē*] **1** *also* **-chae·tes** \ˈkē(ˌ)ēz, -ēˌtēz\ *or* **-chae·tus** \ˈkēd·əs, -ētəs\ **:** haired one **:** hairlike one — in generic names ⟨*Spirochaeta*⟩ ⟨*Connochaetes*⟩ **2** *pl* **-chae·tae** \ˈkēd·(ˌ)ē, -ēˌtē\ **:** bristle (of a specified type) ⟨*microchaeta*⟩

chae·tal \ˈkēd·ᵊl, -ētᵊl\ *adj* [NL *chaeta* + E *-al*] **:** of or relating to bristles or setae

chae·te·tes \kē'tēd·ēz\ *n, cap* [NL, irreg. fr. Gk *chaitē* long flowing hair] **:** a genus (the type of the large extinct family Chaetetidae) of fossil corals that have the skeleton composed of slender closely contiguous tubes and are common in the Carboniferous limestones — **chae·te·tid** \-tēd·ə̇d\ *adj or n*

chae·tig·er·ous \kē'tij(ə)rəs\ *adj* [NL *chaeta* + E *-i-* + *-gerous*] **:** bearing bristles or setae

chae·to·cer·cus \,kēd·ō'sərkəs\ *n, cap* [NL, fr. *chaet-* + Gk *kerkos* tail] **:** a genus of Australian desert-dwelling marsupial mice

chae·to·dip·ter·us \-'diptərəs\ *n, cap* [NL, fr. *chaet-* + Gk *dipteros* two-winged — more at DIPTEROUS] **:** a genus of spadefishes (family Ephippidae) found in warm seas along both coasts of America and distinguished by protractile premaxillaries and dorsal spines of unequal length

chae·to·don \'⸗⸗,dän\ *n* [NL, fr. *chaet-* + *-odon*] **1** *cap* **:** the type genus of Chaetodontidae **2** -s **:** any fish of the genus *Chaetodon*

chaetodon

chae·to·don·ti·dae \,⸗⸗'däntə,dē\ *n pl, cap* [NL, fr. *Chaetodont-, Chaetodon,* type genus + *-idae*] **:** a large family of percoid tropical marine fishes common about coral reefs that includes the butterfly fishes

chae·to·gas·ter \'⸗⸗,gastə(r), ,⸗⸗'⸗⸗\ *n, cap* [NL, fr. *chaet-* + *-gaster*] **:** a common widely distributed genus of small transparent oligochaete worms (family Naididae) that are parasites on gastropods or free-living in fresh water

¹chae·tog·nath \'kēd,äg,nath, -d·əg-\ *n* -s [NL *Chaetognatha*] **:** one of the Chaetognatha **:** ARROWWORM

²chaetognath \"\ *adj* **:** of or relating to the Chaetognatha

chae·tog·na·tha \kē'tägnəthə\ *n pl, cap* [NL, fr. *chaet-* + *-gnatha*] **:** a group of small active transparent marine worms of uncertain systematic position with horizontal lateral and caudal fins and a row of movable curved spines at each side of the mouth and comprising the arrowworms — see SAGITTA, SPADELLA — **chae·tog·na·than** \-thən\ *adj* — **chae·tog·na·thous** \-thəs\ *adj*

chae·to·mi·um \kē'tōmēəm\ *n, cap* [NL, fr. Gk *chaitōma* plume (fr. *chaitē* hair) + NL *-ium* — more at CHAETA] **:** a genus (the type of the family Chaetomiaceae) of ascomycetous fungi that are characterized by long straight, curled, or branched hairs on the usu. dull-colored perithecia esp. on their upper surfaces and that include several fungi destructive to paper and other materials and to some plastics

chae·toph·o·ra \-'täf(ə)rə\ *n, cap* [NL, fr. *chaet-* + *-phora*] **:** the type genus of Chaetophoraceae

chae·toph·o·ra·ce·ae \⸗,⸗ə'rāsē,ē\ *n pl, cap* [NL, fr. *Chaetophora,* type genus + *-aceae*] **:** a large family of widely distributed green algae (order Ulotrichales) — see CHAETOPHORALES — **chae·toph·o·ra·ceous** \⸗;⸗⸗;⸗shəs\ *adj*

chae·toph·o·ra·les \-(,)lēz\ *n pl, cap* [NL, fr. *Chaetophora* + *-ales*] *in some classifications* **:** a large order of green algae that includes the families Chaetophoraceae, Trentepohliaceae, Coleochaetaceae, and related families and also the Oedogoniaceae and that is characterized by a plant body typically consisting of two systems of branching filaments one of which is prostrate and attached to the substratum and the other upright and often possessing hairs or bristles — compare ULOTRICHALES

chae·toph·o·rous \kē'täf(ə)rəs\ *adj* [*chaet-* + *-phorous*] **:** CHAETIGEROUS

chae·to·pod *or* **che·to·pod** \'kēd·ə,päd\ *n* -s [NL *Chaetopoda*] **:** one of the Chaetopoda

chae·top·o·da \kē'täpədə\ *n pl, cap* [NL, fr. *chaet-* + *-poda*] *in many classifications* **:** a major division (usu. a class) of annelid worms containing the Polychaeta and Oligochaeta as subdivisions — **chae·top·o·dan** \-dən, -dᵊn\ *adj* — **chae·top·o·dous** \-dəs\ *adj*

chae·top·ter·us \⸗'tərəs\ *n, cap* [NL, fr. *chaet-* + *-pterus*] **:** a genus (the type of the small family Chaetopteridae) of large marine polychaete worms that inhabit parchmentlike U-shaped tubes open at both ends, are highly bioluminescent, and have one pair of large lateral appendages and several broad fanlike membranous folds by which they maintain a current of water within the tube

chae·to·tac·tic \¦kēd·ō¦taktik\ *adj* [*chaet-* + *-tactic*] **:** of or relating to chaetotaxy

chae·to·taxy \'kēd·ō,taksē\ *n* -ES [*chaet-* + *-taxy*] **1 :** the arrangement or pattern of bristles on an arthropod (as a mosquito, mite, or larva) **2 :** the study of chaetotaxy

chae·tu·ra \kē'türə, kē'tyü-\ *n, cap* [NL, fr. *chaet-* + *-ura*] **:** a genus of swifts having stiff spinelike projecting shafts to the tail feathers and including the chimney swift

chaetura black *n, often cap C* **:** a nearly neutral slightly olive black that is very slightly darker and more neutral than London smoke

chaetura drab *n, often cap C* **:** BEAR 6

-chaetus — see -CHAETA

¹chafe \'chāf, *esp dial* -af\ *vb* -ED/-ING/-S [ME *chaufen* to warm, fr. MF *chaufer,* fr. (assumed) VL *calfare,* alter. of L *calefacere,* fr. *calēre* to be warm + *facere* to make — more at CALDRON, DO] *vt* **1** *obs* **:** to make warm (as the emotions) **:** EXCITE ⟨~ the blood and spirits⟩ **2 :** IRRITATE, ANNOY, VEX ⟨the noise of the children playing *chafed* her⟩ **3 :** to warm by rubbing esp. with the hands ⟨*chafing* his hands together as though they were cold —Elizabeth Bowen⟩ **4 a :** to rub so as to wear away **:** ABRADE ⟨the schooner *chafed* her sides against the dock⟩ **b :** to irritate or make sore by or as if by rubbing ⟨the tight collar *chafed* his neck⟩ ~ *vi* **1 :** to feel irritation or discontent **:** be impatient (as with restraint or restriction) **:** FRET ⟨he *chafed* at the forced inaction —F.Tennyson Jesse⟩ **2 :** to rub with such pressure (as of one body against another) that much wear or irritation is caused ⟨a rope weakened by *chafing* against the rail⟩ **3 :** to dash or toss violently (as of the sea) **:** press or strain esp. against restraint ⟨the river ~*s* against the rocky shore⟩

²chafe \"\ *n* -s **1 :** a state of vexation **:** PASSION, RAGE ⟨the cardinal in a ~ sent for him —William Camden⟩ **2 :** injury or wear caused by friction; *also* **:** RUBBING, FRICTION **3 :** the usu. leather shield that covers the ring of a saddle cinch to prevent it from chafing the horse

chafe iron *n* **:** CRAMP IRON 2

¹cha·fer \'chāfə(r), -af-, -aif-\ *n* -s [ME *cheafer,* fr. OE *ceafor;* akin to OHG *kevar* beetle, OE *ceafl* jowl — more at JOWL] **:** any of various beetles of Scarabaeidae and closely related families esp. of large or medium size, clumsy in flight, and slow in movement (as the june beetle, the rose chafer, and esp. the cockchafer)

²chafer *n* -s [ME *chaufour,* modif. of MF *chaufoire,* fr. *chaufer* to warm — more at CHAFE] *obs* **:** a portable grate **:** CHAFING DISH

³chaf·er \'chāfə(r)\ *n* -s [¹*chafe* + *-er*] **:** a strip of rubberized fabric covering the bead of a tire as a protection from chafing against the rim

chafe·wax \'chāf,waks\ *or* **chaff·wax** \-af-\ *n* [¹*chafe* (to heat) + *wax;* trans. of F *chauffe-cire*] **:** the holder of a now abolished English chancery office whose duty was to prepare wax for sealing documents

¹chaff \'chaf, -aa(ə)f,-aif,-āf\ *n* -s [ME *chaf, chef,* fr. OE *ceaf;* akin to MD *caf* chaff, OHG *cheva* husk] **1 :** the glumes, husks, or other seed coverings or small pieces of stems or leaves (as of grains and grasses) separated from the seed in threshing or processing **2 :** straw or hay cut up fine for the food of cattle **3 :** something comparatively light and worthless **:** a worthless or useless product of an endeavor ⟨in the book are a few practical suggestions; all else is ~⟩ **4 :** the scales borne on the receptacle among the florets in the heads of many composite plants **5 :** WINDOW 4

²chaff \"\ *vt* -ED/-ING/-S **:** to cut into chaff

³chaff \"\ *archaic var of* CHAFE

⁴chaff \"\ *n* -s [prob. fr. ¹*chaff*] **:** light jesting talk **:** BANTER, TEASING, RAILLERY ⟨no end of ~ about my way of speaking —G.B.Shaw⟩

⁵chaff \"\ *vb* -ED/-ING/-S [prob. fr. ⁴*chaff*] *vt* **:** to make fun of in a good-natured way **:** tease good-naturedly ⟨they ~*ed* me for leaving so early —Lucien Price⟩ ~ *vi* **:** to make fun of or joke about someone or something **:** JEST, BANTER

chaffcutter \'⸗,⸗⸗\ *n* **:** a machine for cutting up straw or hay for fodder

¹chaf·fer \'chafə(r), -aif-\ *n* -s [ME *chaffare, cheffare, cheapfare,* fr. *chep* trade, bargaining + *fare* journey — more at CHEAP, FARE] **1** *obs* **a :** buying and selling **:** TRADE **b :** articles of merchandise **:** WARES **2** *archaic* **:** a haggling about price **:** BARGAINING

²chaffer \"\ *vb* **chaffered; chaffered; chaffering** \-f(ə)riŋ\ **chaffers** [ME *chaffaren,* fr. *chaffare,* bargain, n.] *vi* **1** *obs* **:** to buy and sell **:** do business **:** TRADE **2 :** to discuss terms **:** haggle esp. over a price **:** BARGAIN ⟨the . . . ruffian with whom he had ~*ed* to move in the piano —Marcia Davenport⟩ ⟨~ over the price of the room —C.S.Forester⟩ **3** *Brit* **:** to exchange small talk **:** CHAT, CHATTER ~ *vt* **1** *obs* **a :** to buy or sell **:** deal in trading ⟨~ high offices of state⟩ **b :** EXCHANGE, BARTER ⟨~ honor for gold⟩ **2 :** to bargain for **:** alter (as a price) by bargaining — often used with *down* ⟨slash prices in half and ~ them down to nothing —*Johannesburg Sunday Express*⟩

³chaff·er \'chafə(r), -aaf-,-aif-,-āf-\ *n* -s [¹*chaff* + *-er*] **:** a usu. adjustable sieve at the rear end of the grain pan of a threshing machine

chaff–flower \'⸗,⸗\ *n* [¹*chaff*] **:** a tropical herb (*Achyranthes aspera*) having slender chaffy somewhat prickly flower spikes

chaf·finch \'cha(,)finch\ *n* -ES [ME *chaffynche,* fr. OE *ceaffinc,* fr. *ceaf* chaff + *finc* finch] **:** a common Old World finch (*Fringilla coelebs*) often kept as a cage bird and having in the male a reddish breast plumage and a cheerful but not much varied song

chaff·ing·ly *adv* **:** in a chaffing manner

chaff·less \'⸗ləs\ *adj* **:** being without chaff

chaffron *or* **chafron** *var of* CHAMFRON

chaff scale *n* **1 :** a chaffy or chafflike scale **:** PALEA **2 :** a small pale rounded scale insect (*Parlatoria pergandii*) injurious to citrus and other cultivated plants

chaffseed \'⸗,⸗\ *n* [¹*chaff* + *seed*] **:** a leafy maritime herb (*Schwalbea americana*) of the family Scrophulariaceae that is native to eastern No. America, has irregular yellowish purple flowers in showy sparse spikes, and produces chaffy seeds

chaffwax *var of* CHAFEWAX

chaffweed \'⸗,⸗\ *n* [¹*chaff* + *weed*] **:** a low glabrous weedy branching herb (*Centunculus minimus*) of the family Primulaceae having short dry chafflike leaves — called also *bastard pimpernel, false pimpernel*

chaffy \'chafē, -aaf-,-aif-,-āf-, -fi\ *adj* -ER/-EST [¹*chaff* + *-y*] **1 a :** abounding in or covered with chaff **b :** consisting of or resembling chaff **2 a :** LIGHT, WORTHLESS ⟨an empty ~ book by a foolish ~ fellow⟩ **b :** having a bantering quality **:** CHAFFING ⟨teasing in a ~ tone⟩ **3 a :** like paleae **b :** covered with scales

chafing *n* -s **:** inflammation on opposing skin surfaces resulting from friction

chaf·ing dish \'chāfiŋ-\ *n* [ME, fr. *chafing,* fr. pres. part. of *chafen, chaufen* to warm — more at CHAFE] **1** *archaic* **:** a dish holding burning coals used esp. for cooking or warming food **2 :** a cooking utensil supplied with a source of heat (as electricity or an alcohol lamp) and used to cook food at the table

chafing dish 2

chafing gear *n* **:** a usu. rope or canvas covering placed on a line or spar to protect it from chafe

chaft \'chaft\ *n* -s [ME, prob. fr. ON *kjaptr* — more at JOWL] *dial Brit* **:** JAW, CHAP

cha·ga *or* **chag·ga** \'chägə\ *n, pl* **chaga** *or* **chagas** *or* **chagga** *or* **chaggas** *usu cap* **1 a :** a tall agricultural Negro people of the slopes of Mt. Kilimanjaro, Tanganyika **b :** a member of such people **2 :** a Bantu language of the Chaga people

cha·gas' disease \'shägəs(əz)-, -ag-\ *n, usu cap C* [after Carlos *Chagas* †1934 Braz. physician who described it] **:** a trypanosomiasis of tropical America marked by prolonged high fever, edema, and enlargement of spleen, liver, and lymph nodes and caused by a flagellate (*Trypanosoma cruzi*) which is transmitted by reduviid bugs and occurs in flagellated form in the blood and as leishmanial reproductive forms in tissue (as heart muscle)

chagigah *var of* HAGIGAH

cha·go·ma \shə'gōmə\ *n, pl* **chagomas** \-məz\ *or* **chago·ma·ta** \-məd·ə\ [NL, fr. Carlos *Chagas* + NL *-oma*] **:** a tumorlike swelling that appears at the site of infection in Chagas' disease

cha·gres fever \'chägrə̇s-, -ag-\ *n, usu cap C* [fr. *Chagres* river, Panama, where it occurs] **:** a malignant malarial fever occurring along the Chagres river in Panama

¹cha·grin \shə'grin, *Brit usu* 'shagrin *or* shə'grēn\ *n* -s [F, fr. *chagrin,* adj.] **1** *obs* **:** disturbance of mind resulting from care or anxiety **:** WORRY **:** depression of spirits **:** MELANCHOLY **2 a :** vexation, disquietude, or distress of mind brought on by humiliation, hurt pride, disappointment, or consciousness of failure or error ⟨the unhappy defects of her family, a subject of yet heavier ~ —Jane Austen⟩ **b chagrins** *pl, archaic* **:** circumstances causing chagrin **:** TROUBLES, VEXATIONS ⟨so many additional inconveniences and ~*s* —Alexander Pope⟩

²chagrin *adj* [F, sad] *obs* **:** CHAGRINED

³cha·grin \shə'grin, *Brit usu* shə'grēn *or* 'shagrin\ *vt* **chagrined** *also* **chagrinned; chagrined** *also* **chagrinned; chagrining** *also* **chagrinning; chagrins** [prob. fr. F *chagriner,* fr. *chagrin,* adj.] **1** *archaic* **:** to cause to feel anxiety **:** TROUBLE, GRIEVE **2 :** to vex through humiliation, hurt pride, or disappointment ⟨their increasing neglect of his welfare ~*s* him⟩

chagrined *adj* **:** feeling or made to feel chagrin **:** DISAPPOINTED, MORTIFIED ⟨you are ~ at having lost that dowry —Willa Cather⟩ **syn** see ASHAMED

cha·gual gum \(')chä¦gwäl-\ *n* [AmerSp *chagual*] **:** gum obtained in Chile from various plants of the genus *Puya*

cha·guar \(')chä¦gwär\ *n* -s [AmerSp *chaguar, cháguar, chagual,* prob. fr. Quechua *ch'ahuar* vegetable fiber] **:** CARAGUATA

cha·gul *or* **cha·gal** \'chägəl\ *n* -s [Hindi *chāgal,* fr. Skt *chāgala* coming from a goat, fr. *chāga* he-goat] **:** a leather water bag of goatskin used in India

chahar \'(')chä¦här\ *n, pl* **chahar** *or* **chahars** *usu cap* **:** a Mongol people inhabiting the Inner Mongolian steppes northwest of Peking

chahi *var of* SHAHI

chai·ma *or* **chay·ma** \'chīmə\ *n, pl* **chaima** *or* **chaimas** *or* **chayma** *or* **chaymas** *usu cap* [Sp *chaima,* of AmerInd origin] **1 a :** a Cariban people of the coast of Venezuela **b :** a member of such people **2 :** the language of the Chaima people

¹chain \'chān\ *n* -s [ME *cheyne,* fr. OF *chaeine,* fr. L *catena* chain, brace; akin to L *cassis* net and perh. to OE *heathor* confinement, ON *hadda* chain of rings] **1 a** (1) **:** a series of usu. metal links or rings connected to or fitted into one another so as to move freely, forming a flexible ligament used for various purposes (as support, restraint, or transmission of mechanical power), and made in many forms and sizes, the size usu. being designated by the thickness of the links (as a half-inch chain made of bar metal half an inch in diameter) ⟨cable ~⟩ ⟨bicycle ~⟩ ⟨a bridle with a ~ snaffle⟩ ⟨a harness with a ~ trace⟩ — see BICYCLE illustration (2) **:** a mesh of interconnected rods and plates that is often in the form of a belt and is used esp. for transmission of power or as a conveyor **b :** a series of links used or worn as an ornament or insignia **:** COLLAR 1g ⟨he wore a gold ~ of office around his neck⟩ **c** (1) **:** a measuring instrument that consists of 100 links joined together by rings and is used in surveying — see ENGINEER'S CHAIN, GUNTER'S CHAIN; compare TAPE 2c (2) **:** a unit of length equal to 66 feet — see GUNTER'S CHAIN **d :** TIRE CHAIN — usu. used in pl. **e :** a chain 10 yards in length used for measuring the first-down distance in football **2 a :** a chain used as an obstruction to the passage of traffic (as in a street, river, or harbor entrance) — compare ²BOOM 6 **b :** something that confines, restrains, or secures **:** BOND, FETTER ⟨ignorance is . . . a ~ on your mind —Lyman Bryson⟩ **c chains** *pl* **:** manacles or fetters linked with chain; *also* **:** IMPRISONMENT, CAPTIVITY ⟨wept with me when I returned in ~*s* —Alfred Tennyson⟩ **d :** DOOR CHAIN **3 a :** a continuous series of things, events, or conceptions in which each succeeding member depends upon (as for causal agency or motive impulse), derives from, or interrelates with the preceding ⟨a vast ~ of creatures stretching down from . . . the Deity . . . to the grades of men, animals, plants, and minerals —S.F.Mason⟩ ⟨~ of events⟩ ⟨~ of thought⟩ ⟨~ reasoning in which the conclusion of one argument is used in the premise of the next⟩ **b :** a continuous line or series of things connected or adjacent to one another: as (1) **:** a range of mountains (2) **:** a series of events in a temporal order usu. connected causally ⟨a ~ of strikes in the steel industry⟩ (3) **:** a diagonal arrangement of connected pawns in chess (4) **:** a line of dancers with hands linked (5) **:** LADIES CHAIN **c** (1) **:** a group of enterprises, establishments, institutions, or constructions of the same kind or function linked together into a single system usu. under a single ownership, management, or control ⟨a ~ of 100 grocery stores⟩ ⟨a ~ of weather stations⟩ ⟨a ~ of highways⟩ (2) **:** NETWORK 5a **d :** a number of atoms united like links in a chain; *esp* **:** OPEN CHAIN — see BRANCHED CHAIN, SIDE CHAIN, STRAIGHT CHAIN; compare ¹RING 18 **e :** a system of rigid links (sense 2c) pivoted or otherwise movably connected each to one or more others in such a way that their motions are interdependent **4 chains** *pl* **:** the structure composed of channels, chain plates, and deadeyes to which the shrouds of a mast are fastened and in which the leadsman stands in making a cast of the lead — see SHIP illustration **5 :** ¹WARP 1a

²chain \"\ *vb* -ED/-ING/-S [ME *cheynen,* fr. *cheyne,* n.] *vt* **1 :** to fasten, bind, or connect with a chain **:** fetter or restrain with a chain **:** put in chains **2 a :** to bind, fasten, or hold fast as if with a chain ⟨the audience, ~*ed* to their seats by terror⟩ **b :** to hold back, repress, or restrict the movement, function, or change of ⟨you may ~ the law down with all manner of clamps and bonds —B.N.Cardozo⟩ **:** make or hold captive **:** CONFINE ⟨buried now and lost in silent pools, now in strong eddies ~*ed* —William Wordsworth⟩ **3 :** to obstruct or protect (as a harbor) by a chain **4 :** to measure with a surveying chain **5 :** to make a series of (chain stitches) in crocheting —abbr. *ch* ~ *vi* **1 :** to form or join in a chain **2 :** to perform a ladies chain in square dancing

³chain \"\ *adj* [¹*chain*] **1 :** performed, occurring, or acting in a connected series ⟨~ reader of murder mysteries —Louise Mace⟩ **2 :** gathering force or increasing with each successive step **:** CUMULATIVE ⟨~ effects that may ultimately affect the whole country⟩ **3 :** characterized by uniformity **:** STEREOTYPED ⟨strive against ~ thinking and acting —Harlow Shapley⟩

chain armor *n* **:** CHAIN MAIL

chain banking *n* **:** the possession of stock control of two or more banks by one or a few individuals

chain bearer *n* **:** CHAINMAN 4

chain belt *n* **:** a belt constructed of links of metal or other material (as leather) and used in chain gearing or as a conveyor

piece of a chain belt

chain block *n* **:** CHAIN HOIST

chain bolt *n* **:** a bolt with a chain attached for drawing it out

chain bond *n* **:** a bond formed in masonry by building in a tie (as a metal chain, bar, or strap) or a timber

chain boom *n* **:** ²BOOM 6

chain break *n* **:** a brief radio or television commercial given during one of the station-identification intervals in a network program

chain bridge *n* **:** a suspension bridge suspended from chains

chain cable *n* **:** an anchor chain

chain conveyor *n* **:** CONVEYER 2a(3)

chain coral *n* **:** a fossil coral (genus *Halysites*) common in the upper Ordovician and Silurian rocks having tubular corallites of oval section united by their narrow sides and looking like links of chain

chain course *n, masonry* **:** a bond course of stone headers fastened together continuously by cramps

chain discount *n* **:** a series of discounts allowed from the list price of an article of merchandise

chain drive *n* **:** a mechanical drive consisting of chain gears and a driving chain ⟨an automotive *chain drive*⟩ — called also *chain transmission*

chain–driven \'⸗;⸗⸗\ *adj* **:** having a chain drive

chaî·né \she'nā, shā-\ *n* -s [F, fr. past part. of *chaîner* to chain, fr. *chaîne,* n., fr. L *catena* — more at CHAIN] **:** a series of small regular turns by which a ballet dancer moves across the stage

chained *adj* **:** furnished, fitted, or adorned with a chain

chain envelope *n* **:** a business envelope usu. for interdepartmental use that may be readdressed and reused many times

chain·er \'chānə(r)\ *n* -s [¹*chain* + *-er*] **1 :** CHOKERMAN **2 :** a clipper in a coal mine **3 :** one that arranges the pattern chain on a dobby loom **4 :** a worker who ties skeins of yarn into a continuous chain for processing

chain feed *vt* **:** to feed (as envelopes) into a typewriter so that each successive piece is held in place by the preceding one

chain fern *n* **:** a fern having the sori in chainlike rows (as members of the genus *Woodwardia*)

chain gang *n* **1 :** a gang of convicts chained together esp. as an outside working party **2** *slang* **:** one of two or more railroad train crews taking turns in the operation of extra trains in addition to regular trains

chain gear *or* **chain gearing** *n* **:** a gear through which motion is transmitted by a chain that runs in a groove or engages the cogs of a sprocket wheel

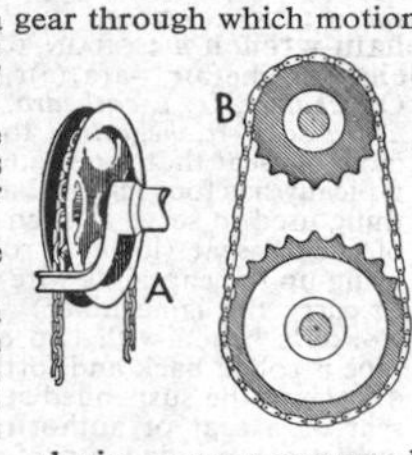

chain gears: grooved wheel with chain, *A;* sprocket wheels with chain, *B*

chain-grate stoker *n* **:** a wide endless traveling chain that feeds and supports the fuel in a boiler furnace

chain harrow *n* **:** a harrow made of linked chainwork

chain hoist *also* **chain fall** *n* **:** a tackle employing an endless chain instead of a rope and operated esp. in workshops from an overhead track for hoisting heavy weights — called also *chain block*

chain hook *n* **:** a hook used for dragging or lifting cables

chaining *pres part of* CHAIN

chain isomerism *n* **:** isomerism involving atoms in a chain (as in butane and isobutane)

chain knot *n* **:** a knot resembling a chain or a link of a chain

chain·less \'chānlə̇s\ *adj* **:** being without a chain

chain·let \'chānlə̇t\ *n* -s [¹*chain* + *-let*] **:** a small chain

chain letter *n* **:** a letter sent to a number of recipients requesting each to write similar letters to an equal number of recipients and often employed as a moneymaking scheme by the inclusion with each letter of a list of persons to whom money is to be sent

chain lightning *n* **:** lightning that appears to move very rapidly in a long angular, zigzag, or forked course

chain line *or* **chain mark** *n* **:** one of the wider-spaced parallel watermark lines in a laid paper made by the chain wires and running with the grain — compare LAID LINE

chain link fence *n* **:** a fence of heavy steel wire woven in continuous spirals so that when the spirals are integrated with each other a diamond-shaped mesh is formed

chain locker *n* **:** a forward compartment in the lower part of a ship for stowing the chain cable

chain mail *n* **:** flexible armor of interlinked metal rings — called also *chain armor*

chain·man \'chānmən, -,man\ *n, pl* **chainmen** [*chain* + *man*] **1 :** one who searches tax and assessment records in order to compile lists of mortgages, deeds, contracts, and other instruments pertaining to real-estate titles **2 :** a sawmill worker who removes lumber from a conveyor and sorts and stacks it according to grade markings **3 :** CHOKERMAN **4 :** a surveyor's assistant who measures distances, marks measuring points, and performs related duties — called also *lineman, rodman, tapeman*

chain of being : a hierarchical order of all entities; *esp* **:** an uninterrupted hierarchy of all beings arranged according to an order of perfection
chain of causation 1 : a series of events or situations interrelated and leading to a particular effect **2** *often cap both Cs, Buddhism* **:** the chain of cause and effect leading in 12 stages from ignorance of the vanity of existence to suffering
chain of command : a series of executive positions or of officers and subordinates in order of authority esp. with respect to the passing on of orders, responsibility, reports, or requests from higher to lower or lower to higher
chain of title : the succession of conveyances from some accepted starting point whereby the present holder of real property derives his title
chain·o·mat·ic \ˌchānəˌmad·ik\ *adj* [fr. *Chainomatic*, a trademark] *of a balance or scale* **:** having suspended from the beam an adjustable fine chain the length of which is measured to determine minute weights
chain pickerel *also* **chain pike** *n* **:** a large greenish black pickerel (*Esox niger*) with dark chainlike markings along the sides that is common in quiet waters of eastern No. America
chain pin *n* **:** ARROW 2c
chain pipe *n* **:** the pipe through which the cable chain passes from the windlass to the chain locker
chain plate *n* **:** a metal plate which is bolted to the channels or to the side of a ship and to which the shrouds are fastened by means of a deadeye or turnbuckle — see ¹CHAIN 4
chain pump *n* **:** a pump consisting of a sprocket-operated endless chain fitted at close intervals with disks that lift the water by moving rapidly through a pipe in the direction of the desired flow
chain-react \ˈ=ˌ=ˌ=\ *vi* [back-formation fr. *chain reaction*] **:** to take part in or undergo chain reaction
chain-reacting pile *n* **:** REACTOR
chain reaction *n* **1 :** a series of events so related to each other that each one initiates the succeeding one esp. in such a manner as to produce a cumulative effect ⟨the employee with more retention points can and does bump the employee with fewer points, setting off a costly *chain reaction* down the line —Sam Stavisky⟩ **2 :** a chemical reaction (as polymerization) that once started can maintain itself by interaction of the starting materials with transitory reactive products (as atoms or free radicals), more of the transitory products being formed as they are consumed **3 :** a self-propagating fission of atomic nuclei continued by the further action of one of the products (as in the fission of a uranium nucleus by a neutron that causes the release of more neutrons that cause further fissions and so on)
chain reactor *n* **:** REACTOR
chain reflex *n, psychol* **:** a series of responses each serving as a stimulus that evokes the next response
chain riveting *n* **:** riveting in which the rivets in rows along the seam are set one behind the other
chains *pl of* CHAIN, *pres 3d sing of* CHAIN
chain saw *n* **:** a portable power saw that has teeth linked together to form an endless chain and is usu. used for the cutting of timber

chain saw

chain scale *n* **:** an engineer's or draftsman's scale graduated in inches that are subdivided by 10 and multiples of 10
chain shot *n* **:** a cannon shot consisting of two balls or half balls united by a short chain and formerly used in naval warfare to cut a ship's rigging; *also* **:** a discharge of such shot
chainsmith \ˈ=ˌ=\ *n* **:** a smith who makes chains
chain-smoke *vi* **:** to smoke cigarettes or cigars continually esp. by lighting each from the previous one ⟨*chain-smoked* all during the conference⟩ ~ *vt* **:** to smoke (as cigarettes) almost without interruption ⟨rolled cigarettes and *chain-smoked* them all afternoon out of nervousness⟩ — **chain smoker** *n*
chain snake *n* **:** KING SNAKE
chain splice *n* **:** a splice for joining a rope to the end link of a chain
chain stitch *n* **1 :** an ornamental stitch that resembles the links of a chain and is used in crocheting, sewing, and embroidery **2 :** a stitch in machine sewing in which the looping of the thread forms a chain on the underside of the work
chain stopper *n* **:** a device (as a hook) that secures the anchor chain (as when the anchor is raised) thus taking the strain from the windlass
chain store *n* **:** a retail store that is a unit of a chain
chain timber *n* **:** a timber used to form a chain bond
chain tongs *n pl* **:** tongs for turning large pipe that consist of a lever with notched head whose teeth engage the pipe and an adjustable short chain which encircles the pipe and whose ends are secured to the head
chain transmission *n* **:** CHAIN DRIVE
chain vise *n* **:** a vise in which round work (as a pipe) is held in a V-shaped support by a chain clamped tightly around the work
chain·wale \ˈchān,wāl, ˈchanᵊl\ *n* -S [¹*chain* + *wale*] **:** ³CHANNEL
chain wire *n* **:** any of the wires running around the circumference of a dandy roll — compare LAID WIRE
chainwork \ˈ=ˌ=\ *n* **1 :** work consisting of esp. metal units looped or linked together in the manner of a chain **2 :** a decorative pattern of links and loops resembling a chain; *specif* **:** CHAIN STITCH
chain wrench *n* **:** CHAIN TONGS
¹**chair** \ˈche(ə)r, -a(ə)(ə)r,-eə,-a(ə)ə\ *n* -S [ME *chayere*, fr. OF *chaiere*, fr. L *cathedra*, fr. Gk *kathedra*, fr. *kata-* cata- + *hedra* seat, fr. *hezesthai* to sit — more at SIT] **1 a :** a usu. movable seat that is designed to accommodate one person and typically has four legs and a back and often has arms **b :** something that is used to serve as such a seat or to support in the manner of such a seat ⟨lower a rope ~ over the side of the ship to bring up the captain's wife⟩ ⟨made a ~ of their clasped hands to carry the lame hiker⟩ **c :** ELECTRIC CHAIR **d :** a glassworker's bench with two extended arms on which the blowpipe is rolled back and forth while the glass is being fashioned **e :** one of the suspended seats on a chair lift **2 a :** an official seat or a seat of authority, state, or dignity (as of a chief magistrate, a judge, a professor, or a bishop) **b :** an office or position of authority or dignity (as of a bishop, a mayor of an English corporate town, a professor, or one who presides on a committee or at a meeting) ⟨the gubernatorial ~⟩ ⟨the ~ of comparative literature at the university⟩ **c** *obs* **:** PULPIT **d :** CHAIRMAN ⟨it is polite to address the ~ in a large meeting⟩ **3 a :** SEDAN CHAIR **b :** a formerly popular light one-horse carriage (as a chaise or gig) **4 a :** an office in a society (as a fraternal organization) **b :** a position of employment usu. of one occupying a chair or desk ⟨a ~ as editorial writer⟩; *specif* **:** the position of a player in an orchestra or band ⟨the first viola ~⟩ ⟨auditioning for the drum ~⟩ **5 :** one of a number of devices that hold up or support: as **a :** a support or carriage of a railroad rail; *specif* **:** an iron or steel block or plate forming a kind of socket or clutch supporting a rail or securing it to a sleeper or tie **b :** a supporting block or socket for a pipe where it passes over a wall or pier **c :** a support for holding reinforcing bars in position while concrete is being placed, the supports and bars becoming part of the permanent structure **6 :** a team of three or more glassworkers who make glass by hand — see FOOTMAKER, GAFFER, SERVITOR
²**chair** \"\ *vt* -ED/-ING/-S **1 a :** to place in a chair **b :** to install formally in a chair of office or honor; *specif* **:** to install (the successful competitor) at a Welsh eisteddfod in a chair of honor **2 a** (1) **:** to carry in or as if in a chair (2) *chiefly Brit* **:** to carry orig. in a chair, now usu. on the shoulders of several members of a group as an expression of acclaim ⟨the time you won your town the race we ~*ed* you through the market place —A.E. Housman⟩ **b :** to wheel in a chair **3 :** to provide with a chair or chairs **4 :** to preside at (a meeting or program) ⟨the president of the society, who ~*s* the proceedings —Robert Craft⟩ **5 :** to be the chief officer of (a committee or any group whose chief officer is customarily called *chairman*)
³**chair** \"\ *n* -S [alter. (influenced by ¹*chair*) of ME *chare*, fr. OF *char*, fr. L *carrus* — more at CAR] **:** CHARIOT

chairback \ˈ=ˌ=\ *n* **1 :** ¹BACK 2d **2 :** TIDY a
chairbed \ˈ=ˌ=\ *n* **:** a living-room chair convertible into a bed usu. by means of a retractable seat extension and a back that may be lowered
chairborne \ˈ=ˌ=\ *adj* [blend of ¹*chair* and *airborne*] **:** assigned to a desk job **:** not serving in the field or esp. in combat — used orig. and esp. of military officers
chair car *n* **1 :** a railroad passenger car having pairs of chairs with individually adjustable backs on each side of the aisle **2 :** PARLOR CAR
chair desk *n* **:** a chair with an arm whose top surface is made wide enough to serve as a writing table or small table or with board attachment usu. for one of the arms to serve the same purpose
chaired *adj* [¹*chair* + *-ed*] **:** seated in a chair
chair form *n* **:** one of the stereochemical conformations of a strainless 6-membered ring (as a cyclohexane ring) in which two atoms directly opposite each other in the ring are outside the plane containing the other four atoms, one of the two atoms being above the plane and the other below the plane — compare BOAT FORM
chairlady \ˈ=ˌ==\ *n* **:** a female chairman **:** CHAIRWOMAN
chair lift *n* **:** a power-driven conveyor consisting of seats hung from an endless cable for carrying skiers and sightseers up or down a mountain slope
chairmaker's rush \ˈ=ˌ==-\ *n* **:** a tall coarse sedge (*Scirpus americanus*) used for making chair bottoms
¹**chair·man** \ˈ=mən\ *n, pl* **chairmen 1 :** one who occupies a chair: as **a :** the presiding officer of a meeting or assembly **b :** the head officer of an organization or committee who is entitled to preside at its meetings and usu. to exercise some authority in carrying on its affairs; *specif* **:** CHAIRMAN OF THE BOARD **c :** a professor or instructor who is chief officer of a department of instruction; *often* **:** one who has relatively little power to determine policy and exercise authority except with the approval of his colleagues or of a committee of them — distinguished from *head* **2 a :** one who serves as a carrier of a sedan chair **b :** one who wheels an invalid's chair **3 :** one in charge **:** SUPERVISOR, DIRECTOR ⟨~ of refreshments for a club meeting⟩ ⟨hospitality ~⟩ ⟨legislative ~⟩ ⟨~ of freshman history courses⟩ **4 :** a master of ceremonies of music-hall entertainments
²**chairman** \"\ *vt* **chairmaned** *or* **chairmanned; chairmaned** *or* **chairmanned; chairmaning** *or* **chairmanning; chairmans** [¹*chairman*] **1 :** to act as chairman of (a meeting or assembly) **2 :** to be chairman of (an organization or committee)
chairman of the board : the principal officer of a corporation who presides over its board of directors and oversees its activity (1) by bringing forward for discussion and action problems arising from conflict of interest, problems stressing financial stewardship, policy questions growing out of operating decisions and (2) by setting up sound board procedures and securing competent board members
chair·man·ship \-ˌship\ *n* -S **:** the office or status of a chairman
chair·o·plane \ˈ=rə,plān\ *n* -S [blend of ¹*chair* and *aeroplane*] **:** an amusement park device usu. for children consisting of a high revolving wheel from which seats hang on chains that swing out when the wheel revolves
chair organ *n* [perh. so called fr. the fact that such organs often formed the back of the organist's seat] **1** *obs* **:** a second organ added to the great organ **2 :** CHOIR ORGAN
chair post *n* **:** a chair leg
chair rail *n* **:** a wooden molding on a wall around a room to protect the wall from being damaged by the backs of chairs
chairs *pl of* CHAIR, *pres 3d sing of* CHAIR
chair swing *n* **:** a swing for young children that has a back, arms, and a protective bar across the front
chair table *n* **:** a table convertible into a chair or settle by raising the hinged top to form the back of a chair whose seat lies between the upright supports
chairwarmer \ˈ=ˌ==\ *n, slang* **:** one who habitually lounges in a chair **:** LOAFER: **a :** a person (as one not registered as a guest) who sits for prolonged periods in hotel lobbies **b :** an employee (as one in a sedentary occupation) who is superfluous or who makes little effort to apply himself to his work ⟨the seniority rule . . . discourages ability and efficiency, and encourages the ~ —S.T.Williamson & Herbert Harris⟩

chair table

chairway \ˈ=ˌ=\ *n* [*chair* + *-way* (as in *tramway*)] **:** CHAIR LIFT
chairwoman \ˈ=ˌ==\ *n, pl* **chairwomen :** a female chairman
chaise \ˈshāz\ *n* -S [F, chair, sedan chair, chaise, fr. MF, chair, alter. of *chaire*, fr. OF *chaiere* — more at CHAIR] **1 :** any of various traveling or pleasure carriages usu. of a chair-backed type: as **a :** a 2-wheeled carriage for one or two persons with a calash top and the body hung on leather straps or thoroughbraces and usu. drawn by one horse **b :** a similar 4-wheeled pleasure carriage **c :** POST CHAISE **2 :** any light carriage or pleasure cart **3 :** CHAISE LONGUE

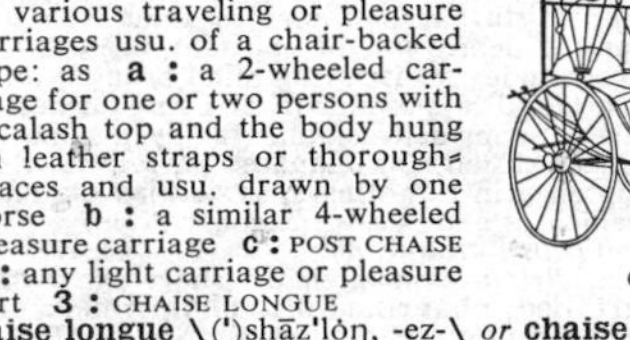

chaise 1a

chaise longue \(ˈ)shāz'lȯŋ, -ez-\ *or* **chaise lounge** \(ˈ)shāz'laünj, (ˈ)chāz-,(ˈ)chās-\ *n, pl* **chaise longues** \-ŋz\ *or* **chaise loung·es** \-njəz\ *also* **chaises longues** \-z'lȯŋz\ [*chaise longue* fr. F, lit., long chair; *chaise lounge* by folk etymology fr. F *chaise longue*] **:** an elongated couchlike seat with a raised back support at one end — called also *chaise*
chait \ˈchīt\ *or* **chai·tra** \-ī·trə\ *n* -S *usu cap* [Hindi *Cait*, fr. Skt *Caitra*] **:** a month of the Hindu year — see MONTH table
chait·ya \ˈchītyə, -īchə\ *n* -S [Skt *caitya*, fr. *citā* funeral pile, fr. *cinoti* he piles up; akin to Gk *poiein* to make, do — more at POET] *India* **:** a sacred place **:** SHRINE, MONUMENT — compare DAGOBA, STUPA, TOPE
cha·ja \chəˈhä, chäˈ-\ *n* -S [Sp *chajá*, prob. fr. Guarani *chahâ*] **:** the largest of the crested screamers (*Chauna torquata*) native to southern Brazil and Argentina
cha·kar \ˈchäkə(r)\ *n* -S [Hindi *cākor*, fr. Per *chākar*] *India* **:** a person in domestic service **:** SERVANT; *also* **:** a clerical worker
cha·ka·ri \ˈchäkə(,)rē\ *n* -S [Hindi *cākarī*, fr. Per *chākarī*, fr. *chākar*] *India* **:** domestic or more commonly clerical service
chak·dar \(,)chəkˈdär, ˈchək,d-\ *n* -S [Panjabi *cakdār*, fr. *cak* tenure (fr. Skt *cakra*) + Per *-dār* having] **:** a native land tenant of India intermediate in position between the proprietor and cultivator
chak·ra *also* **cak·ra** \ˈchəkrə\ *n* -S [Skt *cakra*, lit., wheel — more at WHEEL] **1 :** a disk representing the sun and sovereignty **2 a :** a sharp-edged circular missile weapon carried as an attribute by Vishnu **b :** such a weapon used by the Sikhs
chak·ram *also* **chuck·ram** *or* **chuck·rum** \ˈchəkrəm\ *n* -S [Malayalam *cakram*, fr. Skt *cakra* wheel] **1 :** a very small silver coin formerly issued by the state of Travancore, southern India **2 :** the value of one chakram **:** a unit of value equivalent to 1⁄32 of a rupee or ¼ of a fanam
chak·ra·var·tin \,chəkrəˈvärtᵊn\ *n* -S [Skt *cakravartin*, fr. *cakra* wheel + *-vartin* one who turns, fr. *vartate* he turns — more at WORTH] *India* **:** a universal sovereign **:** an ideal ruler
cha·la·co \chəˈlä(,)kō\ *n* -ES [AmerSp, perh. aug. of Sp *chala* cornhusk, fr. Quechua] **:** a goby (*Dormitator maculatus*) of eastern So. America extensively used in mosquito control
cha·lan \ˈchəlan\ *n* -S [Hindi *calan*] *India* **:** VOUCHER, INVOICE
chal·a·ra \ˈkalərə\ *n, cap* [NL, fr. fem. sing. of Gk *chalaros* slack, loose, fr. *chalan* to loosen, relax; akin to Gk *kichanein* to attain, reach — more at GO] **:** a genus of imperfect fungi (family Dematiaceae) that reproduce by terminally discharged endospores, one species (*C. quercina*) causing the destructive oak wilt disease

chal·a·rop·sis \,kaləˈräpsəs\ *n, cap* [NL, fr. Gk *chalaros* slack, loose + NL *-opsis*] **:** a genus of imperfect fungi (family Dematiaceae) one species of which (*C. thielavioides*) causes black mold of rose grafts
cha·las·to·gas·tra \kə,lastəˈgastrə\ *n pl, cap* [NL, fr. LGk *chalastos* loose + NL *-gastra* (fr. Gk *gastr-, gastēr* belly) — more at GASTRIC] **:** a suborder of Hymenoptera including the sawflies and horntails and characterized by the caterpillarlike larvae and by having the abdomen attached to the thorax by a broad base
cha·la·za \kəˈlāzə\ *n, pl* **chala·zae** \-,zē\ *or* **chalazas** [NL, fr. Gk, hailstone, hard lump, chalazion; akin to OSlav *žlědica* frozen rain, Per *zhāla* hail] **1 :** either of a pair of spiral bands of thickened albuminous substance in the white of a bird's egg that extend out from opposite sides of the yolk to the ends of the egg and are there attached to the lining membrane — called also *treadle;* see EGG illustration **2 :** the region at the base of an ovule where the seedstalk is attached and from which the integuments arise — **cha·la·zi·an** \-ˌzēən\ *adj*
cha·la·zal \-zəl\ *adj* [NL *chalaza* + E *-al*] **:** of or relating to the chalaza; *specif* **:** located or facing toward the chalaza of a seed
chal·a·zif·er·ous \ˌkaləˌzif(ə)rəs\ *adj* [ISV *chalaz-* (fr. NL *chalaza*) + *-i-* + *-ferous*] **:** having chalazas
cha·la·zi·on \kəˈlāzēən, -ē,än\ *n, pl* **chala·zia** \-zēə\ [NL, fr. Gk *chalazion* small lump, chalazion, dim. of *chalaza* hailstone, hard lump, chalazion — more at CHALAZA] **:** a small circumscribed tumor of the eyelid formed by retention of the Meibomian-gland secretions and sometimes accompanied by inflammation
chal·a·zog·a·my \,kaləˈzägəmē\ *n* -ES [ISV *chalaz-* (fr. NL *chalaza*) + *-o-* + *-gamy;* prob. orig. formed as F *chalazogamie*] **:** a process of fertilization in which the pollen tube penetrates to the embryo sac through the tissue of the chalaza
chal·a·zoid·ite \ˈkalə,zȯi,dīt, ,==ˈ==\ *n* -S [Gk *chalaza* hailstone + E *-oid* + *-ite*] **:** a spherical body formed during some volcanic eruptions by concentric accretion of pumiceous dust upon a pellet of mud blown into the air from the volcano
chalc- *or* **chalco-** *also* **chalk-** *or* **chalko-** *comb form* [F & L, fr. Gk *chalk-, chalko-*, fr. *chalkos* copper, prob. akin to Lith *geležis* iron, Russ *zhelezo*] **:** copper **:** brass **:** bronze ⟨*chalco*menite⟩ ⟨*chalco*mancy⟩
chal·can·thite \kalˈkan,thīt, ˈkalkən-\ *n* -S [G *chalkanthit*, fr. L *chalcanthum* copper sulfate solution (fr. Gk *chalkanthon*, fr. *chalk-* chalc- + *-anthon*, fr. *anthos* flower) + G *-it* -ite — more at ANTHOLOGY] **:** a mineral $CuSO_4.5H_2O$ consisting of native copper sulfate — called also *cyanose*
chal·ce·don *or* **chalcedon butterfly** \(ˈ)kalˈsēdᵊn, ˈkalsə,dän\ *n* -S [NL *chalcedona* (specific epithet of *Euphydryas chalcedona*), prob. irreg. fr. LL *chalcedonius* chalcedony — more at CHALCEDONY] **:** a common butterfly (*Euphydryas chalcedona*) of western No. America having black wings speckled with yellow and brownish orange
¹**chal·ce·do·ni·an** \ˌkalsəˈdōnēən, -nyən\ *adj, usu cap* [*Chalcedon*, ancient city (now *Kadıköy*) in Asia Minor opposite Byzantium (fr. L, fr. Gk *Kalchēdōn*) + E *-ian*] **:** of or relating to Chalcedon, the ecumenical council held there in A.D. 451, or the teachings of the council
²**chalcedonian** \"\ *n* -S *usu cap* **:** one who adheres to the doctrinal decisions of the ecumenical council held in Chalcedon in A.D. 451; *esp* **:** a non-Monophysite orthodox Christian
chal·ce·don·ic \ˌkalsəˈdänik\ *also* **chal·ced·o·nous** \(ˈ)kalˈsedᵊnəs\ *adj* [*chalcedony* + *-ic* or *-ous*] **:** of or relating to chalcedony
chal·ced·o·ny *also* **cal·ced·o·ny** \kalˈsedᵊnē, -ni\ *n* -ES [ME *calcedonie*, a precious stone, fr. LL *chalcedonius*, fr. Gk *chalkēdōn*] **:** a cryptocrystalline translucent mineral constituting a variety of quartz and commonly of a pale blue or gray color, uniform tint, and nearly waxlike luster — see AGATE, CARNELIAN, CHRYSOPRASE, ONYX
chal·ce·don·yx \,kalsəˈdäniks, kalˈsedᵊniks\ *n* -ES [*chalcedony* + *onyx*] **:** a mineral that consists of onyx in which the bands are white to gray and that is valued as a semiprecious stone
chalcedony yellow *n* **:** a pale to light greenish yellow — called also *reed yellow*
chal·chi·huitl \,chälˈchēˈwēd·ᵊl\ *n* -S [Nahuatl] **:** CHALCHUITE
chal·chu·ite \,chälchəˈwēd·ē\ *n* -S [AmerSp *chalchihuite*, fr. Nahuatl *chalchihuitl*] **:** a blue or green turquoise
¹**chal·cid** \ˈkalsəd\ *adj* [NL *Chalcid-, Chalcis*] **:** of or relating to the Chalcididae
²**chalcid** \"\ *n* -S **:** CHALCID FLY
chal·ci·dae \ˈkalsə,dē\ [NL, fr. *Chalcis*, type genus + *-idae*] *syn of* CHALCIDIDAE
chalcid fly *or* **chalcid wasp** *n* **:** a usu. minute insect of a large superfamily (Chalcidoidea) of Hymenoptera, a few being gall wasps or seed infesters but most being in their larval state parasitic on the eggs, larvae, or pupae of other insects, some living within and others upon the bodies of their hosts, feeding on their juices and tissues, and thus benefiting man by destroying many injurious insects — see CLOVER SEED CHALCID
¹**chal·cid·i·an** \kalˈsidēən\ *n, usu cap* [L *Chalcidi-, Chalcis*, city on Euboea Island, Greece (fr. Gk *Chalkid-, Chalkis*) + E *-ian*] **:** a native or inhabitant of the city of Chalcis, Greece
²**chalcidian** \(ˈ)=ˌ===\ *adj, usu cap* **:** of or relating to the city of Chalcis ⟨*Chalcidian* culture⟩ ⟨*Chalcidian* colonies⟩
chalcidian alphabet *n, usu cap C* **:** any of the non-Ionic Greek alphabets; *specif* **:** that of the Chalcidian colonies of lower Italy and Sicily from which the Latin alphabet was developed
chal·cid·i·cum \kalˈsidəkəm\ *or* **chal·cid·ic** \-dik\ *n, pl* **chalcidi·ca** \-əkə\ *or* **chalcidics** [L *chalcidicum*, fr. neut. of *Chalcidicus* Chalcidian, fr. *Chalcid-, Chalcis* + L *-icus* -ic] **1 a :** a porch of entrance esp. to a Roman basilica **b :** a vestibule of a Christian basilica **:** NARTHEX **2 :** a building attached to a Roman basilica **3 :** a large Roman building for judicial functions
chal·cid·i·dae \-ə,dē\ *n pl, cap* [NL, fr. *Chalcid-, Chalcis*, type genus + *-idae*] **:** a family of chalcid flies now restricted to certain typical forms but formerly somewhat coextensive with the superfamily Chalcidoidea
¹**chal·ci·doid** \ˈkalsə,dȯid\ *n* -S [NL *Chalcidoidea*] **:** one of the Chalcidoidea **:** CHALCID FLY
²**chalcidoid** \"\ *adj* **:** of or relating to Chalcidoidea **:** resembling a chalcid fly
chal·ci·doi·dea \,kalsəˈdȯidēə\ *n pl, cap* [NL, fr. *Chalcid-, Chalcis* + *-oidea*] **:** a superfamily of Hymenoptera comprising the chalcid flies
chal·cis \ˈkalsəs\ *n, cap* [NL, irreg. fr. Gk *chalkos* copper; fr. the metallic color of insects of this genus — more at CHALC-] **:** the type genus of Chalcididae comprising chalcid flies with the abdomen sessile and the hind femora greatly swollen and toothed below
chalcis fly *n* [NL *Chalcis*] **:** CHALCID FLY
chalco- — see CHALC-
chal·co·al·u·mite \ˌkal(,)kōˈ-\ *n* -S [*chalc-* + *alumite*] **:** a turquoise-green to pale blue mineral $CuAl_4(SO_4)(OH)_{12}.3H_2O$ consisting of a hydrous basic sulfate of copper and aluminum
chal·co·cite \ˈkalkə,sīt\ *n* -S [irreg. fr. F *chalcosine* chalcocite + E *-ite* — more at CHALCOSINE] **:** a black or dark gray mineral Cu_2S of metallic luster consisting of native cuprous sulfide occurring in orthorhombic crystals or massive (hardness 2.5–3, sp. gr. 5.5–5.8)
chal·co·cy·a·nite \ˌkal(,)kōˈ-\ *n* -S [ISV *chalc-* + *cyanite;* orig. formed as It *calcocianite*] **:** a mineral $CuSO_4$ consisting of anhydrous sulfate of copper
chal·co·gen \ˈkalkəjən, -,jen\ *n* -S [ISV *chalc-* + *-gen*] **:** any of the four elements oxygen, sulfur, selenium, and tellurium forming part of group VI of the periodic table
chal·co·gen·ide \ˈkalkəjə,nīd, kalˈkäjə-\ *n* -S [*chalcogen* + *-ide*] **:** a binary compound of a chalcogen with a more electropositive element or radical
chal·co·lite \ˈkalkə,līt\ *n* -S [G *chalkolith*, fr. *chalk-* chalc- + *-lith* -lite] **:** TORBERNITE
chal·co·lith·ic \ˌkalkəˈlithik\ *adj, usu cap* [*chalc-* + *-lithic*] **:** AENEOLITHIC
chal·co·me·nite \,kalkəˈmē,nīt\ *n* -S [F *chalcoménite*, fr. *chalc-* + Gk *mēnē* moon + F *-ite;* fr. its being a compound of selenium, which is named for the moon — more at MOON] **:** a mineral $CuSeO_3.2H_2O$ consisting of copper selenite and occurring in blue crystals
chal·cone *also* **chal·kone** \ˈkal,kōn\ *n* -S [G *chalkon*, fr.

chalk- chalc- + *-on* -one; fr. its use in producing reddish yellow dyestuffs] **:** a yellow crystalline ketone C_6H_5CH-$CHCOC_6H_5$ made by the condensation of benzaldehyde and acetophenone; *also* **:** any of various derivatives of this compound, several of which are plant pigments related to the flavones

chal·coph·a·nite \kal'käfə,nīt\ *n* -S [*chalc-* + *phan-* (fr. Gk *phainein* to show) + *-ite;* fr. its change to a copper color when heated] **:** a mineral $(Zn,Mn,Fe)Mn_2O_5.nH_2O$ consisting of black hydrous manganese and zinc oxide and having a metallic luster

chal·co·phile \'kalkə,fīl\ *adj* [*chalc-* + *-phile*] **:** having such an affinity for sulfur that in a molten mass the greatest concentration (as of an element) is found in the sulfide phase

chal·co·phyl·lite \,kalkō'fi,līt\ *n* -S [G *chalkophyllit,* fr. *chalk-* chalc- + *phyll-* + *-it* -ite] **:** a highly basic arsenate and sulfate of copper and aluminum $Cu_{18}Al_2(AsO_4)_3(SO_4)_3$-$(OH)_{27}.33H_2O$ of various shades of green that occurs in tabular crystals or foliated masses

chal·co·py·rite \-'pī,rīt\ *n* -S [NL *chalcopyrites,* fr. *chalc-* + L *pyrites* sulfide of metallic appearance — more at PYRITES] **:** a bright brass-yellow mineral $CuFeS_2$ consisting of copper-iron sulfide that crystallizes in the tetragonal system but usu. occurs massive and that is one of the most important ores of copper (hardness 3.5–4, sp. gr. 4.1–4.3)

chal·co·sid·er·ite \;kal(,)kō'sidə,rīt\ *n* -S [G *chalkosiderit* fr. *chalk-* chalc- + *sider-* + *-it* -ite] **:** a mineral $Cu(Fe, Al)_6$-$(PO_4)_4(OH)_8.4H_2O$ consisting of a hydrous basic green phosphate of copper, iron, and aluminum, closely related to turquoise, and containing more aluminum than iron

chal·co·sine \'kalkə,sēn\ *n* -S [F, fr. Gk *chalkos* + F *-ine* — more at CHALC-] **:** CHALCOCITE

chal·co·stib·ite \,kalkō'sti,bīt\ *n* -S [G *chalkostibit,* fr. *chalk-* chalc- + *stib-* + *-it* -ite] **:** a lead-gray mineral $CuSbS_2$ consisting of antimony copper sulfide (sp. gr. 4.75–3.0)

chal·co·trich·ite \,kalkō'tri,kīt, kal'kä·trə,kīt\ *n* -S [G *chalkotrichit,* fr. *chalk-* chalc- + *trich-* + *-it* -ite] **:** a mineral consisting of a capillary variety of cuprite

chal·dae-pah·la·vi \;kal,dē'pälə(,)vē\ *n* -S *usu cap C&P* [*Chaldaean* + *Pahlavi*] **:** the variety of Pahlavi using an alphabet found only on inscriptions

chal·da·ic \(')kal'dāik\ *adj or n, usu cap* [L *Chaldaicus,* fr. Gk *Chaldaikos,* fr. *Chaldaia* + Gk *-ikos* -ic] **:** CHALDEAN

[1]**chal·de·an** *also* **chal·dae·an** \kal'dēən\ *n* -S *usu cap* [L *Chaldaeus* Chaldean, astrologer (fr. Gk *Chaldaios,* fr. *Chaldaia* Chaldea, region of ancient Babylonia) + E *-an*] **1 a :** one of an ancient Semitic people that orig. occupied the low alluvial land about the estuaries of the Tigris and Euphrates and that gradually became the dominant people of Babylonia **b :** the original Semitic language of the Chaldeans — called also *neo-Babylonian* **2 :** a person versed in the occult arts (as astrology and sooth-saying) **3 :** a member of a Uniate church in Iraq and Iran converted from Nestorianism in the 16th century

[2]**chaldean** *also* **chaldaean** \(')=;==\ *adj, usu cap* **:** of or belonging to Chaldea or to the language, culture, or occult arts of the Chaldeans

chal·dee \'kal,dē *also* (')kal'dē\ *n* -S *usu cap* [ME *Caldey,* prob. fr. MF *chaldée,* fr. L *Chaldaicus*] **:** the Aramaic vernacular that was the original language of some parts of the Bible (as passages in Daniel, Ezra, and Jeremiah) and that superseded Hebrew among the Jews of Palestine and Babylon

chal·der \'chȯdər, -ȧd-\ *n* -S [ME *chaldre,* fr. MF *chaldere, chaudière* kettle, pot, fr. LL *caldaria* — more at CALDRON] **1 :** a unit of capacity for dry measure formerly used in Scotland equal to 12 quarters or about 96 Winchester bushels **2 :** CHALDRON

chal·dron \'chȯldrən, 'chȧd-\ *n* -S [alter. (influenced by *caldron*) of earlier *chawdron,* fr. MF *chauderon,* fr. *chaudere, chaudière* kettle, pot] **:** any of various old units of measure (as for coal and lime) varying from 32 to 72 imperial bushels; *esp* **:** a unit of measure for coal equal to 36 bushels or 25½ hundredweight

cha·let \'sha,lā, sha'lā *sometimes* 'shalē\ *n* -S [F, fr. F dial. (Switzerland and Savoy); akin to OProv & Catal *cala* cove, inlet; basic meaning: sheltered place] **1 :** a remote herdsman's hut in the Alps **2 a :** a Swiss dwelling characterized by unconcealed structural members that are emphasized by decorative carving, a roof with a wide overhang at the front and sides, and balconies and an exterior staircase under the eaves **b :** a cottage or house built in the style of such a dwelling

chalet 2a

chal·ice \'chaləs\ *n* -S [ME, fr. AF, fr. L *calix* cup; akin to Gk *kalyx* calyx of a flower, Skt *kalaśa* pot, and prob. to Gk *skallein* to hoe — more at SHELL] **1 :** a drinking cup **:** GOBLET; *esp* **:** the cup used in the sacrament of the Lord's supper **2 :** FLOWER CUP 2

chalice 1

chalice cell *n* **:** GOBLET CELL

chal·iced \'chaləst\ *adj, of a flower* **:** having a cup-shaped blossom

chalice vine *n* **:** a climbing strong-branching shrub (*Solandra guttata*) of the family Solanaceae having elliptic-oblong leaves and large solitary terminal funnelform fragrant yellow flowers with purple-brown ridges in the throat

chal·i·co·sis \,kalə'kōsəs\ *n, pl* **chalico·ses** \-ō,sēz\ [NL, fr. Gk *chalik-, chalix* pebble, gravel + NL *-osis* — more at CHALK] **:** a pulmonary affection occurring among stonecutters that is caused by inhalation of stone dust

chal·i·co·there \'kalə(,)kō,thi(ə)r\ *n* -S [NL *Chalicotherium*] **:** one of the Chalicotheriidae

chal·i·co·the·ri·idae \,kalə,kōthə'rīə,dē\ *n pl, cap* [NL, fr. *Chalicotherium,* type genus (fr. Gk *chalik-, chalix* gravel + NL *-therium*) + *-idae*] **:** a family, coextensive with Chalicotherioidea, of Tertiary perissodactyls of worldwide distribution having cleft clawlike toes

chal·i·co·the·ri·oi·dea \;kalə,kō,thirē'ȯidēə\ *n pl, cap* [NL, fr. *Chalicotherium* + *-oidea*] **:** the Ancylopoda regarded as a superfamily of the Perissodactyla — see CHALICOTHERIIDAE

cha·li·na \kə'līnə, -ēnə\ *n, cap* [NL, modif. of Gk *chalinos* bridle, strap] **:** a genus (the type of the family Chalinidae) of sponges that includes the finger sponge and dead-man's-fingers

[1]**chalk** \'chȯk\ *n* -S [ME, fr. OE *cealc;* akin to OHG & MLG *kalk* lime; all fr. a prehistoric WGmc word borrowed fr. L *calc-, calx* limestone, lime, fr. Gk *chalix* small stone, pebble; akin to Gk *skallein* to hoe — more at SHELL] **1 a :** a soft friable limestone of marine origin earthy in texture and white, gray, or buff in color, found widely distributed in Europe and America chiefly in the Cretaceous system, and composed for the most part of the minute shells of Foraminifera — compare CALCIUM CARBONATE, WHITING 2 **b :** chalk or a chalky material in prepared form (as for filler or for marking or drawing purposes) ⟨one twirl or whisk of the ~ is enough —*Billiard Player*⟩ ⟨hand ~ to keep your hands dry —Margery Shaughnessy⟩ ⟨apply liquid ~ to white canvas shoes⟩ ⟨rub a cord with ~ to mark a line⟩ — sometimes used in pl. ⟨some colored ~*s* by the blackboard —Adrian Bell⟩ ⟨only white and transparent ~*s* should be used on a garment fabric —Evelyn A. Mansfield⟩ **2 a :** a mark or line made with chalk ⟨cut a plank to the ~⟩ **b** *Brit* **:** a point scored in a game ⟨winning with 30 ~*s* more than any other player⟩ **3 a :** a drawing done in chalk **b :** a line on a tennis court ⟨the drive hit the ~⟩ **4** *usu cap* **:** the Chalk stage **5 :** the late odds of a horse race, often posted in chalk; *also* **:** a favorite as indicated by such posting — **by a long chalk** *Brit* **:** by any means — usu. used after a negative ⟨that isn't the last of our financial problems *by a long chalk*⟩

[2]**chalk** \"\ *vb* -ED/-ING/-S *vt* **1 :** to treat, process, or prepare with chalk: as **a :** to rub or mark with chalk; *specif* **:** to apply chalk to (the tip of a billiard cue) to prevent slippage **b** *Brit* **:** to fertilize (land) with chalk **2 a :** to write, draw, sketch, or outline with chalk ⟨~ one's name on a wall⟩ **b :** to mark with a sign, number, label, or symbol with or as if with chalk ⟨warehouse goods ~*ed* for export⟩ **3 a :** to delineate roughly with or as if with chalk **:** OUTLINE — usu. used with *out* ⟨~ out a plan of attack⟩ **b :** to set down, add up, or record with or as if with chalk — usu. used with *up* ⟨~*ing* up his good points and ticking off the bad —Hamilton Basso⟩; see CHALK UP ~ *vi* **:** to become chalky; *specif, of paint* **:** to develop a powdery surface due to disintegration of binder — **chalk the door** *Scots law* **:** to make a chalk mark on a door as a notice (as in warning out a tenant)

[3]**chalk** \"\ *adj* **1 :** CHALKY ⟨in the ~ earth of our garden —Clare Leighton⟩ **2** *usu cap* **:** of or belonging to the Upper Cretaceous of Britain and western Europe

chalk- *or* **chalko-** — see CHALC-

chalk blue *n* **:** a pale blue that is lighter than average powder blue, greener and paler than Sistine, and greener, lighter, and stronger than average cadet gray

chalkboard \'=,=\ *n* **:** BLACKBOARD

chalk·er \'chȯkə(r)\ *n* -S **1 :** a worker who applies liquid chalk or wax to shoe parts to prevent their sticking during the lasting process **2 :** a worker who sprinkles chalk over the surface of white leather to improve its appearance

chalkland \'=,=\ *n* **:** an area underlain by chalk

chalklike \'=,=\ *adj* **:** resembling chalk

chalk line *n* **:** a cord rubbed with chalk and used for marking a guide line (as on cement work or on a board); *also* **:** the line marked by such a cord

chalk manner *n* **:** CRAYON MANNER

chalk maple *n* **:** a shade tree (*Acer leucoderme*) of the southeastern U.S. distinguished by its light gray bark

chalk mixture *n* **:** an antacid preparation of chalk, bentonite magma, saccharin sodium, cinnamon water, and distilled water used to combat some diarrheal conditions

chal·kog·ra·phy \kal'kägrəfē\ *n* -ES [G *chalkographie,* fr. Gk *chalkos* copper, anything made of metal + G *-graphie* -graphy — more at CHALC-] **:** the study of opaque minerals under the microscope by means of incident light

chalkone *var of* CHALCONE

chal·ko·si·der·ic \;kal(,)kō,sī;derik, -ōsə;-\ *adj, usu cap* [*chalk-* + *sider-* + *-ic*] **:** of or belonging to the transitional period between the Bronze and Iron ages

chalk pink *n* **:** a moderate pink that is yellower and duller than arbutus pink, yellower and less strong than blossom pink, and deeper than hydrangea pink

chalk plant *n* **:** BABY'S BREATH 1a

chalks *pl of* CHALK, *pres 3d sing of* CHALK

chalkstone \'=,=\ *n* **:** a chalklike concretion mainly of urate of sodium found esp. in and about the small joints of persons suffering from gout **:** TOPHUS

chalk stream *n* **:** a brook or river flowing across or among beds of chalk

chalk stripe *n* **:** a textile design consisting of fine white lines against a dark background

chalk-surfaced paper *n* **:** CHALKY PAPER

chalk-talk \'=,=\ *n* **:** a talk usu. illustrated by impromptu pictures ⟨a *chalk-talk* on malaria control⟩ ⟨a *chalk-talk* for children given by a cartoonist⟩; *specif* **:** a talk designed to brief a group for concerted action ⟨before the attack all noncoms were given *chalk-talks*⟩

chalk up *vt* **1 :** ASCRIBE, CREDIT ⟨why the invasion was not launched still puzzles the field marshal, but he *chalks* it *up* to . . . grudging fondness for the English —*Time*⟩ **2 :** ATTAIN, ACHIEVE ⟨the company will *chalk up* enormous profits⟩ ⟨*chalk up* a record score⟩

chalkware \'=,=\ *n* **:** cheap painted plaster ornamental figures (as of animals, birds, or fruit) made in the 19th century after Staffordshire prototypes

chalky \'chȯkē, -ki\ *adj, often* -ER/-EST **1 :** consisting of, abounding in, or characterized by chalk **:** CRETACEOUS ⟨~ soil⟩ **2 :** having the consistency of chalk **:** POWDERY ⟨~ bread⟩ **3 a :** having the color of chalk ⟨a ~ complexion⟩ **b :** *photog* **:** having excessive contrast and lacking detail in the highlights ⟨~ prints⟩ — compare CONTRASTY

chalky paper *n* **:** a coated paper used in some issues of postage stamps, its sensitive surface making impossible the removal of cancellation marks without removal of the design — called also *chalk-surfaced paper*

challah *n, pl* **challoth** *or* **challot** *or* **challahs** *var of* HALLAH

[1]**chal·lenge** \'chalənj, -ēnj\ *vb* -ED/-ING/-S [ME *chalengen, calengen* to accuse, claim, fr. OF *chalengier* & ONF *calengier,* fr. L *calumniari* to accuse falsely — more at CALUMNIATE] *vt* **1** *obs* **:** to bring a charge against **:** ACCUSE ⟨~ the enemy to be the aggressor⟩ **2 a** *obs* **:** to assert a right, title, or claim to ⟨he *challenged* half the ransom⟩ **b :** to call for, often as if possessing a natural right **:** REQUIRE, DEMAND ⟨an event that ~*s* explanation⟩ ⟨Homer of all Greek poets ~*s* first place⟩ — often used of an attitude, ability, or psychological response ⟨survival in enemy territory ~*s* skill⟩ **3 a :** to call into question esp. for verification, explanation, or justification **:** QUESTION, EXAMINE ⟨I have constantly *challenged* my own principles —A.L.Guérard⟩ ⟨by *challenging* the opinions current among young people —M.R.Cohen⟩ **b** *of a sentry* **:** HALT ⟨~ an unknown person⟩ **4 a :** to dispute esp. as being unjust, invalid, or outmoded **:** take exception to **:** IMPUGN ⟨with recent discoveries *challenging* our former notions not only of the Neanderthal . . . fossils but of *Homo sapiens* as well —R.W.Murray⟩ **b :** to question formally the legality or legal qualifications of (as a vote or voter during elections, a juror or member of a court) **5 a :** to summon boldly or defiantly **:** DARE — used with the infinitive ⟨~ an opponent to show his evidence⟩ **b :** to summon to fight or duel, often in answer to an affront **c :** to invite into competition ⟨the Australian team *challenged* the Americans to meet them next summer⟩ ⟨Germany *challenged* the world in science and then, alas, in arms —G.C.Sellery⟩ **6 :** AROUSE ⟨new ideas to ~ your interest⟩ **:** STIMULATE, EXCITE ⟨temptation ~*s* them at every turn⟩ ⟨we must bring the discussion back to . . . where once again it ~*s* the imagination —A.E.Stevenson b. 1900⟩ **7 :** to administer a challenge (sense 6) to (a person) **:** test (immunity) by administration of infective material ~ *vi* **1** *of a hound* **:** to give tongue on finding scent **2 :** to make, present, or appear as a challenge ⟨when the appropriate moment *challenged,* he was capable of . . . leadership —C.H. Driver⟩ **3 :** to take legal exception **:** OBJECT **syn** see FACE

[2]**challenge** \"\ *n* -S [ME *chalenge, calenge* claim, accusation, challenge, fr. OF *chalenge* & ONF *calenge,* fr. OF *chalengier* & ONF *calengier,* v.] **1** *obs* **:** the act or action of accusing **:** REPROACH, OBJECTION **2** *obs* **:** a demand of a right **:** CLAIM **3 a :** a calling to account or into question (as to obtain justification, verification, or information) ⟨a ~ to the chairman to explain a ruling⟩ **:** EXCEPTION, PROTEST ⟨a ~ to unauthorized use of public funds⟩ **b :** a formal exception taken to a juror or jurors arrayed for the trial of a cause but before they are sworn; *also* **:** a similar exception to a member of a court-martial **c :** words or distinctive sounds used by a sentry to cause an unidentified individual to halt and establish identity **d :** an exception taken to a voter or vote at the polls as not being legally qualified or valid **4 a :** a summons often threatening, provocative, stimulating, or inciting ⟨an unholy ~ to peace and security⟩ ⟨a ~ to uphold the spirit of democracy⟩; *specif* **:** a summons to a duel esp. as answer to an affront **b :** an invitation to compete esp. in a sport ⟨a ~ tennis match⟩ **c :** the crying of a hound when first scenting game **5 :** something that is to be striven for ⟨the ~ today is not merely to improve the material standards of living, but actually to maintain existing standards —S.G.Hanson⟩ **6** *immunol* **:** TEST; *specif* **:** a test of immunity by exposure to virulent infective material after specific immunization

challenge cup *or* **challenge trophy** *n* **:** a cup that must be competed for more than once before passing into the permanent possession of a winner

chal·leng·er \-jə(r)\ *n* -S [ME *chalenger,* fr. *chalengen* + *-er*] **:** one that challenges; *specif* **:** a contender for a championship (as in boxing)

challenging *adj* **1 :** arousing interest, thought, or action that is often contentious or competitive ⟨a ~ hypothesis⟩ ⟨a ~ divergence of opinion⟩ **2 :** inviting often alluringly or enticingly **:** pleasingly or disturbingly provocative **:** FASCINATING ⟨a ~ smile⟩ ⟨a ~ personality⟩

chal·leng·ing·ly *adv* **:** in a challenging manner **:** so as to be challenging

chal·lis \'shalē, *esp Brit* -ləs\ *also* **chal·lie** \-lē\ *n, pl* **challises** \'shalēz, *esp Brit* -ləsəz\ *also* **challies** \-lēz\ [prob. fr. the name *Challis*] **:** a lightweight soft clothing fabric made of cotton, wool, or synthetic yarns in a plain or twill weave in solid colors or small floral prints

challoth *or* **challot** *pl of* CHALLAH

chal·mer \'chämər, -ȯm-\ *n* -S [ME *chalmer, chamer,* alter. of *chambre* chamber — more at CHAMBER] *Scot* **:** CHAMBER

chal·mers·ite \'chalmə(r),zīt\ *n* -S [G *chalmersit,* fr. G. *Chalmers* fl1902 superintendent of the Brazilian mine where it was found + G *-it* -ite] **:** CUBANITE

chal·one \'ka,lōn\ *n* -S [Gk *chalōn,* pres. part. of *chalan* to slacken — more at CALANDO] **:** an internal secretion that depresses activity — compare HORMONE

cha·loupe \shə'lüp\ *n* -S [F; perh. akin to OProv *calup* small boat] **:** a small French boat (as a ship's boat or harbor craft); *specif* **:** an obsolete French lug-rigged fishing boat

chaluka *or* **chalukah** *var of* HALUKKAH

cha·lu·kya \'chälәkyə\ *n, pl* **chalukya** *or* **chalukyas** *usu cap* [Skt *Calukya*] **:** either of two dynasties of Central India: Early Chalukya, 6th century to A.D. 753, and Later Chalukya, A.D. 973 to the 11th century

cha·lu·kyan \-yən\ *adj, usu cap* **:** of or belonging to the Chalukya or to their architectural styles

cha·lu·meau \;shalə;mō\ *n, pl* **chalu·meaux** \-ōz\ [F, fr. LL *calamellus* little reed — more at CALUMET] **1 a :** a medieval wind instrument consisting of an upright tube surmounted by a small tube in which was fixed a double reed **:** SHAWM **b :** an obsolete single-reed wind instrument of varying size that after progressive modifications became the clarinet **2 :** CHANTER 3 **3 :** the lowest register of the clarinet — often used as a direction to play a passage an octave lower **4 :** a reed organ pipe usu. of 8-foot pitch and of clarinetlike tone — called also *schalmei*

chalutz *var of* HALUTZ

chalutziut *var of* HALUTZIUT

chal·y·be·an \;kalə;bēən, kə'libēən\ *adj, usu cap* [L *Chalybes* (fr. Gk) + E *-an*] **:** of or belonging to the Chalybes

[1]**cha·lyb·e·ate** \kə'libēət, -lēb-\ *adj* [prob. fr. NL *chalybeatus,* irreg. fr. L *chalybs* steel (fr. Gk *chalyb-, chalyps,* fr. *Chalybes*) + *-atus* -ate] **:** impregnated with salts of iron **:** having a taste due to iron ⟨a ~ spring⟩

[2]**chalybeate** \"\ *n* -S **:** a chalybeate liquid or medicine

cha·lyb·e·ous \-ēəs\ *adj* [L *chalybeius* of steel, fr. Gk *chalybeios,* fr. *chalyb-, chalyps* steel] **:** bluish black with a steely luster

chal·y·bes \'kalə,bēz\ *n pl, usu cap* [L, fr. Gk] **:** an early people living in northeastern Asia Minor and known to the ancient Greeks as ironworkers

chal·y·bite \-,bīt\ *n* -S [G *chalybit,* fr. L *chalyb-, chalybs* steel + G *-it* -ite] **:** SIDERITE

[1]**cham** \'cham\ *vt* **chammed; chammed; chamming; chams** [ME *chammen,* perh. of imit. origin] *dial Eng* **:** CHEW, BITE

[2]**cham** *var of* KHAN

[3]**cham** \chəm, (;)cham\ [alter. of ME *ich am*] *dial Eng* **:** I am

[4]**cham** \'chäm\ *or* **chi·am** \'chē,äm\ *n, pl* **cham** *or* **chams** *or* **chiam** *or* **chiams** *usu cap* **1 a :** a people of an ancient kingdom in the central coastal part of Annam that reached its peak of power in the 7th and 8th centuries and was absorbed by Annam in 1471 **b :** a member of such people **2 a** (1) **:** a people in central coastal Annam linguistically related to the Cambodians (2) **:** a member of such people **b :** the language of the Cham people

[1]**cha·ma** \'kāmə\ *n* [NL, fr. L *chama, chema* cockle, fr. Gk *chēmē;* akin to Gk *chaskein* to yawn, gape, L *hiare* — more at YAWN] **1** *cap* **:** a genus (the type of the family Chamidae) of eulamellibranchiate bivalve mollusks of warm or tropical seas having fixed massive irregular inequivalve shells and comprising the rock oysters and extinct related forms **2** -S **:** a member of the genus *Chama* **:** ROCK OYSTER

[2]**cha·ma** \'chämə\ *n, pl* **chama** *or* **chamas** *usu cap* [Sp, of AmerInd origin] **1 a :** a Panoan people of northeastern Peru **b :** a member of such people — called also *Chuncho* **2 :** the language of the Chama people

cha·ma·co·co \,chämə'kō(,)kō\ *n, pl* **chamacoco** *or* **chamacocos** *usu cap* [Sp, of AmerInd origin] **1 a :** a Zamuco people of Bolivia **b :** a member of such people **2 :** the language of the Chamacoco people

cha·made \shə'mäd\ *n* -S [F, prob. fr. Pg *chamada,* fr. *chamar* to call, fr. L *clamare* to cry out — more at CLAIM] **:** a drum or trumpet signal for a parley with the enemy

chamae- *or* **chame-** *in pronunciations below,* ;== = ;kamē *or* -mə\ *comb form* [NL, fr. Gk *chamai* on the ground — more at HUMBLE] **:** low **:** ground ⟨*Chamaerops*⟩ ⟨*Chamaesaura*⟩ — used chiefly in generic names of plants and animals

cham·ae·ba·tia \,==;bāsh(ē)ə\ *n, cap* [NL, fr. Gk *chamaibatos* blackberry (fr. *chamai-* chamae- + *batos* blackberry) + NL *-ia*] **:** a small genus of low heavy-scented California evergreen shrubs of the family Rosaceae with fernlike foliage and white flowers in loose terminal cymes

cham·ae·ce·phal·ic \;==sə;falik\ *adj* [ISV *chamae-* + *cephalic*] *anthrop* **:** having a flattened receding head with a length-height index of 70 or less — **cham·ae·ceph·a·ly** \,=='sefəlē\ *n* -ES

cham·ae·conch \'==,käŋk, -änch\ *adj* [*chamae-* + *-conch* (fr. L *concha* shell) — more at CONCH] *anthrop* **:** having low wide orbits with an orbital index of less than 83 — **cham·ae·con·chy** \-äŋkē, -änchē\ *n* -ES

cham·ae·cra·ni·al \;==;krānēəl\ *adj* [G *chamäkran* chamaecranial (fr. *chamä-* chamae- + Gk *kranion* cranium) + E *-ial* — more at CRANIUM] *anthrop* **:** having a low flat skull with a length-height index of less than 70 — **cham·ae·cra·nic** \-;kranik\ *adj* — **cham·ae·cra·ny** \'==,krānē\ *n*

cham·ae·cris·ta \,=='kristə\ *n, cap* [NL, fr. *chamae-* + *crista* (fr. *crista pavonis,* lit., peacock's crest, the pre-Linnaean name of a certain plant of the family Leguminosae) — more at CREST] *in some classifications* **:** a genus of herbs or low shrubs characterized by sensitive leaves and suddenly and forcibly dehiscing pods, now included in the genus *Cassia*

cham·ae·cyp·a·ris \,==;sipərəs\ *n, cap* [NL, fr. *chamae-* + *-cyparis* (fr. Gk *kyparissos* cypress) — more at CYPRESS] **:** a small genus of important timber trees of the family Pinaceae native to No. America and Japan — see SOUTHERN WHITE CEDAR

cha·mae·leon \kə'mēlyən, -lēən\ *n, cap* [NL, fr. L, chameleon — more at CHAMELEON] **:** a large genus (the type of the family Chamaeleontidae) of lizards including most of the Old World chameleons — compare RHIPTOGLOSSA

cha·mae·le·on·i·da \kə,mēlē'änədə\ *or* **cha·mae·le·on·tes** \-'än(,)tēz\ [*Chamaeleonida* fr. NL, fr. *Chamaeleon* + *-ida; Chamaeleontes* fr. NL, fr. L *chamaeleontes,* pl. of *chamaeleont-, chamaeleon* chameleon] *syn of* RHIPTOGLOSSA

cham·ae·lir·i·um \,kamə'lirēəm\ *n* [NL, fr. *chamae-* + Gk *leirion* lily — more at LILY] **1** *cap* **:** a genus of plants (family Melanthaceae) of eastern No. America with flowers in a spikelike raceme **2** *pl* **chamaelir·ia** \-rēə\ **:** HELONIAS

cham·ae·ne·ri·on \,=='nirē,än, -ēən\ *n, cap* [NL, fr. *chamae-* + Gk *nērion* oleander] *in some classifications* **:** a small genus of herbs of the family Onagraceae that is usu included in the genus *Epilobium*

cham·ae·phyte \'kamə,fīt\ *n* -S [*chamae-* + *-phyte*] **:** a perennial plant that bears its over-wintering buds above the surface of but within a few inches of the soil — compare GEOPHYTE, PHANEROPHYTE

cham·ae·pro·so·pic \;==prə;sōpik, -äpik\ *adj* [G *chamäprosop* (fr. *chamä-* chamae- + Gk *prosōpon* face) + E *-ic* — more at PROSOP-] *anthrop* **:** having a low broad face with a facial index of 90 or below — **cham·ae·pros·o·py** \,==-'präsəpē, -prə'sōpē\ *n* -ES

cha·mae·rops \kə'mē,räps\ *n, cap* [NL, fr. L, fr. Gk *chamairōps* wall germander, fr. *chamai-* chamae- + *rhōps* shrub, bush; akin to Gk *rhabdos* rod — more at VERVAIN] **:** a genus of dwarf fan palms of the Mediterranean region having petioles with long straight teeth on their margins usu. for their whole length — see HEMP PALM

cham·aer·rhine \'kamə,rīn\ *adj* [ISV *chamae-* + *-rrhine;* orig. formed as G *chamärrhin*] *anthrop* **:** having a short broad nose with a nasal index of 51–57.9 on the skull, of 85–99.9 on the living — **cham·aer·rhi·ny** \-īnē\ *n* -ES

cham·ae·sau·ra \,kamē'sȯrə, -mə-\ *n, cap* [NL, fr. *chamae-* + *-saura*] **:** a genus of African snakelike lizards (family Cordylidae) without limbs or with one or both pairs of limbs reduced to scaly vestiges

cham·ae·si·phon \-'sīfən, -,fän\ *n, cap* [NL, fr. *chamae-* +

Gk *siphōn* tube] **:** a genus (the type of the family Chamaesiphonaceae) of one-celled blue-green algae characterized by epiphytic habit and formation of endospores that are released by early breakdown of the cell wall at the apex and by successive abstriction

cham·ae·sy·ce \ˌ==ˈsī(ˌ)sē\ *n, cap* [NL, fr. L, fr. Gk *chamaisykē*, fr. *chamai-* chamae- + *sykē* fig tree, fr. *sykon* fig — more at FIG] *in some classifications* **:** a genus of herbs or shrubs (family Euphorbiaceae) now usu. included in the genus *Euphorbia*

cha·ma fox \ˈkämə-\ *n* [part trans. of NL *Vulpes chama*, fr. *Vulpes* + *chama*, modif. of E *caama*] **:** CAAMA 1

[1]cha·mar \chəˈmär\ *n* -S *often cap* [Hindi *camār*, fr. Skt *carmakāra* leather worker, fr. *carman* skin, leather + *-kāra* worker, fr. *kṛṇoti* he does, makes; akin to L *corium* leather — more at CUIRASS, KARMA] **:** a member of a low Indian caste whose caste occupation is leatherworking

[2]cha·mar \ˈchəmə(r)\ *n* -S [Hindi *camar*, fr. Skt *camara*] **:** a fan, typically made of a yak's tail or peacock feathers, used in the Indian subcontinent as a mark of royalty or in temples

chamas *pl of* CHAMA

[1]cham·ber \ˈchāmbə(r)\ *n* -S [ME *chambre*, fr. OF, fr. LL *camera*, fr. L, arched roof, fr. Gk *kamara* vault; akin to L *camur* curved, Av *kamarā* girdle] **1 :** a room usu. in a house and typically with some special feature or distinguishing characteristic: **a :** a private room: as (1) **:** BEDROOM (2) **:** a room situated above the ground floor of a house **b** *chiefly Brit* **:** a suite of rooms **:** APARTMENT — used in pl. ⟨he lived in ~s which had once belonged to his deceased partner —Charles Dickens⟩ **c** *South* **:** a ground-floor sitting room usu. furnished with a bed **d :** *chiefly New Eng* **:** a storage room on an upper floor of a house or barn **e :** the upper level of the inner stage of an Elizabethan playhouse typically used to represent a room of intimate or domestic character — compare STUDY **2 :** an enclosed or compartmented space within the body of an animal ⟨anterior and posterior ~s of the eye⟩ **3 :** an often large room devoted to some special or unusual purpose ⟨the reception hall, a magnificent ~ two stories high . . . executed in a manner that could be called palatial —Lewis Mumford⟩: **a :** a hall for the meetings of a deliberative, legislative, or judicial body or assembly ⟨senate ~⟩ ⟨council ~⟩ **b :** a chamberlain's office **:** a treasury or room where government moneys are received and kept **c :** a room to which a judge retires for consultation (as with opposing counsel) or for official proceedings that may be conducted out of court — usu. used in pl. ⟨Judge Winters reentered the courtroom from his ~s —Erle Stanley Gardner⟩ **d :** the reception room of a person of high rank or authority ⟨the king's audience ~⟩ **4 a :** a legislative or judicial body; *esp* **:** either of the houses of a bicameral legislature **b :** a voluntary board or council (as for some business purpose) **5 a** *obs* **:** a detached plug containing the charge inserted at the breech of heavy firearms **b** *obs* **:** a short cannon that stood on its breech and that was used for celebrations and in the theater **c :** the part of the bore of a gun that holds the charge — see CANNON illustration **d :** the part of a firearm tooled to receive the cartridge: as (1) **:** any of the barrels containing the cartridge in an old revolver (2) **:** a compartment in the cartridge cylinder of a revolver **6 :** an enclosed or compartmented space designed for some special purpose ⟨a dyeing ~⟩ ⟨a gear ~⟩ **7 :** a canal lock **8 :** CHAMBER POT — **chambered** *adj*

[2]chamber \"\ *vt* **chambered; chambered; chambering** \-b(ə)riŋ\ **chambers** [ME *chambren*, fr. *chambre*, n.] **1 :** to place in or as if in a chamber **:** SHELTER, HOUSE, CONFINE ⟨~*ed* in a narrow cave⟩ **2 :** to furnish with a chamber ⟨~*ed* corridors⟩ **3 :** to serve as a chamber for; *esp* **:** to accommodate in the chamber of a firearm ⟨a rifle that will ~ short, long, or long-rifle cartridges⟩ **4 :** to enlarge the bottom of (a drill hole) by one or more light preliminary shots so that a sufficient blasting charge may be loaded for the final shot

[3]chamber \"\ *adj* [[1]*chamber*] **1 :** conducted with or marked by privacy or secrecy ⟨personal ~ studies⟩ ⟨the king's ~ council⟩ **2 :** intended for performance by a few musicians for a small audience **:** INTIMATE ⟨~ works⟩ ⟨~ opera⟩

chamber acid *n* [*chamber (process)*] **:** sulfuric acid made by the chamber process; *esp* **:** the acid of less than 70 percent strength as it leaves the lead chambers before being concentrated

chamber composer *n* [*chamber (music)*] **:** a musician attached to a noble household to compose and direct music

chamber crystals *n* [*chamber (process)*] **:** nitrosylsulfuric acid formed as crystals in the chamber process of making sulfuric acid

chamberdeacon *n* -S [ME *chambredeken*, fr. *chambre* chamber + *deken* deacon] **:** any of certain impoverished Irish scholars at a 15th century English university

chambered nautilus *n* **:** NAUTILUS 1a

[1]chamberer *n* -S [ME *chamberere, chambrier*, fr. MF *chamberiere*, fem. of *chamberier* chamberlain, fr. LL *camerarius*, fr. LL *camera* + L *-arius* -er] *obs* **:** CHAMBERMAID

[2]chamberer *n* -S [ME, chamberlain, fr. MF *chamberier*] *archaic* **:** GALLANT, LOVER, CAVALIER

chamber filter *n* **:** a filter press in which the spaces for the filter cake are formed by raised edges on the plates

cham·be·ri \ˈchämbərē\ *n, pl* **chamberi** *or* **chamberis** *usu cap* **:** TCHAMBULI

cham·ber·ing \ˈchāmb(ə)riŋ\ *n* -S [ME *chambring*, fr. gerund of *chambren*] **:** WANTONNESS, FORNICATION

chamber kiln *n* **:** a kiln with chambers heated separately

cham·ber·lain \ˈchāmbə(r)lən\ *n* -S [ME *chamberleyn*, fr. OF *chamberlenc, chamberlayn*, of Gmc origin; akin to OHG *chamarling* chamberlain, fr. *chamara* chamber (fr. LL *camera*) + *-ling* (akin to OE *-ling*) — more at CHAMBER] **1 :** a bedchamber attendant for royalty or nobility **2 a :** a chief officer in the household of a king or nobleman **b :** one in charge of moneys **:** TREASURER ⟨the town ~⟩ **3** *archaic* **:** an inn attendant in charge of bedchambers

cham·ber·land filter \ˈchāmbə(r)lən(d)-, *F* shäⁿberläⁿ-\ *n, usu cap C* [after Charles-Édouard *Chamberland* †1908 Fr. scientist, its inventor] **:** a candle-shaped porcelain filter used chiefly to filter out microorganisms (as from culture media)

chamber lye *n* [*chamber (pot)*] *now dial* **:** URINE

chambermaid \ˈ==ˌ=\ *n* [[1]*chamber* + *maid*] **1 :** a maid who makes beds and does general cleaning of bedrooms and bathrooms in a home, hotel, or motel **2** *obs* **:** a lady's maid

cham·ber·man \ˈ==mən, -ˌman\ *n, pl* **chambermen** [*chamber (process)* + *man*] **:** a skilled worker engaged in the making of sulfuric acid by the chamber process

chamber music *n* [trans. of It *musica da camera*] **:** art music, usu. instrumental, intended for performance in a private room or small audience hall **:** intimate music as distinguished esp. from operatic and symphonic music

chamber of commerce : an association of businessmen to promote the commercial and industrial interests of a community, state, or nation — compare BOARD OF TRADE

chamber of deputies : the lower or popular branch of certain legislatures

chamber of horrors 1 : a hall in which various things of macabre interest (as relics of criminals and instruments of torture) are exhibited; *also* **:** a collection of such exhibits **2 :** an assemblage of things of macabre interest

chamber orchestra *n* [*chamber (music)*] **:** a small orchestra usu. with one player for each instrumental part **:** SINFONIETTA

chamber organ *n* **:** a small pipe organ

chamber pot *n* **:** a bedroom vessel for urine or other waste

chamber practice *n* **:** the part of the practice of lawyers that is conducted in their offices as distinguished from that involved in appearing in court

chamber process *n* **1 :** a process of making sulfuric acid in which sulfur dioxide is oxidized by moist air with nitrogen oxides as catalyst in a series of lead-lined chambers — see GAY-LUSSAC TOWER, GLOVER TOWER **2 :** a process of making basic carbonate white lead in which lead strips are exposed to carbon dioxide, moist air, and acetic acid vapor in brick chambers

chambers *pl of* CHAMBER, *pres 3d sing of* CHAMBER

chamber sonata *n* [trans. of It *sonata da camera*] **:** SONATA DA CAMERA

cham·ber·tin \shäⁿbertaⁿ\ *n* -S *usu cap* [F, fr. *Chambertin*, vineyard near Dijon, France, where it is produced] **:** a red Burgundy wine

chamberwoman \ˈ==ˌ==\ *n* **:** CHAMBERMAID

cham·be·ry \shäⁿbārē\ *n* -ES *usu cap* [fr. *Chambéry*, France, where it is made] **:** a dry vermouth

chamblet *obs var of* CAMLET

cham·bray \ˈshamˌbrā, -ˌbrē, shamˈbrā, -aam-\ *n* -S [irreg. fr. *Cambrai*, city of France] **:** a lightweight clothing fabric of plain weave made of cotton, silk, linen, or synthetic yarns and having a frosted appearance due to the interweaving of colored warp and white filling yarns

chame- — see CHAMAE-

cha·me·leon *also* **ca·me·leon** \kəˈmēlyən, -lēən *sometimes* shə-\ *n* -S *often attrib* [modif. (influenced by L *chamaeleon*) of ME *camelion*, fr. MF *camelion, camelion*, fr. L *chamaeleon*, fr. Gk *chamaileōn*, fr. *chamai-* chamae- + *leōn* lion — more at LION] **1 :** any of a group (Rhiptoglossa) of specialized slow-moving Old World acrodont lizards that have a laterally compressed body with the skin covered with small granules, a prehensile tail, opposed digits, very large independently movable eyeballs behind eyelids partially fused to leave only a small central opening, and an extremely elastic extensible tongue which can be shot out nearly the length of the animal to take the insects on which it feeds, and that display unusual ability to change the color of the skin in response to both external stimuli and internal factors **2 a :** a fickle person; *esp* **:** a person given to expedient or facile change in ideas or character ⟨he was a ~ and his rare capacity for recognizing what was required of him . . . was equalled only by his capacity for becoming it —Anthony West⟩ **b :** something subject to quick or frequent change esp. in appearance ⟨his goodness was a ~ that changed its hue to the hue of the situation in which he found himself —Peggy Bennett⟩ **3 :** any of various American lizards capable of changing their color; *esp* **:** any of several members of the common genus *Anolis*

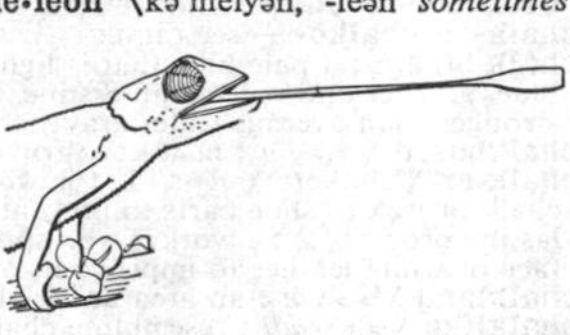

common chameleon 1

cha·me·le·on·ic \kəˌmēlēˈänik\ *adj* **:** like a chameleon in changeability **:** assuming varying hues **:** INCONSTANT

chameleon tree frog *n* **:** TREE TOAD

chametz *var of* HAMETZ

[1]cham·fer \ˈcham(p)fə(r), -aam-, -mpə(r)\ *n* -S [modif. of MF *chanfrein*, alter. of *chanfreint* beveled edge, fr. past part. of *chanfraindre* to bevel, fr. *chant* edge (fr. L *canthus* iron ring round a carriage wheel) + *fraindre* to break, fr. L *frangere* — more at CANT, BREAK] **1 :** a small groove **:** FURROW **2 :** the surface formed by cutting away the angle at the intersection of two faces of a piece of timber, stone, or metal **:** a beveled edge

[2]chamfer \"\ *vt* **chamfered; chamfered; chamfering** \-f(ə)riŋ, -p(ə)r-\ **chamfers 1 a :** to cut a furrow in (as in a column) **:** GROOVE, CHANNEL, FLUTE **b :** to cut off corners or edges (as of timber columns and beams) **2 :** to make a chamfer on **:** cut or reduce (as an angle) to a chamfer **:** BEVEL

chamfer angle *n* **:** the angle between a chamfered surface and one of the original surfaces from which the chamfer is cut

chamfer bit *n* **:** a bit formed to bevel the edge of a hole

cham·fer·er \-m(p)fərə(r), -mpər-\ *n* -S **:** one that chamfers

chamfer plane *n* **:** a carpenter's plane having a V-grooved bottom and used for chamfering the edges of woodwork

chamfron *also* **chaffron** *or* **chafron** *or* **chamfrain** *or* **chanfron** *n* -S [ME *shamfron*, fr. MF *chanfrein*, fr. OF, irreg. fr. *chafresner* to subdue, make obedient, fr. *chief* head (fr. L *caput*) + *frener* to bridle, fr. L *frenare*, fr. *frenum* bridle — more at HEAD, REFRAIN] **:** the headpiece of a horse's bard

cha·mi·cu·ra \ˌchämēˈkürə\ *also* **cha·mi·cu·ro** \-ü(ˌ)rō\ *n, pl* **chamicura** *or* **chamicuras** *also* **chamicuro** *or* **chamicuros** *usu cap* [Sp *chamicuro*, of AmerInd origin] **1 a :** a people of northern Peru considered by some Americanists to be Panoan **b :** a member of such people **2 :** the language of the Chamicura people

cham·i·sal \ˌshaməˈsal\ *n* -S [AmerSp, fr. *chamiso*] **:** a California chaparral of chamiso

cha·mi·so \shəˈmē(ˌ)sō, ch-, -ēsə\ *or* **cha·mise** \-ēs\ *also* **cha·mi·sa** \-ēsə\ *n* -S [AmerSp *chamiso, chamis*, alter. of Sp *chamizo* half-burned wood, fr. Pg *chamiço* stick, wood, fr. *chamiça* small dry pieces of wood — more at CHAMIZA] **1 :** a California shrub (*Adenostoma fasciculatum*) that forms a dense chaparral — see CHAMISAL **2 :** TOYON **3** *Puerto Rico* **:** AKEAKE 1 **4** *Southwest* **:** CHAMIZA

cha·mite \ˈkāˌmīt\ *n* -S [NL *Chama* + E *-ite*] **:** a fossil shell of the genus *Chama* or a related genus

cha·mi·za \shəˈmēzə, ch-\ *n* -S [MexSp, fr. Sp, a grass used in thatching, brushwood, fr. Pg *chamiça* small dry pieces of wood, a cane, a heather, fr. *chama* flame, fr. L *flamma*; akin to L *flagrare* to burn] **:** a semidesert evergreen shrub (*Atriplex canescens*) that has greenish gray foliage and is important as a browse plant in the southern U.S. — called also *chamiso*

chamlet *obs var of* CAMLET

cham·ma \ˈshamə\ *n* -S [Amharic *shamma*] **:** a cotton togalike usu. white garment worn in Ethiopia

chammed *past of* CHAM

chamming *pres part of* CHAM

[1]cham·ois \ˈshamē, -mi, *in sense 1 also* (ˈ)shamˈwä\ *n, pl* **cham·ois** *also* **cha·moix** *in sense 1* -ē(z) *or* -i(z) *or* -wä(z); *in other senses* -ēz *or* -iz\ [MF, fr. LL *camox*, prob. of non-IE origin; akin to the source of OHG *gamiza* chamois] **1 :** a small agile goatlike antelope (*Rupicapra rupicapra*) that lives on the loftiest mountain ridges of Europe and in the Caucasus and is a favorite quarry of hunters **2** *also* **cham·my** *or* **sham·my** *or* **sha·moy** \ˈshamē, -mi\ **a :** a soft pliant leather prepared from the skin of the chamois **b :** an oil-tanned suede-finished leather prepared from the flesher of sheepskins **3** *or* **shammy** -ES **:** a piece of chamois; *esp* **:** a cloth used for washing or polishing **4** *or* **chamois yellow** *also* **chamois skin :** a grayish yellow that is redder, stronger, and slightly lighter than crash, lighter, stronger, and slightly redder than old ivory, and stronger and slightly redder than flax

chamois

[2]cham·ois \ˈshamē, -mi\ *vt* **chamoised** \-mēd, -id\ **chamoised** \-mēd, -id\ **chamoising** \-mēiŋ, -ēēŋ, -i·iŋ\ **chamoises** \-mēz, -iz\ **1** *also* **sha·moy** \ˈshamē, -mi\ **:** to prepare or dress like chamois **2** *or* **sham·my** \ˈshamē, -mi\ **:** to clean or polish with a chamois

chamois cloth *n* **:** a soft cloth fabric made in imitation of chamois leather

cham·o·line \ˈshaməˌlēn, ˌ==ˈ=\ *n* -S [perh. irreg. fr. *chamois*] **:** BUCKTHORN BROWN

cham·o·mile *or* **cam·o·mile** \ˈkaməˌmīl, -ī(ə)l *also* -ēl *or* -ē(ə)l\ *n* -S [ME *camemille*, fr. ML *camomilla*, fr. LL *chamomilla*, modif. of L *chamaemelon*, fr. Gk *chamaimēlon*, fr. *chamai-* chamae- + *mēlon* apple; fr. the applelike smell of its flower — more at MALUS] **1 a :** a plant of the genus *Anthemis* (esp. the common European *A. nobilis*) having strong-scented foliage and flower heads that contain a bitter medicinal principle used as an antispasmodic or a diaphoretic **b :** a plant of the related genus *Matricaria* (esp. *M. chamomilla*) having foliage and flower heads that contain the bitter principle found in plants of the genus *Anthemis* **2 :** the dried flower heads of either of two plants of the genera *Anthemis* and *Matricaria* (*A. nobilis* and *M. chamomilla*) used as aromatic bitters

chamomile oil *n* **:** a blue aromatic essential oil obtained from the flower heads of either of two plants: **a :** such an oil obtained from the common European chamomile and used in perfumes and in medicine — called also *Roman chamomile oil* **b :** such an oil obtained from a related plant (*Matricaria chamomilla*) and used in perfumes — called also *German chamomile oil*

cha·mor·ro \chəˈmȯ(ˌ)rō\ *n, pl* **chamorro** *or* **chamorros** *usu cap* [Sp, lit., man with a shorn head, perh. of Iberian origin; akin to Basque *samur, samurr* tender] **1 a :** a people of the Mariana islands **b :** a member of such people **2 :** the language of the Chamorro people

cham·o·site \ˈshaməˌzīt\ *or* **cham·oi·site** \-m(w)əˌz-\ *n* -S [F, fr. *Chamoson, Chamoison*, Valais canton, Switzerland, its locality + F *-ite*] **:** a mineral consisting of a greenish gray or black silicate (sp. gr. 3–3.4) — **cham·o·sit·ic** \ˌ==ˈzid·ik\ *adj*

cha·motte \shəˈmät\ *n* -S [prob. fr. F, fr. G *schamotte*] **:** GROG 2

[1]champ \ˈchamp, -aa(ə)-, -ai-\ *vb* -ED/-ING/-S [perh. imit.] *vt* **1 a :** to chew on with noisy vigor ⟨~*ing* his food with the gusto of a healthy young animal —*MacLean's Mag.*⟩ **b :** to bite on repeatedly or grind the teeth forcefully against ⟨~*ing* the stem of his pipe in his teeth —Marcia Davenport⟩ **2 :** to open and close with force and noise **:** GNASH ⟨a green crab . . . ~*ing* enormous claws —I.L.Idriess⟩ **3 :** MASH, TRAMPLE ⟨~*ing* soil and water into mud⟩ ~ *vi* **1 :** to make biting or gnashing movements or gestures **:** BITE ⟨a race horse ~*ing* behind a barrier —Upton Sinclair⟩ ⟨little caterpillars . . . ~*ing* on leaves —Peggy Bennett⟩ **2 :** to show restive impatience of delay or restraint ⟨for years industrial psychologists had been ~*ing* to apply scientific methods —W.H.Whyte⟩ — **champ at the bit** *or* **champ the bit 1** *of a horse* **:** to bite or gnash a bit in unruliness or impatience ⟨the mustang snorted and *champed the bit* . . . ready to bolt —Zane Grey⟩ **2 :** to be impatient of restraint or inactivity ⟨Gaul may *champ the bit* and foam in fetters —Lord Byron⟩

[2]champ \"\ *n* -S **:** the act or action of champing

[3]champ *adj* -ER/-EST [origin unknown] *dial Eng* **:** FIRM, HARD

[4]champ \"\ *n* -S [by shortening] **:** CHAMPION

[5]champ \"\ *n* -S [by shortening] **:** CHAMPAC

cham·pa \ˈchampə\ *n, pl* **champa** *or* **champas** *usu cap* **1 :** a Tibetan people of eastern Kashmir **2 :** a member of the Champa people

cham·pac *also* **cham·pak** \ˈchamˌpak, -əm(ˌ)pək\ *or* **cham·pa·ca** *or* **cham·pa·ka** \-pəkə\ *n* -S [Hindi & Skt; Hindi *campak*, fr. Skt *campaka*, of Dravidian origin; akin to Tamil *canpakam, cenpakam*] **:** an East Indian tree (*Michelia champaca*) the yellow flowers of which yield an oil used as a perfume

cham·pa·col \ˈchampəˌkȯl, -ōl\ *n* -S [*champac* + *-ol*] **:** GUAIOL

cham·pagne \(ˈ)shamˈpān, -aam-\ *n* -S *often attrib* [F, fr *Champagne*, region (formerly province) of northeastern France where it was first produced, fr. LL *campania* level country] **1 :** a white sparkling wine that undergoes one fermentation in a cask and a second fermentation in a bottle, the latter generating carbon dioxide that makes the wine sparkle **2 a :** a wine of the champagne type; *broadly* **:** an effervescent white wine **3 :** a pale orange yellow to light grayish yellowish brown — called also *belleek*

champagne cider *n* **:** a sparkling cider that is matured in vats and then fermented in bottles to produce effervescence

champagne cocktail *n* **:** a cocktail consisting of champagne flavored with sugar and bitters, garnished with a twist of lemon peel, and usu. served in a saucer champagne glass

champagne d'ar·gent \-ˌdärˈzhäⁿ, *F* shäⁿpänʸdärzhäⁿ\ *n, usu cap C&A* [F, lit., silver champagne] **:** a French breed of large hardy productive domestic rabbits having silvery blue fur

cham·pagn·i·za·tion \(ˌ)shamˌpānəˈzāshən\ *n* -S **:** the process of making a wine sparkling

cham·pagn·ize \shamˈpāˌnīz\ *vt* -ED/-ING/-S [F *champagniser*, fr. *champagne* + *-iser* -ize] **:** to make (a wine) sparkling by retaining the carbon dioxide generated during fermentation

[1]cham·paign *often* ˈchamˌpān *during its floruit; today prob usu* (ˈ)shamˈp-\ *n* -S [ME *champayne*, fr. MF *champagne*, fr. LL *campania* level country — more at CAMPAIGN] **1 a :** an expanse of level open country **:** PLAIN ⟨the wide ~ around the city⟩ **b :** level open country ⟨traversing the ~ and avoiding the mountains⟩ **2** *archaic* **:** an area of army operations **:** BATTLEGROUND **3 a :** an open expanse ⟨the ~ of the broad sea⟩ **b :** an encompassed expanse **:** FIELD ⟨the ~ of science⟩

[2]champaign \"\ *adj* **1 :** flat and open like a champaign **:** constituting a champaign ⟨a ~ region⟩ **2 :** occurring in a champaign ⟨~ sports⟩ of a champaign ⟨~ scenery⟩

champed *past of* CHAMP

cham·per·tor \ˈchampə(r)d·ə(r)\ *n* -S [earlier *champartour, champertour*, fr. MF *champarteor*, fr. *champart* + *-eor* -or] **:** one that engages in champerty

cham·per·tous \-d·əs\ *adj* [*champerty* + *-ous*] **:** of, relating to, or involving champerty ⟨a ~ contract⟩

cham·per·ty *also* **cham·par·ty** \-d·ē\ *n* -ES [ME *champartie*, modif. (prob. influenced by ME *partie* part) of MF *champart* field rent, fr. *champ* field (fr. L *campus*) + *part* portion — more at CAMP, PART] **:** a proceeding, illegal in many jurisdictions, by which a person not a party in a suit bargains to aid in or carry on its prosecution or defense by furnishing money or personal services in consideration of his receiving a share of the matter in suit **:** maintenance with the addition of an agreement to divide the thing in suit

champest *superlative of* CHAMP

champian *n or adj* [by alter.] *obs* **:** CHAMPAIGN

cham·pi·gnon \shamˈpinyən, -pē- *also* ch-; *F* shäⁿpēnʸōⁿ\ *n* -S [MF, alter. of *champigneul*, fr. *champagne* level country — more at CHAMPAIGN] **1** *obs* **:** FUNGUS **2 :** an edible fungus; *esp* **:** the common meadow mushroom **3 :** a fairy ring (*Marasmius oreades*)

champing *pres part of* CHAMP

[1]cham·pi·on \ˈchampēən, -aam-, -aim-, *chiefly dial or substand* (ˈ)=ˈpēn\ *n* -S [ME *champioun*, fr. OF *champion*, fr. ML *campion-, campio*, of WGmc origin; akin to OE *cempa* warrior, soldier, OHG *kempho* — more at KEMP] **1 :** WARRIOR, FIGHTER, COMBATANT ⟨~s arming for battle⟩ **2 :** a militant advocate or defender ⟨a royalist, always a ~ of his king⟩ **3 :** one that fights, often in single formal combat, for another's rights, honor, or fame ⟨the lady's ~ entered the lists⟩ **4 a :** one whose supremacy or superiority is formally acknowledged esp. after a test, contest, or series of tests or contests ⟨individual and team ~s at the Olympics⟩ ⟨the conference ~s⟩ ⟨the world's chess ~⟩ **b :** a show animal that has won a certain number of points in open competition ⟨this collie puppy is already a ~⟩ **c :** a plant or plant part (as a fruit or flower) that has received a first prize in a competitive exhibit ⟨these tomatoes are ~s⟩ **d :** one showing a marked superiority ⟨a ~ at telling tall tales⟩ **5** *or* **champion oak :** RED OAK 1a

[2]champion \"\ *vt* -ED/-ING/-S **1** *archaic* **:** CHALLENGE, DEFY ⟨~*ing* one to speak⟩ **2 :** to protect or fight for as a champion ⟨~*ing* his lady in the lists⟩ **3 :** to act as militant supporter of **:** DEFEND, UPHOLD, ADVOCATE ⟨faithful to Jefferson's principles, ~*ed* states' rights —*Amer. Guide Series: Va.*⟩

[3]champion \"\ *adj* **1 :** acknowledged as supreme over contestants or rivals ⟨the ~ team of the league⟩ ⟨the ~ speller of the class⟩ **2 a :** FIRST-RATE, SPLENDID ⟨if you'll drop me at the next corner, my lord, that'll do me ~ —Dorothy L. Sayers⟩ **b :** FOREMOST, UNSURPASSED ⟨the ~ liar of the club⟩

[4]champion *obs var of* CHAMPAIGN

cham·pi·on·less \-ləs\ *adj* **:** being without a champion

cham·pi·on·ship \-ˌship\ *n* -S *often attrib* **1 :** the position of a champion **:** acknowledged supremacy; *specif* **:** the title of champion in a competitive sport or game ⟨won four ~s in five years⟩ **2 :** the act of championing **:** ADVOCACY, DEFENSE, SUPPORT ⟨his ~ of the new theory⟩ ⟨~ of the small nations against the Big Four —Vera M. Dean⟩ **3 :** a contest held to determine a champion ⟨colleges represented in the NCAA ~s⟩

champion tooth *n* **:** a form of double tooth for crosscut saws

cham·plain·ian \(ˈ)shamˈplānēən\ *adj, usu cap* [Lake *Champlain*, N. Y. + E *-ian*] **:** of or relating to a subdivision of the No. American Ordovician — see GEOLOGIC TIME table

[1]champ·le·vé \ˌshäⁿləˈvā\ *adj* [F, fr. past part. of *champlever* to engrave depressions in a smooth surface, fr. *champ* field, ground of an engraving (fr. L *campus* field) + *lever* to raise, remove — more at CAMP, LEVER] **:** having the metal ground engraved, cut out, or depressed and the resultant spaces filled in with enamel pastes and fired — used of enamel work; compare CLOISONNÉ

[2]champlevé \"\ *n* -S **1 :** a piece of champlevé enamel **2 :** the art or process of making champlevé enamel **:** champlevé work

champ·ney rose \ˈchampnē-\ *n, usu cap C* [after John *Champney* *fl*1801 Am. horticulturist who developed it] **:** NOISETTE ROSE

champs *pl of* CHAMP, *pres 3d sing of* CHAMP
chams *pres 3d sing of* CHAM, *pl of* CHAM
chamsin *var of* KHAMSIN
ch'an \'chän\ *n* -S *usu cap* [prob. fr. Chin *ch'an*² meditation] **:** a Chinese school of Mahayana Buddhism founded in the 6th century A.D. by the Indian teacher Bodhidharma that emphasizes meditation and higher contemplation as a method of salvation — the Chinese equivalent of the Japanese *Zen* or the Indian *Dhyana*
chan *abbr* channel
cha·ná \chə'nä, chä'-\ *n, pl* **chaná** or **chanás** *usu cap* [Sp, of AmerInd origin] **:** one of a number of groups of Indian peoples of various language affiliation: **a :** the Charrua peoples of Uruguay **b :** some Arawakan peoples; *esp* **:** LAYANÁ **c :** some Tupi-Guaranian peoples
cha·ña·bal \ˌchänyəˈbäl\ *also* **cha·ne·abal** \", -nēə-\ *n, pl* **chañabal** \-äl\ *or* **chañaba·les** \-ä(ˌ)läs\ *or* **chañabals** \-älz\ *usu cap* [Sp *chaneabal, chañabal,* of AmerInd origin] **:** TOJOLABAL
cha·nar \chän'yär\ *n, pl* **chana·res** \-ä(ˌ)rās\ [Sp *chañar*] **:** a thorny shrub or small tree (*Geoffraea decorticans*) of the family Leguminosae common in central Argentina which bears sweet edible berries
chanc *abbr* chancellor; chancery
¹**chance** \'chan(t)s, -aa(ə)-,-ai-,-ȧ-\ *n* -S [ME, fr. OF *cheance, chance,* fr. (assumed) VL *cadentia* fall, fr. L *cadent-, cadens,* pres. part. of *cadere* to fall; akin to Skt *śad* to fall and prob. to W *cesair* hailstones] **1 a :** something that happens unpredictably without any discernible human intention or direction and in dissociation from any observable pattern, causal relation, natural necessity, or providential dispensation ⟨this is a strange ~ that throws you and me together —Charles Dickens⟩ ⟨when the ~*s* of war make him again the spokesman of the majority —B.N.Cardozo⟩ **b** *archaic* **:** such a happening or happenings affecting human well-being in a particular way ⟨hard ~ they had, and lots of 'em died, I guess —Sarah O. Jewett⟩ **c :** the assumed impersonal purposeless determiner of such unaccountable happenings and of the outcome of uncertain situations involving alternatives unavailable to human choice **:** LUCK ⟨whatever be my ~ or my mischance —Robert Browning⟩ ⟨sane persons who by ~ or by evil design have been confined in a lunatic asylum —C.H.Grandgent⟩ ⟨my experience as a historian is that more documents survive by ~ than by intention —Robert Graves⟩ ⟨games in which ~ predominates over skill are used for gambling⟩ **d :** the fortuitous or incalculable element in phenomenal existence **:** CONTINGENT — compare TYCHISM **2 :** a circumstantial situation affording the possibility of effectuating some objective **:** OPPORTUNITY: **a :** an opportunity typically offering problematical success if taken and afforded either by luck or accident or by an equitable arrangement ⟨a ~ for the community to take a hand in punishing a somewhat contemptible malefactor —Agnes Repplier⟩ ⟨the feeling that the system under which we live deprives the majority of the ~ of a decent life —C.D.Lewis⟩ **b :** an opening for a try, venture, or grasp ⟨10 years after his death historians will get a ~ at his personal file⟩ **c :** a suitable space of time or set of conditions for allowing some process to take place **:** OPPORTUNITY ⟨the people had not had a ~ to become indoctrinated⟩ ⟨giving the wound a ~ to heal⟩ **d :** an opportunity given by a batsman to a fielder in cricket to put the batsman out **e :** a fielding opportunity in baseball ⟨the shortstop fumbled on a hard ~⟩; *specif* **:** any play by a player on defense that is scored as a put-out, assist, or error ⟨handling 200 ~*s* without an error⟩ **3 a** (1) **:** the possibility of an indicated or a favorable outcome in an uncertain situation (2) **:** the measure or strength of possibility or degree of likelihood of such an outcome ⟨what ~ has he of pulling through⟩ ⟨we have practically no ~ of winning⟩ — often used in pl. ⟨dubious of his ~*s* on the lottery ticket⟩ — compare PROBABILITY 3 **b :** a possibility that an indicated or likely future happening, condition, or combination of circumstances will come to pass ⟨until I thought I had eliminated all ~ of error —David Fairchild⟩ ⟨and if you guarantee a ~, it is no longer a ~; it is a sinecure —C.W.Mills⟩ ⟨go ahead with the printing on the ~ that no major correction may prove necessary⟩ **c :** at least a tenuous possibility of experiencing a favorable outcome or an escape from a hazard ⟨well, no matter what they think they have on me, I stand a ~ in court —William Faulkner⟩ **d :** ground for hope or expectation **:** PROSPECT ⟨to me, the best ~ for future society lies through apathy, uninventiveness, and inertia —E.M.Forster⟩ **e chances** *pl* **:** the more likely or weighty indications issuing from an overall estimate of the various possible outcomes or facts eventually to emerge — often used without the definite article ⟨the ~*s* are that no one who opens the book will skip a page⟩ ⟨~*s* are he has already heard the news⟩ **4 :** a gamble or risk of a looked-for or a favorable but quite indeterminable outcome of a hazardous situation entered voluntarily or involuntarily — usu. following the verb *take* ⟨a man bold enough to take his ~*s* —F.B.Gipson⟩ ⟨they took a long ~, and they made it —Shine Philips⟩; *esp* **:** such a risk voluntarily undertaken in a gambling game ⟨lost his money taking ~*s* in local lotteries⟩ **5** *Midland* **a :** a quantity, number, or distance usu. specified as large ⟨a right smart ~ of corn⟩ **b :** SAMPLE, SPECIMEN **6 a :** a forest location suitable for a logging operation **b :** a unit of such operation
syn FORTUNE, LUCK, HAP, HAZARD, ACCIDENT: CHANCE is a general term indicating the force that governs issues unpredictably, unanalyzably, without being determined by strict causes or by causes determined by human intent or consideration ⟨we may say that two or more phenomena are conjoined by *chance* . . . meaning that they are in no way related by causation —J.S.Mill⟩ CHANCE may stress blind, random, utter unpredictability ⟨he had felt no will to resist, but had let *chance* take its way —Willa Cather⟩ ⟨the gun . . . wavered as he raised it and fired, but *chance* came to his assistance —Sherwood Anderson⟩ FORTUNE in this sense may be associated with the notion of the goddess Fortuna, a subdeity who capriciously and inconsistently apportioned men's differing allotments of wealth and power ⟨not only, to carry out Bacon's conception, does a man who marries give hostages to *fortune,* but also he who accumulates objects of value; for each affords occasions for Fortune's malice —Herbert Spencer⟩ LUCK is quite similar to FORTUNE in this sense; it differs mainly in being less formal and bookish than FORTUNE and, sometimes, in being more applicable to one specific situation ⟨*luck* operates in most departments of human affairs . . . Read the autobiographies of businessmen and gather from those who are frank their examples of the lucky break —Lydia Strong⟩ Without modification, LUCK is likely to indicate a favoring force, a beneficial one ⟨with *luck* and the help of atomic research, our children may be safe from this grim disease —A.E.Stevenson b. 1900⟩ HAP, now rare, is rather colorless and neutral, and is limited in its use to reference to things past ⟨we had the good *hap* to meet with some young deer, a thing we had long wished for —Daniel Defoe⟩ HAZARD indicates either more or less pure chance ⟨the choice has been determined more by the *hazards* of my recent reading than by anything else —Aldous Huxley⟩ or chance involving much risk or danger ⟨it is much more difficult for small business to survive the *hazards* which come from trade recessions and widespread unemployment —H.S.Truman⟩ ACCIDENT stresses lack of essential cause; it may differ from CHANCE in suggesting an occurrence or event rather than the blind force motivating it ⟨only an occasional *accident,* such as the discovery of some chemically preserved textiles —*Amer. Guide Series: Ind.*⟩ **syn** see in addition OPPORTUNITY
— **by chance** *adv* **:** unaccountably, without premeditation, prearrangement, or any sign of motivation and without observable causal relation to attendant circumstances **:** FORTUITOUSLY ⟨*by chance* the moment of his entrance was also a big moment in the life of the man he had come to see —Sherwood Anderson⟩ **:** in the casual, undirected, haphazard course of events ⟨did you by *chance* see my fountain pen⟩
²**chance** \"\ *vb* -ED/-ING/-S [ME *chancen,* fr. *chance,* n.] *vi* **1 a :** to take place or come about by chance without intention or direction **:** HAPPEN ⟨it *chanced* that the winter of 1783–84 was a very severe one —H.E.Scudder⟩ **b :** to be found or to prove by chance or fortuitous occurrence ⟨let me know if there should ~ to be another book with the same title⟩ **c :** to have the luck, the ill fortune, or the indifferent fortune ⟨a mumbled conversation I *chanced* to hear in the subway⟩ **d** *obs* **:** to come about — used after interrogative *how* ⟨how ~ this was not done before —Christopher Marlowe⟩ **2 :** to come or light by chance esp. casually and unexpectedly — used with *upon* ⟨Shakespeare *chanced* upon the best time and country in which to live —G.M.Trevelyan⟩ ~ *vt* **1 :** to leave to chance the outcome, disposal, or ordering of ⟨I know the course has dangerous curves but I'll ~ one descent⟩ **2 a :** to accept whatever may through chance eventuate from (an action or choice) ⟨hesitant whether to ~ commitment to a world government⟩ **b** *Brit* **:** to accept the uncertainties of (one's luck) **3 :** to accept the hazard of **:** RISK ⟨it was decided to withdraw rather than ~ defeat in enemy territory —T.R. Hay⟩ **syn** see HAPPEN, VENTURE — **chance one's arm** *Brit* **:** to take a position involving possible or probable disastrous loss
³**chance** \"\ *adv* [prob. by shortening] *archaic* **:** by chance
⁴**chance** \"\ *adj* [¹*chance*] **:** happening, made, experienced, or encountered by chance, without forethought, plan, or intention **:** ACCIDENTAL, CONTINGENT ⟨by a charming accident he had disposed of them to a ~ buyer in Bainbridge —Arnold Bennett⟩ ⟨living on the ~ presents of his friends —Anthony Trollope⟩ **syn** see RANDOM
chance·a·ble \-əbəl\ *adj* [²*chance* + *-able*] *archaic* **:** FORTUITOUS, CASUAL, ACCIDENTAL
chance child *n* **:** an illegitimate child
chance·ful \-fəl\ *adj* **1 a** *archaic* **:** dependent on chance **:** CASUAL **b** *obs* **:** HAZARDOUS **2 :** full of chance or chances — **chance·ful·ly** \-fəlē\ *adv*
chan·cel \'chan(t)səl, -aan-,-ain-,-ȧn-\ *n* -S [ME, fr. MF, chancel, lattice separating the chancel from the nave, fr. LL *cancellus* lattice in front of the altar, fr. L *cancelli* lattice — more at CANCEL] **1 :** the part of a church in which is located the altar or communion table, pulpit, and lectern, which is occupied by the clergy and usu. the choir during religious services, and which is customarily on a higher level than the nave and separated from it by steps **2 :** a section similar to a chancel in a building other than a church
chan·ce·lade man \ˌshäⁿsəˈläd, (ˈ)shäⁿsˌl-\ *n, usu cap C* [trans. of F *homme de Chancelade,* fr. *Chancelade,* France, where remains were unearthed] **:** a short-statured long-nosed late paleolithic man known from a skeleton found associated with Magdalenian artifacts and having some affinities with modern Eskimos
chance·less \ˈ=ləs\ *adj* **:** giving or receiving no chance
chan·cel·lery *or* **chan·cel·lory** \chan(t)s(ə)lərē, -aan-,-ain-, -ȧn-, -səlrē, -ri\ *n* -ES [*chancellery* fr. ME *chancellerie,* fr. OF, fr. *chancelier* chancellor + *-ie* -y, *chancellory,* alter. (influenced by *-ory*) of *chancellery*] **1 a :** the position, court, or department of a chancellor **b :** the building or room where a chancellor has his office **2 :** the office of secretary of the court of a person high in authority **3 a :** the office and official residence of a diplomatic minister at a foreign seat of government or the office where a consul conducts business **b :** the official personnel of an embassy or consulate ⟨mounting tension among the *chancelleries* of Europe⟩
chan·cel·lor \-s(ə)lə(r)\ *n* -S [ME *chanceler,* fr. OF *chancelier,* fr. LL *cancellarius* doorkeeper, secretary, fr. *cancellus* lattice, fr. L *cancelli*] **1 a** *obs* **:** a secretary esp. of a nobleman, prince, or king; *specif* **:** the chief secretary of the king of England **b :** the lord chancellor of Great Britain **c :** an official esp. in England who keeps a record of proceedings and does other official acts in a chapter of an order of knighthood **d :** one of four chief dignitaries of Anglican cathedrals of the old foundation some of whose duties are to arrange services, to lecture in theology, and to keep the books **e :** CHARTOPHYLAX **f** *Brit* **:** the chief secretary of an embassy **g :** a Roman Catholic priest in the U.S. appointed by a bishop to take charge of a chancery **h :** an officer in some fraternal or sororal orders having any of varying duties, responsibilities, or privileges **2 :** a university officer of high rank: **a :** the titular head of a British university **b :** PRESIDENT **c :** the chief executive officer of some state systems of higher education **d :** an officer in charge of a certain branch or certain administrative functions of a university **3 a :** a clerical or lay law officer of a bishop or diocese in the Church of England or Protestant Episcopal Church who acts for a bishop esp. in cases relating to ecclesiastical law **b :** a judge in a court of chancery or equity in various states of the U.S.; *specif* **:** the presiding judge in such a court as distinguished from the vice-chancellors **4 :** the chief minister of state in any of certain European countries who is charged with responsibilities corresponding to those of a prime minister **5 :** the foreman of a jury in Scotland
chan·cel·lor·ate \-s(ə)ləˌrāt, -ˌrət\ *n* -S **:** CHANCELLORSHIP
chan·cel·lor·ism \-s(ə)ləˌrizəm\ *n* -S **:** government with a chancellor as responsible head
chancellor of the exchequer *often cap C&E* **:** a member of the British cabinet who, as the highest finance minister of the government, is in charge of the public income and expenditure, submitting to Parliament an annual budget with proposals to extend or curtail taxation
chan·cel·lor·ship \-s(ə)lə(r)ˌship\ *n* -S [ME *chancelershipe,* fr. *chanceler* chancellor + *-shipe* -ship] **:** the office or the term of a chancellor
chancel organ *n* **:** a division of a pipe organ for accompanying a choir
chan·cel·ry \-səlrē\ *archaic var of* CHANCELLERY
chancels *pl of* CHANCEL
chancel table *n* **:** a communion table
chance·man \ˈ=ˌman\ *n, pl* **chancemen :** a regular member of certain police forces who does only auxiliary or emergency police duty
chance–med·ley \ˈ=ˌmedlē\ *n* [AF *chance medlee* mingled chance, fr. MF *chance* + *medlée,* fem. of *medlé,* past part. of *medler* to mix, mingle — more at CHANCE, MEDDLE] **1 a :** the killing of another in self-defense in a sudden and unpremeditated encounter **b :** any accidental homicide in a sudden encounter where the killer is partly at fault but where there was no premeditation or evil intent — see CHAUD-MEDLEY **2 :** HAPHAZARDNESS ⟨abandoning himself to the *chance-medley* of carnival revelry⟩
chance–met \ˈ=ˈ=\ *adj* **:** having met or been met with by chance
chance process \'chan(t)s-, -aa-,-ai-,-ȧ-\ *n, usu cap C* [after Thomas M. *Chance* †1887 Am. mining engineer] **:** a method of cleaning coal by using a fluid mixture of sand and water which floats off a clean coal product but allows slate and other impurities to sink
¹**chan·cer** \-sə(r)\ *vt* -ED/-ING/-S [prob. back-formation fr. *chancery*] **:** ABATE, REDUCE, TAX, ADJUST ⟨~ a bill of costs⟩ ⟨~ an account⟩ **:** make an equitable settlement of (an obligation)
²**chanc·er** \"\ *n* -S [¹*chance* + *-er*] *Africa* **:** a transient job seeker from another country intent on quick profit
chance–ridden \ˈ=ˌ==\ *adj* **:** ruled by chance
¹**chan·cery** \'chan(t)s(ə)rē, -aan-,-ain-,-ȧn-, -ri\ *n* -ES [ME *chancerie,* alter. of *chancellerie* chancellery] **1 a** *usu cap* **:** a former high court having jurisdiction in England and Wales over causes in equity and various common-law functions and now forming the Chancery Division of the High Court of Justice with jurisdiction over causes in equity **b :** a court of equity in the American judicial system **c :** the principles and practice of judicial administration of causes on grounds of conscience and equity where strict law cannot afford relief **d** *obs* **:** a judicial adjustment (as a curtailment) on grounds of equitability of a claim, bond, or similar matter of dispute **2 :** a record office orig. for issuance and preservation of a sovereign's diplomas, charters, and bulls and later for the collection, arrangement, and safekeeping of public archives and ecclesiastical, legal, or diplomatic proceedings ⟨the papal ~⟩ ⟨organize a ~ for a consulate⟩ ⟨the various *chanceries* of the orders of knighthood —F.J.Grant⟩ **3 a :** a chancellor's court or office or the building in which he has his office **b :** an office or department of the Roman curia now charged mainly with the sending of bulls for consistorial benefices and new dioceses **c :** the office in which the business of a diocese is transacted and recorded **d :** the office of a foreign embassy **:** CHANCELLERY 3 **4 :** a style of cursive handwriting used by papal secretaries from the middle of the 15th century and imitated in early italic type **5 :** a wrestling hold that imprisons the head or encircles the neck **:** STRANGLEHOLD — **in chancery 1 :** in litigation in a court of chancery; *also* **:** under the superintendence of the lord chancellor ⟨a ward *in chancery*⟩ **2 :** caught in a chancery hold in boxing or wrestling **3 :** in an inextricable predicament
²**chancery** *vt* -ED/-ING/-ES *obs* **:** CHANCER
chances *pl of* CHANCE, *pres 3d sing of* CHANCE
chance·wise \ˈ=ˌ=\ *adv* **:** by chance **:** in a random manner
chan·chi·to \chän'chēd·(ˌ)ō\ *n* -S [AmerSp, dim. of *chancho* pig] **:** a small black-banded yellow cichlid fish (*Cichlasoma facetum*) of the Plata river that is often kept in an aquarium
chanc·i·ly \'chan(t)səlē, -aan-,-ain-,-ȧn-, -li\ *adv* [*chancy* + *-ly*] **:** without avoiding chance perils **:** HAZARDOUSLY, RISKILY, VENTURESOMELY
chanc·i·ness \-sēnəs, -in-\ *n* -ES **:** uncertainty or risk due to chance **:** FORTUITOUSNESS
chancing *adj* **:** relying on or inviting the risks of chance
chan·co \'chaŋ(ˌ)kō, -äŋ-\ *n* -S [Lepcha *chaṅk'u* wolf] **:** an Asiatic wolf closely related to or possibly a variety of the common wolf
chan·cre \'shaŋkə(r), -aiŋ-\ *n* -S [F, chancre, canker, cancer, fr. L *cancer* — more at CANCER] **:** the primary sore or ulcer formed at the site of entry of an infecting organism in some diseases (as tularemia); *specif* **:** the initial lesion of syphilis
chan·cri·form \'shaŋkrəˌfȯrm\ *adj* [ISV *chancre* + *-i-* + *-form;* prob. orig. formed as F *chancriforme*] **:** resembling a chancre
chan·croid \'shaŋˌkrȯid\ *n* -S [F *chancroïde,* fr. *chancre* + *-oïde* -oid] **:** a venereal sore resembling a chancre in its seat and some external characters but differing from it in being the starting point of a purely local process and never a systemic disease and in being caused by a different microorganism (*Hemophilus ducreyi*) — called also *soft chancre* — **chan·croi·dal** \(ˈ)=ˈkrȯidᵊl\ *adj*
chan·crous \'shaŋkrəs, -aiŋ-\ *adj* [F *chancreux,* fr. MF, fr. *chancre* + *-eux* -ous] **:** of the nature of a chancre **:** having chancres
chancy *also* **chanc·ey** \'chan(t)sē, -aan-,-ain-,-ȧn-, -si\ *adj* **chancier; chanciest** [¹*chance* + *-y*] **1** *Scot* **:** bringing good luck **:** AUSPICIOUS — often used with a negative ⟨whistling maidens and crawing hens were ne'er very ~ —*Henderson's Scottish Proverbs*⟩ **2 a :** marked by uncertainty of outcome or prospect **:** open to unpredictable developments or contingencies or to eventualities entirely subject to chance ⟨a ~ appeal, at best, to the shifting and unguessable sympathies of their readers —Robert Morse⟩ **b :** showing erratic inconsistent traits **:** unpredictable or capricious in decisions and actions **:** given to taking chances ⟨she was a brilliant, if ~ player —Rose Macaulay⟩ **c :** attended with doubtful or adverse chances **:** RISKY, HAZARDOUS ⟨virgin country, untamed forest, no road but a ~ track —Thomas Wood †1950⟩ **syn** see RANDOM
chan·da·la \(ˌ)chənˈdälə\ *n* -S [Skt *caṇḍāla*] **:** an Indian of low caste **:** OUTCAST, UNTOUCHABLE; *esp* **:** the son of a Sudra by a Brahman woman
chan·de·lier \ˌshandəˈli(ə)r, -aan-, -iə *sometimes* ˌch-\ *n* -S [F, lit., candlestick, modif. of L *candelabrum* — more at CANDELABRUM] **:** a lighting fixture suspended from the ceiling and having two or more usu. upcurving arms bearing lights, orig. candles, or two or more pendent lights

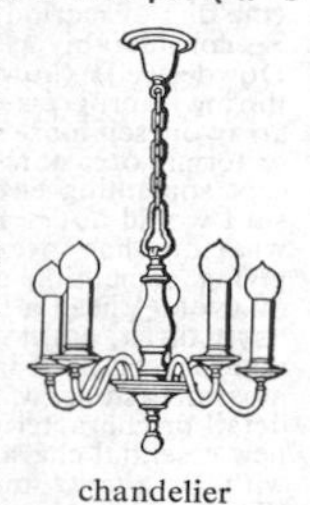
chandelier

chandelier tree *n* **:** CANDELABRUM TREE
¹**chan·delle** \(ˈ)shanˈdel, -än-, -äⁿ ˌ-\ *n* -S [F, lit., candle] **:** an abrupt climbing turn of an airplane in which the momentum of the plane is used to attain a higher rate of climb than would be possible in unaccelerated flight
²**chandelle** \"\ *vi* -ED/-ING/-S **:** to execute a chandelle
chan·dler \'chandlə(r), -aan-,-ȧn-, *rap.* -nl-\ *n* -S [ME *chandeler,* fr. MF *chandelier,* fr. OF, fr. *chandelle* candle, fr. L *candela* — more at CANDLE] **1 :** a maker or seller of tallow or wax candles and usu. soap **2 :** a retail dealer in provisions and usu. supplies, equipment, and knickknacks esp. of a specified kind ⟨a chart of tides obtainable from any yacht ~⟩ ⟨a series of cheap lodgings, laundries, lunches, tattoo parlors, and small trinket ~*s* —Christopher Morley⟩ — compare CORN CHANDLER, SHIP CHANDLER
chan·dler·chaft·ed \-ˌchaftəd\ *adj* [Sc *chandler* candlestick, lantern (fr. ME *chandeler* candlestick, fr. MF *chandelier*) + *chaft* + E *-ed* — more at CHANDELIER] *Scot* **:** LANTERN JAWED
chan·dler·ess \-lərəs\ *n* -ES **:** a female chandler
chan·dler·ing \-ləriŋ\ *or* **chan·dling** \-liŋ\ *n* -S **:** the business of a chandler
chan·dlery \-lərē, -ri\ *n* -ES [*chandler* + *-y*] **1 :** a place where candles are kept **2 :** the business of a chandler **3 :** commodities sold by a chandler — often used in pl.
chan·du *also* **chan·doo** \chən(ˌ)dü\ *n* -S [Hindi *caṇḍū*] **:** prepared opium in India and China
chan·dul \'chəndᵊl, -än-\ *n* -S [origin unknown] **:** a fiber derived from the inner bark of the upas tree (*Antiaris toxicaria*) used for making sacking
cha·né \'chä(ˌ)nā, *in sense 1* " *or* 'shänə\ *n, pl* **chané** *or* **chanés** *usu cap* [Sp & Pg, of AmerInd origin] **1 :** ²GUANÁ **2 a :** an Arawakan people of the Paraná river valley **b :** a member of such people **3 :** the language of the Chané people
chaneabal *usu cap, var of* CHAÑABAL
chanfron *var of* CHAMFRON
¹**chang** \'chaŋ\ *n* -S [imit.] *dial Brit* **:** a loud confused noise (as of talk or complaint) **:** UPROAR
²**chang** \'chaŋ, -äŋ\ *n* -S [Tibetan *chaṅ* beer, wine] **:** a Tibetan beer made from malted barley or rice
³**chang** \"\ *n, pl* **chang** *or* **changs** *usu cap* **1 :** a Naga people in the southern part of the Naga hills in the India-Burma frontier region **2 :** a member of the Chang people
chan·ga \'changə, -äŋ-\ *n* -S [AmerSp] **:** a large brown mole cricket (*Scapteriscus vicinus*) native to So. America but now widely distributed in the West Indies and southeastern U. S. where it is a destructive pest of many cultivated crops, feeding on crowns and stems and damaging roots by its burrowing
chang·chun \'chäŋˈchün, -ùn\ *adj, usu cap* [fr. *Changchun,* Manchuria] **:** of or from Changchun, a city of Manchuria **:** of the kind or style prevalent in Changchun
¹**change** \'chānj\ *vb* -ED/-ING/-S [ME *changen,* fr. OF *changier,* fr. L *cambiare* to exchange, of Celt origin; akin to OIr *camm* crooked; akin to Gk *skambos* crooked and prob. to Sw *skimpa* to hop, Lith *kibti* to hook on] *vt* **1 :** to make different: **a :** to make different in some particular but short of conversion into something else **:** ALTER, MODIFY ⟨on advice of counsel she never bothered to ~ the will —Alan Hynd⟩ ⟨can the Ethiopian ~ his skin, or the leopard his spots —Jer 13: 23 (AV)⟩ ⟨sorrow has *changed* him in mental attitude⟩ **b :** to make over to a radically different form, composition, state, or disposition **:** TRANSFORM, CONVERT ⟨the airplane simply ~*s* the map of a territory as vast and as little built up as the Congo —Tom Marvel⟩ ⟨you can't ~ human nature⟩ ⟨he is not moved . . . he is not *changed* by his experience —Herbert Read⟩; *specif* **:** to lead (a person) to religious conversion **c :** to dispose of or give up toward the substituting of something roughly equivalent — used with *into* ⟨she had to ~ the family jewels into land⟩ ⟨~ a monarchy into a republic⟩ **d :** to give a different position, status, course, or direction to ⟨*changing* residence from Switzerland to Portugal⟩ ⟨the electrolytic refining process that was to ~ aluminum from a scientific curiosity to a widely used material —*Amer. Guide Series: Ark.*⟩ ⟨he seldom ~*s* his itinerary⟩ ⟨*changed* our thinking about parole⟩ **e :** to shift or transfer in position — used with *to* ⟨Netta *changed* her weight from one foot to the other —Stuart Cloete⟩ ⟨he was *changed* from KP to guard duty⟩ **f :** to give a contrary character or trend to **:** REVERSE ⟨~ one's vote⟩ ⟨*changed* his stand⟩ ⟨abruptly *changing* his policy⟩ **g :** CASTRATE, SPAY ⟨our cat has been *changed*⟩ **2 :** to substitute another or others in place of (something under consideration) **:** make substitution for or among: **a :** to replace with another or others of the same kind or class **:** remove, discard, or withdraw and replace with another ⟨*changing* the school's name⟩ ⟨the movie made of the novel ~*s* the ending⟩ ⟨let's ~ the subject⟩ ⟨intended for the

law, he *changed* plans before graduation⟩ ⟨frequently *changing* hands in turning the crank⟩ **b :** to switch to another ⟨he *changed* his seat⟩ ⟨official permission to ~ occupation⟩ ⟨the right to hold or ~ faith⟩ ⟨not till you ~ your attitude⟩ **:** make a shift from one to another of two ⟨forced to ~ planes by bad weather⟩ ⟨one does not ~ parties as he ~*s* tailors⟩ ⟨weakly *changing* sides in the argument⟩ **c :** to give or receive an equivalent sum in bank notes or coins of other (as smaller) denomination or of a different national currency in return for ⟨~ a 20-dollar bill⟩ **d :** to undergo a loss or modification of (some property or aspect) ⟨we arrived in time to find the foliage rapidly *changing* color⟩ ⟨when confronted with the photograph the accused *changed* countenance⟩ **e :** to put a fresh covering on to replace that or those in use (as a diaper on a baby, garments on a bed patient, covers on a bed) **3 a :** to give (something) to another, taking in return something corresponding **:** give and receive reciprocally **:** INTERCHANGE — now used chiefly in colloquial applications ⟨wilt thou ~ fathers? I will give thee mine —Shak.⟩ ⟨this chamber ~ for one more holy —E.A.Poe⟩ ⟨I wouldn't ~ places with him⟩ ⟨let's ~ seats⟩ ⟨he and I *changed* shifts so he could attend his son's graduation⟩ **b :** to give up, taking in return something of a different kind **:** EXCHANGE, TRADE — used with *for* ⟨'tis a fault I will not ~ for your best virtues —Shak.⟩ ⟨for a new name . . . to ~ the honors of abandoned Rome —P.B.Shelley⟩ ⟨~ a uniform for mufti⟩ ⟨unwilling to ~ independence for the comforts of wealth⟩ **~ *vi* 1 :** to become different in one or more respects without becoming something else: **a :** to lose or to acquire some characteristic, property, or tendency **:** ALTER ⟨the *changing* foliage of autumn⟩ ⟨with the threat of war the popular mood *changed*⟩ ⟨racial relations seem to be *changing* for the better⟩ **b** (1) **:** to pass from one form, appearance, position, state, or stage to another **:** SHIFT ⟨the country has survived *changing* governments⟩ ⟨wait till the light ~*s*⟩ ⟨*changing* world conditions⟩ ⟨fashions ~ like the weather⟩ (2) *obs* **:** to pale or blush ⟨how they ~! Their cheeks are paper —Shak.⟩ **c :** to increase or decrease ⟨prices ~ overnight⟩ **d :** to adopt different customs, methods, attitudes ⟨people don't like to ~ —J.P.Blank⟩; *specif* **:** to experience a religious conversion **e** *of the moon* **:** to pass from one phase to another; *specif* **:** to pass through the phase of new moon **f** *chiefly dial* **:** to turn sour **:** become tainted **g :** to shift one's means of conveyance **:** TRANSFER ⟨there we *changed* to a local train⟩ **h** *of the voice* **:** to shift to lower register **:** BREAK **i** *Brit* **:** to shift gears **2 :** to turn into or become something materially different from before: **a :** to undergo transformation or conversion — used with *into* ⟨but the truth is that after a certain point quantity of money does indeed ~ into a quality of personality —Lionel Trilling⟩ **b :** to pass over from one character or state **:** undergo transition — used with *to* ⟨winter *changed* to spring⟩ ⟨the terrain *changed* gradually from rolling farm land to rugged mining country⟩ ⟨the chilly sensations ~ to discomfort and the acuity of touch sensations and muscular reactions are dulled —H.G. Armstrong⟩ **c :** to undergo substantial substitution or replacement or to be wholly replaced ⟨external circumstances may ~ catastrophically, as during a war —Aldous Huxley⟩ ⟨the diet of marine species is generally very varied, and often ~*s* considerably as the animals grow older and larger —W.H. Dowdeswell⟩ ⟨how the objects of a war may ~ completely during its progress —Zechariah Chafee⟩ **3 :** to disrobe and rearray oneself more suitably esp. in clothes suitable for a social or formal occasion ⟨prepared to ~ for dinner⟩ **4 a** *obs* **:** to accept something else in return ⟨but might I of Jove's nectar sip I would not ~ for thine —Ben Jonson⟩ **b** *obs* **:** to give up what one has in exchange— used with *for* **c :** to engage in giving something and receiving something in return **:** EXCHANGE ⟨I need a lighter ax; I'll ~ with you⟩

syn ALTER, MODIFY, VARY: CHANGE is wide in use and meaning and may be used in place of any of the others in this set on most occasions. ALTER may suggest changes only in a single detail or characteristic, without an ensuing loss of identity or new essential character ⟨he looked . . . with clouded eyes and with an *altered* manner of breathing —Charles Dickens⟩ ⟨Tockwotton House, the grounds of which, somewhat *altered* with the passing years, now form Tockwotton Park —*Amer. Guide Series: R. I.*⟩ MODIFY may indicate a change away from an extreme or a minor change made in the interest of adapting to a new use, function, or significance ⟨Boner, refusing to *modify* his politics, found all doors closed to him in his own state —Tremaine McDowell⟩ ⟨all of these have their respiratory organs *modified* to suit their mode of respiration —Joyce Allan⟩ VARY stresses a breaking away from sameness, from identity, duplication, exact repetition ⟨this is not a proceeding which may be *varied* . . . but is a precise course accurately marked out by law and is to be strictly preserved —John Marshall⟩ ⟨tasks may be *varied* slightly, as when a worker in a cigarette factory is shifted from the job of feeding tobacco into a machine to the job of packing and weighing —Aldous Huxley⟩ — **change color :** to undergo a blanching or a diffusion of color in one's face usu. revealing a sudden emotion (as pallor from fear, a blush of shame or embarrassment, or a flush of anger) — **change ends** *of a hunting dog* **:** to reverse direction in scent-following — **change gears** *Brit* **:** to shift gears — **change hands :** to pass from the possession of one person or owner to another or from one of two contesting teams or armies to the other — **change one's feet** *Scot* **:** to put on other shoes or other shoes and stockings — **change step :** to reverse the order in which the feet are advanced in walking esp. by bringing one foot almost up to the other and then stepping off with the foot that is in advance — **change the leg** *of a horse* **:** to change gait

²**change** \"\ *n* -s [ME, fr. OF, fr. *changier*, v. — more at ¹CHANGE] **1 :** the action of making something different in form, quality, or state **:** the fact of becoming different **:** introduction of novelty ⟨~ consists in realizing a potentiality that is not real already —W.T.Harris⟩ ⟨things and processes are the sort of entities of which ~ is predicable —Arthur Pap⟩ ⟨in other words, ~ is concomitant variation in time and some other respect —Nelson Goodman⟩ — used often without implication as to bettering or worsening and often with an implication of undirection or haphazardness **2 a :** an instance of making or becoming different in some particular **:** a departure from a norm **:** a deviation from established character, sequence, or condition **:** a divergence from uniformity or constancy in any quality, quantity, or degree **:** ALTERATION, MODIFICATION, VARIATION, MUTATION ⟨but in the daily routine of their business there was little ~ —Thomas Hardy⟩ ⟨for while there have been several clear and distinct ~*s* in the pattern, the essence of the university tradition has through all the years remained constant —J.B.Conant⟩ ⟨quite clearly, there is no ~ in phenomenal any more than in physical time —Nelson Goodman⟩ **b :** a passing from one state to another marked by radically different makeup, character, or operation, whether by sudden mutation or gradually by evolution **:** TRANSFORMATION, CONVERSION ⟨there is always the danger that people who are impatient when ~ comes too slowly will attempt violent solutions —P.E.James⟩ ⟨the semantics of functional ~⟩ ⟨since the beginning of the 20th century, however, the time span of social ~ is shorter than a human life —Maurice Graney⟩ ⟨another kind of evidence for the ubiquitousness of ~ in culture can be drawn from our own everyday experience as well as from nonliterate societies —M.J.Herskovits⟩ **c :** a shift in relation to surroundings (as to a different place, situation, course level) ⟨prices are subject to ~ without notice⟩ **d :** a switch to contrasting character or trend **:** REVERSAL **e :** CHANGE OF LIFE **f** *obs* **:** INCONSTANCY ⟨it is the woman's part . . . ambitions, covetings, ~ of prides, disdain, nice longing, slanders, mutability . . . for even to vice they are not constant —Shak.⟩ **g :** a religious or moral conversion **h :** any step in the manufacture of soap by boiling including drawing off and addition of liquid (as lye or brine) ⟨strong ~⟩ ⟨salt ~⟩ **3 :** the action of replacing something with something else of the same kind or with something that serves as a substitute **:** SUBSTITUTION ⟨beware of sudden ~ in any great point of diet —Francis Bacon⟩ ⟨but ~ of air changes not the mind —John Milton⟩: **a :** a replacing of some agent, method, means, material, or other subject of regard with a different one ⟨wore out four ~*s* of horses as he galloped all night —Dorothy C. Fisher⟩ ⟨striking for ~*s* in working conditions⟩ **b :** a shift from some mode of personal action or disposition or matter of concern to a different one ⟨American expansion into the Pacific and into the Caribbean, however, represented a ~ in American thinking —Carol L. Thompson⟩ **c** (1) **:** the passage of the moon from one monthly revolution to another (2) **:** the coming of the new moon (3) **:** the passage of the moon from one phase to another (as crescent to quarter) **d :** a spare or reserve outfit of clothing or article of wear to replace one in use; *also* **:** the act of making a transfer from one of these to the other ⟨management supplies each worker with three ~*s* a week⟩ ⟨time for a quick ~ before dinner⟩ **e :** a succeeding or superseding of some activity, condition, circumstance, or other phenomenon or relationship by a different one ⟨on the occasion of her recent tour it was, for a ~, a beautiful summer evening —G.W.Talbot⟩ **f :** a transfer from one point to another in time, space, or measure ⟨a ~ of venue to an adjoining county⟩ ⟨sudden ~*s* of temperature⟩ **g :** a shift of weight from one foot to the other in dancing **4 a** *obs* **:** reciprocal giving and receiving **:** EXCHANGE **b** *Brit* **:** something that is due or obtained in return (as by way of retaliation, by way of advantage over another, or by way of desired cooperation or disclosure) **5** *Brit* **:** a place where merchants, brokers, bankers meet to transact business — used with a prefixed apostrophe as if an abbreviation of *exchange* ⟨with sensational press campaigns and stocks and shares on *'change* —William Irvine⟩ **6 a :** the equivalent in money of small denominations of a sum of money in higher denominations or the equivalent in money of one currency of a sum in another currency ⟨to get ~ at a bank to facilitate cash sales⟩ ⟨supplying ~ for a tourist's dollars⟩ **b :** money returned to one making a payment consisting of the difference between the amount of money given in payment and the amount due ⟨to receive 11 cents in ~⟩ ⟨a cashier quick at making ~⟩ **c :** coins esp. of low denominations ⟨jingling a pocketful of ~⟩ **d** *slang* **:** money in hand **:** DOUGH **7 :** any order in which a set of bells is struck in change ringing properly other than that of the diatonic scale but loosely including it ⟨in ringing the ~*s* a bell may shift one place in position or keep its position⟩ **8 a** (1) **:** FIGURE 13a (2) *in square dancing* **:** a dancing of the figure around the set **b :** CALL 14

³**change** \"\ *adj* [¹*change*] *archaic* **:** serving or held ready to serve as a substitute

change·abil·i·ty \ˌchānjəˈbiləd.ē, -ətē, -i\ *n* [ME *changeabilite*, fr. *changeabil, changeable* changeable + *-ite* -ity] **:** the capacity of being changeable or changed **:** CHANGEABLENESS

change·able \ˈchānjəbəl\ *adj* [ME, fr. MF, fr. OF, fr. *changier* to change + *-able*] **1 :** liable to change; *specif* **:** having a marked tendency to change esp. as a property (as in form, quality, action) **:** fluctuating in direction or tendency **:** MUTABLE, VARIABLE **2 :** capable of being changed **:** subject to change **:** ALTERABLE ⟨a provision ~ at will⟩ **3 :** given or prone to change esp. as a characteristic **:** erratic in disposition **:** CAPRICIOUS, FICKLE, INCONSTANT, MERCURIAL, UNSTABLE **4 :** varying in color with the change of light or point of view; *specif* **:** having such a color effect produced in certain fabrics (as taffeta) by weaving contrasting colors in warp and weft

change·able·ness \-nəs\ *n* -ES [ME *changeablenesse*, fr. *changeable* + *-nesse* -ness] **:** the quality or state of being changeable

change·ably \-əblē, -li\ *adv* [ME, alternately, fr. *changeable* + *-ly*] **1** *obs* **:** in exchange **2** *obs* **:** in alternation **3** *archaic* **:** with the possibility of changing or being changed ⟨events scheduled ~ depending on weather conditions⟩ **4 :** with frequent changing or shifting **:** VARIABLY, INCONSTANTLY ⟨the instrument needle flicking ~⟩ ⟨~ disposed on successive ballots⟩ **5 :** with changing shades or hues ⟨feathers on the drake's neck glinting ~⟩

change·about \ˈ=ˌ=ˌ=\ *n* -s [²*change* + *about*, adv.] **:** a reversal esp. in position or direction

change bowler *n* [³*change*] **:** a relief bowler in cricket

changed *past of* CHANGE

change·ful \-fəl\ *adj* **:** given to or full of frequent changes — **change·ful·ly** \-fəlē\ *adv*

change gear *n* **1 :** a gear by means of which the speed of a mechanism or of a vehicle may be changed while the speed of its driving agent is constant **2 :** any of a set of interchangeable gears for varying the speed ratio between two shafts (as on a screw-cutting lathe) — called also *change wheel*

change house *n* [prob. so called fr. its original use as a station where horses were changed] **1** *Scot* **:** a small inn or alehouse **2 :** a locker building in which workers may wash and change their clothes — called also *dryhouse*

change key *n* **:** a key that operates only one lock of a master= keyed lock system

change·less \ləs\ *adj* **:** that does not change **:** UNCHANGING, CONSTANT — **change·less·ly** *adv* — **change·less·ness** *n* -ES

¹**change·ling** \ˈchānjliŋ, -lēŋ\ *n* -s [¹*change* + *-ling*] **1** *archaic* **:** one that wavers **:** one marked by fickleness or inconstancy; *esp* **:** TRAITOR, TURNCOAT **2 a** *obs* **:** a fraudulent substitute surreptitiously left in place of a valued object or personage **b** (1) **:** a child left in place of another child carried away surreptitiously in early infancy (as a lowborn substitute for one of noble birth) (2) *in folk tradition* **:** a deformed or weak= witted offspring of fairies or elves substituted by them surreptitiously for a comely human child — called also *elf child* **3** *archaic* **:** IMBECILE **4 :** COLOR CHANGELING

²**changeling** \"\ *adj* **1** *archaic* **:** WAVERING, INCONSTANT **2 :** markedly altered from an original or native condition ⟨his return to his family in Bombay . . ., half a stranger in dress and speech, wholly ~ in his un-Indian attitudes —John Woodburn⟩

changemaker \ˈ=ˌ==\ *n* [²*change* (money) + *maker*] **:** a device that mechanically supplies change in coins of desired denominations upon the operation of the proper levers or keys

change·ment \-mənt\ *n* -s [MF, fr. *changier* to change + *-ment* — more at CHANGE] *archaic* **:** CHANGE 1, 2, 3

change·ment de pied \shäⁿzhmäⁿtpyā\ *n, pl* **changements de pied** \"\ [F, lit., change of foot] *ballet dancing* **:** a jump starting and ending with the feet crossed but with their positions interchanged

change note *n* [²*change* (money)] **:** a note of irregular issue in a low denomination serviceable as small change locally and redeemable in regular notes of larger denominations

change-of-day line *n* **:** DATELINE 2

change of edge : a skating figure or maneuver in which the skater shifts from one edge of the blade to the other — compare SERPENTINE

change off *vi* **1 :** to alternate with another at performing an act **2 :** to alternate between two different acts or instruments or between an action and a rest period

change of heart : a full reversal in position or attitude

change of life 1 : CLIMACTERIUM **2 :** MENOPAUSE

change of pace 1 : an interruption of continuity by a sudden and usu. temporary shift to a sharply different manner of action (as for relief from monotony) ⟨he found the work tedious, so . . . for a *change of pace*, he joined the army —John Kobler⟩ **2 :** a slow pitch in baseball that is thrown for deception with the same motion as a fast ball — called also *change-up*

change of voice : the gradual change in quality and pitch of voice occurring in boys about the age of puberty

change over *vt* **:** to convert to a different purpose or system or from use of one method or technique to another ⟨*change over* a plant to production of jet engines⟩ **~ *vi* :** to make a transfer, abrupt transition, or conversion ⟨the industry *changed over* from steam to electricity⟩

change·over \ˈ=ˌ==\ *n* -s [*change over*] **1 :** the action of changing over ⟨the point of ~ from low to high pressure⟩ **2 :** an instance of changing over: **a :** a shift from one operation, one set of equipment or facilities, or one production model to another **b :** a conversion to a different system, program, or method **c :** a change to a different group of personnel **3 :** a transition from one set of economic or social conditions or cultural standards or ideals to another **4 :** the changing from one projector to another between reels during the continuous screening of a motion picture or program of motion pictures

change pocket *n* [²*change* (money)] **:** a small pocket often within a larger pocket (as in a woman's purse or a man's jacket) for holding small change

chang·er \ˈchānjə(r)\ *n* -s [ME *changere*, alter. (*influenced* by ME *-ere* -er) of *changeour*, fr. MF *changeor* money changer, fr. *changier* to change + *-eor* -or] **:** one that changes: as **a :** one that changes or alters the form of something **b :** one that exchanges one thing for another; *esp* **:** RECORD CHANGER **c** *obs* **:** MONEY CHANGER **d :** one that wavers; *esp* **:** one inconstant in his views

change ringer *n* **:** one skilled at change ringing

change ringing *n* **:** the art or practice of ringing a set of tuned bells in continually varying order in such a way as to avoid (1) shifting the place of any one bell in the striking order by more than one step at each change and (2) repeating any order before completing the whole series — used in strict terminology of the ringing of hung tower bells by a team with one man assigned to each bell; called also *peal ringing*; see PEAL

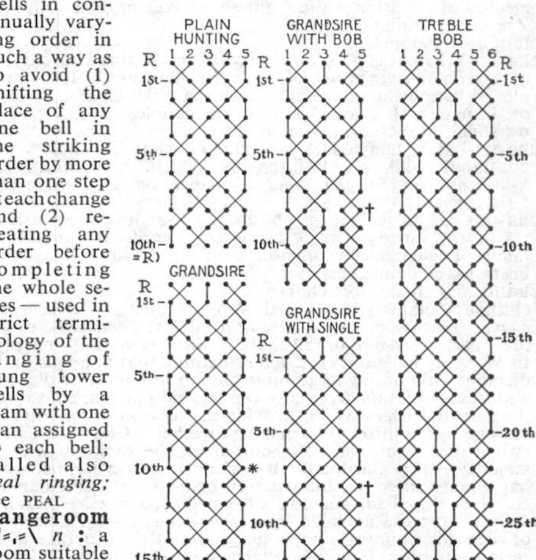

change ringing: diagram showing the order in which the bells (indicated by numbers) are struck in successive changes, beginning in rounds (at R), each horizontal row of dots representing a change

changeroom \ˈ=ˌ=\ *n* **:** a room suitable for changing one's clothes

changes *pres 3d sing of* CHANGE, *pl of* CHANGE

change three *n* **:** a three-lobed fancy skating figure consisting of a right forward outside-to-inside change of edge with an inside three, a left outside-to-inside change of edge followed by an inside back three

change-up \ˈ=ˌ=\ *n* -s **:** CHANGE OF PACE 2 ⟨a fast ball that moves, a fine slider and a good *change-up* —Arthur & Milton Richman⟩

change wheel *n* **:** CHANGE GEAR 2

changing *pres part of* CHANGE

changing bag *n* **:** a lighttight bag with sleeves to fit the arms in which procedures such as loading film holders may be carried out without a darkroom

changing box *n* **:** a holder for a number of sheet films or plates that can be attached to a camera and permits exposure in turn

changing note *or* **changing tone** *n* **1 :** an accented passing note or tone in old strict musical counterpoint **2 :** a usu. unaccented nonharmonic note or tone that resolves to its neighboring chord tone after touching an intervening tone typically a third distant **:** CAMBIATA — compare ESCAPE NOTE

chan·go \ˈchäŋ(ˌ)gō, -äŋ-\ *n, pl* **chango** *or* **changos** *usu cap* [Sp, of AmerInd origin] **1 a :** an extinct people of the north Chilean coast **b :** a member of such people **2 :** the language of the Chango people

chan·go·an \-ˌgōən\ *n* -s *usu cap* [Sp *chango* (of AmerInd origin) + E *-an*] **:** a language family consisting of Chango

changs *pl of* CHANG

chang·sha \ˈchäŋˈshä\ *adj, usu cap* [fr. *Changsha*, China] **:** of or from the city of Changsha, China **:** of the kind or style prevalent in Changsha

ch'ang shan \ˈchäŋˈshän\ *n* -s [prob. fr. Chin] **:** a shrub (*Dichroa febrifuga*) of the family Saxifragaceae found in China, northeastern India, Java, and the Philippines, with opposite serrate leaves, paniculate blue flowers and blue fruits, and roots that have long been used by the Chinese in the manufacture of a home remedy for malaria

chan·i·dae \ˈkanəˌdē\ *n pl, cap* [NL, fr. *Chanos*, type genus (fr. Gk *chanos* mouth) + NL *-idae*] **:** a family of rather large brilliant silvery toothless fishes related to the herrings and including among its present forms only a milkfish (*Chanos chanos*)

ch'an·ism \ˈchäˌnizəm\ *n* -s *usu cap* [²*ch'an* + *-ism*] **:** Ch'an Buddhism

ch'an·ist \-ˌnəst\ *n* -s *usu cap* [²*ch'an* + *-ist*] **:** an adherent of the Ch'an school of Buddhism

¹**chank** \ˈchaŋk, -ȯ-,-ä-\ *vb* -ED/-ING/-S [prob. alter of ¹*champ*] *dial* **:** chew noisily **:** CHAMP

²**chank** \ˈchaŋk\ *also* **chank shell** *n* -s [Skt *śaṅkha* — more at CONCH] **:** any of a family (Xancidae) of tropical heavy-shelled pear-shaped gastropod mollusks; *esp* **:** a species (*Xancus pyrum*) commonly appearing in Hindu religious pictures and writings

chank·ings \ˈchaŋkənz, -ȯŋ-,-äŋ-, -kiŋz\ *n pl* [pl. of *chanking*, gerund of ¹*chank*] *dial* **:** scraps or rejected parts of fruit or nuts (as chewed pieces or parings)

¹**chan·nel** \ˈchanᵊl\ *n* -s [ME *chanel*, fr. OF, fr. L *canalis* pipe, channel — more at CANAL] **1 a :** the hollow bed where a natural body or stream of water runs or may run **b :** the deeper part of a moving body of water (as a river, harbor, or strait) where the main current flows or which affords the best passage **c :** a strait or narrow sea between two close land masses ⟨the English *Channel*⟩ ⟨the Mozambique *Channel*⟩ **d :** a means or instrumentality aiding communication or expression or commercial exchange ⟨alongside the familiar press, radio, and film media . . . other ~*s* have multiplied —E.D.Canham⟩ **e channels** *pl* **:** a fixed, accustomed, or official course of communication or transmission of information or of commercial interchange ⟨submitting material to the Defense Department without going through prescribed . . . Army ~*s* —*N.Y.Times*⟩ **f :** a person through whom information is transmitted ⟨he . . . appears to have been one of Beckford's ~*s* for communication with Courtenay —*Times Lit. Supp.*⟩ **g :** a way, course, or direction of thought or action ⟨the accident which directed my curiosity originally into this ~ —Charles Lamb⟩; *specif* **:** a restricted path of movement (as of traffic directed between islands at an intersection) **h :** RIVER 4 **i :** a band of frequencies of sufficient width for a single radio or television communication being as little as a few cycles per second wide for telegraphy or as great as several megacycles wide for television **j :** the mechanism providing a single path in multiple-path systems for simultaneously and separately recording or transmitting sounds from more than one source; *also* **:** the complete system from microphone to recorder in single-path systems **2 a :** an esp. tubular enclosed passage **:** CONDUIT, PIPE, DUCT ⟨the poison ~ in a snake's fangs⟩ **b :** any of the chambers holding identical matrices in a circulating-matrix typesetting machine **3 :** a long gutter, groove, or furrow: as **a :** a street or road gutter **b :** CANAL 4 **c :** a flute in a column **d :** a groove cut along the line where rock is to be split **e :** a slanting groove cut around the edge of an outsole of a shoe on the grain surface for embedding stitches; *also* **:** one of two parallel grooves cut around the edge of an insole on the flesh surface forming a ridge to which the welt is sewed **f :** the track for the rope in a tackle block **g :** a metal beam or strip having a U-shaped section **syn** see MEAN

²**channel** \"\ *vb* **channeled** *or* **channelled**; **channeled** *or* **channelled**; **channeling** *or* **channelling**; **channels** *vt* **1 a :** to form, cut, or wear a channel in ⟨spring freshets may ~ the fields⟩ ⟨the river ~*ed* a new course⟩ **b :** to incise with a series of parallel flutes **:** GROOVE ⟨~ a chair leg⟩ **c :** to lower (an automobile body) by rebuilding with channels which fit around the frame rails — compare ¹CHOP *vt* 4 **2 :** to traverse by or as if by channels ⟨moors ~*ed* by pastoral valleys⟩ **3 a :** to send or convey through or as if through a channel ⟨~ materials and labor into housing⟩; *specif* **:** to direct through or into a fixed or official course **b :** to direct (feelings

or human drives) into particular channels of behavior or action ⟨~ the aggressive impulses of adolescents into sports activity⟩ **4 :** to confine in or as if in a channel ⟨troops ~*ed* in a narrow road with blocks at either end⟩ **5 :** to shape or stamp (as a metal strip) into a form having a U-shaped section ~ *vi* **1 :** to move in or as if in a channel ⟨the molten metal ~*s* into a belt of troughs⟩ **2 :** to have a channel cut in ⟨gear lubricants may congeal and ~ in cold weather⟩

³channel \"\ *n* -s [alter. of *chainwale*] **:** one of the flat ledges of heavy plank or metal to which the chain plates are fastened and which are bolted edgewise to the outside of a ship, serving to increase the spread of the shrouds and carry them clear of the bulwarks

⁴channel \"\ *adj* [¹*channel*] **:** CHANNELED ⟨~ molding⟩

channel–back *adj* **:** having deep vertical channels in the back-rest — used of an upholstered chair

channel bass \-¦bas, -aa(ə)s,-ais\ *n* **:** a large coppery drum (*Sciaenops ocellatus*) with a black spot at the base of the tail that is an outstanding game fish of the Atlantic coast of No. and So. America and is used as food when young — called also *red drum*

channelbill \'==,=\ *or* **channelbill cuckoo** *n* [so called fr. its grooved bill] **:** a large Australian cuckoo (*Seythrops novaehollandiae*)

channel black *n* [*channel* (*iron*)] **:** a fine carbon black obtained as soot by impingement of small natural-gas flames on a metal surface (as a channel iron) — called also *gas black*

channel-back chair

channel bone *n, now dial Eng* **:** CLAVICLE

channel cat *or* **channel catfish** *n* **:** any of several large catfishes (esp. of the genus *Ictalurus*): of deep fresh waters of interior No. America that are important food fishes of the Mississippi drainage and the Gulf states as **a :** a spotted cat (*I. lacustris punctatus*) **b :** BLUE CAT

channeled wrack *n* **:** a brown alga (*Pelvetia canaliculata*) every part of which is grooved on one side

chan·nel·er *or* **chan·nel·ler** \'chanᵊlə(r)\ *n* -s **:** one that cuts channels or grooves: as **a :** one who hand-feeds insoles or outsoles of shoes into a channeling machine **b :** one who operates a channeling machine in a mine or quarry

channel fever *n* [prob. fr. English *Channel*, strait between southern England & northern France] **:** an unusual excitement or restlessness common among a ship's crew when the ship nears port after a voyage

channel goose *n* **:** the common gannet

channeling *or* **channelling** *n* -s **1 :** a channel or a system of channels **:** GROOVING, FLUTING **2 :** channeled work (as a grooved architectural member)

channel iron *n* **:** ¹CHANNEL 3g

chan·nel·i·za·tion \,chanᵊlə'zāshən, -,ī'z-\ *n* -s **1 :** the act or process of channeling **2 :** CHANNELING 1

chan·nel·ize \'chanᵊl,īz\ *vb* -ED/-ING/-S **:** CHANNEL

channelized intersection *n* **:** a road intersection where raised or colored islands have been installed to direct vehicles or pedestrians into fixed channels

channel of distribution : the course taken by the title to goods from the point of origin or production to the point of consumption by an industrial or commercial user or by the ultimate consumer including all agencies that facilitate the transfer of title (as brokers) as well as those who actually take title to the goods (as wholesalers and retailers)

channel piloting *n* **:** piloting by nonmathematical methods (as by buoys, beacons, or landmarks) near shoal waters

channel pin *n* **:** a tapered metal plug with one or two grooves used to fasten one or two bond wires (as to a railroad rail)

channels *pl of* CHANNEL, *pres 3d sing of* CHANNEL

channel section *n* **:** a part of a structure composed of a channel iron — compare CHANNEL 3g

channel stone *also* **channel stane** *n* **1** *Scot* **:** CURLING STONE **2** *Scot* **:** CURLING

channelure *var of* CANNELURE

channelwale *n* [³*channel* + *wale*] **:** one of several strakes worked between the upper and lower deck ports in 2-decked ships and between the upper and middle deck ports in 3-decked ships to strengthen the topside

channelway \'==,=\ *n* **:** CHANNEL: as **a :** a crack, intergranular space, or other opening in rocks through which fluids or gases may pass **b :** a tunnel or other opening in a glacier through which water may flow

channel wing *n* **:** an airplane wing having an engine with a rear propeller mounted in a downward-curved semicylindrical section near the fuselage

chan·ner \'chanə(r)\ *vi* -ED/-ING/-S [ME *channeren*, prob. of imit. origin] *dial Brit* **:** to scold complainingly **:** MUTTER, GRUMBLE

cha·no·yu \¦chänō¦yü\ *n* -s [Jap, fr. *cha* tea (fr. Chin *ch'a²*) + *no* of + *yu* hot water — more at TEA] **:** a Japanese ceremony consisting of the serving and taking of tea in accordance with an elaborate ritual

chan·son \shäⁿsōⁿ\ *n, pl* **chansons** \-ōⁿ(z)\ [F, fr. L *cantion-, cantio* — more at CANZONE] **:** a lyric intended for singing **:** SONG; *specif* **:** a music-hall or cabaret song or recitative often French or in the French manner

chan·son de geste \-d(ə)zhest\ *n, pl* **chansons de geste** \", -ōⁿzdəzh-\ [F, lit., song of heroic deeds] **:** any of several Old French epic poems of the 11th to the 13th centuries about real or legendary events or exploits written orig. in assonant verse usu. of 10 or 12 syllables

chan·son·nette \¦shäⁿsən¦et; -ān(t)sən-, -an(-\ *n* -s [F, fr. *chanson* + *-ette*] **:** a little song

chan·son·nier \¦shäⁿsən¦yā\ *n* -s [F, fr. *chanson*] **1 :** a writer or singer of chansons; *esp* **:** a cabaret singer **2 :** a collection of songs or of verses for singing

chanst \'chan(t)st\ *n* [by alter.] *dial* **:** CHANCE

¹chant \'chant, -aa(ə)-,-ai-,-ä-\ *or archaic* **chaunt** \-ȯ-,-ȯ-,-ä-\ *vb* -ED/-ING/-S [ME *chanten*, fr. MF *chanter*, fr. L *cantare*, fr. *cantus*, past part. of *canere*] *vi* **1 :** to make melodic sounds with the voice **:** SING, WARBLE, INTONE; *esp* **:** to sing a chant or something resembling a chant **2 :** to utter a statement in a monotonous tone esp. repetitively **:** recite monotonously or with insistent repetition ~ *vt* **1 :** to utter as in chanting **:** SING, WARBLE, INTONE **:** recite monotonously ⟨singers ~*ed* some of the Psalms —K.S.Latourette⟩ ⟨the auctioneer . . . ~*ing* his peculiar singsong jargon —*Amer. Guide Series: Mo.*⟩ **2 :** to celebrate or praise in song or chant ⟨~*ing* the virtues of patriotism⟩ ⟨~*ing* one's love⟩

²chant \"\ *n* -s [F, fr. L *cantus*, fr. *cantus*, past part. of *canere* to sing; akin to OE *hana* rooster, OHG *hano*, ON *hani*, Goth *hana*, Gk *kanachē* ringing sound, and prob. to Russ *kanya*, a bird of prey with a harsh voice] **1 :** SONG, SINGING ⟨with ~ of tuneful birds resounding loud —John Milton⟩ **2 a :** a hymnlike repetitive melody used in liturgical singing (as of psalms, canticles, or anthems) to which the successive nonmetrical verses are fitted by assigning as many syllables to each tone as required ⟨neither the magnificence of the church . . . nor the harmony of the ~ form the substance of religion —Valentine Ughet & Eleanor Davis⟩ **b :** a singing or speaking in monotone often with strongly marked rhythmic stresses and usu. repetitively ⟨the rhythmical ~ of an auctioneer⟩ **c :** a composition serving for or designed for such singing or speaking **d :** WAY 19 **3 :** the act, practice, or art of performing liturgical chants **4 :** a statement of opinion that has been frequently repeated ⟨the consumer's ~ for lower prices⟩

chant·a·ble \-əbəl\ *adj* **:** capable of being chanted **:** lending itself easily to chanting ⟨a clearly ~ rhyme⟩

chan·tage \shäⁿtäazh\ *n* -s [F, fr. *chanter* to yield to extortion, be compliant, lit., to sing + *-age*] **:** BLACKMAIL, EXTORTION

chan·tant \shäⁿtäⁿ\ *adj* [F, fr. pres. part. of *chanter* to sing] **:** of a melodious and singing style **:** TUNEFUL

¹chantecler *var of* CHANTICLEER

²chan·te·cler \¦chantə¦kli(ə)r, -aan-,-ain-, -le(ə)r,-liə,-leə *also* ¦sh-\ *n, usu cap* [CanF, fr. F *Chantecler* Chanticleer — more at CHANTICLEER] **:** a breed of robust general-purpose fowls of Canadian origin with small comb and wattles and white or partridge plumage

chant·er \'chantə(r), -aan-,-ain-,-ân-\ *n* -s [ME *chantour*, fr. OF *chanteor*, fr. L *cantator*, fr. *cantatus* (past part of *cantare* to sing) + *-or* — more at CHANT] **1 :** one that chants: **a :** CHORISTER **b :** CANTOR **2 :** the chief singer in a chantry **3 :** the reed pipe of a bagpipe with finger holes on which the melody is played **4** *obs slang* **:** a deceitful horse dealer

¹chan·te·relle *also* **chan·ta·relle** \¦shantə¦rel, -ān-\ *n* -s [F, fr. NL *cantharella*, dim. of L *cantharus* drinking vessel — more at CANTHARUS] **:** a widely distributed edible mushroom (*Cantharellus cibarius*) that is rich yellow in color and has a pleasant apricotlike aroma

²chan·te·relle *also* **chan·ta·relle** \"\ *or* **chan·ta·rel·la** \,==rela\ *n* -s [F *chanterelle*, fr. *chanter* to sing — more at CHANT] **:** the highest string of various stringed musical instruments (as the violin or banjo)

chant·er·ship \'==,ship\ *n* -s [*chanter* (chief singer) + *-ship*] **:** the office of chanter (sense 2)

chan·teur \(')shäⁿ¦tə(r)z, -tə\ *n* -s [F, fr. *chanter* to sing + *-eur* -or — more at CHANT] **:** SINGER; *esp* **:** a singer of ballads

chan·teuse \(')shäⁿ¦tə(r)z, -än-¦-, -tə̄z, -tüz; (')shan-¦tüz\ *n, pl* **chan·teuses** \-ə(r)z(əz),-ə̄z(əz),-üzəz\ [F, fem. of *chanteur*] **:** a female singer; *esp* **:** a woman who sings in concert halls or nightclubs

chan·tey *or* **chan·ty** \'shantē, -aan-,-ain-,-än-, -ti *also* 'ch-\ *also* **shan·tey** *or* **shan·ty** \'sh-\ *n, pl* **chanteys** *or* **chanties** [modif. of F *chanter* to sing] **:** a song orig. sung by sailors in rhythm with their work (as when heaving at a capstan)

chan·tey·man *or* **shan·tey·man** *also* **shan·ty·man** \-mən\ *n, pl* **chanteymen** *or* **shantymen 1 :** one who sings the verses of chanteys and thereby sets the time and rhythm for them and for the work they accompany **2 :** one noted for singing of chanteys often with improvisations

chan·ti·cleer \¦chantə¦kli(ə)r, -aan-,-ain-, -iə *also* ¦sh-\ *also* **chan·te·cler** \", -le(ə)r,-leə\ *n* -s [ME *Chantecleer*, rooster appearing as a character in verse narratives, fr. OF *Chantecler*, rooster in the *Roman de Renart* (Reynard the Fox), fr. *chanter* to sing + *cler* clear — more at CLEAR] **:** ¹COCK 1

chan·tier \shäⁿtyā\ *n, pl* **chantiers** \-ā(z)\ [CanF — more at SHANTY] *in southern Quebec* **:** a hut esp. in a lumber camp; *also* **:** a lumber camp

¹chan·til·ly \(')shan¦tilē *also* (')shän-; *F* shäⁿtēyē\ *adj, usu cap* [F (in *crème à la Chantilly* cream in the Chantilly manner), fr. *Chantilly*, France] **1** *of cream* **:** whipped and usu. sweetened and flavored with vanilla ⟨crème *Chantilly*⟩ **2** *of foods* **:** prepared or garnished with whipped cream ⟨*Chantilly* potatoes⟩

²chantilly \"\ *or* **chantilly lace** *n* -ES *usu cap C* [*Chantilly* fr. F, short for *dentelle de Chantilly; Chantilly lace*, trans. of F *dentelle de Chantilly*, fr. *Chantilly*, France, where it was first made] **:** a delicate sometimes white but usu. black silk or linen bobbin-type lace made by hand or machine and having a 6-sided mesh ground and a scrolled and floral design outlined in cordonnet

³chantilly \"\ *n* -ES *usu cap* [F, fr. *Chantilly*, France, where it was produced] **:** an 18th century soft-paste porcelain

chanting *adj* [fr. pres. part. of ¹*chant*] **:** SINGSONG — **chant·ing·ly** *adv*

chanting falcon *or* **chanting goshawk** *n* **:** any of several African hawks (genus *Melierax*) noted for their whistling song

chantment *n* -s [ME *chantement*, short for *enchantement* enchantment] *archaic* **:** ENCHANTMENT, INCANTATION

chant roy·al \shäⁿrwäyäl\ *n, pl* **chants roy·aux** \shäⁿrwäyō\ [F, lit., royal song] **:** an elaboration of the ballade that was favored for serious poetry in France in the late middle ages

chan·try \'chan·trē, -ân-, -ri\ *n* -ES [ME *chanterie*, fr. MF, singing, fr. *chanter* to sing — more at CHANT] **1 :** an endowment or foundation for the chanting of masses and offering of prayers commonly for the founder **2 :** a chapel, altar, or part of a church endowed by a chantry

chantry priest *n* [ME *chanterie prest*, fr. *chanterie* chantry + *prest* priest] **:** the incumbent of a chantry endowment

chants *pres 3d sing of* CHANT, *pl of* CHANT

chanukah *also* **chanukkah** *usu cap, var of* HANUKKAH

cha·obor·i·dae \,kāə'bȯrə,dē, -är-\ *n pl, cap* [NL, fr. *Chaoborus*, type genus (fr. LGk *chaoun* to destroy utterly — fr. Gk *chaos* space, abyss — + NL *-borus* — fr. Gk *bora* food, meat) + *-idae* — more at VORACIOUS] **:** a family of gnats related to and often included as a subfamily of Culicidae but distinguished by the short mouth parts, nonbiting habit, and absence of scales on the wing veins and with larvae that are aquatic and predaceous on other insect larvae (as those of mosquitoes) — **cha·ob·o·rine** \kā'äbə,rīn\ *n* -s

¹cha·os \'kā,äs *sometimes* -āəs *or* -ā,ōs\ *n* -ES [L, fr. Gk — more at GUM] **1** *obs* **:** CHASM, GULF, ABYSS **2 a** *sometimes cap* **:** a state of things in which chance is supreme **:** nature that is subject to no law or that is not necessarily uniform; *esp* **:** the confused unorganized state of primordial matter before the creation of distinct and orderly forms — contrasted with *cosmos* **b :** a state of utter confusion completely wanting in order, sequence, organization, or predictable operation ⟨a process calculated to reduce the orderly life of our complicated societies to ~ —Aldous Huxley⟩ ⟨the ~ of a subjectivity that lacks objective control —John Dewey⟩ **c :** a confused mass or agglomerate of matters or heterogeneous items that are hard to distinguish, isolate, or interpret ⟨a work where nothing's just or fit, one glaring ~ and wild heap of wit —Alexander Pope⟩ **syn** see CONFUSION

²chaos \"\ *n, cap* [NL, fr. L] **:** a genus of large amoebas variously delimited and sometimes regarded as equivalent to *Amoeba* or to *Pelomyxa*

cha·ot·ic \kā'äd·ik, -ätik, -ēk, *attrib sometimes* '=,==\ *adj* [fr. *chaos*, after such pairs as Gk *eros* love: E *erotic*] **1 :** of or belonging to chaos **2 :** in a state of or marked by chaos **:** completely confused or disordered ⟨objects . . . piled up in a ~profusion —David Sylvester⟩ ⟨a ~ battle ground —Marion Wilhelm⟩ ⟨a ~ mind⟩ — **cha·ot·i·cal·ly** \-ək(ə)lē, -ēk-, -li\ *adv* — **cha·ot·ic·ness** \-iknə̇s, -ēk-\ *n* -ES

¹chap \'chap\ *vb* **chapped; chapped; chapping; chaps** [prob. fr. ME *chappen, chapien*, fr. OE *cēapian* — more at CHEAP] **1** *dial Eng* **:** BUY, BARTER **2** *Scot* **:** to fix upon **:** CHOOSE

²chap \"\ *n* -s [short for *chapman*] **1** *now dial Eng* **:** BUYER, CUSTOMER, CHAPMAN **2 :** MAN, BOY, FELLOW ⟨a rare plum for a ~ of 25 —F.B.Vickers⟩ ⟨the newspaper ~*s* —Erle Stanley Gardner⟩ **3** *South & Midland* **:** CHILD, BABY

³chap \"\ *vb* **chapped; chapped; chapping; chaps** [ME *chappen*; akin to MD *cappen* to cut down, G dial. (southern Alsatian) *kchapfe* to chop up; all prob. fr. a prehistoric E-D-G word borrowed fr. (assumed) VL *cappare* to castrate, cut, chop (whence ML *cappare* to cut), fr. (assumed) VL *cappo* capon, fr. L *capo* — more at CAPON] *vt* **1** *Scot* **:** to break into small pieces **:** CHOP, POUND **2 a :** to cause to open in slits or chinks **:** SPLIT, CRACK **b :** to cause the skin of (as the face) to crack or become rough **3** *chiefly Scot* **:** STRIKE ⟨~ the hour⟩ **:** BEAT ~ *vi* **1 :** to crack or open in slits ⟨the hands or lips ~⟩ **2** *chiefly Scot* **:** STRIKE, KNOCK, RAP

⁴chap \"\ *n* -s [ME, fr. *chappen* to chop, become cracked] **1 :** a crack in or a sore roughening of the skin from exposure to wind or cold **2** *Scot* **:** BLOW, RAP, KNOCK, STROKE

⁵chap \'chäp, -ap\ *n* -s [³*chap*] **1** *usu pl* **a :** one of the jaws or the fleshy covering of a jaw ⟨the animal's ~*s* were smeared with blood⟩ **b :** the forepart of the face ⟨a dog hairless around the ~*s*⟩ ⟨puckered a little about the ~*s* —Christopher Morley⟩ — called also *chop* **2 :** one of the jaws or cheeks of a clamping tool (as a vise)

chap *abbr* **1** chaplain **2** chapter

chap and lie *n, pl* **chap and lies** [Sc *chap* to strike] **:** the bowling of a bowl or a curling stone so that it hits another bowl or stone and remains in or near its place

chapaneca *or* **chapanecas** *var of* CHIAPANECAS

chap·a·ra·jos *or* **chap·a·re·jos** \,shapə'rā(,)ōs, -,əs *sometimes* ,ch-\ *n pl* [modif. (prob. influenced by Sp *aparejo* equipment, gear) of MexSp *chaparreras*, fr. *chaparro*] **:** CHAPS

chap·ar·ral *also* **chap·pa·ral** \¦shapə¦ral, -el *sometimes* ¦ch-\ *n* -s [Sp, fr. *chaparro* dwarf evergreen oak, fr. Basque *txapar*, dim. of *saphar* thicket] **1 :** a thicket of dwarf evergreen oaks **2 :** a dense impenetrable thicket of stiff or thorny shrubs or dwarf trees **3 :** a community comprising shrubby plants widely distributed in southern California that are esp. adapted to dry sunny summers and moist winters

chaparral bird *or* **chaparral cock** *n* **:** ROAD RUNNER; *esp* **:** the male roadrunner

chaparral broom *n* **:** COYOTE BRUSH

chaparral pea *n* **:** a thorny California shrub (*Pickeringia montana*) of the family Leguminosae having showy rose-purple flowers and forming dense thickets in tracts of chaparral

chap·ar·re·ras *or* **chap·ar·re·ros** \,shapə'rerəs *sometimes* ,ch-\ *n pl* [MexSp *chaparreras*, fr. *chaparro*] **:** CHAPS

cha·par·ro \shə'pä(,)rō, ch-\ *n* -s [AmerSp, fr. Sp, dwarf evergreen oak] **1 :** a Mexican oak (*Quercus reticulata*) with close-grained hard brown wood **2** *or* **chaparro prieto :** a Mexican acacia (*Acacia amentacea*) with sweet-scented yellow flowers **3 :** a tropical American tree (*Curatella americana*) of the family Dilleniaceae distinguished by very rough leaves that are widely used for polishing and scouring — called also *sandpaper tree* **4 :** any of several trees of the genus *Byrsonima* most of which have edible fruits and bark useful for tanning

cha·pa·ti *or* **cha·pat·ti** *n, pl* **chapati** *or* **chapaties** *or* **chapatti** *or* **chapatties** \chə'päd·ē, -pa-\ [Hindi *capati*, fr. Skt *carpaṭī* thin cake, fr. *carpaṭa* flat] **:** a pancake-shaped unleavened bread that is usu. made of wheat flour and baked on a griddle and is common in northern India

chap·book \'chap,bu̇k\ *n* [*chapman* + *book*] **1 :** a small book or pamphlet of a kind formerly sold by chapmen containing popular tales, treatises, ballads, or nursery rhymes **2 :** a small book or pamphlet resembling a chapbook

chape \'chāp, -ap\ *n* -s [ME, fr. MF, cape, cover, chape of a scabbard, fr. LL *cappa* head covering, cloak — more at CAP] **1 a** *obs* **:** SCABBARD, SHEATH **b :** the metal mounting or trimming of a scabbard or sheath at its upper end that bears the ring or hook for attaching it to the belt **c :** the metal trimming that covers the point of a scabbard or sheath **2 :** the tip of a fox's brush **3 :** the metal piece at the back of a buckle that fastens it to a strap **4 :** the outer case of a foundry mold

cha·peau \(')sha¦pō\ *n, pl* **chapeaus** \-ōz\ *or* **cha·peaux** \-ō(z)\ [MF, fr. OF *chapel* hat — more at CHAPLET] **1 :** CAP OF MAINTENANCE 3 **2 :** HAT

chapeau bras \(,)=,='bräˌ\ *n, pl* **cha·peaux bras** \-ō(z)'b-\ [F *chapeau* hat + *bras* arm, fr. L *brachium* — more at BRACE] **:** a bicorne or a modified tricorne that is often folded and carried under the arm as part of ceremonial, diplomatic, or naval dress

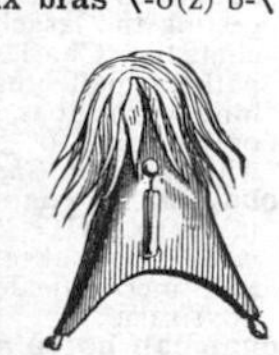
chapeau bras, 18th century

chapeau chi·nois \(,)=,=,shēn'wä\ *n, pl* **cha·peaux chinois** \-ō,sh-, -ōz(h),sh-\ [F, lit., Chinese hat] **:** PAVILLON CHINOIS

¹chap·el \'chapəl\ *n* -s [ME, fr. OF *chapele*, fr. ML *cappella* chapel, short cloak, dim. of LL *cappa* cloak; fr. the preservation of the cloak of St. Martin of Tours as a sacred relic in an oratory specially built for that purpose — more at CAP] **1 a :** a small or subordinate place of worship; *esp* **:** a Christian sanctuary other than a parish or cathedral church **b :** a church subordinate to and dependent on the principal parish church to which it is a supplement of some kind **2 :** a private place of worship: **a :** a building or portion of a building or institution (as a palace, hospital, prison, college) set apart for private devotions and often also for private religious services **b :** a room or recess in a church that often contains an altar and is separately dedicated and that is designed esp. for meditation and prayer but is sometimes used also for small religious services **3 a :** a choir of singers belonging to a chapel (as of a prince) **b :** the choir or the orchestra attached to the court of a prince or nobleman **4 a :** a chapel service or assembly esp. at an educational institution and often only semireligious **b :** attendance at chapel services ⟨~ is required of all students⟩ **5 a** *obs* **:** a printing office **b :** an association or meeting of the workmen (as the compositors) in a printing office for dealing with matters or questions affecting their interests **6 :** a place of worship used by members of a religious denomination or faith other than that of the established church ⟨Anglican churches and nonconformist ~*s* of England⟩ **7 a :** FUNERAL HOME **b :** a room or section of rooms in a funeral home where funeral services are conducted **c :** a place in a cemetery for holding funeral services in inclement weather

²chapel \"\ *vt* **chapeled** *or* **chapelled; chapeled** *or* **chapelled; chapeling** *or* **chapelling** \-p(ə)liŋ\ **chapels :** to cause (a ship taken aback in a light breeze) to recover the original tack by the use of the helm alone without bracing the yards

³chapel \"\ *adj, chiefly Brit* **:** of or belonging to a Protestant nonconformist church ⟨~ I was born and . . . bred —Angela Thirkell⟩

cha·pel-de-fer \(,)sha,peldə'fe(ə)r\ *n, pl* **chapels–de–fer** \-l(z)d-\ [OF *chapel de fer*, lit., hat of iron] **:** an iron or steel skullcap that was worn with a coif of mail in medieval armor

chap·el·man \'chapəlmən\ *n, pl* **chapelmen :** a clergyman or official of a chapel

chapelmaster \'==,=\ *n* [trans. of F *maître de chapelle* or G *kapellmeister*] **:** CHOIRMASTER

chapel of ease : a chapel or dependent church built for the accommodation of an increasing parish

chapel royal *n, pl* **chapels royal 1 :** a chapel officially connected with the court of a Christian sovereign or attached to a royal palace **2** *usu cap C&R* **:** a Church of England establishment that consists usu. of dean, subdean, canons, chaplains, and choir, some of whom attend the king, and is located with his court

chap·el·ry \'chapəlrē\ *n* -ES **1 a :** the territorial district assigned to a chapel or having its own chapel **b :** a chapel with its precinct and appurtenances **2** *obs* **:** the congregation of a nonconformist chapel

¹chap·er·on *or* **chap·er·one** \'shapə,rōn\ *n* -s [ME, fr. MF, fr. *chape* cape — more at CHAPE] **1** *chaperon* **:** a round stuffed covering for the head with folds of cloth falling from the crown that was esp. popular in the 15th century **2** [F, lit., hood] **a :** a person (as a matron) who accompanies one or more young unmarried women in public or in mixed company for propriety and esp. formerly as a protector **b :** an older person who accompanies young people esp. in attendance at a dance, party, or other social gathering to ensure proper behavior ⟨their English teacher who accompanied them as ~ —Christopher Morley⟩ **c :** one delegated to ensure proper behavior ⟨in his guarded cell, was allowed to see no visitors . . . without a Navy ~ present —Drew Pearson⟩

²chaperon *or* **chaperone** \"\ *vb* **chaperoned; chaperoned; chaperoning; chaperons** *or* **chaperones** *vt* **1 :** to attend upon **:** ESCORT, GUIDE ⟨~ a sightseer around the park⟩ ⟨personally ~*ing* a confidential communication to the president's desk⟩ **2 a :** to act as chaperon to or for ⟨~ a college dance⟩ ⟨~ a group of young ladies on tour⟩ **b :** to take care of **:** SUPERVISE ⟨a job ~*ing* cattle to So. Africa —J.T.Winterich⟩ ⟨a . . . salesgirl . . . should ~ the cart . . . and be responsible for restocking it daily —*Lingerie Merchandising*⟩ ~ *vi* **:** to act as a chaperon ⟨part of the work of all sorority dances⟩

chaperon 1

chap·er·on·age \'==,=nij, ,=='==\ *n* -s [²*chaperon* + *-age*] **:** the act or the practice of chaperoning **:** attendance or supervision by or as if by a chaperon ⟨strict ~ of girls⟩ ⟨wise in their ~ of the camera —John Mason Brown⟩

chap·er·on·less \-lə̇s\ *adj* **:** having no chaperon

chapes *pl of* CHAPE

chap·fall·en \'chap,- *also* -ä-\ *or* **chop·fall·en** \'chäp,-\ *adj* [⁵*chap* or ⁴*chop* + *fallen*] **1 :** having the lower jaw hanging loosely ⟨a tired and ~ hound⟩ **2 :** DEJECTED, DEPRESSED ⟨sallied forth . . . with an air quite desolate and ~ —Washington Irving⟩

cha·pin \chə'pēn\ *n* -s [Sp *chapin*, lit., chopine — more at CHOPINE] **:** BOXFISH; *esp* **:** one of a common species (*Lactophrys triqueter*) of the eastern coast of No. America

chap·i·ter \'chapəd·ə(r)\ *n* -s [ME *chapiter, chapitre* — more at CHAPTER] **:** the capital of a column

chap·lain \'chaplə̇n\ *n* -s [ME *chapeleyn*, fr. OF *chapelain*, fr. ML *cappellanus* chaplain, secretary of a king or noble, custodian of sacred relics, fr. *cappella* chapel, short cloak — more at CHAPEL] **1 a :** a clergyman appointed to officiate in a chapel **b** : a Church of England clergyman without a title or benefice in the place where he officiates who performs religious services in a chapel, cathedral, or collegiate church **2** : a clergyman officially attached to the army or navy, to some public institution, or to a family or court **3** : any person chosen to conduct religious exercises (as for a society)

chap·lain·cy \-sē, -i\ *n* -ES : the office, position, or station of a chaplain

chaplain in ordinary : one of the 36 honorary chaplains to the king of England

chap·lain·ry \-rē, -i\ *obs var of* CHAPLAINCY

chap·less \'chäpləs, -ap-\ *adj* [⁵*chap* + *-less*] : having no lower jaw ⟨a ~ skull⟩

chap·let \'chaplət, *usu* -əd+V\ *n* -s [ME *chapelet*, fr. MF, fr. OF, dim. of *chapel* garland, hat, fr. ML *cappellus* head covering, fr. LL *cappa* head covering, cloak — more at CAP] **1 a** : a garland or wreath to be worn on the head **b** : a heraldic bearing consisting of a garland of leaves or of leaves and flowers; *specif* : a heraldic garland of leaves with four roses placed at equal distances around the circle **2 a** : a string of beads; *esp* : a part of a rosary or usu. 55 beads used in praying by Roman Catholics **b** : the prayers recited over such a string of beads **c** : something resembling a string of beads ⟨the most northerly of the ~ of large lakes —*Chambers's Encyc.*⟩ **3** : a small molding (as an astragal or baguette) carved with small decorative forms (as beads, pearls, or olives) **4** : any of various metal devices for holding a core or section of a foundry mold in place

chaplet 1a

chap·let·ed \'chapləd·əd\ *adj* : provided with or having a chaplet

chap·lin·esque \ˌchaplə'nesk\ *adj, usu cap* [Charles S. *Chaplin* b1889 Eng.-born comedian + E *-esque*] : resembling or suggesting the largely pantomime comedy of the motion-picture comedian Charles Chaplin, esp. its central comedy figure, a pathetic ineffectual good-hearted tramp with torn baggy pants, long-worn shoes, cane and bowler hat, an odd jerky walk, and pretensions to gentility ⟨*Chaplinesque* comedy⟩ ⟨waddling with all their *Chaplinesque* style —Russell Owen⟩

chap·man \'chapmən\ *n, pl* **chapmen** [ME, fr. OE *cēapman* (akin to OHG *koufman*, ON *kaupmathr*), fr. *cēap* trade + *man* — more at CHEAP] **1** *archaic* : MERCHANT, TRADER **2** *Brit* : an itinerant dealer : PEDDLER, HAWKER **3** *archaic* : PURCHASER, CUSTOMER

chapman horse *n* [so called fr. its former popularity among chapmen] : CLEVELAND BAY

chap·man·ite \'chapmə,nīt\ *n* -s [Edward *Chapman* †1904 Eng. mineralogist + E *-ite*] : a mineral $Fe_5Sb_2Si_5O_{20}.2H_2O$ consisting of a silicate of iron and antimony

chap·man's zebra \-mən(z)'zē-\ *n, usu cap C* [after James *Chapman* †1872 Eng. traveler in Africa] : a variety (*Equus burchelli chapmanni*) of the Burchell's zebra distinguished by distinct shadow striping on the body and largely restricted to northern Bechuanaland and western Matabeleland — compare GRANT'S ZEBRA

cha·pon \(')sha¦pōⁿ\ *n* -s [F, lit., capon, fr. L *capon-, capo* — more at CAPON] : a piece of bread rubbed with garlic and placed in a salad for flavor

cha·po·te \chə'pōd·ē\ *n* -s [MexSp, alter. of Sp *zapote* sapodilla — more at SAPODILLA] : MEXICAN PERSIMMON

chapparal *var of* CHAPARRAL

chappati *var of* CHAPATI

chap·paul \chə'pȯl\ *n* -s [origin unknown] : SQUAWFISH

chappe *var of* SCHAPPE

¹**chapped** \'chapt\ *also* **chopped** \-ä-\ *adj* [ME *chapped*, fr. past part. of *chappen* to chap — more at CHAP (to split)] **1** : CRACKED, FISSURED, ROUGHENED ⟨~ hands⟩ **2** *Scot* : CHOPPED, MASHED

²**chapped** \¦chäpt, -apt\ *also* **chopped** \-äpt\ *adj* [⁵*chap* or ⁴*chop* + *-ed*] : having a jaw — used in combination with a qualifying adjective ⟨a sour long-*chapped* face⟩

chap·pie *also* **chap·py** \'chapē, -pi\ *n, pl* **chappies** [²*chap* + *-ie*] : FELLOW, CHAP ⟨that other ~ had come back from Africa with money —Donn Byrne⟩

chap·pin \'chapən, -äp-\ *var of* CHOPIN

chapping *pres part of* CHAP

chap·pow \chə'pau̇\ *n* -s [Per *chapū* pillage or *chāpaul* raid] *India* : RAID, FORAY

chap·py \'chapē\ *adj* ER/-EST [⁴*chap* + *-y*] : CHAPPED

cha·pras·si *also* **cha·pra·si** \chə'präsē\ *n* -s [Hindi *caprāsī, caprāsī*, fr. *caprās, caprās* badge] *India* : an official messenger : FUNCTIONARY, OVERSEER, SERVANT, PORTER, BEARER

¹**chaps** *pl of* CHAP, *pres 3d sing of* CHAP

²**chaps** \'shaps *sometimes* 'ch-\ *n pl* [modif. of MexSp *chaparreras* — more at CHAPAREJOS] : leather leggings resembling trousers without a seat and often with fringed and decorated extensions in the width of the outer part of the leg that are worn over regular pants as a leg protection esp. by western ranch hands for riding through brush

chapt *archaic var of* CHAPPED

chap·tal·i·za·tion \ˌ==lə'zāshən, -ˌlī'z-\ *n* -s : the act or process of chaptalizing

chap·tal·ize \'shaptə,līz\ *vi* -ED/ -ING/ -S [F *chaptaliser*, fr. Jean-Antoine *Chaptal* †1832 Fr. chemist + F *-iser* -ize] : to normalize the composition of a wine before fermentation by adding a neutralizer if the must is too acid or by adding sugar if there is not enough to produce the desired alcohol

chaps

chap·ter \'chaptə(r)\ *n* -s [ME *chapitre* division of a book, meeting of canons, body of canons, fr. OF, fr. LL *capitulum* division of a book & ML *capitulum* meeting place of canons (where the meetings were frequently opened by the reading of a chapter from the Scriptures), fr. L, small head, dim. of *capit-, caput* head — more at HEAD] **1 a** : a main division of a book or treatise usu. beginning on a new page **b** : a significant portion of anything conceived as adaptable to presentation in such divisions ⟨begin a new ~ in one's life⟩ ⟨with his death a ~ in the development of the north . . . was closed —Harold Griffin⟩ **2** : a regular meeting or assembly for business or conference of the canons of a cathedral or collegiate church or of canonesses, monks, or members of a religious or nonreligious order **3 a** : the body of canons of a cathedral or collegiate church who are presided over by a dean **b** : an organized esp. local branch or unit of a society or fraternity **4** : one of the hour numerals on a clock or watch dial **5** : a short passage of scripture between the last psalm and the hymn in lauds and the little hours

¹**chapter and verse** *n, pl* **chapters and verses** [so called fr. the tradition of citing biblical sources by chapter and verse number] **1** : the exact reference or source of information or justification for what one has said or written ⟨he claims, and gives *chapter and verse* for it, that he was an accurate and skillful rhymer —*Modern Language Notes*⟩ **2** : full precise information or detail ⟨giving *chapter and verse* for what was already known in general terms —*Newsweek*⟩ ⟨impressed her with the far-reaching program and gave her *chapter and verse* to prove its value —*N.Y. Herald Tribune Bk. Rev.*⟩

²**chapter and verse** *adv* **1** : with precise exactness ⟨repeat *chapter and verse* the ideas Croly had advanced —C.B.Forcey⟩ **2** : in full precise detail ⟨explain slowly, *chapter and verse*, what we were to do⟩

chapter head *n* : printed matter (as the chapter number or title, quotations, illustrations, or decorative letters) preceding the text at the beginning of a chapter

chapter house *n* [ME *chapitre hous*, fr. *chapitre* chapter + *hous* house] **1** : a building, room, or suite of rooms where a chapter meets or transacts its business **2** : a meeting place or residence of a local chapter of a college fraternity or sorority

chapter of accidents : the succession of unforeseen events ⟨make no plans but leave things to the *chapter of accidents*⟩

chap·trel \'chaptrəl\ *n* -s [irreg. fr. *chapiter* + *-el*] : ³IMPOST

chap·wom·an \'chap,-\ *n, pl* **chapwomen** [¹*chap* + *woman*] : a female peddler or hawker

¹**char** *var of* CHARE

²**char** *or* **charr** \'chär, -ȧ(r\ *n, pl* **char** *or* **chars** *or* **charr** *or* **charrs** [origin unknown] : a trout of the genus *Salvelinus*

³**char** \"\ *vb* **charred; charred; charring; chars** [back-formation fr. *charcoal*] *vt* **1** : to convert to charcoal or carbon usu. by exposing to heat ⟨heat ~s wood and paper⟩ **2** : to burn partly, usu. on the outside, with a blackened carbonized effect ⟨the beams badly *charred* and unsafe⟩ ~ *vi* : to burn to charcoal : BURN ⟨sugar ~s at 400°C⟩ **syn** see BURN

⁴**char** \"\ *n* -s : a charred substance or charred remains : CHARCOAL; *esp* : animal or vegetable charcoal used in decolorizing the sugar in sugar manufacturing

⁵**char** \'chär, -ȧ(r\ *vi* **chared** *or* **charred; chared** *or* **charred; charing** *or* **charring; chars** [partly fr. *chare, char* (to do or complete), partly back-formation fr. *charwoman*] : to work as a charwoman or at the tasks often assigned to a charwoman

⁶**char** \'chär, -ȧ(r\ *n* -s [short for *charwoman*] **1** *Brit* : a woman who does domestic cleaning or the cleaning of public buildings or offices for a living, often by the day : CHARWOMAN ⟨the domestic staff . . . reduced to an occasional ~ —Agnes M. Miall⟩ **2** : the work of routine housecleaning or the cleaning of public buildings or offices as a livelihood ⟨~ employees —*U.S. Post Office Manual*⟩

⁷**char** \"\ *n* -s [Hindi *cā*, fr. Chin (Pek) *ch'a²*] *slang Brit* : TEA

char *abbr* **1** character; characteristic **2** charity **3** charter

chara \'ka(a)rə\ *n* [NL, fr. L, a plant] **1** *cap* : a genus (the type of the family Characeae) of plants common in freshwater lakes of limestone districts and usu. having the central internodal cells of the stem, often encrusted with calcareous deposits, sheathed by smaller cells — see NITELLA **2** -s : any plant of the genus *Chara*

char·a·banc *or* **char-à-banc** \'sharə,baŋ, -bäⁿ\ *n, pl* **charabancs** *or* **char-à-bancs** \-aŋz, -äⁿz\ [modif. of F *char à bancs*, lit., wagon with benches] *Brit* : a horse-drawn vehicle or a motor coach usu. open and orig. having several rows of seats extending across its width and facing forward; *specif* : a sight-seeing motor coach

cha·ra·ce·ae \kə'rāsē,ē\ *n pl, cap* [NL, fr. *Chara*, type genus + *-aceae*] : a family of aquatic green algae (order Charales) comprising the stoneworts, resembling the horsetails in general appearance, and having jointed stems with whorls of slender branchlike leaves at the joints — see CHARA, NITELLA — **cha·ra·ceous** \-shəs\ *adj*

cha·rac·i·dae \kə'rasə,dē\ *n pl, cap* [NL, fr. *Charac-, Charax*, type genus, fr. Gk *charak-, charax* pointed stake, or a fish, prob. the sea bream) + *-idae*] : a large family of freshwater fishes of Africa and tropical America typically having a deep scaly body and strong jaws but exhibiting many lines of specialization and with related forms commonly constituting a division of the Cyprinoidea — see CARIBE

¹**char·a·cin** \'karəsən\ *n* -s [ISV *charac* (fr. NL *Characeae*) + *-in*] : a white substance with a moldy odor found in members of the genus *Chara* and some other fatty algae

²**characin** \"\ *also* **cha·rac·i·nid** \kə'rasənəd\ *n* -s [NL *Characinidae*] : a fish of the family Characidae often kept in tropical aquariums for varied form and bright colors

char·a·cin·i·dae \ˌkarə'sinə,dē\ [NL, fr. *Characinus*, type genus (fr. Gk *charak-, charax* pointed stake, or a fish, prob. the sea bream) + *-idae*; akin to Gk *charassein* to sharpen] *syn of* CHARACIDAE

char·act \'ka,rakt, kə'r-\ *n* -s [ME *charecte* mark, prob. alter. (influenced by L *character* mark, sign) of *carecte* — more at CARACT] : CHARACTER 1g

¹**char·ac·ter** \'karəktə(r), -rēk- *also* 'ker-\ *n* -s [alter. (influenced by L *character*) of earlier *caracter*, fr. ME, fr. MF *caractère*, fr. L *character* mark, sign, distinctive quality, fr. Gk *charaktēr*, fr. *charassein* to sharpen, cut into furrows, engrave; akin to Lith *žerti* to scratch, scrape] **1** : a distinctive differentiating mark: **a** : a conventionalized graphic device, token, or symbol typically single or simple in form esp. impressed or engraved as an indication of ownership or origin or capable of being impressed or engraved **b** : a device indicating a special characteristic or relationship ⟨the ~ of the fish is often used to indicate early Christians⟩ **c** : a graphic symbol (as a hieroglyph, ideograph, alphabet letter, punctuation mark, or shorthand mark) used as a unit in writing or printing ⟨a typewriter keyboard with special ~s⟩ ⟨mathematical ~s⟩ **d** : a conventionalized figure, representation, or expression ⟨a medieval ~ of Christ⟩ **e characters** *pl, obs* : SHORTHAND **f** *Roman Catholicism* : an indelible mark impressed on the soul by the sacraments of baptism, confirmation, and holy orders by which the recipient is empowered to produce or receive something sacred **g** : a cabalistic, magical, or astrological emblem ⟨charms, images, ~s stamped of sundry metals —Robert Burton⟩ **h** : a particular set of letters or other symbols used in writing : ALPHABET **2** : CHARACTERISTIC: as **a** (1) : one of the essentials of structure, form, materials, or function that together make up and usu. distinguish the individual : any feature used to separate distinguishable things (as organisms) into categories (2) : the detectable expression of the action of a gene or group of genes — see UNIT CHARACTER (3) : the aggregate of distinctive qualities characteristic of a breed, strain, or type **b** : the complex of accustomed mental and moral characteristics and habitual ethical traits marking a person, group, or nation or serving to individualize it ⟨it depended wholly on the governors' individual ~s whether their terms of office were equitable or oppressive —John Buchan⟩ ⟨to comprehend the full ~ of these United States —Ruth Suckow⟩ **c** : main or essential nature esp. as strongly marked and serving to distinguish : individual composite of salient traits, consequential characteristics, features giving distinctive tone ⟨each town came to have a ~ of its own —Sherwood Anderson⟩ ⟨the president had taken those measures which gave to Union war policy its controlling ~ —*Dict. of Amer. History*⟩ **3 a** : WRITING, INSCRIPTION, PRINTING; *also* : what is represented in such writing, inscription, or printing **b** : style of writing or printing esp. in physical qualities ⟨you know the ~ to be your brother's —Shak.⟩ **c** : a private mode of communication in writing : CIPHER **4** *obs* : APPEARANCE : outward and visible quality or trait **5** : a piece of printer's type that produces a character **6** : POSITION, RANK, CAPACITY, STATUS ⟨in the ~ of a slave⟩ ⟨his ~ as a town official⟩ **7 a** *archaic* : a description, delineation, or detailed account of the qualities or peculiarities — now used of a person, but formerly of a thing ⟨give the police a ~ of the thief⟩ **b** [trans. of Gk *charaktēr*] : a descriptive often satiric analysis usu. in the form of a short literary sketch of a human virtue or vice as embodied in a representative human being, of a general type of human character (as a busybody, an old man, a country bumpkin), or of a quality of a particular place or thing — most frequently applied to the form as it developed in 17th century English and French literature **c** : a written statement as to the behavior, habits, and competence of an employee given by an employer **8 a** : a person regarded as characterized by or exemplifying distinctive or notable traits : PERSONAGE, PERSONALITY ⟨Caesar is a great historical ~⟩ ⟨the Toronto financier . . . an almost fabulous ~ in Canadian mining circles —J.D.Hillaby⟩ **b** : personality as represented or realized in fiction or drama ⟨a play weak in ~ but strong in plot⟩; *also* : a given representation or realization of this kind ⟨the main ~ in the novel⟩ **c** : the personality or part which an actor recreates **d** : characterization esp. in fiction or drama ⟨a novelist good in both ~ and setting⟩ **e** : a unique, extraordinary, or eccentric person ⟨the cheery, cheeky, undefeatable ~ — the cockney —*London Calling*⟩; *esp* : a dramatic role calling for the representation of such a person **f** *slang* : PERSON, INDIVIDUAL, MAN ⟨an underworld ~⟩ ⟨romantic ~s will often camp out on the site —Jacquetta & Christopher Hawkes⟩ **9** : reputation esp. when good ⟨his association with evil companions detracted from his ~⟩ **10** : a composite of good moral qualities typically of moral excellence and firmness blended with resolution, self-discipline, high ethics, force, and judgment ⟨that stiffening of the moral fiber which we call ~ —F.A.Swinnerton⟩ ⟨his eldest brother . . . had not ~ enough to reproach me —John Galsworthy⟩ **11** : the crimp of wool fiber esp. with respect to its evenness **12** *of a dog* : style of action or deportment in field trial

syn SYMBOL, SIGN, MARK, NOTE: CHARACTER is likely to suggest a simple form or shape, sometimes the individual forms or devices that constitute signs or symbols. CHARACTER is likely to be used in reference to familiar conventionalized patterns. ⟨*characters* include letters of the alphabet, digits, simple musical notes, and so on⟩ SYMBOL, sometimes interchangeable with CHARACTER, is likely to stress the fact that the device in question means or stands for something ⟨a *symbol* is a sign, figure, or physical object the meaning of which is established by convention —Kurt Seligmann⟩ ⟨in the expression *Cu*, the *C* and the *u* are *characters; Cu* is the *symbol* for copper⟩ SIGN may be used to designate something less arbitrary and conventional than CHARACTER, something that hints by its form at what is meant, as arrows as direction markers ⟨*symbols* and *signs*, then, may be seen to differ in this wise: signs are proxy for the objects they represent; symbols are "vehicles for the conception of objects" —W.V.O'Connor⟩ MARK may be close to CHARACTER in suggesting simplicity; it usu. indicates something that is arbitrarily and conventionally adopted ⟨consignee *mark* — a symbol placed on packages for export, generally consisting of a square, triangle, diamond, circle, cross, etc., with designated letters . . . for the purpose of identification —*Marine Corps Manual*⟩ NOTE, except in reference to musical notation or perhaps to punctuation marks, is now uncommon as a synonym for CHARACTER. In various subjects use of these words is determined more by convention than by consideration of exact meanings and shades of connotation.

syn see in addition DISPOSITION, QUALITY, TYPE

— **in character** **1** : in accord with a person's normal or usual qualities or traits **2** : befitting a role or character type

— **out of character** **1** : not in accord with a person's normal or usual qualities or traits ⟨his rude behavior was quite *out of character;* he was generally meticulously well-bred⟩ **2** : unbefitting a role or character type ⟨the protagonist's curtain speech in act II was so *out of character* it was omitted after the first performance⟩

²**character** \"\ *vt* -ED/-ING/-S **1** : ENGRAVE, INSCRIBE, WRITE **2 a** *archaic* : REPRESENT, PORTRAY **b** : CHARACTERIZE

³**character** \"\ *adj* **1** : portraying or adept at portraying a usu. subordinate dramatic role whose distinctive mental or moral qualities are of first dramatic interest; *esp* : portraying an unusual or eccentric personality often markedly different (as in age) from the player ⟨a ~ actor⟩ ⟨a ~ actress⟩ **2** : calling for the qualities of a character actor ⟨a ~ part⟩ ⟨~ acting⟩

character assassination *n* : the slandering of another person (as a public figure) with the intention of destroying public trust in him

character dance *n* **1** : a mimetic dance esp. in ballet representing a character **2** : a characteristic national dance

char·ac·ter·ful \-fəl\ *adj* **1** : markedly expressive of character ⟨the ~ high-cheekboned face of a Tataric Abraham Lincoln —James Cerruti⟩ **2** : marked by character ⟨~ as the fluent grace of Sterne's prose —*Times Lit. Supp.*⟩

character-gradient \'===,===\ *n* : CLINE

¹**char·ac·ter·is·tic** \ˌkarəktə¦ristik, -rēk-, -tēk *also* ¦ker-\ *adj* [Gk *charaktēristikos*, fr. *charaktēr* + *-istikos* -istic] : belonging to or esp. typical or distinctive of the character or essential nature of ⟨the gaiety ~ of children on a holiday⟩ ⟨the white cliffs ~ of the coast at Dover⟩ ⟨a poetic style ~ of the epic⟩ ⟨folklore is ~ only of the group which creates it —Abram Kardiner⟩

syn CHARACTERISTIC, INDIVIDUAL, PECULIAR, and DISTINCTIVE all describe special or identifying qualities or traits. CHARACTERISTIC often stresses the typical nature of the qualities mentioned but is likely also to indicate that they distinguish the item described ⟨the dispersed settlement, large plantations, loose government, and individualism *characteristic* of the South, as compact village communities were *characteristic* of New England —S.E.Morison & H.S.Commager⟩ ⟨having nothing in them that is *characteristic*, or that discriminates them from the letters of any other young man —William Cowper⟩ INDIVIDUAL stresses distinguishing or identifying qualities ⟨the *individual* idiosyncrasies of each member of the great family —Sherwood Anderson⟩ ⟨his letters to her . . . are a simple, perfectly *individual*, daily record of a great passion —Arthur Symons⟩ PECULIAR, sometimes interchangeable with INDIVIDUAL, may stress the uncommon and may have a wider application and less force ⟨in these aspects or parts of his work we pretend to find what is *individual*, what is the *peculiar* essence of the man —T.S.Eliot⟩ ⟨the product of a force which was not *peculiar* to England but was operative in England and in France simultaneously —A.J.Toynbee⟩ ⟨habits both universal among mankind and *peculiar* to individuals —F.H. Allport⟩ DISTINCTIVE, less individualizing than PECULIAR or INDIVIDUAL indicates uncommon distinguishing characteristics, often praiseworthy ones ⟨it is rather the exquisite craftsmanship of France . . . that has given to free verse . . . its most *distinctive* qualities —J.L.Lowes⟩ ⟨lacks *distinctive* personal traits —M.R.Cohen⟩

²**characteristic** \"\ *n* -s **1** : a trait, quality, or property or a group of them distinguishing an individual, group, or type : that which characterizes or is characteristic ⟨the Welsh ~s are indelibly stamped —Wilfrid Goatman⟩ ⟨the usual ~s of matter — mass, rigidity, etc. —A.S.Eddington⟩ ⟨reptilian ~s⟩ **2** *physics* **a** : any of the variables pertaining to the normal performance of a device (as the grid voltage, plate current, or tube resistance of a vacuum tube or the voltage and watt rating of a lamp) **b** : CHARACTERISTIC CURVE **3** : the integral part of a common logarithm, being for a number greater than unity one less than the number of digits to the left of the decimal point, and for a number less than unity negative and numerically one more than the number of zeros between the decimal point and the first digit

char·ac·ter·is·ti·cal·ly \-ək(ə)lē, -ēk-, -li\ *adv* : in a characteristic manner

characteristic curve *n* : the graphic curve or the graph picturing it that shows the relation between two variables ⟨a *characteristic curve* plotting the variations of grid potential and plate current in the normal operation of a vacuum tube⟩ ⟨the patient's fever chart showed the *characteristic curve* for the disease⟩: **a** : the curve indicating the variation of density in a developed photographic image that results from the increase of exposure expressed logarithmically — called also *H and D curve, sensitometric curve* **b** : a curve showing the relationship between frequency and recording intensity or frequency and reproducing intensity in sound recording

characteristic function *n* : EIGENFUNCTION

characteristic impedance *n* : the impedance of a uniform alternating-current transmission line of indefinite length (as a long telephone cable) measured at the input end where the voltage is applied

char·ac·ter·is·tic·ness *n* -ES : the quality or state of being characteristic

characteristic radiation *n* : radiation in the form of light or X rays of wavelengths peculiar to the substance emitting or absorbing it

characteristic temperature *n* : DEBYE TEMPERATURE

characteristic x rays *n pl, usu cap X* : X rays of definite wavelengths characteristic of a pure substance and emitted by it under proper excitation

char·ac·ter·iz·a·ble \'karəktə,rīzəbəl, -rēk- *also* 'ker-\ *adj* : capable of being characterized

char·ac·ter·i·za·tion \ˌ==tərə'zāshən, -ˌrī'z-\ *n* -s [ML *characterizatus* (past part. of *characterizare*) + E *-ion*] : the act, process, or result of characterizing; *esp* : the representation of human character or personality (as in fiction or drama)

char·ac·ter·ize \'===,rīz\ *vb* -ED/-ING/-S *see -ize in Explan Notes* [ML *characterizare* to write, print, fr. Gk *charaktērizein* to engrave, inscribe, fr. *charaktēr* character + *-izein* -ize] *vt* **1** *obs* : ³EXPRESS 1 **2** : to describe the essential character or quality of : DELINEATE ⟨~ a friend in a few words⟩ ⟨~ an action as childish⟩ **3** : to be a distinguishing characteristic of : DISTINGUISH ⟨metaphor ~s the language of poetry —R.M. Weaver⟩ ~ *vi* : to portray, delineate, or represent character (as in a work of art) ⟨a writer excellent at *characterizing*⟩

char·ac·ter·less \'==tə(r)ləs\ *adj* : lacking character

character loan *n* : an unsecured loan made by a bank or loan company because of the known integrity of the borrower

character neurosis *n* : a personality disturbance in which character traits are thought to be the functional equivalent of neurotic symptoms

character note *n* : SHAPE NOTE

char·ac·ter·o·log·i·cal \ˌ==tərə¦läjəkəl\ *also* **char·ac·ter·o·log·ic** \-jik\ *adj* : of, relating to, or based on character or characterology

char·ac·ter·ol·o·gist \ˌ===ˈräləjəst\ *n* -s **:** a specialist in characterology

char·ac·ter·ol·o·gy \-jē\ *n* -ES [ISV ¹*character* + *-o-* + *-logy*; orig. formed as G *charakterologie*] **:** the study of character including its development and its differences in different individuals

character piece *n* [trans. of G *charakterstück*] **:** a short musical composition esp. for piano conveying a single mood or impression — compare PROGRAM MUSIC

characters *pl of* CHARACTER, *pres 3d sing of* CHARACTER

character sketch *n* **:** a sketch devoted to an analysis or representation of a character esp. of peculiar, eccentric, or strongly marked individuality or to a description stressing the character of a place

character study *n* **1 :** analysis or portrayal in literature of the traits of character of an individual **2 a :** a brief narrative or sketch devoted primarily to character study **b :** a realistic portrait in one of the plastic arts or in photography typically of an anonymous sitter whose face or figure reveals strong personality or character traits

character witness *n* **:** one that gives evidence concerning the reputation, conduct, and moral nature of a party to a legal action

char·ac·tery \ˈkarəkt(ə)rē, kəˈrak-\ *also* **char·ac·try** \ˈkarəktrē\ *n* -ES [¹*character* + *-y*] **:** characters or symbols esp. unusual used in the expression of thought

cha·rade \shəˈrād, *US sometimes & Brit usu* -ād *or* -ad\ *n* -s [F, fr. Prov *charrado* chat, fr. *charra* to chatter, of imit. origin] **1 a :** a word represented in riddling verse or by picture, tableau, or dramatic action (as *intrusion* represented by depiction of *inn, true,* and *shun*) **b charades** *pl but sing or pl in constr* **:** a game in which a group is divided into two sides each alternately devising charades to be guessed by the other **2 :** something resembling or felt to resemble a charade: as **a :** an almost transparent pretense **b :** a symbolic action ⟨sleepwalkers acting out some fantastic Freudian ~ of their own illusions —J.R.Ullman⟩

cha·rad·rii \kəˈradrēˌī\ *n pl, cap* [NL, fr. pl. of *Charadrius*, type genus] **:** the suborder of Charadriiformes comprising the shorebirds

char·a·dri·i·dae \ˌkarəˈdrīəˌdē\ *n pl, cap* [NL, fr. *Charadrius*, type genus + *-idae*] **:** the family of Charadrii consisting of the plovers, turnstones, and surfbirds and sometimes the related snipes, sandpipers, and woodcocks (family Scolopacidae) — **char·a·drine** \ˈkarəˌdrīn\ *adj* — **cha·rad·ri·oid** \kəˈradrēˌȯid\ *adj or n*

cha·rad·ri·i·form \kəˈradrēəˌfȯrm\ *adj* [NL *Charadriiformes*] **:** of or relating to Charadriiformes or to Charadrii

cha·rad·ri·i·for·mes \kəˌradrēəˈfȯrˌmēz\ *n pl, cap* [NL, fr. *Charadrius*, type genus + *-iformes*] **:** an order of birds including the shorebirds, auks, gulls, and related forms

cha·rad·ri·us \kəˈradrēəs\ *n, cap* [NL, fr. LL, a bird, perh. the thick-knee, fr. Gk *charadrios*, fr. *charadra* ravine; akin to Gk *charassein* to sharpen, cut into furrows — more at CHARACTER] **:** a genus (the type of the family Charadriidae) of plovers comprising small or medium-sized birds (as the piping plover) but sometimes (as formerly) including also the golden plovers

cha·ra·les \kəˈrā(ˌ)lēz\ *n pl, cap* [NL, fr. *Chara* + *-ales*] **:** an order of algae (division Chorophyta) containing the single family Characeae — see CHAROPHYTA

cha·ran·go \chəˈraŋ(ˌ)gō\ *n* -s [Sp, alter. of *charanga* out-of-tune orchestra, military music made by wind instruments, of imit. origin] **:** a small guitar of Spanish America with a body typically made of an animal shell

¹**charas** *pl of* CHARA

²**cha·ras** \ˈchärəs\ *or* **chur·rus** *also* **chur·us** \ˈchərəs\ *n* -ES [Hindi *caras*] **:** a narcotic and intoxicating resin that exudes esp. from the flower heads of hemp — compare CANNABIN; *also* **:** a smoking mixture containing this resin

char·bon \ˈshärbən, -ˌbän, *F* shårbōⁿ\ *n* -s [F, lit., ember, charcoal (trans. of Gk *anthrax* charcoal, ember, carbuncle, malignant pustule), fr. L *carbon-, carbo* ember, charcoal — more at HEARTH] **:** ANTHRAX 2

char·bray \ˈshär(ˌ)brā\ *n, usu cap* [irreg. fr. *Charolais* + *Brahman* (zebu)] **:** a type or breed of beef cattle developed in the southern U.S. by intercrossing animals of the Charolais breed with Brahmans

char·co \ˈchär(ˌ)kō\ *n* -s [Sp] *Southwest* **:** a usu. small natural depression in which water collects **:** WATER HOLE

char·coal \ˈchärˌkōl, -ˌåk-\ *n* -s [ME *charcole*, perh. fr. MF *charbon* charcoal + ME *cole* coal — more at CHARBON, COAL] **1 :** a dark-colored or black porous form of carbon made from vegetable or animal substances (as from wood by charring in a kiln or retort from which air is excluded) and used for fuel and in various mechanical, artistic, and chemical processes **2 a :** a piece or pencil of fine charcoal used as a drawing implement **b :** a charcoal drawing **3 :** a dark purplish gray that is bluer and duller than slate, pigeon, taupe gray, or dusk (sense 3b)

charcoal black *n* **:** a black pigment consisting of a charred substance (as wood charcoal or bone black)

charcoal burner *n* **:** a person whose work is making charcoal

charcoal burning *n* **:** the making of charcoal

charcoal gray *n* **1 :** a nearly neutral slightly greenish black **2 :** PELICAN 4

charcoal iron *n* **:** iron made in a furnace burning charcoal

charcoal pencil *n* **:** a strip or cylinder of artist's charcoal often in a slender wooden casing

charcoal plate *n* **1 :** tin plate made from charcoal iron **2 :** tin plate having the heaviest coating and highest polish

charcoal powder *n* **1 :** powdered charcoal **2 :** GUNPOWDER 1a

charcoal rot *n* **:** a disease of plants that is common in the southern U.S. and destructive to sweet and white potatoes and to corn and is caused by a fungus (*Macrophomina phaseoli*) which attacks the lower stem and roots destroying much of the tissues and forming myriads of tiny black sclerotia on what remains

char·cot joint \(ˈ)shärˌkō-\ *n, usu cap C* [after J. M. *Charcot* †1893 Fr. neurologist] **:** a destructive condition affecting one or more joints, occurring in diseases of the spinal cord, and ultimately resulting in a flail joint

char·cu·te·rie \(ˌ)shärˌküd·əˈrē, ˌ=ˈ==(ˌ)=\ *n* -s [F, fr. MF *chaircuiterie*, fr. *chaircuitier*] **1 :** a French pork butcher's shop **2 a :** a delicatessen in France specializing in dressed meats and meat dishes (as cold cuts and sausages) **b :** the cold cuts and meat dishes sold in such a shop; *also* **:** a single item of such meats

char·cu·tier \(ˌ)shärˌküd·ēˈā, ˌ=ˈ==ˌ=\ *n* -s [F, fr. MF *chaircuitier*, fr. *chair cuite* cooked meat, fr. *chair* meat, flesh (fr. L *carn-, caro*) + *cuite*, fem. of *cuit*, past part. of *cuire* to cook, fr. L *coquere* — more at CARNAL, COOK] **1 :** a pork butcher **2 :** one that prepares or sells charcuterie (sense 2b)

chard \ˈchärd, -ȧd\ *n* -s [modif. (prob. influenced by F *chardon* thistle) of F *carde* edible leafstalk of the cardoon or the artichoke, fr. MF, cardoon with edible leafstalks, fr. OProv *cardo*, fr. L *carduus* thistle, artichoke; akin to MLG *harst* rake, L *carrere* to card, Skt *kaṣati* he scratches] **:** a beet (*Beta vulgaris cicla*) producing large yellowish green leaves with thick succulent stalks and often cooked as a potherb — called also *seakale beet, Swiss chard*

char·don·nay \ˌshärdᵊnˈā\ *n* -s *usu cap* [F] **:** a dry white table wine of Chablis type — called also *Pinot Chardonnay*

¹**chare** \ˈcha(a)(ə)r, -e(ə)r, -a(a)ə, -eə\ *or* **char** \ˈchär, chȧ(r\ *n* -s [ME *cherre, char* turn, time, piece of work, fr. OE *cierr, cyrr*; akin to OE *cierran* to turn, ON *kjarr* underbrush, Gk *gerron* wicker shield, wicker body of a cart; basic meaning: turn, bend, twist] **1 :** an occasional piece of work **:** an odd job or task esp. of housework **:** CHORE **2** *dial Eng* **:** a narrow lane, alley, or street

²**chare** \"\ *or* **char** \"\ *vt* **chared** *or* **charred**; **chared** *or* **charred**; **charing** *or* **charring**; **chares** *or* **chars** [ME *charren, charen* to turn, fr. OE *cierran*] *archaic* **:** to finish off (as a job)

chared *past of* CHAR *or of* CHARE

charet *n* -s [ME *charette*, fr. MF, cart] *obs* **:** a wheeled vehicle **:** CART, CHARIOT

¹**cha·rette** *or* **char·rette** \shəˈret\ *n* -s [F *charrette* cart (used to transport drawings), fr. OF, cart, fr. *char* wheeled vehicle + *-ette* — more at CHARIOT] **:** the intense final effort made by architectural students to complete their solutions to a given architectural problem in an allotted time or the period in which such an effort is made

²**charette** *or* **charrette** \"\ *vi* **charetted** *or* **charretted**; **charetted** *or* **charretted**; **charetting** *or* **charretting**; **charettes** *or* **charrettes :** to exert oneself in a charette

¹**charge** \ˈchärj, ˈchȧj\ *vb* -ED/-ING/-s [ME *chargen*, fr. OF *chargier*, fr. LL *carricare*, fr. L *carrus* wheeled vehicle — more at CAR] *vt* **1 a** *archaic* (1) **:** to put a load on or in ⟨horses *charged* with heavy burdens⟩ (2) **:** to place as a load ⟨all the servants . . . to ~ the Saratoga trunk upon the dickey —R.L.Stevenson⟩ **b** (1) *obs* **:** to place too heavy a burden on **:** OVERLOAD (2) **:** to weigh down with a heavy burden (as of guilt, sickness, or expense) ⟨his spirit was *charged* with sorrow⟩ (3) **:** EMPHASIZE, EXAGGERATE; *esp* **:** to render more striking (a detail in a work of art) ⟨~ a line by reinforcing with black⟩ **c** (1) **:** to place a charge (as of materials to be treated or consumed) in ⟨~ the magazine with three rounds⟩ **:** load or fill to capacity or up to the required amount ⟨~ a blast furnace with ore⟩ (2) **:** to impart an electric charge to (3) **:** to restore the active materials in (a storage battery) by the passage of a direct current through in the opposite direction to that of discharge (4) **:** to load (a charge) into something ⟨granulated cork is *charged* into suitable molds and heat is applied —G.B.Cooke⟩ (5) **:** to fill or load (as a brush or pen) with pigment or ink (6) **:** to fill (as a fire hose) with water under pressure (7) **:** EMBED ⟨~ abrasive grains in a metal disk for grinding⟩ **d** (1) **:** to assume as a heraldic bearing ⟨he ~s three roses or⟩ (2) **:** to place a heraldic bearing on ⟨he ~s his shield with three roses or⟩ **e** (1) **:** to fill full **:** furnish fully ⟨a brain *charged* with fancies⟩; *esp* **:** to fill with a particular mood, tone, or spirit ⟨~s the air with its cosmopolitan sense of freedom —Harry Levin⟩ (2) **:** to cause to be mixed or saturated **:** IMPREGNATE ⟨warehouses ~*ing* the air with odors of spice and coffee⟩ **2 a** (1) **:** to impose a particular duty or task on **:** entrust with a responsibility, duty, or task ⟨chairman specifically *charged* with leading the board —G.B.Huff⟩ (2) **:** to entrust with the care, custody, or management of something or someone ⟨I ~ myself with him . . . I will take care of him —Charles Dickens⟩ **b :** to command or exhort with authority ⟨Badoglio was *charged* by the king to form a new cabinet —Sir Winston Churchill⟩ **:** urge earnestly ⟨I ~ thee be not thou more grieved than I am —Shak.⟩ **c** *of a judge* **:** to give a charge to (a jury) **3 a :** to bring an accusation against **:** call to account **:** BLAME ⟨*charged* him as the instigator of the disorder⟩ **b :** to make an assertion against esp. by ascribing guilt or blame for an offense or wrong **:** ACCUSE — used with *with* ⟨reluctant to ~ a dead man with an offense from which he could not clear himself —Edith Wharton⟩ **c :** to place the blame or guilt for (a fault or wrongdoing) — now usu. used with *to* ⟨he *charged* the fiasco to overconfidence⟩ **d :** to assert as an accusation ⟨*charged* that the . . . line would tend to become a monopoly —*Current Biog.*⟩ **4 a :** to bring (a weapon) to a position suited for attack **:** LEVEL ⟨~ a lance⟩ **b :** to drive upon, rush against, or bear down upon rapidly and violently ⟨~ an enemy position⟩ ⟨the car *charged* the bank and broke through the fence⟩ **5 a** (1) **:** to impose a pecuniary burden on ⟨~ his estate with any debts incurred⟩ (2) **:** to impose or record as a pecuniary obligation ⟨~ debts to an estate⟩ **b** (1) **:** to fix or ask (a sum) as a fee or payment ⟨~ $10 for his services⟩ (2) **:** to ask payment of (a person) ⟨~ a client for expenses⟩ — often used with a double object ⟨~ a student $50 for meals⟩ **c** (1) **:** to record (an item) as an expense, debt, obligation, or liability — usu. used with *to* or *against* ⟨~ a purchase to a customer⟩ ⟨~ a library book to a borrower⟩ ⟨~ a mistake against a person⟩ (2) **:** to record a debt, obligation, or liability against ⟨~ your account with the goods ordered⟩ ⟨~ a person with a book borrowed from a library⟩ ⟨~ a fielder with an error⟩ (3) **:** to enter on the debit side of an account ⟨~ a sum against income for depreciation⟩ ⟨~ rent and phone bill to administration⟩ **~** *vi* **1 :** to drive or rush violently forward typically in attack ⟨the cavalry *charged* to the flank⟩ ⟨came *charging* through the door, wearing a baseball mitt on one hand —Jean Stafford⟩ **2 :** to ask or set a price ⟨~ high for goods⟩ **:** ask payment ⟨he doesn't ~ at all for it⟩ **3** *of a judge* **:** to give a charge to the jury **4** *of a dog* **:** to lie down with head on forepaws **syn** see ACCUSE, ASCRIBE, BURDEN, COMMAND, RUSH — **charge to capital :** to debit a capital asset account ⟨additions and betterments should be *charged to capital* and not to expense⟩ — **charge to revenue :** to debit an expense account

²**charge** \"\ *n* -s [ME, fr. OF, fr. *chargier*, v.] **1 a** *obs* **:** a material load or weight **b :** a figure borne on a heraldic field **:** BEARING **c :** a plaster or ointment used on a domestic animal **d** (1) **:** the quantity of explosive used in a single discharge ⟨a cartridge with a powder ~ of 70 grains⟩ ⟨an artillery shell with an explosive bursting ~⟩ ⟨a ~ of dynamite under the stump⟩ (2) **:** the powder and shot in a cartridge **e :** the quantity of material to be used or consumed that is loaded at one time into an apparatus or that a mechanism is intended to receive in any single operation ⟨the ~ of chemicals in a fire extinguisher⟩ ⟨the ~ of mixed fuel and air in the cylinder of a gas engine⟩ ⟨the ~ of coal placed in a coal-gas retort⟩ **f** (1) **:** ELECTRIC CHARGE (2) **:** the quantity of electricity that a storage battery is capable of yielding expressed usu. in ampere-hours (3) **:** the process of charging a storage battery **g** (1) **:** a store or accumulation of force (as emotion, excitement, or affective power) ⟨poetry with an emotional ~, deeply felt and communicated to the reader⟩ **:** impelling esp. emotional force **:** DRIVE ⟨a man with a high emotional ~⟩ (2) **:** CATHEXIS 2 (3) *slang* **:** a strong feeling of amusement, pleasure, or excitement **:** KICK ⟨the children got a big ~ out of the clown⟩ **h :** the abrasive powder or grains in the surface of a lap used for grinding, polishing, or sawing **2** *obs* **:** CONSEQUENCE, IMPORTANCE ⟨this army of such mass and ~ —Shak.⟩ **3 a :** something that one is obligated for **:** a duty or task laid upon one **:** OBLIGATION ⟨to maintain this readiness . . . is . . . a first ~ upon our military effort —Sir Winston Churchill⟩ **b :** control of the acts, workings, or disposition of something **:** MANAGEMENT, SUPERVISION ⟨he assumed full ~ of the business⟩ **:** CARE, CUSTODY ⟨remained under his uncle's ~ during his minority⟩ **c :** the parish, church, district, or congregations regularly served by a clergyman **d :** a person or thing committed or entrusted to the care, custody, management, or support of another ⟨nursemaids sunning their ~s by the sea —D.G.Gerahty⟩ ⟨he entered the poorhouse, becoming a county ~⟩ **4 a :** INSTRUCTION, COMMAND, ORDER, INJUNCTION ⟨he gave them ~ about the queen to guard and foster her forevermore —Alfred Tennyson⟩ **b :** a formal address containing instruction or exhortation: as (1) **:** an official address of instruction by a senior church official to his clergy or upon the ordination of a minister (2) **:** an instruction given by the court to the jury in order to govern their action in coming to or making their decision; *specif* **:** the statement made by the judge to the jury at the close of a trial of the principles of law that the latter are bound to apply to the facts as determined by them in deciding upon their verdict **5 a :** expenditure or incurred expense ⟨living at the ~ of his brother⟩: as (1) **:** payment of costs **:** money paid out (2) **:** a pecuniary liability (as rents or taxes) against property, a person, or an organization ⟨~s upon the estate⟩ ⟨smoking has become . . . a fixed ~ on the expenditures of every family —Morris Fishbein⟩ — often used in pl. **b :** the price demanded for a thing or service ⟨a 10-cent admission ~⟩ — often used in pl. ⟨reverse the ~s for a telephone call⟩ **c :** a debit to an account ⟨a ~ to expense account⟩ **:** an entry in an account of what is due from one party to another ⟨a ~ to a customer's account⟩ **:** something that is debited ⟨the purchase was a ~⟩ **d :** the record of a loan (as of a book from a library) **6 a :** an accusation of a wrong or offense **:** ALLEGATION, INDICTMENT ⟨arrested on the ~ of bribery⟩ **b :** a statement of complaint or hostile criticism ⟨the ~ that earned incomes are based upon no principle of equity⟩ **7 a** *of a weapon* **:** a position of readiness for attack ⟨pikes held in ~⟩ **b** (1) **:** a violent and impetuous rush toward or upon some person or object ⟨the lion's ~ carried him past the antelope⟩; *specif* **:** an attack with the intent of closing with an enemy ⟨a tank ~⟩ — compare ¹ASSAULT 2 (2) **:** the signal for attack ⟨the bugle sounds the ~⟩ **c :** a lunge used chiefly in gymnastics in which the trunk and stationary leg form a straight line — **in charge 1 :** having the control or custody of something ⟨the assistant manager was placed *in charge* of the shop⟩ **2** *or* **in the charge** *or* **in one's charge :** into or under the control or custody ⟨given these pills *in charge* of Mrs. Sylk —Gabrielle Long⟩ ⟨the papers were *in the charge* of the custodian of documents⟩ **3 :** under supervision ⟨the boy was taken *in charge* by his grandmother⟩ **4** *Brit* **:** into the hands of the police to be charged with violation of the law ⟨caught the thief and gave him *in charge*⟩

³**char·gé** \(ˈ)shärˈzhā *also* (ˈ)chärˈjā; -ä\ˈ-\ *n* -s [by shortening] **:** CHARGÉ D'AFFAIRES

charge·able \ˈchärjəbəl, ˈchȧj-\ *adj* [ME, weighty, important, burdensome, fr. ¹*charge* (load) + *-able*] **1** *obs* **:** involving burdensome expense **:** EXPENSIVE, COSTLY **2 a** [¹*charge* + *-able*] **:** liable to be charged: as (1) **:** liable to be accused or held responsible ⟨a man ~ for assault⟩ (2) **:** capable of being charged to a particular account or as an expense or liability ⟨~ to printing expense⟩ ⟨debts ~ on the estate⟩ **b** [²*charge* (person committed to care of the parish) + *-able*] **:** qualified to be made a charge on the county or parish — **charge·able·ness** *n* -ES

charge account *n* [²*charge* (debit)] **1 :** a customer's account with a creditor (as a merchant) to which the purchase of goods is charged **2 :** ACCOUNT RECEIVABLE

charge–a–plate \ˈchärjəˌplāt, -ȧj-\ *or* **charge plate** *n* [fr. *Charga-plate*, a trademark] **:** an embossed plate (as of metal) used to identify a customer having a charge account

charge–back \ˈ=ˌ=\ *n* -s **:** a debit to a depositor's account that offsets a previous credit that was not collected

charged *adj* [ME, loaded, fr. past part. of *chargen* to charge] **1 a :** showing or possessing strong emotion or vigorous purpose ⟨attacking the author in an emotionally ~ review⟩ **b :** tensely expectant **:** INTENSE ⟨the ~ atmosphere of the room⟩ **2 :** capable of arousing violence, emotion, or strong opinion ⟨a highly ~ political theme⟩

char·gé d'af·faires \(ˌ)shärˌzhādəˈfa(a)(ə)r, -ȧˌzh-, -zhā(ˌ)da'-, -fe(ə)r, -a(a)ə, -eə *also* (ˌ)chärˌjā- *or* -ȧˌj- *or* -rz *or* -əz\ *n, pl* **chargés d'affaires** \-zhā(z)(ˌ)d-, -jāz(ˌ)d-\ [F, lit., one charged with affairs] **1 :** a lower-ranking member of the diplomatic corps who directs diplomatic affairs during the absence of the ambassador or minister **2 :** a diplomatic representative inferior in rank to an ambassador or minister accredited by the government of one country to the minister of foreign affairs of another

charge down *vt* **:** to stop with one's body (a football kicked by an opponent, as in rugby)

charged water *n* **:** SODA WATER 2a

charge·ful *adj, obs* **:** COSTLY

chargehand \ˈ=ˌ=\ *n* [²charge (supervision)] *Brit* **:** FOREMAN, SUBFOREMAN **:** STRAW BOSS

charge·less \ˈ=ləs\ *adj* **:** being without a charge

charge·man \ˈ=mən, -ˌman\ *n, pl* **chargemen** [²*charge* (supervision) + *man*] **1 :** one placed in charge; *esp* **:** a workman placed in charge of other workmen **2 :** one that tends the devulcanizer that removes the fabric content and partially restores the original properties of scrap rubber **3 :** BLASTER a **4 :** BATTERYMAN 1

charge off *vt* **:** to reduce (the value at which an asset has been carried on the books) by an amount representing a loss, partial or complete ⟨*charge off* obsolete inventory⟩

charge–off \ˈ=ˌ=\ *n* -s [*charge off*] **1 :** the reduction of the value at which an asset has been carried on the books ⟨bad debt *charge-offs*⟩ **2 :** the amount by which an account is reduced by charging off decline in value

charge of quarters [²*charge* (supervision)] **:** a noncommissioned officer designated usu. for a 24-hour period to maintain order and handle administrative matters esp. after duty hours in the area of his unit — abbr. *CQ*

charge plate *var of* CHARGE-A-PLATE

¹**char·ger** \ˈchärjər, -ȧjə\ *n* -s [ME *chargeour*; akin to ME *chargen* to charge — more at CHARGE] **:** a large flat dish or platter for carrying meat

²**charg·er** \"\ *n* -s [ME *chargere* one that charges, fr. *chargen* to charge + *-ere* -er] **1 :** a device for charging: as **a :** an appliance for holding or inserting a charge of powder or shot in a gun **b :** a cartridge clip **c :** a device for charging storage batteries — called also *battery charger* **2 :** a horse suitable for cavalry use **:** a mount for battle or parade **3 a :** a workman who charges materials (as ore) into a receptacle or operating unit (as a furnace) for processing **b :** BATTERYMAN 1 **c :** a workman who applies decorative pastes to jewelry or who prepares the parts for soldering

¹**charges** *pres 3d sing of* CHARGE, *pl of* CHARGE

²**chargés** *pl of* CHARGÉ

charges forward *n pl* **:** charges connected with the collection of a draft and paid by the drawee — contrasted with *charges here*

charge sheet *n* **1 :** a memorandum of the names of those to be tried in police and magistrates' courts with a summary statement of the charge against each **2 :** a statement of charges against one brought for trial before a court-martial

charges here *n pl* **:** charges connected with the collection of a draft that are paid by the drawer — contrasted with *charges forward*

charge sister *n* [²*charge* (supervision)] *Brit* **:** a trained nurse who has charge of a ward in an infirmary or hospital

charging *pres part of* CHARGE

charging order *n, Brit* **:** an order of court making a judgment debt a charge upon the stocks or funds of the debtor

charier *comparative of* CHARY

chariest *superlative of* CHARY

char·i·ly \ˈcha(a)rəlē, ˈcher-, -li\ *adv* [*chary* + *-ly*] **:** in a chary manner

char·i·ness \-rēnəs, -rin-\ *n* -ES [*chary* + *-ness*] **1 :** the quality or state of being chary **2** *archaic* **:** carefully preserved state **:** INTEGRITY

charing *pres part of* CHAR *or of* CHARE

cha·ri–nile \ˈshärēˌnīl, -īəl\ *n, usu cap C&N* [fr. *Chari* + *Nile*, rivers in Africa] **:** a family of African languages of which the Nilotic, Nubian, Kunama, and Central Sudanic groups are branches — called also *Macrosudanic*

¹**char·i·ot** \ˈcharēət *also* -er-; *often* -əd·+V\ *n* -s [ME, fr. MF, fr. OF, fr. *char* wheeled vehicle, fr. L *carrus* — more at CAR] **1 :** a vehicle (as a cart or wagon) for transporting goods **2 :** a vehicle for conveying persons esp. in state (as a triumphal car or a coach of state) **3 :** a 2-wheeled vehicle usu. drawn by two horses and used in ancient warfare and also in processions and races **4 :** a light 4-wheeled carriage having a coach box and back seats only

ancient Greek chariot (biga)

²**chariot** \"\ *vb* -ED/-ING/-s *vt* **:** to convey or carry in or as if in a chariot ⟨they . . . were ~*ed* swiftly up that thronging noble street —Thomas Wolfe⟩ **~** *vi* **:** to drive, ride, or go in or as if in a chariot

char·i·ot·ed \-əd·əd, -ətəd\ *adj* **:** furnished with a chariot

char·i·o·tee \ˌ===ˈtē\ *n* -s [irreg. fr. ¹*chariot*] **:** a light covered 4-wheeled pleasure carriage with two seats

¹**char·i·o·teer** \ˌ===ˈti(ə)r, -iə\ *n* -s [alter. (influenced by E *-eer*) of earlier *charioter*, fr. ME *charietere*, modif. (prob. influenced by MF *chariot*) of MF *charretier*, fr. OF, fr. *charrette* cart — more at CHARETTE] **:** one that drives a chariot

²**charioteer** \"\ *vb* -ED/-ING/-s *vi* **:** to act as charioteer **:** drive a chariot or other vehicle **~** *vt* **1 :** DRIVE ⟨~ a vehicle⟩ **2 :** to drive (a person) in a vehicle

char·i·ot·ry \ˈ==ətrē\ *n* -ES **:** the part of a military force that fights from chariots ⟨the Egyptian ~⟩

cha·ris·ma \kəˈrizmə\ *or* **char·ism** \ˈkaˌrizəm\ *n, pl* **cha·ris·ma·ta** \kəˈrizməd·ə\ *or* **char·isms** [Gk *charisma* favor, gift, fr. *charizesthai* to favor, fr. *charis* grace; akin to Gk *chairein* to rejoice — more at YEARN] **1 :** a spiritual gift or talent regarded as divinely granted to a person as a token of grace and favor and exemplified in early Christianity by the power of healing, gift of tongues, or prophesying **2 a :** a personal magic of leadership arousing special popular loyalty or enthusiasm for a public figure (as a political leader or military commander) ⟨already potential presidents are waiting hopefully in the wings, and while none of them possesses the general's ~, at least one or two are both widely popular and highly competent —L.H. Clark, Jr.⟩ **b :** a special magnetic charm or appeal ⟨offers solutions that are independent of the personal ~ of the teacher —*Psychology Today*⟩

char·is·mat·ic \ˌkarəzˈmad·ik\ *adj* [Gk *charismat-, charisma* + E *-ic*] **1 :** constituting or resulting from charisma ⟨~ gifts⟩ **2 :** exhibiting or based on charisma ⟨~ sects⟩ **:** possessing charisma ⟨~ leaders⟩

cha·ris·ti·cary \kəˈristəˌkerē\ *n* -ES [perh. fr. MGk *charistikarios*, fr. Gk *charistikos* bounteous (fr. *charizesthai* to favor, give freely) + MGk *-arios* -ary, fr. L *-arius*] **:** a medieval Greek official who received the revenue from a monastery or benefice

char·i·ta·ble \ˈcharəd·əbəl, -rətəb- *also* -er-\ *adj* [ME, fr. MF, fr. OF, fr. *charité* charity + *-ité* -ity — more at CHARITY] **1 :** exhibiting the virtue of Christian love **:** full of love and goodwill for others **:** BENEVOLENT, KINDLY **2 a :** practicing or showing charity **:** generous in assistance to the poor ⟨a man ~ to all in need⟩ **b :** of, for, or relating to charity ⟨~ gifts⟩ **:** having the quality of charity ⟨a ~ impulse⟩ ⟨money spent for ~ purposes⟩ **:** administering charity ⟨~ institutions⟩ **3 :** liberal in judging others **:** inclined to look on the best side and to avoid harsh judgment ⟨it is more ~ to suspend judgment —Ellen Glasgow⟩ **:** arising from or dictated by kindness ⟨a ~ interpretation of his actions⟩ — **char·i·ta·ble·ness** \-bəlnəs\ *n* -ES — **char·i·ta·bly** \-əblē, -li\ *adv*

charitable trust *n* **:** a trust set up for the benefit of the public usu. setting out a definite charitable purpose for an undetermined number of beneficiaries

char·i·tar·i·an \ˌ⸗⸗ˈterēən\ *n* -S [*charity* + *-arian* (as in *humanitarian*)] **:** a charitable person **:** one that aids or supports charitable enterprises

char·i·ty \ˈcharəd·ē, -ətē, -i *also* -er-\ *n* -ES *often attrib* [ME *charite*, fr. OF *charité*, fr. LL *caritat-, caritas* Christian love, fr. L, costliness, high regard, love, fr. *carus* dear, costly, loved + *-itat-, -itas* -ity; akin to OIr *caraim* I love, Skt *kāma* love, desire] **1 :** Christian love: **a :** the virtue or act of loving God with a love which transcends that for creatures and of loving others for the sake of God **b :** divine love for man **:** love in its perfection **c :** the act of loving or the disposition to love all men as brothers because they are sons of God **:** love of fellow men **2 a :** the kindly and sympathetic disposition to aid the needy or suffering **:** liberality to the poor, to benevolent institutions, or to worthy causes ⟨the ~ of the neighbors was exhausted and there was no more food in the house —Vicki Baum⟩ **b:** an act or series of acts of aid to the needy ⟨performed many *charities* among her neighbors⟩ **c :** whatever is given to the needy or suffering for their relief **:** ALMS ⟨give her a ~⟩ **d :** an organization or institution engaged in the free assistance of the poor, the suffering, or the distressed ⟨a list of deserving *charities*⟩ **e :** public provision for the care or relief of the needy ⟨too proud to accept ~⟩ **f :** the recipient of charitable assistance ⟨he is one of my father's *charities*⟩ **3 a** (1) **:** love or affection for others **:** a disposition to good will, kindliness, and sympathy ⟨no one minded him laughing at them when they saw the endless ~ of his eyes —Mary Webb⟩ (2) **:** an act or instance of good will or affection **b :** an eleemosynary gift **:** a gift (as by grant or devise) of real or personal property to the use of the public or any portion of it as distinct from specific individuals for any beneficial or salutary purpose **c :** an institution (as a hospital, library, or school) founded by a gift and intended for the use of the public **4 :** a disposition to liberal lenient tolerant judgment and toward minimizing shortcomings and putting the best possible construction on the characteristics or actions of others ⟨a kindly critic liked for his ~ and moderation⟩ **5 :** a refreshment dispensed between meals in a monastery **6 :** JACOB'S LADDER 1a **7 :** CHARITY STAMP **syn** see MERCY

charity school *n* **:** a school for poor children that is supported by charitable bequests or contributions

charity stamp *n* **1 :** a semipostal stamp the surcharge on which goes for some charity **2 :** a charity seal

¹cha·ri·va·ri \ˌshivəˈrē, ˈ⸗⸗ˌ⸗, *Brit* ˌshārəˈvāri *or* ˌshär-\ *or* **chiv·a·ree** *or* **chiv·a·ri** \ˌshivəˈrē, ˈ⸗⸗ˌ⸗\ *n* -S [F *charivari*, fr. LL *caribaria* headache, fr. Gk *karēbaria*, fr. *karē, kara* head + *-baria* heaviness (fr. *barys* heavy) — more at CEREBRAL, GRIEVE] **1 :** SHIVAREE 1 **2 a :** a confusion of noises **b :** MEDLEY, HODGEPODGE

²charivari \ˌshivəˈrē, ˈ⸗⸗ˌ⸗\ *vb* **charivaried; charivaried; charivariing; charivaries :** SHIVAREE

¹chark \ˈchärk\ *vt* -ED/-ING/-S [back-formation fr. obs. *chark-coal*, alter. of *charcoal*] **:** to burn to charcoal or coke **:** CHAR

²chark \"\ *n* -S *now dial Eng* **:** charred wood or coal **:** CHARCOAL, COKE, CINDER

char·ka *or* **char·kha** \ˈchərkə, -är-\ *n* -S [Hindi *carkhā*, fr. Per *charkha, charkh* wheel, fr. MPer *chark;* akin to Av *chaxra-* wheel, Skt *cakra* — more at WHEEL] **:** a domestic spinning wheel used in India chiefly for cotton

charlady \ˈ⸗,⸗⸗\ *n* [¹*chare* + *lady*] *Brit* **:** CHARWOMAN

char·la·tan \ˈshärlətən, -ətᵊn, -äl- *sometimes* ˈch-\ *n* -S [It *ciarlatano*, alter. (influenced by It *ciarlare* to chatter, of imit. origin) of *cerretano*, lit., inhabitant of Cerreto, fr. *Cerreto*, village near Spoleto, Italy + It *-ano* -an] **1** *archaic* **:** a barker of dubious remedies ⟨~*s* at a county fair⟩ **2 a :** a pretender to medical knowledge **:** QUACK ⟨~*s* killing their patients by empiric procedures⟩ **b :** one making esp. noisy or showy pretenses to knowledge or ability **:** FRAUD ⟨replaced by the ~*s* and the rogues — by those without learning, without scruples, or both —Asher Moore⟩

char·la·tan·ic \ˌ⸗⸗ˈtanik, -ēk\ *or* **char·la·tan·i·cal** \-ə̇kəl, -ēk-\ *adj* **:** of or like a charlatan **:** marked by or given to pretension and quackery

char·la·tan·ish \ˈ⸗⸗ˌtə(ˌ)nish, -tᵊn(ˌ)i-\ *adj* **:** CHARLATANIC

char·la·tan·ism \ˈ⸗⸗ˌtəˌnizəm, -tᵊn,i-\ *n* -S **:** CHARLATANRY ⟨the dross of fraud and ~ —Lewis Mumford⟩

char·la·tan·ry \ˈ⸗⸗⸗rē, -ri\ *also* **char·la·tan·ery** *like first, or* ˈ⸗⸗ˌtan(ə)rē *or* -ri *or* ˌ⸗⸗ˈ⸗(ə)⸗\ *or* **char·la·tan·e·rie** *like second, or* ˌ⸗⸗ˌtan(ə)ˈrē\ *n* -ES **1 :** the practice of a charlatan **:** QUACKERY, IMPOSTURE ⟨a man given to absurd freaks of intellectual ~ —P.E.More⟩ **2 :** an act or instance of charlatanry

charles's law \ˈchärlzə̇z-, -äl-\ *n, usu cap C* [after Jacques A.C. *Charles* †1823 Fr. physicist, its formulator] **:** a statement in physics: the volume of a given mass of gas at a constant pressure varies directly as its absolute temperature — called also *Gay-Lussac's law*

¹charles·ton \ˈchärlztən, -äl-, -lst-\ *adj, usu cap* [fr. *Charleston*, S.C. & *Charleston*, W.Va.] **1 :** of or from Charleston, S.C. **:** of the kind or style prevalent in Charleston, S.C. ⟨a *Charleston* custom⟩ **2 :** of or from Charleston, the capital of West Virginia ⟨a *Charleston* resident⟩ **:** of the kind or style prevalent in Charleston, W.Va.

²charleston \"\ *n* -S *usu cap* [fr. *Charleston*, S.C.] **:** a ballroom dance in which the knees are twisted in and out and the heels are swung sharply outward on each step

³charleston \"\ *vi* -ED/-ING/-S *often cap* **:** to dance the Charleston

charles·to·ni·an \chärlzˈtōnēən, -äl-, -lˈst-, -nyən\ *n* -S *cap* [*Charleston*, S.C. *or Charleston*, W.Va. + E *-ian*] **:** a native or resident of Charleston, esp. Charleston, S. C., or Charleston, W.Va.

char·ley *or* **char·lie** \ˈchärlē, -älē, -li\ *n* -S *often cap* [dim. of *Charles*, proper name] **1** [perh. after *Charles* I †1649 king of England, who in 1640 improved the watchman system in London] *slang* **:** NIGHT WATCHMAN **2** [after *Charles* I, who wore such a beard] **:** a short pointed beard **3 :** a usu. black-faced or toothbrush-mustached clown whose forte is lugubrious pathos **4** [perh. after *Charlie* Chan, fictional Chin. detective created by Earl Derr Biggers †1933 Am. novelist] **:** an Oriental person

charley horse *n, sometimes cap C* [fr. *Charley* (the name) + *horse;* perh. fr. the occurrence of Charley as a typical name for old lame horses kept for family use] **1 :** pain and stiffness resulting from a bruise usu. of a thigh muscle followed by hardening of the bruised tissue **2 :** muscular strain or soreness esp. in a leg

charley no·ble *or* **charlie noble** \ˌ⸗⸗ˈnōbəl\ *n, usu cap C&N* [prob. fr. the name *Charlie Noble*] **:** the galley smoke pipe

charley pitcher *n, usu cap C* [*Charley* + *pitcher* (vender)] *slang Brit* **:** a vagrant sharper

char·lie \ˈchärlē, -älē, -li\ *usu cap* [fr. the name *Charlie*] — a communications code word for the letter *c*

charlie mc·car·thy \ˌ⸗⸗məˈkär\thē, -kȧ\, \thi *also* \d·ē *or* \tē *or* -i\ *n, pl* **charlie mccarthys** *usu cap 1st C&M&3dC* [after *Charlie McCarthy*, ventriloquist's dummy made famous by Edgar Bergen *b*1903 Am. ventriloquist & comedian] **:** one under the complete domination of another often while enjoying apparent independence **:** STOOGE, YES-MAN, DUMMY ⟨uses him as a *Charlie McCarthy* to prove that even a schoolboy can see through the fallacious arithmetic of the opposition —Elmer Davis⟩

char·lier shoe \ˈshärlēˌā-, -lˌyā-\ *n, often cap C* [prob. fr. the name *Charlier*] **:** a narrow light horseshoe without a toe clip that is nailed in a groove made in the lower edge of the wall of a horse's hoof

char·lock \ˈchärˌläk, -ˌlək\ *or* **chad·lock** \ˈchad-\ *n* -S [ME *cherlok, carlok*, fr. OE *cerlic*] **:** any of several yellow-flowered weeds of the family Cruciferae; *specif* **:** a wild mustard (*Brassica kaber*) that is often troublesome in grainfields

¹char·lotte \ˈshärlət, ˈshäl-, *usu* -əd·+V\ *n* -S [F, prob. fr. the name *Charlotte*] **:** a dessert made by lining a dish with strips of bread, cake, or ladyfingers and filling it with fruit, whipped cream, custard, or other filling

²charlotte \"\ *adj, usu cap* [fr. *Charlotte*, N.C.] **:** of or from the city of Charlotte, N.C. ⟨a *Charlotte* suburb⟩ **:** of the kind or style prevalent in Charlotte

charlotte russe \ˌ⸗lət·ˈrüs\ *n, pl* **charlotte russ·es** \-sə̇z\ [F, lit., Russian charlotte] **:** a charlotte made with sponge cake or ladyfingers and a whipped-cream or custard-gelatin filling

char·lotte·town \ˈ⸗lətˌtau̇n\ *adj, usu cap* [fr. *Charlottetown*, Prince Edward Island, Canada] **:** of or from Charlottetown, the capital of Prince Edward Island, Canada **:** of the kind or style prevalent in Charlottetown

charl·ton white \ˈchärltᵊn-, -tən-\ *n, often cap C* [prob. fr. the name *Charlton*] **:** LITHOPONE

¹charm \ˈchärm, -ȧm\ *n* -S *often attrib* [ME *charme*, fr. OF, fr. L *carmen* song, incantation, fr. *canere* to sing — more at CHANT] **1 a :** the chanting or reciting of a verse supposed to have magic or occult power **:** INCANTATION **b :** an action, process, or thing (as a word, phrase, or verse) believed to have such power **:** a magic spell **2 :** something worn about the person to ward off evil or ensure good fortune **:** AMULET **3 a :** a trait that fascinates, allures, or delights **:** a combination of entirely attractive and delightful traits ⟨a new and even greater ~ — the fascination of the unknown and mysterious —W.H.Hudson †1922⟩ ⟨one of the great ~*s* of Lawrence . . . was that he could never be bored —Aldous Huxley⟩ **b :** an alluring physical attribute — used in pl. ⟨a dancer revealing her ~*s*⟩ **c :** compelling attractiveness and appeal dispelling any possible reserved or antagonistic feeling ⟨Alan, whose educated ~ had enabled him to marry an heiress —John Galsworthy⟩ ⟨an island of great ~, with its pleasing Mediterranean climate, its forest-clad mountains, its vineyards —Charles Woolley⟩ **4 :** a small ornament worn usu. on a bracelet or chain; *esp* **:** a metal miniature replica so worn ⟨a ~ bracelet⟩ — **like a charm :** as if by magic **:** most successfully and effectively ⟨a machine working *like a charm*⟩

²charm \"\ *vb* -ED/-ING/-S [ME *charmen*, fr. OF *charmer*, fr. LL *carminare* to enchant, sing, make verses, fr. L *carmin-, carmen* song, incantation] *vt* **1 :** to influence or control by or as if by charms: **a :** to subdue, dominate, change, or hold under a spell by magic power or power like magic in its supposed effectiveness **b :** to summon or sway by an attraction magical or otherwise compelling ⟨only his daughter had the power of ~*ing* this black brooding from his mind —Charles Dickens⟩ **c :** to please, soothe, or delight by compelling attraction ⟨what had ~*ed* her in it would still ~ her, even though . . . against her will —Edith Wharton⟩ **d :** to check, assuage, or calm as if by magic ⟨~ his rage with soft answers⟩ ⟨~ his grief⟩ **2 :** to endow with supernatural powers by means of charms; *esp* **:** to protect by spells, charms, or supernatural influences ⟨Milo brought an action against him for violence, but Clodius was ~*ed* even against forms of law —J.A.Froude⟩ **3** *obs* **:** to conjure or exhort (a person) typically with a special appeal ⟨~ a woman, by her husband's love, to speak⟩ **4 :** to summon, guide, control, or inveigle (an animal) typically by charms, music, or blandishment ⟨an early Norwich Pied Piper used a violin to ~ rattlesnakes —*Amer. Guide Series: Conn.*⟩ ⟨you can still ~ a bird off a tree —Philip Barry⟩ ~ *vi* **1 :** to use enchantments and spells **:** practice magic and enchantment ⟨no fairy takes, nor witch hath power to ~ —Shak.⟩ **2 :** to have the effect of a charm **:** PLEASE, DELIGHT, FASCINATE ⟨a philosophy that ~*s* by its completeness —H.O.Taylor⟩ **syn** see ATTRACT

³charm \"\ *n* -S [prob. by folk etymology fr. ¹*chirm*] **1** *now dial Eng* **:** a blended or confused noise (as of voices or bird songs) **:** CHIRM **2** *of finches* **:** FLOCK

⁴charm *vt* -ED/-ING/-S *obs* **:** to make music upon **:** PLAY, TUNE

char·man \ˈchärmən, -ˌman\ *n, pl* **charmen** [¹*chare* + *man*] **:** a man who does janitor's odd jobs

char·mat process \(ˈ)shärˈmä-\ *n, usu cap C* [after Eugene *Charmat fl*1907, its inventor] **:** a process for producing champagne in which the second fermentation takes place in a large glass-lined tank instead of in the bottle

charmed *adj* **:** extremely pleased or gratified **:** ENTRANCED ⟨how ~ I was with these new acquaintances —L.P.Smith⟩ — **charmed·ly** \ˈchärm(ə̇)dlē, -ȧm-, -li\ *adv*

charmed circle *n* **:** a group or coterie marked by severe exclusiveness ⟨only if they amassed very vast riches did they . . . find their way into the *charmed circle* of gentility —J.H. Plumb⟩

charmed life *n* **:** a life protected as if by magic charms **:** a life unusually unaffected by dangers and difficulties

charm·er \ˈchärmər, -ȧmə\ *n* -S [ME *charmere*, fr. *charmen* to charm + *-ere* -er] **:** one that charms: **a :** ENCHANTER, MAGICIAN **b :** one that pleases, intrigues, fascinates, or overcomes hostile, harsh, or dubious feeling; *esp* **:** an attractive woman

Char·meuse \(ˈ)shärˈm(y)üz, -ȧˈm-, -müs; -ärˈmə(r)z, -äˈməz\ *trademark* — used for a fine semilustrous crepe in satin weave

charm·ful \ˈchärmfəl, -ȧm-\ *adj* **:** employing charms **:** concerned with magic

charming *adj, sometimes* -ER/-EST [ME, fr. pres. part. of *charmen* to charm] **1 :** employing magic ⟨~ spells⟩ **2** *obs* **:** MELODIOUS, HARMONIOUS ⟨~ pipes⟩ **3 :** fascinating and delighting **:** extremely pleasing **:** marked by compelling attraction or appeal ⟨~ tapestries of rose and green —Elinor Wylie⟩ ⟨endowed with ~ manners, . . . he fascinated all whom he met —V.L.Parrington⟩ — **charm·ing·ly** *adv* — **charm·ing·ness** *n* -ES

charm·less \-mlə̇s\ *adj* **:** lacking charm

charm school *n* **:** a school in which social graces are taught

charmstone \ˈ⸗,⸗\ *n* **:** a smoothed stone often pointed at both ends and used as a ceremonial object by Indian shamans

char·ne·co \shärˈnā(ˌ)kü, -kō\ *n* -ES [prob. fr. *Charneco*, Portugal] **:** a sweet wine popular in Elizabethan and Jacobean England

¹char·nel \ˈchärnᵊl, -ȧn-\ *n* -S [ME, fr. MF, fr. ML *carnale*, fr. LL, neut. of *carnalis* fleshly — more at CARNAL] **1** *obs* **:** CEMETERY **2 a** *or* **charnel house :** a building, chamber, or other area in which bodies or bones are deposited **b :** a mortuary chapel

²charnel \"\ *adj* **1 :** constituting a charnel **2 :** gruesomely indicative or suggestive of death **:** SEPULCHRAL, GHASTLY ⟨a chest filled full of dead men's bones. A ~ smell came from them —Hope Muntz⟩ ⟨devices to which the ~ superstition of the monks has given rise —E.A.Poe⟩

³charnel *n* -S [ME, fr. MF *chernel*, fr. L *cardinalis* of a hinge — more at CARDINAL] *obs* **:** a hinge esp. of a helmet

char·nock·ite \ˈchärnəˌkīt\ *n* -S [Job *Charnock* †1693 Eng. founder of Calcutta + E *-ite;* fr. the fact that his tombstone is made of this rock] **1 :** any of a series of rocks ranging from granite to norite and pyroxenite all containing hypersthene **2 :** hypersthene-granite

cha·ro·lais *or* **cha·rol·lais** \ˌsharəˈlā\ *n, usu cap* [F (*boeuf*) *charolais, charollais*, fr. *Charolais, Charollais*, district in France] **:** a breed of large white cattle developed in France for draft purposes but now kept chiefly as a beef breed and important in crossbreeding — see CHARBRAY

cha·roles cattle *or* **cha·rolles cattle** \shəˈrōl-, -ȯl-\ *n, often cap 1st C* [fr. *Charoles, Charolles*, town in the Charolais district] **:** cattle of the Charolais breed

char·on's staircase \ˈka(a)rənz-, ˈkär-, -ˌränz-\ *n, usu cap C* [after *Charon*, ferryman of the dead in Hades, fr. L, fr. Gk *Charōn;* trans. of Gk *Charōnioi klimakes;* fr. the steps' supposedly leading to the underworld] **:** a flight of steps from the middle of the stage to the orchestra of an early Greek theater

char·o·phy·ce·ae \ˌkarəˈfīsēˌē, -fis-\ *n pl, cap* [NL, fr. *Chara* + *-o-* + *-phyceae*] **:** a class of green algae (division Chlorophyta) coextensive with the order Charales

cha·roph·y·ta \kəˈräfəd·ə\ *n pl, cap* [NL fr. *Chara* + *-o-* + *-phyta*] *in some classifications* **:** a group of plants equivalent to the order Charales and variously treated as a division, subdivision, or often as a class of the green algae — **char·o·phyte** \ˈkarəˌfīt\ *n* -S

charoseth *or* **charoset** *or* **charoses** *var of* HAROSETH

char·pie \(ˈ)shärˈpē, ˈshärpē\ *n* -S [F, fr. MF, fr. fem. of *charpi*, past part. of *charpir* to card, ravel out, modif. of L *carpere* to pluck — more at HARVEST] **:** LINT; *esp* **:** scraped lint

¹charpit \ˈ⸗,⸗\ *n* [³*char* + *pit*] **:** a pit in which wood is charred; *esp* **:** a pit between tree roots for burning out stumps

²charpit \"\ *vt* **charpitted; charpitted; charpitting; charpits :** to burn or burn out with a charpit ⟨*charpitting* stumps⟩

char·poy \ˈchärˌpȯi\ *also* **char·pai** \-ˌpī\ *n* -S [Hindi *cārpāī*, fr. Per *chārpāī*, lit., four-footed, fr. *chahār, chār* four (fr. MPer) + *pāī* foot, fr. MPer; akin to Av *chathwārō* four, Skt *catvāra* and to Av *pad-, pād-* foot, Skt *pāda* — more at FOUR, FOOT] **:** a bed consisting of a frame strung with tapes or light rope used esp. in India

char·py machine \ˈshär(ˌ)pē-\ *n, usu cap C* [after A. G. A. *Charpy* †1945 Fr. engineer] **:** a machine for measuring the breaking strength of materials under impact

charpy test *n, usu cap C* **:** a test made with a Charpy machine

char·qui *also* **char·que** \ˈchärkē, ˈsh-\ *n* -S [Sp, fr. Quechua *ch'arki* dried meat] **:** jerked meat; *esp* **:** jerked beef

charr *var of* CHAR

charred *past of* CHAR *or of* CHARE

char·rer \ˈchärər, -ärə\ *n* -S [³*char* + *-er*] **:** one that chars the interiors of barrels in which whiskey is to be aged

charrette *var of* CHARETTE

charring *pres part of* CHAR *or of* CHARE

char·ro \ˈchä(ˌ)rō\ *n* -S [MexSp, fr. Sp, rude, coarse, rustic, of poor taste, fr. Basque *txar* bad, defective, weak] **:** a Mexican horseman or cowboy typically dressed in an elaborately decorated outfit of close-fitting pants, jacket or sarape, and sombrero

char·ro·nia \kəˈrōnēə\ *n, cap* [NL] **:** a genus of mammals consisting of the yellow-throated marten

char·rua \chəˈrüə\ *n, pl* **charrua** *or* **charruas** *usu cap* [Sp *charrúa;* of AmerInd origin] **1 a :** an extinct Indian people of Uruguay and adjacent parts of Argentina and Brazil **b :** a member of such people **2 :** the language of the Charrua people

char·ry \ˈchärē\ *adj, usu* -ER/-EST [⁴*char* + *-y*] **1 :** forming or constituting charcoal **2 :** suggestive of charring or charcoal ⟨there was a ~ smell in the air —Booth Tarkington⟩

chars *pres 3d sing of* CHAR, *pl of* CHAR

¹chart \ˈchärt, -ät, *usu* -d·+V\ *n* -S [MF *charte* map, charter, fr. L *charta* document, piece of papyrus — more at CARD] **1 a** *obs* **:** MAP **b :** an outline map for conveying information about something other than the purely geographic ⟨a ~ of temperature variations⟩ ⟨a ~ showing military maneuvers⟩ ⟨a ~ of the town lots⟩ **c :** a hydrographic map **:** a map on which is projected a portion of water and usu. adjacent or included land intended esp. for use by navigators ⟨the U. S. Coast Survey ~*s*⟩ ⟨the British Admiralty ~*s*⟩ **d :** a small-scale representation of an area of the earth's surface, its culture and relief, and various aeronautical aids intended for use in air navigation **2** *archaic* **:** CHARTER, GRANT, DEED **3** *archaic* **:** CARD, PLAYING CARD **4 :** a form designed to record or provide information quickly and simply esp. about something fluctuating or changing **:** TABLE, GRAPH, DIAGRAM ⟨a ~ of rainfall for the past year⟩ ⟨a ~ of price changes⟩ ⟨a clinical ~ for a hospital patient⟩ **5 :** a summary of a racehorse's form

²chart \"\ *vt* -ED/-ING/-S **1 :** to make a map or chart of **:** record or indicate by map, chart, outline, or graph **:** DELINEATE ⟨the 1728 expedition that ~*ed* the dividing line between the two colonies —*Amer. Guide Series: N. C.*⟩ ⟨above the boiling cloud cap of a hurricane, an Air Force plane ~*s* the size of the disturbance —*N. Y. Times Mag.*⟩ **2 :** to lay out a plan for typically in orderly outline **:** PLAN, PROJECT ⟨we have ~*ed* the course to a stable world peace —H.S.Truman⟩ ⟨Churchill and Roosevelt met to ~ strategy —*N. Y. Times Mag.*⟩

char·ta \ˈkärd·ə\ *n, pl* **char·tae** \-ˌrˌtē\ [NL, fr. L, leaf of paper, writing, letter] **1 :** a strip of paper impregnated or coated with a medicinal substance and used for external application **2 :** a paper folded to contain a medicinal powder

char·ta·ceous \(ˈ)kärˈtāshəs\ *adj* [LL *chartaceus*, fr. L *charta* + *-aceus* -aceous] **:** resembling paper **:** made of paper ⟨a ~ plant tissue⟩

¹char·ter \ˈchärd·ər, -ȧd·ə, \tə(r)\ *n* -S [ME *chartre*, fr. OF, fr. L *chartula* little paper, dim. of *charta*] **1 :** a written evidence, instrument, or contract executed in due form between man and man **:** DEED, CONVEYANCE **2 a :** an instrument in writing from the sovereign power of a state or country granting or guaranteeing rights, franchises, or privileges **b :** an instrument in writing creating and defining the franchises of a city, university, company, or other public or private corporation **c :** CONSTITUTION ⟨the *Charter* of the United Nations⟩ **3 :** an instrument in writing from the constituted authorities of an order or society creating a lodge, branch, or local unit and defining its powers **4 :** a special privilege, immunity, or exemption that is usu. publicly conceded or generally understood ⟨a ~ to speak freely⟩ **5** *or* **charter party :** a mercantile lease of a ship **:** a specific contract by which the owners of a ship let the entire ship or some principal part of it to another person to be used by him in transportation for his own account either under their charge or under his charge

²charter \"\ *vt* **chartered; chartered; chartering** \-d·ərin, -tər- *also* -ərtrin *or* -ȧ·tr-\ **charters** [ME *charteren*, fr. *charter*, n.] **1 :** to grant or issue a charter to: **a :** to establish or call into being by charter **:** acknowledge the existence of by charter ⟨a state university ~*ed* in 1825⟩ **b :** to endow with certain rights or functions by charter **:** assign a given status to by charter **:** FRANCHISE ⟨an organization ~*ed* to undertake the work⟩ **c :** to convey by charter ⟨Lyndon was ~*ed* in 1780 to Jonathan Arnold —*Amer. Guide Series: Vt.*⟩ **d** *Brit* **:** to certify or authorize (a person) as qualified ⟨a ~*ed* mechanical engineer⟩ **2 :** to grant special privilege or license to ⟨~*ed* libertines of imperial Rome⟩ **3 :** to hire, rent, or lease (as a ship, airplane, or bus) esp. for exclusive use

charter chest *n* **:** a chest used esp. in Scotland as a repository for family papers and documents (as charters or deeds) ⟨from the private *charter chest* the next step was to the public records of the kingdom —A.R.Wagner⟩

charter colony *n, often cap 1st C* **:** one of the three British colonies in America (Massachusetts, Connecticut, and Rhode Island) governed by royal charter without direct interference from the crown — compare PROPRIETARY COLONY, ROYAL COLONY

chartered accountant *n, Brit* **:** a member of an institute of chartered or accredited accountants — compare CERTIFIED PUBLIC ACCOUNTANT

chartered company *n, Brit* **:** a corporation created by charter

char·ter·er \-d·ərə(r), -tər-\ *n* -S **:** one that charters; *esp* **:** one that charters a ship

charter hand *n* **:** COURT HAND

char·ter·house \ˈ⸗⸗,⸗\ *n* [by folk etymology fr. MF *chartrouse*, fr. OF, fr. *Chartreuse, Chartrouse* (now Saint-Pierre-de-*Chartreuse*), locality near Grenoble, France, the site of the first Carthusian monastery] **:** a Carthusian monastery

char·ter·ite \-əˌrīt\ *n* -S **:** an advocate or supporter of a charter

charter member *n* **:** an original member of a society or corporation; *esp* **:** one named in a charter

charter party *n* [by folk etymology fr. ML *charta partita*, lit., divided charter, one part being kept by each of the contractors] **:** CHARTER 5

charter school *n, usu cap C* [fr. *Charter* (*Society*), Irish educational organization founded 1733] **:** any of the schools established in Ireland in the 18th century to furnish Protestant education for the Roman Catholic poor

chart house *n* **:** a compartment on or near the bridge of a ship where charts and other navigational equipment are kept and used — called also *chart room*

charting *pres part of* CHART

char·tism \'chär\|d·,izəm, -ȧ\|, \|,ti-\ *n* -s *usu cap* [charter + *-ism*] **:** the principles and practices of a body of 19th century English political reformers advocating better social and industrial conditions for the working classes

[1]**char·tist** \\|d·əst,\|tə-\ *n* -s *usu cap* [charter + *-ist*] **:** an advocate of Chartism

[2]**chartist** \"\ *n* -s [[1]chart + *-ist*] **1 :** CARTOGRAPHER **2 :** one that studies, interprets, and makes predictions as to stock-market action from charts and graphic records

chart·less \-tləs\ *adj* **:** UNCHARTED ⟨a ~ sea⟩

chart of accounts : a list of account names arranged systematically and usu. coded numerically or alphabetically or both to form the general framework of the accounting system of a specific business and to establish a scheme of account classification

chart·og·ra·pher \chärd·'ägrəfər, -r'tä-; kär'tä-\ *or* **chart·og·ra·phist** \-fəst\ *n* -s [by alter.] **:** CARTOGRAPHER

chart·ol·o·gy \chärd·'äləjē, -r'tä-; kär'tä-\ *n* -ES [[1]chart + *-o-* + *-logy*] **:** CARTOGRAPHY

chart·om·e·ter \-ämәd·ər, -ətər\ *n* -s [[1]chart + *-o-* + *-meter*] **:** an instrument for measuring distances on charts or maps

char·toph·y·lax \kär'täfəˌlaks\ *n* -ES [LGk, fr. Gk *charto-* (fr. *chartēs* paper) + Gk *phylax* guard — more at CARD] **:** a chancellor of a bishop or diocese of the Eastern Orthodox Church who serves as an archivist and has certain administrative and judicial duties

[1]**char·treuse** \(')shär¦trüz, -ä¦t-, -üs, *sometimes* -är¦trə(r)z *or* -ä¦trəz\ *n* -s [*Chartreuse*; fr. the color of Chartreuse liqueurs] **1 :** a variable color averaging a brilliant yellow green — see CHARTREUSE GREEN **2 :** a strong greenish yellow — see CHARTREUSE YELLOW

[2]**chartreuse** \"\ *n* -s [F, fr. La Grande *Chartreuse*, chief monastery of the Carthusian order near Grenoble, France] **1 :** several vegetables arranged and cooked in a mold **2 :** a mold of two or more foods with meat or fish in the center

Chartreuse \"\ *trademark* — used for a liqueur usu. green or yellow in color flavored with orange peel, hyssop, peppermint, and other ingredients

chartreuse green *n* **:** a dark greenish yellow that is redder, less strong, and very slightly lighter than average olive yellow

chartreuse tint *n* **:** a pale yellow green that is yellower, lighter, and slightly stronger than smoke gray, lighter than oyster gray, and yellower, less strong, and much lighter than average Nile

chartreuse yellow *n* **1 :** a variable color averaging a strong greenish yellow that is duller than bright chartreuse yellow **2 :** a light to moderate greenish yellow that is greener and slightly stronger than primrose yellow or canary

chartreux *n, pl* **chartreux** *usu cap*, [F, back-formation fr. *chartreuse* monastery, fr. MF *chartrouse* — more at CHARTERHOUSE] *obs* **:** CARTHUSIAN

chart room *n* **:** CHART HOUSE

charts *pl of* CHART, *pres 3d sing of* CHART

char·tu·la \'kärchələ\ *n, pl* **char·tu·lae** \-,lē\ [L, little paper —more at CHARTER] **:** a folded paper containing a single dose of a medicinal powder

[1]**char·tu·lary** \'kärchə,lerē\ *n* -ES [ML *chartularium* case for storing papers, fr. L *chartula* little paper + *-arium* -ary] **:** CARTULARY

[2]**chartulary** \"\ *n* -ES [LL *chartularius*, fr. L *chartula* + *-arius* -ary] **:** a keeper of archives

charwoman \'ˌ=ˌ=\ *n, pl* **charwomen** [[1]chare + *woman*] **:** a cleaning woman usu. in a large building

chary \'cha(ə)rē, -er-, -ār-, -ri\ *adj, often* -ER/-EST [ME *charry, chary* sorrowful, dear, fr. OE *cearig* sorrowful, fr. *cearu* sorrow; akin to OHG *charag* sorrowful — more at CARE] **1** *archaic* **:** PRECIOUS, TREASURED, DEAR **2 :** marked by discreet caution: **a :** hesitant and vigilant about dangers and risks **:** unwilling to proceed without much consideration ⟨a ~ investor⟩ ⟨the hunter was ~⟩ ⟨yet let us be ~ of casting the first stone —J.L.Lowes⟩ **b :** FASTIDIOUS ⟨~ about the food he eats⟩ **c :** DIFFIDENT, RESERVED ⟨the chariest maid is prodigal enough if she unmask her beauty to the moon —Shak.⟩ **d :** sparing and reluctant in granting, accepting, or expending **:** tending to withhold, preserve, or guard ⟨a busy man ~ of his time⟩ ⟨I wanted my father's good opinion because he was ~ of his compliments and shy in his affection —W.A.White⟩ **syn** see CAUTIOUS

cha·ryb·dis \kə'ribdəs\ *n* -ES *usu cap* [fr. *Charybdis* (now *Galofalo*), whirlpool off the northeastern extremity of Sicily, fr. L, fr. Gk] **:** a destructive peril — usu. used as the alternative to *Scylla* ⟨between the Scylla of national parochialism and the *Charybdis* of complete exoticism —Bernard Smith⟩

chas·a·ble *or* **chase·a·ble** \'chāsəbəl\ *adj* [ME *chaceable*, fr. *chacen, chasen* to chase + *-able*] **:** suitable for being chased **:** fit for hunting

[1]**chase** \'chās\ *vb* -ED/-ING/-S [ME *chacen, chasen*, fr. MF *chasser*, fr. OF *chacier*, fr. (assumed) VL *captiare*, fr. L *captare* to seize, strive after — more at CATCH] *vt* **1 a :** to follow usu. rapidly and intently in order to or as if to trail or overtake, seize, molest, or do violence to **:** PURSUE ⟨some police *chasing* a criminal in a taxi⟩ ⟨a dog *chasing* a rabbit⟩ ⟨the pirates *chased* the treasure galleon⟩ ⟨children *chasing* each other in play⟩ ⟨waves *chased* each other up the beach⟩ **b :** HUNT ⟨rose to ~ the deer at five —Alfred Tennyson⟩ **c :** to follow or attend upon usu. persistently and hopefully with the intention of attracting, alluring, or persuading into companionship or intimacy ⟨a bobby-soxer *chasing* boys⟩ ⟨a middle-aged man *chasing* women half his age⟩ **d :** to follow (as an ambulance) to the scene of an accident in order to solicit business **e :** to follow up (a strong drink) with a chaser **2** *obs* **:** PERSECUTE, HARASS **3 :** to move usu. rapidly in the direction of in order to observe, obtain, or find out about ⟨children *chasing* a fire⟩ ⟨library attendants *chasing* books called for by readers⟩ ⟨salesmen *chasing* new orders⟩ — sometimes used with *down* ⟨detectives *chased* down all possible clues to the murder⟩ **4 a :** to cause to depart or flee esp. by the use of or threat of violence or other harassment **:** DRIVE, EXPEL, DISPEL ⟨love hath *chased* sleep from my enthralled eyes —Shak.⟩ ⟨I'll ~ the whole rebel army all the way to South Carolina —Kenneth Roberts⟩ ⟨~ cattle out of a wheat field⟩ **b** *slang* **:** to take (oneself) off ⟨go ~ yourself; you're too small to play with us⟩ **c** *baseball* **:** to cause the removal of (as a pitcher by a batting rally) or oust from a game ~ *vi* **1 :** to chase an animal, person, or thing — usu. used with *after* ⟨the children of Israel returned from *chasing* after the Philistines —1 Sam 17: 53 (AV)⟩ ⟨*chasing* after material possessions⟩ ⟨a girl who ~*s* after boys⟩ **2 :** RUSH, HASTEN ⟨*chasing* all over town looking for a place to stay⟩ **syn** see FOLLOW

[2]**chase** *also* **chace** \"\ *n* -s [ME *chace, chase*, fr. OF *chace*, fr. *chacier*, v.] **1 a :** the act of pursuing for the purpose of seizing, capturing, molesting, doing violence, or killing **:** PURSUIT **b :** the searching out and pursuit of wild animals for the purpose of killing them as an occupation or sport — used with *the;* see HUNTING **c :** the act of pursuing for the purpose of putting to flight **:** ROUT **d :** a usu. earnest or frenzied seeking after something greatly desired ⟨this mad ~ of fame —John Dryden⟩ ⟨the excitements of the intellectual ~ —R.W. Southern⟩ **2 :** something pursued (as a hunted animal or a ship) **:** QUARRY **3 a** *Eng law* **:** a liberty or franchise to hunt within certain limits of land not necessarily owned by the one having the liberty or of keeping beasts of chase therein **b** *in England* **:** a tract of unenclosed land used as a game preserve usu. distinguished from a forest in being smaller, having fewer law-enforcement officers, and being sometimes private property — compare FOREST, PARK, WARREN **4 :** a stroke in court tennis similar to a placement in lawn tennis which requires that the players replay the point; *also* **:** the point so replayed **5** *dial* **:** a lane between fields on a farm **6** *obs* **:** the chase guns of a ship; *also* **:** the part of a ship in which the chase ports are **7 :** the length of yarn in one traverse of the winding faller in winding the cop in cotton spinning **8** [by shortening] **:** STEEPLECHASE **9 :** a sequence of a melodrama or now usu. of a motion picture representing the pursuit of one character by others

[3]**chase** \"\ *vt* -ED/-ING/-S [ME *chasen*, modif. of MF *enchasser* to set (as a jewel) — more at ENCHASE] **1 a :** to ornament (a metal, esp. silver, surface) by indenting with a hammer and tools without a cutting edge **b :** to make (as a decoration) by such indentation **c :** to set esp. with gems **2 :** to cut (a thread) with a chaser

[4]**chase** \"\ *n* -s [F *chas* eye of a needle, space between beams, compartment of a house, fr. OF, fr. LL *capsus* enclosed space in a house, nave of a church, bladder, fr. L, cage, part of a wagon, alter. of *capsa* box — more at CASE] **1 a** *obs* **:** the furrow on a crossbow in which the arrow lies **b** *obs* **:** the bore of a cannon **c :** the part of a cannon from the trunnions or part where trunnions would be if the piece had them to the mouth or the swell of the muzzle — see CANNON illustration **2 :** a groove or channel for something to lie in or pass through: as **a :** TRENCH **b :** a channel in the inner face of a masonry wall of a building to provide space for pipes, ducts, or wiring **c :** a groove cut lengthwise for the reception of a part to make a joint **3 :** a kind of joint in ship building by which an overlap joint is changed to a flush joint by means of a gradually deepening rabbet (as at the ends of clinker-built boats)

[5]**chase** \"\ *vt* **:** GROOVE, INDENT

[6]**chase** \"\ *n* -s [prob. fr. F *châsse* frame — more at CHASSE] **1 a :** a rectangular steel or iron frame into which letterpress matter is locked for printing or plating — compare FORM **b :** any of certain analogous devices (as for holding work in photocomposing and duplicating machines or for holding carton-cutting dies) **2 :** typeset matter before it is placed in a chase

chaseable *var of* CHASABLE

chase around *vi* **:** to rush from one diversion to another esp. with one of the opposite sex — often used to imply illicit sexual relations

chased *past of* CHASE

chase doll \'chās-\ *n, usu cap C* [after Martha J. *Chase* †1925 Am. manufacturer] **:** a dummy used for teaching purposes in hospitals maintaining training schools for nurses

chase gun \chās\ *or* **chase piece** *n* **:** a cannon at the bow or stern of an armed ship used in pursuit

chase literature *n* **:** literature in which suspense is created by a chase of one person or group by another

chase mortise *n* [[4]chase] **:** a mortise one or both ends of which slope from the bottom to the surface to permit the insertion of the tenon when the clearance outside is limited

chase mortise

chase port *n* [*chase (gun)*] **:** a porthole from which a chase gun is fired

[1]**chas·er** \'chāsə(r)\ *n* -s [ME *chasur*, fr. OF *chaceour*, fr. *chacier* to chase + *-eour* -or — more at CHASE] **1 :** one that chases: as **a :** HUNTER **b :** SUBMARINE CHASER **c :** PHILANDERER **d :** a piece of music played or an inferior vaudeville act or motion picture presented to induce an audience to leave **e** *slang* **:** a prison guard **2 :** CHASE GUN ⟨a bow ~⟩ ⟨a stern ~⟩ **3 a :** one that follows logs out of the forest in order to signal the yarder engineer to stop them if they become fouled — called also *frogger* **b :** one that unhooks the cable used to drag logs from the forest to the yard and readies the equipment to be sent back **4 a :** a drink or occas. food taken after a drink of strong alcoholic content **b :** something (as a literary work or portion of a literary work) that is of a light or mollifying nature in comparison with that which it follows or accompanies **5** [by shortening] **:** STEEPLECHASER

[2]**chaser** \"\ *n* -s [[3]chase + *-er*] **:** one that ornaments by chasing: as **a :** a skilled worker who produces raised designs on silver or similar metals **b :** a skilled worker who cuts the design and finishes the shaping of molds used to cast jewelry articles

[3]**chaser** \"\ *n* -s [[5]chase + *-er*] **1 a :** a threading tool either many-toothed or having a single cutting edge shaped for cutting or finishing external or internal screw threads of specified pitch and standard usu. on work revolving in a lathe **b :** one of the cutting bits in a composite die or tap **2 :** a grinding machine used in ore dressing and made with a revolving pan or base and fixed rollers **3 :** a lathe operator whose specialty is cutting screw threads

chaser stone *n* [[2]chaser] **:** a flat circular stone set on edge and rolled on a stone pavement to pulverize minerals

chases *pres 3d sing of* CHASE

chasid *n, pl* **chasidim** *usu cap, var of* HASID

[1]**chasing** *n* -s [by shortening] **:** STEEPLECHASING

[2]**chasing** *n* -s [fr. gerund of [3]chase] **1 a :** the act or art of ornamenting by chasing **b :** the design produced by chasing or the work chased **2 :** the process of finishing the surface of castings by polishing and removing small imperfections **3 :** a calendered finish for improving the luster and appearance of fabrics (as cotton or linen)

chasm \'kazəm\ *n* -s [L *chasma*, fr. Gk; akin to L *hiare* to gape, yawn — more at YAWN] **1 a :** a deep opening (as in the earth) **:** a narrow deep steep-walled valley, gorge, or canyon **:** a yawning abyss **:** a deep gap impassable by ordinary means ⟨the brink of a precipice, of a ~ in the earth over two hundred feet deep, the sides sheer cliffs —Willa Cather⟩ **b :** CLEFT, FISSURE, RAVINE **c :** BLANK, OMISSION, HIATUS ⟨if I leave anywhere a ~ in my narrative, tell me —Sheridan Le Fanu⟩ **2 :** a marked esp. irreconcilable division, separation, or difference ⟨our only way of closing the ~ between the magnificent richness of human potentiality and the paltriness of human achievement —Paul Pickrel⟩; *esp* **:** one due to a marked opposition of attitude, opinion, belief, or loyalty ⟨trade between the two countries had attained a considerable volume despite the . . . political ~ between them —*Collier's Yr. Bk.*⟩ ⟨the rifts that seemed to cleave soldier from civilian, in habit and state of mind, tempting the former to make the ~ permanent —Dixon Wecter⟩

chasma *n* -s [L] **1** *obs* **:** a gaping or yawning esp. of the earth or sea **2** *obs* **:** a large rent or fissure in the earth **3** *obs* **:** a wide gap or breach

chas·mal \'kazməl\ *adj* **:** resembling a chasm

chasmed \-zəmd\ *adj* **:** having chasms

chas·mic \-zmik\ *adj* **:** resembling a chasm (as in grandeur or proportions) ⟨"Revolutionary warfare," about which we still display ~ ignorance —C.L.Sulzberger⟩

chas·mo·gam·ic \¦kazmə¦gamik\ *also* **chas·mog·a·mous** \(')kaz¦mägəməs\ *adj* **:** characterized by chasmogamy

chas·mog·a·my \kaz'mägəmē\ *n* -ES [ISV *chasm-* (fr. Gk *chasma* opening) + *-o-* + *-gamy*] **:** the opening of the perianth at maturity for the purpose of fertilization (as in most flowers) — compare CLEISTOGAMY

chas·mo·phyte \'kazmə,fīt\ *n* -s [ISV *chasm-* + *-o-* + *-phyte;* prob. orig. formed as G *chasmophyt*] **:** a plant that grows in the crevices of rocks

chasmy \'kaz(ə)mē\ *adj* **1 :** abounding with chasms **2 :** CHASMIC

[1]**chasse** \'shäs\ *n* -s [F *châsse*, fr. OF *chasse*, fr. L *capsa* box, case — more at CASE] **:** a reliquary or shrine of a saint

[2]**chas·sé** \(')sha¦sā\ *vi* **chasséd; chasséd; chasséing; chassés** [F, n.] **1 :** to make the dance movement called *chassé* **2 :** SASHAY

[3]**chas·sé** \"\ *n* -s [F, fr. past part. of *chasser* to chase, fr. OF *chacier* — more at CHASE] **1 :** a dance step in which a slide on one foot is followed closely by a slide on the other foot in a rhythm resembling that of the galop **2 :** a chassé step in figure skating

[4]**chasse** \'shas, -ä-\ *n* -s [F] **:** a liqueur taken after coffee

chasse-ca·fé \¦=(,)ka¦fā\ *n* -s [F, lit., coffee-chaser, fr. *chasser* to chase + *café* coffee, fr. Turk *kahve* — more at COFFEE] *archaic* **:** [4]CHASSE

chas·sé-croi·sé \sha¦sākr(ə)wä¦zā\ *n, pl* **chassé-croisés** [F, lit., crossed chassé, fr. *chassé* the dance + *croisé*, past part. of *croiser* to cross, fr. OF, fr. *crois* cross, fr. L *cruc-, crux* — more at CROSS] **:** a movement in a quadrille or country-dance in which partners exchange places by means of a chassé

chasse-ma·rée \¦shasmə¦rā\ *n* -s [F, lit., tide-chaser, fr. *chasser* to chase + *marée* tide, fr. OF, fr. *mer* sea, fr. L *mare* — more at MARINE] **:** a French coasting lugger

chasse·pot \'sha,spō\ *n* -s [F, fr. Antoine A. *Chassepot* †1905 Fr. inventor who designed it] **:** a bolt-action rifle firing a paper cartridge having in its base a percussion cap exploded by a firing pin

chas·seur \sha'sər, +V -ər-\ *n* -s [F, fr. OF *chaceour* — more at CHASER] **1 :** HUNTER, HUNTSMAN **2 :** one of a body of light cavalry or infantry trained for rapid maneuvering **3 a :** an attendant upon persons of rank or wealth who wears a plume and sword **b :** an employee in a continental European hotel having any of various duties (as those of a bellboy or doorman)

chas·sez \(')sha¦sā\ *n, pl* **chassez·es** \sha'sā(zə)z\ [by alter.] **:** [3]CHASSÉ

chassid *n, pl* **chassidim** *usu cap, var of* HASID

chas·si·gnite \'shasᵊn,yīt, sha'sēn-\ *n* -s [G *chassignit*, fr. *Chassigny*, eastern France + G *-it* -ite] **:** an achondritic meteorite of olivine and chromite

chas·sis \'chasē, 'sh-, -aasē, -si *sometimes* -səs\ *n, pl* **chassis** \-a(a)sēz, -iz\ *also* **chassises** \-a(a)səsəz\ [F *châssis*, fr. OF *chassiz*, fr. (assumed) VL *capsicium*, fr. L *capsa* box, case — more at CASE] **1** *obs* **:** a wooden frame fitted or to be fitted with a sheet of paper, linen, or glass **:** a sash esp. of a window **2 a :** the frame upon which is mounted the body (as of an automobile or airplane), the working parts (as of a radio or other electronic device), the barrel and other recoiling parts (of a cannon), or the roof, walls, floors, and facing (as of a building) **b :** the frame and working parts as opposed to the body (as of an automobile) or cabinet (as of a radio or television set) **c** *slang, of a woman* **:** FIGURE 8b **3 :** a calibrated frame used by a sculptor in making an enlarged or reduced copy of his plaster model

chas·ta·cos·ta \,shastə'kȯstə\ *n, pl* **chastacosta** *or* **chastacostas** *usu cap* [Chastacosta *Shista-Kwŭsta*] **1 a :** an Athapaskan people in the Illinois and Rogue river valleys, Oregon **b :** a member of such people **2 :** the language of the Chastacosta people

chaste \'chāst\ *adj, usu* -ER/-EST [ME, fr. OF, fr. L *castus* pure, chaste — more at CASTE] **1 a :** abstaining from sexual intercourse that is reprobated by religion or condemned by morality ⟨~ behavior⟩ **b :** abstaining from such intercourse and in addition from any willful acts or thoughts that are likely to lead to its occurrence **2 a :** abstaining from all sexual relations ⟨Galahad's ~ life⟩ **b :** CLEAN, PURE, STAINLESS ⟨~ stars —Shak.⟩ **c :** free from lewdness, obscenity, indecency, suggestiveness, or offensiveness **:** MODEST, DECENT ⟨his conversation is ~ —Ernest Dimnet⟩ **d :** free of connection or association with anything crass, sordid, impure, or debasing ⟨the ~ and abstracted intellect of the scholar —Elinor Wylie⟩ **3 a** *archaic* **:** RESTRAINED, SUBDUED ⟨her tastes were, however, too feminine and ~ ever to render her eccentric —E.G.Bulwer-Lytton⟩ **b :** lacking that which provides sensual pleasure **:** severely simple **:** AUSTERE, ASCETIC, PLAIN ⟨a ~ meal⟩ **c :** decorous and somewhat severe in design or expression **:** free of anything meretricious, florid, or tawdry **:** REFINED, SIMPLE ⟨a ~ border of conventionalized flowers⟩

syn PURE, MODEST, DECENT: CHASTE stresses absence of immorality or sexuality in acts or behavior and sometimes even in thoughts or suggestions, and connotes a complete avoidance of anything meretricious ⟨all virtuous persons who hear this song whose lives are *chaste* and placid —Elinor Wylie⟩ ⟨she . . . withdrew to the *chaste* darkness of her own room where she knelt before a plaster virgin —Louis Bromfield⟩ PURE indicates avoidance of immoral action and lustful thoughts and desires ⟨it may have been that . . . he had never known any woman, that he had been *pure* as a saint —Louis Bromfield⟩ ⟨as down she knelt for heaven's grace and boon . . . she seem'd a splendid angel . . . so *pure* a thing, so free from mortal taint —John Keats⟩ MODEST stresses avoidance of anything brazen, bold, wanton, or suggestive in behavior, speech, or appearance ⟨she had previously made a respectful virginlike curtsey to the gentleman, and her *modest* eyes gazed so perseveringly on the carpet that it was a wonder how she should have found an opportunity to see him —W.M.Thackeray⟩ ⟨to suggest that it [the infidelity of Antony] had been largely Octavia's own fault in dressing in so *modest* a way and behaving with such decorum —Robert Graves⟩ DECENT indicates accord with conventions of what is seemly or proper in behavior or language ⟨sex must be treated from the first as natural, delightful, and *decent* —Bertrand Russell⟩ ⟨after only a *decent* period of mourning, Mr. Murdock married Marie Antoinette O'Daniel —W.A.White⟩ ⟨filthy beyond all powers of *decent* expression —Leslie Stephen⟩

chas·tek paralysis \'cha,stek-\ *n, usu cap C* [after John S. *Chastek* †1954 Am. fur farmer] **:** a fatal paralysis of ranch-raised foxes and minks fed raw freshwater fish that is due to inactivation of thiamine by an enzyme (thiaminase) present in fish

chaste·ly \'chāstlē, -li\ *adv* [ME, fr. *chaste* + *-ly*] **:** in a chaste manner

chas·ten \'chāsᵊn\ *vt* **chastened; chastened; chastening** \-s(ᵊ)niŋ\ **chastens** [alter. of obs. E *chaste* to chasten, fr. ME *chasten, chastien*, fr. OF *chastier*, fr. L *castigare* to punish, fr. *castus* pure + *-igare* (fr. *agere* to lead, drive) — more at CHASTE, ACT] **1 a :** to subject to pain, suffering, deprivation, or misfortune in order to correct, strengthen, or perfect in character, in mental or spiritual qualities, or in conduct **:** DISCIPLINE ⟨whom the Lord loveth he ~*eth* —Heb 12:6(AV)⟩ **b :** to act upon or affect in any way so as to correct, strengthen, or perfect (as in character, conduct, or mental or spiritual qualities) **2 a :** to make (a work of art or literature, an artistic or literary style, or some natural object regarded with respect to its aesthetic qualities) more decorous, restrained, or refined **:** remove floridity, excessive exuberance or luxuriance, or irregularity from **:** CORRECT, PURIFY **b :** to increase the purity or refinement of (the mind or mental faculties) ⟨~ and enlarge the mind —A.H.Layard⟩ ⟨the once common practice of making children commit passages to memory had a ~*ing* effect on the general ear and literary conscience —George Sampson⟩ **c :** to keep from being excessive or overintense **:** RESTRAIN, TEMPER ⟨his air of ~*ed* triumph —Dorothy Sayers⟩ **d :** to cause to be more humble, modest, restrained, or cautious **:** SUBDUE **syn** see PUNISH

chas·ten·er \-s(ᵊ)nə(r)\ *n* -s **:** one that chastens

chaste·ness \-s(t)nəs\ *n* -ES **:** the state or quality of being chaste

chas·ten·ing·ly *adv* **:** in a chastening manner

chas·ten·ment \'chāsᵊnmənt\ *n* -s **:** the action of chastening

chaster *comparative of* CHASTE

chastest *superlative of* CHASTE

chaste tree \'=,=\ *n* [trans. of L *agnus castus*, by folk etymology (influence of L *agnus* lamb) fr. Gk *agnos* (associated with chastity rites because of influence of *hagnos* chaste, sacred)] **:** AGNUS CASTUS

chas·tise \(')cha¦stīz, -aas-\ *vt* -ED/-ING/-S [ME *chastisen*, alter. of *chastien* — more at CHASTEN] **1 :** to inflict pain or suffering on for punishment or reformation ⟨~ children by spanking⟩ **2 a** *now dial* **:** REPROVE, REBUKE, SCOLD **b :** to censure severely in denunciation or in an attempt to correct or improve **:** CASTIGATE ⟨the world of moral and intellectual weaklings that she felt herself appointed to ~ —Tennessee Williams⟩ **3** *archaic* **:** CHASTEN 2 **syn** see PUNISH

chas·tise·ment \cha'stīzmənt *also* 'cha,stīz- *or* 'chastəz-; -aas-\ *n* -s [ME, fr. *chastisen* + *-ment*] **:** the action, an act, or the means of chastising; *esp* **:** PUNISHMENT

chas·tis·er \(')chastəd·ə, -aas-, -əte, -i\ *n* -s [alter. of ME *chastysowre*, fr. *chastisen* + *-owre* -or] **:** one that chastises

chas·ti·ty \'chastəd·ē, -aas-, -ətē, -i\ *n* -ES [ME *chastete, chastitie*, fr. OF *chasteté*, fr. L *castitat-, castitas*, fr. *castus* pure + *-itat-, -itas* -ity — more at CHASTE] **1 :** the quality or state of being chaste: as **a :** abstention from any sexual intercourse reprobated by religion or condemned by morality **b :** abstention from all sexual intercourse **c :** freedom from immorality and lewdness in act and intention **:** purity in act and will **:** DECENCY, MODESTY **d :** decorousness in design or expression often tending toward the severe **:** freedom from meretricious ornament, floridity, or tawdriness **2 :** the obligation of lifelong celibacy and continence assumed in some monastic vows **3 :** ethical integrity

chastity belt *n* **:** a belt device esp. of earlier times designed to prevent sexual intercourse on the part of the woman wearing it

chas·tush·ka \cha'stüshkə\ *n* -s [Russ, fr. *chasty* often, fr. ORuss *častŭ*; akin to OSlav *čęstŭ* often, Lith *kimštas* stuffed] **:** a rhymed folk verse usu. of four lines traditional in form but often having political or topical content

chas·u·ble \ˈchazəbəl, -asə-, -azhə- *sometimes* -azyə- *or* -asyə- *or* -ˈäz(y)ə-\ *n* -s [F, fr. OF, fr. LL *casubla* hooded garment, prob. alter. of LL *casula* cloak, fr. L, dim. of *casa* small house, hut — more at CASA] **:** an outer ecclesiastical vestment in the form of a wide sleeveless cloak or mantle that slips over the wearer's head but remains open at the sides, the color of which varies with either the season or the occasion, worn by the celebrant at eucharistic services in the Roman Catholic and Eastern Orthodox churches and some churches of the Anglican Communion

chasubles: Gothic (left) and fiddleback (right)

¹chat \ˈchat, *usu* -ad·+V\ *n* -s [ME *chatte* catkin, fr. MF, lit., female cat, fr. *chat* cat, fr. LL *cattus;* prob. fr. its resemblance to a cat's tail — more at CAT] **1 a :** the inflorescence or seed of various plants (as an ament or a samara) **b** *now dial* **:** STROBILE, CONE **2** *dial Eng* **:** a twig or little branch suitable for kindling **3** *Brit* **:** a small inferior potato **4 :** TAILING 2c — often used in pl.

²chat \ˈ"\ *vb* **chatted; chatted; chatting; chats** [ME *chatten,* short for *chatteren* to chatter] *vi* **1 :** CHATTER, PRATTLE **2 :** to talk in a light and familiar manner **:** converse without ceremony or stiffness ⟨~ about trifles⟩ ~ *vt* **1** *obs* **:** CHATTER, PRATTLE **2** *dial Brit* **:** to talk to; *esp* **:** to address in a tentative manner **:** APPROACH

³chat \ˈ"\ *n* -s **1 :** idle unimportant talk **:** PRATTLE, CHATTER **2 a :** light familiar talk ⟨a magazine devoted to ~ about the arts⟩; *esp* **:** CONVERSATION ⟨kept up a continual ~ with the lady —Michael McLaverty⟩ **b :** an instance of such talk ⟨a TV ~ broadcast at intervals⟩ ⟨a long ~ between old friends⟩ **3** [imit.] **:** any of several songbirds: as **a :** a bird of the genus *Saxicola* (as the stonechat and whinchat of Europe) **b :** a bird of an Australian genus *Epthianura* (family Turdidae) **c :** a bird of an American genus *Icteria* (family Parulidae) — see YELLOW-BREASTED CHAT

châ·teau \(ˈ)shaˌtō *sometimes* -ˈä;- *or* -ˈä;-\ *n, pl* **châteaus** \-ōz\ *or* **châ·teaux** \-ō(z)\ [F, fr. OF *chastel,* fr. L *castellum* — more at CASTLE] **1 :** a feudal castle or fortress in France **2 :** a large country house **:** MANSION **3 :** a French vineyard estate esp. in the Bordeaux wine region — often used prepositively in compounds naming such estates and their wines (as *Château-Haut-Brion,* the name of a vineyard in the Graves district in the Gironde and the red wine produced from its grapes) — compare CLOS, CÔTE

château bottled *adj* **:** ESTATE BOTTLED

cha·teau·bri·and \ˌsha,tōbrēˈäⁿ\ *n* -s *often cap* [after François René, vicomte de *Chateaubriand* †1848 Fr. writer and statesman] **1 :** a steak in which a pocket is cut and stuffed with shallots, chives, cayenne, and salt **2 :** a thick tenderloin steak

châ·teau d'eau \ˌsha,tōˈdō\ *n, pl* **château d'eaus** \-dōz\ *or* **cha·teaux d'eau** \-tō(z)ˈdō\ [F, lit., castle of water] **:** a fountain terminating an aqueduct and having an architectural background

chateau gray *n* **:** FROST GRAY

châ·teau·neuf-du-pape \shätōnœfdüpȧp\ *n* -s *usu cap C&P* [fr. *Châteauneuf-du-Pape,* commune near Avignon, France] **:** a usu. red wine produced in the Rhone valley north of Avignon

chateau potatoes *n pl* **:** potato balls parboiled briefly and then braised in butter

cha·te·lain \ˈshad·ᵊl,ān, ˌ==ˈ=\ *n* -s [MF *châtelain,* fr. L *castellanus* occupant of a castle — more at CASTELLAN] **:** CASTELLAN

cha·te·laine \ˈ"\ *n* -s [F *châtelaine,* fem. of *châtelain*] **1 a :** the wife of a castellan **:** the mistress of a château **b :** the mistress of the household, esp. of a large establishment **2 :** an ornamental chain, pin, or clasp usu. worn at a woman's waist to which trinkets, keys, a purse, or other articles are attached

cha·te·let \ˈshad·ᵊl,ā, ˌ==ˈ=\ *n* -s [F *châtelet,* fr. OF *chastelet,* dim. of *chastel* castle — more at CHÂTEAU] **:** a small castle

chat·el·lany \ˈshad·ᵊl,anē, -,ānē,-,ōnē, shaˈtelənē\ *n* -ES [F *châtellenie,* fr. OF *chastelenie*] **:** CASTELLANY

châ·tel·per·ro·ni·an \ˌsha,telpəˈrōnēən\ *adj, usu cap* [fr. *Châtelperron,* Allier dept., France + E *-ian*] **:** of or relating to the first phase of the Aurignacian epoch characterized by a special flint-chipping technique and a blade tool with one straight sharp edge and one curved over to the point and blunted

chat·e·nay pink \ˈshatᵊn,ā-\ *n, often cap C* [so called fr. Mme. Abel *Chatenay,* a variety of rose] **:** a light to moderate yellowish pink that is stronger and much redder than seashell pink

chat·ham·ite \ˈchad·ə,mīt\ *n* -s [*Chatham,* Conn., its locality + E *-ite*] **:** a mineral consisting of a variety of chloanthite containing much iron

cha·ti·no \chəˈtē(,)nō\ *n, pl* **chatino** *or* **chatinos** *usu cap* [Sp, of AmerInd origin] **1 a :** an Indian people of Oaxaca state, Mexico **b :** a member of such people **2 :** a Zapotecan language of the Chatino people

cha·ton \(ˈ)shaˌtōⁿ\ *n, pl* **chatons** \-ōⁿ(z)\ [F, fr. OF *chastun,* of Gmc origin; akin to OHG *kasto* container, MD *kaste* barn, OE *bēocere* beekeeper, OHG *kar* vessel, ON *ker,* Goth *kas*] **1 :** the head of a ring in which a stone is set or on which a device is engraved **2 :** the stone set in a chaton **3** *or* **chaton foil :** a coating (as a foil or lacquer) applied to the back of a cheap gemstone to give it greater brilliancy

cha·tot \(ˈ)shaˌtō\ *n, pl* **chatot** *or* **chatots** *usu cap* [F, fr. Choctaw *Chahta* Choctaw] **1 :** an extinct Muskogean people of Florida west of the Apalachicola river **2 :** a member of the Chatot people

cha·toy·ance \shəˈtȯiən(t)s, ˌsha·,twäˈyäⁿs\ *or* **cha·toy·an·cy** \shəˈtȯiənsē\ *n, pl* **chatoyances** *or* **chatoyancies :** the quality or state of being chatoyant ⟨the blue *chatoyancy* of moonstone — G.P.Merrill & W.F.Foshag⟩

¹cha·toy·ant \shəˈtȯiənt, ˌsha·,twäˈyäⁿ\ *adj* [F, fr. pres. part. of *chatoyer* to shine like a cat's eyes, fr. *chat* cat, fr. LL *cattus* — more at CAT] **:** having a changeable luster or color esp. marked by an undulating narrow band of white light ⟨a dress of ~ silk⟩ ⟨a cat's eye ~ in the dark⟩ ⟨an unusual ~ aquamarine — *Jour. of Gemmology*⟩

²chatoyant \ˈ"\ *n* -s **:** a chatoyant gem

chats *pres 3d sing of* CHAT, *pl of* CHAT

chat·ta \ˈchad·ə, -ädə\ *n* -s [Hindi *chātā,* fr. Skt *chattraka*] *India* **:** UMBRELLA

chattak *or* **chattack** *var of* CHITTAK

chat·ta·noo·ga \ˌchad·əˈnüga, -atᵊnˈü-,-atəˈnü-\ *adj, usu cap* [fr. *Chattanooga,* Tenn.] **:** of or from the city of Chattanooga, Tenn. ⟨*Chattanooga* physicians⟩ **:** of the kind or style prevalent in Chattanooga

chat·ta·noo·gan \ˌ===ˈ=gən\ *n* -s *cap* [*Chattanooga,* Tenn. + E *-an*] **:** a native or resident of Chattanooga, Tenn.

chatted *past of* CHAT

chat·tel \ˈchad·ᵊl, -atᵊl\ *n* -s [ME *chatel* goods, property, fr. OF, fr. ML *capitale* — more at CATTLE] **1 :** an item of tangible movable or immovable property except real estate, freehold, and that movable property which is by its nature considered to be essential to such an estate **2 :** SLAVE, BONDSMAN

chattel corporeal *n, pl* **chattels corporeal :** a chattel having a physical body visible and tangible and of substantial value as distinguished from an incorporeal chattel (as a chose in action)

chattel interest *n* **:** a legal interest in land less than a freehold estate

chat·tel·ism \-,izəm\ *n* -s **1 :** the state or quality of being a chattel **2 :** the treatment of things or esp. persons as chattels

chat·tel·i·za·tion \ˌ==,əˈzāshən, -,īˈz-\ *n* -s **:** the act of chattelizing a person or thing

chat·tel·ize \ˈ==,īz\ *vt* -ED/-ING/-S **:** to make a chattel of

chattel mortgage *n* **:** a mortgage of chattel property as opposed to estate

chattel personal *n, pl* **chattels personal :** a movable chattel (as goods, plate, or money) — distinguished from *chattel real*

chattel real *n, pl* **chattels real :** a chattel consisting of a right in land that is less than a freehold (as a lease or a growing crop) — distinguished from *chattel personal*

¹chat·ter \ˈchad·ə(r), -atə-\ *vb* -ED/-ING/-S [ME *chatteren,* of imit. origin] *vi* **1 a :** to utter rapidly succeeding sounds somewhat like language but inarticulate and indistinct — orig. used of birds ⟨~*ing* like a flock of blackbirds —Ellen Glasgow⟩ ⟨squirrels and chipmunks came to ~ and play about them —Sherwood Anderson⟩ ⟨the leaves began to ~ —George Meredith⟩ ⟨a tiny stream that ~*s* and twists through dells and dingles —*Amer. Guide Series: Conn.*⟩ **b** *of a pickup cartridge* **:** to produce unwanted sound acoustically **2 :** to talk idly, carelessly, incessantly, or with undue rapidity **:** JABBER ⟨men who followed the sea were always ~*ing* about the ease and security of life in the country —L.C.Douglas⟩ ⟨all through the rest of the meal I ~*ed* of the cottage —Adrian Bell⟩ ⟨men who are silent are set against men who ~ —*Times Lit. Supp.*⟩ **3 a :** to make the sound of or as if of rapidly repeated noisy contacts (as of the teeth of one who is extremely cold or frightened) ⟨master's teeth ~*ed* with horror —Donn Byrne⟩ ⟨~ like castanets in a Spanish dance⟩ ⟨skis will ~ in a turn if they are edged too much —*Operations in Snow & Extreme Cold* (U.S. War Dept.)⟩ ⟨machine guns ~*ing* —Philip Wylie⟩ **b** *of a cutting tool* **:** to vibrate rapidly in the action of cutting so as to form ridges or nicks ⟨the plane ~*ed* along the edge of the plank⟩ **c :** to operate or perform with any irregularity that causes rapid intermittent noise or vibration ⟨the motor ~*ed* in reverse⟩ ~ *vt* **1 :** to utter or speak rapidly, idly, or indistinctly ⟨English is ~*ed* here —Claudia Cassidy⟩ ⟨the woman ~*ed* her silly tale⟩ **2** *dial Eng* **:** TEAR, SHATTER **3** *of a cutting tool* **:** to cut unevenly because of vibration ⟨variation in the thickness of an oil film produces ~*ed* work —*New Departure Handbook*⟩

²chatter \ˈ"\ *n* -s [ME *chatere,* fr. *chatteren,* v.] **1 :** the action or sound of chattering ⟨the ~ of magpies⟩ ⟨the ~ of rivet guns⟩ ⟨the ~ of the plane along the wood⟩ ⟨the ~ of the worn clutch trying to take hold⟩ **2 :** idle talk **:** PRATTLE ⟨my ~ was as gay and sprightly as a bird song —R.P.Warren⟩ ⟨the ~ of small voices around him —M.W.Fishwick⟩

chatterbox \ˈ==,=\ *n* **:** one who talks incessantly and idly **:** a habitual chatterer

chatterbox tree *n* [so called fr. the clatter made by its dry pods] **:** LEBBEK

chat·ter·er \-ərə(r)\ *n* -s **1 :** one that chatters **2 :** any of various passerine birds, esp. the waxwings and members of the Cotingidae

chat·ter·ing·ly *adv* **:** in a chattering manner

chatter mark *n* **1 :** a fine undulation or ripple formed on the surface of work by a chattering tool **2 :** one of a series of short curved cracks on a glaciated rock surface roughly transverse to the glacial striae

chatter water *n, Brit* **:** weak tea

chat·ti·ly \ˈchad·ᵊlē, -atᵊl, ˌəlē, -lī\ *adv* **:** in a chatty manner ⟨writes ~ of his pet canaries —R.K.Buehrle⟩

chat·ti·ness \-d·ēnəs, -tē-, -in-\ *n* **:** the quality or state of being chatty

chatting *pres part of* CHAT

chat·ting·ly *adv* **:** in a chatting manner

¹chat·ty \ˈchad·ē, -atē, -i\ *adj, often* -ER/-EST **1 :** given to chat **:** informal, friendly, and talkative ⟨a ~ woman⟩ **2 :** being or resembling chat ⟨a ~ letter⟩ ⟨a ~ magazine article⟩

²chat·ty \ˈ"\ *also* **chat·ti** \ˈ"\ *n, pl* **chatties** *also* **chattis** [Tamil-Malayalam *caṭṭi*] **:** an earthenware water jar used in India

¹chau·ce·ri·an \(ˈ)chȯˈsirēən, -ˈer-\ *adj, usu cap* [Geoffrey *Chaucer* †1400 Eng. poet + E *-ian*] **:** of, relating to, befitting, or resembling the English medieval writer Geoffrey Chaucer or his writings

²chaucerian \ˈ"\ *n, usu cap* **1 :** an imitator of Chaucer; *esp* **:** one of a group of Scottish imitators of the 15th century **2 :** an admirer of Chaucer's writings **3 :** a scholar or teacher specializing in the study or the teaching of Chaucer

chau·cer·ism \ˈchȯsə,rizəm\ *n, usu cap* [*Chaucer* + E *-ism*] **:** a word, expression, or quality of style characteristic of or imitative of the writings of Chaucer ⟨Spenser's ~*s*⟩

chaud-froid \(ˈ)shōˌfrwä, -ōfrəˈwä\ *n* -s [F, lit., hot-cold, fr. *chaud* hot (fr. L *calidus*) + *froid* cold, fr. L *frigidus* — more at CALDRON, FRIGID] **1 :** a jellied sauce (as a white or brown sauce fortified with gelatin) used as a garnish esp. for meat or fish **2 :** food (as meat or fish) covered with a chaudfroid sauce usu. molded into shapes after cooking, and served cold

chaud-medley *or* **chaud-melle** *or* **chaud-mella** *n* -s [*chaud-medley, chaud-mella,* alter. of *chaud-melle; chaud-melle* fr. ME *chaudmellee, chawdmelle,* fr. MF *chaude mellee,* lit., hot fight] **1** *Scots law* **:** an affray in the heat of passion **2** *Scots law* **:** the wounding or killing of a person in a chaud-medley without premeditation

chau·dron \(ˈ)shōˌdrōⁿ\ *n* -s [F, kettle, fr. OF *chauderon,* dim. of *chaudiere,* fr. LL *caldaria* — more at CALDRON] **:** ANTIQUE RED

chauf·fer \ˈchȯfə(r)\ *n* -s [alter. (prob. influenced by F *chauffer* to heat, warm, fr. OF *chaufer*) of ²*chafer* — more at CHAFE] **:** a portable stove usu. with a grate at the bottom and an open top

¹chauf·feur \ˈshōfə(r); (ˈ)shōˌfər, +V -ˌfər-; (ˈ)shōˌfə̄, +V -ˌfər- *also* -ˌfər\ *n* -s [F, lit., stoker, fr. *chauffer* to heat, warm + *-eur* -er] **1 :** one that is employed to operate a motor vehicle for the transportation of persons or property **2 :** one that transports (as persons) by operating a motor vehicle ⟨to be ~ for a group of friends who could not drive⟩

²chauffeur \ˈ"\ *vb* **chauffeured; chauffeured; chauffeuring** \-f(ə)riŋ, -ˌfəriŋ *also* -ˌfəriŋ\ **chauffeurs** *vi* **:** to do the work of a chauffeur ⟨~ for a livelihood⟩ ~ *vt* **1 :** to transport in the manner of a chauffeur ⟨has time to garden, ~ the kids to school, and sleep —Bernard Kalb⟩ ⟨at twelve I ~*ed* him around the country—C.A.Lindbergh b. 1902⟩ **2 a :** to operate (as an automobile) as chauffeur ⟨~ a sporty town car for a crippled relative⟩ ⟨~*ing* a plane for a millionaire candy magnate —*Newsweek*⟩ **b :** to operate (a motor vehicle) by means of a chauffeur ⟨two company cars, both ~*ed* —Pearl Buck⟩

¹chauf·feuse \(ˈ)shōˌfə(r)z, -ˌfəz\ *n* -s [F, fr. *chauffer* to heat, warm] **:** a low-seated French fireside chair

²chauffeuse \ˈ"\ *n* -s [F, fem. of *chauffeur*] **:** a female chauffeur

chau·ki·dar \ˌchaukēˈdär\ *var of* CHOKIDAR

chau·li·o·don·ti·dae \kȯ,lēəˈdäntə,dē, ˌkȯlēōˈd-\ *n pl, cap* [NL, fr. *Chauliodont-, Chauliodus,* type genus (fr. Gk *chauliodont-, chauliodous* with projecting teeth, fr. *chauli-* — irreg. fr. *chaunos* wide open, loose, foolish, fr. the stem of *chaos* space, abyss, gen. *chaous* — + *-odont-, -odous,* fr. *odont-, odōn* tooth) + *-idae* — more at GUM, TOOTH] **:** a widely distributed family (order Isospondyli) of large-headed long-bodied deep-sea fishes with large mouths and greatly enlarged fangs

chaul·moo·gra *also* **chaul·mu·gra** \chȯlˈmügrə\ *or* **chaulmau·gra** \-mȯ-\ *n* -s [Beng *cāulmugrā, cālmugrā,* fr. *cāul, cāl* rice + *mugrā* bowstring hemp (*Sansevieria zeylanica*)] **:** any of several East Indian trees of the family Flacourtiaceae that yield chaulmoogra oil: **a :** a large-fruited tree (*Taraktogenos kurzii*) **b :** any of several trees of the genus *Hydnocarpus* (esp. *H. anthelminticus* and *H. wightiana*)

chaulmoogra oil *n* **:** any of several fixed oils or fats similar in physical and chemical properties that are expressed from seeds of certain trees of the family Flacourtiaceae and used esp. formerly in the treatment of leprosy and skin diseases: **a :** an oil or soft fat from seeds of any chaulmoogra tree composed chiefly of glycerides of chaulmoogric, hydnocarpic, and gorlic acids **b :** GORLI OIL

chaul·moo·grate \-grət, -,grāt\ *n* -s [*chaulmoogric* + *-ate*] **:** a salt or ester of chaulmoogric acid

chaul·moo·gric acid \(ˈ)chȯlˈmügrik-\ *n* **:** a crystalline unsaturated acid $C_5H_7(CH_2)_{12}COOH$ found as an ester in chaulmoogra oil and hydnocarpus oil; 13-(2-cyclopenten-1-yl)= tridecanoic acid

chau·mer \ˈchämər, -ōm-\ *Scot var of* CHAMBER

chaunt *archaic var of* CHANT

chaunter *archaic var of* CHANTER

chauntry *obs var of* CHANTRY

chauri *var of* CHOWRIE

chaus \ˈkaüs, ˈch-\ *n, pl* **chaus** [origin unknown] **:** an Old World wildcat, possibly the Kaffir cat

chaus·sée \(ˈ)shōˌsā\ *n* -s [F, fr. ML *calciata* paved road — more at CAUSEY] **:** a paved road **:** CAUSEWAY, HIGHWAY

chausses \ˈshōs\ *n pl* [F, pl. of *chausse,* fr. ML *calcea,* fr. L *calceus* shoe, fr. *calc-, calx* heel — more at CALCANEUM] **1 :** a medieval tight-fitting garment worn by men to cover the legs and feet and sometimes the body below the waist **2 :** the early medieval armor of linked mail that fitted like chausses

chaus·sure \shōˈsü(ə)r\ *n* -s [ME *chauceore, chaucer,* fr. MF *chaussure,* fr. *chausser* to put on footwear, fr. L *calceare,* fr. *calceus* shoe] **1 :** FOOTGEAR **2 chaussures** *pl* **:** SHOES

chau·tau·qua \shəˈtȯkwə\ *n* -s *sometimes cap* [fr. *Chautauqua* lake, western New York, where it was founded] **1 a :** a stationary or traveling institution that flourished in the late 19th and early 20th centuries providing popular education usu. combined with entertainment in the form of lectures, concerts, or dramatic performances often presented outdoors or in a tent ⟨~ is no more, its place taken by the radio everywhere —Lancaster Pollard⟩ **b :** a particular instance of meetings belonging to this institution as held in any one place or a single traveling unit of such lectures or concerts ⟨lecture circuits usually suggest canvas-topped ~*s* —*Infantry Jour.*⟩ **2 :** any institution or series of popular presentations similar to a chautauqua in purpose or organization ⟨in six states, ~ courses were held at various times throughout the states in four to twelve centers —*Jour. Amer. Med. Assoc.*⟩

chautauqua muskellunge *n, usu cap C* [fr. *Chautauqua* Lake, N. Y.] **:** a muskellunge of a variety (*Esox masquinongy ohiensis*) distinguished by dark crossbars and paucity of spots and found chiefly in the Ohio and St. Lawrence river drainages

chau·tau·quan \-wən\ *adj, usu cap* [in sense 1, fr. *Chautauqua* + *-an;* in sense 2, fr. *Chautauqua* lake + E *-an*] **1 :** *sometimes cap* **:** of or relating to a chautauqua or chautauquas **2 :** of or relating to a subdivision of the No. American Devonian — see GEOLOGIC TIME table

chauve-sou·ris \ˌshōvsüˈrē\ *n, pl* **chauve-sou·rises** \-ˈrēz\ [F, fr. OF *chauve soriz,* fr. ML *calva sorex,* fr. L *calva* bald (fem. of *calvus*) + *sorex* shrew — more at CALVARIUM, SOREX] **:** ³BAT 1

chau·vin·ism \ˈshōvə,nizəm\ *n* -s [F *chauvinisme,* fr. *chauvin* warmonger (after *Chauvin,* a very patriotic soldier in *La Cocarde tricolore,* play written 1831 by Charles T. and Jean Hippolyte Cogniard, after Nicolas *Chauvin fl* 1815 legendary French soldier very devoted to Napoleon) + *-isme* -ism] **1 :** excessive esp. blind patriotism — compare JINGOISM **2 :** undue esp. invidious attachment or partiality for a group or place to which one belongs or has belonged ⟨professional ~*s* —Wilbur Zelinsky⟩ ⟨the passionate ~ of a child away from home —John Woodburn⟩

¹chau·vin·ist \-ˌnəst\ *n* -s **:** one who practices chauvinism

²chauvinist \ˈ"\ *or* **chau·vin·is·tic** \ˌshōvəˈnistik, -ēk\ *adj* **:** marked by chauvinism — **chau·vin·is·ti·cal·ly** \-tək(ə)lē, -ēk-, -lī\ *adv*

cha·van·te \shəˈvantē\ *n, pl* **chavante** *or* **chavantes** *usu cap* [Pg, of AmerInd origin] **1 :** OTI **2 a :** an Indian people of Mato Grosso state, Brazil **b :** a member of such people **3 a :** a Gesan people of Goiaz state, Brazil **b :** a member of such people — **cha·van·te·an** \-ēan\ *adj, usu cap*

chav·el \ˈchavəl\ *vb* -ED/-ING/-S [ME *chavlen, chaulen,* fr. *chavel, chauel* jaw — more at JOWL] *now dial Eng* **:** NIBBLE, GNAW

chav·en·der \ˈchavəndə(r)\ *n* -s [ME *chevender,* irreg. fr. *cheveyne* chevin] **:** CHUB 1

cha·ver \ˈkävər\ *n, pl* **chave·rim** \käˈvärim\ *var of* HAVER

chav·i·be·tol \ˌchavəˈbē,tōl, -ōl\ *n* -s [ISV *chavi-* (fr. NL *chavica* — prob. modif. of Skt *cavika,* a pepper (*Piper chaba*) — genus name of *Chavica betle,* syn. of *Piper betle*) + *bet-* (fr. NL *betle,* prob. fr. Pg) + *-ol* (fr. L *oleum* oil); prob. orig. formed in G — more at BETEL, OIL] **:** an oily phenol $C_3H_5C_6H_3(OCH_3)OH$ found in the essential oil from the leaves of the betel pepper; 5-allyl-guaiacol

chav·i·cine \ˈchavə,sēn, -sən\ *n* -s [ISV *chavic-* (fr. NL *Chavica*) + *-ine*] **:** an alkaloid $C_{17}H_{19}NO_3$, isomeric with piperine obtained from black pepper as a pungent greenish resinous substance

chav·i·col \-,kōl, -ōl\ *n* -s [ISV *chavic-* (fr. NL *Chavica*) + *-ol* (fr. L *oleum*); prob. orig. formed as G *chavikol*] **:** a colorless oily phenol $C_3H_5C_6H_4OH$ found esp. in the oil from the leaves of the betel pepper and in bay oil; *para*-allyl-phenol

cha·vin \chəˈvēn\ *adj, usu cap* [fr. *Chavín* or *Chavín* de Huantar, town in central Peru, its type station] **:** of or relating to a Peruvian culture of the 1st to the 6th centuries A.D. characterized by a platform type of stone building with masonry in alternating thick and thin courses, sculpture of human, animal, and monster heads in the round and outlines on slabs, and monochrome pottery decorated in relief or by incision with feline or geometric designs

cha·vish \ˈchävish\ *n* -ES [prob. imit.] *dial Eng* **:** CHATTERING, PRATTLING

¹chaw \ˈchȯ\ *vb* **chawed; chawed; chawing** \-ȯ(·)iŋ\ **chaws** [alter. of ¹*chew*] *vt* **1** *now dial* **:** to grind with the teeth **:** CHEW **2** *now dial* **:** mull over **:** PONDER **3** *dial* **:** VEX, EMBARRASS ~ *vi, now dial* **:** CHEW

²chaw \ˈ"\ *n* -s *now dial* **:** a chew esp. of tobacco

³chaw *n* -s [alter. (influenced by ²*chaw*) of ¹*jaw*] *obs* **:** JAW — usu. used in pl.

cha·wa·sha \chəˈwȯshə -ˈwä-\ *n, pl* **chawasha** *or* **chawashas** *usu cap* **1 :** a Chitimachan people of Louisiana at the mouth of the Mississippi **2 :** a member of the Chawasha people

chawbacon \ˈ=,==\ *n* -s [¹*chaw* + *bacon*] **:** RUSTIC, BUMPKIN, HICK, YOKEL

¹chawbuck *n* [Hindi *cābuk,* fr. Per *chābuk*] *archaic, chiefly India* **:** a large whip

²chawbuck *vt, archaic, chiefly India* **:** to flog with a chawbuck

chaw·dron \ˈchȯdrən\ *n* -s [ME *chawdoun, chaudern,* fr. MF *chaudun* tripe, fr. ML *calduna* intestine, prob. fr. L *calidus* warm — more at CALDRON] *archaic* **:** the entrails of an animal used as a food

chawl \ˈchȯl\ *n* -s [Hindi *cāl* thatched roof] **:** a large tenement house esp. in the factory cities of India

chawn \ˈchȯn\ *n* -s [prob. irreg. fr. obs. *chine,* v., to crack, fr. ME *chinen,* fr. OE *cīnan* — more at CAUL] *now dial Eng* **:** GAP, CLEFT

chawng *var of* CHUANG

chawstick \ˈ=,=\ *n* -s [²*chaw* + *stick*] **:** a woody vine (*Gouania lupuloides*) of the buckthorn family the twigs of which are chewed as a stomachic — called also *chewstick*

¹chay \ˈchī\ *or* **chaya** \ˈchī(y)ə\ *also* **choy** \ˈchȯi\ *or* **choya** \ˈchȯi(y)ə\ *n* -s [Tamil-Malayalam *cāya-vēr,* perh. fr. Skt *chāyā* color, shadow — more at SCENE] **:** the root of an East Indian herb (*Oldenlandia umbellata*) that yields a red dye

²chay \ˈshā\ *n* -s [back-formation fr. *chaise,* taken as pl.] **:** CHAISE

chayaroot \ˈ==,=\ *also* **choyroot** \ˈ=,=\ *n* -s [*chaya, choy* + *root*] **:** ¹CHAY

chayma *usu cap, var of* CHAIMA

cha·yo·te \chīˈyōd·ē, chīˈō-\ *n* -s [Sp, fr. Nahuatl *chayotli*] **1 :** the rounded or pear-shaped fruit of a West Indian annual vine (*Sechium edule*) of the cucumber family that is widely cultivated as a vegetable **2 :** the plant bearing the chayote

chazan *or* **chazzan** *n, pl* **chazanim** *or* **chazzanim** *var of* HAZAN

chazanuth *or* **chazanut** *or* **chazzanuth** *or* **chazzanut** *var of* HAZANUTH

chazar *usu cap, var of* KHAZAR

CHB *abbr* center halfback

chd *abbr* **1** chaldron **2** chord

che *pron* [alter. of *'ch,* fr. ME *ich* — more at I] *obs dial Eng* **:** I

ChE *abbr or n* -s chemical engineer

¹cheap *vt* -ED/-ING/-S [ME *chepen,* fr. OE *cēapian* to buy; akin to OHG *koufōn,* ON *kaupa,* Goth *kaupōn*] **1** *obs* **:** to ask the price of **:** PRICE **2** *obs* **:** to bid or offer for

²cheap \ˈchēp\ *n* -s [ME *chep,* fr. OE *cēap* trade, purchase, sale; akin to OHG *kouf* trade, *koufo* merchant, ON *kaup* bargain, Goth *kaupōn* to trade; all fr. a prehistoric Gmc word stem borrowed fr. L *caupo* tradesman, innkeeper; perh. akin to Gk *kapēlos* tradesman, innkeeper] *obs Brit* **:** BARGAIN — now used only in the phrase *on the cheap* — **on the cheap** *adv* **:** at minimum expense **:** CHEAPLY ⟨called the "Penny Crowning" because it was done *on the cheap* —H.V.Morton⟩

³cheap \ˈ"\ *adj* -ER/-EST [²*cheap* (in such phrases as *at good cheap* at a bargain)] **1 a :** of small cost **:** inexpensive esp. as compared with the going price or the real value ⟨living is ~*er*

during the summer than in winter) — formerly used with *good* or *great* ⟨food is good ~ in a time of plenty⟩ **b :** charging a comparatively low price ⟨the ~*er* stores⟩ **c :** dealing in low-priced goods ⟨the ~ stores along the waterfront⟩ **d :** depreciated in value (as by currency inflation) ⟨~ dollars⟩ **2 :** costing little labor or effort or involving little trouble to obtain **:** easily obtained or attained ⟨a ~ victory⟩ ⟨~ kisses⟩ — formerly used with *good* or *great* ⟨compliments are good ~⟩ **3 a :** of inferior quality **:** of small intrinsic worth **:** SHODDY, TAWDRY, MERETRICIOUS ⟨the ~ novel does not itself turn back to reality —Bernard De Voto⟩ ⟨nothing is ~ about this volume but its price —S.L.Faison⟩ ⟨~ publicity⟩ **b :** worthy of scorn or rejection **:** unredeemed by any fine or lofty qualities **:** CONTEMPTIBLE ⟨a ~ and nasty life —G.B.Shaw⟩ ⟨a ~ and vulgar remark⟩ ⟨he feels pretty ~⟩ **4 a :** yielding small satisfaction ⟨~ entertainment⟩ **b :** paying or able to pay less than given amounts ⟨a ~*er* class of customers⟩ **5** *of money* **:** obtainable at a low rate of interest **6** *Brit* **:** specially reduced in price ⟨a ~ day ticket to Manchester —S.P.B.Mais⟩ **syn** see CONTEMPTIBLE — **cheap of** *Scot* **:** getting no more than one's deserts **:** well deserving of

⁴cheap \"\ *adv* **:** CHEAPLY ⟨bought the article ~⟩

cheap·en \'chēpən\ *vb* **cheapened; cheapened; cheapening** \-p(ə)niŋ\ **cheapens** [¹, ², or ³*cheap* + *-en*] *vt* **1 a :** to ask the price of **b :** to bid or bargain for **2 :** to make cheap: as **a :** to lessen the price or the value of ⟨a glutted market ~*s* the goods in all categories⟩ **b :** to lower in general esteem **c :** to make tawdry, vulgar, or inferior in some moral sense ⟨how a group of human beings can be ~*ed* by the constant waterdrop of shabbiness . . . during the depression —Henry Hewes⟩ ~ *vi* **:** to become cheap ⟨food ~*s* in summer⟩

cheap·ie \'chēpē\ *n* -s [³*cheap* + *-ie*] **:** something that costs relatively little in money or effort to produce; *esp* **:** an inexpensive motion picture

¹cheap–jack \'=,jak\ *also* **cheap–john** \'=,jän\ *n* -s *sometimes cap J* [³*cheap* + *Jack* or *John* (the names) — more at JACK, JOHN] **1 :** a hawker or peddler **:** HUCKSTER; *esp* **:** a hawker who bargains over his goods ⟨*cheap-jacks* have mingled with showmen, especially on fairgrounds, since the 18th century —Eric Partridge⟩ **2 :** a dealer in cheap often inferior or worthless merchandise ⟨so many *cheap-jacks* with their bottled, spiritual cure-alls —G.S.Fraser⟩

²cheap–jack \"\ *also* **cheap–john** \"\ *adj, sometimes cap J* **:** of, relating to, or befitting a cheap-jack: as **a :** often inferior, cheap, or worthless ⟨*cheap-jack* wares⟩ ⟨*cheap-jack* dramaturgy⟩ **b :** opportunistic esp. unscrupulously or in dealing in inferior goods ⟨the *cheap-jack* speculators . . . destroying the beauty of London —Robert Lutyens⟩

cheap·ly \-lē,-li\ *adv* [³*cheap* + *-ly*] **:** in a cheap manner: as **a :** INEXPENSIVELY ⟨borrow as ~ as possible⟩ ⟨if their products are ~ and well produced —Brian Inglis⟩ **b :** VULGARLY ⟨rather ~ dressed⟩ **c :** with little expenditure of effort or time ⟨if we seek peace ~ or meanly —A.E.Stevenson †1965⟩

cheap·ness \-pnəs\ *n* -ES **:** the quality or state of being cheap

cheap·skate \'=,=\ *n* [³*cheap* + *skate* (miserly person)] **:** a miserly or ungenerous person; *esp* **:** one who tries to avoid his share of costs ⟨if we were courageous enough to demur at the price we were made to feel in no uncertain terms that we were *cheapskates* —Frances W. Browin⟩

chear *archaic var of* CHEER

¹cheat \'chēt, *usu* -ēd·+V\ *n* -s [earlier *cheat* forfeited property, booty, fr. ME *chet* escheat, short for *achet*, alter. of *eschet* — more at ESCHEAT] **1 a :** the act or action of cheating or fraudulently deceiving **:** DECEPTION, FRAUD ⟨his financial activity turned out to be a great ~⟩ **b :** a means of cheating, misleading, tricking, or deluding one putting credence in seeming honesty or genuineness **:** whatever invites disappointment ⟨the elaborate ~ that the positivistic movement has perpetrated upon the human spirit —Allen Tate⟩ **c :** an act or instance of cheating ⟨tax ~*s* being discovered⟩ **d :** one that cheats esp. habitually **:** PRETENDER, DECEIVER, SHARPER ⟨if I passed myself off . . . as a gentleman, I should deserve to be exposed as a ~ —G.B.Shaw⟩ **2** *archaic* **:** THING, ARTICLE — usu. used with a distinguishing modifier ⟨a smelling ~ is a nose⟩ ⟨a nubbing ~ is the gallows⟩ **3** [prob. so called fr. its resemblance to grain among which it grows] **a :** the common chess (*Bromus secalinus*) **b :** DOWNY BROME **c :** BEARDED DARNEL **4** *law* **:** the obtaining of property from another by an intentional active distortion of the truth; *esp* **:** the common-law offense later enlarged by statute consisting in defrauding numbers of people by means of deceitful or illegal symbols or tokens but not so as to constitute a felony — compare ¹FRAUD 1 **syn** see IMPOSTURE

²cheat \"\ *vb* -ED/-ING/-S [earlier *cheat* to confiscate, fr. ME *cheten* to escheat, short for *acheten*, alter. of *escheten* — more at ESCHEAT] *vt* **1 :** to deprive of something valuable by the use of deceit or fraud **:** DEFRAUD, SWINDLE ⟨~ a man out of his savings⟩ ⟨suspicious . . . lest she should be ~*ed* out of the salary she had come resolved to demand —G.B.Shaw⟩ **2 :** to condition, influence, or lead by or as if by deceit, trick, or artifice ⟨~*ed* into cordial admiration by the splendor of the verses —Thomas De Quincey⟩ **3 :** to defeat in an expectation or purpose by or as if by deceit and trickery **:** DISAPPOINT, FOIL ⟨by God's mercy Ludendorff was ~*ed* of the Channel Ports —S.L.A.Marshall⟩ ⟨then I ~*ed* my despair. I said that you were safe —Maurice Baring⟩ **4** *archaic* **:** to obtain by fraud or trickery ~ *vi* **1 a :** to practice fraud or trickery **b :** to violate rules dishonestly (as at cards) **2 :** to be sexually unfaithful ⟨the divorce suit alleged that he had been ~*ing* on his wife⟩

syn SWINDLE, DEFRAUD, COZEN, OVERREACH: CHEAT is a general term indicating dishonest and deceitful trickery and is likely to imply censure, blame, or contempt ⟨Jane Orange . . . was not liked. She was called stingy and it was said that she and her husband had *cheated* every one with whom they had dealings —Sherwood Anderson⟩ SWINDLE implies gross and large-scale cheating for gain by means of imposture or mean abuse of confidence ⟨the despised Chinese, who were cuffed and maltreated and *swindled* by the Californians —Van Wyck Brooks⟩ ⟨Barnum knew the American public loved to be gulled . . . His genius consisted in knowing how to *swindle* them —W.L.Phelps⟩ DEFRAUD, a more legalistic word, indicates taking away from or withholding from another his rights or possessions by calculated perversion of truth, chicanery, or coercive pressure ⟨she ever claimed more than she could receive; they, as constantly, called themselves robbed and *defrauded* —Hilaire Belloc⟩ COZEN implies artful or tricky persuading, wheedling, bamboozling, or chiseling in deluding or obtaining ⟨I fought . . . to save my niche . . . Old Gandolf *cozened* me, despite my call —Robert Browning⟩ ⟨the Popular Front — that famous opportunity for men of good will to be *cozened* by the Communists —C.G.Poore⟩ OVERREACH indicates outwitting, as in dealing or bargaining, or cheating, by crafty dishonesty ⟨the suspicion that most of the talk they [the deaf] cannot hear consists in plottings and schemings to *overreach* or get around them —J.G.Cozzens⟩

³cheat *n* -s [ME *chet*] *obs* **:** wheat bread inferior to manchet

cheat·er \'chēd·ə(r), -ētə-\ *n* -s [ME *chetour*, modif. of AF *eschetour* — more at ESCHEATOR] **1** *obs* **:** ESCHEATOR **2 :** one that cheats **3 cheaters** *pl, slang* **:** SPECTACLES ⟨through heavy horn-rimmed ~*s* —*Time*⟩ **4 cheaters** *pl, slang* **:** FALSIES

cheat·ery \'chēd·ərē, -ētə-\ *or* **cheat·ry** \'chētrē\ *n* -ES **:** CHEATING, SWINDLING

cheatgrass \'=,=\ *n* **:** DOWNY BROME

cheat·ing·ly *adv* **:** in a cheating manner

cheats *pl of* CHEAT, *pres 3d sing of* CHEAT

cheat shot *n* **:** a motion-picture camera shot in which a part of the action necessary for filming a scene is suppressed in the finished picture in order to create or sustain a desired illusion

che·bac·co boat \shə'ba(,)kō-, -akə-\ *n* [fr. *Chebacco*, former parish of Ipswich, Mass., (now in the town of Essex), where it originated] **:** a narrow-sterned boat formerly much used in Newfoundland fisheries

¹che·bec \shə'bek\ *or* **che·beck** \"\ *n* -s [F *chebec, chébec* — more at XEBEC] **:** XEBEC

²che·bec \chē'bek, chə-\ *n* -s [imit.] **:** LEAST FLYCATCHER

ché·be·ro \'chebə,rō, 'chä-\ *n, pl* **chébero** *or* **chéberos** *usu cap* [Sp, of AmerInd origin] **1 a :** a Cahuapana people of northern Peru **b :** a member of such people **2 :** the language of the Chébero people

che·bog \'ch ,bäg, -ôg, =' =\ *n* -s [prob. fr. Natick *chippeog*, lit., they are separated or dead; fr. its use as manure by the Indians] **:** MENHADEN

che·bule \kə'b(y)ül\ *n* -s [F *chébule*, fr. Pashto *halīla-ī-kābulī* myrobalan from Kabul, fr. *Kabul*, city in Afghanistan] **:** the dried astringent fruit of an East Indian tree (*Terminalia chebula*)

cheb·u·lin·ic acid \¦kebyə¦linik-\ *n* [ISV *chebulinic* (fr. NL *chebula*, specific epithet of *Terminalia chebula* — fr. F *chébule* — + ISV *-in* + *-ic*) + *acid*; orig. formed as G *chebulinsäure*] **:** a crystalline tannin $C_{41}H_{32}O_{27}$ found in dried fruits of an East Indian tree (*Terminalia chebula*)

chechako *or* **chechaqua** *var of* CHEECHAKO

che·che·het \¦chächə¦het, -ech-\ *n, pl* **chechehet** *or* **chechehets** *usu cap* [Sp *chechehet, chechaet*, of AmerInd origin] **1 a :** an extinct people of central Argentina **b :** a member of such people **2 :** the language of the Chechehet people constituting a linguistic family — called also *Het*

che·chem \chə'chem\ *n* -s [prob. native name in the West Indies] **:** a tree (*Metopium brownii*) of British Honduras, Cuba, and Santo Domingo yielding a dark wood used in cabinet and furniture making and for interior finishes

che·chen \chə'chen\ *n, pl* **chechen** *or* **chechens** *usu cap* [modif. of Russ *chechenets*, prob. fr. *chechenit' sya* to talk mincingly, of imit. origin] **1 a :** a Japhetic people living north of Dagestan, U.S.S.R. **b :** a member of such people **2 :** the North Caucasic language of the Chechen people

che·chia \(')shäsh¦yä\ *n* -s [F *chéchia*, fr. Maghribi *shāshiya*, fr. *Shāsh*, town in Persia where it was manufactured in medieval times] **:** a cylindrical brimless cap of Arab origin often having a tassel on the crown

chechia

¹check \'chek\ *interj* [ME *chek*, interj. & n.] — used to warn a chess opponent that his king is attacked

²check \"\ *n* -s [ME *chek* check at chess, attack, quarrel, reproof, fr. OF *eschec, eschac* check at chess, repulse, fr. Ar *shāh* check at chess, fr. Per, lit., king; akin to Av *xshayeti* he rules, has power, Skt *kṣayati* he possesses, rules, Gk *ktasthai* to acquire] **1 :** exposure of a chess king to an opponent's piece in such a way that if it were not the king and not immediately protected (as by interposing another piece) it could be captured on the next move ⟨with his king in ~⟩ ⟨relieving the ~⟩ — see DISCOVERED CHECK **2 a :** a sudden stoppage of a forward course or progress **:** a condition of impeded progress **:** ARREST, REPULSE, STOP ⟨the outbreak of war in 1939 gave a sudden ~ to the sculptor's work —Herbert Read⟩ **b** *obs* **:** a fine imposed on servants of the royal household for neglect of duty **c :** ²STOP 9 **d** *of a hunting dog* **:** a temporary loss of scent while in pursuit of quarry **e :** a legal or illegal checking of an opposing player or play in ice hockey — see BACK-CHECK, BOARD CHECK, BODY CHECK, CROSS-CHECK, HOOK CHECK, POKE CHECK, SWEEP CHECK **3 :** the interruption by a hawk of its pursuit of the proper quarry in order to pursue inferior game; *also* **:** the inferior game it pursues **4 :** a typically sudden and sharp pause in a course **:** a break in a progression ⟨the invaders coming in without a ~⟩ **5** *archaic* **:** REPRIMAND, REBUKE **6 :** an agency, force, condition, or provision likely to arrest progress, limit action, restrain power, or curb excess **:** RESTRAINT ⟨a small minority of men of high character who acted as a ~ upon this irresponsible majority —Warren Grice⟩ ⟨I must put a ~ on these roving fancies of mine —T.B.Costain⟩: **a :** a person who acts to restrain or counter another ⟨using one earl as a ~ on the other⟩ **b :** a provision conferring power on a governmental branch or agency to restrain others ⟨the ~*s* and balances of republican governments —John Adams⟩ **c** [by shortening] **:** CHECKREIN **d :** a mechanical device for curbing, braking, or otherwise limiting action ⟨a door ~ preventing slamming⟩ **e :** a rope for checking the motion of a ship **f :** DAMPER 1a **g :** a device in a fishing reel to control the running out of the line **h :** the act of checking in poker **7 a :** supervision insuring accuracy, fitness, or due performance **:** CONTROL ⟨under the ~ of the superintendent⟩ **b :** a standard for testing and evaluation **:** CRITERION ⟨any arbitrary formula too rigidly adhered to may endanger good writing, but a good set of principles used as a ~ and an aid may be very useful —F.L.Mott⟩ **c :** an examination, test, or other device for determining progress, condition, value, or accuracy; *sometimes* **:** a test performed by quick sampling ⟨a ~ on a student's progress⟩ **d :** INSPECTION, INVESTIGATION ⟨a loyalty ~ on government employees⟩ **e :** a ready source of information used in investigating or verifying ⟨graphs serving as a ~ on our standing⟩ **f :** act of testing or verifying ⟨making a ~ on the data⟩; *also* **:** the material, sample, or unit used for such testing or verifying **8 a :** an area of land enclosed by embankments that confine irrigation water admitted by flooding **b :** a gate for controlling water flow in an irrigation ditch **9** *dial* **:** a light meal **:** SNACK **10** [so called fr. the use of the counterfoil to check forgery] **a** *obs* **:** the counterfoil of a bank draft; *also* **:** a draft form with a counterfoil **b :** a written order directing a bank or banker to pay money as therein stated **:** a draft drawn on a bank or banker payable on demand **11 a :** a card or small metal piece showing ownership, indicating payment of a charge or fee, identifying a person, or enabling him to make certain demands or claims **:** TICKET, CERTIFICATE ⟨a baggage ~⟩ ⟨a hat ~⟩ ⟨a baseball rain ~⟩ **b :** a token used in trade as a piece of money or as evidence of credit ⟨an army post exchange ~⟩ ⟨a ~ good for a bottle of beer⟩ **c :** a counter in various games (as card games) that is often cashed or otherwise turned in on leaving a game **:** CHIP ⟨the piles of ~*s* before the roulette players⟩ **d :** a tab or slip indicating an amount due **:** BILL ⟨our waitress finally brought the ~⟩ **e :** CHECKROOM ⟨there's a hat ~ in the hotel lobby⟩ **12** [ME *chek*, short for *cheker* checker (chessboard)] **a :** a pattern in squares **:** a design that resembles a checkerboard **b :** a fabric woven or printed with such a design **c :** a square in such a design **d :** a square made by vertical and horizontal lines to facilitate planned planting ⟨planting the trees in ~*s*⟩ **13 :** a mark typically √ placed beside an item to show its having been noted, examined, or verified **14 a :** CRACK, CHINK, BREAK: (1) **:** a lengthwise separation in wood that usu. extends across the annual growth rings and commonly results from stresses set up during seasoning — compare SHAKE (2) **:** an almost imperceptible crack in steel caused by uneven quenching in hardening (3) **:** a short shallow crack in a paint, varnish, or lacquer film occurring as a result of age and disintegration of film **b** *pl* **checks** *also* **chex** \-ks\ **:** a poultry egg with a minuscule break in the shell due to improper sealing but with unbroken membrane — contrasted with *crack* (sense 13) **15 :** a rabbet-shaped cutting **:** RABBET, REBATE — **in check :** in restraint **:** in a situation precluding free activity or development **:** under control ⟨Lee held the left of the Union army *in check* —G.J. Fiebeger⟩

³check \"\ *vb* -ED/-ING/-S [ME *cheken*, fr. MF *eschequier* to play chess, put in check, defeat, fr. *eschecs* chess or *eschec* check] *vt* **1 :** to place (a chess king) in check — see CHECKMATE **2 :** CHECKROW **3** *now chiefly dial* **:** REBUKE, REPRIMAND **4 a** *archaic* **:** to penalize, fine, or mulct by withholding wages ⟨~ a delinquent servant⟩ **b :** GARNISHEE, MULCT ⟨~ a delinquent's salary⟩ **5 a :** to bring to a sudden stop and halt the course, progress, or action of often abruptly, forcefully, and certainly ⟨the army of the Huns under Attila had been ~*ed* and turned back at Châlons —Tom Wintringham⟩ ⟨he . . . went on pacing . . . but suddenly he ~*ed* himself, stood still for a moment —Joseph Conrad⟩ **b :** to block the progress of (an opposing hockey player or a hockey play) by a check **6 a :** to restrain or abate the course, action, or force of **:** cause to act more slowly with less force or effect **:** have the power or ability to restrain or control ⟨the Parliament Act of 1911, which made our House of Lords less able to thwart or ~ the purposes of the House of Commons —Ernest Barker⟩ **b :** to slack or ease off and then belay again (as a purchase or rope) **:** STOPPER ⟨~ a cable when it's running out⟩ **7 a** *obs* **:** DRIVE ⟨~ thy fiery steeds —Shak.⟩ **b :** to hold in restraint **:** CONTROL **:** act as a check, curb, or counter to ⟨~ for a time the inward sweeping waves of melancholy —Louis Bromfield⟩ **8 a :** to compare with source of information (as an original, another version, a record, or body of data) **:** VERIFY ⟨we ~*ed* our information by looking up meteorological records —V.G. Heiser⟩ ⟨numerous scholars do not ~ quotations, references, or bibliographies —E.S.McCartney⟩ — often used with *with* or *against* **b :** to inspect and ascertain the condition of esp. in order to determine that the condition is satisfactory **:** find out about **:** investigate and ensure accuracy, authenticity, reliability, safety, or satisfactory performance of ⟨the applicant must be ~*ed*, much as a bank ~*s* the credit rating of a would-be borrower —Craig Thompson⟩ ⟨incoming fishing boats were ~*ed* for radiation —*Time*⟩ ⟨I ~*ed* the ship out, testing the engine at full power —B.T.Guyton⟩ **c :** to note or mark often with a check as examined, verified, present, satisfactory, finished, or in order ⟨~ an inventory list⟩ — often used with *off* ⟨~ off the names of men reporting⟩ **9 a :** to consign for shipment typically as a service extended to the holder of a passenger ticket ⟨~ the trunk at the station⟩ **b :** to ship or accept for shipment under such a consignment arrangement ⟨the agent ~*ed* our baggage through⟩ **10 a** [ME *cheken*, fr. *chek* (square)] **:** to mark into squares **:** mark with a pattern of crossing lines **:** CHECKER ⟨~ the cloth⟩ **b :** to mark (ground) to facilitate planting in squares ⟨~ the field with a marker⟩ **11** [²*check* (token)] **a :** to leave in safekeeping typically with receipt of a check or token indicating ownership ⟨~ your hat and coat at the theater⟩ **b :** to accept for safekeeping under such an arrangement ⟨working in a nightclub ~*ing* hats⟩ **12** [²*check* (crack)] **:** to make checks or chinks in **:** cause to crack ⟨the sun ~*s* timber⟩ **13** [²*check* (draft)] **:** to use checks to withdraw or pay over (money held in a bank) — usu. used with *out* ⟨~ out over a thousand dollars⟩ ~ *vi* **1** *obs* **:** to come into jarring conflict **:** CLASH ⟨heat ~*ing* against cold⟩ **2** *falconry* **:** to turn when in pursuit of proper game and fly after inferior game — used with *at* **3** *obs* **:** to take offense **:** become offended **4 a** *of a dog* **:** to stop in a chase esp. when scent is lost **b :** to halt suddenly **:** pause in one's procedure often through caution, uncertainty, or fear **:** STOP ⟨she ~*ed* for a moment in the dance and missed a step —Monica Ewer⟩ ⟨the train ~*ed* with a jolt —B.A.Williams⟩ **5 :** to prevent or hinder (as by a pad, cup, or ring) the escape of gas in a gun **6 a :** to investigate and make sure about conditions or circumstances **:** obtain confirmation or substantiation ⟨~*ing* on her passengers' safety belts —E.K.Gann⟩ ⟨he ~*ed* to be sure the *Savo's* deck was ready —J.A.Michener⟩ **b :** to correspond often detail for detail **:** AGREE, CONCUR, TALLY ⟨the description ~*s* with the photograph⟩ **7 :** to draw a check (as upon a bank or banker) **8** *poker* **a :** to bet one chip of lowest value in games in which one must bet or drop in each turn **b :** to announce one's intention of postponing his right to bet with privilege of betting later in games in which this is permitted **9 :** CRACK, SPLIT: **a :** to crack open (as of wood in drying or as biscuits in cooling) **b :** to develop small cracks (as of varnish or eggs) **10 a :** to check off or tally items in a list or group esp. of prices **b :** to place a check beside items in tallying, listing, or otherwise accounting for them **syn** see ARREST, RESTRAIN — **check into :** to check in at ⟨*check into* a hotel⟩ — **check on :** to examine or inspect to discover the condition of **:** find the facts about

⁴check \"\ *adj* [in sense 1, fr. ²*check* (square); in sense 2 & 3, fr. ²&³*check*] **1 :** marked with checks **:** showing a check pattern **:** CHECKED, CHECKERED **2 :** serving to check, stop, baffle, or regulate ⟨a ~ valve⟩ **3 :** serving as a control **:** affording a likely means of verifying, correcting, codifying, or measuring ⟨~ areas in soils research projects⟩

⁵check \"\ *interj* [²*check* (mark)] — used to express assent or agreement

check·a·ble \'chekəbəl\ *adj* **1 :** capable of being checked ⟨a ~ statement⟩ **2 :** suitable for being checked on a passenger ticket ⟨~ baggage⟩

check·age \-ij\ *n* -s **1 :** act of checking **2 :** items or amount checked

checkback \'=,=\ *n* -s **:** a check on or verification of something already completed, once figured, or presumably accounted for; *esp* **:** a check of this kind that goes over the matter in reverse order

check beam *n* **:** a radio beam for use of pilots in checking exact position preparatory to landing airplanes

check binding *n* [²*check* (draft); fr. its use in commercial checkbooks] **:** a simple and inexpensive style of bookbinding featuring paper-covered board sides with edges trimmed flush

checkbite \'=,=\ *n* -s [³*check* + *bite*; fr. its function of checking or testing] **1 a :** an act of biting into a sheet of wax or other material to record the relation between the opposing surfaces of upper and lower teeth **b :** the record obtained **2 :** wax or other material for checkbites

check block *n* **:** a delaying block in football

checkbook \'=,=\ *n* -s **1 :** a book containing items by which other items are checked or verified (as a book with a bank's record of checks issued to customers) **2 :** a book containing blank checks on a bank

checkbook money *n* **:** demand bank deposits subject to check

check certifier *n* **:** a machine used in banking that certifies checks by printing on them a form of endorsement

check collar *n* [³*check*] **:** a collar that chokes when pulled upon and that is used in breaking horses or training dogs

check dam *n* **:** an often improvised barrier in a channel to retard the flow of water esp. for controlling soil erosion

check damper *n* **:** DAMPER 1a

checked *adj* [fr. past part. of ³*check*] **1 :** consisting of, provided with, or subject to a check or checks **:** CHECKERED **2** *phonetics* **a** *of a syllable* **:** ended by a consonant **b** *of a vowel* **:** standing in such a syllable — opposed to *free* **syn** see VARIEGATED

¹check·er \'chekə(r)\ *n* -s *often attrib* [ME *cheker*, fr. OF *eschequier* chessboard, fr. *eschec* check in the game of chess + *-ier* -er — more at CHECK] **1** *archaic* **:** CHESSBOARD **2** *obs* **:** TREASURY, EXCHEQUER **3 :** a square, other rectangle, mark, or spot resembling checkerboard markings ⟨an aerial view of the country showing ~*s* of green and brown⟩ **4** [so called fr. the checkered appearance of the fruit] **:** the fruit of the service tree **5 a :** a European service tree (*Sorbus domestica*) **b :** a wild service tree (*S. torminalis*) **6** *also* **checkerman** [back-formation fr. *checkers*] **:** one of a set of disks used in the game of checkers **7 checkers** *pl* **:** CHECKERWORK 3 **8** *slang* **:** the fit thing **:** the most appropriate condition — used with *the*

²checker \"\ *vt* **checkered; checkered; checkering** \-k(ə)riŋ\ **checkers** [ME *chekeren*, fr. *cheker* chessboard — more at CHECKER] **1 a :** to variegate with different colors or shades typically with a small square or diamond pattern throughout ⟨his face ~*ed* by the shadow of the grating —William Faulkner⟩ **b :** to vary with differing or contrasting elements or situations (as alternating prosperity and hardship) ⟨life's ~*ed* scene of joy and sorrow —Sir Walter Scott⟩ ⟨pride ~*ed* by many painful feelings —T.B.Macaulay⟩ **2 a :** to mark into different colored squares, diamonds, or more or less rectangular figures ⟨farm lands that are ~*ed* with dense tracts of timber —*Amer. Guide Series: Mich.*⟩ **b :** to mark into squares irrespective of color; *esp* **:** to lay out (land) in checks or squares before planting **c :** to intersperse in a fashion suggestive of squares on a chessboard ⟨~ veteran units in the ranks of an inexperienced army⟩ **3 :** to ornament with a pattern of diamond-shaped projections by intersecting grooves ⟨a ~*ed* rifle stock⟩

³checker \"\ *n* -s [³*check* + *-er*] **:** one that checks: as **a :** one that marks, counts, or tallies ⟨a freight ~ in a shipping house⟩ **b :** one that examines materials or products for completeness and conformity to standards, checks data or articles against records for verification, or observes and records the presence or condition of things for purposes of comparison and administration **c :** one that checks articles of personal property for the patrons of an establishment **d :** one that totals purchases and usu. accepts payment (as in a supermarket) **:** CASHIER

checkerbelly \'=,==\ *or* **checkerbreast** *n, in California* **:** WHITE-FRONTED GOOSE

checkerberry \'==,==\ *n* [*checker* (wild service tree) + *berry*] **1 :** any of several reddish berries: as **a :** the spicy red berry-like fruit of a wintergreen (*Gaultheria procumbens*) **b :** PARTRIDGEBERRY 2 **2 :** a plant producing checkerberries

checkerbloom \'==,=\ *n* [prob. fr. ¹*checker* + *bloom*] **:** a perennial purple-flowered mallow (*Sidalcea malvaeflora*) that occurs wild in the western U.S. and is also cultivated

1checkerboard \R -kə(r),b-, -R -kə,b-\ *n* [1*checker* + *board*] **1 :** a board used in checkers, chess, and other games with a typical pattern of 64 squares in 2 alternating colors arranged in 8 rows of 8 squares each **2 :** a pattern or arrangement like a checkerboard ⟨a ~ of cultivated fields, pasture lands and wooded tracts —*Amer. Guide Series: Texas*⟩

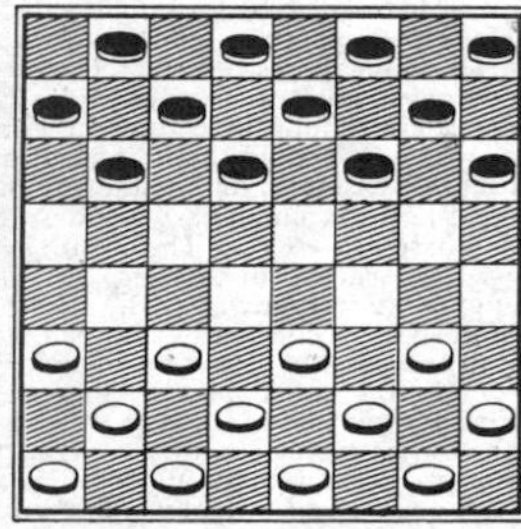
checkerboard with checkers arranged as at the beginning of a game

2checkerboard \"\ *vt* -ED/-ING/-S **:** to arrange, mark, line, or split up into a checkerboard pattern ⟨with fields and forests ~*ed* around —*Amer. Guide Series: Ark.*⟩; *specif* **:** to purchase or lease (scattered parcels of land) in acquiring oil rights in a given area ⟨the company's holdings are ~*ed* over the prospective oil territory⟩
checker-brick \ˈ=,=\ *n* **:** CHECKERWORK 3; *also* **:** the material composing it or an individual brick in it
checkered *adj, sometimes* -ER/-EST **1 :** marked by alternating squares of different colors, shades, or materials in checkerboard fashion **:** showing a pattern of alternating rectangles differing in color or shade ⟨hills ~ with pastures among small forests —Sinclair Lewis⟩ **2 :** marked by alternation, contrast, vicissitude, or diversity esp. of fortune ⟨a man with a ~ business career, but who survived all storms —George Santayana⟩ **3 :** provided with checkerwork **syn** see VARIEGATED
checkered adder *n* **:** MILK SNAKE
checkered lily *or* **checkered daffodil** *n* **:** a plant of the genus *Fritillaria; esp* **:** GUINEA-HEN FLOWER
checkering *pres part of* CHECKER
check·er·ist \ˈchekərəst\ *n* -S **:** a checker player or enthusiast
check·er·man \-mən\ *n, pl* **checkermen :** 1CHECKER 6
checker roll *n* [ME *chekerrolle*, fr. *cheker* + *rolle* — more at CHECKER, ROLL] *obs* **:** a list of persons (as of those to be paid from the royal exchequer)
check·ers \ˈchekə(r)z\ *n pl but sing in constr* [pl. of 1*checker* (chessboard)] **:** a game played on a checkerboard by two players each having 12 men that move diagonally forward one square at a time or backward as well if crowned, the object being to capture or block all the opponent's men
checkerspot \ˈ==,=\ *or* **checkerspot butterfly** *n* **:** CHALCEDON
checker-up \ˈ==ˈ=\ *n* -S [3*checker* + *up*] **:** one that checks up
checkerwise \ˈ==,=\ *adv* **:** in the form or pattern of a checkerboard **:** in alternating squares
checkerwork \ˈ==,=\ *n* **1 :** work with a checkered pattern **:** work marked by checks **:** checkered design ⟨a ~ of light and shadow⟩ **2 :** sequence of changing fortune **:** VICISSITUDE ⟨the ~ of our lives⟩ **3 :** a structure of firebrick (as in a regenerative furnace) built so that the bricks alternate with open spaces permitting the passage of gases which give heat to or receive heat from the firebrick
check·hook \ˈche,ku̇k, -ek,hu̇k\ *n* [3*check*] **:** a hook on the saddle of a harness over which a checkrein is looped
check in *vi* **:** to register esp. at a hotel **:** show or report one's presence or arrival by satisfying requisite forms ⟨*check in* at a convention⟩ ⟨*check in* for a certain flight⟩ **~** *vt* **:** to make a record of **:** REGISTER ⟨records were *checked in* and verified⟩
check-in \ˈ=,=\ *n* -S [*check in*] **:** an act, instance, or occasion of checking in
checking *pres part of* CHECK
checking account *n* **:** an account in a bank against which the depositor can draw checks without giving notice or presenting a passbook — distinguished from *savings account*
check key *n* [4*check;* fr. its function of hindering entry] *Brit* **:** LATCHKEY
checkle *vi* -ED/-ING/-S [prob. imit.] *obs* **:** to laugh violently or hysterically
check·less \ˈchekləs\ *adj* **:** being without a check
check ligament *n* [4*check*] **:** either of a pair of strong fibrous bands passing upward and outward from the upper part of the odontoid process to the inner side of the corresponding occipital condyle and limiting the rotation of the head
checkline \ˈ=,=\ *n* [4*check* + *line*] **:** a hawser made fast on a dock and checked on a ship's bitts and used when coming alongside a wharf for taking off way or snubbing toward the wharf
checklist \ˈ=,=\ *n* [4*check* + *list*] **:** a list intended for ready checking and reference **:** INVENTORY, CATALOG; *often* **:** a complete list ⟨a ~ of voters' names⟩ ⟨a ~ of editions of an author⟩ ⟨a ~ of reptiles of the island⟩
check lock *n* [4*check*] **:** a small lock for checking or securing a large lock (as by closing its keyhole)
check mark *n* [4*check*] **:** a mark indicating that a thing has been checked, noted, examined, or approved
1check·mate \ˈchek,māt\ *interj* [ME *chekmate*, fr. MF *eschec mat*, fr. Ar *shāh māt*, fr. Per, lit., the king is left unable to escape, fr. *shāh* king + *māt* left, perplexed, fr. *māndan* to remain, fr. MPer, fr. OPer *man-*; akin to Av *man-* to remain — more at CHECK, MANSION] — used in chess to tell an opponent that his king has been checkmated
2checkmate \", *usu* -ād+V\ *vt* -ED/-ING/-S [ME *chekmaten*, fr. *chekmate*, n.] **1 :** to arrest, check, thwart, or counter completely ⟨for several centuries Britain *checkmated* the rise of rival powers on the continent of Europe by a balance-of-power policy —H.W.Baldwin⟩ **2 :** to check (a chess opponent's king) so that escape from or capture of the attacking piece is impossible
3checkmate \"\ *n* -S [ME *chekmate*, fr. *chekmate*, interj.] **1 a :** the act of checkmating **b :** the situation of a checkmated king — called also *mate* **2 :** a complete check **:** an utter defeat **:** effective thwarting or countering ⟨to give ~ to an old adversary⟩
check nut *n* [4*check*] **:** LOCK NUT
check off *vt* **1 :** to check or mark as noted **:** tick off **:** note item by item **2 :** to eliminate from further consideration ⟨robbery was *checked off* as a motive⟩ **3 :** to handle by the checkoff ⟨*check off* each miner's dues⟩
checkoff \ˈ=,=\ *n, often attrib* [*check off*] **:** an authorized withholding of union dues, fees, fines, and assessments from the wages of union members and a turning of such withheld money over to the union
check out *vi* **1 :** to satisfy requisite forms in departing ⟨*check out* of a hotel⟩ ⟨*check out* of an office⟩ **2** *slang* **:** DIE ⟨really *checked out* the hard way —Charles Burgess⟩ **3 :** to become substantiated or verified **:** ACCORD ⟨his story *checked out* with the facts⟩ **4 :** to satisfy requirements **:** pass a competency test **:** QUALIFY ⟨the trainee *checked out* all right on his first flight⟩ **~** *vt* **1 :** to satisfy all requirements in taking away (as in borrowing a library book or withdrawing money from a bank account) ⟨he *checked out* two books from the library⟩ ⟨would deposit sufficient cash in the bank to cover the premium, and then *check it out* —Mary R. Rinehart⟩ **2 :** to submit to examination **:** verify, substantiate, or gain approval for ⟨an electronics man assigned to *check out* carefully the new plane's radio and radar system⟩ ⟨all . . . testimony which could be *checked out* has turned out to be correct —Arthur Schlesinger b.1917⟩ ⟨*checked out* his ideas with an expert⟩ **3 :** to itemize and reckon up the total cost of and receive payment for (outgoing merchandise or services) esp. in a self-service store ⟨*checking out* groceries in a supermarket⟩ ⟨employed in *checking out* cleaned suits in a dry-cleaning establishment⟩
check-out \ˈ=,=\ *n* -S [*check out*] **1 a :** the completion of the usu. fixed procedure or requirements (as the paying of one's bill) in relinquishing or vacating a hotel room **b :** the time at which a hotel guest must relinquish his room or be charged for retaining it ⟨*check-out* is at 12 noon⟩ **2 a :** a satisfactory performance in a competency test **b :** itemization and receiving of amounts due ⟨taking care of *check-outs* in the supermarket⟩ ⟨a *check-out* counter in a self-service department store⟩
check over *vt* **:** EXAMINE, INVESTIGATE
check-over \ˈ=,==\ *n* -S [*check over*] **:** EXAMINATION, INSPECTION, INVESTIGATION
check paper *n* [2*check*] **:** a paper treated with chemicals that make alteration in writing very difficult
check passer *n* [2*check* (draft)] **:** one that passes worthless checks
check pinochle *n* [2*check*] **:** partnership pinochle in which, after the play of each hand, settlement is made in chips for each particular scoring feature (as melds and bids that are fulfilled)
checkpoint \ˈ=,=\ *n* [4*check* + *point*] **1 :** a point at which vehicular traffic is halted for examination, inspection, or clearance ⟨allowing Allied traffic to move through Russian ~*s* —*N.Y.Times*⟩ **2 :** a geographical feature used by a flier to determine his location ⟨he glanced at the terrain below, looking for a ~ —Walt Sheldon⟩
check protector *n* [2*check* (draft)] **:** CHECKWRITER
check rail *n* [4*check* + *rail;* prob. fr. its hindering the entrance of rain or snow] **:** MEETING RAIL
check rate *n* [2*check* (draft)] **:** the rate at which sight drafts payable in foreign currency are bought and sold **:** the basic quotation of foreign exchanges at a particular time
1checkrein \ˈ=,=\ *n* [4*check* + *rein*] **1 a :** a short rein looped over the checkhook to hold a horse's head up or back — called also *bearing rein;* see HARNESS illustration **b :** a branch rein connecting the driving rein of one horse of a span or pair with the bit of the other horse **2 :** measures calculated to check or govern **:** CONTROL ⟨he held a tight administrative ~ upon expenditures —*Current Biog.*⟩ ⟨new import controls and other ~*s* seem to have worked . . . overseas trade into at least a temporarily favorable balance —*Newsweek*⟩
2checkrein \"\ *vt* **:** hold in check **:** CONTROL ⟨civilian authority ~*ing* the military⟩
checkroll \ˈ=,=\ *n* [ME *chekrolle*, prob. alter. of *chekerrolle* — more at CHECKER ROLL] **1** *archaic* **:** CHECKER ROLL **2** *obs* **:** a list of household servants **3 :** MUSTER ROLL, CHECKLIST
check roller *n* [2*check* (crack)] **:** a tool used in graining for imitating the cracks of weathered wood
checkroom \ˈ=,=\ *n* [3*check* (to deposit)] **:** a room at which baggage, parcels, clothing, or other personal articles are checked
1checkrow \ˈ=,=\ *n* [2*check* (square) + *row*] **:** one of a series of rows (as of corn) dividing land into squares to permit cultivation both between and across the rows
2checkrow \"\ *vt* **:** to plant or set in checkrows
check·row·er \-ō(ə)r\ *n* **:** a device in a corn-planting machine for dropping the seed so that the hills will lie in checkrows
checks *pres 3d sing of* CHECK, *pl of* CHECK
check sheet *n* **:** a form prepared to facilitate ready checking off or marking
check side *n* [2*check*] *Brit* **:** REVERSE ENGLISH 1
checkstones \ˈ=,=\ *n pl but usu sing in constr* [perh. fr. *check* (short for *checker*)] *Brit* **:** a children's game like jackstones usu. played with pebbles
check stopper *n* [4*check*] **:** one of a series of light cables that are fastened to a heavier cable (as an anchor cable) and are designed to check a ship's speed esp. during launching by holding for a moment before breaking as the heavier main cable runs out
checkstrap \ˈ=,=\ *n* [4*check*] **:** a strap designed to check, control, or secure: as **a :** a helmet fastening consisting of a strap passing under the chin **b :** a leather or composition strap for checking the motion of the picker stick in a loom
check system *n* [2*check*] **:** irrigation of checks
check up *vb* **:** EXAMINE, INSPECT, TEST, INVESTIGATE ⟨the police became suspicious and *checked up*⟩ ⟨*check up* some doubtful points⟩ — often used with *on* ⟨*check up* on his alibi⟩
checkup \ˈ=,=\ *n* -S [*check up*] **:** act of checking up **:** EXAMINATION, INSPECTION, VERIFICATION ⟨a ~ is made of the physical condition of every child —*School & Society*⟩; *esp* **:** a general physical examination ⟨went to the hospital every year for a ~⟩
checkup man *n* **:** an editor who examines illustration layouts to detect and remedy inaccuracies of detail or color
check valve *n* [4*check*] **:** a valve that permits flow in one direction but prevents a return flow
check viewer *n* [4*check*] **:** one that inspects leased portions of mines to see that all agreements and safety precautions are observed
check washer *n* [4*check*] **:** LOCK WASHER
check weave *n* [2*check* (pattern)] **:** a simple weave in basketry or rushwork in which one cane strip or rush is woven alternately under and over the parallel canes or rushes at right angles to it
checkweigher \ˈ=,==\ *or* **checkweighman** \ˈ=,==\ *n* [4*check* + *weigher* or *weighman*] **:** one that checks weight; *specif* **:** one employed by miners or unions to check weighing of coal or ore by a company weighmaster
checkwork \ˈ=,=\ *n* [2*check* (pattern) + *work*] **:** CHECKERWORK
checkwriter \ˈ=,==\ *n* [2*check* (draft)] **:** a device (as a machine) that imprints figures or amounts on the faces of bank checks or drafts in such a way (as by perforation or embossing) as to prevent fraud by alteration or erasure
checky *also* **chequ·ey** *or* **chequy** \ˈchekē\ *adj, usu* -ER/-EST [modif. of MF *eschequé*, past part. of *eschequer* to mark with checks, fr. *eschec* check — more at CHECK] **1 :** CHECKERED **2** *heraldry* **:** divided into usu. equilateral rectangles of alternate tinctures
1ched·dar \ˈchedə(r)\ *or* **cheddar cheese** *n* -S *often cap Cheddar* [fr. *Cheddar*, England, where it was first made] **:** a hard pressed cheese of smooth texture widely made esp. in America as standard factory cheese — called also *American cheddar, American cheese, store cheese*
2cheddar \"\ *vt* -ED/-ING/-S **:** to pile and repile (slices of curd) so as to expel any remaining free whey in cheddar-making
cheddar pink *n, usu cap C* [fr. *Cheddar*, England] **:** a European pink (*Dianthus gratianopolitanus*) with pale rose-colored flowers
chedd·ite \ˈshed,īt, chˈ-\ *n* -S [*Chedde*, town in Haute-Savoie, France, where it was first made + E *-ite*] **:** a blasting explosive consisting essentially of a mixture of a chlorate or perchlorate (as of potassium) with an aromatic nitro compound (as nitronaphthalene) and usu. a fatty substance (as castor oil)
cheder *also* **chedar** *n, pl* **chadarim** *also* **cheders** *or* **chedars** |*var of* HEDER
chee·cha \ˈchēchə\ *n* -S [native name in Ceylon] **:** a small Ceylonese lizard (*Hemidactylus frenatus*) of the family Gekkonidae found about houses
chee·cha·ko *or* **chee·cha·co** *or* **che·cha·ko** \chēˈchä(,)kō\ *or* **che·cha·qua** \-äkə\ *n* -S [Chinook Jargon *chee chahco*, fr. Chinook *t'shi* new + Nootka *chako* to come] **:** a tenderfoot in Alaska or the Pacific northwest
chee-chee \ˈchē(,)chē\ *n* -S [prob. fr. Hindi *chī-chī* fie!, lit., dirt] **:** a Eurasian half-caste — usu. taken to be offensive
1cheek \ˈchēk\ *n* -S [ME *cheke* jawbone, cheek, fr. OE *cēace;* akin to OFris *ziāke* jawbone, MLG *kāke*, OE *acēocian* to suffocate, strangle, and perh. to OE *cēowan* to chew — more at CHEW] **1 a :** the fleshy wall or side of the mouth in man and mammals **:** the side of the face below the eye and above and to the side of the mouth **b :** the lateral aspect of the head of a lower vertebrate or an invertebrate (as an insect) **:** GENA **c :** the portion of a hide corresponding to the cheek of the animal — see HIDE illustration **d :** the lateral part of the cephalic shield of a trilobite **2 :** a lateral side of any mass, structure, or opening: as **a :** either of the side posts of a door or gate **b :** a sidepiece around the eye of the head of a pike, hammer, or pick by which it is secured to the staff or handle **c :** a sidepiece on a mast, supporting a crosstree **d :** one of two laterally paired parts of a mechanism or structure ⟨the ~*s* of a vise⟩ ⟨the ~ of a mortise⟩ ⟨the ~ of a pulley block⟩ **e :** a wall of a mineral vein **f :** one of the vertical side faces of a dormer window **g :** a middle part of a foundry flask **3 a** *of a bridle* **:** CHEEK STRAP **b** *of a bit* **:** CHEEKPIECE **4 :** the shoulder of an artificial fly — see FLY illustration **5 :** BUTTOCK 1 **6 :** insolent boldness and flaunted self-assurance in speech or action **:** IMPUDENCE ⟨he has plenty of ~⟩ **syn** see TEMERITY — **cheek by jowl :** with cheeks close together **:** in close proximity or intimate relationship ⟨people who live *cheek by jowl* and breathe the same air —Virginia Woolf⟩
2cheek \"\ *vt* -ED/-ING/-S **1** *obs* **:** to form a side to **2 :** to place in or against the cheek **3 a :** to speak impudently or saucily to **b :** TEASE
cheekbone \ˈ=ˌ=\ *n* **:** the prominence below the eye that is formed by the zygomatic bone; *also* **:** ZYGOMATIC BONE
cheek·er \-kə(r)\ *n* -S [1*cheek* + *-er*] **:** a slaughterhouse worker who cuts loosened meat from hog heads and sometimes also removes tongue and brain
cheek·i·ly \-ələ̄, -li\ *adv* **:** IMPUDENTLY, BOLDLY
cheek·i·ness \-kēnəs, -in-\ *n* -ES **:** insolence or impudence of speech or behavior
cheek knee *n* **:** one of the knees worked horizontally above and below the hawseholes in the angle of the bow and cutwater of a ship
cheek·less \ˈchēkləs\ *adj* **:** having no cheek
cheekpiece \ˈ=,=\ *n* **:** a piece or part forming, crossing, or covering a cheek: as **a** (1) *of a bridle* **:** CHEEK STRAP (2) *of a bit* **:** either of the sidepieces at the ends of the mouthpiece **b :** the portion of the stock of certain firearms that is specially constructed to offer a convenient rest for the firer's cheek
cheek pouch *n* **:** a saclike dilatation of the cheeks of certain monkeys and rodents used for holding food
cheek strap *n* **:** either of those straps of a bridle that pass down the sides of the horse's head connecting the crownpiece with the bit or noseband — called also *cheekpiece;* see BRIDLE illustration
cheek tooth *n* **:** 1MOLAR
cheeky \ˈchēkē, -i\ *adj* -ER/-EST **1 :** having or showing cheek **:** BRAZENFACED, IMPUDENT **2 :** having well-developed cheeks — used esp. of a bulldog
chee·ny *or* **chee·ney** \ˈchēni, -āni\ *dial Brit var of* 1CHINA 1
1cheep \ˈchēp\ *vb* -ED/-ING/-S [imit.] *vi* **1 :** to utter faint shrill sounds esp. of a young bird **:** CHIRP, PEEP **:** SQUEAK ⟨a mouse ~*ed*⟩ **2 :** to make a small sound **:** utter a word — often used with negative ⟨he didn't even ~⟩ **~** *vt* **:** CHIRP
2cheep \"\ *n* -S **1 :** a feeble shrill sound (as by a young bird or mouse) **:** CHIRP, PEEP, SQUEAK **2 :** HINT, WORD, SOUND — usu. used with negative ⟨not a ~ out of him⟩
cheep·er \-pə(r)\ *n* -S **:** one that cheeps: as **a :** a young partridge, grouse, or quail **b** *in England* **:** MEADOW PIPIT
cheepy \-pē\ *adj* -ER/-EST **:** inclined to cheep
1cheer \ˈchi(ə)r, -iə\ *n* -S [ME *chere* face, welcome, cheer, fr. OF *chiere, chere* face, perh. fr. LL *cara* head, fr. Gk *kara* head, face — more at CEREBRAL] **1 a** *obs* **:** FACE **b** *archaic* **:** facial expression ⟨meek and mild of ~ —Edmund Spenser⟩ **2 :** state of mind or heart **:** FEELING, SPIRIT ⟨be of good ~ —Mt 9:2(AV)⟩ **3 :** lightness of mind and feeling **:** GAIETY ⟨the wives of the officers came to the camp, and these brave women gave of their ~ to its dreary life —H.E.Scudder⟩ **4 :** hospitable entertainment **:** WELCOME **5 :** something that is provided for entertainment esp. at table **:** food and drink prepared for a feast **:** FARE ⟨the fewer the better ~⟩ **6 :** something that gladdens ⟨words of ~⟩ **7 a :** a shout or acclamation expressing enthusiasm, applause, favor, encouragement ⟨~*s* from the audience⟩ **b :** a set form of words for this purpose ⟨the college ~⟩
2cheer \"\ *vb* -ED/-ING/-S [ME *cheren*, fr. *chere*, n.] *vt* **1 a :** to give new hope to **:** lift from discouragement, dejection, or sadness to a more happy state **:** SOLACE, COMFORT ⟨and through all Europe ~ desponding men with new-born hope —William Wordsworth⟩ **b :** to instill with gladness **:** make glad or cause to be happy with or as if with gaiety or festivity ⟨a fandango usually ~*ed* the weary legislators . . . after strenuous hours of deliberation —*Amer. Guide Series: Calif.*⟩ **2** *obs* **:** to supply with good cheer **:** FEAST **3 :** COMFORT, INSPIRIT, INVIGORATE ⟨food ~*s*⟩ ⟨cups that ~ but not inebriate —William Cowper⟩ **4 :** to instill with courage, good spirits, and optimism and to inspire to continue or persevere by or as if by cheers, applause, commendation, aid ⟨~ the survivors of the attack⟩ — often used with *on* ⟨~ on the team⟩ **5 :** to salute or applaud with shouts ⟨the contest winner was ~*ed* as she came in sight⟩ **~** *vi* **1** *obs* **:** to be mentally or emotionally disposed ⟨how *cheer'st* thou, Jessica —Shak.⟩ **2 :** to grow or be cheerful **:** make merry **:** become glad or joyous **:** REJOICE **:** take or pluck up courage — used now only with *up*, often imperatively **3 :** to utter a shout of applause or triumph ⟨what is there to ~ about⟩ **syn** see ENCOURAGE
3cheer \"\ *dial var of* CHAIR
4cheer \"\ *or* **cheer pheasant** *n* -S [Garhwali *chīr*, perh. of imit. origin] **:** a buff or grayish pheasant (*Catreus wallichi*) of the lower Himalayan mountains distinguished by a bare red eye patch and a long narrow dark-barred tail
cheer·er \ˈchirə(r)\ *n* -S *dial Brit* **:** a cheering drink or cup (as of spirits)
cheer·ful \ˈchirfəl, -iəf-\ *adj, sometimes* **cheerfuller** \-f(ə)lə(r)\ *sometimes* **cheerfullest** \-f(ə)ləst\ [ME *cherefull*, fr. *chere* + *-full* -ful] **1 :** marked by cheer or by spontaneous good spirits arising from a carefree sanguine attitude and a hearty bright lively disposition ⟨the incessant warble of the red-eyed vireo, ~ . . . as the merry whistle of a schoolboy —John Burroughs⟩ **2 :** conducive to cheer **:** likely to brighten, encourage, and dispel gloom or worry ⟨her flat was always . . . ~, gay with flowers, and the chintzes in the drawing room were bright and pretty —W.S.Maugham⟩ **syn** see GLAD
cheer·ful·ize \-fə,līz\ *vt* -ED/-ING/-S **:** to render cheerful
cheer·ful·ly \-f(ə)lē, -li\ *adv* **:** in a cheerful manner **:** GLADLY
cheer·ful·ness \-fəlnəs\ *n* -ES **:** the quality or state of being cheerful
cheer·i·ly \ˈchirəlē, -li\ *adv* **:** in a cheery manner **:** CHEERFULLY
cheer·i·ness \-rēnəs, -rin-\ *n* -ES **:** the quality or state of being cheery
cheer·ing·ly *adv* **:** in a cheering manner
cheering section *n* **:** a section of a grandstand reserved for rooters for one of the contending teams; *also* **:** rooters esp. when led by a cheerleader ⟨the *cheering section* went wild⟩
cheer·io \ˌchi(ə)rēˈō\ *also* **cheero** \ˈchi(ə)(,)rō\ *interj* [*cheery*, 1*cheer* + *-o*] *chiefly Brit* — usu. used as a farewell, sometimes as a greeting or a toast
cheerleader \ˈ=,==\ *n* **:** one that calls for and directs organized cheering (as at a football game) — **cheerleading** \ˈ=,==\ *n*
cheer·less \ˈchirləs, -iəl-\ *adj* **:** lacking anything cheering, comforting, gladdening, or heartening **:** BLEAK, DISPIRITING ⟨there was something ~ and stiff about the room which had always seemed so friendly —W.S.Maugham⟩ **syn** see DISMAL
cheer·less·ly \-slē, -li\ *adv* **:** in a cheerless manner **:** DISMALLY
cheer·less·ness \-snəs\ *n* -ES **:** the quality or state of being cheerless
1cheer·ly \-irlē, -iəlē\ *adj, archaic* **:** GAY, CHEERFUL
2cheerly \"\ *adv* **1 :** with a will **:** CHEERILY, HEARTILY — now used chiefly as a cry of encouragement among sailors **2 :** CHEERFULLY
cheer pine *var of* CHIR PINE
cheers \-i(ə)rz, -iəz\ *interj* [fr. pl. of 1*cheer*] *chiefly Brit* — used as a toast
cheery \ˈchirē, -ri\ *adj* -ER/-EST **:** causing or suggesting lightness of spirits **:** lively in voice, manner, or appearance **:** GAY, UNTROUBLED ⟨his heart belied the ~ flippancy of his tone —Donn Byrne⟩
1cheese \ˈchēz\ *n* -S *often attrib* [ME *chese*, fr. OE *cēse;* akin to OHG & OS *kāsi;* all fr. a prehistoric WGmc word borrowed fr. L *caseus;* akin to OSlav *kvasŭ* sour dough, OE *hwatherian* to foam, ON *hvethnir* milker, Goth *hwatho* foam, Skt *kvathati* he boils] **1 a :** curd that has been separated from whey, consolidated by molding for soft cheese or subjected to pressure for hard cheese, and ripened for use as a food **b :** a cake of this food typically in the shape of a wheel or of a flat cylinder **c :** CHEDDAR **2 :** something shaped like a cheese: as **a :** a mass of pomace in a cider press **b :** a package in which yarn is commonly wound **c :** a batch of raw fiber stock as it leaves the dyeing kettle **d :** SKITTLE BALL **e :** a compressed mass of tobacco to be cut up by machine into smoking or chewing tobacco **3 :** something like cheese in texture (as soft wood or paraffin wax saturated with oil) or odor — often used as a generalized term of disapproval ⟨surveys, generally speaking, are the ~ —*Atlantic Bull.*⟩ ⟨a lawyer simply has to convince the poor ~*s* on the jury —Sinclair Lewis⟩ **4 :** DWARF MALLOW; *also* **:** the flat fruits of the dwarf mallow or of the cheeseflower — usu. used in pl.
2cheese \"\ *vt* -ED/-ING/-S **1 :** to form (a rope end) into a tight neat coil — usu. used with *down* **2 :** to wind (yarn) onto a cheese **:** SPOOL
3cheese \"\ *vt* -ED/-ING/-S [origin unknown] *slang* **:** to leave off **:** STOP — **cheese it 1** *slang* **:** look out **:** be quiet **:** STOP **2** *slang* **:** get out **:** get away **:** VAMOOSE

4**cheese** \"\ *n* -s [perh. fr. Urdu *chīz* thing, fr. Per] **1** *slang* **:** something first-rate ⟨this car is certainly the ~⟩ **2** *slang* **:** someone important **:** BOSS ⟨thought himself a bit of a ~⟩
cheese bolt *n* [1*cheese* + *bolt;* fr. the round flat head] **:** a cheese-head bolt
cheesebox \'=,=\ *n* **1 :** a box or case (as a low cylinder) for holding a cheese **2 :** something shaped like a cylindrical cheesebox (as a gun turret, a tank, or a building)
cheese·burg·er \-,bərgə(r), -bəgə(r), -bəigə(r)\ *n* -s [1*cheese* + *hamburger*] **:** a hamburger with a slice of toasted cheese
cheesecake \'=,=\ *n* **1 :** a dessert made by baking a mixture of cottage cheese, eggs, and sugar or a filling of similar texture in a pastry shell or a mold lined with sweet crumbs **2 a :** photography or photographs (as in advertisements or publicity) featuring the natural curves of shapely female legs, thighs, or trunk, usu. scantily clothed — called also *leg art* **b :** something resembling such cheesecake
cheese cement *n* **:** a kind of casein glue made from cheese or milk curd and used for mending earthenware
cheesecloth \'=,=\ *n* -s **:** a very lightweight unsized cotton fabric loosely woven in plain weave and used orig. in cheese-making and now also for surgical gauze, costumes, curtains, and wrapping for food — compare TOBACCO CLOTH
cheese color *n* **:** ANNATTO 1a
cheese cutter *n* **:** a slicing implement whose cutting edge is a wire stretched on a frame furnished with one or two handles
cheesed off *adj* [prob. fr. past. part. of 3*cheese*] *slang chiefly Brit* **:** extremely discontented **:** very indignant
cheese dream *n* **:** a toasted or sautéed cheese sandwich
cheese-eater \'=,==\ *n, slang* **:** INFORMER, STOOL PIGEON, RAT
cheeseflower \'=,=\ *n* [so called fr. the shape of the fruit] **:** the common tall mallow (*Malva sylvestris*) adventive from Europe in the U.S., Canada, and Mexico
cheese fly *n* **:** a black two-winged fly (*Piophila casei*) that is the adult of the cheese skipper
cheese food *n* **:** cheese (as cheddar) finely ground and mixed with seasoning and other ingredients (as cream, milk solids, preservative agents)
cheese-head \'=¦=\ *or* **cheese-headed** \'=¦==\ *adj, of a screw or bolt* **:** having a raised cylindrical head
cheese hoop *n* **:** a broad usu. wood hoop or cylinder in which the curd is pressed in making cheese
cheese knife *n* **1 :** a large spatula used to break down the curd in making cheese **2 :** a knife with a curved blade for cutting cheese **3 :** CHEESE CUTTER
cheese·lip \'chēz,lip, -,ləp\ *or* **cheese·lep** \-,lep, -,ləp\ *n* -s [ME *cheslypp, cheslep,* fr. OE *cēselybb,* fr. *cēse* cheese + *lybb* medicinal herb, poison, magic; akin to OHG *luppi* sap, poison, magic, ON *lyf* medicinal herb, poison, magic, Goth *lubja*leisei magic, OIr *luib* herb, OE *lēaf* leaf — more at LEAF] **1** *dial Brit* **:** RENNET **2** *dial Brit* **:** the dried stomach of a calf
cheese mite *n* **:** a minute whitish mite (*Acarus siro*) infesting cheese or dried meat and sometimes causing grocer's itch
cheese·par·er \'=,==\ *n* **:** a parsimonious person **:** SKINFLINT
1**cheese·par·ing** \'=,==\ *n* -s **1 :** something saved or valued only by a parsimonious or very needy person **:** a worthless bit **:** an insignificant quantity **2 :** miserly or petty economizing ⟨administrative ~ that could not have plugged up more than a pinhole in France's leaking economy —Ray Alan⟩
2**cheeseparing** \"\ *adj* **:** given to or marked by mean economies and picayune frugality **syn** see STINGY
cheese pitch *n* **:** asphalt in a mass whose surface has dried and formed a skin
cheese press *n* **:** an appliance for pressing cheese curd in a mold or hoop
cheese rennet *n* [so called fr. its use as a milk coagulant] **:** YELLOW BEDSTRAW
chees·ery \'chēz(ə)rē, -ri\ *n* -ES **:** an establishment in which cheese is made
cheeses *pl of* CHEESE, *pres 3d sing of* CHEESE
cheese scoop *n* **:** a pointed spoonlike table implement for scooping out cheese
cheese skipper *or* **cheese hopper** *or* **cheese maggot** *n* **:** the cheese fly larva that lives in cheese, ham, and smoked beef and that can jump several inches
cheese spread *n* **:** a cheese food soft enough to spread
cheese-starter \'=,==\ *n* **:** a culture of lactic acid-producing bacteria used in the preliminary fermentation of milk for cheese production
cheese straw *or* **cheese stick** *n* **:** a narrow strip of puff paste sprinkled with grated cheese before baking
cheese vat *also* **cheese tub** *n* **:** a round vat in which the curd is formed and cut or broken in cheese making
cheese week *n, usu cap C&W, Eastern Church* **:** the week from Monday through Sunday preceding the first day of Lent during which period cheese and eggs may be eaten for the last time before Easter
cheesewood \'=,=\ *n* [so called fr. its yellowish white appearance] **1 :** either of two Australasian timber trees (*Pittosporum bicolor* and *P. undulatum*) — called also *bonewood* **2 :** the hard yellowish wood of either of the cheesewoods
chees·i·ness \'chēzēnəs, -zin-\ *n* -ES **:** the quality or state of being cheesy
cheesing *pres part of* CHEESE
1**cheesy** *also* **chees·ey** \-zē, -zi\ *adj* **cheesier; cheesiest** [ME *chesy,* fr. *chese* + *-y*] **1 a :** resembling or suggesting cheese esp. in consistency or odor **b** *slang* **:** SHABBY, CHEAP ⟨~ comedy⟩ **2 :** CASEOUS
2**cheesy** \"\ *adj* -ER/-EST [4*cheese* + *-y*] *slang* **:** STYLISH
chee·tah *or* **chee·ta** *also* **che·tah** *or* **chi·ta** \'chēd·ə, -ētə\ *n* -s [Hindi *cītā,* fr. Skt *citrakāya* tiger, panther, fr. *citra* variegated, bright, speckled + *kāya* body; akin to Skt *cinoti* he gathers, heaps up — more at -HOOD, POET] **:** a long-legged swift-moving somewhat doglike African and formerly Asiatic cat (*Acinonyx jubatus*) about the size of a small leopard that has a tawny pelt spotted with dark brown or black and blunt nonretractile claws and is often tamed and trained to run down antelopes and other game
cheetal *or* **cheetul** *var of* CHITAL
chewink *var of* CHEWINK
chef \'shef\ *n* -s [F, chief, head — more at CHIEF] **1 :** a chief or head person — now used only in French phrases **2** [F, short for *chef de cuisine* head of the kitchen] **a :** a man skilled in food preparation who has charge of the kitchen and kitchen personnel in a large establishment (as a hotel or restaurant), planning menus, ordering foodstuffs, directing and assisting cooks, preparing special dishes **b :** COOK
chef de ca·bi·net \¦shefdə,kabē'nā\ *n, pl* **chefs de cabinet** \-f(s)d-\ [F, lit., office head] **:** the chief secretary of a French minister or prefect
chef d'é·cole \¦shefdā'kȯl, -ōl\ *n, pl* **chefs d'école** \-f(s)d-\ [F] **:** a leader of a school (as of painters, musicians, writers)
chef de cui·sine \¦shefdəkwē'zēn\ *n, pl* **chefs de cuisine** \-f(s)d-\ [F, lit., kitchen head] **:** CHEF 2a
chef d'oeu·vre \shā'də(r)v(rᵊ), -dōv-, -vrə, (')shef'd-, *F* shedœvr(ᵊ) *or* -v(rə)\ *n, pl* **chefs d'oeuvre** \"\ [F *chef-d'oeuvre,* lit., leading work] **:** a masterpiece esp. in art or literature
cheffonier *var of* CHIFFONIER
che·foo \'jə¦fü\ *adj, usu cap* [fr. *Chefoo,* China] **:** of or from the city of Chefoo, China **:** of the kind or style prevalent in Chefoo
chegoe *or* **chegre** *var of* CHIGOE
che·ha·lis \chə'hāləs\ *n, pl* **chehalis** *or* **chehalises** *usu cap* [fr. *Chehalis,* one of their villages on Grays Harbor, Wash., fr. *Chehalis,* lit., sand] **1 a :** a Salishan people of the Chehalis river valley and Grays Harbor, Washington **b :** a member of such people **2 :** the language of the Chehalis people
cheil- *or* **cheilo-** — see CHIL-
chei·lan·thes \kī'lan(,)thēz\ *n, cap* [NL, fr. *chil-* + *-anthes*] **:** a widely distributed genus of ferns (family Polypodiaceae) having indusia with whitish reflexed margins — see LIP FERN — **chei·lan·thoid** \-,thȯid\ *adj*
cheil·ec·tro·pi·on *also* **chil·ec·tro·pi·on** \,kī,lek'trōpē,än, -,ən\ *n* -s [NL, fr. *chil-* + *ectropion*] **:** an abnormal turning outward of one or both lips
-chei·lia \'kīlēə\ *also* **-chi·lia** \", 'kil-\ *n comb form* -s [NL, fr. Gk *-cheilēs* having (such) lips (fr. *cheilos* lip) + NL *-ia* — more at CHIL-] **:** lip formation (of a specified type) ⟨macro*cheilia*⟩

chei·li·on \'kīlē,än, -,ən\ *n* -s [NL, fr. *chil-* + Gk *-ion* (dim. suffix)] **:** the lateralmost point at the angle of the lips
chei·li·tis *or* **chi·li·tis** \kī'līd·əs\ *n* -ES [NL, fr. *chil-* + *-itis*] **:** inflammation of the lip
chei·lo·dac·tyl·i·dae \,kī(,)lō,dak'tilə,dē\ *n pl, cap* [NL, fr. *Cheilodactylus,* type genus (fr. *chil-* + Gk *daktylos* finger) + *-idae* — more at DACTYL] **:** a family of marine percoid fishes resembling members of the family Serranidae and widely distributed in the southern Pacific — see MORWONG
chei·lo·plas·ty \'kīlō,plastē\ *n* [*chil-* + *-plasty*] **:** plastic surgery to repair lip defects
chei·los·chi·sis \kī'läskəsəs\ *n, pl* **cheiloschi·ses** \-,sēz\ [NL, fr. *chil-* + *-schisis*] **:** HARELIP
chei·lo·sis \kī'lōsəs\ *n, pl* **cheilo·ses** \-ō,sēz\ [NL, fr. *chil-* + *-osis*] **:** an abnormal condition of the lips characterized by scaling of the surface and fissuring in the corners of the mouth
chei·lo·spi·ru·ra \¦kī(,)lō,spī'rürə\ [NL, fr. *chil-* + *Spirura* genus of nematode worms, fr. *spir-* + *-ura*] *syn of* ACUARIA
chei·lo·sto·ma·ta \,kīlə'stōməd·ə\ *n pl, cap* [NL, fr. *chil-* + *-stomata*] **:** a large order of bryozoans (class Gymnolaemata) having the colony erect or encrusting, the zooecia more or less tubular, and the aperture closed by a chitinous operculum when the polypide is retracted
chei·lo·stom·a·tous *or* **chi·lo·stom·a·tous** \¦=¦stäməd·əs, -ōm-\ *adj* [NL *Cheilostomata* + E *-ous*] **:** of or relating to the Cheilostomata
cheir- *or* **cheiro-** — see CHIR-
chei·ran·thus \kī'ran(t)thəs\ *n, cap* [NL, fr. *cheir-* (fr. Ar *khīrī* wallflower) + *-anthus*] **:** a genus of perennial herbs (family Cruciferae) including the true wallflower
-cheiria — see -CHIRIA
chei·ro·ga·le·us \,kīrō'gālēəs\ *n* [NL, fr. *chir-* + Gk *galeē, galē* weasel — more at GALEA] **1** *cap* **:** a genus of small arboreal Malagasy lemurs **2** -ES **:** a lemur of the genus *Cheirogaleus* **3** -ES **:** MOUSE LEMUR
chei·ro·glos·sa \,==='gläsə, -ȯsə\ *n, cap* [NL, fr. *chir-* + *-glossa*] **:** a small genus of epiphytic ferns (family Ophioglossaceae) having palmately divided fronds bearing pendent spikes near their bases
chei·ro·lin \'== ,lən\ *n* -s [ISV *cheir-* (fr. NL *Cheiranthus* genus of herbs, fr. Gk *chir-* + *-anthus*) + *-ol* + *-in;* orig. formed in G] **:** a colorless crystalline sulfone $CH_3SO_2(CH_2)_3$-NCS occurring as a glucoside in seeds of a wallflower (*Cheiranthus cheiri*) and in those of plants of the genus *Erysimum*
cheiromancy *var of* CHIROMANCY
chei·ro·mys \'kīrō,mis\ [NL, fr. *chir-* + *-mys*] *syn of* DAUBENTONIA
cheironomy *var of* CHIRONOMY
chei·ro·pom·pho·lyx \,kīrō'pämfə,liks\ *n* -ES [NL, fr. *chir-* + *pompholyx*] **:** a skin disease characterized by itching vesicles or blebs occurring in groups on the hands or feet
cheiropterophilous *var of* CHIROPTEROPHILOUS
chei·ros·tro·bus \kī'rästrəbəs\ *n, cap* [NL, fr. *chir-* + L *strobus* labdanum] **:** a form genus of sphenopsid fossil plants based on only the strobilus which consists of numerous crowded verticils of sporophylls, each sporophyll being divided in two planes
che·ka \'chā(,)kä\ *n* -s [Russ, fr. *che* + *ka,* names of initial letters of *Chrezvychainaya Kommissiya* extraordinary commission] **:** secret police (as in a Communist-dominated country) having virtually unrestrained power over life and death
che·kho·vi·an \che'kōvēən, -ȯv, -äv-, 'che,kȯfē-\ *adj, usu cap* [Anton Pavlovich *Chekhov* †1904 Russ. writer + E *-ian*] **:** suggestive of the characterization or atmosphere (as of frustration and introspective complexity) in the plays and short stories of the Russian writer Chekhov ⟨a worrier of *Chekhovian* proportions —Herbert Mitgang⟩
che·kist \'chäkəst\ *n* -s [Russ, fr. *cheka* + *-ist*] **:** a member of a cheka
chek·ker \'chekə(r)\ *n* -s [origin unknown] **:** a stringed keyboard instrument of the 14th and 15th centuries
chel- *or* **cheli-** *comb form* [NL, fr. 1*chela*] **:** claw ⟨*chelicera*⟩
1**che·la** \'kēlə\ *n, pl* **che·lae** \-(,)lē\ [NL, modif. of obs. E *chely,* fr. Gk *chēlē* claw] **1 :** the pincerlike organ or claw borne by certain of the limbs of Crustacea and Arachnida **2 :** a somewhat curved sponge spicule with recurved processes at each end
2**che·la** \'chā(,)lä\ *n* -s [Hindi *celā,* fr. Skt *ceṭa, ceṭaka* servant, slave; akin to Pali *ceṭo* servant, boy, Prakrit *ceḍa, cilla* boy] **:** a disciple (as of a mahatma) **:** a follower (as of an occult philosopher or esoteric philosophy)
chel·a·mela \,chelə'melə\ *n, pl* **chelamela** *or* **chelamelas** *usu cap* [Kalapooia] **1 :** a Kalapooian people in western Oregon **2 :** a member of the Chelamela people

chela of a lobster

1**che·late** \'kē,lāt\ *adj* [NL 1*chela* + E *-ate*] **1 :** like or having chelae **2** [Gk *chēlē* hoof, claw + E *-ate*] **a :** relating to, producing, or characterized by a cyclic structure usu. containing five or six atoms in a ring in which a central metallic ion (as bivalent copper or bivalent or trivalent iron) is held in a coordination complex by one or more groups (as citrate or ethylenediamine) each of which can attach itself to the central ion by at least two bonds ⟨a ~ ring⟩ ⟨chlorophyll and hemoglobin are ~ compounds⟩ **b :** relating to or characterized by a cyclic structure (as of the ring formed by salicylaldehyde) resulting from the formation of a hydrogen bond
2**chelate** \"\ *vb* -ED/-ING/-S *vt* **:** to combine with (a metal) so as to form a chelate ring or rings — compare SEQUESTER **~** *vi* **:** to react so as to form a chelate ring or rings
3**chelate** \"\ *n* -s **:** a compound formed by chelation **:** a chelate compound
che·la·tion \kē'lāshən\ *n* -s [2*chelate* + *-ion*] **:** the process of chelating or the quality or state of being chelated ⟨~ of trace metals in nutrient solutions⟩
chel·e·ryth·rine \,kelə'ri,thrēn, kə'lerə,-, -,thrən\ *n* -s [ISV *chelerythr-* (fr. Gk *chelidonion* celandine + *erythros* red) + *-ine;* orig. formed as G *chelerythrin* — more at CELANDINE, RED] **:** a colorless crystalline poisonous alkaloid $C_{21}H_{19}NO_5$ obtained from celandine and other papaveraceous plants and forming yellow salts with a violet fluorescence
che·lic·era \kə'lisərə\ *also* **chel·i·cer** \'keləsər\ *or* **chel·i·cere** \-,si(ə)r\ *n, pl* **chelicer·ae** \-sə,rē\ *also* **chelicers** \-sərz\ *or* **cheliceres** \-,si(ə)rz\ [*chelicera,* NL, modif. of F *chélicère,* fr. *chél-* chel- + *-cère* (fr. Gk *keras* horn); *chelicer, chelicere* fr. F *chélicère* — more at CEREBRAL] **:** one of the anterior pair of appendages of an arachnid prob. derived from antennae, distinguished in scorpions by being short, chelate, and lacking a poison gland, in spiders by terminating in a sharp-pointed tip near which a venom duct opens, and in ticks by being modified into piercing and attachment organs — **che·lic·er·al** \kə'lisərəl\ *adj*
che·lic·er·ata \kə,lisə'rād·ə, -ād·ə\ *n pl, cap* [NL, fr. *chelicera* + *-ata*] *in some classifications* **:** a subphylum or superclass of Arthropoda comprising forms having chelicerate appendages and lacking antennae and including the king crabs and eurypterids, spiders, scorpions, and sea spiders — compare ARACHNIDA, MEROSTOMATA, PYCNOGONIDA
che·lic·er·ate \kə'lisə,rāt, -,rət\ *adj* [NL *chelicera* + E *-ate*] **1 :** provided with chelicerae **2 :** having the form of a chelicera
chel·i·dam·ic acid \¦kelə¦damik-\ *n* [ISV *chelidonic* + *ammonia* + *-ic*] **:** a crystalline acid $C_7H_5NO_6$ prepared from chelidonic acid and ammonia; 4-pyridone-2,6-dicarboxylic acid
chel·i·don·ic acid \¦kelə¦dänik-\ *n* [ISV *chelidonic* (fr. Gk. *chelidonion* celandine + ISV *-ic*) + acid; orig. formed as G *chelidonsäure*] **:** a crystalline acid $C_7H_4O_6$ occurring combined in celandine sap and in white hellebore roots; 4-pyrone-2,6-dicarboxylic acid
chel·i·do·nine \,kelə'dō,nēn, kə'lidᵊn,ēn\ *n* -s [ISV *chelidon-* (fr. Gk *chelidonion* celandine) + *-ine;* orig. formed as F *chélidonine*] **:** a crystalline alkaloid $C_{20}H_{19}NO_5$ found in celandine and other papaveraceous plants
chel·i·do·ni·um \,kelə'dōnēəm\ *n, cap* [NL, fr. Gk *chelidonion* celandine, fr. *chelidonion,* neut. of *chelidonios* of the swallow — more at CELANDINE] **:** a genus of herbs of the family Papaveraceae characterized by brittle stems, yellowish acrid juice, pinnately divided leaves, and small yellow flowers in pedunculate umbels — see CELANDINE

chel·i·fer \'keləfə(r)\ *n, cap* [NL, fr. *chel-* + *-fer*] **:** the genus of the common book scorpion (order Pseudoscorpiones)
chel·i·fer·id·ea \,keləfə'rideə\ [NL, fr. *Chelifer* + *-idea*] *syn of* PSEUDOSCORPIONES
che·lif·er·ous \kə'lifərəs\ *adj* [*chel-* + *-ferous*] **:** bearing a chela or chelae
che·li·form \'kēlə,fȯrm, 'ke-\ *adj* [*chel-* + *-form*] **:** having a movable joint or finger closing against the adjacent segment so as to form a forcepslike organ — used esp. of a crab's claw
Che·lin·ga \chə'liŋgə\ *or* **che·lin·go** \-(,)gō\ *n* -s [Tamil *calaṅku,* perh. fr. Skt *jalaṅga* water-going, fr. *jalaṁ* (nom. & acc. of *jala* water) + *-ga* (akin to *gam* to go, come) — more at COME] **:** a boat of light draft pointed at both ends and used on the Coromandel coast
che·li·ped \'kēlə,ped, 'ke-\ *n* -s [*chel-* + *-ped*] **:** one of the pair of legs that bears the large chelae in decapod crustaceans
chel·le·an *or* **chel·li·an** \'shelēən\ *adj, usu cap* [F *chelléen,* fr. *Chelles,* France + F *-éen* -ean] **1 :** of or relating to Chelles, France **2 :** ABBEVILLIAN
chel·o·di·na \,kelə'dīnə\ *n, cap* [NL, prob. fr. *chelo-* (fr. Gk *chelys* tortoise) + *-dina* (fr. Gk *deinos* terrible) — more at CHELYS, DIRE] **:** a genus of freshwater turtles of Australia including the long-necked turtle — **chel·o·dine** \'kelə,dīn, -,dən\ *adj or n*
cheloid *var of* KELOID
1**che·lo·ne** \ke'lōnē\ *n* [NL, fr. Gk *chelōnē* tortoise] **1** *cap* **:** a small genus of perennial herbs (family Scrophulariaceae) of the eastern U.S. having serrate leaves and large white or purple flowers in nearly sessile spikes **2** -s **:** any plant of the genus *Chelone* — called also *turtlehead*
2**chelone** \"\ [NL, fr. Gk *chelōnē*] *syn of* 2CHELONIA
chel·o·ne·thi \,kelə'nē,thī\ *also* **chel·o·neth·i·da** \-'nethədə\ *or* **chel·o·ne·thid·ea** \-lōnə'thideə\ [*Chelonethi* fr. NL, fr. *chel-* + *-nethi* (fr. Gk *nēthein* to spin); *Chelonethida, Chelonethidea* fr. NL, fr. *chel-* + Gk *nēthein* + NL *-ida, -idea;* akin to Gk *nēn* to spin — more at NEEDLE] *syn of* PSEUDOSCORPIONES
chel·o·ne·thid \,kelə'nēthəd, -eth-\ *n* -s [NL *Chelonethida, Chelonethidea*] **:** PSEUDOSCORPION
1**che·lo·nia** \ke'lōnēə, -nyə\ [NL, fr. Gk *chelōnē* + NL *-ia*] *syn of* TESTUDINATA
2**chelonia** \"\ *n, cap* [NL, fr. Gk *chelōnē* + NL *-ia*] **:** the genus of Cheloniidae comprising the green turtles
1**che·lo·ni·an** \-nēən, -nyən\ *adj* [NL 2*Chelonia* + E *-an*] **:** resembling, having the characteristics of, or being a tortoise or turtle
2**chelonian** \"\ *n* -s **:** TORTOISE, TURTLE
chel·o·nib·ia \,kelə'nibēə\ *n, cap* [NL, fr. *cheloni-* (fr. Gk *chelōnē* tortoise) + *-bia*] **:** a widely distributed genus of turtle barnacles
che·lon·i·dae \kə'länə,dē\ [NL, fr. 2*Chelonia,* type genus + *-idae*] *syn of* CHELONIIDAE
che·lo·ni·id \kə'lōnēəd\ *also* **chel·o·nid** \'kelə,nid, kə'lōnəd\ *n* -s [NL *Cheloniidae, Chelonidae*] **:** one of the Cheloniidae
chel·o·ni·i·dae \,kelə'nīə,dē\ *n pl, cap* [NL, fr. 2*Chelonia,* type genus + *-idae*] **:** a family of large marine turtles including the commercially important green turtle and hawksbill
che·lo·nus \kə'lōnəs\ *n, cap* [NL, fr. Gk *chelōnos* turtle; fr. the shape of the abdomen] **:** a genus of small ichneumon flies (family Braconidae) parasitic on various lepidopterous larvae and introduced in many regions in attempts at biological control of plant-eating larvae
1**chelp** \'chelp\ *vi* -ED/-ING/-S [prob. of imit. origin] **1** *dial Eng* **:** CHIRP **2** *dial Eng* **:** to talk pertly
2**chelp** \"\ *n* -s **1** *dial Eng* **:** the chirp of a young bird **2** *dial Eng* **:** pert talk
chel·sea china \'chelsē-\ *n, usu cap 1st C* [fr. *Chelsea,* England, where it was made] **:** soft-paste porcelain made from about 1745 until 1770
chelsea-der·by ware \-'därbē-, -'dər-\ *n, usu cap C&D* [fr. *Chelsea* and *Derby,* England] **:** soft paste porcelain made at Chelsea or Derby from the taking over of the Chelsea works by Derby in 1770 to their closing in 1784
chel·ten·ham \'chelt(ᵊ)nam\ *n* -s *usu cap* [fr. *Cheltenham,* town in Gloucestershire, England] **:** a large family of printing types orig. designed by Bertram G. Goodhue in 1900
che·lu·ra \kə'lürə\ *n, cap* [NL, fr. *chel-* + *-ura*] **:** a genus of marine amphipod Crustacea that bore into and sometimes destroy timber
che·lus \'kēləs, 'ke-\ *n, cap* [NL, irreg. fr. Gk *chelys* tortoise] **:** a genus of turtles including solely the matamata
che·lya·binsk \chel'yäbənsk\ *adj, usu cap* [fr. *Chelyabinsk,* U.S.S.R.] **:** of or from the city of Chelyabinsk, U.S.S.R. **:** of the kind or style prevalent in Chelyabinsk
che·lyd·i·dae \kə'lidə,dē\ *n pl, cap* [NL, fr. *Chelyd-* (irreg. fr. *Chelys,* type genus) + *-idae*] **:** a family of side-necked freshwater turtles inhabiting So. America and Australasia
chel·y·dra \'kelədrə\ *n, cap* [NL, modif. of Gk *chelydros* amphibious serpent, tortoise] **:** the type genus of Chelydridae comprising the common snapping turtles — **chel·y·droid** \-,drȯid\ *adj*
che·lyd·ri·dae \kə'lidrə,dē\ *n pl, cap* [NL, fr. *Chelydra,* type genus + *-idae*] **:** a family of large powerful freshwater turtles of No. America and Central America including the snapping turtles (sense 1) and the alligator turtle
che·lys \'kēləs, 'ke-\ [NL, fr. Gk, tortoise; akin to OSlav *želŭvĭ* tortoise] *syn of* CHELUS
chem- *or* **chemo-** *or* **chemico-** *also* **chemi-** *or* **chemio-** *comb form* [*chem-* & *chemo-* fr. NL, fr. LGk *chēmeia* alchemy; *chemico-* fr. *chemical; chemi-* & *chemio-* prob. fr. Dan *kemi-,* fr. *kemi* chemistry, fr. LGk *chēmeia* — more at ALCHEMY] **1 :** chemical **:** chemistry ⟨*chemo*smosis⟩ ⟨*chemo*taxis⟩ **2 :** chemically ⟨*chemi*sorb⟩ ⟨*chemio*tropic⟩ **:** chemical and ⟨*chemico*-physical⟩
chem·a·ku·an \¦chemə¦küən\ *or* **chim·a·ku·an** \¦chim-\ *n, pl* **chemakuan** *or* **chemakuans** *or* **chimakuan** *or* **chimakuans** *usu cap* [*Chemakum* + *-an*] **:** a language stock of the Mosan phylum in Washington comprising Chemakum and Quileute
chem·a·kum \'cheməkəm\ *or* **chim·a·kum** \'chim-\ *n, pl* **chemakum** *or* **chemakums** *or* **chimakum** *or* **chimakums** *usu cap* **1 a :** a Salishan people of northwestern Washington **b :** a member of such people **2 :** a Chemakuan language of the Chemakum people
che·ma·wi·nite \chə'mäwə,nīt\ *n* -s [*Chemahawin, Chemayin,* the Indian name of a Hudson Bay post near which it was found + E *-ite*] **:** a fossil resin similar to amber
chem·e·hue·vi \,chemə'wāvē\ *n, pl* **chemehuevi** *or* **chemehuevis** *usu cap* [Sp, fr. Yuma] **1 a :** a Shoshonean people resident in ancient times in the Mojave desert and later in the Colorado river valley, California **b :** a member of such people **2 :** the language of the Chemehuevi people
chem·i·at·ric \¦kemē¦a·trik\ *adj* [NL *chemiatria* iatrochemistry (fr. *chem-* + *-iatria* -iatry) + E *-ic*] **:** IATROCHEMICAL
1**chem·ic** \'kemik, -ēk\ *adj* [alter. (influenced by LGk *chēmeia* alchemy) of earlier *chimic,* fr. NL *chimicus* alchemist, fr. ML *alchimicus,* fr. *alchimia, alchymia* alchemy + L *-icus* -ic — more at ALCHEMY] **1** *archaic* **:** of or relating to alchemy **2 :** of or relating to chemistry **:** CHEMICAL
2**chemic** *also* **chem·ick** \"\ *n* -s **1** *obs* **a :** ALCHEMIST **b :** CHEMIST **2** *textile manuf* **a** *usu chemick, archaic* **:** a bleaching powder or a solution of bleaching powder or of calcium hypochlorite **b :** a dilute solution of sodium hypochlorite
3**chemic** *var of* CHEMICK
1**chem·i·cal** \'keməkəl, -ēk-\ *adj* [alter. of earlier *chimical,* fr. *chimic* (earlier form of *chemic*) + *-al*] **1 a** *obs* **:** ALCHEMICAL **b** *archaic* **:** of or relating to Paracelsian medicine specif. as it opposes Galenic medicine **2 :** relating to applications of chemistry: as **a :** acting or operated by chemical means ⟨a ~ extinguisher⟩ **b :** treated with or performed by the aid of chemicals ⟨~ development in photography⟩ **c :** produced by chemical means or synthesized from chemicals ⟨~ fiber⟩ ⟨~ rubber⟩ **d :** suitable for use in or used for operations in chemistry ⟨a ~ laboratory⟩ ⟨a ~ plant⟩ **3 :** having reference to or relating to the science of chemistry: as **a :** occupied with chemistry ⟨a ~ researcher⟩ ⟨~ societies⟩ **b :** dealing with chemistry ⟨a ~ journal⟩ ⟨~ nomenclature⟩ **c :** characterized by the phenomena of chemistry ⟨~ changes⟩ ⟨~ forces⟩ **4 :** of or relating to rocks (as gypsum, salt, and most limestones) that are deposited from solution

²chemical \"\ *n* -s [alter. of earlier *chemical*, fr. *chemical*, adj.] **:** a substance (as an acid, alkali, salt, synthetic organic compound) obtained by a chemical process, prepared for use in chemical manufacture, or used for producing a chemical effect — see FINE CHEMICAL, HEAVY CHEMICAL

³chemical \"\ *vt* -ED/-ING/-S **:** CHEMICALIZE

chemical balance *n* **:** a balance used in chemical work; *esp* **:** an analytical balance

chemical cellulose *n* **:** CELLULOSE 2e

chemical closet *n* **:** CHEMICAL TOILET

chemical cotton *n* **:** a pure form of cellulose obtained from cotton linters by treatment with dilute sodium hydroxide solution

chemical engineer *n* **:** a specialist in chemical engineering

chemical engineering *n* **:** a branch of engineering that deals with the development and application of manufacturing processes in which materials undergo changes in properties and that deals esp. with the design and operation of plants and equipment to perform such work

chemical focus *n* **:** ACTINIC FOCUS

chem·i·cal·i·za·tion \ˌkeməkələ'zāshən, -mēk-, -ˌlī'z-\ *n* -s **:** the act or process of chemicalizing ⟨~ of agriculture⟩

chem·i·cal·ize \'≈≈≈ˌlīz\ *vt* -ED/-ING/-S [²*chemical* + *-ize*] **:** to treat with chemicals **:** use chemicals extensively in

chemical kinetics *or* **chemical dynamics** *n* **:** REACTION KINETICS

chemical lead *n* **:** lead of sufficient purity for use in tanks, pipes, and other apparatus in chemical manufacture; *specif* **:** lead of this character made from the ores of southeastern Missouri

chem·i·cal·ly \'kemək(ə)lē, -mēk-, -li\ *adv* **1 :** by a chemical process or processes ⟨vitamin A can be estimated biologically, optically, or ~ —*Science*⟩ **2 :** according to chemical principles or from the chemist's standpoint ⟨a ~ impossible formula⟩

chemically pure *adj* **:** free from all impurities detectable by chemical analysis — used in commerce rather indefinitely of chemicals of a relatively high degree of purity

chemical mediation theory *n* **:** a theory in physiology: nervous transmission is due to the release of specific substances (as acetylcholine) at nerve endings and synapses — compare NEUROHUMORAL THEORY

chemical microscopy *n* **:** microscopy for the purpose of chemical identification and also recognition of physical structures and phases — compare MICROANALYSIS

chemical pneumonia *n* **:** an acute generalized inflammation of the lungs occurring in warfare and industry and caused by the inhalation of irritating gases or soluble dusts

chemical porcelain *n* **:** a porcelain that has low expansibility and acid-resisting glaze and is used in chemical laboratories and plants

chemical property *n* **:** a property of a substance relating to its chemical reactivity (as the explosive property of nitroglycerin)

chemical pulp *n* **:** pulp from chemically digested wood used chiefly for making paper and rayon and acetate fibers — compare GROUNDWOOD

chemicals *pl of* CHEMICAL, *pres 3d sing of* CHEMICAL

chemical sense *n* **:** a nervous mechanism for the physiological reception of and response to chemical stimulation; *specif* **:** the central nervous process (as in smelling and tasting) initiated by excitation of special receptors sensitive to chemical substances in solution — see COMMON CHEMICAL SENSE; compare CHEMORECEPTOR

chemical telegraph *n* **:** a telegraphic apparatus by which a message is recorded on a moving slip of paper moistened with a solution having a chemical composition that is altered on the passage of current through a stylus

chemical telephone *n* **:** a telephone operating by chemical or electrolytic action

chemical toilet *n* **:** a toilet rendering waste matter innocuous by chemical decomposition and employed where running water is not available — called also *chemical closet*

chemical warfare *n* **:** warfare in which incendiary mixtures, smokes, or irritant, burning, or asphyxiating gases are used for tactical purposes

chemical wood *n* **1 :** the wood of any of various trees used as a chemical raw material (as for the production of acetic acid, wood alcohol, or acetone by carbonization) **2 :** CHEMICAL PULP

chemic blue *n* **:** INDIGO CARMINE 2

chemic green *n* **:** BREMEN BLUE 1

¹chemick *var of* CHEMIC

²chem·ick *also* **chem·ic** \'kemik, -mēk\ *vt* **chemicked; chemicked; chemicking; chemicks :** to treat (textile materials) with chemic

chemico- — see CHEM-

chemics *pl of* CHEMIC

chem·i·graph \'keməˌgraf\ *n* -s [ISV *chem-* + *-graph*; orig. formed in G] **:** an engraving made by chemigraphy

che·mig·ra·phy \ke'migrəfē\ *n* -ES [ISV *chem-* + *-graphy*; orig. formed as G *chemigraphie*] **:** a process of etching on metal (as zinc) in which photography is not used

chemi·ground·wood pulp \ˌkemē'≈ˌ≈-\ *n* [*chem-* + *groundwood*] **:** wood pulp produced by treating wood chemically before it is ground up

chemi·luminescence \ˌkemē+\ *n* -s [ISV *chem-* + *luminescence*; prob. orig. formed as G *chemilumineszenz*] **:** luminescence due to chemical reaction; *esp* **:** luminescence due to the formation of new compounds (as the oxidation of phosphorus vapor or of luciferin in fireflies) — **chemi·luminescent** \"+\ *adj*

che·min de fer \shəˌmandə'fe(ə)r\ *n, pl* **chemins de fer** [F, lit., railroad] **:** a card game in which any number of players may participate in betting against the dealer, in which the dealer and one other player each receive two cards and may draw one additional card, the winning hand being the one totaling closest to 9, 19, or 29, and in which aces count one each, face cards 10 each, and other cards their numerical value — compare BACCARAT

chemio- — see CHEM-

chemi·photic \ˌkemē+¦-\ *adj* [*chem-* + *photic*] **:** relating to a change of chemical energy to light — contrasted with *photochemical*

che·mise \shə'mēz\ *n* -s [ME, fr. OF, shirt, fr. LL *camisa*, *camisia* shirt, thin dress, prob. of Gmc origin; akin to OE *hemethe* shirt, OS *hemithi*, OHG *hemidi*, OE *hama* cover, skin — more at HAME] **1** *archaic* **:** a shirtlike outer garment or undergarment usu. with long sleeves and of linen and formerly worn by both men and women **2 :** a woman's one-piece undergarment consisting usu. of panties and straight-hanging vest with straps **3 :** a loose straight-hanging dress sometimes belted

chem·i·sette \ˌshemē¦zet, -mə¦-\ *n* -s [F, dim. of *chemise*] **:** a woman's vestlike outergarment or undergarment; *esp* **:** one (as of lace) used as a fill-in for the open front of a dress

chem·ism \'keˌmizəm\ *n* -s [modif. (influenced by E *chemistry*) of F *chimisme*, fr. *chimie* chemistry (fr. ML *chimia*, fr. *alchimia* alchemy) + *-isme* -ism — more at ALCHEMY] **1 :** chemical activity or affinity **2 :** chemical property or relationship

chem·i·sorb \'keməˌsȯrb, -mē-\ *or* **chem·o·sorb** \-mə-,-\ *vt* [*chem-* + *sorb*] **:** to take up and hold by chemisorption

chem·i·sorp·tion *also* **chem·o·sorp·tion** \ˌ≈≈'sȯrpshən\ *n* -s [*chem-* + *sorption*] **:** adsorption, esp. when irreversible, by means of chemical forces in contrast with physical forces ⟨~ of gaseous nitrogen on iron catalysts⟩

chem·ist \'keməst\ *n* -s [alter. (influenced by LGk *chēmeia* alchemy) of earlier *chimist*, *chymist*, fr. NL *chimista*, *chymista*, short for ML *alchimista* — more at ALCHEMIST] **1 a** *obs* **:** ALCHEMIST **b :** one trained in or engaged in chemistry **2** *Brit* **:** DRUGGIST

chem·is·try \-trē, -i\ *n* -ES [alter. (influenced by LGk *chēmeia* alchemy) of earlier *chimistry*, *chymistry*, fr. *chimist*, *chymist* + *-ry*] **1 a** *obs* **:** ALCHEMY **b** *obs* **:** IATROCHEMISTRY **c :** a science that deals with the composition, structure, and properties of substances and of the transformations that they undergo — see INORGANIC CHEMISTRY, ORGANIC CHEMISTRY **2 a :** the composition and chemical properties of a substance ⟨the ~ of iron⟩ **b :** chemical processes and phenomena (as of an organism) ⟨blood ~⟩ ⟨the ~ of fungi⟩ **3 a :** peculiar makeup ⟨the ~ of modern diplomacy⟩ **b :** AGITATION, UNREST ⟨there was a ~ in his blood stirring him on to write —E.A.Weeks⟩ **c :** an often inexplicable or intangible function or process ⟨struggle against the *chemistries* . . . of desire and self-love —Bruce Marshall⟩

chemist's shop *n, Brit* **:** DRUGSTORE

chem·my \'shemē\ *n* -ES [by shortening & alter.] **:** CHEMIN DE FER

chem·nitz \'kemˌnits, -nə-\ *adj, usu cap* [fr. *Chemnitz*, Germany] **:** of or from the city of Chemnitz, Germany **:** of the kind or style prevalent in Chemnitz

che·mo- *in pronunciations below*, ¦≈≈ = ¦kēmō *or* -mə *or sometimes* ¦ke-\ — see CHEM-

chemo·autotroph \ˌ≈≈+\ *n* -s [*chem-* + *autotroph*] **:** an organism having a chemoautotrophic method of nutrition

chemo·autotrophic \¦≈≈+\ *adj* [*chem-* + *autotrophic*] **:** autotrophic and oxidizing some inorganic compound as a source of available energy ⟨a number of bacteria and a few protozoans are ~⟩ — compare PHOTOAUTOTROPHIC — **chemo·autotrophically** *adv* — **chemo·au·to·trophy** \+'ȯd·əˌtrāfē, -ōfē, ˌō'tä·trəfē\ *n* -ES

chemo·differentiation \¦≈≈+\ *n* -s [*chem-* + *differentiation*] **:** differentiation at the molecular level assumed to precede morphological differentiation in embryogenesis

che·mo·gen·ic \¦≈≈+¦jenik\ *or* **che·mog·e·nous** \ke'mäjənəs\ *adj* [*chem-* + *-genic*, *-genous*] **:** arising in or resulting from chemical action ⟨~ humus⟩

chemo·kinesis \¦≈≈*at* CHEMO- +\ *n, pl* **chemokineses** [NL, fr. *chem-* + *-kinesis*] **:** increased activity of free-moving organisms produced by a chemical agency — **chemo·kinetic** \+(ˌ)≈¦≈≈\ *adj*

chemo·organotrophic \¦≈≈+\ *adj* [*chem-* + *organotrophic*] **:** requiring an organic source of carbon and metabolic energy — compare AUTOTROPHIC

chemo·prophylactic \¦≈≈+\ *adj* [*chem-* + *prophylactic*] **:** of or relating to chemoprophylaxis

chemo·prophylaxis \¦≈≈+\ *n, pl* **chemoprophylaxes** [*chem-* + *prophylaxis*] **:** the prevention of infectious disease by the use of chemical agents

chemo·reception \¦≈≈+\ *n* -s [ISV *chem-* + *reception*] **:** the physiological reception of chemical stimuli — compare CHEMICAL SENSE — **chemo·receptive** \+≈¦≈≈\ *adj* — **chemo·receptivity** \¦≈≈+\ *n* -ES

chemo·receptor \¦≈≈+\ *n* -s [ISV *chem-* + *receptor*] **:** any sense organ responding to chemical stimuli (as a taste or smell receptor or one of the carotid body receptors that react to changes in the chemical composition of the blood)

¹chemo·reflex \¦≈≈+\ *n* -ES [*chem-* + *reflex*] **:** a physiological reflex initiated by a chemical stimulus or in a chemoreceptor

²chemo·reflex \¦≈≈+¦-\ *adj* **:** of, relating to, or dependent on a chemoreflex

chemo·resistance \ˌ≈≈+\ *n* -s [*chem-* + *resistance*] **:** the quality or state of being chemoresistant

chemo·resistant \¦≈≈+¦≈≈\ *adj* [*chem-* + *resistant*] **:** resistant to the action of a (particular) chemical — used esp. of certain insects

chemo·sensitive \¦≈≈+¦-\ *adj* [*chem-* + *sensitive*] **:** susceptible to the action of a (particular) chemical — used esp. of strains of bacteria) — **chemo·sensitivity** \¦≈≈+\ *n* -ES

che·mo·sis \kə'mōsəs\ *n, pl* **che·mo·ses** \-ōˌsēz\ [NL, fr. Gk *chēmōsis* swelling of the cornea resembling a cockleshell, fr. *chēmē* cockle + *-ōsis* -osis — more at CHAMA] **:** swelling of the conjunctival tissue around the cornea

chem·osmosis \¦kem, ¦kem+\ *n, pl* **chemosmoses** [NL, fr. *chem-* + *osmosis*] **:** chemical action taking place through an intervening membrane — **chem·osmotic** \"+\ *adj*

chemosorption *var of* CHEMISORPTION

che·mo·stat \'≈≈ *at* CHEMO- +ˌstat\ *n* -s [*chem-* + *-stat* (as in *thermostat*)] **:** a device in which bacteria are kept uniformly suspended in a culture medium constantly renewed and maintained chemically unaltered by a continuous flow of new medium through it and which is used esp. in quantitative studies of mutation rates

chemo·synthesis \ˌ≈≈+\ *n* [ISV *chem-* + *synthesis*; orig. formed as G *chemosynthese*] **:** synthesis of organic compounds by energy derived from chemical reactions (as in certain autotrophic bacteria) — opposed to *photosynthesis* — **chemo·synthetic** \¦≈≈+(ˌ)≈¦≈≈\ *adj*

chemosynthetic bacteria *n pl* **:** bacteria that obtain energy required for metabolic processes from exothermic oxidation of inorganic or simple organic compounds without the aid of light

chemo·tactic \¦≈≈+¦-\ *adj* [ISV *chem-* + *-tactic*; prob. orig. formed as G *chemotaktisch*] **1 :** involving chemotaxis ⟨~ response⟩ **2 :** exhibiting chemotaxis ⟨slime molds ~ to dextrose⟩ — **chemotactically** *adv*

che·mo·tax·is \ˌ≈≈+'taksəs\ *also* **che·mo·taxy** \'≈≈+ˌtaksē\ *n, pl* **chemotax·es** \-'takˌsēz\ *also* **chemotax·ies** \-ˌtak¸sēz\ [*chemotaxis*, NL, fr. *chem-* + *-taxis*; *chemotaxy*, ISV *chem-* + *-taxy*] **:** orientation or movement of cells or organisms in relation to chemical agents — compare TAXIS 2

chemo·therapeusis \¦≈≈+\ *n* [NL, fr. *chem-* + *therapeusis*] **:** CHEMOTHERAPY

che·mo·ther·a·peu·tant \¦≈≈+ˌtherə'pyüt°nt\ *n* -s [*chemotherapeutic* + *-ant*] **:** a chemotherapeutic agent

¹chemo·therapeutic \¦≈≈+\ *or* **chemo·therapeutical** \¦≈≈+\ *adj* [*chem-* + *therapeutic*, *therapeutical*] **:** of or belonging to chemotherapy — **chemotherapeutically** *adv*

²chemotherapeutic \"\ *or* **chemotherapeutical** \"\ *n* -s **:** an agent used in chemotherapy

chemotherapeutic index *n* **:** the ratio of the maximum tolerated dose of a chemical agent used in chemotherapy to its minimum effective dose

chemo·therapeutics \¦≈≈ *at* CHEMO- +\ *n pl but sing or pl in constr* **:** CHEMOTHERAPY

chemo·therapist \¦≈≈+\ *n* **:** a specialist in chemotherapy

chemo·therapy \ˌ≈≈ *at* CHEMO- +\ *n* [ISV *chem-* + *-therapy*; orig. formed as G *chemotherapie*; *chemotherapeutics*, fr. *chem-* + *therapeutics*; *chemotherapeusis*, NL, fr. *chem-* + *therapeusis*] **:** the prevention or treatment of esp. infectious disease in man, animals, or plants by the use of chemical agents

che·mot·ic \kə'mäd·ik\ *adj* [fr. NL *chemosis*, after such pairs as NL *sclerosis*: E *sclerotic*] **:** marked by or belonging to chemosis

chemo·trophic \¦≈≈ *at* CHEMO- +\ *adj* [*chem-* + *-trophic*] **:** CHEMOAUTOTROPHIC

chemo·tropic \¦≈≈+\ *adj* [ISV *chem-* + *-tropic*] **:** involving or exhibiting chemotropism — **chemotropically** *adv*

che·mot·ro·pism \ke'mä·trəˌpizəm, kə'-\ *n* -s [ISV *chem-* + *tropism*; orig. formed as G *chemotropismus*] **:** orientation of cells or organisms in relation to chemical stimuli — compare TROPISM

che·mur·gic \(')ke¦mərjik, kə'm-\ *adj* **:** relating to or produced by chemurgy — **che·mur·gi·cal·ly** \-jək(ə)lē\ *adv*

chem·ur·gist \'ke(ˌ)mərjəst; ke'm-, kə'm-\ *n* -s **:** a specialist in chemurgy

chem·ur·gy \'ke(ˌ)mərjē *sometimes* ke'm- *or* kə'm-\ *n* -ES [*chem-* + *-urgy*] **:** a branch of applied chemistry that deals with industrial utilization of organic raw materials esp. from farm products (as in the use of soybean oil for paints and varnishes and of southern pine for paper pulp)

chen \'ken\ *n, cap* [NL, fr. Gk *chēn* goose — more at GOOSE] **:** a genus (or subgenus of *Anser*) of geese having the adult plumage chiefly white — see SNOW GOOSE

chen- *or* **cheno-** *comb form* [Gk *chēn-*, *chēno-*, fr. *chēn*] **:** goose ⟨*Cheno*podium⟩

che·na \'chānə, -(ˌ)nä\ *n* -s [Hindi *cenā*, fr. Skt *cīna*, *cīnaka*, *ciṇaka*] **:** an area of virgin or secondary timberland in a tropical region cleared and cultivated for only a few years and then abandoned

chenango *var of* SHENANGO

chenar *var of* CHINAR

chen·chu \'chen(ˌ)chü\ *n, pl* **chenchu** *or* **chenchus** *usu cap* [native name in India] **1 :** a primitive people of Hyderabad in central India most of whom have been influenced by the Telugu population but some of whom cling to a food-gathering economy and represent, racially and culturally, survivals of ancient India **2 :** a member of the Chenchu people

che·neau \shā'nō\ *n* -s [F *chéneau*, fr. L *canalis* canal, channel — more at CANAL] **:** a cresting above a cornice or at the ends of eaves

che·net \shə'nā\ *n, pl* **chenets** \-'nā(z)\ [F, fr. OF, prob. dim. of *chien* dog, fr. L *canis*; fr. the dog heads frequently ornamenting them — more at HOUND] **:** ANDIRON

chen·e·vix·ite \¦shenə¦vikˌsīt\ *n* -s [F, fr. Richard *Chenevix* †1830 Irish chemist and mineralogist + F *-ite*] **:** a mineral $Cu_2Fe_2(AsO_4)_2(OH)_4.H_2O$(?) consisting of a hydrous copper iron arsenate occurring in greenish masses

chen·fish \'chen,-\ *n* [origin unknown] **:** KINGFISH 1a (2)

cheng *var of* SHENG

chen·gal \'cheŋgəl\ *n* -s [Malay *chĕngal*] **1 :** the hard heavy durable wood of a large Malayan tree (*Balanocarpus heimii*) **2 :** the tree that produces chengal and from which a damar is obtained **3 :** the wood of a tree (*Balanocarpus maximus*) related to the chengal

cheng·tu \'chəŋ¦dü, 'cheŋ¦tü\ *adj, usu cap* [fr. *Chengtu*, China] **:** of or from the city of Chengtu, China **:** of the kind or style prevalent in Chengtu

ch'eng-tzu-yai \¦cheŋ(t)ˌsü'yī\ *adj, usu cap* [prob. fr. a place name in China] **:** of or relating to a late Neolithic culture of China from Shantung southward and inland of about 1000 B.C. characterized by black pottery

che·nier *or* **chê·nière** \'shinərē, -ri\ *n* -s [AmerF (La.) *chênière*, fr. F *chêne* oak] **:** a wooded ridge or sandy hummock in a swampy region — compare SHINNERY

che·nille \shə'nēl, *esp before pause or consonant* -ēəl\ *n* -s [F, lit., caterpillar (so called fr. the appearance of the cord), fr. L *canicula*, dim. of *canis* dog; fr. its hairy appearance — more at HOUND] **1 a :** a wool, cotton, silk, or rayon yarn with pile protruding all around made by weaving a cloth with warp threads about soft filling threads and cutting it into narrow strips that are used esp. for tufting and fringes **b :** a pile-face fabric made with a filling of this yarn and commonly used for curtains, bedspreads, and rugs **c :** an imitation of this yarn or fabric **2** *also* **chenille plant :** an East Indian herb (*Acalypha hispida*) having long pendent spikes of crimson flowers resembling pieces of chenille

chenille axminster *n, usu cap A* **:** AXMINSTER

chenille carpet *or* **chenille rug** *n* **:** a carpet or rug with a chenille weft

chenille weed *n* **:** a common red alga (*Dasya elegans*) of the family Rhodomelaceae of the U.S. Atlantic coast

cheno- -see CHEN-

che·no·de·oxy·cho·lic acid \¦kē(ˌ)nōˌdēˌäksē¦kōlik-, ¦ke-, -äl-\ *or* **che·no·des·oxy·cho·lic acid** \-ˌdeˌzäksē\ *n* [ISV *chenodesoxycholic* or *chenodeoxycholic* (fr. *chen-* + *desoxy-*, *deoxy-* + *cholic*) + *acid*; orig. formed as G *chenodesoxycholsäure*] **:** a bile acid $C_{23}H_{37}(OH)_2COOH$ found in the bile of man, goose, hen, and ox; 3,7-dihydroxy-cholanic acid

che·no·pod \'kēnəˌpäd, 'ke-\ *n* -s [NL *Chenopodiaceae*] **:** a plant of the family Chenopodiaceae

che·no·po·di·a·ce·ae \ˌ≈≈ˌpōdē'āsēˌē\ *n pl, cap* [NL, fr. *Chenopodium*, type genus + *-aceae*] **:** a family of plants (order Caryophyllales) distinguished by small inconspicuous apetalous greenish flowers and utricular fruit — see GOOSEFOOT

che·no·po·di·a·ceous \¦≈≈ˌ≈≈¦āshəs\ *adj* **:** of or relating to the family Chenopodiaceae

che·no·po·di·a·les \-'ā(ˌ)lēz\ [NL, fr. *Chenopodium* + *-ales*] *syn of* CARYOPHYLLALES

che·no·po·di·um \-'pōdēəm\ *n, cap* [NL, fr. *chen-* + *-podium*] **:** a large genus (the type of the family Chenopodiaceae) of glabrous or mealy herbs having a 4-parted or 5-parted calyx, including the goosefoots, and occurring in temperate regions of the world — see LAMB'S-QUARTERS, WORMSEED

chenopodium oil *n* **:** a colorless or pale yellow toxic essential oil of unpleasant odor and taste obtained from Mexican tea plants and formerly used as an anthelmintic

che·o·plastic \¦kēō+¦-\ *adj* **:** of, relating to, or used in cheoplasty

che·o·plas·ty \'≈≈ˌplastē\ *n* -ES [*cheo-* (fr. Gk *chein* to pour) + *-plasty* — more at FOUND] **:** a process of molding artificial teeth by the use of low-fusing metals or alloys

che·pen·a·fa \chə'penəˌfō\ *n, pl* **chepenafa** *or* **chepenafas** *usu cap* [Calapooya *Chep-en-a-pho*] **1 :** a Kalapooian people near present Corvallis, Oregon **2 :** a member of the Chepenafa people

cheque \'chek\ *chiefly Brit var of* ²CHECK 10

che·queen *or* **che·quin** \chə'kēn\ *n* -s [alter. of earlier *chikino*, modif. of It *zecchino* — more at SEQUIN] **:** SEQUIN 1

che·quer \'chekə(r)\ *chiefly Brit var of* CHECKER

che·quered \'chekə(r)d\ *chiefly Brit var of* CHECKERED

chequ·ey *or* **chequy** \'cheki\ *var of* CHECKY

che·raw \chē'rȯ, '≈ˌ≈\ *n, pl* **cheraw** *or* **cheraws** *usu cap* [alter. of earlier *Saraw*, prob. modif. of Cherokee *Suala*] **1 :** a people of the Carolinas tentatively assigned to the Siouan language family **2 :** a member of the Cheraw people

cherem *var of* HEREM

cher·e·mis *or* **cher·e·miss** \¦cherə¦mis, -mēs\ *n, pl* **cheremis** *or* **cheremises** *or* **cheremiss** *or* **cheremisses** *usu cap* [Russ *Cheremis*, fr. ORuss *Čermisy*, prob. fr. Chuvash *Śarmĭś*] **1 :** one of a Finnish people of eastern Russia that are farmers and forest dwellers in the Mari and Bashkir republics of the U.S.S.R. — called also *Mari* **2 :** the Finno-Ugric language of the Cheremis people — see URALIC LANGUAGES table

¹cher·e·mis·si·an \¦cherə¦misēən\ *adj, usu cap* [*Cheremis* + *-ian*] **:** of or relating to the Cheremis

²cheremissian *n* -s *usu cap* **:** CHEREMIS

cherenkov radiation *usu cap C, var of* CERENKOV RADIATION

cher·e·thim \'kerəˌthim\ *or* **cher·e·thims** \-mz\ *n pl, cap* [Heb *Kĕrēthīm*, pl. of *Kĕrēthī*] **:** CHERETHITES

cher·e·thite \-ˌthīt\ *n* -s *cap* [Heb *Kĕrēthī* + E *-ite*] **:** a member of a group of the ancient Philistines from which the bodyguard of Israel's King David was recruited

cher·i·moya \ˌcherə'mȯiə\ *also* **cher·i·moy·er** \-ə(r)\ *or* **chir·i·moya** \ˌchir-\ *n* -s [Sp *chirimoya*, prob. fr. Quechua *chirimúya*, *chirimóya*] **:** a small widely cultivated tropical American tree (*Annona cherimola*) with 3-petaled yellowish brown flowers and round, oblong, or heart-shaped fruit with pitted rind that somewhat resembles the custard apple

cher·ish \'cherish, -ēsh, *esp in pres part* -əsh\ *vt* -ED/-ING/-ES [ME *cherisshen*, fr. MF *cheriss-*, stem of *cherir* to cherish, fr. OF, fr. *chier* dear, fr. L *carus* — more at CHARITY] **1 a :** to hold dear **:** feel or show fond affection for ⟨he admired them . . . ~*ed* and protected them like pets —Edmund Wilson⟩ **b :** to keep or guard with care and affection ⟨a birthright of freedom to be ~*ed* and fought for⟩ ⟨to ~ an illusion⟩ ⟨to love and to ~, till death us do part —*Bk. of Com. Prayer*⟩ **c :** to care for, tend, cultivate, or nurture usu. with care, affection, or love ⟨sought to ~ whatever of these forms could be made to work —John Buchan⟩ ⟨~ the seeds of love⟩ **d** *archaic* **:** PAT, FONDLE **2** *obs* **:** ENTERTAIN **3** *archaic* **:** WARM **4 a :** to have at heart **:** think of fondly or reverentially ⟨Socrates would have men ~ preciously this fraction of knowledge —Irving Babbitt⟩ **b :** to contemplate, imagine, or recall fondly with joy or pleasure ⟨she only ~*es* his illness as an instrument of power —Scott Fitzgerald⟩ **c :** to entertain or harbor in one's mind deeply and resolutely, often tacitly and often pleasurably ⟨a large school of thought ~*es* a curious animus against what it calls intellectualism —W.R.Inge⟩ ⟨few of us who do not ~ a feeling of self-complacency —Jane Austen⟩ **syn** see APPRECIATE, NURSE

cher·ish·ing·ly *adv* **:** in a cherishing manner

cher·kess \chə(r)'kes\ *n, pl* **cherkess** *or* **cherkesses** *usu cap* [Russ *Cherkes*] **:** CIRCASSIAN

cher maî·tre \sher'mātr(°), -t(rə)\ *n* [F, lit., dear master] **:** a person regarded as a master or model in his art or profession — often used as a form of address to such a person

cher·mes \['kər(ˌ)mēz\ [NL, fr. Ar *qirmiz* kermes — more at CRIMSON] *syn of* ADELGES, PSYLLA

cher·mi·dae \'kərməˌdē\ [NL, fr. *Chermes*, type genus + *-idae*] *syn of* PSYLLIDAE

cher·na \'chernə, -(ˌ)nä\ *n* -s [Sp, fr. LL *acernia*, prob. fr. LGk *acherna*] **1 :** any of several groupers (sense 1) **2 :** PRIEST-FISH **3 :** ³GAR c

cher·ne·vi·ye tatar \chə(r)'nāvē(y)ə-\ *n, usu cap C&T* [Russ *cherneviye*, nom. pl. of *cherny* black] **:** a member of a Tatar subdivision of the Altai mountains

cher·nov·tsy \cher'nȯftsē, chər-\ *adj, usu cap* [fr. *Chernovtsy*, Ukraine, U.S.S.R.] **:** of or from the city of Chernovtsy, Ukraine, U.S.S.R. **:** of the kind or style prevalent in Chernovtsy

cher·no·zem \ˌchernəˈzyȯm\ *n* -S [Russ, lit., black earth, fr. *cherno-* (fr. *cherny* black) + *-zem* earth (fr. ORuss *zem* earth); akin to Lith *žė́rszas* black and white spotted, Skt *kṛṣna* black, and to OSlav *zemlja* earth, L *humus* — more at HUMBLE] **:** any of a group of dark-colored zonal soils with a deep rich humus horizon found in regions (as the grasslands of central No. America) of temperate to cool climate — **cher·no·zem·ic** \ˌ=ˌ=ˈ=mik\ *adj*

cherogril *n* -S [LL *choerogryllus*, fr. Gk *choirogryllos*, fr. *choiros* young pig + *gryllos* young pig; akin to Gk *gryzein* to grunt — more at CHAEROPUS, GRUNT] *obs* **:** HYRAX

cher·o·kee \ˈcherə(ˌ)kē, ˌ=ˈ=\ *n, pl* **cherokee** *or* **cherokees** [prob. fr. Creek *tciloki* people of a different speech] **1** *usu cap* **a :** an Iroquoian people orig. of the Appalachian mountains of Tennessee and No. Carolina, later spreading as far south as Alabama and Georgia and as far west as Texas and Oklahoma **b :** a member of such people **2** *usu cap* **:** the language of the Cherokee people **3 :** TILE RED 2

cherokee rose *n, usu cap C* **:** a Chinese climbing rose (*Rosa laevigata*) with a fragrant white blossom

che·roon·jie nut \chəˈrünjē-\ *n* [Hindi *cirañjī*] **:** the seed of a medium-sized East Indian tree (*Buchanania latifolia*) of the family Anacardiaceae used in the unripe state as an ingredient of curry

che·root \shəˈrüt, chə-\ *n* -S [Tamil *curuṭṭu*, lit., roll, fr. *curuḷ* to become coiled, rolled, curled] **:** a cigar cut off square at both ends

¹cher·ry \ˈcherē, -ri\ *n* -ES [ME *chery*, modif. of ONF *cherise* (taken as a plural), fr. LL *ceresia*, fr. L *cerasus* cherry tree, cherry, fr. Gk *kerasos* cherry tree — more at CORNEL] **1 a :** any of numerous trees and shrubs of the genus *Prunus* that have pale yellow to deep red or blackish smooth-skinned nearly globular rather small fruits which are drupes enclosing a smooth seed and that include various improved forms cultivated for their fruits or for their ornamental flowers — see JAPANESE FLOWERING CHERRY, SOUR CHERRY, SWEET CHERRY; compare PEACH, PLUM **b :** the fruit of the cherry **c :** the reddish brown wood of any of the larger cherry trees (as the sweet cherry or the American black cherry) much used in cabinetmaking **2 :** BARBADOS CHERRY **3 :** COFFEE CHERRY **4 :** a variable color averaging a moderate red that is yellower, lighter, and stronger than cerise, claret (sense 3a), Turkey red, or average strawberry (sense 2a) and bluer, lighter, and stronger than catsup **5** *slang* **a :** ²HYMEN **b :** VIRGINITY **6 a :** milling cutter used to make small circular or spherical cavities (as in bullet molds) **7 :** the knocking down of only the front pin or pins in trying for a spare in bowling

²cherry \"\ *adj* **1 :** of or resembling a cherry: as **a :** of the color cherry ⟨~ cheeks⟩ **b :** made of cherry wood ⟨a ~ table⟩ **2** *slang* **:** ¹VIRGINAL 2

³cherry \"\ *vt* -ED/-ING/-ES **:** to mill with a cherry

cherry aphid *n* **:** a large dark aphid (*Myzus cerasi*) infesting the cherry tree and making the leaves crumple and roll

cherry apple *n* **:** SIBERIAN CRAB

cherry birch *n* **:** SWEET BIRCH

cherry blossom *n* **:** a moderate red that is bluer and paler than cerise, claret (sense 3a), Turkey red, or average strawberry (sense 2a) and deeper than carnation red

cherry bomb *n* [so called fr. its cherrylike shape & color] **:** a powerful globular red firecracker detonated by lighting a relatively long fuse

cherry bounce *n* **1** *Brit* **:** CHERRY BRANDY 1 **2 :** an often homemade American cherry-flavored liqueur concocted from rum or whiskey and sometimes cider

cherry brandy *n* **1 :** a liqueur made from brandy flavored with cherries and sweetened with sugar **2 :** a brandy distilled from fermented cherry juice

cherry casebearer *n* **:** a casebearer (*Coleophora pruniella*) closely related to and similar in habits to the pistol casebearer but chiefly attacking wild and cultivated cherries

cherry coal *n* [so called fr. its size] **:** a soft noncaking coal that burns readily

cherry crab *n* **:** SIBERIAN CRAB

cherry currant *n* **:** a variety of the red currant having a very large berry

cherry fruit fly *n* **:** a small brown trypetid fly (*Rhagoletis cingulata*) whose larva lives in the fruit of the cherry

cherry fruit sawfly *n* **:** an American sawfly (*Hoplocampa cookei*) whose larva feeds on the cherry and plum

cherry fruitworm *n* **:** the larva of a small mottled gray moth (*Grapholitha packardi*) that feeds in the fruits of cherries and blueberries

cherry gum *n* **:** CHERRY-TREE GUM

cherry holly *n* **:** ISLAY

cherry laurel *n* **1 :** a European evergreen shrub (*Prunus laurocerasus*) common in cultivation — called also *laurel* **2 :** an evergreen shrub (*Prunus caroliniana*) of the southern U.S. — called also *laurel cherry*

cherry leaf beetle *n* **:** a small red beetle (*Pyrrhalta cavicollis*) that attacks the leaves of cherry and peach trees

cherry leaf spot *n* **:** a disease of the cherry caused by a fungus (*Higginsia hyemalis*) that produces localized dead spots on the foliage, fruit, and pedicels, a general chlorosis often occurring and the dead spots on the leaves often dropping out — called also *yellow leaf*; compare SHOT HOLE 3a

cherrylike \ˈ==ˌ=\ *adj* **:** resembling or like a cherry

cherry liqueur *n* **:** a liqueur whose base is grape brandy or neutral spirits and whose flavor derives from wild black cherries

cherry maggot *n* **:** the larva of the cherry fruit fly

cherry mahogany *n* **:** MAKORE

cherry mildew *n* **:** a powdery mildew (*Podosphaera oxycanthae*) esp. destructive of the cherry

cherry orange *n* **1 :** KUMQUAT **2 :** a shrub of the genus *Citropsis*

cherry pepper *n* **1 :** a hot pepper (*Capsicum frutescens cerasiforme*) with small rounded extremely pungent fruits **2 :** the fruit of the cherry pepper

cherry picker *n* **:** any of various small traveling cranes; *esp* **:** one suitable for holding a passenger at the end of the boom

cherry pie *n* **1** *chiefly Brit* **:** GARDEN HELIOTROPE 2 **2 :** HAIRY WILLOW HERB

cherry pink *n* **:** BLOSSOM PINK

cherry pit *n* **1 :** CHERRYSTONE **2 :** an old game consisting of throwing cherrystones into a small hole in the ground

cherry plum *n* **1 :** an Asiatic plum (*Prunus cerasifera*) used extensively in Europe as a stock on which to bud domestic varieties — called also *myrobalan* **2 :** EUROPEAN BIRD CHERRY

cherry red *n* **:** a variable color averaging a strong red that is yellower and lighter than geranium red, yellower and paler than Goya, and yellower and darker than geranium (sense 3a) — compare CHERRY

cherry rose *n* **:** a deep pink that is bluer and stronger than average coral (sense 3b) and bluer and deeper than fiesta or begonia

cherry scab *n* **:** PEACH SCAB

cherry scale *n* **:** FORBES SCALE

cherry slug *n* **:** PEAR SLUG

cherrystone \ˈ==ˌ=\ *n* **1 :** the stone or endocarp of the cherry **2 :** something of little or no value ⟨I wouldn't give a ~ for his opinion⟩ **3 :** a small quahog ⟨a ~ clam⟩

cherry tomato *n* **1 :** any of several tomatoes bearing bunches of small fruits that resemble cherries: as **a :** a thin-leaved tomato (*Lycopersicon esculentum cerasiforme*) with globular to oblong red or yellow fruits **b :** CURRANT TOMATO **2 :** GROUND-CHERRY **3 :** the fruit of a cherry tomato

cherry-tree gum *n* **:** a gum that resembles gum arabic and is formed as an exudation from various trees of the genus *Prunus*

cherry wine *n* **:** a deep red

cherrywood \ˈ==ˌ=\ *n, often attrib* **:** CHERRY 1c

cher·so·nese \ˈkərsəˌnēz, -ēs\ *n* -S [L *chersonesus*, fr. Gk *chersonēsos*, fr. *chersos* dry land + *nēsos* island; akin to L *horrēre* to bristle, and to L *nare* to swim — more at HORROR, NATANT] **:** PENINSULA ⟨Thracian ~⟩

cher·syd·ri·dae \(ˌ)kərˈsidrəˌdē\ [NL, fr. *Chersydrus*, type genus (fr. Gk *chersydros* amphibious snake, fr. *chersos* dry land + *hydros* water snake) + *-idae*; akin to Gk *hydōr* water — more at WATER] *syn of* ACROCHORDIDAE

chert \ˈchərt, ˈchat\ *n* -S [origin unknown] **:** an impure flintlike rock essentially of cryptocrystalline quartz or fibrous chalcedony and usu. dark in color

chert·y \ˈchərd·ē, ˈchad·ē\ *adj, usu* -ER/-EST **1 :** like chert **2 :** containing chert **:** FLINTY

cher·ub \ˈcherəb\ *also* **cher·u·bim** \-r(y)əˌbim *also* -ēm *sometimes* ˈker- *or* ˌ==ˈ=\ *or* **cher·u·bin** \-in,-ēn\ *n, pl* **cherubs** *or* **cherubim** *also* **cherubims** *or* **cherubins** [Heb *kĕrūbh*] **1 :** a biblical figure frequently represented as a composite being with large wings, a human head, and an animal body and regarded as a guardian of a sacred place and as a servant of God **2 a :** one of an order of angels ordinarily symbolizing divine wisdom or justice and variously placed in the heavenly hierarchies usu. below the seraphim — see CELESTIAL HIERARCHY **b** *cherubin* **:** a beautiful or beloved woman ⟨thou young and rose-lipped cherubin —Shak.⟩ **3** *pl cherubs* **a** *in painting or sculpture* **:** a beautiful child, generally winged **:** CUPID **b** *in painting* **:** a child's head with wings **c :** an innocent-looking esp. chubby and rosy child **d :** an adult resembling or suggesting an innocent-looking, chubby, or rosy child **4 :** a moderate yellowish pink that is yellower and paler than coral pink, yellower and less strong than peach pink, and redder and slightly paler than average peach

che·ru·bic \chəˈrübik, che-, -bēk *sometimes* -ˈrəb- *or* ˈcherə(ˌ)bik\ *adj* [*cherub* + *-ic*] **:** of, resembling, or befitting a cherub ⟨a ~ face⟩ ⟨a ~ smile⟩

cherup *archaic var of* CHIRRUP

cher·vil \ˈchərvəl\ *n* -S [ME *chervell, cherville*, fr. OE *cerfelle, cerfille*; akin to OHG *kervila, kervola*; both fr. a prehistoric WGmc word borrowed fr. (assumed) VL *cerfolia*, fr. L *caerefolium*, part trans. of Gk *chairephyllon*, fr. *chairein* to take pleasure in + *phyllon* leaf — more at YEARN, BLADE] **1 :** an aromatic annual Old World herb (*Anthriscus cerefolium*) that is cultivated for its finely divided often curled leaves which are used esp. in soups and salads — called also *beaked parsley* **2 :** any of several plants that are related to chervil — usu. used with a qualifying term ⟨wild ~⟩ ⟨cow ~⟩

cher·vo·nets *or* **cher·vo·netz** \chərˈvȯnəts\ *n, pl* **cher·von·tsi** *or* **chervon·tzi** \-ntsē\ [Russ *chervonets*, alter. of ORuss *červonyi*, fr. OPol *czerwony* golden, purple] **1 :** the gold 10-ruble coin of Soviet Russia authorized by decree 1922 and struck 1923 **2 :** a unit of value equivalent to one gold chervonets designated by law of 1924 as the basic monetary unit but never such in practice **3 :** a currency note representing one chervonets

ches·a·peake bay retriever \ˈchesəˌpēk-, *rapid* -eˌspēk-\ *or* **chesapeake bay dog** *also* **chesapeake** *n, usu cap C&B* [fr. *Chesapeake Bay*, inlet of the Atlantic ocean in Virginia and Maryland] **:** a large powerful sporting dog that was developed in Maryland apparently by crossing Newfoundlands with native retrievers, is broad-headed and deep-chested with a short muscular neck, and has a coat, short but very dense and slightly waved on the back, varying from straw-colored to dark brown

chesapeake canoe *n, usu cap 1st C* **:** a fishing and working craft of Chesapeake Bay, from 20 feet to 40 feet long, rigged with one or two masts and leg-of-mutton sails spread by means of sprits, and sometimes with a jib of peculiar shape, orig. built from a single log and later from three, five, or seven logs bolted together — compare BUGEYE

¹chesh·ire \ˈcheshə(r) *also* -ˌshi(ə)r *or* -ˌshiə\ *adj, usu cap* [fr. *Cheshire*, county of England] **:** of or from the county of Chester, England **:** of the kind or style prevalent in the county of Chester

²cheshire \"\ *n* -S *usu cap* **:** an American breed of medium-sized white swine

cheshire cat *n, usu cap 1st C* **:** a fictitious cat with a broad grin

cheshire cheese *n, usu cap 1st C* **:** a cheese similar to cheddar and made chiefly in Cheshire, England

cheshvan *usu cap, var of* HESHVAN

chesnut *archaic var of* CHESTNUT 1

¹chess \ˈches\ *n* -ES [ME *ches*, fr. OF *esches*, acc. pl. of *eschec* check at chess — more at CHECK] **:** a game of ancient origin for two played on a chessboard in which each player moves his chessmen according to fixed types of movements for each across the board in such a way as to try to checkmate the opponent's king

²chess \"\ *n* -ES [ME *ches* tier, modif. of MF *chasse* frame, mounting — more at CHASSE] **1** *now dial Eng* **a :** TIER, LAYER **b :** ⁴ROW **2** *pl* **chess** *or* **chesses :** one of the boards placed transversely on the balk of a pontoon bridge to form the flooring

³chess \"\ *n* -ES [origin unknown] **:** a weedy annual bromegrass (*Bromus secalinus*) native to Europe but widely distributed as a weed esp. in grain and sometimes popularly believed to be a degenerate wheat; *broadly* **:** any of several weedy bromegrasses

chessboard \ˈ=ˌ=\ *n* **1 :** a checkerboard used in the game of chess **2 :** the scene of any contest like chess in requiring subtle scheming and cautious manipulation ⟨the political ~⟩

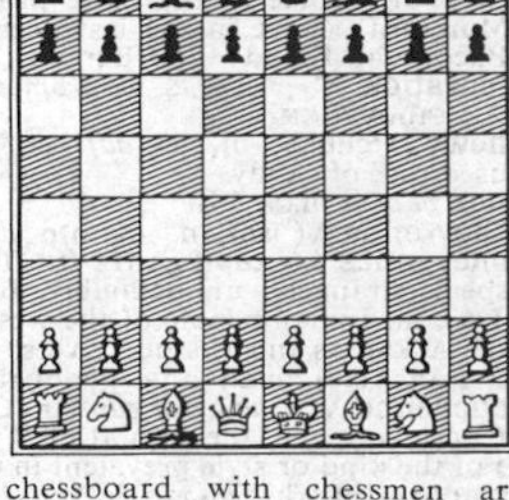

chessboard with chessmen arranged as at the beginning of a game

ches·sel \ˈchesəl\ *n* -S [prob. fr. ¹*cheese* + *well*] **:** CHEESE VAT

ches·set \ˈchesət\ *n* -S [by alter.] *Scot* **:** CHEESE VAT

chess·man \ˈchesˌman, -ˌmən, -ˌmaa(ə)n\ *n, pl* **chessmen** [by folk etymology fr. earlier *chesse meyne*, fr. *chesse* chess + *meyne* company, fr. MF *meyné, mesniée* company, servants, fr. L *mansio* house — more at MANSION] **:** one of 32 men used in chess with each player having a set of 16 consisting of 8 pieces and 8 pawns

chessom *adj* [*chess-* (perh. alter. of *cheese*) + *-som* (alter. of *-some*)] *obs, of soil* **:** loose, friable, and free from stones

chess pie *also* **chess cake** \ˈches-\ *n* [prob. alter. of *cheese pie, cheese cake*] **:** a dessert consisting essentially of a filling made of eggs, butter, and sugar and baked in individual tart shells of rich pastry

chess rook *n, heraldry* **:** a representation of the rook in chess in a shape now obsolete

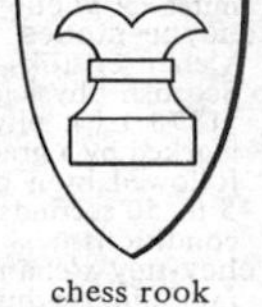

chess rook

chess-tree \ˈchesˌtrē\ *n* [perh. by folk etymology fr. F *châssis* framework — more at CHASSIS] **:** a piece of wood with a sheave or sheaves formerly bolted in the topsides of a ship and through which a tack or sheet was rove

ches·sy cat \ˈchesē-\ *sometimes cap 1st C, slang var of* CHESHIRE CAT

ches·sy·lite \ˈshesəˌlīt\ *or* **ches·sy copper** \ˈshesē-, sheˈsē-\ *n* -S *usu cap 1st C* [*Chessy*, France, one of its localities + E *-lite*] **:** AZURITE

chessylite blue *n* **:** AZURITE BLUE

¹chest \ˈchest\ *n* -S [ME, fr. OE *cest, cist* chest, box, basket, coffin; akin to OFris *kiste* box, chest, OHG & ON *kista*; all fr. a prehistoric NGmc-WGmc word borrowed fr. L *cista* box, basket, fr. Gk *kistē* box, basket, hamper; perh. akin to OIr *cess, ciss* basket] **1 :** any of various containers for storage: as **a :** a box usu. with a hinged lid esp. for the safekeeping of valuables or the storing of tools or belongings ⟨a tool ~⟩ ⟨a jewel ~⟩ ⟨a ~ lock⟩ **b :** a cupboard esp. for the storing of medicines or first-aid supplies ⟨a medicine ~⟩ **c :** a reusable storage or shipping container generally made or fitted for a special commodity or group of items **d :** CHEST OF DRAWERS **e :** a storage tank for pulp during processing in papermaking **2** *now dial* **:** COFFIN **3 a :** the place for the keeping of the money of a public institution **:** TREASURY, COFFER **b :** a fund of money esp. in or from such a chest — see COMMUNITY CHEST **4 :** the part of the body enclosed by the ribs and breastbone **:** THORAX — see DOG illustration **5 :** the seat of the emotions **6 :** the breast of an arrow

²chest \"\ *vt* -ED/-ING/-S [ME *chesten* to put into a coffin, fr. *chest*, n.] *now dial Brit* **:** to place in a coffin

chest beating *n* **:** the striking of overly dramatic attitudes esp. in personal confession of errors ⟨the ritualistic *chest beating* of self-criticism⟩

chest·ed \ˈchestəd\ *adj, of an arrow* **:** thickest at the breast, tapering toward the point and usu. also toward the nock

¹ches·ter \ˈchestə(r)\ *adj, usu cap* [fr. *Chester*, England] **1 :** of or from the county borough of Chester, England **:** of the kind or style prevalent in the county borough of Chester **2 :** CHESHIRE

²chester \"\ *n, usu cap* **:** CHESHIRE CHEESE

ches·ter·field \ˈchestə(r)ˌfēld\ *n* -S *sometimes cap* [after a 19th cent. Earl of *Chesterfield*] **1 :** a semifitted overcoat of dark plain woolen fabrics made in single-breasted or double-breasted style with a velvet collar, flap pockets, a fly-front closure, and no belt, orig. for men's wear, and adapted for women **2 a :** a style of davenport usu. having upright armrests at both ends **b** *Brit & West* **:** DAVENPORT, SOFA

ches·ter·field·i·an \ˌ==ˈ=dēən\ *adj, usu cap* [Philip Dormer Stanhope, fourth Earl of *Chesterfield* †1773 Eng. statesman & man of letters + E *-ian*] **:** of, relating to, or befitting the writings or the attitudes of Chesterfield, distinguished for his elegant manners and for his *Letters* to his son in which he expounded his principles of conduct said to reflect sharply the pragmatic morality of the age

chesterfield suite *n, sometimes cap C, Brit* **:** a matching suite of davenport and easy chairs

ches·te·ri·an \(ˈ)cheˈstirēən\ *adj, usu cap* [*Chester*, Ill. + E *-ian*] **:** of or relating to a division of the Mississippian geologic period — see GEOLOGIC TIME table

chester white *n, usu cap C&W* [fr. *Chester* county, Pa., where it originated] **:** a breed of large white swine of the lard type

chest founder *n* **:** a hollow appearance of the chest and a stiff gait, suggesting a painful chest, sometimes seen in older horses and dogs, esp. those lacking exercise or suffering from strain or injury of the shoulder area

chestier *comparative of* CHESTY

chestiest *superlative of* CHESTY

chest·i·ly \ˈchestəlē, -li\ *adv* **:** in a chesty manner

chest·i·ness \-tēnəs, -tin-\ *n* -ES **:** the quality or state of being chesty ⟨with the ~ of a town bully⟩

¹chest·nut \ˈches(ˌ)nət, *usu* -əd.+V\ *n* -S [earlier *chesten nut*, fr. ME *chesten, chesteine, chasteine*, fr. MF *chastaigne*, fr. L *castanea*, fr. Gk *kastanea, kastanon*] **1 a :** the sweet edible nut produced by any shrub or tree of the genus *Castanea* **b :** any plant bearing this nut: (1) **:** a European tree (*C. sativa*) (2) **:** a closely related American tree (*C. dentata*) — see JAPANESE CHESTNUT **c :** the light coarse-grained wood of this tree **d :** any of numerous trees having edible nuts: as (1) **:** CAPE CHESTNUT (2) **:** MORETON BAY CHESTNUT — usu. used with an attributive modifier **2 a :** a color like or close to that of a chestnut **b :** a grayish brown that is slightly redder than coconut and redder and slightly darker than new cocoa — called also *brown bay, brownstone*; compare CHESTNUT BROWN **3 :** HORSE CHESTNUT **1 4 :** an animal of a chestnut color; *specif* **:** a horse having a body color of any shade of pure or reddish brown with mane, tail, and points of the same or a lighter shade — compare ²BAY 1; see ¹SORREL 1a **5 :** one of the small round or oval horny callosities on the inner sides of the forelegs and hind legs of the horse and on the forelegs of asses and zebras **6 a :** an old usu. stale joke or story ⟨a comedy act trying to get by with nothing but ~s⟩ **b :** something repeated (as a generalization, a musical piece, or a play) or hashed over (as a philosophic problem or concept) very frequently esp. to the point of staleness ⟨Thursday's philharmonic program . . . contained a couple of . . . old ~s that could have been lent interest only by brilliant performances —Winthrop Sargeant⟩ ⟨then tackle the age-old ~s — so traditionally chewed over that they have capitalized names: the Problem of Being, the Problem of Evil —Susanne K. Langer⟩ **7** *Puerto Rico* **:** BREADFRUIT 1, 2

²chestnut \"\ *adj* **:** of, relating to, or like chestnut or a chestnut; *esp* **:** of the color chestnut

chestnut-backed chickadee *n* **:** a brown-backed chickadee (*Penthestes rufescens*) of the western U.S.

chestnut bean *n* **:** CHICK-PEA

chestnut blight *or* **chestnut-bark disease** *or* **chestnut canker** *n* **:** a destructive disease of the American chestnut caused by a fungus (*Endothia parasitica*) and attacking the bark and cambium to produce sunken or swollen cankers that ultimately girdle and kill the affected part

chestnut borer *n* **:** an insect that bores in the wood of the chestnut tree; *specif* **:** a small blue-black yellow-striped beetle (*Agrilus bilineatus*) having a flattened larva that bores in various deciduous trees — called also *two-lined chestnut borer*

chestnut-breasted finch *n* **:** a small Australian finch (*Donacola castaneothorax*) that is ashy brown above shading into rich chestnut on the back and wings with lighter chestnut breast and tail and white underparts and is often kept in aviaries though something of a pest in its native habitat, feeding on various seed crops

chestnut brown *n* **:** a moderate brown that is yellower and duller than toast brown, yellower, less strong, and slightly lighter than bay, redder and lighter than coffee, and yellower and slightly duller than auburn — compare CHESTNUT 2b

chestnut coal *n* **:** anthracite coal of medium size — see ANTHRACITE table

chestnut-collared longspur *n* **:** a longspur (*Calcarius ornatus*) of the central prairies of the U.S.

chestnut-eared finch *n* **:** ZEBRA FINCH

chestnut extract *n* **:** an extract of chestnut wood esp. from the European chestnut or American chestnut oak that is used chiefly in tanning heavy leathers (as sole and belting leathers)

chestnut oak *n* **:** an oak having leaves resembling those of the chestnut: as **a :** DURMAST **b :** CHINQUAPIN OAK **c :** a large oak (*Quercus montana*) of eastern No. America having oblong leaves with rounded teeth that are shiny yellow-green above and paler beneath and large acorns

chestnut rail *n* **:** a fence with rails made of chestnut wood

chestnut-sided warbler *n* **:** a common warbler (*Dendroica pensylvanica*) of eastern No. America

chestnut soil *n* **:** any of an agriculturally important group of zonal soils typically having a dark-brown surface horizon that grades downward into a lighter zone and then into a horizon of lime accumulation and being characteristic of certain cool semiarid grasslands and steppes (as in the northern U.S. prairie states)

chest·nut·ty \ˈches(ˌ)nəd·ē, -ətē, -i\ *adj* **1 :** tinged with or resembling the color chestnut **2 :** of or like a chestnut

chestnut weevil *n* **:** either of two brownish weevils (*Curculio auriger* and *C. proboscideus*) that lay eggs in the nut of the chestnut tree, the larvae feeding in and destroying the fruit

chest of drawers : a piece of case furniture designed almost solely to contain drawers

chest of viols : a set of matching viols of different sizes (as treble, tenor, gamba)

chest-on-chest *n* -S **:** a double chest of drawers, the lower section with short feet and the upper slightly smaller than the lower

chest-on-frame *n* -S **:** a chest of drawers raised on a frame with legs **:** HIGHBOY

chest-on-chest

chest pulse *n* **:** a sudden expiratory movement of the chest muscles or the impulse of breath so produced

chest register *n* **:** the lower register of the voice

chests *pl of* CHEST, *pres 3d sing of* CHEST

chest server *n* **:** a chest of drawers that serves also as a sideboard

chest shot *n* **:** a two-handed basketball set shot from chest height

chest thumping *n* **:** conduct or expression marked by pompous or arrogant self-assertion

chest tone *n* **:** a tone in the chest register

chest weight *n* **:** a weight (as one of a pair of weights) raised by a cord-and-pulley device for exercising and developing the muscles of the chest, back, and arms

chesty \'chestē, -ti\ *adj* -ER/-EST **1 :** marked by a large or well-developed chest **2** *slang* **:** arrogantly or pridefully self-assertive ⟨~ as a peacock —Milton Mezzrow & Bernard Wolfe⟩ **3 :** marked by chest tones — used of a singer or his tone quality

chesvan *usu cap, var of* HESHVAN

chetah *var of* CHEETAH

chet·co \'chet,kō\ *n, pl* **chetco** *or* **chetcos** *usu cap* [Chetco *Cheti*, lit., close to the mouth of the stream] **1 :** an Athapaskan people in the Chetco river valley of Oregon **2 :** a member of the Chetco people

cheth *var of* HETH

chet·nik \(')chet¦nēk, -ik\ *n* -s *usu cap* [Serb *četnik*, fr. *četa* band, troop; perh. akin to L *caterva* band, troop, IrGael *cethern* troop, battalion] **:** a member of a Pan-Serbian movement or home-defense band for resistance to oppressors by guerrilla tactics

chetopod *var of* CHAETOPOD

chet·ty *or* **chet·tie** \'ched·ē\ *n, pl* **chet·tis** *or* **chetties** \-d·ēz\ *or* **chetty·ars** \-d·ē,ärz\ *often cap* [Tamil-Malayalam *cetti*, fr. Skt *śreṣṭhin*] **:** a member of a caste of Tamil moneylenders or merchants in southern India, Ceylon, Burma, Malaya, Fiji, and So. Africa

chet·ty·ar \'ched·ē,är\ *adj, often cap* **:** of or relating to the Chettyars

chet·vert \'chetvə(r)t\ *n* -s [Russ *chetvert'*, lit., quarter, fr. *chetverty* fourth; akin to Skt *catur* four — more at FOUR] **:** a Russian unit of capacity equal to about 5.96 bushels

chev *abbr* **1** chevalier **2** chevron

che·vage \'chēvij\ *or* **chiv·age** \'chiv-\ *n* -s [ME *chyvage*, fr. MF *chevage*, fr. OF, fr. *chief* head + *-age* — more at CHIEF] **:** a capitation tax or tribute formerly paid to a lord or a superior

chevaine *var of* CHEVIN

che·val-de-frise \shə¦valdə¦frēz\ *also* **che·vaux-de-frise** \-¦vōd-\ *n, pl* **chevaux-de-frise** \-¦vōd-\ [F, lit., horse or horses from Friesland; fr. its being first used there] **1 :** a piece of timber or an iron barrel from which iron-pointed spikes, spears, or pointed poles project five or six feet long, used in warfare to defend a passage, stop a breach, or impede cavalry — usu. used in pl. **2 :** a protecting line of sharp points (as of spikes or nails) set firmly into the top of a fence or wall — usu. used in pl.

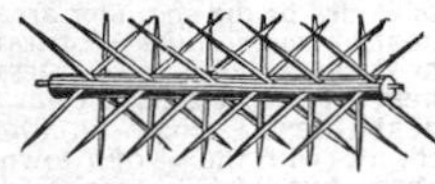
cheval-de-frise 1

chevaleresque *var of* CHIVALRESQUE

che·va·let \shə'va(,)lā, ¦shevə¦lā\ *n* -s [F, dim. of *cheval* horse, fr. L *caballus* — more at CAVALCADE] **:** the bridge of a stringed musical instrument

che·val glass \shə'val-\ *n* [F *cheval*, lit., horse; fr. the resemblance of the frame to a horse] **:** a full-length mirror in a frame by which it may be moved or tilted

cheva·lier \¦shevə¦li(ə)r, -liə *or (esp in senses other than 1a & 3)* shə'val,yā *or* -äl- *or* -àl- *or* ¦=¦=\ *n* -s [ME *chevaler*, fr. MF *chevalier*, fr. LL *caballarius* horseman — more at CAVALIER] **1 a** *archaic* **:** HORSEMAN; *esp* **:** CAVALIER 3 **b (1) :** a member of certain orders of knighthood **(2) :** a member of the lowest rank of a French order of merit ⟨the coveted ribbon of the ~ of the Legion of Honor —W.H.Downes⟩ **2 a :** a member of the lowest rank of French nobility **b :** a cadet of the French nobility **3 :** a chivalrous man

cheval glass

cheva·lier crab \¦shevə¦li(ə)r-, -liə-\ *n* [so called fr. its rapid pace] **:** a swift-running seacoast crab (genus *Ocypode*)

chev·a·line \'shevə,lēn\ *adj* [MF, fem. of *chevalin*, fr. OProv *cavalin*, fr. L *caballinus*, fr. *caballus* horse + *-inus* -ine — more at CAVALCADE] **:** of or relating to horses

che·vee \shə'vā\ *n* -s [F *chevée*, fr. fem. of *chevé*, past part. of *chever* to hollow out, fr. L *cavare*, fr. *cavus* hollow — more at CAVE] **:** a flat gemstone with a smooth depression — compare CUVETTE

cheve·lure \¦shevə¦lů(ə)r, shəv'l-\ *n* -s [F, lit., head of hair, wig, fr. L *capillatura*, fr. *capillus* hair] **1 :** hair of the head **:** head of hair **2 :** a nebulous envelope (as around the nucleus of a comet or of a nebulous star) **:** COMA

chev·er·el \'shev(ə)rəl\ *or* **chev·er·il** \-əl\ *n* -s [ME *chevrelle*, fr. MF *chevrele* kid, dim. of *chèvre, chievre*, fr. L *capra* she-goat, fem. of *capr-, caper* goat — more at CAPRIOLE] **:** soft elastic leather made of kidskin **:** KID LEATHER

cheveron *var of* CHEVRON

cheveronel *var of* CHEVRONEL

cheveronny *var of* CHEVRONY

chev·e·saile \'shevə,sāl\ *n* -s [ME, fr. MF *cheveçaille* opening for the head in a garment, fr. OF, fr. *chevesce* head opening, fr. (assumed) VL *capitia*, pl. (taken as sing.) of L *capitium* opening for the head] **:** the ornamented collar of a medieval garment

che·vet \shə'vā\ *n* -s [F, alter. of OF *chevez*, fr. L *capitium* head covering, opening for the head, fr. *caput* head — more at HEAD] **:** the apsidal eastern termination of a church choir typically having a surrounding ambulatory that opens onto a number of radiating apses or chapels — used esp. of French Gothic architecture

che·ville \shə'vē\ *n* -s [F, lit., peg, fr. L *clavicula*, dim. of *clavis* key — more at CLAVICLE] **1 :** a redundant word or phrase used to fill out a sentence or verse **2 :** a peg of a stringed musical instrument

chev·in \'chevən\ *also* **che·vaine** *or* **che·vesne** \shə'vān\ *or* **chiv·en** \'chivən\ *n* -s [ME *chevin, cheveyne*, fr. MF *chevenne, chevesne*, fr. (assumed) VL *capitin-, capito*, fr. LL *capiton-, capito*, fr. L, large-headed one, fr. *caput* head] **:** the chub of Europe

chev·i·ot \'shevēət, *Brit usu & US sometimes* 'ch-\ *n* [fr. the Cheviot hills, England and Scotland] **1** *usu cap* **:** a breed of very hardy hornless medium-wooled meat-type sheep originating in the Cheviot hills **2** -s *sometimes cap* **a :** a fabric of Cheviot wool **b :** a heavy rough napped suiting and coating having a plain or twill weave and made of coarse wool or worsted often mixed with mungo **c** -s *broadly* **:** any of several fabrics resembling this suiting; *esp* **:** a sturdy soft-finished cotton shirting of a plain or twill weave **3** -s **:** a lightweight paper decorated to simulate the weave of cheviot fabric and used for covering and ornamenting boxes

chev·i·sance \'shevəsən(t)s, -zən-\ *n* -s [ME *chevisaunce* achievement, resource, supply, booty (whence by misunderstanding the meaning "enterprise"), fr. MF *chevisance*, fr. OF, fr. *chevir* to come to an end, perform, fr. *chief* head — more at CHIEF] **1** *archaic* **:** UNDERTAKING, ENTERPRISE; *esp* **:** chivalrous enterprise or prowess **:** CHIVALRY **2 :** an unlawful transaction or contract; *esp* **:** a transaction intended to evade the statutes against usury

chev·kin·ite \'chefkə,nīt, -evk-\ *n* -s [G *tschewkinit*, fr. Konstantin V. Chevkin (*Tschewkin*) †1875 Russ. general and chief of Dept. of Mines of Russia + G *-it* -ite] **:** a mineral approximately $(Fe,Ca)(Ce,La)_2(Si,Ti)_2O_8$ consisting of silicotitanate of iron, calcium, and rare-earth elements

chev·on \'shevən\ *n* -s [F *chèvre* goat (fr. L *capra* she-goat, fem. of *capr-, caper* goat) + E *mutton*, fr. ME *motoun*, fr. OF *moton* ram — more at CAPRIOLE, MUTTON] **:** the flesh of the goat used as food ⟨to many inhabitants of the tropics ~ is as palatable as mutton⟩

chev·ret \shəv'rā\ *also* **chè·vre** \'shevr(ᵊ), -v(rə)\ *or* **chev·ro·tin** \'shevrə,tan\ *n* -s [F, fr. *chèvre* goat] **:** a cheese made from goats' milk

chev·rette \shəv'ret\ *n* -s [F, kid, dim. of *chèvre* goat] **:** a thin goatskin

¹chev·ron \'shevrən\ *n* -s [ME, fr. MF, fr. (assumed) VL *caprion-, caprio*, fr. L *capra*] **1** *or* **chev·er·on** \-v(ə)rən\ *heraldry* **:** a charge consisting of two diagonal stripes meeting at an angle, the point up unless a different position is specified **2 :** a chevron-shaped figure, pattern, or object; *esp* **:** an ornamental unit of this shape often used (as in a chevron molding) as one of a number of attached identical units forming a continuous zigzag **3 :** a sleeve badge awarded or worn usu. as an indication of rank or of a completed term of service or used esp. formerly in the armed services as an indication that one has been wounded, usu. consisting of one or more V-shaped stripes sometimes with arcs, bars, and other devices, and distinctive in detail in the various organizations that employ them — compare ¹BAR 4d — **in chevron** *of a pair of heraldic charges* **:** one bendwise and the other bendwise sinister with the upper ends approaching or touching each other in the midline of the field ⟨on a chevron azure two swords *in chevron* proper⟩

chevron 1

chevrons 3: *1* marine staff sergeant; *2* air force staff sergeant; *3* army staff sergeant

²chevron \"\ *n* -s [perh. fr. MF, kid, dim. of *chèvre* goat; fr. their being orig. made of kidskin — more at CHEVEREL] *archaic* **:** GLOVE

chevron bone *n* [¹*chevron*] **:** HEMAL ARCH b(2)

chev·ron·el \¦shevrə¦nel\ *or* **chev·er·on·el** \-v(ə)rə-\ *n* -s [¹*chevron* + *-el*] *heraldry* **:** a narrow chevron

chevron molding *n* [¹*chevron*] **:** a molding ornamented with chevrons (as in Norman architecture) **:** a zigzag molding

chevron rattler [¹*chevron* + *rattler*; fr. its markings] *n* **:** TIMBER RATTLESNAKE

chev·ron·wise \'shevrən,wīz\ *also* **chev·ron·ways** \-,wāz\ *adv* **:** in chevron

chev·rony *or* **chev·ron·ny** \'shevrənē\ *or* **chev·er·on·ny** \-v(ə)rə-\ *adj* [F *chevronné*, past part. of *chevronner* to adorn with chevrons, fr. *chevron*, n.] *heraldry* **:** divided into chevrons

chev·ro·tain \'shevrə,tān\ *also* **chev·ro·tin** \-,tan\ *n* -s [F, dim. of *chevrot* kid, fawn, fr. MF, dim. of *chèvre* goat — more at CHEVEREL] **:** any of several very small hornless deer-like ruminant mammals of tropical Asia, the Malay archipelago, and West Africa superficially resembling the musk deer, the male having short tusks, and being among the smallest known ruminants, standing only about a foot high — called also *mouse deer*; see WATER CHEVROTAIN

chevy *var of* CHIVY

¹chew \'chü\ *vb* -ED/-ING/-S [ME *chewen*, fr. OE *cēowan* to chew, gnaw, eat; akin to OHG *kiuwan* to chew, ON *tyggva* to chew, OSlav *žïvati*] *vt* **1 a :** to crush or grind (as food) in the mouth by continued action of the teeth with the help of the tongue and other masticatory organs usu. in preparation for swallowing **:** MASTICATE **b :** to injure, destroy, or consume as if by chewing ⟨logs ~*ed* up for paper⟩ ⟨a weather-*chewed* white flag —Ivan Innerst⟩ **2 :** to utter indistinctly **:** MUMBLE **3** *slang* **:** UPBRAID, REPRIMAND ⟨not going to ~ him just because he cuts out now and then —J.G.Cozzens⟩ ~ *vi* **:** to chew something; *specif* **:** to chew tobacco — **chew the rag** *or* **chew the fat** *slang* **:** to make friendly familiar conversation **:** CHAT ⟨sitting in an old chair in front of the warehouse on the St. Paul levee . . . *chewing the rag* with anybody who came up the river —Meridel Le Sueur⟩ — **chew the scenery :** to act a stage or screen part with undue or inappropriate violence **:** OVERACT

²chew \"\ *n* -s **1 :** the act of chewing **2 a :** something that is chewed **:** a portion (as of tobacco) suitable for chewing **:** QUID, CUD **b :** a piece of chewy candy ⟨a molasses ~⟩

che·wa *also* **ce·wa** \'chā(,)wä\ *n, pl* **chewa** *or* **chewas** *also* **cewa** *or* **cewas** *usu cap* **1 :** a Bantu-speaking agricultural people of Nyasaland **2 :** a member of the Chewa people

chew·er \'chüə(r), -ü(ə)r, -üə\ *n* -s **:** one that chews; *esp* **:** one that chews tobacco habitually

chew·et \'chüət\ *n* -s [MF *chouette* owl, chough, of imit. origin] **1 :** CHOUGH **2 :** CHATTERER

chewing gum *n* **:** a preparation of chicle sometimes mixed with other plastic insoluble substances, sweetened and flavored for chewing

chew·ings fescue \'chüiŋz, -üi-\ *n, often cap C* [after Charles *Chewings* †1937 Australian scientist] **:** a perennial pasture and turf grass (*Festuca rubra commutata*) closely related to red fescue but producing a closer firmer sod and tolerating partial shade

chewing the cud *n* **:** RUMINATION

chewing tobacco *n* **:** tobacco, usu. in the form of a plug, that contains a large percentage of flavoring material

che·wink *also* **chee·wink** \chə'wiŋk, chē-\ *n* -s [imit.] **:** the common towhee (*Pipilo erythrophthalmus*) of eastern No. America

chew out *vt, slang* **:** to bawl out **:** REPRIMAND, UPBRAID ⟨some niggling Quartermaster lieutenant *chewed* them *out* because they were a few hundred cases short —A.J.Leibling⟩ ⟨watched him *chew out* an umpire —*Time*⟩

chew over *vt* **:** to meditate on **:** think about reflectively ⟨likes to *chew over* some of the basic problems of our lives —Lewis Mumford⟩ ⟨have in the last decades *chewed over* Plato and Bacon and Freud —J.M.Barzun⟩

chewstick \'=,=\ *n* -s **1** *tropical America* **:** BOARWOOD 1 **2 :** CHAWSTICK

chewy \'chüē, -üi, |i\ *adj* -ER/-EST **:** requiring chewing — used esp. of candy

chex *pl of* ²CHECK 14b

¹chey·enne \(')shī¦an, -aa(ə)n *also* -en\ *n, pl* **cheyenne** *or* **cheyennes** *usu cap* [CanF, fr. Dakota *Shaiyena*, fr. *shaia* to speak strangely, unintelligibly, fr. *sha* red + *ya* to speak] **1 a :** an Indian people of the western plains ranging between the Arkansas and Missouri rivers **b :** a member of such people **2 :** an Algonquian language of the Cheyenne people

²cheyenne \"\ *adj, usu cap* [fr. *Cheyenne*, Wyoming] **:** of or from Cheyenne, the capital of Wyoming ⟨a *Cheyenne* street⟩ **:** of the kind or style prevalent in Cheyenne

¹chey·le·tid \kī'lēd·əd, -le-\ *adj* [NL *Cheyletidae*] **:** of or relating to the Cheyletidae

²cheyletid \"\ *n* -s **:** one of the Cheyletidae

chey·let·i·dae \-'led·ə,dē\ *n pl, cap* [NL, fr. *Cheyletus*, type genus + *-idae*] **:** a small family of minute chiefly ectoparasitic mites distinguished by a pair of immense palpi attached to an anterior beak that are usu. ultimately beneficial because of feeding on debris and other ectoparasites of their bird or mammal hosts

chey·le·tus \-'lēd·əs\ *n* [NL, irreg. fr. Gk *chēlē* claw — more at CHELA] **1** *cap* **:** the type genus of Cheyletidae comprising certain free-living predatory mites that feed chiefly on grain mites **2** *pl* **cheyletus :** a mite of the genus *Cheyletus*

cheyne-stokes respiration *or* **cheyne-stokes breathing** \'chān(ē)'stōks-\ *n, usu cap C&S* [after John *Cheyne* †1836 Scottish physician who first described it, and William *Stokes* †1878 Irish physician who also noted it] **:** cyclic breathing marked by a gradual increase in the rapidity of the respirations followed by a gradual decrease and total cessation for from 5 to 50 seconds observed in cardiac and cerebral and other conditions

chey·ney \'chānē\ *n* -s [prob. fr. Per *chīnī* Chinese] **:** a woolen fabric in use during the 17th and 18th centuries

chez \(')shā\ *prep* [F, fr. L *casae* at home, locative of *casa* house — more at CASA] **:** at or in the home or business place of ⟨hair dressed ~ Pierre⟩ **:** WITH — used with a French personal pronoun ⟨will you dine ~ nous⟩ or a proper name ⟨a British politician lunched ~ Hitler —John Gunther⟩

chf *abbr* chief

chg *abbr* **1** change **2** charge

chgd *abbr* **1** changed **2** charged

chha·tri \'chə·trē\ *n* -s [Hindi *chatrī*] *India* **1 :** a funerary monument **:** a chapel built over a tomb **2 :** a resthouse for visitors to a temple or other sacred site

chhat·tis·gar·hi \,chəd·ēs'gärē\ *n, usu cap* [Hindi *Chattīsgarhī*, fr. *Chattīsgarh*, district in India] **:** a dialect of Hindi spoken by the peoples of Madhya Pradesh and Orissa in northeast India

chi \'kī\ *n* -s [Gk] **:** the 22d letter of the Greek alphabet — symbol X or χ; see ALPHABET table

chia \'chēə\ *n* -s [Sp *chia*, fr. Nahuatl *chia, chian*, fr. Maya *chihàan* strong, strengthening] **1 :** any of several plants of the genus *Salvia* of Mexico and the southwestern U. S. (*Salvia columbariae, S. hispanica, S. tiliaefolia*, and *S. chia*) from the seeds of which the natives prepare a beverage **2 :** a beverage prepared from chia seeds **3** *also* **chia oil :** an edible oil made from chia seeds

chi·ack \'chīək\ *vt* -ED/-ING/-S [prob. alter. of *cheek*] *Austral* **:** to jeer at **:** RAZZ ⟨the spectators continued to ~ him⟩

chiam *usu cap, var of* CHAM

¹chi·an \'kīən\ *adj, usu cap* [*Chios*, island in the Aegean sea (fr. Gk) + E *-an*] **:** of, relating to, or characteristic of Chios (modern Khíos), island in the Aegean sea

²chian \"\ *n* -s *cap* **:** a native or inhabitant of Chios

chi·an·ti \kē'antē, -än-, *Ital* 'kyän-\ *n* -s *usu cap* [It, fr. the *Chianti* mt. area, Italy, where it was first made] **:** a still dry usu. red table wine often bottled in squat green wicker-covered bottles and orig. produced in the Chianti mountain region of Italy but now also elsewhere (as in California)

chian turpentine *n, usu cap C* **:** TURPENTINE 1a

chia·pa·nec \chē'äpə,nek\ *or* **cha·pa·nec** \'chäp-\ *n, pl* **chiapanec** *or* **chiapanecs** *or* **chapanec** *or* **chapanecs** *usu cap* [Sp *chiapaneca, chapaneca*, of AmerInd origin] **1 a :** a Chorotegan people of western Chiapas, Mexico **b :** a member of such people **2 :** the language of the Chiapanec people

chia·pa·nec·an \chē¦äpə¦nekən\ *n, usu cap* **:** CHOROTEGAN

chia·pa·ne·cas \chē,äpə'nākəs\ *or* **cha·pa·ne·cas** \-kəs\ *also* **cha·pa·ne·ca** \,chäpə'nākə\ *n, pl* **chiapanecas** *or* **chapanecas** [Sp, fem. pl. (*chiapanecas*) or sing. (*chiapaneca*) of *chiapaneco* of Chiapas, fr. *Chiapas*, state of Mexico] **:** a mestizo girls' dance from the Mexican state of Chiapas with hops, waltz steps, and hand clapping

chia·ro·scu·rist \,kyärə'sk(y)ůrəst, kē,är-, -ar-, -rō'sk-, -ürə-\ *n* -s [*chiaroscuro* + *-ist*] **:** an artist in chiaroscuro

chia·ro·scu·ro \-ür(,)ō, -ü(,)rō\ *also* **chia·ro·oscu·ro** \-rō·ō's-, -rōə's-\ *n* -s *often attrib* [It, fr. *chiaro* light (fr. L *clarus*) + *oscuro* dark, fr. L *obscurus* — more at CLEAR, OBSCURE] **1 :** pictorial representation in terms of light and shade without regard for or use of colors in the objects depicted ⟨a sketch in ~⟩; *specif* **:** drawing or painting in black and white **2 a :** the arrangement or treatment of the light and dark parts in a pictorial work of art **b :** interplay, variety, or contrast of dissimilar qualities (as of mood, style, character, or spirit) thought of as lightness and darkness ⟨Mynheer had little ~ in his composition; he was prone to call a spade a spade —Norman Douglas⟩ **3 a :** a 16th century woodcut technique in which forms are defined in terms of light and shade through the use of several blocks one of which is used to print deep, sometimes black, shadows and the others moderated shades of a single color **b :** a print produced by this technique **4 :** the use of marked light and shade contrasts for decorative or dramatic effect in painting ⟨the great power of high light and deep shadow that we today call ~ —*Christian Science Monitor*⟩ — compare SFUMATO, TENEBROSO **5 :** interplay of light and shadow on or as if on a surface ⟨a spotlight revealing a ~ of ridges and craters on a mountainside⟩ **6 :** the quality of being veiled or partly in shadow

chi·asm \'kī,azəm\ *n* -s [in sense 1, fr. NL *chiasma;* in sense 2, fr. NL *chiasmus*] **1 :** CHIASMA **2 :** CHIASMUS

chi·as·ma \kī'azmə\ *n, pl* **chiasma·ta** \-məd·ə\ *or* **chiasmas** [NL, fr. Gk, crosspiece of wood, cross bandage, fr. *chiazein* to mark with a chi, fr. *chi* (X)] **1** *anat* **:** a decussation or intersection ⟨the optic ~⟩ **2** *biol* **:** a fusion and exchange of segments of chromatids occurring between members of a bivalent during diplotene **:** the source of genetic crossovers — **chi·as·mal** \(')kī¦azməl\ *adj* — **chi·as·mat·ic** \,kīaz¦mad·ik, -ī,az-\ *adj* — **chi·as·mic** \(')kī¦azmik\ *adj*

chi·as·ma·type \kī'azmə,tīp-\ *adj* [back-formation fr. *chiasmatypy*] **:** of or relating to chiasmatypy

chiasmatype theory *n* **:** a theory in biology: genetic crossing over and chiasma formation are causally related — compare CHIASMATYPY

chi·as·ma·typy \-,tīpē\ *n* -ES [ISV *chiasma-* (fr. NL *chiasma*) + *-typy*; orig. formed as F *chiasmatypie*] **:** the spiral twisting of homologous chromosomes during zygotene that results in intimate association of chromatids with chiasma formation and provides the mechanism for crossing over

chi·as·mo·don \kī'azmə,dän\ *n, cap* [NL, fr. Gk *chiasma* + NL *-odon*] **:** a genus of deep-sea percoid fishes — see BLACK SWALLOWER — **chi·as·mo·don·tid** \¦=¦=¦=tәd\ *n or adj*

chi·as·mus \kī'azməs\ *n, pl* **chias·mi** \-,mī\ [NL, fr. Gk *chiasmos*, fr. *chiazein* to mark with a chi] **:** the inversion of the order of syntactical elements in the second of two juxtaposed and syntactically parallel phrases or clauses (as *a superman in physique but in intellect a fool*); *also* **:** an instance of this — **chi·as·tic** \(')kī¦astik\ *adj*

chiasto- *comb form* [G, fr. Gk *chiastos*] **:** marked with or characterized by a cross **:** crossed at right angles ⟨*chiasto*basidium⟩

chi·as·to·basidial \kī¦astō+\ *adj* [*chiasto-* + *basidial*] **:** having the nuclear spindles of the basidia at right angles to the longitudinal axis — compare STICHOBASIDIAL — **chi·as·to·basidium** \"+\ *n*

chi·as·to·lite \kī'astə,līt\ *n* -s [G *chiastolith*, fr. *chiasto-* + *-lith* -lite] **:** a mineral consisting of a variety of andalusite whose crystals have a tessellated appearance in cross section due to the arrangement of impurities — called also *macle*

chiaus \'chaůs(h)\ *n* -ES [Turk *çavuş* sergeant, doorkeeper, messenger, fr. *çav* voice, news] **1 :** a Turkish messenger or sergeant **2 :** CHEAT, SWINDLER

chia·vet·ta \kyə'ved·ə, kyä'-\ *n, pl* **chiavet·te** \-ed·ē\ [It, dim. of *chiave* key, clef, fr. L *clavis* key — more at CLAVICLE] **:** a clef (as one of the C clefs) formerly used to shift temporarily the pitch range of a staff carrying a voice part and so avoid the use of ledger lines

chi·ba \'chēbə\ *adj, usu cap* [fr. *Chiba*, Japan] **:** of or from the city of Chiba, Japan **:** of the kind or style prevalent in Chiba

chib·cha \'chibchə\ *n, pl* **chibcha** *or* **chibchas** *usu cap* [Sp, of AmerInd origin] **1 a :** a people of central Colombia constituting one of the peoples of the Chibchan language family — called also *Muisca* **b :** a member of such people **2 :** the extinct language of the Chibcha people

chib·chan \-chən\ *adj, usu cap* **1 :** of or relating to a language stock of Colombia and Central America including Andaki, Barbacoa, Bribri, Cabecar, Cágaba, Chibcha, Coiba, Colima, Cueva, Cuna, Guatuso, Guaymi Guetar, Ica, Paez, Rama, San Blas, Tulamanca, and Valiente **2 :** of or relating to the peoples speaking Chibchan languages

chi·bi·gou·a·zou \,shēbē,gü'ä(,)zü\ *n* -s [Pg, fr. Guarani] **:** a brightly marked ocelot (*Felis pardalis chibigouazou*) of the Mato Grosso

chib·ol \'chibəl\ *dial Brit var of* CIBOL

chi·bouk *or* **chi·bouque** \chə'bük, -ük\ *n* -s [F *chibouque*, fr. Turk *çıbuk, çubuk*] **:** a Turkish tobacco pipe having a clay or meerschaum bowl and a long stem with a mouthpiece often of amber

¹chic \'shēk *also* -ik\ *n* -s [F, perh. fr. G *schick* fitness, order, skill, fr. LG, fr. *schicken* to put into order, fr. MLG; akin to MHG *schicken* to prepare, arrange, send] **1 :** artistic cleverness and dexterity esp. in painting **2 :** easy elegance and sophistication of dress or manner **:** STYLE, SWANK, CHARM **3 :** VOGUE, FASHION, MODISHNESS ⟨the ~ of the latest hats⟩

²chic \"\ *adj* [F, fr. *chic*, n.] **1 :** cleverly stylish **:** having chic **2 :** in vogue **:** currently fashionable **:** MODISH

¹chica *var of* CHICHA

²chi·ca \'chēkə\ *n* -s [AmerSp] **:** CARAJURA 2

chicadee *var of* CHICKADEE

¹chi·ca·go \shə'kä(,)gō, -'kȯ(- *sometimes* -'kà(- *or* -gə — *natives of the city prob most often use* ȯ *in the second syllable*\ *adj, usu cap* [fr. *Chicago*, Ill.] **:** of or from the city of Chicago, Ill. **:** of the kind or style prevalent in Chicago

²chicago \"\ *n* -s *usu cap* [fr. *Chicago*, Ill.] **1 :** a method of playing contract bridge in sets of four deals rather than rubbers **2 :** MICHIGAN

chicago acid *n, usu cap C* **:** a crystalline acid $NH_2C_{10}H_4(OH)(SO_3H)_2$ used as an intermediate in making azo dyes; 8-amino-1-naphthol-5,7-disulfonic acid

chi·ca·go·an \-,gōwən\ *n* -s *cap* [*Chicago* + E *-an*] **:** a native or inhabitant of Chicago

chicago blue *n, usu cap C & often cap B* **:** any of several direct dyes — see DYE table I (under *Direct Blue 1, 4, and 22*)

chicago piano *n, usu cap C, slang* **:** POM-POM

chicago pool *n, usu cap C* **:** rotation pool in which at the start of play the object balls are placed around the table at the diamonds in numerical order

chicago style *n, usu cap C* **:** a widely used method of butchering animal carcasses

chi·ca·lo·te \ˌchikəˈlōd·ē\ *n* -s [Sp, fr. Nahuatl *chicalotl*] **:** a white-flowered prickly poppy (*Argemone platyceras*) of Mexico and the southwestern U.S.

¹chi·cane \shəˈkān, chə-\ *vb* -ED/-ING/-S [F *chicaner*, fr. MF, to quibble, prevent justice] *vi* **:** to use chicanery **:** employ shifts, subterfuges, or artifices ⟨a wretch he had taught to lie and ~ —George Meredith⟩ ~ *vt* **:** to cavil at **:** quibble over; *also* **:** TRICK, CHEAT, DUPE ⟨he *chicaned* the widow out of her property⟩

²chicane \"\ *n* -s [F, fr. MF, fr. *chicaner*] **1 a :** deception usu. by legalistic subterfuge **:** CHICANERY ⟨the lawyer is exclusively occupied with the details of predatory fraud, either in achieving or checkmating ~ —Thorstein Veblen⟩ **b :** an instance of chicane **:** SUBTERFUGE, QUIBBLE **2 :** an obstacle esp. on a racecourse **3 :** the absence of any trumps in a hand of cards just dealt, in some forms of bridge formerly scoring as simple honors **syn** see DECEPTION

³chicane \"\ *adj* [²*chicane*] **1 :** having no trumps — used of a player or his hand of cards **2** *slang* **:** having no money **:** BROKE

chi·can·er \-nə(r)\ *n* -s [earlier *chicaneur*, fr. F, fr. MF, fr. *chicaner* + *-eur* -or] **:** one that uses chicanery

chi·ca·nery \-n(ə)rē, -i\ *n* -ES [F *chicanerie*, fr. MF, fr. *chicaner* + *-erie* -ery] **1 :** deception by artful subterfuge, sophistry, pettifogging, misrepresentation, conniving, or similar artifice ⟨the administrative ~ of governments —*New Republic*⟩ **2 :** a piece of sharp practice (as at law) **:** TRICK — usu. used in pl. **syn** see DECEPTION

chic·a·ric \ˈchikəˌrik, ˌ==ˈ=\ *n* -s [imit.] **:** TURNSTONE

chiccory *var of* CHICORY

chich \ˈchich\ *n* -ES [ME *chiche*, fr. MF, fr. L *cicer*; akin to Arm *siseṙn* chick-pea] **:** CHICK-PEA

chi·cha \ˈchēchə\ *or* **chi·ca** \-ēkə\ *n* -s [Sp, prob. fr. Cuna *chichah* (*co-pah*), lit., corn drink] **:** a So. American and Central American beer made chiefly from fermented maize

chi·char·ro \chēˈchä(ˌ)rō\ *n* -s [Sp] **:** BIG-EYED SCAD

chiches *pl of* CHICH

¹chi·chi \ˈchē(ˌ)chē, ˈshē(ˌ)shē *sometimes* shēˈshē\ *adj* [F] **1 :** elaborately or conspicuously ornamented or ornamental **:** FRILLY, SHOWY **2 :** limited in appeal to a small artistic or intellectual cult **:** ARTY, PRECIOUS, AFFECTED **3 :** placing excessive emphasis on fashion or elegance **:** CHIC

²chichi \"\ *n* -s **:** something that is chichi **:** ORNAMENTATION, FRILLINESS, SHOW, AFFECTATION

ch'i-chia \ˈchēˈjyä\ *adj, usu cap 1st C* [prob. fr. a place name in China] **:** of or relating to the earliest Neolithic stage in China characterized by a distinctive painted pottery

chi·chi·mec \ˈchēchəˌmek\ *or* **chi·chi·me·ca** \ˌ==ˈmākə\ *or* **chi·chi·me·co** \-ˈmā(ˌ)kō\ *n, pl* **chichimec** *or* **chichimecs** *or* **chichimeca** *or* **chichimecas** *or* **chichimeco** *or* **chichimecos** *usu cap* [Sp *chichimeca*, fr. Nahuatl *chichimecatl*] **1 a :** any one of the Nahuatlan peoples in Mexico before the rise of the Aztec empire **b :** a warlike people of northern Mexico **c :** a member of any such people **2 :** the language of the Chichimec people — **chi·chi·mecan** \ˌ==ˈmākən, -mek-\ *adj, usu cap*

chi·chi·pa·te \ˌchichəˈpäd·ē\ *n* -s [AmerSp, fr. Nahuatl *chichipatli*, lit., bitter medicine, fr. *chichic* bitter + *patli* medicine] **:** a tropical American timber tree (*Sweetia panamensis*) of the family Leguminosae

chi·chi·pe \chəˈchēpē\ *n* -s [MexSp *chichipe, chichibe*] **:** a tall treelike Mexican cactus (*Lemaireocereus chichipe*) with edible red fruits

chi·chi·tu·na \ˌchēchəˈtünə\ *n* -s [MexSp] **:** the fruit of the chichipe

¹chick \ˈchik\ *n* -s [ME *chike, chiken* — more at CHICKEN] **1 a :** CHICKEN; *esp* **:** one newly hatched or still downy **b :** the young of any bird **2 :** CHILD — often used as a term of endearment **3** *slang* **:** a young woman

²chick \"\ *vi* -ED/-ING/-S [ME *chicken, chykkyn*, perh. of imit. origin; fr. the cracking of seeds when they germinate] *dial Eng* **:** SPROUT

³chick \"\ *n* -s [Hindi *ciq*, fr. Per *chiq*] **:** a screen used in India and southeast Asia esp. for a doorway and constructed of bamboo slips loosely bound by vertical strings and often painted

⁴chick \"\ *n* -s [short for earlier *chickeen, chickino*, fr. It *zecchino* — more at SEQUIN] *India* **:** a sequin formerly current at the ports of India at the value of four rupees

chick·a·bid·dy \ˈchikəˌbidē, -di\ *n* -ES [¹*chick* + connective *-a-* + *biddy*] **1 :** CHICKEN — a child's term **2 :** CHILD — a term of endearment

chick·a·dee *also* **chic·a·dee** \ˈchikə(ˌ)dē, -ˌdi\ *n* -s [imit.] **:** any of several crestless American titmice (genus *Penthestes* or *Parus*) usu. having the crown of the head sharply demarked and darker than the body plumage — see ACADIAN CHICKADEE, BLACK-CAPPED CHICKADEE

chick·a·mau·ga \ˌchikəˈmȯgə\ *n, pl* **chickamauga** *or* **chickamaugas** *usu cap* **1 :** a Cherokee people living near the present location of Chattanooga, Tenn. **2 :** a member of the Chickamauga people

chick·a·ree \ˈchikəˌrē\ *n* -s [imit.] **:** the American red squirrel or certain related squirrels

chick·a·saw \ˈchikəˌsȯ *also* -kˌsȯ\ *n, pl* **chickasaw** *or* **chickasaws** *usu cap* **1 a :** a Muskogean people of northern Mississippi and Alabama **b :** a member of such people **2 :** a dialect of Choctaw spoken by the Chickasaw

chickasaw plum *n, usu cap C* **:** a native American shrub or small tree (*Prunus angustifolia*) that has red or yellowish cherrylike fruit and has given rise to several cultivated varieties in the southern U.S.

chick bronchitis *n* [¹*chick*] **:** INFECTIOUS BRONCHITIS 1

chick disease *n* [¹*chick*] **:** a virus infection of young chicks that is of uncertain relationship to the avian leukosis complex and is characterized by focal lesions in liver and heart muscle

chickee *var of* CHIKEE

chick·ell \ˈchikəl\ *n* -s [imit.] *Brit* **:** WHEATEAR

¹chick·en \ˈchikən *sometimes* -kᵊŋ *esp when another word, as "coop" or "pie", follows without pause*\ *n* -s [ME *chiken*, fr. OE *cicen, cycen* young chicken; akin to MHG *kuchen* young chicken, ON *kjūklingr* gosling, OE *cocc* cock — more at COCK] **1 a :** the common domestic fowl (*Gallus gallus*); *also, now Brit* **:** the young of this bird when less than one year old **b :** the flesh esp. of the young of such fowl used as food **2 :** the young of any of various esp. gallinaceous birds whose young run about soon after hatching **3** *slang* **:** a young person, esp. a woman **:** ¹CHICK 3 **4 :** COWARD, SISSY **5** *slang* **:** a young woman of easy familiarity **6** *slang* **:** the details of duty or discipline considered unnecessary or an imposition **:** petty detail rigorously emphasized

²chicken \"\ *adj* [prob. short for *chickenhearted* or *chicken-livered*] **1** *slang* **:** CHICKENHEARTED, COWARDLY **2** *slang* **:** insistent on petty or irksome esp. military discipline

³chicken \"\ *vi* **chickened; chickened; chickening** \-k(ə)niŋ\ **chickens** *slang* **:** to lose one's nerve **:** show cowardice **:** DESERT — often used with *out* ⟨~*ed* out on an earlier plan to march into a package store wearing a mask —*Springfield (Mass.) Union*⟩

chickenberry \ˈ==ˌ==\ *n* **1 :** WINTERGREEN 2a **2 :** PARTRIDGEBERRY

chicken body louse *n* **:** a common yellowish biting louse (*Menacanthus stramineus*) of poultry

chicken breast *n* **:** PIGEON BREAST — **chicken-breasted** *adj*

chicken bug *n* **:** ADOBE BUG

chicken cac·cia·to·re \-ˌkächəˈtōrē, -ˌkach-\ *n* **:** chicken fried in olive oil, seasoned with herbs, and simmered in tomato and white wine liquor

chicken cholera *n* **:** FOWL CHOLERA

chicken colonel *n* [so called fr. the eagle worn on the shoulders] *slang* **:** a colonel as distinguished from a lieutenant colonel

chicken corn *n* **:** an annual nonsaccharine sorghum (*Sorghum vulgare drummondii*) that is often a troublesome weed in the southern U.S.

chicken feed *n, slang* **:** a trifling or contemptible sum (as in profit or wages) **:** SMALL CHANGE

chicken-fighters \ˈ==ˌ==\ *also* **chicken-fights** *n pl* [so called fr. a children's game in which each of two participants tries to decapitate the other's flower by pulling on the stem of his own, one spurred petal (likened to a cock's spur) of which is interlocked with that of his adversary's flower] **:** the flowers of several violets (as *Viola cucullata*) one petal of which is spurred

chicken flu *n* **:** INFECTIOUS LARYNGOTRACHEITIS

chicken grape *n* **:** a stout tall-growing grape (*Vitis vulpina*) of the eastern and central U.S. with small shining black fruits that sweeten with the first frosts —called also *frost grape*

chicken gumbo *n* **:** a gumbo made with chicken

chicken halibut *n* **:** a young halibut

chicken hawk *n* **:** any of various hawks that sometimes prey or are reputed to prey on chickens: as **a :** SHARP-SHINNED HAWK **b :** COOPER'S HAWK

chickenhearted \ˈ==ˈ==\ *adj* **1 :** TIMID, COWARDLY **2 :** lacking in necessary sternness **:** SOFT-HEARTED — **chickenheartedly** \ˈ==ˈ===\ *adv*

chicken-livered \ˈ==ˈ==\ *adj* **:** FAINTHEARTED, COWARDLY

chicken lobster *n* **:** a young lobster

chicken mite *n* **:** a small mite (*Dermanyssus gallinae*) infesting poultry esp. in warm regions

chicken pepper *n* **:** a common small-flowered buttercup (*Ranunculus abortivus*) of the eastern U.S.

chicken pest *n* **:** FOWL PEST 1

chicken pox *n* **1 :** an acute contagious disease principally of children and not commonly dangerous caused by a virus and characterized by low-grade fever and other symptoms and blisterlike vesicles **2 :** FOWL POX

chicken pull *n* **:** a contest in horsemanship in which the rider tries at full gallop to snatch up a half-buried chicken

chickens *pl of* CHICKEN, *pres 3d sing of* CHICKEN

chicken septicemia *n* **:** hemorrhagic septicemia of poultry

chicken skin *n* [so called fr. the pin-point marks resembling chicken skin] **:** a fine thin vellum used in covering fans

chicken's-meat \ˈ==ˌ=\ *n, dial Eng* **:** CHICKWEED

chicken snake *n* **1 :** any of a number of large harmless No. American colubrid snakes (genus *Elaphe*) — called also *rat snake* **2 :** the tropical rat snake (*Spilotes pullatus*), a large colubrid closely related to the indigo snake

chicken's-toes \ˈ==ˌ=\ *n pl but sing or pl in constr* [so called fr. the shape of its roots] **:** a coralroot (*Corallorhiza odontorhiza*)

chicken terrapin *or* **chicken tortoise** *or* **chicken turtle** *n* **1 :** a small or medium-sized edible aquatic turtle (*Deirochelys reticularia*) of the southern Atlantic states having a long snakelike neck and an elongated carapace marked with a network of yellow lines **2 :** the young of the green turtle

chicken tick *n* **:** an argasid tick (*Argas persicus* syn. *miniatus*) attacking fowls in the warmer parts of the world and transmitting the fowl spirochetosis organism (*Spirochaeta gallinae*)

chickenweed \ˈ==ˌ=\ *n* [ME *chikenwede*, fr. *chiken* chicken + *wede* weed] **:** CHICKWEED

chicken wire *n* [so called fr. its use in fencing chicken pens] **:** a light galvanized wire netting of hexagonal mesh

chick·ery \ˈchik(ə)rē\ *n* -ES [¹*chick* + *-ery*] **:** a poultry hatchery

chicking *pres part of* CHICK

chick·ling \ˈchikliŋ\ *or* **chickling vetch** *n* -s [by folk etymology (prob. influence of ¹*chick*) fr. earlier *chichling*, fr. *chich* + *-ling*] **:** the grass pea (*Lathyrus sativus*) of Europe cultivated for seeds and forage

chick-pea \ˈ=ˌ=\ *n* [by folk etymology (prob. influence of ¹*chick*) fr. earlier *chich-pea*, fr. *chich* + *pea*] **1 :** an Asiatic herb (*Cicer arietinum*) now widespread in the western hemisphere that bears short pods with one or two seeds somewhat resembling peas in flavor **2 :** the seed of the chick-pea constituting an important article of diet esp. in southern Europe and in India — called also *chestnut bean, chich, dwarf pea, garbanzo, garavance* and in India *gram* or *Bengal gram*

chicks *pl of* CHICK, *pres 3d sing of* CHICK

chickweed \ˈ=ˌ=\ *n* -s [alter. of *chickenweed*] **1 :** any of various low-growing small-leaved weedy plants of the family Caryophyllaceae (as members of the genera *Arenaria, Cerastium*, and *Stellaria*) several of which are relished by birds or used as potherbs **2 :** any of various plants of families other than Caryophyllaceae that resemble chickweeds — usu. used in combination ⟨red ~⟩; compare CARPETWEED

chickweed phlox *n* **:** a diffuse herb (*Phlox stellaria*) found in rocky places in the U.S. and having small linear leaves and bluish white flowers

chickweed wintergreen *n* **:** an American starflower (*Trientalis americana*) or its Eurasian relative (*T. europaea*)

chi·cle \ˈchikəl *sometimes* ˈchēkəl *or* ˈchiklē\ *n* -s [Sp, fr. Nahuatl *chictli, tzictli*] **1 :** a gum reported to contain both rubber and gutta-percha obtained as pinkish to reddish brown pieces from the latex of the sapodilla largely from Yucatan and Central America and used as the chief ingredient of chewing gum **2 :** any of several gums derived from tropical So. American trees of the families Moraceae and Apocynaceae

chicle bleeder *n* **:** CHICLERO

chi·cle·ro \chiˈkle(ˌ)rō\ *n* -s [AmerSp, fr. Sp *chicle* + *-ero* -er] **:** a gatherer of chicle

chiclero ulcer *n* **:** leishmaniasis of the mouth, nose, and throat

¹chi·co \ˈchē(ˌ)kō\ *n* -s [MexSp (*juego*) *chico*, lit., small game, fr. Sp *juego* game + *chico* small, baby talk modif. of L *ciccum* pomegranate core, integument, trifle, fr. Gk *kikkos*] **:** the game played in the composite card game frog when the bid is won by the player naming as trumps any suit but hearts, the widow being set aside but belonging finally to the bidder — compare ²GRAND 4a (2)

²chico \"\ *n* -s [modif. of Sp *chicalote* — more at CHICALOTE] **:** the common greasewood (*Sarcobatus vermiculatus*) of the western U.S.

³chico \"\ *n* -s [in sense 1, fr. AmerSp, short for Sp *chicozapote*, fr. Nahuatl *xicatzapotl*, fr. *xicotl* juice + *tzapotl* sapote; in sense 2, PhilSp, fr. AmerSp] **1** *Philippines* **:** SAPODILLA 2 **2** *Philippines* **:** MARMALADE TREE

chico mamey *n* [PhilSp, fr. AmerSp *chico* sapodilla, marmalade tree + Sp *mamey* mammee — more at CHICO, MAMMEE] *Philippines* **:** the fruit of the marmalade tree; *also* **:** MARMALADE TREE

chi·co·mu·cel·tec \ˌchēkōˈmüsəlˌtek\ *n, pl* **chicomuceltec** *or* **chicomuceltecs** *usu cap* [Sp *Chicomuceltecа*, of AmerInd origin] **1 a :** an Indian people of southern Chiapas, Mexico **b :** a member of such people **2 :** a Mayan language of the Chicomuceltec people

chic·o·ry *also* **chic·co·ry** *or* **chick·o·ry** \ˈchik(ə)rē, -ri\ *n* -ES [alter. (influenced by F *chicorée*) of ME *cicoree*, fr. MF *chicorée, cichorée*, fr. L *cichoreum, cichorium*, fr. Gk *kichora, kichoreia*] **1 :** a thick-rooted usu. blue-flowered perennial herb (*Cichorium intybus*) that is native to Europe but widely grown for its young leaves which are used as salad greens and for its roots and that in many areas (as in parts of Australia and the U.S.) has escaped to become a serious weed pest — called also *witloof;* see ENDIVE **2 :** the dried ground roasted root of chicory used to flavor or adulterate coffee **3** *or* **chicory blue :** a light bluish gray that is greener and deeper than sky gray — called also *succory blue*

chicory family *n* **:** CICHORIACEAE

chi·cot \shēˈkō\ *n* -s [AmerF, fr. F, stub, stump] **:** KENTUCKY COFFEE TREE

chi·co·te \chiˈkōd·ē\ *n* -s [AmerSp, fr. Sp, end of a rope, piece of rope, perh. fr. MF *chicot* stump] *West* **:** a long whip that has a wooden handle and is used by cowboys

chi·co·za·po·te \ˌchēkōzəˈpōd·ē, ōsə-\ *n* -s [Sp, fr. Nahuatl *xicotzapotl*, fr. *xico* bee + *tzapotl* sapote] **:** SAPODILLA

chics *pl of* CHIC

chi-dan *usu cap C, var of* KHITAN

chide \ˈchīd\ *vb* **chid** \ˈchid\ *or* **chid·ed** \ˈchīdəd\ *or archaic* **chode** \ˈchōd\ **chid** \ˈchid\ *or* **chid·den** \ˈchidᵊn\ *or* **chided; chid·ing** \ˈchīdiŋ\ **chides** [ME *chiden*, fr. OE *cīdan* to quarrel, chide, fr. *cīd* strife] *vi* **1 :** to speak out in angry or displeased rebuke **:** CONTEND, BRAWL, WRANGLE **:** clamor stridently ⟨the people did ~ with Moses —Exod 17:2 (AV)⟩ **2 :** to make an uproar or clamor (as of a tempest or the sea) suggesting violent anger ⟨the *chiding* flood —Shak.⟩ **3 :** to express disapproval in correcting or appealing for change and improvement ⟨*chiding* against the king for his blind infatuation⟩ ~ *vt* **1 :** to voice disapproval to (for some shortcoming) now often mildly and charitably as a parent, mentor, or friendly critic in the interests of amendment or improvement **:** SCOLD ⟨*chiding* the child for his inattention⟩ ⟨*chiding* the maid for her carelessness⟩ **2 :** to seem to scold, complain against, rebuke, or threaten with strident or brawling sound ⟨the sea that ~*s* the banks of England —Shak.⟩ **syn** see REPROVE

chiding *n* -s [ME, fr. OE *cīding*, fr. *cīdan* + *-ing*] **1** *archaic* **:** CONTENTION, QUARRELING **2 :** REPROOF, REBUKE

chid·ing·ly *adv* **:** in a chiding manner

chi·dra \ˈchēdrə\ *n* -s [AmerSp] **:** JIPIJAPA

¹chief \ˈchēf\ *n, pl* **chiefs** \ˈchēfs *sometimes* -ēvz\ [ME *chief, chef*, fr. OF *chief, chef*, fr. L *caput* head — more at HEAD] **1 a** *obs* **:** the top or uppermost part **:** HEAD **b** *heraldry* (1) **:** the upper part of the field — compare ESCUTCHEON 1 (2) **:** a horizontal band at the top of the field **2 a :** the head or leader of any body of men **:** a commander (as of an army) or a headman (as of a tribe, clan, or family) **b :** the directing head of a political party, government bureau or department, or office organization ⟨~ of mission⟩; *also* **:** one's superior in such a body **c :** an officer in charge of any of certain branches or departments of the service — used in titles ⟨*Chief* of Staff⟩ ⟨*Chief* of Ordnance⟩ **d :** a chief officer of a department of government ⟨*Chief* of Police⟩ ⟨Fire *Chief*⟩ **e :** CHIEF PETTY OFFICER **3 :** the principal part **:** the most valuable portion ⟨this London where the ~ of his life must pass —John Galsworthy⟩ — **in chief 1** *feudal law* **a :** of tenure or holding directly from the lord paramount, that is, in England, the king, to whom the tenure service is rendered personally **b :** by perpetual ground rent or feu duty as distinguished from the limited lease **2** *heraldry* **:** borne on the part of the field that would be occupied by a chief **3 :** in the chief position or place — often used in titles ⟨Commander-*in-Chief*⟩

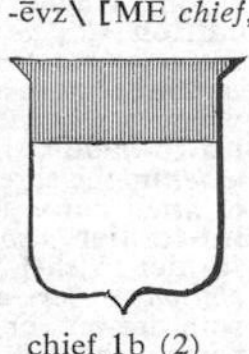

chief 1b (2)

²chief \"\ *adj* -ER/-EST [ME *chef, chief*, fr. *chef, chief*, n.] **1 :** accorded highest rank, office, or rating ⟨~ executive⟩ **:** superior in authority, power, or influence ⟨~ prelate of our church, archbishop, first in council —Alfred Tennyson⟩ **2 :** marked by greatest importance, significance, influence **:** SALIENT **:** subordinating other persons, things, items of the same kind or class ⟨his ~ fame rests on his important volumes —A.V.W.Jackson⟩ **3** *now chiefly Scot* **:** INTIMATE, FRIENDLY, CLOSE ⟨a whisperer separates ~ friends —Prov 16:28 (RSV)⟩

syn PRINCIPAL, MAIN, LEADING, FOREMOST, CAPITAL all indicate first in importance and are often interchangeable. CHIEF may stress the fact of the existence of subordinate matters ⟨so many young people of today have lost sight of the fact that duty, not pleasure, is the *chief* aim of living —Ellen Glasgow⟩ ⟨one of the performances I remember extremely vividly, because the *chief* turn consisted of four performing elephants —Osbert Sitwell⟩ PRINCIPAL is likely to indicate greatest importance or power and influence, with other matters as minor ⟨after summing all the rest, religion ruling in the breast, a *principal* ingredient —William Cowper⟩ ⟨the central point of interest, unforgotten, absorbing, *principal* —Matthew Arnold⟩ ⟨the country of the Shilluk is almost entirely in grass, hence the *principal* wealth of the people consists in their flocks and herds —J.G.Frazer⟩ MAIN stresses greater size, power, or importance ⟨the *main* line express services tended to further this concentration, and the feeder lines and cross country services ran down, died out, or were deliberately extirpated —Lewis Mumford⟩ ⟨the literary critic . . . will yet find, like the historian, his *main* subject-matter in the past —L.P.Smith⟩ LEADING stresses precedence or coming before others in a series, sequence, or progression ⟨if John of Gaunt was fallen from his old power he was still the *leading* noble in the realm —J.R.Green⟩ ⟨Massachusetts furnished one of the *leading* defenders of the disturbing views of Darwin in the person of Asa Gray Fisher, professor of botany at Harvard —*Amer. Guide Series: Mass.*⟩ FOREMOST is often the equivalent of LEADING but may more strongly suggest the notion of a course, race, chase, or contest ⟨within a year the Bulletin had outstripped all other papers in the city, winning recognition as the *foremost* champion of the people's right —*Amer. Guide Series: Calif.*⟩ ⟨the clock has been the *foremost* machine in modern technics: and at each period it has remained in the lead: it marks a perfection toward which other machines aspire —Lewis Mumford⟩ CAPITAL stresses the idea of major significance or importance ⟨the *capital* as well as the trivial sins —Henry Miller⟩

³chief \"\ *adv* [²*chief*] *archaic* **:** CHIEFLY, PRINCIPALLY

chief cell *n* **1 :** one of the cells that line the lumen of the fundic glands of the stomach: **a :** a small cell with granular cytoplasm that secretes pepsin **b :** a larger cell with hyaline cytoplasm and a mucoid secretion — compare PARIETAL CELL **2 :** one of the secretory cells of the parathyroid glands

chief·dom \-dəm\ *n* -s **1 :** the position or office of chief **:** LEADERSHIP **2 :** a region or a people ruled by a chief

chief·ery \ˈchēf(ə)rē\ *or* **chief·ry** \-frē\ *n* -ES [¹*chief* + *-ery, -ry*] **1 :** CHIEFTAINCY — used mostly of Celtic institutions **2 :** dues, tribute, or rent belonging to a chief

chief·ess \ˈchēfəs\ *n* -ES [¹*chief* + *-ess*] **:** a female chief — used esp. in Polynesia

chief hare *n* **:** LITTLE CHIEF HARE

chief justice *n* **:** the justice who is the official head of a judicial body (as the head of one of the supreme courts of the various states or of the Supreme Court of the U.S.) — **chief-justiceship** \ˈ=ˈ===ˌ=\ *n*

chief·less \ˈchēfləs\ *adj* **:** being without a chief

¹chief·ly \ˈchēflē, -li\ *adv* [ME *chefly, chiefly*, fr. *chef, chief*, adj. + *-ly*] **1 :** most importantly **:** above all **:** PRINCIPALLY, PREEMINENTLY, ESPECIALLY **2 :** for the most part **:** MOSTLY, MAINLY

²chiefly \"\ *adj* [¹*chief* + *-ly*] **:** relating or belonging to a chief

chief master sergeant *n* **:** an air force noncommissioned officer rating just above a senior master sergeant

chief master sergeant of the air force : a noncommissioned officer of the highest enlisted rank in the air force — see RANK table

chief of state : the formal head of a national state as distinguished from the head of the government

chief petty officer n **:** a petty officer ranking just below senior chief petty officer and just above petty officer first class

chief point *n* **1 :** MIDDLE CHIEF POINT **2 :** DEXTER CHIEF POINT

chiefs *pl of* CHIEF

chief·tain \ˈchēftən *also* -tin *sometimes* -ˌtān\ *n* -s [ME *cheftaine, chieftaine*, fr. MF *chevetain*, alter. (influenced by MF *chev-*, fr. ML *capi-*, fr. L *caput* head) of OF *chastain*, fr. LL *capitaneus* commander, fr. *capitaneus*, adj., outstanding, fr. L *caput* — more at HEAD] **1 :** CHIEF, RULER **2** *archaic* **:** the leader of a troop or army **:** CAPTAIN **3 :** the leader or headman of a band (as of robbers) or gang (as of thieves) **4 a :** the head of a branch of a Scottish clan; *also* **:** the chief of a Scottish clan **b :** a chief ruling a primitive tribe or people

chief·tain·cy \-tənsē, -tin-, -si\ *n* -ES **1 :** the rank, dignity, office, or rule of a chieftain **2 :** a subdivision of the land in early England ruled over by a chieftain **3 :** CHIEFDOM

chief·tain·ess \-nəs\ *n* -ES **:** a female chieftain

chief·tain·ry \-nrē\ *n* -ES **1 :** the office or territory of a chieftain **2 :** a collective body of chieftains

chief·tain·ship \-nˌship\ *n* -s **:** CHIEFTAINCY

chief·tess \ˈchēftəs\ *n* -ES [contr. of *chieftainess*] **:** CHIEFESS

chief warrant officer *n* **:** a senior warrant officer in the armed forces

chiel \ˈchē(ə)l\ *or* **chield** \-l(d)\ *n* -s [ME *cheld*, var. of *child* —more at CHILD] *chiefly Scot* **:** FELLOW, LAD, CHILD

ch'ien lung \ˈchēenˈlu̇ŋ\ *adj, usu cap C&L* [after *Ch'ien Lung* (Kien Lung) †1799 Chinese emperor, fourth of the Ch'ing dynasty] **:** of, relating to, or having the characteristics of Chinese ceramic art or Chinese porcelain wares of the latter half of the 18th century

chieve \ˈchēv\ *vi* -ED/-ING/-S [ME *cheven, chieven* to reach an end, succeed, thrive, fr. OF *chevir* to reach an end, finish, satisfy, come to terms, fr. *chief, chef* end, extremity, head — more at CHIEF] *now dial Eng* **:** THRIVE, PROSPER

chiff·chaff \ˈchifˌchaf\ *n* -s [imit.] **:** a small grayish European warbler (*Phylloscopus collybita*) related to the common willow warbler

chif·fer *also* **chif·fre** \'shifə(r)\ *n* -s [F *chiffre,* fr. It *cifra* figure, fr. ML, zero — more at CIPHER] **:** FIGURE, NUMBER; *specif* **:** a figure in a music score indicating the harmony (as in a figured bass)

¹chif·fon \shi'fän, 'shif,än *sometimes* -ōn\ *n* -s [F, lit., rag, fr. *chiffe* old rag, alter. (influenced by *chiffre* thing of no value, zero) of MF *chipe,* fr. ME *chip* — more at CHIP] **1 :** any of various ornamental additions to a woman's dress (as a knot of ribbons) **2 :** a sheer plain-weave very lightweight clothing fabric made of hard-twisted single yarns of wool, silk, cotton, rayon, or nylon and usu. given a dull soft finish

²chiffon \"\ *adj* **1 :** like the fabric chiffon in sheerness or softness ⟨~ taffeta⟩ **2** *of pie, cake, or pudding* **:** having a light delicate texture achieved usu. by adding whipped egg whites or whipped gelatin ⟨lemon ~ pie⟩

chif·fo·nade \,shifə'näd, -ād\ *n* -s [F *chiffonnade,* fr. *chiffon* + *-ade;* fr. the shredded vegetables, resembling rags] **:** shredded or finely cut vegetables used in soup or salad dressing

chif·fo·nier *also* **chif·fon·nier** \¦shifə¦ni(ə)r, -iə\ *or* **chef·fo·nier** \¦shef-\ *n* -s [F *chiffonnier,* fr. *chiffon* + *-ier* -er] **1 :** an ornamental cabinet with drawers or shelves; *specif* **:** a high and narrow chest of drawers **2 :** RAGPICKER

chif·fo·robe \'shifə,rōb\ *n* -s [*chiffonier* + *wardrobe*] **:** a combination of wardrobe and chest of drawers

chiffonier

chig·e·tai \'chigə,tī\ *or* **dzeg·ge·tai** \'jeg-\ *n* -s [Mongolian *tchikhitei,* lit., long-eared, fr. *tchikhi* ear] **:** a wild ass of Mongolia being prob. a variety of the kiang

chig·ger \'chigə(r) *also* 'ji-\ *also* **chig·ga** \-gə\ *n* -s [of African origin; akin to Wolof *jiga* insect, Yoruba *jì¹ga³* jigger] **1** [influenced in meaning by *chigoe*] **:** CHIGOE 1 **2 :** one of many 6-legged larval mites (family Trombiculidae) that attach themselves to various vertebrates including man to suck blood causing intense itching and local irritation and in some instances serving as vectors of scrub typhus or other infectious diseases — called also *chigoe, harvest mite, jigger, red bug*

chi·gnon \'shēn,yän, ⸗'⸗ *also* -ōn\ *n* -s [F, alter. (influenced by MF *tignon* chignon, fr. *tigne, teigne* moth, scurf, fr. L *tinea* moth) of MF *chaignon* chain, collar, nape of the neck, fr. (assumed) VL *catenion-, catenio,* fr. L *catena* chain — more at CHAIN] **:** a smooth knot, twist, or arrangement of hair, either natural or artificial that is worn at the back of the head esp. at the nape of the neck

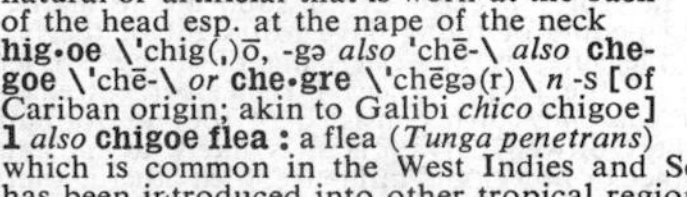

chignon

chig·oe \'chig(,)ō, -gə *also* 'chē-\ *also* **che·goe** \'chē-\ *or* **che·gre** \'chēgə(r)\ *n* -s [of Cariban origin; akin to Galibi *chico* chigoe] **1** *also* **chigoe flea :** a flea (*Tunga penetrans*) which is common in the West Indies and So. America and has been introduced into other tropical regions and of which the fertile female burrows under the skin of the foot or other exposed part of the body of man and animals causing great discomfort — called also *chigger* **2** [influenced in meaning by *chigger*] **:** CHIGGER 2

chi·hua·hua \chə'wä(,)wä, shə-, -'wä(,)wə, -wə\ *n* -s *usu cap* [MexSp, fr. *Chihuahua,* state and city in Mexico] **:** a very small round-headed large-eared short-coated dog (average weight two to six pounds) reputed to antedate Aztec civilization

chihuahua pine *n, usu cap C* [fr. *Chihuahua* state, its locality] **:** a coniferous tree (*Pinus leiophylla chihuahuana*) forming extensive forests chiefly in Mexico and yielding soft durable wood

chi·ka·ra \chə'kärə\ *n* -s [Hindi *cikārā,* fr. Skt *chikkāra,* a kind of antelope, prob. of Dravidian origin; akin to Kannada *cigari, cigare* black antelope] **1** *or* **chin·ka·ra** \chiŋ'-, -in'-\ **:** the common gazelle (*Gazella benettii*) of India **2 :** FOUR-HORNED ANTELOPE

chi·kee \chə'kē; 'chikē, 'chē-\ *or* **chic·kee** \chə'kē, 'chikē\ *n* -s [prob. fr. Creek] **:** a stilt house of the Seminole Indians that is built open on all sides and thatched usu. with palmetto leaves

chil \'chēl\ *n* -s [Panjabi *cīl* pine; akin to Hindi *cīr* pine] **:** CHIR PINE

chil- *or* **chilo-** *also* **cheil-** *or* **cheilo-** *comb form* [NL, fr. Gk *cheil-, cheilo-,* fr. *cheilos* — more at GILL] **:** lip ⟨*Chilopsis*⟩ ⟨*Chilomastix*⟩

chi·la·ca·yo·te *or* **chi·li·co·jo·te** \,chiləkə'yōd·ē\ *n* -s [AmerSp, fr. Nahuatl *tzilakayútli,* perh. fr. *tzilak* smooth + *ayútli* gourd] **1 :** any of several gourds of Mexico and the southwestern U.S. (as *Echinocystis fabacea, E. marah, Cucurbita ficifolia,* and *C. foetidissima*) or their fruits **2 :** the pulp of a chilacayote fruit

chi·lar·i·um \kī'la(a)rēəm\ *n, pl* **chilar·ia** \-ēə\ [NL, fr. *chil-* + *-arium*] **:** one of a pair of anatomical processes between the bases of the last (fourth) pair of walking legs in the king crab

chil·blain \'chil,blān\ *n* -s [³*chill* + *blain*] **:** a redness and swelling of toes, fingers, nose, or ears or sometimes cheeks in cold weather accompanied by itching and burning and sometimes followed by cracking of skin and ulceration and believed to be based on a constitutional instability of the local circulation

chilcat *usu cap, var of* CHILKAT

chil·co·tin \chil'kōt·ᵊn\ *n, pl* **chilcotin** *or* **chilcotins** *usu cap* [fr. *Chilcotin* river, British Columbia, Canada] **1 a :** an Athapaskan people in the Chilcotin river valley, British Columbia **b :** a member of such people **2 :** the language of the Chilcotin people

¹child \'chīld, *esp before pause or consonant* -īəld\ *n, pl* **children** \'childrən, -dərn *also* -dən *sometimes* -ůl-\ [ME, fr. OE *cild;* akin to OSw *kulder* all the children of the same marriage, litter, Goth *kilthei* womb, *inkiltho* pregnant, Skt *jaṭhara* belly, L *galla* gallnut — more at GALL] **1 a :** an unborn or recently born human being **:** FETUS, INFANT, BABY **b** *now dial* **:** a female infant **2 a :** a young person of either sex esp. between infancy and youth ⟨a play for both *children* and adults⟩ ⟨a ~ bride⟩ ⟨these ~ authors —Louis Auchincloss⟩ **b :** one who exhibits the characteristics of a very young person (as innocence or lack of restraint) ⟨she would stay what she was — a placid grownup ~ until she died —Ida A.R.Wylie⟩ ⟨I am a ~ in most matters of practical business —O.W.Holmes †1935⟩ **c :** a person who has not yet come of age — compare AGE 1d(2), AGE OF CONSENT, AGE OF DISCRETION **3** *usu* **childe** \'chī(ə)ld\, *usu cap, archaic* **:** a child or youth wellborn or of noble birth — usu. used as a title esp. in early English ballads and romances ⟨*Childe* Harold⟩ ⟨*Childe* Roland⟩ **4 a :** a son or a daughter **:** a male or female descendant in the first degree **:** the immediate progeny of human parents **b :** an adopted child **c :** any specified direct descendant (as a grandchild) — used esp. in wills **5 :** DESCENDANT **:** a member of the tribe or clan — usu. used in pl. ⟨the *children* of Israel⟩ **6 a :** one who in character or practices shows strong signs of the relationship to or the influence of another (as a disciple of a teacher) ⟨a ~ of God⟩ **b :** one who has been strongly conditioned by a place, a type of action or occupation, or a state of affairs ⟨a ~ of New York⟩ ⟨a ~ of toil⟩ ⟨a ~ of the depression⟩ **7 :** something in a relationship suggesting that of child to parent: as **a :** PRODUCT, RESULT ⟨technical development, the *children* of British brains and ingenuity —Roy Lewis & Angus Maude⟩ ⟨barbed wire . . . is truly a ~ of the plains —W.P.Webb⟩ ⟨Holland is the ~ of its rivers and of the sea —S.L.A.Marshall⟩ **b :** DEPENDENT, SUBSIDIARY ⟨another ~ of both competing outfits was marketing their products in the Middle East and Africa —E.O.Hauser⟩ — **this child** *dial* **:** I, ME — **with child 1 :** PREGNANT ⟨she is *with child*⟩ **2** *obs* **:** EAGER, IMPATIENT

²child *vb* -ED/-ING/-S [ME *childen,* fr. *child,* n.] *obs* **:** to bear young **:** give birth

¹childbearing \'⸗,⸗⸗\ *n* -s [ME *childbering,* fr. *child* + *bering,* fr. gerund of *beren* to bear — more at BEAR] **:** the act of producing or bringing forth children **:** PARTURITION

²childbearing \"\ *adj* **:** of, relating to, or suitable for childbearing ⟨the ~ period of life⟩ ⟨women of ~ age⟩

childbed \'⸗,⸗\ *n* [ME, fr. *child* + *bed*] **:** the condition of a woman in childbirth **:** PARTURITION, LYING-IN ⟨women in ~⟩ ⟨visiting her the first week after her ~ —Samuel Putnam⟩

childbed fever *n* **:** PUERPERAL FEVER

childbirth \'⸗,⸗\ *n* -s **:** the act of bringing forth a child or offspring **:** LABOR, PARTURITION, TRAVAIL

child-centered \'⸗¦⸗⸗\ *adj* **:** designed to develop the individual and social qualities of a student rather than provide a generalized information or training by way of prescribed subject matter — used of elementary or secondary education or schools ⟨a *child-centered* curriculum⟩ ⟨today, the school is more and more *child-centered* —Kimball Young⟩

childcrowing \'⸗,⸗⸗\ *n* **:** the loud crowing sound made by an infant or child with spasmodic croup

childe *var of* ¹CHILD 3

chil·der \'childə(r)\ *chiefly dial pl of* CHILD

child guidance *n* **1 :** the clinical study and treatment of the personality and behavior problems of esp. maladjusted and delinquent children by a staff of specialists usu. comprising a physician or psychiatrist, a clinical psychologist, and a psychiatric social worker **2 :** the field of study or practice of child guidance or the movement devoted to it

child·hood \'chīld,hůd\ *n* -s [ME *childhod,* fr. OE *cildhād,* fr. *cild* child + *-hād* -hood] **1 :** the period of being a child ⟨a happy ~ but an adulthood fraught with troubles⟩ **2 :** the quality or state of being a child ⟨the ignorance and infirmities of ~ stand in need of restraint and correction — John Locke⟩ ⟨reach manhood without having experienced ~⟩ ⟨experience the bonds of ~ and parental love⟩ **3 :** CHILDREN ⟨a toy designed to appeal to ~⟩ **4 :** the early period in the development of something ⟨there was a ~ of religion as there was a ~ of science —*Times Lit. Supp.*⟩ ⟨industrial hygiene in America had an uneasy ~ —Victor Robinson⟩

child·ing \'chīldiŋ\ *adj* [ME, fr. pres. part. of ²*child*] **1 :** bearing children or young **:** PREGNANT, PARTURIENT **2 :** PRODUCTIVE, FRUITFUL **3** *of flowers* **:** producing younger or smaller blossoms around an older blossom

childing pink *n* **:** an annual pink (*Dianthus prolifer*) naturalized from Europe with small flowers in terminal bracted heads

child·ish \'chīldish, -ēsh\ *adj* [ME *childishe,* fr. OE *cildisc,* fr. *cild* child + *-isc* -ish] **1 :** of, relating to, befitting, or resembling a child ⟨a ~ simplicity⟩ ⟨I fell sick with some ~ complaint —Corra Harris⟩ ⟨a ~ face⟩ **2 :** marked by immaturity or simplemindedness **:** PUERILE, PETTY ⟨a ~ and spiteful remark⟩ — **child·ish·ly** *adv* — **child·ish·ness** *n* -ES

child labor *n* **:** the employment of a child in a business or industry esp. in violation of state or federal statutes prohibiting the employment of children under a specified age

child·less \'chī(ə)l(d)ləs\ *adj* **:** having no offspring ⟨till he dies ~; and the family will die out with him —J.C.Powys⟩ — **child·less·ness** *n* -ES

¹childlike \'⸗,⸗\ *adj* [¹*child* + *-like*] **:** of, relating to, or having the characteristics of a child or childhood; *esp* **:** marked by innocence, trust, frankness, and ingenuousness

²childlike \"\ *adv* **:** in the manner of a child — **child·like·ness** *n* -ES

child·ly \'chī(ə)l(d)lē\ *adj* -ER/-EST [ME, fr. OE *cildlīc,* fr. *cild* child + *-līc* -ly] **:** CHILDLIKE, CHILDISH 1

childminder \'⸗,⸗⸗\ *n* -S *Brit* **:** BABY-SITTER

child psychiatry *n* **:** psychiatry applied to the treatment of children — compare CHILD PSYCHOLOGY

child psychology *n* **:** the study of the psychological characteristics of infants and children and the application of general psychological principles to infancy and childhood

children *pl of* CHILD

chil·dren·ite \'childrə,nīt\ *n* -s [John George *Children* †1852 Eng. scientist + E *-ite*] **:** a mineral $(Fe,Mn)Al(PO_4)(OH)_2\cdot2H_2O$ consisting of a hydrous basic iron aluminum phosphate in translucent pale yellowish to dark brown orthorhombic crystals (hardness 4.5–5, sp. gr. 3.18–3.24)

children of Israel : the Jewish people

children of light [trans. of Gk *huioi ton phōtos*] **1 :** Christians as having received the divine light or being enlightened by it — in allusion to Luke 16: 8 (RSV) **2 :** a name assumed by the early Quakers

children's-bane \'⸗⸗,⸗\ *n* **:** a water hemlock (*Cicuta maculata*)

children's court *n* **:** JUVENILE COURT

children's day *n, usu cap C&D* **:** a special day (usu. the second Sunday in June) observed throughout the world by Protestant churches with exercises for children

childs *pres 3d sing of* CHILD

child's play *n* **1 :** extremely simple work **:** an extremely simple task ⟨nor will it be exactly *child's play* . . . to dispose of 197 ships —*N.Y.Times*⟩ **2 :** an act of small importance ⟨his injury was *child's play* compared with the damage he inflicted⟩

child welfare *n* **:** social work centered upon the welfare of children (as upon improvement in health and home conditions) and upon vocational training

¹chile *var of* CHILI

²chile \'chilē, -li\ *adj, usu cap* [fr. *Chile,* country in So. America] **:** of or from Chile **:** of the kind or style prevalent in Chile **:** CHILEAN

¹chil·ean *or* **chil·ian** \'chilēən *also* -lyən\ *adj, usu cap* [*Chile,* country in So. America + E *-an* or *-ian*] **1 :** of, relating to, or characteristic of Chile **2 :** of, relating to, or being the subregion of the Neotropical biogeographic region that includes temperate So. America

²chilean \"\ *n* -s *cap* **:** a native or inhabitant of Chile

chilean bellflower *n, usu cap C* **1 :** CHILE-BELLS **2 :** a prostrate perennial herb (*Nolana atriplicifolia*) of southwestern So. America that is sometimes cultivated for its large bell-shaped flowers which are usu. blue with a yellow and white throat

chilean guava *n, usu cap C* **:** a Chilean shrub (*Myrtus ugni*) bearing an edible berry with a pleasant flavor

chilean jasmine *n, usu cap C* **:** a showy woody vine (*Mandevilla laxa*) of the family Apocynaceae used as an ornamental and having axillary or terminal racemes of white or blush flowers each of which may be two inches across

chilean laurel *n, usu cap C* **:** PERUVIAN NUTMEG

chilean nitrate *n, usu cap C* **:** sodium nitrate from Chile

chilean nut *n, usu cap C* **:** a Chilean shrub (*Guevina heterophylla*) of the family Proteaceae; *also* **:** its coral-red fruit containing an edible seed like the hazelnut — called also *Chile hazel*

chilean strawberry *n, usu cap C* **:** a New World strawberry (*Fragaria chiloensis*) from a variety of which (*F. chiloensis ananassa*) many of the common cultivated strawberries originated — called also *beach strawberry*

chile-bells \'chilē-\ *n pl but sing or pl in constr, usu cap C* **:** a showy Chilean twining vine (*Lapageria rosea*) that is related to the smilax, has leathery alternate leaves, and produces deep rosy red trumpet-shaped blossoms followed by oval edible yellowish fruits

chile bonito *also* **chilean bonito** *n, usu cap C* **:** a common bonito (*Sarda chiliensis*) of the Pacific coast of the Americas being metallic blue above and silvery below with dark oily flesh that cans esp. well — compare ATLANTIC BONITO

chilectropion *var of* CHEILECTROPION

chile hazel *n, usu cap C* **:** CHILEAN NUT

chile mill *or* **chilean mill** *n, usu cap C* **:** a machine for crushing substances (as ore) by means of heavy rollers moving in a circle

chile nettle *n, usu cap C* **:** a plant of the family Loasaceae

¹chi·le·no \chə'lā(,)nō, -ān(,)yō\ *n* -s *cap* [Sp, adj. & n., fr. *Chile*] **:** a native or inhabitant of Chile

²chileno \"\ *n* -s *often cap* [MexSp, fr. Sp, adj., of Chile] **:** a severe curb bit with the curb strap replaced by a metal ring

chile pine *or* **chilean pine** *n, usu cap C* **:** MONKEY PUZZLE

chile saltpeter *also* **chile niter** *n, usu cap C* **:** sodium nitrate esp. occurring naturally (as in caliche)

chili *or* **chile** *or* **chil·li** \'chilē, -li\ *n, pl* **chilies** *or* **chiles** *or* **chillies** [Sp *chile,* fr. Nahuatl *chīlli*] **1 a :** HOT PEPPER 1; *esp* **:** LONG PEPPER 2b **b** *usu* **chilli,** *chiefly Brit* **:** a pepper whether hot or sweet **2 :** HOT PEPPER 2 **3 a :** a thick sauce made principally of meat and chilies **b :** CHILI CON CARNE **4 :** a moderate reddish orange that is yellower and duller than flamingo and duller and very slightly yellower than crab apple **5 :** a hot dry southerly wind in Tunisia

-chilia — see -CHEILIA

chil·i·ad \'kilē,ad\ *n* -s [LL *chiliad-, chilias,* fr. Gk *chilias,* fr. *chilioi* thousand; akin to Skt *sahasra* thousand, and perh. L *mille* — more at MILE] **1 :** a group of 1000 ⟨a ~ of errors⟩ ⟨~s of years⟩ **2 :** a period of 1000 years **:** MILLENNIUM

chil·i·ad·al \¦⸗⸗¦adᵊl\ *also* **chil·i·ad·ic** \-dik\ *adj* **:** of or relating to a chiliad

chilian *usu cap, var of* CHILEAN

chil·i·arch \'kilē,ärk\ *n* -s [Gk *chiliarchēs, chiliarchos,* fr. *chilioi* thousand + *-archēs, -archos* -arch] **:** the commander of a thousand men in ancient Greece

chil·i·asm \-azəm\ *n* -s [NL *chiliasmus,* fr. LL *chiliastes* chiliast (after such pairs as Gk *enthousiastēs* enthusiast: *enthousiasmos* enthusiasm), fr. (*assumed*) Gk *chiliastēs,* fr. *chilioi* thousand] **:** the theological doctrine that Christ will come to earth in a visible form and set up a theocratic kingdom over all the world and thus usher in the millennium

chil·i·ast \-,ast\ *n* -s [LL *chiliastes*] **:** one that believes in chiliasm **:** MILLENARIAN

chil·i·as·tic \¦⸗⸗¦astik\ *adj* **:** MILLENARIAN — **chil·i·as·ti·cal·ly** \-tək(ə)lē\ *adv*

chilicojote *var of* CHILACAYOTE

chili con car·ne \¦chilē¦,kän'kärnē, -lil, ¦,kən-, -'kän-, -ni\ *n* [Sp *chile con carne* chili with meat] **:** a highly spiced stew of chopped or ground beef and minced chilies or chili powder and usu. served with beans

chil·i·co·the \,chilə'kōthē\ *n* -s [modif. of MexSp *chilicote*] **:** a Californian herbaceous vine (*Echinocystis macrocarpa*) of the family Cucurbitaceae having ball-like prickly fruit

chi·lid·i·al \kī'lidēəl\ *adj* [NL *chilidium* + E *-al*] **:** of or relating to a chilidium

chi·lid·i·um \-ēəm\ *n* -s [NL, fr. *chil-* + *-idium*] **:** the convex plate that covers the cardinal process of the dorsal valve of certain brachiopods

chil·i·pep·per \'chilē,pepə(r)\ *n* [so called fr. its color] **:** a common rockfish (*Sebastodes goodei*), brick-red above and pink below, that is a well-known market fish of the California coast

chili pepper *n* [*chili* + *pepper*] **:** CHILI

chili powder *n* **:** a condiment made of chilies ground to a powder

chili sauce *n* **:** a condiment sauce consisting of pureed tomatoes, seasonings, and spices orig. made with chilies but now usu. prepared with red and green sweet peppers

chilitis *var of* CHEILITIS

chili vinegar *n* **:** PEPPER SAUCE

chil·kat *or* **chil·cat** \'chil,kat\ *n, pl* **chilkat** *or* **chilkats** *or* **chilcat** *or* **chilcats** *usu cap* [prob. fr. Tlingit *tcīl-xāt,* lit., storehouses for salmon] **1 :** a Tlingit people of southeastern Alaska **2 :** a member of the Chilkat people

¹chill \'chil\ *vb* -ED/-ING/-S [ME *chillen, chilen,* fr. *chile, chele* cold (n.), frost, fr. OE *cele, ciele;* akin to OE *ceald, cald* cold (adj.) — more at COLD] *vi* **1 a :** to grow or become cold or chill often rapidly ⟨as the hot mixture ~s, it begins to thicken⟩ **b :** to shiver or quake with cold or as if with cold ⟨awake up in the morning alternately sweating and ~*ing* in an¦emotional seizure —R.E.McGill⟩ **2 :** to become taken with a chill (sense 1a) **3** *of a metal* **:** to become surface-hardened by sudden cooling while solidifying **~** *vt* **1 a :** to make cold or chilly ⟨the cold wind from the north ~*ed* the day⟩ ⟨the water ~*ed* the swimmer to the marrow⟩ **b :** to treat (as a food or beverage) by cooling ⟨~ the wine before serving⟩ **c :** to refrigerate (as food) without freezing **2 :** to affect as if with cold **:** CHECK ⟨was forced to ~ his enthusiasm⟩ **:** DAMPEN, DEPRESS, DISCOURAGE, DISPIRIT ⟨rain ~*ed* the glittering pageant —Bill Sumner⟩ **3 :** to cool (metal) suddenly at the surface so as to effect a change in solidification that often increases the hardness **4 :** to produce a dull or clouded appearance upon (a varnished surface) by cold **:** ³BLOOM *vt* 2 **5** *dial Eng* **:** to take the chill off (a liquid)

²chill \"\ *adj, usu* -ER/-EST **1 a :** moderately but unpleasantly cold ⟨a ~ night⟩ **b :** COLD, RAW ⟨a ~ wind⟩ **2 :** affected by a penetrating cold **:** benumbed or shivering with cold **:** CHILLED ⟨~ travelers⟩ **3 :** cool in manner or feeling **:** lacking warmth **:** DISTANT, FORMAL, UNFRIENDLY ⟨a ~ reception⟩ **4 :** DISCOURAGING, DEPRESSING, DISPIRITING ⟨~ penury —Thomas Gray⟩

³chill \"\ *n* -s [¹*chill*] **1 a :** a sensation of cold attended with shivering or convulsive shaking of the body due to a disturbance of the temperature-regulating mechanism of the body resulting from exposure to cold, from infection accompanied by fever, or from a reaction to adverse nervous stimuli ⟨nervous ~⟩ **b :** a disagreeable sensation of coldness ⟨feel a ~ in both hands and feet⟩ ⟨she felt the ~ of fear —E.T.Thurston⟩ **c** *chiefly Brit* **:** a usu. respiratory illness resulting esp. from exposure to cold or damp ⟨he caught a ~ from sitting in a draft⟩ ⟨take a ~⟩ **2 a :** a degree of cold that would induce shivering in a lightly dressed person ⟨an autumn ~ in the air⟩ **b :** a cold atmospheric condition ⟨the ~ of the night⟩ **3 :** a check to enthusiasm or warmth of feeling **:** an atmosphere of discouragement **:** a depressing influence or effect upon the feelings or spirit ⟨a ~ spread over the group at the sad news⟩ ⟨a ~ in his attitude toward opponents⟩ **4 a :** a metal mold or portion of a mold serving to cool rapidly and often to harden the surface of molten metal brought in contact with it **b :** the hardened part of a casting (as the tread of a car wheel) **5 :** a jointed steel bar that actuates the platen in some hand printing presses

⁴chill \,chəl\ [contr. of ME *ich wille* I will] *now dial* **:** I will

chil·la·gite \'chilə,gīt\ *n* -s [*Chillagoe,* Queensland, Australia, + E *-ite*] **:** a mineral consisting of a tungstic wulfenite

chill-cast \'⸗¦⸗\ *adj, of a metal or alloy* **:** cast with a chill (sense 4a) — **chill casting** *n*

chilled iron *n* **:** chilled cast iron — compare CAST IRON

chilled shot *n* **:** lead shot that has an antimony content of 3 to 6 percent

chill·er \'chilə(r)\ *n* -s [¹*chill* + *-er*] **1 :** an eerie or frightening story of murder, violence, or the supernatural **2 :** a refrigerator compartment for chilling foods **3 :** an apparatus used in petroleum refineries to remove wax from paraffin distillates by chilling **4 :** a coolerman in a meat-packing establishment

chilli *var of* CHILI

chill·i·ly \'chiləlē, -li\ *adv* **:** CHILLY

chill·i·ness \'chilēnəs, -in-\ *n* -ES [¹*chilly* + *-ness*] **:** the quality or state of being chilly

chillingly *adv* **:** in a chilling manner

chill mold *n* **:** CHILL 4a

chill·ness \-lnəs\ *n* -ES **:** CHILLINESS

chill plow *or* **chilled plow** *n* **:** a plow having the share and moldboard of chilled semisteel or cast iron

chillproof \'⸗¦⸗\ *vt* [³*chill* + *proof*] **:** to treat (beer) so as to prevent the development of turbidity on exposure to cold — **chillproofing** \'⸗¦⸗⸗\ *n*

chillroom \'⸗,⸗\ *n* [¹*chill* + *room*] **:** a room for refrigeration usu. at temperatures above freezing

chills and fever *n* **:** MALARIA 2

chill·some \'chilsəm\ *adj* **:** CHILLY, COLD ⟨a ~ November⟩

chil·lum \'chiləm\ *n* -s [Hindi *cilam,* fr. Per *chilam*] **:** the part of a hookah containing the tobacco or the charge of tobacco used in it ⟨it was the bitterest ~ I ever smoked —W.M.Thackeray⟩

chil·lum·chee \-,chē\ *n* -s [Hindi *cilamcī,* fr. Per *chilamchī*] *India* **:** a metal wash basin

¹chilly \'chilē, -li\ *adj, usu* -ER/-EST [²*chill* + *-y*] **1 a :** noticeably cold **:** cold enough to chill **:** CHILLING ⟨~ weather⟩ ⟨a ~ drink⟩ **b :** CHILL 1 ⟨a ~ wind, cold, damp, and miserable⟩ **2 :** unpleasantly affected by cold ⟨in the thin coat the boy was manifestly ~⟩ **3 :** having a tendency to chill: as **a :** lacking humanly warm qualities, esp. warmth of feeling ⟨a . . . model of . . . ~ virtues —John Buchan⟩ ⟨a female figure in marble — a ~ but ideal medium for depicting abstract virtues —C.W. Cunnington⟩ ⟨a ~ personality⟩ ⟨a ~ laugh⟩ **b :** UNFRIENDLY ⟨a ~ reception⟩ **c :** coldly critical ⟨a calm and ~ mind —G.N. Shuster⟩ **4 :** having a tendency to arouse fear or apprehension ⟨a giggling, degenerate handyman . . . a ~ thing to watch —Wolcott Gibbs⟩ ⟨this study of a mind for which reality has . . . ceased to exist is a nice ~ piece of work —*New Yorker*⟩

²chil·ly \'chil(l)ē, -l(l)i\ *adv* **:** in a chilly manner ⟨the whole landscape of Asia to which I had hitherto been so ~ indifferent —Edmond Taylor⟩

chill zone *n* **:** a border zone in intrusive igneous rocks that are fine-grained because of rapid cooling

chi·lo \'kī(,)lō\ *n, cap* [NL, fr. L *Chilo,* a nickname, lit., having large lips, prob. modif. of Gk *cheilos* lip] **:** a genus of small slender dull colored nocturnal moths (family Pyralididae) the larvae of which are borers in cereals and other grasses

chilo- — see CHIL-

chi·lo·don \ˈkīlə,dän\ [NL, fr. *chil-* + *-odon*] *syn of* CHILODONELLA

chi·lo·do·nel·la \,kīlədəˈnelə\ *n, cap* [NL, fr. *Chilodon* + *-ella*] **:** a large genus of freshwater or brackish water holotrichous ciliates that are ovoid and dorsoventrally flattened and that include a number of ectoparasites some of which are destructive pests of the skin and gills of cyprinoid fishes

chi·log·nath \ˈkīləg,nath\ *n* -S [NL *Chilognatha*] **:** one of the Chilognatha

¹**chi·log·na·tha** \kīˈlägnəthə\ *n pl, cap* [NL, fr. *chil-* + *-gnatha*] **:** a subclass of Diplopoda that includes the typical millipedes with chitinous exoskeleton reinforced with calcareous deposits — compare PSELAPHOGNATHA — **chi·log·na·than** \(ˈ)═¦══thən\ *adj or n* — **chi·log·na·thous** \(ˈ)═¦══thəs\ *adj*

²**chilognatha** \"\ [NL, fr. *chil-* + *-gnatha*] *syn of* DIPLOPODA

chi·lo·mas·tix \,kīlōˈmastiks\ *n, cap* [NL, fr. *chil-* + *-mastix*] **:** a genus (often made the type of the family Chilomastigidae) of small pear-shaped 4-flagellated protozoans (order Polymastigina) commensal in the intestines of various vertebrates including man

chi·lom·o·nad \kīˈlämə,nad\ *n* -S [NL *Chilomonad-, Chilomonas*] **:** a flagellate of the genus *Chilomonas*

chi·lom·o·nas \kīˈlämənəs\ *n, cap* [NL, fr. *chil-* + *-monas*] **:** genus of small colorless freshwater plantlike flagellates (family Cryptomonadidae) with two anterior flagella and without pyrenoids that have been much used in biological research

chi·lop·la·cus \kīˈläpləkəs\ *n, cap* [NL, fr. *chil-* + *-placus* (fr. Gk *plak-, plax* anything flat and broad) — more at PLEASE] **:** a genus of usu. saprophagous soil-dwelling nematode worms (family Cephalobidae) sometimes associated with root blindness of seedling plants and with failure of cuttings to root

chi·lo·pod \ˈkīlə,päd\ *n* -S [NL *Chilopoda*] **:** one of the Chilopoda **:** CENTIPEDE

chi·lop·o·da \kīˈläpədə\ *n pl, cap* [NL, fr. *chil-* + *-poda*; fr. their foot jaws] **:** a class of arthropods comprising the centipedes — **chi·lop·o·dan** \(ˈ)═¦══dən, -dᵊn\ *adj or n* — **chi·lop·o·dous** \-dəs\ *adj*

chi·los·to·ma \kīˈlästəmə\ *or* **chi·lo·sto·ma·ta** \,kīləˈstōmədə\ *n, pl, cap* [NL, fr. *chil-* + *-stoma, -stomata*] *syn of* CHEILOSTOMATA

chilostomatous *var of* CHEILOSTOMATOUS

chi·lo·stome \ˈkīlə,stōm\ *n* -S [NL *Chilostoma*] **:** a bryozoan of the suborder Cheilostomata

chil·te \ˈchiltē\ *n* -S [MexSp] **:** a bushlike Mexican tree (*Jatropha tepiquensis*) of the spurge family yielding a latex and also a chicle used as a chewing-gum base

chil·tern \ˈchiltə(r)n\ *adj, usu cap* [fr. *Chiltern* hills, range of chalk hills in south-central England] **:** of, relating to, or being chalky, sandy, gravelly, and loamy soils of England that are naturally dry and lie in dry situations

chil·u·la \ˈchilələ\ *n, pl* **chilula** *or* **chilulas** *usu cap* [modif. of Yurok *Tsulu-la*, lit., people of the Bald hills] **1 a :** an Athapaskan people of northwestern California **b :** a member of such people **2 :** a dialect of Hupa spoken by the Chilula people

chil·ver \ˈchilvə(r)\ *n* -S [fr. (assumed) ME, fr. OE *cilforlamb*; akin to OHG *kilbur, kilburra* ewe lamb, OE *cealf* calf — more at CALF] *now dial Eng* **:** a ewe lamb

¹**chimaera** *var of* CHIMERA

²**chi·mae·ra** \kīˈmirə, -mē- *also* kə-\ *n* [NL, fr. L] **1** *cap* **:** a widely distributed genus (type of the family Chimaeridae) of marine elasmobranch fishes that sometimes includes all holocephalans with a blunt snout and a prolonged or threadlike tail but is now usu. restricted to forms having also a true anal fin **2** -S **:** any fish of the family Chimaeridae

chi·mae·rae \-ir(,)ē, -ē(,)rē\ *n pl, cap* [NL, fr. pl. of *Chimaera*] **:** an order of marine elasmobranch fishes comprising the chimaeras and extinct related forms and being coextensive with the subclass Holocephali — see CHIMAERIDAE

chi·mae·ri·dae \-mirə,dē, -mer-\ *n pl, cap* [NL, fr. *Chimaera*, type genus + *-idae*] **:** a family of Holocephali that includes the chimaeras and with extinct related forms constitutes the order Chimaerae

¹**chi·mae·roid** \-mir,ȯid, -mē,rȯid\ *adj* [NL *chimaera* + E *-oid*] **:** of, relating to, or like a chimaera

²**chimaeroid** \"\ *n* -S **:** a fish of the subclass Holocephali

chi·mae·roi·dei \,kīməˈrȯidē,ī\ [NL, fr. *Chimaera* + *-oidei*] *syn of* CHIMAERAE

chimakuan *usu cap, var of* CHEMAKUAN

chimakum *usu cap, var of* CHEMAKUM

chi·man \chəˈmän\ *n, pl* **chima·nes** \-ä(ˈ)nās\ [AmerSp *chimán*, fr. Mam] **:** a shaman-priest of the Mam Indians whose function is to mediate between man and the supernatural through prayers, soothsaying, and divination

chi·maph·i·la \kīˈmafələ\ *n, cap* [NL, fr. Gk *cheima* winter + NL *-phila*; akin to Gk *cheimōn* winter — more at HIBERNATE] **:** a small genus of herbs (family Pyrolaceae) having long creeping subterranean shoots, thick shining leaves, and white or pinkish flowers in terminal clusters — see PIPSISSEWA

chim·a·ri·kan \,chiməˈrēkən\ *n* -S *usu cap* [*Chimariko* + *-an*] **:** a language family of the Hokan stock in California comprising the Chimariko language

chim·a·ri·ko \-(,)kō\ *n, pl* **chimariko** *or* **chimarikos** *usu cap* [modif. of Chimariko *Djimaliko*, fr. *djimar* man] **1 a :** an extinct Indian people of the Trinity river valley, California **b :** a member of such people **2 :** a Chimarikan language of the Chimariko people

chim·ar·rog·a·le \,kiməˈrägə(,)lē\ *n* [NL, fr. *chimarro-* (fr. Gk *cheimarrhos* torrent, fr. *cheimarrhos*, adj., winter-flowing, fr. *cheima* winter + *-rhos*, fr. *rhein* to flow) + Gk *galē* weasel; akin to Skt *giri, girikā* mouse — more at HIBERNATE, STREAM] **1** *cap* **:** a genus of Asiatic water shrews **2** -S **:** any shrew of the genus *Chimarrogale*

chim·bly \ˈchim(b)lē, -lī\ *dial var of* CHIMNEY

¹**chime** \ˈchīm\ *n* -S [ME *chime, chimbe* cymbal, fr. OF *chimbe, cymbe*, fr. L *cymbalum* — more at CYMBAL] **1 :** a mechanical or electrical apparatus for chiming a bell or set of bells ⟨wind a clock ~⟩; *specif* **:** an electrically operated chime used in place of a doorbell **2 a :** a set of bells tuned in a scale and capable of playing melody but not properly harmony — compare CARILLON **b :** one of a set of objects giving a bell-like sound when struck — usu. used in pl. ⟨stone ~s⟩ ⟨gong ~s⟩ ⟨organ ~s⟩ **c :** BELL 6a **3 a :** the sound of a set of bells — usu. used in pl. ⟨we have heard the ~s at midnight —Shak.⟩ **b :** a musical sound resembling or suggesting that of bells **c :** a sequence of musical or harmonious sounds **4 :** order and proportion **:** ACCORD, HARMONY ⟨nature's ~⟩ ⟨each keeping ~ with the other⟩

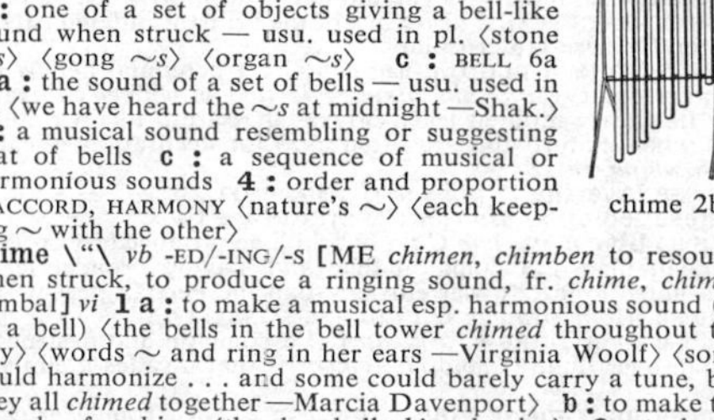
chime 2b

²**chime** \"\ *vb* -ED/-ING/-S [ME *chimen, chimben* to resound when struck, to produce a ringing sound, fr. *chime, chimbe* cymbal] *vi* **1 a :** to make a musical esp. harmonious sound (as of a bell) ⟨the bells in the bell tower *chimed* throughout the day⟩ ⟨words ~ and ring in her ears —Virginia Woolf⟩ ⟨some could harmonize . . . and some could barely carry a tune, but they all *chimed* together —Marcia Davenport⟩ **b :** to make the sounds of a chime ⟨the doorbell *chimed* twice⟩ **2 :** to be or act in harmonious accord ⟨the music and the mood *chimed* well together⟩ — usu. used with *with* ⟨the swan singing before death . . . ~s so perfectly with Yeats's conception of pride —D.A.Stauffer⟩ **3 :** to call by means of bells or chimes ⟨churches and chapels that ~ to services all day —J.P. O'Donnell⟩ ~ *vt* **1 a :** to strike (as a bell or set of bells) so as to produce a musical sound or a chime ⟨a device to ~ bells for morning service⟩; *specif* **:** to sound (a bell) by striking from the outside or by swinging only a bell clapper or by describing only a small arc in sounding — distinguished from *ring* and *peal* **b :** to cause to sound or chime esp. harmoniously in this way ⟨he ~s one note against another —Virginia Woolf⟩ **2 :** to produce by chiming **:** give forth (as sound or music) in chimes ⟨a church bell tower *chiming* hymns⟩ **3 :** to indicate (an hour of the day) by chiming ⟨a clock *chiming* midnight⟩ **4 :** to call or bring to a place or condition by chiming ⟨bells *chiming* a congregation to church⟩ ⟨the soft sounds of the distant city *chimed* her to sleep⟩ **5 :** to utter repetitively or mechanically **:** DIN 2 ⟨~ the same phrases over and over⟩ ⟨~ a foolish slogan into our ears⟩

³**chime** \ˈchīm\ *or* **chine** \ˈchīn\ *also* **chimb** \ˈchīm\ *n* -S [ME *chimbe*, fr. OE *cimb-* (in *cimbstān* base of a pillar); akin to MD *kimme* edge of a cask, MLG, outer edge, horizon, OE *camb* comb — more at COMB] **1 a :** the portion of the staves of a cask that extend from the croze to the rim **b :** the rim of a cask or of any casklike container **2 :** the chamfer on the rim of a cask or on a single cask stave

⁴**chime** \"\ *vt* -ED/-ING/-S **:** to chamfer the ends of the staves to form the chime of (a cask)

chime clock *n* [¹*chime*] **:** a clock that indicates the half and quarter hours by playing short melodies on bells or gongs in addition to striking the hours

chime in *vb* [²*chime*] *vi* **1 a :** to join in (as in singing) ⟨the audience *chimed in* on the chorus⟩ ⟨the shrill of grasshoppers *chiming in* with the monotonous hum of the auctioneer's voice —Ellen Glasgow⟩ **b :** to join in in expression of unanimity or agreement ⟨dealers denounced the stricter installment regulations . . . and certain labor unions *chimed in* for fear of a drop in employment —John Harriman⟩ **2 :** to be consistent or harmonious — used with *with* ⟨asserted that deep feeling *chimed in* with Christian morals and religion —Roy Pascal⟩ ⟨the artist's illustrations *chime in* perfectly with the text —*Book Production*⟩ **3 :** to break into the conversation or discussion to express oneself ⟨critics *chiming in* every few minutes⟩ ~ *vt* **:** to remark while chiming in ⟨"but he was busy," *chimed in* Miss Parton —Dorothy Sayers⟩

chime maul *n* [³*chime*] **:** a hammer or mallet designed esp. for driving head hoops on casks

chi·me·ra *or* **chi·mae·ra** \kīˈmirə, -mē- *also* kə-\ *n* -S [L *chimaera*, fr. Gk *chimaira* chimera, she-goat; akin to ON *gymbr* yearling ewe, L *bimus* two years (winters) old, *hiems* winter — more at HIBERNATE] **1 a** *usu cap* **:** a she-monster in Greek mythology represented as vomiting flames and usu. as having a lion's head, goat's body, and dragon's or serpent's tail or a lion's body and head together with a goat's head rising from the back — compare GRYLLUS **b :** a similar imaginary monster; *specif* **:** a grotesque animal form in painting or sculpture compounded from parts of different real or imaginary animals **c :** a horrible or frightening manifestation **d :** an often fantastic combination of incongruous parts, esp. a fabrication **2 :** an illusion or fabrication of the mind or fancy ⟨that unintelligible ~—substance —Frank Thilly⟩; *esp* **:** a utopian or unrealizable dream or aim ⟨concluded that the democratic hope of rational policy . . . was a ~ —C.B. Forcey⟩ ⟨universal justice and equality . . . were ~s one could chase for generations and never capture —Victor Canning⟩ **3 :** an individual, organ, or part consisting of tissues of diverse genetic constitution occurring esp. in plants and most frequently at a graft union, the tissues from both stock and cion retaining their distinctness in the chimera — see MERICLINAL, PERICLINAL, SECTORIAL

¹**chi·mere** \shəˈmi(ə)r, chə-, -miə\ *also* **chim·er** \ˈchimə(r), ˈsh-\ *n* -S [ME *chimmer, chemer*, prob. fr. ML *chimera*] **:** a loose sleeveless robe often with balloon sleeves of lawn attached worn by some bishops of the Anglican communion

²**chi·mere** \kīˈmi(ə)r, kə-, -iə\ *n* -S [ME, fr. MF, fr. L *chimaera*] **:** CHIMERA

chi·mer·i·cal \kəˈmerəkəl, -rēk- *also* kə- *or* -mir-\ *or* **chi·mer·ic** \-rik, -ēk\ *or* **chi·me·ral** \-mirəl, -mē-\ *adj* [*chimera* + *-ic, -ical or -al*] **1 :** being, relating to, or like a chimera; *esp* **:** unreal and existing only as the product of wild unrestrained imagination ⟨his Utopia is not a ~ commonwealth but a practicable improvement on what already exists —Douglas Bush⟩ **2 :** inclined to or indicative of unrestrained imagination **:** UNREALISTIC ⟨~ to demand that a government . . . should exercise the art of governing purely for its own sake —George Santayana⟩ **3** *usu chimeral or chimeric* **:** of, relating to, or being a chimera ⟨a *chimeric* tetraploid⟩ ⟨the *chimeral* nature of some ornamental plants⟩ **syn** see IMAGINARY

chimesmaster \ˈ═,══\ *n* **:** the chief performer on a chime of bells, esp. tower bells

chim·ic *or* **chim·ick** \ˈkimik\ *archaic var of* CHEMIC

chi·mi·la \chəˈmēlə\ *n, pl* **chimila** *or* **chimilas** *usu cap* [Sp, of AmerInd origin] **1 a :** an Indian people of Colombia classified by some Americanists as Chibchan and by others as Arawakan **b :** a member of such people **2 :** the language of the Chimila people

chiming bell *n* [so called fr. its bell-shaped flowers] **:** a plant of the genus *Mertensia*

chim·ist \ˈkiməst\ *archaic var of* CHEMIST

chim·la \ˈchim(,)lä\ *or* **chim·ley** \-lē\ *dial var of* CHIMNEY

chimley lug *n, chiefly Scot* **:** CHIMNEY CORNER

chimley neuck *or* **chimley nuik** \-¦nyük\ *n* [Sc *neuck, nuick*, var. of *nook*] *Scot* **:** CHIMNEY CORNER

chimmesyan *usu cap, var of* TSIMSHIAN

¹**chim·ney** \ˈchimnē, -ni\ *n* -S *often attrib* [ME, fr. MF *cheminée*, fr. LL *caminata*, fr. L *caminus* furnace, fireplace, fr. Gk *kaminos*; akin to Gk *kamara* vault — more at CHAMBER] **1** *dial* **:** FIREPLACE, HEARTH — compare CHIMNEY CORNER **2 a :** a vertical structure incorporated into a building and enclosing a flue or flues that carry off smoke or other undesirable fumes or gases; *esp* **:** the part of such a structure extending above a roof — compare CHIMNEY BREAST **b :** a pipelike more or less vertical natural vent or opening in the earth: (1) **:** the conduit of a volcano (2) **:** a passage or shaft in the roof or floor of a cave (3) **:** a moulin of small diameter **c :** a columnar geological erosion feature that is smaller than a stack on a wave-cut platform **3** *Brit* **:** the smokestack of a locomotive **4 a :** a tube usu. of glass and usu. shaped placed around a flame (as of a lamp) to serve as a shield and to create a draft and promote combustion **b :** a glass shield made to resemble or resembling such a tube and enclosing an electric light **5 :** a steep and very narrow cleft or gully in the face of a cliff or mountain **6 :** a small tube through the top of a stopped metal pipe of an organ permitting air to escape to sharpen the pitch **7 :** a vertical or steeply inclined shoot of roughly columnar shape in a body of ore

chimney 4a

²**chimney** \"\ *vt* -ED/-ING/-S **:** to climb (a chimney) in mountaineering by the use of body pressure against the sides

chimney back *n* **:** the back or the backing of a fireplace

chimney bar *n* **:** a bar to support the masonry above a fireplace

chimney bellflower *n* **:** CHIMNEY PLANT

chimney block *n* **:** a concrete block made to form a continuous round flue when a number of such blocks are placed in position one on top of another

chimney breast *n* **1 :** the projection of a chimney from a wall into a room **2 :** an ornamental casing (as paneling) that surrounds or covers a chimney breast over and around a fireplace opening **:** CHIMNEYPIECE

chimney cap *n* **:** a cap or cover for a chimney; *specif* **:** a device fitted to the top of a chimney to improve the draft by presenting an exit aperture to leeward

chimney cloth *n* **:** a valance hung around the mantel of a fireplace for decoration or to impede smoke

chimney–corner \ˈ══¦══\ *adj* **:** such as might be devised by one sitting idly in a chimney corner ⟨a *chimney-corner* legend⟩ ⟨*chimney-corner* law⟩ ⟨*chimney-corner* philosophy⟩

chimney corner *n* **1 a :** the area to the side of a large open fireplace **b :** FIRESIDE **2 :** the settle or bench often formerly occupying the chimney corner

chimney flute *n* [prob. trans. of F *flûte à cheminé*] **:** ROHRFLÖTE

chimney glass *n* **:** a mirror placed over a chimney piece

chimneyhead \ˈ══,═\ *n* **:** the upper end of a chimney

chimney hood *n* **:** an ornamental or protective covering over a chimneyhead

chimney hook *n* **:** a hook attached to the inside, back, or side walls of a fireplace for holding pots and kettles over a fire or one esp. in the side wall for holding implements (as fire tongs)

chim·ney·less \ˈ══-ləs\ *adj* **:** lacking a chimney

chimney money *n* **:** HEARTH MONEY

chimneypiece \ˈ══,═\ *n* **1** *obs* **:** a picture or piece of tapestry hung as an ornament over a fireplace **2 a :** an ornamental construction above and around a fireplace opening embracing the mantel and the ornament or casing of the chimney breast **b :** MANTEL 2

chimney pink *n* **:** SOAPWORT

chimney plant *n* [so called fr. its use as a fireplace ornament] **:** a bellflower (*Campanula pyramidalis*) of southeastern Europe cultivated in gardens

chimney pot *n* **:** a cylindrical or prismoidal pipe of earthenware or metal placed at the top of a chimney to increase the draft and carry off the smoke

chimney red *n* **:** a moderate to deep red that is yellower than cadmium purple or burnt carmine

chimney rock *n* **1 :** a column of rock rising above its surroundings or isolated on the face of a slope **2 :** a porous phosphate rock that hardens on exposure to the air and is used esp. in construction of chimneys

chimney shelf *n, dial* **:** a mantel shelf

chimney stack *n* **1 :** a number of flues embodied in one chimney; *esp* **:** the part of a multiple-flue chimney rising above a roof **2 :** a chimney shaft containing only one flue

chimney stalk *Brit var of* CHIMNEY STACK

chimney swallow *n* **1 :** CHIMNEY SWIFT **2 :** the European barn swallow

chimney sweep *or* **chimney sweeper** *n* **1 :** one whose occupation is the removal of soot by means of scraper, brushes, or vacuum cleaner from the flues of a chimney and from pipes connecting with a furnace **2** *dial* **:** CHIMNEY SWIFT

chimney swift *n* **:** a small sooty-gray American swift (*Chaetura pelagica*) commonly called a swallow and noted for its habit of attaching its nest inside of a chimney

chimney tax *n* **:** HEARTH MONEY

chimney throat *n* **:** a part of a chimney immediately above the fireplace where the walls of the flue are gathered or brought close together to increase the draft

chimney top *n* **1 :** the upper part of a chimney: **a :** the part of a chimney extending above a roof **b :** CHIMNEY POT **2 :** CHIMNEY 6

chi·mo·nan·thus \,kīməˈnan(t)thəs\ *n* [NL, fr. Gk *cheimōn* winter + NL *-anthus* — more at HIBERNATE] **1** *cap* **:** a genus of evergreen or deciduous Asiatic shrubs (family Calycanthaceae) often included in the genus *Calycanthus* but having scaly buds and yellow flowers with five or six stamens **2** -S **:** any plant of the genus *Chimonanthus*; *esp* **:** JAPAN ALLSPICE

chi·mo·pelagic \¦kīmō+\ *adj* [*chim-* (fr. Gk. *cheima, cheimōn* winter) + *-o-* + *pelagic*] **:** being or belonging to marine organisms which live in the depths of the sea except in winter when they rise to the surface

chimp \ˈchimp, ˈsh-\ *n* -S [by shortening] **:** CHIMPANZEE

chim·pan·zee \¦chim,pan¦zē, ¦shim-; chimˈpanzē, shim-, -zi; -paan-; *also* ¦chimpən¦zē *or* ¦shimpən- *sometimes* ˈ═(,)═zē *or* ˈ═(,)═zi *or* (*prob by dissimilation of nasals*) chəˈpanzē *or* shə- *or* -zi\ *n* -S [Kongo dial. *chimpenzi, kimpenzi*] **:** an anthropoid ape (*Pan troglodytes* syn. *Anthropopithecus troglodytes* or *Simia satyrus*) of the equatorial forests of Africa that rarely stands erect, habitually uses its arms in walking, rests on the knuckles, and that is smaller and more arboreal in habit than the gorilla, less fierce, being easily tamed when taken young, and having a rounder head with large ears

chimpanzee

chim·pan·zoid \ˈchim,pan,zȯid, ˈshim-; chimˈp-,shimˈp-; -aan-; ˈchimpən-, ˈshimpən-\ *adj* [ISV *chimpanzee* + *-oid*] **:** belonging to or resembling a chimpanzee

¹**chi·mu** \chēˈmü\ *n, pl* **chimu** *or* **chimus** *usu cap* [Sp *chimú*, of AmerInd origin] **1 a :** an extinct Yuncan people of the northwest coast of Peru **b :** a member of such people **2 :** the language of the Chimu people — compare YUNCA

²**chimu** \"\ *adj, usu cap* **:** of or relating to a pre-Inca Peruvian culture characterized by the construction of large cities and by white and red pottery portrait vases and metalworking

chi·myl alcohol \ˈkīməl-\ *n* [NL *Chimaera* + E *-yl*] **:** a crystalline alcohol $C_{16}H_{33}OCH_2CH(OH)CH_2OH$ obtained esp. from shark-liver oil and other fish-liver oils and from the yellow marrow of cattle bones; glycerol α-cetyl ether

¹**chin** \ˈchin\ *n* -S *often attrib* [ME, fr. OE *cinn*; akin to OHG *kinni* chin, ON *kinn* cheek, Goth *kinnus*, L *gena*, Gk *genys* jaw, cheek, Skt *hanu* jaw] **1 :** the lower portion of the face lying below the lower lip and including the prominence of the lower jaw and the overlying soft tissues **2 :** the surface lying beneath the lower jaw or between the branches of the jaw — used chiefly of lower vertebrates in which a mental prominence is lacking from the jawbone **3 :** a casual or random conversation **:** CHAT ⟨get together for a ~ —C.G.Norris⟩ — **chin up :** courage or spirits high — used chiefly in the expression *keep your chin up*

²**chin** \"\ *vb* **chinned**; **chinned**; **chinning**; **chins** *vt* **1 :** to bring to or hold with the chin ⟨the weary fiddler *chinning* his violin —Christopher Morley⟩ **2 a :** to raise oneself on (as a horizontal bar) while hanging by the hands from a position in which the arms are fully extended to a position in which the chin is level with or above the support ⟨he *chinned* the bar 12 times⟩ **b :** to raise (oneself) in this manner ⟨looked up at the top of the doorway, and . . . it was in his mind to leap up and seize it and ~ himself on it —Kenneth Roberts⟩ **3 :** to talk to esp. volubly or boldly **:** chatter to ~ *vi* **:** to talk esp. idly or casually **:** CHATTER ⟨the janitor can come in and ~ with me any time he wants —W.H.Whyte⟩

³**chin** \"\ *n, pl* **chin** *or* **chins** *usu cap* [Burmese, lit., hill-man] **1 a :** a people in Burma differing from the Burmese in shorter stature and darker skin that inhabit the Chin hills and the Arakan Yoma in the southern part of the India-Burma frontier **b :** a member of such people **2 :** the language of the Chin people similar to the Naga language and including numerous dialects

⁴**chin** \"\ *n* -S *usu cap* [by shortening] **:** CHINCHILLA 5

chin- *or* **chino-** *comb form* [alter. (influenced by G *chin-, chino-*, fr. *chinin* quinine) of *quin-, quino-*] **:** quinine ⟨*chino*toxine⟩ ⟨*chin*ol⟩

¹**chi·na** \ˈchīnə\ *n* -S [modif. (influenced by *China*, the country) of Per *chīnī* (Chinese) porcelain] **1 a :** PORCELAIN 1a; *also* **:** vitreous porcelain wares (as dishes, vases, ornaments) for domestic use as distinguished from industrial whitewares **b :** earthenware or porcelain tableware ⟨set the table with the good ~⟩ **c :** CROCKERY **2 a** [by shortening] **:** CHINAROOT **b** [fr. *China*, the country] **:** SWEET ORANGE

²**china** \"\ *adj* [fr. *China*, country in Asia] **1** *usu cap* **:** of, from, or native to China ⟨a *China* pig⟩ ⟨a *China* pheasant⟩ **:** produced in or of a kind or type prevalent or orig. produced in China ⟨*China* silk⟩ **:** CHINESE **2** [¹*china*] **a :** made of china **b :** resembling porcelain (as in hardness or finish) ⟨a woman with a set ~ face⟩; *also* **:** of the opaque blue characteristic of certain chinas ⟨a *china*-eyed dog⟩

³**chi·na** \ˈkēnə\ *n* -S [modif. of Sp *quina*, perh. fr. Quechua *kina*] **:** CINCHONA

⁴**chi·na** \ˈchīnə\ *n* -S [perh. short for *china plate*, rhyming slang for *mate*] *slang Brit* **:** COMPANION, PAL ⟨swapping yarns with my two old ~s⟩

chi·na ale \ˈchīnə-\ *n* **:** ale flavored with chinaroot

china aster *n, usu cap C* **:** an annual aster (*Callistephus chinensis*) which is native to rocky uplands of northern China and from which have been developed under cultivation numerous varieties differing in flower and petal form and occurring in white and shades of blue, red, or purple

chinaball \'==,=\ *n* : CHINABERRY 2
china bean *n, usu cap C* : COWPEA
china bedbug *n, usu cap C* : CONENOSE
chinaberry \'==,==\ *n* -ES **1** : a soapberry (*Sapindus saponaria*) of the southern U. S. and Mexico **2** *also* **chinaberry tree** : a small rapid-growing Asiatic tree (*Melia azedarach*) that has large twice-compound leaves and fragrant purplish flowers in open clusters, the latter followed by smooth yellow berries, and that is naturalized in the southern U. S. where it is widely planted as a shade or ornamental tree **3** : the fruit of the chinaberry
china blue *n, often cap C* : a grayish to moderate blue — called also *Nikko*
china brier *n, usu cap C* [so called fr. its similarity to *chinaroot*] : a bullbrier (*Smilax bona-nox*) with scurfy stem bases
china cantharides *n pl but sing or pl in constr, usu cap 1st C* : cantharides obtained from bruchid beetles of the genus *Mylabris* and chiefly produced in eastern Asia
china cinnamon *n, usu cap 1st C* : CASSIA BARK
china clay *n* [¹*china*] : KAOLIN; *esp* : English plastic kaolin
china clay rock *n, sometimes cap 1st C* [¹*china*] : CHINA STONE
china closet *also* **china cabinet** *n* [¹*china*] : a cupboard or cabinet for the storage and often display of household crockery or china
chinacrin *also* **chinacrine** *var of* QUINACRINE
china eye *n* : WALLEYE 1a
china fir *n, usu cap C* : an Asiatic tree (*Cunninghamia lanceolata*) with brownish outer bark that scales off in irregular plates exposing the reddish inner bark and having sharply pointed leaves
chinafish \'==,=\ *n, often cap* **1** : SNAKEHEAD 3 **2** : any of several rockfishes (genus *Sebastodes*) of the Pacific coast of No. America
chi·na·fy \'chīnə,fī\ *vt* -ED/-ING/-ES *often cap* [*China* (country) + E *-fy*; fr. the political impotence of China in 1915, when it was coined] : to reduce (as a country) to a state of passivity and helplessness
chi·na·graph pencil \'chīnə,graf-\ *n* [¹*china* + *-graph*] : a pencil for marking on porcelain or other hard glazed surfaces that do not take lead or wax pencil marks satisfactorily
china grass *n, usu cap C* **1** : the stiff dried hand-cleaned but not completely degummed fiber of ramie — called also *bon* **2** : RAMIE 1
china hat *n, usu cap C&H* [by folk etymology fr. Kwakiutl *Xāexaes*] : one of the five Indian peoples comprising the Heiltsuk group
china ink *n, usu cap C* : INDIA INK
china jute *n, usu cap C* : CHINGMA
¹**chi·na·man** \'chīnəmən\ *n, pl* **chinamen** [¹*china* + *man*] *archaic* : a dealer in or manufacturer of porcelain
²**chinaman** \"\ *n, pl* **chinamen** [*China* (the country) + E *man*] **1** *cap* : a native of China : CHINESE — often taken to be offensive **2** *usu* **china man** *usu cap C* : PEKING MAN
chi·na·man's chance *n, usu cap 1st C, slang* : the slightest or barest chance — usu. used in negative constructions ⟨he hasn't a *Chinaman's chance* of winning⟩
china mark \'chīnə-\ *n, usu cap C* [origin unknown] : any of various moths commonly placed in the family Pyraustidae whose larvae live in floating cases and feed on water plants
china mink *n, usu cap C* : JAPANESE MINK 2
chi·nam·pa \chə'nampə, -äm-\ *n* -S [MexSp, fr. Nahuatl, fr. *chinamitl* reed or twig mat + *pa* on] : a Mexican artificial meadow or garden reclaimed from a lake or pond by piling soil dredged from the bottom onto a mat of twigs and planting thereon
chi·nan·tec \'chinən,tek\ *n, pl* **chinantec** *or* **chinantecs** *usu cap* [Sp *chinanteca*, of AmerInd origin] **1** : an Indian people of the state of Oaxaca, Mexico **2** : a member of the Chinantec people
chi·nan·tec·an \,==ˈtäkən, -ekən\ *n* -S *usu cap* : the language of the Chinantec people constituting a Mexican Indian language family
china orange *n, usu cap C* : CALAMONDIN
chi·naphthol \kē, ki+'-\ *n* -S [ISV, blend of *chin-* and *naphthol*; orig. formed in G] : a bitter yellow powder formerly used as an intestinal antiseptic — called also *quinaphthol*
china pink *n, usu cap C* : a biennial or short-lived perennial pink (*Dianthus chinensis*) often grown as an annual and having little or no basal branching, stiff stems, and usu. whitish or rosy lilac flowers often with a purplish eye — called also *rainbow pink*; see JAPANESE PINK
chi·na po·bla·na \ˌchēnəpə'blänə\ *n, sometimes cap C&P* [MexSp, lit., bold and attractive mestizo woman of Puebla] : a colorful Mexican costume consisting of an embroidered white blouse and a red and green skirt with sequins
china press *n* [¹*china*] : CHINA CLOSET
chi·nar *also* **chinar tree** *or* **che·nar** \chə'när\ *n* -S [Hindi *cinār*, *canār*, fr. Per *chanār*] : ORIENTAL PLANE
china rooster *n, usu cap C, dial* : a ring-necked pheasant cock
chinaroot \'==,=\ *n* [perh. trans. of Pg *raiz de China*] : the rootstock of an East Indian climbing shrub (*Smilax china*)
china rose *n, usu cap C* **1 a** : a shrubby Chinese rose (*Rosa chinensis* — called also *Bengal rose* **b** : any of numerous garden roses derived from this rose having single or double flowers of white, pink, or red and tending to be recurrent blooming **2** : a large showy-flowered Asiatic shrub (*Hibiscus rosa-sinensis*)
chi·nar·ra \chə'närə\ *n, pl* **chinarra** *or* **chinarras** *usu cap* [Sp, of AmerInd origin] **1** : an Indian people comprising a major subdivision of the Concho group **2** : a member of the Chinarra people
chinas *pl of* CHINA
china shot *n, usu cap C* : INDIAN SHOT
china silk *n, usu cap C* : a lightweight silk made in China; *broadly* : any of various soft thin silks in plain weave with irregular threads
china stone *n* [¹*china*] : a partly decomposed granite (as Cornish stone) frequently used as a flux to produce vitrification and translucency or mixed with silica and lime to form a glaze in the manufacture of porcelain
china tea *n, usu cap C* : a tea prepared from a small-leaved dwarf variety (*Camellia sinensis bohea*) of the tea plant grown chiefly in southern China
chinatown \'==,=\ *n, usu cap* : the Chinese quarter of a city
china tree *n, usu cap C* **1** : CHINABERRY 1, 2 **2** : GOLDENRAIN TREE
chinaware \'==,=\ *n* [¹*china*] : CHINA 1
china wax *n, usu cap C* : CHINESE WAX
china wood oil *n, usu cap C* : TUNG OIL 1
chinbeak molding \'=,=-\ *n* [¹*chin* + *beak*] : a molding consisting of a convex followed below by a concave profile with or without a fillet below or between
chinbone \'=ˌ=\ *n* [ME, fr. OE *cinbān*, fr. *cin* chin + *bān* bone] : MANDIBLE; *esp* : the median anterior part of the human mandible
chincapin *var of* CHINQUAPIN
chin·cha \'chēn(,)chä\ *n, pl* **chincha** *or* **chinchas** *usu cap* [Sp, of AmerInd origin] : a subdivision of the Yunca
chin·chai·su·yu \,chēn,chī'sü(,)yü\ *or* **chin·cha·su·yu** \-,chə's-\ *n, pl* **chinchaisuyu** *or* **chinchaisuyus** *or* **chinchasuyu** *or* **chinchasuyus** *usu cap* [Quechua *chinchaysúyu*] **1** : the peoples of a territorial division of the Inca empire occupying most of central and northern Peru and Ecuador and their present-day descendants **2** : the dialects of Quechua spoken by the Chinchaisuyu peoples
chin·cha·yo·te \,chinchə'yōd-ē\ *n* -S [MexSp, fr. Nahuatl *tzinchayotli*, fr. *tzintli* rear or bottom part + *chayotli* chayote] : CHAYOTE
chinch bug *also* **chinch** \'chinch\ *or* **chintz** \-n(t)s\ *n* -ES [Sp *chinche*, fr. L *cimic-, cimex*; akin to Lith *šemas* blue-gray, Skt *śyāma* black, dark, OE *hār* gray, old — more at HOAR] **1** : a small bug (*Blissus leucopterus*) of the family Lygaeidae that is black and white in color when adult and very destructive to grass, wheat, corn, and other grains esp. in the central U.S. during dry seasons **2** *chinch or sometimes chintz* : BEDBUG
chin·che·rin·chee \,chinchə'rinchē\ *or* **chin·che·rich·ee** \-richē\ *or* **chin·ke·rich·ee** *also* **chin·ke·rin·chee** \,chiŋkə-\ *n, pl* **chincherinchee** *or* **chincherinchees** *or* **chincherichee** *or* **chincherichees** *or* **chinkerichee** *or* **chinkerichees** *also* **chinkerinchee** *or* **chinkerinchees** [origin unknown] : a southern African perennial bulbous herb (*Ornithogalum thyrsoides*) with long-lasting spikes of starry white blossoms that are shipped in quantity to Europe and America for use as winter cut flowers — called also *star-of-Bethlehem*
chin·chil·la \chin'chilə\ *n* [Sp, prob. fr. Aimara or Quechua] **1** -S : a small rodent (*Chinchilla laniger*) the size of a large squirrel having very soft fur of a pearly gray color and native to the mountains of Peru and Chile but now extensively bred in captivity **2** -S : the fur of the chinchilla **3** *cap* [NL, fr. Sp] : a genus (the type of the family Chinchillidae) of hystricomorph rodents comprising the chinchillas **4** -S : a heavy twilled woolen coating with double cloth construction and with deep napping that is rubbed into curled tufts and nubs **5** -S *often cap* : a domestic rabbit of a breed distinguished by dense soft fur each hair of which is banded with slate blue, pearl gray, and white and tipped with black **6** -S *often cap* : a domestic long-haired cat having green eyes and a pale silver coat sometimes tipped with black **7** : genetic lack of ability to produce yellow pigment occurring as a member of a polygenic series of variants in mammalian coat= color, dominant to albinism and Himalayan but recessive to wild type, and resulting in a silvery coat suggesting that of the chinchilla

chinchilla

chinchilla rat *n* : ABROCOME
chin·chil·li·dae \=ˈ=lə,dē\ *n pl, cap* [NL, fr. *Chinchilla*, type genus + *-idae*] : a family of small bushy-tailed burrowing hystricomorph rodents of the uplands of So. America that includes the chinchillas, the vizcachas, and extinct related forms
chin·chil·lon *or* **chin·chil·lone** \ˌchinchə'lōn, -chə'yōn\ *n* -S [Sp *chinchillón*, aug. of *chinchilla*] : VIZCACHA
¹**chin-chin** \'chin,chin\ *interj* [Chin (Pek) *ch'ing³*, *ch'ing³* -*ch'ing³*, an expression of courtesy] — used to express greeting or farewell
²**chin-chin** \"\ *vi* **chin-chinned**; **chin-chinned**; **chin= chinning**; **chin-chins** **1** : to make a request ceremoniously : converse politely **2** : to talk esp. casually or at random
³**chin-chin** \"\ *n* -S **1** : ceremonious talk : SALUTATION **2** : casual or trivial talk : CHATTER ⟨idle *chin-chin* to pass a hot afternoon⟩
chinchona *or* **chincona** *var of* CINCHONA
chin·chow \'jin¦jō\ *adj, usu cap* [fr. *Chinchow*, Manchuria] : of or from the city of Chinchow, Manchuria : of the kind or style prevalent in Chinchow
chinch·weed \'chinch,wēd\ *n* [prob. fr. *chinch* + *weed*; fr. its unpleasant odor] : a slender or wiry glandular-dotted strongly-scented herb (*Pectis papposa*) of the family Compositae having narrow opposite leaves and flower heads with yellow rays
chinchy \'chinchē\ *adj* -ER/-EST [ME, fr. *chinche* miser, miserly (fr. OF *chinche*, *chiche*, fr. — assumed — VL *ciccus*, fr. L *ciccum* trifle) + ME *-y* — more at CHICO] *chiefly South & Midland* : STINGY
chinc·ing iron \'chin(t)siŋ-\ *n* [fr. pres. part. of *chince*, *chinse* to caulk, prob. var. of *chink*] : a tool used by coopers to insert cooper's flag between the head and staves of a barrel after the head is in place
chin·cough \'chin,kȯf, -äf\ *n* [by folk etymology fr. ⁵*chink* + *cough*] *dial Brit* : WHOOPING COUGH
chin·di *also* **chin·dee** \'chində\ *n* -S [Navaho *chindi*] : a Navaho evil spirit of the dead
¹**chine** \'chīn\ *n* -S [ME *chin*, *chine* crack, fissure, chasm, fr. OE *cine*, *cinu*; akin to OE *cīnan* to gape, yawn, crack, OHG *kīnan*, *chīnan* to sprout, split open, Sw *kina* to sprout, Goth *keinan*, OHG *kīmo*, *chīmo* sprout, *kīl* wedge, OE *cīth* sprout, shoot, and perh. to Arm *cil*, *ciul*, *cel* stem, Latvian *ziêt* to bloom; basic meaning: to sprout, split apart] *dial Eng* : a narrow and deep ravine or gorge
²**chine** \"\ *n* -S [ME *chyne*, fr. MF *eschine*, of Gmc origin; akin to OHG *scina* needle, shinbone — more at SHIN] **1 a** *archaic* : the back or spine of an animal or man **b** : a piece of the backbone of an animal carcass with the adjoining parts cut for cooking : a saddle or a portion of it — see COW illustration **2** : RIDGE, CREST ⟨walking carefully along the ~*s* of the rocks⟩ **3 a** : the thick part of the waterway of a ship projecting above the deck and hollowed on the inboard edge to form a watercourse **b** : the intersection of the bottom and the sides of a flat or V-bottomed boat; *also* : a longitudinal member lying along the bilge at this point
³**chine** \"\ *vt* -ED/ -ING/ -S **1** : to cut through the backbone of: **a** : to split (as a carcass) through the length of the backbone **b** : to cut up (as a salmon or other fish) **2** : to break the back of
⁴**chine** *var of* CHIME
⁵**chi·né** \shə'nā, shē-\ *adj* [F, past part. of *chiner* to dye threads of a fabric in different colors so as to produce a figure, fr. *Chine* China] *of a fabric* : having a mottled pattern of a supposed Chinese fashion produced by printing, dyeing, or painting the stretched warp, sometimes the warp or weft threads, before weaving
⁶**chiné** \"\ *n* -S : a fabric with a chiné design
chi·nee \chī'nē *also* '=,=\ *n, usu cap* [back-formation fr. *Chinese*, pl.] *substand* : CHINESE
chine hoop *n* [⁴*chine*] : the hoop round each end of a cask
chi·ne·la *also* **chi·ne·le** \chə'nālə\ *n* -S [Sp *chinela*, alter. of *chanela*, prob. fr. It dial. *cianella*, var. of *pianella*, fr. *piano* flat (fr. L *planus*) + *-ella* fem. dim. suffix — more at FLOOR] : SLIPPER; *esp* : a flat slipper with no heel worn by Philippine women
¹**chi·nese** \(')chī¦nēz, -ēs\ *adj, usu cap* [*China* + E *-ese*] **1 a** : of, relating to, or characteristic of China **b** : of, relating to, or characteristic of the Chinese **2** : of, relating to, or characteristic of a Chinese language or of the Chinese branch of the Sino-Tibetan language family
²**chinese** \"\ *n, cap* **1** *pl* **chinese** : a native or inhabitant of China or one of his descendants **2** -S : a group of related languages mutually unintelligible in their spoken form but sharing a single system of writing in which the visual symbols directly represent words regardless of the sounds involved used by the people of China and constituting a branch of the Sino-Tibetan language family; *specif* : MANDARIN — see AMOY, CANTONESE, FOOCHOW, HAKKA, PEKINGESE, SWATOW, WU
chinese air plant *n, usu cap C* : a red-flowered epiphytic orchid (*Renanthera coccinea*) of Indochina
chinese alligator *n, usu cap C* : a small alligator (*Alligator sinensis*) of the Yangtze valley distinguished from the American alligator by its completely unwebbed fingers
chinese angelica *n, usu cap C* : an Asiatic shrub (*Aralia chinensis*) resembling Hercules'-club but less prickly and with a long inflorescence
chinese anise *n, usu cap C* : an evergreen tree (*Illicium verum*) of southern China — see BADIAN
chinese arborvitae *n, usu cap C* : an Asiatic evergreen tree (*Thuja orientalis*) widely planted for ornament
chinese artichoke *n, usu cap C* : a hardy perennial (*Stachys sieboldii*) native to China and Japan that is cultivated for its crisp edible tubers eaten either raw or cooked — called also *chorogi*, *crosnes*, *Japanese artichoke*, *knotroot*
chinese azalea *n, usu cap C* : a deciduous shrub (*Rhododendron molle*) having leaves two to six inches long and golden yellow clustered flowers up to two inches across
chinese banana *n, usu cap C* : DWARF BANANA
chinese bean oil *n, usu cap C* : SOYBEAN OIL
chinese bellflower *n, usu cap C* : any of several plants of the genus *Platycodon*; *specif* : BALLOONFLOWER
chinese bezique *n, usu cap C* : SIX-PACK BEZIQUE
chinese bladdernut *n, usu cap C* : GOLDENRAIN TREE
chinese blister fly *or* **chinese blistering fly** *or* **chinese blistering beetle** *n, usu cap C* : a beetle (genus *Mylabris*) that yields China cantharides
chinese block *n, usu cap C* : CHINESE TEMPLE BLOCK
chinese blue *n, usu cap C* **1** : any of various blue pigments: as **a** : an iron blue esp. having a relatively greenish tint **b** : a mixture of ultramarine or of cobalt blue with white lead **2** : PRUSSIAN BLUE 2
chinese boxes *n pl, usu cap C* : a set of graduated boxes each fitting into the one next larger
chinese bridge *n, usu cap C* **1** : CHINESE WHIST **2** : a variety of whist in which the object is to win not tricks but scoring cards, the ace and ten counting 10 each and the five counting 5
chinese bush cherry *n, usu cap 1st C* : a flowering almond (*Prunus japonica*)
chinese cabbage *n, usu cap 1st C* : either of two Asiatic brassicas (*Brassica pekinensis* and *B. chinensis*) somewhat resembling cabbage and widely used as greens, the first forming an elongated compact head of broad light green leaves, the second a loose chardlike head of dark green leaves — called also respectively *pe-tsai* and *pakchoi* and together *celery cabbage*, *lettuce cabbage*
chinese checkers *n pl but sing or pl in constr, usu cap 1st C* : a game for from two to six people played on a pitted board the object being for each player in turn to transfer a set of marbles from a home point to the opposite point of a 6-pointed star by a series of moves similar to those in checkers
chinese chestnut *n, usu cap 1st C* : an Asiatic chestnut (*Castanea mollissima*) of importance chiefly for its resistance to chestnut blight
chinese chippendale *n, usu cap both Cs* : Chippendale furniture employing chiefly straight lines, bamboo turnings, and as surface decoration fluting and fretwork in a variety of lattice patterns
chinese cinnamon *n, usu cap 1st C* : the bark of a Chinese tree (*Cinnamomum cassia*) generally considered less agreeable in flavor or fragrance than Ceylon and Saigon cinnamon — called also *cassia bark*
chinese cinnamon oil *n, usu cap 1st C* : CASSIA OIL
chinese civet *n, usu cap 1st C* : a civet cat (*Viverra zibetha ashtoni*) of southern China
chinese copy *n, usu cap 1st C* : an exact imitation or duplicate made without discrimination reproducing defects as well as desired qualities
chinese cork tree *n, usu cap 1st C* : an eastern Asiatic tree (*Phellodendron amurense*) that has light-gray corky bark and is cultivated as an ornamental and shade tree
chinese crescent *n, usu cap 1st C* : PAVILLON CHINOIS
chinese crested dog *n, usu cap 1st C* : a small now nearly extinct dog of a breed native to northern Tibet and China and distinguished by slender greyhoundlike build, naked body, and head crest and tail brush of long usu. white hairs
chinese date *n, usu cap C* **1** : a tree (*Ziziphus jujuba*) with leaves used in China as food for the tussah silkworm **2** : the edible plumlike fruit of the Chinese date — called also *jujube*
chinese dogskin *n, usu cap C* : MANCHURIAN DOG
chinese drum *n, usu cap C* : a small gaily decorated drum with two thick heads used chiefly in dance orchestras
chinese elm *n, usu cap C* **1** : a small rapid-growing tree or shrub (*Ulmus parvifolia*) that is native to eastern Asia, has shining coriaceous leaves, and is used widely for shelterbelts and hedges **2** : SIBERIAN ELM
chinese evergreen *n, usu cap C* : an erect or semiclimbing herb (*Aglaonema modestum*) often kept as a house plant for its green or variegated drought-resisting leaves — called also *Japanese leaf*
chinese export porcelain *n, usu cap C* : LOWESTOFT WARE 2
chinese fan palm *n, usu cap C* : a fan palm (*Livistona chinensis*) of China growing up to six feet in height and sold as a pot or tub plant in cultivation under the name of *Latania borbonica*
chinese fiddle *n, usu cap C* : a Chinese or central Asian bowed lute having two strings and no fingerboard
chinese fir *n, usu cap C* : an ornamental east Asian evergreen tree (*Cunninghamia lanceolata*) with narrow flat leaves close= set along the spreading branches
chinese fleecevine \,=,=ˈ=,=\ *n, usu cap C* : SILVER-LACE VINE
chinese forget-me-not *n, usu cap C* : any of several plants of the genus *Cynoglossum*; *esp* : a biennial herb (*C. amabile*) grown for its usu. bright blue flowers
chinese gall *n, usu cap C* : a gall very rich in tannin produced by insects on an Asian sumac (*Rhus semialata*)
chinese gelatin *n, usu cap C* : AGAR 1a
chinese ginger *n, usu cap C* : GALINGALE 1b(1)
chinese gong *n, usu cap C* : GONG 1
chinese goose *n, usu cap C* **1** : a very large wild goose (*Anser cygnoides* syn. *Cygnopsis cygnoides*) of northeastern Asia that interbreeds freely with the grayleg and is probably an ancestor of various eastern domesticated geese **2** : a brown or white goose of a breed that originated in China probably from the Chinese goose and is distinguished by upright carriage, large knob at the base of the bill, and small size
chinese gooseberry *n, usu cap C* : a vigorous chiefly subtropical twining vine (*Actinidia chinensis*) the brownish hairy fruit of which is eaten fresh or in preserves esp. in New Zealand
chinese green *n, usu cap C* : LOKAO
chinese hat plant *n, usu cap C* [so called fr. its large spreading calyx] : a straggling evergreen Himalayan shrub (*Holmskioldia sanguinea*) of the family Verbenaceae sometimes cultivated in the southern U.S.
chinese hibiscus *n, usu cap C* : CHINA ROSE 2
chinese holly *n, usu cap C* : a dense rounded evergreen shrub (*Ilex cornuta*) native to China, widely used as an ornamental, and distinguished by its quadrangular oblong leaves each usu. with three strong spines at its dilated apex
chinese homer *n, usu cap C, slang* : a cheap home run; *specif* : a fly ball that is barely over a barrier or into stands that are unusually close to home plate
chinese horn *n, usu cap C* : an oboe with a flaring end
chinese ink *n, usu cap C* : INDIA INK
chinese insect wax *n, usu cap C* : CHINESE WAX
chinese isinglass *n, usu cap C* : AGAR 1a
chinese jujube *n, usu cap C* : any of several large-fruited jujubes developed in China from the common jujube (*Ziziphus jujuba*) and cultivated in warm regions (as California)
chinese jute *n, usu cap C* : CHINGMA
chinese lacquer *n, usu cap C* : LACQUER 1b
chinese lake *n, often cap C* : CARMINE 2
chinese lantern *n, usu cap C* **1** : a collapsible lantern of thin colored paper mostly for ceremonial or decorative use **2** : CHINESE LANTERN PLANT; *also* : one of the brilliant inflated calyxes of the Chinese lantern plant
chinese lantern plant *n, usu cap C* : a perennial Old World ground-cherry (*Physalis alkekengi*) that is widely cultivated for its showy inflated leafy calyxes that are brilliant orange= red when mature and are often used for decoration — called also *winter cherry*
chinese layering *n, usu cap C* : MARCOTTAGE
chinese lemon *n, usu cap C* : CITRON 1a, 1b
chinese lilac *n, usu cap C* : a hybrid lilac produced by crossing Persian lilac and common lilac and having broader leaves and much longer flower clusters than the Persian parent
chinese lily *n, usu cap C* : CHINESE SACRED LILY
chinese liver fluke *n, usu cap C* : a common and destructive Asian liver fluke (*Clonorchis sinensis*) that invades the human liver
chinese matrimony vine *n, usu cap C* : a strongly growing vinelike shrub (*Lycium chinense*) having purplish flowers and red berries
chinese millet *n, usu cap C* **1** : the common sorghum (*Sorghum vulgare*) **2** *Austral* : MILLET 1a **3** : a foxtail (*Setaria faberii*)
chinese money plant *n, usu cap C* : HONESTY 3
chinese musk *n, usu cap C* : MUSK 1
chinese mustard *n, usu cap C* : INDIAN MUSTARD; *also* : any of several Asiatic brassicas sometimes used as potherbs
chinese nut *n, usu cap C* : LITCHI 1
chinese olive *n, usu cap C* : JAVA ALMOND
chinese orange *n, usu cap C* **1** : a kumquat (*Fortunella japonica*) having globular fruit **2** : a vivid yellowish pink to strong reddish orange that is very slightly redder than capucine red — called also *Japanese yellow*
chinese parasol tree *also* **chinese parasol** *n, usu cap C* : an Asiatic tree (*Firmiana simplex*) of the family Sterculiaceae now widely planted as an ornamental in warmer parts of the U.S. having large maplelike leaves and greenish white flowers in clusters

chinese pavilion *n, usu cap C* [trans. of F *pavillon chinois*] : PAVILLON CHINOIS

chinese pear *n, usu cap C* : SAND PEAR 2a

chinese pea tree *n, usu cap C* : a bushy shrub (*Caragana sinica*) with angular branches, stipules that become stiff thorns, and solitary reddish yellow flowers

chinese peel *n, usu cap C* : rattan interwoven with grasses ⟨*Chinese peel* furniture⟩

chinese pheasant *n, usu cap C* : RING-NECKED PHEASANT

chinese preserving melon *n, usu cap C* : WAX GOURD

chinese primrose *n, usu cap C* : a cultivated Asiatic primrose (*Primula sinensis*); *sometimes* : any of several related cultivated Asiatic primroses

chinese pusley *also* **chinese pussley** *n, usu cap C* : SEASIDE HELIOTROPE

chinese puzzle *n, usu cap C* **1** : an intricate or ingenious puzzle such as those made by the Chinese — see TANGRAM **2** : something intricate and obscure ⟨the rules of taxonomy are a *Chinese puzzle* to the novice⟩

chinese quince *n, usu cap C* : a half-evergreen medium-sized tree (*Chaenomeles sinensis*) resembling dwarf Japanese quince but with solitary pink flowers

chinese red *n, usu cap C* **1** : any of various red pigments: as **a** : a basic lead chromate (as chrome red) **b** : VERMILION 1a **c** : an iron red **2 a** : VERMILION 2b **b** : INDIAN RED 2b **c** : a deep reddish orange that is slightly yellower and stronger than average tomato

chinese rhubarb *n, usu cap C* : a rhubarb (*Rheum officinale*) from whose thick caudex medicinal rhubarb is obtained

chinese rose *n, usu cap C* : CHINA ROSE 2

chinese rose beetle *n, usu cap C* : a common leaf-eating beetle (*Adoretus sinicus*) of southeast Asia accidentally introduced into Hawaii where it is a serious pest on many cultivated plants

chinese rouge *n, often cap C* [³*rouge*] : CARTHAMUS RED

chi·nes·ery \chī'nēz(ə)rē\ *n* -ES *usu cap* [modif. of F *chinoiserie*] : CHINOISERIE

chinese sacred lily *n, usu cap C* : a narcissus (*Narcissus tazetta orientalis*) that constitutes a variety of yellow polyanthus narcissus

chinese scale *n, usu cap C* : SAN JOSE SCALE

chinese scholartree *n, usu cap C* : JAPANESE PAGODA TREE

chinese silk plant *n, usu cap C* : RAMIE 1

chinese snowball *n, usu cap C* : a shrub (*Viburnum macrocephalum sterile*) that is a cultivated variety of a Chinese shrub with ball-like white flowers

chinese squill *n, usu cap C* : an herb (*Scilla scilloides*) native to China having elongated racemes of pink flowers

chinese stick *n, usu cap C* : a black pigment in stick form used to make India ink

chinese sumac *n, usu cap C* : TREE OF HEAVEN

chinese tallow *or* **chinese vegetable tallow** *n, usu cap C* : a hard white fat obtained from the surface of the seeds of the Chinese tallow tree and used for making candles and soap

chinese tallow tree *n, usu cap C* : an Asiatic tree (*Sapium sebiferum* or *Stillingia sebifera*) that yields a hard wood used for engraving and from its seeds a drying oil and vegetable tallow — called also *stillingia;* see CHINESE TALLOW

chinese temple block *n, usu cap C* : a hollow slotted wooden box struck with a drumstick or hammer adapted by jazz bands from the wooden fish used by Buddhist priests — called also *clog box, tap box*

chinese tree wax *n, usu cap C* : CHINESE WAX

chinese trumpet creeper *or* **chinese trumpet vine** *n, usu cap 1st C* : a deciduous vine (*Campsis grandiflora*) having orange or scarlet flowers shorter and broader than those of the common trumpet creeper

chinese vampire *n, usu cap C* : an Asiatic big-eared bat (*Lyroderma lyra sinensis*) that is not a true vampire but an insectivorous bat

chinese varnish tree *n, usu cap C* : CANDLENUT 2

chinese vermilion *n, usu cap C* **1** : VERMILION 1a **2** : a vivid red that is yellower, lighter, and slightly stronger than apple red, yellower, lighter, and stronger than carmine or scarlet, and yellower and lighter than madder crimson — called also *Harrison red, signal red*

chinese violet *n, often cap C* : a moderate purple that is redder and paler than heliotrope (sense 4a), bluer and lighter than average amethyst, and paler than manganese violet

chinese wall *n, usu cap C & sometimes cap W* [fr. the *Chinese Wall,* a defensive wall built in the 3d cent. B.C. & extending 1500 miles between China and Mongolia] : a strong barrier; *esp* : a serious obstacle to free intercourse or understanding (as between individuals or nations) ⟨go backwards towards an old *Chinese wall* policy of isolation —F.D.Roosevelt⟩

chinese watermelon *n, usu cap C* : WAX GOURD

chinese wax *n, usu cap C* : a white or yellowish white crystalline wax resembling spermaceti but harder, more friable, and higher melting that is deposited on certain trees by a scale (*Ceroplastes ceriferus*) common in China and India or a related scale (*Ericerus pela*) of China and Japan and is used chiefly for making candles, polishing materials, and sizes for paper — called also *Chinese insect wax, insect wax*

chinese whist *n, usu cap C* : a card game for two, three, or four players resembling whist except that six of each player's cards are dealt face down on the table and a like number of cards face up upon them, the lower cards being revealed only as the cards above them are removed in the course of the play

chinese white *n, usu cap C* : ZINC WHITE; *esp* : a dense form of it

chinese windlass *n, usu cap C* : DIFFERENTIAL WINDLASS

chinese wistaria *n, usu cap C* : a wistaria (*Wisteria chinensis*) with nearly glabrous mature leaves, blue-violet flowers, and velvety pubescent pods

chinese witch hazel *n, usu cap C* : either of two plants of the family Hamamelidaceae that are native to China: **a** : a white-flowered evergreen shrub or small tree (*Loropetalum chinense*) **b** : a large deciduous shrub (*Hamamelis mollis*) having large fragrant yellow flowers

chinese wood oil *n, usu cap C* : TUNG OIL 1

chinese yam *n, usu cap C* : CINNAMON VINE

chinese yellow *n, usu cap C* **1** : either of two pigments: **a** : KING'S YELLOW **b** : YELLOW OCHER 1 **2 a** : YELLOW OCHER 2 **b** : LEMON YELLOW 1b

chinfest \'=,=\ *n* [*chin* + *fest*] *slang* : an instance of talking together or conferring esp. informally : DISCUSSION, GAB

chin fly *n* [so called fr. its laying its eggs about the mouth of the horse] : THROAT BOTFLY

¹**ch'ing** \'chiŋ\ *n, often cap* [Chin (Pek) *ch'ing* azure] : a vivid blue that is redder and duller than Cleopatra and greener and duller than ultramarine

²**ching** \'jiŋ\ *n* -S [Chin (Pek) *ching*¹ classic (book), the classics] : a Chinese authoritative or canonical book; *specif* : a Chinese scripture

ching·ma \'chiŋ'mä\ *n* -S [Chin (Pek) *ch'ing*³*ma*²] : the bast fiber of Indian mallow used for cordage — called also *China jute, Chinese jute*

ch'ing ming \'chiŋ'miŋ\ *n, usu cap C&M* [Chin (Pek) *ch'ing*¹ *ming*², lit., clear and bright] : a spring festival in China when graves are put in order and special offerings are made to the dead

ching·paw \'chiŋ,pō\ *n, pl* **chingpaw** *or* **chingpaws** *usu cap* **1** : a Tibeto-Burman ethnic group inhabiting upper Burma and the north Burma-Chinese frontier region, esp. the Irrawaddy drainage above Myitkyina known as "the Triangle" and the Hukawng valley — called also *Singpho;* see KACHIN **2** : a member of the Chingpaw

chin·hsien \'jinshē'en\ *adj, usu cap* [fr. *Chinhsien* (Chinchow), China] : CHINCHOW

chinidine *var of* QUINIDINE

chi·nin \chə'nēn\ *n* -S [MexSp *chinin,* fr. Nahuatl *xinene*] : COYO

chining *pres part of* CHINE

chi·ni·o·fon \kə'nīə,fän\ *n* -S [*chin-* + *iodine* + *sulfonic*] : a yellow powder composed of a sulfonic acid $C_9H_4NI(OH)SO_3H$ derived from quinoline, the sodium salt of this acid, and sodium bicarbonate and used in the treatment of amebiasis

chi·ni·pa \chə'nēpə\ *n, pl* **chinipa** *or* **chinipas** *usu cap* [Sp, of AmerInd origin] **1** : a Taracahitian people in Chihuahua state, Mexico **2** : a member of the Chinipa people

¹**chink** \'chiŋk\ *n* -S [prob. alter. of ME *chin, chine* crack, fissure, chasm] **1 a** : an opening, space, break, or hole typically of greater length than breadth (as between planks in a wall) : CRACK, CREVICE, CRANNY, INTERSTICE **b** : a means of evasion or escape : LOOPHOLE : a weak spot (as in a plan or system) ⟨he was indicted but his lawyers found a ~ in the law⟩ **2** : something used to fill a chink; *specif* : a strip of wood used to close the crevice between adjoining logs in a log cabin **3** : a beam of light of similar form to or perceived through a chink **4** *or* **chink shell** : any of several gastropod mollusks: **a** : KEYHOLE LIMPET **b** : any of a family (Lacunidae) of conical thin-shelled marine snails having a slit on the columella opposite the aperture **syn** see CRACK

²**chink** \"\ *vb* -ED/-ING/-S *vi, obs* : to open in cracks : CRACK ~ *vt* **1** *obs* : to cause to open in cracks : CRACK **2** : to fill the chinks of (as by caulking) : stop up ⟨~ and daub a log cabin⟩

³**chink** \"\ *n* -S [imit.] **1** : a short sharp sound (as of metal or small sonorous bodies struck with a slight tap) **2 a chinks** *pl, obs* : pieces of money : COINS **b** *slang* : COIN, MONEY, CASH

⁴**chink** \"\ *vb* -ED/-ING/-S *vi* : to make a slight sharp metallic sound (as of coins or glasses in collision) : strike or strike together with a chink ⟨the sound . . . of ~*ing* china —Nancy Hale⟩ ~ *vt* : to cause (as coins) to make a chink

⁵**chink** \"\ *vi* -ED/-ING/-S [perh. fr. (assumed) ME *chinken;* akin to ME *kinken* to gasp convulsively, OE *cincung* hearty laughter, obs. D *kincken* to pant, MHG *kīchen* to breathe heavily, prob. of imit. origin] *dial Eng* : to catch one's breath : gasp convulsively

⁶**chink** \"\ *n* -S [imit.] **1** : CHAFFINCH **2** : REED BUNTING

⁷**chink** \"\ *n* -S *often cap* [alter. (prob. influenced by *chink* small cleft) of *Chinese;* fr. their slant eyes] : CHINESE — usu. taken to be offensive

chinkapin *var of* CHINQUAPIN

chinkara *var of* CHIKARA

chink·er \'chiŋkə(r)\ *n* -S [²*chink* + *-er*] **1** : something that fills or can be used to fill chinks **2 chinkers** *pl, slang* : pieces of money : COIN 5

chinkerichee *also* **chinkerinchee** *var of* CHINCHERINCHEE

chin·kiang \'jinjē'äŋ\ *adj, usu cap* [fr. *Chinkiang,* China] : of or from the city of Chinkiang, China : of the kind or style prevalent in Chinkiang

chinking *n* -S [¹*chink* + *-ing*] : material (as mud or chips) to fill chinks

chin·kle \'chiŋkəl\ *vb* -ED/-ING/-S [freq. of ⁴*chink*] : CHINK JINGLE

chinks \'chiŋks\ *n* [origin unknown] : WINTERGREEN 2a

chink shell *n* : ¹CHINK 4

chinky \'chiŋkē, -i\ *adj* -ER/-EST [¹*chink* + *-y*] : having chinks : full of chinks

chin·less \'chinləs\ *adj* : lacking a chin : having a receding chin

chin music *n, slang* : idle talk : CHATTER, GABBLE

chinned \'chind\ *adj* [¹*chin* + *-ed*] : having a chin of a specified kind ⟨weak-*chinned*⟩

chinning *pres part of* CHIN

¹**chi·no** \'chē(,)nō\ *n* -S [AmerSp, masc. of *china* Indian woman, woman of mixed blood, fr. Quechua & Aymara, female animal, servant] : a Spanish-American of mixed blood; *esp* : one with one quarter Indian and three quarters Negro blood

²**chino** \"\ *n* -S [modif. of AmerSp *china,* short for Sp *naranja china* Chinese orange] : SWEET ORANGE

³**chino** \" *sometimes* 'shē-\ *n* -S [AmerSp] **1** : a usu. khaki-colored cotton twill of the type used for military uniforms **2** : an article of clothing made of chino — usu. used in pl.

¹**chi·no-** \'chī(,)nō\ *comb form, usu cap* [*China*] : Chinese and ⟨*Chino*-Japanese⟩ — compare SINO-

²**chino-** — see CHIN-

chi·noi·se·rie \,shēn,wäz(ə)'rē, shēn'wäzərē\ *n* -S *sometimes cap* [F, fr. *chinois* Chinese (fr. *Chine* China) + *-erie* -ery] **1 a** : a style in art (as in decoration) reflecting or felt to reflect Chinese artistic esp. decorative qualities or motifs (as in costume, furniture, objects of virtu, or architecture); *esp* : such a style akin to the rococo in decorative intricacy popular in 18th century Europe — compare CHINESE CHIPPENDALE **b** : an art object or instance of decoration in this style **2** : conduct felt to suggest the Chinese

chinoline *var of* QUINOLINE

chinone *var of* QUINONE

chi·nook \shə'nu̇k *sometimes* chə- *or* -ük\ *n, pl* **chinook** *or* **chinooks** [Chehalis *Tsinúk*] **1** *usu cap* **a** : an Indian people of the north shore of the Columbia river at its mouth **b** : a member of such people **2** *usu cap* : a Chinookan language of the Chinook and other nearby peoples — see LOWER CHINOOK, UPPER CHINOOK **3 a** : a warm moist southwest wind of the Pacific coastal region of No. America from Oregon northward **b** : a warm dry foehnlike wind that descends the eastern slopes of the Rocky mountains

¹**chi·nook·an** \-ən\ *adj, usu cap* : of or relating to Chinook or a Chinook or to Chinookan

²**chinookan** \"\ *or* **chinook** *n* -S *usu cap* : a language family of the Penutian phylum in Washington and Oregon comprising Lower Chinook and Upper Chinook

chinook jargon *also* **chinook** *n, usu cap C&J* : a pidgin language based on Lower Chinook and other Indian languages, French, and English and at one time used as a lingua franca in the northwestern U.S. and on the Pacific coast of Canada and Alaska — called also *Jargon, Oregon Jargon*

chinook licorice *n, usu cap C* : a silky blue-flowered American herb (*Lupinus littoralis*) found in the Pacific coastal dunes

chinook salmon *also* **chinook** *n* -S *usu cap C* : KING SALMON

chi·not·to \kē'nȯd·(,)ō\ *or* **chinotto orange** *n, pl* **chinot·ti** \-d·ē\ [It, fr. obs. *China* China] : SOUR ORANGE; *esp* : a broad-leafed variety of the sour orange tree

chinovic acid *var of* QUINOVIC ACID

chinovin *var of* QUINOVIN

chi·nov·nik \chə'nȯvnik\ *n* -S [Russ, fr. *chinovny* having rank (fr. *chin* rank + *-ovny,* adj. suffix) + *-ik* (nominal suffix); akin to Russ *chinit'* to do, OSlav *činiti* to arrange — more at POET] : a minor official in czarist Russia

chinovose *var of* QUINOVOSE

chinpiece \'=,=\ *n* : a piece (as of armor) to fit around and usu. protect the chin

chin·qua·pin *also* **chin·ca·pin** *or* **chin·ka·pin** \'chiŋkə,pin, -kē-\ *n* -S [alter. of earlier *chincomen,* of Algonquian origin; akin to *chechinkamin* chestnut (in some Algonquian language of Virginia); perh. akin to Delaware *chinqua* large, great and to Delaware *mihn* berry, Natick *min* berry, nut] **1 a** : any of several trees (genus *Castanea*); *esp* : a dwarf chestnut (*C. pumila*) of the U. S. **b** : the sweet edible nut of this tree usu. solitary in the bur **2** : CHINQUAPIN OAK **3 a** : any of several trees of a genus (*Castanopsis*) closely related to *Castanea; esp* : a tree (*Castanopsis chrysophylla*) of California and Oregon **b** : the nut of any of these trees **4** : WATER CHINQUAPIN **5** *or* **chinquapin perch** : WHITE CRAPPIE

chinquapin oak *n* : either of two No. American chestnut oaks: **a** : a medium to large oak (*Quercus muhlenbergii*) of the eastern U.S. that yields a strong durable timber — called also *yellow oak* **b** : a small shrubby oak (*Q. prinoides*) of the same area that has a sweet edible acorn and often forms dense thickets — called also *dwarf chinquapin oak, scrub oak, yellow chestnut oak*

chin rest *n* : a device for the top of a violin or viola to enable a player to hold the instrument more firmly under his chin

chins *pres 3d sing of* CHIN, *pl of* CHIN

chinse *or* **chintze** \'chin(t)s\ *vb* -ED/-ING/-S [alter. of E dial. *chinch* to fill up cracks, perh. var. of ²*chink*] : to calk in a makeshift or temporary fashion

chin shield *n* : one of certain paired elongate scales below the lower labials on the chin in some reptiles

chin stay *n* : a stay or supporting band passing under the chin

chin strap *n* **1** : a strap worn under or in front of the chin esp. as a means of holding a hat on the head **2** : a strap connecting the throatlatch and noseband of a halter or bridle

¹**chintz** \'chin(t)s\ *n* -ES *often attrib* [earlier *chints,* pl. (taken as sing.) of earlier *chint,* fr. Hindi *chīṭ*] **1** : a printed calico from India **2** : a firm usu. glazed cotton fabric of plain weave commonly with colorful printed designs generally in not less than five colors used for clothing and for interior decoration

²**chintz** *var of* CHINCH BUG

¹**chintzy** \'chin(t)sē, -si\ *adj, usu* -ER/-EST [¹*chintz* + *-y*] **1** : decorated with or like chintz **2 a** : GAUDY, CHEAP ⟨a ~ spa town in the Shakespeare country —J.P.O'Donnell⟩ **b** : STINGY ⟨~ set-manufacturers haven't left any room in the set for a decent-sized loudspeaker —David Lachenbruch⟩

²**chintzy** \"\ *var of* CHINCHY

¹**chin-up** *also* **chins-up** \'=,=\ *adj* : COURAGEOUS ⟨the *chin-up* British spirit⟩

²**chin-up** \"\ *n* -S [*chin up* to chin oneself] : the act of chinning oneself ⟨doing a dozen *chin-ups* each morning⟩

chin-wag \'=,=\ *n or vi, slang* : GOSSIP

chi·nyan·ja \chə'nyanjə\ *n, usu cap* : NYANJA

chi·o·coc·ca \,kīə'käkə\ *n, cap* [NL, fr. *chion-* + *-cocca* (fr. L *coccum* berry, fr. Gk *kokkos* kermes berry, seed)] : a small genus of tropical American shrubs (family Rubiaceae) having white or yellowish flowers and a white 2-seeded berry and usu. having roots with purgative properties — see CAHINCA ROOT

chi·og·e·nes \kī'äjə,nēz\ *n, cap* [NL, fr. *chion-* + Gk *-genēs* born — more at -GEN] *in some classifications* : a genus of creeping evergreens containing solely the creeping snowberry that is commonly placed in *Gaultheria*

chi·o·lite \'kīə,līt\ *n* -S [G *chiolith,* fr. *chion-* + *-lith* -lite] : a mineral $Na_5Al_3F_{14}$ resembling cryolite in color and composition

chion- *or* **chiono-** *also* **chio-** *comb form* [NL, fr. *chion-, chiono-* fr. NL, fr. Gk, fr. *chiōn* snow; *chio-* fr. G & NL, fr. Gk *chiōn;* akin to Gk *cheimōn* winter — more at HIBERNATE] : snow ⟨*chion*anthus⟩ ⟨*chio*lite⟩ ⟨*chiono*doxa⟩

chi·on·ablep·sia \,kī,änə'blepsēə\ *n* -S [NL, fr. *chion-* + *ablepsia*] : SNOW BLINDNESS

chi·o·nan·thus \,kīə'nan(t)thəs\ *n, cap* [NL, fr. *chion-* + *-anthus*] : a genus of low trees or shrubs (family Oleaceae) having drooping panicles of fragrant flowers with narrow petals — see FRINGE TREE

chi·o·nas·pis \-'naspəs\ *n, cap* [NL, fr. *chion-* + *-aspis*] : a genus of scales with elongate often white scales — see SCURFY SCALE

chi·o·ne \'kīə,nē\ *n, cap* [NL, fr. *Chione,* a mythological character shot by Diana, fr. L] : a genus of rock cockles (family Veneridae)

chi·o·nid·i·dae \,kīə'nidə,dē\ *n pl, cap* [NL, fr. *Chionid-, Chionis,* type genus (irreg. fr. Gk *chiōn* snow) + *-idae*] : a family of birds (order Charadriiformes) containing a single genus (*Chionis*) consisting of the sheathbills

chi·o·no·doxa \,kīənō'däksə, kī,änə'd-\ *n* [NL, fr. *chion-* + Gk *doxa* glory; akin to Gk *dokein* to seem good — more at DECENT] **1** *cap* : a genus of small bulbous herbs of the family Liliaceae having narrow leaves and the perianth segments united below — see GLORY-OF-THE-SNOW **2** -S : any plant of the genus *Chionodoxa*

chiot *usu cap, var of* SCIOT

¹**chip** \'chip\ *n* -S [ME; prob. akin to OE *-cippian* to cut] **1 a** : a small usu. somewhat thin and flat piece of wood, stone, or other material separated by a quick blow (as with a cutting or striking instrument) or by natural flaking : FRAGMENT, FLAKE **b** : a small piece of food ⟨chocolate ~*s*⟩: as (1) : a thin slice of cooked or uncooked food ⟨orange ~*s*⟩; *esp* : POTATO CHIP (2) : FRENCH FRY **c** : palm leaf, straw, or wood split into thin pieces for making women's hats **d** (1) : a metal often continuous fragment or curl cut during machining from material being machined (2) : the thread of material cut from a blank during the process of disc recording **e** (1) : a small piece from a crystal (2) : a piece of usu. uncut diamond weighing less than three fourths of a carat ⟨wearing a diamond ~ ring —Betty Smith⟩ **f** *chiefly Brit* (1) *or* **chip basket** : a ventilated container (as for fruit) made of thin sheets of split wood commonly overlapped at the bottom and secured at the upper edge by a band of similar wood (2) : the contents of such a container ⟨strawberries at two shillings a ~⟩ **g** (1) : CHIPBOARD (2) : logged wood for use in pulp manufacture **h chips** *pl* : soap in flakes or granules **i** : one of the thin slices or shreds into which beets are cut in sugar making — called also *cossette* **j** : a small piece of bark (as of cinchona or cinnamon) **2 a** (1) : something valueless or trivial ⟨I don't care a ~ for his views⟩ (2) : something small of its kind : BIT ⟨a ~ of a lad⟩ **b** : something dried up, withered, or flavorless ⟨meat roasted to a ~⟩ **3** : something having the distinctive qualities of that from which it is derived or taken — used chiefly of persons with reference to resemblance of child to parent ⟨Jack's exactly like his father, he's a real ~ off the old block⟩ **4** : the triangular piece of wood attached to the end of a log line **5** : a coin or a unit (as a small disk) equivalent to a coin in value: **a** : one of the counters used as a token for money in poker and other games of chance and usu. of a distinctive color to indicate its relative value : CHECK 11c **b** : a playing counter in such games as tiddledywinks **c chips** *pl, slang* : MONEY — used esp. in the phrase *in the chips* **d** *slang Brit* : any of various coins (as a shilling, rupee, or sovereign) **e** : something that is hazarded on some issue or the interest that one holds in some venture ⟨the industrialists that had their ~*s* on Hitler⟩ ⟨bargaining ~⟩ **6** : a piece of dried dung — usu. used in combination ⟨a cow ~⟩ ⟨buffalo ~*s*⟩ **7** : a flaw in a surface remaining after a chip has been removed ⟨a cup with a ~ in its rim⟩ **8** : CHIP SHOT **9** : BEACH **3** — **chip on one's shoulder** [so called fr. the allusion to a chip of wood placed on the shoulder to be knocked off as a challenge to fight] : a challenging or bellicose attitude

²**chip** \"\ *vb* **chipped; chipped; chipping; chips** [ME *chippen,* fr. OE *-cippian* (as in *forcippian* to cut off); akin to obs. G *kipfen* to cut the point off, MLG *kēp* notch, ON *keipr* oarlock] *vt* **1** *obs* : to cut the crust from (bread) **2** *now dial Eng* : to fissure the surface of : CRACK, CHAP **3 a** : to cut or hew with or as if with an ax, chisel, or other edged tool : CHOP, HACK **b** : to cut or break (a small piece) from something ⟨~ a piece off the rock⟩ : cut or break a fragment from ⟨~ my best platter⟩ ⟨with the egg tooth the young bird ~*s* the shell⟩ **c** : to shape (a material or an object) by cutting or breaking away a little at a time ⟨~ flint to a point⟩ ⟨~ an arrowhead out of flint⟩ **d** : to cut or break up into fragments ⟨~ ice⟩ : reduce to chips (as wood for pulping) **e** : to decorate (as silver or enamel) by cutting chips from or chasing **4** : to cut a piece or pieces of bark from (a tree) esp. in tapping for turpentine **5** *Austral* : HOE, HARROW **6** *slang Brit* : CHAFF, BANTER, TAUNT ~ *vi* **1** *obs* : to break into bud, shoot, or blossom : GERMINATE **2** : to break or fly off in small pieces ⟨fine porcelain often ~*s* less readily than softer ware⟩ **3 a** : to bet one chip or a minimum amount in a poker game : CHECK *vi* 8a **b** : to play a chip (as in stops) when unable to play a card **4** : to play a chip shot **5** *of an egg* : PIP 2b

³**chip** \"\ *vb* **chipped; chipped; chipping; chips** [perh. fr. ²*chip*] *vt, dial Eng* : to trip or throw in wrestling ~ *vi* **1** *dial Eng* : to trip along nimbly **2** *dial Eng* : QUARREL — often used with *out*

⁴**chip** \"\ *n* -S : a trick or special attack for throwing a wrestling opponent

⁵**chip** \"\ *vi* **chipped; chipped; chipping; chips** [imit.] : ¹CHEEP

⁶**chip** \"\ *n* -S : ²CHEEP

chip away *vt* [²*chip*] : to remove, take away, or withdraw gradually ⟨might restore the magnificence that man has *chipped away* —Brooks Atkinson⟩ ~ *vi* : to chip away something — often used with *at* ⟨men who *chip away* at the American way of life⟩

chip ax *n* [²*chip*] : a small ax for chipping timber or stone into shape

chi·paya \chə'pīə\ *n, pl* **chipaya** *or* **chipayas** *usu cap* [Sp, of AmerInd origin] **1 a** : a people of Bolivia **b** : a member of such people **2** : the language of the Chipaya people

chip basket *n* : CHIP 1 f (1)

chip bird *n* [⁶*chip*] : CHIPPING SPARROW

chip-blower \'=,==\ *n* : a dental instrument typically consisting of a rubber bulb with a long metal tube and used to blow drilling debris from a tooth cavity that is being prepared for filling

chipboard \'=,=\ *n* [*chip* "kind of paper stock" (fr. ¹*chip*) + *board*] : a paperboard made from waste paper — called also *chip*

chip breaker *n* : a shoulder in a machine tool made by grinding a groove parallel to the cutting edge or by attaching a plate to the top to form a wall against which the chip produced in turning or other machining will be broken up

chip budding *n* **:** budding that is effected by the insertion of a bud on a chip of bark and wood into a mortise cut in the stock and that is used esp. for budding small grapevines

chip cap *n* **:** a plate fitted to the upper side of the cutting iron of a carpenter's plane and shaped to give the iron rigidity and break up the shavings

chip carving *n* **1 a :** hand carving of soft wood by cutting chips with a knife or other instrument usu. in simple geometric designs **b :** the decoration wrought by such carving **2 :** a surface decoration imitating chip carving

chip·e·wy·an *or* **chip·pe·wai·an** *or* **chip·pe·wy·an** \ˌchipəˈwīən\ *n, pl* **chipewyan** *or* **chipewyans** *or* **chippewaian** *or* **chippewaians** *or* **chippewyan** *or* **chippewyans** *usu cap* [Cree *Chipwayanawok,* lit., pointed skins, fr. *chipwa* pointed + *weyanaw* skin + *-ok* (suffix denoting pl.); fr. their pointed skin shirts or parkas] **1 a :** an Athapaskan people closely related to the Slave and Yellowknife people and living north of the Churchill river between the Great Slave lake and the Slave and Athabaska rivers on the west and Hudson Bay on the east **b :** a member of such people **2 :** the language of the Chipewyan people

chip hat palm *n* **:** a medium-sized fan palm (*Thrinax microcarpa*) of southern Florida and the Bahamas the leaves of which are used in making hats and baskets

chip in *vb* [²*chip*] *vi* **1 :** to put up a chip or chips as one's stake at cards **2 :** to contribute money or assistance to an enterprise ⟨all our people *chipped in* generously⟩ **3 :** to interject a comment into a conversation **:** INTERPOSE ~ *vt* **:** CONTRIBUTE ⟨*chip in* my time⟩ ⟨each of us *chipped* 10 dollars *in* to help pay for the damage⟩

chip log *n* **:** the common log consisting of a chip and log line

chip·man \ˈchipmən, -ˌman\ *n, pl* **chipmen** [*chip* + *man*] **1 :** a worker who cleans up metal chips and shavings from machining processes — called also *scrapman* **2 :** a worker who removes the flavor-giving wooden chips from beer-fermenting tanks and washes them for reuse

chip·muck \ˈchip,mək\ [by alter.] *now dial var of* CHIPMUNK

chip·munk *also* **chip·monk** \ˈchip,məŋk\ *n* -s [alter. (prob. influenced by *chipping squirrel*) of earlier *chitmunk,* of Algonquian origin; akin to Ojibwa *atchitamō* squirrel] **1 :** any of numerous small striped American squirrels (genera *Tamias* and *Eutamias*) that are semiterrestrial in habits and intermediate between the typical tree squirrels and the true ground squirrels — called also *ground squirrel, striped squirrel* **2 :** any of various other squirrels of similar habits or appearance (as the mantled ground squirrel)

chip·o·la·ta \ˌchipəˈlädə\ *n* -s [F, fr. It *cipollata,* fr. fem. of *cipollato* with onions, fr. *cipolla* onion (fr. LL *cepulla,* dim. of L *cepa, caepa* onion) + *-ato* -ate] **:** a small spicy sausage used chiefly as a garnish or hors d'oeuvre; *also* **:** a dish (as a ragout) of which such sausages are an ingredient

chip·pa·ble \ˈchipəbəl\ *adj* [²*chip* + *-able*] **:** capable of being chipped

chip·page \ˈchipij\ *n* -s [²*chip* + *-age*] **:** wood lost in felling trees with an ax

chipped *adj* [fr. past part. of ²*chip*] *of glass* **:** having a fernlike design resulting from fine chipping induced by coating the clear glass surface with glue and allowing it to dry

chipped beef \-p(t)ˈb-\ *also* **chip beef** *n* **:** smoked dried beef sliced thin

¹**chip·pen·dale** \ˈchipən,dāl *sometimes* -pᵊm,d-\ *adj, usu cap* [after Thomas *Chippendale* †1779 English cabinetmaker] **:** of, relating to, or closely imitating a style of furniture originating in late 18th century England that in its earlier forms closely resembled the Queen Anne style but in its more typical form is characterized by a graceful outline but often ornate rococo ornamentation, its chairs, in which the style is esp. typified, usu. distinguished by a seat wider at the front than back, by relatively sharp corners, and by a back usu. widened toward the top with carvings at the corners — see CHINESE CHIPPENDALE, FRENCH CHIPPENDALE, GOTHIC CHIPPENDALE

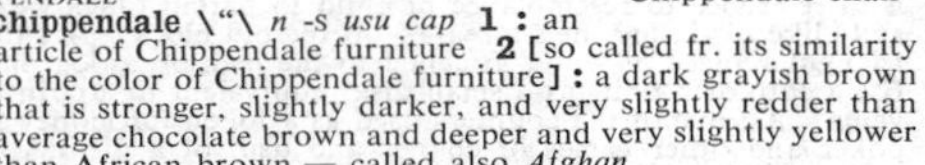
Chippendale chair

²**chippendale** \ˈ"\ *n* -s *usu cap* **1 :** an article of Chippendale furniture **2** [so called fr. its similarity to the color of Chippendale furniture] **:** a dark grayish brown that is stronger, slightly darker, and very slightly redder than average chocolate brown and deeper and very slightly yellower than African brown — called also *Afghan*

¹**chip·per** \ˈchipə(r)\ *n* -s [²*chip* + *-er*] **:** one that chips: as **a :** a tool, device, or machine used for removing unwanted material or surface roughness by chipping (as in finishing castings or forgings or cleaning painted metal); *specif* **:** a narrow blade with diametrically opposite and broad cutting points to be fitted between two circular saw blades in a dado head and designed to cut out the wood between the grooves cut by the circular blades **b :** a machine for reducing something (as pulpwood) to chips **c :** a workman who dresses, cleans, or finishes something by chipping or grinding ⟨ore ~⟩ ⟨pottery ~⟩ ⟨tire ~⟩ **:** an operator of a chipper **d :** a worker who chips trees for turpentine

²**chipper** \ˈ"\ *vi* -ED/-ING/-S [⁵*chip* + *-er*] **1** *of a bird* **:** CHIRP, TWITTER **2** *of a person* **:** CHATTER, BABBLE — see CHIPPER UP

³**chipper** *adj* [perh. var. of *kipper*] **:** being in high spirits **:** CHEERFUL, GAY, SPRIGHTLY ⟨looked ~, like a man who has been diverted by his own wit — Frances G. Patton⟩ **:** TRIM, TRIG ⟨a ~ man with a bandbox look⟩ **:** being in good health **:** being in a state of physical well-being **:** VIGOROUS ⟨as ~ as when I had last seen him, ten years before —James Thurber⟩

chipper up *vb* [³*chipper*] *vt* **:** to cause to be or become cheerful ~ *vi* **:** to cheer up

chip·pe·wa \ˈchipə,wȯ, -,wä, -,wā, -wə *also* -p(,)w-\ *n, pl* **chippewa** *or* **chippewas** *usu cap* **:** OJIBWA

chippewaian *or* **chippewyan** *var of* CHIPEWYAN

chipping *n* -s [fr. gerund of ²*chip*] **1 a :** the action of a chipper (as in dressing or shaping an object of iron, timber, or stone) **b :** the breaking off in small pieces (as of the edges of pottery or glassware) **2 :** a small piece separated in the process of chipping **:** CHIP, FRAGMENT **3 a :** the process of making chipped glass **b :** the decorative effect wrought by this process

chipping chisel *n* [fr. pres. part. of ²*chip*] **:** COLD CHISEL

chipping hammer *n* [fr. pres. part. of ²*chip*] **:** a pneumatically operated chisel

chipping sparrow *n* [fr. pres. part. of ⁵*chip*] **:** a small sparrow (*Spizella passerina*) that is one of the most familiar No. American birds, often building its nest sometimes lined with horsehair in the immediate vicinity of dwellings and having a weak monotonous trilling song — called also *chippy*

chipping squirrel *n* [fr. pres. part. of ⁵*chip*] **:** CHIPMUNK

chip potato *n* **:** FRENCH FRY

chip–proof \ˈ=,=\ *adj* **:** not subject to chipping ⟨a *chip-proof* enamel finish⟩

¹**chip·py** \ˈchipē, -pi\ *adj* -ER/-EST [¹*chip* + *-y*] **1 :** like a chip esp. in dryness **2** *slang* **:** UNWELL; *specif* **:** suffering from a hangover

²**chippy** *or* **chip·pie** \ˈ"\ *n, pl* **chippies** [⁵*chip* + *-y, -ie*] **1 :** CHIPPING SPARROW **2** *slang* **:** a boldly flirtatious or sexually promiscuous woman; *sometimes* **:** PROSTITUTE **3** [by shortening and alter.] **:** CHIPMUNK **4 :** a narrow-gage railroad car

chipre *var of* CHYPRE

chips \ˈchips\ *n pl but sing in constr* [prob. fr. pl. of ¹*chip*] *slang* **:** a ship's carpenter

chip shop \ˈ=,=\ *n, Brit* **:** a fish-and-chip shop

chip shot *n* **:** a short usu. low approach shot in golf that lofts the ball to the green and allows it to roll — called also *pitch-and-run shot;* compare PITCH SHOT

chipyard \ˈ=,=\ *n* [¹*chip* + *yard*] **:** an area or enclosure where wood is cut up for fuel

chi·que·ro \chəˈker(,)ō\ *n* -s [Sp, fr. Ar dial. (Spain) *shirkair*] **:** TORIL

chi·qui·chi·qui palm \ˌchēkēˌchēkē-\ *n* [Sp *chiquichique,* fr. Tupi] **:** either of two So. American palms (*Leopoldinia piassaba* and *Attalea funifera*) yielding piassava fiber

chi·qui·to \chəˈkēd·(,)ō\ *n, pl* **chiquito** *or* **chiquitos** *usu cap* [Sp, dim. of *chico* little — more at CHICO] **1 a :** a people of southeastern Bolivia **b :** a member of such people **2 :** the language of the Chiquito people

chi·qui·to·an \-ēd·əwən\ *n, pl* **chiquitoan** *or* **chiquitoans** *usu cap* **:** a language family comprising Chiquito and including Manasi, Pinoki and Pinyoca

chir *var of* CHIR PINE

chir- *or* **chiro-** *also* **cheir-** *or* **cheiro-** *comb form* [L *chir-, chiro-,* fr. Gk *cheir-, cheiro-,* fr. *cheir;* akin to Alb *dore* hand, Hitt *kesar,* Toch A *tsar*] **:** hand ⟨*chiragra*⟩ ⟨*chiromancy*⟩ ⟨*cheirology*⟩

chi·rag·ra \kīˈragrə\ *n* -s [L, fr. Gk *cheiragra,* fr. *cheir-* chir- + *-agra*] **:** pain in the hand

chi·rap·sia \kīˈrapsēə\ *n* -s [NL, fr. Gk *cheirapsia* rough handling, fr. *cheir-* chir + *-apsia* (fr. *hapsis* contact, touching, fr. *haptein* to touch)] — more at APSIS] **:** friction with the hand **:** MASSAGE

chi·ra·ta \chəˈräd·ə\ *also* **chi·ret·ta** \-red·ə\ *n* -s [Hindi *ciraitā,* fr. Skt *cirātikta, ciratikta,* perh. fr. *cira* long-lasting (perh. akin to Skt *cinoti* he gathers, heaps up) + *tikta* sharp, pungent; akin to Skt *tejate* it is sharp — more at POET, STICK] **:** the dried tissues of a green gentian (*Swertia chirata*) of northern India that has been used as a bitter tonic

chi–rho \ˈkēˈrō, ˈkī-\ *n* -s *usu cap C & R* [*chi* + *rho,* names of the 1st two letters of Gk *Christos* Christ] **:** a Christian monogram and symbol formed of the first two letters, *chi* (X) and *rho* (P), of the Greek word for *Christ* — called also *chrismon, christogram;* compare LABARUM

-chi·ria \ˈkīrēə, ˈkir- *or* **-chei·ria** \ˈkīr-\ *n comb form* -s [NL, fr. Gk *-cheiria,* fr. *cheir* hand — more at CHIR-] **:** -handedness ⟨allo*chiria*⟩ ⟨macro*chiria*⟩

chir·i·ca·hua \ˌchirəˈkäwə\ *n, pl* **chiricahua** *or* **chiricahuas** *usu cap* [modif. of Sp *chiricahue,* fr. Apache, lit., great mountain; fr. their former residence around the Chiricahua mountains in southeastern Arizona] **1 a :** an American Indian people constituting a subdivision of the Gileños **b :** a member of such people **2 :** the language of the Chiricahua people

chir·i·gua·no \ˌchirəˈgwä(,)nō\ *n, pl* **chiriguano** *or* **chiriguanos** *usu cap* [Sp, of AmerInd origin] **1 a :** a Guaranian people inhabiting the slopes of the Bolivian cordillera and including the Guarayú, Pauserna, and Sirionó **b :** a member of the Chiriguano people **2 :** the language of the Chiriguano people

chi·ri·mia \ˌchirəˈmēə\ *or* **chi·ri·mi·lla** \-ē(y)ə\ *n* -s [Sp *chirimía, chirimilla,* modif. (influenced by *charamela,* a wind instrument) of MF *chalemie* — more at SHAWM] **:** a high-pitched oboe of Spain and Spanish America, esp. of the more remote areas of these countries

chirimoya *var of* CHERIMOYA

chi·ri·no \chəˈrē(,)nō\ *n, pl* **chirino** *or* **chirinos** *usu cap* [Sp, of AmerInd origin] **1 a :** an extinct people of western Ecuador **b :** a member of such people **2 :** the language of the Chirino people

¹**chi·ri·pa** \ˌchirəˈpä\ *n* -s [AmerSp *chiripá,* fr. Quechua *chiripak,* lit., for the cold, fr. *chiri* cold + *-pak* for] **:** a man's woolen garment rectangular in shape, usu. tucked in at the belt and wrapped in various ways around the hips and thighs, and worn by gauchos and Indians in southern So. America

²**chi·ri·pá** \ˈ"\ *n, pl* **chiripá** *or* **chiripás** *usu cap* [Sp & Pg, of AmerInd origin] **:** a significant subdivision of the Cayuá people of Brazil and Paraguay

chi·ri·qui \ˌchirəˈkē\ *also* **chi·ri·qui·an** \-ēən\ *adj, usu cap* [fr. *Chiriquí,* province of Panama] **:** of or relating to a prehistoric culture of western Panama noted for its pottery on which a design is produced by removing areas of a surface layer of pigment so that the original color of the pottery shows through

chi·ri·vi·ta \ˌchirəˈvēd·ə\ *n* -s [Sp *chiribita*] **:** the black angelfish or a related form

¹**chirk** \ˈchərk, -ək\ *vb* -ED/-ING/-S [ME *chirken, charken,* fr. OE *cearcian* to creak, gnash — more at CRACK] *vi* **1 :** to make a shrill creaking, squeaking, or chirping noise (as of a door, a mouse, or a bird) ⟨the birds ceased from cheeping and ~*ing* —Gwyn Jones⟩ **2** *archaic* **:** to chirp like a bird **:** CHIRRUP **3 :** to become cheerful **:** CHEER — usu. used with *up* ~ *vt* **:** to make cheerful **:** CHEER — usu. used with *up*

²**chirk** \ˈ"\ *adj* -ER/-EST [prob. fr. ¹*chirk*] *dial* **:** in good spirits **:** LIVELY, CHEERFUL

¹**chirl** \ˈchir(ə)l, -ər(-ə)l\ *n* -s [imit.] **1** *Scot* **:** CHIRP, WARBLE **2** *Scot* **:** a low melancholy sound

²**chirl** \ˈ"\ *vi* -ED/-ING/-S **1** *Scot* **:** CHIRP, SING, WARBLE **2** *Scot* **:** to emit a low melancholy sound

¹**chirm** \ˈchərm, ˈchi(ə)rm\ *n* -s [ME, fr. OE *cirm;* akin to OIr *gairm* cry, shout, OE *cearu* anxiety, sorrow — more at CARE] *dial* **:** NOISE, DIN; *esp* **:** confused noise, clamor, or hum (as of voices or insects)

²**chirm** \ˈ"\ *vi* -ED/-ING/-S [ME *chirmen,* fr. OE *cirman,* fr. *cirm*] **1** *dial* **:** to make a chirm **:** CHIRP **2** *dial* **:** CROON

chi·ro \ˈchē(,)rō\ *n* -s [origin unknown] **:** TENPOUNDER

chiro- — see CHIR-

chi·ro·cen·trus \ˌkīrōˈsen·trəs\ *n, cap* [NL, fr. *chir-* + *-centrus* (fr. L *centrum* center) — more at CENTER] **:** a genus of clupeoid fishes comprising the wolf herrings

chi·rog·a·le \kīˈrägəlē\ [F *chéirogale,* fr. NL *cheirogaleus*] *syn of* CHEIROGALEUS 1

chi·rog·no·mist \kīˈrägnəməst\ *n* -s **:** PALMIST

chi·rog·no·my \-mē\ *n* -ES [modif. (influenced by *-gnomy*) of F *chirognomonie,* fr. *chir-* + *-gnomonie,* fr. Gk *-gnōmonia* judging (as in *physiognōmonia* physiognomy) — more at -GNOMY] **:** PALMISTRY

chi·ro·graph \ˈkīrə,graf\ *n* -s [MF *chirographe,* fr. L *chirographum* autograph, that which is written with one's own hand, fr. neut. of Gk *cheirographos* written with the hand, fr. *cheir-* chir- + *-graphos* -graph] **1 :** any of various legal instruments formally written or signed: as **a :** an indenture formerly made in duplicate on one sheet, the sheet or parchment being divided and often the word *chirographum* written in where the division was made **b :** the indenture of a fine of lands; *also* **:** one of the counterparts of such an indenture **c :** an obligation (as a bond or note) given in one's own handwriting **2 :** a genus of apostolic letter in the handwriting and with the signature of the pope

chi·rog·ra·phary \kīˈrägrə,ferē, ˌkīrəˈgrafərē\ *adj* [LL *chirographarius,* fr. L *chirographum* chirograph + L *-arius* -ary] *of a legal entity* **:** created or evidenced by means of a chirograph ⟨a ~ debt⟩ ⟨a ~ creditor⟩

chi·rog·ra·pher \kīˈrägrəfə(r)\ *n* -s [alter. (influenced by LL *chirographarius*) of earlier *cirographer,* fr. AF or ML; AF *cirogrofer* fr. ML *chirographarius,* fr. LL, signed, of handwriting, fr. *chirographus* + *-arius* -er] **:** one who studies or practices chirography

chi·ro·graph·ic \ˌkīrəˈgrafik\ *or* **chi·ro·graph·i·cal** \-əkəl\ *adj* [*chirograph* + *-ic, -ical*] **:** of, relating to, or in handwriting

chi·rog·ra·phy \kīˈrägrəfē\ *n* -ES [*chirograph* + *-y*] **1 :** HANDWRITING, PENMANSHIP ⟨a document in the ~ of the late governor⟩ **2 :** CALLIGRAPHY 1 ⟨skilled in ~⟩

chi·ro·man·cer \ˈkīrə,man(t)sə(r)\ *also* **chi·ro·man·cist** \-səst\ *n* -s [*chiromancy* + *-er* or *-ist*] **:** one who practices chiromancy

chi·ro·man·cy *also* **chei·ro·man·cy** \-sē\ *n* -ES [prob. fr. MF *chiromancie, cyromancie,* fr. ML *chiromantia,* fr. (assumed) MGk *cheiromanteia* (after Gk *cheiromantis* chiromancer), fr. Gk *cheir-* chir- + *manteia* divination — more at -MANCY] **:** divination by examination of the hand **:** PALMISTRY

chi·ro·man·tic \ˌkīrəˈmantik\ *or* **chi·ro·man·ti·cal** \-əkəl\ *adj* [MF *chiromantique,* fr. ML *chiromantia* chiromancy + MF *-ique* -ic] **:** of or relating to chiromancy or chiromancers

chi·ro·meg·a·ly \ˌkīrəˈmegəlē\ *n* -ES [ISV *chir-* + *-megaly*] **:** abnormal increase in the size of the hands

chi·ro·mys \ˈkīrə,mis\ [NL, fr. *chir-* + *-mys*] *syn of* DAUBENTONIA

chi·ro·nec·tes \ˌkīrəˈnek,tēz\ *n, cap* [NL, fr. *chir-* + *-nectes*] **:** a genus of tropical American marsupial mammals consisting of the yapok

chi·ro·nom·ic *or* **chei·ro·nom·ic** \ˌkīrəˈnämik\ *adj* [*chironomy* + *-ic*] **:** related to or based upon chironomy — used of musical notation, esp. neumes

¹**chi·ron·o·mid** \kīˈränəməd\ *adj* [NL *Chironomidae*] **:** of or relating to the Chironomidae

²**chironomid** \ˈ"\ *n* -s **:** an insect of the family Chironomidae

chi·ro·nom·i·dae \ˌkīrəˈnämə,dē\ *n pl, cap* [NL, fr. *Chironomus,* type genus + *-idae*] **:** a family of minute long-legged nematocerous two-winged flies that is now usu. restricted to forms without piercing mouthparts but formerly also including the biting midges and related forms

chi·ron·o·mus \kīˈränəməs\ *n, cap* [NL, fr. LGk *cheironomos* one who gestures with the hands, fr. Gk *cheir-* chir- + *-nomos* manager (fr. *nemein* to manage)] **:** the type genus of Chironomidae

chi·ron·o·my *or* **chei·ron·o·my** \kīˈränəmē\ *n* -ES [L *chironomia,* fr. Gk *cheironomia,* fr. *cheir-* chir- + *-nomia* management, fr. *nemein* to distribute, manage — more at NIMBLE] **:** a method of directing the singing of Gregorian chant by hand gestures indicating the rise and fall of the melody

chi·ro·patagium \ˌkīrə+\ *n, pl* **chiropatagia** [NL, fr. *chir-* + *patagium*] **:** the wing membrane between the fingers in bats

chi·ro·plast \ˈkīrə,plast\ *n* -s [*chir-* + *-plast*] **:** a mechanical device for teaching hand position at the piano

chi·ro·plasty \-ē\ *n* -ES [*chir-* + *-plasty*] **:** plastic surgery of the hand

chi·ro·po·di·al \ˌkīrəˈpōdēəl\ *adj* [*chiropody* + *-al*] **:** of or relating to chiropody

chi·rop·o·dist \kəˈräpədəst *also* ÷ shəˈr- *sometimes* kīˈr-\ *n* -s [*chir-* + *-pod* + *-ist*] **:** one who practices chiropody — called also *podiatrist*

chi·rop·o·dous \kīˈräpədəs\ *adj* [*chiropod-* (fr. obs. NL *Cheiropoda,* former name for mammals with handlike feet, fr. *cheir-* chir- + *-poda*) + *-ous*] **:** having the feet modified for grasping and climbing

chi·rop·o·dy \kəˈräpədē *also* ÷ shəˈr- *sometimes* kīˈr-\ *n* -ES [*chiropodist* + *-y*] **:** the care and treatment of the human foot in health and disease — called also *podiatry*

chi·ro·prac·tic \ˈkīrə,praktik, ˌ==ˈ==\ *n* -s [*chir-* + Gk *praktikos* effective, practical — more at PRACTICAL] **:** a system of healing based upon the theory that disease results from a lack of normal nerve function and employing treatment by scientific manipulation and specific adjustment of body structures (as the spinal column) and utilizing physical therapy when necessary

chi·ro·prac·tor \ˈ==,=tə(r)\ *n* -s [*chiropractic* + *-or*] **:** a practitioner of chiropractic

chi·ro·prax·is \ˈ==,praksəs, ˌ==ˈ==\ *n, pl* **chiroprax·es** \-sēz\ [NL, fr. *chir-* + *-praxis*] **:** CHIROPRACTIC

chi·rop·sal·mus \ˌkī,räpˈsalməs\ *n, cap* [NL, fr. *chir-* + Gk *psalmos* twitching, plucking, string music, psalm, fr. *psallein* to pluck, twitch — more at PSALM] **:** a genus of Cubomedusae comprising the fire medusae

chi·rop·ter \kīˈräptə(r), =ˈ==\ *n* -s [NL *Chiroptera*] **:** ³BAT 1

chi·rop·tera \=ˈ=tərə\ *n pl, cap* [NL, fr. *chir-* + *-ptera*] **:** an order of eutherian mammals modified for true flight comprising the recent and extinct bats, all believed to have differentiated from an ancestral insectivore line during the early Eocene — **chi·rop·ter·an** \(ˈ)=ˈ==rən\ *adj or n* — **chi·rop·ter·ous** \(ˈ)=ˈ==rəs\ *adj*

chi·rop·ter·ite \=ˈ==,rīt\ *n* -s [NL *Chiroptera* + E *-ite*] **:** guano formed by bats in prehistoric times

chi·rop·ter·oph·i·lous \(ˈ)kīˌräptəˈräfələs\ *adj* [NL *Chiroptera* + E *-o-* + *-philous*] **:** pollinated by bats

chi·rop·te·ryg·i·um \ˌkīˌräptəˈrijēəm\ *n* -s [NL, fr. *chir-* + *pterygium*] **:** the typical jointed and fingered limb of a vertebrate animal conceived of as having developed from a finlike appendage — compare ICHTHYOPTERYGIUM

chi·ros·o·phy \kīˈräsəfē\ *n* -ES [*chir-* + *-sophy*] **:** CHIROMANCY

chi·ro·spasm \ˈkīrə+,-\ *n* [*chir-* + *spasm*] **:** WRITER'S CRAMP

chi·ro·tes \kīˈrōd·ēz\ *n, cap* [NL, irreg. fr. Gk *cheir* hand — more at CHIR-] **:** a genus of wormlike burrowing lizards related to *Amphisbaena* having small forelimbs but no hind limbs

chi·ro·the·sia \ˌkīrōˈthēzh(ē)ə\ *n* -s [LGk *cheirothesia,* fr. Gk *cheir-* chir- + *-thesia* (fr. *thesis* setting, placing, fr. *tithenai* to set, place) — more at DO] **:** imposition of hands as in the ecclesiastical rites of confirmation and ordination

chi·rot·o·ny \kīˈrätˀnē\ *n* -ES [Gk *cheirotonia,* fr. *cheir-* chir- + *-tonia* (fr. *tonos* stretching, tension) — more at TONE] **:** the extension of hands in bestowing a blessing in an ecclesiastical rite

¹**chirp** \ˈchərp, -əp\ *vb* -ED/-ING/-S [imit.] *vi* **1 :** to make a usu. repetitive short sharp sound (as of small birds or crickets) **:** CHIRRUP ⟨grasshoppers ~*ing* and birds singing —G.B.Shaw⟩ **2 :** to make a sound imitating or resembling the chirping of a bird esp. in speaking ⟨someone turned on the water down the hall and all the second floor faucets ~*ed* at once —Nelson Algren⟩ ~ *vt* **:** to say or utter with a sound of chirping ⟨wait until the boldest ~*s:* "It was tonight, dear, wasn't it?" —Archibald MacLeish⟩

²**chirp** \ˈ"\ *n* -s **1 :** a short sharp note natural to some birds or insects (as crickets) **:** CHIRRUP **2 :** a sound imitating or resembling a chirp

chirp·i·ly \-əlē, -li\ *adv* **:** in a chirpy manner

chir pine *or* **chir** *also* **cheer pine** \ˈchi(ə)r-\ *n* [Hindi *cīr* pine] **:** an East Indian resinous timber pine (*Pinus roxburghii*) the wood of which is used as a substitute for northern pine or fir

chirp·i·ness \ˈchərpēnəs, -əp-, -pin-\ *n* -ES **:** the quality or state of being chirpy

chirping *adj* **1 :** noisily lively as from high spirits ⟨a ~ and merry companion⟩ **2 :** CHEERING, ENLIVENING ⟨a ~ drink⟩ — **chirp·ing·ly** *adv*

chirpy \ˈchərpē, -əp-, -pi\ *adj* -ER/-EST **1 a :** given to chirping ⟨as ~ as a sparrow —Ruth Park⟩ **b :** resembling or suggesting chirping **:** marked by a quality similar to that of chirping ⟨the average coloratura's ~ twitter —Irving Kolodin⟩ ⟨~ little voices⟩ **2 :** cheerfully lively **:** CHEERFUL ⟨a ~ indifference to reality —*Times Lit. Supp.*⟩

¹**chirr** \ˈchər, +V -ər-; ˈchə, +V -ər- *also* -ər\ *n* -s [imit.] **:** the short esp. vibrant or trilled and repetitive sound characteristic of certain insects (as grasshoppers and cicadas) and some birds and animals and often suggesting the rubbing together of two rough surfaces **2 :** a sound like a chirr

²**chirr** \ˈ"\ *vi* -ED/-ING/-S **:** to make a chirr ⟨the ~*ing* of a squirrel —Archie Binns⟩ ⟨the crickets never ~*ed* so blithely —Rex Ingamells⟩ ⟨the endless ~*ing* of their bills against the rice grains —Archibald Rutledge⟩

¹**chir·rup** \ˈchər·əp, ˈchirəp\ *vb* -ED/-ING/-S [imit.] *vi* **1 :** CHIRP **2 :** to make a sound like a chirrup esp. by sucking in air through compressed lips (as in urging on a horse) ⟨~ to a pony⟩ ⟨the bullets ~*ed* by in the soft buzzing sound of insects on the wing —Norman Mailer⟩ ~ *vt* **:** to utter by chirruping

²**chirrup** \ˈ"\ *n* -s **:** the act or the sound of chirruping ⟨the house sparrow's metallic ~ —*British Birds in Colour*⟩ ⟨the sudden ~ of police whistles —Dan Wickenden⟩

chir·rupy \-ē, -i\ *adj* **1 :** CHEERFUL, LIVELY, CHIRPY ⟨standing, gay and ~ before the footlights, eyes twinkling from audience to fellow actors in enjoyment —*Fortnight*⟩ **2 :** CHATTY ⟨a ~ chronicle of how Hollywood romped and played —Gordon Kahn⟩

chirs *pres 3d sing of* CHIR, *pl of* CHIR

chiru \ˈchir(,)ü\ *n* -s [prob. native name in Tibet] **:** a pinkish-fawn goat antelope (*Pantholops hodgsoni*) of the Tibetan plateau the male being distinguished by a laterally swollen muzzle and very long nearly straight horns

chirurgeon *n* -s [alter. (influenced by L *chirurgia* surgery) of ME *cirurgian,* fr. OF *cirurgien,* fr. *cirurgie* surgery + *-ien* -ian] *archaic* **:** SURGEON

chirurgery *n* -ES [alter. (influenced by L *chirurgia* surgery) of earlier *cyrurgery,* fr. ME *syrurgery,* fr. OF *cirurgerie* — more at SURGERY] *archaic* **:** SURGERY

-chi·rur·gia \ˌkīˈrərjēə, -ˈrərj-,-ˈrəij-\ *n comb form* -s [NL, fr. L *chirurgia*] **:** surgery **:** cutting ⟨entero*chirurgia*⟩ ⟨pneumo*chirurgia*⟩

chirurgic *or* **chirurgical** *adj* [*chirurgic,* fr. F or L; F *chirurgique* fr. L *chirurgicus,* fr. *chirurgia* + *-icus* -ic; *chirurgical,* alter. of earlier *cyrurgical,* fr. MF or ML; MF *cirurgical* fr. ML *cirurgicalis, chirurgicalis,* fr. L *chirurgicus* + *-alis* -al] *archaic* **:** of, concerned with, or treating of surgery **:** SURGICAL

chis *pl of* CHI

¹**chis·el** \ˈchizəl\ *n* -s [obs. *chisel, chesil* gravel, fr. ME, fr. OE *cisel, ceosel;* akin to OHG *kisil* pebble, OPruss *sixdo* sand, Lith *žiezdrà* gravel, grain] *dial Eng* **:** BRAN **:** coarse flour

²chisel \"\ *n* -s [ME, fr. ONF, prob. alter. of *chisoir* gold-

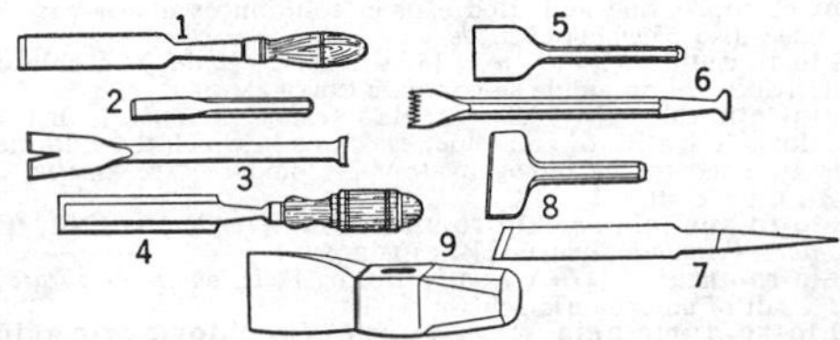

chisels: *1* socket paring chisel, *2* cold chisel, *3* box chisel, *4* beveled firmer chisel, *5* floor chisel, *6* stonecutter's tooth chisel, *7* turning chisel, *8* bricklayer's chisel, *9* blacksmith's chisel

smith's chisel, fr. (assumed) VL *caesorium* cutting instrument, fr. L *caesus* (past part. of *caedere* to cut) + *-orium* -ory — more at CONCISE] **1** : a tool consisting of a metal bar with a sharpened edge at one end used for working on the surface of various materials by chipping, carving, turning, or other cutting action and often driven by a mallet **2** : a strong heavy tractor-drawn tillage tool with curved points used for deep stirring without turning the soil

³**chisel** \"\ *vb* **chiseled** *or* **chiselled; chiseled** *or* **chiselled; chiseling** *or* **chiselling** \-z(ə)liŋ\ **chisels** *vt* **1** : to cut, pare, gouge, engrave, or shape with or as if with a chisel — often used with *out* ⟨~ a block of marble into a statue⟩ **2 a** : to cut close (as in a bargain) : CHEAT **b** : to employ shrewd sometimes unfair practices on (as a person) to obtain one's end; *also* : to obtain by such practices **3** : to stir (soil) with a chisel ~ *vi* **1** : to work with a chisel ⟨the actual cutter merely ~*ed* within the outlines of a preliminary drawing —F.W. Goudy⟩ **2 a** : to employ shrewd sometimes unfair practices to obtain an end ⟨~ for good marks in a college course⟩ **b** : to thrust oneself : INTRUDE — used with *in* or *in on* ⟨trying to ~ in on the beer racket —Polly Adler⟩

chiseled *or* **chiselled** *adj* **1** : cut, shaped, or wrought with a chisel **2** : appearing as if chiseled : CLEAR-CUT, CARVEN ⟨~ phrases⟩ **3** : shaped like a chisel ⟨a ~ face⟩ **3** : shaped like a chisel ⟨a ~ crowbar⟩

chis·el·er *or* **chis·el·ler** \'chiz(ə)lə(r)\ *n* -s **1** : one that chisels : CHEAT : petty crook : GOUGER **2** *Irish* : CHILD

chis·el·ly \-lē\ *adj* [obs. E *chisel* gravel + *-y* — more at CHISEL (bran)] **1** *dial Eng* : GRAVELLY, GRITTY **2** *dial* : UNPLEASANT, DISAGREEABLE

chiselmouth \'ˌˌˌ\ *n* -s : a cyprinoid fish (*Acrocheilus alutaceus*) of the Columbia river having a large straight-edged horny plate in each jaw

chisel tooth *n* : a tooth shaped like a chisel; *esp* : one of the incisor teeth of a rodent

chisel-tooth saw *n* : a circular wood saw having inserted teeth with chisel-shaped cutting edges

chish·ti \'chishtē\ *n, usu cap* [after Mu'īn al-Din Muhammad *Chishti*, saint of India †1236, its founder] : a Sufi brotherhood centered in India

chislev *usu cap, var of* KISLEV

chi-square \'kī,-\ *n* : the sum of the quotients obtained by dividing the square of the difference between the observed and theoretical values of a quantity by the theoretical value

chis·set \'chizət\ *var of* CHESSET

chist \'chist\ *dial var of* CHEST

chis·te·ra \chi'sterə\ *n* -s [Sp, fr. Basque *xistera* basket, chistera, fr. L *cistella*, dim. of *cista* box, chest, basket — more at CHEST] : a wicker scoop used by a jai alai player

chist·ka \'chis(t)kə\ *n* -s [Russ, lit., cleaning, cleansing, fr. *chistit'* to clean, fr. *chisty* clean, fr. ORuss *čistŭ*; akin to L *scindere* to split — more at SHED] : a political purge

¹**chit** \'chit, *usu* -id·+V\ *n* -s [ME *chitte* kitten, cub, perh. alter. (influenced by such pairs as *church: kirk*) of *kit*, short for *kitling*] **1** *obs* : the offspring of an animal (as a cub or whelp) : KIT **2 a** : CHILD **b** : a person likened to a child; *esp* : a pert or forward young woman ⟨has no use for young ~*s* of girls —Christopher Isherwood⟩

²**chit** \"\ *n* -s [prob. alter. of ME *chithe* sprout, fr. OE *cīth*; akin to OS *kīth* bud, young shoot, OHG *-kīdi* shoot — more at CHINE] **1 chits** *pl, obs* : rice of second or third grade **2** : SHOOT, SPROUT

³**chit** \"\ *vb* **chitted; chitted; chitting; chits** *vi, dial Eng* : GERMINATE, SPROUT ⟨after a period of about 48 hours, the grain begins to ~ —Norman Wymer⟩ ~ *vt* : to remove chits from (as potatoes)

⁴**chit** \"\ *n* -s [short for *chitty* fr. Hindi *ciṭṭhī*] **1** : a short letter or note : a written message : MEMORANDUM ⟨a ~ written by the president specifically to be read to them —*Time*⟩; *esp* : a certificate of recommendation (as one given to a servant) **2 a** : a signed voucher or memorandum of a small debt (as for food or drinks) ⟨seldom carries money; signing a ~ is so much easier —Nancy B. Shea⟩ **b** : CHECK, DRAFT, ORDER, BILL, RECEIPT ⟨put in a ~ for ninety cents' fare —McKenzie Porter⟩ ⟨23 percent of your bill is added automatically to the ~ as the tip —Tad Szulc⟩ : a small slip of paper with writing on it

¹**chita** *var of* CHEETAH

²**chi·ta** \chə'tä\ *adj, usu cap* [fr. *Chita*, U.S.S.R.] : of or from the city of Chita, U.S.S.R. : of the kind or style prevalent in Chita

chi·tal *also* **chee·tal** *or* **chee·tul** \'chēd·ᵊl\ *n, pl* **chital** *also* **cheetal** *or* **cheetul** [Hindi *cītal*, fr. Skt *citrala* variegated, fr. *citra* spotted, bright — more at -HOOD] : AXIS DEER

chi-tan *usu cap C, var of* KHITAN

chi·tar·ri·no \ˌkēd·ə'rē(ˌ)nō\ *n, pl* **chitarri·ni** \-(ˌ)nē\ [It, dim. of *chitarra*, fr. Gk *kithara* lyre] : a small guitar

chi·tar·ro·ne \ˌkēd·ə'rō(ˌ)nā\ *n, pl* **chitarro·ni** \-(ˌ)nē\ [It, aug. of *chitarra*] : a bass or a contrabass of the lute family

¹**chit·chat** \'chit,chat, *usu* -ad·+V\ *n* [redupl. of *chat*] : familiar or trifling talk or conversation : SMALL TALK, GOSSIP ⟨the ~ between contestant and quizmaster —*Time*⟩

²**chitchat** \"\ *vi* : to make chitchat : indulge in small talk : GOSSIP ⟨a girl can't get along anymore just by *chitchatting* on the dance floor —Louis Auchincloss⟩ ⟨*chitchatted*, swopping experiences —Rose Thurburn⟩

chit·chat·ty \-ad·ē\ *adj, usu* -ER/-EST : given to or full of chitchat

chit·i·ma·cha \ˌchid·ə'mäshə\ *n, pl* **chitimacha** *or* **chitimachas** *usu cap* [perh. Choctaw *Chutimasha*, lit., they have cooking pots, fr. *chuti* cooking pot + *másha* they possess] **1 a** : an Indian people of the Mississippi delta **b** : a member of such people **2** : the language of the Chitimacha people

¹**chit·i·ma·chan** \ˌˌˌ'ˌshən\ *adj, usu cap* : of or relating to the Chitimacha or their language

²**chitimachan** \"\ *n, pl* **chitimachan** *or* **chitimachans** *usu cap* [¹*Chitimachan*] : a language family of the Gulf phylum in Louisiana comprising the Chitimacha language

chi·tin \'kītᵊn\ *n* -s [F *chitine*, fr. Gk *chitōn*, chiton, tunic + F *-ine* -in] : a white or colorless amorphous horny substance that forms part of the hard outer integument of insects, crustaceans, and some other invertebrates and occurs also in fungi, being a polysaccharide structurally similar to cellulose except that the repeating unit is derived from acetylglucosamine instead of glucose

chi·tin·i·za·tion \ˌkītᵊnə'zāshən\ *n* -s [*chitin* + *-ization*] : the process of becoming chitinous : the state of being chitinous

chi·tin·ized \'kītᵊn,īzd\ *adj* [*chitin* + *-ized*] : filled in with chitin esp. with a hardening effect ⟨elytra strongly ~⟩

chi·tin·og·e·nous \ˌkītᵊn'äjənəs\ *adj* [*chitin* + *-o-* + *-genous*] : producing chitin ⟨~ hypodermal cells of arthropods⟩

chi·tin·oid \'kītᵊn,ȯid\ *adj* [*chitin* + *-oid*] : resembling chitin esp. in physical properties

chi·tin·o·phosphatic \ˌkītᵊn,ō+\ *adj* [*chitin* + *-o-* + *phosphatic*] *of certain marine shells* : made up of chitin and calcium phosphates — used chiefly of inarticulate brachiopods

chi·tin·ous \'kītᵊnəs\ *adj* [*chitin* + *-ous*] : of or like chitin

chitlings *or* **chitlins** *var of* CHITTERLINGS

chit-munk \'chit,məŋk\ *dial var of* CHIPMUNK

chi·to melon \'kē,tō-\ *n* [NL *chito*, specific epithet of *Cucumis chito*] : MANGO MELON

chi·ton \'kītᵊn, -ˌtän\ *n* [NL, fr. Gk *chitōn* tunic, of Sem origin; akin to Heb *kuttōneth* coat, Syr *kettānā* linen, Assyr-Bab *kitū*, *kitinnu* linen] **1** *cap* : a large genus (the type of the family Chitonidae) of mollusks of the order Polyplacophora (class Amphineura) having the girdle covered with imbricating scales, no eyes, and gills extending the length of the foot **2** -s : a mollusk of the order Polyplacophora **3** -s [Gk *chitōn*] : the basic garment of ancient Greece worn usu. knee-length by men and full-length by women and made in two styles: **a** : an oblong of usu. wool cloth with a wide turndown at the top to form a double waist, folded in half about the body, pinned once on each shoulder with a fibula, and girdled at the waist in the Doric style **b** : a garment usu. of wool or linen differing from the Doric in being fuller and more elaborate and in having sewn sides and sleeves formed by a series of pins along the upper fold in the later Ionic style

Doric chiton

chi·to·sa·mine \kī'tōsə,mēn, -ˌmən\ *n* -s [ISV *chitin* + *-ose* + *-amine*; orig. formed as G *chitosamin*] : glucosamine esp. as obtained from chitin by hydrolysis

chi·to·san \'kīd·ə,san\ *n* -s [ISV *chit-* (fr. *chitin*) + *-ose* + *-an*] : a substance formed from chitin by partial deacetylation with alkali

chi·tose \'kī,tōs *also* -ōz\ *n* -s [*chitin* + *-ose*] : a nonfermentable sugar formed from glucosamine by the action of nitrous acid

chi·tra \'chi·trə\ *n, pl* **chitra** [Hindi *citra* spotted, fr. Skt, spotted, bright — more at -HOOD] : AXIS DEER

chi·tra·li \chi'trälē\ *n, pl* **chitrali** *or* **chitralis** *usu cap* [fr. *Chitral*, state in Pakistan] **1 a** : a people living on the slopes of the Hindu Kush, Afghanistan **b** : a member of such people **2** : the language of the Chitrali people

chits *pl of* CHIT, *pres 3d sing of* CHIT

chit·ta·gong \'chid·ə,gäŋ, -ȯŋ\ *adj, usu cap* [fr. *Chittagong*, Pakistan] : of or from the city of Chittagong, Pakistan : of the kind or style prevalent in Chittagong

chittagong wood *n, usu cap C* [fr. *Chittagong*, division of East Bengal, Pakistan] : the wood of either of two Indian trees (*Chukrasia tabularis* and *Toona ciliata*) of the family Meliaceae used for its mahoganylike qualities in cabinetwork

chit·tak *or* **chit·tack** *or* **chat·tak** *or* **chat·tack** \chə'täk\ *n* -s [Bengali *cha-ṭāk*] : an Indian unit of weight equal to ¹⁄₁₆ seer or 900 grains

chit·tam bark *also* **chit·tem bark** *or* **chit·tim bark** \'chid-əm-\ *n* [perh. of Muskogean origin; akin to Choctaw *shitimmi* puff, swell] : the bark of the cascara buckthorn

chittamwood *or* **chittimwood** \'ˌˌˌˌ\ *n* **1** : SMOKE TREE 1b **2** : CASCARA BUCKTHORN **3** : BUCKTHORN 2; *esp* : FALSE BUCKTHORN

chitted *past of* CHIT

¹**chit·ter** \'chid·ə(r)\ *vi* -ED/-ING/-S [ME *chiteren*, prob. of imit. origin] **1** : to twitter like a bird : CHIRP : chatter like a squirrel **2** *dial Brit* : to shiver or chatter esp. with cold

²**chitter** \"\ *n* -s : the act or sound of chittering : TWITTER

chit·ter-chat·ter \'chid·ə(r),chad·ə(r)\ *n* -s [redupl. (prob. influenced by *chit-chat*) of ²*chatter*] **1** : light and lively discussion **2** : trivial, nonsensical, or incessant talk

chit·ter·lings \'chitlənz *sometimes* -id·|ᵊlənz *or* -id·|ᵊliŋz *or* -id·|ə(r)liŋz *or* -itl|ənz *or* -itliŋz\ *or* **chit·lings** \'chitlənz *sometimes* -liŋz\ *or* **chit·lins** \'chitlənz\ *n pl* [ME *chitirling*; prob. akin to MHG *kutel* tripe, OE *cwith* womb, OHG *quiti* vulva, ON *kviðr* belly, Goth *qithus* womb, L *botulus* intestine, sausage, Skt *guda* intestine, Gk *gyros* round — more at COWER] : the intestines of hogs esp. prepared as food

chitting *pres part of* CHIT

chiurm *n* -s [F & It; F *chiourme* fr. It *ciurma*, fr. L *celeusma*, command given by head oarsman so that rowers can keep in time, fr. Gk *keleusma*, *keleuma* command, command given to rowers, fr. *keleuein* to command, incite; akin to Gk *kellein* to land a ship, drive on — more at HOLD] *obs* : a gang of galley slaves

¹**chiv** \'chiv, 'sh-\ *var of* ²·³CHIVE

²**chiv** \"\ *n* -s [perh. short for E dial. *Chivy Chase*, *Chevy Chase* chase, pursuit, noise, confusion (used in rhyming slang to mean "face") — more at CHIVY] *slang Austral* : FACE

chivage *var of* CHEVAGE

chiv·al·resque \ˌshivəl'resk, shə'ˌvalə'resk\ *or* **che·va·le·resque** \shə'ˌvalə'resk, F shəvalresk\ *adj* [*chivalry* + *-esque* (after F *chevaleresque*, after It *cavalleresco*)] **1** : of, relating to, or befitting chivalry ⟨~ knights⟩ ⟨~ manners⟩ **2** : having the spirit or manners of chivalry ⟨a ~ romance⟩ ⟨a ~ gentleman⟩

chi·val·ric \shə'valrik, -ēk *sometimes* 'shivəl(ˌ)rik\ *adj* [*chivalry* + *-ic*] : relating to chivalry : CHIVALROUS

chivalric rite *n, usu cap C & often cap R* : the ceremonial observed by the Knights Templar body of Freemasons

chiv·al·rous \'shivəlrəs *sometimes* shə'val-\ *adj* [ME, fr. MF *chevalereus*, fr. *chevalier* knight + *-eus* -ous — more at CHEVALIER] **1** : characteristic of or like a knight of feudal times esp. in valor : VALIANT, WARLIKE ⟨in brave pursuit of ~ emprise —Edmund Spenser⟩ **2** : relating to, according with, or suggestive of the system of chivalry and knight-errantry obtaining in the age of chivalry in the later medieval period ⟨the austere inspection of . . . these battlemented city walls and these dark churches could not have been more ~ —George Santayana⟩ **3 a** : characteristic of or relating to the ideal knight of feudal and Renaissance times according to modern romantic tradition **b** : marked by honor, fairness, generosity, and kindliness esp. to foes, the weak and lowly, and the vanquished according to knightly tradition ⟨Robert E. Lee, the great Southern general, ~, gentle —S.V.Benét⟩ **c** : marked by especial courtesy and high-minded disinterested consideration to women ⟨a broken heart made an irresistible appeal to a ~ mind —Ellen Glasgow⟩ **4** : of or relating to a knight : KNIGHTLY ⟨~ rank⟩ **syn** see CIVIL

chivalrously *adv* : in a chivalrous manner

chiv·al·rous·ness \-nəs\ *n* -ES : quality of being chivalrous : COURTESY

chiv·al·ry \'shivəlrē, -ri\ *n* -ES [ME *chivalrie*, fr. OF *chevalerie*, fr. *chevalier* + *-ie* -y] **1 a** : mounted men at arms : heavy cavalry of the middle ages; *also* : a medieval army whose strength was in its mounted men **b** : cavalry of ancient times **2** *archaic* **a** : the rank, position, or characteristics of a feudal knight; *esp* : martial valor **b** : a gallant deed : EXPLOIT **c** : knightly skill : dexterity in arms ⟨the glory of our Troy this day doth lie on his fair worth and single ~ —Shak.⟩ **3** : a body of knights or illustrious mounted soldiers : gallant and distinguished warriors or brave gentlemen ⟨Belgium's capital had gathered then her beauty and her ~ —Lord Byron⟩ **4** : the dignity or system of knighthood : the spirit, usages, or manners of knighthood : the practice of knight-errantry ⟨but Lancelot on him urged all the devisings of their ~ —Alfred Tennyson⟩ **5** : the qualifications or character of the ideal knight of the age of chivalry according to the romantic traditions (as honor, protective kindness to the weak, generosity to foes, and gallantry) : CHIVALROUSNESS ⟨~ demanded of him that he be conspicuous through his gallant, courteous, and generous behavior —H.W.Van Loon⟩ **6** : the slaveholding class of southern society before the Civil War

chivaree *or* **chivari** *var of* CHARIVARI

¹**chive** \'chīv *sometimes* 'sh-\ *n* -s [ME *chyve*, fr. ONF *chive*, fr. L *cepa*, *cepe* onion] **1** : a perennial plant (*Allium schoenoprasum*) related to the onion and having slender rushlike leaves that are used for seasoning (as in soups and omelets) — usu. used in pl. **2** *archaic* : BULBIL 1a; *esp* : a clove of garlic

²**chive** \'chiv, 'sh-, -īv\ *n* -s [perh. fr Romany *chiv* blade] *slang* : KNIFE — compare SHIV

³**chive** \"\ *vt* -ED/-ING/-S *slang* : KNIFE

chiven *var of* CHEVIN

chivey *var of* CHIVY

²**chiv·ey** \'shivē\ *n* -s [prob. fr. Natick *chippe*, lit., it is separated or dead; fr. its use as manure by the Indians] : MENOMINEE WHITEFISH

chiv·i·a·tite \ˌchivē'ä,tīt\ *n* -s [G *chiviatit*, fr. *Chiviato*, Peru, its locality + G *-it* -ite] : a mineral $Pb_2Bi_6S_{11}$ consisting of a lead bismuth sulfide in lead-gray foliated masses

¹**chivy** \'chivē, -vi\ *or* **chevy** \" *sometimes* -ev-\ *n* -ES [prob. short for E dial. *Chevy Chase* chase, pursuit, noise, confusion, fr. the name of a ballad describing the Battle of Otterburn (1388), prob. alter. of *Cheviot Chase*, fr. *Cheviot* hills, range of hills in northern England and Scotland, near which the battle took place] **1** *Brit* **a** : ²HUNT 1, ²CHASE 1 **b** : ¹FLIGHT **2** *Brit* : PRISONER'S BASE

²**chivy** \"\ *or* **chevy** \"\ *or* **chiv·vy** *also* **chiv·ey** \-iv-\ *vt* -ED/-ING/-ES **1** : CHASE, PURSUE **2 a** : to harass, annoy, or tease esp. with persistence and by petty vexations and often for a specific purpose : HARRY ⟨he drove his staff hard but never nagged or *chivied* his writers —*Time*⟩ ⟨the skua *chivies* the herring gull and makes it surrender the booty —J.A.Thomson⟩ **b** : to acquire, attain, direct, or manipulate by persistent petty maneuvering ⟨*chivying* the polo ball with small strokes — George Orwell⟩ ⟨~ an olive out of a bottle⟩ **syn** see BAIT

chi·were \chə'werē\ *n, pl* **chiwere** *usu cap* [Chiwere *Che-waerae*, lit., belonging to this place] : a Siouan language of the Iowa, Missouri, and Oto peoples

chi·zo \'chē(ˌ)zō, -sō\ *n, pl* **chizo** *or* **chizos** *usu cap* [Sp, of AmerInd origin] **1** : a people constituting a major subdivision of the Concho **2** : a member of the Chizo people

chk *abbr* check

chka·lov \chə'kälə|f, -ˌlȯ|f, |v\ *adj, usu cap* [fr. *Chkalov*, U.S.S.R.] : of or from the city of Chkalov, U.S.S.R. : of the kind or style prevalent in Chkalov

chka·lov·ite \chə'kälə,vīt\ *n* -s [Russ *chkalovit*, fr. *Chkalov*, city of Chkalov region, U.S.S.R. + Russ *-it* -ite] : a mineral $Na_2BeSi_2O_6$ that consists of a rare silicate of sodium and beryllium

chlad·ni figures \'klädnē-, -ad-\ *n pl, usu cap C* [trans. of G *Chladnische figuren*, after Ernst F. *Chladni* †1827 Ger. physicist] : SONOROUS FIGURES

chlad·nite \'klad,nīt\ *n* -s [Ernst F. *Chladni* + E *-ite*] **1** : meteoritic material composed of enstatite **2** : pure enstatite

chlamyd- *or* **chlamydo-** *comb form* [NL, fr. Gk *chlamyd-*, *chlamys*] : mantle ⟨*chlamydospore*⟩ ⟨*Chlamydozoa*⟩

chlam·y·date \'klamə,dāt, -ˌdət\ *adj* [L *chlamydatus* dressed in a chlamys, fr. *chlamyd-*, *chlamys* + *-atus* -ate] : having a mantle ⟨a ~ mollusk⟩

chla·myd·e·ous \klə'midēəs\ *adj* [prob. back-formation fr. *achlamydeous*, *archichlamydeous*, *metachlamydeous*, *monochlamydeous*] **1** : relating to the floral envelope of a plant — used chiefly in combinations ⟨*archichlamydeous*⟩ ⟨*metachlamydeous*⟩ **2** : having a perianth — opposed to *achlamydeous*

chla·myd·ia \klə'midēə\ *n, cap* [NL, fr. Gk *chlamyd-*, *chlamys* mantle + NL *-ia*] : the type genus of Chlamydiaceae comprising coccoid to spherical gram-negative intracellular parasites and including the causative agent of trachoma

chla·myd·i·a·ce·ae \ˌˌˌdē'āsē,ē\ *n pl, cap* [NL, fr. *Chlamydia*, type genus (fr. Gk *chlamyd-*, *chlamys* mantle + NL *-ia*) + *-aceae*] : a family of rickettsiae that are obligate parasites in the cells of warm-blooded vertebrates, that esp. attack the conjunctiva, and that include the causative agents of trachoma and of lymphogranuloma inguinale

chlam·y·do·bac·te·ri·a·ce·ae \ˌklamə,dō(ˌ)bak,tirē'āsē,ē\ *n pl, cap* [NL, fr. *chlamyd-* + *bacterium* + *-aceae*] : a family (order Chlamydobacteriales) of free-floating filamentous alga-like bacteria that contain no sulfur granules and occur chiefly in stagnant water

chlam·y·do·bac·te·ri·a·les \-'ā(ˌ)lēz\ *n pl, cap* [NL, fr. *Chlamydobacteriaceae*, typical family + *-ales*] : an order of chiefly free-living aquatic filamentous bacteria that are commonly ensheathed by an organic matrix which may contain oxides of iron or manganese, that produce no endospores but reproduce by conidia or flagellated swarm spores, and that may exhibit gliding motility like that of certain blue-green algae

chlam·y·do·bac·te·ri·um \-'tirēəm\ *n, pl* **chlamydobacteria** \-rēə\ [NL, fr. *chlamyd-* + *bacterium*] : a higher bacterium of the family Chlamydobacteriaceae or the order Chlamydobacteriales

chlam·y·do·mon·a·da·ce·ae \-ˌmänə'dāsē,ē\ *n pl, cap* [NL, fr. *Chlamydomonad-*, *Chlamydomonas*, type genus + *-aceae*] : a family of green algae (order Volvocales) that in botanical classifications includes *Chlamydomonas* and related algae some of which are colored red by hematochrome

chlam·y·dom·o·nas \ˌklamə'dämənəs\ *n, cap* [NL, fr. *chlamyd-* + *-monas*] : a genus of solitary biflagellated plant-like flagellates or algae common in fresh water and damp soil and sometimes multiplying so freely as to be a pest about filtration plants — see CHLAMYDOMONADACEAE

chlam·y·do·sau·rus \ˌklamədō'sȯrəs\ *n, cap* [NL, fr. *chlamyd-* + *-saurus*] : a genus of reptiles containing the frilled lizard of Australia

chlam·y·do·sel·a·chus \-'seləkəs\ *n, cap* [NL, fr. *chlamyd-* + *Selachus* (syn. of *Cetorhinus*), fr. Gk *selachos* cartilaginous fish — more at SELACHII] : a genus (coextensive with the family Chlamydoselachidae) comprising sharks with diplospondylic vertebrae, including the frilled shark and certain extinct related forms, and being placed with the Hexanchidae in the suborder Notidanoidea or isolated in a separate suborder

chla·myd·o·spore \klə'midə,spō(ə)r\ *n* -s [ISV *chlamyd-* + *spore*; prob. orig. formed in F] : a thick-walled spore: as **a** : a unicellular resting spore in certain fungi usu. borne terminally on a hypha and rich in stored reserves — called also *gemma*; compare AKINETE **b** : the usu. black or dark brown zygote of a smut — see USTILAGINALES **c** : a bacterial cell transformed into a resting spore by accumulation of reserves and thickening of the cell wall — compare ENDOSPORE — **chla·myd·o·spor·ic** \ˌˌˌˌ'spōrik\ *adj*

chlam·y·do·zo·a·ce·ae \ˌklamə,dōzō'āsē,ē\ *n pl, cap* [NL, fr. *Chlamydozoon*, type genus + *-aceae*] *syn of* CHLAMYDIACEAE

¹**chlam·y·do·zo·on** \ˌˌˌˌ'zō,än\ *n, cap* [NL, fr. *chlamyd-* + *-zoon*] *syn of* CHLAMYDIA

²**chlamydozoon** *n, pl* **chlamydo·zoa** \-'zōə\ **1** : INCLUSION BODY **2** : any of certain microorganisms related to the typical rickettsias; *esp* : an organism of the family Chlamydiaceae

chlam·y·phore \'klamə,fō(ə)r\ *also* **chla·myd·o·phore** \klə'midə,f-\ *n* -s [*chlamyphore* fr. NL *chlamyphorus*, fr. Gk *chlamys* mantle + L *-phorus* -phore; *chlamydophore* fr. NL *chlamydophorus*, fr. *chlamyd-* + L *-phorus*] : PICHICIAGO

chla·myph·o·rus \klə'mifərəs\ *n, cap* [NL, fr. *chlamy-* (fr. L *chlamys* mantle) + *-phorus*] : a genus of So. American armadillos comprising the pichiciago and related forms

chlam·ys \'klaməs, -ām-\ *n, pl* **chla·my·ses** \-məsəz\ *or* **chlam·y·des** \'klamə,dēz\ [L, fr. Gk] : a short oblong mantle fastened with a fibula usu. at the right shoulder or in front and worn chiefly by young men of ancient Greece

chleuh \shə'lü, 'shlü\ *n, pl* **chleuh** *or* **chleuhs** *usu cap* : SHILHA

chlo·an·thite \klō'an,thīt\ *n* -s [G *chloanthit*, fr. Gk *chloanthēs* budding, pale (fr. *chloos* light green color + *-anthēs* blooming, flowered) + G *-it* -ite; fr. its frequent green coating — more at GLOW, -ANTHES] : a mineral $NiAs_{2-3}$ consisting of nickel arsenide isomorphous with skutterudite, smaltite, and nickel-skutterudite and being white or grayish with metallic luster and usu. massive

chlamys

chlo·as·ma \klō'azmə\ *n, pl* **chloasma·ta** \-məd·ə\ [NL, fr. LGk, greenness, fr. Gk *chloazein* to be green, fr. *chloos* light green color] : a skin discoloration marked by yellowish brown pigmented patches or spots — called also *liver spots*

chlor \'klō(ə)r, -ō(ə)r\ *n* -s [Gk *chlōros*] : a hue between yellow and green; *specif* : yellowish green

chlor- *or* **chloro-** *comb form* [NL, fr. Gk, fr. *chlōros* greenish yellow — more at YELLOW] **1** : green ⟨*chlorophyll*⟩ ⟨*chlorophane*⟩ **2** : yellowish green : pale green : anemic ⟨*chlorosis*⟩ **3 a** : chlorine ⟨*chlorhydrate*⟩ ⟨*chloroform*⟩ **b** *now usu chloro-* : containing chlorine in place of hydrogen — in names of organic compounds ⟨*chloroaniline*⟩ **c** *now usu chloro-* : containing chlorine regarded as replacing hydroxyl or oxygen or as coordinated to a central atom — in names of inorganic acids and salts ⟨*chloro*auric acid⟩ ⟨*chloro*chromate⟩ **d :** containing chlorine as chloride sometimes replacing another element or group — in names of minerals and salts occurring as minerals ⟨*chloro*sulfate⟩

chloracetic acid *var of* CHLOROACETIC ACID

chloracetophenone *var of* CHLOROACETOPHENONE

chlor·ac·ne \(ˈ)klōrˌaknē\ *n* -s [*chlor-* + *acne*] **:** an eruption on the skin resembling acne and resulting from exposure to chlorine or its compounds — compare HYPERKERATOSIS

chloraemia *var of* CHLOREMIA

chlor·a·go·cyte \ˈklōrəgəˌsīt\ *n* -s [*chloragogen* + *-cyte*] **:** a chloragogen cell

chlor·a·go·gen \ˌklōrəˌgōjən, -ōgən\ *or* **chlor·a·gogue** \ˈklōrəˌgäg\ *adj* [*chloragogen,* fr. *chlor-* + Gk *agōgos* leading (fr. *agein* to lead) + E *-en; chloragogue,* fr. *chlor-* + Gk *agōgos* — more at AGENT] **:** of, relating to, or being certain cells that line the outer surface of the alimentary tract in earthworms and other annelids and are believed to function in excretion and waste storage

chlo·ral \ˈklōrəl, -ȯr-, -ˌral\ *n* -s [F, fr. *chlor-* + *al*cool alcohol] **1 :** a colorless oily aldehyde CCl_3CHO having a pungent odor, obtained by the action of chlorine on ethyl alcohol, and used in making DDT and chloral hydrate; trichloro-acetaldehyde **2 :** CHLORAL HYDRATE

chlo·ral·formamide \ˌ≈≈+\ *n* [ISV *chloral* + *formamide*] **:** a colorless crystalline compound $C_3H_4Cl_3NO_2$ of chloral and formamide used as a hypnotic

chloral hydrate *n* **:** a bitter colorless crystalline compound $CCl_3CH(OH)_2$ formed by treating chloral with water and used usu. by oral administration for producing sleep

chlo·ral·ide \ˈklōrəˌlīd, -ˌləd\ *n* -s [ISV *chloral* + *-ide;* orig. formed as G *chloralid*] **1 :** a white crystalline cyclic compound $C_5H_2Cl_6O_3$ formed by heating chloral with trichloro-lactic acid **2 :** a compound formed by the condensation of chloral with an alpha-hydroxy acid

chlo·ral·o·sane \ˌklōrəˈlōˌsān\ *also* **chlo·ral·o·san** \-ˌsan\ *n* -s [*chloralose* + *-ane*] **:** CHLORALOSE

chlo·ra·lose \ˈklōrəˌlōs *also* -ōz\ *n* -s [ISV *chloral* + *-ose;* orig. formed in F] **1 :** a bitter crystalline compound $C_8H_{11}Cl_3O_6$ formed by heating chloral with dextrose and used as a hypnotic **2 :** a condensation product of chloral with a sugar similar to chloralose

chlo·ra·losed \-ōst,-ōzd\ *adj* **:** treated with chloralose

[1]**chlor·al·um** \klōrˈaləm\ *n* [ISV *chlor-* + *alum*inum] **:** aluminum chloride in the form of yellowish white to colorless deliquescent crystals or powder of the hydrate $AlCl_3.6H_2O$ or its aqueous solution used esp. in salting out glycerin lyes in soapmaking, in carbonizing wool, and as a disinfectant, deodorant, and astringent

[2]**chlo·ra·lum** \ˈklōrələm, klōrˈal-\ *n* [NL, fr. ISV *chloral* + NL *-um*] **:** CHLORAL

chlor·alu·mi·nite \ˌklōrəˈlüməˌnīt\ *n* [ISV *chlor-* + *aluminite;* orig. formed as It *coralluminite*] **:** a mineral $AlCl_3.6H_2O$ consisting of hydrous aluminum chloride

chlor·am·ide \klōrˈaˌmīd, -ˌməd, ˈklōrə,-\ *n* -s [*chlor-* + *amide*] **1 :** an organic amide in which chlorine has replaced hydrogen attached to the nitrogen atom (as in chloramine-T); an *N*-chloroamide — called also *chloramine* **2 :** the chloramine NH_2Cl

chlor·am·ine \klōrˈaˌmēn, -ˌmən, ˈklōrəˌmēn\ *n* -s [ISV *chlor-* + *am*monia + *-ine*] **1 :** any of three compounds formed by the reaction of dilute hypochlorous acid with ammonia; *esp* **:** a colorless oily bactericidal compound NH_2Cl having an ammoniacal odor and being formed in one process of water purification by the interaction of ammonia, chlorine, and water — compare DICHLORAMINE 1, NITROGEN TRICHLORIDE **2 :** any of various organic compounds containing nitrogen and chlorine, esp. having the chlorine attached to the nitrogen atom (as in the groups $-NHCl$ and $-NCl_2$): as **a :** CHLOROAMINE 1 **b :** any of various chloramides (sense 1); *esp* **:** CHLORAMINE-T **c :** CHLORIMIDE

chloramine–B *n* **:** a white crystalline compound $C_6H_5SO_2NClNa.2H_2O$ used as an antiseptic **:** sodium benzene-sulfonchloramide

chloramine–T *n* **:** a white or faintly yellow crystalline compound $CH_3C_6H_4SO_2NClNa.3H_2O$ used as an antiseptic (as in treating wounds) **:** sodium *para*-toluene-sulfonchloramide — called also *chloramine;* compare DICHLORAMINE-T

chlor·am·phen·i·col \ˌklōrˌamˈfenəˌkȯl, -ōl\ *n* -s [*chlor-* + *amid-* + *phen-* + *nitr-* + *glycol*] **:** a colorless crystalline antibiotic $C_{11}H_{12}Cl_2N_2O_5$ isolated from cultures of a soil microorganism (*Streptomyces venezuelae*) and also prepared synthetically (as from *p*-nitro-acetophenone) that is effective against certain diseases caused by bacteria, rickettsiae, or viruses

chlor·ane·mia *or* **chlor·anae·mia** \ˌklōr+\ *n* -s [NL, fr. *chlor-* + *anemia, anaemia*] **:** CHLOROSIS — **chlor·anemic** \"+\ *adj*

chlor·an·il \klōrˈanᵊl, ˈklorəˌnil\ *n* -s [G, fr. *chlor-* + *anil*in aniline] **:** a bright yellow crystalline compound $C_6Cl_4O_2$ made usu. by chlorination and oxidation of phenol or aniline and used chiefly in dye manufacture and as a seed disinfectant; tetrachloro-quinone

chlo·ran·tha·ce·ae \ˌklōrˌanˈthāsēˌē\ *n pl, cap* [NL, fr. *Chloranthus,* type genus + *-aceae*] **:** a small family of tropical herbs, shrubs, or trees (order Piperales) distinguished by opposite stipulate leaves and united petiole bases — **chlo·ran·tha·ceous** \ˌ≈ˌ≈ˌ≈shəs\ *adj*

chlo·ran·thy \ˈklōrˌan(t)thē\ *n* -ES [F *chloranthie,* fr. *chlor-* + Gk *anthos* flower + F *-ie* -y — more at ANTHOLOGY] **:** reversion of normally colored floral leaves to green foliage leaves

chlor·apatite \(ˈ)klōr+\ *n* -s [ISV *chlor-* + *apatite*] **:** a common apatite containing chlorine: as **a :** apatite in which chlorine predominates over fluorine, hydroxyl, and carbonate **b :** calcium phosphate chloride $Ca_5Cl(PO_4)_3$

chlor·argyrite \(ˈ)klōr+\ *n* -s [ISV *chlor-* + *argyr-* + *-ite;* orig. formed as G *chlorargyrit*] **:** CERARGYRITE

chlor·ar·sen \klōrˈärsᵊn\ *n* -s [*chlor-* + *arsen* (alter. of *arsine*)] **:** the hydrochloride of dichlorophenarsine

chlor·as·tro·lite \klōrˈastrəˌlīt\ *n* -s [*chlor-* + *astr-* + *-lite*] **:** a mineral like prehnite that occurs as green pebbles of a stellate structure and is found near Lake Superior

chlo·rate \ˈklōrˌāt, -lȯˌr-, -ˌrət\ *n* -s [*chlor-* + *-ate*] **:** a salt (as the potassium or the sodium salt) of chloric acid

chlorate of potash : POTASSIUM CHLORATE

chlorauric acid *var of* CHLOROAURIC ACID

chlor·az·ide \klōrˈaˌzīd, -ˌzəd, ˈklōrə-\ *n* -s [ISV *chlor-* + *azide;* prob. orig. formed as G *chlorazid*] **:** a colorless highly explosive gas ClN_3 made by the reaction of sodium azide with sodium hypochlorite; chlorine azide

chlo·ra·zol black E \ˈklōrəˌzȯl-, -ōl-\ *n, usu cap C & often cap B* [*chlor-* + *az-* + *-ol*] **:** DIRECT DEEP BLACK EW

chlorbenzene *var of* CHLOROBENZENE

chlorbutanol *var of* CHLOROBUTANOL

chlor·bu·tol \ˈklōrbyəˌtȯl, -ōl\ *n* -s [by contr.] **:** CHLOROBUTANOL

chlor·co·sane \ˈklōrkōˌsān\ *n* -s [*chlor-* + *-cosane* (as in tetra*cosane*)] **:** a yellow oily liquid consisting of chlorinated paraffins and used chiefly as a solvent for dichloramine-T

chlor·cy·cli·zine \(ˈ)klōrˈsīkləˌzēn, -ˌzən\ *n* -s [*chlor-* + *cycl-* + *i-* + pipera*zine*] **:** a cyclic antihistaminic agent $C_{18}H_{21}ClN_2$, administered as the hydrochloride; 1-(*p*-chloro-benzhydryl)-4-methyl-piperazine

chlor·dane \ˈklōrˌdān\ *or* **chlor·dan** \-ˌdan\ *n* -s [*chlor-* + *indane, indan*] **:** a viscous usu. amber-colored volatile liquid insecticide $C_{10}H_6Cl_8$ consisting of a highly chlorinated compound derived from indan or of a mixture of this compound with related compounds

chlore \ˈklō(ə)r\ *vt* -ED/-ING/-s [short for [2]*chlorine*] **:** to treat with a dilute solution of bleaching powder **:** CHLORINATE

chlo·rel·la \kləˈrelə\ *n* [NL, fr. *chlor-* + *-ella*] **1** *cap* **:** a genus (the type of the family Chlorellaceae) of nonmotile unicellular green algae (order Chlorococcales) potentially important as a cheap source of high grade protein and B-complex vitamins **2** -s **:** any alga of the genus *Chlorella* — **chlo·rel·la·ceous** \ˌklōrəˈlāshəs\ *adj*

chlor·e·mia *or* **chlor·ae·mia** \klōrˈēmēə\ *n* -s [NL, fr. *chlor-* + *-emia, -aemia*] **1 :** CHLOROSIS **2 :** excess of chlorides in the blood

chlor·en·chy·ma \klōrˈeŋkəmə\ *n* -s [NL, fr. *chlor-* (fr. ISV *chlorophyll*) + *-enchyma*] **:** chlorophyll-containing tissue — **chlor·en·chym·a·tous** \ˌklōrˌenˌkimədəs, -eŋ-\ *adj* — **chlo·ren·chy·mous** \(ˈ)klōrˈeŋkəməs\ *adj*

Chlo·re·tone \ˈklōrəˌtōn\ *trademark* — used for chlorobutanol (sense 2)

chlorguanide *var of* CHLOROGUANIDE

chlorhydrin *var of* CHLOROHYDRIN

chlo·ric acid \ˈklōrik-, -ȯr-, -rēk-\ *n* [*chlor-* + *-ic*] **:** a strong acid $HClO_3$ like nitric acid in oxidizing properties but far less stable that is obtained from its salts (as sodium chlorate) as a colorless aqueous solution

chlo·ride \ˈklōrˌīd, -ȯˌr-, -ˌrəd\ *n* -s [G *chlorid,* fr. *chlor* chlorine (fr. Gk *chlōros* greenish yellow) + *-id* -ide — more at YELLOW] **1 :** a compound of chlorine with another element or radical **:** a salt or ester of hydrochloric acid ⟨sodium ~⟩ ⟨ethyl ~⟩ **2 :** chloride paper or a photographic print made on it

chlo·ri·del·la \ˌklōrəˈdelə\ [NL, fr. L *Chlorid-, Chloris* the goddess Flora (fr. Gk *Chlōrid-, Chlōris,* a feminine name) + NL *-ella*] *syn of* SQUILLA

chlo·ri·del·li·dae \-ləˌdē\ [NL, fr. *Chloridella,* type genus + *-idae*] *syn of* SQUILLIDAE

chloride of lime : BLEACHING POWDER

chloride paper *n* **:** paper coated with silver chloride and used in photography chiefly for contact printing

chlo·rid·er \ˈklōrˌīdə(r)\ *n* -s **:** one that mines on a small scale for ore (as silver) in the form of a chloride

chloride shift *n* **:** the passage of chloride ions from the plasma into the red blood cells when carbon dioxide enters the plasma from the tissues and their return to the plasma when the carbon dioxide is discharged in the lungs, a major factor both in maintenance of blood pH and in transport of carbon dioxide

chlo·ri·dize \ˈklōrəˌdīz\ *also* **chlo·ri·date** \ˈ≈≈ˌdāt, *usu* -ād·+V\ *vt* -ED/-ING/-s **:** to treat with chlorine or with a chloride; *esp* **:** to convert (the metal of an ore) into chloride

chlor·im·ide \klōrˈiˌmīd, -ˌməd\ *n* -s [*chlor-* + *imide*] **1 :** an organic imide in which chlorine has replaced the hydrogen attached to the nitrogen atom (as in succinchlorimide); an *N*-chloro-imide — called also *chloramine* **2 :** DICHLORAMINE 1

chlo·rin \ˈklōrən, -ȯr-\ *also* **chlo·rine** \", -ōrˌēn, -ȯˌrēn\ *n* -s [*chloro*phyll + *-in, -ine*] **:** any of several derivatives of chlorophyll obtained by hydrolysis, removal of the magnesium, sometimes with replacement by another metal (as copper), and opening of the carbocyclic ring — see CHLOROPHYLLIN 2

[1]**chlo·rin·ate** \ˈ≈rəˌnāt, *usu* -ād· + V\ *also* **chlo·rin·ize** \-ˌnīz\ *vt* -ED/-ING/-s [[2]*chlorine* + *-ate* or *-ize*] **:** to treat or cause to combine with chlorine or a compound of chlorine: as **a :** to treat (paper pulp) with chlorine for the purpose of bleaching **b :** to apply chlorine or a hypochlorite to (water, sewage, or wastes) esp. for purposes of disinfection, oxidation of organic matter, or retardation of putrefaction **c :** to treat (wool) with a solution usu. of a hypochlorite and acid for the purpose of increasing resistance to shrinking **d :** CHLORIDIZE **e :** to introduce chlorine into (a compound); *specif* **:** to cause substitution of chlorine for hydrogen in (an organic compound)

[2]**chlo·rin·ate** \ˈ≈rəˌnāt, -ˌnət, *usu* -d·+V\ *n* -s **:** a chlorinated product

chlorinated camphene *n* **:** TOXAPHENE

chlo·rin·at·ed lime *n* **:** BLEACHING POWDER

chlorinated paraffin *also* **chlorinated paraffin wax** *n* **:** any of various pale yellow viscous liquids or resinous solids obtained by treating molten paraffin wax with chlorine and used chiefly as plasticizers, as additives for lubricants, and as weatherproofing and flameproofing agents for textiles

chlorinated rubber *n* **:** an odorless tasteless nonflammable white powder that is resistant to many chemicals, is usu. obtained by treating a solution of rubber (as in carbon tetrachloride) with chlorine, and is used chiefly in coatings, inks, and adhesives

chlo·rin·a·tion \ˌklōrəˈnāshən, -ȯr-\ *n* -s **:** the act or process of chlorinating

chlo·rin·a·tor \ˈ≈≈ˌnād·ə(r), -atə\ *n* -s **:** an apparatus (as a cylindrical tank) for chlorinating

[1]**chlo·rine** \ˈklōrˌēn, -ȯˌr-, -ˌrən\ *adj* **:** of the color grass green

[2]**chlorine** \"\ *n* -s [*chlor-* + *-ine*] **:** a common nonmetallic univalent and polyvalent element belonging to the halogens that is best known as a heavy greenish yellow irritating toxic gas of disagreeable odor, is usu. made by electrolysis of aqueous solutions of sodium chloride, and is used chiefly as a powerful bleaching, oxidizing, and disinfecting agent in water purification and in making numerous products (as bleaching powder, chlorinated solvents, military gases, insecticides, herbicides, and synthetic resins and plastics) — symbol *Cl;* see ELEMENT table

chlorine demand *n* **:** the greatest amount of chlorine that added to water is completely utilized in the process of sterilizing the water

chlorine dioxide *also* **chlorine peroxide** *n* **:** a heavy reddish yellow odorous explosive gas ClO_2 made by the action of chlorine on sodium chlorite and used chiefly in bleaching (as of paper pulp, flour, starch, and soap) and in water purification

chlorine water *n* **:** a yellowish aqueous solution of chlorine used for bleaching

chlo·rin·i·ty \klōˈrinədē, -ȯˈr-\ *n* -ES [[1]*chlorine* + *-ity*] **:** the quality or degree of being chlorinous

chlo·rin·ol·y·sis \ˈ≈≈ˈnäləsəs\ *n, pl* **chlorinoly·ses** \-əˌsēz\ [NL, fr. ISV *chlorine* + NL *-o-* + *-lysis*] **:** a chemical reaction analogous to hydrolysis in which chlorine plays a role similar to that of water

chlo·rin·ous \ˈklōrənəs, -ȯr-\ *adj* **:** of, relating to, or like chlorine ⟨~ tastes in water⟩

chloriodide [*chlor-* + *iodide*] *var of* CHLOROIODIDE

chlo·ri·on \ˈklōrēˌän, -ˌən\ *n, cap* [NL, fr. Gk *chlōriōn,* a kind of yellow bird, fr. *chlōros* greenish yellow — more at YELLOW] **:** a genus of digger wasps (family Sphecidae)

chlo·ris \ˈklōrəs\ *n, cap* [NL, fr. L, the goddess Flora, fr. Gk *Chlōris,* a feminine name] **:** a genus of grasses with spikelets in two rows along one side of the rachis and with the spikes being arranged digitately — see FINGER GRASS

[1]**chlo·rite** \ˈklōrˌīt, -ȯˌrīt\ *n* -s [G *chlorit,* fr. L *chloritis,* a kind of green stone, fr. Gk *chlōritis,* fr. *chlōros* greenish yellow] **:** any of a group of monoclinic minerals of extensive occurrence that are essentially hydrous silicates of aluminum, ferrous iron, and magnesium, include clinochlore, penninite, prochlorite, and corundophilite, are associated with and resemble the micas, and are usu. green in color — **chlo·rit·ic** \klōˈrid·ik, -ȯˈr-\ *adj*

[2]**chlorite** \"\ *n* -s [prob. fr. F, fr. *chlor-* + *-ite*] **:** a salt of chlorous acid

chlo·rit·i·za·tion \ˌklōrˌīd·əˈzāshən, -rətəˈz-\ *n* -s **:** production of or conversion into chlorite

chlo·ri·tize \ˈklōrəˌtīz\ *vt* -ED/-ING/-s [[1,2]*chlorite* + *-ize*] **1 :** to introduce chlorite in **2 :** to alter into mineral chlorite

chlo·ri·toid \-rəˌtȯid\ *n* -s [G, fr. *chlorit* chlorite (mineral) + *-oid*] **:** a mineral $(Mg,Fe)AlSiAlO_5(OH)_2$ consisting of a silicate of aluminum and ferrous iron with magnesium occurring usu. in dull green to gray or grayish black masses of brittle folia and related to the brittle micas (as clintonite)

chlor·man·ga·no·ka·lite \ˈklōrˌmaŋgəˌnōˈkāˌlīt\ *n* -s [*chlor-* + *mangan-* + *kal*ium + *-ite*] **:** a rare chloride of potassium and manganese found in blocks of rock ejected from Vesuvius in 1906

chlo·ro \ˈklōr(ˌ)ō, -ō(ˌ)rō\ *adj* [*chlor-*] **:** containing chlorine — used esp. of organic compounds; compare CHLOR- 3

chloro- *in pronunciations below,* ˌ≈≈ = ˌklōrō *or* ˌklȯrō *or* -rə\ — see CHLOR-

chlo·ro·acetate \ˌ≈≈+\ *n* -s [ISV *chlor-* + *acetate*] **:** a salt or ester of chloroacetic acid

chlo·ro·ace·tic acid \ˌ≈≈+ . . . -\ *also* **chlor·ace·tic acid** \ˌklōr, -ȯr + . . . -\ *n* [ISV *chlor-* + *acetic*] **:** a crystalline acid $ClCH_2COOH$ obtained by direct chlorination of acetic acid and used in organic synthesis — called also *monochloroacetic acid;* compare DICHLOROACETIC ACID, TRICHLOROACETIC ACID

chlo·ro·acetophenone \ˌ≈≈+\ *or* **chlor·acetophenone** \(ˌ)klōr, -ȯr+\ *n* -s [*chlor-* + *acetophenone*] **:** a chlorine derivative of acetophenone; *specif* **:** the alpha derivative $C_6H_5COCH_2Cl$ obtained as irritating white crystals by reaction of benzene and chloro-acetyl chloride or by chlorination of acetophenone and used esp. in solution as a tear gas — called also *phenacyl chloride*

chlo·ro·amide \ˌ≈≈+\ *n* -s [ISV *chlor-* + *amide*] **:** a chloro derivative of an amide — compare CHLORAMIDE

chlo·ro·amine \ˌ≈≈+\ *n* -s [ISV *chlor-* + *amine*] **1 :** a chloro derivative of an amine; *esp* **:** one in which the chlorine is attached to the nitrogen atom — compare CHLORAMINE 2 **2 :** CHLORAMINE 1

chlo·ro·ane·mia *or* **chlo·ro·anae·mia** \ˌ≈≈+\ *n* -s [NL, fr. *chlor-* + *anemia, anaemia*] **:** CHLOROSIS 1

chlo·ro·aurate \ˌ≈≈+\ *n* -s [prob. fr. F, fr. *chlor-* + *aurate*] **:** a salt of chloroauric acid

chlo·ro·auric acid \ˌ≈≈+ . . . -\ *also* **chlor·auric acid** \(ˈ)klōr, -ȯr+ . . .-\ *n* [ISV *chlor-* + *auric*] **:** an acid $HAuCl_4$ formed when gold is dissolved in aqua regia and obtainable as long yellow deliquescent crystals

chlo·ro·az·o·din \ˌ≈≈ˈazədən\ *n* -s [blend of *chloro-formamidine* and *az-*] **:** a yellow crystalline compound $C_2H_4Cl_2N_6$ used in solution as a surgical antiseptic; α,α'-azo-bis-(chloro-formamidine)

chlo·ro·bacteriaceae \ˌ≈≈+\ *n pl, cap* [NL, fr. *Chlorobacterium,* type genus + *-aceae*] **:** a family of eubacteria (suborder Rhodobacteriinae) comprising the green sulfur bacteria and distinguished by a photosynthetic pigment related to but distinct from both the chlorophyll of higher plants and the bacterio-chlorophyll of the purple sulfur bacteria

chlo·ro·bacterium \ˌ≈≈+\ *n, cap* [NL, fr. *chlor-* + *bacterium*] **:** the type genus of Chlorobacteriaceae comprising green sulfur bacteria that live symbiotically with various protozoans

chlo·ro·benzene \ˌ≈≈+\ *also* **chlor·benzene** \(ˈ)klōr, -ȯr+\ *n* -s [ISV *chlor-* + *benzene*] **:** a colorless flammable volatile toxic liquid C_6H_5Cl with an almondlike odor made usu. by direct chlorination of benzene and used in organic synthesis and as a solvent — called also *monochlorobenzene;* compare DICHLOROBENZENE

chlo·ro·bromide *also* **chlo·ro·bromid** \ˌ≈≈+\ *n* -s [*chlor-* + *bromide, bromid*] **1 :** a compound of chlorine and bromine with an element or radical **2 :** chlorobromide paper or a photographic print made on it

chlo·ro·butanol \ˌ≈≈+\ *also* **chlor·butanol** \(ˈ)klōr, -ȯr+\ *n* -s [*chlor-* + *butanol*] **1 :** a monochloro derivative of 1- or 2-butanol **2 :** a white crystalline alcohol $CCl_3C(CH_3)_2OH$ with a camphorlike odor and taste that is made by the reaction of acetone and chloroform in the presence of alkali and is used as a local anesthetic, sedative, and preservative (as for hypodermic solutions); β,β,β-trichloro-*tert*-butyl alcohol — called also *chlorbutol*

chlo·ro·calcite \ˌ≈≈+\ *n* -s [ISV *chlor-* + *calcite;* orig. formed in It] **:** HYDROPHILITE

chlo·ro·carbonate \ˌ≈≈+\ *n* -s [ISV *chlor-* + *carbonate*] **:** CHLOROFORMATE

chlo·ro·carbonic acid \ˌ≈≈+ . . .-\ *n* [*chlor-* + *carbonic*] **1** *obs* **:** PHOSGENE **2 :** CHLOROFORMIC ACID

chlo·roch·ro·us \klōˈräkrəwəs\ *adj* [*chlor-* + *-chrous* (alter. of *-chroous*)] **:** of a hue approximating green

chlo·ro·chy·tri·um \ˌ≈≈ *at* CHLORO- + ˈkītrēəm, ˈki-\ *n, cap* [NL, fr. *chlor-* + *-chytrium* (fr. Gk *chytrion* cup, dim. of *chytra* earthen pot)] **:** a genus of unicellular green algae (family Endosphaeraceae) living within the tissues of red algae, mosses, and certain aquatic flowering plants (as the duckweed)

chlo·ro·coc·ca·les \ˌ≈≈(ˌ)käˈkā(ˌ)lēz\ *n pl, cap* [NL, fr. *Chlorococcum* + *-ales*] **:** an order of unicellular green algae (class Chlorophyceae) distinguished from other similar forms in not dividing vegetatively but reproducing only by spores

chlo·ro·coc·cine \ˌ≈≈ˌkäkˌsīn, -ēn\ *adj* [NL *Chlorococcum* + E *ine*] **:** lacking motility except in reproductive cells and having no capacity for vegetative division ⟨~ algae⟩

chlo·ro·coc·cum \ˌ≈≈ˌkäkəm\ *n, cap* [NL, fr. *chlor-* + *-coccum* (fr. L *coccum* berry, fr. Gk *kokkos* kermes, grain, seed)] **:** a genus (the type of the family Chlorococcaceae) of unicellular green algae (order Chlorococcales) occurring singly or in a layer on soil or damp rock, reproducing only by spores, and varying greatly in size of the vegetative cells — compare PROTOCOCCUS

chlo·ro·cresol \ˌ≈≈+\ *n* -s [*chlor-* + *cresol*] **:** any of several chlorine derivatives of the cresols; *esp* **:** the para derivative $Cl(CH_3)C_6H_3OH$ obtained as colorless crystals by chlorination of *meta*-cresol and used as an antiseptic and preservative (as for glue and leather)

chlo·ro·cru·o·rin \ˌ≈≈ˈkrüərən\ *n* -s [*chlor-* + *cruorin* (old name for hemoglobin), fr. L *cruor* blood) + E *-in* — more at RAW] **:** a green iron-containing respiratory pigment related chemically to hemoglobin and found in the blood of certain marine polychaete worms

chlo·ro·dyne \ˈ≈≈ˌdīn\ *n* -s [fr. *Chlorodyne,* a trademark] **:** a preparation of varying composition containing numerous narcotic and sedative drugs

chlo·ro·ethane \ˌ≈≈+\ *n* [*chlor-* + *ethane*] **:** ETHYL CHLORIDE

chlo·ro·ethyl \ˌ≈≈+\ *n* -s [ISV *chlor-* + *ethyl*] **:** a chloro derivative of ethyl; *esp* **:** the beta or 2-derivative $ClCH_2CH_2-$

[1]**chlo·ro·form** \ˈklōrəˌfȯrm, -lȯr-\ *n* -s [F *chloroforme,* fr. *chlor-* + *-forme* (fr. *formyle* formyl); fr. its having been regarded as a trichloride of this radical] **:** a colorless volatile heavy toxic liquid $CHCl_3$ of ethereal odor and sweetish taste made usu. by chlorination and oxidation of acetone or by chlorination of methane or methyl chloride and used chiefly as a solvent and esp. formerly as a general anesthetic or as a carminative and anodyne; trichloro-methane

[2]**chloroform** \"\ *vt* -ED/-ING/-s **:** to treat with chloroform or to place under its influence esp. so as to produce insensibility or anesthesia; *also* **:** to kill with chloroform

chlo·ro·form·ate \ˌ≈≈ˈfȯrmət, -ˌmāt\ *n* -s [ISV [1]*chloroform* + *-ate*] **:** a salt or ester of chloroformic acid — called also *chlorocarbonate*

chlo·ro·for·mic acid \ˌ≈≈ˌfȯrmik-\ *n* [ISV *chloroform* + *-ic*] **:** an acid $ClCOOH$ best known in the form of its esters — called also *chlorocarbonic acid*

chloroformic ester *n* **:** an ester (as ethyl chloroformate $ClCOOC_2H_5$) of chloroformic acid made by reaction of phosgene on an alcohol or phenol and used in organic synthesis (as of esters of carbonic acid)

chlo·ro·form·ize \ˈ≈≈ˌfȯrˌmīz\ *vt* -ED/-ING/-s [[1]*chloroform* + *-ize*] *immunol* **:** to treat with chloroform (esp. a living antigen for purposes of attenuation)

chlo·ro·for·myl \ˈ≈≈ˌfȯrməl\ *n* -s [*chloroformic* + *-yl*] **:** the univalent radical $ClCO-$ of chloroformic acid

chlo·ro·gen·ic acid \ˌ≈≈ˌjenik-\ *n* [ISV *chlor-* + *-genic;* orig. formed as F *chlorogénique*] **:** a crystalline acid $C_{15}H_{17}O_7COOH$ occurring in coffee beans as the potassium caffeine salt, in potatoes, and in other plant products and yielding caffeic acid and quinic acid on hydrolysis

chlo·ro·gen·in \ˌ≈≈+ˈjenən\ *n* -s [ISV *chloro-* (fr. NL *chlorogalum pomeridianum*) + *-genin*] **:** a steroidal sapogenin $C_{27}H_{44}O_4$ obtained from a soap plant (*Chlorogalum pomeridianum*)

chlo·rog·e·nine \klōˈräjəˌnēn, -ˌnən\ *n* -s [ISV *chlor-* + *-genine*] **:** ALSTONINE

chlo·ro·go·gen *or* **chlo·ro·gogue** *adj* [by alter.] **:** CHLORAGOGEN

chlo·ro·gua·nide \ˌ≈≈+ˌgwäˌnīd, -ˌnəd\ *or* **chlor·gua·nide** \(ˈ)klōr, -ȯr+\ *n* -s [*chlor-* + *biguanide*] **:** an antimalarial drug $C_{11}H_{16}N_5Cl$ derived from biguanide and administered as the bitter crystalline hydrochloride

chlo·ro·hy·drin \ˌ≈≈+ˈhīdrən\ *also* **chlor·hy·drin** \klōr, -ȯr+\ *n* -s [ISV *chlor-* + *-hydrin*] **:** any of a class of organic compounds derived from glycols or polyhydroxy alcohols (as glycerol) by substitution of chlorine for part of the hydroxyl groups: as **a :** either of the two syrupy liquid mono-chlorohydrins of glycerol distinguished as alpha-chlorohydrin $CH_2ClCHOHCH_2OH$ and beta-chlorohydrin $CH_2OHCHClCH_2OH$ and used chiefly in organic synthesis and as solvents **b :** ETHYLENE CHLOROHYDRIN

chlo·ro·hydrocarbon \ˌ≈≈+\ *n* -s [*chlor-* + *hydrocarbon*] **:** a chlorine derivative of a hydrocarbon

chlo·ro·io·dide \ˌ≈≈+\ *also* **chlor·io·dide** \(ˈ)klōr, -ȯr+\ *n* -s [*chlor-* + *iodide*] **:** a compound of chlorine and iodine with an element or radical — called also *iodochloride*

chlo·ro·leucite \ˌ⸗⸗+\ *n* -s [ISV *chlor-* + *leucite;* orig. formed in F] : CHLOROPLAST

chlo·ro·leukemia *or* **chlo·ro·leukaemia** \ˌ⸗⸗+\ *n* -s [NL, fr. *chlor-* + *leukemia, leukaemia*] : CHLOROMA

chlo·ro·ma \klə'rōmə\ *n, pl* **chloromas** \-məz\ *or* **chloro·ma·ta** \-məd·ə\ [NL, fr. *chlor-* + *-oma*] : leukemia originating in the bone marrow and marked by the formation of tumorlike growths of myeloid tissue beneath the periosteum of flat bones (as the skull, ribs, or pelvis) — **chlo·rom·a·tous** \-'rämədəs, -ōm-\ *adj*

chlo·ro·magnesite \ˌ⸗⸗+\ *n* -s [ISV *chlor-* + *magnesite;* orig. formed as It *cloromagnesite*] : a mineral $MgCl_2$ found on Vesuvius and consisting of a deliquescent anhydrous chloride of magnesium

chlo·ro·melanite \ˌ⸗⸗+\ *n* -s [ISV *chlor-* + *melan-* + *-ite;* orig. formed as F *chloromélanite*] : a dark green or nearly black variety of jadeite

chlo·rom·e·ter \klō'rämə̇d·ə(r)\ *n* -s [F *chloromètre,* fr. *chlor-* + *-mètre* -meter] : a device for measuring chlorine

chlo·ro·methane \ˌ⸗⸗ *at* CHLORO- +\ *n* -s [ISV *chlor-* + *methane*] : METHYL CHLORIDE

chlo·ro·methyl \ˌ⸗⸗+\ *n* -s [*chlor-* + *methyl*] : the univalent radical $ClCH_2$— formed by removal of one hydrogen atom from methyl chloride

chlo·ro·methylation \ˌ⸗⸗+\ *n* -s [*chlor-* + *methylation*] : the introduction of a chloromethyl group into a compound usu. by use of formaldehyde and hydrogen chloride

chlo·rom·e·try \klō'rämə·trē\ *n* -ES [prob. fr. F *chlorométrie,* fr. *chlor-* + *-métrie* -metry] : the measurement of chlorine: as **a** : the determination of available chlorine (as in bleaching powder) **b** : analysis by the use or liberation of chlorine similar to iodometry

chlo·ro·monadina \ˌ⸗⸗ *at* CHLORO- +\ *n pl, cap* [NL, fr. *chlor-* + *Monadina*] : a small order of biflagellate plantlike flagellates distinguished from the euglenoids by production of oily reserve products

Chlo·ro·my·ce·tin \ˌ⸗⸗+ˌmī'sēt³n\ *trademark* — used for chloramphenicol

chlor·opal \(')klōrˌōpəl, -lȯˌrō-\ *n* -s [G, fr. *chlor-* + *opal*] : a yellowish green or greenish yellow clay mineral consisting of hydrous silicate of iron and aluminum and occurring in compact masses or earthy forms resembling opal

chlo·ro·pal·la·date \ˌ⸗⸗ *at* CHLORO- + 'paləˌdāt\ *n* -s [*chlor-* + *palladium* + *-ate*] : a salt analogous to a chloroplatinate containing the anion $PdCl_6^{--}$

chlo·ro·phane \'⸗⸗ˌfān\ *n* -s [F, fr. *chlor-* + *-phane*] : a variety of fluorite that when heated emits a beautiful green light

chlo·ro·phenol \ˌ⸗⸗+\ *also* **chlor·phenol** \(')klōr, -ȯr+\ *n* -s [ISV *chlor-* + *phenol*] **1** : any of three monochloro derivatives ClC_6H_4OH of phenol distinguished as *ortho*-chlorophenol, *meta*-chlorophenol, and *para*-chlorophenol and used chiefly as dye intermediates **2** : a chlorine derivative of a phenol — compare PENTACHLOROPHENOL

chlorophenol red *also* **chlorphenol red** *n* : a dye $C_{19}H_{12}Cl_2O_5S$ used as an acid-base indicator; dichloro-phenolsulfonephthalein

chlo·ro·phen·o·thane \ˌ⸗⸗+'fenəˌthān\ *n* -s [di*chloro*⸗di*phen*yl-trichlor*o-ethane*] : DDT

chlo·ro·phoe·ni·cite \ˌ⸗⸗+'fēnəˌsīt\ *n* -s [*chlor-* + *phoenic-* (fr. Gk *phoinik-, phoinix* purple) + *-ite;* fr. its colors by daylight and by artificial light — more at PHOENICIAN] : a mineral $(Mn,Zn)_5AsO_4(OH_7)$ consisting of a basic arsenate of manganese and zinc and occurring in monoclinic crystals

chlo·roph·o·ra \klō'räfərə\ *n, cap* [NL, fr. *chlor-* + *-phora*] : a small genus of tropical timber trees (family Moraceae) with rather hard heavy wood — see FUSTIC, IROKO

chlo·ro·phy·ce·ae \ˌ⸗⸗ *at* CHLORO- + 'fīsēˌē, 'fis-\ *n pl, cap* [NL, fr. *chlor-* + *-phyceae*] : a class of algae (division Chlorophyta) distinguished chiefly by having a clear green color, their chlorophyll being masked or altered little or not at all by other pigments — **chlo·ro·phy·cean** \ˌ⸗⸗ˌfīshən, -ˌfish-\ *adj*

chlo·ro·phyll *also* **chlo·ro·phyl** \'klōrəˌfil, -ȯr-, -ˌfəl *sometimes* -är-\ *n* -s [F *chlorophylle,* fr. *chlor-* + *-phylle* -phyll] **1 a** : the green coloring material of plants that is essential to photosynthesis, occurs usu. in discrete bodies and only in the presence of light and where iron is available in the living cell, and is extractable as a mixture of chlorophyll a and chlorophyll b together with various amounts of other pigments (as carotene and xanthophyll) — see CHLOROPLAST **b** : any of several oil-soluble pigments making up this green coloring matter: as (1) : an ester $C_{55}H_{72}MgN_4O_5$ obtained as a blue-black powder that is a magnesium-containing porphyrin derivative related structurally to heme and that yields phytol and methanol on hydrolysis — called also *chlorophyll a* (2) : an ester $C_{55}H_{70}MgN_4O_6$ obtained as a dark green powder and very closely related structurally to chlorophyll a — called also *chlorophyll b* **2** : a dark green waxy substance obtained by extraction of green plants (as nettles or alfalfa) that contains chlorophyll or chlorophyll derivatives and often other plant constituents and is used esp. as a coloring agent or for its claimed deodorant properties

chlo·ro·phyl·la·ceous \ˌ⸗⸗ˌfiˌlāshəs, -ˌfəˌ-\ *adj* : consisting of or containing chlorophyll : CHLOROPHYLLOSE

chlo·ro·phyl·lase \'⸗⸗fə̇ˌlās, -āz, ˌ⸗⸗'fiˌl-\ *n* -s [ISV *chlorophyll* + *-ase;* orig. formed in G] : an enzyme present in leaves that hydrolyzes chlorophyll to chlorophyllides and phytol

chlo·ro·phyl·lide \'⸗⸗fə̇ˌlīd, ˌ⸗⸗'fiˌl-\ *n* -s [ISV *chlorophyll* + *-ide;* orig. formed as G *chlorophyllid*] : any of the pigments obtained from chlorophyll by removal of the phytyl radical

chlo·ro·phyl·lin \'⸗⸗ˌfilə̇n, ˌ⸗⸗'⸗⸗\ *n* -s [*chlorophyll* + *-in*] **1** : any of several water-soluble pigments derived from chlorophyll by hydrolysis with alkali with replacement of both the methyl and phytyl radicals by hydrogen or a metal **2** : any of various derivatives of chlorophyll (as copper chlorins) used as breath and body deodorants

chlo·ro·phyl·lite \'⸗⸗fə̇ˌlīt, ˌ⸗⸗'fiˌl-\ *n* -s [*chlor-* + *-phyll* + *-ite*] : a mineral consisting of a green foliated alteration product of cordierite

chlo·ro·phyl·lose \'⸗⸗fə̇ˌlōs, ˌ⸗⸗ˌfiˌlōs\ *also* **chlo·ro·phyl·lous** \ˌ⸗⸗ˌfiləs\ *adj* : relating to, being, or containing chlorophyll

chlo·roph·y·ta \klō'räfəd·ə\ *n pl, cap* [NL, fr. *chlor-* + *-phyta*] : a division or other category of lower plants including the true green algae and the stoneworts

chlo·ro·phyte \'⸗⸗ *at* CHLORO-+ˌfīt\ *n* -s [*chlor-* + *-phyte*] : a green-pigmented flagellate

chlo·ro·pia \klō'rōpēə\ *n* -s [NL, fr. *chlor-* + *-opia*] : CHLOROPSIA

chlo·ro·pic·rin \ˌ⸗⸗ *at* CHLORO- + 'pikrə̇n\ *also* **chlor·pic·rin** \klōr, -ȯr+\ *n* -s [G *chlorpikrin,* fr. *chlor-* + *-pikrin* -picrin] : a heavy colorless liquid CCl_3NO_2 that has a sweetish odor, causes tears and vomiting, is now usu. made by reaction of nitromethane and a hypochlorite, and is used chiefly as a soil fumigant: trichloro-nitromethane — called also *nitrochloroform*

[1]chlo·ro·pid \'⸗⸗+ˌpid\ *adj* [NL *Chloropidae*] : of or relating to the Chloropidae

[2]chloropid \"\ *n* -s : an insect of the family Chloropidae : FRIT FLY

chlo·rop·i·dae \klō'räpəˌdē\ *n pl, cap* [NL, fr. *Chlorops,* type genus (fr. *chlor-* + *-ops*) + *-idae*] : a family of small nearly hairless acalyptrate flies with broad heads and short antennae comprising the frit flies some of which have larvae that are borers in various cereals and other grasses, others being irritating though nonbiting pests about the eyes of man and various animals and sometimes implicated in the transmission of diseases (as yaws)

chlo·ro·plast \'⸗⸗ *at* CHLORO-+ˌplast\ *n* -s [ISV *chlor-* + *plast;* orig. formed in G] : a plastid containing chlorophyll being the seat of photosynthesis and starch formation, in higher plants having commonly the form of a minute flattened granule, and in algae occurring in varied sizes and shapes that are often diagnostic for particular forms

chlo·ro·platinate \ˌ⸗⸗+\ *n* -s [*chlor-* + *platinate*] : a salt of chloroplatinic acid

chlo·ro·platinic acid \ˌ⸗⸗+ . . . -\ *n* [*chlor-* + *platinic*] : an acid H_2PtCl_6 obtained usu. as red-brown deliquescent crystals of the hexahydrate by the action of aqua regia on metallic platinum and used chiefly in analysis — called also *platinic chloride*

chlo·ro·plat·i·nite \ˌ⸗⸗+'plat³nˌīt\ *n* -s [*chlor-* + *platinum* + *-ite*] : a salt of chloroplatinous acid

chlo·ro·platinous acid \ˌ⸗⸗+ . . . -\ *n* [*chlor-* + *platinous*] : an acid H_2PtCl_4 formed in solution by dissolving platinous chloride in aqueous hydrochloric acid

chlo·ro·prene \'⸗⸗ˌprēn\ *n* -s [*chlor-* + iso*prene*] : a colorless liquid $CH_2{=}CClCH{=}CH_2$ made from acetylene and hydrochloric acid and used esp. in making neoprene by polymerization; 2-chloro-butadiene

chlo·ro·procaine \ˌ⸗⸗+\ *n* -s [*chlor-* + *procaine*] : a local anesthetic $C_{13}H_{19}ClN_2O_2$ used chiefly in the form of a salt (as the white powdery hydrochloride)

chlo·rop·sia \klō'räpsēə\ *n* -s [NL, fr. *chlor-* + *-opsia*] : a visual defect in which all visible objects appear green

chlo·rop·sis \-psə̇s\ *n* [NL, fr. *chlor-* + *-opsis*] **1** *cap* : a genus of passerine birds comprising the green bulbuls and included in the family Pycnotidae or placed with a few related forms in a separate family Aegithinidae **2** *pl* **chloropsis** : GREEN BULBUL

chlo·ro·quine \'⸗⸗ *at* CHLORO- + ·ˌkwīn, -ēn\ *also* **chlo·ro·quin** \-·ˌkwin\ *n* -s [*chlor-* + *-quine, -quin* (fr. *quinoline*)] : an antimalarial drug $C_{18}H_{26}ClN_3$ derived from quinoline that is administered as the bitter crystalline diphosphate

chlo·ro·silane \ˌ⸗⸗+\ *n* -s [*chlor-* + *silane*] **1** : a gas SiH_3Cl derived from monosilane — called also *monochlorosilane* **2** : a chlorine derivative of a silane; *esp* : a derivative [as dimethyl-dichloro-silane $(CH_3)_2SiCl_2$] of an organic silane used in making silicones — called also *organochlorosilane*

chlo·ro·sis \klə'rōsə̇s\ *n, pl* **chloro·ses** \-ōˌsēz\ [NL, fr. *chlor-* + *-osis*] **1** : an iron-deficiency anemia in young girls characterized by a greenish color of the skin, weakness, and menstrual disturbances — called also GREENSICKNESS **2** *plant pathol* : a diseased condition in chlorophyll-bearing plants manifested as yellowing or blanching of the normally green parts due to causes other than the absence of light (as attacks of parasites or mineral deficiencies) — compare ETIOLATE — **chlo·rot·ic** \-'räd·ik\ *adj* — **chlo·rot·i·cal·ly** \-ə̇k(ə)lē\ *adv*

chlo·ro·spinel \ˌ⸗⸗ *at* CHLORO- +\ *n* -s [ISV *chlor-* + *spinel;* orig. formed as G *chlorospinell*] : a grass-green spinel

chlo·ro·sulfonate \ˌ⸗⸗+\ *n* -s [*chlor-* + *sulfonate*] : a salt or ester of chlorosulfonic acid

chlo·ro·sulfonic acid \ˌ⸗⸗+ . . . -\ *also* **chlor·sulfonic acid** \ˌklōr, -ȯr+\ *n* [*chlor-* + *sulfonic*] : a colorless fuming corrosive liquid $ClSO_3H$ made usu. by reaction of gaseous hydrogen chloride with sulfur trioxide and used chiefly in organic synthesis (as of sulfa drugs, saccharin, and sulfonic acids)

chlo·ro·then \'⸗⸗+ˌthen\ *n* -s [*chlor-* + *thenyl*] : an antihistaminic agent $C_{14}H_{19}Cl_2N_3S$ usu. administered in the form of its crystalline mono-citrate

chlo·ro·thi·o·nite \ˌ⸗⸗+'thīəˌnīt\ *n* -s [ISV *chlor-* + *thion-* + *-ite*] : a mineral $K_2Cu(SO_4)Cl_2$ consisting of potassium copper sulfate chloride found on Vesuvius

chlo·ro·thymol \ˌ⸗⸗+\ *n* -s [ISV *chlor-* + *thymol*] : any of several chlorine derivatives of thymol; *esp* : the para derivative $Cl(CH_3)(C_3H_7)C_6H_2OH$ obtained as colorless crystals with a pungent taste and used as a germicide (as in mouthwashes)

chlorotic streak *n* : a systemic disease of sugar cane caused by a virus and characterized by striking yellow or whitish streaks on the leaves

chlo·rous acid \'klōrəs-\ *n* [F *chloreux,* fr. *chlor-* + *-eux* -ous] : a strongly oxidizing acid $HClO_2$ known only in solution and in the form of its salts (as sodium chlorite)

chlo·rox·i·phite \klō'räksəˌfīt\ *n* -s [*chlor-* + Gk *xiphos* sword + E *-ite;* fr. the bladed crystals] : a mineral $Pb_3CuO_2(OH)_2Cl_2$(?) consisting of a basic chloride of lead and copper found in the Mendip hills of England

chlo·ro·xylenol \ˌ⸗⸗ *at* CHLORO- +\ *n* -s [*chlor-* + *xylenol*] : any of several chlorine derivatives of the xylenols; *esp* : the para derivative $Cl(CH_3)_2C_6H_2OH$ obtained as colorless crystals by chlorination of 3,5-xylenol and used as an antiseptic and germicide

chlo·ro·zincate \ˌ⸗⸗+\ *n* -s [*chlor-* + *zincate*] : a compound with zinc chloride; *specif* : one containing the anion $ZnCl_4^{--}$

chlorphenol *var of* CHLOROPHENOL

chlorphenol red *var of* CHLOROPHENOL RED

chlorpicrin *var of* CHLOROPICRIN

chlor·prom·a·zine \klōr'präməˌzēn, -ȯr-, -ˌzə̇n\ *n* -s [*chlor-* + *promethazine*] : a gray-white crystalline compound $C_{17}H_{19}ClN_2S$ derived from phenothiazine and administered as the hydrochloride in the treatment esp. of vomiting and of anxiety states and mental disorders

chlors *pl of* CHLOR

chlor·tetracycline \ˌklōr, -ȯr+\ *n* -s [*chlor-* + *tetracycline*] : a yellow crystalline antibiotic $C_{22}H_{23}ClN_2O_8$ produced by one strain of a soil actinomycete (*Streptomyces aureofaciens*), administered usu. in the form of its hydrochloride in the treatment of certain bacterial, rickettsial, and viral diseases and added in crude form to animal feeds for stimulating growth

chm *abbr* **1** chairman **2** checkmate

chmn *or* **chn** *abbr* chairman

cho \'chō\ *n, pl* **cho** [Jap *chō*] : a Japanese unit of land measure equal to about 2½ acres

choak *obs var of* CHOKE

choan- *or* **choano-** *comb form* [NL, fr. Gk *choanē* funnel, fr. *chein* to pour — more at FOUND] : funnel : funnel-shaped opening or part ⟨*choan*ate⟩ ⟨*choano*cyte⟩

cho·a·na \'kōənə\ *n, pl* **choa·nae** \-ˌnē\ [NL, fr. Gk *choanē* funnel] **1** *anat* : a funnellike opening; *esp* : either of the posterior nares **2** : a collarlike contractile protoplasmic cup or rim surrounding the flagellum of certain flagellates and the endoderm cells of sponges

[1]cho·a·nate \-ˌnāt\ *adj* [*choan-* + *-ate*] : having a choana; *specif* : having internal nares — compare CHOANICHTHYES

[2]choanate \"\ *n* -s : a choanate fish : one of the Choanichthyes

cho·a·neph·o·ra \ˌkōə'nefərə\ *n, cap* [NL, fr. Gk *choanē* funnel + *-phora*] : a genus of fungi typifying the family Choanephoraceae

cho·a·neph·o·ra·ce·ae \-ˌnefə'rāsēˌē\ *n pl, cap* [NL, fr. *Choanephora,* type genus + *-aceae*] : a family of fungi (order Mucorales) with both sporangiophores and conidiophores swollen at their tips and with naked zygospores

cho·a·nich·thy·es \ˌkōə'nikthēˌēz\ *n pl, cap* [NL, fr. *choan-* + Gk *ichthyes,* pl. of *ichthys* fish — more at ICHTHUS] : a subclass of Teleostomi comprising fishes with internal nares that were dominant life-forms in the Devonian but are now nearly extinct and including the Crossopterygii and the aberrant Dipnoi — compare LATIMERIA — **cho·a·nich·thys** \-thə̇s\ *n, pl* **choa·nichthys**

cho·a·no·cy·tal \ˌkōə(ˌ)nōˌsīd·³l, kōˌanəˌs-\ *adj* : of or relating to a choanocyte

cho·a·no·cyte \'kōə(ˌ)nōˌsīt, kō'anəˌs-\ *n* -s [ISV *choan-* + *-cyte*] : one of the choanate and flagellate endodermal cells lining the cavity of a sponge

cho·a·no·flagellata \ˌkōə(ˌ)nō+\ *n pl, cap* [NL, fr. *choan-* + *Flagellata*] *in some classifications* : an order or other major division of Mastigophora comprising the choanoflagellates — compare LISSOFLAGELLATA

cho·a·no·flagellate \"+\ *n* -s [NL *Choanoflagellata*] : any of numerous small solitary or colonial aquatic flagellates constituting three families (Phalansteriidae, Codosigidae, and Bicosoecidae) of the order Protomonadina and distinguished from all other flagellates by possession of a contractile protoplasmic collar about the single anterior flagellum — compare CHOANOCYTE

cho·a·no·fla·gel·li·da \"+flə'jelədə\ [NL, fr. *choan-* + *flagellum* + *-ida*] *syn of* CHOANOFLAGELLATA

cho·a·no·fla·gel·li·dae \-ˌdē\ *n pl, cap* [NL, fr. *choan-* + *flagellum* + *-idae*] *in some esp former classifications* : a family comprising the choanoflagellates — invalid because it lacks a type

cho·a·noph·o·rous \ˌkōəˌnäf(ə)rəs\ *adj* [*choan-* + *-phorous*] : CHOANATE

cho·a·no·som·al \ˌkōə(ˌ)nōˌsōməl, kōˌanəˌs-\ *adj* : of or relating to a choanosome

cho·a·no·some \'kōə(ˌ)nōˌsōm, kō'anəˌs-\ *n* -s [*choan-* + *-some*] : the inner layer containing the choanocytes of a sponge

cho·a·no·tae·nia \ˌkōə(ˌ)nō'tēnēə\ *n, cap* [NL, fr. *choan-* + *Taenia*] : a genus of taenioid tapeworms including a number of intestinal parasites of birds that utilize various insects as intermediate hosts

cho·ate \'kōə̇t, 'kōˌāt\ *adj* [fr. *inchoate,* after such pairs as E *invisible: visible*] : COMPLETE

chob·dar \'chōbˌdär\ *n* -s [Hindi *cobdār,* fr. Per *chōbdār, chūbdār,* fr. *chōb, chūb* staff, wood (fr. MPer *chōp* wood) + *-dār* having] *India* : USHER, ATTENDANT

cho·bie \'chōbē\ *n* -s [origin unknown] : TRIPLETAIL

cho·ca·lho \shü'kal(ˌ)yü\ *n* -s [Pg, cowbell, rattle, fr. (assumed) VL *cloccaculum,* fr. ML *clocca* bell — more at CLOCK] : a Brazilian rattle commonly consisting of a gourd with its dried seeds inside or a metal sphere with pellets and used as a rhythm instrument

cho·chem \'k̲ȯk̲əm\ *n, pl* **cha·cha·mim** \ˌk̲äk̲ä'mēm\ *or* **cha·cho·mim** \k̲ä'k̲ȯmim\ *var of* HAKAM

[1]cho·cho \'chō(ˌ)chō\ *or* **cho·ko** \-(ˌ)kō\ *n* -s [AmerSp] : CHAYOTE

[2]cho·cho \'chō(ˌ)chō\ *n, pl* **chocho** *or* **chochos** *usu cap* [Sp, of AmerInd origin] **1 a** : a Popolocan people of northern Oaxaca, Mexico **b** : a member of such people **2 a** : a Popolocan people of southern Puebla, Mexico — called also *Popoloca* **b** : a member of such people **3** : the language of a Chocho people

[1]chock \'chäk\ *n* -s [origin unknown] **1** *also* **chuck** \'chək\ : a wedge or block (as of wood or metal) for steadying a body (as a cask or boat) and holding it motionless, or for filling in an unwanted space, or for blocking the movement of a wheel (as of a vehicle) **2** *Brit* : [8]COG 2 **3** : a heavy metal casting fitted usu. at the sides of the upper deck and at the bow and stern of a ship and having two short horn-shaped arms curving inward between which ropes or hawsers may pass for mooring or towing — compare [1]CLEAT 1b

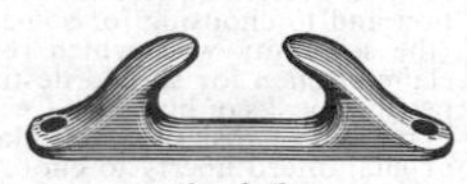
chock 3

[2]chock \"\ *vb* -ED/-ING/-S *vt* **1** : to provide, fit, stop, or make fast with or as if with chocks — often used with *off* **2** : to raise or support with chocks **3** : CHOKE ⟨caves and inlets ~*ed* up with cinders — Norman Douglas⟩ ~ *vi* : to fit closely — used with *in* or *into*

[3]chock \"\ *or* **chuck** \'chək\ *adv* : as close as possible ⟨~ aft⟩ ⟨~ up against the wall⟩ : as nearly or as completely as possible ⟨a wagon ~ full of chunks of wood⟩ — usu. used with another adverb or an adjective

[4]chock \"\ *n* -s [imit.] : a sharp somewhat hollow sound (as of wooden blocks striking together) ⟨the loud ~ of croquet balls⟩

[1]chock·a·block \ˌchäkəˌbläk\ *adj* [[1]*chock* + [1]*a-* + *block;* fr. the position of a tackle when hoisting has reached its limit, with both blocks touching] **1** : brought close together ⟨the two blocks of a tackle in hoisting or hauling are ~⟩ : fully hoisted : hauled tight **2** : very full : CROWDED, CRAMMED ⟨exhibition floors were ~ with racing and sports cars —*New Yorker*⟩

[2]chockablock \"\ *adv* : in a crowded or overflowing manner ⟨families living ~⟩

chock·er·man \'chäkə(r)mən\ *n, pl* **chockermen** [by alter.] : CHOKERMAN

chock–full *or* **chock·ful** \'chəkˌfu̇l, 'chäk-\ *or* **chuck–full** \'chək-\ *also* **choke–full** \'chōk-\ *adj* [ME *chokkefulle, chekefull,* prob. fr. *choken, cheken* to choke + *full*] : full to the extreme limit : CRAMMED ⟨the hotels were *chock-full*⟩ — compare [3]CHOCK

chockstone \'⸗ˌ⸗\ *n* -s [[1]*chock* + *stone*] : a mass of rock wedged in a mountain chimney

[1]cho·co \chə'kō\ *n, pl* **choco** *or* **chocos** *usu cap* [Sp *chocó, chocoa, chocoe,* of AmerInd origin] **1 a** : a people of northwestern Colombia and Panama **b** : a member of such people **2** : the language of the Choco people, prob. Cariban

[2]choco \'chä(ˌ)kō, 'chȯ-\ *n* -s [short for *chocolate soldier;* prob. fr. the new uniforms worn by recruits] *Austral* : a militiaman or a conscript in World War II

[1]choc·o·late \'chäklə̇t, 'chȯk- *also* -kəl-\ *n* -s [Sp, fr. Nahuatl *xocoatl,* perh. fr. *xococ* sour, bitter + *atl* water, drink] **1** : a food obtained by grinding roasted cacao beans that have been freed from germ and shell — sometimes called *plain chocolate, bitter chocolate, cooking chocolate;* see CACAO, COCOA **2** : a beverage made by cooking a portion of chocolate in water or milk **3** : a small candy with a center (as of fondant, nougat, or nut) and a coating of chocolate — distinguished from *bonbon* **4** : a variable color averaging a brownish gray that is deeper and slightly redder than taupe, redder and darker than mouse gray, and redder and deeper than castor **5** : a warm light brown approximating the color of fresh milk chocolate and occurring as a variant coat color in certain mammals (as the Siamese cat or the mink) **6** *also* **chocolate root** : WATER AVENS

[2]chocolate \"\ *adj* **1** : composed of chocolate : flavored or coated with chocolate **2** : of the color chocolate

chocolate–box \'⸗(⸗)⸗ˌ⸗\ *adj, of a painting* : superficially pretty or sentimental ⟨his fiancée wanted him to paint her, and always in a *chocolate-box* pose —L.S.Gannett⟩

chocolate brown *n* : a variable color averaging a dark grayish brown that is very slightly yellower and duller than African brown and redder than cordovan (sense 3a) — compare CHOCOLATE 4

chocolate cream *n* : a chocolate with a creamy fondant center

chocolate flower *n* : a wild geranium (*Geranium maculatum*)

chocolate house *n* : a public house or room serving chocolate

chocolate maroon *n* : OLD ROSELEAF

chocolate moth *n* : ALMOND MOTH

chocolate prune *n* : a prune dried to the color of chocolate

chocolate soldier *n* **1** : a soldier that does not fight **2** : [2]CHOCO

chocolate spot *n* : a disease of beans and other legumes caused by fungi of the genus *Botrytis* and characterized by brown spotting of leaves and stems and withering of shoots

chocolate tree *n* : a cacao (*Theobroma cacao*)

choc·o·laty \-lə̇d·ē, -ə̇tē, -i\ *adj* : made of or like chocolate

choc·taw \'chäkˌtȯ\ *n, pl* **choctaw** *or* **choctaws** *usu cap* [Choctaw *Chahta*] **1 a** : a Muskogean people of Mississippi, Alabama, and Louisiana **b** : a member of such people **2 a** : the language of the Choctaw and Chickasaw people **b** : strange or incomprehensible language : JARGON, GIBBERISH **3** *sometimes cap, in fancy skating* : a stroke forward on either edge of either skate followed by a stroke backward on the opposite edge of the other skate

choctaw beer *n, usu cap C* : a bootleg beer made in the southwestern U.S. during national prohibition

chode [ME, alter. (influenced by *rode,* past of *riden* to ride) of *chidde,* past of *chiden* to chide] *archaic past of* CHIDE

choe·ro·pus \'kirəpəs\ *syn of* CHAEROPUS

-choe·rus \'kirəs, 'kēr-\ *n comb form* [NL, fr. Gk *choiros* pig; akin to L *horrēre* to bristle — more at HORROR] : pig : piglike animal — in generic names in zoology ⟨Hydro*choerus*⟩

chof·fer \'chäfər\ *n* -s [alter. of ME *chaufour* — more at CHAFER] *Scot* : a portable heater or chafing dish

cho·ga \'chōgə\ *n* -s [Sindhi, of Altaic origin; akin to Turk *çuha* cloth] : a long-sleeved long-skirted cloak for men worn mainly in India and Pakistan

chog·set \'chägsə̇t, -gzə̇t\ *n* -s [of Algonquian origin; akin to Pequot *cachauxet* cunner, Natick *chohchohkesit* striped, spotted] : CUNNER b

[1]choice \'chȯis\ *n* -s [ME *chois,* fr. OF, fr. *choisir* to choose, of Gmc origin; akin to Goth *kausjan* to examine, test, *kiusan* to choose — more at CHOOSE] **1** : the act of choosing; *typically* : the voluntary and purposive or deliberate action of picking, singling out, or selecting from two or more that which is favored or superior : the decision reached by such action ⟨the ~ made by the voters⟩ ⟨Lincoln's ~ of Grant as general⟩ **2 a** : the right, privilege, opportunity, or faculty of freely choosing, picking out, or deciding : freedom to pick or decide : OPTION ⟨a captive has little ~⟩ **b** : situation demanding choosing or justifying consideration of alternatives ⟨there is no ~ between right and wrong⟩ **3 a** : a person, thing, part, way, or characteristic chosen, singled out, or favored typically as best or most likely, fit, or advantageous ⟨New York was the delegates' first ~ as capital⟩ **b** : an example, part, or instance worthy of being chosen as excellent or best : PRIME, PICK, FLOWER, CREAM, ELITE ⟨of the cavalry the king's own was the ~⟩ **c** : a person or thing available, fit, or likely to be picked out or designated ⟨several ~s for the nomination⟩ **4 :** a sufficient or ample number or variety for wide or free selection ⟨more ~ of fruits at the larger market⟩ **5 :** care and judgment in choosing : DISCRIMINATION ⟨pick words with ~⟩ **6 :** a dilemma involving a decision between alternatives; *also* **:** the one way, person, or thing to be preferred to another ⟨death or exile was the ~⟩

syn PREFERENCE, SELECTION, ELECTION, OPTION, ALTERNATIVE: CHOICE may suggest freedom in picking out, valuing, or deciding ⟨the oracle has no *choice;* it must produce an answer — W.D.Howells⟩ Specifically it may suggest individual modifications in obvious or logical criteria ⟨the *choice* of a cook not for their culinary skill but for her ability to make pretty dishes — Herbert Spencer⟩ PREFERENCE may heighten notions of personal bias, predilection, or individuality of judgment; it is less likely to suggest a single act of picking, choosing, or deciding ⟨a sterilization of the self, an elimination . . . of the human bias and *preference* —Lewis Mumford⟩ ⟨his *preferences* betray him more than his aversions —J.E.E.Acton-Dalburg⟩ SELECTION may suggest careful or wise judgment and discrimination in picking out from a sizable number ⟨when schools attempted, at least, to cultivate discrimination and to furnish the material on which *selection* can be founded —C.H.Grandgent⟩ ELECTION may refer to a definitive or formal choosing after deliberation and to choosing for some explicit role, duty, or function ⟨the solemnity with which religious and ideological groups claim *election* for special destinies beyond the grave or upon peculiar peaks of history —Cecil Sprigge⟩ In nontechnical uses in today's English OPTION is likely to suggest genuine conferred or guaranteed liberty to choose deliberately ⟨it was the privilege of the English parent to choose whether his children should be instructed or not . . . the Education Act of 1870 abolished this *option* —George Sampson⟩ ALTERNATIVE stresses the idea that things not chosen must necessarily be rejected and vice versa ⟨the necessary *alternative* was to deny it altogether —O.W.Holmes †1935⟩ Although objected to, it is quite common in situations involving more than two choices ⟨our three *alternatives* —T.E.Lawrence⟩ ⟨no third *alternative* —Walter Moberly⟩ ⟨other *alternatives* existed —Sidney Hook⟩ — **by choice** *or* **for choice :** by preference ⟨Austrian by birth and French *by choice* —A.E.Wier⟩ ⟨in the evening sat *for choice* without a light —H.W.Glover⟩; *also* **:** most usually ⟨hired outlaws *for choice* to skin and drive and cook for him on the buffalo range —W.S.Campbell⟩ — **of choice :** to be chosen first : PREFERRED, RECOMMENDED — used esp. of drugs and treatments

²choice \"\ *adj* -ER/-EST [ME *chois,* fr. *chois,* n.] **1 :** worthy of being chosen above others **:** of highest quality **:** without blemish, demerit, or disadvantage : FINE, SELECT ⟨Monseigneur . . . sat down alone to his sumptuous and ~ supper —Charles Dickens⟩ ⟨accepting *choicest* candidates⟩ ⟨stamps in ~ condition⟩ **2 :** well-chosen **:** selected by keen intuition or by care and deliberation **:** most appropriate ⟨sinister stories of Paris landlords . . . told . . . with singularly ~ words —F.M.Ford⟩ **3 a :** FASTIDIOUS, DISCRIMINATING ⟨~ of his food⟩ **b :** CAREFUL, FOND ⟨uncommon ~ over her daughters —*West Somerset Word Bk.*⟩ **4 a** *of meat and other products* **:** of highest or next highest quality **b** *of beef* **:** of a grade between prime and good

syn EXQUISITE, ELEGANT, RARE, RECHERCHÉ, DAINTY, DELICATE: CHOICE indicates preeminence or superiority and may or may not connote the idea of being selected ⟨as from the beds and borders of a garden *choice* flowers are gathered —William Wordsworth⟩ ⟨when education in America began, it was intended for the fit and designed to produce a *choice* type —C.H. Grandgent⟩ EXQUISITE implies near perfection, esp. in craftsmanship, and may also imply an especial appeal to the discriminating ⟨selected for their beauty . . . and beautified with the numerous Indian cosmetics, these girls were of the most *exquisite* loveliness —C.B.Nordhoff & J.N.Hall⟩ ⟨an *exquisite* skill of eye and hand which gave them their unique success in that artistic craftsmanship —C.W.Eliot⟩ ELEGANT applies to a refined luxury or richness restrained by good taste ⟨they [the Cavaliers] had more both of profound and of polite learning than the Puritans. Their tempers were more engaging . . . their tastes more *elegant* —T.B.Macaulay⟩ ⟨his trousers were extremely *elegant*, a light cloth, black and white check, hung on his legs —George Moore⟩ RARE, in this sense, may apply to any uncommon excellence ⟨the *rarest* cordials old monks ever schemed to coax from pulpy grapes —Amy Lowell⟩ ⟨nowhere else do we find such *rare* and costly marbles —H.T. Buckle⟩ RECHERCHÉ may apply to a studied opulent elegance ⟨the sangfroid, grace, abandon, and *recherché* nonchalance with which Charles Yates ushers ladies and gentlemen to their seats in the opera house —O.Henry⟩ DAINTY may apply to the graceful and fragile; it usually applies to what pleases the fastidious ⟨the touch is so light, the fancy so *dainty*, and the conceit so delicate that the poem remains immortally fresh and young —J.W.Draper⟩ ⟨this *dainty* and somewhat supercilious guest has been brought to the supper by a young Roman — Agnes Repplier⟩ DELICATE, in this sense, suggests subtlety and fineness and either sensuous or intellectual appeal ⟨the *delicate* fan tracery and crenellated molding of the screen —Dorothy Sayers⟩ ⟨not, however, an effervescing wine, although its *delicate* piquancy produced a somewhat similar effect — Nathaniel Hawthorne⟩ ⟨the exquisite transparency and *delicate* finish of her work —P.E.More⟩

choice–drawn *adj, obs* **:** chosen with care : PICKED

choice·less \-ləs\ *adj* **:** offering or permitting no choice **:** unable to choose

choice·ly \-lē, -i\ *adv* [ME *choisly,* fr. *chois,* adj. + *-ly*] **:** in a choice manner: **a :** with care in choosing : CAREFULLY, DISCRIMINATINGLY **b :** in a preferable or excellent manner : DAINTILY, EXQUISITELY

choice·ness \-nəs\ *n* -ES **:** the quality or state of being choice

choicy \'chȯisē, -si\ *adj, usu* -ER/-EST [¹*choice* + -*y*] *slang* **:** FASTIDIOUS, CHOOSY

¹choil \'chȯi(ə)l\ *n* -S [origin unknown] **:** the angle in a pocketknife blade at the junction of the wedge-shaped cutting part with the tang or the corresponding part of any knife

²choil \"\ *vt* -ED/-ING/-S **:** to form a choil on (a knife blade)

¹choir *also* **quire** \'kwī(ə)r, -īə\ *n* -S [ME *quer,* fr. OF *cuer,* fr. ML *chorus* body of singers in church, place for singers in church, fr. L, chorus, choral dance — more at CHORUS] **1 :** an organized company of singers esp. in church service **:** a choral society **:** a chorus or a subdivision of a chorus **2 :** a group of instruments of the same class (as in an orchestra) ⟨the wood-wind ~⟩ **3 :** an organized assemblage **:** a band of persons **:** a group or rank of things ⟨Illilouette Fall, one of the most beautiful of all the Yosemite ~ —John Muir †1914⟩ **4 :** an order or division of angels **5 :** a company of dancers or of dancers and singers **6 :** the part of a church appropriated to the singers: **a :** such a part separated from the nave on the one hand and the sanctuary on the other **b** *of a large church* **:** the entire section in which the choir (sense a) is situated **7 :** CHOIR ORGAN **8 :** a group organized for ensemble speaking — compare CHORAL SPEAKING

²choir *also* **quire** \"\ *vb* -ED/-ING/-S **:** to sing or sound in chorus or concert ⟨what company, in masks, can ~ it with the naked wind —Wallace Stevens⟩

³choir \"\ *adj* [¹*choir*] **:** specially deputed to community recitation or singing of the divine office — distinguished from *lay* ⟨~ nuns⟩

choir aisle *n* **:** an aisle flanking the choir of a church

choirboy \'=,=\ *n* **:** a boy member of a church choir — called also *chorister*

choir loft *n* **:** a gallery appropriated to a choir

choir manual *n* **:** the manual of a choir organ

choirmaster \'=,==\ *n* **:** the director of a choir (as in a church)

choi·ro·pot·a·mus \,kȯirō'pädəməs\ *syn of* KOIROPOTAMUS

choir organ *n* **:** a division of a pipe organ designed for accompanying singing

choir rail *n* **:** a rail enclosing the choir of a church

choir school *n* **:** a school for the general education of choirboys maintained by a cathedral or large church esp. of the Anglican Communion

choir screen *n* **1 :** a screen (as of ornamental woodwork or wrought iron) enclosing the choir (sense 6a) **2 :** the part of a choir screen that closes the western end of the choir and separates it from the crossing or the nave

choir stall *n* **:** a seat in the choir of a church enclosed wholly or partly at the back and sides and often canopied and elaborately carved

choir wall *n* **:** a wall enclosing the choir (sense 6a) often built in between the columns surrounding the choir

choirwise \'=,=\ *adv* [¹*choir* + *-wise*] **:** by choirs : ANTIPHONALLY

¹choke \'chōk\ *vb* -ED/-ING/-S [ME *cheken, choken,* alter. of *acheken, achoken,* fr. OE *aceōcian* to suffocate, strangle — more at CHEEK] *vt* **1 :** to make normal breathing difficult or impossible for (a person or animal) (1) by compressing the throat with strong external pressure ⟨an unwary guard *choked* to death by a murderous prisoner⟩, (2) by obstructing or clogging the windpipe ⟨a fish bone *choking* a kitten⟩, (3) by poisoning (as with gas) or otherwise adulterating air being breathed ⟨gas fumes were *choking* the rescue squad⟩, or (4) through nervous agitation ⟨rage *choked* him as he tried to speak⟩ **2 :** to check, suppress, or repress expression or delivery of (as an utterance) ⟨a cloture rule designed to ~ off discussion⟩ ⟨trying to ~ down my laughter⟩ **:** suppress or check manifestation of (as an emotion) ⟨~ down his rage⟩; *also* **:** to check or suppress utterance by (as a speaker) **:** shut up : SILENCE ⟨the moderator could not ~ her off⟩ ⟨fear of . . . punishment may often ~ those who would otherwise speak out —Zechariah Chafee⟩ — often used with *off, back, down* **3 a :** to check or stop the growth, development, activity, or vitality of with or as if with forceful constriction ⟨antagonism to an environment whose complications are *choking* his life —C.D.Lewis⟩ **b :** to check or obstruct flow, motion, progress, or other activity through (as a pipe) by clogging, congesting, crowding, filling densely, or sometimes external constriction ⟨the drifting ice which *choked* the bay —R.E.Byrd⟩ ⟨the channels are nearly *choked* with weeds and reeds —C.S. Forester⟩ ⟨the hallway . . . was *choked* with rubbish —Liam O'Flaherty⟩ **c :** to fill completely or chock-full : PACK, GLUT, JAM ⟨windows were *choked* with the merchandise of a summer sale —William McFee⟩ **4 :** to make a choke in (as a cartridge or the barrel of a shotgun) **5 :** to check or stop the motion or action of (as a cable, rudder, or machine) by clogging or jamming **6 :** to enrich the fuel mixture of (a motor) by partially shutting off the air intake of the carburetor **7** *sports* **:** to grip (a bat, club, racket, or stick) some distance from the end of the handle **:** shorten one's grip on (a bat or other implement) in order to alter the effective length — often used with *up* ⟨the power hitter seldom ~s up his bat very much⟩ ~ *vi* **1 :** to suffer from interference with breathing typically by having the windpipe obstructed or irritated with resulting throat spasms ⟨we *choked* in the dust of the desert —T.B.Costain⟩ ⟨he *choked* on a fish bone⟩ **2 :** to become obstructed, stopped, or checked by or as if by constriction or obstruction ⟨the words *choked* in his throat —Sir Walter Scott⟩ **3 :** to shorten one's grip on the handle of a bat or similar implement **syn** see SUFFOCATE

²choke \"\ *n* -S **1 a :** the act of choking : SUFFOCATION **:** partial or complete obstruction that prevents the passage of air through the throat to the lungs **b chokes** *pl* **:** caisson disease when marked by suffocation — used with *the* **2 :** an obstruction to passage or flow: **a :** a valve for choking a gasoline engine **b :** a constriction in an outlet (as of a gas or oil well) to limit the flow **c :** REACTOR 3 **3 a :** a narrowing of the bore immediately before the muzzle of a shotgun that serves to concentrate the shot pellets as they leave the muzzle of the gun **b :** an attachment that allows variation of muzzle constriction of a shotgun **4 :** the filamentous or scaly center of an artichoke head **5 :** an interference with the development of the inflorescence of certain grasses caused by growth of the cattail fungus while the flowers are still in the leaf sheath **6** *in judo* **:** an application of pressure on the jugular vein

³choke \"\ *adj* [¹*choke*] *sports* **:** shortening the effective length of (a bat, racket, or club) ⟨a ~ grip⟩ **:** using a shortening grip ⟨a ~ hitter⟩

⁴choke \"\ *n* -S [ME, perh. fr. ON *kjālki* jawbone; akin to *kjölr* keel — more at KEEL] *chiefly Scot* **:** JAW, CHEEK, NECK — usu. used in pl.

chokeberry \'=,==\ *n* [so called fr. the bitter taste] **1 :** the small berrylike astringent fruit of any plant of the genus *Aronia* **2 :** a plant of the genus *Aronia*

¹chokebore \'=,=\ *n* [²*choke* + *bore*] **1 :** ²CHOKE 3 **2 :** a shotgun with a choke

²chokebore \"\ *vt* -ED/-ING/-S **:** to provide with a choke

³chokebore \"\ *adj, of a dog* **:** having a keen accurate nose

chokecherry \'=,==\ *n* [so called fr. the bitter taste] **1 a :** a common cherry (*Prunus virginiana*) of eastern No. America **b :** a cherry (*P. demissa*) of the western U.S. **c :** BLACK CHERRY 2 **2 :** the astringent fruit of any chokecherry

choke coil *n* **:** REACTOR 3

choke collar *n* **:** a collar that may be tightened as a noose used esp. in training and controlling powerful or fractious dogs

choked *past of* CHOKE

chokedamp \'=,=\ *n* **:** BLACKDAMP

choked disk \chōkt-\ *n* **:** swelling and protrusion of the optic disk caused by edema and occurring in various diseases, esp. brain tumor — called also *papilledema*

choke–full *var of* CHOCK-FULL

choke pear *n* **1 a :** a pear with an astringent taste **b :** CHOKEBERRY **2** *obs* **:** a sarcasm by which one is put to silence **:** something that cannot be answered

choke point *n* **1 :** THROAT 2f(3) **2 :** BOTTLENECK

¹chok·er \'chōkə(r)\ *n* -S [¹*choke* + *-er*] **1 :** one that chokes **2 :** something worn closely about the throat or neck: **a :** a wide neckcloth; *esp* **:** STOCK **b :** a formal white necktie **c :** a very high usu. stiffened collar **d :** a short necklace or jeweled collar **e :** a narrow fur piece for women **3 :** a noose of wire rope for hauling a log

²choker \"\ *adj* **:** worn closely about the throat or neck ⟨~ beads⟩

chok·ered \'chōkə(r)d\ *adj* **:** wearing a choker

chok·er·man \'chōkə(r)mən\ *n*, pl **chokermen :** one who puts chokers around logs and gets them ready for hauling — called also *choker setter*

chokes *pres 3d sing of* CHOKE, *pl of* CHOKE

chokestrap \'=,=\ *n* [alter. of *checkstrap*] **:** a checkstrap on a horse's harness

choke up *vi* **1 :** to become or feel constricted in the throat (as from a strong emotion) ⟨rising to answer their tribute he *choked up* and could not utter a word⟩ **2** *of an athlete or performer* **:** to become hampered by nervousness or overeagerness (as in competition)

¹cho·key \'chōkē\ *n* -S [Hindi *caukī,* dim. of *cauk* market place, fr. Skt *catuṣka* consisting of four, quadrangular, fr. *catur* four — more at FOUR] **1** *India* **:** a station or post esp. for collection of customs or for palanquin bearers or police **2** *slang Brit* **:** JAIL, LOCKUP

²chokey *var of* CHOKY

cho·ki·dar \'chōkē,där\ *n* -S [Hindi *caukīdār,* fr. *caukī* police station, guard's post + *-dār* possessing — more at CHOKEY] *India* **:** WATCHMAN; *esp* **:** a private watchman (as at a gate)

choking *adj* [fr. pres. part. of ¹*choke*] **1 :** producing the feeling of strangulation ⟨a ~ cloud of dust⟩ **2 :** indistinct in utterance —used esp. of the voice of a person affected with strong emotion — **chok·ing·ly** *adv*

choking coil *n* **:** REACTOR

chokmah *usu cap, var of* HOKHMAH

choko *var of* CHOCHO

cho·kra \'chōkrə\ *n* -S [Hindi *chokrā*] *India* **:** a boy employed as a servant

chok·we \'chäkwē\ *n, pl* **chokwe** *or* **chokwes** *usu cap* [Chokwe] **1 a :** a scattered people of the southern Congo and northern Angola noted for the religious masks that they produce **b :** a member of such people **2 :** a Bantu language of the Chokwe people closely related to or perhaps a dialect of Lwena

choky *or* **chok·ey** \'chōkē, -ki\ *adj* **chokier; chokiest** [¹*choke* + *-y*] **1 :** tending to choke or suffocate **:** having power to choke ⟨the air was ~ with wood smoke⟩ **2 :** inclined or having a tendency to choke — used esp. of one moved by strong emotion

chol \'chōl\ *n, pl* **chol** \"\ *or* **cho·les** \-ō,lās\ *usu cap* [Sp, of AmerInd origin] **1 a :** an Indian people of northern Chiapas, Mexico **b :** a member of such people **2 :** a Mayan language of the Chol people

chol- *or* **chole-** *or* **cholo-** *comb form* [Gk *chol-, cholē-, cholo-,* fr. *cholē, cholos* — more at GALL] **:** bile **:** gall ⟨*cholane*⟩ ⟨*cholelith*⟩ ⟨*chologenetic*⟩

cho·la \'chōlə, -,lä\ *n* -S [AmerSp, fem. of *cholo*] **:** a woman of mixed Spanish and Indian ancestry

cholaemia *var of* CHOLEMIA

chol·a·gog·ic \¦kälə¦gäjik, -ōl-\ *adj* **:** being a cholagogue **:** inducing a flow of bile

chol·a·gogue \'kälə,gäg, -ōl-\ *n* -S [F, fr. Gk *cholagōgos,* leading off bile, fr. *chol-* + *-agōgos* -agogue] **:** an agent that promotes an increased flow of bile — compare CHOLERESIS

cho·lam \'chōləm\ *n* -S [Tamil *cōḷam*] *India* **:** GRAIN SORGHUM

cho·lane \'kō,lān\ *n* -S [*chol-* + *-ane*] **:** a crystalline steroid hydrocarbon $C_{24}H_{42}$ from which the bile acids are derived

cholangiogram \kō'l+an . . .\ *n* -S [ISV *chol-* + *angiogram*] **:** a roentgenogram of the bile ducts made after the ingestion or injection of a radiopaque substance

chol·an·gi·o·graph·ic \kō¦lanjēə¦grafik\ *adj* [ISV *cholangiography* + *-ic*] **:** of or relating to cholangiography

chol·an·gi·og·ra·phy \=,=='ägrəfē\ *n* -ES [ISV *chol-* + *angiography*] **:** roentgenographic visualization of the bile ducts after ingestion or injection of a radiopaque substance

chol·an·gi·ole \kō'lanjē,ōl\ *n* -S [NL *cholangiola*] **:** a bile canaliculus

chol·an·gi·o·lit·ic \=¦==ə¦lid·ik\ *adj* [NL *cholangiolitis* + E *-ic*] **:** relating to or involving cholangiolitis ⟨~ cirrhosis⟩

chol·an·gi·o·li·tis \=,==='līd·əs\ *n, pl* **cholangiolit·i·des** \-'lid·ə,dēz\ [NL, fr. *cholangiola* bile canaliculus (fr. *chol-* + *angi-* + L *-ola* -ole) + *-itis*] **:** inflammation of bile capillaries

chol·an·gi·o·ma \kō,lanjē'ōmə\ *n, pl* **cholangiomas** \-məz\ *also* **cholangioma·ta** \-məd·ə\ [NL, fr. *chol-* + *angioma*] **:** carcinoma of a bile duct

chol·an·gi·tis \,kō,lan'jīd·əs\ *n, pl* **cholangit·i·des** \-'jid·ə,dēz\ [NL, fr. *chol-* + *angitis*] **:** inflammation of one or more bile ducts

cho·lan·ic acid \(')kō¦lanik-\ *n* [ISV *chol-* + *-an-* + *-ic*] **:** a colorless crystalline acid $C_{23}H_{39}COOH$ some of whose hydroxy and keto derivatives constitute the bile acids

chol·an·threne \kō'lan,thrēn\ *n* -S [*chol-* + *-anthrene*] **:** a pale yellow crystalline pentacyclic carcinogenic hydrocarbon $C_{20}H_{14}$ that can be made from deoxycholic acid; 7,8-ethylene-benz[a]anthracene — compare METHYLCHOLANTHRENE

cho·late \'kō,lāt\ *n* -S [*chol-* + *-ate*] **:** a salt or ester of cholic acid

chole- — see CHOL-

c–hole \'=,=\ *n, usu cap C* [so called fr. its shape] **:** the sound hole in the body of viols and guitars

cho·le·ate \'kōlē,āt\ *n* -S [prob. fr. G *choleat,* fr. *chol-* + *-at* -ate] **:** a salt or ester of choleic acid

cho·le·cal·cif·er·ol \,kōlə,kal'sifə,rōl, ,käl-, -rōl\ *n* -S [ISV *chol-* + *calci-* + *-fer* + *-ol*] **:** VITAMIN D_3

cho·le·cyst \'kōlə,sist, 'käl-\ *also* **cho·le·cys·tis** \,=='sistəs\ *n, pl* **cholecysts** [NL *cholecystis,* fr. *chol-* + *-cystis*] **:** GALLBLADDER — **cho·le·cys·tic** \¦==¦=tik\ *adj*

cho·le·cys·tec·to·my \,==si'stektəmē\ *n* -ES [ISV *cholecyst* + *-ectomy*] **:** surgical excision of the gallbladder

cho·le·cys·ti·tis \-'stīd·əs\ *n, pl* **cholecystit·i·des** \-'stid·ə,dēz\ [NL, fr. *cholecystis* + *-itis*] **:** inflammation of the gallbladder

cho·le·cys·to·gram \-'sistə,gram\ *n* -S [*cholecyst* + *-o-* + *-gram*] **:** a roentgenogram of the gallbladder made after ingestion or injection of a radiopaque substance

cho·le·cys·to·graph·ic \¦==,==¦grafik\ *adj* [ISV *cholecystography* + *-ic*] **:** of or relating to cholecystography

cho·le·cys·tog·ra·phy \,=,='stägrəfē\ *n* -ES [ISV *cholecyst* + *-o-* + *-graphy*] **:** the roentgenographic visualization of the gallbladder after ingestion or injection of a radiopaque substance

cho·le·cys·to·ki·nin \,==,sistə'kīnən\ *n* -S [*cholecyst* + *-o-* + Gk *kinein* to move + E *-in*] **:** a hormone produced in the mucosa of the upper intestine that stimulates contraction of the gallbladder

cho·le·cys·tos·to·my \,==,si'stästəmē\ *n* -ES [ISV *chol-* + *cystostomy* "operation into the bladder", fr. *cyst-* + *-stomy*] **:** surgical incision of the gallbladder usu. to effect drainage

cho·le·doch \'kōlə,däk, 'käl-\ *or* **cho·le·doch·al** \¦==¦däkəl, kə'ledəkəl\ *adj* [*choledoch* fr. NL *choledochus,* fr. Gk *cholēdochos,* fr. *cholē* bile + *dochos* containing; *choledochal* fr. *choledoch* + *-al;* akin to Gk *dechesthai* to receive, *dokein* to seem good — more at GALL, DECENT] **:** conveying bile ⟨the ~ duct is the common bile duct⟩

cho·led·o·cho·li·thi·a·sis \kə¦ledə(,)kōlə'thīəsəs\ *n* [NL, fr. *choledochus* + *-o-* + *lithiasis*] **:** a condition marked by presence of calculi in the gallbladder and common bile duct

cho·led·o·chos·to·my \=,=='kästəmē; ,kōlə,dä'k-, ,kälə-\ *n* -ES [*choledoch-* + *-o-* + *-stomy*] **:** surgical incision of the common bile duct usu. to effect drainage

cho·led·o·chus \kə'ledəkəs\ *n, pl* **choledo·chi** \-,kī, -,kē\ [NL, short for *ductus choledochus* choledoch duct] **:** the common bile duct

cho·le·glo·bin \¦kōlə¦glōbən, ¦käl-\ *n* -S [*chol-* + *globin*] **:** a green pigment that occurs in bile, is a combination of globin and a ferric salt of biliverdin, and is formed by breakdown of hemoglobin

cho·le·ic \kə'lēik, kō-\ *adj* [ISV *chol-* + *-ic*] **:** of, relating to, or derived from bile

choleic acid *n* **:** DEOXYCHOLIC ACID; *also* **:** a molecular compound of this acid (as with a fatty acid or a hydrocarbon)

cho·le·lith \'kōlə,lith, 'käl-\ *n* -S [ISV *chol-* + *-lith*] **:** GALLSTONE

cho·le·li·thi·a·sis \,kōlələ'thīəsəs, ,kä-\ *n* [NL, fr. *chol-* + *lithiasis*] **1 :** the production of gallstones ⟨stasis and inflammation usu. precede ~⟩ **2 :** an abnormal state characterized by the presence of gallstones ⟨the obese are particularly subject to ~⟩

cho·le·mia *or* **cho·lae·mia** \kō'lēmēə\ *n* -S [NL, fr. *chol-* + *-emia, -aemia*] **:** the presence of excess bile in the blood usu. indicative of liver disease — **cho·lem·ic** \-mik\ *adj*

cho·lent \'chȯlənt, 'chəl- *also* 'sh-\ *n* -S [Yiddish *tsholnt, tshont, shalet, shalent*] **:** a Jewish Sabbath-day dish of slow-baked meat and vegetables

cho·le·poi·e·sis \,kōlə,pȯi'ēsəs, ,käl-\ *n, pl* **cholepoie·ses** \-ē,sēz\ [NL, fr. *chol-* + Gk *poiēsis* creation, manufacture, fr. *poiein* to make — more at POET] **:** production of bile — compare CHOLERESIS — **cho·le·poi·et·ic** \¦==,=¦ed·ik\ *adj*

chol·er \'kälə(r), 'kōl-\ *n* -S [ME *coler,* fr. MF *colere,* fr. L *cholera* bilious disease, fr. Gk, fr. *cholē* bile; akin to IrGael *galar* disease — more at GALL] **1 a** *archaic* **:** YELLOW BILE **b** *obs* **:** BILE 1a **2** *obs* **:** BILIOUSNESS **3 :** IRASCIBILITY **:** ready disposition to anger and irritation ⟨my ~ rising at the virulence of her invective —Ellery Sedgwick⟩

chol·era \'kälərə *also* -lrə\ *n* -S *often attrib* [ME *colera* bile, fr. ML, fr. L *cholera* bilious disease] **:** any of several diseases of man and domestic animals usu. marked by severe gastrointestinal symptoms: as **a :** ASIATIC CHOLERA **b :** FOWL CHOLERA **c :** HOG CHOLERA

cholera belt *n* **:** a flannel or wool band or cincture around the waist

chol·er·a·ic \¦kälə¦rāik\ *also* **chol·er·ic** \'kälərik; kə'lerik, kä'-, -rēk\ *adj* [*cholera* + *-ic*] **:** relating to, resulting from, or resembling cholera

cholera in·fan·tum \-in'fantəm\ *n* [NL, lit., cholera of infants] **:** an acute noncontagious intestinal disturbance of infants formerly common in congested areas of high humidity and temperature but now rare

cholera mor·bus \-'mȯrbəs, -ȯ(ə)b-\ *n* [NL, lit., the disease cholera] **:** a gastrointestinal disturbance characterized by griping, diarrhea, and sometimes vomiting and usu. resulting from overeating or from contaminated foods

cholera vib·rio \-'vibrē,ō\ *n* [NL] **:** the bacterium (*Vibrio comma*) that causes Asiatic cholera

cho·le·re·sis \,kōlə'rēsəs, ,käl-\ *n, pl* **choleres** \-ē,sēz\ [NL, fr. *chol-* + *-resis* (modif. — influenced by such words as *diuresis*— of Gk *rhysis* flowing) — more at STREAM] **:** the flow of bile from the liver esp. when increased above a previous or normal level — compare CHOLAGOGUE, CHOLEPOIESIS

¹cho·le·ret·ic \¦==¦red·ik\ *adj* [fr. NL *choleresis,* after such pairs as NL *diuresis:* E *diuretic*] **:** of or relating to choleresis

2**cho·le·ret·ic** \¦≈≈¦red·ik\ *n* -s : an agent that induces choleresis

1**chol·er·ic** \'käl̇ərik; kə'lerik, kä'-, -rēk; *sometimes* 'kōlərik\ *adj* [ME *colerik*, fr. MF *colerique*, fr. L *cholericus* bilious, fr. Gk *cholerikos*, fr. *cholera* + *-ikos* -ic] **1** *obs* : having yellow bile as the predominating bodily humor; *also* : having the bodily conformation and temperament thought to be characteristic of such predominance **2 a** : easily moved to anger : HOT-TEMPERED, IRASCIBLE ⟨where melancholic men abandon effort, men of the ~ type take to kicking and smashing —H.G.Wells⟩ ⟨a ~ disposition⟩ **b** : ANGRY, IRATE, WRATHFUL ⟨a ~ outburst⟩ ⟨the book is clear, convinced and combative, even ~ in places —*Times Lit. Supp.*⟩ **syn** see IRASCIBLE

2**choleric** *var of* CHOLERAIC

chol·er·i·cal·ly \-lərəklē, -li; -lerək(ə)l-, -rēk-\ *or* **cho·ler·ic·ly** \-rəklē, -rēk-, -li\ *adv* : in a choleric manner

chol·er·i·form \'käl(ə)rə,fȯrm\ *adj* [ISV *cholera* + *-iform*; prob. orig. formed as F *cholériforme*] : resembling cholera

choles *pl of* CHOL

cho·les·tane \kə'le,stān\ *n* -s [*cholest*erol + *-ane*] : a crystalline saturated steroid hydrocarbon $C_{27}H_{48}$ obtained from cholesterol by reduction

cho·les·ta·nol \-,stə,nȯl, -ōl\ *n* -s [ISV *cholestane* + *-ol*; orig. formed in G] : a monohydroxy alcohol $C_{27}H_{47}OH$ derived from cholestane

cho·les·te·a·to·ma \kə,lestēə'tōmə, ,kōlə,stē-, ,kälə,-\ *n, pl* **cholesteatomas** \-məz\ *or* **cholesteatoma·ta** \-məd·ə\ [NL, fr. *chol-* + *steatoma*] **1** : an epidermoid cyst usu. in the brain arising from aberrant embryonic rests and appearing as a compact shiny flaky mass — called also *pearly tumor* **2** : a tumor usu. growing in a confined space (as the middle ear or mastoid) and often as a sequel to chronic otitis media

cho·les·tene \kə'le,stēn\ *n* -s [ISV *cholest*erol + *-ene*] : any of several crystalline hydrocarbons $C_{27}H_{46}$ differing from cholestane by having one double bond in the molecule, 5-cholestene being the parent hydrocarbon of cholesterol

cho·les·ter·ic \kə'lestərik; ¦kōlə¦ster-, ¦käl-\ *adj* [F *cholestérique*, fr. *cholestér*ine cholesterin + *-ique* -ic] **1** : of, relating to, or resembling cholesterol or its derivatives **2** : of, relating to, or being the phase of a liquid crystal characterized by arrangement of molecules in layers with the long molecular axes parallel to one another in the plane of each layer and incrementally displaced in successive layers to give helical stacking — compare NEMATIC, SMECTIC

cho·les·ter·in \kə'lestərən\ *n* -s [F *cholestérine*, fr. *chol-* + *stérine*, fr. Gk *stereos* solid + F *-ine* -in — more at STARE] : CHOLESTEROL

cho·les·ter·ol \-,rȯl, -,rōl\ *n* -s [ISV *cholester*in + *-ol*] : a

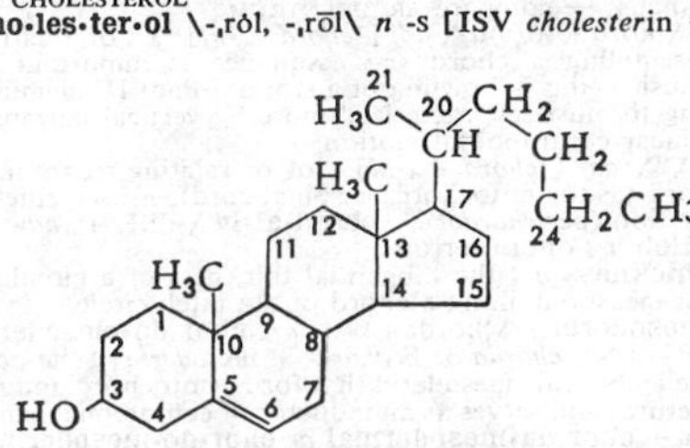

cholesterol

fat-soluble crystalline steroid alcohol $C_{27}H_{45}OH$ that occurs as an essential constituent of animal cells and body fluids, is important in physiological processes, has been implicated experimentally as a factor in arteriosclerosis, is synthesized in the body esp. in the liver and adrenal cortex, is usu. extracted from beef spinal cord and wool grease, and is used in the synthesis of vitamin D_3 and steroid hormones (as testosterone) and in the making of ointments and lotions — compare STRUCTURAL FORMULA

cho·les·ter·ol·emia *also* **cho·les·ter·ol·ae·mia** \kə,lestə(,)rȯ'lēmēə, -(,)rō'-\ *or* **cho·les·ter·emia** *or* **cho·les·ter·ae·mia** \kə,lestə'rēmēə\ *n* -s [NL, fr. ISV *cholesterol* + NL *-emia, -aemia*] : the presence of cholesterol in the blood

cho·les·ter·o·sis \kə,lestə'rōsəs\ *n, pl* **cholestero·ses** \-ō,sēz\ [NL, fr. ISV *cholesterol* + NL *-osis*] : abnormal deposition of cholesterol (as in blood vessels or gallbladder)

cho·les·ter·yl \kə'lestərəl, -,rēl\ *n* -s [ISV *cholester*in + *-yl*] : the radical $C_{27}H_{45}$ formed by removal of the hydroxyl group from cholesterol

chol hamoed *sometimes cap, var of* HOL HAMOED

cho·li \'chōlē\ *n* -s [Hindi *colī*, fr. Skt *cola*, *coḍa*, prob. of Dravidian origin; akin to Tamil *coli* bark, Malayalam *toli*] : a short-sleeved bodice with a very low neckline worn esp. in India

cho·li·amb \'kōlē,am(b)\ *or* **cho·li·am·bus** \,kōlē'ambəs\ *n, pl* **choliambs** \-,amz\ *or* **choliam·bi** \-'am,bī, -(,)bē\ [LL *choliambus*, fr. Gk *choliambos*, fr. *chōlos* lame + *iambos* iamb] : a quantitative iambic trimeter verse of six feet having a spondee or trochee in the last foot — called also *scazon*

cho·li·am·bic \¦kōlē¦ambik\ *adj* [LL *choliamb*us choliamb + E *-ic*] : of or belonging to a choliamb : consisting of choliambic lines

cho·lic acid \'kōlik-, -äl-\ *n* [Gk *cholikos*, fr. *chol-* + *-ikos* -ic] : a crystalline bile acid $C_{23}H_{36}(OH)_3COOH$ obtained by hydrolysis of taurocholic or glycocholic acid; 3,7,12-trihydroxy-cholanic acid

cho·line \'kō,lēn, 'kä-\ *n* -s [ISV *chol-* + *-ine*, *-in*; orig. formed as G *cholin*] : a crystalline or syrupy liquid base $(CH_3)_3N(CH_2CH_2OH)OH$ that is widely distributed among animal and plant products, in which it is combined in lecithins, that can be made synthetically, that constitutes a vitamin of the B complex and is essential to the metabolism of fat esp. in the liver, and that is used in the form of its salts in the treatment of certain liver disorders and in the feeding of animals, esp. poultry; (β-hydroxyethyl)-trimethyl-ammonium hydroxide — compare ACETYLCHOLINE

cho·lin·er·gic \¦kōlə¦nərjik, -äl-\ *adj* [ISV acetyl*choline* + *erg-* (fr. Gk *ergon* work) + *-ic* — more at WORK] **1** *of autonomic nerve fibers* **a** : liberating acetylcholine **b** : activated by acetylcholine — compare ADRENERGIC **2** : resembling acetylcholine or simulating its physiologic action **3** : involving or induced by the physiologic action of acetylcholine — **cho·lin·er·gi·cal·ly** \-jək(ə)lē\ *adv*

cho·lin·es·ter·ase \,kōlə'nestə,rās, -äl-, -āz\ *also* **choline esterase** *n* -s [*choline* + *esterase*] **1** : ACETYLCHOLINESTERASE **2** : an enzyme that hydrolyzes choline esters and that is found in blood plasma and in the liver in man — compare CHOLINERGIC; see ANTICHOLINESTERASE

chol·la \'chȯiə; 'chōyə, -(,)yä\ *n* -s [MexSp, fr. Sp, head, perh. fr. OF dial. *cholle* ball, of Gmc origin; akin to MHG *kiule* club, *kūle* ball, ON *kūla* knob, ball, OE *cēol* ship — more at KEEL] : any of several arborescent very spiny cacti of the southwestern U.S. and Mexico esp. of the genus *Opuntia* (as *O. cholla*)

chol·ler \'chälə(r)\ *n* -s [fr. (assumed) ME, fr. OE *ceolor* throat; akin to OHG *kelur* throat, OE *ceole* — more at KEEL] *dial Brit* : the flesh on the lower jaw esp. when fat and hanging : DOUBLE CHIN

cho·lo \'chō(,)lō\ *n* -s [AmerSp] **1** *sometimes cap* : a Spanish-American Indian; *esp* : an acculturated Quechuan of Peru and Bolivia **2** : a person of mixed Spanish and Indian blood : MESTIZO **3** *Southwest* : a lower-class Mexican or person of Mexican ancestry — often used disparagingly

cholo- — see CHOL-

cho·loe·pus \kō'lēpəs\ *n, cap* [NL, irreg. fr. LGk *chōlopous* lame-footed, fr. Gk *chōlos* lame + *pous* foot — more at FOOT] : the genus consisting of the two-toed sloth

cho·lón \chə'lōn\ *also* **cho·lo·na** \-nə\ *n, pl* **cholón** \-ōn\ *or* **cholo·nes** \-ō,nās\ *also* **cholonas** \-ōnəz\ *usu cap* [Sp, of AmerInd origin] : a language family of central Peru consisting of two dialects — **cho·lo·nan** \-ōnən\ *adj, usu cap*

chol·uria \kōl'yu̇rēə, kō'lü-, kä-,kə-\ *n* -s [NL, fr. *chol-* + *-uria*] : presence of bile in urine

chomer *var of* HOMER

chometz *var of* HAMETZ

chomp \'chämp, 'chȯmp\ *vb* [alter. of *champ*] *vt* : to chew or bite on : CHAMP ~ *vi* : to chew or bite on something

1**chon** \'chōn\ *n, pl* **chon** [Korean] **1** : a Korean subsidiary unit of value equal to 1/100 won or 1/100 hwan — see MONEY table **2** : a coin representing one chon

2**chon** \"\ *n, pl* **chon** *or* **chons** *usu cap* [Sp *chona*, of AmerInd origin] **1** : a language family of southern Argentina and Tierra del Fuego comprising the languages spoken by the Tehuelche and the Ona people **2 a** : a people speaking a Chonan language **b** : a member of any such people — **cho·nan** \'chōnən\ *adj, usu cap*

chondr- *or* **chondri-** *or* **chondro-** *comb form* [NL, fr. Gk *chondr-*, *chondro-*, fr. *chondros* grain, cartilage — more at GRIND] **1** : cartilage : cartilaginous and ⟨*chondr*ectomy⟩ ⟨*chondr*ify⟩ ⟨*chondro*-osseous⟩ ⟨*chondro*cele⟩ **2** : grain ⟨*chondr*ite⟩

chon·dral \'kändrəl\ *adj* [*chondr-* + *-al*] : of or relating to cartilage or a cartilage

chon·dre \'kändə(r)\ *n* -s [Gk *chondros* grain, cartilage] : CHONDRULE

chondri *pl of* CHONDRUS

1**chondri-** — see CHONDR-

2**chondri-** *or* **chondrio-** *comb form* [G, fr. Gk *chondrion* small grain, dim. of *chondros*] : grain : granular ⟨*chondrio*some⟩ ⟨*chondrio*somal⟩ ⟨*chondrio*cont⟩ ⟨*chondri*ome⟩

chon·dric \'kändrik\ *adj* [*chondr-* + *-ic*] : CHONDRAL, CARTILAGINOUS

chon·drich·thi·an \kän'drikthēən\ *n* -s [NL *Chondrichthyes* + E *-ian*] : a member of the class Chondrichthyes : an elasmobranch fish

chon·drich·thy·es \-thē,ēz\ *n pl, cap* [NL, fr. *chondr-* + Gk *ichthyes*, pl. of *ichthys* fish — more at ICHTHUS] : a class comprising cartilaginous fishes with well-developed jaws and including the sharks, skates, and rays, chimaeras, and extinct related forms — *compare* AGNATHA, CYCLOSTOMI, PLACODERMI

chon·dri·fi·ca·tion \,kändrəfə'kāshən\ *n* -s [*chondr-* + *-fication*] : formation of or conversion into cartilage

chon·dri·fy \'kändrə,fī\ *vb* -ED/ -ING/ -ES [*chondr-* + *-ify*] *vt* : to convert into cartilage ~ *vi* : to become converted into cartilage

chon·dril·la \kän'drilə\ *n, cap* [NL, fr. L *chondrille*, fr. Gk *chondrilē*] : a genus of Old World herbs (family Compositae) having large basal mostly pinnatifid leaves, small stem leaves, and few-flowered heads with spinulose achenes — see GUM SUCCORY

chon·drin \'kändrən\ *n* -s [*chondr-* + *-in*; orig. formed in G] : a horny substance obtainable from cartilage and similar to and often associated with gelatin — compare CHONDROMUCOID

chon·drio·cont \'kändrēō,känt\ *n* -s [ISV *chondri-* + *-cont* (fr. Gk *kontos* pole); orig. formed as G *chondriokont* — more at -KONT] : a rod-shaped or fibrillar chondriosome

chon·drio·gene \-,jēn\ *n* -s [ISV *chondri-* + *-gene*] : a hypothetical cytoplasmic determiner responsible for maintaining the continuity of mitochondria

chon·drio·kinesis \¦kändrē(,)ō+\ *n, pl* **chondriokineses** [NL, fr. *chondri-* + *kinesis*] : division of the chondriome

chon·dri·ome \'kändrē,ōm\ *also* **chon·dri·o·ma** \,≈≈'ōmə\ *n* -s [ISV *chondri-* + *-ome*; orig. formed as G *chondriom*] : the chondriosomes of a cell regarded as a functional unit

chon·drio·mere \'kändrēō,mi(ə)r\ *n* -s [ISV *chondri-* + *-mere*; orig. formed as G *chondriomer*] : the chondriosomal portion of a sperm cell

chon·drio·mite \-,mīt\ *n* -s [ISV *chondri-* + Gk *mitos* thread; orig. formed as G *chondriomit* — more at DIMITY] : a chain of granular chondriosomes; *also* : one such chondriosome

chon·drio·som·al \¦kändrēō¦sōməl\ *adj* : of or relating to chondriosomes or the chondriome

chon·drio·some \'≈≈≈,sōm\ *n* -s [ISV *chondri-* + *-some*; orig. formed as G *chondriosom*] *biol* : any of a class of minute granular, rodlike, or threadlike apparently self-perpetuating lipoprotein complexes in the cytoplasm of most cells that are thought to function in cellular metabolism and secretion : MITOCHONDRION

chon·drio·sphere \-,sfi(ə)r\ *n* -s [ISV *chondri-* + *sphere*; orig. formed as G *chondriosphäre*] : a large or aggregated spherical chondriosome

chon·drite \'kän,drīt\ *n* -s [ISV *chondr-* + *-ite*; orig. formed as G *chondrit*] : a meteoric stone characterized by the presence of chondrules

chon·drit·ic \(')kän¦drid·ik\ *adj, of minerals* : relating to or having the granular structure characteristic of chondrites : GRANULAR

chondro- *in pronunciations below*, ¦≈≈ = ¦kändrō *or* -rə\ — see CHONDR-

chon·dro·blast \'≈≈,blast\ *n* -s [ISV *chondr-* + *-blast*] : a cell that produces cartilage — **chon·dro·blas·tic** \¦≈≈¦blastik\ *adj*

chon·dro·clast \'≈≈,klast\ *n* -s [ISV *chondr-* + *-clast*] : a cell that absorbs cartilage — compare OSTEOCLAST

chon·dro·coc·cus \,≈≈'käkəs\ *n, cap* [NL, fr. *chondr-* + *-coccus*] : a genus of chiefly soil-inhabiting and dung-inhabiting myxobacteria including one (*C. columnaris*) causing columnaris disease of trout and salmon

chon·dro·costal \¦≈≈+\ *adj* [ISV *chondr-* + *costal*] : of or relating to the costal cartilages and the ribs

chon·dro·cranium \¦≈≈+\ *n, pl* **chondrocrania** [*chondr-* + *cranium*] : the cartilaginous cranium; *also* : the part of the adult skull derived therefrom — compare OSTEOCRANIUM

chon·dro·cyte \'≈≈,sīt\ *n* -s [*chondr-* + *-cyte*] : a cartilage cell

chon·dro·dite *also* **con·dro·dite** \'≈≈,dīt\ *n* -s [Sw *kondrodit*, fr. Gk *chondrōdēs* granular (fr. *chondros* grain) + *-it* -ite — more at CHONDR-] : a mineral $(Mg,Fe)_3SiO_4(OH,F)$ consisting of basic silicate of magnesium and sometimes iron belonging to the humite group and found in certain metamorphic rocks

chon·dro·dit·ic \¦≈≈¦did·ik\ *adj, of minerals* : characterized by the presence of chondrodite ⟨a ~ limestone⟩

chon·dro·dys·pla·sia \¦≈≈də'splāzh(ē)ə\ *n* -s [NL, fr. *chondr-* + *dys-* + *-plasia*] : a hereditary skeletal disorder characterized by the formation of exostoses at the epiphyses and resulting in arrested development and deformity — called also DYSCHONDROPLASIA

chon·dro·dystrophia \¦≈≈+\ *n* -s [NL, fr. *chondr-* + *dystrophia*] : ACHONDROPLASIA

chon·dro·dystrophic \¦≈≈+\ *adj* [ISV *chondrodystrophy* + *-ic*] : characterized by chondrodystrophy

chon·dro·dystrophy \¦≈≈+\ *n* -ES [ISV *chondr-* + *dystrophy*] : ACHONDROPLASIA

chon·dro·ganoidei \¦≈≈+\ [NL, fr. *chondr-* + *Ganoidei*] *syn of* CHONDROSTEI

chon·dro·genesis \¦≈≈+\ *n, pl* **chondrogeneses** [ISV *chondr-* + *genesis*] : the development of cartilage — **chon·dro·genetic** \"+\ *adj*

chon·dro·gen·ic \¦≈≈¦jenik\ *or* **chon·drog·e·nous** \(')kän¦dräjənəs\ *adj* [*chondr-* + *-genic*, *-genous*] : CHONDROGENETIC

chon·drog·e·ny \kän'dräjənē\ *n* -ES [*chondr-* + *-geny*] : CHONDROGENESIS

chon·dro·glos·sus \,≈≈ *at* CHONDRO- + 'gläsəs\ *n, pl* **chondroglos·si** \-ä,sī, -(,)sē\ [NL, fr. *chondr-* + *-glossus* (fr. Gk *glōssa* tongue) — more at GLOSS] : a muscle arising from the lesser cornu of the hyoid bone and blending with the intrinsic muscles of the tongue

chon·droid \'kän,drȯid\ *adj* [*chondr-* + *-oid*] : resembling cartilage

chon·dro·it·ic acid \¦kändrə¦wid·ik-\ *n* [ISV *chondroitic* (fr. *chondr-* + *-itic*) + *acid*; orig. formed as G *chondroitsäure*] : CHONDROITINSULFURIC ACID

chon·dro·i·tin \kän'drōətən\ *n* -s [ISV *chondroit*ic + *-in*; orig. formed in G] : a gummy nitrogenous polysaccharide acid occurring as chondroitinsulfuric acid

chon·dro·i·tin·sulfuric acid \"+. . .-\ *n* [*chondroitin* + *sulfuric*] : a white amorphous acid found esp. in cartilage that is a derivative of glucuronic acid and chondrosamine and constitutes the polysaccharide portion of one class of mucoproteins

chon·drol·o·gy \kän'dräləjē\ *n* -ES [F *chondrologie*, fr. *chondr-* + *-logie* -logy] : the branch of anatomy that treats of cartilages

chon·dro·ma \kän'drōmə\ *n, pl* **chondromas** \-məz\ *also* **chondroma·ta** \-məd·ə\ [NL, fr. *chondr-* + *-oma*] : a benign tumor containing the structural elements of cartilage — compare CHONDROSARCOMA — **chon·drom·a·tous** \(')kän¦drämədəs, -ōm-\ *adj*

chon·dro·mucoid \¦≈≈ *at* CHONDRO- +\ *n* -s [ISV *chondr-* + *mucoid*; orig. formed as G *chondromukoid*] : a white amorphous substance obtainable from the matrix of cartilage and consisting of a protein that resembles gelatin and is combined with chondroitinsulfuric acid — compare CHONDRIN

chon·dro·my·ces \,≈≈+'mī,sēz\ *n, cap* [NL, fr. *chondr-* + *-myces*] : a genus of saprophytic myxobacteria (family Polyangiaceae) occurring in soil or on decaying organic matter

chon·dro·pha·ryn·ge·us \¦≈≈+fə'rinjēəs, *or* ,farən¦jēəs\ *n, pl* **chondropharyn·gei** \-ē,ī\ [NL, fr. *chondr-* + *pharyngeus* pharyngeal (fr. *pharynx*)] : the muscle arising from the lesser cornu of the hyoid bone and forming part of the middle constrictor of the pharynx

chon·droph·o·ra \kän'dräfərə\ *n pl, cap* [NL, fr. *chondr-* + *-phora*] *in some classifications* : a suborder of Decapoda comprising the squids

chon·dro·phore \'≈≈ *at* CHONDRO-+,fō(ə)r\ *n* -s [*chondr-* + *-phore*] : a cavity or process that supports the internal hinge cartilage of the shell of a bivalve mollusk

chon·dro·phyte \'≈≈,fīt\ *n* -s [ISV *chondr-* + *-phyte*] : an outgrowth or spur of cartilage

chon·dro·plast \'≈≈,plast\ *n* -s [*chondr-* + *-plast*] : CHONDROBLAST

chon·dro·protein \¦≈≈+\ *n* -s [ISV *chondr-* + *protein*] **1** : any of various glycoproteins (as chondromucoid) that yield on hydrolysis chondroitinsulfuric acid and a protein **2** : any glycoprotein whose carbohydrate radical is combined with sulfuric acid — not used systematically

chon·drop·te·ryg·ii \,kän,dräptə'rijē,ī\ *n pl, cap* [NL, fr. *chondr-* + *-pterygii*] *in former classifications* : a group of fishes including the elasmobranchs, sturgeons, and lampreys

chon·dro·sa·mine \kän'drōsə,mēn, -,mən\ *n* -s [ISV *chondr-* + *osamine*] : an amino sugar $H(CHOH)_4CH(NH_2)CHO$ obtained from chondroitinsulfuric acid and related compounds; 2-deoxy-2-amino-D-galactose

chon·dro·sarcoma \¦≈≈ *at* CHONDRO- +\ *n, pl* **chondrosarcomas** *also* **chondrosarcomata** [NL, fr. *chondr-* + *sarcoma*] : a sarcoma containing cartilage cells rarely arising as a primary neoplasm but more frequently developing as a secondary growth by malignant degeneration of a chondroma

chon·dro·septum \¦≈≈+\ *n* -s [NL, fr. *chondr-* + *septum*] : the part of the nasal septum formed of cartilage

chon·dro·sin \'kändrəsən\ *n* -s [G, fr. Gk *chondros* grain, cartilage + G *-in* — more at GRIND] : a gummy nitrogenous monobasic acid with strong reducing power obtained by hydrolysis of chondroitin

chon·dro·sis \kän'drōsəs\ *n, pl* **chondro·ses** \-ō,sēz\ [NL, fr. *chondr-* + *-osis*] : CHONDROGENESIS

chon·dro·skeleton \¦≈≈+\ *n* [*chondr-* + *skeleton*] **1** : a cartilaginous skeleton **2 a** : the cartilaginous parts of a skeleton **b** : the parts of a bony skeleton that originated in cartilage

1**chon·dros·te·an** \(')kän¦drästēən\ *adj* [NL *Chondrostei* + E *-an*] **1** : having a cartilaginous skeleton **2** : of or relating to the Chondrostei

2**chondrostean** \"\ *n* -s : one of the Chondrostei

chon·dros·tei \kän'drästē,ī\ *n pl, cap* [NL, fr. *chondr-* + *-ostei* (pl. of *-osteus*)] : an order of Teleostomi comprising fishes having a largely cartilaginous skeleton and skin that is scaleless or bears bony bucklers and including the sturgeons, paddlefishes, and extinct related fishes — compare GLANIOSTOMI, SELACHOSTOMI

chon·dro·sternal \¦≈≈ *at* CHONDRO- +\ *adj* [*chondr-* + *sternal*] : of or relating to the costal cartilages and sternum

chon·dro·xiphoid \¦≈≈+\ *adj* [*chondr-* + *xiphoid*] : connecting a costal cartilage and the xiphoid process

chon·drule \'kän,drül\ *n* -s [NL *chondr*us (mineral) + E *-ule*] : a rounded granule of cosmic origin usu. consisting of enstatite or chrysolite and occurring embedded more or less abundantly in the mass of many meteoric stones and sometimes free in marine sediments

chon·drus \'kändrəs\ *n* [NL, fr. Gk *chondros* grain, cartilage] **1** *pl* **chon·dri** \-,drī\ : CHONDRULE **2** *cap* : a small genus of red algae (family Gigartinaceae) having rather coarse branching fronds **3** *pl* **chondri** : IRISH MOSS 1

chong·jin \'chȯŋ¦jin\ *adj, usu cap* [fr. *Chongjin*, No. Korea] : of or from the city of Chongjin, No. Korea : of the kind or style prevalent in Chongjin

chon·ju \'jȯn¦jü\ *adj, usu cap* [fr. *Chonju*, So. Korea] : of or from the city of Chonju, So. Korea : of the kind or style prevalent in Chonju

chonk \'chȯŋk\ *vt* -ED/-ING/-S [alter. of *chomp*] *dial* : to chew energetically : CHAMP

cho·no \'chō(,)nō\ *n, pl* **chono** *or* **chonos** *usu cap* [Sp, of AmerInd origin] **1** : an extinct Indian people that formerly inhabited the Chonos archipelago and the adjacent coast of Chile **2** : a member of the Chono people — **cho·no·an** \'chōnəwən\ *adj or n, usu cap*

cho·no·lith \'kōnə,lith, -än-\ *n* -s [Gk *chōnē* mold, crucible (fr. *chein* to pour) + E *-o-* + *-lith* — more at FOUND] : an intrusive igneous rock mass of wholly irregular form

cho·no·trich \-,trik\ *n* -s [NL *Chonotricha*] : one of the Chonotricha

cho·not·ri·cha \kō'nä·trəkə\ *n pl, cap* [NL, fr. *chono-* (irreg. fr. Gk *chonnos* copper cup) + *-tricha*] : a small order of euciliate protozoans that are commensal on the surface of aquatic invertebrates, have a more or less vasiform body with reduced ciliation and complex terminal peristome, and reproduce by budding and in some cases by conjugation — **cho·not·ri·chous** \-kəs\ *adj*

chon·ta \'chäntə, -ȯn-\ *n* -s [AmerSp, fr. Quechua *chunta* palm tree] **1** : any of several palms with hard durable wood used in making implements and weapons: as **a** : any of various tropical American palms of the genera *Guilielma* and *Astrocaryum* — compare TUCUM **b** : a palm (*Juania australis*) of the southern Pacific **2** *also* **chontawood** \-,≈\ : the wood of a chonta

chon·tal \chȯn·'täl\ *n, pl* **chontal** \"\ *or* **chonta·les** \-ä,lās\ *usu cap* [Sp, fr. Nahuatl *chontalli* stranger] **1 a** : an Indian people of the state of Tabasco, Mexico **b** : a member of such people **2** : a Mayan language of the Chontal people **3** : TEQUISTLATEC

chon·ta·qui·ro \,chäntə'kē(,)rō, -ȯn-\ *n* -s *usu cap* [Sp *chontaquiro*, *chontapiro*, of AmerInd origin] : PIRO

choo-choo \'chü,chü\ *n* -s [imit.] : LOCOMOTIVE, TRAIN

chook \'chu̇k, -ük\ *n* -s [imit.] *chiefly Austral* : CHICKEN

chookchie *usu cap, var of* CHUKCHI

chook·ie \'chu̇ki, -üki\ *n* -s [*chook* + *-ie*] *slang Brit* : a child or young person; *specif* : SWEETHEART

choop \'chüp\ *n* -s [prob. of Scand origin; akin to Icel (dial.) *kjupa* hip of the rose, Icel *hjupa*, OE *hēope* — more at HIP] *dial Brit* : the hip of the wild rose

1**choose** \'chüz\ *vb* **chose** \'chōz\ **cho·sen** \'chōzᵊn\ *or obs* **chose**; **choosing**; **chooses** [ME *chesen*, *chosen*, *chusen*, fr. OE *cēosan*; akin to OHG *kiosan* to choose, ON *kjōsa*, Goth *kiusan* to choose, test, L *gustare* to taste, enjoy, Gk *geuesthai* to taste, Skt *juṣate* he enjoys, tastes, loves] *vt* **1 a** : to select (as one thing over another) esp. with free will and by exercise of judgment ⟨~ the lesser of two evils⟩ **b** : to decide upon esp. by vote : ELECT ⟨the town twice *chose* him as mayor⟩ **2 a** : to consider or assume as fitting, proper, or advantageous esp. from personal preference ⟨for recreation he ~*s* tennis and swimming⟩ **b** : to be inclined to (as by arbitrary decision or personal preference) — often used with the infinitive ⟨I do not ~ to enter into particulars —Tobias Smollett⟩ **3** *now dial* : to wish to have : WANT ⟨the landlady now returned to know if we did not ~ a more genteel apartment —Oliver Goldsmith⟩ ~ *vi* **1** : to make a selection ⟨he may ~ as best he can⟩ **2** *archaic* : to do as one pleases ⟨if you will not have me, ~ —Shak.⟩ **3** : to take an alternative — used only after *can* in the negative ⟨they go because they cannot ~⟩ and often followed by *but* plus infinitive ⟨he can't ~ but to listen⟩ **4** : to see fit : have the inclination ⟨you can take them all if you ~⟩

2**choose** \"\ *n* -s [ME *chose*, alter. (influenced by *chosen* to choose) of *chois* choice] **1** *obs* : SELECTION **2** *dial* : turn to choose : CHOICE

choos·er \-zə(r)\ *n* -s [ME *cheser,* fr. *chesen* to choose + *-er*] **1 :** one that chooses **2** *archaic* **:** VOTER, ELECTOR

choose up *vt* **:** to form (sides) for a game esp. by having opposing captains choose their players ~ *vi* **:** to form sides for a game ⟨let's *choose up* and play ball⟩

choosy *or* **choos·ey** \'chüzē, -zi\ *adj* **choos·i·er; choos·i·est** [1*choose* + *-y*] **:** fastidiously selective **:** PARTICULAR ⟨~ with food⟩ **:** hesitant or reluctant esp. in accepting or receiving ⟨pretty ~ about making new friends⟩ **:** difficult to satisfy ⟨~ customers⟩

1**chop** \'chäp\ *vb* **chopped; chopped; chopping; chops** [ME *choppen,* var. of *chappen* — more at CHAP (to split)] *vt* **1 a :** to cut into or esp. through with or as if with a heavy implement (as an ax or cleaver) usu. by a forceful slanting blow ⟨~ off a length of rope⟩ or by a series of such blows ⟨~ down a tree⟩ **b :** to mince, dice, or cut into small pieces ⟨*chopped* vegetables⟩ — often used with *up* ⟨~ the meat up⟩ **2 :** to work at or labor over with a heavy cleaving or hewing implement ⟨~ wood⟩; *specif* **:** to weed and thin out (young cotton) usu. with a hoe **3 a** *obs* **:** to thrust quickly and forcibly **:** STICK, DART **b :** to hit or strike (as a ball in tennis, baseball, or cricket) esp. with a short quick downward glancing blow — compare DRIVE 10 **4 :** to cut metal from the corner posts of (an automobile) to lower the body profile ⟨~ a top⟩ ⟨~ a sedan⟩ **:** cut metal from (part of an automobile) to reduce weight ⟨~ a flywheel⟩ — compare 2CHANNEL 1c **5 a :** to reduce the power, influence, or extent of — usu. used with *down* **b :** to retard or close (an airplane throttle) with a sudden motion **:** diminish or shut off the flow of fuel to (an airplane engine) ~ *vi* **1 :** to strike with or as if with a heavy implement (as an ax or cleaver) using a forceful slanting blow or a series of such blows ⟨he was *chopping* at an old stump⟩ **2** *archaic* **:** to go, come, or make some movement suddenly or violently **:** SWOOP, POUNCE ⟨the hawk ~*s* upon its prey⟩ **:** intervene or interpose **:** INTERRUPT — used with *in* or *into* ⟨~ into a conversation⟩ **3** *now dial* **:** to break open in fissures **:** CHAP **4 :** to strike something (as a ball in tennis, baseball, or cricket or an opponent in boxing) with a chopping blow **5** *of a hound* **:** to bay in chops **syn** see CUT

2**chop** \"\ *n* -s [ME *choppe,* fr. *choppen,* v.] **1 a :** a forceful often slanting blow made with or as if with a heavy implement (as an ax or cleaver) **:** a cutting stroke **:** SWIPE ⟨the prowler took a ~ at the dog with his stick⟩ **b :** a sharp downward blow (as in boxing) or stroke (as in baseball and tennis) **2** *archaic* **:** a crack or cleft (esp. on the lips and hands, on stone, or in the crust of dry earth **3 :** a small slice or cut of meat often including a part of a rib and usu. served individually — see LAMB illustration **4 :** a cut or indentation made by or as if by a cleaving or hewing stroke ⟨a hoe ~⟩ ⟨we left ~*s* in every tenth tree to mark the trail⟩ **5 :** material that has been chopped up: as **a :** ground or chopped feed usu. of one or more cereal grains or by-products — often used in pl. ⟨milo ~*s*⟩ ⟨corn ~*s*⟩ **b :** crushed unbolted particles of grain that are the product of an individual break in milling (as in the milling of flour) **c chops** *pl* **:** slices of apple that are usu. of inferior grade (as culls) and are dried by evaporation **6 a :** a short abrupt motion (as of waves) **:** CHOPPINESS **b :** a stretch of choppy sea; *esp* **:** one caused by a current or tide opposed in direction to the wind or to another current **7 :** the sharp clipped bay of a hound **8 :** 1CHERRY 7

3**chop** \"\ *vb* **chopped; chopped; chopping; chops** [ME *choppen,* var. of *chappen* — more at CHAP (to barter)] *vt* **1** *dial Eng* **:** TRADE, SWAP ⟨~ horses⟩ **2** *obs* **:** to bandy back and forth **:** EXCHANGE ~ *vi* **1** *obs* **:** to make an exchange **:** BARTER **2** *obs* **:** to bandy words **:** answer back **3 a :** to change direction ⟨the wind *chopped* round to the north⟩ **b :** veer or change with or as if with the wind ⟨the next day he *chopped* about and accepted the plan he had previously rejected⟩ — **chop logic :** to make unnecessary distinctions or dispute with an affected use of logical terms

4**chop** \"\ *n* -s [var. of 5*chap*] **1 :** JAW — now used only in the pl. ⟨his ~*s* fell in astonishment⟩ **2 chops** *pl* **a :** MOUTH ⟨he never opens his ~*s* unless someone speaks to him⟩ **b :** the fleshy covering of the jaws **:** the jowls or chaps ⟨the fox left the henyard licking his ~*s*⟩ — sometimes sing. of the flews of a dog ⟨a bulldog with a fine ~⟩ **3 chops** *pl* **:** the passage into something (as the straits leading to a large body of water, the entrance to a valley, the muzzle of a cannon) **4 a :** 5CHAP 2 **b :** either of a pair of metal jaws that grip the end of the pendulum suspension spring in a pendulum clock **5 chops** *pl, slang* **:** EMBOUCHURE, LIP ⟨the trumpet player had no ~*s* after a bout with pneumonia⟩

5**chop** \"\ *vt* **chopped; chopped; chopping; chops 1** *obs* **:** to seize with the jaws and eat **:** SNAP **2** *Brit* **:** to come upon and kill (prey) esp. without chase ⟨the hounds *chopped* the fox in its covert⟩

6**chop** \"\ *n* -s [Hindi *chāp* stamp, brand] **1** *in the India and China trade* **a :** a seal or its impression **:** an official stamp **b :** a license rendered valid by a seal **:** PERMIT, CLEARANCE — see GRAND CHOP **2 a :** a mark used on goods or coins in the China trade to indicate nature or quality **b :** a particular kind, brand, or lot of goods bearing the same chop **c :** quality, class, or grade ⟨first-*chop* tea⟩ ⟨an author of the first ~⟩

7**chop** \"\ *vt* **chopped; chopped; chopping; chops 1** *in the China trade* **:** to attest the legality of ⟨~ passengers⟩ ⟨~ a ship's papers⟩ **2 :** to stamp (a coin) with a seal or indentation usu. as evidence of legality — used esp. of coins often of non-Oriental origin circulated in China ⟨a *chopped* dollar⟩

8**chop** \"\ *n* -s [prob. native word in W. Africa] *slang Brit* **:** FOOD — used chiefly in African colonial areas

cho·pa \'chōpə, -äpə\ *n* -s [Sp, fr. Pg *choupa,* fr. L *clupea,* a fish] **:** any of several rudderfishes (family Kyphosidae)

1**chop and change** *vi* [ME *choppen and chaungen* to barter, fr. *choppen* to chop (barter) + *and* + *chaungen* to change, exchange] **1** *archaic* **:** to buy and sell **2 :** to change esp. pointlessly or capriciously ⟨a book which, however fashions may *chop and change,* must hold its place among the great English novels —Virginia Woolf⟩

2**chop and change** *n, pl* **chops and changes :** CHANGE, FLUCTUATION, VICISSITUDE ⟨the *chops and changes* of a political career⟩

cho·part's joint \(')shō¦pärz-\ *n, usu cap C* [after François *Chopart* †1795 French surgeon] **:** a tarsal joint comprising the talonavicular and calcaneocuboid articulations

chop box *n* [8*chop*] **:** a box used in Africa (as on a safari) to transport food

chop–cherry *n* [5*chop*] *obs* **:** a game of trying to catch a suspended cherry between the teeth

chop–chop \'chäp¦chäp\ *adv* [pidgin E, fr. a Chin dial. word akin to Cant *kap⁴kap⁴*] **:** QUICKLY, PROMPTLY

chop·dar \'chōp,där\ *var of* CHOBDAR

chop dollar *n* [6*chop*] **:** a chopped dollar — see 7CHOP 2

chopfallen *var of* CHAPFALLEN

chop hill *n* [prob. fr. 1*chop*] *in Nebraska* **:** SAND HILL

chop·house \'chäp,haüs, -ä,paüs\ *n* [2*chop* (cut of meat)] **:** RESTAURANT

cho·pi *or* **cho·pe** \'chōpē\ *n, pl* **chopi** *or* **chopis** *or* **chope** *or* **chopes** *usu cap* **1 a :** a Bantu-speaking people of northern Mozambique on the borders of Tanganyika **b :** a member of such people **2 :** a Bantu language of the Chopi people

chop·in \'chäpən\ *n* -s [ME, fr. MF *chopine,* a liquid measure, fr. MLG *schōpe, schōpen* scoop, ladle or MD *schoepe* scoop — more at SCOOP] **:** an old Scottish unit of liquid capacity equal to half a Scottish pint or about an English quart

cho·pine \chō'pēn, 'chäpən\ *n* -s [MF *chapin,* fr. OSp *chapín,* prob. of imit. origin] **:** a woman's shoe of the 16th and 17th centuries having a high often stiltlike sole designed to increase stature and protect the feet from mud and dirt — compare 1PATTEN 1

1**chop·log·ic** \'=,==\ *n* [3*chop*] **1 :** involved and often specious argumentation **2** *obs* **:** an absurdly argumentative person

2**choplogic** \"\ *also* **choplogical** \'=,===\ *adj* **:** given to complex often erroneous and absurd argumentation ⟨a ~ speech⟩

chop mark *n* [6*chop*] **:** an indentation or stamp made (as by a Chinese banking or business firm) on a coin to attest weight, silver content, or legality — see 6CHOP 2a — **chop–marked** *adj*

1**chopped** *past of* CHOP

2**chopped** *var of* CHAPPED

1**chop·per** \'chäpə(r)\ *n* -s [1*chop* + *-er*] **1 a :** a person who cuts something (as wood) off, up, or into segments (as with an ax or knife); *specif* **:** a logger that fells and lops trees **b :** a person who chops or cuts into segments with a machine-driven implement (as a slaughterhouse worker who operates a meat-chopping machine or a worker who operates a machine that cuts fur from pelts) **2 :** an implement (as an ax or knife) or mechanical device worked by machine or by hand and designed to chop or cut into segments: as **a :** a tool for thinning out plants in drills **b** (1) **:** any domestic or commercial tool that chops food (2) **choppers** *pl, slang* **:** TEETH **c** *or* **chopper tool :** a stone tool with a handhold end rounded or unfinished and a lower end chipped to an edge which in the early Paleolithic of Asia takes the place of the biface hand ax of Europe **3 :** a meat animal not esp. suitable for sale in fresh butcher's cuts — used of an overweight or aged hog in Australia and New Zealand or an aged ewe in poor to moderate flesh in the U.S. **4 :** a device that interrupts an electric current, a beam of light, or other radiation at short regular intervals **5 :** a canary having a song with loud trills, each component note being distinct — distinguished from *roller* **6 :** a gangster armed with a machine gun; *also* **:** a gangster's machine gun **7** *slang* **:** HELICOPTER

2**chopper** \"\ *n* -s [Hindi *chappar* sloping thatch, thatched roof, shed, hut, tester of a bed, fr. Skt *chattvara* house] **:** a thatched roof

chopper cot \-,kät\ *n* [Hindi *chappar-khāṭ,* fr. *chappar* tester of a bed + *khāṭ* bedstead — more at COT] *India* **:** a bedstead having curtains

chop·pi·ness \'chäpēnəs, -pin-\ *n* -ES **:** the quality or state of being choppy

1**chopping** *adj* [fr. pres. part. of 1*chop*] **1 :** characterized by fits and starts **:** JERKY ⟨a ~ manner of speaking⟩ **2 a** (1) **:** having a tumbling dashing movement ⟨a ~ tide⟩ (2) **:** breaking in short abrupt waves ⟨a ~ sea⟩ **b :** shifting or changing suddenly ⟨a ~ wind⟩ **3** *archaic* **:** large and vigorous **:** STRAPPING

2**chopping** *n* -s [fr. gerund of 1*chop*] **:** an area where trees are being felled or have been felled

chopping block *n* **:** a wooden block on which material (as meat, wood, or vegetables) is cut, split, or diced

chopping knife *n* **:** a knife often with a crescent-shaped blade for chopping or mincing (as meat or vegetables)

1**chop·py** \'chäpē, -pi\ *adj* -ER/-EST [2*chop* (crack) + *-y*] **:** 1CHAPPED 1 ⟨her ~ finger laying upon her skinny lips —Shak.⟩

2**choppy** \"\ *adj* -ER/-EST [2*chop* (of waves) + *-y*] *of the wind* **:** repeatedly veering about **:** CHANGEABLE, VARIABLE

3**choppy** \"\ *adj* -ER/-EST [1*chop* + *-y*] **1 :** somewhat chopping ⟨a ~ sea⟩ ⟨a ~ lake⟩ **2 a :** interrupted by ups and downs ⟨~ countryside⟩ **b :** abrupt in transition **:** JERKY ⟨a ~ style⟩ **c :** marked by poorly integrated components **:** DISCONNECTED ⟨a ~ novel⟩

chops *pl of* CHOP, *pres 3d sing of* CHOP

1**chop·stick** \'=,=\ *n* [perh. fr. 1*chop* + *stick*] **:** the crosspiece (as of wire or whalebone) from which the hooks hang on a deep-sea fishing line

2**chopstick** \"\ *n* [pidgin E, fr. *chop* fast (fr. a Chin dial. word akin to Cant *kap*) + E *stick;* trans. of Chin (Cant) *faai tsź*] **:** one of a pair of slender sticks held between the thumb and fingers of one hand and used chiefly in Oriental countries to lift food to the mouth

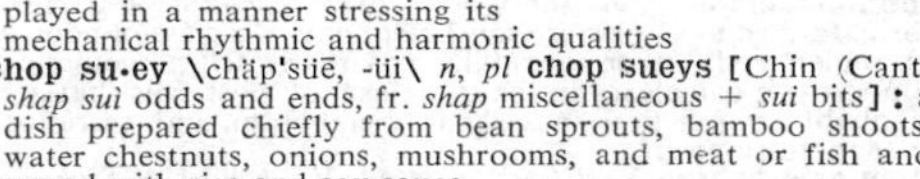

chopsticks

chop·sticks \'=,=\ *n pl but sing in constr* [perh. fr. pl. of 2*chopstick;* fr. the manner of playing with straight fingers] **:** music played in a mechanical or expressionless way; *esp* **:** a simple old fast waltz for four hands played in a manner stressing its mechanical rhythmic and harmonic qualities

chop su·ey \chäp'süē, -üi\ *n, pl* **chop sueys** [Chin (Cant) *shap sui* odds and ends, fr. *shap* miscellaneous + *sui* bits] **:** a dish prepared chiefly from bean sprouts, bamboo shoots, water chestnuts, onions, mushrooms, and meat or fish and served with rice and soy sauce

chop·tank \'chäp,taŋk\ *n, pl* **choptank** *or* **choptanks** *usu cap* [perh. fr. *Choptank* river, Maryland, where they settled] **1 :** an Algonquian people once resident on the Choptank river in Maryland — compare NANTICOKE **2 :** a member of the Choptank people

cho·pun·nish \chō'pənish\ *n, pl* **chopunnish** *or* **chopunnishes** *usu cap* [perh. modif. of Nez Percé *Tsútpēli*] **:** NEZ PERCÉ

chor- *or* **choro-** *comb form* [L, fr. Gk *chōr-, chōro-,* fr. *chōros* place, clear space; akin to Gk *chēros* left, bereaved — more at HEIR] **:** place **:** land ⟨*chor*episcopus⟩ ⟨*choro*logy⟩

cho·rag·ic \kə'rajik\ *adj* [Gk *choragikos, chorēgikos,* fr. *choragos, chorēgos*] **:** of or relating to a choragus; *esp* **:** honoring a successful choragus ⟨a ~ monument⟩

cho·ra·gus \kə'rāgəs\ *or* **cho·re·gus** \-rē-\ *also* **cho·ra·gos** -rā,gäs, -gəs\ *n, pl* **chora·gi** \-,jī, -,gī\ *or* **choraguses** \-gəsəz\ *or* **chore·gi** \-,jī, -,gī\ *or* **choreguses** \-gəsəz\ *also* **chora·goi** \-,gȯi\ [L & Gk; L *choragus,* fr. Gk *choragos, chorēgos,* fr. *choros* chorus + *-agos, -ēgos* (fr. *agein* to lead) — more at CHORUS, AGENT] **1 :** the leader of a chorus or choir; *broadly* **:** the leader of any group or movement ⟨the ~ of the Victorian poets⟩ **2 a :** a leader of a dramatic chorus in ancient Greece — called also at later periods *coryphaeus* **b :** an Athenian who provided a dramatic chorus at his own expense

1**cho·ral** \'kōrəl, -ȯr- *sometimes* -är-\ *adj* [F or ML; F *choral,* fr. ML *choralis,* fr. L *chorus* + *-alis* -al — more at CHORUS] **1 a :** of or belonging to a choir or chorus **:** performed by a chorus or in chorus **b :** accompanied with song ⟨a ~ dance⟩ **2 :** sung or intended for singing by a chorus ⟨a ~ arrangement⟩ ⟨~ counterpoint⟩ **:** containing a chorus ⟨Beethoven's ~ symphony⟩ — **cho·ral·ism** \-rə,lizəm\ *n* -s — **cho·ral·ist** \-rələst\ *n* -s — **cho·ral·ly** \-rəlē, -li\ *adv*

2**choral** *var of* CHORALE

choral bass *n* [1*choral*] **:** a flue pedal stop in a pipe organ usu. of 4-foot pitch and prominently voiced to sustain the melodic line in a choral prelude

cho·ral·celo \,==che(,)lō\ *n* -s [1*choral* + *-celo* (alter. of *cello*)] **:** a keyboard instrument like the piano but with electromagnets vibrating the strings and producing an organlike effect with string quality

cho·rale *also* **cho·ral** \kə'ral, kȯ-,kō-; kə'räl, kō-,kȯ-, -räl\ *n* -s *often attrib* [G *choral,* short for *choralgesang,* part trans. of ML *cantus choralis,* lit., choral song, fr. L *cantus* song + ML *choralis* choral] **1 a :** a hymn or psalm sung by choir or congregation or both to a traditional or composed melody in a church service; *also* **:** a hymn tune or sacred melody or a harmonization of a traditional melody ⟨a Bach ~⟩ **b :** a group formed to sing such music **:** CHORUS, CHOIR **2 :** something resembling a chorale; *esp* **:** a song in high praise ⟨the singing of paeans and *chorals* —P.L.Dunbar⟩ ⟨the novel, a passionate ~ on the themes of sin and salvation —*Time*⟩

chorale prelude *n* **1 :** an improvisatory organ prelude to the congregational singing of the hymn in the Protestant churches of 17th and 18th century Germany **2 :** a composition, usu. for organ, based upon a chorale or hymn tune

choral service *n* **:** a church service in which a part or all of the liturgy is intoned and sung by clergy, choir, and congregation

choral speaking *n* **:** ensemble speaking by a group often using various voice combinations and contrasts to bring out the meaning or the tonal beauty of a passage of poetry or prose

1**cho·ras·mi·an** \kə'razmēən\ *adj, usu cap* [*Chorasmia,* province of ancient Persia + E *-an*] **:** of or relating to Chorasmia

2**chorasmian** \"\ *n* -s *usu cap* **:** a native or inhabitant of ancient Chorasmia

chor bishop \'kō(ə)r-\ *n* [part trans. of LL *chorepiscopus* — more at CHOREPISCOPUS] **:** CHOREPISCOPUS

1**chord** \'kō(ə)rd, -ȯ(ə)d\ *n* -s [alter. (influenced by 3*chord*) of *cord,* fr. ME, short for *accord*] **:** a combination of two or more tones sounded together, esp. tones that blend harmoniously because of the simple ratios of their pitch frequencies; *specif* **:** COMMON CHORD

2**chord** \"\ *vb* -ED/-ING/-S *vi* **1 :** to harmonize together **:** ACCORD ⟨this tone ~*s* with that⟩; *also* **:** to sound together in harmony **2 :** to play chords on a stringed instrument usu. as an accompaniment ⟨when she played something . . . , Mother ~*ed* for her on the piano —Frances Judge⟩ ~ *vt* **1 :** to make chords on (a musical instrument) by stopping the strings **2 :** to furnish (a melody) with chords **:** HARMONIZE

3**chord** \"\ *n* -s [alter. (influenced by L *chorda*) of 1*cord*] **1 :** CORD 3a **2 a :** a straight line joining two points on a curve; *specif* **:** the segment of a secant between the two points of its intersection with a curve **b** *of an arch* **:** 2SPAN 3b **3 a** *obs* **:** CORD 1a **b** *archaic* **:** a string of a musical instrument **c :** a particular emotional or intellectual response ⟨the story struck a popular ~⟩ **:** a particular disposition or orientation of mind or spirit ⟨surrealism . . . touched old ~*s* of native, creative eccentricity —*Saturday Rev.*⟩ **4 :** either of the two outside members of a truss connected and braced by the web members **5 :** an arbitrary datum line from which the ordinates and position angles of an airfoil are measured; *esp* **:** the straight line joining the leading and trailing edges

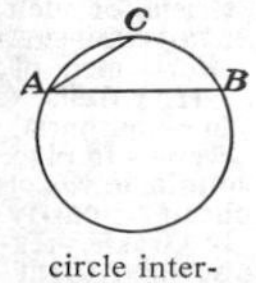

circle intersected by chords *AB* and *AC*

chord- *or* **chordo-** *comb form* [NL, fr. Gk *chordē* gut, string — more at YARN] **:** an anatomical cord: as **a :** vocal cord ⟨*chord*itis⟩ **b :** spinal cord ⟨*chordo*tomy⟩ **c :** notochord ⟨*Chorda*ta⟩

1**-chord** \,kȯrd, -ȯ(ə)d\ *n comb form* -s [partly fr. ME *-corde* (in *monacorde* monochord), fr. MF, fr. LL *-chordon,* fr. Gk, fr. *-chordos* stringed, fr. *chordē* string; partly fr. ML *-chordium* (in *clavichordium* clavichord), fr. L *chorda* string, fr. Gk *chordē*] **1 :** musical instrument having (such or so many) strings ⟨lyri*chord*⟩ **2 :** musical scale or interval (of a specified extent) ⟨hexa*chord*⟩

2**-chord** \"\ *adj comb form* [LL *-chordus,* fr. Gk *-chordos*] **:** having (so many) strings ⟨septi*chord*⟩

chor·da \'kȯrdə\ *n* [NL, fr. L — more at CORD] **1** *cap* **:** a genus of brown algae typifying the family Chordaceae and having usu. hollow blackish fronds **2** *pl* **chor·dae** \-,dē\ **:** CORD 3a; *specif* **:** NOTOCHORD

chor·da·ce·ae \kȯr'dāsē,ē\ *n pl, cap* [NL, fr. *Chorda,* type genus + *-aceae*] **:** a family of brown algae (order Laminariales) having slender cordlike fronds

chor·da·centrum \¦kȯrdə+\ *n* [NL, fr. *chorda* (anat.) + *centrum*] **:** a centrum of a vertebra formed by segmentation of the cartilaginous or calcified sheath of the notochord (as in elasmobranchs) — compare ARCOCENTRUM

1**chord·al** \'kȯrdᵊl, -ȯ(ə)d-\ *adj* [1*chord* + *-al*] **1 :** of, relating to, or resembling a chord ⟨~ assonance is important in modern music⟩ ⟨the ~ howling of a storm —Paul Hindemith⟩ **2 :** relating to music characterized more by vertical harmony than by linear contrapuntal motion

2**chordal** \"\ *adj* [3*chord* + *-al*] **:** of or relating to an anatomical cord (as the notochord or spinal cord) — used chiefly in combination ⟨peri*chordal*⟩ — **chord·al·ly** \-dᵊlē, -i\ *adv*

chordal pitch *n* **:** CHORD PITCH

chordal thickness *n* **:** the tangential thickness of a circular-gear tooth measured along a chord of the pitch circle

chor·da·mesoderm \¦kȯrdə+\ *or* **chor·do·mesoderm** \-dō+\ *n* -s [NL *chorda* or E *chord-* + *mesoderm*] **:** the portion of the embryonic mesoderm that forms notochord and related structures and serves as an inductor of ectodermic neural structures — **chor·da·mesodermal** *or* **chor·do·mesodermal** \"+\ *adj*

chor·dar·i·a·les \(,)kȯr,darē'ā(,)lēz\ *n pl, cap* [NL, fr. *Chordaria* genus of algae (fr. *chord-* + *-aria*) + *-ales*] **:** an order of brown algae (class Heterogeneratae) having a branched filamentous sporophyte that is not markedly compacted with a pseudoparenchymatous mass

chor·da·ta \kȯr'dād·ə, -äd·ə\ *n pl, cap* [NL, fr. L *chorda* cord + NL *-ata* — more at CORD] **:** a phylum or subkingdom comprising animals having at least at some stage of development a more or less well-developed notochord, dorsally situated central nervous system, and gill clefts in the walls of the pharynx and including the vertebrates, lancelets, tunicates, and usu. the hemichordates

1**chor·date** \'kȯrdət, -,dāt\ *adj* [NL *chorda* + E *-ate*] **1 :** having a notochord **2** [NL *Chordata*] **:** of or relating to the Chordata

2**chordate** \"\ *n* -s **:** a chordate animal

chorda ten·din·ea \-,ten'dinēə\ *n, pl* **chordae tendine·ae** \-nē,ē\ [NL, lit., tendinous cord] **:** any of the delicate tendinous cords that are attached to the edges of the auriculoventricular valves of the heart and to the papillary muscles and serve to prevent the valves from being pushed into the auricle during the ventricular contraction

chord·ed \'kȯrdəd, -ȯ(ə)d-\ *adj* **:** having or combined in chords

chor·dee \'kȯr,dē, -,dā, ='=\ *n* -s [F *cordée,* fem. of *cordé* corded (in *chaude-pisse cordée* corded gonorrhea), fr. *corde* cord — more at CORD] **:** painful erection of the penis often with a downward curvature, common as a lesion of gonorrhea

chor·dei·les \kȯr'dī(,)lēz\ *n, cap* [NL, irreg. fr. Gk *chordē* string of a lyre or harp + *deilē* afternoon, evening; fr. its cry at twilight — more at YARN] **:** a genus of nocturnal birds (family Caprimulgidae) consisting of the nighthawks

chording *pres part of* CHORD

chor·di·tis \kȯr'dīd·əs\ *n* -ES [NL, fr. *chord-* + *-itis*] **:** inflammation of a cord or cords (as the vocal or spermatic cords)

chordo- — see CHORD-

chor·doid \'kȯr,dȯid\ *adj* [*chord-* + *-oid*] **:** like a chorda ⟨a ~ notochord⟩

chor·do·mesoblast \kȯr(,)dō +\ *also* **chor·da·mesoblast** \-,də +\ *n* -s [ISV *chord-* or *chorda-* (fr. NL *chorda*) + *mesoblast*] **:** CHORDAMESODERM — **chor·do·mesoblastic** \"+\ *adj*

chor·do·nia \kȯr'dōnēə\ *n pl, cap* [NL, fr. *chordon-* (irreg. fr. L *chorda*) + *-ia*] **:** the Chordata exclusive of the hemichordates

chor·do·phone \'kȯrdə,fōn\ *n* -s [ISV *chord-* + *-phone*] **:** a member of the class of musical instruments having strings and including for classifying purposes the zithers, lutes, lyres, and harps — **chor·do·phon·ic** \¦==¦fänik\ *adj*

chor·do·plasm \'kȯrdə,plazəm\ *n* -s [*chord-* + *-plasm*] **:** the portion of a mosaic egg that consists of potential notochord

chor·dot·o·my *or* **cor·dot·o·my** \kȯr'däd·əmē\ *n* -ES [ISV *chord-* + *-tomy*] **:** the surgical division of certain areas of the spinal cord for relief of severe intractable pain

chor·do·tonal \¦kȯrdə +\ *adj* [ISV *chord-* + *tonal;* orig. formed in G] **:** relating to or being certain sensory organs found in various parts of the bodies of insects and believed to be receptors of auditory or other vibrational stimuli

chord pitch *or* **chordal pitch** *n* [1*chord*] **:** distance between corresponding points of consecutive gear teeth measured in a straight line

chords *pl of* CHORD, *pres 3d sing of* CHORD

-chords *pl of* -CHORD

chordwise \'=,=\ *adj* **:** directed, moving, or placed along the chord of an airfoil section — compare SPANWISE

1**chore** \'chō(ə)r, -ȯ(ə)r,-ōə,-ȯ(ə)\ *n* -s [alter. of *chare, char* — more at CHARE] **1 chores** *pl* **:** recurrent tasks performed at more or less regular intervals in the operation or maintenance of a farm, home, or business; *specif* **:** the morning and evening care of the livestock on a farm **2 :** a usu. routine or accustomed small task or odd job **3 :** a task or duty; *esp* **:** one that is dull, difficult, or disagreeable ⟨make the job more exciting and less of a ~⟩ ⟨to get across its lanes of skidding traffic is a perilous ~ —Truman Capote⟩ **syn** see TASK

2**chore** \"\ *vb* -ED/-ING/-S *vi* **:** to do chores ~ *vt* **:** to win, work, or gain by doing odd jobs ⟨he *chored* his way through school⟩

chore- — see CHOREO-

-chore \,kō(ə)r, -ȯ(ə)r,-ōə,-ȯ(ə)\ *n comb form* -s [Gk *chōrein* to withdraw, advance, go, spread; akin to Gk *chēros* left, bereaved — more at HEIR] **:** plant distributed by a (specified) means or agency ⟨zoo*chore*⟩ — **-cho·rous** \¦kōrəs, -ȯr-\ *adj comb form* — **-cho·ry** \,kōrē, -ȯr-, -ri\ *n comb form* -ES

cho·rea \kə'rēə\ *n* -s [NL, fr. L, dance, fr. Gk *choreia,* fr. *choros* — more at CHORUS] **:** any of various nervous disorders of infectious or organic origin in man and dogs having as common features involuntary uncontrollable purposeless movements of body and face and marked incoordination of limbs — see CANINE CHOREA, HUNTINGTON'S CHOREA, SYDENHAM'S

CHOREA — **cho·re·al** \-ēəl\ *adj* — **cho·re·at·ic** \¦kōrē¦ad·ik\ *adj* — **cho·re·ic** \kə'rēik\ *adj*

chore boy *n* **1 :** one who does chores; *esp* **:** a man who does the domestic maintenance tasks and helps the cook in a lumber camp **2 :** a person who assumes responsibility for onerous detail in any situation

cho·ree \'kōr,ē, kə'rē\ *n* -s [F *chorée*, fr. L *choreus*, fr. Gk *choreios*, fr. *choreios*, adj., of a dance, of a chorus, fr. *choros* dancing area, dance, chorus — more at CHORUS] **:** CHOREUS — **cho·re·ic** \kə'rēik\ *adj*

choregus *var of* CHORAGUS

cho·re·i·form \kə'rēə,fȯrm\ *adj* [ISV *chorea* (fr. NL) + *-iform*] **:** resembling chorea ⟨~ convulsions⟩

chore·man \'chōrmən, -ȯr-, -,man\ *n, pl* **choremen :** a worker who performs any of numerous menial jobs in a factory or camp (as a leather factory or a logging, mining, or construction camp) — compare BULL COOK

choreo- *also* **chore-** *or* **chorio-** *comb form* [choreo-, chore-, fr. F *choréo-*, *choré-*, fr. Gk *choreia* dance, fr. *choros* dance, place for dancing; *chorio-*, alter. of *choreo-* — more at CHORUS] **:** dance ⟨*choreo*mania⟩ ⟨*choreo*graphy⟩

cho·reo·ath·e·toid \¦kōrē(,)ō¦athə,tȯid\ *or* **cho·reo·ath·e·tot·ic** \-¦athə¦täd·ik\ *adj* [*choreoathetoid* fr. NL *choreoathetosis* + E *-oid*; *choreoathetotic* fr. NL *choreoathetosis*, after such pairs as NL *sclerosis*: E *sclerotic*] **:** resembling choreoathetosis

cho·reo·ath·e·to·sis \-,athə'tōsəs\ *n* [NL, fr. *chorea* + -o- + *athetosis*] **:** a nervous disturbance marked by the involuntary purposeless and uncontrollable movements characteristic of chorea and athetosis

cho·reo·drama \¦kōrē(,)ō +\ *n* -s [*choreo-* + *drama*] **:** a dance drama for large groups

cho·re·o·graph \'kōrēə,graf, -ȯr-, -rēō,-, -raa(ə)f,-raif,-räf, *Brit often & US sometimes* 'kär-\ *vb* -ED/-ING/-S [back-formation fr. *choreography*] *vt* **:** to undertake or compose the choreography of (as a ballet or a poem) ⟨has ~*ed* a lively string of . . . musicals —R.L.Taylor⟩ ~ *vi* **:** to serve as choreographer **:** engage in choreography

cho·re·og·ra·pher \,≈≈'ägrəfə(r)\ *n* -s **:** one engaging in the composing and often the teaching of choreography

cho·re·o·graph·ic \¦≈≈¦grafik, -ō¦-, -fēk\ *also* **cho·re·o·graph·i·cal** \-fəkəl, -ēk-\ *adj* **:** of, belonging to, or concerned with choreography — **cho·re·o·graph·i·cal·ly** \-fək(ə)lē, -ēk-, -li\ *adv*

cho·re·og·ra·phy \,≈≈'ägrəfē, -fi\ *or* **cho·reg·ra·phy** \kə'reg-\ *n* -ES [F *chorégraphie*, fr. *choré-* choreo- + *-graphie* -graphy] **1 :** the art of representing dancing by signs as music is represented by notes **2 :** DANCING; *esp* **:** stage dancing as distinguished from social or ballroom dancing **3 :** the composition and arrangement of dance movements and patterns (as for a ballet) created usu. to accompany a particular piece of music or to develop a theme or a pantomime; *also* **:** a composition created by this art

cho·re·oid \'kōrē,ȯid\ *adj* [NL *chorea* + E *-oid*] **:** CHOREIFORM

chor·episcopal \¦kōr+\ *adj* **:** of, performed by, or relating to a chorepiscopus

chor·epis·co·pus \,kȯrə'piskəpəs\ *n, pl* **chorepisco·pi** \-,pī, -pē\ *or* **chorepiscopuses** [LL, fr. LGk *chōrepiskopos*, fr. Gk *chōr-* chor- + *episkopos* overseer, bishop — more at BISHOP] **:** a bishop who is appointed by a diocesan bishop to assist him in the exercise of his episcopal jurisdiction in a rural district

chores *pl of* CHORE, *pres 3d sing of* CHORE

cho·re·us \kə'rēəs\ *n, pl* **cho·rei** \-ē,ī\ [L, fr. Gk *choreios*, lit., of a chorus, fr. *choros* chorus — more at CHORUS] **:** a trochee in classical prosody — used at first esp. of the trochee when resolved into the tribrach

cho·reu·tic \kə'rüd·ik\ *adj* [Gk *choreutikos*, fr. *choreutēs* choral dancer, fr. *choreuein* to dance, fr. *choros*] **:** of or belonging to a chorus

¹chori- *or* **chorio-** *comb form* [NL, fr. Gk *chorio-*, fr. *chorion*] **1 :** chorion **:** chorionic ⟨*chorio*carcinoma⟩ ⟨*chori*oma⟩ **2 :** choroid **:** choroid and ⟨*chorio*cele⟩ ⟨*chorio*retinal⟩

²chori- *comb form* [NL, fr. Gk *chōri*, *chōris* apart; akin to Gk *chēros* left, bereaved — more at HEIR] **:** separated **:** distinct ⟨*chori*petalous⟩

cho·ri·al \'kōrēəl\ *adj* [ISV ¹*chori-* + *-al*] **:** of or relating to a chorion **:** CHORIONIC

cho·ri·amb \'kōrē,am(b)\ *n, pl* **choriambs** \-mz\ [LL *choriambus*, fr. Gk *choriambos*, fr. *choreios* choreus + *iambos* iambus] **:** CHORIAMBUS

cho·ri·am·bic \¦kōrē¦ambik\ *adj* [LL *choriambicus*, fr. Gk *choriambikos*, fr. *choriambos* + *-ikos* -ic] **:** of, relating to, consisting of, or containing choriambuses

cho·ri·am·bus \,kōrē'ambəs\ *n, pl* **choriambuses** \-bəsəz\ *or* **choriam·bi** \-,bī\ [LL] **:** a foot of four syllables in classical prosody in which the cadence of the trochee is followed by that of the iambus (- ◡ ◡ -) the corresponding pattern of cadence in accentual prosody (ó o o ó) consisting of the combination of trochee and iambus in succession

cho·ric \'kōrik, -ȯr-, -ēk *also* -är-\ *adj* [LL *choricus*, fr. Gk *chorikos*, fr. *choros* chorus] **:** of, relating to, or in the style of a chorus ⟨a ~ Greek tragedy⟩ or sometimes of a choir

choric speaking *n* **:** CHORAL SPEAKING

-chories *pl of* -CHORY

cho·rine \'kōr,ēn, 'kȯ,rēn\ *n* -s [*chorus* + *-ine*] **:** CHORUS GIRL

choring *pres part of* CHORE

¹chorio- — see CHOREO-

²chorio- — see ¹CHORI-

cho·rio·allantoic \¦kōrē,ō+\ *or* **cho·rio·allantoid** \"+\ *adj* [NL *chorioallantois* + E *-ic* or *-oid*] **:** of, relating to, or produced by chorioallantois

cho·rio·allantois \"+\ *n* -ES [NL, fr. ¹*chori-* + *allantois*] **:** a very vascular fetal membrane composed of the more or less fused chorion and adjacent wall of the allantois, that of the developing hen's egg being used as a living culture medium for a number of viruses pathogenic to man or animals and for certain tissues — called also *chorioallantoic membrane*

cho·rio·carcinoma \"+\ *n* [NL, fr. ¹*chori-* + *carcinoma*] **:** a malignant tumor derived from chorionic tissue arising spontaneously in the testis, in the ovary following pregnancy, or extragenitally in the mediastinum — called also *chorioepithelioma*

cho·rio·epithelioma \"+\ *n* [NL, fr. ¹*chori-* + *epithelioma*] **:** CHORIOCARCINOMA — **cho·rio·epitheliomatous** \"+\ *adj*

chorioid *or* **chorioidal** *var of* CHOROID

cho·ri·oi·dea \,kōrē'ȯidēə\ *n* -s [NL, alter. of *choroides* — more at CHOROID] **:** CHOROID

chorioiditis *var of* CHOROIDITIS

cho·ri·o·ma \,kōrē'ōmə\ *n, pl* **choriomas** \-məz\ *also* **chorioma·ta** \-məd·ə\ [NL, fr. ¹*chori-* + *-oma*] **:** a tumor formed of chorionic tissue (as a choriocarcinoma)

cho·rio·meningitis \¦kōrē(,)ō+\ *n* [NL, fr. ¹*chori-* + *meningitis*] **:** cerebral meningitis; *specif* **:** LYMPHOCYTIC CHORIOMENINGITIS

cho·ri·on \'kōrē,än, -ȯr-, -ēən\ *n* -s [NL, fr. Gk] **1 :** the highly vascular outer embryonic membrane of higher vertebrates (reptiles, birds, and mammals) that in the more advanced placental mammals is associated with the allantois in the formation of the placenta and is commonly separable into (1) a villous part that enters into the placenta and (2) a smooth part that does not — called also respectively (1) *chorion frondosum* and (2) *chorion laeve*; see AMNION **2 :** any of various envelopes (not homologous with the chorion of mammals) of the eggs of different animals; *esp* **:** a membrane of the eggs of many insects secreted by the follicular cells surrounding the egg in the ovary — **cho·ri·on·ic** \¦≈≈¦änik\ *adj*

cho·ri·on·epithelioma \"+\ *n* [NL, fr. *chorion* + *epithelioma*] **:** CHORIOCARCINOMA

cho·ri·op·tes \,kōrē'äp,tēz\ *n, cap* [NL, prob. fr. Gk *chorion* chorion, leather (hence taken here to mean animal skin) + NL *-optes* (as in *Sarcoptes*)] **:** a genus of small parasitic mites infesting domestic animals and causing certain forms of mange — **cho·ri·op·tic** \¦≈≈¦tik\ *adj*

chorioptic mange *n* [NL *Chorioptes* + E *-ic*] **:** mange caused by mites (genus *Chorioptes*) that usu. attack only the surface of the skin esp. about the feet and lower legs or in cattle at the base of the tail — compare DEMODECTIC MANGE, SARCOPTIC MANGE

cho·rio·retinitis \¦kōrē(,)ō +\ *also* **cho·roido·retinitis** \kə¦rȯi(,)dō +\ *n* [NL, fr. ¹*chori-* or *choroido-* (fr. *choroides*) + *retinitis*] **:** inflammation of the retina and choroid coat of the eye

cho·ri·pet·a·lae \,kōrə'ped·ᵊl,ē\ *n pl, cap* [NL, fr. ²*chori-* + *-petalae*] *in some classifications* **:** a group of Archichlamydeae comprising plants with the floral corolla divided into distinct petals — compare APETALAE, METACHLAMYDEAE

cho·ri·petalous \¦kōrə+\ *adj* [²*chori-* + *-petalous*] **1 :** POLYPETALOUS **2** [NL *Choripetalae* + E *-ous*] **:** belonging to the Choripetalae

cho·ri·sis \'kōrəsəs\ *n, pl* **chori·ses** \-ə,sēz\ [LGk *chōrisis* separation, fr. Gk *chōrizein* to separate, fr. *chōris* apart — more at CHORI-] **:** the separation of a leaf or floral organ into two or more parts by division during development — called also *collateral chorisis* when the parts are side by side and *parallel chorisis* or *median chorisis* when they are one in front of another

cho·rist \'kōrəst\ *n* -s [F or ML; F *choriste* fr. ML *chorista*, fr. L *chorus* + *-ista* -ist — more at CHORUS] *archaic* **:** a member of a chorus or choir

chorist- *or* **choristo-** *comb form* [NL, fr. Gk *chōristos* separable] **:** separated **:** misplaced ⟨*chorist*oblastoma⟩ ⟨*chorist*oma⟩

cho·ris·tate \kə'ristət, -,stāt\ *adj* [Gk *chōristos* separable, separate (fr. *chōrizein* to separate) + E *-ate*] **:** exhibiting chorisis

cho·ris·ter \'kȯrəstə(r), 'kōr-,'kär-\ *n* -s [ME *querister*, fr. AF *cueristre*, *cueriste*, fr. ML *chorista*] **1 :** one of a choir or chorus of singers; *specif* **:** CHOIRBOY **2** *obs* **:** SINGER **3 :** the singer in a church choir who leads the singing and in the absence of instrumental accompaniment sets the pitch and tempo

cho·ri·zo *also* **cho·ri·so** \chə'rē(,)zō, -sō\ *n* -s [Sp *chorizo*] **:** pork sausage highly seasoned with cayenne pepper, pimientos, and garlic

c–horizon \'sē≈¦≈≈\ *n, usu cap C* **:** the layer of a soil profile lying beneath the B-horizon and consisting essentially of more or less weathered rock of the kind that has contributed the major mineral part of the A-horizon and B-horizon

cho·ro \'shōr(,)ü\ *n* -s [Pg *chôro*, lit., weeping, fr. *chorar* to weep, fr. L *plorare* to cry out, to bewail, prob. of imit. origin] **1 :** a Brazilian dance band; *also* **:** a piece played by such a band **2 :** a musical piece in the style of or suggesting Brazilian folk music

choro- — see CHOR-

cho·ro·gi \'chōrō,gē\ *n* -s [Jap] **:** CHINESE ARTICHOKE

cho·rog·ra·pher \kə'rägrəfə(r)\ *n* -s [*chorography* + *-er*] **:** a specialist in chorography

cho·ro·graph·ic \¦kȯrə¦grafik\ *also* **cho·ro·graph·i·cal** \-fəkəl\ *adj* **:** of, relating to, or employing the methods of chorography — **cho·ro·graph·i·cal·ly** \-fək(ə)lē\ *adv*

cho·rog·ra·phy \kə'rägrəfē\ *n* -ES [L *chorographia*, fr. Gk *chōrographia*, fr. *chōr-* chor- + *-graphia* -graphy] **1 :** the art of describing or mapping a particular region or district esp. one larger than that considered by topography but smaller than that by geography **2 :** a description, map, or chart of a particular region or district; *also* **:** the physical conformation and features of such an area

¹cho·roid \'kōr,ȯid, 'kȯ,rȯid\ *or* **cho·ri·oid** \'kōrē,ȯid, -ȯr-\ *n* -s [NL *choroides*, fr. Gk *choroeidēs*, MS var. of *chorioeidēs*, fr. *chori-* ¹chori- + *-oeidēs* -oid] **:** the choroid coat of the eye — see EYE illustration

²choroid \"\ *or* **cho·roi·dal** \kə'rȯidᵊl\ *also* **cho·ri·oid** \'kōrē,ȯid, -ȯr-\ *or* **cho·ri·oi·dal** \¦≈≈¦≈ᵊl\ *adj* **1 :** resembling a chorion esp. in being of highly vascular membranous structure — see CHOROID COAT, CHOROID PLEXUS **2** *usu choroidal* **:** of or relating to a choroid part ⟨~ arteries⟩

choroid coat *also* **choroid membrane** *n* **:** a vascular membrane containing large branched pigment cells that lies between the retina and the sclerotic coat of the vertebrate eye

cho·roid·itis \,kōr,ȯi'dīd·əs\ *or* **cho·ri·oid·itis** \,kōrē,ȯi'd-\ *n* -ES [NL, fr. *choroides* or *chorioidea* + *-itis*] **:** inflammation of the choroid coat of the eye

choroidoretinitis *var of* CHORIORETINITIS

choroid plexus *n* **:** a highly vascular portion of the pia mater that projects into the ventricles of the brain and is thought to secrete the cerebrospinal fluid

cho·ro·log·ic \¦kōrə¦läjik\ *or* **cho·ro·log·i·cal** \-jəkəl\ *adj* **:** of or relating to chorology — **cho·ro·log·i·cal·ly** \-jək(ə)lē\ *adv*

cho·rol·o·gy \kə'räləjē\ *n* -ES [ISV *chor-* + *-logy*; orig. formed as G *chorologie*] **:** biogeography esp. as concerned with the migrations and areas of distribution of organisms

cho·ro·te·ga \,chōrə'tāgə\ *n, pl* **chorotega** *or* **chorotegas** *usu cap* [Sp, of AmerInd origin] **1 a :** a people of Honduras, Nicaragua, and Costa Rica **b :** a member of such people **2 :** the language of the Chorotega people

cho·ro·te·gan \¦≈≈¦gən\ *n, pl* **chorotegan** *or* **chorotegans** *usu cap* **:** a language family of Mexico and Central America, including the languages of the Chiapanecs, Chorotegas, Mangues, and Orotiñas

cho·ro·ti \chə'rōd·ē\ *n, pl* **choroti** *or* **chorotis** *usu cap* [Sp *choroti*, *choroté*, of AmerInd origin] **1 a :** a Matacan people of northwestern Paraguay and southeastern Bolivia **b :** a member of such people **2 :** the language of the Choroti people

-chorous — see -CHORE

chor·ten \'chȯr,ten\ *n* -s [Tibetan *chörten*, alter. of *mchod rten*, fr. *mchod* offering + *rten* holder] **:** a Lamaist shrine or monument

chor·ti \'chȯrd·ē\ *n, pl* **chorti** *or* **chortis** *usu cap* [Sp, of AmerInd origin] **1 a :** an Indian people of eastern Guatemala and western Honduras **b :** a member of such people **2 :** a Mayan language of the Chorti people

¹chor·tle \'chȯr\|d·ᵊl, -ō(ə)\|, \|tᵊl\ *vb* **chortled; chortled; chortling** \|d·ᵊliŋ, \|t(ᵊ)l-\ **chortles** [blend of ¹*chuckle* and *snort*] *vi* **1 :** to sing or chant exultantly ⟨he *chortled* in his joy —Lewis Carroll⟩ **2 :** to utter a chuckling laugh or a sound like a chortle **:** speak with a chuckling laugh ⟨~ over the team's defeat⟩ **3** *of a motor vehicle* **:** to progress noisily ⟨flivvers *chortling* up the avenue⟩ **4 :** to express usu. somewhat contemptuous amusement ~ *vt* **:** to express effervescently or with a chortling intonation ⟨~ one's joy⟩

²chortle \"\ *n* -s **:** a sound expressive of pleasure or exultation; *also* **:** an act or instance of chortling

chor·toi·ce·tes \,kȯr,tȯi'sēd·ēz, ,kȯrd·ə's-\ *n, cap* [NL, fr. Gk *chortos* pasturage, grass, enclosure + *oiketēs* dweller, fr. *oikos* house — more at YARD, VICINITY] **:** a genus of grasshoppers including a very destructive Australian migratory plague grasshopper (*C. terminifera*)

¹cho·rus \'kōrəs, -ȯr-\ *n* -ES [L, ring dance, dance accompanied with singing, group of dancers and singers, fr. Gk *choros*; prob. akin to Lith *žaras* course, way] **1 a :** a company of singers and dancers acting as a unit and in the developed Athenian drama acting as participants in or commenters on the action; *also* **:** a similar company in later plays imitating or adapted from Greek models **b :** a character in the Elizabethan drama who speaks the prologue and epilogue and comments on the action **c :** an organized company of singers who sing in concert **:** CHOIR; *specif* **:** a body of singers who sing choral parts (as in opera) — distinguished from *soloist* **d :** a company of singers who join a soloist in singing a refrain **e :** a group of dancers and usu. singers supporting the featured players in a musical comedy or revue **2 :** something suitable for or intended for performance by a choral group: as **a :** a part of a song or hymn recurring at intervals (as the refrain at the end of stanzas) **b :** the part of a drama sung or spoken by the chorus, typically consisting in Greek drama of a series of odes for antiphonal singing interspersed between the scenes of the play **c :** a composition usu. of two or more parts in harmony intended to be sung by a number of voices in concert ⟨a double ~ of eight parts⟩ **d :** the main or characteristic part of a popular song as distinguished from the introductory verse **3 :** something performed by or as if by a choral group: as **a :** the simultaneous singing or song of a number of persons **b :** the simultaneous utterance (as of speech, laughter, or cries) by a number of persons or animals ⟨the ~ of dogs in the chase⟩; *also* **:** sounds so uttered ⟨the insects . . . raising a ~ from the woods and grasses —D.C.Peattie⟩ **c :** any utterance that follows immediately upon another or that comes as a response to another, suggesting the refrain to a song ⟨their laughter was a ~ to his stories⟩ **d :** a unanimous utterance by the members of a group, giving the impression of a chorus ⟨the ~ of critical praise⟩ ⟨a ~ of boos⟩ — **in chorus** *adv* **:** in unison **:** by all giving utterance simultaneously

²chorus \"\ *vb* **chorused** *also* **chorussed; chorused** *also* **chorussed; chorusing** *also* **chorussing; choruses** *also* **chorusses** *vi* **:** to sing or make utterance in chorus ~ *vt* **1 :** to furnish with a chorus **2 :** to sing (a song) in chorus **3 :** to utter (as a greeting) together or simultaneously **:** ECHO ⟨they ~*ed* their agreement with his views⟩

chorus boy *or* **chorus man** *n* **:** a usu. young man who sings or dances in the chorus of a theatrical production (as a musical comedy or revue)

chorus girl *n* **:** a usu. young woman who sings or dances in the chorus of a theatrical production (as a musical comedy or revue)

chorus master *n* **:** the director of a chorus; *specif* **:** one who directs and rehearses the singing chorus of an opera company

chorus reed *n* **:** a heavy reed pipe-organ stop of brass-wind quality and of 16-foot, 8-foot, or 4-foot pitch and usu. one of a group

chor·wat \kȯr'vät\ *n* -s *usu cap* [Russ *Khorvat*] **:** CROAT

-chory — see -CHORE

cho·rzow \'kō(,)zhüf, 'k-\ *adj, usu cap* [fr. *Chorzów*, Poland] **:** of or from the city of Chorzow, Poland **:** of the kind or style prevalent in Chorzow

¹chose *past or obs past part of* CHOOSE

²chose \'shōz\ *n* -s [F, fr. L *causa* cause, reason — more at CAUSE] **:** a piece of personal property **:** THING — see CHOSE IN ACTION

chose in action [²*chose*] **1 :** any right to a personal as opposed to a real thing that is not in one's possession or actual enjoyment but is recoverable by suit at law; *esp* **:** any right to an act or forbearance (as in case of debts, stocks, shares, and negotiable instruments or claim of reparation for a tort) **2 :** the thing (as a bond or note) that is the subject of chose in action — compare CHOSE IN POSSESSION

chose in possession [²*chose*] **:** a thing in one's actual possession — compare CHOSE IN ACTION

chose ju·gée \shōz·zhüezhā\ *n* [F] **:** a matter that has been settled **:** RES JUDICATA

chose local \(')shōz'lōkəl\ *n, pl* **choses local** \-z(əz)'-\ [²*chose*] **:** a thing annexed to a place (as a house) as distinguished from something movable — distinguished from *chose transitory*

¹cho·sen \'chōzᵊn\ *adj* [ME, fr. past part. of *chesen*, *chosen* to choose — more at CHOOSE] **1 :** selected or marked for favor or to receive special privilege ⟨privileges granted to a ~ few⟩ **2 :** selected by God **:** ELECT

²chosen \"\ *n, pl* **chosen :** one who is the object of choice or of divine favor **:** an elect person ⟨this prophet, the ~ of the Most High⟩ ⟨the ~ are freed of all sin⟩

cho·sen·ese \¦chō,se¦nēz, chō¦s-, -ēs\ *adj or n, usu cap* [*Chosen*, former official name for Korea (fr. Jap *Chōsen*) + E *-ese*] **:** KOREAN

chosen freeholder *n* **:** one of a board of county officers in New Jersey having charge of county finances and similar to county commissioners or county supervisors in other states

chosen instrument *n* **:** a person or agency favored by an individual, group, or government in furtherance of the latter's own interests; *specif* **:** a commercial airline sponsored or subsidized by its national government for foreign transport esp. in a given part of the world

chosen people *n, often cap C&P* **:** a people that is considered or that considers itself to be chosen esp. by God as his people and specially consecrated to holy purposes; *specif* **:** ISRAELITES

chose transitory *n, pl* **choses transitory** [²*chose*] *law*: MOVABLE

cho·ta \'chōd·ə, -ō(,)tä\ *adj* [Hindi *choṭā*] *India* **:** LITTLE

chota haz·ri \-'häzrē\ *n* [Hindi *choṭā hāzirī* small breakfast] *India* **:** a light meal eaten very early in the morning

cho·ta·peg \'chōd·ə,peg\ *n* -s [Hindi *choṭā* small + E *peg*] *India* **:** a half-sized drink esp. of whiskey or whiskey and soda

chott *or* **shott** \'shät\ *n* -s [F & Ar; F *chott*, fr. Ar *shaṭṭ*] **:** a shallow saline lake of northern Africa; *also* **:** the dried bed of such a lake

chou \'shü\ *n, pl* **choux** *in sense* 1 -üz, *in other senses* -ü\ [F, lit., cabbage, fr. L *caulis* stalk — more at HOLE] **1 :** a soft cabbage-shaped ornament or rosette of fabric used in women's wear (as a knot of ribbons on a dress or a crushed crown on a hat) **2 :** CABBAGE 1 **3 :** DARLING — used as a term of endearment

chou·an \'shü,än, ≈'≈, *F* shwäⁿ\ *n, pl* **chouans** \-änz,-äⁿ\ *usu cap* [after Jean *Chouan* (nickname of Jean *Cottereau* †1794 Fr. revolutionary, one of the leaders), fr. F dial. *chouan* owl, alter. of MF *javan*, fr. LL *cavannus*, of Celt origin; akin to W *cwan* owl, Bret *kaouenn*] **:** one of the royalist insurgents in western France during and after the French revolution

chou·croute \shü·krüt\ *n* -s [F, by folk etymology (influence of *chou* cabbage), fr. G *sauerkraut* — more at SAUERKRAUT] **1 :** SAUERKRAUT **2** *or* **choucroute gar·nie** \-gärnē\ **:** sauerkraut cooked and served with meat

chou·ette \shü'et, 'shwet\ *n* -s [F, fr. *faire la chouette* to play a lone hand at cards, lit., to act like a barn owl, fr. *chouette* barn owl, alter. of OF *çuete*, of imit. origin] **:** a method of scoring by which more than two persons can participate in a two-handed game (as backgammon), one player accepting the bets of all other players on the result of a game between himself and one other active player — see *in the box* at ²BOX, CAPTAIN 1p

chough \'chəf\ *n* -s [ME *chough*, *choge*, *chowe*; prob. akin to OE *cēo*, *cīo* jackdaw, jay, chough, MD *cauwe* rook, OHG *kāa*, *kā* jackdaw, jay, Toch A *kāk* he called, Skt *gāyati* he sings] **1 :** a bird of the Old World genus *Pyrrhocorax* (family Corvidae) of small or medium size with red legs and glossy black plumage — see ALPINE CHOUGH, CORNISH CHOUGH **2 :** any of various related or similar birds (as a jackdaw)

chou·kou·tien \¦jō,kō¦tyen\ *or* **chou·kou·tien·ian** \-nēən\ *adj, usu cap* [fr. *Choukoutien*, town near Peking, China, its type station] **:** of or relating to a middle Pleistocene culture of China characterized by rude chopper tools produced from cores or large flakes

choul·try \'chau̇l·trē\ *n* -ES [modif. of Tamil-Malayalam *cāvaṭi*] **1** *India* **:** INN, CARAVANSARY **2** *India* **:** a pillared hall or colonnade of a temple

chou·moel·lier \shə'mälyə(r)\ *n* -s [F, lit., marrow cabbage] **:** a hybrid of cabbage, kohlrabi, and kale that is used for forage and feed esp. in New Zealand and Australia — called also *marrow cabbage*

chounse *also* **chounce** \'chau̇n(t)s\ *vt* -ED/-ING/-S [prob. alter. of *jounce*] *South & Midland* **:** SHAKE, BOUNCE; *esp* **:** to freshen (as a pillow or tick) by shaking

choup \'chüp\ *var of* CHOOP

chou·pique *also* **chou·pic** \'shü,pik\ *n* -s [AmerF (La.) *choupique*, fr. Choctaw *shupik*] **:** BOWFIN

¹chouse *also* **chowse** \'chau̇s\ *n* -s [Turk *çavuş* sergeant, doorkeeper, messenger, fr. *çav* voice, news] **1** *obs* **:** CHIAUS **2** *obs* **:** one easily cheated **:** GULL, DUPE **3 :** TRICK, SHAM, IMPOSITION

²chouse \"\ *vt* -ED/-ING/-S **:** CHEAT, TRICK, DEFRAUD ⟨~ him out of his money⟩

³chouse \'chau̇s\ *vt* -ED/-ING/-S [origin unknown] *West* **:** to drive or herd (as livestock) roughly; *also* **:** to chase, harass, or stir up (livestock, esp. cattle)

choux *pl of* CHOU

¹chow \'chau̇\ *n* -s [perh. fr. Chin (Pek) *chiao³* meat dumpling] **1** *slang* **:** FOOD, VICTUALS; *also* **:** a meal or mealtime **2** *often cap, Austral* **:** CHINESE 1 — often used disparagingly

²chow \"\ *vi* -ED/-ING/-S **:** EAT

Chow \'chau̇\ *trademark* — used for a mixed balanced animal ration

³chow *var of* CHOW CHOW

¹chow·chow \'chau̇,chau̇\ *adj* [pidgin E] **:** consisting of several kinds mingled together **:** ASSORTED, MIXED, MISCELLANEOUS

²chowchow \"\ *n* -s [pidgin E] **:** something mixed or commingled: **a** (1) **:** a Chinese preserve or confection of ginger, fruits, and peels in heavy syrup (2) **:** a spicy relish of chopped mixed pickles in mustard sauce **b :** HODGEPODGE, MISCELLANY

³chowchow \"\ *n* -s [prob. imit.] **:** YELLOW-BILLED CUCKOO

chow chow \"\ *or* **chow** *n* -s *often cap both Cs* [fr. a Chin dial. word akin to Cant *kau̇* dog] **:** a heavy-coated blocky powerfully built dog that is believed to have originated in north China and that has a broad flat head and short broad muzzle set off by a very full ruff of long hair usu. somewhat lighter than the rest of the coat, which may be of any clear solid color, and a distinctive blue-black tongue and black-lined mouth

¹chow·der \'chaùdə(r)\ *n* -S [F *chaudière* kettle, pot, its contents, fr. LL *caldaria* — more at CALDRON] **1 :** a soup or stew of seafood (as clams or white-fleshed sea fishes) usu. made with milk and containing salt pork or bacon, onions, and potatoes and sometimes other vegetables **2 :** any of various soups more or less resembling chowders — used often in combination ⟨corn ~⟩

²chowder \"\ *vt* **chowdered; chowdered; chowdering** \-d(ə)riŋ\ **chowders :** to make a chowder of

chow·der·head \'chaùdə(r),hed\ *n* [alter. of *jolter-head*] **:** DOLT, BLOCKHEAD — **chow·der·head·ed** \-¦hedəd\ *adj*

chowhound \'⸗,⸗\ *n, slang* **:** one excessively fond of food **:** GLUTTON, GOURMAND

chowk \'chaùk\ *n* -S [Hindi *cauk* — more at CHOKEY] *India* **:** MARKETPLACE, BAZAAR; *also* **:** a main street

chow·ki·dar \¦chaùkē¦där\ *var of* CHOKIDAR

chow line *n* **:** a queue waiting to be served food (as in a military mess)

chow mein \(')chaù'mān\ *n, pl* **chow meins** [Chin (Pek) *ch'ao³ mien⁴*, fr. *ch'ao³* to fry + *mien⁴* flour, dough, vermicelli] **1 :** fried noodles **2 :** a thick stew of shredded or finely diced meat, mushrooms, vegetables, and seasonings that is served with fried noodles

chow·rie *also* **cau·ri** *or* **chau·ri** \'chaùrē\ *n* -S [Hindi *caurī*, fr. Skt *camara* yak, yak tail employed as whisk] **:** a whisk to keep off flies that is used in the East esp. as a mark of rank

chowse *var of* CHOUSE

choy *or* **choya** *var of* CHAY

choyroot *var of* CHAYAROOT

chp *abbr* championship

chq *abbr* cheque

chrem·a·tis·tic \¦kremə¦tistik, -ēm-\ *adj* [Gk *chrēmatistikos* of business or moneymaking, fr. *chrēmatistēs* businessman (fr. *chrēmatizein* to deal, transact business, make money — fr. *chrēmat-*, *chrēma* thing, possession, fr. *chrēsthai* to need, use — + *-istēs* -ist) + *-ikos* -ic] **:** of, relating to, or occupied in the gaining of wealth

chrem·a·tis·tics \,⸗⸗'⸗stiks\ *n pl but sing in constr, also* **chrem·a·tis·tic** \-stik\ [F *chrématistique*, fr. Gk *chrēmatistikē*, fr. fem. of *chrēmatistikos*] **:** the study of wealth or a particular theory of wealth as measured in money

chrem·sel \'kremzəl, 'kr-\ *also* **chrim·sel** \-rim-\ *n, pl* **chrems·lach** \-emzlək, -,läk, -k̲\ [Yiddish *chremzel*] **:** a flat fried cake made with matzoth meal and filled usu. with prunes

chre·sard \'krē,särd\ *n* -S [Gk *chrēsis* use + *ardein* to water; akin to Gk *chreō* need — more at CHRESTOMATHY, ARDELLA] **:** the soil water available for plant growth — compare ECHARD, HOLARD

chres·to·math·ic \¦krestə¦mathik\ *adj* [*chrestomath-* (fr. F, G, or Gk; F *chrestomathie*, fr. G, fr. Gk *chrēstomatheia*) + *-ic*] **:** belonging to or devoted to useful knowledge or learning

chres·tom·a·thy \kre'stäməthē, -thi\ *n* -ES [NL *chrestomathia*, fr. Gk *chrēstomatheia*, fr. *chrēstos* useful (fr. *chrēsthai* to need, use) + *-matheia* (fr. *mathein*, *manthanein* to learn); akin to Gk *chreō* need, necessity, OIr *gair* short, Skt *hrasva* short, small; basic meaning: small, scarce — more at MATHEMATICAL] **1 :** a selection of passages from various authors compiled as an aid to learning a language **2 :** a volume of selected passages or stories of an author

¹chrism \'krizəm\ *n* -S [ME *crisme*, fr. OE *crisma*, fr. LL *chrisma*, fr. Gk, ointment, fr. *chriein* to anoint; akin to OE *grēot* sand — more at GRIT] **1 a :** consecrated oil that is generally mixed with balm or balm and spices and used by some liturgical churches in the administration of certain sacraments (as baptism, confirmation, or ordination) and sometimes in other ceremonies (as the consecration of churches or altars) **b :** OINTMENT, UNGUENT **2 a :** a sacramental anointing **:** UNCTION **b** *usu cap* **:** a sacrament of the Eastern Orthodox Church corresponding to confirmation in the Western Church

²chrism *vt* -ED/-ING/-S *obs* **:** to anoint with chrism

chris·ma \'krizmə\ *n, pl* **chrisma·ta** \-məd·ə,-mətə\ [alter. of *chrismon*] **:** CHRISMON

¹chris·mal \'krizməl\ *adj* [ML *chrismalis*, fr. LL *chrisma* chrism] **:** of or relating to chrism

²chrismal \"\ *n* -S [ML *chrismale*, fr. LL *chrisma* chrism] **:** a vessel or flask for holding the chrism

chris·ma·tion \kriz'māshən\ *n* -S *usu cap* [ML *chrismation-*, *chrismatio*, fr. LL *chrismare* to chrism] **:** a confirmatory sacrament of the Eastern Orthodox Church in which a baptized member is anointed with chrism and which corresponds to confirmation in the West

¹chris·ma·to·ry \'krizmə,tōrē\ *n* -ES [ME *crismatorie*, fr. ML *chrismatorium*, fr. LL *chrismat-*, *chrisma* chrism + L *-orium* -ory] **1 :** a cruet or vessel or a place in which the chrism is kept **2 :** sacramental anointment **:** UNCTION

²chrismatory \"\ *adj* **:** of or relating to sacramental unction

chris·mon \'kriz,män\ *n, pl* **chrismons** *or* **chris·ma** \-mə, -,mä\ [ML, fr. *chris-* (fr. L *Christus* Christ) + *-mon* (fr. LL *monogramma* monogram)] **:** CHI-RHO

chris·om *also* **chrys·om** *or* **chrys·ome** \'krizəm\ *n* -S [ME *crisom*, alter of *crisme* — more at CHRISM] **1 :** CHRISM **2** [ME *crisom*, short for *crisom cloth*] **:** a white cloth, robe, or mantle put upon a person at baptism as a symbol of innocence **3** [by shortening] **:** CHRISOM CHILD

chrisom child *n* **1 :** an innocent child **:** INFANT **2 :** a child that dies in its first month

christ \'krīst\ *n* -S [after Jesus *Christ* †*ab* A.D.29, fr. ME *Crist*, fr. OE, fr. L *Christus*, fr. Gk *Christos*, lit., anointed (fr. *chriein* to anoint), trans. of Heb *māshīaḥ* anointed, Messiah — more at CHRISM, MESSIAH] **1** *cap* **:** one who is accepted as the Messiah ⟨this Jesus, whom I proclaim to you, is the *Christ* — Acts 17:3 (RSV)⟩ **2** *usu cap* **a :** one who in his outlook or activities resembles Jesus ⟨the legend of Thunupa, the Andean *Christ*, who was stoned to death and abandoned on a drifting raft for preaching virtue and goodness —F.D. de Medina⟩ **b :** an ideal and perfect type of humanity **3** *cap, Christian Science* **:** the ideal truth that comes as a divine manifestation of God to destroy incarnate error

¹chris·ta·del·phi·an \,kristə'delfēən\ *n* -S *usu cap* [*Christ* + Gk *adelphos* brother + E *-ian* — more at ADELPHOUS] **:** one of a premillennial religious sect that was founded in the U. S. about 1850 and that rejects the doctrine of the Trinity in favor of a Unitarian and Adventist theology

²christadelphian \¦⸗⸗¦⸗⸗⸗\ *adj, usu cap* **:** of or relating to Christadelphians ⟨*Christadelphian* doctrine⟩

chris·ta·del·phi·an·ism \,⸗⸗'⸗⸗ə,nizəm\ *n* -S *cap* **:** the beliefs and practices of Christadelphians

christ·church \'krīs(t),chərch\ *adj, usu cap* [fr. *Christchurch*, New Zealand] **:** of or from the city of Christchurch, New Zealand **:** of the kind or style prevalent in Christchurch

christ·cross \'kri,skrȯs *also* -äs\ *n* [ME *Crist cross*, fr. *Crist* Christ + *cross*] **:** the mark of the cross formerly put before the alphabet or as the sign of 12 o'clock on a dial **:** a crosslike mark or figure used as a signature by one unable to write

christ·cross-row \¦⸗,⸗¦rō\ *n* [so called fr. the figure of a cross heading it in old hornbooks] **:** ALPHABET

¹christen *adj or n, cap* [ME *cristen*, fr. OE] *obs* **:** CHRISTIAN

²chris·ten \'kris³n\ *vb* **christened; christened; christening** \-s(³)niŋ\ **christens** [ME *cristnen*, *cristen*, fr. OE *cristnian*, fr. *cristen* Christian, fr. L *christianus*] *vt* **1** *obs* **:** CHRISTIANIZE **2 a :** to receive or initiate into a Christian church by the rite of baptism **:** BAPTIZE **b :** to name at baptism **3** *obs* **:** to stand sponsor to (a child) at baptism **4 :** to name or dedicate in naming (as a ship) by a ceremony suggestive of baptism **5 :** to give a name to **:** NAME, DENOMINATE ⟨the latter hill they ~*ed* Mount Joy —*Amer. Guide Series: Pa.*⟩ **6 :** to use for the first time esp. with a sense of the formality of the occasion ⟨~ a new car by taking a Sunday drive⟩ ~ *vi* **:** to administer baptism

chris·ten·die \¦kris³n¦dē\ *n, cap* [alter. (prob. influenced by *christendom*) of ME *cristentie*, fr. OF *crestienté* — more at CHRISTIANITY] *Scot* **:** CHRISTENDOM

chris·ten·dom \'kris³ndəm\ *n* -S [ME *cristendom*, fr. OE *cristendōm*, fr. *cristen* Christian + *-dōm* -dom] **1 a** *often cap*, *obs* **:** CHRISTIANITY 3 **b** *usu cap* **:** CHRISTIANITY 1,2 ⟨across the first thousand years of *Christendom* the principal church was the Roman Catholic Church —F.S.Mead⟩ **2** *usu cap* **:** the portion of the world in which Christianity prevails or which is governed principally under Christian institutions

chris·ten·ing \'kris(³)niŋ\ *n* -S [ME *cristening*, fr. gerund of *cristnen*] **1 :** the ceremony of baptizing and officially naming a child often including following festivities **2 :** the esp. official or ceremonial naming of something ⟨the colorful ~ of an aircraft carrier⟩

christ·er \'krīstə(r)\ *n* -S *cap* [*Christ* + *-er*] **1** *slang* **:** one thought to associate himself too prominently or overpiously with the Christian church or its principles (as with the stricter forms) or with organizations or activity dedicated to spreading such principles **2** *slang* **:** one who is overly pious or prudish

christ·hood \'krīst,hu̇d, 'krīst,hu̇d\ *n* -S *usu cap* [ME *Cristhod*, fr. *Crist* + *-hod* -hood] **:** the quality or state of being a Christ

¹chris·tian \'kris(h)chən, *Brit often & US sometimes* -styən *or* -stēən; *in sense 1b sometimes* 'krī- *by nonmembers of these groups*\ *n* -S *usu cap* [L *christianus*, adj. or n., fr. Gk *christianos*, fr. *Christos* Christ] **1 a :** one who believes or professes or is assumed to believe in Jesus Christ and the truth as taught by him **:** an adherent of Christianity **:** one who has accepted the Christian religious and moral principles of life **:** one who has faith in and has pledged allegiance to God thought of as revealed in Christ **:** one whose life is conformed to the doctrines of Christ ⟨in Antioch the disciples were for the first time called *Christians* —Acts 11:26 (RSV)⟩ **b :** a member of a church or group professing Christian doctrine or belief: as (1) **:** a member of the Disciples of Christ (2) **:** a member of one of the Churches of Christ, a body of churches dedicated to the restoring of New Testament Christianity and the promotion of Christian unity by dispensing with creeds and sectarian names and relying on the Bible as the sole rule of faith and practice (3) **:** a member of the Christian Church that united with Congregationalists in 1931 to form the Congregational Christian Churches (4) **:** one of the Plymouth Brethren **2** *now chiefly dial* **:** a human being as distinguished from a lower animal **3 :** one born in a Christian country or of Christian parents who has not definitely adhered to an opposing system

²christian \"\ *adj, usu cap* [alter. (influenced by L *christianus*) of earlier *cristen*, fr. ME — more at CHRISTEN] **1 :** professing or belonging to Christianity ⟨a *Christian* people⟩ ⟨a *Christian* country⟩ **2 a :** of or relating to Jesus Christ ⟨*Christian* religion⟩ **b :** of or based on Christianity **:** according to Christian principles ⟨*Christian* art⟩ ⟨a *Christian* burial⟩ **c :** of or relating to a Christian or Christians ⟨one drop of *Christian* blood —Shak.⟩ **d :** representing Christianity ⟨his most *Christian* majesty, the king⟩ **3 a :** characteristic of Christian people **:** following Christ's precepts and example **b** *now chiefly dial* **:** human as distinguished from brutish **c :** DECENT, CIVILIZED ⟨act in a *Christian* fashion⟩ **4** *obs* **:** relating to the church **:** ECCLESIASTICAL — used chiefly in the phrase *court Christian* or *Christian court* **5** *of a door* **:** having the panels so placed that the design of a Latin cross is formed, formerly as a deterrent to evil spirits

christian brethren *n, cap C&B* **:** PLYMOUTH BRETHREN

christian brother *n, usu cap C&B* **:** BROTHER OF THE CHRISTIAN SCHOOLS

christian d'or \¦krist,yän¦dȯ(ə)r, -stē,än-\ *n, pl* **christian d'ors** \-rz\ [F, fr. *Christian* VII †1808 king of Denmark and duke of Holstein, under whom it was struck + *d'or* of gold (as in *louis d'or*)] **:** a Danish gold coin of the 19th century

christian era *n, usu cap C* **:** the era used in Christian countries for numbering the years since the birth of Christ, its first year corresponding with the Roman year 754, Christ's birth having been placed by Dionysius Exiguus († *ab* 540), who first used this era, at December 25 in Roman year 753

christian existentialism *n, usu cap C* **:** a form of existentialism stressing subjective aspects of the human person considered as a creature of God; *esp* **:** such a theory emphasizing (1) the natural desire of the creature to seek his creator (as in the philosophers and thinkers Augustine, Pascal, Nikolai Berdyaev, and Gabriel Marcel) or (2) the distance between guilty man and omnipotent God (as in Kierkegaard and the dialectical or crisis theology of Karl Barth and Emil Brunner) — called also respectively (1) *Catholic existentialism* (2) *Protestant existentialism*

chris·ti·an·ia \,kris(h)chē'anēə, -stē- *also* -än-\ *or* **chris·ty** *or* **chris·tie** \'kristē\ *also* **chris·ti·ana** \,kris(h)chē'anə, -stē- *also* -än-\ *n, pl* **christianias** *or* **christies** *also* **christianas** *often cap* [*christiania* fr. *Christiania* (now Oslo), Norway; *christy*, *christie*, *christiana*, by shortening and alter. fr. *Christiania*] **:** a skiing turn used for altering the direction of hill descent usu. from one diagonally transverse direction to the other or for checking or stopping and executed usu. at relatively high speed largely by shifting the body weight forward and skidding into a turn with parallel skis — see STEM CHRISTIANIA

chris·tian·ism \'kris(h)chə,nizəm *sometimes* -styə,n- *or* -stēə,n-\ *n* -S *cap* [MF *christianisme*, fr. LL *christianismus*, fr. Gk *christianismos*, fr. *christianos* Christian + *-ismos* -ism — more at CHRISTIAN] **:** the religious system, tenets, or practices of Christians

chris·ti·an·i·ty \,kris(h)chē'anəd·ē, -nətē, -i *also* ,kristē'a- *or* kris(h)'cha- *sometimes* krist'ya-\ *n* -ES [ME *cristiente*, *cristianitee*, fr. MF *crestienté*, fr. LL *christianitat-*, *christianitas*, fr. L *christianus* Christian + *-itat-*, *-itas* -ity — more at CHRISTIAN] **1** *usu cap* **:** the whole body of Christian believers **:** CHRISTENDOM **2** *cap* **:** the religion of Christians **:** the religion stemming from the life, teachings, and death of Jesus Christ **:** the religion that believes in God as the Father Almighty who as a just and merciful creator and sustainer of the universe works redemptively through the Holy Spirit for men's salvation and that affirms Jesus Christ as Lord and Savior who proclaimed to man the gospel of salvation **:** the religion that recognizes the New Testament as its book of sacred scripture **3** *usu cap* **:** the quality or state of being a Christian **:** Christian character or spirit **:** practical conformity of one's inward and outward life to the spirit of the Christian religion

chris·tian·iza·tion \,kris(h)chənə'zāshən, -,nī'z- *sometimes* -styə- *or* -stēə-\ *n* -S *usu cap* **:** the act or process of christianizing or being christianized

chris·tian·ize \'⸗(⸗)⸗,nīz\ *vb* -ED/-ING/-S *often cap* [¹*christian* + *-ize*] *vt* **1 :** to make Christian **:** convert to Christianity **2 :** to imbue with or deeply affect by Christian principles ~ *vi* **:** to adopt the character or beliefs of a Christian **:** become Christian

chris·tian·iz·er \-zə(r)\ *n* -S *often cap* **:** one that christianizes

chris·tian·ly *adj, usu cap* **:** belonging to or befitting a Christian **:** Christian in spirit **:** GENTLE, GENEROUS, CHARITABLE ⟨moderate and *Christianly* of attitude⟩ ⟨a *Christianly* greeting⟩

christian name *n, often cap C* **:** the name given at birth or christening as distinct from the family name **:** FIRST NAME, FORENAME

chris·tian·ness \-n(n)əs\ *n* -ES *usu cap* **:** the state or the quality of being Christian

christian reformed *adj, usu cap C&R* **:** of or relating to the Christian Reformed Church formed in the Netherlands in 1834 by dissenters from the Netherlands Reformed Church or to the Christian Reformed Church formed in the U.S. in 1857 by dissenters from the Reformed Church in America

christian science *n, cap C&S* **:** a religion discovered by Mary Baker Eddy in 1866 that was organized under the official name of the Church of Christ, Scientist, that derives its teachings from the Scriptures as understood by its adherents, and that includes a practice of spiritual healing based upon the teaching that cause and effect are mental and that sin, sickness, and death will be destroyed by a full understanding of the divine principle of Jesus's teaching and healing

christian scientist *n, usu cap C&S* **:** a believer in Christian Science **:** one who practices the teachings of Christian Science

christian year *n, usu cap C* **1 :** a year of the Christian era **:** a Gregorian year **2 :** the year as it is observed by Christian churches marked by various festivals or commemorations at special seasons and on special days — called also *church year*

christ·less \'krīstləs\ *adj, usu cap* **:** without faith in the teachings of Christ **:** UNCHRISTIAN

christ·like \'krīst,līk\ *adj, usu cap* **1 :** like or like that of Christ in character, spirit, or action ⟨dedicated men leading *Christlike* lives⟩ **2 :** in accord with the teaching and example of Christ ⟨in behalf of virtue, holiness, brotherly love, and whatsoever else is *Christlike* and Godlike —W.F.Tillett⟩

christ·ly \-lē,-li\ *adj, usu cap* **:** like Christ or like that of Christ in spirit ⟨*Christly* self-denial —*Emporia (Kans.) Gaz.*⟩ ⟨*Christly* activities⟩ — sometimes used as a generalized term of disparagement ⟨a *Christly* mess⟩

¹christ·mas \'krisməs\ *n* -ES *cap* [ME *Cristemasse*, *Cristes masse*, fr. OE *Cristes mæsse*, fr. *Cristes* (gen. of *Crist* Christ) + *mæsse* mass — more at CHRIST, MASS] **1 :** an annual church festival kept on December 25 or by some Eastern churches on January 7 in memory of the birth of Christ, celebrated generally by a particular church service, special gifts, and greetings, and observed in most Christian communities as a legal holiday **2 :** the Christmas season **:** CHRISTMASTIDE **3** *dial Eng* **:** evergreens used for decorations at Christmas

²christmas \"\ *vi* -ED/-ING/-ES *cap* **:** to celebrate Christmas ⟨an evening of *Christmasing*⟩

christmas begonia *n, usu cap C* **:** any of various bulbous begonias usu. considered as of a single species (*Begonia cheimantha*) but derived chiefly from an Asiatic form (*B. socotrana*) either directly as sports or by hybridization with a southern African form (*B. dregei*) or other species

christmas bell *n, usu cap C* **1 :** any of several plants of the genus *Blandfordia* — usu. used in pl. **2 :** the flower of the Christmas-bell plant

christmasberry \'⸗⸗,⸗⸗\ *n, usu cap* **:** the fruit of the toyon; *also* **:** the shrub itself

christmas bush *n, usu cap C* **:** an Australian tree (*Ceratopetalum gummiferum*) of the family Cunoniaceae often used in Christmas decorations — called also *Christmas tree*

christmas cactus *n, usu cap 1st C* **:** CRAB CACTUS

christmas card *n, usu cap 1st C* **:** an ornamental card with a greeting sent at Christmas

christmas club *n, usu cap 1st C* **:** a savings account in which regular usu. weekly deposits are made throughout the year to provide money for Christmas shopping in December

christmas disease *n, usu cap C* [after Stephen *Christmas*, 20th cent. English boy who was first patient found with the disease] **:** a hereditary sex-linked hemorrhagic disease involving absence of a coagulation factor in the blood and failure of the clotting mechanism — compare HEMOPHILIA

christmas fern *n, usu cap C* **:** a No. American evergreen fern (*Polystichum acrostichoides*) used for decoration in winter and having the fertile terminal pinnae much smaller than the sterile ones

christmas flower *n, usu cap C* **1 :** CHRISTMAS ROSE **2 :** AMERICAN HELLEBORE **3 :** a poinsettia (*Euphorbia pulcherrima*) of Mexico

christmas gift \¦⸗⸗'⸗, *with exclamatory intonation*\ *interj, usu cap C, South & Midland* — used as a Christmas greeting and sometimes esp. formerly as part of a custom requiring that the first person to speak the greeting to another on Christmas morning be given a gift by the other

christmas green *n, usu cap C* **:** GROUND PINE 2

christmas holly *n, usu cap C* **:** any of several shrubs or trees of the genus *Ilex*: as **a :** ENGLISH HOLLY **b :** AMERICAN HOLLY

christmas pepper *n, usu cap C* **:** an annual pepper (*Capsicum frutescens*) grown for its ornamental round or cone-shaped red or purple fruits

christmas pie *n, usu cap C, chiefly Brit* **:** MINCE PIE

christmas rose *n, usu cap C* **:** a European herb (*Helleborus niger*) having white or purplish roselike flowers produced in winter

christmas stocking *n, usu cap C* **:** a stocking or sometimes a pillowcase customarily hung up usu. on the mantel of a fireplace by children on Christmas eve to hold Christmas presents

christmastide \'⸗⸗,⸗\ *n, usu cap* [¹*Christmas* + *tide* (time)] **:** the festival season from Christmas eve till after New Year's or esp. in England till Epiphany

christmastime \'⸗⸗,⸗\ *n, usu cap* **:** CHRISTMASTIDE

christmas tree *n, usu cap C* [trans. of G *weihnachtsbaum* or *Christbaum*] **1 :** a usu. small evergreen tree customarily decorated at Christmas with ornaments and lights and often when in the home with Christmas presents around the base **2 a :** CHRISTMAS BUSH **b** *NewZeal* **:** POHUTUKAWA **c :** any of several evergreen trees of the north temperate zone esp. of the genera *Abies* and *Picea* **3** *dial* **:** a Christmas gathering or celebration **4 :** an oil-well control manifold consisting of an assembly of fittings (as valves, clamps, anchors, and connections) placed on the casinghead of a flowing well to control its production **5** *slang* **:** a submarine control-room panel of red and green lights that flash on and off to indicate valve conditions

christ·masy *or* **christ·mas·sy** \'krisməsē, -si\ *adj, usu cap* **:** befitting Christmas or the Christmas season; *esp* **:** colorful, cheerful, or festive in a way usu. associated with the celebration of Christmas or with the bustle of preparing for it ⟨a *Christmasy* glitter⟩

chris·to- *comb form, cap* [LGk, fr. Gk *Christos*] **:** Christ ⟨*Christocentric*⟩ ⟨*Christolatry*⟩ ⟨*Christocracy*⟩

chris·to·cen·trism \,kristə'sen,trizəm\ *n* -S *usu cap* [*Christo-* + *centr-* + *-ism*] **:** the placing of Christ at the center of one's thought, actions, or theological system

chris·to·gram \'⸗⸗,gram\ *n* -S *usu cap* [*Christo-* + *-gram*] **:** a graphic symbol of Christ; *esp* **:** CHI-RHO

chris·to·log·i·cal \¦⸗⸗¦läjəkəl\ *adj, often cap* **:** of or relating to Christology

chris·tol·o·gy \kri'stäləjē\ *n* -ES *usu cap* [*Christo-* + *-logy*] **1 :** the theological interpretation of the person and work of Christ often expressed doctrinally **2 :** the branch of theology that deals with the person and work of Christ

Christogram

christom child *n* [by alter.] *obs* **:** CHRISOM CHILD

chris·toph·a·ny \kri'stäfənē\ *n* -ES *usu cap* [*Christo-* + *-phany*] **:** an appearance of Christ after resurrection esp. as recorded in the Gospels

chris·to·phine \'kristə,fēn\ *n* -S [AmerF, prob. fr. *Christophe* Christopher + F *-ine*] **:** CHAYOTE

christs *pl of* CHRIST

christ's-thorn \'krīs(t)+, -īs(t)s+\ *n, pl* **christ's-thorns** *usu cap C* **:** any of several prickly or thorny shrubs of Palestine (esp. the shrub *Paliurus spina-christi* or the jujube *Ziziphus jujuba*)

christ within *n, usu cap C&W* **:** INNER LIGHT

christy *often cap, var of* CHRISTIANIA

-chroia \'krȯiə *also* -ōiyə\ *n comb form* -S [NL, fr. Gk, fr. *-chroos* -chroous + *-ia*] **:** coloration ⟨*cyanochroia*⟩ **:** discoloration ⟨*cyanochroia*⟩

-chro·ic \¦krōik\ *adj comb form* [Gk *-chroos* -chroous + ISV *-ic*] **:** -CHROOUS ⟨*erythrochroic*⟩

chrom- *or* **chromo-** *comb form* [F, fr. Gk *chrōma* color] **1 :** chromium⟨*chromammine*⟩ ⟨*chromoarsenate*⟩ **2 a :** color **:** colored ⟨*chromidrosis*⟩ ⟨*chromometer*⟩ **b :** pigment **:** pigmented ⟨*chromocyte*⟩ ⟨*chromogen*⟩

chro·ma \'krōmə\ *n* -S [Gk *chrōma* color — more at CHROMATIC] **1 :** SATURATION 4a **2 :** the color dimension on the Munsell scales that correlates most closely with saturation — see the Color Charts explanation at COLOR **syn** see COLOR

chro·ma·ble \'krōməbəl\ *adj* [*chrom-* + *-able*] **:** capable of combining with chromium or a chromium compound — used of a mordant ⟨~ dyes⟩

chro·ma·dor·i·da \,krōmə'dȯrədə\ *n pl, cap* [NL, fr. *Chromadora*, genus of nematode worms (fr. Gk *chrōma* color + *dora* skin) + *-ida*; akin to Gk *derein* to skin, flay — more at CHROMATIC, TEAR] **:** an order of Aphasmidia comprising free-living or occas. commensal nematode worms having the esophagus divisible into three regions and the amphids spiral, vesicular, or circular — compare ENOPLIDA

chro·maf·fin \krō'mafən, 'krōmə-\ *also* **chro·maf·fine** \-(,)fēn, -,fən\ *adj* [ISV *chrom-* + L *affinis* associated with, related by marriage; prob. orig. formed in G — more at AFFINITY] **:** staining deeply with chromium salts ⟨~ tissue⟩; *specif* **:** indicating, relating to, or made up of certain pigmented cells derived from the sympathetic ganglia and capable of secreting adrenaline and forming in higher vertebrates the medulla of the suprarenal glands and the paraganglia — **chro·maf·fin·ic** \¦krōmə¦finik, -,ma¦-\ *adj*

chromaffin body *n* **:** PARAGANGLION

chrom·am·mine \ˈkrōmˌaˌmēn,-ˌmən; ¦krōmə¦mēn\ *n* -s [ISV *chrom-* + *ammine*; orig. formed as F *chromamine*] **:** an ammine of chromium

chro·man \ˈkrōˌman\ *n* -s [ISV *chrom-* (color) + *-an*] **:** a bicyclic heterocyclic compound $C_9H_{10}O$ that is the parent nucleus of the tocopherols; dihydro-benzo-pyran

chro·ma·phil \ˈkrōməˌfil\ *adj* [Gk *chrōma* color + E *-phil*] **:** CHROMAFFIN

chro·ma·scope \ˈ==ˌskōp\ *n* -s [Gk *chrōma* color + E *-scope*] **:** an instrument for testing the optical effects of color

-chro·ma·sia \krōˈmāzh(ē)ə\ *n comb form* -s [NL, fr. Gk *chrōmat-, chrōma* color + NL *-ia*] **1 :** color ⟨*achromasia*⟩ **2 :** stainability **:** colorability ⟨*polychromasia*⟩

chromat- *or* **chromato-** *comb form* [Gk *chrōmat-, chrōma* color] **1 :** color ⟨*chromatology*⟩ **:** colored ⟨*chromatopsia*⟩ **2 :** chromatin ⟨*chromatolysis*⟩

[1]**chro·mate** \ˈkrōˌmāt, -mət\ *n* -s [F, fr. *chrom-* + *-ate*] **:** a salt or ester of chromic acid

[2]**chro·mate** \-ˌmāt\ *vt* -ED/-ING/-S **:** to treat or impregnate with a chromate or dichromate esp. with potassium dichromate

chromate method *n* **:** the metachrome method in dyeing

[1]**chro·mat·ic** \krōˈmad·|ik, krə-, -at|, |ēk, *attrib also* ˈkrōˌm-\ *adj* [Gk *chrōmatikos*, fr. *chrōmat-, chrōma* skin, color, modification of diatonic music consisting of the use of tones altered in pitch; akin to Gk *chrōs* skin, color, OE *grēot* sand; basic meaning: to rub, grind — more at GRIT] **1 a :** having to do with color **:** with respect to color phenomena **b :** evoking, resulting from, or associated with color sensations **c :** full of color **:** highly colored **2 a :** having or manifesting chroma **b :** exhibiting hues or embracing the hues **c :** with respect to hue or saturation **3 a** *of a Greek tetrachord* **:** comprising successive steps of 1½, ½, and ½ — distinguished from *diatonic* and *enharmonic* **b :** of, relating to, or giving all the tones of the chromatic scale ⟨a ~ harmonica⟩ ⟨~ intervals⟩ **c** *of harmony* **:** characterized by frequent use of tones foreign to the basic mode or key of the piece containing the harmony **4** *biol* **a :** capable of being colored by staining agents **b :** of, like, or relating to chromatin **5** *of language or prose* **:** of, relating to, or having colorful connotations or evocative power ⟨the full ~ and diatonic possibilities of the prose medium —G.M.Hopkins⟩ ⟨~ words —F.R.Leavis⟩ **6 :** executed in fine usu. colorful detail ⟨~ coverage of the Dark Continent —*Newsweek*⟩ ⟨a masterpiece of ~ mendacity —J.J.Ingalls⟩ — **chro·mat·i·cal·ly** \-ək(ə)lē, -ēk-, -li\ *adv*

[2]**chromatic** \"\ *n* -s [F *chromatique*, fr. *chromatique*, adj., fr. Gk *chrōmatikos*] **:** [2]ACCIDENTAL 3

chromatic aberration *n* **:** aberration caused by the different refrangibilities of the colored rays of the spectrum

chromatic alteration *n* **:** the raising or lowering of a musical tone by a half step

chromatic chord *n* **:** a chord having tones foreign to a given key or mode

chromatic figure *n* **:** the mitotic or meiotic chromosomes — compare ACHROMATIC FIGURE

chromatic interval *n* **:** a normal musical scale interval raised or lowered by a half step

chro·mat·i·cism \=ˈ=əˌsizəm\ *n* -s **1 :** the quality or state of being chromatic **2 a :** the act or action of chromaticizing **:** the use of chromatic notes or tones ⟨excessive ~ means excessive increase in harmonic tension —Mosco Carner⟩ — contrasted with *diatonicism* **b :** an instance of this use

chro·ma·tic·i·ty \ˌkrōməˈtisəd·ē, -ətē, -i\ *n* -ES **1 :** the quality or state of being chromatic **2 :** the quality of color characterized by its dominant or complementary wavelength and purity taken together

chromaticity coordinate *n* **:** the ratio of the amount of one primary color to the total amount of all three necessary to reproduce a given color

chromaticity diagram *n* **:** a triangular graph on which points for all chromaticity coordinates may be systematically plotted, the apexes of the triangle representing the primary colors — called also *color triangle, Maxwell triangle*

chro·mat·i·ci·za·tion \krōˌmadəsəˈzāshən, krə-, -atə-, -ˌsīˈz-\ *n* -s **:** CHROMATICISM 2

chro·mat·i·cize \=ˈ=əˌsīz\ *vb* -ED/-ING/-S *vi* **:** to use in chords and progressions notes that are foreign to a given tonality **:** use the tones of the chromatic scale ~ *vt* **:** to make chromatic in harmonic structure

chro·mat·ic·ness \-iknəs, -ēk-\ *n* -ES **:** the quality of color characterized by its hue and saturation taken together

chro·mat·ics \-ks\ *n pl but sing in constr* **1 :** the part of optics that deals with the properties of colors **2 :** the branch of colorimetry that deals with hue and saturation

chromatic scale *n* **:** any musical sequence of half steps **:** all the notes, in series, possible to a keyboard or wind instrument with fixed tempered intervals

chromatic sign *n* **:** [2]ACCIDENTAL

chromatic vision *n* **1 :** normal color vision in which the colors of the spectrum are distinguished and evaluated — opposed to *color blindness* **2 :** CHROMATOPSIA

chro·ma·tid \ˈkrōmətəd\ *n* -s [ISV *chromat-* + *-id*] **:** one of the paired complex constituent strands of a chromosome — compare CHROMONEMA — **chro·mat·i·dal** \krōˈmad·ədᵊl, ¦krōmə¦tīdᵊl\ *adj*

chro·ma·tin \ˈkrōmətən, -məd·ən\ *n* -s [ISV *chromat-* + *-in*; orig. formed in G] **1 a (1) :** the part of a cell nucleus that stains intensely with basic dyes and is usu. divisible into more stainable basichromatin and less stainable oxychromatin and linin — not used technically **(2) :** a cytoplasmic constituent that because of similar staining reactions is considered identical with nuclear chromatin — not used technically **b :** an ampholytic complex of highly polymerized deoxyribose nucleic acid with basic proteins of protamine or histone type that exhibits differential staining of various parts of the complex at different periods in the nuclear cycle prob. due to fluctuation in the degree of polymerization, that is regarded as the physical carrier of genes, and that is typically manifest in chromomeres which in mitosis form chromosomes **2 :** KARYOTIN — **chro·ma·tin·ic** \¦==¦tinik\ *adj*

chromatin diminution *n* **:** elimination of parts of the chromosomes from prospective soma during early cleavage

chro·ma·tism \ˈkrōməˌtizəm\ *n* -s [Gk *chrōmatismos* coloring, fr. *chrōmatizein* to color, fr. *chrōmat-, chrōma* color] **1 :** COLORING 1c; *esp* **:** abnormal pigmentation **2 :** CHROMATIC ABERRATION **3 :** CHROMESTHESIA

chro·ma·tist \-məd·əst\ *n* -s **:** a specialist in chromatics — compare COLORIST

chro·ma·ti·um \krōˈmāshēəm\ *n, cap* [NL, fr. *chromat-* + *-ium*] **:** a genus of purple sulfur bacteria (family Thiorhodaceae) that are ovoid to bean-shaped or rod-shaped, motile by polar flagella, reddish from a mixture of bacteriochlorophyll and carotenoid pigments, and widely distributed in fresh or salt water, some having been reported also from soil

chro·ma·tize \ˈkrōməˌtīz\ *vt* -ED/-ING/-S [*chromat-* + *-ize*] **:** CHROMATE

chromato- *in pronunciations below*, =¦== = ¦krōˌmad·ə *or* krə- *or* -atə, ¦=== = ¦krōməd·|ə *or* -ət| *or* |ō\ — see CHROMAT-

chro·mato·cyte \=ˈ==+ˌsīt\ *n* -s [ISV *chromat-* + *-cyte*] **:** a unicellular chromatophore **:** a pigment cell

chro·mato·gram \-ˌgram\ *n* -s [*chromat-* + *-gram*] **:** the series of separate zones on an adsorbent medium into which the different substances in a mixture are separated by chromatography

[1]**chro·mato·graph** \-ˌgraf\ *n* -s [*chromat-* + *-graph*] *archaic* **:** a colored print

[2]**chromatograph** \"\ *vt* -ED/-ING/-S **1 :** to make a chromatic representation or reproduction of **2 :** to separate into components by chromatography

chro·mato·graph·ic \=¦==, ¦===+¦grafik\ *adj* **:** of or relating to chromatography — **chro·mato·graph·i·cal·ly** \-fək(ə)lē\ *adv*

chro·ma·tog·ra·phy \ˌkrōməˈtägrəfē\ *n* -ES [*chromat-* + *-graphy*] **:** a process of separating gases, liquids, or solids in a mixture or solution by adsorption (as selective adsorption on clay, silica gel, or alumina or on paper) as the mixture flows over the adsorbent medium, often in a column, each substance finally appearing in the medium at a different level or band that is often colored and then being recoverable (as by washing out with pure solvent)

chro·ma·toid \ˈkrōməˌtȯid\ *adj* [ISV *chromat-* + *-oid*; orig. formed in G] **:** resembling chromatin esp. in affinity for stains

chro·ma·tol·y·sis \ˌkrōməˈtäləsəs\ *n, pl* **chromatoly·ses** \-əˌsēz\ [NL, fr. *chromat-* + *-lysis*] **:** the dissolution and breaking up of chromophil material (as Nissl bodies or chromatin) of a cell — **chro·mato·lyt·ic** \=¦==, ¦=== *at* CHROMATO- +¦lid·ik\ *adj*

chro·ma·tom·e·ter \ˌkrōməˈtäməd·ə(r)\ *n* -s [F *chromatomètre*, fr. *chromat-* + *-mètre* -meter] **1 :** a color diagram or chart so arranged as to serve as a scale of colors **2 :** an instrument for measuring color perception **3 :** CHROMOMETER

chro·ma·tone process \ˈkrōməˌtōn-\ *n* [Gk *chrōma* color + E *tone*] **:** a photographic color process in which three colored images are formed separately by toning, stripped from their special paper, and superimposed in register

chromatophil *or* **chromatophile** *var of* CHROMOPHIL

chro·mato·phil·ia \=ˌ==, ˌ=== *at* CHROMATO-+ˈfilēə\ *also* **chro·moph·i·ly** \krōˈmäfəlē\ *n, pl* **chromatophilias** *also* **chromophilies** [NL *chromatophilia*, fr. *chromat-* + *-philia*] **:** the quality or state of being chromophil

chro·ma·toph·o·ral \ˌkrōməˈtäf(ə)rəl, krōˌmad·əˈfōrəl\ *adj* **:** of or belonging to a chromatophore

chro·mato·phore \=ˈ==, ˈ=== *at* CHROMATO- + ˌfō(ə)r\ *n* -s [ISV *chromat-* + *-phore*] **1 :** a pigment-bearing cell; *esp* **:** one of those cells in the integument of various animals capable of changing the apparent pigmentation of the skin by expanding or contracting **2 :** a chromoplast or chloroplast — **chro·mato·phor·ic** \=ˈ==, ¦===+¦fōrik\ *or* **chro·ma·toph·o·rous** \¦krōmə¦täf(ə)rəs\ *adj*

chro·mato·plasm \=ˈ==, ˈ=== *at* CHROMATO- + ˌplazəm\ *also* **chro·mo·plasm** \ˈkrōməˌp-\ *n* -s [ISV *chromat-* or *chrom-* + *-plasm*; orig. formed as G *chromatoplasma*] **:** the peripheral protoplasm of a blue-green alga containing chlorophyll and accessory pigments together with stored substances

chro·ma·top·sia \ˌkrōməˈtäpsēə\ *n* -s [NL, fr. *chromat-* + *-opsia*] **:** a disturbance of vision which is sometimes caused by drugs and in which colorless objects appear colored

chro·mato·scope \=ˈ==, ˈ=== *at* CHROMATO- + ˌskōp\ *n* -s [ISV *chromat-* + *-scope*; prob. orig. formed in F] **:** an instrument for the mixing of color stimuli by means of light beams

chro·ma·to·sis \ˌkrōməˈtōsəs\ *n, pl* **chromato·ses** \-ōˌsēz\ [NL, fr. *chromat-* + *-osis*] **:** PIGMENTATION; *specif* **:** deposit of pigment in a normally unpigmented area or excessive pigmentation in a normally pigmented site

chro·ma·trope \ˈkrōmə·ˌtrōp\ *n* -s [ISV *chroma-* (fr. Gk *chrōma* color) + *-trope* — more at CHROMATIC] **:** CHROMOTROPE

chro·ma·type \-məˌtīp\ *n* -s [Gk *chrōma* + E *type*] **1 :** a photograph made upon paper sensitized with potassium bichromate and a metallic sulfate (as copper sulfate) **2 :** the process of making a chromatype — compare CARBON PROCESS

[1]**chrome** \ˈkrōm\ *n* -s [F, fr. Gk *chrōma* color, fr. the beautiful colors of its compounds — more at CHROMATIC] **1 :** CHROMIUM **2 :** CHROME YELLOW **3 :** CHROME LEATHER

[2]**chrome** \"\ *vb* -ED/-ING/-S *vt* **1 :** to treat with a compound of chromium: **a** *in dyeing* **:** to treat with a solution of a dichromate (as sodium dichromate) or complex chromium chromate **b :** to subject to chrome tanning **2 :** to give chroma to ⟨~ a neutral background⟩ **3 :** to surface (as an electrotype) with chromium ~ *vi* **:** to acquire or to increase in chroma

-chrome \(ˌ)ˌkrōm\ *n comb form or adj comb form* [ML *-chromat-, chroma* colored thing, fr. Gk *chrōmat-, chrōma* color] **1 :** colored thing **:** colored ⟨*monochrome*⟩ **2 :** coloring matter ⟨*endochrome*⟩

chrome alum *n* **:** an alum in which chromium is the trivalent metal; *esp* **:** potassium chromium sulfate $KCr(SO_4)_2.12H_2O$ obtained as dark purple crystals by treating potassium dichromate with sulfur dioxide and used in tanning, as a mordant, and as a hardening agent for gelatin in photography

chrome black *n* **:** a black produced by dyeing with logwood after chroming

chrome brick *n* **:** a refractory brick manufactured substantially or entirely of chrome ore

chrome cake *n* **:** sodium sulfate containing some chromium, obtained as a by-product in the manufacture of sodium dichromate, and used in the paper industry

chrome dye *n* **:** any of a class of mordant acid dyes applied usu. to wool with a chromium compound as the mordant — see DYE table I (under *Mordant*)

chrome green *n* **1 a** *Brit* **(1) :** a chromic oxide either anhydrous or hydrated **(2) :** any of several similar green pigments consisting essentially of some chromic salt (as the phosphate) — compare CHROME OXIDE GREEN **b :** any of various brilliant green pigments essentially mixtures of chrome yellow and iron blue, often with barite or clay, used as oil colors, in printing inks, and in textile printing — called also *Brunswick green* **2 :** any of several mordant acid dyes **3 a :** any of several yellowish greens that are mixtures of characteristic colors of iron blue and chrome yellow including three with varying amounts of white pigment: **(1) :** DEEP CHROME GREEN **(2) :** MEDIUM CHROME GREEN **(3) :** LIGHT CHROME GREEN **b :** VIRIDIAN 2 **c :** the color of chromic oxide

chrome iron *or* **chrome iron ore** *n* **:** CHROMITE 1

chrome leather *n* **:** chrome-tanned leather used largely in the manufacture of shoe uppers

chrome leather fast black S *n, usu cap C&L&F&B* **:** a direct dye — see DYE table I (under *Direct Black 41*)

chrome lemon *or* **chrome citron** *n* **:** a light yellow that is greener, lighter, and stronger than average maize, greener and slightly paler than jasmine, and lighter and stronger than popcorn

chrome liquor *n* **:** a solution of a chromium compound that is used in chrome tanning

chrome-mordant \=¦==\ *adj* **:** relating to a method of dyeing esp. wool by applying a chromium mordant before the dye

chrome orange *n* **1 :** any of several pigments varying from reddish yellow to deep orange and consisting essentially of varying proportions of normal and basic lead chromates that are usu. prepared similarly to chrome yellows **2 :** any of several mordant acid dyes **3 :** a vivid reddish orange that is yellower, less strong, and much lighter than international orange and duller and slightly yellower than golden poppy — called also *orange chrome yellow*

chrome oxide green *n* **:** chromic oxide used as a pigment — compare CHROME GREEN 1a

chrome primrose *n* **:** a light to brilliant yellow

chrome red *n* **1 :** any of several pigments consisting essentially of basic lead chromate **2 :** any of several mordant acid dyes **3 :** vermilion or a color resembling it

chrome re·tan \-ˈrēˌtan\ *n* **:** a leather produced by a combination of chrome tanning and vegetable tanning and usu. used for boots and heavy shoes

chrome scarlet *n* **:** a moderate to strong reddish orange — called also *deep chrome orange, midnight sun, russet orange*

chrome sole *n* **:** a heavy greenish gray leather tanned with chromium salts and used for making soles of boots and shoes

chrome spinel *n* **:** PICOTITE

chrom·esthesia \¦krōm+\ *n* -s [NL, fr. *chrom-* + *esthesia*] **:** synesthesia in which color is seen in response to nonchromatic stimuli (as words or numbers) — called also *color hearing*

chrome tan *vt* **:** to tan (an animal skin) by impregnating with chromium salts — **chrome-tanned** *adj* — **chrome tanning** *n*

chrome tannage *n* **:** the process or the product of chrome tanning

chrome vermilion *n* **:** a variety of chrome red

chrome yellow *n* **1 :** any of several bright pigments with good hiding power that vary from light greenish yellow to reddish medium yellow, consist essentially of normal lead chromate now usu. without extenders (as barite or clay) but often contain other lead compounds (as lead sulfate) for the lighter shades, and are prepared by precipitation from solutions of a lead salt (as lead nitrate) and sodium chromate or dichromate **2 :** any of several mordant acid dyes **3 a :** DEEP CHROME YELLOW **b :** LIGHT CHROME YELLOW

chrome yellow orange *n* **:** DEEP CHROME YELLOW

chro·mia \ˈkrōmēə\ *n* -s [NL, fr. *chromium* + *-a*] **:** CHROMIC OXIDE

-chro·mia \ˈkrōmēə\ *n comb form* -s [NL, fr. LGk *-chrōmia*, fr. Gk *-chrōmos* colored (fr. *chrōma* color) + *-ia* — more at CHROMATIC] **:** state of pigmentation ⟨*anisochromia*⟩

chro·mic \ˈkrōmik, -mēk\ *adj* [F *chromique*, fr. *chrome* + *-ique* -ic] **1 :** of, relating to, or derived from chromium — used esp. of compounds in which this element is trivalent and of the acid in which it is hexavalent; compare CHROMOUS **2 :** subjected to chrome tanning

chromic acid *n* **1 :** an acid H_2CrO_4 analogous to sulfuric acid but known only in solution and esp. in the form of its salts (as lead chromate) most of which are yellow and are toxic causing ulcers on the skin or mucous membranes **2 :** CHROMIC ANHYDRIDE — used chiefly commercially

chromic anhydride *n* **:** a brilliant red crystalline substance essentially CrO_3 that is made from sodium dichromate and sulfuric acid and that is used esp. in chromium plating and as an oxidizing agent — called also *chromium trioxide, chromic acid*

chromic hydroxide *n* **:** a substance obtained as a gray-green gelatinous precipitate or bluish amorphous powder by reaction of a chromic salt with alkali that is usu. assigned the formula $Cr(OH)_3$ but is better considered a hydrated chromic oxide $Cr_2O_3.xH_2O$ — compare GUIGNET'S GREEN

chromic iron *n* **:** CHROMITE 1

chro·mi·cize \ˈkrōməˌsīz\ *vt* -ED/-ING/-S [*chromic* + *-ize*] **:** to treat (catgut) with a compound of chromium

chromic oxide *n* **:** an oxide Cr_2O_3 obtained as a green powder by thermal decomposition of most chromium compounds or by reduction of sodium dichromate or sodium chromate and used as the very permanent pigment chrome oxide green, as a coloring agent for glass and ceramic ware, and as a catalyst — compare CHROMIC HYDROXIDE

chro·mi·dae \ˈkrōməˌdē\ [NL, fr. *Chromis* + *-idae*] *syn of* CICHLIDAE

chro·mide \ˈkrōˌmīd\ *n* -s [NL *Chromides*] **:** any of several small brightly colored African fishes (family Cichlidae); *esp* **:** a brilliant orange or yellow fish (*Etroplus maculatus*) that is spotted with red, has a large black spot on either side, and is frequently kept in the tropical aquarium — called also *orange chromide*

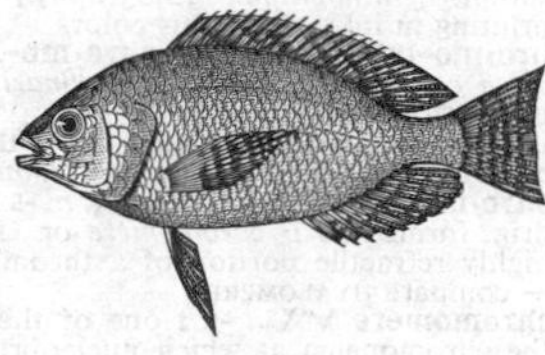

chromide

chro·mi·des \ˈkrōmə-ˌdēz, -räm-\ *n pl, cap* [NL, irreg. fr. *Chromis*, genus of fishes, fr. L *chromis*, a sea fish, fr. Gk; perh. akin to Gk *chremizein* to neigh — more at GRIM] *in some classifications* **:** an order of spiny-finned fishes comprising the percoid families Cichlidae and Pomacentridae and sometimes related forms

chro·mid·i·al \krōˈmidēəl\ *adj* [NL *chromidium* + E *-al*] **:** of or relating to chromidia

chro·mid·i·um \krōˈmidēəm\ *n, pl* **chromid·ia** \-ēə\ [NL, fr. *chrom-* + *-idium*] **:** a chromatin or chromatinlike granule in the cytoplasm of a cell; *esp* **:** one of nuclear origin

chro·mi·dro·sis \ˌkrōməˈdrōsəs\ *also* **chrom·hi·dro·sis** \-m(h)ə-\ *n, pl* **chromidro·ses** *or* **chromhidro·ses** \-ōˌsēz\ [NL, fr. *chrom-* + *-idrosis*] **:** secretion of colored sweat

-chromies *pl of* -CHROMY

chro·mif·er·ous \(ˈ)krōˈmif(ə)rəs\ *adj* [ISV *chrom-* + *-i-* + *-ferous*; prob. orig. formed as F *chromifère*] *of a mineral* **:** containing chromium

chro·mi·nance \ˈkrōmənən(t)s\ *n* -s [*chrom-* + *luminance*] *color television* **:** the difference determined by quantitative measurements between a color and a chosen reference color of the same luminous intensity, the reference color having a specified color quality **:** the quality of a color without reference to brightness

chroming *pres part of* CHROME

chro·mi·ole \ˈkrōmēˌōl\ *n* -s [*chrom-* + *-i-* + *-ole*] **1 :** a hypothetical subdivision of a chromomere **2 :** CHROMIDIUM

chro·mite \-ˌmīt\ *n* -s [in sense 1, fr. G *chromit*, fr. *chrom-* + *-it* -ite; in sense 2, *chrom-* + *-ite*] **1 :** a mineral of the spinel group consisting of an oxide of iron and chromium $FeCr_2O_4$, occurring massive, and valuable as a source of chromium and refractories **2 :** a compound of chromic oxide and a metal oxide (as sodium chromite $Na_2Cr_2O_4$)

chromite series *n* **:** a series of isomorphous minerals in the spinel group consisting of magnesiochromite and chromite

chro·mi·tite \-məˌtīt\ *n* -s [ISV *chromite* + *-ite*; orig. formed as G *chromitit*] **:** a rock composed chiefly of the mineral chromite

chro·mi·um \ˈkrōmēəm, *esp Brit* -myəm\ *n* -s [NL, fr. F *chrome* + NL *-ium* — more at CHROME] **:** a blue-white multivalent metallic element hard and brittle as usu. prepared and resistant to corrosion that is found only in combination and principally in the mineral chromite from which it is separated by the aluminothermic, silicothermic, or electrolytic process and that is used chiefly in alloys (as ferrochromium for use in chromium steel or as nickel-chromium electrical resistance alloys) and in electroplating (as for automobile bumpers and trim and for cutting tools) — symbol *Cr*; see ELEMENT table

chromium green *n* **1 :** CHROME GREEN 1 **2 a :** CHROME GREEN 3a **b :** a moderate yellow green that is greener and deeper than average moss green and yellower and duller than average pea green or apple green (sense 1)

chromium oxide *n* **:** an oxide of chromium; *specif* **:** CHROMIC OXIDE

chromium oxide green *n* **:** CHROME OXIDE GREEN

chromium sesquioxide *n* **:** CHROMIC OXIDE

chromium trioxide *n* **:** CHROMIC ANHYDRIDE

chromium yellow *n* **:** CHROME YELLOW

chro·mize \ˈkrōˌmīz\ *vt* -ED/-ING/-S [*chrom-* + *-ize*] **:** to treat (a metal, esp. steel) with chromium or a chromium compound to form a protective surface alloy

chro·mo \ˈkrō(ˌ)mō\ *n* -s [short for *chromolithograph*] **1 :** CHROMOLITHOGRAPH **2 :** an often badly executed or garish picture printed in colors

chromo- *in pronunciations below*, ¦== = ¦krōmə *or* -mō\ — see CHROM-

chro·mo·bacterium \¦==+\ *n* [NL, fr. *chrom-* + *bacterium*] **1** *cap* **:** a genus of aerobic gram-negative saprophytic soil and water bacteria (family Rhizobiaceae) producing a violet pigment **2** *pl* **chromobacteria :** a bacterium of the genus *Chromobacterium*

chro·mo·blast \¦==+ˌblast\ *n* -s [ISV *chrom-* + *-blast*] **:** an anatomical cell that develops into a pigment cell

chro·mo·blastomycosis \¦==+\ *n, pl* **chromoblastomycoses** [NL *chrom-* + *blastomycosis*] **:** a skin disease that is caused by any of several pigmented fungi esp. of the genera *Hormodendrium* or *Phialophora* and is marked by the formation of warty colored nodules usu. on the legs

chro·mo·center *also* **chro·mo·centre** \ˈ==+ˌ-\ *n* -s [ISV *chrom-* + *center, centre*; orig. formed as It *cromocentro*] **:** a densely staining nuclear body associated with the chromatin of certain cells — **chro·mo·centric** \¦==+\ *adj*

chro·mo·citronine R *n, usu cap* [*chrom-* + *citron* + *-ine*] **:** a mordant dye — see DYE table I (under *Mordant Yellow 26*)

chro·mo·collograph \¦==+\ *n* -s [*chrom-* + *collograph*, a kind of duplicating machine, fr. *coll-* + *-graph*] **:** CHROMOCOLLOTYPE — **chro·mo·collographic** \"+\ *adj* — **chro·mocollography** \"+\ *n* -ES

chro·mo·collotype \¦==+\ *n* -s [*chrom-* + *collotype*] **:** collotype in two or more colors — **chro·mo·collotypy** \"+\ *n* -ES

chro·mo·cyte \ˈ==+ˌsīt\ *n* -s [ISV *chrom-* + *-cyte*] **:** a pigmented anatomical cell — called also *color cell*

chro·mo·gen \ˈ==+ˌjen, -jən\ *n* -s [ISV *chrom-* + *-gen*] **1** *biochem* **:** a precursor (as urobilinogen) of a pigment (as urobilin) **2 :** a compound containing a chromophore that is not itself a dye but is capable of becoming one on introduction of an auxochromic group into the molecule **3 :** a pigment-producing microorganism ⟨many bacteria are ~*s*⟩

chromogene \ˈ==+ˌ-\ *n* -s [ISV *chrom-* + *gene*] **:** GENE — used to distinguish the nuclear gene from the cytogene in an otherwise ambiguous context

chro·mo·genesis \¦==+\ *n* [NL, fr. *chrom-* + *genesis*] **:** color production (as by the metabolic activities of microorganisms, esp. bacteria and fungi)

[1]**chro·mo·gen·ic** \¦krōmə¦jenik\ *adj* [*chromogen* + *-ic*] **:** of or relating to a chromogen

[2]**chromogenic** \"\ *also* **chro·mo·ge·net·ic** \-jə¦ned·ik\ *or* **chro·mog·e·nous** \krōˈmäjənəs\ *adj* [*chrom-* + *-genic, -genetic, -genous*] **:** producing color ⟨~ bacteria⟩
[3]**chromogenic** \¦krōmə¦jenik\ *adj* [*chromogene* + *-ic*] **:** of, relating to, or involving the action of chromogenes ⟨~ inheritance⟩ ⟨~ bacteria⟩
chro·mo·gram \ˈ⸗⸗+ˌgram\ *n* -s [*chrom-* + *-gram*] **1 :** a stereoscopic pair of positive images used in some processes of color photography **2 :** KROMOGRAM
chro·mo·graph \ˈ⸗⸗+ˌgraf\ *n* -s [ISV *chrom-* + *-graph*] **1 :** CHROMOLITHOGRAPH **2 :** a compact device for making quick semiquantitative tests for one or more chemical elements — **chro·mo·graph·ic** \¦⸗⸗¦grafik\ *adj*
chro·mo·iso·mer \¦⸗⸗+\ *n* -s [*chrom-* + *isomer*] **:** a compound that is chromoisomeric with another or others
chro·mo·iso·mer·ic \¦⸗⸗+\ *adj* **:** of, relating to, or exhibiting chromoisomerism
chro·mo·isom·er·ism \¦⸗⸗+\ *n* -s **:** isomerism in which the isomers are of different colors — used esp. of cases in which the isomers are tautomeric
chro·mo·lipoid \¦⸗⸗+\ *n* -s [*chrom-* + *lipoid*] **:** LIPOCHROME
chro·mo·lith \ˈ⸗⸗+ˌlith\ *n* -s [by shortening] **:** CHROMOLITHOGRAPH — **chro·mo·lith·ic** \¦⸗⸗¦lithik\ *adj*
[1]**chro·mo·lithograph** \¦⸗⸗+\ *n* -s [back-formation fr. *chromolithography*] **:** a picture printed by chromolithography
[2]**chromolithograph** \"\ *vt* **:** to print or reproduce by chromolithography
chro·mo·lithographic \¦⸗⸗+\ *adj* **:** of or relating to chromolithography
chro·mo·lithography \¦⸗⸗+\ *n* -ES [F *chromolithographie*, fr. *chrom-* + *lithographie* lithography] **:** lithography adapted to printing in inks of various colors
chro·mo–luminarism *or* **chro·mo–luminism** \¦⸗⸗+\ *n* -s *often cap C&L* [*chrom-* + *luminarism* or *luminism*] **:** NEO-IMPRESSIONISM
chro·mo–luminarist *or* **chro·mo–luminist** \¦⸗⸗+\ *n* -s *often cap C&L* [*chrom-* + *luminarist* or *luminist*] **:** NEO-IMPRESSIONIST
[1]**chro·mo·mere** \ˈ⸗⸗+ˌmi(ə)r\ *n* -s [ISV *chrom-* + *-mere*; orig. formed as F *chromomère* or G *chromomer*] *anat* **:** the highly refractile portion of a thrombocyte or blood platelet — compare HYALOMERE
[2]**chromomere** \"\ *n* -s **:** one of the visible enlargements of the chromonema at which nucleoproteins appear to be concentrated, by some held to be the physical seat of the genes and by others considered optical artifacts due to the coiled state of the chromonema — compare CHROMOSOME — **chro·mo·mer·ic** \¦⸗⸗+¦merik, -mir-\ *adj*
chro·mom·e·ter \krōˈmäməd·ə(r), krə-\ *n* -s [*chrom-* + *-meter*] **:** an apparatus for comparing the color of a substance (as a refined ore) with a standard esp. to determine the degree of purity or percentage of a constituent **:** COLORIMETER
chro·mone \ˈkrōˌmōn\ *n* -s [ISV *chrom-* + *-one*] **:** a colorless crystalline cyclic ketone $C_9H_6O_2$; 1,4-benzo-pyrone; *also* **:** a derivative (as flavone) of this ketone
chro·mo·ne·ma \ˌ⸗⸗ *at* CHROMO- + ˈnēmə\ *n, pl* **chromone·ma·ta** \-məd·ə\ [NL, fr. *chrom-* + *-nema*] *biol* **:** the coiled threadlike core of a chromatid commonly regarded as the actual carrier of the genes **:** GENE-STRING — **chro·mo·ne·mal** \¦⸗⸗¦nēməl\ *or* **chro·mo·ne·mat·ic** \-nə¦mad·ik, -nē-\ *or* **chro·mo·ne·mic** \-¦nēmik\ *adj*
chromo paper *n* **:** a coated paper suitable for color printing
chro·mop·a·rous \(ˈ)krōˈmäpərəs\ *adj* [*chrom-* + *-parous*] *bacteriol* **:** excreting pigment either soluble or insoluble in water — compare PARACHROMOPHOROUS
chro·mo·pexy \ˈ⸗⸗ *at* CHROMO- + ˌpeksē\ *n* -ES [ISV *chrom-* + *-pexy*] **:** the capacity of certain living cells to take up and store dyes
[1]**chro·mo·phil** \ˈ⸗⸗+ˌfil\ *or* **chro·mato·phil** \⸗ˈ⸗⸗, ˈ⸗⸗⸗ *at* CHROMATO- +\ *also* **chro·mo·phile** \"+ˌfīl\ *or* **chro·mato·phile** \⸗ˈ⸗⸗, ˈ⸗⸗⸗ *at* CHROMATO- +\ *or* **chro·mo·phil·ic** \¦⸗⸗+¦filik\ *adj* [ISV *chrom-* or *chromat-* + *-phil, -phile, -philic*] **1** *biol* **:** staining readily **2 :** CHROMAFFIN
[2]**chromophil** \" *or* **chromophile** \" *or* **chro·mato·phil** *or* **chro·mato·phile** \(ˈ)⸗¦⸗⸗, ˈ⸗⸗⸗ *at* CHROMATO- + ˌ-\ *n* -s **:** a chromophil cell or substance
chromophily *var of* CHROMATOPHILIA
[1]**chro·mo·phobe** \ˈ⸗⸗ *at* CHROMO- + ˌfōb\ *or* **chro·mo·pho·bic** \¦⸗⸗¦fōbik *also* -äb-\ *adj* [ISV *chrom-* + *-phobe, -phobic*] *biol* **:** not readily absorbing stains **:** difficult to stain — **chro·mo·pho·by** \ˈ⸗⸗ˌfōbē, krōˈmäfəbē\ *n* -ES
[2]**chromophobe** \"\ *n* -s **:** a chromophobe cell esp. in the pituitary gland
chro·mo·phore \ˈ⸗⸗+ˌfō(ə)r\ *n* -s [ISV *chrom-* + *-phore*; orig. formed as G *chromophor*] **:** a functional group (as nitroso, nitro, azo, or the conjugated unsaturated grouping of quinone) that gives rise to color in a molecule and that with the assistance of an auxochrome (as a hydroxyl or amino group) produces a dye
chro·mo·phor·ic \¦⸗⸗¦fȯrik\ *adj* **:** color-bearing; *esp* **:** relating to a chromophore ⟨~ groups⟩ ⟨~ function⟩
chro·moph·o·rous \(ˈ)krō¦mäf(ə)rəs\ *adj* [*chrom-* + *-phorous*] *bacteriol* **:** containing pigment as an integral part of the protoplasm
chro·mo·phyll \ˈ⸗⸗ *at* CHROMO- + ˌfil\ *n* -s [ISV *chrom-* + *-phyll*] **:** a plant pigment (as chlorophyll)
chromoplasm *var of* CHROMATOPLASM
chro·mo·plast \ˈ⸗⸗+ˌplast\ *n* -s [ISV *chrom-* + *-plast*; orig. formed as G *chromoplastid*] **1 :** a colored plastid usu. not including chloroplasts **2 :** a chromatin nucleolus
chro·mo·plas·tid \¦⸗⸗¦plastəd\ *n* -s [ISV *chrom-* + *-plastid*; orig. formed as G *chromoplastid*] **:** CHROMOPLAST 1
chro·mo·protein \¦⸗⸗+\ *n* -s [*chrom-* + *protein*] **:** any of a class of compounds (as hemoglobin) of a protein with a metal-containing pigment (as heme) or with a carotenoid
chro·mo·scope \ˈ⸗⸗+ˌskōp\ *n* -s [ISV *chrom-* + *-scope*] **:** an optical instrument for combining colored images so as to produce a picture in natural colors — **chro·mo·scop·ic** \¦⸗⸗¦skäpik\ *adj* — **chro·mos·co·py** \krōˈmäskəpē\ *n* -ES
chro·mo·som·al \¦krōmə¦sōməl\ *adj* **:** of or relating to chromosomes ⟨the geographic distribution of ~ prime types —*New York Times*⟩ — **chro·mo·som·al·ly** \-məlē\ *adv*
chromosomal vesicle *n* **:** KARYOMERE
chro·mo·some \ˈkrōməˌsōm\ *n* -s [ISV *chrom-* + *-some*; orig. formed as G *chromosom*] **:** one of the more or less rodlike chromatin-containing basophilic bodies constituting the genome and chiefly detectable in the mitotic or meiotic nucleus that are regarded as the seat of the genes, consist of one or more intimately associated chromatids functioning as a unit, and are relatively constant in number in the cells of any one kind of plant or animal — see SEX — **chro·mo·so·mic** \¦⸗⸗¦sōmik\ *adj*
chromosome complement *n* **1 :** the entire group of chromosomes in a nucleus **2 :** the chromosomes received from one parent without regard to ploidy
chromosome number *n* **:** the number of chromosomes characteristic of a particular kind of plant or animal
chromosome set *n* **:** a group of chromosomes in a polyploid nucleus presumably constituting a haploid component derived from some diploid ancestor **:** GENOME
chro·mo·so·min \ˌkrōməˈsōmən\ *n* -s [*chromosome* + *-in*] **:** an acid protein rich in tryptophan isolated from fish sperm and regarded by some as a major component of the chromosomes
chro·mo·som·ol·o·gy \ˌ⸗⸗(ˌ)sōˈmäləjē\ *n* -ES [*chromosome* + *-o-* + *-logy*] **:** the branch of cytology devoted to study of the chromosomes
chro·mo·sphere \ˈ⸗⸗+ˌ-\ *n* -s [*chrom-* + *sphere*] **:** the lower part of the atmosphere of the sun thousands of miles thick and composed predominantly of hydrogen gas that is responsible for its rosy color; *also* **:** a similar portion of the atmosphere of any star — **chro·mo·spheric** \¦⸗⸗+\ *adj*
chro·mo·therapy \¦⸗⸗+\ *n* -ES [*chrom-* + *therapy*] **:** treatment of disease by colored lights
chro·mo·trich·i·al \¦⸗⸗+¦trikēəl\ *adj* [NL *chromotrichia* hair pigmentation (fr. *chrom-* + *-trichia*) + E *-al*] **:** concerned with or modifying hair color
chro·mo·trope \ˈ⸗⸗+ˌtrōp\ *also* **chro·mo·trop** \-äp\ *n* -s *often cap* [ISV *chrom-* + *-trope*; orig. formed as G *chromotrop*] **:** any of several acid dyes — see DYE table I (under *Acid Red 29, Acid Violet 6* and *13*)
chro·mo·trop·ic \¦⸗⸗+¦träpik\ *adj* **:** relating to or causing chromotropism
chromotropic acid *also* **chromotrope acid** *n* [ISV *chromotropic, chromotrope* (fr. *chrom-* + *-tropic, -trope*) + *acid*; orig. formed as G *chromotropsäure*] **:** a colorless crystalline acid $C_{10}H_4(OH)_2(SO_3H)_2$ used as a dye intermediate and as an analytical reagent
chro·mot·ro·pism \krōˈmä·trəˌpizəm\ *also* **chro·mot·ro·py** \-pē\ *n, pl* **chromotropisms** *also* **chromotropies** **1 :** change of color esp. of certain salts known in differently colored modifications — compare CHROMOISOMERISM **2 :** the orientation of living organisms in relation to color stimuli — compare TROPISM
chro·mo·type \ˈ⸗⸗ *at* CHROMO- + ˌtīp\ *n* -s [*chrom-* + *type*] **:** a sheet printed in colors by any process (as chromolithography)
chro·mo·typ·ic \¦⸗⸗¦tipik\ *adj* **:** CHROMOTYPOGRAPHIC
chro·mo·typographic \¦⸗⸗+\ *adj* **:** used in or produced by chromotypography
chro·mo·typography \¦⸗⸗+\ *n* [F or G *chromotypographie*, fr. *chrom-* + *typographie* typography] **:** the art or the process of printing in chromatic colors
chro·mo·typy \ˈ⸗⸗+ˌtīpē\ *n* -ES [ISV *chrom-* — *-typy*] CHROMOTYPOGRAPHY
chro·mous \ˈkrōməs\ *adj* [[1]*chrome* + *-ous*] **:** of, relating to, or derived from chromium — used esp. of chemical compounds in which this element is bivalent; compare CHROMIC
chro·mo·xylograph \¦⸗⸗ *at* CHROMO- +\ *n* -s [*chrom-* + *xylograph*] **:** a print made by chromoxylography
chro·mo·xylography \¦⸗⸗+\ *n* -ES [*chrom-* + *xylography*] **:** the art or process of printing in colors from wooden blocks
[1]**-chro·my** \ˌkrōmē\ *n comb form* -ES [Gk *chrōma* color + ISV *-y*; prob. orig. formed as G *-chromie* — more at CHROMATIC] **:** painting **:** coloring ⟨litho*chromy*⟩ ⟨stereo*chromy*⟩
[2]**-chromy** \"\ *n comb form* -ES [NL *-chromia*] **:** -CHROMIA
chro·myl \ˈkrōməl, -ˌmēl\ *n* -s [ISV *chrom-* + *-yl*] **:** the bivalent radical CrO_2 analogous to sulfuryl
chromyl chloride *n* **:** a red fuming toxic liquid compound CrO_2Cl_2 obtained by distilling a chromate or dichromate with a soluble chloride and concentrated sulfuric acid
chron- *or* **chrono-** *comb form* [Gk, fr. *chronos*] **:** time ⟨*chron*axie⟩ ⟨*chrono*gram⟩
chron *abbr* **1** chronicle **2** chronological; chronology
chro·nal \ˈkrōnᵊl\ *adj* [*chron-* + *-al*] **:** of or relating to time
chron·anagram \(ˈ)krän+\ *n* -s [NL *chronanagramma*, fr. *chron-* + *anagramma* anagram — more at ANAGRAM] **:** an anagram of a chronogram
chro·nax·ie \ˈkrōˌnaksē, ˈkrä-, ⸗ˈ⸗⸗\ *also* **chro·nax·ia** \⸗ˈ⸗sēə\ *or* **chro·naxy** \ˈ⸗ˌ⸗sē, ⸗ˈ⸗⸗\ *n, pl* **chronaxies** *also* **chronaxias** [F *chronaxie*, fr. *chron-* + Gk *axia* value, fr. *axios* worthy, weighing as much as — more at AXIOM] *physiol* **:** the minimum time required for excitation of an excitable structure (as a nerve cell) by a constant electric current of twice the threshold voltage — compare RHEOBASE
chro·nax·im·e·ter \ˌkrōˌnakˈsimədˑə(r), ˌkrä-\ *n* [*chronaxie* + *-meter*] **:** a device for measuring chronaxie
chro·nax·i·met·ric \(¦)krō¦naksə¦me·trik, (¦)krä¦-\ *adj* [ISV *chronaxie* + *metric*] **:** of or relating to measurement of the duration of chronaxie — **chro·nax·i·me·tri·cal·ly** \(¦)⸗¦⸗sə¦me·trək(ə)lē\ *adv*
chro·nax·im·e·try \ˌkrōˌnakˈsimə·trē, ˌkrä-\ *n* -ES [ISV, fr. *chronaxie* + *-metry*] **:** the measurement of chronaxie
[1]**chron·ic** \ˈkränik, -nēk\ *adj* [F *chronique*, fr. L *chronicus*, fr. Gk *chronikos* of time, fr. *chronos* time + *-ikos* -ic] **1 a :** marked by long duration, by frequent recurrence over a long time, and often by slowly progressing seriousness **:** not acute ⟨~ indigestion⟩ ⟨her hallucinations became ~⟩ **b :** suffering from a disease or ailment of long duration or frequent recurrence ⟨~ arthritic⟩ ⟨~ sufferers from asthma⟩ **2 a :** marked by long continuation or frequent recurrence **:** always present or encountered **:** long-lasting **:** UNENDING; *esp* **:** constantly vexing, weakening, or troubling ⟨war between states and civil war within a nation — the ~ state of affairs when Hobbes lived —John Dewey⟩ ⟨the ~ financial predicament of American colleges and universities — *Nation*⟩ **b :** given to steady or frequently repeated behaving or acting **:** given to being habitually **:** HABITUAL, ACCUSTOMED ⟨the ~ amateur of causes — always eager, always profoundly convinced . . . never quite expert —James Gray⟩ ⟨a ~ grumbler⟩ ⟨a ~ joiner⟩ **3** *of a pathologic process* **:** characterized by a slow progressive course of indefinite duration — used esp. of degenerative invasive diseases, some infections, psychoses, inflammations, and the carrier state ⟨~ heart disease⟩ ⟨~ arthritis⟩ ⟨~ tuberculosis⟩ ⟨~ carrier⟩ — compare ACUTE 5a (2) **4** *slang Brit* **:** INTENSE, SEVERE, DISAGREEABLE ⟨she started howling and carrying on . . . something ~ —Richard Llewellyn⟩ **syn** see INVETERATE
[2]**chronic** \"\ *n* -s **:** one that suffers from a chronic disease
chron·i·cal \ˈkränəkəl, -nēk-\ *adj* [F *chronique* + E *-al*] **:** CHRONIC ⟨~ dysentery⟩
chronic alcoholism *n* **:** a symptom or disease that involves complex psychologic factors characterized by compulsive drinking or the inability to stop drinking once started and that results if long continued in neurologic, psychiatric, and nutritional disturbances — compare ACUTE ALCOHOLISM
chron·i·cal·ly \ˈkränək(ə)lē, -nēk-, -li\ *adv* **:** in a chronic manner **:** CONTINUALLY, REPEATEDLY
chro·nic·i·ty \kräˈnisəd·ē\ *n* -ES [[1]*chronic* + *-ity*] **:** the quality or state of being chronic ⟨~ of a disease⟩
[1]**chron·i·cle** \ˈkränəkəl, -nēk-\ *n* -s [ME *cronicle*, fr. AF, alter. (prob. influenced by such words as OF *article*) of OF *chronique*, fr. L *chronica*, fr. Gk *chronika*, fr. neut. pl. of *chronikos*, adj.] **:** an esp. historical account of facts or events that are arranged in order of time and usu. continuous and detailed but without analysis or interpretation; *broadly* **:** HISTORY, NARRATIVE
[2]**chronicle** \"\ *vt* **chronicled**; **chronicled**; **chronicling** \-k(ə)liŋ\ **chronicles** [ME *cronicle*n, fr. *cronicle*, n.] **1 :** to record or present in or as if in a chronicle ⟨the greater French novelists from Stendhal to Proust ~ the rise, the regime, and the decay of the upper bourgeoisie in France —T.S.Eliot⟩ **2 :** LIST, DESCRIBE ⟨it is impossible to ~ all the splendors and humbler delights to be found in these volumes —*Times Lit. Supp.*⟩
chronicle drama *n* **:** CHRONICLE PLAY; *collectively* **:** CHRONICLE PLAYS
chronicle play *or* **chronicle history** *n* **:** a play with a theme from history consisting usu. of rather loosely connected episodes chronologically arranged
chron·i·cler \-k(ə)lə(r)\ *n* -s [ME *cronicler*, fr. *croniclen* + *-er*] **:** a writer or compiler of a chronicle ⟨a historian without philosophy is but a ~ —John Mason Brown⟩ ⟨disillusioned ~ of social disintegration —Carlos Baker⟩ ⟨successful ~ of the upper middle class —Taliaferro Boatwright⟩
chro·nique scan·da·leuse \krȯnēkskäⁿdälœ̄z\ *n, pl* **chroniques scandaleuses** \"\ [F, lit., scandalous story] **:** a history, biography, or report that stresses scandalous details
chron·ist \ˈkränəst\ *n* -s [*chron-* + *-ist*] **1 :** CHRONOLOGIST **2 :** CHRONICLER
chrono- *in pronunciations below*, ¦⸗⸗ = ¦kränə *or* ¦krōnə *or* -nō\ — see CHRON-
chrono·cinematography \¦⸗⸗+\ *n* -ES [blend of *chronography* and *cinematography*] **:** chronography (sense 2) by means of motion-picture photography
chrono·cline \ˈ⸗⸗+ˌ-\ *n* -s [*chron-* + *cline*] **:** a cline manifested by successive changes in the members of a natural group (as a species) in successive fossiliferous strata
chrono·ge·neous \¦⸗⸗+¦jēnyəs, -nēəs\ *adj* [*chron-* + *-geneous* (as in *homogeneous*)] *psychol* **:** appearing at a given chronological age — compare PHASOGENEOUS
chrono·genesis \¦⸗⸗+\ *n, pl* **chronogeneses** [NL, fr. *chron-* + *-genesis*] *biol* **:** the history of the development of a group of organisms
chrono·genetic \¦⸗⸗+\ *adj* [*chron-* + *-genetic*] **:** of or relating to chronogenesis
chron·o·gram \ˈ⸗⸗+ˌgram\ *n* -s [*chron-* + *-gram*] **1 :** an inscription, sentence, or phrase in which certain numeral letters usu. made specially conspicuous express a particular date or epoch on being added together (as in the motto of a medal struck by Gustavus Adolphus in 1632 — ChrIstVs DVX; ergo trIVMphVs — the capitals of which, added as numerals, make 1632) **2 :** the record made by a chronograph
chron·o·gram·mat·ic \¦⸗⸗+grə¦mad·ik\ *or* **chron·o·gram·mat·i·cal** \-d·əkəl\ *adj* [fr. *chronogram*, after such pairs as E *anagram: anagrammatic, anagrammatical*] **:** containing or bearing a chronogram — **chron·o·gram·mat·i·cal·ly** \-d·ək(ə)lē\ *adv*
chron·o·gram·ma·tist \ˌ⸗⸗+ˈgramədˑəst\ *n* -s [fr. *chronogram*, after such pairs as E *anagram: anagrammatist*] **:** a writer or maker of chronograms
chron·o·gram·mic \¦⸗⸗+¦gramik\ *adj* [*chronogram* + *-ic*] **:** CHRONOGRAMMATIC
[1]**chron·o·graph** \ˈ⸗⸗+ˌgraf\ *n* -s [*chron-* + *-graph*] **:** an instrument for measuring and recording time: **a :** an instrument consisting of a recording apparatus (as a stylus and revolving drum) connected with a clock or chronometer and used for recording the precise clock time of astronomical and other occurrences **b :** a watch having in addition to conventional hour, minute, and second hands a center sweep-second hand that can be stopped, started, or reset to zero and that indicates intervals of time as small as ⅕ second **c :** an instrument used for measuring the time of flight of projectiles — **chron·o·graph·ic** \¦⸗⸗¦grafik\ *adj* — **chron·o·graph·i·cal·ly** \-fək(ə)lē\ *adv*
[2]**chronograph** \"\ *vt* -ED/-ING/-S **:** to measure (velocity) by means of a chronograph (sense c)
chro·nog·ra·pher \krəˈnägrəfə(r)\ *n* -s [*chron-* + *-grapher*] *obs* **:** CHRONOLOGIST, CHRONICLER
chro·nog·ra·phy \-fē\ *n* -ES [MF *chronographie*, fr. Gk *chronographia*, fr. *chron-* + *-graphia* -graphy] **1** *obs* **:** a record of past time **:** HISTORY **2 :** the measurement by graphic methods of intervals of time (as in studying the successive phases of a rapid and complex motion) **:** the use of the chronograph
chrono·iso·ther·mal \¦⸗⸗ *at* CHRONO- +\ *adj* [*chron-* + *isothermal*] *meteorol* **:** relating to a diagram exhibiting the course of the mean monthly temperature of a place for each hour of the day
chro·nol·o·ger \krəˈnäləjə(r)\ *n* -s [NL *chronologia* + E *-er*] **:** CHRONOLOGIST
chron·o·log·ic \¦kränᵊl¦äjik, -ōn-, -jēk\ *adj* **:** of or relating to chronology **:** CHRONOLOGICAL ⟨the first principle of ~ reconstruction —Edward Sapir⟩
chron·o·log·i·cal \-jəkəl, -ēk-\ *adj* **:** relating to or dealing with chronology **:** arranged in order of time ⟨~ tables⟩ **:** reckoned in units of time ⟨~ age⟩ — **chron·o·log·i·cal·ly** \-jək(ə)lē, -ēk-, -li\ *adv*
chro·nol·o·gist \krəˈnäləjəst\ *n* -s [F *chronologiste*, fr. NL *chronologista*, fr. *chronologia* + *-ista* -ist] **:** a person who investigates dates and records of events **:** one expert in chronology
chro·nol·o·gize \-ˌjīz\ *vt* -ED/-ING/-S [*chronology* + *-ize*] **:** to arrange chronologically **:** establish the order in time of (as events, documents)
chro·nol·o·gy \krəˈnäləjē, krō-, krä-\ *n* -ES [NL *chronologia*, fr. *chron-* + *-logia* -logy] **1 :** the science that treats of measuring or computing time by regular divisions or periods and that assigns to events or transactions their proper dates **2 :** a chronological table or list **3 :** an arrangement (as of data, events) in the order of time of occurrence or appearance **:** chronological relation ⟨his ~ of the facts is confused⟩; *specif* **:** the classification of archaeological sites or prehistoric periods of culture according to their time relationship by stratigraphy, typology, or actual dating
chron·o·man·cy \ˈ⸗⸗ *at* CHRONO- + ˌman(t)sē\ *n* -ES [*chron-* + *-mancy*] **:** divination to determine the favorable time for action formerly practiced esp. in China
chron·o·man·tic \¦⸗⸗+¦mantik\ *adj* [fr. *chronomancy*, after such pairs as E *necromancy: necromantic*] **:** of or relating to chronomancy
chro·nom·e·ter \krəˈnämədˑə(r), krō-,krä-, -ətə(r)\ *n* -s [*chron-* + *-meter*] **:** an instrument for measuring time: **a :** a portable timepiece usu. having a detent escapement and compensation balance and beating half seconds for keeping time where great accuracy is essential (as in determining longitude at sea) — called also *box chronometer, marine chronometer* **b :** a watch of great esp. officially certified accuracy **c** *obs* **:** METRONOME
chron·o·met·ric \¦⸗⸗ *at* CHRONO- + ¦me·trik\ *or* **chron·o·met·ri·cal** \-trəkəl, -ēk-\ *adj* [*chron-* + *-metric*] **:** relating to a chronometer or chronometry **:** measured by a chronometer — **chron·o·met·ri·cal·ly** \-trək(ə)lē, -ēk-, -li\ *adv*
chro·nom·e·try \krəˈnämə·trē, krō-,krä-\ *n* -ES [*chron-* + *-metry*] **:** the science of measuring time **:** the measuring of time by periods or divisions (as by a chronometer or chronograph)
chro·non·o·my \-ˈnänəmē\ *n* -ES [*chron-* + *-nomy*] **:** method of reckoning and measuring time
chron·o·pher \ˈ⸗⸗ *at* CHRONO- + fə(r)\ *n* -s [*chron-* + *-pher*] **:** an instrument signaling the correct time to distant points by electricity
chrono·photograph \¦⸗⸗ +\ *n* -s [*chron-* + *photograph*; part trans. of F *chronophotographie*] **:** one of a set or a set of photographs of a moving object taken to record and exhibit successive phases of the motion — **chrono·photographic** \" +\ *adj* — **chrono·photography** \" +\ *n* -ES
chron·o·scope \ˈ⸗⸗ + ˌskōp\ *n* -s [*chron-* + *-scope*] **:** an instrument for the precise measurement of small time intervals (as by means of a falling rod, released pendulum, or an electronic device) — **chron·o·scop·ic** \¦⸗⸗¦skäpik\ *adj* — **chron·o·scop·i·cal·ly** \-pək(ə)lē\ *adv*
chro·nos·co·py \krəˈnäskəpē\ *n* -ES [F *chronoscopie*, fr. *chron-* + *-scopie* scopy] **:** the study of very brief intervals of time by means of a chronoscope
chrono·se·mic \¦⸗⸗ *at* CHRONO- + ¦sēmik\ *adj* [*chron-* + Gk *sēma* sign + E *-ic* — more at SEMANTICS] **:** employing intervals of time with a fixed significance (as in a system of signaling) by exposing visual objects or sounding audible signals for selected intervals of time
chrono·thermal \¦⸗⸗ *at* CHRONO- +\ *adj* [*chron-* + *thermal*] **:** relating to both time and temperature ⟨~ equation⟩
chrono·thermometer \¦⸗⸗ +\ *n* [*chron-* + *thermometer*] **:** a timepiece so constructed as to exaggerate the effect of changes of temperature upon its rate and used to indicate mean temperature
chron·o·tron \ˈ⸗⸗ + ˌträn\ *n* -s [*chron-* + *-tron*] **:** a device for measuring very small intervals of time by observing on an indicator the distance between electric pulses
chron·o·trop·ic \¦⸗⸗ + ¦träpik\ *adj* [*chron-* + *-tropic*] **:** influencing the rate esp. of the heartbeat — used esp. of the inhibitory and accelerator cardiac nerves and of certain drugs
chro·not·ro·pism \krəˈnä·trəˌpizəm\ *n* -s [*chron-* + *-tropism*] **:** interference with the rate of the heartbeat
-chro·nous \krənəs\ *adj comb form* [Gk *-chronos*, fr. *chronos* time] **:** of (such) a time or period ⟨homeo*chronous*⟩ ⟨iso*chronous*⟩
chro·o·coc·ca·ce·ae \ˌkrōəˌkäˈkāsēˌē\ *n pl, cap* [NL, fr. *Chroococcus*, type genus + *-aceae*] **:** a family of usu. colonial, ensheathed marine or freshwater blue-green algae that reproduce by colonial fragmentation and simple cell division and are usu. isolated in a distinct order — see GLOEOCAPSA — **chro·o·coc·ca·ceous** *adj* \¦⸗⸗¦⸗¦kāshəs\ — **chro·o·coc·coid** \¦⸗⸗¦käˌkȯid\ *adj*
chro·o·coc·ca·les \ˌkrōəˌkäˈkā(ˌ)lēz\ *n pl, cap* [NL, fr. *Chroococcus* + *-ales*] **:** an order of Myxophyceae coextensive with the family Chroococcaceae
chro·o·coc·cus \¦krōə¦käkəs\ *n, cap* [NL, fr. Gk *chrōs* color + NL *-o-* + *-coccus*] **:** the type genus of Chroococcaceae
-chro·ous \krəwəs\ *adj comb form* [Gk *-chroos*, fr. *chrōs* skin, color — more at CHROMATIC] **:** -colored ⟨iso*chroous*⟩
chrot·ta \ˈkräd·ə\ *n* -s [LL *crotta, chrotta*, of Celt origin; akin to W *crwth* fiddle, MIr *crott* harp — more at CROWD] **1 :** CRWTH **2 :** a small medieval harp
chrs *abbr* chambers
chrys- *or* **chryso-** *comb form* [Gk, fr. *chrysos* gold — more at CHRYSALIS] **:** gold **:** golden **:** yellow ⟨*chrys*amine⟩ ⟨*chryso*phyll⟩
chrys·al *also* **crys·al** \ˈkrisəl\ *n* -s [origin unknown] **:** a transverse line of crushed fibers in the belly of an archery bow beginning as a pinch — called also *fret*
[1]**chrys·a·lid** \ˈkrisələd\ *n* -s [L *chrysallid-, chrysallis*] **:** CHRYSALIS
[2]**chrysalid** \"\ *adj* **:** relating to or like a chrysalis — **chry·sal·i·dal** \krəˈsaləd ᵊl\ *adj* — **chrys·a·lid·i·an** \¦krisə¦lidēən\ *adj*

chrys·a·lis \'krisələs\ *n, pl* **chry·sal·i·des** \krə'saləˌdēz\ *or* **chrysalises** \'krisələsəz\ [L *chrysallis* gold-colored pupa of butterflies, fr. Gk, fr. *chrysos* gold, of Sem origin; akin to Heb *hārūṣ* gold, Assyr-Bab *khurāṣu*] **1 :** the pupa of insects (as of butterflies) that pass the pupal stage in a quiescent and helpless condition without taking food, being enclosed in a more or less firm integument; *also* **:** the enclosing integument or case of a pupa **2 :** a protecting covering **:** a sheltered state or stage of being or growth

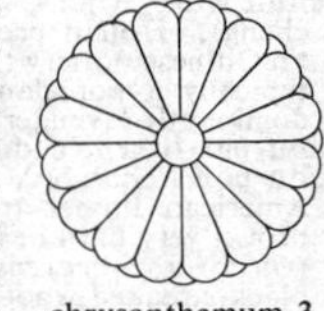
chrysalis 1

chrys·a·loid \'krisəˌlȯid\ *adj* [*chrysalis* + *-oid*] **:** like a chrysalis

chrysamine G \'krisəˌmēn-\ *n, usu cap C* [ISV *chrys-* + *amine*] **:** a direct dye — see DYE table I (under *Direct Yellow 1*)

chrys·amphora \krəs +\ [NL, fr. *chrys-* + *amphora*] *syn of* DARLINGTONIA

chrys·aniline \krəs +\ *n* -S [ISV *chrys-* + *aniline;* orig. formed as G *chrysanilin*] **:** a yellow crystalline base $C_{19}H_{15}N_3$ obtained as a by-product in the manufacture of fuchsine — see PHOSPHINE

chrys·anisic acid \ˈkris + . . . -\ *n* [ISV *chrys-* + *anisic;* orig. formed as F *chrysanisique*] **:** a golden yellow crystalline acid $C_6H_2(NO_2)_2(NH_2)CO_2H$ obtained indirectly from anisic acid and used in preparing some dyes

chry·san·the·min \krə'san(t)thəmən *also* kri'z-\ *n* -S [ISV *chrysanthem-* (fr. NL *Chrysanthemum*) + *-in;* orig. formed in G] **:** an anthocyanin pigment $C_{21}H_{20}O_{11}$ obtained from a chrysanthemum (*Chrysanthemum indicum*) and other plants; the 3-glucoside of cyanidin

chry·san·the·mum \krə'san(t)thəməm, -aan- *also* kri'z-\ *n* [L, fr. Gk *chrysanthemon*, fr. *chrys-* + *anthemon* flower, fr. *anthos* — more at ANTHOLOGY] **1** -S **a :** CORN MARIGOLD **b :** any of various cultivated plants of the genus *Chrysanthemum; also* **:** one of the large double flower heads **2** [NL, fr. L] **a** *cap* **:** a large genus of perennial herbs (family Compositae) that are widely distributed in the Old World and that include many plants derived chiefly from two species (*C. morifolium* and *C. indicum*) which are prob. Asiatic though known only in cultivation and are cultivated for their showy often double and brightly colored flower heads, others that are pernicious weeds, and still others that are of economic importance as sources of medicinals and insecticides — see MARGUERITE, PYRETHRUM **b** -S **:** any plant or flower of the genus *Chrysanthemum* **3** -S **:** a chrysanthemum flower in a conventionalized form with 16 complete rays used as the chief badge of the Japanese imperial family — called also *kikumon;* compare MON **4** -S **:** a dark to deep red that is yellower and slightly lighter than garnet red — called also *Turkish-crescent red*

chrysanthemum 3

chrysanthemum-dicarboxylic acid *n* **:** an acid $C_{10}H_{14}O_4$ derived from chrysanthemumic acid that occurs in the form of esters in pyrethrum flowers — compare PYRETHRIN

chrysanthemum dog *n* **:** TIBETAN TERRIER

chrysanthemum eelworm *or* **chrysanthemum leaf nematode** *n* **:** a plant-parasitic nematode worm (*Aphelenchoides ritzema-bosi*) of the family Aphelenchidae that damages the leaves and buds of chrysanthemums

chrysanthemum gall midge *or* **chrysanthemum midge** *also* **chrysanthemum gall fly** *n* **:** a small orange fly (*Diarthronomyia chrysanthemi*) forming galls on the flowers and leaves of chrysanthemums esp. in greenhouses

chry·san·the·mum·ic acid \(ˌ)=ˌ==ˌ==ˌməmik-\ *n* [NL *Chrysanthemum* + E *-ic*] **:** an acid $C_9H_{15}COOH$ that occurs in the form of esters in pyrethrum flowers — called also *chrysanthemummonocarboxylic acid;* compare PYRETHRIN

chrysanthemum rust *n* **:** a rust of chrysanthemums caused by a fungus (*Puccinia chrysanthemi*)

chrys·a·ro·bin \ˌkrisə'rōbən\ *n* -S [*chrys-* + *araroba* (Goa powder) + *-in*] **1 :** a brownish to orange-yellow powder that is a mixture of neutral principles obtained from Goa powder and is used in the treatment of skin diseases **2 :** a yellow crystalline compound $C_{15}H_{12}O_3$

chrys·a·zin \'krisəzən\ *n* -S [ISV *chrysammic* + *alizarin*] **:** an orange or reddish brown compound $C_{14}H_6O_2(OH)_2$ used as a dye intermediate; 1,8-dihydroxy-anthraquinone

chrys·elephantine \(ˌ)kris + \ *adj* [Gk *chryselephantinos*, fr. *chrys-* + *elephantinos* made of ivory, fr. *elephant-, elephas* ivory, elephant] **:** composed of or adorned with gold and ivory ⟨she might have been ~ — made, that is, like some old Greek statues, out of ivory and gold —G.K.Chesterton⟩

chrys·e·mys \'krisəməs\ *n, cap* [NL, fr. *chrys-* + *Emys*] **:** a genus of small brightly marked American freshwater turtles or terrapins — see PAINTED TURTLE

chry·sene \'krīˌsēn\ *n* -S [F *chrysène*, fr. *chrys-* + *-ène* -ene] **:** a white crystalline hydrocarbon $C_{18}H_{12}$ with violet fluorescence obtained from coal-tar fractions and from petroleum by cracking and prepared from indene by catalytic dehydrogenation; 1,2-benzo-phenanthrene

chrys·i·del·la \ˌkrisə'delə\ *n, cap* [NL, fr. Gk *chrysid-, chrysis* vessel of gold (fr. *chrysos* gold) + NL *-ella* — more at CHRYSALIS] **:** a genus of symbiotic plantlike flagellates (order Cryptomonadina) with yellow chromatophores that are often considered algae and are the zooxanthellae of the protoplasm of certain higher protozoans (as many radiolarians)

chry·sid·i·dae \krə'sidəˌdē, krī'-\ *n pl, cap* [NL, fr. *Chrysid-, Chrysis*, type genus + *-idae*] **:** a family comprising brilliantly colored wasps of medium size with a shining metallic luster and with a few related forms commonly constituting a superfamily of the hymenopterous suborder Clistogastra — see CUCKOO WASP

chry·sin \'krīsᵊn\ *n* -S [ISV *chrys-* + *-in;* orig. formed in G] **:** a yellow crystalline flavone pigment $C_{15}H_{10}O_4$ found esp. in the buds of species of poplar; 5,7-dihydroxy-flavone

chry·sis \'krīsəs, -ris-\ *n, cap* [NL, fr. Gk *chrysid-, chrysis* vessel of gold, fr. *chrysos* gold — more at CHRYSALIS] **:** the type genus of Chrysididae

chryso- *in pronunciations below,* ˈ== = ˈkrisə *or* -sō\ — see CHRYS-

chrys·o·bal·a·nus \ˌ==+'balənəs\ *n, cap* [NL, fr. *chrys-* + L *balanus* acorn, fr. Gk *balanos* — more at GLAND] **:** a small genus of tropical shrubs or trees (family Rosaceae) having a pulpy drupe with a ridged stone — see COCO PLUM

chryso·beryl \'==+ˌ-\ *n* [L *chrysoberyllus*, fr. Gk *chrysobēryllos*, fr. *chrys-* + *bēryllos* beryl] **1** *obs* **:** beryl that has a yellow tinge **2** [G *krisoberil, chrysoberyll*, fr. L *chrysoberyllus*] **:** a hard mineral $BeAl_2O_4$ usu. yellow or pale green consisting of beryllium aluminum oxide with a small amount of iron and occurring in tabular orthorhombic crystals that when transparent are used as gems — see ALEXANDRITE, CAT'S-EYE

chryso·bull \'==+ˌbu̇l\ *n* [ML *chrysobulium*, MGk *chrysoboullon*, fr. ML & MGk *chrys-* + ML *-bulium*, MGk *-boullon* (respectively alter. & modif. of ML *bulla* seal, bull) — more at BULL] **1 :** a pendent seal made of gold — compare BULLA 2 **2 :** a document issued under a chrysobull

chrys·o·cap·sa·les \ˌ==ˌkap'sā(ˌ)lēz\ *n pl, cap* [NL, fr. *Chrysocapsa*, type genus (fr. *chrys-* + L *capsa* box) + *-ales* — more at CASE] **:** an order of yellow-green algae (class Chrysophyceae) having nonmotile vegetative cells in palmelloid colonies within a gelatinous matrix

chryso·car·pous \ˌ==+ˈkärpəs\ *adj* [L *chrysocarpus*, fr. Gk *chrysokarpos*, fr. *chrys-* + *-karpos* -carpous] **:** having or bearing yellow fruits

chrys·o·chlore \'==+ˌklō(ə)r\ *n* -S [NL *Chrysochloris*] **:** a mole of the genus *Chrysochloris*

chrys·o·chlo·ris \ˌ==ˈklōrəs\ *n, cap* [NL, fr. *chrys-* + *-chloris* (modif. of Gk *chlōros* greenish yellow) — more at YELLOW] **:** a genus (the type of the family Chrysochloridae) of African golden moles

chrys·o·chlo·rous \ˌ==+ˈklōrəs\ *adj* [*chrys-* + Gk *chlōros* greenish yellow] **:** of the color golden green

chrys·o·col·la \ˌ==+ˈkälə\ *n* -S [L, fr. Gk *chrysokolla*, fr. *chrys-* + *kolla* glue — more at PROTOCOL] **1 :** a mineral $CuSiO_3.2H_2O$ consisting of a hydrous silicate of copper occurring massive and of a blue to green color **2 :** MALACHITE GREEN

chryso·er·i·ol \ˌ==+'erēˌȯl, -ˌōl\ *n* -S [*chrys-* + NL *Eriodictyon* + E *-ol*] **:** a yellow crystalline flavone pigment $C_{16}H_{12}O_6$ found in the leaves of yerba santa

chrys·o·gen \'==+ˌjen, -jən\ *n* -S [ISV *chrys-* + *-gen;* orig. formed in G] **:** NAPHTHACENE

chrys·o·graph \'==+ˌgraf\ *vt* [Gk *chrysographia* writing with gold letters, fr. *chrys-* + *-graphia* -graphy] **:** to write in letters of gold

chry·sog·ra·phy \krə'sägrəfē\ *n* -ES [Gk *chrysographia*] **:** writing executed in gold letters

chry·so·idine \krə'sōədən, -ˌdēn\ *n* -S [ISV *chrysoid-* (fr. Gk *chrysoeidēs* like gold, fr. *chrys-* + *-oeidēs* -oid) + *-ine;* orig. formed as G *chrysoidin*] **1 :** a yellow crystalline base $C_6H_5N{=}NC_6H_3(NH_2)_2$ made from diazotized aniline and meta-phenylenediamine — see DYE table I (under *Solvent Orange 3*) **2** *usu cap* **a :** the reddish brown crystalline monohydrochloride of chrysoidine base used chiefly for dyeing leather and paper and as a biological stain — called also *Chrysoidine G, Chrysoidine Y;* see DYE table I (under *Basic Orange 2*) **b :** any of certain other basic azo dyes — see DYE table I (under *Basic Orange 1*)

chry·sol·i·na \krə'sälənə\ *n, cap* [NL, modif. of Gk *chrysolinon* gold thread, fr. *chrys-* + *linon* cord, thread, flax — more at LINEN] **:** a genus of small leaf-eating beetles (family Chrysomelidae) that have been extensively used in biological control of Klamath weed and other species of *Hypericum*

chrys·o·lite \'== *at* CHRYSO- + ˌlīt\ *n* -S [ME *crisolite*, fr. OF *crisolite*, fr. L *chrysolithos*, fr. Gk *chrysolithos*, fr. *chrys-* + *-lithos* -lite] **1 :** any of several yellow or greenish gems (as chrysoberyl) — not now used technically **2 :** OLIVINE; *specif* **:** olivine in which the ratio of magnesium to total magnesium plus iron is between 0.90 and 0.70 — **chrys·o·lit·ic** \ˌ==ˈlid-ik\ *adj*

chrysolite green *n* **:** a moderate yellow green that is lighter, stronger, and slightly yellower than average moss green, yellower and lighter than average pea green, and yellower, lighter, and slightly stronger than spinach green

chry·sol·o·phus \krə'sälәfəs\ *n, cap* [NL, fr. Gk *chrysolophos* golden crested, fr. *chrys-* + *lophos* nape, crest] **:** the genus consisting of the golden pheasant and Lady Amherst's pheasant

chrysom *or* **chrysome** *var of* CHRISOM

¹chrys·o·mel·id \ˈ== *at* CHRYSO- + ˈmeləd, -ēl-\ *adj* [NL *Chrysomelidae*] **:** of or relating to the Chrysomelidae

²chrysomelid \"\ *n* -S **:** one of the Chrysomelidae

chrys·o·mel·i·dae \ˌ==+'meləˌdē\ *n pl, cap* [NL, fr. *Chrysomela*, type genus (modif. of Gk *chrysomēlon* quince, fr. *chrys-* + *mēlon* apple, tree-fruit, influenced in meaning by Gk *chrysomēlolonthion* little golden cockchafer, fr. *chrys-* + *mēlolonthē* cockchafer + dim. suff. *-ion*) + *-idae*] **:** a large family of small usu. oval or rounded and often smooth, shining and brightly colored beetles comprising the leaf beetles having small heads, short antennae, and inconspicuous mouthparts and feeding on leaves both as larvae and adults with some (as the cucumber beetles and the Colorado potato beetle) being serious pests of cultivated plants

¹chry·som·o·nad \krə'sämәˌnad\ *also* **chrys·o·mon·a·dine** \ˌkrisō'mänəˌdīn\ *adj* [NL *Chrysomonad-, Chrysomonas* & *Chrysomonadina*] **:** of or relating to the Chrysomonadina

²chrysomonad \"\ *also* **chrysomonadine** \"\ *n* -S **:** a flagellate of the order Chrysomonadina

chrys·o·mon·a·da·les \ˌkrisōˌmänə'dā(ˌ)lēz\ *n pl, cap* [NL, fr. *Chrysomonad-, Chrysomonas*, genus of algae (fr. *chrys-* + *-monas*) + *-ales*] **:** the Chrysomonadina regarded as an order of yellow-green algae

chrys·o·mo·nad·i·da \-mə'nadədə\ [NL, fr. *Chrysomonad-, Chrysomonas* + *-ida*] *syn of* CHRYSOMONADINA

chrys·o·mon·a·di·na \-ˌmänə'dīnə, -ēnə\ *n pl, cap* [NL, fr. *Chrysomonad-, Chrysomonas* + *-ina*] **:** an order of minute plastic often ameboid plantlike flagellates usu. with yellow or brown chromatophores, solitary or forming palmella colonies, and commonly producing calcareous or siliceous skeletons that is treated by botanists as an order of the class Chrysophyceae — see COCCOLITHOPHORIDAE, SILICOFLAGELLATA

chrys·o·mya \ˌ==ˈmīə\ *n, cap* [NL, fr. *chrys-* + *-mya*] **:** the genus of blowflies including the Old World screwworms

¹chrys·o·my·ia \-'mī(y)ə\ [NL, fr. *chrys-* + *-myia*] *syn of* CHRYSOMYA

²chrysomyia \"\ [NL, fr. *chrys-* + *-myia*] *syn of* CALLITROGA

chrys·opal \kri'sōpəl\ *n* [F *chrysopale*, fr. *chrys-* + *opale* opal] **1 :** CHRYSOBERYL **2 :** opalescent chrysolite

chrys·o·phan·ic acid \ˌ== *at* CHRYSO- + ˈfanik\ *n* [*chrysophanic* ISV *chrysophan-* (fr. Gk *chrysophanēs* shining like gold, fr. *chrys-* + *-phanēs* shining) + *-ic* — more at -PHANE] **:** a yellow crystalline phenol $C_{15}H_{10}O_4$ obtained from rhubarb, senna leaves, and chrysarobin; 1, 8-dihydroxy-3-methylanthraquinone

chry·soph·a·nol \krə'säfəˌnōl, -ōl\ *n* -S [ISV *chrysophanic* + *-ol*] **:** CHRYSOPHANIC ACID

chry·soph·e·nine \krə'säfəˌnēn, -ˌnən\ *n* -S *often cap* [ISV *chrys-* + *phenine*] **:** a direct disazo stilbene dye that dyes cotton and viscose rayon yellow — called also *Chrysophenine G;* see DYE table I (under *Direct Yellow 12*)

chry·soph·i·list \krə'säfələst\ *or* **chry·soph·i·lite** \-əˌlīt\ *n* -S [LGk *chrysophilos* gold-loving (fr. Gk *chrys-* + *-philos* -phile) + E *-ist* or *-ite*] **:** a lover of gold

chrys·o·phlyc·tis \ˌ== *at* CHRYSO- + 'fliktəs\ [NL, fr. *chrys-* + Gk *phlyktis* blister; akin to L *fluere* to flow — more at FLUID] *syn of* SYNCHYTRIUM

chrys·o·phy·ce·ae \ˌ==+'fīsēˌē\ *n pl, cap* [NL, fr. *chrys-* + *-phyceae*] **:** a class of the yellow-green algae (division Chrysophyta) having cells solitary or in colonies of definite form, with few yellow or golden brown chromatophores in each cell, reserves occurring as fats and leucosin but not as starch, and motile cells when present having the flagella at their anterior end and more or less equal in length

chrys·o·phyll \'==+ˌfil\ *n* -S [*chrys-* + *-phyll*] **:** a yellow coloring matter in plants that is prob. a decomposition product of chlorophyll — compare XANTHOPHYLL

chrys·o·phyl·lum \ˌ==+'filəm\ *n, cap* [NL, fr. *chrys-* + *-phyllum*] **:** a large genus of tropical American trees (family Sapotaceae) having the leaves oblong and silky golden beneath and the flowers small and clustered chiefly in the leaf axils

chry·soph·y·ta \krə'säfəd·ə\ *n pl, cap* [NL, fr. *chrys-* + *-phyta*] **:** a division or other category of lower plants that comprises algae with pigments localized in yellowish green to golden brown chromatophores and usu. with a cell wall made up of overlapping halves and that includes the classes Xanthophyceae, Chrysophyceae, and Bacillariophyceae

¹chry·so·pid \krə'sōpəd\ *adj* [NL *Chrysopidae*] **:** of or relating to the Chrysopidae

²chrysopid \"\ *n* -S **:** a chrysopid fly **:** GOLDENEYE, STINK FLY

chry·so·pi·dae \krə'sōpəˌdē\ *n pl, cap* [NL, fr. *Chrysopa*, type genus (fr. *chrys-* + *-opa*, fr. Gk *ōp-, ōps* face) + *-idae*] **:** a family of pale green golden-eyed unpleasant-smelling lacewing flies having carnivorous larvae called aphis lions

chrys·o·prase \'krisəˌprāz\ *n* -S [alter. (influenced by F *chrysoprase*) of ME *crisopace*, fr. OF *crisopace, crisoprase*, fr. L *chrysoprasus*, fr. Gk *chrysoprasos*, fr. *chrys-* + *prasos* (fr. *prason* leek) — more at PRASINE] **1 :** an apple-green variety of chalcedony valued as a gem **2** *or* **chrysoprase green :** a brilliant to light green that is very slightly darker than seafoam

chrysoprasus *n, pl* **chrysoprasi** [L] *obs* **:** CHRYSOPRASE

chrys·ops \'kriˌsäps\ *n, cap* [NL, fr. Gk *chrysōps* gold-colored, fr. *chrys-* + *ōps* eye, face — more at OPTIC] **:** a widely distributed genus of small pestiferous sometimes disease-transmitting horseflies (family Tabanidae) including the deerflies of America and the mango flies of Africa

chry·sop·sis \krə'säpsəs\ *n, cap* [NL, fr. *chrys-* + *-opsis*] **:** a genus of No. American chiefly perennial woolly, hairy, or glutinous herbs (family Compositae) having large often corymbose heads — see GOLDEN ASTER

chrys·o·sphae·ra·les \ˌ== *at* CHRYSO- + sfə'rā(ˌ)lēz\ *n pl, cap* [NL, fr. *Chrysosphaera* genus of algae (fr. *chrys-* + *-sphaera*) + *-ales*] **:** an order of yellow-green unicellular or nonfilamentous colonial algae (class Chrysophyceae) having the cell content not transformed directly into a zoospore or other motile form

chrys·o·sple·ni·um \ˌ==+'splēnēəm\ *n, cap* [NL, fr. *chrys-* + L *splenium* spleenwort (fr. Gk *splēnion*, fr. *splēn* spleen)] **:** a small genus of widely distributed semiaquatic herbs (family Saxifragaceae) having minute greenish yellow apetalous flowers

chrys·o·tham·nus \ˌ==+'thamnəs\ *n, cap* [NL, fr. *chrys-* + Gk *thamnos* shrub — more at THAMN-] **:** a genus of low branching shrubs (family Compositae) of the alkali plains of western No. America comprising some of the rayless goldenrods and characterized by linear entire leaves and clusters of golden yellow flowers

chryso·therapy \ˌ==+\ *n* -ES [ISV *chrys-* + *therapy*] **:** treatment (as of arthritis) by injection of gold salts

chrys·o·thrix \'==+ˌthriks\ [NL, fr. *chrys-* + *-thrix*] *syn of* SAIMIRI

chrys·o·tile \'==+ˌtīl\ *n* -S [G *chrysotil*, fr. *chrys-* + Gk *tilos* anything plucked (as hair or fiber), fr. *tillein* to pluck] **:** a fibrous silky serpentine $Mg_3Si_2O_5(OH)_4$ constituting one kind of asbestos

chrys·o·tri·cha·les \ˌ==+trə'kā(ˌ)lēz\ *n pl, cap* [NL, fr. *Chrysotrich-, Chrysothrix*, + *-ales*] **:** an order of yellow-green algae (class Chrysophyceae) distinguished by their branching filamentous form

chrys·to·crene \'kristəˌkrēn\ *n* -S [*chrysto-* (prob. irreg. fr. *crystal*) + Gk *krēnē* spring, well] **:** a mass of loose rock fragments remarkably similar to a glacier **:** ROCK GLACIER

cht *abbr* **1** chemist **2** chest

chthon·ic \'thänik\ *or* **chtho·ni·an** \'thōnēən\ *adj* [*chthonic* fr. Gk *chthon-, chthōn* earth + E *-ic; chthonian* fr. Gk *chthonios* in or under the earth (fr. *chthon-, chthōn*) + E *-an* — more at HUMBLE] **1** *of a divinity or a spirit* **:** dwelling or reigning in the underworld **:** INFERNAL ⟨Pluto was the ~ counterpart of Zeus⟩ **2 :** relating to infernal deities or spirits **:** GHOSTLY ⟨~ worship⟩

chtr *abbr* charter

CHU *abbr* centigrade heat unit

chuana *usu cap, var of* TSWANA

chuang \'jwäŋ\ *or* **chawng** \'jōŋ\ *n, pl* **chuang** *or* **chuangs** *or* **chawng** *or* **chawngs** *usu cap* **:** any of a large number of tribal peoples of southern China under a variety of names but all having cultural and linguistic affiliation with the Thai or Siamese

chub \'chəb\ *n, pl* **chub** *or* **chubs** [ME *chubbe*] **1 :** a common European freshwater cyprinoid fish (*Leuciscus cephalus*) little valued as food — called also *chevin* **2 a :** any of various cyprinoid fishes (as the fallfish, horned dace, golden shiner, squawfish, hornyhead) **b :** any of several marine species (as the tautog, Bermuda chub or related forms, spot, pinfish) **c :** LARGEMOUTH BLACK BASS **d** *in the Great Lakes region* **:** LAKE HERRING **e :** CHUB SUCKER

chu·ba \'chübə\ *n* -S [origin unknown] **:** a game adapted in America from mancala using a board with 4 rows of 11 holes each

chu·bas·co \chü'bäˌskō\ *n* -S [Sp, fr. Pg *chuvasco*, fr. *chuva* rain, fr. L *pluvia*, fr. *pluere* to rain — more at FLOW] **:** a severe squall of rain and wind esp. along the west coast of Central America

chub·bi·ly \'chəbəlē, -li\ *adv* **:** in the manner of one who is chubby

chub·bi·ness \'chəbēnəs, -in-\ *n* -ES **:** the quality or state of being chubby **:** PLUMPNESS

chub·by \'chəbē, -bi\ *adj* -ER/-EST [*chub* + *-y*] **:** short, thick, and well-rounded **:** CHUNKY, PLUMP ⟨a ~ cigar⟩ ⟨a ~ boat⟩; *esp* **:** marked wholesomely by ample flesh **:** well-fed and not lean or wiry ⟨of middle height . . . stocky though not ~ —W. A.White⟩ ⟨a ~ little boy⟩ **syn** see FAT

chub mackerel *n* **:** a small mackerel (*Pneumatophorus japonicus* syn. *Scomber japonicus*) of the Atlantic and northeastern Pacific oceans that has a well-developed swim bladder — called also *tinker mackerel*

chub sucker *n* **:** either of two common suckers (*Erimyzon sucetta* and *E. oblongus*) of stout build widely distributed in the eastern and central U. S.

chucalho *var of* CHOCALHO

chu·cho \'chüˌchō\ *n* -S [Sp, perh. fr. *chucho* dog, owl, of imit. origin] **:** EAGLE RAY

¹chuck \'chək\ *vb* -ED/-ING/-S [ME *chukken*, of imit. origin] *vi* **1 a** *of a hen* **:** to make a clucking noise **b :** to make a noise suggesting the chucking of a hen **2** *obs* **:** CHUCKLE **:** laugh inwardly ~ *vt* **1 :** to call (as chickens) by clucking **2 :** to urge (a horse) forward by a cluck or palatal click

²chuck \"\ *n* -S [ME *chuk*, fr. *chukken*, v.] **1 :** DEAR — used as a term of endearment ⟨sweet ~⟩ **2** *dial Brit* **:** FOWL, CHICKEN

³chuck \"\ *vt* -ED/-ING/-S [origin unknown] **1 :** to give a pat or caress to under the chin orig. to make the mouth close ⟨~*ed* the barmaid under the chin —Washington Irving⟩ **2 a** (1) **:** to toss or jerk out of the hand **:** throw with a short action of the arm and usu. in an easy or careless manner (2) **:** to throw (a baseball) to a batter or fielder **b :** to throw away **:** DISCARD ⟨he had ~*ed* his old suit⟩ **c :** DISMISS, EJECT, OUST — used esp. with *out* ⟨~*ed out* of office⟩ **3 :** to give up **:** have done with — often used with *up* ⟨~ *up* a job⟩ **4 :** to clear (the ground) of obstructions with horses or machinery in logging — **chuck it :** QUIT, YIELD

⁴chuck \"\ *n* -S **1 :** a pat or nudge under the chin **2 :** TOSS, JERK; *esp* **:** a toss or short cast (as of a stone) from the hand **3 :** CHUCK-FARTHING **4** *slang Brit* **:** DISMISSAL ⟨to get the ~⟩

⁵chuck \"\ *n* -S [prob. var. of *chock*] **1** *now dial* **:** a log or lump **:** CHUNK **2 a :** a portion of a side of dressed beef including most of the neck, the parts about the shoulder blade, and those about the first three ribs ⟨a ~ roast⟩ — see BEEF illustration **b :** a similar cut from a carcass of dressed veal or lamb **3** *chiefly West* **:** FOOD, GRUB **4 :** a tapered piece of wood used in founding to stiffen the bars of a flask or connect them with parts below the joint **5 a :** an attachment for holding a workpiece or tool in a machine (as a drill press or lathe) usu. by means of adjustable jaws or setscrews — see COLLET CHUCK, DRILL CHUCK, INDEPENDENT CHUCK, MAGNETIC CHUCK, UNIVERSAL CHUCK **b :** a hydrant carried on fire apparatus for attaching to a chuck hydrant

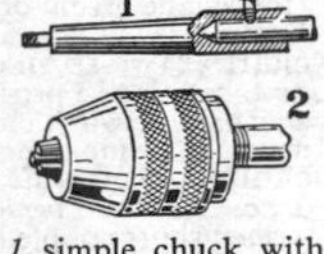

1 simple chuck with setscrew; *2* drill chuck

⁶chuck \"\ *vt* -ED/-ING/-S **:** to place in a chuck **:** hold by means of a chuck

⁷chuck \"\ *var of* CHOCK

⁸chuck \"\ *n* -S [by shortening] **:** WOODCHUCK

⁹chuck \'chu̇k, 'chək\ *n* -S [alter. (prob. influenced by ³*chuck*) of ²*check* (checkstone)] *dial Brit* **:** CHECKSTONE

¹⁰chuck \'chək\ *n* -S [Chinook Jargon, water, river, stream, sea, prob. fr. Nootka *chauk*] *Northwest* **:** INLET, HARBOR ⟨salmon caught right in front of the ~ entrance⟩ ⟨a sizable stream . . . met the salt ~ —N.C.McDonald⟩

chuck-a-luck \'chəkəˌlək\ *also* **chuck-luck** \'=ˌ=\ *n* [prob. fr. ³*chuck* (throw) + connective *-a-* + *luck*] **:** a banking game played with three dice in which players bet that a certain number will appear on one or more of the dice, that the sum of the three dice will make a certain number, or that all three dice will turn up alike — called also *birdcage;* compare RAFFLE

chuckawalla *var of* CHUCKWALLA

chuckchee *usu cap, var of* CHUKCHI

chucked *past of* CHUCK

¹chuck·er \'chəkə(r)\ *n* -S [³*chuck* (throw) + *-er*] **:** one that chucks: as **a :** BOUNCER **b :** a baseball pitcher

²chucker \"\ *var of* CHUKKER

³chucker \"\ *n* -S [⁶*chuck* + *-er*] **1 :** one that chucks **2 :** an operator of a crozing machine that cuts, grooves, and trims ends of staves in a headless barrel while it is held in chucks — called also *crozer*

chucker-out \'=ˌ=\ *n, pl* **chuckers-out** [¹*chucker*] *Brit* **:** BOUNCER

chuck-farthing \'=ˌ==\ *n* [³*chuck*] **:** an old game in which the player who pitched coins nearest to a mark tossed all the coins at a hole and won those that went into it — called also *pitch-farthing;* compare PITCH-PENNY

chuck-full *var of* CHOCK-FULL

chuckhole \'=ˌ=\ *n* [³*chuck* + *hole*] **:** a hole, depression, or rut in a road **:** MUDHOLE ⟨washouts and the biggest ~*s* were filled up —Bernard De Voto⟩

chuck hydrant *n* [5*chuck*] **:** a fire hydrant having a cover set flush with the pavement and to which a chuck can be attached — called also *flush hydrant*

1**chuck·ie** \'chəkē, -ki\ *n* -s [2*chuck* (chicken) + *-ie*] *Scot* **:** 2CHUCK 2

2**chuckie** \"\ *or* **chuckie stane** \-,stān\ *n* -s [9*chuck* + *-ie*] *Scot* **:** a small pebble (as one used in checkstones)

chuck·ing·ly \'chəkiŋlē, -li\ *adv* [fr. pres. part. of 2*chuck* + *-ly*] **:** CHUCKLINGLY

chucking reamer *n* [fr. pres. part. of 6*chuck*] **:** a reamer (as a twist drill) held in a chuck and usu. being stationary while the workpiece revolves

1**chuck·le** \'chəkəl\ **chuckled; chuckled; chuckling** \-k(ə)liŋ\ **chuckles** *vi* -ED/-ING/-S [prob. freq. of 1*chuck*] **1 :** to laugh convulsively (as with marked heaving of the shoulders) ⟨this breezy approach . . . soon had the reader racing along, *chuckling* —J.M.Chase⟩ **2 :** to laugh inwardly or quietly ⟨hummed snatches of some vagrant melody and *chuckled* at some private joke —Harold Sinclair⟩ **3 :** to make a continuous gentle sound resembling suppressed mirth (as of a wobbling millstone or a brook over stones) ⟨sometimes there were sunny rips where the clear bright water *chuckled* over gravel —B.A.Williams⟩

2**chuckle** \"\ *n* -s **:** a quiet hardly audible laugh (as of satisfaction, appreciation of humor, exultation, or derision) **:** CHUCKLING ⟨the gladsome ~ of the announcer as he archly nears the commercial —Bergen Evans⟩ ⟨a photographer gets a picture that gives a ~ to thousands of perspiring readers —F.L. Mott⟩

3**chuckle** *adj* [perh. irreg. fr. 5*chuck*] *obs* **:** CLUMSY, STUPID

chucklehead \'==,=\ *n* -s [3*chuckle* + *head*] **1 :** BLOCKHEAD, DOLT ⟨a ~ advertising his stupidity to thousands of TV viewers⟩ **2 :** a rockfish (*Sebastodes chlorostictus*) of the California coast **3** *or* **chucklehead cat :** BLUE CAT

chuck·le·head·ed \;==;==\ *adj* **:** BLOCKHEADED, STUPID ⟨a ~ play cost them the game⟩

chuck·ler \'chəklə(r)\ *n* -s [Tamil-Malayalam *cakkiliyar*, honorific pl. of *cakkiliyan*] *India* **:** a worker in leather **:** COBBLER

chuck line *n* [5*chuck* (food)] *West* **:** ranch houses visited for free meals — usu. used in the phrase *ride the chuck line* with reference to an unemployed cowboy

chuck·ling·ly \'chək(ə)liŋlē, -li\ *adv* [fr. pres. part. of 1*chuckle* + *-ly*] **:** with a chuckle

chuck-luck *var of* CHUCK-A-LUCK

chuck plate *n* [5*chuck*] **1 :** a plate on which a chuck is fastened and which is arranged for attaching to a lathe spindle (as by a screw thread) **2 :** a lathe faceplate

chuckram *or* **chuckrum** *var of* CHAKRAM

chuck ring *n* [5*chuck*] **:** one of a pair of heavy steel rings that form a chuck for holding a keg when turning grooves in the ends of staves

1**chucks** *pres 3d sing of* CHUCK, *pl of* CHUCK

2**chucks** \'chüks, 'chəks\ *n pl but sing or pl in constr* [pl. of 9*chuck*] *dial Brit* **:** CHECKSTONES

chuck wagon *n* [5*chuck* (food)] **:** a wagon that is equipped with a stove and provisions for cooking (as on a ranch or in a lumber camp)

chuck·wal·la \'chək,wälə\ *or* **chuck·a·wal·la** \'chəkə-\ *n* -s [modif. of MexSp *chacahuala*, fr. Cahuilla *tcáxxwal*] **:** a large harmless herbivorous iguanid lizard (*Sauromalus ater*) of the desert regions of the southwestern U.S. sometimes eaten by the Indians

chuck-will's-widow \'chək,wilz,==\ *n, pl* **chuck-will's-widows** [so called fr. its note] **:** a goatsucker (*Caprimulgus carolinensis*) of the southern U.S. resembling but larger than the whippoorwill

chucky \'chəkē, -ki\ *n* -ES [2*chuck* + *-y*] *dial Brit* **:** 2CHUCK

chu·cu·na·que \,chükü'nä,kwā\ *n, pl* **chucunaque** *or* **chucunaques** *usu cap* [Sp, of AmerInd origin] **1 :** a Cunan people of the Mulatas islands, Panama **2 :** a member of the Chucunaque people

chud \'chüd\ [alter. of ME *ich wolde* I would] *dial Eng* **:** I would

chuddar *or* **chudder** *var of* CHADOR

chud·ic \'chüdik\ *adj, usu cap* [Russ *Chud'* Chud, Finn (perh. of Gmc origin; akin to Goth *thiuda* people) + E *-ic* — more at DUTCH] **:** constituting or belonging to the West Finnic languages

chue·ta \'chwād·ə\ *n* -s [Sp, fr. Catal *juéuet*, dim. of *jueu* Jew, fr. L *Judaeus* — more at JEW] **1** *in the Balearic islands* **:** a descendant of a Christianized Jew **2** [AmerSp, fr. Sp] *in Puerto Rico* **:** a descendant of the Majorcan Jews

chu·fa \'chüfə\ *n* -s [Sp, fr. OSp, tidbit, trifle, joke, fr. *chufar* to joke, alter. (influenced by *trufar* to fib) of *chuflar* to ridicule, whistle, fr. (assumed) VL *sufilare* to whistle, alter. of L *sibilare* — more at SIBILANT] **:** a European sedge (*Cyperus esculentus*) with small edible nutlike tubers — called also *earth almond, ground almond, rush nut*

1**chuff** \'chəf\ *n* -s [ME *chuffe, choffe*] **1 :** BOOR, CHURL ⟨coarse country ~*s*⟩ **2 :** MISER

2**chuff** \'chəf, -üf\ *adj* -ER/-EST *dial* **:** SURLY, SULLEN

3**chuff** \"\ *adj* -ER/-EST [perh. fr. 1*chuff*] **1** *dial Brit* **:** PLUMP **2** *dial Eng* **a :** HAPPY **b :** PROUD, CONCEITED

4**chuff** \'chəf\ *n* -s [origin unknown] **:** a brick cracked by rain during burning

5**chuff** \"\ *n* -s [imit.] **:** a sound made by or suggestive of noisy exhaust or exhalation; *typically* **:** the sound of a steam engine ⟨the engine giving off quiet ~*s* like a giant breathing —Helen Eustis⟩

6**chuff** \"\ *vi* -ED/-ING/-S **:** to make chuffs **:** emit noisy exhaust or exhalations **:** proceed or operate with chuffs ⟨the ~*ing* and snorting of switch engines —Paul Gallico⟩ ⟨the ferryboat ~*ed* across the wide river —Walter Havighurst⟩

1**chuffy** \'chəfē, -üfē, -fi\ *adj* -ER/-EST [perh. fr. 3*chuff* + *-y*] **1** *now dial, of a person* **:** short and stout **:** FAT, CHUBBY **2** *of swine* **:** short-coupled and fat ⟨a new boar . . . with heftier ham, but not so ~ —*Breeder's Gazette*⟩ — opposed to *rangy*

2**chuffy** \"\ *adj* -ER/-EST [1*chuff* + *-y*] *now dial Eng* **:** CHUFF, SURLY

1**chug** \'chəg\ *also* **chug-chug** \'=,=\ *n* -s [imit.] **:** a sound made by or suggestive of the muffled firing of an engine; *typically* **:** one of a series of dull explosive sounds made by a laboring engine

2**chug** \"\ *vi* **chugged; chugged; chugging; chugs 1 :** to make chugs **:** make the intermittent explosive sound of a firing motor ⟨*chugging* overladen old cars —Russell Lord⟩ **2 :** to proceed or operate with or as if with chugs **:** travel in a vehicle or ship that chugs ⟨with 75 pounds of steam from her wood-fired boiler she puffed and *chugged* —Tom Marvel⟩ ⟨over these highways the farmers *chugged* to market —*Amer. Guide Series: Wash.*⟩

chug·ger \'chəgə(r)\ *n* -s [E dial *chug* to pull, jerk + *-er*] **:** a surface casting plug used in angling

chug·hole \'chəg,hōl\ *dial var of* CHUCKHOLE

chug step *n* **:** a forward push on one foot in dancing

chuh·ra \'chürə\ *n, pl* **chuhra** *or* **chuhras** [Hindi *cūhṛā*] **:** a member of a lower caste of India now usu. engaged in agriculture

chuj \'chü(k), -üē\ *n, pl* **chuj** \"\ *or* **chu·jes** \'chü,kās\ *usu cap* [Sp, of AmerInd origin] **1 a :** an Indian people of northwestern Guatemala **b :** a member of such people **2 :** a Mayan language of the Chuj people

chu·kar \chə'kär\ *or* **chukar partridge** *also* **chu·kor** \-ōr, -ȯr\ *n, pl* **chukar** *or* **chukars** [Hindi *cakor*, fr. Skt *cakora*, prob. of imit. origin] **:** an Indian rock partridge (*Alectoris graeca chukar*) that is gray with black and white bars on the sides and with red bill and legs and that has been introduced into dry parts of the western U.S. where it is rapidly becoming established and is highly esteemed as a game bird; *broadly* **:** any rock partridge

chuk·chi *or* **chuk·chee** *also* **chook·chie** \'chük,chē\ *n, pl* **chukchi** *or* **chukchis** *or* **chukchee** *or* **chukchees** *also* **chookchie** *or* **chookchies** *usu cap* [Russ *Chukcha*] **1 a :** a Siberian Americanoid people allied to the Kamchadal and Koryak and inhabiting the Chukchi peninsula **b :** a member of such people **2 :** the Luorawetlan language of the Chukchi people frequently cited for its extreme differentiation in pronunciation between men and women

1**chukka** *var of* CHUKKER

2**chuk·ka** \'chəkə\ *or* **chukka boot** *n* -s [1*chukka*; fr. a similar boot's being worn by polo players] **:** a short leather boot usu. ankle-length and having two pairs of eyelets — compare JODHPUR

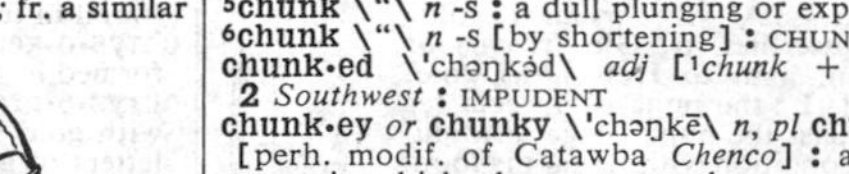

chukka boot

chuk·ker *or* **chuk·kar** \'chəkə(r)\ *n* -s [Hindi *cakkar*, *cakar*, fr. Skt *cakra* wheel, circle — more at WHEEL] **1** *India* **:** a circular course **:** WHEEL, CIRCLE **2** *or* **chuk·ka** \'chəkə\ *or* **chuck·er** \'chəkə(r)\ **:** a playing period of a polo game

chukker brown *n* **:** MUMMY BROWN 2b

chul·ha *also* **chu·la** \'chülə\ *n* -s [Hindi *cūlhā*, *cūlā*, fr. Skt *cullī* fireplace, hearth, prob. of Dravidian origin; akin to Tamil *cuḷḷai*, *cūḷai* hearth] *India* **:** a small earthen or brick stove

chu·llo \'chü,lyō\ *n* -s [AmerSp] **:** a knitted wool cap with ear flaps worn in Peru

chull·pa *or* **chul·pa** \'chülpə\ *n* -s [AmerSp *chulpa*, fr. Aymara *chullpa*] **:** a stone tower or tomb erected by the pre-Incan inhabitants of Peru and Bolivia

chu·lo \'chü(,)lō\ *n* -s [Sp, fr. OSp, boy, fr. OIt *ciullo*, short for *fanciullo*, dim. of *fante*, fr. L *infant-, infans* young child — more at INFANT] **:** a matador's assistant in the ring

chul·tun \'chül,tün\ *n, pl* **chultu·nes** \chül'tü,näs\ [Maya] **:** a circular or bottle-shaped stone cistern constructed by the Mayas of Yucatán

chu·ly·ma tatar \chü'limə-\ *n, usu cap C&T* [fr. *Chulym*, river in Siberia, U.S.S.R.] **1 :** a people inhabiting the Tomsk and Yeniseisk areas of Siberia **2 :** a member of the Chulyma Tatar people

1**chum** \'chəm\ *n* -s [perh. by shortening & alter. fr. *chamber fellow*] **1** *archaic* **:** ROOMMATE **2 :** an habitual intimate companion **:** a close friend ⟨a boyhood ~ of his⟩

2**chum** \"\ *vb* **chummed; chummed; chumming; chums** *vi* **1 :** to share quarters **:** room together ⟨the two bedrooms to each study favored the pleasant custom of *chumming* —George Santayana⟩ **2 a :** to be a chum **:** be on terms of intimate friendship — usu. used with *with* ⟨he soon *chummed* with du Maurier and me in several languages and became one of our set —Felix Moscheles⟩ **b :** to show affable friendliness **:** form close friendship — usu. used with *up* ⟨two husbands might ~ up and slip out for a light ale —Elizabeth Taylor⟩ ~ *vt* **:** to place in the same quarters with another — usu. used with *on* ⟨the college *chummed* him on a student from Duluth⟩

3**chum** \"\ *n* -s [origin unknown] **1 :** chopped fish, vegetable matter, or small live fish thrown overboard to draw fish to a fishing boat **2 a :** refuse or scrap fish (as in a fish cannery) **b :** the pulp left after expressing oil from menhaden

4**chum** \"\ *vb* **chummed; chummed; chumming; chums** *vi* **:** to attract fish with chum ~ *vt* **:** to attract by chumming ⟨*chumming* the fish with cut-up shrimp⟩

5**chum** \"\ *n* -s [perh. fr. Chinook Jargon *tsum, tzum* spots, writing, fr. Chinook] **:** a dog salmon (*Oncorhynchus keta*)

6**chum** \"\ *n* -s [perh. alter. of 1*chump*] **:** a cradle used in ceramics for turning a form

7**chum** \'chüm, 'chəm\ *n* -s [Russ, of Finnic origin; akin to Zyrian *t'śom* tent, hut, Votyak *tśum*] **:** a tepeelike shelter esp. of skins, turf, or fibers used as a summer dwelling by the Samoyeds, Buryats, Tungus, and other peoples of northern Eurasia — compare YURT

chu·mash \'chü,mash\ *n, pl* **chumash** *or* **chumashes** *usu cap* **1 a :** an Indian people of southwestern California **b :** a member of such people **2 :** the Chumashan language of the Chumash people **3 :** CHUMASHAN

chu·mash·an \(')chü'mashən\ *n* -s *usu cap* [*Chumash* + E *-an*] **:** a language family of the Hokan stock comprising only the Chumash language

chum·ble \'chəmbəl\ *vb* **chumbled; chumbled; chumbling** \-b(ə)liŋ\ **chumbles** [prob. freq. of 2*chump*] **:** GNAW, CHEW ⟨clashing jaws of moth *chumbling* holes in cloth —Robert Graves⟩

chum·mage \'chəmij\ *n* -s [2*chum* + *-age*] **:** the quartering of persons together in the same room (~ of various collegians together)

chum·mer \'chəmə(r)\ *n* -s [4*chum* + *-er*] **:** one that scatters chum in fishing

chum·mery \'chəm(ə)rē, -ri\ *n* -ES [1*chum* + *-ery*] *India* **:** the living quarters of chums ⟨a ~ he shared with another bachelor —John Masters⟩

chum·mi·ly \'chəmə̇lē, -li\ *adv* [3*chummy* + *-ly*] **:** in a chummy manner

chum·mi·ness \-ēnə̇s\ *n* -ES [3*chummy* + *-ness*] **:** the quality or state of being chummy

1**chum·my** \'chəmē, -mi\ *n* -ES [perh. alter. of *chimney*] *slang Brit* **:** CHIMNEY SWEEP **:** a boy helper to a chimney sweep

2**chummy** \"\ *n* -ES [*chum* + *-y*] **:** 1CHUM

3**chummy** \"\ *adj* -ER/-EST [1*chum* + *-y*] **:** marked by or affording easy familiarity, companionableness, and shared interests **:** intimately sociable ⟨the secretary is on ~ terms with a host of congressmen —Philip Hamburger⟩ ⟨a ~ little cocktail lounge⟩ **syn** see FAMILIAR

1**chump** \'chəmp\ *n* -s [perh. blend of 1*chunk* and *lump*] **1 :** a short thick heavy piece of wood **2** *slang chiefly Brit* **:** HEAD **3 a :** stupid lout **:** BLOCKHEAD, FOOL **b :** GULL, DUPE; *specif* **:** intended victim — **off one's chump** *slang chiefly Brit* **:** out of one's mind **:** CRAZY

2**chump** \"\ *vb* -ED/-ING/-S [alter. of 1*champ*] **:** MUNCH, CHAMP

chum·pa \'chəmpə\ *n* -s [perh. fr. Choctaw *chumpa* purchase] *West* **:** a faggot of pine kindling

chump chop *n* [1*chump*] *Brit* **:** a mutton chop from the thick end of a loin

chumpy \'chəmpē, -pi\ *adj* -ER/-EST [1*chump* + *-y*] *dial* **:** THICK, THICKSET

chums *pl of* CHUM, *pres 3d sing of* CHUM

chum salmon *n* [5*chum*] **:** DOG SALMON

chu·nam \chü'nam\ *n* -s [Tamil *cuṇṇam*, fr. Skt *cūrṇa* powder, flour, fr. *carvati* he grinds, chews; perh. akin to Slovak *čren* jaw, cheekbone, Latvian *ceruoklis* molar] **1** *India* **:** lime used esp. with betel leaf in making pan **2 :** a cement or plaster used in India that is usu. highly polished and decorated with paintings

chun·cho \'chün,chō\ *n, pl* **chuncho** *or* **chunchos** *usu cap* [Sp, fr. Quechua *ch'unchu* uncivilized Indian of the eastern forests] **:** a member of any jungle people of So. America

chun·ga \'chəŋgə\ *n* -s [alter. of AmerSp *chuña*] **:** a cariama (*Chunga burmeisteri*) of northern Argentina that is smaller and darker than the crested cariama, has a shorter crest, and frequents more wooded terrain

chung·chia \'jüŋ'jyä\ *n pl, usu cap* **:** the Tai-related valley-dwelling people numbering over a million and inhabiting the plateau province of Kweichow in southern China

chung·king \'chüŋ'kiŋ, -üŋ'ch-\ *adj, usu cap* [fr. *Chungking*, China] **:** of or from the city of Chungking, China **:** of the kind or style prevalent in Chungking

1**chunk** \'chəŋk\ *n* -s [perh. alter. of 5*chuck*] **1 a** *dial* **:** LOG, STUMP **:** a heavy piece of wood, esp. of firewood; *sometimes* **:** a piece of firewood made by splitting a log in quarters **b :** a piece of burning wood ⟨get a ~ from a neighbor's fire⟩ **c :** a short thick piece often crudely or roughly formed **:** LUMP ⟨a ~ of meat⟩ ⟨a sizzling summer day holds few finer refreshments than a great ~ of cold watermelon —Jane Nickerson⟩ **2 :** a sizable amount **:** a noteworthy quantity **:** a large portion ⟨six months is a ~ out of any man's life —Upton Sinclair⟩ **3 a :** a strong thickset horse usu. smaller than a typical draft horse **b :** a person and esp. a child who is large or stocky ⟨the chubby little ~ who had played in the sandpile —Dorothy C. Fisher⟩ — often used with *of* ⟨a fine ~ of a man⟩

2**chunk** \"\ *vt* -ED/-ING/-S [prob. fr. 1*chunk*] **1** *chiefly South* **:** THROW ⟨~ sticks at grazing cows⟩ ⟨~*ed* three more stones into the water —Dan Wickenden⟩; *also* **:** throw things at **:** PELT **2** *dial* **:** to build or revive (a fire) by throwing on fuel or by raking or stirring — sometimes used with *up* **3 :** to remove chunks from (a skid road) — usu. used with *out*

3**chunk** \"\ *vt* -ED/-ING/-S [perh. by alter.] **:** 2CHINK 2

4**chunk** \"\ *vi* -ED/-ING/-S [imit.] **:** to make a dull plunging or explosive sound **:** proceed while making dull plunging sounds

5**chunk** \"\ *n* -s **:** a dull plunging or explosive sound

6**chunk** \"\ *n* -s [by shortening] **:** CHUNKEY

chunk·ed \'chəŋkə̇d\ *adj* [1*chunk* + *-ed*] **1 :** CHUNKY **2** *Southwest* **:** IMPUDENT

chunk·ey *or* **chunky** \'chəŋkē\ *n, pl* **chunkeys** *or* **chunkies** [perh. modif. of Catawba *Chenco*] **:** a Muskogean Indian game in which players try to throw or slide a pole so that a crook at one end curves around a disk

chunk honey *n* [1*chunk*] **:** mixed extracted and comb honey

chunk·i·ly \'chəŋkəlē, -li\ *adv* [1*chunky* + *-ly*] **:** in a chunky manner ⟨another man — brown-suited, ~ built, with a square face and rather heavy features —R.M.Coates⟩

chunk·i·ness \'chəŋkēnə̇s\ *n* -ES **:** the quality or state of being chunky

1**chunky** \'chəŋkē, -ki\ *adj* -ER/-EST [1*chunk* + *-y*] **:** short and thick or broad; *esp* **:** having or characterized by a stout robust solid body ⟨short, ~ . . . far removed from the elegant, willowy statesmen —Mollie Panter-Downes⟩ ⟨a ~ topcoat —*New Yorker*⟩ **syn** see STOCKY

2**chunky** *var of* CHUNKEY

chu·ño \'chü,nyō\ *also* **chu·ñu** \-,nyü\ *n* -s [AmerSp, fr. Quechua *ch'uñu*] **:** potatoes processed by successive freezing, thawing, and dehydrating prepared and eaten esp. by the native peoples of the Andes

chun·ter \'chəntə(r), -ünt-\ *or* **chun·ner** \'chənə(r), -ün-\ *vi* -ED/-ING/-S [prob. of imit. origin] **1** *dial Brit, of a person* **:** to talk in a low inarticulate way **:** MUTTER; *also* **:** COMPLAIN, GRUMBLE **2** *dial Brit, of an animal* **:** to emit typical outcries

chu·nu·pí \,chünü'pē\ *n, pl* **chunupí** *or* **chunupis** *usu cap* [Sp, of AmerInd origin] **1 :** a people of the Vilela group **2 :** a member of the Chunupí

chün ware \'jün-, 'jüen-\ *n, usu cap* [fr. *Chün* Chon (Fangcheng), Honan province, China, where it was orig. made] **:** a Chinese pottery that originated in the Sung period and has typically a porcelaneous stoneware body and a thick predominantly lavender flambé glaze

chu·pat·ti \chə'päd·ē, -pa-\ *var of* CHAPATI

chu·pon \chü'pōn\ *n* -s [AmerSp *chupón*] **1 a :** a tropical American timber tree (*Bumelia obtusifolia*) with yellowish brown very hard heavy wood **b :** a So. American timber tree (*Gustavia yaracuyensis*) of the family Lecythidaceae with dark black-streaked wood **2 :** a sucker of the chocolate tree

chuppah *also* **chupah** *n, pl* **chuppoth** *or* **chuppot** *also* **chuppahs** *var of* HUPPAH

chu·pras·si \chə'präsē\ *var of* CHAPRASSI

chu·ra·pa \chə'räpə\ *n, pl* **churapa** *or* **churapas** *usu cap* [Sp, of AmerInd origin] **1 :** an Indian people of the Chiquitoan group now found in or near Buenavista, Bolivia **2 :** a member of such people

1**church** \'chərch, -əch, -əich\ *n* -ES [ME *chirche*, fr. OE *cirice*; akin to OS *kirika*, OHG *kirihha*; all fr. a prehistoric WGmc word borrowed fr. (assumed) Goth *kyriko* (whence OSlav *crŭky*), fr. LGk *kyrikon*, alter. of *kyriakon*, short for *kyriakon dōma* the Lord's house, fr. Gk *kyriakon* (neut. of *kyriakos* of the lord or master, fr. *kyrios* lord, master, fr. *kyros* power) + *dōma* house; akin to W *cawr* giant, Skt *śūra* strong, L *cavus* hollow — more at CAVE] **1 :** a building set apart for public esp. Christian worship ⟨visit the ~*es* of a city⟩: as **a :** the principal house of a parish **b :** a house of worship in Great Britain for members of the established or formerly established church as distinguished from those of nonconformists and Roman Catholics — compare CHAPEL 6 **2 :** a place of worship of any religion ⟨a Muslim ~⟩ **3 :** church service **:** divine worship or religious service in a church **:** the church building with the service going on in it ⟨go to ~⟩ ⟨attend ~⟩ **4** *often cap* **a :** the organization of Christianity or of an association of Christians; *esp* **:** an historical institution composed of believing Christians **b :** the clergy or officers of such an organization **c :** a body of Christian believers holding the same creed, observing the same rites, and acknowledging the same ecclesiastical authority regarded either as the only true representative of or as a separate branch of the church universal and often confined to territorial or historical limits **:** DENOMINATION ⟨the Presbyterian *Church*⟩ **d :** the total body of Christians regarded as a spiritual society **e :** a formally organized body of Christian believers worshiping together **:** a local Christian congregation ⟨they had appointed elders for them in every ~ — Acts 14:23 (RSV)⟩ **f :** ecclesiastical power, authority, or government **5 :** the clerical profession ⟨to go into the ~⟩ ⟨the youngest son was destined for the ~⟩ **6 :** a body of worshipers **:** a religious society or organization: as **a :** the congregation or company of God's worshipers under the old dispensation or in Old Testament times, the analogue and precursor of the Christian church **b :** a society, school, or the like resembling the Christian church (as in having a set of opinions held in common) ⟨the Jewish ~⟩ **syn** see RELIGION

2**church** \"\ *vt* -ED/-ING/-ES [ME *chirchen*, fr. *chirche*, n.] **1 :** to bring or conduct to church to receive one of its rites **2** *in some high liturgical churches* **:** to perform the rite of blessing (a woman) after childbirth — see CHURCHING **3** *Midland* **:** to discipline by church action

3**church** \"\ *adj* [1*church*] **1 :** of or relating to a church ⟨~ work⟩ ⟨~ government⟩ **2 :** composed of or conducted by members of a church ⟨~ socials⟩ **3** *chiefly Brit* **:** of or relating to the established or formerly established church ⟨we were ~ not chapel —E.L.Thomas⟩

church-ale \'=;=\ *n* [ME *chirche ale*, fr. *chirche* church + *ale* (festival)] **:** a festival formerly held in English country parishes at which ale was sold to raise money for church expenses and relief of the poor

church assembly *n, usu cap C&A* **:** the Church of England body for the governance of the church consisting of a house of clergy and a house of laity which since 1919 have together had the power to pass measures relating to the church for submission to Parliament for approval or rejection

church bell *n* **1 :** a large metal bell; *esp* **:** one cast in traditional shape and producing a true bell tone **2 :** an instrument (as an organ stop) imitating the sound of church bells — usu. used in pl.; compare CATHEDRAL CHIMES

church book *n* **:** any of several books used in or by a church (as a service book, a record of church proceedings, or a parish register of births, marriages, and deaths)

church concerto *n* **:** CONCERTO 1

church congress *n, usu cap both Cs* **:** a semiofficial annual conference of the clergy and laity of the Church of England

church council *n* **:** a lay group appointed in certain Lutheran churches to assume responsibility with and assist the pastor in spiritual guidance and in such practical matters as the handling of church property and the collection and distribution of money for benevolences

church father *n, sometimes cap C&F* **:** FATHER 4

churchgoer \'=,==\ *n* -s **:** one who attends church; *esp* **:** one who attends habitually or zealously

1**churchgoing** \'=,==\ *n* -s **:** church attendance esp. when habitual

2**churchgoing** \;=;==\ *adj* **:** attending church esp. habitually

church hand *n* **:** TEXT HAND

church house *n* [ME *chirche hous*, fr. *chirche* church + *hous* house] **1 :** a house belonging to a church (as a rectory or a parish house) **2** *South & Midland* **:** CHURCH, MEETINGHOUSE

church·i·an·i·ty \,chərchē'anəd·ē, -əch-, -əich-, -ətē, -i\ *also* **church·an·i·ty** \=ˈchan-\ *n* -ES [1*church* + *-ianity, -anity* (as in *Christianity*)] **:** the usu. excessive or sectarian attachment to the practices and interests of a particular church

churchier *comparative of* CHURCHY

churchiest *superlative of* CHURCHY

church·i·fied \'chərchə,fīd, -əch-,-əich-\ *adj* [fr. past part. of *churchify*, fr. 1*church* + *-ify*] **:** brought into accord or sympathy with church principles or forms

church·il·li·an *also* **church·ill·e·an** \chər'chilēən\ *adj, usu cap* [Sir Winston *Churchill* †1965 Brit. statesman and author + E *-ian, -ean*] **:** relating to or suggestive of Sir Winston Churchill

church·ing \'chərchiŋ, -əch-, -əich-\ *n* -s [fr. gerund of 2*church*] **:** the administration or reception of a rite of the church; *specif* **:** a ceremony in some high liturgical churches by which after childbirth women are received in the church with prayers, blessings, and thanksgiving

church invisible *n* **:** the entire company of those on earth and in afterlife who whether members of the church visible or not belong to the faithful for whom it is believed God has destined salvation

church·ism \'chər,chizəm, -ə̄,ch-,-əi,ch-\ *n* -s [¹*church* + *-ism*] **:** strong adherence to church practices or beliefs, esp. sectarian practices or beliefs

¹**church·ite** \-,chīt, *usu* -īd.+V\ *n* -s [¹*church* + *-ite*] **:** a church supporter or advocate

²**churchite** \"\ *n* -s [Arthur H. *Church* †1915 Eng. chemist + E *-ite*] **:** a mineral (Ce,Ca) $(PO_4).2H_2O$ consisting of a hydrous cerium calcium phosphate occurring in thin drusy crusts of small light gray to pink crystals (sp. gr. 3.1)

church·less \-ləs\ *adj* [¹*church* + *-less*] **:** having no church **:** not affiliated or connected with a church

church·ly \-lē, -li\ *adj, sometimes* -ER/-EST [¹*church* + *-ly*] **1 :** of or relating to a church **:** suitable to or suggestive of a church ⟨~ custom⟩ ⟨~ truth⟩ **2 :** adhering to a church **:** inclined to religion ⟨~ people⟩

churchman \'=mən\ *n, pl* **churchmen 1 :** ECCLESIASTIC, CLERGYMAN, PRIEST **2 :** an adherent or member of a church

church·man·ly \-lē\ *adj* **:** ECCLESIASTICAL

church·man·ship \'==,ship\ *n* -s **:** the attitude, belief, or practice of a churchman

church militant *n, often cap C&M* [trans. of ML *ecclesia militans*] **:** the Christian church on earth regarded as engaged in a constant warfare against its enemies, the powers of evil — distinguished from *church triumphant*

church mode *n* **:** ECCLESIASTICAL MODE

church papist *n* **:** a Roman Catholic who was a conformist to the Church of England in England in the 17th century

church pennant *n* **:** a pennant flown on a ship during church service, in the U.S. Navy being white with a blue Latin cross and flown above the ensign

church rate *n* **:** a rate upon the lands and houses in a parish in England or Ireland assessed on the occupiers for the maintenance of the church and its services compulsory by law until 1868 but now payable voluntarily or fixed at the request of the annual vestry meeting

church register *n* **:** a parish register of baptisms, marriages, and deaths

church school *n* **1 a :** a school providing a general education but supported by a particular church in contrast to one supported by the public authority or a nondenominational private school **b** *Brit* **:** a school providing a general education but in which denominational religious teaching is also given and where certain rights are vested in a board of managers composed of church people with the incumbent of the parish as chairman **2 :** an organization of officers, teachers, and pupils for purposes of moral and religious education under the supervision of a local church

church·scot \'chərch,skät, -ə̄ch-,-əich-\ *or* **church·shot** \-,shät\ *n* -s [alter. & part trans. of OE *ciricsceat*, fr. *cirice* church + *sceatt* payment, treasure; akin to OHG *scaz* money, ON *skattr*, Goth *skatts*, L *scatere* to bubble up, Gk *skatamizein* to jump, Lith *skasti*] **:** a tribute formerly collected by the clergy for their support or as a due prob. orig. in the form of a portion of grain

church slavic *or* **church slavonic** *n, cap C&S* **:** OLD CHURCH SLAVONIC

church suffering *n, often cap C&S, Roman Catholicism* **:** the souls in purgatory

church triumphant *n, often cap C&T* **:** members of the church who have died and are regarded as enjoying eternal happiness through union with God — compare CHURCH MILITANT, CHURCH SUFFERING

church visible *n* **:** the whole body of actually professed Christians on earth — distinguished from *church invisible*

church·ward·en \'chərch'wȯrdᵊn, -ə̄ch-,-əich-, -ō(ə)d-\ *n* [ME *chirche wardein*] **1 :** a lay honorary parish official in the Church of England whose duties include the protection of the church building and property, the making and executing of various parochial regulations, and criticism though not control with respect to divine worship **2 :** a church officer in the Protestant Episcopal Church whose duties though they vary in the different dioceses now relate chiefly to the oversight and management of the temporal affairs of the parish (as the care of the parish property and the raising of money) **3** *Brit* **:** a long-stemmed clay pipe

churchway \'=,=\ *n* **:** the way leading to a church

churchwoman \'=,==\ *n, pl* **churchwomen :** a woman who is a member of a church

church work *n* **:** work in behalf of a church esp. in furtherance of its purpose (as in charity, visitation of the sick, or support of the church's world mission)

churchy \'chərchē, -ə̄ch-,-əich-, -chi\ *adj, usu* -ER/-EST **:** of or suggesting a church; *esp* **:** marked by strict conformity or zealous adherence to the forms or beliefs of a church

churchyard \'=,=\ *n* [ME *chircheyerd*] **:** a yard which belongs to a church and which is often used as a burial ground

churchyard beetle *n* **:** a large dull black European beetle (*Blaps mortisaga*)

church year *n, usu cap C* **:** CHRISTIAN YEAR

chu·rel \chü'rāl\ *n* -s [Hindi *curail*] *India* **:** GOBLIN; *specif* **:** the ghost of a woman who has died while pregnant that haunts lonely places

chu·rin·ga \chü'riŋgə\ *also* **tju·run·ga** \tyü'rəŋgə\ *or* **tju·rin·ga** \-'riŋgə\ *n, pl* **churingas** *or* **churinga** [native name in Australia] **:** an object of wood or stone that is considered sacred by various aboriginal tribes of Central Australia and that is often elliptical in shape, bears incised designs, is believed to represent either the spiritual double of a living native or the embodiment of the spirit of a totemic ancestor, and is generally regarded as secret; *sometimes* **:** the quality of sacredness — compare BULL-ROARER

churl \'chərl, -ə̄l, -əil\ *n* -s [ME *cherl, churl*, fr. OE *ceorl* man, husband, freeman of the lowest rank; akin to OHG *karal* man, husband, ON *karl*, Gk *gerōn* old man, *geras* old age — more at CORN] **1 a** *obs* **:** a male person **:** MAN, HUSBAND **b :** VILLEIN, SERF, BONDMAN **2** *in early England* **:** a man without rank **:** a man in the lowest rank of freemen below the earl and thane **:** YEOMAN 2a **3 :** RUSTIC, COUNTRYMAN, PEASANT ⟨not framed for village ~s, but for high dames and mighty earls —Sir Walter Scott⟩ **4 a :** a person (as a rustic) who is ungracious, mean, ill-bred, and rude ⟨the boy might well believe this ~ was lying —George Meredith⟩ **b :** a stingy, grasping, and morose person ⟨when a few words can rescue misery . . . I hate a man who can be a ~ of them —Tobias Smollett⟩ **syn** see BOOR

churl·ish \-lish,-lēsh\ *adj* [ME *churlish, cherlish*, fr. OE *ceorlisc, cierlisc*, fr. *ceorl* + *-isc* -ish] **1 :** of or like a churl **:** having the position or rank of a churl **:** RUSTIC, VULGAR, MEAN **2 :** characteristic of or befitting a churl **:** BASE, RUDE, ILL-BRED **:** lacking refinement or higher feelings **3 :** difficult to work with or deal with **:** UNMANAGEABLE, UNYIELDING, INTRACTABLE ⟨~ soil⟩ ⟨~ intractable minerals⟩ — **churl·ish·ly** *adv* — **churl·ish·ness** *n* -ES

churly \-lē,-li\ *adj* [*churl* + *-y*] **:** CHURLISH

churm \'chərm, -ə̄m\ *chiefly Scot var of* CHIRM

¹**churn** \'chərn, -ə̄n, -əin\ *n* -s [ME *chyrne, cherne*, fr. OE *cyrin, cyrn*; akin to MHG *kern* churn, G dial. *kern* cream, ON *kjarni* churn, OE *cyrnel* kernel, dim. of *corn* grain; fr. the granular appearance of cream as it turns to butter — more at CORN] **1 :** a vessel in which milk or cream is stirred, beaten, or otherwise agitated (as by a plunging or revolving dasher or by shaking) in order to separate the oily globules from the other parts and thus to obtain butter **2 :** an agitated state (as of water) **:** CHURNING ⟨the ground is a ~ of straw and mud —John Galsworthy⟩ **3** *Brit* **:** a large metal can for conveying milk

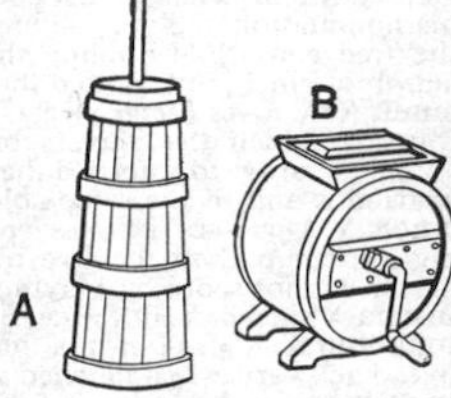

churns: *A* with plunging dasher, *B* cylinder churn

²**churn** \"\ *vb* -ED/-ING/-S [ME *chyrnen*, fr. *chyrne*] *vt* **1 :** to stir, beat, or agitate (milk or cream) in a churn in order to make butter **:** make (butter) by churning **2 a :** to stir or agitate violently, heavily, or continuously **b :** to make (as foam) by thus doing **3 :** to produce by vigorous or continuous mental activity ⟨whose head was ~*ing* ideas for social change —*Saturday Rev.*⟩ ~ *vi* **1 :** to work a churn (as in making butter) **2 a :** to produce or be in violent or continuous agitation ⟨the steamer's screw ~*s*⟩ **b :** to proceed by means of rotating members (as wheels or propellers) ⟨the tug ~*s* down the bay⟩ ⟨the car veered into a snowdrift and ~*ed* to a halt⟩

churn·a·bil·i·ty \-nə'bilədē, -ətē, -i\ *n* -ES **1** *of milk or cream* **:** ease of churning **2 :** completeness of formation of butter in churning

churn barrel *adj, of an animal* **:** having the trunk or body deep and capacious with well-sprung ribs

churn-butted \'=;==\ *adj, of a tree* **:** SWELL-BUTTED

churn drill *n* **:** a piece of drilling equipment in which the drill is raised by a rope or cable and allowed to drop, pulverizing the rock with successive blows

churning *n* -s [fr. gerund of ²*churn*] **:** the making of a batch of butter; *also* **:** the quantity of butter made at one operation

churnmilk \'=,=\ *n, chiefly dial* **:** BUTTERMILK

churn supper *n* **:** a feast at the end of the hay harvest

churn up *vt* **:** to dig into (as a driveway) with spinning wheels

chu·ro·ya \chü'rōyə\ *n, pl* **churoya** *or* **churoyas** *usu cap* [Sp *churoy*, of AmerInd origin] **1 a :** a Guahiban people of eastern Colombia **b :** a member of such people **2 :** the language of the Churoya people

chu·ro·yan \-yən\ *adj, usu cap* **:** relating or belonging to a branch of Guahiban formerly considered a distinct stock

¹**churr** \'chər, +V -ər-; 'chə̄, +V -ər- *also* -ə̄r\ *vi* -ED/-ING/-S [imit.] **:** to make a churr

²**churr** \"\ *n* -s **:** a vibrant or whirring noise such as that made by some insects (as the cockchafer) or by some birds (as the nightjar or the partridge)

chur·ras·co \chü'räˌskō\ *n* -s [AmerSp] **:** beef broiled on a spit over an open fire or grilled under an oven flame

chur·ri·gue·resque \¦chürēgə¦resk\ *adj* [Sp *churrigueresco*, fr. José *Churriguera* †1723 Spanish architect + Sp *-esco* -esque] **1 :** relating or belonging to a Spanish baroque architectural style characterized by elaborate surface decoration **2 :** of or relating to the Latin-American adaptation of Spanish churrigueresque forms esp. as executed by native craftsmen

chur·ro \'chü,rō\ *n* -s [Sp, coarse, coarse-wooled, coarse-wooled sheep; akin to Sp *churre* thick grease, Pg *churro, surro* dirty, unprocessed (of wool), miserable, lowly; all prob. of Iberian origin; akin to Basque *txur* miserly, economical] **:** a hardy coarse-wooled sheep originating in northwest Spain but surviving chiefly in Mexico and among the Navahos of the southwestern U.S.

churr-owl \'=,=\ *n, dial Eng* **:** the European nightjar

¹**chur·rus** \'chərəs\ *n* -ES [Hindi *caras*] **:** a device used in India for drawing water from deep wells that consists of a leather bag hung on a rope running over a pulley and drawn by oxen

²**churrus** *also* **churus** *var of* CHARAS

chuse *archaic var of* CHOOSE

chut \a *t sound formed by suction rather than pressure, or* cht, *or* sht *with prolonged* sh; *often read as* 'chət\ *interj* [F, of imit. origin] — used to express impatience

¹**chute** *also* **shute** \'shüt, *usu* -üd+V\ *n* -s [F, fr. OF, fem. of *chu*, past part. of *cheoir* to fall, fr. L *cadere* — more at CHANCE] **1 a :** FALL 3b **b :** a quick descent (as in a river), steep channel, or narrow sloping passage by which water falls to a lower level **:** RAPID **2 :** an artificial or natural inclined plane, sloping channel, or partially or completely covered passage (as a trough, framework) down or through which substances or bodies (as water, coal, ore, grain, or logs) may pass or slide usu. to a lower level **:** FLUME, SLIDE **3 a :** a narrow high-walled passageway or similar device for holding or restraining animals (as cattle for branding or dehorning) **b :** a straight extension of the home stretch of a race track **:** an extension of the straightaway portion of an oval running track **c :** ORE SHOOT **4** [by shortening] **:** PARACHUTE

²**chute** \"\ *vb* -ED/-ING/-S *vt* **:** to convey by a chute ~ *vi* **1 :** to go in or as if in a chute **2 :** to utilize a chute (as by passing ore down it) — **chute the chutes :** to go down a chute, esp. a steep slide made for amusement

chute man *n* **:** one who tends chutes esp. by receiving and disposing of loads from or into them: as **a :** a worker in a metal mine who loads mine cars underground **b :** a coal miner who tends chutes from tipple to railroad cars **c :** a millworker who receives sacks of flour, meal, or feed and readies them for storage **d :** a collector of soiled laundry in an institution

chute-the-chute *or* **chute-the-chutes** \'=='=\ *n* **1 :** a slide (as in an amusement park) often ending in a pool of water **2 :** ROLLER COASTER

chut·ing board \'shüd-iŋ-, -ütiŋ-\ *n* [by alter.] **:** SHOOTING BOARD

chut·ist \'shüd-əst, -ütəst\ *n* -s [by shortening] **:** PARACHUTIST

chut·ney \'chətnē, -ni\ *n* -s [Hindi *caṭnī*, fr. *caṭnā* to be licked, tasted, fr. *cāṭnā* to lick, taste, fr. Prakrit *caṭṭei* he licks] **:** a condiment that has the consistency of jam and is made of acid fruits with added raisins, dates, and onions and seasoned to taste with spices and vinegar ⟨apple ~⟩

chu·vash \'chü,väsh, chü'väsh\ *n, pl* **chuvash·es** \-əz\ *or* **chuvash** *or* **chu·va·shi** \chü'väshē\ *usu cap* [Russ, fr. Chuvash *Tsǝvaš*; akin to Turk *yavaş* gentle, mild, docile] **1 a :** a people related to Mordvin and Cheremis inhabiting the Chuvash Republic of eastern Russia **b :** a member of such people **2 :** the Turkish dialect spoken by the Chuvash people

chuz·wi \'chəz,wē\ *n, pl* **chuzwi** *or* **chuzwis** [of African origin; akin to Umbundu *ochisovo, ochisema* waterbuck] **:** an iron-gray or blackish gray medium-sized waterbuck (*Kobus crawshayi*) of central Africa

chwdn *abbr* churchwarden

chy *abbr* chimney

chyack \'chīək\ *var of* CHIACK

chyl- *or* **chyli-** *or* **chylo-** *comb form* [F or NL, fr. Gk *chyl-*, *chylo-*, fr. *chylos*] **1 :** chyle ⟨chyluria⟩ ⟨chyliform⟩ ⟨chylocyst⟩ **2 :** juice ⟨chylocauly⟩

chy·la·ceous \(')kī¦lāshəs\ *adj* [*chyl-* + *-aceous*] **:** possessed of the properties of chyle **:** consisting of chyle

chyle \'kīl, *esp bef pause or cons* -īəl\ *n* -s [earlier *chylus*, fr. LL, fr. Gk *chylos* juice, chyle, fr. *chein* to pour — more at FOUND] **:** lymph that is milky in appearance due to the presence of emulsified fats, that is characteristically present in the lacteals, and that is most apparent during intestinal absorption of ingested fats which pass to the blood and tissues largely by way of the lacteals and the thoracic duct

-chy·lia \¦kīlēə\ *n comb form* -s [NL, fr. Gk, fr. *chyl-* + *-ia*] **:** condition of having (such) chyle ⟨achylia⟩

chy·li·fac·tion \¦kīlə¦fakshən, ¦kil-\ *n* -s [by alter.] **:** CHYLIFICATION

chy·li·fac·tive \-tiv\ *or* **chy·li·fac·to·ry** \-t(ə)rē, -ri\ *or* **chy·lif·ic** \(')kī¦lifik\ *or* **chy·lif·i·ca·to·ry** \(')=¦fəkə,tōrē, -ȯr-, =¦==¦kād-ərē\ *adj* [*chylifactive* fr. *chyl-* + *-factive*; *chylifactory* fr. *chyl-* + *-factory* (fr. L *factus* — past part. of *facere* to do — + E *-ory*); *chylific* fr. NL *chylificus*, fr. *chyl-* + L *-ficus* -fic; *chylificatory* alter. (influenced by *chylification*) of *chylifactory* — more at DO] **:** producing or converting into chyle **:** having the power to form chyle

chy·lif·er·ous \(')kī¦lif(ə)rəs\ *adj* [*chyl-* + *-ferous*] **:** transmitting or conveying chyle ⟨~ vessels⟩

chy·li·fi·ca·tion \,kīləfə'kāshən, ,kil-\ *n* -s [NL *chylification-, chylificatio*, fr. *chyl-* + *-fication-, -ficatio* -fication] **:** the formation of chyle

chy·li·form \'kīlə,fȯrm\ *adj* [ISV *chyl-* + *-form*] **:** resembling chyle

chy·li·fy \-,fī\ *vb* -ED/-ING/-ES [F *chylifier*, fr. *chyl-* + *-fier* -fy] *vt* **:** to make chyle of ~ *vi* **:** to become converted into chyle

chy·lo·cau·lous \¦kīlə¦kȯləs\ *adj* [Gk *chylocaul* chylocaulous (fr. *chyl-* + Gk. *kaulos* stem) + E *-ous* — more at HOLE] **:** having fleshy or succulent stems — used of cacti and similar plants — **chy·lo·cau·ly** \-lē, -li\ *n* -ES

chy·lo·cyst \'kīlə,sist\ *n* -s [*chyl-* + *-cyst*] **:** CISTERNA CHYLI

chy·loid \'kī,lȯid\ *adj* [*chyl-* + *-oid*] **:** CHYLIFORM

chy·lo·mi·cron \,kīlə'mī,krän, -'mi,k-\ *n* [*chyl-* + Gk *mikron* (neut. of *mikros* small) — more at MICR-] **:** a microscopic particle of fat common in the blood during the digestion and assimilation of ingested fat

chy·lo·phyl·lous \¦==¦filəs\ *adj* [*chyl-* + *-phyllous*] **:** having fleshy or succulent leaves ⟨~ desert plants⟩ — **chy·lo·phylly** \'==,filē, -li\ *n* -ES

chy·lo·poi·e·sis \¦==pȯi'ēsəs\ *n, pl* **chylopoie·ses** \-,sēz\ [NL, fr. *chyl-* + *-poiesis*] **:** CHYLIFICATION — **chy·lo·poi·et·ic** \-¦ed·ik\ *or* **chy·lo·po·et·ic** \-pō¦ed-\ *adj*

chy·lo·sis \kī'lōsəs\ *n, pl* **chylo·ses** \-,sēz\ [NL, fr. Gk *chylōsis*, fr. *chyl-* + *-ōsis* -osis] **:** CHYLIFICATION

chy·lous \'kīləs\ *adj* [prob. fr. F *chyleux*, fr. MF, fr. *chyl-* + *-eux* -ous] **:** consisting of or like chyle ⟨~ ascites⟩

chy·lu·ria \kī'lürēə, kīl'yü-\ *n* -s [NL, fr. *chyl-* + *-uria*] **:** the presence of chyle in the urine as a result of organic disease (as of the kidney) or of mechanical lymphatic esp. parasitic obstruction

chy·mase \'kī,mās, -āz\ *n* -s [*chyme* + *-ase*] **:** RENNIN

chyme \'kīm\ *n* -s [NL *chymus*, fr. LL, chyle, fr. Gk *chymos* juice, fr. *chein* to pour — more at FOUND] **:** the semifluid mass of partly digested food resulting from the action of the gastric juice and expelled by the stomach into the duodenum

chymic *obs var of* CHEMIC

chy·mif·er·ous \(')kī¦mif(ə)rəs\ *adj* [ISV *chyme* + *-i-* + *-ferous*; prob. orig. formed as F *chymifère*] **:** bearing or containing chyme

chy·mi·fi·ca·tion \,kīməfə'kāshən, ,kim-\ *n* -s [*chyme* + *-i-* + *-fication*] **:** the conversion of food into chyme by the digestive action of gastric juice

chy·mi·fy \'kīmə,fī\ *vt* -ED/-ING/-ES [*chyme* + *-ify*] **:** to convert into chyme

chymist *archaic var of* CHEMIST

chy·mo·plasm \'kīmə,plazəm\ *n* -s [*chyme* + *-o-* + *plasm*] **:** a portion of a mosaic egg consisting of potential mesenchyme

chy·mo·sin \'kīməsə̇n\ *n* -s [F *chymosine*, fr. *chyme* (fr. NL *chymus*) + *-ose* + *-ine* -in] **:** RENNIN

chy·mo·trypsin \,kīmə +\ *n* -s [*chyme* +*-o-* + *trypsin*] **:** a crystalline proteinase known in several forms that occurs in the pancreas as chymotrypsinogen and differs from crystalline trypsin in its ability to clot milk

chy·mo·trypsinogen \,kīmə +\ *n* -s [ISV *chyme* + *-o-* + *trypsinogen*] **:** a precursor of a chymotrypsin prepared in crystalline form usu. from the pancreas of cattle or hogs and converted by trypsin into a chymotrypsin

chy·mous \'kīməs\ *adj* **:** of or relating to chyme

chy·pre *also* **chi·pre** \'shēprᵊ\ *n* -s [F *Chypre* Cyprus] **:** a nonalcoholic perfume containing oils and resins

chy·tra \'kī·trə, 'ki-·\ *n, pl* **chy·trae** \-(,)trē\ *or* **chy·trai** \-,trī\ [Gk, fr. *chein* to pour — more at FOUND] **:** a usu. earthenware cooking pot of ancient Greece

chy·trid \-,trəd\ *n* -s [NL *Chytridiales*] **:** one of the Chytridiales

chy·trid·i·a·ce·ae \kī-,tridē'āsē,ē, kə̇-\ *n pl, cap* [NL, fr. *Chytridium*, type genus (fr. Gk *chytra* + NL *-idium*) + *-aceae*] **:** a family of aquatic fungi (order Chytridiales) having a monocentric thallus

chy·tri·di·a·ceous \(')=¦==¦āshəs\ *adj* [NL *Chytridiaceae* + E *-ous*] **:** of, resembling, or relating to the Chytridiales

chy·tri·di·a·les \=,=='ā(,)lēz\ *n pl, cap* [NL, fr. *Chytridium* + *-ales*] **:** an order of simple aquatic fungi (subclass Oomycetes) that have little or no mycelium, that have zoospores with single flagella posterior or lacking, and that are mostly saprophytic except for several which are parasitic on higher plants, animals, or freshwater fungi

chy·trid·i·o·sis \kə̇,tridē'ōsəs\ *also* **chy·trid·i·ose** \='==,ōs\ *n, pl* **chy·trid·i·o·ses** \=,=='ō,sēz\ [*chytridiosis*, NL, fr. *Chytridium* + *-osis*; *chytridiose* fr. NL *Chytridium* + E *-ose*] **:** a disease caused by a chytrid

CI *abbr* **1** cast iron **2** cephalic index **3** certificate of insurance **4** chief inspector **5** color index **6** consular invoice **7** cost and insurance **8** counterintelligence

Ci·ba·cron \'sēbə,krän\ *trademark* — used for any of several fiber-reactive dyes; see DYE table I

¹**ci·bar·i·al** \sə̇'ba(a)rēəl\ *adj* [L *cibarius* of food (fr. *cibus* food, fodder, perh. of Gk origin; akin to dial. Gk *kibba* fodder bag) + E *-al*] **:** relating to food

²**cibarial** \"\ *adj* [NL *cibarium* + E *-al*] **1 :** relating to the cibarium **2 :** CIBARIAN

ci·bar·i·an \-ēən\ *adj* [NL *cibarium* + E *-an*] **:** of or relating to the mouthparts of an insect — used chiefly in the phrase *cibarian system of classification*

ci·bar·i·um \-ēəm\ *n, pl* **cibaria** \-ēə\ [NL, fr. L *cibus* food + *-arium*] **:** the space anterior to the true mouth cavity in which the food of an insect is chewed

cibation *n* -s [ME *cibacioun*, fr. LL *cibation-, cibatio* feeding, meal, fr. L *cibatus* (past part. of *cibare* to feed, fr. *cibus* food) + *-ion-, -io* -ion] *obs* **:** the process of feeding the alchemical crucible with fresh material during the course of an operation

cib·e·cue \'sibə,kyü\ *n, pl* **cibecue** *or* **cibecues** *usu cap* **1 :** an Apache people belonging to the San Carlos subdivision **2 :** a member of the Cibecue people

cib·ol *also* **cib·oul** *or* **cib·oule** \'sibəl\ *n* -s [F *ciboule*, fr. Prov *cebula*, fr. LL *cepulla*, dim. of L *cepa, cepe* onion] **1 :** WELSH ONION **2 :** SHALLOT 1a

cibolan *n or adj, usu cap* [Sp *Cíbola*, land of the Zuñis in New Mexico and Arizona (fr. Zuñi *šiwona*) + E *-an*] *obs* **:** ZUÑI

cib·o·le·ro \,sibə'le,rō\ *n* -s [MexSp, fr. Sp *cíbolo* buffalo (fr. *Cíbola*) + *-ero* -er (fr. L *-arius*)] *Southwest* **:** a buffalo hunter

ci·bo·ney *also* **si·bo·ney** \,sēbə'nā, -bō-\ *n, pl* **ciboney** \"\ *or* **cibo·neys** \-z\ *or* **cibone·yes** \-'nā,yās\ *usu cap* [Sp, perh. fr. Arawak *siba-eyeri*, fr. *siba* rock + *eyeri* man] **1 a :** an aboriginal people of Cuba closely related to or a division of the Arawaks **b :** a member of the Ciboney people — compare TAINO **2 :** the Arawakan language of the Ciboney people

ci·bo·ri·um \sə̇'bōrēəm, -ȯr-\ *n, pl* **cibo·ria** \-ēə\ *or* **cibo·riums** [ML, fr. L, cup, fr. Gk *kibōrion* seed vessel of the Indian lotus, cup made of or shaped like this seed vessel] **1 :** a usu. covered goblet-shaped ecclesiastical vessel holding the consecrated eucharistic bread **:** PYX **2** *archit* **:** BALDACHIN; *specif* **:** a freestanding vaulted canopy supported by four columns (as that over the high altar in some churches)

ciborium

ci·bo·ti·um \sə̇'bōd-ēəm\ *n, cap* [NL, fr. Gk *kibōtion*, dim. of *kibōtos* box, chest] **:** a genus of ornamental tree ferns (family Cyatheaceae) with coarse gracefully drooping fronds bluish green on the under side and with 2-valved indusia (as the Scythian lamb)

CIC *abbr* commander in chief

cic·ad \'sikəd, -,kad, 'sī,kad\ *n* -s [L *cicada*] **:** CICADA

ci·ca·da \sə̇'kādə, -ādə,-ädə *also* sī- *sometimes* 'sikədə\ *n* [NL, fr. L] **1** *cap* **:** a genus (the type of the family Cicadidae) of homopterous insects with a stout body, wide blunt head, and large transparent wings **2** *pl* **cicadas** *also* **cica·dae** \-(,)dē\ **:** any insect of the family Cicadidae (order Hemiptera) — called also *harvest fly, locust*

cicada bird *n* **:** a common cuckoo shrike (*Edolisoma tenuirostre*) of Australia and islands of the southwestern Pacific having the male largely bluish gray and the female olive brown

cicada killer *n* **:** a large black or rusty yellow-marked American digger wasp (*Sphecius speciosus*) that provisions its nests with cicadas

cicada

cic·a·del·la \,sikə'delə\ *n, cap* [NL, fr. L *cicada* + NL *-ella*] **:** the type genus of Cicadellidae

ci·ca·del·lid \-əd\ *n* -s [NL *Cicadellidae*] **:** a leafhopper of the family Tettigellidae; *broadly* **:** LEAFHOPPER

ci·ca·del·li·dae \-ə,dē\ *n pl, cap* [NL, fr. *Cicadella*, type genus + *-idae*] *in some esp formerly classifications* **:** a large family of leafhoppers: **a :** a very large family comprising all the leafhoppers and certain related insects **b :** a family more or less exactly coextensive with Tettigellidae

ci·cad·i·dae \sə̇'kadə,dē\ *n pl, cap* [NL, fr. L *cicada*, type genus + *-idae*] **:** a family of large insects comprising the cicadas and with the spittle insects, treehoppers, and leafhoppers commonly constituting a superfamily of Homoptera

ci·ca·la \sə'kälə\ *n* -s [It, fr. ML, alter. of L *cicada*] **1 :** CICADA **2 :** GRASSHOPPER

cic·a·trice \'sikə·trəs, -ˌtrēs\ *n* -s [ME, fr. MF, fr. L *cicatric-, cicatrix*] **:** CICATRIX

cicatrices *pl of* CICATRIX

cic·a·tri·cial \ˌsikə'trishəl\ *adj* [*cicatrice* + *-ial*] **:** relating to or having the character of a cicatrix ⟨~ tissue⟩

cic·a·tri·cle \'sikə·ˌtrikəl\ *n* -s [L *cicatricula* small scar, dim. of *cicatric-, cicatrix*] **1 :** CICATRIX 2b **2 :** BLASTODISC

ci·cat·ri·cose \sə'ka·trə·ˌkōs, 'sikə·trə-\ *adj* [L *cicatricosus*, fr. *cicatric-, cicatrix* + *-osus* -ose] *bot* **:** marked with or as if with scars

cic·a·tri·sive \ˌsikə'trīsiv\ *adj* [irreg. fr. *cicatrize* (after such words as *incisive, decisive*)] **:** CICATRIZANT

cic·a·trix \'sikə·ˌtriks *also* sə'kā·triks\ *n, pl* **cic·a·tri·ces** \ˌsikə'trī(ˌ)sēz, sə'kā·trə·ˌsēz\ *also* **cic·a·trix·es** \'sikə-ˌtriksəz *also* sə'kā·triksəz\ [L, scar] **1 :** a scar resulting from cicatrization of a flesh wound **2 :** a scarlike mark esp. when caused by the previous attachment of a part or organ: as **a :** the impression on the inside of a bivalve shell caused by the insertion of the adductor muscle **b** (1) **:** the permanent mark left on the stem after the fall of a leaf or bract (2) **:** the hilum of a seed

cic·a·tri·zant \ˌsikə·¦trīzᵊnt\ *adj* [F *cicatrisant*, pres. part. of *cicatriser* to scar, fr. ML *cicatrizare*, fr. L *cicatric-, cicatrix*] **:** promoting the healing of a wound or the formation of a cicatrix

cic·a·tri·za·tion \ˌsikə·trə'zāshən, -ə-,trī'z-\ *n* -s [MF *cicatrisation*, fr. *cicatriser* + *-ation*] **:** the formation of a scar at the site of a healing wound by replacement of the fibroblasts of the granulation tissue by collagenous fibrous tissue followed by overgrowth of epithelium from the margin of the wound, contraction of fibrous tissue, and reduction of blood supply

cic·a·trize \'sikə·ˌtrīz\ *vb* -ED/-ING/-S [MF or ML; MF *cicatriser*, fr. ML *cicatrizare*, fr. L *cicatrix* + ML *-izare* -ize] *vt* **1 :** to induce the formation of a scar in (a wound) **:** heal by cicatrization **2 :** SCAR ~ *vi* **:** to heal by forming a scar

cic·a·trose \-ˌtrōs\ *adj* [by contr.] **:** CICATRICOSE

ci·ce·ly \'sisᵊlē, -li\ *n* -ES [by folk etymology (influence of proper name *Cicely*) fr. *seseli*] **:** any of several herbs of the family Umbelliferae (as of the genus *Myrrhis* or *Osmorhiza*) — see SWEET CICELY

ci·cer \'sīsə(r)\ *n* [ME *cycer*, fr. L *cicer;* akin to Gk *krios* chick-pea, LGk (Maced. dial.) *kikerros*, a kind of pea (prob. *Lathyrus ochrus*), Arm *siseṙn* chick-pea] **1** -S *obs* **:** CHICK-PEA **2** *cap* [NL, fr. L, chick-pea] **:** a genus of Asiatic herbs (family Leguminosae) having odd-pinnate leaves of several small dentate leaflets and solitary white or pink-tinged flowers

cic·e·ro·nage \ˌsisə'rōnij, ˌchichə-, ˌchēchə-\ *n* -s **:** the act or office of a cicerone **:** GUIDANCE

¹cic·e·ro·ne \ˌsisə'rōnē, ˌchichə-, ˌchēchə-, -ni\ *n, pl* **cicero·ni** \-(ˌ)nē, _ni\ *or* **cicerones** [It, after *Cicerone* Cicero; fr. the talkativeness of guides] **1 :** a guide who conducts sightseers to places or objects of interest (as a museum or a monument) **2 :** GUIDE, MENTOR

²cic·e·rone \"·¦=¦rōn\ *vt* **ciceroned; ciceroned; cicerone·ing** \-'rōniŋ\ *or* **cice·ron·ing** \-¦rōniŋ\ **cicerones :** to act as cicerone to **:** show the sights to

¹cic·e·ro·nian \ˌsisə¦rōnēən, -ōnyən\ *adj, usu cap* [L *Ciceronianus*, after Marcus Tullius *Cicero* †43 B.C. Roman orator] **:** of or relating to Cicero; *specif* **:** resembling Cicero esp. in the rhythm and cadence of his periodic sentences, the balance of antitheses, or any more general oratorical or literary qualities ⟨*Ciceronian* eloquence⟩

²ciceronian \"\ *n* -s *usu cap* **:** one that admires or imitates the style of Cicero (as in purity and elegance of diction)

cic·e·ro·nian·ism \ˌ==¦=nēə,nizəm, -nyə,-\ *n* -s *usu cap* **:** imitation of or resemblance to the oratorical or literary style of Cicero esp. as practiced or produced by the Ciceronians of the early Renaissance; *also* **:** any use of language characteristic of Cicero's writings

cic·e·ro·nian·ist \-ˌnəst\ *n* -s *usu cap* **:** one characterized by Ciceronianism

cic·e·ro·nism \ˌsisə'rō,nizəm, ˌchichə-, ˌchēchə-\ *n* -s **:** the practice or office of guiding

cich·la·so·ma \ˌsiklə'sōmə\ *n, cap* [NL, fr. Gk *kichlē*, a wrasse + NL *-soma*] **:** a genus of small cichlid fishes including several brightly marked African species popular in the tropical aquarium

¹cich·lid \'sikləd\ *adj* [NL *Cichlidae*] **:** of or relating to the family Cichlidae **:** characteristic of a fish of this family

²cichlid \"\ *n* -s **:** a fish of the family Cichlidae

cich·li·dae \'siklə,dē\ *n pl, cap* [NL, fr. *Cichla*, type genus (fr. Gk *kichlē* thrush, also, a kind of wrasse) + *-idae;* akin to Gk *chelidōn* swallow — more at CELANDINE] **:** a large family of chiefly tropical freshwater percoid fishes similar in many respects to the American sunfishes, some (as the bolti) being important food fishes while a number of small forms are favored for the tropical aquarium

ci·cho·ri·a·ce·ae \sə,kōrē'āsē,ē, -ȯr-\ *n pl, cap* [NL, fr. *Cichorium*, type genus + *-aceae*] *in some classifications* **:** a family of herbs or shrubs comprising all the composites (as chicories) that have milky juice and flower heads made up of only ligulate flowers — see COMPOSITAE — **ci·cho·ri·a·ceous** \¦=¦=¦āshəs\ *adj*

ci·cho·ri·um \sə'kōrēəm, -ȯr-\ *n, cap* [NL, fr. L — more at CHICORY] **:** a genus of deep-rooted biennial or perennial herbs (family Compositae) having flowers bright blue or occas. pink or white all ligulate and with flower heads solitary or in twos or threes — see CHICORY, ENDIVE

cic·in·del·i·dae \ˌsisən'delə,dē\ *n pl, cap* [NL, fr. *Cicindela*, type genus (fr. L, glowworm) + *-idae;* akin to L *candēre* to shine — more at CANDID] **:** a family of active free-flying usu. bright colored diurnal predaceous beetles comprising the tiger beetles

ci·cis·be·ism \ˌchēchəz'bā,izəm\ *n* -s [It *cicisbeismo*, fr. *cicisbeo* + *-ismo* -ism] **:** the social institution of the cicisbeo

ci·cis·beo \-'bā(,)ō\ *n, pl* **cicis·bei** \-ā,ē\ [It] **:** the recognized gallant of a married woman in Italy esp. in the 18th century **:** CAVALIER SERVENTE

ci·co·nia \sə'kōnēə\ *n, cap* [NL, fr. L, stork; prob. akin to L *canere* to sing — more at CHANT] **:** the type genus of Ciconiidae including the common stork of Europe

cic·o·ni·i·dae \ˌsikə'nīə,dē\ *n pl, cap* [NL, fr. *Ciconia*, type genus + *-idae*] **:** a family of birds comprising the storks and jabirus and with the ibises, spoonbills, and a few related forms constituting a suborder of the order Ciconiiformes

ci·co·ni·ifor·mes \sə,kōnēə'fȯr,mēz\ *n pl, cap* [NL, fr. *Ciconia* + *-iformes*] **:** an order of chiefly tropical fish-eating wading birds including the herons, storks, spoonbills, flamingos, and related forms all relatively large and usu. with long legs and bills, upright carriage, and excepting the flamingos unwebbed feet

cic·o·nine \'sikə,nīn, -,nən\ *adj* [L *ciconia* + E *-ine*] **:** of, relating to, or resembling the storks

cicurate *vt* -ED/-ING/-S [L *cicuratus*, past part. of *cicurare* to tame, fr. *cicur* tame; akin to Skt *śakura* tame] *obs* **:** to make mild or innocuous **:** TAME

ci·cu·ta \sə'kyüd·ə\ *n* [NL, fr. L, poison hemlock (prob. *Conium maculatum*)] **1** *cap* **:** a small genus of perennial herbs (family Umbelliferae) having tuberous usu. fascicled deadly poisonous roots and the leaves twice or thrice pinnate or ternate — see POISON HEMLOCK, WATER HEMLOCK **2** -S [L] **:** POISON HEMLOCK 1

cic·u·tox·in \ˌsikyə+\ *n* [ISV *cicu-* (fr. NL *Cicuta*) + *toxin*] **:** an amorphous poisonous principle $C_{19}H_{26}O_3$ in plants of the genus *Cicuta*

CID *abbr* criminal investigation department; criminal investigation detachment; criminal investigation division

-cidal \ˌsīdᵊl\ *adj comb form* [LL *-cidalis*, fr. L *-cida* + *-alis* -al — more at -CIDE] **1 :** killing **:** having power to kill ⟨*filaricidal*⟩ **2 :** cutting ⟨*loculicidal*⟩

cid·a·rid \'sidərəd\ *n* -s [NL *Cidaridae*] **:** a sea urchin of the family Cidaridae

ci·dar·i·dae \sə'darə,dē\ *n pl, cap* [NL, fr. *Cidaris*, type genus + *-idae*] **:** a family of sea urchins including all recent members of the order Cidaroida and comprising a number of forms that are widely distributed in warm seas

cid·a·ris \'sidərəs\ *n* **1** *pl* **cida·res** \-,rēz\ [L, fr. Gk *kidaris*, prob. of Sem origin; akin to Heb *kether* crown] **:** the royal tiara of the ancient Persian kings **2** *cap* [NL, fr. L] **:** the type genus of Cidaridae

cid·a·roi·da \ˌsidə'rȯidə\ *n pl, cap* [NL, fr. *Cidaris* + *-oida*] **:** the oldest surviving order of sea urchins containing the most primitive of living forms, all lacking peristomial gills and sphaeridia but having an apically located anus — see CIDARIDAE

-cide \ˌsīd\ *n comb form* -S [MF, fr. L *-cida*, fr. *caedere* to kill — more at CONCISE] **1 :** killer ⟨*fratricide*⟩ ⟨*insecticide*⟩ **2** [MF, fr. L *-cidium*, fr. *caedere*] **:** killing ⟨*homicide*⟩ ⟨*suicide*⟩

ci·der \'sīdə(r)\ *n* -S [ME *sidre, sider, cidre*, fr. OF *sidre*, fr. LL *sicera* strong drink, fr. LGk *sikera*, of Sem origin; akin to Heb *shēkhār* strong drink] **1 :** the expressed juice of apples or sometimes other fruits used as a beverage or for making other products (as applejack, vinegar, and apple butter) — called also *sweet cider* **2** *Brit* **:** fermented apple juice often made sparkling by carbonation or fermentation in a sealed container

cider apple *n* **1 :** an apple grown esp. because it produces a superior cider **2 :** an apple below marketable grade for eating or storage but suitable for making cider

cider gum *or* **cider tree** *n* **:** an Australian tree (*Eucalyptus gunnii*) from the sap of which a ciderlike beverage is made

ci·der·kin \'sīdə(r)kən\ *n* -s [*cider* + *-kin*] **:** weak cider made by steeping the refuse pomace from cider making

cider royal *also* **cider oil** *n* **:** concentrated cider with honey

cider vinegar *n* **:** vinegar made from fermented cider

cider wine *n, dial Eng* **:** hard cider sugared and spiced

ci·dery \'sīdərē, -ri\ *adj* **:** smelling or tasting of or like cider or rotting apples

¹ci–de·vant \sēdᵊväⁿ\ *adj* [F, lit., hitherto, formerly] **:** FORMER, LATE, EX- ⟨*ci-devant* governor⟩

²ci–devant \"\ *n* -s **1 :** one that had been a noble before titles were abolished during the French Revolution **2 :** a person or thing of the past **3 :** one retired or no longer having power or influence **:** HAS-BEEN

¹ciel *obs var of* CEIL

²ciel \'sēl, 'syel\ *n* -s [F, sky, fr. L *caelum* — more at -HOOD] **:** a pale or light blue like that of the clear sky

cieling *obs var of* CEILING

cié·na·ga *or* **cie·ne·ga** \'syānəgə, 'syen- 'sin-, -,gä\ *n* -s [Sp *ciénaga*, fr. *cieno* mud, slime, fr. L *caenum* dirt, filth — more at OBSCENE] *Southwest* **:** SWAMP, MARSH; *esp* **:** one formed by hillside springs

-cies *pl of* -CY

CIF *abbr* cost, insurance, and freight

CIFC *abbr* cost, insurance, freight, and charges; cost, insurance, freight, and commission

CIFE *abbr* cost, insurance, freight, and exchange

CIFI *abbr* cost, insurance, freight, and interest

cig \'sig\ *n* -s [by shortening] *slang* **:** CIGARETTE

ci·ga·la \sə'gälə\ *or* **ci·gale** \-'gäl\ *n* -s [F & Prov; F *cigale*, fr. Prov *cigala*, fr. ML *cicala*, alter. of L *cicada*] **:** CICADA

ci·gar *also* **se·gar** \sə'gär, -gȧ(r *sometimes* 'si,g-, *chiefly substand* 'sē,g-\ *n* -s [Sp *cigarro*, perh. of Mayan origin; akin to Maya *sī'c* tobacco, cigar, pipe, *sicar* to perfume, smoke] **:** a tubular roll of tobacco designed for smoking usu. consisting of a core bound together by a leaf with the whole being encased in another leaf of smooth and even texture — see BINDER, FILLER, WRAPPER

cigar–box cedar \·=·=,=·\ *n* **:** SPANISH CEDAR

cigar casebearer *n* **:** a larval moth (*Coleophora serratella*) that is enclosed in a brown cigar-shaped case and that feeds on apple-tree and other fruit-tree foliage

cig·a·resque \¦sigə¦resk; sə¦gä¦resk, -gȧ-\ *adj* **:** featured by a cigar

cig·a·rette *also* **cig·a·ret** \ˌsigə'ret, '==,=, *usu* -ed·+V\ *n* -s [F *cigarette*, dim. of *cigare* cigar, fr. Sp *cigarro*] **1 a :** a tube of finely cut tobacco enclosed in paper, designed for smoking, and usu. narrower and shorter than a cigar **b :** a similar tube for smoking filled wholly or partly with some substance other than tobacco **2 :** ANTIQUE BROWN

cigarette beetle *n* **:** a small brown beetle (*Lasioderma serricorne*) of the family Anobiidae often very destructive to stored tobacco products, other vegetable materials, and animal materials

cigarette drain *n* **:** a cigarette-shaped gauze wick enclosed in rubber dam tissue or rubber tubing for draining wounds

cigarette girl *n* **:** a girl who walks about a dining room or nightclub selling cigarettes

cigarette paper *n* **:** a thin strong tissue paper that burns evenly and is of the proper porosity to control the burning of the tobacco it surrounds

cigarfish \·=·,=\ *n* [so called fr. its shape] **:** ROUND SCAD; *also* **:** the related mackerel scad (*Decapterus macarellus*)

cigar flower *also* **cigar plant** *n* [so called fr. the shape of the flower] **:** a tender spreading perennial (*Cuphea ignea*) used as a pot plant and having solitary bright-red tubular flowers with a dark ring at the end and a white mouth

cig·a·ril·lo \ˌsigə'ril,ō\ *also* **cig·a·ri·to** \-'rēd·,ō\ *n* -s [Sp *cigarrillo, cigarrito*, dim. of *cigarro* cigar] **1 :** a very small cigar **2 :** a cigarette wrapped in tobacco rather than paper

ci·gar·less *pronunc at* CIGAR +ləs\ *adj* **:** lacking a cigar

ci·gar·ro \sə'gär,ō\ *n* -s [Sp] **:** CIGAR, CIGARILLO

cigar spot *n* **:** frogeye of tobacco

cigar store *n* **:** a shop selling tobacco products and related items

cigar–store indian \·=·,=·=\ *n, usu cap I* **:** a wooden effigy of an American Indian at a cigar-store door

cigar tree *n* [so called fr. the shape of the pods] **:** WESTERN CATALPA

ci·gua \'sēgwə\ *n* -s [Sp *cigua, sigua*, fr. Taino] **:** a lancewood (*Ocotea coriacea*)

ci·gua·te·ra \ˌsēgwə'terə\ *n* -s [AmerSp, prob. fr. *cigua* sea snail, fr. Taino] **:** poisoning caused by eating fish or mollusks with flesh toxic to man

cilery *or* **cillery** *n* -ES [alter. of earlier *celure* bed canopy, bed hangings, tapestry, fr. ME *celure, sillour, siller*, fr. OF *celeure* ceiling, canopy, fr. ML *celatura* canopy, carved ceiling, fr. L *caelatura* carving, fr. *caelare* to carve — more at CEIL] *obs* **:** the carved ornamentation of the capital of a column

cili– *or* **cilio–** *comb form* [NL, fr. *cilium*] **1 :** ciliary body ⟨*ciliotomy*⟩ **:** ciliary body and ⟨*cilioretinal*⟩ **2 :** cilia ⟨*ciliferous*⟩ ⟨*ciliiform*⟩ ⟨*ciliograde*⟩

cilia [NL, pl. of *cilium*, fr. L, eyelid, prob. back-formation fr. *supercilium* eyebrow — more at SUPERCILIOUS] *pl of* CILIUM

cil·i·ary \'silē,erē, -i\ *adj* [F *ciliaire*, fr. L *cilia* + E *-ary;* F *ciliaire* fr. L *cilia* + F *-aire* -ary — more at CILIA] **1 :** of or relating to cilia **2** *of ocular structures* **:** of, relating to, or being the ciliary body ⟨a ~ arteriole⟩ ⟨the ~ zonule⟩

ciliary body *n* **:** an annular structure on the inner surface of the anterior wall of the eyeball composed largely of the ciliary muscle and bearing the ciliary processes

ciliary flame *n* **:** a tuft of cilia functioning in excretion (as in the nephrostomes of annelids or the flame cells of flatworms)

ciliary ganglion *n* **:** a small autonomic ganglion on the nasociliary branch of the ophthalmic nerve receiving preganglionic fibers from the oculomotor nerve and sending postganglionic fibers to the ciliary muscle and to the circular muscle of the iris

ciliary muscle *n* **:** an annular muscle composed of nonstriated fibers situated in the ciliary body and serving as the chief agent in accommodation — see EYE illustration

ciliary process *n* **:** any one of the vascular folds on the inner surface of the ciliary body that give attachment to the suspensory ligament of the lens

cil·i·a·ta \ˌsilē'ād·ə\ *n pl, cap* [NL, fr. *cilium* + *-ata* — more at CILIA] **:** a large class (commonly divided into the subclasses Protociliata and Euciliata) of chiefly free-living and holozoic protozoans distinguished by possession of cilia or cirri throughout the vegetative stages of the life cycle and usu. having nuclei of two kinds

¹cil·i·ate \'silēət, -ˌāt, *usu* -d·+V\ *or* **cil·i·at·ed** \¦==¦ād·əd\ *adj* [*ciliate* fr. NL *ciliatus*, fr. *cilium* + L *-atus* -ate; *ciliated* fr. NL *ciliatus* + E *-ed*] **:** provided with cilia ⟨a ~ leaf⟩ ⟨~ infusorians⟩ — **cil·i·ate·ly** *adv*

²ciliate \"\ *n* -s **:** a protozoan of the subphylum Ciliophora

cil·i·a·tion \ˌ==·'āshən\ *n* -s **:** the state or degree of being ciliate **:** the cilia of a part

cil·ice \'siləs\ *n* -s [F, fr. L *cilicium*, fr. *Cilicius* Cilician, fr. *Cilicia*, ancient region in Asia Minor] **1 :** HAIRCLOTH **2 :** a hair shirt or undergarment

¹ci·li·cian \sə'lishən\ *adj, usu cap* [*Cilicia*, ancient region in Asia Minor (fr. L) + E *-an*] **1 :** of, relating to, or characteristic of Cilicia, an ancient country and region in southeast Asia Minor **2 :** of, relating to, or characteristic of Cilicians

²cilician \"\ *n* -s *cap* **:** a native or inhabitant of ancient Cilicia

cilii– *or* **cilio–** — see CILI-

cil·io·flag·el·la·ta \ˌsilēə,flajə'lād·ə\ [NL, fr. *cili-* + *Flagellata*] *syn of* DINOFLAGELLATA

cil·io·late \'silēə,lāt, -,lət\ *adj* [NL *ciliolum* + E *-ate*] **:** minutely ciliate

ci·li·o·lum \sə'līələm\ *n, pl* **cilio·la** \-lə\ [NL, dim. of *cilium*] **:** a minute or secondary cilium

¹cil·i·oph·o·ra \ˌsilē'äf(ə)rə\ *n pl, cap* [NL, fr. *cili-* + *-phora*] **:** a subphylum of Protozoa including those protozoans that possess cilia during some phase of the life cycle and usu. have nuclei of two kinds and comprising the classes Ciliata and Suctoria — compare PLASMODROMA — **cil·i·oph·o·ran** \¦==¦äf(ə)rən\ *adj or n*

²ciliophora \"\ [NL, fr. *cili-* + *-phora*] *syn of* CILIATA

cil·i·um \'silēəm\ *n, pl* **cil·ia** \-ēə\ *also* **ciliums** [NL, fr. L, eyelid — more at CILIA] **1 :** EYELASH **2 :** a minute hairlike process often forming a fringe (as between the teeth of the moss peristome or on the margins of many leaves) **3 :** a hairlike process found on many cells that is capable of vibratory or lashing movement and that serves in free-swimming unicellular organisms and in some small multicellular forms as an organ of locomotion or in the higher animal as a producer of a current of fluid (as in the human external nares, trachea, and bronchi where ciliated cells beating constantly toward the nose assist in removal of mucus and dust particles) **4 :** a barbicel of a feather

cill *var of* SILL

cillery *var of* CILERY

¹cima *var of* CYMA

²ci·ma \'chēmə\ *n* -s [It, top, summit, mountain peak, fr. L *cyma* young sprout of a cabbage, the tip of the stalk — more at CYME] **:** a mountain peak or dome

cim·ar·ron *also* **cim·ma·ron** \'simə,rän, -,rōn, ,==·'=; '==,rən\ *or* **cim·a·roon** \¦==¦rün\ *n, pl* **cimarrons** \-nz\ *or* **cimarrones** \,==·'rō(,)nēz, -(,)nās\ *sometimes cap* [AmerSp *cimarrón* — more at MAROON] **1 a :** a fugitive slave **:** a descendant of an escaped slave **:** MAROON ⟨the ~s of the West Indies and Central America⟩ **b :** a feral animal **2** *West* **:** BIGHORN

cim·ba·lom *also* **cym·ba·lom** \'simbələm\ *or* **cymbalon** \-lən\ *or* **cem·ba·lon** \'sem-\ *n* -s [Hung *cimbalom*, fr. It *cembalo* dulcimer, cymbal, fr. L *cymbalum* cymbal — more at CYMBAL] **:** a Hungarian gypsy dulcimer

cimbia *n* -s [It, fr. ML *cymbius* arch, vault, fr. LL, canopy, fr. L *cymbium* small cup, fr. Gk *kymbion*, dim. of *kymbē* cup, boat — more at CYMBA] *obs* **:** a fillet or band around the shaft of a column

cimblin *var of* CYMLING

cim·bo·rio \sim'bōrē,ō\ *n* -s [Sp, fr. ML *ciborium* — more at CIBORIUM] *in Spanish architecture* **:** a raised structure like a dome or a cupola; *specif* **:** a lantern usu. octagonal in plan built over the crossing of a Gothic cathedral

cim·bri \'sim,brī, 'kim(,)brē\ *n pl, usu cap* [L] **:** a prob. Celtic or Teutonic people that invaded Italy and were destroyed by the Romans in 101 B.C. — **cim·bri·an** \-,brēən\ *adj or n, usu cap* — **cim·bric** \-,brik\ *adj, usu cap*

ci·me·lia \sə'mēlē·ə, -lyə\ *n pl* [ML, fr. Gk *keimēlia*, pl. of *keimēlion;* akin to Gk *keisthai* to lie — more at CEMETERY] **:** TREASURES: **a :** HEIRLOOMS **b :** church treasures

cimeter *var of* SCIMITAR

ci·mex \'sī,meks\ *n* [L — more at CHINCH] **1** *pl* **cim·i·ces** \'simə,sēz\ **:** BEDBUG **2** *cap* [NL, fr. L] **:** the type genus of Cimicidae comprising the common bedbug and a few related insects

ci·mi·cid \'sīməsəd, 'sim-, -,sid\ *n* -s [NL *Cimicidae*] **:** a bug of the family Cimicidae

ci·mic·i·dae \sī'misə,dē, sə'-\ *n pl, cap* [NL, fr. *Cimic-, Cimex*, type genus + *-idae*] **:** a small family of flat-bodied wingless bloodsucking bugs (order Hemiptera) including the bedbug and certain pests of birds and bats

cim·i·cif·u·ga \ˌsimə'sifyəgə\ *n, cap* [NL, fr. *Cimic-, Cimex* + *-i-* + *-fuga* -fuge] **:** a small genus of perennial herbs (family Ranunculaceae) having two or three ternately divided serrate leaves and white flowers in long rodlike racemes — see BUGBANE

cim·i·cif·u·gin \-jən\ *n* -s [NL *cimicifuga* + E *-in*] **:** an eclectic resinoid prepared from the bugbane (*Cimicifuga racemosa*) and used as a nerve tonic and antispasmodic

ci·mi·coid \'sīmə,kȯid, 'sim-\ *adj* [prob. fr. F *cimicoïde*, fr. L *cimic-, cimex* bug + F *-oïde* -oid] **:** of or resembling the Cimicidae

cim·i·nite \'chimə,nīt, 'sim-\ *n* -s [Monti *Cimini* (Ciminian hills), Italy, its locality + E *-ite*] **:** an extrusive rock intermediate between trachyte and andesite that is marked by the presence of olivine

cimmaron *var of* CIMARRON

¹cim·me·ri·an \sə'mirēən, -mēr-\ *adj, usu cap* [L *Cimmerii*, a mythical people (fr. Gk *Kimmerioi*) + E *-an*] **1 :** of or suggestive of the Cimmerians **2 :** suggestive of the fabled home of the Cimmerians **:** marked by intensity of darkness or gloom **:** STYGIAN ⟨in ~ gloom, darker than starless midnight — a darkness that could be felt —Norman Douglas⟩

²cimmerian \"\ *n* -s, *usu cap* **1 :** one of a mythical people described by Homer as dwelling in a remote realm of mist and gloom **2 :** one of a nomadic people of antiquity dwelling about the Crimea who overran Asia Minor about 635 B.C. and were succeeded in southern Russia by the Sarmatians and Scythians

cim·o·lite \'simə,līt, sə'mō,l-\ *n* -s [G *zimolit*, fr. *Cimolus*, island in the Aegean sea + G *-it* -ite] **:** a mineral $2Al_2O_3.9SiO_2.6H_2O$ consisting of a hydrous aluminum silicate occurring in soft white to reddish claylike masses

cin– — see KIN-

C in C *abbr* commander in chief

¹cinch \'sinch\ *n* -ES [Sp *cincha*, fr. L *cingula* girdle, girth, fr. *cingere* to gird — more at CINCTURE] **1 :** a strong girth often of braided horsehair or canvas for a pack or saddle **2 :** a tight clinched hold or grasp ⟨a ~ on what was going on⟩ **3 a :** a thing accomplished with great ease **:** a thing obtained or condition attained to very easily ⟨the country's flatness makes cycling a ~ —Israel Shenker⟩ **b :** a certainty as indicated **:** a person or thing sure to do as predicted — often used with an infinitive or dependent clause ⟨not only political naturals but surefire ~*es* to make newspaper headlines —Andy Logan⟩ ⟨it's a ~ that the Blues will win⟩

²cinch \"\ *vb* -ED/-ING/-ES *vt* **1 a :** to put a cinch or girth on ⟨~ a horse⟩ **:** GIRTH **b :** to bind closely **:** fasten tightly or snugly with or as if with a belt ⟨~ his arms fast⟩ ⟨a waistline ~*ed* with a belt⟩ **c :** to get a sure hold on **:** place (one) in a tight situation, in difficulties, or at a disadvantage ⟨these grafters ~*ing* honest businessmen⟩ **d :** to secure firmly **:** TIGHTEN — used with *up* or *on* ⟨~ up your belt⟩ **2 :** to make utterly certain **:** GUARANTEE, ASSURE ⟨his speed ~*ed* the victory for his team⟩ ⟨this speech by the candidate has ~*ed* his nomination⟩ **3 :** to tighten (a roll of film) by pulling on the free end while holding the spool ~ *vi* **:** to perform the action of cinching **:** tighten the cinch — often used with *up*

³cinch \"\ *n* -ES [¹*cinch*] **:** a variety of the card game of all fours in which the players bid for the privilege of naming trump, a draw to improve the hand is permitted, and the five of trumps and of the same-colored suit have special values

⁴cinch \"\ *vt* -ED/-ING/-ES *in the game of cinch* **:** to play a higher trump than the five on (a trick) so that a following player cannot score by playing a five

cin·cha \'sinchə, 'sēn-\ *n* -s [Sp — more at CINCH] **:** ¹CINCH 1

cinchbinder \'=,==\ *n* **:** a horse that balks, rears, or falls over backward when cinched too tight

cinch mark *n* **:** a scratch formed on the emulsion by friction between adjacent layers of a photographic film during cinching

cin·cho·caine \'siŋkə,kān, 'sin-\ *n* -s [NL *Cinchona* + E *-caine* (as in *cocaine*)] **:** DIBUCAINE

cin·cho·loi·pon \ˌsiŋkə'lȯi,pän, ,sin-\ *n* -s [ISV *cinchonine* + Gk *loipon*, *loipos* remainder, fr. *leipein* to leave — more at LOAN] **:** a yellow crystalline acid $C_5H_9N(C_2H_5)CH_2COOH$ obtained esp. by oxidation of cinchonine

cin·cho·me·ron·ic acid \¦==mə¦ränik-\ *n* [ISV *cinchomeronic* (fr. *cinchonine* + *mer-* + *-onic*) + *acid;* orig. formed as G *cinchomeronsäure*] **:** a colorless crystalline acid $C_5H_3N(COOH)_2$ made by oxidizing cinchonine, quinine, or isoquinoline; 3,4-pyridine-dicarboxylic acid

cin·cho·na \siŋ'kōnə, sin- *also* -n'chō-\ *n* [NL, after Doña Francisca Henríquez de Ribera, countess of *Chinchón* †1641 vicereine of Peru, who was said to have introduced the bark to Europe] **1** *cap* **:** a large genus of trees (family Rubiaceae) native to the Andean region of northwestern So. America and now extensively cultivated both there and in Indonesia and having panicled flowers with a salver-shaped corolla and an ovary crowned with a fleshy disk **2** *also* **chin·cho·na** \chin'ch-\ *or* **chin·co·na** \chin'k-\ -s **:** a tree of the genus *Cinchona* **3** *or* **cinchona bark** *also* **chinchona** *or* **chincona** -s **:** the dried bark of any of several trees of the genus *Cinchona* (esp. *C. ledgeriana* and *C. succirubra* or their hybrids) containing alkaloids (as quinine, cinchonine, quinidine, and cinchonidine) and being used esp. formerly as a specific in malaria, an antipyretic in other fevers, and a tonic and stomachic — called also *Jesuits' bark, Peruvian bark*

cin·chon·a·mine \-'känə,mēn, -kōn-, -,mən\ *n* -s [ISV *cinchon-* (fr. NL *Cinchona*) + *amine;* orig. formed in F] **:** a white crystalline alkaloid $C_{19}H_{24}N_2O$ obtained from certain So. American shrubs (genus *Remijia*) that has been used as a substitute for and is more toxic than quinine

¹cin·chon·ic \(')siŋ¦känik, (')sin¦-\ *adj* [NL *Cinchona* + E *-ic*] **:** belonging to or obtained from cinchona

²cinchonic \"\ *n* -s **:** a constituent or preparation of cinchona used in medicine

cin·chon·i·cine \siŋ'känə,sēn, sin'k-, -kōn-, -,sən\ *n* -s [ISV *cinchonic* + *-ine;* orig. formed in F] **:** CINCHOTOXINE

cin·chon·i·dine \-,dēn, -,dən\ *n* -s [ISV *cinchon-* (fr. NL *Cinchona*) + *-idine;* orig. formed in F] **:** a bitter crystalline levorotatory alkaloid $C_{19}H_{22}N_2O$ stereoisomeric with cinchonine that is found in cinchona bark and used like quinine

cin·cho·nine \'=kə,nēn, -,nən\ *n* -s [F, fr. NL *cinchona* + F *-ine*] **:** a bitter white crystalline dextrorotatory alkaloid $C_{19}H_{22}N_2O$ stereoisomeric with cinchonidine that is found in cinchona bark and cuprea bark and used like quinine

cin·cho·nin·ic acid \¦==¦ninik-\ *n* [ISV *cinchonine* + *-ic;* orig. formed as G *cinchoninsäure*] **:** a white crystalline acid C_9H_6NCOOH made by reaction of isatin and a pyruvic salt or by oxidation of cinchonine; 4-quinoline-carboxylic acid

cin·cho·nism \'siŋkə,nizəm, 'sin-\ *n* -s [ISV *cinchon-* (fr. NL *Cinchona*) + *-ism*] **:** a condition either produced by excessive or long-continued use of or activated by sensitivity to cinchona or its alkaloids (as quinine) and marked by temporary deafness, ringing in the ears, headache, dizziness, and rash

cin·cho·nize \-,nīz\ *vt* -ED/-ING/-S [NL *Cinchona* + E *-ize*] **:** to treat (as a malarial patient) with cinchona or its alkaloids (as quinine)

cin·cho·nol·o·gy \,siŋkə'näləjē, sin-, -ji\ *n* -ES [NL *Cinchona* + E *-logy*] **:** a branch of pharmacology dealing with cinchona and its derivatives

cin·cho·phen \'==,fen, -,fən\ *n* -s [*cinchoninic* + *phenyl*] **:** a bitter white crystalline compound $C_9H_5N(C_6H_5)COOH$ made synthetically and used for treating gout and rheumatism but damaging to the liver; 2-phenyl-cinchoninic acid

cin·cho·tine \-,tēn, -,tən\ *n* -s [F, irreg. fr. NL *Cinchona* + F *-ine*] **:** a crystalline alkaloid $C_{19}H_{24}N_2O$ in cinchona bark — called also *hydrocinchonine*

cin·cho·tox·ine \,siŋkə'täk,sēn, ,sin-, -,sən\ *n* -s [ISV *cincho-* (fr. NL *Cinchona*) + *toxine,* alter. of *toxin*] **:** a crystalline alkaloid $C_{19}H_{22}N_2O$ obtained from cinchonine or cinchonidine by heating — called also *cinchonicine*

cinch ring *n* [¹*cinch*] **:** a metal ring terminating a cinch and used to make it fast to a saddle

¹cin·cin·nati \¦sin(t)sə¦nad·|ē, -at|, |i, |ə\ *adj, usu cap* [fr. *Cincinnati,* Ohio] **:** of or from the city of Cincinnati, Ohio **:** of the kind or style prevalent in Cincinnati

²cincinnati \"\ *n, usu cap* [fr. *Cincinnati,* Ohio] **:** a wild-card poker game

¹cin·cin·nat·i·an \|ēən\ *n* -s *cap* [*Cincinnati,* Ohio + E *-an*] **:** a native or resident of Cincinnati, Ohio

²cincinnatian \"\ *adj, usu cap* **1 :** CINCINNATI **2** [so called fr. the succession of formations found in the region of Cincinnati] **:** of or relating to a division of the American Ordovician — see GEOLOGIC TIME table

cin·clus \'siŋkləs\ *n, cap* [NL, fr. Gk *kinklos,* a kind of bird] **:** the genus consisting of the water ouzels sometimes placed in the Turdidae or isolated in a separate family

cinct \'siŋ(k)t\ *adj* [ME *cincte,* fr. L *cinctus*] **:** ENGIRDLED

¹cinc·ture \'siŋ(k)chə(r), -)shə(r)\ *n* -s [L *cinctura* girdle, fr. *cinctus,* past part. of *cingere* to gird; akin to Gk *kakala* walls, Skt *kāñcī* girdle, Lith *kinkyti* to harness a horse] **1 :** GIRDING, ENCOMPASSING, ENCLOSURE **:** act of encircling ⟨an island in the ~ of the sea⟩ **2 :** GIRDLE, BELT ⟨a robe gathered with a ~⟩ **3 :** the fillet, list, or band next to the apophyge at the extremity of the shaft of a column

²cincture \"\ *vt* **cinctured; cinctured; cincturing** \-chəriŋ, -sh(ə)riŋ\ **cinctures :** to girdle with or as if with a cincture **:** GIRD, ENCIRCLE ⟨a valley *cinctured* with mountains⟩ ⟨her hair *cinctured* with a band⟩

¹cin·der \'sində(r)\ *n* -s *often attrib* [ME *cinder,* alter. (influenced by MF *cendre* ash) of *sinder,* fr. OE; akin to OHG *sintar* dross, slag, ON *sindr,* OSlav *sędra* stalactite] **1 a :** the slag from a metal furnace **:** DROSS, SCORIA **b :** a scale thrown off in forging metal **2 cinders** *pl* **a :** ASHES **:** the incombustible residue of something burnt; *esp* **:** small fragments of clinker left by burning soft coal **b** *obs* **:** the residue of a human body following cremation or decomposition **3 a :** a partly burned combustible in which fire is extinct or which no longer gives off flame — often distinguished from *ash* and *ashes* **b :** a hot coal without flame **:** EMBER **c :** a piece of partly burned coal capable of further burning without flame **4 :** one of the small commonly vesicular fragments of lava that are projected from an erupting volcano, are about ¼ to 1½ inches in diameter, and are coarser than volcanic ash and smaller than volcanic bombs — compare LAPILLUS, SCORIA **5** *or* **cinder gray :** a purplish gray that is redder and lighter than crane, slightly less strong than dove gray, lighter than granite, and redder than zinc — called also *crystal gray, silverwing* **6 cinders** *pl* **:** a cinder running track **:** an outdoor track ⟨faster in indoor races than on ~s⟩

²cinder \"\ *vt* **cindered; cindered; cindering** \-d(ə)riŋ\ **cinders** [ME *scindern,* fr. *cinder, sinder,* n.] **1** *archaic* **:** to burn or reduce to cinders **2 :** to sprinkle with cinders

cinder block *n* **1 :** a block closing the front of a blast furnace and containing the cinder notch **2 :** a hollow rectangular unit made of cinder concrete and used in walls, partitions, and foundations of buildings

cinder concrete *n* **:** portland-cement concrete in which clean well-burned coal cinders are used as coarse aggregate

cinder cone *n* **:** a conical hill formed by the accumulation of volcanic debris around a vent

cinder dick *n, slang* **:** a railroad policeman or special agent

cin·der·el·la \,sində'relə, *attrib* ¦==¦=\ *n* -s *often cap* [after *Cinderella,* heroine of a fairy tale who is mistreated by her stepmother but elevated to happiness and affluence through the intervention of her fairy godmother] **:** a person, place, or thing likened to Cinderella of the fairy tale: **a :** one suffering neglect usu. undeservedly in a lowly despised position ⟨bats are the ~s of the mammal world⟩ **b :** one suddenly lifted often fortuitously from obscurity and neglect to honor and significance ⟨uranium is a ~ among the world's metals⟩

cinderella dance *n, usu cap C* [so called fr. the episode in the Cinderella fairy tale in which Cinderella's fine raiment and equipage, metamorphosed by her fairy godmother from baser materials to enable her to attend a royal ball, are converted to their original state at the stroke of midnight] *Brit* **:** a dancing party that is to end at midnight

cin·der·man \'==,man, -,maa(ə)n, -,mən\ *n, pl* **cindermen** **1 :** a worker who removes ashes or slag **2** [*cinder* (track) + *man*] **:** FOOT RACER

cinder notch *also* **cinder tap** *n* **:** the opening in a blast furnace through which molten slag flows out

cin·der·ous \'sind(ə)rəs\ *adj* **:** composed of or suggestive of cinders **:** CINDERY

cinder path *n* **:** a path or running track surfaced with cinders

cinder pig *n* **:** pig iron made from a mixture of mill cinder with ore or crude metal

cinder track *n* **:** a running track surfaced with hard-packed cinders

cin·dery \'sind(ə)rē, -ri\ *adj* **1 :** like a cinder **2 :** composed of or full of cinders **:** sprinkled or begrimed with cinders

cine *also* **ciné** \'sinē, -nā\ *n* -s [partly short for *cinema,* partly fr. F *ciné,* short for *cinématographe*] **1 :** MOTION PICTURE **2** [Sp, It & F; Sp & It *cine,* fr. F *ciné*] **:** a motion-picture theater

cine- *comb form* [*cinema*] **:** motion picture ⟨*cine*camera⟩ ⟨*cine*film⟩ ⟨*cine*-X ray⟩

cin·e·ast *also* **cin·é·aste** \'sinē,ast, -nā-, -,əst\ *n* -s [F *cinéaste* scenario writer, movie fan, fr. *ciné* + *-aste* (as in *enthousiaste* enthusiast)] **:** a devotee of motion pictures

cin·e·dance \'sinə,=\ *n* [*cine-* + *dance*] **:** a dance composition or performance esp. devised for motion-picture photography

cin·e·fluorogram \¦sinə+\ *n* [*cine-* + *fluorogram*] **:** a motion picture produced by cinefluorography

cin·e·fluorographic \"+\ *adj* **:** of, used in, or relating to cinefluorography

cin·e·fluorography \"+\ *n* [*cine-* + *fluorography*] **:** the process of making motion pictures of images of objects by means of X rays with the aid of a fluorescent screen (as for revealing the motions of organs in the body or the movement of inanimate objects) — compare CINERADIOGRAPHY

cin·e·ma \'sinəmə *sometimes* -,mä\ *n* -s [short for *cinematograph*] **1** *chiefly Brit* **a :** MOTION PICTURE **b :** a motion-picture showing **c :** a motion-picture theater **2 a :** the art or technique of making motion pictures — usu. used with *the* **b :** the production and distribution of motion pictures or the industry devoted to their production and distribution — usu. used with *the* **c :** motion pictures exhibited as a medium of communication and entertainment — usu. used with *the* **3 :** material or method of a specified suitability for motion-picture production ⟨this story is good ~⟩

cinemagoer \'===,==\ *n* -s **:** one that attends motion pictures with frequency

cin·e·mat·ic \¦sinə¦mad·ik, -atik, -ēk\ *adj* [*cinematograph* + *-ic*] **1 :** played, narrated, or otherwise presented for photographing with a motion-picture camera and projection on a screen or suited or adapted for such reproduction ⟨a ~ fantasy on a musical theme⟩ ⟨his first ~ appearance⟩ ⟨the most ~ Shakespeare yet brought to the screen —Arthur Knight⟩ **2 a :** peculiar to the art and technique of making motion pictures ⟨replacing period background with fast ~ action⟩ ⟨all his films therefore lacked a ~ continuity —Lewis Jacobs⟩ ⟨tension between the dramatic and ~ principles cannot always be avoided —E.R.Bentley⟩ **b :** having essential technical and aesthetic qualities of motion-picture art (as episodic composition, sustained movement, pictorial brilliance, suspense, the spotlighting of dramatic moments) **3 :** using methods or devices or obtaining effects suggestive of motion-picture technique ⟨some stream of consciousness fiction is notably ~⟩ ⟨gave stilted and generally ~ performances in the leading roles —Wolcott Gibbs⟩ **4 :** relating to the production or showing of motion pictures ⟨has had a great deal of ~ training and experience⟩ ⟨the ~ fortunes of a novel or stage play⟩

cin·e·mat·i·cal·ly \-ək(ə)lē, -li\ *adv* **1 :** in or for cinematic production **2 :** from the point of view of cinematic art or technique **3 :** according to cinematic principles

¹cinematics *var of* KINEMATICS

²cin·e·mat·ics \,sinə'mad·iks, -atiks\ *n pl but usu sing in constr* **:** the art or technique of cinematic presentation

cin·e·mat·i·za·tion \¦sinəmad·ə'zāshən, -,mad·-, -ī'z-\ *n* -s **1 :** the making of a motion picture from a narrative or dramatic work **2 :** an adaptation for presenting as a motion picture

cin·e·ma·tize \'sinəmə,tīz, -ə,tīz\ *vt* -ED/-ING/-S [*cinema* + *-tize* (as in *dramatize*)] **:** to make a motion picture of (as a novel or stage play) **:** adapt for motion pictures

¹cin·e·mat·o·graph \,=='mad·ə,graf, -atə-, -aa(ə)f,-äf\ *n* -s [F *cinématographe,* fr. Gk *kinēmat-, kinēma* movement (fr. *kinein* to move) + F *-o-* + *-graphe* -graph; akin to Gk *kiein* to go — more at CITE] **1** *now chiefly Brit* **:** a motion-picture camera, projector, theater, or show **2** *now chiefly Brit* **:** the art and techniques of producing motion pictures — often used with *the*

²cinematograph \"\ *vt* -ED/-ING/-S *now chiefly Brit* **:** to photograph with a motion-picture camera

cin·e·ma·tog·ra·pher \,==mə'tägrəfə(r)\ *n* -s **1 :** a motion-picture cameraman **2 :** a motion-picture projectionist

cin·e·mat·o·graph·ic \¦==,mad·ə¦grafik, -atə-, -aaf-,-äf-, -ēk\ *also* **cin·e·mat·o·graph·i·cal** \-fəkəl\ *adj* [*cinematography* + *-ic, -ical*] **1 a :** peculiar to, used in, or connected with cinematography **b :** skilled in cinematography **2 :** filmed for or reproduced by means of motion-picture projection **3 a :** conveyed or evoked by motion pictures **b :** having qualities in common with cinematography; *specif* **:** using devices suggestive of motion-picture technique — **cin·e·mat·o·graph·i·cal·ly** \-fək(ə)lē, -li\ *adv*

cin·e·ma·tog·ra·phist \,==mə'tägrəfəst\ *n* -s *Brit* **:** CINEMATOGRAPHER

cin·e·ma·tog·ra·phy \-fē, -fi\ *n* -ES **:** the art or science of motion-picture photography

cinema van *n, Brit* **:** CINEMOBILE

cin·e·ma·za·tion \,sinəmə'zāshən\ *n* -s [*cinema* + *-zation* (as in *dramatization*)] **:** CINEMATIZATION

cin·e·micrograph \¦sinə+\ *n* [*cine-* + *micrograph*] **:** a motion picture produced by cinemicrography

cin·e·micrography \¦==+\ *n* [*cine-* + *micrography*] **:** CINEPHOTOMICROGRAPHY

cin·e·mize \'sinə,mīz\ *vt* -ED/-ING/-S [*cinema* + *-ize*] **:** CINEMATIZE

cin·e·mo·bile \'sinəmə¦bēl, ,=='mō,bēl, *esp bef pause or cons* -ēəl\ *n* -s [*cine-* + *automobile*] **:** a truck or trailer that carries the film and equipment necessary for showing outdoor movies

ci·ne·mo·graph \sə'nēmə,graf, 'sinəmə-\ *n* -s [Gk *kinēma* movement + E *-graph* — more at CINEMATOGRAPH] **:** an instrument for registering velocity (as of the wind)

cin·e·ole \'sinē,ōl\ *also* **cin·e·ol** \-,ōl, -ōl\ *n* -s [ISV *cine-* (fr. NL *cina* — in *oleum cinae* wormseed oil, *semen cinae* Levant wormseed) + *-ole, -ol;* orig. formed as G *cyneol*] **:** a syrupy liquid $C_{10}H_{18}O$ of camphorlike odor found in many essential oils (as Levant wormseed, eucalyptus, and cajeput) and used esp. as an expectorant — called also *1,8-cineole, eucalyptole*

cin·e·photomicrograph \¦sinə+\ *n* [*cine-* + *photomicrograph*] **:** a motion picture made by cinephotomicrography

cin·e·photomicrography \"+\ *n* [*cine-* + *photomicrography*] **:** photomicrography in which the product is a motion picture

cin·e·plas·tic \¦sinə¦plastik\ *adj* [ISV *cineplasty* + *-ic*] **:** of, relating to, or used in cineplasty

cin·e·plasty \'==,=tē\ *n* -ES [ISV *cine-* (var. of *kine-*) + *-plasty*] **1 :** surgical fitting of a lever to a muscle in an amputation stump to facilitate the operation of an artificial hand **2 :** surgical isolation of a loop of muscle of chest or arm, covering it with skin, and attaching to it a prosthetic device to be operated by contraction of the muscle in the loop

cin·er·a·ceous \¦sinə¦rāshəs\ *adj* [L *cineraceus,* fr. *ciner-, cinis* ashes + *-aceus* -aceous — more at INCINERATE] **:** CINEREOUS

cin·e·radiography \¦sinə+\ *n* [*cine-* + *radiography*] **:** the process of making radiographs of moving objects in sufficiently rapid sequence so that the radiographs or copies made from them may be projected as motion pictures — compare CINEFLUOROGRAPHY

cin·e·rar·ia \,sinə'ra(a)rēə\ *n* -s [NL, fr. fem. of L *cinerarius* of ashes, fr. *ciner-, cinis* ashes + *-arius* -ary; fr. the ash-colored down on the leaves] **:** any of several pot plants derived from a perennial herb (*Senecio cruentus*) of the Canary islands and having heart-shaped leaves and large clusters of flower heads with white, red, blue, or purple rays

cin·e·rar·i·um \-ēəm\ *n, pl* **cinerar·ia** \-ēə\ [L, fr. *ciner-, cinis* + *-arium*] **:** a place to receive the ashes of the cremated dead

cin·er·ary \'sinə,rerē\ *adj* [L *cinerarius*] **:** containing or used for ashes esp. of the cremated dead

cin·er·a·tor \'sinə,rād·ə(r), -ātə(r)\ *n* -s [obs. *cineration* + *-or*] **:** a crematory furnace

ci·ne·rea \sə'nirēə\ *n* -s [NL, fr. fem. of L *cinereus*] **:** the gray matter of nerve tissue

ci·ne·re·al \-ēəl\ *adj* [L *cinereus* ash-colored + E *-al*] **:** CINEREOUS

ci·ne·re·ous \-ēəs\ *adj* [L *cinereus,* fr. *ciner-, cinis* ashes + *-eus* -eous — more at INCINERATE] **1 a :** ASHEN 2 **b :** gray tinged or shaded with black — used esp. in technical descriptions in biology **2 :** like ashes esp. in inert and powdery quality **:** consisting of ash

cinereous vulture *n* **:** a large vulture (*Aegypius monachus*) that has entirely dark brown plumage and that is found from southern Europe and northern Africa east to northern India and China

cin·er·in \'sinərən\ *n* -s [L *ciner-, cinis* ashes + E *-in*] **:** either of two oily liquid esters $C_{20}H_{28}O_3$ and $C_{21}H_{28}O_5$ of cinerolone having high insecticidal properties and occurring in pyrethrum flowers and distinguished by the numerals I and II

cin·er·i·tious \¦sinə¦rishəs\ *adj* [L *cineritius, cinericius,* fr. *ciner-, cinis* ashes] *archaic* **:** CINEREOUS

cin·e·roentgenography \¦sinə+\ *n* [*cine-* + *roentgenography*] **:** CINERADIOGRAPHY

cin·er·ol·one \'sinə(,)rō,lōn, -,rə-\ *n* -s [*cinerin* + *-ol* + *-one*] **:** an oily keto alcohol $C_{10}H_{14}O_2$ derived from cyclopentene and obtained by hydrolysis of the cinerins — compare PYRETHROLONE

cin·er·ous \'sinərəs\ *n* -ES [L *ciner-, cinis* ashes + E *-ous*] **:** a light bluish gray to light gray that is redder and darker than skimmed-milk white and very slightly redder than glaucous gray

cines *pl of* CINE

-cinesia — see -KINESIA

cinesis *var of* KINESIS

cinet- *or* **cineto-** — see KINET-

cinetoplast *var of* KINETOPLAST

cingalese *also* **cinghalese** *usu cap, var of* SINHALESE

cin·gle \'siŋgəl\ *n* -s [ME *syngle, sengle,* fr. MF & L; MF *cengle,* fr. L *cingula,* fr. *cingere* to gird — more at CINCTURE] *archaic* **:** GIRTH, BELT

cin·gu·lar \'siŋgyələ(r)\ *adj* [L *cingulum, cingula* girdle + E *-ar*] **:** ANNULAR

cin·gu·la·ta \,siŋgyə'lād·ə, -ād·ə\ *n pl, cap* [NL, fr. L *cingulum, cingula* girdle + NL *-ata*] *in some classifications* **:** a major division of Edentata comprising armadillos and extinct related forms

cin·gu·late \'siŋgyələt, -,lāt, *usu* -d·+V\ *adj* [NL *cingulatus,* fr. L *cingulum, cingula* girdle + *-atus* -ate] **:** having a girdle esp. of transverse bands or markings

cin·gu·lum \'siŋgyələm\ *n, pl* **cingu·la** \-lə\ [NL, fr. L, girdle, fr. *cingere* to gird — more at CINCTURE] **1 :** a ridge about the base of the crown of a tooth **2 :** the clitellum of an annelid **3 :** a tract of association fibers running chiefly in the substance of and connecting the callosal and hippocampal convolutions of the brain **4 :** a band of color or raised spiral line (as on certain gastropod shells) **5 :** the outer zone of cilia on the disk of certain rotifers **6 :** the girdle of a diatom

cin·na·bar \'sinə,bär, -ā(r\ *n* -s [ME *cynoper, cynabare,* fr. MF & L; MF *cenobre,* fr. L *cinnabaris,* fr. Gk *kinnabari,* of non-IE origin; akin to Ar *zinjafr* cinnabar] **1 :** a mineral HgS consisting of mercuric sulfide occurring in brilliant red crystals or in red or brownish masses and being the only important ore of mercury **2 :** artificial red mercuric sulfide used principally as a pigment **:** VERMILION 1a **3** *or* **cinnabar moth :** a European moth (*Tyria jacobeae*) having grayish black fore wings marked with red, hind wings clear reddish pink, and larvae that feed on the leaves of ragwort which it was introduced into several areas of the U.S. to control

cinnabar green *n* **1 :** a mixture of Prussian blue and chrome yellow **2 :** the color of the cinnabar-green mixture **:** DEEP CHROME GREEN

cin·na·bar·ine \'sinə,bä,rīn, ,sinə'bärən\ *also* **cin·na·bar·ic** \¦==¦barik\ *adj* [*cinnabar* + *-ine* or *-ic*] **:** like, relating to, consisting of, or containing cinnabar ⟨~ sand⟩

cinnabar red *n* **:** GOYA

cinnam- *or* **cinnamo-** *comb form* [F, fr. L *cinnamum*] **1 :** cinnamon ⟨*cinnamo*dendron⟩ **2 :** cinnamic acid ⟨*cinnam*oyl⟩

cin·na·mal \'sinə,mal, ,=='=\ *n* -s [prob. short for *cinnamaldehyde*] **:** the bivalent radical $C_6H_5CH{:}CHCH<$ derived from cinnamaldehyde by removal of the oxygen atom

cin·na·mal·de·hyde \,sinə'maldə,hīd\ *n* -s [ISV *cinnam-* + *aldehyde*] **:** an aromatic oily aldehyde $C_6H_5CH{:}CHCHO$ occurring as the chief constituent of cinnamon-bark oil and cassia oil and used as a flavor

cin·na·mate \'sinə,māt, si'namət, *usu* -d·+V\ *n* -s [F, fr. *cinnam-* + *-ate*] **:** a salt or ester of cinnamic acid

cin·nam·e·in \sə'namēən\ *n* -s [ISV *cinnam-* + *-ein;* orig. formed as F *cinnaméine*] **:** benzyl cinnamate or a mixture of this ester with other esters

cin·na·mene \'sinə,mēn\ *n* -s [ISV *cinnam-* + *-ene;* orig. formed as G *zinnamen*] **:** STYRENE

cin·nam·e·nyl \sə'namə,nil, -ēl\ *n* -s [*cinnamene* + *-yl*] **:** STYRYL

cin·nam·ic acid \sə'namik- *also* 'sinəmik-\ *n* [F *cinnamique,* fr. *cinnam-* + *-ique* -ic] **:** a white crystalline odorless acid $C_6H_5CH{:}CHCOOH$ found esp. in cinnamon oil and storax and made synthetically for preparing esters for perfumes

cinnamic alcohol *n* **:** CINNAMYL ALCOHOL

cinnamic aldehyde *n* **:** CINNAMALDEHYDE

cin·na·mo·den·dron \,sinəmə'dendrən\ *n, cap* [NL, fr. *cinnam-* + *-dendron*] **:** a small genus of tropical American shrubs or small trees (order Parietales) having pungent aromatic bark resembling canella bark

cin·na·mo·mum \,sinə'mōməm\ *n, cap* [NL, fr. L, cinnamon (the tree and the bark)] **:** a large genus of Asiatic and Australian aromatic trees and shrubs of the family Lauraceae having mostly opposite leaves with three to five prominent longitudinal veins and small flowers in panicles — see CAMPHOR TREE, CHINESE CINNAMON, CINNAMON

cin·na·mon \'sinəmən\ *n* -s *often attrib* [ME *cynamone, cynamum,* fr. MF & L; MF *cinnamome,* fr. L *cinnamomum, cinnamon, cinnamum,* fr. Gk *kinnamōmon, kinnamon,* of non-IE origin; akin to Heb *qinnāmōn* cinnamon] **1 a :** the highly aromatic bark of any of several trees of the genus *Cinnamomum* yielding cinnamaldehyde and other aromatic products in the form of cinnamon oil — see CEYLON CINNAMON, CHINESE CINNAMON, SAIGON CINNAMON **b :** a culinary spice prepared from cinnamon either by powdering or by drying in small rolls **2 :** a tree that yields cinnamon **3 :** a light yellowish brown that is redder and stronger than khaki, deeper and slightly redder than walnut brown, and redder and deeper than fallow or manila

cinnamon apple *n* **:** SWEETSOP

cinnamon bark *n* **1 :** CANELLA BARK **2 :** CINNAMON 1a

cinnamon-bark oil \'===,=-\ *n* **:** a light-yellow essential oil obtained from the bark of Ceylon cinnamon and used in medicine, flavoring, and perfumery — called also *cinnamon oil*

cinnamon bat *n* **:** a tropical American cave bat (genus *Mormoops*) often living in great flocks

cinnamon bear *n* **:** a dark chestnut color phase of the American black bear

cinnamon brown *n* **:** a moderate yellowish brown that is duller and slightly redder than maple sugar, lighter and redder than bronze, and slightly redder and slightly less strong than Bismarck brown

cin·na·moned \'sinəmənd\ *adj* **:** spiced with cinnamon

cinnamon fern *n* **:** a large No. American fern (*Osmunda cinnamomea*) having woolly rich cinnamon-colored spore-bearing fronds shorter than and produced separately from the green foliage fronds

cinnamon flower *n* **:** CASSIA BUD

cinnamon honeysuckle *n* **:** SWAMP AZALEA

cin·na·mon·ic \¦sinə¦mänik\ *adj* **:** of or like cinnamon

cinnamon-leaf oil \'==,=-\ *n* **:** a pale yellow essential oil obtained from the leaves of Ceylon cinnamon and used chiefly as a source of eugenol

cinnamon oak *n* **:** BLUEJACK 2

cinnamon oil *n* **:** an oil obtained from a tree or shrub of the genus *Cinnamomum:* as **a :** CINNAMON-BARK OIL **b :** CASSIA OIL

cinnamon rose *n* **:** a Eurasian rose (*Rosa cinnamomea*) with slender stems and solitary fragrant flowers

cinnamon sedge *n* : SWEET FLAG
cinnamon stone *n* : ESSONITE
cinnamon teal *n* : a small wild duck (*Anas cyanoptera*) of western No. America much resembling the blue-winged teal in appearance and habits but having the male more markedly brownish red about the head and body
cinnamon vine *n* : a hardy Chinese vine (*Dioscorea batatas*) cultivated as an ornamental climber for its glossy heart-shaped leaves and in the tropics for its edible tubers — called also *Chinese yam*
cinnamon water *n* : a saturated solution of cinnamon oil in distilled water used as a vehicle for certain drugs
cinnamonwood \ˈ==,=\ *n* : SASSAFRAS 1b
cin·na·mony \ˈsinəmənē, -ni\ *adj* : like or like that of cinnamon : due to cinnamon ⟨a warm ~ fragrance⟩
cin·nam·o·yl \sə̇ˈnamə,wil, -ēl\ *or* **cin·na·myl** \-məl; ˈsinə,mil, -el\ *n* -S [ISV *cinnam-* + *-yl*] : the acid radical $C_6H_5CH{=}CHCO{-}$ of cinnamic acid
cin·na·myl \sə̇ˈnaməl; ˈsinə,mil, -ēl\ *n* -S [F *cinnamyle*, fr. *cinnam-* + *-yle* -yl] : the univalent radical $C_6H_5CH{=}CHCH_2{-}$
cinnamyl alcohol *n* : a crystalline alcohol $C_6H_5CH{=}CHCH_2OH$ of hyacinth odor occurring as an ester in liquid storax and balsam of Peru and used in synthetic perfumes — called also *cinnamic alcohol*
cin·na·myl·i·dene \,sinəˈmilə,dēn\ *n* -S [ISV *cinnamyl* + *-id* + *-ene*] : CINNAMAL
cin·no·line \ˈsinə,lēn, -,lən\ *n* -S [G *cinnolin*, alter. of *chinolin* quinoline, fr. *chin-* + *-ol* + *-in*] : a poisonous crystalline base $C_8H_6N_2$; 1,2-benzo-diazine
cino- — see KIN-
cin·o·bufagin \,sinə, ,sīnə+\ *n* [*cino-* (prob. fr. NL *Bufo chinensis*, species of toad from which senso is produced) + *bufagin*] : a bufagin $C_{26}H_{34}O_6$ obtained from senso
cin·o·ster·ni·dae \,sinəˈstərnə,dē, ,sī-\ *syn of* KINOSTERNIDAE
cin·o·ster·non \-,nän\ *syn of* KINOSTERNON
cinq-cents \saⁿsäⁿ\ *n pl but sing in constr* [F, lit., five hundred, fr. *cinq* five (fr. L *quinque*) + *cents*, pl. of *cent* hundred, fr. L *centum* — more at FIVE, HUNDRED] : a card game like bézique but played with one 32-card pack
cin·quain \siŋˈkān, ˈ=,=\ *n* -S [F, fr. *cinq* + *-ain* (as in *quatrain*)] : a five-line stanza; *specif* : the five-line verse form that is analogous to the Japanese tanka and that has two syllables in its first and last lines, four, six, and eight in the intervening three lines, and generally iambic cadence
cinque \ˈsiŋk, ˈsaŋk\ *n* -S [ME *cink*, fr. MF *cinq*, fr. L *quinque* — more at FIVE] **1** : FIVE; *esp* : the number five in dice or cards **2 cinques** *pl* : change ringing on 11 bells that are treated as 5 pairs, the tenor bell added after each change
cin·que·cen·tist \,chiŋkwəˈchentə̇st, ,chēŋkwā-\ *n*, *pl* **cinquecentists** \-ə̇s(t)s\ *or* **cinquecentis·ti** \-(,)chenˈti(,)stē\ [It *cinquecentista*, fr. *cinquecento* + *-ista* -ist] **1** : an Italian of the cinquecento; *usu* : a poet or artist of this period **2** : a student of the art or literature of the cinquecento
cin·que·cen·to \-ˈchen(,)tō\ *n* -S *sometimes cap* [It, lit., five hundred (abbr. of fifteen hundred), fr. *cinque* five (fr. L *quinque*) + *cento* hundred, fr. L *centum* — more at FIVE, HUNDRED] : the 16th century; *specif* : the 16th century period in Italian literature and art
cin·que·dea \,chiŋkwə̇ˈdēə, -dāə\ *n* -S [It, fr. *cinque* five (fr. L *quinque*) + It dial. *dea* fingers; akin to It *dita*, pl. of *dito* finger, fr. L *digitus* — more at FIVE, TOE] : a heavy broad-bladed medieval dagger
cinque·foil \ˈsiŋk,fȯil, ˈsaŋ-, *dial* ˈsiŋkē,f-\ *also* **cinq·foil** \-ŋk,f-\ *n* -S [ME *sink foil*, fr. MF *cincfoille*, fr. L *quinquefolium* (trans. of Gk *pentaphyllon*), fr. *quinque* five + *folium* leaf — more at FIVE, BLADE] **1** : a plant of the genus *Potentilla* **2** : a figure enclosed by five joined foils; *specif* : a 5-lobed foliation in Gothic tracery **3** : a conventionalized heraldic flower showing five lobelike petals

cinquefoil 2

cinque·foiled \-ld\ *adj* : made like a cinquefoil : made with a cinquefoil or cinquefoils
cinque·pace \ˈsiŋk(ə)pās\ *or* **cinque·pas** \-,pas, saⁿk(ə)päˈ\ *n*, *pl* **cinquepaces** \-āsə̇z\ *or* **cinquepas** \-pas,-päˈ\ [alter. of earlier *cinquepas*, fr. MF *cinq pas*, fr. *cinq* five + *pas* dance step, pace — more at CINQUE, PACE] : a 16th century dance with steps regulated by the number five prob. related to the galliard
cion *var of* SCION
cion- *or* **ciono-** *comb form* [NL, fr. Gk *kion-*, *kiono-*, fr. *kion-*, *kiōn* pillar, uvula] **1** : uvula ⟨*cionitis*⟩ ⟨*cionotomy*⟩ **2** : pillar ⟨*cionocranial*⟩
ci·o·na \ˈsīənə\ *n*, *cap* [NL, fr. Gk *kion-*, *kiōn* pillar; akin to Arm *siun* pillar] : a genus (coextensive with the family Cionidae) comprising relatively large simple ascidians and including a single cosmopolitan species (*C. intestinalis*) — **ci·o·nid** \ˈsīənə̇d, -,nid\ *adj or n*
ci·o·no·cranial \,sīənō+\ *or* **ci·o·no·cranian** \"+\ *adj* [*cion-* + *cranial*] : having a rodlike epipterygoid bone in the skull — used of some lizards
¹cioppino *obs var of* CHOPINE
²ciop·pi·no \chəˈpē(,)nō\ *n* -S [It] : a dish of fish and shellfish cooked in tomato sauce and usu. seasoned with wine, spices, and herbs
¹ci·pher \ˈsīfə(r)\ *n* -S *often attrib* [ME, fr. MF *cifre*, fr. ML *cifra* zero, fr. Ar *ṣifr* empty, cipher, zero] **1** : the symbol 0 denoting the absence of all magnitude or quantity : NAUGHT, ZERO — see NUMBER table **2 a** : a method of transforming a text in order to conceal its meaning (1) by systematically replacing the letters of the plaintext by substitutes in the same sequence either singly or in pairs or other polygraphs (as by writing 1 for A, 2 for B, etc., or F for A, S for B, etc., or QL for AB, etc.) or (2) by systematically rearranging the plaintext letters into another sequence (as by writing them normally in a rectangle and then copying them off from the columns taken in an arbitrary succession) — called also respectively (1) *substitution cipher* and (2) *transposition cipher;* compare CODE 3 **b** : a prescription for a cipher system : a key or memorandum that enables decipherment **c** : a message in cipher : a text in secret writing **3** : an arabic numeral : NUMBER, FIGURE **4 a** *obs* : a symbolic character (as a letter, hieroglyph, or astrological sign) **b** : a combination of symbolic letters; *esp* : the interwoven initials of a name : DEVICE, MONOGRAM ⟨an engraver's ~⟩ **c** : a sign in Karl Jaspers' existentialism serving to mediate between the existent and the transcendent **5** : one that has no weight, worth, or influence : NONENTITY ⟨doomed to die as a ~ in some vast statistical operation in which our teeth would be counted . . . but our death itself would be unknown — Norman Mailer⟩ **6** : the sounding of an organ pipe caused by a mechanical defect

cipher 4b: the initials represented are Noah Webster's

²cipher \"\ *vb* **ciphered; ciphered; ciphering** \-f(ə)riŋ\ **ciphers** *vi* **1** : to use figures in a mathematical process : do sums in arithmetic : FIGURE **2** : to produce a cipher — used of an organ pipe ~ *vt* **1 a** *archaic* : to express (as thoughts or words) by written or graven characters **b** *obs* : to show forth : make plain by visible evidence : PORTRAY **c** : ENCIPHER **d** *obs* : DECIPHER **2** *in shipbuilding* : BEVEL, CHAMFER **3 a** : to compute in figures : calculate or figure arithmetically — sometimes used with *out* ⟨a sum ~*ed* out⟩ **b** *dial* : to figure out as if by calculation : solve by pondering
cipher clerk *n* : a person who routinely encrypts and decrypts messages — called also *code clerk*
cipher component *or* **cipher sequence** *n* : the sequence of a substitution alphabet that identifies the ciphertext letters — compare ALPHABET 1j
cipher disk *or* **cipher wheel** *n* : a device for enciphering and deciphering in substitution cipher consisting of two movable concentric disks with the letters of the alphabet written around the margin of each
ci·pher·dom \-fə(r)dəm\ *n* -S : the state of being a nonentity
ci·pher·er \-fərə(r)\ *n* -S : one that ciphers : one skilled in the use of cipher
cipher machine *n* : an enciphering and deciphering instrument : CRYPTOGRAPH; *esp* : one that telegraphs or prints its output — see CONVERTER e (1)
cipher square *n* : VIGENÈRE TABLEAU
ciphertext \ˈ==,=\ *n* : the cipher form of a text or of its elements ⟨this message looks like ~⟩ ⟨in the Playfair scheme no ~ J is possible⟩ — compare PLAINTEXT; ³C 4
ci·po \sēˈpō\ *n* -S [Sp *cipó*, *sipó*, *isipó*, fr. Guarani *icipó*] : LIANA
cipo·lin \ˈsipələn, ¦sēpəˈlaⁿ\ *or* **ci·pol·li·no** \,chēpəˈlē(,)nō\ *n* -S [F & It; F *cipolin*, fr. It *cipollino*, dim. of *cipolla* onion, fr. LL *cepulla*, dim. of L *cepa*, *cepe* onion] : a light-colored Roman marble containing layers of micaceous minerals and abundant silicates
ci·pol·let·ti weir \¦chēpə¦led·ē-\ *n*, *usu cap C* [after Cesare *Cipolletti*, 20th cent. Ital. engineer] : a weir that is trapezoidal in shape with the sides inclining outward from the base
cippi *pl of* CIPPUS
cip·pus \ˈsipəs\ *n*, *pl* **cip·pi** \-,pī\ [L — more at CEPE] : a small low pillar usu. inscribed and used in ancient Rome and Greece as a gravestone or landmark
cir *or* **circ** *abbr* **1** circa **2** circle; circular **3** circuit **4** circulation **5** circumference
¹cir·ca \ˈsərkə, ˈkir(,)kä\ *prep* [L, fr. *circum* round about — more at CIRCUM-] : ABOUT, AROUND — often used with numerals ⟨~ 1740⟩ — abbr. *ca*, *c*
²circa \"\ *n* -S : APPROXIMATION ⟨a ~ of reasonable probability —George Saintsbury⟩
cir·caea \(,)sərˈsēə\ *n*, *cap* [NL, fr. L, fem. of *Circaeus* of Circe — more at CIRCEAN] : a genus of low perennial herbs (family Onagraceae) with whitish to roseate flowers in racemes and an indehiscent fruit covered with bristly hooked hairs that are widely distributed in cool and temperate regions of the northern hemisphere and that comprise the enchanter's nightshades
circ·aetus \(,)sərˈkādəs\ *n*, *cap* [NL, fr. Gk *kirkos* hawk + NL *-aëtus*; akin to L *crocire* to croak (as of a raven), Skt *krkara*, a kind of partridge, OE *hringan* to ring — more at RING] : a genus of large Old World hawks intermediate in characters between the eagles and the harriers
circar *often cap*, *var of* SIRCAR
¹cir·cas·sian \(,)sərˈkashən, səˈ-,sə̇ˈ-, -aash-,-aish-\ *n* -S *cap* [*Circassia*, region in Russia (fr. NL or ML, alter. of Russ *Cherkes* Circassian + L *-ia*) + E *-an*] **1** : a member of a group of peoples of the Caucasus of Caucasian race but not of Indo-European speech noted for their physical beauty and being tall with oval face, brown eyes, and chestnut hair **2** : the North Caucasic language of the Circassian peoples
²circassian \¦==¦==\ *adj*, *usu cap* : of, relating to, or characteristic of Circassia or the Circassians
circassian seed *n*, *usu cap C* : the seed of a red sandalwood tree (*Adenanthera pavonina*) used for ornament in the Orient
circassian walnut *n*, *usu cap C* **1** : the light-brown but irregularly black-veined wood of the English walnut much used for veneer and cabinetwork **2** : ENGLISH WALNUT
circe *abbr* circumstance
cir·ce·an \ˈsərsēən, ,sərˈs-\ *adj*, *usu cap* [L *circaeus* (fr. *Circe*, sorceress deity who transformed men into beasts, fr. Gk *Kirkē*) + E *-an*] **1** : relating to or resembling Circe **2** : having the quality of a fascinating sorceress : dangerously or fatally attractive or misleading : LULLING
cir·cen·sian \(,)sərˈsenchən\ *adj*, *sometimes cap* [L *circensis* of the circus (fr. *circus*) + E *-an* — more at CIRCUS] : of or relating to the Circus in ancient Rome
cir·ci·nate \ˈsərsᵊn,āt\ *adj* [L *circinatus*, past part. of *circinare* to make round, fr. *circinus* pair of compasses, fr. *circus* circle] : rounded in outline: as **a** : characterized by or having the form of a flat coil of which the apex is the center ⟨the retracted tongue of a butterfly forms a ~ coil⟩ — used esp. of arrangements of plant parts in vernation and of developing fern fronds ⟨~ bracken fronds unfolding⟩; see SCORPIOID **b** *med*, *of lesions* : having a sharply circumscribed and somewhat circular margin — **cir·ci·nate·ly** *adv*
circingle *var of* SURCINGLE
cir·ci·ter \ˈsərsəd·ər, ˈkirkə,te(ə)r\ *prep* [L] : ABOUT
¹cir·cle \ˈsərkəl, -ōk-,-əik-\ *n* -S [alter. (influenced by L *circulus*) of ME *cercle*, fr. OF, fr. L *circulus*, dim. of *circus* ring, fr. or akin to Gk *kirkos*, *krikos* ring; perh. akin to Lith *kreĩvas* crooked, Russ *kriv'*, Gk *korōnē* ring — more at CROWN] **1 a** : a bright ring (as around the moon) : HALO **b** : a closed plane curve every point of which is equidistant from a fixed point within the curve : CIRCUMFERENCE, RING — see DIAMETER, RADIUS **c** : the plane surface bounded by such a curve — see AREA table, PI 2a **2 a** *obs* : the sphere in which a celestial body was thought to revolve **b** : the orbit of revolution of such a sphere **c** : the period of revolution through the orbit of such a sphere **3** : something having the shape of a closed curve or a section of one; as: **a** : RING, CIRCLET **b** : CROWN, DIADEM **c** : an instrument of astronomical observation the graduated limb of which consists of an entire circle **d** : a balcony or tier of seats in a theater or opera house **e** : a group of people (as dancers) or things (as stones, campfires) forming a ring **f** : a circle of latitude or longitude **g** : a small circular park or garden **h** : ROTARY **4** : something having the shape of an area enclosed by a circle: as **a** : a circus ring **b** : a round plate or sheet ⟨cutting cloth into ~*s*⟩ **5 a** *obs* : a region thought of as bounded by a circle ⟨in the ~ of this forest —Shak.⟩ **b** : an area of action or influence : REALM — compare SPHERE **6 a** : a series ending at its starting point : CYCLE, ROUND ⟨the ~ of 24 hours⟩ ⟨the wheel has come full ~⟩ **b** *logic* : fallacious reasoning in which something that ostensibly is being proved or demonstrated is taken for granted or covertly assumed esp. in the premises ⟨arguments in a ~ are instances of begging the question⟩ **7 a** : things grouped in or as if in a system of coordinate members ⟨a ~ of sciences⟩ **b** : a group of people thought of as held together by a common point of interest ⟨theatrical ~*s*⟩ : an exclusive group : COTERIE, CLIQUE, ELITE ⟨the gossip of court ~*s*⟩ ⟨the charmed ~ of 20-game winners⟩ **c** : a chapter or local group of any of various societies **8 a** : territorial or administrative division or district: **a** : any one of the 10 territorial divisions of Germany under the Holy Roman Empire **b** : KREIS **c** : a district in India for the issue of government paper currency **9** *bookbinding* : ROLL **10 a** : a circular course or path of movement; *specif* : the operation of rounding up cattle ⟨he would . . . take the lead for the morning's ~ —Will James⟩

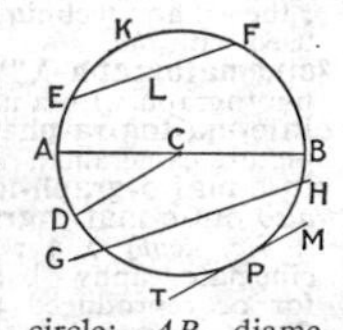

circle: *AB* diameter; *C* center; *CD*, *CA*, *CB* radii; *EKF* arc on chord *EF; ACD* (area) sector; *GH* secant; *TPM* tangent at point *P; EKFBPDAE* circumference

²circle \"\ *vb* **circled; circled; circling** \-k(ə)liŋ\ **circles** [ME *cerclen*, fr. *cercle*, n.] *vt* **1** : to enclose in or as if in a circle : form a circle or oval around ⟨the gridiron was *circled* with a cinder track⟩; *specif* : to draw a circle around for special attention (as for correction or deletion) ⟨~ the misspelled words⟩ **2 a** : to move or revolve around : travel around or traverse so as to describe a circle, arc, or curved figure ⟨fast planes *circling* the earth⟩ **b** : to cause to move in a circle **c** : to proceed in an arc or curve around (as for avoiding or eluding) ⟨the ship *circled* the cape⟩ ⟨~ an opposing end in football⟩ **3** : to form into a circle : make circular ~ *vi* **1 a** : to move around or proceed in or as if in a circle or circles ⟨~ around over a landing strip⟩; *sometimes* : to meander or proceed aimlessly ⟨grass-mounds where water *circled*, running from scoops and cups to curves and brook streams —George Meredith⟩ ⟨winding and *circling*, at last it reaches a conclusion from some point unforeseen —H.O. Taylor⟩ **b** : CIRCULATE **c** : to turn in a usu. wide loop esp. in reversing one's course — often used with *back* ⟨~ back toward home⟩ **2** : to form, describe, or extend in a circle ⟨the lighthouse sent out its slow steady *circling* beam —R.O. Bowen⟩ **syn** see SURROUND, TURN
circle brick *n* : an arc-shaped brick used in making arches or other curved forms
circle dance *n* : a dance in which the dancers join hands and move in a circular direction; *esp* : a dance in which women form a circle and move clockwise, men form a circle around them and move counterclockwise, the man and woman opposite one another when the music stops becoming partners for the next dance
circle eight *n*, *figure skating* : a figure comprised of two tangent circles, the first usu. skated on the right foot, the second on the left foot
circle graph *n* : PIE CHART
circle of ap·ol·lo·nius \-,apəˈlōnyəs, -nēəs\ *usu cap A* [after *Apollonius* of Perga, 3d cent. B.C. Greek mathematician] : a circle that is the locus of points the ratio of whose distances from two given fixed points is constant
circle of confusion : the indistinct circular patch formed by a lens representing the out-of-focus image of a single object point — called also *blur circle;* compare CIRCLE OF LEAST CONFUSION
circle of curvature : the osculating circle of a curve
circle of fifths : keys or tonalities ordered by ascending (for sharp keys) or descending (for flat keys) intervals of a fifth
circle of latitude 1 : a great circle perpendicular to the plane of the ecliptic **2** : a meridian of the terrestrial sphere along which latitude is measured; *sometimes* : PARALLEL OF LATITUDE
circle of least confusion *physics* : the minimum cross section of a symmetrical bundle of rays that have no common focus because of spherical aberration
circle of position *navigation* : a circle on the earth whose center is the point directly under a celestial body and whose radius is the zenith distance of the celestial body, the observer's location being somewhere on this circle — compare SUMNER LINE
circle of wil·lis \-ˈwilə̇s\ *usu cap W* [after Thomas *Willis* †1675 Eng. anatomist who described it] : a complete ring of arteries formed by the anastomosing branches of the carotid and basilar arteries at the base of the brain
circle rider *n* : one of a group of cowpunchers who cover a range in search of cattle by riding from outlying points to a central meeting place
circle shear *n* : a machine that cuts circular disks by rotating the sheet stock between cutting wheels
cir·clet \ˈsərklə̇t, -ōk-,-əik-\ *n* -S [ME *serclett* ornamental band, fr. MF *cerclet*, dim. of *cercle*] **1 a** : a little circle; *esp* : an ornament for the person having the form of a circle **b** : something that encircles (as a ring, a bracelet, or a headband) **c** : a circular or oval ring about the central medallion of a badge of an order of knighthood or a baronet's badge usu. inscribed with the motto of the order; *also* : a representation of this ring placed about the escutcheon in the coat of arms of a knight or baronet **2** : a small horseshoe-shaped tubelet of steel driven into the top lift of a shoe heel to lessen wear
circle turn *n* : a turn in ballroom dancing in which the feet of the couple trace a circle
circ·line \ˈsər,klīn\ *n* -S [prob. blend of *circle* and *line*] : a fluorescent lamp in the form of a ring
circling *pres part of* CIRCLE
circling disease *n* [so called fr. the typical circling ambulations of affected animals] : listerellosis of sheep or cattle
circ·o·var·i·an \,sərk+\ *adj* [*circ-* (irreg. fr. *circum-*) + *ovarian*] : around the ovary
circs \sōks\ *n pl* [by shortening] *chiefly Brit* : CIRCUMSTANCES ⟨I hope to see you again in better ~⟩
¹cir·cuit \ˈsərkə̇t, -ōk-,-əik-, *usu* -kə̇d·+V\ *n* -S *often attrib* [ME, fr. MF *circuite*, fr. L *circuitus*, fr. past part. of *circuire*, *circumire* to go around, fr. *circum-* + *ire* to go — more at ISSUE] **1 a** : a usu. more or less circular line encompassing an area : CIRCUMFERENCE ⟨a swamp about 10 miles in ~⟩ **b** : the course around the four bases in baseball ⟨he hit for the ~⟩ **2** : the act of moving around typically in an orbit or a circular course : a circular route : a course around a periphery : REVOLUTION ⟨the periodic ~ of the earth around the sun⟩ ⟨the sightseeing newcomer makes the ~ of the state —*Amer. Guide Series: Fla.*⟩ **3 a** : a roundabout way : a circuitous or indirect course ⟨describing a ~ rather than a straight course⟩ **b** *obs* : roundabout speech : CIRCUMLOCUTION **4** : space enclosed within a circumference or periphery : AREA, SCOPE ⟨the ~ of the duke's lands⟩ **5 a** : an appointed or accustomed course from place to place in following a calling ⟨the old "mail rider", who was just returning on his ~ of twenty-six miles —Ellen Glasgow⟩ **b** : the route of a traveling judge or preacher around a district or territory assigned to him ⟨lawyers rode the ~*s* like the backwoods preachers of the day —*Amer. Guide Series: Tenn.*⟩ **c** : a judicial district legally established ⟨the state shall be divided into thirteen circuits —*W.Va.Constitution*⟩; *also* : the judges and lawyers making a circuit **d** : a group of church congregations ministered to or under the supervision of one pastor (as in the Methodist Church) **6 a** : the complete path of an electric current including any displacement current **b** : a specified portion of a circuit ⟨external ~⟩ ⟨generator ~⟩ **c** : the region through which the magnetic flux from any source extends esp. when largely confined within a ferromagnetic body (as a magnet) **7 a** : ASSOCIATION, CONFERENCE, LEAGUE ⟨baseball ~⟩ ⟨football ~⟩ **b** : a series of harness races held at associated tracks according to a more or less permanent schedule **c** : a group of motion-picture theaters owned by one company **d** : a number of associated theaters at which productions are presented in turn **e** : an association, ring, or coterie sharing common interests or similar practices and gathering or performing at various places at different times ⟨the nightclub ~⟩ ⟨the small college ~⟩ **8 a** : an assemblage of electronic elements : HOOKUP **b** : a system for two-way communication between two places (as by telegraph, telephone, or radio) **9** : a closed path followed by a fluid in a mechanical system ⟨hydraulic ~⟩ ⟨oil ~⟩
²circuit \"\ *vb* -ED/-ING/-S *vt* : to make a circuit about ⟨an automobile route ~*ing* the Back Bay section of Portland —*Amer. Guide Series: Maine*⟩ : go or move in a circuit about ~ *vi* : to go or move over a circuit ⟨while five of my brethren are ~*ing* about the state —O.W.Holmes †1935⟩
cir·cuit·al \-kə̇d·ᵊl\ *adj* : concerning a circuit : resembling a circuit
circuital field *n* : a vector field having the nature of a circuit ⟨the *circuital field* of a magnet⟩
circuit binding *n* : DIVINITY CIRCUIT BINDING
circuit breaker *n* : a switch that automatically interrupts an electric circuit under an infrequent abnormal condition (as overload)
circuit court *n* : a court that sits at two or more places within one judicial district: as **a** : an English court authorized by commission from the crown that is held in one of the seven circuits of the kingdom by a judge designated by the lord chancellor to hold assizes to try civil and criminal cases **b** : any of several courts in the U.S.: as (1) : a court of original common-law jurisdiction sitting with a jury (2) : an intermediate appellate court (3) : a court with both original and appellate jurisdiction (4) : a court having equity or probate jurisdiction or both (5) : any of the U.S. courts of appeal — not used technically (6) : a former court of original jurisdiction existing in each of the seven judicial circuits of the U.S. and its territories until abolished by law in 1912
circuit edges *n pl* : the projecting flaps in a divinity circuit binding
cir·cui·teer \¦sərkə¦ti(ə)r\ *vi* -ED/-ING/-S *archaic* : to travel in a circuit
circuit element *n* **1** : a part of an electric circuit or network (as a generator, switch, lamp, or vacuum tube) **2** : one of the three quantitative attributes (resistance, inductance, capacitance) characteristic of an electric circuit
cir·cuit·er \ˈ=kə̇d·ər\ *also* **cir·cui·teer** \¦=kə¦ti(ə)r\ *n* -S : one that makes or travels a circuit (as the judge of an English circuit court)
cir·cu·i·tion \,sərkyəˈwishən\ *n* -S [L *circuition-*, *circuitio*, fr. *circuitus* (past part. of *circuire* to go around) + *-ion-*, *-io* -ion — more at CIRCUIT] **1** *archaic* : the act of circuiting **2** *archaic* : a circuitous mode of reasoning or arguing : CIRCUMLOCUTION
circuit judge *n* : a judge who holds a circuit court
cir·cuit·or \ˈsərkə̇d·ər\ *n* -S [L, fr. *circuitus* (past part. of *circuire*) + *-or*] *archaic* : one that makes a circuit
cir·cu·i·tous \,sər¦kyüəd·əs, (ˈ)sə̇¦-,(ˈ)səi¦-, ,sə(r)ˈk-, -ətəs\ *adj* [ML *circuitosus*, fr. L *circuitus* circuit + *-osus* -ous —

more at CIRCUIT] **1 :** being a circular or winding course **:** INDIRECT, ROUNDABOUT ⟨two lines possible — the one direct by sea, the other ~ through Gaul —A.T.Mahan⟩ ⟨in one ~ mile through the business district it [the San Antonio river] ends up less than eight hundred yards from where it started —Green Peyton⟩ **2 :** marked by roundabout, indirect, or devious procedure ⟨~ actions⟩ **:** not forthright, direct, or to the point ⟨~ in speech⟩ — **cir·cu·i·tous·ly** *adv* — **cir·cu·i·tous·ness** *n* -ES

circuit rider *n* **:** a typically Methodist preacher assigned to a circuit esp. on the frontier

cir·cuit·ry \ˈsərkə̇trē, -ə̇k-,-əik-, -tri\ *n* -ES **1 :** the detailed plan of an electric circuit or network (as of a radio or television receiver) **2 :** the components of an electric circuit or network (as tubes and resistors)

circuits *pl of* CIRCUIT, *pres 3d sing of* CIRCUIT

circuit steward *n* **:** a church official of certain Methodist bodies charged with ushering and advising the minister and church board concerning the temporal interests of the circuit

cir·cu·i·ty \ˌsər-ˈkyüəd·ē, ˌsər'k-\ *n* -ES [irreg. fr. *circuit*] **:** roundabout circuitous procedure **:** INDIRECTION **:** lack of straightforwardness ⟨mired so deeply in its own complicated ~ of words —C.O.Gregory⟩

circuity of action : an unnecessarily long course of proceedings

cir·cu·lant \ˈsərkyələnt, -ə̇k-,|-əik-\ *n* -S [L *circulant-, circulans,* pres. part. of *circulare* to make round — more at CIRCULATE] **:** a mathematical determinant in which each row is derived from the preceding by cyclic permutation, each constituent being pushed into the next column and the last into the first so that constituents of the principal diagonal are all the same

[1]**cir·cu·lar** \ˈsərkyələr, ˈsə̄kyələ(r, ˈsəik-\ *adj* [alter. (influenced by LL *circularis*) of earlier *circuler*, fr. ME, fr. MF *circuler, circulier*, fr. LL *circularis*, fr. L *circulus* circle — more at CIRCLE] **1 a :** having the exact or approximate form or outline of a circle **:** ROUND ⟨a ~ orbit⟩ ⟨a ~ cavity⟩ ⟨a ~ area⟩ **b :** made in round shape or tubular form **:** so made as to form a circle when spread flat ⟨a ~ cape⟩ **2 :** marked by motion in a circle ⟨a ~ dance⟩ **:** describing a circle or spiral ⟨a ~ staircase⟩ **:** going in a circle **:** operating with a circular arrangement ⟨a ~ machine for knitting⟩ **3 :** relating to the circle or its properties ⟨a ~ arc⟩ **4** *obs* **:** PERFECT, COMPLETE **5 :** CIRCUITOUS, INDIRECT ⟨a ~ treatment of the problem⟩ **6 :** marked by or similar to reasoning or arguing in a circle ⟨paucity of evidence tends to make the arguments ~ —*Times Lit. Supp.*⟩ **7 :** marked by or moving in a cycle of repetition **8 :** intended for circulation either widely or within a particular group ⟨a subcommittee drafted a ~ letter to all the disaffected groups⟩ — **cir·cu·lar·ly** *adv* — **cir·cu·lar·ness** *n* -ES

[2]**circular** \"\ *n* -S **1 :** an announcement, advertisement, or directive typically in the form of a printed leaflet intended to be sent to many persons or otherwise distributed widely ⟨the first government ~ relative to the medical examination of aviators —H.G.Armstrong⟩ ⟨a ~ to be sent to the police of the areas in which the twenty-nine men lived —F.W.Crofts⟩ **2** *also* **circular cloak :** a long full often fur-lined cape popular in the 19th century

circular canal *n* **:** a canal running around the circumference of the bell of a jellyfish

circular canon *n* **1 :** a musical canon in which the subject leads back to its own beginning so that it may be endlessly repeated — called also *perpetual canon* **2 :** a canon in which the repetitions modulate through a succession of fifths

circular error *n* **:** the error in a timepiece resulting from variations in extent of the arc described by a pendulum

circular flow *n* **:** the continuing and recurrent transfers of money and goods among producers and consumers

circular function *n* **:** TRIGONOMETRIC FUNCTION

circular insanity *or* **circular psychosis** *n* **:** manic-depressive psychosis specif. involving the alternation of manic and depressive states

cir·cu·lar·i·ty \ˌsərkyəˈlarəd·ē, -ə̇k-,-əik-, -ətē, -i *also* -ler-\ *n* -ES [ML *circularitas*, fr. LL *circularis* circular + L *-itas* -ity — more at CIRCULAR] **:** the quality or state of being circular esp. in thought or expression

cir·cu·lar·i·za·tion \ˌsərkyələrə̇ˈzāshən, -ə̇k-, -əik-, -ˌrīˈz-\ *n* -S **:** the act of circularizing

cir·cu·lar·ize \ˈsərkyələˌrīz, -ə̇k-,-əik-\ *vt* -ED/ -ING/ -S *see -ize in Explan Notes* **1 a :** to send circulars to **:** ply with circulars ⟨all the retail outlets were *circularized* well ahead of time⟩ **b :** to send questionnaires to **:** poll by questioning **:** ascertain the knowledge or beliefs of (a number of persons) ⟨farmers, who were recently *circularized* on the subject, indicated that they wanted 200,000 additional tractors —D.C.McKay⟩ **2 :** to announce or advertise by circular or circulars **:** PUBLICIZE ⟨took the unusual step of seeing that this opinion was *circularized* throughout the United States —C.B.Swisher⟩

circular–knit \ˈ≈≈≈ˈ≈\ *adj* **:** knitted in tubular form by machine and usu. later shaped or cut ⟨*circular-knit* sweaters and seamless hosiery⟩ — contrasted with *flat-knit*

circular knitting machine *n* **:** a machine with needles and yarn feeds arranged in a circle for knitting fabrics, hosiery, sweaters, and underwear

circular level *n* **:** BOX LEVEL

circular measure *n* **:** the measure of an angle in radians

circular mil *n* **:** a unit of area used esp. for the cross section of wire equal to the area of a circle having a diameter of one mil and equivalent to 0.000000785 square inch

circular note *n* **:** LETTER OF CREDIT

circular pitch *n* **:** the distance between corresponding points of consecutive gear teeth measured along the pitch circle

circular plane *n* **:** a woodworking plane with flexible face adjustable for planing convex or concave surfaces — called also *compass plane*

circular reaction *or* **circular response** *n, psychol* **:** a chain reflex in which the final response acts as stimulus for the initial response

circular saw *n* **:** a saw in the form of a thin steel disk with teeth on its periphery that revolves upon a spindle

circular sinus *n* **:** a circular venous channel at the base of the brain formed by the intercavernous sinuses

circular tale *n* **:** a factitious jocular narrative indefinitely repeated in which the last element leads to repetition of the first

circular tour *n, Brit* **:** ROUND TRIP

circular vamp *n* **:** a shoe vamp that covers the forepart of the foot and extends to the shank

circular velocity *n* **:** VELOCITY OF CIRCULATION

circular saws

cir·cu·late \ˈsərkyəˌlāt, ˈsə̄k-,ˈsəik-, *usu* -ād·+V\ *vb* -ED/-ING/-S [L *circulatus*, past part. of *circulari, circulare* to go around in a circle, make round, fr. *circulus* circle — more at CIRCLE] *vi* **1** *of a vital fluid* **:** to flow or become propelled naturally (as of blood, lymph, or sap) **2 :** to move in a circle, circuit, or orbit **:** move along a course having curves or bends; *esp* **:** to move around and return to the same point ⟨steam *circulating* through the pipes⟩ ⟨the wine decanter *circulated* around the table⟩ **3 :** to move, pass, or go around freely from person to person or from place to place: **a :** to move or flow without obstruction ⟨air *circulating* through the boards being seasoned⟩ **b :** to spread widely **:** become widespread **:** become known or familiar to many ⟨the news made its way up to Airlie and *circulated* through the village —William Black⟩ ⟨the obscene tales that *circulated* so widely in the Italian Renaissance —R.A.Hall b. 1911⟩ **c :** to go from person to person or group to group greeting, chatting, and talking ⟨our host and hostess *circulated* diligently from guest to guest —Nora Waln⟩ ⟨no one can ~ among members of Congress without hearing frequent and sharp criticism —Harold Zink⟩ **d :** to come into the hands of readers; *often* **:** to become sold or distributed ⟨the satire, *circulating* in manuscript copies, had a great local vogue —E.V.Lucas⟩ ⟨these magazines ~ mostly in rural areas⟩ ~ *vt* **1** *chem, obs* **:** to subject to continuous redistillation in a closed vessel **2 :** to cause to move in a circle or circuit **:** REVOLVE, ROTATE ⟨fans ~ the air through the pipes⟩ **3 :** to cause to pass from person to person and usu. to become widely known **:** DISSEMINATE ⟨this evidence of weakening enemy morale was instantly *circulated* to our own people —D.D.Eisenhower⟩ **syn** see SPREAD

circulating assets *n pl* **:** CURRENT ASSETS

circulating capital *n* **:** capital consumed in the process of production (as fuel, power, and raw materials) — contrasted with *fixed capital*

circulating decimal *n* **:** REPEATING DECIMAL

circulating fan *n* **:** a motor-driven fan used to maintain air circulation (as in a building, automobile, or air-conditioning system)

circulating library *n* **1 :** RENTAL LIBRARY **2 :** a collection of books rotated among a group of institutions (as small public libraries or schools)

circulating medium *n* **:** a medium of exchange (as coin, bank notes, or government notes) that passes from hand to hand without endorsement

cir·cu·la·tion \ˌsərkyəˈlāshən, -ə̇k-,-əik-\ *n* -S [MF or L; MF, fr. L *circulation-, circulatio*, fr. *circulatus* + *-ion-, -io* -ion] **1 :** movement or passage in a circuit or other curving or bending course typically with return to a starting point ⟨~ of air through the building⟩ ⟨~ of water in the lake⟩ **2 :** the orderly movement of liquid or dissolved matter through a living body: **a :** the movement of blood through the vessels of the body that is induced by the pumping action of the heart and serves to distribute nutrients and oxygen to and remove waste products from all parts of the body; in man, other mammals, and birds being double, the blood making two distinct circuits and the arterial and venous blood being completely separated by capillary networks; in amphibians and reptiles the circuits being imperfect with some mixing of blood in the single ventricle; and in fishes, a single circuit occurring, the blood passing over the gills and thence to the tissues and back to the heart — see PULMONARY CIRCULATION, SYSTEMIC CIRCULATION **b :** analogous movement of fluid through defined channels and tissue spaces in the bodies of various invertebrates **c :** the flow of sap in a plant **3** *obs* **:** continuous repetition of actions in a set order ⟨a daily ~ of sorrow —Daniel Defoe⟩ **4 :** the act of circulating or being circulated **:** passage or transmission from person to person or place to place: **a :** popular dissemination **:** DISTRIBUTION **:** widespread transmission ⟨the book had wide ~ and its first publication was followed by many successive editions —J.T.Howard⟩ ⟨the report which was in general ~ within five minutes after his entrance —Jane Austen⟩ **b :** passage of money or other means of exchange from person to person throughout a group or society ⟨calling in gold coins in ~⟩ **:** money so circulated **:** CURRENCY ⟨the ~ was again so worn and clipped that the sixth recoinage followed —John Craig⟩ **5 a :** the average number of copies of a publication sold or less frequently distributed over a given period ⟨a country paper with little more than five hundred ~ —W.A.White⟩ **b :** the number of persons exposed to an advertisement or sales message by the use of a certain advertising medium; *esp* **:** potential audience with available receiving sets ⟨the ~ of a radio program⟩ ⟨increasing TV ~⟩ **6 a :** the elements of communication within a building (as foyers, halls, corridors, stairways, and elevators) **b :** unhindered passage or motion about an area ⟨this arrangement of doors permits easy ~⟩ ⟨a parking garage with free ~ of cars⟩ **7 :** the line integral of a vector field around a closed curve **8 a :** the lending of books or other library materials for outside use **b :** the total number of items taken by borrowers from a library **c :** a single borrowing of a library book ⟨a strong binding good for 100 ~s⟩ **9 :** free active social life with different persons or groups ⟨getting back into ~ after her divorce⟩

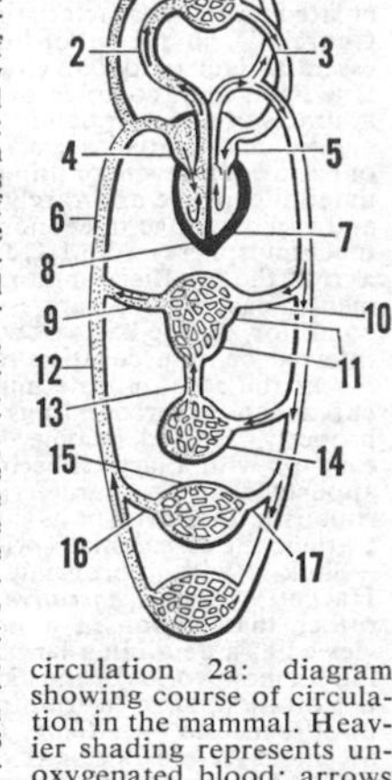

circulation 2a: diagram showing course of circulation in the mammal. Heavier shading represents unoxygenated blood; arrows indicate direction of flow. *1* capillaries of head, *2* pulmonary arteries, *3* pulmonary veins, *4* right auricle, *5* left auricle, *6, 12* postcaval veins, *7* left ventricle, *8* right ventricle, *9* hepatic vein, *10* hepatic artery, *11* capillaries of the liver, *13* portal vein, *14* capillaries of digestive tract, *15* capillaries of kidney, *16* renal veins, *17* renal arteries

cir·cu·la·tive \ˈ≈≈ˌlā|d·iv, -ˌlə|, |tiv\ *adj* [L *circulatus* (past part. of *circulari*) + E *-ive*] **:** marked by circulation **:** CIRCULATING **:** promoting circulation

cir·cu·la·tor \-ˌlād·ə(r), -ātə-\ *n* -S [L, peddler, mountebank, fr. *circulatus* (past part. of *circulari* to go around) + *-or* — more at CIRCULATE] **:** one that circulates: **a** *obs* **:** MOUNTEBANK, QUACK **b :** GOSSIP, SCANDALMONGER **c :** a machine for circulating fluids or heating by convection **d :** a worker in a copper refinery who maintains circulation in electrolysis tanks and removes copper incrustations

[1]**cir·cu·la·to·ry** \-ləˌtōrē, -ór-, -ri\ *n* -ES [NL *circulatorium*, fr. L *circulatus* + *-orium* -ory] *chem, obs* **:** a vessel (as a pelican) in which to circulate liquids

[2]**circulatory** \"\ *adj* [prob. fr. NL *circulatorius*, fr. L *circulatus* + *-orius* -ory — more at CIRCULATE] **1 :** of or relating to circulation (as of the blood, air, or traffic) **:** causing or concerned in circulation **2** *chem, obs* **:** of or relating to the process of circulating liquids

circulatory system *n* **:** the system of blood, blood vessels, lymphatics, and heart concerned with the circulation of the blood and lymph

cir·cu·lin \ˈsərkyələ̇n\ *n* -S [NL *circulans* (specific epithet of NL *Bacillus circulans*) + E *-in*] **:** an antibiotic consisting of a mixture of polypeptides related to polymyxin that is obtained from a soil bacterium (*Bacillus circulans*) and is active esp. against gram-negative bacteria (as colon bacilli)

cir·cu·lus \-ləs\ *n, pl* **circu·li** \-ˌlī\ [NL, fr. L, circle — more at CIRCLE] **:** one of the usu. concentric ridges on a fish scale each representing an increment of growth

circulus in de·fin·i·en·do \-ˌində̇ˌfinēˈen(ˌ)dō\ *n* [NL, circle in definition] *logic* **:** a vicious circle in definition

circulus in pro·ban·do \-prōˈban(ˌ)dō\ *n* [NL] *logic* **:** a circle in proof — compare CIRCLE 6b

cir·cum \ˈsərkəm, ˈkirkəm\ *prep* [L] **:** AROUND, ABOUT, SURROUNDING

circum- *in pronunciations below,* ˈ≈≈ = ˈsərkəm *or* -ə̇k- *or* -əik-\ *prefix* [OF or L; OF, fr. L, fr. *circum* round about, fr. *circus* circle — more at CIRCLE] **1** *adverbially* **:** around **:** about **:** on all sides ⟨*circum*rotate⟩ ⟨*circum*gyration⟩ **2** *prepositionally* **:** around **:** surrounding ⟨*circum*basal⟩ ⟨*circum*corneal⟩ ⟨*circum*lunar⟩ **:** revolving around ⟨*circum*solar⟩ **3 :** circumscribed ⟨*circum*polygon⟩

cir·cum·ambages \ˈ≈≈+\ *n pl* [*circum-* + *ambages*, pl. of *ambage*] **:** instances of indirectness or deviousness in speaking or writing **:** CIRCUMLOCUTIONS — **cir·cum·ambagious** \ˈ≈≈+\ *adj*

cir·cum·ambience *or* **cir·cum·ambiency** \ˈ≈≈+\ *n, pl* **circumambiences** *or* **circumambiencies :** the quality or state of being circumambient

cir·cum·ambient \ˈ≈≈+\ *adj* [LL *circumambient-, circumambiens*, pres. part. of *circumambire* to surround in a circle, fr. L *circum-* + *ambire* to go around — more at AMBIENT] **1 :** going around **:** ENCIRCLING ⟨~ black lines that are intended . . . to reveal the construction of the picture —Clive Bell⟩ **2 :** SURROUNDING, ENCOMPASSING **:** being on all sides ⟨the ~ air⟩ ⟨the ~ Unknown —C.D.Lewis⟩

cir·cum·ambulate \ˈ≈≈+\ *vb* -ED/-ING/-S [L *circum ambulatus*, past part. of *circum ambulare* to walk around, fr. *circum* + *ambulare* — more at CIRCUM-, AMBLE] *vi* **1 :** to walk or go around; *esp* **:** to walk or go around an object of worship or reverence or in a ritual circular course ⟨one ~s with the object of worship as one's physical as well as spiritual focus —S.W.Nakamura⟩ **2 :** to wander about at leisure without definite purpose or as a result of indirection ~ *vt* **:** to walk around esp. ritualistically ⟨she might have gone and *circumambulated* the Yeobrights' premises at Blooms-End —Thomas Hardy⟩ ⟨the stupa which the worshipers *circumambulated* —W.N.Brown⟩ — **cir·cum·ambulation** \"+\ *n* -S — **cir·cum·ambulator** \"+\ *n* -S

cir·cum·ambulatory \ˈ≈≈+\ *adj* [L *circum ambulatus* + E *-ory*] **1 :** CIRCUMAMBULATING ⟨the ~ scholar⟩ **2 :** designed for esp. ritualistic circumambulation ⟨the ~ passage made of lime concrete —H.D.Sankalia⟩

cir·cum·bend·i·bus \ˌ≈≈+ˈbendə̇bəs\ *n* -ES [L *circum* round about + E *bend* + L *-ibus*, abl. pl. ending — more at CIRCUM] **:** an indirect or roundabout course esp. in writing or speaking **:** CIRCUMLOCUTION

cir·cum·boreal \ˈ≈≈+\ *adj* [*circum-* + *boreal*] **:** throughout the boreal regions

cir·cum·cel·lion \ˌ≈≈+ˈselyən\ *n* -S *usu cap* [LL *circumcellion-, circumcellio*, fr. L *circum-* + LL *-cellion-* *-cellio* (fr. L *cella* cell) — more at CELL] **:** one of a group of the Donatists composed of runaway slaves, ruined peasants, and the non≈ Roman population of northern Africa who combining social with ecclesiastical revolt and courting martyrdom were suppressed by the government

cir·cum·center \ˈ≈≈+\ *n* [*circum-* + *center*] **:** the center of the circle circumscribing a triangle or a regular polygon of more than three sides

cir·cum·circle \ˈ≈≈+\ *n* [*circum-* + *circle*] **:** a circumscribed circle

cir·cum·cise \ˈ≈≈+ˌsīz\ *vt* -ED/-ING/-S [ME *circumcisen*, fr. L *circumcisus*, past part. of *circumcidere* to cut around, circumcise, fr. *circum-* + *caedere* to cut — more at CONCISE] **1 a :** to cut off the prepuce of (a male) or the clitoris of (a female) **b :** to cut around, off, or away — now used only in medicine **2 :** to purify spiritually ⟨~ therefore the foreskin of your heart, and be no longer stubborn —Deut 10:16 (RSV)⟩

cir·cum·cis·er *or* **cir·cum·ci·sor** \-zə(r)\ *n* -S **:** one that circumcises

cir·cum·ci·sion \ˌ≈≈+ˈsizhən\ *n* -S [ME *circumcisioun*, fr. OF *circumcision, circoncision*, fr. LL *circumcision-, circumcisio*, fr. L *circumcisus* + *-ion-, -io* -ion] **1 :** the act of circumcising or being circumcised: **a :** the cutting off of the prepuce of males being practiced as a religious rite by Jews and Muslims and as a sanitary measure in modern surgery **b :** the cutting off of prepuce and clitoris being practiced as religious rites or as a practical or punitive measure by some primitive peoples **2 :** spiritual purification **3** *usu cap* **:** a feast commemorating the circumcision of Jesus held on January 1 in the Roman Catholic, Eastern, and Anglican churches

cir·cum·cres·cence \ˈ≈≈+ˈkresᵊn(t)s\ *n* -S [*circum-* + obs. E *crescence* "growth", fr. L *crescentia*, fr. *crescere* to grow — more at CRESCENT] **:** a growing around or over **:** EPIBOLY — **cir·cum·cres·cent** \-ᵊnt\ *adj*

cir·cum·denudation \ˈ≈≈+\ *n* -S [*circum-* + *denudation*] **:** denudation or erosion around an object leaving it isolated

cir·cum·duce \ˈ≈≈+ˈdyüs\ *vt* -ED/-ING/-S [LL *circumducere* to annul, cancel, fr. L, to lead around, fr. *circum-* + *ducere* to lead — more at TOW] *Scots law* **:** to set a limit to or declare to be at an end by a judicial decision

cir·cum·duct \ˈ≈≈+ˌdəkt\ *vt* -ED/-ING/-S [L *circumductus*, past part. of *circumducere* to lead around, fr. *circum-* + *ducere* to lead — more at CIRCUM-, TOW] **1 :** to turn about an axis **:** REVOLVE, ROTATE; *esp* **:** to move (as a leg) so that the distal end describes a circle with the proximal end remaining fixed **2 a** *law* **:** to put a limit or end to **b** *civil law* **:** ABROGATE, ANNUL ⟨~ a law or citation⟩

cir·cum·duc·tion \ˌ≈≈+ˈdəkshən\ *n* -S [L *circumduction-, circumductio*, fr. *circumductus* + *-ion-, -io* -ion] **:** the act or action of circumducting; *specif* **:** TERMINATION, ABROGATION, CANCELLATION

cir·cum·ero·sion \ˈ≈≈+\ *n* -S [*circum-* + *erosion*] **:** CIRCUMDENUDATION

circumesophageal ring \ˈ≈≈+ . . .-\ *n* [*circum* + *esophageal*] **:** ESOPHAGEAL RING

cir·cum·e·ter \ˌsərˈkəməd·ər\ *n* -S [blend of *circum-* and *-meter*] **:** a device for measuring the circumference esp. of a fruit

cir·cum·fer·ence \sərˈkəm(p)f(ə)rən(t)s, -f(ə)rən(t)s, *-R & often R* səˈk-\ *n* -S [ME, fr. MF *circumference, circonference*, fr. L *circumferentia*, fr. *circumferre* to carry around, fr. *circum-* + *ferre* to carry — more at BEAR] **1 :** the line that bounds a circular plane surface or the length of this line equal to π times the diameter **:** PERIMETER; *broadly* **:** PERIPHERY, CIRCUIT **2 a :** the surface or outer limits of a sphere or rounded body **:** the measure of the perimeter of a great circle or sphere ⟨from the center to the ~ of the spheroid⟩ **b :** LIMITS, BOUNDS ⟨within the ~ of a grain of sand⟩ ⟨that mysterious intellectual magnetism that enlarges the ~ of his ego —J.C.Powys⟩

cir·cum·fer·en·tial \sə(r)ˌkəm(p)fəˈrenchəl; ˌsər,≈≈≈, ˌsə̄,-, ˌsəi,-\ *adj* [L *circumferentia* circumference + E *-al*] **:** of or relating to the circumference esp. of a town or city: as **a :** ENCIRCLING ⟨~ seam welding —*Industrial Equipment News*⟩ ⟨a ~ highway around a city —*U.S. Code*⟩ **b :** PERIPHERAL, SKIRTING ⟨bypass or ~ roads to enable through traffic to keep out of cities —*New Internat'l Yr. Bk.*⟩ ⟨parkways and ~ drives —*Amer. Builder*⟩ ⟨these efforts . . . are nevertheless peripheral, ~, apart from the curricular body of knowledge which is central to any educational institution —K.I. Brown⟩ — **cir·cum·fer·en·tial·ly** \-ch(ə)lē, -li\ *adv*

cir·cum·fer·en·tor \sə(r)ˈkəm(p)fəˌrentə(r)\ *n* -S [L *circumferentia* circumference + E *-or*] **1 :** a surveyor's compass with diametral projecting arms each carrying a vertical slit sight **2 :** a graduated wheel formerly used to measure tires

[1]**cir·cum·flex** \ˈsərkəmˌfleks, ˈsə̄k-,ˈsəik-\ *vt* -ED/-ING/-ES [L *circumflexus*, past part. of *circumflectere* to bend around, mark with a circumflex, fr. *circum-* + *flectere* to bend] **:** to mark with a circumflex

[2]**circumflex** \"\ *adj* [L *circumflexus*; in ref. to accent, approximate trans. of Gk *perispōmenos*, pres. middle part. of *perispan* to draw off, divert, fr. *peri-* + *span* to draw — more at SPAN] **1 a :** characterized by the pitch, quantity, or quality indicated by a circumflex (sense 1); *esp* **:** first rising and then falling in pitch ⟨a ~ intonation⟩ ⟨the long *o* of Greek *dōron* "gift" is spoken with a ~ accent⟩ **b :** being a circumflex (sense 1) ⟨the *a* of French *bâtir* "to build" is written with a ~ accent⟩ **c :** marked with a circumflex (sense 1) ⟨~ *e*⟩ **2** *of nerves and blood vessels* **:** bending around

[3]**circumflex** *n* -ES **1** *or* **circumflex accent :** a mark ˆ, ˜, or ˜ orig. used in Greek over long vowels to indicate a rising-falling tone and thence in other languages to mark length, contraction, or a falling-rising tone and in still others and in phonetic notation to indicate a particular vowel quality — see ACCENT 5; compare TILDE **2 :** a rising-falling or falling-rising intonation of a vocalic or syllable

circumflex artery *n* **:** any of several paired curving arteries as: **a :** either of two branches of the deep femoral artery, an external supplying the front of the thigh and an internal the adductor muscles and adjacent parts **b :** either of two branches of the axillary artery that wind around the neck of the humerus **c :** either circumflex iliac artery **d :** a branch of the subscapular artery supplying the muscles of the shoulder

circumflex iliac artery *n* **:** either of two arteries arching anteriorly near Poupart's ligament: **a :** an artery lying internal to the iliac crest and arising from the external iliac artery **b :** a more superficially located artery that is a branch of the femoral artery

circumflex nerve *n* **:** AXILLARY NERVE

cir·cum·flu·ent \(ˌ)sərˈkəmfləwənt\ *also* **cir·cum·flu·ous** \-wəs\ *adj* [*circumfluent* fr. L *circumfluent-, circumfluens*, pres. part. of *circumfluere* to flow around, surround, fr. *circum-* + *fluere* to flow; *circumfluous* fr. L *circumfluus*, fr. *circum-* + *-fluus* (fr. *fluere*) — more at FLUENT] **:** flowing round or surrounding in the manner of a fluid ⟨the earth and its ~ air⟩

cir·cum·fo·ra·ne·ous \ˌsərkəmfəˈrānēəs, sər¦k-\ *adj* [L *circumforaneus*, fr. *circum-* + *-foraneus* (fr. *forum* market place) — more at FORUM] **:** going about from market to market **:** wandering from place to place ⟨a ~ jester⟩

cir·cum·fuse \¦=≡ *at* CIRCUM- + ¦fyüz\ *vt* -ED/-ING/-S [L *circumfusus*, past part. of *circumfundere* to pour around, fr. *circum-* + *fundere* to pour — more at FOUND] **1 :** to spread or diffuse around ⟨his army, *circumfused* on either wing —John Milton⟩ **2 :** to surround, envelop, or bathe esp. by a pouring or diffusing around ⟨education and civilization are gradually *circumfusing* the earth —L.M.Winters⟩ ⟨a face all *circumfused* with light —Ben Jonson⟩

cir·cum·fu·sion \ˌ=≡+ˈfyüzhən\ *n* -S [LL *circumfusion-, circumfusio*, fr. L *circumfusus* + *-ion-, -io* -ion] **:** the act of circumfusing or state of being circumfused ⟨the ~ of the smoke⟩ ⟨the ~ of the island by fog⟩

cir·cum·gyration \¦=≡+\ *n* -S [LL *circumgyratus* (past part. of *circumgyrare* to turn around, fr. L *circum-* + *gyrare* to turn) + E *-ion* — more at GYRATE] **1 :** GYRATION **2 :** movement in a circular course ⟨Aristotle's view that all the heavenly bodies . . . move in circular orbits in which each ~ is an exact repetition of every one that has preceded it —A.J.Toynbee⟩

cir·cum·horizontal arc \¦=≡+ . . -\ *n* **:** a colored halo of 90° extent or less that is red on the upper side, parallel to the horizon and 46° or a little more below the sun, and produced by the refraction of light across 90° angles at the undersides of ice crystals in suspension in the air

cir·cum·in·ces·sion *also* **cir·cum·in·ses·sion** \ˌ=≡+in-ˈseshən\ *n* -S [ML *circumincession-, circumincessio* (fr. L *circum-* + ML *incessio*, fr. L *incessus*, past part. of *incedere* to go along, fr. *in-* + *cedere* to go), trans. of MGk *perichōrēsis*, fr. Gk *perichōrein* to go around, rotate, fr. *peri-* + *chōrein* to go, withdraw (akin to *chēros* left, bereaved) — more at IN-, CEDE, HEIR] **:** the theological doctrine of the reciprocal existence in each other of the three persons of the Trinity

cir·cum·ja·cen·cies \ˌ=≡+¦jāsᵊnsēz\ *n pl* **:** adjacent parts **:** areas that surround **:** SURROUNDINGS ⟨the ~ of the school⟩

cir·cum·ja·cent \¦=≡+¦jāsᵊnt\ *adj* [L *circumjacent-, circumjacens*, pres. part. of *circumjacēre*, fr. *circum-* + *jacēre* to lie — more at CIRCUM-, GIST] **:** lying adjacent on all sides **:** SURROUNDING ⟨the ~ hills —John Buchan⟩ ⟨the whole ~ region of which it is the capital —George Borrow⟩

cir·cum·len·tal \¦=≡+¦lentᵊl\ *adj* [*circum-* + NL *lent-, lens* lens (fr. L, lentil) + E *-al* — more at LENS] **:** encircling a lens

cir·cum·lo·cu·tion \ˌ=≡+lōˈkyüshən\ *n* -S [L *circumlocution-, circumlocutio* (fr. *circum-* + *locutio* speaking, speech, fr. *locutus*, past part. of *loqui* to speak), trans. of Gk *periphrasis* — more at PERIPHRASIS] **1 a :** the use of an unnecessarily large number of words to express an idea **:** indirect or roundabout expression ⟨the gift of the pamphleteer, who cuts through academic ~ —Vera M. Dean⟩ **b :** evasion in speech ⟨a preference for ~ rather than forthrightness⟩ **2 :** an instance of circumlocution — **cir·cum·lo·cu·tion·al** \¦=≡+¦=≡shənᵊl, -shnəl\ *or* **cir·cum·lo·cu·tion·ary** \-shə,nerē, -ri\ *adj*

cir·cum·lo·cu·tion·ist \ˌ=≡≡ˈsh(ə)nəst\ *n* -S **:** one who uses circumlocution

cir·cum·lo·cu·tious \¦=≡+¦=≡shəs\ *adj* [*circumlocution* + *-ous*] **:** CIRCUMLOCUTORY

cir·cum·loc·u·to·ry \¦=≡+¦läkyə,tōrē, -ȯr-, -ri\ *adj* [*circumlocution* + *-ory*] **:** marked by or exhibiting circumlocution ⟨~ detail —Dorothy Sayers⟩ ⟨~ remarks⟩

cir·cum·lunar \¦=≡+\ *adj* [*circum-* + *lunar*] **:** revolving about or surrounding the moon

cir·cum·meridian \¦=≡+\ *adj* [*circum-* + *meridian*] **:** at or in relation to the meridian — used of a celestial body or the observation of it

cir·cum·mure \¦=≡+¦myů(ə)r\ *vt* -ED/-ING/-S [*circum-* + *mure*] **:** to encompass with a wall

cir·cum·navigable \¦=≡+\ *adj* [*circumnavigate* + *-able*] **:** capable of being circumnavigated

cir·cum·navigate \¦=≡+\ *vt* -ED/-ING/-S [L *circumnavigatus*, past part. of *circumnavigare* to sail around, fr. *circum-* + *navigare* to sail — more at CIRCUM-, NAVIGATE] **1 :** to go or travel completely around (as the earth) esp. by water ⟨~ the globe in a small craft⟩ **2 :** to go around as opposed to going through (as a congested area) **:** SKIRT, BYPASS ⟨roads . . . which neatly ~ industrial areas —Joseph Wechsberg⟩

cir·cum·navigation \¦=≡+\ *n* -S **:** the act or process of circumnavigating an object (as the earth) ⟨when Malacca Henry arrived . . . he had been around the world although Magellan's men had not yet finished their ~ —R.P.Ludlum⟩

cir·cum·navigator \¦=≡+\ *n* -S **:** one that circumnavigates an object (as the earth) ⟨disputed that Magellan was the first ~⟩

cir·cum·navigato·ry \¦=≡+\ *adj* **:** consisting of circumnavigation ⟨Magellan's ~ voyage⟩

cir·cum·neutral \¦=≡+\ *adj* [*circum-* + *neutral*] *of soil* **:** nearly neutral **:** having a pH between 6.5 and 7.5

cir·cum·nutate \¦=≡+\ *vi* -ED/-ING/-S [*circum-* + *nutate*] **:** to grow in a way characteristic of circumnutation

cir·cum·nutation \¦=≡+\ *n* -S [*circum-* + *nutation* (influenced by G *rotierende nutation*, lit., revolving nutation)] **:** a movement of the growing portions of a plant to form spirals, irregular curves, or ellipses — compare NUTATION

cir·cum·oral \¦=≡+\ *adj* [*circum-* + *oral*] **:** surrounding the mouth

cir·cum·polar \¦=≡+\ *adj* [*circum-* + *polar*] **1** *of a celestial body* **:** remaining above the horizon during the entire 360 degrees of daily travel **2 :** surrounding, lying near, or found in the vicinity of a terrestrial pole

cir·cum·position \¦=≡+\ *n* -S [LL *circumposition-, circumpositio*, fr. L *circumpositus*, past part. of *circumponere* to place around (fr. *circum-* + *ponere* to place) + *-ion-, -io* — more at CIRCUM-, POSITION] **:** AIR LAYERING

cir·cum·radius \¦=≡+\ *n* [*circum-* + *radius*] **:** the radius of a circumscribed circle

cir·cum·scissile \¦=≡+\ *adj* [L *circumscissus* (past part. of *circumscindere* to tear or cleave around, fr. *circum-* + *scindere* to cleave) + E *-ile* — more at SHED] *bot* **:** dehiscing by a transverse fissure around the circumference — compare LOCULICIDAL, PYXIDIUM; see FRUIT illustration

cir·cum·scrib·a·ble \¦sərkəmz¦skrībəbəl, ¦sōk-, ¦sȯik-, -m¦sk-\ *adj* **:** capable of being circumscribed

cir·cum·scribe \ˈ=kəmz,krīb, -m,sk-, ˌ=≡ˈ=\ *vt* -ED/-ING/-S [L *circumscribere*, fr. *circum-* + *scribere* to write, draw — more at SCRIBE] **1 a :** to draw a line around **:** encompass with or as if with a line ⟨~ a word on a page⟩ ⟨a voyage that ~s the world⟩ **b :** to surround by or as if by a boundary **:** BOUND ⟨that the American nation was not to be *circumscribed* by narrow isthmuses and gulf streams —*Encyc. Americana*⟩ **2 :** to set limits or bounds to: as **a :** to constrict the range or activity of ⟨~ a heart patient's activity⟩ ⟨a London physician whose round of practice remained among the poor and was *circumscribed* by poverty —H.V.Gregory⟩ **b :** to define, mark off, or demarcate carefully ⟨rulership by the best and wisest under well-considered laws, *circumscribed* by a written constitution —V.L.Parrington⟩ **3 a :** to be drawn around (as a geometrical figure) so as to touch at as many points as possible ⟨a curve *circumscribing* a polygon⟩ **b :** to draw (as a line) around something ⟨~ a circle around a triangle⟩ — compare INSCRIBE 4 **syn** see LIMIT

cir·cum·scrip·tion \ˌ=kəmˈskripshən, -mˈsk-\ *n* -S [L *circumscription-, circumscriptio*, fr. *circumscriptus* (past part. of *circumscribere*) + *-ion-, -io* -ion] **1 :** the quality or state of being circumscribed: as **a** *obs* **:** the property of having limitation in space as opposed to omnipresence or infiniteness **b** *obs* **:** CONFINEMENT **2 :** something that circumscribes or encloses: **a :** LIMIT, BOUNDARY **b :** RESTRICTION ⟨rigid ~ of tradition⟩ **c :** an esp. clearly defined outline ⟨the oval ~ of the man's head⟩ **3 :** the act or action of circumscribing: as **a :** DELIMITATION, DEFINITION ⟨an idea that does not lend itself easily to ~⟩ **b :** LIMITATION ⟨the ~ of a patient's movements during convalescence⟩ **4 :** a circumscribed area or district ⟨a ~ controlled by a given political group⟩

cir·cum·spect \ˈ=kəmz,pekt, -m,sp-, ˌ=≡ˈ=\ *adj* [ME, fr. MF or L; MF *circonspect*, fr. L *circumspectus*, past part. of *circumspicere* to look around, be cautious, fr. *circum-* + *specere* to look — more at CIRCUM-, SPY] **:** marked by caution and earnest attention to all significant circumstances and possible consequences of action (as action to be undertaken) and usu. by prudence and discretion ⟨a ~ investor⟩ ⟨a ~ action⟩ ⟨the wicked are always alert and ~ —George Meredith⟩ **syn** see CAUTIOUS

cir·cum·spec·tion \ˌ=kəmzˈpekshən, -mˈsp-\ *n* -S [ME *circumspeccioun*, fr. MF or L; MF *circonspection*, fr. L *circumspection-, circumspectio*, fr. *circumspectus* + *-ion-, -io* -ion] **:** the quality or state of being circumspect ⟨I was followed or watched by one or other of the Indians, so that great ~ was needed —W.H.Hudson †1922⟩

cir·cum·spec·tive \¦=≡¦=tiv\ *adj* [*circumspection* + *-ive*] **:** CIRCUMSPECT

cir·cum·spect·ly *adv* [ME, fr. *circumspect* + *-ly*] **:** in a circumspect manner

cir·cum·spect·ness *n* -ES **:** CIRCUMSPECTION

cir·cum·stance \ˈsərkəmz,tan(t)s, ˈsōk-, ˈsȯik-, -m,st-, -taa(ə)n-, -tain- *Brit usu & US also* -,tən- *or* -,stən-; *sometimes* -,tȧn- *or* -,stȧn-\ *n* -S [ME, fr. MF, fr. L *circumstantia*, fr. *circumstant-, circumstans*, pres. part. of *circumstare* to stand around, fr. *circum-* + *stare* to stand — more at STAND] **1 a :** a specific part, phase, or attribute of the surroundings or background of an event, fact, or thing or of the prevailing conditions in which it exists or takes place **:** a condition, fact, or event accompanying, conditioning, or determining another **:** an adjunct or concomitant that is present or logically likely to be present ⟨it was late but he overlooked that ~⟩ ⟨the time, place, and other ~s of an action⟩ ⟨the ~ that the man was happy raised the presumption that he was prosperous enough⟩ ⟨every ~ of calculated and characteristic . . . treachery —Sir Winston Churchill⟩ **b :** a subordinate detail **:** an adventitious nonessential fact or detail ⟨the gist of the matter, not the ~s⟩ **2 a :** the total complex of essential attributes and attendant adjuncts of a fact or action **:** the sum of essential and environmental characteristics **:** arrangement, situation, composition, or nature of an event or thing — usu. used in singular without the indefinite article and rarely with the definite article ⟨constant and rapid change in economic ~, social custom, and intellectual atmosphere —G.M.Trevelyan⟩ **b :** OCCURRENCE, EVENTUALITY ⟨the unofficial minority voted solidly against a government measure — a rare ~ —W.T.Stace⟩ **c :** an evidential condition on the basis of which an event (as a crime) may be inferred or an accusation made probable or improbable ⟨the ~s of the case indicate murder⟩ ⟨the ~s tell against the accused⟩ **d :** surroundings or situation as regards wealth, property, assured income — usu. used in pl. ⟨a bachelor in easy ~s with a large inheritance to draw on⟩ **e** *obs* **:** a likely appurtenance **:** a characteristic property **3 :** formalities and ritualistic display esp. as contrasted with essential procedure **:** attendant ceremonial ⟨pride, pomp, and ~ of glorious war —Shak.⟩ ⟨with appropriate ducal and episcopal ~ —Francis Hackett⟩ **4** *in a narrative* **:** circumstantial detail ⟨stress ~ rather than action in a novel⟩ **5 :** an occurrence or fact viewed as a detail in a larger continuum ⟨the conqueror weeping for new worlds or the like ~s in history —Joseph Addison⟩ **6 :** CHANCE, FATE ⟨a training in self-reliance, endurance, and indifference to ~ —*Geog. Rev.*⟩ ⟨a mere victim of ~ —Fritz Stern⟩ **syn** see OCCURRENCE — **in the circumstances** *or* **under the circumstances :** as matters stand **:** things being the way they are ⟨we had no means of transportation to the picnic so *in the circumstances* we stayed home⟩ — **not a circumstance to** *slang* **:** insignificant by comparison with ⟨a squall is *not a circumstance to* a hurricane wind⟩ — **under no circumstances :** under no conditions ⟨*under no circumstances* were they to go unattended⟩

cir·cum·stanced \-n(t)st\ *adj* **:** being or placed in a particular condition or in certain circumstances esp. in regard to property or income ⟨comfortably ~ and for the first time in her life commanding ready money —Thomas Hardy⟩ ⟨those more happily ~ in their birth —Reginald Hargreaves⟩

¹cir·cum·stan·tial \¦=kəmz¦tanchəl, -m¦st-, -aan-, -ain-\ *adj* [L *circumstantia* circumstance + E *-al*] **1 :** belonging to, consisting in, influenced by, or dependent on circumstances ⟨a historical novel . . . full of ~ life —Jean Garrigue⟩ ⟨~ developments not covered in the main plan⟩ ⟨a purely ~ outcome to the play⟩ **2 :** pertinent but not essential **:** ACCOMPANYING, INCIDENTAL, ADVENTITIOUS ⟨a hard life, stripped of every ~ grace —Isabel Paterson⟩ ⟨the forces which thrust him down are ~ rather than inevitable —C.C.Walcutt⟩ **3 :** marked strongly by attention to small incidents and details, esp. attendant circumstances or conditions ⟨his ~ accounts of his adventures —Richard Griffith⟩ **4 :** marked by ceremony and pomp ⟨the ~ splendor of the coronation⟩

syn MINUTE, PARTICULAR, PARTICULARIZED, DETAILED, ITEMIZED: CIRCUMSTANTIAL may suggest precise or detailed treatment (as that of an acute eyewitness) of circumstances and secondary incidents and items ⟨I solemnly declare that I am at this time in the possession of my right mind — that my memory is exact and *circumstantial* —Charles Dickens⟩ ⟨the story of the rattlesnake chasing the squirrel was too *circumstantial* to have been invented —Constance M. Rourke⟩ MINUTE suggests searching, close attention even the smallest details ⟨she was interested in the little details and writes with *minute* care about the change of fashion —Gamaliel Bradford⟩ ⟨Plato, the foe of the mechanical, in the Laws . . . provides for the state a perfect jumble of *minute* regulations —John Buchan⟩ PARTICULAR implies a zealous care about and attention to details ⟨I should have been more *particular* in my account of Miss Unwin if I had had materials for a minute description —William Cowper⟩ PARTICULARIZED, that is, treated or presented with full particulars, has pretty much superseded PARTICULAR in reference to accounts, descriptions, and so on ⟨a most concrete, *particularized*, earthy series of small diurnal recognitions —J.C. Powys⟩ DETAILED simply indicates treatment with a wealth of detail and lacks any special connotation ⟨his [Ruskin's] *detailed* criticisms of architecture and painting —Bliss Perry⟩ ITEMIZED, mostly commercial in use and suggestion, indicates a specific and separate listing or inclusion of each item, as each charge, cost, or deduction ⟨an *itemized* bill from the hotel⟩ ⟨an *itemized* list of stock losses accompanying the tax return⟩

²circumstantial \"\ *n* -S **:** an attendant circumstance **:** DETAIL; *esp* **:** something incidental to the main subject — usu. used in pl. ⟨the main point of an argument and the ~s⟩

circumstantial evidence *n* **:** evidence that tends to prove a fact in issue by proving other events or circumstances which according to the common experience of mankind are usu. or always attended by the fact in issue and that therefore affords a basis for a reasonable inference by the jury or court of the occurrence of the fact in issue

cir·cum·stan·ti·al·i·ty \ˌ=kəmz,tanchēˈaləd·ē, -m,st-, -aan-, -ain-, -ətē, -i\ *n* -ES **1 :** the quality or state of being circumstantial: as **a :** particularity or minuteness of detail ⟨a legend arose of such ~ that the wise historian would hesitate to attack it —W.S.Maugham⟩ **b :** a conversational pattern (as in some manic states) exhibiting excessive attention to irrelevant and digressive details **2 :** a circumstantial matter **:** DETAIL ⟨the *circumstantialities* of the event⟩

cir·cum·stan·tial·ly \¦=≡chəlē, -li\ *adv* **:** in a circumstantial manner: as **a :** in respect to circumstances ⟨an account that was ~ accurate though incomplete⟩ **b :** not essentially **:** ACCIDENTALLY ⟨a mere acquaintance only ~ related to the victim⟩ **c :** in detail **:** MINUTELY ⟨sit down, and compose herself, and tell him ~ what had been done —George Meredith⟩ **d :** according to or by means of circumstantial evidence ⟨finally convicted not by eyewitnesses but ~⟩

cir·cum·stan·tial·ness *n* -ES **:** CIRCUMSTANTIALITY

¹cir·cum·stan·ti·ate \ˌ=≡ˈ=chē,āt, *usu* -ād.+V\ *vt* -ED/-ING/-S [L *circumstantia* circumstance + E *-ate*] **:** to provide the circumstantial evidence or support for ⟨~ a theory⟩ ⟨~ a claim⟩ — **cir·cum·stan·ti·a·tion** \ˌ=≡,=≡ˈāshən\ *n* -S

²cir·cum·stan·ti·ate \¦=≡¦=≡ət, -,āt\ *adj* [L *circumstantia* + E *-ate*] *archaic* **:** CIRCUMSTANTIATED

cir·cum·tropical \¦=≡ *at* CIRCUM- +\ *adj* [*circum-* + *tropical*] **:** surrounding or distributed throughout the tropics — compare TROPICOPOLITAN

¹cir·cum·val·late \¦=≡+¦va,lāt, -lət\ *adj* [L *circumvallatus*] **1 :** surrounded or enclosed by or as if by a rampart **2** *anat* **:** surrounded by a ridge or elevation

²cir·cum·val·late \ˌ=≡+ˈ=,lāt\ *vt* -ED/-ING/-S [L *circumvallatus*, past part. of *circumvallare* to surround with a wall, fr. *circum-* + *vallare* to surround with a wall, fr. *vallum* rampart — more at CIRCUM-, WALL] **1 :** to surround or enclose with or as if with a rampart ⟨a fir copse . . . *circumvallated* by a stout wire fence —Rose Macaulay⟩ **2** *of a rampart* **:** to surround or enclose ⟨ramparts . . . ~ more than an obscure village —D.C.Peattie⟩

circumvallate papilla *n* **:** any of approximately 12 large papillae each surrounded with a marginal sulcus and richly supplied with taste buds chiefly responsive to bitter flavors and arranged in a V-shaped row near the back of the tongue — called also *vallate papilla*

cir·cum·val·la·tion \ˌ=≡,vaˈlāshən\ *n* -S [L *circumvallatus* + E *-ion*] **1 :** the act of circumvallating **2 :** something that circumvallates; *esp* **:** ramparts or entrenchments around a besieged place or a besieging army

cir·cum·vene \¦=≡¦vēn\ *vt* -ED/-ING/-S [F *circonvenir*, fr. L *circumvenire* to surround, afflict, cheat] **:** CIRCUMVENT

cir·cum·vent \ˌsərkəm¦vent, ¦sōk-, ¦sȯik-\ *vt* -ED/-ING/-S [L *circumventus*, past part. of *circumvenire* to surround, afflict, cheat, fr. *circum-* + *venire* to come — more at COME] **1 a :** to surround and cut off the escape of **:** hem in and capture ⟨~*ed* by the enemy, he had to yield⟩ **b :** ENCIRCLE **:** form a circling boundary around ⟨little islands ~*ed* by a river⟩ **c :** to encompass with evils, difficulties, or enemies ⟨the melodrama's heroine ~*ed* with perils⟩ **d :** to go around **:** make a full circuit around or bypass without going through ⟨a lake allows an average father, walking slowly, to ~ it in an afternoon —W.H.Auden⟩ ⟨an alternative path, ~*ing* Kentucky through the states to its north —*New Republic*⟩ **2 :** to overcome or avoid the intent, effect, or force of **:** anticipate and escape, check, or defeat by ingenuity or stratagem **:** make inoperative or nullify the purpose or power of esp. by craft or scheme ⟨~*ing* his enemies by craft and driving them out . . . by force —P.N.Ure⟩ ⟨rules which they ~ or openly violate —Jerome Frank⟩ **syn** see FRUSTRATE

cir·cum·ven·tion \ˌ=≡ˈvenchən\ *n* -S [LL *circumvention-, circumventio*, fr. L *circumventus* + *-ion-, -io* -ion] **:** the act or action, instance, or means of circumventing ⟨~ of the law⟩ ⟨the ~ of an enemy's clever plan⟩

cir·cum·vo·lute \(,)sərˈkəmvə,lüt, ¦sərkəmvō¦lüt\ *vb* -ED/-ING/-S [L *circumvolutus*, past part. of *circumvolvere* to revolve, roll around, fr. *circum-* + *volvere* to roll — more at VOLUBLE] *vi* **:** to wind or turn in volutions esp. in an inward spiral (as a snail shell or the capital scroll of an Ionic column) **~** *vt* **:** to encircle or entangle with something twisted or wound around

cir·cum·vo·lu·tion \(,)sər,kəmvəˈlüshən, ,sərkəmvōˈlüshən\ *n* -S [ME *circumvolucioun*, fr. ML *circumvolution-, circumvolutio*, fr. L *circumvolutus* + *-ion-, -io* -ion] **1 a :** a turning or winding around a center or axis **:** ROTATION, GYRATION **b :** a single revolution or rotation **2 a :** a folding or twisting of one thing about another **b :** a winding in an inward spiral (as in the scroll of an Ionic capital) **c :** a single turn of such a folding or winding ⟨the ~s of a boa constrictor⟩ ⟨the ~s of a snail's shell⟩

circumvolve *vt* -ED/-ING/-S [L *circumvolvere*] *obs* **:** to wind, wrap, or bend round **:** SURROUND, ENVELOP

cir·cum·zenithal arc \¦=≡ *at* CIRCUM- + . . . -\ *n* [ISV *circum-* + *zenithal*; orig. formed as F *circumzénithal*] **:** a bright rainbow-colored circular halo arc about the zenith as center convex to the sun and about 46 degrees above it

¹cir·cus \ˈsərkəs, -ōk-, -ȯik-\ *n* -ES *often attrib* [L, circle, ring, circus (sense 1) — more at CIRCLE] **1 a :** a large oblong or circular structure similar to an amphitheater and enclosed by tiers of seats on three or all four sides and used for athletic contests, exhibitions of horsemanship or in ancient times chariot racing and public esp. gladiatorial spectacles — compare HIPPODROME, STADIUM **b :** a spectacle presented in such an area or structure **c (1) :** a spectacular public entertainment given usu. in a large tent and made up of acts of physical skill (as horsemanship) and daring (as gymnastic and aerial acrobatics) and acts with trained wild animals (as lions, tigers, and elephants) interspersed with showing off elaborate and colorful costumes and trappings and with informally interjected comedy by clowns and often accompanied by menageries and sideshows held in separate tents featuring biological freaks, trick acts (as sword swallowing and fire eating), and rather crude girly shows **(2) :** the physical plant, livestock, and personnel of such a circus ⟨the ~ moved out of winter quarters in its special train⟩ **d :** an activity suggesting a circus ⟨loudspeakers, parades, jazz records, rallies . . . made a ~ of the noon hour —*New Republic*⟩ **e** *slang* **:** an esp. lively or diverting entertainment ⟨so funny it was a ~⟩ ⟨men in boats are having a ~ with mackerel, yellowtails, barracuda, and dolphin —*Ford Times*⟩ **2 a** *obs* **:** CIRCLE, RING **b** *Brit* **:** an esp. circular area at an intersection of streets — often used in proper names ⟨Piccadilly *Circus*⟩ **c :** CIRQUE 3 **3 :** FLYING CIRCUS

²circus \"\ *n, cap* [NL, fr. Gk *kirkos* hawk — more at CIRCAETUS] **:** a genus of hawks comprising the harriers — see MARSH HAWK

³circus \"\ *vi* -ED/-ING/-ES [back-formation fr. *circus movement*] **:** to exhibit circus movements after an injury

circus catch *n* **:** a catch (as in baseball) requiring an extraordinary or spectacular effort

circus duck *n* [so called fr. its plumage] **:** HARLEQUIN DUCK

circus makeup *n* **:** an extreme variegated makeup of a newspaper page featuring a profusion of sizes and kinds of attention-catching headlines, cuts, and boxes in unbalanced array

circus movement *n* [L *circus* (circle)] **1 :** involuntary circling in one direction due to injury to the central nervous system, esp. to the cerebellum or the semicircular canals — compare NYSTAGMUS **2 :** movement of a wave of excitation through excitable tissue in such a manner that it makes and repeats more or less indefinitely a complete circuit back to the point of origin, considered to be a possible cause of auricular fibrillation in man

cir·cusy \-kəsē\ *adj* **:** befitting or suggesting a circus esp. in having spectacular qualities (as highly colored or ornate ornamentation)

ci·ré *also* **ci·re** \səˈrā\ *n* -S [F, fr. past part. of *cirer* to wax, fr. *cire*, n., wax, fr. L *cera* — more at CEREUS] **1 :** a brilliant highly glazed finish for fabrics usu. achieved by applying wax to the fabric and subjecting it to hot calendering **2 :** a fabric with a ciré finish — **ci·réd** \səˈrād\ *adj*

cire per·due \ˈsir,perˈd(y)ü, F sēerperdüe\ *n* [F (*moulage à*) *cire perdue*, lit., lost wax casting] **:** a process used in metal casting that consists of making a wax model (as of a statuette), coating it with a refractory (as clay) to form a mold, heating until the wax melts and runs out of small holes left in the mold, and then pouring metal into the space left vacant

cir·io \ˈsirē,ō\ *n* -S [AmerSp, fr. Sp, thick candle, fr. L *cereus* waxen, fr. *cera* wax] **:** a Mexican candlewood (*Fouquieria columnaris*) having tall columnar stems

cirl bunting \ˈsər(-ə)l-\ *n* [NL *cirlus* (specific epithet of *Emberiza cirlus*), fr. It *cirlo*, of imit. origin] **:** a small European finch (*Emberiza cirlus*) brightly marked with yellow, olive, and black

cir·o·grille \ˈsirə,gril\ *n* -S [ME, fr. LL *choerogryllos*, fr. LGk *choirogryllos*, fr. Gk *choiros* pig, young pig + *gryllos* young pig; akin to Gk *gryzein* to grunt — more at -CHOERUS, GRUNT] **:** SYRIAN HYRAX

ci·ro·lana \,sirəˈlanə, -lä-, -lā-\ *n, cap* [NL, coined *ab*1818 by William E. Leach †1836 Brit. naturalist] **:** a widely distributed genus (the type of the family Cirolanidae) of small more or less ovate gregarious marine isopods with setose palps and maxillipeds that are sometimes pests at bathing beaches because of their vicious biting

cirque \ˈsərk\ *n* -S [F, fr. L *circus* — more at CIRCUS] **1 :** CIRCUS 1a **2 :** CIRCLE, CIRCLET — used chiefly in poetry **3 :** a deep steep-walled basin high on a mountain usu. shaped like half a bowl and often containing a small lake, caused esp. by glacial erosion, and usu. forming the blunt head of a valley

cirr- *or* **cirri-** *or* **cirro-** *also* **cirrhi-** *or* **cirrho-** *comb form* [L *cirrus* curl] **1 :** cirrus of a plant or animal ⟨*cirri*ferous⟩ ⟨*cirri*grade⟩ **2 :** cirrus cloud ⟨*cirro*stratus⟩

cir·ral \ˈsirəl\ *adj* [ISV *cirr-* + *-al*] **:** of or relating to a cirrus

cir·rate \ˈsi,rāt, -rət\ *adj* [L *cirratus* having ringlets, fr. *cirrus* curl + *-atus* -ate] **1 :** bearing a cirrus **2 :** curled like a cirrus — used esp. of a leaf tipped with a tendril

cir·rat·u·lid \səˈrachələd\ *adj* [NL *Cirratulidae* family of marine worms, fr. *Cirratulus*, type genus + *-idae*] **:** of or relating to the genus *Cirratulus* or family Cirratulidae

cir·rat·u·lus \-ləs\ *n, cap* [NL, fr. L *cirratus* + *-ulus*] **:** a genus (the type of the family Cirratulidae) of marine burrowing polychaete worms

cir·rhit·i·dae \sə'ridə,dē\ *n pl, cap* [NL, fr. *Cirrhitus*, type genus (irreg. fr. L *cirritus* having filaments, fr. *cirrus* curl) + *-idae*] **:** a family of small brilliantly colored percoid fishes of the tropical Indian and Pacific oceans esp. abundant about coral reefs

cirrhose *var of* CIRROSE

cir·rhosed \sə'rōst, 'si,r-\ *adj* [NL *cirrhosis* + E *-ed*] **:** affected with cirrhosis

cir·rho·sis \sə'rōsəs\ *n, pl* **cirrho·ses** \-ō,sēz\ [NL, fr. Gk *kirrhos* orange-colored + NL *-osis*; fr. the yellowish appearance which the diseased liver often presents when cut] **1 :** a chronic progressive disease of the liver that is characterized by an excessive formation of connective tissue followed by hardening and contraction and that results from unknown cause or from toxemia, nutritional deficiency, or parasites **2 :** a condition of other organs than the liver resembling cirrhosis — now used chiefly in veterinary medicine

1**cir·rhot·ic** \sə'räd·ik\ *adj* [ISV *cirrhotic*, fr. NL *cirrhosis*, after such pairs as NL *neurosis*: ISV *neurotic*] **:** of, relating to, caused by, or affected with cirrhosis ⟨~ degeneration⟩ ⟨a ~ liver⟩

2**cirrhotic** \"\ *n* -s **:** an individual affected with cirrhosis

cir·rhous \'sirəs\ *adj* [alter. of *cirrous*] **:** CIRROSE

cirrhus *var of* CIRRUS

cirri *pl of* CIRRUS

cirri- — see CIRR-

cir·ri·form \'sirə,fȯrm\ *adj* [*cirr-* + *-form*] **:** having the form of a cirrus **:** slender and prolonged and usu. curved — used of processes ⟨a mollusk having a foot with a ~ tip⟩

cir·rip·e·da \sə'ripədə\ *syn of* CIRRIPEDIA

1**cir·ri·pede** \'sirə,pēd\ *or* **cir·ri·ped** \-,ped\ *adj* [NL *Cirripedia*] **:** of or relating to the Cirripedia

2**cirripede** \"\ *or* **cirriped** \"\ *n* -s **:** one of the Cirripedia

cir·ri·pe·dia \,sirə'pēdēə\ *n pl, cap* [NL, fr. *cirr-* + *-pedia* footed ones (fr. L *ped-*, *pes* foot) — more at FOOT] **:** a subclass of Crustacea comprising the barnacles, goose barnacles, and a few highly modified parasitic related forms, all being free-swimming in the larval stages but permanently attached or parasitic as adults — **cir·ri·pe·di·al** \¦==¦dēəl\ *adj*

cirro- — see CIRR-

cir·ro·cumular *or* **cir·ro·cumulative** *or* **cir·ro·cumulous** \¦si(,)rō +\ *adj* [NL *cirrocumulus* + E *-ar* or *-ative* or *-ous*] **:** of, relating to, or consisting of cirrocumulus

cir·ro·cumulus \¦si(,)rō+\ *n, pl* **cirrocumuli** [NL, fr. *cirr-* + *cumulus*] **:** a cloud form of small white rounded masses at a high altitude usu. in lines and regular groupings forming a mackerel sky and often preceding a change in the weather esp. from calm to windy — see CLOUD illustration

cir·ro·lite \'sirə,līt\ *n* -s [ISV *cirro-* (fr. Gk *kirrhos* orange-colored) + *-lite*; orig. formed as Sw *kirrolit*] **:** a mineral consisting of pale yellow alkaline calcium aluminum phosphate

cir·ro·nebula \¦si(,)rō +\ *n, pl* **cirronebulae** *or* **cirronebulas** [NL, fr. *cirr-* + *nebula*] **:** a thin cirrus veil without structure

cir·rop·o·dous \sə'räpədəs\ *adj* [*cirr-* + *-podous*] **:** CIRRIPEDE

cir·rose *or* **cir·rhose** \'si,rōs\ *adj* [NL *cirrosus*, fr. *cirr-* + L *-osus* -ose] **:** CIRRATE

cir·ros·to·mi \sə'rästə,mī\ *n pl, cap* [NL, fr. *cirr-* + *-stomi*] **:** the order comprising the lancelets — compare AMPHIOXUS

cir·ro·stra·tive \¦si(,)rō¦strād·iv\ *or* **cir·ro·stra·tous** \-ād·əs\ *adj* [NL *cirrostratus* + E *-ive* or *-ous*] **:** having the character of cirrostratus

cir·ro·stratus \¦si(,)rō+\ *n, pl* **cirrostrati** [NL, fr. *cirr-* + *stratus*] **:** a fairly uniform layer of high whitish stratus darker than the white cirrus

cir·rous \'sirəs\ *adj* [L *cirrus* curl + E *-ous*] **1 :** CIRRATE **2 :** resembling cirrus clouds

cir·ro·ve·lum \¦si(,)rō'vēləm\ *n, pl* **cirro·ve·la** \-lə\ [NL, fr. *cirr-* + L *velum* veil] **:** cirrus in sheet form veiling the whole sky **:** a continuous cirrostratus

cir·rus *also* **cir·rhus** \'sirəs\ *n, pl* **cir·ri** \-,rī\ [NL, fr. L *cirrus* curl, ringlet, bird's crest] **1 :** a curllike tuft **:** TENDRIL **2 :** any of various slender usu. flexible appendages of animals: as **a :** any of the curved many-jointed arms of barnacles **b :** any of the filaments growing from the stalk and sometimes from the aboral surface of crinoids **c :** any of the tactile barbels about the mouth of many fishes **d :** any of certain tufts of hair on the legs or antennae of many insects **e :** a fused limblike group of cilia on certain protozoans **f :** the male copulatory organ of various invertebrate animals (as certain worms and mollusks) **3 :** a white filmy variety of cloud usu. formed in the highest cloud region at altitudes of 20,000 to 40,000 feet and normally consisting of minute ice crystals — see CLOUD illustration

cirs- *or* **cirso-** *comb form* [MF, fr. Gk *kirs-*, *kirso-*, fr. *kirsos*] **:** swollen vein **:** varix ⟨*cirsoid*⟩ ⟨*cirsotomy*⟩

cir·si·um \'sərs(h)ēəm\ *n, cap* [NL, fr. Gk *kirsion*, a thistle, prob. fr. *kirsos* swollen vein; fr. the use of the thistle in antiquity in the treatment of swollen veins] **:** a widely distributed genus of prickly herbs (family Compositae) having the bristles of the pappus plumose — compare CARDUUS; see BULL THISTLE

cir·soid \'sər,sȯid\ *adj* [*cirs-* + *-oid*] **:** resembling a dilated tortuous vein

ciru·e·la \,sirə'wālə\ *n* -s [AmerSp, fr. Sp, plum, fr. L *cereola (pruna)* wax-colored plums, fr. *cereolus* wax-colored, fr. *cereus* waxen, fr. *cera* wax — more at CEREUS] **:** the plumlike fruit of any of several tropical American trees belonging to the genus *Spondias* — compare HOG PLUM, OTAHEITE APPLE

cis \'sis\ *adj* [L, on this side] **:** having or characterized by certain atoms or groups on the same side of the molecule ⟨~ fusion of two steroid rings⟩ — opposed to *trans*

cis- *prefix* [L, fr. *cis* — more at HE] **1 :** on this side **:** on the nearer side — often joined to second element with a hyphen ⟨*cisalpine*⟩ ⟨*cis-*Alleghany⟩; compare TRANS-, ULTRA- **2 :** nearer in time **:** since ⟨*cisatomic*⟩ **3** *usu ital* **:** cis ⟨*cis*-dichloroethylene⟩ — opposed to *trans-*; see CIS-TRANS ISOMERISM

1**cis·alpine** \sis+\ *adj* [L *cisalpinus*, fr. *cis-* + *Alpinus* of the Alps, Alpine] **1 a :** of, relating to, or situated on this side of the Alps **b :** situated on the southern side of the Alps **:** nearer Rome ⟨~ Gaul⟩ **c :** situated on the northern side of the Alps **:** nearer France — opposed to *transalpine* **2 :** holding a doctrine of limited papal power **:** GALLICAN

2**cisalpine** \"\ *n* -s *usu cap* [L *cisalpinus*] **:** 2GALLICAN

cis·andine \sis +\ *adj* [*cis-* + *Andine* (after Sp *cisandino*)] **:** situated on this or the nearer side of the Andes mountains ⟨~ forests⟩

cis·co \'si(,)skō\ *n* -ES [short for CanF *ciscoette* — more at SISCOWET] **:** any of various whitefishes of the genus *Leucichthys* which are important food fishes of the Great Lakes region (esp. *L. artedi*) — see LAKE HERRING

ci·seaux \sē'zō\ *n pl but usu sing in constr* [F, lit., scissors, fr. OF, pl. of *cisel* chisel, scissors, alter. of (assumed) OF *cisoir* goldsmith's chisel, fr. (assumed) VL *caesorium* cutting instrument — more at CHISEL] **:** a ballet jump in which the legs are opened to a wide second position in the air

ci·se·lé \¦sēzə¦lā, (')sēz¦lā\ *adj* [F, fr. past part. of *ciseler* to chisel, shear velvet, fr. OF, to chisel, fr. *cisel* chisel] **:** having a chased or chiseled appearance ⟨velvet ~⟩

cis·gangetic \¦sis +\ *adj* [*cis-* + *Gangetic*] **:** situated on this esp. the western side of the Ganges river

cis·jurane \sis +\ *adj* [F *cisjuran*, fr. ML *cisjuranus*, fr. L *cis-* + ML *Juranus* Jurane] **:** situated on this esp. the western side of the Jura mountains

cis·lei·than \(')si¦slīthən\ *adj* [modif. of G *zisleithanisch*, fr. *zis-* cis- + *Leitha*, river in eastern Austria + G *-anisch* (fr. L *-anus* -ane + G *-isch* -ish)] **:** situated on this esp. the western or Austrian side of the Leitha river

cis·mon·tane \(')si¦smän,tān\ *adj* [F or L; F *cismontain*, fr. L *cismontanus*, fr. *cis-* + *montanus* mountainous, fr. *mont-*, *mons* mountain — more at MOUNT] **1 :** CISALPINE — compare TRAMONTANE, ULTRAMONTANE **2 :** situated on the nearer side of any mountains ⟨~ California⟩

cis·pa·dane \¦sispə¦dān, (')si¦spā,dān\ *adj* [F *cispadan*, fr. *cis-* + *padane*, fr. L *padanus* of the Po, fr. *Padus* Po, river in Italy] **:** situated on this esp. the Roman side of the Po river

cis·pon·tine \(')si¦spän·,tīn\ *adj* [*cis-* + L *pont-*, *pons* bridge + E *-ine* — more at FIND] **:** situated on this or the nearer side of the bridge

cis·rhe·nane \¦sisrə¦nān; sis'rē,nān, -re,n-\ *adj* [L *cisrhenanus*, fr. *cis-* + *rhenanus* of the Rhine, fr. *Rhenus* Rhine] **:** situated on this or the nearer side of the Rhine river

cis·sa \'sisə\ *n* -s [NL (old syn. of *Kitta*), fr. Gk *kissa*, *kitta* jay] **:** any of several green or blue magpies (genus *Kitta*) of southeast Asia

cis·sam·pe·los \si'sampə,läs\ *n, cap* [NL, fr. Gk *kissos* ivy + *ampelos* vine] **:** a genus of tropical woody vines (family Menispermaceae) having alternate simple leaves and dioecious mostly tetramerous flowers — see FALSE PAREIRA, VELVETLEAF

cis·sie *or* **cis·sy** \'sisi\ *Brit var of* SISSY

cis·sing \'sisiŋ\ *n* -s [origin unknown] **:** the gathering of a wet film (as of varnish) into drops or streaks leaving parts of the surface bare or imperfectly covered

cis·soid \'si,sȯid\ *n* -s [LGk *kissoeidēs*, fr. Gk, like ivy, fr. *kissos* ivy + *-oeidēs* -oid] **:** a plane curve with two branches meeting at a cusp at one end of a diameter of a fixed circle, each point of the cissoid being obtained by going from the cusp along any chord to its intersection when extended with the tangent diametrically opposite the cusp and then returning along the extended chord a distance equal to the length of the chord — **cis·soi·dal** \(')si¦sȯidᵊl\ *adj*

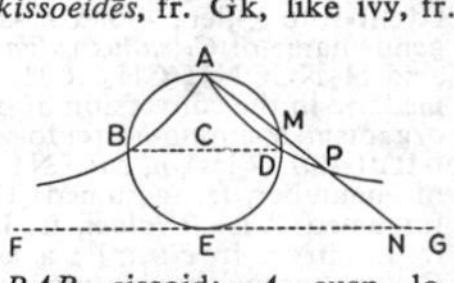

BAP cissoid; *A* cusp located on generating circle *ABEDM*; *AMPN* secant; *FENG* tangent; *AMP* = *MPN*

cis·sus \'sisəs\ *n* [NL, fr. Gk *kissos* ivy] **1** *cap* **:** a large genus of widely distributed chiefly tropical woody vines (family Vitaceae) related to the grape but differing esp. in having tetramerous flowers with expanding separate petals and largely persistent foliage and often fleshy or somewhat succulent leaves **2** *pl* **cissus :** any plant of the genus *Cissus* — see MARINE IVY

1**cist** \'sist, 'kist\ *also* **kist** \'k-\ *n* -s [W *cist* chest, fr. L *cista* — more at CHEST] **1 :** a Neolithic grave lined with stone slabs **2 :** a roofed storage pit often lined with stones found in the southwestern U.S. in Basket Maker sites

2**cist** \'sist\ *or* **cis·ta** \'sistə, 'ki-\ *n, pl* **cists** \'sis(t)s\ *or* **cis·tae** \'si,stē, 'ki,stī\ [L *cista*] **:** a receptacle orig. made of wicker for carrying sacred utensils in procession in ancient Rome

cis·ta·ce·ae \si'stāsē,ē\ *n pl, cap* [NL, fr. *Cistus*, type genus + *-aceae*] **:** a family of shrubs or somewhat woody herbs (order Parietales) with simple entire leaves and a capsular fruit — **cis·ta·ceous** \(')si¦stāshəs\ *adj*

1**cis·ter·cian** \(')si¦stərshən, -ə̄sh-, -əish-\ *adj, usu cap* [ML *Cistercium* (now *Cîteaux*) site of the abbey near Dijon, France + E *-an*] **:** of or relating to Cistercians or Cistercianism

2**cistercian** \"\ *n* -s *usu cap* **:** a member of an austere order founded on the Benedictine rule as adapted by Robert de Molesme at Cîteaux, France, in 1098, the order being now divided into a group that follows a mitigated rule and a group that follows a more strictly interpreted rule — compare TRAPPIST

cistercian of the common observance *usu cap both Cs&2dO* **:** a Cistercian who follows the mitigated rule

cistercian of the strict observance *usu cap C&S&2dO* **:** a Cistercian who follows the more strictly interpreted rule

cis·ter·cian·ism \-,nizəm\ *n* -s *usu cap* **:** the state, system, or practices of Cistercians

cis·tern \'sistə(r)n\ *n* -s [ME, fr. OF *cisterne*, fr. L *cisterna*, fr. *cista* box, chest — more at CHEST] **1 :** an artificial reservoir or tank for holding or storing water or other liquids; *specif* **:** an often underground tank for storing rainwater collected from a roof **2 a** *obs* **:** LAVER **b** *obs* **:** a large vessel for use (as in cooling wine) at the dining table **3 :** a natural reservoir **:** a hollow place containing water **4 :** a fluid-containing sac or cavity in an organism

cis·ter·na \si'stərnə\ *n, pl* **cister·nae** \-,nē\ [NL, fr. L, cistern] **:** CISTERN 4: as **a :** CISTERNA MAGNA **b :** CISTERNA CHYLI

cisterna chy·li \-'kī,lī\ *n, pl* **cisternae chyli** [NL, lit., cistern of the chyle] **:** a dilated lymph channel usu. opposite the 1st and 2d lumbar vertebrae and marking the beginning of the thoracic duct

cis·ter·nal \(')si¦stərnᵊl\ *adj* [ISV *cistern-* (fr. NL *cisterna*) + *-al*] **:** of or relating to a cisterna, esp. the cisterna magna ⟨~ puncture⟩ — **cis·ter·nal·ly** \-ᵊlē, -ᵊli\ *adv*

cisterna mag·na \-'magnə\ *n, pl* **cisternae mag·nae** \-,nē\ [NL, lit., large cistern] **:** a large subarachnoid space between the caudal part of the cerebellum and the medulla oblongata

cistern of pec·quet \-pə'kā\ *usu cap P* [after Jean *Pecquet* †1674 French physician and anatomist] **:** CISTERNA CHYLI

cist grave *n* [1*cist*] **:** CIST 1

cis·to·phor·ic \¦sistə¦fȯrik\ *adj* **:** relating to a cistophorus

cis·toph·o·rus \si'stäfərəs\ *n, pl* **cistopho·ri** \-,rī\ [L, fr. Gk *kistophoros*, fr. *kisto-* (fr. *kistē* basket) + *-phoros* -phorous — more at CHEST] **:** any of certain silver coins of the 2d and 1st centuries B.C. chiefly of Pergamum bearing the picture of the sacred basket that was carried in the worship of Dionysus

cis-trans \¦si¦stran(t)s, -nz\ *adj* [*cis-* + *trans-*] **:** relating to, exhibiting, or being a particular type of stereoisomerism — see CIS-TRANS ISOMERISM

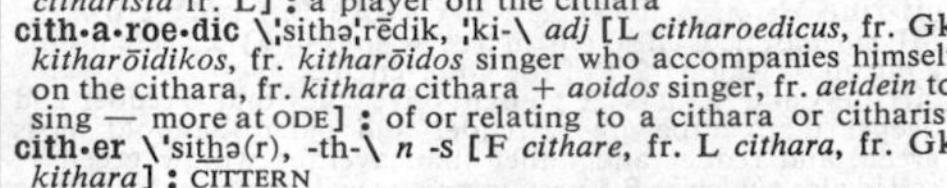

cis-trans isomerism *n* **:** geometric isomerism in unsaturated compounds or cyclic compounds depending usu. on the presence in the molecule of a pair of substituted groups (as unsymmetrically substituted methylene groups) so that the isomers have comparable substituents on either the same or opposite sides of the molecule: as **a :** stereoisomerism in compounds (as maleic and fumaric acids) containing one or more carbon-to-carbon double bonds **b :** SYN-ANTI ISOMERISM **c :** stereoisomerism in various cyclic compounds (as disubstituted cyclohexanes) which in many cases may also exhibit optical isomerism

R-C-X ‖ R-C-X
cis form

R-C-X ‖ X-C-R
trans form

cis·tu·do \si'st(y)ü(,)dō\ [NL, fr. L *cista* box + *-udo* (as in *testudo* tortoise)] — more at CHEST, TESTUDO] *syn of* TERRAPENE

cis·tus \'sistəs\ *n* [NL, fr. Gk *kistos*, *kisthos* rockrose] **1** *cap* **:** a genus (the type of the family Cistaceae) of shrubs or woody herbs widely distributed in the Mediterranean region and the Orient and distinguished by opposite leaves and capsular fruits with 5 or 10 valves — see ROCKROSE **2** -ES **:** any plant of the genus *Cistus* **:** ROCKROSE

cit \'sit\ *n* -s [short for *citizen*] **1 :** an inhabitant of a city **:** TOWNSMAN, TRADESMAN, SHOPKEEPER **2** *slang* **a :** one not in the armed forces **b cits** *pl* **:** civilian clothes as opposed to military uniform **:** CIVVIES

cit *abbr* **1** citation; cited **2** citizen **3** citrate

cit·a·del \'sid·əd°l, -itə-, -,del\ *n* -s [MF *citadelle*, fr. OIt *cittadella*, dim. of *cittade* city, fr. L *civitat-*, *civitas* — more at CITY] **1 :** a fortress that commands a city both for control and defense; *broadly* **:** a strong fortress **:** STRONGHOLD **2** *archaic* **:** the protected central structure in heavily armored ships of war that contains the engines, boilers, magazines and in and upon which the broadside battery is mounted **3 :** a mission hall of the Salvation Army

cital *n* -s [by shortening] *obs* **:** RECITAL

ci·ta·tion \sī'tāshən\ *n* -s [ME *citacioun* summoning, fr. OF *citation*, fr. L *citation-*, *citatio*, fr. *citatus* (past part. of *citare* to put in movement, summon) + *-ion-*, *-io* -ion] **1 a :** an official summons giving notice to a person to appear (as before a tribunal of justice) ⟨the congressional committee issued several contempt ~s⟩; *broadly* **:** SUMMONS **b :** the paper embodying such a summons ⟨gave a certified copy of the ~⟩ **2 a :** the act of citing verbatim the spoken, written, or printed words of another **b :** the act of citing a previously settled case or a recognized legal authority as support for a point of view or course of action; *also* **:** the formal caption by which such a case is designated in citation **c :** a quoted word or passage **3 :** ENUMERATION, MENTION: as **a :** a formal statement of the justifying merits or achievements of a person receiving an academic honor (as an honorary degree) **b :** specific mention in military orders or dispatches; *often* **:** a written narrative statement of an act or of meritorious performance of duty for which a military decoration is awarded **c :** a formal commendation (as by an organization) for action adjudged meritorious

citation form *n* **:** HYPOSTASIS 7b

ci·ta·tor \sī'tād·ə(r), '=,==\ *n* -s **:** one that cites; *specif* **:** a record or indexed list of legal decisions and cases ⟨there is a ~ for statutes and for cases —*Brit. Book News*⟩

ci·ta·to·ry \'sīd·ə,tōrē\ *adj* [ML *citatorius*, fr. L *citatus* + *-orius* -ory] **:** relating to citing or summoning **:** being or constituting a citation or summons ⟨letters ~⟩ ⟨a body with ~ powers⟩

cite \'sīt, *usu* -īd·+V\ *vt* -ED/-ING/-S [MF *citer* to cite, summon, fr. L *citare* to put in motion, summon, fr. *citus* quick, fr. past part. of *cire*, *ciēre* to put in motion, excite — more at HIGHT] **1 a :** to call upon officially or authoritatively to appear before a court **:** SUMMON **b** *obs* **:** to summon to some action **:** AROUSE, EXCITE ⟨~ the young desires —William Shenstone⟩ **2 :** to quote by way of evidence, authority, proof ⟨a list of Biblical phrases *cited* in a recent volume —J.L.Lowes⟩ **3 a :** to bring to mind **:** RECALL ⟨*citing* praise⟩ ⟨~ his virtuous life⟩ **:** refer to **:** KNOW ⟨these irregulars, *cited* as the duke's scouts⟩ **b :** to name formally, typically in commendation or praise ⟨*cited* by the trustees for his work in public health⟩ **c :** to name in a citation **4 :** to bring forward, mention, call to another's attention esp. as an example, proof, or precedent ⟨one could ~ other examples without number —B.N.Cardozo⟩ **5** [Sp *citar*, fr. L *citare*] *of a bullfighter* **:** to challenge or provoke (a bull) esp. by a movement of the cape

syn ADVANCE, ADDUCE, ALLEGE: CITE indicates bringing forward as relevant, cogent, and specific in an argument, inquiry, or discussion ⟨many works also have been the product of extensive consultation . . . , Child's *English and Scottish Ballads*, to *cite* . . . one of the very great monuments —F.N.Robinson⟩ ⟨Columbus had also some objective evidence to *cite* —G.C. Sellery⟩ ADVANCE stresses the notion of bringing forward for or as if for consideration, discussion, analysis without implications about its validity ⟨once or twice psychoanalysts have *advanced* that idea to me as a theoretical possibility —Bernard De Voto⟩ ⟨the story may well be regarded as untrue, as it was not *advanced* until six centuries after Amr's death —*Encyc. Americana*⟩ ADDUCE is close to CITE in its suggestions about bringing forth as evidence; it may lack some of the specific suggestion of the latter ⟨the old arguments from miracle and prophecy are now seldom *adduced* —W.R.Inge⟩ ⟨numerous examples to the contrary might be *adduced* from the history of the Catholic church or of the socialist movement —M.R. Cohen⟩ ALLEGE may indicate bringing forward and stating or affirming without proving ⟨younger scholars nevertheless can *allege* a very strong point on their side and win at least a debater's victory —Howard M. Jones⟩ ALLEGE may stress doubt about an assertion and convey a warning and a disclaimer of responsibility for the truth of whatever is under discussion ⟨the presence, real or *alleged*, of some hostile group —John Dewey⟩ **syn** see in addition QUOTE

ci·tel·lus \sī'teləs\ *n, cap* [NL, prob. modif. of G *ziesel* suslik, fr. MHG *zisel*, *zisemūs*, fr. OHG *zisimūs*, *sisimūs*, of Slavic origin; akin to Pol *susel*, Russ *suslik* — more at SUSLIK] **:** a genus of rodents (family Sciuridae) consisting of the typical ground squirrels

cith·a·ra \'sithərə, 'ki-; ki'thärə\ *n* -s [L — more at ZITHER] **1 :** an ancient Greek musical instrument of the lyre class having a wooden sounding board **2 :** an early medieval instrument prob. resembling the harp

cith·a·rex·y·lum \,sithə'reksələm\ *n, cap* [NL, fr. *cithare-* (irreg. fr. L *cithara*) + *-xylum*] **:** a genus of tropical American trees and shrubs (family Verbenaceae) often cultivated for their small panicled flowers and berrylike drupes seated in the persistent calyx

cith·a·rist \'sithərəst, 'ki-; ki'thärəst\ *also* **cith·a·ris·ta** \,sithə'ristə, ,ki-\ *n* -s [*citharist* fr. ME, fr. MF *cithariste*, fr. L *citharista*, fr. Gk *kitharistēs*, fr. *kithara* cithara + *-istēs* -ist; *citharista* fr. L] **:** a player on the cithara

cithara 1

cith·a·roe·dic \¦sithə¦rēdik, ¦ki-\ *adj* [L *citharoedicus*, fr. Gk *kitharōidikos*, fr. *kitharōidos* singer who accompanies himself on the cithara, fr. *kithara* cithara + *aoidos* singer, fr. *aeidein* to sing — more at ODE] **:** of or relating to a cithara or citharist

cith·er \'sithə(r), -th-\ *n* -s [F *cithare*, fr. L *cithara*, fr. Gk *kithara*] **:** CITTERN

cith·e·ro·nia \,sithə'rōnyə\ *n, cap* [NL, fr. *Citheron*, *Cithaeron*, mountain in Boeotia (fr. L, fr. Gk *Kithairōn*) + NL *-ia*] **:** a genus (the type of the family Citheroniidae) including the regal moth and certain other large moths

cith·e·ro·ni·idae \,sithərə'nīə,dē\ *n pl, cap* [NL, fr. *Citheronia*, type genus + *-idae*] **:** a family of large No. American moths lacking a frenulum, having small maxillary and labial palpi, and having larvae commonly armed with hairs and spines that feed on the leaves of deciduous trees

cit·ied \'sid·ēd, -it|, |id\ *adj* [*city* + *-ed*] **1 :** resembling or made into a city **2 :** containing or occupied by a city

cities *pl of* CITY

cit·i·fi·ca·tion \,sid·əfə'kāshən, -itəf-\ *n* -s **:** growth or transformation into the status or character of a city **:** the action or process of becoming citified

cit·i·fied \-,fīd\ *adj* **:** marked by the manners and general behavior of a city dweller **:** accustomed to city life — usu. used disparagingly

cit·i·fy \-,fī\ *vt* -ED/-ING/-ES [*city* + *-fy*] **1 :** to make citylike **:** cause to become urban ⟨the wooded glens gone, the stream bank straightened and *citified*⟩ **2 :** to stamp with or conform to city ways, manners, and customs

ci·tig·ra·dae \sə'tigrə,dē\ *n pl, cap* [NL, fr. *citi-* (fr. L *citus* swift) + *-gradae* (nom. pl. fem. of *-gradus* -grade) — more at CITE] *in former classifications* **:** a group comprising running spiders that chase their prey and including the wolf spiders and related forms — **cit·i·grade** \'sid·ə,grād\ *adj or n*

citing *pres part of* CITE

cit·i·zen \'sid·əzən, -itə- *also* -əsən\ *n* -s [ME *citizein*, fr. AF *citezein*, alter. of OF *citeien*, fr. *cité* city + *-ien* -ian — more at CITY] **1 a :** an inhabitant of a city or town; *esp* **:** one that is entitled to the civic rights and privileges of a freeman **b :** a townsman as contrasted with a rustic ⟨both ~s and peasants⟩ **2 a :** a member of a state **:** one who is claimed as a member of a state **b :** a native or naturalized person of either sex who owes allegiance to a government and is entitled to reciprocal protection from it and to enjoyment of the rights of citizenship ⟨all persons born or naturalized in the U.S., and subject to the jurisdiction thereof, are ~s of the U.S. and of the state wherein they reside —*U.S. Constitution*⟩ — compare ALIEN, SUBJECT **3 :** a resident in or member of a community or institution (as a school) — compare INHABITANT **4 :** a civilian as opposed to a soldier, policeman, or other specialized servant or functionary of the state **:** a commoner without the interests or affiliations of any special group ⟨not only by professionals but also by parents and ~s —J.B.Conant⟩

syn SUBJECT, NATIONAL: CITIZEN may indicate being a member of a sovereign state, esp. one showing democratic forms and usages, owing it allegiance, and, usu., sharing in individual political rights. SUBJECT may imply a state of subjection to a person, as a monarch, without much sense of membership in a political community or sharing in political rights ⟨the line of distinction between the citizen and the *subject*, the free and the subjugated races —R.B.Taney⟩ It may on the other hand simply indicate membership in a political community with a personal sovereign to whom allegiance is owed ⟨*subjects* of Saxon Aella —William Wordsworth⟩ NATIONAL, a more general word, may apply to anyone owing permanent allegiance to a nation and usu. indicates one belonging to a broad category that includes both people who are legally citizens or subjects and also people who have not attained such legal status ⟨Polish *nationals* in this country⟩

cit·i·zen·ess \-nəs\ *n* -ES **:** a female citizen

cit·i·zen·ly \-nlē, -li\ *adj* **:** belonging to or characteristic of a citizen

cit·i·zen·ry \-nrē, -ri\ *n* -ES **:** citizens often as distinguished from soldiery or sometimes from the official or intellectual class

cit·i·zen·ship \-n,ship\ *n* -s **1 :** the status of being a citizen

2 a : membership in a community **b :** the quality of an individual's adjustment, responsibility, or contribution to his community **:** social conduct ⟨a pupil's ~ in his school⟩

citizens' ticket *n* **:** a nonpartisan ticket esp. of reform candidates for local or municipal offices

ci·tole \sə'tōl, 'si,tōl\ *n* -s [ME *citole*, fr. MF, prob. fr. L *cithara*, fr. Gk *kithara*] **:** a small flat-backed lute of late medieval times

ci·tol·er \sə'tōlə(r), 'si,t-\ *n* -s **:** one that plays the citole

citr- *or* **citri-** *or* **citro-** *comb form* [NL, fr. *Citrus*] **1 :** citrus ⟨*citropsis*⟩ ⟨*citri*culture⟩ **2 a :** citric acid ⟨*citr*amide⟩ **b :** citrate ⟨*citro*chloride⟩

citra- *prefix* [ML, fr. L *citra* — more at HE] **:** cis- ⟨*citra*montane⟩ — opposed to *ultra-*

cit·ra·con·ate \,si·trə'kä,nāt, sə'trakə,n-\ *n* -s [ISV *citraconic* + *-ate*] **:** a salt or ester of citraconic acid

cit·ra·con·ic acid \¦si·trə¦känik-\ *n* [ISV *citr-* + *aconic;* prob. orig. formed as F *citraconique*] **:** a white crystalline deliquescent dicarboxylic acid $CH_3C(COOH){=}CHCOOH$ obtained by distillation of citric acid; methyl-maleic acid

cit·ral \'si,tral\ *n* -s [ISV *citr-* + *-al*] **:** an unsaturated liquid aldehyde $C_9H_{15}CHO$ that has a strong lemon and verbena odor, is found in many essential oils (as lemon oil and citronella oil), is used in flavoring and perfumery, and consists of a mixture of two stereoisomeric forms (1) the form obtained by the oxidation of geraniol and (2) the form obtained by the oxidation of nerol — called also respectively (1) *citral a*, *geranial* (2) *citral b*, *neral*

cit·range \'si·trənj\ *n* -s [*citr-* + *orange*] **:** a citrus fruit resulting from a cross between the sweet orange and the trifoliate orange and having a more acid flavor and a more pronounced aroma than the orange

ci·tran·ge·din \sə·'tranjədən\ *n* -s [*citrange* + calamon*din*] **:** a citrus fruit resulting from a cross between the citrange and the calamondin and having fruit suggestive in flavor of the lime

cit·range·quat \'si·trənj,kwät\ *n* -s [*citrange* + kum*quat*] **:** a citrus fruit resulting from a cross between the citrange and the kumquat and having small acid limelike fruits

¹cit·rate \'si·,trāt, 'sī-,trāt, 'si·trət\ *n* -s [ISV *citr-* + *-ate*] **:** a salt or ester of citric acid

²cit·rate \-·,trāt\ *vt* -ED/-ING/-s **:** to treat with a citrate esp. of sodium or potassium ⟨to ~ blood to prevent coagulation⟩

citrated caffeine *n* **:** a mixture of caffeine and citric acid — called also *caffeine citrate*

cit·re·an \'si·trēən\ *adj* [L *citreus* citreous + E *-an*] **:** CITRINE

cit·rene \'si·,trēn\ *n* -s [ISV *citr-* + *-ene*] **:** dextrorotatory limonene

cit·re·ous \'si·trēəs\ *adj* [L *citreus*, fr. *citrus* citron tree] **:** of the color citron yellow

cit·ric acid \'si·trik-, -ēk-\ *n* [*citric* ISV *citr-* + *-ic*] **:** a colorless crystalline or white powdery tricarboxylic acid $HOOCCH_2C(OH)COOHCH_2COOH$ that has a pleasant acid taste, occurs widely in plants (as citrus fruits), is extracted from lemon and lime juices or obtained by fermentation of sugars, and is used as a flavoring agent in foods, carbonated beverages, and pharmaceuticals

citric acid cycle *n* **:** KREBS CYCLE

ci·tric·o·la scale \sə'trikələ-\ *also* **citricola** *n* -s [NL, fr. *citr-* + *-cola*] **:** a scale (*Coccus pseudomagnoliarum*) believed to be native to Japan but injurious to citrus fruit trees in California

cit·ri·culture \'si·trə+,-\ *n* -s [*citr-* + *-culture*] **:** the cultivation of citrus fruits (as oranges, lemons, and grapefruit)

cit·ri·culturist \¦si·trə+\ *n* -s **:** a pomologist who specializes in the cultivation of citrus fruits

cit·rin \'si·trən\ *n* -s [ISV *citr-* + *-in;* orig. formed in G] **:** a crystalline water-soluble flavonoid concentrate that was orig. prepared from lemons and considered to be a source of vitamin P and to consist of hesperidin and eriodictyol glycoside and that is now used as a source of bioflavonoids

cit·ri·na·tion \,si·trə'nāshən\ *n* -s [ME *citrinacioun*, fr. ML *citrination-, citrinatio*, fr. *citrinus* + L *-ation-, -atio* -ation] *obs* **:** an alchemical operation in which a base metal was made more yellow and therefore thought to have been brought nearer to gold

¹cit·rine \'si-,trēn *sometimes* -īn\ *adj* [ME, fr. MF *citrin*, fr. ML *citrinus*, fr. L *citrus* citron tree + *-inus* -ine] **1 :** resembling a citron or lemon **2 :** of the color citrine

²citrine \si·'trēn\ *n* -s **1 :** a light olive color that is redder and deeper than grape green, redder and paler than old moss green, and redder and duller than average willow green — called also *rhubarb* **2 :** a semiprecious yellow stone resembling topaz but actually black quartz changed in color by heating

citrine ointment *n* **:** a yellow ointment of mercuric nitrate and lard used as an antiparasitic

ci·tri·nin \sə'trīnən\ *n* -s [NL *citrinum* (specific epithet of *Penicillium citrinum*) + E *-in*] **:** a toxic antibiotic $C_{13}H_{14}O_5$ that is produced by certain molds (esp. *Penicillium citrinum*) and is bactericidal towards some gram-positive bacteria

cit·ri·nous \'si·trənəs\ *adj* [ML *citrinus* — more at CITRINE] **:** CITRINE

citro- — see CITR-

cit·ro·my·ces \,si·trō'mī(,)sēz\ *n*, *cap* [NL, fr. *citr-* + *-myces*] *in some classifications* **:** a genus of molds comprising those species of the genus *Penicillium* as usu. understood that are monoverticillate and that change sugar into citric acid

cit·ron \'si·trən\ *n* -s [ME, fr. MF, fr. OProv, modif. of L *citrus* citron tree, sandarac tree (*Tetraclinis articulata*); akin to Gk *kedros* cedar — more at CEDAR] **1 a :** a citrus fruit that resembles the lemon in appearance and structure but is larger and without a terminal nipple **b :** a small shrubby citrus tree (*Citrus medica*) that produces citrons **c** *also* **citron melon :** any of various melons derived from a variety (*Citrullus vulgaris citroides*) of the watermelon having the hard fruit often mottled and with white flesh **2 :** the preserved rind of the citron used in cakes, breads, and puddings **3 a :** a grayish greenish yellow **b :** a light yellow

cit·ro·nel·la \,si·trə'nelə, *attrib* ¦==¦==\ *n* -s [NL, fr. F *citronnelle* lemon balm, Barbados water (a cordial), fr. *citron*] **1 :** CITRONELLA OIL **2** *also* **citronella grass :** a fragrant grass (*Cymbopogon nardus*) of southern Asia **3 :** HORSE BALM 1

cit·ro·nel·lal \,==='=,lal, -ləl\ *n* -s [ISV *citronell-* (fr. NL *citronella*) + *-al*] **:** an unsaturated liquid aldehyde $C_9H_{17}CHO$ that has a lemonlike odor, is found in two optically active forms in many essential oils (as Java citronella oil), is formed by oxidation of citronellol, and is used in perfumery and organic synthesis

citronella oil *n* **:** a yellowish essential oil with lemonlike odor obtained from either of two grasses and used esp. as an insect repellent: **a :** an oil from citronella grass containing chiefly geraniol **b :** an oil from a related grass (*Cymbopogon winterianus*) containing citronellal, citronellol, and geraniol — called also *Java citronella oil*

cit·ro·nelle \¦si·trə¦nel\ *n* -s [*citron* + *-elle* (fr. F, dim. suffix, fr. L *-ella*)] *Austral* **:** ROUGH LEMON

cit·ro·nel·lol \,si·trə'ne,lōl, -ōl\ *n* -s [ISV *citronell-* (fr. NL *citronella*) + *-ol*] **:** an unsaturated liquid alcohol $C_{10}H_{19}OH$ that has a roselike odor, is found in two optically active forms in many essential oils (as geranium and rose oils), and is used in perfumery and soaps; 3,7-dimethyl-6-octen-1-ol; *esp* **:** the dextrorotatory form found in Java citronella oil and a gland secretion of the alligator and prepared by reduction of citronellal — see RHODINOL

citron gray *n* **:** a variable color averaging a light grayish olive that is greener and lighter than Quaker gray, greener and paler than hemp, and greener and lighter than twine

citron green *n* **:** a grayish to moderate greenish yellow that is greener and lighter than russet green

citronwood \'==,=\ *n* **1 :** the wood of the citron tree **2 :** the wood of the sandarac tree used in cabinetwork

citron yellow *n* **1 :** a variable color averaging a moderate greenish yellow that is redder, stronger, and slightly lighter than linden green and redder, lighter, and stronger than Javel green or oil yellow **2 :** ZINC YELLOW

ci·troph·i·lous mealybug *also* **ci·troph·i·lus mealybug** \sə·'träfələs-\ *n* [*citrophilus* fr. NL, fr. *citr-* + *-philus; citrophilous* alter. (influenced by *-philous*) of *citrophilus*] **:** a mealybug (*Pseudococcus fragilis*) esp. destructive to citrus

ci·trop·sis \sə·'träpsəs\ *n*, *cap* [NL, fr. *citr-* + *-opsis*] **:** a small genus of spiny evergreen African shrubs or trees (family Rutaceae) differing from the closely related *Citrus* in having compound leaves — see CHERRY ORANGE

ci·trop·ten \sə'träptən\ *also* **ci·trop·tene** \-,tēn\ *n* -s [ISV *citr-* + stear*opten*, stear*optene*] **:** a colorless crystalline compound $C_{11}H_{10}O_4$ found in some essential oils (as lime and lemon oils); 5,7-dimethoxy-coumarin — called also *limettin*

cit·rous \'si·trəs\ *adj* [in sense 1, fr. NL *Citrus;* in sense 2, fr. *citrus* + *-ous*] **1 :** of or relating to the genus *Citrus* ⟨a hardier strain of ~ trees⟩ **2 :** of, relating to, devoted to the production of, or affecting plants or fruit of the genus *Citrus* ⟨a ~ disease⟩ ⟨an important ~ area⟩

ci·trov·o·rum factor \sə·'trävərəm-\ *n* [NL *citrovorum* (specific epithet of *Leuconostoc citrovorum*), fr. *citr-* + *-vorum* (neut. sing. of L *-vorus* -vorous)] **:** FOLINIC ACID

ci·trul·lin \sə·'trələn\ *n* -s [NL *Citrullus* (genus name of *Citrullus colocynthis*) + E *-in*] **:** a purgative yellow resinous preparation of the colocynth

ci·trul·line \-,lēn, -lən\ *n* -s [ISV *citrull-* (fr. NL *Citrullus*, genus name of *Citrullus vulgaris*) + *-ine*] **:** a crystalline amino acid $H_2NCONH(CH_2)_3CH(NH_2)COOH$ formed as an intermediate in the conversion of ornithine to arginine in the living organism; α-amino-δ-ureido-valeric acid

ci·trul·lus \-ləs\ *n*, *cap* [NL, fr. ML *citrullus, citrolus*, a kind of cucumber, fr. (assumed) OIt dial. *citrulo* (It. *cetriolo*), fr. (assumed) VL *citriolum*, fr. LL *citrium*, a kind of cucumber, fr. L, citron, fr. *citrus*] **:** a genus of African plants (family Cucurbitaceae) having pinnatifid leaves, small sepals, solitary staminate flowers, a corolla 5-parted to the base, and fleshy succulent fruits and including the widely cultivated watermelon and the colocynth

cit·rus \'si·trəs\ *n*, *often attrib* [NL, fr. L, citron tree — more at CITRON] **1** *cap* **:** a genus of often thorny trees and shrubs (family Rutaceae) having alternate unifoliolate leaves with a winged petiole, tetramerous flowers with many stamens, and large baccate fruits with pulpy endocarp and firm exocarp, including the orange, lemon, lime, and related fruits, and being native to tropical Asia but now widely cultivated for their fruits — compare CITRANGE, KUMQUAT, MANDARIN, SHADDOCK, TANGELO **2** *pl* **citruses** *or* **citrus :** any plant or fruit of the genus *Citrus* or related genera **3 :** SULPHUR YELLOW 2

citrus anthracnose *n* **:** a disease of various citrus plants (as orange, lemon, and grapefruit) caused by a fungus (*Colletotrichum gloeosporioides*) and characterized by twig blight of mature tips, leaf spots, and fruit stains, spots, or rots — compare TEARSTAIN

citrus blackfly *n* **:** an insect (*Aleurocanthus woglumi*) of the family Aleyrodidae that is destructive to citrus, coffee, and other plants

citrus blast *n* **:** a disease of citrus trees caused by a bacterium (*Pseudomonas syringae*) and characterized by a drying out and browning of leaves and twigs and a black pitting of the fruit

citrus bud mite *n* **:** a widely distributed eriophyid mite (*Aceria sheldoni*) feeding on new growth and flower buds of citrus and esp. destructive to the lemon in California

citrus butterfly *n*, *Austral* **:** either of two swallowtail butterflies (*Papilio aegeus* and *P. anactus*) the larvae of which feed on the foliage of citrus trees

citrus canker *n* **:** a destructive disease of citrus fruits caused by a bacterium (*Xanthomonas citri*) producing lesions on the leaves, twigs, and fruits

citrus fruit *n* **:** any of several edible fruits (as the orange, lemon, and grapefruit) produced by plants of *Citrus* and related genera

citrus gall wasp *n* **:** a chalcid fly (*Eurytoma fellis*) producing twig galls on citrus in Australia

citrus mealybug *n* **:** a widely distributed mealybug (*Planococcus citri*) feeding on a wide variety of cultivated plants but esp. destructive to citrus

citrus molasses *n* **:** molasses made from citrus fruit wastes and commonly fed to livestock

citrus nematode *n* **:** a microscopic roundworm (*Tylenchulus semipenetrans*) that infests the roots of citrus trees causing malnutrition and dwarfing

citrus red mite *or* **citrus red spider** *n* **:** a comparatively large mite (*Panonychus citri*) resembling the European red mite and being a destructive pest of citrus, feeding on the foliage and turning the leaves speckled or silvery by extracting the chlorophyll

citrus rust mite *n* **:** a rust mite (*Phyllocoptruta oleivorus*) that is esp. destructive to growing fruits, causing a russeting of oranges and a silvering of lemons by its feeding

citrus scab *n* **:** a disease of citrus plants caused by an imperfect fungus (*Elsinoë fawcettii*) producing scablike or warty lesions on trees, leaves, and fruits

citrus thrips *n* **:** a small yellow thrips (*Scirtothrips citri*) that is a major pest of citrus, esp. the orange, in the southwestern U.S.

citrus whitefly *n* **:** a widely distributed whitefly (*Dialeurodes citri*) having a scalelike larva that is a destructive pest of citrus

ci·tryl·i·dene \sə·'trilə,dēn\ *n* -s [*citral* + *-ylidene*] **:** the bivalent radical $C_9H_{15}CH<$ formed by removal of the oxygen atom from citral

cits *pl of* CIT

cit·tern \'sidə(r)n\ *or* **cith·ern** \-ithə(r)n, -th-\ *or* **cith·ren** \-ithrən\ *n* -s [blend of *cither* and *gittern*] **:** a guitar with a pear-shaped flat-backed body and wire strings popular esp. in Renaissance England

cittern

citternhead *n*, *obs* **:** BLOCKHEAD, DUNCE

cit·to·tae·nia \,sidə'tēnēə\ *n*, *cap* [NL] **:** a genus of taenioid tapeworms parasitic in rodents

city \'sid·ē, -itē, -i\ *n* -ES *often attrib* [ME *citie*, fr. OF *cité*, fr. L *civitat-, civitas*, fr. *civis* citizen + *-itat-, -itas* -ity — more at HOME] **1** *archaic* **:** an inhabited place **:** HAMLET, VILLAGE **2 a :** a large or important incorporated town or borough in Great Britain holding a royal charter and usu. being the seat of an episcopacy — a title bearing traditional and honorary significance but not specific legal significance **b :** a populous place **:** a place larger than a village or town **:** a large, prominent, or important center of population ⟨the *cities* of the ancient world⟩; *specif* **:** a relatively permanent and highly organized center having a population with varied skills, lacking self-sufficiency in the production of food, and usu. depending primarily on manufacture and commerce to satisfy the wants of its inhabitants ⟨the ~ offers real cultural advantages⟩ **c :** CITY-STATE **d :** a municipal corporation in the U.S. occupying a definite area and subject to the state from which it derives its powers and for which it exists as an area of local government governed under a legal charter by a mayor and council, by a commission, or by a city manager and council and being usu. more populous than a town, borough, or village — see COMMISSION PLAN, COUNCIL-MANAGER PLAN **e :** a Canadian municipality of the highest class varying in character in the different provinces **f :** an administrative area centering in a municipality and set up under the protection of an international body (as the League of Nations) chiefly for the purpose of insuring freedom of trade and communication — see FREE CITY c **3 :** the inhabitants or citizens of a city **4 :** an aggregation of dwellings or other structures that is of such size or importance as to suggest a city ⟨a trailer ~ of construction workers⟩ ⟨Radio *City*⟩

city central *n* **:** an organization made up of locals of several labor unions within a city

city chicken *n* **:** pieces of boneless veal on skewers cooked by braising

city council *n* **:** the legislative body of a city

city crop *n* **:** the part of the annual crop of cotton, statistically considered, that has been rebaled and that consists of samples, sweepings, and pickings from damaged bales

city desk *n* **:** a department or section of a newspaper editorial office where local news is edited

city edition *n* **:** an edition of a usu. metropolitan newspaper that is designed for sale within the city and that is later than and distinguished from a suburban edition or mail edition — called also *home edition*

city editor *n* **1** *often cap C* [fr. (The) *City*, the financial section of London, England] *Brit* **:** the editor of financial and commercial news on a newspaper **2 :** a newspaper editor with varying functions but usu. in charge of local news and staff assignments

city father *n* **:** a member of the governing body of a city (as an alderman or councilman)

city hall *n* **1 :** the chief municipal building of a city **2 :** a city government **:** city officialdom or bureaucracy

city·ite \'==,īt\ *n* -s **:** a resident of a city

city·less \-ləs\ *adj* **:** lacking a city

city manager *n* **:** an official employed by an elected council to direct the administration of a city government — see COUNCIL-MANAGER PLAN

city-manager plan *n* **:** COUNCIL-MANAGER PLAN

city·ness *n* -ES **:** the quality or state of being citified

city of god *cap C&G* [trans. of LL *Civitas Dei*, an ideal heavenly city described by Saint Augustine (*Aurelius Augustinus*) †430 early Christian church father in his work *De Civitate Dei* (*The City of God*)] **:** NEW JERUSALEM **:** PARADISE, HEAVEN

city of refuge : a city in ancient Israel appointed as a place of asylum for unintentional murderers

city plan *n* **:** an organized arrangement or laying out (as of the streets, parks, and business sections) of a city with a view to general convenience, attractiveness of appearance, and the encouragement of healthier living

city planner *n* **:** one that makes city plans; *esp* **:** a professional who participates in such activity

city room *n* **1 a :** the room or department where local news is handled in a newspaper editorial office **b :** the personnel of such a room or department **2 :** a newspaper editorial room

city·scape \'==,skāp\ *n* -s [*city* + *-scape*] **1 :** a pictorial representation of a city **2 :** a city viewed as a scene or picture ⟨the skyscrapers which now bedizen the American ~ —*Amer. Mercury*⟩ **3 :** a pictorial composition of urban elements

city slicker *n* **:** SLICKER 3; *broadly* **:** someone regarded as sophisticated or effete

city-state \'==¦=\ *n* [trans. of Gk *polis* & L *civitas*] **:** a state (as in classical antiquity) in which the sovereignty is vested in the free citizens of an independent city and extends over the territories under its direct control — compare FREE CITY a

city·ward \'==wə(r)d\ *or* **city·wards** \-wə(r)dz\ *adj* (*or adv*) [ME *cite-ward*, fr. *cite, citie* city + *-ward* — more at CITY] **:** to or toward the city ⟨~ migration⟩ ⟨hastening ~⟩

ciu·dad juá·rez *or* **ciudad juarez** \,sēü,thä'wärəs, -ü,dad'-, -'(h)wär,ez\ *adj*, *usu cap C&J* [fr. *Ciudad Juárez*, Mexico] **:** of or from Ciudad Juárez, Mexico **:** of the kind or style prevalent in Ciudad Juárez

ciudad tru·ji·llo \-trü'hi(,)lō, -'hē(,)yō\ *adj*, *usu cap C&T* [fr. *Ciudad Trujillo*, former name of Santo Domingo, Dominican Republic] **:** of or from Ciudad Trujillo, Dominican Republic **:** of the kind or style prevalent in Ciudad Trujillo

civ *abbr* civil; civilian

cive \'sīv\ *n* -s [ME, fr. MF, chives, onion, fr. L *cepa, cepe* onion] **:** ¹CHIVE 1

¹civ·et \'sivət\ *n* -s [MF *civette*, fr. It *zibetto*, fr. Ar. *zabād* civet perfume] **1 :** CIVET CAT **2 :** a substance found in a pouch near the sexual organs of the true civet cats that is of the consistency of butter or honey, clear yellowish or brownish in color, with a strong musky odor, used in perfume, and chemically a complex mixture chiefly of fats and volatile oils **3 :** the fur of a civet or of a little spotted skunk

²ci·vet \sēvā\ *n* -s [F, alter. of OF *civé* hare or venison stew cooked in onion-flavored wine sauce, fr. *cive* onion, chives] **:** a highly seasoned stew of game

civ·et bean \'sivət-\ *n* [prob. by folk etymology fr. *Sieva bean*] **:** SIEVA BEAN

civet cat *n* **1 a :** any of various carnivorous mammals of the family Viverridae; *esp* **:** a brownish gray black-marked African animal (*Civettictis civetta*) two to three feet long that produces most of the civet of commerce — compare BUSH CAT 2, PALM CIVET, VIVERRA **b :** the cacomistle or any other animal of the genus *Bassariscus* **c :** LITTLE SPOTTED SKUNK **2 :** the fur of a civet cat

civ·e·tone \'sivə,tōn\ *n* -s [ISV *civet* + *-one;* prob. orig. formed as G *zibeton*] **:** a crystalline ketone $C_{17}H_{30}O$ that constitutes the characteristic odorous constituent of civet and that is used in perfumes, the odor becoming sweet on dilution

ci·vet·ta \sə'ved·ə\ *n* -s [NL, fr. *Civetta*, old genus including the civet, fr. F *civette* civet] **:** CIVET 2

ci·vette green \sə'vet-\ *n* [F *civette* civet] **:** a dark yellowish green that is yellower and paler than average hunter green or holly green (sense 1) and yellower, lighter, and stronger than deep chrome green

civ·ic \'sivik, -ēk\ *adj* [L *civicus*, fr. *civis* citizen — more at CITY] **1 :** inherent in or owing or accruing to the individual citizen **:** attendant on citizenship ⟨pledged by treaty to observe ~ liberties⟩ ⟨giving dissidents full ~ rights⟩ — used less commonly than *civil* in this sense **2 :** forming a component of or connected with the functioning, integration, and development of a civilized community (as a town or city) involving the common public activities and interests of the body of citizens ⟨the mayor urged low-cost housing as a prime ~ project⟩ ⟨~ pride⟩ ⟨~ opera⟩ ⟨this suburb is growing gradually with deepening ~ consciousness⟩ **3 :** concerned with or contributory to general welfare and the betterment of life for the citizenry of a community or enhancement of its facilities; *esp* **:** devoted to improving health, education, safety, recreation, and morale of the general public through nonpolitical means ⟨giving generously to various ~ clubs and causes⟩ ⟨lacking ~ initiative⟩ ⟨architectural congruity calls for ~ imagination⟩ ⟨a real sense of ~ and social responsibilities⟩ **4 :** essential to or obligatory on citizens in connection with the administration of laws and regulations **:** relating to government ⟨public office as a ~ duty⟩

civ·i·cal·ly \-vək(ə)lē, -ēk-, -li\ *adv* **1 :** with respect to or regard for civic demands and activities ⟨~ aroused about housing conditions⟩ **2 :** into one civic unit

civic center *n* **:** a section of a city or town usu. near the center where administration buildings, courts, libraries, galleries, and other public buildings are grouped

civic crown *also* **civic wreath** *n* [trans. of L *corona civica*] **1 :** a crown or garland of oak leaves and acorns bestowed by the Romans for saving the life of a citizen in battle **2 :** a representation of a civic crown esp. in architecture or heraldry

civ·i·cism \'sivə,sizəm\ *n* -s [*civic* + *-ism*] **:** devotion to civic interests and causes **:** CIVIC-MINDEDNESS

civ·i·cize \-,sīz\ *vt* -ED/-ING/-s **:** to infuse with civic consciousness

civic-minded \¦==¦==\ *adj* **:** disposed to look after civic needs and interests — **civ·ic-mind·ed·ness** *n* -ES

civ·ics \'siviks, -ēks\ *n pl but usu sing in constr* **:** study of the workings of the national and local government esp. as the subject of a secondary school course suited as training for citizenship

civic university *n* **:** one of the modern universities in Great Britain founded since the early 19th century orig. designed for the education of middle-class youth and therefore usu. nonresidential and situated in a large city

civie *var of* CIVVY

civ·il \'sivəl, *esp Brit sometimes* -(,)vil\ *adj* [ME, fr. MF, fr. L *civilis*, fr. *civis* citizen — more at CITY] **1 a :** relating to, growing out of, or involving the relations of citizens one with another or with the body politic or organized state or its divisions and departments ⟨~ institutions⟩ ⟨interested in ~ affairs⟩ ⟨a contribution to ~ philosophy⟩ **b :** concerned with or pertinent to internal affairs of a state or its citizenry in contrast to external affairs ⟨~ strife between two political groups⟩ ⟨~ embargo⟩ **2 a :** composed of or shared by individuals living and participating in a community ⟨the oldest form of ~ society were the early city-states of oriental antiquity —H.E.Barnes⟩ **b :** given to or marked by group activity or organization ⟨man is a ~ creature⟩ **3 :** concerning, befitting, or applying to the collective citizenry or the individual citizen ⟨a ~ duty⟩ ⟨the individual's ~ right of free speech⟩ — see CIVIL LIBERTY, CIVIL RIGHTS **4 a :** living in or exhibiting a condition of social advancement marked by organization and stability of community life or government **:** not uncivilized or primitive ⟨tribal anarchy giving way to ~ order⟩ **b :** marked by public order **:** quiet and peaceable in behavior ⟨areas still ~ in the turbulent country⟩ **c :** educated, cultured, or sophisticated **:** not rustic and unlettered ⟨a ~ philosophy⟩ ⟨~ jests⟩ **5 a :** based on or skilled in the Roman civil law ⟨a ~ doctor —Shak.⟩ **b :** relating to private rights and to legal proceedings in connection with them : relating to rights and remedies sought by action or suit distinct from criminal proceedings — distinguished from *criminal* and *political* ⟨a ~ liability⟩ ⟨~ jurisdiction⟩ ⟨a ~ suit⟩ ⟨a ~ remedy⟩; see CIVIL LAW **c** : as defined by law : having to do with legal rights or status ⟨~ disabilities⟩ — compare NATURAL 5; see CIVIL DEATH **6 a** *sometimes* -ER/-EST : adequate in courtesy and politeness : marked by satisfactory adherence to social usage and sufficient but not noteworthy consideration for others : MANNERLY ⟨even if he didn't like them he should have been ~ —W.S.Maugham⟩ ⟨it was all he could do to be ~ to her —Mary Austin⟩ ⟨I asked a ~ question, and I expect a ~ answer —D.H.Lawrence⟩ **b** *sometimes* -ER/-EST : showing goodwill, humaneness, or clemency : not savage or fierce ⟨the *civilest* and most friendly people that we met with —Daniel Defoe⟩ **c** *obs* : SOBER, STAID : not showy or audacious : QUIET **d** : seemly in aspect : compatible with human sensibilities : PRESENTABLE, SHIPSHAPE **e** *dial, of weather* : not inclement : FAVORABLE **7** *of time* : based on the mean sun and legally recognized for use by the general public in ordinary affairs — distinguished from *sidereal* ⟨the ~ calendar⟩ ⟨a ~ day begins at mean midnight⟩ **8 a** : belonging or relating to the general public, the pursuits, experiences, ways, and interests of the citizenry, or to civic or temporal affairs as distinguished from military, naval, ecclesiastical, or like specialized membership or affairs : CIVILIAN ⟨new educational techniques, learned in the war just ended, should be put into ~ use —Henry Wallace⟩ ⟨the old conflict between the ~ and the sacerdotal powers —Edward Clodd⟩ **b** : representing or serving the general public in the sphere of political rule or administration; *esp* : belonging to or sanctioned by an executive department of a nation, state, or municipality ⟨officials of a ~ board⟩ ⟨prohibiting a member of Congress from being appointed to any ~ office⟩ ⟨rates and hours set by ~ regulations⟩ **9** *obs* : virtuous by nature but not regenerate : moral as distinguished from religious ⟨~ righteousness⟩

syn POLITE, COURTEOUS, COURTLY, GALLANT, CHIVALROUS: CIVIL now implies adequate consideration of others and forbearance from rudeness or unpleasantness ⟨remember, then, that to be *civil* . . . is the only way to be beloved and well received in company, that to be ill-bred . . . is intolerable —Earl of Chesterfield⟩ ⟨I mean to return his visit tomorrow. It will be only *civil* in return for his politeness, to ask to see him —Sheridan Le Fanu⟩ POLITE may imply cold, formal, perfunctory deference to etiquette ⟨let's be *polite*, but act as though she didn't exist —Sherwood Anderson⟩ Often it differs from CIVIL in suggesting somewhat warmer or more sincere consideration of others ⟨the bishop seldom questioned Jacinto about his thoughts or beliefs. He didn't think it *polite* —Willa Cather⟩ ⟨under ordinary circumstances he would have tried to be *polite*. As it was, he could hardly bring himself to give them a *civil* word of welcome —Norman Douglas⟩ COURTEOUS may suggest a certain polish and delicacy of action; it may connote either mere formal deference, however perfect, to custom, or a genuine sincere consideration and regard ⟨the baronet peeped at his grandson with the *courteous* indifference of one who merely wishes to compliment that mother of anybody's child —George Meredith⟩ ⟨M. Laval owns a fine old historical painting in Chateldon, and he was *courteous* enough to permit me to view it —Upton Sinclair⟩ COURTLY suggests the stately or ceremonious ⟨Pitt Crawley treated her to a profound *courtly* bow, such as he had used to H. H. the Duchess of Pumpernickel, when he was attaché at that court —W.M. Thackeray⟩ GALLANT and CHIVALROUS, in this sense, indicate esp. courtesy and attention to women, the former often suggesting either the spirited and dashing or the elaborate and over-attentive ⟨the qualities . . . of surface chivalry and *gallant* attentiveness in her brilliant American friend had for a moment seemed to reveal a lack in me —Havelock Ellis⟩ CHIVALROUS in this sense often connotes high-mindedness and disinterested attention ⟨ladies were supposed to be without sexual desire . . . gracious beings they were, without a sordid thought, according to the *chivalrous* notions of the time —W.E.Woodward⟩ ⟨she had fainted from weakness, and he had felt strangely *chivalrous* and paternal —Ellen Glasgow⟩

civil affairs *n pl* : affairs and operations of the civil population of a territory that are supervised and directed by a friendly occupying power

civil airway *n* : an airway designated by the national civil aeronautic authority as suitable for interstate or foreign air commerce

civil architecture *n* : ARCHITECTURE 1

civil authority clause *n* : a clause in fire and similar insurance policies excluding loss caused by order of civil authorities unless destruction is for the purpose of checking the progress of the hazard insured against

civil bond *n, Brit* : a security issued by a sovereign or quasi-sovereign state and usu. not secured by collateral

civil contempt *n* : willful disobedience to a lawful order or decree entered as a civil remedy for the benefit of a party to a lawsuit

civil corporation *n* : a corporation organized for business purposes — contrasted with *eleemosynary corporation*

civil day *n* : a day adopted for time reckoning in civil affairs; *usu* : the mean solar day of 24 hours beginning at mean midnight

civil death *n* : a change of status of a person equivalent in its legal consequences to natural death : deprivation of rights and privileges as a citizen or a member of society

civil defense *n* : protective measures and emergency relief activities conducted by civilians under civilian authority for minimizing civilian casualties and property damage and for maintaining vital facilities and services in case of hostile attack or natural disaster

civil disobedience *n* : refusal to obey the demands or commands of the government esp. as a nonviolent collective means of forcing concessions from the government — see NONCOOPERATION

civil district *n* : a district formed for administrative purposes; *specif* : a minor political division of a county in certain states

civil embargo *n* : a government's embargo on the movement of ships under its own registry — compare HOSTILE EMBARGO

civil engineer *n* : an engineer whose training or occupation is in civil engineering —abbr. *C.E.*

civil engineering *n* : a branch of engineering concerned primarily with public works (as land surveying, the building of highways, bridges, waterways, or harbors, or the provision of artificial water supply, sewage disposal, irrigation) but also embracing private enterprises (as railroad and airport building, private building construction, farm drainage)

¹ci·vil·ian \sə'vilyən\ *n* -S [ME, fr. *civile* civil law (fr. L, short for *jus civile*) + *-ian*] **1 a** : one who practices or has made a special study of the Roman or modern civil law esp. as distinguished from the canon law and the English common law **b** : one esp. skilled in or devoted to the law affecting civil rights and remedies **2** : an employee in the former imperial civil service of India **3 a** : a resident of a country who is not on active duty in one of the armed services **b** : a resident not an active member of a police or fire-fighting force organized with ranks like military ranks **4 civilians** *pl* : CIVVIES

²civilian \"\ *adj* **1 a** : made up of civilians ⟨the ~ population⟩ **b** : belonging to or issuing from the aggregate body of civilians ⟨~ customers⟩ ⟨~ demands⟩ : peculiar to civilians ⟨~ habits of mind⟩ **c** : having the status of a civilian ⟨a ~ pilot⟩ **2 a** : operated or controlled by civilians ⟨~ industry⟩ : possessed by or vested in civilians ⟨~ authority⟩ **b** : undergone or sustained by civilians ⟨~ sacrifices⟩ **3 a** : intended or allotted for use or consumption by civilians ⟨~ goods⟩ **b** : suitable for civilians

ci·vil·ian·ism \-,nizəm\ *n* -S : dominance of civilian interests and their independence over military force

ci·vil·ian·i·za·tion \ˌ=,==nə'zāshən, -,nī'z-\ *n* -S : the action of civilianizing

ci·vil·ian·ize \=ˈ==,nīz\ *vt* -ED/-ING/-S *see -ize in Explan Notes* : to convert from military to civilian status or control

civil imprisonment *n* : imprisonment by civil process

civ·i·lise *Brit var of* CIVILIZE

civ·i·list \'sivəlǝst\ *n* -S [ML *civilista*, fr. L *civile* civil law + *-ista* -ist] *archaic* : CIVILIAN 1

ci·vil·i·té \sə'vilə(,)tā, =,==ˈ=\ *n* -S [F, lit., civility] : an early French cursive hand; *also* : a type styled therefrom

ci·vi·li·ter mor·tu·us \sə'vilətər'mȯrchəwəs, kə'vilə,ter-'mȯrd·əwəs\ *adj* [NL] : civilly dead

ci·vil·i·ty \sə'viləd·ē, -ətē, -i\ *n* -ES [ME *civylite*, fr. MF *civilité*, fr. L *civilitat-, civilitas*, fr. *civilis* + *-itat-, -itas* -ity] **1 a** *obs* : decency or allegiance to the social order befitting a citizen **b** *obs* : civil government or polity **c** : solidarity of civil rights and obligations and civil justice in the civil order ⟨our great traditions of ~, the liberties western man has won for himself after centuries of struggle —Walter Lippmann⟩ **2** : the state of being civilized : CIVILIZATION 3 ⟨I have heard ladies say that the measure of a people's ~ is the position it accords to women —Clive Bell⟩ **3** *archaic* : training in the humanities **4 a** : civil conduct; *esp* : bare observance of the forms of accepted social behavior or adequate perfunctory politeness **b** *obs* : decent behavior or treatment : PROPRIETY **c** : an act or expression conforming to conventional patterns of social behavior

civ·i·liz·a·ble \'sivə,līzəbəl\ *adj* [F *civilisable*, fr. *civiliser* to civilize + *-able*] : capable of being civilized

civ·i·li·za·tion *or* **civ·i·li·sa·tion** \ˌsivələ'zāshən, sivə,lī'zāshən, *Brit often & US sometimes* -vi-\ *n* -S [*civilize* + *-ation*, prob. influenced in meaning by F *civilisation*] **1** *obs* : the act of making a criminal process civil **2 a** : an ideal state of human culture characterized by complete absence of barbarism and nonrational behavior, optimum utilization of physical, cultural, spiritual, and human resources, and perfect adjustment of the individual within the social framework ⟨true ~ is an ideal to be striven for⟩ **b** : a particular state or stage of human advance toward civilization: as (1) : the culture characteristic of a particular time or place ⟨medieval ~⟩ ⟨the impact of European ~ on primitive peoples⟩; *sometimes* : a widely diffused long-lived culture often with subcultures ⟨the Aegean ~ was a confluence of many Bronze Age cultures⟩ (2) : the stage of cultural development at which writing and the keeping of written records is attained; *also* : the stage marked by urbanization, advanced techniques (as of agriculture and industry), expanded population, and complex social organization ⟨modern ~ with its helpless dependence on technology⟩ **3** : the process of becoming civilized : progressive development of arts, sciences, statescraft, and human aspirations and spirituality ⟨~ is a slow process marked by many failures and setbacks⟩ **4** : the act of civilizing; *esp* : the forcing of a particular cultural pattern on a population to which it is foreign ⟨much of the nation's strength was wasted on the bloody ~ of unwilling peoples⟩ **5** : the whole of the advances of human culture and aspirations beyond the purely animal level ⟨~ is the descriptive inventory of all the modifications brought about in . . . the normal life of man in society —Pierre Lecomte du Noüy⟩ ⟨the first man to chip a stone into a better tool took a great step forward in ~⟩ **6** : conformity to conventional patterns of behavior or expression : refinement of thought, manners, or taste **7 a** : the parts of the earth characterized by a relatively high level of cultural and technological development ⟨made his way across the lands of two hostile tribes to reach ~⟩ **b** : a situation of urban comfort : city life ⟨we enjoy our country weekends but it's good to get back to ~ and hot running water⟩

civ·i·li·za·tion·al \ˌ==(,)=ˈzāshən°l, -shnəl\ *adj* : dealing with or relating to civilization — **civ·i·li·za·tion·al·ly** \-shən°lē, -shnəlē, -i\ *adv*

civ·i·liz·a·to·ry \ˈ==,līzə,tōrē\ *adj* [*civilization* + *-ory*] : tending to advance civilization : CIVILIZING

civ·i·lize \'sivə,līz, *Brit often & US sometimes* -vi-\ *vb* -ED/-ING/-S *see -ize in Explan Notes* [F *civiliser*, fr. *civil* + *-iser* -ize] *vt* **1** : to give a civil character to: **a** : to cause (as a people) to develop out of a primitive state through establishment of a system of social custom and political organization : instruct in the rules and standards of a civil order **b** : to bring (a people) to a technically advanced and rationally ordered stage of development of knowledge, polity, and international relations **2** : to raise up to a rationally and aesthetically refined and humanely oriented level of adjustment to the collective relations of mankind: **a** : to instruct in the sophisticated attitudes, polished elegance, and polite observances of elite society and good breeding : train in urbanity **b** : to instruct in or bring into line with the standards of self-control, uprightness, and impartial consideration of common needs and aspirations of humankind that are essential to social harmony and security of human freedoms : SOCIALIZE 2 **c** : to bring to recognition of or to accord with cultivated and refined aesthetic standards of classic literature and the fine arts **3** *obs* : to bring under civil authority **4** *obs* : to declare or treat as socially permissible or acceptable ~ *vi* **1** : to acquire the customs and amenities of a civil community **2** *dial* : to array or tidy oneself according to the standard of seemliness acceptable in a community

civilized *adj* **1** : advanced in social culture : characterized by progress esp. in statecraft and in the arts and sciences ⟨the essential characteristic of a highly ~ society is . . . that it is appreciative —Clive Bell⟩ **2** : of or relating to peoples or nations in a state of civilization ⟨must not be supposed that there is any essential stability in a ~ way of life —Bertrand Russell⟩ **3 a** : characterized by politeness, refinement, or good breeding ⟨had become a ~ chivalrous Christian knight —Charles Kingsley⟩ **b** : characterized by sophistication or urbanity ⟨he is humorous, ironic, and penetrating in a dispassionate ~ way —Marvin Lowenthal⟩ — **civ·i·lized·ness** \ˈ==,līzədnəs, -z(d)n-\ *n* -ES

civ·i·liz·ee \ˌ==,lī'zē\ *n* -S : a civilized person

civ·i·liz·er \ˈ==,līzə(r)\ *n* -S : one that civilizes

civil law *n, sometimes cap C&L* [ME *lawe civile*, trans. of L *jus civile*] **1** *Roman law* **a** : the local law of a state or of Rome — distinguished from *jus gentium* and *jus naturae* **b** : the strict law as distinguished from the praetorian law established by edicts **2** : Roman law as applied in the middle ages and set forth chiefly in the Justinian Code **3 a** : the body of private law that has developed from the Roman law in the states where the legal system is still substantially Roman but has been influenced by Germanic, ecclesiastical, and purely modern institutions — compare COMMON LAW **b** : the law of private rights — distinguished from *criminal law*

civil libertarian *n* : one who upholds the principles of civil liberty; *esp* : one who defends civil liberties against invasion

civil liberty *n* : freedom from arbitrary governmental interference (as with the right of free speech) specif. by denial of governmental power and in the U.S. esp. as guaranteed by the Bill of Rights — usu. used in pl.

civil list *n* **1** *British Commonwealth* : a list of sums appropriated annually to pay members of the civil government (as judges, ambassadors, secretaries) and civil servants — obs. in U.S. **2** : a list of sums appropriated by a parliament to pay expenses of the sovereign and his household

civ·il·ly \'sivəl(l)ē, -ivi-, -)i\ *adv* **1** : with just ordinary cool or perfunctory politeness **2 a** : in connection with civil rights and liabilities or civil affairs **b** : in civil relations ⟨a ~ united Europe⟩ **3** : in accordance with civil law or obligation

civilly dead *adj* : dead in the eyes of the law

civil marriage *n* : a marriage solemnized before a civil magistrate as distinguished from one before a clergyman

civil process *n* : a writ or order of court in a civil action; *esp* : a writ for arrest in a civil proceeding

civil rights *n pl* **1** : those rights the enjoyment of which does not involve participation in the establishment, support, or management of the government; *specif* : the rights secured to citizens of the U.S. by the 13th and 14th amendments to the constitution and certain acts passed by Congress April 9, 1866, May 31, 1870, and March 1, 1875, abolishing the civil incidents of involuntary servitude **2** : rights that guarantee to all citizens equal opportunities (as for employment, schooling, housing, or voting) regardless of race, religion, sex, or national origin

civils *n pl, obs* : civil affairs

civil servant *n* **1** : a member of a civil service **2** : a member of the administrative staff of an international agency

civil service *n* **1 a** : the branch of the service of the East India Company conducted by covenanted servants not belonging to the army or navy **b** : the whole public administrative service of a government including all branches except the armed services **c** : the whole body of public servants employed by a government other than those in the armed services **2** : government service in which appointments and status are determined by merit or examination rather than by political patronage

civil-spoken \ˈ==ˈ==\ *adj* : given to speaking courteously

civil time *n* : clock time reckoned in mean solar hours, minutes, and seconds and commonly divided into 12-hour periods beginning alternately at midnight and noon of each civil day — see STANDARD TIME

civil twilight *n* : the period after sunset or before sunrise ending or beginning when the sun is about 6 degrees below the horizon and during which on clear days there is enough light for ordinary outdoor occupations

civil war *n* : a war between different sections or parties of the same country or nation

civ·ism \'si,vizəm\ *n* -S [F *civisme*, fr. L *civis* citizen + F *-isme* -ism — more at HOME] : the virtues and sentiments of a good citizen — used orig. of devotion to the cause of the French revolution of 1789

ci·vi·tas \'kēwē,täs\ *n, pl* **civi·ta·tes** \ˌkēwē'tä,tās\ [L — more at CITY] : a body of people constituting a politically organized community : STATE; *esp* : CITY-STATE

civitas dei \-'dā,ē\ *n, usu cap C&D* [LL — more at CITY OF GOD] : CITY OF GOD

civ·vy *also* **civ·ie** \'sivē, -vi\ *n, pl* **civvies** *also* **civies** [by shortening and alter. fr. *civilian*] **1** *civvies pl* : civilian clothes as distinguished from military or naval uniform **2** : CIVILIAN

civvy street *n, Brit* : civilian life

cixi·id \'siksēəd\ *n* -S [NL *Cixiidae*] : an insect of the family Cixiidae

cixi·idae \sik'sīə,dē\ *n pl, cap* [NL, fr. *Cixius*, type genus (fr. LGk *kixios* cicada) + *-idae*] : a family of small elongated somewhat depressed insects (suborder Homoptera) related to the lantern flies

CJ *abbr* chief judge; chief justice

ck *abbr* **1** cake **2** cask **3** chalk **4** check **5** cook **6** countersink

CKD *abbr* completely knocked down

ckw *abbr* clockwise

cl *abbr* **1** centiliter **2** claim; claiming **3** class; classification **4** classical **5** clause **6** clearance **7** clergyman **8** clerk **9** close; closure **10** cloth **11** clove **12** clutch **13** coil

CL *abbr* **1** carload; carload lot **2** cash letter **3** center line **4** civil law **5** common law **6** connecting line

Cl *symbol* chlorine

¹clab·ber \'klabə(r) *sometimes* -läb-\ *also* **clabbered milk** *or* **clabber milk** *n* -S [short for *bonnyclabber*] *now chiefly dial* : sour milk that has thickened or curdled

²clabber \"\ *vb* **clabbered; clabbered; clabbering** \-b(ə)riŋ\ **clabbers** *chiefly Midland* : CURDLE, LOPPER

³clab·ber \'klabə(r), -läb-,-läb-\ *n* -S [ScGael & IrGael *clābar*] *dial Brit* : MUD, MIRE

⁴clab·ber \'kläbə(r), 'klab-\ *n* -S [by shortening & alter. fr. *klaberjass*] : klaberjass or a similar card game derived from it

clabber cheese *n* [¹*clabber*] *dial* : COTTAGE CHEESE

cla·chan \'klakən\ *n* -S [ME, fr. ScGael, hamlet, stepping-stones, prob. fr. *clach* stone; akin to OIr *cloch* stone] *Scot & Irish* : HAMLET

¹clack \'klak\ *vb* -ED/-ING/-S [ME *clacken*, of imit. origin] *vi* **1** : to utter words or sounds rapidly and continually : let the tongue run on : CHATTER ⟨just get her started and she'll ~ all day —J.C.Lincoln⟩ **2** : to make a sharp abrupt noise ⟨the whiplash ~*ed*, the jog-trot sharpened —Edmund Blunden⟩ or succession of such noises ⟨teletypes ~*ed* in all police stations —*Time*⟩ : CLATTER ⟨she ~*ed* up the aisle and entered a front pew —Bruce Marshall⟩ **3** *of fowl* : CACKLE, CLUCK ⟨hen voices ~*ing* —Edith Sitwell⟩ ~ *vt* **1** : to cause to make a sharp noise : make clatter ⟨grasshoppers . . . ~*ing* their desiccate wings —William Goyen⟩ **2** : to produce with a cracking or clapping sound; *specif* : BLAB, BABBLE ⟨all sorts of rumors were ~*ed* about⟩

²clack "\ *n* -S [ME *clakke*, fr. *clacken*, v.] **1** : loud confused noise (as of many voices) : loud continual, importunate, or foolish talk : CHATTER, PRATTLE ⟨nothing but a farrago of the ~ of nurses —Laurence Sterne⟩ **2** *archaic* : an object (as a rattle or clack valve) that produces clapping or cracking noises usu. in regular rapid sequence **3** : a sharp abrupt noise or succession of such noises often produced by the striking together of objects ⟨dull ~*s* of plates and cups —Elizabeth M. Roberts⟩ **4 a** : a gossiping tongue ⟨her ~ was going all day —Mark Twain⟩ **b** : one having such a tongue ⟨that old ~⟩

clack·a·mas *or* **clak·a·mas** \'klakəməs\ *n, pl* **clackamas** *or* **clakamas** *usu cap* [modif. of Clackamas *Guithlákimas*] **1 a** : an Indian people of the Clackamas river valley of northwestern Oregon **b** : a member of such people **2** : a dialect of Upper Chinook

clack·dish \'klak,dish\ *n* [so called fr. the sound made by the lid] : CLAPDISH

clack·er \'klakə(r)\ *n* -S : one that clacks: as **a** *dial Brit* : a gossiping tongue **b** *dial Brit* : a rattle to frighten away birds

clack·et \'klakət\ *vb* [MF *claqueter*, fr. *claquet* clapper of a mill, fr. *claque* slap, clatter, of imit. origin] *dial* : CLACK

clack goose \'klak-\ *var of* CLAIK GOOSE

clack·man·nan·shire \(')klak'manən,shi(ə)r, -,shər\ *or* **clack·man·nan** \(')=ˈ==\ *adj, usu cap* [fr. *Clackmannanshire* or *Clackmannan* county, Scotland] : of or from the county of Clackmannan, Scotland : of the kind or style prevalent in Clackmannan

clack valve *n* : a valve usu. hinged at one edge that permits flow of fluid in one direction only and that closes with a clacking sound — called also *clapper valve*

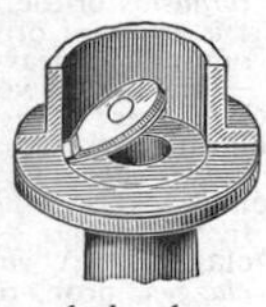

clack valve (open)

cla·co \'klä(,)kō\ *n* -S [MexSp, alter. of Sp *tlaco*] : TLACO

clac·to·ni·an \(')klak'tōnēən, -nyən\ *adj, usu cap* [*Clacton*-on-Sea, England, where the flaking tools were first found + E *-ian*] : of or relating to a lower Paleolithic culture of England characterized by a peculiar method of flaking stone that resulted in flakes having a half cone at the point where the hammerstone struck

¹clad \'klad, -aa(ə)d\ [ME *clad, cladde*, fr. OE *clǣthde*, past of *clǣthan* to clothe, fr. *clāth* garment, cloth — more at CLOTH] *past of* CLOTHE

²clad \"\ *adj* [ME *cladd*, fr. OE *geclǣthd*, past part. of *clǣthan* to clothe] **1 a** : CLOTHED ⟨well-*clad* children⟩ **b** : DECKED, ADORNED ⟨ivy-*clad* buildings⟩ **2 a** : SHEATHED, COVERED ⟨an armor-*clad* car⟩ **b** *of a metal* : overlaid on one or both sides with a metal coating of a different composition to promote electrical conductivity or corrosion resistance or to impart other special properties ⟨copper-*clad* steel⟩ ⟨~ coins⟩

³clad \"\ *vt* **clad; clad; cladding; clads** [ME *claden*, fr. *cladd*, adj] **1** : CLOTHE ⟨*cladding* himself with the ornaments belonging to his degree —Edward Dacres⟩ **2** : SHEATHE, FACE ⟨the long wall . . . ~ in vertical boarding of walnut —Michael Rosenauer⟩; *specif* : to cover (a metal) with another metal by bonding

clad- *or* **clado-** *comb form* [NL, fr. Gk *klad-, klado-*, fr. *klados* — more at GLADIATOR] : slip : sprout ⟨*clad*anthous⟩ ⟨*clado*phyll⟩

cla·dan·thous \klə'dan(t)thəs\ *adj* [*clad-* + *-anthous*] : PLEUROCARPOUS

clad·au·toi·cous \ˌkladə'tȯikəs, -ad,dȯ't-\ *adj* [*clad-* + *autoicous*] *of mosses* : having the male sexual organ on a special branch

clad·ding \'kladiŋ, -aad-, -ēŋ\ *n* -S [fr. gerund of *clad*] : something that covers or overlays; *specif* : metal coating bonded to a metal core by heat and pressure or by casting — compare ²CLAD 2b

cladi *pl of* CLADUS

cla·dis·tia \klə'distēə\ *n pl, cap* [NL, fr. *clad-* + *-istia* (fr. Gk *histia*, pl. of *histion* web, cloth, sail, fr. *histanai* to make stand, stand) — more at STAND] : an order of Teleostomi comprising primitive bony freshwater African fishes that have scales, head skeleton, and pectoral arch which resemble those of the extinct Archistia and that include the bichir and the reedfish — compare POLYPTERUS

clad·o·car·pous \ˌkladəˈkärpəs\ *adj* [*clad-* + *-carpous*] **:** PLEUROCARPOUS

cla·doc·era \kləˈdäsərə\ *n pl, cap* [NL, fr. *clad-* + *-cera*] **:** an order of minute chiefly freshwater branchiopod crustaceans comprising the water fleas

¹cla·doc·er·an \-rən\ *or* **cla·doc·er·ous** \-rəs\ *adj* [NL *Cladocera* + E *-an* or *-ous*] **:** of or relating to the Cladocera

²cladoceran \"\ *n* -S **:** a crustacean of the order Cladocera

clad·o·chyt·ri·a·ce·ae \ˌkladō,kiˈtrēˈāsē,ē\ *n pl, cap* [NL, fr. *Cladochytrium*, type genus (fr. *clad-* + Gk *chytrion*, dim. of *chytris, chytra* pot) + NL *-aceae*] **:** a family of fungi (order Chytridiales) characterized by uniflagellate zoospores and a rhizomycelial plant body with frequent enlargements into spindle bodies, several species esp. in the type genus *Cladochytrium* being parasitic in algae, aquatic seed plants, and some plants of economic importance (as alfalfa, corn, beets)

clad·o·chyt·ri·a·ceous \¦==¦==¦āshəs\ *adj* [NL *Cladochytriaceae* + E *-ous*] **:** of or relating to the Cladochytriaceae

clad·ode \ˈklaˌdōd\ *n* -S [NL *cladodium*, fr. LGk *kladōdēs* having many sprouts (fr. Gk *klad-* clad- + *-ōdēs* -odes) + NL *-ium*] **:** CLADOPHYLL — **cla·do·di·al** \kləˈdōdēəl, (ˈ)klaˈd-\ *adj*

clad·o·dus \ˈkladədəs\ *n, cap* [NL, fr. *clad-* + *-odus*] *in some classifications* **:** a genus of primitive Carboniferous sharks supposedly distinguished by teeth with a tall central cusp, a broad base, and one or more pairs of lateral tubercles, a character now known to have occurred widely in early elasmobranchs

cla·do·nia \kləˈdōnyə, -nēə\ *n, cap* [NL, fr. LGk *kladon-, kladōn* sprout (fr. Gk *klados*) + NL *-ia* — more at CLAD-] **:** a genus (the type of the family Cladoniaceae) of lichens characterized by its crustose plant body and capitate fruiting bodies borne on simple or branched podetia — see REINDEER MOSS

cla·do·ni·a·ceous \klə¦dōnē¦āshəs\ *adj* [NL *Cladonia* + *-aceous*] **:** CLADONIOID

cla·do·ni·oid \kləˈdōnē,ȯid\ *adj* [NL *Cladonia* + E *-oid*] **:** of or relating to the genus *Cladonia*

cla·doph·o·ra \kləˈdäfərə\ *n, cap* [NL, fr. *clad-* + *-phora*] **:** a genus (the type of the family Cladophoraceae of the order Cladophorales) of branched filamentous septate green algae usu. firmly attached and with the branches arising from the upper end of the cells each of which has a reticulate chloroplast and several nuclei, the genus also being placed sometimes in the order Siphonocladales and sometimes in Ulotrichales

cla·doph·o·ra·ceous \klə¦däfə¦rāshəs\ *adj* [NL *Cladophora* + E *-aceous*] **:** of or relating to the genus *Cladophora* or family Cladophoraceae

cla·doph·o·ra·les \klə,däfəˈrā(,)lēz\ *n pl, cap* [NL, fr. *Cladophora* + *-ales*] **:** an order of green algae (class Chlorophyceae) having a simple or branching thallus and containing a single family — see CLADOPHORA

clad·o·phyll \ˈkladə,fil\ *also* **clad·o·phyl·lum** \ˈkladəˈfiləm\ *n, pl* **clado·phylls** \-,filz\ *also* **cladophyl·la** \-ˈfilə\ [NL *cladophyllum*, fr. *clad-* + *-phyllum*] **:** a branch assuming the form of and closely resembling an ordinary foliage leaf and borne in the axil of a true leaf, often bearing leaves or flowers on its margins (as in butcher's-broom) — called also *cladode;* see PHYLLOCLADE

clad·op·to·sis \ˌkla,däpˈtōsəs\ *n, pl* **cladopto·ses** \-ō,sēz\ [NL, fr. *clad-* + *ptosis*] **:** an annual dropping of twigs or branches instead of leaves in plants of various genera (as *Thuja* and *Taxodium*)

cla·dose \ˈkla,dōs, -lā,d-\ *adj* [*clad-* + *-ose*] **:** BRANCHED, RAMOSE

clad·o·sel·a·che \ˌkladəˈselə(,)kē\ *n, cap* [NL, fr. *clad-* + *-selache* (fr. Gk *selachos* fish with cartilaginous skeleton) — more at SELACHII] **:** a genus (the type of the family Cladoselachidae) comprising the most primitive known sharklike fishes, restricted to the upper Devonian and with a few other extinct forms constituting the subclass Pleuropterygii — **cladoselachian** \¦kladōsə¦lākēən\ *adj or n*

clad·o·se·la·chii \ˌkladōsəˈlākē,ī\ *also* **clad·o·se·la·chea** \-kēə\ *or* **clad·o·se·la·chi·for·mes** \¦kladōsə,lākəˈfȯr,mēz\ *or* **clad·o·sel·a·choi·dea** \ˌkladō,seləˈkȯidēə\ [NL, fr. *Cladoselache*] *syn of* PLEUROPTERYGII

clad·o·spo·ri·um \ˌkladəˈspōrēəm\ *n, cap* [NL, fr. *clad-* + *-sporium*] **:** a form genus of imperfect fungi (family Dematiaceae) having conidia borne on branched conidiophores and the conidia with usu. one or in age two or three septa and including some economically important plant parasites

¹clad·o·thrix \ˈkladə,thriks\ [NL, fr. *clad-* + *-thrix*] *syn of* ACTINOMYCES

²cladothrix \"\ [NL, fr. *clad-* + *-thrix*] *syn of* SPHAEROTILUS

-cla·dous \ˌklədəs\ *adj comb form* [NL *-cladus*, fr. Gk *-klados*, fr. *klados* sprout, twig — more at GLADIATOR] **:** branched ⟨acanth*oclado*us⟩

cla·dox·y·la·ce·ae \klə,däksəˈlāsē,ē\ *n pl, cap* [NL, fr. *Cladoxylon*, type genus + *-aceae*] **:** a family of fossil plants that is coextensive with the genus *Cladoxylon* and is placed in the order Psilophytales or Cladoxylales

cla·dox·y·la·les \-ā(,)lēz\ *n pl, cap* [NL, fr. *Cladoxylon* + *-ales*] *in some classifications* **:** an order of fossil plants (class Filicineae) coextensive with the family Cladoxylaceae

cla·dox·y·lon \kləˈdäksə,län\ *n, cap* [NL, fr. *clad-* + *-xylon*] **:** a genus (the type of the family Cladoxylaceae) of Devonian to mid-Carboniferous fossil plants having dichotomously branched stems and leaves, each forking of the fertile segments bearing a single sporangium

cla·dras·tis \kləˈdrastəs\ *n, cap* [NL, irreg. fr. *clad-* + Gk *thraustos* brittle (fr. *thrauein* to shatter) — more at DREARY] **:** a genus of ornamental trees (family Leguminosae) having odd-pinnate leaves and white flowers borne in showy panicles — see YELLOWWOOD 1a

clads *pres 3d sing of* CLAD

cla·dus \ˈklādəs, -lad-\ *n, pl* **cla·di** \-,dī\ [NL, fr. Gk *klados* sprout] **:** a branch of a ramose spicule

claes \ˈklāz\ *n pl* [ME (northern dial.) *clais, claithes, clathes*, fr. OE *clāthas* — more at CLOTHES] *chiefly Scot* **:** CLOTHES

¹clag \ˈklag\ *vb* **clagged; clagged; clagging; clags** [ME *claggen*, prob. of Scand origin; akin to Dan *klagge* sticky mud, ON *kleggi* horsefly; akin to OE *clǣg* clay — more at CLAY] *vt* **1** *dial Brit* **:** to bedaub usu. with a sticky substance (as mud or dirt) **2** *dial Brit* **:** CLOG, CLOT **3** *dial Brit* **:** to cause to adhere ~ *vi, dial Brit* **:** ADHERE, STICK

²clag \"\ *n* -S *dial Brit* **:** a clot or lump esp. of dirt or snow

clag·gum \ˈklagəm\ *n* -S [prob. fr. ¹*clag* + *-um* (as in *medium*)] *dial Brit* **:** a gummy sweetmeat; *esp* **:** taffy made with molasses or treacle

clag·gy \ˈklagi, -aigi\ *adj* -ER/-EST [²*clag* + *-y*] **1** *dial* **:** STICKY, GUMMY **2** *dial* **:** MUDDY

claik \ˈklāk\ *Scot var of* CLACK

claik goose \"-\ *n, Scot* **:** BARNACLE GOOSE

¹claim \ˈklām\ *vb* -ED/-ING/-S [ME *claimen*, fr. *claim-*, pres. ind. sing. stem of OF *clamer*, fr. L *clamare* to call, to cry out, call; akin to L *calare* to call, summon — more at LOW] *vt* **1** *obs* **:** NAME, ANNOUNCE, PROCLAIM **2 a :** to demand recognition of (as a title, distinction, possession, or power) esp. as a right ⟨the papal-imperial partnership which *~ed* universal rule over all Christendom —W.K.Ferguson⟩; *also* **:** to have as a property or quality ⟨each rhyme in the verse *~s* four lines⟩ ⟨the small child *~s* the family red hair⟩ **b :** to call for **:** REQUIRE ⟨public health must ~ everyone's attention⟩ **:** demand esp. as a consequence ⟨the plague *~ed* thousands of lives⟩ **3 a** (1) **:** to demand delivery or possession of by or as if by right ⟨he went to ~ their bags at the station⟩ (2) **:** BUY ⟨*~ed* a fine horse after the race⟩ **b :** to recognize the fact of or assert often proudly the right to a close or special relationship with (as by reason of birth, residence, common circumstances, or special affinity) ⟨Paris can ~ many significant writers and artists⟩ ⟨the city can ~ the highest accident rate in 10 years⟩ **4 :** to assert esp. with conviction and in the face of possible contradiction or doubt **:** MAINTAIN ⟨*~ed* he saw a ghost⟩ ⟨some people ~ to see beauty in a puddle —Andrew Buchanan⟩ ~ *vi, obs* **:** to assert or establish a right or privilege **syn** see DEMAND

²claim \"\ *n* -S [ME *claim, claime*, fr. OF *claim*, fr. *clamer*] **1 a** (1) **:** an authoritative or challenging request **:** DEMAND ⟨the present age makes great *~s* upon us —Matthew Arnold⟩ (2) **:** a demand of a right or supposed right ⟨Holland withdrew her ~ to the annexation of German territory⟩ (3) **:** a calling on another for something due or supposed to be due ⟨the speaker laid no ~ on the intelligence of his audience⟩ **b :** a demand for compensation, benefits, or payment (as one made in conformity with provisions of the Social Security Act or of a workmen's compensation law, one made under an insurance policy upon the happening of the contingency against which it is issued, or one made against a transportation line because of loss occasioned by carrier negligence or overcharge); *also* **:** the amount or payment of such a demand **2 :** a privilege to something **:** RIGHT ⟨his ~ to be called Europe's leading spokesman⟩ ⟨a ~ to fame⟩ ⟨liberty itself became . . . a principle of anarchy rather than a body of *~s* to be read in the context of the social process —H.J.Laski⟩; *specif* **:** a title to any debt, privilege, or other thing in the possession of another ⟨an applicant has a special ~ on . . . funds listed —*Official Register of Harvard Univ.*⟩ **3 :** an assertion, statement, or implication (as of value, effectiveness, qualification, eligibility) often made or likely to be suspected of being made without adequate justification ⟨his *~s* to sound scholarship⟩ ⟨appraising the authenticity of some dealer's ~ —Edith Diehl⟩; *specif* **:** the formal assertion of novelty and patentability with specification of particulars made by an applicant for a patent **4 a :** an assertion of title made (as by a settler, lumberman, prospector) on a tract of land (as one in the public domain) and evidenced by staking or otherwise marking as required by law; *also* **:** the tract of land for which such an assertion is made

claim adjuster *n* **:** ADJUSTER 2

claim agent *or* **claim man** *n* **1 :** one who investigates and adjusts claims for shortage, damage, loss, or overcharge on shipments of goods **2 :** one who acts as agent in transactions with holders of property on which pipelines are to be laid or oil or gas wells drilled and who investigates and adjusts their claims

claim·ant \ˈklāmənt\ *n* -S [¹*claim* + *-ant*] **:** one that asserts a right or title ⟨the ~ to an estate⟩

claim·er \ˈklāmə(r)\ *n* -S [ME, fr. *claimen* + *-er*] **1 :** one that claims **:** CLAIMANT **2 a :** CLAIMING RACE **b :** a horse entered in a claiming race **:** PLATER

claiming race *n* **:** a horse race before which each owner pledges to sell a horse he enters at a given price and after which must sell it if so requested usu. by someone who has entered a horse in a race at the same meeting

claim·less \ˈklāmləs\ *adj* **:** being without a claim

claim shanty *n* **:** a cabin built hastily on a land claim to legalize possession of the land

claims·man \ˈklāmzmən\ *n, pl* **claimsmen** [*claims* (pl. of ²*claim*) + *man*] **:** ADJUSTER 2

clair·audience \kla(a)r, kler + \ *n* [*clair-* (as in *clairvoyance*) + *audience* (act of hearing)] **:** the act or the power of hearing something not present to the ear but regarded as having objective reality

clair·audient \(ˈ)=+\ *adj* **:** of, relating to, or having clairaudience — **clair·au·di·ent·ly** *adv*

clair de lune \ˌkla(a)rdᵊlˈün, -ler-\ *n, pl* **clair de lunes** [F, lit., moonlight] **1 :** a pale blue or green-blue glaze used on porcelain; *also* **:** porcelain of this color **2 :** a bluish gray that is greener and paler than average dusk (sense 3a), lighter than Medici blue, and stronger than puritan gray

claire \ˈkla(a)(ə)r, -le(ə)r\ *n* -S [F, fr. fem. of *clair*, adj.] **:** a small enclosed pond for growing or observing the growth of oysters

clair-obscure *also* **clare-obscure** \¦kla(a)r, -ler-+\ *n* [F *clair-obscur* — more at CLEAR-OBSCURE] **:** CHIAROSCURO

clai·ron \klārōⁿ\ *n* -S [F — more at CLARION] **:** CLARION 3

clairschach *var of* CLARSACH

clair·sentience \kla(a)r, -ler+\ *n* -S [*clair-* (as in *clairvoyance*) + *sentience*] **:** perception of what is not normally perceptible

clair·sentient \(ˈ)=+\ *adj* **:** having clairsentience

clair·voy·ance \kla(a)rˈvȯiən(t)s, klerˈv-,kla(a)əˈv-,kleəˈv- *also* -ȯiyə-\ *also* **clair·voy·an·cy** \-nsē, -si\ *n, pl* **clairvoyanc·es** *also* **clairvoyan·cies** [F *clairvoyance*, fr. *clairvoyant*] **1 :** the act or power professed by certain persons of discerning objects hidden from sight or at a great distance **2 :** ability to perceive matters beyond the range of ordinary perception **:** PENETRATION, DISCERNMENT, CLEAR-SIGHTEDNESS

¹clair·voy·ant \(ˈ)=¦=(y)ənt\ *adj* [F, adj. & n., fr. *clair* clear (fr. L *clarus*) + *voyant*, pres. part. of *voir* to see, fr. L *vidēre* — more at CLEAR, VIEW] **1 :** able to perceive matters beyond the range of ordinary perception **:** CLEAR-SIGHTED, DISCERNING ⟨if the poet is not ~ he is nothing —C.D.Lewis⟩ **2 :** of or relating to clairvoyance ⟨the ~ revelations of a medium⟩ — **clair·voy·ant·ly** *adv*

²clairvoyant \"\ *n* -S [F] **:** one held to possess the power of clairvoyance

clair·voy·ante \-nt\ *n* -S [F, fem. of *clairvoyant*] **:** a female clairvoyant

clai·sen flask \ˈklīsᵊn-, ˈklīzᵊn-\ *n, usu cap C* [after Ludwig *Claisen* b1851 Ger. chemist] **:** a distilling flask with a branched neck esp. designed for vacuum distillation — see DISTILLING FLASK illustration

clakamas *usu cap, var of* CLACKAMAS

clal·lam \ˈklaləm\ *n, pl* **clallam** *or* **clallams** *usu cap* [Clallam, lit., strong people] **1 a :** a Salishan people of the south shore of the straits of Juan de Fuca, Washington **b :** a member of such people **2 :** the language of the Clallam people

¹clam \ˈklam, -aa(ə)m\ *n* -S [ME, fr. OE *clamm* bond, fetter; akin to OHG *klamma* constriction, ON *klām* obscene language, L *glomus* ball, Gk *glamōn* blear-eyed, L *galla* gall on a plant — more at GALL] **:** a viselike or pincerlike device designed to hold or constrict something **:** CLAMP: as **a :** a tight ligature used in bloodless castration of domestic animals **b :** a comblike frame used for holding feathers for clothing decoration

²clam \"\ *vt* **clammed; clammed; clamming; clams** *dial Brit* **:** to grasp with the hand **:** GROPE, CLUTCH

³clam \"\ *vb* **clammed; clammed; clamming; clams** [ME *clammen*, alter. of *clemen* to smear, fr. OE *clǣman* — more at CLOAM] *vt, dial Eng* **:** to daub, smear, or clog esp. with glutinous or viscous matter; *specif* **:** to plug up (a kiln) with wet clay ~ *vi, dial Eng* **:** to become clammy **:** STICK, ADHERE

⁴clam \"\ *adj* [ME; akin to *clammen*, v.] **1** *dial chiefly Brit* **:** STICKY, ADHESIVE **2** *dial chiefly Brit* **:** damp and cold

⁵clam \"\ *n* -S *often attrib* [¹*clam* (clamp); fr. the clamping action of the shells] **1 a :** any of a number of bivalve mollusks; *esp* **:** any of various equivalved edible marine mollusks that live wholly or partially buried in sand or mud — see BUTTER CLAM, QUAHOG, RAZOR CLAM, SOFT-SHELL CLAM **b :** a freshwater mussel **c :** the flesh of a clam used as food — usu. used in pl. **2 :** a stolid or closemouthed person **3 :** CLAMSHELL 2

clam: *1* siphon, *2* incurrent orifice, *3* excurrent orifice, *4* mantle, *5* shell, *6* foot

⁶clam \"\ *vb* **clammed; clammed; clamming; clams** *vi* **:** to gather clams esp. by digging ~ *vt* **:** to harvest clams from ⟨these beds are *clammed* mostly by summer people⟩

⁷clam \"\ *var of* ¹CLEM

cla·mant \ˈklāmənt, -lam-\ *adj* [L *clamant-, clamans*, pres. part. of *clamare* to call — more at CLAIM] **1 :** crying out **:** CLAMOROUS, LOUD ⟨a world distracted everywhere by ~ national creeds —*Times Lit. Supp.*⟩ **2 :** demanding notice **:** PRESSING, URGENT ⟨~ need⟩ — **cla·mant·ly** *adv*

clam·a·roo \¦klamə¦rü\ *n* -S [irreg. fr. ⁵*clam*] **:** CLAMBAKE 2a

clam·a·to·res \ˌklaməˈtōr(,)ēz\ *n pl, cap* [NL, fr. L, pl. of *clamator* bawler, fr. *clamatus*, past part. of *clamare* + *-or*] *in some classifications* **:** a suborder or superfamily of Passeriformes nearly coextensive with the modern suborder Tyranni

clam·a·to·ri·al \¦klamə¦tōrēəl\ *adj* [NL *Clamatores* + E *-ial*] **:** of or relating to Clamatores

clambake \ˈ=,=\ *n* [⁵*clam* + *bake*] **1 a :** a social gathering where food is prepared and eaten outdoors; *specif* **:** a seashore outing where clams and fish are baked (as on heated rocks covered by seaweed) **b** *slang* **:** an often noisy and pretentious social entertainment esp. attended by a great many people ⟨seldom attend the fancier *~s* in which Washington abounds —*N.Y. Times*⟩; *esp* **:** a political rally ⟨the party faithful gathered . . . for the great New York ~ —*Time*⟩ **2** *slang* **a :** a radio or television program or rehearsal that is confused, badly organized, or full of mistakes **b :** JAM SESSION; *esp* **:** one that is disorganized or unsuccessful

¹clam·ber \ˈklam(b)ə(r), -aambə(r)\ *vb* **clambered; clambered; clambering** \-m(b)əriŋ,-m(b)riŋ\ **clambers** [ME *clambren;* akin to MHG *klamben* to fit together tightly, ON *klembra* to clamber, OE *climban* to climb — more at CLIMB] *vi* **:** to move (as up, around, through, or under something) by or as if by catching hold with the hands and feet **:** CRAWL, STRUGGLE, CLIMB ⟨~ into a tank⟩ ⟨~ out of an overcoat⟩ ⟨~ to emotional heights⟩ ⟨construction workers *~ed* down from their scaffolding —Robert Shaplen⟩ ~ *vt* **:** to scramble up **:** CLIMB ⟨hodmen, *~ing* a ladder —Washington Irving⟩

²clamber \"\ *n* -S **:** the act or action of clambering

clam·ber·er \-m(b)ərə(r)\ *n* -S **:** one that clambers; *esp* **:** a clambering plant

clam catcher *n, usu cap both Cs* [⁵*clam*] **:** NEW JERSEYITE — used as a nickname

¹clame \ˈklām\ *var of* ³CLAM

²clame \"\ *var of* CLEAM

clam·e·hew·it \ˌklaməˈh(y)üət\ *n* -S [origin unknown] *Scot* **:** BLOW, DRUBBING

clamflat \ˈ=,=\ *n* [⁵*clam* + *flat*] **:** a flat often muddy tidal area where clams are abundant

clam·jam·fry *or* **clam·jam·frey** \klamˈjamfri\ *n, pl* **clamjamfrys** *or* **clamjamfries** *or* **clamjamfreys** [perh. fr. obs. *clam* base, mean + Sc *jamph* to sneer, scoff + E *-ry*] **1** *chiefly Scot* **:** RABBLE, MOB **2** *chiefly Scot* **:** ODDS AND ENDS, RUBBISH

clammed *past of* CLAM

¹clam·mer \ˈklamə(r), -aam-\ *n* -S [⁶*clam* + *-er*] **:** one that digs, dredges, tongs, or rakes for clams

²clammer \"\ *n* -S [²*clam* + *-er*] **:** ⁴CLAMPER

clam·mer·some \ˈklamə(r)səm\ *var of* CLAMOURSOME

clam·mi·ly \-məlē, -li\ *adv* **:** in a clammy manner

clam·mi·ness \-mēnəs, -min-\ *n* -ES **:** the quality or state of being clammy

clamming *n* -S [fr. gerund of ⁶*clam*] **:** the harvesting of clams ⟨the ~ industry⟩

clammish *adj* [⁴*clam* + *-ish*] *obs* **:** CLAMMY

clam·my \ˈklamē, -mi\ *adj* -ER/-EST [ME, prob. fr. *clammen, clemen* to stick + *-y* — more at CLAM] **1 a** (1) **:** moist and sticky ⟨~ flesh⟩ ⟨a plant with a ~ stem⟩ (2) **:** drearily sticky and wet ⟨a ~ and intensely cold mist —Charles Dickens⟩ **b** (1) **:** damp and cold ⟨~ air⟩ **:** suffused or covered with a cool sticky dampness ⟨a ~ uniform⟩ (2) **:** unpleasantly sticky and cold ⟨the ~ moisture of the Burma night —Ed Cunningham⟩ **2 a** (1) **:** lacking normal human warmth ⟨~ statistics⟩ ⟨the ~ atmosphere of an institution⟩ (2) **:** unnaturally or perversely cold **:** OFFISH ⟨that American captain was a bit on the ~ side —Bennett Cerf⟩ **b :** unpleasantly or uncomfortably sickly, furtive, or aberrant **:** UNNATURAL ⟨a rather ~ sense of humor⟩ ⟨~ fear that once held the country in its grip —H.H.Martin⟩

clammy azalea *also* **clammy honeysuckle** *n* **:** SWAMP AZALEA

clammy cherry *n* **:** a tall West Indian tree (*Cordia collococca*) with soft wood and cherrylike fruit

clammy chickweed *n* **1 :** MOUSE-EAR CHICKWEED **2 :** a fleshy-leaved stitchwort (*Stellaria crassifolia*) of the western U.S.

clammy cuphea *n* **:** WAXWEED

clammy everlasting *n* **:** an aromatic silvery herb (*Gnaphalium macounii*) of Canada and the U.S.

clammy locust *n* **:** a small rough-barked locust (*Robinia viscosa*) native to the southeastern U.S. and cultivated elsewhere and having glandular twigs and racemes of pale pink flowers

clammy sage *n* **:** ²CLARY

clammyweed \ˈ==,=\ *n* **:** any of several plants of the genus *Polanisia; esp* **:** a strong-scented herb (*P. graveolens*) having glandular-pubescent foliage and being common in the western U.S.

¹clam·or \ˈklamə(r)\ *n* -S *see -or in Explan Notes* [ME, fr. MF *clamur, clamour*, fr. L *clamor*, fr. *clamare* to cry out — more at CLAIM] **1 a :** the loud and continued uproar of many human voices **:** HUBBUB, RUMPUS ⟨the ~ of children at play⟩ **b :** a loud continued and usu. confused noise (as of animals, birds, musical instruments, or a storm) **:** TUMULT, DIN ⟨finches and flickers . . . gave out a dissonant and reedy ~ —Jean Stafford⟩ ⟨the even ~ of a waterfall⟩ **2 :** a loud and insistent expression (as of dissatisfaction, support, indignation) **:** popular outcry ⟨~ against exorbitant taxes⟩ ⟨~ for home rule⟩

²clamor \"\ *vb* **clamored; clamored; clamoring** \-m(ə)riŋ\ **clamors** *see -or in Explan Notes, vi* **1 :** to make a din **:** utter loud, mixed, and confused outcries or sounds ⟨a *~ing* group whose voices were like the squalling of gulls —Kenneth Roberts⟩ **2 :** to appeal, demand, or protest by sustained noisy outcry ⟨threatening him with impeachment . . . and *~ing* for the suppression of his command —J.A.Froude⟩ ⟨he can borrow no more, and his debtors are *~ing* —Gertrude Atherton⟩ ~ *vt* **1 :** to utter or proclaim insistently and noisily ⟨*~ed* their piteous prayer incessantly —H.W.Longfellow⟩ **2 :** to reduce to a certain condition or to effect a certain objective from by means of clamor **syn** see ROAR

³clamor *vt* -ED/-ING/-S *see -or in Explan Notes* [prob. fr. ²*clam* + *-or*] *obs* **:** to put an end to the noise of **:** SILENCE ⟨~ your tongues, and not a word more —Shak.⟩

clam·or·ous \ˈklam(ə)rəs\ *adj* [¹*clamor* + *-ous*] **1 a :** marked by din or outcry ⟨the ~ streets⟩ **:** NOISY, TUMULTUOUS ⟨our theater has to be brassier, more ~ and more audacious —Brooks Atkinson⟩ **b :** RESONANT, VIBRANT ⟨iron is strong and heavy, ~ when struck —D.C.Peattie⟩ ⟨tales . . . with the surge of Antarctic seas —Clifton Fadiman⟩ **2 a :** crying out ⟨we'll be ~ for something to do —Jack London⟩ **:** IMPORTUNATE, PRESSING ⟨~ demands⟩ ⟨hounded by ~ bill collectors⟩ **b :** DEMONSTRATIVE, EFFUSIVE ⟨the death penalty will seem . . . an anachronism . . . mocking . . . our ~ professions of the sanctity of life —B.N.Cardozo⟩ **syn** see VOCIFEROUS

clam·or·ous·ly *adv* **:** in a clamorous manner

clam·or·ous·ness *n* -ES **:** the quality or state of being clamorous

clam·our·some \ˈklamə(r)səm\ *adj* [*clamour, clammer* (vars. of ¹*clamor*) + *-some*] *dial chiefly Brit* **:** CLAMOROUS

¹clamp \ˈklamp, -aa(ə)mp, -aimp\ *n* -S [ME, prob. fr. (assumed) MD *klampe* (whence D *klamp*); akin to OHG *klampfer* clamp, ON *kleppr* lump, OE *clamm* bond, fetter — more at CLAM] **1 a :** a device (as a band or brace) designed to bind or constrict or to press two or more parts together so as to hold them firmly in their relative position **b :** any of various instruments or appliances having parts brought together (as by a screw) for holding or compressing something: as (1) **:** an instrument used to hold, compress, or crush vessels and hollow organs and to aid in surgical excision of parts (2) **:** one of a pair of false jaws **2** *obs* **:** CLAM, MOLLUSK **3** *also* **clamp strake :** a structural member of a ship running inside the frames from the stempost to the transom or sternpost and fastened to the frames and deck beams or shelf and serving to increase longitudinal stiffness of the hull — see SHIP illustration **4 a :** STOP, OBSTACLE ⟨a ~ on debate⟩ **b :** HOLD, GRIP ⟨takes a firm ~ on the reader's imagination —Martin Levin⟩

²clamp \"\ *vt* -ED/-ING/-S **1 a :** to fasten or press with or as if with a clamp ⟨~ two boards together⟩ ⟨a pipe *~ed* between his teeth⟩ **b :** to grasp firmly **:** HOLD ⟨the town was *~ed* by winter —A.J.Cronin⟩ **2 :** to force or impress authoritatively — often used with *on* or *upon* ⟨*~ed* a censorship on the news of his defeat —*Nation*⟩ ⟨controls were *~ed* on bank lending —E.L.Dale⟩

³clamp \"\ *n* -S [prob. fr. D *klamp* heap; akin to OE *clympre* lump of metal — more at CLUMP] **:** a compact pile or heaped-up mass of materials: as **a :** a number of bricks piled up in a particular form for burning **b** *Brit* **:** a heap of produce covered over usu. with straw or earth to prevent freezing

⁴clamp \"\ *vt* -ED/-ING/-S *Brit* **:** to heap or stack (as bricks or root crops) in a clamp

⁵clamp \"\ *n* -S [imit.] **:** ¹CLUMP 4

⁶clamp \"\ *vi* -ED/-ING/-S **:** ²CLUMP 1

clamp connection *or* **clamp cell** *also* **clamp** *n* **:** a bulgelike hyphal outgrowth in many basidiomycetous fungi that is formed at cell division over the cross wall between the two daughter cells and provides a connection through which one of the involved nuclei may pass in order to maintain the binucleate state of the resulting cells — called also *buckle*

clamp down *vb* [²*clamp*] *vt* **1 :** to clean (the deck of a boat) by spraying with water and swabbing down **2 :** to impose (as a curfew, blackout, censorship) esp. in a sudden, arbitrary, or violent manner ⟨the police *clamped down* a deadline after which all slot machines were to disappear⟩ ~ *vi* **:** to become suddenly or violently repressive, dire, or dictatorial ⟨a military adventurer took over control of a free people and then *clamped down* —*New Yorker*⟩ — usu. used with *on* ⟨the government was *clamping down* on Moslem activities —*N.Y. Times*⟩
clampdown \ˈ=,=\ *n* -s [*clamp down*] **:** the act or action of making regulations and restrictions more stringent or infractions thereof liable to greater punishment **:** CRACKDOWN ⟨a ~ on charge accounts, bank loans, and other inflationary influences —*Time*⟩
¹**clamp·er** \ˈklampər\ *vt* -ED/-ING/-S [freq. of ²*clamp*] *now chiefly Scot* **:** to patch together esp. clumsily or hastily ⟨I can ~ up the story —J.G.Lockhart⟩
²**clamper** \"\ *n* -s *now chiefly Scot* **:** a patched-together argument or charge ⟨his defense was a mere ~⟩
³**clamp·er** \ˈklampə(r), -laam-\ *n* -s [²*clamp* + *-er*] **:** CREEPER 5a
⁴**clamper** \"\ *n* -s [¹*clamp* + *-er*] **:** a skilled workman who operates a special rotary press that transfers an engraved design from one small steel roller to another in raised form so that it can later be impressed in a large copper roller for printing cloth — called also *clammer*
clamping *pres part of* CLAMP
clamping circuit *n* **:** a device that maintains at a constant value the positive or the negative extreme of voltage in an alternating-current circuit
clamps *pl of* CLAMP, *pres 3d sing of* CLAMP
clamp screw *or* **clamping screw** *n* **:** a screw used to hold some part tightly in place by forcing it against an immovable part (as one used to secure a drill or other tool in a simple chuck) — compare SETSCREW
clamp strake *n* **:** CLAMP 3
clams *pl of* CLAM, *pres 3d sing of* CLAM
clamshell \ˈ=,=\ *n* [⁵*clam* + *shell*] **1 :** the shell of a clam **2 :** an object or esp. a piece of equipment or apparatus resembling or having a part that resembles a clam or the valves of a clam (as in mechanical operation): as **a :** a bucket or grapple (as on a crane, dredge, or shovel) having two hinged jaws — called also *grab bucket* **b :** either of a pair of doors in the nose or tail of an airplane that open outward and away from each other when loading or unloading ⟨~ cargo doors⟩
clam up *vi* [⁵*clam*] *slang* **:** to become silent ⟨the people on the porches all *clammed up* and watched him go by —R.O. Bowen⟩; *esp* **:** to refuse further talk or divulging of information ⟨news sources suddenly seemed to be *clamming up* all over town —*Newsweek*⟩
clam worm *n* [⁵*clam*] **:** any of several large burrowing polychaete worms often used as bait and usu. of the genus *Nereis*
¹**clan** \ˈklan, -aa(ə)n\ *n* -s [ME, fr. ScGael *clann* offspring, clan, akin to OIr *cland* plant, offspring, fr. L *planta* sprout, cutting — more at PLANT] **1 :** a social unit smaller than a tribe and larger than the family and claiming descent from a common ancestor: **a :** a Celtic group esp. in the Scottish Highlands comprising a number of households the heads of which claim descent from a common ancestor, bear a common surname, and acknowledge the preeminence of a chief who bears a distinctive title — compare SEPT, TARTAN **b :** an exogamous tribal division that traces descent in either the male or the female line from a common real, totemic, or mythological ancestor, that has a common name and often a common territory, and that constitutes the chief political, religious, and social unit of tribal society — used by some ethnologists of such a tribal division tracing descent in the female line only; compare GENS, MOIETY, PHRATRY **2 :** a group united by a common trait, qualification, or program and often appearing self-interested, overexclusive, or narrow ⟨a whole ~ of cousins, aunts, uncles, and in-laws⟩ ⟨a ~ of poets⟩ **3 a :** a collection of animals, plants, or inanimate things **b :** a minute ecological community being typically a climax formation covering an area of a few square yards and having a single dominant species
²**clan** \"\ *vi* **clanned; clanned; clanning; clans :** to unite in or as if in a clan **:** form a clique **:** GATHER — used esp. with *together* ⟨the whole family used to ~ together at Christmas⟩
clancular *adj* [L *clancularius*, fr. *clanculum* secretly, fr. *clam*] *obs* **:** secret and often underhanded **:** CLANDESTINE ⟨the ~ whispering of temptation⟩ — **clancularly** *adv, obs*
clan·des·tine \klanˈdestən, klaan-\ *adj* [MF or L; MF *clandestin*, fr. L *clandestinus*, fr. (assumed) L *clamde* secretly (fr. L *clam* secretly) + L *-stinus* (as in *intestinus* internal); akin to L *celare* to hide — more at HELL, INTESTINE] **:** marked by, held in, or conducted with secrecy and concealment **:** not openly avowed or generally known **:** given to wary concealment ⟨a ~ love affair⟩ ⟨to elude the vigilance of church and state . . . a number of Tolstoy's pamphlets were printed by a ~ press —*New Republic*⟩ **syn** see SECRET
clandestine evolution *n* **:** evolutionary change affecting only developmental stages of an organism and not readily detectable in the mature organism or phylogenetically effective
clan·des·tine·ly *adv* **:** in a clandestine manner
clan·des·tine·ness \-ən(n)əs\ *n* -ES **:** the quality or state of being clandestine
clan·des·tin·i·ty \,kla(a)n,deˈstinəd-ē\ *n* -ES [perh. fr. F *clandestinité*, fr. *clandestin* + *-ité* -ity] **:** the quality or state of being secret esp. in political or social activities normally overt, manifest, or apparent
¹**clang** \ˈklaŋ, -aiŋ\ *now dial past of* CLING
²**clang** \"\ *vb* -ED/-ING/-S [L *clangere* to sound (as of a trumpet), scream (as of an eagle); akin to Gk *klazein* to scream, bark, roar, Lith *klagėti* to cackle, cluck, and OE *hlōwan* to moo — more at LOW] *vi* **1 a :** to make a loud resounding sound like that of a trumpet or esp. like pieces of metal struck together ⟨~*ing* anvils⟩ ⟨every steeple . . . began to ~ joyfully —Dorothy C. Fisher⟩ **b :** to proceed or function in such a way as to produce a loud resounding noise ⟨a cable car ~*ed* up the hill —J.B.Clayton⟩ ⟨the convoy . . . ~*ed* over cobblestones —Earle Birney⟩ **2** *of a bird* **:** to produce a harsh cry or scream ⟨wedges of ~*ing* geese —*Nature Mag.*⟩ ⟨a stream of ducks flowed ~*ing* by —Eileen Duggan⟩ ~ *vt* **:** to produce a resonant noise with or on **:** RING ⟨~ a bell⟩ ⟨the gates of the elevator are ~*ed* in his face —Rebecca West⟩
³**clang** \"\ *n* -s **:** a loud resounding sound or noise like that made by a trumpet or esp. by metal objects struck together **:** RING ⟨the ~ of a gong⟩ ⟨the ~ and bang of a boiler factory —*Lamp*⟩; *specif* **:** the resonant cry of a bird (as a crane or goose)
clang association *n* **:** association through the sound and not the meaning of words (as in psychological word-association tests)
¹**clang·or** \ˈklaŋə(r), -aiŋ- *sometimes* -ŋgə-\ *n* -s *see -or in Explan Notes* [L, noise, sound, clang, fr. *clangere* to clang — more at CLANG] **:** a loud deeply resounding sound like that made by a trumpet or esp. by metal objects struck together ⟨the ~ of hammers⟩ or a loud medley of such sound ⟨the ~ of battle⟩
²**clangor** \"\ *vi* **clangored; clangored; clangoring** \-ŋ(ə)riŋ *sometimes* -ŋg(ə)r-\ **clangors** *see -or in Explan Notes* **:** to make a clanging noise ⟨the long train . . . ~*ed* through the night —J.W.Vandercook⟩
clang·or·ous \-ŋərəs *sometimes* -ŋgə-\ *adj* **:** noisy and resounding ⟨~ locomotive works —C.V.Hancock⟩ **:** filled with usu. confused noise ⟨jammed streets and ~ air —R.H.Rovere⟩ — **clang·or·ous·ly** *adv*
clang tint *n* [part trans. of G *klangfarbe*, fr. *klang* noise, sound (fr. OHG *klanc*) + *farbe* color] **:** the quality of a complex sound **:** TIMBRE
clan·gu·la \ˈklaŋgyələ\ *n, cap* [NL, fr. Gk *klangē* scream + NL *-ula*; akin to L *clangere* to scream — more at CLANG] **:** a genus containing such ducks as the old-squaw and formerly also the goldeneye
clan·jam·frey \klanˈj-\ *var of* CLAMJAMFRY
¹**clank** \ˈklaŋk, -aiŋk\ *vb* -ED/-ING/-S [prob. imit.] *vi* **1 :** to make a sharp abrupt ringing sound like a piece of heavy metal striking a hard surface ⟨the prison gate ~*ed* shut⟩ or series of such sounds ⟨the steam radiators . . . ~*ed* and spewed —Robert Hazel⟩ **2 :** to proceed or function with a sharp abrupt ringing sound or series of such sounds ⟨armored cars ~*ed* through the streets⟩ ~ *vt* **1 :** to put or set with a sharp abrupt ringing sound or series of such sounds ⟨~ a pail down⟩ **2 :** to cause to make a sharp abrupt ringing sound or series of such sounds ⟨~ chains⟩
²**clank** \"\ *n* -s **:** a sharp abrupt ringing sound like a piece of heavy metal striking a hard surface ⟨the hammer fell with a ~⟩
clank·ety-clank \ˌkla(i)ŋkəd-ēˈkla(i)ŋk\ *n* [redupl. of ²*clank*] **:** sharp successive often metallic and ringing noises ⟨the *clankety-clank* of a windlass hoisting anchor⟩
clank·ing·ly *adv* **:** in a clanking manner
clan·less \ˈklanləs, -aa(ə),n-\ *adj* **:** being without a clan
clanned *past of* CLAN
clanning *pres part of* CLAN
clan·nish \ˈklanish, -aan-, -nēsh\ *adj* **1** *archaic* **:** of or relating to a clan ⟨~ ceremonies⟩ **2 :** characteristic or suggestive of clan psychology or organization ⟨~ loyalty⟩; *specif* **:** tending to associate only with others of like origins, sympathies, and prejudices ⟨~ immigrants⟩ ⟨~ party members⟩ — **clan·nish·ness** *n* -ES
clans *pl of* CLAN, *pres 3d sing of* CLAN
clan·ship \-n,ship\ *n* -s **1 a :** the clan system ⟨the ~ of the Highlands⟩ **b :** the state of belonging to a clan ⟨to reckon ~ by matrilineal descent⟩ **2 :** a tendency to stick together **:** clannish spirit ⟨the ~ of mountain climbers⟩
clans·man \ˈklanzmən, -laanz-\ *n, pl* **clansmen :** one belonging to a clan or clanlike group
clan·wil·liam cedar \(ˈ)klanˈwilyəm-\ *n, usu cap 1st C* [fr. *Clanwilliam*, town in western Cape Province, Union of South Africa] **:** a southern African evergreen tree (*Callitris arborea*) yielding timber and gum
cla·o·sau·rus \,klāəˈsȯrəs\ *n, cap* [NL, fr. *clao-* (fr. Gk *klan* to break off, as shoots of a vine) + *-saurus* — more at GLADIATOR] **:** a genus of dinosaurs (suborder Ornithopoda) from the Upper Cretaceous of No. America — compare IGUANODON
¹**clap** \ˈklap\ *vb* **clapped** *also* **clapt; clapped** *also* **clapt; clapping; claps** [ME *clappen*, *cleppen*, fr. OE *clappian*, *clæppan* to clap, beat, throb; akin to OHG *klaphōn* to beat, ON *klappa*, L *glēba* clod — more at CLIP] *vt* **1 a :** to strike together (as two flat hard surfaces) so as to produce a sharp percussive noise or series of such noises ⟨*clapped* his head on a rafter⟩ ⟨~ shut a book⟩ ⟨~ a stick along a picket fence⟩ **b** *of a bird* **:** to beat (the wings) so as to strike each other, the sides, or the air noisily **2 a :** to beat (one's hands usu. flat or slightly cupped palm against palm) together repeatedly so as to produce a series of sharp percussive noises ⟨the children *clapped* hands as they danced⟩ often as a sign of pleasure or approval ⟨the curtain went up and everyone *clapped* hands⟩ **b :** to show pleasure at or approval of (as a performer or performance) by making such noises esp. with one's hands **:** APPLAUD ⟨they *clapped* the speaker⟩ **3 a** (1) **:** to strike with the flat of the hand and often as a gesture of friendship or encouragement ⟨*clapped* his friend on the back⟩ (2) *dial Brit* **:** to pat endearingly **:** STROKE, CARESS **b** (1) *obs* **:** to strike (hands) with someone as a sign of closing a bargain (2) *obs* **:** PLEDGE ⟨ere I could make thee open thy white hand and ~ thyself my love —Shak.⟩ **4 :** to strike (as bread dough or laundry) with a flat surface esp. to smooth or flatten **5 a :** to place, put, or set esp. with haste or energy ⟨*clapped* a piece of candy into his mouth⟩ ⟨~ him into jail⟩ ⟨~ eyes on a person⟩ ⟨~ an awning up⟩ **b :** to put on and fasten securely ⟨~ a muzzle on a dog⟩ **6 :** to make, contrive, or provide in a hasty or botched-up manner — used with *together* or *up* ⟨they *clapped* the house together⟩ ⟨~ up a conspiracy⟩ **7 :** to lay or apply (as a legal action or writ) — often used with *on* or *upon* ⟨~ an attachment on a person's house⟩ ~ *vi* **1 :** to produce a percussive or explosive noise or series of such noises ⟨the loose shutters *clapped* against the house⟩ ⟨the thunder *clapped* against the valley walls⟩ **2 :** to close noisily **:** SLAM ⟨the windows *clapped* shut⟩ ⟨the doors *clapped* to⟩ **3 :** to talk noisily **:** chatter on **:** PRATE ⟨her tongue could ~ until midnight⟩ **4 :** to begin, move, or act briskly or energetically ⟨~ into a song⟩ ⟨his hand *clapped* over my mouth⟩; *specif* **:** to rush precipitously **:** throw oneself **:** POUNCE ⟨he *clapped* out the door after the thief⟩ **5 :** to produce a series of sharp percussive noises by clapping the hands esp. as a sign of pleasure or approval ⟨the curtain rose and the audience *clapped*⟩ **6** *dial Brit* **:** to sit down abruptly ⟨~ down in a chair⟩ **:** crouch suddenly
²**clap** \"\ *n* -s [ME *clappe*, *cleppe*, prob. fr. ME *clappen*, *cleppen*, v.] **1 :** a device (as the clapper of a mill) that makes a clapping noise **2** *obs* **:** the human tongue **3** *obs* **:** a sudden stroke or turn of fortune, esp. ill fortune **4 :** a loud percussive or explosive noise: as **a** *obs* **:** the report of a gun ⟨the ~ of a musket⟩ **b :** a sudden crash of thunder **5 a :** a sudden sometimes resounding blow or stroke ⟨the guard gave him a ~ in the ribs with his stick⟩ or series of such blows or strokes ⟨the flock rose with a great ~ of wings⟩ **b :** a blow (as with the flat of the hand) given as a gesture of encouragement or friendship ⟨he gave his pal a ~ on the back⟩ **6 :** the lower part of the beak of a hawk **7 :** the noise made by clapping the hands ⟨the ~ and cry of children at play⟩ or esp. by clapping one's hands as a token of pleasure or approval ⟨the audience gave him a good ~⟩ — **at a clap :** at once **:** TOGETHER — **in a clap :** in a moment **:** IMMEDIATELY
³**clap** \"\ *n* -s [MF *clapoir* bubo, prob. fr. *clapoire*, *clapier* rabbit warren, house of prostitution, fr. OProv *clapier* rabbit warren, heap of stones] **1 :** GONORRHEA — often used with *the* **2 a :** a swelling in the legs of horses caused by a disease **b :** the disease producing such a swelling **3 :** bovine mastitis
⁴**clap** \"\ *vt* **clapped; clapped; clapping; claps :** to infect with gonorrhea — sometimes used with *up*
¹**clap·board** \ˈklabə(r)d; ˈkla,bōrd, ˈklap,bōrd, -ȯrd,-ōəd, -ȯ(ə)d\ *n* -s [part trans. of D *klaphout* stave wood, fr. MD *clapholt*, prob. fr. *clappen* to clap, hit + *holt* wood; akin to OE *clæppan* to throb and to OE *holt* wood — more at CLAP, HOLT] **1** *archaic* **:** a size of board esp. of split oak used for making staves and wainscoting **2 :** a narrow board that is usu. thicker at one edge than the other and is used for weatherboarding outside walls ⟨a ~ house⟩ **3 :** material for clapboards; *collectively* **:** CLAPBOARDS
²**clapboard** \"\ *vt* -ED/-ING/-S **:** to cover (as an outside wall) with clapboards ⟨the house was ~*ed* and then painted white⟩
clap·bread \ˈklap,bred\ *n* [¹*clap* + *bread*] *dial Eng* **:** oatmeal cake clapped or patted out thin and baked
clapdish \ˈ=,=\ *n* [²*clap* "lid" + *dish*] **:** a wooden dish once carried by alms seekers having a lid that could be clapped to attract attention and also, if carried by a leper, to warn of approach
cla·pey·ron equation \ˌklapəˌrōn-, -rän-\ *or* **clapeyron's equation** *n, usu cap C* [after B.P.E. *Clapeyron* †1864 Fr. physicist] **:** an equation relating to change of phase in a pure substance (as vaporization of a liquid) that gives the rate of change with temperature of the pressure at equilibrium between the phases in terms of the heat of transition and the volumes of the phases before and after the transition — compare CLAUSIUS-CLAPEYRON EQUATION
clap-in-clap-out \=ˈ=ˈ=\ *n* -s **:** a parlor game in which a player who has been sent from the room returns and tries to guess which of the other players has chosen him for a partner, the other players clapping when his guess is right
clapmatch *var of* KLAPMATCH
clapnest \ˈ=,=\ *n* [¹*clap* + *nest*] **:** a net or other enclosure designed to be dropped over a nest or pool for the capture of ground-nesting or water birds
clapnet \ˈ=,=\ *n* [¹*clap* + *net*] **:** a net made to close or clap together suddenly for capturing birds
clapped *past of* CLAP
¹**clap·per** \ˈklapə(r)\ *n* -s [ME *clapper*, *clepper*, fr. *clappen*, *cleppen* to clap + *-er*] **1 a** (1) **:** a mendicant's noisemaking device (as the lid of a clapdish or a leper's rattle) (2) **:** a wooden rattle used in some Christian churches instead of a bell on the last three days of Holy Week **b** *Brit* **:** a rattle used to frighten away birds **c** (1) **:** a noisemaker having a metal plate and two balls on flexible wires attached to a stick (2) **:** one of a pair of flat sticks held between the fingers and clapped usu. rhythmically **:** KNACKER — usu. used in pl. **2 a** (1) **:** the tongue of a bell — see BELL illustration (2) *slang* **:** the tongue of a talkative person **b :** the piece of wood or metal that strikes a mill hopper so as to cause the grain to pass down **:** CLAP **3 :** a piece of board with a handle for dressing and flattening newly molded bricks

clapper 1a(2)

²**clapper** \"\ *vt* **clappered; clappered; clappering** \-p(ə)riŋ\ **clappers :** to ring (a bell) by moving the clapper
clapper boards *n pl* **:** a pair of boards hinged at one end and banged together in front of a motion-picture camera before or after a take to facilitate synchronization of sound and picture prints
clapper box *n* **:** a hinged part on the toolhead of a reciprocating machine (as a planer or shaper) that permits the tool to clear the workpiece on the return stroke
clapper boy *n* **:** a member of a motion-picture camera crew who works the clapper boards and holds the slate up to be photographed
clapperclaw \ˈ==,=\ *vt* [perh. fr. ¹*clapper* + *claw* (v.)] **1** *now dial chiefly Eng* **:** to thrash or abuse clumsily by or as if by striking with the hand and clawing with the nails **2** *dial Eng* **:** to abuse with scolding **:** REVILE
clap·per·dud·geon \ˈklapə(r),dəjən\ *n* -s [perh. fr. ¹*clapper* + *dudgeon* (dagger)] **:** BEGGAR
clapper rail *n* [¹*clapper* + *rail*] **:** any of several large long-billed New World rails; *specif* **:** a dull-plumaged form (*Rallus longirostris*) common on salt marshes of the Atlantic coast of the U.S. — see CALIFORNIA CLAPPER RAIL
clapper valve *n* **:** CLACK VALVE
clapping *pres part of* CLAP
claps *pres 3d sing of* CLAP, *pl of* CLAP
clapstick \ˈ=,=\ *n* **:** CLAPPER BOARDS — often used in pl.
clapt *past of* CLAP
¹**claptrap** \ˈ=,=\ *n* [¹*clap* + *trap*] **:** literature or other expression that attempts to convince or gain applause, credit, or recognition by the use of cheap, empty, or meretricious means **:** pretentious nonsense **:** TRASH ⟨speeches full of ~⟩ ⟨~ selling as science fiction⟩
²**claptrap** \"\ *adj* **:** characterized by or suggestive of claptrap esp. in showiness of a cheap nature, spiritual emptiness, or poor technique ⟨~ eloquence⟩ ⟨~ sentiment⟩ ⟨a ~ plot⟩
clap up *vt* **:** to imprison hastily ⟨they *clapped* the smugglers *up* without trial⟩
clapwort \ˈ=,=\ *n* -s [³*clap* + *wort*] **:** SQUAWROOT a
claque \ˈklak\ *n* -s [F, fr. *claquer* to applaud, fr. *claque* clap; of imit. origin] **1 :** an opera hat with a collapsible crown **:** CRUSH HAT **2 a :** a group hired to applaud at a performance (as an opera, play, recital) in order to promote its success or the success of a performer ⟨the ~ gave her three curtain calls⟩ **b :** a group of often demonstrative or self-seeking supporters or adherents ⟨surrounded by a ~ of fair-weather friends⟩
cla·queur \klaˈkər(·)\ *also* **claqu·er** \ˈklakər\ *n* -s [F *claqueur*, fr. *claquer* + *-eur* -or] **:** a member of a claque
clar *abbr* clarinet
clar·a·bel·la *or* **clar·i·bel·la** \,klarəˈbelə\ *n* -s [L *clara* (fem. of *clarus* clear) + *bella*, fem. of *bellus* beautiful — more at CLEAR, BEAUTY] **:** an 8-foot organ stop with open wooden pipes — called also *claribel flute*
clar·ain \ˈkla(a),rān\ *n* -s [F, fr. L *clarus* bright + F *-ain* (as in *fusain*, *durain*) — more at CLEAR] **:** one of the materials composing the lustrous layers present in some coals — compare DURAIN, FUSAIN, VITRAIN
¹**clare** \ˈkla(ə)r, -le(ə)r\ *adj, usu cap* [fr. County *Clare*, Ireland] **:** of or from County Clare, Ireland **:** of the kind or style prevalent in County Clare
²**clare** *n* -s *usu cap* **:** POOR CLARE
clar·ence \ˈklarən(t)s\ *n* -s [after the duke of *Clarence*, later William IV of England (†1837)] **:** a closed 4-wheeled carriage with seats for four inside and a seat for the driver outside — called also *growler*

clarence

clar·en·ceux king of arms *also* **clarenceux** *or* **clar·en·cieux king of arms** *or* **clarencieux** \ˈklarən,sü(·)\ *n, pl* **clarenceux kings of arms** \-,sü-\ *also* **clarenceux** \-,sü(z)\ *or* **clarencieux kings of arms** \-,sü-\ *or* **clarencieux** \-,sü(z)\ *usu cap C&K&A* [trans. of AF *Roy d'Armes de Clarenceux*, fr. *Clarenceux*, English dukedom, fr. *Clare*, Suffolk, England] **:** an English king of arms having jurisdiction south of the river Trent — compare COLLEGE OF ARMS, GARTER KING OF ARMS, NORROY AND ULSTER KING OF ARMS, NORROY KING OF ARMS
clare-obscure *var of* CLAIR-OBSCURE
clar·et \ˈklarət *also* -ler- *sometimes* -(,)rā\ *n* -s [ME, fr. MF (*vin*) *claret* clear wine, fr. *vin* wine + *claret* clear, fr. *cler* clear — more at CLEAR] **1 a :** a dry red table wine from the Bordeaux wine district of France **b :** any dry red table wine — often used with a term designating origin ⟨California ~⟩ ⟨New Zealand ~⟩ **2** *slang* **:** BLOOD **3 a** *or* **claret red** *or* **claret brown :** a moderate red that is slightly lighter than cerise, lighter than Harvard crimson (sense 1), very slightly bluer and paler than average strawberry (sense 2a), bluer and lighter than Turkey red, and bluer and stronger than pepper red — called also *Bordeaux* **b** *of textiles* **:** a dark purplish red that is redder and duller than pansy purple
¹**cla·re·tian** \kləˈrēshən, kla(a)ˈr-\ *adj, usu cap* [Anthony *Claret* (Antonio Maria Claret y Clara) †1870 Spanish priest who founded the order + E *-ian*] **:** of or relating to the Claretians
²**claretian** \"\ *n* -s *usu cap* **:** a member of the Congregation of the Missionary Sons of the Immaculate Heart of Mary founded in Vich, Spain, in 1849
claret wine *n* [part trans. of MF *vin claret* — more at CLARET] **:** a variable color averaging a dark red that is yellower and slightly duller than average wine, yellower and duller than cranberry, and yellower and less strong than average garnet
clar·ety \ˈklarəd-ē\ *adj* [*claret* + *-y*] **:** having a color resembling or suggesting the color of claret wine ⟨a *clarety*-complexioned, opinionated country gentleman —P.H.Newby⟩
clar·i·as \kla(a)rēəs\ *n, cap* [NL, modif. of Gk *Klarios*, an epithet of Apollo, lit., of Klaros, fr. *Klaros* city of ancient Greece near Colophon] **:** a genus of large eellike freshwater catfishes of Africa and southern Asia that survive the dry season buried deep in the mud
clar·i·bel flute \ˈklarə,bel-\ *n* [by alter.] **:** CLARABELLA
clar·i·fi·a·ble \-,fīəbəl — *see* CLARIFY\ *adj* **:** capable of being clarified
cla·rif·i·cant \kləˈrifəkənt\ *n* -s [LL *clarificant-*, *clarificans*, pres. part. of *clarificare*] **:** a clarifying substance **:** CLARIFIER
clar·i·fi·ca·tion \,klarəfəˈkāshən *also* ,kler-\ *n* -s [F or LL; F, fr. LL *clarification-*, *clarificatio* glorification, fr. *clarificatus* (past part. of *clarificare*) + L *-ion-*, *-io* -ion] **:** the act or process of clarifying
clar·i·fi·er \ˈ==,fī(ə)r, -īə\ *n* -s **:** one that clarifies: as **a :** one that filters a substance (as paint, varnish, or wine) to remove impurities **b :** one that purifies oleo stock by straining and skimming it while it is heated in a tank **c :** one that changes the filters that strain cellulose solution before it is spun into rayon yarn or made into transparent wrapping material — called also *filterer*
clar·i·fy \ˈklarə,fī *also* ˈkler-\ *vb* -ED/-ING/-ES [ME *clarifien*, fr. MF *clarifier*, fr. LL *clarificare*, fr. L *clarus* clear + *-i-* + *-ficare* -fy — more at CLEAR] *vt* **1 a** *archaic* **:** to make clear and bright by lightening the darkness and obscurity of ⟨the sun *clarifies* the earth⟩ **b :** to clear (the air or atmosphere) of clouds or fog **c** *obs* **:** GLORIFY, TRANSFIGURE **2 :** to make (a liquid or something liquefied) clear, pure, or pellucid **:** free from unwanted solid matter ⟨~ coffee with eggshells⟩ ⟨~ syrup⟩ ⟨~ sewage⟩ **3 a :** to free (the mind or understanding) of confusion, doubt, or uncertainty ⟨the conference did help to harmonize, as well as ~, the thinking of the leaders of the republics on a number of controversial questions —*Atlantic*⟩ ⟨the cold night air *clarified* his muddled brain⟩ ⟨hoped a long rest would ~ his mind⟩ **b :** to explain clearly **:** make understandable **:** REVEAL, INTERPRET ⟨~ a process by the use of diagrams⟩ **4 :** to make less complex or less ambiguous **:** put in order **:** DEFINE ⟨~ one's life⟩ ⟨~ an issue⟩ ~ *vi* **:** to grow or become clear ⟨waiting for the present muddled diplomatic situation to ~ —*Newsweek*⟩
cla·rin \kləˈrēn\ *n* -s [Sp *clarín* trumpet, prob. modif. of F

clairon, claron] **:** a very long trumpetlike wind instrument used by the aborigines in Mexico

cla·ri·na \klə'rēnə\ *n* -S [G, alter. of It *clarino* trumpet] **:** a wind instrument combining the qualities of oboe and clarinet invented by Heckel in 1891

clar·i·net \ˌklarəˌnet *also* -ler- *sometimes* '≈≈ˌnət; *usu* -d·+V\ *also* **clar·i·o·net** \ˌ≈rēəˌne-\ *n* -S [F *clarinette*, prob. fr. It *clarinetto*, dim. of *clarino* trumpet] **1 :** a single-reed woodwind instrument; *specif* **:** an orchestral and band instrument having a cylindrical tube with moderately flaring end, a chromatic-scale compass of about 3½ octaves upward from the written D below middle C, and a strong flexible violinlike tone **2 :** a usu. 8-foot reed organ stop with a clarinetlike tone

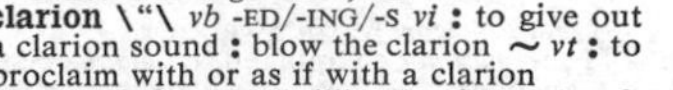
clarinet 1

clar·i·net·ist *or* **clar·i·net·tist** \ˌ≈≈'ned·əst, -etəst\ *n* -S [G *klarinettist*, fr. *klarinette* clarinet (fr. F *clarinette*) + *-ist*] **:** a performer on the clarinet

¹cla·ri·no \klə'rē(ˌ)nō\ *n, pl* **clari·ni** \-(ˌ)nē\ *or* **clarinos** [It, trumpet, prob. fr. Sp *clarín*] **1 :** CLARION **2 a :** the trumpet as played in the 17th century in its high range without valves — compare OVERBLOW **b :** the first trumpet part — called also *clarin trumpet* **3 :** the middle register of the clarinet — called also *clarion*

²clarino \"\ *n* -S [modif. of Sp *clarín*, lit., trumpet] **:** SOLITAIRE 5b — used esp. of aviary or cage birds kept for their song

¹clar·i·on \'klarēən *also* 'kler-\ *n* -S [ME *clarioun*, fr. MF &ML; MF *clairon, claron*, fr. ML *clarion-, clario*, fr. L *clarus*] **1 :** a medieval trumpet; *specif* **:** one capable of melody as distinguished from a field or military trumpet **2 :** the sound of a clarion or a similar sound **3 :** a 4-foot reed organ stop of trumpetlike quality **4 :** CLARINO 3 **5 :** a heraldic bearing somewhat resembling a panpipe and understood to represent an organ — called also *organ rest, rest*

clarion 5

²clarion \"\ *vb* -ED/-ING/-S *vi* **:** to give out a clarion sound **:** blow the clarion ~ *vt* **:** to proclaim with or as if with a clarion

³clarion \"\ *adj* **:** brilliantly clear ⟨the clean ~ sky —R.M. Coates⟩; *esp* **:** having a loud clear tone ⟨issued a ~ call to action⟩

clar·i·ty \'klarəd·ē, -ətē, -i *also* 'kler-\ *n* -ES [ME *clarte, clarite*, fr. MF & L; MF *clarté*, fr. L *claritat-, claritas*, fr. *clarus* + *-itat-, -itas* -ity] **1** *obs* **:** BRILLIANCY, BRIGHTNESS, SPLENDOR, GLORY **2 a :** CLEARNESS, PELLUCIDNESS ⟨the ~ of the atmosphere⟩ ⟨the ~ of the wine⟩ **b :** distinctness of shape, outline, or sound ⟨the ~ of the drawing⟩ ⟨a great ~ of speech⟩ ⟨~ of tone⟩ **3 :** directness, orderliness, and precision of thought or expression ⟨he relied more on a forceful ~ to convince his readers than on the brilliant and exciting ambiguities of propagandist eloquence —Aldous Huxley⟩

clark \'klärk, -åk\ *now dial var of* CLERK

clark cell *or* **clark standard cell** \"-\ *n, usu cap 1st C* [after Josiah L. *Clark* †1898 Eng. engineer] **:** a voltaic cell in early use as a standard of electromotive force having zinc amalgam and mercury as electrodes and zinc sulfate as electrolyte with an electromotive force at 15° C of 1.4328 volts

clarke·ite \'klär,kīt\ *n* -S [Frank W. *Clarke* †1931 Am. chemist + E *-ite*] **:** a rare dark brown radioactive mineral whose chief constituent is uranium oxide (sp. gr. 6.39)

clarke's column *or* **clarke's nucleus** \'klärks-\ *n, usu cap 1st C* [after Jacob A. L. *Clarke* †1880 Eng. physician] **:** NUCLEUS DORSALIS

clarke's gazelle *n, usu cap C* [perh. after George S. *Clarke*, Baron Sydenham †1933 colonial administrator in Egypt and Sudan] **:** DIBATAG

clarke's spheroid *n, usu cap C* [after Alexander R. *Clarke* †1914 Eng. geodesist] **:** an ideal oblate spheroid generally recognized as representing the figure of the earth at average sea level

clark·ia \'klärkēə\ *n* [NL, fr. William *Clark* †1838 Am. explorer + NL *-ia*] **1** *cap* **:** a small genus of showy annual herbs (family Onagraceae) of the Pacific slope of No. America having petals with a distinct claw and fruit capsulate **2** -S **:** any plant of the genus *Clarkia*

clark nutcracker *or* **clark's nutcracker** *also* **clark's crow** \'klärk(s)-\ *n, usu cap C* [after William *Clark* †1838 Am. explorer] **:** a grayish white bird (*Nucifraga columbiana*) of the family Corvidae of western No. America with black-and-white wings and tail

cla·ro \'klä(ˌ)rō\ *n* -S [Sp, fr. L *clarus*] **:** a light-colored generally mild cigar

cla·ro·ne \klə'rōnē, -ō(ˌ)nā\ *n, pl* **claro·ni** \-(ˌ)nē\ [It, fr. F *claron, clairon* — more at CLARION] **1 :** BASS CLARINET **2 :** BASSET HORN

clar·sach *or* **clar·seach** *or* **clar·seth** *or* **clar·sech** *or* **clar·shech** *or* **clair·schach** \'kla(a)r,s(h)ak, -är-,-er-,-ār-,-ōi(ə)r-, ˌs(h)ək\ *n, pl* **clar·saich** \"\ [alter. (influenced by ScGael *clārsach* & IrGael *clāirseach*) of ME *clareschaw*, modif. of ScGael *clārsach;* akin to MIr *clāirseach* harp] **:** the ancient small harp of Ireland and Scotland

clarsach or Irish harp of the early 13th century

¹clart \'klärt, -åt\ *n* -S [akin to ME *biclarten* to soil] **1** *dial Brit* **:** a clot or daub of mud or other sticky substance **2** *dial Brit* **:** MUD, MIRE — often used in pl. **3** *dial Brit* **:** SLOVEN

²clart \"\ *vt* -ED/-ING/-S *dial Brit* **:** to daub or smear esp. with mud or dirt

clarty \-tī\ *adj* -ER/-EST *dial* **:** bedaubed with sticky dirt **:** DIRTY, MUDDY; *also* **:** STICKY, GOOEY

¹clary \'kla(a)rē\ *n* -ES [ME *clare, clarrie*, fr. OF *claré*, fr. *clar, cler* clear — more at CLEAR] **:** a beverage consisting of a mixture of wine, honey, and spices strained till clear

²clary \"\ *also* **clary sage** *n* -ES [ME *clare, clarie*, fr. MF *sclaree*, fr. ML *sclareia, scarleia*] **:** any of several aromatic herbs of the genus *Salvia* (esp. *S. sclarea*) of southern Europe cultivated esp. in England as a potherb and widely as an ornamental

³clary \"\ *n* -ES [by alter. and shortening] *slang* **:** CLARINET

-clase \ˌklās, -āz\ *n comb form* -S [F, fr. Gk *klasis* breaking, fr. *klan* to break — more at GLADIATOR] **:** a mineral having a (specified) kind of cleavage ⟨clino*clase*⟩ ⟨plagio*clase*⟩

¹clash \'klash, -aa(ə)sh,-aish\ *vb* -ED/-ING/-ES [imit.] *vi* **1 a :** to make a jarring resounding metallic noise by or as if by striking or ringing ⟨the bells of St. Paul's ~*ed* out —Rose Macaulay⟩ ⟨gears ~*ed* loudly as the truck moved on⟩ **b :** to meet and hit together violently usu. with a metallic noise ⟨the swords ~*ed* together⟩ ⟨the empty oil drums ~*ed* as the truck sped along⟩ **2 :** to meet in opposition, controversy, or variance **:** CONFLICT: **a :** to fight or engage in conflict esp. in sharp skirmish or rough brawl — often used with *with* ⟨the settlers often ~*ed* with the Indians⟩ **b :** to compete sharply **:** be completely and sharply in disagreement, incompatibility, discord, or inconsistency ⟨American and British interests ~*ed* in the fur-producing areas⟩ ⟨colors that ~ badly⟩ ⟨political expediency and the law of morality frequently ~ —V.L.Parrington⟩ **3** *chiefly Scot* **:** GOSSIP ~ *vt* **1 :** to strike together **:** hit, thrust, dash, or hurl against sharply and forcefully typically with a loud ringing noise ⟨dark and passionate shapes . . . ~ their weapons —Norman Douglas⟩ ⟨when two males [wildebeest] are engaged in single combat, they rush together, ~*ing* their horns —James Stevenson-Hamilton⟩ **2** *now dial Brit* **:** DASH, SLAM **syn** see BUMP

²clash \"\ *n* -ES **1 :** a loud harsh esp. metallic jangling sound or series of sounds produced esp. by striking or grinding together **:** a noisy collision ⟨the ~ of swords⟩ ⟨a ~ of cymbals⟩ ⟨the ~ of gears⟩ **2 a :** a meeting in conflict or opposition **:** a sharp affray **:** BRAWL, SKIRMISH ⟨the ~*es* of minutemen and British at Lexington and Concord⟩ **b :** a situation sharply marked by disagreement, incompatibility, discord, rivalry, or opposition **:** a sharp usu. jarring or unpleasant contrast ⟨the tragedy of politics is not the ~ of right and wrong but the ~ of one right with another —H.J.Laski⟩ ⟨buildings marked by a ~ of architectural styles⟩ **3** *dial Brit* **:** a quantity or mass esp. of mud or water **4** *dial* **:** NEWS, GOSSIP, SCANDAL — often used in pl. **syn** see IMPACT

clash·ing·ly *adv* **:** in a clashing manner

clashy \-shi\ *adj* -ER/-EST *dial Eng* **:** WET, SHOWERY

-cla·sia \'klāzh(ē)ə\ *n comb form* -S [NL, fr. Gk *klasis* breaking (fr. *klan* to break) + NL *-ia* — more at GLADIATOR] **:** breaking ⟨arthro*clasia*⟩ **:** breaking up ⟨hemo*clasia*⟩

-cla·sis \kləsəs\ *n comb form, pl* **-cla·ses** \kləˌsēz\ [NL, fr. Gk *klasis*] **:** -CLASIA ⟨dia*clasis*⟩

-cla·site \'klāˌsīt, ˌkləˌ-, -zīt, *usu* -īd· + V\ *n comb form* -S [ISV *-clase* + *-ite;* orig. formed as G *-klasit*] **:** -CLASE

clas·mat·o·cyte \klaz'mad·əˌsīt\ *n* -S [ISV *clasmat-* (fr. Gk *klasmat-, klasma* fragment, fr. *klan* to break) + *-o-* + *-cyte* — more at GLADIATOR] **:** HISTIOCYTE — **clas·mat·o·cyt·ic** \(ˌ)≈ˌ≈≈ˌsid·ik\ *adj*

clas·ma·to·sis \ˌklazmə'tōsəs\ *n, pl* **clasmato·ses** \-ō,sēz\ [NL, fr. Gk *klasmat-, klasma* fragment + NL *-osis*] *biol* **:** fragmentation esp. of cells

¹clasp \'klasp, -aa(ə)sp,-aisp,-åsp\ *n* -S [ME *claspe, clapse;* perh. akin to OE *clyppan* to embrace — more at CLIP] **1 a :** a releasable catch for holding together two or more objects (as necktie and shirt) or complementary parts of something (as of a book, necklace, or handbag) **b :** a device designed to encircle a tooth to hold a denture in place **c** *mil* **:** a bar of metal attached across the suspension ribbon of a service medal inscribed with the name of (1) an action or (2) a country or area — called also respectively *battle clasp, service clasp* **2 a** *obs* **:** TENDRIL **b :** the tenaculum of a collembolan **3 :** a holding or enveloping with or as if with the arms or hands: **a :** EMBRACE **b :** GRIP ⟨the hearty ~ of his hand⟩ ⟨the iron ~ of never-ending cold —Walter O'Meara⟩

²clasp \"\ *vb* **clasped** *or archaic* **claspt; clasped** *or archaic* **claspt; clasping; clasps** [ME *claspen, clapsen*, fr. *claspe, clapse*, n.] *vt* **1 a :** to fasten or shut together with or as if with a clasp ⟨a robe ~*ed* with a brooch⟩ **b :** to furnish with a clasp ⟨a ~*ed* binding of a book⟩ **2 :** to surround and hold **:** hold (as a large object) against the body ⟨~*ing* a bulging briefcase⟩ **:** entwine about **:** cling to ⟨~*ing* ivy⟩ **3 a :** to enclose and hold or press with the arms **:** EMBRACE, ENWRAP **b :** to encircle within joined hands usu. with interlocked fingers ⟨her hands ~*ed* round one knee —George Meredith⟩ **4 :** to press (the hands) together esp. with interlocked fingers (as in prayer, grief, supplication, or anxiety) ⟨~*ing* her hands tightly in her lap⟩ **5 :** to seize or hold (another's hand) firmly (as in greeting, show of affection, congratulation, or encouragement) **:** grasp cherishingly or protectively ⟨~*ing* her baby to her bosom⟩ **6 :** to engage in a clasp **:** WRAP — used with *around, round,* or *over* ⟨~*ed* his enormous fingers tight around the chair arm —Kenneth Roberts⟩ ~ *vi* **1 :** CLING, EMBRACE **2** *of lower animals* **:** MATE, COPULATE

clasp·er \-pə(r)\ *n* -S **:** any of various structures modified to assist in copulation (as the gonapophyses of many male insects); *specif* **:** one of a pair of male copulatory organs on the anterior of the pelvic fins of sharks, rays, and chimaeroids

clasping *adj* [fr. pres. part. of ²*clasp*] *of a leaf or petiole* **:** partly or wholly surrounding the stem — compare PERFOLIATE

clasp knife *n* **:** a large pocketknife the blade or blades of which fold or shut into the handle **:** JACKKNIFE; *esp* **:** a large one-bladed folding knife having a catch to hold the blade open rigidly

clasp lock *n* **:** a self-locking spring lock

clasp nail *n* **:** CUT NAIL

clasp nut *n* **:** a split nut arranged so that it grips its mating screw when closed

¹class \'klas, -aa(ə)s,-ais,-ås\ *n* -ES *often attrib* [F *classe*, fr. L *classis* class, men called to arms, fleet; akin to L *calare* to call, summon — more at LOW] **1 a :** one group of a usu. society-wide grouping of people according to social status, political or economic similarities, or interests or ways of life in common ⟨the ruling ~⟩ ⟨the upper and lower ~*es*⟩ ⟨the entrepreneurial ~⟩ ⟨these occupational ~*es* are admittedly not internally homogeneous in respect to such ~ criteria as "income", "prestige" or "social equality" —Louis Schneider⟩ ⟨*class*-conscious behavior⟩ — see CASTE **b :** social rank; *esp* **:** high social rank ⟨a feeling of ~⟩ **c :** an economic or social rank above that of the proletariat ⟨the ~*es* as opposed to the masses⟩ — usu. used in pl. **d :** high quality or outstanding ability **:** METTLE ⟨the actors were adequate but without real ~⟩ **e** *slang* **:** elegance in appearance or outward behavior **:** OSTENTATION — usu. used to express naïve admiration ⟨this hotel certainly has ~⟩ or ironic appraisal; see CLASSY **2 a :** a course of instruction esp. considered apart from other courses ⟨education can no longer be separated into courses or ~*es* in half a dozen main subjects⟩ **b :** a body of students meeting regularly to study the same subject under the guidance of an instructor, to listen to lectures, or to engage in guided discussions or in recitations ⟨a Spanish ~⟩ ⟨a Bible ~⟩ **c :** the period during which such a body meets or the meeting itself **d** *at Brit universities* **:** the final rating achieved by a student reading for Honours ⟨a First-*Class* Honours degree⟩ — distinguished from *pass* **e :** a body of alumni who have graduated or of students who expect to graduate in the same year from the same institution **:** a body of students having similar academic standing ⟨donated by the ~ of 1925⟩ **f :** a church group consisting of approximately 12 members under the direction of a class leader formed for religious study and instruction in early Methodism and continued in some Methodist bodies today **3 :** a group, set, or kind marked by common attributes or a common attribute ⟨any ~ or description of persons —R.B. Taney⟩ ⟨such contraptions are symbolic of a whole ~ of labor-saving devices —F.L.Allen⟩: as **a :** a major category in biological taxonomy ranking above the order, in modern taxonomy falling below the phylum or division and in the Linnaean system being the highest category ⟨the ~ Musci includes all the mosses⟩ **b :** SET 44b **4 :** a group, division, distinction, or rating based on quality, degree of competence, or condition ⟨a ~ of travel accommodation⟩ ⟨a ~ A movie⟩ ⟨a ~ B tuberculosis patient⟩ **5 :** one of the genders usu. not associated with sex and often greatly exceeding three in number into which nouns are divided in the Bantu languages and some others

syn CATEGORY, GENUS, SPECIES, DENOMINATION, GENRE, PREDICAMENT: these words are herein discussed only in their general, nonspecialized use, and the following comments may be inapplicable to such studies as philosophy and the sciences. CLASS is a very general term for a group including all individuals with a common characteristic ⟨as soon as we employ a name to connote attributes, the things . . . which happen to possess those attributes are constituted ipso facto a *class* —J.S.Mill⟩ CLASS sometimes suggests a value judgment as a basis of classification ⟨a libel of the lowest *class*, both in sentiment and language —T.B.Macaulay⟩ ⟨the *class* of nominal Christians for whom there might be a chance —R.M.Lovett⟩ CATEGORY may be interchangeable with CLASS but is sometimes more precise in suggesting classification or grouping on the basis of a certain readily perceived criterion or on a predication, often an explicit one ⟨we cannot approach a work of art with our laws and *categories*. We have to comprehend the artist's own values —Havelock Ellis⟩ ⟨none of the writings of the fathers of the English Church belongs to the *category* of speculative philosophy —T.S.Eliot⟩ GENUS and SPECIES, scientific in their suggestion, may differ in that the first may imply a larger, less specific group, the latter a smaller, more specific one ⟨English society, in other words, is . . . a *species* of a larger cultural *genus* —Morris Watnick⟩ ⟨the word "infringement" is almost never used to describe acts of the *genus*, unfair competition. It is applied only to the *species*, namely trademark misuse —Beverly W. Pattishall⟩ DENOMINATION usu. indicates that the group under consideration has been or may be named explicitly and clearly; it is common in religious use ⟨Methodist, Presbyterian, and other *denominations*⟩ and use with a series of closely related units ⟨*denominations* of currency⟩ GENRE refers to a specific, named type; its use is mainly restricted to literature and art ⟨some of his prose poems, a *genre* . . . which he invented —*Saturday Rev.*⟩ ⟨the larger literary types or *genres*, such as the drama or novel —Max Lerner & Edwin Mims⟩ PREDICAMENT is a rather uncommon synonym for CATEGORY, esp. in situations showing a close Aristotelian connection.

²class \"\ *vt* -ED/-ING/-ES **1 :** to divide or distribute into classes **:** CLASSIFY ⟨~ wool by grade and staple⟩ **2 :** to place in a class — often used with *with* or *among* ⟨~*ed* as one of the world's greatest men⟩

class a \(')≈'ā\ *adj, cap A* **:** FIRST-CLASS

class-angle \'≈,≈≈\ *vt* **:** to present or treat (as a news story) in such a way as to point up or emphasize class interests or social conflict

class cleavage *n* **:** the occurrence of a linguistic form in more than one form class (as *one* in "one hat", "if one only knew", "the other one")

class-conscious \'≈,≈≈\ *adj* **:** actively aware of one's position or of one's responsibilities or privileges as a member of a particular social or economic class or of one's identity of interest or common status with others of the same class usu. as against other such classes; *esp* **:** actively aware in this way of one's membership in the proletariat — **class consciousness** *n*

class day *n* **:** a day of the commencement season in American universities, colleges, and schools on which the senior class holds exercises usu. consisting of the reading of a class history and poem, or the delivery of a class oration, and other similar observances

classed *past of* CLASS

classed catalog *n* [²*class*] **:** CLASSIFIED CATALOG

class·er \'≈ə(r)\ *n* -S **:** one that classifies (as wool, cotton, or tobacco) — called also *grader*

classes *pl of* CLASS *or of* CLASSIS, *pres 3d sing of* CLASS

¹clas·sic \'klasik, -aas-, -ēk\ *adj* [F or L; F *classique*, fr. L *classicus* of the classes of the Roman people, of the first class, of the first rank, fr. *classis* class — more at CLASS] **1 a :** of the highest quality or rank **:** having recognized and permanent value **:** of enduring interest and appeal — used esp. of literature, art, and music ⟨his achievement as a writer was that out of his knowledge of common speech he forged a ~ prose⟩ ⟨a ~ quartet for strings⟩ **b :** forming part of the permanent cultural achievement of mankind **:** felt to be among the great works esp. literary and artistic of mankind ⟨the annals of the Jews and the Scots have become a ~ heritage⟩ ⟨the really ~ products of the human imagination endure for all time⟩ **c :** characterized by simple tailored lines correct for a variety of places and occasions and basically in fashion year after year — used of wearing apparel **2 :** ²CLASSICAL 2 **3 a :** ²CLASSICAL 3a, 3b(5), 3c **b** *usu cap* (1) **:** of or belonging to the Hohokam culture of the period A.D. 1150–1400 characterized by polished red pottery, houses having solid walls and contiguous rooms, and artifacts for use rather than ornament (2) **:** of or relating to the culture of the Old Empire period of the Maya **c** *of a postage stamp* **:** obsolete and scarce and having special significance in postal or philatelic history; *esp* **:** dating from mid-19th century when postage stamps first came into use **4 a :** historically memorable ⟨their execution became a ~ national tragedy⟩ **b :** noted because of special literary or historical associations ⟨the ~ districts of London⟩ **c :** well known as customary or traditional ⟨Paris, the ~ refuge of expatriates⟩ **5 :** particularly definitive, reliable, or authoritative — used generally of reference works and scholarly studies ⟨a ~ study of the American Indian⟩ **6 a :** standard or recognized esp. because of great frequency or consistency of occurrence ⟨~ symptoms of pneumonia⟩ ⟨a ~ appeal to patriotism⟩ **b :** typical or regarded as typical **:** ideally illustrative ⟨a ~ instance of guilt by association⟩ ⟨he had the ~ eccentricities of the absent-minded professor⟩ **7 a :** particularly appropriate or effective (to a given end) ⟨his appointment was a ~ answer to many problems⟩ **b :** basic and often traditional to an art or skill ⟨he demonstrated the five ~ passes in bullfighting⟩

²classic \"\ *n* -S **1 a :** a work of literature of ancient Greece or Rome **b :** the body of such writings ⟨study of the ~*s* is no longer required for a college degree⟩ — usu. used in pl. and with *the* **c** *archaic* **:** a student of the literature of Greece and Rome **2 a :** a work that is classic ⟨his manual of botany has become a ~ among scientists⟩ **b :** a work esp. of literature, art, or music meriting the highest respect ⟨a ~ of operettas⟩ **c :** the author of any such work ⟨he had already become a ~ many years before his death⟩ **3 :** something regarded as perfect of its kind or fitting to serve as a model ⟨his march through the wilderness of Maine has been regarded as a ~ of perseverance⟩ **4 :** a traditional contest or race having special significance and honorific value ⟨the racing ~ at Churchill Downs⟩ **5 :** a classic article of clothing **6 :** a classic postage stamp

¹clas·si·cal \-səkəl, -sēk-\ *adj* [NL *classis* + E *-ical*] **:** of or relating to a classis esp. in the Reformed Church or to the system of polity of which it is a part

²classical \"\ *adj* [L *classicus* + E *-al*] **1 :** ¹CLASSIC 1a, 1b **2 a :** of or relating to the ancient Greek and Roman world, esp. to its literature, art, architecture, or ideals ⟨the strong influence of ~ civilization upon the western world⟩ **b :** having order, balance, restraint or other qualities felt to derive from or suggest those characteristic of the literature, art, architecture, or ideals of ancient Greece and Rome ⟨a ~ serenity of mood⟩ ⟨a ~ integration of artistic elements⟩ **:** conforming to the models or of the rules derived from or felt to be derived from the Greek and Roman classics; *esp* **:** NEOCLASSIC — compare ROMANTIC **c :** specializing in or devoted to the literature or the languages of ancient Greece and Rome ⟨a ~ scholar⟩ **d :** of or relating to places inhabited by the Greeks and Romans or rendered famous by their deeds, art, or writings ⟨a trip to the ~ islands of the Aegean⟩ **e** (1) **:** appealing to critical interest or developed musical taste or conforming to an established and elaborated form of the art (as the fugue, suite, or sonata) — compare ROMANTIC (2) **:** relating to a musical composition characterized by classicism or to a composer of such music (3) **:** relating to art music or all music other than popular music or music for entertainment **3 a :** regarded as of first historical significance — used of a coherent and authoritative theory, method, or body of ideas commonly after new developments or general change of view have made it less authoritative **b :** of or relating to a form or system felt to be of first significance before modern times: as (1) **:** based on formerly generally accepted concepts in physics, esp. the mechanics of Newton and the electromagnetic theories of Maxwell **:** not involving relativity, wave mechanics, or quantum theory (2) **:** of or relating to the evolutionist school of anthropologists (3) **:** of or relating to the economics doctrines that were developed largely in England by Adam Smith, David Ricardo, T. R. Malthus, and J. S. Mill prior to 1848 and that constituted the first unified explanation of the capitalist system (4) **:** relating to the theory of penal reform mainly associated with the Italian jurist Beccaria (1738–?1794) and notable for its emphasis on deterrence and punishment proportional to the grievousness of the criminal act (5) **:** of, relating to, or felt to suggest traditional ballet (as in formality or grace of movement) **c :** of any form or system felt to be the authentic, authoritative, or time-tested one in comparison with later modified or more radical forms deriving from it ⟨the ~ goals of socialism⟩ ⟨a ~ folk dance⟩ ⟨a ~ golf swing⟩ **d :** ¹CLASSIC 5 ⟨a ~ study of juvenile delinquency⟩ **4 :** ¹CLASSIC 4 **5 :** ¹CLASSIC 6 ⟨the ~ symptoms of alcoholism⟩ **6 :** ¹CLASSIC 7 ⟨the ~ cure for malaria⟩ **7** *of language* **:** conforming to a pattern of usage sanctioned by a body of literature rather than by everyday speech ⟨~ Arabic⟩ **8 :** concerned with or giving instruction in the humanities, the fine arts, and the broad aspects of science ⟨a ~ high school⟩ ⟨a ~ curriculum⟩

classical humanism *n* **:** HUMANISM 1

clas·si·cal·ism \-ˌlizəm\ *n* -S **:** CLASSICISM

clas·si·cal·ist \-ˌləst\ *n* -S **:** CLASSICIST

clas·si·cal·i·ty \ˌ≈sə'kaləd·ē, -ətē, -i\ *n* -ES **1 :** the quality or state of being classic (as in literary or artistic style); *also* **:** classical scholarship **2 :** a piece or example of classicality **:** a classical feature

clas·si·cal·ize \'≈sikəˌlīz, -sē-\ *vb* -ED/-ING/-S **:** to imitate or cause to imitate Greek or Roman antiquity **:** CLASSICIZE ⟨the names of many towns in New York state were *classicalized*⟩

clas·si·cal·ly \-ək(ə)lē, -ēk-, -li\ *adv* **1 :** in a classic or classical manner: as **a :** according to the manner or style of classical authors **b :** in or by the study of the classics **2 :** in a traditionally accepted or prescribed manner **:** TYPICALLY ⟨the experiment as ~ performed⟩

classical suite *n* **:** a form of instrumental composition prevalent in the 18th century consisting strictly of the allemande, courante, saraband, and gigue often with the interpolation of gavotte, bourrée, minuet, musette, and passepied

clas·si·cism \ˈ≈sə,sizəm\ *n* -s [¹*classic* + *-ism*] **1 a :** the principles or the style of classical literature, art, or architecture **b :** classical scholarship **2 :** an ancient Greek or Roman word or expression esp. in an English context; *also* **:** a word or expression closely akin to the ancient Greek or Roman form **3 :** adherence to or practice of the virtues thought to be characteristic of classical art, literature, and in modern times music or to be universally and enduringly valid (as formal elegance and correctness, simplicity, dignity, restraint, order, proportion) — often opposed to *romanticism;* compare HELLENISM

clas·si·cist \-sə̇st\ *n* -s [¹*classic* + *-ist*] **1 :** an advocate or follower of classical style, rules, or models — often opposed to *romanticist* **2 :** one learned in the classics **:** a classical scholar **3 :** an advocate of the school study of the classics

clas·si·cis·tic \ˌ≈≈ˈsistik\ *adj* **:** adhering to or influenced by classical models or precepts ⟨~ architecture⟩ ⟨~ drama⟩

clas·si·cize \ˈ≈≈,sīz\ *vb* -ED/-ING/-S [¹*classic* + *-ize*] *vt* **:** to make classic or classical ~ *vi* **:** to follow or affect classic style or form

classico- *comb form* [F, fr. *classique* — more at CLASSIC] **1 :** classical **:** classical and ⟨*classico*-Lombardic⟩ **2 :** the classics ⟨*classicolatry*⟩

classic pitch *also* **classical pitch** *n* **:** a tuning standard in use during the latter half of the 18th century of 415 to 429 vibrations per second for A above middle C

classic revival *or* **classical revival** *n, usu cap C&R* **:** an artistic style inspired by or imitative of classical modes of expression — used esp. of works of art of the 15th and the 19th centuries

classics *pl of* CLASSIC

classier *comparative of* CLASSY

classiest *superlative of* CLASSY

clas·si·fi·a·ble \ˈklasə,fīəbəl, -laas-\ *adj* **:** capable of being classified or discriminated

clas·si·fi·ca·tion \ˌ≈səfəˈkāshən, *rap.* -sf-\ *n* -s [prob. fr. F, fr. *classe* class + *-i-* + *-fication*] **1 :** the act or a method of classifying **:** the act or a method of distributing into groups, classes, or families **:** an assigning to a proper class **:** SORTING: as **a :** the systematic arrangement or method of arrangement of animals and plants in groups or categories according to a definite plan or in a definite sequence either as in earlier practice by assuming static morphological relationships among the various groups and so producing typically broadly inclusive categories or as in modern practice by recognizing the dynamic evolutionary quality of biologic relationship and with the aid of physiology, ecology, and cytogenetics in analyzing underlying relations producing an ever-increasing subdivision of categories into groups expressive of natural relationships **:** TAXONOMY — compare CLASS, DIVISION, FAMILY, GENUS, ORDER, PHYLUM, SPECIES; LUMPER, SPLITTER **b :** a system for the arrangement of books or other library material according to subject or form — see DECIMAL CLASSIFICATION, EXPANSIVE CLASSIFICATION, LIBRARY OF CONGRESS CLASSIFICATION, UNIVERSAL DECIMAL CLASSIFICATION **c :** the classifying of ships by a classification society **d :** the arrangement of positions in public service or in an occupational catalog into classes on the basis of duties and qualification requirements **e :** a systematic assignment of prisoners in a penal institution to a program of prison treatment appropriate to their individual needs after study and examination by a staff of specialists — compare INDIVIDUALIZATION **f :** the classifying of esp. documentary information into groupings (in the U.S. usu. designated top secret, secret, and confidential) according to the stringency of the measures to be taken to prevent its falling into the hands of an enemy or potential enemy **g :** the grouping of articles of freight or express into classes for rate-making purposes **2 :** the result of classifying **:** a system of classes or groups or a systematic division of a series of related phenomena; *also* **:** one of such classes **:** CATEGORY, RATING **3 :** a publication containing for the purpose of tariff assessment a list of articles, the classes to which they are assigned, and the rules and regulations governing the application of class rates

clas·si·fi·ca·tion·ist \-sh(ə)nə̇st\ *n* -s **:** one skilled in or primarily interested in classification

classification number *n* **:** CLASS NUMBER

classification rating *n* **:** the class to which an article is assigned in the process of making or determining a class rate for freight or express charges

classification society *n* **:** a society for the promulgation of rules for the construction of vessels, the supervision of such construction, the classification of vessels according to merit, and the publication of a register listing them and classifying their essential features

classification track *n* **:** any track of a group of railroad tracks in a freight yard used in the separation of cars esp. according to destination or contents and their arrangement in preparation for train movement

classification yard *n* **:** a railroad yard consisting of classification tracks

clas·si·fi·ca·to·ri·ly \ˌklasəfəkəˌtōrəlē, klaˌsif-, *esp Brit* ˈklasifi,kātərəli\ *adv* **:** in a manner that accords with the terminology of a classificatory system

clas·si·fi·ca·to·ry \ˈklasəfəkə,tōrē, klaˈsif-, *esp Brit* ˈklasifi,kātəri\ *adj* [fr. *classify*, after such pairs as E *justify: justificatory*] **1 :** relating to or involving classification **:** tending or designed to classify **:** TAXONOMIC **2** *ethnol* **a :** characterized by a small number of kinship terms grouping in one kinship name class not only lineal relatives but also collateral relatives and even individuals having only a remote genetic relationship or none — compare DESCRIPTIVE **b :** included in a name class in a system of this kind

classified *adj* [fr. past part. of *classify*] **1 a :** consisting of classes **b :** divided into classes or placed in a class **2 :** forbidden to be disclosed outside a specified ring of secrecy for reasons of national security; *specif* **:** having a particular security classification

classified advertisement *n* **:** a single advertisement in a classified advertising section (as of a newspaper) — usu. called *classified ad*

classified advertising *n* **:** advertisements grouped by subject usu. appearing under categorical headings in a section of a publication given over to such advertisements and consisting chiefly of descriptive listings in text type

classified catalog *n* **:** a catalog having entries arranged according to subject or class — compare DICTIONARY CATALOG

classified station *n* **:** a postal station occupying government quarters and operated by government employees — compare CONTRACT STATION

clas·si·fi·er \ˈklasə,fī(ə)r, -laas-, -īə\ *n* -s [*classify* + ²*-er*] **1 :** one that classifies or sorts; *specif* **:** a machine or device for separating the constituents of a material (as ore, coal, sand) according to relative sizes and densities thus facilitating concentration and treatment **2 :** a word or morpheme used with nouns designating countable or measurable objects or with numerals and often indicating a class to which the object designated by the noun is assignable on the basis of shape or function (as Japanese *hon* in *empitsu ni hon* "two pencils", literally, "pencil two cylindrical-object", or Chinese *pen*³ in *san*¹ *pen*³ *shu*¹ "three books", literally, "three origin book") **3 :** RADICAL 2c, ²DETERMINATIVE 2

clas·si·fy \-,fī\ *vt* -ED/-ING/-ES [¹*class*, + *-ify*] **1 :** to group or segregate in classes that have systematic relations usu. founded on common properties or characters **:** SORT **2 :** to put into a class, classification, or category **:** RATE; *specif* **:** to assign (as a document) to one of the graded categories of matter restricted for national security

class interval *n, statistics* **:** an interval setting bounds to a class of a frequency distribution

clas·sis \ˈklasə̇s\ *n, pl* **clas·ses** \-a,sēz\ [NL, fr. L, class — more at CLASS] **1 :** an ecclesiastical governing body of a district in certain churches of presbyterian polity (as Dutch and German Reformed churches in Europe and America) consisting of the ministers and representative elders of the district **2 :** the ecclesiastical district governed by a classis and corresponding to a presbytery

class·less \ˈklasləs, ˈklaa-,ˈklai-,ˈklȧ-\ *adj* **1** *of a society* **:** free from distinctions of social class **2** *of a person* **:** belonging to no particular social class

class lottery *n* **:** DUTCH LOTTERY

class mark *n, statistics* **:** a value represented by the mid-value of a class interval

classmate \ˈ≈,≈\ *n* [¹*class* + *mate*] **:** one belonging to the same class (with another) at school or college

class meaning *n, linguistics* **:** the meaning common to all forms belonging to the same form class ⟨the words *cars, departures,* and *ideas* as members of the form class of plurals have the *class meaning* "more than one"⟩

class number *or* **class letter** *n* **:** a number or letter (from a classification scheme) assigned to a book or other library material to show its location on the library shelf

class publication *n* **:** a publication other than a trade journal designed for a group of readers with a common interest

class rate *n* **:** the transportation charge applicable to ratings of articles listed in class tariffs of common carriers and distinguished from commodity rates

classroom \ˈ≈,≈\ *n, often attrib* **:** a place for conducting formal instruction of students by a teacher in a school or college

class struggle *or* **class war** *or* **class warfare** *n* **:** opposition of and contention between social or economic classes; *esp* **:** such a struggle between or felt to exist between the proletariat and the capitalist classes

class suit *or* **class action** *n, law* **:** a suit or action by one or more persons for their own benefit and considered to be ultimately for the benefit of all persons who are for the purposes of the suit considered to be in the same class or group (as the taxpayers of a city)

class tariff *n* **:** a printed schedule of charges and related rules applicable to classes of articles transported by common carrier

classwork \ˈ≈,≈\ *n* **:** the part of a student's work that is done in class **:** the combined work of a class and teacher ⟨the book would be suitable for ~⟩ ⟨student responsibility is even more important in homeroom activities than it is in ~⟩ — often used in contrast with *homework* or *nonacademic student activity*

classy \ˈklasē, -aas-, -ais-, -ȧs-, -si\ *adj* -ER/-EST [¹*class* + *-y*] **1** *slang* **:** of superior type **:** notably excellent **:** HIGH-CLASS ⟨~ fielding⟩ ⟨a ~ suburb⟩ **2** *slang* **:** ostentatiously elegant **:** SLICK, STYLISH ⟨a ~ dresser⟩

¹-clast \,klast, -aa(ə)st,-aist\ *n comb form* -s [ML *-clastes*, fr. MGk *-klastēs*, fr. Gk *klan* to break — more at GLADIATOR] **1 :** one that breaks or destroys ⟨icono*clast*⟩ ⟨biblio*clast*⟩ **2** [G *-klast*, fr. ML *-clastes*] **:** something that breaks or destroys; *esp* **:** a tool for breaking ⟨cranio*clast*⟩

²-clast \"\ *n comb form* -s [back-formation fr. ²*-clastic*] **:** rock composed of fragmental material (of a specified type) ⟨pyro*clast*⟩ ⟨cata*clast*⟩

clas·tic \ˈklastik, -aas-,-ais-\ *adj* [ISV *clast-* (fr. Gk *klastos* broken, fr. *klan* to break) + *-ic;* orig. formed as G *klastisch* — more at GLADIATOR] **1 :** capable of being taken apart — used of anatomical models made of detachable pieces **2 :** of, belonging to, or being a rock (as a conglomerate or a sandstone) made up of fragments of preexisting rocks

¹-clastic \ˌ≈≈\ *adj comb form* [¹*-clast* + *-ic*] **1 a :** breaking, destroying ⟨icono*clastic*⟩ ⟨mytho*clastic*⟩ **b :** disintegrating ⟨proteo*clastic*⟩ **2** [Gk *klastos* broken (fr. *klan* to break) + E *-ic*] **:** curved ⟨anti*clastic*⟩

²-clastic \ˌ≈≈\ *n comb form* -s **:** breaker **:** destroyer ⟨dendro*clastic*⟩ ⟨pan*clastic*⟩

³-clastic \ˌ≈≈\ *adj comb form* [ISV *-clast* (fr. Gk *klastos* broken) + *-ic;* orig. formed as G *-klastisch*] **:** composed of fragmental material (of a specified type) — used in names of rocks ⟨crypto*clastic*⟩ ⟨pyro*clastic*⟩

¹clat \ˈklat\ *n* -s [perh. var. of ¹*clot*] *dial Brit* **:** a clot or clod (as of dirt or dung); *also* **:** a dirty condition **:** MESS

²clat \"\ *vt* **clatted; clatted; clatting; clats** *dial Brit* **:** DIRTY, BEDAUB

³clat \"\ *n* -s [short for ²*clatter*] *dial chiefly Eng* **:** CHATTER, GOSSIP

⁴clat \"\ *vi* **clatted; clatted; clatting; clats** *dial Eng* **:** CHATTER, GOSSIP, PRATE

clatch \ˈklach\ *n* -ES [prob. alter. of ¹*clat*] **1 :** a clod (as of mud) **:** DAUB, MESS **2** *Scot* **:** a sluttish or slipshod woman

clatchy \-chē,-chi\ *adj, Scot* **:** MUDDY

clath·ra·ce·ae \klaˈthrāsē,ē\ *n pl, cap* [NL, fr. *Clathrus*, type genus (fr. L *Clathri* lattice) + *-aceae*] **:** a family of fleshy fungi (order Phallales) typified by the genus *Clathrus* and distinguished from the true stinkhorns (family Phallaceae) by having the spore-bearing region enclosed or between the arms of the latticed receptacle — **clathraceous** \(ˈ)≈ˈ≈shəs\ *adj*

clath·rar·ia \klaˈthra(a)rēə\ *n, cap* [NL, fr. L *clathri* lattice + NL *-aria*] **:** a genus of fossil cycadlike plants known only from their tree trunks with clathrate markings — **clath·rar·i·an** \(ˈ)≈ˈrēən\ *adj*

clath·rate \ˈkla,thrāt, -,thrət\ *adj* [L *clathratus*, past part. of *clathrare* to furnish with lattice, fr. *clathri* lattice, fr. Gk *klēthra*, pl. of *klēthron, kleithron* bar, fr. *kleiein* to shut — more at CLOSE] **1** *biol* **:** shaped like a lattice **:** CANCELLATE **2 :** relating to a type of solid molecular compound in which one component (as argon or heptane) is trapped in cavities of cagelike crystals of another component (as hydroquinone or urea)

clath·ri·na \klaˈthrīnə, -ēnə\ *n, cap* [NL, fr. L *clathri* lattice + NL *-ina*] **:** a genus (the type of the family Clathrinidae) of primitive ascon sponges

clath·ro·cys·tis \,klathrōˈsistə̇s\ [NL, fr. *clathro-* (fr. L *clathri* lattice) + *-cystis*] *syn of* POLYCYSTIS

clath·roid \ˈkla,thrȯid\ *adj* [L *clathri* lattice + E *-oid*] **:** CLATHRATE

clath·rose \-,thrōs\ *adj* [L *clathri* lattice + E *-ose* — more at CLATHRATE] **:** marked with latticelike furrows

clath·ru·late \-,thrə,lāt\ *adj* [NL *clathruli* (dim. of L *clathri* lattice) + E *-ate*] **:** minutely clathrate

clats·ka·nie \ˈklatskə,nī\ *n, pl* **clatskanie** *or* **clatskanies** *usu cap* **1 :** an Athapaskan people of the Chehalis and Clatskanie river valleys, Oregon **2 :** a member of the Clatskanie people

clat·sop \ˈklatsəp\ *n, pl* **clatsop** *or* **clatsops** *usu cap* [modif. of Upper Chinook *tlaak'eelak*, lit., dried salmon] **1 a :** an Indian people of northwestern Oregon **b :** a member of such people **2 :** a dialect of Lower Chinook

¹clat·ter \ˈklad·ə(r), -atə-\ *vb* -ED/-ING/-S [ME *clatren*, fr. (assumed) OE *clatrian;* akin to OE *clatrung* clattering, MD *clateren* to rattle, Norw *klatra* to beat; of imit. origin] *vi* **1 :** to make a loud rattling sound by striking hard bodies together **:** RATTLE **2 :** to move or go rapidly and noisily ⟨~*ing* over the cobblestones⟩ **3 a :** CHATTER, PRATTLE **b** *Scot* **:** TATTLE, GOSSIP ~ *vt* **:** to cause to clatter **:** make a rattling noise with ⟨~*ing* the dishes on the tray⟩

²clatter \"\ *n* -s [ME, noisy talk, fr. *clatren*, v.] **1 :** a loud rattling noise esp. when made by the collision of hard bodies **:** a series of sharp clashes ⟨the ~ of pots and pans⟩ ⟨~ of a typewriter⟩ **2 :** COMMOTION, DISTURBANCE ⟨the midday ~ of the business district⟩ **3 a :** rapid, noisy, or idle talk **:** BABBLE, CHATTER, GABBLE **b** *Scot* **:** a piece of gossip **:** TATTLE, RUMOR

clat·ter·ing·ly *adv* [fr. pres. part of ¹*clatter* + *-ly*] **:** with clattering

clat·tery \-ərē,-əri\ *adj* [²*clatter* + *-y*] **:** marked by clatter **:** CLATTERING, NOISY

clat·ty \ˈklad·ē\ *adj* [¹*clat* + *-y*] *dial* **:** DIRTY, SLOVENLY, CLUTTERED

clau·ber \ˈklōbər\ *Scot var of* CLABBER

claude lor·raine glass \ˌklōdlə̇ˈrān-, -ōd-, -lȯˈr-\ *or* **claude glass** \ˈ≈-\ *n, usu cap C&L* [*Claude Lorraine* (earlier E spelling of *Lorrain*) pseudonym of Claude Gellée †1682 Fr. landscape painter; fr. the similarity of the effects it gives to those of a picture by him] **:** a convex hand mirror of dark or colored glass that reflects an image of diminished size and subdued color

claude process \ˈklōd-, -ōd-\ *n, usu cap C* [after Georges *Claude b*1870 French chemist and physicist] **:** a synthetic ammonia process characterized by higher operating pressures than other processes and by the use of a train of converters

clau·de·tite \ˈklōdə,tīt\ *n* -s [F *claudétite*, fr. F. *Claudet*, 19th cent. Fr. chemist, its discoverer + F *-ite*] **:** a mineral consisting of a native arsenic trioxide As_2O_3 crystallizing in the monoclinic system — compare ARSENOLITE

clau·di·an \ˈklōdēən\ *adj, usu cap* [L *Claudius*, a Roman gens name + E *-an*] **:** of or relating to any of several celebrated Romans of the name of Claudius or the gentes, one patrician and the other plebeian, to which they belonged; *esp* **:** of, belonging to, or characteristic of the emperors who belonged to the patrician gens (Tiberius, Caligula, Claudius, and Nero) or their time

clau·di·ca·tion \,klōdəˈkāshən\ *n* -s [L *claudication-, claudicatio* (fr. *claudicatus*, past part. of *claudicare* to limp, fr. *claudus* lame) + *-ion-*, *-io* -ion; akin to L *claudere* to close — more at CLOSE] **1** *med* **:** LAMENESS, LIMPING **2 :** INTERMITTENT CLAUDICATION

¹claught *or* **claucht** *past of* CLEEK

²claught *or* **claucht** \ˈklȯkt\ *n* -s [¹*claught, claucht*] *Scot* **:** CLUTCH, GRASP, HANDFUL

claus·al \ˈklȯzəl\ *adj* [¹*clause* + *-al*] **:** relating to or of the nature of a clause or clauses

clause \ˈklȯz\ *n* -s [ME, fr. OF, clause, fr. ML *clausa* close (of a rhetorical period), fr. L, fem. of *clausus*, past part. of *claudere* to close, shut — more at CLOSE] **1 :** a short sentence **:** a distinct section of a discourse or writing; *specif* **:** a distinct article, stipulation, or proviso in a formal document ⟨the attestation ~ to a will⟩ **2 a :** a group of words containing a finite verb but not constituting a whole sentence either because it functions as a noun (as in "I don't know *how he got there*"), adjective (as in "the account *that he gave was true*"), or adverb (as in "he stopped *when he saw the signal*") in the larger sentence to which it is subordinate or because it contains or is modified by one or more clauses subordinate to it (as in "*I don't know* how he got there") or because it is joined to another clause of equal rank with itself (as the two clauses in "*he stopped the car* and *they got out*") **b :** a group of words containing a nonfinite verb and functioning in its sentence somewhat like a subordinate clause (as in "he saw *the man leave*" and in "*his tire fixed*, the man drove off") — compare PHRASE

clau·se·witz \ˈklauzə,vits\ *n* -ES *usu cap* [after Karl von *Clausewitz* †1831 Prussian army officer and expert on military science] **:** an expert on military strategy

clau·sil·ia \klȯˈzilēə, -ˈsi-\ *n, cap* [NL, irreg. fr. L *clausus* closed] **:** the type genus of Clausiliidae comprising a large number of Old World land snails

clau·si·li·i·dae \,klȯzəˈlīə,dē, -ōsə-\ *n pl, cap* [NL, fr. *Clausilia*, type genus + *-idae*] **:** a family of terrestrial pulmonate snails having a fusiform sinistral spiral shell in which a rodlike clausilium functions as an operculum

clau·sil·i·um \klȯˈzilēəm, -si-\ *n, pl* **clausil·ia** \-lēə\ [NL, irreg. fr. L *clausus* closed + NL *-ium*] **:** the rodlike closure of the aperture of a mollusk of the family Clausiliidae

clau·si·us-clapeyron equation \ˌklōzēəs-ˈklapā,rōn-, -,rän-\ *n, usu cap both Cs* [after Rudolf J. E. *Clausius* †1888 German mathematical physicist and B. P. E. *Clapeyron* †1864 French engineer] **:** the Clapeyron equation as modified for liquid-vapor phases by assuming that the vapor is an ideal gas and that the volume of the liquid phase is negligible in comparison with the volume of the vapor

clausius cycle \ˈ≈≈≈-\ *n, usu cap 1st C* [after Rudolf J. E. *Clausius* †1888 Ger. physicist] **:** RANKINE CYCLE

claus process \ˈklaus,-\ *n, usu cap C* [after C. F. *Claus fl*1885 Eng. chemist who helped develop it] **:** a process for converting hydrogen sulfide to elemental sulfur by oxidation with air

claus·thal·ite \ˈklaustə,līt\ *n* -s [F *clausthalie* clausthalite (fr. *Clausthal*, Germany, its locality + F *-ie*) + E *-ite*] **:** a mineral consisting of lead selenide PbSe and resembling galena in appearance (sp. gr. 7.6–8.8)

claustra *pl of* CLAUSTRUM

claus·tral \ˈklȯstrəl\ *adj* [ME, fr. ML *claustralis*, fr. LL, of a fortress, fr. L *claustrum* bar, bolt, barricade — more at CLOISTER] **:** of or belonging to a cloister **:** like or savoring of the cloister **:** CLOISTRAL

claustral prior *n* **:** the coadjutor of an abbot ranking next to him in a monastery

claus·tra·tion \klȯˈstrāshən\ *n* -s [prob. fr. F, fr. ML *claustrum* monastery + F *-ation* — more at CLOISTER] **:** the act of confining in or as if in a cloister

claus·tro·phobe \ˈklȯstrə,fōb *sometimes* ˈklaus-\ *n* -s [back-formation fr. *claustrophobia*] **:** one having claustrophobia

claus·tro·pho·bia \ˌ≈≈ˈfōbēə\ *n* -s [NL, fr. *claustro-* (fr. L *claustrum* bar, bolt) + *-phobia*] **:** abnormal dread of being in closed or narrow spaces — contrasted with *agoraphobia*

claus·tro·pho·bic \ˌ≈≈ˈfōbik, -ēk *also* -ȧb-\ *or* **claus·tro·pho·bi·ac** \-ˈfōbē,ak\ *adj* **1 :** suffering from or inclined to claustrophobia **2 :** inducing or suggesting claustrophobia ⟨the ~ confines of the urban detective novel —*Times Lit. Supp.*⟩

claus·trum \ˈklȯstrəm, ˈklaus-\ *n, pl* **claus·tra** \-rə\ [NL, fr. L, bar] **:** a thin lamina of gray matter in each cerebral hemisphere between the lenticular nucleus and the island of Reil

clau·su·la \ˈklȯzhələ\ *n, pl* **clausu·lae** \-,lē\ [ML, fr. L, end, close of a rhetorical period, fr. *clausus*, past part. of *claudere* to close — more at CLOSE] **1 :** a rhythmic close or terminal cadence esp. in ancient and medieval Latin prose rhythm — see CURSUS **2** *in medieval music* **:** an ornamented cadence or close **3 :** a composition in descant style developed from a melismatic phrase of plainsong — **clau·su·lar** \-lə(r)\ *adj*

clausure *n* -s [ME, fr. L *clausura* — more at CLOSURE] *obs* **:** CLOSURE

¹claut \ˈklȯt, -ōt\ *vb* -ED/-ING/-S [origin unknown] *chiefly Scot* **:** SCRATCH, TEAR; *also* **:** SCRAPE, RAKE

²claut \"\ *n* -s **1** *Scot* **:** GRASP, CLUTCH **2** *Scot* **:** HANDFUL, LUMP, CHUNK **3** *Scot* **:** RAKE

cla·va \ˈklāvə, -ävə\ *n, pl* **cla·vae** \-ā,vē,-ä,vī\ [NL, fr. L, club — more at CLAVI-] **:** a clublike structure: as **a :** the club-shaped end of certain insect antennae **b :** the fruiting body of certain fungi **c :** a slight bulbous enlargement that forms part of the wall of the 4th ventricle of the brain and is the seat of a nucleus contributing axons to the lemniscus

clav·a·cin \ˈklavəsə̇n, ˈklä-\ *n* -s [*clava-* (fr. NL *clavatus*, specific epithet of *Aspergillus clavatus*, a species of fungus) + *-cin* (as in *actinomycin, streptothricin*)] **:** a colorless crystalline very toxic antibiotic $C_7H_6O_4$ produced by several molds (as *Aspergillus clavatus* and *Penicillium patulum*) — called also *clavatin, claviformin, patulin*

cla·val \ˈklāvəl, ˈklä-\ *adj* [NL *clava* + E *-al*] *anat* **:** of or relating to the clava

cla·var·ia \klə'va(a)rēə\ *n, cap* [NL, fr. L *clava* club + NL *-aria*] **:** a genus (the type of the family Clavariaceae) of fleshy mostly saprophytic and edible fungi having the hymenium over the surface of simple or branched club-shaped or corallike sporophores

cla·var·i·a·ce·ae \≈,≈≈ˈāsē,ē\ *n pl, cap* [NL, fr. *Clavaria*, type genus + *-aceae*] **:** a family of fleshy fungi (order Polyporales) having the characters of the genus *Clavaria* — **cla·var·i·a·ceous** \ˌ≈≈≈ˈāshəs\ *adj*

cla·vate \ˈklā,vāt\ *also* **cla·vat·ed** \-vād·ə̇d\ *adj* [NL *clavatus*, fr. L *clava* club + *-atus* -ate, -ated; akin to L *claudere* to close — more at CLOSE] *biol* **:** gradually thickening near the distal end **:** shaped like a club — see ANTENNA illustration — **cla·vate·ly** *adv*

clav·a·tin \ˈklavətə̇n, ˈklā-\ *n* -s [*clavat-* (fr. NL *clavatus*, specific epithet of *Aspergillus clavatus*, a species of fungus) + *-in*] **:** CLAVACIN

cla·va·tion \klāˈvāshən\ *n* -s **:** the condition of being clavate

¹clave [ME, var. of *clove*, past of *cleven* to cleave (split) and of *clevede*, past of *clevien* to cleave (stick)] *past of* ¹CLEAVE, *archaic past of* ²CLEAVE

²cla·ve \ˈklä(,)vā\ *n* -s [AmerSp, fr. Sp, keystone, clef, fr. L *clavis* key — more at CLAVICLE] **:** one of a pair of small cylindrical wooden sticks used as percussion instruments by being struck together while held in cupped hands (as in accompaniment to the rumba) — usu. used in pl.

clav·e·cin \ˈklavəsə̇n\ *n* -s [F, short for MF *clavycimbale*, fr. ML *clavicymbalum* — more at CLAVICYMBAL] **:** HARPSICHORD

clav·e·cin·ist \-nə̇st\ *n* -s **:** a performer on the clavecin

clav·el \ˈklavəl\ *n* -s [MF *clavel* keystone of an arch, fr. L *clavis* key — more at CLAVICLE] *now dial Eng* **:** the lintel over a fireplace **:** MANTEL

clav·e·li·za·tion \,klavələˈzāshən\ *n* -s [F *clavelisation*, fr. *claveliser* to clavelize (inoculate with sheep virus) (fr. *clavelée* sheep pox, fr. MF, fr. *clavel*, fr. LL *clavellus* nail-shaped pustule, dim. of L *clavus* nail) + *-ation* — more at CLAVUS] **:** inoculation with virus from sheep pox **:** OVINATION

clav·el·lat·ed \'klavə,lād·əd\ *adj* [ML *clavellatus* (fr. *clavellus* nail — fr. LL, small sore resembling the head of a nail, dim. of L *clavus* nail — + L *-atus* -ate) + E *-ed* — prob. fr. the nail-studded appearance of the surface of clavellated ashes — more at CLAVUS] *old chem* **:** made of the dried and burned lees or dregs of wine or vegetable matter ⟨~ ashes⟩

¹cla·ver \'klāvə(r), -av-\ *vb* -ED/-ING/-S [ME *claveren;* akin to D *klaveren* to clamber, Dan *klavre*, OE *clifian* to cling — more at CLEAVE] *dial Eng* **:** CLAMBER

²clav·er \'klavə(r), -āv-\ *n* -S [ME — more at CLOVER] *dial Brit* **:** CLOVER

³cla·ver \'klāvər\ *vi* -ED/-ING/-S [prob. of Celtic origin; akin to ScGael & IrGael *clabaire* babbler, IrGael *claibéir* chatter, W *clebar, clebran* to chatter, prate] *chiefly Scot* **:** PRATE, GOSSIP

⁴claver \"\ *n* -S *chiefly Scot* **:** idle talk **:** CHATTER, GOSSIP — usu. used in pl.

cla·ver grass \'klāvə(r)-\ *n* [by alter.] **:** CLEAVERS

claves *pl of* CLAVE *or of* CLAVIS

clavi *pl of* CLAVUS

¹clavi- *or* **clavo-** *comb form* [ML *clavi-*, fr. L, fr. *clavis* key — more at CLAVICLE] **1 :** key **:** keyboard ⟨*clavi*chord⟩ ⟨*clavi*lux⟩ **2** [NL *clavi-, clavo-*, fr. L *clavi-*] **:** clavicle **:** clavicular **:** clavicular and ⟨*clavi*pectoral⟩ ⟨*clavo*deltoid⟩

²clavi- *comb form* [NL, fr. L, fr. *clava;* perh. akin to L *clavis*] **:** club ⟨*Clavi*cornia⟩ ⟨*clavi*form⟩

cla·vi·al *var of* CLAVIOL

clav·i·a·ture \'klavēə,chu̇(ə)r, -āv-\ *n* -S [G *klaviatur*, fr. L *clavis* key — more at CLAVICLE] **1 :** the keyboard of a piano or organ **2 :** a system of fingering a keyboard instrument

clavi·cembalo \,klavə +\ *n, pl* **clavicembali** [It, fr. ML *clavicymbalum* — more at CLAVICYMBAL] **:** HARPSICHORD

clav·i·ceps \'klavə,seps\ *n, cap* [NL, fr. ²*clavi-* + L *-ceps* headed (fr. L *caput* head) — more at HEAD] **:** a genus of ascomycetous fungi (family Hypocreaceae) parasitic upon the ovaries of various grasses and forming characteristic sclerotia from which arise the ascus-bearing stromatal heads

clav·i·chord \'klavə,kȯrd, -ō(ə)d\ *n* -S [ML *clavichordium*, fr. *clavi-* ¹clavi- + *-chordium* -chord] **:** an early keyboard instrument smaller and much weaker in tone than the piano, having strings pressed by tangents attached directly to the key ends, the pitch produced by any one string being determined by the point at which it was divided by the tangent — compare MONOCHORD

clav·i·chord·ist \-dəst\ *n* -S **:** a performer on the clavichord

clav·i·cle \'klavəkəl, -vēk-\ *n* -S [F *clavicule*, fr. NL *clavicula*, fr. L, dim. of *clavis* key; akin to L *claudere* to close — more at CLOSE] **:** a bone of the vertebrate shoulder girdle typically serving to link the scapula and sternum: **a :** a bone in man situated just above the first rib on either side of the neck and having the form of a narrow elongated S — called also *collarbone* **b :** a corresponding but rudimentary bone in some of the ungulates and carnivores **c :** one of the two bones fused into the wishbone of a bird **d :** a large crescent-shaped bone under the pectoral fin of many teleost fishes

clav·i·cor \'klavə,kȯ(ə)r\ *n* -S [F, fr. *clavi-* + *cor* horn, trumpet, fr. L *cornu* horn — more at HORN] **:** BASS HORN 2

clav·i·corn \-ȯrn\ *adj* [ISV ²*clavi-* + *-corn*] **:** having club-shaped antennae

clav·i·cor·nia \,==ˈkȯrnēə\ *n pl, cap* [NL, fr. ²*clavi-* + *-cornia* (neut. pl. of L *-cornis* -corn)] *in some classifications* **:** a superfamily or other group of beetles having the antennae usu. club-shaped or capitate

cla·vic·u·la \klə'vikyələ, kla-\ *n, pl* **clavicu·lae** \-,lē, -,lī\ [NL, fr. L, small key — more at CLAVICLE] **:** CLAVICLE

cla·vic·u·lar \-lə(r)\ *adj* [prob. fr. F *claviculaire*, fr. *clavicule* clavicle + *-aire* -ar — more at CLAVICLE] **:** of or relating to the clavicle

cla·vic·u·lar·i·um \klə,vikyə'la(a)rēəm, kla-\ *n, pl* **clavicu·lar·ia** \-rēə\ [NL, fr. *clavicula* clavicle + *-arium*] **:** the epiplastron of turtles regarded as representing the clavicle

cla·vic·u·late \=ˈ==,lət, -,lāt\ *adj* [NL *clavicula* clavicle + E *-ate* — more at CLAVICLE] *anat* **:** having clavicles

claviculo- *comb form* [NL *clavicula* clavicle] **:** clavicular and ⟨*claviculo*humeral⟩

clavi·cylinder \'klavə +\ *n* -S [G *klavizylinder*, fr. *klavi-* ¹clavi- + *zylinder* cylinder, fr. L *cylindrus* — more at CYLINDER] **:** a keyboard instrument producing its tones by the friction of metal rods against a set of glass cylinders

clavi·cymbal \"+\ *n* -S [ME *clavysymbal*, fr. MF *clavycimbale*, fr. ML *clavicymbalum*, fr. *clavi-* ¹clavi- + L *cymbalum* cymbal] **:** an early Italian harpsichord

clavi·cy·the·ri·um \,klavə,sī'thirēəm\ *n, pl* **clavicythe·ria** \-rēə\ [NL, fr. *clavi-* ¹clavi- + *-cytherium, -citerium* (fr. L *cithara*) — more at ZITHER] **:** an early upright spinet

cla·vier \klə'vi(ə)r, kla-, -iə; 'klavēə(r), -av-; *sometimes* klåvyā\ *n* -S [F, fr. OF, key bearer, fr. L *clavis* key + OF *-ier* -er] **1 :** the keyboard of a musical instrument ⟨the ~ of a carillon⟩ **2** [G *klavier*, fr. F *clavier*] **:** one of the family of stringed instruments having a keyboard **3 :** a dummy keyboard for practice

cla·vier·ist \-'virəst, -ˈvēərəst\ *n* -S **:** a performer on the clavier

cla·vier·is·tic \klə,vi'ristik; ;klavēə;r-, -av-\ *adj* [prob. fr. G *klavieristisch* suitable for a piano, fr. *klavier* piano + *-istisch* -istic] **:** suited to or suggesting a keyboard stringed instrument

clav·i·form \'klavə,fȯrm\ *adj* [L *clava* club + E *-iform*] **:** shaped like a club

clav·i·for·min \,klavə'fȯrmən\ *n* -S [NL *claviforme* (specific epithet of *Penicillium claviforme*, a species of fungus) + E *-in*] **:** CLAVACIN

clav·i·ger \'klavəjə(r)\ *n* -S [L, fr. *clavi-* ¹clavi- + *-ger* bearing, bearer — more at -GEROUS] **:** one that keeps the key or keys **:** CUSTODIAN, WARDEN

clav·i·lux \-və,ləks\ *n* -ES [¹*clavi-* + L *lux* light — more at LIGHT] **:** an instrument for throwing upon a screen varying patterns of light and color that permit combinations analogous to the successive phrases and themes of music — called also *color organ*

clav·i·ol *or* **clav·i·ole** \'klavē,ōl, -āv-\ *or* **cla·vi·al** \'klāvēəl\ *n* -S [blend of ¹*clavi-* and *viol, viole*] **:** a viollike instrument played from a keyboard by means of a rotary bow — compare SOSTINENTE PIANOFORTE

clavi·pectoral \,klavə +\ *adj* [ISV *clavi-* + *pectoral;* orig. formed in F] **:** relating to the clavicle and pectoral muscles

cla·vis \'klāvəs, -āv-\ *n, pl* **cla·ves** \-,vēz\ *or* **clavises** [L — more at CLAVICLE] **:** a key or glossary serving as an aid to interpretation

clavo- — see ¹CLAVI-

clav·o·la \'klavələ\ *n, pl* **clavo·lae** \-,lē, -,lī\ [NL, fr. L, dim. of *clava* club — more at CLAVI-] **:** CLAVA a

cla·vus \'klāvəs, -āv-\ *n, pl* **cla·vi** \-ā,vī, -ä,vē\ [L, lit., nail; akin to L *claudere* to shut — more at CLOSE] **1 :** ³CORN 1 **2 :** a vertical stripe or band of purple on a tunic worn broad by early Roman senators and narrow by the equites as a mark of rank **3** [NL, fr. L] *zool* **:** any of various rounded or fingerlike parts or processes: as **a :** the pointed anal area of the hemelytron of a bug **b :** the club of an insect's antenna

clavy \'klavi\ *var of* CLAVEL

¹claw \'klȯ\ *n* -S *often attrib* [ME *clawe*, fr. OE *clawu*, alter. of *clēa*, gen. dat. acc. *clawe;* akin to OHG *klāwa, chlōa* claw, ON *klō*, OE *cliewen* sphere, ball, ball of yarn — more at CLEW] **1 :** a sharp nail on the toe of an animal esp. when such a nail is slender and curved (as that of a bird or cat); *also* **:** either lateral half of the hoof of a cloven-footed mammal — see COCK illustration **2 :** any of various similar sharp curved processes esp. if at the end of a limb (as those on the legs of insects); *sometimes* **:** the limb if it ends in such a process **3 :** one of the pincerlike organs terminating certain limbs of some arthropods (as the lobsters and scorpions) **4 :** something shaped like or grasping in a way felt to suggest an animal's claw: as **a :** the curved and forked end of a hammer or nail puller **b :** the slender projecting part of a jewelry setting that holds a stone **c :** the slender prolonged basal portion of certain petals (as in the pink) — compare BLADE 1c(2) **d :** a pronged grasp at the end of a derrick hoist **e :** a gardening tool for loosening soil **f :** a part of the intermittent mechanism of a motion-picture camera, printer, or projector that engages the perforations of and moves the film **5 :** a wound from or as if from a claw

²claw \"\ *vb* -ED/-ING/-S [ME *clawen*, fr. OE *clawan, clawian;* akin to MD *klouwen*, OHG *klāwēn;* denominative fr. the root of E ¹*claw*] *vt* **1 :** to pull, tear, scratch, scrape, seize, clutch, or dig with or as if with claws or nails **2** *chiefly Scot* **:** to scratch softly esp. in order to relieve itching or uneasiness **3 :** to force forward or upward as if with claws ⟨~*ed* his way to the top of the mountain⟩ or at the expense of others ⟨~ his way to the top of his profession⟩ **4 :** to attack spitefully, treacherously, or unexpectedly (as with a veiled insult) ⟨an actress ~*ing* her rival⟩ ~ *vi* **1 :** to scrape, scratch, dig, or pull with a claw or with the hand as a claw **2 :** to grope or clutch in desperation or panic ⟨~*ing* for the door handle⟩ **3** *of a boat* **:** to work to windward (as from a lee shore)

claw-and-ball foot *n* **:** a foot on a piece of furniture shaped like a bird's or animal's claw grasping a ball — see FOOT illustration

clawback \'=,=\ *n* -S [²*claw* (scratch softly) + *back*] *now dial* **:** FLATTERER, SYCOPHANT

claw bar *n* **:** a ripping bar or crowbar with a forked claw for drawing spikes (as from railroad ties)

claw chisel *n* **:** a stonecutter's toothed chisel

claw clutch *n* **:** a mechanical clutch in which jaws or claws interlock when pushed together — called also *positive clutch*

simple claw clutch

clawed *adj* [¹*claw* + *-ed*] **:** furnished with or having claws — used chiefly in compounds ⟨bare-*clawed*⟩ ⟨sharp-*clawed*⟩

clawed frog *or* **clawed toad** *n* **:** a frog (*Xenopus laevis*) of southern Africa that is much used in pregnancy tests — see XENOPUS

claw foot *n* **1 :** a foot that is or that resembles or is felt to resemble a claw; *specif* **:** a foot on a piece of furniture in the shape of a claw ⟨a *claw-foot* chair⟩ **2 :** a deformity of the foot characterized by an exaggerated curvature of the longitudinal arch — **claw-footed** \'=;==\ *adj*

claw hammer *n* **1 :** a hammer with one end of the head forked for use in extracting nails **2** *also* **claw-hammer coat :** TAILCOAT

claw hammer

claw hand *n* **:** a deformity of the hand characterized by extreme extension of the wrist and first phalanges and extreme flexion of the other phalanges

claw hatchet *n* **:** a hatchet with one end of the head forked for nail pulling — see HATCHET illustration

clawk \'klȯk\ *vt* -ED/-ING/-S [alter. (prob. influenced by *claw*) of ME *cloke, cluke*] *dial Eng* **:** CLAW, SCRATCH; *also* **:** SNATCH

claw·less \'klȯləs\ *adj* **:** having no claw **:** having the claws reduced or rudimentary

clawless otter *n* **1 :** a small southern Asiatic otter (*Amblyonyx cinerea*) with claws weakly developed **2 :** a large easily domesticated otter (*Aonyx capensis*) of western and southern Africa with the claws reduced or wanting

claw nut *n* **:** CLASP NUT

claw off *vi, of a boat* **:** to beat to windward to prevent going aground on a lee shore

claws *pl of* CLAW, *pres 3d sing of* CLAW

claw-tailed \'=;=\ *adj* **:** having a tail resembling a claw

claw toe *n* **:** HAMMERTOE

claw tool *n* **:** a fireman's implement for forcible entry or demolition consisting of a bar or pole with a hook at one end and a 2-pronged claw at the other

clax·on \'klaksən\ *n* -S [alter. of *Klaxon*] **:** a Klaxon horn

¹clay \'klā\ *n* -S [ME, fr. OE *clǣg;* akin to OS *klei* clay, MD *clei*, OHG *klīwa* bran, LL *glut-, glus* glue, MGk *glia*, Lith *glitùs* slippery and prob. to L *galla* gall on a plant — more at GALL] **1 a :** a widely distributed colloidal lusterless earthy substance, plastic when moist but permanently hard when fired, that is composed primarily of decomposed igneous and metamorphic rocks rich in the mineral feldspar in the form of crystalline grains less than .002 mm in diameter, whose essential constituents are kaolinite and other hydrous aluminous minerals and fine particles, and that is used widely in the manufacture of such articles as porcelain, building blocks, sewer pipe, tile, and earthenware or in its raw form in paper manufacture, filtration, and oil refining **b :** CLAY SOIL **c :** earth esp. when moist **2 a :** a claylike substance; *esp* **:** one used by a potter or sculptor **b :** the mortal human body as distinguished from an immortal spirit animating it **c :** the human character regarded as serving the purpose of a divine creator ⟨aspirants to be noble ~ plastic under the Almighty effort —R.W.Emerson⟩ **d :** NATURE 3, ABILITY, ENDOWMENT ⟨common ~⟩ ⟨the stupid feeling of employers that they are of a different ~ —O.W. Holmes †1935⟩ **3 a :** PIPE CLAY **b :** a clay tobacco pipe **4 :** CLAY PIGEON **5 :** a moderate to strong yellowish brown that is lighter than tobacco brown and slightly yellower and lighter than Aztec

²clay \"\ *vt* -ED/-ING/-S **:** to treat with clay: as **a :** to cover, daub, plaster, or dress with clay — often used with *up* ⟨~ up an auto body model⟩ **b :** to apply clay to (soil) **:** mix clay into **c :** to filter through clay

³clay \"\ *var of* CLEE

claybank \'=,=\ *n* **1 :** a brownish orange that is yellower and paler than leather or spice and yellower and lighter than gold pheasant **2 :** a horse of yellowish color produced by a mixture of sorrel and dun coloration

clayboard *n* **:** SCRATCHBOARD

claybrained \'=;=\ *adj* [¹*clay* + *brained*] **:** STUPID, DULL

clay burning *n* **:** the burning or roasting of clay esp. in Great Britain for use in improving the soil

clay-colored sparrow \'=,==-\ *n* **:** a small sparrow (*Spizella pallida*) of the dry interior of western No. America that resembles the chipping sparrow but has a buffy-brown rump

clay court *n* **:** a tennis court with a clay or dirt surface ⟨*clay-court* championship⟩ — compare GRASS COURT, HARD COURT

clay·den effect \'klādᵊn-\ *n, usu cap C* [after Arthur W. *Clayden* †1944 Eng. meteorologist] **:** partial desensitization of the emulsion layer of a photographic material by an initial high-intensity exposure of very short duration so that a later exposure of lower intensity and longer duration produces less effect than expected from the combined exposures, sometimes resulting in reversal of an image — compare DARK LIGHTNING

clay digger *n* **:** a spade held in the hands but power-driven (as by compressed air) and used to dig hard soil or soft rock

clay drab *n* **:** a moderate yellowish brown to light olive brown that is duller than Isabella and very slightly redder than medal bronze

clayen *adj* [ME, fr. *clay* + *-en*] *obs* **:** made of clay **:** EARTHENWARE

clay·ey \'klāē, -āi\ *adj* [ME *claiy*, fr. ¹*clay* + *-y*] **1 :** consisting of or characterized by the presence of clay **:** abounding in or being clay **:** like clay **2 :** covered, daubed, or soiled with clay **3 :** resembling that of clay ⟨a ~ color⟩

clay fever *n* [prob. so called fr. its being contracted under muddy conditions] *of a horse* **:** GREASE HEEL

clay·i·ness *also* **clay·ey·ness** \-ēnəs, -āin-\ *n* -ES [*clayey* + *-ness*] **:** clayey state or quality **:** STICKINESS

clay ironstone *n* **:** siderite ore occurring admixed with clayey rock material

clay·ish \-āish,-ēsh\ *adj* [¹*clay* + *-ish*] **:** like clay or containing particles of it ⟨~ soil⟩ **:** somewhat clayey (as in color)

clay loam *n* **:** a loam consisting of from 20 to 30 percent clay, from 20 to 50 percent silt, and from 20 to 50 percent sand

clay·man \'klāmən, -,man\ *n, pl* **claymen :** one that works with or digs clay; *specif* **:** one that mixes clay, water, and dispersing agents for use in papermaking

clay marl *n* **:** a whitish smooth chalky clay **:** a marl in which clay largely predominates

clay mill *n* **:** PUG MILL

clay mineral *n* **:** one of a group of hydrous silicates of aluminum and sometimes other metals (as magnesium and iron) formed chiefly in weathering processes, found in clays, soils, shales and other rocks, and characterized by small particle size and ability to adsorb substantial amounts of water, other molecules, and ions on the surface of the particles

clay·more \'klā,mō(ə)r, =ˈ=\ *n* -S [ScGael *claidheamh mōr*, lit., great sword] **1 :** a large 2-edged occas. 2-handed sword used formerly by the Scottish Highlanders **2 :** a basket-hilted often one-edged broadsword first used in the 16th century by the Scottish Highlanders

clay·o·quot \'klāə,kwät\ *n, pl* **clayoquot** *or* **clayoquots** *usu cap* **1 :** a subdivision of the Nootka people of western Vancouver Island, British Columbia **2 :** a member of the Clayoquot people

claypan \'=,=\ *n* -S [¹*clay* + *pan*] **1 :** hardpan consisting mainly of clay **2** *Austral* **:** a shallow silted depression in which water collects after rain

clay pigeon *n* **:** a saucer-shaped target composed of baked clay and pitch or similar substances and thrown from a trap in skeet and trapshooting

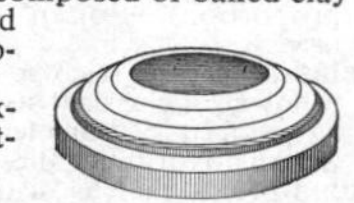

clay pigeon

clay press *n* **:** a filter press used for expressing excess water from slip in pottery making

clays *pl of* CLAY, *pres 3d sing of* CLAY

clay slip *n* **:** a slurry of clay and water used in casting ware as an engobe and with certain clays (as Albany slip) as a high-fire glaze

clay soil *n* **:** a soil that contains a high percentage of fine particles and colloidal substance and becomes sticky when wet

clay stone *n* **1 :** a calcareous concretion formed in a bed of clay **2 :** a dull earthy feldspathic rock containing clay

clay·ton fern \'klātᵊn-\ *n, usu cap C* [after John *Clayton* †1773 Am. botanist] **:** INTERRUPTED FERN

clayton gas *n, usu cap C* [after T. A. *Clayton*, Eng. chemist] **:** a gaseous mixture used esp. in fumigating ships for exterminating vermin

clay·to·nia \klā'tōnēə\ *n* [NL, fr. John *Clayton* + NL *-ia*] **1** *cap* **:** a genus of mainly No. American succulent herbs (family Portulacaceae) having cormlike or thickened roots and a single pair of leaves **2** -S **:** any plant of the genus *Claytonia*

clay·ver-grass \'klāvə(r),=\ *n* [alter. of *claver grass*] **:** CLEAVERS

clayware \'=,=\ *n* [¹*clay* + *ware*] **:** an article made of fired clay; *collectively* **:** such articles (as crockery or bricks)

clayweed \'=,=\ *n* [¹*clay* + *weed*] **:** COLTSFOOT a

cld *abbr* **1** called **2** canceled **3** cleared **4** cloud **5** colored **6** cooled

CLD *abbr* cost laid down

-cle \kəl\ *n suffix* -S [ME, fr. OF, fr. L *-culus, -cula, -culum*] **:** little one ⟨denti*cle*⟩ ⟨corpus*cle*⟩ ⟨funi*cle*⟩ — **-cu·lar** \kyələ(r)\ *adj suffix*

clea \'klē\ *var of* CLEE

clead \'klēd\ *vt* -ED/-ING/-S [ME *clethen, cleden*, fr. ON or OE; ON *klǣtha*, fr. OE *clǣthan*, fr. *clāth* garment, cloth — more at CLOTH] *dial Brit* **:** CLOTHE

clead·ing \'klēdiŋ\ *n* -S [ME *clething, cleding*, fr. the gerund of *clethen, cleden* to clothe] **1** *chiefly Scot* **:** CLOTHING, ATTIRE **2 :** a lining or covering of boards, planks, battens, or nonconducting material (as for lining a ship's cabin or a mine shaft or for insulating a boiler or engine cylinder) **:** LAGGING

cleam \'klēm, -ām\ *vb* -ED/-ING/-S [ME *clemen* — more at CLAM] **1** *dial Eng* **:** SMEAR, DAUB, SPREAD **2** *dial Eng* **:** ADHERE, STICK

¹clean \'klēn\ *adj* -ER/-EST [ME *clene*, fr. OE *clǣne* pure, clear; akin to OS *klēni* delicate, dainty, fine, OHG *kleini*, Gk *glainoi* ornaments, Arm *calr* laughter; basic meaning: bright, gay] **1 a :** free from matter that adulterates, contaminates, or pollutes ⟨add ~ mercury to the solution⟩ **b :** free from admixture with whatever diminishes the distinctive quality or essential character ⟨the ~ thrill of one's first flight⟩ ⟨the ~ satisfaction that comes from the stern performance of duty —F.D.Roosevelt⟩ **c** *of a precious stone* **:** having no interior flaws visible to the unaided eye **d** *of stock* **:** free of slow-moving goods or inventory **2 a :** free from or freed of dirt, filth, refuse, or remains ⟨wearing ~ linen⟩ ⟨requested a ~ plate⟩ **:** free from any putrefying or infecting agent ⟨fowl reared on ~ litter⟩ **b :** free from disease, often from a specified disease ⟨a pullorum-*clean* flock⟩ ⟨keep installations ~ of TB infection⟩ **c :** accustomed to keep free of dirt and foulness ⟨raccoons are ~*er* than other cage animals⟩ **d** *of a domestic animal* **:** that has never been bred **e** *of a ship* **:** having the bottom free from fouling accumulation **f** (1) **:** free from smudges or anything that tends to obscure ⟨a ~ set of fingerprints⟩ (2) *of copy* **:** easy to read with corrections clearly and neatly made (3) *of typesetting or a proof* **:** relatively free from error — opposed to *dirty* (4) *of a proof* **:** pulled from type in which errors detected on a previous proof have been corrected for sending to the author — compare FOUL **g** *of a deer or antlers, Brit* **:** having shed the velvet **h :** freeing or freed of weeds and other harmful growth and rubbish and of growth that hinders tillage ⟨the pros and cons of ~ culture between fruit trees⟩ ⟨~ farming is detrimental to wild life⟩ **3 a :** free from moral taint or corruption or sinister connections of any kind **:** GUILTLESS ⟨police confirmed he had had a ~ record for two years⟩ ⟨~ candidates are needed for ~ government⟩ **b :** free from looseness in sex relations **:** free from offensive treatment of sexual subjects and from the use of obscenity **c :** observing the rules **:** SPORTSMANLIKE, FAIR ⟨a ~ fighter⟩ ⟨~ rivalry⟩ **d** *slang* **:** free from involvement in a matter under police investigation **e** *slang* **:** carrying no concealed weapons **4 :** ceremonially or spiritually pure ⟨. . . and took of every ~ animal . . . and offered burnt offerings on the altar —Gen 8:20 (RSV)⟩ ⟨and all who are ~ may eat flesh —Lev 7:19 (RSV)⟩ **5 a :** so decisive, complete, or thoroughgoing as to leave no remainder, loose ends, or uncertainty ⟨a ~ sweep in the challenge round⟩ ⟨making a ~ break with his past⟩ **:** OUTRIGHT, UNRESERVED, INCONTESTABLE ⟨a ~ beat for his paper⟩ ⟨a ~ miss with a torpedo⟩ **b :** precisely, deftly, or unerringly directed or executed esp. without a trace of strain or awkwardness **:** FAULTLESS ⟨every hunter, if he is a real sportsman, wants quick, ~ kills —R.R.Camp⟩ ⟨~ sword work required of a matador⟩ ⟨some ~ ballet technique⟩ **:** showing no deficiency or deviation from a high standard of skill ⟨a steeplechaser must be a ~ jumper⟩ **c** *sports* **:** swiftly, skillfully, and decisively executed **:** free from error or misjudgment ⟨a ~ double play⟩ or played or scored with a decided margin of success or safety ⟨a ~ single over second base⟩ ⟨a ~ backhand shot⟩ **6 a :** free from obstruction or encumbrance ⟨and I envy the ~ straight sweep of your mind —H.J.Laski⟩ **b** *of cash* **:** in hand subject to no deduction or further liability **c** (1) *of a bond* **:** free from any endorsement or marks (2) *of a bill of lading or ship's receipt* **:** free from any statement about damage or poor condition of goods or containers (3) *of a draft or bill of exchange* **:** free from attached documents **7 a :** having simplicity, definiteness, articulateness, and usu. gracefulness of form ⟨architecture with ~ almost forbiddingly austere lines⟩; *specif* **:** constructed on fine sharp lines ⟨a ship with a ~ body slips through the water with little or no disturbance⟩ **b** *in the arts* **:** marked by straightforward presentation or concise composition **:** free from nonessential elements or affectation ⟨a ~, spare, expressive prose style⟩; *specif* **:** precise and flawless in execution or reproduction ⟨efforts to obtain a ~ bass in orchestral recordings⟩ **c :** free from unevenness or irregularity of outline or partition ⟨this saw leaves a ~ edge⟩ ⟨a sharp blow causing a ~ break⟩ **d** *archaic, of a party ticket* **:** STRAIGHT **e** *of a horse's leg* **:** free from curbs or bunches below the hock **f** *of an airplane* **:** well streamlined and free from external protuberances or projections that give rise to increased aerodynamic drag **g** *radio & television* **:** sharply defined and unwavering **:** free from distortion and interference ⟨a speaker providing ~ output⟩ **8 a :** empty esp. of what might be expected to be carried or stocked ⟨the whaling ship returned with a ~ hold⟩ **b** *slang* **:** cleaned out of one's money **:** without funds **9 a :** having a distinctive, unmixed, and fresh quality to the senses ⟨the ~ scent of pine⟩ ⟨a ~ yellow⟩ **b :** marked by no failure or deficiency ⟨a ~ record of victories⟩ **10** *of an atom bomb or hydrogen bomb* **:** having little or no fallout

²clean \"\ *adv, sometimes* -ER/-EST [ME *clene*, fr. OE *clǣne* clearly, purely, fr. *clǣne*, adj.] **1 a :** in such a manner as to keep or leave free of dirt or refuse ⟨a new broom sweeps ~⟩ **:** without distortion or error ⟨played the difficult piano accompaniment very ~⟩ **b :** in a manner free from cheating or unsportsmanlike conduct ⟨play the game ~⟩ ⟨he doesn't fight ~⟩ **c** *archaic* **:** PRECISELY, UNERRINGLY ⟨the arrow flew ~ to the center of the target⟩ **2 :** without qualification **:** THOROUGHLY, ENTIRELY, COMPLETELY ⟨an area burned over ~⟩

⟨gone ~ out of his head⟩ ⟨thrown ~ off balance⟩ ⟨my own view is ~ contrary —F.R.Leavis⟩ : all the way ⟨a bullet ~ through the chest⟩ ⟨~ back to colonial times⟩ : far or remotely ⟨living ~ out in the sticks⟩

³**clean** \"\ *vb* -ED/-ING/-S [ME *clenen*, fr. *clene* clean] *vt* **1 :** to make clean or free of dirt or any foreign or offensive matter: as **a :** to wash with water and soap or with any aqueous liquid medium **b :** to bathe, brush, or treat with an acid, alkaline, or organic agent, rub with an oil or cream, or sponge or swab with a disinfectant for removing undesired matter ⟨~ a wound⟩ **c :** to wipe or polish esp. with a solvent for removing grime ⟨~ the domestic silver⟩ **d :** to free of dirt, refuse, or litter and set in order — often used with *up* ⟨~ up the attic⟩ **e :** DRY-CLEAN **2 a :** to rid (land) of weeds and rubbish by cultivation — often used with *up* **b :** to scrape (a ship's bottom) free of accretions of barnacles and fouling matter **c :** to brush, scrape, or blow clean of dirt or other accumulation — often used with *out* ⟨~ one's shoes before entering⟩ ⟨specimens from an archaeological excavation need expert ~*ing*⟩ ⟨~ out a drain⟩ **d** (1) **:** to brush (the teeth) with a cleanser, esp. a dentifrice (2) **:** to perform dental prophylaxis on (the teeth) **e :** to blast with grit for removing undesired accumulations ⟨~ a brick wall of layers of paint⟩ **f :** to free (a surface) of what adheres, covers, or obstructs (as by brushing, wiping, or scraping) — often used with *off* ⟨~ off a slate⟩ ⟨~ flues⟩ ⟨earning pocket money by ~*ing* sidewalks⟩ ⟨hard to ~ a windshield of a coating of sleet⟩ **g :** to remove cancellation marks from (a stamp) so as to give an appearance of being unused **3 a :** to remove the outer shell, husk, hull, or hairy appendages from ⟨rough rice is ~*ed* before milling⟩ **b :** to free (as by screening) of dirt, chaff, stray weed seeds, and other foreign matter ⟨~ grain coming from the thresher⟩ **c :** to gin (cotton) **4 a :** to remove the entrails from **:** GUT, DRESS ⟨~ fish, fowl, or game⟩ **b :** to strip bare or to empty of contents ⟨the lumberjacks quickly ~*ed* the platter⟩ ⟨the tree was ~*ed* of fruit by hurricane winds⟩ ⟨a play that ~*ed* the board of the opponent's checkers⟩ **c** *slang* **:** to defeat decisively in a contest or competition — sometimes used with *up* ⟨we took on their best bridge players and ~*ed* them⟩ **d** *slang* **:** to deprive wholly of money or possessions in a gambling game, by robbery, or through skulduggery or stock-market speculation — often used with *out* ⟨they started ~*ing* him . . . bit by bit they were taking everything he had, his banks, his factories —Louis Bromfield⟩ ⟨a few disastrous plunges and he found himself ~*ed* out⟩ **e :** to exhaust or strip clean ⟨carp may ~ a pond of indigenous fish⟩ **:** PRUNE ⟨~ a roster of inactive members⟩ **f** *baseball* **:** to empty (the bases) by enabling all base runners to score ~ *vi* **:** to undergo or perform a process of cleaning **:** become clean — often used with *up* — **clean house :** to eradicate by stern vigorous thoroughgoing measures whatever is obstructive, thwarting, or degrading ⟨the industry is full of troublemakers and must *clean house*⟩ ⟨in departments where graft was rife the new mayor began to *clean house*⟩

⁴**clean** \"\ *n* -S **:** an act of cleaning dirt esp. from the surface of something ⟨give footwear a daily ~ with polish⟩

clean·a·bil·i·ty \ˌklēnəˈbiləd.ē\ *n* -ES **:** the property of being cleanable or accessible to cleaning

clean·a·ble \ˌklēnəbəl\ *adj* **:** capable of being cleaned

clean and jerk *n* **:** a lift in weight lifting in which the weight is momentarily raised from the floor, held at shoulder height, and then jerked overhead — compare PRESS, SNATCH

clean bill *n* **1 :** a legislative resolution introduced by a committee incorporating provisions of an original bill and embodying amendments adopted by the committee **2 :** CLEAN BILL OF HEALTH 2

clean bill of health 1 : a bill of health certifying absence of infectious disease **2 :** an unqualified finding or certification of the moral or political soundness of ⟨dismissing charges of racketeering, the committee gave the organization a *clean bill of health*⟩

clean bill of lading : a bill of lading free from statements about damage or poor condition of goods or containers

clean–boled \ˈ=ˌbōld\ *adj* **:** having a bole free or trimmed of branches

clean–bowled \ˈ=ˌ=\ *adj, cricket* **:** bowled by a ball that does not touch the bat or any part of the batsman's person

clean–built \ˈ=ˌ=\ *adj* **:** of trim shapely build

clean–cut \ˈ=ˌ=\ *adj* **1 :** having a clean and distinct outline as if evenly and precisely cut along the border **:** seen in high relief as if chiseled, sculptured, or shaped in a mold ⟨the skyline stands out *clean-cut* —G.R.Stewart⟩ ⟨he had *clean-cut* features and piercing eyes⟩ ⟨the *clean-cut* youthful figure leaning over her friend —Ellen Glasgow⟩ **2 a :** accomplished or attained through precision so as to give clear demarcation or distinctness of effect or result ⟨the habit of *clean-cut* articulation⟩ **b :** explicit and unmistakable in intent and distinct in detail ⟨the difficulties that have beset investigators in getting *clean-cut* answers —J.B.Conant⟩ **c :** narrowly limiting or limited in range **:** quite definite ⟨his responsibility in the matter is *clean-cut*⟩ **3 :** presented concisely and vividly by avoidance of vagueness, oversubtlety, or diverting embellishment and a minimum of shading and transition ⟨detectives have made a *clean-cut* case⟩ ⟨one of the *cleanest-cut* of all his stories⟩ **4 :** wholesome and uncontaminated **:** wholly up to standard in sterling qualities ⟨a *clean-cut* and well-bred young man⟩

clean cutting *n* **:** CLEAR-CUTTING

clean dollar *n, in the China trade* **:** a dollar that has not been chopped

cleaned *past of* CLEAN

¹**cleaner** *comparative of* CLEAN

²**clean·er** \ˈklēnə(r)\ *n* -S **1 :** one whose work is cleaning: as **a :** one employed to do cleaning esp. of the interiors of buildings or transportation vehicles **b :** a worker who cleans materials, equipment, or working areas either for the sake of neatness or as part of a manufacturing process **c :** a worker who cleans spots from such materials as fabrics or tinware by washing, scraping, or any means suitable to the material **d :** one whose business is the dry cleaning of garments, rugs, upholstery, or other articles not normally washed **e :** a worker who examines completed garments for defects, cuts off loose threads, cleans soiled spots, and folds or hangs the garments — called also *clipper, folder* **f :** a worker who cleans radio condenser terminals and moistureproofs them with chemicals **2 :** a preparation for cleaning, cleaning off, or cleaning out something; *specif* **:** a liquid preparation for household use in removing dirt and spots from clothing or furnishings **3 :** an implement or machine for cleaning: as **a :** a currier's 2-handled knife **b :** a contrivance for cleaning a steam boiler **c :** a molder's tool having a long flat blade with a turned-up end **d :** a machine for cleaning the air of dirt or other foreign matter **e :** VACUUM CLEANER **4 :** a flotation machine used in mining that re-treats concentrates and produces a clean finished product (as coal) — **to the cleaners** *adv, slang* **:** to or through an experience of being deprived of all one's money (as in a game of chance or a confidence game) ⟨some sharpies took him *to the cleaners*⟩

cleaner tooth *n* **:** a special tooth on a circular saw for cleaning out the kerf

cleaner–up \ˈ==ˈ=\ *n, pl* **cleaners–up :** one that cleans up refuse or cleans the surface of some product

cleanest *superlative of* CLEAN

clean fallow *n* **:** uncropped land kept free of weeds and other growth by frequent cultivation

clean–fingered \ˈ=ˈ==\ *adj* **1 :** SCRUPULOUS **2 :** DEFT

cleanhanded \ˈ=ˈ==\ *adj* **:** innocent of wrongdoing

clean hands *n* **1 :** freedom from guilt, esp. from dishonesty in money matters or elections **2 :** the condition of being free from wrongdoing, misconduct, or deceit as a prerequisite of application for relief in a court of equity

clean–hewn \ˈ=ˈ=\ *adj* **:** CLEAN-CUT 1

¹**cleaning** *pres part of* CLEAN

²**cleaning** *n* -S **1** *Brit* **:** CLEANSING 2 — usu. used in pl. **2 cleanings** *pl* **:** things collected by cleaning **3** *slang* **:** a decisive defeat ⟨gave the visiting team a ~⟩; *also* **:** a total loss of resources in a business venture or in speculation or gambling ⟨got a good ~ on the stock market⟩ **4 :** a thinning of a young stand (as of trees) **5 :** a large profit or gain **:** KILLING ⟨makes his little ~ and then leaves us all flat —George Abbott & J.C.Holm⟩

cleaning crop *n, Brit* **:** any crop (as turnips or potatoes) adapted to cultivation and suitable for cleaning weedy land

cleaning hinge *n* **:** a sliding hinge for a window sash that permits the sash to swing to such a position that the outside of the glass may be cleaned from within the room

cleaning mark *n* **:** an indelible identification mark applied to an article in a cleaning establishment

cleaning shoe *n* **:** a threshing-machine mechanism that consists of sieves and a fan and that separates the clean grain from the dirt and refuse

cleaning tissue *n* **:** CLEANSING TISSUE

cleaning woman *n* **:** a woman who hires herself out for housecleaning

clean–legged \ˈ=ˌleg(ə)d\ *adj* **1** *of poultry* **:** having legs free from feathers **2 :** having legs free from a feathery fringe or tuft of hair — used esp. of a horse or dog

clean·li·ly \ˈklenləlē, -əli\ *adv* **1 :** in a cleanly or neat manner **2 :** in a clean-cut manner **:** accurately and smoothly **:** so as to fit or blend neatly **3 :** CHASTELY, INNOCENTLY ⟨I, too, might have lived ~ —J.B.Cabell⟩

clean–limbed \ˈ=ˈlimd\ *adj* **:** with well-proportioned or shapely limbs or parts likened to limbs **:** TRIM ⟨*clean-limbed* youths⟩ ⟨the *clean-limbed* racers tacked and put about gracefully⟩

clean·li·ness \ˈklenlēnəs, -lin-\ *n* -ES [ME *clenlynesse*, fr. *clenly* cleanly + -*nesse* -ness] **:** the quality or state of being cleanly: **a :** freedom from superficial foulness or imperfections (as dust, grease, incrustation, mechanical burrs) **b :** the condition or habit of being clean; *specif* **:** diligence in keeping clean in person and dress ⟨~ is indeed next to godliness —John Wesley⟩ **c :** unalloyed or unblemished quality or purity ⟨Huxley's effort to introduce fresh air and intellectual ~ into the Augean stables of official science —M.R.Cohen⟩; *specif* **:** freedom from moral frailty or impurity of motive ⟨as he spoke of the ~ of Washington's soul —Van Wyck Brooks⟩

clean–living \ˈ=ˈ==\ *adj* **:** leading a life free from immorality

¹**cleanly** \ˈklenlē, -li\ *adj, often* -ER/-EST [ME *clenly*, fr. OE *clǣnlic* pure, fr. *clǣne* pure + -*lic* -ly — more at CLEAN] **1** *obs* **:** clean morally or ceremonially ⟨the *cleanlier* in his office for his new-washed surplice —John Milton⟩ **2 :** free from dirt or litter **3 a :** careful to keep clean ⟨~ in their persons and habitations —Meriwether Lewis⟩ ⟨the badger is a most ~ animal⟩ **b :** habitually kept clean **c :** chaste and refined in quality ⟨turn the jargon into ~ English⟩ **4** *obs* **:** cleverly devised or deftly executed ⟨~ knavery —Edmund Spenser⟩ **5** *archaic* **:** conducive to cleanness

²**cleanly** \ˈklēnlē, -li\ *adv* [ME *clenly*, fr. OE *clǣnlīce* purely, fr. *clǣne* pure + -*lice* -ly] **:** in a clean manner

clean–mouthed \ˈ=ˈ=\ *adj* **:** given to propriety of speech

clean·ness \ˈklēnnəs\ *n* -ES **:** the state or condition of being clean

clean out *vt* [³*clean* + *out*] **1 :** to strip or exhaust of all contents, supplies, or resources ⟨the redecorating job *cleaned out* the club treasury⟩ **2 a :** to eliminate, dismiss, or expel (as from a group or organization) ⟨intent on *cleaning out* inefficient personnel in the department⟩ ⟨*cleaned out* both open foes and lukewarm friends in the old cabinet⟩ **b :** to rout out or exterminate the occupants of ⟨*clean out* an enemy machine-gun nest⟩ **3 :** to exhaust the stock of ⟨tourists *cleaned out* the shops⟩ ⟨heavy rains *cleaned* us *out* of boots⟩

cleanout \ˈ=ˌ=\ *n* -S **1 :** the act of cleaning out ⟨a ~ of his predecessor's assistants⟩ **2 :** an opening that is usu. covered by a cap, plate, or door and is provided for cleaning out an enclosure (as a furnace dome, chimney, or plumbing trap)

clean–run \ˈ=ˈ=\ *adj* **1** *of a salmon* **:** having the bright color and healthy plumpness characteristic of a recent arrival in fresh water for spawning **2** *Brit* **:** redolent of health and fresh vitality

cleans *pres 3d sing of* CLEAN, *pl of* CLEAN

cleans·a·ble \ˈklenzəbəl\ *adj* **:** capable of being cleansed

cleanse \ˈklenz\ *vb* -ED/-ING/-S [ME *clensen*, fr. OE *clǣnsian* to purify, fr. *clǣne* pure] *vt* **1 a :** to release, deliver, or absolve from sin or guilt **:** rid of any moral blemish ⟨a group of sinners reveal their wickedness and are *cleansed* and redeemed —A.M. Sullivan⟩ ⟨seeking for that which shall ~ me —George Meredith⟩; *also* **:** FREE, ABSOLVE ⟨our hearts *cleansed* of all evil⟩ **b :** to rid one of (moral or spiritual taint) as if by washing — sometimes used with *away* ⟨mysterious means of purification by which they proposed to ~ away the defilements of the soul —W.R.Inge⟩ **c :** to free or purge of what is spurious, degrading, or vitiating ⟨a city *cleansed* of graft, gangsterism, and prostitution⟩; *also* **:** to eradicate as spurious, degrading, or vitiating — used with *from* ⟨all feeling of pity had been *cleansed* from him⟩ **d :** to free or rid of any undesirable feature or condition ⟨a smile *cleansing* his face of all severities —R.P.Warren⟩; *esp* **:** to purge (a political party or other organization) of disruptive or dissident elements ⟨found it necessary to ~ party ranks⟩ **2 a :** to wash, brush, or scrub with water or a detergent solution ⟨a floor covering that is easily *cleansed*⟩; *also* **:** to wipe clean (as with oil or cosmetic cream) **b :** to wipe free of surface accumulation (as with absorbent waste or tissues) **c :** to free of extraneous or undesired matter; *esp* **:** to rid (air) of foul or noxious gases **d** *archaic* **:** to cause to recover from disease or injury to health **:** HEAL ⟨raise the dead, ~ lepers —Mt 10:8(RSV)⟩ ⟨and immediately his leprosy was *cleansed* —Mt 8:3(RSV)⟩ **e** *Brit* **:** to sweep and clean (streets) of refuse and snow **:** SCAVENGE **f :** to wash or flush out or dislodge ⟨~ nematodes from the intestines of sheep⟩ ⟨~ dirt from a wound⟩ **3 :** to make ceremonially clean **:** free from pollution or purify in a religious sense ⟨*cleansed* through baptism⟩ ⟨*cleansed* from the effects of a ritual oath⟩ ~ *vi* **:** to undergo a cleansing process **:** become clean ⟨utensils that ~ easily⟩

cleans·er \ˈklenzə(r)\ *n* -S [*cleanse* + -*er*] **1 :** one whose work is cleansing something: **a** *Brit* **:** STREET CLEANER **b :** DRY CLEANER **2 a :** a preparation including a solvent or other cleaning agent for cleansing the skin, the teeth, or glass surfaces **b :** a powdered cleaning agent for scouring the dampened surface of kitchen utensils, sinks, or flooring material

clean–shaven \ˈ=ˈ==\ *adj* **:** having the hair shaved from cheeks, lips, chin, and throat

¹**cleans·ing** \ˈklenziŋ, -zēŋ\ *n* -S [ME *clensing*, fr. gerund of *clensen* to cleanse] **1 :** the action or an act of cleansing; *esp* **:** moral or spiritual purification **2 :** the afterbirth and sometimes also the fetal membranes of a domesticated mammal — usu. used in pl.

²**cleansing** \"\ *adj* [ME *clensing*, fr. pres. part. of *clensen* to cleanse] **:** serving to dispel (as shams or illusions) ⟨a mordant . . . wit which is at once ~ and devastating —H.G. Laski⟩ or to relieve (as emotional tension) ⟨how often during my life have I turned back and back to the ~ comfort of technique —Agnes de Mille⟩

cleansing tissue *n* **:** a square piece of soft absorbent tissue paper for use chiefly in wiping skin cream, cosmetics, and moisture from the face or hands

cleanskin \ˈ=ˌ=\ *n, Austral* **:** an unbranded animal — compare MAVERICK

clean–till \ˈ=ˈ=\ *vt* **:** to cultivate by stripping the soil clean of weeds and other harmful growth — compare CLEAN 2a

clean–timbered \ˈ=ˈ==\ *adj, obs* **:** CLEAN-LIMBED

clean up *vt* **1 :** to make in clear profit **:** NET ⟨by selling when prices rose he *cleaned up* a small fortune⟩ **2** *archaic* **:** to catch and collect (grains of valuable mineral) from an accumulation in a sluice or stamping mill **3 a :** to strip or empty of the whole of the contents or supply ⟨taught to *clean up* his plate⟩ **b :** to extinguish or eliminate remaining enemy resistance from ⟨marines sent to *clean up* the atoll⟩ **c :** to sweep clean (as of political corruption or organized vice) ⟨a reform administration pledged to *clean up* the city⟩ **:** root out as a social evil ⟨helped the district attorney *clean up* the rackets⟩ **:** rid of debasing or harmful features or elements ⟨demand for *cleaning up* the movies⟩ **4 a :** to free from a state of ruin or disorder **:** rid of accumulated debris ⟨a section *cleaned up* of bomb damage⟩ **b :** to make final disposal of **:** SETTLE ⟨*clean up* pending cases⟩ ⟨*clean up* past-due bills⟩ **c :** to free from defects of performance **:** eliminate any remaining faults from ⟨*clean up* the stage business in early rehearsals⟩ ~ *vi* **1 :** to wash up, change or arrange one's clothes, and tidy oneself ⟨*clean up* for dinner⟩ **2 :** to make a spectacular or sensational profit in a business enterprise or a killing in speculation or gambling **3** *slang* **:** to inflict a severe thrashing or decisive defeat — used with *on* ⟨a chance to *clean up* on his critics⟩ **4 :** to make a sweep of wins ⟨to *clean up* in a series of yacht races⟩

cleanup \ˈ=ˌ=\ *n* -S [*clean up*] **1 a :** a selling off of remaining stock **b :** the disposal of final details or making of final trials or a tidying up of litter (as when completing an undertaking) **c :** removal of residual gas from an incandescent lamp or vacuum tube due to the action of the getter, the absorption of gas by the anodes, or the driving of gas molecules into the electrodes **d :** the fourth position in the batting order of a baseball team **2 a :** a periodical cleaning up in a gold or silver mill or placer mine or dredge; *also* **:** the material thus collected **b :** an extraordinarily large return or profit on a shrewdly or opportunely timed sale; *specif* **:** KILLING **3 a :** a cleaning up or stamping out (as of vice, crime, or other undesirable conditions); *also* **:** a clearing out or purging (as of gangsters or other undesirable elements) **b :** a cleaning out or liquidation of remaining enemy resistance ⟨the ~ of enemy machine-gun nests⟩ **c** *slang* **:** a decisive defeat of a competitor

clean–up fund *n* **:** a personal fund usu. provided by life insurance to pay debts and final expenses incident to death

¹**clear** \ˈkli(ə)r, -iə\ *adj* -ER/-EST [ME *clere*, fr. OF *cler*, fr. L *clarus* clear, bright, loud, distinct, renowned; akin to L *calare* to call — more at LOW] **1 a** (1) **:** shining brightly **:** GLEAMING, LUSTROUS ⟨bonfires ~ and bright —Shak.⟩ (2) **:** entirely light **:** UNDIMMED, UNDARKENED, BRIGHT ⟨it is almost ~ dawn —Shak.⟩ **b** (1) **:** having the sky free from clouds ⟨watching the stars on ~ nights⟩ **:** having the air free from mist, haze, or dust ⟨on a ~ day one could see for miles⟩ (2) *meteorol* **:** relating to the sky when it is less than one-tenth covered with clouds (3) **:** unclouded or serene as if undisturbed by doubt, uncertainty, or guilt ⟨eyes so straight and ~ that everybody loved him —Stark Young⟩ **c :** giving free passage to light or to the sight **:** easily seen through **:** not cloudy, turbid, or opaque ⟨fish seen swimming through water ~ as air⟩ ⟨~ glass⟩ **d** (1) *of the skin or complexion* **:** good in texture and color and without blemish or discoloration (2) *of an animal coat* **:** of uniform shade throughout **:** UNSPOTTED — sometimes opposed to *ticked* **e :** having no color, smoke, or suspended matter to impede the passage of light **:** TRANSLUCENT ⟨~ varnish⟩ ⟨~ soup⟩ ⟨a candle burning with a ~ flame⟩ **f** *of color* **:** without admixture of other color **:** PURE ⟨~ reds and blues⟩ **2 a :** easily or distinctly heard **:** distinct and audible in detail ⟨her speech was ~ and easy to understand⟩ **:** having purity of tone **:** free from roughness or harshness ⟨you could hear ~ laughter like a waterfall —Edith Sitwell⟩ **b** *of an l sound* **:** formed with the tip of the tongue on the teethridge and the rest of the tongue in a position similar to that of a front vowel — compare DARK **3 a :** easily understood **:** without obscurity or ambiguity ⟨a ~ description of his point of view⟩ **:** thoroughly understood or comprehended ⟨the consequences of his act were not ~ at the time⟩ ⟨make it ~ that there will be no discussion⟩ **:** easy to perceive or determine with certainty ⟨it is ~ that you were wrong⟩ **:** sharply distinguished **:** readily recognized **:** UNMISTAKABLE ⟨a ~ instance of favoritism⟩ **b :** easily visible or distinguishable without blurring or becoming obscure **:** sharp and distinct in outline ⟨though the gloom had increased . . . the white surface of the road remained almost as ~ as ever —Thomas Hardy⟩ **:** readily seen **:** in plain sight ⟨~ identification of the product on the label⟩ **4 a :** having no doubt, uncertainty, or confusion of mind **:** straight-thinking ⟨a complex problem requiring a ~ brain⟩ **:** having a sure understanding or a confident certainty ⟨we are not ~ about what we are going to do⟩ **:** without misconception, error, or vagueness ⟨a ~*er* understanding of the issue⟩ **b :** undistorted or unweakened in perception or vision ⟨~ sight⟩ ⟨~ eyes⟩ **5 :** free from obstruction, burden, limitation, defect, or other restricting features: as **a :** free from guile, guilt, or stain **:** UNSULLIED, INNOCENT ⟨in action faithful, and in honor ~ —Alexander Pope⟩ ⟨a ~ conscience⟩ **b :** free from pecuniary liabilities, charges, or deductions ⟨a good income ~ for life⟩ ⟨a ~ profit of 6 percent⟩ **c :** free from qualification or limitation **:** UNQUESTIONED, ABSOLUTE ⟨a ~ victory over his opponent⟩ ⟨that wall is a ~ 20 feet high⟩ **d :** free from anything that impedes movement or action ⟨a road ~ for traffic⟩ ⟨a field ~ of trees⟩; *also* **:** indicating freedom from obstruction ⟨a ~ signal on a railroad⟩ **e :** freed or emptied of burden, contents, or cargo ⟨a ship is ~ after unloading⟩ **f** (1) *of tree boles or timbers* **:** free of knots, branches, or other projections (2) *of lumber* **:** free of defect or blemish **g :** free from contact **:** out of the way ⟨~ of the hose⟩; *esp* **:** free from contact or association with anything that encumbers, impedes, entangles, or obscures ⟨the moon was ~ of the trees⟩ ⟨~ of the storm area⟩ ⟨~ of trouble⟩ **h** *of a measurement of space or time* **:** without deduction or diminution **:** FULL ⟨a ~ 15 yards from side to side⟩ — compare CLEAR DAYS **i** (1) **:** having nothing within or upon **:** empty of content **:** free of occupancy ⟨walls ~ of ornament⟩ ⟨a mind ~ of all such notions⟩ (2) *of a fabric* **:** having a finished surface free of nap, fuzz, or loose fibers (3) *of an egg* **:** INFERTILE **j :** NORMAL; *specif* **:** free from abnormal sounds — used esp. in auscultation of the chest or lungs **k :** having won no hearts or other penalty card in tricks in the game of hearts

syn TRANSPARENT, TRANSLUCENT, LUCID, PELLUCID, DIAPHANOUS, LIMPID: CLEAR stresses absence of clouding or other obscuring of vision ⟨the launch moved slowly through water *clear* as air —C.B.Nordhoff & J.N.Hall⟩ TRANSPARENT stresses complete absence of obstruction to vision ⟨guavas, with the shadows of their crimson pulp flushing through a *transparent* skin —Herman Melville⟩ TRANSLUCENT applies to that which permits passage of light but bars clear and complete vision ⟨*translucent* amber that cages flies —Elinor Wylie⟩ ⟨poured out a goblet full of the *translucent* crimson liquid —Joseph Hergesheimer⟩ LUCID, a rather romantic and literary word, may suggest luminous transparency ⟨changed . . . their hue (like clouds of sunset) into *lucid* amber —William Wordsworth⟩ PELLUCID intensifies the idea of CLEAR ⟨a *pellucid* plain of waters, azure with the noontide day —P.B.Shelley⟩ DIAPHANOUS suggests a gossamer translucency, a virtual transparency ⟨in her flowery loveliness, she looked *diaphanous*, ethereal —Maurice Hewlett⟩ LIMPID usu. suggests soft clearness ⟨the eyes are of that soft, *limpid*, turquoise blue so often sung by the poets —Wilkie Collins⟩ ⟨in the light of the dawn, growing more *limpid* rather than brighter —Joseph Conrad⟩ Applied to intangibles in more figurative senses, CLEAR stresses freedom from obscurity or possibility of misunderstanding ⟨making our age one of bewildered groping where our ancestors walked in the *clear* daylight of unquestioning certainty —Bertrand Russell⟩ ⟨experience in India had made it abundantly *clear* that the government of a great empire required special training and disinterested selection —Felix Frankfurter⟩ TRANSPARENT implies either commendable utter clarity or obvious, easily perceived deception ⟨*transparent* and disprovable untruths . . . and histories far-fetched a million miles —Elinor Wylie⟩ LUCID, more common in this use, suggests especial clearness, sometimes of order and arrangement ⟨he thought little of recasting a chapter in order to obtain a more *lucid* arrangement —G.O.Trevelyan⟩ PELLUCID and LIMPID stress simple complete clarity ⟨[Goldsmith's] *pellucid* simplicity —Frederic Harrison⟩ ⟨utter simplicity, *limpid* clearness . . . these are the salient qualities of the diction of the men who wrote the Bible —J.L.Lowes⟩

syn LUCID, PERSPICUOUS: CLEAR and LUCID have been dealt with in the preceding synonymy. PERSPICUOUS may stress the clearness and understandability of the general style of a passage ⟨the ode is not wholly *perspicuous*. Wordsworth himself seems to have thought it difficult —Lionel Trilling⟩ **syn** see in addition EVIDENT

²**clear** \"\ *adv* -ER/-EST [ME *clere*, fr. *clere*, adj.] **1 :** in a clear manner: as **a :** without confusion or obscurity **:** DISTINCTLY ⟨now ~ I understand —John Milton⟩ **b :** with clear voice or sound ⟨to cry loud and ~⟩ **c :** all the way **:** for the entire distance, extent, or time ⟨beyond the fence was open country ~ to the skyline —Hartley Howard⟩ **:** WHOLLY, ENTIRELY ⟨I was sore ~ through at myself —W.A.White⟩

³**clear** \"\ *vb* -ED/-ING/-S [ME *cleren*, fr. *clere*, adj.] *vt* **1 a** (1) **:** to make clear, transparent, or translucent **:** free from darkening elements, turbidness, muddiness, clouds, or cloudiness ⟨~ the river water by filtering⟩ (2) **:** to free (sugar

crystals) from mother liquor by spraying with water or steam (3) **:** to free or almost free (the emulsion of a photographic film or plate) from silver halide during fixing so that unexposed parts are transparent (4) **:** to render (a specimen for microscopic examination) transparent by the use of an agent (as an essential oil) that modifies the refractive index **b** (1) *obs* **:** to remove guilt or the stain of sin from **:** make pure **:** wash away (as a sin) **:** ABSOLVE (2) **:** to free from imputation of guilt or from accusation or blame **:** JUSTIFY, VINDICATE ⟨to take the stand, tell the truth, and ~ his name —S.H.Adams⟩ ⟨his accusers never gave him an opportunity to ~ himself⟩ — often used with *of* or *from* before the thing imputed ⟨he is ~*ed* of suspicion of duplicity⟩ (3) **:** to certify (as by investigation of one's personal history and background) as loyal to the national interest and safely to be trusted with secret information or employed in responsible work ⟨~ a man for top-secret military work⟩ **c** (1) **:** to make clear mentally **:** give clear understanding to **:** ENLIGHTEN ⟨~ my mind about the new arrangement⟩ (2) **:** to make intelligible **:** free from obscurity or ambiguity **:** EXPLAIN ⟨many knotty points there are which all discuss but few can ~ —Matthew Prior⟩ **d :** to make (the eyes or sight) clear or keen (as by strengthening or cleaning) **e** *obs* **:** to prove the truth of **:** DEMONSTRATE **2 a :** to remove from (as a space) all that occupies or encumbers or that impedes or restricts use, passage, or action ⟨~*ed* his calendar in order to give full time to the problem⟩ ⟨~ a room upstairs for the guest⟩ ⟨~ two downtown blocks for the new civic center⟩ ⟨~ the way for the landing forces⟩ ⟨~ an acre of woodland with a bulldozer⟩ **b :** to free, rid, or empty (as an area or object) of accumulated, intruding, or encumbering things ⟨~ your mind of foolish fancies⟩ ⟨~ land of trees and brush⟩ ⟨~ a ship of her cargo⟩ ⟨~ an equation of fractions⟩ **c :** to remove (something that occupies, intrudes, obstructs, or encumbers) from an area or place ⟨spend a week ~*ing* timber⟩ ⟨~ snow from the walk⟩ ⟨~ the plates and serve dessert⟩ — often used with *away, off, out* **d :** to establish one's remaining cards in (a specified suit) by forcing the opponents to play all their cards or all their remaining cards in that suit ⟨he ~*ed* the spade suit in two leads⟩ ⟨the ace ~*ed* the trump suit⟩ **e :** to clear for action **f :** to de-energize (an electric circuit) manually or by means of an automatic circuit-interrupting device **g** (1) **:** to make (the voice) free from harshness or huskiness (2) **:** to rid (the throat) of phlegm or of something that makes the voice indistinct or husky (3) **:** to make a rasping noise in (the throat) as if clearing phlegm — used often as a nonlinguistic sound esp. to call attention to something said or done **h :** to exhaust the available market supply of (a commodity) by purchase or sale ⟨buyers ~*ed* the day's cattle run at steady rates⟩ **:** dispose of the supply on hand of (a commodity) often by special sale ⟨unsold stock was ~*ed* at a loss⟩ **i :** to move (as a hockey puck or soccer ball) out of the defensive zone **j :** to classify and distribute, transmit, or dispatch (as messages, mail, or freight) to the intended destination ⟨that post office ~*s* 300 pieces of mail an hour⟩ ⟨~*ed* messages for the state police over his shortwave set —Mary H. Vorse⟩ **k :** to remove accumulated totals, stored information, or previously made settings from (a business or calculating machine) **:** replace stored information by zero in (a computing machine) **3 :** to make clear or free from obligation, esp. from pecuniary liability: as **a :** SETTLE, PAY, DISCHARGE ⟨~ an account⟩ ⟨money sent to ~ our debts⟩ **:** make free from debt or pecuniary encumbrance ⟨money paid to ~ his estate⟩ **b** (1) **:** to free (a ship or shipment) for passage by payment of customs duties or harbor fees **:** pass through (customs) by conforming to regulations ⟨the baggage ~*ed* customs⟩ (2) **:** to leave (a port) after conforming to customs and port regulations ⟨the ship ~*ed* New York harbor⟩ **c :** to gain without deduction **:** earn as a net profit ⟨~ a good profit on the sale⟩ ⟨~ $1500 a year on the investment⟩ **d :** to pass (as a check) through a clearinghouse; *sometimes* **:** to get the cash for (a check) — compare CLEARING 3 **4 a :** to free (as from contact or entanglement) **:** DISENTANGLE ⟨~ a hawser⟩ ⟨~ a fishing line⟩ **b :** to leap over ⟨the horse ~*ed* the fence in a bound⟩ or pass by or over ⟨~*ing* the ridge, we saw below us a great valley⟩ **:** go over or by without touching, colliding, or getting entangled ⟨the planes barely ~*ed* the tops of the trees⟩ **c :** to pass free of, out of, or away from ⟨the tax bill ~*ed* the legislature a week ago⟩ **5 a :** to submit (something proposed or intended) to an authority for review and approval before placing in effect ⟨important appointments are first ~*ed* with the committee⟩; *also* **:** to review and approve (as a proposal) **:** give approval to **:** AUTHORIZE ⟨the chairman ~*ed* the article for publication⟩ **b :** to obtain official permission to use (as a song) in broadcasting **c :** to authorize (an aircraft) to proceed under specified traffic conditions ⟨~*ed* the plane for landing⟩ ~ *vi* **1 :** to become clear, bright, or transparent: as **a :** to become free of clouds, mist, fog, or rain **:** become fair — often used with *up* or *off* ⟨it ~*ed* up quickly after the rain⟩ **b :** to become transparent, translucent, or free of sediment or turbidity ⟨the muddy water ~*s*⟩ **c :** to become free of care, doubt, uncertainty, disorder, or of anything that puzzles or troubles the mind or obscures or confuses the situation ⟨his face ~*ed* as he heard my explanation⟩ ⟨with the improvement in sales the business prospect ~*s*⟩ **2 a** *obs* **:** to adjust differences **:** pay claims **:** make a settlement — used with *with* **b :** to conform to the customs and other port regulations by payment of duties and fees so as to obtain permission to leave port ⟨the ship ~*ed* yesterday and is ready to leave⟩; *also* **:** to leave port with clearance papers ⟨ships ~*ed* from Boston with cargoes for the west⟩ **c :** to pass for clearing or collection through a clearinghouse or through another bank (as of a check) — see CLEARING 3a **3 a :** to go away **:** DISAPPEAR, VANISH ⟨these symptoms should ~ gradually⟩ ⟨the crowds ~*ed* rapidly, leaving the streets deserted⟩ — often used with *away, up, off* **b** *of a commodity* **:** to become sold out ⟨hogs ~*ed* at steady rates⟩ **c :** to remove the dishes, food, and other remains of a meal (as from a table or a room) ⟨you are to ~ after every meal⟩ **d :** to move a puck or ball away from the goal area ⟨the goalie ~*ed* to an open teammate⟩ **4 a :** to go to an authority (as for scrutiny, review, or approval) before becoming effective ⟨all tax bills must ~ through our committee⟩ **b :** to pass through or undergo handling by a single authority or office usu. with the purpose of achieving efficiency or consistency of handling ⟨outgoing letters ~ through this office where they are checked against our files⟩ **syn** see RID — **clear for action :** to clear a ship's decks and fighting spaces of unnecessary encumbrances and fire hazards and make ready in all respects for battle — **clear hawse :** to untwist anchor cables when a ship that is riding to two anchors has fouled her cables by shifting with the tide — **clear one's skirts :** to clear oneself of accusation of guilt or one's character of a stigma — **clear the air** *also* **clear the atmosphere :** to remove elements of hostility, tension, confusion, or uncertainty from the mood or temper of the time **:** remove the confusions or ambiguities from a conception or a problem ⟨the government announcement *cleared the air* of speculation and suspicion⟩ — **clear the decks 1 :** to clear for action **2 :** to remove all impediments to or make everything ready for a particular course of action or series of developments ⟨*clearing the decks* so that we can now set about attacking the real problems —*Times Lit. Supp.*⟩ — **clear the land** *of a ship* **:** to gain such a distance from shore as to have sea room — **clear the way :** to make preparations **:** get everything out of the way in order to be ready for new developments or a new course of action ⟨*clear the way* for the entertainment of the visitor⟩

[4]**clear** \"\ *n* -S [[1]*clear*] **1** [trans. of It *chiaro*] **clears** *pl* **:** the parts of a painting shown in a state of illumination as opposed to those in shadow **2 clears** *pl* **:** a less refined flour consisting of the bolted portion of the meal recovered in the manufacture of patent flour and graded in several grades according to the quality resulting from further milling **3 :** a board or piece of lumber free from defects **4 :** an infertile hatching egg **5 :** a bird or animal having clear plumage or coat **6 :** a deep shot over the opponent's head in badminton **7 :** plain or unencrypted language ⟨a message sent in ~⟩ **:** PLAINTEXT ⟨~ alphabet⟩ — **in the clear** *adv (or adj)* **1 :** in inside measurement ⟨corridors three feet *in the clear*⟩ **2 :** free of resistance, obstruction, obligation, or anything that restricts or impedes action ⟨the airplane had just passed through a squall and was *in the clear*⟩ **3 :** free of guilt or not subject to suspicion or imputation of guilt ⟨as for the charge of cowardice, he was now *in the clear*⟩ **4 :** in plaintext **:** not in code or cipher ⟨a message sent *in the clear*⟩

clear·age \ˈklirij\ *n* -S **:** the act of clearing **:** CLEARANCE

clear·ance \ˈklirən(t)s\ *n* -S **1 :** the act of making clear of whatever may obstruct, occupy, encumber, or hinder: as **a :** the removal of buildings from an area (as a city slum) in order to permit new construction **b** (1) **:** the act or an instance of clearing a ship at the customhouse (2) *or* **clearance papers :** the papers showing that a ship has cleared **c :** the offsetting of checks and other claims among banks through a clearinghouse, the Federal Reserve banks, or other agencies **d :** approval or certification as clear of objection, prohibition, suspicion, or guilt ⟨security ~ of those with access to secret atomic information —J.G.Palfrey⟩ ⟨given ~ by the FBI⟩ **:** permission to proceed without objection, check, or reservation ⟨you have to have the general's personal ~ —J.G.Cozzens⟩ **e :** the sale usu. at reduced prices of stock (as excess inventory) which it is desired to move from the store ⟨a January ~ of men's suits⟩ **f :** authorization for an airplane to proceed under specified traffic conditions **2 :** the distance by which one object clears another or the clear space between them ⟨a car with a road ~ of 7⅛ inches⟩ ⟨a bridge with a 100 foot ~ above water⟩: as **a** (1) **:** the distance between the piston and the cylinder head at the end of a stroke in an engine (2) **:** the total volume (as of steam) remaining in the cylinder and ports at the end of the exhaust or compression stroke; *also* **:** the line or area on an indicator diagram noting this distance or volume **b :** the space between adjacent structural members or their component parts to allow for inaccuracies in cutting and to permit them to be placed in a structure **c :** the distance by which the top of a gear tooth clears the bottom of the space between two teeth on the mating gear **d :** the margin of space between the structures along a railroad track (as poles, buildings, or tunnel walls) and the periphery of the largest locomotive or car that will pass over that track **e** *or* **clearance angle :** the angle between the face of a cutting tool and the work **f :** the interval stipulated in the lease of a motion picture that must elapse after the film's exhibition in a first-run theater before it can be leased to other theaters within a specified surrounding area **g :** a quantitative measure of renal efficiency in the transfer of any solute from the blood to the urine, being determined as the volume of blood that would be freed of a specified constituent by removal of a quantity equal to the measured renal excretion of that constituent during one minute — called also *renal clearance* **3 :** a space or area that has been cleared of that which formerly occupied it (as trees or brush) ⟨a ~ in the forest⟩ ⟨~*s*, the Highland equivalent of enclosures, in which the . . . peasants were treated . . . as mere squatters —Russell Kirk⟩ **4 :** a permission-to-work order to a line crew after a power line has been de-energized for the crew's safety **5 :** a part of a foundry mold or core beveled off to prevent contact of friable surfaces when closing the mold **syn** see ROOM

clearance fit *n* **:** a fit (as of mechanical parts) in which there is clearance

clearance lamp *n* **:** one of the usu. colored lamps on the left and right of the front and rear of a truck that indicate the extreme sides of the vehicle

clearance loan *n* **:** DAY LOAN

clear and present danger *n* **:** such danger as satisfies a court that the invasion of freedom of speech and press by legislation is justified by the gravity and degree of probability of a substantial evil (as overthrow of the government) that the legislature in the exercise of its lawful powers is seeking to prevent

clear away *vt* **1 :** to remove or dispose of (something that obstructs, impedes, or inconveniences) ⟨the recent adjudication *cleared away* all obstacles to the bond issue⟩ **2 :** to free from entanglement or obstruction so as to make ready for use ⟨*clear away* an anchor ready to let go⟩ ~ *vi* **:** to remove from a table or a room the dishes, food, and other remains of a meal

clear belly *n* **:** a square bacon slab without pigmentation (as from the mammary gland)

clear board *n* **:** a signal to an approaching railroad train that the block ahead is clear

[1]**clear·cole** \ˈklir,kōl\ *n* -S [part trans. of F *claire colle*, fr. *claire* clear + *colle* glue, fr. (assumed) VL *colla*, fr. Gk *kolla* — more at PROTOCOL] **:** a priming of size mixed with whiting or white lead used esp. in house painting; *also* **:** a size upon which gold leaf is applied in gilding

[2]**clearcole** \"\ *vt* -ED/-ING/-S **:** to coat or paint with clearcole

[1]**clear-cut** \ˈ=ˈ=\ *adj* **1 :** having a sharp clear outline with regular distinct lines **:** not obscure, hazy, softened, or shadowed ⟨a *clear-cut* pattern⟩ ⟨a cold and *clear-cut* face . . . perfectly beautiful —Alfred Tennyson⟩ **2 a :** showing distinct lucid analysis, plan, or presentation **:** having unmistakable clarity and definiteness **:** not vague, ambiguous, or confused ⟨the Hoosier novels, simple in plot, *clear-cut* in characterization, concise and lucid in language —Carl Van Doren⟩ **b :** marked by certainty, definiteness, unmistakableness **:** beyond reservation or doubt ⟨a *clear-cut* victory⟩ ⟨the decision of the court was *clear-cut* and final⟩ ⟨the announcement may be *clear-cut* or again it may be somewhat equivocal⟩ **syn** see INCISIVE

[2]**clear-cut** \"\ *vt* **:** to remove all timber from (an area) **:** cut all the trees in (a stand of timber)

clear-cutting \ˈ=ˈ==\ *n* **:** removal of all timber from an area; *also* **:** the area so treated

clear days *n pl* **:** days reckoned from one day to another with exclusion of both the first and the last day ⟨from Sunday to Sunday there are six *clear days*⟩

cleared *past of* CLEAR

clearedness *n* -ES **:** the quality or state of being cleared

[1]**clear·er** \ˈklirə(r)\ *comparative of* CLEAR

[2]**clearer** \"\ *n* -S **1 :** a person or worker who clears: as **a :** a worker who clears goods of faults or working places of debris and objects not in use **b :** one who bleaches extract-tanned hides by brushing with weak acid solution **c :** PROPERTY MAN **2 :** an instrument, device, apparatus, or agent that clears esp. as part of a manufacturing process: as **a :** CLEARING AGENT **b :** a reservoir into which the brine is conveyed in the manufacture of salt **c** (1) **:** one of the small rapidly revolving rollers in a carding machine the teeth of which catch the material from the worker rollers (2) **:** a contrivance (as a roller or flat board covered with flannel or as an endless flannel band) in a drawing, roving, or spinning frame to collect the fly from the rollers (3) **:** a device in a ring spinner consisting of an upward projecting piece of metal that catches the fly on the traveler and removes it

clearest *superlative of* CLEAR

clear-eyed \ˈ=ˈ=\ *adj* **1 :** having clear eyes **:** seeing clearly **2 :** perceiving, thinking, or analyzing clearly **:** not subject to self-deception or misinterpretation of facts or evidence

clear-fell \ˈ=ˈ=\ *vt* **:** CLEAR-CUT

clear fork \ˈ=,=\ *adj, usu cap C&F* [fr. *Clear Fork* river, Texas, near which the artifacts were discovered] **:** ABILENE

clear-hawse pendant \ˈ=,=-\ *n* **:** a heavy chain having a pelican hook and tailed with a hemp hawser or wire rope used in mooring and clearing hawse

clearheaded \ˈ=ˈ==\ *adj* **:** having a clear understanding **:** quick of perception **:** not confused in mind **:** not subject to misinterpretation of fact — **clear·head·ed·ly** \ˈ=ˈ===\ *adv*

clear ice *n* **:** a transparent ice coating or glaze

clear in *vi* **:** to obtain permission to discharge cargo by conforming to customs or port regulations

clearing *n* -S [ME *clering*, fr. gerund of *cleren* to clear] **1 :** the act or process of making or becoming clear **2 :** a tract of land cleared of wood and brush (as for cultivation) **3 a :** a method adopted by banks and bankers for making an exchange of checks and bills held by each against the others in which checks deposited in the banks of a particular area are set off against each other with cash settlement only of the balances due after the clearing **b :** a similar method adopted by railroads and by buyers and sellers of merchandise for adjusting their accounts with each other; *also* **:** the machinery or procedure established under this method **c clearings** *pl* **:** the gross amount of balances so adjusted **4 a :** NATURAL PRUNING **b :** the cutting of all mature trees at one time **5 :** the collection, classification, and distribution of information or other matter requiring wide distribution ⟨an agency for the ~ of reconstruction projects and plans⟩ ⟨a ~ center for management ideas⟩

clearing agent *n* **:** any substance used to clear a specimen or preparation for microscopic examination

clearing agreement *n* **:** an agreement between nations as to the method of settlement of commercial accounts that is usu. designed to avoid transfer of foreign exchange; *specif* **:** an agreement between two countries designed to force a balance of trade between them with exports being offset by imports and the use of cash remittances minimized

clearing bath *n* **:** a solution for bathing photographic negatives or prints to remove stains, unwanted or foreign deposits, or oxidizing substances

clearinghouse \ˈ==,=\ *n* **1 :** an institution or establishment for carrying on the business of clearing **2 :** an agency for collection, classification, and distribution esp. of information or other matter or items requiring wide distribution ⟨functioning as a ~, the committee farms out for special study the questions that must be settled —*Newsweek*⟩ ⟨a ~ for information on management problems⟩

clearinghouse agent *n* **:** a clearinghouse member bank that clears checks for nonmember banks

clearinghouse stock *n* **:** a security in which transactions may be settled through the stock exchange's clearing department

clearing nut *n* **:** the seed of an East Indian tree (*Strychnos potatorum*) that is used in the Orient for clearing muddy water

clearing shower *n* **:** the final and usu. heaviest shower of a storm; *specif* **:** a line-squall shower of a cyclone

clearing station *n* **:** a medical installation in a combat area where casualties are received from collecting stations, given additional treatment, classified, and if necessary evacuated

clear lake gnat \ˈ=,=ˈ=\ *n, usu cap C&L* [fr. *Clear Lake*, Calif.] **:** a minute nonbiting fly (*Chaoborus asticopus*) that is a major pest about Clear Lake, Calif., where it swarms in great numbers — compare CHAOBORIDAE

clear lead *n* **:** FAIRLEAD

clear length *n* **:** the part of a tree trunk that is clear of branches or of branches of a specified size

clear·ly \ˈkli(ə)rlē, -iəlē, -li\ *adv* **1 :** in a clear manner ⟨that which is ~ and distinctly conceived as the truth —C.W.Hendel⟩ **2** *of something asserted or observed* **:** without doubt or question ⟨~ we are in a transitional stage —Vera M.Dean⟩ ⟨its dominance was ~ waning —Louise Pound⟩

clear·ness \ˈkli(ə)rnəs, -iən-\ *n* -ES **1 :** the quality or state of being clear **:** freedom from confusion or obstruction **:** DISTINCTNESS **2 :** precise unambiguous transmission of meaning in writing or speaking **:** LUCIDITY, CLARITY

clear obscure *n* [trans. of F or It; F *clair-obscur*, fr. It *chiaroscuro* — more at CHIAROSCURO] **:** CHIAROSCURO

clear off *vt* **:** to get rid of or dispose of (troublesome, burdensome, or encumbering things); *specif* **:** to pay off (a debt or other financial obligation) ~ *vi* **:** to go or run away **:** leave esp. in a hurry ⟨*clear off* as fast as you can⟩

clear out *vi* **1 :** to go through the procedure of clearing from a port **2 :** to go or run away often suddenly or secretly **:** DECAMP, DESERT **:** get or move out ~ *vt* **:** to drive out or away usu. forcibly ⟨*cleared* the Persians *out* of Europe⟩

clear plate *n* **:** the layer of fat on top of the butt of a pork shoulder

clears *pres 3d sing of* CLEAR, *pl of* CLEAR

clearsach *var of* CLARSACH

clear-sighted \ˈ=ˈ==\ *adj* **:** having clear vision, discernment, or judgment — **clear-sight·ed·ly** \ˈ=ˈ===\ *adv* — **clear-sight·ed·ness** \ˈ=ˈ===\ *n* -ES

clearskin \ˈ=,=\ *n* [[1]*clear* + *skin*] *Austral* **:** CLEANSKIN

clear·starch \ˈ=ˈ=\ *vi* **:** to stiffen fabrics with clear translucent starch ~ *vt* **:** to starch (clothes) with a clear starch

clearstory *var of* CLERESTORY

clear tare *n* **:** a tare established by weighing all of the packages of a shipment

clear up *vt* **1 :** to explain or make clear ⟨*cleared up* the doubtful points in his story⟩ **:** SOLVE ⟨*clearing up* the mystery⟩ **2 :** to remove, dispose of, or set right (a source of trouble or dissatisfaction) ⟨arbitrators *cleared up* the controversy⟩ **:** bring or restore to a normal, ordered, or acceptable condition ⟨*clear up* the disturbed condition of the market⟩ ⟨*clear* the rubbish *up*⟩

clear-up \ˈ=,=\ *n* -S [*clear up*] **:** a clearing up or settlement (as of accounts)

clearweed \ˈ=,=\ *n* [so called fr. the translucence of the leaves and stems] **:** RICHWEED 1

clearwing \ˈ=,=\ *n* **:** a moth having the wings largely devoid of scales and transparent: as **a :** a moth of the family Aegeriidae **b :** any of various hawkmoths (as the bumblebee hawkmoth)

clear-winged grasshopper \ˈ=,=-\ *n* **:** a widely distributed and very destructive No. American grasshopper (*Camnula pellucida*) distinguished by its small size and colorless nearly transparent hindwings

clearwing moth \ˈ=,=-\ *n* **:** a clearwing (family Aegeriidae)

[1]**cleat** \ˈklēt, *usu* -ēd· + V\ *n* -S [ME *cleete, clete* wedge, fr. (assumed) OE *clēat*; akin to MHG *klōz* lump — more at CLOUT] **1 a :** a wedge-shaped piece of wood or other material fastened to or projecting from something and serving as a support or check **b :** a wooden or metal fitting usu. with two projecting horns around which a rope may be made fast (as by belaying it) **2 :** a strip of wood, iron, or other material fastened across something to give strength, hold in position, or furnish a grip: as **a :** a projecting strip or cone usu. of leather, rubber, or metal fastened to or built into the sole or heel of a shoe to increase traction or provide a firm grip; *also* **:** a plate of metal on the heel or sole of a shoe for minimizing wear **b :** a similar projection on any surface demanding traction (as on a tractor tread or a machine belt) **c :** an often porcelain support with grooves or channels for electric wiring — see INSULATOR illustration **d** (1) **:** a strip usu. of wood but sometimes of metal or paperboard used to align and hold several boards (as in a barrelhead or box) or to connect adjacent panels or sides of a box (2) **:** BATTEN 2b(3) (3) **:** a piece of metal attached to a can or drum to secure a handle or a cover **3 :** a system of joints along which coal breaks when mined; *also* **:** a single joint of cleavage

cleat 1b

[2]**cleat** \"\ *vt* -ED/-ING/-S **1 :** to secure to or by a cleat **2 :** to provide or strengthen with a cleat

cleat·er \-ə(r)\ *n* -S **:** one that saws out cleats or attaches cleats (as to shipping cases)

cleating *n* -S [fr. gerund of *cleat*] **:** CLEAT 3

cleats \ˈklēts\ *n pl* [origin unknown] **:** COLTSFOOT a

cleav·a·bil·i·ty \,klēvəˈbiləd·ē, -ətē, -i\ *n* -ES **:** the degree of ease with which a material can be split

cleav·a·ble \ˈklēvəbəl\ *adj* [[2]*cleave* + *-able*] **:** capable of being cleaved or divided

cleav·age \ˈklēvij, -ēj\ *n* -S *often attrib* [[2]*cleave* + *-age*] **1 a :** the quality possessed by many crystallized substances of splitting readily in one or more definite directions and yielding surfaces always parallel to actual or possible crystal faces ⟨~ planes⟩; *also* **:** the direction of the dividing plane — compare PARTING **b :** the structure possessed by some rocks by virtue of which they break more readily and more persistently in one direction or in certain directions than in others — compare SCHIST, SLATE **2 :** the action of cleaving or splitting **:** the state of being cleft **:** DIVISION; *specif* **:** a division into distinct and often opposed or hostile groups ⟨a sharp ~ of fundamental interests that kept farmers and wage earners separate —F.L.Paxson⟩ **3 :** a fragment (as of a diamond) obtained by splitting **4 :** cell division: **a :** the series of mitotic divisions of the egg that results in the formation of the blastomeres and changes the single-celled zygote into a multicellular embryo **:** SEGMENTATION — see DETERMINATE CLEAVAGE, INDETERMINATE CLEAVAGE; DISCOIDAL CLEAVAGE, SUPERFICIAL CLEAVAGE; HOLOBLASTIC, MEROBLASTIC **b :** any division belonging to this series **c :** a process of cell formation in which the whole mass of cytoplasm is segmented progressively into small usu. uninucleate portions leaving no epiplasm (as in spore formation in certain fungi, esp. Phycomycetes) — compare FREE CELL FORMATION **5 :** the splitting of a molecule into simpler molecules ⟨hydrolytic ~⟩ **6 :** the depression between a woman's breasts esp. when made visible by the wearing of low-cut dresses

cleavage cavity *n* **:** BLASTOCOEL

cleavage cell *n* **:** BLASTOMERE

cleavage crystal *n* **:** a crystal fragment having a regular form because bounded by cleavage faces

cleavage nucleus *n* **:** the zygote nucleus formed by the fusion of male and female pronuclei

¹cleave \ˈklēv\ *vi* **cleaved** \-vd\ *also* **clave** \ˈklāv\ *or* **clove** \ˈklōv\ **cleaved; cleaving; cleaves** [ME *cleven, clivien,* fr. OE *clifian, cleofian;* akin to OHG *kleben* to stick, ON *klīfa* to clamber, cling to, Serb *glib* filth, OE *clǣg* clay — more at CLAY] **1 :** to adhere firmly and closely as though evenly and securely glued ⟨the rain continued . . . their uniforms *cleaved* uncomfortably to their bodies —Norman Mailer⟩ ⟨the homespun shirt . . . was sodden and *clove* coldly to her shivering body —Florette Henri⟩ **2 :** to adhere firmly, loyally, or unwaveringly ⟨the creed . . . embodied doctrines to which the believer must ~ —Frank Thilly⟩ ⟨insisted that his students ~ to the facts⟩ ⟨a man . . . shall ~ unto his wife —Gen 2:24 (AV)⟩ **syn** see ADHERE

²cleave \"\ *vb* **cleaved** \-vd\ *also* **cleft** \ˈkleft\ *or* **clove** \ˈklōv\ *or archaic* **clave** \ˈklāv\ **cleaved** *also* **cleft** *or* **clo·ven** \ˈklōvən\ **cleaving; cleaves** [ME *cleven, cleoven,* fr. OE *clēofan;* akin to OHG *klioban* to split, ON *kljūfa,* L *glubere* to peel, Gk *glyphein* to carve or hollow out, and perh. to OPruss *gleuptene* smoothing board of a plow] *vt* **1 a :** to divide into two parts by a cutting blow **:** SPLIT ⟨the final blow *cleaving* the archbishop's skull —E.V.Lucas⟩ **:** pass swiftly through (as water or air) as if by cutting ⟨our bow . . . *cleaving* . . . the surface of the deep blue water —Ernest Beaglehole⟩ **b :** to divide into distinct parts or portions esp. into groups having divergent or opposing views or interests **c :** to cause to undergo cleavage **2 a :** to sever or separate by cutting or splitting off **b :** to separate (as a person) from the group or (a part) from the whole ⟨rifts that seemed to ~ soldier from civilian in habit and state of mind —Dixon Wecter⟩ **3 :** to penetrate, pierce, or drive a way through ⟨her slim body . . . *clove* the water like a straight gold sword —Elinor Wylie⟩ **:** force (a passage) as if by cutting or hewing ⟨~ one's way through thick underbrush⟩ ~ *vi* **1 :** to split open or apart esp. along the grain ⟨pine fir wood ~*s* easily⟩ **2 :** to penetrate, pierce, or pass through something usu. swiftly as if by cutting or hewing ⟨a ship *cleaving* through the water⟩ ⟨his acumen *clove* clean to the heart of a piece of writing —D.G.Mandelbaum⟩ **3 :** to undergo cleavage **syn** see TEAR

³cleave \"\ *n* -S [IrGael *cliabh,* fr. MIr *cliab*] *Irish* **:** BASKET

cleave·land·ite *or* **cleve·land·ite** \ˈklēvlən,dīt\ *n* -S [Parker *Cleaveland* †1858 Am. mineralogist + E *-ite*] **:** a white lamellar variety of albite

cleav·er \ˈklēvə(r)\ *n* -S [ME *clever,* fr. *cleven* to split + *-er*] **1 :** one that cleaves: as **a :** a tool for cutting animal bodies into joints or pieces (as in butchering) **b :** one who prepares gems by cleaving off imperfect pieces **2 :** a prehistoric ax-like stone implement having a sharp somewhat straight cutting edge at one end

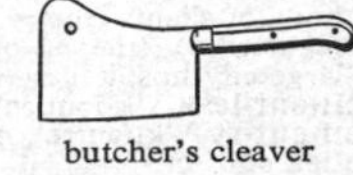

butcher's cleaver

cleav·ers \-(r)z\ *also* **cliv·ers** \ˈklivə(r)z\ *n pl but usu sing in constr* [ME *clivre,* alter. of OE *clife* cleavers, burdock; akin to OHG *chliba,* OE *clifian* to stick — more at CLEAVE] **:** any of several plants of the genus *Galium* (esp. *G. aparine*) having the stems beset with curved prickles — called also *catchweed, goose grass*

cleav·er·wort \ˈklēvə(r) +\ *n* [*cleavers* + *wort*] **:** CLEAVERS

cleav·ing·ly *adv* **:** in a cleaving manner

cle·chée *also* **cle·ché** \kläˈshā, kleˈ-, ˈkleshē\ *or* **clechy** \ˈkleshē\ *adj* [F *cléché,* fr. (assumed) VL *clavicatus,* fr. L *clavis* key — more at CLAVICLE] *of a heraldic cross* **:** voided and having each extremity shaped like the handle of a medieval key — compare URDÉE; see CROSS illustration

cleck \ˈklek\ *vb* -ED/-ING/-S [ME *clekken,* fr. ON *klekja;* perh. akin to OE *clyccan* to clutch — more at CLUTCH] *chiefly Scot* **:** HATCH

clee \ˈklē\ *n* -S [ME *clee, cleu, clea,* fr. OE *clēa* — more at CLAW] *now dial Eng* **:** CLAW

cleed \ˈklēd\ *var of* CLEAD

¹cleek \ˈklēk\ *vb* **claught** \ˈklȯkt\ *or* **cleeked** \ˈklēkt\ *or* **claucht** \ˈklȯkt\ **cleeked; cleeking; cleeks** [ME (northern dial.) *cleken;* prob. akin to OE *clyccan* to clutch — more at CLUTCH] *vt* **1** *chiefly Scot* **:** to seize or clutch **:** SNATCH, PLUCK **2** *chiefly Scot* **:** to catch or draw out **:** HOOK ~ *vi, chiefly Scot* **:** to link arms **:** go arm in arm

²cleek \"\ *n* -S [ME (northern dial.) *cleke* hook, act of clutching, fr. *cleken,* v.] **1** *chiefly Scot* **a :** a large hook or crook (as for a pot over a fire) **b :** FISHHOOK **2 :** either of two golf clubs: **a :** a narrow-bladed driving iron formerly in use for short drives **b :** a number four wood

cleeve \ˈklēv\ *var of* CLEVE

clef \ˈklef\ *n* -S [F, key, a key in music, fr. L *clavis* key — more at CLAVICLE] **:** a character placed at the beginning of the musical staff to determine the position of the notes

G, or Treble, Clef Soprano Clef Alto Clef Tenor Clef

F, or Bass, Clef C Clef

¹cleft \ˈkleft\ *n* -S [alter. of ME *clift,* fr. OE *geclyft;* akin to OS *kluht* tongs, OHG *kluft* gap, tongs, ON *Kluftir,* a place name, OE *clēofan* to split — more at CLEAVE] **1 a :** a space or opening made by or as if by splitting **:** SPLIT, CLEAVAGE, INDENTATION ⟨a spring bubbling out of a ~ in the rock⟩ **b :** an abrupt defile, chasm, or cut ⟨a ~ in the mountains⟩ **c :** a usu. V-shaped indented formation **:** a hollow between ridges or protuberances ⟨the anal ~ of the human body⟩ **d :** the hollow space between the two branches of the frog or the frog and bars or between the bulbs of the heel of a horse's hoof **e :** a crack on the bend of the pastern of a horse **f :** a wide, deep, or insurmountable division (as of belief or opinion) ⟨a ~ opened between sacred and profane science, which has not yet been closed —W.R.Inge⟩ **2 :** a piece or part separated by or as if by cleaving **:** DIVISION; *specif* **:** a division of the cleft foot of an animal **syn** see CRACK

²cleft \"\ *adj* [ME, fr. the past part. of *cleven* to cleave (split)] **1 :** split or divided for a part of the depth or length **:** formed with a partial division ⟨his nose ends in a puggy knob, ~ at the tip —N.M.Clark⟩ **2** *of a leaf* **:** divided about halfway to the midrib often with narrow lobes or sinuses — compare DIVIDED, PARTED — **in a cleft stick :** in an inextricable position **:** in a dilemma **:** in a fix ⟨I never saw his equal to put a fellow *in a cleft stick* —Charles Lever⟩

cleft·ed \ˈkleftəd\ *adj* **:** having clefts **:** FISSURED, CLEFT

cleft-footed \ˈ≡ˌ≡≡\ *adj* **:** having a cloven foot

cleft graft *n* **:** a plant graft made by cutting the stock squarely across, splitting the cut end, and inserting one or two scions in the split so that the cambiums of stock and scion are in contact — see GRAFT illustration

cleft lip *n* **:** HARELIP

cleft palate *n* **:** congenital partial or complete fissure of the roof of the mouth often associated with harelip

cleftstone \ˈ≡ˌ≡\ *n* [²*cleft* + *stone*] **:** FLAGSTONE

cleft weld *n* **:** a weld made by upsetting the ends of the work by cutting a V-shaped opening in the end of one piece, by forming the end of the other piece to fit the first, and by joining the pieces by welding

cleg *or* **clegg** \ˈkleg\ *n* -S [ME, fr. ON *kleggi;* akin to Norw *klegg* burr, OE *clǣg* clay — more at CLAY] *Brit* **:** a horsefly or gadfly

cleid- *or* **cleido-** *comb form* [NL, fr. Gk *kleid-, kleido-,* fr. *kleid-, kleis* key; akin to L *clavis* key — more at CLAVICLE] **1 a :** clavicle **:** clavicular ⟨*cleid*agra⟩ **b :** clavicular and ⟨*cleido*scapular⟩ **2 :** key ⟨*cleido*mancy⟩

clei·do·ic \(ˈ)klīˈdōik\ *adj* [Gk *kleidoun* to fasten, lock in (fr. *kleid-, kleis* key, bolt) + E *-ic*] *of an egg* **:** cut off or isolated from free exchange with the environment by reason of a more or less impervious shell ⟨the eggs of birds are ~⟩

cleik \ˈklēk\ *var of* CLEEK

-clei·sis *or* **-cli·sis** \ˈklīsəs\ *n comb form, pl* **-clei·ses** *or* **-cli·ses** \-ī,sēz\ [NL, fr. Gk *kleisis,* kleisis, fr. *kleiein* to close — more at CLOSE] **:** closure **:** occlusion ⟨arthro*cleisis*⟩ ⟨entero*clisis*⟩

cleist- *or* **cleisto-** *also* **clist-** *or* **clisto-** *comb form* [G *kleist-, kleisto-,* fr. Gk *kleistos;* akin to Gk *kleis* key] **:** closed ⟨*cleisto*carp⟩ ⟨*cleisto*gamy⟩

cleis·to·carp \ˈklīstə,kärp\ *also* **clis·to·carp** \", ˈklis-\ *n* -S [*cleist-* + *-carp*] **:** CLEISTOTHECIUM

cleis·to·car·pous *also* **clis·to·car·pous** \ˌ≡≡ˈkärpəs\ *adj* [*cleist-* + *-carpous*] **1** *of mosses* **:** having the capsule opening irregularly without an operculum **2** *of fungi* **:** having or forming cleistothecia

cleis·to·gam·ic *also* **clis·to·gam·ic** \-ˈgamik\ *adj* [ISV *cleist-* + *-gamic*] **:** CLEISTOGAMOUS — **cleis·to·gam·i·cal·ly** \-mək(ə)lē\ *adv*

cleis·tog·a·mous \(ˈ)klīˈstägəməs\ *also* **clis·tog·a·mous** \", (ˈ)kliˈs-\ *adj* [*cleist-* + *-gamous*] **:** exhibiting or relating to cleistogamy — **cleis·tog·a·mous·ly** *adv*

cleis·tog·a·my *also* **clis·tog·a·my** \≡ˈ≡≡mē\ *n* -ES [ISV *cleist-* + *-gamy;* orig. formed as G *kleist gamismus*] **:** the production (as in violets and pansies) of small inconspicuous nonopening self-pollinating flowers additional to and often bearing more seeds than the showier type — compare CHASMOGAMY

cleis·to·gene \ˈklīstə,jēn\ *also* **clis·to·gene** \", ˈklis-\ *n* -S [*cleist-* + *-gene*] **1 :** a plant producing cleistogamous flowers **2 :** a cleistogamous flower

cleis·tog·e·nous \(ˈ)klīˈstäjənəs\ *adj* [*cleist-* + *-genous*] **:** bearing cleistogamous flowers

cleis·to·the·ci·um \ˌklīstəˈthēs(h)ēəm\ *n, pl* **cleistothe·cia** \-ēə\ [NL, fr. *cleist-* + *-thecium*] **:** a closed spore-bearing structure in ascomycetous fungi (as the Aspergillaceae and Erysiphaceae) from which the asci and spores are released only by decay or disintegration — called also *cleistocarp*

clei·thral \ˈklīthrəl\ *adj* [Gk *kleithra* lattice + E *-al* — more at CLATHRATE] *of a temple* **:** having a roofed central space — opposed to *hypaethral*

clei·thrum \-rəm\ *n, pl* **clei·thra** \-rə\ [NL, fr. Gk *kleithron*] **:** a bone external to and beside the clavicle in the pectoral arch of some fishes, stegocephalians, and primitive reptiles

¹clem \ˈklem\ *vb* **clemmed; clemmed; clemming; clems** [ME *clemmen* to pinch — more at CLAM] *vt, dial Eng* **:** to cause to suffer from hunger, thirst, or cold **:** STARVE ~ *vi, dial Eng* **:** to suffer from hunger, thirst, or cold

²clem \"\ *n* -S [origin unknown] *slang* **:** a fight or brawl esp. between circus or carnival workers and the local townsfolk

clem·a·tis \ˈklemədˌəs, ˌtəs; kləˈma-, -ˈmä-,-ˈmā-,-ˈmà-\ *n* [NL, fr. L, periwinkle, fr. Gk *klēmatis* brushwood, clematis, fr. *klēmat-, klēma* twig; akin to Gk *klan* to break — more at GLADIATOR] **1** *cap* **:** a genus of opposite-leaved slightly woody vines or erect herbs (family Ranunculaceae) having elongate plumose styles — see TRAVELER'S-JOY, VIRGIN'S BOWER **2** *pl* **clematises** *or* **clematis :** a plant of the genus *Clematis* or of the related genera *Atragene* and *Viorna* **3** *pl* **clematises :** a strong violet that is redder and paler than pansy, redder, stronger, and slightly lighter than royal purple (sense 2), and redder than lobelia

clem·en·cy \ˈklemənsē, -si\ *n* -ES [L *clementia,* fr. *clement-, clemens* mild, calm + *-ia* -y] **1 a :** disposition to be clement, mild, and compassionate and to moderate possible severity of judgment and punishment ⟨show ~ to first offenders⟩ **b :** an act or instance of leniency **2 :** mildness and moderateness esp. of weather **syn** see MERCY

clem·ent \ˈklemənt\ *adj* [ME, fr. L *clement-, clemens;* prob. akin to Gk *klinein* to lean — more at LEAN] **1 a :** characterized by mercy and humaneness in the exercise of power to judge or punish ⟨a master as intelligent, as cultivated, and as ~ as Caesar —R.P.Oliver⟩ **b :** giving the impression or creating an effect of mildness, gentleness, or tenderness ⟨a bright and ~ star shining through the powdery bloom of the dusk —Ellen Glasgow⟩ **2** *of weather* **:** MILD ⟨birds that . . . seek the ~ South —Edna S. V. Millay⟩ **syn** see FORBEARING

¹clem·en·tine \ˈklemən,tēn, -tīn\ *adj, usu cap* [ML & NL *clementinus,* fr. L, ML, & NL *Clement-, Clemens* Clement (the name) + L *-inus* -ine] **:** of or relating to Clement: **a** [after *Clement* I (Clemens Romanus) †*ab* A.D. 100 bishop of Rome] **:** relating to the homilies and liturgies falsely attributed to Clement I, bishop of Rome **b** [after Pope *Clement* V (Bertrand de Got) †1314 Fr. prelate] **:** relating to the compilations of canon law made by Pope Clement V **c** [after Pope *Clement* VIII (Ippolito Aldobrandini) †1605 Ital. prelate] **:** relating to the revised edition of the Vulgate issued under the direction of Pope Clement VIII

²clementine \"\ *n* -S *usu cap* **:** a follower of any of various leaders named Clement (as Clement of Alexandria or Clement VII of Avignon)

clem·ent·ly *adv* **:** in a clement manner

clem·men·sen reduction \ˈklemənsən-\ *n, usu cap C* [after Erik *Clemmensen* †1941 Dan. chemist] **:** the reduction of a ketone or aldehyde directly to a hydrocarbon by the action of amalgamated zinc and hydrochloric acid

clem·mys \ˈkleməs\ *n, cap* [NL, fr. Gk *klemmys* tortoise] **:** a genus of nearly cosmopolitan semiaquatic turtles (family Testudinidae) that includes the No. American wood tortoise and spotted turtle

¹clench \ˈklench\ *vb* -ED/-ING/-ES [ME *clenchen,* fr. OE *-clencan* (in *beclencan* to hold fast); akin to OHG *klenken* to tie, MHG *klank* snare, OE *clingan* to cling — more at CLING] *vt* **1 :** CLINCH *vt* 1 **2 :** to hold fast by or as if by grasping tightly **:** CLUTCH ⟨he ~*ed* the arms of his chair⟩ **3 a :** to set or strain (as the jaws) closely or tightly together ⟨~*ed* his teeth⟩ **:** close tightly ⟨~*ed* his fists⟩ **b :** to strain tight or tense (as the body or mind) under or as if under the stress of emotion ⟨you are always ~*ed* against me —D.H.Lawrence⟩ **4 :** CLINCH *vt* 3 **5 :** CLINCH *vt* 4 ~ *vi* **1 :** CLINCH *vi* 2 **2 :** to set together or close tightly **:** strain tight or tense ⟨her hands ~*ed* in her pockets⟩ ⟨your stomach ~*es* and unclenches —Alvah Bessie⟩

²clench \"\ *n* -ES **1 a :** the end of a nail or other fastening that is turned back in clinching it **b :** a strong fitting (as on the deck of a ship) designed to provide anchorage for cables or shackles under heavy strain **2** *archaic* **:** a play on words **:** PUN **3 :** the action of clenching

clench-built \ˈ≡ˌ≡\ *adj* **:** CLINKER-BUILT

cle·oid \ˈklē,ȯid\ *n* -S [Gk *kleis* key, catch, hook + E *-oid* — more at CLOSE] **:** an excavator with a claw-shaped working point used in dentistry

cle·o·me \klēˈōmē\ *n* [NL] **1** *cap* **:** a large genus of herbs or low shrubs (family Capparidaceae) having showy flowers with clawed petals and an elongate-linear stalked pod — see SPIDER FLOWER **2** -S **:** any plant of the genus *Cleome*

cle·o·nus \klēˈōnəs\ *n, cap* [NL, fr. L *Cleon,* a proper name (fr. Gk *Kleōn*) + NL *-us*] **:** a genus of Old World weevils (family Curculionidae) including one (*Cleonus punctiventris*) that is a destructive pest of sugar beet, the adults feeding on the leaves and the larvae on the roots

cle·o·pat·ra \ˌklēəˈpa·trə *also* -pä- *or* -pā- *or* -pà-\ *n* -S *often cap* [prob. after *Cleopatra* VII (or VI) †30 B.C. queen of Egypt] **:** a vivid blue that is greener, lighter, and stronger than Ch'ing and greener than ultramarine

clepe \ˈklēp\ *vt* **cleped** \-ēpt,-ept\ **cleped** \"\ *or* **ycleped** \iˈklēpt, ēˈk-, -ept\ *or* **yclept** \-ept\ **clep·ing** \-ēpiŋ\ **clepes** \-ēps\ [ME *clepen,* fr. OE *clipian, cleopian* to speak, cry out, call; akin to OFris *kleppa, klippa* to ring, knock, MLG *kleperen* to clatter and perh. to OE *clæppan* to clap — more at CLAP] *archaic* **:** to call by the name of **:** NAME, CALL ⟨they ~ us drunkards —Shak.⟩ ⟨a loose lady *yclept* Julie —Will Cuppy⟩

clepht *var of* KLEPHT

clep·si·ne \klepˈsīnē\ [NL] *syn of* GLOSSIPHONIA

clep·sy·dra \ˈklepsədrə\ *n, pl* **clepsydras** \-rəz\ *or* **clepsy·drae** \-,drē\ [L, fr. Gk *klepsydra,* fr. *kleps-* (fr. *kleptein* to steal) + *-ydra* (fr. *hydōr* water) — more at KLEPT-, WATER] **:** WATER CLOCK

clep·to·biosis \ˌkleptō+\ *n, pl* **cleptobioses** [NL, fr. *clepto-* (fr. Gk *klepto-* theft, fr. *kleptein* to steal) + *-biosis*] **:** a mutual relation in which members of one species (as of ants) habitually steal food from another — see LESTOBIOSIS — **clep·to·biotic** \"+\ *adj*

cleptomania *var of* KLEPTOMANIA

clere·storied \ˈklir, -iə+\ *adj* **:** having a clerestory ⟨~ roof⟩

clere·story *or* **clear·story** \ˈklir, -iə+,-\ *n* -ES [ME, fr. *clere* clear + *story*] **1 :** an outside wall of a room or building (as a church) carried above an adjoining roof and pierced with windows which admit light to the interior **2 :** interior space on the level of the clerestory in a room or building **:** GALLERY **3 :** a raised section of a railroad car roof having windows or openings for ventilation on the sides

building exterior showing clerestory, *1*

clergical *adj, obs* **:** of or belonging to the clergy

cler·gy \ˈklərjē, -ōj-, -əij-, -ji\ *n* -ES [ME *clergie,* fr. OF, fr. *clerg-* (alter. — influenced by *clergié* body of ecclesiastics — of *clerc* clergyman) + *-ie* -y — more at CLERK] **1 :** LEARNING, KNOWLEDGE — used chiefly in the proverb *an ounce of mother wit is worth a pound of clergy* **2 :** the body of men and women duly ordained to the service of God in the Christian church **:** the body of ordained ministers **:** clergymen and clergywomen **3 :** a body of religious officials or functionaries prepared and authorized to conduct religious services and attend to other religious duties ⟨the Taoist ~⟩ ⟨the Jewish ~⟩ **4 :** BENEFIT OF CLERGY 1

cler·gy·able *also* **cler·gi·a·ble** \-jēəbəl\ *adj* **:** entitled to or admitting the benefit of clergy ⟨a ~ felony⟩

cler·gy·man \-jəmən, -jē\ *n, pl* **clergymen 1 :** a member of the clergy **:** an ordained minister **:** a man regularly authorized to preach the gospel and administer its ordinances **:** one in holy orders **2** *Brit* **:** a minister of the Church of England

clergyman's sore throat *n* **:** chronic inflammation of the pharynx often occurring in persons who habitually overstrain or misuse the voice (as in public speaking)

cler·gy·woman \-jə, -jē+,-\ *n, pl* **clergywomen 1** *archaic* **:** a woman member of a religious order **:** NUN **2 :** a woman who is an ordained minister **3** *archaic* **:** a clergyman's wife or female relative esp. when officiously meddlesome

¹cler·ic \ˈklerik, -rēk\ *n* -S [LL *clericus,* adj. & n. — more at CLERK] **1 :** CLERGYMAN **2 :** one who has received the ecclesiastical tonsure **:** CLERK

²cleric \"\ *adj* [LL *clericus*] **:** CLERICAL

¹cler·i·cal \-rəkəl, -ēk-\ *adj* [LL *clericalis,* fr. *clericus*] **1 :** of, belonging to, or characteristic of the clergy, a clergyman, or a cleric ⟨~ vows⟩ **2 :** of, suitable to, or belonging to a clerk in an office or business ⟨~ occupations such as bookkeeping⟩ **:** being or consisting of an office clerk or clerks ⟨~ staff⟩ **3 :** governed by or supporting the principles of clericalism ⟨a ~ party⟩ — **cler·i·cal·ly** \-rək(ə)lē, -ēk-, -li\ *adv*

²clerical \"\ *n* -S **1 :** a clergyman or cleric **2 :** one who believes in or supports clericalism **:** a member of a clerical party ⟨the ~*s* proposed compulsory religious education in the public schools⟩ **3 clericals** *pl* **:** clerical garments **4 :** one who does clerical work in an office or business ⟨permanent jobs as secretaries, ~*s,* typists —*N.Y. Times*⟩

clerical collar *n* **:** a narrow stiffly upright white collar buttoned at the back of the neck and worn by various clergymen — called also *reversed collar*

clerical error *n* **:** an error made in copying or writing

cler·i·cal·ism \-,lizəm\ *n* -S **1 :** a policy that attempts to maintain or augment the temporal power (as the political power) of a church or religious hierarchy **2 a :** a policy favoring the maintenance or increase of power over religious matters by an ecclesiastical hierarchy or clergy **b :** dogmatic and authoritarian control of religious matters by clergy

cler·i·cal·ist \-,ləst\ *n* -S **:** one who favors the increase of ecclesiastical power and influence

cler·i·cal·i·ty \ˌklerəˈkalədˌē\ *n* -ES **:** clerical quality, state, or characteristic

cler·i·cal·ize \ˈklerəkə,līz, -rēk-\ *vt* -ED/-ING/-S [F *cléricaliser,* fr. *clérical* + *-iser* -ize] **:** to cause to become clerical or be influenced by clericalism

clerical technician *n* **:** one who studies the clerical and statistical procedures of business establishments for the purpose of improving the methods used

cler·i·ca·ture \ˈklerəkə,chù(ə)r\ *n* -S [F *cléricature,* fr. ML *clericatura,* fr. *clericatus* (past part. of *clericare* to make a cleric, fr. LL *clericus*) + L *-ura* -ure] **:** clerical position or function

cle·ri·ci solution \kləˈrēchē-\ *n, usu cap C* [fr. the name *Clerici*] **:** a water solution of thallium malonate and thallium formate used as a liquid of high specific gravity to separate mixtures of solids into their components

clerico- *comb form* [LL *clericus* priest] **:** clerical (sense 1) **:** clerical and ⟨*clerico*political⟩ ⟨*clerico*fascist⟩

cler·id \ˈklerəd\ *n* -S [NL *Cleridae*] **:** a beetle of the family Cleridae

cler·i·dae \ˈklerə,dē\ *n pl, cap* [NL, fr. *Clerus,* type genus (fr. Gk *klēros,* a kind of beetle, prob. of the genus *Clerus*) + *-idae*] **:** a family of beetles related to the soldier beetles and fireflies and usu. of bright checkered colors or metallic luster and predaceous on other insects

cler·i·hew \ˈklerə,hyü\ *n* -S [after Edmund *Clerihew* Bentley †1956 Eng. writer of detective fiction, its originator] **:** a light verse quatrain in lines usu. of varying length, rhyming *aabb,* and making a statement usu. concerning a person whose name typically supplies the initial rhyme

cler·i·sy \ˈklerəsē\ *n* -ES [G *klerisei* clergy (often used contemptuously), fr. ML *clericia,* fr. LL *clericus* priest] **:** the well-educated or learned class **:** the academic class **:** INTELLIGENTSIA ⟨the ~ of a nation . . . whether poets or philosophers or scholars —S.T.Coleridge⟩

¹clerk \ˈklərk, -ōk,-əik, *Brit usu* ˈklàk\ *n* -S [ME, fr. OF *clerc* & OE *clerc, cleric,* both fr. LL *clericus,* fr. Gk *klērikos,* fr. Gk *klēros* lot, allotment, clergy + *-ikos* -ic; akin to Gk *klan* to break — more at GLADIATOR] **1 :** a clergyman or cleric: as **a :** an ordained minister of the Church of England ⟨a ~ in holy orders⟩ **b** *Roman Catholicism* (1) **:** one who has received the ecclesiastical tonsure (2) **:** a person who under canon law enjoys benefit of clergy (as a monk or nun) **2** *archaic* **a :** a person who can read or read and write **b :** a learned person **:** SCHOLAR, MAN OF LETTERS **3 a :** an employee or official responsible (as to a corporation or a government agency) for correspondence, the keeping of records and accounts, and the management of routine affairs and vested with certain specified powers or authority (as to issue writs or other processes as ordered by a court) **:** SECRETARY ⟨~ of a court⟩ ⟨town ~⟩ ⟨~ of the society⟩ **b** (1) **:** one employed (as in a business office) to keep records or accounts or to perform more or less routine office tasks ⟨tally ~⟩ ⟨filing ~⟩ (2) **:** one in charge of records and accounts on a steamboat **:** purser of a steamboat **c** (1) **:** a postal employee who works at the sales and service windows in a post office and esp. in a small post office sometimes performs operations connected with the sorting of mail (2) **:** one who sorts mail in a railway post office **d :** a hotel employee usu. stationed at the desk who serves the hotel and its guests esp. by assigning rooms and performing small services (as giving guests their mail and holding their keys when they are out of the hotel) **4 :** a layman who performs some ecclesiastical office: **a :** a Church of England minister regarded in civil law as a layman whose office is to assist the clergy, lead the responses, and teach in schools — called also *parish clerk* **b :** a layman or laywoman in the Protestant Episcopal Church serving as the scribe of the vestry and sometimes also of the parish or parish meeting **c :** a chief official appointed to serve at a regularly organized meeting of the Society of Friends **5 :** a salesperson in a store **:** one who shows and sells articles of merchandise in a store ⟨a grocery ~⟩ **6 :** one who holds a clerkship (sense 3)

²clerk \"\ *vb* -ED/-ING/-S *vi* **:** to act or work as a clerk ⟨~*ing* in the feed store at six dollars a week —Elmer Davis⟩ ~ *vt, chiefly Scot* **:** WRITE, COMPOSE

clerk·ess \-kəs\ *n* -ES *chiefly Scot* **:** a female clerk

clerk·ish \-kish\ *adj* **1 :** CLERICAL **2 a :** suggesting a clerk or the work of a clerk **b :** overprecise or particular of detail
clerk·less \-ləs\ *adj* **:** having no clerk
¹clerk·ly \-lē\ *adv* [ME, fr. *clerk* + *-ly*] **:** in a clerkly manner; *esp* **:** LEARNEDLY
²clerkly \"\ *adj* -ER/-EST [*clerk* + *-ly*] **:** of, relating to, suitable to, or characteristic of a clerk: as **a :** belonging to or befitting the clergy ⟨~ privilege⟩ ⟨the Wife of Bath's ~ husband —G.G.Coulton⟩ **b** *archaic* **:** LEARNED, SCHOLARLY **c :** showing skill in penmanship ⟨to write a ~ hand⟩ **d :** quiet or studious in conduct **:** precise or modest in appearance ⟨a timid ~ fellow⟩ **e :** of or in the capacity of a clerk ⟨pursuing a ~ career⟩
clerk of the course : an official who acts as executive secretary to the board of judges of races or track athletics
clerk of the scales : an official who weighs jockeys and their gear before and after a horse race
clerk regular *n* [trans. of ML *canonicus regularis*] **:** a religious combining monastic life with the ministry of a diocesan priest
clerk·ship \-,ship\ *n* -S **1 :** the office or business of a clerk **:** a position as a clerk **2** *archaic* **:** LEARNING, SCHOLARSHIP **3 :** the part of the undergraduate medical curriculum during which the student under supervision serves as a clerk performing routine clinical work for stated periods in a hospital that is affiliated with a medical school
clerk vicar *n* **:** a layman in the Church of England who is employed in a cathedral to take those parts of the liturgy not reserved to the clergy — called also *lay vicar, secular vicar*
cler·mont-fer·rand \¦klermōⁿfe¦räⁿ\ *adj, usu cap C&F* [fr. *Clermont-Ferrand*, France] **:** of or from the city of Clermont-Ferrand, France **:** of the kind or style prevalent in Clermont-Ferrand
cle·ro·den·dron \,klirə'dendrən, ,kler-\ *n, cap* [NL, fr. *clero-* (fr. Gk *klēros* lot) + *-dendron* — more at CLERK] **:** a genus of chiefly Old World tropical sometimes climbing shrubs and trees (family Verbenaceae) that are often cultivated esp. in greenhouses and have opposite simple leaves, irregular flowers in headlike clusters, and a drupelike fruit enclosed in the calyx
cle·ro·den·drum \-drəm\ *syn of* CLERODENDRON
cle·ro·man·cy \'==,man(t)sē\ *n* -ES [MF or ML; MF *cleromancie*, fr. ML *cleromantia*, fr. *clero-* + *-mantia* -mancy] **:** divination by means of casting lots
cle·ruch \'kli,rük, -lē,r-, -,rək\ *n* -S [Gk *klērouchos*, fr. *klēro-* (fr. *klēros* lot, allotment) + *-ochos* holder (fr. *echein* to have, hold) — more at SCHEME] **:** a citizen of ancient Greece who received an allotment of land in a conquered country and usu. migrated to it without loss of his citizenship — **cle·ru·chi·al** \klə'rükēəl\ *or* **cle·ru·chic** \-kik\ *adj*
cle·ru·chy \'kli,rükē, -lē,r-, -,rəkē\ *n* -ES [Gk *klērouchia*, fr. *klērouchos*] **:** a body or settlement of cleruchs
cle·rus \'klirəs\ *n, cap* [NL, fr. Gk *klēros*, a beetle (*Clerus apiarius*)] **:** the type genus of the family Cleridae
cless \'kles\ *Scot var of* CLASS
cletch \'klech\ *n* -ES [alter. (perh. influenced by ³*clutch*) of *cleck*] **1** *dial Eng* **:** HATCHING, CLUTCH, BROOD **2** *dial Eng* **:** a brood of persons **:** FAMILY
cle·thra \'klēthrə, -eth-\ *n, cap* [NL, fr. Gk *klēthra* alder; akin to G (Tirolese dial.) *lutter* green alder (*Alnus viridis*)] **:** a genus (coextensive with the family Clethraceae) of deciduous shrubs or trees with stellate pubescence and capsular fruits of three locules — see SWEET PEPPERBUSH, WHITE ALDER
cle·thra·ce·ae \klə'thrāsē,ē, kle-\ *n pl, cap* [NL, fr. *Clethra*, type genus + *-aceae*] **:** a family of dicotyledonous plants (order Ericales) coextensive with the genus *Clethra*
cleth·ri·on·o·mys \,klethrē'änəməs\ *n, cap* [NL, fr. *clethri-ono-* (modif. of Gk *kleithrion*, dim. of *kleithron* entrance of the windpipe, fr. *kleiein* to close) + *-mys* — more at CLOSE] **:** a genus of rodents consisting of the red-backed mice
cleuch *or* **cleugh** \'klük\ *n* -S [ME (Sc), fr. (assumed) OE *clōh* — more at CLOUGH] *chiefly Scot* **:** CLOUGH
cleuk \'kl(y)ük\ *n* -S [ME (northern dial.) *cluk, cluke, cloke*; akin to ME *cleken* to catch or snatch — more at CLEEK] *chiefly Scot* **:** CLAW, HAND **:** GRASP, CLUTCH
cleve \'klēv\ *n* -S [ME *cleve, cleove*, fr. OE *clif*, nom. & acc. pl. *cleofu* — more at CLIFF] **1** *dial Eng* **:** CLIFF **2** *dial Eng* **:** steep sloping ground **:** BRAE
cleve·ite \'klē,vīt, 'klāvə,īt\ *n* -S [Sw *cleveit*, fr. P. T. *Cleve* †1905 Swed. chemist + Sw *-it* -ite] **:** URANINITE
cleve·land \'klēvlənd\ *adj, usu cap* [fr. *Cleveland*, Ohio] **:** of or from the city of Cleveland, Ohio ⟨a *Cleveland* terminal⟩ **:** of the kind or style prevalent in Cleveland
cleveland bay *n, usu cap C & often cap B* [fr. *Cleveland*, district in Yorkshire, England, where it was developed] **:** a horse of a breed developed for light draft and carriage use, being uniformly bay in color with black points and legs and of good conformation and strong constitution
cleve·land·er \-ləndə(r)\ *n* -S *cap* [*Cleveland*, Ohio + E *-er*] **:** a native or resident of Cleveland, esp. Cleveland, Ohio
clevelandite *var of* CLEAVELANDITE
¹clev·er \'klevə(r)\ *adj* -ER/-EST [ME *cliver*, prob. of Scand origin; akin to Dan dial. *kløver* clever, skillful, alert, ON *kljūfa* to split, pierce — more at CLEAVE] **1 :** showing deftness, skill, or adroitness in using the hands or in other bodily movements **:** NIMBLE ⟨~ with the gloves⟩ **2 :** having mental quickness, intelligence, resourcefulness in improvising often accompanied by craft, wit, or physical dexterity ⟨you are a ~ man, . . . you reason well, and your wit is bold —Bram Stoker⟩ ⟨through the porcelain . . . a ~ artisan had thrust a rivet —Elinor Wylie⟩; *often* **:** intelligent, quick, ingenious, and resourceful but lacking in depth, soundness, wisdom, or morality ⟨too ~ to be sound —Van Wyck Brooks⟩ ⟨an exercise in ~ film-making without ever striking fire as a film —Arthur Knight⟩ **3 :** characterized by the display of wit or ingenuity ⟨a ~ poem⟩ ⟨his judgments were wise rather than ~ —James Hilton⟩ ⟨applauded his ~ sparkling speech⟩ **4** *now dial* **a :** in good health ⟨wasn't looking too ~ —Thomas Wood †1950⟩ **b :** well-shaped **:** CLEAN-LIMBED — used esp. of an animal ⟨a right ~ horse⟩ **c :** well-made **:** carefully constructed ⟨a ~ spade⟩ **5** *now chiefly dial* **:** convenient or easy to use or handle ⟨a sweet craft, trim, staunch, and ~ to handle —S.H. Adams⟩ **:** SATISFACTORY, PLEASING ⟨~ land for farming⟩ — a generalized expression of approval **6** *dial* **:** GOOD-NATURED, OBLIGING, AMIABLE, HOSPITABLE ⟨good ~ man —Elizabeth M. Roberts⟩
syn ADROIT, CUNNING, INGENIOUS: although CLEVER still occas. retains its old meaning of physical dexterity, agility, and deftness, it usu. indicates mental alertness and resourcefulness ⟨curiously *clever* at all kinds of things . . . a sort of impromptu conjuring, making fifteen matches set fire to each other like a regular firework —G.K.Chesterton⟩ ⟨"who invented the story — you or her?" "He did, monsieur. He was very *clever*. He thought of everything" —Dorothy Sayers⟩ ⟨Austin was not *clever* like Adrian: he seldom divined other people's ideas and always went the direct road to his object —George Meredith⟩ ADROIT suggests shrewd and wily or alert and agile expedients ⟨the cool prudence, the sensitive selfishness, the quick perception of what is possible, which distinguish the *adroit* politician —J.R.Green⟩ ⟨'tis said he could shave himself with the axe — so all *adroit* . . . does he work and play at once —Robert Browning⟩ CUNNING may apply to high creative skill or low guileful craft ⟨he knew how . . . to construct a plot, he was *cunning* in his manipulation of stage effects —T.S.Eliot⟩ ⟨it is, of course, possible that a *cunning* man might change the tire of his bicycle in order to leave unfamiliar tracks —A. Conan Doyle⟩ INGENIOUS suggests brilliant or notable inventiveness and resourcefulness ⟨the batteries being kept recharged by an *ingenious* device —Dorothy Sayers⟩ ⟨the *ingenious* Yankee, quick to adapt himself everywhere, easily extricating himself from situations —Matthew Josephson⟩ **syn** see in addition INTELLIGENT
²clever \"\ *adv* **1** *now dial* **:** very well **:** EXCELLENTLY ⟨treated him real ~ —Willa Cather⟩ **2** *dial Brit* **:** DIRECTLY, STRAIGHT ⟨you must go ~ through the city⟩ ⟨the dog jumped ~ over the hedge⟩
clev·er·al·i·ty \,klevə'ralətī\ *n* -ES [¹*clever* + *-ality* (as in *comicality*)] *chiefly Scot* **:** CLEVERNESS
clev·er·ish \'klev(ə)rish\ *adj* **:** somewhat clever — **clev·er·ish·ly** *adv*
clev·er·ly *adv* **1 :** in a clever manner **2** *dial* **:** FULLY, COMPLETELY ⟨as soon as he was ~ out of hearing —T.C.Haliburton⟩ **:** ENTIRELY, QUITE ⟨the boy wasn't ~ grown⟩ **3** *dial* **:** SATISFACTORILY, CONVENIENTLY
clev·er·ness \-və(r)nəs\ *n* -ES **:** the quality of being clever; *esp* **:** ADROITNESS
cle·ve's acid \'klāvəz-, 'klēvz-\ *n, usu cap C* [after P.T. *Cleve* — more at CLEVEITE] **:** either of two colorless crystalline isomeric monosulfonic acids $NH_2C_{10}H_6SO_3H$ derived from alpha-naphthylamine and used as intermediates in making azo dyes; *also* **:** a mixture of these acids
clev·is \'klevəs\ *n* -ES [earlier *clevi* (akin to Sc *clivvie, clevie* cleft branch, cleft instrument), prob. of Scand origin; akin to ON *klofi* cleft stick, groove for a door, ON *kljūfa* to split — more at CLEAVE] **1 :** a fitting for attaching or suspending parts (as a cable to another structural member of a bridge or a hanger for supporting pipe) that consists usu. of a U-shaped piece of metal with the ends drilled to receive a pin or bolt **2 :** any of various connections in which one part is fitted between the forked ends of another and fastened by means of a bolt or pin passing through the forked ends

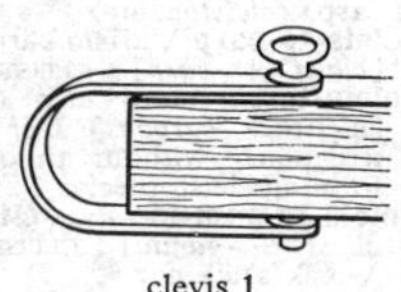
clevis 1

clevy \'klevē, -vi\ *n* -ES [back-formation fr. *clevis*, taken as pl.] **:** CLEVIS
¹clew *or* **clue** \'klü\ *n* -S [ME *clewe*, fr. OE *cliewen*; akin to OHG *kliuwa* ball, ON *klō* claw, Gk *ginglymos* hinge, Skt *glau* round lump — more at GALL] **1 :** a ball of thread, yarn, or cord **2** *usu clue* **a :** the information or key that guides through an intricate procedure or a maze of difficulties ⟨provide a ~ through the complex negotiations⟩ **b :** the thread of narrative (as in a story) or of thought or argument **c :** a piece of evidence tending to lead one toward the solution of a problem **:** an indication that properly interpreted may lead to full understanding of something or to the discovery of something unknown or hidden ⟨the flight of birds might furnish a valuable *clue* to the problem of blind flying —H.G.Armstrong⟩ ⟨possess a rough *clue* as to what the conversation has previously been about —Paul Dehn⟩ **3 a :** a lower corner of a square sail or the after lower corner of a fore-and-aft sail — see SAIL illustration **b clews** *pl* **:** a combination of lines or nettles by which a hammock is suspended
²clew *or* **clue** \"\ *vt* **clewed** *or* **clued; clewed** *or* **clued; clewing** *or* **clueing** *or* **cluing; clews** *or* **clues 1 :** to roll into a ball **2** *usu clue* **a :** to provide with a clue (as to something hidden or unknown) ⟨nothing to ~ us to what happened⟩ **b** *slang* **:** to give reliable information to ⟨~ me on how it works⟩ **3 a :** to haul (a sail) by means of the clew garnets or clew lines up to a yard or mast — used with *up* **b :** to force (a yard) down by hauling on the clew lines — used with *down*
clew garnet *n* **:** one of the ropes by which the clews of the courses of square-rigged ships are hauled up to lower yards
clew jigger *n* **:** a small tackle used instead of clew lines to trice up the clew of a sail
clew line *n* **:** a rope by which a clew of an upper square sail is hauled up to its yard — see SAIL illustration
clg *abbr* ceiling
CLI *abbr* cost-of-living index
cli·an·thus \klī'an(t)thəs\ *n* [NL, fr. *cli-* (irreg. fr. Gk *kleos* glory) + *-anthus*; akin to Gk *klytos* famous — more at LOUD] **1** *cap* **:** a genus of Australasian semiprostrate shrubs or vines (family Leguminosae) with compound leaves and pealike red flowers in drooping racemes **2** -ES **:** any plant of the genus *Clianthus* (esp. *C. dampieri*) — see GLORY PEA
¹cli·ché \klē'shā, '=,=, kli'shā\ *n* -S [F, fr. past part. of *clicher* to stereotype, of imit. origin; fr. the noise of the die striking the metal] **1 :** a stereotype or electrotype; *esp* **:** a single stamp of which a number are joined to form a plate for printing a whole sheet of stamps at once **2 a :** a trite or stereotyped phrase or expression; *also* **:** the idea expressed by it **b :** a hackneyed theme, plot, or situation in fiction or drama **:** an overworked idea or its expression in music or one of the other arts ⟨such photographic ~s as indicating change of seasons by the transition from snow to fruit in the orchards —John McCarten⟩
²cliché \"\ *adj* **:** HACKNEYED ⟨those desperate perceptions of our life which . . . have become so obvious and ~ that they seem to close for us the possibility of thought and imagination —Lionel Trilling⟩
cli·chéd \-ād\ *adj* **1 :** marked by or abounding in clichés ⟨the ~ pattern of her mind —Russell Thacher⟩ **2 :** CLICHÉ ⟨the somewhat ~ phrase, *horrified fascination* —Neville Braybrooke⟩
¹click \'klik\ *vb* -ED/-ING/-S *vt* **1 a :** to strike or move with a click **:** cause to click ⟨~ his heels together⟩ ⟨~*ed* down the lid of the card file —Emilie Glen⟩ **b :** to produce with clicks — usu. used with *out* ⟨~ out a rhythm on castanets⟩ ⟨~ out a message on a typewriter⟩ **2 :** to cut out (as parts of a shoe upper) by using a small knife or by operating a die-cutting machine ~ *vi* **1 a :** to make a click ⟨the latch ~*ed* as the door closed⟩ ⟨billiard balls ~*ed* in the next room⟩ **b :** to move with a click ⟨hearing her heels ~ across the kitchen tiles —Leslie Ford⟩ ⟨the camera adjustment lever ~*ed* into position⟩ **2 a :** to fit or agree exactly ⟨personal opinions have their value particularly when they ~ with experimental results —W.C. Allee⟩ **b :** to fit together **:** hit it off ⟨the thought of Dornford and Dinny and whether they would ~ —John Galsworthy⟩ ⟨explores the nature of the diversity of human beings and their compulsions, what makes them ~ as mates —David Tilden⟩ ⟨we were sitting on the . . . big town bridge trying to ~ with a few girls —Walter Macken⟩ **c :** to function or operate efficiently, smoothly, and successfully esp. in or as one of a team ⟨the platoon's teamwork was still ~*ing* —Mack Morriss⟩ **d :** SUCCEED; *esp* **:** to make a hit ⟨the selling aid that ~s . . . for any promotional effort —*Retailing Daily*⟩ ⟨a movie that ~s⟩ ⟨a bit player who finally ~*ed* in a first-rate Broadway play⟩ **3 :** FORGE *vi* 3 **4 :** to emphasize a musical beat by suddenly quickening the baton's motion toward the end of its stroke
²click \"\ *n* -S [prob. of imit. origin] **1 a :** a slight sharp noise (as that made by the cocking of a pistol or the latching of a door) ⟨the ~ of billiard balls⟩ **b** (1) **:** a sound that in some languages is a speech sound made by enclosing air between two stop articulations of the tongue, enlarging the enclosure to rarefy the air, and suddenly opening the enclosure **:** a velaric suction stop (2) *usu cap* **:** a language family of Africa including Khoisan, Sandawe, and Hatsa characterized by extensive employment of clicks **c :** the audible movement from one graduation to another in the rear sight of a firearm; *also* **:** such a graduation in a sight **2 :** a part (as a ratchet catch or lock tumbler) to control the movement of a mechanism or the movable part of a device: as **a :** DETENT **b :** a pawl esp. of small size **3** *dial Eng* **:** a sharp unexpected blow or rap **4** *of a horse* **:** the act of forging **5 :** a sudden flick of a conductor's baton marking an emphatic musical beat
³click \"\ *vb* -ED/-ING/-S [alter. of ¹*cleek*] *dial Brit* **:** CLUTCH, SEIZE, SNATCH
click beetle *n* [²*click*] **:** an adult beetle of the family Elateridae — called also *skipjack, snapping beetle*; compare WIREWORM
¹click-clack \'klik,klak\ *n* [reduplic. of ²*click*] **:** a succession of clicks or of alternating clicks and clacks ⟨the *click-clack* of the pendulum of the old grandfather clock⟩
²click-clack \"\ *vi* **:** to make a click-clack sound (as in walking) ⟨*click-clacked* out of the room⟩
click·er \'klikə(r)\ *n* -S [¹*click* + *-er*] **1 :** a horse that forges **2** *Brit* **:** PULLER-IN **3 :** one that operates a die-cutting machine which cuts small shapes from materials (as cloth, paper, cardboard, or leather) **4** *chiefly Brit* **:** the chargehand of a companionship or comparable group of compositors
¹click·et \'klikət\ *n* -S [ME *cliket*, fr. MF *cliquet*, fr. *cliquer* — more at CLICK] *now dial Eng* **:** LATCH, LATCHKEY
²clicket \"\ *vi* -ED/-ING/-S [origin unknown] **:** to be in heat **:** COPULATE — used chiefly of the fox or hare
click·ety-clack \¦klikəd·ē¦klak\ *or* **click·ety-click** \-klik\ *n* [alter. of ¹*click-clack*] **:** a rhythmic usu. fast click-clack ⟨the *clickety-click* of the wheels along the railroad track⟩ ⟨the *clickety-clack* of typewriters⟩
click hook *n* [³*click*] *dial Eng* **:** a large barbed hook for catching or landing fish
click·less \'kliklas\ *adj* **:** lacking a click
click off *vt* **1 :** to click out ⟨*click off* a message on the typewriter⟩ **2 :** to record usu. with clicks ⟨the speedometer *clicked off* the miles⟩ **3 :** to list or enumerate unhesitatingly or with unerring precision ⟨*clicked off* his facts and figures without a slip —E.P.Snow⟩
click stop *n* **:** a diaphragm setting device on a camera or enlarger for selecting desired apertures by means of a series of audible clicks
cli·das·tes \klī'da(,)stēz\ *n, cap* [NL, prob. irreg. fr. Gk *kleid-, kleis* key; akin to L *claudere* to shut — more at CLOSE] **:** a genus of large extinct No. American Cretaceous fish-eating marine lizards in many respects resembling the recent monitors — compare MOSASAURUS, VARANIDAE
cli·ent \'klīənt\ *n* -S [ME, fr. MF & L; MF *client*, fr. L *client-, cliens* client, dependent, lit., one who has someone to lean on; akin to ON *hlīta* to be satisfied with, L *clinare* to lean — more at LEAN] **1 :** a person under the protection of another **:** VASSAL, DEPENDENT ⟨an impecunious ~ and favored dinner companion of Lorenzo the Magnificent and his court —G.C. Sellery⟩ ⟨a first-rate power, able to defend her political ~s in central and eastern Europe —W.W.Kulski⟩; *esp* **:** a dependent (as a freed slave or one of the plebs) in ancient Rome who was obliged to perform certain services in return for the protection he received from his patrician patron **2 a :** a person who engages the professional advice or services of another ⟨results . . . discouraging to the ~ as well as the veterinarian —O.V. Brumley⟩ ⟨professional relationship of architect and ~⟩; *specif* **:** a person who consults or engages the services of a legal advisor **b :** PATRON, CUSTOMER ⟨hotel ~s⟩ ⟨the single ~ examining the secondhand books on the stand outside the paper shop —Kay Boyle⟩ **c :** a person served by or utilizing the services of a social agency or a public institution ⟨one set of laws for ~s of social agencies and another for the rest of our citizens —Jane Rinck⟩ ⟨relief and old-age ~s —*N. Y. State Legislative Committee on Problems of the Aging*⟩ ⟨was spreading for the benefit of new ~s —F.L.Paxson⟩
cli·ent·age \-tij\ *n* -S **1 :** a body of clients **:** CLIENTELE ⟨the ~ of a Roman nobleman⟩ ⟨one of those little shops . . . where they sell such smart things so cheaply to a ~ of minor actresses and cocottes —Aldous Huxley⟩ **2 :** the relationship of a client to a patron or benefactor ⟨the specific tie which bound the herdsmen to their leader was in the nature of ~ —Kalervo Oberg⟩
cli·en·tal \(')klī¦entᵊl, 'klīən-\ *adj* **:** of or relating to a client ⟨I sat down in the ~ chair —Charles Dickens⟩
cli·en·tele \¦klīən·¦tel, -lēən- *also* -lē,än-\ *n* -S [F *clientèle*, fr. L *clientela*, fr. *client-, cliens*] **1** *archaic* **:** the quality or state of being a client (sense 1) **:** the institution of clientship **2 :** a body of clients ⟨the ~ of an advertising agency⟩ ⟨the theater's regular ~⟩ ⟨the ~ of our colleges —R.W.Livingstone⟩ ⟨a large city hospital ~ —*Jour. Amer. Med. Assoc.*⟩
cli·ent·less \'klīəntləs\ *adj* **:** having no clients
cli·ent·ry \'klīəntrē\ *n* -ES *archaic* **:** CLIENTELE
clies *pl of* CLY
¹cliff \'klif\ *n* -S [ME *clif*, fr. OE; akin to OS *klif*, OHG *klep*, ON *klif*, OE *clīfan, clifian* to adhere to — more at CLEAVE] **1 :** a very steep, perpendicular, or overhanging face of rock, earth, or glacial ice of considerable height **:** PRECIPICE — see FAULT-LINE SCARP, FAULT SCARP, SCARP; compare ESCARPMENT **2** *Brit* **:** a steep slope or hill **:** CLEVE
²cliff \"\ *vb* -ED/-ING/-S **:** to erode so as to form a cliff ⟨the shores of both mainland and continental islands are ~*ed* and drowned —*Jour. of Geol.*⟩ ⟨postglacial ~*ing* —F.P.Shepard⟩
cliff brake *n* **:** a fern of the genus *Pellaea* (esp. *P. atropurpurea*) growing usu. on cliffs and walls
cliff dweller *n* **1** *often cap C&D* **a :** one of the people of the Anasazi culture of the American southwest who erected their dwellings on rock ledges or in the recesses of canyon walls and cliffs **b :** a member of any cliff-dwelling people **2 :** a person who lives in a large usu. metropolitan apartment building ⟨the *cliff dwellers* of Chicago —M.D.Geismar⟩ — **cliff dwelling** *n*
cliffed \-ft\ *adj* **:** consisting of or marked by the presence of a cliff ⟨a commanding scarp . . . , ~ at the top —P.E.James⟩
cliff-green \'=,=\ *n* **:** MOUNTAIN LOVER
cliff-hang \'=,=\ *vi* **:** to end an installment of a cliff-hanger with a suspenseful usu. melodramatic unresolved conflict designed to entice the audience to read or view the succeeding installment to discover the resolution of the conflict ⟨to forbid *cliff-hanging* in children's radio serials⟩
cliff-hanger \'=,==\ *n* **1 :** an adventure serial or melodrama; *esp* **:** one presented in installments each of which ends in suspense ⟨*cliff-hangers* on radio⟩ **2 :** a contest whose outcome is in doubt up to the very end ⟨the election was a *cliff-hanger*⟩
cliff·less \'kliflas\ *adj* **:** lacking cliffs
cliff rose *n* **1 :** a thrift (*Armeria maritima*) **2 :** a small evergreen shrub (*Cowania stansburiana*) of the family Rosaceae common on the desert ranges of the southern U.S. and Mexico, useful as a browse plant, and characterized by briliant golden-yellow flowers followed by clusters of achenes with long feathery tails — called also *quinine bush*
cliffside \'=,=\ *n* **:** the steep side of a cliff or of any abrupt natural incline of considerable size ⟨picking his way up the dangerous ~⟩ ⟨~ caves⟩
cliff swallow *n* **:** any of a number of chiefly No. American swallows (genus *Petrochelidon*) that build their bottlelike nests of mud against cliffs or under eaves — called also *eaves swallow*
cliffy \-fē\ *adj* -ER/-EST **:** characterized by or abounding in cliffs **:** STEEP, CRAGGY ⟨a ~ shore⟩
¹clift \'klift\ *archaic or dial var of* CLEFT
²clift \"\ *n* -S [ME, alter. (influenced by *clift* cleft) of *clif* cliff — more at CLIFF, CLEFT] *now chiefly dial* **:** CLIFF
clif·ton·ite \'kliftə,nīt\ *n* -S [Robert B. *Clifton* †1921 Eng. physicist + E *-ite*] **:** carbon found in minute cubic crystals in meteoric iron
clifty \'kliftē\ *adj* [²*clift* + *-y*] **:** CLIFFY
clim *dial past of* CLIMB
cli·ma·ci·um \klī'mās(h)ēəm\ *n, cap* [NL, fr. Gk *klimak-, klimax* ladder + NL *-ium* — more at CLIMAX] **:** a small genus (the type of the family Climaciaceae) of treelike branching true mosses — compare BRYALES; see TREE MOSS
climacter *n* -S [L, fr. Gk *klimaktēr*, lit., rung of a ladder, fr. *klimak-, klimax* ladder] *obs* **:** a climacteric period
cli·mac·te·ri·al \¦klī,mak¦tirēəl\ *adj* [NL *climacterium* + E *-al*] **:** relating to or involving the climacterium
¹cli·mac·ter·ic \(')klī¦maktərik *also* ¦klī,mak¦terik\ *also* **cli·mac·ter·i·cal** \¦=,=¦terəkəl\ *adj* [*climacteric* fr. L *climactericus*, fr. Gk *klimaktērikos*, fr. *klimaktēr*; *climacterical* fr. L *climactericus* + E *-al*] **1 :** constituting or relating to a climacteric (as a climacterium) **2 :** CRITICAL, CRUCIAL, CLIMACTIC
²climacteric \"\ *n* -S **1 a :** a major turning point or critical stage in a person's life ⟨the first ~ of his maturity —W.H. Gardner⟩; *also* **:** a decisive or critical period or stage in any course, career, or developmental process ⟨the Middle Ages advanced to their ~ —H.O.Taylor⟩ **b :** MENOPAUSE; *also* **:** a corresponding phenomenon of reduced sexual activity and competence in the male **2 :** an individual passing through a climacteric (as a climacterium) **3 :** the maximum to which the respiratory rate of fruit rises just prior to full ripening and from which it falls during senescence
cli·mac·te·ri·um \,=,='tirēəm\ *n, pl* **climacte·ria** \-ēə\ [NL, fr. L *climacter* climacteric + NL *-ium*] **:** the bodily and psychic changes (as in reproductive and endocrine function) accompanying the transition from middle life to old age; *specif* **:** menopause and the bodily and mental changes that accompany it
cli·mac·tic \(')klī¦maktik, -tēk *sometimes* klə'm-\ *also* **cli·mac·ti·cal** \-təkəl, -ēk-\ *adj* [fr. *climax*, after such pairs as E *syntax: syntactic, syntactical*] **:** of, being, or relating to a climax **:** forming or involving a climax ⟨a year of great decisions and ~ events ending in triumph —*Saturday Rev.*⟩ ⟨the ~ stunt of a time of marvelous stunts —John Lardner⟩ ⟨a story, witty and ~⟩ ⟨the ~ assault of outraged creditors . . . upon the beleaguered man —Arthur Knight⟩ — **cli·mac·ti·cal·ly** \-tək(ə)lē, -ēk-, -li\ *adv*
climagraph *var of* CLIMOGRAPH
¹cli·mate \'klīmət, *usu* -d·+V\ *n* -S [ME *climat*, fr. MF *climat*, fr. LL *climat-, clima*, fr. Gk *klimat-, klima* inclination, the supposed slope of the earth toward the pole, region, clime, fr.

klinein to slope, incline — more at LEAN] **1** *in ancient and old geography* **a :** any of seven astrological belts or zones of the earth each presided over by a planet **b :** any of the 30 zones (24 between the equator and either polar circle) into which the surface of the earth was divided according to the successive increase of half an hour in the length of the longest day within successive zones **2 :** a region of the earth esp. considered with reference to its climatic conditions : CLIME ⟨his physician advised moving to another ~⟩ **3 a :** the average course or condition of the weather at a particular place over a period of many years as exhibited in absolute extremes, means, and frequencies of given departures from these means, of temperature, wind velocity, precipitation, and other weather elements **b :** the prevailing set of conditions (as of temperature, humidity, or freshness of atmosphere) in any place ⟨the ~ maintained inside our houses —E.L.Ullman⟩ ⟨the ~ in the vault has to be carefully controlled —Joseph Wechsberg⟩ **4 :** the prevailing temper, outlook, set of attitudes, or environmental conditions (as in regard to a particular activity or concern) characterizing a group or period : MILIEU ⟨a financial ~ favorable to the nation's economic health —*Economist*⟩ ⟨a petty and bickering office ~⟩ ⟨the 19th century ~ of opinion⟩ ⟨a ~ of fear⟩

²climate *vi* -ED/-ING/-S *obs* **:** to dwell or visit for a period in a particular climate or region

cli·mat·ic \(ˈ)klīˈmad·ik, -atik, -ēk *sometimes* kləˈm-\ *also* **cli·mat·i·cal** \-ə̇kəl, -ēk-\ *or* **cli·mat·al** \ˈklīmə̇d·ᵊl, -mə̇tᵊl\ *adj* **1 :** of or relating to a climate ⟨a ~ position more or less similar to that . . . of the Gulf Coast of Texas —P.E.James⟩ ⟨~ variations⟩ ⟨sensitive to the ~ changes of feeling —V.S. Pritchett⟩ **2** *of ecological formations* **:** resulting from climatic differences ⟨forests that had reverted to the ~ type⟩ — opposed to *edaphic* — **cli·mat·i·cal·ly** \(ˈ)klīˈmad·ə̇k(ə)lē, -atə̇k-, -ēk-, -li *sometimes* kləˈm-\ *adv*

climatic climax *n* **1 :** CLIMAX 4 **2 :** the ecological climax of those possible in a particular climatic area whose stability is directly due to the influence of climate — compare EDAPHIC CLIMAX

cli·ma·ti·us \klīˈmāsh(ē)əs\ *n, cap* [NL, fr. Gk *klimat-, klima* slope — more at CLIMATE] **:** a genus of small Devonian acanthodian fishes (family Diplacanthidae) — see DIPLACANTHUS

cli·ma·tize \ˈklīmə,tīz\ *vb* -ED/-ING/-S [by shortening] **:** ACCLIMATIZE

climatograph *var of* CLIMOGRAPH

cli·ma·tog·ra·pher \ˌklīməˈtägrəfə(r)\ *n* -S **:** a specialist in climatography

cli·ma·to·graph·i·cal \ˌklīmə̇d·əˌgrafə̇kəl, (ˈ)klīˌmad·-\ *adj* **:** of or relating to climatography

cli·ma·tog·ra·phy \ˌklīməˈtägrəfē\ *n* -ES [ISV *climat-* (fr. LL *climat-, clima* climate) + *-o-* + *-graphy*] **:** the description or study of climates

cli·ma·to·log·i·cal \ˌklīmə̇d·ᵊlˈäjə̇kəl, (ˈ)klīˌmad·-\ *also* **cli·ma·to·log·ic** \-jik\ *adj* **:** relating to climatology

cli·ma·tol·o·gist \ˌkliməˈtäləjə̇st\ *n* -S **:** a specialist in climatology

cli·ma·tol·o·gy \-jē,-ji\ *n* -ES [¹*climate* + *-o-* + *-logy*] **:** the science that deals with climates and investigates their phenomena and causes

cli·ma·tom·e·ter \-ˈtämə̇d·ə(r)\ *n* -S [¹*climate* + *-o-* + *-meter*] **:** an instrument for measuring the sensible temperature of the atmosphere

cli·ma·to·physiological \ˌklīmə,tō+\ *adj* [¹*climate* + *-o-* + *physiological*] **:** of, relating to, or caused by interaction of climatic and physiologic factors

cli·ma·to·therapy \ˌklīmə̇d·ō+\ *n* [ISV *climat-* (fr. LL *climat-, clima* climate) + *-o-* + *therapy*] **:** treatment of disease by means of residence in a suitable climate

cli·ma·ture \ˈklīmə,chu̇(ə)r\ *n* -S [*climate* + *-ure* (as in *temperature*)] **1** *obs* **:** REGION **2 :** climatic conditions **:** CLIMATE

cli·ma·type \ˈklīmə,tīp\ *n* [LL *clima* climate + E *type* — more at CLIMATE] **:** a climatic ecotype ⟨in grasses . . . there are definite ~*s* which each characterize a particular climatic zone —Julian Huxley⟩

¹cli·max \ˈklī,maks\ *n* -ES [L, fr. Gk *klimax* ladder, fr. *klinein* to lean — more at LEAN] **1 :** a figure of speech in which a number of phrases or sentences are arranged in ascending order of rhetorical forcefulness **2 a :** the last and highest member of a rhetorical climax **b :** the highest point or one of a number of high points (as of significance, intensity, or achievements) in anything conceived as growing, developing, or unfolding ⟨this group of brilliant paintings marks the ~ of the artist's career⟩ ⟨the revolutionary upsurge reached its ~ in bitter street fighting⟩ **c :** the point of highest dramatic tension or a major turning point in the action of a play, story, or other literary composition **d :** ORGASM **e :** CLIMACTERIUM, MENOPAUSE **f :** the focus or center of interest in an artistic (as architectural) composition **3 :** the peak or point of maximum development of a cultural tradition in a given area and period of time **4 :** the relatively stable stage or community attained by an available population of organisms in a given environment, often constituting the culminating development in a natural succession or being one of the transitory stable states through which many populations pass before attaining such culminating development — see CLIMATIC CLIMAX, DISCLIMAX, EDAPHIC CLIMAX, POSTCLIMAX, PRECLIMAX, SUBCLIMAX

²climax \"\ *vb* -ED/-ING/-ES *vi* **:** to come or ascend to a climax ⟨that decade which ~*ed* in 1912 was a time of tremendous change in our national life —W.A.White⟩ ⟨~*ing* in the hair-raising death of Rasputin —*Publisher's Weekly*⟩ ~ *vt* **:** to bring to a climax **:** provide a culminating event for ⟨he ~*ed* his school career . . . by winning the Barbados Scholarship —Gordon Bell⟩ ⟨scenic interest . . . is ~*ed* in the Goat Rocks Primitive Area —*Amer. Guide Series: Wash.*⟩ ⟨~*ing* bitter hardship, an epidemic took 156 of the 600 settlers —*Amer. Guide Series: Texas*⟩

climax basket *n* [*climax* "kind of plum", prob. fr. ¹*climax*] **:** a small oblong veneer basket with rounded ends, a solid-wood bottom, usu. a veneer or wire handle across the midpoint, and sometimes a cover

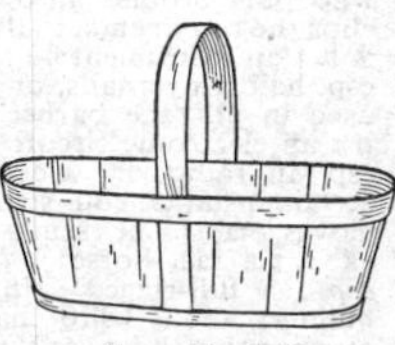
climax basket

¹climb \ˈklīm\ *vb* **climbed** \-md\ *or dial* **clim** \ˈklim\ *or now dial* **clomb** \ˈklōm\ *or chiefly Midland* **clum** \ˈkləm\ **climbed** *or dial* **clim** *or now dial* **clomb** *or chiefly Midland* **clum; climbing; climbs** [ME *climben*, fr. OE *climban;* akin to OHG *klimban,* ON *klembra* to clamber, OE *clamm* bond, fetter — more at CLAM] *vi* **1 a** (1) **:** to rise or go upward with gradual or continuous motion ⟨watching the smoke ~⟩ (2) **:** to gain altitude ⟨the airplane ~*ed* suddenly⟩ **b :** to increase gradually ⟨stock-market prices ~*ing* a little each day⟩ **c :** to slope upward **:** form an upward or rising grade **:** serve as way or means of going up or higher ⟨the road ~*s* steadily until . . . you are high up on the mountain —Norman Cousins⟩ ⟨a staircase, which ~*ed*, steep and slender, to the upper story —Ellen Glasgow⟩ **d :** to become situated on a rising grade ⟨pleasant middle-class houses ~*ing* up the hill —R.M.Lovett⟩ **2 a :** to go upwards, rise, or raise oneself esp. by grasping or clutching with the hands ⟨~*ed* up a steep hill⟩ ⟨~ aboard a car⟩ ⟨~*ed* upon her father's knee⟩ **b** *of a plant* **:** to ascend in growth by twining about or scrambling over a support or by the attachment thereto of tendrils or aerial roots **3 :** to rise or seek to rise in dignity, rank, or eminence **:** come to rate more highly or occupy a higher state ⟨from this humble beginning he ~*ed* to a position at the very top —J.M.England⟩ **4 :** to go about or down usu. by grasping, clinging, or holding with the hands to facilitate progress or ensure safety ⟨~ down a ladder⟩ ⟨~*ing* around in a haymow⟩ ⟨~ out on a limb⟩ **5 :** to get into or out of clothing or an article of dress typically with some haste or effort ⟨the firemen ~*ed* into their clothes⟩ ⟨the diver ~*ed* out of his heavy suit⟩ ~ *vt* **1 a :** to go or proceed upwards upon or along, to the top of, or over **:** get to the top of or go over typically with some effort ⟨~ a hill⟩ ⟨energy spent ~*ing* stairs⟩ ⟨the car ~*ed* the long hill⟩ **b :** to reach by climbing ⟨~ the summit of a hill⟩ **2 :** to draw or pull oneself up, over, or to the top of by using hands and feet ⟨~ a ladder⟩ ⟨children ~*ing* the tree⟩ **3 :** to ascend through or to the higher parts of ⟨the sun ~*ing* the eastern sky⟩ **4 :** to grow up or creep up to the top of typically by twisting, twining, or cleaving ⟨ivy ~*ing* the western wall⟩ **5 :** to occupy or be situated on the ascending slope of ⟨the battlemented town . . . ~*s* a high hill crowned by the cathedral —Ellery Sedgwick⟩ **6 :** to cause (an aircraft) to climb **syn** see ASCEND

²climb \"\ *n* -S **1 :** a place (as a steep incline) where climbing is necessary to progress; *esp* **:** a trail up a mountain designed or mapped out for mountain climbers ⟨the approach to the Westmore mountain ~ —*Amer. Guide Series: Vt.*⟩ ⟨the commandos . . . began to rename many of the ~*s* —R.W.Clark⟩ **2 :** the act or an instance of climbing **:** ascent by climbing ⟨the slow ~ up the steep hills —E.H.Collis⟩ ⟨farm prices showed an upward ~⟩ ⟨an airplane with a rapid rate of ~⟩ ⟨its program includes several mountain ~*s* —*Bull. of Bates Coll.*⟩

climb·able \ˈklīməbəl\ *adj* **:** capable of being climbed ⟨some thought the mountain was not ~⟩

climb down *vi* **:** to retreat from a position previously taken ⟨after taking a bold stand on foreign policy, the ambassador *climbed down* at the first sign of opposition⟩

climb-down \ˈ=,=\ *n* -S **:** the act or an instance of climbing down ⟨a last minute *climb-down* by the government⟩

climb·er \ˈklīmə(r)\ *n* -S [ME, fr. *climben* + *-er*] **1 :** one that climbs: as **a :** one that cuts limbs and tops from tall trees chosen for use as spar trees — called also *topper* **b :** RIGGER **c :** HIGH RIGGER **d :** one that climbs about scaffolding to assist in construction work **e :** SOCIAL CLIMBER **f :** a vine or twining plant that readily grows up a support (as a trellis) or over other plants **2 :** a device to assist one in climbing esp. up steep places: as **a :** CLIMBING IRON **b :** a strip of material (as sealskin or mohair) attachable to the running surface of a ski to prevent sliding backward while going uphill — called also *creeper* **3 :** JUNGLE GYM

climbing bindweed *or* **climbing buckwheat** *n* **:** BLACK BINDWEED 1

climbing-boy \ˈ==,=\ *n* **:** a small child formerly employed by a chimney sweep to ascend and clean flues

climbing cutworm *n* **:** any of various cutworms that feed on the foliage of trees and other plants

climbing false buckwheat *n* **:** a slender twining annual (*Polygonum scandens*) characterized esp. by thin scarious brown or rosy wings on the mature fruiting calyx

climbing fern *n* **:** any of several ferns of the genus *Lygodium; esp* **:** a delicate No. American fern (*L. palmatum*) having a twining stem, palmately lobed sterile fronds, and sporiferous fronds that are much forked, form a terminal panicle, and are highly valued for decoration — called also *creeping fern*

climbing fig *n* **:** CREEPING FIG

climbing fumitory *n* **:** an herbaceous vine (*Adlumia fungosa*) having feathery leaves and white or pinkish flowers

climbing hardfern *n* **:** a high-climbing New Zealand fern (*Lomaria filiformis*) of the family Polypodiaceae with upper pinnae that are often two feet long

climbing hempweed *also* **climbing boneset** *n* **:** a plant of the genus *Mikania; esp* **:** an herb (*M. scandens*) that climbs up trees

climbing hydrangea *n* **1 :** a climbing vine (*Schizophragma hydrangeoides*) of the family Saxifragaceae having flowers with only one style, the sterile marginal flowers in each cluster having only one sepal **2 :** any of certain climbing plants of the related genus *Hydrangea* (esp. *H. petiolaris*)

climbing iron *n* **:** any of various steel frameworks with spikes attached that may be affixed to one's boots for climbing trees, poles, or snow-covered mountains — see CRAMPON 2; compare CREEPER 5

climbing lily *n* **:** GLORIOSA 2

climbing maidenhair *n* **:** a climbing fern (*Lygodium scandens*) — compare NITO

climbing milkweed *n* **:** SAND VINE

climbing nightshade *n* **:** BITTERSWEET 2a

climbing onion *n* **:** a much-branched leafless twining southern African herb (*Bowiea volubilis*) of the family Liliaceae sometimes cultivated as an ornamental for its bright green stems that arise from large aboveground bulbs

climbing perch *n* **:** a small perchlike Indian fish (*Anabas scandens*) that has part of the gill apparatus modified into leaflike expansions for the breathing of air, often travels overland by means of its spiny projecting fin rays, and is said to climb trees

climbing rope *n* **:** a rope used in mountain climbing

climbing rose *n* **:** any of numerous rather strong-growing garden roses that produce long flexible canes by which they cling to and scramble over any available support — see RAMBLER 2

climbing sumac *n* **:** POISON IVY 1

climbing tea rose *n* **:** any of certain climbing garden roses derived from the tea rose

climb milling *n* **:** milling in which the cutting motion of the tool is in the same direction as the feeding direction of the work — called also *down milling;* compare UPCUT

climbs *pres 3d sing of* CLIMB, *pl of* CLIMB

clime \ˈklīm\ *n* -S [L *clima* — more at CLIMATE] **:** CLIMATE

cli·mo·graph \ˈklīmə,graf\ *also* **cli·mat·o·graph** \klīˈmad·ə-\ *or* **cli·ma·graph** \ˈklīmə,graf\ *n* -S [*climo-* or *climato-* (fr. *climate*) + *-graph*] **:** a graphic representation of the relation of two climatic elements (as temperature and humidity) plotted at monthly intervals throughout the year — **cli·mo·graph·ic** \ˌklīməˈgrafik\ *adj* — **cli·mo·graph·i·cal·ly** \-fə̇k(ə)lē\ *adv*

clin- *or* **clino-** *comb form* [NL, fr. Gk *klin-, klino-,* fr. *klinē* couch; akin to Gk *klinein* to lean — more at LEAN] **1 :** bed ⟨*clinium*⟩ ⟨*clinoid*⟩ **2 :** lean **:** slant ⟨*clinochlore*⟩ ⟨*clinometer*⟩ **3 :** decline ⟨*clinology*⟩ **4** *clino-, mineralogy* **:** monoclinic

clin *abbr* clinical

clin·al \ˈklīnᵊl\ *adj* [*cline* + *-al*] **:** of or relating to a cline — **clin·al·ly** \-nᵊlē\ *adv*

-cli·nal \ˌklīnᵊl\ *adj comb form or n comb form* [ISV *-clin-* (fr. Gk *-klinēs* leaning, fr. *klinein* to lean) + *-al*] **1 :** sloping **:** slope ⟨*centroclinal*⟩ **2 :** ²-CLINOUS ⟨*matroclinal*⟩

cli·na·men \klīˈnāmən\ *n, pl* **clinam·i·na** \-ˈnamənə\ [L, fr. *clinare* to bend — more at LEAN] **:** TURN, BIAS, TWIST

cli·nan·dri·um \klīˈnandrēəm\ *n, pl* **clinan·dria** \-ēə\ [NL, fr. *clin-* + *andr-* + *-ium*] **:** a cavity or area in which the anther is situated on the column in flowers of the Orchidaceae

¹clinch \ˈklinch\ *vb* -ED/-ING/-ES [prob. alter. of ¹*clench*] *vt* **1 a :** to turn over or flatten the protruding pointed end of (a driven nail) in order to secure; *also* **:** to treat (a screw, bolt, or rivet) in a similar way **b :** to fasten by means of a nail, bolt, or similar article treated in this way ⟨~ two planks together⟩ **c :** to fasten firmly in a manner resembling this way or as if in this way ⟨this new method takes regular flat stitching wire . . . then drives and ~*es* the stitch⟩ ⟨~*ed* their hold⟩ **2 :** CLENCH 2 ⟨he spoke between his ~*ed* teeth —W.F.Davis⟩ **3 a :** to settle or make final, irrefutable, definite, or beyond dispute ⟨~ an argument⟩ ⟨~ a sale⟩ ⟨the rain ~*ed* the matter — we would have to stay indoors⟩ ⟨~ a bargain⟩ ⟨the many laboratory tests which finally ~*ed* his suspicions —*Brit. Book News*⟩ **b :** to secure or gain conclusively or beyond question **:** WIN ⟨~ a basketball title⟩ ⟨~ the governorship⟩ **4 :** to fasten (as a rope) by means of a clinch ~ *vi* **1 a :** to grasp and struggle at close quarters (as in wrestling) **b :** to hold an opponent (as in boxing) at close quarters (as by the arms or around the waist) with one or both arms so that no blows or only blows at short range can be exchanged ⟨after a furious trading of punches, the fighters ~*ed*⟩ **c** *slang* **:** to embrace esp. passionately ⟨lovers about to ~ —Bernard Hollowood⟩ **2 :** to hold fast or firmly — usu. used of a nail, bolt, or rivet that has been clinched ⟨if the floor is cement, clout nails will ~ automatically —Herbert Philippi⟩

²clinch \"\ *n* -ES **1 a :** a slip noose consisting of a small loop made with seizings in the end of a line around its own standing part — compare INSIDE CLINCH, OUTSIDE CLINCH **b :** the part of the rope fastened with this type of noose **2 a :** a fastening by means of a clinched nail, rivet, or bolt (as a rivet or bolt with the protruding end flattened down over a ring put around it for the purpose); *also* **:** the clinched part of a nail, bolt, or rivet **b :** a device that grips or fastens securely **:** CLAMP **3** *archaic* **:** a pun or play on words **4 :** the act or an instance of clinching (as an argument, case, sale, or title) **5 a :** a scuffle involving clinching between two persons **b :** the act or fact of clinching in boxing **c** *slang* **:** a passionate embrace

A B C D

clinch 1a: *A* simple clinch with two seizings, *B* inside clinch, *C* outside clinch, *D* double clinch

³clinch \"\ *or* **clinch·er** \-chə(r)\ *adj* [*clinch* fr. ²*clinch* (fastening); *clincher* fr. *clincher,* n., "fastener"] **:** LAP-JOINTED, LAPSTRAKE

clinch bolt *or* **clink bolt** *n* **:** RIVET

clinch-built \ˈ=,=\ *or* **clincher-built** \ˈ==,=\ *adj* **:** CLINKER-BUILT

clinch·er \ˈklinchə(r)\ *n* -S **:** one that clinches: as **a :** a decisive fact, argument, act, or remark ⟨the expense was the ~ that persuaded us to give up the enterprise⟩ **b :** a machine in commercial canning for positioning a lid loosely on the can prior to sealing it **c** *or* **clincher tire :** an automobile tire with flanged beads fitting into the wheel rim

clinching iron *n* **:** a tool for clinching nails

clinch·ing·ly *adv* **:** in a clinching manner

clinch joint *n* [³*clinch*] **:** LAP JOINT

clinch knot *n* **:** a knot used to tie a fishing leader or spinning line to a hook or fly and made by passing the end through the eye of the hook and twisting it around the standing part several times before pushing it back through the loop that holds the hook or fly

clinch nail *n* **:** a nail made of soft metal or so cut that the pointed end may be bent over easily for clinching

clinch nut *n* **:** a nut intended to be riveted into position in sheet metal

cline \ˈklīn\ *n* -S [Gk *klinein* to lean] **:** a graded series of characters (as morphological or physiological differences) exhibited by a species or other group of related organisms usu. along a line of environmental or geographic transition — see STEP-CLINE

-cline \ˌklīn\ *n comb form* -S [back-formation fr. *-clinal*] **1 :** slope ⟨anti*cline*⟩ **2 :** gradient **:** layer ⟨thermo*cline*⟩

cli·ner \ˈklīnə(r)\ *n* -S [origin unknown] *slang Austral* **:** GIRL

¹cling \ˈkliŋ\ *vb* **clung** \ˈkləŋ\ *also now dial* **clang** \ˈklaŋ, -aiŋ\ **clung; clinging; clings** [ME *clingen,* fr. OE *clingan;* akin to OHG *klunga* tangled ball of thread, ON *klungr* hip, haw, MIr *glacc* hand, Gk *gelgis* head of garlic, Skt *gr̥ñja* kind of garlic, L *galla* gallnut — more at GALL] *vi* **1 a :** to hold to each other cohesively and firmly **:** resist forces or influences acting to separate or disperse — often used with *together* ⟨the fused particles ~ together⟩ ⟨all our vessels *clung* together, as if for company —Kenneth Roberts⟩ **b :** to hold or hold on tightly or tenaciously (as with the hands or feet) and to resist pressure to separate or dislodge ⟨the sailors were obliged to ~, to prevent being washed away —Frederick Marryat⟩ **:** to adhere closely and firmly as if glued ⟨their soaked garments ~*ing* to the curves of their figures —J.C.Powys⟩ **c :** to become situated as if holding firmly and resisting pressure to dislodge or separate ⟨a bluff to which hotels and residences ~⟩ ⟨parched plants ~*ing* to the drought-stricken soil⟩ **2** *now dial Brit* **:** to become emaciated **:** SHRINK, SHRIVEL, WITHER **3 a :** to have a strong emotional attachment or dependence ⟨weak-willed and purposeless he *clung* to all who offered the least sign of sympathy⟩ **b** (1) **:** to have or continue to have strong emotional or intellectual loyalty or stubborn attachment or belief ⟨~*ing* pathetically to his worn-out creeds and dogmas⟩ ⟨*clung* to the hope that her son had survived⟩ (2) **:** to continue on a course of action or policy as if resisting efforts to interrupt or distract ⟨*clung* resolutely to his work —J.A.Froude⟩ (3) **:** to hold on tenaciously as if resisting dispossession ⟨~*ing* grimly to his few wretched acres⟩ **c :** to remain or linger as if resisting complete dissipation or dispersal ⟨the odor of mignonette still *clung* to the room⟩ **:** remain habitually or continuously associated ⟨the nickname *clung* to him throughout his life⟩ **d :** to become retained and survive as a practice or belief ⟨this habit of saving . . . would ~ to her for the rest of her life —Ellen Glasgow⟩ ~ *vt* **1** *now dial Eng* **:** to stick (objects) together **:** cause to adhere **2** *obs* **:** to cause (as one's fingers) to hold tightly **syn** see ADHERE

²cling \"\ *n* -S **1 :** the act or an instance of clinging **:** ADHERENCE **2 :** CLINGSTONE

³cling \"\ *n* -S [prob. alter. of ²*clink*] **:** a sharp high metallic ringing sound ⟨the ~ of the coin as it fell on the stone floor⟩ ⟨the ~ of the busy till —John Prebble⟩

⁴cling \"\ *vi* -ED/-ING/-S **:** to make a cling ⟨the coin ~*ed* as it hit the stone floor⟩

cling-clang \ˈ=ˌ=\ *n* -S [³*cling* + *clang*] **:** a repeated metallic ringing sound (as of a bell) ⟨the buoys toll a slow *cling-clang* —D.C.Peattie⟩

clingfish \ˈ=,=\ *n* [¹*cling* + *fish*] **:** any of various fishes (as of the order Xenopterygii) having a sucker on the underside of the body by which they cling to objects (as stones)

cling·i·ness \ˈkliŋēnə̇s\ *n* -ES **:** the quality of being clingy ⟨the ~ of certain types of dress material⟩

cling·ing·ly *adv* **:** in a clinging manner

cling·ing·ness *n* -ES **:** CLINGINESS

cling·stone \ˈkliŋz,tōn, -ŋ,st-\ *n* -S [¹*cling* + *stone*] **:** a fruit (as a peach or plum) in which the flesh adheres strongly to the pit — compare FREESTONE

clingy \ˈkliŋē, -ŋi\ *adj, often* -ER/-EST [¹*cling* + *-y*] **:** having the quality of clinging ⟨a soft and ~ dress⟩

-clinia *pl of* -CLINIUM

clin·ic \ˈklinik, -nēk\ *n* -S [F *clinique,* fr. Gk *klinikē* medical practice at the sickbed, fr. *klinikos* physician who attends bedridden patients, fr. *klinikos,* adj., of a bed, fr. *klinē* bed, fr. *klinein* to lean, recline — more at LEAN] **1 a :** a session or class of medical instruction in a hospital held at the bedside of patients serving as case studies **b :** a group of selected patients presented with discussion before doctors (as at a convention) for purposes of instruction **2 :** a class, session, or group meeting devoted to the presentation, analysis, and treatment or solution of actual cases and concrete problems in some special field or discipline ⟨writing ~*s* for feeble students were established here and there —H.L.Creek⟩ ⟨holding ~*s* with businessmen on their troubles —W.B.Barnes⟩ ⟨a monthly fashion ~ —*Time*⟩ **3 a :** an institution connected with a hospital or medical school where diagnosis and treatment are made available to outpatients **b :** a form of group practice in which several physicians (as specialists) work in cooperative association

-clin·ic \ˈ==\ *adj comb form* [ISV *-clin-* (fr. Gk *-klinēs* leaning, bending, fr. *klinein* to lean) + *-ic*] **1 :** inclining **:** dipping ⟨iso*clinic*⟩ **2 :** having (a certain number of) oblique intersections of the axes ⟨mono*clinic*⟩ ⟨tri*clinic*⟩ **3 :** ²-CLINOUS ⟨matro*clinic*⟩

clin·i·cal \ˈklinə̇kəl, -nēk-\ *adj* [*clinic* + *-al*] **1 :** of, relating to, or conducted in or as if in a clinic (as a medical clinic): as **a :** involving or depending on direct observation of the living patient ⟨~ diagnosis⟩ ⟨~ examination⟩ **b :** observable by clinical inspection ⟨~ tuberculosis⟩ **c :** based on clinical observation ⟨~ picture⟩ ⟨~ treatment⟩ **d :** applying objective or standardized methods (as interviews and personality or intelligence tests) to the description, evaluation, and modification of human behavior ⟨~ psychology⟩ **2 a** *of a sacrament* **:** administered on a sickbed or deathbed ⟨~ baptism⟩ **b** *of a religious convert or conversion* **:** made on a sickbed or deathbed **3 :** analytical, detached, or coolly dispassionate (as in attitude, judgment, or description) ⟨the direct and unabashed appeal to the emotions . . . has been . . . diminished in favor of studied impersonality, a ~ detachment —Louis Untermeyer⟩ ⟨writes with intensity, insight, and a ~ sense of scrutiny —Catherine M. Brown⟩ ⟨a largely ~ analysis of the whole "loyalty program" —W.S.White⟩

clin·i·cal·ly \-nə̇k(ə)lē, -nēk-, -li\ *adv* **:** in a clinical manner ⟨classical literature also was subjected to ~ detailed examination —Gilbert Highet⟩ ⟨~portrayed —W.J.Schultz⟩

clinical clerk *n* **:** one who holds a clerkship (sense 3)

clinical thermometer *n* **:** a self-registering thermometer for determining the temperature of a human or animal body

cli·ni·cian \kləˈnishən\ *n* -S [F *clinicien,* fr. *clinique* clinic + *-ien* -ian] **:** one who directs, is closely allied with, or works in or

through a clinic or with clinical methods; *esp* : one qualified or engaged in the clinical practice of medicine, psychiatry, or psychology as distinguished from one specializing in laboratory or research techniques in the same fields
clinico- *comb form* [*clinical*] : clinical : clinical and ⟨*clinico*pathology⟩
clin·i·co·pathologic *also* **clin·i·co·pathological** \ˌklinə̇ˌkō+\ *adj* [*clinico-* + *pathologic, pathological*] : involving both clinical and pathologic factors, aspects, or approaches ⟨~ analysis⟩
clin·i·dae \ˈklinəˌdē\ *n pl, cap* [NL, fr. *Clinus,* type genus + *-idae*] : a family of viviparous blennies widely distributed in the intertidal zone of temperate and tropical seas and esp. abundant in California and southern Africa
-clinies *pl of* -CLINY
-cli·nism \ˈklīˌnizəm\ *n comb form* -s [ISV *-clin-* (fr. NL *-clinus*) + *-ism*] : the state of having the androecium and gynoecium in a (single or different) flower or (two separate) flowers ⟨*diclinism*⟩
-clin·i·um \ˈklinēəm\ *n comb form, pl* **-clinia** [NL, fr. Gk *klinion,* dim. of *klinē* couch — more at CLIN-] *bot* : receptacle ⟨*anthoclinium*⟩
¹**clink** \ˈkliŋk\ *vb* -ED/-ING/-s [ME *clinken,* prob. fr. MD, of imit. origin] *vi* **1 a** : to give out a slight sharp short metallic sound ⟨the coin ~*ed* as it hit the floor⟩ ⟨swished the highball gently around in his glass so that the ice ~*ed* —Leslie Charteris⟩ **b** : to move or act so that such a sound is given out (as by the heels) ⟨a man in hobnailed boots ~*ed* in at the door⟩ **2** *of words or verses, archaic* : RHYME, JINGLE **3** *dial Brit* : to move or throw oneself quickly and abruptly — usu. used with *down* ⟨~*ed* down beside her on the sofa⟩ or *off* ⟨~*ed off* . . . and jumped safe over hedge —Thomas Hardy⟩ ~ *vt* **1** : to cause to clink : strike together so as to produce a clinking sound ⟨~*ed* the coins in his purse —T.B.Costain⟩ **2** *archaic* : to make (words or lines) rhyme or jingle **3** *dial Brit* : to strike or beat sharply : SLAP
²**clink** \"\ *n* -s [ME, fr. *clinken,* v.] **1 a** : a clinking sound ⟨the ~ of glasses⟩ ⟨the ~ of coins⟩ **b** *chiefly Scot* : MONEY, CASH, COIN **2** : RHYME, ASSONANCE, JINGLE **3** : the sharp note of certain birds (as the stonechat) **4 a** *dial Brit* : a quick sharp blow : RAP **b** *dial* : INSTANT, MOMENT ⟨in a ~⟩
³**clink** \"\ *vt* -ED/-ING/-s [ME *clinken,* perh. fr. OE *-clencan* (in *beclencan* to hold fast) — more at CLENCH] *chiefly Scot* : to clinch esp. with nails or rivets
⁴**clink** \"\ *n* -s [fr. *Clink,* a prison in Southwark, borough of London, England, prob. fr. *Clink,* a part of the Manor of Southwark] *slang* : JAIL, PRISON : prison cell : GUARDHOUSE ⟨put in the ~ for petty thievery⟩ ⟨safeguards the reputation of the arresting policeman by riding with him when he takes the girl to the county ~ —G.S.Perry⟩
clink bolt *var of* CLINCH BOLT
clink-clank \ˈ=ˌ=\ *n* [²*clink* + *clank*] : a usu. repeated noise made up of generally alternating clinks and clanks
¹**clink·er** \ˈkliŋkə(r)\ *n* -s [earlier *klincard,* fr. obs. D *klinkaard* (now *klinker*), fr. *klinken* to clink, fr. MD *clinken;* fr. its resonance when struck — more at CLINK] **1** : DUTCH CLINKER **2 a** *or* **clinker brick** : a brick that has been overburned in the kiln **b** : a quantity of bricks of this kind **c** : stony matter vitrified or fused together (as that formed in a furnace from impurities in the coal or that ejected from a volcano) : SLAG; *also* : a lump of such matter — see CEMENT CLINKER **3** : a scale of iron oxide formed in forging
²**clinker** \"\ *vb* **clinkered; clinkered; clinkering** \-k(ə)riŋ\ **clinkers** *vt* **1** : to cause to form clinker ⟨a piece of ~*ed* coke⟩ **2** : to clear out the clinkers from ⟨fires were not ~*ed* as frequently as desirable —*Amer. Gas Jour.*⟩ ~ *vi* : to turn to clinker under heat
³**clinker** \"\ *n* -s [³*clink* + *-er*] : CLINCH
⁴**clinker** \"\ *n* -s [¹*clink* + *-er*] **1** : a shoemaker's nail usu. driven into the shoe sole as a protective stud **2** *Brit* : one that is first-rate or of extraordinary quality ⟨a good dog — a real well-bred ~⟩ **3** *slang* : a wrong note or a badly sounded note played or sung by a performer ⟨a couple of ~*s* and Sol would know that he was no clarinet player —Harold Sinclair⟩ **4** *slang* **a** : a serious mistake or error or notably inferior performance (as in music, drama, or sports) : BONER ⟨dropping the ball, a ~ that cost his team the game⟩ **b** : one that is regarded as a notable failure or of poor quality ⟨the play turned out to be a ~ —*Springfield (Mass.) Daily News*⟩
clinker beech *n* [¹*clinker;* fr. the color of the wood] : RED BIRCH 3
clinker boat *n* [³*clinker*] : a clinker-built boat
clinker-built \ˈ=ˌ=ˌ=\ *adj* [³*clinker*] : having the external planks (as on a boat) or plates (as on a boiler) lap-jointed : LAPSTRAKE — compare CARVEL-BUILT
clinkered *adj* [⁴*clinker* + *-ed*] : studded with nails (as clinkers) ⟨a climber, noisy in ~ boots —Wilfred Noyce⟩
clink·er·er \ˈkliŋkərə(r)\ *n* -s [²*clinker* + *-er*] : one whose occupation is the removing of clinkers from furnaces or gas generators
clink·ery \-k(ə)rē, -ri\ *adj* [¹*clinker* + *-y*] : consisting of or resembling clinkers ⟨the surfaces of volcanic lavas show the . . . smooth, ropy, and ~ structures —E.B.Branson & W.A. Tarr⟩
clink·ety-clank \ˌkliŋkəd·ēˈklaŋk, -aiŋk\ *n* [*clinkety* (alter. of ²*clink*) + *clank*] : a repeated usu. rhythmic clanking sound ⟨the *clinkety-clank* of a loose chain on an automobile wheel⟩
clink·ety-clink \-ˈkliŋk\ *n* [*clinkety* + ²*clink*] : a repeated usu. rhythmic clinking sound ⟨the *clinkety-clink* of coins in his pocket as he walked⟩ — compare CLINKETY-CLANK
clink·ing \ˈkliŋkiŋ\ *adv* [prob. fr. pres. part. of ¹*clink*] *slang* : VERY, EXTREMELY ⟨it's going to be a ~ fine day —John Buchan⟩
clinks *pres 3d sing of* CLINK, *pl of* CLINK
clink shell *n* [¹*clink*] : JINGLE SHELL
clinkstone \ˈ=ˌ=\ *n* -s [¹*clink* + *stone*] : PHONOLITE
clin·kum clan·kum \ˈkliŋkəmˈklaŋkəm, -laiŋkəm\ *n* [alter. of *clink-clank*] : a rhythmic clink-clank
clino- — see CLIN-
cli·no·axis \ˌklīnō+\ *n, pl* **clinoaxes** [*clin-* + *axis*] : the diagonal or lateral axis that makes an oblique angle with the vertical axis in the monoclinic system of crystallography
cli·no·chlore \ˌklīnəˌklō(ə)r\ *or* **cli·no·chlorite** \ˌ=ˌ=ˈklōrˌīt\ *n* -s [*clin-* + Gk *chlōros* pale green or E *chlorite* — more at YELLOW] : a mineral $(Mg,Fe,Al)_3(Si,Al)_2O_5(OH)_4$, of the chlorite group consisting of magnesium aluminum silicate usu. containing iron, and occurring in monoclinic pseudohexagonal crystals, in folia or scales, or massive and commonly of a green color — called also *ripidolite*
cli·no·clase \ˈklīnəˌklās, -āz\ *or* **cli·no·cla·site** \ˌklīnəˈklāˌsīt, klīˈnäkləˌ-\ *n* -s [*clinoclase* fr. G *klinoklas,* fr. *klin-* clin- + *-klas* -clase; *clinoclasite* fr. G *klinoklas* + E *-ite*] : a mineral $Cu_3(AsO_4)_2.3Cu(OH)_2$ consisting of basic copper arsenate and being dark green and translucent in prismatic crystals or massive
¹**cli·no·diagonal** \ˌklī(ˌ)nō+\ *n* -s [*clin-* + *diagonal*] : CLINOAXIS
²**clinodiagonal** \"\ *adj* [ISV *clin-* + *diagonal*] : being or belonging to a clinoaxis
cli·no·do·mat·ic \ˌklīnə(ˌ)dōˈmad·ik\ *adj* [*clinodome* + *-atic* (as in *prismatic*)] : being or belonging to a clinodome
cli·no·dome \ˈklīnəˌdōm\ *n* -s [ISV *clin-* + *dome*] : a dome in which the planes are parallel to the inclined axis in a monoclinic crystal — compare BRACHYDOME, MACRODOME, ORTHODOME
cli·no·enstatite \ˌ=(ˌ)=+\ *n* -s [ISV *clin-* + *enstatite;* orig. formed as G *klinoenstatit*] : a monoclinic magnesium-iron pyroxene with magnesium substantially in excess of iron; *specif* : the magnesium silicate $MgSiO_3$
cli·no·ferrosilite \ˌklī(ˌ)nō +\ *n* [*clin-* + *ferrosilite*] : a mineral $FeSiO_3$ consisting of iron silicate in the monoclinic form — compare FERROSILITE, ORTHOFERROSILITE
cli·no·graph \ˈklīnəˌgraf\ *n* -s [*clin-* + *-graph*] **1** : an instrument for ascertaining the deviation from the vertical of a bore-hole, well, or shaft **2** : a drawing instrument having two straight edges united by a hinge and capable of being set at any desired angle
cli·no·graph·ic \ˌ=ˌ=ˈgrafik\ *adj* [*clin-* + *-graphic*] : representing by so locating the object with reference to the plane of projection that no face will be projected as a line — used of a system of oblique projection that is used esp. for representing crystals
cli·no·he·dral \ˌklīnōˈhēdrəl\ *adj* [*clin-* + *-hedral*] : of or relating to a rare class of crystals of the monoclinic system having a plane but not an axis of symmetry
cli·no·he·drite \-ˈhēˌdrīt\ *also* **cli·no·edrite** \-ōˈē-\ *n* -s [ISV *clin-* + Gk *hedra* seat, base + ISV *-ite;* orig. formed as G *klinoëdrit* — more at SIT] : a calcium zinc silicate $CaZnSiO_3(OH)_2$ occurring in the form of colorless, white, or purplish monoclinic crystals (hardness 5.5, sp. gr. 3.33)
cli·no·humite \ˌklīnō+\ *n* [ISV *clin-* + *humite*] : a mineral $Mg_9Si_4O_{16}(F,OH)_2$ of the humite group crystallizing in the monoclinic system
cli·no·hypersthene \ˌklīnō +\ *n* [ISV *clin* + *hypersthene;* orig. formed as G *klinohypersthen*] : a monoclinic magnesium-iron pyroxene $(Mg,Fe)_2Si_2O_6$ common in certain basaltic rocks
cli·noid process \ˈklīˌnȯid-\ *n* [NL *clinoīdes,* fr. *clin-* + *-oīdes* -oid] : any of certain processes of the sphenoid bone
cli·no·lim·ni·on \ˌklīnəˈlimnēˌän\ *n, pl* **clinolim·nia** \-nēə\ [NL, fr. *clin-* + *-limnion*] : the upper layers of a hypolimnion in which the rate of warming falls off exponentially with depth — compare BATHYLIMNION
cli·nom·e·ter \klīˈnäməd·ə(r), klə̇-\ *n* -s [*clin-* + *-meter*] : any of various instruments (as the short telescope, bubble tube, and graduated vertical arc used by surveyors) for measuring or indicating angles of slope, elevation, or inclination (as the dip of geological beds or strata, the slope of an embankment or cutting, or the angle of elevation of a gun) — compare ABNEY LEVEL — **cli·nom·e·try** \-ə·trē\ *n* -ES
cli·no·metric \ˌ=ˌ=+\ *also* **cli·no·metrical** \ˌ=ˌ=+\ *adj* : of, relating to, or ascertained by a clinometer

clinometer: *1* clamp nut, *2* cross hairs, *3* eyepiece, *4* quadrant, *5* index

cli·no·pinacoid \ˌklīnō+\ *n* -s [ISV *clin-* + *pinacoid*] : a pinacoid whose planes are parallel to the inclined and vertical axes in a monoclinic crystal
cli·no·po·di·um \ˌklīnəˈpōdēəm\ [NL, fr. *clin-* + *-podium*] *syn of* SATUREIA
cli·no·stat \ˈklīnəˌstat\ *n* -s [ISV *clin-* + *-stat;* orig. formed as G *klinostat*] : an apparatus consisting of a slowly revolving disk usu. regulated by clockwork by means of which the action of external agents (as light and gravity) on the movements of growing plants mounted on the disk may be modified or eliminated by the change of direction
cli·nos·to·mum \klīˈnästəməm\ *n* [NL, fr. *clin-* + *-stomum*] **1** *cap* : a genus of digenetic trematodes occurring as adults in the mouth and esophagus of fish-eating birds and as metacercaria encysting in the muscles of various fishes and other aquatic vertebrates **2** *pl* **clinostoma** \-mə\ : any worm of the genus *Clinostomum; esp* : YELLOW GRUB
cli·no·ungemachite \ˌklīˌnō+\ *n* -s [*clin-* + *ungemachite*] : a rare mineral consisting of a sulfate of iron and alkalis and prob. dimorphous with ungemachite
¹**-cli·nous** \ˌklīnəs\ *adj comb form* [prob. fr. NL *-clinus,* fr. Gk *klinē* couch — more at CLIN-] : having the androecium and gynoecium in a (single or different) flower or (two separate) flowers ⟨di*clinous*⟩ ⟨hetero*clinous*⟩ ⟨mono*clinous*⟩
²**-clinous** \"\ *adj comb form* [ISV *-clin-* (fr. Gk *-klinēs* leaning, bending, fr. *klinein* to lean) + *-ous* — more at LEAN] : inherited from : having characteristics inherited from ⟨matro*clinous*⟩ ⟨patro*clinous*⟩
cli·no·zoisite \ˌklīnə+\ *n* -s [ISV *clin-* + *zoisite;* orig. formed as G *klinozoisit*] : a monoclinic mineral $Ca_2Al_3Si_3O_{12}(OH)$ consisting of a basic silicate of calcium and aluminum — compare ZOISITE
¹**clin·quant** \ˈkliŋkənt\ *adj* [MF, glittering, making a clinking sound, fr. pres. part. of *clinquer,* of imit. origin] : glittering esp. with gold decoration : SPANGLED : showily ornate
²**clinquant** \"\ *n* -s [F, short for *or clinquant,* gold in leaf or thin plates, lit., glittering or clinking gold] **1** : imitation gold leaf : TINSEL, DUTCH METAL **2** : something with a false and showy glitter
clint \ˈklint\ *n* -s [ME, perh. fr. MLG *klint* cliff, crag; akin to OSw *klinter* mountain top, ON *klettr* cliff, crag, L *galla* gallnut — more at GALL] **1** *chiefly Scot* : a hard or flinty rock : a rocky cliff : a projecting rock or ledge **2** *dial Eng* : a crevice or gully in limestone rocks
clin·to·nia \klinˈtōnēə\ *n* [NL, fr. DeWitt *Clinton* †1828 Am. statesman + NL *-ia*] **1** *cap* : a genus of perennial herbs (family Liliaceae) having yellow or white flowers on a naked stalk in early summer with the stalk sheathed below by the bases of two to four oblong or ovate leaves **2** -s : any plant of the genus *Clintonia* — called also *Clinton's lily*
clin·ton·ite \ˈklintᵊnˌīt\ *n* -s [DeWitt *Clinton* + E *-ite*] **1** : SEYBERTITE **2** : a group of micas that contain calcium instead of potassium — see BRITTLE MICA
-cli·ny \ˌklīnē, -ni\ *n comb form* -ES [ISV ²*-clinous* + *-y*] : fact or condition of having characteristics inherited from ⟨matro*cliny*⟩
clio \ˈklī(ˌ)ō\ *n, cap* [NL, fr. *Clio,* one of the Muses, also, a sea nymph, fr. L, fr. Gk *Kleiō,* one of the Muses, fr. *kleiein* to make famous; akin to Gk *klytos* famous — more at LOUD] : a genus of pteropod mollusks having an external symmetrical shell
cli·o·na \klīˈōnə\ *n, cap* [NL, irreg. fr. *Clio,* the Muse] : a genus (the type of the family Clionidae) of boring sponges
cli·o·ne \-ˌnē\ *n, cap* [NL, irreg. fr. *Clio*] : a genus (the type of the family Clionidae) of naked pelagic pteropod mollusks that are abundant in the Arctic ocean and that constitute a large part of the food of the Greenland whale
¹**cli·on·i·dae** \klīˈänəˌdē, -īˈōn-\ *n pl, cap* [NL, fr. *Cliona,* type genus + *-idae*] : a family (order Hadromerina) of small sponges with monaxon spicules that bore in shells and soft limestone rocks — see CLIONA
²**clionidae** \"\ *n pl, cap* [NL, fr. *Clione,* type genus + *-idae*] : a family of naked pteropod mollusks comprising forms intermediate in many characters between typical pteropods and nudibranchs
¹**clip** \ˈklip\ *vb* **clipped; clipped; clipping; clips** [ME *clippen,* fr. OE *clyppan;* akin to OHG *klāftra* fathom, ON *klafi* yoke, L *galla* gall on a tree, *gleba* clod, *globus* globe, Lith. *globti* to embrace — more at GALL] *vt* **1 a** *now dial Brit* : EMBRACE, HUG **b** : to encircle closely : ENCOMPASS ⟨a belt *clipped* her waist⟩ **2 a** : to hold in a tight grip : CLUTCH **b** : to clasp or fasten with a clip
²**clip** \"\ *n* -s [ME *clipp,* fr. *clippen* to clip (embrace)] : any of a number of devices which grip, clasp, or hook or with which one grips, clasps, or hooks: as **a** : GRAPPLING IRON **b** : an encircling often metal strap for connecting parts (as the metal strap of a whiffletree) **c** : the upward projection at the extreme front or at the side of a horseshoe over the margin of the hoof **d** : a holder or container (as for letters, bills, or music) consisting wholly or partly of a metal spring clamp **e** : a device to hold cartridges for charging the magazines of some rifles; *also* : a magazine from which ammunition is fed into the chamber of a firearm **f** : a device for confining the bottom of a trouser leg used esp. when riding a bicycle without a chain guard **g** : a device used to arrest bleeding from vessels or tissues during operations **h** : a wire resembling and applied like a staple and used to hold together wound margins or tissues or structures separated or opened during operations **i** : a metal device to connect up angle and T irons to rolled beams without drilling or bolting **j** : a clamplike wire or cable terminal for temporary electrical connections **k** : a piece of jewelry (as a pin or an earring) that is held in position by a spring clip

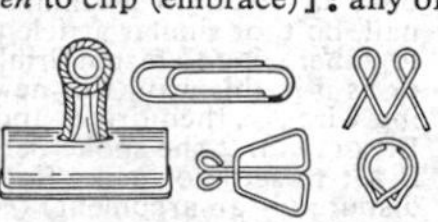
clips for paper

³**clip** \"\ *vb* **clipped; clipped** *also* **clipt; clipping; clips** [ME *clippen,* fr. ON *klippa*] *vt* **1 a** : to cut or cut off with or as if with shears ⟨~ a string in two⟩ ⟨~ the wool of a sheep⟩ ⟨~ her hair close⟩ ⟨~ an hour off traveling time⟩ **b** : to cut off the margins, ends, or a small portion of : PARE, TRIM ⟨~ rosebushes⟩ ⟨~ a coin⟩ ⟨~ a bird's wings⟩ : cut or snip off a part of the hair or surface growth of : SHEAR ⟨~ a sheep⟩ : MOW ⟨~ a lawn⟩ **c** (1) : EXCISE ⟨~ imperfect passages from the recording⟩ (2) : to cut items out of (as a newspaper) ⟨*clipped* a week's papers⟩ (3) : to cut out of esp. a publication **d** *of a radio or television circuit* : REJECT ⟨~ the instantaneous signals above or below a predetermined amplitude or frequency⟩ **2 a** : CURTAIL, DIMINISH ⟨*clipping* his power or authority⟩ ⟨worked to ~ the senator's influence⟩ **b** : to abbreviate (as a word or a customary sequence of sounds) in speech or writing in some way (as *ad* for *advertisement,* \ˈnesəsri\ for \ˈnesəˌseri\) ⟨the *clipped* "n'kyou" of the bus conductors and the ticket collectors —Richard Joseph⟩ ⟨*clipped* dialogue —D.M.Friedenberg⟩ ⟨to most unsophisticated users of the language "a short circuit" has nothing to do with either "short" or "circuit" (except insofar as the phrase itself has been *clipped* to "a short") —D.L.Bolinger⟩ **c** : REDUCE ⟨appliance stores . . . were *clipping* prices for people with ready cash —*Newsweek*⟩ ⟨the company *clipped* his wages two dollars a week⟩ **3 a** *slang* : to hit esp. with a short sharp blow ⟨*clipped* him with a left hook —Ernest Hemingway⟩ ⟨both got *clipped* by drunk drivers —*Pasadena (Calif.) Independent*⟩ **b** : to block (an opposing football player other than the ball-carrier) illegally by hitting with the body from behind **4** : to take money from unfairly or dishonestly esp. by charging exorbitant prices or by deception ⟨the nightclub *clipped* the diner for $23⟩ ⟨~ a patient by excessive charges for surgery⟩ **5** : to touch or go very close to esp. in moving past ⟨the bearings should just ~ the shaft —John Southward⟩ ⟨~ the edge of the cliff as closely as possible —F.W.Booth⟩ ~ *vi* **1** : to clip something ⟨remove a portion of it by *clipping*⟩ ⟨the record was made by a good deal of *clipping*⟩ **2 a** *archaic* : to move the wings swiftly : fly swiftly ⟨some falcon . . . ~*s* it down the wind —John Dryden⟩ **b** : to travel or pass rapidly ⟨a rock *clipped* through the air —Max Steele⟩ ⟨the half hour *clipped* along with pace and movement —Goodman Ace⟩ **3** : to block an opposing football player from behind — **clip one's wings** : to place an effectual check on the ambitions or efforts of : make powerless : RESTRAIN
⁴**clip** \"\ *n* -s **1 a clips** *pl, Scot* : SHEARS **b** : a 2-bladed instrument for cutting esp. the nails ⟨a wire ~⟩ **2** : something that is clipped: as **a** : a clipping esp. from a newspaper **b** : the product of a single shearing (as of sheep) **c** : a season's crop of wool of a sheep, a flock, or a region **d** : a section of filmed material (as a stock shot or a portion of a newsreel); *esp* : a fragment of film deleted during the editing of a motion picture **3** : an act of clipping : CUTTING, SHEARING **4** : a sharp blow esp. with the fist ⟨hit someone a ~ on the jaw⟩ **5** : a rapid gait or pace ⟨the train was snaking along at a brisk ~ —Robert Shaplen⟩ **6** : TIME : a single instance or occasion ⟨he charged $10 a ~⟩ — often used in the phrase *at a clip* ⟨to train 1000 workers at a ~⟩
clipboard \ˈ=ˌ=\ *n* [²*clip* + *board*] : a small portable rectangle of wood or other stiff backing material to one end of which is attached a spring clip for holding sheets of paper or a writing tablet securely
clip bond *n* [³*clip*] : a masonry wall bond formed by clipping off the inner corners of face bricks and used to unite diagonal bond with a face composed entirely of stretchers — see PLUMB BOND
¹**clip-clop** \(ˈ)klipˈkläp\ *n* [imit.] : the sound of or a sound suggesting the hoofbeats of a horse walking or trotting on a hard surface

clipboard

²**clip-clop** \"\ *vi* : to make a clip-clop (as in walking) ⟨*clip-clopping* in slippers across the floor —Elizabeth Bowen⟩
clipfish *var of* KLIPFISH
clip hook *n* : SISTER HOOK
clip joint *n* [³*clip*] *slang* **1** : a place of public entertainment (as a café or nightclub) that makes a practice of defrauding patrons (as by gross overcharging) **2** : a business establishment regarded as making a practice of overcharging
clip man *n* [⁴*clip*] : a clerk who keeps track of the sales on the tobacco auction floor and prepares a seller's bill covering each lot sold
clip off *vt* [³*clip*] : to make (as a fast run) or cover rapidly (as a distance) ⟨some of the fastest runs *clipped off* on the Ohio river —Frederick Way⟩ ⟨his long legs *clipped off* the distance⟩
clip on *vi* [¹*clip*] : to fasten on or be capable of being fastened by an attached clip ⟨the medal has no pin but merely *clips on* to the coat lapel⟩
clip-on \ˈ=ˌ=\ *adj* : that clips on ⟨a *clip-on* bow tie⟩ ⟨*clip-on* earrings⟩
clipped *adj* [fr. past part. of ³*clip*] : characterized by more fortis articulation, more frequent syncope, and often more rapid tempo than the usual speech in another dialect or language (as southern British speech in comparison with most U.S. speech, the former often having for example a full stop \t\ instead of a flap \d·\ for the *t* of *city,* a vigorously flapped consonantal sound instead of the more laxly articulated vocalic or vowellike sound for the *r* of *very,* an \i\ instead of the laxer \ə\ for the *e* of *naked,* and \ˌtri\ instead of unsyncopated \ˌterē\ for the *-tery* of *cemetery*) ⟨a ~ crackling elliptical French —Dorothy C. Fisher⟩
clipped gable *n* [³*clip*] : JERKINHEAD
¹**clip·per** \ˈklipə(r)\ *n* -s [ME *clippere,* fr. *clippen* to clip (cut) + *-ere* -er] **1** : one that clips esp. as a livelihood: as **a** : one that clips coins **b** : one that shears sheep **c** : any of various workers who cut fur from pelts, ravelings from cloth, or threads from garments or inspect stitching and other details of garments **d** : a worker who puts brooms into a machine that clips the rough ends to the desired length **2 a** : an instrument or tool for clipping esp. hair, fingernails, or toenails — usu. used in pl. ⟨the barber's ~*s* hummed⟩ **b** : an electronic circuit or part of one esp. in radio or television that clips certain instantaneous signals **3** : one that moves, runs, or scuds along swiftly: as **a** : a fast horse **b** *or* **clipper ship** : a fast sailing ship; *esp* : a full-rigged ship of a type developed by American builders about 1840 characterized by long slender lines, an overhanging bow, tall raking masts, and a large sail area **4** : a short sheep **5** : HELLGRAMITE

animal clipper

²**clipper** \"\ *n* -s [¹*clip* + *-er*] : one that grasps or clips on: as **a** : a mining worker who attaches receptacles to or detaches them from haulage ropes **b clippers** *pl* : SISTER HOOKS
³**clipper** \"\ *adj* [¹*clipper* (ship)] : CLIPPER-BUILT ⟨~ schooner⟩ ⟨~ packet⟩
clipper bow *n* [³*clipper*] : an overhanging ship's bow with a concave profile
clipper-built \ˈ=ˌ=ˌ=\ *adj* [³*clipper*] : built like a clipper esp. on slender fast lines
clipper man *n* [³*clip* + *-er*] **1** : one who feeds sheet steel from which a pipe is to be made into a machine that tapers and cups the end **2** : one who operates a power shear to cut veneer to size and to cut out imperfections
clip·pe·ty-clop \ˌklipəd·ēˈkläp\ *n* -s [imit.] : a rhythmic usu. repeated sound resembling a clip-clop but having one or two more beats in its basic rhythm ⟨the *clippety-clop* of the horse and hansom cab going by⟩
clip·pie \ˈklipē, -pi\ *n* -s [³*clip* "to punch a hole" + *-ie*] *slang Brit* : a woman conductor and ticket-taker on a bus
clipping *n* -s [fr. gerund of ³*clip*] : something that is clipped off or out of something : a piece severed or removed by clipping ⟨the barber swept up the hair ~*s*⟩; *esp* : an item clipped from a publication ⟨a newspaper ~⟩
clipping bureau *or* **clipping service** *n* : an organization or business that supplies to order clippings on any given subject cut from publications
clip·ping·ly *adv* : in a clipping manner
clips *pl of* CLIP, *pres 3d sing of* CLIP
clipsheet \ˈ=ˌ=\ *n* [³*clip* + *sheet;* fr. their being printed on

one side for convenience in cutting] **:** a sheet of newspaper material (as news items, features, interviews, fillers, or cartoons) issued by a publisher, publicity bureau, or other organization and usu. printed on only one side of the sheet to facilitate clipping and reprinting by newspapers and periodicals

clipt *past part of* CLIP

clique \'klēk, 'klik\ *n* -S [F, perh. fr. MF, latch, fr. *cliquer* to click; fr. the secrecy involved in some such groups] **:** a narrow exclusive circle or group of persons; *esp* **:** one held together by a presumed identity of interests, views, or purposes ⟨a number of ~*s* developed within the union leadership⟩ ⟨the court ~⟩ ⟨~*s* within the student body⟩

clique·less \-ləs\ *adj* **:** lacking a clique

cli·quey *also* **cli·quy** \'klēkē, 'klikē, -ki\ *adj, often* **cli·qui·er**; *usu* **cli·qui·est** **:** CLIQUISH 1

cli·quish *also* **clique·ish** \'klēkish, 'klik-, -kēsh\ *adj* **1 :** tending toward narrow exclusiveness or to form a clique ⟨~ attitudes developed among children coming from the fashionable west side⟩ ⟨newly arrived immigrants tend to be ~ for a while⟩ **2 :** marked by a tendency to divide into cliques ⟨ballet companies by reputation are . . . ~ —Al Hine⟩

cli·quism \'klē,kizəm, 'kli,k-\ *n* -S **:** the tendency to form cliques **:** a cliquish spirit

cli·se·ral \'klīsərəl\ *adj* **:** of, relating to, or typical of a clisere

cli·sere \'klī,si(ə)r\ *n* [*climate* + *sere* (cycle)] **:** the succession of ecological communities that results from climatic changes; *esp* **:** one preceding the reestablishment of a stable state following an intense climatic change (as the advance or recession of a major glaciation)

clish·ma·cla·ver \ˌklishməˈklāvər, ˌklēsh-\ *n* -S [Sc *clish* to gossip (of imit. origin) + connective *-ma-* + *claver*] *chiefly Scot* **:** idle talk **:** GOSSIP

-clisis — see -CLEISIS

clist- *or* **clisto-** — see CLEIST-

clistocarp *var of* CLEISTOCARP

clistogamy *var of* CLEISTOGAMY

clis·to·gas·tra \ˌklistəˈgastrə, ˌklis-\ *n pl, cap* [NL, fr. *cleist-* + *-gastra* (fr. Gk *gastr-, gastēr* belly)] **:** a suborder of Hymenoptera including the ants, typical wasps, and bees, all having a legless grub as larva and a constricted second abdominal segment that forms a narrow waist or petiole — compare CHALASTROGASTRA

clistogene *var of* CLEISTOGENE

clit \'klit\ *adj* [perh. fr. ME *clyht,* past part. of *clicchen*] *dial Eng* **:** HEAVY, DOUGHY, CAKED, STICKY

clitch \'klich\ *vb* -ED/-ING/-ES [ME *clicchen, clycchen,* fr. OE *clyccan* — more at CLUTCH] *vt* **1** *dial Eng* **:** to grasp tightly **:** CLUTCH **2** *dial Eng* **:** to cause to adhere **:** stick together ~ *vi, dial Eng* **:** to stick together **:** ADHERE

cli·tel·la·ta \ˌklīd·əlˈläd·ə, -lˈād·ə\ *n pl, cap* [NL, fr. *clitellum* + *-ata*] *in certain classifications* **:** a major division of annelid worms comprising the Oligochaeta and Hirudinea

cli·tel·late \klə'telət, (ˈ)klī;t-\ *adj* [NL *clitellum* + E *-ate*] **:** having a clitellum

cli·tel·lum \klə'teləm, klī-\ *n, pl* **clitel·la** \-elə\ [NL, modif. of L *clitellae* packsaddle; akin to Gk *klinein* to lean — more at LEAN] **:** a thickened glandular section of the body wall of certain annelid worms that functions as an accessory reproductive organ secreting a viscid material that forms the cocoon in which the eggs are deposited

clit·ic \'klid·ik\ *n or adj* [back-formation fr. *enclitic* & *proclitic*] **:** ENCLITIC, PROCLITIC

clit·i·on \'klid·ē,än\ *n, pl* **clit·ia** \-ēə\ [NL, fr. Gk *klitos* slope; akin to Gk *klinein* to lean] **:** the median point of the anterior margin of the clivus

cli·tocy·be \klī'täsə,bē\ *n, cap* [NL, fr. *clito-* (fr. Gk *klitos* slope) + MGk *kybē* head; perh. akin to Gk *kyphos* bent, humpbacked — more at CYPHELLA] **:** a genus of white-spored agarics (family Agaricaceae) with flat or funnel-shaped pileus and elastic stem — see JACK-O'-LANTERN

clit·o·ral \'kli|d·ərəl, 'klī|, |tərəl\ *or* **clit·o·ric** \'kli|d·ərik, 'klī|, |tərik\ *adj* [NL *clitoris* + E *-al* or *-ic*] **:** of or relating to the clitoris

cli·to·ria \klī'tōrēə, -tȯr-, klə'-\ *n, cap* [NL, fr. *clitoris* + *-ia;* — fr. the appearance of the flower] **:** a genus of herbs or woody vines (family Leguminosae) having pinnate leaves and large axillary flowers often in short racemes — see BUTTERFLY PEA

clitorid- *or* **clitorido-** *comb form* [NL, fr. *clitorid-, clitoris*] **:** clitoris ⟨*clitoridauxe*⟩ ⟨*clitoridotomy*⟩

clit·o·rid·e·an \ˌklid·əˈridēən, ˌklīd·-\ *adj* [*clitorid-* + *-ean*] **:** CLITORAL

clit·o·ri·dec·to·my \ˌklid·ərəˈdektəmē, ˌklīd·-\ *n* -ES [*clitorid-* + *-ectomy*] **:** excision of the clitoris **:** female circumcision

clit·o·ris \'kli|d·ərəs, 'klī|, |tərəs, klə'tōrəs, -'tȯr-\ *n* -ES [NL, fr. Gk *kleitoris*] **:** a small organ at the anterior or ventral part of the vulva homologous to the penis in the male

¹clit·ter \'klid·ə(r)\ *vi* -ED/-ING/-S [prob. alter. of *clatter*] **:** to make a frictional or rattling sound **:** stridulate esp. softly ⟨a cicada ~*ing*⟩ ⟨her breath made in her throat a little ~*ing* sound —F.M.Ford⟩

²clitter \'klitə(r)\ *n* -S *dial Eng* **:** a mass of loose stones ⟨tumbled ~*s* of granite⟩

cliv \'kliv\ *Scot var of* CLOOF

clivers *var of* CLEAVERS

cli·via \'klīvēə, -iv-\ *n, cap* [NL, fr. Lady Charlotte *Clive* †1866 duchess of Northumberland + NL *-ia*] **:** a small genus of fleshy southern African herbs (family Amaryllidaceae) having distichous leaves and large funnel-shaped flowers — see KAFIR LILY

cli·vis \'klīvəs, 'klēv-\ *n* -ES [ML] **:** a neume denoting two notes or tones with the first higher in pitch than the second

cli·vus \'klīvəs\ *n, pl* **cli·vi** \-ˌvī\ [NL, fr. L, hill; akin to Gk *klinein* to lean — more at LEAN] **:** the smooth sloping surface on the upper posterior part of the body of the sphenoid bone supporting the pons

clk *abbr* **1** clerk **2** clock

clkg *abbr* calking

clmg *abbr* claiming

clo·a·ca \klō'ākə\ *n, pl* **cloa·cae** \-'ā(ˌ)sē\ [L; akin to Gk *klyzein* to wash — more at CLYSTER] **1 :** ³SEWER 2 **2** [NL, fr. L] **a :** the common chamber into which the intestinal, urinary, and generative canals discharge in birds, reptiles, amphibians, and many fishes **b :** a chamber or passage having similar functions in invertebrates

clo·a·cal \klō'ākəl\ *adj* [L *cloacalis,* fr. *cloaca* + *-alis* -al] **1 :** constituting or carried by a cloaca **2 :** having a cloaca **3 :** concerned with or replete with obscenity or out-and-out indecency ⟨a writer with a ~ obsession⟩

cloacal gland *n* **:** any of several glands located in the cloaca of lower vertebrates: as **a :** one of the glands producing foul-smelling defensive secretions in certain snakes **b :** one of several glands believed to have hedonic function in many caudate amphibians

clo·ac·a·line \klō'akələn, -'āk-, -ˌlīn\ *adj* [*cloacal* + *-ine*] **:** CLOACAL

cloacal membrane *n, anat* **:** a plate of fused ectoderm and endoderm closing the fetal anus in the vertebrate embryo

cloaca max·i·ma \-'maksəmə\ *n, pl* **cloacae maxi·mae** \-ˌmē\ [L, largest sewer, fr. the main drain of ancient Rome] **:** a general repository of filth

clo·a·ci·nal \ˌklōə'sīnᵊl\ *adj* [*cloaca* + *-ine* + *-al*] **:** CLOACAL

clo·a·ci·tis \ˌ==ˈsīd·əs\ *n* -ES [NL, fr. *cloaca* + *-itis*] **:** a venereal disease of the common fowl occurring as an ulcerative inflammation of the vent and cloaca and having no known etiology but apparently transmitted by copulation — called also *vent gleet*

¹cloak \'klōk\ *n* -S [ME *cloke,* fr. ONF *cloque* cloak, bell, fr. ML *clocca* bell; fr. the bell-like shape — more at CLOCK] **1 :** a loose outer garment (as a cape or an overcoat) **2 :** something resembling or suggesting an outer garment: as **a :** a distinctive character or role ⟨laying aside the ~ of military commander⟩ ⟨a ~ of martyrdom had no appeal for the rebel leader⟩ **b :** an encompassing veil serving to exclude interruption or interference ⟨a ~ of secrecy around ships' movements⟩ ⟨draped himself in a ~ of heavy thoughtfulness —Hamilton Basso⟩ **c :** a deceptive pretense or disguise to screen an unpalatable fact, devious action, or ulterior design ⟨use by the unscrupulous of watchwords of western democracy as a ~⟩ ⟨onslaughts of a populace using liberty as a ~ for an attack upon order and stability —John Dewey⟩

²cloak \"\ *vt* -ED/-ING/-S **1 :** to cover with or as if with a cloak ⟨the inside of the church was ~*ed* with black drapes⟩ ⟨hills ~*ed* with heather⟩ **2 a :** HIDE, DISGUISE, SCREEN ⟨preparations ~*ed* in secrecy⟩ ⟨~*ed* by diplomatic immunity⟩ ⟨the attack upon Germany appeared to ~ an assault upon China —F.L.Paxson⟩ **b :** to clothe in a given often false or misleading form or appearance ⟨the stories . . . perhaps ~ in symbolic form an old quarrel —Catharine McClellan⟩ ⟨self-assurance ~*ed* by a quiet, repressed, and rather deadly manner —W.A. White⟩ **syn** see DISGUISE

cloak-and-dagger \ˌ==ˈ==\ *adj* **1 a :** dealing in intrigue and action of a romantic and melodramatic kind usu. with characters in a colorful historical setting and involving espionage, duels, pursuit, and rescue **b :** resembling or suggesting such intrigue or action **2 :** concerned with espionage; *specif* **:** engaged in or connected with undercover activities of secret agents of a national intelligence or counterintelligence service behind enemy lines

cloak-and-sword \ˌ==ˈ=\ *adj* [trans. of Sp. (*comedia de*) *capa y espada* cloak-and-sword comedy] **:** dealing in fictional or semifictional romance and adventure of the nobility in a period when swordplay and colorful elaborate dress were common

cloak-and-sworder \ˌ==ˈ==\ *n* -S **:** a cloak-and-sword novel or drama

cloak fern *n* **:** a fern of the genus *Notholaena*

cloaking *n* -S **:** material of which cloaks are made

cloak·less \'klōkləs\ *adj* **:** lacking a cloak

cloak·let \'klōklət\ *n* -S **:** a little cloak

cloakroom \'=ˌ=\ *n* **1 :** a room in which outdoor wraps may be placed during one's stay **2 :** an anteroom of a legislative chamber where members may keep their wraps, rest, and confer with colleagues **3 :** a room or cubicle where garments, parcels, and luggage may be checked for temporary safekeeping (as in a theater, cabaret, or hotel) **:** CHECKROOM **4** *Brit* **:** a room with lavatory and toilet

cloam \'klōm\ *n* -S [ME *clome,* fr. OE *clām;* akin to OE *clǣman* to smear, daub, MD *clēm* mud, OE *clǣg* clay — more at CLAY] *dial Eng* **:** EARTHENWARE, CROCKERY

cloam·en \'klōmən\ *adj* [*cloam* + *-en*] *dial Eng* **:** of earthenware **:** EARTHEN

¹clob \'kläb\ *dial Eng var of* ⁴COB

²clob \"\ *n* -S [by shortening & alter.] **:** KLABERJASS

¹clob·ber \'kläbə(r)\ *n* -S [prob. alter. of *clothes*] **1** *slang Brit* **:** wearing apparel ⟨dressed in his bathing ~⟩ **2** *slang Brit* **:** GEAR ⟨loaded himself with a lot of ~⟩

²clobber \"\ *vt* **clobbered; clobbered; clobbering** \-b(ə)riŋ\

clobbers *slang Brit* **:** DRESS, TOG — often used with *up*

³clobber \"\ *chiefly dial var of* ¹CLABBER

⁴clobber \"\ *chiefly Midland var of* ²CLABBER

⁵clobber \"\ *n* -S [by alter. and shortening] **:** KLABERJASS

⁶clobber \"\ *vt* **clobbered; clobbered; clobbering** \-b(ə)riŋ\

clobbers [obs. *clobber* to patch, fr. obs. *clobber* paste to fill cracks, fr. ScGael *clābar* mud] **:** to load (already decorated porcelain) with added overglaze enameling

⁷clobber \"\ *vb* **clobbered; clobbered; clobbering** \-b(ə)riŋ\

clobbers [origin unknown] *vt* **1 a** *slang* **:** to pound mercilessly **:** beat up **:** knock out **:** knock down **b :** to strike with crushing force **2** *slang* **:** to defeat overwhelmingly **:** SMEAR **3 :** to hit and demolish or severely damage (the target) ~ *vi* **:** to crash in an aircraft **:** make a crash landing

clob·ber·er \'kläbərə(r)\ *n* -S [obs. *clobber* to patch + *-er*] *Brit* **:** a repairer of clothes and shoes

¹clo·chard \'klōshə(r)d, klō'shär\ *n* -S [by alter.] **:** CLOCHER

²clochard \"\ *n* -S [F, fr. *clocher* to limp (fr. — assumed — VL *cloppicare,* fr. LL *cloppus* lame) + *-ard*] **:** TRAMP, BUM, HOBO ⟨a ~'s views on Parisian life⟩

cloche \'klōsh, 'klash, 'klȯsh\ *n* -S [F, lit., bell, fr. ML *clocca*] **1 :** a translucent cover for a young plant or shoot often used to force plants in the early part of the growing season **2 :** a woman's small helmetlike hat usu. with deep rounded crown and very narrow brim **3 :** BELL 6a **4 :** BELL 5g

clo·cher \'klōshə(r), klō'shā\ *n* -S [ME, fr. MF, fr. *cloche*] **:** BELL TOWER

clo·chette \klō'shet, klō-\ *n* -S [F, dim. of *cloche*] **:** a small bell-shaped ornament

¹clock \'kläk\ *n* -S *often attrib* [ME *clok,* fr. MD *clocke* clock, bell, fr. ONF or ML; ONF *cloque* bell, fr. ML *clocca,* of Celt origin; akin to MIr *clocc* bell, W *cloch;* akin to OE *hliehhan* to laugh — more at LAUGH] **1 a :** a device other than a watch for indicating or measuring time chiefly consisting of a train of wheels actuated by various devices (as falling weights, a tensed spring, changes in temperature, or electrical impulses), regulated through an escapement in various ways (as by a pendulum, dripping water, a synchronized electrical motor, or the vibrations of atoms), and indicating time most commonly by means of hands moving on a dial often with accompanying bells made to strike at regular intervals (as once each hour) — see ELECTRIC CLOCK, PROGRAM CLOCK, SIDEREAL CLOCK, TURRET CLOCK, WATCHMAN'S CLOCK, WATER CLOCK; compare CHRONOMETER, HOUR GLASS, WATCH **b** *obs* **:** WATCH; *esp* **:** one that strikes **c :** the downy fruiting head of the common dandelion **d :** a form of solitaire in which packets of cards are laid out in a circle to resemble the dial of a clock **2** *obs* **a :** a stroke of a clock sounding the hour **b :** the hour indicated by strokes of a clock **3 :** a registering device with a dial and indicator attached to a mechanism to measure or gauge its functioning or to record its output ⟨a pick ~ on a loom⟩ ⟨a hank ~ on a roving frame⟩; *specif* **a :** TAXIMETER **b :** SPEEDOMETER **4 :** TIME CLOCK ⟨punched the ~ at 8:45⟩ **5 :** an inflexible time schedule or timing plan ⟨uranium and thorium are also wasting assets, but to a much slower ~ —Stuart Chase⟩ ⟨he threw the whole weight of his genius into an effort to stop the ~ of history —J.T.Farrell⟩ **6** *slang Brit* **:** the human face — **around the clock 1 :** continuously for 24 hours **:** day and night without cessation **2 :** without relaxation and heedless of time — **hold the clock on :** to time (as a racer in a workout) with a stopwatch — **turn back the clock :** to revert to a condition existing well in the past — usu. with an implication of surrendering progress or improvement ⟨would not such a "Balkanization of the United States" be a clear *turning back of the clock* —E.N.Griswold⟩

²clock \"\ *vb* -ED/-ING/-S *vt* **1 a :** to time (a person or a performance) with a stopwatch or by an electric timing device ⟨~*ed* his practice quarter mile at 48 seconds⟩ **b :** to be timed at ⟨other Americans had ~*ed* 8:55.7 in the two-mile⟩ **c :** to register (time, distance, rate, velocity, or number) on a mechanical recording device ⟨wind velocities were ~*ed* at 80 miles per hour⟩ ⟨~*ed* an average of 4000 visitors a day⟩ **d :** to determine the timing of ⟨a station ~*ed* to broadcast one minute in each hour⟩ **2 :** to sound (a bell) either by pulling the clapper or by striking with a hammer from outside and without swinging ~ *vi* **:** to register on a time sheet or time clock **:** PUNCH — used with *in, out, on, off* ⟨it would be too late to load after the driver ~*s* in at eight⟩ ⟨a workshop where workers are required to ~ on and off⟩

³clock \"\ *vb* -ED/-ING/-S [ME *clokken,* fr. OE *cloccian* to cluck; like MD *klucke* brood hen, OHG *cloccōn* to beat, ON *klaka* to gossip, L *glocire* to cluck, Gk *klōzein,* Lith *klukšeti* of imit. origin] *vi, now dial Brit* **1 :** CALL, CLUCK — used esp. of a hen **2 :** SET, BROOD ~ *vt, now dial Brit* **:** SET, INCUBATE

⁴clock \"\ *n* -S [prob. fr. ¹*clock* (bell); fr. its original shape] **:** an ornamental figure or figured work on the ankle or side of a stocking or sock

⁵clock \"\ *vt* -ED/-ING/-S **:** to ornament with figured work

⁶clock \"\ *n* -S [prob. of Scand. origin; akin to Sw dial. *klocka* beetle] **:** BEETLE

clockbird \'=ˌ=\ *n, Austral* [¹*clock* + *bird;* fr. its calling regularly at dawn and dusk] **:** KOOKABURRA

clock calm *n, archaic* **:** a dead calm

clock card *n* **:** a card on which the periods an employee has worked are recorded by a time clock

¹clock·er \'kläkə(r)\ *n* -S [²*clock* + *-er*] **1 :** one that times racehorses during workouts and records information that will be useful in grouping and handicapping the horses **2 :** one that times a race or measures a flow (as of traffic) **3 :** a worker who measures lens blanks for conformance to specified dimensions, verifies their focal strength, and inspects and sorts them — called also *neutralizer, sizer*

²clocker \"\ *n* -S [⁵*clock* + *-er*] **:** one that embroiders clocks on stockings

clockface \'=ˌ=\ *n* **:** the dial face of a clock

clockface method *n* **:** a method of target designation and marking by reference to a known description point conceived as the center of a clockface, the targets being pointed out as on the hour radii of the imaginary dial

clock golf *n* **:** a lawn game that is played and scored like golf but confined to putting and that uses a single cup placed eccentrically within a circle of 12 tee positions

clock hour *n* **:** a full sixty minutes ⟨the certificate required a minimum of forty *clock hours* of instruction which could not be satisfied by forty class hours of only fifty minutes each⟩

clocking *n* -S [fr. gerund of ²*clock*] **:** the time used to traverse a measured course (as in a race) ⟨a near world record ~ for the mile⟩

clock·less \'kläkləs\ *adj* **:** lacking a clock

clock·like \'=ˌlīk\ *adj* **:** unusually regular, undeviating, and precise ⟨do his job with ~ efficiency⟩

clockmaker \'=ˌ==\ *n* [ME *clokmaker,* fr. *clok* clock + *maker*] **:** one that makes or repairs clocks

clock plant *n* **:** TELEGRAPH PLANT

clock stamp *n* **:** a combination clock and dating stamp for stamping the exact time

clockstar \'=ˌ=\ *n* **:** a star of accurately known right ascension used to ascertain the correction of an astronomical clock

clock·ster \'kläkstə(r)\ *n* -S **:** HOROLOGER

clock vine *n* **:** a plant of the genus *Thunbergia* (esp. *T. alata*)

clock watch *n* **:** a watch that strikes the hours consecutively

clock watcher *n* **:** a worker having the habit of overfrequently consulting a timepiece

¹clock·wise \'kläk,wīz\ *adv* **:** in the direction in which the hands of a clock rotate as viewed from in front, circularly from horizontal left, up or away, down or approaching, to horizontal right **:** with the sun — opposed to *counterclockwise*

²clockwise \"\ *adj* **:** moving or directed clockwise **:** RIGHT-HANDED, DEXTROROTATORY, POSITIVE

clockwork \'=ˌ=\ *n* **1 :** machinery composed of or containing a train of wheels of small size; *esp* **:** a mechanism of delicate construction that operates with unfailing regularity and minute accuracy (as in a meter) **2 :** a timing device similar to the works of a clock and operated usu. by a spring esp. for actuating a signal, a set of motions in a toy, or a bomb **3 :** something that by its effects seems to perform in response to clockwork or to be controlled by clockwork ⟨Emil Ludwig adapted psychoanalytic methods in exposing the psychical ~ of his subjects —Siegfried Mandel⟩ ⟨like a waxen lady with ~ breathing —Elizabeth Bowen⟩

¹clod \'kläd\ *n* -S [ME *clodde,* alter. of *clot, clotte* — more at CLOT] **1** *obs* **:** CLOT **2 a :** a lump or mass esp. of earth, turf, or clay **b :** SOIL, GROUND, EARTH; *also* **:** a spot of earth or turf **c :** something as unfeeling or as insensitive as a clod of earth **:** one that is gross and stupid **:** DOLT ⟨remind oneself that the lifeless ~ he is writing about is the author of some . . . most important novels —J.W.Aldridge⟩ **3 :** a part of the shoulder of a beef or of the neck piece near the shoulder **4 :** soft shale esp. over a coal seam

²clod \"\ *vb* **clodded; clodded; clodding; clods** [ME *clodden,* fr. *clodde,* n.] *vt* **1 a :** to throw clods of earth at ⟨caught Henry on the outside stairs and *clodded* him vivaciously —Dixon Wecter⟩ **b :** to drive by pelting with clods ⟨came a turtle, and I *clodded* it back into the water —W.A.White⟩ **2** *dial Brit* **:** to throw violently **:** HURL ~ *vi* **:** to form into clods

clod·di·ness \'klädēnəs\ *n* -ES **:** the quality or state of being cloddy

clodding press *n* [*clodding* (pres. part. of *clod* to make clods of) + *press*] **:** a press used for squeezing the oil from meal made from flax and other seeds

clod·dish \'klädish\ *adj* **1 :** heavy and spiritless ⟨our thoughts ~ from unending toil⟩ **2 :** stolid and boorish ⟨set apart from the ~ world about them by their heightened capacity for feeling —Mark Schorer⟩

clod·dy \'klädē\ *adj, sometimes* -ER/-EST [¹*clod* + *-y*] **1 :** consisting of clods **:** full of clods **:** like a clod **2 :** of low stature and heavily set — used of an animal, esp. a dog

clod·hop·per \'kläd,häpə(r)\ *n* -S **1 a :** a rustic (as a plowman) typically clumsy, heavy-footed, uncouth, and uninformed esp. of urbane ways ⟨~*s* . . . that never handled a sword —Mark Twain⟩ **b :** a clumsy heavy-footed cloddish person **:** DOLT **2 :** a large heavy shoe **syn** see BOOR

clod·hop·per·ish \-pərish\ *adj* **:** LOUTISH

clod·hop·ping \-piŋ\ *adj* **1 :** suitable for or serving a farm laborer **2 :** BOORISH ⟨Mr. Lewis . . . with this ~ blaring potwalloper —Ezra Pound⟩

clodknocker \'=ˌ==\ *n* **:** CLODHOPPER

clod·let \'klädlət\ *n* -S **:** a small clod

clod·ly \'klädlē\ *adv* [¹*clod* (dolt) + *-ly*] **:** clumsily and insensibly

clod·pate \'kläd,pāt\ *n* -S [¹*clod* (lump) + *pate*] **:** BLOCKHEAD 2

clod·pat·ed \'=ˌpād·əd\ *adj* **:** THICKHEADED

clodpoll \'=ˌ=\ *also* **clodpole** \'=ˌ=\ *n* -S [¹*clod* (lump) + *poll* (head) or *pole,* alter. of *poll*] **:** CLODPATE

clod smasher *or* **clod crusher** *n* **:** ¹FLOAT 5d(1)

cloff \'kläf\ *n* -S [perh. alter. of *²clove*] **:** an allowance of two pounds in every three hundredweight formerly given on certain goods to cover small losses in retailing

¹clog \'kläg *also* -ȯg-\ *n* -S [ME *clogge*] **1** *dial Brit* **:** a short thick piece of wood (as of a tree trunk or root) **:** LOG **2 a :** a weight attached to a man or an animal to hinder motion **b :** something that shackles, restricts, or impedes motion or desired freedom of action **:** ENCUMBRANCE 2 ⟨there are two inconsistent passions, which . . . are commonly ~*s* upon each other . . . ambition and avarice —Earl of Chesterfield⟩ **3 :** a heavy shoe, sandal, or overshoe having a thick typically wooden sole — compare CHOPINE, GETA, PATTEN, PLATFORM, SABOT **4 :** CLOG ALMANAC **5 :** CLOG DANCE

²clog \"\ *vb* **clogged; clogged; clogging; clogs** [ME *cloggen* to fasten a clog to, to fetter, fr. *clogge,* n.] *vt* **1 :** ENCUMBER: **a :** to impede the motion of (as with a chain or a burden) ⟨mustangs are tamed by being *clogged* until they have run themselves footsore⟩ ⟨her sides were *clogged* with the lazy weed that spawns in the Eastern seas —Rudyard Kipling⟩ **b :** to halt or retard operation, progress, or growth of ⟨restraints that have been *clogging* the market —T.W.Arnold⟩ ⟨all common ambitions, rank, possessions, power, the things which ~ man's feet —John Buchan⟩ **2 a :** to obstruct so as to hinder motion in or through **:** fill beyond capacity (as a limited space or narrow thoroughfare) ⟨for . . . years drovers *clogged* the turnpikes with herds —*Amer. Guide Series: N.Y.*⟩ ⟨the telephone lines were *clogged* —F.L.Allen⟩ ⟨the jury system has undergone serious criticism in recent years, due in part to the *clogging* of the courts —C.B.Swisher⟩ **b :** to fill or block up the hollows, interior, interstices, or working parts of with an adhesive accumulation ⟨excessive ink ~*s* the type⟩ ⟨valves *clogged* with carbon⟩ **3 a :** to fill (as the mind or the senses) so as to impair function ⟨fear ~*s* the mind —Jawaharlal Nehru⟩ **b :** to overload (as a work of art) with irrelevant matter so as to obscure the essence ⟨a great deal of . . . philosophizing ~*s* such movement as the book has —Elizabeth Janeway⟩ **4 a :** to put clogs on **b :** to make into clogs **:** put wooden soles on (as on shoes) ~ *vi* **1 :** to become clogged **:** become filled with extraneous matter ⟨the heater *clogged* with dust, preventing proper circulation⟩ **2 :** to coalesce or unite in a mass **:** come together ⟨they meant to run him until his blood *clogged* on his heart as his brush with mud —John Masefield⟩ **3 a :** to dance a clog dance ⟨began to ~ on the brick fireplace —Scott Fitzgerald⟩ **b :** to walk heavily **:** walk wearing or as if wearing clogs ⟨he grabbed a towel and *clogged* out to take a shower —Thomas Gallagher⟩ **syn** see HAMPER

clog almanac *n* **:** a calendar formerly used in England made by cutting notches and figures on the four edges of a square block of hard wood

clog box *n* **:** CHINESE TEMPLE BLOCK

clog dance *n* **:** a dance in which the performer wears clogs and beats out a clattering rhythm upon the floor — **clog dancer** *n* — **clog dancing** *n*

clog·gage \'klägij *also* -ȯg-\ *n* -S **:** condition of being clogged

clog·ger \ˈkläg·ə(r) *also* -ȯg-\ *n* -s [¹*clog* (shoe) + *-er*] **1** *dial Eng* : CLOGMAKER **2** : CLOG DANCER

clog·gy \ˈkläge *also* -ȯgē\ *adj, sometimes* -ER/-EST **1** : like a clog : characterized by clogs or lumps **2** : clogging or having power to clog : STICKY

clogwheel \ˈ=,=\ *n, dial Eng* : a cartwheel of solid wood fixed firmly on its axle

clogwood \ˈ=,=\ *n* : wood (as the wood of the yamanai) used for making clogs

clog·wyn \ˈklȯg(,)wēn, -äg-, -(,)win\ *n* -s [W *clogwyn, clog;* akin to OIr *cloch* stone — more at CLACHAN] : PRECIPICE, CLIFF

cloi·son \ˈklȯizᵊn, *F* klwàzōⁿ\ *n* -s [F, partition, fr. (assumed) VL *clausion-, clausio,* fr. L *clausus,* past part. of *claudere* to close — more at CLOSE] : one of the wire fillets or metal dividing strips used in cloisonné

¹**cloi·son·né** \ˌklȯizᵊnˈā, *F* klwàzȯnā\ *adj* [F, fr. past part. of *cloisonner,* to partition, fr. *cloison*] : consisting of, used in, or forming cloisonné

²**cloisonné** \"\ *n* -s : a multicolored decoration made of enamels poured into the divided areas in a design outlined with bent wire fillets or metal strips secured to a usu. metal ground — compare CHAMPLEVÉ

¹**clois·ter** \ˈklȯistə(r)\ *n* -s [ME *cloistre,* fr. OF, alter. (influenced by *cloison* partition) of *clostre,* fr. ML *claustrum* room in a monastery, fr. L, bar, bolt, enclosure, fr. *clausus,* past part. of *claudere* to close — more at CLOSE] **1** *obs* : an enclosed space (as in a ring of stones or within a seed or nut) **2** : a monastic establishment : a monastery or convent; *also* : monastic life **3 a** : a covered passage or ambulatory on the side of a court usu. having one side walled and the other an open arcade or colonnade and typically connecting different buildings of a group or running round an open court esp. of a monastery or college **b** : a covered walk, passageway, or arcade (as along a street) **4** : the status of being cloistered ⟨he ordered the ~ of the new monastery to become effective —*Springfield* (*Mass.*) *Daily News*⟩

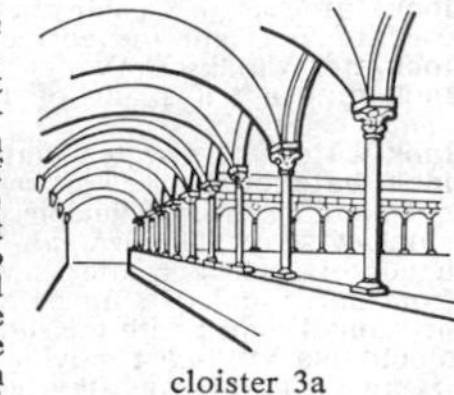
cloister 3a

²**cloister** \"\ *vt* **cloistered; cloistered; cloistering** \-t(ə)riŋ\ **cloisters** **1** : to confine in or as if in a cloister : seclude from the world : IMMURE ⟨a physicist who ~*s* himself in his laboratory⟩ **2** : to surround with a cloister : make a cloister of ⟨a small hill-*cloistered* college town⟩

cloistered *adj* **1** : living or remaining in seclusion and aloof from normal social participation or secular concerns or from public notice or public affairs ⟨he is not a ~ intellectual —Clifton Daniel⟩ ⟨men with burning causes are generally more eloquent than ~ dons —Heywood Broun⟩ **2** : narrowly restricted or insulated in outlook and interests : preoccupied and detached ⟨the phenomenon of a college professor leaving his ~ life to enter a political fight⟩ ⟨the ~ thinking of certain isolationists⟩ **3 a** : sheltered or providing shelter from contact with common life and relations with the outer world : intent on its own affairs to the exclusion of external affairs ⟨you might have expected such a man to end his days in the ~ academic world of books and blackboards —Philip Pollack⟩ **b** : such as is provided by the isolation of a cloister ⟨to recapture the ~ serenity in his work which he had grown to love —Marcia Davenport⟩ **c** : cultivated or conducted in the privacy of seclusion sheltered from outside interference and the bustle of mundane life ⟨a fugitive and ~ poetry that never at any time heard the chimes at midnight —J.L.Lowes⟩

cloistered arch *or* **cloistered vault** *n* : CLOISTER VAULT

cloistered heart *n* : CLOSED GENTIAN

clois·ter·er \ˈklȯistərə(r)\ *n* -s [ME *cloistrer,* fr. MF *cloistrier,* fr. *cloistre* + *-ier* -er] : one belonging to or living in a cloister : RECLUSE

cloister garth *n* : an open court surrounded by cloisters esp. in a group of buildings of a monastery or college

clois·ter·less \ˈklȯistə(r)ləs\ *adj* : lacking a cloister

clois·ter·ly \ˈklȯistə(r)lē\ *adj* : proper to a cloister : CLOISTRAL

cloister vault *n* : a cupolalike vault on a square or polygonal base with diminishing courses to the top and of similar horizontal section throughout and in shape like a pyramid or frustum of a pyramid with sides curved convexly outward

clois·tral \ˈklȯistrəl\ *also* **clois·ter·al** \-t(ə)rəl\ *adj* **1** : belonging to a cloister or suggestive of a cloister or the austerity of a cloister **2** : such as is characteristic of cloistered recluses or scholars **3** : closely limited in outlook as if isolated in a cloister

cloistress *n* -ES *obs* : NUN

¹**cloit** \ˈklȯit\ *vi* [origin unknown] *Scot* : to fall down heavily

²**cloit** \"\ *n* -s *Scot* : a heavy fall

cloke *archaic var of* CLOAK

cloky *var of* CLOQUE

¹**clomb** [*clomb,* past, fr. ME, alter. of *clamb,* fr. OE, past of *climban* to climb; *clomb,* past part., fr. ME, alter. of *clomben, clumben,* fr. OE *clumben,* past part. of *climban* — more at CLIMB] *now dial past of* CLIMB

²**clomb** *var of* CLOAM

¹**clomp** \ˈklämp\ *vi* -ED/-ING/-S [by alter.] : ²CLUMP *vi* 1

²**clomp** \"\ *n* -s [by alter.] : ¹CLUMP 4

clo·nal \ˈklōnᵊl\ *adj* [*clone* + *-al*] : of, relating to, or occurring in or as a clone — **clo·nal·ly** \-nəlē\ *adv*

clone \ˈklōn\ *also* **clon** \ˈklōn, -än\ *n* -s [Gk *klōn* twig, slip; akin to Gk *klan* to break — more at GLADIATOR] *biol* : the aggregate of the asexually produced progeny of an individual whether natural (as the products of repeated fission of a protozoan) or otherwise (as in the propagation of a particular plant by budding or by cuttings through many vegetative generations)

clo·nic \ˈklōnik, ˈklän-\ *adj* [NL *clonus* + E *-ic*] : exhibiting, relating to, or involving clonus ⟨~ contraction⟩ ⟨~ spasm⟩ — **clo·nic·i·ty** \klōˈnisəd·ē, klä'-\ *n* -ES

clo·nism \ˈklō,nizəm, ˈklä,-\ *n* -s [NL *clonismus,* fr. *clonus* + L *-ismus* -ism] : the condition of being affected with clonus

¹**clonk** \ˈklȯŋk, ˈkläŋk\ *vb* -ED/-ING/-S [alter. of ¹*clank*] *vi* : to make a dull echoless thumping sound as if from impact of a hard object on a hard but hollow surface ~ *vt* : to produce or cause to make clonks or clonks on

²**clonk** \"\ *n* -s : a clonking sound

clo·nor·chi·a·sis \ˌklōˌnȯrˈkīəsəs\ *also* **clo·nor·chi·o·sis** \ˌklō,nȯrkīˈōsəs\ *n, pl* **clonorchia·ses** \-ˈkīə,sēz\ *also* **clonorchio·ses** \-kīˈō,sēz\ [NL, fr. *Clonorchis,* type genus + *-iasis*] : infestation with or disease caused by an oriental liver fluke (*Clonorchis sinensis*) that invades the bile ducts of the liver and when present in numbers causes severe systemic reactions including edema, liver enlargement, and diarrhea

clo·nor·chis \klōˈnȯrkəs\ *n, cap* [NL, fr. Gk *klōn* twig + *orchis* testis — more at ORCHIS] : a genus of trematode worms (family Opisthorchiidae) containing the Chinese liver fluke (*C. sinensis*), having a complex life cycle involving a mollusk and a fish as intermediate hosts, and constituting a serious parasite of man in eastern and southeastern Asia with human infection resulting from consumption of raw infected fish

clo·no·thrix \ˈklōnō,thriks\ *n, cap* [NL, fr. *clono-* (fr. Gk *klōn* twig) + *-thrix*] : a genus of chlamydobacteria that have organic sheaths encrusted with iron or manganese, that reproduce by spherical conidia borne in chains, and that are known chiefly from waterworks and pipes

clo·nus \ˈklōnəs\ *n* -ES [NL, fr. Gk *klonos* turmoil; akin to L *celer* swift — more at CELERITY] : a series of alternating contractions and partial relaxations of a muscle that in certain nervous diseases occurs in the form of convulsive spasms involving complex groups of muscles and is believed to result from alteration of the normal pattern of motor neuron discharge — compare TONUS

cloof \ˈklüf\ *n* -s [prob. of Scand origin; akin to ON *klauf* cleft, cloven hoof, *klof* cleft, *kljūfa* to split — more at CLEAVE] *dial Brit* : HOOF

¹**clook** \ˈklük\ *var of* CLEUK

²**clook** \"\ *n* -s [PaG *gluck,* fr. MHG *kluck,* of imit. origin] *Midland* : ²CLUCK 2

¹**cloop** \ˈklüp\ *n* -s [imit.] : the sound made when a cork is forcibly drawn from a bottle

²**cloop** \"\ *vi* : to make a cloop

cloot \ˈklüt\ *n* -s [prob. of Scand origin; akin to ON *klō* claw — more at CLAW] **1** *chiefly Scot* : a cloven hoof **2** *usu cap, chiefly Scot* : DEVIL — usu. used in pl.

cloot·ie \ˈklütē, -i\ *n* -s *usu cap* [dim. of *cloot*] *chiefly Scot* : DEVIL

¹**clop** \ˈkläp\ *n* -s [imit.] : a sound made by or as if by a hoof or wooden shoe against pavement

²**clop** \"\ *vi* **clopped; clopped; clopping; clops** : to make or move with a succession of clops ⟨a milkman's horse *clopping* down an empty city street —M.D.Geismer⟩ ⟨*clopped* over to the bar in her wooden-soled sandals —Dawn Powell⟩

¹**clop-clop** \ˈ=ˌ=\ *n* -s [redupl. of ¹*clop*] : a sound of rhythmically repeated clops

²**clop-clop** \"\ *vi* : to move with a clop-clop

clop·py \ˈkläpē, -pi\ *adj* : marked by the sound of successive clops

clo·que \klōˈkā, ˈ=(,)=\ *also* **clo·ky** \ˈklōkē\ *n, pl* **cloques** *also* **clokies** *often attrib* [F *cloqué,* fr. *cloqué,* adj., with an embossed design, fr. past part. of *cloquer* to become blistered, fr. F dial. *cloque* bell, blister, fr. ML *clocca* bell — more at CLOCK] **1** : a fabric with an embossed design **2** : a fabric esp. of piqué with small woven figures

clos \ˈklō\ *n, pl* **clos** \"\ [F, fr. OF, enclosure — more at ³CLOSE] : a French vineyard; *esp* : one enclosed by a wall — often used prepositively in a compound naming such a vineyard or its wine (as *Clos-Vougeot,* a vineyard in the Côte-d'Or, or the red Burgundy produced from its grapes); compare CHÂTEAU 3, CÔTE

clos·a·ble *or* **close·a·ble** \ˈklōzəbəl\ *adj* : capable of being closed

¹**close** \ˈklōz\ *vb* -ED/-ING/-S [ME *closen,* fr. OF *clos-,* stem of *clore,* fr. L *claudere* — more at ⁴CLOSE] *vt* **1 a** : to move (some part, esp. some hinged or sliding part) so as to bar passage through something ⟨~ the gate of the plant⟩ ⟨keep this valve *closed*⟩ **b** (1) : to block or shut off (a channel, path, or area) against entry or passage ⟨~ a street for snow removal⟩ ⟨~ a range to settlers⟩ (2) : to stop or deny access to or prohibit use of ⟨~ a firing area during target practice⟩ ⟨an attempt to ~ the mails to communist propaganda periodicals⟩ (3) *linguistics* : to make (a morphological or syntactic construction) incapable of having an additional constituent of a particular kind (as an adjective or a derivational suffix) ⟨the addition of *all* before *these young men* ~*s* the construction⟩ ⟨the addition of *-s* to *normalize* ~*s* the construction⟩ **c** (1) : to block or refuse admission to the inside, interior, or contents of ⟨keep the drawer *closed*⟩ ⟨continued drought caused the governor to ~ the woods⟩ ⟨volumes kept on *closed* shelves⟩ ⟨a seal used in Charlemagne's time to ~ letters and wills⟩ (2) : to exclude outside blood from (a herd, strain, or breed) **d** : to block out : SCREEN, EXCLUDE ⟨~ a view⟩ : form a boundary to ⟨a church ~*s* the vista⟩ **e** : to make or keep inaccessible, imperceptive, or inscrutable ⟨even a neutral cannot be asked to ~ his mind or his conscience —F.D.Roosevelt⟩ ⟨magazines *closed* to inexperienced writers⟩ **f** (1) : to suspend or stop the services, sessions, or operations of ⟨snow and high wind *closed* the airport⟩ ⟨~ school because of an outbreak of polio⟩ ⟨a theater *closed* for repairs⟩ (2) : to force to discontinue or end a business enterprise ⟨a manufacturer *closed* by his creditors⟩ (3) : to exclude the public from ⟨health authorities *closed* the swimming pools⟩ **2 a** *archaic* : ENCLOSE, ENCOMPASS, CONTAIN ⟨leaving the whole establishment to her, *closing* only himself in invisible bonds —F.M.Ford⟩ **b** : to arrange (the strands of a wire rope) spirally around a center **3 a** : to bring to an end or period : shut off or preclude further continuation of ⟨the Peace of Westphalia . . . which *closed* the Thirty Years' War —Stringfellow Barr⟩ ⟨he *closed* his military career with an idealized concept —Jeannette P. Nichols⟩ ⟨he *closed* his business and moved away⟩ **b** : to serve as last, final, or ultimate in (a series, sequence, or development) ⟨Madame Defarge going first . . . Mr. Lorry *closing* the little procession —Charles Dickens⟩ ⟨the . . . duet which ~*s* the first act —*Saturday Rev.*⟩ **c** : to conclude discussion or negotiation about : terminate or bring to agreement, decision, or settlement ⟨questions that have been *closed* for centuries suddenly yawn wide open —G.B. Shaw⟩ ⟨~ a deal or bargain⟩ ⟨~ a real estate transfer of title⟩ **d** : to render (an account) no longer current **4 a** : to bring or bind together the parts or edges of ⟨a *closed* fist⟩ ⟨cut the sides and back to fit and ~ them with a slide fastener⟩ ⟨after amputation ~ the stump for good scar line⟩ ⟨in no hurry to ~ the wound⟩ ⟨*closing* the break in the metal bar by welding⟩ **b** : to fill up (as a hole or opening) with something serving as a sealer, filler, or stopper ⟨first ~ the cracks with plaster of paris⟩ ⟨~ a grave⟩ **c** : to fill (a gap) so as to attain full continuity or smooth integration ⟨help them to ~ their dollar gap⟩ ⟨efforts to ~ the sharp division within the alliance⟩ ⟨tax loopholes that should be *closed*⟩ **d** : to complete by way of circling or enveloping or by making circumferentially or circuitously continuous ⟨the centripetal force constraining the planets to move in *closed* orbits —S.F.Mason⟩ ⟨to connect electric conductors so as to ~ a circuit⟩ **e** : to stitch together parts forming the upper of (a shoe) **f** : to reduce to nil ⟨milers fast *closing* the distance to the tape⟩ ⟨the ferry *closed* the last few feet of water between it and the ship⟩ **5** *of a ship* : to come close to ⟨the minesweeper *closed* the island under cover of darkness⟩ **6** : to convert (granular soap) into a homogeneous pasty form (as by adding water and boiling) **7** : to alter (a stance in golf or baseball batting) so that the left foot is closer to the line of play than the right ~ *vi* **1** : to close itself or become closed: **a** : to contract, fold, swing, or slide so as to leave no opening ⟨a camera shutter adjusted to ~ after 1/50 second⟩ ⟨the jackknife *closed* on my finger⟩; *also* : to admit of being closed ⟨this valve won't ~⟩ **b** : to cease operation ⟨forced the mine to ~⟩ : discontinue institutional activities ⟨banks and schools ~ for the holiday⟩ — often used with *down, up* **c** : to suspend business or end the business day ⟨this store ~*s* at 5 p.m.⟩ — often used with *down, up; also* : to remain closed ⟨barbershops ~ Mondays⟩ **d** : to end a theatrical run or tour ⟨the play *closed* after two weeks⟩ **e** : to cease to be passable for boats because of an ice cover ⟨the river has the appearance of *closing* for the winter⟩ **2 a** : to come near or approach close ⟨radar showed a plane *closing* fast⟩ ⟨a ship fast *closing* with the land⟩ **b** *of a racehorse* : to lessen the gap with the lead horse or horses esp. near the finish of a race ⟨*closing* fast in the home stretch⟩ **c** : to engage in a struggle at close quarters : GRAPPLE ⟨forbidding terrain prevented our *closing* with the enemy⟩ **3 a** : to join together : MEET, UNITE ⟨the jaws of the vise imperceptibly *closing*⟩; *also* : to tighten in a grasping or crushing motion ⟨a hand *closed* on my collar⟩ ⟨sullen anger *closed* down on the community⟩ **b** : to become filled in ⟨find themselves in a tight place when the gaps begin to ~ —W.R.Inge⟩; *also* : DIMINISH ⟨the distance between us rapidly *closed*⟩ **c** : to draw together, join, or gather so as to cover, conceal, or confine something ⟨clouds soon ~ over the sun⟩ ⟨just as the sea *closed* over the sinking ship⟩ **d** : to form or approach in a tight or diminishing circle ⟨his comrades *closed* around him protectively⟩ **e** : to tighten fingers or jaws in a grasping motion — used often with *on* ⟨seeing a rope dangling I *closed* on it⟩ ⟨the clamshell bucket *closed* on a load of dirt⟩ ⟨the idea faded before I could ~ on it⟩ **f** *dancing* : to draw the free foot up to and into contact with the supporting foot **4** : to enter into or complete an agreement : make a contract ⟨before I can ~ with a new employer⟩ **5 a** : to come to an end or period : cease from further continuation ⟨his diplomatic career *closed* with this incident⟩ ⟨the services *closed* with a short prayer⟩ **b** : to bring one's discourse or a debate to a conclusion ⟨I ~ with this warning⟩ ⟨the senior debater of each team is to ~⟩ **c** : to make an announcement or play in certain card games that ends some phase of the game; *esp* : to turn the trump card face down in a game of sixty-six in order to stop the draw from the stock and compel players to follow suit **6** *civil engin* : to give a closed figure when plotted ⟨this survey of the tract fails to ~⟩ — see ERROR OF CLOSURE **7 a** : to become priced in the last recorded sale of the trading day in an exchange ⟨to compensate for stock opened at 126, *closed* at 128⟩ ⟨hogs *closed* strong⟩ **b** : to show an overall price average at the end of a trading period ⟨the market managed to ~ slightly lower⟩

syn END, CONCLUDE, FINISH, TERMINATE, COMPLETE: all of these words, along with CLOSE, are near in meaning and often interchangeable. CLOSE may suggest that the matter in question is no longer open to further continuation ⟨the case is now *closed* and needs no further discussion⟩ ⟨these discoveries *closed* his career in the church⟩ END may more strongly connote finality; likely to contrast with *begin,* it may imply a certain progress, sequence, or development ⟨difficulties in determining when the medieval period *ends*⟩ ⟨the book *ends* on a happier note⟩ CONCLUDE may be more formal in suggestion ⟨the meeting *concluded* with a vote of thanks to the hostess⟩ FINISH may suggest full execution or resolution of the last steps or stages of a continued action or process ⟨the War of the Confederacy over but not *finished* —Elizabeth M. Roberts⟩ ⟨at three o'clock his business was *finished* and he was ready to return —Sherwood Anderson⟩ TERMINATE may suggest a definite term or limit involved, an attaining definitively to that term, with or without completing or fulfilling ⟨the old arrangement with the company, now *terminated*⟩ ⟨the interim appointments having *terminated*⟩ COMPLETE may indicate an ending marked by fulfilling, perfecting, leaving nothing undone ⟨he did not *complete* the picture until three years later⟩ Words of this series are often close synonyms, and any one of this set may be substituted for CLOSE in a sentence like "singing the Alma Mater *closes* the services".

—close its doors **1** : to bar entrance or refuse admission ⟨keeping *its doors closed* to immigrants⟩ **2** : to cease operation : go out of business ⟨a school forced by economic considerations to *close its doors*⟩ **— close one's eyes to** : to deliberately ignore : decline to acknowledge **— close ranks** : to unite in a militant attitude and submerge differences esp. to meet a challenge **— close the books** **1 a** : to cease accepting subscriptions to a new security offering because orders have been received in excess of the amount offered **b** : to intermit the use of certain books of account or record of a corporation or business concern (as prior to the payment of a dividend) **2** *accounting* : to transfer periodically after adjustment to the proprietorship accounts the balances of the income and expense accounts **— close the door** : to take a determined and uncompromising obstructive position ⟨an action that *closes the door* on any amicable settlement⟩

²**close** \"\ *n* -s [ME *clos,* fr. *closen* to close — more at ¹CLOSE] **1 a** : a coming or bringing of something to a conclusion or end ⟨the things that a busy life and its premature ~ left him no time to give —D.M.Davin⟩ ⟨at the ~ of hostilities⟩ **b** : a conclusion or end in time or existence : CESSATION ⟨as the decade drew to a ~⟩ ⟨bring the chapter to a ~⟩ ⟨after the ~ of the war⟩ **c** : a final stage, outcome, or finish ⟨conduct the negotiations to a satisfactory ~⟩ **d** : the concluding passage (as of a speech or play) **e** : COMPLIMENTARY CLOSE **2** : the conclusion of a musical strain or period : CADENCE **3** *archaic* : a bringing together : MEETING, JOINING ⟨attested by the holy ~ of lips —Shak.⟩ **4** *archaic* : a hostile encounter ⟨unwounded from the dreadful ~ —Sir Walter Scott⟩ **5** : the closing price on a stock or a commodity or the closing prices on an exchange or over-the-counter market **6** *dancing* : the movement of a free foot towards and into contact with the supporting foot, with or without transfer of weight

³**close** \ˈklōs *sometimes* -ōz\ *n* -s [ME *clos,* fr. OF *clos,* fr. L *clausum* enclosure, fr. neut. of *clausus,* past part. of *claudere*] **1** : ENCLOSURE: **a** *dial Brit* : an enclosed field esp. near a farmhouse : FARMYARD **b** *Brit* : the precinct of a cathedral or abbey; *esp* : an enclosed space close to a cathedral bordered by the archdeanery, deanery, and residences (as of the canons) **c** *Brit* : a walled enclosure (as a paddock or school playground) **d** *Brit* : an open space (as a quadrangle) that is partially or wholly closed in by a group of dwellings **2** *chiefly Brit* **a** : a narrow passage or entry leading from a street to a court and the houses within or to the common stairway of tenements **b** : a road closed at one end **3 a** : a parcel of land in which a person has an interest involving at least a right of present possession whether enclosed or not, an ideal boundary being there in legal fiction **b** : the interest itself entitling the owner to an action of trespass for breach of the close

⁴**close** \ˈklōs\ *adj* -ER/-EST [ME *clos,* fr. MF *clos,* fr. L *clausus,* past part. of *claudere* to close; akin to Gk *kleid-, kleis* key, bolt, *kleiein* to close, OIr *clō* nail, OSlav *ključiti* to close, MLG *slūten* to close, OHG *sliozan,* OFris *slūta*] **1 a** : having no openings : CLOSED ⟨a ~ hatch⟩ ⟨drove off in a ~ carriage⟩ **b** *heraldry* (1) : with wings folded to the body — used of a bird (2) : with the visor down — used of a helmet **2** *archaic* : closed in or around by or as if by walls or hills ⟨~ streets of the old city⟩ **3 a** : confined or confining strictly : narrowly restricting or restricted ⟨a ~ prisoner⟩ ⟨~ quarters⟩ ⟨five days of ~ arrest⟩ ⟨so ~ was her hold upon his arm that he feared to detach himself lest he should hurt her —Charles Dickens⟩ ⟨to escape from a ~, systematic, cultivated life into an open and relatively barbarous existence —Lewis Mumford⟩ **b** (1) *of a vowel* : ¹HIGH 1a(6) (2) : formed with the tongue in a higher position than for another vowel — used of one of two vowels constituting a pair because similar in articulation or identical in orthography ⟨Italian has a ~ and an open *e*⟩ (3) *of lip rounding* : EXTREME **c** : restricted (as in membership, prerogatives, admission to competition) to a privileged class ⟨a ~ scholarship⟩ **d** : CLOSED 3g ⟨the ~ season for hunting deer⟩ **e** : *of a chess game* : characterized by a restricted development of pieces behind the pawns **4 a** : out of the way of observation : SECLUDED, SECRET ⟨the bandits kept ~ during the day⟩ **b** : marked by a disposition to secrecy, taciturnity, or extreme discreetness about divulging information ⟨she could tell us something if she would . . . but she was as ~ as wax —A. Conan Doyle⟩ **5** : maintained or achieved by virtue of unrelaxing scrutiny, acute discernment, and exacting minuteness : STRICT, RIGOROUS ⟨keeping a ~ watch on expenditures⟩ ⟨~ control over the credit structure⟩ ⟨keeping records in ~ accord with facts⟩ ⟨nothing short of a ~ critical analysis will do⟩ ⟨a prisoner in ~ custody⟩ **6** : causing a sensation of being slightly smothered or stifled : SULTRY, STUFFY ⟨it seemed from the dreadfully ~ atmosphere that no window had been opened in it for weeks past —Anthony Trollope⟩ ⟨I lolled on the couch and breathed its ~ smell of cloth in hot weather —Edmund Wilson⟩ **7** : reluctant to part with money or possessions : stingy or cautious about expenditures ⟨a ~ buyer and a good marketer —W.A.White⟩ **8** : marked by an arrangement leaving little space between items or units ⟨~ texture⟩ ⟨~ grain in wood⟩: **a** : having individuals pressed, arranged, or arrayed quite near each other ⟨in so ~ and murderous a conflict the valor of no single individual could decide the day —J.L.Motley⟩ ⟨flying in ~ formation⟩ **b** : having characters written or inscribed with a minimum of space between ⟨she was handicapped by her almost illegible ~ handwriting⟩ **c** *of type* : set with minimum spacing between words or lines **d** *of a library classification* : having relatively small subdivisions — compare BROAD **e** *of an animal's coat* : sleek and smooth with the hairs more or less parallel and close to the body : not loose or fluffy ⟨a *close*-coated dog is better for working briery uplands⟩ **9 a** : fitting quite tightly or exactly with very little looseness, play, or ease ⟨a ~ gown⟩ ⟨a bathing suit skintight and ~⟩ **b** : very short or near to the ground, skin, or other surface ⟨the fall mowing of the grass was too ~⟩ ⟨the barber gave him a ~ shave⟩ **c** : accurately matching or blending without interval or gap : PRECISE ⟨a concession that brought him into ~ harmony with his colleagues⟩ ⟨unable to escape the force of ~ reasoning⟩ **d** *of a tolerance* : MINUTE **10** : marked by being near, by nearness of any sort, or by adjacency, proximity, approach, or approximation in space ⟨as ~ together as bungalows in a suburban town —*Amer. Guide Series: Calif.*⟩ ⟨St. Louis is *closer* to Chicago than it is to Detroit⟩ ⟨an . . . ibis, strikingly colorful at ~ range —*Amer. Guide Series: Fla.*⟩ or in time ⟨these dates come ~ to the Christmas holidays⟩ or in kind ⟨a strong intense smell ~ to that of burning garbage —Norman Mailer⟩ ⟨Spanish is ~ to French and Italian⟩ or in feeling ⟨Whittier was ~ in spirit to the Rhode Island Quakers —*Amer. Guide Series: R.I.*⟩ ⟨farmers in overalls . . . proclaim again how ~ to the soil is Minneapolis —*Amer. Guide Series: Minn.*⟩ or in effect ⟨*crude* and *vulgar* are ~ synonyms⟩ ⟨the banker has got to be ~ to the property he is financing —*Encyc. Americana*⟩ or in degree ⟨a speed ~ to that of sound⟩ ⟨a salary ~ to the presi-

dent's) or in action ⟨his reply left her ~ to tears⟩ or in relationship ⟨first cousins are ~ relatives⟩ **11 a :** marked by, given to, or enjoying strong liking or regard, mutual ready confidence, general accord, or constant association ⟨you loved your mother and your sister, all the ~ circle that was bound to you by blood and habit —Mary Austin⟩ ⟨too ~ to Theodore Roosevelt ever to receive the confidence of Woodrow Wilson —F.L.Paxson⟩ **b :** marked by or given to compatibility or conformity of interests, aims, pursuits, preferences, or by cordiality, accord, cooperation, or alliance ⟨the ~ ties that bind them together⟩ ⟨~ relations between Norway and Sweden⟩ **12 a :** marked by careful or searching attention to details and their relationships or by consideration of or familiarity with details ⟨many of the 18th century policemen of usage were not ~ students of the language —Charlton Laird⟩ ⟨a ~ study⟩ ⟨~ knowledge of French⟩ ⟨~ questioning about his activities⟩ ⟨a ~ observer of weather conditions⟩ **b :** marked by fidelity in details esp. to an original ⟨a ~ copy of an old master⟩ ⟨a ~ analogy between their customs and ours⟩ **c :** marked by terse economical expression of details ⟨his exact, ~, sober classical style —Edmund Wilson⟩ **13 a :** decided by a narrow margin or a slight edge **:** long undecided because almost evenly balanced **:** marked by or showing opposed tendencies nearly even ⟨a ~ baseball game ending with a score of 10–9⟩ ⟨the base runner was safe at second on a ~ play⟩ ⟨the ~ election of 1916⟩ ⟨Minnesota was ~, with twelve votes whose disposition must await final count —F.L.Paxson⟩ ⟨a ~ race won by a nose⟩ **b :** taking a favorable turn only by a very small margin (as just barely in time or missing disaster by a hair) ⟨looking at the vanishing train, he breathed "that was ~"⟩ **c :** having given the winning candidate only a slight majority (as less than 60 percent) in a two-party vote ⟨a congressman from a ~ district⟩ ⟨dividing the seats in the legislature into sure and ~ seats⟩ **14** *Eng law* **:** CLOSED, SEALED — used esp. of writs or letters directed to particular persons for particular purposes and therefore not left open; opposed to *patent* **15** *finance* **:** difficult to obtain ⟨money is ~⟩ **16 :** CLOSED 1j **17 a** *of punctuation* **:** characterized by liberal use of punctuation marks, esp. commas **b** *of the punctuation of a letter* **:** characterized by the use of a comma at the end of each line of the heading and inside address except the last and after the complimentary close and of a period at the end of the last line of the heading and the inside address and after the signature — opposed to *open*

syn DENSE, COMPACT, THICK: indicating a tight massing together with little intervening empty space, these words may be interchangeable in many contexts. CLOSE typically suggests a pressing together of things separable or often separated ⟨*close* stitching⟩ ⟨*close* formations⟩ ⟨between the *close* moss violet-inwoven —P.B.Shelley⟩ ⟨a *close* impervious soil —*Amer. Guide Series: N.C.*⟩ In literary criticism it may indicate effective compression into few words ⟨a relief to turn back to the austere, *close* language of Everyman, the simplicity of the mysteries —T.S.Eliot⟩ DENSE describes an aggregation of particles or component units set very near each other and making penetration or perception difficult ⟨the *dense* trees of the avenue rendered the road dark as a tunnel —Thomas Hardy⟩ ⟨surrounded by a throng so *dense* that I could scarcely breathe —C.B.Nordhoff & J.N.Hall⟩ ⟨Proust's book is a gigantic *dense* mesh of complicated relations —Edmund Wilson⟩ COMPACT may suggest a consolidation within a circumscribed area or space making for order, firmness, efficiency, or strength ⟨the village has ceased to be a *compact* unit and it is no longer easy to find its center —*Times Lit. Supp.*⟩ ⟨below the ordinary height . . . he was all *compact* and under his swart, tattooed skin the muscles worked like steel rods —Herman Melville⟩ THICK may suggest a concentrated abundance ⟨chestnuts near, that hung in masses *thick* —Alfred Tennyson⟩ ⟨what the dry weather doesn't spoil, the tobacco worms will. They were *thick* as hops —Ellen Glasgow⟩ ⟨sometimes the isle was *thick* with savages . . . sometimes full of dangerous animals —R.L. Stevenson⟩ **syn** see in addition FAMILIAR, SILENT, STINGY

— **close to home :** within one's strong personal interests so that one is affected esp. strongly ⟨the audience felt that the speaker's remarks were pretty *close to home*⟩ ⟨if . . . this book might not be too *close to home* for the average teen-age boy to appreciate —L.T.Bulman⟩

[5]**close** \"\ *adv* -ER/-EST [ME *clos*, fr. *clos*, adj.] **1 a :** in proximity of space or time ⟨in fog stick ~ to the white guideline⟩ ⟨strangers draw ~ and ask each other two questions —E.W. Smith⟩ ⟨its nucleons draw *closer* to one another —G.W.Gray b.1886⟩ ⟨~ to my cheek⟩ ⟨~ under the roof⟩ ⟨building a school ~ by⟩ ⟨overlooking the tasks lying ~ at hand⟩ ⟨it is only ~ up that the impact of his power-charged personality makes itself felt —R.C.Doty⟩ ⟨having their babies *closer* together⟩ — often used in combination ⟨*close*-set⟩ **b :** in proximity of approach ⟨anxious to come *closer* to the truth of life⟩ ⟨as for solving the problem, we haven't come ~⟩ **2** *archaic* **:** SECRETLY, COVERTLY ⟨His Royal Highness must lie very ~ here till tomorrow evening —John Buchan⟩ **3 :** in a close state **:** TIGHTLY ⟨there is not a door, nor a window, that shuts ~ —Tobias Smollett⟩ **4 :** in a close manner ⟨on looking *closer*, it struck me that Hamlet often does one thing instead of another —Karl Polanyi⟩ **5 :** in close likeness or conformity ⟨sticking ~ to the classic models⟩ **6 :** in a close or intimate association ⟨the cause that touches me *closest*⟩ ⟨there is something in the heart of street dogs that draws them ~ to men —William Saroyan⟩ ⟨it is up to the illustrator to get as ~ as he can to the spirit of the text —Mervyn Peake⟩ — **close to the wind** *of a ship* **:** with the head directed as nearly to the point from which the wind blows as it is possible to sail

closeable *var of* CLOSABLE

close–at–hand \'klōs-ə-'\ *adj* **1 :** lying in the immediate vicinity **2 :** approaching in the immediate future

close attack \'klōs-\ *n* **:** the three forward attacking positions on a lacrosse team

close bolt \'klōs-\ *n* **:** a wall or layer composed of bricks laid close together in brickmaking (as for the casing of a clamp)

close bolting \'=-\ *n* **1 :** the stacking of bricks without leaving any spaces between them **2 :** the bricks stacked in a close bolt

close borough \'=-\ *n, Brit* **:** a borough with a restricted electorate and self-perpetuating council

close breeding \'=-\ *n* **:** breeding from closely related individuals — used esp. of relationships less close than in inbreeding

close–by \'=¦=\ *adj* **:** being close at hand **:** ADJACENT

close call \'=-\ *n* **:** a narrow escape

close chair \'klōz-, 'klōs-\ *n, Brit* [[1]*close*] **:** a closestool equipped with the back and arms of a chair

close communion \'klōs-\ *or* **closed communion** \-ōzd-\ *n* **:** Communion in the Lord's Supper restricted to the baptized members belonging to the same denomination or the same church — opposed to *open communion* — **close communionist** *n*

close corporation \'klōs-\ *n* **1 :** a self-perpetuating body each part of which fills its own vacancies **2 :** a corporation whose stock is held by a few persons who are often those active in the management **3 :** a small tightly exclusive group cool to outsiders

close–coupled \'=¦==\ *adj* **1** *of an animal* **:** short in loins and back **2** *of an automobile* **:** having the space between front and rear seats restricted **3 :** directly united — used of a closed and an open electrical circuit in combination

close coupling \'=-\ *n* **:** a coupling of two electrical circuits such that any change of current in one produces a relatively large change in the other

close–cropped \'=¦=\ *adj* **1 :** clipped short **2 :** having the hair clipped short

[1]**closecross** \'=,=\ *n* **1 :** a cross between individuals of related strains **2 :** the progeny of a closecross

[2]**closecross** \"\ *vt* -ED/-ING/-ES [[1]*closecross*] **:** to breed (animals) from closely related individuals, esp. members of related strains within a breed

closed \'klōzd\ *adj* [ME, past part. of *closen* to close] **1 a** *of a vehicle* **:** having a permanently enclosed body with stationary back, side panels, and top **b :** structurally enclosed or closed in ⟨a ~ porch⟩ ⟨a ~ freight car⟩ ⟨a ~ stairway⟩ **c :** covered over ⟨bake in a ~ dish⟩ **d :** blocked up or blocked in ⟨~ valleys⟩ **e :** barring or barred to traffic ⟨illegally entering a ~ port⟩ ⟨a ~ street⟩ **f** *phonetics* **:** CHECKED **g :** kept secret ⟨a ~ file on suspects⟩ ⟨the ~ ballot⟩ **h** *of the face of an animal* **:** covered esp. with wool or hair **i (1) :** covered by unbroken skin ⟨~ fracture⟩ **(2) :** not discharging pathogenic organisms to the outside ⟨a case of ~ tuberculosis⟩ — compare OPEN **j :** not free **:** COVERED — used of a tone in music, specif. a tone of the upper register; opposed to *open* **2 a (1) :** forming a self-contained unit admitting of no additions ⟨a ~ collection of documents⟩ ⟨organisms are not self-sufficient ~ systems —Weston La Barre⟩ **(2)** *of habitats or communities* **:** so completely stocked as to offer no opportunity for additional kinds of organisms to enter and establish themselves ⟨a ~ association⟩ **b :** lacking boundaries and having no point or element that has an infinite coordinate — used of lines, surfaces, and extents of any number of dimensions ⟨the ~ circumference of a circle⟩ **c :** existing with few external relations ⟨treating atomic physics as a ~ subject⟩; *specif* **:** having only limited foreign trade and approaching economic self-sufficiency ⟨a ~ economy⟩ **d (1)** *of a flock or herd* **:** bred from a single strain **(2)** *of a stud book* **:** permitting solely the registration of animals of which both sire and dam are registered therein — compare OPEN **e** *of a racetrack* **:** having the same starting and finishing point **f :** characterized by continuous return and reuse of the working medium — used esp. of water in a heating system or of air in a cooling system **g :** established in an invariable pattern ⟨a ~ program⟩ **h (1)** *dancing* **:** placing the free foot up to and in contact with the supporting foot **(2)** *ballroom dancing* **:** facing each other with the man's right arm around the woman's waist, the woman's left hand on the man's right shoulder, and their free hands joined **3 a :** rigidly excluding outside influence **:** having minimum contact ⟨to any but the most ~ of minds —R.E.McGill⟩ **b :** excluding participation of outsiders and witnesses **:** conducted in strict secrecy ⟨taking part in ~ international conferences⟩ **c :** confined to a few **:** restricted to selective membership ⟨a ~ hospital staff⟩ ⟨a ~ circle of believers⟩ **d :** intolerant of the influx of new members and ideas and approaching a state of social immobility and self-containment with respect to customs and traditions ⟨a ~ society⟩ ⟨a ~ class system⟩ **e :** not accessible to other nations ⟨unlimited sovereignty implies the policy of the ~ sky⟩ **f** *sports* **:** restricted to entrants of a specified kind or class ⟨a women's ~ golf tournament⟩ ⟨a ~ event for amateurs only⟩ — contrasted with *open* **g :** restricted with respect to the time or place for taking game **:** CLOSE ⟨woods ~ to hunters⟩ ⟨a ~ season for trout⟩ **4 :** having no cambium in the bundle, all meristematic tissue having been differentiated into xylem and phloem — used of certain vascular bundles; compare OPEN **5** *logic, of an expression* **:** containing variables all of which are bound — contrasted with *open* **6** *of the punctuation of a letter* **:** [4]CLOSE 17b **7 :** COMPLETED — used of a canasta meld containing seven or more cards esp. when it has been turned facedown

closed account *n* **1 :** an account whose total debit and total credit entries are equal and show no balance **2 :** an activity that has definitely ended

closed bank note *n* **:** BROKEN BANK NOTE

closed bolt *n* **:** a bookbinding in which the edge folds of the sections are left uncut

closed book *n* **:** something beyond comprehension ⟨railway operation is a *closed book* for many people —O.S.Nock⟩ **:** something that resists clarification ⟨a modern age in which the law is a *closed book* —B.N.Cardozo⟩

closed chain *n* **:** [1]RING 22 — opposed to *open chain*

closed circuit *n* **:** a circuit whose path carries completely around a course or through a cycle without break in continuity: **a :** an electric circuit made up of a continuous endless conductor or series of conductors with electrically conducting connections **b :** a television installation in which picture and sound are not broadcast but transmitted over a closed channel to a limited number of interconnected receivers ⟨*closed-circuit* television⟩

closed–circuit cell \'=¦==-\ *n* **:** a voltaic cell that is used where the duty is continuous and that does not polarize when furnishing current

closed–circuit winding \"-\ *n* **:** a mesh winding

closed corporation *n* **:** CLOSE CORPORATION ⟨many boroughs had previously been *closed corporations* in which aldermen co-opted whom they pleased to fill vacancies —W.H.Wickwar⟩ ⟨snobbish to the core and its society is still a *closed corporation* —J.E.Jennings⟩

closed couplet *n* **:** a rhymed couplet in which the sense is relatively complete or independent

closed–door \'=¦=\ *adj* **:** done or carried on in a closed session barring public and press ⟨a *closed-door* session of the investigating committee⟩

close defense \'klōs-\ *n* **:** the three defending positions closest to the goalie on a lacrosse team

closed–end \'klōzd+\ *adj* **1 :** having a fixed capitalization of shares that are traded on the open market instead of being redeemed daily by the company at the demand of the holders ⟨a *closed-end* investment company⟩ — opposed to *open-end* **2 :** issued to the full amount authorized or substantially the full amount ⟨a *closed-end* bond issue⟩

closed fold *n* **1 :** ISOCLINAL FOLD **2 :** a quaquaversal flexure around which a structure-contour line will close upon itself

closed form *n, crystallog* **:** a form whose faces enclose a space (as an octahedron)

closed gate *n* **:** a slalom obstacle consisting of two poles set one directly below the other in line with the vertical descent of the ski slope — compare OPEN GATE

closed gentian *n* **:** any of several fall-blooming No. American plants of the genus *Gentiana* (esp. *G. andrewsii* and *G. clausa*) having tubular usu. blue flowers that open little or not at all

closed hand *n* **:** the declarer's hand in bridge

closed issue *n* **:** an issue, question, or problem on which a decision has been reached and announced

closed–minded \'=¦==\ *adj* **:** obstinately resistant to argument or to unfamiliar or unwelcome ideas

closed mortgage *n* **:** a mortgage under which no or virtually no additional bonds can be sold under the indenture — contrasted with *open-end mortgage*

close down \'klōz-\ *vi* **1 :** to settle or appear close around so as to block any outward view ⟨fog presently *closed down*⟩ **2 :** to put a stern curb (as on an illegal operation by raids and arrests) ⟨a campaign to *close down* on slot machines⟩

closedown \'=,=\ *n* -S [*close down*] **1 :** a closing down (as of night) **2 :** a stoppage of operations **3** *Brit* **:** a signing off of a radiobroadcasting station

closed pair *n, physics* **:** a pair of bodies in which the relative motion is completely constrained

closed planer *n* **:** a planer having the crossrail supported by housings on each of the two sides

closed poker *n* **:** a game of poker in which all cards are dealt facedown and are not legally exposed until the showdown

closed pouch *n* **:** a mail pouch transported in a baggage car or by trolley line or truck and not opened for distribution en route as is done in a railway post office

closed primary *n* **:** a primary at which members of only one political party vote — compare OPEN PRIMARY

closed reduction *n, med* **:** the reduction of a displaced part (as a fractured bone) by manipulation without incision

closed rule *n* **:** a parliamentary rule barring amendments from the floor

closed sea *n* **:** MARE CLAUSUM

closed shop *n* **:** an establishment in which the employer by agreement hires and retains in employment only union members in good standing except that by some agreements when union members are unavailable the employer may hire nonunion workers provided they apply for union membership or obtain work permits before beginning work — compare MAINTENANCE OF MEMBERSHIP, OPEN SHOP, UNION SHOP

closed stance *n* **:** a preparatory position (as in baseball batting or golf) in which the left foot of a right-handed person is closer to the line of play than the right foot — contrasted with *open stance*

closed string *n* **:** CLOSE STRING

closed union *n* **:** a labor union that limits its size to guard against an oversupply of available workers

close fertilization \'klōs-\ *n* **:** fertilization in seed plants of the ovules of a flower by pollen from the same flower

close–fertilize \(')=¦==,=\ *vt* **:** to subject to close fertilization

close–fights \'=,=\ *n pl* **:** barriers with loopholes formerly erected on the deck of a ship to shelter men in a close engagement with boarders — called also *close quarters*

closefisted \'=¦==\ *adj* **:** not openhanded or liberal **:** TIGHTFISTED, CLOSE ⟨~ deacons objecting to expenses⟩ **syn** see STINGY

close–fitting \'=¦==\ *adj* **:** fitting snugly to the body or limbs

close girl \'klōs-, 'klōz-\ *n* **:** JOINER 1b

closegirt \'klōs+\ *adj* **:** fitting or fitted snugly round the waist

close–grained \'=¦=\ *also* **close–grain** \'=¦=\ *adj* **1 :** having fine and closely arranged fibers, crystals, or particles **:** having a closely compacted smooth texture; *specif, of wood* **:** having narrow annual rings or small wood elements or both **2 :** careful and precise as to order and articulation ⟨a book of fairly *close-grained* reasoning —N.M.Lawrence⟩

closehanded \'=¦==\ *adj, archaic* **:** CLOSEFISTED

close harmony \'klōs-\ *n* **1** *in traditional harmony* **:** the arrangement or distribution of the notes or tones of a chord so that the three upper parts lie within an octave — compare OPEN HARMONY **2 :** BARBERSHOP 2

close–hauled \'=¦=\ *adj, of a sailing ship* **:** having the yards braced up sharp and sheets aft if square-rigged or having the boom hauled in close to the center line if fore-and-aft rigged and sailing as nearly against the wind as the ship will go

close helm *or* **close helmet** \'klōz-\ *n* **:** ARMET

close–herd \'klōs+\ *vt* [[5]*close*] *West* **:** to herd (cattle) in a close group

close in \'klōz-\ *vb* [[1]*close*] *vi* **1 :** to gather in close all around with an oppressing or isolating effect ⟨the suffocating heaviness of New York's summer had already *closed in* —Marcia Davenport⟩ ⟨a brief bloom of fortune . . . before adversity *closed in* —Dixon Wecter⟩ ⟨despair *closed in* on her⟩ **2 :** to approach from various directions to close quarters esp. for an attack, raid, or arrest ⟨military intelligence agents *closed in* on him⟩ **3 :** to grow dark; *often* **:** to grow dark early — used of the day or the evening ⟨the short November day was already *closing in* —Ellen Glasgow⟩ **~** *vt* **1 :** to encircle closely and isolate **2 :** to enshroud to such an extent as to preclude approach or egress ⟨scouts report target *closed in*⟩ ⟨the airport is *closed in*⟩ **3 :** to shut off the flow of (an oil well)

close–in \'klōs+\ *adj* [[5]*close*] **1 :** near to a central part esp. of a city ⟨need for a *close-in* landing field⟩ **2 :** operating or delivered from close quarters ⟨*close-in* bombardment⟩

close juncture \"-\ *or* **close internal juncture** *n* **:** a juncture between two consecutive sounds in speech of the kind found in a simplex word (as between \t\ and \r\ in the pronunciation of *trait* or *nitrate* or between \ī\ and \n\ in the pronunciation of *mine* or *minus* — compare OPEN JUNCTURE, TERMINAL JUNCTURE

close–knit \'=¦=\ *adj* **1 :** bound together by intimate social or cultural ties or closely bound by economical or political ties ⟨the immigrants had left their *close-knit* little villages —Oscar Handlin⟩ **2 :** having the elements firmly and logically joined together ⟨the argument is *close-knit*⟩

close–lipped \'=¦=\ *adj* **:** TIGHT-LIPPED ⟨*close-lipped* and silent about the misadventure⟩ **syn** see SILENT

close·ly \'klōslē, -li\ *adv, sometimes* -ER/-EST [[4]*close* + *-ly*] **:** in a close position, state, manner, or relation: **a :** with close attention or scrutiny ⟨now listen ~⟩ ⟨ability to read ~⟩ **b** *obs* **:** SECRETLY, COVERTLY **c :** in close proximity ⟨a ~ built-up area⟩ ⟨~ held to his desk⟩ ⟨~ printed⟩ **d :** in a close state **:** TIGHTLY **:** in the hands of a few ⟨~ held private companies⟩ ⟨~ knit into the Soviet orbit⟩ **e :** in close conformity to a model ⟨~ resembling our housefly⟩ ⟨a coating most ~ matching the cover⟩ **f :** in close relation **:** INTIMATELY ⟨incidents in the book are quite ~ connected⟩ ⟨the two had worked ~ during the war⟩ ⟨made friends quickly but not ~⟩ **g :** ACCURATELY, MINUTELY ⟨indicating fairly ~ the true conditions⟩ ⟨questioned ~ and at length⟩ **h :** STRICTLY ⟨a ~ reasoned argument⟩ ⟨~ controlled sources of supply⟩

closemouthed \'klōs+\ *adj* **:** marked by customary caution against disclosing much information in speaking ⟨a ~ private secretary⟩ **syn** see SILENT

clos·en \'klōsᵊn\ *vb* **closened; closened; closening** \'klōs(ᵊ)niŋ\ **closens** [[4]*close* + *-en*] *vt* **:** to make close **~** *vi* **:** to become close or more close ⟨the ~*ing* bonds between two countries⟩

close·ness \'klōsnəs\ *n* -ES [ME, fr. [4]*close* + *-ness*] **:** the quality or state of being close

close off \'klōz-\ *vt* **1 :** to isolate or keep in seclusion **2 :** to stop the flow of

close on \'klōs-\ *or* **close onto** *prep* [[5]*close*] **1 :** within a very short time or distance of ⟨*close on* fifty years ago⟩ ⟨for *close on* five miles⟩ **:** within a very small number, amount, or quantity of ⟨housing *close on* a million volumes⟩ **:** just short of ⟨a deficit *close on* four billion dollars⟩ **2 :** closely approaching ⟨respect *close on* veneration⟩

close order \"-\ *n* **:** an arrangement of troops for formations, drill, or marching according to an exact scheme prescribing fixed distances and intervals — distinguished from *extended order*

close out \'klōz-\ *vt* **1 a :** EXCLUDE **b :** PRECLUDE ⟨*close out* his chances⟩ **2 a :** to dispose of a whole stock of by sale often at a concession **b :** to make final disposal of (a business) **c :** SELL ⟨*closed out* his share of the business⟩ **d :** to put (an account) in order for disposal or transfer **3 a :** to bring to a rapid or abrupt conclusion **:** TERMINATE **b :** to withdraw from operation **:** dismantle and discontinue **~** *vi* **1 :** to sell out a business **2 :** to buy or sell securities or commodities in order to terminate an account (as when margin is exhausted)

close·out \'klō,zau̇t\ *n* -S [*close out*] **1 :** a closing out; *specif* **:** a clearing out by a sale usu. at reduced price of the whole remaining stock whether of a closing business or of a particular discontinued item **2 :** an article offered or bought at a closeout

close position \'klōs-\ *n* **:** CLOSE HARMONY 1

close price \"-\ *n* **:** a price in a stock exchange showing slight variation between bid and asked prices or between successive transactions

close–price \'=,=\ *vi* [*close price*] **:** to limit prices so as to allow only a slight margin of profit esp. through government negotiation with manufacturers when competition is not effective

close–quarter \'=¦==\ *or* **close–quartered** \'=¦==\ *adj* **:** done or used at close quarters or in a narrowly restricted space

close quarters \klōs-\ *n pl* **1 :** CLOSE-FIGHTS **2 a :** immediate contact or close range ⟨fighting at *close quarters* with gun butts and fists⟩ **b :** an attitude of intently searching scrutiny ⟨coming to *close quarters* with a theory⟩

[1]**closer** *comparative of* CLOSE

[2]**clos·er** \'klōzə(r)\ *n* -S [[1]*close* + *-er*] **1 :** one that closes by hand or by machine: as **a :** a lid closer **b :** one that operates a sewing machine for joining the parts of a shoe upper esp. at the back seam or for stitching lining parts **c :** a sewing-machine operator who sews the seams of garments, gloves, and mattresses **2 :** something that closes: **a** *masonry* **(1) :** the last stone in a horizontal course if smaller than the others or a piece of brick finishing a course **(2) :** a piece of brick inserted in each alternate course to enable a bond to be formed by preventing two headers from exactly superimposing on a stretcher **b :** a device for closing something (as a door) **c :** an act, number, or play that brings a program to a close

close reach \'klōs-\ *n* **:** a reach sailed by a ship with the wind well forward of the beam but not as close-hauled as possible

close reading \"-\ *n* **:** detailed and careful analysis of a written work; *also* **:** the product of such analysis

close reef \'klōs-, 'klōz-\ *n* **:** the last ordinary reef that can be put in a sail — compare BALANCE REEF

close–reef \'=¦=\ *vt* [*close reef*] **:** to reduce the area of (a sail) as much as possible

close–reefed \'=¦=\ *adj* **:** having all the reefs taken in — used of a sail

close–rounded \'klōs+\ *adj, of a vowel sound* **:** made with great rounding of the lips ⟨the vowel in "boot" is *close-rounded*⟩

closes *pres 3d sing of* CLOSE, *pl of* CLOSE

close score \'klōs-\ *n* **:** a musical score in which two or more parts are put on the same staff — compare OPEN SCORE

close shake \"-\ *n* **:** BEBUNG

close shave \"-\ *n* **:** a narrow escape

close shot \"-\ *n* **:** a motion-picture shot made with the camera near the person or object but far enough away to include some of the background
closest *superlative of* CLOSE
close·stool \'klōz, 'klōs + ,-\ *n* [ME *close stol*, fr. *closen* to close + *stol* stool] **:** a stool or chair holding a chamber pot — compare COMMODE
close stretto \'klōs-\ *n* **:** a stretto in which the answer follows very closely after the subject
close string \'klōs-\ *n* **:** a string of a stair having its upper edge straight and usu. parallel with the lower edge so that the outer ends of the steps are entirely enclosed
close support \"-\ *n* **:** close-in fire or bombing delivered by a ground unit or by an air unit to assist another unit
¹clos·et \'kläzət *also* -lōz-; *usu* -əd·+V\ *n* -s [ME, fr. MF, dim. of *clos* enclosure — more at CLOSE] **1 :** an apartment or small room for retirement or privacy: as **a :** a monarch's, statesman's, or official's private chamber for counsel or devotions ⟨that diplomacy at critical stages is something for the ~ and not a mass meeting —C.G.Bowers⟩ **b** *chiefly Midland* **:** PRIVY **2 :** a cabinet or recess for china, household utensils, or clothing **:** CUPBOARD **3 :** a place of retreat or privacy ⟨~ of the heart⟩ **4 :** a diminutive of the bar in heraldry of one half its width **5 :** the bowl of a water closet
²closet \"\ *adj* **1 :** closely private ⟨a ~ utterance⟩ ⟨~ vows⟩ **2** *archaic* **:** suited to a closet ⟨~ prayer⟩ **3 a :** theoretical as opposed to practical ⟨a ~ politician⟩ **b :** working in or fitted for use or enjoyment only in the closet as the place of seclusion, study, or speculation ⟨the danger of intellectual anemia which threatens all ~ philosophers —M.R.Cohen⟩ ⟨the universe refutes our ~ rationalizations —W.L.Sullivan⟩
³closet \"\ *vt* -ED/-ING/-S **1 :** to shut up in or as if in a closet ⟨he ~*ed* himself in a phone booth⟩ **2 :** to take into a closet for a secret interview ⟨the inspector was ~*ed* with the district attorney⟩
close tail \'klōs-\ *n* **:** a tailing by a detective close on the heels of his subject; *also* **:** the detective doing this
closet drama *n* **:** drama suited primarily for reading rather than production; *also* **:** a play of this type
closeted *adj* **:** ²CLOSET 3b
close time \'klōs-\ *n, chiefly Brit* **:** a closed season
close–tongued \'=;=\ *adj* **:** CLOSEMOUTHED
close·up \'klō,səp\ *adj* [*close up*, adv.] **:** detailed and intimate from or as if from a point of vantage in close proximity
close–up \"\ *n* -s [*close up*, adv.] **1 a :** a motion picture taken very near an object or person to emphasize detail strongly or accentuate mood **b :** a photograph taken at close range **c :** photographic presentation produced with camera and object in close proximity ⟨television is mostly in *close-up*⟩ **2 a :** a close or intimate view or examination of anything **b :** a voice amplified to give the effect of issuing from close proximity **c :** a theatrical scene in which action is focused on the facial expression and emotional tension of certain characters **d :** a compact intimate biography ⟨it affords unique *close-ups* of key actors in political melodrama being played in Europe⟩
close up \-ōz-\ *vb* [¹*close*] *vt* **1 :** to bring to a complete conclusion or settlement **2 :** to restrain by legal measures from further business operations **3** *printing* **a :** to remove or reduce the spacing material between (units of set type matter) **b :** to assemble (type matter set in separate takes) ~ *vi* **1 :** to converge in close array **2 :** to discontinue business operations **3 :** to retreat into complete silence **:** become uncommunicative —**close up shop** \"-\ **1 :** to shut up shop **2 :** to cease all activities
close with \'klōz-\ *vt* **1 :** to approach close to **2 :** to engage in hostile encounter at close quarters **3 :** to ratify an agreement with
closh \'kläsh\ *n* -ES [origin unknown] **:** a post on a whaling ship fitted with hooks for hanging blubber to be sliced
¹clos·ing \'klōziŋ, -zēŋ\ *n* -s [ME, fr. gerund of *closen* to close] **1 a :** the concluding portion of a speech or debate **:** PERORATION **b :** a complimentary close of a letter **2 a :** a closable gap in an article of wear or luggage; *specif* **:** the section of an article that opens and closes for convenience of use (as a placket in a garment or the fastening of a bag)
²closing \"\ *adj* [fr. pres. part. of ¹*close*] **:** constituting the last stage or the final portion or item ⟨the ~ years of the century⟩ ⟨the ~ campaign of the revolution⟩
closing entry *n* **:** any one of a series of journal entries necessary to close the books of a business
closing error *n* **:** ERROR OF CLOSURE
closing layer *n, bot* **:** one of the layers of small compact cells that subdivide the complementary cells
closing line *n, math* **:** the line vector that is necessary to complete the polygon representing a vector sum and thus to render the sum zero (as in obtaining the equilibrant of a set of forces); *esp* **:** the closing side of a plane traverse
closing machine *n* **:** a machine that sews a lock stitch with two threads in heavy material
closing membrane *n* **:** PIT MEMBRANE
closing price *n* **:** the final price quoted for a bond, stock, or commodity on a stock exchange or produce exchange for a given day
clos·ish \'klōsish\ *adj* [⁴*close* + *-ish*] **:** rather close
clost \'klōst\ *dial var of* CLOSE
clos·te·ri·um \klä'stirēəm\ *n, cap* [NL, fr. Gk *klōstēr* spindle + NL *-ium*] **:** a genus of crescent-shaped desmids
clos·trid·i·al \(')klä;stridēəl\ *or* **clos·trid·i·an** \-ēən\ *adj* [NL *clostridium* + E *-al* or *-an*] **:** of, relating to, produced by, or resembling a clostridium
clos·trid·i·um \=';=ēəm\ *n* [NL, fr. *clostr-* (fr. Gk *klōstēr* spindle) + *-idium*] **1** *cap* **:** a genus of anaerobic or microaerophilic saprophytic rod-shaped or spindle-shaped bacteria (family Bacillaceae) that are nearly cosmopolitan in soil, animal intestines, and dung, that are distinguished from members of the genus *Bacillus* by the swollen drumstick shape assumed during spore formation, by the absence of aerobic growth, and by lack of the enzyme catalase, that are very actively biochemically comprising numerous fermenters of carbohydrates with vigorous production of acid and gas, many nitrogen fixers, and others which rapidly putrefy proteins, and that include forms of considerable importance to man in certain industrial fermentations (as *C. butyricum* or *C. acetobutylicum*) or as pathogens of himself, his domestic animals, or his cultivated plants — compare BLACKLEG, BOTULISM, GAS GANGRENE, LIMBERNECK, TETANUS **2** *pl* **clostrid·ia** \-ēə\ **a :** any bacterium of the genus *Clostridium* **b :** a spindle-shaped or ovoid bacterial cell; *esp* **:** one swollen at the center by an endospore
¹clo·sure \'klōzhə(r)\ *n* -s [ME, fr. MF, fr. L *clausura*, fr. *clausus* (past part. of *claudere* to close) + *-ura* -ure — more at CLOSE] **1 a** *archaic* **:** means of enclosing ⟨formed a ~ around a plot of land⟩ **b** *obs* **:** FORT **c** *obs* **:** encircling bounds ⟨within the guilty ~ of thy walls —Shak.⟩ **d** *obs* **:** a space enclosed **e** *civil engin* **:** a giving of a closed figure when plotted — compare CLOSE *vi* 6 **2 a** *obs* **:** the action of confining or condition of being confined in an enclosing place **b :** the absence of social mobility in a social group **:** social self-containment of a group **3 a :** a bringing to a point of completion **b** *cricket* **:** an act or right of declaring an innings closed **c** *linguistics* **:** a closed construction — compare CLOSE *vt* 1b (3) **4 a :** an act of closing up or condition of being closed up ⟨~ of the eyelids⟩ ⟨the captain checked the ship's ~ for the pending attack⟩ **b :** a filling up of a space to seal or render impervious ⟨be sure the container has a tight ~ to keep it free from contamination⟩ **c :** a drawing together of edges or parts to form a united integument ⟨wound ~ by suture immediately after laceration⟩ **d** *phonetics* (1) **:** the extent to which an articulation blocks the passage of air (2) **:** the outer and the inner closure in a consonant articulation **5 a :** a means of filling a space or gap esp. by sealing it or of closing an opening (as in a garment or luggage): as (1) **:** FASTENER, CLOSING ⟨styled with fly-front ~⟩ ⟨pocket with zipper ~⟩ ⟨~ buttons for tubular furniture⟩ (2) **:** CLOSER 2 (3) **:** a cap, lid, or other form of stopper on or in a container esp. for sealing it **b :** the part of a container where the final seal is made **6** *archaic* **:** a coming to an agreement ⟨a precipitate ~ with this gentleman's proposals —Jane Austen⟩ **7** [trans. of F *clôture* — more at CLOTURE] **:** CLOTURE **8 a :** the vertical distance between the highest point in a quaquaversal flexure or doubly plunging anticline and the lowest structure-contour line that closes around it **b** *Brit* **:** a fold of a close-textured rock over a layer of porous rock to form a trap **9 :** a bringing of some activity to a stop ⟨a ~ on smoking in the woods during a dry spell⟩ **:** cessation of operation ⟨~ of foreign-owned industries⟩ **10 :** a closing with a particular destination on the part of a ship **11** *psychol* **:** the perception of incomplete figures or situations as though complete by ignoring the missing parts or by compensating for them by projection based on past experience
²closure \"\ *vt* **closured; closured; closuring** \-zh(ə)riŋ\ **closures :** CLOTURE ⟨debate was *closured* so the bill could be put to an almost immediate vote⟩
¹clot \'klät, *usu* -äd·+V\ *n* -s [ME, fr. OE *clott* lump, mass; akin to MHG *kloz* lumpy mass, ball, *klōz* lump, ball — more at CLOUT] **1 a :** a portion of a substance cleaving together in a thick nondescript mass (as of clay or gum) ⟨dodging ~*s* of dirt from the horse's hoofs⟩ **b** *archaic* **:** a hard lump **:** CLOD **2 a :** a roundish viscous lump formed by coagulation of a portion of liquid or by melting **:** a sizable blob or gob ⟨~*s* of cream forming in the churn⟩ **b :** a semisolid coagulum produced by entrapment of formed elements of the blood in a meshwork of precipitated fibrin filaments **c :** something seen esp. from some distance as an amorphous patch (as of color or light) or group ⟨coloring the ridges with ~*s* of shadow —H.L.Davis⟩ ⟨a small ~ of officials at the door⟩ **d :** an intangible knot resulting from a congealing and separating out from some moving stream ⟨public opinion is beginning to congeal in two ~*s*⟩ **3** *dial Eng* **:** BLOCKHEAD 2 **4 :** a closely grouped or intertwined or interweaving assemblage of living beings **:** CLUSTER, CLUMP ⟨~*s* of black ducks migrating south⟩ ⟨the Filipinos lived and worked in ~*s* of five or six —John Steinbeck⟩ ⟨almost a hundred marines, soldiers, and sailors drawn up into a ~ in the street —E.L.Burdick⟩
²clot \"\ *vb* **clotted; clotted; clotting; clots** *vi* **1 :** to form into a clot ⟨*clotting* masses of hydrocarbon molecules⟩ ⟨spectators *clotted* around the more closely contested field events⟩ ⟨when darkness seeped across the hill and *clotted* in the valley below us —H.D.Skidmore⟩ **2 :** to undergo a sequence of complex chemical and physical reactions that results in conversion of fluid blood into a coagulum and that in vertebrates prob. involves the following course: shedding of blood, release of thromboplastin from blood platelets and injured tissues, inactivation of heparin by thromboplastin permitting calcium ions of the plasma to convert prothrombin to thrombin, interaction of thrombin with fibrinogen to form an insoluble fibrin network in which blood cells and plasma are trapped, and contraction of the network to squeeze out excess fluid **:** COAGULATE ~ *vt* **1 :** to gather, press, or stick together in a clot ⟨perspiration *clotted* his hair⟩ ⟨the milk was *clotted* by the addition of a coagulant before it was used⟩ **2 :** to fill, strew, or overspread with clots ⟨streets *clotted* with traffic⟩ ⟨a mud-*clotted* pony⟩ ⟨an elder grew leaning forward, its branches *clotted* with waxen blossom —Elizabeth Bowen⟩ ⟨fruit and flower paintings that *clotted* the walls —Truman Capote⟩ **3 :** to cause to form into a clot or clump that halts, obstructs, or stagnates ⟨each night *clotted* the intership phones with "alerts", warnings, and alarms —John Mason Brown⟩ ⟨the meaning is often *clotted* by metaphor —Edmund Wilson⟩ ⟨a people whose new, raw culture was not yet *clotted* with inhibition —R.L.Taylor⟩
clot·bur \'klät +,-\ *n* [*clote* + *bur*] **:** BURDOCK
clote \'klōt\ *n* -s [ME, fr. OE *clāte* burr, burdock; akin to L *glut-, glus* glue, Lith *gliēti* to grease — more at CLAY] *dial Eng* **:** any of several plants related to the burdocks (as the cleavers, the butterbur, the coltsfoot, and the SPATTERDOCK)
¹cloth \'klȯth *also* -läth\ *n, pl* **cloths** \-thz,-ths\ *often attrib* [ME, fr. OE *clāth;* akin to OFris *klāth*, MD *cleet*, MHG *kleit*, OE *clīthan* to adhere to, Lith *glitùs* slippery — more at CLAY] **1 a :** something made by weaving, felting, knitting, knotting, bonding, or crocheting natural or synthetic fibers and filaments and used in variations of texture, finish, weight, width for clothing, upholstery, rugs, and industrial purposes or treated so that it will serve a special purpose (as made semirigid for bookbinding) **b :** a similar material (as of plastic, wire, or glass) **2 a :** a piece of cloth of varying length esp. as taken from a loom, as measured in a bolt, or as required for a garment **b :** a particular kind of cloth ⟨velvet is a ~ with a pile face⟩ ⟨cotton is the commonest woven ~⟩ **c :** a piece of cloth adapted by size, texture, or finish for a particular purpose — often used in combination ⟨dust*cloth*⟩ ⟨face*cloth*⟩ **d :** TABLECLOTH **e** *obs* **:** a piece of fabric of a standard quantity or length **f** (1) **:** canvas made into a sail (2) **:** one of the breadths of canvas sewed together to make a sail **g** *archaic* **:** canvas for a painting **h** *theater* **:** a painted cloth drop **3 a** *obs* **:** wearing apparel **:** CLOTHING **b** *archaic* **:** LIVERY **c :** a piece of cloth worn as a garment **4 a :** distinctive dress esp. of any profession or calling ⟨how any naval officer who respected his ~ could go fishing on equal terms with enlisted men —Fletcher Pratt⟩ **b :** the dress of the clergy or the clerical profession; *also* **:** CLERGY
²cloth *vt, obs* **:** to make into cloth
cloth beam *n* **:** the cylinder of a loom on which cloth is rolled as it is woven — called also FORE BEAM
clothbound \'=;=\ *adj, of a book* **:** bound in full cloth with stiff boards
clothe \'klōth\ *vb* **clothed** *or* **clad** \'klad, -aa(ə)d\ **clothed** *or* **clad; clothing; clothes** \'klō(th)z\ [ME *clothen*, fr. OE *clāthian*, fr. *clāth* garment, cloth — more at CLOTH] *vt* **1 a :** to put garments on **:** cover with clothes **b :** to provide with clothes ⟨trying to feed and ~ a family⟩ **c** *obs* **:** to hang or spread cloth over ⟨they *clothed* the royal bed with purple⟩ **d :** to fit out ⟨horses heavily *clothed* with armor⟩ ⟨natives *clothed* in ritual beads⟩ ⟨gold and diamonds to ~ their harlots⟩ **e :** to invest with the habit of a religious or the robes of a dignitary ⟨to attend the *clothing* of two lay sisters⟩ **f :** RIG ⟨~ a ship⟩ ⟨~ a mast⟩ **g :** to cover (carding equipment) with card clothing **h :** to cover (a sieve in milling equipment) with silk or woven wire **i :** to house in an intimate protective sheath suggestive of a garment ⟨a simple coffin to ~ the body of their friend —D.V.Steere⟩ ⟨*clothed* in its complicated shell⟩ **2 a :** to serve as a blanket overspreading the surface of esp. as adding or emphasizing some visual effect ⟨dense coniferous forests ~ the high bordering ridges —C.D.Forde⟩ ⟨foothills *clothed* in magnificent jungle⟩ **b :** to cover or overspread the integument or exterior of ⟨their bodies and wings densely *clothed* with hair⟩ ⟨scales ~ its whole body⟩ ⟨apple trees *clothed* in blossoms⟩ **3 :** to express, convey, or enhance by suitably significant language **:** COUCH ⟨treaties *clothed* in stately phraseology⟩ ⟨the sweep of its ideas and the something akin to perfection of form in which they are *clothed* —H.J.Laski⟩ **4 a :** to envelop, finish out, or flesh out ⟨the roof and sides of the cavern begin to ~ themselves with that quivering violet sheen —Norman Douglas⟩ ⟨to ~ the dry bones of the law⟩ **b :** to wrap or cloak esp. in a way to provide delusion or borrow prestige ⟨by no whit lessened his agitation, which he sought to ~ with a semblance of debonair indifference —Osbert Sitwell⟩ ⟨~ themselves in Bismarck's conception of a nation standing between East and West —M.W.Straight⟩ **c :** PRESENT, REPRESENT, PORTRAY ⟨*clothing* its message in allegory⟩ ⟨meticulously *clothing* the period with authenticity⟩ **:** to present or represent through an illustrative or interpretive medium ⟨her innate tact, *clothed* in tender warmth and naturalness —Marcia Davenport⟩ **5 :** to endow esp. with power or a quality ⟨an act *clothing* Indians with U. S. citizenship⟩ ⟨~ a commission with power to fix utility rates⟩ ~ *vi, archaic* **:** to clothe oneself
clothes \'klō(th)z\ *n pl, often attrib* [ME, fr. OE *clāthas*, pl. of *clāth* cloth, article of clothing — more at CLOTH] **1 :** CLOTHING 1a **2 :** BEDCLOTHES **3 :** all the cloth articles of personal and household use that can be washed ⟨I always wash ~ on Mondays⟩ **4 a :** distinctive style **:** GUISE ⟨old theories in contemporary verbal ~⟩ **b :** CHARACTER, ROLE ⟨stepping into the ~ of the departed leader⟩
clothes basket *n* **:** a deep open usu. oval-shaped basket for carrying clothes and household linen to and from the place of laundering or drying **:** HAMPER
clothes closet *n* **:** a small room for hanging clothes
clothes hanger *n* **:** COAT HANGER
clothes·horse \'=,=\ *n* **1 :** a frame on which to hang clothes or household linen (as for airing or drying) **2 a :** one whose marked or often sole claim to attention is in undue variety or conspicuous fashionableness of dress **b :** one overly concerned with appearing fashionable in dress esp. by conspicuously frequent changes

clotheshorse

clothesline \'=,=\ *n* **:** a line (as a length of cord or wire) stretched over some distance for hanging and drying clothes
clothes louse *n* **:** BODY LOUSE
clothes maid *or* **clothes maiden** *n, dial Brit* **:** CLOTHESHORSE 1
clothes moth *n* **:** any of several small yellowish or buff-colored tineid moths whose larvae eat organic matter (as woolen goods, furs, or feathers) — see CASEMAKING CLOTHES MOTH, WEBBING CLOTHES MOTH
clothes–peg \'=,=\ *n, Brit* **:** CLOTHESPIN
clothes·pin \'=,=\ *n* **:** a forked piece of wood or plastic or a small spring clamp used for fastening clothes on a line
clothespin graft *n* **:** a piece of bone shaped like a clothespin and used as a bone graft in spine fusion operations to bridge several vertebrae

clothespins

clothes·pole \'=,=\ *n* **:** a pole forked at the top for propping up a clothesline
clothes·press \'=,=\ *n* **1 :** a receptacle for clothes: as **a :** a tall piece of furniture having a compartment in which clothes may be hung **b :** a piece of case furniture with sliding trays to hold clothes **2** *North & Midland* **:** CLOTHES CLOSET
clothes screen *n* **:** CLOTHESHORSE 1
clothes stick *n* **:** a staff or bat with forked tip for turning and handling clothes being boiled or rinsed
clothes stop *n* **:** cotton line used for fastening washed clothes to a line or for tying up rolled clothes in bags or lockers
clothes tree *n* **:** an upright postlike stand with hooks or pegs around the top on which to hang clothes — called also *costumer, hall tree, hatstand, hat tree*
clothesyard \'=,=\ *n* **:** a section of a yard of a dwelling used for hanging clothes to dry or air
cloth hall *n* [trans. of F *halle aux draps*] **:** a building serving as a medieval exchange for the cloth merchants
cloth house *n* **:** a flat-topped shelter of loosely woven cloth used to protect growing plants (as tobacco) from insects, fungus pests, heavy rain, and wind and to reduce light intensity and evaporation and hence induce greater stem length and larger blooms or a thinner or higher quality of leaf
cloth·ier \'klōthyə(r), -thēə-\ *n* -s [ME, alter. of earlier *clother*, fr. ¹*cloth* + *-er*] **1** *obs* **:** a maker of cloth **2** *archaic* **:** a fuller of cloth **3 a :** a retailer of cloth and often also a tailor **b :** a retailer of men's clothes **4 :** one that covers with cloth the steel drawing rollers of textile machines
cloth·ier's–brush \'=,=,=\ *n, pl* **clothier's–brushes :** WILD TEASEL
cloth·i·fy \'klōthə,fī\ *vt* -ED/-ING/-ES [¹*cloth* + *-ify*] *archaic* **:** CLOTHE

clothes tree

cloth·ing \'klōthiŋ, -ēŋ *but see sense 5*\ *n* -s [ME, fr. gerund of *clothen* to clothe] **1 a :** covering for the human body or garments in general **:** all the garments and accessories worn by a person at any one time **b** *obs* **:** LIVERY **c :** the equipment (as blankets, hoods, or bandages) used to cover and protect a domestic animal (as a horse) **d :** characteristic exterior properties and aspects, style, and atmosphere in which something intangible is discerned ⟨the moral ~ of legislation⟩ **2 :** CLEADING 2 **3 a :** SAILS **b :** the bowsprit rigging **4 :** CLOTHING WOOL **5** \'klōth- *also* 'kläth-\ **:** CARD CLOTHING **6 :** the felts and wires of papermaking machines
clothing wool \'klōthiŋ-, -ēŋ-\ *n* **1 :** short staple wool usu. under 1¾ inches in length and suitable only for carding and woolen goods — called also *carding wool* **2 :** wool used in apparel fabrics as distinguished from wool used in carpets
cloth measure *n* **:** a unit or system of units for measuring cloth; *specif* **:** a system of ells, quarters, and nails
cloth of gold : a fabric woven wholly or partly of gold thread esp. for ceremonial use
cloth–of–gold cone \;=;=;=-\ *n* **:** TEXTILE CONE
cloth of silver : a cloth wholly or partly of silver thread
cloth of state : a rich cloth forming a canopy and background to a throne or chair of state
cloth oil *n* **:** WOOL OIL 1
cloth plate *n* **:** the metal plate in a sewing machine through which the needle passes and on which the work rests
cloth red B *n, usu cap C&R* **:** an acid dye — see DYE table I (under *Acid Red 115*)
cloths *pl of* CLOTH
cloth scarlet G *n, usu cap C&S* **:** an acid dye — see DYE table I (under *Acid Red 151*)
cloth wheel *n* **:** a polishing wheel consisting of built-up layers of cloth charged with an abrasive or polishing material
clothworker \'=,=,=\ *n* **:** a textile worker or manufacturer
clothy \'klōthē *also* -äthē\ *adj* **:** resembling cloth
cloth yard *n* **:** a yard esp. for measuring cloth; *specif* **:** a unit of 37 inches equal to the Scotch ell and used also as a length for arrows ⟨*cloth yard* shafts used by English archers at Crécy⟩
clot molder *n, Brit* **:** a molder's assistant who works clots of clay and rough-shapes them into bricks
clot·poll \'klät,pōl\ *n* [by alter.] **:** CLODPOLL
clot retraction time *n* **:** the time required for the fibrin of a fresh blood clot to contract and squeeze out excess serum
clots *pl of* CLOT, *pres 3d sing of* CLOT
clot·ta·ble \'kläd·əbəl, -lätə-\ *adj* **:** capable of being clotted
clotted *adj* [fr. past part. of ²*clot*] **1 :** choked with thickened masses or compact assemblages suggestive of gobbets **:** CLUTTERED, CLOGGED ⟨roads ~ with trucks and tanks⟩ **2** *Brit* **:** UNQUALIFIED, SHEER ⟨~ nonsense⟩ — **clot·ted·ness** *n* -ES
clotted cream *n* **:** DEVONSHIRE CREAM
clot·ter \'klätə(r)\ *vi* [ME *cloteren*, fr. ¹*clot* + *-eren* (freq. suffix)] *now dial Brit* **:** CLOT, COAGULATE
clotting *pres part of* CLOT
clot·ty \'kläd·ē, -lätē\ *adj* **:** clotted or inclined to clot
¹clo·ture \'klōchə(r)\ *n* -s [F *clôture*, alter. (influenced by such words as *fermeture* closing, *ouverture* opening) of OF *closture* — more at CLOSURE] **:** the closing or limitation of debate in a legislative body by calling for a vote or by other authorized methods — compare GUILLOTINE, KANGAROO CLOSURE
²cloture \"\ *vt* -ED/-ING/-S **:** to end debate of by cloture
clotweed \'=,=\ *n* [*clote* + *weed*] **:** COCKLEBUR 1
clou \'klü\ *n* -s [F, lit., nail, fr. L *clavus* — more at CLAVUS] **:** the point of chief interest or attraction
¹cloud \'klaud\ *n* -s *often attrib* [ME, rock, hill, cloud, fr. OE *clūd;* akin to Gk *gloutos* buttock, Slovenian *glúta* bump, Skt *glau* round lump — more at GALL] **1 a :** a visible assemblage of particles of water or ice in the form of fog, mist, or haze formed by the condensation of vapor in the air and suspended in the air generally at a considerable height — see CIRRUS, CUMULUS, NIMBUS, STRATUS **b :** the material of which such a mass is composed **c :** a light filmy, puffy, or billowy mass seeming to float in the air ⟨a clipper ship under a

clouds, 1a: *1* cirrus, *2* cirrostratus, *3* cirrocumulus, *4* altostratus, *5* altocumulus, *6* stratocumulus, *7* nimbostratus, *8* cumulus, *9* cumulonimbus, *10* stratus

~ of sail⟩ ⟨a girl with a lustrous ~ of long golden hair⟩ **2 a :** a usu. visible assemblage of minute particles of a substance suspended in the surrounding air or in a gas ⟨enveloped in a ~ of steam⟩ ⟨when the wind drops, the sand ~ disappears with it —R.A.Bagnold⟩ ⟨the mushroom ~ arising from an atomic blast⟩ ⟨the flower smell came up in a heavy invisible ~ from the bed —Paul Bowles⟩ **b :** one of the aggregations of obscuring matter in space that reveal themselves as dark areas against the background of more distant bright objects or by stationary lines in stellar spectra ⟨fine yellow dust forming the ~*s* of the morning star⟩ **c :** a group of microscopic waves or electrically charged particles ⟨a ~ of electrons exists in the space surrounding the cathode —A.V. Eastman⟩ **3 a :** a flying swarm (as of birds, insects, or airplanes) **b :** a great crowd or multitude ⟨a host of individual geniuses and a ~ of admirable painters notwithstanding —Clive Bell⟩ ⟨in a mystifying ~ of words⟩ **4 a :** something that has a dark, lowering, or threatening aspect ⟨the ~*s* of World War II began to loom over the horizon⟩ **b :** something that temporarily overshadows or depresses ⟨occasionally a ~ darkens my reflections —P.E.More⟩ **5 a :** something that obscures or disrupts ⟨tried to veil his testimony in a ~ of sanctity —L.P.Stryker⟩ **b :** something that impairs, detracts, subjects to suspicion or controversy **:** BLEMISH ⟨justice demands removal of the ~ on the title to this land⟩ ⟨ a ~ rests over the transaction⟩ ⟨emerging from under the ~ of international disapprobation⟩ **6 a :** a dark or opaque vein or spot on a lighter or transparent material (as in marble) **b :** a similar spot of any shade or color against a different ground ⟨precipitated as a reddish ~ in the bottle⟩; *specif* **:** a patch of color marking ⟨a blackish ~ on the mare's forehead⟩ **7 :** a large lightweight loosely knitted head scarf — **in the clouds :** given over to or in a state of impractical fancy; *specif* **:** rapt in abstruse cogitation, nebulous theorizing, or aesthetic transport — **under a cloud 1 :** in disfavor or disgrace **2 :** subject to a stigma or to suspicion as not fully cleared of a damaging charge **3 :** suffering repression or derangement

²**cloud** \"\ *vb* -ED/-ING/-S *vi* **1 a :** to grow cloudy **:** become overcast — usu. used with *over* or *up* ⟨~ over before a rain⟩ **b** *of a transparent surface* **:** to become overspread or obscured with spots or streaks ⟨a windshield often ~*s* in winter with condensation of the breath⟩ **2 a** *of facial features* **:** to become troubled, apprehensive, or distressed in appearance ⟨his eyes ~*ed* with indignation⟩ **b :** to become blurry, dubious, or ominous ⟨the outlook . . . ~*ed* abruptly —Michael Clark⟩ **3 :** to billow up in the form of a cloud ~ *vt* **1 a :** to envelop or hide with a cloud or as if by a cloud ⟨the mountain peak was ~*ed* all day⟩ ⟨the smog ~*ed* our view⟩ **b :** to make opaque (as a mirror or window) esp. by condensation of moisture ⟨the steam from the shower ~*ed* the windows⟩ **c :** to darken or make murky esp. with smoke or mist ⟨smoke ~*ed* the sky and the atmosphere of the hillside⟩ **d :** to darken or overshadow with a dispirited or dispiriting cast (as of perplexity, gloom, shame) ⟨with a distressing melancholy ~*ing* her features⟩ **2 :** to make unclear **:** OBSCURE, CONFUSE: **a :** to make uncertain or disputable (as a title or an issue) ⟨both the title and the legal right are ~*ed* by the loss⟩ ⟨~ the issue of fault and blame⟩ **b :** to make indistinct or difficult to discern or clarify ⟨language which will not ~ the nature of the problem⟩ **c :** to make (the mind or the reasoning) confused or illogical ⟨a religiosity which ~*ed* their minds⟩ **d :** to make torpid ⟨a disease characterized by a ~*ing* of consciousness⟩ **3 a :** TAINT, SULLY ⟨a ~*ed* reputation⟩ ⟨a ~*ed* character⟩ ⟨the slightly dishonest deed ~*ed* his good name all his life⟩ ⟨no misunderstanding ever ~*ed* their friendship —John Buchan⟩ **b :** to impair or distort the sound state or purity of ⟨letting his feelings ~ his sense of justice⟩ **c :** to cast gloom over or put a blighting influence on — usu. implying a certain persistence of the cause ⟨the latter part of his life was ~*ed* by disillusionment⟩ ⟨discouragements ~ the life of every man at some time⟩ **d :** to impoverish of spirit or morale ⟨his future was ~*ed* by poor eyesight⟩ **4 :** to mark with or darken in patches or spots ⟨the hot water ~*ed* the surface of the table⟩ ⟨the wind ~*ed* the lake⟩ **syn** see OBSCURE

cloud·age \'klau̇dij\ *n* -S [¹*cloud* + *-age*] **:** a mass of clouds

cloud band *n* **:** a sinuous stylization of a cloud used as a motif in Chinese art and esp. in Persian and other oriental rugs

cloud banner *n* **:** BANNER CLOUD

cloudberry \'=-— *see* BERRY\ *n* -ES [¹*cloud* + *berry;* prob. fr. its shape] **1 :** a creeping herbaceous raspberry (*Rubus chamaemorus*) of north temperate regions bearing large white flowers and edible fruit — called also *dwarf mulberry* **2 :** the reddish amber-colored fruit of the cloudberry

cloud blower *n* **:** a straight clay pipe used by Pueblo Indians for sending symbolic puffs of smoke in different directions during rites

cloud blue *n* **:** a very pale blue that is less strong and slightly redder and lighter than baby blue (sense 1) and greener and paler than pastel blue (sense 2)

cloud-built \'=,=\ *adj* **:** UNSUBSTANTIAL, IMAGINARY

cloudburst \'=,=\ *n* -S **1 :** a sudden copious rainfall as if a whole cloud had been precipitated at once **2 :** DELUGE 2 **3 :** pseudopregnancy of the goat

cloudcap \'=,=\ *n* **:** CAP CLOUD

cloud-capped \'=;=\ *adj* **:** having clouds about the top or peaks **:** reaching to the clouds

cloud chamber *n* **:** a closed vessel containing air saturated with water vapor in which ionizing particles (as electrons or protons) passing through the vessel simultaneously with the sudden expansion and resultant cooling of the vapor leave visible white tracks of droplets condensed on the ions created by the particles, these tracks usu. being photographed — called also *expansion chamber*

cloud-cuckoo-land \'=;=;=,=\ *n, sometimes cap C&C&L* [trans. of Gk *nephelokokkygia*] **:** a whimsically conceived realm of utopian fantasy

cloud drift *n* **1 :** a mass of drifting clouds **2 :** a method of distributing by airplane a powdered insecticide that drifts slowly like a cloud over the area under treatment

cloud·ed \'klau̇dəd\ *adj* **1 :** of variegated material **:** MOTTLED **2 :** obscure or obscured in form or expression **:** BLURRED ⟨sometimes one understood clearly and sometimes the meaning was ~ —H.G.Wells⟩ **3 :** mentally confused **:** DISORDERED **4** *of title to land* **:** having some defect that constitutes a cloud on title **5 :** QUESTIONABLE 4

clouded leopard *n* **:** a medium-sized arboreal cat (*Felis nebulosa*) of southeastern Asia and the East Indies that is mottled and striped with black on a brownish gray ground

clouded sulphur *n* **:** a medium-sized yellow butterfly (*Colias philodice*) with black-bordered wings that is common in most of the U.S. and has a larva that feeds on several economic leguminous plants — compare ALFALFA CATERPILLAR

clouded tiger *n* **:** CLOUDED LEOPARD

clouded ware *n* **:** glazed ware dabbed with spots colored by metallic oxides

cloud forest *n* **:** a dense forest esp. on coastal slopes in the rainy regions of low latitudes that is almost constantly under clouds and differing from tropical rain forest mainly in being cooler and more humid

cloud funnel *n* **:** the funnel-shaped pendent cloud of a tornado

cloud grass *n* **:** a Spanish grass (*Agrostis nebulosa*) with a light feathery panicle cultivated for dried bouquets

cloud gray *n* **:** ZINC 2

cloud·i·ly \'klau̇dᵊlē, -dəlē\ *adv* **:** in a cloudy or clouded manner **:** INDISTINCTLY, OBSCURELY

cloud·i·ness \-dēnəs, -din-\ *n* -ES **:** cloudy or clouded condition or appearance; *esp* **:** the amount of cloud formation covering the sky — usu. expressed in tenths or eighths

cloud·ing \-diŋ\ *n* -S **1 :** a cloudy marking or appearance **:** fogginess esp. of shadows in an X ray **2 :** dull blurry and usu. mottled coloration

clouding of consciousness : mental confusion with impaired awareness of the environment

cloud·land \'klau̇d,land, -lənd\ *n* **1 :** a region in the upper atmosphere occupied by clouds **2 :** the realm of visionary hypothesis or uncertain speculation **3 :** the realm of poetic imagination

cloud·less \'klau̇dləs\ *adj* **:** free from any cloud ⟨one of the most ~ loves in life, this for books —Mary Stolz⟩

cloud·less·ly *adv* **:** in a cloudless manner

cloud·less·ness *n* -ES **:** the quality or state of being cloudless

cloudless sulphur *n* **:** a widely distributed New World butterfly (*Phoebis sennae*) resembling the clouded sulphur but lacking the broad black margin on the wings and being a strong migrant with a larva that is a pest on senna

cloud·let \'klau̇dlət\ *n* -S [¹*cloud* + *-let*] **:** a small cloud

cloud·ling \-dliŋ\ *n* -S [¹*cloud* + *-ling*] **:** a little cloud

cloud meter *n* **:** an instrument for measuring rates of collection of atmospheric water and ice by means of a porous plug through which the moisture is drawn and then measured to give an indication of liquid water content

cloud on title : a defect in the owner's title to a piece of land arising from a written instrument, a judgment, or an order of court purporting to create an interest in or lien upon the land and therefore impairing the marketability of the owner's title though it may be shown to be invalid by evidence

cloud pink *n* **:** a grayish yellowish pink that is redder and slightly stronger than iris mauve

cloud point *n* **:** the temperature at which a liquid (as a petroleum oil) begins to cloud (as from the separation of wax on cooling)

cloud rack *n* **:** ¹RACK 2a

cloud rat *n* [so called fr. their mountain habitation] **:** any of several large long-haired mountain-dwelling rats of two Philippine genera (*Crateromys* and *Phloeomys*) that may attain a length of 30 inches nearly half of which is made up by the bushy hairy tail — called also *bushy-tailed rat*

cloud ring *n* **:** a ring of clouds; *specif* **:** the nearly permanent belt of clouds along the equator

clouds *pl of* CLOUD, *pres 3d sing of* CLOUD

cloud·scape \'klau̇d,skāp\ *n* -S [¹*cloud* + *-scape*] **:** a view or pictorial representation of a cloud formation

cloud street *n* **:** a group of cumulus clouds arranged in rows

cloud track *n* **:** a slender train of minute water droplets left in the path of an ionizing particle that passes through saturated vapor in a cloud chamber

cloud·ward \'klau̇dwə(r)d\ *or* **cloud·wards** \-dz\ *adv* **1 :** toward the clouds **2 :** upward in aspiration or achievement esp. to lofty heights

cloudy \'klau̇dē, -di\ *adj* -ER/-EST [ME, fr. OE *clūdig* rocky, fr. *clūd* rock, hill — more at CLOUD] **1 :** made or consisting of cloud ⟨the mountain with its ~ veil⟩ **:** like cloud in appearance ⟨~ smoke⟩ **2 :** darkened (as in mood or spirit) by gloom, anxiety, ill temper, or other emotion ⟨a ~ mood⟩ ⟨a ~ eye⟩ **3 :** overcast with clouds ⟨a ~ sky⟩ ⟨~ moon⟩ **:** having the sky overcast ⟨~ morning⟩ ⟨~ day⟩; *specif, in meteorology* **:** with clouds obscuring six tenths to nine tenths of the sky **4 :** obscure in meaning **:** hard to perceive, understand, or comprehend ⟨gropes among ~ issues toward a feeble conclusion —H.T.Moore⟩ **:** uncertain as to fact or outcome ⟨a ~ future⟩ **:** vague or inexact in thought or meaning **:** HAZY ⟨his ~ obsessions and obstinacies —F.M.Ford⟩ **5 :** dimmed or dulled or made obscure as if by clouds **:** lacking clearness, brightness, or luster ⟨a ~ diamond⟩ ⟨a ~ mirror⟩ ⟨the violins had a rather ~ tone⟩ **6 :** like cloud in being light or floating in a light, airy, or translucent mass ⟨dream faces, pale, with ~ hair —G.W. Russell⟩ **7 :** having irregular light and dark areas or markings **:** uneven in color or texture **8 :** having visible material in suspension **:** MURKY ⟨a ~ liquid⟩

cloudy amber *n* **:** GOLDEN GREEN

cloudy swelling *n* **:** a form of degeneration in the tissues of various organs (as the liver, the kidneys, or the heart) marked by swelling and a cloudy appearance of the cells from a deposition in them of granules of protein nature

cloudy-winged whitefly \'=;=;=\ *n* **:** a common whitefly (*Dialeurodes citrifolii*) important in Florida as a destructive sap-sucking pest of citrus

cloué *also* **clou·ée** \(')klü¦ā\ *adj* [F, past part. of *clouer* to nail, fr. *clou* nail — more at CLOU] *heraldry* **:** emblazoned with nailheads ⟨a trellis gules ~ argent⟩

clough \'kləf *also* 'klau̇\ *n* -S [ME *clough, cloge, clou*, fr. (assumed) OE *clōh;* akin to OHG *Clāh*uelde, a place name, *klingo, klinga* ravine, mountain brook and perh. to OE *clingan* to cling — more at CLING] **:** a cleft in a hill **:** a narrow valley **:** RAVINE

¹**clour** \'klü(ə)r\ *n* -S [origin unknown] *chiefly Scot* **:** a bump on the head made by a blow; *also* **:** the blow itself

²**clour** \"\ *vt* -ED/-ING/-S *chiefly Scot* **:** BATTER, THUMP

clous *pl of* CLOU

¹**clout** \'klau̇t, *usu* -d·+V\ *n* -S [ME, fr. OE *clūt;* akin to MHG *klōz* lump, ON *klūtr* kerchief, Russ *gluda* lump, L *galla* gall on a plant — more at GALL] **1 a** *now dial Brit* **:** a patch esp. of cloth or leather **:** a shred or rag esp. of cloth **b :** CLOTH; *esp* **:** a cloth for household use (as a towel or cover) **c :** an article of clothing (as for infants); *specif* **:** DIAPER **2 a :** an iron plate on an axletree or other wood to keep it from wearing **b :** CLOUT NAIL **3 :** a blow esp. with the fist ⟨gave him a ~ on his old head —Arnold Bennett⟩ **:** a hit esp. in baseball ⟨a long ~ over the fence⟩ **4 a :** the mark shot at in archery; *specif* **:** a white cloth placed on a stake or stretched on a hoop or frame used as a target in distance shooting — see CLOUT SHOOTING **b :** a hit in the clout

²**clout** \"\ *vt* -ED/-ING/-S [ME *clouten*, fr. *clout* patch — more at CLOUT] **1 a :** to mend with a patch **:** PATCH **b :** to stud with nails **:** protect (as shoe soles) by studding with nails **c :** to protect (an axletree) with a clout **d :** to cover with or as if with a cloth **2 :** to strike forcefully esp. with the hand or fist ⟨the troublesome boy whose mother has just ~*ed* his head —G.B.Shaw⟩ **:** hit (as a ball) with force ⟨~ the ball into the bleachers⟩ **3** *slang* **:** STEAL **syn** see STRIKE

¹**clout·ed** \'klau̇d·əd\ *adj* [ME, fr. past part. of *clouten*] **:** protected or patched with clouts **:** PATCHED ⟨dark wool dresses and ~ boots —Anne Green⟩

²**clouted** \"\ *adj* [obs. *clout* curds (fr. ME) + *-ed;* akin to ME *clott* lump — more at CLOT] *dial Brit* **:** CLOTTED — used esp. of cream

clouterly *adj* [obs. *clouter* cobbler, botcher (fr. ME, fr. *clouten* + *-er*) + *-ly*] *archaic* **:** CLUMSY, AWKWARD

clout nail *n* **:** a nail having a large flat head used for fastening clouts to axletrees, studding timber, or fastening down sheet metal

clout-shoe *n* [¹*clout* (iron plate) + *shoe*] *obs* **:** a wearer of clouted shoes **:** RUSTIC

clout shooting *n* [¹*clout* (white cloth)] **:** archery shooting in contest in which rounds of arrows are shot from long range at a very large circular target marked on the ground

¹**clove** \'klōv\ *n* -S [ME, fr. OE *clufu;* akin to OS *cluflōc* garlic, OHG *chlobilouh*, ON *klofi* cleft, OE *clēofan* to split — more at CLEAVE] **:** one of the small bulbs developed in the axils of the scales of a large bulb (as in garlic)

²**clove** \"\ *past of* CLEAVE

³**clove** \"\ *n* -S [modif. (influenced by L *clavus*) of AF *clou*, lit., nail, fr. L *clavus* — more at CLAVUS] **:** any of various old English units of weight (as for wool, cheese); *esp* **:** one equal to eight pounds

⁴**clove** \"\ *n* -S [alter. (prob. influenced by ¹*clove*) of ME *clowe, cloue*, fr. OF *clou (de girofle)*, lit., nail of clove, fr. L *clavus* nail] **1 a :** the pungent fragrant aromatic reddish brown dried flower bud of a tropical tree **b :** a spice consisting of whole or ground cloves — usu. used in pl.; see CLOVE OIL **2 :** a moderate-sized very symmetrical red-flowered tropical evergreen tree (*Eugenia caryophyllata* or *Syzygium aromaticum*) of the family Myrtaceae that is probably native to the Moluccas but is now widely cultivated in the tropics (as Zanzibar and Madagascar) for its flower buds which are the source of cloves **3 :** SHERRY 2

⁵**clove** \"\ *n* -S [D *klove, kloof;* akin to OE *clēofan* to split — more at CLEAVE] **:** CLEFT, GAP, RAVINE — used chiefly in place names

clove brown *n* [⁴*clove*] **1 :** a dark yellowish brown **2 :** a brownish gray that is yellower and lighter than average chocolate and yellower and deeper than taupe (sense 1) — called also *eagle*

clove carnation *n* [⁴*clove*] **:** CLOVE PINK 1

clove cassia *n* [⁴*clove*] **:** the bark of a Brazilian tree (*Dicypellium caryophyllatum*) used for mixing with other spices

clove cinnamon *n* [⁴*clove*] **:** CLOVE CASSIA

clove currant *n* [⁴*clove*] **1 :** BUFFALO CURRANT 1 **2 :** GOLDEN CURRANT 1

clove gillyflower *n* [⁴*clove*] **:** CLOVE PINK 1

clove hitch *n* [*clove* (var. of *cloven*) + *hitch*] **:** a knot used to secure a rope temporarily to an object (as a post or spar) and consisting of a turn around the object, over the standing part, around the object again, and under the last turn

clove hitch

clove hook *n* [*clove* (var. of *cloven*)] **:** SISTER HOOK

¹**cloven** *past part of* ²CLEAVE

²**cloven** *adj* [ME, fr. OE *clofen*, past part. of *clēofan* to split — more at CLEAVE] **:** divided or split esp. to a certain depth

clo·vene \'klō,vēn, =ˈ=\ *n* -S [⁴*clove* + *-ene*] **:** a liquid sesquiterpene $C_{15}H_{24}$ obtained from caryophyllene

clo·ven foot *or* **cloven hoof** \'klōvən-\ *n* **1 :** a foot (as of an ox or sheep) that is divided or cleft into two or more parts esp. at its distal extremity — compare SOLID HOOF **2** [fr. the traditional representation of Satan as cloven-footed] **:** the sign of devilish character ⟨show the *cloven hoof*⟩ — **cloven-footed** \¦==¦=\ *or* **cloven-hoofed** \¦==¦=\ *adj*

clove nutmeg *n* [⁴*clove*] **1 :** a tree (*Ravensara aromatica*) of Madagascar resembling a nutmeg and having small leathery leaves **2 :** the nutmeglike fruit of this tree

clove oil *n* [⁴*clove*] **:** a colorless to pale yellow essential oil obtained from cloves and used in medicine as a flavor and perfume and as a source of eugenol

clove pepper *n* [⁴*clove*] **:** ALLSPICE 1

clove pink *n* [⁴*clove*] **1 :** a pink (*Dianthus caryophyllus*) or any of several varieties developed therefrom having a rich clovelike fragrance — see CARNATION **2 :** a dark red that is yellower, less strong, and slightly darker than cranberry, lighter, stronger, and slightly yellower than average garnet, and bluer, lighter, and stronger than average wine

clo·ver \'klōvə(r)\ *n* -S [ME *claver, clovere*, fr. OE *clāfre, clǣfre;* akin to MLG *klēver* clover, MD *clāver*, OHG *klēo*, and perh. to OE *clifian* to stick to — more at CLEAVE] **1 :** an herb of the genus *Trifolium* characterized by trifoliolate leaves and flowers in dense heads — see ALSIKE CLOVER, CRIMSON CLOVER, RED CLOVER, WHITE CLOVER **2 :** any of several plants of the family Leguminosae (as sweet clover, bush clover, prairie clover, or spotted clover) — **in clover** *or* **in the clover :** in prosperity or in pleasant circumstances ⟨the farmers were *in clover*, and it was about time —F.L.Allen⟩

clover-and-alfalfa disease \¦===¦==-\ *n* **:** CLOVER DISEASE 1

clover aphid *n* **:** a common aphid (*Nearctaphis bakeri*) chiefly of western and northwestern U.S. that in early spring feeds on apple and later on clover to which it is often very destructive

clover broom *n* **:** INDIGO BROOM

clover broomrape *n* **:** a European broomrape (*Orobanche minor*) parasitic on clover roots

clover butterfly *n* **:** SULPHUR

clover casebearer *n* **:** a casebearer moth (*Coleophora spissicomis*) the larvae of which feed on the developing seeds of clover esp. in New Zealand

clover club *also* **clover club cocktail** *n* [fr. *Clover Club*, name of a legal and literary club of Philadelphia] **:** a cocktail consisting of gin, white of egg, and lemon or lime juice flavored with grenadine and sweetened

clover disease *also* **clover sickness** *n* **1 :** an acute photosensitization of white or light-skinned animals feeding on certain clovers and other leguminous plants characterized by swelling and inflammation esp. of the skin of the face and the mucous membranes of the mouth **2 :** SWEET CLOVER DISEASE

clover dodder *n* **:** a common dodder (*Cuscuta epithymum*) that infests clover

clover fern *n* **:** a water fern of the genus *Marsilea* distinguished by four cloverlike leaflets

clover hay worm *n* **:** the larva of a small moth (*Hypsopygia costalis*) of the family Pyralididae that is often destructive to clover hay

clover head caterpillar *n* **:** a larval moth (*Grapholitha interstinctana*) that feeds on the flower heads or foliage of various clovers

¹**cloverleaf** \'==,=\ *adj* **:** resembling a clover leaf in shape ⟨a ~ roll⟩

²**cloverleaf** \"\ *n, often attrib* **:** something resembling a clover leaf in shape; *specif* **:** a road plan passing one highway over another and routing turning traffic onto connecting roadways which branch only to the right and lead around in a circle to enter the other highway from the right and thus merging traffic without left-hand turns or direct crossings

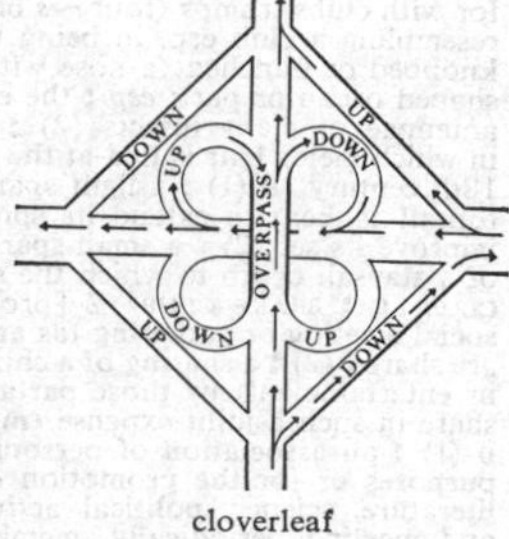

cloverleaf

clover leafhopper *n* **:** a widely distributed leafhopper (*Aceratagallia sanguinolenta*) feeding chiefly on clovers and related plants but sometimes a vector of certain virus diseases of potatoes

clover leaf midge \'==,=-\ *n* **:** a small two-winged fly (*Dasyneura trifolii*) whose larvae develop on the leaves of clover and fold together the halves of the leaflets

clover leaf weevil *n* **:** a small brownish or blackish widely distributed weevil (*Hypera punctata*) native to Europe and sometimes highly destructive both as adult and larva to clovers and other leguminous plants

cloverlike \'==,=\ *adj* **:** resembling clover

clover mite *n* **:** a small reddish mite (*Bryobia praetiosa*) that is seriously destructive to legumes, wheat, fruits, and other crops and often a pest in houses into which it may enter in great numbers esp. in the spring of the year — called also *brown mite, house mite*

clove-root \'klōv+,-\ *n* [⁴*clove* + *root;* fr. its odor] **:** HERB BENNET

clover pink *n* **:** a dark purplish pink that is bluer than Persian lilac and bluer and stronger than rhodonite pink

clover root borer *n* **:** a small brown weevil (*Hylastinus obscurus*) of the family Scolytidae that bores in clover roots

clover root curculio *n* **:** a small dark broad-snouted weevil (*Sitona hispidula* or a closely related species) that feeds on clovers, alfalfa, and other legumes, the larva on the root surface, scoring and girdling the roots, and the adult on the leaves

clover rootworm *n* **:** GRAPE COLASPIS

clover rot *or* **clover wilt** *n* **:** a disease of clover plants caused by a fungus (*Sclerotinia trifoliorum*)

clover rust *n* **1 :** a disease of clovers caused by fungi of the genus *Uromyces* and characterized by rusty brown pustules **2 :** any of the fungi causing clover rust

clover seed chalcid *n* **:** a tiny dark chalcid fly (*Bruchophagus platyptera*) the larva of which feeds on the developing seeds of clovers and alfalfa and is in certain areas a major factor restricting production of clover seed

clover seed midge \'==,=-\ *n* **:** a small two-winged fly (*Dasyneura leguminicola*) that infests the heads of red and white clover destroying the flower and is in certain areas a chief factor limiting clover-seed production

clover seed weevil *n* **:** a tiny grayish brown weevil (*Microtrogus picirostris*) the larva of which feeds on developing seeds of various clovers

clover-sick \'==,=\ *adj, of soil* **:** incapable of yielding profitable crops of clover because of the presence of an organism capable of causing disease — **clover sickness** *n*

clover weevil *n* **:** a small European weevil (*Apion apricans* or related species) that feeds on clover

clo·very \'klōv(ə)rē\ *adj* **:** like clover or abounding in clover

cloves *pl of* CLOVE

cloves-strip \'=,=\ *n* **:** a primrose willow (*Jussiaea diffusa*) of eastern No. America

clove tree *n* [⁴*clove*] **:** ⁴CLOVE 2

clovewort \'=,=\ *n* -S [fr. (assumed) ME, fr. OE *clufwyrt*, fr. *clufu* clove + *wyrt* -wort] **1** *dial chiefly Eng* **:** a crowfoot (*Ranunculus acris*) **2** *obs* **:** HERB BENNET

clow \'klau̇\ *n* -S [alter. of ME *clowse* (taken as pl.), fr. OE *clūs, clūse* bar, bolt, enclosure, fr. ML *clusa* enclosure, fr. L, fem. of *clusus, clausus,* past part. of *claudere* to close — more at CLOSE] **1 :** an outfall sluice for water from a tidal river after it has deposited its sediment on flooded land **2 :** a floodgate esp. for a lock or water mill

clowd·er \'klau̇də(r)\ *n* -s [prob. var. of ²*clutter*] **:** a group of cats

¹**clown** \'klau̇n\ *n* -s [perh. fr. MF *coulon* settler, fr. L *colonus* colonist, farmer — more at COLONY] **1 :** a husbandman or farmer **:** COUNTRYMAN, RUSTIC **2 :** a man of coarse nature and manners **:** a rude, ill-bred person **:** BOOR ⟨thou art mated with a ~ and the grossness of his nature will have weight to drag thee down —Alfred Tennyson⟩ **3 a :** a fool, jester, or comedian in a play or other entertainment; *specif* **:** a comedy performer in a circus grotesquely made up and dressed **b :** one who frequently or habitually plays the buffoon or engages in comedy **:** JOKER ⟨practical jokes by the office ~⟩ **4 :** a dancer who performs ridiculous or satirical dances usu. in disguise and often for magical or ritualistic purposes **syn** see BOOR

²**clown** \"\ *vb* -ED/-ING/-S *vi* **:** to act as a clown **:** play the clown **:** jest ridiculously ~ *vt* **:** to jest at or ridicule grotesquely **:** act out or perform in burlesque or farcical manner ⟨the actor ~*ed* his part splendidly⟩

clown·age \'klau̇nij\ *n* -s **:** the behavior or function of a clown

clown·ery \'klau̇nərē\ *n* -ES **:** clownish behavior or an instance of clownishness **:** BUFFOONERY

clown fish *n* **:** a small brilliantly colored barb (*Barbus everetti*) of southeastern Asia and Borneo that is often kept in the tropical aquarium

clownheal \'ₛ,ₛ\ *n* -s [*clown* (countryman) + *heal;* fr. its use in rustic remedies] **:** a hedge nettle (*Stachys palustris*)

clown·ish \'klau̇nish, -ēsh\ *adj* **:** of or resembling a clown **:** having the characteristics of a clown

clownishly *adv* **:** in a clownish manner

clown·ish·ness \-nəs\ *n* -ES **:** clownish quality **:** RUDENESS, BUFFOONERY

clown's allheal *n* **:** CLOWNHEAL

cloy \'klȯi\ *vb* -ED/-ING/-S [short for *accloy*] *vt* **1** *obs* **:** to prick (a horse) with a nail in shoeing **2** *obs* **:** to fill or choke up **:** stop up **:** CLOG **3 :** to surfeit or make weary with an excess usu. of something orig. pleasing ⟨Cordelia has been ~*ed* by her sisters' excessive protestations of affection —Rebecca West⟩ ~ *vi* **:** to cause surfeit **:** be or become insipid or distasteful usu. through an excess of an orig. pleasurable quality (as sweetness) ⟨persons and places had begun to ~ —*Time*⟩ ⟨few pleasures sooner ~ than reading what the reviewers say —A.T.Quiller-Couch⟩ **syn** see SATIATE

cloyed·ness \'klȯidnəs\ *n* -ES **:** the state of being cloyed

cloy·ing \'klȯi·iŋ\ *adj* **:** having an excess of a quality (as sweetness or sentimentality) to the point of arousing distaste or disgust ⟨a sweet but not ~ manner —W.A.White⟩ ⟨sentiment more real and less ~ —Katherine G. Jackson⟩ — **cloy·ing·ly** *adv* — **cloy·ing·ness** *n* -ES

cloy·less \'klȯiləs\ *adj* **:** that does not cloy

cloy·some \'klȯisəm\ *adj* **:** tending to cloy **:** CLOYING

clr *abbr* **1** clear; clearance **2** color

clt *abbr* **1** claimant **2** collateral

CLU *abbr* certified life underwriter; chartered life underwriter

¹**club** \'kləb\ *n* -s [ME *clubbe,* fr. ON *klubba;* akin to OHG *kolbo* club, OE *clympre* lump of metal, *clamm* bond, fetter — more at CLAM] **1 a** (1) **:** a heavy staff esp. of wood usu. tapering and sometimes having an attached head of stone or metal wielded with the hand as a striking weapon ⟨struck down by a blow from his great ~⟩ — see BOOMERANG, MACE, POGAMOGGAN (2) **:** something (as a threat, an argument, or a concept) used as a weapon of attack or intimidation ⟨his threat of resignation becomes a . . . ~ to beat a dissenting majority into line —M.R.Cohen⟩ **b :** a stick or bat used to hit a ball with in any of various games (as golf and hockey) **c** (1) **:** a playing card, in a pack of playing cards, of the suit having a figure like the trefoil or clover leaf represented by the symbol ♣ (2) **:** the figure on such a card (3) **clubs** *pl* **:** the suit of cards having such figure (4) **:** an odd trick won or contracted for with clubs trumps ⟨four ~s bid and made⟩ **d :** something resembling a club esp. in being tapered, short and thick, or knobbed or bunched ⟨a nose with a red ~⟩: as (1) **:** a club-shaped organ or part; *esp* **:** the enlarged terminal part of the antennae of many insects (2) **:** a club-shaped tail or knot in which men's hair is tied at the back, fashionable in the late 18th century **e** (1) **:** a light spar to which the foot of a gaff topsail is bent to extend its spread beyond the gaff and to improve its set (2) **:** a small spar at the after part of the foot of a staysail or jib to which the sheet is attached **f :** INDIAN CLUB **g :** BRAKE CLUB **2** [prob. fr. ²*club*] **a** *obs* (1) **:** a social meeting or gathering (as at a tavern) at which expenses are shared (2) **:** a sharing of a charge or expense (as for a meal or entertainment) by those partaking; *also* **:** one individual's share in such a joint expense ⟨my ~ came to three shillings⟩ **b** (1) **:** an association of persons for social and recreational purposes or for the promotion of some common object (as literature, science, political activity) usu. jointly supported and meeting periodically, membership in social clubs usu. being conferred by ballot and carrying the privilege of use of the club property (2) *obs* **:** a periodical meeting of a society (3) **:** the building, rooms, or other property owned by a club ⟨the dock at the yacht ~⟩ **:** the meeting place of a club ⟨a livery stable . . . served also as a ~ for the male population —Agnes S. Turnbull⟩ **c** *obs* **:** a set or group of persons having common opinions or aims ⟨to bear up under the . . . condemnation of his own ~ —John Locke⟩ **d :** an association of persons participating in a plan by which they agree to make regular payments (as into a savings account) or regular purchases in order to secure some advantage (as price reduction) ⟨book ~⟩ ⟨savings ~⟩ **e :** a commercial establishment serving food and liquor and often featuring music, dancing, or other entertainment **:** NIGHTCLUB ⟨singing at a ~ in Miami —Mary Deasy⟩ **f :** an amateur or professional athletic organization devoted to a particular sport; *also* **:** the team representing such an organization ⟨a major league baseball ~⟩ ⟨a boxing ~⟩

²**club** \"\ *vb* **clubbed; clubbed; clubbing; clubs** *vt* **1 a :** to beat or strike with or as if with a club ⟨*clubbed* him with the butt of a riding crop⟩ **b :** to gather or combine into a clublike mass or body ⟨~ the hair⟩ **c :** to hold like a club ⟨*clubbed* his newspaper⟩; *esp* **:** to turn (as a musket or rifle) butt uppermost so as to use as a club **2 :** to unite or combine for a common cause or goal ⟨*clubbed* their small means together —Thomas Carlyle⟩ **:** contribute to a common stock, supply, or fund ⟨each ~*s* his penny toward the purchase⟩ **3** *chiefly Brit* **:** to throw (a body of troops) into confusion ⟨~ a battalion⟩ ~ *vi* **1 :** to come together to form a club or mass **2 :** to combine for the promotion of some common object or joint action ⟨~ together and work out a plan —Julian Huxley⟩ **3 :** to pay an equal or proportionate share of a common charge or expense **:** pay for something by contribution ⟨the owl, the raven, and the bat, *clubbed* for a feather to his hat —Jonathan Swift⟩ **4 :** to drift in a current with an anchor down to ensure control — usu. used with *down*

³**club** \"\ *adj* **1 :** of or relating to a club **2 :** consisting of foods in a fixed combination offered on a menu at a set price ⟨~ breakfast⟩ ⟨a ~ luncheon⟩

club·ba·ble *also* **club·a·ble** \'kləbəbəl\ *adj* [¹*club* + *-able*] **:** inclined to club together with others **:** SOCIABLE, COMPANIONABLE ⟨a ~ man⟩

club bag *n* **:** a rectangular usu. leather traveling bag that tapers to a purselike opening at the top and that is often zippered

club bag

clubbed \'kləbd\ *adj* [ME, fr. ¹*club* + *-ed*] **:** shaped like a club: as **a** *of a finger* **:** having a bulbous enlargement of the tip with convex overhanging nail **b** *of a foot* **:** exhibiting the deformity clubfoot **c :** thickened to clublike form at the top — used of the tall letters of Carolingian minuscule writing **d :** affected with the disease clubroot ⟨~ cabbages⟩

club·ber \'kləbə(r)\ *n* -s [¹*club* + *-er*] **:** a member of a club

club·bi·ly \-bəlē\ *adv* [*clubby* + *-ly*] **:** in a clubby manner

clubbing *n* -s **:** the condition of being clubbed

club·bish \-bish,-bēsh\ *adj* [¹*club* + *-ish*] **:** disposed to club together ⟨a ~ set⟩

club·bist \-bəst\ *n* -s [F *clubiste,* fr. *club* (fr. E) + *-iste* -ist] **:** an advocate of the principles of a political club (as French revolutionary clubs)

club·by \-bē,-bi\ *adj* -ER/-EST [¹*club* + *-y*] **:** characteristic of a club or club members: as **a :** displaying or offering informality, cordiality, or friendliness esp. to other members of the same set or social group **:** SOCIABLE ⟨we got rather ~ —Raymond Chandler⟩ **b :** open only to qualified or approved persons **:** SELECT ⟨the legitimate theater . . . is an uncommonly ~ field of enterprise —E.J.Kahn⟩

club car *n* **:** LOUNGE CAR

club chair *n* **:** a deep low thickly upholstered easy chair often with rather low back and heavy sides and arms

club cheese *n* **:** a process cheese made by grinding cheddar and other cheeses usu. with added condiments and seasonings

club convention *n* [¹*club* (suit)] **:** a system of bidding in contract bridge employing an artificial bid of one club to show a strong hand with 3½ or more quick tricks and an artificial response of one diamond to show a hand with less than 2 quick tricks

club coupe *n* **:** an automobile resembling a coupe in having only two doors but with a full-width rear seat accessible by tilting the front-seat backs forward

club dance *n* [¹*club* (weapon)] **:** a group dance by men armed with clubs and similar to stick and sword dances

clubfoot \'ₛ,ₛ\ *n* [¹*club* + *foot*] **1** *pl* **clubfeet a :** a congenital deformity of the foot in which the forepart of the foot is twisted into one of several directions — called also *talipes* **b :** a foot with such a deformity **2** *pl* **clubfoots :** CLUBROOT — **clubfooted** *adj*

club foot *n* [¹*club*] **:** a rounded foot on a flat base on a furniture leg — compare DUTCH FOOT; see FOOT illustration

clubfoot moss *n* **:** CLUB MOSS

club fungus *n* **:** a fungus of the family Clavariaceae

clubhand \'ₛ,ₛ\ *n* [¹*club* + *hand*] **1 :** a congenital deformity in which the hand is short and distorted **2 :** a hand with such a deformity

clubhaul \'ₛ,ₛ\ *vt* [¹*club* (spar) + *haul*] **:** to put (a ship) on the other tack when in danger of going into irons by dropping the lee anchor as the vessel's head comes to the wind and hauling on a hawser from the lee quarter to the anchor until the vessel pays off on the other tack

clubhouse \'ₛ,ₛ\ *n* [¹*club* (association) + *house*] **1 :** a house occupied by a club or commonly used for club activities **2 :** a section of a racetrack pavilion reserved for special ticket holders **3 :** dressing or locker rooms used by an athletic team (as a baseball team) **4 :** a communal dwelling for the unmarried men of certain primitive tribes

club·i·on·i·dae \,kləbē'änə,dē\ *n pl, cap* [NL, fr. *Clubiona,* type genus (irreg. fr. Gk *kleos* glory + *bioun* to live) + *-idae;* akin to Gk *klytos* famous, Gk *bios* life — more at LOUD, QUICK] **:** a family of terrestrial tube-weaving spiders lacking cribellum, calamistrum, and colulus

clubland \'ₛlənd, -,land\ *n* [¹*club* (association) + *land*] **:** the region or realm of clubs and esp. social clubs

club link *n* **:** a specially formed link which with two or three other links is permanently shackled to the ring of the anchor and by which the anchor is secured to the chain

club·man \'ₛmən-,-,man,-,maa(ə)n\ *n, pl* **clubmen** [¹*club* (association) + *man*] **:** a man given to club life; *esp* **:** a usu. wealthy man belonging to one or more exclusive clubs

club·mo·bile \'kləbmō,bēl\ *n* -s [¹*club* (association) + *-mobile*] **:** a trailer equipped like a clubroom for serving hot coffee, doughnuts, candy, and cigarettes and supplying recreational equipment to troops or workers

club link

club mold *n* [prob. so called fr. the swollen apex of the conidiophore] **:** a fungus of the genus *Aspergillus*

club moss *n* [trans. of NL *muscus clavatus*] **:** a plant of the order Lycopodiales esp. of the genus *Lycopodium* or the closely related *Selaginella* in some species of which the sporangia are borne in club-shaped strobili

club–moss family \'ₛ,ₛ-\ *n* **:** LYCOPODIACEAE

club palm *n* [¹*club*] **:** a plant of the genus *Cordyline*

clubroom \'ₛ,ₛ\ *n* **:** a room designed for or as if for the use of a club

clubroot \'ₛ,ₛ\ *n* -s [¹*club* + *root*] **:** a common disease of cabbages and related plants caused by a slime mold (*Plasmodiophora brassicae*) producing swellings or distortions of the root followed often by decline in vigor or by death

club rush *n* [¹*club* (weapon) + *rush*] **1 :** a cattail (*Typha latifolia*) **2 :** a sedge of the genus *Scirpus* **:** BULRUSH

clubs *pl of* CLUB, *pres 3d sing of* CLUB

club sandwich *n* **:** a sandwich usu. of three slices of toast with chicken or turkey, lettuce, tomato, bacon or ham, and mayonnaise

club–shaped \'ₛ'ₛ\ *adj* **:** cylindrical and enlarging gradually toward the end

club shell *n* **:** a mollusk of the genus *Cerithium* **:** HORN SHELL

club skate *n* [prob. short for *New York Club skate,* after a New York skating organization of the 1860s] **:** a skate made to fasten to the shoe by means of clamps or screws

club soda *n* **:** SODA WATER 2a

club sofa *n* **:** a sofa of the same style as a club chair

clubstart \'klùb,stärt, 'kləb-, -stȧt\ *n* -s [¹*club* + *start* (tail)] *dial Eng* **:** STOAT

club steak *n* **:** a small steak cut from the end of the short loin and containing no part of the tenderloin — see BEEF illustration

club·ster \'klùbstə(r)\ *n* -s [alter. of *clubstart*] *dial Eng* **:** STOAT

club stripe *n* **:** an arrangement of stripes of two or more colors on an article of dress (as a scarf or blazer) orig. representing the colors of a particular club and worn by a club member — compare CLUB TIE

club tie *n* **1 :** a necktie worn by members of a club and bearing the club's colors, usu. in stripes, or the club emblem — compare CLUB STRIPE **2 :** a silk necktie having diagonal stripes of two or more colors

club tooth *n* [¹*club*] **:** a club-shaped tooth used in lever escapement wheels in timepieces designed esp. to retain oil

clubweed \'ₛ,ₛ\ *n* [¹*club* + *weed*] **:** a knapweed (*Centaurea nigra*)

club wheat *n* [¹*club*] **:** a wheat (*Triticum compactum*) or any of its varieties used either as spring wheat or winter wheat and having short thick compact club-shaped spikes and grain that does not shatter and that may be harvested long after it is ripe

clubwoman \'ₛ,ₛₛ\ *n, pl* **clubwomen :** a woman belonging to a club or active in club and other social or community affairs

clubwood \'ₛ,ₛ\ *n* [¹*club* + *wood*] **1 :** the wood of any species of *Casuarina* **2 :** WAMARA

¹**cluck** \'klək\ *vb* -ED/-ING/-S [imit.] *vi* **1 :** to make the noise of a brooding hen or a similar sound **2 :** to make a clicking sound with the tongue often expressive of alarm, distress, or concern; *also* **:** to express interest or concern ⟨critics ~*ed* over the new developments⟩ ~ *vt* **1 :** to call together, urge, or impel as a hen does her chicks ⟨his mother ~*ed* them hastily to their feet —T.H.Jones⟩ **2 :** to express usu. with interest or concern ⟨~*ed* his approval of the victory⟩ **3 :** to move (the tongue) in such a way as to produce clucks ⟨the driver ~*ed* his tongue and the horse started forward at a sharp trot⟩

²**cluck** \"\ *n* -s **1 :** the characteristic sound made by a hen esp. in calling her chicks; *also* **:** a sound resembling this **2** *also* **cluck hen :** a broody fowl **3** *slang* **:** a stupid or naïve person

clue *var of* CLEW

cluif \'klüf\ *Scot var of* CLOOF

cluj \'klüzh\ *adj, usu cap* [fr. *Cluj,* Romania] **:** of or from the city of Cluj, Romania **:** of the kind or style prevalent in Cluj

clum *chiefly Midland past of* CLIMB

clum·ber spaniel \'kləmbə(r)-\ *n, often cap C&S* [fr. *Clumber,* estate in Nottinghamshire, Eng.] **:** a large spaniel of a breed brought to England from France about 1720 that is massive, heavyset, and somewhat slow-moving but an expert game finder and very steady and reliable and has a dense silky coat of moderate length lemon and white or orange and white in color, the color preferably being restricted to the head

¹**clump** \'kləmp\ *n* -s [prob. fr. LG *klump;* akin to OE *clympre* lump of metal, OE *clamm* bond, fetter — more at CLAM] **1 :** a group of things clustered together ⟨a ~ of bushes⟩ ⟨people standing around in little ~*s*⟩ ⟨a ~ of buildings along the road⟩ **2 :** a compact mass **:** a closely compact group or lump ⟨a ~ of roots⟩ ⟨a ~ of dates⟩ **3 :** an aggregation or mass of particles (as of bacteria or blood cells) — compare AGGLUTINATION **4 :** a heavy tramping sound **5 clumps** *pl* **:** a team game in which two players, one from each side, are sent out to agree upon some object, then upon their return each is surrounded by the members of the opposing team who try to guess the chosen object by asking questions to which the answers may be only "Yes," "No," or "I don't know" **6** *Brit* **:** a less-than-type-high slug used as spacing material

²**clump** \"\ *vb* -ED/-ING/-S *vi* **1 :** to tread clumsily and noisily **2 :** to cluster together in clumps **:** form clumps ⟨the molecules tended to ~⟩ ~ *vt* **1 :** to arrange or cluster in a clump ⟨ships are ~*ed* in the harbor like sitting ducks —*Newsweek*⟩ **:** cause to form clumps ⟨the serum ~*s* the bacteria⟩ **2 :** to strike heavily **3 :** to group together indiscriminately **:** LUMP ⟨~*ing* the various classes under one heading⟩

clump block *n* **:** a short thick strongly made block with a thick metal sheave having a large opening

clump foot *n* **:** CLUBFOOT 1

clump–head grass \'ₛ,ₛ-\ *n* **:** WOOL GRASS 1

clumproot \'ₛ,ₛ\ *n* **:** CLUBROOT

clumpy \'kləmpē\ *adj* -ER/-EST [¹*clump* + *-y*] **:** composed of clumps **:** abounding in clumps **:** growing in clumps

clum·si·ly \'kləmzəlē, -li\ *adv* **:** in a clumsy manner

clum·si·ness \'kləmzēnəs, -zən-\ *n* -ES **:** the quality of being clumsy

clum·sy \'kləmzē, -zi\ *adj* -ER/-EST [prob. fr. obs. E *clumse* benumbed with cold + E *-y;* of Scand origin (like ME *clumsen* to become stiff); akin to Icel *klumsa* lock-jawed, Sw dial. *klumsen* benumbed; akin to OE *clamm* bandage, bond, fetter — more at CLAM] **1 a :** lacking dexterity, skill, nimbleness, or grace (as in the use of the body or limbs or the performance of an action) **:** stiff or awkward in motion ⟨he was a ~ dissector because of his injury —H.G.Wells⟩ **b :** lacking intellectual skill or adroitness, grace or elegance (as in handling words or ideas) **:** lacking tact or subtlety ⟨a ~ joke⟩ ⟨~ diplomacy⟩ **2 :** heavy and unwieldy **:** awkwardly or poorly made ⟨roads were very bad, wagons very slow and ~ —Tom Wintringham⟩ **:** inconvenient, inefficient, or ineffective in use ⟨~ as it was . . . the Aztec picture writing seems to have been adequate —W.H.Prescott⟩ **syn** see AWKWARD

clunch \'klənch, 'klùn-\ *n* -ES [origin unknown] **1** *dial Eng* **:** indurated clay **2** *dial Eng* **:** a soft limestone

¹**clung** *past of* CLING

²**clung** \'kləŋ\ *adj* [ME *clung, clungen,* fr. OE *clungen,* past part. of *clingan* to shrivel, adhere — more at CLING] **1** *dial Brit* **a :** SHRUNKEN, SHRIVELED **b :** lean from hunger **:** EMACIATED **2** *dial Eng, of soil* **:** stiff and clinging

¹**clu·ni·ac** \'klünē,ak\ *adj, usu cap* [ML *Cluniacus,* fr. Abbey of *Cluny,* Cluny, France + L *-acus,* adj. suffix, fr. Gk *-akos*] **:** of or relating to the Cluniacs

²**cluniac** \"\ *n* -s *usu cap* **:** a monk of a reformed Benedictine congregation established in 910 at Cluny, France

¹**clunk** \'kləŋk\ *n* -s [imit.] **1** *chiefly Scot* **:** a sound such as is made when a cork is quickly drawn or when liquid flows intermittently from a bottle **2 :** a blow or the sound of a blow **:** THUMP **3 :** a dull or stupid person

²**clunk** \"\ *vb* -ED/-ING/-S *vi* **1 :** to make a clunk, esp. a dull thumping or bumping **2 :** to hit something with a clunk ⟨the gun . . . ~*ed* on the floor —Mickey Spillane⟩ ~ *vt* **1** *dial Eng* **:** to swallow with audible effort **2 :** to strike or hit with a clunk

clunk·er \-kə(r)\ *n* -s [prob. fr. ²*clunk* + *-er*] **:** a dilapidated rattling old machine; *esp* **:** JALOPY

clun·ter \'klùntə(r)\ *vi* -ED/-ING/-S [origin unknown] *dial Eng* **:** to make a clumping or clattering noise

clu·ny lace \'klünē-, ₛ'ₛ-\ *n, usu cap C* [fr. the Abbey of *Cluny,* Cluny, France, where it was used by the monks] **:** a sturdy bobbin lace for clothing and interior decoration made by hand or machine of linen or cotton thread and characterized by wheat or wheel designs on a coarse mesh

clu·pan·o·don·ic acid \(')klü;panə;dänik-, ;klüpə(,)nō;-\ *n* [ISV *clupanodon-* (fr. NL *Clupanodon* genus name of the small Japanese fish *Clupanodon melanosticta,* fr. L *clupea,* a small fish + Gk *anodōn* toothless, fr. *an-* an- + *odōn* tooth) + *-ic* — more at TOOTH] **:** a highly unsaturated acid $C_{21}H_{33}COOH$ obtained as a light yellow oil from fish or fish liver oils and blubber oil

clu·pea \'klüpēə\ *n, cap* [NL, fr. L, a small river fish] **:** the type genus of Clupeidae comprising the typical herrings

¹**clu·pe·id** \'klüpēəd, -,id\ *adj* [NL *Clupeidae*] **:** of or relating to the Clupeidae

²**clupeid** \"\ *n* -s **:** a fish of the family Clupeidae

clu·pe·i·dae \klü'pēə,dē\ *n pl, cap* [NL, fr. *Clupea,* type genus + *-idae*] **:** a large family of soft-finned teleost fishes (order Isospondyli) including the herrings, sardines, shads, menhaden, and related forms all having a narrow compressed body and forked tail

clu·pe·ine \'klüpēən, -,ēn\ *also* **clu·pe·in** \-ēən\ *n* -s [ISV *clup-* (fr. NL *Clupea*) + *-ine, -in*] **:** a protamine contained in the spermatozoa of the herring

¹**clu·pe·oid** \-pē,ȯid\ *adj* [NL *Clupeoidea*] **:** of or relating to or like the herrings or the Clupeoidea

²**clupeoid** \"\ *n* -s **:** a clupeoid fish

clu·pe·oi·dea \,klüpē'ȯidēə\ *n pl, cap* [NL, fr. *Clupea* + *-oidea*] **:** a large suborder (order Isospondyli) comprising the herrings and related fishes

clu·pe·oi·dei \-dē,ī\ *syn of* CLUPEOIDEA

cluse \'klüz\ *n* -s [F, fr. MF (dial.), fr. ML *clusa,* fr. L, fem. of *clusus, clausus,* past part. of *claudere* to close — more at CLOSE] **:** a narrow gorge cutting transversely through an otherwise continuous ridge

clu·sia \'klüzh(ē)ə\ *n* [NL, fr. Charles de Lécluse (Carolus *Clusius*) †1609 Fr. botanist + NL *-ia*] **1** *cap* **:** a large genus of tropical American aromatic trees or shrubs (family Guttiferae) having opposite coriaceous leaves and large white, yellow, or pink flowers **2** -s **:** any tree of the genus *Clusia* — see WAXFLOWER, WILD FIG

clu·si·a·ce·ae \,klüz(h)ē'āsē,ē\ [NL, fr. *Clusia,* type genus + *-aceae*] *syn of* GUTTIFERAE

¹**clus·ter** \'kləstə(r)\ *n* -s [ME *cluster, clustre,* fr. OE *clyster, cluster;* akin to LG *kluster* cluster, OE *clott* lump, mass — more at CLOT] **1 :** a number of things of the same kind (as fruit or flowers) growing closely together **:** BUNCH ⟨a flower ~⟩ ⟨a ~ of coral animals⟩ **2 :** a number of similar things grouped together in association or in physical proximity ⟨a ~ of houses⟩ ⟨little ~*s* of settlers scattered along the coast⟩: as **a :** a number of honeybees clinging together in a solid mass **b :** an aggregation of stars, galaxies, or supergalaxies that appear close together in the sky and seem to have common properties (as distance and motion) — see GLOBULAR CLUSTER, MOVING CLUSTER **c :** two or more electric lamps grouped together on a single fixture **d :** the group of four cups that connect the teats of a cow to a milking machine **3 :** a number of similar things considered as a group because of their relation to each other or their simultaneity of occurrence or for convenience in treatment or discussion ⟨tone ~*s* which are known as blue —Rudi Blesh⟩ ⟨the great ~ of inventions of the last quarter of the 19th century —Bruce Bliven b.1889⟩ ⟨a ~ of characteristics⟩ **4 :** two or more consecutive consonants or vowels in a segment of speech ⟨the consonant sounds for the italics in "wi*nch spr*ocket" are a ~⟩

²**cluster** \"\ *vb* **clustered; clustered; clustering** \-t(ə)riŋ\ **clusters** [ME *clusteren,* fr. *cluster,* n.] *vt* **1 :** to collect into a cluster or clusters **:** gather into a bunch ⟨~ ten or a dozen of these together, with several smaller sheds and tents —Walt Whitman⟩ **2 :** to furnish or cover with clusters ⟨the bridge was ~*ed* with men and officers —Herman Wouk⟩ ~ *vi* **:** to grow in clusters or assemble in groups **:** collect, gather, or unite in a cluster or clusters ⟨men ~ around the stove⟩ ⟨legends have already ~*ed* about his name⟩

cluster bean *n* **:** GUAR

clusterberry \'ₛₛ- — *see* BERRY\ *n* **:** MOUNTAIN CRANBERRY

cluster clover *also* **clustered clover** *n* **:** an annual clover (*Trifolium glomeratum*) having globular purplish heads native to Europe but now grown elsewhere esp. in No. America and Australasia as a hay and forage plant

cluster cup *n* : AECIUM
cluster–cup stage \'==,=-\ *n* : the aecial stage of a rust fungus
clustered *adj* [ME, fr. ¹*cluster* + *-ed*] **1** : formed or located in clusters — compare SOLITARY 5a **2** : composed or apparently composed of several similar elements clustered together ⟨a ~ pier⟩ ⟨a ~ column⟩

clustered pier

clustered bluet *n* : a weed (*Oldenlandia uniflora*) having buttonlike clusters of tiny flowers
clustered poppy mallow *n* : a perennial herb (*Callirhoë triangulata*) of the prairie regions of the U.S. with purple flowers in panicled clusters
cluster fig *n* : an East Indian fig (*Ficus glomerata*) often planted as a shade tree having tapering leaves, small clusters of red fruit, and astringent bark — called also *country fig*
cluster flower *n* : a plant of the genus *Cestrum*
cluster fly *n* : a large dark-brown fly (*Pollenia rudis*) related to the bluebottles and often gathering in large clusters in attics and other sheltered places during cool autumn weather
cluster gear *n* : a set of gears of different sizes mounted as a unit on the same shaft — called also *gear cluster*
clus·ter·ing·ly *adv* : in a clustering manner
cluster pepper *n* **1** : a hot pepper (*Capsicum frutescens fasciculatum*) with slender elongated bright red and extremely pungent fruits borne erect in clusters **2** : the fruit of a cluster pepper
cluster piles *n pl* : piles driven in a close bundle and usu. lashed together with chains or steel bands
cluster pine *also* **cluster fir** *n* [so called fr. its cones] : a pyramidal pine (*Pinus pinaster*) of the Mediterranean region with reflexed bud scales and needles in pairs
clusters *pl of* CLUSTER, *pres 3d sing of* CLUSTER
cluster variable *n* : a short-period variable star of Cepheid characteristics and a period of light fluctuations not longer than a day orig. found in globular clusters but abundant elsewhere in the Milky Way galaxy — called also *cluster-type Cepheid*
cluster wheat *n* : CLUB WHEAT
¹clutch \'kləch\ *vb* -ED/-ING/-ES [ME *clucchen*, fr. OE *clyccan*; akin to OFris *kletsie* spear, Sw *klyka* fork, crotch, MHG *klok* spot, ON *klakkr* lump, MIr *glacc* hand — more at CLING] *vt* **1 a** : to seize, grip, or hold with the hand or claws usu. strongly, tightly, or suddenly ⟨sleeps . . . with his musket . . . ~*ed* tightly —S.V.Benét⟩ ⟨~*ed* his arm fiercely⟩ **b** : to hold or try to retain control or possession of : SEIZE ⟨~ power⟩ **2** *obs* : to close tightly : CLENCH ⟨~*ing* hands⟩ ~ *vi* **1** : to seek to hold or retain possession ⟨~*ed* at her son's devotion —Andrea Parke⟩ : take immediate advantage or make immediate use (as of an idea or an opportunity) — often used with *at* ⟨~ at remedies that her calmer self would have put by —H.O.Taylor⟩ **2** : GRASP, HOLD ⟨roots that ~ deeply into the earth⟩ **3** : to operate a clutch (sense 3) **syn** see TAKE
²clutch \"\ *adj* **1** *of a woman's coat* : lacking fasteners and suitable for holding closed with the hand or arm **2** *of a woman's handbag* : lacking handles and of a size and shape suitable for clasping in the hand
³clutch \"\ *n* -ES [ME *cloche, clowche*, alter. (influenced by ME *clucchen* to clutch) of *cloke, cluke*; akin to OE *clyccan* to clutch] **1 a** : the claws or a hand in the act of grasping or seizing firmly ⟨a rabbit in the ~ of a hawk⟩ **b** : control, power, or possession esp. of a rapacious or cruel person or an unrelenting force ⟨in the dry, womanless ~ of the army —Irwin Shaw⟩ ⟨the fell ~ of circumstance —W.E.Henley⟩ — often used in pl. ⟨in the ~*es* of a desperate infatuation —Delmore Schwartz⟩ **c** : the act of grasping, holding, or restraining : GRASP, GRIP ⟨the gravitational ~ of the earth —*N.Y. Times*⟩ **2** : a device for gripping an object, as at the end of a chain or tackle **3 a** : a coupling used to connect and disconnect a driving and a driven part of a mechanism esp. one that permits the former part to engage the latter gradually and without shock — see BAND CLUTCH, CENTRIFUGAL CLUTCH, CONE CLUTCH, DISK CLUTCH, FRICTION CLUTCH, MAGNETIC CLUTCH, MAGNETIC FLUID CLUTCH **b** : a lever operating such a clutch **4** : a tight or critical situation (as when the outcome of a game is at stake) : PINCH ⟨a batter able to come through with a hit in the ~⟩ ⟨a good ~ hitter⟩
⁴clutch \"\ *n* -ES [alter. of *cletch*] **1 a** : a nest of eggs or a brood of chicks **b** : a group of offspring produced at a birth **2** : the eggs laid by a bird at regular consecutive intervals without intervening longer pauses **3** : GROUP, BUNCH ⟨a whole ~ of people trooped in together —Mollie Panter-Downes⟩
clutch·man \'=mən, -,man\ *n, pl* **clutchmen** [³*clutch* + *man*] : one who operates a clutch; *specif* : one operating a clutch on a beet-slicing machine — called also *cutterman*
cluth·er \'klu̇thə(r), -th-\ *n* -s [var. of ²*clutter*] *dial Brit* : a large quantity : CLUSTER, BUNCH
¹clut·ter \'klətə(r), -ətə-\ *vb* -ED/-ING/-s [alter. of earlier *clotter*, fr. ME *clotteren* to clot, fr. *clot* + *-eren* (freq. suffix) — more at CLOT] *vt* **1** *dial* : to crowd together in disorder **2** : to fill or cover with things in disorder or scattered at random or with things that impede movement or action or reduce effectiveness ⟨a ~*ed* room⟩ ⟨an author . . . may ~ his explanations with digressive evidence that delays the reader —G.W.Sherburn⟩ — often used with *up* ⟨the roads of France ~*ed* up with refugees —Henri Peyre⟩ ~ *vi* **1** *now chiefly dial* **a** : to run together in knots or confused crowds : run in disorder **b** : to make a confused noise : BUSTLE **2** *archaic* : to speak confusedly or inarticulately : jumble words
²clutter \"\ *n* -s **1 a** : a crowded or confused mass or collection ⟨a ~ of shops and tenements⟩ : a mass of disorderly or distracting objects or details ⟨pure and noble design, unspoiled by ~ or ornament —E.K.Brown⟩ ⟨steaming . . . seaward among a ~ of sister ships—K.M.Dodson⟩ **b** : LITTER, DISORDER ⟨photographs . . . propped up amid a ~ of china ornaments —Hamilton Basso⟩ ⟨pushing aside the ~ on the table —Harriet LaBarre⟩ **c** : the visual indication on a radar screen of interference or echo from objects other than the target tending to obscure target indication — compare SEA RETURN **2** *now dial* : turmoil or confusion of movement or activity : DISTURBANCE, HUBBUB : confused noise ⟨ladies who were apt to make the greatest ~ upon such occasions—Jonathan Swift⟩ **syn** see CONFUSION
clut·ter·er \-ərə(r)\ *n* -s : one whose speech is defective by reason of cluttering
cluttering *n* -s : a speech defect in which phonetic units are dropped, condensed, or otherwise distorted as a result of overly rapid agitated utterance
¹cly \'klī\ *vt* [perh. fr. LG *kleien* to scratch, fr. MLG; akin to Flem *klauwen* to scratch, steal, G *klauen*, OHG *klāwa* claw — more at CLAW] *slang* : SEIZE, STEAL
²cly \"\ *n* -ES [perh. fr. ¹*cly*] *slang* : POCKET, PURSE
clydes·dale \'klīdz,dāl\ *n* -s *usu cap* [fr. *Clydesdale*, valley in Scotland where it originated] : a heavy draft horse of a breed orig. from Clydesdale, Scotland, distinguished by a dark brown or black coat, white blaze and stockings, and heavy feathering about the fetlock
clydesdale terrier *n, usu cap C* [fr. *Clydesdale*, valley in Scotland where it originated] : a small terrier of a breed resulting from selective breeding of the Skye terrier and distinguished by tiny erect ears, a long and silky coat, and short legs
clyde·side \'klīd,sīd\ *adj, usu cap* [*Clyde*, river in Scotland + *E side*] : of or relating to the region along the Clyde in Scotland; *esp* : having to do with shipbuilding, the chief industry of this region
clyde·sider \-də(r)\ *n* -s *cap* : a native or resident of the region along the Clyde in Scotland
cly·er \'klī(ə)r\ *n* -s [D *klier* gland, scrofula, fr. MD *cliere*; akin to Fris *klīr* gland] **1** : a tuberculous lymph gland in cattle **2 clyers** *pl* : tuberculosis of the bovine lymphatic system
cly·me·nel·la \,klīmə'nelə, ,klim-\ *n, cap* [NL, fr. *Clymene*, an Oceanid (fr. L, fr. Gk *Klymenē*) + NL *-ella*] : a genus of polychaete worms common in shallow waters of the northern Atlantic coasts — see BAMBOO WORM
¹clym·e·nid \'klīmənəd, -,nid\ *adj* [NL *Clymenidae*] : of or relating to the Clymenidae
²clymenid \"\ *n* -s : a clymenid ammonoid
cly·men·i·dae \klī'menə,dē, klə'-\ *n pl, cap* [NL, fr. *Clymenia*, type genus (fr. *Clymene* + NL *-ia*) + *-idae*] : a family of extinct Devonian ammonoids having the siphuncle at the dorsal margin of the whorls
clype \'klīp\ *vi* -ED/-ING/-s [alter. of earlier *cleip*, fr. ME *clepien* to call — more at CLEPE] *Scot* : to tell secrets : TATTLE
clyp·e·al \'klipēəl\ *adj* [NL *clypeus* + E *-al*] : of or relating to a clypeus
clyp·e·as·ter \,klipē'astə(r)\ *n, cap* [NL, fr. L *clypeus* round shield + NL *-aster*] : a widely distributed genus (the type of the family Clypeastridae) of large burrowing cake urchins
clyp·e·as·trid·ea \,=pēə'stridēə\ [NL, fr. *Clypeastr-, Clypeaster* + *-idea*] *syn of* CLYPEASTRINA
clyp·e·as·tri·na \-ə'strīnə, -rēnə\ *n pl, cap* [NL, fr. *Clypeaster* + *-ina*] : a suborder of sea urchins (order Exocycloida) comprising a large number of flattened more or less discoidal sea urchins (as the cake urchins and sand dollars) — compare SPATANGINA
¹clyp·e·as·troid \'==ˌa,strȯid\ *adj* [NL *Clypeastroida*] : of or relating to the Clypeastrina
²clypeastroid \"\ *n* -s : one of the Clypeastrina : CAKE URCHIN
clyp·e·as·troi·da \,==ə'strȯidə\ *or* **clyp·e·as·troi·dea** \-dēə\ [NL *Clypeastroida*, alter. of *Clypeastroidea*, fr. *Clypeaster* + *-oidea*] *syn of* CLYPEASTRINA
clyp·e·ate \'klipēət, -ē,āt, *usu* -d· + V\ *or* **clyp·e·at·ed** \-,ād·əd\ *or* **clyp·e·i·form** \-pēə,fȯrm\ *adj* [*clypeate* fr. L *clypeus* round shield + E *-ate*; *clypeated* fr. L *clypeus* + E *-ate* + *-ed*; *clypeiform* fr. L *clypeus* + E *-iform*] **1** *biol* : shaped like a round buckler or shield : SCUTATE **2** *biol* : furnished with a clypeus or with a shieldlike plate or process
clyp·e·ole \-,ōl\ *also* **clyp·e·o·la** \klə'pēələ\ *n, pl* **clypeoles** \-lz\ *or* **clypeo·lae** \-ə,lē\ [NL *clypeola*, fr. L *clypeus* round shield + *-ola* -ole] : one of the shield-shaped sporophylls composing the fertile spike in members of the genus *Equisetum*
clyp·e·us \'klipēəs\ *n, pl* **clyp·ei** \-ē,ī\ [NL, fr. L *clipeus, clupeus, clypeus* round shield] **1** : a plate or shield on the anterior median aspect of an insect's head that commonly consists of two fused sclerites and bears the labrum on its anterior margin **2** *bot* : a black disklike tissue formed about the mouth of the perithecia in certain ascomycetes **3** : the area on the front of a spider's head bounded by the eyes and the first pair of appendages
cly·sis \'klīsəs\ *n, pl* **cly·ses** \-,sēz\ [NL, fr. Gk *klysis*, fr. *klyzein* to wash] : the introduction of large amounts of fluid into the body usu. by parenteral injection to replace that lost (as from hemorrhage or in dysentery or burns), to provide nutrients, or to maintain blood pressure — see HYPODERMOCLYSIS, PHLEBOCLYSIS, PROCTOCLYSIS
clys·ma \'klizmə\ *n, pl* **clysma·ta** \-məd·ə\ [NL, fr. Gk *klysma*, fr. *klyzein*] : ENEMA
clys·sus \'klisəs\ *n, pl* **clys·si** \-,sī\ [NL] : a quintessence or efficacious principle
clys·ter \'klistə(r)\ *n* -s [ME, fr. MF or L; MF *clistere*, fr. L *clyster*, fr. Gk *klystēr*, fr. *klyzein* to wash out; akin to OE *hlūtor* clean, pure, OHG *hlūttar*, ON *hlēr* sea, Goth *hlutrs* pure, clean, L *cluere* to purge, W *clir* clear, clean, Lith *šlúoti* to sweep] : ENEMA
clyte \'klīt\ *var of* CLOIT
cm *abbr* **1** centimeter **2** cumulative
CM *abbr* **1** *often not cap* [L *causa mortis*] by reason of death **2** center matched **3** certificated master; certificated mistress **4** circular measure **5** *often not cap* circular mil **6** common meter **7** corresponding member **8** countermark; countermarked **9** court-martial
Cm *symbol* curium
c major *n, usu cap C* : the major musical key having neither sharps nor flats in its signature
cmd *abbr* command
CMD *abbr* common meter double
cmdg *abbr* commanding
cmdr *abbr* commander
cmdre *abbr* commodore
c melody *n, usu cap C* : a tenor saxophone in C instead of the usual B flat
c minor *n, usu cap C* : the minor musical key having a signature of three flats
c–mitosis \'sē+\ *n* [colchicine + *mitosis*] : an artificially induced abortive nuclear division in which the chromosome number is doubled (as that caused by exposure of cells to colchicine)
c–mitotic \" +\ *adj* : of, like, or inducing c-mitosis
cml *abbr* commercial
cn *abbr* **1** canon **2** consolidated
CN *abbr* **1** case of need **2** circular note **3** compass north **4** consignment note **5** cover note **6** credit note
-cne·mia \(k)'nēmēə\ *n comb form* -s [NL, fr. F *-cnémie*, fr. Gk *knēmē* shin + F *-ie* -y] : -shinnedness ⟨platycnemia⟩
cne·mi·al \'nēmēəl\ *adj* [Gk *knēmē* shin + E *-ial*] : relating to the shin or shinbone
-cne·mic \(k)|nēmik\ *adj comb form* [ISV *-cnem-* (fr. Gk *knēmē* shin) + *-ic*; prob. orig. formed as F *-cnémique*] : -shinned ⟨platycnemic⟩
cne·mi·do·cop·tes \,nēmə(,)dō'käp,tēz\ [NL, alter. of *knemidokoptes*, fr. Gk *knēmid-, knēmis* greave (fr. *knēmē* shin) + MGk *koptēs* cutter, fr. Gk *koptein* to cut — more at CAPON] *syn of* KNEMIDOKOPTES
cne·mi·doph·o·rus \,nēmə'däfərəs\ *n, cap* [NL, fr. Gk *knēmidophoros* wearing greaves, fr. *knēmid-, knēmis* greave + *-phoros* -phorous] : a genus of American lizards of the family Teiidae — see RACE RUNNER
cne·mis \'nēməs\ *n, pl* **cnem·i·des** \'nemə,dēz\ [NL, fr. Gk *knēmis* greave, fr. *knēmē* shin] : SHIN, TIBIA
-cne·mus \(k)'nēməs\ *n comb form* [NL, modif. of Gk. *knēmē* shin] : -legged one — in generic names of animals ⟨Octacnemus⟩
cne·o·rum \nē'ōrəm, -ȯr-\ *n, cap* [NL, fr. Gk *kneōron*, a plant, prob. spurge flax (*Daphne gnidium*); prob. akin to Goth *hnasqus* soft, Skt *kiknasa* grits, and L *cinis* ashes — more at INCINERATE] : a small genus (constituting a family Cneoraceae of the order Geraniales) of low evergreen shrubs of the Mediterranean region having oblong or spatulate coriaceous leaves and small axillary cymose or solitary flowers
cni·cus \'nīkəs\ *n, cap* [NL, fr. L *cnicus, cnecus* safflower, fr. Gk *knēkos* safflower, thistle, yellow — more at HONEY] : a genus of European herbs of the family Compositae — see BLESSED THISTLE
cnid- *or* **cnido-** *comb form* [NL, fr. *cnida*] : cnida ⟨cnidosac⟩ ⟨cnidoglandular⟩ ⟨Cnidaria⟩
cni·da \'nīdə\ *n, pl* **cni·dae** \-(,)dē\ [NL, fr. Gk *knidē* nettle, sea nettle; akin to L *nidor* smell of roasting meat — more at NIDOR] : NEMATOCYST
cni·dar·ia \nī'da(a)rēə\ [NL, fr. *cnid-* + *-aria*] *syn of* COELENTERATA — used esp. to distinguish the narrow from the more inclusive scope of Coelenterata
¹cni·dar·i·an \(')=¦=rēən\ *adj* [NL *Cnidaria* + E *-an*] : of or relating to a cnida or the Cnidaria
²cnidarian \"\ *n* -s : one of the Cnidaria
cni·do·blast \'nīdə,blast\ *n* -s [ISV *cnid-* + *-blast*; orig. formed in G] : a cell that develops a nematocyst or develops into a nematocyst
cni·do·cell \-,sel\ *n* -s [*cnid-* + *cell*] : NEMATOCYST
cni·do·cil \-,sil\ *n* -s [ISV *cnid-* + NL *cilium* hairlike process — more at CILIA] : a minute process of a nematocyst that when touched is believed to cause the projection of the stinging thread
cni·do·cyst \-,sist\ *n* -s [ISV *cnid-* + *-cyst*] : NEMATOCYST
cni·do·phore \-,fō(ə)r\ *n* -s [*cnid-* + *-phore*] : a structure bearing nematocysts — **cni·doph·o·rous** \(')nī¦däfərəs\ *adj*
cni·do·pod \-,päd\ *n* -s [*cnid-* + *-pod*] : the stalklike base of a nematocyst
cni·do·sco·lus \,=='skōləs\ *n, cap* [NL, fr. *cnido-* (fr. Gk *knidē* nettle) + Gk *skōlos* thorn, pointed stake; akin to Gk *skallein* to hoe — more at CNIDA, SHELL] : a genus of stinging perennial herbaceous or shrubby plants (family Euphorbiaceae) characterized by alternate mostly long-petioled palmately veined and often lobed or divided leaves and stipules armed with stinging bristles
cni·do·spo·rid·ia \-spə'ridēə\ *n pl, cap* [NL, fr. *cnid-* + *-sporidia*] : a subclass of Sporozoa comprising protozoans that have complex spores with polar capsules and coiled polar filaments and are single-host parasites of lower vertebrates and invertebrates — see ACTINOMYXIDIA, MICROSPORIDIA, MYXOSPORIDIA — **cni·do·spo·rid·i·an** \¦===¦ridēən\ *adj or n*
cnossian *usu cap, var of* KNOSSIAN
c–note \'sē + ,-\ *n* -s *usu cap C, slang* : a 100-dollar bill
cnr *abbr* corner
CNS *abbr* central nervous system
co- *prefix* [ME, fr. L, fr. *com-*; akin to OE *ge-*, perfective, associative, and collective prefix, OHG *gi-, ga-*, Goth *ga-*, OIr *com-, con-* with, together, Alb *kë-*, Gk *koinos* common] **1** : with : together : joint : jointly : shared : mutual : mutually ⟨coexist⟩ ⟨coinheritance⟩ ⟨cosustain⟩ ⟨cooperate⟩ **2** : in or to the same degree ⟨coextensive⟩ ⟨coeval⟩ **3 a** : fellow : partner ⟨coauthor⟩ ⟨co-worker⟩ **b** : having a usu. lesser share in duty or responsibility : alternate : deputy ⟨cochairman⟩ ⟨copilot⟩ **4 a** : operating together or reciprocally ⟨coterm⟩ **b** : of the complement of an angle ⟨cosine⟩ ⟨codeclination⟩
co *abbr* **1** colon **2** company **3** container **4** coral **5** county
CO \'sē'ō\ *abbr or n* -s **1** commanding officer **2** conscientious objector
CO *abbr* **1** *often not cap* care of — usu. separated by a virgule **2** carried over **3** cash order **4** certificate of origin **5** colonial office **6** commissioner for oaths **7** communications officer **8** cut out
Co *symbol* cobalt
¹co·ac·er·vate \kō'asər,vāt, ,kōə'sər,-\ *vt* -ED/-ING/-s [L *coacervatus*] : to heap up : gather together in a heap or group : COLLECT; *esp* : to cause to form a coacervate
²co·acer·vate \,kōə'sərvət, (')kō¦asər,vāt\ *adj* [L *coacervatus*, past part. of *coacervare* to heap up, fr. *co-* + *acervare* (fr. *acervus* heap); perh. akin to L *acus* chaff — more at EAR] **1** : piled up : collected into a crowd **2** : growing in dense clusters
³coacervate \"\ *n* -s : an aggregate of colloidal droplets (as of two hydrophilic sols or of a sol and ions of opposite charge) held together by electrostatic attractive forces
co·ac·er·va·tion \(,)kō,asə(r)'vāshən\ *n* -s : the process of becoming a coacervate : mutual precipitation : AGGREGATION ⟨~ of gelatin and gum arabic⟩
¹coach \'kōch\ *n* -ES *often attrib* [ME *coche*, fr. MF, fr. G *kutsche*, prob. fr. Hung *kocsi* (*szekér*) wagon from Kocs, fr. *Kocs*, village in Hungary] **1 a** : a large usu. closed 4-wheeled carriage having doors in the sides and generally a front and a back seat inside and an elevated seat in front for the driver **b** *Brit* : a railway passenger or mail car **c** : a railroad passenger car with reclining or nonreclining seats that is intended primarily for day travel **d** : BABY CARRIAGE **e** : a closed 2-door single-compartment automobile with permanent back panel and top and in front two separate seats which may be turned down and in the rear a full-width cross seat **f** : MOTOR COACH **g** : HOUSE TRAILER **h** : an automobile body esp. of a closed model **i** : a class of passenger air transportation at a lower fare than first class **2** : a cabin on the afterpart of the quarterdeck of a man-of-war usu. occupied by the captain **3 a** [so called fr. the tutor's being regarded as a means for conveying the student through his examinations] : a private tutor who assists students esp. in preparing for examination **b** : one who instructs or trains a performer or a team of performers (as in debating or in musical or dramatic performance); *specif* : one who instructs players in the fundamentals of a competitive sport and directs team strategy ⟨fencing ~⟩ ⟨football ~⟩ — compare MANAGER, TRAINER **c** : a manual with a condensed body of information on a subject to be committed to memory **d** : a member of a team at bat in baseball who is posted near first or third base to direct base runners and signal to batters **4** *Austral* : a decoy bullock used to catch wild cattle **5** : SPONSOR 4b

coach 1a

²coach \"\ *vb* -ED/-ING/-ES *vt* **1** *archaic* : to transport in, place in, or provide with a coach **2 a** : to train intensively by detailed instruction, frequent demonstration, and repeated practice (as for an examination, a dramatic performance, or a public appearance) ⟨~ pupils⟩ ⟨there never was a witness so obviously ~*ed*⟩ **b** : to act as coach to (an athletic team or performer) **c** : to direct the movements of (a base runner) **d** : to give instructions, directions, or prompting to (one performing or attempting something) ⟨two escort vessels, the first maintaining sound contact . . . while it ~*ed* the second . . . by signals —J.P.Baxter b.1893⟩ ~ *vi* **1** : to go in a coach ⟨he ~*ed* to that licentious city —S.H.Adams⟩ **2 a** : to instruct as a coach : receive instruction from a coach **b** : to direct the movements of a base runner **syn** see TEACH
coach–and–four \¦==¦=\ *n* -s : a coach with four horses
coach box *n* : the driver's seat on a coach
coachbuilding \'=,==\ *n, Brit* : the design and manufacture of automobile bodies
coach dog *n* [so called fr. its formerly being used to run in attendance on a coach] : DALMATIAN
coach·ee \kō'chē *often and in sense 2 usu* '=(,)=\ *n* -s **1** : an American carriage shaped like a coach but longer and open in front **2** : COACHMAN
coach·er \'kōchə(r)\ *n* -s [In sense 1, fr. MF *cocher*, fr. *coche*; in sense 2, fr. ¹*coach* + *-er*; in sense 3, fr. ²*coach* + *-er*] **1** *obs* : COACHMAN **2** : COACH HORSE **3** : one that coaches; *specif* : COACH 3d
coach horn *n* : a long straight tapering copper horn with slight flare — compare POST HORN
coach horse *n* : a horse used or adapted for drawing a coach, being typically heavier and of more compact build than a road horse and exhibiting good style and action
coach house *n* : an outbuilding for a coach or carriage
coaching *n* -s **1 a** : traveling by coach **b** : pleasure driving in a coach (as in a tallyho) **2 a** : the profession or occupation of a coach **b** : instruction given esp. in private by or as if by a coach ⟨she learned while under the ~ of her mother⟩
coaching house *n* : an inn serving coach travelers
coaching traffic *n* [¹*coach* (railroad car) + *-ing*] *Brit* : railroad passenger traffic
¹coach·man \'=mən\ *n, pl* **coachmen** [¹*coach* + *man*] **1** : a man whose business is to drive a coach or carriage **2** *angling* : an artificial fly with white wings, peacock herl body, brown hackle, and gold tag
²coachman \"\ *adj, of women's clothing* : imitative of the double-breasted coat with fitted waist and wide lapels formerly worn by coachmen
coach roof *n, chiefly Brit* : the roof of the cabin on a small boat
coach screw *n* : LAG SCREW
coachwhip \'=,=\ *n* **1** : a whip usu. provided with a long lash and used in driving a coach **2** : OCOTILLO 1 **3** : COACHWHIP SNAKE **4** : LONG PENNANT
coachwhip bird *n* : a babblerlike Australian passerine bird of the genus *Psophodes*; *esp* : a bird (*P. olivaceus*) having a note resembling the crack of a whip
coachwhip snake *n* : a long slender active colubrid snake (*Coluber*, syn. *Masticophis, flagellum*) of the southern U.S. of which the scale pattern resembles a braided whip
coachwood \'=,=\ *n* [so called fr. its use in coachbuilding] **1** : either of two Australian trees of the family Cunoniaceae: **a** : a medium-sized tree (*Ceratopetalum apetalum*) with grayish bark and dry hard fruits surrounded by winglike calyx lobes — called also *leatherjacket* **b** : a medium-sized to large tree (*Schizomeria ovata*) with a succulent egg-shaped fruit — called also *white cherry* **2** : the heavy tough fine-grained wood of the coachwood (sense 1a) pinkish in color but darkening on exposure and used chiefly for veneers and in cabinetwork — called also *scented satinwood*
coachwork \'=,=\ *n* : the design, building, and finishing of automobile bodies
¹coachy \'kōchē, -chi\ *n* -ES [alter. of *coachee*] : COACHMAN
²coachy \"\ *adj* [¹*coach* (*horse*) + *-y*] : like a coach horse esp. in configuration
¹co·act \kō'akt\ *vt* -ED/-ING/-s [ME *coacten*, fr. L *coactus*, past part. of *cogere* to compel — more at COGENT] : FORCE, COMPEL, DRIVE, CONTROL

²**coact** \(ˈ)kō +\ *vi* -ED/-ING/-S [*co-* + *act* (verb)] **:** to act or work together

co·act·ee \ˌkō,akˈtē, kō¦akˈtē\ *n* -S [²*coact* + *-ee*] **:** an organism that passively participates in coaction (as a food species in a food chain)

¹**co·ac·tion** \kōˈakshən\ *n* -S [ME *coaccioun*, fr. MF *coaction*, fr. L *coaction-*, *coactio* collection, fr. *coactus* (past part. of *cogere* to collect, compel) + *-ion-*, *-io* -ion — more at COGENT] **:** force or compulsion in restraining or impelling **:** CONTROL

²**coaction** \(ˈ)kō + \ *n* [*co-* + *action*] **1 :** action taken together **:** joint action **:** an acting together **2 :** the relation or interaction that exists between individuals or kinds of organisms (as species) in an ecological community and typically takes the form of cooperation, disoperation, or competition — compare REACTION

¹**co·ac·tive** \(ˈ)kō¦aktiv\ *adj* [¹*coact* + *-ive*] **:** serving to compel or constrain **:** of compulsory nature **:** RESTRICTIVE ⟨any ~ power of the civil kind —William Warburton⟩ — **co·ac·tive·ly** *adv* — **co·ac·tiv·i·ty** \ˌkōakˈtivəd·ē\ *n* -ES

²**co·active** \(ˈ)kō + \ *adj* [*co-* + *active*] **:** acting in concurrence or together — **co·actively** \" +\ *adv* — **co·activity** \" +\ *n*

co·ac·tor \ˌkō,akˈtō(r); kō¦akˈtō(r), ˌ==tə(r)\ *n* [*co-* + *actor*] **:** an organism that participates in ecological coaction; *esp* **:** one (as a predator) that actively initiates coaction with another — compare COACTEE

co·adaptation \¦kō +\ *n* [*co-* + *adaptation*] **:** mutual adaptation (as of a flower and the insect that pollinates it)

coade stone \ˈkōd-\ *n*, *usu cap C* [after Eleanor *Coade*, 19th cent. Brit. manufacturer] **:** a very durable artificial stone made in London from 1760 to about 1840 apparently from ground stone and clay

co·adjacent \¦kō +\ *adj* [*co-* + *adjacent*] **:** mutually adjacent; *specif* **:** contiguous in thought

co·adjust \¦kō +\ *vt* [*co-* + *adjust*] **:** to adjust by mutual adaptation — **co·adjustment** \" +\ *n* -S

¹**co·adjutant** \(ˈ)kō +\ *adj* [*co-* + *adjutant*] **:** mutually assisting

²**coadjutant** \"\ *n* -S **:** ASSISTANT, HELPER

co·ad·jute \ˌkōəˈjüt\ *vb* -ED/-ING/-S [back-formation fr. *coadjutor*] *vi* **:** COOPERATE ~ *vt* **:** to cooperate with

co·ad·ju·tor \ˌkōəˈjüd·ə(r), -ütə(r) *also* kōˈajəd·ə(r) *or* -ətə(r)\ *n* -S [ME *coadjutour*, fr. MF *coadjuteur*, fr. L *coadjutor*, fr. *co-* + *adjutor*, fr. *adjutare* to help — more at AID] **1 :** one who works together with another usu. in a somewhat subordinate position **:** fellow worker **:** ASSISTANT **2** *or* **coadjutor bishop :** BISHOP COADJUTOR

co·ad·ju·tor·ship \-ˌship\ *n* -S **:** the office of a coadjutor

co·ad·ju·tress \ˌkōəˈjütrəs *also* kōˈajətrəs\ *n* -ES [*coadjutor* + *-ess*] **:** COADJUTRIX

co·ad·ju·trix \-ˌtriks\ *n*, *pl* **coadjutri·ces** \kō,ajəˈtrī,sēz\ [NL, fem. of *coadjutor* — more at -TRIX] **:** a female coadjutor

co·adjuvancy \(ˈ)kō+\ *n* -ES [*co-* + *adjuvancy*] **:** COOPERATION

co·adsorbent \¦kō+\ *n* [*co-* + *adsorbent*] **:** an agent that increases the effectiveness of an adsorbent

¹**co·ad·u·nate** \kōˈajə,nāt\ *vt* -ED/-ING/-S [LL *coadunatus*, past part. of *coadunare*, fr. L *co-* + LL *adunare*, fr. L *ad-* + LL *unare*, fr. L *unus* one — more at ONE] **:** to unite into one **:** COMBINE

²**coadunate** \(ˈ)=¦==nət, -ˌnāt\ *adj* [L *coadunatus*] **:** grown together and confluent **:** UNITED

co·ad·u·na·tion \=,==ˈnāshən\ *n* -S [LL *coadunation-*, *coadunatio*, fr. *coadunatus* + *-ion-*, *-io* -ion] **:** the union (as of dissimilar substances) in one body or mass

co·ad·u·na·tive \(ˈ)=¦==,nād·iv, -ātiv\ *adj* [L *coadunatus* + E *-ive*] **:** concerning, producing, or tending to produce coadunation — **co·ad·u·na·tive·ly** *adv*

coaetaneous *var of* COETANEOUS

co·a·gel \ˈkōə,jel\ *n* -S [blend of *coagulate* and *gel*] **:** a gelatinous precipitate (as of aluminum hydroxide) formed by coagulation of a sol — compare GEL

co·agency \(ˈ)kō+\ *n* [*co-* + *agency*] **:** combined or joint agency

co·agent \"+\ *n* [*co-* + *agent*] **:** a person, force, cause, or other agency working together with another

co·ag·ment \ˌkōagˈment\ *vt* -ED/-ING/-S [L *coagmentare*, fr. *coagmentum* act of joining together, joint, fr. *cogere* to drive together — more at COGENT] **:** to join together (as parts into a whole) **:** UNITE

coagmentate *vt* -ED/-ING/-S [L *coagmentatus*, past part. of *coagmentare*] *obs* **:** COAGMENT — **coagmentation** *n* -S *obs*

coagula *pl of* COAGULUM

co·ag·u·la·bil·i·ty \=,===ˈbiləd·ē, -ətē, -i\ *n* -ES **:** the quality or state of being coagulable

co·ag·u·la·ble \kōˈagyələbəl\ *adj* [F, fr. *coaguler* to coagulate (fr. L *coagulare*) + *-able*] **:** capable of being coagulated

co·ag·u·lant \kōˈagyələnt\ *n* -S [L *coagulant-*, *coagulans*, pres. part. of *coagulare*] **:** something that produces coagulation

co·ag·u·lase \-ˌlās\ *n* -S [ISV *coagulate* + *-ase*] **:** any of several enzymes that cause coagulation (as of blood) ⟨the antigenic ~*s* of some staphylococci⟩

¹**co·ag·u·late** \kōˈagyələt, -ˌlāt, *usu* -d·+V\ *adj* [ME *coagulat*, fr. L *coagulatus*] **:** COAGULATED

²**co·ag·u·late** \-ˌlāt, *usu* -d·+V\ *vb* -ED/-ING/-S [L *coagulatus*, past part. of *coagulare* to curdle, fr. *coagulum* curdling agent, rennet, fr. *cogere* to drive together — more at COGENT] *vt* **1 :** to cause or bring about the coagulation of **:** CURDLE, CLOT ⟨~ the blood⟩ ⟨rennet ~*s* milk⟩ **2 :** to gather together or form into a mass or a group ⟨~ all these many programs into one general program⟩ ⟨smaller particles can be *coagulated* into lumps of matter⟩ ~ *vi* **1 :** to undergo coagulation **2 :** to gather together into a mass or group ⟨industry has *coagulated* in dense masses along the railroad lines —W.D. Teague⟩ **:** take form or shape ⟨vague uneasy feelings *coagulated* into a desire for action⟩

³**co·ag·u·late** \-lət, -ˌlāt, *usu* -d·+V\ *n* -S [¹*coagulate*] **:** COAGULUM 2

co·ag·u·la·tion \=,==ˈlāshən\ *n* -S [F or L; F *coagulation*, fr. L *coagulation-*, *coagulatio*, fr. *coagulatus* + *-ion-*, *-io-* -ion] **1 a :** the process of becoming viscous, jellylike, or solid or of uniting into a coherent mass; *esp* **:** the change from a liquid to a thickened curdlike state not by evaporation but by chemical reaction ⟨the spontaneous ~ of freshly drawn blood⟩ ⟨the ~ of egg albumen by heat⟩ **b :** the process by which such change of state takes place consisting of the alteration of a soluble substance, usu. protein, into an insoluble form or of the flocculation or separation of colloidal or suspended matter **2 :** a substance or body formed by coagulation **:** COAGULUM 2

coagulation time *n* **:** the time required by shed blood to clot, being a measure of the normality of the blood

co·ag·u·la·tive \=ˈ==,lād·iv, -ātiv\ *adj* [*coagulate* + *-ive*] *obs* **:** having the power to cause coagulation or the property of coagulating

co·ag·u·la·tor \=ˈ==,lād·ə(r), -ātə(r)\ *n* -S [*coagulate* + *-or*] **:** an agent that causes coagulation — **co·ag·u·la·to·ry** \-lə,tōrē, -tȯrē\ *adj*

co·ag·u·lin \kōˈagyələn\ *n* -S [*coagulate* + *-in*] **1 :** PRECIPITIN **2 a :** a hypothetical tissue constituent able to induce conversion of fibrinogen to fibrin in the absence of prothrombin or thrombin **b :** THROMBOPLASTIN

co·ag·u·lom·e·ter \kō,agyəˈläməd·ə(r), -ətə(r)\ *n* -S [*coagulate* + *-o-* + *-meter*] **:** an apparatus for measuring the time required for a sample of fluid (as blood) to coagulate

co·ag·u·lum \kōˈagyələm\ *n*, *pl* **coagu·la** \-lə\ [L — more at COAGULATE] **1** *obs* **:** COAGULANT **2 :** a coagulated mass or substance **:** CLOT, CURD — called also *coagulate*

co·a·huil·tec \kōəˈwēl,tek\ *n*, *pl* **coahuiltec** *or* **coahuiltecs** *usu cap* [Sp *coahuilteca*, fr. *Coahuila* state in Mexico + Sp *-teca* (as in *azteca* Aztec)] **1a :** an Indian people of northeastern Mexico and Texas **b :** a member of such people **2 :** a Coahuiltecan language of the Coahuiltec people

co·a·huil·tec·an \ˌkōə¦wēl¦tekən\ *n*, *pl* **coahuiltecan** *or* **coahuiltecans** *usu cap* **:** a presumed language family of possible Hokan relationship of northeastern Mexico and southern Texas including Coahuiltec, Comecrudo, Cotoname, and Tamaulipec

co·ai·ta \kü,īˈtä\ *n* -S [obs. Pg *coaitá* (now *coatá*), fr. Tupi *coaitá*, *coatá*] **:** any of various spider monkeys (esp. *Ateles paniscus*)

¹**coak** *obs var of* COKE

²**coak** \ˈkōk\ *n* -S [prob. fr. (assumed) ONF *coque* notch, fr. L *coccum* excrescence on a tree, berry of the scarlet oak (whence OF *coche* notch), fr. Gk *kokkos* berry of the scarlet oak, core of fruit] **1 a :** a projecting tenon connecting the face of a scarfed timber with the similarly scarfed face of another timber — compare SCARF JOINT **b :** a dowel of hard wood or metal let into timbers to unite them or keep them from slipping — compare COG **2 :** a metallic bushing or strengthening piece in the center of a wooden block sheave

³**coak** \"\ *vt* -ED/-ING/-S **:** to unite by a coak

coak·um \ˈkōkəm\ *n* -S [origin unknown] **:** POKEWEED

¹**coal** \ˈkōl\ *n* -S *often attrib* [ME *cole*, fr. OE *col*; akin to OHG & ON *kol* coal of fire, IrGael *gual* coal, Arm *krak* glowing coals] **1 a :** a piece of carbon or charred wood or other combustible substance glowing without flame **:** a hot ember ⟨food cooked on the ~*s*⟩ ⟨burned by a ~ from the grate⟩ ⟨heated by a bed of hot ~*s*⟩ **b :** a piece of charred wood or other combustible substance more or less completely consumed **:** CINDER **2 :** CHARCOAL 1 **3 a :** a black or brownish black solid combustible mineral substance formed by the partial decomposition of vegetable matter without free access of air and under the influence of moisture and in many cases increased pressure and temperature, the substance being widely used as a natural fuel and containing carbon, hydrogen, oxygen, nitrogen, and sulfur as well as inorganic constituents that are left behind as ash after burning — see ANTHRACITE, BITUMINOUS COAL, COKE, LIGNITE; compare PEAT **b coals** *pl*, *Brit* **:** pieces or a quantity of the fuel broken up for burning ⟨a ton of ~*s*⟩ **c :** a particular kind or size of coal ⟨a good stove ~⟩

²**coal** \"\ *vb* -ED/-ING/-S *vt* **1 :** to convert to charcoal by burning **:** CHAR ⟨~ a cord of wood in one day⟩ **2 :** to supply with coal for fuel ⟨~ a steamer⟩ ~ *vi* **:** to take in coal ⟨the steamer ~*ed* as soon as she reached port⟩

coala *var of* KOALA

coal ball *n* **:** a nodule found in coal usu. composed of calcite or silica and carbonaceous matter and having fragmentary or microscopic plant remains

coal black *n* **:** a very dark black

coal blacking *n* **:** iron founders' blacking made from ground coal

coal brass *or* **coal blende** *n* **:** pyrite found with coal

coal·brook·dale \ˈkōl,bru̇k,dāl\ *n* -S *usu cap* [after *Coalbrookdale*, Shropshire, England] **:** COALPORT

coal bucket *n*, *chiefly Midland* **:** COAL SCUTTLE

coal cutter *n* **:** a hand-manipulated but power-driven machine that is used to detach coal from the vein usu. by sawing or drilling

coal·er \ˈkōlə(r)\ *n* -S [¹*coal* + *-er*] **:** something (as a railroad or ship) wholly or chiefly employed in transporting or supplying coal

co·a·lesce \ˌkōəˈles\ *vb* -ED/-ING/-S [L *coalescere*, fr. *co-* + *alescere* to grow — more at OLD] *vi* **1 :** to grow together ⟨the edges of a wound ~⟩ **:** unite by growth into one body ⟨the outer suburbs of the two neighboring cities have now almost *coalesced*⟩ **2 a :** to unite or join together into one body or product **:** become integrated into a whole ⟨the tables . . . have . . . *coalesced* and . . . the customers who came in by twos and fours and sixes have become one big party —*N.Y. Times*⟩ **b :** to unite for a common end **:** join forces **:** agree in principle or effect ⟨all the divergent forces of the insurrection had *coalesced* for the final thrust —Paul Willen⟩ ⟨these two political parties often ~ on a candidate⟩ ~ *vt* **:** to cause to unite **:** bring together to form a unit or a single body ⟨~*s* moralities hardly ever found together —Randall Jarrell⟩ **syn** see MIX

co·a·les·cence \-ˈlesᵊn(t)s\ *n* -S [L *coalescere* + E *-ence*] **:** a growing together or union in one body, form, or group **:** COMBINATION ⟨~ of cloud dust, gas, or small particles in interstellar space —A.E.Benfield⟩ ⟨~ of two similar theories into one great system⟩

coalescency *n* -ES *obs* **:** COALESCENCE

¹**co·a·les·cent** \¦kōə¦lesᵊnt\ *adj* [L *coalescent-*, *coalescens*, pres. part. of *coalescere*] **:** growing together **:** COHERING, COALESCING

²**coalescent** \"\ *n* -S **:** one that coalesces

coalfield \ˈ=,=\ *n* [¹*coal* + *field*] **1 :** a region in which deposits of coal occur ⟨the rich ~*s* of the U.S.⟩ **2 :** the coal mines of a region — often used in pl. ⟨industrial peace in the ~*s*⟩

coalfish \ˈ=,=\ *n* [so called fr. its color] **:** any of several blackish or dark-backed fishes: as **a :** POLLACK **b :** COBIA **c :** SABLEFISH

coal gas *n* **:** gas made from coal: as **a :** the mixture of gases thrown off by burning coal (as in the furnace of a house) **b :** the gas consisting chiefly of hydrogen and methane made by carbonizing bituminous coal in retorts and used for heating and lighting — see COKE-OVEN GAS

coal hod *n*, *chiefly Northeast* **:** COAL SCUTTLE

coalhole \ˈ=,=\ *n* **1 :** a hole for coal (as a trap or opening in a sidewalk leading to a coal bin) **2** *Brit* **:** a compartment for storing coal

coal house *n* **:** a building (as a shed) or an enclosed place (as a bin) for storage of coal

coalier *comparative of* COALY

coalies *pl of* COALY

coaliest *superlative of* COALY

coal·i·fi·ca·tion \ˌkōləfəˈkāshən\ *n* -S **:** the process in which vegetable matter becomes converted into coal of increasingly higher rank with anthracite as the final product

coal·i·fy \ˈkōlə,fī\ *vb* -ED/-ING/-ES [*coal* + *-ify*] **:** to change into coal by the process of coalification

coaling *pres part of* COAL

coaling station *n* [fr. pres. part. of ²*coal*] **:** a port at which vessels may coal

Coal·ite \ˈkō,līt\ *trademark* — used for a smokeless fuel made by heating bituminous coal in a retort until much of the volatile matter has been given off

co·a·li·tion \ˌkōəˈlishən\ *n* -S *often attrib* [MF, fr. L *coalitus* + *-ion-*, *-io* -ion] **1 a :** the act of coalescing **:** the union of things separate into a single body or group ⟨~ of water vapor into raindrops⟩ **b :** a group or body formed by the coalescing of orig. distinct elements **:** COMBINATION ⟨they formed a ~ with the theater owners⟩ **2** *in government or politics* **:** a temporary alliance of distinct parties, persons, or states for joint action or to achieve a common purpose ⟨the party could keep control only by ~ with two smaller parties⟩ ⟨the parties of the right formed a ~ against the Communists⟩ ⟨a ~ of free nations⟩

co·a·li·tion·al \-shənᵊl, -shnəl\ *adj* **:** of or concerning coalition

co·a·li·tion·ist \-shənəst\ *or* **co·a·li·tion·er** \-shənə(r)\ *n* -S **:** one who joins, aids, or favors a coalition

coal·less \ˈkōlləs\ *adj* **:** lacking coal

coal measures *n pl* **:** beds of coal with the associated rocks varying in thickness from a few feet to several thousand feet and consisting of shales, sandstones, limestones, and conglomerates with interstratified beds of coal and occas. of iron ore

coal·mouse \ˈkōl,mau̇s\ *n*, *pl* **coal·mice** \-ˌmīs\ [by folk etymology fr. ME *colmose*, fr. OE *colmāse*, fr. *col* coal + *māse* titmouse; fr. its dark color — more at COAL, TITMOUSE] **:** COAL TIT

coal oil *n* **1 :** petroleum or a refined oil prepared from it **2** *chiefly Midland & South* **:** KEROSENE

coal-oil brush \ˈ=,=-\ *n* **:** a low spreading horsebrush (*Tetradymia glabrata*) chiefly of the Intermountain region and a leading cause of bighead

coal passer *n* **:** one that brings coal from a ship's bunkers to furnaces and removes ashes

coal pipe *n* **:** a very thin and irregular seam of coal

coalpit \ˈ=,=\ *n* [ME *colpit*, fr. OE *colpytt*, fr. *col* coal + *pytt* pit — more at COAL, PIT] **1** *dial* **:** a place where charcoal is made **2 :** a pit where coal is dug **:** a coal mine

coal plant *n* **:** one of the impressions or fossilized remains of plants found in the coal measures

coal pocket *n* **:** a plant equipped for the storage and loading of coal esp. for retail distribution

coal·port \ˈkōl,pōrt, -pȯrt\ *n* -S *usu cap* [fr. *Coalport*, near Shrewsbury, England, where it was produced] **:** a soft paste porcelain and later bone china ware produced both in table wares and in elaborate ornamental pieces often in the manner of Meissen or Sèvres

coalrake \ˈ=,=\ *n* [ME (northern dial.) *colrake*, fr. *cole* coal + *rake*] **:** a pronged instrument for stirring ashes or coals in an oven or furnace

coal road *n* **:** a railroad concerned primarily with the transportation of coal

coals *pl of* COAL, *pres 3d sing of* COAL

coal scuttle *n* **:** a metal pail for holding and carrying coal typically having a bail and a sloping lip for ease in pouring

coal-scuttle bonnet \ˈ=,==-\ *n* **:** a woman's bonnet with flat back and stiff projecting brim somewhat resembling a coal scuttle

coal scuttle

coal seam *n* **:** a bed of coal usu. thick enough to be mined with profit

coal tar *n* **:** tar obtained by the destructive distillation of bituminous coal usu. in coke ovens or retorts and consisting of numerous constituents (as benzene, xylenes, naphthalene, pyridine, quinoline, phenol, cresols, light oil, creosote) that may be obtained by distillation

coal-tar dye \ˈ=,=-\ *n* **:** a dye made from a coal-tar derivative; *broadly* **:** any synthetic organic dye — compare ANILINE DYE

co·alternate \(ˈ)kō, ¦kō+\ *adj* [*co-* + *alternate*] *logic* **:** related so as to express alternatives which taken together exhaust the possibilities — used of propositions and judgments — **co·alternation** \(ˈ)kō+\ *n* — **co·alternative** \¦kō+\ *adj*

coal tit *or* **cole·tit** \ˈkōl,tit\ *n* [*coal*, *cole* + *tit*] **:** a small European tit (*Parus ater*) greenish gray with black cap and white patch on the neck

co·altitude \(ˈ)kō+\ *n* [*co-* + *altitude*] **:** the complement of the altitude **:** the zenith distance

coal-whipper \ˈ=,==\ *n*, *Brit* **:** one (as a laborer or a machine) that raises coal out of the hold of a ship

¹**coaly** \ˈkōlē, -li\ *adj* -ER/-EST [¹*coal* + *-y*] **:** covered or impregnated with coal **:** containing or resembling coal ⟨~ shale⟩

²**coaly** \"\ *n* -ES [¹*coal* + *-y*] **:** a coal heaver

coa·ming \ˈkōmiŋ\ *n* -S [prob. fr. *coam-* (alter. of ¹*comb*) + *-ing*] **1 a :** the raised frame of wood or steel around a hatchway, skylight, or other opening in the deck of a ship to prevent water from running below — sometimes used in pl. **b :** the raised frame along the sides of the cockpit of a boat **c :** the lower strake of plating on a deckhouse or casing **2 :** a raised frame around a floor or roof opening or esp. a scuttle to keep water from running in — sometimes used in pl.

co·an \ˈkōən\ *adj*, *usu cap* [Cos, (now *Kos*), an island of the Dodecanese in the Aegean sea + E *-an*] **:** of or relating to the island of Kos

co·appear \¦kō+\ *vi* [*co-* + *appear*] **:** to appear together or at the same time — **co·appearance** \"+\ *n*

co·apt \kōˈapt\ *vt* -ED/-ING/-S [LL *coaptare* (past part. *coaptatus*), fr. L *co-* + *aptare*, fr. *aptus* fit — more at APT] **1 :** to fit or join to each other **2 :** to close or fasten together **:** cause to adhere ⟨the margins of the wound were then closely ~*ed* with sutures —*Biol. Abstracts*⟩

co·ap·ta·tion \ˌkōapˈtāshən\ *n* -S [LL *coaptation-*, *coaptatio*, fr. *coaptatus* + *-ion-*, *-io* -ion] **:** the adaptation or adjustment of parts to each other **:** the joining or fitting together (as of the ends of a broken bone or the edges of a wound)

co·a·ra·tion \ˌkōəˈrāshən\ *n* -S [*co-* + obs. *aration* tilling of the soil, fr. L *aration-*, *aratio*, fr. *aratus* (past part. of *arare* to plow) + *-ion-*, *-io* -ion — more at EAR] **:** cooperative tilling of the soil as practiced by early village communities

co·arb \ˈkō,ärb\ *n* -S [IrGael *comharba* successor, fr. OIr *comarbe* heir, fr. *com-* with, together + *orbe* inheritance; akin to Gk *orphanos* orphan — more at CO-, ORPHAN] *in the early Irish and Scottish churches* **:** the incumbent of an abbey or bishopric as successor to the patron saint or founder

co·arct \kōˈärkt, -ˈäkt\ *vt* -ED/-ING/-S [ME *coarten*, *coharten*, fr. L *coarctare*, *coartare* — more at COARCTATE] **1 a** *obs* **:** to press or draw together **b :** to cause (the aorta) to become narrow or (the heart) to constrict **2 :** to restrict the action of **:** CONFINE, RESTRAIN

co·arc·tate \(ˈ)kō¦ärk,tāt, -ˌtət\ *adj* [L *coarctatus*, past part. of *coarctare*, *coartare* to press together, contract, fr. *co-* + *artare*, fr. *artus* narrow, confined; akin to L *artus* joint — more at ARTICLE] *biol* **:** pressed together **:** closely connected; *specif* **:** enclosed in a rigid case formed from the last larval skin — used of insect pupae

co·arc·ta·tion \ˌ==ˈtāshən\ *n* -S [L *coarctation-*, *coarctatio*, fr. *coarctatus* + *-ion-*, *-io* -ion] **1** *obs* **:** confinement to a narrow space **:** COMPRESSION, RESTRICTION **2 :** a stricture or narrowing (as of a vessel or canal, esp. the aorta)

coarse \ˈkō(ə)rs, -ȯ(ə)rs, -ōəs, -ȯ(ə)s\ *adj* -ER/-EST [ME *cors*, *corse* common, fr. *cors*, *corse*, n., customary sequence of events — more at COURSE] **1 :** of ordinary or inferior quality or value **:** COMMON, BASE ⟨of what ~ metal ye are molded —Shak.⟩ **2 a :** composed of relatively large parts or particles ⟨~ sand⟩ **:** loose or rough in texture ⟨~ skin⟩ ⟨the Southern textile industry developed first in . . . ~ goods; the North went in for medium and fine grade yarns —*Amer. Guide Series: R.I.*⟩ **b :** of crude, unskilled, or careless workmanship or design **:** roughly or crudely formed **:** without delicacy or grace of feature ⟨~ imitations, completely lacking in the original delicacy⟩ ⟨a ~ heavy face, loose-featured, red and sensual —Thomas Wolfe⟩ **c** *of paper* **:** of a grade suitable for wrapping or industrial use **d :** adjusted, set, or designed for heavy, fast, or less delicate work ⟨a ~ saw with large teeth⟩ ⟨a high-speed milling cutter with ~ pitch⟩ **e :** not precise or detailed with respect to adjustment, classification, discrimination **:** roughly approximate ⟨to fill in the details of the rather ~ picture obtained by the earlier studies⟩ ⟨one dial for ~ adjustment, one for fine⟩ **f** *med*, *of a tremor* **:** of wide excursion ⟨a ~ tremor of the extremities⟩ **3 a :** crude or unrefined in taste, manners, or sensibilities **:** without cultivation of taste, politeness or civility of manner, or delicacy of feeling ⟨many of the muckraking novels . . . were simple parables of the ~ businessman and the sensitive intellectual —Bernard De Voto⟩ **b :** crude and indelicate of language or idea esp. with violation of social taboos on language **:** OBSCENE, PROFANE **4 a** *dial*, *of the weather* **:** ROUGH, STORMY **b** *dial Brit*, *of persons or circumstances* **:** BRUTAL, HARSH **5 :** harsh, raucous, or rough in tone **:** not melodious or mellow ⟨the ~ jangling of ordinary bells —G.B.Shaw⟩ — used also of certain sounds heard in auscultation in pathological states of the chest ⟨~ rales⟩

syn VULGAR, GROSS, OBSCENE, RIBALD: COARSE suggests unrefined crudeness, indelicacy, or robust roughness ⟨he was forever making eyes at me — a *coarse*, puffy-faced, red= moustached young man, with his hair plastered down on each side of his forehead. I thought he was perfectly hateful . . . —A. Conan Doyle⟩ ⟨the landlady who had tyrannized over her when ill-humoured and unpaid, or when pleased had treated her with a *coarse* familiarity scarcely less odious —W.M.Thackeray⟩ In this sense, VULGAR, a stronger term, describes what offends good taste or decency and may suggest boorishness ⟨his passion for physical luxury nakedly revealed itself as simply the *vulgar* longing of the idle rich for conspicuous waste —Granville Hicks⟩ ⟨her father is a . . . *vulgar* person, mean in his ideals and obtuse in his manners —John Erskine †1951⟩ ⟨it was, in fact, the mouth that gave his face its sensual, sly, and ugly look, for a loose and *vulgar* smile seemed constantly to hover about its thick coarse edges —Thomas Wolfe⟩ GROSS stresses crude animal inclinations and lack of refinement ⟨merely *gross*, a scatological rather than a pornographic impropriety —Aldous Huxley⟩ ⟨Clif Clawson, at forty, was *gross*. His face was sweaty, and puffy with pale flesh; his voice was raw; he fancied checked Norfolk jackets, tight across his swollen shoulders and his beefy hips —Sinclair Lewis⟩ ⟨a spirituelle amoureuse, she is repelled by the *gross* or the voluptuary —S.N.Behrman⟩ OBSCENE is the strongest of this group in stressing impropriety, indecency, or nastiness ⟨it was, of course, easy to pick out a line here and there . . . which was frank to indecency, yet certainly not *obscene* —H.S. Canby⟩ ⟨his innate belief that human flesh is in some way *obscene*. In the old days artists . . . had painted decently and had draped their figures —Ellen Glasgow⟩ ⟨there are depths beneath depths in what happened last night — obscure fetid chambers of the human soul. Black hatreds, unnatural desires, hideous impulses, *obscene* ambitions are at the bottom of it —W.H.Wright› RIBALD suggests rough merriment or crude humor at the irreverent, scurrilous, or vulgar ‹they had their backs to him, shaking with the loose laughter which punctuates a *ribald* description —Mary Austin› ‹a *ribald* folksong about fleas in straw —J.L.Lowes›

coarse aggregate *n* **:** the portion of the aggregate used in concrete that is larger than about 3⁄16 inch

coarse fish *n* **1 :** ROUGH FISH **2** *chiefly Brit* **:** a freshwater fish not belonging to the family Salmonidae

coarse fodder *n* **:** a feeding stuff containing a relatively large percentage of crude fiber or water (as grass, hay, corn fodder, mangel-wurzels) — called also *roughage*

coarse–grained \ˈ=ˌ=\ *adj* **1 :** of a coarse grain or texture; *esp, of wood* **:** having wide annual rings, large wood elements, or both **2 :** lacking in culture **:** CRUDE, UNREFINED

coarsely *adv* **:** in a coarse manner

coars·en \ˈkōrsᵊn, -ȯr-,-ōəs-,-ȯ(ə)s-\ *vb* **coarsened; coarsening** \-sᵊniŋ, -sniŋ\ **coarsens** [*coarse* + *-en*] *vt* **:** to make coarse ~ *vi* **:** to become coarse

coarse·ness *n* -ES **:** the quality or state of being coarse

coarser *comparative of* COARSE

coarsest *superlative of* COARSE

coarse stuff *n* **:** the mixture of plastering materials consisting of lime, sand, and hair used in the scratch and brown coats

coarse wool *or* **coarse–wooled sheep** *n* **:** a sheep having long strong coarse-fibered wool esp. suitable for carpet weaving (as those of various large mutton breeds of English origin)

co·articulation \ˌkō+\ *n* -S [*co-* + *articulation*] *phonetics* **:** action or position of such part of an articulator as is not directly participating in an articulation

¹**coast** \ˈkōst\ *n* -S [ME *cost*, fr. MF *coste*, fr. L *costa* rib, side; akin to OSlav *kostĭ* bone] **1** *obs* **a :** a region or area esp. of the earth ‹through all the ~s of dark destruction —John Milton› **b :** the border or frontier of a country **:** the land near a border **c :** a point of the compass **:** DIRECTION **2 a :** the seashore or land near it **:** sea margin **:** SEABOARD **:** the land immediately abutting the sea ‹they saw across the water the English ~› **b :** the littoral or coastal region **:** that area of a country regarded as near the coast, sometimes including the whole of the coastal plain ‹a plant native to the Pacific ~› **c** *dial* **:** the border or bank of any body of water **d** *often cap* **:** the Pacific coast of the U.S. **3 :** a hill or slope suited to coasting (as on a sled); *also* **:** a slide or run down a slope on a coasting vehicle — **coast is clear :** no enemies or obstacles in sight

²**coast** \"\ *vb* -ED/-ING/-S [ME *costen*, fr. *cost*, n.] *vt* **1 a** *obs* **:** to move along or past the side of **:** SKIRT ‹~*ing* the wall of Heaven —John Milton› **b** *obs* **:** to move along in company with or at the side of **c :** to sail along the shore of **:** follow the coastline of ‹the entire shoreline of the Gulf of Mexico had been ~*ed* —Bernard DeVoto› **2** *obs* **a :** BORDER, ADJOIN **b :** to go throughout **:** traverse all parts of (a country) **3** *obs* **:** to locate with reference to or to mark with the points of the compass **4 :** to cause to go or move without continual application of propulsive power (as by momentum or gravity) ‹~ a car down the hill› ~ *vi* **1** *obs* **a :** to come near or approximate (as in nature or time) **b :** to draw near or approach **2 a** *archaic* **:** to travel on land along a coast or along or past the side of something **b** *obs* **:** to make a tour **:** travel around ‹~ up and down the country —Henry Blount› **c :** to sail along the shore **:** sail from port to port along the coast ‹~*ing* steadily southward along the margin of the lake —C.S. Forester› **3 a :** to slide, run, or glide down hill by the force of gravity (as on a sled or a bicycle) **b :** to move along without further application of propulsive power (as by momentum or by gravity) ‹to ~ from Earth to the moon . . . we must achieve a velocity of 25,000 mph —A.C.Clarke› **c :** to proceed without further application of effort **:** drift easily along without special effort or concern ‹the country . . . seems in a mood to ~ along —*U.S.News & World Report*›

coast·al \ˈkōstᵊl\ *adj* [¹*coast* + *-al*] **:** of or relating to a coast **:** located on or near a coast ‹~ marshes› ‹~ traffic› **:** bordering on a coast ‹the Atlantic ~ plain› ‹~ waters› — **coast·al·ly** \-təlē, -li\ *adv*

coastal erysipelas *n* **:** ONCHOCERCIASIS

coastal fever *n* **:** EAST COAST FEVER

coastal plain *n* **:** a plain extending inland from a seashore commonly the result of geologically recent emergence of the land

coastal staggers *n pl but sing in constr* **:** an ataxia of uncertain origin affecting Australian horses possibly as a result of ingestion of toxic plant matter or of a trace-element deficiency

coast artillery *n* **:** artillery esp. organized and equipped to defend a coastline

coast disease *n* **:** a disease of Australian sheep caused by deficiency of dietary copper and cobalt and marked by general debility and severe hypochromic anemia — compare ¹PINE 3

coast·er \ˈkōstə(r)\ *n* -S **1 :** one that coasts: as **a :** a person engaged in coastal traffic or commerce **b :** a vessel employed in sailing along a coast or engaged in the coasting trade; *specif, in statute law* **:** a vessel carrying to a port a cargo taken in at another port of the same country **2 a :** a resident of a seacoast **b :** one of the longhorn cattle of Texas esp. of the coastal region **c** (1) **:** a very large brook trout found along the northern shores of Lake Superior and Lake Michigan (2) **:** RAINBOW TROUT **3 a :** a round tray usu. of silver and often on wheels that is used for circulating a decanter after a meal **b :** a shallow container or a plate or mat to protect a surface (as a table from moisture from drinking vessels) **c** [²*coast* + *-er*] **:** a small vehicle (as a sled or wagon) on or in which a child may coast **d :** ROLLER COASTER

coaster brake *n* **:** a brake in the hub of the rear wheel of a bicycle that is applied by back pressure on the pedals and released by moving the pedals forward

coaster wagon *n* **:** a child's toy wagon often used for coasting

coast fever *n* **:** EAST COAST FEVER

coast gorilla *n* **:** a gorilla found in southeastern Nigeria usu. regarded as forming a subspecies (*Gorilla gorilla gorilla*) — compare MOUNTAIN GORILLA

coast guard *n* -S **1** *Brit* **:** a body of men orig. employed along the coast to prevent smuggling and later established as a naval reserve **2 :** a military or naval force employed in guarding a coast or responsible for the safety, order, and effective operation of maritime traffic in neighboring waters **3 :** a member of a coast guard

coast guard cutter *n* **:** CUTTER 5c

coastguardsman \ˈ=ˌ=mən\ *or* **coastguardman** \ˈ=ˌ=mən\ *n*, *pl* **coastguardsmen** *or* **coastguardmen :** a member of a coast guard

coast·ing \ˈkōstiŋ\ *n* -S **:** configuration of a coast **:** COASTLINE

coasting trade *n* **:** trade along a coast esp. as regulated by the laws of a particular country

coastland \ˈ=ˌ=\ *n* **:** land bordering the sea **:** a section of seacoast

coast lily *n* **:** a lily (*Lilium maritimum*) of the Pacific coast of the U.S. having orange flowers

coastline \ˈ=ˌ=\ *n* **1 a :** the line that forms the boundary between the land and the water esp. of a sea or ocean **b :** a broad zone of land and water extending indefinitely both landward and seaward from a shoreline **2 :** the general configuration of the land along a coast

coast live oak *n* **:** a highly variable evergreen oak (*Quercus agrifolia*) of the coastal zone of western No. America from Puget Sound to Lower California with rather small thick usu. spiny-toothed leaves that are dark green above but paler and somewhat shining below — called also *California live oak*

coast pilot *n* **1 :** one who pilots coasting vessels **2 :** an official publication giving a description of a particular section of coast and usu. sailing directions for coastal navigation

coast rat *n* **:** a southern African rodent (*Bathyergus maritimus*) that is about the size of a rat and is noted for its extensive burrows

coast redwood *n* **:** REDWOOD 3a

coast rhododendron *n* **:** a medium-sized rhododendron (*Rhododendron californicum*) of the Pacific coast of No. America with large rosy brown-spotted flowers

coasts *pl of* COAST, *pres 3d sing of* COAST

coastwaiter \ˈ=ˌ=\ *n*, *Brit* **:** a landwaiter over coastal shipping

¹**coast·ward** \ˈkōstwə(r)d\ *or* **coastwards** \-dz\ *adv* **:** toward the coast

²**coastward** \"\ *adj* **:** situated near or directed toward the coast

coast·ways \-ˌwāz\ *archaic var of* COASTWISE

¹**coast·wise** \-ˌwīz\ *adv* **:** by way of the coast **:** along the coast

²**coastwise** \"\ *adj* **:** moving along the coast **:** carried on by water between places on a coast ‹~ business› **:** engaged in commerce between places on a coast **:** COASTAL ‹~ shipping›

¹**coat** \ˈkōt, *usu* -d·+V\ *n* -S *often attrib* [ME *cote*, fr. OF *cote*, *cotte*, of Gmc origin; akin to OHG *kozza*, *kozzo* coarse mantle, OS *kot* woolen coat, and prob. to G dial. *chūz* disheveled hair, *chūder*, *kauder* oakum; perh. akin to Gk *beudos* feminine attire] **1 a :** an outer garment (as a raincoat) usu. with long sleeves, a collar, and a single-breasted or double-breasted front opening made of fabric, fur, or plastic and varying in length and style according to fashion and use **b** (1) *now dial* **:** PETTICOAT, SKIRT — usu. used in pl. (2) *South* **:** DRESS 3 **c** *archaic* **:** habit or clothing indicating the order, class, profession, or office **:** CLOTH, PROFESSION ‹men of his ~ should be minding their prayers —Jonathan Swift› **d :** something resembling a coat in covering ‹a ~ of tan› or pervading ‹a thick ~ of gloom enveloped the prairies —J.H.Gray› or serving as an article of dress ‹if malice and vanity wear the ~ of philanthropy —R.W.Emerson› **2 :** COAT OF ARMS **3 :** the external growth on animals like a garment (as of fur, skin, wool, or feathers) ‹the horses' ~s were sleek› **4 :** a layer of any substance covering another: as **a :** a cover or lining esp. of an animal organ **:** MEMBRANE **:** HUSK, BARK ‹the ~ of the eyeball› ‹the ~s of an onion› **b :** a layer of a protective or ornamental substance (as paint or plaster) laid on in a single application ‹three ~s of paint on the wall› **5** *obs* **:** COAT MONEY **6** *obs* **:** FACE CARD **7** *naut* **:** a piece of tarred or painted canvas to keep out water fastened about the mast, bowsprit, or pumps where they pass through the deck or about the rudder casing

²**coat** \"\ *vt* -ED/-ING/-S [ME *coten*, fr. *cote*, n.] **1 :** to cover or dress with a coat or outer garment **2 :** to cover or spread with a finishing, protecting, or enclosing layer of any substance ‹~ a surface with paraffin› ‹frost ~s the window› ‹~ glass with silver to make a mirror›

coat armor *n* [alter. of *cote-armour*] **1** *obs* **:** COAT OF ARMS 1 **2** *obs* **:** COAT OF ARMS 2a **3 :** COATS OF ARMS 2b **:** armorial ensigns

coat arms *n* [modif. of MF *cote d'armes*] *archaic* **:** COAT ARMOR 3

coat card *n* [so called fr. the coated figure drawn on the card] **:** FACE CARD

coatdress \ˈ=ˌ=\ *n* **:** a dress made on coat lines usu. with a front buttoning from neckline to hemline

coatdress

coated *adj* **:** covered with or dressed in a coat: as **a** *of paper or paper board* **:** faced with a surface coating (as of china clay and an adhesive) and made smooth by calendering ‹~ paper is specially suitable for halftone printing› **b** *of the tongue* **:** covered with a yellowish white deposit of desquamated cells, bacteria, and debris usu. as an accompaniment of digestive disorder **c** *of cloth* **:** covered or impregnated with a durable chemical or rubber compound (as of oilcloth) **d** *of an optical lens* **:** covered with a thin coating of a substance to reduce reflection and increase light transmission

coated ginger *n* **:** BLACK GINGER

coated rice *n* **:** rice coated with glucose and talc to give it a pearly luster

coat·ee \ˌkōˈtē\ *n* -S [¹*coat* + *-ee*] **:** a short coat; *esp* **:** a close-fitting coat with short skirts or tails

coat·er \ˈkōd·ə(r), -ōtə-\ *n* -S **:** one that coats surfaces: as **a :** a workman or a machine that applies a coating to materials in manufacture (as the chemical emulsion on photographic paper) **b :** a workman or a machine that forms or finishes material in sheets by dispersing a liquid film of the material usu. onto a drying surface

coat flower *n* [perh. trans. of L *tunica*; fr. the shape of its bracts] **:** a tufted spreading perennial garden herb (*Tunica saxifraga*) of the family Caryophyllaceae with very slender hairlike stems, narrow leaves, and small pink or pale purple flowers

coat hanger *n* **:** a slender arched device (as of wood, metal, or plastic) which is shaped typically somewhat like a person's shoulders, over which a coat or dress may be hung, and which is usu. fitted with a crossbar for hanging trousers or a skirt

co·a·ti \kəˈwäd·ē\ *n* -S [Pg *coati*, fr. Tupi *coati*, *cuati*] **:** a mammal of tropical America of the genus *Nasua* that is related to the raccoon but with a longer body and tail and a long flexible snout

co·a·ti·mun·di *or* **co·a·ti·mon·di** \=ˌ==ˈmən,dē\ *n* -S [Tupi] **:** COATI

coating *n* -S **1 :** a layer of any substance used as cover, protection, decoration, or finish ‹porcelain enamel is widely used as a ~› ‹~s applied for ceramic glazes› ‹a thin ~ of soil over the ore› **:** COAT, COVERING ‹a protective ~ of cynicism› **2 :** cloth for coats ‹new woolen ~s›

coat·less \ˈkōtləs\ *adj* **:** having or wearing no coat

coat money *n* **:** money to provide coats for men in British military service esp. as exacted by Charles I — used esp. in the phrase *coat and conduct money*

coat of arms [tr. of F *cotte d'armes*] **1 :** a tabard or surcoat embroidered with armorial bearings **2 a :** a heraldic achievement **b :** any emblem or group of emblems whether or not inclusive of an escutcheon of arms that is regarded as having a symbolic function equivalent or comparable to that of a heraldic achievement ‹the *coats of arms* of all the sovereign nations›

coat of mail : a defensive garment of metal scales or chain mail **:** HAUBERK — compare CHAIN MAIL

coat–of–mail shell \ˌ===ˈ=-\ *n* **:** CHITON

coat·rack \ˈkōt-+ˌ-\ *n* **:** a stand or rack fitted with pegs, hooks, or hangers and used for the temporary storage of outdoor garments (as coats, cloaks, or rain gear)

coatroom \"+ˌ-\ *n* **:** CLOAKROOM

coats *pl of* COAT, *pres 3d sing of* COAT

coattail \ˈkō(t)+ˌ-\ *n* -S **1 :** the rear flap of a man's coat **2 coattails** *pl* **:** the skirts of a dress coat, cutaway, or frock coat — **on one's coattails :** in a state of dependence on another for assistance ‹a lazy man still riding *on his* father's *coattails*› **:** with the help of another; *esp* **:** with the benefit of another's political prestige ‹congressmen riding into office *on the coattails* of a popular president›

coattailed \"+\ *adj* **:** having or wearing coattails

coat–tree \"+ˌ-\ *n* **:** a coatrack with a vertical shaft from the upper part of which pegs or hooks diverge like branches

¹**co·author** \(ˈ)kō+\ *n* [*co-* + *author*] **:** one who collaborates with another in the production of a literary or dramatic work, a document, or other composition ‹~s of many books and plays› ‹~s of the new tax bill›

²**coauthor** \"\ *vt* **:** to be coauthor of ‹the two ~*ed* a charter›

¹**coax** \ˈkōks\ *vb* -ED/-ING/-ES [earlier *cokes*, fr. *cokes*, n.] *vt* **1** *obs* **:** to make a fool of **:** DUPE **2** *obs* **:** FONDLE, PET **:** treat lovingly **3 :** to influence or persuade by gentle urging, caressing, or flattering **:** WHEEDLE ‹some sisters would have ~*ed* him for a sight of it —George Meredith› ‹tried to ~ her into arranging her nursery elsewhere —Mary S. Broome› **4 :** to draw, gain, or persuade forth (a desired object from its possessor or its place) by means of gentle urging or flattery or by persistent effort ‹~ bits of raw meat from the cook —Edita Morris› ‹how many isolated facts can be ~*ed* out of an overstuffed memory by the offer of a washing machine —J.M. Barzun› **5 :** to manipulate with great perseverance and usu. with considerable effort toward a desired state or activity ‹~ a fire to burn› ‹~ a cold engine to start› ~ *vi* **:** to persuade or influence a person by gentle urging or flattery

²**coax** \"\ *n* -ES **:** a coaxing speech or act

³**co·ax** \(ˈ)kōˌaks\ *n* -ES [by shortening] **:** COAXIAL CABLE

co·axal \(ˈ)kō+\ *adj* [*co-* + *axal*] **:** COAXIAL: as **a** *of circles* **:** having collinear centers and the same radical axis **b** *of triangles* **:** having the intersections of corresponding sides on a straight line called the axis of the triangles

co·ax·a·tion \ˌkōakˈsāshən\ *n* -S [L *coaxatus* (past part. of *coaxare* to croak, prob. fr. Gk *koax* noise made by a frog, of imit. origin) + E *-ion*] **:** a croaking esp. of frogs

co·axial \(ˈ)kō+\ *adj* [*co-* + *axial*] **1 :** having coincident axes ‹~ ellipses› ‹~ cylinders› **2 :** referred to the same set of coordinate axes **3 :** mounted on concentric shafts — used esp. of airplane propellers or rotors driven independently and in different directions —**co·axially** \"+\

coaxial cable *also* **coaxial** *n* **:** a cable consisting of a tube of conducting material surrounding a central conductor held in place by insulators with the whole assembly being covered with insulation and used to transmit telegraph, telephone, and television signals of high frequency — called also *concentric cable*

coaxial speaker *n* **:** a loudspeaker in which the high-frequency reproducer is mounted at the center of and on the same axis as the low frequency reproducer (as a high-frequency horn mounted in a paper cone speaker)

¹**cob** \ˈkäb\ *vt* **cobbed; cobbed; cobbing; cobs** [ME *cobben* to fight, give blows; akin to Icel *kubba* to chop, Norw *kubbe* log, ME *cobbe* big man, leader — more at ³COB] **1 :** STRIKE, THUMP: as **a** *archaic* **:** to beat on the buttocks (as with a flat stick) **b** *dial Eng* **:** THRESH ‹~ grain› **2** *dial Eng* **:** to toss effortlessly or carelessly **3 :** to break (ore) into small pieces preliminary to sorting; *esp* **:** to break off waste or low-grade material from (lumps of ore) with hand hammers **4 :** SURPASS, EXCEL, BEAT, OUTDO

²**cob** \"\ *or* **cobb** \"\ *n* -S **:** a blow or a beating esp. upon the buttocks

³**cob** \"\ *n* -S [ME *cobbe*; akin to ON *kobbi* seal (the animal), OE *cot* den, cottage — more at COT] **1** *now dial Eng* **:** an eminent person **:** LEADER, TOPMAN **2 :** a male swan — compare ⁵PEN **3** *dial Eng* **:** a lump or piece (as of coal or stone) or a rounded heap or mass: as **a :** COBNUT **b :** a nut used in the game of cobnut or conker **c cobs** *pl* **:** TESTES **d :** a small stack of grain or hay **e :** a small loaf of bread **4** *obs* **:** the head of a herring **5 a :** a piece of eight or a Spanish-American dollar — used in Ireland and the British colonies during the period when Spanish-American gold and silver coins were irregularly shaped and crudely struck **b :** any crude, irregularly shaped coin of early Spanish-American issue ‹a ~ dollar› ‹~ money› ‹~ gold› **6 a :** CORNCOB 1 **b** *chiefly Africa* **:** an ear of Indian corn **7 :** a short-legged stocky horse; *esp* **:** one having an artificially high stylish action **8** *Brit* **:** the seed head of clover **9 :** a string of crystals of sugar of milk usu. cylindrical in shape — compare LACTOSE

⁴**cob** \"\ *n* -S [prob. fr. ³*cob* (lump)] *Brit* **:** a mixture that consists of unburned clay usu. with straw as a binder and is used for constructing walls of small buildings ‹windows set in ~ walls three foot thick —Clemence Dane›

⁵**cob** \"\ *or* **cobb** \"\ *n* -S [prob. fr. D *kobbe*, *kob* sea gull, fr. MD *cobbe* crested bird or animal; akin to Fris *kobbe* sea gull and prob. to Icel *kobbi* seal — more at ³COB] **:** SEA GULL; *esp* **:** GREAT BLACK-BACKED GULL

⁶**cob** \"\ *or* **cobb** \"\ *n* -S [origin unknown] *dial Eng* **:** a wicker basket

⁷**cob** \"\ *n* -S [modif. of NL *Kobus*] **:** a waterbuck of the genus *Kobus*

co·baea \kōˈbēə, kəˈ-\ *n*, *cap* [NL, irreg. fr. Bernabé *Cobo* †1657 Span. naturalist] **:** a small genus of woody tendril-climbing tropical American vines (family Polemoniaceae) with pinnate leaves and large bell-shaped purple or white flowers — see CATHEDRAL BELLS

co·bal·a·min \kōˈbȯləˌmən, kəˈ-; ˌkō(ˌ)bȯˈlamən, -ˌbȯˈl-\ *n* -S [*cobalt* + *-amin* (as in *vitamin*)] **:** a member of the vitamin B_{12} group; *broadly* **:** the vitamin B_{12} group

co·balt \ˈkōˌbȯlt *also* -bält *or chiefly Brit* kəˈbȯlt\ *n* -S [G *kobalt*, alter. (influenced by NL *cobaltum*, modif. of G *kobold*) of G *kobold* cobalt, kobold, fr. MHG *kobolt* kobold, fr. *kobe* hut, cage + *-olt* (prob. akin to OHG *holdo* spirit, fr. *hold* gracious); fr. its appearance in silver ore where it was believed to have been placed by silver-stealing goblins; akin to OE *cofa* den and to OHG *hald* inclined — more at COVE, HEEL] **1 :** a hard magnetic silver-white bivalent and trivalent metallic element belonging to the same family as iron and nickel, occurring usu. with nickel or copper either native in nickel-iron alloys (as in meteors) or combined in minerals from which it is isolated chiefly as a by-product, being essential as a trace element in animal and plant nutrition, and being used to produce magnetic alloys and hard alloys resistant to abrasion, corrosion, and high temperatures — symbol *Co*; see COBALT 60, ELEMENT table **2 :** the azure of the cloudless sky

cobaltammine \ˌ=ˌ=, =ˈ=+\ *n* -S [ISV *cobalt* + *ammine*; prob. orig. formed as G *kobaltammin*] **:** any of numerous ammines of cobalt

cobalt bloom *n* **:** ERYTHRITE 2

cobalt blue *n* **1 a :** a permanent greenish blue pigment consisting essentially of cobalt oxide and alumina — called also *cobalt ultramarine*, *King's blue* **b :** POWDER BLUE **2 :** a strong greenish blue that is bluer and deeper than grotto, greener, lighter, and stronger than average cerulean blue (sense 1a), and bluer, lighter, and stronger than indigo carmine — called also *cobalt ultramarine*, *Hungary blue*, *Leithner's blue*, *Leyden blue*, *Olympic blue*, *Thenard's blue*, *Venetian blue*

cobalt bronze *n* **:** a violet colored cobalt double salt of bronze-like luster; cobalt ammonium phosphate

cobalt chloride *n* **:** a chloride of cobalt; *usu* **:** the dichloride $CoCl_2$ crystallizing ordinarily with six molecules of water, being dark red when hydrated, blue when dehydrated, and used in solution as a secret ink

cobalt fluoride *n* **:** either of two fluorides of cobalt: **a :** the difluoride CoF_2 obtained as a rose colored granular powder — called also *cobaltous fluoride* **b :** the trifluoride CoF_3 obtained as a brown crystalline material and used as a carrier of fluorine in the preparation of fluorocarbons — called also *cobaltic fluoride*

cobalt glance *n* **:** COBALTITE

cobalt glass *n* **:** SMALT 2

cobalt green *n* **1 :** a permanent green pigment consisting essentially of cobalt and zinc oxides — called also *zinc green* **2 :** a moderate yellowish green that is greener and stronger than tarragon and yellower and deeper than malachite green or verdigris — called also *Rinnemann's green*, *Saxony green*, *smalt green*, *zinc green*

co·bal·ti- *comb form* [*cobalt*] **:** trivalent cobalt **:** cobaltic ‹*cobalti*nitrite›

co·bal·tic \(ˈ)kōˈbȯltik, kəˈb-, -ēk\ *adj* [ISV *cobalt* + *-ic*] **:** of, relating to, or containing cobalt — used esp. of compounds in which this element is trivalent; compare COBALTOUS

cobaltic fluoride *n* **:** COBALT FLUORIDE b

co·bal·ti·cyanic acid \kōˌbȯltə+-\ *n* [ISV *cobalti-* + *cyanic*] **:** a stable complex colorless crystalline acid $H_3Co(CN)_6.xH_2O$

co·bal·ti·cyanide \kōˌbȯltə+\ *n* [ISV *cobalti-* + *cyanide*] **:** a salt of cobalticyanic acid

co·balt·if·er·ous \ˌkō(ˌ)bȯlˈtif(ə)rəs\ *adj* [*cobalti-* + *-ferous*] **:** containing cobalt ‹~ ores›

co·bal·ti·nitrite \ˌkō(ˌ)bȯltə+\ *n* -S [*cobalti-* + *nitrite*] **:** any of a series of complex salts of cobalt having the general formula $M_3Co(NO_2)_6$ — see POTASSIUM COBALTINITRITE

co·bal·tite \kəˈbȯlˌtīt, kōˈ-, ˈkōˌ-\ *or* **co·balt·ine** \ˈkōˌbȯlˌtēn, -ˌtən\ *n* -S [*cobaltite*, alter. of *cobaltine*; *cobaltine*, fr. F, fr. *cobalt* + *-ine*] **:** a mineral consisting of a grayish to silver-white cobalt sulfarsenide CoAsS used in the manufacture of smalt and occurring massive and in isometric crystals related to those of pyrite

co·balt·ized *or* **co·balt·ised** \ˈkōˌbȯlˌtīzd\ *adj*, *of fertilizers* **:** treated with a compound of cobalt (as cobalt sulfate)

co·bal·to- *comb form* [*cobalt*] **:** bivalent cobalt **:** cobaltous ‹*cobalto*cyanic›

co·bal·to·calcite \kəˌbȯl(ˌ)tō+\ *n* -S [*cobalto-* + *calcite*] **:** a mineral consisting of carbonate of cobalt $CoCO_3$ isomorphous with calcite

co·bal·tom·e·nite \ˌkōˌbȯlˈtämə,nīt\ *n* -S [ISV *cobalto-* + Gk *mēnē* moon + ISV *-ite*; orig. formed in F] **:** a mineral consisting of cobalt selenium oxide of uncertain composition, possibly hydrous

co·bal·tous \(ˈ)kōˈbȯltəs\ *adj* [*cobalt* + *-ous*] **:** of, relating to, or containing cobalt — used esp. of cobalt compounds in which this element is bivalent; compare COBALTIC

cobaltous chloride *n* **:** the cobalt chloride $CoCl_2$

cobaltous fluoride *n* **:** COBALT FLUORIDE a
cobaltous sulfate *n* **:** the cobalt sulfate $CoSO_4$
cobalt oxide *n* **:** an oxide of cobalt: as **a :** the monoxide CoO obtained usu. as a grayish powder — called also *cobaltous oxide* **b :** a gray to blue-black powder containing cobalt monoxide and higher oxides (as tricobalt tetroxide Co_3O_4) and used chiefly in coloring glass and ceramic ware blue
cobalt pyrites *n* **:** LINNAEITE
cobalt red *n* **:** a moderate purplish red that is bluer and deeper than average rose or violine pink and bluer and lighter than magenta rose
cobalt 60 \-'sikstē\ *n* **:** a heavy radioactive isotope of cobalt having the mass number 60 produced in nuclear reactors and used as a source of gamma rays esp. in place of radium (as in the treatment of cancer and in radiography) — called also *radiocobalt*; symbol Co^{60} or ^{60}Co
cobalt sulfate *n* **:** a sulfate of cobalt; *usu* **:** the salt $CoSO_4$ crystallizing in pale red monoclinic prisms containing seven molecules of water and occurring native as bieberite
cobalt ultramarine *n* **:** COBALT BLUE 1a, 2
cobalt violet *n* **1 :** any of several purple pigments containing a compound of cobalt (as cobalt phosphate) **2 :** a moderate purple that is redder and duller than heliotrope (sense 4a), redder, lighter, and stronger than average amethyst, redder and less strong than manganese violet, redder and deeper than average lilac (sense 3a), and redder and stronger than mignon — called also *thistle*
cobalt vitriol *n* **:** the cobalt sulfate $CoSO_4$
cobalt yellow *n* **1 :** a bright yellow pigment consisting essentially of potassium cobaltinitrite — called also *aureolin* **2 :** a strong to brilliant yellow — called also *aureolin*
cobang *var of* KOBAN
cobb *var of* COB
cobbed *past of* COB
[1]**cob·ber** \'käbə(r)\ *n* -s [[1]*cob* + *-er*] **:** a worker who breaks asbestos fibers away from asbestos-bearing rock or chips waste rock from lumps of ore
[2]**cobber** \"\ *n* -s [origin unknown] *Austral* **:** a close friend and companion ⟨staunchest ~ a man could have —Rex Ingamells⟩
cob·bing *pres part of* COB
[1]**cob·ble** \'käbəl\ *vt* **cobbled; cobbled; cobbling** \-b(ə)liŋ\ **cobbles** [ME *coblen*, perh. back-formation fr. *cobelere* cobbler] **1** *Brit* **:** to mend, patch, or repair coarsely or roughly ⟨any holes he would ~ with sack-needle and string —Adrian Bell⟩ **2 a :** MEND, REPAIR **b :** MAKE ⟨*cobbled* shoes⟩ **3 :** to make or put together roughly, clumsily, or hastily often in a temporary or improvised fashion — often used with *up*
[2]**cobble** \"\ *n* -s **:** a cobbled place **:** a coarse mending
[3]**cobble** \"\ *n* -s [back-formation fr. *cobblestone*] **1 a :** a naturally rounded stone larger than a pebble and smaller than a boulder often arbitrarily limited by geologists to a size ranging from 64 to 256 millimeters in diameter **b :** such a stone used in paving a street or in other construction **2 cobbles** *pl, also* **cobble coal** *chiefly Brit* **:** lump coal about the size of small cobblestones **3 :** a ball or piece of waste iron or steel
[4]**cobble** \"\ *vt* **:** to pave with cobblestones
[5]**cobble** \"\ *n* -s [perh. fr. [3]*cobble*] *Northeast* **:** a rounded hill usu. of moderate elevation
[6]**cobble** \"\ *n* -s [perh. fr. [3]*cob* (swan) + *-le* (dim. suffix)] **:** a common loon (*Gavia immer*); *also* **:** RED-THROATED LOON
cobbled *adj* [fr. past part. of [4]*cobble*] **:** paved or covered with cobblestones
cobble gravel *n* [[3]*cobble*] **:** gravel containing rounded fragments of rock usu. ranging in size between 64 and 256 millimeters in diameter
cob·bler \'käblə(r)\ *n* -s [ME *cobelere*] **1 :** a repairer or maker of shoes and often of other leather goods **2** *archaic* **:** one that does clumsy or coarse work **:** BOTCHER **3 :** a tall drink that consists usu. of wine, rum, or whiskey and sugar and is served esp. in a goblet filled with shaved ice and garnished with a sprig of mint or slice of lemon or orange ⟨claret ~⟩ ⟨whiskey ~⟩ **4 :** a deep-dish fruit pie without a bottom crust and with a thick biscuit top crust **5 a :** a spiny Australian catfish (*Cnidoglanis macrocephalus*) **b :** THREADFISH 1 **c :** a long-spined European sea scorpion (*Cottus bubalis*) **d :** a scaleless So. Australian scorpaenid fish (*Gymnopistes marmoratus*) related to and greatly resembling the fortescue **e :** POMPANO 1 **6** *chiefly Austral* **:** a sheep left to the last at shearing time; *also* **:** a sheep difficult to handle
cobblerfish \'==,=\ *n* **1** [so called fr. the fancied resemblance of their rays to a cobbler's strings] **:** THREADFISH 1 **2 :** POMPANO 1
cobbler's-awl \'käblə(r)z + ,-\ *n, pl* **cobbler's-awls 1 :** AVOCET **2** *Austral* **:** a spinebill (*Acanthorhynchus tenuirostris*)
cobbler's bench *n* **:** a low 4-legged bench formerly used by cobblers that has a seat at one end, compartments for tools and supplies, and a working area; *also* **:** an occasional table suggesting a cobbler's bench
cobbler's peg *n* [prob. fr. the appearance of the pappi] **:** either of two chiefly Australian weedy composite herbs (*Erigeron linifolius* and *Bidens pilosa*) — often used in pl. but sing. or pl. in constr.
cobblestone \'==,=\ *n* [ME, fr. *cobble-* (prob. fr. [3]*cob* (lump) + *-le*) + *stone*] **:** [3]COBBLE 1b
cob·bly \'käb(ə)lē, -li\ *adj* [[3]*cobble* + *-y*] **:** containing cobbles **:** STONY, ROUGH, LUMPY
cob·bra \'käbrə\ *n* -s [native name in New So. Wales] *Austral* **:** HEAD, SKULL
cobb's disease \'käbz-\ *n, usu cap C* [after Nathan A. *Cobb* †1932 Am. biologist] **:** a disease of sugarcane caused by a bacterium (*Xanthomonas vascularum*) and characterized by a slime in the vascular bundles accompanied by dwarfing, streaking of leaves, and decay — called also *sugarcane gummosis*
cob·by \'käbē, -bi\ *adj* -ER/-EST [[3]*cob* + *-y*] **1** *dial Eng* **a :** HEARTY, LIVELY **b :** HEADSTRONG **2 :** like a cob horse in shape **:** having a deep strong short-coupled body and relatively short sturdy legs ⟨a ~ cat⟩ **:** STOCKY ⟨~ in build⟩
cob cactus *n* [[3]*cob* (corncob); fr. its shape] **:** STRAWBERRY CACTUS
cob coal *n* [[3]*cob* (lump)] **:** coal in rounded lumps from the size of an egg to that of a football
cob·den·ism \'käbdə,nizəm\ *n* -s *usu cap* [Richard *Cobden* †1865 Eng. statesman and economist + E *-ism*] **:** the political and economic doctrines of Richard Cobden, 19th century English statesman and economist whose national policy was for peace, for withdrawal from the European competition for balance of power, and for free trade
cob·den·ite \-,nīt\ *n* -s *usu cap* [Richard *Cobden* †1865 + E *-ite*] **:** an adherent of Cobdenism
co·be·go \kə'bē(,)gō\ *n* -s [modif. of Malay *kubong*] **:** FLYING LEMUR
co·belligerency \¦kō+\ *n* -ES [*co-* + *belligerency*] **:** the state of being a cobelligerent
[1]**co·belligerent** \¦kō+\ *n* -s [*co-* + *belligerent*] **:** a country fighting together with another power against a common enemy often without a formal alliance — usu. distinguished from *ally*
[2]**cobelligerent** \"\ *adj* **:** having the status of or fighting as a cobelligerent
cobhouse \'=,=\ *n* [[3]*cob* (corncob) + *house*] **1 :** a toy house of corncobs or sticks laid in parallel pairs piled on one another each at right angles to the preceding pair **2 :** a flimsy unstable structure or arrangement ⟨a ~ of lies ready to fall⟩
co·bia \'kōbēə\ *also* **ca·bio** \'käbē(,)ō\ *n* -s [origin unknown] **:** a large percoid fish (*Rachycentron canadum*) cream to brown above fading to white below with one or more longitudinal dark stripes along the sides that is widely distributed in warm seas and regarded as an outstanding food and game fish
cob·iron \'kä,bī(ə)rn, -īən\ *n* -s [ME *cobiren*, fr. [3]*cob* (lump) + *iren* iron; fr. the knobs on the ends] **:** an iron for supporting a spit **2 :** ANDIRON
co·bit·i·dae \kə'bid·ə,dē\ *n pl, cap* [NL, fr. *Cobitis*, type genus (fr. Gk *kōbitis* like the gudgeon, fr. *kōbios* gudgeon) + *-idae*] **:** a family of slender Old World cyprinoid fishes having long barbels at the mouth and living at the bottom of flowing waters where they feed on small invertebrates
co·ble \'kōbəl, 'käb-\ *n* -s [ME, prob. of Celt origin; akin to W *ceubal* ferryboat, skiff, OBret *caubal*; perh. akin to L *cavus* hollow — more at CAVE] **1** *Scot* **:** a short flat-bottomed boat **2 :** a flat-floored fishing boat with a drop rudder extending below the keel, bilge keels beneath the stern, and a dipping lugsail on a raking mast that is used chiefly in the North sea
co·blenz·ian \(')kō¦blen(t)sēən, -nzē-\ *adj, usu cap* [*Koblenz, Coblenz*, city in western Germany + E *-an*] **:** of or relating to a division of the European Devonian — see GEOLOGIC TIME table
cob·less \'käbləs\ *adj* **:** being without a cob
cob meal *n* [[3]*cob* (corncob)] **:** corn meal in which the cob is also ground
cob-nosed \'=¦=\ *adj* [[3]*cob* (lump)] **:** having a large and bulbous nose
cobnut \'=,=\ *n* -s [[3]*cob* (lump) + *nut*] **1 a :** a filbertlike fruit yielded by a variety (*Corylus avellana grandis*) of the hazel much grown in Europe **b :** a plant bearing this fruit **2 a :** a game in which a player pitches a nut at a pile of nuts and wins any that he knocks down **b :** a game played with nuts tied on a string in which one tries to strike and break his opponent's nut with one of his own
co·bo·la \kə'bōlə\ *n* -s [AmerSp] **:** a Central American tree of the genus *Podocarpus*
co·boss \'kō, 'kə(m) + ,-\ *v imper* [alter. of *come, Boss*] — a call to cows
cob pipe *n* [[3]*cob* (corncob)] **:** CORNCOB PIPE
[1]**co·bra** \'kōbrə\ *n* -s [Pg *cobra* (*de capello*), lit., hooded snake, fr. L *colubra*, fem. of *coluber* snake — more at COLUBER] **1 :** any of several very venomous Asiatic and African elapid snakes of the genus *Naja* that, when excited, expand the skin of the neck into a broad hood by movement of the anterior ribs — see INDIAN COBRA, KING COBRA **2 :** either of two African snakes that spit their venom from a distance: **a :** BLACK-NECKED COBRA **b :** RINGHALS **3 :** MAMBA

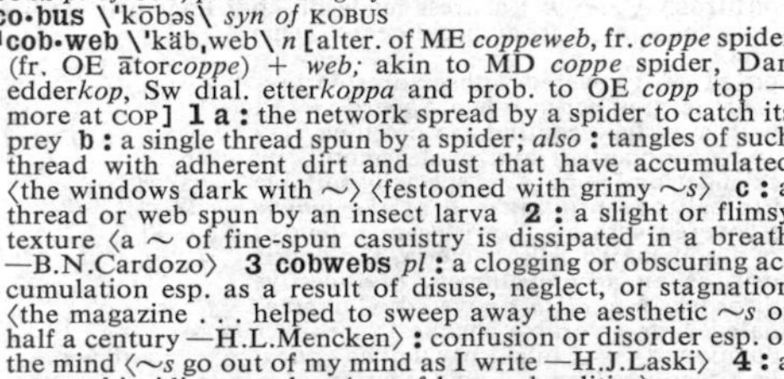
cobra (*Naja naja*)

[2]**cobra** \"\ *n* -s *Austral* **:** SHIPWORM
cobra de ca·pel·lo \-dēkə'pe(,)lō\ *n, pl* **cobras de capello** [Pg] **:** INDIAN COBRA
cobra plant *n* **:** CALIFORNIA PITCHER PLANT
co·bri·form \'kōbrə,fȯrm\ *adj* [*cobra* + *-iform*] **:** like or related to the cobras
cob rot *n* [[3]*cob* (corncob)] **:** a disease of corn due to a fungus (*Nigrospora sphaerica*) of the family Dematiaceae that causes yellowish basal rot and shredding of the ear
cobs *pl of* COB, *pres 3d sing of* COB
co·bus \'kōbəs\ *syn of* KOBUS
[1]**cob·web** \'käb,web\ *n* [alter. of ME *coppeweb*, fr. *coppe* spider (fr. OE ātor*coppe*) + *web*; akin to MD *coppe* spider, Dan edder*kop*, Sw dial. etter*koppa* and prob. to OE *copp* top — more at COP] **1 a :** the network spread by a spider to catch its prey **b :** a single thread spun by a spider; *also* **:** tangles of such thread with adherent dirt and dust that have accumulated ⟨the windows dark with ~⟩ ⟨festooned with grimy ~s⟩ **c :** a thread or web spun by an insect larva **2 :** a slight or flimsy texture ⟨a ~ of fine-spun casuistry is dissipated in a breath —B.N.Cardozo⟩ **3 cobwebs** *pl* **:** a clogging or obscuring accumulation esp. as a result of disuse, neglect, or stagnation ⟨the magazine . . . helped to sweep away the aesthetic ~s of half a century —H.L.Mencken⟩ **:** confusion or disorder esp. of the mind ⟨~s go out of my mind as I write —H.J.Laski⟩ **4 :** a snare of insidious meshes ⟨~s of law and politics⟩
[2]**cobweb** \"\ *vt* **cobwebbed; cobwebbed; cobwebbing; cobwebs 1 :** to obscure (as a mind or a subject) by confusion or stagnation ⟨the drunk whose mind is *cobwebbed* and confused —Lucius Garvin⟩ **2 :** to cover with a network resembling cobwebs ⟨*cobwebbed* with ropes —Osbert Sitwell⟩
cobwebbed *adj* **:** covered or filled with cobwebs
cobweb bird *also* **cobweb** *n* [so called fr. its use of cobwebs in its nest] *dial Eng* **:** SPOTTED FLYCATCHER
cob·web·by \-,webē\ *adj* -ER/-EST **1 :** covered with cobwebs **2 :** resembling, suggesting, or having the character of cobwebs ⟨Corot painted thousands of such ~ canvases —*Time*⟩ **3 :** MUSTY, STAGNANT, COBWEBBED ⟨~ brain⟩
cobweb disease *n* **:** a disease of cultivated mushrooms caused by a fungus (*Dactylium dendroides*) that produces a white or pink-tinted coating of mycelium over the fruiting bodies
cobweb houseleek *n* **:** a low European herb (*Sempervivum arachnoideum*) having bright red flowers and a basal rosette of small succulent leaves connected by cobwebby strands
cobweb theorem *n* **:** a theorem in economics: in some cases successive adjustments of supply and demand amplify rather than diminish price fluctuations
cobwork \'=,=\ *n* [prob. fr. *cob* (*house*) log cabin (formerly, mud hut; fr. [4]*cob*) + *work*] **:** construction or a structure of elements (as logs) laid horizontally with the ends joined at the corners
[1]**co·ca** \'kōkə\ *n* -s [Sp, fr. Quechua *kúka*] **1 :** any of several So. American shrubs of the genus *Erythroxylon*; *esp* **:** a shrub (*E. coca*) with leaves resembling tea leaves that are chewed with alkali by natives of the Andean uplands to impart endurance **2 :** the dried leaves of either of two cocas both containing several alkaloids of which cocaine is the most important: **a :** those of the coca (*Erythroxylon coca*) — called also *Bolivian coca, Huanuco coca* **b :** those of the related plant (*E. novagranatense*) — called also *Peruvian coca, Truxillo coca*
[2]**coca** \"\ *usu cap* — a communications code word for the letter *c*
co·caine \kō'kān, kə'-, 'kō,k- *sometimes* 'kōkə,ēn *or* -k(ə)in\ *n* -s [ISV *coca* + *-ine*; orig. formed as G *kokain*] **1 :** a bitter crystalline alkaloid $C_{17}H_{21}NO_4$ obtained from coca leaves and synthesized from ecgonine that has first a stimulating then a narcotic effect if taken internally, in large doses produces intoxication like that from hemp, and acts as a local anesthetic and mydriatic; methyl-benzoyl-ecgonine **2 :** any of several alkaloids found in coca that are derived from ecgonine
cocaine family *n* **:** ERYTHROXYLACEAE
cocaine plant *n* **:** COCA 1
co·cain·ism \kō'kā(ə),nizəm, kə'k-; 'kō,kā(ə),n-, -,kə,n-\ *n* -s [ISV *cocaine* + *-ism*] **:** addiction to cocaine
co·cain·i·za·tion \¦kō,kā(ə)nə¦zāshən, kə¦k-, -nī'-\ *n* -s **:** the act of cocainizing or the state of being cocainized
co·cain·ize \kō'kā(ə),nīz, kə'k-, 'kō,k-\ *vt* -ED/-ING/-S [*cocaine* + *-ize*] **:** to treat or anesthetize with cocaine
co·ca·ma \kō'kāmə, kə'-\ *n, pl* **cocama** *or* **cocamas** *usu cap* [Sp, of AmerInd origin] **1 a :** a group of Tupian peoples of Peru including the Omagua **b :** a member of such peoples **2 :** the language of the Cocama
co·carboxylase \(')kō + \ *n* -s [*co-* + *carboxylase*] **:** a coenzyme $C_{12}H_{19}ClN_4O_7P_2S{\cdot}H_2O$ that is the pyrophosphate of thiamine, functions in conjunction with various carboxylases, and is physiologically important esp. in the decarboxylation of pyruvic acid
co·carcinogen \(')kō + \ *n* -s [*co-* + *carcinogen*] **:** an agent that acts synergistically with one or more carcinogens to produce a cancer — **co·carcinogenic** \¦kō + \ *adj*
co·carde \kō'kärd, kə'-, -kád\ *n* -s [F — more at COCKADE] **1 :** a distinguishing mark worn usu. on the hat to indicate esp. military status **:** COCKADE; *also* **:** a similar distinguishing mark on an airplane **2 :** an ornament often of pleated ribbon for a woman's hat

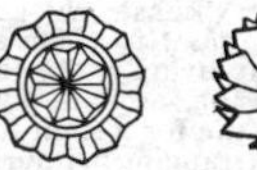
cocardes 2

co·cash \kə'kash\ *n* -ES [of Algonquian origin; akin to Natick *kôshki* it is rough] **1 :** a No. American herb (*Aster puniceus*) having red or purple flower heads in terminal clusters **2 :** HORSEWEED 1
cocashweed \'=,=\ *n* **:** GOLDEN RAGWORT
cocc- *or* **cocci-** *or* **cocco-** *comb form* [NL, fr. *coccus* & L *coccum* kermes berry, both fr. Gk *kokkos* grain, seed, kermes berry] **:** grain **:** seed **:** berry **:** coccus ⟨*cocc*oid⟩ ⟨*cocci*form⟩ ⟨*cocco*lith⟩
coc·ca·ce·ae \kä'kāsē,ē, kä'-\ *n pl, cap* [NL, fr. *cocc-* + *-aceae*] *in some classifications* **:** a family of bacteria comprising those more or less spherical in shape now rarely regarded as a natural assemblage — compare BACILLACEAE, BACTERIACEAE — **coc·ca·ceous** \-'kāshəs\ *adj*
coc·ca·gee \,käkə'jē\ *n* -s [IrGael *cac a' ghēidh* goose dung; fr. its color] **1 :** a cider apple formerly popular in England **2 :** cider made from the coccagee
coc·cal \'käkəl\ *adj* [NL *coccus* + E *-al*] **:** of or relating to a coccus
coc·ce·ian \käk'sēyən\ *n* -s *usu cap* [Johannes *Cocceius* (Koch) †1669 Ger. theologian + E *-an*] **:** an adherent of Cocceianism
coc·ce·ian·ism \-,nizəm\ *n* -s *usu cap* [Johannes *Cocceius* (Koch) †1669 + E *-an* + *-ism*] **:** the theological belief that the whole history of the Christian church is foreshadowed in the Old Testament
coc·ce·rin \'käksərən\ *n* -s [*cocceryl* + *-in*] **:** a wax $C_{92}H_{182}O_6$ found in cochineal
cocci *pl of* COCCUS
-cocci *pl of* -COCCUS
coc·cid \'käksəd, -,sid\ *n* -s [NL *Coccidae*] **:** a scale or mealybug **:** any member of the superfamily Coccoidea
coc·ci·dae \'käksə,dē\ *n pl, cap* [NL, fr. *Coccus*, type genus + *-idae*] **:** an important family of homopterous insects mostly of small size, sometimes including all the scales, mealybugs, and related forms but now often restricted to the soft and tortoise scales
coccidi- *or* **coccidio-** *comb form* [*coccidium*] **:** Coccidia ⟨*coccidio*cide⟩ ⟨*coccidio*stasis⟩
[1]**coc·cid·ia** \käk'sidēə\ *pl of* COCCIDIUM
[2]**coccidia** \"\ *n pl, cap* [NL, fr. pl. of [1]*Coccidium*] **:** a large order of schizogonous telosporidian protozoans, typically parasites of the digestive epithelium of vertebrates and higher invertebrates and including several forms of great economic importance — see EIMERIA — **coc·cid·i·al** \(')käk¦sidēəl\ *adj* — **coc·cid·i·an** \-dēən\ *adj or n*
coc·ci·di·ida \,käksə'dīədə\ *or* **coc·cid·i·id·ea** \käk,sidē'idēə\ [NL, fr. [1]*Coccidium* + *-ida* or *-idea*] *syn of* COCCIDIA
coc·cid·i·oi·dal \(')käk¦sidē¦ȯid°l\ *adj* [NL *Coccidioides* + E *-al*] **:** belonging to, like, or caused by fungi of the genus *Coccidioides*
coccidioidal granuloma *n* **:** COCCIDIOIDOMYCOSIS — now used chiefly of the generalized form or stage characterized by formation of nodular lesions throughout the body
coc·cid·i·oi·des \käk,sidē'ȯi,dēz\ *n, cap* [NL, fr. *coccidi-* + *-oides* -oid] *in some classifications* **:** a genus of parasitic zygomycetous fungi usu. included in Blastomycetes but of doubtful taxonomic position, having septate mycelium and endospores — see COCCIDIOIDOMYCOSIS
coc·cid·i·oi·din \(')=¦=dē¦ȯid°n, -ȯi(,)din\ *n* -s [NL *Coccidioides* (genus name of *Coccidioides immitis*) + E *-in*] **:** an antigen prepared from asparagine-synthetic cultures of a fungus (*Coccidioides immitis*) and used to detect skin sensitivity to and, by inference, infection with this organism
coc·cid·i·oi·do·mycosis \(')käk¦sidē¦ȯidō, -ȯidə +\ *also* **coc·cid·i·o·mycosis** \(')käk¦sidē(,)ō, -sideə +\ *n* [NL, fr. *Coccidioides* (genus name of *Coccidioides immitis*) + *mycosis*] **:** an infective disease of man and various wild and domestic animals caused by a fungus (*Coccidioides immitis*) usu. inhaled as spores and marked by fever and localized pulmonary symptoms but sometimes becoming generalized with granulomatous nodular lesions in various parts of the body
coc·cid·io·mor·pha \(')käk¦sidē(,)ō¦mȯrfə, -sideə¦-\ *n pl, cap* [NL, fr. *coccidi-* + *-morpha*] *in some classifications* **:** a subdivision of Sporozoa comprising the schizogonous forms (orders Coccidia and Haemosporidia) and being equivalent to Telosporidia with the gregarines omitted
coc·cid·io·sis \(')käk¦sidē¦ōsəs\ *n, pl* **coccidio·ses** \-,sēz\ [NL, fr. *coccidi-* + *-osis*] **:** infestation with or disease caused by coccidia — compare EIMERIA, ISOSPORA
coc·cid·io·stat \(')käk¦sideō,stat, -dēə,-\ *n* -s [*coccidi-* + *-stat*] **:** an agent that serves to retard the life cycle or reduce the population of a pathogenic coccidium to the point that disease is minimized and immunity is developed by the host
coc·cid·io·stat·ic \(')=¦===¦stad·ik\ *adj* [*coccidi-* + *-o-* + Gk *statikos* causing to stand — more at STATIC] **:** inhibiting the growth and development of coccidia
[1]**coc·cid·i·um** \käk'sidēəm\ [NL, fr. *cocc-* + *-idium*] *syn of* EIMERIA
[2]**coccidium** \"\ *n, pl* **coccid·ia** \-dēə\ **:** a protozoan of the order Coccidia
coc·ci·dol·o·gy \,käksə'däləjē\ *n* -ES [NL *Coccidae* + E *-o-* + *-logy*] **:** the branch of zoology that treats of the scales, mealybugs, and other members of the superfamily Coccoidea
coc·ci·doph·a·gous \¦==¦däfəgəs\ *adj* [*coccid* + *-o-* + *-phagous*] **:** feeding on scales ⟨~ ladybugs⟩ — compare VEDALIA
coc·ci·nel·la \,käksə'nelə\ *n, cap* [NL, fr. L *coccinus* scarlet-colored (fr. Gk *kokkinos*, fr. *kokkos* kermes berry) + *-ella*] **:** a cosmopolitan genus of small beetles that is the type of the family Coccinellidae and includes a number of typical ladybugs
[1]**coc·ci·nel·lid** \¦==¦=ləd\ *adj* [NL *Coccinellidae*] **:** of or relating to the Coccinellidae
[2]**coccinellid** \"\ *n* -s **:** a beetle of the family Coccinellidae **:** LADYBUG
coc·ci·nel·li·dae \-'nelə,dē\ *n pl, cap* [NL, fr. *Coccinella*, type genus + *-idae*] **:** a family of small usu. hemispherical beetles that are known as ladybugs and that have larvae which are mostly beneficial predators of aphids and other small insects — compare MEXICAN BEAN BEETLE
coccineous *adj* [L *coccineus*, var. of *coccinus*] *obs* **:** SCARLET
coc·cin·ic acid \(')käk¦sinik-\ *n* [F *coccinique*, fr. *coccine* carmine (fr. L *coccinus* scarlet, fr. Gk *kokkinos*, fr. *kokkos* grain, seed) + *-ique* -ic] **:** any of three isomeric crystalline diacids $C_6H_2(OH)(CH_3)(COOH)_2$ distinguished as alpha, beta, and gamma with the alpha acid being obtained by oxidizing cochineal
coc·ci·nite \'käksə,nīt\ *n* -s [G *kokzinit*, fr. L *coccinus* scarlet + G *-it* -ite] **:** a native mercury iodide HgI_2 found esp. at Broken Hill, New So. Wales, and in Mexico
cocco- — see COCC-
coc·co·bacillary \¦kä(,)kō, ¦käkə +\ *adj* [NL *coccobacillus* + E *-ary*] **:** of, relating to, or being a coccobacillus
coc·co·bacilliform \" + \ *adj* [NL *coccobacillus* + E *-iform*] **:** resembling a coccobacillus — used esp. of certain small bacillary organisms recovered chiefly from respiratory infections of poultry and regarded as related to the pleuropneumonia group
[1]**coc·co·bacillus** \" + \ *n* [NL, fr. *cocc-* + *bacillus*] **:** a very short coccuslike bacillus esp. of the genus *Pasteurella*
[2]**coccobacillus** \"\ [NL, fr. *cocc-* + *bacillus*] *syn of* PASTEURELLA
coc·co·gen·ic \¦käkō¦jenik, -kə¦j-\ *or* **coc·ci·gen·ic** \¦käksə¦-\ *adj* [*cocc-* + *-genic*] **:** caused by a coccus
[1]**coc·coid** \'kä,kȯid\ *or* **coc·coi·dal** \(')kä¦kȯid°l\ *adj* [*cocc-* + *-oid, -oidal*] **:** belonging to or resembling a coccus **:** GLOBOSE — compare -COCCUS 2
[2]**coccoid** \"\ *n* -s **:** a coccoid cell or body
coc·coi·dea \kä'kȯidēə\ *n pl, cap* [NL, fr. *cocc-* + *-oidea*] **:** a superfamily of Hemiptera including scales and mealybugs and being equivalent to Coccidae in the broadest sense
coc·co·lite \'käkə,līt\ *n* -s [F, fr. *cocc-* + *-lite*] **:** a granular variety of pyroxene of various colors
coc·co·lith \-,lith\ *n* -s [*cocc-* + *-lith*] **:** a minute calcareous body found in chalk and deep-sea ooze and constituting the skeletal remains of a coccolithophore — **coc·co·lith·ic** \¦==¦lithik\ *adj*
coc·co·lith·o·phore \,käkō'lithə,fō(ə)r, ,käkə'-\ *n* -s [NL *Coccolithophora*] **:** any of numerous minute mostly marine planktonic biflagellated organisms with brown chromatophores and complex calcareous, less commonly siliceous, shells that are sometimes considered to constitute the family Coccolithophoridae of the order Chrysomonadina — **coc·co·li·thoph·o·rid** \¦==lə¦thäfərəd, -,rid\ *adj or n*
coc·co·lith·o·phor·i·dae \,==,lithə'fȯrə,dē\ *n pl, cap* [NL, fr. *Coccolithophora*, type genus (fr. E *coccolith* + NL *-o-* + *-phora*) + *-idae*] **:** a family of minute marine chrysomonad flagellates having a skeleton of calcareous plates — see COCCOLITHOPHORE
coc·col·o·ba \kə'käləbə\ *n, cap* [NL, alter. of *Coccolobis*, fr. *cocc-* + *-lobis* (fr. Gk *lobos* lobe, capsule, pod) — more at SLEEP] **:** a genus of tropical and subtropical American evergreen trees, shrubs, and woody vines (family Polygonaceae) having greenish flowers in axillary spikes or racemes — see SEA GRAPE

coc·col·o·bis \-bə̇s\ [NL, fr. L, a kind of Spanish grape] *syn of* COCCOLOBA

coc·co·my·ces \ˌkäkōˈmīˌsēz, ˌkäkə'-\ *n, cap* [NL, fr. *cocc-* + *-myces*] **:** a genus of ascomycetous fungi (family Phacidiaceae) with filiform 1-celled, 2-celled, or many-celled ascospores and with conidial stages that are often referred to the form genus *Cylindrosporium*

coc·co·sphere \ˈkäkō, ˈkäkə + ˌ-\ *n* -s [*cocc-* + *-sphere*] **:** a coccolithophore or its skeleton

coc·cos·te·an \kəˈkästēən\ *n* -s [NL *Coccosteus* + E *-an*] **:** a fish of the genus *Coccosteus* or family Coccosteidae

coc·co·ste·i·dae \ˌkäkōˈstēəˌdē, ˌkäkə'-\ *n pl, cap* [NL, fr. *Coccosteus,* type genus + *-idae*] **:** a family (subclass Arthrodira) of armored extinct fishes — see COCCOSTEUS

coc·cos·te·us \kəˈkästēəs\ *n, cap* [NL, fr. *cocc-* + *-osteus*] **:** a genus of Devonian fishes having broad armored plates about the head and being the type of the family Coccosteidae

coc·co·thraus·tes \ˌkäkōˈthrȯˌstēz, ˌkäkə'-\ *n, cap* [NL, fr. *cocc-* + Gk *thraustēs* crusher (fr. *thrauein* to shatter) — more at DREARY] **:** a genus of large finches comprising the hawfinches and in some classifications the evening grosbeaks — **coc·co·thraus·tine** \ˌ==ˈ=ˌstīn, -ˌstən\ *adj*

coc·co·thri·nax \-ˈthrīˌnaks\ *n, cap* [NL, fr. *cocc-* + *Thrinax*] **:** a small genus of West Indian and Floridian fan palms having short unarmed trunks and small white flowers in dense sheathed clusters

coc·cous \ˈkäkəs\ *adj* [NL *coccus* + E *-ous*] **:** composed of cocci **:** COCCOID

coc·cu·lin \ˈkäkyələn\ *n* -s [ISV *coccul-* (fr. NL *cocculus,* specific epithet of *Anamirta cocculus*) + *-in;* orig. formed as G *kokkulin*] **:** PICROTOXIN

¹**coc·cu·lus** \-ləs\ *n, cap* [NL, lit., small berry, fr. *cocc-* + *-ulus*] **:** a small genus of slender woody vines (family Menispermaceae) with alternate leaves, paniculate flowers, and drupaceous fruits — see CAROLINA MOONSEED

²**cocculus** \"\ *or* **cocculus in·di·cus** \-ˈində̇kəs\ *n, pl* **cocculus** [NL *cocculus indicus,* fr. *cocculus* small berry + L *indicus* of India — more at INDIC] **:** the very poisonous bean-shaped berry of a woody vine (*Anamirta cocculus*) of the East Indies that yields picrotoxin and is used locally to stupefy fishes and in an ointment to control vermin

coc·cus \ˈkäkəs\ *n* [NL, fr. Gk *kokkos* grain, seed, kermes berry] **1** *pl* **coc·ci** \ˈkäˌkī, -ˌkē, -äkˌsī, -ˌäksē\ **:** MERICARP **2** *pl* **cocci :** a spherical bacterium **3** *cap* **:** the type genus of Coccidae formerly including most scales, lac insects, and cochineal insects but now restricted to certain typical scales **4** *pl* **cocci :** COCHINEAL 1

-coccus \ˈkäkəs\ *n comb form, pl* **-cocci** \ˈkäˌkī, ˈkäˌkē, ˈkäkˌsī, ˈkäksē\ [NL, fr. Gk *kokkos*] **1 :** plant having berries, seeds, or cocci (of a specified type) — usu. in generic names ⟨Oxycoccus⟩ ⟨Pterococcus⟩ **2 :** berry-shaped organism — esp. in generic names of algae and bacteria ⟨*Protococcus*⟩ ⟨Micro*coccus*⟩ ⟨Strepto*coccus*⟩ ⟨Staphylo*coccus*⟩

coc·cy·dyn·ia \ˌkäksəˈdinēə\ *n* -s [NL, by shortening] **:** COCCYGODYNIA

coccyg- *or* **coccygo-** *comb form* [NL, fr. *coccyg-, coccyx*] **:** coccyx ⟨*coccyg*ectomy⟩ ⟨*coccyg*otomy⟩

coc·cy·geal \(ˈ)käkˈsijēəl\ *adj* [ML *coccygeus* of the coccyx (fr. *coccyg-, coccyx*) + E *-al*] **:** of or relating to the coccyx

coccygeal ganglion *n* **:** a small ganglion anterior to the coccyx at the caudal junction of the two gangliated cords of the sympathetic nervous system

coccygeal gland *n* **1** *also* **coccygeal body :** a small mass of vascular tissue situated near the tip of the coccyx **2 :** the oil gland near the base of the tail of a bird

coc·cy·gec·to·my \ˌkäksə̇ˈjektəmē\ *n* -ES [*coccyg-* + *-ectomy*] **:** the surgical removal of the coccyx

coccygeo- *comb form* [NL, fr. *coccygeus*] **:** coccygeal and ⟨*coccygeo*anal⟩ ⟨*coccygeo*mesenteric⟩

coc·cy·geus \käkˈsijēəs\ *n, pl* **coccyg·ei** \-jēˌī\ [NL, fr. *coccyg-, coccyx*] **:** a muscle arising from the ischium and sacrospinous ligament and inserted into the coccyx and sacrum

coc·cy·go·dyn·ia \ˌkäksə̇(ˌ)gōˈdinēə\ *n* -s [NL, fr. *coccyg-* + *-odynia*] **:** pain in the coccyx and adjacent regions

coc·cyx \ˈkäksiks\ *n, pl* **coccy·ges** \ˈkäksəˌjēz, käkˈsī(ˌ)j-\ *also* **coccyxes** \ˈkäksiksə̇z\ [NL (L, cuckoo), fr. Gk *kokkyx* cuckoo, coccyx; fr. its resemblance to a cuckoo's beak — more at CUCKOO] **1 :** the end of the vertebral column beyond the sacrum in man and certain other primates comprising usu. four small vertebrae that are more or less completely fused in the adult and represent a vestigial tail **2 :** a bone in vertebrates (as birds) corresponding to the primate coccyx; *sometimes* **:** UROSTYLE

coc·cy·zus \käkˈsīzəs\ *n, cap* [NL, irreg. fr. Gk *kokkyx* cuckoo] **:** a genus of American arboreal cuckoos

coch *abbr* [L *cochleare*] spoonful

co·cha·both \kōˈchäbəth\ *n, pl* **cochaboth** *or* **cochaboths** *usu cap* **1 :** MACÁ **2 :** a division of the Macá language family

co·chairman \(ˈ)kō+\ *n, pl* **cochairmen** [*co-* + *chairman*] **:** joint chairman, vice-chairman, or assistant chairman

co·chal \kōˈchäl\ *n* -s [MexSp] **:** the edible fruit of a tall cactus (*Myrtillocactus cochal*) of Lower California; *also* **:** the plant producing this fruit

co·che \ˈkō(ˌ)chā\ *n* -s *usu cap* [Sp] **:** a language family of Colombia and Ecuador comprising Sebundoy, Quillacinga, and Patoco — called also *Mocoa*

co·cher \kōˈshā, kȯshā\ *n* -s [F, fr. *coche* cab — more at COACH] **:** CABDRIVER

co·chief \(ˈ)kō+\ *n* [*co-* + *chief*] **:** joint chief, alternate chief, or vice-chief

co·chil sa·po·ta \kōˈchēlsəˈpōd·ə\ *n* [Sp *cochilzapote,* fr. Nahuatl *cochiztzapotl,* fr. *cochitl* sleep + *tzapotl* sapote; fr. the belief that eating the fruit would put one to sleep] **1 :** a large Mexican tree (*Casimiroa edulis*) with fruit about the size of a large apple and resembling the peach in flavor **2 :** the fruit of the cochil sapota

co·chi·mi \ˌkōchə̇ˈmē\ *n, pl* **cochimi** *or* **cochimis** *usu cap* [Sp *cochimí,* of AmerInd origin] **1 a :** an Indian people of central Lower California, Mexico **b :** a member of such people **2 :** a Yuman language of the Cochimi people

co·chin \ˈkōchən, ˈkäch-\ *n* -s [fr. *Cochin* China, a region of Vietnam] **1** *or* **cochin china** *often Cochin & usu Cochin China* **:** a large domestic fowl of an Asian breed having soft thick plumage of white, black, buff, or partridge, small wings and tail, and densely feathered legs and feet **2 :** ARGUS BROWN

coch·i·neal \ˈkächəˌnēl, ˌ==ˈ= *sometimes* -öch-, *esp bef pause or cons* -nēəl\ *n* -s [MF & Sp; MF *cochenille,* fr. OSp *cochinilla* cochineal, wood louse] **1 a :** a red dyestuff consisting of the dried bodies of females of the cochineal insect that is obtained in various grades (as silver cochineal and black cochineal, according to whether dry heat or boiling water is used to kill the insects) and that was formerly used as a mordant wool dye and food color and is now used as a biological stain and as an indicator — see CARMINE, CARMINIC ACID; DYE table I (under *Natural Red 4*) **b :** a synthetic product resembling cochineal — see DYE table I (under *Acid Red 18*) **2 :** CASTILIAN RED **3** [by shortening] **:** COCHINEAL INSECT

cochineal fig *or* **cochineal cactus** *or* **cochineal plant** *n* **:** a cactus (*Nopalea cochinellifera*) of Central and So. America that is widely cultivated as food for the cochineal insect

cochineal insect *n* **1 :** a small bright red insect (*Dactylopius coccus*) that is related to and resembles the mealybug in appearance and habits, feeds on cactus (esp. of the genera *Nopalia* and *Opuntia*), and has long been a source of red dyes **2 :** any of certain other insects closely related to the cochineal insect and usu. of similar coloring

cochin ginger *n, usu cap C* [fr. *Cochin* China, where it is produced] **:** WHITE GINGER

cochin kino *n, usu cap C* [fr. *Cochin,* India] **:** a commercial variety of kino

cochin oil *n, often cap C* [fr. *Cochin,* India] **:** a fine grade of coconut oil

co·chise \(ˈ)kōˈchēs, -ēz\ *adj, usu cap* [fr. *Cochise* county, Arizona] **:** of or belonging to a prehistoric culture of southeastern Arizona and adjacent New Mexico characterized by an abundance of flat milling slabs and lack of defensive weapons in the first stage and evidences of change from a seed-gathering to a hunting economy in the later stages

co·chi·ti \ˌkōchə̇ˈtē, ˈ==ˌ=\ *n, pl* **cochiti** *or* **cochitis** *usu cap* **1 a :** a subdivision of the Keresan-speaking Indian people of New Mexico **b :** a member of such people **2 :** the language of the Cochiti

cochl *abbr* [L *cochleare*] spoonful

co·chlea \ˈkōklēə, ˈkä-\ *n, pl* **cochle·ae** \-ēˌē, -lēˌī\ *or* **cochle·as** \-ēəz\ [NL, fr. L, snail, snail shell, Archimedean screw, spiral stairway, fr. Gk *kochlias,* fr. *kochlos* land snail (also, a kind of shellfish with a spiral shell); akin to Gk *konchē* mussel, cockle — more at CONCH] **:** a division of the labyrinth of the ear wanting or rudimentary in the lower vertebrates but well developed in birds and mammals and in all the latter except the monotremes coiled into the form of a snail shell, in man consisting of a spiral canal in the petrous part of the temporal bone in which lies a smaller membranous spiral passage that communicates with the sacculus at the base of the spiral, ends blindly near its apex, and contains the organ of Corti — see EAR illustration

¹**co·chle·ar** \-ēə(r)\ *adj* [NL *cochlea* + E *-ar*] **:** of or belonging to the cochlea

²**cochlear** \"\ *n* -s [L *cochlear, cochleare* spoon] **:** the spoon used in the Eastern Church in serving the consecrated wine sometimes with a particle of the Host

co·chle·ar·ia \ˌkōklēˈa(a)rēə, ˌkä-, -ˈärēə\ *n, cap* [NL, fr. L *cochleare* spoon + NL *-ia;* fr. the shape of the leaves] **:** a genus of fleshy maritime herbs (family Cruciferae) with thick leaves and globose seed pods — see SCURVY GRASS

co·chle·ar·i·form \ˌ==ˈa(a)rə̇ˌfȯrm\ *adj* [ISV *cochlear* (fr. L *cochlear* spoon) + *-iform*] **:** shaped like a spoon

cochleariform process *n* **:** the thin plate of bone between the eustachian tube and the canal for the muscle that adjusts the tension of the tympanic membrane

co·chle·a·ri·idae \ˌkōklēəˈrīəˌdē, ˌkä-\ *n pl, cap* [NL, fr. *Cochlearius,* type genus (fr. L *cochleare*) + *-idae*] **:** a family of neotropical wading birds (order Ciconiiformes) comprising the boat-billed herons

cochlear nerve *n* **:** the branch of the auditory nerve supplying the cochlea and subserving the sense of hearing

cochlear nucleus *n* **:** the nucleus of the cochlear nerve in the floor of the fourth ventricle of the brain

co·chle·ate \ˈkōklēət, ˈkä-, -lēˌāt\ *or* **co·chle·at·ed** \-lēˌād·ə̇d\ *adj* [L *cochleatus* spiral, fr. *cochlea* snail + *-atus* -ate — more at COCHLEA] **:** having the form of a snail shell

co·chle·i·form \(ˈ)kōkˈlēəˌfȯrm, (ˈ)kä-\ *adj* [ISV *cochlea* (fr. L) + *-iform*] **:** COCHLEATE

¹**co·chli·di·idae** \ˌkōkləˈdīəˌdē, ˌkä-\ *n pl, cap* [NL, fr. *Cochlidium,* type genus (fr. Gk *kochlidion,* dim. of *kochlos* land snail) + *-idae* — more at COCHLEA] *syn of* EUCLEIDAE

²**cochlidiidae** \"\ [NL, fr. *Cochlidium,* type genus + *-idae*] *syn of* EUCLEIDAE

co·chli·o·dont \ˈkōklēəˌdänt, ˈkä-\ *n* -s [NL *Cochliodontidae*] **:** a fish of the family Cochliodontidae

co·chli·o·don·ti·dae \ˌ===ˈdäntəˌdē\ *n pl, cap* [NL, fr. *Cochliodont-, Cochliodus,* type genus (fr. *cochli-,* fr. Gk *kochlos,* a kind of shellfish + NL *-odus*) + *-idae* — more at COCHLEA] **:** a family of Carboniferous and Permian tectospondylic elasmobranch fishes having the few teeth broad and arched

¹**co·chli·o·my·ia** \ˌ===ˈmīyə\ [NL, fr. Gk *kochlios* anything spiral, screw + NL *-myia*] *syn of* CALLITROGA

²**cochliomyia** \"\ *n, cap* [NL, fr. Gk *kochlios* anything spiral, screw + NL *-myia*] *in some classifications* **:** a genus of two-winged flies comprising the secondary screwworm

co·chlo·so·ma \ˌkōkləˈsōmə, ˌkä-\ *n, cap* [NL, fr. Gk *kochlos* shellfish with a spiral shell + NL *-soma;* akin to Gk *konchē* mussel — more at CONCH] **:** a genus of endocommensal flagellated protozoans known from the intestines of various vertebrates and possibly implicated in diarrheal conditions of young turkeys

co·chlo·sper·mum \-ˈspərməm\ *n, cap* [NL, fr. *cochlo-* (fr. Gk *kochlos,* a kind of shellfish with a spiral shell) + *-spermum;* fr. the coiled embryo — more at COCHLEA] **:** a genus (typifying the family Cochlospermaceae of the order Parietales) of trees native to tropical America and Africa and having palmate leaves and seeds covered with a silky down — see STERCULIA GUM

co·cil·lana \ˌkōsəˈlanə, -länə *also* -lānə\ *n* -s [prob. fr. AmerSp] **:** the dried bark of a So. American tree (*Guarea rusbyi*) used as an expectorant

co·cin·er·ite \ˌkōsəˈneˌrīt\ *n* -s [*Cocinera,* mine at Ramos, San Luis Potosi, Mexico, where it was found + E *-ite*] **:** a rare mineral consisting of sulfide of copper and silver Cu_4AgS

co·ci·ne·ro \-ˈne(ˌ)rō, -nā-\ *n* -s [Sp, fr. L *coquinarius,* fr. *coquina* kitchen + *-arius* -ary] *Southwest* **:** COOK

¹**cock** \ˈkäk\ *n* -s [ME *cok,* fr. OE *cocc;* prob. akin to obs. D *cocke* cock, ON *kokr;* all of imit. origin] **1 a :** the adult male of the domestic fowl (*Gallus gallus*) — distinguished from *cockerel* **b :** the male of birds other than the domestic fowl, esp. of other than gallinaceous birds **c :** WOODCOCK — usu. used without regard to sex **d** *archaic* **:** the crowing of a cock; *also* **:** COCKCROW 1 **e :** a representation of a cock; *specif* **:** WEATHERCOCK **2 :** a faucet, tap, valve, or similar device for starting, stopping, or regulating the flow of a liquid ⟨a ball ~⟩ ⟨a sill ~⟩ ⟨an automobile radiator ~⟩; *sometimes* **:** the amount of opening permitted by or as if by a cock ⟨a faucet turned on full ~⟩ **3 a :** one occupying a position of success and control **:** VICTOR; *often* **:** one dominating some field or leading some circle usu. through determined aggressive individual effort **b :** a person of pluck and spirit and often a certain swagger or arrogance ⟨all the young ~*s* dashing in new uniforms⟩ — often esp. formerly used as a term of intimate address ⟨you're sure doing fine, old ~⟩ **4 a** *in older firearms* **:** the hammer in the lock of a firearm **b :** the cocked position of the hammer ⟨a gun at half ~⟩ **5 a :** PENIS — usu. considered vulgar **b** *chiefly South & Midland* **:** the female pudenda — usu. considered vulgar **6 a :** GNOMON 1a **b :** an overhanging bracket containing a bearing for a watch or clock arbor or a wheel bridge supported at one end only **7** [perh. short for *cock-and-bull story*] *slang Brit* **:** NONSENSE, POPPYCOCK ⟨"you were talking some awful ~ about righteousness," the brigadier said —Bruce Marshall⟩ — **cock of the walk :** one that dominates a group or situation esp. overbearingly ⟨a rather boastful gentleman in a high collar and red suspenders appeared to be *cock of the walk* —R.H.Schauffler⟩

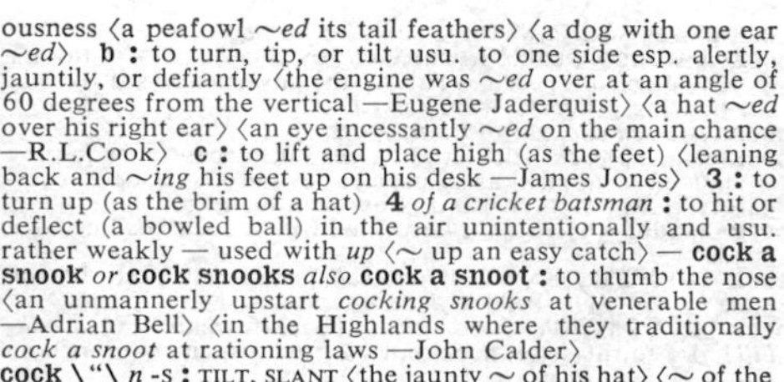

cock 1a: diagram of a male fowl showing parts: *1* main tail, *2* sickles, *3* saddle, *4* back, *5* cape, *6* ear lobe, *7* ear, *8* eye, *9* blade, *10* points, *11* base, *12* comb, *13* beak, *14* wattles, *15* hackle, *16* wing bow, *17* breast, *18* wing bar, *19* secondaries, *20* primaries or flight feathers, *21* hock, *22* claw, *23* spur, *24* shank, *25* fluff, *26* saddle feathers, *27* tail coverts, *28* lesser sickles

²**cock** \"\ *adj* **1 :** MALE — used of birds and sometimes of other animals ⟨~ lobster⟩ **2 :** CHIEF, LEADING, TOP ⟨a ~ swordsman⟩ ⟨a ~ wencher⟩ ⟨his house, having been ~ house at football for three years running, is very likely to be beaten next winter —Joyce Cary⟩

³**cock** \"\ *vb* -ED/-ING/-S [ME *cocken,* fr. ¹*cok* cock, male fowl] *vi* **1 :** to act big, arrogant, or menacing **:** STRUT, SWAGGER ⟨did a lot of bragging and ~*ing* after winning the game⟩ **2 :** to turn, tip, or stick up ⟨the show horse's abbreviated tail ~*ing* almost straight up⟩ ⟨[tubes] may be badly scratched in handling and mounting and may ~ in the fixture —C.J.Phillips⟩ ⟨a common failing with two-wheeled traps was ~*ing,* a tendency to tip up when in use so that the shafts pointed upwards and the tailboard down —Hugh McCausland⟩ **3 :** to position the hammer of a firearm for firing ~ *vt* **1 a** *obs* **:** to put (the match) into the cock of a matchlock gun **b :** to draw the hammer of (a firearm) fully back and set it for firing; *also* **:** to set (the trigger) for firing **c :** to draw or bend back (as the arm, the wrist, or by extension something held in the hand) in preparation to throw or hit ⟨a boxer with his fist ~*ed*⟩ ⟨a forward passer ~*ing* his arm to throw⟩ ⟨a ballplayer at the plate with his bat ~*ed*⟩ ⟨~ the wrists at the top of the backswing in golf⟩ **d :** to set a trip mechanism (as a camera shutter) for tripping **2 a :** to set erect esp. with a certain jaunty conspicuousness ⟨a peafowl ~*ed* its tail feathers⟩ ⟨a dog with one ear ~*ed*⟩ **b :** to turn, tip, or tilt usu. to one side esp. alertly, jauntily, or defiantly ⟨the engine was ~*ed* over at an angle of 60 degrees from the vertical —Eugene Jaderquist⟩ ⟨a hat ~*ed* over his right ear⟩ ⟨an eye incessantly ~*ed* on the main chance —R.L.Cook⟩ **c :** to lift and place high (as the feet) ⟨leaning back and ~*ing* his feet up on his desk —James Jones⟩ **3 :** to turn up (as the brim of a hat) **4** *of a cricket batsman* **:** to hit or deflect (a bowled ball) in the air unintentionally and usu. rather weakly — used with *up* ⟨~ up an easy catch⟩ — **cock a snook** *or* **cock snooks** *also* **cock a snoot :** to thumb the nose ⟨an unmannerly upstart *cocking snooks* at venerable men —Adrian Bell⟩ ⟨in the Highlands where they traditionally *cock a snoot* at rationing laws —John Calder⟩

⁴**cock** \"\ *n* -s **:** TILT, SLANT ⟨the jaunty ~ of his hat⟩ ⟨~ of the head⟩

⁵**cock** \"\ *n* -s [ME *cok,* alter. (influenced by *cok* cock, male fowl) of *God*] *obs* **:** GOD — used in oaths often in the possessive form which is sometimes spelled *cox* ⟨by *Cock!*⟩ ⟨by *Cock's* soul!⟩ ⟨by *Cox*bones!⟩

⁶**cock** \"\ *n* -s [ME *cok,* of Scand origin; akin to Dan *kok* pile; akin to OHG *coccho* pile, Lith *guga* pommel of a saddle, OE *cot* den, cottage — more at COT] **:** a small pile esp. of hay, dung, or turf

⁷**cock** \"\ *vt* -ED/-ING/-S **:** to put (as hay) into cocks

⁸**cock** \"\ *n* -s [ME *cok,* fr. OF *coque, coche,* fr. ML *caudica,* fr. L *caudic-, caudex* trunk of a tree — more at CODE] *obs* **:** COCKBOAT

⁹**cock** \"\ *vb* -ED/-ING/-S [prob. fr. (assumed) ONF *coquer* to notch, fr. (assumed) ONF, *coque,* n., notch — more at COAK] **:** ⁷COG

¹**cock·ade** \käˈkād\ *n* -s [modif. of F *cocarde,* fr. the fem. of *cocard* vain, proud, fr. *coq* cock (of imit. origin) + *-ard*] **:** a rosette or knot of ribbons or leather or any similar ornament worn usu. on the hat as a badge of office, of party allegiance, or of livery service or as a decoration

²**cockade** \"\ *adj, of an ore* **:** like a comb **:** having a profile like that of a cock's comb ⟨~ ore⟩ ⟨~ structure⟩

cock·ad·ed \-ˈkād·ə̇d\ *adj* **1 :** wearing a cockade ⟨~ guards patrolling the presidential palace —Claudia Cassidy⟩ **2 :** decorated with a cockade ⟨plumed helmets and ~ top hats —James Laver⟩

¹**cock-a-doo·dle-doo** \ˌkäkəˌdüdᵊlˈdü\ *n* -s [imit.] **:** ³CROW

²**cock-a-doodle-doo** \"\ *also* **cock-a-doodle** \ˌ==ˈ==\ *vi* -ED/-ING/-S **1 :** ²CROW 1 ⟨a rooster *cock-a-doodle-dooing* at dawn⟩ **2 :** ²CROW 3 ⟨all the papers were *cock-a-doodle-dooing* over the wonderful performance —*Sydney (Australia) Bulletin*⟩

cock-a-hoop \ˌkäkəˈhüp, -ˈhu̇p\ *adj* [perh. fr. ¹*cock* (male fowl) + ³*a* + *hoop* (measure of grain); fr. the phrase *to set the cock a hoop,* to live extravagantly, lit., to put the cock on the (full) measure of grain] **1 a :** elated and exulting esp. with abandon **:** triumphantly boastful ⟨exaggeratedly *cock-a-hoop* and strutting deportment —R.H.Rovere⟩ ⟨*cock-a-hoop* with success⟩ **b :** in buoyant spirits **:** LIVELY ⟨the cat . . . just went off into the bush and probably ate something, for he came back in a few days quite *cock-a-hoop* and as ready to eat snakes as ever —R.A.W.Hughes⟩ **2 :** AWRY, COCKEYED ⟨porch askew, chimneys all *cock-a-hoop* —Kenneth Roberts⟩ ⟨knock an argument *cock-a-hoop*⟩

cock·aigne *also* **cock·ayne** \käˈkān, kəˈ-\ *n* -s *usu cap* [ME *cokaygne,* fr. MF *(pais de) cocaigne* land of plenty] **1 :** an imaginary land of extreme luxury and ease where physical comforts and pleasures are always immediately at hand **2 :** any actual place resembling or suggesting such an imaginary land

cock·al \ˈkäkəl\ *n* -s [origin unknown] **1** *obs* **:** the knucklebone esp. of a sheep **2 :** a game played with knucklebones **:** DIBS

cock ale *n* [¹*cock* (male fowl)] *obs* **:** ale fermented with fruits, spices, and the jelly or mincemeat of a boiled cock

cock-a-leek·ie *or* **cock·ie-leek·ie** *or* **cock·y·leek·ie** *or* **cock·y·leeky** \ˌkäkəˈlēkē\ *n, pl* **cock-a-leekies** *or* **cockie-leekies** *or* **cockyleekies** [alter. of *cockieleekie,* fr. *cockie* (dim. of ¹*cock*) + *leekie,* dim. of *leek*] **:** a soup made of chicken boiled with leeks

cock·a·lo·rum \ˌkäkəˈlōrəm, -lȯr-\ *n* -s [prob. modif. (influenced by the L gen. pl. ending *-orum*) of obs. Flem *kockeloeren* to crow, of imit. origin; akin to OE *cocc* cock — more at COCK] **1 :** a strutting little fellow **:** a small boastful or self-important person **2 :** the game of leapfrog **3 :** boasting talk **:** BRAGGARTISM ⟨the crowing ~ of the pioneer —D.G.Hoffman⟩

cock·a·ma·roo \ˌkäkəməˈrü\ *n* -s [origin unknown] **:** RUSSIAN BAGATELLE

cock-and-bull story \ˈ==ˈ=-\ *n* [perh. so called fr. the legendary sexual prowess of cocks and bulls] **:** a fabricated tale passed off as true esp. in self-glorification ⟨*cock-and-bull stories* about the big jobs he had held⟩

cock-and-hen \ˈ==ˈ=\ *adj* **:** including both men and women ⟨a *cock-and-hen* party⟩

cock·an·dy \käˈkandē\ *n* -ES [perh. fr. ¹*cock* + *Andy,* the name] *Scot* **:** PUFFIN

cock·a·pert \ˈkäkəˌpərt\ *adj* [prob. fr. ¹*cock* + *apert* (bold)] *archaic* **:** IMPUDENT

cock·a·rouse *or* **cock·e·rouse** \ˈkäkəˌrau̇s\ *n* -s [of Algonquian origin; akin to *caucauasu* elder (in some Algonquian language of Virginia) — more at CAUCUS] **:** a person of consequence among the American colonists

cock·a·tiel *also* **cock·a·teel** \ˌkäkəˈtē(ə)l\ *n* -s [modif. (influenced by ¹*cock*) of D *kaketielje,* prob. fr. Pg *cacatilha,* dim. of *cacatua* cockatoo, fr. Malay *kakatua*] **:** a small crested Australian parrot (*Nymphicus hollandicus*) that is gray with a yellow head — called also *cockatoo parrot*

cock·a·too \ˈkäkəˌtü, ˌ==ˈ=\ *n* -s [modif. (influenced by ¹*cock*) of D *kaketoe,* fr. Malay *kakatua, kakak-tua,* fr. *kakak* elder sibling + *tua* old] **1 :** any of numerous large noisy chiefly Australasian parrots esp. of the genus *Kakatoe* that are often kept as cage birds, many (as the pink cockatoo) having large erectile crests and most (as the sulphur-crested cockatoo) having basically white plumage more or less tinged or marked with red, orange, or yellow — see GREAT BLACK COCKATOO **2 :** ³COCKY 1 **3** *slang Austral* **:** a lookout or sentinel (as one that warns criminals of approaching police) **4 :** a light yellow that is greener, less strong, and slightly lighter than average maize and greener, less strong, and very slightly darker than jasmine

pink cockatoo

cockatoo bush *n* **:** BLUEBERRY

cockatoo fence *n, Austral* **:** a rough fence of logs and saplings

cockatoo-parrot \ˌ==ˌ=ˈ==\ *n* **:** COCKATIEL

cock·a·touche *or* **cock·a·tush** \ˈkäkəˌtüsh, -təsh\ *n, pl* **cockatouches** *or* **cockatushes** [origin unknown] **:** a small freshwater fish (*Triglopsis thompsoni*) of the family Cottidae living in deep waters of the Great lakes and Canadian arctic streams

cock·a·trice \ˈkäkəˌtrə̇s, -ˌtrīs, *chiefly Brit* -rīs\ *n* -s [ME *cocatrice,* fr. MF *cocatris* ichneumon, crocodile, cockatrice, fr. ML *cocatric-, cocatrix* ichneumon, perh. alter. (influenced by L *cocodrilus, crocodilus* crocodile) of LL *calcatric-, calcatrix* trampler, fr. L *calcare* to tread, fr. *calc-, calx* heel — more at CALK] **1 :** a legendary serpent with deadly glance said to be hatched by a reptile from a cock's egg on a dunghill and often conceived of and represented esp. in heraldry as having the head, wings, and legs of a cock and the tail of a serpent — compare BASILISK **2 :** an extremely offensive esp. pernicious person **3** *obs* **:** PROSTITUTE

cockatrice

cock·a·wee \'käkə,wē\ *n* -s [imit.] : OLD-SQUAW
cock–a–whoop \ˌkäkə(h)wüp\ *adj* [by alter.] : COCK-A-HOOP 1 ⟨a *cock-a-whoop* speech . . . about the government's success in the housing program —*Economist*⟩
cockayne *usu cap, var of* COCKAIGNE
cock bead *n* [³*cock* (stick up)] : a bead in carpentry or joinery so molded or applied as to project beyond a surface — compare ASTRAGAL, QUIRK BEAD; see BEAD illustration
cock–beaded \'ˌ=ˌ=\ *adj* : decorated with a cock bead or cock beads
cock·bell \'käk,bel\ *n* [ME *cokbelle* small bell, perh. fr. *cok* male fowl + *belle* bell] *dial Eng* : ICICLE
cock·bill \'käk,bil\ *vt* -ED/-ING/-S [back-formation fr. *acockbill*] **1** : to tilt or set acockbill **2** : to suspend (an anchor) by the ring stopper esp. before dropping
cockbird \'=,=\ *n* [¹*cock* + *bird*] : a male bird
cock·boat \'käk,bōt\ *n* [ME *cokbote*, fr. *cok* cockboat + *bote* boat — more at COCK] : a small boat; *esp* : one used as a tender to a larger boat
cock–brained \'ˌ=ˌ=\ *adj* [¹*cock*] : FOOLISH, SCATTERBRAINED
cockchafer \'=,==\ *n* -s [¹*cock* + *chafer*; perh. fr. its size] : a large European scarablike beetle (*Melolontha melolontha*) that is destructive to vegetation, the larva feeding on roots, the adult on the foliage; *also* : any of various related beetles of similar habits formerly constituting a subfamily of Scarabeidae but now often made a separate family, Melolonthidae (as the pasture cockchafers or the New World rose chafer) — compare JUNE BEETLE; see GRASS-GRUB
cockcrow \'=,=\ *n* [ME *cokcrowe*, fr. *cok* rooster + *crowe* crow (crowing)] **1** : DAWN ⟨arise each morning at ~ to be ready for the sunrise⟩ **2** : any utterance or other kind of expression suggesting the triumphant crowing of a cock ⟨bawled a triumphant ~ to the rising sun —I.L.Idriess⟩
cockcrowing \'=,==\ *n* -s [ME *cokcrowing*, fr. *cok* cock + *crowing*, fr. gerund of *crowen* to crow] : COCKCROW
cocked *adj* [fr. past part. of ³*cock*] *of dice* : resting unevenly after a throw so that it is difficult to tell which face is up
cocked ankle *n* : an ankle (as of a horse) in which the relative position of the pastern to the cannon is changed, the former becoming too upright and causing a partial dislocation of the joint — used chiefly in pl.; called also *knuckling*
cocked hat *n* **1 a** : a hat with brim turned up at three places to give a three-cornered appearance — called also *tricorne* **b** : a hat with brim turned up on two sides to give a two-cornered shape and worn either front to back or sideways — called also *bicorne* **2** : a bowling game in which only the three corner pins are set up

cocked hat, 18th century

¹**cock·er** \'käkə(r)\ *n* -s [ME *coker* quiver, boot, fr. OE *cocer* quiver; akin to OHG *kohhari* quiver] **1** *archery* : a ground quiver **2** *now dial Eng* : a half boot or legging
²**cocker** \"\ *vt* **cockered; cockered; cockering** \-k(ə)riŋ\ **cockers** [ME *cokeren*, prob. fr. *cok* male fowl + *-eren* (freq. suffix) — more at COCK] **1** : INDULGE, PAMPER ⟨~ a child⟩ ⟨~ oneself too much⟩ ⟨~ foolishness⟩ **2** : to nurture or foster indulgently or encouragingly — used with *up* ⟨be cared for and ~*ed* up in an illness by good friends⟩
³**cocker** \"\ *n* -s [¹*cock* + *-er*] : one that keeps or handles fighting cocks
⁴**cocker** \"\ *n* -s [¹*cock*ing (woodcock hunting) + *-er*; fr. their having been used to flush woodcocks & similar game] : COCKER SPANIEL
cock·er·el \'käk(ə)rəl\ *n* -s [ME *cokerelle*, fr. OF dial. *kokerel*, dim. of OF *coc* cock, fr. LL *coccus*, of imit. origin like OE *cocc* cock — more at COCK] : a young male domestic fowl; *esp* : one less than a year old — compare COCK
cock·er·meg \'käkə(r),meg\ *n* -s [E dial. *cocker* prop, support (fr. ³*cock* — to set erect, turn or tip — + *-er*) + *Meg*, nickname for *Margaret* (as in *roaring Meg*, a cannon)] : a set of props used for the temporary support of a coal face in an upwardly inclined mine working
cock·er·nony *or* **cock·er·non·nie** \'käkər'nänē\ *n, pl* **cock·erno·nies** *or* **cockernon·nies** [origin unknown] *Scot* : the gathering of a young woman's hair under the snood or fillet
cocker spaniel *n* [⁴*cocker*] : a small spaniel of a breed believed to have originated in Spain that is of medium length with fairly short legs, long low-set ears, a square muzzle, and a flat or slightly waved silky coat which is usu. red, black, buff, or parti-colored and that is bred particularly for work in heavy cover
¹**cock·et** \'käkət\ *n* -s [ME *cocquet*, fr. AF *cokkette* or ML *coketa, coketum* customhouse seal] **1 a** : a seal formerly of the English or Scottish king's customhouse **b** : any one of certain other seals formerly used to seal permits **2** : a certified document given to a shipper as a warrant that his goods have been duly entered and have paid duty
²**cocket** \"\ *n* -s [ME *cocket, coket*] *obs* : fine wheaten leavened bread
³**cocket** \"\ *adj* [MF *coquet* coquettish — more at COQUETTE] *now dial Eng* **1** : PERT, SAUCY **2** : LIVELY, BRISK, MERRY
cocket center *or* **cocket centering** *n* [obs. E *cocket* to mortise, join, fr. It *cocchetta*, dim. of *cocca* notch, knot, prob. fr. L *coccum* excrescence on a tree, berry of the scarlet oak — more at COAK] : an arch center or centering in which the horizontal tie beam is replaced by bracing that allows headway above the springers to permit passage through while building
¹**cockeye** \'=,=\ *n* [³*cock* + *eye*] **1** : a squinting eye : STRABISMUS **2** : COCKEYE PILOT
²**cockeye** \"\ *n* [¹*cock* + *eye*] **1** : the loop at the end of a trace by which it is attached to the carriage or to the singletree **2** : the socket in the underside of a millstone balance rind and resting on the cockhead
cockeye bob *also* **cockeyed bob** *n* [prob. modif. of native name in Australia] *Austral* : a sudden violent storm ⟨a *cockeye bob* roared out of the north and tore the front veranda off —Xavier Herbert⟩
cock–eyed \'kä,kīd\ *adj* **1** : having a cockeye or cockeyes **2 a** : turned, slanted, or twisted off the proper line : ASKEW, AWRY ⟨his hat is always a little ~⟩ ⟨after the house settled, most of the door frames were ~⟩ ⟨knock a lamp ~⟩ **b** : slightly crazy : CONFUSED, WRONG, INCOMPREHENSIBLE : TOPSY-TURVY ⟨in this ~ realm of matter where temperatures are close to absolute zero, tough steel turns brittle, rubber loses its elasticity, and a kind of liquid helium runs straight up —*Springfield (Mass.) Union*⟩ ⟨a ~, willful quite unjustified inference from something said —J.M.Barzun⟩ ⟨a ~ scheme⟩ **c** : DRUNK ⟨gets wonderfully ~ in the neighborhood bar —Jane Cobb⟩
cockeye pilot *n* : BEAU GREGORY
cockeyes \'=,=\ *n pl* [prob. fr. pl. of ¹*cockeye*] *in craps* : a throw of three
cock feather *n* [prob. fr. ³*cock*] : the feather of an arrow that is at right angles to the nock — compare HEN FEATHER
cock–feathered \'ˌ=ˌ==\ *adj* [¹*cock*] : having plumage of the pattern characteristic of a cock bird — distinguished from *hen-feathered*
¹**cockfight** \'=,=\ *n* [¹*cock* + *fight*] **1** : a match or contest of gamecocks usu. heeled with metal gaffs and set at each other in a cockpit **2** : a boy's game in which the contestants, trussed into a squatting position or maintaining an awkward position on one leg, try to knock one another off balance
²**cockfight** \"\ *vi* : to engage in a cockfight ⟨~ with knees and hands tied together⟩
cockfight chair *n* [so called fr. its use for viewing sports] : READING CHAIR
cockfighting \'=,==\ *n* -s : the sport of matching gamecocks in a cockfight; *also* : the patronizing of such matches esp. for the purpose of betting on the outcome ⟨addicted to card playing, ~, and drinking —H.E.Starr⟩
cockhead \'=,=\ *n* [¹*cock* + *head*] : the rounded or pointed top of a grinding-mill spindle forming a support for the stone
¹**cockhorse** \'=ˌ=\ *n* [perh. fr. ²*cock* + *horse*] **1** : something (as an adult's knee, a broomstick, or a hobbyhorse) on which a child may sit astride and pretend to ride as if on a horse ⟨ride a ~⟩ **2** : an extra horse led behind a coach to be hitched before the regular team to assist in passing over steep or difficult terrain
²**cockhorse** \"\ *adv* : ASTRIDE, ALOFT ⟨ride ~ on a broomstick⟩ ⟨emaciated beasts that were lame and blindfolded and padded, but ridden ~ —J.H.Allen⟩
cockie *var of* COCKY
cockieleekie *var of* COCK-A-LEEKIE
cockier *comparative of* COCKY
cockies *pl of* COCKY
cockiest *superlative of* COCKY
cock·i·ly \'käkəlē, -li\ *adv* [²*cocky* + *-ly*] : in a cocky manner
cock·i·ness \'käkēnəs\ *n* -ES [²*cocky* + *-ness*] : the quality or state of being cocky ⟨self-confidence, variously called ~ and courage —N.M.Clark⟩
¹**cocking** *n* -s [ME *cokking* fighting, fr. gerund of *cocken* to fight — more at COCK] **1** : COCKFIGHTING **2** [¹*cock* (woodcock) + *-ing*] : woodcock shooting
²**cocking** *adj* [fr. pres. part. of ³*cock*] *obs* : STRUTTING, COCKY
³**cocking** *n* -s [fr. gerund of ⁹*cock*] : COGGING
cocking cart *n* [¹*cocking* (woodcock shooting)] : a short-bodied high 2-wheeled sporting cart used for tandem driving and having a seat for a groom behind the box
cocking dog *n* [¹*cocking* (woodcock shooting)] : COCKER SPANIEL
cocking main *n* [¹*cocking* (cockfighting)] : ³MAIN 3
cocklaird \'=,=\ *n* [¹*cock* + *laird*] *Scot* : one who owns and cultivates a small plot
¹**cock·le** \'käkəl, 'kək-\ *n* -s [ME *cockel, cockle*, fr. OE *coccel*] **1 a** : BEARDED DARNEL **b** : CORN COCKLE **c** : any of several other plants growing in grainfields (as the cowherb, corn poppy, or cocklebur) **2** : a small gall resembling a seed of the corn cockle that is produced on wheat by a nematode worm (*Anguina tritici*)
²**cockle** \'käkəl\ *n* -s [ME *cokille*, fr. MF *coquille* shell, modif. (influenced by *coque* shell, fr. L *coccum* excrescence on a tree) of L *conchylia*, pl. of *conchylium*, fr. Gk *konchylion*, fr. *konchē* shell — more at COAK, CONCH] **1 a** : a bivalve mollusk of the family Cardiidae characterized by a shell that has convex radially ribbed valves and prominent umbones and is somewhat heart-shaped as seen from one end; *esp* : a common edible European bivalve (*Cardium edule*) **b** : any of many small or medium bivalves more or less resembling members of the Cardiidae — used usu. with a qualifying word ⟨beaked ~*s*⟩ ⟨false ~*s*⟩ **2** : COCKLESHELL **3** : a confection inscribed with a motto **4 cockles** *pl* : COCKLES OF THE HEART
³**cockle** \"\ *n* -s [MF *coquille*] **1** : PUCKER, WRINKLE, BULGE, RIPPLE ⟨a ~ in glass⟩ ⟨~*s* in paper⟩ **2** : a warty outgrowth constituting a defect on sheepskins
⁴**cockle** \"\ *vb* **cockled; cockled; cockling** \-k(ə)liŋ\ **cockles** [MF *coquiller*, fr. *coquille*, n.] *vi* **1** : to contract, pucker, or bulge so as to produce cockles esp. (of fabrics or paper) after wetting or (of fabrics) because of the uneven tension of the yarn during weaving ⟨vellum leaves ~ badly with atmospheric changes —*All the King's Horses*⟩ **2** : RIPPLE ⟨the *cockling* waves along the shore⟩ ~ *vt* : to cause to cockle ⟨the humidity of the room *cockled* the documents⟩
⁵**cockle** \"\ *adj* [prob. fr. ²*cockle* (shell)] *Scot* : WHIMSICAL, QUEER — used in compounds ⟨*cockle*-headed⟩
⁶**cockle** \"\ *n* -s [modif. (influenced by ²*cockle*) of D *kachel* (obs. D also *kaeckel*), short for *kacheloven*, fr. MHG, earthen oven, fr. *kachel* earthen pot (fr. OHG *chachala*, fr. — assumed — VL *caculus, cacculus*, alter. of LL *cacabulus, caccabulus*, dim. of *cacabus, caccabus* cooking pot, fr. Gk *kakkabos*, perh. fr. a Sem word akin to Assyr *kukubu* a vessel) + *oven*, fr. OHG *ovan* — more at OVEN] **1** : any of various stoves or heaters now largely disused: as **a** : COCKLE OAST **b** : COCKLE STOVE **2 a** : the fire chamber of an air stove or certain furnaces **b** : the dome of a heating furnace
⁷**cockle** \"\ *vi* **cockled; cockled; cockling** \-k(ə)liŋ\ **cockles** [perh. fr. ²*cockle* ("boat")] *dial Brit* : WOBBLE
cock·le·bur *or* **cock·le·burr** \'käkəl, 'kəkəl + ,-\ *n* -s [¹*cockle* + *bur*] **1** : a plant of the genus *Xanthium* **2** : the prickly fruit of a cocklebur that readily attaches itself to any passing object by means of the stiff hooked spines with which it is clothed
cockle button *n* [¹*cockle*] : BURDOCK 1
cockled *adj* **1** [²*cockle* + *-ed*] : having a shell **2** [fr. past part. of ⁴*cockle*] : WRINKLED, PUCKERED, CURLED
cockle hat *n* [²*cockle* (shell)] : a hat bearing a cockleshell as the badge of a pilgrim esp. to the shrine of St. James of Compostela in Spain
cockleloft \'==,=\ *n* [by alter.] : COCK LOFT
cockle oast *n* [⁶*cockle*] : a hop-drying kiln
cock·ler \'käk(ə)lə(r)\ *n* -s **1** : one that gathers and sells cockles **2** : a cockler's boat
cockleshell \'==,=\ *n* [ME *cokille shelle*, fr. *cokille* cockle + *shelle* shell] **1 a** : the shell or one of the shell valves of a cockle **b** : any shell suggesting this (as a scallop shell) **2** : something resembling a cockleshell ⟨the ~*s* of fair hair —Roger Senhouse⟩; *specif* : a light usu. flimsy boat

cockleshell

cockles of the heart [perh. fr. ²*cockle*, with influence of NL *cochlea* ventricle, fr. L, snail, snail shell — more at COCHLEA] : the center or core of one's sentient being — usu. used in the phrase *to warm the cockles of the heart*
cockle stove *n* [⁶*cockle*] : a large heating stove in which the air currents are conducted around the fire chamber before passing into the apartments to be warmed
cocklight \'=,=\ *n* [*cock* + *light*] *dial Eng* : twilight at cockcrow or roosting time
cockling *pres part of* COCKLE
cock·loche \'kä,klōch\ *n* -s [origin unknown] : a silly or contemptible fellow
cockloft \'=,=\ *n* [prob. fr. ¹*cock*; fr. the use of attics as roosting places for fowls] **1** : a small garret; *esp* : one immediately under the ridgepole of a roof and accessible by ladder **2** *slang* : the cupola of a railroad caboose
cock·ly \'kak(ə)lē, -li\ *adj* [³*cockle* + *-y*] : marked by or abounding in cockles ⟨a ~ fabric⟩
¹**cock·ney** \'käknē, -ni\ *n* -s [ME *cokenay, cokeney* misshapen egg, spoiled child, effeminate person, lit., cocks' egg, fr. *coken* (gen. pl. of *cok* cock) + *ey, ay* egg, fr. OE *æg* — more at COCK, EGG] **1** *obs* **a** : a spoiled child **b** : an effeminate man : MILKSOP **c** : a townsman as opposed to a sturdy manly countryman — used disparagingly to suggest effeminacy **d** : a squeamish or affected woman **2** *often cap* **a** : someone born within the range of sound of the bells of Bow Church, London : a native or a long-established resident of London **b** : the dialect of London or of the East End of London **3** : a young Australian snapper — **cock·ney·ish** \-nē(,)ish\ *adj*
²**cockney** \"\ *adj, sometimes cap* : of, relating to, or resembling a cockney
cock·ney·fy *or* **cock·ni·fy** \'käknə,fī\ *vt* -ED/-ING/-ES [²*cockney* + *-fy, -ify*] : to make cockney or what may be regarded as cockney in quality or characteristics; *esp* : to make vulgar or showy
cock·ney·ism \-nē,izəm\ *n* -s [¹*cockney* + *-ism*] **1 a** : cockney manners, speech, or attitudes **b** : the writing or the qualities of the writing esp. the poetry of the 19th century English writers John Keats, Percy B. Shelley, William Hazlitt, and Leigh Hunt — used disparagingly by some contemporaries, esp. the Scottish critic John Lockhart **2** : a feature of cockney dialect ⟨~*s* found in London records⟩
cock of the rock [so called fr. the location of its nest] : a bird (*Rupicola rupicola*) of the family Cotingidae of northern So. America the male being chiefly orange in color with a high disklike crest; *sometimes* : a related bird (*R. peruviana*) of the Andean forests
cock of the wood **1** : PILEATED WOODPECKER **2** : CAPERCAILLIE
cockpaddle \'=,==\ *n* [¹*cock* + *paddle*; prob. fr. the resemblance of its dorsal ridge to a cock's comb] *Scot* : LUMPFISH
cock penny *n* [¹*cock*] : a payment formerly made at Shrovetide to masters of certain schools in northern England and orig. spent for cockfighting or cockthrowing
cockpit \'=,=\ *n* [¹*cock* + *pit*] **1 a** : a pit or enclosure for cockfights **b** : any place noted for esp. bloody, violent, or long-continued conflict ⟨Italy . . . was wearied by the long years when she had been the ~ of war —John Buchan⟩ ⟨its capital city . . . is a ~ of East-West intrigue —W.M.Healy⟩ **2** *obs* : the pit of a theater **3 a** : an apartment of an old sailing warship usu. on the after part of the orlop deck below the waterline used as quarters for junior officers and for treatment of the wounded in an engagement **b** : an open space aft of a decked area from which a yacht or other small vessel is steered **c** : a space in the fuselage of an airplane for the seating of the pilot or the pilot and passengers or in large passenger planes the pilot and crew **d** : any space (as in a sports car) resembling such a place in an airplane ⟨a racing driver hunched over in the ~ of his car⟩
cock·roach \'kä,krōch\ *n* [by folk etymology fr. Sp *cucaracha* cockroach, scolopendra, irreg. fr. *cuca* caterpillar, moth] : an insect of the order Blattaria a few of which are troublesome pests esp. in warm countries, being generally flat and with the head directed downward and covered dorsally by the pronotum, having long many-jointed antennae, sometimes having long wings and flying freely but often having wings short and of little use or, esp. in the female, absent, and being chiefly nocturnal, hiding in dark, moist places during the daytime — see AMERICAN COCKROACH, AUSTRALIAN COCKROACH, GERMAN COCKROACH, GIANT COCKROACH, ORIENTAL COCKROACH

cockroach

cock robin *n* [²*cock*] **1** : the male of the robin, esp. of the European robin **2** : HOODED MERGANSER
cocks *pl of* COCK, *pres 3d sing of* COCK
cocks·comb \'käks + ,-\ *n* [ME *cokkes comb*, fr. *cokkes* (gen. of *cok* cock) + *comb*] **1** : a cock's comb **2** : something resembling or suggesting a cockscomb: as **a** : COXCOMB 1a **b** : a garden plant of the genus *Celosia* cultivated for its showy usu. red, purplish, or yellow inflorescence **3** : COXCOMB 1b, 2
cockscomb oyster *n* : a very large tropical edible oyster (*Pycnodonta hyotis* or *Ostrea cristi-galli*) having the margins of both valves strongly scalloped

cockscomb 2b

cockscomb pyrites *n* : a crestlike variety of marcasite
cock's egg *n* [¹*cock* (male fowl); fr. its small size] : a small usu. yolkless egg — see COCKATRICE
cock's–eggs \'=,=\ *n, pl* **cock's–eggs** **1** : the egg-shaped white or yellow fruit of a weedy herbaceous vine (*Salpichroa rhomboidea*) of the family Solanaceae of Argentina **2** : the plant bearing cock's-eggs
cocks–foot \'käks+,-\ *n, pl* **cocksfoots** [so called fr. the shape of its spikes] : ORCHARD GRASS
cock–shut \'käk,shu̇t, -shət\ *n* -s [¹*cock* + *shut*; fr. the time poultry are shut in to rest] *now dial Eng* : evening twilight
cockshy \'=,=\ *n* -ES [¹*cock* + *shy* (throw)] **1 a** : a throw at an object set up or taken as a mark **b** : a mark or target so set up or taken **c** : any object or person taken as a butt (as of constant or persistent criticism or ridicule) ⟨another of his favorite *cockshies* . . . was Respectability —*Manchester Guardian Weekly*⟩ ⟨our public men . . . in moments of annoyance. . . are our first *cockshies* —John Buchan⟩ **2 a** *chiefly Brit* : an arrangement or construction of usu. balanced coconuts or other objects set up (as at a fair) to be thrown at with sticks or balls **b** : a booth (as at a fair) in which a cockshy is set up
cock snapper *n* [¹*cock* + *snapper* (fish)] : a young Australian snapper
cock sparrow *n* [²*cock*] : a cocky little man
cockspur \'=,=\ *n* [¹*cock* + *spur*] **1** : a cock's spur **2 a** : COCKSPUR THORN **b** : a small West Indian tree (*Pisonia aculeata*) **c** *in Honduras* : any of several spiny trees of the genus *Acacia* **d** : a bur grass (*Cenchrus echinatus*) **e** : an annual European weed (*Centaurea melitensis*) naturalized in No. and So. America **f** : ORCHARD GRASS **3** : SPUR 5e
cockspur flower *n* : any of several tropical plants of the genus *Plectranthus* (family Labiatae)
cockspur grass *n* : a grass of the genus *Echinochloa*; *esp* : BARNYARD GRASS
cockspur thorn *or* **cockspur hawthorn** *n* : a hawthorn (*Crataegus crus-galli*) having long straight thorns
cock–stride \'=,=\ *n* [¹*cock*] : a short distance ⟨not far from Brisbane — that is, only a matter of six hundred miles, a *cock-stride* in Australia —*Manchester Guardian Weekly*⟩
¹**cocksure** \'=ˌ=\ *adj* [prob. fr. ¹*cock* + *sure*] **1** *obs* **a** : quite safe **b** : of certain outcome **c** : sure of doing, receiving, or acting as indicated **2 a** : marked by firmly and conviction with no doubt or reservation : perfectly sure ⟨not being ~ of my position, [I] have often lacked the passionate conviction —W.A.White⟩ **b** : given to or marked by overconfidence, presumptuousness, lack of thoroughness, or cockiness ⟨how cautious and profound a thinker he was — how very far from being that arrogant and ~ materialist —Aldous Huxley⟩ **syn** see SURE
²**cocksure** \"\ *adv* : with complete security or certainty
cock·sure·ly *adv* [¹*cocksure* + *-ly*] : in a cocksure manner ⟨answer a question a bit too ~⟩
cock·surety \'käk +\ *n* : the state of being cocksure
cockswain *var of* COXSWAIN
cocksy \'käksē, -si\ *var of* COXY
¹**cocktail** \'=,=\ *n* [¹*cock* + *tail*] **1 a** : a horse with its tail docked **b** : a horse (as a race horse) not of pure breed **c** : a person passing for a gentleman but underbred **2** : a form of cirrus cloud suggesting the tail of a cock
²**cocktail** \"\ *n* [prob. fr. ¹*cock* + *tail*] **1 a** : a short iced drink containing a strong alcoholic base (as rum, whiskey, or gin) or occas. wine with the admixture either by stirring or shaking of flavoring and sometimes coloring ingredients (as fruit juice, egg, bitters, liqueur, or sugar) and often garnished (as with a sprig of mint or slice of lemon) **b** : something resembling or suggesting such a drink esp. as being a mixture of notably diverse elements ⟨fog and smoke in equal parts — a city ~ familiar to all —*New Yorker*⟩ ⟨a musical ~⟩ **2** : an appetizer (as tomato juice, fruit in a syrup, or shrimp in a sauce of catsup, chili sauce, tabasco, and other seasoning) served as a first course at a meal
³**cocktail** \"\ *adj* **1** : of, belonging to, or set aside for a cocktail ⟨a ~ cherry⟩ ⟨the ~ hour⟩ **2** *of women's clothing* : designed for semiformal wear ⟨a ~ dress⟩ ⟨a series of ~ hats in white felt —*Women's Wear Daily*⟩
⁴**cocktail** \"\ *vb* -ED/-ING/-S *vt* : to entertain by a cocktail party esp. as a guest of honor ⟨finds himself ~*ed*, partied, and dined like the year's most eligible bachelor —Ray Josephs⟩ ~ *vi* : to drink cocktails
cocktail cabinet *n, Brit* : LIQUOR CABINET
cock–tailed \'=ˌ=\ *adj* [¹*cock*] *of an animal* : with the tail or hinder part of the body cocked up; *esp, of a horse* : docked and nicked in the tail so that the stump sticks up
cocktail glass *n* : a bell-shaped drinking glass usu. having a foot and stem and holding about three ounces
cocktail hour *n* : the hour when cocktails are customarily served usu. just before dinner or between four and six in the afternoon
cocktail lounge *n* : a public room in a hotel, club, or restaurant where cocktails and other drinks are served
cocktail party *n* : an informal or semiformal party or gathering, usu. for conversation and during the cocktail hour, at which drinks, esp. alcoholic drinks, are a major item
cocktail ring *n* : DINNER RING
cocktail table *n* : COFFEE TABLE
cock–throttled \'=ˌthrät°ld\ *or* **cock–thropple d** \-ˌthräp°ld\ *adj* [¹*cock*] *of a horse* : having a long neck with the head carried high like that of a fowl
cockthrowing \'=,==\ *n* [¹*cock* + *throwing*] : an old sport of throwing sticks at a cock tied to a stake popular esp. at Shrovetide

1cockup \ˈ=,=\ *n* -S [3*cock* + *up*] **1 :** a hat or cap turned up in front **2** [2*cockup*] **:** a cockup letter or character in printing **3 :** BEGTI

2cockup \"\ *adj* [3*cock* + *up*] **1 :** markedly taller than the text capitals but aligning with them at the bottom — used of an ornamental initial **2 :** SUPERIOR 5

cock up *vt* [3*cock*] *Brit* **:** to cheer up **:** INSPIRIT ⟨disencourage any attempt to *cock* them *up* with any kind of comfort —Sean O'Casey⟩

cock–up splint \ˈ=,=-\ *n* [*cock up*] **:** a splint designed to immobilize the hand in the position of function (dorsal extension) during healing (as of a fracture)

1cocky \ˈkäkē, -ki\ *n* -ES [1*cock* (fowl) + *-y*] **:** a little cock —used formerly as a term of endearment

2cocky \"\ *adj* -ER/-EST [1*cock* + *-y*] **1 :** PERT, ARROGANT ⟨like a ~ little bird, waxed, ruffling, wonderfully insolent, he would stand his ground —Mollie Panter-Downes⟩ ⟨lean on the news, but ~, caustic, brilliantly written —W.A.Swanberg⟩ **2 :** JAUNTY

3cocky *or* **cock·ie** \ˈkäkē, -ki\ *n, pl* **cockies** [by shortening & alter. fr. *cockatoo*] **1** *chiefly Austral* **:** a farmer who farms on a small scale **2 a :** COCKATOO 1 **b :** COCKATIEL

4cocky \ˈkäkē, -ki\ *adj* [1*cock* + *-y*] **:** of, belonging to, or proper to a cock ⟨customary to speak of the plumage of adult birds as either ~ or henny —L.V.Domm⟩

cockyleekie *or* **cockyleeky** *var of* COCK-A-LEEKIE

cocky·ol·ly bird *or* **cocky·oly bird** \ˌkäkēˈälē,-\ *n* [baby= talk, perh. fr. 1*cock* + *yellow*] **:** any small bird — used as a pet name

cocky's joy \ˈkäkēz-, -kiz-\ *n* [3*cocky*] *slang Austral* **:** TREACLE

co·clé \(ˈ)kōˈklā\ *adj, usu cap* [fr. *Coclé*, province of Panama] **:** of or relating to the prehistoric culture of central Panama

1co·co *also* **co·coa** \ˈkō(ˌ)kō\ *n* -S [Sp & Pg; Sp *coco*, fr. Pg *côco*, lit., bogeyman, prob. baby-talk redupl. of (assumed) *co!* boo!; fr. the resemblance of a coconut to a grotesque head] **1 a :** COCONUT PALM **b :** COCONUT 1 **2** *slang* **:** COCONUT 2 **3 a :** NUT GRASS 1 **b :** TARO **c :** YAUTIA a **d :** an Argentine timber tree (*Zanthoxylon coco*) with a green light wood **e :** SAPUCAIA

2coco *also* **cocoa** \"\ *adj* **:** made from the fibrous husk of the coconut ⟨~ matting⟩

co·coa \"\ *n* -S [modif. (influenced by 1*coco*) of Sp *cacao* — more at CACAO] **1 :** CACAO 2 **2 a :** chocolate (sense 1) deprived of a portion of its fat and pulverized **b :** a beverage prepared by cooking the resulting powder with water or milk **3 :** a moderate brown that is stronger and slightly redder and lighter than bay, redder and stronger than chestnut brown, and redder and deeper than average cocoa brown

cocoa bean *n* **:** CACAO 1

cocoa brown *n* **:** a variable color averaging a moderate brown that is paler and slightly yellower than bay, redder and slightly lighter than chestnut brown, and yellower and paler than cocoa

cocoa butter *or* **cacao butter** *n* **:** a yellowish or white brittle but low-melting fat with a chocolatelike odor and taste obtained from cacao beans and used in the manufacture of chocolate candy, cosmetics, and pharmaceutical preparations — called also *theobroma oil*

cocoanut *var of* COCONUT

cocoa palm *var of* COCONUT PALM

cocoa plant *n* **1 :** the cacao tree **2 :** COCA 1

cocoa plum *var of* COCO PLUM

cocoa powder *n* **1 :** BROWN POWDER **2 :** COCOA 2a

cocoa red *n* **:** the brown-red coloring matter of cocoa and chocolate formed by oxidation of tannin in the cacao bean

cocoa sedge *n* **:** NUT GRASS 1

cocoas *pl of* COCOA

cocoa shells *n pl* **:** the husks of cacao beans used as a stock feed or fertilizer or in the preparation of a beverage

cocoawood *var of* COCOWOOD

co·co·bo·lo \ˌkōkəˈbō(ˌ)lō\ *also* **co·co·bo·la** \-ˌlə\ *n* -S [Sp, fr. Arawak *kakabali*] **:** any of several valuable tropical American timber trees of the genus *Dalbergia* (esp. *D. retusa*)

co·co–de–mer \ˌkō(ˌ)kōdəˈma(a)(ə)r\ *n* -S *sometimes cap* [F] **:** SEA COCONUT 1b

co·co·dette \ˌkōkəˈdet\ *n* -S [F, alter. of *cocodète*, fem. of *cocodès* fop, dandy, fr. *coq* cock — more at COCK] **:** a French prostitute esp. in fashionable society

coco grass *or* **cocoa grass** *n* [1*coco, cocoa;* prob. fr. the appearance of the fruit] **:** NUT GRASS

co·com \kōˈkōm\ *n, pl* **cocom** *or* **cocoms** *usu cap* [Sp, of AmerInd origin] **1 :** a ruling Mayan people that dominated Yucatán until the war of 1201 along with the Itza and then became the sole overlords of the peninsula from 1201 to the revolution of 1485 **2 :** a member of the Cocom people — compare ITZA

co·co·mat \ˈkō(ˌ)kōˌmat\ *n* -S [*coconut mat*] **1 :** a matting made of coconut fiber **2 :** a doormat having a stiff bristly pile made of coconut fiber

co·co·na \kəˈkōnə\ *n* -S [AmerSp] **:** the tart applelike fruit of a shrubby plant (*Solanum hyporhodium*) of the upper Amazon

1co·conscious \(ˈ)kō+\ *adj* [*co-* + *conscious*] **1 :** experiencing or aware of the same things **2 :** of or belonging to the coconscious

2coconscious \"\ *or* **co·consciousness** *n* -ES **:** mental processes outside the main stream of consciousness but sometimes available to it **:** secondary consciousness

co·conspirator \ˌkō+\ *n* -S [*co-* + *conspirator*] **:** CONSPIRATOR

co·co·nu·can \ˌkōkəˈnükən\ *adj, usu cap* **1 :** of, relating to, or characteristic of the Coconuco peoples **2 :** of, relating to, or characteristic of the Coconuco language

co·co·nu·co \ˌ==ˈ=(ˌ)kō\ *also* **coconu·ca** \-ˌkə\ *n, pl* **coconuco** *or* **coconucos** *also* **coconuca** *or* **coconucas** *usu cap* [Sp, of AmerInd origin] **1 a :** a group of Chibchan peoples of the department of Cauca, Colombia **b :** a member of any people in this group **2 :** the language of the Coconuco people constituting a language family of Chibchan stock

1co·co·nut *also* **co·coa·nut** \ˈkōkə(ˌ)nət\ *n* [1*coco, cocoa* + *nut*] **1 :** the fruit of the coconut palm that is a drupe consisting of an outer fibrous husk that yields coir and a large nut containing the thick edible meat and, in the fresh fruit, a clear fluid called coconut milk — see COCONUT PALM, COIR, COPRA **2** *also* **co·co** \ˈkō(ˌ)kō\ *slang* **:** HEAD; *esp* **:** the human head ⟨hit on the ~ with a hockey stick⟩ **3 :** a hollow shell often half a coconut shell used to make the sound of hoofbeats esp. in an orchestra **4 :** a grayish brown that is slightly redder and darker than new cocoa and slightly yellower than chestnut — called also *Ascot tan, brown stone, Kermanshah, warm sepia*

2coconut *also* **cocoanut** \"\ *adj* **:** made from or involving as an element any of the various products of the coconut palm (as the fiber or the fruit or its meat) ⟨~ matting⟩ ⟨~ baskets⟩ ⟨a ~ cake⟩

coconut brown *n* **:** a moderate brown that is yellower and slightly deeper than toast brown, yellower, lighter, and stronger than bay or auburn, and lighter, stronger, and slightly redder than chestnut brown — called also *burnt almond*

coconut bud rot *n* **:** a disease of the coconut palm caused by a fungus (*Phytophthora palmivora*) that destroys the terminal bud and adjacent leaves finally killing the tree

coconut cake *n* **:** a palatable oil cake obtained as a residue in the production of coconut oil and used esp. in animal feeds — called also *copra cake*

coconut crab *n* **:** PURSE CRAB

coconut cream *n* **:** the white liquid obtained from the compressed meat of fresh coconuts and constituting the principal sauce and flavoring of the Pacific islands

coconut meal *n* **:** ground coconut cake — called also *copra meal*

coconut mealybug *n* **:** a short-tailed mealybug (*Nipaecoccus nipae*) that is destructive to coconut, avocado, fig, and other fruiting plants

coconut milk *or* **coconut water** *n* **:** the clear liquid within the fruit of the fresh coconut

coconut oil *n* **:** a nearly colorless fatty oil or white semisolid fat, lathering readily in water, extracted from fresh coconuts or from copra, and used chiefly in making soap, in foods, and as a raw material for the production of fatty acids and of lauryl alcohol and related alcohols by reduction

coconut palm *or* **coconut tree** *or* **coco palm** *or* **cocoa palm** *n* **:** a tall pinnate-leaved palm (*Cocos nucifera*) found throughout the tropics but believed to have originated in tropical America and bearing a large edible fruit and leaves that are used in thatching or are split for use in weaving (as hats, baskets, and matting) — see COCONUT 1

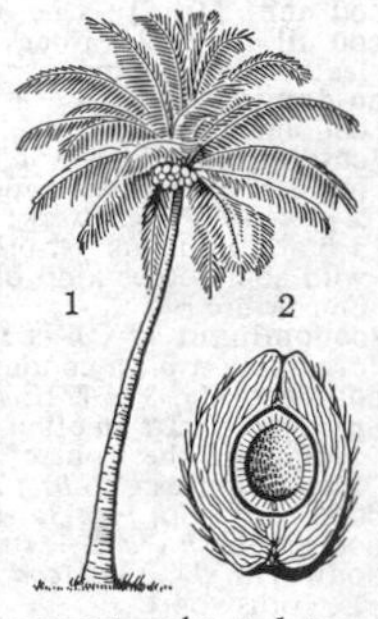

coconut palm **:** *1* tree, *2* section of fruit

coconut shy *n, chiefly Brit* **:** a cockshy with coconuts as the targets

1co·coon \kəˈkün *also* kuˈk- *or sometimes esp Brit* käˈk-\ *n* -S [F *cocon*, fr. Prov *coucoun* cocoon, eggshell, fr. *coco* shell, fr. L *coccum* excrescence on a tree — more at COAK] **1 a :** the envelope often composed largely of silk which the larvae of many insects form about themselves previous to changing to a pupa and in which they pass the pupa stage, those of silkworms being the source of the silk of commerce **b :** any of various other protective coverings produced by animals (as the cases of silk made by spiders or the egg cases of mucus secreted by leeches and earthworms) **2 :** any covering resembling or suggesting a cocoon ⟨soon we two old fellows were stuffed into a tight ~ of buffalo robes —Austin Strong⟩; *specif* **:** a long-term protective covering usu. plastic placed or sprayed over a gun or other military or naval equipment in storage

2cocoon \"\ *vb* -ED/-ING/-S *vi* **:** to form a cocoon ~ *vt* **1 :** to wrap or envelop esp. tightly as if in a cocoon ⟨~*ed* in several layers of shawls and scarves —*Time*⟩ ⟨the aircraft having been ~*ed* at the U.S. Navy base —*Crowsnest*⟩ **2 :** to fit into or enclose in esp. snugly as if in a cocoon ⟨once having ~*ed* myself in Quongdong, I could never pluck up enough courage to go forth —Rex Ingamells⟩ ⟨a sense of . . . being in a steel box packed against another steel box, inhumanly ~*ed*, came over her —William Sansom⟩

co·coon·ery \-n(ə)rē\ *n* -ES [1*cocoon* + *-ery*] **:** a place for raising silkworms

co·co·pa *or* **co·co·pah** \ˈkōkəˌpä\ *n, pl* **cocopa** *or* **cocopas** *or* **cocopah** *or* **cocopahs** *usu cap* [Sp *cocopa*, of AmerInd origin] **1 a :** a Yuman people living around the mouth of the Colorado river **b :** a member of such people **2 :** a Yuman language of the Cocopa and Halyikwamai peoples

coco palm *var of* COCONUT PALM

co·co·pan \ˈkō(ˌ)kōˌpan, ˈkōkəˌ-\ *n* -S [prob. by folk etymology fr. Afrik *koekpan*, lit., cake pan, fr. *koek* cake (fr. MD *coeke, couke*) + *pan*, fr. MD *panne;* akin to OHG *kuocho* cake and to OHG *pfanna* pan — more at CAKE, PAN] *Africa* **:** a mining tipcart

coco plum *also* **cocoa plum** *n* [*coco* by folk etymology fr. Sp *icaco, hicaco* — more at ICACO] **1 :** a small spreading tree (*Chrysobalanus icaco*) of tropical America **2 :** the plum= shaped fruit of the coco plum tree varying from nearly white to almost black and used for preserves

co·co·ra \kəˈkōrə, -ȯrə\ *n, pl* **cocora** *or* **cocoras** *usu cap* [Sp, of AmerInd origin] **1 :** a Chibchan people of the Rio Cocora valley in southeastern Nicaragua **2 :** a member of the Cocora people

co·co·ri·co \ˌkōkəˈrē(ˌ)kō, kəˌkōrēˈkō\ *n* -S [F, of imit. origin] **:** a small game bird (*Ortalis ruficauda*) of Trinidad

co·cos \ˈkōˌkäs\ *n, cap* [NL, fr. Pg *côco* — more at COCO] **:** a genus of pinnate-leaved palms of which all except possibly the coconut palm are natives of tropical So. America and all are characterized by a large fruit with thick fibrous pericarp enclosing a bony nut — see COCONUT

coco sedge *n* [1*coco;* prob. fr. the appearance of the fruit] **:** NUT GRASS 1

cocoswood *var of* COCUSWOOD

co·cotte \kōˈkät, kəˈk-\ *n* -S [F, fr. (baby-talk) *cocotte* hen, of imit. origin] **1 :** PROSTITUTE **2** [F, alter. of *cocasse*, a kind of pot, alter. of *coquemar*, a kind of pot, fr. L *cucuma* cooking pot] **:** a small shallow individual baking dish usu. with one or two handles

cocowood *also* **cocoawood** \ˈ=(ˌ)=ˌ=\ *n* [1*coco, cocoa* + *wood*] **1 :** the hard dark brown wood of an East Indian tree (*Aporosa dioica*) of the family Euphorbiaceae — called also *kokra wood* **2 a :** a wood somewhat similar to cocowood from a West Indian tree (*Inga vera*) **3 :** PORCUPINE WOOD

cocoyam \ˈ=(ˌ)=ˌ=\ *n* -S [*cocoa* + *yam;* fr. its being planted in cocoa groves] **:** EDDO

coc·o·zel·le \ˌkäkəˈzelē\ *n* -S [prob. fr. an It dial. word akin to It *cocuzza* squash, fr. ML *cocutia*] **:** a smooth cylindrical dark green summer squash usu. with lighter green to yellow stripes or mottlings and firm white to greenish flesh growing over a foot in length and four to five inches thick but usu. used when half that size — called also *Italian vegetable marrow;* compare ZUCCHINI

coct *vt* -ED/-ING/-S [L *coctus*, past part. of *coquere* to cook, boil — more at COOK] *obs* **:** BOIL

coc·tile \ˈkäktəl, -ˌtīl\ *adj* [L *coctilis*, fr. *coctus*, past part. of *coquere* to cook, bake + *-ilis* -ile] **:** made by baking or exposing to heat (as a brick)

coc·tion \ˈkäkshən\ *n* -S [L *coction-, coctio* cooking, digestion, fr. *coctus* + *-ion-, -io* -ion] **1** *archaic* **:** the act or process of attaining a more perfect, more mature, or more desirable condition either through natural processes or by the intervention of foreign agents (as heat); *specif* **:** digestion of food **2** *archaic* **:** suppuration conceived of esp. by humoralists as a stage in the normal process of wound healing or as a phase in the development of any disease

cocto *usu cap, var of* COTO

cocto- *comb form* [L *coctus*, past part. of *coquere* to cook] **:** boiled **:** modified by heat ⟨*cocto*antigen⟩ ⟨*cocto*protein⟩ **:** at boiling point ⟨*cocto*stable⟩

cocum *var of* KOKUM BUTTER

co·current \(ˈ)kō+\ *adj* [*co-* + *current*] **:** involving flow of materials in the same direction ⟨acetic acid separated from chloroform by ~ extraction with water⟩

co·curricular \ˌkō+\ *adj* [*co-* + *curricular*] **:** outside of but usu. complementing the regular curriculum — usu. contrasted with *extracurricular*

co·cus·wood *also* **co·cos·wood** \ˈkōkəs + ˌ-\ *n* [NL *Cocos* + E *wood*] **:** the wood of the granadilla tree used for making clarinets and other musical instruments

1cod \ˈkäd\ *n* -S [ME, fr. OE *codd;* akin to ON *koddi* pillow, testicle, OHG *kutti* herd, Hitt *ku-u-tar* nape of the neck, upper arm, L *guttur* throat — more at COT] **1 obs :** a small bag esp. for perfume **2** *now dial Eng* **:** HUSK, POD — compare PEASECOD **3 a :** SCROTUM **b cods** *pl, dial* **:** TESTES **4** *or* **cod end :** the closed saclike terminal part of a trawl (sense 1) in which fish are trapped **5** *now dial* **:** a bag-shaped area of water or land; *esp* **:** the inmost recess of a bay, marsh, or meadow

2cod \"\ *n* -S [ME, fr. ON *koddi*] *chiefly Scot* **:** a pillow or cushion

3cod \"\ *n, pl* **cod** *also* **cods** [ME] **1 a :** a soft-finned fish

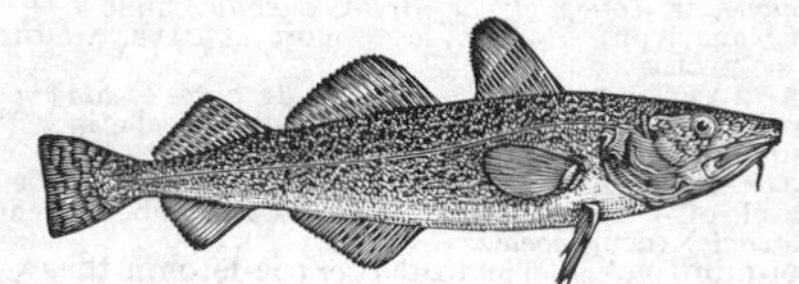
cod 1a

(*Gadus morrhua*) of the colder parts of the North Atlantic, being one of the leading food fishes of the world, living near the bottom of comparatively shallow water and averaging 10 to 35 pounds though occas. attaining very large size, and being taken, chiefly with hand lines or trawl lines, mainly from certain restricted areas, as off the Norwegian and New England coasts and on the Banks of Newfoundland, where the fishes congregate at certain seasons in waters of 20 to 40 fathoms' depth **b :** any fish of the family Gadidae; *esp* **:** a member of a Pacific species (*Gadus macrocephalus*) that is closely related to the cod of the Atlantic but less common and of less commercial importance **2 :** any of a number of spiny= finned fishes (esp. of the groups Percoidea and Scleroparei) more or less resembling members of the Gadidae — often used with a qualifying word; see BLUE COD, LINGCOD, RED COD, ROCK COD, TOMCOD

4cod \"\ *vb* **codded; codded; codding; cods** [origin unknown] *dial* **:** TEASE, HOAX, BANTER, KID

5cod \"\ *n* -S *dial* **:** HOAX

cod *abbr* codex

COD *abbr* cash on delivery; collect on delivery

co·da \ˈkōdə\ *n* -S [It, lit., tail, fr. L *coda, cauda* — more at COWARD] **1 a :** a final or concluding musical section that is formally distinct from the main structure of a composition or movement (as a fugue or rondo) **b :** a concluding portion of a literary or dramatic work; *usu* **:** a portion or scene that rounds off or integrates preceding themes or ideas ⟨a generalized discussion falling into two divisions . . . a third part entitled "dedication" forming a sort of ~ for the whole —Howard M. Jones⟩ **c :** anything that serves to round out, conclude, or summarize yet has an interest of its own ⟨the penetration of the ionosphere . . . in making radar contact with the moon, is a magnificent ~ to the invalidation of all that once insulated and protected human life —J.H.Spigelman⟩ **d :** the finale of a classical ballet; *also* **:** the third part of a pas de deux in which the male and female dancers dance together after completion of their respective variations **2 :** a tail (sense 16) added to a stanza (as a sonnet)

coda mark *or* **coda sign** *n* **:** a character consisting of a circle superimposed on a cross used in music to mark a part to be omitted in a repeated section and to direct the performer to skip from the sign to the coda

co·da·mine \ˈkōdəˌmēn, -ˌmən\ *n* -S [ISV *codeine* + *amine;* orig. formed as G *kodamin*] **:** a crystalline alkaloid $C_{20}H_{25}NO_4$ found in the aqueous extract of opium

codbait \ˈ=,=\ *n* [1*cod* + *bait*] **:** CADDISWORM

codbank \ˈ=,=\ *n* [3*cod* + *bank*] **:** a submarine bank frequented by cod

codd *abbr* codices

codding *adj* [prob. fr. *cod* (scrotum) + *-ing*] *obs* **:** LECHEROUS

cod·ding·ton lens \ˈkädiŋtən-\ *n, usu cap C* [after Henry *Coddington* †1845 Eng. mathematician] **:** a hand magnifier consisting of a lens made from a glass sphere around which a deep equatorial groove acting as a diaphragm has been cut

1cod·dle \ˈkädᵊl\ *vt* **coddled; coddled; coddling** \-d(ᵊ)liŋ\ **coddles** [perh. alter. of 1*caudle*] **1 :** to cook (as eggs) in liquid slowly and gently just below the boiling point **2 :** to treat with extreme usu. excessive care **:** PAMPER

2coddle \"\ *n* -S **:** a coddled or self-indulged person

1code \ˈkōd\ *n* -S [ME, fr. MF *code*, fr. L *codex, caudex* trunk of a tree, split block of wood, tablet of wood covered with wax on which the ancients wrote, book, a writing; akin to L *cudere* to beat — more at HEW] **1** *law* **a** *in ancient times* **:** any written collection of laws **b** *in more modern times* **:** a systematic complete written collection of law arranged logically with index and table of contents and covering fully one or more subjects of law ⟨The Internal Revenue *Code*⟩ **c** *in the jurisdictions following the common law* **:** a written compilation periodically amended of the existing statutes of general and permanent importance, sometimes expressly repealing all prior laws inconsistent with the compilation, sometimes being only a restatement of the existing statutes and only prima-facie evidence of the true laws passed by the legislature ⟨The *Code* of Laws of the U.S.⟩ **d :** a written revision of all existing statutory laws of permanent and general importance eliminating clerical errors and obsolete portions and occas. including amendments and new provisions **e** *in the jurisdictions following the most advanced theory of the civil law* **:** a written complete logical systematic statement of the entire law in effect in the jurisdiction with complete index and table of contents and repealing all prior laws ⟨the Napoleonic *Code*⟩ **2 :** any of various systems or collections of principles, rules, or regulations that do not constitute a legal code: as **a :** any set of traditional rules of conduct that are considered morally binding upon the individual as a member of a particular group, a resident of a particular place, or a participant in a particular activity ⟨the ~ of a gentleman⟩ ⟨the ~ of the West⟩ ⟨the ~ of organized crime⟩; *broadly* **:** customary socially acceptable behavior (as of an individual or group) ⟨a complex fashion ~ also requires that women have more clothes than men —*Time*⟩ **b :** a set of rules for or standards of professional practices or behavior set up by an organized group (as an association of manufacturers) and usu. reinforced by certain police and punitive powers of the group against nonconforming members ⟨the medical association may close the hospitals to physicians who transgress its ethical ~⟩; *often* **:** a formal statement of such a set of rules or standards ⟨the International *Code* of Botanical Nomenclature⟩ **c :** a set of rules of procedure and standards of materials designed to secure uniformity and protect the public interest in such matters as building construction and public health established usu. by a public agency and commonly having the force of law in a particular jurisdiction ⟨a building ~⟩ ⟨changes in the sanitary ~⟩ **3 :** any system of symbols for meaningful communication: **a :** a system of standardized signals for mechanically conveying information (as by telegraph, heliograph, flags, drums, or smoke) between points separated by a finite distance **b :** a system of symbols designed primarily to restrict comprehension (as of a message) to particular individuals: (1) **:** a system in which arbitrary meanings are assigned to letters, numbers, words, or other symbols and often used to procure brevity or system as well as secrecy ⟨each case history written up in a simple ~⟩; *specif* **:** a complete cryptographic system employing code groups of standard lengths (as 3742 or XEQSJ) each group representing a plaintext segment of any convenient length (as a sentence, phrase, word, or affix, or a letter of the alphabet for spelling out words otherwise unprovided for) and normally embodied in a code book — see AGENT CODE, BOOK CODE, CODE BOOK; PERMUTATION TABLE (2) **:** a record of such a system **:** CODE BOOK (3) **:** CIPHER 2 — not used technically **c :** language conceived as a stock of signals from which the speaker or writer chooses certain ones with which to convey his message **d :** any system of symbols for introducing information and instructions into an automatic computer or tabulating machine; *also* **:** a recording of such symbols (as by punching cards or magnetizing spots on magnetic tape) **4 a :** a word or other symbol used in a code system instead of a plaintext term ⟨"hocus" was the ~ for the city editor⟩ **b :** a group of numbers indicating the order, position, and form of the wards required on a key to draw the bolt of a particular lock **c :** a symbol used to identify something that lacks a specific name ⟨several of the new fibers, esp. ~*s* 500, 610, and 687, look promising⟩

2code \"\ *vt* -ED/-ING/-S **1 :** to put in or into the form or symbols of a code ⟨~ a system of laws⟩ ⟨~ a message for transmission by shortwave radio⟩ **2 :** to classify or categorize by a code esp. to facilitate tabulation ⟨*coded* the information⟩ ⟨*coding* . . . words into numbers so that answers to questions may be punched on tabulating cards and tabulated by machine —J.H. Platten⟩ ⟨personnel who ~ diseases and operations according to standard nomenclature —*Jour. Amer. Med. Assoc.*⟩ ⟨nearly 800 other treated patients have been *coded* and analyzed —P.H.Wilcox⟩

code book *n* **:** a list of code groups and their meanings arranged as a dictionary

co·decarboxylase \ˌkō+\ *n* [*co-* + *decarboxylase*] **:** the coenzyme $C_8H_{10}NO_6P$ of various amino acid decarboxylases and transaminases; pyridoxal phosphate

code clerk *n* **:** CIPHER CLERK

co·declination \(ˌ)kō+\ *n* [*co-* + *declination*] **:** the complement of the declination

code duello *n, pl* **codes duello** *or* **code duellos** [*code* + *duello;* after such terms as *Code Napoléon*] **:** the rules of etiquette governing duels

co·defendant \ˌkō+\ *n* **:** a joint defendant

code flag *n* **:** one of the flags patterned for maximum visibility that are used to exchange messages between ships at sea, the distinctive pattern of each flag symbolizing a particular letter, word, or phrase

code group *n, cryptology* **:** the significant unit of code text usu. a group of letters or numerals (as XEQSJ)

co·dehydrogenase I \ˌkō+ . . . ˈwən\ *n* [*co-* + *dehydrogenase*] **:** DIPHOSPHOPYRIDINE NUCLEOTIDE

co·dehydrogenase II \" + . . . ˈtü\ *n* **:** TRIPHOSPHOPYRIDINE NUCLEOTIDE

co·deine \ˈkō(ˌ)dēn, -ˌdēən, -dē,ēn\ *n* -s [F *codéine*, fr. Gk *kōdeia* poppyhead (fr. *kōos* cavity) + F *-ine* -ine; akin to Gk *koilos* hollow — more at CAVE] **:** a crystalline alkaloid $C_{18}H_{21}NO_3.H_2O$ associated in opium with morphine, usu. made from morphine, and similar to the latter but feebler in its action; morphine methyl ether

code·less \ˈkōdləs\ *adj* **:** lacking a code **:** not regulated by a code

co·den \ˈkōdᵊn\ *n, pl* **coden** [irreg. fr. ¹*code*] **:** a code classification assigned to a document or other library item consisting typically of four capital letters followed by two hyphenated groups of arabic numerals

code name *n* **:** a word made to serve as a code designation disguising single items in otherwise intelligible discourse

cod end *n* [¹*cod*] **:** COD 4

code pennant *n* **:** an answering pennant used in the International Signal Code when hoisted under the ensign to denote a signal taken from the International Code

code pleading *n, law* **:** pleading done in accordance with the rules set forth in a code

cod·er \ˈkōdə(r)\ *n* -s **1 :** one that codes: as **a :** a device for putting information into a form (as on the perforated tape fed into an automatic telegraph keyer) that facilitates its transmission in code over a communication circuit **b :** one that translates information or instructions into the code of an automatic computer **2 :** any of a number of esp. electronic devices that translate one set of impulses into another set often of a different kind: as **a :** a device to change or modulate an electric current (as on a track) so that it will operate corresponding controls on a car or other apparatus **b :** a telephone relay device by which a given set of signals (as a dialed telephone number) actuates a selective set of electronic processes **c :** an electronic device by which a number of single-pole single-throw switches can actuate a number of parallel, overlapping, or interrelated circuits **d :** an electronic device used in airplanes for sending coded identification signals **e :** a unit in a radar receiver that translates a simple impulse from a receiver into several impulses

codes *pl of* CODE, *pres 3d sing of* CODE

co·determination \ˌkō+\ *n* [*co-* + *determination*] **:** the participation of labor with management in the determination of business policy; *specif* **:** the legally required participation of labor representatives in the ultimate decision-making body (as a board of directors) of large West German industrial corporations

co·det·ta \kōˈdedə, -etə\ *n* -s [It, dim. of *coda* tail — more at CODA] **1 :** a short coda **2 :** a musical passage connecting the parts of a movement or the entries in a fugue

code wheel *n* **:** CIPHER DISK

code word *n* **1 :** CODE NAME **2 :** CODE GROUP

co·dex \ˈkō,deks\ *n, pl* **co·di·ces** \ˈkōdə,sēz, ˈkäd-\ [L — more at CODE] **1** *obs* **:** CODE 1, 2 **2 :** a usu. ancient book or unbound sheets in manuscript esp. of Scripture, Greek and Latin classics, or ancient mythological or historical annals — distinguished from *scroll* **3 :** a collection of drug formulas ⟨a ~ similar to the British Pharmaceutical Codex⟩

codex re·scrip·tus \-rəˈskriptəs, -rē-\ *n* [NL, lit., rewritten codex] **:** PALIMPSEST 2

cod family *or* **codfish family** *n* [³*cod*] **:** GADIDAE

codfish \ˈ=,=\ *n* [³*cod* + *fish*] **1 :** ³COD **2 :** the flesh of the cod used as food esp. when cured or salted

codfish aristocracy *n* **1 :** the social aristocracy of the Massachusetts families enriched from the trade in codfish **2 :** an esp. parvenu aristocracy based on commercial success

codg·er \ˈkäjə(r)\ *n* -s [prob. var. of *cadger*] **:** FELLOW, CHAP — usu. used of the aged as an affectionate or mildly derogatory term ⟨a nice old ~⟩ ⟨pompous old ~ —Claud Cockburn⟩

codhead \ˈ=,=\ *n* [³*cod* + *head*; fr. the shape of the flowers] **:** TURTLEHEAD

co·di·a·ce·ae \ˌkōdēˈāsē,ē\ *n pl, cap* [NL, fr. *Codium*, type genus + *-aceae*] **:** a family of marine coenocytic green algae (order Siphonales) — **co·di·a·ceous** \ˌ=ˌ=ˈshəs\ *adj*

co·di·ae·um \ˌ==ˈēəm\ *n, cap* [NL, prob. fr. Malay *kodiho*] **:** a small genus of Indo-Malayan trees and shrubs of the family Euphorbiaceae having thick leathery highly colored often variegated leaves — see CROTON 2

co·di·a·les \-ˈā(ˌ)lēz\ [NL, fr. *Codium* + *-ales*] *syn of* SIPHONALES

cod·i·cal \ˈkädəkəl\ *adj* [L *codic-*, *codex* + E *-al*] **:** of or relating to a codex or code

codices *pl of* CODEX

cod·i·cil \ˈkädəsəl\ *n* -s [MF *codicille*, fr. L *codicillus*, dim. of *codic-*, *codex* book — more at CODE] **1 a :** a legal instrument made subsequently to a will and modifying it in some respects, executed in the same manner as the will itself and forming a part of it, superseding it so far as inconsistent with it **b** *Roman law* **:** an informal will that could not institute an heir but could set forth instructions binding upon the heirs and could give legacies, that was initially free from specific requirements (as the appointment of executors) and made orally or in writing often before a public official, but that was later required to be witnessed by five citizens if oral or signed if in writing **c :** a provision, as of a document, made subsequently to and appended to the original **d :** APPENDIX, SUPPLEMENT **2 a** *obs* **:** a writing tablet **b** *archaic* **:** ³LETTER 2

cod·i·cil·lary \ˌ==ˈsilərē, -ri\ *adj* [F *codicillaire*, fr. *codicille* codicil + *-aire* -ary] **:** of, being, or belonging to a codicil

cod·i·fi·ca·tion \ˌkädəfəˈkāshən, -ōd-\ *n* -s **:** the act of codifying or being codified

cod·i·fy \ˈkädə,fī, ˈkōd-\ *vt* -ED/-ING/-ES [¹*code* (body of laws) + *-ify*] **1 :** to reduce to a code (as laws) **2 a :** SYSTEMATIZE **:** arrange in systematic or comprehensible order **b :** to make an appropriate part of a system or classification **:** CLASSIFY

co·di·mer \(ˈ)kōˈdīmə(r)\ *n* -s [*co-* + *dimer*] **:** a copolymer formed from two dissimilar molecules (as two olefins); *specif, in petroleum refining* **:** the mixture of hydrocarbons formed by the copolymerization of the butylenes which on hydrogenation yields a mixture of octanes used as a blending agent in aviation gasoline

coding *pres part of* CODE

co·directional \ˌkō +\ *adj* [*co-* + *directional*] **:** coinciding in direction

co·di·um \ˈkōdēəm\ *n, cap* [NL, fr. Gk *kōdion* fleece, dim. of *kōas*; fr. the fleecy thallus; perh. akin to L *cutis* skin — more at HIDE] **:** a genus (the type of the family Codiaceae) of green algae having a tubular thallus made up of interwoven threads that often end in club-shaped cells and often branching or forming spherical or cushion-shaped masses

codl *abbr* codicil

cod line *n* [³*cod*] **:** an 18-thread line used esp. in cod fishing

¹cod·ling \ˈkädliŋ\ *n, pl* **codlings** *also* **codling** [ME, fr. ³*cod* + *-ling*] **1 :** a young cod **2 :** ¹HAKE 2

²codling \" *or* **codlin** \-lən\ *n* -s [alter. of ME *querdlyng*] **:** a small immature or inferior apple used chiefly for cooking; *also* **:** any of several elongated greenish English cooking apples — compare COSTARD, PIPPIN

³codling \-liŋ\ *n* -s [origin unknown] **:** a balk sawed in lengths to be cleft into staves

codling moth *or* **codlin moth** *n* [²*codling*] **:** a small moth (*Carpocapsa*, or *Cydia, pomonella*) having a larva that lives in apples, pears, quinces, and English walnuts, often doing great damage, leaves the fruit to hibernate, and pupates in the spring

cod·lins and cream \-lənz-\ *n* [alter. of ²*codling*; fr. the smell of the leaves and flowers when crushed] *dial Eng* **:** FIREWEED b

cod–liver meal *n* [³*cod*] **:** the ground residue of the cod liver after the extraction of the oil

cod–liver oil *n* **:** a pale yellow fatty oil obtained from the liver of the cod and related fishes and used in medicine chiefly as a source of vitamins A and D in conditions due to abnormal calcium and phosphorus metabolism (as rickets, infantile tetany, osteomalacia) — see COD OIL

cod·man \ˈkädmən\ *n, pl* **codmen** [³*cod* + *man* (vessel)] **:** a ship used in fishing for cod

cod net *n* [¹*cod*] **:** a net with a cod (sense 4)

cod oil *n* [³*cod*] **:** a dark-colored inferior cod-liver oil used in leather manufacture

co·dominance \(ˈ)kō +\ *n* -s **:** the quality or state of being codominant

¹co·dominant \" +\ *adj* [*co-* + *dominant*] **1** *of trees* **:** forming part of the main canopy of a forest — compare DOMINANT **2** *of kinds of organisms* **:** sharing in the controlling influence of a biotic community **:** present in equal and highest frequency with some other kind of organism ⟨a forest in which spruce and fir are ~⟩

²codominant \" \ *n* -s **:** a codominant individual or kind of organism; *esp* **:** a codominant plant

codpiece \ˈ=,=\ *n* [ME *kodpese*, fr. *kod*, *cod* (testis) + *pese*, *pece* piece] **1 :** an often ornamented flap or bag concealing an opening in the front of men's breeches esp. in the 15th and 16th centuries **2** *obs* **:** PENIS

cods *pl of* COD, *pres 3d sing of* COD

cod smack *n* [³*cod* + *smack* (vessel)] **:** CODMAN

codworm \ˈ=,=\ *n* [¹*cod*; fr. the case or tube in which it lives] **:** CADDISWORM

¹coe \ˈkō\ *n* -s [D *kooi*, lit., cage, fr. MD *cōie*, *coie*, fr. L *cavea* cage, den, cave, fr. *cavus* hollow — more at CAVE] *dial Eng* **:** a small hut or shack over a mine shaft

²coe \", ˈkȯ\ *n* -s [ME *cothe*, fr. OE *cothu*] *dial Eng* **:** a disease of sheep; *usu* **:** LIVER ROT

³coe \"\ *vt* -ED/-ING/-S *dial Eng* **:** to infest with coe

COE *abbr* cab-over-engine

coecilian *var of* CAECILIAN

coecum *var of* CECUM

¹co–ed \ˈkō¦ed *sometimes* =ˈ=\ *n* -s [short for *coeducational* (*student*)] **:** a female student in a coeducational institution

²co–ed \"\ *adj* **1 :** COEDUCATIONAL ⟨*co-ed* schools⟩ **2 :** of, for, relating to, or being a co-ed ⟨*co-ed* hairdos⟩ **3 :** for both men and women ⟨a bill that would make the Army and Air National Guard *co-ed* —*Springfield* (*Mass.*) *Union*⟩

co·editor \(ˈ)kō+\ *n* [*co-* + *editor*] **:** one who collaborates with another in editing a newspaper, magazine, or book

co·educate \(ˈ)kō+\ *vt* [back-formation fr. *coeducation*] **1 :** to subject to coeducation **2 :** to train (the different senses) to coordinated reaction

co·education \(ˌ)kō+\ *n* -s [*co-* + *education*] **:** the education of students of both sexes at the same institution, esp. a college or university — **co·educational** \" +\ *adj* — **co·educationally** \" +\ *adv*

¹co·efficient \ˌkō+\ *adj* [*co-* + *efficient*] **:** acting together to produce an effect — **co·efficiently** \" +\ *adv*

²coefficient \"\ *n* -s [NL *coefficient-*, *coefficiens*, fr. L *co-* + *efficient-*, *efficiens* — more at EFFICIENT] **1 :** something that unites in action to produce an effect **:** a joint agent **2 :** any of the factors (as constants) of a product considered in relation to another factor (as a variable) ⟨in $6x$, bx, $x(a+b)$, $3xyz$ the ~*s* of x are respectively 6, b, $(a+b)$, $3yz$⟩ **3 a :** a number that serves as a measure of some property (as of a substance or body) or characteristic (as of a device or process) and that is commonly used as a factor in computations ⟨the ~ of expansion of a metal⟩ ⟨the absorption ~ of a medium for light⟩ ⟨the coupling ~ of a transformer⟩ **b :** MEASURE, DEGREE ⟨a ~ of culture that greatly surpassed the cultural mean —V.V.Nabokov⟩ ⟨~*s* of feeling —C.I.Glicksberg⟩

coefficient of absorption : ABSORPTION COEFFICIENT

coefficient of compressibility : the decrease in volume per unit volume (as of a gas) produced by a unit change in pressure

coefficient of contingency : a measure of association between statistical variables which have quantitative categories of unequal magnitude or at least one of which can be classified only qualitatively

coefficient of contraction *physics* **:** the ratio of the cross-sectional area of the first vena contracta to the area of the discharge aperture

coefficient of correlation : CORRELATION COEFFICIENT

coefficient of discharge : the ratio of the actual discharge to the ideal discharge, assuming unit coefficients of contraction and velocity, equal to the product of these coefficients

coefficient of elasticity : MODULUS OF ELASTICITY

coefficient of expansion : the ratio of the increase of length, area, or volume of a body per degree rise in temperature to its length, area, or volume, respectively, at some specified temperature, commonly 0°C, the pressure being kept constant — called also *expansivity*

coefficient of friction : the ratio of the tangential force that is needed to start or to maintain uniform relative motion between two contacting surfaces to the perpendicular force holding them in contact, the ratio usu. being larger for starting than for moving friction

coefficient of inbreeding *or* **coefficient of relation :** a measure of the degree of inbreeding of an individual expressed as the percentage homozygous in that individual of characters heterozygous in the general population of its kind

coefficient of kinematic viscosity : the ratio of the coefficient of viscosity to the density of a fluid — compare ²STOKE

coefficient of leakage : the ratio of total magnetic flux to useful flux

coefficient of racial likeness : a measure of the resemblance between two races as determined by a comparison of measurements taken on two or more series of skulls

coefficient of resistance : the ratio of the loss of head to the remaining head of a fluid discharging through an orifice or over a weir

coefficient of restitution : the ratio of the relative velocity of two elastic bodies after rebounding to that before impact

coefficient of variation *or* **coefficient of variability :** the ratio of the measure of variability, usu. the standard deviation, to an average, usu. the arithmetical mean, about which the variation occurs

coefficient of velocity : the ratio of the actual velocity to the theoretical velocity of a fluid jet

coefficient of viscosity : the ratio of the tangential frictional force per unit area to the velocity gradient perpendicular to the direction of flow of a liquid **:** the ratio of the shearing stress in a moving fluid to the time rate of shearing strain

coehorn *var of* COHORN

coeing *pres part of* COE

coel– *or* **coelo–** *also* **cel–** *or* **celo–** *comb form* [NL, fr. Gk *koil-*, *koilo-*, fr. *koilos* hollow — more at CAVE] **:** hollow **:** cavity ⟨*coelodont*⟩ ⟨*coelozoic*⟩

¹coe·la·canth \ˈsēlə,kanth\ *or* **coe·la·can·thid** \ˌ=ˌ=ˈkan(t)thəd\ *adj* [NL *Coelacanthidae*] **:** of or belonging to the family Coelacanthidae

²coelacanth \" *also* **coelacanthid** \"\ *n* -s **:** a fish or fossil of the family Coelacanthidae

coe·la·can·thi·dae \ˌsēləˈkan(t)thə,dē\ *n pl, cap* [NL, fr. *Coelacanthus*, type genus (fr. *coel-* + *-acanthus*) + *-idae*] **:** a family of crossopterygian fishes usu. regarded as coextensive with the order Actinistia — compare LATIMERIA — **coe·la·can·thine** \ˌ=ˌ=ˈkan,thīn, -an(t)thən\ *adj* — **coe·la·can·thoid** \-an,thȯid\ *adj or n* — **coelacanthous** \-an(t)_thəs\ *adj*

coe·la·can·thi·ni \-thə,nī\ [NL, fr. *coel-* + *acanth-* + *-ini*] *syn of* ACTINISTIA

coe·lan·a·glyph·ic relief \(ˈ)sē¦lanəˈglifik-\ *n* [F *coilanaglyphique*, fr. *coilanaglyphe* (fr. Gk *koilos* hollow + *anaglyphe* anaglyph) + *-ique* -ic — more at CAVE, ANAGLYPH] **:** SUNK RELIEF

coe·la·ta \səˈlād·ə, sē-\ *n pl, cap* [NL, fr. *coel-* + *-ata*] *in some classifications* **:** a group comprising all Turbellaria with an intestine — distinguished from *Acoela*

-coele *or* **-coel** *also* **-cele** *n comb form* -s [prob. fr. NL *-coela*, fr. neut. pl. of *-coelus* -coelous)] **:** cavity **:** chamber **:** ventricle ⟨*endocoele*⟩ ⟨*neurocoele*⟩

coe·lel·min·tha \ˌsēlelˈmin(t)thə\ *or* **coe·lel·min·thes** \-min(ˌ)thēz\ *syn of* COELHELMINTHES

coe·len·tera \səˈlentərə, sē-\ [NL, by shortening] *syn of* COELENTERATA

coe·len·ter·a·ta \səˌlentəˈräd·ə, sē-\ *n pl, cap* [NL, fr. *coel-* + Gk *enteron* intestine + NL *-ata* — more at INTER-] **:** a phylum or other major division of more or less radially symmetrical invertebrate animals lacking a true body cavity and including hydroids, jellyfishes, sea anemones, corals, and formerly sponges and ctenophores — see ANTHOZOA, HYDROZOA, SCYPHOZOA — **coe·len·ter·ate** \(ˈ)sē¦lentə,rāt, sə¦-\ *adj or n* — **coe·len·ter·ic** \¦sē=¦terik\ *adj*

coe·len·ter·on *or* **ce·len·ter·on** \=ˈlentə,rän\ *n, pl* **coelentera** *or* **ce·len·tera** \-rə\ [NL, fr. *coel-* + Gk *enteron* intestine] **:** the internal cavity of a coelenterate

coelestine *var of* CELESTINE

coel·hel·minth \(ˈ)sēl¦helmin(t)th\ *n* -s [NL *Coelhelminthes*] **:** one of the Coelhelminthes

coel·hel·min·thes \¦sēl+\ *n pl, cap* [NL, fr. *coel-* + *Helminthes*] *in some classifications* **:** a major division of Metazoa including diverse coelomate vermiform invertebrate animals — **coel·hel·min·thic** \" +\ *adj*

coeli– *or* **coelio–** *also* **celi–** *or* **celio–** *comb form* [Gk *koili-*, *koilio-*, fr. *koilia* cavity of the body, belly] **:** belly **:** abdomen ⟨*coelialgia*⟩ ⟨*coelioscopy*⟩

coe·lia \ˈsēlēə\ *n, pl* **coeli·ae** \-ē,ē,-ē,ī\ [NL, fr. Gk *koilia*] **:** a body cavity esp. of the brain

¹coe·li·ac *or* **ce·li·ac** \ˈsēlē,ak\ *adj* [L *coeliacus*, fr. Gk *koiliakos*, fr. *koilia* cavity, belly, fr. *koilos* hollow — more at CAVE] **:** of, located in, or belonging to the cavity of the abdomen

²coeliac *n* -s **:** a coeliac part (as an artery or nerve)

coeliac artery *or* **coeliac axis** *n* **:** a short thick artery arising from the aorta just below the diaphragm and dividing almost immediately into the gastric, hepatic, and splenic branches

coeliac ganglion *n* **:** either of a pair of collateral sympathetic ganglia, the largest of the autonomic system, lying one on each side of the coeliac artery near the suprarenal gland

coeliac plexus *n* **:** SOLAR PLEXUS

coe·lic·o·list \səˈlikələst, sē-\ *n* -s *usu cap* [L *coelicola*, *caelicola* heaven-worshiper (fr. *coelum*, *caelum* heaven, sky + *colere* to worship, cultivate, dwell) + E *-ist* — more at -HOOD, WHEEL] **:** one of an obscure heretical sect of the 4th and 5th centuries combining Jewish and Christian doctrines

coe·lin \ˈsēlən\ *or* **coe·line** \-,lēn,-,lən\ *n* -s [ISV *coel-* (fr. L *coelum*, *caelum* sky) + *-in* or *-ine*] **:** CERULEAN BLUE 1b

coelo– — see COEL-

coe·lo·blast \ˈsēlə,blast, -lō,-\ *n* -s [*coel-* + *-blast*; trans. of G *darmdrüsenblatt*] **:** HYPOBLAST

coe·lo·blas·tic \¦=ˌ=¦blastik\ *adj* **:** of, relating to, or derived from the hypoblast

coe·lo·blastula \ˌ== + \ *n* [NL, fr. *coel-* + *blastula*] **:** a hollow blastula — compare BLASTOCOEL

coe·lo·coc·cus \ˈ==,käkəs\ *n, cap* [NL, fr. *coel-* + *-coccus*] **:** a small genus of Polynesian pinnate-leaved palms — see APPLENUT

coe·lo·gastrula \ˌ== + \ *n* [NL, fr. *coel-* + *gastrula*] **:** a typical gastrula derived from a coeloblastula

coe·log·y·ne \səˈläjə(ˌ)nē, sē-\ *n* [NL, fr. *coel-* + Gk *gynē* woman; fr. the hollow stigma — more at QUEEN] **1** *cap* **:** a large genus of tropical Asiatic epiphytic orchids having mostly yellow or white flowers with membranaceous perianth **2** -s **:** a plant of the genus *Coelogyne*

coe·lo·lep·id \ˈsēlə,lepəd, -lō,-\ *n* -s [NL *Coelolepida*] **:** an ostracoderm of the order Coelolepida

coe·lo·lep·i·da \ˌ==ˈlepədə\ *n pl, cap* [NL, fr. *Coelolepid-*, *Coelolepis*, genus of ostracoderms (fr. *coel-* + *-lepis*) + *-ida*] *in some classifications* **:** an order of very small scaly Silurian and Lower Devonian ostracoderms

coe·lom \ˈsēləm\ *also* **coe·lome** \-,lōm,-ləm\ *or* **ce·lom** \-ləm\ *n, pl* **coeloms** \-mz\ *or* **coe·lo·ma·ta** \səˈlōmədə, -ām-\ [G *zölom*, *coelom*, fr. Gk *koilōma* cavity, fr. *koilos* hollow — more at CAVE] **:** the body cavity or perivisceral cavity of metazoans above the lower worms usu. being lined by a distinct epithelium and where well developed forming a large space between the alimentary viscera and the body walls — compare HEMOCOEL, HEMOCOELOM, PSEUDOCOEL

coe·lo·ma·ta \səˈlōməd·ə, sē-, -ām-\ *n pl, cap* [NL, fr. *coeloma* coelom (fr. Gk *koilōma* cavity) + *-ata*] *in some classifications* **:** a group including all Metazoa except sponges and coelenterates

¹coe·lo·mate \ˈsēlə,māt, sēˈlōmət\ *or* **coe·lom·a·tous** \(ˈ)sē¦lämədəs, -ōm-\ *adj* **:** having a coelom

²coelomate \"\ *n* -s [NL *Coelomata*] **:** a coelomate animal **:** one of the Coelomata

¹coe·lo·mat·ic \ˌsēlə¦mad·ik, -lō-\ *adj* **:** COELOMIC

²coelomatic \"\ *n* -s [NL *Coelomata* + E *-ic*] **:** COELOMATE

coe·lo·mesoblast \ˌsēlō, -lə + \ *n* [*coel-* + *mesoblast*] **:** MESOTHELIUM

coe·lom·ic *or* **ce·lom·ic** \səˈlämik, (ˈ)sē¦-\ *adj* [ISV *coelom*, *celom* + *-ic*] **:** of, relating to, or found in the coelom

coe·lo·mo·coe·la \ˌsēlōməˈsēlə, -ləm- sə¦lō-\ *n pl, cap* [NL, fr. *coelom* + *-o-* + *-coela* (neut. pl. of *-coelus*)] *syn of* COELOMATA

coe·lo·mo·cyte \ˈsē(ˌ)lōmə,sīt, -lə-, səˈlō-\ *n* -s [ISV *coelom* + *-o-* + *-cyte*] **:** a cell free in the coelom esp. of an invertebrate animal — compare AMOEBOCYTE, ELEOCYTE

coe·lo·mo·duct \-,dəkt\ *n* [*coelom* + *-o-* + *duct*] **:** an excretory and genital duct that is typical of certain invertebrates (as annelid worms) and has a wide and usu. ciliated lumen opening into the coelom by a broad funnel and terminating externally by a small pore in the body wall

coe·lo·mo·my·ces \ˌsē(ˌ)lōməˈmī,sēz, -ˌlə-, sə,lō-\ *n, cap* [NL, fr. ISV *coelom* + NL *-o-* + *-myces*] **:** a genus (coextensive with the family Coelomomycetaceae of the order Blastocladiales) of water molds that have naked mycelium without rhizoids and that live as parasites on insects (as mosquitoes)

coe·lo·mo·stome \ˈsē(ˌ)lōmə,stōm, -lə-, səˈlō-\ *n* -s [*coelom* + *-o-* + *-stome*] **:** the coelomic opening of a coelomoduct

coe·lo·my·ar·i·an \¦=(ˌ)=mī¦a(a)rēən\ *adj* [*coel-* + *my-* + *-arian*] *of nematode muscle cells* **:** having the myofibrils extending centrally in the periphery of the cell and partially enclosing the sarcoplasm — compare PLATYMYARIAN

coe·lo·phy·sis \sēˈläfəsəs, -ləf-, -səs\ *n, cap* [NL, fr. *coel-* + Gk *physis* nature, appearance — more at PHYSIC] **:** a genus of small primitive carnivorous saurischian dinosaurs (suborder Theropoda) of the Upper Triassic of No. America

coe·lo·pi·dae \səˈlōpə,dē, sē-\ *n pl, cap* [NL, fr. *Coelopa*, type genus (fr. *coel-* + *-opa*, fr. Gk *ōp-*, *ōps* face, eye) + *-idae* — more at EYE] **:** a small family of acalyptrate muscoid flies that have flattened bodies and frequent seashores — see KELP FLY

coe·lo·planula \ˌsēlə, -lō + \ *n* [NL, fr. *coel-* + *planula*] *zool* **:** a hollow planula with a wall of two layers

coe·lo·stat \ˈ==,stat\ *n* -s [ISV *coelo-* (fr. ML *caelum* sky, heaven, fr. L *caelum* heaven) + *-stat*] **:** an instrument consisting of an adjustable plane mirror clock-driven on an axis parallel to the axis of the earth and a second fixed mirror that act together to send light from a celestial body in a fixed direction — compare HELIOSTAT

-coelous *adj comb form* [NL *-coelus*, fr. Gk *-koilos* hollow, concave, fr. *koilos* — more at CAVE] **1 :** cavitied ⟨dendrocoelous⟩ **2 :** concave ⟨procoelous⟩ ⟨opisthocoelous⟩

coe·lo·zoic \ˌsēləˈzōik, -lō-\ *adj* [*coel-* + *-zoic*] **:** inhabiting a cavity of an animal's body

coe·lur·o·saur \səˈlu̇rə,sȯ(ə)r, sē-\ *also* **coe·lur·o·sau·ri·an** \=¦==ˈsȯrēən\ *n* -s [NL *Coelurosauria*] **:** a dinosaur of the subdivision Coelurosauria

coe·lur·o·sau·ria \=,==ˈsȯrēə\ *n pl, cap* [NL, fr. *coel-* + *ur-* + *-sauria*] **:** a subdivision of Theropoda (order Saurischia) comprising a number of small primitive generalized bipedal dinosaurs of the Upper Triassic, Jurassic, and Cretaceous

co·emp·tio \kōˈempshē(ˌ)ō, -emptē-\ *n* -s [L] *Roman law* **:** a ceremony symbolizing the sale of a woman to a man and bringing the woman under the manus of the man usu. (1) as a plebeian marriage but sometimes (2) as a device of the woman to displace her guardian — called also respectively (1) *coemptio matrimoni causa*, (2) *coemptio fiduciae causa*

co·emp·tion \kōˈempshən\ *n* -s [L *coemption-*, *coemptio* coemption, coemptio, fr. *coemptus*, past part. of *coemere* to buy up (fr. *co-* + *emere* to buy) + *-ion-*, *-io* -ion — more at REDEEM] *obs* **:** purchase of all supplies of a commodity in the market esp. to gain a monopoly — **co·emp·tive** \(ˈ)kō¦emptiv, -ēv\ *adj*

coen– *or* **coeno–** *also* **cen–** *or* **ceno–** *or* **caen–** *or* **caeno–** *comb form* [NL, fr. Gk *koin-*, *koino-*, fr. *koinos* — more at CO-] **:** common **:** general ⟨*coenoblast*⟩ ⟨*coenesthesia*⟩

coe·na·gri·idae \ˌsēnəˈgrīə,dē, ,sen-\ *n pl, cap* [NL, fr. *Coenagria*, type genus (fr. *coen-* + *-agria*, fr. Gk *agrios* wild) + *-idae*] **:** a large cosmopolitan family of damselflies

coe·na·gri·on·i·dae \-,grīˈänə,dē\ [NL] *syn of* COENAGRIIDAE
co·en·di·dae \kōˈendə,dē\ [NL, fr. *Coendou*, type genus + *-idae*] *syn of* ERETHIZONTIDAE
co·en·dou \kōˈen(,)dü\ *n* [NL, fr. Tupi *coendu*] **1** *cap* **:** a genus (family Erethizontidae) comprising the prehensile-tailed porcupines of Central and So. America **2** -s **:** a member of the genus *Coendou*
coe·nen·chy·ma \sə̇ˈneŋkəmə, sē-\ *n, pl* **coenen·chym·a·ta** \,sēneŋˈkiməd·ə\ [NL, fr. *coen-* + *-enchyma*] **:** COENENCHYME
coe·nen·chy·mal \sə̇ˈneŋkəməl, ˈsē;-\ *or* **coe·nen·chym·a·tous** \;sēneŋ;kiməd·əs\ *adj* [*coenenchymal* fr. *coenenchyme* + *-al*; *coenenchymatous* fr. NL *coenenchymat-, coenenchyma* + E *-ous*] **:** of, relating to, or being coenenchyme
coe·nen·chyme \sə̇ˈneŋ,kīm, sē-\ *or* **coe·nen·chym** \-,kə̇m\ *n* -s [NL *coenenchyma*] **:** the complex mesogloea uniting the polyps of a compound anthozoan
coe·nes·the·sia \,sēnesˈthēzh(ē)ə, ,sen-\ *or* **coe·nes·the·sis** \-thēsə̇s\ *or* **ce·nes·the·sia** \-ˈthēzh(ē)ə\ *n, pl* **coenesthesias** \-əz\ *or* **coenesthe·ses** \-ē,sēz\ *or* **cenesthesias** \-əz\ [NL, fr. *coen-* + *esthesia, esthesis*] **:** the totality of sensations arising from bodily organs through which one perceives his own body
coe·nes·thet·ic \;==;thed·ik\ *adj* **:** of or relating to coenesthesia
coe·no·bi·ar *or* **ce·no·bi·ar** \sə̇ˈnōbēə(r), (ˈ)sē;-\ *adj* [NL *coenobium*, *cenobium* + E *-ar*] **:** of or relating to a coenobium
coe·no·bi·oid \-,ȯid\ *adj* [NL *coenobium* + E *-oid*] **:** like a coenobium
coenobite *var of* CENOBITE
coe·no·bi·um *or* **ce·no·bi·um** \sə̇ˈnōbēəm, sē-\ *n, pl* **coenobia** *or* **ceno·bia** \-ēə\ [LL *coenobium* — more at CENOBY] **1 :** CENOBY **2** *also* **coe·nobe** *or* **ce·nobe** \ˈsē(,)nōb, ˈse(,)-\ -s [NL, fr. LL] **:** a usu. spherical colony of unicellular organisms surrounded by a common investment; *esp* **:** a colony having a definite number and specific arrangement of cells
coe·no·blast \ˈsēnə,blast, -en-, -nō-\ *n* -s [ISV *coen-* + *-blast*; orig. formed as G *zönoblastem*] **:** MESENDODERM — **coe·no·blas·tic** \;==;=ik\ *adj*
coenoby *var of* CENOBY
coe·no·car·pic \;==;kärpik\ *also* **coe·no·car·pous** \-pəs\ *adj* [*coen-* + *-carp* + *-ic* or *-ous*] **:** SYNCARPOUS — **coe·no·car·py** \ˈ==,=pē\ *n* -ES
coe·no·cen·trum \,==ˈsen·trəm\ *n, pl* **coenocen·tra** \-trə\ [NL, fr. *coen-* + L *centrum* center] **:** a dense deep-staining cytoplasmic structure in the egg cells of certain fungi
coe·no·cyte \ˈ==,sīt\ *n* -s [ISV *coen-* + *-cyte*] **1 a :** a multinucleate mass of protoplasm resulting from repeated nuclear division unaccompanied by cell fission **b :** an organism (as certain algae) consisting of such a structure — compare PLASMODIUM **2 :** SYNCYTIUM 1 — **coe·no·cyt·ic** \;==;sid·ik, -itik\ *adj*
coe·noe·ci·um \sə̇ˈnēs(h)ēəm, sē-\ *n, pl* **coenoe·cia** \-ēə\ [NL, fr. *coen-* + Gk *oikion* house (fr. *oikos*) — more at VICINITY] **:** the common often chitinous or calcareous investment of a bryozoan colony
coe·no·gamete \;sēnə, -enə, -nō+\ *n* [*coen-* + *gamete*] *bot* **:** a multinucleate gamete
coenogenesis *var of* CENOGENESIS
coenogonous *var of* CENOGONOUS
coe·no·les·tes \,==ˈle(,)stēz\ *syn of* CAENOLESTES
coe·nop·ter·i·da·les \,sē(,)näp,terəˈdā(,)lēz, ,se-\ *n pl, cap* [NL, fr. *coen-* + Gk *pterid-, pteris* fern + NL *-ales* — more at PTERIS] **:** an order of extinct Devonian and Carboniferous ferns that is usu. considered as part of or coextensive with the subclass Primofilices and that has both simple and pinnate leaves with the latter having pinnae at an angle to the plane of the leaf blade
coe·no·sarc \ˈsēnə,särk, -en-, -nō-\ *n* -s [*coen-* + Gk *sark-, sarx* flesh — more at SARCASM] **1 :** the hollow living tube consisting of hydrocaulus and stolons that connects the zooids of a hydroid colony **2 :** COENENCHYME
coenospecies *var of* CENOSPECIES
coe·nos·te·um \sə̇ˈnästēəm, sē-\ *n, pl* **coenos·tea** \-ēə\ [NL, fr. *coen-* + Gk *osteon* bone — more at OSSEOUS] **:** the calcareous skeleton of a compound coral or a bryozoan colony
coe·no·the·ca·lia \,sēnəthəˈkālēə, -en- -nō-\ *n pl, cap* [NL, fr. *coen-* + *thec-* + *-alia*] **:** an order of massive calcareous corals including solely the blue corals of the Indo-Pacific
coe·no·type \ˈ==,tīp\ *n* [*coen-* + *type*] *biol* **:** an organism having the type of structure fundamental to a group — **coe·no·typ·ic** \;==;tipik\ *adj*
coe·no·zygote \,==+\ *n* [*coen-* + *zygote*] **:** the product of fusion of two coenogametes
coe·nu·ro·sis \,sēnyəˈrōsə̇s, -en-\ *or* **coe·nu·ri·a·sis** \-ˈrīəsə̇s\ *n, pl* **coenuro·ses** \-ō,sēz\ *or* **coenuria·ses** \-ə,sēz\ [NL *coenurus* + *-osis* or *-iasis*] **:** infestation with or disease caused by coenuri (as gid of sheep)
coe·nu·rus \sə̇ˈn(y)ürəs, sē-\ *n, pl* **coenu·ri** \-,rī,-(,)rē\ [NL, fr. *coen-* + *-urus*] **:** a complex tapeworm larva growing interstitially in vertebrate tissues and consisting of a large fluid-filled sac from the inner wall of which numerous scolices develop — see GID, MULTICEPS; compare CYSTICERCOID, CYSTICERCUS, HYDATID
co·enzyme \(ˈ)kō+\ *n* [*co-* + *enzyme*] **:** any thermostable nonprotein compound (as cocarboxylase) that forms the active portion of an enzyme system after combination with an apoenzyme — compare PROSTHETIC
coenzyme A \-ˈā\ *n* **:** a coenzyme $C_{21}H_{36}N_7O_{16}P_3S$ occurring in all living cells that is essential to the metabolism of carbohydrates, fats, and some amino acids and in the form of its acetyl or other acyl derivatives promotes biological acetylations or other acylations and that is a nucleotide consisting of a pyrophosphoric ester of both adenylic acid and pantetheine — called also *CoA*
coenzyme I \-ˈwən\ *n* **:** DIPHOSPHOPYRIDINE NUCLEOTIDE
coenzyme R *n* **:** BIOTIN
coenzyme II \-ˈtü\ *n* **:** TRIPHOSPHOPYRIDINE NUCLEOTIDE
co·equal \(ˈ)kō+\ *adj* [ME, fr. *co-* + *equal*] **:** equal with one another (as in rank, power, age, or extent) ⟨a confederacy of ~ sovereign states —S.E.Morison & H.S.Commager⟩ — **co·equality** \;kō+\ *n* -ES — **coequally** \(ˈ)kō+\ *adv*
co·erce \kōˈərs, -ˈəs, -ˈəis\ *vt* -ED/-ING/-S [L *coercēre*, fr. *co-* + *arcēre* to shut up, enclose — more at ARK] **1 :** to restrain, control, or dominate, nullifying individual will or desire (as by force, power, violence, or intimidation) ⟨religion has in the past tried to ~ the irreligious, by garish promises and terrifying threats —W.R.Inge⟩ **2 :** to compel to an act or choice by force, threat, or other pressure ⟨a person might no longer be *coerced* into an agreement not to join an union —*Amer. Guide Series: Mass.*⟩ **3 :** to effect, bring about, establish, or enforce by force, threat, or other pressure ⟨struggles to ~ uniformity of sentiment —Felix Frankfurter⟩ **syn** see FORCE
co·erc·i·ble \-səbəl\ *adj* [*coerce* + *-ible*] **1 :** capable of being coerced **2 :** COMPRESSIBLE; *specif* **:** condensable to a liquid state
co·er·cion \-ˈərzhən, -ˈəl, -ˈəil, |shən\ *n* -s [ME *cohercion*, fr. MF, fr. L *coertion-, coertio* (also *coerction-, coercitio*), alter. of *coercitio*, fr. *coercitus*, past part. of *coercēre* + *-ion-, -io* -ion] **1 a :** the act of coercing **:** use of physical or moral force to compel to act or assent ⟨some form of ~, overt or covert, which encroaches upon the natural freedom of individuals —John Dewey⟩ **b :** a power or force that coerces ⟨the submissive way of one long accustomed to obey under ~ —Charles Dickens⟩ **2 :** the application of sanctions or force by a government usu. accompanied by the suppression of constitutional liberties in order to compel dissenters to conform ⟨~ acts⟩ **3 :** physical force tending to constrict or compress ⟨the ~ of the ice around the ship's bows⟩ **syn** see FORCE
co·er·cive \|siv,|sēv\ *adj* [*coerce* + *-ive*] **:** serving or intended to coerce **:** being or exerting coercion ⟨self-created will rather than ~ force —Adrienne Koch⟩ ⟨~ measures for compelling a restitution —C.G.Bowers⟩ ⟨authority is directional instead of ~ —Theodore Bienenstok⟩ — **co·er·cive·ly** *adv*
coercive force *also* **coercive field** *n* **:** the opposing magnetic intensity that must be applied to a magnetized substance to reduce the residual magnetic induction in the material to zero — compare COERCIVITY
co·er·civ·i·ty \,kō,ərˈsivəd·ē\ *n* -ES [*coercive* + *-ity*] **:** the property of a material determined by the value of the coercive force when the material has been magnetized to saturation
coe·reb·i·dae \səˈrebə,dē\ *n pl, cap* [NL, fr. *Coereba*, type genus (fr. Tupi *guira coereba*, a bird) + *-idae*] **:** a family of songbirds comprising the honeycreepers
coe·ru·le·in *also* **ce·ru·le·in** \səˈrülēən\ *n* -s *often cap* [ISV *coerul-, cerul-* (fr. L *coeruleus, caeruleus* cerulean) + *-in*] **:** a xanthene dye $C_{20}H_{10}O_6$ that is obtained by heating gallein with concentrated sulfuric acid and that dyes mordanted cotton, silk, and wool green
coe·ru·le·o·lac·tite \sə̇,rülē(,)ōˈlak,tīt\ *n* -s [*coeruleo-* (fr. L *coeruleus, caeruleus* cerulean) + *-lactite*, fr. L *lact-, lac* milk + E *-ite* — more at CERULEAN, GALAXY] **:** a mineral consisting of an aluminum phosphate $Al_3(PO_4)_2(OH)_3.4H_2O$ of a milk-white to sky-blue color
coerulignol *var of* CERULIGNOL
coerulignone *var of* CERULIGNONE
coes *pl of* COE, *pres 3d sing of* COE
co·essential \;kō+\ *adj* [ME, fr. *co-* + *essential*] **:** being of one essence ⟨a prophet who considers himself as ~ with God⟩ — **co·essentially** \ˈ"+\ *adv*
co·e·ta·ne·i·ty \,kōəd·əˈnēəd·ē\ *n* -ES [L *coaetaneus* of the same age (fr. *co-* + *aetas* age) + E *-ity* — more at AGE] **:** the quality or state of being coetaneous
co·e·ta·ne·ous *or* **co·ae·ta·ne·ous** \;kōə;tānēəs\ *adj* [L *coaetaneus*, fr. *co-* + *-aetaneus* (fr. *aetas* age) — more at AGE] **:** COEVAL ⟨to far surpass her peers, the ~ dames —Robert Browning⟩ **syn** see CONTEMPORARY
coeteris paribus *var of* CETERIS PARIBUS
co·eternal \;kō+\ *adj* [ME, fr. *co-* + *eternal*] **:** equally or jointly eternal ⟨the three Persons of the Trinity are believed ~⟩ — **co·eternally** \ˈ"+\ *adv* — **co·eternity** \ˈ"+\ *n* -ES
coeur à la crème \,kər·,äləˈkrem\ *n* [F, lit., heart with cream] **:** a dessert of cream cheese molded in small heart shapes served with cream and fine preserves
coeur d'a·lene \,kərdᵊlˈān\ *n, pl* **coeur d'alene** *or* **coeur d'alenes** *usu cap C&A* [F *cœur d'alêne*, lit., awl-heart; fr. a tribal chief's characterization of the size of a trader's heart] **1 a :** a Salishan people of northern Idaho — called also *Skitswish* **b :** a member of such people **2 :** a language of the Coeur d'Alene people
¹co·e·val \(ˈ)kō;ēvəl\ *adj* [L *coaevus* of the same age (fr. *co-* + *aevum* age) + E *-al* — more at AGE] **:** of the same or equal age or antiquity **:** originating or occurring in and often lasting through the same era or epoch ⟨the theory requires that these ~ stars should be nearly the same in mass and brightness —A.S.Eddington⟩ ⟨California, too, has its ranches, many of them of Mexican genesis and ~ with those of Texas —P.A. Rollins⟩ **syn** see CONTEMPORARY
²coeval *n* -s **:** one of the same age **:** CONTEMPORARY ⟨the American actor seems "younger" than his ~s abroad —H.E. Clurman⟩ ⟨he spoke and wrote to children as a ~ —John Buchan⟩
co·e·val·i·ty \,kōēˈvaləd·ē\ *n* -ES **:** the quality or state of being coeval
co·exist \;kō+\ *vi* [*co-* + *exist*] **1 :** to exist together or at the same time ⟨its educational and manufacturing interests ~ without friction —*Amer. Guide Series: Mich.*⟩ **2 :** to live in peace with each other esp. as a matter of policy — used esp. of countries with seemingly incompatible policies — **co·existence** \ˈ"+\ *n* -s
¹co·existent \ˈ"+\ *adj* [*coexist* + *-ent*] **:** existing at the same time or in conjunction with **:** COEXISTING
²coexistent \ˈ"\ *n* -s **:** something that coexists **:** CONCOMITANT
co·extended \;kō+\ *adj* **:** COEXTENSIVE
co·extension \ˈ"+\ *n* [*co-* + *extension*] **:** the quality or state of coextending or being coextensive
co·extensive \ˈ"+\ *adj* [*co-* + *extensive*] **:** having the same scope or boundaries **:** occupying the same space or period of time — **co·extensively** \ˈ"+\ *adv*
co·factor \(ˈ)kō+\ *n* [*co-* + *factor*] **1 :** a factor occurring in multiplication with another factor or factors; *specif* **:** the determinant multiplier of any constituent of a determinant in expansion of the determinant **2 :** a substance (as coenzyme) that acts with another substance to bring about certain effects
co·fán \kōˈfän\ *n, pl* **cofán** *usu cap* [Sp, of AmerInd origin] **1 a :** a nearly or wholly extinct people of western Ecuador **b :** a member of this people **2 :** the language of the Cofán people sometimes considered to constitute a language family
C of B *abbr* confirmation of balance
C of C *abbr* chamber of commerce
¹co·feature \(ˈ)kō+\ *n* [*co-* + *feature*] **:** a feature (as in an entertainment) accompanying but usu. presumed subordinate in interest to a main attraction
²cofeature \ˈ"\ *vt* [*co-* + *feature*] **1 :** to give equal prominence to esp. in an entertainment **:** feature equally **2 :** to present as a cofeature
co·ferment \(ˈ)kō+\ *n* [*co-* + *ferment*] **:** COENZYME
coff \ˈkäf\ *vt* **coft** \-ft\ **coft**; **coffing**; **coffs** [back-formation fr. *coft* (past tense and past part.), fr. ME (Sc), fr. MD *coft*, *cocht* bought, past tense of *copen* to buy — more at COPE] *Scot* **:** BUY
cof·fea \ˈkȯfēə\ *n, cap* [NL, fr. obs. Sw *coffe, coffé* (now *kaffe*), fr. obs. G or E; obs. G *coffée, coffee* (now *kaffee*) fr. E *coffee*] **:** a genus of small trees and shrubs of the family Rubiaceae native to the tropical Old World (as Africa) having white fragrant flowers borne in clusters at the base of the shining evergreen leaves, and including several species (esp. *C. arabica, C. liberica*, and *C. robusta*) that are widely grown in tropical and subtropical uplands for their cherrylike fruits which contain seeds from which coffee is prepared
cof·fee \ˈkȯfē, -fi *also* ˈkäf-\ *n* -s *often attrib* [It & Turk; It *caffè*, fr. Turk *kahve* coffee, café, fr. Ar *qahwah* wine, coffee] **1 a :** a drink made by infusion or decoction from the roasted and ground or pounded seeds of plants of the genus *Coffea* **b :** a cup of coffee ⟨the waitress brought two ~s⟩ **c :** any social occasion at which coffee is served esp. for informal entertaining or during a rest period of a workday — see COFFEE BREAK **2 :** the edible green or roasted seeds obtained from the fruit of various plants of the genus *Coffea* — compare COFFEE CHERRY **3 :** a plant of the genus *Coffea* **4 :** a drink or substance used as a substitute for coffee — usu. used with an identifying modifier ⟨barley ~⟩ ⟨acorn ~⟩ **5 :** a moderate brown that is yellower and duller than bay, auburn, or toast brown, darker and slightly yellower than chestnut brown, and yellower, less strong, and slightly lighter than tobacco **6 :** seeds of the Kentucky coffee tree

coffee: *1* flowering and fruiting branch with leaves, *2* fruit, *3* fruit with pericarp partly removed to show seeds

coffee-and \;=ˈand\ *n* [by shortening] *slang* **:** coffee and doughnuts
coffee bean *n* **:** the seed of any plant of the genus *Coffea* or of the Kentucky coffee tree
coffee-bean weevil *n* **:** a small stocky dark brown weevil (*Araecerus fasciculatus*) prob. native to India but now nearly cosmopolitan in warm regions where it feeds and breeds in a great variety of products (as dried fruits, coffee beans, grains, or cornstalks
coffeeberry \ˈ==,==\ *n* **1 :** any of several California shrubs with fruits suggesting coffee cherries: **a** (1) **:** CASCARA BUCKTHORN (2) **:** CALIFORNIA COFFEE 2 **b :** a chaparral shrub (*Ceanothus divaricatus*) **c :** JOJOBA **2 :** SOYBEAN **3 :** either of two shrubs (genus *Coprosma*) related to coffee: **a :** a New Zealand shrub (*C. lucida*) **b :** a Tasmanian shrub (*C. hirtella*) **4 :** the fruit of a coffeeberry
coffee berry *n* **:** COFFEE CHERRY
coffee bread *n* **:** COFFEE CAKE
coffee break *n* **:** a short rest period (as in the mid-morning or mid-afternoon) during which coffee or other refreshment is often consumed
coffeebush \ˈ==,=\ *n* **:** any of several coffeeberries
coffee cake *n* **1 a :** a breakfast bread of yeast dough enriched with eggs, butter, and sugar, baked in a sheet topped with streusel or with added fruit and spices shaped into any of various forms (as rings, braids, rolls, or pinwheels), and glazed with melted sugar after baking **b :** a similar bread leavened with baking powder **2 :** a dark fruited raised bread
coffee cherry *n* **:** the fruit of any plant of the genus *Coffea* being cherrylike in shape, color, and size and containing two seeds enclosed by pulp and an outer skin — compare COFFEE BEAN
coffee cocktail *n* [prob. so called fr. the color] **:** a cocktail consisting of equal parts of port wine and brandy into which are shaken sweetening and an egg
coffee cooler *n, obs slang* **:** a petty crook or opportunist
coffee cream *n* **:** cream that is legally required to contain at least 18 percent but less than 30 percent of butterfat — compare WHIPPING CREAM
coffee disease *n* **:** LEAF DISEASE
coffee fern *n* **:** a Californian evergreen fern (*Pellaea andromedaefolia*)
coffee-ground vomit \ˈ==,=-\ *n* **:** BLACK VOMIT
coffee hour *n* **1 :** a usu. fixed occasion of informal meeting and chatting at which coffee and other refreshment is served **2 :** COFFEE BREAK
¹coffeehouse \ˈ==,=\ *n* **1 :** a place where coffee and other refreshments are sold often (as in 17th and 18th century England) resembling a club and being a center for the dissemination of news and for informal discussion (as of politics or literature) **2 :** CAFÉ
²coffeehouse \ˈ"\ *vi* -ED/-ING/-S [¹*coffeehouse*] **:** to make aimless conversation
coffee klatch *or* **coffee klatsch** \-,klach, -ä-\ *n* [G *kaffeeklatsch*, fr. *kaffee* coffee + *klatsch* gossip] **:** a meeting, often over coffee, for informal conversation
coffeeleaf \ˈ==,=\ *n* **:** SHINLEAF
coffee maker *n* **:** any of various utensils in which coffee is brewed
coffee mill *n* **:** a small mill for grinding coffee beans
coffee nib *n* **:** COFFEE BEAN
coffee nut *n* **1 :** KENTUCKY COFFEE TREE **2 :** the fruit of the Kentucky coffee tree
coffee party *n* **:** a social occasion usu. in the afternoon and often with a guest of honor at which coffee and other light refreshment are served
coffee pea *n* [so called fr. the use of its seeds as a substitute for coffee] **:** CHICK-PEA
coffee plant *n* **1 :** COFFEE 3 **2 :** SOYBEAN **3 :** an evening primrose (*Oenothera biennis*)

coffee mill

coffeepot \ˈ==,=\ *n* **1 a :** a covered pot with a spout and handle in which coffee is prepared **b :** a utensil from which coffee is served ⟨a silver ~⟩ **2 :** a small lunchroom; *esp* **:** one that stays open all night
coffee ring *n* **:** a coffee cake in the shape of a ring that is plain or fruited and often glazed with melted sugar
coffee roll *n* **:** coffee cake or similar sweet raised bread shaped into rolls with or without raisins, nuts, and spices and sometimes glazed with melted sugar
coffee royal *n* **:** a drink of black coffee and a liquor (as brandy or rum) often sweetened with sugar
coffee sack *n, Midland* **:** a large burlap sack
coffee senna *n* **:** a tropical weed (*Cassia occidentalis*) having rank-scented foliage and seeds that have been used as an adulterant for coffee — called also *mogdad coffee, negro coffee*
coffee service *n* **:** a usu. sterling silver or silverplate service consisting of coffeepot, sugar bowl, creamer, and tray — compare TEA SERVICE
coffee set *n* **1 :** COFFEE SERVICE **2 :** a set of porcelain or pottery for the serving of coffee consisting typically of coffeepot, cream pitcher, and sugar bowl together with a number of matching cups and saucers
coffee shell *n* **:** any of several small ear snails (genus *Melampus*) chiefly of tropical seas
coffee shop *n* **:** a small restaurant that is either independent or attached to a hotel and where light refreshments or regular meals are served
coffee spoon *n* **:** a small spoon for use with after-dinner coffee cups — see SPOON illustration
coffee table *n* **:** any low table customarily placed in front of a sofa; *esp* **:** such a table used to accommodate a coffee or other service while serving
coffee tree *n* **1 :** COFFEE 3 **2 :** KENTUCKY COFFEE TREE **3 :** CASCARA BUCKTHORN
coffeeweed \ˈ==,=\ *n* **1** [so called fr. its use as a substitute for coffee] **:** CHICORY **2 a :** either of two herbs (*Cassia marylandica* and *C. tora*) having seeds that resemble coffee beans **b :** COFFEE SENNA **3 :** CURLED DOCK
coffee wit *n, obs* **:** a coffeehouse wit
coffeewood \ˈ==,=\ *n* [so called fr. its color] **1 :** GRANADILLA WOOD **2:** wood from coffee (sense 3)
¹cof·fer \ˈkȯfə(r), ˈkäf-\ *n* -s [ME *coffre*, fr. OF *cofre, coffre*, fr. L *cophinus* basket, fr. Gk *kophinos*] **1 :** CHEST, CASKET, BOX; *esp* **:** a strongbox for the safe storage of money or other valuables **2 :** TREASURY, EXCHEQUER, FUNDS — usu. used in pl. ⟨captives . . . whose ransoms did the general ~s fill —Shak.⟩ ⟨working children contribute to the household ~s —D.G.Bettison⟩ **3 a :** the chamber of a canal lock **b :** CAISSON **c :** FLOATING DOCK **d :** COFFERDAM **4 a :** a recessed panel usu. forming with other panels a continuous pattern in a vault, ceiling, or soffit **b :** a space (as in a wall or pier) filled with concrete, rubble, or other materials

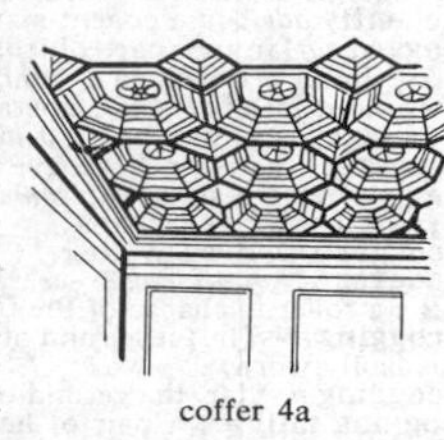
coffer 4a

²coffer \ˈ"\ *vt* **coffered; coffered; coffering** \-f(ə)riŋ\ **coffers** [ME *cofren*, fr. *cofer*, n.] **1 :** to put into, store, or hoard up in a coffer; *broadly* **:** to keep securely **:** treasure up **:** HOARD **2 :** to form (as a ceiling) with recessed panels; *sometimes* **:** to recess (as a panel) **3 :** to secure (as a mining shaft) from leaking by ramming clay behind the masonry or timbering
cofferdam \ˈ==,=\ *n* [¹*coffer* + *dam*] **1 a :** a temporary watertight enclosure (as of piles packed with clay or of metal plates) from which the water is pumped to expose the bottom of a body of water and permit construction (as of foundations or piers) **b :** a watertight structure for making repairs below the waterline of a ship **2 a :** a compartment formerly provided near the waterline of a man-of-war and filled with cellulose which would swell on contact with water and plug a hole **b :** the space between two closely located bulkheads in a ship
cof·fer·er \ˈ==(r)\ *n* -s [MF *coffrier*, fr. *coffre* + *-ier* -er] *archaic* **:** TREASURER; *esp* **:** a former officer of the British royal household subordinate to the controller
cofferfish \ˈ==,=\ *n* [so called fr. its boxlike body] **:** BOXFISH
cof·fer·ing \ˈkȯf(ə)riŋ, ˈkäf-\ *n* -s [¹*coffer* + *-ing*] **:** a system or structure of coffers ⟨carved and gilded ceiling ~⟩
¹cof·fin \ˈkȯfə̇n *also* ˈkäf-\ *n* -s [ME, basket, receptacle, fr. MF *cofin*, fr. L *cophinus* — more at COFFER] **1** *obs* **a :** BASKET, CHEST, CASE **b :** a casing, crust, or mold of pastry (as for a pie); *also* **:** a pie dish **c :** BIER **2 :** a box or chest for a corpse to be buried in formerly often of a hexagonal or wedge shape, wider at the head than at the foot — compare CASKET **3** *archaic* **:** a paper cornucopia (as for groceries or filtration) **4 :** the horny body forming the hoof of a horse's foot **5** *printing* **a :** the bed or carriage of a handpress **b :** a wooden frame enclosing an imposing stone
²coffin \ˈ"\ *vt* -ED/-ING/-S **:** to enclose in or as if in a coffin
coffin bone *n* **:** the foot bone enclosed within the hoof of the horse and other equines
coffin corner *n* **:** one of the corners formed by a goal line and a sideline on a football field into which a punt is often aimed so that it may go out of bounds close to the defenders' goal line
coffing *pres part of* COFF
coffin joint *n* **:** the joint next above the coffin bone
cof·fin·less \ˈkȯfə̇nlə̇s *also* ˈkäf-\ *adj* **:** lacking a coffin
coffin nail *n* [so called fr. the presumed pernicious effects of smoking, each cigarette being likened to a nail driven into one's coffin] *slang* **:** CIGARETTE

coffin ship *n* **:** an unseaworthy ship
coffin stool *n* **:** JOINT STOOL
coffin text *n* **:** any of many inscriptions on coffins of the Middle Kingdom in Egypt consisting usu. of charms or prayers and forming a stage between the Pyramid Texts and the Book of the Dead
cof·fle \'kȯfəl, -äf-\ *n* -S [Ar *qāfila* caravan] **:** a gang of men or a train of animals fastened together; *esp* **:** a group of slaves chained together (as when traveling)
cof·fre *like* ¹COFFER\ *n* -S [ME — more at COFFER] **:** COFFER 1
cof·fret \'kȯfrət, 'käf-\ *n* -S [F, dim. of *coffre* coffer — more at COFFER] **:** a small coffer
coffs *pres 3d sing of* COFF
C of M *abbr* certificate of merit
co·fra·dia \,kōfrə'dēə, -rä'-\ *n* -S [Sp *cofradía*, fr. *cofrade* member of a confraternity (fr. OSp *confrade*, fr. *con-* — fr. L *com-* — + *frade* brother, monk, priest, fr. L *fratr-, frater*) + *-ia* (fr. L *-ia*) — more at BROTHER] **:** a group or organization of Roman Catholic laymen in Mexico and Central America responsible for the material care of religious images, pilgrimages, and ceremonies
C of S *abbr* **1** chief of section **2** chief of staff
coft *past of* COFF
co·function \'kō+,==\ *n* [*co-* + *function*] **:** the corresponding trigonometric function of the complement of an angle ⟨the ~ of the tangent is the cotangent⟩
¹**cog** \'käg *also* 'kȯg\ *n* -S [ME *cogge*, of Scand origin; akin to Norw *kug* cog, Sw *kugge*; akin to OE *cycgel* cudgel — more at CUDGEL] **1 :** a tooth on the rim of a wheel **:** a gear tooth **2 :** one that functions as a necessary but subordinate part of a larger process, organization, or system ⟨the jobber is an important ~ in the scheme of distribution —*Marketing Toys*⟩ ⟨the Malayan tiger . . . constitutes an important and necessary ~ in the natural balance wheel of Malaya —R.R.Camp⟩
²**cog** \"\ *vt* **cogged; cogged; cogging; cogs** [ME *coggen*, fr. *cogge*, n.] **:** to furnish with a cog
³**cog** \"\ *n* -S [ME *cogge*, fr. MD *cogghe*, fr. MF *coque* — more at COCK] **:** any of several boats: **a :** a broadly built ship with bluff prow and stern used prior to the 16th century chiefly for freighting and transport **b** *obs* **:** a British riverboat **c** *also* **cogboat** \'=,=\ **:** COCKBOAT
⁴**cog** \"\ *n* -S [origin unknown] *obs* **:** an act of trickery or deception esp. at dice **:** TRICK, DECEPTION, FALSEHOOD; *sometimes* **:** something (as a piece of money) used as bait for dupes **:** COME-ON
⁵**cog** \"\ *vb* **cogged; cogged; cogging; cogs** *vi* **1** *obs* **:** to use any of certain tricks in throwing dice **2** *obs* **:** DECEIVE, CHEAT **3** *obs* **:** to use venal flattery **:** FAWN ~ *vt* **1 :** to direct the fall of (dice) fraudulently **2** *obs* **:** ENTICE **:** get by flattery or cajolery **:** WHEEDLE
⁶**cog** \'käg, 'kōg\ *n* -S [origin unknown] *chiefly Scot* **:** a wooden vessel varying as to size and usu. having a handle formed by an extension of one or two of the staves
⁷**cog** \'käg *also* 'kȯg\ *vt* **cogged; cogged; cogging; cogs** [prob. alter. (influenced by ¹*cog*) of ⁸*cock*] **:** to connect (as timbers or joists) by means of tenons
⁸**cog** \"\ *n* -S **1 a :** a tenon on the face or side of a beam or timber received into a mortise in another beam to secure the two together: as **a :** the tabular projection at the end of a scarfed timber **:** COAK **b :** a tenon (as a dovetail) in a beam or joist resting in a notch in the bearing surface of another so that the two are flush (as in the corner joints of wall plates) **c :** a tongue in the upper surface of a beam to fit into a notch in the lower surface of a beam crossing it **2** *Brit* **:** a pillar or column consisting of blocks of wood or stone set vertically upon each other or of timbers set crosswise two by two upon each other to support the roof of a mine — called also *chock*
⁹**cog** \"\ *vt* **cogged; cogged; cogging; cogs** [E dial. *cog* to beat] **:** to consolidate (iron or steel) by hammering or rolling; *sometimes* **:** to rough (iron or steel) to shape by rolling — see COGGING MILL
cog *abbr* cognate
cog and round *n* [¹*cog*] **:** a device common in clocks consisting of a cogwheel working into the trundles of a lantern pinion
co·gen·cy \'kōjənsē, -si\ *also* **co·gence** \-n(t)s\ *n, pl* **cogencies** *also* **cogenc·es :** the quality or state of being cogent
cogener *var of* CONGENER
co·gent \'kōjənt\ *adj* [L *cogent-, cogens*, pres. part. of *cogere* to drive together, collect, compel, fr. *co-* + *agere* to drive — more at AGENT] **1 :** having the power of compelling or constraining ⟨the ~ forces of nature⟩ **2 a :** appealing persuasively to the mind or reason **:** CONVINCING ⟨a ~ argument⟩ ⟨a ~ description⟩ ⟨criticism that shows his argumentative style at its most ~ —Edmund Wilson⟩ **b :** being pertinent, concise, and often timely **:** to the point **:** RELEVANT ⟨a ~ analysis of the problem⟩ ⟨studied writing . . . in order to be able to write ~ and expert briefs —*Current Biog.*⟩ ⟨the 14th chapter of St. Luke's Gospel, which says some ~ things about the futility of aspiration —C.B.Marshall⟩ **syn** see VALID
cogently *adv* **:** in a cogent manner
cogged *adj* [fr. past part. of ²*cog*] **1 :** provided with a cog or cogs ⟨~ rim of a wheel⟩ ⟨a ~ timber dressed to join firmly with a mortised member⟩ **2 :** operated by means of cogged wheels ⟨a ~ railway running up a mountain⟩
¹**cog·ger** \'käg(ə)r\ *n* -S [⁵*cog* + *-er*] *archaic* **:** a cheat or deceiver esp. at dice **:** SHARPER; *sometimes* **:** a false fawning person **:** SYCOPHANT, FLATTERER
²**cogger** \"\ *n* -S [by alter.] **:** ¹COCKER 2
³**cogger** \"\ *n* -S [⁸*cog* + *-er*] **1** *Brit* **:** one that erects mine cogs **2 :** a roller in charge of the first set of rolls in a steelworks
¹**cogging** *n* -S [fr. the gerund of ²*cog*] **:** COGS ⟨the ~ of the wheel is badly worn⟩
²**cogging** *n* -S [fr. the gerund of ⁷*cog*] **:** a cogged joint
cogging mill *n* **:** a pair of heavy rolls through which heated steel ingots are passed
¹**cog·gle** \'kägəl\ *vi* -ED/-ING/-S [perh. alter. of ⁷*cockle*] *dial Brit* **:** WOBBLE, TOTTER
²**coggle** \"\ *vt* -ED/-ING/-S [perh. alter. of ¹*cobble*] *dial* **:** to repair roughly **:** COBBLE — usu. used with *up*
³**coggle** \"\ *n* -S [perh. fr. ¹*cog* + *-le*] **:** a ceramics tool that consists mainly of a wheel or disk and is used to make indentations or grooves in the outer edges of plates
cog·gly \'käglē, -li\ *adj* [¹*coggle* + *-y*] *dial chiefly Brit* **:** UNSTEADY, WOBBLY
co·gi·da \kō'hēthə\ *n* -S [Sp, fr. fem of *cogido*, past part. of *coger* to receive, seize, get, fr. L *colligere* to bind together — more at COLLECT] **:** a tossing of a bullfighter by a bull
cog·ie \'kägi, 'kōgi\ *n* -S [⁶*cog* + *-ie*] *Scot* **:** ⁶COG
cog·i·ta·ble \'käjəd·əbəl, -ətəb-\ *adj* [L *cogitabilis*, fr. *cogitare* to think + *-bilis* -able] **:** capable of being brought before the mind as a thought or idea **:** THINKABLE ⟨the practical steps to achieve the maximum utilization of heat become more ~ —*Times Rev. of Industry*⟩
cog·i·ta·bund \-,bənd\ *adj* [L *cogitabundus*, fr. *cogitare*] *archaic* **:** given to deep thought **:** having the appearance of being in deep meditation **:** PENSIVE
cog·i·tate \'käjə,tāt, *usu* -ād.+V\ *vb* -ED/-ING/-S [L *cogitatus*, past part. of *cogitare* to think, think about, fr. *co-* + *agitare* to drive, agitate, turn over in the mind — more at AGITATE] *vt* **:** to ponder on or meditate upon usu. with intentness and objectivity ⟨cogitating what they should do⟩ ⟨cogitating how to answer⟩; *sometimes* **:** PLAN, PLOT ⟨he sat and *cogitated* the trick he would play on his big brother⟩ ~ *vi* **:** to ponder, meditate, or think deeply, intently, or objectively ⟨~ on his previous mistakes⟩ ⟨the three of us were silent, *cogitating* —Kenneth Roberts⟩ **syn** see THINK
cog·i·ta·tion \,käjə'tāshən\ *n* -S [ME *cogitacioun*, fr. OF or L; OF *cogitation*, fr. L *cogitation-, cogitatio*, fr. *cogitatus* + *-ion-, -io* -ion] **1 a :** the act of cogitating **:** REFLECTION, MEDITATION ⟨agree to a plan after considerable ~⟩ **b :** the capacity to think or reflect ⟨some people think animals not capable of ~⟩ **2 a :** THOUGHT ⟨agreeable ~*s*⟩ ⟨present her ~*s* in the form of a treatise⟩ **b** *obs* **:** PLAN, PURPOSE ⟨evil ~*s* and nefarious designs⟩ **c** *obs* **:** CONCEPTION, IDEA ⟨he dislikes other people's ~*s* of God⟩
cog·i·ta·tive \'käjə,tād·iv, -,tət|, |tiv, -ēv\ *adj* [MF or ML; MF *cogitatif*, fr. ML *cogitativus*, fr. L *cogitatus* + *-ivus* -ive] **1 a :** of or relating to cogitation ⟨the ~ faculty⟩ **b :** possessing the faculty or power of thinking or meditating ⟨man is a ~ being⟩ **2 :** marked by or given to cogitation ⟨eyes . . . hardly ~ in their gaze —Anne D. Sedgwick⟩ ⟨the mere ~ pagans of the twenties —Wylie Sypher⟩
co·gi·to \'kōgə,tō, 'käjə-\ *n* -S [L, I think (as in NL *cogito ergo sum* I think, therefore I am), 1st pers. sing. pres. ind. of *cogitare*] **1 :** the philosophic principle that one's existence is demonstrated by the fact that one thinks **2 :** the intellectual processes of the self or ego
cog·man *n, pl* **cogmen** \'=mən\ [⁸*cog* + *man*] **:** ³COGGER
co·gnac \'kōn,yak *also* 'kän- *or* 'kȯn-\ *n* -S [F, fr. *Cognac*, Charente department, France, where it is made] **1** *usu cap* **:** a brandy from the departments of Charente and Charente-Maritime, France, distilled from white wine **2 :** BRANDY; *esp.* **:** a French brandy — not used technically **3 :** a moderate brown that is yellower, lighter, and stronger than bay or auburn and lighter, stronger, and slightly yellower than chestnut brown
¹**cog·nate** \'käg,nāt, *usu* -ād.+V\ *adj* [L *cognatus*, fr. *co-* + *gnatus, natus*, past part. of *nasci* to be born; akin to L *gignere* to beget — more at KIN] **1 a :** related by blood **:** kindred by birth ⟨~ families⟩ ⟨a family ~ with another⟩ ⟨a boy ~ to several royal families⟩ **b :** related on the mother's side — used in some legal systems **2 a** *of a language* **:** related by descent from the same recorded or assumed ancestral language ⟨Spanish and French are ~ languages⟩ — often used with *with*, sometimes with *to* ⟨English is ~ to German⟩ **b** *of a word or morpheme* **:** related by descent from the same root or affixal element in a recorded or assumed ancestral language ⟨English *eat* and German *essen* are ~⟩ ⟨Latin *-us* and Old Norse *-r* are ~⟩ or by the processes of derivation or composition within a single language ⟨English *boyish* and *boyhood* are ~⟩ — often used with *with*, sometimes with *to* ⟨English *foot* is ~ with Greek *pous*⟩ **c** *of a word* **:** related in a manner that involves borrowing rather than descent from or as well as descent from an ancestral language ⟨English *tobacco* and French *tabac* are ~⟩ — often used with *with*, sometimes with *to* ⟨German *panzer* is ~ with English *paunch*⟩ **d** *of a substantive* **:** related usu. in derivation but sometimes only in meaning to the verb of which it is the object (as *song* in "she sang the song"; *race* in "he ran the race") ⟨~ object⟩ ⟨~ accusative⟩ **3 :** related, akin, or similar esp. in having the same or common or similar nature, elements, qualities, or origin ⟨illustrated books and ~ reference materials —*Current Biog.*⟩ ⟨you know exactly how a man looks and behaves and, with ~ clarity, something of what he feels and thinks —Thomas Dozier⟩ ⟨action engendered in regard to drugs may spill over into the ~ problem of the alcoholic —*New Republic*⟩ **4 a :** closely related logically through certain specifiable factors; *esp, of propositions* **:** having the same subject or predicate **b :** belonging to volcanic fragments in solidified lava which are part of the same extrusion **c :** HOMORGANIC — **cognate·ly** *adv*
²**cog·nate** \"\ *n* -S [L *cognatus*, fr. *cognatus*, adj.] **:** one that is cognate with another: as **a :** a person related to another on the mother's side — compare AGNATE **b :** a cognate word or morpheme
cognate inclusion *n* **:** AUTOLITH
cog·nat·ic \käg'nad·ik\ *adj* [F *cognatique*, fr. *cognat* cognate (fr. L *cognatus*) + *-ique* -ic] **:** of or relating to cognates or to the maternal line
cog·na·tion \käg'nāshən\ *n* -S [ME *cognacioun*, fr. L *cognation-, cognatio*, fr. *cognatus* cognate + *-ion-, -io* -ion] **:** cognate relationship esp. of words
cog·na·tus \-'nād·əs\ *n, pl* **cogna·ti** \-d·,ī, -ē\ [L — more at COGNATE] **:** a relative by blood esp. on the mother's side — usu. used in pl.
cog·ni·tion \käg'nishən\ *n* -S [ME *cognicioun*, fr. L *cognition-, cognitio*, fr. *cognitus* (past part. of *cognoscere* to become acquainted with, know, fr. *co-* + *gnoscere, noscere*) + *-ion-, -io* -ion — more at KNOW] **1 a :** cognitive mental processes; *specif* **:** the intellectual process by which knowledge is gained about perceptions or ideas — distinguished from *affection* and *conation* **b :** a conscious intellectual act ⟨conflict between ~*s*⟩ **2** *Scots law* **:** the act or process of cognoscing **:** adjudication of rights
cog·ni·tion·al \-shən°l, -shnəl\ *adj* **:** being, belonging to, or based on cognition
cog·ni·tive \'kägnəd·iv, -ətiv\ *adj* [*cognition* + *-ive*] **1 :** of, relating to, or being conscious intellectual activity (as thinking, reasoning, remembering, imagining, or learning words) ⟨the ~ elements of perception —C.H.Hamburg⟩ **2 :** based on or capable of being reduced to empirical factual knowledge ⟨to debate whether normative statements can be ~⟩ — **cognitively** *adv*
cog·ni·tiv·ism \-,vizəm\ *n* -S **:** the ethical theory of a cognitivist
cog·ni·tiv·ist \-,vəst\ *n* -S **:** an ethicist who holds that genuine ethical judgments are cognitive or empirically confirmable; *usu* **:** UTILITARIAN, PRAGMATIST
cog·ni·za·ble *or* **cog·ni·sa·ble** \'kägnəzəbəl, (')käg'nīz- *sometimes* 'känəz- *esp in sense 2*\ *adj* [*cognizance* + *-able*] **1 :** capable of being known ⟨~ events⟩ **2 :** competent as a subject of judicial investigation **:** capable of being judicially heard and determined — **cog·ni·za·bly** \-blē, -i\ *adv*
cog·ni·zance *or* **cog·ni·sance** \'kägnəzən(t)s *sometimes* 'känə- *esp in sense 3*\ *n* -S [alter. (influenced by *cognition*) of ME *conisaunce*, fr. OF *conoissance*, fr. *conoistre* to know, fr. L *cognoscere* — more at COGNITION] **1 :** a distinguishing mark or emblem (as a heraldic bearing, crest, or cockade); *specif* **:** the badge worn by an armed knight and his followers **2 a** *obs* **:** knowledge or understanding in general **b :** SURVEILLANCE, CONTROL ⟨the engineering department also has ~ over all engineering compartments —A.A.Ageton⟩ ⟨reserves them to his own jurisdiction unless he chooses to give ~ of them to anyone as a mark of unusual honor —F.W. Stenton⟩ **c :** particular knowledge **:** conscious recognition **:** APPREHENSION, PERCEPTION ⟨the officer's power to arrest without a warrant depends upon his own sensory ~ that a crime has been committed —Paul Wilson⟩ ⟨seemed to have no ~ of the crime⟩ **d :** range of apprehension or perception ⟨beyond the children's ~⟩ **e :** NOTICE, OBSERVANCE ⟨nothing could happen, among a certain class of society, without the ~ of some philanthropic agency —Arnold Bennett⟩ ⟨to take ~ of a fault⟩ **3 a :** the right and power to hear and decide controversies **:** JURISDICTION **b :** the judicial hearing of a matter **4 a :** an admission made by one levying a fine that the lands in question belong to the plaintiff **:** a plea admitting the facts alleged **b :** a justification by the defendant in replevin that the goods were taken by him by command of another lawfully entitled to their possession
cog·ni·zant \'kägnəzənt *sometimes* 'känə- *esp in sense b*\ *adj* [fr. *cognizance*, after such pairs as E *abundance: abundant*] **:** having cognizance: **a :** AWARE, CONSCIOUS ⟨~ of the facts⟩ ⟨~ of the fascinated gaze I bent upon him —Jack London⟩ **b :** having the surveillance, responsibility, or jurisdiction ⟨legislative proposals have been introduced in the Congress and referred to the ~ congressional committees —*U.S. Code*⟩ **syn** see AWARE
cognize \(')käg'nīz\ *vt* -ED/-ING/-S *see -ize in Explan Notes* [back-formation (influence of *recognize*) fr. *cognizance*] **:** KNOW, PERCEIVE **:** have cognizance of esp. in any philosophically fundamental or ultimate sense ⟨to doubt whether we ~ anything as it really is⟩
cog·no·men \käg'nōmən\ *n, pl* **cognomens** \-ənz\ *or* **cog·nom·i·na** \-nämənə, -nōm-\ [L, fr. *co-* + *-gnomen*, alter. (influenced by *gnoscere* to know) of *nomen* name — more at NAME, KNOW] **1 :** SURNAME ⟨having the ~ Smith⟩; *esp* **:** the third of the usual three names of a person among the ancient Romans — compare PRAENOMEN, NOMEN; see AGNOMEN **2 :** NAME; *esp* **:** a distinguishing nickname or epithet ⟨who gained, and richly earned, the ~ of Tom-Tom —G.W.Johnson⟩
cog·nom·i·nal \(')käg'nämən°l, -nōm-\ *adj* [L *cognomin-, cognomen* + E *-al*] **:** of, relating to, or being a cognomen
cog·nom·i·na·tion \(,)=,==='nāshən\ *n* -S [L *cognomination-, cognominatio*, fr. *cognominatus* + *-ion-* *-io* -ion] **:** COGNOMEN
cognosce \(')käg'näs\ *vt* -ED/-ING/-S [L *cognoscere* to become acquainted with — more at COGNITION] *Scots law* **:** to determine judicially esp. with respect to insanity
cog·nos·cent \(')=;=°nt\ *adj* [L *cognoscent-, cognoscens*, pres. part. of *cognoscere*] *archaic* **:** COGNIZANT
co·gno·scen·te \,känyō'shentē, ,kägnə'-\ *also* **co·no·scen·te** \,känə-\ *n, pl* **cognoscen·ti** \-tē\ *also* **conoscen·ti** [obs. It (now *conoscente*), fr. *cognoscente*, adj., wise, having good judgment, fr. L *cognoscent-, cognoscens*, pres. part. of *cognoscere* to know] **:** a person having or claiming expert knowledge in one or more realms of the fine arts or of fashion **:** CONNOISSEUR ⟨art dealers, collectors, and other *cognoscenti* —Janet Flanner⟩
¹**cog·nos·ci·ble** \(')käg'näsəbəl\ *adj* [LL *cognoscibilis*, fr. L *cognoscere* + *-ibilis* -ible] **:** COGNIZABLE, KNOWABLE
²**cognoscible** \"\ *n* -S **:** a cognizable thing
cog·nos·ci·tive \-səd·iv\ *adj* [L *cognoscere* to know + E *-itive*] **:** having the power of knowing ⟨~ abilities⟩
cog·no·vit note \(')käg'nōvət-\ *n* [L *cognovit*, lit., he has acknowledged] **1 :** a note authorizing an attorney to confess judgment **2 a :** a note indicating that its maker acknowledges a debt **b** *in some jurisdictions* **:** PROMISSORY NOTE
co·gon \kō'gōn\ *also* **co·gon·grass** \(')=;=,=\ *or* **ko·gon** \=\ *n* -S [Sp *cogón*, fr. Tag, Bisayan, Bikol *kugon*] **:** any of several grasses of the genus *Imperata*; *esp* **:** either of two coarse tall grasses (*I. cylindrica koenigii* and *I. exaltata*) used in the Philippines and adjacent lands for thatching — called also *alang-alang*
co·go·nal \,kōgō'näl, -gō'-, '==,=\ *n, pl* **cogona·les** \-(,)lās\ [Sp, fr. *cogón*] *Philippines* **:** an area overgrown with cogon
cograil \'=,=\ *n* [¹*cog* + *rail*] **:** a cogged rail — called also *rack rail*
cog railway *also* **cog railroad** *n* **:** a steep mountain railroad that has in the middle or on the side of its track a cograil that engages a cogwheel on the locomotive to ensure traction
cogroad \'=,=\ *n* [¹*cog* + *road*] **:** COG RAILWAY
cogs *pl of* COG, *pres 3d sing of* COG
cogs·well chair *also* **cogswell** \'kägz,wel-, -,wəl-\ *or* **cox·well chair** \'käk,swel-, -,swəl-\ *n, often cap 1st C* [fr. the name *Cogswell*] **:** an upholstered easy chair with inclined back, seat cushion, thin open arms, and often cabriole front legs
cogs·wel·lia \käg'zwelēə\ [NL, fr. Joseph G. *Cogswell* †1871 Am. librarian + NL *-ia*] *syn of* LOMATIUM
cogue \'käg, 'kōg\ *n* -S *chiefly Scot* **:** ⁶COG
cogway \'=,=\ *n* [by contr.] **:** COG RAILWAY
cogwheel \'=,=\ *n* [ME *cogwhele*, fr. *cogge* cog + *whele* wheel] **:** a wheel with cogs or teeth
cogwheel ore *n* **:** BOURNONITE
cogwood \'=,=\ *n* [¹*cog* + *wood*] **:** the hard tough wood of a West Indian tree (*Zizyphus chloroxylon*)

cogwheel

co·hab \'kō,hab, ='=\ *n* -S [short for *cohabitant*] *slang* **:** one living in illegal cohabitation; *esp* **:** a polygamous Mormon
co·hab·it \kō'habət, *usu* -əd·+V\ *vb* -ED/-ING/-S [LL *cohabitare*, fr. L *co-* + *habitare* to inhabit, dwell, fr. *habitus*, past part. of *habēre* to have — more at HABIT] *vi* **1 :** to live together as or as if as husband and wife ⟨~*ed* without formal marriage⟩ **2 a :** to live together or in company ⟨buffaloes ~*ing* with crossbred cows —*Biol. Abstracts*⟩ **b :** to be intimately together or in company ⟨two strains in his philosophy . . . ~ in each of his major works —Justus Buchler⟩ ~ *vt* **:** to live together in ⟨two closely related species of freshwater cottids . . . ~ the Arrow lakes in British Columbia —*Copeia*⟩ — **co·hab·i·tant** \-bəd·ənt, -bətə- *also* -bət°nt\ *n* -S
co·hab·i·ta·tion \(,)kō,habə'tāshən\ *n* -S [ME *cohabitacioun*, fr. LL *cohabitation-, cohabitatio*, fr. *cohabitatus* (past part. of *cohabitare*) + *-ion-, -io* -ion] **1 :** act or state of cohabiting esp. as or as if husband and wife **2 :** COITUS
co·hee \'kō,hē\ *or* **coo·hee** \'kü,-\ *n* -S *cap* [origin unknown] **:** an inhabitant of western Pennsylvania or western Virginia
co·heir \(')kō+\ *n* [*co-* + *heir*] **:** a joint heir
co·heiress \(')kō+\ *n* [*co-* + *heiress*] **:** a joint heiress
co·hen *or* **ko·hen** \'kō(h)ən\ *n, pl* **co·ha·nim** \-nəm, ,kō(h)ə'nēm\ *also* **cohens** *usu cap* [Heb *kōhēn* priest] **:** a member of one of the families or clans descended from the high priest Aaron having certain hereditary religious privileges and responsibilities
co·hen·ite \'kōə,nīt\ *n* -S [G *cohenit*, fr. Emil *Cohen* †1905 Ger. mineralogist + G *-it* -ite] **:** a tin-white crystalline mineral $(Fe,Ni,Co)_3C$ consisting of a carbide of iron, nickel, and cobalt and occurring in some meteorites
co·here \kō'hi(ə)r, -iə\ *vb* -ED/-ING/-S [L *cohaerēre*, fr. *co-* + *haerēre* to stick, cling — more at HESITATE] *vi* **1 a :** to hold together firmly, solidly, stickily, with resistance to separation (as of ingredients in a conglomeration or similar particles in a mass) ⟨particles of wet sand ~⟩ ⟨the two sticky surfaces ~⟩; *often* **:** STICK, ADHERE — usu. used of a substance stuck to a similar substance **b** *bot* **:** to display cohesion **2 a :** to consist of or become marked by parts, ingredients, or elements which cohere ⟨despite the addition of a bonding agent the mass would not ~⟩ **b** (1) *of a group or community* **:** to become harmoniously united by common interests or sense of social membership or by emotional ties and esp. with the cooperative playing down of any individual differences or disagreements ⟨torn by personal animosities, the town did not ~ in any of its endeavors⟩ (2) *of an individual* **:** to be a cooperative part of a group or community united in this way ⟨the necessity that he shall conform, that he shall ~ —T.S.Eliot⟩ **c :** to have unambiguous connectedness and logical or aesthetic interrelation of parts **:** fit together naturally and consistently with suitable order, proportion, and similarity of tone without jar or wrench ⟨did not the whole composition ~, were its unity broken, it would be not one picture —Irwin Edman⟩ **d :** to become fittingly connected or unified by certain principles, relationships, or themes esp. in the study or presentation of one purpose or idea ⟨pure arithmetic ~*s* with its basal elements given in whole numbers —Samuel Alexander⟩ **3 :** to be consistent **:** SUIT, FIT ⟨the account ~*s*⟩ ⟨the adornments ~ with the base design⟩ ~ *vt* **:** to make (parts or components) fit or stick together in a suitable or orderly way ⟨amends, ~*s*, and sharpens our map —*Times Lit. Supp.*⟩ **syn** see ADHERE
co·her·ence \kō'hirən(t)s *also* -her- *or* -hēr-\ *n* -S [MF & L; MF *cohérence*, fr. L *cohaerentia*, fr. *cohaerent-, cohaerens* (pres. part. of *cohaerēre*) + *-ia*] **1 :** the quality or state of cohering: as **a :** systematic or methodical connectedness or interrelatedness esp. when governed by logical principles **:** CONSISTENCY, CONGRUITY **b :** integration of social and cultural elements based on a consistent pattern of values and a congruous set of ideological principles **2** *obs* **:** mutual understanding **:** fellow feeling
coherence theory *n* **:** the theory that the ultimate criterion of truth is the coherence of all its separate parts with one another and with experience — contrasted with *correspondence theory*
co·her·en·cy \-nsē, -i\ *n* -ES [L *cohaerentia*] **:** COHERENCE
co·her·ent \-nt\ *adj* [MF or L; MF *cohérent*, fr. L *cohaerent-, cohaerens*] **1 :** having the quality of cohering ⟨two ~ substances⟩ ⟨the felting of the individual fibers into a ~ sheet requires the use of a bonding agent —A.C.Morrison⟩ ⟨a ~ plan⟩ ⟨a ~ speech⟩ ⟨a place and time ~ with a plan of action⟩; *specif, bot* **:** displaying cohesion — compare ADNATE 1 **2 :** logically consistent and ordered ⟨a ~ way of explaining⟩ ⟨a ~ thinker⟩ **3 :** relating to electromagnetic waves that have a definite relationship to each other: as **a :** composed of two wave trains with a constant difference in phase **b :** producing coherent light ⟨a ~ source⟩ — **co·her·ent·ly** *adv*
co·her·er \-hirə(r)\ *n* -S [so called fr. the assumption that the current caused the loosely connected points to cohere] **:** a radio detector in which an imperfectly conducting contact between pieces of metal or other conductors loosely resting against each other is materially improved in conductance by the passage of high-frequency current
co·he·sion \kō'hēzhən\ *n* -S [fr. *cohere*, after such pairs as E *adhere: adhesion*] **1 :** the act, quality, or state of cohering (as tangibly or morally) **:** a sticking together ⟨the ~ of two substances⟩ ⟨the ~ of the tribal group —D'Arcy McNickle⟩ ⟨the ~ of the free nations —Dean Acheson⟩ ⟨cultural ~⟩ **2 :** union between similar plant parts or organs (as between petals of a flower) — compare ADHESION **3 :** molecular attraction by which the particles of a body are united throughout the mass whether like or unlike — distinguished from *adhesion*
co·he·sive \-hēsiv, -sēv *also* -hēz-\ *adj* [*cohesion* + *-ive*] **1 :** COHERING ⟨a beautifully ~ whole —Arthur Knight⟩ ⟨a ~ family unit⟩ **2 :** causing to cohere ⟨~ forces⟩ — **co·he·sive·ly** *adv* — **co·he·sive·ness** *n* -ES
co·hib·it \kō'hibət\ *vt* -ED/-ING/-S [L *cohibitus*, past part. of

cohibēre, fr. *co-* + *habēre* to have, hold — more at HABIT] *archaic* : RESTRAIN, RESTRICT

co·hi·tre \kō'hē-(,)trā\ *n* -S [Sp *cojitre*] : a dayflower (*Commelina longicaulis*) troublesome as a weed esp. in Puerto Rico

cohn·heim's area \'kōn,hīmz-\ *n, usu cap C* [trans. of G *Cohnheimsche felder*, after Julius F. *Cohnheim* †1884 Ger. pathologist] : one of the polygonal areas seen in transverse sections of a striated muscle fiber representing a bundle of cut ends of fibrils surrounded by sarcoplasm

co·ho *or* **co·hoe** \'kō(,)(h)ō\ *or* **coho salmon** *or* **cohoe salmon** *n, pl* **cohos** *or* **coho** *or* **cohoes** [origin unknown] : SILVER SALMON

co·ho·ba \kō'hōbə\ *n* -S [AmerSp *cohoba, cojoba*, of Arawakan origin; akin to Taino *cohoba* tobacco, cohoba] : a narcotic snuff made from the seeds of a tropical American tree (*Piptadenia peregrina*)

co·ho·bate \'kōə,bāt, -ō(h)ō,-, kə'hō,-\ *vt* -ED/-ING/-S [NL *cohobatus*, past part. of *cohobare*, perh. fr. Ar *ka'aba* to repeat an action, double a number] : to redistill formerly esp. by pouring a distillate back upon the matter from which it was distilled but now usu. by subjecting a distillate to a new act of distillation — **co·ho·ba·tion** \,==ˈbāshən\ *n* -S

cohol *var of* KOHL

co·ho·ni·na \,kō(h)ə'nēnə\ *adj, usu cap* [fr. the name *Cohonina*] : of or relating to a prehistoric Indian culture which flourished in northwestern Arizona from the 8th to the 11th centuries

co·horn \'kō,hȯrn\ *also* **coe·horn** \'kōō,-, 'kō,-\ *n* -S [fr. earlier *Coehorn mortar*, part trans. of D *Coe-hoorn-mortier*, after Baron Menno van *Coehoorn* †1704 Dutch engineer, its inventor] : a small bronze mortar that was mounted on a wooden block with handles and used for throwing light shells

co·hort \'kō,hȯ(ə)rt, -ō(ə)t, *usu* -d·+V\ *n* -S [MF & L; MF *cohorte*, fr. L *cohort-, cohors* enclosure, cohort — more at COURT] **1 a** : one of ten divisions of an ancient Roman legion comprising at first 300 but later 500 to 600 soldiers **b** : a similar subdivision in some organizations of Roman cavalry or auxiliary troops **c** : a group of warriors or soldiers **d** : COMPANY, BAND, GROUP ⟨a loyal ~ of adherents —S.N.Behrman⟩ **e** : a group of individuals or vital statistics about them having a statistical factor in common in a demographic study (as year of birth) ⟨data that tells what happened to a ~ of patients admitted in a specific year —*Diagnostic & Statistical Manual*⟩ ⟨a ~ of 100,000 females starting life together⟩ **2** : a taxonomic category of somewhat indefinite rank: **a** *bot* : a category nearly equivalent to and now generally replaced by the modern order **b** *zool* : SUBORDER **3 a** : COMPANION, ACCOMPLICE ⟨he and three alleged housebreaking ~s were arraigned on attempted burglary charges —*Springfield (Mass.) Republican*⟩ **b** : FOLLOWER, SUPPORTER ⟨a congressman accompanied by a group of loyal ~s⟩

co·hor·ta·tion \,kō,hȯ(r)'tāshən\ *n* -S [L *cohortation-, cohortatio*, fr. *cohortatus*, past part. of *cohortari* to exhort (fr. *co-* + *hortari* to urge) + *-ion-, -io* -ion — more at YEARN] : EXHORTATION

¹co·hor·ta·tive \kō'hȯ(r)d·əd·iv\ *n* -S [ISV *cohortat-* (fr. L *cohortatus*) + *-ive*; prob. orig. formed as G *kohortativ*] : a set of verb forms expressing exhortation; *also* : a form belonging to such a set

²cohortative \(')=¦===\ *adj* : belonging to or constituting a set of verb forms expressing exhortation

co·hosh \'kō,häsh, ='=, kə'häsh\ *n* -ES [of Algonquian origin; akin to Natick *kôshki* it is rough] : any of several American medicinal plants: as **a** : a bugbane (*Cimicifuga racemosa*) **b** : BLUE COHOSH **c** : WHITE BANEBERRY **d** : RED BANEBERRY

cohow *or* **cohowe** *var of* CAHOW

co·hune \kō'hün\ *or* **cohune palm** \(')=¦=-\ *n* -S [AmerSp, fr. Mosquito *óchuñ, uchúñ*] : a commercially important Central and So. American pinnate-leaved palm (*Orbignya cohune*) valued esp. for the oil and the hard ivory-nutlike shell of its fruit

cohune oil *also* **cohune-nut oil** *or* **cohune fat** *n* : a yellowish semisolid fat obtained from cohune fruits and used in cooking and in soapmaking

coi·ba \'kōivə\ *n, pl* **coiba** *or* **coibas** *usu cap* [Sp, of AmerInd origin] **1 a** : a Cunan people of southwestern Panama **b** : a member of such people **2** : the Chibchan language of the Coiba people

co·identity \¦kō+\ *n* [*co-* + *identity*] : identity between two or more things

¹coif *also* **coiffe** \'kȯif, *in sense 4 usu* 'kwäf *or* -af *or* -aa(ə)f *or* -âf\ *n* -S [ME *coyfe*, fr. MF *coife, coiffe*, fr. LL *cofea, cofia*] **1** : a cap covering the sides of the head like a small hood, having various shapes and sizes, and worn at various periods of history by men and women ⟨a nun's ~⟩ **2** : a defensive usu. iron or steel skullcap formerly worn by soldiers (as under the hood of mail); *also* : a hood of mail **3** : a white cap formerly worn by lawyers in England, esp. serjeants-at-law; *also* : the order or rank of a serjeant-at-law **4** : COIFFURE **5** : a small close-fitting woman's hat worn on the crown or the back of the head

²coif *also* **coiffe** \'kȯif, *in sense 3 usu* 'kwäf *or* -af *or* -aa(ə)f *or* -âf\ *vt* **coiffed** *or* **coifed**; **coiffed** *or* **coifed**; **coiffing** *or* **coifing**; **coifs** [MF *coiffer*, fr. *coiffe*, n.] **1** : to cover or dress with or as if with a coif **2** : to invest with a coif **3** : to arrange (hair) by combing, brushing, or curling

coif·feur \kwä'fər, kwa-,kwá-, +V -ər-; -'fə̄, +V -ər- *also* -ər\ *n* -S [F, fr. *coiffer* + *-eur* -er] : a male hairdresser

coif·feuse \kwä'fə(r)z, kwa'-kwá'-, -'fə̄z\ *n* -S [F, fem. of *coiffeur*] : a female hairdresser

¹coif·fure \kwä'fyů(ə)r, kwa'-,kwá'-, -ůə, '=,=(ə), *F* kwáfüːr\ *n* -S [F, fr. *coiffer* + *-ure*] : a manner of arranging or styling the hair : HEADDRESS

²coiffure \"\ *vt* -ED/-ING/-S : ²COIF 3

¹coign *var of* QUOIN

²coign \'kȯin\ *n* -S [earlier spelling of ¹*coin*] : a projecting corner; *specif* : a corner of a crystal formed by the intersection of three or more faces at a point

coign of vantage : a position advantageous for action or observation ⟨from the *coign of vantage* which the present age affords . . . we will . . . retell the history of Christianity —K.S.Latourette⟩

coigny *var of* COYNYE

coi·gue \kȯi'gā, '=,=\ *or* **coi·hue** \kȯi'wā, '=,=\ *n* -S [Sp *coigué, coihué*, fr. Araucan *coyhue*] : a Chilean evergreen tree (*Nothofagus dombeyi*) the leafy boughs of which are used for thatching

¹coil \'kȯil, *esp before pause or consonant* -ȯiəl\ *n* -S [origin unknown] **1** : noisy disturbance : TUMULT, TURMOIL **2 a** : a troublesome activity or disturbance esp. over a trifling matter : a great ado : FUSS ⟨here's a ~ raised, a pother and for what —Robert Browning⟩ **b** : worldly activities, affairs, or troubles ⟨in that sleep of death . . . when we have shuffled off this mortal ~ —Shak.⟩

²coil \"\ *vb* -ED/-ING/-S [MF *coillir* to collect, gather together — more at CULL] *vt* **1** : to wind (something long and pliable, as a rope) into rings laid within or on top of one another or wound spirally about an object ⟨the snake ~*ed* itself about its victim⟩ ⟨she ~*ed* her hair at the back of her head⟩ **2** : to encircle and hold with or as if with coils **3** : to roll or twist (as oneself) into a shape resembling a coil ⟨she ~*ed* herself upon the bed with a book⟩ ~ *vi* : to move in a circular, spiral, or winding course ⟨under the image on the water the water ~s and goes —R.P.Warren⟩ : form a coil : lie in coils : WIND **syn** see WIND

³coil \"\ *n* -S **1 a** : a series of loops or a spiral (as of a flexible strand or sheet) ⟨her hair hung in neat ~s⟩ : an arrangement of something in a spiral or in concentric rings ⟨large ~s of sheet metal⟩ **b** : a single loop or part of such a coil ⟨the town nearly enclosed by a ~ of the river⟩ **2** : a helix or spiral of insulated wire wound on a spool or other structure usu. for electromagnetic effect or for providing resistance **3 a** : series of connected pipes in rows, layers, or windings (as in steam-heating or water-heating apparatus) **4** : a roll of postage stamps for use in a stamp machine or other type of stamps dispenser; *also* : a stamp from such a roll **5 a** : the action of coiling, winding up, or tensing (as of a spring) ⟨the better ~ in the legs, the greater spring for lift —H.O. Crisler⟩ **b coils** *pl* : something resembling a coil or a coiling (as of rope) in that it binds, restricts, or entangles ⟨wrestling with the ~s of convention —Clive Bell⟩

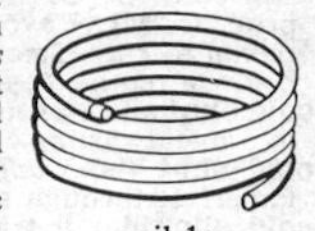

coil 1a

⁴coil \"\ *n* -S [origin unknown] *dial* : HAYCOCK

⁵coil \"\ *vt* -ED/-ING/-S : COCK ⟨~*ing* hay⟩

coil antenna *n* [³*coil*] : a radio antenna of one or more complete turns of wire or other conductor functioning as an inductance rather than as a capacity — compare LOOP ANTENNA

coiled *adj* [fr. past part. of ²*coil*] **1** : under tension : straining to be released ⟨an impression of ~ power⟩ **2** *of a basket* : of a close weave, circular in form and made by coiling the fiber

coil·er \'kȯilə(r)\ *n* -S [²*coil* + *-er*] **1** : an apparatus used in spinning cotton and other fibers that coils the sliver by feeding it through a tube attached to an annular revolving plate into oppositely revolving cans **2** : one that makes coils (as by winding wire to form springs)

coiling *n* -S [fr. gerund of ²*coil*] : the construction of coil pottery

coil pottery *or* **coiled pottery** *n* [³*coil*] : a pottery common among American Indians made by building up sides of pots with successive rolls of clay

coil spring *n* [³*coil*] : a flat-spiral, volute, or helical spring

coil waste *n* [³*coil*] : postage stamps intended orig. to be coils but constituting remnants sold as sheet stamps

coim·ba·tore \¦kōimbə¦tō(ə)r, -tȯ(ə)r\ *adj, usu cap* [fr. *Coimbatore*, India] : of or from the city of Coimbatore, India : of the kind or style prevalent in Coimbatore

co·implicant \(')kō+\ *adj* [*co-* + *implicant*] *logic* : mutually implying : EQUIVALENT 2b

¹coin \'kȯin\ *n* -S [ME *coyne*, fr. MF *coing, coin* wedge, stamp, corner, fr. L *cuneus* wedge; perh. akin to L *culex* gnat — more at CULEX] **1 a** *archaic* : CORNER, CORNERSTONE, QUOIN **b** *archaic* : a wedge used for blocking, securing, or tightening **c** : a small corner cupboard esp. of the 18th century **2** *obs* : the stamped device or impress on coined money **3** : a piece of metal or rarely of some other material (as leather or porcelain) certified by a mark or marks upon it as being of a specific intrinsic or exchange value; *specif* : such a piece issued by governmental authority to circulate as lawful money — see MINOR COIN, STANDARD COIN, SUBSIDIARY COIN, TOKEN, TOKEN COIN **4** : something accepted as having value or validity ⟨perhaps wisecracks . . . are respectable literary ~ in the U.S. —*Times Lit. Supp.*⟩ : something given or offered in an exchange ⟨too much softened . . . to answer his obstinacy in like ~ —J.C.Powys⟩; *specif* : a unit (as an expression or idea) of intellectual or social exchange ⟨they exchanged a few small ~s of country talk —Mollie Panter-Downes⟩ **5** *slang* : MONEY

²coin \"\ *vt* -ED/-ING/-S [ME *coynen*, fr. MF *coignier*, fr. *coin, coing*, n.] **1 a** : to make (a coin) by stamping the design onto the planchet ⟨~ pennies⟩ : convert (metal) into coins ⟨~ silver⟩ **b** : to make (a coin) by any process or series of processes : MINT, STRIKE ⟨~ dimes⟩ : manufacture or issue (money) in the form of coins **c** : to shape (a piece of metal) in a mold or die by applying great pressure **2** : to make up or invent (something false or spurious) ⟨~ smile and fair words⟩ **3** : CREATE, INVENT ⟨~ a phrase⟩ **4** : to make money out of ⟨~ your brains⟩ : convert into something valuable ⟨~ his talent into verses⟩ **5** : to make or earn (money) rapidly and in large quantity ⟨~*ed* a small fortune . . . in the real estate boom —Irving Dilliard⟩

³coin \"\ *adj* **1** : of or relating to coins ⟨a ~ show⟩ **2** : operated by coins ⟨a ~ laundry⟩

coin·age \'kȯinij, -ēj\ *n* -S [ME, fr. MF *coignaige*, fr. *coin, coing* + *-age*] **1 a** : the act or process of coining (as money) : the manufacture of coins **b** : the official stamping of tin blocks of standard weight **c** : the fabricating or inventing esp. of new words ⟨a word of recent ~⟩ **2** : something that has been coined: as **a** : COINS **b** : a quantity of coins produced at one time from a particular metal or by a particular mint : a series of coins minted under a particular ruler, government, or dynasty or in a particular country or city ⟨the Jubilee ~ of 1887⟩ **c** : something that is made up or invented ⟨this is the very ~ of your brain —Shak.⟩; *specif* : a coined word ⟨*chortle* is a ~ of Lewis Carroll's⟩ **d** : something that passes current (as in the language of a group) or is of recognized worth ⟨the term has become common ~⟩

coinage ratio *n* : RATIO 2c

coin box *n* : a locked receptacle to store the coins inserted in a coin-operated device (as in a pay phone)

coin changer *n* : a key-operated machine which from a store of coins drops into a coin tray a required number of coins in required denominations (as in making change for paper money)

co·in·cide \,kōən'sīd, '=,=,=\ *vi* -ED/-ING/-S [ML *coincidere*, fr. L *co-* + *incidere* to fall on, fr. *in* + *cadere* to fall — more at CHANCE] **1 a** : to occupy the same place in space ⟨the base of the triangle ~s with one side of the square⟩ **b** : to occur at the same time or occupy the same period of time ⟨the fall of Granada *coincided* with the discovery of America⟩ **c** : to occupy exactly corresponding or equivalent positions on a scale or in a series ⟨100° centigrade ~s with 212° Fahrenheit⟩ **2** : to be identical or correspond in nature, character, or function : be in harmony ⟨our sentiments *coincided* in every particular —Jane Austen⟩ ⟨engaged in a work which *coincided* with his own inclinations —H.W.H.Knott⟩ **3** : to be in accord or agreement : CONCUR ⟨she *coincided* with his views on most subjects⟩ **syn** see AGREE

co·in·ci·dence \kō'in(t)sədən(t)s\ *n* -S [F *coïncidence*, fr. MF *coincidance*, fr. *coincider* (fr. ML *coincidere*) + *-ance*] **1** : the occupation of the same position in space ⟨the ~ of a point in space with another point⟩, in time ⟨~ of two events⟩, or in a series or on a scale ⟨~ of the readings on two thermometers⟩ : the coming together or simultaneous occurrence or existence of things or events ⟨the ~ of the last note of the violin with the sound of the bell⟩ **2** : correspondence or agreement in nature, character, or detail ⟨a perfect ~ between truth and goodness —Robert South⟩ **3** : an instance of coinciding or corresponding ⟨the ~s between the Arabic and the Sanskrit versions —F.M.Müller⟩ **4** : the concurrence of events or circumstances appropriate to one another or having significance in relation to one another but between which there is no apparent causal connection ⟨the ~ that Mr. Baines should have died while there was a show of mourning goods in his establishment —Arnold Bennett⟩ **5** *biol* : the ratio between the observed number of double crossovers and the number predicted on a random basis — compare INTERFERENCE **6** : the simultaneous indication by two or more counting tubes of the passage presumably of the same ionizing particle through both or all of them (as in a cosmic-ray telescope) — compare ANTICOINCIDENCE

coincidence method *n* : a precise method of comparing the frequencies of two periodic phenomena (as the ticking of two clocks) by observing the interval between their successive coincidences, the interval being the least common multiple of the periods compared

co·in·ci·den·cy \-dənsē, -si\ *n* -ES [F *coincidence* + E *-y*] *archaic* : COINCIDENCE

¹co·in·ci·dent \(')kō¦insədənt, -,dent\ *adj* [F *coïncident*, fr. MF, fr. *coincider* + *-ent*] : marked by or showing coincidence: **a** : occurring or operating at the same time : CONCOMITANT, ATTENDING ⟨hand weaves and their ~ expense —*New Yorker*⟩ **b** : occupying the same space : having the same position, direction, or setting ⟨the culture areas . . . would be essentially ~ with language areas —Harry Hoijer⟩ **c** : having accordant characteristics or nature : HARMONIOUS ⟨they had a sincere affection for each other and ~ opinions on the proper conduct of life —A.T.Quiller-Couch⟩ **syn** see CONTEMPORARY

²coincident \"\ *n* -S *archaic* : a coincident thing or event

co·in·ci·den·tal \(')=¦==¦dentᵊl\ *adj* [²*coincident* + *-al*] **1** : being or resulting from a coincidence ⟨similarity between the two texts is too consistent to be ~⟩ : characterized by coincidence : occurring or existing at the same time ⟨rebellion in Burma was ~ with . . . insurrection in Malaya —W.B. Hamilton⟩ — **co·in·ci·den·tal·ly** \-t(ə)lē, -li\ *adv*

co·in·ci·dent·ly \(')kō¦insə¦dentlē, -sədəntlē, -li\ *adv* : COINCIDENTALLY

co·indicate \(')kō+\ *vt* [*co-* + *indicate*] : to provide conjoint indications of — **co·indication** \¦kō+\ *n*

coin dot *n* : a pattern (as on a fabric) resembling a polka dot but usu. with large dots

coin·er \'kȯinə(r)\ *n* -S [ME *coyner*, fr. *coynen* + *-er*] : one that coins: as **a** : a maker of coins **b** : one that performs the stamping operation in the manufacture of a coin **c** *chiefly Brit* : one that makes coins illegally : COUNTERFEITER **d** : an inventor or fabricator esp. of new words or expressions

co·infinite \(')kō+\ *adj* [*co-* + *infinite*] : equally infinite : conjointly infinite

coin gold *n* : gold of the fineness legalized for coins (as .900 fine in the U. S., .9166 or ¹¹⁄₁₂ fine in Great Britain)

co·inhabit \¦kō+\ *vi* [*co-* + *inhabit*] : to dwell together — **co·inhabitant** \¦kō+\ *n*

coining *n* -S [fr. gerund of ²*coin*] **1** : the stamping or manufacture of coins **2** *chiefly Brit* : the counterfeiting or illegal manufacture of coin

coining die *n* : one of a set of dies between which a piece of metal is squeezed in or as if in coining money

coin lesion *n* : a round well-circumscribed nodule in a lung that is seen in the roentgenogram as a shadow the size and shape of a coin

coin lock *n* : a lock released by the insertion of a coin; *also* : a lock operated by inserting a coin which releases the key

coin machine *n* : SLOT MACHINE

coin note *n* : a currency note bearing a statement that promises redemption in coin; *specif* : one from either of two series of U. S. treasury notes issued in 1863–65 and in 1890–91

coin of the realm : the legal money of a country

coins *pl of* COIN, *pres 3d sing of* COIN

coin seal \'=,=\ *n* : a metal seal with a design on both face and back

coin silver *n* : silver of the fineness legalized for coins (as .900 fine in the U. S., .500 fine for Great Britain since 1920)

co·instantaneity \¦kō+\ *n* -ES [*coinstantaneous* + *-ity*] : the quality or state of being coinstantaneous

co·instantaneous \(')kō+\ *adj* [*co-* + *instantaneous*] : happening at the same instant — **co·instantaneously** \(')kō+\ *adv*

co·insurance \¦kō+\ *n* [*co-* + *insurance*] **1** : joint assumption of risk with another or others (as the sharing of a risk jointly by two or more underwriters) **2** : a system of insurance (as fire insurance) in which the insured is obligated to maintain coverage on a risk at a stipulated percentage of its total value or in the event of loss suffer a penalty in proportion to the deficiency

co·insure \¦kō+\ *vb* [*co-* + *insure*] *vi* : to insure a property jointly or upon the basis of coinsurance ~ *vt* : to insure (a property) jointly or with another or others

co·insurer \¦kō+\ *n* [*co-* + *insurer*] : one that assumes liability as an insurer jointly with another : one subject to penalty under a coinsurance clause

coin·tise \kwan'tēz\ *n* -S [ME (also, wisdom, skill), fr. OF, fr. *cointe* wise, skillful, elegantly dressed — more at QUAINT] : a fanciful or symbolical article of apparel; *esp* : a scarf worn on a lady's headdress or as a token of favor on a knight's helmet

Coin·treau \kwaⁿ·trō\ *trademark* — used for a sweet colorless orange-flavored liqueur

coin weight *n* : a weight (sense 3b) used in judging coins

coir \'kȯi(ə)r, -ȯiə\ *n* -S [Tamil *kayiṟu* rope] : a stiff coarse fiber from the outer husk of the coconut

cois·trel \'kȯistrəl\ *n* -S [MF *coustillier* soldier carrying a short sword, squire of a knight, fr. *coustille* short sword (alter. of *coustele* knife, fr. L *cultellus*) + *-ier* -er — more at CUTLASS] **1** *archaic* : a groom employed to care for a knight's horses **2** *archaic* : a mean fellow : VARLET

co·i·tal \'kōəd·ᵊl, -ōtᵊl\ *adj* [L *coitus* + E *-al*] : of or relating to coitus

coital exanthema *n* : a highly contagious virus disease of horses and cattle transmitted chiefly by copulation and marked by the formation of vesicles and pustules on the mucous membranes of the genital tract, the viruses in horses and in cattle being commonly considered distinct

co·i·tion \kō'ishən\ *n* -S [L *coition-, coitio*, fr. *coitus* (past part. of *coire* to come together, fr. *co-* + *ire* to go) + *-ion-*, *-io* -ion — more at ISSUE] **1** *obs* : a coming together or meeting : conjunction esp. of planets **2** *obs* : mutual attraction esp. of iron and a magnet **3** [LL *coition-, coitio*, fr. L] : COITUS — **co·i·tion·al** \-shənᵊl, -shnəl\ *adj*

co·i·tus \'kōəd·əs, -ōtəs\ *n* -ES [L, fr. *coitus*, past part. of *coire*] : physical union of male and female genitalia accompanied by rhythmic movements leading to the ejaculation of semen from the penis into the female reproductive tract; *also* : INTERCOURSE 3 — compare ORGASM

coitus in·ter·rup·tus \-,intə'rəptəs\ *also* **coitus re·ser·va·tus** \-,rezər'vād·əs\ *n, pl* **coitus interrup·ti** \-,tī,-(,)tē\ *also* **coitus reserva·ti** \-d·,ī,-d·(,)ē\ [NL, interrupted coitus] : coitus which is purposely interrupted in order to prevent ejaculation of semen into the vagina

co·ix \'kōəks\ *n* [NL, fr. Gk *koix* doom palm] **1** *cap* : a small genus of coarse Asiatic monoecious grasses having the pistillate flowers and seeds enclosed in a shining capsulelike involucre **2** -ES : any plant of the genus *Coix*; *esp* : JOB'S-TEARS

co·jo·nes \kə'hō,nās\ *n pl* [Sp, pl. of *cojón* testis, fr. (assumed) VL *coleon-, coleo* — more at CULLION] **1** : TESTES **2** : COURAGE, GUTS

co·juror \(')kō+\ *n* [*co-* + *juror*] : COMPURGATOR

¹coke \'kōk\ *n* -S [ME *coke, colke*; akin to Sw *kälk* pith, Gk *gelgis* bulb of garlic, Skt *gṛñjana* garlic, L *galla* gall on a plant — more at GALL] **1** *dial Eng* : the core esp. of a fruit **2 a** : the infusible cellular coherent residue from carbonized coal that consists mainly of carbon, is hard, porous, and gray with a submetallic luster, and is used as a fuel (as in blast furnaces and domestic furnaces) **b** : a similar residue from various other carbonized substances (as petroleum, shale oil, or copal) **c** : a piece of coke ⟨put a ~ on the fire⟩

²coke \"\ *vb* -ED/-ING/-S *vt* : to change into coke ⟨a uniform controlled heat makes it impossible to ~ or char the material⟩ ~ *vi* : to become coky ⟨the *coking* of petroleum oils on distillation —R.F.Goldstein⟩

³coke \"\ *n* -S [by alter. and shortening] *slang* : COCAINE

Coke \"\ *trademark* — used for a cola drink

coke breeze *n* : fine coke separated by screening from the larger sizes before or after crushing

coked *adj* [³*coke* + *-ed*] *slang* : stimulated by an addicting drug (as cocaine) — often used with *up* ⟨a *coked*-up gunman⟩

coke dust *n* : powdered coke

coke iron *n* : iron made in a furnace using coke as fuel

coke oven *n* : an oven made usu. of refractory brick and blocks and used for carbonization (as of coal) for the production of coke — see BEEHIVE OVEN, BY-PRODUCT OVEN

coke-oven gas \'=,==-\ *n* : a gas that is similar in composition to coal gas and that is obtained in the carbonization of coal esp. at high temperatures for the production of coke

coke plate *or* **coke tin** *n* **1** : tin plate made from coke iron **2** : tin plate having lighter coating than charcoal plate

co·ker \'kōkə(r)\ *n* -S [alter. of *coco*] : COCO — used in the port of London to avoid confusion with *cocoa*

co·ker·nut \'kōkə(r),nət\ *n* [alter. of *coconut*] **1** : COCONUT 1 **2** : the edible seed of the coquito palm (*Jubaea spectabilis*) of Chile enclosed in a fruit like a small coconut

cok·ery \'kōk(ə)rē\ *n* -ES [¹*coke* + *-ery*] : a plant for making coke

cokes *n* [orig. unknown] *obs* : SIMPLETON, GULL

¹cok·ie *also* **cok·ey** \'kōkē\ *n* -S [³*coke* + *-ie, -y*] *slang* : a cocaine addict

²cokie *also* **cokey** \"\ *adj, slang* : addicted to cocaine

coking coal *n* [fr. pres. part. of ²*coke*] : a bituminous coal suitable for making into coke

coky \'kōkē\ *adj* -ER/-EST [¹*coke* + *-y*] : resembling coke (as in physical properties)

col \'käl\ *n* -S [F, fr. MF, neck, fr. L *collum* — more at COLLAR] **1 a** : a high pass in a mountain range generally across a watershed **b** : a saddlelike depression in the crest of a ridge **2** : a neck of low pressure between two anticyclones

¹col- — see COM-

²col- *or* **coli-** *or* **colo-** *comb form* [NL, fr. L *colon*] **1** : large intestine ⟨*colitis*⟩ ⟨*colostomy*⟩ **2** : colon bacillus ⟨*coliform*⟩

³col *abbr* **1** *often cap* colonel **2** colonial; colony **3** colophon **4** color; colored **5** column **6** counsel

²col *or* **coll** *abbr* **1** collated **2** collateral **3** colleague **4** collect; collected; collective; collector **5** college; collegiate **6** colloquial; colloquialism

COL *abbr* cost of living

¹cola *pl of* COLON

²co·la \ˈkōlə\ *n* [of African origin; akin to Temne *k'ola* kola nut, Mandingo *kolo*] **1** *cap* **:** a large genus of African trees (family Sterculiaceae) having capsular fruits containing large seeds **2** -s **a** *or* **ko·la** \"\ a tonic extract derived from the kola nut **b** [fr. *Coca-Cola*, a trademark] **:** a carbonated soft drink flavored with extract from coca leaves, kola nut, sugar, caramel, and acid and aromatic substances

³co·la \ˈkōlə\ *n* -s [Sp, lit., tail, fr. L *coda, cauda*] **:** LINE, QUEUE ⟨a ~ of ticket holders⟩

-co·la \kələ, kōlə\ *n comb form* -s [NL, fr. L — more at -COLOUS] **:** inhabitant ⟨*Arenicola, Rupicola*⟩

co·la·ci·a·les \kə,lāsēˈā(,)lēz\ *n pl, cap* [NL, fr. *Colacium* (fr. Gk *kolak-, kolax* parasite, flatterer + NL *-ium*) + *-ales;* perh. akin to Gk *kēlein* to beguile — more at CALUMNY] **:** an order of algae (class Euglenophyceae) comprising those forms that have immobile cells with an encapsulating wall and that develop amorphous or dendroid colonies with sometimes temporary naked flagellate stages, the members of some of its genera (as *Colacium*) occurring on rotifers, copepods, and other minute aquatic animals

col·a·co·bi·o·sis \,kälə,kōbīˈōsəs, -bēˈ-\ *n, pl* **colacobio·ses** \-,sēz\ [NL, fr. Gk *kolak-, kolax* parasite + NL *-o-* + *-biosis*] *zool* **:** permanent social parasitism (as that between certain species of ants)

co·la·mine \ˌkōlə¦mēn, kōˈlamən\ *n* -s [ISV al*col*ohol + *amine*] **:** ethanolamine esp. as a component of certain phosphatides (as cephalin)

col·an·der \ˈkələndə(r), ˈkäl-\ *also* **cul·len·der** \ˈkəl-\ *n* -s [ME *colyndore*, prob. modif. of OProv *colador*, fr. ML *colatorium*, fr. L *colatus*, past part of *colare* to filter, strain, sieve, fr. *colum* sieve — more at HEDGE] **:** a bowl-shaped usu. metal utensil having perforations permitting use as a strainer

colander

co·lane \kōˈlān\ *n* -s [origin unknown] **:** EMU APPLE

cola nut *var of* KOLA NUT

colarian *usu cap, var of* KOLARIAN

co·la·scio·ne \,kōläˈshōnē, -nā\ *n, pl* **colascio·nes** \-,nēz\ [It] **:** an Italian long-necked lute of the 16th and 17th centuries

cola seed *n* **:** KOLA NUT

co·la·tion \kəˈlāshən\ *n* -s [L *colatus* + E *-ion*] **:** removal of solids from a liquid by straining esp. through filter paper

co·latitude \(ˈ)kō+\ *n* -s [*co-* + *latitude*] **:** the complement of the latitude

cola tree *var of* KOLA TREE

col·a·ture \ˈkäləchə(r)\ *n* -s [LL *colatura*, fr. L *colatus* (past part. of *colare* to strain) + *-ura* -ure] **:** STRAINING

col bas·so \kōlˈbä(,)sō\ *adv* [It] **:** with the bass — used as a direction in music to play the same part as the bass

col·ber·teen *or* **col·ber·tine** \ˈkälbə(r),tēn, ˈkōl-\ *n* -s [after Jean B. *Colbert* †1683 Fr. statesman + E *-een* or *-ine*] **:** a lace with a coarse network of open square mesh

col·bert·ism \ˈkälbə(r),tizəm, ˈkōl-, kōlˈbā(ə),rizəm\ *n* -s *usu cap* [Jean B. *Colbert* + E *-ism*] **:** the mercantilistic policies and practices of Colbert

col·by \ˈkōlbē\ *also* **colby cheese** *n* -ES *sometimes Colby* [prob. fr. the name *Colby*] **:** a porous soft moist mild cheese

col·can·non \kəlˈkanən, ˈkäl,k-\ *n* -s [IrGael *cāl ceannan*, lit., white-headed cabbage, fr. *cāl* cabbage, kale (fr. OIr, fr. L *caulis*) + *ceannan* white-headed, bald, fr. *ceann* head (fr. OIr *cend, cenn*) + *fionn* white, fr. OIr *find* — more at COLE, ARPENT, FINNOCK] **:** potatoes and cabbage or other greens boiled and mashed together

col·cha \ˈkōlchə\ *n* -s [Sp, bedspread, quilt, fr. OSp, bed, couch, fr. OF *colche, couche* — more at COUCH] **:** a wool-embroidered coverlet of Mexican origin

col·ches·tri·an \(ˈ)kōl¦chestrēən\ *n* -s *cap* [*Colchester*, Essex, England + E *-ian*] **:** a native or resident of Colchester

¹col·chi·an \ˈkälkēən\ *adj, usu cap* [L *Colchis* (fr. Gk *Kolchis*) + E *-an*] **1 :** of, relating to, or characteristic of Colchis, an ancient region in Asia **2 :** of, relating to, or characteristic of Colchians

²colchian \"\ *n* -s *usu cap* **:** a native or inhabitant of Colchis

col·chi·ce·ine \käl'chisēən, -ˈkis-; ¦kälchə¦sēən, -lkə¦-\ *n* -s [ISV, fr. *colchicine*] **:** a crystalline compound $C_{21}H_{23}NO_6$ of which colchicine is the methyl ether

col·chi·cine \ˈkälchə,sēn, ˈkälkə-, -sən\ *n* -s [G *kolchizin*, fr. NL *Colchicum* + G *-in* -ine] **:** a poisonous yellow crystalline alkaloid $C_{22}H_{25}NO_6$ extracted from the seed and corm of the meadow saffron that on application to mitotic cells induces polyploidy, an effect used experimentally and commercially to create new plant varieties, and that is used medicinally in the treatment of acute attacks of gout

col·chi·cin·ize \ˈ==sə,nīz\ *vt* -ED/-ING/-s **:** to treat with colchicine in order to induce c-mitosis ⟨*colchicinized* root-tips — *Biol. Abstracts*⟩

col·chi·cum \ˈkälchəkəm, -älkə-\ *n* [NL, fr. L, a kind of plant with a poisonous root, fr. Gk *kolchikon*, fr. *kolchikos* Colchian, fr. *Kolchis* Colchis] **1** *cap* **:** a genus of chiefly fall-blooming Old World cormous herbs (family Liliaceae) having crocuslike flowers with a very long perianth tube and six stamens — see MEADOW SAFFRON; compare CROCUS **2** -s **:** a plant, bulb, or flower of the genus *Colchicum* **3** *or* **colchicum root** -s **:** the dried corm or dried ripe seeds of autumn crocus that contain the alkaloid colchicine and possess an emetic, diuretic, and cathartic action used chiefly for gout and rheumatism

col·co·thar \ˈkälkəthə(r)\ *n* -s [ML, fr. MF or OSp; MF *colcotar*, fr. OSp *cólcotar* (now *colcótar*), fr. Ar dial. *qulqutār*, prob. modif. of Gk *chalkanthos* — more at CHALCANTHITE] **1 :** a reddish brown iron oxide left as a residue when ferrous sulfate is highly heated and used formerly in polishing glass and as a pigment **2 :** a moderate reddish brown that is yellower and deeper than roan, yellower, stronger, and slightly darker than mahogany, and yellower, less strong, and slightly darker than oxblood — called also *angel red, Coromandel, English red, Mars red, Prussian red, Tuscany*

¹cold \ˈkōld\ *adj* -ER/-EST [ME, fr. OE *cald, ceald;* akin to OHG *kalt* cold, ON *kaldr*, Goth *kalds*, L *gelu* frost, *gelare* to freeze, congeal] **1 a :** having a temperature notably below an accustomed norm, often notably below that of the human body or below that compatible with human comfort **:** notably lacking in warmth **:** having a low temperature ⟨quite ~ weather⟩ ⟨it was ~ yesterday⟩ ⟨the rain was very ~ now, almost frigid, and they shuddered —Norman Mailer⟩ ⟨a ~ and drafty hallway⟩ ⟨~ arctic seas⟩ ⟨have trouble starting with a ~ motor⟩ — distinguished from *cool* **b :** likely to lose heat quickly **:** likely to feel cool ⟨a ~ metallic substance⟩ **c :** receptive to the sensation of coldness **:** stimulated by cold ⟨a ~ spot is the typical ~ receptor in higher vertebrates⟩ **2 a :** naturally without heat — used in ancient and medieval sciences to describe one of the qualities of the four elements **b** *of a sign of the zodiac* **:** having a cold complexion **3 a :** marked by lack of warm feeling **:** without ardor, zeal, or sympathy **:** DISTANT ⟨he's a pretty ~ one —Ernest Hemingway⟩ ⟨the ~, correct, regular, narrow poetry of Pope —A.L.Kroeber⟩ ⟨this novel leaves the reader ~⟩ **b :** free from emotion or passion, esp. sexual passion **:** FRIGID, INHIBITED ⟨one of the ~ kisses that he disliked so much —Archibald Marshall⟩ **c :** lacking cordiality, heartiness, friendliness, or affability **:** UNFRIENDLY **:** forbiddingly reserved **:** ALOOF, CHILLING ⟨his ~, mean, selfish policy toward those whom he liked to segregate and hate as his enemies —W.A.White⟩ ⟨the court becomes a ~ place for the self-exiled queen —H.O.Taylor⟩ **d :** lacking feeling **:** EMOTIONLESS, DETACHED, INDIFFERENT, APATHETIC, COLD-BLOODED ⟨the ~ neutrality of an impartial judge —Edmund Burke⟩ ⟨~, sullen, unreliable, brusque, unconventional, grasping, a man of iron will —C.L.Jones⟩ **e :** feeling or showing no interest, excitement, or sympathy **:** UNENTHUSIASTIC ⟨the discouragement of playing to a ~ audience⟩ ⟨the mawkish appeal left him ~⟩ ⟨to his astonishment, he finds the people of his village ~ to this noble and time-honored sentiment —Arthur Knight⟩ **f :** marked by deliberate intent or plan **:** not shaped or influenced by passion or strong feeling **:** activated or executed deliberately ⟨a ~ calculated punishing punch in the mouth —John Steinbeck⟩ ⟨that a goodly part of the illegal drug supply is grown and processed in China; that it is spread with ~ deliberation to other countries —Meyer Berger⟩ **g :** unemotionally calculated or calculating **:** marked by analysis and calculation uninfluenced by warmer feelings **:** UNFEELING ⟨how ~ economic considerations and calculations prevail in all matters of international importance —H.W.Van Loon⟩ ⟨the ~ argument and unhurried process of trial in the courts of law —W.C.Dickinson⟩ **4 a :** previously cooked but served or eaten cold ⟨a ~ collation⟩ ⟨~ boiled ham⟩ **b :** not hot enough **:** heated insufficiently or permitted to cool ⟨the soup was ~⟩ **c :** not heated ⟨stored in a ~ cellar⟩ **d :** made cold **:** COOLED, ICED ⟨~ soft drinks⟩ **e :** unheated while being worked ⟨drive rivets ~⟩ ⟨a *cold*-bent iron pipe⟩ ⟨*cold*-forged steel⟩ **5 a :** inducing discouragement **:** DEPRESSING, CHEERLESS, DISPIRITING, GLOOMY ⟨a ~ correctness in the way he put his bicycle in its place that made her heart sink —D.H. Lawrence⟩ ⟨the ~ respectability of a Pharisee's dining room —W.L.Sullivan⟩ **b :** producing a sensation of cold **:** CHILLING ⟨I hold a key in my hand and it is ~ —Muriel Rukeyser⟩ ⟨~ blank walls⟩ **c** *of a color* **:** COOL; *esp* **:** having a cool hue and low value **6 a :** DEAD ⟨lay ~ in his coffin —Margaret A. Barnes⟩ **b :** unconscious typically from a blow or shock or from complete intoxication **:** INSENSIBLE ⟨knocked out ~⟩ ⟨pass out ~⟩ **c :** completely at one's mercy **:** without hope of escape **:** DEFENSELESS ⟨you're as good as found guilty because they never crack down unless they have you ~ —Polly Adler⟩ **d :** marked by complete knowledge or errorless familiarity **:** CERTAIN, SURE ⟨the actors had their lines ~ a week before the opening night⟩ **e** *slang* **:** sure to be fulfilled — used of a contract in a card game **7 a** *of a soil* **:** retentive of moisture, often compact and clayey, and responding only slowly to atmospheric temperature changes **b** *of a manure* **:** decaying slowly with little evolution of heat ⟨~ pig manure⟩ **8 :** feeling cold **:** made uncomfortable by cold — usu. used postpositively ⟨the children came back in when they were ~⟩ **9** *obs, of foods* **:** BLAND, MILD **:** not strong, hot, or pungent ⟨~ plants⟩ **10 :** lacking power to influence, incite, animate, inspire, impassion, or affect in other ways ⟨the Roman copy is almost inevitably ~er, less alive, less emotional, and (above all) less expressive than the Greek —Hunter Mead⟩ ⟨a ~ traffic of minds and ideas and, for all the melodrama, not a clash of living people —J.R.Newman⟩**: a :** FAINT **:** not strong; *usu* **:** old and being obscured ⟨dogs trying to follow the ~ scent⟩ **:** retaining only faint scents, traces, or clues ⟨the trail had become ~⟩ **b :** STALE, UNINTERESTING; *often* **:** having undergone loss of timeliness ⟨the story is now too ~ to be newsworthy⟩ **c :** old and showing lack of power to communicate ⟨a stenographer trying to transcribe ~ notes⟩ **d :** not illegal or involved in a crime **:** not suspect ⟨trading the hot car for a ~ one⟩ **e :** allowing little or no possibility of contact with radioactivity — used esp. of area in a plant or laboratory; opposed to *hot* **11 :** presented or regarded in a straightforward, blunt, or matter-of-fact way **:** not influenced or relieved by emotional presentation or persuasive appeal **:** IMPERSONAL ⟨competing on a basis of sheer ~ efficiency —T.W.Arnold⟩ ⟨the ~ facts of the case⟩ ⟨presenting ~ statistics⟩ **12 a :** far from finding, discovering, or solving **b :** marked by poor or unlucky performance ⟨an erratic bowler, sometimes hot, sometimes ~⟩ ⟨hot and ~ periods even fall . . . upon writers —C.B.Davis⟩ **c :** not in operation **:** IDLE ⟨a ~ munitions plant in peace times⟩ **d** *slang, of dice* **:** not producing many passes or results that win for the shooter **13 a :** marked by lack of preparation, rehearsal, preliminary performance, preliminary exercise or operation, introduction, or knowledge and familiarity ⟨instead of opening ~ in New York, all the productions have had a week of preliminary performing in Hartford —Brooks Atkinson⟩ ⟨they came here ~, years ago, not knowing many people —J.P.Marquand⟩ ⟨a substitute entering the game ~⟩ **b** *in radio & television* **:** without music or embellishments ⟨a program that comes on ~⟩ ⟨~ drama⟩ ⟨the salesman had to approach the prospective customer ~⟩ ⟨~ selling⟩ **14 :** certain to be indicated **:** ASSURED ⟨a ~ five thousand dollars⟩ **15 :** lacking in thoroughbred blood ⟨a ~ cross⟩ **16 :** designed for use in cutting cold metal **17 :** living in or characteristic of a cold environment ⟨the ~ fauna of glacial epochs⟩ **18 a :** intense and barely controlled ⟨a ~ fury⟩ ⟨a ~ irritation⟩ **b :** checked short of sustained overt violence (as military action) but marked by deep antagonism and conducted with all available economic, political, or social means ⟨a ~ pogrom⟩ ⟨~ revolution⟩ **19 a :** intended for use without being heated ⟨a ~ glue⟩ **b :** using or produced by cold type ⟨~ composition⟩ — **in cold blood** *adv* **:** with premeditation **:** DELIBERATELY — used of an action generally avoided or condemned ⟨kill a man *in cold blood*⟩

²cold \"\ *n* -s [ME, fr. OE *cald*, fr. *cald*, adj. — more at COLD] **1 a :** a condition of low temperature **:** COLDNESS ⟨the ~ was intense⟩ **b :** cold weather **2 :** bodily sensation produced by loss or lack of heat **:** CHILL ⟨they groan with pain and shudder with the ~ —S.T.Coleridge⟩ **3 :** a respiratory infection: **a** *in man* **:** COMMON COLD ⟨to catch ~⟩ ⟨he has a ~⟩ **b** *in domestic animals* **:** CORYZA b **4 :** chill discouragement **:** a feeling of blended fear, crushing disappointment, shock, depression, or despair — **in the cold :** without heating — **out in the cold :** NEGLECTED, IGNORED **:** left unconsidered **:** deprived of benefits given others ⟨the plan helps engineers and firemen but leaves brakemen *out in the cold*⟩

³cold \"\ *vb* -ED/-ING/-s [ME *colden*, fr. (assumed) OE *caldian, cealdian*, fr. *cald* cold — more at COLD] *vi* **:** to become cold ⟨the nights were ~*ing* —Maristan Chapman⟩ ~ *vt* **:** to make cold ⟨~ his blood with the thought of dying —John Masefield⟩

⁴cold \"\ *adv* -ER/-EST [¹*cold*] **1 :** with utter finality **:** in a completely unmitigated way **:** TOTALLY, ABSOLUTELY ⟨he was stopped ~⟩ ⟨be turned down ~⟩ ⟨know the answers ~⟩ **2 :** while cold or without the application of heat — used esp. of metalworking processes ⟨*cold*-hammer a bar of iron⟩ ⟨*cold*-roll steel⟩ ⟨*cold*-swage metal parts⟩

cold abscess *n* **:** a chronic often tuberculous abscess of slow formation and with little evidence of inflammation

cold agglutination *n* **:** AUTOAGGLUTINATION

cold agglutinin *also* **cold hemagglutinin** *n* **:** any of certain agglutinins present in some bloods (as those of many patients with primary atypical pneumonia) that at low temperatures agglutinate compatible as well as incompatible erythrocytes, including the patient's own

coldbar \ˈ=,=\ *adj* [²*cold* + *bar*] **:** providing protection against extreme cold — used of a suit or uniform, esp. military

coldblood \ˈ=,=\ *n* -s [back-formation fr. *cold-blooded*] **:** an animal that is cold-blooded (senses 2, 3)

cold-blooded \ˈ=¦==\ *adj* **1 a :** marked by absence of warm feelings **:** without consideration, compunction, or clemency **:** UNFEELING, CALLOUS, HARDENED, CRUEL ⟨of *cold-blooded* expediency and sometimes of unscrupulous self-interest —Douglas Bush⟩ ⟨*cold-blooded* executions of innocent people —Sir Winston Churchill⟩ **b :** MATTER-OF-FACT, EMOTIONLESS ⟨the literary evidence must be tested by sidelights from *cold-blooded* documents —G.G.Coulton⟩ **2 :** having cold blood; *specif* **:** having a body temperature not internally regulated but approximating that of the environment ⟨*cold-blooded* amphibians and reptiles⟩ **:** POIKILOTHERMIC, HETEROTHERMIC **3** *or* **coldblood a** *of horses* **:** not possessing Arab or Thoroughbred ancestry — used esp. of members of the heavy draft breeds **b** *of horses and other livestock* **:** of mixed or inferior breeding **:** MONGREL **4 :** noticeably sensitive to cold ⟨too *cold-blooded* to enjoy skating⟩ — **cold-blood·ed·ly** *adv* — **cold-blood·ed·ness** *n* -ES

cold cash *n* **:** cash viewed as readily fluid or expendable, indicative of real value, or assured as gain or income ⟨enough *cold cash* to close the purchase⟩

cold cathode *n* **:** a cathode in an electron tube or fluorescent lamp that is unheated and that emits electrons when bombarded by ions or subjected to light, infrared, or ultraviolet rays ⟨*cold-cathode* tube⟩

cold cellar *n, Northeast* **:** a room or section of a cellar where root crops may be stored over winter at temperatures slightly above freezing

cold chisel *n* **:** a chisel made of tool steel of a strength, shape, and temper suitable for chipping or cutting cold metal — see CHISEL illustration

coldcock \ˈ=,=\ *vt* [perh. fr. ¹*cold* + *cock* (penis)] **:** to knock unconscious

cold comfort *n* **:** scant consolation **:** quite limited sympathy or encouragement

cold cream *n* **:** a soothing and cleansing ointmentlike usu. white cosmetic consisting typically of a perfumed emulsion of a bland vegetable oil or heavy mineral oil and other ingredients

cold cure *n* **:** the vulcanization esp. of thin rubber products by treatment at ordinary temperatures with a solution or vapors of a sulfur compound, usu. sulfur monochloride

cold-cut \ˈ=,=\ *adj* [⁴*cold*] *of a varnish or lacquer* **:** manufactured by dissolving one ingredient in another without the application of heat

cold cuts *n pl* **:** sliced assorted cold meats and cheeses — compare DUTCH LUNCH

cold deck *n* **1 :** a stacked pack of playing cards; *esp* **:** one prepared for surreptitious substitution for the pack in play **2 :** a pile of logs assembled when cut and left for later transportation to a mill — compare HOT DECK

cold-deck \ˈ=¦=\ *vt* [*cold deck*] **:** CHEAT, DEFRAUD, SWINDLE

cold-draw \ˈ=¦=\ *vt* **1 :** to draw (as metal or nylon) while cold or without the application of heat **2 :** to cold-press (vegetable oil) — **cold-drawing** \ˈ=,==\ *n* -s

cold emission *n* **:** FIELD EMISSION

cold enamel *n* **:** a solution of bichromated shellac or other colloid that does not require heating or burning in and is used as a sensitizer in photoengraving — called also *cold top*

¹colder *comparative of* COLD

²col·der \ˈkäldə(r), ˈkōd-\ *n* -s [origin unknown] *dial Eng* **:** refuse from threshing **:** HUSK

coldest *superlative of* COLD

cold feet *n pl* **:** apprehension, misgiving, doubt, or fear strong enough to prevent a planned course of action ⟨wanted to complain to the boss but at the last minute got *cold feet*⟩

cold fish *n* **:** a cold aloof emotionless person ⟨a *cold fish*, reserved and calculating —Polly Adler⟩

cold flour *n, dial* **:** sugared pulverized corn

cold flow *n* **1 :** the viscous flow of a solid at ordinary temperatures **2 :** the distortion of a solid under sustained pressure esp. with an accompanying inability to return to its original dimensions when the pressure is removed

cold-flow \ˈ=¦=\ *vi* [*cold flow*] **:** to exhibit cold flow

cold frame *n* **:** an outdoor shallow rectangular frame of boards or concrete with a usu. glass cover to protect small plants from wind and low temperature esp. early in the growing season — compare HOTBED

cold front *n* **:** an advancing edge of a cold air mass that is displacing warm air in its path often recognized by a wind shift and drop in air temperature as it passes — see FRONT illustration

cold hands *n pl* **:** poker in which each player is dealt five cards face up and the highest hand wins without betting or draw

cold-head \ˈ=,=\ *vt* **:** to upset a head on a rod or wire without heating the metal (as in forming bolts, screws, and rivets)

coldhearted \ˈ=¦==\ *adj* **:** marked by lack of sympathy, interest, normal sensitivity, kindliness, or mercy ⟨a ~ judge⟩ ⟨a ~ refusal⟩ — **cold·heart·ed·ly** *adv* — **cold·heart·ed·ness** *n* -ES

cold house *n* **:** a greenhouse (as for grapes) maintained at a low temperature

cold·ish \ˈkōldish, -dēsh\ *adj* **:** somewhat cold ⟨~ weather⟩

cold-jaw \ˈ=¦=\ *vi, West* **:** to become hard-mouthed ⟨when a horse *cold-jaws* on you and wants to run, let him go till he runs down his mainspring —R.F.Adams⟩

cold-jawed \ˈ=¦=\ *adj, West* **:** HARDMOUTHED

cold light *n* **1 :** light emitted by any body whose temperature is below that of incandescence — compare LUMINESCENCE **2 :** visible light from whatever source unaccompanied by appreciable amounts of infrared and having therefore little heating effect

coldly *adv* [ME, fr. ¹*cold* + *-ly*] **:** in a cold manner ⟨he answered ~⟩ ⟨staying ~ aloof⟩

cold meat *n, slang* **:** CORPSES, CORPSE

cold-meat fork \ˈ=¦=-\ *n* **:** a large serving fork with flat pointed tines

cold nail *n* **:** a cut nail

cold·ness *n* -ES [ME, fr. ¹*cold* + *-ness*] **:** the quality or state of being cold

cold pack *n* **:** a sheet or blanket wrung out of cold water, wrapped around the patient's body, and covered with dry blankets

cold-pack \ˈ=¦=\ *vt* **:** to can or tin by the cold-pack method ⟨*cold-pack* peaches⟩

cold-pack method \ˈ=¦=-\ *n* **1 :** a method of canning fruits or vegetables that consists of (1) scalding or blanching, (2) packing immediately into hot containers and covering or sealing, (3) processing or sterilizing in a hot-water bath or pressure cooker, and (4) sealing or resealing at once while contents are still hot — called also *raw-pack method* **2 :** FROZEN-PACK

cold patch *n* **1 :** a mixture of crushed stone and bituminous binder that may be used cold for mending pavement **2 :** a rubber patch cemented without vulcanizing to a pneumatic tire tube

cold-patch *vt* [*cold patch*] **:** to repair with a cold patch

cold peace *n* **:** an unstable peace among nations formerly engaged in a cold war

cold pig *n, slang Brit* **:** a wetting with cold water to awaken one

cold pit *n* **:** an excavation with walls that is usu. covered with glass and is used for rooting potted bulbs and resting half-hardy plants

cold plague *n, archaic* **:** a severe ague

cold pole *n* **:** POLE OF COLD

cold-press \ˈ=¦=\ *vt* **:** to subject to pressure or to express without heating ⟨*cold-press* metal⟩ ⟨*cold-press* petroleum oil for separation of wax by filtration⟩

cold pressor test *n* **:** the response of a person's blood pressure to immersion of one hand in ice water for one minute, an excessive rise or slow return to normal being considered an indication of susceptibility to the development of hypertension

cold process *n* **:** a soapmaking process in which melted fats are treated with lye without further heating

cold prophet *var of* COLEPROPHET

cold-roll \ˈ=¦=\ *vt* **:** to roll (metal) without applying heat

cold room *n* **:** a room in which a low temperature is maintained (as for refrigeration)

cold rubber *n* **:** a synthetic rubber of the GR-S type that is made at a relatively low temperature (as 41°F) and is characterized by a lowered viscosity and usu. by increased resistance to wear (as in tire treads)

colds *pl of* COLD, *pres 3d sing of* COLD

cold saw *n* **1 :** a saw (as a circular saw) for cutting cold metal — distinguished from *hot saw* **2 :** a soft-steel or iron disk operated at such an angular velocity, corresponding to a velocity of a point on its periphery of about 15,000 feet per minute, that it grinds off metal by friction — compare FUSING DISK

cold seeds *n pl* [²*cold*] **:** the seeds of various cucurbitaceous fruits (as the melon or cucumber) sometimes used as emollients

cold set *n* **:** a chisel ground to a flat edge and used in metalworking esp. for flattening seams

cold-set \ˈ=¦=\ *adj* [⁴*cold*] **:** used in a method of printing in which ink is kept fluid by heat until it contacts the cold paper when it quickly solidifies ⟨*cold-set* ink⟩; *also* **:** using or done by this method ⟨the *cold-set* process⟩ ⟨*cold-set* printing⟩

cold shape *n* **:** a blancmange pudding that is molded and chilled

cold-short \ˈ=¦=\ *adj* [by folk etymology fr. Sw *kallskör*, fr. *kall* cold (fr. ON *kaldr*) + *skör* brittle, fr. OSw *skör, skyr*, prob. fr. MLG *skōr;* akin to MLG *schoren* to break, OHG *sceran* to cut — more at COLD, SHEAR] *of metal* **:** brittle when below a red heat — compare HOT-SHORT

cold shot *n* **1 :** round shotlike particles formed by a cold shut in a metal casting **2 :** COLD SHUT 1

cold-shot \ˈ=¦=\ *adj* [⁴*cold*] **:** chilled by the mold in casting or imperfect through such chilling — used of a foundry casting

cold shoulder *n* **:** intentionally cold or unsympathetic treatment **:** scornful neglect **:** deliberate coldness ⟨hurt at getting the *cold shoulder* from an old friend⟩

cold-shoulder \ˈ=¦==\ *vt* [*cold shoulder*] **:** to give the cold shoulder to ⟨insulted in the streets, *cold-shouldered* by his friends —Bertrand Russell⟩

cold-shut \'=¦=\ *adj* [⁴*cold*] **:** closed while too cold to become thoroughly welded — used of a forging; compare COLD SHUT 2

cold shut *n* [*cold-shut*] **1 :** the freezing of the surface of liquid metal during the pouring of an ingot or casting due to interrupted or improper pouring; *also* **:** an imperfection thus caused **2 :** the imperfect weld caused in a forging by the inadequate heat of one surface under working or by an oxide film **3 :** a split ring or link used to mend or fasten chains

cold·slaw \'kōl(d),slȯ\ *n* -s [by folk etymology fr. D *koolsla*, fr. *kool* cabbage + *sla* salad, fr. *salade*, fr. F; akin to OE *cāl* cabbage — more at COLE, SALAD] **:** COLESLAW

cold-smoke \'=¦=\ *vt* [⁴*cold*] **:** to smoke (as ham) at a temperature between 70 and 90 degrees F

cold soldering *n* **:** soldering in which two pieces are joined without heat (as by means of a copper amalgam)

cold sore *n* [²*cold*] **:** the group of blisters appearing about or within the mouth in herpes simplex

cold steel *n* **:** a steel weapon (as a sword or bayonet)

cold stoking *n* **:** the operation in glass manufacturing of reducing the glass to the proper degree of viscosity for being worked

cold storage *n* **1 :** storage esp. of food in a place kept cold often by refrigeration for preservative purposes ⟨meats in *cold storage*⟩ — compare DRY STORAGE **2 :** a condition of being held or continued without being acted on **:** ABEYANCE ⟨the second world war effectively put the question into *cold storage* —Leo Marquard⟩

cold-storage training \'=¦=-\ *n* **:** the training of workers for positions usu. of relatively high levels in advance of need

cold store *n* [short for *cold storage*] **:** a building for cold storage

cold-store \'=¦=\ *vt* [back-formation fr. *cold storage*] **:** to place or hold in cold storage ⟨the excess eggs are *cold-stored*⟩

cold sweat *n* [¹*cold*] **:** perspiration accompanied by feelings of chill or cold and usu. induced or accompanied by dread, fear, or shock ⟨the blush of embarrassment or the *cold sweat* of fear —*Jour. Amer. Med. Assoc.*⟩

cold-sweat \'=¦=\ *vi* [⁴*cold*] **:** to sweat (as hides) in cold water

cold test *n* **:** a test of oils (as lubricating oils) to determine the temperature at which a cooled sample begins to deposit solid material or becomes too viscous to flow; *also* **:** the temperature so determined

cold top *n* **:** COLD ENAMEL

cold-trail \'=¦=\ *vb* **:** to follow on a cold trail ⟨a dog *cold-trailing* more than a mile⟩

cold trailing *n* **:** a method of controlling smoldering forest fires by feeling the edge of a burning area with the hand and digging out or trenching round burning spots

cold turkey *n* **1 :** unrelieved blunt matter-of-fact statement or procedure **:** statement with irrevocable finality ⟨I'm talking *cold turkey* to you . . . I think it wise if your relationship has ended —J.B.Clayton⟩ **2 :** a sure victim **:** one facing certain defeat, punishment, or destruction ⟨a *cold turkey* for the enemy⟩ **3 :** abrupt complete cessation without medication of the use of drugs by a drug addict ⟨trying the *cold-turkey* cure⟩ **4 :** a cold aloof person ⟨the head nurse was a *cold turkey*⟩

cold type *n* **:** composition or typesetting (as photocomposition) done without the casting of metal; *specif* **:** such composition produced directly on paper by a typewriter mechanism

cold war *n* **1 :** conflict between two nations or groups of nations by means of power politics, economic pressures, spy activities, or hostile propaganda and often sabotage and exclusion of opposing nationals but without engagement by arms **2 :** conflict short of violence esp. between power groups (as labor and management)

cold water *n* **:** deprecation (as of a plan or an expectation) as being ill-advised, unwarranted, or worthless **:** DISCOURAGEMENT, DISPARAGEMENT ⟨throw *cold water* on our hopes⟩ ⟨pour *cold water* on a scheme⟩

cold-water \'=¦==\ *adj* [*cold water*] **1 :** of or relating to temperance groups **:** preferring cold water to alcoholic beverages **2 a :** provided only with running cold water **b :** not having all modern plumbing or heating facilities ⟨a *cold-water* flat⟩

cold-wa·ter paint *n* **:** a paint consisting of a pigment held in suspension by a binder dissolved in cold water

¹**cold wave** *n* **:** a sudden large drop in temperature; *broadly* **:** a period of unusually cold weather

²**cold wave** *n* **:** a machineless permanent wave set by a chemical preparation usu. containing a salt of thioglycolic acid

cold-weld \'=¦=\ *vt* [⁴*cold*] **:** to weld (metal) cold by pressure without the application of heat

cold-work \'=¦=\ *vt* [*cold work*] **:** to work (metal) without using heat

¹**cole** \'kōl\ *n* -s [ME, fr. OE *cāl*, *cawel*, fr. L *caulis* stalk of a plant, cabbage — more at HOLE] **1 :** a plant of the genus *Brassica*; *esp* **:** RAPE **2** *Brit* **:** SEA KALE

²**cole** *obs var of* COAL

-cole \kōl\ *adj comb form* [by alter. (influenced by F *-cole*)] **:** -COLOUS ⟨saxicole⟩

cole- *or* **coleo-** *comb form* [NL, fr. Gk *koleo-*, fr. *koleon*] **:** sheath **:** covering ⟨coleitis⟩ ⟨Coleoptera⟩ ⟨coleorhiza⟩

co·lec·ti·vo \,kōlek'tē(,)vō\ *n* -s [AmerSp, fr. Sp, adj., collective, fr. L *collectivus* — more at COLLECTIVE] **:** a small bus, a station wagon, or a limousine serving as a public conveyance

col·ec·to·my \kə'lektəmē, kō-, -mi\ *n* -ES [ISV *col-* + *-ectomy*] **:** excision of a portion or all of the colon

co·legatee \,kō +\ *n* [*co-* + *legatee*] **:** a joint legatee

co·le·gio \kə'lāhē,ō, -hyō\ *n* -s [Sp, fr. ML *collegium* college — more at COLLEGE] **:** SECONDARY SCHOOL

cole·man·ite \'kōlmə,nīt\ *n* -s [William T. *Coleman* †1893 owner of mine where mineral was discovered + E *-ite*] **:** a mineral $Ca_2B_6O_{11}.5H_2O$ consisting of a hydrous calcium borate occurring in brilliant colorless or white massive monoclinic crystals

co·le·o·chae·ta·ce·ae \,kōlē,ōkē'tāsē,ē, ,käl-\ *n pl, cap* [NL, fr. *Coleochaete*, type genus + *-aceae*] **:** a family of green algae (order Ulotrichales) having the features of *Coleochaete* — **co·le·o·chae·ta·ceous** \¦==¦==¦tāshəs\ *adj*

co·le·o·chae·te \-'kēd·,ē\ *n, cap* [NL, fr. *cole-* + Gk *chaitē* hair — more at CHAETA] **:** a genus (the type of the family Coleochaetaceae) of aquatic epiphytic green algae having cells solitary or in branching filaments that in some members form cushionlike masses

co·le·on·yx \,==¦änəks\ *n, cap* [NL, fr. *cole-* + *-onyx*] **:** a genus of lizards comprising the ground geckos of the western U.S.

co·le·oph·o·ra \-'äf(ə)rə\ *n, cap* [NL, fr. *cole-* + *-phora*] **:** a genus (the type of the family Coleophoridae) of small moths comprising the casebearer moths — **co·le·oph·o·rid** \-rəd, -,rid\ *adj or n*

co·le·op·te·ra \-'äptərə\ *n pl, cap* [NL, fr. Gk *koleoptera*, neut. pl. of *koleopteros* sheath-winged, fr. *koleo-* cole- + *-pteros* -pterous] **:** the largest order of insects comprising the beetles and weevils and sometimes the Strepsiptera, being distinguished by an anterior pair of wings that are usu. hard and rigid, are never used for flight, and serve as a protective covering for the delicate membranous flight wings and the upper surface of the abdomen, having usu. a heavily armored body and strong mouthparts that are always of the chewing type, typically producing larvae that are grubs and pass into an inactive pupal stage with a pupa in which the appendages are not cemented to the body and which is rarely enclosed in a cocoon, varying in size from tropical goliath beetles several inches in length to minute forms that pass their lives within the spore tubes of polypore fungi, and including numerous destructive pests of economic plants and of stored products as well as others (as the ladybugs or the fireflies) that are of economic or aesthetic value to man

co·le·op·ter·ist \-rəst\ *n* -s [NL *Coleoptera* + E *-ist*] **:** a specialist in the Coleoptera

¹**co·le·op·ter·oid** \¦kōlē¦äptə,rȯid, ¦käl-\ *adj* [ISV *coleopter-* (fr. NL *Coleoptera*) + *-oid*] **:** like the Coleoptera **:** like a beetle

²**coleopteroid** \"\ *n* -s **:** a coleopteroid insect

co·le·op·ter·o·log·i·cal \¦==¦==rə¦läjəkəl\ *adj* **:** of or relating to coleopterology

co·le·op·ter·ol·o·gy \,==¦==¦räləjē\ *n* -ES [ISV *coleopter-* (fr. NL *Coleoptera*) + *-o-* + *-logy*] **:** a branch of zoology that deals with the Coleoptera

co·le·op·te·ron \,==¦äptə,rän, -,rən\ *n, pl* **coleop·te·ra** \-tərə\ [NL, sing. of *Coleoptera*] **:** one of the Coleoptera **:** BEETLE

co·le·op·te·rous \¦==¦äptərəs\ *adj* [NL *Coleoptera* + E *-ous*] **1 :** of or relating to the beetles **2** *of an insect* **:** SHEATH-WINGED

co·le·op·ti·lar \-¦äptələ(r)\ *adj* **:** of or relating to a coleoptile

co·le·op·tile \,kōlē'äptəl, ,käl-\ *also* **co·le·op·ti·lum** \-tələm\ *n, pl* **coleop·tiles** \-təlz\ *also* **coleopti·la** \-tələ\ [NL *coleoptilum*, fr. *cole-* + *-ptilum* (fr. Gk *ptilon* down) — more at PTIL-] **:** the first leaf of a monocotyledon forming a protective sheath about the plumule

co·le·o·rhi·za \-lēə'rīzə\ *n, pl* **coleorhi·zae** \-(,)zē\ [NL, fr. *cole-* + *-rhiza*] **:** the sheath investing the hypocotyl in some plants through which the roots burst

co·le·o·spo·ri·um \-lēə'spōrēəm, -spȯr-\ *n, cap* [NL, fr. *cole-* + *-sporium*] **:** a genus of rusts (family Melampsoraceae) having the teliospores united in a single-layered or double-layered waxy cushion

coleprophet *n* [obs. *cole* trick, deceiver, cheat (fr. ME) + *prophet*] *obs* **:** DIVINER, SOOTHSAYER

¹**cole·ridg·e·an** *also* **cole·ridg·i·an** \¦kōl¦rijēən\ *adj, usu cap* [Samuel Taylor *Coleridge* †1834 Eng. poet and critic + E *-an*, *-ian*] **:** of, relating to, or suggestive of Coleridge or his writings ⟨critical treatment along *Coleridgean* lines⟩

²**coleridgean** *also* **coleridgian** \"\ *n* -s *usu cap* **:** an admirer or follower of Coleridge

cole·seed \'kōl,sēd\ *n* [trans. of D *koolzaad*] **:** the seed of the rape; *also* **:** ²RAPE 2

cole·slaw \'kōl,slȯ\ *n* -s [alter. (influenced by D *kool* cabbage) of *coldslaw*] **:** a salad made of raw sliced or chopped cabbage

co·le·ta \kə'lād·ə\ *n* -s [Sp, dim. of *cola* tail — more at COLA] **:** the pigtail worn by a bullfighter

coletit *var of* COAL TIT

co·le·us \'kōlēəs\ *n* [NL, fr. Gk *koleos*, *koleon* sheath; fr. the manner in which the stamens are united] **1** *cap* **:** a large genus of herbs (family Labiatae) having showy and often highly variegated leaves and spicate blue flowers **2** -ES **:** a plant of the genus *Coleus* (esp of *C. blumei* and its garden varieties)

colewort \'=,=\ *n* [ME, fr. *cole* + *wort*] **1 :** COLE 1 **2 :** a cabbage in which the leaves do not form a compact head **3 :** a young cabbage

co·li \'kō,lī\ *adj* [L, of the colon, gen. of *colon*] **:** of or relating to bacteria normally inhabiting the intestine or colon, esp. to species of the genus *Escherichia* (as *E. coli*)

coli- — see COL-

co·li-aerogenes \,kōlē +\ *adj* [NL, fr. ²*col-* + *aerogenes*, any of several bacterial species, fr. *aer-* + *-genes*] **:** of, relating to, or being bacteria of the genera *Escherichia* and *Aerobacter*

co·li·as \'kōlē,as\ *n, cap* [NL, fr. Gk *Kōlias*, Attic goddess] **:** a large cosmopolitan genus of butterflies (family Pieridae) which have primarily yellow or orange wings and whose larvae feed mostly on legumes but sometimes on willows or blueberries — see ALFALFA BUTTERFLY, CLOUDED SULPHUR

co·li·bacillary \¦kōlə +\ *adj* [ISV ²*col-* + *bacillary*] **:** of, relating to, or caused by the colon bacillus

co·li·bacillosis \,kōlə +\ *n, pl* **colibacilloses** [NL, fr. ²*col-* + *bacil-* + *-osis*] **:** infection with or disease caused by colon bacilli (esp. *Escherichia coli*)

coli bacillus *also* **coli** *n* **:** COLON BACILLUS

¹**col·ic** \'kälik, -ēk\ *n* -s [ME *colike*, fr. MF *colique*, fr. L *colicus* sick with the colic, fr. Gk *kōlikos*, fr. *kōlon* (alter. of *kolon* colon) + *-ikos* -ic; fr. being seated in or near the colon — more at COLON] **:** a paroxysm of acute abdominal pain in man or animals localized in a hollow organ or tube and caused by spasm, obstruction, or twisting ⟨biliary ~⟩ ⟨ureteral ~⟩

²**colic** \"\ *adj* **:** of or relating to colic **:** COLICKY

³**co·lic** \'kōlik, -äl-, -ēk\ *adj* [²*col-* + *-ic*] **:** of or relating to the colon

col·i·cal \'käləkəl\ *adj* [¹*colic* + *-al*] **1 :** likely to have colic **2 :** relating to or resembling colic

colic artery *n* [³*colic*] **:** any of three arteries supplying the large intestine, the right and middle colic arteries being branches of the superior mesenteric and serving the ascending and transverse colon and the left colic artery deriving from the inferior mesenteric and supplying the descending colon — called also respectively *colica dextra*, *colica media*, and *colica sinistra*

co·liche·marde \¦kō(,)lēsh'märd\ *n* -s [F *colismarde*, *colichemarde*, after Otto Wilhelm, Count von *Königsmark* †1688 Ger. soldier and statesman, its inventor] **:** a long sword with a large forte narrowing abruptly into a slender foible

co·li·cin *or* **col·i·cine** \'kōləsən, 'käl-, -,sēn\ *n* -s [NL *coli* (specific epithet of *Escherichia coli*, a bacterium that produces it) + E connective *-c-* + *-in*, *-ine*] **:** any of certain antibacterial substances produced by some strains of intestinal bacteria and considered to have possible affinity with the coliphages

col·ick·er \'käləkə(r)\ *n* -s [¹*colic* + *-er*] **:** a horse esp. subject to colic

col·icky \-kē,-ki\ *adj* [¹*colic* + *-y*] **1 :** relating to or resembling colic **:** attended by colic ⟨~ disorders⟩ **2 :** suffering from colic ⟨a ~ child⟩ **3 :** causing colic ⟨~ foods⟩

coli count *n* **:** a test of freedom of water from fecal contamination based on determining the number of colon bacteria in a specified volume

colicroot \'==,=\ *n* [¹*colic* + *root*] **1 :** any of certain plants having roots reputed to cure colic; *esp* **:** either of two bitter herbs (*Aletris farinosa* and *A. aurea*) — called also *crow corn* **2 a :** the dried rhizome and roots of the colicroot (*Aletris farinosa*) **b :** the rhizome of a wild yam (*Dioscorea paniculata*)

colicweed \'==,=\ *n* [¹*colic* + *weed*] **:** SQUIRREL CORN

colicwort \'==,=\ *n* [¹*colic* + *wort*] **:** a colicroot (*Aletris farinosa*)

colies *pl of* COLY

¹**col·i·form** \'kälə,fȯrm, 'kōl-\ *adj* [²*col-* + *-form*] **:** relating to, resembling, or being the colon bacillus

²**coliform** \"\ *n* -s [by shortening] **:** a coliform bacillus

coliform index *or* **coli index** *n* **:** an index of the purity of water based on a coli count

co·li·idae \kə'līə,dē\ *n pl, cap* [NL, fr. *Colius*, type genus + *-idae*] **:** a family of birds comprising the colies

co·li·ifor·mes \,==¦fȯr,mēz\ *n pl, cap* [NL, fr. *Colius* + *-iformes*] **:** an order of birds comprising the colies

¹**co·li·ma** \kə'lēmə\ *n* -s [MexSp] **:** a prickly tropical American shrub or small tree (*Zanthoxylum fagara*) — called also *wild lime*

²**colima** \"\ *n, pl* **colima** *or* **colimas** *usu cap* [Sp, of AmerInd origin] **1 a :** a Chibchan people of southern Colombia **b :** a member of such people **2 :** a language of the Colima people

col·in \'kälən; kə'lin, -lēn\ *n* -s [Sp *colin*, modif. of Nahuatl *çolin*] **:** the bobwhite or any of several related New World game birds

-co·line \kə,līn, -,lən\ *adj comb form* [NL *-colinae*, fr. *-cola* + *-inae*] **:** -COLOUS ⟨fluvicoline⟩

co·lin·e·ar \(')kō¦linēə(r)\ *adj* [by alter.] **:** COLLINEAR

co·lingual \¦kō+\ *n* -s [*co-* + *lingual*] **:** one speaking the same native language as another ⟨a poet who has done so much to set the taste of his ~s as has Shakespeare —Allan Gilbert⟩

co·li·nus \kə'līnəs\ *n, cap* [NL, fr. Sp *colin*] **:** the genus of birds (family Phasianidae) consisting of the bobwhites

col·i·phage \'kälə,fāj\ *n* -s [²*col-* + *-phage*] **:** a bacteriophage active against the colon bacillus

col·i·se·um \,kälə'sēəm\ *n* -s [ML *Colisseum*, *Colyseus*, modif. of L *colosseum*, neut. of *colosseus* colossal, fr. *colossus*] **:** a large building designed to hold many spectators or activities calling for a good deal of room (as a basketball game or horse show) **:** a large assembly hall **:** STADIUM

coliseum ivy *n* **:** KENILWORTH IVY

co·lit·ic \kə'lid·ik, -itik, -ēk\ *adj* [NL *colitis* + E *-ic*] **:** belonging to or affected with colitis ⟨~ pain⟩ ⟨~ patient⟩

co·li·tis \kə'līd·əs, -ītəs\ *n* -ES [NL, fr. ²*col-* + *-itis*] **:** inflammation of the colon — see MUCOUS COLITIS, ULCERATIVE COLITIS

co·li·us \'kōlēəs\ *n, cap* [NL, fr. Gk *kolios* green woodpecker] **:** a genus of birds comprising the colies

colk \'kōk\ *n* -s [ScGael *colc*] *dial Eng* **:** EIDER DUCK

¹**coll** \'käl, 'kal\ *vt* -ED/-ING/-S [ME *collen*, fr. OF *coler*, fr. *col* neck, fr. L *collum* — more at COLLAR] *dial* **:** EMBRACE, HUG

²**coll** \'käl, 'kōl\ *vt* -ED/-ING/-S [perh. fr. ON *kollr* rounded point, head; akin to MLG *kol*, *kolle* head, top of a plant, OE *cēol* ship — more at KEEL] *chiefly Scot* **:** CLIP, POLL

coll- *or* **collo-** *comb form* [NL, fr. Gk *koll-*, *kollo-*, fr. *kolla* — more at PROTOCOL] **1 :** glue ⟨collenchyma⟩ ⟨Collocalia⟩ **2 :** colloid ⟨collochemistry⟩

-coll \,käl\ *n comb form* -s [ME *-col* (in *sarcocol*), fr. L *-colla*, fr. Gk *-kolla*, fr. *kolla*] **:** glue ⟨glycocoll⟩ ⟨pyrocoll⟩

coll *abbr* — see COL

¹**colla** *pl of* COLLUM

²**col·la** \'kōlyə\ *n* -s [Sp] *Philippines* **:** a period of rainy windy weather from the southwest

col·la·bent \(')kō¦lābənt, kə'l-\ *adj* [L *collabent-*, *collabens*, pres. part. of *collabi* to collapse — more at COLLAPSE] **:** sunken or falling in **:** collapsing in the middle

col·labo \kə'la(,)bō\ *n* -s [short for *collaborator*] **:** one who collaborates with an enemy

col·lab·o·rate \kə'labə,rāt, *usu* -ād· + V\ *vi* -ED/-ING/-S [LL *collaboratus*, past part. of *collaborare* to labor together, fr. L *com-* + *laborare* to labor] **1 :** to work jointly esp. with one or a limited number of others in a project involving composition or a research to be jointly accredited ⟨Beaumont and Fletcher *collaborated* in writing plays⟩ ⟨Sullivan *collaborated* with Gilbert to produce operettas⟩ **2 :** to cooperate with or assist usu. willingly an enemy of one's country (as an invading or occupying force) ⟨Frenchmen who *collaborated* with the Nazis⟩ **3 :** to cooperate usu. willingly with an agency or instrumentality with which one is not immediately connected often in some political or economic effort ⟨attempts of the West to ~ with Russia⟩ ⟨the two universities ~ on library services⟩

col·lab·o·ra·teur \==¦=rə'tər, + V -ər-; -tō, + V -or- *also* -ər\ *n* -s [F, fr. ML *collaborator*] **:** COLLABORATOR

col·lab·o·ra·tion \kə,labə'rāshən\ *n* -s [F, fr. L *collaboratus* (past part. of *collaborare*) + F *-ion*] **1 :** the act of collaborating or a situation marked by collaborating ⟨either in ~ or independently⟩ ⟨the machinery of international ~ —Vera M. Dean⟩; *esp* **:** collaborating with an enemy or an opposed group rather than struggling or resisting ⟨a Norwegian accused of ~⟩ ⟨the ~ of less militant unionists⟩ **2 :** a product of collaboration ⟨this play is a ~⟩

col·lab·o·ra·tion·ism \-shə,nizəm\ *n* -s **:** the theory or practice of collaboration **:** advocacy of collaboration

¹**col·lab·o·ra·tion·ist** \-,nəst\ *n* -s [*collaboration* + *-ist*] **:** one that advocates or practices collaboration with an enemy (as an invader or part of an occupying force) or with some other group opposed or antagonistic to his own ⟨punishment for ~s after the liberation⟩

²**collaborationist** \"\ *adj* **:** of or relating to a collaborationist ⟨the ~ tricks by which the success of the occupation was assured —Ann F. Wolfe⟩

col·lab·o·ra·tive \kə'labə,rād·iv, -ātiv; -lab(ə)rəd·iv, -ətiv\ *adj* **:** marked or produced by collaboration ⟨a ~ research project⟩ — **col·lab·o·ra·tive·ly** *adv*

col·lab·o·ra·tor \kə'labə,rādə(r), -ātə\ *n* -s [F *collaborateur*, fr. ML *collaborator*, fr. L *collaboratus* + *-or*] **:** one that collaborates esp. in some composition or research ⟨they were ~s on this book⟩ or with an enemy or opposed group ⟨purging ~s from the newly established government⟩

col·la des·tra \¦kōlə'destrə\ *adv (or adj)* [It] **:** with the right hand — used as a direction in music

col·lage \kə'läzh\ *n* -s [F, gluing, pasting, fr. *coller* to glue (fr. *colle* glue, fr. — assumed — VL *colla*, fr. Gk *kolla*) + *-age* — more at PROTOCOL] **1 :** an artistic composition of fragments of printed matter and other materials pasted on a picture surface: as **a :** a cubist composition in which pieces of paper, string, and textile are used to represent planes and textures **b :** a surrealist pictorial composition in which figures from engravings, photographs, and printed illustrations are shown in an incongruous environment **2 :** the art of making collages **3 :** PHOTOMONTAGE **4 :** an assembly of diverse fragments ⟨a weekly ~ of cartoons, satirical sketches, and interviews that calls attention to the madness of our time —Ben Harte⟩

col·la·gen *also* **col·lo·gen** \'käləjən, -,jen\ *n* -s [ISV *colla-* (fr. Gk *kolla* glue) or *coll-* + *-gen* — more at PROTOCOL] **:** an insoluble fibrous protein that occurs in vertebrates as the chief constituent of the fibrils of connective tissue (as in skin and tendons) and of the organic substance of the bones and that is characterized by swelling in water solutions, by conversion to gelatin and glue on prolonged heating with water, and by conversion to leather on tanning — compare ELASTIN — **col·la·gen·ic** \¦==¦jenik\ *adj* — **col·lag·e·nous** \kə'lajənəs, (')kä¦l-\ *adj*

col·la·gen·ase \-jə,nās, -nāz\ *n* -s [ISV *collagen* + *-ase*] **:** any of a group of proteolytic enzymes that decompose collagen and gelatin and have been found in some bacteria of the genus *Clostridium* and in a few insect larvae

collagen disease *n* **:** any of various diseases or abnormal states marked by changes in connective tissue presumably involving destruction of collagen (as rheumatoid arthritis, rheumatic fever, or scleroderma)

col·la·gen·o·sis \,==jə'nōsəs\ *n, pl* **collageno·ses** \-,sēz\ [NL, fr. ISV *collagen* + NL *-osis*] **:** COLLAGEN DISEASE

col·lag·ist \kə'läzhəst\ *n* -s **:** one who makes collages; *specif* **:** an artist who works in collage

col·la par·te \¦kōlə'pär(,)tā\ *adv (or adj)* [It, with the part] **:** with the solo part in tempo and phrasing — used as a direction in musical accompaniment

¹**col·lapse** \kə'laps\ *vb* -ED/-ING/-S [L *collapsus*, past part. of *collabi* to collapse, fr. *com-* + *labi* to fall, slide — more at SLEEP] *vi* **1 :** to break down completely **:** fall apart in confused disorganization **:** crumble into insignificance or nothingness **:** DISINTEGRATE ⟨his case had *collapsed* in a mass of legal wreckage —Erle Stanley Gardner⟩ ⟨a flimsy banking enterprise which *collapsed* —R.A.Billington⟩ **2 :** to fall or shrink together abruptly and completely **:** fall into a jumbled or flattened mass through the force of external pressure **:** fall in ⟨the sides of a limp empty boat ~⟩ ⟨our interest ~s like a pricked balloon —G.M.Trevelyan⟩ ⟨a blood vessel that *collapsed*⟩ **3 :** to cave in, fall in, or give way **:** undergo ruin or destruction by or as if by falling down **:** become dispersed ⟨its passage ripped away the crown of the arch and immediately the whole bridge *collapsed* —O.S.Nock⟩ ⟨a magnetic field *collapsing*⟩ **4 :** to suddenly lose force, significance, effectiveness, or worth ⟨all his annoyance *collapsed* in a heap —Hamilton Basso⟩ ⟨*collapsing* currencies of unstable countries⟩ **5 :** to break down in vital energy, stamina, or self-control through exhaustion or disease **:** lose ability to perform accustomed activities **:** fall helpless or unconscious ⟨a fireman *collapsing* from the fumes⟩ ⟨several oarsmen *collapsing* after the hard race⟩ ⟨*collapsed* into tears⟩ **6 :** to fold down into a more compact shape **:** close together ⟨a *collapsing* opera hat⟩ ⟨a telescope that ~s⟩ ~ *vt* **:** to cause to collapse ⟨~ the movement⟩ ⟨*collapsing* an infected lung⟩ ⟨the explosion *collapsed* several buildings⟩ ⟨~ an opera hat⟩

²**collapse** \"\ *n* -s **1 a :** a breakdown in vital energy, strength, or stamina **:** complete sudden enervation **:** sudden loss of accustomed abilities ⟨the daughter's mental ~ through mounting frustration —Leslie Rees⟩ **b :** a state of extreme prostration and physical depression resulting from circulatory failure, great loss of body fluids, or heart disease and occurring terminally in diseases such as cholera, typhoid fever, pneumonia — compare SHOCK **c :** an airless state of a lung in whole or in part of spontaneous origin or induced surgically — see ATELECTASIS **d :** an abnormal falling together of the walls of an organ ⟨~ of blood vessels⟩ **2 :** the action of collapsing **:** the act or action of drawing together or permitting or causing a falling together ⟨the cutting of many tent ropes, the ~ of the canvas —Rudyard Kipling⟩ **3 a :** BREAKDOWN **:** sudden failure **:** DISINTEGRATION, RUIN, DESTRUCTION ⟨the speedy disruption and eventual ~ of our entire society —Lewis Mumford⟩ ⟨the panic . . . with its attendant ~ of grandiose dreams —*Amer. Guide Series: Minn.*⟩ **b :** sudden loss of force, value, effect, or significance ⟨the ~ of respect for ancient law and custom —L.S.B.Leakey⟩ ⟨to save the pound sterling from ~ —Leon Halden⟩ **4 :** a defect in wood due to abnormal and irregular shrinkage and resulting in a wrinkled or corrugated appearance of the surface and sometimes also an internal honeycombing **5 :** the sum of postbreeding regressive changes in the testes of a seasonal breeding male animal

collapse breccia *n* **:** a breccia formed by the collapse of rock overlying an opening
collapse therapy *n* **:** a surgical procedure that collapses a lung and is now used almost solely in the treatment of tuberculosis to rest an infected lung by immobilization
col·laps·i·ble *also* **col·laps·a·ble** \kə'lapsəbəl\ *adj* **:** capable of collapsing or being collapsed ⟨a ~ boat⟩ ⟨a false bag, ~ so that it may be concealed —Valentine Williams⟩
collapsible corporation *n* **:** a corporation that plans to liquidate or whose shares are to be sold to others before sale of goods produced so as to turn what should be taxable income into a capital gain for shareholders
col·lap·sion \kə'lapshən\ *n* -s [LL *collapsion-, collapsio,* fr. L *collapsus* + *-ion-, -io*] *archaic* **:** COLLAPSE
¹col·lar \'kälə(r)\ *n* -s *often attrib* [ME *coller, coler,* fr. OF *coler, colier* necklace, collar, fr. L *collare,* fr. *collum* neck; akin to OE *heals* neck, OHG, ON, & Goth *hals* neck, OE *hwēol* wheel — more at WHEEL] **1 :** a band, strip, or chain worn or placed around the neck: as **a** *obs* **:** neck armor **:** a hauberk neckpiece **b :** an attached or separate band that varies in shape and size and serves to finish or decorate the neckline of a garment or costume — see RUFF, SHAWL COLLAR, WING COLLAR **c :** a short necklace **:** an ornamental band or chain **d :** a band placed around the neck of a dog, cat, or other animal to lead, restrain, identify, or adorn **e :** a part of the harness of draft animals fitted over the shoulders and taking the strain when a load is being drawn **f :** a band often of iron placed around a prisoner's or slave's neck to confine or identify **g :** an ornament or badge (as a necklace) used as an insignia of an order of knighthood **h :** an indication of control **:** a token that another is subservient to one ⟨an independent refusing to wear any man's ~⟩ **i :** a bandage, brace, cast, or other protecting or supporting device worn around the neck **2 :** an encircling band, strap, or ring to check, guide, guard, or adorn: as **a :** an eye in the bight or end of a stay or shroud to go over the masthead **b :** a strap or grommet to secure a heart or deadeye **c :** a filler plate or shape fitted around a structural shape (as an angle or beam) passing through a bulkhead or deck **d :** a ring or round flange upon, around, or against an object chiefly to restrain motion within given limits, to hold something in place, or to cover an opening (as on a shaft to prevent endwise motion or around a pipe where it enters a wall) **e** (1) **:** a curb around the mouth of a mine shaft **:** the immediate vicinity of the mouth of a shaft (2) **:** the rock surrounding the mouth of a drill hole **f :** a piece of leather, fur, or fabric stitched around the top of a shoe or boot upper usu. for ornament — compare CUFF; see SHOE illustration **g :** a ring on a coining press confining a planchet while it is being struck and impressing a milling or edge lettering **h :** a narrow molding near the top or bottom of the leg of a piece of furniture **3 a** *Brit* **:** a piece of meat or fish rolled or coiled and tied close **b** *zool* **:** any of various structures or markings likened to a collar: as (1) **:** a band of specially colored feathers about a bird's neck (2) **:** the prothorax of an insect esp. when lengthened, narrowed, or specially modified (3) **:** the choana of a choanocyte or a choanate flagellate **c** (1) **:** RING, CINCTURE (2) **:** a necking in certain orders (as the classic Tuscan) (3) **:** COLLAR BEAM **d** (1) **:** ¹COLLET 3 (2) **:** the annulus of a mushroom (3) **:** a ringlike mass of tissue around the base of the ovule in ginkgo **e :** an abrupt increase in the thickness of the rim of a pottery vessel or a change of direction in the vessel wall that serves to set off a band near the top **f :** the layer of foam on top of a glass of beer **g :** a band of rocks encircling rocks of another kind or of different structure ⟨a ~ of sedimentary rock⟩ **4 :** an act of collaring **:** ARREST, CAPTURE

collars 2d on a shaft

²collar \"\ *vb* -ED/-ING/-S *vt* **1 a :** to seize by the collar or neck **:** obtain a hold on the neck of ⟨a wrestler ~*ing* an opponent⟩ **b :** CAPTURE, TACKLE, NAB ⟨to dart among the crowd and ~ the delinquent —Sheridan Le Fanu⟩ **c :** to attain to forceful possession of **:** GRASP, GRAB ⟨the circle broke up, each ~*ing* his own jug —Thomas Hughes⟩ **d :** to take or gain possession or control esp. of what is not rightfully one's own ⟨~ his partner's share of the profits⟩ **e :** to stop or corner and detain in unwilling conversation ⟨~ the guest of honor⟩ **f :** to draw up to and pass ⟨the favorite ~*ed* the tiring longshot in the stretch⟩ **2 a :** to put a collar on **:** adorn with a collar ⟨~ a coat⟩ **:** form a collar around **b :** to fasten a collar on (an animal) **3 :** to roll up and tie (meat or fish) for cooking; *specif* **:** to roll up and fit into a mold and cook with herbs and spices ⟨~*ed* eels⟩ **~** *vi* **:** to wind around a roll instead of moving straight through — used of a steel bar in a rolling mill
collarband \'≈,≈\ *n* **:** NECKBAND
collar beam *n* **:** a tie beam connecting the rafters at a level considerably above the wall plate in a roof truss
collar bearing *n* **:** a thrust bearing having a suitably formed face or faces that resist the axial pressure of one or more collars on a rotating shaft
collar blight *n* **:** pear and apple blight affecting the trunk base
collarbone \'≈≈,≈\ *n* [ME (Sc) *colar bane,* fr. *colar* collar (fr. ME *coler*) + *bane* bone, fr. OE *bān*] **:** CLAVICLE
collar button *n* **:** a button-sized stud consisting of a disk joined by a shank to a smaller disk, knob, or hinged flap and used for buttoning a collar to a shirt
collar cell *n* **:** CHOANOCYTE
coll' ar·co \(')kō¦lär(,)kō\ *adv (or adj)* [It] **:** with the bow — used as a direction following a pizzicato passage in a musical score for strings
col·lard \'kälə(r)d\ *n* -s [alter. of *colewort*] **:** a stalked smooth-leaved kale (spinach and ~ greens) — usu. used in pl. when applied to the food ⟨potatoes and ~s for supper⟩
col·lared \¦kälə(r)d\ *adj* [ME *colleryd, colered,* fr. *coller, coler* collar + *-yd, -ed* -ed] **1 :** wearing, having, or depicted with a collar ⟨~ executives⟩ **2 :** having a marking or part that resembles a collar ⟨a ~ jug⟩ ⟨a crimson-*collared* bird⟩
collared dove *n* **:** RINGDOVE 2
collared lemming *n* **:** a stout-bodied murine rodent (*Dicrostonyx hudsonius*) of arctic America that is white-pelted in winter and more or less brown in summer
collared lizard *n* **:** a brightly colored iguanid lizard (*Crotaphytus collaris*) of the south-central U.S. and Mexico — called also *mountain boomer, ring-necked lizard*
collared monad *or* **collared flagellate** *n* **:** CHOANOFLAGELLATE
collared peccary *n* **:** a peccary (*Tayassu angulatus*) about three feet long and marked with an indistinct white collar
col·lar·et *or* **col·lar·ette** \,kälə'ret, '≈≈,≈\ *n* -s [F *collerette,* dim. of *collier* collar — more at COLLAR] **1 :** a usu. small or tight collar **2 :** jewelry worn on or near a collar **:** NECKLACE
collarette dahlia *n* **:** any of various dahlias having flower heads with one row of true ray florets and with shorter rays forming a collarlike fringe around the disk
col·lar·less \'kälə(r)ləs\ *adj* **:** lacking a collar
collar nut *n* **:** a screw-thread nut and collar
collar of SS \-'es'es\ **:** a heraldic collar with the letter S continually repeated that was orig. a badge of adherents of the house of Lancaster and is now part of certain official costumes — called also *SS collar*
collar roof *n* **:** a roof using collar beams
collar rot *or* **collar girdle** *n* **:** any of various plant diseases in which the lesion is localized at or about the collet between stem and root
collars *pl of* COLLAR, *pres 3d sing of* COLLAR
collar tie *n* **:** a board used to prevent the roof framing from spreading or sagging
collar-to-collar \¦≈≈≈¦≈≈\ *adj* **:** PORTAL-TO-PORTAL
collar work *n* **:** hard work (as that causing a horse to strain against a collar)
collas *pl of* COLLA
col·la si·nis·tra \¦kōləsə'nistrə\ *adv (or adj)* [It] **:** with the left hand — used as a direction in keyboard music
col·late \kə'lāt, kä-; 'kä,lāt, 'kō-, *usu* -ād.+V\ *vb* -ED/-ING/-S [partly fr. L *collatus,* used as past part. of *conferre* to bring together, partly back-formation fr. *collation*] *vt* **1** *obs* **:** CONFER, BESTOW, GRANT **2 a :** to bring together for close comparison **:** compare critically with careful attention to particulars and minute points **:** verify fidelity of to an original **b :** to collect, compare carefully in order to verify, and often to integrate or arrange into informative or significant order ⟨the data gathered by the local study groups are being *collated* for publication —*Saturday Rev.*⟩ **c :** ¹GATHER 2d **d** *printing* **:** to assemble in final order (as matter set in more than one typeface or by more than one typesetter) **3 :** to admit and institute (a cleric) to a benefice — compare COLLATION 4a **4 a :** to examine (a set of gathered sheets or a book) to verify the order and number of signatures, pages, plates, or maps **b :** to arrange or assemble (paper, sheets, or forms) according to an orderly system ⟨*collating* the pages of the report⟩ **5** *civil law* **:** to bring into an estate for equal division **~** *vi* **1 :** to appoint a cleric to a benefice **2** *civil law* **:** to bring goods into an estate for equal division **syn** see COMPARE
¹col·lat·er·al \kə'lad·ərəl, -latərəl, -la·trəl\ *adj* [ME, prob. fr. MF, fr. ML *collateralis,* fr. L *com-* + *lateralis* lateral] **1 a :** accompanying as a secondary fact, activity, or agency but usu. extrinsic to a main consideration **:** similar but subordinate **:** CONCOMITANT, SUBSIDIARY ⟨wrong on the main question and on all the ~ questions springing out of it —T.B.Macaulay⟩ ⟨digress into ~ matters⟩ **b :** INDIRECT ⟨no direct objection, but several ~ ones⟩ **c :** serving to support or reinforce **:** ANCILLARY ⟨sometimes literature will provide the historian of art with a pretty piece of ~ evidence —Clive Bell⟩ **2 :** belonging to the same ancestral stock but not in a direct line of descent ⟨brothers, cousins, uncles, and nephews are ~ kinsmen⟩ — distinguished from *lineal;* compare CONSANGUINITY **3 :** placed or regarded as side by side **:** parallel, coordinate, or corresponding in position, order, time, or significance ⟨~ mountain ranges⟩ ⟨~ states like Athens and Sparta⟩ **4 a :** being or belonging to an obligation or security attached to another to secure its performance ⟨a ~ assurance to a deed⟩ ⟨~ funds⟩ **b :** secured or guaranteed by additional security, esp. by personal as opposed to real property ⟨a ~ loan secured by stocks and bonds deposited with the lender⟩ ⟨a ~ loan from a finance company on one's promissory note⟩ **5** *bot, of a vascular bundle* **:** having phloem only external to the xylem — compare BICOLLATERAL
²collateral \"\ *n* -s **1 :** one that is collateral: as **a :** a collateral relative ⟨a greedy ~ who inherited the estate —J.G. Lockhart⟩ **b :** COLLATERAL SUBJECT **2 :** something used as collateral security **3 a :** a branch esp. of a blood vessel, nerve, or the axon of a nerve cell **b :** a bodily part that is lateral in position (as a ligament) **4** *chiefly NewEng* **a :** a miscellaneous clutter of personal belongings ⟨got your ~ packed⟩ **b :** odds and ends of trash **:** RUBBISH ⟨a woodshed full of ~⟩
collateral circulation *n* **:** circulation of blood established through enlargement of minor vessels and anastomosis of vessels with those of adjacent parts when a major vein or artery is functionally impaired (as by obstruction); *also* **:** the modified vessels through which such circulation occurs
collateral fact *n, law* **:** a fact that has no direct relation to or immediate bearing on the cause or matter in question
collateral fissure *n* **:** a fissure of the tentorial surface of the cerebrum lying below and external to the calcarine fissure and causing an elevation on the floor of the lateral ventricle between the hippocampi
collateral fraud *n* **:** EXTRINSIC FRAUD
collateral ganglion *n* **:** any of several autonomic ganglia not in the sympathetic chain (as the coeliac ganglion)
collateral issue *n* **:** an issue taken upon a matter aside from the general issue or the merits of a law case
col·lat·er·al·i·ty \kə,lad·ə'raləd·ē, -latə'r-, -ralətē, -i\ *n* -ES **1 :** the quality or state of being collateral **2 :** use in kinship classification of terms for collateral relatives distinct from those for lineal relatives of the same generation
col·lat·er·al·ize \kə'lad·ərə,līz, -latər-, -la·trə,l-\ *vt* -ED/-ING/-S **1 :** to make secure (as a loan) by pledge of collateral ⟨loans *collateralized* by government securities —*Mag. of Wall Street*⟩ **2 :** to use as collateral for a loan
col·lat·er·al·ly \kə'lad·ərəlē, -latər-, -la·trə-, -li\ *adv* [ME, fr. ¹*collateral* + *-ly*] **1 :** side by side **2 :** in an auxiliary or subordinate manner **:** INDIRECTLY **3 :** in collateral relation **:** not lineally
collateral power *n* **:** a power granted to one who has no interest or estate in the property to which the power relates (as a power of sale granted to an executor who is not a legatee or devisee) — called also *naked power, power in gross;* distinguished from *power coupled with an interest*
collateral reading *n* **:** required or recommended reading to supplement school or college class assignments
collateral subject *n* **:** a subject complementary to a student's major field of concentration
collateral trust bond *n* **:** a bond secured by negotiable securities deposited with a trustee
collates *pres 3d sing of* COLLATE
collating *pres part of* COLLATE
collating mark *n* **:** a black mark differently positioned on the outside fold of each different signature in bookbinding to aid in collating
col·la·tio bo·no·rum \kə'lāsh(ē)ōbə'nōrəm, -ȯr-\ *n, pl* **collatio·nes bonorum** \≈,≈shē'ō,nēz-\ *or* **collatio bonorums** [LL] *civil law* **:** collation of goods
¹col·la·tion \kə'lāshən, kä-, kō-\ *n* -s [ME *collacioun* bringing together, comparison, fr. L *collation-, collatio,* fr. *collatus* (used as past part. of *conferre* to bring together) (fr. *com-* + *latus*) + *-ion-, -io* -ion — more at TOLERATE] **1** [ME, fr. LL, fr. L, bringing together] **a :** a reading from or conference upon some edifying book at a gathering of the members of a monastery at close of day **b** *obs* **:** an often informal conference **2** [ME, fr. ML, fr. LL, conference] **a :** the refreshment taken at a monastic collation **b :** a light meal allowed on fast days in place of lunch or supper **c :** a light meal or other refreshment at an unusual hour served in connection with a ceremony or meeting ⟨a ~ after the church services⟩ **3 a :** the act of bringing together for comparing **:** a usu. close, detailed, and careful comparison **:** comparative scrutiny **:** ordered arrangement made by comparison **b :** comparison of manuscripts or editions of a text to determine the original or the condition or authenticity of a particular copy; *also* **:** the conclusions drawn and recorded from such comparison **c :** the act of collating a book or set of sheets; *also* **:** the bibliographical description of a book expressed in a formula in which information about size, signatures, and pagination is represented by symbols **d :** the verification of a telegraphic message by repetition **4 a :** the bestowal of a living or other preferment upon a clergyman; *specif* **:** the bestowal of a living in the Church of England where the bishop is the patron **b :** the right of bestowing such a living **5 :** the act of an heir or legatee under civil or Scots law in giving back to his ancestor's or testator's estate the property received from him during the ancestor's or testator's lifetime in order to bring about an equal distribution of property among those entitled **:** the return of advancements to an estate **:** HOTCHPOT **syn** see COMPARISON
²collation *vb* -ED/-ING/-S *vt, obs* **:** COLLATE **~** *vi, obs* **:** to eat a collation
col·la·tion·al \-'lāshən°l, -shnəl\ *adj* **:** of or relating to a collation
collation in·ter hae·re·des \-'intərhe'rē,dēz\ *n* [part trans. of NL *collatio inter haeredes* collation among heirs] *Scots law* **:** collation by an heir to heritable property who is also entitled to share in the movable property to prevent unfair diminution in the shares of those taking the movable property
collation in·ter li·be·ros \-'libə,rōs, -lē-\ *n* [part trans. of NL *collatio inter liberos* collation among the children (descendants)] *Scots law* **:** collation by one entitled to legitim in order to preserve equality among all entitled to legitim
col·la·tive \kə'lād·iv, (')kä¦l-, (')kō¦l-, -ātiv\ *adj* [L *collativus* brought together, fr. *collatus* + *-ivus* -ive] **1 :** having the quality or power of conferring **2 :** passing, held, or conferred by collation (sense 4a) **3 :** marked by collation or systematic comparison ⟨a ~ act or function⟩
col·la·tor \-lād·ə(r), -ātə-\ *n* -s [L, fr. *collatus* + *-or*] **:** one that collates or makes a collation: as **a :** a punch-card machine that matches, selects, and files identical cards of two sets fed into the machine **b :** a machine that gathers or gathers and glues printed sheets from separate groupings
col·la vo·ce \'kōlə¦vō(,)chā\ *adv (or adj)* [It, with the voice] **:** COLLA PARTE
¹col·league \'kä,lēg *sometimes* 'kō,lēg *or* kä'lēg *or* kə'lēg\ *n* -s [MF *collegue,* fr. L *collega* one chosen at the same time with another, partner in office, fr. *com-* + *-lega* (fr. *legare* to choose or send as deputy) — more at LEGATE] **:** an associate or coworker typically in a profession or a civil or ecclesiastical office and often of similar rank or state
²colleague *vb* -ED/-ING/-S [MF *colliguer, colleguer* to unite, ally, fr. L *colligare* to bind together — more at COLLIGATE] *vt, obs* **:** become allied with **:** JOIN, UNITE **~** *vi* **:** to enter into an alliance **:** COOPERATE, CONSPIRE ⟨*colleaguing* with a score of petty kings —Alfred Tennyson⟩
³col·league \'kä'lēg\ *Scot var of* COLLOGUE
¹col·lect \'kälikt, -(,)lekt\ *n* -s [ME *collecte,* fr. OF, fr. ML *collecta* (short for *oratio ad collectam* prayer upon assembly), fr. LL, assembly, fr. L, collection, assemblage, fr. fem. of *collectus,* past part. of *colligere* to collect, fr. *com-* + *-ligere* (fr. *legere* to gather) — more at LEGEND] **1 :** a short prayer comprising an invocation, petition, and conclusion; *specif, often cap* **:** one preceding the Eucharistic epistle and varying with the day **2** [ME *collecte,* fr. L *collecta*] *archaic* **:** COLLECTION, GATHERING **3** [prob. fr. ²*collect*] *dial* **:** a place where water collects **:** SINKHOLE
²col·lect \kə'lekt\ *vb* -ED/-ING/-S [ME, adj., collected, fr. L *collectus*] *vt* **1 a :** to bring together into a band, group, assortment, or mass **:** GATHER ⟨~ an army⟩ ⟨~ all the available chairs⟩ ⟨~*ing* facts about immigration⟩ **b :** to receive, gather, or exact from a number of persons or other sources ⟨the Congress shall have power to lay and ~ taxes on incomes, from whatever source derived —*U.S. Constitution*⟩ **c :** to serve as a point of attraction or focus for (a crowd or accumulation) ⟨a positive genius for ~*ing* impossible people —Ngaio Marsh⟩ **2 :** INFER, DEDUCE, CONCLUDE ⟨he ~s our destination from the way in which things appear to have gone in the past 150 years —*Times Lit. Supp.*⟩ ⟨I ~ thou art to be my fatal enemy —John Milton⟩ **3 :** to regain control of **:** gather or summon up **:** overcome distraction of ⟨they were excited and unsteady and . . . required time to ~ themselves —J.A.Froude⟩ ⟨~ his thoughts, before setting to work, in a quiet room —Laurence Binyon⟩ **4 :** to bring together esp. in accordance with a principle of selection or an informative or profitable end **:** come to own as a collection or part of a collection **:** include as part of one's experience ⟨a volume of 122 ballads . . . which he had ~*ed* in the mountains —*Amer. Guide Series: N.C.*⟩ ⟨having spent some months in successfully ~*ing* and arranging my materials —Mary W. Shelley⟩ ⟨in the matter of ~*ing* books — I mean owning them —J.C.Powys⟩ ⟨I tried to ~ lakes —O.S.J. Gogarty⟩ **5 a :** to bring (a saddle horse) into a state of collection by use of the aids **b** *of a horse* **:** to bring (himself) into a state of collection — compare EXTEND **6 a :** to claim and receive in payment or fair recompense ⟨unable to ~ his wife's retirement benefits⟩ ⟨~*ing* social security payments⟩ **b :** to present as due and receive payment for ⟨~ a bill⟩ **c :** to call for **:** pick up **:** take or bring with one **:** ESCORT ⟨waited only long enough to ~ a letter of introduction —Harvey Graham⟩ ⟨~ his girl and bring her in to the cinema —F.T.B.Macartney⟩ **7 :** to unite (two or more lines of fire hose) to form a more powerful jet of water **~** *vi* **1 :** to come together in a band or group **:** form into or as if into a crowd ⟨crowds of folk used to ~ on the beach to see the fun —Norman Douglas⟩ **2 :** form a layer, heap, or mass **:** ACCUMULATE ⟨dust ~s on the furniture⟩ ⟨junk will ~ in the attic⟩ **3 a :** to collect matter or objects ⟨the botanists were out ~*ing* in full force⟩ **b :** to receive payment, remuneration, or other return — often used with *on* ⟨~*ing* on his insurance⟩ **syn** see GATHER
³collect \"\ *adv (or adj)* **:** to be paid for by the receiver ⟨send the package ~⟩ ⟨a ~ telephone call⟩
col·lec·ta·nea \,kä(,)lek'tānēə\ *n pl* [L, neut. pl. of *collectaneus* collected, fr. *collectus,* past part. of *colligere* to collect] **:** collected writings **:** literary items forming a collection ⟨its past development, as partly revealed by present ~ —S.P. Bayard⟩
col·lec·tar·i·um \-'ta(a)rēəm\ *n, pl* **collectariums** \-ēəmz\ *or* **collectar·ia** \-ēə\ [ML, fr. *collecta* collect + L *-arium*] **:** a service book containing collects
collected *adj* **1 :** gathered together ⟨the ~ works of Scott⟩ **2 :** freed from agitation, excitement, or distraction **:** possessed of calmness and composure often through concentrated effort ⟨such an intellect . . . cannot be at a loss, cannot but be patient, ~, majestically calm —J.H.Newman⟩ **3** *of a gait* **:** performed or performable by a horse from a state of collection ⟨~ gaits include the trot, canter, and rack⟩ **syn** see COOL
collected edition *n* **:** a uniform usu. complete edition of an author's work
col·lect·ed·ly *adv* **1 :** all together **:** in an assembled or collected state **:** COLLECTIVELY **2 :** with coolness and composure **:** in a collected way
col·lect·ed·ness *n* -ES **:** the quality or state of being collected
collect for the day \'kälikt, -(,)lekt\ **:** a collect appropriate for a particular day of the church year
col·lect·i·bil·i·ty *or* **col·lect·a·bil·i·ty** \kə,lektə'biləd·ē, -'lətē, -i\ *n* -ES **:** the quality or state of being collectible or readily exchangeable for money ⟨the ~ of the debt⟩
col·lect·i·ble *or* **col·lect·a·ble** \kə'lektəbəl\ *adj* **1 :** suitable for a collection **:** fit for being collected ⟨~ specimens⟩ **2 :** due for present payment **:** capable of being collected **:** exchangeable for cash **:** PAYABLE ⟨a ~ bill⟩ ⟨a ~ account⟩
collecting cell *n* **:** one of the spongy parenchyma cells having dilated ends and underlying the palisade cells of leaves and reputedly conveying the products of photosynthesis from the palisade cells to the vascular system of the plant
collecting station *n* **:** a medical installation in a forward combat area where casualties are received from aid stations, treated, classified, and either returned to duty or prepared for evacuation to a clearing station in the rear
collecting tubule *n* **:** a nonsecretory tubule that receives urine from several nephrons and discharges it into the pelvis of the kidney — called also *collecting duct*
col·lec·tion \kə'lekshən\ *n* -s *often attrib* [ME *collectioun,* fr. MF *collection,* fr. L *collection-, collectio,* fr. *collectus* (past part. of *colligere* to collect, amass) + *-ion-, -io* -ion — more at COLLECT] **1 :** the act of collecting (as taxes by a tax collector); *specif* **:** the securing of payment of a check, bond coupon, or other credit instrument by presentation to the payer for cash **2 :** a number of objects or persons or a quantity of a substance that has been collected or has collected often according to some unifying principle or orderly arrangement: as **a :** an assembly of objects or specimens for the purposes of education, research, or interest ⟨the magnificent ~ of trees —Edmund Wilson⟩ **b :** AGGREGATION, GROUP, NUMBER ⟨a ~ of buffalo-hide huts —*Amer. Guide Series: Texas*⟩ ⟨a ~ of different personalities —Warwick Braithwaite⟩ **c :** apparel that is displayed for sale in a particular season (as by a particular designer) **3** *obs* **:** DEDUCTION, INFERENCE, INTERPRETATION ⟨wrong ~s have been hitherto made out of those words by modern divines —John Milton⟩ **4 a :** an attaining to composure **:** a becoming collected **:** a bringing under control ⟨some time was required for the ~ of her faculties⟩ **b :** a standard pose of a well-handled saddle horse in which it is brought well up to the bit and flexion of the body predominates with jaw relaxed, head arched at the poll, and hocks tucked under the body so that the center of gravity is shifted toward the rear quarters; *also* **:** the act of bringing a horse into a state of collection **5 collections** *pl* **:** a term examination at some English colleges **6 :** ³AGGREGATE 5
collection at source : STOPPAGE AT SOURCE
collection line *n* **:** HOUSE DRAIN
collection plate *n* **:** ¹PLATE 3e(1)
collection station *n* **:** COLLECTING STATION
¹col·lec·tive \kə'lektiv, -ēv *also* -əv\ *adj* [MF or L; MF *collectif,* fr. L *collectivus,* fr. *collectus* + *-ivus* -ive] **1 a** *of a word or term* **:** indicating a number of persons or things considered as constituting one group or aggregate ⟨*family* and *flock* are ~ words⟩ **b** *of a noun or pronoun* **:** singular in form but sometimes or always plural in construction ⟨*family* in "the family were proud" is a ~ word⟩ **2 a :** formed by collecting **:** gathered into a mass, sum, or body **:** AGGREGATED **b** *of fruit* **:** MULTIPLE **3 :** by, characteristic of, or relating to a group of individuals, esp. a public group such as a social class or a whole society ⟨the ~ interests of the society⟩ **4 :** originating in, authorized by, or composed of a group (as a governing

group) ⟨~ leadership⟩ **5 :** involving or characterized by the united action or cooperative endeavors of all members of an aggregation or group as distinct from that of individuals ⟨~ work⟩ **6 :** marked by simultaneity, uniformity, or similarity (as of a response to a stimulus) among all the members of a group (as a whole society) ⟨~ feeling⟩ ⟨the ~ opinion of all Americans —F.D.Roosevelt⟩ **7 :** collectivized or characterized by collectivism **8 a :** having the same general characteristics as the group and thus tending to lack any individual personal traits **:** DEPERSONALIZED ⟨~ man⟩ **:** TYPICAL, REPRESENTATIVE ⟨the ~ New Yorker⟩ **b :** shared or assumed by all members of the group ⟨the ~ responsibility of the cabinet⟩ ⟨the ~ guilt of all party members⟩ **9 :** comprising a number of imperfectly differentiated entities — used esp. of a species made up of several imperfectly separable types

[2]**collective** \"\ *n* -s **1 :** a collective word or term **2 :** a collective body **:** GROUP ⟨a social ~⟩ **3 :** a cooperative unit or organization; *specif* **:** COLLECTIVE FARM

collective action *n* **:** united action by an association (as of nations against an aggressor)

collective agreement *n* **:** an agreement between an employer and a union usu. reached through collective bargaining and establishing wage rates, hours of labor, and working conditions

collective bargaining *n* **:** negotiation for the settlement of the terms of a collective agreement between an employer or group of employers on one side and a union or number of unions on the other; *broadly* **:** any union-management negotiation

collective behavior *n* **:** the mass behavior of a group whether animal or human (as mob action) **:** the unified action of an assembly of persons whether organized or not; *also* **:** the like or similar response of the members of a society to a given stimulus or suggestion

collective biography *n* **:** a volume containing biographies of a number of people

collective farm *n* **:** a farm (as in a communist country) formed from many small holdings collected into a single unit for joint operation under governmental supervision

col·lect·ive·ly \-tə̇vlē, -li\ *adv* [[1]*collective* + *-ly*] **:** in a collective sense or manner **:** in a mass or body **:** in a collected state **:** in the aggregate **:** by collective acts

collective mark *n* **:** a trademark or a service mark of a group (as a cooperative or other association)

col·lect·ive·ness *n* -ES **:** the quality or state of being collective

collective psychology *n* **:** SOCIAL PSYCHOLOGY

collective representation *n* **:** a symbol that articulates and embodies the collective beliefs, sentiments, and values of a social group

collective security *n* **1 :** a policy by an association of nations to maintain international peace through a league or confederation that would oppose by united action violations of the peace by an aggressor **2 :** security of all members of an association of nations from aggression by collective action

collective unconscious *n* **:** the genetically determined part of the unconscious that esp. in the psychoanalytic theory of C.G. Jung occurs in all the members of a people or race — called also *racial unconscious*

col·lec·tiv·ism \kə'lektə̇,vizəm\ *n* -s [F *collectivisme*, fr. *collectif* collective + *-isme* -ism] **1 a :** a politico-economic system characterized by collective control esp. over production and distribution of goods and services in contrast to free enterprise ⟨forces that have led to individualism have in the last fifty years been successfully opposed by the forces of ~ —M.R.Cohen⟩ **b :** extreme control of the economic, political, and social life of its subjects by an authoritarian state (as under communism or fascism) **c :** a doctrine or system that makes the group or the state actively responsible for the social and economic welfare of its members **2 :** a social theory or doctrine that emphasizes the importance of the collective (as the society or state) in contrast to the individual and that tends to analyze society in terms of collective behavior — see HOLISM **3 :** [2]COLLECTIVE 2, 3

[1]**col·lec·tiv·ist** \-_və̇st\ *n* -s [F *collectiviste*, fr. *collectivisme* + *-iste* -ist] **1 :** an advocate or adherent of collectivism **2 :** a member of a collective or collectivity

syn SOCIALIST, COMMUNIST: COLLECTIVIST is likely to apply to a person approving or desiring greater control or outright ownership of major industries and resources by the state, presumably in the interests of a degree of economic equality among the whole people, this control or ownership to be achieved gradually and without violence but with some restriction on individual action. SOCIALIST is a close synonym for COLLECTIVIST in this sense, but is likely to evoke more of an emotional reaction than COLLECTIVIST. COMMUNIST is likely to suggest one desiring more rigid and far-reaching control, often control achieved by force. The words SOCIALIST and COMMUNIST are naturally affected in their connotations by whatever particular Socialist or Communist Party or Socialism or Communism happens to be prominent in world affairs at the moment. In matters historical or philosophical, the two words, esp. the latter, may be used without praise or stigma to refer to persons favoring or accepting conditions in which the wishes and activities of the individual are checked and guided by the interests of the group, as in Plato's ideal republic, in ancient Sparta, or in some of the earliest Christian communities

[2]**collectivist** \"\ *also* **col·lec·tiv·is·tic** \=¦==¦vistik, -ēk\ *adj* **1 :** favoring collectivism **:** based on the principles of collectivism **2 :** relating to or having the characteristics of collectivism

col·lec·tiv·i·ty \,kä(,)lek'tivəd·ē, -_lə̇k-, -vətē, -i\ *n* -ES **1 :** the quality or state of being collective **2 a :** collective sum **:** totality esp. of persons in social organization **:** AGGREGATE ⟨great *collectivities* that bury, if they do not destroy, individuality —Robert Lindner⟩ **b :** a group of persons acting in concert or considered as a single unit (as a state, corporation, or class) **3 :** the processes or results of collectivism

col·lec·ti·vi·za·tion \kə,lektə̇və̇'zāshən, -,vī'-\ *n* -s **:** the action or process of collectivizing **:** the state of being collectivized

col·lec·tiv·ize \kə'lektə̇,vīz\ *vt* -ED/-ING/-S *see -ize in Explan Notes* **1 :** to organize according to the principles of collectivism ⟨institute a *collectivized* society⟩ **:** influence by or as if by a collective process or method with decrease of individualism **2 :** to bring into a system of or under the control of collective farms ⟨~ the land⟩ **3 :** to make collective **:** consider as collective ⟨the *collectivized* emotions of the people⟩

collect on delivery *adj* (*or adv*) **:** to be paid for in cash at the time of delivery to the buyer — abbr. *COD*

col·lec·tor \kə'lektə(r)\ *n* -s [ME *colector*, *collectour*, fr. MF & ML; MF *collecteur*, fr. ML *collector* one who collects, fr. L *collectus* (past part. of *colligere* to bring together) + *-or* — more at COLLECT] **1 :** an official who collects funds or moneys: as **a :** an officer commissioned to collect and receive revenues **b** *Brit* **:** one that collects parish alms **c :** the administrative head of a district in some provinces of British India **d :** one authorized to collect debts and accounts due: as (1) **:** a clerk or agent who by telephone, correspondence, or personal visits attempts to collect delinquent accounts and sometimes cuts off service or repossesses merchandise if payment is not made (2) **:** one that makes collection at regular intervals of installment payments or insurance premiums **e :** a messenger who acts as a bank's agent in presenting checks, drafts, and money orders to local banks for payment or acceptance **f :** one that collects money from coin boxes of public and private pay telephones and computes and pays a percentage refund to subscribers when cash exceeds the maximum guarantee **2 :** one that makes a collection ⟨a stamp ~⟩ ⟨a ~ of first editions⟩ **3 :** an object or device that collects ⟨the statuette was a fine dust ~⟩ ⟨a ~ lowered overboard to gather plankton specimens⟩ **4 a :** a conductor maintaining contact between moving and stationary parts of an electric circuit (as one of the tinsel brushes on an induction machine or the third-rail shoe of an electric-railway car) **b :** a device (as an electrode) that collects moving electrons **c :** the output terminal of a transistor **5** *in the flotation process of ore dressing* **:** a chemical used to increase the floating capacity of a mineral

col·lec·to·rate \='=tərə̇t\ *n* -s **:** COLLECTORSHIP 1

collector ring *n* **1 :** one or more continuous conducting rings in a dynamo or motor from which the brushes take or to which they deliver current **2 :** the ring-shaped exhaust manifold of a radial airplane engine

col·lec·tor·ship \='==,ship\ *n* -s **1 :** the jurisdiction, residence, office, or staff of a collector **2 :** the practice of one that collects

collector's item *n* **:** an item whose rarity or perfection makes it esp. worth collecting

collects *pl of* COLLECT, *pres 3d sing of* COLLECT

colled *past of* COLL

col·leen \kä'lēn, kə̄-; 'kä,lēn\ *n* -s [IrGael *cailīn*, dim. of *caile*, prob. fr. L *paelex* concubine — more at PERI] **1** *Irish* **:** a young girl **2 :** an Irish girl

col·lege \'kälij, -ēj\ *n* -s *often attrib* [ME, fr. MF, fr. L *collegium* society, fr. *collega* colleague — more at COLLEAGUE] **1 :** a body of clergy living in common on a foundation **2 :** a building or a number of buildings used in connection with some specific educational or religious purpose: as **a :** the precinct of an English cathedral **b :** a dormitory for students **3** [ME, fr. ML *collegium*, fr. L, society] **a :** a self-governing constituent body of a university offering living quarters and instruction, sometimes limited, but not granting degrees ⟨Balliol and Magdalen *Colleges* at Oxford⟩ **b :** UNIVERSITY ⟨Edinburgh *College*⟩ **c :** preparatory or high school ⟨Eton *College*⟩ ⟨Girard *College*⟩ **d :** an independent institution of higher learning offering a course of general studies and usu. preprofessional training leading to a bachelor's degree **e :** a part of a university offering a specialized group of courses ⟨this university has a ~ of dentistry⟩ ⟨the ~ of engineering at the university⟩ **f :** an institution offering instruction usu. in a professional, vocational, or technical field ⟨teachers ~⟩ ⟨business ~⟩ ⟨army war ~⟩ ⟨barber ~⟩ ⟨~ of embalming⟩ **4 a :** COMPANY, ASSEMBLAGE, COTERIE, CLUB ⟨a ~ of courtesans⟩ ⟨some dusty ~ of pedants⟩ **b :** a meeting or reunion of companions or associates ⟨a ~ of Collegiants⟩ **5 :** an organized body, guild, society, or group of persons engaged in a common pursuit, having common interests or a common duty or role and sometimes a charter or special rights and privileges ⟨a ~ of cardinals serving as papal councillors and electors⟩ ⟨a ~ of craftsmen⟩ ⟨a ~ of witches was entrusted with the duty of annually choosing a beautiful girl to be the bride of the water-god —J.G.Frazer⟩; *specif* **:** COLLEGE OF ARMS **6 a :** a collection of persons treated in law in one or more respects as a unit **b :** a body of electors — see ELECTORAL COLLEGE **7** *slang* **:** PRISON, REFORMATORY **8 :** a course of study or of lectures ⟨taking three ~*s* a year⟩ **9 :** a charitable foundation in England providing residence and care **:** ASYLUM, HOSPITAL **10 :** the faculty, students, or administrative body of a college ⟨the ~ stood behind any move to improve education⟩ ⟨the ~ was at the football game in force⟩

College Board *service mark* — used for administration of tests of aptitude and achievement considered by some colleges in determining admission and placement of students

college-bred \'==¦=\ *adj* **:** educated in a college ⟨forgotten who of their gownsmen was *college-bred* —R.W.Emerson⟩

college ice *n*, *NewEng* **:** SUNDAE

college of arms *or* **college of heralds 1** *usu cap C&A&H* **a :** a corporation in England dependent upon the crown and consisting of three kings of arms, six heralds, and four pursuivants under the earl marshal's headship who have retained from the middle ages certain of the ceremonial duties of heralds but whose principal responsibility in modern times is the designing, grant, and registration of armorial bearings **b :** the building occupied by this corporation **2 :** an officially incorporated body of officers of arms of any nation

college-preparatory \¦kälij+\ *adj* **:** of or relating to a school or course of studies designed to qualify students for admission to a college — compare COMMERCIAL, GENERAL

col·leg·er \'kälə̇jə(r)\ *n* -s **1 :** a student at Eton College who lives on the original foundation — compare OPPIDAN 3 **2 :** a college student

college scrip *n* **:** scrip issued to facilitate the establishment of colleges

college spirit *n* **:** demonstrative enthusiastic zeal for one's college esp. in matters athletic

college try *n* **:** a zealous all-out uninhibited effort for complete success without expedient compromise ⟨an outfielder making the old *college try* for a low liner⟩

college widow *n* **:** a young woman in a college town who dates students of successive college classes

collegia *pl of* COLLEGIUM

col·le·gi·al \kə'lēj(ē)əl, *esp for 2 also* -'lēgēəl\ *adj* [MF or L; MF *collegial*, fr. L *collegialis*, fr. *collegium* society — more at COLLEGE] **1 :** of or relating to a college or university **:** COLLEGIATE **2 :** of or relating to a collegium or group of colleagues ⟨an increasing tendency to turn from ~ to one-man management —Merle Fainsod⟩ — **col·le·gi·al·ly** *adv*

col·le·gi·al·ism \-,lizəm\ *n* -s [G *kollegialismus*, fr. *kollegial* (fr. L *collegialis*) + *-ismus* -ism] **:** a theory of church polity that defines the church as a society of voluntary members independent of the state, self-governing, and with authority vested in the members

col·le·gi·al·i·ty \kə,lējē'aləd·ē, -ətē\ *n* -ES [F *collégial* of a colleague (fr. MF, fr. L *collegialis*) + E *-ity*] **:** the relationship of colleagues ⟨the impediment of ~, under which in old days one tribune could nullify the work of another —John Buchan⟩

collegial system *n* **:** COLLEGIALISM

col·le·gian \kə'lēj(ē)ən\ *n* -s [ME, fr. ML *collegianus*, fr. *collegium* + *-anus* -an] **:** a member of a college **:** a college student or recent college graduate

col·le·gian·er \-ə(r)\ *n* -s *Scot* **:** a student at a university **:** COLLEGIAN

col·le·gi·ant \-jēənt, -jə̇nt\ *n* -s *usu cap* [D, fr. NL *collegium* congregation (fr. L, society) + D *-ant* (fr. L *-ant-*, *ans* -ant — more at COLLEGE] **:** a member of an Arminian sect started in 1619 by Jan, Adrian, and Gilbert van der Kodde and forming congregations in Holland

[1]**col·le·giate** \-j(ē)ə̇t, *usu* -d·+V\ *adj* [ML *collegiatus*, fr. ML *collegium* + L *-atus* -ate — more at COLLEGE] **1 :** of or relating to a collegiate church ⟨a ~ pastor⟩ ⟨a ~ charge⟩ ⟨monasteries and other ~ bodies such as the cathedral churches —R.W. Southern⟩ **2 :** of, relating to, or comprising a college or colleges: **a :** having college rank or standards ⟨a ~ education⟩ **b :** resembling that of a college ⟨~ architecture⟩ ⟨~ living⟩ **c** *of a university* **:** composed of several autonomous colleges **3 :** marked by power or authority vested equally in each of a number of colleagues **:** COLLEGIAL ⟨abolished the ~ executive and restored full powers to the presidency —M.I. Vanger⟩ **4 a :** characteristic of college students (as in appearance, attitude, or behavior) ⟨~ clothes⟩ ⟨~ humor⟩ **b :** designed for the use or relevant to the life of college students often on the nonacademic side ⟨~ athletics⟩ — **col·le·giate·ly** *adv* — **col·le·giate·ness** *n* -ES

[2]**col·le·gi·ate** \-jē,āt, *usu* -d·+V\ *vt* -ED/-ING/-S **:** to constitute or organize as a college or as a collegiate church

[3]**col·le·giate** \-j(ē)ə̇t, *usu* -d·+V\ *n* -s **1 :** COLLEGIAN **2 :** a British or Canadian secondary school

collegiate church *n* **1 :** a church that although not a cathedral or bishop's church has a college or chapter of canons and, in the Church of England, a dean (as Westminster Abbey or St. George's Chapel at Windsor) **2 :** a Presbyterian church that regularly has two or more ministers of equal rank **3 :** a church or an association of churches in the U.S. possessing common revenues administered under the joint pastorate of several ministers

collegiate gothic *n*, *usu cap G* **:** the style of Gothic architecture exemplified in English college buildings (as at Oxford)

col·le·gi·enne \kə¦lējē¦en\ *n* -s [fr. *collegian*, after such pairs as E *comedian: comedienne*] **:** a female college student — used esp. in fashion advertisements

col·le·gi·um \kə'legēəm, -'(āg- *also* -'lejē-\ *n*, *pl* **colle·gia** \-gēə, -jēə, -jə\ *or* **collegi·ums** \-əmz\ [L — more at COLLEGE] **1 a :** COLLEGE 5 **b** *Roman & civil law* **:** an association of individuals of the same class or rank formed to promote their common interest in some business pursuit or enterprise **2** [modif. (influenced by L *collegium*) of Russ *kollegya*, fr. L *collegium*] **:** an executive body with each member having approximately equal power and authority; *specif*, *often cap* **:** a board or committee responsible for the work of a commissariat or a nationalized industry under a soviet system of government

col legno \kō'lān(,)yō\ *adv* [It] **:** with the wood — used as a direction in music to players of bowed instruments to use the wood and not the hair of the bow in playing

col·lem·bo·la \kə'lembələ\ *n pl*, *cap* [NL, fr. *coll-* + *-embola* (fr. Gk *embolos*, *embolon* peg, wedge); fr. their collophore — more at EMBOL-] **:** an order of small primitively wingless arthropods that are related to or sometimes classed among the true insects, are characterized by possession of a median collophore, not more than 6 abdominal segments, 3 pairs of legs, and usu. a forked caudal furcula, are found esp. in soil rich in organic debris or on the surface of snow or water, and comprise the springtails — **col·lem·bo·lan** \-lən\ *adj or n* — **col·lem·bo·lous** \-ləs\ *adj*

col·len·chy·ma \kə'leŋkəmə\ *n*, *pl* **col·len·chym·a·ta** \,kälən'kimad·ə\ [NL, fr. *coll-* + *-enchyma*] **1 :** a tissue that is found chiefly in the outer parts of young stems, petioles, and leaf midribs, consists of elongated living cells with rectangular, oblique, or tapering ends and walls variously thickened esp. in the angles, and provides temporary support and elasticity prior to differentiation of the vascular elements — compare SCLERENCHYMA **2 :** COLLENCHYME

col·len·chym·a·tous \¦kälən¦kimad·əs\ *adj* [NL *collenchymat-*, *collenchyma* + E *-ous*] **1 :** of, relating to, or resembling collenchyma **2 :** of or relating to collenchyme — **col·len·chym·a·tous·ly** *adv*

col·len·chyme \'kälən,kīm\ *n* -s [NL *collenchyma*] **:** a loose mesenchyme containing few cells and much gelatinous material that occupies the space between the ectoderm and endoderm of the body wall of many lower invertebrates (as sponges)

col·len·cyte \'kälən,sīt\ *n* -s [*collen*chyme + *-cyte*] **:** one of the branched cells of collenchyme

col·lery \'kälərē\ *n*, *pl* **collery** *or* **colleries** *usu cap* [prob. modif. of Tamil *kaḷḷar* thieves, fr. *kaḷ* to steal] **1 :** a Dravidian people of southern India **2 :** a member of the Collery people

col·les' fracture \'käləs-,-ə̇z-,'kä,lēz-\ *n*, *usu cap C* [after Abraham *Colles* †1843 Irish surgeon] **:** a fracture of the lower end of the radius with backward displacement of the lower fragment and radial deviation of the hand at the wrist that produces a characteristic deformity

[1]**col·let** \'kälə̇t, *usu* -d·+V\ *n* -s [MF, dim. of *col* collar, neck, fr. L *collum* neck — more at COLLAR] **1 :** a metal band, collar, ferrule, or flange: **a :** a small collar pierced to receive the inner end of a balance spring and fixed friction-tight on the balance staff of a watch or chronometer **b** (1) **:** a casing or socket for holding a drill or other tool **:** COLLET CHUCK (2) **:** a bushing that keeps stuffing-box packing in place (3) **:** a ring forming part of or secured to a spindle or arbor **c :** a circle or flange in a ring or other piece of jewelry in which a precious stone is set **2 :** a nonmetallic insert that interrupts the conduction of heat through a metal teapot handle **3 :** the often hypothetical although sometimes physically identifiable boundary between the stem and root of a plant — called also *collar* **4** [modif. (influenced by *collet*) of F *culet* — more at CULET] **:** CULET 1

[2]**collet** \"\ *vt* -ED/-ING/-S **:** to furnish or surround with a collet

collet chuck *n* **:** a chuck consisting of a collet that grips the workpiece (as a bar of metal to be shaped)

[1]**col·le·ter** \kə'lēd·ə(r)\ *n* -s [G *kolleter*, irreg. fr. Gk *kollan* to glue, fr. *kolla* glue — more at PROTOCOL] **:** one of the mucilage-secreting hairs that clothe many plant surfaces esp. on various winter buds (as those of the horse chestnut)

[2]**col·let·er** \'kälə̇d·ə(r)\ *n* -s [*collet* + *-er*] **:** a worker who attaches the inner coil of a watch hairspring to a collet for assembly to the balance wheel

col·le·te·ri·al gland \¦kälə¦tirēəl-\ *n* [*colleterial* fr. *colleterium* + *-al*] **:** COLLETERIUM

col·le·te·ri·um \-rēəm\ *n*, *pl* **collete·ria** \-rēə\ [NL, irreg. fr. Gk *kollan* to glue] **:** a gland in female insects that secretes a cement by which the eggs are glued together

col·le·tia \kə'lēsh(ē)ə, -lēd·ēə\ *n*, *cap* [NL, fr. Philibert *Collet* †1718 Fr. jurisconsult and botanist + NL *-ia*] **:** a small genus of spiny So. American shrubs (family Rhamnaceae) often quite leafless and with small white or yellow flowers — see ANCHOR PLANT

col·let·in \'kälət[ə]n, -,tin\ *n* -s [F, fr. *collet*] **:** plate armor for neck and shoulders

col·le·tot·ri·chum \,kälə'tä·trə̇kəm\ *n*, *cap* [NL, fr. *colleto-* (fr. Gk *kollētos* glued, fr. *kollan* to glue) + *-trichum* (fr. Gk *trich-*, *thrix* hairs) — more at TRICH-] **:** large and widely distributed form genus of imperfect fungi (family Melanconiaceae) having the conidia borne in erumpent acervuli surrounded by setae — compare ANTHRACNOSE

colletside \'==,=\ *n* -s [[1]*collet* + *side*] **:** PAVILION 4

col·ley \'kälē, -li\ *var of* [4]COLLY

col·li·bert \'kälə,bərt\ *n* -s [F, fr. ML *collibertus*, fr. L, fellow freedman, fr. *com-* + *libertus* one made free, fr. *liber* free — more at LIBERAL] **:** a peasant tenant next superior to the serfs

col·li·cle \'kälə̇kəl\ *n* -s [NL *colliculus*] **:** COLLICULUS; *specif* **:** VERUMONTANUM — **col·lic·u·lar** \kə'likyələ(r)\ *adj*

col·lic·u·late \kə'likyələ̇t, ,lāt\ *adj* [L *colliculus* (dim. of *collis* hill) + E *-ate* — more at HILL] *zool* **:** having small elevations

col·lic·u·lus \-yələs\ *n*, *pl* **collicu·li** \-,lī, -lē\ [NL, fr. L] *anat* **:** PROMINENCE; *specif* **:** any of the four prominences constituting the corpora quadrigemina — see INFERIOR COLLICULUS, SUPERIOR COLLICULUS

col·lide \kə'līd\ *vb* -ED/-ING/-S [L *collidere*, fr. *com-* + *laedere* to injure] *vt*, *archaic* **:** to strike against ~ *vi* **1 a :** to become impelled into violent contact ⟨waves *colliding* with the rocks⟩ **b :** to strike or dash together in collision typically by accident with a degree of force and shock and with solid rather than glancing or sideswiping impact ⟨the car and truck *collided*⟩ ⟨the car *collided* with the truck⟩ **2 :** to meet in sharp direct opposition **:** be sharply, forcefully, and directly at variance, in discord, disagreement, or conflict ⟨liberty, equality, fraternity . . . these three ideas *collided* with the vested interests of decaying monarchy and feudal privilege —Stringfellow Barr⟩ **syn** see BUMP

col·li·dine \'kälə,dēn, -_də̇n\ *n* -s [ISV *coll-* + *-idine*] **:** any of a number of organic bases $C_8H_{11}N$ that are the trimethyl, methyl-ethyl, and propyl homologues of pyridine, that are in general pungent oily poisonous liquids, and are obtained chiefly as by-products in the coking process or are synthesized: as **a :** the liquid symmetrical trimethyl homolog made by reaction of acetone and ammonia and used as a solvent in chromatography — called also *s-collidine*, *2,4,6-collidine*, *2,4,6-trimethylpyridine* **b :** METHYLETHYLPYRIDINE

col·lie \'kälē, -li\ *n* -s [prob. fr. [2]*colly*] **1 :** a dog of a breed developed in Scotland and used for generations in herding sheep, standing 20 to 24 inches at the shoulder, weighing 50 to 60 pounds, having a long pointed muzzle with little or no stop, and occurring in two varieties, the long-haired with profuse coat, very full ruff and feathering, and plumy tail, and the less common short-haired with somewhat harsh close coat **2 :** OLIVE WOOD

collied *adj* [fr. past part. of [1]*colly*] *now chiefly dial Brit* **:** blackened as if by colly **:** SOOTY

[1]**col·lier** \'kälyə(r), *chiefly Brit* -lēə(r)\ *n* -s [ME *colier*, fr. *col* coal + *-ier* — more at COAL] **1 :** one that produces charcoal by burning wood in a beehive kiln **2 a** *obs* **:** a charcoal or coal dealer **b :** a coal miner **3 :** a ship employed in transporting coal **4 a :** BEAN APHID **b** *dial Eng* **:** a swift (*Apus apus*) **c :** WILSON'S PLOVER

[2]**collier** *comparative of* COLLY

col·liery \'kälyərē, -ri\ *n* -ES [*collier* + *-y*] **:** a coal mine and the buildings connected with it

collies *pres 3d sing of* COLLY, *pl of* COLLY

col·lie·shang·ie \'kälē,shaŋē\ *n* -s [perh. fr. *collie* (cur) + *shang* kind of meal (perh. fr. ScGael *seang* thin, hungry-looking) + *-ie*; akin to OIr *seng* thin, OE *swancor* pliable, MHG *swanger* swaying, ON *svangr* thin, hungry, OE *swingan* to beat, flog — more at SWING] *Scot* **:** SQUABBLE, BRAWL, UPROAR

colliest *superlative of* COLLY

col·li·gate \'kälə̇,gāt, *usu* -ād·+V\ *vt* -ED/-ING/-S [L *colligatus*, past part. of *colligare*, fr. *com-* + *ligare* to tie — more at LIGATURE] **1 :** to bind, unite, or group together often according to a subsuming principle ⟨*colligating* a number of instances⟩ **2 :** to bring together (isolated facts) inductively to organize under one conception or elicit a general principle

col·li·ga·tion \,=='gāshən\ *n* -s [L *colligation-*, *colligatio*, fr. *colligatus* + *-ion-*, *-io* -ion] **1 :** CONNECTION, CONJUNCTION

2 : the act or process of colligating ⟨the truth emerges spontaneously and directly from a sufficiently thorough ~ of particular instances —*Times Lit. Supp.*⟩

col·li·ga·tive \ˈkälə,gād·iv, kəˈligəd-·\ *adj* [ISV *colligat-* (fr. L *colligatus*) + *-ive;* orig. formed as G *kolligativ*] **:** depending on or varying according to the number of particles (as molecules, atoms, and ions) and not on or according to nature ⟨gaseous pressure is a ~ property⟩

col·li·mate \ˈkälə,māt, *usu* -ād.+V\ *vt* -ED/-ING/-S [NL *collimatus*, past part. of *collimare*, var. reading in some editions for L *collineare*] **1 a :** to render parallel to a certain line or direction **b :** to render parallel (as rays of light) **2 :** to adjust the line of sight of (a transit or level) to proper position relative to the other parts **3 :** to set the fiducial marks of (a surveying camera) so that they define the principal point (as in photogrammetry)

collimating lens *n* **:** a lens used for producing parallel rays of light

col·li·ma·tion \,==ˈmāshən\ *n* -S [NL *collimatus* + E *-ion*] **1 :** the act of collimating **2 :** the state of being collimated

col·li·ma·tor \ˈ==,mād·ə(r)\ *n* -S **1 :** a device for producing a beam of parallel rays of light or other radiation or for forming an infinitely distant virtual image that can be viewed without parallax usu. consisting of a tube having an objective lens at the end toward the observer and a slit or cross hairs in the objective focal plane at the other end — see SPECTROMETER illustration **2 :** a device for obtaining a beam of molecules, atoms, or nuclear particles of limited cross section and moving in parallel lines

col·lin·ear \kəˈlinēə(r), (ˈ)kōˈl-, (ˈ)käˈl-\ *adj* [ISV *com-* + *linear*] **1 :** lying in the same straight line **2 :** having a straight line in common ⟨~ intersecting planes⟩ — **col·lin·ear·ly** *adv*

col·lin·ea·tion \=,==ˈāshən\ *n* -S [NL *collineation-, collineatio*, fr. L *collineatus* (past part. of *collineare* to direct in a straight line, fr. *com-* + *lineare* to make straight, fr. *linea* line) + *-ion-*, *-io* -ion — more at LINE] **:** a mathematical transformation in which collinear elements (as points or lines) are transferred as corresponding elements to another plane or space

colling *n* -S [fr. pres. part. of ¹*coll*] *now dial Eng* **:** EMBRACING, PETTING

col·lin·gual \kəˈliŋgwəl, (ˈ)kōˈl-, (ˈ)käˈl-\ *adj* [*com-* + *lingual*] **:** using the same language

¹**col·lins** \ˈkälənz\ *n* -ES *sometimes cap* [prob. fr. the name *Collins*] **:** a tall drink that is served iced in a large tumbler and that has a gin, whiskey, rum, brandy, or vodka base to which are added sugar, carbonated water, and lemon or lime juice

²**collins** \"\ *n* -ES [after William *Collins*, character in *Pride and Prejudice* (1813), by Jane Austen †1817 Eng. novelist] *Brit* **:** a bread-and-butter letter

col·lin·sia \kəˈlinzēə, -sēə\ *n* [NL, fr. Zaccheus *Collins* †1831 Am. botanist + NL *-ia*] **1** *cap* **:** a genus of U.S. biennial or annual herbs (family Scrophulariaceae) with irregular whorled flowers **2** -S **:** any plant of the genus *Collinsia*

col·lins·ite \ˈkälən,zīt\ *n* -S [William H. *Collins* †1937 Can. geologist + E *-ite*] **:** a mineral consisting of a hydrous phosphate of calcium, magnesium, and iron $Ca_2(Mg,Fe)(PO_4)_2 \cdot 2H_2O$ occurring in concentric layers in phosphorite nodules

col·lin·so·nia \,kälənˈsōnēə\ *n* [NL, fr. Peter *Collinson* †1768 Eng. naturalist + NL *-ia*] **1** *cap* **:** a genus of aromatic herbs (family Labiatae) with large ovate leaves and terminal spikes of yellow flowers — see HORSE BALM **2** -S **:** any plant of the genus *Collinsonia*

colliquate *vt* -ED/-ING/-S [NL *colliquatus*, past part. of *colliquare*, fr. L *com-* + *liquare* to melt; akin to *liquor* liquid — more at LIQUID] *obs* **:** MELT

col·li·qua·tion \,käləˈkwāzhən, -āsh-\ *n* -S [F, fr. MF, fr. NL *colliquatus* + MF *-ion*] **1** *obs* **:** the action or process of melting, liquefying, or fusing **2** *med* **:** the breakdown and liquefaction of tissue

col·liq·ua·tive \ˈkälə,kwād·iv, kəˈlikwəd·iv\ *adj* [F *colliquatif*, fr. MF, fr. NL *colliquatus* + MF *-if* -ive] **:** causing colliquation

col·li·sion \kəˈlizhən\ *n* -S *often attrib* [ME, fr. L *collision-, collisio*, fr. *collisus* (past part. of *collidere* to collide) + *-ion-*, *-io* -ion] **1 :** the action or an instance of colliding, violent encounter, or forceful striking together typically by accident and so as to harm or impede ⟨a ~ between the two ships⟩ ⟨the ~ of the car with the trolley⟩ **2 :** a clashing meeting **:** a coming together of things opposed or diverse **:** ENCOUNTER: **a :** a meeting in sharp direct opposition **:** DISAGREEMENT ⟨when the English expansion had at length come into ~ with the borders of the French forest preserve —*Encyc. Americana*⟩ **b :** an unpleasant discordant juxtaposition of sounds ⟨the ~ of difficult consonant clusters in some words⟩ **c :** an encounter or impingement marked by activity or consequence; *sometimes* **:** a noteworthy accidental juxtaposition ⟨the fruits that spring from an intercourse and ~ with other minds from other mental regions —Van Wyck Brooks⟩ ⟨the unexpected ~ of incidents —Thomas Hardy⟩ **d :** an encounter between particles (as atoms or molecules) resulting in exchange or transformation of energy **syn** see IMPACT

col·li·sion·al \-zhənᵊl, -zhnəl\ *adj* **:** marked by or ensuing from a collision

collision bulkhead *n* **:** the first watertight bulkhead in the forward part of a ship designed to keep out water in the event of a collision

collision clause *n* **:** a policy provision that the insurer agrees to assume the legal liability of an insured shipowner to owners of another vessel and its cargo for loss resulting from collision with the insured ship

collision course *n* **:** a course (as of a ship, plane, or antiaircraft shell) that will result in a collision if continued unaltered

collision insurance *n* **:** insurance provided for a motor-vehicle owner against damage to the motor vehicle due to collision with another object

collision mat *n* **:** a large canvas or heavy rope mat used to close a hole made in a ship's side (as by collision or explosion)

collo- — see COLL-

col·lo·blast \ˈkälə,blast\ *n* -S (*coll-* + *-blast*) **:** ADHESIVE CELL

col·lo·cal \kəˈlōkəl, (ˈ)kōˈl-\ *adj* [*com-* + *local*] **:** present in or belonging to the same place with another

col·lo·ca·lia \,käləˈkālēə\ *n, cap* [NL, fr. *coll-* + Gk *kalia* nest — more at HALL] **:** a genus of small chiefly cave-nesting swifts (family Apodidae) which produce the edible bird's nests

col·lo·cate \ˈkälə,kāt, *usu* -ād.+V\ *vt* -ED/-ING/-S [L *collocatus*, past part. of *collocare*, fr. *com-* + *locare* to place, fr. *locus* place — more at STALL] **:** to set or arrange in a place or position; *esp* **:** to set side by side

col·lo·ca·tion \,==ˈkāshən\ *n* -S [L *collocation-, collocatio*, fr. *collocatus* + *-ion-*, *-io* -ion] **:** the act or result of placing or arranging esp. with something else ⟨outcome of accidental ~s of atoms —Bertrand Russell⟩; *often* **:** a noticeable arrangement or conjoining of words or other linguistic elements ⟨the ~ of these two names — that of an elderly French marquise and of an English actor —L.P.Smith⟩

col·lo·ca·tive \ˈ==,kād·iv\ *adj* [*collocate* + *-ive*] **:** of, relating to, or tending to collocation **:** tending to collocate

col·lo·chore \ˈkälə,kō(ə)r\ *n* -S [*coll-* + Gk *chōros* place — more at CHOR-] **:** a specialized segment of certain chromosomes that functions like a chiasma in bivalent formation and is thought to be lacking in genes and comparable to a centromere

col·loc·u·tor \kəˈläkyəd·ə(r), kōˈ- ˈkälə,kyüd·ə(r)\ *n* -S [It & LL; It *collocutore*, fr. LL *collocutor*, fr. L *collocutus* (past part. of *colloqui* to converse, fr. *com-* + *loqui* to speak) + *-or*] **:** a person to or with whom one speaks

collodio- *comb form* [*collodion*] **:** collodion ⟨*collodio*type⟩

col·lo·di·on \kəˈlōdēən\ *n* -S *often attrib* [modif. of NL *collodium*, fr. Gk *kollōdēs* glutinous (fr. *kolla* glue + *-eidēs* -oid) + NL *-ium* — more at COLL-] **:** a viscous solution of pyroxylin in a mixture of alcohol and ether or sometimes in some other solvent (as acetone) used chiefly as a coating for wounds and for photographic films and plates and as a membrane (as for dialysis)

collodion cotton *n* **:** PYROXYLIN 1

col·lo·di·on·ize \-dēə,nīz\ *vt* -ED/-ING/-S [*collodion* + *-ize*] **:** to treat with collodion

collodion process *n* **:** a photographic process in which collodion is used as a vehicle for sensitive salts; *specif* **:** an early process in which the negative is prepared by coating a glass plate with collodion containing iodide, exposing in a camera while wet, developing with pyrogallol or acidified ferrous sulfate, and fixing in a cyanide solution or hypo

col·lo·di·um \kəˈlōdēəm\ *n* -S [NL — more at COLLODION] **:** COLLODION

col·lo·form \ˈkälə,fȯrm\ *adj* [*coll-* + *-form*] **:** having the form or shape of a colloidal deposit **:** botryoidal, mammillary, and usu. internally banded concentrically

collogen *var of* COLLAGEN

col·logue \kəˈlōg\ *vi* -ED/-ING/-S [origin unknown] **1** *obs* **:** to employ flattery **:** speak cajolingly ⟨fawn on and ~ with some leader⟩ **2** *obs* **:** to feign assent or adherence **3** *dial* **:** INTRIGUE, CONSPIRE ⟨that villain . . . had been in the works *colloguing* with one of the men —Charles Reade⟩ **4 :** to talk privately **:** CONFER ⟨he *collogued* long of nights with the head-priest —Rudyard Kipling⟩

¹**col·loid** \ˈkä,lȯid\ *adj* [*coll-* + *-oid*] **:** COLLOIDAL

²**colloid** \"\ *n* -S [ISV *coll-* + *-oid;* prob. orig. formed as F *colloïde*] **1 a :** a substance (as gelatin, albumin, or starch) that, when apparently dissolved in water or other liquid, diffuses not at all or very slowly through a membrane and shows other special properties (as lack of pronounced effect on the freezing point or vapor pressure of the liquid); *also* **:** any substance (as an aggregate of atoms or molecules), whether a gas, liquid, or solid, in a fine state of subdivision with particles too small to be visible in an ordinary optical microscope that is dispersed in a continuous gaseous, liquid, or solid medium and does not settle or settles very slowly (as the liquid droplets in fog, solid particles in smoke, bubbles in foam, or gold particles in ruby glass) **b :** matter consisting of a colloid and the medium in which it is dispersed **:** DISPERSE SYSTEM — compare AEROSOL, CRYSTALLOID, EMULSION, GEL, MICELLE, SOIL COLLOID, SOL, SUSPENSION **2 :** a gelatinous or mucinous substance found in colloid degeneration and colloid carcinoma **3 :** a gelatinous substance in the vesicles in the thyroid gland and occas. in the interstices between the secreting cells that is thought to be the stored secretion

³**colloid** \", kəˈlȯid\ *vt* -ED/-ING/-S **:** to convert (cellulose nitrate in smokeless powder) into a colloidal state (as by treating with a mixture of ether and alcohol)

col·loi·dal \kəˈlȯidᵊl, (ˈ)käˈl-\ *adj* [²*colloid* + *-al*] **:** of, relating to, or having the properties of a colloid ⟨~ state⟩ ⟨~ graphite⟩ — **col·loid·al·i·ty** \,käl,ȯiˈdaləd·ē, ˈ==,===, -ətē, -i\ *n* -ES — **col·loi·dal·ly** \kəˈlȯidᵊlē, (ˈ)käˈl-, -i\ *adv*

colloidal fuel *n* **:** a stabilized suspension of a solid fuel (as powdered coal) in an oil (as fuel oil)

colloidal gold test *n* **:** GOLD SOL TEST

colloid carcinoma *or* **colloid cancer** *n* **:** carcinoma characterized by excessive production of a colloidal or mucinous material

colloid chemistry *n* **1 :** the branch of chemistry that deals with colloids and colloidal phenomena **2 :** the branch of chemistry that deals with surfaces and large molecular particles

col·loid·er \ˈkä,lȯidə(r), kəˈl-\ *n* -S [³*colloid* + *-er*] **:** a mechanical device (as a filter) used to remove or coagulate colloidal matter in sewage or industrial wastes

col·loid·ize \-,dīz\ *vt* -ED/-ING/-S [²*colloid* + *-ize*] **:** to change into a colloid **:** COLLOID

colloid mill *n* **:** a machine utilizing shearing action for very fine grinding and dispersion esp. by breaking down the particles in an emulsion or paste to extremely fine dispersions of liquid or solid — compare HOMOGENIZER

col·loi·do·pexy \kəˈlȯidə,peksē, ˈkä,l-\ *n* -ES [ISV *colloid* + *-o-* + *-pexy;* orig. formed as F *colloïdopexie*] **:** the capacity of certain cells to ingest colloidal material

col·lo·mia \kəˈlōmēə\ *n* [NL, irreg. fr. Gk *kolla* glue; fr. the nature of the seed — more at PROTOCOL] **1** *cap* **:** a genus of herbs (family Polemoniaceae) found in western No. America with alternate leaves and terminal clusters of phloxlike flowers **2** -S **:** any plant or flower of the genus *Collomia*

¹**col·lop** \ˈkäləp\ *n* -S [ME *colope, colhoppe* egg fried on bacon] **1 :** a small piece or slice of meat; *sometimes* **:** a rasher of bacon **2 :** a fold of fat flesh **3 :** SLICE, PIECE, PORTION

²**col·lop** \ˈkäləp, ˈkōl-\ *also* **colp** \ˈkälp, ˈkōlp\ *n* -S [IrGael *colpa*, lit., full-grown horse or cow] **1 :** an Irish measure of quantity or quality of land based on the grazing requirements of an adult cow or horse (reckoned as an acre of good land) **2 a :** a cow or horse or a grazing equivalent in sheep **b :** the pasturage for one of these for a year

col·loped \ˈkäləpt\ *adj* [¹*collop* + *-ed*] **:** cut up into collops ⟨~ venison⟩

col·lo·phane \ˈkälə,fān\ *or* **col·loph·a·nite** \kəˈläfə,nīt, ˈkäləf-\ *n* -S [ISV *coll-* + *-phan* or *-phane* + *-ite;* orig. formed as G *kollophan*] **:** any of the massive cryptocrystalline varieties of apatite, often opaline or horny in appearance, used as a source of phosphate for fertilizers; *usu* **:** a hydroxylapatite containing carbonate

col·lo·phore \ˈkälə,fō(ə)r\ *n* -S [*coll-* + *-phore*] **:** a thick median tubular pouch usu. terminating in a bilobate vesicle and projecting from the ventral surface of the first abdominal segment of all members of the order Collembola

col·loque \kəˈlōk\ *vi* -ED/-ING/-S [L *colloqui* — more at COLLOQUY] **:** CONVERSE

colloquia [L] *pl of* COLLOQUIUM

¹**col·lo·qui·al** \kəˈlōkwēəl\ *adj* [*colloquy* + *-al*] **1 :** of or relating to conversation **:** expressed in conversation **:** CONVERSATIONAL **2 :** used in or characteristic of conversation, esp. familiar and informal conversation ⟨~ English⟩ ⟨a letter written in ~ style⟩ ⟨the great majority [of the common words of English are] at once literary and ~ —*Oxford English Dict.*⟩ **:** using or characterized by conversational style ⟨a ~ poet⟩

²**colloquial** \"\ *n* -S **:** colloquial style or diction **:** a colloquial language or dialect ⟨literary Chinese and the various ~s⟩

col·lo·qui·al·ism \-,lizəm\ *n* -S **1 a :** an expression considered more appropriate to familiar conversation than to formal speech or to formal writing ⟨slang words frequently rise to the rank of ~s —G.L.Kittredge⟩ **b :** an expression belonging to local or regional dialect — not used technically **2 :** informal or conversational style in language ⟨the appeal of Wordsworth's ~⟩

col·lo·qui·al·ist \-ləst\ *n* -S **:** CONVERSATIONALIST

col·lo·qui·al·i·ty \kə,lōkwēˈaləd·ē, -ətē, -i\ *n* -ES **:** colloquial quality or style; *also* **:** an instance of this

col·lo·qui·al·ize \kəˈlōkwēə,līz\ *vb* -ED/-ING/-S **:** to write employing colloquialisms

col·lo·qui·al·ly \-əlē, -i\ *adv* **:** in a colloquial manner **:** with use of colloquial expressions **:** CONVERSATIONALLY

col·lo·qui·al·ness *n* -ES **:** the quality or state of being colloquial

col·lo·quist \ˈkäləkwəst\ *n* -S [*colloquy* + *-ist*] **:** COLLOCUTOR, TALKER

col·lo·qui·um \kəˈlōkwēəm\ *n, pl* **colloqui·ums** \-ēəmz\ *or* **collo·quia** \-ēə\ [L] **1** *obs* **:** CONVERSATION **2 :** the part of the plaintiff's pleading in an action for slander that avers that the defendant spoke the slanderous words concerning the plaintiff or the subject matter in question in a certain conversation **3 a :** discussion meeting **:** CONFERENCE; *specif* **:** a seminar that several lecturers take turns in leading **b :** a lecture prepared for such a seminar

col·lo·quize \ˈkälə,kwīz\ *vi* -ED/-ING/-S [L *colloquium* + E *-ize*] **:** to hold colloquy **:** CONVERSE

col·lo·quy \ˈkäləkwē, -i\ *n* -ES [L *colloquium* conversation, fr. *colloqui* to converse, fr. *com-* + *loqui* to speak] **1 a :** CONVERSATION, DIALOGUE ⟨a ~ between two old Connecticut codgers gossiping —Dixon Wecter⟩ ⟨a ~ between senators⟩ **b :** high-level serious discussion **:** CONFERENCE ⟨the Sino-Soviet ~ for drafting new treaties —*Current Biog.*⟩ **2 :** an ecclesiastical court much like the presbytery of Presbyterian churches formerly existing in certain churches with a presbyterian polity (as the Reformed Church in France)

coll'ot·ta·va \(ˈ)kōlōˈtävə, -lə̇ˈ-\ *adv (or adj)* [It, with the octave] **:** with the addition of the octave above or the octave below the note on the written score — used as a direction in music; abbr. *coll' 8*

col·lo·type \ˈkälə,tīp\ *n* -S [ISV *coll-* + *type*] **1 :** a photomechanical process for making prints directly from a hardened film of gelatin or other colloid, the sensitized film being exposed under a reversed negative, desensitized, and then soaked in glycerin and salt water to cause swelling in the parts that have not been exposed to light, the swelled parts becoming ink-repellent and the unswelled parts ink-receptive, thereby forming a printing surface that functions on the lithographic principle — called also *photogelatin process* **2 :** a print made by collotype

col·low \ˈkälō\ *dial Eng var of* COLLY

colls *pres 3d sing of* COLL

col·luc·ta·tion \,käləkˈtāshən\ *n* -S [L *colluctation-, colluctatio*, fr. *colluctatus* (past part. of *colluctari* to struggle, fr. *com-* + *luctari*) + *-ion-*, *-io* -ion — more at LOCK] **:** STRUGGLE

col·lude \kəˈlüd\ *vi* -ED/-ING/-S [L *colludere*, fr. *com-* + *ludere* to play, fr. *ludus* game — more at LUDICROUS] **:** to connive with another **:** CONSPIRE, PLOT

col·lum \ˈkäləm\ *n, pl* **col·la** \-lə\ [L, neck — more at COLLAR] **1** *anat* **:** a neck or necklike part or process **2 :** COLLET 3

col·lu·nar·i·um \,käləˈna(a)rēəm\ *n, pl* **collunar·ia** \-ēə\ [NL, fr. L *colluere* to wash out, rinse + *nares* nostrils, nose + NL *-ium* — more at COLLUVIES, NOSE] **:** a medicated solution for instillation into the nostrils as a wash or spray or as drops

col·lu·sion \kəˈlüzhən\ *n* -S [ME *collucioun*, fr. MF *collusion*, fr. L *collusion-, collusio*, fr. *collusus* (past part. of *colludere*) + *-ion-*, *-io* -ion] **:** secret agreement **:** secret cooperation for a fraudulent or deceitful purpose ⟨acting in ~ with the enemy⟩: as **a :** a secret agreement between two or more persons to defraud a person of his rights often by the forms of law **b :** agreement between parties considered adversaries at the law (as in a divorce proceeding) **c :** a secret agreement considered illegal for any reason

col·lu·sive \-ˈlüsiv, -lüz|, |ēv *also* |əv\ *adj* [*collusion* + *-ive*] **1 :** constituting, marked by, or done with collusion **:** FRAUDULENT ⟨~ agreement between pope and king —G.M.Trevelyan⟩ ⟨~ bidding arrangements by contractors ostensibly competing⟩ **2 :** given to or acting in collusion ⟨~ parties —Edmund Burke⟩ — **col·lu·sive·ly** *adv*

col·lu·so·ry \-|ərē\ *adj* [F *collusoire*, fr. *collusion* + *-oire* -ory] **:** COLLUSIVE

col·lu·to·ri·um \,käləˈtōrēəm, -tȯr-\ *n, pl* **colluto·ria** \-rēə\ [NL, fr. L *collutus* (past part. of *colluere*) + *-orium*] **:** MOUTHWASH

col·lu·vi·al \kəˈlüvēəl\ *adj* [*colluvies* + *-al*] **:** indicating, relating to, or marked by colluvium

col·lu·vi·a·tion \kə,lüvēˈāshən\ *n* -S [*colluvies* + *-ation*] **:** a process that produces colluvial deposits

col·lu·vi·es \kəˈlüvē,ēz\ *n, pl* **colluvies** [L, collection of washings, dregs, offscourings, fr. *colluere* to wash, fr. *com-* + *-luere* (fr. *lavere* to wash) — more at LYE] **:** COLLECTION, GATHERING: **a :** an accumulation of foulness **b :** HOTCHPOTCH, JUMBLE ⟨a ~ of low characters⟩

col·lu·vi·um \-vēəm\ *n, pl* **collu·via** \-vēə\ *or* **colluvi·ums** \-mz\ [ML, alter. of L *colluvies*] **:** a heterogeneous mass of rock detritus or soil material emplaced primarily by gravitational processes on or at the foot of slopes; *also* **:** alluvium emplaced at the foot of slopes by creek and slope wash

¹**col·ly** \ˈkälē, -li\ *vt* -ED/-ING/-ES [alter. (influenced by ²*colly*) of ME *colwen*, fr. (assumed) OE *colgian*, fr. *col* coal — more at COAL] *dial chiefly Brit* **:** to blacken with or as if with soot or smut

²**colly** \"\ *adj, often* -ER/-EST [earlier *colie*, fr. (assumed) ME *coly*, fr. ME *cole* coal + *-y*] *dial chiefly Brit* **:** grimed with or as if with coal dust or soot **:** BLACK

³**colly** \"\ *n* -ES *chiefly dial Brit* **:** SOOT, SMUT

⁴**colly** \"\ *n* -ES *dial Eng* **:** BLACKBIRD

col·ly·ba *or* **col·y·ba** \ˈkäləbə\ *n pl* [Gk *kollyba* sweet cakes, pl. of *kollybon*, prob. alter. of *kollybos* small coin] **:** small sweet cakes made of crushed wheat, raisins, nuts, almonds, and honey, and blessed and distributed on certain commemorative occasions in the Eastern Church

col·lyb·ia \kəˈlibēə\ *n, cap* [NL, fr. Gk *kollybos* small coin + NL *-ia*] **:** a genus of white-spored agarics (family Agaricaceae) lacking both volva and ring, having the thin fleshy cap incurved when young, and including some forms that are on tree roots

collyria *pl of* COLLYRIUM

col·lyr·i·clum \kəˈlirə̇kləm\ *n, cap* [NL, alter. of L *collyriolum* (prob. read as *collyriclum*), dim. of *collyrium*] **:** a genus of digenetic trematodes (family Troglotrematidae) including a form (*C. faba*) commonly encountered encysted in the skin of chickens, turkeys, and various wild birds exposed to marshy environment

col·ly·rid·i·an \,käləˈridēən\ *n* -S *usu cap* [ML *Collyridianus*, fr. LL *collyrida* thin cake of bread, fr. Gk *kollyrid-, kollyris*, dim. of *kollyra* roll of bread] **:** one of a heretical sect in the 4th and 5th centuries chiefly in Arabia that employed women as priestesses to offer sacrifices in the form of rolls of bread to the Virgin Mary

col·lyr·i·um \kəˈlirēəm\ *n, pl* **collyr·ia** \-rēə\ *or* **collyri·ums** \-mz\ [L, fr. Gk *kollyrion* eye salve, pessary, suppository, dim. of *kollyra* roll of bread] **:** an eye lotion **:** EYEWASH

col·ly·wob·bles \ˈkälē,wäbᵊlz\ *n pl but sing or pl in constr* [prob. by folk etymology (influence of *colic* and *wobble*) fr. NL *cholera morbus*] **:** a slight intestinal usu. diarrheal disturbance accompanied by abdominal cramps **:** BELLYACHE

col·mar \ˈkälmə(r)\ *n* -S *sometimes cap* [perh. fr. *Colmar*, France] **:** a fan in fashion in Queen Anne's reign

col·ma·tage \,kälməˈd·ij\ *n* -S [F, fr. *colmater* to impound silt-laden water (fr. *colmate* silt, fr. It *colmata*, fr. *colmare* to heap up, to build up by silt-laden water, fr. *colmo* top, summit, fr. L *culmin-, culmen*) + *-age* — more at HILL] *NewZeal* **:** the impounding of silt-laden water to build up low-lying areas

coln *abbr* column

colo *abbr* colophon

colo- — see ²COL-

colobi *pl of* COLOBUS

col·o·bin \ˈkäləbə̇n\ *n* -S [F, fr. NL *Colobinae* (subfamily of apes), fr. *Colobus* type genus + *-inae*] **:** a monkey of the genus *Colobus*

co·lo·bi·um \kəˈlōbēəm\ *n, pl* **colo·bia** \-bēə\ [LL, fr. LGk *kolobion*, fr. Gk *kolobos* docked, curtailed — more at HALT] **:** a sleeveless or short-sleeved tunic used as an ecclesiastical vestment **:** a similar garment worn as a coronation robe

col·o·bo·ma \,käləˈbōmə\ *n, pl* **coloboma·ta** \-məd·ə\ [NL, fr. Gk *kolobōma* part taken away in mutilation, fr. *koloboun* to mutilate, fr. *kolobos* docked] **:** a fissure of the eye usu. of congenital origin — **col·o·bo·ma·tous** \ˌ==ˈbōməd·əs\ *adj*

col·o·bus \ˈkäləbəs\ *n* [NL, fr. Gk *kolobos* docked, mutilated; fr. the rudimentary thumbs] **1** *cap* **:** a genus of slender long-tailed African monkeys sometimes made the type of a separate family but usu. included in the Cercopithecidae **2** *pl* **colobi** \-,bī, -,bē\ **:** GUEREZA

col·o·ca·sia \,käləˈkāzh(ē)ə\ *n, cap* [NL, fr. L, East Indian lotus, fr. Gk *kolokasia, kolokasion*, lit., root of the East Indian lotus] **:** a small genus of Asiatic and Polynesian tuberous-rooted aroids having the spadix terminated by a club-shaped or subulate appendage — see TARO

col·o·ceph·a·li \,käləˈsefə,lī\ *n pl, cap* [NL, fr. *colo-* (fr. Gk *kolos* docked, hornless) + *-cephali* (pl. of *-cephalus* -cephalous) — more at HALT] *in some classifications* **:** a suborder of Apodes consisting of the morays — **col·o·ceph·a·lous** \ˌ==ˈsefələs\ *adj*

co·lo·col·ic \ˌkäləˈkälik, ˌkōl-\ *adj* [²*col-* + *colic*] **:** relating to two parts of the colon

col·o·cynth \ˈkälə,sinth\ *n* -S [L *colocynthis*, fr. Gk *kolokynthis*] **1** *or* **colocynth apple :** a Mediterranean and African herbaceous vine (*Citrullus colocynthis*) which is related to the watermelon and from which a powerful cathartic is prepared — called also *bitter apple, bitter cucumber, bitter gourd* **2 :** the spongy fruit of the colocynth

co·logarithm \(ˈ)kō+\ *n* -S [*co-* + *logarithm*] **:** the logarithm of the reciprocal

¹**co·logne** \kəˈlōn\ *adj, usu cap* [fr. *Cologne*, Germany] **:** of or from the city of Cologne, Germany **:** of the kind or style prevalent in Cologne

²**cologne** \"\ *n* -S [short for *Cologne water*, trans. of F *eau de Cologne*, fr. *Cologne*, Germany, where it was manufactured] **1** *also* **cologne water** *sometimes cap C* **:** a perfumed liquid composed of alcohol and certain aromatic oils chiefly derived from the citrus family and used as a toilet water — called also *eau de Cologne* **2 :** a cream or paste of cologne sometimes formed into a semisolid stick

cologne brown *n, usu cap C* [trans. of G *Kölner braun, Kölner erde*, fr. *Cologne* (*Köln*), Germany, where it was discov-

ered] 1 *or* **cologne earth** : VANDYKE BROWN 1b 2 : VANDYKE BROWN 2
cologne plant *n* [[2]cologne] : COSTMARY
cologne spirit *or* **cologne spirits** *n, usu cap C* [[2]cologne] : ethyl alcohol in 95 percent concentration
cologne ware *n, usu cap C* : a glazed stoneware mottled with gray and brown and made into tankards and jugs esp. in the 16th and 17th centuries — called also *grès de Flandres*
cologne yellow *n* 1 *usu cap C* : a pigment composed essentially of chrome yellow containing lead chromate and lead sulfate 2 *often cap C* : LIGHT CHROME YELLOW
colomba *var of* CALUMBA
co·lom·bia \kəˈlәmbēә, -ˈlōm-\ *adj, usu cap* [fr. *Colombia*, country in So. America] : of or from Colombia : of the kind or style prevalent in Colombia : COLOMBIAN
[1]co·lom·bi·an \-bēən\ *adj, usu cap* [*Colombia*, country in So. America + E *-an*] 1 : of, relating to, or characteristic of Colombia 2 : of, relating to, or characteristic of Colombians
[2]colombian \"\ *n* -s *cap* : a native or resident of Colombia
colombian mahogany *n, usu cap C* 1 : a tropical American timber tree (*Cariniana pyriformis*) 2 : the wood of the Colombian mahogany often sold as true mahogany — called also *albarco*
colombin *var of* COLUMBIN
[1]colombo *var of* CALUMBA
[2]co·lom·bo \kəˈləm(ˌ)bō\ *adj, usu cap* [fr. *Colombo*, Ceylon] 1 : of or from Colombo, the capital of Ceylon : of the kind or style prevalent in Colombo 2 [fr. the first conference's having taken place in Colombo] : of, concerning, or participated in by India, Pakistan, Burma, Ceylon, and Indonesia ⟨the *Colombo* plan⟩
co·lo·met·ric \ˌkōləˈme·trik, ˈkäl-\ *adj* : of or relating to colometry — **co·lo·met·ric·al·ly** \-trək(ə)lē, -li\ *adv*
co·lom·e·trize \kəˈlämə·ˌtrīz, ˈkōləm-, ˈkäləm-\ *vt* -ED/-ING/-S : to analyze or divide into cola : apply colometry to ⟨a ~ manuscript or verse⟩
co·lom·e·try \kəˈlämə·trē, -ri\ *n* -ES [MGk *kōlometria*, fr. Gk *kōlo-* (fr. *kōlon* part of a strophe) + *-metria* -metry — more at COLON] : measurement or division (as of a manuscript or a rhythmic utterance) by cola
[1]co·lon \ˈkōlən, -ˌlän\ *n, pl* **colons** \-nz\ *or* **co·la** \-lə\ [L, large intestine, fr. Gk *kolon*; perh. akin to Lith *skilvis* belly, Arm *kʻaird* guts] 1 : the part of the large intestine that extends from the cecum to the rectum and in man is divided into an initial portion which passes up on the right side of the abdomen, a midportion which passes across to the left side, a descending portion which passes downward on the left side, and a terminal tortuous portion continuous with the rectum — called respectively (1) *ascending colon*, (2) *transverse colon*, (3) *descending colon*, (4) *sigmoid flexure* — see DIGESTION illustration 2 : the second division of an insect's intestine
[2]colon \"\ *n, pl* **colons** *or* **cola** *see numbered senses* [L, part of a poem, fr. Gk *kōlon* limb, part of a strophe, clause of a sentence — more at CALK] 1 *pl* **cola a** : a rhythmical unit of an utterance: (1) *in Greek or Latin verse* : a system or series of from two to not more than six feet having a principal accent and forming part of a line (2) : a division of an utterance by sense or rhythm that is smaller and less independent than the sentence and larger and less dependent than the phrase — compare COMMA, PERIOD **b** : a unit that is used in measuring the length of manuscripts and that is equal to what was regarded as the average length of a colon 2 *pl* **colons a** : the punctuation mark : used before an explanation, example, definition, restatement, recapitulation, quotation, appositive, or list and esp. after or in place of such expressions as *namely, as follows* or sometimes between the clauses of a compound sentence esp. when no conjunction is used and when the clauses balance each other antithetically **b** : the sign : used between the parts of a numerical expression of time in hours and minutes (as in 1:15) or in hours, minutes, and seconds (as in 8:25:30), of a bibliographical reference (as in *Nation* 130:20), a ratio where it is usually read as "to" (as in 4:1 read "four to one"), or a proportion where it is usually read as "is to" or when doubled as "as" (as in 2:1::8:4 read "two is to one as eight is to four")
[3]co·lon \ˈkōˌlän, kəˈlōn\ *n* -s [L *colonus* colonist, farmer, inhabitant — more at COLONY] : a colonial farmer, planter, or plantation owner
[4]co·lon \kəˈlōn, kōˈl-\ *n, pl* **co·lo·nes** \-nās\ *also* **colons** \-nz\ [Sp *colón*, after Cristóbal *Colón* Christopher Columbus — more at COLUMBIAN] 1 : the basic monetary unit of Costa Rica and El Salvador — see MONEY table 2 : a coin representing one colon 3 : a Salvadoran note representing one colon
colon bacillus *n* [[1]colon] : any of a number of bacilli esp. of the genera *Escherichia* and *Aerobacter* normally commensal in vertebrate intestines or living in soil and only occas. of pathogenic significance although one species (*E. coli*) may be implicated in urinary tract and biliary infections and in a variety of suppurative lesions esp. in the tropics and another (*A. aerogenes*) has been reported as a cause of cystitis
colon crayfish *n, often cap first C* [[1]colon] : a common Central American crayfish (*Macrobrachium jamaicense*)
col·o·nel \ˈkərnᵊl, ˈkōnᵊl\ *n* -s [alter. (influenced by MF or OIt; MF *colonel*, fr. OIt *colonnello*) of earlier *coronel*, fr. MF, modif. of OIt *colonnello* column of soldiers, colonel, dim. of *colonna* column, fr. L *columna* — more at COLUMN] 1 : an army, marine, or air force officer ranking below a brigadier general and above a lieutenant colonel and entitled to the insignia of a silver eagle 2 : a minor purely titular officer or official of a state or similar instrumentality esp. in southern or midland U.S. — used as an honorific title without much significance and without military rating; used sometimes of an auctioneer or drummer 3 : a Salvation Army officer ranking above a lieutenant colonel and below a lieutenant commissioner
colonel blimp *n, cap C&B* [after *Colonel Blimp*, a cartoon character created by David Low *b*1891 British cartoonist] : an army officer or government official notoriously stuffy, pompous, short-sighted, and unobservant of or hostile to up-to-date procedures; *broadly* : an elderly pompous reactionary
col·o·nel·cy \-sē, -si\ *n* -ES : the office, rank, or commission of a colonel
colonel general *n, pl* **colonels general** *or* **colonel generals** : an officer in some foreign armies usu. equivalent to a U.S. full general
colonel-in-chief *n, pl* **colonels-in-chief** *or* **colonel-in-chiefs** : an honorary rank in some corps or regiments of foreign armies (as the British) usu. held by a member of a royal family or a distinguished military leader
co·longitude \(ˈ)kō+\ *n* -s [*co-* + *longitude*] : the complement of a longitude
coloni *pl of* COLONUS
[1]co·lo·ni·al \kəˈlōnyəl, -nēəl\ *adj* [F, fr. *colonie* colony (fr. OF) + *-al* — more at COLONY] 1 **a** : of, for, or relating to a colony : having the characteristics or status of a colony ⟨~ possessions⟩ ⟨~ administration⟩ **b** *often cap* : of or relating to the 13 English colonies that first formed the United States of America: as (1) : made or prevailing in America during the colonial period ⟨a ~ spoon dated 1730⟩ ⟨~ architecture was a modification of English Georgian⟩ (2) : adapted from or reminiscent of an American colonial mode of design ⟨a ~ piano⟩ **c** : possessing colonies : composed of colonies ⟨Britain's ~ empire⟩ **d** (1) : of or relating to the period of A.D. 500–900 in southwestern U.S. characterized by Hohokam expansion (2) : of or relating to the period of Spanish overlordship in Mexico about 1535–1821 (3) : of or relating to the period about 1544–1824 in Peru characterized by a continuation of Spanish conquest and merging of native states 2 *biol* : forming, existing in, consisting of, or used by a colony ⟨a ~ organism (as *Volvox*)⟩ ⟨~ burrows⟩ — **co·lo·ni·al·ly** \-ēlē, -li\ *adv* — **co·lo·ni·al·ness** *n* -ES
[2]colonial \"\ *n* -s 1 : a member or inhabitant of a colony ⟨battles between Indians and the ~s⟩ ⟨British ~s in India⟩ 2 : a low shoe with a broad flaring tongue and usu. a large buckle worn in the colonial days of America 3 **a** : a product made for use in a colony; *specif* : a coin or stamp issued for use in a colony; *esp* : a coin of colonial America **b** : a security involving a colonial enterprise or development — usu. used in pl. **c** : a product showing colonial style
colonial bent *n* : RHODE ISLAND BENT
colonial blue *n* : a variable color averaging a moderate greenish blue that is bluer and paler than average peacock, greener and duller than Brittany, and bluer and duller than larkspur
colonial bouquet *n* : a small round bouquet with a paper backing showing
colonial buff *n* : BARIUM YELLOW 2
colonial dollar *n* : HOLEY DOLLAR
colonial furniture *n* : furniture made in the American colonies before the end of the Revolution and largely influenced by contemporary European styles (as the Queen Anne and Georgian) but having some indigenous features (as greater variety in woods and more extensive use of turnings)
colonial goose *n, Austral* : a boned leg of mutton stuffed with savory herbs
co·lo·ni·al·ism \kəˈlōnēəˌlizəm, -nyəˌl-\ *n* -s 1 : the quality or state of being colonial 2 : a custom, idiom, idea, notion, or style characteristic of a colony : PROVINCIALISM 3 : the aggregate of various economic, political, and social policies by which an imperial power maintains or extends its control over other areas or peoples : practice of or belief in acquiring and retaining colonies
[1]co·lo·ni·al·ist \-ələst\ *n* -s [[1]colonial + *-ist*] : an adherent or advocate of colonialism
[2]colonialist \"\ *adj* : marked by belief in or support or practice of colonialism
co·lo·ni·al·is·tic \kəˌlōnēəˈlistik, -nyəˈl-\ *adj* 1 : [2]COLONIALIST 2 : factitiously colonial in style or characteristics ⟨a building that is ~ rather than colonial⟩
co·lo·ni·al·i·za·tion \kəˌlōnēələˈzāshən\ *n* -s : the act of colonializing or being colonialized; *esp* : subjugation by colonial policies ⟨outcries against ~ and economic imperialism —*Economist*⟩
co·lo·ni·al·ize \kəˈlōnēəˌlīz, -nyəˌl-\ *vt* -ED/-ING/-S [[1]colonial + *-ize*] : to make colonial
colonial pine *n* : an Australian evergreen tree (*Araucaria cunninghamii*) that yields a soft timber
colonial rose *n* : a variable color averaging a dark pink that is less strong and slightly darker than wild rose and bluer and darker than dusty coral
colonial teak *n* : FLINDOSA
colonial yellow *n* : a moderate yellow that is greener, lighter, and stronger than brass, lighter and stronger than mustard yellow, and redder and lighter than quince yellow
co·lon·ic \(ˈ)kōˈlänik, kəˈl-\ *adj* [[1]colon + *-ic*] *anat* : of or relating to the colon
col·o·nist \ˈkälənəst\ *n* -s [*colony* + *-ist*] 1 : a member or inhabitant of a colony 2 : one that colonizes or settles in a new country
col·o·ni·za·tion \ˌkälənəˈzāshən, -ˌnīˈz-\ *n* -s 1 : the act of establishing colonies : the state of being colonized ⟨English ~ of America in the 17th century⟩ 2 **a** : the placing of nonresidents in doubtful electoral districts and qualifying them to vote **b** : infiltration of zealous militants into a neutral, opposed, or uncertain group to alter its orientation ⟨left-wing ~ of the society⟩ 3 : the resettlement chiefly in Africa of freed American Negro slaves by interested organizations 4 : the spread and development of a species or other natural group in a new area
col·o·ni·za·tion·ist \-shənəst\ *n* -s : one that advocates resettling American Negroes in Africa
col·o·nize \ˈkäləˌnīz\ *vb* -ED/-ING/-S *see -ize in Explan Notes* [*colony* + *-ize*] *vt* 1 **a** : to establish a colony in or on : send out colonists to ⟨it may happen . . . that Venus may be *colonized* by the earth as America was once *colonized* by Europe —Waldemar Kaempffert⟩ **b** : to migrate to and settle in ⟨the French who *colonized* Canada⟩ 2 : to send illegal or irregularly qualified voters into ⟨the machine was *colonizing* doubtful districts⟩ 3 : to migrate to : come to live in as a new species ⟨forms which have been able to ~ cold regions —S.A. Cain⟩ 4 : to infiltrate with usu. subversive militants for propaganda and strategy reasons ⟨the left-wingers *colonized* key industries with trusted party members⟩ 5 : to isolate (as the feeble-minded) in supervised groups ⟨the chronic alcoholics, the psychopaths . . . some of these should be hospitalized and some *colonized* —L.N.Robinson⟩ ~ *vi* 1 : to make or establish a colony : SETTLE ⟨~ in Africa⟩ 2 *of microorganisms* : to become established in a habitat (as a host or a wound) ⟨these bacteria in turn ~ in other parts of the body —R.A.Runnells⟩
col·o·niz·er \-zə(r)\ *n* -s : one that colonizes
col·on·nade \ˌkäləˈnād, ˈ==ˌ=\ *n* -s [F, alter. of *collonate*, fr. It *colonnato*, fr. *colonna* column + *-ato* -ade — more at COLONEL] 1 : a series or range of columns placed at regular intervals usu. with an architrave and sometimes with adjuncts (as pavement, stylobate, or roof) — see PERISTYLE, PORTICO 2 : a row of trees, posts or other uprights suggestive of columns

colonnade 1

col·on·nad·ed \-ādəd\ *adj* : having a colonnade
col·on·nette \ˌkäləˈnet\ *n* -s [F, dim. of *colonne* column, fr. L *columna* — more at COLUMN] : a small column esp. in a group in a parapet, balustrade, or clustered column
colons *pl of* COLON
co·lo·nus \kəˈlōnəs\ *n, pl* **colo·ni** \-ˌnī, -(ˌ)nē\ [L] : a freeborn serf or tenant farmer in the later Roman Empire who could sometimes own property but who was bound to the land and obliged to pay a rent usu. in produce
col·o·ny \ˈkälənē, -ni *sometimes* ˈkäln-\ *n* -ES *often attrib* [ME *colonie*, fr. MF & L; MF *colonie*, fr. L *colonia*, fr. *colonus* colonist, farmer, inhabitant (fr. *colere* to cultivate, dwell) + *-ia* -y — more at WHEEL] 1 : a body of people settled in a new territory, foreign and often distant, retaining ties with their motherland or parent state : a settlement in a new country : the territory inhabited by such a body or occupied by such a settlement : the body of descendants of settlers wholly or partially retaining their ideology and organization: **a** : a settlement made in hostile, newly conquered, or unstable country as a means of facilitating established occupation and governed by the parent state ⟨the Roman *colonies* in Gaul⟩ **b** : a settlement in a new territory enjoying a degree of autonomy or semiresponsible government without severing ties with the parent state and without attaining the more free status of a dominion — see CROWN COLONY; compare MANDATE, PROTECTORATE **c** : such a settlement including in its control autochthonous groups in any of a number of statuses 2 **a** : a distinguishable localized population within a species (as a community of termites or bees) ⟨bird *colonies* on the islands and promontories —P.E.James⟩ **b** : a group of two or more kinds of organisms (as species or clones) usu. migrant into and developing in a barren area or the interstices of an existent ecological community; *often* : an incompletely developed community consisting of two or more kinds of organisms **c** : an assemblage of fossils apparently contained in rocks older than those in which they normally belong 3 **a** : a circumscribed mass of microorganisms developed from a single cell or small cluster of cells, usu. growing in or upon a solid or semisolid medium — compare FAMILY **b** : the aggregation of zooids of a compound animal **c** : COENOBIUM 4 **a** : a group of persons united by a common characteristic or interest living in a limited section surrounded by others not so united ⟨the American ~ in Paris⟩ ⟨New York City's Syrian ~⟩ ⟨an artist ~⟩ ⟨the film ~⟩; *also* : the section or quarter occupied by such a group **b** : a group of persons institutionalized away from others for some particular kind of care, treatment, correction, or punishment ⟨a leper ~⟩ ⟨a ~ for epileptics⟩ ⟨a penal ~⟩; *also* : the land or buildings occupied by such a group **c** : a cluster or somewhat discrete group (as of dwellings) usu. with common characteristics or functions ⟨a ~ of ranch houses⟩ ⟨crowded *colonies* of tiny shingled shacks —F.L.Allen⟩ **d** : a group of institution inmates quartered away from main buildings or centers ⟨the children's ~⟩ **e** : a nucleus of militants infiltrated into a group or organization ⟨a Communist ~ at the power plant⟩
colony house *n* : a small usu. somewhat isolated building used to accommodate a group of animals (as chickens or pigs) esp. when on range
col·o·pexy \ˈkäləˌpeksē\ *n* -ES [NL *colopexia*, fr. [2]*col-* + *-pexia* -pexy] : the operation of suturing the sigmoid flexure to the abdominal wall
col·o·phene \ˈkäləˌfēn\ *n* -s [ISV *colophony* + *-ene*; orig. formed as F *colophène*] : an oily liquid that is a high-boiling component of the mixture obtained by treating turpentine (sense 2) with sulfuric acid
col·o·phon \ˈkäləfən, -ˌfän\ *n* -s [L, fr. Gk *kolophōn* summit, finishing touch; prob. akin to L *collis* hill — more at HILL] 1 : an inscription usu. placed at the end of a book or manuscript and usu. containing facts relative to its production (as the designer's, artist's, and printer's names and the type faces and paper used) 2 : an identifying mark, emblem, or device used by a printer or a publisher sometimes on the title page, cover, shelfback, or jacket
col·o·pho·nite \ˈkäləfəˌnīt, kəˈläfə-\ *n* -s [G *kolophonit*, fr. *kolophonium* colophony + *-it* -ite] : a coarse garnet of the variety andradite
col·o·pho·ny \ˈkälə(ˌ)fōnē, kəˈläfə-\ *also* **col·o·pho·ni·um** \ˌkäləˈfōnēəm\ *n, pl* **colophonies** *also* **colophoniums** [*colophony* fr. ME *colophonie*, fr. L *colophonia*, fr. Gk *kolophōnia*, fem. of *kolophōnios* colophonian, fr. *Kolophōn* Colophon, an Ionian city; *colophonium*, NL, alter. of L *colophonia*] : ROSIN
col·o·quin·ti·da \ˌkäləˈkwintədə\ *n* -s [ML *coloquintida*, alter. of L *colocynthis* — more at COLOCYNTH] : COLOCYNTH
[1]col·or \ˈkələ(r)\ *n* -s *see -or in Explan Notes* [ME *colour*, fr. OF *color, colour*, fr. L *color*; akin to L *celare* to conceal — more at HELL] 1 **a** : any of manifold phenomena of light (as red, brown, pink, gray, green, blue, white) or of visual sensation or perception that enables one to differentiate objects even though the objects may appear otherwise identical (as in size, form, or texture) **b** : the aspect of the appearance of objects and light sources that may be described and specified in terms derivable wholly from one's perceptions most conveniently involving hue, lightness, and saturation for objects and hue, brightness, and saturation for light sources — used in this sense as the psychological basis for definitions of color in this dictionary **c** : the characteristic of light by means of which two areas of identical size and shape that are juxtaposed, structure-free, and steadily and uniformly illuminated may be distinguished by a human observer and which is commonly identified for spectral colors by dominant wavelength, luminance, and purity and for nonspectral colors (as purples) by complementary wavelength, luminance, and purity — used in this sense as the psychophysical basis for measuring color which in turn makes it possible to define the limits for each color definition used in this dictionary; see the Color Charts **d** : a hue as contrasted to black, white, or gray **e** : a hue or tint noticeable as different, not prevalent, unusual, unexpected 2 **a** : an outward show often concealing an underlying true character : ASPECT, APPEARANCE, SEMBLANCE, GUISE ⟨related processes of thought, beliefs, and standards prevailed and imparted a spiritual ~ to the time —H.O.Taylor⟩ ⟨he suddenly, to give his conclusions the ~ of religion, slips in a false analogy —P.E.More⟩ **b** : a legal claim to or appearance of a right, authority, or office **c** : appearance or pretense offered as justification or extenuation : show of reason : PRETEXT ⟨she could have drawn from the Versailles treaty the ~ of legality for any action she chose —*Yale Rev.*⟩ : qualified justification **d** : appearance of validity or authenticity : PLAUSIBILITY ⟨lending ~ to this notion⟩ ⟨army officers spread the word that this ship had brought 800 troops, and to give ~ to the story, they ordered tents pitched —*Amer. Guide Series: Md.*⟩ **e** : CHARACTER, COMPLEXION, TONE, QUALITY, NATURE ⟨something was happening that changed the whole ~ of the political scene —H.L.Mencken⟩ ⟨England was up against a foe of its own weight and ~ —O.S.J.Gogarty⟩ : nature as regards genuineness ⟨see the ~ of one's money⟩ 3 : complexion tint: **a** : the tint characteristic of good health and spirits or of at least a normal amount of outdoor activity ⟨to bring the ~ back to her pale cheeks⟩ ⟨the prisoners had lost ~ during their confinement⟩ **b** : the ruddy suffusion of or as if of a blush ⟨she had recovered some of her poise but her ~ showed beneath her makeup —Hartley Howard⟩ 4 **a colors** *pl, archaic* : rhetorical ornaments of language : stylistic decorations; *esp* : figures of speech **b** : vividness or variety of emotional effects of language (as of sound and image) in prose or poetry ⟨that ~ and force of style which were later to make him outstanding —Arthur Krock⟩ **c** : LOCAL COLOR 5 **a** (1) : a distinctively colored badge or device or distinctively colored clothing distinguishing one as a member of a particular group or organization, a follower or representative of a particular person or thing, or a partisan of a particular cause — usu. used in pl. ⟨wearing the college ~*s*⟩ ⟨a jockey riding under the ~*s* of a stable⟩ ⟨the ~*s* of the prince's household —Sir Walter Scott⟩ (2) : COGNIZANCE 1 — usu. used in pl. **b** *Brit* : an athlete or player awarded the right to a color in recognition of status as a team member **c colors** *pl* (1) : position with reference to a question or course of action : STAND, POINT OF VIEW ⟨we did not know how to act until our antagonist had clearly shown his ~*s*⟩ (2) : appearance or conduct in respect to its reflecting a person's character or nature ⟨showing himself finally in his true ~*s*⟩ 6 **a** (1) : a color usu. used in armory excepting those classified as metals : a heraldic tincture that is not a metal or a fur (2) **colors** *pl* : LIVERY COLORS 2a **b** : a variegation of hues, tints, or shades or a basic hue marked with spots, patches, bands, or streaks of one or more shades ⟨of tabby ~⟩ **c** : a striking hue or combination of hues in foliage esp. other than or in combination or contrast with green **d** (1) : the use or combination of colors; *esp* : the use of color regarded as determining the total effect of a painting ⟨Titian is a master of ~⟩ (2) : an effect of a variety of colors produced with a monochrome medium (as an etching or engraving) (3) : two or more hues employed in a medium of presentation ⟨movies in ~⟩ ⟨~ printing⟩ ⟨~ television⟩ (4) : one hue of two or more used in a printing job **e** : the general overall shade or tone of ink on a page of printed matter **f** : contrast between what is printed, whatever its hue, and what it is printed on ⟨this print lacks ~; it is too gray⟩; *also* : ability of a typeface to achieve such contrast **g** : ink regardless of its hue ⟨the pressman calls out for ~ when he needs more ink —Howard Lockwood⟩ 7 **a** : a flag, ensign, or pennant usu. symbolic (as of a country): as (1) : one carried by an army regiment — see KING'S COLOR, REGIMENTAL COLOR (2) **colors** *pl, in the British navy* : the ensign, jack, and pennant or distinguishing flag flown instead of the pennant : the ensign and jack (3) **colors** *pl* : a set of two or more flags that are customarily displayed together (as on parade) by any group or organized body or a group representing such an organization and that includes typically at least one civic flag (as the national, state, or municipal flag) and one organizational flag (4) **colors** *pl, usu cap* : the national flag **b** : the regiment or service distinguished by the color **c colors** *pl* : a navy or nautical salute to a flag when it is hoisted **d colors** *pl* : the armed forces of one's country — usu. used in the phrase *serve with the colors* 8 : VITALITY, VIVIDNESS, INTEREST ⟨the play had a good deal of ~ to it⟩ ⟨the wonderful ~ of a foreign market place⟩ 9 : something that is used to give color : coloring matter : PIGMENT, DYE ⟨oil ~*s*⟩ ⟨butter ~⟩ 10 **a** : TIMBRE 1b **b** : the tonal quality of a voice or instrument or the effect produced by a combination of such qualities in the performance of music — called also *tone color* 11 **a** : skin pigmentation other than white characteristic of race (as of the Negro race) ⟨a person of ~⟩ ⟨~ prejudices⟩ **b** : the members of a race or group with such pigmentation; *esp* : NEGROES 12 : a small particle of gold in a gold miner's pan after most of the waste has been washed away 13 : animating, striking, or vividly picturesque character : attendant features evoking interest or stimulating the imagination : striking quality commanding attention ⟨the ~ of the Mardi Gras⟩ ⟨a ballplayer with ~⟩; *specif* : such quality or character as a marked characteristic of a composition ⟨having all the ~ of a romantic tale⟩ ⟨add ~ to the event in recounting it⟩ 14 : a coating mixture of pigment and adhesive, whether colored or not, used in papermaking 15 **a** : all the red cards (hearts and diamonds) or all the black cards (spades and

Color samples arranged in a systematic order exhibit certain marked differences from each other. They may be arranged according to the characteristics of their appearance or according to variations in the spectral composition of the light reflected or transmitted by them. The hue variation in the normal solar spectrum is illustrated in A. The numbers on the bottom of the diagram refer to the length of the light waves that are associated with characteristically different parts of the spectrum, 400 millimicrons for the blue end of the spectrum to 700 millimicrons for the red end. Measurements of the spectral composition of light in wavelengths require instruments, but an analysis of colors by their appearance may be made in terms based wholly on perception.

As analyzed in terms of appearance, most colors have a *hue* that more or less resembles one of the hues in the spectrum illustrated in A or in the hue circle illustrated in B. The purple hues, while not found in the spectrum itself, show a resemblance to the blue and red ends and complete the hue circuit. Such colors are *chromatic* and differ characteristically from those illustrated in the black-to-white scale of C, which have no hue and hence are called *achromatic* or *neutral*.

If colors, either chromatic or achromatic, are arranged in further order, as in the black-to-white scale in C, some colors appear to be light, others dark, and still others are intermediate in *lightness*. Some light colors may be described as *very* light, some dark colors as *very* dark.

If a number of chromatic colors are selected to be constant in hue and lightness, as is the intention with the series of reds illustrated in C, some of these red colors stand out more vividly than others. Such a series may be arranged in an order of difference that increases from the grayest color to the most vivid. This difference is one of *saturation*.

These three attributes — hue, lightness, and saturation — may be thought of as dimensions of color which can be related in the three-dimensional form suggested in D (skeleton form) and E (solid form). In this color solid *hue* extends in a circular direction about the neutral axis, *lightness* extends in the vertical direction from black at the bottom through a series of grays to white at the top, and *saturation* extends in a radial direction horizontally from the central neutral axis at which the saturation is zero out to the strongest saturation, as far as this may extend from the central axis.

This dictionary defines color names by a method that depends upon this three-dimensional analysis of color. The method is one standardized, developed, and published by the Inter-Society Color Council and the National Bureau of Standards as the ISCC-NBS Method of Designating Colors and a Dictionary of Color Names (NBS Circular 553, National Bureau of Standards, Washington, 1955). The method is simple in principle. The terms *light, medium*, and *dark* designate decreasing degrees of lightness, and the adverb *very* extends the lightness scale to *very light* and *very dark*. The adjectives *grayish, moderate, strong*, and *vivid* designate increasing degrees of saturation. These and a series of hue names, used both as nouns and in adjective forms, are combined to form names for describing color in terms of its three perceptual attributes. Certain other adjectives cover combinations of lightness and saturation, as *brilliant* for "light, strong", *pale* for "light, grayish", and *deep* for "dark, strong".

There are 267 ISCC-NBS name blocks in the complete system and each defines a block in the color solid. This number is sufficient for naming colors from memory, but since it is estimated that man can distinguish several million surface colors, it necessarily follows that each name block contains a number of distinguishable colors. The important thing about this method that distinguishes it from all others is that the boundaries of each color term are specified. These boundaries are in terms of the numerical scales of hue, value, and chroma of the Munsell color notation, illustrated in B and C. (Under standard daylight conditions these scales correlate closely with the hue, lightness, and saturation scales of color perception: see footnote definitions [1] and [2] for Munsell and C.I.E. color systems.) Each ISCC-NBS color designation defines a block in the color solid bounded by vertical planes of constant hue, horizontal planes of constant value, and cylindrical surfaces of constant chroma.

The following table contains the hue names and abbrs. used in the ISCC-NBS system; Fig. 1 shows the scheme of hue modifiers, the "-ish" grays and the neutrals with their modifiers.

[1]MUNSELL COLOR SYSTEM : a system of specifying colors in terms of appearance on scales of hue, value, and chroma, exemplified first in 1915 by a collection of color chips (later, 1943, standardized and defined to the theoretical limits by tables and diagrams, July 1943 *Journal Opt. Soc. Amer*., in terms of the internationally adopted C.I.E. color mixture system), these chips forming an atlas of charts that shows scales in which two of the three variables are constant, the hue scale containing five principal and five intermediate hues (to provide a color notation in the decimal system), the value scale containing ten steps from black to white, and the chroma scales showing 10 or more steps from the equivalent gray, all three scales intended to represent equal visual (not physical) intervals for a normal observer and daylight viewing with gray to white surroundings, so that under these conditions hue, value, and chroma of the color chips correlate closely with hue, lightness, and saturation of the color perception, though under other conditions the correlation for these chips is lost, and their hue value, and chroma designations become terms of psychophysical significance since they refer to their appearance only under these standard conditions.

[2]C.I.E. COLOR SYSTEM : a world-known and world-used color mixture system for specifying any color, recommended in 1931 by the International Commission on Illumination (Commission Internationale de l'Eclairage, C.I.E.) (1) by giving the amounts (tristimulus values) X, Y, Z of three primary colors required by a standard observer to match it, which are calculable from the spectral composition of the radiant energy leaving the color specimen or (2) by giving one of the tristimulus values Y, expressing the luminous value of the color, combined with two of the fractions: X/ (X+Y+Z), Y/ (X+Y+Z), Z/ (X+Y+Z), known as chromaticity coordinates x, y, z, respectively.

HUE NAMES AND ABBREVIATIONS

NAME	ABBREVIATION	NAME	ABBREVIATION
red	R	purple	P
reddish orange	rO	reddish purple	rP
orange	O	purplish red	pR
orange yellow	OY	purplish pink	pPk
yellow	Y	pink	Pk
greenish yellow	gY	yellowish pink	yPk
yellow green	YG	brownish pink	brPk
yellowish green	yG	brownish orange	brO
green	G	reddish brown	rBr
bluish green	bG	brown	Br
greenish blue	gB	yellowish brown	yBr
blue	B	olive brown	OlBr
purplish blue	pB	olive	Ol
violet	V	olive green	OlG

The color solid, extended to the pigment limits available today, is illustrated in the black and white diagrams E and F and in color in H and I. The drawing in F shows one quarter of the solid removed to demonstrate the relation of the interior sampling for color charts of constant hue, in which lightness (value) changes in a vertical direction and saturation (chroma) varies in a horizontal direction from the center to outside limits. The color illustrations H and I show the general appearance of the outside colors from two sides of the solid, 180° apart. One side (H) illustrates the progression from purplish blue through blues and greens to the yellows, and the other side (I) starts with the yellows and progresses through the yellowish reds to reds and purples, back to the purplish blues. Actually this color solid has no rigid boundary for saturation (except in terms of theoretical limits, which are not approached today in any except yellow pigments and dyes). To illustrate the relation of ISCC-NBS color names to the color solid, a diagram of the purple section is shown in G. (The outside limits would have to be expanded if colors were found saturated enough to extend beyond the surface indicated.) The name limits are set up in relation to Munsell value-chroma charts which represent vertical slices cut through the neutral center of the solid, as illustrated in F. Two diagrams illustrate how this is done: Figure 2 represents an uncomplicated name diagram in the Munsell 3P to 9P hue range, and Figure 3 represents a complicated diagram in the 5YR to 7YR hue range in which the pale colors are *yellowish pinks*, the light and strong yellow-reds are *oranges*, and the dark yellow-reds are *browns*.

This ISCC-NBS naming method does not provide for describing colors to a close tolerance, but it does provide a description that is understandable. For colorimetry, when it is important to distinguish to a very close tolerance among the thousands of colors that in the ISCC-NBS system might bear an identical designation, a numerical notation must be used, preferably one that is as internationally standardized as the C.I.E. colorimetric coordinate system or the Munsell system of notation, both of which are included in the group of standards adopted in 1951 by the American Standards Association to specify a method of measuring and specifying color (ASA-Z58.7.1,2,3).

Following is a list of the 267 color name pockets grouped by hue names. The relationships are as shown in Figure 1 for such modifiers as are used with each hue name. Color matches, within tolerances close enough if they are to be useful in illustrating these names, are not possible with usual conditions of color printing. The color illustrations on these pages have been limited therefore to those that would aid in developing the concepts involved in describing or naming colors. Color names are defined in this dictionary in terms of the 267 color name pockets of the ISCC-NBS system.

COLOR NAME POCKETS

pinks
1—vivid Pk
2—strong Pk
3—deep Pk
4—light Pk
5—moderate Pk
6—dark Pk
7—pale Pk
8—grayish Pk
9—pinkish white
10—pinkish gray

reds
11—vivid R
12—strong R
13—deep R
14—very deep R
15—moderate R
16—dark R
17—very dark R
18—light grayish R
19—grayish R
20—dark grayish R
21—blackish R
22—reddish gray
23—dark reddish gray
24—reddish black

yellowish pinks
25—vivid yPk
26—strong yPk
27—deep yPk
28—light yPk
29—moderate yPk
30—dark yPk
31—pale yPk
32—grayish yPk

33—brownish pink

reddish oranges
34—vivid rO
35—strong rO
36—deep rO
37—moderate rO
38—dark rO
39—grayish rO

reddish browns
40—strong rBr
41—deep rBr
42—light rBr
43—moderate rBr
44—dark rBr
45—light grayish rBr
46—grayish rBr
47—dark grayish rBr

oranges
48—vivid O
49—brilliant O
50—strong O
51—deep O
52—light O
53—moderate O

54—brownish orange

browns
55—strong Br
56—deep Br
57—light Br
58—moderate Br
59—dark Br
60—light grayish Br
61—grayish Br
62—dark grayish Br
63—light brownish gray
64—brownish gray
65—brownish black

orange yellows
66—vivid OY
67—brilliant OY
68—strong OY
69—deep OY
70—light OY
71—moderate OY
72—dark OY
73—pale OY

yellowish browns
74—strong yBr
75—deep yBr
76—light yBr
77—moderate yBr
78—dark yBr
79—light grayish yBr
80—grayish yBr
81—dark grayish yBr

yellows
82—vivid Y
83—brilliant Y
84—strong Y
85—deep Y
86—light Y
87—moderate Y
88—dark Y
89—pale Y
90—grayish Y
91—dark grayish Y
92—yellowish white
93—yellowish gray

olive browns
94—light OlBr
95—moderate OlBr
96—dark OlBr

greenish yellows
97—vivid gY
98—brilliant gY
99—strong gY
100—deep gY
101—light gY
102—moderate gY
103—dark gY
104—pale gY
105—grayish gY

olives
106—light Ol
107—moderate Ol
108—dark Ol
109—light grayish Ol
110—grayish Ol
111—dark grayish Ol
112—light Ol gray
113—Ol gray
114—Ol black

yellow greens
115—vivid YG
116—brilliant YG
117—strong YG
118—deep YG
119—light YG
120—moderate YG
121—pale YG
122—grayish YG

olive greens
123—strong OlG
124—deep OlG
125—moderate OlG
126—dark OlG
127—grayish OlG
128—dark grayish OlG

yellowish greens
129—vivid yG
130—brilliant yG
131—strong yG
132—deep yG
133—very deep yG
134—very light yG
135—light yG
136—moderate yG
137—dark yG
138—very dark yG

greens
139—vivid G
140—brilliant G
141—strong G
142—deep G
143—very light G
144—light G
145—moderate G
146—dark G
147—very dark G
148—very pale G
149—pale G
150—grayish G
151—dark grayish G
152—blackish G
153—greenish white
154—light greenish gray
155—greenish gray
156—dark greenish gray
157—greenish black

bluish greens
158—vivid bG
159—brilliant bG
160—strong bG
161—deep bG
162—very light bG
163—light bG
164—moderate bG
165—dark bG
166—very dark bG

greenish blues
167—vivid gB
168—brilliant gB
169—strong gB
170—deep gB
171—very light gB
172—light gB
173—moderate gB
174—dark gB
175—very dark gB

blues
176—vivid B
177—brilliant B
178—strong B
179—deep B
180—very light B
181—light B
182—moderate B
183—dark B
184—very pale B
185—pale B
186—grayish B
187—dark grayish B
188—blackish B
189—bluish white
190—light bluish gray
191—bluish gray
192—dark bluish gray
193—bluish black

purplish blues
194—vivid pB
195—brilliant pB
196—strong pB
197—deep pB
198—very light pB
199—light pB
200—moderate pB
201—dark pB
202—very pale pB
203—pale pB
204—grayish pB

violets
205—vivid V
206—brilliant V
207—strong V
208—deep V
209—very light V
210—light V
211—moderate V
212—dark V
213—very pale V
214—pale V
215—grayish V

purples
216—vivid P
217—brilliant P
218—strong P
219—deep P
220—very deep P
221—very light P
222—light P
223—moderate P
224—dark P
225—very dark P
226—very pale P
227—pale P
228—grayish P
229—dark grayish P
230—blackish P
231—purplish white
232—light purplish gray
233—purplish gray
234—dark purplish gray
235—purplish black

reddish purples
236—vivid rP
237—strong rP
238—deep rP
239—very deep rP
240—light rP
241—moderate rP
242—dark rP
243—very dark rP
244—pale rP
245—grayish rP

purplish pinks
246—brilliant pPk
247—strong pPk
248—deep pPk
249—light pPk
250—moderate pPk
251—dark pPk
252—pale pPk
253—grayish pPk

purplish reds
254—vivid pR
255—strong pR
256—deep pR
257—very deep pR
258—moderate pR
259—dark pR
260—very dark pR
261—light grayish pR
262—grayish pR

neutrals
263—white
264—light gray
265—medium gray
266—dark gray
267—black

FIGURE 1

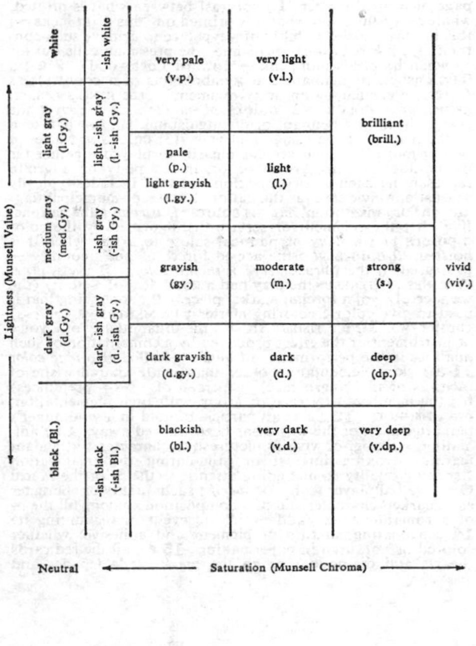

Lightness (Munsell Value)
white | -ish white | very pale (v.p.) | very light (v.l.)
light gray (l.Gy.) | light -ish gray (l. -ish Gy.) | pale (p.) light grayish (l.gy.) | light (l.) | brilliant (brill.)
medium gray (med.Gy.) | -ish gray (-ish Gy.) | grayish (gy.) | moderate (m.) | strong (s.) | vivid (viv.)
dark gray (d.Gy.) | dark -ish gray (d. -ish Gy.) | dark grayish (d.gy.) | dark (d.) | deep (dp.)
black (Bl.) | -ish black (-ish Bl.) | blackish (bl.) | very dark (v.d.) | very deep (v.dp.)
Neutral ← Saturation (Munsell Chroma) →

FIGURE 2

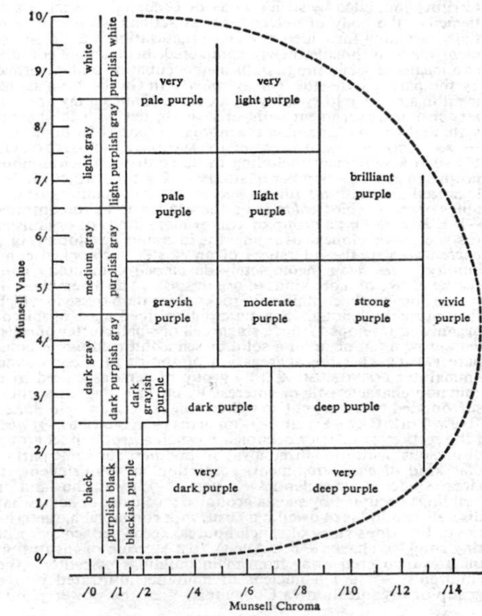

FIGURE 3

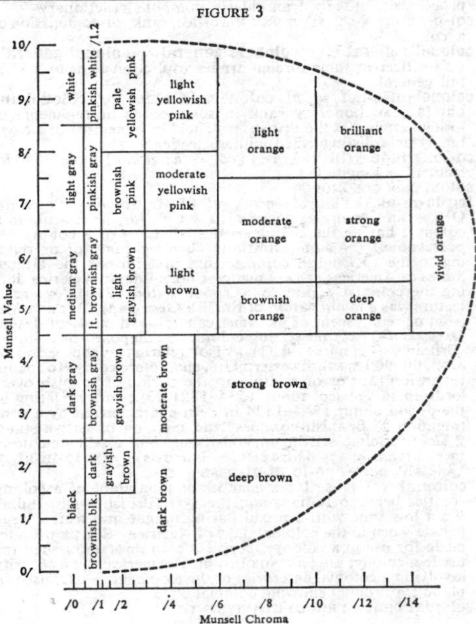

COLOR

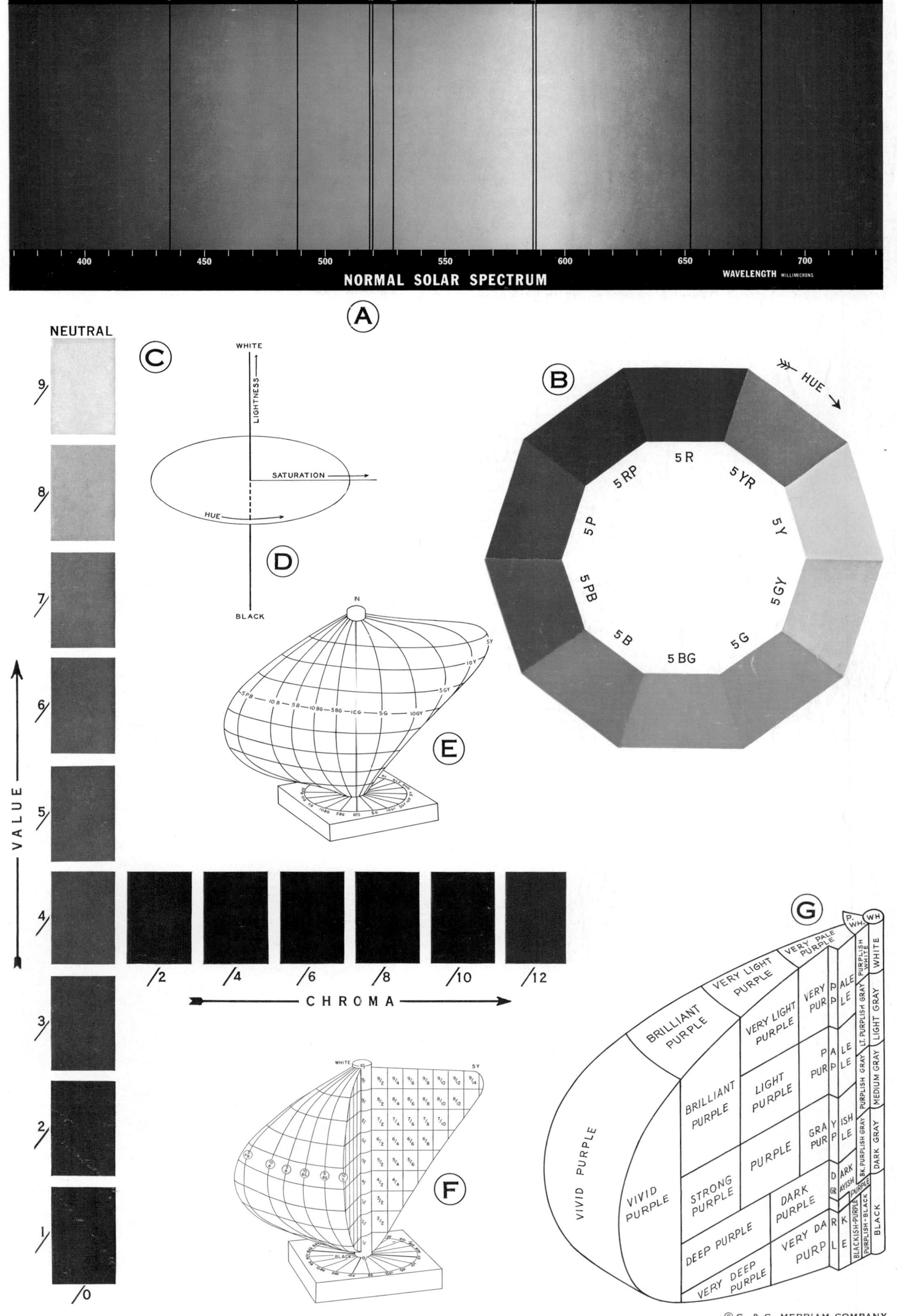

FRAUNHOFER LINES
G
F
b
E
D
C
B
400
450
500
550
600
650
700
NORMAL SOLAR SPECTRUM
WAVELENGTH MILLIMICRONS
A
NEUTRAL
C
WHITE
LIGHTNESS
SATURATION
HUE
D
BLACK
B
HUE
5 R
5 RP
5 YR
5 P
5 Y
5 PB
5 GY
5 B
5 G
5 BG
E
F
VALUE
CHROMA
/2
/4
/6
/8
/10
/12
G
VIVID PURPLE
BRILLIANT PURPLE
VERY LIGHT PURPLE
VERY PALE PURPLE
LIGHT PURPLE
PURPLE
STRONG PURPLE
DEEP PURPLE
VERY DEEP PURPLE
DARK PURPLE
VERY DARK PURPLE
WHITE
LIGHT GRAY
MEDIUM GRAY
DARK GRAY
BLACK

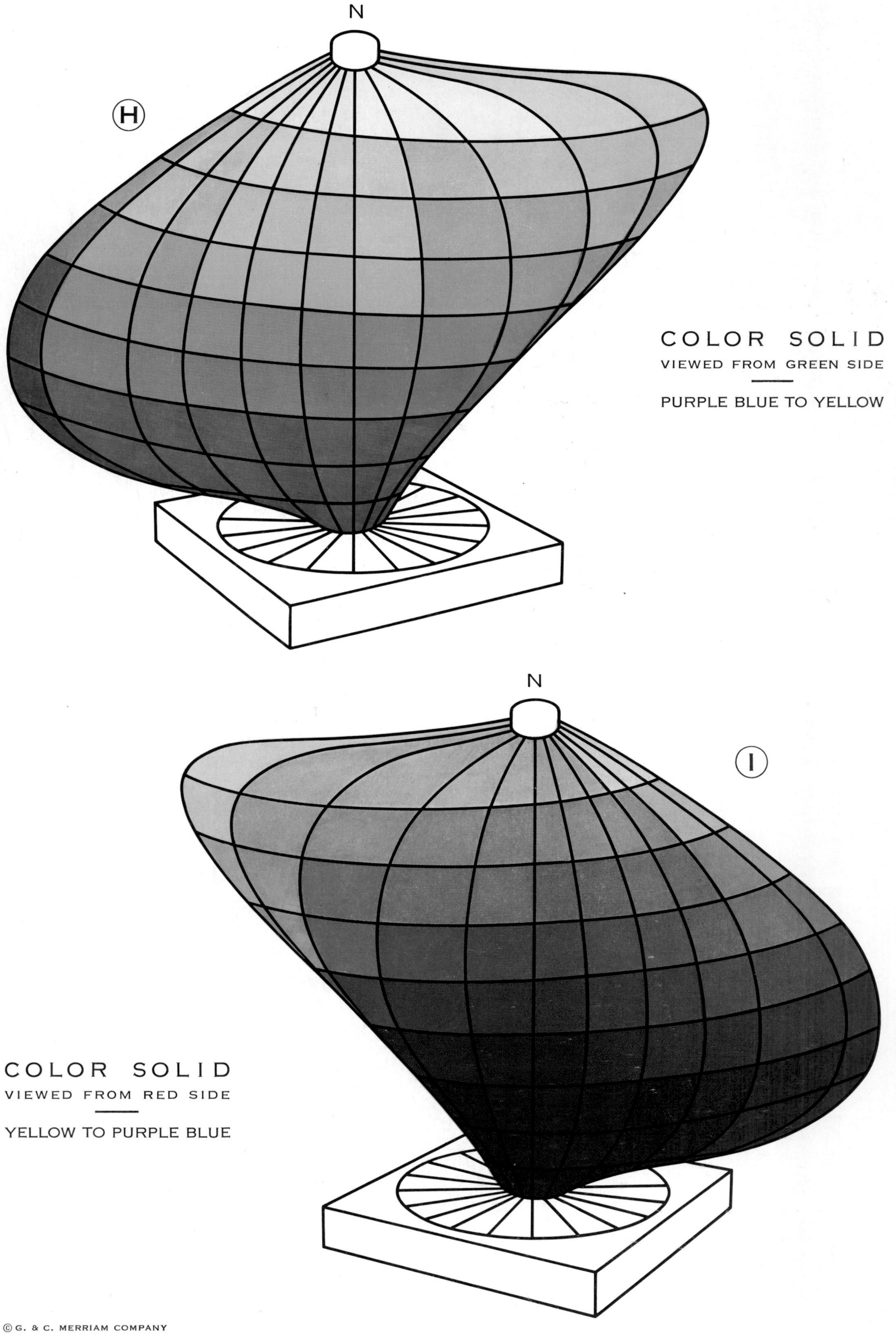

COLOR SOLID
VIEWED FROM GREEN SIDE
PURPLE BLUE TO YELLOW

COLOR SOLID
VIEWED FROM RED SIDE
YELLOW TO PURPLE BLUE

clubs) **b :** the other suit of the same color as the trump suit **c :** SUIT 7a(1) **d :** COULEUR 2b
syn CHROMA, HUE, SHADE, TINT, TINGE, TONE: COLOR is the generic and most general term in this set. CHROMA, usu. limited to scientific or technical writing, may stress the attributes of hue and saturation, as in bright red or dull green, in contrast to white, grays, or black, which do not possess these attributes. HUE may suggest that property by which colors of the spectrum are distinguished one from another and from corresponding grays ⟨all the gradational *hues* of the spectrum from red through yellow, green, blue, to violet —*Scientific Monthly*⟩ In less scientific use it indicates merely color or gradation or modification of color ⟨livid with the *hue* of death —Mary W. Shelley⟩ ⟨their shining green has changed to a less vivid *hue* —Lafcadio Hearn⟩ SHADE is usu. used to indicate a gradation of a color or hue according to lightness or brightness. It often but not always suggests a darker rather than lighter gradation. TINT indicates a gradation of a color or hue, usu. either a lighter gradation, one oriented toward white, or a gradation of a light color ⟨Father Latour had often remarked that this tree seemed especially designed in shape and color for the adobe village. The sprays of bloom which adorn it are merely another *shade* of the red earth walls, and its fibrous trunk is full of gold and lavender *tints* —Willa Cather⟩ TINGE suggests an interfusion or an overlay, stain, dappling, or freaking of one color over or into another general background color ⟨in ore it [copper] is red in color, but a freshly fractured surface of the pure metal has a pinkish or yellowish *tinge* —*New Yorker*⟩ In nontechnical writing COLOR, HUE, SHADE, and TINT are often interchangeable ⟨flowing . . . now over rocks of greenish *hue* and again over those of brownish *tint* —*Amer. Guide Series: N. H.*⟩ TONE, while often equivalent to COLOR, suggests more particularly hue or a modification of hue, as tint or shade ⟨from strand to cloud-capped peak, the *tone* was purple —William Beebe⟩ ⟨it [dun] was also very much used as a couplet to other terms, like brown, red, yellow, etc., to express dull, grayed *tones* of such colors —A.J.Maerz & M.R.Paul⟩ **syn** see in addition FLAG
— **under colors** *of a horse* **:** in an official race ⟨the colt . . . made his first appearance *under colors* at Hialeah —G.F.T. Ryall⟩ — **with flying colors :** eminently successful **:** VICTORIOUS, UNDEFEATED, IRREPROACHABLE

²color \"\ *vb* **colored; colored; coloring** \'kəl(ə)riŋ\ **colors** *see -or in Explan Notes* [ME *colouren*, fr. OF *colorer*, fr. L *colorare*, fr. *color*, n.] *vt* **1 a :** to give color to **:** imbue with color **b :** to change or alter the color of (as by dyeing, staining, or painting) **:** DYE, TINGE, TINT, SHADE, PAINT, STAIN **2 :** to change or alter as if by dyeing or painting: as **a :** MISREPRESENT, DISGUISE, DISTORT, BIAS ⟨a highly ~*ed* version of the facts⟩ **b :** GLOSS, PALLIATE, EXCUSE ⟨~ a lie⟩ **3** *obs* **:** to misrepresent as one's own **4 :** INFLUENCE, SHAPE, CONDITION, AFFECT ⟨the lives of most of us have been ~*ed* by politics —Christine Weston⟩ ⟨how much the contemplation of death has ~*ed* human thought —H.L.Mencken⟩ **5 :** to imbue (as a piece of writing) with a subjective quality or cause to produce a particular emotional effect ⟨his writings were ~*ed* by his feelings⟩ **6 :** to produce a fine finish on (a metal) by polishing with rouge or lime **7 :** to modify the articulation or acoustic quality of (a speech sound) ⟨an r-*colored* vowel⟩ ~ *vi* **:** to take on or acquire a color: **a :** to take on the color of ripeness (as of grapes) **b :** BLUSH, FLUSH ⟨~*ed* as though she had said something very daring —Willard Robertson⟩

³color \"\ *adj* — *see -or in Explan Notes* [¹*color*] **:** showing or dealing with or concerned with color: **a :** concerned with skin pigmentation **:** RACIST ⟨the ~ line⟩ **b :** capable of reproducing color **:** showing things in color ⟨~ photography⟩ **:** capable of producing more than one color at a single operation ⟨a two-*color* press⟩; *also* **:** used to print one color in a job printed in two or more colors ⟨a ~ cut⟩ ⟨a ~ border⟩

col·or·a·bil·i·ty \ˌkəl(ə)rəˈbiləd·ē, -ətē, -i\ *n* -ES **:** the quality of being colorable

col·or·a·ble \'kəl(ə)rəbəl\ *adj* [ME, fr. MF *colorable*, fr. *color* + *-able*] **1 :** seemingly valid and genuine **:** having an appearance of truth, right, or justice **:** PLAUSIBLE ⟨any ~ pretext for refusing —Bertrand Russell⟩ **2 :** FEIGNED, FACTITIOUS, COUNTERFEIT ⟨~ and false pretenses⟩ — **col·or·a·bly** \-blē, -bli\ *adv*

¹col·o·rad·an \ˌkäləˈradᵊn, -rä-, -rā- *archaic* -rā-\ *or* **col·o·rad·o·an** \-dəwən\ *adj, usu cap* [*Colorado*, state of U.S. + E *-an*] **1 :** of, relating to, or characteristic of the state of Colorado **2 :** of, relating to, or characteristic of Coloradans

²coloradan \"\ *or* **coloradoan** \"\ *n* -S *cap* **:** a native or resident of the state of Colorado

¹col·o·rado \-(ˌ)dō,-də\ *adj, usu cap* [fr. *Colorado*, state of U.S., fr. the *Colorado* river, fr. Sp, lit., red, reddish (past part. of *colorar* to color) fr. L *coloratus*, past part. of *colorare* to color — more at COLOR] **1 :** of or from the state of Colorado ⟨the *Colorado* mountains⟩ **:** of the kind or style prevalent in Colorado **:** COLORADAN **2 :** of or relating to a subdivision of the American Upper Cretaceous — see GEOLOGIC TIME table

²colorado \"\ *n, pl* **colorado** *or* **colorados** *usu cap* [Sp, lit., red, reddish] **1 a :** a Barbacoan people at the foot of the western Andes, Ecuador **b :** a member of such people **2 :** the language of the Colorado people

³colorado \"\ *n* -ES [AmerSp, fr. Sp *colorado*, adj.] **:** a cigar of medium color and strength

colorado blue spruce *n, usu cap C* **:** COLORADO SPRUCE; *esp* **:** a pendulous-branched spruce (*Picea pungens kosteriana*) that is a variety of this tree

colorado bur *n, usu cap C* **:** BUFFALO BUR

colorado fir *n, usu cap C* **:** WHITE FIR 1a(1)

colorado grass *n, usu cap C* **:** TEXAS MILLET

col·o·rad·o·ite \-də,wīt\ *n* -S [*Colorado*, its locality + E *-ite*] **:** a grayish black mineral with metallic luster consisting of mercury telluride HgTe (sp. gr. 8.6)

colorado manroot *n, usu cap C* **:** MAN-OF-THE-EARTH

colorado potato beetle *or* **colorado beetle** *n, usu cap C* **:** a black-and-yellow striped beetle (*Leptinotarsa decemlineata*) orig. found in the eastern foothills of the Rocky mountains where it fed on the sandbur (*Solanum rostratum*) but now feeding in both the larval and adult stages on the leaves of the potato, often doing great damage, and spread into most potato-growing regions of the world

colorado ranger *n, usu cap C* [¹*Colorado*] **:** a parti-colored horse of a breed developed in the western U.S. by interbreeding barbs with native stock ultimately of Spanish origin

colorado river hemp *n, usu cap C&R* **:** a tall-growing annual legume (*Sesbania exaltata*) of the southwestern U.S. that produces a strong tough bast fiber formerly used by the Indians for cordage and that is widely used as a green manure esp. on heavy moist soils — called also *sesbania*

colorado rubber plant *or* **colorado rubber weed** *n, usu cap C* **:** any of several herbs of the genus *Hymenoxys* (family Compositae) of the western U.S. that contain small quantities of rubber

colorado spruce *n, usu cap C* **:** a tall wide-spreading evergreen tree (*Picea pungens*) often planted for ornament — called also *blue spruce, Colorado blue spruce, silver spruce*

colorado steer hide *or* **colorado steer** *n, usu cap C* **:** a hide from a side-branded steer

colorado tick fever *n, usu cap C* **:** a mild nonruptive disease that is characterized by intermittent fever, short course, and long convalescence and that is caused by a virus transmitted by a wood tick (*Dermacentor andersoni*)

colorado white balsam *or* **colorado white fir** *n, usu cap C* **:** WHITE FIR 1a(1)

colorado wild potato *n, usu cap C* **:** an herb (*Solanum jamesii*) of Colorado and adjacent states with white flowers and small tubers

col·or·ant \'kəl(ə)rənt\ *n* -S [F, fr. pres. part. of *colorer* to color, fr. L *colorare* — more at COLOR] **:** a substance capable of or used for coloring a material **:** DYE, PIGMENT

col·or·a·tion \ˌkələˈrāshən\ *n* -S [F, fr. MF, fr. *colorer* to color + *-ation*] **1 a :** the state of being colored **:** COLORING 1c ⟨a rock with a strange and interesting ~⟩ ⟨the ~ of the skin from a bruise⟩ **b :** use or choice of colors (as by an artist) ⟨Millet's subdued ~⟩; *specif* **:** arrangement or combination of colors ⟨the brilliant ~ of a butterfly's wing⟩ **2 a :** characteristic quality **:** TIMBRE ⟨the newspapers . . . took on the former ~ of the magazines —L.B.Seltzer⟩ **b :** aspect suggesting an attitude **:** PERSUASION, ATTITUDE, INCLINATION ⟨the chameleon talent for taking on the intellectual ~ of whatever idea he happened to fasten onto —Budd Schulberg⟩ **3 :** subtle variation of intensity or quality of tone ⟨a haunting ~ in the string passages of the concerto⟩ ⟨a certain odd ~ in his voice⟩

col·or·a·tion·al \ˌ≠≠ˈrāsh(ə)nəl\ *adj* **:** of, relating to, or depending on coloration

col·or·a·tive \'kələˌrād·iv\ *adj* [*coloration* + *-ive*] **1 :** that colors **2 :** consisting of or depending upon coloration ⟨the ~ protection of certain animals⟩

col·or·a·tu·ra \ˌkələrəˈtu̇rə, ˌkäl-, ˌkōl-\ *n* -S *often attrib* [obs. It, lit., coloring, fr. LL, fr. L *coloratus* + *-ura* -ure] **1 :** the florid ornamentation in vocal music (as runs, trills, arpeggios); *broadly* **:** music characterized by ornate figuration **2 :** one that sings or has the ability to sing coloratura; *usu* **:** a soprano singer of coloratura

col·or·a·ture \'kələrəchə(r)\ *n* -S [G or It; G *koloratur*, fr. It *coloratura*] **:** COLORATURA

color balance *n* **1 :** a distribution of colors (as in a painting) resulting in a feeling of fitness, satisfaction, and beauty **2 :** the chromatic characteristics of the reproduction of gray tones in a color photograph

color-ball pool \'≠≠,≠-\ *n* **:** ENGLISH POOL

color bar *n* **:** a bar or barrier hindering or preventing colored persons from participating with whites in various activities and ranging in severity from social discrimination and conventional debarring from some occupations to a strict legally enforced exclusion from any skilled occupations (as in the Union of So. Africa)

color base *n* **:** DYE BASE

color-bearer \'≠≠ˌ≠≠\ *n* **:** one that carries a color or standard esp. in a military parade or drill

color-blind \'≠≠ˌ≠\ *adj* **1 a :** afflicted with a congenital or acquired partial or total inability to distinguish one or more chromatic colors **b :** not noticing or considering **:** BLIND, INSENSITIVE, OBLIVIOUS ⟨laws *color-blind* to economic reality⟩ **2** *of a photographic film or emulsion* **:** sensitive only to blue, violet, and ultraviolet light

color blindness *n* **:** the state of being color-blind **:** inability or marked difficulty in distinguishing chromatic color — compare CHROMATIC VISION; DICHROMATISM, MONOCHROMATISM, TRICHROMATISM

colorbreed \'≠≠,≠\ *vt* **:** to breed selectively for the development of particular colors ⟨~*ing* canaries for red⟩

color camera *n* **:** a camera of special design for making color≠separation negatives (as a beam-splitter camera or a one-shot camera)

¹colorcast \'≠≠,≠\ *n* -S [*color* + tele*cast*] **:** a television broadcast in color

²colorcast \"\ *vb* **colorcast** *also* **colorcasted; colorcast** *also* **colorcasted; colorcasting; colorcasts :** to broadcast in color over television

color cell *n* **:** CHROMOCYTE

color change *n* **:** a fraudulent or accidental change in the color of a particular postage stamp; *also* **:** an authorized change in a particular denomination of stamps

color changeling *n* **:** a postage stamp whose color has changed as a result of chemical action

color chart *n* **:** a systematic arrangement of colors or their representations with respect to either the attributes of the colors or the mixing relations of their stimuli

color chest *n* **:** a chest for signal flags (as on a ship)

color chip *n* **:** a small usu. paper sample representing a color

color cinematography *n* **:** cinematography that uses a color photography process

color circle *n* **:** an arrangement of hues in their natural spectrum order (red, orange, yellow, green, blue, violet plus the purples) about the circumference of a circle usu. with pairs of complementary hues represented on the opposite ends of diameters

color collotype *n* **:** collotype in more than one color; *often* **:** collotype in four or more colors

color company *n* **:** the company with which the colors are posted for military ceremonies and drills

color constancy *n* **:** tendency of the colors perceived as belonging to objects to remain invariable in spite of changes in amount and spectral quality of illumination

color cycle *n* **1 :** COLOR CIRCLE **2 :** recurrence of colors as they reach peak in fashion

color developer *n* **:** a developer in color photography that after becoming oxidized combines with a coupler to form a dye that is deposited along with the developed silver in the image, the silver image being then bleached to leave the colored image

color diagram *n* **:** a diagram showing relations between colors or facts of color mixture; *specif* **:** COLOR CHART

color dimension *n* **:** one in any set of three dimensions used for describing or denoting color — compare COLOR SOLID

¹col·ored \'kələ(r)d\ *adj* [ME *coloured*, fr. past part. of *colouren* to color — more at COLOR] **1 :** marked by color **:** having or showing usu. chromatic color ⟨white and ~ lights⟩ ⟨advertisements on ~ paper⟩; *sometimes* **:** having a color other than the accustomed or expected ⟨~ glass⟩ ⟨a green and a ~ leaf⟩ **2 a :** FEIGNED, PRETENDED ⟨a ~ ally⟩ **b :** glossed over **:** made to appear less extreme **:** PALLIATED ⟨his ~ crimes⟩ **c :** ADORNED, EMBELLISHED ⟨the ~ verse of Claudian —Arthur Symons⟩ **:** made colorful ⟨the pictures, ~ and racy, which Captain Nichols' vivid account offered —W.S.Maugham⟩ **:** EXAGGERATED, SLANTED, BIASED ⟨~ political news —F.L.Mott⟩ ⟨the prosecutor's well-*colored* evidence —Arthur Morrison⟩ **d :** ORIENTED, ALIGNED ⟨politically ~ labor unions⟩ **3** *sometimes cap* **a :** of some other race than the white; *often* **:** Negro or having some proportion of Negro blood **b :** of, for, or relating to colored persons ⟨a teacher in ~ schools⟩ **4** *sometimes cap* **a :** of mixed race ⟨the ~ people, as contrasted with the Negroes of St. Thomas⟩ **b** *Africa* **:** of or relating to the Cape Colored

²colored \"\ *n* -S *sometimes cap* **1 :** colored people ⟨education of the ~⟩ **2 :** a colored person ⟨a school for ~*s*⟩

colored corpuscle *n* **:** a red blood cell

colored vision *n* **:** CHROMATOPSIA

color emissivity *n* **:** monochromatic emissivity

col·or·er \'kəl(ə)rə(r)\ *n* -S **:** one that colors: as **a :** one that coats gold articles with zinc or gold to secure uniform color **b :** one that applies colored glaze to tiles using a bulb pen **c :** a worker who brushes coloring fluid over hides

colorfast \'≠≠,≠\ *adj* **:** having color that retains its original hue esp. without fading or running in washing, cleaning, wearing, or long exposure to light — **col·or·fast·ness** *n* -ES

color-feed \'≠≠,≠\ *vt* **:** to feed (as canaries) elements intended to enrich the color of plumage

color film *n* **:** a photographic film used for making color pictures

color filter *n* **:** a filter (as of glass, gelatin, or liquid) that absorbs light of certain wavelengths or colors selectively and is used for modifying the light that reaches a sensitized material esp. for increasing contrast, photographing through haze, or making color-separation negatives — called also *color screen, light filter*

col·or·ful \'kələ(r)fəl\ *adj* **1 :** marked by much color or many colors esp. those that are bright or vivid ⟨the ~ scenery of the area⟩ **:** attractively colored **2 :** compelling attention or interest **:** striking because of lively animation, diverting variety, compelling individual manner, distinctive procedure, or unusual content often exaggerated ⟨a ~ pageant⟩ ⟨a ~ athlete⟩ ⟨version . . . garnished with boasts of his own exploits, is a ~ . . . account —*Amer. Guide Series: Calif.*⟩ — **col·or·ful·ly** \-f(ə)lē, -li\ *adv* — **col·or·ful·ness** *n* -ES

col·or·gravure \ˌkələ(r)+\ *n* -S **:** gravure printed in more than one color

color guard *n* **:** a guard of honor for the colors of an organization, in the armed forces consisting of four men of which two are senior noncommissioned officers who carry the colors — compare GUARD OF THE STANDARD

color hearing *n* **:** CHROMESTHESIA

colories *pl of* COLORY

col·or·if·ic \ˌkələˈrifik\ *adj* **1 :** capable of communicating color **2** *archaic* **:** with respect to color **3** *archaic* **:** abounding in literary color

col·or·im·e·ter \ˌkələˈrimədə(r)\ *n* -S [ISV *color* + *-i-* + *-meter*] **1 :** an instrument or device for determining and specifying colors by reference either to other colors or to complex stimuli not in general identical with the actual color stimulus and giving results not independent of abnormalities in the observer's color vision — distinguished from *spectrophotometer* and *spectroradiometer* **2 :** an instrument for chemical analysis of liquids by comparison of the color of the given liquid with standard colors — compare COMPARATOR

col·or·i·met·ric \ˌkələrəˈme·trik\ *or* **col·or·i·met·ri·cal** \-trəkəl\ *adj* **:** of or relating to colorimetry ⟨a ~ procedure⟩; *also* **:** determined or to be determined by the use of a colorimeter ⟨~ analysis⟩ — **col·or·i·met·ri·cal·ly** \-trək(ə)lē, -li\ *adv*

colorimetric photometer *n* **:** a photometer measuring light intensities for several spectral regions by means of filters successively interposed in the path of the light

colorimetric purity *n* **:** purity (sense 2a) found by evaluating the components in luminance terms

colorimetric quality *n* **:** CHROMATICNESS

col·or·i·met·rics \ˌkələrəˈmetriks\ *n pl but usu sing in constr* **:** COLORIMETRY

col·or·im·e·trist \ˌkələˈrimə·trəst\ *n* -S **:** a specialist in colorimetry

col·or·im·e·try \ˌkələˈrimə·trē, -tri\ *n* -ES [ISV *color* + *-i-* + *-metry*] **1 :** the science and practice of determining and specifying colors — compare COLORIMETER **2 :** quantitative chemical analysis by color comparison (as by a colorimeter)

col·or·in \'kələrən, ˌkələˈrēn, ˌkōl-\ *n* -S [MexSp *colorín*, fr. Sp, linnet, bright color, fr. *color*, fr. L — more at COLOR] **:** a spiny Mexican tree (*Erythrina americana*) with showy red flowers and brilliant scarlet seeds

color index *n* **1 a :** the photographic magnitude of a star or other celestial body minus visual magnitude **b :** the difference between the magnitudes of a star or other celestial body as measured in two distinct wavelength regions of the spectrum and intended to indicate the object's color **2 :** a figure representing the ratio of the amount of hemoglobin to the number of red cells in a given volume of blood and being a measure of the normality of the hemoglobin content of the individual cells

coloring *n* -S [ME *colouring*, fr. gerund of *colouren* to color — more at COLOR] **1 a :** the act of applying colorants **:** the application of color **b :** something that produces color or color effects ⟨pouring the ~ into the paint before mixing⟩ **c** (1) **:** the effect produced by applying or combining colors or shades ⟨a painting with startling ~⟩ (2) **:** natural color or a combination of natural colors ⟨the dun ~ of the mole⟩ ⟨the startling ~ of the peacock⟩ ⟨a sunset with vivid ~⟩ (3) **:** COMPLEXION 3a ⟨the ~ of a blonde⟩ **d :** the final stage in buffing a metallic surface wherein a high polish is imparted **2 a :** false semblance **:** SHOW, DISGUISE; *esp* **:** a pleasing masking of something bad ⟨lies under the ~ of truth⟩ **b :** a slanting or suggesting added extrinsically **:** ORIENTATION, SLANT, BIAS ⟨although given a Christian ~ here and there . . . this poetry is essentially heathen —*Encyc. Americana*⟩ **3 a :** COLOR 4b **b :** COLOR 13 **c :** the indirect disclosure of sympathies or point of view in writing or speaking **4 a :** TIMBRE, QUALITY **b :** COLORATURA, ORNAMENTATION

col·or·ism \'kələˌrizəm\ *n* -S **:** COLORATION, COLORING

col·or·ist \'kələrəst\ *n* -S [F *coloriste*, fr. *colorer* to color + *-iste* -ist — more at COLOR] **1 :** one that colors: **a :** an artist, designer, or composer who excels in the use of color or to whom color is of prime importance **b :** one who duplicates the exact colors of customers' samples used in printing cloth to order **2 a :** a chemist who develops color formulas for plastics to match customer specifications **b :** one who advises about fashionable color shades and combinations **c :** one who colors photographs

col·or·is·tic \ˌkələˈristik\ *adj* **:** relating to color or coloring ⟨~ truth in a landscape⟩ ⟨a concept formulated in ~ terms⟩ ⟨~ treatment of orchestral instruments⟩ — **col·or·is·ti·cal·ly** \-tək(ə)lē\ *adv*

color lake *n* **:** ⁴LAKE 1b

col·or·less \'kələ(r)ləs\ *adj* [ME *colourless*, fr. *colour* + *-less*] **1 :** without color: **a :** transparent and not distinguished by any hue ⟨a ~ gas⟩ **b :** PALLID, BLANCHED ⟨a ~ sallow complexion⟩ **2 :** without distinctive character: as **a :** lacking variety and contrast, energetic individuality, animating qualities such as spontaneity, or ability to command interest ⟨~ histories, so passionless and so lacking in distinctive mark or motive —Woodrow Wilson⟩ **b :** free from any manifestation of partial or peculiar feeling **:** NEUTRAL ⟨did not try to write a ~ story —W.A.White⟩ — **col·or·less·ly** *adv*

colorless corpuscle *n* **:** LEUKOCYTE

col·or·less·ness *n* -ES **:** the quality or state of having no color

color line *n* **1 :** a line of stacked rifles on which the colors rest while troops are engaged in activities without arms **2 :** the line of social demarcation that some people maintain between the white race and colored races (as between whites and Negroes); *also* **:** a similar line between groups of lighter and darker colored people

col·or·man \'kələ(r)mən, -ˌman\ *n, pl* **colormen 1** *Brit* **:** a dealer in colors and paints **2 a :** a workman who mixes dyes (as in leather manufacturing) **b :** one that plans, supervises, or carries out dyeing processes in manufacturing **3 :** one that distributes identifying silks and numbers to jockeys **4 :** one that obtains colored finishes in the electroplating of metal objects by the use of various plating solutions

color mixer *n* **:** an apparatus for color mixture; *esp* **:** a wheel provided with concentric colored disks slit along a radius and dovetailed so as to reveal differently colored sectors which when whirled rapidly blend into a circle of uniform color

color music *n* **:** the portrayal (as on a screen) of successive shades of color often in patterns and with rhythm similar to that of sounds in music; *also* **:** the artistic effect so produced — compare CLAVILUX

color of office : the pretense or appearance of official authority in one who being an officer in law or fact is without the authority claimed

color of title 1 : an apparent but invalid title based upon a written instrument or record; *also* **:** the instrument itself **2 :** an apparent ownership claimed by adverse possession

color organ *n* **:** CLAVILUX

col·o·ro·to \ˌkələˈrōd·ō\ *n* -S [blend of *color* and *roto*] **:** rotogravure printed in more than one color

color party *n, Brit* **:** the color guard of a regiment

color phase *n* **1 a :** a genetic variant manifested by the occurrence of a skin or pelage color unlike the wild type of the animal group in which it appears and usu. produced by a number of different factors interacting in accord with Mendel's laws ⟨the silver *color phase* of the red fox⟩ **b :** an individual exhibiting or a pelt or skin that is the result of such a genetic variant ⟨these foxes are all *color phases*⟩ — compare MUTATION **2 :** a seasonally variant pelage color ⟨the drab summer *color phase* of the ermine⟩

col·or·pho·bia \ˌkələ(r)ˈfōbēə\ *n* -S **:** hatred of Negroes

col·or·pho·to \'≠≠ˌfōd·ō\ *n* **:** a photograph produced by color photography

color photography *n* **:** photographic production of pictures in nearly natural colors

col·or·plate \'kələ(r)ˌplāt, *usu* -ād·+V\ *n* **:** any of a set of process color printing plates; *also* **:** a print made from a complete set of such plates

color point *n* **:** HONOR POINT

color print *n* **:** a print in two or more colors

color printing *n* **:** the making of color prints esp. in three or more colors

color quality *n* **:** CHROMA

color question *n* **:** the problem of race antagonisms and their elimination in human relations esp. as affecting whites and Negroes

color ratio *n* **:** the volumetric ratio of dark minerals to light in igneous rocks

colors *pl of* COLOR, *pres 3d sing of* COLOR

color salute *n* **:** a salute made by dipping the colors

color scheme *n* **:** a combination or arrangement of colors regarded as elements in a systematic conception ⟨the *color scheme* of a costume⟩ ⟨a room with a blue and green *color scheme*⟩

color screen *n* **:** COLOR FILTER

color-sensitize \'≠≠ˈ≠≠,≠\ *vt* **:** to make (a photographic material) sensitive to colors other than those to which the material is naturally sensitive

color separation *n* **:** the isolation on separate photographic negatives by the use of color filters of the parts of a picture or design that are to be printed in the given colors; *also* **:** any of these separate negatives

color sergeant *n* **1 :** a sergeant in a color guard who carries one of the colors **2 :** a Salvation Army soldier appointed as a flag bearer

color slab *n* **:** a tile of white china on which a palette of colors has been burned

color·slide \ˈ==,=\ *n* **:** a color transparency for projection

color solid *or* **color space** *n* **:** three-dimensional space each point of which represents a color

color striker *n* **:** one that makes color-ants

color temperature *n* **:** the temperature at which a blackbody emits radiant energy competent to evoke a color of the same hue and saturation as that evoked by radiant energy from a given source (as a lamp)

color tone *n* **1 :** TONE 8 **2 :** the general effect of a pleasing color harmony

color top *n* **:** COLOR MIXER

color transparency *n* **:** a color photograph to be examined by transmitted light

color trial *n* **:** a proof of a stamp that was made for testing the use of a certain color subsequently rejected — called also *trial color proof*

color triangle *n* **:** CHROMATICITY DIAGRAM

color solid

col·or·type \ˈkələ(r),tīp\ *n* **1 :** a color print produced by process plates; *also* **:** a process by which such prints are produced — compare COLOR SEPARATION **2 :** a halftone print in three or more colors

color vision *n* **:** perception of and ability to distinguish colors

color wash *n* **:** a whitewash or a cold-water paint tinted with colored pigments

color weakness *n* **:** a partial inability to distinguish colors that is not so marked as in color blindness

color wheel *n* **:** a color mixer using a wheel of colored disks

¹col·ory \ˈkəl(ə)rē, -ri\ *adj* [¹*color* + *-y*] **1 :** characterized by color **:** showing color **:** COLORFUL **2 :** having a color indicating good quality ⟨~ coffee⟩

²colory \"\ *n* -ES **:** a colory product; *specif* **:** leaf tobacco with the lightest color of the type

color zone *n, in some theories of vision* **:** one of the three concentric areas of the retina as distinguished on the basis of their color sense, the outer zone giving practically only the grays, the intermediate zone adding yellow and blue, and the central zone adding red and green so that only the central zone is sensitive to all colors

co·loss *or* **co·losse** \kəˈläs\ *n, pl* **colosses** [MF & L; MF *colosse,* fr. L *colossus*] *archaic* **:** COLOSSUS

co·los·sal \kəˈläsəl\ *adj* [F, fr. L *colossus* + F *-al* — more at COLOSSUS] **1 :** like or relating to a colossus **:** of very great size ⟨a ~ statue⟩ **2 :** characterized by extremely great bulk, extent, force, strength, power, or effect, approaching or suggesting the stupendous or incredible ⟨the ~ speed of 15,000 miles a second —James Jeans⟩ ⟨their wars have now become so ~ that every woman's husband, father, son, brother, or sweetheart . . . must go to the trenches —G.B.Shaw⟩ **3 :** characterized by an exceptional or astonishing degree ⟨~ impudence⟩ **syn** see HUGE

col·os·sal·i·ty \,kälə'saləd·ē\ *n* -ES **:** colossal nature or characteristics ⟨the ~ of the skyscraper⟩

co·los·sal·ly \kəˈläs(ə)lē, -li\ *adv* **:** in a colossal manner

colossal order *n* **:** an architectural order extending in height beyond one interior story; *esp* **:** with the columns or pilasters reaching from the basement to nearly the top of the wall

col·os·se·um \,käləˈsēəm\ *n* -S [ML, fr. L *colosseum,* neut. of *colosseus* colossal, fr. *colossus*] **:** COLISEUM

co·los·si \kəˈläsē, -,sī\ *pl of* COLOSSUS

¹co·los·si·an \kəˈläsh(ē)ən, -äsēən, -äsyən\ *adj, usu cap* [*Colossæ,* ancient city in Phrygia, Asia Minor + E *-ian*] **1 :** of, relating to, or characteristic of Colossae, an ancient city of Phrygia in Asia Minor where there was an early Christian church **2 :** of, relating to, or characteristic of Colossians

²colossian \"\ *n* -S *usu cap* **:** a native or inhabitant of Colossae; *esp* **:** a member of its Christian church

colosso *n, pl* **colossos** *or* **colossoes** [It, fr. L *colossus*] *obs* **:** COLOSSUS

col·os·soch·e·lys \,käləˈsäkələs\ *n, cap* [NL, fr. Gk *kolosso-* (fr. *kolossos* colossus) + *chelys* tortoise — more at CHELYS] **:** a genus of gigantic extinct Pliocene tortoises of India

co·los·sus \kəˈläsəs\ *n, pl* **colossuses** \-səsəz\ *or* **colossi** \-,sī, -,sē\ [L, fr. Gk *kolossos*] **1 :** a huge statue of greater than heroic size and proportions ⟨fronting the Amon temple four gigantic *colossi* were erected —D.A.Mackenzie⟩ **2 :** one marked by great size, scope, strength, power, or effect and able to dwarf or dominate others: **a :** a nation vastly larger and more powerful than those near it ⟨Latin-American distrust and fear of the ~ to the north⟩ **b :** a huge and powerful industrial concern ⟨a ~ with eight plants, some 44,000 employees —*Time*⟩ **c :** one remarkably outstanding and preeminent over others ⟨such an artistic ~ as Michelangelo —Hunter Mead⟩

co·los·to·mize \kəˈlästə,mīz\ *vt* -ED/-ING/-S **:** to perform a colostomy on

co·los·to·my \kəˈlästəmē\ *n* -ES [ISV *col-* + *-stomy*] **1 :** the surgical formation of an artificial anus by making an opening from the colon through the abdominal wall; *also* **:** the orifice so made **2 :** a surgical joining of one part of the colon with another part of the intestine (as ileum)

colostomy bag *or* **colostomy pouch** *n* **:** a container kept constantly in position to receive feces discharged through a colostomy

colostomy belt *n* **:** a belt or girdle designed to hold a colostomy bag securely against a colostomy

co·los·tral \kəˈlästrəl\ *or* **co·los·tric** \-rik\ *or* **co·los·trous** \-rəs\ *adj* [*colostrum* + *-al* or *-ic* or *-ous*] **:** of, relating to, or caused by colostrum

co·los·trum \kəˈlästrəm\ *n* -S [L, beastings] **:** a specialized secretion of the mammary glands that is produced during the first few days after parturition, that differs from typical milk in its higher content of protein (as albumin and globulins) and antibodies, vitamins, and minerals and its lower content of sugars and fats, and that supplies essential immune bodies to the young animal and aids in the establishment of the intestinal function

colostrum corpuscle *n* **:** a cell in the colostrum supposed to be a degenerated cell of the mammary alveoli

co·lot·lan \,kōlōtˈlän\ *n, pl* **colotlan** *or* **colotlans** *usu cap* [Sp *colotlán,* of AmerInd origin] **1 :** a Piman people in Jalisco, Mexico **2 :** a member of the Colotlan people

co·lot·o·my \kəˈläd·əmē\ *n* -ES [ISV ²*col-* + *-tomy*] **:** surgical incision of the colon — compare COLOSTOMY

colour \ˈkələ(r)\ *chiefly Brit var of* COLOR

-co·lous \k(ə)ləs\ *adj comb form* [L *-cola* inhabitant + E *-ous;* akin to L *colere* to cultivate, inhabit — more at WHEEL] **:** living or growing in or on ⟨arenicolous⟩ ⟨saxicolous⟩

colp *var of* COLLOP

colp- *or* **colpo-** *comb form* [NL, fr. Gk *kolp-, kolpo-,* fr. *kolpos* bosom, fold, vagina, womb — more at GULF] **:** vagina ⟨*colpitis*⟩ ⟨*colposcope*⟩

col·pate \ˈkäl(,)pāt, -,pət\ *adj* [Gk *kolpos* + E *-ate*] *of pollen grains* **:** having longitudinal germinal furrows in the exine

col·peo \kälˈpāō\ *n* -S [Sp *culpeo,* fr. Araucanian *culpeu*] **:** a So. American dog (*Pseudalopex culpaeus*) somewhat resembling a fox; *also* **:** any of various closely related dogs

col·pid·i·um \kälˈpidēəm\ *n* [NL, fr. Gk *kolpos* bosom, fold, vagina, womb + NL *-idium* — more at GULF] **1** *cap* **:** a genus of small aquatic holotrichous ciliates that are much used in biological research **2** *pl* **colpidia :** a member of the genus *Colpidium*

col·pin·dach \ˈkōlpəndə̇k\ *n* -S [ME, prob. modif. of ScGael *colpach*] *early Scots law* **:** a yearling heifer

col·pi·tis \kälˈpīd·əs\ *n* -ES [NL, fr. *colp-* + *-itis*] **:** VAGINITIS

col·po·clei·sis \,kälpōˈklīsəs\ *n, pl* **colpoclei·ses** \-,sēz\ [NL, fr. *colp-* + *-cleisis*] **:** the suturing of posterior and anterior walls of the vagina to prevent uterine prolapse

col·po·da \ˈkälpōdə\ *n, cap* [NL, fr. Gk *kolpōdēs* embosomed, embayed, winding, fr. *kolpos* bosom, fold, vagina, womb + *-ōdēs* -ode — more at GULF] **:** a genus (the type of the family Colpodidae) of small flattened reniform holotrichous freshwater ciliates

col·po·di·dae \kälˈpōdə,dē\ *n pl, cap* [NL, fr. *Colpoda,* type genus + *-idae*] **:** a large family of common and widely distributed chiefly aquatic free-living holotrichous ciliates

col·por·tage \ˈkäl,pōrd·ij, -,pȯr-, kȯlpȯrtäzh\ *n* -S [F, fr. *colporter* (alter. of MF *comporter*) + *-age*] **:** a colporteur's work

col·por·teur \ˈkäl,pōrd·ər, -,pȯr-, kȯlpȯrtœr\ *also* **col·por·ter** \ˈkäl,pōrd·ər, -,pȯr-\ *n* -S [F *colporteur,* alter. (influenced by *porter à col* to carry on one's back, lit., neck) of MF *comporteur* (fr. *comporter* to hawk, peddle, carry, bring together) + *-eur* -or — more at COMPORT] **:** a peddler of books, esp. of bibles and religious books and tracts; *also* **:** a missionary or publicist for some usu. religious cause

-col·pos \ˈkälpəs, -,päs\ *n comb form* -ES *also* **-col·pus** \ˈkälpəs\ [NL, fr. Gk *kolpos* bosom, fold, vagina, womb — more at GULF] **:** vaginal disorder (of a specified type) ⟨hematocolpos⟩

col·po·scope \ˈkälpə,skōp\ *n* -S [ISV *colp-* + *-scope*] **:** an instrument designed to facilitate visual inspection of the vagina — **col·po·scop·i·cal** \ˈ==ˈskäpəkəl\ *adj* — **col·po·scop·i·cal·ly** \-pək(ə)lē, -li\ *adv* — **col·pos·co·py** \kälˈpäskəpē\ *n* -ES

col·po·stat \ˈkälpə,stat\ *n* -S [*colp-* + *-stat*] **:** a medical appliance or instrument (as a radium applicator) designed to facilitate vaginal treatment

col·pot·o·my \kälˈpäd·əmē\ *n* -ES [ISV *colp-* + *-tomy*] **:** surgical incision of the vagina

cols *pl of* COL

¹colt \ˈkōlt\ *n* -S [ME, fr. OE; akin to Sw (dial.) *kult* half-grown pig, ON *kjolta* lap, skirt, Skt *gadi* young bull, OE *cild* child — more at CHILD] **1 a :** the young of the camel — obs. except in Scripture **b :** the young of the horse or any other equine (as a zebra or an ass) — not used technically **c :** a male horse or other equine that has not attained sexual maturity or been gelded **d :** a young male horse before the attainment of an arbitrarily designated age (as three, four, or five years) — used esp. of racehorses **2 :** a young untried person **:** NOVICE, ROOKIE, TYRO; *specif* **:** a novice cricketer esp. when trying for a place on a team **3 :** a short rope knotted or with something heavy attached to the end formerly used as an instrument of punishment in the navy

²colt \"\ *vt* -ED/-ING/-S **1** *obs* **:** CHEAT, BEFOOL **2 :** to beat or punish with a colt

colt distemper *n* **:** STRANGLES

col·ter *also* **coul·ter** \ˈkōltə(r)\ *n* -S [ME *colter,* fr. OE *culter* & OF *coltre,* both fr. L *culter* plowshare, knife; akin to OHG *scala* husk, ON *skilja* to separate, Goth *skilja* butcher, Gk *skalis* hoe, mattock, Lith *skélti* to split — more at SHELL] **:** a knife, sharp disc, or other cutting tool that is attached to the beam of a plow to cut the sward in advance of the plowshare and moldboard

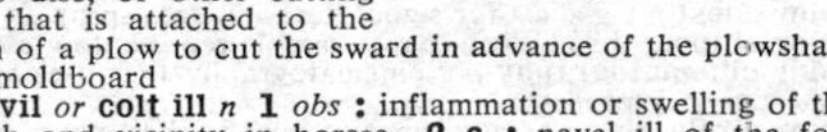

1 notched colter

colt evil *or* **colt ill** *n* **1** *obs* **:** inflammation or swelling of the sheath and vicinity in horses **2 a :** navel ill of the foal **b :** STRANGLES

colt·ish \ˈkōltish, -tēsh\ *adj* **1 :** UNDISCIPLINED: **a** *obs* **:** WANTON **b :** FRISKY, PLAYFUL, SPORTIVE ⟨~ antics of children⟩ **2 :** of, relating to, or resembling a colt — **colt·ish·ly** *adv* — **colt·ish·ness** *n* -ES

colt·pix·ie *or* **colt·pixy** \ˈkōlt,piksē\ *n, pl* **coltpixies :** a mischievous hobgoblin supposed to appear as a colt and mislead men or horses into bogs

colts·foot \ˈkōlts,fu̇t\ *n, pl* **coltsfoots :** any of various plants with large rounded leaves resembling the foot of a colt: **a :** a perennial herb (*Tussilago farfara*) native to Europe but now nearly cosmopolitan, having yellow heads of flowers appearing before the leaves and being used esp. formerly in pharmacy and as a flavoring agent **b** *also* **coltsfoot snakeroot :** WILD GINGER 2a **c :** GALAX 2 **d :** OCONEE BELLS **e :** a tropical American herb (*Pothomorphe peltata*) of the family Piperaceae with inconspicuous flowers in spikes **f :** SWEET COLTSFOOT

colt·skin \ˈ=,=\ *n* **:** leather made of the skin of a colt

colt's-tail \ˈ=,=\ *n, pl* **colt's-tails 1 :** HORSEWEED 1 **2 :** FIELD HORSETAIL

colt's tooth *n* **1 :** youthful wantonness **:** concupiscent desire **2 :** wolf tooth in horses

col·u·ber \ˈkäləbə(r), -lyə-\ *n* [NL, fr. L *coluber, colubra* snake; perh. akin to Gk *kōlon* limb — more at CALK] **1** *cap* **:** an extensive genus (the type of the family Colubridae) of nonpoisonous snakes **2** -S **:** any snake of the genus *Coluber*

¹col·u·brid \-brəd\ *adj* [NL *Colubridae*] **:** of or relating to Colubridae or to a snake of this family

²colubrid \"\ *n* -S **:** a snake of the family Colubridae

co·lu·bri·dae \kəˈlübrə,dē\ *n, pl, cap* [NL, fr. *Colubr-, Coluber,* type genus + *-idae*] **1 :** a very large cosmopolitan family of nonvenomous terrestrial, arboreal, or sometimes aquatic snakes with aglyphous teeth in both jaws, imbricating scales, and reduced postfrontal bones **2** *in some esp former classifications* **:** a more inclusive family in which Colubridae is merged as a subfamily as are also the families Acrochordidae and Dasypeltidae of aglyphous snakes, Boigidae, Elachistodontidae, and Homalopsidae of venomous opisthoglyphous snakes, and sometimes Elapidae and Hydrophidae of venomous proteroglyphous snakes

co·lu·bri·form \-brə,fȯrm\ *adj* [ISV *colubr-* (fr. L *colubr-, coluber*) + *-iform*] **:** being or resembling a colubrine snake

col·u·bri·na \,käl(y)əˈbrīnə, -brēnə\ *n, cap* [NL, fr. LL, a plant, fr. fem. of L *colubrinus* snakelike] **:** a genus of mostly tropical American shrubs or small trees (family Rhamnaceae) with small yellowish flowers and yellow or red fruits

col·u·bri·nae \-nē\ *n pl, cap* [NL, fr. *Colubr-, Coluber,* type genus + *-inae*] **:** a subfamily of Colubridae (sense 2) almost exactly coextensive with Colubridae (sense 1)

¹col·u·brine \ˈkäl(y)ə,brīn, -,brən\ *adj* [L *colubrinus,* fr. *colubra* snake + *-inus* -ine — more at COLUBER] **1 :** relating or similar to a snake ⟨his ~ nature⟩ **2** [NL *Colubrinae*] **:** of or relating to the subfamily Colubrinae

²colubrine \-,brēn, -,brən\ *n* -S [blend of NL *Colubrina* and E *-ine*] **:** either of two colorless crystalline alkaloids $C_{22}H_{24}N_2O_3$ occurring with strychnine and distinguished as alpha-colubrine and beta-colubrine

¹col·u·broid \ˈkäl(y)ə,brȯid\ *adj* [ISV *colubr-* (fr. L *coluber, colubra* snake) + *-oid* — more at COLUBER] **:** COLUBRINE, COLUBRIFORM

²colubroid \"\ *n* -S **:** a snake of the family Colubridae

co·lu·go \kəˈlügō\ *n* -S [prob. native name in Malaya] **:** FLYING LEMUR

col·u·lus \ˈkäl(y)ələs\ *n, pl* **colu·li** \-,lī,-,lē\ [NL, dim. of L *colus* distaff; akin to L *colere* to cultivate, dwell — more at WHEEL] **:** an apparently vestigial organ consisting of a slender process between the bases of the anterior spinnerets of spiders lacking a cribellum

¹columba *var of* CALUMBA

²co·lum·ba \kəˈləmbə\ *n, cap* [NL, fr. L, dove, pigeon — more at COLUMBINE] **:** a large genus consisting of the typical pigeons and including the rock pigeon and band-tailed pigeon

col·um·ba·ceous \,käləmˈbāshəs\ *adj* [L *columba* + E *-aceous*] **:** of or relating to pigeons

co·lum·bae \kəˈləmbē\ *n pl, cap* [NL, fr. L, pl. of *columba*] **:** a suborder of birds (order Columbiformes) consisting of the doves and pigeons and the extinct dodo and solitaire

co·lum·ba·mine \kə,ləmbəˈmēn, =ˈ=,=\ *n* -S [ISV, blend of ¹*columba* and *amine*] **:** an alkaloid $C_{20}H_{21}NO_5$ that occurs in calumba and is related in structure to berberine

co·lum·ban \kəˈləmbən\ *adj, usu cap* [St. *Columba* †597 Ir. missionary + E *-an*] **:** of, relating to, or founded by Saint Columba or his disciples

col·um·ba·ri·um \,käləmˈba(a)rēəm\ *n, pl* **columba·ria** \-rēə\ [L, lit., dovecote, fr. *columba* dove — more at COLUMBINE] **1 :** a structure of vaults lined with recesses for cinerary urns ⟨a ~ containing glass-doored marble compartments for the ashes of cremated bodies —*Amer. Guide Series: N.Y.City*⟩ **2 :** a recess in a columbarium

col·um·bary \ˈkäləm,berē\ *n* -ES [L *columbarium*] **:** DOVECOTE 1

co·lum·bate \kəˈləm(,)bāt, -,bət\ *n* -S [NL *columbium* + E *-ate*] **:** NIOBATE

col·um·batz fly \ˈkäləm,bats-\ *n, usu cap C* [fr. Hung *Kolumbács* (Serbo-Croatian *Golubac*), town in Yugoslavia] **:** a black fly (*Simulium columbatczense*) of the Balkan region said to be sometimes present in such numbers as to be fatal to children or animals

col·um·bel·la \,käləmˈbelə\ *n, cap* [NL, fr. L *columba* dove + NL *-ella;* fr. the color of the shell — more at COLUMBINE] **:** a genus (the type of the family Columbellidae) of small marine gastropods having a thick fusiform shell and being abundant in tropical seas

col·um·bel·li·dae \,käləmˈbelə,dē\ *n pl, cap* [NL, fr. *Columbella,* type genus + *-idae*] **:** a family (order Pectinibranchia) of marine gastropods comprising the dove shells some of which were formerly used as ornaments or as money

¹co·lum·bia \kəˈləmbēə\ *adj, usu cap* [fr. *Columbia,* S.C.] **:** of or from Columbia, the capital of So. Carolina ⟨a *Columbia* resident⟩ **:** of the kind or style prevalent in Columbia

²columbia \"\ *n, pl* **columbia** *or* **columbias** *usu cap* [fr. *Columbia* river, southwestern Canada & northwestern U.S., near which they dwelt] **1 a :** a Salishan people of eastern Washington **b :** a member of such people **2 :** a language of the Columbia and Wenatchee peoples — called also *Sinkiuse*

columbia black *n, usu cap C, often cap B* **:** any of several direct dyes — see DYE table I (under *Direct Black 9 and 38*)

columbia blue *n, often cap C* [prob. fr. NL *Columbia* United States] **:** a pale blue that is redder and deeper than average powder blue or Sistine and redder, stronger, and slightly darker than average cadet gray

co·lum·bi·ad \kəˈləmbē,ad\ *n* -S [F *colombiade,* fr. NL *Columbia* United States + F *-ade* -ad] **1** *cap* **:** any of certain epics recounting the beginning and growth of the U.S.; *also* **:** any epic with similar subject matter **2 :** an obsolete heavy long-chambered muzzle-loading gun that is very thick behind the trunnions and designed for throwing shells and shot at high angles of elevation

¹co·lum·bi·an \kəˈləmbēən\ *adj* [NL *Columbia* United States (fr. Christopher *Columbus* †1506) + E *-an*] **1** *usu cap* **:** of or relating to America, the U. S., or Christopher Columbus **2** *sometimes cap* **:** having or indicating a color pattern characteristic of the plumage of certain varieties of poultry in which the head, body, and leg feathers are white and the tail, neck, and parts of the wing are black or black with white edging

²columbian \"\ *n* -S *cap* **:** AMERICAN; *specif* **:** a native of the U.S.

columbian ground squirrel *n, usu cap C* [*Columbia* river + E *-an*] **:** a mottled-gray burrowing squirrel (*Citellus columbianus*) with rusty-colored muzzle common in the Columbia river region of Washington

columbian pine *n, usu cap C* [*Columbia* river + E *-an*] **:** DOUGLAS FIR

columbian red *n, often cap C* [¹*Columbian*] **:** CASTILIAN BROWN

columbian spirit *n, usu cap C* [¹*Columbian*] **:** METHANOL — often used in pl.

columbia river salmon *n, usu cap C&R* [fr. *Columbia river,* southwestern Canada & northwestern U.S.] **:** KING SALMON

columbia river sucker *n, usu cap C&R* **:** a large sucker (*Catostomus macrocheilus*) of the Columbia river basin

columbia sheep *n, usu cap C* [fr. NL *Columbia* United States; fr. its being the first breed of sheep developed in America] **:** a large hardy open-faced utility sheep of an American breed developed by crossing Lincoln and Rambouillet and distinguished by a high yield of fine wool longer than that of the Rambouillet and by satisfactory mutton conformation

¹co·lum·bic \kəˈləmbik\ *adj* [¹*columba* + *-ic*] **:** relating to or derived from the columba root

²columbic \"\ *adj* [NL *columbium* + E *-ic*] **:** NIOBIC

columbic acid *n* **:** NIOBIC ACID

co·lum·bi·dae \kəˈləmbə,dē\ *n pl, cap* [NL, fr. *Columba,* type genus + *-idae*] **:** a family of game birds comprising the doves and pigeons

col·um·bif·er·ous \,käləmˈbif(ə)rəs\ *adj* [NL *columbium* + E *-i-* + *-ferous*] **:** containing columbium

co·lum·bi·for·mes \kə,ləmbəˈfȯr,mēz\ *n pl, cap* [NL, fr. *Columba* + *-iformes*] **:** a cosmopolitan order of land birds with four unwebbed toes, short legs, small heads, and usu. little visible difference between the sexes that includes the sandgrouse and the pigeons and doves together with their extinct relatives, the dodo and solitaire

co·lum·bin *or* **co·lom·bin** \kəˈləmbən\ *n* -S [alter. of earlier *calumbin,* fr. *calumba* + *-in*] **:** a bitter crystalline constituent of calumba

¹col·um·bine \ˈkäləm,bīn, -,bən\ *n* -S [ME, fr. ML *columbina,* fr. fem. of L *columbinus* dovelike, fr. *columba* dove + *-inus* -ine; fr. the fancied resemblance of the inverted bloom to a group of five doves; akin to Gk *kolymbos,* a bird (prob. a grebe), OHG *holuntar* elder tree, OSw *hylle* elder, Gk *kelainos* black, Skt *kalanka* spot, nest; basic meaning: spot] **1 :** a plant of the genus *Aquilegia:* as **a :** a red-flowered plant (*A. canadensis*) of eastern No. America **b :** a blue-flowered plant (*A. coerulea*) of the Rocky mountains **2** *or* **columbine blue :** a moderate purplish blue to violet

²columbine \"\ *adj* [ME, fr. MF *colombin,* fr. L *columbinus*] **:** of, relating to, or similar to a dove ⟨a ~ form⟩ ⟨~ innocence⟩

³columbine \", -,bēn\ *n* -S *usu cap* [It *Colombina,* dim. of *colomba* dove, fr. L *columba*] **:** the pert and adroit young girl in English harlequinade and in the later commedia dell' arte, in the English harlequinade usu. being Pantaloon's daughter or ward in love with Harlequin

co·lum·bite \kəˈləm,bīt\ *n* -S [NL *columbium* + E *-ite*] **:** a black mineral that is essentially an iron columbate (Fe,Mn)-$(Cb,Ta)_2O_6$ grading into tantalite and having a bright submetallic luster (hardness 6, sp. gr. 5.4–6.5)

co·lum·bi·um \kəˈləmbēəm\ *n* -S [NL, fr. *Columbia* United States + *-ium* — more at COLUMBIAN] **:** NIOBIUM — used chiefly in America esp. by metallurgists; symbol *Cb*

columbium pentoxide *n* **:** NIOBIUM PENTOXIDE

¹columbo *var of* CALUMBA

²co·lum·bo \kəˈləmbō\ *n* -S **:** AMERICAN COLUMBO

co·lum·boid \kəˈləm,bȯid\ *adj* [L *columba* dove + E *-oid* — more at COLUMBINE] **:** relating to or resembling pigeons

columbo wood *n* [¹*Columbo*] **:** an East Indian plant (*Coscinium fenestratum*) of the family Menispermaceae that possesses a bitter property and is medicinally like calumba

¹co·lum·bus \kəˈləmbəs\ *adj, usu cap* [fr. *Columbus,* Ohio] **:** of or from Columbus, the capital of Ohio ⟨our *Columbus* office⟩ **:** of the kind or style prevalent in Columbus

²columbus \"\ *n* -ES [after Christopher *Columbus* †1506 Ital. explorer, discoverer of America] **:** EXPLORER, DISCOVERER

columbus day *n, usu cap C&D* [after Christopher *Columbus*] **1 :** October 12 observed as a legal holiday in some states of the U.S. and in most of the countries of Latin America in celebration of the anniversary of the landing of Columbus in the Bahamas in 1492 — called also *Discovery Day* **2 :** the second Monday in October observed as a legal holiday in many states of the U.S.

columbus's crab *or* **columbus crab** *n, cap 1st C* [after Christopher *Columbus*] **:** GULFWEED CRAB

col·u·mel·la \,käl(y)əˈmelə\ *n, pl* **columel·lae** \-lē, -,lī\ [NL, fr. L, small column, dim. of *columna* column — more at COLUMN] **1 :** any of various anatomical parts likened to a column: as **a** *or* **columella cra·nii** \-ˈkrānē,ī\ **:** the epipterygoid bone of the skull of many lizards **b** *or* **columella au·ris** \-ˈȯrəs, -ˈau̇r-\ **:** the bony or partly cartilaginous rod, often with several distinct parts, connecting the tympanic membrane with the internal ear in birds and many reptiles and amphibians **c :** the bony central axis of the cochlea **d :** the central column or axis of a spiral univalve shell **e :** the central pillar in the calyx of many corals **2 a :** the carpophore of various seed plants **b :** the axis of the capsule in mosses and in some of the liverworts (as those of the genus *Anthoceros*) consisting of sterile tissue **c :** the central sterile portion of the sporangium in fungi of *Mucor* and related genera **d :** STALACE **3 :** a columnar thickening of the peripheral protoplasm of spirochetes

col·u·mel·lar \ˌ⁼⁼ˈmelə(r)\ *adj* [L *columellaris* pillar-shaped, fr. *columella* + *-aris* -ar] **:** of, relating to, or like a columella

columellar muscle *n* **:** a muscle that has its origin on the columella of a gastropod mollusk shell and serves to retract the animal into the shell

col·u·mel·late \ˌ⁼⁼ˈmelət, -me(ˌ)lāt\ *adj* [NL *columella* + E *-ate*] **:** possessing or forming a columella

col·u·mel·lia \ˌkäl(y)əˈmelēə\ *n, cap* [NL, fr. Lucius J.M. *Columella* 1st cent. A.D. Roman agricultural writer + NL *-ia*] **:** a small genus (coextensive with a family Columelliaceae of the order Polemoniales) of bitter evergreen shrubs of the northern Andes that have yellow cymose flowers with two stamens and capsular fruit enclosed by the calyx

col·u·mel·li·a·ceous \ˌ⁼⁼ˌmelēˈāshəs\ *adj* [NL *Columellia* + E *-aceous*] **:** of or relating to the genus *Columellia* or the family Columelliaceae

col·u·mel·li·form \ˌ⁼⁼ˈmeləˌfȯrm\ *adj* [NL *columella* + E *-iform*] **:** like a columella

col·umn \ˈkäləm, *sometimes* ÷ -lyəm\ *n* -s [ME *columne*, fr. MF *colonne*, fr. L *columna*, fr. *columen* top, summit; akin to L *collis* hill — more at HILL] **1 a :** a vertical arrangement of items printed or written on a page or otherwise inscribed **:** a vertical list ⟨with students' names in ~*s*⟩ ⟨adding a ~ of figures⟩ **b :** one of two or more vertical sections of a printed page or table that are separated by a rule or blank space **c :** an accumulation arranged vertically **:** STACK **d :** a special department or feature (as of humor, sports, literary reviewing, or gossip) in a newspaper or periodical under a permanent title and generally reflecting the writer's individual tastes and point of view **e :** a list of those showing, favoring, or approving something ⟨swinging the state into the Republican ~⟩ **f :** a vertical set of positions on a punch card in which a character may be punched **2 :** a supporting pillar: as **a :** a pillar consisting of a shaft, a capital, and usu. a base, the shaft being of circular section except as it is fluted or channeled **b :** one of a building's vertical supporting members made of steel, cast iron, reinforced concrete, timber, or stone and often extending from the foundation through several floors, which it supports, to the roof **c :** a hollow steel cylinder with a jackscrew base usu. set up between the floor and roof of mining workings to serve as a mounting for rock drills, light hoists, and other equipment **3 :** a form, structure, or formation shaped like a column: as **a :** an upright mass **:** a somewhat cylindrical upright body ⟨the springs occasionally spouted ~*s* of water far into the air —*Amer. Guide Series: Mich.*⟩ ⟨the metal ~ of the water spout⟩ ⟨a ~ of smoke from the burning ship⟩; *specif* **:** a cylindrical dripstone formation made by union of stalactite and stalagmite **b :** a tower or other cylindrical construction **c :** a mass of air conceived of as columnar in shape but not necessarily vertical ⟨a ~ of air sweeping through the tunnel⟩ **d :** a vertical tube or tower through which gases or vapors are passed to purify them; *esp* **:** one used in connection with distillation equipment for effecting a fractionation of the vapors (as by the use of plates with bubble caps or of packing) **4 a :** a military, naval, or aeronautic formation in which elements (as soldiers, vehicles, ships, or planes) proceed one after another — contrasted with *line* **b :** an arrangement of elements moving or placed one after another **:** an active group likened to such a column ⟨a ~ of strikers picketing the mill⟩ ⟨a ~ of cars crossing the bridge⟩ — see FIFTH COLUMN **5 a :** the united monadelphous stamens in mallows **b :** the united androecium and gynoecium in orchids **c :** PROP, SUPPORT **d :** a decorative element made to resemble a pillar ⟨a cabinet with ~*s* running up the length of each corner⟩ **6 :** any of various bodily parts or structures likened to a column or pillar: as **a :** the body of an actinian as distinguished from the base and disk **b :** the stalk of a crinoid **c :** a longitudinal subdivision of the spinal cord: as (1) **:** any of the principal longitudinal bundles of nerve fibers disposed as the anterior, the lateral, and the posterior divisions of white matter on each side and separated by the median fissures and spinal nerve roots — called also *funiculus* (2) **:** any of a number of smaller bundles of spinal nerve fibers **:** FASCICULUS ⟨the ~ of Burdach⟩ (3) **:** any of the confluent longitudinal masses of nerve cells constituting the gray matter of each side — called also *gray column, gray horn;* see DORSAL COLUMN, LATERAL COLUMN, VENTRAL COLUMN **7 :** one of the vertical lines of a determinant or matrix in mathematics **8 :** the vertical or chronologic succession of geologic formations in a region

column 2a showing *1* base, *2* shaft, *3* capital

co·lum·na \kəˈləmnə\ *n, pl* **co·lum·nae** \-ˌnē, -nī\ *also* **columnas** [L] **:** an anatomical structure that suggests a column in form — usu. used in combination

¹co·lum·nal \kəˈləmnəl\ *adj* [*column* + *-al*] **:** COLUMNAR

²columnal \"\ *n* -s **:** a columnar part or structure; *specif* **:** one of the vertical segments that make up the stem of a crinoid

co·lum·nar \kəˈləmnə(r)\ *adj* [LL *columnaris*, fr. L *columna* column + *-aris* -ar] **1 :** formed in columns **:** having the form of a column **:** like the shaft of a column ⟨~ forms⟩ **2 :** of, relating to, or characterized by columns ⟨~ construction⟩: as **a** *cryptology* **:** in columns **:** VERTICAL ⟨~ writing⟩ **b :** by columns ⟨~ transposition⟩ **3 :** of, derived from, or appearing in a newspaper column ⟨a popular ~ character⟩

columnar epithelium *n* **:** epithelium consisting of or having the superficial layer composed of tall narrow somewhat cylindrical or prismatic cells and occurring in man chiefly in the digestive tract from the esophageal end of the stomach to the anus and in various glands and in parts of the kidneys — compare SQUAMOUS EPITHELIUM

col·um·nar·ia \ˌkäləmˈna(a)rēə\ *n, cap* [NL, fr. L *columna* column + NL *-aria*] **:** a genus of Silurian and Devonian compound tetracorals with small prismatic septate corallites

columnaris disease *also* **col·um·na·ris** \ˌkäləmˈna(a)rəs\ *n* -ES [NL *columnaris*, specific epithet of *Chondrococcus columnaris*, species causing the disease, fr. LL, columnar] **:** a highly fatal disease of fingerling trout and salmon esp. when concentrated in hatchery ponds that is caused by a myxobacterium (*Chondrococcus columnaris*)

co·lum·nar·ized \kəˈləmnəˌrīzd\ *adj* [*columnar* + *-ize* + *-ed*] **:** arranged in columns

co·lum·nar·ly *adv* **:** by means of a columnar transposition

columnar root *n* **:** PROP ROOT

columnar structure *n* **1 :** the structure of a mineral aggregate that is made up of nearly parallel slender columns and that is intermediate between an equant and acicular structure (as in some amphiboles) **2 :** a geologic structure common in basalts and other lavas that is characterized by the division of the rock into more or less regular often vertical prisms or columns which ordinarily have six but may have from three to eight sides and which may be nearly vertical or nearly horizontal

columnar transposition *n* **:** encipherment in which letters of the alphabet or of a message first written normally in the cells of a rectangle are copied out of it by reading down the columns in an agreed or keyed sequence to form a mixed alphabet or a ciphertext of the message — compare ROUTE TRANSPOSITION

column bone *n* **:** ²EPIPTERYGOID

column chart *n* **:** a chart representing comparative periods of fluctuation or the comparative size, length, value, or endurance of a group of things by means of juxtaposed proportional columns

co·lum·nea \kəˈləmnēə\ *n* [NL, after Fabio Colonna (Latinized as *Columna*) †*ab* 1640 It. scholar] **1** *cap* **:** a genus of tropical American evergreen herbs or subshrubs (family Gesneriaceae) that are often creeping or climbing, have thick opposite hairy leaves frequently unequal and somewhat toothed, produce axillary solitary or clustered yellow to scarlet flowers, and include several forms cultivated for their flowers and ornamental foliage **2** -s **:** any plant of the genus *Columnea*

col·umned \ˈkäləmd\ *adj* **:** having columns ⟨a ~ portico⟩ **:** made in the form of or resembling a column ⟨trees with ~ trunks⟩ **:** made up of columnar elements ⟨the ~ foreshore⟩

co·lum·ni·a·tion \kəˌləmnēˈāshən\ *n* -s [modif. (influenced

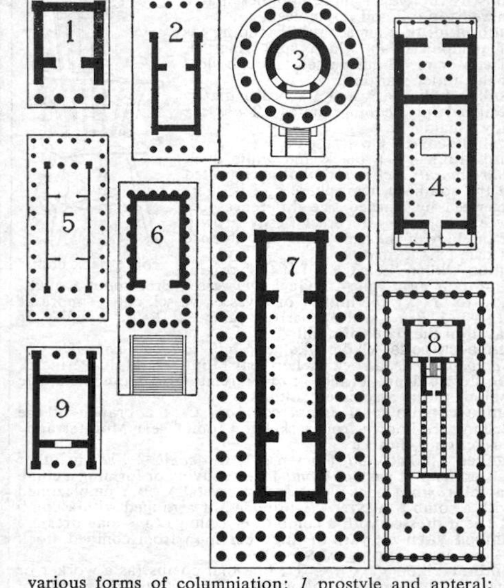

various forms of columniation: *1* prostyle and apteral; *2* amphiprostyle, amphistylar, and apteral; *3* monopteral; *4* and *5* peripteral; *6* pseudoperipteral; *7* dipteral; *8* pseudodipteral; *9* in antis

by E *intercolumniation*) of L *columnation-, columnatio*, fr. *columna* + *-ation-, -atio* -ation] **:** the employment or the arrangement of columns and esp. of free columns in a structure — see AMPHISTYLAR, APTERAL, DIPTERAL, DISTYLE, INTERCOLUMNIATION, MONOPTERAL, PERISTYLAR, PROSTYLE

co·lum·ni·form \kəˈləmnəˌfȯrm\ *adj* [L *columni-* (fr. *columna*) + E *-form*] **:** marked by column form **:** COLUMNAR

column inch *n* **:** a unit of measure for printed matter one column wide and one inch deep

col·um·nist \ˈkäləmnəst, -ləməst *sometimes* ÷ -lyəm-\ *n* -s **:** one that writes a newspaper column or conducts a radio or television program resembling such a column in its material and style ⟨a newspaper ~⟩ ⟨a radio ~⟩

column of ber·tin \bertaⁿ\ *usu cap B* [after Exupère-Joseph *Bertin* †1781 Fr. anatomist] **:** any of the masses of cortical tissue extending between the sides of the Malpighian pyramids of the kidney as far as the pelvis

column of lis·sau·er \ˈliˌsau̇ə(r)\ *cap L* [after Heinrich *Lissauer* †1891 Ger. neurologist] **:** LISSAUER'S TRACT

column of the fornix : either of the anterior pillars of the fornix

column of türck \tu̇erk\ *usu cap T* [trans. of G *Türcksche Säule*, after Ludwig *Türck* †1868 Austrian physician] **:** the direct pyramidal tract in the spinal cord

column rule *n* **:** a rule usu. of exact column length used between columns of a page or table

columns *pl of* COLUMN

column still *n* **:** a still equipped with a column (sense 3 d)

co·lure \kəˈlu̇(ə)r, ˈkōˌl-\ *n* -s [LL *coluri*, pl., fr. Gk *kolouroi* colures, pl. of *kolouros* stump-tailed, fr. *kol-* (fr. *kolos* docked) + *-ouros* -urous; fr. the fact that in temperate latitudes a part is always below the horizon — more at HALT] **:** a great circle on the celestial sphere passing through the poles and the equinoxes or the solstices

co·lu·site \kəˈlüˌsīt\ *n* -s [*Colusa*, mining claim near Butte, Montana + E *-ite*] **:** a mineral consisting of a sulfide of copper and arsenic, tin, vanadium, iron, tellurium $Cu_3(As,Sn,V,Fe,Te)S_4$ occurring in tetrahedral crystals of bronze color

co·lu·tea \kəˈlüd·ēə\ *n, cap* [NL, fr. Gk *koloutea, koloitia*, a kind of tree or shrub (perh. a species of *Cytisus*)] **:** a small genus of Eurasian shrubs (family Leguminosae) with yellow flowers and a bladdery inflated fruit pod — see BLADDER SENNA

col·ville \ˈkälvəl\ *n, pl* **colville** *or* **colvilles** *usu cap* [fr. Fort *Colville*, old trading post near Kettle Falls, Wash.] **1 a :** a Salishan people of the Colville and Columbia river valleys, Washington **b :** a member of such people **2 :** a dialect of Okanagon, a Salishan language

colwort *obs var of* COLEWORT

co·ly \ˈkōlē\ *n* -ES [NL *colius*, prob. fr. Gk *kolios* green woodpecker] **:** any of a small group of fruit-eating African birds with long tails and soft somewhat hairy grayish brown plumage comprising the genus *Colius* (family Coliidae) and ranking as a distinct order (Coliiformes) — called also *mousebird*

colyba *var of* COLLYBA

co·lym·bi·dae \kəˈlimbəˌdē\ *n pl, cap* [NL, fr. *Colymbus*, type genus + *-idae*] **:** a family (coextensive with the order Colymbiformes) of aquatic birds that comprise the grebes and are closely related to the loons

co·lym·bi·form \kəˈlimbəˌfȯrm\ *adj* [NL *Colymbiformes*] **:** of, relating to, or like the Colymbiformes

co·lym·bi·for·mes \⁼ˌ⁼⁼ˈfȯrˌmēz\ *n pl, cap* [NL, fr. *Colymbus* + *-iformes*] **:** a small cosmopolitan order of strong-flying water birds comprising the grebes that are distinguished from the related loons by their generally smaller size and their lack of webbed feet

co·lym·bus \kəˈlimbəs\ *n, cap* [NL, fr. Gk *kolymbos*, a kind of bird (prob. a grebe) — more at COLUMBINE] **:** the type genus of the family Colymbidae

co·lyt·ic \kəˈlid·ik\ *adj* [Gk *kōlytikos* hindering, preventive, fr. *kōlyein* to hinder] **1 :** INHIBITORY **2 :** ANTISEPTIC

col·yum \ˈkälyəm\ *n* -s [by alter.] **:** COLUMN 1d — **col·yum·ist** \-məst\ *n* -s

col·za \ˈkälzə, ˈkōl-\ *n* -s [F, fr. D *koolzaad*, fr. MD *coolsaet*, fr. *coole* cabbage + *saet* seed; akin to OHG *chōlo* cabbage and to OE *sǣd* seed — more at COLE, SEED] **1 :** any of several coles: as **a :** ²RAPE 2 **b :** any of several Asiatic coles resembling rape and producing seed that is used esp. in India as a source of oil **2 :** rapeseed esp. when used as a source of rape oil

colza oil *n* **:** rape oil esp. of a refined grade

com \ˈkäm\ *n* -s [by shortening] *slang Austral* **:** COMMUNIST

com- *or* **col-** *or* **con-** *or* **cor-** *in words having the stress pattern seen in "complain", "collect", "congratulation", "correct"* ä *rather than* ə *is sometimes the vowel in these prefixes, and* ŋ *rather than* n *is esp in Brit speech sometimes the second consonant in con- words before a syllable beginning with a* g *or* k *sound, as in "congratulate", "conclude"; the* ä *and* ŋ *variants have usu not been shown at individual entries*\ *prefix* [*com-* fr. ME, fr. OF, fr. L; *col-* fr. ME, fr. L, fr. *com-; con-* fr. ME, fr. OE (in *consolde* comfrey), fr. OF, fr. L, fr. *com-; cor-* fr. ME, fr. MF, fr. L, fr. *com-* — more at CO-] **:** with **:** together **:** jointly — usu. *com-* before *b* ⟨*com*burgess⟩ and *p* ⟨*com*panion⟩ or *m* ⟨*com*mingle⟩, *col-* before *l* ⟨*col*lingual⟩, *cor-* before *r* ⟨*cor*relation⟩, and *con-* before other sounds ⟨*con*cyclic⟩

¹com *abbr* **1** comedy; comic **2** comma

²com *or* **comm** *abbr* **1** command; commandant; commander; commanding **2** commemorative **3** commentary **4** commerce; commercial **5** commissary **6** commission; commissioned; commissioner **7** committee **8** commodore **9** common; commoner **10** commonwealth **11** communication **12** communist **13** community

¹co·ma \ˈkōmə\ *n* -s [NL, fr. Gk *kōma* deep sleep; perh. akin to MIr *cuma* sorrow, Gk *kamnein* to work, be weary, Skt *śamati* he works] **1 :** a state of profound unconsciousness caused by disease (as diabetes or uremia), injury, or poison **2 :** a state of mental or physical sluggishness **:** TORPOR ⟨lay in a ~ of repletion⟩ ⟨they will rouse Western civilization from the ~ of the Dark Ages —A.W.Griswold⟩

²coma \"\ *n, pl* **co·mae** \-ˌmē, -ˌmī\ [NL, hair, fr. Gk *komē*] **1** *bot* **:** a tuft or bunch: as **a :** an assemblage of branches forming a leafy crown (as in many palms) **b :** a cluster of empty bracts terminating an inflorescence (as in the pineapple) **c :** a tuft of hairs on certain seeds (as of cotton or milkweed) **2 :** the head of a comet usu. containing a nucleus **3 :** an optical aberration in which the image of a point source not on the axis of a lens or mirror is a comet-shaped blur of light being produced by the varying magnification of the lens or mirror with varying distance from the axis **4** *Southwest* **:** SOUTHERN BUCKTHORN

-co·ma \-ˌkəmə\ *n comb form* [NL, fr. Gk *komē* hair] **:** one having (such) hair — in generic names ⟨Pycno*coma*⟩

co·ma·cine \ˈkōməˌchēn, -ˌsēn\ *n* -s [It *comacino*, fr. ML *comacinus, commacinus*, fr. LL *comacenus*, adj., of Como, irreg. fr. L *Comum* Como, city in Italy] **:** an early medieval Italian mason; *esp* **:** a member of a guild of medieval Italian masons supposedly persistent from classical times

comacine masters *n pl, usu cap C* **:** the Lombard master builders of the middle ages who influenced architecture of the period

co·magmatic \ˌkō+\ *adj* [*co-* + *magmatic*] *of igneous rocks* **:** having mineral or chemical peculiarities indicative of a closely similar magmatic source; *also* **:** indicating a region, district, or province in which such rocks occur

co·maker \(ˈ)kō+\ *n* -s [*co-* + *maker*] **:** one that participates in the preparation or formulation of something (as a treaty); *specif* **:** a person who formally accepts responsibility for the payment of a loan made to another if the latter fails to pay

¹co·mal \ˈkōməl\ *adj* [²*coma* + *-al*] *bot* **:** having or being a coma ⟨a ~ tuft⟩

²co·mal \kōˈmäl\ *n, pl* **comals** \-lz\ *or* **coma·les** \-(ˌ)läs\ [AmerSp, fr. Nahuatl *comalli*] **1 :** a flat slab of sandstone used as a griddle **2 :** a griddle of earthenware or metal

coman *usu cap, var of* CUMAN

¹co·man·che \kəˈma(a)nchē\ *n, pl* **comanche** *or* **comanches** *usu cap* [Sp, of Shoshonean origin; perh. akin to Hopi *kománči* scalp lock, fr. *kópa* top of the head + *mánči* tied lock of hair] **1 a :** a Shoshonean people orig. in Wyoming and later ranging from Wyoming and Nebraska south into New Mexico and northwestern Texas **b :** a member of such people **2 :** the language of the Comanche people

²comanche \"\ *adj or n, usu cap* [fr. *Comanche*, town and county in Texas, locality of its type station] **:** COMANCHEAN

¹co·man·che·an \-chēən\ *adj, usu cap* [*Comanche*, Tex. + E *-an*] **1 :** of or relating to a period of the Mesozoic between the Jurassic and the Upper Cretaceous during which the great expansion of reptiles was the most striking feature of animal life and the appearance and spread of angiosperms the most notable fact connected with plant life **2 :** of, or relating to the system of rocks deposited during the Comanchean period ⟨~ fossils⟩ — see GEOLOGIC TIME table

²comanchean \"\ *n* -s *usu cap* **:** the Comanchean period or system

co·man·che·ro \kəˌma(a)nˈche(ˌ)rō, ˌkō,⁼-\ *n* -s *often cap* [MexSp, fr. Sp *comanche* + *-ero* -er] **:** a trader with the Indians of the southwest during the unsettled period of the 19th century

co·man·dan·cia \ˌkämənˈdanch(ē)ə; kōmänˈdänthyä *or* -dänsyä\ *n* -s [Sp, fr. *comandante*] **:** a province or district under military control; *also* **:** the headquarters of the commander of such a district

co·man·dan·te \ˌkämənˈdantē, kōmänˈdäntā\ *n* -s [Sp, fr. (assumed) VL *commandant-, commandans*, pres. part. of (assumed) VL *commandare* — more at COMMAND] **:** COMMANDANT

co·man·dra \kəˈmandrə\ *n, cap* [NL, fr. L *coma* hair + NL *-andra;* fr. the hairy calyx lobes that are attached to the anthers — more at COMA] **:** a small genus of chiefly No. American herbs (family Santalaceae) that are usu. partial parasites attaching to other plants by underground holdfasts and that have creeping stems, whitish flowers in terminal clusters, and a dry nut as fruit

co·man·ic acid \(ˈ)kōˌmanik-\ *n* [ISV, alter. of *comenic acid*] **:** a crystalline acid $C_5H_3O_2COOH$ obtained by partial decarboxylation of chelidonic acid; 1,4-pyrone-2-carboxylic acid

co·ma·ni·to \ˌkōməˈnēd·(ˌ)ō\ *n, pl* **comanito** *or* **comanitos** *usu cap* [Sp] **1 :** a Taracahitian people of Sinaloa, Mexico **2 :** a member of the Comanito people

co·mar·ca \kōˈmärkə\ *n* -s [Sp, fr. ML *commarca* boundary, confines, fr. *com-* + *marca* boundary, border territory, of Gmc origin; akin to OHG *marca* border, border region — more at MARK] **1 :** a territorial subdivision (as a district or circuit) of a state — used chiefly of administrative units of certain Latin-American nations

co·mart \kōˈmärt\ *n* [prob. misprint of *cov'nant*] **:** COVENANT — used in the 1605 quarto of Shakespeare's *Hamlet* I. i. 93, but in later versions often considered a misprint and emended to *covenant or compact*

comas *pl of* COMA

¹co·mate \(ˈ)kō+\ *n* [*co-* + *mate*] **:** COMPANION

²co·mate \ˈkōˌmāt\ *adj* [L *comatus*, fr. *coma* hair + *-atus* -ate — more at COMA] **:** covered with hair or filaments **:** HAIRY, SHAGGY

co·mat·ic \(ˈ)kōˈmad·ik\ *adj* [irreg. (influence of *comatose*) fr. ²*coma* (blur) + *-ic*] *of an optical image* **:** blurred as a result of coma

co·ma·tose \ˈkōməˌtōs, ˈkäm-\ *also* **co·ma·tous** \-məd·əs, -təs\ *adj* [F *comateux*, fr. Gk *kōmat-, kōma* deep sleep + F *-eux* -ose, -ous — more at COMA] **1 :** relating to, resembling, or affected with coma ⟨~ breathing⟩ ⟨a ~ state⟩ ⟨~ patients⟩ **2 :** dull and inactive **:** LETHARGIC, TORPID, DROWSY ⟨stout old men ~ on the sunny porch⟩ ⟨the market has been ~ for several days⟩ ⟨Broadway was theatrically ~ that summer⟩ **syn** see LETHARGIC

co·mat·u·la \kōˈmachələ\ *n, pl* **comatulae** \-ˌlē\ [NL, former generic name (now *Antedon*), fem. of LL *comatulus* having hair neatly curled, fr. L *comatus* hairy] **:** COMATULID

co·mat·u·lid \-ləd\ *n* -s [NL *Comatulidae*, former family name (now *Antedonidae*), fr. *Comatula*, type genus + *-idae*] **:** a free-swimming stalkless crinoid — called also *feather star*

coma vigil *n* [¹*coma*] **:** a state of coma in which the patient lies unconscious but with the eyes open

¹comb \ˈkōm\ *n, pl* **combs** \-mz\ [ME, fr. OE *camb;* akin

combs 2: *1* single, *2* pea, *3* rose, *4* V-shaped, *5* strawberry

to OHG *kamb*, ON *kambr* comb, Gk *gomphos* tooth, peg, Skt *jambha* molar, fang] **1 a :** an instrument consisting of a thin strip (as of plastic, metal, or bone) with a row of teeth on one or both edges or sides that is used for adjusting, cleaning, or confining the hair or for adornment **b :** any of several toothed devices used in handling or ordering textile fibers: (1) **:** a toothed instrument for separating, ordering, and cleansing fibers (as of wool, flax, or hair); *also* **:** the machine of which it is the basic part (2) **:** the serrated vibratory device used to strip fiber from the doffer of a carding machine (3) **:** a reed of a loom and esp. of a hand loom **c :** a toothed instrument for currying hairy animals or cleansing and smoothing their coats **:** CURRYCOMB **d :** the collector of an electrostatic machine **e** (1) **:** a toothed instrument used to form patterns on a painted surface that typically resemble grained wood or marbled paper (2) **:** a pattern so formed **f :** a tool having teeth similar to those on a saw and used in finishing stone **2 :** the fleshy crest or caruncle on the head of the domestic fowl and certain other gallinaceous birds usu. best developed in the male — see PEA COMB, ROSE COMB, SINGLE COMB, STRAWBERRY COMB **3 :** something resembling or suggesting the comb of a cock: as **a :** the crest of a helmet; *esp* **:** the upright blade on a morion **b** *dial* **:** the crest or ridge of a mountain or hill **c :** the ridge of a roof **d :** a ridge or crest of hair **e :** the upper edge of the buttstock of a shoulder firearm against which the firer's cheek rests during firing **f :** the curling crest of a wave **g :** a hook on which bacon slabs are hung for smoking **4 :** a structure resembling a comb (sense 1a): as **a :** the pecten of a scorpion **b :** the pecten of a bird's eye **c :** one of the ciliated swimming plates of a ctenophore **d :** STRIGIL 2 **e :** CTENIDIUM 2 **5 a :** HONEYCOMB; *also* **:** one of the somewhat similar masses of cells built by social wasps **b :** an aggregate of crystals resembling a honeycomb that have grown outward from the walls of a vein or cavity so that their closely set points or ends project

²comb \ˈ"\ *vb* **combed** \-md\ **combed** \ˈ"\ **combing** \-miŋ\ **combs** \-mz\ [ME *comben,* fr. *comb,* n.] *vt* **1 :** to draw a comb through **:** disentangle with or as if with a comb: **a :** to lay straight **:** DRESS, ARRANGE ⟨~ one's hair⟩ **b :** to cleanse, disentangle, and collect together (animal or vegetable fibers) by the use of a comb preparatory to spinning so that only the longer fibers are collected, the short staple being combed away — compare ¹CARD 1 **c :** to dress or finish (stone) with a comb **2 :** THRASH, BEAT **3 a :** RAKE ⟨~ the grass⟩ **b :** to afflict or assault as if by raking: as (1) **:** to pass over with violent force ⟨the city was ~*ed* by rain and high winds⟩ (2) **:** FLATTEN, ERODE ⟨huge waves ~*ing* down the dunes⟩ (3) **:** to shell systematically ⟨~*ing* the enemy's position with our guns⟩ **4 a :** to remove or eliminate with or as if with a comb ⟨~ out snarls⟩ ⟨~ out head lice⟩ ⟨~ subversives out of the organization⟩ **:** treat with or as if with a comb in order to remove anything undesirable — usu. used with *out* ⟨~ out a staff in search of dishonest persons⟩ **b :** SEPARATE, SORT ⟨~*ing* out of the tangle the right elements⟩ ⟨~ army recruits from industries⟩ **5 a :** to search or examine systematically and thoroughly omitting or ignoring no part or detail ⟨~ all the evidence⟩ ⟨~ the whole trial record for reasons for appeal⟩ ⟨~ the woodland for traces of the lost children⟩ ⟨police ~*ing* the city for the killer⟩ **b :** to seek out and collect from — used esp. of one that gathers flotsam cast up by the sea ⟨added to his income by ~*ing* the little beach beyond the point⟩ **6 :** to use in the manner of a comb ⟨~*ing* his fingers through his long red beard⟩ **~** *vi* **1** *of a wave or its crest* **:** to roll over **:** break into foam **2 :** to flow or come over like a combing wave **syn** see SEEK

³comb \ˈküm, ˈkōm\ *var of* COMBE

comb *abbr* **1** combination; combined; combining **2** combustion

com·bas·sou *also* **com·ba·sou** \kəmˈba(ˌ)sü\ *n* -s [native name in southern Africa] **:** a small southern African seed-eating finch (*Hypochera funerea*) with white bill and red feet, the male bluish black and the female brownish, that is often kept as a cage or aviary bird

¹com·bat \kəmˈbat, ˈkäm,bat *sometimes* ˈkəm,bat *or* kämˈbat *or* ˈkəmbət; *Brit usu & US sometimes* ˈkämbət; *usu* -d·+V\ *vb* **combated** *or* **combatted; combated** *or* **combatted; combating** *or* **combatting; combats** [MF *combattre,* fr. (assumed) VL *combattere,* fr. L *com-* + *-battere* (fr. *battuere* to beat) — more at BAT] *vi* **:** STRUGGLE, CONTEND, FIGHT ⟨~ fiercely with an enemy⟩ ⟨nations ~ to make one submit — Lord Byron⟩ ⟨fiercely ~*ed* with death —Amy Lowell⟩ **~** *vt* **1 :** to fight with **:** BATTLE **2 :** to struggle against or oppose esp. by argument ⟨there was nobody to ~ that royal will —Edith Sitwell⟩ **:** work against **:** strive to reduce or eliminate ⟨~ malnutrition and disease⟩ ⟨~ inflation⟩ **syn** see ¹CONTEST

²com·bat \ˈkäm,bat *sometimes* ˈkəm-; *Brit usu & US sometimes* -bət; *usu* -d·+V\ *n* -s *often attrib* [MF, fr. *combattre,* v.] **1 :** a fight, encounter, or contest between individuals or groups ⟨furious ~ of antlered stags⟩ **:** DUEL; *specif* **:** an engagement between contending armed forces esp. when of lesser extent than a battle **2 :** CONFLICT, STRUGGLE, CONTROVERSY ⟨two years of almost continuous parliamentary ~ —F.L.Paxson⟩ ⟨such strenuous ~s as the humanist-naturalist or the aesthetic-sociological controversies —F.B.Millett⟩ **3 :** actual fighting engagement of military forces as distinguished from other military duties or periods of active service without fighting **:** ACTION **syn** see ²CONTEST

¹com·bat·ant \kəmˈbatᵊnt, -ad·ənt *sometimes* ˈkäm,ba-; *Brit usu & US also* ˈkämbətənt *or* -bəd·ənt *or* -bətᵊnt, *Brit sometimes* ˈkəmbə-\ *n* -s [MF *combattant,* fr. *combattant,* adj.] **:** one that engages in combat

²combatant \ˈ"\ *adj* [MF *combattant,* fr. pres. part. of *combattre*] **:** contending or disposed to contend: as **a :** taking part in or prepared to take part in active fighting ⟨a ~ officer⟩ **b** *also* **com·bat·tant** \ˈ"\ *heraldry* **:** rampant and facing each other as if in combat — used of representations of two animals ⟨two lions ~⟩

combat boot *n* **:** a heavy laced leather boot esp. with a wide cuff buckled above the ankle

combat command *n* **:** a major tactical unit within an armored division consisting of a headquarters and headquarters company and a variable number of attached units (as of armor, infantry, and artillery)

combat fatigue *also* **combat exhaustion** *n* **:** a traumatic psychoneurotic reaction (as of the anxiety type) or an acute psychotic reaction occurring during wartime combat or under conditions causing stress similar to that of combat — called also *fatigue syndrome*

combat intelligence *n* **:** military intelligence for use in a combat area gathered by combat units in the field or furnished to them from other sources

com·bat·ive \kəmˈbad·iv, |tiv, -ēv *also* -əv, *Brit usu & US sometimes* ˈkämbə|, *esp Brit sometimes* ˈkəmbə| \ *adj* **:** disposed to combat **:** marked by belligerence **:** PUGNACIOUS **syn** see BELLIGERENT

combative accent *n* **:** a speech accent that does not coincide with metrical ictus in classical verse

com·bat·ive·ly \-əvlē, -li\ *adv* **:** in a combative manner **:** BELLIGERENTLY

com·bat·ive·ness \-ivnəs, -ēv-\ *n* -ES **:** the state or quality of being combative **:** PUGNACITY, BELLIGERENCE ⟨admitting that man's nature will never lose the ~, hostility, and animosity which are so large a part of it —Norman Angell⟩

com·ba·tiv·i·ty \,kämbəˈtivəd·ē, *esp Brit sometimes* ,kəm-\ *n* -ES **:** COMBATIVENESS

combat jacket *n* **:** BATTLE JACKET 1

combat load *vt* **:** to load (a ship) so that combat supplies and materiel may be more readily unloaded (as by amphibious assault troops) than noncombat supplies and materiel

combat orders *n pl* **:** orders containing instructions for operations in a military campaign (as letters of instruction, operation orders, and administrative orders)

combat practice *n* **:** an individual or small-unit tactical problem that must be solved under simulated combat conditions and that requires firing live ammunition at appropriate targets

combat team *n* **:** a tactical nonorganic grouping of military forces capable of maintaining independent operation with its own weapons and supplies, usu. combining infantry and artillery, air and tank forces or surface craft, aircraft, and submarines; *specif* **:** an infantry regiment or battalion reinforced by the attachment of artillery, engineers, or medical or other troops for a particular combat mission

combat unit *n* **:** a military unit whose organization, equipment, and training are designed to fit it to engage in combat

combat zone *n* **:** the forward part of a theater of military operations extending from the front line to the forward boundary of the communications zone

comb–back \ˈ=,=\ *adj, of a Windsor chair* **:** having above the arm rail an extension of the back that consists of five or more spindles and a curved top rail and resembles a comb

comb-back chair

comb binding *n* **:** mechanical binding (as of pamphlets) in which split rings of plastic or metal are passed through slots at the gutter margin

comb–brush \ˈ=,=\ *n* **1 :** a brush that is designed for cleaning combs **2** *obs* **:** a lady's maid

comb disease *n* **:** WHITECOMB

comb duck *n* **:** a black and white duck (*Sarkidiornis melanotos*) that is restricted to the southern hemisphere and is characterized by marked size differences between the sexes, an erect fleshy growth at the base of the male's bill, and absence of true pair formation

combe \ˈküm, ˈkōm\ *n* -s [of Celt origin; akin to W *cwm* valley, IrGael *cum* vessel, Bret *komm* trough; akin to Gk *kymbē* hollow of a vessel, vessel, cup — more at HUMP] **1** *Brit* **:** a deep narrow valley **2** *Brit* **:** a valley or basin on the flank of a hill

combe–ca·pelle \ˌkōm(ˌ)kaˈpel\ *adj, usu cap both Cs* [fr. *Combe-Capelle,* a rock shelter near Montferrand-du-Périgord, Dordogne dept., France] **:** of or relating to Combe-Capelle man or to the associated culture

combe–capelle man *n, usu cap both Cs* **:** a branch of the Brünn race known from a skeleton found near Montferrand-du-Périgord, France

combed \ˈkōmd\ *adj* [in sense 1, fr. ¹*comb* + *-ed;* in other senses, fr. past part. of ²*comb*] **1 a :** having or forming a comb ⟨a tall-*combed* cock⟩ ⟨~ quartz crystals⟩ **b :** emblazoned with a comb **:** CRESTED **2 :** dressed or arranged with a comb **3 :** as if dressed with a comb ⟨a ~ ceiling⟩ ⟨a ~ oak dresser⟩

combed yarn *n* **:** yarn of any fiber spun from combed stock — compare CARDED YARN

comb·er \ˈkōmə(r)\ *n* -s **1 :** one that combs (as a worker or machine that combs wool or flax) **2 :** a long curling wave of the sea **3 :** cotton of a staple length and grade suitable for combing

comber board *n* **:** a perforated wooden frame in a loom through which the lower ends of the harness cords are passed to keep them separate

comber leather *n* **:** a heavily greased cattlehide leather used in combing machines in the textile industry

comb fern *n* **:** CURLY GRASS

combflower \ˈ=,=\ *n* **1 :** COMMON SUNFLOWER **2 :** PURPLE CONEFLOWER

comb–footed \ˈ=ˈ=\ *adj, of a spider* **:** having calamistra

comb foundation *n* **:** FOUNDATION 5g

comb grain *n* **:** grain in quarter-sawed lumber of plainly marked narrow nearly parallel stripes of darker and lighter color — **comb–grained** \ˈ=ˈ=\ *adj*

comb honey *n* **:** honey kept intact in the honeycomb

combier *comparative of* COMBY

combiest *superlative of* COMBY

com·bin·abil·i·ty \kəm,bīnəˈbiləd·ē, -ətē, -i\ *n* -ES **:** ability (as relative ability) to enter into combination

com·bin·able \kəmˈbīnəbəl\ *adj* **:** that can be combined

¹com·bi·nate \ˈkämbə,nāt\ *vt* -ED/-ING/-S [LL *combinatus,* past part. of *combinare*] **1 :** COMBINE **2 :** to form (the teeth of a self-distributing linotype matrix) so that the matrix will fall into its proper channel **3 :** to set up the combination of (a lock)

²combinate *adj* [LL *combinatus*] *obs* **:** COMBINED, BETROTHED

¹com·bi·na·tion \,kämbəˈnāshən\ *n* -s [MF, fr. LL *combination-, combinatio* union, fr. *combinatus* (past part. of *combinare* to combine) + L *-ion-, -io* -ion — more at COMBINE] **1 :** the result or product of combining **:** a union or aggregate made by combining one thing with another: as **a** (1) **:** a union or alliance of individuals, corporations, or states for some special purpose formerly often to achieve a result contrary to law or public welfare but now usu. to achieve a legitimate social, political, or economic end — see COMBINATION IN RESTRAINT OF TRADE (2) **:** a binomial taxonomic name formed by combining a specific epithet with a generic name (3) **:** two or more members of a team in competitive sports who perform esp. well together (4) **:** a small jazz band esp. when playing without elaborate arrangements; *also* **:** any dance band **b :** a series of events or results occurring in an ordered sequence: as (1) **:** a sequence of moves in chess so planned as to force the responses of the opponent and gain a decisive advantage often at the expense of an initial sacrifice (2) **:** a sequence of letters or numbers in a particular order chosen in setting a combination lock; *also* **:** the mechanism operating or moved by the sequence (3) **:** any one of the different sets into which a number of individuals (as letters) may be grouped without regard to the order of arrangement within the group — compare PERMUTATION 3b (4) **:** a sequence of synchronized blows delivered by a boxer in rapid succession **c :** a union of mechanical parts so arranged that they interact to produce a practical result — compare AGGREGATION **d :** any of various one-piece garments covering the upper and lower parts of the body; *esp* **:** UNION SUIT — usu. used in pl. **e :** an instrument designed to perform two or more tasks ⟨a radio-phonograph ~⟩; *specif* **:** a haulage tractor and one or more trailers that it draws **2 a :** the act or process of combining **:** the quality or state of being combined **b :** the act or process of uniting to form a chemical compound; *sometimes* **:** the compound so formed **3 :** a group of organ stops used in performance at one or more specific points; *also* **:** the tonal effect produced by such a group

²combination \ˈ===ˈ==\ *adj* **1 :** of, relating to, or exhibiting combination **:** used in combination **:** resulting from combination **2 :** serving more than one purpose ⟨a ~ saddle and harness horse⟩ ⟨a ~ bed-sitting room⟩ **3 a** *of a plied yarn* **:** made of single yarns of different fibers, size, or twist **b** *of a fabric* **:** made of combination yarns or of two different yarns

com·bi·na·tion·al \ˈ==ˈnāshənᵊl, -shnəl\ *adj* **:** of or relating to combination **:** having the quality of combining

com·bi·na·tion·al·ism \,==ˈnāshənᵊl,izəm, -shnə,li-\ *n* -s **:** the practice of combining varying intellectual elements esp. without sufficient attention to systematic integration

combination board *n, papermaking* **:** a board made on a cylinder machine in which one or both of the outer plies differ from the middle ply as to color or material

combination by volume : the action, process, or ratio by which gaseous elements and compounds unite in definite proportions by volume to form distinct compounds

combination by weight : the action, process, or ratio by which substances unite (in compounds) in proportions by weight, relatively fixed and exact — see LAW OF DEFINITE PROPORTIONS

combination chuck *n* **:** a chuck with jaws that may be moved simultaneously or independently

combination door *n* **:** an outer door with interchangeable panels, one screened for warm-weather use, the other glazed for cold-weather use

combination in restraint of trade : any monopoly or attempt at monopoly or any contract, combination, or conspiracy intended to restrain trade or commerce among the states or with the territories, the District of Columbia, or foreign nations, all such, excepting resale price-maintenance agreements permitted by fair-trade laws, being declared illegal by the antitrust laws of the U.S. — compare COMBINATION

combination last *n* **:** a shoe last in which there is a variation from the standard measurements, the heel or instep portion being narrower than normal

combination lock *n* **:** a lock whose mechanism is controlled by one or more movable dials or rings inscribed with letters or figures and that may only be opened after the dial has been so turned as to combine the characters in a certain order

combination package *n* **:** a package of fourth-class mail to the outside of which is affixed a letter or other piece of first-class mail matter — used in the U.S. postal system

combination piston *n* **:** a device that acts on a combination of organ stops and allows the combination to be thrown on or off with a single movement

combination plane *n* **:** a plane that has interchangeable cutters of various shapes and is usable for rabbeting, grooving, making moldings, and other special processes

combination plate *n* **:** a photoengraving plate produced by more than one process; *specif* **:** a photomechanical engraving in which the printing surface contains both line and halftone images

combination pliers *n pl but sing or pl in constr* **:** slip-joint pliers with a notched inner grip for holding and grasping round objects and cutting and bending wire

combination plow *n* **:** a moldboard plow with interchangeable bottom parts suitable for different soil conditions

combination rate *n* **:** a through rate formed by combining two or more rates

combination room *n* **:** a common room at Cambridge University

combination rubber *n* **:** sheet rubber with a linen web or webs through it used esp. to pack pipe joints

combination sale *n* **:** a sale coupling two products at a unit price slightly higher than the price of one

combination shot *n* **1 :** a pool shot in which a ball is pocketed by causing another object ball to strike it **2 :** an English billiards shot in which a player scores in two ways (as by cannoning and pocketing the red ball)

combination square *n* **:** a measuring tool consisting of a steel rule that slides through an adjustable protractor head or level or a center head which can be fixed at any point on the rule by a lock bolt and being usable as an inside or outside try square, a marking or depth gauge, level, miter square, plumb, and straightedge

combination stacker *n* **:** a combined buck rake and hay stacker

combination tone *also* **combination note** *n* **:** a subjective tone heard by many observers when two pure tones of widely different frequency are sounded together and thought to be due to the fact that the human ear does not in general give a linear response to sound waves — compare AURAL HARMONIC, DIFFERENCE TONE, SUMMATION TONE

combination wrench *n* **:** a wrench with one open end and one socket end

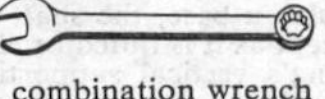
combination wrench

com·bi·na·tive \ˈkämbə,nā|d·iv, kəmˈbīnə| \ *adj* [*combination* + *-ive*] **:** tending or able to combine **:** marked by, relating to, or resulting from combination; *specif, of sound change* **:** dependent on phonetic environment ⟨the change of an orig. short vowel into a long vowel in the ancestors of English *field* is ~ because of the vowel's being followed by a liquid and a homorganic voiced stop⟩

com·bi·na·to·ri·al \,kämbənəˈtōrēəl, kəmˈbī-, -tȯr-\ *adj* [*combinatory* + *-al*] **:** of or relating to combination or combinations **:** involving combination

combinatorial analysis *n* **:** the mathematical study of permutations and combinations of finite sets of objects

com·bi·na·to·ry \kəmˈbīnə,tōrē\ *adj* [*combination* + *-ory*] **:** COMBINATIVE, COMBINATORIAL

combinatory logic *n* **:** a branch of symbolic logic that deals esp. with the notion of substitution and the eliminability of variables in favor of special function symbols

¹com·bine \kəmˈbīn\ *vb* -ED/-ING/-S [ME *combynen,* fr. MF *combiner,* fr. LL *combinare,* fr. L *com-* + *bini* two by two — more at BINARY] *vt* **1 :** to bring into close relationship: **a :** to join in physical or chemical union (as two substances) ⟨~ toxin and living tissue to produce antitoxin⟩; *specif* **:** to cause to unite into a chemical compound ⟨*combining* hydrogen with sulfur⟩ **b :** to cause to unite or associate harmoniously (as in a joint action or into an organic whole) ⟨~ their efforts to a common end⟩ ⟨the growing town of South Bethlehem was . . . to be *combined* with the mother town —*Amer. Guide Series: Pa.*⟩ **2 :** to cause (as two or more things or ideas) to mix together **:** MINGLE, BLEND ⟨*combining* the language of the gutter with ideas of undoubted worth⟩ ⟨~ the sugar, flour, and butter⟩ **3 :** to possess or exhibit (as qualities or attributes) in combination ⟨one who ~s creative imagination with true scholarliness⟩ **~** *vi* **1 a :** to become one **:** COALESCE, INTEGRATE ⟨the two papers *combined* as the *Chronicle*⟩ **b :** to unite in definite proportions by weight to form a distinct chemical compound **2 :** to come together or join forces (as for a common purpose) **:** act together to accomplish an aim ⟨the foreign powers *combined* in a note reprimanding the aggressor's action⟩ ⟨~ to raise wages in an industry⟩ **syn** see JOIN, UNITE

²com·bine \ˈkäm,bīn\ *n* -s **1 :** an act or result of combining **2 :** a combination (as of persons) to effect some object; *sometimes* **:** one having a purpose that is illegal or against the public interest **3** *also* **combine harvester :** a harvesting machine that heads, threshes, and cleans grain while moving over the field **4 :** a passenger-train car divided into two or more parts for handling different classes of items (as passengers and baggage)

³combine \ˈ"\ *vb* -ED/-ING/-S [²*combine*] *vt* **:** to harvest with a combine **~** *vi* **:** to combine a crop

com·bined \kəmˈbīnd\ *adj* **1 a :** formed by combination **:** joined together into one **:** UNITED **b :** formed into a chemical compound **2 :** performed by agents in combination **3 :** concerned with or consisting of a combination — used of previously or usu. separate items or considerations ⟨a ~ intelligence service —A.L.Funk⟩ **4 :** considered as a whole **:** added together ⟨mercenaries outnumbered all other troops ~⟩ ⟨his talents and looks ~ got him the job⟩ — **com·bined·ly** \-n(ə)dlē\ *adv* — **com·bined·ness** \-nədnəs, -n(d)nəs\ *n* -ES

combined carbon *n* **:** the portion of the carbon in iron and steel that is chemically united in the form of carbides — distinguished from *graphitic carbon*

combined experience table *n* **:** a mortality table based on the experience of 17 British companies that was used in the U.S. prior to 1901

combined method *n* **:** a method of teaching the deaf in which features of both the manual method and the oral method are used

combined operation *n* **1 :** a military operation in which several allies coordinate their armed forces to accomplish a single mission, effect a defense, or gain some other goal **2** *Brit* **:** an often amphibious operation requiring the coordinated efforts of two or more services — often used in pl

com·bine·ment \kəmˈbīnmənt\ *n* -s *archaic* **:** COMBINATION

com·bin·er \-nə(r)\ *n* -s **:** one that combines: as **a :** a machine that applies adhesive to the plies of paper or board and presses them together to produce laminated board **b :** one that arranges plastics sheets in desired combinations and finishes and cements them and presses them in a hydraulic press

com·bi·net \ˈkämbəˈnet\ *n* -s [*combination* + *-et*] **:** a handled lidded pail usu. of enameled metal combining the function of chamber pot and slop jar

combine type *n* **:** a class or variety of a crop adapted to harvesting with a combine

combing *n* -s *often attrib* **1 :** the action or process of using a comb or combs: as **a :** the straightening and ordering of wool or other fibers of long staple by a combing machine with elimination of shorter fibers **b :** a method of decorating pottery in the wet state by scratching with a comb **2 combings** *pl* **:** loose hair removed with a comb **3 :** COMBING WOOL **4 :** an action of combing or like combing esp. in thoroughness ⟨a skillful ~ of the salvage incidents . . . for the stories that bear retelling —Alfred Stanford⟩

combing machine *n* **:** a machine for combing wool, flax, cotton, or other fibers and separating the longer and more valuable fiber from the shorter — compare CARDING MACHINE

combing wool *n* **:** long-stapled strong-fibered wool suitable for combing and used esp. in the manufacture of worsteds

combining *pres part of* COMBINE

combining form *n* **:** a linguistic form that occurs only in compounds or derivatives and can be distinguished descriptively from an affix by its ability to occur as one immediate constituent of a form whose only other immediate constituent is an affix (as *cephal-* in *cephalic*) or by its being an allomorph of a morpheme that has another allomorph that may occur alone (as *electro-* representing *electric* in *electromagnet, resini-* representing *resin* in *resiniferous, forma-* representing *formaldehyde* in *formalith, para-* representing *parachute* in *paratrooper*) or can be distinguished historically from an affix by

the fact that it is borrowed from another language in which it is descriptively a word (as French *mal* giving English *mal-* in *malodorous*) or a combining form (as Greek *kako-*, combining form of *kakos*, giving English *caco-* in *cacography*)
combining weight *n* **:** EQUIVALENT 2a
com·bite \käm'bēt\ *also* **coum·bite** \küm-\ *n* -s [AmerF (Haiti)] **:** an informal cooperative group of Haitians helping a neighbor in his work to the accompaniment of drumming and singing
comb jelly *n* **:** CTENOPHORE
com·ble \kōⁿbl(ᵊ), -b(lə)\ *n* -s [F, fr. L *cumulus* heap, summit; akin to L *cavus* hollow — more at CAVE] **:** culminating point **:** ACME
combmaker \'=,==\ *n* -s **:** one who makes combs
comb marbling *n, papermaking* **:** marbling in patterns produced by use of the comb — called also *drawn edge*
comb–mouth bryozoan *n* **:** one of the Ctenostomata
com·bo \'käm(,)bō\ *n* -s [*comb-* (fr. *combination*) + *-o*] **1** *slang* **:** COMBINATION; *esp* **:** COMBINATION 1a(4) **2** *Austral* **:** a white man living with an aboriginal woman
comb–out \'=,=\ *n* -s [fr. *comb out*, v.] **:** an act of combing (as of an industry for workers fit for military service or of criminals from a district)
com·boy \'käm,bȯi\ *n* -s [Sinhalese *kambāya*, perh. fr. *Cambay*, India, where it is produced] *Ceylon* **:** SARONG
comb perforation *n* **:** a stamp perforation made by a machine that punches at one stroke the vertical perforations between the stamps in a single row across a sheet and the horizontal perforations at the top of this row
comb piece \'=,=\ *n* **:** the extension of the back characteristic of a comb-back Windsor chair
comb pottery *n* **:** a late neolithic pottery found in Baltic countries that is ornamented by combing
comb rat *n* [so called fr. the comblike bristles of the hind feet] **:** the gundi or a related rodent
com·bre·ta·ce·ae \,kämbrə'tāsē,ē\ *n pl, cap* [NL, fr. *Combretum*, type genus + *-aceae*] **:** a family of tropical shrubs and trees (order Myrtales) with usu. entire often terminal leaves, mostly perfect flowers with 4 to 6 ovules, and a single-celled indehiscent fruit — **com·bre·ta·ceous** \;==;=shəs\ *adj*
com·bre·tum \kəm'brēd·əm\ *n* [NL, fr. L, a kind of plant; akin to ON *hvōnn* wild angelica, Ir *cuinneog*, Lith *švendrai* cattail] **1** *cap* **:** the type genus of the family Combretaceae, comprising numerous tropical and subtropical small shrubs and trees typically with hard tough wood, bark rich in tannins, flowers with bell-shaped calyces in spikes or racemes, and winged one-seeded fruits **2** -s **:** a plant of the genus *Combretum*
comb ridge *n* **:** a jagged steep-sided mountain ridge with pinnacles and notches along its crest like a cockscomb **:** ARÊTE; *esp* **:** the sharp divide between opposing cirques in a vigorously glaciated mountain range
combs *pl of* COMB, *pres 3 sing of* COMB
comb scab *n* **:** WHITECOMB
comb shell *n* **:** PECTEN 2b
comb speedwell *n* **:** a prostrate Asiatic herb (*Veronica pectinata*) with often pectinate or divided leaves
comb–toothed shark \'=,=-\ *n* **:** a shark of the family Hexanchidae; *esp* **:** a cow shark (*Hexanchus griseus*)
¹com·bu·rent *also* **com·bu·rant** \kəm'byürənt\ *adj* [L *comburent-, comburens*, pres. part. of *comburere* to burn up — more at COMBUSTION] **:** burning or supporting combustion — distinguished from *combustible*
²comburent *also* **combur ant** \"\ *n* -s **:** a substance that burns or that aids combustion
com·burgess \(')käm+\ *n* -ES [*com-* + *burgess*; trans. of ML *comburgensis*] **1 :** a fellow burgess **2 :** a onetime magistrate elected in certain English boroughs and associated with the alderman
com·bu·rim·e·ter \,kämbyə'rimǝd·ǝ(r)\ *n* -s [ISV *combur-* (fr. L *comburere* to burn up) + *-i-* + *-meter* — more at COMBUSTION] **:** an apparatus for determining the proportion of air required for the ideal combustion of a gas — **com·bu·rim·e·try** \-mə·trē\ *n* -ES
com·bu·riv·o·rous \;kämbyə;rivərəs\ *adj* [L *comburere* to burn + E *-i-* + *-vorous*] **:** consuming by combustion ⟨the ~ power of a gas⟩ — compare COMBURENT
¹com·bust \kəm'bəst\ *adj* [ME, fr. MF, fr. L *combustus*, past part. of *comburere* to burn up — more at COMBUSTION] **1** *of a planet* **:** so near the sun as to be obscured or overpowered by its light **2** *obs* **:** BURNED, CONSUMED
²combust \"\ *vb* -ED/-ING/-S *vt* **:** BURN, CONSUME ⟨machines are delivering up to 25 percent of the fuel they ~ —D.C. Peattie⟩ ~ *vi* **1 :** to burn fuel ⟨the engine regularly ~*ed* —Andy Logan⟩ **2 :** BURN **:** become consumed — used chiefly of fuels
com·bus·ti·bil·i·ty \kəm,bəstə'biləd·ē, -ətē, -i\ *n* -ES [ME *combustebyllyte*, fr. MF *combustible* + ME *-ite* -ity] **:** the quality or state of being combustible
¹com·bus·ti·ble \kəm'bəstəbəl\ *adj* [MF, fr. *combustion* + *-ible*] **1 :** capable of undergoing combustion or of burning — used esp. of materials that catch fire and burn when subjected to fire; compare FLAMMABLE **2 a :** easily kindled or excited ⟨the concentrated ~ essence of sex —Claudia Cassidy⟩ **b :** QUICK, FIERY, IRASCIBLE — **com·bus·ti·bly** \-təblē, -li\ *adv*
²combustible \"\ *n* -s **:** a thing that is combustible
combustible shale *n* **:** TASMANITE
com·bus·tion \kəm'bəschən\ *n* -s [ME, fr. MF or LL; MF, fr. LL *combustion-, combustio*, fr. L *combustus* (past part. of *comburere* to burn up, irreg. — influenced by *amburere* to burn up, fr. *ambi-* + *urere* — fr. *com-* + *urere* to burn) + *-ion-, -io* -ion — more at EMBER] **1 :** a process or instance of burning: as **a :** any chemical process accompanied by the evolution of light and heat, being typically a vigorous union of substances with oxygen; *sometimes* **:** slower oxidation (as in the animal body) **b** *in quantitative analysis* **:** the entire operation of burning a measured portion of a substance to be analyzed and collecting the products — see COMBUSTION METHOD **2 :** violent agitation **:** CONFUSION, TUMULT ⟨the wasteful, uncontrolled ~ of Nasser's early career —R.C.Doty⟩
combustion chamber *n* **:** a chamber within which combustion occurs: as **a :** the space in some boiler furnaces where the gases from the fire become more thoroughly mixed with air and burned **b :** the clearance space in the cylinder of an internal-combustion engine where the charge is compressed and ignited **c :** the part of a jet engine or gas turbine in which the propulsive power is developed by combustion of the injected fuel and the expansive force of the resulting gases
combustion engine *n* **:** an engine that derives its motive force from the energy of combustion — compare EXTERNAL-COMBUSTION ENGINE, INTERNAL-COMBUSTION ENGINE
combustion method *n* **:** a method for the quantitative determination of certain elements (as carbon, hydrogen, and nitrogen) in organic compounds by combustion
combustion spoon *n* **:** DEFLAGRATION SPOON
combustion starter *n* **:** CARTRIDGE STARTER
com·bus·tious \kəm'bəschəs\ *adj, obs* **:** FLAMMABLE, COMBUSTIBLE **:** being in combustion **:** TURBULENT
com·bus·tive \-bəstiv, -tēv\ *adj* **:** tending or able to effect combustion **:** relating to or marked by combustion — **com·bus·tive·ly** \-təvlē, -li\ *adv*
com·bus·tor \-stə(r)\ *n* -s [²*combust* + *-or*] **:** the combustion chamber of a gas turbine or a jet engine along with associated burners, igniters, and injection devices
comb wheat grass *n* [so called fr. the comblike arrangement of the spikelets] **:** a European grass (*Agropyron pectinatum*) introduced into New Zealand and Australia
comby \'kōmē\ *adj* -ER/-EST [¹*comb* + *-y*] **:** resembling a comb in structure ⟨~ veins of quartz⟩ **:** HONEYCOMBED
comd *abbr* **1** command; commander; commanding **2** commissioned
comdg *abbr* commanding
comdr *abbr* commander
comdt *abbr* commandant
¹come \'kəm; *often when a stressed syllable, esp an adverb or preposition syllable, follows without pause* ,kəm\ *vb* **came** \(')kām\ *or substand* **come** \(')kəm\ *or* **comed** \-md\ *or dial Brit* **cam** \(')kam\ **come** *or substand* **comed** *or dial Brit* **cam**; **coming** \'kəmiŋ\ **comes** \(')kəmz\ *or archaic* **cometh** \'kəməth\ [ME *comen*, fr. OE *cuman*; akin to OHG *queman* to come, ON *koma*, Goth *qiman*, L *venire* to come, Gk *bainein* to walk, go, Skt *gamati* he goes] *vi* **1 a :** to move toward or away from something **:** pass from one point toward another nearer or more central **:** APPROACH ⟨do ~ to church today⟩ ⟨he *came* quietly into the room⟩ ⟨when will they ~⟩ — distinguished from and sometimes opposed to *go*; usu. used with a preposition (as *toward, on, before, behind*) or an adverb (as *away, down, forth, up*) when the point of departure or terminus is expressed ⟨~ toward me slowly⟩ ⟨the babe *came* forth from the womb⟩ **b :** to move toward or enter a scene of action or into a field of interest whether partly physical or wholly ideal — usu. used with an implication of purpose that may be expressed by an infinitive or participle or a coordinate verb introduced by *and* ⟨he *came* to see us⟩ ⟨a man *came* asking after wisdom⟩ ⟨~ and help us set the table⟩ or by a prepositional phrase ⟨they'll ~ to the rescue when they hear⟩ **c :** to approach or reach a particular station in an expressed or implied series ⟨day is *coming*⟩ ⟨now we ~ to the section on health⟩: (1) **:** to approach in kind or quality — usu. used with *near* ⟨this ~*s* near perfection⟩ ⟨the pure in heart ~ near to God⟩ (2) **:** to result in or progress — often used with *to* ⟨all our good planning *came* to naught⟩ (3) **:** to approach or reach a condition through or as if through change ⟨their fury *came* quickly to a boil⟩ **d** (1) **:** to advance toward maturity or a culminating state or stage — often used with *on* or *along* ⟨the gray filly is *coming* nicely⟩ ⟨that corn will ~ along better if it rains⟩ (2) **:** to advance in a particular manner ⟨~ running when I call⟩ ⟨the referee *came* between the clinching boxers⟩ (3) **:** to advance, rise, or improve in rank or condition — often used with *up* ⟨a general who had *come* up through the ranks⟩ ⟨the neighborhood, after declining for years, was *coming* up again⟩ **e :** FARE **:** come along ⟨how're you *coming* now?⟩ **f** (1) **:** to reach or extend ⟨trousers scarcely *coming* to his shoe tops⟩ (2) **:** to extend along or occupy a denoted or understood space or situation ⟨a path ~*s* through the valley⟩ ⟨at high tide water ~*s* over the lower end of the walk⟩ (3) **:** to reach through the intellect or emotions ⟨this ~*s* very near to me⟩ ⟨the arguments ~ home forcibly⟩ **2 a** (1) **:** to arrive at a particular place, end, result, or conclusion ⟨he *came* slowly to his senses⟩ ⟨she *came* tired to bed each night⟩ ⟨the spirit of true humility ~*s* to those who seek it diligently⟩ (2) **:** to attain by connected or related stages ⟨~ to an understanding⟩ (3) **:** AMOUNT ⟨taxes ~ to more than the property is worth⟩ (4) **:** to appear to the mind **:** become recalled to memory ⟨after much thought the answer *came* to him⟩ ⟨it *came* to her that this was where she first met him⟩ (5) **:** to return in time or space ⟨the good old days never ~ back⟩ **b** (1) *of an event or condition* **:** HAPPEN, BEFALL, OCCUR ⟨no harm will ~ to you⟩ ⟨everything ~*s* to him who waits⟩ (2) **:** to reach a particular state or condition or to happen as the result of chance or of some process or development ⟨~ untied⟩ ⟨how did you ~ to have such an idea⟩ ⟨the whole plan was *coming* clearer and clearer —Willa Cather⟩ — compare COME UPON (3) **:** to come to pass **:** take place — used with inverted subject and verb to express the particular time or occasion concerning which a statement is being made and often in the subjunctive mood with the notion of futurity ⟨*came* Christmas and we had a merry time⟩ ⟨the house burned a year ago ~ March⟩ ⟨~*s* the revolution we'll all live, or hang, high⟩ ⟨~ the end of the war when costs fall⟩ (4) **:** to become merited or owed — usu. used as a present participle ⟨all the credit that's *coming* to him⟩ ⟨I've another dollar *coming* to me⟩ **c** (1) **:** to be the product or result **:** ORIGINATE, ARISE, FOLLOW ⟨pepper ~*s* from a bush⟩ ⟨most wine ~*s* from grapes⟩ ⟨good crops ~ from good soil⟩ ⟨they ~ of sturdy yeoman stock⟩ ⟨do not evil that good may ~⟩ ⟨kind deeds ~ from a kind heart⟩ ⟨after joy ~ sadness⟩ ⟨his wealth ~*s* by inheritance⟩ (2) **:** to be or have been a native or resident — used with *from* ⟨he ~*s* from Toronto, Canada⟩ ⟨she has been here in the city 20 years but who would doubt that she ~*s* from the backwoods?⟩ **d :** to enter or assume a given condition, relation, use, or position ⟨at sundown the artillery *came* into action⟩ ⟨he *came* to the peerage in 1892⟩ **e :** to fall within a field of view, an indicated or implied scope, or a range of application ⟨his follies ~ to mind along with his kindnesses⟩ ⟨this ~*s* within the terms of the treaty⟩ ⟨Connecticut, Rhode Island, then ~*s* Massachusetts⟩ **f** (1) *of an utterance* **:** to become produced **:** issue forth ⟨a dry sob *came* from her constricted throat⟩ ⟨some of the noblest thoughts to ~ from this generation⟩ (2) **:** to take shape **:** assume a given or desired form **:** JELL ⟨in spite of her best efforts the picture would not ~⟩ (3) *of cheese or butter* **:** to be formed by adhesion of particles (4) *of a bow* **:** to bend too much in one place when drawn **g :** to be available ⟨this model ~*s* in several sizes⟩ **:** EXIST ⟨as good as they ~⟩ **h :** to experience orgasm **3 :** to fall to a person in a division of property or as an inheritance ⟨several thousand dollars *came* to him from his uncle⟩ **4 :** pay attention **:** HEED — used only in the imperative and often intensified by repetition to imply rebuke, impatience, or encouragement ⟨~, we must hurry⟩ ⟨~, ~, that's no way to speak to your mother⟩ **5 :** to become moved favorably **:** RELENT ⟨he will relent; he's *coming*; I perceive't —Shak.⟩ **6 :** to command or require a specified exertion or expenditure **:** be possible or be obtainable at a specified cost or by a specified effort ⟨it ~*s* hard for me to accept your views⟩ ⟨good clothes ~ high⟩ ⟨easy ~, easy go⟩ **7 :** RISE — used chiefly in the phrase *come to one's feet* **8 :** to appear to become **:** BECOME ⟨monsters ~ alive from a Goya picture —*New Republic*⟩ ⟨things will ~ clear if we are patient⟩ ~ *vt* **1 :** to approach or be near (an age) ⟨a pretty child *coming* eight years old⟩ **2 a :** to act or play the part of ⟨why should he ~ the dude like that⟩ **b :** PLAY ⟨~ a hand of cards⟩ **c** *Brit* **:** ATTAIN, DO ⟨he cannot ~ that⟩ — **come abroad** *archaic* **:** to appear in public **:** become public or known — **come a cropper 1 :** to fall headlong **2 :** to fail completely ⟨they'll *come a cropper* one of these days if they don't balance their budget⟩ — **come across 1 :** to occur or suggest itself to ⟨the possibility . . . *came across* her —Jane Austen⟩ **2 :** to meet, find, or encounter esp. unexpectedly or by chance ⟨I *came across* grandfather's diary in the attic⟩ ⟨perhaps we will *come across* your sister while we are shopping⟩ — **come again** *slang* **:** REPEAT; *also* **:** to speak further — **come alive :** to show signs of life or awareness ⟨Zack and George *came alive* then, ready to go into the hog business —F.P.Gipson⟩ **:** appear real ⟨careful lighting made the scene *come alive*⟩ — **come a long way :** to make progress **:** SUCCEED ⟨he's *come a long way* since he left the boat at Ellis Island⟩ — **come apart :** to disintegrate physically or mentally ⟨after a good showing in the early rounds the challenger *came apart* in the ninth⟩ — **come at :** to accomplish an understanding or mastery of **:** ATTAIN ⟨art is not something to be *come at* by dint of study —Clive Bell⟩ — **come away 1** *now dial Brit* **:** come with me **:** come along ⟨*come away, come away*, death —Shak.⟩ **2 :** to depart from something or someone expressed or implied **:** LEAVE ⟨*come away* from there before you get dirty⟩ **3 a :** to become detached **:** SEPARATE ⟨the rail *came away* in his hand⟩ **b** *chiefly Brit, of a plant* **:** to come up **:** GROW — **come between :** to cause to be estranged ⟨theirs was a happy home until her mother *came between* them⟩ — **come by 1** *chiefly Midland* **:** to call at **:** VISIT **2 :** to get possession of **:** ACQUIRE ⟨many older recordings are hard to *come by*⟩ ⟨benevolence and selflessness . . . are only indirectly *come by* —C.W.Berenda⟩; *sometimes* **:** to get by or as if by inheritance ⟨he *comes by* his temper naturally⟩ — **come clean** *slang* **:** to tell the whole story **:** CONFESS ⟨after he *comes clean*, I'll do the best for you that I can —Erle Stanley Gardner⟩ — **come close :** to be or arrive near **:** APPROXIMATE ⟨this day has *come close* to perfection⟩ ⟨his quotation *came close* to our bid⟩ — **come compass** *of a bow* **:** to bend in a true arc when drawn — **come forward 1 :** to present oneself (as for candidacy or to public notice) **:** VOLUNTEER **2 :** to attain note or success **:** ADVANCE ⟨light woolens have *come forward* to enjoy marked fashion prestige⟩ — **come home 1 :** to come close or press closely; *esp* **:** to touch the feelings, interest, or reason ⟨the ideal of equality would *come home* with special meaning to men bred up . . . on the frontier —V.L.Parrington⟩ **2 :** to give way under strain (as of an anchor in weighing) — **come home to roost :** to return by way of retribution — **come into :** to enter upon or into possession of **:** acquire esp. as an inheritance ⟨he will *come into* a fortune when his father dies⟩ — **come into case** *or* **come into order** *of tobacco* **:** to acquire such moisture content that the leaf is pliable and readily handled without breaking — **come into one's own :** to acquire something (as rights or a position) that rightfully belongs or is felt to belong to one; *sometimes* **:** to gain recognition ⟨natural gas has *come into its own* —Gardiner Symonds⟩ — **come into play :** to have an effect **:** play a part ⟨his early training in self-expression *came into play* in his new situation⟩ — **come it 1 :** to succeed in doing something **:** attain one's purpose ⟨I meant to pay him last week but I couldn't *come it*⟩ — **come it over 1** *slang* **:** to lord it over **:** DOMINATE, BULLY **2** *slang* **:** DECEIVE, TRICK — **come it strong** *slang* **:** OVERDO, EXAGGERATE — contrasted with *draw it mild* — **come off :** to cease to utter (pretentious or foolish talk) — used chiefly in the phrase *come off it* ⟨*come off it*, you're being silly⟩ — **come on :** to encounter by or as if by chance **:** NEAR ⟨*came on* him in the dark⟩ — **come one's way** *also* **come one's ways :** to fall to one's lot — **come over 1 :** to play or practice (something) upon a person by way of deceiving or taking advantage of him ⟨don't *come* the old soldier *over* me⟩ **2 :** to take advantage of **:** OVERREACH, TRICK ⟨you'll not *come over* me with your innocent looks⟩ **3 :** to take possession of **:** OVERTAKE ⟨quiet *comes over* the market at twilight⟩ — often used of an emotion, idea, or state of mind ⟨what's *come over* you; you're acting so strangely⟩ — **come round :** to circumvent by trickery or flattery ⟨you can't *come round* me that way⟩ — **come through :** to endure successfully **:** SURVIVE ⟨they *came through* that hard winter in good health⟩ — **come to a head 1** *of a pustule or boil* **:** to become distended with pus **:** RIPEN **2** *of affairs* **:** to reach a crisis or a point at which some new course, trend, or decision is inevitable and immediately required — **come to anchor 1** *of a ship* **:** to drop anchor **2 :** to come to rest **:** settle down — **come to blows :** to carry a disagreement to the point of physical violence — **come to grief :** to encounter misfortune (as calamity, defeat, or ruin) esp. when deserved or in some degree the result of one's own actions ⟨were he less self-willed he would be less likely to *come to grief*⟩ — **come to grips 1 :** to engage wholeheartedly and thoroughly **:** get down to business ⟨they could come to terms if they *came* truly *to grips* instead of scolding at each other over a barrier of misunderstanding —Edward Sapir⟩ — often used with *with* ⟨last week the way was opened for the West to *come to grips* with Russia on the atom —*N.Y.Times*⟩ **2 :** to grapple or deal on the most fundamental level — usu. used with *with* ⟨they failed to *come to grips* with the underlying evils of the system⟩ — **come to hand 1 :** to be received ⟨your letter *came to hand* early yesterday morning⟩ ⟨larger quantities of potatoes *came to hand* and values declined somewhat —*Farmer's Weekly* (So. Africa)⟩ **2 :** to come to light **:** be found **:** APPEAR ⟨new evidence has *come to hand* on the authorship of Shakespeare's plays⟩ — **come to life 1 :** to regain consciousness; *also* **:** to exhibit vitality or animation ⟨the birds *coming to life* in song to salute the new day⟩ **2 :** to produce an effect of reality **:** be lifelike ⟨his wife truly *comes to life* in his portrayal⟩ — **come to light :** to come forth **:** be made manifest — **come to nature :** to become pasty and granular — used of iron at the conclusion of the puddling process — **come to nothing** *also* **come to naught :** to be fruitless **:** result in failure ⟨all their efforts *came to nothing*⟩ — **come to oneself :** to come to **:** regain self-control — **come to pass :** HAPPEN — used impersonally with *it* — **come to stay :** to become a fixture or permanency ⟨the automobile has *come to stay*⟩ — **come to terms :** to reach an agreement or a state of comprehension that permits agreement with or adjustment to something ⟨some adaptability is essential if one is to *come to terms* with modern life⟩; *also* **:** SUBMIT — usu. used with *with* — **come to that :** for that matter **:** so far as that goes ⟨*come to that*, you still owe for the car⟩ — **come to time :** to fulfill an obligation — **come true 1 :** to happen as desired or expected **:** attain reality ⟨like a dream *come true*⟩ **2 :** to reproduce the characters of the parent — **come up** *naut* **:** to slacken off gently **:** ease off ⟨*come up* a tackle⟩ — **come upon 1 :** to befall as if descending from above **:** ATTACK, AFFLICT, AFFECT ⟨doubt *came upon* her as she waited⟩ **2** *archaic* **:** to become dependent on esp. financially ⟨he had saved nothing and finally *came upon* the town⟩ **3 :** to meet with **:** chance upon **:** ENCOUNTER ⟨he *came upon* them suddenly at the bend of the path⟩ ⟨not until 1890 did an English missionary *come upon* the curiously carved inscription —Tom Marvel⟩
²come \'kōm, 'küm\ *n* -s [ME; perh. akin to OHG & OS *kīmo* shoot, sprout, OE *cīnan* to gape, yawn, crack — more at CHINE] **:** the dried rootlets produced in malting grain — usu. used in pl.
come about *vi* **1 :** to come to pass **:** attain fulfillment **:** HAPPEN ⟨how did this accident *come about*⟩ **2 :** to change direction **:** come round ⟨the wind has *come about* into the north⟩ **3** *of a sailing craft* **:** TACK
come across *vi* **1 :** to supply or furnish something demanded or requested; *esp* **:** to pay over money **:** CONTRIBUTE — often used with *with* ⟨*come across* now, I've asked for it often enough⟩ ⟨the man *came across* with the price of a drink⟩ **2 :** to succeed in producing a desired effect ⟨he never *came across* as well on the stage as on radio⟩
come–all–ye *also* **come–all–you** \(,)kə'mȯlyə, -yē\ *n, pl* **come–all–ye's** *also* **come–all–you's** [so called fr. the typical opening words] **:** a popular narrative ballad
come along *vi* **1 :** to move on in company ⟨she *came along* with us⟩ or toward one — often used imperatively and with an implication of impatience or irritation ⟨*come along* now, let's have no more dawdling⟩ **2 :** to make progress **:** get along **:** SUCCEED ⟨the paper was *coming along* nicely —S.H.Adams⟩ **3 :** APPEAR ⟨if another dealer *comes along* and offers a better price⟩
come–along \'==,=\ *n* -s [*come along*] **1 :** a gripping device (as for pulling in or stretching wire) consisting of two jaws so attached to a ring that they are closed by pulling on the ring **2 :** any device, method, or hold used to compel an unwilling or resisting person or animal to come along in order to avoid physical discomfort (as a slip noose, a judo hold)
¹come–and–go \;==;=\ *n* -s **:** coming and going; *esp* **:** contraction and expansion
²come–and–go \"\ *adj* **:** APPROXIMATE, VARIABLE ⟨the *come-and-go* dimensions of a piece of glass⟩ ⟨a man of *come-and-go* honesty⟩
come around *vi* **:** to come round
come–at–able \(,)kə'mad·əbəl, 'kə;m-\ *adj* [*come at* + *-able*] **:** capable of being come at or attained **:** ACCESSIBLE
come back *vi* **1 :** to return to life or vitality ⟨of course vampires *come back*⟩ ⟨after lying in a coma for several months he slowly *came back*⟩ **2 :** to return to memory or the mind ⟨it all *comes back* to me now⟩ **3 :** REPLY, RETORT ⟨when questioned, he *came* right *back* with a vehement denial⟩ **4 :** to return to a former condition, state, or position from which one has declined or been deposed **:** stage a comeback ⟨no heavyweight champion has ever *come back*⟩ ⟨rigid closed season may be needed if the birds are to *come back*⟩
¹comeback \'=,=\ *n* -s [*come back*] **1 a :** an answer or retort usu. sharp or biting; *sometimes* **:** REPARTEE **b :** cause for complaint **c :** return of merchandise to a seller usu. because unsatisfactory in quality; *also* **:** the merchandise so returned **2 a** *Austral* **:** a sheep suitable for both wool and meat production that is obtained by breeding a half-breed sheep with one wool-type parent (as a Merino) and one meat-type parent (as a Leicester) to a sheep of one of the parent breeds **b :** the wool from such a sheep **3 :** the act or an instance of coming back esp. to a former state or condition **:** RECOVERY; *also* **:** one that comes back **4 :** any of several shrubs or vines with burs or prickles that catch in one's clothing and impede progress **5 :** money bet by a bookmaker to hedge a bet or to reduce the odds on a heavily backed entry (as in a horse race)
²come·back \,kəm'bak\ *n* -s [imit.] *dial Eng* **:** GUINEA FOWL
come bet \'kəm,bet\ *n* **:** a bet on whether or not a crapshooter engaged in a series of rolls to settle bets previously made will pass from the point of view of treating his next cast as though it were his first
come–between \'==,=\ *n* -s [*come between*] **:** one that comes between
come by *vi* **:** to pay a call ⟨next time you're over this way, *come by*⟩
come–by–chance \'=bə,=\ *n* -s **:** one that comes by chance **:** BASTARD
co·me·chin·gón \,kōməchiŋ'gän\ *n* -s *usu cap* [Sp, of AmerInd

origin] : an extinct language of Argentina that is classed by some Americanists with Huarpean and by others with Calchaqui

co·me·cru·do \ˌkōməˈkrü(ˌ)dō, -(ˌ)thō\ *n, pl* **comecrudo** *or* **comecrudos** *usu cap* [Sp, fr. *comer* to eat, (fr. L *comedere* to eat up) + *crudo* raw, fr. L *crudus* — more at COMESTIBLE, RAW] **1 a :** an Indian people of northeastern Mexico **b :** a member of such people **2 :** a Coahuiltecan language of the Comecrudo people

comed *substand past of* COME

comeddle *vt* -ED/-ING/-S [*co-* + *meddle*] *obs* **:** COMMINGLE

co·me·dia \kəˈmādēə, kōˈmāthyä\ *n* -S [Sp, fr. L *comoedia* — more at COMEDY] **:** a Spanish regular-verse drama or comedy **:** COMEDY

co·me·di·al \kəˈmēdēəl\ *adj* [*comedy* + *-al*] **:** of or relating to comedy

co·me·di·an \kəˈmēdēən\ *n* -S [MF *comédien*, fr. *comédie* comedy, + *-ien* -ian — more at COMEDY] **1 :** a writer of comedy **2 :** an actor who plays comedy; *sometimes* **:** any stage player **3 :** a comical or amusing individual — often used ironically ⟨you're quite the ~ aren't you⟩

co·me·dic \-ˈmēdik, -med-\ *also* **co·me·di·cal** \-dəkəl\ *adj* [*comedic* fr. L *comoedicus*, fr. Gk *kōmōidikos*, fr. *kōmōidia* comedy + *-ikos* -ic; *comedical* fr. L *comoedicus* + E *-al*] **:** of, relating to, or having the attributes of comedy ⟨~ incantations⟩ ⟨a ~ hero⟩ **:** like or like that of comedy ⟨high, ~ raillery —F.A.Swinnerton⟩ — **co·me·di·cal·ly** \-dək(ə)lē\ *adv*

co·me·di·enne \kəˌmēdēˈen *sometimes* -mād; ˌ═ˌ══ˈ═\ *n* -S [F *comédienne*, fem. of *comédien*] **:** an actress who plays comedy

co·me·di·et·ta \kəˌmādēˈed·ə, -mēd-\ *n* -S [obs. It (now *commedietta*), dim. of obs. *comedia* (now *commedia*), fr. L *comoedia*] **:** a light farcical comedy

co·me·dist \ˈkämədəst\ *n* -S [*comedy* + *-ist*] **:** one who writes comedies

com·e·do \ˈkäməˌdō\ *n, pl* **com·e·do·nes** \ˌkäməˈdō(ˌ)nēz\ [NL, fr. L, glutton, fr. *comedere* to eat, fr. *com-* + *edere* — more at EAT] **:** a collection of dead cells and oily secretion that plugs a hair follicle and duct of an oil gland and is usu. covered with a black dot — called also *blackhead;* compare MILIUM

com·e·do·carcinoma \ˈ═ˌ══+\ *n* [NL, fr. *comedo* + *carcinoma*] **:** a breast cancer that arises in the larger ducts and is characterized by slow growth, late metastasis, and the accumulation of solid plugs of atypical and degenerating cells in the ducts

come down *vi* **1 :** to reduce itself **:** AMOUNT — used with *to* ⟨it *comes down* to this⟩ **2 :** to lose or fall esp. in estate or condition — used chiefly in the phrase *come down in the world* **3 a :** to place oneself in opposition esp. in speech or writing ⟨the judge *came down* hard on gambling⟩ **b :** to utter a reprimand **:** inflict punishment or punish — usu. used with *on* **4** *chiefly Brit* **:** to make payment or to make a gift of money ⟨old Mr. Pontifex then *came down* more handsomely than expected and settled £10,000 on his son —Samuel Butler †1902⟩ **5 :** to fall sick **:** become affected or infected — used with *with* ⟨they *came down* with measles⟩

comedown \ˈ═ˌ═\ *n* -S [*come down*] **:** a descent from rank or dignity or from a higher to a lower state or quality **:** a disappointment or humiliation **:** SETBACK

com·e·dy \ˈkämədē, -di\ *n* -ES [ME *comedye*, fr. MF *comedie*, fr. L *comoedia*, fr. Gk *kōmōidia*, fr. *kōmos* revel, village festival, festal procession, ode sung in this procession (fr. *kōmē* village) + *-ōidia* (fr. *aeidein* to sing) — more at HOME, ODE] **1 a :** a drama of light and amusing character and typically with a happy ending **b** *obs* **:** a mystery play or interlude with a happy ending **2 a :** any medieval narrative that ends happily; *esp* **:** one written in a vernacular language **b :** any literary composition written in a comic style or treating a theme suitable for comedy **3 :** the genre of dramatic literature that deals with the light or the amusing or with the serious and profound in a light, familiar, or satirical manner — compare TRAGEDY **4 :** matter suitable for treatment in comedy **:** a ludicrous, farcical, or amusing event or series of events ⟨a ~ of misunderstandings⟩ **5 :** the comic element (as in a play, story, or motion picture) ⟨the ~ was furnished by the parlormaid⟩

comedy ballet *n* **:** ballet with features of comedy, with stress on the dramatic element, and with an overture, recitatives, airs, and choruses

comedy drama *n* **:** serious drama with comedy interspersed

comedy of character : comedy in which the emphasis is on characterization rather than plot or lines — compare COMEDY OF SITUATION

comedy of intrigue : a comedy of situation in which complicated conspiracies and stratagems dominate the plot

comedy of manners : comedy that satirically portrays the manners and fashions of a particular class or set

comedy of situation : comedy in which the comic effect depends chiefly upon the involvement of the main characters in a predicament or ludicrous complex of circumstances — compare COMEDY OF CHARACTER

comedy relief *n* **:** a light tension-breaking interlude in a serious drama; *also* **:** any comparable interruption of a serious, distressing, or ponderous production or situation

come-hith·er \(ˌ)kəmˈhithə(r), (ˌ)kəˈmi-\ *n* -S [fr. *come hither!*, a call to animals] **1 :** an enticing invitation **2** *chiefly Irish* **:** winning talk or ways **:** PERSUASION, BEGUILING ⟨she could put the *come-hither* on any man⟩

come in *vi* **1 :** to place (as in a race or competition) among those finishing ⟨*came in* second in the golf tournament⟩ **2 :** to accrue or come as gain or revenue ⟨we can afford it as long as the money keeps on *coming in* so freely⟩ **3 a :** to become of use ⟨gunpowder first *came in* in China⟩ **b :** to fit in **:** enter into or assume its place or course ⟨this *comes in* pat⟩ **:** take a part or perform a usu. useful service ⟨old newspapers . . . *come in* handy for lighting the fire —Victoria Sackville-West⟩ **c :** to make reply to a signal or call **:** come on to a communication channel **:** RETURN, REPLY — used esp. by communications units ⟨*come in*, San Francisco⟩ **4 :** to be the recipient — used with *for* ⟨the chancellor's policy has *come in* for increasing criticism —Douglas Stuart⟩ **5 a :** to take or perform one's part or function (as in a joint activity) ⟨that's where you *come in*⟩ **b :** to assume official duties or station ⟨if the Republicans *come in* next fall⟩ **:** take possession or command ⟨when his heirs *came in* they found the estate gutted⟩ **6 :** to attain maturity, fruitfulness, or production: **a** *of a crop* **:** to mature and produce a harvest; *also, of a seasonal food* **:** to be in season **b** *of a female mammal* (1) **:** to bring forth young **:** CALVE — used esp. of dairy cattle (2) **:** to be in heat **c** *of an oil well* **:** to begin to yield oil

comelily *adv* [ME *comlyly*, fr. *comly* + *-ly*] *obs* **:** in a suitable or comely manner **:** with propriety or dignity

come·li·ness \ˈkəmlēnəs, -lin- *sometimes* ˈkōm- *or* ˈkäm-\ *n* -ES [ME *comlynesse*, fr. *comly* + *-nesse* -ness] **:** the condition of being comely esp. with respect to grace or beauty of external form

come·ling \ˈkəmliŋ\ *n* -S [ME *comling*, fr. *comen* to come + *-ling* — more at COME] *archaic* **:** one not native to the place where he is **:** NEWCOMER, IMMIGRANT

[1]**come·ly** \ˈkəmlē, -li *sometimes* ˈkōm- *or* ˈkäm-\ *adj, usu* -ER/-EST [ME *comly*, alter. (influenced by *comen* to come) of OE *cȳmlic* lovely, glorious, fr. *cȳme* lovely, fine, glorious + *-lic* -ly; akin to OHG *kūmig* weak, powerless, ON *kȳmiligr* peculiar, ridiculous, OE *ciegan* to cry out, L *gavia* sea gull, Gk *goan* to lament, Skt *gavate* it sounds; basic meaning: crying out] **1 :** having a pleasing appearance **:** attractive through a measure of good looks, good proportions, pleasing coloration, neat or wholesome aspect **:** not homely or plain ⟨those dark-featured ~ womenfolk healthy and tall —Robert Browning⟩ **2 :** generally pleasant and attractive-looking **:** SEEMLY; *specif* **:** pleasurably conforming to notions of fitness, proportion, or decorum ⟨going in with him, they observed that all was neat and ~ —Willa Cather⟩ ⟨the best architect seeks to present . . . the *comeliest* possible fulfillment of certain practical requirements —C.E.Montague⟩ **syn** see BEAUTIFUL

[2]**comely** *adv* [ME *comly*, alter. (influenced by *comen* to come) of OE *cȳmlice*, fr. *cȳmlic*, adj.] *obs* **:** COMELILY

co·men·ic acid \(ˈ)kōˌmenik-, -mēn-\ *n* [ISV *comenic* (anagram of *meconic*) + *acid*] **:** a yellow crystalline acid, $C_5H_3O_3COOH$ formed from meconic acid; 5-hydroxy-1,4-pyrone-2-carboxylic acid

come off *vi* **1 a :** to issue or emerge (as from a contest or situation whose outcome is uncertain) ⟨the American nation has not *come off* untouched —J.S.Dickey⟩ ⟨he *came off* well in the distribution of honors⟩ **b :** to give a performance of an indicated quality **:** acquit oneself ⟨the new player *came off* very well in the match⟩ **2 :** to prove satisfactory **:** SUCCEED ⟨the meeting of the prime ministers *came off* well⟩; *specif* **:** to produce a desired effect (as an illusion of reality) ⟨in spite of excellent lighting and scenery the production of his play did not quite *come off*⟩ **3 :** to take place **:** HAPPEN, OCCUR ⟨the meeting will *come off* a week from Tuesday⟩ **4 :** to turn out to be ⟨the day *came off* fine⟩

come-off \ˈ═ˌ═\ *n* -S [*come off*] **1 :** a conclusion or finish **2 :** an evasion esp. of a duty **:** evasive statement **:** EXCUSE

come-of-will *or* **come-o'-will** \ˈ═ə(v)ˌ═\ *n* -S *Scot* **:** one that comes uninvited and unexpected (as a volunteer plant)

come on *vi* **1 :** to begin by degrees — used esp. of natural phenomena ⟨it *came on* dark⟩ ⟨rain *came on* toward noon⟩ **2 :** to make progress esp. in growth or development **:** THRIVE, IMPROVE ⟨the corn is *coming on* splendidly⟩ ⟨he deserves credit for the way he has *come on* lately⟩ **3 a :** ENTER, APPEAR ⟨lights were beginning to *come on*⟩ **b :** to be brought forward (as a case in court) **4** *of a physical condition or disease* **:** to begin to affect one ⟨a cold may *come on* quite unexpectedly⟩ **5 :** PLEASE — used in cajoling or pleading ⟨*come on*, give me another apple⟩

come-on \ˈ═ˌ═\ *n* -S [*come on*] **1 :** an allurement or bait: as **a :** something designed to induce a person to become a victim of trickery ⟨let him win a few bets as a *come-on*⟩ **b :** a special inducement (as a premium or an article offered at less than cost) intended to attract customers to a store or other selling agency **2 :** the discard of a high card as a signal for one's partner to lead back a card of the same suit **3** *slang* **:** SWINDLER; *also* **:** a person victimized by a swindler **:** EASY MARK

come out *vi* **1 :** to pass to a place thought of as away from or remote from the center of affairs — often used of passage to a remote or unsettled area ⟨my father *came out* to New Zealand in the '60s⟩ **2 :** to come into view **:** EMERGE: as **a :** to become published **b :** to become public ⟨his shameful secret finally *came out*⟩ **c :** to make one's professional or social debut **d :** to break out — used of rashes **3 :** to come to an end **:** TERMINATE; *esp* **:** to turn out ⟨how did the story *come out*⟩ ⟨that cake *came out* splendidly⟩ **4 :** to extend or project ⟨the fireplace *came out* into the room⟩ **5 :** to allow something to appear or become known: as **a :** to declare oneself ⟨he *came out* strongly against the administration⟩ **b :** CONFESS — usu. used with *with* ⟨he *came out* shyly with his regrets⟩

come-out \ˈ═ˌ═\ *n* -S [*come out*] **1 :** a capacity for growth or development **:** EMERGENCE **2 :** a crapshooter's first roll of the dice after new bets are made and faded; *also* **:** the number cast

come-out·er \(ˌ)kəˈmaud·ə(r)\ *n* -S [*come out* + *-er*] **:** one who withdraws from something established or settled (as a religious body or a community); *broadly* **:** one who seeks to replace an existent organization (as a political party) **:** a radical reformer

come over *vi* [[1]*come*] **1 a :** to change from one side (as of a controversy) to the other **b** *of a product of distillation* **:** to rise and pass over from the heated vessel to a collecting system ⟨when the temperature reaches 300°, some of the heavier fractions begin to *come over*⟩ **c :** to visit casually **:** drop in ⟨*come over* when you're through sweeping⟩ **2** *Brit* **:** to experience an indicated feeling or condition **:** BECOME ⟨the sky *came over* dark as a cloud passed before the moon⟩ ⟨she *came over* queer and gasped for breath⟩

come-o'-will *var of* COME-OF-WILL

co·me pri·ma \ˌkō(ˌ)māˈprēmə\ *adv (or adj)* [It, lit., as at first] **:** in the same manner as the first time — used as a direction in music

com·er \ˈkəmə(r)\ *n* -S [ME, fr. *comen* to come + *-er*] **1 a :** one that comes; *esp* **:** one that comes voluntarily or offers or chooses to come (as to a contest) — used chiefly in the pl. and in the phrase *all comers* **b :** one newly arrived **:** ARRIVAL **2 :** one making rapid progress or showing promise esp. of future success or prominence

come round *vi* **1 a :** to recur in regular course **b :** MENSTRUATE **c :** to return to a former condition of body or mind; *esp* **:** to recover from an illness or faint **2 :** to change in direction or opinion ⟨the wind *came round* at dawn⟩ ⟨sooner or later he'll *come round* to our point of view⟩; *also* **:** to come about **:** TACK

[1]**comes** *pres 3d sing of* COME, *pl of* COME

[2]**co·mes** \ˈkōˌmēz, -mes\ *n, pl* **com·i·tes** \ˈkäməˌtēz, -ˌtās\ [L, lit., companion — more at COUNT] **1 :** a legal or military adviser to the Roman emperor; *broadly* **:** any prominent military or civil officer of the Roman empire **2** [ML, fr. L] **a :** a wellborn attendant on a king or chief in medieval Europe subject to the duty of military service **b** *comites, pl* **:** the persons making up the suite of an ambassador **3** [LL, fr. L] **:** a Roman Catholic service book containing a complete index and sometimes the text of all the liturgical lessons **4** [NL, fr. L] **a :** the answer in a fugue **b :** the consequent in a canon — compare DUX **5** [NL, fr. L] **:** VENA COMES

co·me so·pra \ˌkō(ˌ)māˈsōprə\ *adv (or adj)* [It, lit., as above] **:** as previously — used as a direction in music

[1]**co·mes·ti·ble** \kəˈmestəbəl\ *adj* [MF, fr. ML *comestibilis*, fr. L *comestus* (past part. of *comedere* to eat up, fr. *com-* + *edere* to eat) + *-ibilis* -ible — more at EAT] **:** suitable to be eaten **:** EATABLE, EDIBLE

[2]**comestible** \"\ *n* -S **:** something comestible **:** FOOD, DISH — usu. used in pl.

com·et \ˈkämət, *usu* -əd·+V\ *n* -S [ME *comete*, fr. OE *cometa*, fr. L *cometa, cometes*, fr. Gk *komētēs*, lit., long-haired, fr. *koman* to wear long hair, fr. *komē* hair] **1 :** a nebulous celestial body that consists of a fuzzy head usu. surrounding a bright nucleus, that often when in the part of its orbit near the sun develops a long tail which points away from the sun because of radiation pressure, that has an orbit varying in eccentricity between nearly round and parabolic, that has an inclination from zero to 180 degrees, and that has a period from three to thousands of years **2** [prob. trans. of F *comète;* fr. the picture of a comet on one of the cards] **a :** a card game that is a form of stops **b :** the nine of clubs or nine of diamonds when assigned special values in this game **3** *sometimes cap* **:** a goldfish of a fancy breed **4 :** one of a class of racing sloops similar to the star boat but smaller in size **5 :** one that rapidly attains high position but fails to retain it

co·metallic \ˌkō+\ *adj* [*co-* + *metallic*] *of a coin* **:** having a center piece made of different metal from the rest

com·e·tary \ˈkäməˌterē, -ri\ *adj* [*comet* + *-ary*] **:** of or relating to a comet **:** like a comet (as in erratic course or transience) **:** coming from comets ⟨meteors of ~ origin⟩

comet aster *n* **:** any member of a race of garden asters of compact growth with large heads of flowers

cometh *archaic 3d sing of* COME

co·meth·er \kəˈmethə(r)\ *dial var of* COME-HITHER

come through *vi* **1** *chiefly South & Midland* **:** to experience a religious conversion esp. at a revival meeting **2 :** to do what is needed or expected **:** PROVIDE, GIVE, CONTRIBUTE ⟨he knew that he had to *come through*⟩ ⟨after some hesitation they *came through* with the price⟩ **3 :** to attain reality **:** MATERIALIZE, EMERGE ⟨his personality *comes through* in his writing⟩

co·met·ic \kəˈmed·ik, (ˈ)käˌm-\ *also* **co·met·i·cal** \-d·əkəl\ *adj* [*comet* + *-ic*, *-ical*] **:** COMETARY

come to *vi* **1 :** to recover consciousness or vitality **2** *now dial* **:** to reach an agreement or accord **:** become pleasant **:** AGREE, YIELD **3 a :** to bring a ship's head nearer the wind **:** LUFF **b :** to anchor or stop in a certain port

comet seeker *also* **comet finder** *n* **:** a telescope of wide field used in searching the sky for comets

comet tail *n* **:** something suggesting the tail of a comet esp. in brightness or form

cometwise \ˈ═ˌ═\ *adv* [*comet* + *-wise*] **:** in the manner of a comet ⟨a blade curving ~⟩

come up *vi* **1 :** RISE 6a **2 :** to become mentioned **:** arise esp. in conversation **3** *Brit* **:** to enter a university **4 :** to reach something as if by pursuit **:** MEET — used with *with* **5** *of a sailing ship* **:** to come to a certain direction esp. as near as may be to the wind **6 :** to come before an authoritative person, group, or body for consideration or decision ⟨the housing bill *came up* for a vote⟩ ⟨several senators *coming up* for reelection⟩ **7 a :** to be equal **:** compare in quality or worth — usu. used with *to* ⟨few great moments *come up* to expectation⟩ **b :** to draw near ⟨the old man *came up* and welcomed them⟩ **8 :** to start or move along faster — used in the imperative and for directing horses or other draft animals **9 :** to supply what is needed or desired — used with *with* ⟨they *came up* with a solution that cut down on losses from rust⟩ ⟨he *came up* with a check for the swimming pool⟩

come-up·pance *also* **come·up·ance** \(ˌ)kəˈməpən(t)s\ *n* -S [*come up* + *-ance*] **:** a deserved rebuke or penalty **:** DESERTS

comfier *comparative of* COMFY

comfiest *superlative of* COMFY

[1]**com·fit** \ˈkəm(p)fət, ˈkäm-\ *n* -S [ME *confit*, fr. MF, fr. past part. of *confire* to prepare, preserve, pickle, fr. L *conficere* to prepare, fr. *com-* + *-ficere* (fr. *facere* to make) — more at DO] **:** a confection consisting of a solid center (as a piece of fruit, a root, or a seed) that is coated and preserved by layers of sugar

[2]**com·fit** *vt, obs* **:** to make into a comfit **:** PRESERVE

com·fi·ture \-fəˌchů(ə)r\ *n* -S [ME *confiture*, fr. MF, fr. *confit* + *-ure*] **:** a comfit or preserve

com·form·a·ble \kəmˈfȯrməbəl\ *adj* [by alter.] **:** CONFORMABLE

[1]**com·fort** \ˈkəm(p)fə(r)t *sometimes esp by clergymen* -ˌfȯrt *or* -ō(ə)t; *usu* -d·+V\ *n* -S [ME *comfort, confort*, fr. OF *confort*, fr. *conforter*, v.] **1 :** strengthening aid: **a :** ASSISTANCE, SUCCOR, SUPPORT ⟨optimists, those who put their faith in humanity, believers in God . . . will find little ~ anywhere in Jeffers' work —*Time*⟩ ⟨give aid and ~ to the enemies of us all⟩ **b :** consolation in trouble or worry **:** SOLACE ⟨it is a ~ too to have a man tackle his job in the old-fashioned way —O.W. Holmes †1935⟩ ⟨to give ~ to a bereaved parent⟩ **2 a :** state or feeling of having relief, encouragement, or consolation ⟨merely getting to the end of the journey provided some ~⟩ ⟨the sedative gave some small ~ to the patient⟩ **b :** contented enjoyment in physical or mental well-being esp. in freedom from want, anxiety, pain, or trouble ⟨living a life of ease and ~⟩ **3 :** SATISFACTION, ENJOYMENT ⟨I do not find ~ in Greek poetry as I should —H.J.Laski⟩ ⟨having the ~ of a draw on my pipe —Mary Deasy⟩ **4 :** something that gives or brings comfort: **a :** a person or thing that brings aid, support, or satisfaction ⟨the son was the ~ of his parents' old age⟩ **b :** an appurtenance or condition furnishing mental or physical ease ⟨the ~*s* of home life⟩ ⟨bathrooms, water supplies, lighting, heating, and the whole array of domestic ~*s* —Henry Adams⟩ **5** *chiefly South & Midland* **:** COMFORTER 3b **syn** see REST

[2]**comfort** \"\ *vb* -ED/-ING/-S [ME *comforten, conforten*, fr. OF *conforter*, fr. LL *confortare* to strengthen greatly, fr. L *com-* + *fortis* strong — more at FORT] *vt* **1** *obs* **:** to make strong or secure **:** STRENGTHEN, ENCOURAGE **2** *obs* **:** ASSIST, HELP, ABET — once commonly used in law **3 a :** to impart strength and hope to **:** GLADDEN, CHEER **b :** to relieve esp. of mental distress **:** allay the grief or trouble of **:** CONSOLE, EASE **4 :** to make comfortable ⟨~*ed* his aching feet in a tub of hot water⟩ **~** *vi, obs* **:** to take comfort

syn CONSOLE, SOLACE: COMFORT, more intimate in its suggestions than CONSOLE or SOLACE, may connote relieving, soothing, and encouraging with cheer, hope, assurance extended with sympathetic kindness ⟨"This war will go on forever", she would whisper. "It cannot go on for ever", I would *comfort* her —H.G.Wells⟩ ⟨he put the letter away. Later it would *comfort* him, as she meant it to do. Later it might make him happy —Susan Ertz⟩ CONSOLE, less intimate in suggestion, may stress alleviating grief and disappointment rather than cheering and encouraging ⟨his father's letter gave him one of his many fits of melancholy over his own worthlessness, but the thought of the organ *consoled* him —Samuel Butler †1902⟩ ⟨if you really want to *console* me, teach me rather to forget what has happened —Oscar Wilde⟩ ⟨*consoled* herself with going to parties, spoiling her babies, and flirting with other people —Rose Macaulay⟩ SOLACE applies to any agency tending to relieve grief, pain, disappointment, chagrin, weariness, despondency ⟨his father's death left Ariosto at the head of a large family, for which he had to provide out of a scanty patrimony. He *solaced* his cares by classical studies, which made him a fair Latin poet —Richard Garnett⟩ ⟨though you rail against the bar and the imperfect medium of speech, you will be *solaced*, even in your chagrin, by a sense of injured innocence —B.N. Cardozo⟩ ⟨liberals are constantly tempted to depart from their difficult path and either embrace some simple panacea or else *solace* themselves with a rather too easy skepticism —M.R. Cohen⟩

[1]**com·fort·able** \ˈkəm(p)(f)təbəl, -m(p)fə(r)d·əb-, -m(p)fə(r)təb- *also* ÷ -m(p)fə(r)b- *or* ÷ -m(p)(f)tərb-\ *adj* [ME *comfortable, confortable*, fr. MF *confortable*, fr. *conforter* + *-able*] **1 :** affording solace, sustenance, delight **:** COMFORTING: **a :** CONSOLING **:** extending consolation **:** CHEERING, ENCOURAGING **:** dispelling worry ⟨her presence warmed the atmosphere . . . she herself was a most ~ little person —Willa Cather⟩ ⟨for God's sake speak ~ words —Shak.⟩ **b** *obs* **:** REFRESHING, SUSTAINING **c :** uplifting or delighting spiritually or mentally ⟨~ religious contemplation⟩ **2 :** enjoying or showing solace or good cheer ⟨sooner than she could have supposed it possible . . . her spirits became absolutely ~ —Jane Austen⟩ **3 a :** giving or promising physical ease, pleasurable feeling, ample convenience, or cheerful well-being **:** calculated to operate against unpleasant feelings, distress, oppression, difficulty, or want ⟨a ~ fit⟩ ⟨a ~ summer suit⟩ ⟨a more ~ automobile⟩ ⟨~ houses set in spacious grounds —*Amer. Guide Series: Pa.*⟩ ⟨a makeshift arrangement not altogether . . . ~ for either of us —Havelock Ellis⟩ **b :** conducive to mental or spiritual ease, relaxation, placidity **:** occasioning no challenging difficulty, disconcerting obscurity, or worrying uncertainty ⟨the home team had a ~ 7 to 1 lead in the eighth⟩ ⟨irregular war was . . . more exhausting than service in the ~ imitative obedience of an ordered army —T.E.Lawrence⟩ ⟨~ compromises —V.L. Parrington⟩ ⟨the world will probably keep on getting better and better, which is a very nice ~ thought —*Atlantic Monthly*⟩ **c :** assuring or affording an easy tranquillity about money or a convenient, pleasant, and secure way of living, although without great wealth ⟨retiring on a ~ income⟩ ⟨in ~ circumstances by reason of prize money —C.O.Paullin⟩ **4 :** enjoying or showing comfort and ease: **a :** at ease physically **:** in a restful situation **:** without urgent unsatisfied wants **:** free from pain, irritation, stricture, or other unpleasant feelings **:** RELAXED ⟨making himself ~ in an armchair⟩ ⟨treatment by which the person with hay fever may be made more ~ —Morris Fishbein⟩ **b :** at ease mentally or socially **:** free from vexation, worry, doubt, fear **:** not disturbed or perturbed **:** PLACID, UNRUFFLED ⟨~ in his allegiance to his king⟩ ⟨Lamb was ~ in his ignorance of what he did not choose to know —John Mason Brown⟩ **c :** in assured or easy circumstances esp. financially **:** not hard pressed or harried by exigency ⟨a ~, though by no means affluent family —*Times Lit. Supp.*⟩

syn COMFORTABLE, COZY, SNUG, EASY, RESTFUL, and REPOSEFUL describe that which makes for contented tranquil ease and enjoyment. COMFORTABLE stresses absence of matters vexatious, worrisome, irritating, or painful in any way ⟨"I fear I should not be happy in that company . . ." "Then I give in. Do whatever will be most *comfortable* to yourself" —Thomas Hardy⟩ ⟨"Thank God for colonels", thought Mrs. Miniver; "sweet creatures, so easily entertained, so biddably diverted from senseless controversy into *comfortable* monologue" —Jan Struther⟩ COZY suggests warmth, shelter, and ease, and hints tranquillity and friendliness ⟨Wimsey gratefully took in the *cozy* sitting room, with its little tables crowded with ornaments, its fire roaring behind a chaste canopy of velvet overmantel —Dorothy Sayers⟩ SNUG indicates secure and assured warmth and comfort usu. in compact quarters ⟨Lady D. will find us in rather a smaller house than we are accustomed to receive our friends in, but it's *snug* —W.M.Thackeray⟩ EASY implies absence of anything likely to cause physical, social, or mental discomfort ⟨there's a pleasant feel in being gently . . . pinioned fast to the *easy* armchair —Robert Browning⟩ RESTFUL, applicable to indoor and outdoor situations, and the less common REPOSEFUL apply to whatever induces rest or repose ⟨a *restful*, friendly room, fitted to the uses of gentle life, covered, when it must be covered, with beauty —Mary Austin⟩ ⟨I . . . drank in deep, calm gladness from the sweet, *restful* scene—the gray old church with its clustering ivy and its quaint carved wooden porch, the white lane winding down the hill between tall rows of elms —J.K.Jerome⟩ ⟨the secretary's office, which his wife endowed with ship's lamps, ship's bells, crossed naval swords, and a generally *reposeful* colonial decor —*Time*⟩ COMFORTABLE, COZY, SNUG, and EASY may all describe an assured financial position. In reference to persons, COMFORTABLE, COZY, and SNUG may indicate mere absence of discomfort or, more positively, a pleasant, relaxed, warm, contented feeling ⟨we found the doctor and Zeke making themselves *comfortable*. The latter was reclining on the ground, pipe in mouth —Herman Melville⟩ ⟨Mrs. Carewe, faced with impecunious widowhood, had successfully daydreamed herself right out of bleak reality into *cozy* semiinvalidism —Edna Ferber⟩ ⟨there must be no open windows or drafty cracks to disturb his *cozy* reflections —M.R.Cohen⟩ ⟨ere that the fisherfolk were all *snug* under thatch and sheltering wall, breathing the cabin's air of gold, safe from blue storm and nipping cold —G.W.Russell⟩ ⟨all the gypsies and showmen who had remained on the ground lay *snug* within their carts and tents —Thomas Hardy⟩

²comfortable \"\ *n* -s **1** *chiefly Brit* **:** a knitted wristlet **2** *chiefly Brit* **:** COMFORTER 3a **3** *chiefly North* **:** COMFORTER 3b

com·fort·able·ness *n* -ES **:** the condition of being comfortable

com·fort·ably \-blē,-bli\ *adv* [ME, fr. *comfortable* + *-ly*] **:** in a comfortable manner: as **a** *obs* **:** ENCOURAGINGLY, REASSURINGLY, COMFORTINGLY **b :** in comfort **:** in an adequate and comfortable manner ⟨they live plainly but ~⟩ **c :** COMPLACENTLY **:** with calm self-assurance

com·fort·er *R* 'kəm(p)fə(r)d·ər, -fə(r)tər, -*R* -fəd·ə(r,-fətə(r\ *n* -s [ME *comfortoure, confortoure*, fr. MF *conforteor*, fr. *conforter* + *-eor* -or] **1 :** one that gives comfort (as by aid, consolation, cheer) **2** *cap* **:** HOLY SPIRIT **3 a :** a long narrow usu. knitted neck scarf **b :** a warm bedcover **:** QUILT, PUFF **4** *chiefly Brit* **:** PACIFIER a

com·fort·ful \-fə(r)tfəl\ *adj* **:** abounding in comfort

comforting *adj* [ME, fr. pres. part. of *comforten* to comfort] **:** providing or intended to provide comfort **:** CONSOLING, CHEERING — **com·fort·ing·ly** *adv*

com·fort·iza·tion \,kəm(p)fə(r)d·ə'zāshən\ *n* -s **:** the act of rendering (an aircraft) more comfortable (as by adequate heating and pressure control)

com·fort·ize \'kəm(p)fə(r)d·,īz\ *vt* -ED/-ING/-S **:** to make comfortable **:** adapt to the needs of the user **:** ADJUST, FIT

com·fort·less \-(r)tləs\ *adj* [ME, fr. ¹*comfort* + *-less*] **1 :** without comfort **:** DREARY **:** lacking in comforts **2** *obs* **:** offering no comfort — **com·fort·less·ly** *adv* — **com·fort·less·ness** *n* -ES

com·for·tress \-(r)trəs\ *n* -ES [ME *confortouresse*, fr. MF *conforteresse*, fem. of *conforteor*] **:** a female comforter

comfortroot \'⸗⸗,⸗\ *n* -s *in Florida* **:** COONTIE

comforts *pl of* COMFORT, *pres 3d sing of* COMFORT

comfort station *also* **comfort room** *n* **:** a place where toilet and lavatory facilities are available to the public

com·frey *also* **cum·frey** \'kəm(p)frē\ *n* -s [ME *comfirie, confirie*, fr. OF *cumfirie, cunfirie*, fr. L *conferva* — more at CONFERVA] **1 :** a plant of the genus *Symphytum* **2 :** DAISY 1

com·fy \'kəm(p)fē, -fi\ *adj* -ER/-EST [by shortening & alter.] **:** COMFORTABLE

¹com·ic \'kämik, -mēk\ *adj* [L *comicus*, fr. Gk *kōmikos*, fr. *kōmos* festivity with music and dancing — more at COMEDY] **1 a :** dealing or dealt with in comedy as contrasted with tragedy ⟨a standard ~ theme⟩ **b :** composing or acting in comedies ⟨a ~ dramatist⟩ **c :** showing or conveying an attitude of thoughtful mirth or amused detached reflection rather than sorrow, pain, or resolution ⟨the alone in the book has a remarkable ~ sense. He can prick the bubble of any illusion —John Erskine †1951⟩ **2 :** calling forth laughter by intentional wit, humor, or burlesque or by unintentional exaggeration or inappropriateness **:** COMICAL ⟨it would have been ~ if she were making all this fuss for nothing —Joseph Conrad⟩ **3 :** presenting a series of humorous incidents or dramatic adventures in a sequence of pictures usu. accompanied by balloons giving conversation ⟨the ~ section of a newspaper⟩ **syn** see LAUGHABLE

²comic \"\ *n* -s **1 :** an actor of comic roles **:** COMEDIAN **2 a :** the element in art or nature that provokes mirth or humorous reflection ⟨to inquire into the essence of the ~⟩ **b :** the representation of the incongruous (as in character and in conduct or in aim and in method) as amusing; *sometimes* **:** the representation of human error and weakness as provocative of amusement **3 a :** a group of cartoons or drawings arranged in a narrative sequence — compare ¹COMIC 3 **b comics** *pl* **:** the portion of a publication (as a daily or Sunday newspaper) devoted to such groups **4 :** a motion picture presenting broad comedy or farce

com·i·cal \-məkəl, -mēk-\ *adj* [*comic* + *-al*] **1** *obs* **a :** belonging or relating to comedy rather than tragedy **b :** like comedy in its conclusion **:** HAPPY **c :** not elevated or dignified enough to call for serious treatment **:** MEAN, TRIVIAL **2 :** calling forth often intentionally mirth and easy spontaneous laughter **:** FUNNY, HUMOROUS ⟨dancing up to Bligh with such a ~ expression . . . that the tension was relieved —C.B. Nordhoff & J.N.Hall⟩ **3** *dial Eng* **a :** queer in the mind **:** ODD, CRACKED **b :** DISAGREEABLE, CAPRICIOUS, UNCERTAIN **c :** out of sorts **:** UNWELL **syn** see LAUGHABLE

com·i·cal·i·ty \,⸗⸗'kaləd·ē, -ətē, -i\ *n* -ES **:** comical quality; *also* **:** something comical

com·i·cal·ly \'kämək(ə)lē, -mēk-, -li\ *adv* **:** in a comical manner

com·i·cal·ness \-kəlnəs\ *n* -ES **:** COMICALITY

comic book *n* **:** a publication in pamphlet format containing one or more comics

comico- *comb form* [NL, fr. L *comicus* — more at COMIC] **:** comic **:** comic and ⟨*comico*tragedy⟩ ⟨*comico*didactic⟩

comic opera *n* [trans. of F *opéra comique*] **1 :** a musical dramatic work of an amusing nature with or without spoken dialogue **:** OPÉRA BOUFFE, OPERETTA **2 :** a farcical action or behavior on the stage or in life; *typically* **:** a false or absurd display of emotion or excitement

comic paper *n* **:** COMIC 3b

comic relief *n* **:** a relief of emotional or other tension resulting from a comic episode or item interposed in the midst of serious or tragic elements (as in a drama); *also* **:** something that causes such relief

comic spirit *n* **:** the spirit of comedy **:** the point of view of the comic **:** the attitude of one who represents or regards human complications as subjects for mirth

comic strip *n* **:** COMIC 3a

com·in·form·ist \'kämən,fōrməst, -ô(ə)m-\ *n* -s *usu cap* [*Cominform*, an international communist organization formed in 1947 (fr. *Com*munist *Inform*ation Bureau) + E *-ist*] **:** a member of the Russian Cominform organized to spread communism throughout the world

¹coming *n* -s [ME, fr. the gerund of *comen* to come] **:** an act or instance of approaching **:** APPROACH, ARRIVAL, ADVENT, MANIFESTATION

²coming *adj* [ME, fr. the pres. part. of *comen* to come] **:** that comes or is about to come: as **a :** APPROACHING ⟨a fine black studhorse ~ four this spring⟩ **:** lying in the near future **:** NEXT ⟨the ~ week or year⟩ **b** *archaic* **:** ready to offer or meet advances **:** FORWARD **c :** DUE, DESERVED — compare HAVE IT COMING **d :** on the way to attain importance or distinction — **coming and going :** with no escape **:** with no way out ⟨his lies put him in a position where she had him *coming and going*⟩ **:** HELPLESS, DEFENSELESS

coming in *n, pl* **comings in 1** *obs* **:** ENTRY, ENTRANCEWAY **2 :** ENTRANCE, BEGINNING **3 :** INCOME, REVENUE — usu. used in pl.

co·mingle \kə, kō+\ *vt* -ED/-ING/-S [*co-* + *mingle*] **:** COMMINGLE

coming-of-age \'⸗⸗⸗'⸗\ *n, pl* **comings-of-age :** the attainment of legal age; *broadly* **:** the reaching of maturity or the fullness of development ⟨the *coming-of-age* of jazz⟩

coming-on \'⸗⸗'⸗\ *adj* **:** YIELDING, COMPLIANT ⟨a more *coming-on* disposition —Shak.⟩

coming out *n, pl* **comings out :** ISSUANCE; *esp* **:** social debut

comings and goings *n pl* **:** AFFAIRS, DOINGS, ACTIVITIES

co·mi·no \kə'mē(,)nō\ *n* -s [Sp, fr. L *cuminum* — more at CUMIN] **:** CUMIN

co·mique \kō'mēk, kä'-,kə'-,kō'-\ *n* -s [F, fr. *comique*, adj., fr. L *comicus* — more at COMIC] **:** ²COMIC 1

comitadji *var of* KOMITADJI

com·i·tal \'kämәd·ᵊl\ *adj* [ML *comitalis*, fr. *comit-, comes* count (fr. L, companion, overseer, official) + *-alis* -al — more at COMES] **:** of, belonging to, or befitting a count or earl

co·mi·tas gen·ti·um \'kōmə,täs'gentēəm, 'kämə,tas'jench-(ē)əm\ *or* **comitas in·ter gen·tes** \-,sintər'gen·,täs, -ntə(r)-'jen·,tēz\ *n* [NL] **:** COMITY OF NATIONS

co·mi·tat \,kōmə;tät\ *n* -s [G *komitat*, fr. L *comitatus* retinue] **:** an administrative division or county in Hungary

com·i·ta·ten·sian \;kämətə;tenchən\ *adj* [LL *comitatensis* (fr. L *comitatus*) + E *-ian*] **:** of, belonging to, or relating to a comitatus

¹com·i·ta·tive \'kämə,tād·iv, -təd·-\ *adj* [L *comitatus* + E *-ive*] **:** expressing accompaniment ⟨~ case⟩

²comitative \"\ *n* -s *linguistics* **:** a comitative inflectional form or set of inflectional forms; *esp* **:** a comitative case

com·i·ta·tus \,kämə'tād·əs, -tād-\ *n* -ES [L, escort, retinue, imperial court, fr. *comit-, comes* companion + *-atus* -ate — more at COUNT] **1 :** a body of wellborn men attached to a king or chieftain by the duty of military service; *also* **:** the status of the body so attached **2** [ML, fr. L] **:** COUNTY — used chiefly in the phrase *posse comitatus*

comites *pl of* COMES

co·mi·tia \kə'mish(ē)ə\ *n, pl* **comitia** \[L, pl. of *comitium* assembly, assembly place, fr. *com-* + *-itium* (fr. *itus*, past part. of *ire* to go) — more at ISSUE] **:** an assembly at which the ancient Roman people acted on matters submitted by authorized officials

co·mi·tial \-shəl\ *adj* [L *comitialis*, fr. *comitium* + *-alis* -al] **:** of or relating to the Roman comitia

com·i·tje *var of* KOMMETJE

comi·tragedy \;kämə, -mē+\ *n* -ES [alter. of *tragicomedy*] **:** tragedy with a comedy element

com·i·ty \'kämәd·ē, -ətē, -i\ *n* -ES [L *comitat-, comitas*, fr. *comis* courteous (fr. OL *cosmis*, fr. *com-* + *-smis* — akin to Skt *smayate* he smiles) + *-tat-, -tas* -ty — more at SMILE] **1 :** kindly courteous behavior **:** friendly civility **:** mutual consideration between or as if between equals ⟨management should constantly point up every group activity until it actually promotes ~ —W.A.Hamor⟩: as **a :** courteous and friendly agreement and interaction between nations **b :** the informal and nonmandatory courtesy sometimes referred to as a set of rules to which the courts of one sovereignty often defer in determining questions (as of jurisdiction or applicable precedent) where the laws or interests of another sovereignty are involved **c :** the custom among Protestant churches of the U.S. of avoiding direct or indirect proselytizing of one another's members **2 :** association esp. for common and mutually pleasing purposes ⟨the honorable ~ of scholars in Phi Beta Kappa —*Key Reporter*⟩ ⟨a Europe which pretends to have founded its ~ upon brotherhood —Weston La Barre⟩

comity of nations *or* **comity of states** [trans. of NL *comitas gentium*] **1** *law* **:** the comity nations give effect to within their own territory **2 :** the friendly code whereby nations get along together

coml *abbr* commercial

com·ly *or* **comlye** *obs var of* COMELY

comm *abbr* — see COM

com·ma \'kämə\ *n* -s [LL & L; LL, comma (punctuation mark, musical interval) fr. L, part of a sentence, fr. Gk *komma* stamp, coinage, clause, fr. *koptein* to cut off, stamp — more at CAPON] **1 a** *pl also* **comma·ta** \-məd·ə\ **:** a short phrase or word group smaller than a colon **:** a fragment of a few words or feet — used of Greek and Latin prosody or rhetoric **b** *obs* **:** a clause or short section of a treatise or argument **2 a :** a punctuation mark, used esp. as a mark of separation within the sentence generally indicating a slight pause and appearing either singly to separate two related but distinct terms or in a pair, one at each end of a word, phrase, or clause, which the enclosing commas set off as an entity at the same time emphasizing the coherence of the preceding and following terms **b commas** *pl* **:** QUOTATION MARKS — compare INVERTED COMMA **3 :** PAUSE, INTERVAL **4 a :** a pause or break in the phrasing of a melodic line **b :** a mark indicating a pause for taking breath **5 :** a minute interval or difference in the pitches of the same musical tone occasioned by different systems of tuning — compare DITONIC COMMA, SYNTONIC COMMA

comma bacillus *also* **comma** *n* **:** a bacterium (*Vibrio comma* syn. *Spirillum cholerae asiaticae*) that causes Asiatic cholera

comma butterfly *also* **comma** *n* **:** a common No. American anglewing butterfly (*Polygonia comma*) having a silvery comma-shaped mark on the underside of the hind wings and larvae that feed on elm, nettles, and hop; *sometimes* **:** any of several other butterflies of the genus *Polygonia*

comma di·ton·i·cum \-,dī'tänəkəm\ *n, pl* **com·ma·ta di·ton·i·ca** \'kämәd·ə,dī'tänəkə\ [NL] **:** DITONIC COMMA

commadore *obs var of* COMMODORE

comma fault *n* **:** the careless or unjustified use of a comma between coordinate main clauses not connected by a conjunction — called also *comma splice*

¹com·mand \kə'mand, -maa(ə)nd,-mȧnd\ *vb* -ED/-ING/-S [ME *comanden*, fr. OF *comander* to command, commend, fr. (assumed) VL *commandare*, alter. (influenced by L *mandare* to commit to one's charge, order) of L *commendare* to commend, command — more at COMMEND] *vt* **1 :** to direct authoritatively **:** ORDER, ENJOIN ⟨the doctrine of that church ~*ed* man to love God with his whole soul —Stringfellow Barr⟩ **2 :** to exercise a dominating influence over **:** have within one's authority, control, or power: as **a :** to rule over, dominate, control, or govern authoritatively, without question or opposition ⟨England . . . had long ~*ed* the European market for raw wool —G.M.Trevelyan⟩ ⟨those young boys who have inherited great fortunes which they own but cannot ~ —Van Wyck Brooks⟩ **b :** to have at one's immediate bidding or disposal ⟨the produce of other men's labor which it enables him to purchase or ~ —Adam Smith⟩ **c :** to be able readily to call forth, evoke, exact, or compel, typically by some right or due ⟨the courage can scarcely fail to ~ our admiration —Virginia Woolf⟩ ⟨a successful pugilist ~*s* far higher terms for giving tuition in boxing than a tutor at one of the universities —G.B.Shaw⟩ **d :** to face, front on, or overlook so as to afford full view of ⟨the wide and peaceful rural landscape ~*ed* by the cottage —Joseph Conrad⟩ **e :** to dominate by strategic position, by fire, or by observation ⟨Fort Amsterdam, whose four bastions . . . ~*ed* both the North and East rivers —*Amer. Guide Series: N.Y. City*⟩ ⟨this island, which ~*s* one of the principal passages from the Atlantic to the Caribbean sea —F.J.Haskin⟩ **f :** to constitute the passageway or chief passageway to ⟨the hallway ~*s* the entrances to all the upstairs rooms⟩ **g :** to have military or naval command of as senior officer **h :** to hold the controlling cards of (a suit) in a card game **3 :** to cause or direct to come or go **:** SUMMON, DISPATCH, SEND ⟨I will ~ my blessing upon you —Lev 25:21 (RSV)⟩ **4** *obs* **:** to order or request to be given ~ *vi* **1 :** to have or to exercise direct authority **:** GOVERN **2 :** to give an order or orders **3 :** to be commander ⟨the general will ~ in person at the western front⟩ **4 :** to dominate as if from an elevated position ⟨far and wide his eye ~*s* —John Milton⟩

syn CHARGE, ORDER, ENJOIN, DIRECT, INSTRUCT, BID: in the meaning of issuing commands or orders, these words are often interchangeable. COMMAND is used in situations in which great or high authority is involved officially or formally ⟨as sovereign lord he can *command* —S.T.Coleridge⟩ ⟨the chairman *commands* the undertaking —Estes Kefauver⟩ CHARGE suggests a formal or solemn order with connotations of duty and responsibility ⟨the Marine Hospital service was *charged* with the duty of recommending for rejection immigrants afflicted with loathsome or contagious diseases —V.G.Heiser⟩ ⟨Gustavus . . . considered himself *charged* by God with the defense of the true Lutheran faith —Stringfellow Barr⟩ ORDER may indicate a specific or routine command or direction from one having due authority or right ⟨many of the managing posts will be filled up by pig-headed people only because they happen to have the habit of *ordering* poor people about —G.B. Shaw⟩ ENJOIN suggests an order or direction given authoritatively and urgently but with some admonition, sententiousness, or solicitude ⟨I *enjoin* upon all citizens to cooperate with the government in its endeavor to restore greater respect for law and order —F.D.Roosevelt⟩ ⟨St. Peter admirably *enjoins* us to be ready always to give an answer to every man that asks us a reason for the faith that is in us —J.L.Lowes⟩ DIRECT may suggest either a routine or an esp. mandatory order often on specific points of procedure or activity ⟨why otherwise does it [the Constitution] *direct* the judges to take an oath to support it? —John Marshall⟩ ⟨it is hoped that President Eisenhower will *direct* Ambassador Lodge to propose such action —*Nation*⟩ INSTRUCT may suggest an authoritative order, perhaps a formal one, delivered with care about its being fully understood ⟨"Don't waste oil", Miss Hannah had been *instructed* long ago —Margaret Deland⟩ ⟨Marvin was *instructed* . . . to uproot nothing until it was proved to have no remedial property —Mary Austin⟩ BID is likely to sound archaic or literary; it may indicate either a mild or a peremptory command ⟨the . . . Curate doth *bid* the Man to put a Ring on the Woman's fourth finger —George Meredith⟩ ⟨he seized him by the collar and sternly *bade* him cease making a fool of himself —G.B.Shaw⟩

²command \"\ *n* -s [MF *comand, comande*, fr. *comander*, v.] **1 :** the act of commanding ⟨the troops shall march at ~⟩ **2 a :** an order given **:** MANDATE, COMMANDMENT **b :** a word or phrase esp. in a set form by which an order is given ⟨at the ~ "halt" all troops will stop immediately⟩ **3 a :** the ability to control or the faculty of controlling **:** MASTERY ⟨the teacher has given evidence of ~ in her classes⟩ ⟨lose ~ of one's temper⟩ **b :** the authority or right to command conferred by official position ⟨the captain is in ~ of the ship⟩ **c** (1) **:** the power to dominate, control, or overlook ⟨the fort has ~ of the valley⟩ (2) **:** scope of vision **:** PROSPECT ⟨the tower provided a wide ~ of neighboring hills⟩ **d :** facility in use (as of a language) ⟨a good ~ of French⟩ **4 :** a body of persons (as military troops), an area, or a particular unit, usu. military, under one in command ⟨a top-ranking officer in the Middle East ~⟩ ⟨police put all ~*s* on alert against possible disorders or vandalism —*Springfield (Mass.) Union*⟩ — compare AIR COMMAND **5 :** height above the ground or the level commanded by a fortification or a gun **6 a :** the possession of the highest card or cards of a suit in a card game **b :** the highest card remaining unplayed in any suit **7** *contract bridge* **:** DEMAND BID **syn** see POWER — **at command :** ready to be commanded **:** available for service

³command \"\ *adj* **:** presented (as a stage play) or completed (as a study) as a result of a compelling command or request or of great need ⟨a ~ performance of the play for the queen⟩ ⟨a ~ study for the air force of the psychological makeup of good fliers⟩

com·man·dant \'kämən,dant, -dänt,-daa(ə)nt,-dȧnt, ,⸗⸗'⸗\ *n* -s [F, fr. pres. part of *commander*, fr. OF *comander*] **:** the commanding officer of a place or of a military group ⟨the ~ of a naval district⟩ ⟨the ~ of the U.S. Marine Corps⟩

command car *n* **:** an open armored motor vehicle intended for military staff and reconnaissance duties, usu. with radio, six forward speeds, and four-wheel drive

com·man·deer \,kämən'di(ə)r, -iə\ *vb* -ED/-ING/-S [Afrik *kommandeer*, fr. F *commander* to command, fr. OF *comander* — more at COMMAND] *vt* **1 a :** to compel to perform military service **b :** to seize for military purposes **2 :** to take arbitrary or forcible possession of ~ *vi* **:** to commandeer men or goods

com·mand·er \kə'mandə(r), -maan-,-man-\ *n* -s [ME *comander, comandour*, fr. OF *comandeor*, fr. *comander* + *-eor* -or] **1 :** one in an official position of command or control: as **a :** the chief officer in command of a military force or unit **b :** a naval executive officer in command of a ship, station, or installation **c :** a senior naval officer ranking just below a captain and above a lieutenant commander **d :** the administrator or chief officer of a commandery in a medieval religious military order **e :** the presiding officer of certain societies (as the Knights Templars) at the local, regional, or national level — used esp. in secret orders and veterans' organizations **f :** the ranking officer (as a lieutenant or captain) in charge of a division, a district, a precinct, or a squad in certain metropolitan police departments **g :** the officer in charge of a fire company in certain fire departments **2 :** a heavy beetle or wooden mallet **:** RAMMER **3 :** a member of one of the higher grades or divisions in certain honorary orders of knighthood (as the French Legion of Honor)

commander in chief *n, pl* **commanders in chief :** one who holds the supreme command of an armed force often including more than one service and sometimes more than one nation

com·mand·er·ship \-,ship\ *n* **:** the rank or title of commander

com·mand·ery *or* **com·mand·ry** \-d(ə)rē, -ri\ *n* -ES [MF *commanderie*, fr. ML *commendaria*, fr. *commenda* benefice (fr. *commendare* to commend) + *-aria* -ary — more at COMMEND] **1 :** the office or rank of a commander — now used only of orders of knighthood **2 a** (1) **:** a district or a manor with lands and tenements appertaining thereto under the control of a commander of a religious military order of knights **:** PRECEPTORY (2) **:** a pension or benefice attached to a commandership of an order of knighthood **b :** a conventual priory of a religious order **c :** the house of a medieval commandery **3 :** an assembly or lodge in certain secret orders (as the Knights Templars) **4 :** a district under the administration of a commander or governor

command-in-chief \⸗;⸗⸗;⸗\ *vt* **commanded-in-chief; commanded-in-chief; commanding-in-chief; commands-in-chief** [back-formation fr. *commander in chief*] **:** to serve as commander in chief of ⟨he was authorized to *command-in-chief* all the local militia⟩

commanding *adj* [ME *comanding*, fr. pres. part. of *comanden* to command] **:** that commands or has the air of command ⟨he sought a ~ position in all he did⟩ ⟨a ~ view of the valley⟩ ⟨a ~ appearance⟩ — **com·mand·ing·ly** *adv* — **com·mand·ing·ness** *n* -ES

commanding officer *n* **:** an officer in command **:** COMMANDER; *esp* **:** a military officer below the rank of brigadier general who is in command of an organization or installation

com·man·di·taire \kə,mandə;ta(a)(ə)r\ *n* -s [F, fr. *commandite* + *-aire* -ary] *French law* **:** a silent partner in a commandite

com·man·dite \;kämən;dēt, kōⁿmäⁿdēt\ *n* -s [F, fr. It. *accomandita*, fr. fem. of *accomandito*, past part of *accomandare* to deposit in safe custody, fr. *ad-* + (assumed) VL *commandare* to commend, command — more at COMMAND] *civil law* **:** a form of partnership in which there are one or more silent partners who contribute funds but were liable orig. only for the capital invested and later only according to a registered scheme of liability

com·mand·ment \kə'man(d)mənt, -'maan-,-'mȧn-\ *n* -s [ME *comandement*, fr. OF *comandement*, fr. *comander* + *-ment*] **:** the act of commanding, power of command, or what is commanded; *specif* **:** one of the biblical ten commandments

commandment keeper *n, cap C&K* **:** one of a Negro Jewish religious sect of the Harlem section of New York City that practices orthodox Judaism and teaches that Negroes are true Hebrews whose ancestry is traceable back through the kings of Ethiopia to King Solomon — called also *Black Jew*

com·man·do \kə'man(,)dō, -maan-,-mȧn-\ *n, pl* **commandos** *or* **commandoes** [Afrik *kommando* unit of militia, fr. D *commando* command, fr. Sp *comando*, fr. *comandar* to command, fr. F *commander*, fr. OF *comander* — more at COMMAND] **1** *Africa* **a** (1) **:** a raid or expedition — used esp. in the phrase *on commando* (2) **:** militia service in the Boer army **b** (1) **:** a military unit or command of the Boers (2) **:** a member of a Boer military unit **2 a** (1) **:** a military unit of specially trained amphibious shock troops organized for hit-and-run raids into enemy territory for sabotage, destruction of stores and communications, obtaining information, and seizure of captives (2) **:** a member of a commando unit or other specialized raiders' organization — compare RANGER **b** (1) **:** any body of troops (as of frontier fighters or guerrillas) or of insurrectionists or saboteurs that is felt to resemble a commando unit on account of some similarity of function or tactics (as that of engagement in hit-and-run raids) (2) **:** a member of such a body **c :** a raid or attack of the type characteristic of commando units

com·man·do·man \-(,)dō,man,-,dōmən\ *n, pl* **commando-men :** a member of a commando unit

command paper *n* [so called fr. its being by command of the Crown] **:** a document published by the British government or a department at public expense

command pennant *n, in the U.S. Navy* **:** a swallow-tailed pennant flown by an officer below flag rank who is temporarily in command of a division or of a comparable or greater unit — see BROAD COMMAND PENNANT, BURGEE COMMAND PENNANT

command pilot *n* **:** a U. S. Air Force pilot who has had at least 3000 hours in the air and not less than 15 years flying service

command post *n* **:** a post established by the headquarters of a unit at which orders for the command are received and from which the commander of the unit exercises command

command post exercise *n* **:** a field exercise participated in by command, staff, and communication personnel only

com·man·dress \-ndrəs\ *n* -ES [*commander* + *-ess*] **:** a female commander

commands *pres 3d sing of* COMMAND, *pl of* COMMAND

command sergeant major *n* **:** a noncommissioned officer in the army ranking above a first sergeant — see RANK table

commas *pl of* COMMA

comma splice *n* **:** COMMA FAULT

com·ma syn·to·num \ˈkäməˈsintᵊnləm, -ntən-\ *n, pl* **comma·ta syn·to·na** \-äməd·əˈs . . . |ə\ [LL] **:** SYNTONIC COMMA

commata *pl of* COMMA

com·mat·ic \kəˈmad·ik, (ˈ)käˌm-\ *adj* [LL *commat-, comma* musical comma + E *-ic*] **:** of or relating to a musical comma

comma tract *n* **:** a small tract medial to the lateral cervical and upper thoracic tract of the posterior white column of the spinal cord

com·mea·sur·able \kəˈmezh(ə)rəbəl, -māzh-\ *adj* [*com-* + *measurable*] **:** COMMENSURATE

com·mea·sure \-zhə(r)\ *vt* -ED/-ING/-S [*com-* + *measure*] **:** to be commensurate with **:** EQUAL

com·me·dia \kəˈmādēə, -med-\ *n* -S [It, fr. L *comoedia* — more at COMEDY] **1 :** COMEDY 2b **2** [by shortening] **:** COMMEDIA DELL'ARTE

commedia del·l'ar·te \-(ˌ)deˈlärd·ē\ *n, pl* **commedia dell'artes** *or* **commedias dell'arte** [It, lit., comedy of art] **:** Italian comedy as performed in the 16th to 18th centuries by companies of actors trained to improvise dialogue and business from a written plot built around standardized situations and certain stock characters — see ³COLUMBINE, PANTALOON

commedia eru·di·ta \-ˌerəˈdēd·ə, -ärü'-\ *n, pl* **commedia eruditas** *or* **commedias eruditas** [It, lit., erudite comedy] **:** Italian comedy played from a written text — compare COMMEDIA DELL'ARTE

comme il faut \ˌkəˌmēlˈfō\ *adj* [F, lit., as it should be] **:** conforming to accepted social usage **:** PROPER ⟨it never can have been *comme il faut* . . . for a man of note to be constantly asking for money —T.B.Macaulay⟩ **syn** see DECOROUS

com·me·li·na \ˌkäməˈlīnə, -lēnə\ *n* [NL, after Kaspar *Commelin* †1731 Dutch botanist] **1** *cap* **:** a large widely distributed genus (the type of the family Commelinaceae) of herbs of branching or creeping habit with flowers having one petal smaller than the other two **2** -S **:** any plant of the genus *Commelina*

commelina blue *n* **:** a moderate blue that is redder and duller than average copen, redder and stronger than azurite blue, and redder and deeper than Dresden blue

com·me·li·na·ce·ae \ˌkäməlˈnāsēˌē\ *n pl, cap* [NL, fr. *Commelina,* type genus + *-aceae*] **:** a large widely distributed family of herbaceous plants (order Xyridales) that have perfect flowers with a distinct calyx and corolla and upper leaves shaped like a spathe and that comprise the spiderworts — see COMMELINA, TRADESCANTIA — **com·me·li·na·ceous** \ˌkäməlˌīˈnāshəs\ *adj*

com·mem \kəˈmem\ *n* -S [by shortening] **1** *slang Brit* **:** COMMEMORATION **2 :** a commemorative postage stamp

com·mem·o·ra·ble \kəˈmem(ə)rəbəl\ *adj* [F *commémorable,* fr. L *commemorabilis,* fr. *commemorare* + *-abilis* -able] **:** worthy of being commemorated

com·mem·o·rate \kəˈmeməˌrāt, *usu* -ād·+V\ *vt* -ED/-ING/-S [L *commemoratus,* past part. of *commemorare* to remind of, mention, fr. *com-* + *memorare,* fr. *memor* mindful — more at MEMORY] **1 :** to call to remembrance (as by speech, writing, or ceremony) **:** make mention of — now chiefly in ecclesiastical use **2 :** to mark by some ceremony or observation **:** CELEBRATE, OBSERVE ⟨~ a holiday⟩ ⟨~ an anniversary⟩ **3 :** to be a memorial of **:** preserve the remembrance of ⟨a tablet ~*s* his patriotic activities⟩ **syn** see KEEP

com·mem·o·ra·tion \kəˌmeməˈrāshən\ *n* -S [ME *commemoracioun,* fr. L *commemoration-, commemoratio,* fr. *commemoratus* + *-ion-, -io* -ion] **1 :** the act of commemorating **2 :** something that commemorates (as a speech, statue, or ceremony); *specif* **:** a church service to commemorate a saint or sacred event — **com·mem·o·ra·tion·al** \kəˌmeməˈrāshənᵊl, -shnəl\ *adj*

¹com·mem·o·ra·tive \kəˈmem(ə)rəd·iv, -məˌrā|, |tiv, -ēv *also* -əv\ *adj* [F *commémoratif,* fr. MF, fr. *commémoration* (fr. L *commemoration-, commemoratio*) + *-if* -ive] **:** commemorating or intended as a commemoration ⟨a ~ speech in his honor⟩; *specif* **:** issued temporarily in commemoration of some notable event and bearing a design and inscription symbolizing that event ⟨a ~ stamp⟩ — **com·mem·o·ra·tive·ly** *adv*

²commemorative \"\ *n* -S **:** something commemorative; *specif* **:** a commemorative coin or postage stamp

com·mem·o·ra·tor \-eməˌrād·ə(r), -ātə-\ *n* -S [LL, fr. L *commemoratus* + *-or*] **:** one that commemorates

com·mem·o·ra·to·ry \-em(ə)rəˌtōrē, -tȯr-, -ri\ *adj* [*commemorate* + *-ory*] **:** COMMEMORATIVE

com·mence \kəˈmen(t)s\ *vb* -ED/-ING/-S [ME *comencen,* fr. MF *comencer,* fr. (assumed) VL *cominitiare,* fr. L *com-* + LL *initiare* to begin, fr. L, to initiate — more at INITIATE] *vt* **1 :** to enter upon **:** BEGIN, START ⟨~ a literary career⟩ ⟨~ to buy securities⟩ ⟨they sat down and tried to ~ a conversation —George Meredith⟩ **2 :** to initiate formally by performing the first act of ⟨~ legal proceedings⟩ **~** *vi* **1 :** to have a beginning **:** BEGIN, START, ORIGINATE ⟨the program *commenced* with a prayer⟩ ⟨the debate will ~ on Tuesday⟩ **2 :** to begin to be **:** begin to act as **:** assume a role or function as **3** *chiefly Brit* **:** to take a degree at a university — usu. used with prepositional phrase indicating the faculty ⟨~ in arts⟩ or with a complement indicating the degree ⟨~ doctor⟩ **syn** see BEGIN

com·mence·ment \-mənt\ *n* -S [ME *commencement, comencement,* fr. OF *comencement,* fr. *comencer* + *-ment*] **1 :** the act, fact, or time of commencing (as of an era, season, career, or event) **2 a :** the ceremonies at which or the day when degrees or diplomas are conferred by an educational institution **b :** the period of festivities at this time **3 :** the part of a legal declaration that gives the parties and the capacities in which they sue or are sued and the necessary facts as to the summoning of the defendant and the form of action

com·mend \kəˈmend\ *vb* -ED/-ING/-S [ME *commenden,* fr. L *commendare* to entrust, recommend, command, fr. *com-* + *-mendare* (fr. *mandare* to commit to one's charge, order) — more at MANDATE] *vt* **1 :** to commit, entrust, or give in charge for care or preservation ⟨Father, into thy hands I ~ my spirit —Lk 23:46 (AV)⟩ **2 a :** to recommend as worthy of confidence or regard **:** present as worthy of notice or favorable attention ⟨I ~ to you our sister Phoebe —Rom 16:1 (RSV)⟩ **b** *obs* **:** OFFER ⟨I ~ my duty to your lordship —Shak.⟩ **3 :** to mention with approbation **:** PRAISE ⟨they refer to what I am not in the habit of doing and they ~ me —S.M.Crothers⟩ **4** *archaic* **:** to mention with kindly remembrance and good will ⟨~ me to my son —William Robertson †1793⟩ **5** *obs* **:** to set off advantageously **:** GRACE, ADORN **6** *obs* **:** to bestow in commendam **7** *in the feudal system* **:** to commit or place as vassal under the protection of a lord — used of oneself or of land **~** *vi* **:** to commend or serve as a commendation of something — **commend me to :** give me by preference ⟨of all the homes I have been in *commend me to* my own home and fireside⟩

com·men·da \kəˈmendə\ *n* -S [ML, back-formation fr. L *commendare* to entrust, command] **1 :** a form of trust in use in the middle ages in which goods are delivered to another for a particular enterprise (as for marketing abroad) **2 :** COMMENDAM **3 :** the insignia, title, rights, or stipend of membership in a medieval order of chivalry

com·mend·able \kəˈmendəbəl, *archaic* ¦kämənˈdāb-\ *adj* [MF, fr. L *commendabilis,* fr. *commendare* + *-abilis* -able] *adj* **:** worthy of being commended **:** LAUDABLE — **com·mend·able·ness** *n* -ES

com·mend·ably \-dəblē, -li\ *adv* **:** in a commendable manner

com·men·dam \kəˈmenˌdam\ *n* -S [ML, accus. of *commenda* trust (as used in the phrase *dare in commendam* to give in trust)] **1 a :** the custody or holding of a benefice by a cleric or a layman to whom it is given in charge often only until a proper incumbent is provided **b :** the enjoyment of the revenues from such a custody or holding **2 :** a benefice held in commendam

com·men·da·tion \ˌkäˌmenˈdāshən, -mən-\ *n* -S [ME *commendacioun,* fr. MF *commendation,* fr. L *commendation-, commendatio,* fr. *commendatus* + *-ion-, -io* -ion] **1 a :** the act of commending **:** the expression of approval **b :** something that commends ⟨good nature is the most godlike ~ of man —John Dryden⟩; *specif* **:** an award (as to a military unit) for distinction in operations ⟨a meritorious unit ~⟩ **2** *archaic* **:** a message of affection or respect **:** COMPLIMENT, GREETING — usu. used in pl. **3 :** an office commending to God the souls of the dead or dying **4 :** the act of placing as a vassal under the protection of a lord **:** VASSALAGE **5 a :** the act of giving a benefice in commendam **b :** the state of a commendam

com·men·da·tor \ˈ≈(ˌ)≈ˌdād·ə(r)\ *n* -S [ML *commendator* commander, fr. L *commendatus* (past part. of *commendare* to entrust, recommend command) + *-or* — more at COMMEND] **1 :** one who holds a benefice in commendam **2 :** COMMENDATORE

com·men·da·to·re \kəˌmendəˈtōrē, (ˌ)käˌm-\ *n* -S [It, fr. ML *commendator*] **:** a member of an Italian honorary order of chivalry who ranks next above an officer and next below a grand officer

¹com·men·da·to·ry \kəˈmendəˌtōrē, -tȯr-, -ri\ *adj* [LL *commendatorius,* fr. L *commendatus* (past part. of *commendare* to recommend) + *-orius* -ory — more at COMMEND] **1 :** of, relating to, or serving for commendation **2** [alter. of earlier *commendatary,* adj., fr. ML *commendatarius,* fr. L *commendatus* + *-arius* -ary] **:** holding or held in commendam

²commendatory *n* -ES **1** *obs* **:** COMMENDATION, EULOGY **2** *obs* **:** a knight commander of an order of chivalry **3** *obs* **:** COMMENDATOR 1 **4** *obs* **:** COMMANDERY 2a **5** *archaic* **:** COMMENDAM 1

commendatory letter *n* **:** a letter of commendation; *specif* **:** a letter of introduction testifying to an individual's good standing in a church and given by a bishop to a traveling member of his diocese or to a cleric transferring to another diocese

com·mend·ing·ly *adv* **:** in a commending manner

¹com·men·sal \kəˈmen(t)səl\ *adj* [ME, fr. ML *commensalis,* fr. L *com-* + LL *mensalis* of the table, fr. L *mensa* table + *-alis* -al — more at MENSA] **1 :** of or relating to those who habitually eat together ⟨~ pleasures⟩ **2** *biol* **:** living in a state of commensalism — **com·men·sal·ly** \-səlē\ *adv*

²commensal \"\ *n* -S [ME, fr. *commensal,* adj.] **1 :** one who eats at the same table with others **:** MESSMATE **2** *biol* **:** an organism living in a state of commensalism

com·men·sal·ism \-ˌlizəm\ *n* -S **1 :** the relation existing between two kinds of organisms in which one obtains food, protection, or other benefits from the other without damaging or benefiting it — compare PARASITISM, SYMBIOSIS **2 :** intimate association in a social group esp. at meals

com·men·sal·ist \-ləst\ *n* -S **:** COMMENSAL 1 — **com·men·sal·is·tic** \kəˌmen(t)səˈlistik\ *adj*

com·men·sal·i·ty \ˌkäˌmenˈsaləd·ē\ *n* -ES **1 a :** the practice of eating together **b :** a social group that eats together **2 :** COMMENSALISM

com·men·su·ra·bil·i·ty \kəˌmen(t)s(ə)rəˈbiləd·ē *also* -mench(ə)-\ *n* -ES [MF *commensurabilité,* fr. *commensurable* + *-ité* -ity] **:** the quality or state of being commensurable

com·men·su·ra·ble \≈ˈ≈(≈)rəbəl\ *adj* [MF or LL; MF *commensurable,* fr. LL *commensurabilis,* fr. L *com-* + LL *mensurabilis* measurable, fr. *mensurare* to measure, fr. L *mensura* measure — more at MEASURE] **1 :** having a common measure; *specif* **:** divisible by a common measure or unit an integral number of times ⟨10 and 25 are ~ since they have 5 as a common divisor⟩ **2 :** COMMENSURATE 2 ⟨the two punishments must be perfectly ~ —Jeremy Bentham⟩ — **com·men·su·ra·bly** \-blē\ *adv*

com·men·su·rate \kəˈmen(t)s(ə)rət *also* -mench(ə)-; *usu* -əd·+V\ *adj* [LL *commensuratus* equal, fr. L *com-* + LL *mensuratus,* past part. of *mensurare* to measure] **1 :** equal in measure or extent **:** COEXTENSIVE ⟨the life of Burleigh was ~ with one of the most important periods —T.B.Macaulay⟩ ⟨iron has defects almost ~ with its virtues —Lewis Mumford⟩ **2 :** corresponding in size, extent, amount, or degree **:** PROPORTIONATE ⟨an income ~ with his needs⟩ ⟨the child was started in a grade ~ with his mental ability —F.H.Allen⟩ **3** *archaic* **:** corresponding in nature **:** of the same sphere of phenomena **:** essentially interrelated **4 :** COMMENSURABLE 1 — **com·men·su·rate·ly** *adv* — **com·men·su·rate·ness** *n* -ES

com·men·su·ra·tion \kəˌmen(t)səˈrāshən *also* -menchə'-\ *n* -S [MF, fr. LL *commensuration, commensuratio,* fr L *com-* + LL *mensuration-, mensuratio* act of measuring — more at MENSURATION] **1 :** the measuring of things in comparison with one another **2 :** the state of being proportionate ⟨fitness lies in a particular ~ . . . of one thing to another —Robert South⟩

¹com·ment \ˈkäˌment *sometimes* -mənt\ *n* -S [ME, commentary, exposition, fr. LL *commentum* commentary, fr. L, invention, contrivance, fr. neut. of *commentus,* past part. of *comminisci* to invent, contrive, devise, fr. *com-* + *-minisci* (fr. the root of *ment-, mens* mind) — more at MIND] **1 :** an expository treatise **:** COMMENTARY **2 a :** a note or observation intended to explain, illustrate, or criticize the meaning of a writing **:** ANNOTATION ⟨~*s* upon the passage were printed in the margin⟩ **b :** the whole body of such matter ⟨two pages of ~ for every page of text⟩ **3 a :** an observation or remark expressing an opinion or attitude concerning what has been seen or heard or concerning the subject at hand ⟨she listens, and puts in from time to time some critical ~ —Rose Macaulay⟩ **b :** discussion, interpretation, or expression of opinion or attitude ⟨the paper also gave ~ on the news in signed editorials —Jacques Kayser⟩ **:** CRITICISM ⟨the brown tweeds, sir, . . . would have occasioned unfavorable ~ —T.S.Watt⟩ **4 :** a critical observation, interpretation, or expression of opinion conveyed by suggestion, implication, analogy, or other indirect means ⟨the painting is a ~ on the subject's character⟩ ⟨the film is an ironic ~ on the industrial age⟩

²comment \" *sometimes* käˈment\ *vb* -ED/-ING/-S *vi* **:** to explain or interpret by comment **:** make or write comment **:** REMARK, OBSERVE ⟨neither could be induced . . . to ~ during general discussions —Victor Boesen⟩ ⟨~*ing* on the situation in the West⟩ **~** *vt* **1 :** to furnish (a written work) with comments **:** explain or interpret by comment **:** ANNOTATE ⟨translated and ~*ed* the Psalter —G.G.Coulton⟩ **2 :** to make a comment on **:** DISCUSS, CRITICIZE ⟨the discovery . . . is hardly ~*ed* by the press —*Nation*⟩

com·men·tary \ˈkämənˌterē, -ri\ *n* -ES [L *commentarius, commentarium* notebook, commentary, fr. *commentari* to meditate upon (freq. of *comminisci* to invent, contrive, devise) + *-arius, -arium* -ary (n. suffix) — more at COMMENT] **1 a :** a treatise in explanation of some subject — usu. used in pl. ⟨Blackstone's *Commentaries*⟩ **b :** a record of a set of events usu. written by a participant and marked by less formality and elaborateness than a history — usu. used in pl. ⟨Caesar's *Commentaries on the Gallic War*⟩ **2 a :** a systematic series of explanations or interpretations of the text of a writing ⟨a ~ on Dante's *Divine Comedy*⟩ ⟨*commentaries* on the Scriptures⟩ **b :** COMMENT 2a **c :** a spoken description or series of comments accompanying a motion picture or other exhibition **3 a :** something that serves for illustration or explanation ⟨godly persons . . . whose lives might be a fitting ~ on their teaching —W.H.Prescott⟩ **:** a fact or piece of evidence that explains or illustrates a condition or characteristic ⟨the dark, airless apartments and sunless factories . . . are a sad ~ upon our civilization —H.A.Overstreet⟩ **b :** an observation or interpretation conveyed by suggestion, implication, analogy, or other indirect means ⟨both books are *commentaries* with tragic or ironic overtones on certain social groups⟩ ⟨a scene that is a gem of satiric ~ on the world of art —Rose Feld⟩ **4 :** the act of commenting

com·men·tate \ˈkämənˌtāt, -ˌmen-\ *vb* -ED/-ING/-S [back formation fr. *commentator*] *vt* **1 :** to write a commentary upon (as a text) **2 :** to deliver an oral commentary upon (as a fashion show or other exhibition) **~** *vi* **:** COMMENT; *specif* **:** to act as a commentator

com·men·ta·tion \ˌkämənˈtāshən, -ˌmen-\ *n* -S [MF or L; MF, commentary, fr. L *commentation-, commentatio* meditation, treatise, fr. *commentatus* (past part. of *commentari* to meditate upon) + *-ion-, -io* -ion] **1** *obs* **:** a commentary esp. on a text **2** *archaic* **:** the act of commenting **:** interpretation or expression of opinion

com·men·ta·tive \ˈkämənˌtād·iv, käˈmentəd·-\ *adj* [¹*comment* + *-ative*] **:** of or concerning comment or commentary

com·men·ta·tor \ˈkämənˌtād·ə(r), -ātə- *also* -ˌmen-\ *n* -S [LL, fr. L, deviser, contriver, fr. *commentatus* + *-or*] **:** one who comments or makes a commentary: as **a :** one who writes a commentary (as on a literary text) **:** ANNOTATOR **b :** one who reports and discusses current events or daily news esp. on radio or television usu. with interpretation and analysis — called also *news analyst* — **com·men·ta·to·ri·al** \ˌkäˌmentəˈtōrēəl, käˌm-\ *adj*

com·men·ti·tious \ˌkämənˈtishəs\ *adj* [L *commenticius, commentitius,* fr. *commentus* (past part. of *comminisci* to invent, contrive, devise) + *-icius, -itius* -itious — more at COMMENT] *archaic* **:** fictitious or imaginary **:** feigned or lying

¹com·merce \ˈkä(ˌ)mərs, -ˌməs, -ˌmə̄s, -ˌməis\ *n* -S [MF, fr. L *commercium,* fr. *com-* + *merc-, merx* merchandise — more at MARKET] **1 a :** social intercourse **:** dealings between individuals or groups in society **:** interchange of ideas, opinions, or sentiments ⟨their ~ with the ancients appears to me to produce . . . a steadying . . . effect upon their judgment —Matthew Arnold⟩ **b :** dealings of any kind ⟨their conviction that art has no ~ with morality —C.J.Glicksberg⟩ **:** interrelationship, connection, or communication ⟨the ~ between our intellectual . . . interests and the nature of experience —Herbert Feigl & W.S.Sellars⟩ **2 a :** the exchange or buying and selling of commodities esp. on a large scale and involving transportation from place to place — compare TRADE, TRAFFIC **b commerces** *pl, obs* **:** commercial transactions **3 :** mental or spiritual intercourse or relationship **:** COMMUNION ⟨so hold I ~ with the dead —Alfred Tennyson⟩ **4** *obs* **:** an exchange (as of letters) ⟨a ~ of letters between friends⟩ **5 :** SEXUAL INTERCOURSE **6** *obs* **:** means of communication **:** PASSAGE **7 :** an old card game similar to whiskey poker in which each player in succession may exchange one of his three cards for another card until some one refuses, whereupon the best hand wins

²com·merce \", kəˈmərs, käˈ-, -ˈməs,-ˈməis\ *vi* -ED/-ING/-S [MF *commercer,* fr. *commerce,* n.] **:** to hold personal intercourse or communication **:** COMMUNE — used with *with* ⟨less disposed to ~ with my kind —Cornelius Weygandt⟩

com·merce·less *pronunc at* ¹COMMERCE +ləs\ *adj* **:** lacking commerce

commercia *pl of* COMMERCIUM

com·mer·cia bel·li \kəˌmərsh(ē)əˈbeˌlī, -(ˌ)lē; kəˌmerkēəˈbeˌlē\ *n pl* [NL, fr. L, pl. of *commercium belli* stipulation, treaty, lit., intercourse of war] **:** agreements between enemy states (as truces, capitulations, safe-conducts, and cartels)

¹com·mer·cial \kəˈmərshəl, -məsh-, -məish-\ *adj* [¹*commerce* + *-ial*] **1 :** of, in, or relating to commerce: as **a :** occupied with or engaged in commerce ⟨a ~ establishment⟩ ⟨the ~ world⟩ **b :** related to or dealing with commerce ⟨~ treaty⟩ **c :** used in or characteristic of commerce ⟨~ weights⟩ ⟨~ language⟩ ⟨~ ethics⟩ **d :** suitable to or adequate for commerce ⟨found oil in ~ quantities⟩ **e (1) :** of the kind or quality used in commerce **(2) :** of an average or inferior quality ⟨~ oxalic acid⟩ ⟨~ grade of beef⟩ — compare TECHNICAL **f :** produced or producible in large quantities for commerce ⟨relying on a balanced diet rather than ~ vitamin concentrates⟩ **2 a :** from the point of view of profit **:** having profit as the primary aim ⟨~ success⟩ ⟨~ failure⟩ ⟨~ aspect⟩ **b :** sacrificing artistic principles for qualities that bring financial success ⟨~ drama⟩ ⟨~ music⟩ **3** *of a school, a course, or a curriculum* **:** emphasizing skills and subjects considered useful in business occupations — compare BUSINESS EDUCATION, GENERAL **4 :** paid for by an advertiser — used esp. of a radio or television program

²commercial \"\ *n* -S **1** *Brit* **:** TRAVELING SALESMAN **2 a :** an advertisement broadcast during a sponsored radio or television program or between programs **b :** a radio or television program sponsored by an advertiser

commercial agency *n* **:** MERCANTILE AGENCY 2

commercial arbitration *n* **:** arbitration by which disputes arising out of business contracts or transactions may be settled out of court by a special tribunal

commercial art *n* **:** art applied to commercial purposes

commercial attaché *n* **:** an officer in the foreign commerce service of a country who is attached to an embassy or legation in those countries considered important for trade or business

commercial bank *n* **:** a bank including in its functions the acceptance of demand deposits subject to withdrawal by check

commercial blanket bond *n* **:** a fidelity bond or form of insurance issued to business firms that covers all losses due to theft by employees

commercial club *n* **:** CHAMBER OF COMMERCE

commercial code *n* **:** a code designed to achieve brevity or economy of words esp. in order to save telegraph tolls

commercial control *n* **:** insect pest control or crop disease control that is incomplete but adequate to prevent large losses

commercial credit *n* **:** credit granted by a bank to a business concern to finance commercial transaction

commercial credit company *n* **:** a finance company engaged in lending on or buying up accounts receivable or discounting installment contracts

commercial feed *n* **:** any mixed ration for animal feeding offered for sale on the open market

commercial fertilizer *n* **:** a manufactured chemical mixture prepared for use as fertilizer as distinguished from such natural substances as farm manures

commercial geography *n* **:** geography that deals with commodities according to their places of origin and their paths of transportation

commercial hotel *n* **:** a hotel for transients that caters esp. to salesmen (as by providing rooms for the display of samples)

com·mer·cial·ism \-ˌlizəm\ *n* -S **1 :** commercial spirit, institutions, or methods ⟨the vigor of the ~ of New England . . . led . . . to the conflict between Britain and the . . . colonies —W.A.Mackintosh⟩ **2 :** excessive emphasis on profit or financial success ⟨the new ~, the aim to "show results" that was undermining and vulgarizing education —Willa Cather⟩

com·mer·cial·ist \-ləst\ *n* -S **:** one engaged in commerce or devoted to commercialism

com·mer·cial·is·tic \≈ˌ≈shəˈlistik, -tēk\ *adj* **:** marked or motivated by a desire to accumulate wealth through business pursuits

com·mer·cial·i·ty \kəˌmərshēˈaləd·ē, ˌkäˌmərˈshal-\ *n* -ES **:** commercial quality

com·mer·cial·i·za·tion \kəˌmərsh(ə)ləˈzāshən, -məsh-, -məish-, -shəˌlīˈz-\ *n* -S **:** the act of commercializing or the state resulting from such action

com·mer·cial·ize \≈ˈ≈shəˌlīz\ *vt* -ED/-ING/-S **1 a :** to subject to the conditions of commerce **:** make into a form of trade ⟨agriculture . . . has been . . . *commercialized* and become a branch of trade —James Bryce⟩ **b :** to develop commerce in ⟨a highly *commercialized* country⟩ **:** organize for increased commercial efficiency or effectiveness ⟨*commercialized* vice⟩ **2 :** to cause (something having only a potential income-producing value) to be sold, manufactured, displayed, or utilized so as to yield income ⟨raise capital to ~ his invention⟩ ⟨only two of the five caves have been *commercialized*⟩ **3 :** to engage in, conduct, practice, or make use of for profit-seeking purposes as distinguished from participation, practice, or use for spiritual or recreational purposes or for other nonpecuniary satisfactions ⟨~ the celebration of Christmas⟩ ⟨bitterly opposed to *commercialized* Sunday sports⟩ **4 a :** to debase in quality, make more conventional and unoriginal, or employ for inferior purposes in the hope of securing a greater or more certain profit ⟨our somewhat *commercialized* theater —*Amer. Mercury*⟩ ⟨or he may give up poetry for some more popular form of literary entertainment — that is to say, he ~*s* his talent —Herbert Read⟩ **b :** to affect through commercialism so as to debase in quality or make more conventional and unoriginal ⟨our *commercialized* taste —S.H.Horton⟩

commercial law *n* **:** the legal rules or principles bearing esp. on commercial transactions and comprising matters of partnership, joint stock companies, agency, negotiable paper, contracts with carriers, insurance, sale, bottomry and respondentia, debt, guaranty, stoppage in transitu, lien, and bankruptcy

com·mer·cial·ly \-shəlē, -li\ *adv* **:** in a commercial manner

commercial paper *n* **1 :** short-term negotiable instruments (as bills of exchange, checks, and promissory notes) arising out of commercial transactions; *esp* **:** instruments constituting direct obligations of business firms that are sold through note brokers to banks, corporations, and other investors seeking liquid investments **2 commercial papers** *pl, in Universal Postal Union regulations* **:** pieces of mail matter in a classification comprising business papers and documents and including old correspondence, invoices, and bills of lading that have previously served their purpose and are not at the time of shipment being sent as current personal correspondence

commercial pilot *n* **:** a pilot who operates an airplane for transportation of mail, passengers, or freight or for other commercial purposes

commercial policy *n* **:** an accident or health and accident insurance policy sold to persons in such less hazardous occupations as clerical work, business administration, sales, and teaching

commercial room *n, Brit* **:** a public hotel room for use by traveling salesmen

commercials *pl of* COMMERCIAL

commercial traveler *n* **:** TRAVELING SALESMAN

commercial treaty *n* **:** a treaty that defines the conditions under which citizens of one country may do business in another and covers such matters as the right to hold property, mode of enforcing claims, and tariff privileges

commercial vehicle *n* **:** a vehicle that is designed for commercial use (as the transportation of cargo other than passengers)

commercing *pres part of* COMMERCE

com·mer·cium \kə'mərsh(ē)əm\ *n, pl* **commer·cia** \-(ē)ə\ [L — more at COMMERCE] *Roman law* **:** COMMERCE, TRAFFIC **:** commercial transaction **:** business intercourse; *also* **:** JUS COMMERCII

com·merge \kə'mərj, kä'-\ *vb* -ED/-ING/-S [*com-* + *merge*] **:** MERGE

com·mers *or* **kom·mers** *also* **com·merz** \kȯ'mers\ *n* -ES *often cap* [G *kommers,* fr. G dial. *kommers, kommersch* social intercourse, noisy social activity, fr. F *commerce* commerce — more at COMMERCE] **:** a social gathering of students in German universities

[1]**com·mie** *or* **com·my** \'kämē, -mi\ *also* **com·mon·ey** \-mənē, -ni\ *n, pl* **commies** *also* **commoneys** [*commie* & *commy* prob. by shortening & alter. fr. *common* (as in *common marble*); *commoney* fr. *common* + *-ey* (var. of *-y*)] **:** a playing marble made of clay

[2]**commie** *also* **com·my** \'kämē, -mi\ *n, pl* **commies** *often cap* [by shortening and alter.] **:** COMMUNIST 3

com·mi·nate \'kämə,nāt\ *vb* -ED/-ING/-S [back-formation fr. *commination*] **:** to threaten with divine punishment

com·mi·na·tion \,kämə'nāshən\ *n* -S [ME *comminacioun,* fr. MF or L; MF *commination,* fr. L *commination-, comminatio,* fr. *comminatus* (past part. of *comminari* to threaten, fr. *com-* + *minari* to threaten) + *-ion-, -io* -ion — more at MOUNT] **1 a :** an instance or the action of announcing, warning of, or threatening punishment or vengeance, esp. divine punishment or vengeance **b :** DENUNCIATION **:** ANATHEMA ⟨those thunderous ~*s,* that jeering and abuse which make Milton's prose such lively reading —Aldous Huxley⟩ **2 :** a recital of God's anger and judgments against sinners read in the Church of England esp. after the litany on Ash Wednesday; *also* **:** the penitential office which contains this recital

com·mi·na·to·ry \'kämənə,tōrē, kə'min-, kə'mīn-\ *adj* [ML *comminatorius,* fr. L *comminatus* + *-orius* -ory] **1 :** conveying warning or threat of punishment or vengeance **2 :** DENUNCIATORY ⟨had nothing sensible and ~ to say against her —Rebecca West⟩

com·min·gle \kə'miŋgəl, kä'-\ *vb* -ED/-ING/-S [*com-* + *mingle*] *vi* **:** to mingle or mix together ⟨the *commingling* in him of earthiness and sophistication —Robert Pick⟩ ~ *vt* **1 :** to mix together ⟨savage ridicule, *commingled* with resentment —Jean Stafford⟩ **2 :** to combine (the funds or property of several individuals) into a common fund or stock (as for convenience of investment by a trust company) **syn** *see* MIX

com·min·gler \-g(ə)lə(r)\ *n* -S **:** a device for noiseless heating of water by steam in a vessel filled with a porous mass (as of pebbles)

[1]**com·mi·nute** \'kämə,n(y)üt\ *vt* -ED/-ING/-S [L *comminutus,* past part. of *comminuere,* fr. *com-* + *minuere* to lessen — more at MINOR] **:** to reduce to minute particles or fine powder **:** PULVERIZE, TRITURATE; *specif* **:** to break up, chop, or grind (as meat or cheese) into small particles

[2]**comminute** \"\ *adj* [L *comminutus*] **:** COMMINUTED

comminuted fracture *n* **:** a fracture in which the bone is splintered or crushed into numerous pieces

com·mi·nu·tion \,kämə'n(y)üshən\ *n* -S [L *comminutus* + E *-ion*] **1 :** the act or action of comminuting or the fact of being comminuted **:** TRITURATION, PULVERIZATION **2 :** gradual diminution by the removal of small particles at a time **:** wearing away **:** LESSENING ⟨natural and necessary ~ of our lives —Samuel Johnson⟩ **3 :** fracture (as of a bone) into a number of pieces

com·mi·nu·tor \-üd·ə(r)\ *n* -S [[1]*comminute* + *-or*] **:** a machine that cuts up solids in raw sewage in preparation for purifying treatment

com·miph·o·ra \kə'mifərə\ *n, cap* [NL, fr. Gk *kommi* gum + NL *-phora* — more at GUM] **:** a large genus of East Indian and African trees (family Burseraceae) yielding balsamic products (as the resins of *C. schimperi* of Abyssinia, *C. kataf* of Arabia, and others that are used as substitutes for myrrh) — see BALM OF GILEAD, MYRRH

com·mis \,kə'mē, kȯ'-\ *n, pl* **commis** \-ē(z)\ [F, fr. *commis* (past part. of *commettre* to commit, entrust), fr. L *commissus,* past part. of *committere* to connect, entrust — more at COMMIT] **:** DEPUTY, ASSISTANT, CLERK

com·mis·cu·um \kə'miskyəwəm\ *n, pl* **commis·cua** \-wə\ *also* **commiscuums** \-wəmz\ [NL, fr. L, neut. of *commiscuus* common, fr. *commiscere* to mix together — more at COMMIX] **:** a subdivision of a comparium comprising organisms that can interbreed to produce fertile hybrids and being usu. equivalent in scope to a taxonomic species

com·mis·er·a·ble \kə'miz(ə)rəbəl\ *adj* [*commiserate* + *-able*] **:** PITIABLE

[1]**com·mis·er·ate** \kə'mizə,rāt, *usu* -ād·+V\ *vb* -ED/-ING/-S [L *commiseratus,* past part. of *commiserari,* fr. *com-* + *miserari* to pity, fr. *miser* wretched] *vt* **:** to feel or express sorrow, pain, or compassion for **:** express pity for **:** PITY ⟨*commiserating* the state of her poor friend —Jane Austen⟩ ~ *vi* **:** CONDOLE, SYMPATHIZE — used with *with* ⟨set up an altar in the reception room, *commiserated* with the war criminals and their visiting relatives —*Time*⟩

[2]**com·mis·er·ate** \-z(ə)rət, *usu* -əd·+V\ *adj* [L *commiseratus*] **:** showing commiseration ⟨the first ~ touch of a smile —H.E. Bates⟩ — **com·mis·er·ate·ly** *adv*

com·mis·er·a·tion \kə,mizə'rāshən\ *n* -S [MF *commisération,* fr. L *commiseration-, commiseratio* part of an oration intended to excite compassion, fr. *commiseratus* + *-ion-, -io* -ion] **:** the act of commiserating **:** the feeling or showing of sorrow or the expression of condolence for the wants or distresses of another ⟨an adult who falls on the street is the object of . . . ~ —Agnes Repplier⟩ **syn** *see* SYMPATHY

com·mis·er·a·tive \kə'mizə,rād·iv, -z(ə)rəl, -tiv\ *adj* **:** given to commiseration **:** COMPASSIONATE ⟨made ~ clicking sounds with his tongue —Kenneth Roberts⟩

com·mis·sar \'kämə,sär, -sä(r, ,==' \ *n* -S [Russ *komissar,* fr. G *kommissar* commissary, fr. ML *commissarius* one to whom something is entrusted — more at COMMISSARY] **1 a :** a Communist party official assigned to a military unit or sometimes to a civilian group to teach party principles and policies and to ensure party loyalty — called also *political commissar* **b :** one resembling or held to resemble a political commissar esp. in attempting to control public opinion or its expression ⟨would-be ~*s* of culture —G.B.Oxnam⟩ **2 a :** a Soviet government official **b :** the head of a government department in the U.S.S.R. until 1946 ⟨*Commissar* of Justice⟩ ⟨*Commissar* for Foreign Affairs⟩ — called also *people's commissar*

com·mis·sar·i·at \,kämə'serēət *sometimes* -sa(a)r- *or* -ē,at; *in sense 3 also* -sär- *or* -sȧr-; *usu* -d·+V\ *n* -S [NL *commissariatus,* fr. ML *commissarius* + L *-atus* -ate] **1 a :** the organized system by which armies and military posts are supplied with food and daily necessaries **b :** the body of officers charged with such service **2 :** food supplies **:** one's stock of provisions **:** COMMISSARY **3** [Russ *komissariat,* fr. G *kommissariat,* fr. NL *commissariatus*] **:** a government department in the U.S.S.R. until 1946 — compare COLLEGIUM, COMMISSAR 2 **4 :** a board of commissioners **:** COMMISSION

com·mis·sar·i·ot \-rēət\ *n* -S [alter. of *commissariat*] **:** COMMISSARY COURT 2

com·mis·sary \'kämə,serē, -ri\ *n* -ES [ME *commissarie,* fr. ML *commissarius* one to whom something is entrusted, fr. L *commissus,* past part. of *committere* to entrust + *-arius* -ary — more at COMMIT] **1 a :** an officer in the Church of England with spiritual or ecclesiastical jurisdiction who represents a bishop in an esp. distant part of the diocese or who performs the bishop's duties in his absence **b :** a clergyman appointed by a bishop or other official in the Church of England as his deputy for certain specified purposes **2 :** one to whom some charge, duty, or office has been committed by a superior power; *esp* **:** one sent or delegated to execute a duty or an office as the representative of his superior **3 a :** a civilian official or military officer in charge of some special service or department ⟨~ of muster⟩ ⟨~ of Indian affairs⟩ ⟨~ of prisoners⟩; *esp* **:** one in charge of procuring or distributing food and other supplies for military forces **b :** a department or store supplying personal equipment and provisions (as on a military post or in a railroad, lumber, or mining camp) **c :** food supplies **:** one's stock of provisions **:** COMMISSARIAT **d :** a lunchroom or refectory esp. in a motion-picture studio **4 :** a superior French police official **5 :** a judge of a commissary court in Scotland **6 :** COMMISSAR ⟨ordinances of the Council of People's *Commissaries* —W.E.Walling⟩

commissary court *n* **1 :** the court of a bishop's commissary **2 a :** a former supreme probate and divorce court in Scotland absorbed by the Court of Sessions in 1863 **b :** a county or sheriff's court in Scotland that appoints and confirms executors of estates possessing personal property

commissary general *n, pl* **commissaries general 1 :** a supreme representative or deputy **2 :** the chief official or officer in charge of some special army service — compare COMMISSARY 3a

[1]**com·mis·sion** \kə'mishən\ *n* -S [ME *commissioun,* fr. MF *commission,* fr. L *commission-, commissio* act of bringing together, committing, fr. *commissus* + *-ion-, -io* -ion] **1 a :** a formal written warrant or authority granting certain powers or privileges and authorizing or commanding the performance of certain acts or duties ⟨whil'st our ~ from Rome is read, let silence be commanded —Shak.⟩ ⟨a ~ of jail delivery issued by the court⟩ ⟨a ~ to serve as notary public⟩ **b** *obs* **:** a warrant conferring authority to raise and command a body of troops **c :** a certificate conferring military or naval rank and authority on officers above a certain rank; *also* **:** the rank and command so conferred **d :** a document issued to a lay worker in the Salvation Army who undertakes certain duties **2 a :** an authorization or command to act in a prescribed manner or to perform prescribed acts or duties **:** INSTRUCTION, CHARGE ⟨the priest was a custodian of Christ's ~ to his apostles. "Whose sins you shall forgive, they are forgiven them" —M.W.Baldwin⟩ **b :** an order to perform a particular task or carry out a work ⟨provide a young painter with a profitable ~ for a portrait⟩ **3 a :** authority to act for, in behalf of, or in place of another ⟨had summoned all the clans which acknowledged his ~ —T.B.Macaulay⟩ **b :** a task or matter entrusted to one as agent for another ⟨executed a ~ for me while he was in Singapore⟩ **4 a :** a group of persons directed to perform some duty or execute some trust **:** a body of commissioners ⟨U.N. ~ to investigate differences between the two countries⟩ **b :** a government agency having administrative, legislative, or judicial powers ⟨regulatory powers exercised by the Federal Trade *Commission*⟩ **c :** a city council having legislative and executive functions — see COMMISSION PLAN **5 :** the act of committing, performing, or doing (as a crime, misdeed, or other offense) ⟨the ~ of an illegal act⟩ ⟨the sins of omission and ~⟩ **6 :** a fee paid to an agent or employee for transacting a piece of business or performing a service ⟨a broker receives a ~ on each share of stock bought for a customer⟩ ⟨a ~ of 50 cents for each car washed⟩; *esp* **:** a percentage of the money received in a sale or other transaction paid to the agent responsible for the business ⟨a ~ of 9 percent on each sale⟩ — see DEL CREDERE **7 :** the act of entrusting, committing, or giving authority ⟨the ~ of limited powers to the administrator⟩ — **in commission 1** *obs* **:** in the exercise of an authority or the performance of an authorized or delegated act ⟨the Moor himself . . . is *in* full *commission* here for Cyprus —Shak.⟩ **2** *or* **into commission** *of an office or public trust* **:** under the authority of a commission or commissioners (as during the abeyance of the incumbent) ⟨to usurp to itself the executive power of the king and in effect to put the kingship *into commission* —S.B.Chrimes⟩ **3** *of a ship* **:** equipped, manned, and under command in readiness for active service ⟨warships will remain *in commission* when not refitting⟩ **4 :** in use or service or in condition for service ⟨put the old car back *in commission* for a time⟩ — **on commission :** with commissions serving as partial or full remuneration for work or services performed ⟨selling bonds *on commission*⟩ — **out of commission 1 :** out of or retired from active service ⟨the ship was placed *out of commission* after the war⟩ **2 :** out of order **:** not in working order **:** not in use or operation ⟨the bicycle is *out of commission*⟩ ⟨the . . . strike . . . put Alaska's principal ship line *out of commission* —*N.Y. Times*⟩

[2]**commission** \"\ *vt* **commissioned; commissioned; commissioning** \-sh(ə)niŋ\ **commissions 1 :** to give a commission to or for: as **a :** to confer a formal commission on **:** furnish with a written commission ⟨officers will be ~*ed* upon graduation⟩ **b :** to endow with effective right or power **:** AUTHORIZE, EMPOWER ⟨judges are not ~*ed* to make and unmake rules at pleasure —B.N.Cardozo⟩ **c :** to appoint to a certain task, mission, function, or duty ⟨~*ed* to make out a deed of conveyance —Havelock Ellis⟩ **d :** to give an order to (a person) for a work (as an art work) ⟨~*ed* him to paint her portrait⟩ **:** order (as a work of art) made or performed ⟨~ a painting⟩ **2 :** to put in commission (as a ship) **syn** see AUTHORIZE

com·mis·sion·aire \kə,mishə'na(a)(ə)r\ *n* -S [F *commissionnaire,* fr. *commission* commission + *-aire* -ary — more at COMMISSION] **1 a** *chiefly Brit* **:** one (as a messenger or porter) entrusted with small commissions **b :** a member of an association of pensioned soldiers and sailors organized in London in 1859 for employment as doorkeepers, caretakers, or messengers **c** *chiefly Brit* **:** a uniformed attendant; *esp* **:** a doorman at a hotel or theater **2 :** a purchasing agent in the foreign market acting on commission for an importer

com·mis·sion·al \kə'mishən°l, -shnəl\ *adj* **:** of or relating to a commission

commissionate *vt* -ED/-ING/-S [[1]*commission* + *-ate*] *obs* **:** COMMISSION

commission day *n, Brit* **:** the opening day of the assizes when the judge's commission is read

commissioned officer *n* **:** an officer of the armed forces holding by virtue of a commission a rank of second lieutenant or ensign or above

com·mis·sion·er \kə'mish(ə)nə(r)\ *n* -S [ME, fr. *commissioun* + *-er*] **:** a person who has received a commission or has been delegated to perform some service or carry out some business: as **a :** a member of a commission **b :** the representative or agent of the sovereign power or governmental authority in a district, province, or other governmental unit often having both judicial and administrative powers ⟨he was appointed chief ~ of the colony⟩ **c :** the officer in charge of a department or bureau of the public service ⟨~ of patents⟩ ⟨a state ~ of education⟩ ⟨police ~⟩ **d :** one of the administrative officials of an unincorporated town in Scotland **e :** COUNTY COMMISSIONER **f :** the administrative head of an organized professional sport usu. having regulatory or judicial powers ⟨baseball ~⟩ **g :** a Salvation Army officer ranking above a colonel and below the general

commissioner-general \=;=(=)=;=(=)=\ *n, pl* **commissioners-general :** a chief commissioner

commissioners standard ordinary table *n, usu cap C&S&O* **:** a mortality table based on the experience of American life insurance companies during the 1930s and widely used by American companies for premium and reserve calculations for new policies

commission house *n* **1 :** a concern that sells goods for others on commission **2 :** a member firm on an exchange that executes orders to buy and sell listed securities or commodity future contracts

commissioning pennant *n, Brit* **:** COMMISSION PENNANT

commission merchant *n* **:** FACTOR 1a

commission of oyer and terminer : a commission authorizing an English judge (as a High Court judge on circuit) to hear and determine at the assizes all indicted cases of treason, felony, or misdemeanor committed in the county — called also *writ of oyer and terminer*

commission of the peace *English law* **:** a commission under the great seal constituting one or more persons justices of the peace

commission pennant *n* **:** a long pennant flown at the mainmast of a government ship which is in commission but not under the command of an officer entitled to a personal flag or pennant

commission plan *n* **:** a method of city government in which both the executive and legislative powers are held by a small elected commission, each commissioner being directly in charge of one or more municipal departments — compare COUNCIL-MANAGER PLAN

commissions *pl of* COMMISSION, *pres 3d sing of* COMMISSION

com·mis·sur·al \'kämə,shụrəl\ *adj* **:** of, relating to, or having the properties of a commissure

com·mis·sure \-ü(ə)r\ *n* -S [ME, fr. MF or L; MF *commissure,* fr. L *commissura* a joining together, fr. *commissus,* past part. of *committere* to connect + *-ura* -ure — more at COMMIT] **1 :** the place where two bodies or parts of one body meet and unite **:** JOINT, SEAM, CLOSURE, CLEFT, JUNCTURE **2 :** the point or line of union between two parts (as the angles of the lips): **a :** the whole line along which the mandibles of a bird's bill close **b :** a connecting band of nerve tissue (as one connecting corresponding parts of the right and left halves of the brain or spinal cord) **c :** any of certain nerves that link ganglia in certain invertebrates **3 :** the plane of coherence of the two carpels or mericarps in fruits of the family Umbelliferae

com·mis·sur·ot·o·my \,kämə,shụ'rädəmē, -,shə'r-\ *n* -ES [ISV *commissure* + *-o-* + *-tomy*] **:** the operation of cutting through a band of muscle or nerve fibers; *specif* **:** separation of the flaps of a mitral valve by cutting or by use of a finger to relieve mitral stenosis — compare FINGER FRACTURE, VALVULOTOMY

[1]**com·mit** \kə'mit, *usu* -id·+V\ *vb* **committed; committed; committing; commits** [ME *committen,* fr. L *committere* to connect, entrust, fr. *com-* + *mittere* to send — more at SMITE] *vt* **1 a :** to put into charge or keeping **:** give in trust **:** ENTRUST, CONSIGN ⟨~ all executive, legislative, and judicial powers to one man —A.T.Vanderbilt⟩ **b** (1) **:** to place in or send officially to confinement or other place of punishment ⟨~ a criminal to prison⟩ **:** sentence to punishment ⟨*committed* Anne Boleyn to a criminal death —Francis Hackett⟩ (2) **:** to consign legally to a mental institution ⟨a patient *committed* by the court to a state hospital⟩ **c :** to consign to a permanent form or to record for preservation (as by writing down or memorizing) ⟨turning the scenes . . . over in his mind . . . before he started *committing* his ideas to paper —Ernest Newman⟩ ⟨~ a poem to memory⟩ **d :** to put into a place for disposal or safekeeping ⟨~ the papers to the fire⟩ ⟨~ his body to the earth⟩ **e :** to refer (as a legislative bill) to a committee for consideration and report **2 :** DO, PERFORM ⟨convicted of *committing* crimes against the state⟩ ⟨~ suicide⟩ ⟨*committing* an even greater folly —O.S.Nock⟩ **3 a** *obs* **:** CONNECT, JOIN **b :** to bring (a force) into battle **:** assign to a military action ⟨should . . . Company C be unable to take the objectives, then Company A will be *committed* —*Infantry Jour.*⟩ **c :** to expose to risk or danger ⟨*committing* his letters to the dangers of censorship —Marcia Davenport⟩ **d** (1) **:** to obligate or bind to take some moral or intellectual position or course of action ⟨a resolution *committing* the party to build 300,000 houses a year —B.C.L.Keelan⟩ ⟨this belief in science, to which our forefathers then *committed* themselves —A.J.Toynbee⟩ (2) **:** to pledge to some particular course or use **:** contract or bind by obligation to a particular disposition ⟨the government has *committed* 135 million dollars worth of surplus commodities in foreign barter activity⟩ (3) **:** to express the opinion of **:** reveal the views of ⟨cautiously refusing to ~ himself on any controversial subject⟩ ~ *vi* **1** *obs* **:** to perform an act that is an offense (as illicit sexual intercourse) ⟨~ not with man's sworn spouse —Shak.⟩ **2 :** to consign a person to prison ⟨officers without power to ~⟩

syn ENTRUST, CONFIDE, CONSIGN, RELEGATE: COMMIT is the widest term; it may express merely the general idea of delivering into another's charge, or it may have the special sense of transfer to a superior power or to an agency for custody ⟨on landing in Boston in 1872, my father and I were able safely to *commit* our trunk to the expressman —George Santayana⟩ ⟨in some districts of Hungary women . . . run around the herd before they drive it out and *commit* it to the care of the herdsmen —J.G.Frazer⟩ ⟨into thy hands I *commit* my spirit —Ps 31:5 (RSV)⟩ ⟨the principal State institution for the mentally ill, caring for about 1,000 *committed* patients —*Amer. Guide Series: Del.*⟩ ENTRUST is to deliver with trust and confidence, with appeal to or security in another's good faith ⟨all he would do was to put the investigation into the hands of a detective, and *entrust* him with the business of collecting evidence —Rose Macaulay⟩ ⟨the governor is *entrusted* with broad executive powers —*Amer. Guide Series: N.H.*⟩ CONFIDE heightens suggestions of trust and good faith ⟨the right of naturalization was therefore, with one accord, surrendered by the States, and *confided* to the Federal Government —R.B.Taney⟩ ⟨our customers over there seem not to be able to *confide* their property to us fast enough —Charles Dickens⟩ CONSIGN implies a delivering or transferring with or as if with formality, certification, or finality ⟨the gaol to which he was *consigned* by the victorious Cavaliers —T.B.Macaulay⟩ ⟨the orthodox *consigned* the heretics and the heretics consigned the bishops to eternal flames —G.M.Trevelyan⟩ ⟨wrapping the ivory carefully in a handkerchief of fine white silk, he *consigned* it to his pocket —Elinor Wylie⟩ RELEGATE indicates consigning to a particular class, position, or sphere, often a secondary or less favored one ⟨within three years overland staging was *relegated* to a secondary place in frontier life by the coming of the railroad —R.A.Billington⟩ ⟨and it is not inherent in the astronomical category either, though it was for many years *relegated* there —E.M.Forster⟩ ⟨the stylistic and philosophical difficulty of Valéry's art would seem to *relegate* him to a very small circle of initiates —Wallace Fowlie⟩

[2]**com·mit** \'kämət\ *n* -S [alter. of *comet*] **:** the card game comet or another card game similar to and derived from it

com·mit·ment \kə'mitmənt\ *n* -S **1** *obs* **:** the act of doing or performing something **:** COMMISSION **2 a :** the act of committing to the charge, keeping, or trust: as (1) **:** the consignment or sentencing to confinement (as in a prison or mental hospital) (2) **:** the action of referring a matter to a legislative committee **b :** a warrant for imprisonment or confinement **:** MITTIMUS **3 a** (1) **:** the obligation or pledge to carry out some action or policy or to give support to some policy or person ⟨American military ~ to the Asian land mass —William Costello⟩ ⟨a ~ by the British to withdraw . . . from Egyptian territory —R.C. Doty⟩ (2) **:** an engagement by contract or purchase order to assume a financial obligation (as to accept goods at an agreed price, to pay for subscribed stock, or to make a mortgage loan upon the completion of a building) (3) **:** something that has been pledged ⟨their ~ to the alliance was 10 divisions⟩ **b** (1) **:** the state of being obligated or bound (as by intellectual conviction or emotional ties) ⟨~ to a given ideal is not equivalent to provincial intolerance toward other forms of excellence —Ernest Nagel⟩ **:** a state or declaration of adherence or association (as to a doctrine or ideal) (2) *philos* **:** a decisive moral choice that involves a person in a definite course of action

com·mit·ta·ble \kə'mid·əbəl, -itə-\ *adj* **:** capable of being committed **:** legally subject to being committed

com·mit·tal \-d·°l, -t°l\ *n* -S *often attrib* **1 :** COMMITMENT ⟨~ of his wife . . . to the work house —J.C.Snaith⟩ ⟨enthusiastic

~ to the cause⟩ **2 :** the consignment of a body to the grave ⟨a public ~ service was conducted at the cemetery⟩
committed *past of* COMMIT
com·mit·tee *in sense 2* kə'mid·|ē *or* -it| *or* |i, *in sense 1* ˌkämə'tē *or* kəˌmid·'ē *or* kəˌmi'tē\ *n* -s [ME, fr. *committen* to commit, entrust + *-ee* — more at COMMIT] **1 a** *archaic* **:** a person or one of a number of persons to whom some charge or trust is committed or some particular business is delegated **b :** a person to whom another person or his estate is legally given in charge **2 a :** a body of persons delegated to consider, investigate, or take action upon and usu. to report concerning some matter or business; *specif* **:** a body of members chosen by a legislative body to give special consideration to pending legislation or to other legislative matters **b :** COMMITTEE OF ONE **c :** a self-constituted organization for the promotion of some common object ⟨the Northwest Wildlife *Committee*⟩
com·mit·tee·man \kə'mid·|ēmən, -it|, |im-, -ˌman, -maa(ə)n\ *n, pl* **committeemen 1 :** a member of a committee **2 a :** a party leader of a ward or precinct responsible for getting party members to vote and persuading other than party members to vote for his party's candidates or policies **b :** SHOP STEWARD
committee of correspondence : a body established by various towns or assemblies of the American colonies to exchange information with each other, mold public opinion, and take joint action against the British
committee of one : a person delegated to perform the duties of a committee
committee of selection *also* **committee on committees :** a legislative committee empowered to assign members to committee posts
committee of supply : a committee of the whole house in a British parliament for the purpose of considering and voting the ordinary state expenditure of the year
committee of the whole *or* **committee of the whole house :** a committee consisting of the whole membership of a legislative house and operating with its own chairman under informal and flexible rules for the purpose of considering a particular measure or some special business ⟨the house resolved itself into a *committee of the whole*⟩
com·mit·tee·wom·an \-ˌwu̇mən\ *n, pl* **committeewom·en** \-ˌwimən\ **1 :** a woman member of a committee **2 :** a woman doing the work of a committeeman esp. among women voters — compare COMMITTEEMAN 2
com·mix \kə'miks, kä'-\ *vb* [back-formation fr. earlier *commixt* mixed together, fr. ME *comyxt*, fr. L *commixtus*, past part. of *commiscēre* to mix together, fr. *com-* + *miscēre* to mix — more at MIX] **:** to mix or mingle together **:** BLEND
com·mix·tion \-schən\ *n* -s [ME, fr. LL *commixtion-, commixtio*, fr. L *commixtus* + *-ion-, -io* -ion] **1** *obs* **:** COMMIXTURE 1, 2 **2** *Roman, Scots, & civil law* **:** COMMIXTURE 3
com·mix·ture \-schə(r), 'kä,m-\ *n* -s [L *commixtura*, fr. *commixtus* + *-ura* -ure] **1 a :** the act or process of mixing or the state of being mixed **b :** the mass of things mixed **:** the result of mixing **:** COMPOUND, MIXTURE ⟨the Australian terrier is a ~ of several . . . breeds —Idris Davies⟩ **2 :** the act of putting a small piece of the Host into the consecrated wine **3** *common law* **:** the mingling of solid or liquid movables belonging to different owners — compare SPECIFICATION
commn *abbr* commission
commo *abbr* commodore
com·mo·da·ta·ry \ˌkämə'dād·ərē\ *n* -ES [F *commodataire*, fr. *commodat* commodatum (fr. L *commodatum*) + *-aire* -ary] **:** the bailee in a commodatum
com·mo·date \'kämə,dāt\ *n* -s [L *commodatum* loan] **:** COMMODATUM
com·mo·da·tion \ˌkämə'dāshən\ *n* -s [L *commodation-, commodatio*, fr. *commodatus* + *-ion-, -io* -ion] **:** the act of making a loan of commodatum
com·mo·da·tum \-ād·əm\ *n, pl* **commoda·ta** \-ād·ə\ [L, loan, fr. neut. of *commodatus*, past part. of *commodare* to make fit, give, lend, fr. *commodus* fit, convenient] **:** a loan of chattels to be returned without payment for their use — compare BAILMENT 2
[1]**commode** *adj* [F] **1** *obs* **:** CONVENIENT, SUITABLE **2** *obs, of a woman* **:** free with her favors **:** COMPLIANT, ACCOMMODATING — **commodely** *adv, obs*
[2]**com·mode** \kə'mōd\ *n* -s [F, fr. *commode*, adj., convenient, fr. L *commodus*, fr. *com-* + *modus* measure, mode — more at METE] **1 :** a woman's cap made of lace, fine fabric, and ribbons over a high wire framework popular in the late 17th and early 18th centuries **2** *obs* **:** BAWD, PROCURESS **3 a :** a low chest of drawers or a cabinet on legs **b :** a movable sink or washstand with cupboard underneath **c :** a chair or similar framework holding a toilet utensil under an open seat; *also* **:** CHAMBER POT

commode 1

com·mo·di·ous \kə'mōdēəs\ *adj* [ME, fr. MF *commodieux*, fr. ML *commodiosus*, irreg. fr. L *commodum* convenience (fr. neut. of *commodus*) + *-osus* -ous] **1** *obs* **:** BENEFICIAL, USEFUL, ADVANTAGEOUS — often used with *to* or *for* **2 :** adapted to or suitable for use **:** SERVICEABLE — often used with *to* or *for* ⟨the cheapness of the conveyance made it equally ~ for dead fish and lively company —William Cowper⟩ **3 :** affording ample space and room **:** large or roomy and convenient esp. in permitting free motion **:** not narrow or confining ⟨the room . . . was of a ~, well-proportioned size—Jane Austen⟩ ⟨a ~ harbor for that city —*Amer. Guide Series: Del.*⟩ **syn** see AMPLE
com·mo·di·ous·ly *adv* [ME, fr. *commodious* + *-ly*] **:** in a commodious manner
com·mo·di·ous·ness *n* -ES **:** the quality or state of being commodious
com·mod·i·ty \kə'mädəd·ē, -ətē, -i, *rap.* -ädtē *or* -i\ *n* -ES [ME *commoditee*, fr. MF *commodité*, fr. L *commoditat-, commoditas* fitness, convenience, pleasantness, fr. *commodus* + *-itat-, -itas* -ity] **1 a** *archaic* **:** CONVENIENCE, USEFULNESS **b** *archaic* **:** PROFIT, ADVANTAGE, EXPEDIENCY ⟨a good wit will make use of anything. I will turn diseases to ~ —Shak.⟩ **c :** something used or valued esp. when regarded as an article of commerce ⟨transformed from a rather fragile comedy into a durable ~ —John McCarten⟩ ⟨plenty of that ~ known as "temperament" —H.C.Schonberg⟩ **2 a :** an economic good; *esp* **:** a product of agriculture, mining, or sometimes manufacture as distinguished from services ⟨*commodities* such as meat, fats, and sugar —*Americana Annual*⟩ ⟨~ prices⟩ **b :** an article of commerce; *esp* **:** one delivered to a transportation company for shipment **3** *obs* **:** a parcel or quantity of goods **:** LOT ⟨I knew where a ~ of good names were to be bought —Shak.⟩
commodity dollar *n* **:** a unit of a proposed form of currency whose gold value is arbitrarily determined by and whose nominal gold content is periodically adjusted to an index number reflecting market prices of basic commodities — called also *compensated dollar*
commodity exchange *n* **:** an organized market where future delivery contracts for graded commodities (as grains, cotton, sugar, coffee, wool) are bought and sold
commodity paper *n* **:** a note or draft secured by a bill of lading or other document giving a lien upon or title to readily marketable nonperishable staples
commodity rate *n* **:** a common carrier rate distinguished from a class rate and applicable only to a specific commodity or group of related commodities carried between specific points or territories
commodity standard *n* **:** a monetary standard in which the medium of exchange consists of one or more economic goods ⟨the gold standard is one type of *commodity standard*⟩
commodity tariff *n* **:** a tariff containing only commodity rates and related rules for transportation on a common carrier
com·mo·do *var of* COMODO
com·mo·dore \'kämə,dō(ə)r, -dȯ(ə)r,-dōə,-dȯ(ə)\ *n* -s [prob. modif. of D *commandeur* commander, fr. F, fr. OF *comandeor*, fr. *comander* to command + *-eor* -or — more at COMMAND] **1 :** a naval officer usu. ranking next above a captain and below a rear admiral: **a :** a captain holding this rank temporarily while commanding a detached squadron or division of a fleet — used in the British navy **b** (1) **:** a captain in command of a squadron as senior officer — used in the U. S. Navy as a courtesy title prior to 1862 (2) **:** a naval officer commanding a squadron, division, ship of the first class, or naval station and having a rank corresponding to that of brigadier general in the army — used in the U.S. Navy 1862–99 and during World War II (3) **:** a naval captain with Civil War service receiving the rank upon retirement (4) **:** a naval officer of the rank of captain or below commanding a squadron, division, or other subdivision of a fleet esp. when consisting of small ships (as destroyers) — used only as a courtesy form of address **2 a :** the officer commanding a body of merchant ships sailing in company esp. in a convoy ⟨the convoy ~ . . . sees to the internal management of the convoy —J.P.Bishop⟩ **b :** the ranking captain of the fleet operated by a particular shipping company **3 :** the chief officer of a yacht club or boating association **4 :** AIR COMMODORE
[1]**com·mon** \'kämən\ *adj, often* -ER/-EST [ME *commun, comon*, fr. OF *commun, comun*, fr. L *communis* — more at MEAN] **1 a :** of or relating to a community at large (as a family unit, social group, tribe, political organization, or alliance) **:** generally shared or participated in by individuals of a community **:** not limited to one person or special group ⟨we, the people of the U.S., in order to . . . provide for the ~ defense —*U.S. Constitution*⟩ ⟨a sense of ~ interest, a guild feeling in reaction against the extreme competitive individualism —J.M.Barzun⟩ **b :** known to the community; *esp* **:** notorious as an accustomed general vexation ⟨a ~ thief⟩ ⟨punished as a ~ scold⟩ ⟨maintaining a ~ nuisance⟩ **c :** belonging to or typical of all mankind **:** shared with all men ⟨our ~ humanity⟩ ⟨our ~ nature⟩ **2 a :** held, enjoyed, experienced, or participated in equally by a number of individuals **:** possessed or manifested by more than one individual ⟨a ~ attribute⟩ ⟨a ~ characteristic⟩ **:** calling forth, giving rise to as source, or sending out a number of different items **:** marked by the same relationship to a number of persons or things ⟨our ~ rights⟩ ⟨the sharp teeth ~ to all cats⟩ ⟨streets radiating out from a ~ center⟩ ⟨we will help our allies against our ~ enemy⟩ **b :** marked by or resulting from joint action of two or more parties **:** practiced or engaged in by two or more equally ⟨in the partnership of our ~ enterprise we must share in a unified plan —F.D.Roosevelt⟩ ⟨our ~ defense⟩ ⟨by ~ consent the partnership was dissolved⟩ **c :** open freely to the individual use of any member of a society or group ⟨"folk-land", the ~ property of the tribe —J.R.Green⟩ ⟨the front hall, ~ to all the tenants —Dorothy Sayers⟩ **d :** available for indiscriminate or promiscuous use ⟨a ~ woman⟩ ⟨the ~ cup⟩ **e :** belonging to or appointed for the common (sense 6) **f** *math* **:** belonging equally to two or more quantities **g** *anat* **:** formed of or dividing into two or more branches ⟨the ~ carotid artery⟩ ⟨~ iliac vessels⟩ **3 :** ceremonially or religiously unclean or unfit ⟨eating nothing ~ on the holy day⟩ **4 a :** occurring or appearing frequently esp. in the ordinary course of events **:** not unusual **:** known or referred to widely or generally because of frequent occurrence ⟨the ~ is that which is found in the experience of a number of persons —John Dewey⟩ ⟨the ~ judgment which sets tragedy above comedy as the greater art —Samuel Alexander⟩ **b** *archaic* **:** subject to or ensuing from widespread conversation **:** recognized or agreed on through copious discussion ⟨young Arthur's death is ~ in their mouths —Shak.⟩ **c** *chiefly Midland* **:** USUAL ⟨I'm as well as ~ —Ellen Glasgow⟩ **d :** VERNACULAR — used of plant and animal names ⟨cat is the ~ name for *Felis catus*⟩ **5 a :** of, relating to, or typical of the majority or to the many rather than the few **:** GENERAL, PREVALENT ⟨a sentiment ~, but not universal —W.G.Sumner⟩ ⟨this revelation has . . . passed into the ~ consciousness of the civilized world —W.R.Inge⟩ **b :** characterized by a lack of privilege or special status ⟨the ~ people⟩ ⟨was then forced to take on a job as a ~ laborer⟩ **6 a :** characteristic of a usual type or standard **:** representative of a type **:** quite usual and average **:** entirely ordinary and undistinguished esp. by anything superior ⟨the everyday man and woman, the ~ people —I.M.Price⟩ ⟨a ~ man, no holier than you and I —Thomas Hardy⟩ ⟨the great gods . . . were not exempt from the ~ lot. They too grew old and died —J.G.Frazer⟩ **b :** having no claim or showing no pretense to rank, position, polish, learning, or culture ⟨apart . . . from the ~ reader, there is an elite —A.L.Guérard⟩ **c :** satisfying accustomed criteria **:** attaining to an ordinary standard **:** ADEQUATE ⟨the ~ honesty to face it —W.R.Inge⟩ ⟨it was simply ~ courtesy to help him⟩ **d :** falling below ordinary standards **:** INFERIOR, MEAN, SECOND-RATE ⟨O hard is the bed . . . and ~ the blanket and cheap —A.E.Housman⟩ ⟨labor was scarce and ~ at that —*Amer. Guide Series: Del.*⟩ **e :** falling below accustomed standards of conduct **:** lacking polish, learning, or taste **:** marked by or suggestive of the lax, crass, tawdry, earthy, or crude ⟨a very ~ girl snubbed by the others⟩ ⟨as Harris said, in his ~ vulgar way, the city would have to lump it —J.K. Jerome⟩ **f** *of lumber* **:** of or relating to several grades that are inferior to finish lumber **:** DEFECTIVE, KNOTTY **7** *now chiefly dial* **:** easily approachable **:** UNRESERVED, INFORMAL ⟨he's such a nice ~ fellow⟩ **8 :** frequently met with and known better than types less often encountered ⟨~ salt⟩ ⟨the ~ fern⟩; *specif* **:** most frequent and best known of its kind in a particular region — used of plants and animals **9 a** *of gender* (1) **:** either masculine or feminine ⟨the gender of F *enfant* is ~⟩ (2) **:** characterizing words of which in an earlier stage of the language some were masculine and some feminine ⟨Danish has two genders, ~ and neuter⟩ **b** *of a substantive* **:** belonging to the common gender **c** *of a syllable* **:** either short or long ⟨in Greek prosody a syllable is ~ that has a short vowel followed by a stop and a liquid or nasal, as the first syllable of *teknon*⟩ **d** *of a grammatical case* **:** denoting relations by a single form that in a more highly inflected language might be denoted by two or more different case forms ⟨*moon*, as subject in "the moon is shining" and as object in "I see the moon", is in the ~ case⟩
syn ORDINARY, FAMILIAR, POPULAR, VULGAR: COMMON, ORDINARY, AND FAMILIAR all describe something that is very frequently or generally met with and hence is not at all strange or unusual. COMMON stresses lack of distinguishing or exceptional characteristics ⟨Norris quite definitely identified the romantic with that which is peculiar or special as opposed to the *common* —M.R.Cohen⟩ and may connote coarseness or lack of refinement ⟨weavers produced fine muslins, gauzes, calicoes, and the *common* cloths used by the poorer population —C.L.Jones⟩ ORDINARY applies to what is met with in the routine, regular, or accustomed order of events; it may connote lack of rareness or of superiority ⟨the business of the poet is not to find new emotions, but to use the *ordinary* ones —T.S.Eliot⟩ ⟨it is not an *ordinary* war. It is a revolution . . . which threatens all men everywhere —F.D.Roosevelt⟩ ⟨the mass of *ordinary* men, as definitely opposed to exceptional men —W.H.Mallock⟩ FAMILIAR applies to what is well known because encountered often and lacks any suggestion of the foreign or exotic ⟨the *familiar* arrangement of chairs and tables, always the same —Pearl Buck⟩ ⟨the curious impression . . . that she had seen everything and everybody before. Every face was *familiar* to her —Ellen Glasgow⟩ POPULAR indicates the common due to acceptance, sometimes enthusiastic, by the people, esp. commoners; it may imply a lack of qualities pleasing to the elite, upper classes, or learned groups ⟨the *popular* faith in the omnipotence of education —M.R.Cohen⟩ ⟨these brotherhoods were . . . thoroughly *popular*, drawing most of their support from the lower classes —W.R.Inge⟩ ⟨compromise its values by publishing work that could be described as merely cheap or *popular* —H.V.Gregory⟩ VULGAR is used only occas. to mean COMMON; it usu. suggests meanness, bad taste, crudeness, or crassness ⟨the now *vulgar* opinion that [Samuel] Johnson was more distinguished as a talker than as a writer —J.W.Krutch⟩ ⟨he never could have been *vulgar;* there is not in the whole range of English literature quite such a gentleman —George Saintsbury⟩ ⟨not for the *vulgar* gaze but for an aristocratic and urbane inspection⟩ **syn** see in addition RECIPROCAL, UNIVERSAL
[2]**common** \"\ *n* -s [ME *commun*, fr. *commun*, adj.] **1 a** *obs* **:** the common body of people of a place, community, or polity **b commons** *pl but sing or pl in constr* **:** COMMONALTY; *esp* **:** people lacking noble, knightly, or gentle rank ⟨the ~s were pleased⟩ **2 commons** *pl a sing or pl in constr* **:** provisions for a usu. ecclesiastical or collegiate community or company ⟨a modern university ~s⟩ **b** *sing in constr* **:** a common table **:** a dining hall **:** a building housing an institution's dining hall **c** *sing in constr* **:** RATIONS, FARE ⟨were eating an ample ~s⟩ ⟨shortening the ~s when our supply train was intercepted⟩ ⟨subsisting on short ~s⟩ **3 commons** *pl but sing or pl in constr* **a :** the political group or estate comprising the commoners **b** *sometimes cap* **:** parliamentary representatives of the commoners **c** *often cap* **:** a lower house of a parliament **4 :** the legal right that arises either from a grant or contract or from prescription or operation of a statute and that allows the taking of a profit in another's land in common with the owner or in common with other persons **5 a** *sometimes* **commons** *pl* **:** land used in common by people of a community esp. for pasture **b :** a stretch of land that is not enclosed or cultivated **:** WASTE, HEATH; *sometimes* **:** a vacant lot **c** *sometimes* **commons** *pl, chiefly NewEng* **:** a publicly owned typically grass-covered plot usu. in the center of a town or village **:** an open square **6** *sometimes cap* **a :** a religious service suitable for any of various festivals — compare PROPER **b :** the ordinary of the mass **c :** the part of a missal or breviary containing the common offices **7 :** COMMON STOCK **8 :** a common board or piece of lumber — **in common 1 :** that is shared, experienced, or possessed together or equally **:** COMMONLY ⟨the two brothers own a bicycle *in common*⟩ ⟨the boss had much *in common* with his employees⟩ **2 :** in a community — **out of common** *or* **out of the common :** UNUSUAL, UNUSUALLY
[3]**common** *vi* -ED/-ING/-S [ME *communen*, fr. *commun*, adj.] **1** *obs* **:** PARTICIPATE, SHARE **2** *obs* **:** CONFER, TALK **3** *obs* **:** to exercise a right together
com·mon·able \'kämənəbəl\ *adj* [[2]*common* + *-able*] **1** *of an animal* **:** permitted to pasture on public commons **2** *of land* **:** held in common
common adjective *n* **:** a descriptive adjective that is not a proper adjective
com·mon·age \-nij\ *n* -s [[2]*common* + *-age*] **1 :** the right to pasture animals on another's land or on a common **2 :** COMMONALTY **3 :** common or community land **4 :** the condition of being held in common ⟨the ~ of the land⟩
com·mon·al·i·ty \ˌkämə'naləd·ē\ *n* -ES [ME *communalitie*, alter. (influenced by *-itie* -ity) of earlier *communalte, communaltie*] **1 :** possession with another of a certain attribute **:** COMMONNESS **2 :** FREQUENCY
com·mon·al·ty \'kämənəltē\ *n* -ES [ME *comonalte, communalte*, fr. OF *comunalté*, fr. *comunal* communal + *-té* -ty — more at COMMUNAL] **1** *or* **com·mon·al·i·ty** \ˌkämə'naləd·ē\ **:** common people without authority or rank **:** COMMONERS; *esp* **:** the political estate formed by the commons **2 :** body corporate **:** CORPORATION **3 :** the general group or body ⟨the ~ of scholars will welcome his research⟩ **4** *obs* **:** a self-governing commonwealth **:** DEMOCRACY
common appendant *n* **:** the right belonging by common law to the possession of arable land to pasture commonable beasts on another's land (as that of the owner of the manor of which the land possessed forms a part)
common appurtenant *n* **:** a common in the land of another not historically appurtenant to an estate but annexed to it by grant or by prescription from long enjoyment
common ash *n* **:** EUROPEAN ASH
common assumpsit *n* **:** a form of action employing the common counts that is used to recover liquidated damages on quasi contracts and was early extended to most cases where an action of debt would lie and later to nearly all cases where there is a money obligation not payable as damages — called also *general assumpsit, indebitatus assumpsit*
common assurance *n* **:** ASSURANCE 5
common at large : COMMON IN GROSS
common average *n* **:** PARTICULAR AVERAGE
common bail *n* **:** BAIL BELOW
common bar *n* **:** a bar in an action of trespass constituted by the defendant's pleading that the act complained of was on his own freehold
common barberry *n* **:** an upright shrub (*Berberis vulgaris*) that is widely naturalized in the U.S. from Europe, has gray branches, usu. forked prickles, bristle-toothed leaves, and juicy berries in elongate clusters, and is important as the alternate host of the fungus that causes stem rust of wheat — compare JAPANESE BARBERRY
common barrator *n* **:** one who practices barratry
common bile duct *n* **:** the duct formed by the union of the hepatic and cystic ducts and opening into the duodenum — see DIGESTION illustration
common bond *n* **:** AMERICAN BOND
common brick *n* **:** brick made from natural clay and having no special surface treatment; *also* **:** unselected kiln-run brick
common bronzewing *n* **:** an Australian bronzewing (*Phaps chalcoptera*) with a white forehead and chin, a brown back on which each feather is tipped with buff, a mauve breast, and brilliantly metallic bronze and green specula on the wing coverts
common buckthorn *n* **:** a common Eurasian shrub (*Rhamnus cathartica*) with oval leaves and black berries that sometimes are used as a laxative
common buckwheat *n* **:** an Asiatic buckwheat (*Fagopyrum esculentum*) that has short dense flower clusters and sharp-angled fruit and is now widespread esp. in cultivation — compare TARTARIAN BUCKWHEAT
common bundle *n* **:** a vascular bundle that passes from a stem into a leaf — compare CAULINE BUNDLE
common cardinal vein *n* **:** DUCT OF CUVIER
common carotid *also* **common carotid artery** *n* **:** the part of either carotid artery between its point of origin and its division into internal and external branches
common carrier *n* **1 :** one that undertakes for hire the carrying of goods, persons, or messages treating its whole clientele without individual preference or discrimination and being responsible for all losses and injuries except those in consequence of an act of God, of the enemies of the country, or of the owner of the property himself **2 :** a public utility or public service company **3** *in federal regulatory use* **:** a carrier offering its services to all comers for interstate transportation by railroad, motor vehicle, ship, aircraft, or pipeline — compare CONTRACT CARRIER
common chemical sense *n* **:** a chemical sense universally exhibited by body surfaces exposed to certain (as irritant) solutions or vapors that in vertebrates is mediated by both spinal and cranial nerves
common chickweed *n* **:** a Eurasian herb (*Stellaria media*) widely naturalized as a weed in No. America
common chord *n* **:** the major or minor triad
common coin *n* **:** something that is current through being commonly mentioned, discussed, accepted, or sanctioned ⟨his name became *common coin*⟩
common cold *n* **:** an acute contagious disease of the upper respiratory tract caused by a filterable virus and characterized by inflammation of the mucous membranes of the nose, throat, eyes, and eustachian tubes with watery then purulent discharge
common comfrey *n* **:** a European comfrey (*Symphytum officinale*) that is naturalized as a weed in No. America and has the upper part of the stem densely hispid
common cost *n* **:** expense chargeable in accounting to the business as a whole **:** cost assigned to several departments or operations
common council *n* **:** a legislative body or council of a municipal government — **common councilman** *n*
common count *n* **:** any of various technical counts in law that are of a general nature and are used in pleadings to prevent a failure of justice by reason of an inadvertent variance
common cracker *n* **:** BOSTON CRACKER
common curlew *n* **:** a large Old World curlew (*Numenius arquata*) with strong flight somewhat resembling that of a gull
common denominator *n* **1 :** a common multiple of the denominators of a number of fractions **2 a :** something that marks a group of things as alike or that characterizes a group or class **:** a trait or characteristic in common ⟨the essence of religious experience, the actual *common denominator* of the world's great religions —H.J.Muller⟩ ⟨diverse writings whose only *common denominator* was a supposed sophistication —J.D.Hart⟩ ⟨the *common denominator* in this collection of distraught . . . men and women is that they are all Americans who are dissatisfied with their lives —Harrison Smith⟩ **b :** something on which all in a group may agree ⟨trying

to find a *common denominator* that would bring the opposing factions of the party together⟩ **c :** a strain, theme, quality, or trait persisting throughout a mass of material (as the writings of an author) ⟨the *common denominator,* the atmosphere and the whole tempo of a writer's work may be recorded by just one sentence —Paul Potts⟩

common difference *n* **:** the difference between two consecutive terms of an arithmetic progression

common disaster *n* **:** the simultaneous death of an insured and his beneficiary

common divisor *or* **common factor** *n* **:** a number, quantity, or expression that divides each of two or more numbers, quantities, or expressions without remainder

commoned *past of* COMMON

common entrance *n, sometimes cap C&E* **:** the general entrance examination required by British public schools

[1]**commoner** *comparative of* COMMON

[2]**com·mon·er** \ˈkämənə(r)\ *n* -s [ME *communer,* fr. *commun,* adj., + *-er*] **1 :** one of the common people: as **a :** one not of the nobility; *sometimes* **:** one not of the titled nobility or of the peerage **b :** a person without special class distinction **2 :** one having a right of common **:** one having a right to common land **3** *obs* **:** a common prostitute **4 :** a student (as at Oxford University or Winchester) who pays for his own board instead of being dependent on a foundation — compare PENSIONER **5 a :** a member of the House of Commons **b** *usu cap* **:** a member of the Court of Common Council of the City of London

common era *n, usu cap C&E* **:** CHRISTIAN ERA

commonest *superlative of* COMMON

common establishment *n* **:** VULGAR ESTABLISHMENT

commoney *var of* COMMIE

common fig *n* **:** a fig not requiring caprification in order to set fruit — compare SMYRNA FIG

common fishery *n* **1 :** a fishery (sense 4) enjoyed by the public — compare COMMON OF PISCARY **2 :** a right to fish in another's waters with the owner or with others

common flute *n* **:** RECORDER

common form *n* **1** *Scholasticism* **:** a form belonging to a species **2 :** the form of probate of a will where the will is not contested and is proved by the executor's own oath **3 :** one of the forms of pleading used in the common-law actions (as assumpsit, covenant, debt, detinue, replevin, trespass on the case, and trover) in which the allegations were fixed in their general nature

common fraction *n* **:** a fraction in which both numerator and denominator are expressed

common garden *adj* **:** common or garden

common grace *n* **:** grace that relates to temporal concerns only — distinguished from *special grace*

common ground *n* **:** a basis of mutual interest or understanding in human relations ⟨she had no *common ground* with her iron-spirited Presbyterian father —*Times Lit. Supp.*⟩

common hazard *n* **:** a potential cause of fire common to all

common heliotrope *n* **:** GARDEN HELIOTROPE 2

commoning *n* -s [fr. gerund of [3]*common*] **:** the exercise of common rights to land use

common in gross : a common not appendant or appurtenant to the ownership of any land but belonging to a person as an independent subject of property and requiring a deed for its transfer — called also *common at large*

common intendment *or* **common intent** *n* **:** customary or natural meaning as legally construed — compare INTENDMENT

common in the soil : the right to dig and take away a part of the soil or minerals of another's land — called also *common of digging*

com·mo·ni·tion \ˌkäməˈnishən\ *n* -s [L *commonition-, commonitio,* fr. *commonitus* (past part. of *commonēre* to remind, impress upon, fr. *com-* + *monēre* to remind, warn + *-ion-, -io* -ion — more at MIND] **:** ADMONITION

commonitory *adj* [LL *commonitorius,* fr. L *commonitus* + *-orius* -ory] *obs* **:** calling to mind

com·mon·i·za·tion \ˌkämənəˈzāshən, -ˌnīˈz-\ *n* -s **:** the formation or development of a common noun, a common adjective, or a verb from a proper noun (as *mercury, quixotic, to boycott*)

com·mon·ize \ˈkäməˌnīz\ *vt* -ED/-ING/-S [[1]*common* + *-ize*] **:** to make common

common joist *n* **:** one of the ordinary floor beams to which flooring planks are secured

common juniper *n* **:** a small tree or sometimes a shrub (*Juniperus communis*) widespread in northern Europe, Asia, and No. America and the source of many cultivated junipers — see IRISH JUNIPER, SWEDISH JUNIPER

common jury *n* **:** a jury drawn in the ordinary manner for the trial of causes — distinguished from *special jury*

common labor *n* **:** UNSKILLED LABOR

common land *n* **:** [2]COMMON 5a

common law *n* [ME *commun lawe,* trans. of L *jus commune*] **1 :** the system of unwritten law governing the rights and duties of persons that was developed in England in courts of superior jurisdiction having general application throughout the kingdom, that was declared in written opinions by the judges and based either on the general customs or on reason and fixed principles of justice but even in the absence of a precedent capable of being adapted to new situations or of being changed or modified in the light of different circumstances or needs, and that is distinguished both from the written statute laws enacted by the parliament and from other systems of law such as equity, ecclesiastical law, civil law, admiralty law, probate law, + the law merchant **2** *in U.S. state courts and statutes* **:** the common law as it existed in England at the time of the American Revolution or at some other time fixed by state statute with whatever modifications may have been made by the inclusion at that time of doctrines from other systems of law (as equity or civil law) together with such important English statutes of general application as were suitable to the needs and conditions of the state provided no such statute contravened any local statute **3 :** unwritten law as opposed to statute law **4 :** English common law unaffected by doctrines that originated in any system of law (as civil law) having a different tradition **5 :** law of general application throughout a political entity (as a state) as opposed to law having only a special or local application **6 :** the English common law as extended or modified by any doctrines taken from another system of law (as equity or civil law) or even by statutes whenever those doctrines or statutes may be judicially asserted to grant the remedies recognized under the English common law

common-law *adj* [*common law*] **:** of or belonging to a common-law marriage or similar relationship ⟨a *common-law* child⟩ **:** taking part in such an arrangement ⟨a *common-law* wife⟩

common-law estoppel *n* **:** an estoppel by record or by deed or an estoppel in pais whenever recognized in a court of common law (as distinguished from one of equity)

common-law lien *n* **:** a lien arising only in cases of possession of personal property usu. under a bailment (as a carrier's lien)

common-law marriage *n* **:** an agreement now not recognized in many jurisdictions as a legal marriage between a man and a woman to enter into the marriage relation without ecclesiastical or civil ceremony that in many jurisdictions must be followed by cohabitation to be legally valid and is provable by the writings, declarations, or conduct of the parties

common-law right *n* **:** a right that derives from common-law custom and usage

common-law trust *n* **:** MASSACHUSETTS TRUST

common lawyer *n* **:** a lawyer versed in common law

common learning *n* **:** any of certain skills, attitudes, and items of information that by some modern educators are held to be essential for all elementary and secondary pupils in handling life situations likely to arise outside the classroom

common ligament *n* **:** either of two strong fibrous bands, an anterior and a posterior, the latter within the spinal canal, that extend from the axis to the sacrum and are attached to and bind together the bodies of the vertebrae

common logarithm *n* **:** a logarithm whose base is 10

common loon *n* **:** a loon (*Gavia immer*) the size of a small goose having the back black spotted with white, the head and neck nearly all black, and the underparts white, being widely distributed in northern No. America and occurring less frequently in northern Europe and Asia

commonly *adv* [ME *communly,* fr. *commun* common + *-ly*] **1 :** as a general thing **:** often in the usual course of events **:** USUALLY, ORDINARILY **2 :** to a degree that is common

common mallow *n* **1 :** a procumbent biennial plant (*Malva neglecta*) with round-cordate leaves on long petioles and pale-blue flowers in the axils **2** *Brit* **:** an erect plant (*Malva sylvestris*) related to the common mallow

common man *n* **:** the undistinguished commoner lacking class or rank distinction or special attributes

common measure *n* **1 :** COMMON TIME **2** *also* **common meter :** BALLAD METER

common mullein *n* **:** GREAT MULLEIN

common multiple *n* **:** a multiple of each of two or more numbers, quantities, or expressions

com·mon·ness \ˈkämən(n)əs\ *n* -ES **:** the quality or state of being common: as **a :** the quality of being possessed or shared by all mankind or by a group **:** jointness of possession or use; *also* **:** the quality of appealing to the general run of people ⟨although he came from the aristocracy he preserved a certain ~ that made him a successful politician⟩ **b :** the possession of usual, standard, ordinary, or undistinguished qualities or character ⟨the ~ of the common man⟩; *also* **:** the quality of occurring or appearing frequently in the ordinary course of events ⟨they are the familiar folk one can come upon in any town, on any street, and in this book their ~ lends an extraordinary reality to the events that overtake them —Harrison Smith⟩ **c :** the marked display of lack of learning, refinement, or taste ⟨her father's ~ was what offended the daughter most, his habit of sitting in the parlor in his undershirt drinking beer⟩ **d :** INDISCRIMINATENESS, VULGARITY, PROMISCUOUSNESS ⟨behavior marked by the ~ of a prostitute⟩

common nightshade *n* **:** BLACK NIGHTSHADE

common noun *also* **common name** *n* **:** a noun that is used with limiting modifiers (as *a* or *an, some, every, my*) and that designates a being or thing of which more than one specimen exists ⟨in each of the phrases *no horse, such a crowd, some water, his courage, a Mozart,* the last word is a *common noun*⟩

common nuisance *n* **:** PUBLIC NUISANCE

common of digging : COMMON IN THE SOIL

common of estovers : the right to estovers

common of pasture : the right of pasturing animals on another's land

common of piscary *or* **common of fishery :** the right of fishing in waters belonging to another

common orange *n* **:** SWEET ORANGE

common or garden *adj* **:** frequently met with **:** ORDINARY ⟨a *common or garden* variety of nail⟩

common particular meter *or* **common particular measure** *n* **:** a variation of ballad meter in which the four-stress lines are doubled producing a stanza of six lines in tail-rhyme arrangement, the number of stresses in the lines being 4, 4, 3, 4, 4, 3

common pasturage *n, Scots law* **:** COMMON OF PASTURE

[1]**commonplace** \ˈ==ˌ= *sometimes* ˌ==ˈ=\ *n* [trans. of L *locus communis* widely applicable argument or thesis, trans. of Gk *koinos topos*] **1 a** *obs* **:** a passage applicable to particular cases **:** THEME, TOPIC **:** the text of a discourse **b** *archaic* **:** a striking or esp. noticeable passage; *usu* **:** such a passage entered in a commonplace book **c** [by shortening] *obs* **:** COMMONPLACE BOOK **2 a :** an opinion, statement, or other expression lacking originality or freshness and often repeated and generally accepted **:** a stock comment or subject of remark **:** TRUISM, CLICHÉ ⟨a ~ in the study of human nature that men often turn against those who have raised them —Hilaire Belloc⟩ ⟨the superficial ~*s* which pass as axioms in our popular intellectual milieu —M.R.Cohen⟩ **b :** the quality or state of commonness ⟨their originality has become our ~ —Virginia Woolf⟩ **c :** a thing commonly encountered **:** a common ordinary object, occurrence, or practice taken for granted and arousing no interest or curiosity ⟨to most of us railways are one of the ~*s* of life —O.S.Nock⟩

[2]**commonplace** \"\ *adj* **:** having nothing out of common **:** without originality, freshness, or interest **:** commonly encountered **:** ORDINARY, DULL, TRITE, STALE ⟨revolutionary in the seventies, but ~ by 1900 —F.L.Mott⟩ ⟨the lover whose imagination makes a goddess of some ~ young woman —C.E.Montague⟩ — **com·mon·place·ly** *adv* — **com·mon·place·ness** *n* -ES

[3]**commonplace** \"\ *vt* **:** to extract striking or memorable passages from (as for a commonplace book) esp. with arrangement of the passages under general headings ~ *vi* **:** to employ commonplaces in communication

commonplace book *n* [[1]*commonplace*] **:** a book of literary passages, cogent quotations, occasional thoughts, or other memorabilia ⟨transcribing from an old manuscript volume into his *commonplace book* —J.G.Lockhart⟩

com·mon·plac·er \"+ə(r)\ *n* -s [[1]*commonplace* + *-er*] **:** one that keeps a commonplace book

common pleas *n pl* [ME *common place,* fr. AF *communs pletz,* trans. of ML *communia placita*] **1 a** *in English law* **:** those pleas or actions over which the crown did not claim exclusive jurisdiction **b :** civil actions between subjects — distinguished from *pleas of the crown* **2** *usu cap C&P* **:** COURT OF COMMON PLEAS

common prayer *n* **:** prayer in which a congregation unites

common privet *n* **:** PRIVET 1a(1)

common property *n* **1 :** land in which all members of the community hold equal rights **2 :** land or other property in which a person other than the owner holds certain rights in common with the owner — compare ESTOVERS **3 :** information generally known ⟨prevent the events of the evening from becoming *common property* —Hamilton Basso⟩

common pyrites *n* **:** PYRITE

common rafter *n* **:** one of the rafters to which the roofing is secured — see ROOF illustration

common rail *n* **:** a single fuel line that supplies oil under pressure to all the cylinders of a diesel engine **:** HEADER 3c

common ratio *n* **:** the ratio of each term of a geometrical progression to the term preceding it

common recovery *n* **:** a conveyance of real property through the medium of an action and judgment at law formerly widely used in England as a means of giving a tenant in tail an absolute power to dispose of his estate

common room *n* **1** *Brit* **:** a room available to all members of a residential community for relaxation and sociability ⟨the *common room* of an inn⟩ **2 a :** a room in a college reserved for the informal and exclusive use of the teaching staff — see SENIOR COMMON ROOM **b :** a room in a college reserved for the general use of students — see JUNIOR COMMON ROOM

commons *pl of* COMMON, *pres 3d sing of* COMMON

common school *n* **:** a free public school now usu. including primary and secondary grades; *sometimes* **:** a free public elementary school

common scold *n* **:** a woman who disturbs the public peace by noisy and quarrelsome or abusive behavior constituting a public nuisance

common seal *n* **:** a seal adopted and used by a corporation or similar body

common sense *n* [trans. of L or Gk; L *sensus communis,* trans. of Gk *koinē aisthēsis*] **1 :** a sense believed to unite the sensations of all senses in a general sensation or perception **2 :** good sound ordinary sense **:** good judgment or prudence in estimating or managing affairs esp. as free from emotional bias or intellectual subtlety or as not dependent on special or technical knowledge ⟨too absurdly metaphysical for the ears of prudent *common sense* —P.E.More⟩ **3 a** *among Cartesians* **:** something that is evident by the natural light of reason and hence common to all men **b** (1) **:** the intuitions that according to the school of Scottish philosophy are common to all mankind (2) **:** the capacity for such intuitions **c :** the unreflective opinions of ordinary men **:** the ideas and conceptions natural to a man untrained in technical philosophy — used esp. in epistemology **syn** see SENSE

commonsense \ˈ==ˌ=\ *adj* [*common sense*] **1 :** showing practical common sense ⟨canny ~ folk with a shrewd eye to interest —Charles Kingsley⟩ **2 :** perceptible by the ordinary senses **:** understood as commonly interpreted **:** CLEAR, PALPABLE ⟨a ~ object⟩ ⟨the ~ interpretation⟩

commonsense realism *n* **:** the philosophy of Thomas Reid and the Scottish school **:** NATURAL REALISM

common sensibility *n* **:** SENSUS COMMUNIS

com·mon·sen·si·ble \ˈkämənˈsen(t)səbəl\ *adj* **:** marked by or conforming to common sense

com·mon·sen·si·cal \-en(t)səkəl\ *adj* **:** COMMONSENSIBLE ⟨countryfolk, unlearned and ~, were capable of solving problems that beset the more sophisticated —J.D.Hart⟩ — **com·mon·sen·si·cal·ly** \-k(ə)lē\ *adv*

common serjeant *n* **:** a judicial officer of the Corporation of London who is assistant to the recorder

common shell *n* **:** a gun shell having a comparatively large cavity filled with a bursting charge of high explosive intended to explode after passing through light protective armor

common shrew *n* **:** a widely distributed European shrew (*Sorex araneus*)

common sign *n* **:** one of the four zodiacal signs Gemini, Virgo, Sagittarius, and Pisces

common sorghum *n* **:** a strong erect annual grass (*Sorghum vulgare*) that is the source of many of the cultivated varieties of sorghum (as kafir and broomcorn)

common stock *n* **:** capital stock of a corporation having one or more classes of preferred stock that enjoy a preference in dividend distributions

common storage *n* **:** storage or a storage place that uses air at outside temperature for cooling; *specif* **:** a storage place esp. for fruits or vegetables that has openings just above ground level for admission of cool air and at the top for escape of warm air and other gases

common substitution *n* **:** SUBSTITUTION 1a(1)

common sunflower *n* **:** the annual sunflower (*Helianthus annuus*) often grown for silage and for its seeds which yield an edible oil and are used for stock feed — see SUNFLOWER illustration

common time *n* **:** duple or quadruple time; *esp* **:** four quarter notes per bar or its musical equivalent — called also *common measure*

common touch *n* **:** the trait or gift of appealing to or arousing the sympathetic interest of the generality of man esp. by having or giving the appearance of having basic qualities in common with them ⟨come a long way up the ladder of success without losing the *common touch* —Joseph Driscoll⟩ ⟨despite an excellent family and educational background, he has the *common touch* —Bill Wolf⟩

common traverse *n* **:** a legal traverse without the denial of inducement and amounting to a direct denial in common negative language

com·mon·ty \ˈkäməntē\ *n* -ES [ME *comunete, comountee,* fr. MF *comuneté* — more at COMMUNITY] **1 :** a right of ownership in land held in common by two or more persons and under certain servitudes; *also* **:** the land itself **2 :** COMMON OF PASTURE

common vetch *n* **:** a somewhat twining annual herb (*Vicia sativa*) that was introduced from Europe, that is grown esp. as a forage, silage, and green manure crop, and that often escapes to waste places and roadsides

com·mon·weal \ˈkämənˌwēl, ˌ==ˈ=\ *n* -s [ME *commun wele,* fr. *commun* common + *wele* weal] **1 :** the general welfare **2** *archaic* **:** COMMONWEALTH

com·mon·wealth \ˈkämənˌwelth, ˌ==ˈ=\ *n* -s [ME *commen wealthe,* fr. *commen, commun* common + *wealthe, welthe* wealth (well-being)] **1 :** public welfare **:** wealth held in common **2 a :** a whole body of people united by common consent to form a nation, state, or politically organized community **b :** a state esp. conceived as a body politic founded on law and united by compact or by tacit agreement of the people for the common good **c :** a state in which the supreme power resides with the people and their representatives **:** REPUBLIC ⟨the ~ established in England under Oliver Cromwell⟩ **3 a :** a state of the U.S. ⟨~*s* joining the Union after the Civil War⟩ — used in the official designations of Kentucky, Massachusetts, Pennsylvania, and Virginia in preference to the word *state* **b :** a self-governing autonomous state; *usu* **:** a former colony that is associated by treaty or agreement in a loose political federation with a mother country or former colonial power ⟨*Commonwealth* of Australia⟩ **c :** an association of self-governing autonomous states united by a common allegiance to a mother country and forming by treaty or agreement a loose confederation having a somewhat common political and cultural background ⟨a ~ of nations⟩ ⟨the British *Commonwealth*⟩ **4 a :** a group of persons conceived of as united by common interests ⟨the ~ of artists or of literary men⟩ **b :** the range of interests uniting such a group ⟨the ~ of learning⟩

commonwealth day *n, usu cap C&D* **:** May 24 observed in parts of the British Commonwealth as the anniversary of Queen Victoria's birthday

commonwealth's-man \-l(th)smən, -ˌsman\ *n, pl* **commonwealth's-men 1** *obs* **:** a man in his relation to a commonwealth **2 a :** an adherent of a commonwealth (as the 17th century English Commonwealth) **b** *archaic* **:** REPUBLICAN 1

common year *n* **:** a calendar year not containing any intercalary period — see YEAR table

com·mo·ran·cy \ˈkämərənsē\ *n* -ES **:** ordinary residence or dwelling in a place **:** the habitation of a place

com·mo·rant \-rənt\ *adj* [L *commorant-, commorans,* pres. part. of *commorari* to sojourn, tarry, fr. *com-* + *morari* to delay, stay, remain — more at MORATORY] **:** having one's habitation **:** DWELLING ⟨a London man now ~ in Edinburgh⟩

com·mo·ri·ent \kəˈmōrēənt\ *n, pl* **commorients** \-ts\ *or* **commorien·tes** \kəˌmōrēˈenˌtēz\ [L *commorient-, commoriens,* pres. part. of *commori* to die with, fr. *com-* + *mori* to die — more at MURDER] **:** one of two or a number of persons perishing at the same time by the same calamity

commos *var of* KOMMOS

com·mot \ˈkäˌmät\ *or* **com·mote** \-mōt\ *n* -s [ME, fr. ML *commotum,* fr. MW *cymwd*] **:** an early Welsh territorial and administrative unit, two such units being normally equal to a cantred

com·mo·tion \kəˈmōshən\ *n* -s [ME *commocioun,* fr. MF *commotion,* fr. L *commotion-, commotio,* fr. *commotus* (past part. of *commovēre*) + *-ion-, -io* -ion] **1 :** a condition of civil unrest, public disorder, agitation, or insurrection ⟨18 years of ~ had made the majority of the people ready to buy repose at any price —T.B.Macaulay⟩ **2 :** continuous or recurrent motion ⟨the ~ of the steady gentle breeze⟩ ⟨the thermal ~ of the surface atoms —*Physical Rev.*⟩ **3 :** mental excitement, uncertainty, or confusion ⟨startled . . . into no ordinary state of ~ —Arnold Bennett⟩ **4 a :** violent or sharp disturbance **:** noisy, unruly, or tumultuous stir ⟨a gang of hooligans making a ~ in the street⟩ **b :** noisy confusion **:** HUSTLE ⟨there was ~ all over the house at the return of the young heir —George Meredith⟩ **5** *med* **:** CONCUSSION, SHOCK

syn AGITATION, CONFUSION, TUMULT, TURMOIL, TURBULENCE, CONVULSION, UPHEAVAL: COMMOTION may suggest unusual, violent, or disturbing activity usu. accompanied by noise, uproar, hubbub, or activity bringing with it unrest ⟨wakened at midnight by a *commotion* in the street below⟩ ⟨trying to put out a drunk without distracting *commotion*⟩ ⟨agitators keeping up a *commotion* during the speech⟩ AGITATION may suggest a strong swirling, stirring, or seething, an emotional excitation similar to these physical actions, or a sustained effort to stir up excitement about some political or social issue ⟨the panting of the horses communicated a tremulous motion to the coach, as if it were in a state of *agitation* —Charles Dickens⟩ ⟨breathless with *agitation* —Jane Austen⟩ ⟨an anti-Catholic *agitation* that was marked by the destruction of churches —*Amer. Guide Series: N. Y.*⟩ CONFUSION describes a state in which things are mixed, poured, or heaped together in a jumble so that differentiation is hard, a mental condition marked by uncertainty, indecisiveness and doubt, or a social or political situation making for such a condition ⟨tremendous smokestacks rose out of a *confusion* of buildings —*New Yorker*⟩ ⟨if jostled they bowed profusely to the jostlers, and appeared overwhelmed with *confusion* —E.A.Poe⟩ TUMULT applies to commotion and agitation marked by uproar, din, or, more specif., the noise of a great mob in riot or to any similar noisy jarring inescapable confusion ⟨the *tumults* and disorders of the Great Rebellion —T.S.Eliot⟩ ⟨the whole knoll was suddenly in a *tumult* of movement; mounted officers clattered off —Kenneth Roberts⟩ TURMOIL indicates a state in which everything is in agitated disorder and pointless noisy activity, where nothing is at rest or in place ⟨the *turmoil* which attends departure from home —F.A.Swinnerton⟩ ⟨her life had been calm, regular, monotonous. And now it was thrown into an indescribable *turmoil* —Arnold Bennett⟩ ⟨the revolutionary *turmoil* in Mexico in 1913 —*Amer. Guide Series: Texas*⟩ TURBULENCE suggests swirling wild unruly disorder or a disposition to it ⟨scenes of public *turbulence* and crass overriding of parliamentary opinion —Cecil Sprigge⟩ ⟨the *turbulence* normal in a frontier community —R.A.Billington⟩ ⟨plenty of the *turbulence* of passion but none of the gravity of thoughtful emotion —A.T. Quiller-Couch⟩ CONVULSION indicates a violent, spasmodic, or sudden surging confused action — as in the earth's crust, the individual's mind, or the body politic ⟨flourishing cities were demolished by the earth's *convulsion* —Martin Gardner⟩ ⟨the *convulsions* of a soul storm-driven and unreconcilable spiritual conflicts —H.O.Taylor⟩ UPHEAVAL indicates a violent, very forceful thrusting out or up, heaving up, or overthrowing ⟨the vast social *convulsions* of a continent in travail are such a mystery to this type of mind that even the most catastrophic *upheavals* are attributed to mistakes made in our State Department —Reinhold Niebuhr⟩ ⟨new islands rising from the seas as a result of volcanic *upheavals*⟩

com·move \kə'müv, kä'-\ *vt* -ED/-ING/-S [ME *commoeven, commeven*, fr. MF *commuev-*, pres. stem of *commovoir*, fr. L *commovēre*, fr. *com-* + *movēre* to move — more at MOVE] **1** : to move violently : stir up : AGITATE **2** : stir to emotion : EXCITE, IMPASSION

commr *abbr* **1** commissioner **2** commoner

com·mu·na \kə'myünə\ *n, pl* **commu·nae** \-,nē, -,nī\ [ML — more at COMMUNE] : COMMUNE

com·mu·nal \kə'myünəl *also* 'kämyən- *sometimes esp in sense 1* (')kä¦myün-\ *adj* [F, fr. OF *comunal*, fr. LL *communalis*, fr. L *communis* of the community, common + *-alis* -al — more at COMMON] **1 a** : of or relating to a commune or a society characterized by communes ⟨~ electors⟩ ⟨~ organization⟩ **b** : belonging to or produced by the social environment of a primitive commune : characteristic of a simple social life ⟨~ poetry is typified by the ballad⟩ **2** : owned in common : participated in, shared, or used by a whole community : marked by sharing in common by members of a group ⟨a ~ settlement in which all wages, earnings and food were pooled —*Time*⟩ ⟨dipping each his bread into a ~ dish of stew —Paul Roche⟩ **3** : of or relating to rival communities, esp. the communities of India ⟨~ division⟩ ⟨the ~ problem⟩ : involving two or more communities competing (as for political advantage and patronage) ⟨~ strife⟩ — **com·mu·nal·ly** \-əlē,-əli\ *adv*

com·mu·nal·ism \-ə,lizəm\ *n* -S **1** : a principle or system of organization in which the major social or political units of the society are communes or local self-governing communities **2** : belief in or practice of communal living **3** : a system or principle of communal organization in which rival minority groups are devoted to their own interests rather than to those of the whole society : strong loyalty and adherence to one's community and its values sometimes appearing in excess and with nationally divisive effects; *broadly* : ETHNOCENTRISM

com·mu·nal·ist \-ələst\ *n* -S [F *communaliste*, fr. *communal* + *-iste* -ist] : an advocate of communalism

com·mu·nal·i·ty \,kämyə'nalədē\ *n* -ES **1** : communal state or character **2** : the sentiment of community solidarity : concordance or agreement in opinion or feeling throughout a group : group unity

com·mu·nal·i·za·tion \kə,myünələ'zāshən, ,kämyən-, -ə,lī'z-\ *n* -S : act or process of making communal

com·mu·nal·ize \kə'myünə,līz, 'kämyən-\ *vt* -ED/-ING/-S : to make communal; *specif* : to subject to the rights, methods, organization, or ownership of a community

communal marriage *n* : a hypothetical primitive promiscuity in which all the women of a social group belonged to all the men in common — called also *group marriage*; compare PUNALUA

communal ownership *n* : the ownership of land or other property by a community so that each member has a right to use the property or a portion of it

com·mu·nard \'kämyə,närd, ,==ˈ=\ *n* -S [F, fr. *commune* commune + *-ard* — more at COMMUNE] **1** : an adherent of the principles of communalism **2** *usu cap* : one who supported or participated in the Commune of Paris in 1871

[1]**com·mune** \kə'myün, *archaic* 'kä,m-\ *vi* -ED/-ING/-S [ME *comunen, communen*, fr. OF *comuner* to put in common, share, fr. *comun* common — more at COMMON] **1** *archaic* : CONVERSE, CONFER **2** *archaic* : to associate together : have dealings **3** [ME *comunen* to administer Holy Communion, fr. MF *comunier* to administer or receive Communion, fr. LL *communicare* — more at COMMUNICATE] : to receive Communion : partake of the Eucharist **4 a** : to hold converse or intercommunication esp. with great mental or spiritual depth or intensity **b** : to attain to an earnest or deep feeling of unity, appreciation, and receptivity — used with *with* ⟨~ with nature⟩ ⟨~ with precious books, ancient and new, which bear the stamp of eternity —David Ben-Gurion⟩

[2]**com·mune** \'kä,myün\ *n* -S : COMMUNION, CONVERSATION ⟨in ~ with nature⟩

[3]**com·mune** \'kä,myün *also* kə'm- *or* kä'm-\ *n* -S [F, fr. ML *communa, commune*, fr. L *communia*, neut. pl. of *communis* common — more at COMMON] **1** : a small administrative district (as one governed by a mayor and municipal council) usu. in a European country ⟨the provinces and ~s of Belgium⟩ — compare ARRONDISSEMENT **2** : a political or governmental body espousing revolutionary or communist principles **3 a** : COMMONALTY, COMMONS **b** : any of various bodies treated as a unit at law (as the peasantry sharing the common rights and property in a village community) **4 a** : a community in which the inhabitants have close personal ties of friendship and interest **b** : a small collective unit typically rural : a group practicing communal living

com·mu·ni·ca·bil·i·ty \kə,myünəkə'bilədē, -nēk-, -ətē, -i\ *n* -ES : the quality of being readily communicated or of having a message readily understood

com·mu·ni·ca·ble \=ˈ==kəbəl\ *adj* [MF, fr. LL *communicabilis*, fr. L *communicare* + *-abilis* -able] **1** : capable of being communicated: **a** : imparted without undue difficulty ⟨~ knowledge⟩ **b** : transmitted from one to another ⟨a ~ illness⟩ **2** : talkative, open, or frank rather than taciturn : given to communicating : COMMUNICATIVE — **com·mu·ni·ca·ble·ness** *n* -ES — **com·mu·ni·ca·bly** \-blē, -li\ *adv*

communicable disease *n* : an infectious disease transmissible from person to person, animal to animal, animal to man, or man to animal by direct contact with an affected individual or his discharges or by indirect means (as by a vector) — compare CONTAGIOUS DISEASE

[1]**com·mu·ni·cant** \-kənt\ *n* -S [LL & L; LL *communicant-, communicans*, pres. part. of *communicare* to receive Holy Communion, fr. L, to share, impart, partake] **1** : one who partakes of the sacrament of the Lord's Supper or is entitled to partake of it : a church member; *broadly* : a member or adherent of a group **2** : one who communicates or imparts; *specif* : INFORMANT

[2]**communicant** \"\ *adj* [L *communicant-, communicans*] **1** : SHARING, PARTICIPATING **2** [LL *communicant-, communicans*, fr. L] : partaking in a church communion

com·mu·ni·cate \kə'myünə,kāt, *usu* -ād.+V\ *vb* -ED/-ING/-S [L *communicatus*, past part. of *communicare* to share, impart, partake, fr. *communis* common — more at MEAN] *vt* **1** *archaic* : partake of : use or enjoy in common : SHARE ⟨thousands that ~ our loss —Ben Jonson⟩ **2 a** : to make known : inform a person of : convey the knowledge or information of ⟨~ the news⟩ ⟨~ his secret to a friend⟩ **b** : IMPART, TRANSMIT ⟨~ his pleasure to us⟩ ⟨an odor *communicated* to one's fingers⟩ ⟨*communicating* the disease to others⟩ **c** : to make (itself) known — used of an intangible ⟨his tension *communicated* itself to his companion⟩ **3** [LL *communicatus*, fr. L] : to administer the Communion to (a person) ⟨the priest *communicating* him⟩ **4** *archaic* : to put (oneself) into close connection or relationship with — used with *to* **5** *archaic* : to give or deliver over (something material or tangible) : BESTOW ~ *vi* **1** [LL *communicatus*, fr. L] : to partake of the Lord's Supper : receive Communion ⟨Eastern Orthodox Christians ~ in both elements⟩ **2** *obs* : to have a common part : PARTICIPATE, SHARE **3** : to send information or messages sometimes back and forth : speak, gesticulate, or write to another to convey information : interchange thoughts ⟨they *communicated* with each other for years⟩ **4** : be connected : open into each other : afford unbroken passage : JOIN ⟨the two rooms ~⟩ ⟨the pantry ~s with the hall⟩ **5** *philos* : to have something logically in common : be further specifications of a common universal : be overlapping classifications or connotations **6** : to arouse or enlist the sympathetic interest or understanding — used with *with* ⟨old plays that . . . have long since lost their ability to ~ with an audience —Wolcott Gibbs⟩

com·mu·ni·ca·tee \kə'myünəkə¦tē, -nēk-\ *n* -S : one that receives a communication : one that is communicated with

communicating artery *n* : any of three arteries in the brain that complete the circle of Willis, one connecting the anterior cerebral arteries and two connecting the internal carotids with the posterior cerebrals

com·mu·ni·ca·tion \kə,myünə'kāshən\ *n* -S [ME *communicacioun*, fr. MF *communication*, fr. L *communication-, communicatio*, fr. *communicatus* (past part. of *communicare* to communicate) + *-ion-, -io*, -ion] **1** : the act or action of imparting or transmitting ⟨the ~ of the common cold⟩ ⟨the ~ of power to the machine⟩ **2 a** : facts or information communicated **b** : a letter, note, or other instance of written information ⟨he had not yet read the spy's ~⟩ **3 a** *obs* : CONVERSATION, TALK **b** *archaic* : personal dealings **c** *archaic* : SEXUAL INTERCOURSE **4** *archaic* : common participation **5 a** : access between persons or places : opportunity of communicating ⟨maintaining ~ between the regulars and guerrillas⟩ **b communications** *pl* : means of communicating: (1) : a system (as of telephones or telegraphs) for communicating information and orders (as in a naval service) (2) : a system of routes for moving troops, supplies, and vehicles in military operations (3) : the function in an industrial organization that transmits ideas, policies, and orders (4) *sometimes cap* : personnel engaged in communicating **c** : a medium through which information is carried ⟨channels of ~ in industry⟩ **6 a** : interchange of thoughts or opinions : a process by which meanings are exchanged between individuals through a common system of symbols (as language, signs, or gestures) **b** : close or intimate rapport that is sometimes intellectual and often affective **7** : a Masonic lodge meeting **8** *or* **communications** *pl but sing or pl in const* : an art that deals with expressing and exchanging ideas effectively in speech or writing or through the graphic or dramatic arts and that is taught as an integrated program at various levels of education in distinction to traditional separate courses in composition and speech

communication engineering *n* : engineering concerned with the sending and receiving of signals esp. by means of electrical or electroacoustic devices and electromagnetic waves

communications zone *n* : the part of a theater of military operations behind and contiguous to the combat zone

communication trench *n* : a connecting trench

com·mu·ni·ca·tive \kə'myünə,kā|d·iv, -nəkə|, -nēkə|, |tiv, -ēv *also* -əv\ *adj* [ME, fr. MF or ML; MF *communicatif*, fr. ML *communicativus*, fr. L *communicatus* (past part. of *communicare* to communicate) + *-ivus* -ive — more at COMMUNICATE] **1** : marked by the ability or tendency to communicate: **a** *obs* : capable of spreading or transmitting : DIFFUSIVE **b** *archaic* : disposed to give : GENEROUS, BENEFICENT **c** : ready to give information freely : free, unguarded, and open in conversation : TALKATIVE; *sometimes* : SOCIABLE, AFFABLE ⟨a ~ person and quickly told all she knew —W.M.Thackeray⟩ **2 a** *obs* : capable of being communicated : COMMUNICABLE **b** *obs* : commonly applicable **c** *archaic* : well adapted for use in communication **3** : of or relating to communication ⟨~ arts⟩ — **com·mu·ni·ca·tive·ly** *adv* — **com·mu·ni·ca·tive·ness** *n* -ES

com·mu·ni·ca·tor \-nə,kād·ə(r), -ātə-\ *n* -S [LL, fr. L *communicatus* + *-or*] : one that communicates; *sometimes* : a person who works with or on methods or devices used in communication or facilitating communication

com·mu·ni·ca·to·ry \-nəkə,tōrē, -nēk-, -tȯr-, -ri\ *adj* [ML *communicatorius*, fr. L *communicatus* + *-orius* -ory] : tending to communicate

communicatory letters *n pl* : letters of communication between ancient churches; *also* : letters of recommendation to the communion of distant churches

communing *pres part of* COMMUNE

com·mu·nion \kə'myünyən\ *n* -S [ME *comunioun*, fr. MF, LL, & L; MF *communion*, fr. LL *communion-, communio* union of Christians, Eucharist, fr. L, mutual participation, fr. *communis* common + *-ion-, -io* -ion — more at COMMON] **1** : an action or situation involving sharing: **a** : possession in common : joint ownership : the state of possessions thus held ⟨this ~ of goods —William Blackstone⟩ **b** : a function performed jointly : an interrelation in activity : an interdependent working together or cooperation ⟨~ of motion of a bird's wings⟩ **2** *usu cap* **a** : the Eucharist : the Lord's Supper **b** : a celebration of the Eucharist or the Lord's Supper either as a separate service or as a part of a larger service (as the mass in Roman Catholicism or the divine liturgy in Eastern Orthodoxy) **c** : the act of receiving the eucharistic elements **d** : the elements of the Eucharist ⟨take *Communion*⟩ **e** : the psalm or antiphon said or sung at Communion **3 a** : the fellowship of members of the same church **b** : general fellowship : a state marked by fellowship, sympathetic companionship, communication, and understanding : COMMUNICATION, CONVERSE, EXCHANGE ⟨the sentiment of ~ with others, of the breaking down of barriers —John Dewey⟩ **c** : intimate, sympathetic, reverential, or mystic interchange of ideas and feelings esp. dealing with matters innermost and spiritual in order to inspire, strengthen, or solace often as if between man and nature or the supernatural ⟨this ~ with the spirit of love at work in the universe —E.R.Bentley⟩ ⟨no sympathetic ~ between him and the solitude —Ellen Glasgow⟩ **d** : COMMUNICATION, DEALINGS ⟨having only limited ~ with the natives⟩ **4** : a group of religious persons bound together by essential agreement in religious consciousness; *esp* : a body of Christians having one common faith and discipline ⟨the Presbyterian ~⟩ ⟨the Roman Catholic ~⟩ **syn** see RELIGION

com·mu·nion·able \-nyənəbəl\ *adj* : open to or admissible to communion

com·mu·nion·al \-nyənəl\ *adj* : of or relating to communion

communion cloth *n* : [1]CORPORAL

communion cup *n* : a cup used for wine or grape juice in the Lord's Supper or Communion service; *specif* : either a small individual cup furnished each communicant or a single large cup from which all communicants sip

communion glass *n* : a small glass used as an individual communion cup

communion hymn *n* : a hymn sung in a Christian worship service immediately preceding the celebration of Holy Communion

com·mu·nion·ist \-nyənəst\ *n* -S **1** : one who holds a specified theory as to communion ⟨a strict ~⟩ ⟨a free ~⟩ **2** : COMMUNICANT

communion of saints [trans. of ML *communio sanctorum*] : the fellowship of all true Christian believers living and dead

communion rail *n* : the altar rail at which communicants receive Communion

communion sunday *n, usu cap C&S* : a Sunday on which Holy Communion is celebrated in Protestant churches

communion table *n* : the table used in the celebration of the Lord's Supper

com·mu·ni·qué \kə'myünə,kā, =,==ˈ=\ *n* -S [F, fr. past part. of *communiquer* to communicate, fr. L *communicare* — more at COMMUNICATE] : an official announcement; *typically* : a brief formal summation report

com·mu·nism \'kämyə,nizəm, *chiefly in substand speech* -mə,n-\ *n* -S [F *communisme*, fr. *commun* common + *-isme* -ism — more at COMMON] **1 a** : a theory advocating elimination of private ownership of property or capital **b** : a system or condition real or imagined in which goods are owned commonly rather than privately and are available as needed to each one in a unified group sometimes limited, sometimes inclusive, and often composed of members living and working together : a similar system preventing amassing of privately owned goods and assuring equalitarian returns to those working ⟨Plato's aristocratic ~⟩ ⟨the ~ of the early church groups⟩ ⟨the ~ obtaining among the early colonists⟩ **2** *often cap* [Russ & G; Russ *kommunizm*, fr. G *kommunismus*, fr. F *communisme*] **a** : a social and political doctrine or movement based upon revolutionary Marxian socialism that interprets history as a relentless class war eventually to result everywhere in the victory of the proletariat and the social ownership of the means of production with relative social and economic equality for all and ultimately to lead to a classless society **b** : BOLSHEVISM **c** : a totalitarian system of government in which the state as owner of the major industries and acting through the medium of a single authoritarian party controls in large measure the economic, social, and cultural life of the society **3** *often cap* : strong left-wing activity or inclination that is subversive or revolutionary **4** *biol* : COMMENSALISM

[1]**com·mu·nist** \-myənəst, *chiefly in substand speech* -m(ə)n-\ *n* -S [F *communiste*, fr. *commun* + *-iste* -ist] **1 a** : one who believes in or adheres to a theory of communism or communal living ⟨the principle from which the ~s started was the Christian belief, widespread through the middle ages, that common possession was a more perfect way of life than private ownership —G.H.Sabine⟩ **b** : one who practices communism : one living in a society in which goods are owned in common ⟨more rigid sectarians living as ~s⟩ **2** : COMMUNARD **3** *usu cap* [Russ *kommunist*, fr. G, fr. F *communiste*] **a** : a member of a Communist party or movement; *esp* : an official member paying dues and carrying a party membership card — compare BOLSHEVIK **b** : one who consistently adheres to, supports, or aids a Communist government, party, or movement and opposes all others **c** : one who holds to notions or engages in activities conceived to be violently left-wing, subversive, or revolutionary — used rhetorically in political denigration ⟨it was a common habit of the East European dictatorships to denounce as *Communists* all who resolutely criticized social and political abuses —*Economist*⟩ ⟨their definition of a *Communist* is a man who wants reforms —Elmer Davis⟩ **syn** see COLLECTIVIST

[2]**communist** \"\ *adj* **1** : of or relating to communism : marked by communal living : adhering to or favoring communism ⟨a ~ community where possessions were commonly owned⟩ ⟨a ~ philosophy from ancient times⟩ **2** *usu cap* **a** : of or relating to a Communist party : composed of or participated in by Communists ⟨a *Communist* newspaper⟩ ⟨a *Communist* government⟩ ⟨a *Communist* plot⟩ **b** : advocating, aiding, or furthering Communism ⟨a *Communist* sympathizer⟩

com·mu·nis·tic \¦kämyə¦nistik, *chiefly in substand speech* -mə¦n-\ *adj* **1** : living in common : COMMUNIST, COMMUNAL : illustrating or favoring communal living and common ownership of wealth ⟨the ~ teachings of the old Fathers that all have an equal right to property —Frank Thilly⟩ ⟨the ~ sects, which require the renunciation of all personal property —W.L.Sperry⟩ **2** *sometimes cap* : of, relating to, or marked by communism : in accordance with, tending to, or influenced by communism ⟨had heard of ~ propaganda in the area⟩ **3** *of birds* : living or having their nests in common — **com·mu·nis·ti·cal·ly** \-tək(ə)lē, -tēk-, -li\ *adv*

[1]**com·mu·ni·tar·i·an** \kə,myünə'terēən, -taar-, -tār-\ *n* -S [*community* + *-arian*; trans. of F *communautaire*] : an advocate of communitarianism : a member of a community practicing communitarianism

[2]**communitarian** \=¦==¦==\ *adj* : advocating, practicing, or based on communitarianism

com·mu·ni·tar·i·an·ism \=,==ˈ==ə,nizəm\ *n* -S : a communal system of organization based on small cooperative communities practicing some communist principles

com·mu·ni·ty \kə'myünəd·ē, -ətē, -i\ *n* -ES [ME *comunete*, fr. MF *communité, comuneté*, fr. L *communitat-, communitas*, fr. *communis* common + *-itat-, -itas* -ity] **1** : a body of individuals organized into a unit or manifesting usu. with awareness some unifying trait: **a** : STATE, COMMONWEALTH **b** : the people living in a particular place or region and usu. linked by common interests; *broadly* : the region itself : any population cluster ⟨small, compact, homogeneous *communities* such as the Greek city-state or Elizabethan England —C.D.Lewis⟩ **c** : a monastic body or other unified religious group **d** : an interacting population of different kinds of individuals (as species) constituting a society or association or simply an aggregation of mutually related individuals in a given location ⟨a climax ~⟩ **e** : a group of people marked by a common characteristic but living within a larger society that does not share that characteristic ⟨the Chinese ~ in New York⟩ ⟨the artists' ~ downtown⟩ ⟨the Jewish ~ in London⟩; *esp* : such a group politically organized and recognized esp. as a separate voting group for election purposes ⟨Sikh and Muslim *communities* in India⟩ **f** : a group sharing a particular economic or social belief and living communally **g** : any group sharing interests or pursuits ⟨a ~ of scholars⟩ : a group linked by a common policy ⟨a tariff ~ of small nations⟩ **h** : a body of persons or nations united by historical consciousness or by common social, economic, and political interests ⟨the entire Christian ~⟩ ⟨the European coal and steel ~⟩ **2** : society at large : PUBLIC : people in general — used with the definite article ⟨the interests of the ~⟩ **3 a** : common or joint ownership, tenure, experience, or pertinence : COMMONNESS, SHARING, PARTICIPATION ⟨asserts that ~ of goods would be the ideal institution —G.L.Dickinson⟩ ⟨out of the atmosphere of controversy to the ~ of our love again —Mary Austin⟩ ⟨the essential ~ of interests shared by all branches of learning —G.W.Cottrell⟩ **b** : common character : fact of showing a trait or various traits in common : AGREEMENT, CONCORD, LIKENESS ⟨although there are varieties, the ~ of style is still more evident —O. Elfrida Saunders⟩ **c** : shared activity : social intercourse : FELLOWSHIP, COMMUNION; *esp* : social activity marked by a feeling of unity but also individual participation completely willing and not forced or coerced and without loss of individuality ⟨in order that there may be a ~, there must be conscious and purposive sharing —Ernest Barker⟩ **d** *obs* : frequent occurrence **e** : a social or societal state ⟨emerging from feral isolation into ~⟩ **4** : a civil-law partnership or society of property between husband and wife arising by virtue of the fact of marriage or by contract

community center *n* : a building or group of buildings constituting a focal point of educational and recreational activities and serving a whole community; *also* : a concentration of such activities

community chest *or* **community fund** *n* : a general fund accumulated from individual subscriptions to defray demands on a community's private charitable and welfare organizations

community church *n* : an interdenominational or nondenominational church for community use found in the U.S. and Canada

community college *n* : a college or junior college typically nonresidential serving a specific community often by fitting its curriculum to the community's needs

community house *n* **1** : a center consisting often of a single building for a community's social, cultural, recreational, and civic activities **2** : a large building providing separate quarters for families of common descent : PUEBLO

community organization *n* : social work concentrating upon the organized development of community social welfare through coordination of public and private agencies

community property *n* : property held jointly by husband and wife

community school *n* : a school that seeks to integrate children into the community by selected activities other than academic and at the same time serves as a community center for recreation and adult education

community singing *n* : unrehearsed mass singing of familiar songs by any assemblage or audience

community trust *n* : a fund acquired from bequests the income from which is to be used for the general betterment of the inhabitants of a community

community-wide \=¦==¦=\ *adj* : operative or effective throughout the whole community ⟨a *community-wide* service⟩

com·mu·ni·za·tion \,kämyənə'zāshən, -,nī'z- *sometimes* kə,myünə'z- — *see* COMMUNIZE\ *n* -S *often cap* [L *communis* common + E *-ization* — more at COMMON] : the act of communizing : state of being communized

com·mu·nize \'kämyə,nīz *sometimes in sense 1a* kə'myü,n-\ *vb* -ED/-ING/-S [back-formation fr. *communization*] **1 a** : to make common **b** : to make into state-owned property

2 *sometimes cap* **:** to subject to or bring into accord with Communist principles of organization
com·mut·able \kə'myüd·əbəl, -üt·ə-\ *adj* [L *commutabilis,* fr. *commutare* to exchange + *-abilis* -able — more at COMMUTE] **:** capable of being commuted or interchanged
com·mu·tate \'kämyə,tāt, *usu* -ād.+V\ *vb* -ED/-ING/-S [back-formation fr. *commutation*] **1 :** to reverse the direction of (an electric current) by a change of connections **2 :** to reverse every other half cycle of (an alternating current) so as to form a unidirectional current
commutating pole *n* **:** INTERPOLE
com·mu·ta·tion \,kämyə'tāshən\ *n* -S [ME, fr. MF, fr. L *commutation-, commutatio,* fr. *commutatus* (past part. of *commutare* to change) + *-ion-, -io* -ion — more at COMMUTE] **1 :** EXCHANGE, TRADE, BARTER ⟨the transatlantic ~ of experts —*Fortune*⟩ **2** *archaic* **:** CHANGE, ALTERATION **3 :** SUBSTITUTION, INTERCHANGE, REPLACEMENT **4 :** substitution in a charge, assessment, payment, or remuneration of one form, method, schedule, or amount for another **:** an arrangement effecting such substitution **:** money or other value involved ⟨~ by money payment in place of the exacted service⟩ ⟨a ~ whereby the remaining payments were lumped together⟩ ⟨officers living off the post receiving rental allowance ~⟩ **5 a :** change of a legal penalty or punishment to a lesser one ⟨~ of the death sentence to a long prison term⟩ **b :** substitution of one work for another in fulfilling a religious vow **6 :** act of commuting **:** travel back and forth between two points, esp. between home and work, repeated a certain number of times within a given interval **7 a :** reversal or transference of the connections between an armature coil and the external circuit in a direct-current dynamo or motor **b :** the partial overlapping of successive cycles of current from successive anodes in a polyphase rectifier
commutation ticket *n* **:** a transportation ticket for a fixed number of trips back and forth over the same route (as between a city and one of its suburbs) during a limited time (as a month) sold at a reduced rate because of the frequency and regularity of travel
com·mu·ta·tive \'kämyə,tād·iv, kə'myüd·əd·iv\ *adj* [ML *commutativus,* fr. L *commutatus* (past part. of *commutare* to exchange) + *-ivus* -ive — more at COMMUTE] **1 :** of or relating to commutation **:** effecting or showing commutation ⟨a ~ fine⟩ ⟨~ payment plans⟩ **2** *of a mathematical or logical operation* **:** consisting of a step or sequence of steps in which the final result is independent of the order of the elements or steps ⟨~ multiplication⟩ ⟨~ addition⟩
commutative algebra *n* **:** algebra in which the rule of multiplication is such that the product of *a* by *b* is the same as the product of *b* by *a*
commutative contract *n* **:** a civil-law contract in which each party gives and receives an equivalent
commutative justice *n* **:** justice bearing on the relations between individuals esp. in respect to the equitable exchange of goods and fulfillment of contractual obligations
commutative law *n* **:** a law applicable to certain mathematical operations: the order of the elements involved is immaterial
com·mu·ta·tor \'kämyə,tād·ə(r), -,tāt·ə-\ *n* -S [*commutation* + *-or*] **1 :** a switch for reversing the direction of an electric current in a circuit by reversing connections **2 :** a series of bars or segments insulated from each other and so connected to armature coils of a dynamo that rotation of the armature will in conjunction with fixed brushes result in unidirectional current output in the case of a generator and in the reversal of the current into the coils in the case of a motor — see DYNAMO illustration
com·mute \kə'myüt, *usu* -üd.+V\ *vb* -ED/-ING/-S [L *commutare* to change, exchange, fr. *com-* + *mutare* to change — more at MUTABLE] *vt* **1 a :** to place or give (a thing) in exchange for another **:** EXCHANGE, SUBSTITUTE, INTERCHANGE ⟨*commuting* foreign money to domestic⟩ ⟨*commuting* comfort for hardship⟩ **b :** CHANGE, ALTER ⟨*commuting* a base metal into gold⟩ **2 :** to convert (as a particular obligation, assessment, charge, or payment) into another often more convenient form **:** substitute one form of obligation or charge for (another) ⟨the tithe . . . was *commuted* to a rental to be paid in cash —K.S.Latourette⟩ ⟨~ the small debts into a lump sum due one person⟩ ⟨~ fringe benefits into cash⟩ **3 :** to exchange (a penalty) for another; *usu* **:** to revoke (a sentence) and impose something less severe ⟨~ the death sentence for a long prison term⟩ **4 :** COMMUTATE ⟨*commuting* an electric current⟩ ~ *vi* **1 :** to make up for something **:** serve as substitute for something **:** COMPENSATE ⟨*commuting* for her sins⟩ ⟨*commuting* with payments in place of labor⟩ **2 :** to pay or arrange to pay in gross instead of part by part **:** effect commutation of tithes or annuities **3 :** to travel by use of a commutation ticket esp. daily to and from a city and one's suburban residence **:** travel back and forth regularly or frequently ⟨*commuting* between London and New York⟩
commuted value *n* **:** the sum necessary to provide future payments as provided for in an annuity policy
com·mut·er \-üd·ə(r), -üt·ə-\ *n* -S **:** one that commutes (as between suburban home and city work)
com·mutual \kə, (')kä+\ *adj* [*com-* + *mutual*] *archaic* **:** MUTUAL, RECIPROCAL ⟨long ~ friendship —Alexander Pope⟩
commy *often cap, var of* COMMIE
commy *abbr* commissary
com·ne·ni·an \(')käm¦nēnēən\ *adj, cap* [*Comnenus,* Byzantine noble family + E *-ian*] **:** of or belonging to a Byzantine dynasty of the 11th to the 15th centuries
co·mo·bo \kə'mō(,)bō\ *n, pl* **comobo** *or* **comobos** *usu cap* [Sp, of AmerInd origin] **1 a :** a Panoan people of central Peru **b :** a member of such people **2 :** the language of the Comobo people
co·mo·do *or* **com·mo·do** \'kōmə,dō, 'käm-\ *adv* [It *comodo* comfortable, convenient, fr. L *commodus* convenient, suitable — more at COMMODE] **:** in an easy or convenient tempo — a direction in music
co·moid \'kō,mȯid\ *adj* [²*coma* + *-oid*] **:** resembling a tress or tuft of hair
co·monomer \¦kō+\ *n* -S [*co-* + *monomer*] **:** one of the constituents of a copolymer
co·mo·quer \,kōmō'ker, kə'mōkər\ *n* -S [MexSp] **:** a card that can be combined in panguingue and other Mexican forms of rummy only with other cards of the same rank in the same or different suits (as three tens of spades or the tens of spades, hearts, and diamonds) — compare NONCOMOQUER
co·mose \'kō,mōs\ *adj* [L *comosus* hairy, fr. *coma* hair — more at COMA] **:** bearing a tuft of soft hairs ⟨~ seeds⟩
co·mous \'kōməs\ *adj* [L *comosus*] **:** HAIRY, COMOSE ⟨a ~ stalk⟩
co·mox \'kō,mäks\ *n, pl* **comox** *or* **comoxes** *usu cap* **1 a :** a Salishan people of eastern Vancouver Island and the opposite mainland of British Columbia **b :** a member of such people **2 :** the language of the Comox people
¹**comp** \'kämp\ *n* -S [by shortening] *slang* **:** COMPOSITOR
²**comp** \"\ *vb* -ED/-ING/-S *vi, slang* **:** to work as a compositor ~ *vt, slang* **:** COMPOSE *vt* 1c
comp *abbr* **1** companion **2** company **3** comparative; compare **4** compensation **5** compilation; compiled; compiler **6** complement **7** complete **8** composed; composer; composite; composition; compositor **9** compound; compounded **10** comprehensive **11** comprising **12** comptroller
¹**com·pact** \kəm'pakt, (')käm¦pakt\ *adj, sometimes* -ER/-EST [ME *compacte,* fr. L *compactus,* past part. of *compingere* to join, fr. *com-* + *pangere* to fasten — more at PACT] **1** *obs* **:** firmly put together, joined, or integrated **2 :** predominantly formed or filled **:** COMPOSED, MADE — usu. used with *of* ⟨a figure ~ of chivalry and faith⟩ ⟨Miss Austen's novels are ~ of delicate trivialities —Samuel Alexander⟩ **3 :** marked by an arrangement of parts or units closely pressed, packed, grouped, or knit together with very slight intervals or intervening space: as **a :** BRIEF, PITHY ⟨~ language⟩ ⟨a ~ style⟩ ⟨a ~ writer⟩ **:** not diffuse or verbose ⟨a ~ statement⟩ **b :** having the twigs or branches so close together as to form a dense often rounded mass ⟨~ evergreens⟩ **c** *of bone* **:** lacking in obvious interstices **:** DENSE, SOLID — compare CANCELLOUS **d :** DENSE 5 **4 a :** suggesting firmness, soundness, and a degree of strength **:** not gangling, weak, spare, or ill-formed in appearance **:** solid and without excess flesh ⟨he had a small, ~ body that looked full of life —D.H.Lawrence⟩ **b** *of an animal* **:** CLOSE-COUPLED **:** STOCKY, COBBY **5 :** marked by concentration in a limited area **:** homogeneous and located within a limited definite space without straggling or rambling over a wide area ⟨his long narrow strips did not lie next to one another in a ~ farm —G.M.Trevelyan⟩ ⟨downtown San Francisco, ~ and accessible —*Amer. Guide Series: Calif.*⟩ **syn** see CLOSE
²**compact** \"\ *vb* -ED/-ING/-S *vt* **1 a :** to knit or draw together (as into a unified or coherent whole) **:** COMBINE, CONSOLIDATE ⟨racial and religious similarities helped ~ the tribes into a great nation⟩ **b :** to press together (as parts, components, segments) **:** COMPRESS ⟨thousands of crates ~*ed* in a warehouse⟩ ⟨a great human document, ~*ing* the experience and reflection of a . . . unified life —M.R.Cohen⟩ **2 :** to make up (as by uniting, connecting, combining) **:** COMPOSE, CREATE ⟨a mob ~*ed* of all the more violent elements of the underworld⟩ ~ *vi* **:** to become compacted ⟨the old snow had ~*ed* into the hardness of ice⟩ **syn** see UNIFY
³**compact** \'käm,pakt\ *n* -S **1 a :** a compacted body, structure, or unit ⟨the ~ of business families forming the upper classes — Hugh MacLennan⟩ **b :** an object produced by the compression of metal powders **2 :** a small cosmetic case for the purse **3 :** a small automobile
⁴**compact** \"\ *vi* -ED/-ING/-S [MF *compacter,* fr. *compact* agreement, fr. L *compactum*] **:** to make a formal agreement
⁵**compact** \"\ *n* -S [L *compactum* agreement, fr. neut. of *compactus* past part. of *compacisci* to make an agreement, fr. *com-* + *pacisci* to agree, contract — more at PACT] **1** *obs* **:** CONSPIRACY, PLOT **2 :** an agreement, understanding, or covenant between two or more parties ⟨the matrimonial ~⟩ ⟨a ~ with the devil⟩ ⟨a five-nation ~ to control opium traffic⟩; *specif* **:** an interstate agreement entered into to handle a particular problem or task ⟨a Colorado River *Compact* . . . allocating rights to the waters of the Colorado among seven states —F.A.Ogg & P.O.Ray⟩ **3 :** SOCIAL CONTRACT ⟨a man not having the power of his own life cannot by ~ . . . enslave himself to anyone —John Locke⟩
com·pac·ta \kəm'paktə\ *n* -S [NL, fr. L, fem. of *compactus* (past part. of *compingere*)] **:** the part of a bone made up of compact bone (as the shaft wall of a long bone)
com·pact·ed·ly \kəm'paktədlē, -li\ *adv* **:** COMPACTLY
com·pact·ed·ness \-dnəs\ *n* -ES **:** COMPACTNESS
com·pac·tion \kəm'pakshən, käm-\ *n* -S [ME *compaccion,* fr. L *compaction-, compactio,* fr. *compactus* (past part. of *compingere* to join) + *-ion-, -io* -ion — more at COMPACT] **:** the act or action of compacting or being compacted ⟨the ~ of all this material into a single volume —*Natural History*⟩ ⟨a second evil of severe grazing . . . is ~ of the soil surface by trampling —*Conservation & Nevada*⟩
com·pact·ly *pronunc at* ¹COMPACT +lē *or* li\ *adv* **:** in a compact manner
com·pact·ness \"+nəs\ *n* -ES [¹*compact* + *-ness*] **:** the quality or state of being compact
com·pac·tor *or* **compacter** \kəm'paktə(r), (')käm¦p-\ *n* -S [²*compact* + *-or* or *-er*] **:** one that compacts; *specif* **:** a machine (as one having a roller or a vibrating tamper) for crushing or compacting material (as in preparing a seedbed or roadbed)
compacture *n* -S [MF or L; MF, fr. L *compactura,* fr. *compactus* (past part. of *compingere*) + *-ura* -ure] *obs* **:** close union or connection of parts **:** JOINING
com·pa·draz·go \,kȯmpä'dräz(,)gō\ *n* -S [Sp, fr. *compadre*] **:** the reciprocal relationship or the social institution of such relationship existing between a godparent or godparents and the godchild and its parents in the Spanish-speaking world (as in So. America)
com·pa·dre \kəm'pädrē\ *n* -S [Sp, godfather, fr. ML *compater* — more at COMPEER] *chiefly Southwest* **:** a close friend **:** BUDDY
com·pa·ges \kəm'pā,jēz\ *or* **com·page** \'käm,pāj\ *n, pl* **com·pages** \kəm'pā,jēz, 'käm,pājəz\ [L *compages;* akin to L *compingere*] **:** a structure of many parts united into a functioning whole **:** a complex structure; *esp* **:** a large geographic region
com·pag·i·nate \kəm'pajə,nāt\ *vt* -ED/-ING/-S [LL *compaginatus,* past part. of *compaginare,* fr. L *compagin-, compago* connection; akin to L *compingere*] *archaic* **:** to join together
com·pag·i·na·tion \kəm,pajə'nāshən\ *n* -S [LL *compagination-, compaginatio,* fr. *compaginatus* + *-ion-, -io* -ion] *archaic* **:** union of parts **:** STRUCTURE
com·pa·ñe·ro \,kämpən'ye(,)rō\ *n* -S [Sp, fr. obs. Sp *compaña* company (fr. — assumed — VL *compania,* fr. LL *companio* companion) + *-ero* -er] *chiefly Southwest* **:** COMPANION, BUDDY
companiable *adj* [ME, fr. MF *compagnable,* fr. *compain* companion (fr. LL *companio*) + *-able*] *obs* **:** COMPANIONABLE
companied *past of* COMPANY
companies *pl of* COMPANY, *pres 3d sing of* COMPANY
¹**com·pan·ion** \kəm'panyən\ *n* -S *often attrib* [ME *compainoun,* fr. OF *compagnon,* fr. LL *companion-, companio* (prob. trans. of a Gmc word akin to Goth *gahlaiba* companion, fellow soldier, OHG *galeipo* companion), fr. L *com-* + *panis* bread, loaf, food — more at FOOD] **1 :** one that accompanies or is in the company of another **:** one much in the company of another **:** ASSOCIATE, COMRADE ⟨the ~*s* of one's youth⟩ ⟨armor and infighting are close ~*s* throughout warfare —Tom Wintringham⟩ ⟨the report and its ~ recommendations⟩ ⟨the captain and two ~ officers⟩ **2 a** *obs* **:** a partner or associate esp. in some legal or formal relationship (as a spouse or professional colleague) **b (1) :** a member of an order of knighthood or of chivalry ⟨a ~ of the Order of St. Michael and St. George⟩ — compare KNIGHT-COMPANION **(2) :** a member ranking below knight commander in orders having several grades or classes ⟨a ~ of the Bath⟩ **c :** a member of a companionship of compositors — not now in common use **3** *obs* **:** FELLOW, RASCAL **4 a :** one of a pair or set of things that match ⟨a ~ to the Gutenberg Bible is the Giant Bible of Mainz —Elizabeth E. Hamer⟩ ⟨a ~ sketch to the original drawing⟩ **b :** one employed to live with and to serve someone (as an elderly person or an invalid) **c** *usu cap* **:** one of Muhammad's closest associates; *specif* **:** a fellow emigrant from Mecca or one of the citizens of Medina who received and supported Muhammad following the hegira **d** *or* **companion star :** a celestial body attendant upon another but not necessarily associated with it in space (as the fainter component of a double-star system)
²**companion** \"\ *vb* -ED/-ING/-S *vt* **1** *obs* **:** to unite in fellowship **2 :** to attend or accompany in or as if in the manner of a companion ⟨nuns ~*ed* the pilgrims to the shrine⟩ ⟨a true humorist, whose humor is ~*ed* by compassion —B.R.Redman⟩ ~ *vi* **:** to keep company **:** chum with someone ⟨fellows he'd ~*ed* with long ago⟩
³**companion** \"\ *n* -S [by folk etymology fr. D *kampanje* poop deck, perh. fr. It *campagna* navigation on the open sea (in the phrase *camera della campagna* ship's storeroom), lit., open country, fr. LL *campania* level country — more at CAMPAIGN] **1 a :** a structure with frames and sashes formerly incorporated into the deck of a vessel to admit light to a cabin or lower deck **b :** a hood or other covering at the top of a companionway **2** [by shortening] **:** COMPANIONWAY
com·pan·ion·able \-yənəbəl\ *adj* **:** marked by, conducive to, or suggestive of friendly association or companionship **:** agreeable and pleasant through warm but unobtrusive affability ⟨greeted with a ~ wave of the hand⟩ **syn** see SOCIAL
com·pan·ion·able·ness *n* -ES **:** the quality or state of being companionable
com·pan·ion·ably \-blē, -li\ *adv* **:** in a companionable manner
com·pan·ion·age \-yənij\ *n* -S [¹*companion* + *-age*] **:** the companions of an order; also **:** a list of such companions
com·pan·ion·ate \-yənət\ *adj* **:** of, having to do with, or suggestive of a companion or companionship ⟨a ~ dog at one's heels⟩ ⟨a ~ union of words and music⟩; *specif* **:** harmoniously or suitably accompanying ⟨a skirt . . . with two or more ~ blouses —*Women's Wear Daily*⟩ ⟨old silver and ~ bone china⟩
companionate marriage *n* **1 :** a proposed form of marriage in which legalized birth control would be practiced, the divorce of childless couples by mutual consent would be permitted, and neither party would have any financial or economic claim on the other — compare TRIAL MARRIAGE **2 :** an informal association of a man and woman in a connubial relation that is usu. comparatively transitory and without legal status — compare COMMON-LAW MARRIAGE
companion cell *n* **:** one of the elongated parenchyma cells lying next to and supposedly associated physiologically with the sieve tube in many seed plants, developing with the sieve tube from the same mother cell, sometimes extending the full length of the sieve tube, and readily identified by its small size and denser protoplasm
companion crop *n* **:** a secondary crop planted to increase or hasten returns on a plot of land (as lettuce between tomatoes)
companion flange *n* **:** a pipe flange threaded internally to receive a pipe length and drilled so it may be bolted to another like flange; *sometimes* **:** a similar arrangement for coupling two parts of a shaft
companion ladder *n* [³*companion*] **:** COMPANIONWAY; *specif* **:** a companionway esp. on a naval vessel leading down from the quarterdeck to the officers' quarters
com·pan·ion·less \kəm'panyənləs\ *adj* **:** having no companion
companion piece *n* **:** one object that is associated with and has qualities in common with a related object usu. in the same class of objects; *esp* **:** a literary work that complements another work of the same author
companions *pl of* COMPANION, *pres 3d sing of* COMPANION
com·pan·ion·ship \-yən,ship\ *n* -S **1 :** the quality or state of being a companion **:** the fellowship existing among companions ⟨woman must no longer be barred from intellectual ~ with man —Robert Grant †1940⟩ ⟨secure in the ~ of family and friends⟩ **2 a :** a group of companions **b** *chiefly Brit* **:** a group of compositors working under a clicker — sometimes contracted to *'ship*
companion star *n* **:** COMPANION 4d
companionway \=ˈ==,=\ *n* -S [³*companion* + *way*] **:** a ship's stairway running from one deck to another
¹**com·pa·ny** \'kəmp(ə)nē, -ni\ *n* -ES *often attrib* [ME *companie,* fr. OF *compagnie,* fr. *compain* companion (fr. LL *companio*) + *-ie* -y — more at COMPANION] **1 a :** the quality or state of being a companion or associate of another **:** association esp. on terms of intimacy **:** COMPANIONSHIP ⟨enjoy a person's ~⟩ ⟨with only her thoughts for ~ — Polly Adler⟩ ⟨in ~ with others⟩ **b :** persons affording companionship **:** ASSOCIATES ⟨know a person by the ~ he keeps⟩ **c :** visitors esp. to one's house **:** GUESTS ⟨invite ~ for dinner⟩ **2 a :** an assemblage or association of persons or things **:** BAND, RETINUE ⟨a great ~ of priests and monks⟩ ⟨a ~ of ships⟩ ⟨the ~ of sovereign nations⟩ ⟨the whole ~ of thinkers who have written philosophy —W.L. Sullivan⟩ **b :** a body of soldiers: as **(1) :** a tactical and administrative unit (as of infantry) consisting usu. of a headquarters and two or more platoons — compare BATTERY, TROOP **(2) :** a unit that is normally a fifth part of a battle group **c :** a band of musical or dramatic performers; *esp* **:** an organization of actors and singers producing dramatic or operatic compositions — compare STOCK COMPANY **d :** the officers and men of a ship — usu. used in the phrase *ship's company* **e :** a fire-fighting unit of men and apparatus often designed for a special duty ⟨hose ~⟩ ⟨ladder ~⟩ **f** *chiefly Brit* **:** a group or flock of widgeon **g :** a local congregation of Jehovah's Witnesses **h :** a unit of girl guides under the leadership of a captain **3 a :** a unit of a chartered commercial organization (as of merchant adventurers) or a trade guild during the medieval period **b :** an association of persons for carrying on a commercial or industrial enterprise or business (as a partnership or stock company) — see PRIVATE COMPANY **c :** those members of a partnership firm whose names do not appear in the firm name ⟨J. J. Smith and *Company*⟩ — sometimes used of the remaining members of a group represented by one or more named individuals ⟨Caesar, Napoleon, and ~⟩
²**company** \"\ *vb* -ED/-ING/-ES [ME *companien,* fr. MF *compagnier,* fr. OF, fr. *compain* companion (fr. LL *companio*) — more at COMPANION] *vt* **:** to accompany or go with **:** COMPANION ⟨may . . . fair winds ~ your safe return —John Masefield⟩ ~ *vi* **1 :** to keep company **:** associate on terms of intimacy ⟨those who *companied* with our Lord in the days of his flesh —J.C.Swaim⟩ **2** *obs* **:** COHABIT
company man *n* **:** a worker who is felt by his fellows to have the interests of the employer rather than those of the workers at heart; *sometimes* **:** an employee who is or is thought to be a spy upon his fellows — often used as a generalized term of abuse ⟨he's a *company man,* he'd sell his mother for a dime⟩
company officer *n* **:** a captain or lieutenant in the U.S. Army or Marine Corps
company punishment *n* **:** light punishment that may be imposed by a company commander without resort to a court-martial
company servant *n* **:** one who performs the function of a minister to a company of Jehovah's Witnesses
company store *n* **:** a retail store associated with and usu. owned and operated by an industrial company: **a :** a store usu. extending limited amounts of credit from which employees of a company may and are sometimes required to buy their groceries and other merchandise **b :** a store selling the product (as textiles) of a mill at retail — called also *mill outlet, mill store*
company town *n* **:** a community that is dependent on one firm for all or most of the necessary services or functions of town life (as employment, housing, stores, and government)
company union *n* **:** a labor union consisting of the employees of a single firm, having no affiliation with a larger outside union, and often felt to be dominated by the employer
com·pa·ra·bil·i·ty \,kämp(ə)rə'bilәd·ē, -ətē, -i *sometimes* ÷kəm,par- *or* ÷kəm,per-\ *n* -ES **:** the quality or state of being comparable ⟨wrote a monograph on the ~ of related languages⟩ ⟨advocates of Virginia . . . pointed to its ~ in latitude with Palestine . . . encouraging false belief in climatic similarities —R.H.Brown⟩
com·pa·ra·ble \'kämp(ə)rəbəl *sometimes* ÷kəm'par- *or* ÷kəm'per-\ *adj* [ME, fr. MF, fr. L *comparabilis,* fr. *comparare* + *-abilis* -able] **1 :** capable of being compared: **a :** having enough like characteristics or qualities to make comparison appropriate — usu. used with *with* ⟨differing from steel in some of the circumstances . . . but ~ with steel in respect of the necessity for a centralized control —Thorstein Veblen⟩ **b :** permitting or inviting comparison often in one or two salient points only — usu. used with *to* ⟨not too far below Jonson to be ~ to that master's work —T.S.Eliot⟩ ⟨hot cornbread baked with squash seeds — an Indian delicacy ~ to raisin bread —Willa Cather⟩ **2 :** suitable for matching, coordinating, or contrasting **:** EQUIVALENT, SIMILAR ⟨samples of subtlety . . . which made most of the ~ performances of the season sound clumsy —Irving Kolodin⟩ ⟨we have information about Arctic regions but lack ~ data for the Antarctic⟩ **syn** see LIKE
com·pa·ra·ble·ness *n* -ES **:** COMPARABILITY
com·pa·ra·bly \-blē, -li\ *adv* **:** in a comparable manner
comparascope *var of* COMPAROSCOPE
com·par·a·tist \kəm'parəd·əst\ *n* -S [F *comparatiste,* fr. L *comparatus* + F *-iste* -ist] **:** one that uses a comparative method in linguistics or literature
com·par·a·ti·val \kəm¦parə¦tīvəl\ *adj* **:** of or belonging to the comparative degree
¹**com·par·a·tive** \kəm'parəd·iv, -rətiv *also* -per-\ *adj* [ME, fr. L *comparativus,* fr. *comparatus* (past part. of *comparare* to compare) + *-ivus* -ive] **1 :** belonging to or constituting the degree of comparison that is usu. expressed in English by placing *more* before an adjective (as *more natural*) or adverb (as *more clearly*) or by suffixing *-er* to it (*newer, sooner*) and that typically denotes increase in the quality, quantity, or relation expressed by the adjective or adverb ⟨the ~ degree⟩ ⟨the irregular ~ forms *elder* and *better*⟩ — compare COMPARISON 3; POSITIVE, SUPERLATIVE **2** *obs* **:** adept at making comparisons esp. of a scoffing or mocking nature **3 a :** considered as if with something or someone else held up to reveal contrast or likeness **:** seen as if in the light of something or someone implied or suggested **:** RELATIVE ⟨a ~ stranger⟩ ⟨in 1796 when ~ peace came to the frontier —*Amer. Guide Series: Pa.*⟩ **b :** approximating but not quite achieving (as a desired quality or state) **:** NEAR, APPROXIMATE ⟨~ comfort⟩ ⟨a position of mere ~ security⟩ **4 a :** making use of or capable of making use of a method whereby likenesses or dissimilarities are determined by simultaneous examination of two or more items ⟨the ~ viewpoint⟩ ⟨the study of blood types by ~ analysis⟩; *specif* **:** characterized by the comparison of things that have developed divergently from a common origin ⟨~

linguistics⟩ or of things that have developed convergently from different origins or of both ⟨~ anatomy⟩ — compare DESCRIPTIVE **b :** viewed or examined for the purpose of ascertaining or revealing likeness or dissimilarity ⟨the ~ morality of the sexes —Haldane Macfall⟩ **5** *obs* **:** COMPARABLE — **com·par·a·tive·ly** \-tə̇vlē, -li\ *adv* — **com·par·a·tive·ness** \-tivnə̇s\ *n* -ES

²**comparative** \"\ *n* -S [ME, fr. *comparative*, adj.] **1 :** one that compares with another esp. on equal footing **:** RIVAL; *specif* **:** one that makes witty or mocking comparisons **2 a :** the comparative degree in a language **b :** a comparative form of an adjective or adverb

comparative advantage *n* **:** the advantage enjoyed by a person or country in the cost ratio of one commodity to another in comparison with the ratio of costs of these same commodities elsewhere

comparative government *n* **:** the study and analysis of the general structure of governments throughout the world

comparative literature *n* **:** the study of the interrelationship of the literatures of two or more national cultures usu. of differing languages and esp. of the influences of one upon the other; *sometimes* **:** informal study of literary works in translation

comparative method *n* **:** a method of investigation (as of ethnologic phenomena and relations) based on comparison

comparative negligence *n* **:** the doctrine long the rule in admiralty and now adopted by statute for suits at law in a few states under which the negligence of the parties is weighed and the total damages divided up among them in proportion to the fault of each

comparative philosophy *n* **:** the study of philosophies from various cultures, nations, or epochs

comparative psychology *n* **1 :** the branch of psychology endeavoring to understand human behavior through the study of its similarities and differences from infrahuman behavior **2 :** the study of the psychological similarities and differences between different races of humanity **:** FOLK PSYCHOLOGY

comparative religion *n* **:** comparative study of the origin, development, and interrelations of the religious systems of mankind — compare HISTORY OF RELIGIONS

comparative statement *n* **:** a business statement including two or more sets of figures arranged for comparison

com·par·a·tiv·ist \kəm'parədə̇və̇st\ *n* -S [¹*comparative* + *-ist*] **:** COMPARATIST

com·par·a·tor \kəm'parəd·ə(r) *also* 'kämpə,rād·-\ *n* -S [F & L; F *comparateur*, fr. L *comparator* comparer, fr. *comparatus* (past part. of *comparare* to compare) + *-or*] **:** one that compares something to be measured with a standard measure: as **a** (1) **:** a device employing a micrometer screw or a vernier and a microscope in the precise measurement of short lengths (2) **:** any of various devices for the rapid inspection of mechanical parts to detect deviations from a standard piece **b :** an apparatus used for determining concentration of dissolved substances (as hydrogen ions) in solution by color comparison with known standards — compare COLORIMETER 2 **c :** an instrument, device, or set of charts (as for use in chemical analysis and medical diagnosis) for the determination and specification of colors by direct comparison with a standardized system of colors **d :** STEREOCOMPARATOR

¹**com·pare** \kəm'pa(a)(ə)r, -pe(ə)r, -pa(a)ə,-peə\ *vb* -ED/-ING/-S [ME *comparen*, fr. MF *comparer*, fr. L *comparare* to couple together, compare, fr. *compar* like, similar, fr. *com-* + *par* equal — more at PAIR] *vt* **1 :** to represent as similar (as for the purpose of illustration) **:** LIKEN ⟨~ a person's teeth to pearls⟩ — often used negatively in the passive infinitive of something inferior ⟨a drama not to be *compared* with any of Shakespeare's⟩ **2 a :** to examine the character or qualities of (as two or more persons or things) esp. for the purpose of discovering resemblances or differences ⟨~ today's medical costs with the mortality rates of 20 years ago⟩ **b :** to view in relation to something or someone else for the purpose of showing or establishing contrast or similarity — used in the past participle usu. preceded by *as* and followed by *to* or *with* ⟨Calcutta is the home of more than two million people *compared* to less than a million in Madras —*Science & Culture*⟩ ⟨the greater strength of steel as *compared* to cast iron⟩ **3 :** to inflect or modify (an adjective or adverb) according to the degrees of comparison **:** state the positive, comparative, and superlative forms of ~ *vi* **1 :** to bear being equated or likened ⟨his artistry does not ~ to his brother's⟩ ⟨can Dante ~ with Shakespeare and Milton⟩ **2 :** to assume or presume likeness or equality ⟨fools vainly striving to ~ with wise men⟩ **3 :** to make or draw comparisons ⟨if we now go to Italy at all, we go not to learn, but to ~ —Norman Douglas⟩ **4 :** to differ or stand out in some particular respect ⟨steel production this year ~*s* very poorly with the production of manufactured articles⟩ **5 :** to be equal or alike ⟨his performance at bat in 1951 ~*s* with his 1956 performance⟩ — often used in the negative in connection with something so different (as in superiority or inferiority) that anything being likened to it is as if impossible ⟨cannot ~ this year's crop with last year's⟩

syn COLLATE, CONTRAST: COMPARE indicates the placing together and examining of two things to discover resemblances and differences. It may but does not always concentrate on similarities rather than dissimilarities ⟨the discomforts of the road were light when *compared* to the discomforts of the sea, and the fatigue of the road was measurable when *compared* to the suffering and weariness entailed by a sea voyage —Agnes Repplier⟩ ⟨the army will have four armored, or tank, divisions, as *compared* to the single brigade, or less than half a division, available a year ago —H.W.Baldwin⟩ ⟨a hitherto unpublished letter by Hearn offers additional evidence of his independence of mind, his hostility toward the West as *compared* to the Orient, and his curiosity about his mother and her people —*Amer. Literature*⟩ COLLATE indicates painstaking minute orderly comparison, all small variations and differentiations being noted ⟨his books are for the most part built up around tables of statistics, carefully collected and *collated* and subjected to an unwearying critical scrutiny —*Times Lit. Supp.*⟩ CONTRAST always centers attention on differences between juxtaposed items ⟨with their large output of verse we may *contrast* the small amount of literary criticism that has been attempted by the younger poets —C.D.Lewis⟩ ⟨wind-swept dunes *contrast* with the otherwise rugged coastal scenery —*Amer. Guide Series: Maine*⟩

— **compare notes :** to exchange observations and views ⟨the two rival coaches got together after the game to *compare notes*⟩

²**compare** \"\ *n* -S **1 :** COMPARISON ⟨a ruffian in ~ to his comrades⟩ — used esp. in connection with something so superior it cannot be equaled by anything else ⟨her beauty was beyond ~⟩ ⟨a storm past ~ in violence⟩ **2** *obs* **:** illustration by comparison **:** SIMILE

³**compare** *n* -S [alter. (influenced by ¹*compare*) of *compeer*] **:** COMPEER

⁴**compare** *vt* -ED/-ING/-S [L *comparare* to prepare, acquire, buy, fr. *com-* + *parare* to prepare — more at PARE] *obs* **:** PROCURE, ACQUIRE

com·par·i·son \kəm'parəsən *also* -per-, *rap.* -rsən\ *n* -S [ME *comparisoun*, fr. MF *comparaison*, fr. L *comparation-*, *comparatio*, fr. *comparatus* (past part. of *comparare* to compare) + *-ion-*, *-io* -ion — more at COMPARE] **1 :** the act or action of comparing **:** LIKENING, EQUATING: as **a :** the representing of one thing or person as similar to or like another ⟨a ~ of man to a monkey⟩ — often used with *beyond*, *without*, or *out of all* in connection with something or someone so superior that likening to anything or anyone else is impossible ⟨wealth beyond ~⟩ ⟨out of all ~ the more beautiful of the two⟩ **b :** the placing together or juxtaposing of two or more items to ascertain, bring into relief, or establish their similarities and dissimilarities ⟨a ~ between American and British business procedures⟩ ⟨health record of rural areas . . . suffers by ~ with urban centers —*Commonweal*⟩ **2 :** identity (as of one feature or set of features with another) between two or more things or persons **:** SIMILARITY ⟨points of ~ between the two authors are many⟩ — used chiefly with a negative of something or someone decidedly inferior to another or of markedly unequal things or persons ⟨his technique bears no ~ with that of any other artist⟩ ⟨no ~ between the firepower of modern and 19th century armies⟩ **3 :** the modification (as by inflection) of an adjective or adverb to denote different levels of the quality, quantity, or relation expressed by the adjective or adverb — see ¹COMPARATIVE 1, POSITIVE, SUPERLATIVE **4** *obs* **:** a scoffing or mocking similitude

syn CONTRAST, ANTITHESIS, COLLATION, PARALLEL: COMPARISON is the most general term; in its broadest use it may imply no more than an impartial search for resemblances as well as differences ⟨there can be no *comparison* between the intelligence of native-born and foreign-born until differences due to language difficulties have been eliminated⟩ ⟨a *comparison* of many children from diverse backgrounds would yield an understanding of the common characteristics of childhood⟩ In a narrower use COMPARISON means likening ⟨a *comparison* to Sarah Bernhardt is flattering to any actress⟩ and in yet another use it implies a judgment ⟨parents should avoid *comparisons* between their children⟩ CONTRAST emphasizes difference intensified by physical nearness or by the association of the contrasting objects in an organic whole, a logical category, or an actual relationship ⟨the *contrast* the neat bright doctor . . . made with the coltish countryfolk —R.L.Stevenson⟩ ⟨Rembrandt achieves his greatest effect by the *contrast* of light and dark⟩ ⟨the *contrast* between democracy and fascism⟩ ⟨Electra's character given in a moment by the sharp *contrast* to her sister —Edith Hamilton⟩ ANTITHESIS implies comparison for the sake of revealing startling differences. But the objects of an antithesis always appear in pairs or sets of pairs; and antithesis suggests that the members of each pair are at opposite extremes or directly negate each other ⟨the century-old *antithesis* of heavenly justice and earthly fallibility, sin and innocence, Heaven and Hell, God and the Devil dominate Melville's mind —Charles Weir⟩ COLLATION denotes a close and far-going comparison, esp. a scrutiny of manuscripts, records, differing accounts or editions of a text, with the purpose of arriving at the most nearly complete, authentic, or true version of something said, written, or done ⟨this *collation* is relevant . . . to the question of Seneca's influence upon language —T.S.Eliot⟩ PARALLEL implies a similarity in growth, development, or action between people or events separated in time or place, background, or origin ⟨the controversy which raged as an earlier *parallel* to that which Darwin was to start later —W.E. Swinton⟩ ⟨the contribution of the Third Programme . . . is without *parallel* in the history of the art —Dyneley Hussey⟩

comparison lamp *n* **:** an incandescent lamp of constant and not necessarily known luminous intensity against which a working standard lamp and lamps to be tested are successively compared in a photometer

comparison microscope *n* **:** an apparatus consisting essentially of a pair of microscope objective lenses and tubes connected by prisms in such a way that images from both may be viewed side by side through a single ocular lens

comparison shopper *n* **:** a store employee who gathers information through actual visits and purchases about the quality, style, and price of merchandise in competitors' stores and about stock assortments, sales service, and customer response to special promotions

comparison slip *n* **:** EXCHANGE TICKET

comparison spectrum *n* **:** a line spectrum of accurately known wavelengths that is matched wavelength for wavelength with another spectrum for calibration of the latter

comparison star *n* **:** a star used as a reference in the measurement of another star's position, brightness, or other observable characteristic

com·par·i·um \kəm'pa(a)rēəm\ *n*, *pl* **compar·ia** \-ēə\ [NL, fr. L *comparare* to couple together, compare + NL *-ium* — more at COMPARE] **:** a group of organisms capable of direct or indirect interbreeding whether or not fertile hybrids result and being usu. equivalent in scope to a taxonomic genus

com·par·o·scope *also* **com·par·a·scope** \-parə,skōp\ *n* -S [¹*compare* + connective *-o-*, *-a-* + *-scope*] **:** an apparatus used for simultaneous microscopic study of two objects **:** COMPARISON MICROSCOPE

com·par·sa \kəm'pärsə\ *n* -S [AmerSp, fr. Sp, group of revelers costumed alike, entire group of supernumeraries in a play, supernumerary in a play, fr. It, supernumerary in a play, appearance, fr. fem. of *comparso*, past part. of *comparire* to appear, fr. L *comparēre*, fr. L *com-* + *parēre* to be visible — more at APPEAR] **1 :** a folk dance and song of Cuban Negro origin **2 :** a masked company of street dancers in Cuban carnival processions

com·part \kəm'pärt, -pȧt, *usu* -d·+V\ *vt* -ED/-ING/-S [It *compartire* to mark out into parts, share out, fr. LL *compartiri* to share out, fr. L *com-* + *partiri*, *partire* to share, fr. *part-*, *pars* part — more at PART] **:** to mark out into parts or subdivisions; *specif* **:** to lay out in parts according to a plan

com·par·ti·men·to \kəm,pärd·ə'men(,)tō\ *n*, *pl* **comparti·men·ti** \-n(,)tē\ [It] **:** an administrative district or region in Italy

com·par·ti·tion \,kämˌpär'tishən, -mpər-\ *n* -S [ML *compartition-*, *compartitio* apportionment, fr. LL *compartitus* (past part. of *compartiri*) + L *-ion-*, *-io* -ion] **:** distribution esp. of the parts of a design

¹**com·part·ment** \kəm'pärtmənt, -pȧt-\ *n* -S [MF *compartiment*, fr. It *compartimento*, fr. *compartire* + *-mento* -ment] **1 :** a subdivision of a plane surface: as **a :** a separate division of a structure or design (as a panel or coffer in a ceiling or a sculptured subdivision of a portal) **b** *obs* **:** COMPARTITION **2 :** a subdivision esp. of a series of abstractions, an integrated organization, or a body of knowledge **:** SECTION, PART ⟨the ~*s* of your mind⟩ **3 :** a subdivision of three-dimensional space: as **a :** a small chamber, receptacle, or container ⟨the seeds may be found in numerous ~*s* within the pod⟩ ⟨the ~*s* of a roulette wheel⟩ **b** (1) **:** a private room on a sleeping car that has toilet facilities and berths and is larger than a bedroom and smaller than a drawing room (2) *in Europe and elsewhere outside of the U.S.* **:** a private room on a railroad passenger car with or without berths and toilet facilities (3) *in Great Britain* **:** one of the subdivisions of a railroad passenger car having seats that face each other and opening into a side corridor or extending entirely across the car **c :** one of the sections into which the interior of a ship is divided by bulkheads **d** *mil* **:** an area bounded by such topographic features (as woods or ridges) that observation and direct fire into the area are limited — compare CORRIDOR

²**com·part·ment** \-t,ment, -tmənt\ *vt* -ED/-ING/-S **1 :** to break down (as into sections or segments) **:** divide up ⟨a ~*ed* box⟩ ⟨biology is ~*ed* into a host of special sciences —*Scientific American Reader*⟩ **2 :** to separate into mutually isolated units ⟨in the protected and ~*ed* society of Beacon Hill —John Mason Brown⟩ ⟨international treaties must be discussed as a whole; they may not be ~*ed* —H.M.Dorr & H.L.Bretton⟩

com·part·men·tal \kəm¦pärt¦mentᵊl, ¦käm,pärt-, -pȧt-\ *adj* **:** divided or tending to divide into separate or independent compartments ⟨a ~ organization⟩ ⟨~ seed pods⟩ — **com·part·men·tal·ly** \-ᵊlē, -ᵊli\ *adv*

com·part·men·tal·i·za·tion \kəm¦pärt,mentᵊlə̇'zāshən, ¦käm,p-, -pȧt-, -ᵊl,ī'z-\ *n* -S **:** division esp. into units lacking normal interaction or cooperation ⟨the rigid ~ that has done so much to sterilize scientific knowledge by depriving scientific specialists of a broad social vision —T.S.Harding⟩

com·part·men·tal·ize \kəm,pärt'mentᵊl,īz, ,käm-, -pȧt-\ *vt* -ED/-ING/-S **:** to separate into compartments or categories in a manner tending to preclude interrelationships

com·part·men·ta·tion \kəm,pärtmən'tāshən, -pȧt-, -,men-\ *n* -S **:** division into separate sections or units ⟨elaborate ~ in submarines makes them difficult to sink⟩ ⟨~ and specialization go hand in hand with . . . the increasing complexities of civilization —V.D.Tate⟩

com·part·ment·ize \kəm'pärtmən,tīz, -pȧt-\ *vt* -ED/-ING/-S **:** COMPARTMENTALIZE

¹**com·pass** \'kəmpəs *also* 'käm-\ *vb* -ED/-ING/-ES [ME *compassen*, fr. OF *compasser* to measure, arrange, ponder, contrive, fr. (assumed) VL *compassare* to measure off by paces, fr. L *com-* + (assumed) VL *passare* to go, move, fr. L *passus* step, pace — more at PACE] *vt* **1 :** to devise or contrive often in a treacherous manner **:** PLOT **2 a :** to lie around **:** GIRDLE, ENCOMPASS ⟨island ~*ed* by the sea⟩ ⟨the Great Peace beyond all this turmoil and fret ~*ed* me around —L.P.Smith⟩ **b :** to move around **:** travel entirely around (as a circle or curved course) **:** ENCIRCLE ⟨Magellan's ship ~*ed* the earth⟩ **3 :** to hem in or enclose in or as if in a ring **:** SURROUND ⟨suddenly enemies ~*ed* him on all sides⟩ **4 a :** to bring about **:** ACHIEVE, ACCOMPLISH ⟨a writer . . . attempting a higher strain of elevation . . . than his powers can ~ —C.E.Montague⟩ **b :** to get at or within one's power **:** OBTAIN ⟨~ his freedom⟩ **5** *obs* **:** to bend into a circular form **:** CURVE **6** *obs* **:** to get around (someone) esp. for one's own advantage **7 :** GRASP ⟨~*ing* an idea⟩ **:** COMPREHEND ⟨could not ~ the smallest problems⟩ ~ *vi* **:** to assume a circular or curved form **:** CURVE, BEND ⟨a plank ~*ing* under pressure⟩ **syn** see REACH, SURROUND

²**compass** \"\ *n* -ES [ME *compas*, fr. MF, fr. *compasser* to go round, measure, divide] **1 a :** an often rounded or curved boundary limit **:** CIRCUMFERENCE ⟨within the ~ of the outer wall⟩ **b :** an enclosed or delimited space or area often circumscribed ⟨three passengers shut up in the narrow ~ of one lumbering old mail coach —Charles Dickens⟩ ⟨the narrow ~ of 21 pages —V.L.Parrington⟩ **c :** range or limit of perception, cognizance, knowledge, interest, concern, or treatment ⟨impossible within the ~ of this report to do justice to all the projects —J.B.Conant⟩ ⟨disposing of his property . . . within the ~ of the law —John Locke⟩ ⟨works . . . of such ~ and excellence as to supersede those of his predecessors —H.O.Taylor⟩ **d :** the range of pitch covered by a melody or lying within the capacity of a voice or instrument **e** *obs* **:** due bounds **:** limits imposed by moderation and good sense **2** *obs* **:** cunning ingenuity **3 a** *obs* **:** CIRCLE **b** *obs* **:** a ring, globe, or other object with circular outline **c :** a circular motion or course **:** a roundabout way ⟨finishing the ~ of his life⟩ ⟨hawks rising in ~*es* through the air⟩ ⟨a ~ of seven days' journey —2 Kings 3:9 (AV)⟩ **d** (1) **:** the curve of an arrow's flight (2) **:** the angle of elevation determining this curve **4 a :** a device for determining directions on the earth's surface by means of a magnetic needle or group of needles turning freely on a pivot and pointing to the magnetic north **b :** any of certain nonmagnetic devices that serve the same purpose as the magnetic compass (as the gyrocompass and the sky compass) — see GYROCOMPASS, MAGNETIC NEEDLE, MARINER'S COMPASS, SKY COMPASS, SURVEYOR'S COMPASS **c** *usu* **compasses** *pl* **:** an instrument for describing circles, transferring measurements, and similar operations consisting in its simple form of two pointed branches joined at the top by a pivot, one of the branches generally having a pen or pencil point — called also *pair of compasses* **syn** see RANGE

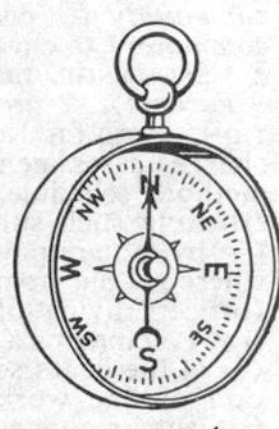

compass 4a

³**compass** \"\ *adj* **:** forming a curve **:** CURVED, CIRCULAR ⟨a ~ timber⟩

⁴**compass** *adv* [³*compass*] *obs* **:** in an arc **:** so as to form an arc or circle

com·pass·able \'kəmpəsəbəl *also* 'käm-\ *adj* **:** that may be compassed or attained ⟨a ~ distance⟩ ⟨materials easily ~⟩

compass bearing *n* **:** a bearing relative to north as indicated by a magnetic compass

compass brick *n* **:** curved or tapering brick for use in curved work (as in arches, shafts, and wells) — compare ARCH BRICK 1

compass calipers *n pl* **:** HERMAPHRODITE CALIPERS

compass card *n* **:** the circular card attached to the needles of a mariner's compass on which are marked the 32 points of the compass and the 360° of the circle

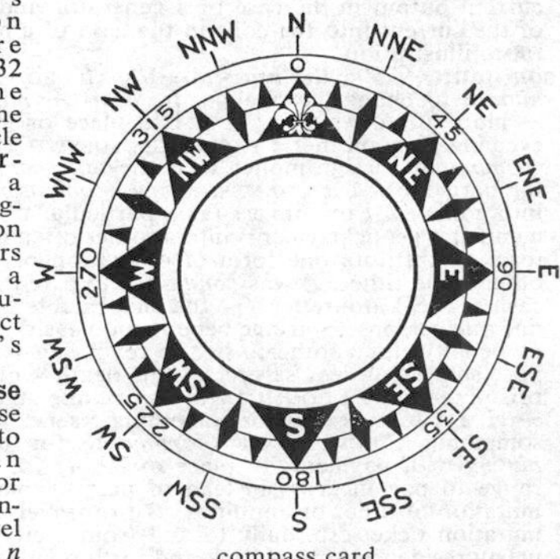

compass card

compass corrector *n* **:** a magnet or magnets or soft iron spheres or bars placed near a compass to neutralize the effect of the ship's magnetism

compass course *n* **:** the course with respect to true north in which a ship or an aircraft is intended to travel

compass dial *n* **:** a small pocket sundial fitted with a compass needle by which the gnomon may be adjusted to tell the hour of the day

compassed *past of* COMPASS

compass error *n* **:** the difference between compass heading and true heading expressed as the algebraic sum of variation and deviation

compasses *pres 3d sing of* COMPASS, *pl of* COMPASS

compass-headed \'==,==\ *adj* **:** having a semicircular head ⟨a *compass-headed* arch⟩

compass heading *n* **:** heading measured clockwise from north as indicated by the compass

compassing *adj* [ME, fr. pres. part. of *compassen* to compass] **1 :** ENCOMPASSING, INCLUSIVE ⟨~ knowledge⟩ **2 :** CURVED, BENT ⟨~ timbers⟩

¹**com·pas·sion** \kəm'pashən, -aash-,-aish-\ *n* -S [ME *compassioun*, fr. MF or LL; MF *compassion*, fr. LL *compassion-*, *compassio*, fr. *compassus* (past part. of *compati* to have compassion, fr. L *com-* + *pati* to bear, suffer) + *-ion-*, *-io* -ion — more at PATIENT] **:** deep feeling for and understanding of misery or suffering and the concomitant desire to promote its alleviation **:** spiritual consciousness of the personal tragedy of another or others and selfless tenderness directed toward it ⟨to have ~ on a person⟩ ⟨with ~ (so different from pity) she shows the sordid impact of this convict settlement on the lives of the natives —Sarah Campion⟩ **syn** see SYMPATHY

²**compassion** \"\ *vt* -ED/-ING/-S *archaic* **:** COMPASSIONATE

com·pas·sion·able \-sh(ə)nəbəl\ *adj* **1** *obs* **:** COMPASSIONATE **2** *archaic* **:** PITIABLE

¹**com·pas·sion·ate** \-sh(ə)nə̇t, *usu* -ə̇d·+V\ *adj* **1 :** marked by compassion, by a ready inclination to pity, sympathy, or tenderness **:** SYMPATHETIC ⟨not cold and blaming . . . but an older and wiser brother, very ~ —Sinclair Lewis⟩ ⟨there was a murmur of commiseration . . . the soft and ~ voices of women were conspicuous —Charles Dickens⟩ **2** *obs* **:** calling forth pity **:** PITIABLE **3 :** granted because of unusual distressing circumstances affecting an individual — used of leaves and other military privileges ⟨considered for a ~ discharge because of his domestic difficulties⟩ **syn** see TENDER

²**com·pas·sion·ate** \-shə,nāt, *usu* -ād·+V\ *vt* -ED/-ING/-S **:** to have compassion for **:** sympathize with **:** PITY ⟨even *compassionating* those who hold in bondage their fellowmen —John Quincy Adams⟩

com·pas·sion·ate·ly \-sh(ə)nə̇tlē, -li\ *adv* **:** in a compassionate manner

com·pas·sion·ate·ness *n* -ES **:** COMPASSION

com·pas·sion·less \-shənlə̇s\ *adj* **:** lacking compassion

com·pas·sive \kəm'pasiv\ *adj* [*compassion* + *-ive*] *archaic* **:** COMPASSIONATE

compass key *n* **:** a small screwdriver or pin wrench for tightening or loosening the joints of compasses

com·pass·less \'kəmpəslə̇s *also* 'käm-\ *adj* **:** lacking a compass

compass man *n* **:** one who accompanies a timber estimator in order to establish for him by use of a compass and other means the correct boundaries of the tract

compass plane *n* **:** CIRCULAR PLANE

compass plant *also* **compass flower** *n* **:** any of several plants whose leaves or branches are arranged on the axis so as to indicate the cardinal points of the compass: as **a :** a rosinweed (*Silphium laciniatum*) **b :** a prickly lettuce (*Lactuca scariola*) **c :** PRAIRIE BIRD'S-FOOT TREFOIL **d :** a low tufted white-woolly yellow-flowered composite herb (*Wyethia ovata*) of California

compass rafter *n* **:** a rafter that is cut to a curve and commonly used in an ornamented roof truss or in a gable framing

compass roof *n* : a timber roof in which each truss has its rafters, collar beams, and braces combined into an arched form
compass rose *n* : a circle graduated to degrees or quarter points and printed on a chart for reference (as of lines and courses) usu. showing both magnetic and true directions
compass saw *n* : a handsaw that has a thin tapering blade for cutting small circles, curves, or irregular edges
compass termite *n* : any of certain Australian termites that build flattened earthen nests which are shaped like steeples and have the broader faces always pointing east and west
compass window *n* : a bay or oriel window of semicircular plan
com·paternity \ˌkäm+\ *n* -ES [ME *compaternite*, fr. ML *compaternitas*, fr. *compater* godfather, after L *pater* father: LL *paternitas* paternity — more at COMPEER] : the spiritual relation between the godparents of a child; *also* : the spiritual relationship between godparents and the child's actual parents
com·pa·thy \ˈkämpəthē\ *n* -ES [*com-* + *-pathy*] : shared feeling (as of joy or sorrow)
com·pat·i·bil·i·ty \kəm,padəˈbilədē, -atə-, -ətē, -i\ *n* -ES [F *compatibilité*, fr. *compatible* + *-ité* -ity] **1** : the quality or state of being compatible : the capacity of two or more entities to combine or remain together without undesirable aftereffects : mutual tolerance : CONGRUITY ⟨the ~ of blood types⟩ ⟨~ between church and state⟩ **2 a** : the capability of cross-fertilizing freely — used chiefly of plants and plant parts **b** : the capability of components (as of an electronic system) to function together; *specif* : the ability of a color television transmission system to provide black-and-white service for monochrome receivers without special modification
com·pat·i·ble \kəmˈpadəbəl, -atə-\ *adj* [MF, fr. ML *compatibilis*, fr. LL *compati* to have compassion + L *-ibilis* -ible — more at COMPASSION] **1** *obs* : sharing in another's suffering **2 a** : capable of existing together without discord or disharmony — used usu. with *with* ⟨slavery, which nowadays . . . we no longer regard as ~ with high civilization —Havelock Ellis⟩ **b** *logic* : so related that both or all may hold or be true : NONCONTRADICTORY **c** (1) : capable of cross-fertilizing freely ⟨some plants are ~⟩ ⟨~ pollens⟩ (2) : uniting readily and usu. permanently — used of certain plant stocks and scions **d** *of drugs or medicines* : not incompatible **e** : having to do with a system in which color television broadcasts may be received in black and white on ordinary receivers without special modification **f** : capable of blending into a homogeneous mixture that neither separates nor is altered by chemical interaction of ingredients **syn** see CONSONANT
com·pat·i·ble·ness *n* -ES : COMPATIBILITY
com·pat·i·bly \-blē, -li\ *adv* : in a compatible manner
com·pat·ric \kəmˈpa·trik, (ˈ)kämˈp-\ *adj* [*com-* + *-patric* (as in *sympatric*)] : SYMPATRIC
com·pa·tri·ot \kəmˈpā·trēət, -ē,ät *also* käm-, *Brit usu* -pa-; *usu* -d·+V\ *n* -S *often attrib* [F *compatriote*, fr. LL *compatriota*, fr. L *com-* + LL *patriota* fellow countryman — more at PATRIOT] **1** : one of the same country : a fellow countryman ⟨our Southern ~s⟩ **2** : COMPEER, COLLEAGUE
com·pa·tri·ot·ic \-ˌ==ˈäd·ik\ *adj* [*compatriot* + *-ic*] : of or having to do with one's native land ⟨a ~ friend⟩ ⟨a ~ hymn⟩
compd *abbr* compound
compear *vi* -ED/-ING/-S [ME *compeiren*, *compeeren*, fr. MF *comper-*, pres. indic. stem of *comparoir*, fr. L *comparēre*, fr. *com-* + *parēre* to be visible — more at APPEAR] *obs* : APPEAR; *specif*, *Scots law* : to appear in court personally or by attorney
com·pear·ance \kəmˈpērən(t)s, -pär-\ *n* -S [ME *compeirance*, fr. *compeiren* + *-ance*] *Scots law* : formal appearance in court
comped *past of* COMP
¹com·peer \ˈkäm,pi(ə)r, kämˈp-,kəmˈp-\ *n* -S [ME (influenced in meaning by ME *peer*), fr. OF *compere* godfather, comrade, fellow, fr. ML *compater* godfather, fr. L *com-* + *pater* father — more at FATHER, PEER] **1** : an equal in rank, age, prowess : PEER ⟨Hitler as a strategist was not the ~ of Washington or Napoleon⟩; *specif* : COLLEAGUE ⟨the specialist and his ~s who examined the patient's heart⟩ **2** : a close associate : COMPANION, COMRADE ⟨as a raw inductee he found himself no better off than any of his ~s⟩
²compeer *vt* -ED/-ING/-S *obs* : to be equal with : MATCH
com·pel \kəmˈpel\ *vb* **compelled**; **compelled**; **compelling**; **compels** [ME *compellen*, fr. MF *compeller*, *compellir*, fr. L *compellere* to drive together, compel, urge, fr. *com-* + *pellere* to drive — more at FELT] *vt* **1** : FORCE, DRIVE, IMPEL: as **a** : to force by physical necessity or evidential fact ⟨poverty *compelled* him to work⟩ — often used in the passive ⟨so lame that he was *compelled* to use a cane —*Amer. Guide Series: N.H.*⟩ ⟨*compelled* to confess that the project was a failure —R.P.Warren⟩ **b** : to urge irresistibly by moral or social pressure ⟨public opinion *compelled* President Lincoln to order McDowell to move forward —*Dict. of Amer. History*⟩ : force by authority, code, or custom **c** : to force by personal temperament or other subjective considerations ⟨*compelled*, as if by inner command, to listen —J.C.Powys⟩ ⟨his sense of order would ~ him to tidy up —Morley Callaghan⟩ **2 a** : to force or cause irresistibly : call upon, require, or command without possibility of withholding or denying ⟨Alexander . . . after the decisive victory at Legnano *compelled* Frederick's submission —*Encyc. Americana*⟩ **b** : to impel or force to appear, come, or go : summon peremptorily ⟨potent spells for *compelling* the Evil One —Charles Dickens⟩ ⟨wedging his tense arm imperatively under mine, Tom Buchanan *compelled* me from the room —Scott Fitzgerald⟩ **c** *archaic* : to cause to congregate : drive together : gather together irresistibly **3 a** : to domineer over so as to force compliance or submission : demand consideration or attention ⟨nobody will ~ you; you are perfectly free —Samuel Butler †1902⟩ **b** : to obtain (a response) by force, violence, or coercion ⟨~ assent at the point of a gun⟩ ~ *vi* : to employ force; *esp* : to exert an irresistible influence ⟨he had a presence that inspired and a voice that *compelled*⟩ **syn** see FORCE
com·pel·la·ble \-ləbəl\ *adj* : capable of being compelled
compellable witness *n* : a person that can claim no exemption from testifying in a legal proceeding
com·pel·la·tion \ˌkämpəˈlāshən, -,peˈ-\ *n* -S [L *compellation-*, *compellatio*, fr. *compellatus* (past part. of *compellare* to accost, fr. *com-* + *-pellare* as in *appellare* to address) + *-ion-*, *-io* -ion — more at APPEAL] **1** : an act or action of addressing someone **2** : the word or words used in addressing someone **3** : APPELLATION 3
com·pel·lent \kəmˈpelənt\ *adj* [L *compellent-*, *compellens*, pres. part. of *compellere*] : COMPELLING ⟨~ example of heroism⟩
compelling *adj* [fr. pres. part. of *compel*] **1** : FORCING, IMPELLING, DRIVING ⟨~ circumstances⟩ ⟨~ ambition⟩ **2** : demanding respect, honor, or admiration ⟨a ~ personality⟩ ⟨her singing was as ~ as her acting —*Time*⟩ **3** : calling for examination, scrutiny, consideration, or thought ⟨new and ~ evidence⟩ **4** : demanding and holding one's attention ⟨a ~ novel⟩ ⟨a ~ manner of speech⟩ **5** : tending to convince or convert by or as if by forcefulness of evidence ⟨though his logic is often unconvincing, his documentation is always ~ —H.J.Muller⟩ — **com·pel·ling·ly** *adv*
com·pend \ˈkäm,pend\ *n* -S [ML *compendium*] : COMPENDIUM, EPITOME
com·pen·di·ary \kəmˈpendē,erē, käm-\ *adj* [L *compendiarius*, fr. *compendium* short cut + *-arius* -ary] : COMPENDIOUS: as **a** : BRIEF ⟨a ~ abridgment⟩ **b** *obs* : EXPEDITIOUS
com·pen·di·ous \-dēəs\ *adj* [ME, fr. L *compendiosus*, fr. *compendium* + *-osus* -ose] **1** : marked by the brief expression of a comprehensive matter : like a compendium : resolving essentials into few words ⟨such looseness cannot be afforded in a short and ~ book —*Times Lit. Supp.*⟩ **2** *obs* : showing saving of time : EXPEDITIOUS, DIRECT **syn** see CONCISE
com·pen·di·ous·ly *adv* [ME, fr. *compendious* + *-ly*] : in a compendious manner
com·pen·di·um \kəmˈpendēəm\ *sometimes* käm-\ *n*, *pl* **compendiums** \-ēəmz\ *or* **compen·dia** \-ēə\ [ML, fr. L, saving, gain, shortcut, fr. *compendere* to weigh, fr. *com-* + *pendere* to weigh — more at PENDANT] **1 a** : a brief compilation or composition consisting of a reduction and condensation of the subject matter of a larger work : ABRIDGMENT, ABSTRACT ⟨a one-volume ~ of the multivolume original⟩ **b** : a work treating in brief form the important features of a whole field of knowledge or subject matter category ⟨a ~ of physics⟩ **c** : a list of a number of brief items : CATALOG, INVENTORY ⟨a ~ of all the fashionable faults likely to be found in a young . . . novelist —*Time*⟩ **2** *archaic* : SAVING, ECONOMY **3** : a folder containing writing paper and envelopes

syn SYLLABUS, DIGEST, PANDECT, SURVEY, SKETCH, PRÉCIS, APERÇU: a COMPENDIUM gathers in brief, orderly, and intelligible form, sometimes outlined, the essential facts ⟨*A Treatise on Epidemic Cholera* which contained little original matter but was published as a *compendium* of the existing knowledge of this disease —W.R.Steiner⟩ A SYLLABUS, often presented with a series of headings, points, or propositions, gives concise statements affording a view of the whole and an indication of its significance ⟨no party program, no official *syllabus* of opinions, which we all have to defend —W.R.Inge⟩ A DIGEST presents a body of information gathered from many sources and arranged and classified for ready accessibility, often alphabetized and indexed; the word also indicates any condensed easy-to-read version ⟨the only hope of gaining such knowledge lies in a summarization and thorough *digest* of the huge body of county statistics already available —D.J.Bogue⟩ ⟨the *Current Digest of the Soviet Press*, now in its fifth year of uninterrupted weekly appearance, a seventy-thousand word a week *digest* of forty Russian newspapers and periodicals —Mortimer Graves⟩ A PANDECT is a systematic digest covering the whole of a monumental subject ⟨no printed body of modern social history, either by purpose or accident, contains a richer *pandect* of the efficient impulses of its age —Christopher Morley⟩ A SURVEY is a brief comprehensive presentation giving main outlines, often as a preliminary aid to later study of more detailed treatment ⟨the policy of the Board and its founder being to make first of all a thorough *survey* of the educational needs of the country —J.D.Greene⟩ ⟨an essay on the Renaissance, not a history of the Renaissance. It omits mention of many interesting details of that vast transformation in an effort to determine, through a broad *survey* of its more salient features, the fundamental nature of the movement —G.C.Sellery⟩ A SKETCH is a slight tentative preliminary presentation subject to much later change, emendation, and amplification ⟨to give anything but the most fragmentary *sketch* of the winter of '94 and '95 in Berlin is impossible —David Fairchild⟩ ⟨*The American Chancery Digest*, including state and federal equity decisions, with an introductory *sketch* of equity courts and their jurisdiction —V.L.Wilkinson⟩ A PRÉCIS is a concise clear-cut statement or restatement of main matters, often a report or a summary suggesting the style or tone of an original ⟨a carefully prepared critical text of Guido, with a short critical introduction, a full critical apparatus, and English *précis* printed concurrently —*Times Lit. Supp.*⟩ An APERÇU is a sketch giving a very quick, perhaps impressionistic compression of the whole, with all details omitted ⟨popular books which give an *aperçu* of recent research, in order to have some idea of the general scientific purpose served by particular facts and laws —Bertrand Russell⟩
com·penetrate \(ˌ)käm+\ *vt* -ED/-ING/-S [*com-* + *penetrate*] : to penetrate throughout : PERVADE
com·penetration \(ˌ)käm+\ *n* -S : pervasive penetration : mutual interfusion ⟨the ~ of two ideas⟩
com·pen·sa·bil·i·ty \kəm,pen(t)səˈbilədē, (,)käm-\ *n* -ES [*compensable* + *-ity*] : the capacity or fitness of something to be made up or made good ⟨the ~ of an unemployment claim⟩
com·pen·sa·ble \kəmˈpen(t)səbəl, (ˈ)kämˈp-\ *adj* [F, fr. *compenser* to compensate + *-able* — more at COMPENSE] : that is to be or can be compensated ⟨hard work ~ by a sense of achievement⟩; *esp* : that can be compensated under the provisions of workmen's compensation laws ⟨~ injury⟩
compensables \-lz\ *n pl* : costs or losses entitling persons covered under social security to benefits
com·pen·sate \ˈkämpən,sāt, -,pen-, *archaic* kəmˈpen- *or* kämˈ-; *usu* -ād·+V\ *vb* -ED/-ING/-S [L *compensatus*, past part. of *compensare*, fr. *compensus*, past part. of *compendere* to weigh] *vt* **1** : to be equivalent to (as in value or effect) : make up for : COUNTERBALANCE ⟨*compensating* evil with good⟩ ⟨her vanity, dearth of brains, and excessive sentimentality were *compensated* by her kindness —E.J.Simmons⟩ **2** : to make proper payment to : requite suitably : REMUNERATE : RECOMPENSE ⟨~ a worker injured on his job⟩; *specif*, *civil law* : to extinguish or satisfy (as a claim) by compensation **3** *physics* : to provide with means of counteracting variation ⟨~ a magnetic needle⟩ : neutralize the effect of (variation or varying parts) **4** : to alter gradient on (curved portions of railroad track) so that total resistance to movement equals that for tangent track ~ *vi* : to make amends : supply an equivalent — used with *for* ⟨~ for his feelings of loneliness by assertions of superiority —W.H.Auden⟩ **syn** see PAY
compensated *adj* [fr. past part. of *compensate*] *of an optically inactive chemical compound* : balanced with respect to asymmetric carbon atoms ⟨*meso*-tartaric acid is an internally ~ form⟩
compensated dollar *n* [*compensated* fr. past part. of *compensate*] : COMMODITY DOLLAR
compensating *adj* [fr. pres. part. of *compensate*] : serving or functioning as a compensation (as for some irregularity or flaw); *esp*, *of an auxiliary electrical or mechanical device* : correcting performance that has been adversely affected by some operating variant (as by friction in a watt-hour meter, pressure in a main cylinder, or variation in an electronic circuit impedance) — **com·pen·sat·ing·ly** \ˈ==ˌ==\ *adv*
compensating balance *n* : COMPENSATION BALANCE
compensating condenser *n* : BALANCING CONDENSER
compensating errors *n pl* : errors equal in amount but opposite in sense that cancel each other
compensating gear *n* : DIFFERENTIAL GEAR
compensating magnet *n* : COMPASS CORRECTOR
compensating winding *n* : a winding embedded in the pole faces of a commutating alternating-current or direct-current machine and connected in series with the armature, the magnetic field of the winding neutralizing the cross-magnetizing field of the armature
com·pen·sa·tion \ˌkämpənˈsāshən, -,pen-\ *n* -S [ME *compensacioun*, fr. L *compensation-*, *compensatio* balancing of accounts, fr. *compensatus* (past part. of *compensare* to compensate) + *-ion-*, *-io* -ion] **1** : the act or action of making up, making good, or counterbalancing : rendering equal : AMENDING: as **a** (1) : the counterbalancing of a defect in bodily structure or limitation in function of an organ by overgrowth of another or by increased function of unimpaired parts of the same organ ⟨cardiac ~⟩ — compare DECOMPENSATION (2) : a psychic mechanism or process whereby an individual compensates for a frustrated drive, inadequacy, or imperfection by substituting or stressing another drive, trait, or function **b** : adjustment of the phase retardation of one light ray with respect to that of another **c** *civil law* : extinction of the mutual debts of two persons that are reciprocally debtors and creditors (as in setoff) **d** *phonetics* : compensatory lengthening or compensatory doubling **2** : something that constitutes an equivalent or recompense: as **a** : something that makes good a lack ⟨rewards which are no ~s for the abandoned gratifications —Abram Kardiner⟩ **b** : something that makes up for a loss ⟨~ will be made by Germany for all damage done to the civilian population of the Allies . . . by the aggression of Germany —J.M.Keynes⟩; *specif* : payment received by a worker or his dependents for claims under a workmen's compensation act or cash benefits received by eligible unemployed as provided for by legislation **c** : something that relieves, equalizes, or neutralizes (as pressure, stress, or stimuli) : means of alleviation ⟨nor did he use letter writing as a ~ for inner tensions —*Yale Rev.*⟩ ⟨for the men who are really up there, the war is a tough and dirty life, without immediate ~ —Walter Bernstein⟩ ⟨jazz began as the ~ music of a shackled race —*Esquire's Jazz Bk.*⟩ **d** : payment for value received or service rendered : REMUNERATION ⟨the ~ of U.S. government employees⟩ ⟨~ to the Indians for the land ceded by them consisted of livestock —D.E.Clark⟩ **e** : moral or spiritual reward or feeling or sense thereof ⟨however shoddy his life an artist knows the ~s of creation and achievement⟩ ⟨there are so many ~s that come from coaching small-time football —Bert LaBrucherie⟩ **f** *physics* : balance or counteraction of opposed forces
com·pen·sa·tion·al \ˌ=(,)=ˈ=shənᵊl, -shnəl\ *adj* : of or relating to compensation
compensation balance *n* : a timepiece balance wheel so constructed (as of two metals of different expansivities) that variations of temperature produce such changes in its mean rim diameter as offset the changes produced in the hairspring
compensation guard *n* : a narrow strip of paper included at the binding margin of a book to compensate for the thickness of items mounted on pages
compensation insurance *n* : WORKMEN'S COMPENSATION INSURANCE
compensation neurosis *n* : a neurosis of work phobias manifested in physical symptoms that persist as long as unemployment compensation continues
compensation pendulum *n* : a clock pendulum so constructed as to remain of the same pendulum length by automatic compensation for the effect of changes of temperature
compensation point *n* : the light intensity at which the amount of carbon dioxide released in respiration equals the amount used in photosynthesis and the amount of oxygen used in respiration equals the amount released in photosynthesis, varying in different species of plants and in response to changes in temperature and other environmental factors
com·pen·sa·tive \ˈkämpən,sād·iv, -,pen-; kəmˈpen(t)səd·-, (ˈ)kämˈp-\ *adj* [*compensate* + *-ive*] : affording compensation : COMPENSATORY
com·pen·sa·tor \ˈkämpən,sād·ə(r), -,pen-\ *n* -S [*compensate* + *-or*] : one that compensates: as **a** : AUTOTRANSFORMER **b** : BALANCER SET 1 **c** : COMPASS CORRECTOR **d** : a combination of quartz plates of wedge shape used to measure the phase difference between the two rectangular vibration components of elliptically polarized light **e** : a photographic device (as a star diaphragm or suitably graded neutral-density filter) for holding back the light in the middle of the field of a wide-angle lens to allow proper exposure at the corners **f** : a portion of a direction finder that automatically applies a correction to the direction indication and that commonly consists of a mechanical arrangement of cams **g** : a device fitted to the muzzle of a firearm that reduces recoil by directing part of the powder gases through a series of lateral vents — compare MUZZLE BRAKE **h** : an electrical equalizer designed to compensate for the recording characteristic of a record and usu. connected between a pickup and an amplifier
com·pen·sa·to·ry \kəmˈpen(t)sə,tōrē, (ˈ)kämˈp-, -tȯr-, -ri\ *adj* [*compensate* + *-ory*] : serving as compensation : making amends : making up for loss ⟨a ~ enlargement of the heart⟩ ⟨to overcome this feeling of inferiority by developing such ~ mechanisms as intelligent aggression or shrewdness —Edward Sapir⟩: as **a** : designed to counteract extreme fluctuations in the business cycle esp. by governmental planning and adjustments in revenue programs and government expenditures ⟨theories of ~ fiscal policy⟩ ⟨a ~ economy⟩ **b** : maintaining the length of a syllable — used esp. of the lengthening of a vowel when a following consonant is lost (Latin *cānus*, earlier *căsnus*) or the doubling of a consonant when a preceding vowel becomes short (Latin *littera*, earlier *lītera*)
compensatory damages *n pl* : damages awarded to make good or compensate for an injury sustained — distinguished from *punitive damages*
compensatory interest *n*, *Roman Dutch law* : interest covering the creditor's direct loss from forgoing use of his money
compense *vb* -ED/-ING/-S [ME *compensen*, fr. MF *compenser*, fr. L *compensare* — more at COMPENSATE] *obs* : COMPENSATE
¹com·pere \ˈkäm,pa(ə)ə, +V -a(ə)(ə)r\ *n* -S [F *compère*, lit., godfather, fr. ML *compater* — more at COMPEER] *chiefly Brit* : the master of ceremonies of an entertainment (as a revue or radio program)
²compere \ˈ"\ *vb* -ED/-ING/-S *vt*, *chiefly Brit* : CONDUCT ⟨~ a radio program⟩ ~ *vi* : to act as a compere ⟨he spent six hours at their studios, rehearsing, editing, and *compering* —*advt*⟩
com·pesce \kəmˈpes\ *vt* -ED/-ING/-S [ME *compessen*, fr. L *compescere*, fr. *com-* + *-pescere* (akin to L *parcere* to spare, abstain) — more at PARSIMONY] *archaic Scot* : to hold in check : RESTRAIN
com·pete \kəmˈpēt, *usu* -ēd·+V\ *vi* -ED/-ING/-S [L *competere* to come together, agree, be suitable, belong, compete for, fr. *com-* + *petere* to go to, head for, seek — more at FEATHER] **1** : to seek or strive for something (as a position, possession, reward) for which others are also contending : vie with another or others for or as if for a prize ⟨~ with top-notch performers⟩ ⟨a team that ~s against other teams⟩ ⟨~ for top honors⟩ ⟨the children *competed* with one another in seeing who could eat the most⟩ **2 a** : to stand comparison (as in fitness or value) ⟨the steam locomotive could no longer ~ with the diesel⟩ **b** : to come into rivalry esp. in economic value, usefulness, or efficiency ⟨rayon is seriously *competing* with wool in . . . fall and winter clothing —Desmond Reilly⟩

syn CONTEND, CONTEST: COMPETE may indicate simply the fact of struggle to win out over others, or to continue to exist despite the strength and efforts of others, or it may be used in reference to organized contests ⟨New Hampshire cannot *compete* with its neighboring State of Maine in raising potatoes —*Amer. Guide Series: N.H.*⟩ ⟨the dinosaurs were unable to *compete* successfully with the smaller mammals⟩ ⟨only at its best does the drama *compete* with the novel in finalities —Bernard De Voto⟩ ⟨the teams *competing* in the tournament⟩ CONTEND may suggest vigorous striving and struggling against an equal or stronger adversary ⟨a gray stone castle, for whose keep Bruces and Comyns and Macdowalls *contended* seven centuries ago —John Buchan⟩ ⟨two Greek schools of thought, the Stoic and the Epicurean, *contended* for the allegiance of Romans who aspired to philosophy —Benjamin Farrington⟩ ⟨the passions and hopes which he had excited had become too strong for him to *contend* against —J.A.Froude⟩ CONTEST is often a close synonym of COMPETE; typically, it may apply to a struggle that is limited, bounded, and definite in outcome, as a debate, race, match, fight, or battle ⟨New Orleans was . . . *contesting* with New York for first place among American ports —*Amer. Guide Series: Louisiana*⟩
com·pe·tence \ˈkämpəd·ən(t)s, -pətən- *also* -pətᵊn-\ *n* -S [MF *compétence*, fr. L *competentia* agreement, fr. *competent-*, *competens* (pres. part. of *competere*) + *-ia* -y] **1** *obs* : a sufficient supply : SUFFICIENCY **2 a** : property or means sufficient for the necessities and conveniences of life : sufficiency without excess ⟨his business acumen . . . provided his family with a comfortable ~ —Rex Ingamells⟩ ⟨those who . . . kept their shares . . . reaped ~s and small fortunes —Jack Alexander⟩ **b** : the condition of possessing or enjoying such sufficiency ⟨living in peace and ~⟩ **3 a** : the quality or state of being functionally adequate or of having sufficient knowledge, judgment, skill, or strength (as for a particular duty or in a particular respect) ⟨drugs that improve the ~ of a failing heart⟩ : range of ability or capability ⟨some ~ in the operation of a drill press⟩ ⟨a technicality beyond his ~ to master⟩; *specif* : legal authority, ability, or admissibility ⟨a matter within the ~ of a judge to adjudicate⟩ ⟨the committee has no actual ~ in criminal matters⟩ **b** : legitimacy or validity of a conclusion, logical process, point of view : ADEQUACY ⟨the schooled ~ of his observations⟩ **4** : the ability of a stream to transport detritus as measured by the size of the largest particle, pebble, or boulder it can move forward — compare CAPACITY 1i **5** : the capacity of living tissue to react; *specif* : the sum of the properties that permit a particular embryonic field to respond in a characteristic manner to the influence of an inductor — compare FIELD, INDUCTOR, POTENCY
com·pe·ten·cy \-nsē, -si\ *n* -ES [ML *competentia*, fr. L, agreement] : COMPETENCE
com·pe·tent \-nt\ *adj* [ME, suitable, appropriate, fr. MF & L; MF *compétent*, fr. L *competent-*, *competens*] **1 a** (1) : possessed of or characterized by marked or sufficient aptitude, skill, strength, or knowledge : SATISFACTORY, ADEQUATE ⟨was generally considered a ~ painter of landscapes⟩ (2) : SUFFICIENT ⟨a ~ income⟩ **b** : satisfactorily or moderately able : without marked weakness or demerit ⟨one way toward the ~ and salable, the other toward excellent and possibly unsalable —H.S.Canby⟩ **c** : possessed of knowledge, judgment, strength, or skill needed to perform an indicated action — followed by an infinitive phrase ⟨one of the finest raiders alive, and most ~ to judge my half-formed scheme —T.E.Lawrence⟩ **2 a** *archaic* : appropriate or suitable esp. to a certain social position or rank ⟨a moiety ~ was gaged by our king —Shak.⟩ **b** : proper or rightly pertinent : rightfully belonging or exercised ⟨if it be ~ for our government to segregate

and impound one group of law-abiding innocent citizens —A.J.Nock⟩ **3** *geol, of a bed or stratum* **:** strong enough to transmit effectively the thrust when strata are folded by lateral compression and capable of sustaining the weight of overlying strata when arched into an anticline **4 :** legally qualified or capable: as **a :** authorized to act or possessed of jurisdiction ⟨a ~ court⟩ ⟨a ~ judge⟩ **b :** legally qualified in mental and physical makeup ⟨a ~ witness⟩ **c :** meeting legal requirements as to validity ⟨~ evidence⟩ **5** *biol* **:** exhibiting competence **:** FUNCTIONAL **syn** see ABLE, SUFFICIENT

com·pe·tent·ly *adv* [ME, fr. *competent* + *-ly*] **:** in a competent manner

competes *pres 3d sing of* COMPETE

competible *adj* [obs. *compete* to be suitable (fr. L *competere* to be suitable, compete for) + *-ible*] **1** *obs* **:** COMPATIBLE, SUITABLE, APPROPRIATE **2** *obs* **:** COMPETENT — used with *to* or *with*

competing *pres part. of* COMPETE

com·pe·ti·tion \\ˌkämpəˈtishən\\ *n* -s [LL *competition-, competitio*, fr. L *competitus* (past part. of *competere* to compete for) + *-ion-, -io* -ion — more at COMPETE] **1 :** the act or action of seeking to gain what another is seeking to gain at the same time and usu. under or as if under fair or equitable rules and circumstances **:** a common struggle for the same object esp. among individuals of relatively equal standing **:** RIVALRY ⟨to prevent the realization that cooperation, not ~, is the road to happiness —Bertrand Russell⟩ **2 :** a contest between rivals **:** a match or trial between contestants ⟨a ~ in essay writing⟩ ⟨a high-diving ~⟩ **3 :** RIVAL, COMPETITOR **4 a :** the effort of two or more parties to secure the custom of a third party by the offer of the most favorable terms **b :** a market condition in which a large number of independent buyers and sellers compete for identical commodities, deal freely with each other, and retain the right of entry and exit from the market **5 :** more or less active demand by two or more organisms or kinds of organisms at the same time for some environmental resource in excess of the supply available, typically resulting in ultimate elimination of the less effective organism from the particular ecologic niche

com·pe·ti·tion·er \\-sh(ə)nə(r)\\ *n* -s **:** one that competes (as to achieve an official position or entrance into a service)

com·pet·i·tive \\kəmˈped·əd·|iv, -etət| *also* |əv\\ *adj* [*competit-* (as in *competitor*) + *-ive*] **:** of or relating to competition: as **a :** characterized by, arising from, or designated to exhibit rivalry among two or more equally matched individuals or forces esp. for a particular goal, position, or reward ⟨~ sports⟩ ⟨~ spirit⟩ ⟨~ tactics⟩ ⟨~ examinations⟩ **b :** produced by, based on, resulting from, or capable of existing in rivalry of economic endeavor and without the presence of monopoly or collusion ⟨a ~ market⟩ ⟨~ bids⟩ ⟨~ prices⟩ ⟨chemical cotton prices are now ~ with wood pulp —*Wall Street Jour.*⟩ — **com·pet·i·tive·ly** *adv* — **com·pet·i·tive·ness** *n* -ES

competitive point *n* **:** a transportation point served by two or more independent lines

com·pet·i·tor \\kəmˈped·əd·ə(r), -etətə(r) *also* -ed·əˌtȯ(ə)r *or* -etəˌtȯ(ə)r *or* -ˌtȯ(ə)\\ *n* -s [MF *competiteur*, fr. L *competitor*, fr. *competitus* (past part. of *competere* to compete for) + *-or*] **1 a :** one that seeks what another seeks or claims what another claims **:** RIVAL; *esp* **:** one on equal footing with another rival or other rivals ⟨a ~ in an election⟩ ⟨a born ~⟩ ⟨a ~ nation⟩ **b :** an organism or kind of organism that lives in competition with another **2 :** one that is engaged in selling or buying goods or services in the same market as another **3** *obs* **:** ASSOCIATE, CONFEDERATE

com·pet·i·to·ry \\-ed·əˌtōrē, -etə-\\ *adj* [*competit-* (as in *competitor*) + *-ory*] **:** COMPETITIVE

com·pi·la·tion \\ˌkämpəˈlāshən\\ *n* -s [ME *compilacioun*, fr. MF & L; MF *compilation*, fr. L *compilation-, compilatio*, fr. *compilatus* (past part. of *compilare*) + *-ion-, -io* -ion] **1 :** the act or action of gathering together written material esp. from various sources ⟨the slow ~ of data⟩ **2 :** something that is a product of the putting together of two or more items: as **a :** a book or document composed of materials gathered from other books or documents ⟨"Italian Cooking" . . . is a businesslike ~ of Italian dishes —Mary Poore⟩ ⟨a ~ of the best bibliography in the field of agriculture or natural sciences —Helen T. Geer⟩ **b :** an accumulation of many things, elements, or influences **:** ACCRETION ⟨a ~ of detrital matter⟩ ⟨like most architecture erected since the Gothic age . . . a ~ rather than a design —Thomas Hardy⟩

com·pi·la·tor \\ˈkämpəˌlād·ə(r), -ātə-\\ *n* -s [ME *compilatour*, fr. LL *compilator* plunderer, plagiarist, fr. L *compilatus* + *-or*] **:** one that compiles **:** COMPILER

com·pi·la·to·ry \\kəmˈpīləˌtōrē, -ˈpil-; ˈkämpələ-\\ *adj* [*compilat-* (as in *compilator*) + *-ory*] **:** of, relating to, or being compilation ⟨a work ~ in nature and not truly original⟩ **:** of or relating to a compiler ⟨~ techniques⟩

com·pile \\kəmˈpīl, *esp before pause or consonant* -īəl\\ *vt* -ED/-ING/-s [ME *compilen*, fr. MF *compiler*, fr. L *compilare* to plunder, rob, fr. *com-* + *-pilare* (perh. akin to L *pila* pillar, pier) — more at PILE] **1 :** to collect and assemble (written material or items from various sources) into a document or volume or a series of documents or volumes ⟨~ authoritative books as well as numerous articles —W.M.Emery⟩ ⟨~ a weather map⟩ ⟨~ a statistical chart⟩ **2** *obs* **:** to compose as an original literary work ⟨~ sharp satires —Christopher Marlowe⟩ **3 a :** to put together ⟨"chlorophyll", a name *compiled* from the Greek words for "green-leaf" —W.E.Swinton⟩ **b :** to pile up ⟨~ a great majority of votes⟩ **:** LIST, ENUMERATE ⟨a whole literature on him that ~s defects as well as virtues⟩

compiled map *n* **:** a small-scale map developed from data not obtained from original surveys conducted in the field

com·pile·ment \\-ī(ə)lmənt\\ *n* -s *archaic* **:** COMPILATION

com·pil·er \\-īlə(r)\\ *n* -s [ME *compilour*, fr. MF *compileur*, fr. LL *compilator*] **:** one that compiles: as **a :** a person who assembles items of information for publication ⟨a ~ of maps⟩ ⟨a ~ of specialized bibliographies⟩ **b :** a person who develops mailing lists for advertisers or gathers and arranges information of a variety of types for use in publications (as catalogs and directories)

comping *pres part of* COMP

com·pi·tal \\ˈkämpəd·ᵊl\\ *adj* [L *compitalis* of crossroads, fr. *compitum* crossroads + *-alis* -al; akin to L *competere* to come together — more at COMPETE] **1** *of a leaf vein* **:** intersecting at a broad angle **2** *of a fern* **:** having the sori borne at the junction of two veins

com·pla·cence \\kəmˈplāsᵊn(t)s\\ *n* -s [ME, fr. ML *complacentia* satisfaction, good will, pleasure, fr. L *complacent-, complacens* + *-ia* -y] **1 :** calm or secure satisfaction with one's self or lot **:** SELF-SATISFACTION ⟨the general's bovine ~ at being after all a general⟩ **2** *obs* **a :** PLEASURE, SATISFACTION **b :** a source of gratification or joy **3** *obs* **:** disposition to give satisfaction **:** AFFABILITY, COMPLAISANCE

com·pla·cen·cy \\-ᵊnsē, -si\\ *n* -ES [ML *complacentia*] **1 a :** the quality or state of being satisfied **:** a calm sense of well-being and security ⟨any momentary ~ was generally sternly dispelled by the harsh criticism of the coach —A.C.Benson⟩; *esp* **:** satisfaction or self-satisfaction accompanied by unawareness of actual dangers or deficiencies ⟨a ~ doubtless engendered by railroading and banking —*Amer. Guide Series: Minn.*⟩ ⟨the immense ~ of our population about civil defense —Reinhold Niebuhr⟩ ⟨~ in the performance of her car⟩ **b :** SELF-SATISFACTION, VANITY ⟨his candor was . . . coated with ~ —John Woodburn⟩ **2** *archaic* **:** complaisance or an instance thereof **3** *obs* **:** passive acquiescence **4** *archaic* **:** PLEASURE, DELIGHT

com·pla·cent \\-ᵊnt\\ *adj* [L *complacent-, complacens* very pleasing, pres. part. of *complacēre* to please greatly, fr. *com-* + *placēre* to please — more at PLEASE] **1 a :** marked by sometimes unwarranted, uncritical, and irritating satisfaction and pleasure at one's own personality, accomplishments, or situation ⟨~ when they should have been self-critical —Allan Nevins & H.S.Commager⟩ ⟨the ~ ones, to those who love themselves much but not too wisely —M.R.Cohen⟩ **b :** marked by or as if by unruffled or blasé satisfaction about the security of one's position or by careless acceptance of events around one **:** disinclined to act, to change, or to guard ⟨the ~ case of obesity —Arnold Bennett⟩ ⟨in that ~ old world . . . youth did not easily feel the impact of national problems —John Buchan⟩ **2 a :** feeling or showing complaisance or desire to please ⟨the University of Colorado courteously released me from my contract, but the Garrett Biblical Institute was less ~ —R.M.Lovett⟩ **b :** marked by smooth even contented ease without notable activity, tension, or stress ⟨townfolk made a ~ living by trading with countryfolk —*Amer. Guide Series: Texas*⟩ **3** *of a tree or a forest* **:** marked by evenness and regularity in the growth of annual rings regardless of different conditions in different years — opposed to *sensitive*

syn SELF-COMPLACENT, SELF-SATISFIED, SMUG, PRIGGISH: COMPLACENT may imply a feeling of assured well-being and absence of worry or complaint ⟨the people who suffer most from their conscience are obviously the sensitive and high-minded, while self-approbation comes most easily to the *complacent* and fortune-favored Jack Horners —M.R.Cohen⟩ It may suggest a gloating superiority or a blameworthy lassitude and lack of drive ⟨his insufferable smile was more *complacent* than ever —A. Conan Doyle⟩ ⟨the chief occasion on which he aspired to rise above the level of *complacent* mediocrity —H.E.Nettles⟩ SELF-COMPLACENT and SELF-SATISFIED stress satisfaction at one's own personality or situation and may suggest ill-based pride, self-deception, depreciation of others, indolent or blind inactivity ⟨the strong, *self-complacent* Luther declares . . . that "God himself cannot do without wise men" —R.W.Emerson⟩ ⟨those flaunting childish family portraits, with their farce of sentiment and smiling lies, and innocence so self-conscious and *self-satisfied* —W.M. Thackeray⟩ ⟨Stroeve, eager for praise and naively *self-satisfied*, could never resist displaying his work —W.S.Maugham⟩ SMUG indicates accustomed feelings about oneself of superiority, rectitude, or utter security ⟨our *smug* conviction that somehow we are more virtuous than the rest of the world, and that everyone should realize it —Richard Watts⟩ ⟨a *smug* and arrogant look about him, as is often the case with men who have unexpectedly acquired great power or great wealth —Kenneth Roberts⟩ SMUG often suggests narrow provincialism. PRIGGISH may suggest finical adherence to one's ideas or notions, perhaps ill-based, and an odious self-righteousness ⟨there is something artificial and even *priggish* about Goethe's healthiness, as there is about Baudelaire's unhealthiness —T.S.Eliot⟩ ⟨that unpromising young man with high collar and pince-nez whose somewhat *priggish* air of superiority infuriated most of the Democrats —A.M.Schlesinger b.1917⟩

complacential *adj* [ML *complacentia* + E *-al*] *obs* **:** COMPLAISANT

com·pla·cent·ly \\kəmˈplāsᵊntlē, -li\\ *adv* **:** in a complacent manner

¹com·plain \\kəmˈplān\\ *vb* -ED/-ING/-s [ME *compleynen*, fr. MF *compleindre, complaindre* (3d pers. pl. pres. indic. *complaignent*), fr. (assumed) VL *complangere*, fr. L *com-* + *plangere* to beat, beat the breast, lament — more at PLAINT] *vi* **1** *obs* **:** to express sorrow with weeping and outcry **:** LAMENT **2 a :** to express discontent, dissatisfaction, protest, resentment, or regret usu. without recalcitrance or threat and as though expecting sympathy ⟨began to ~ of it and lament her being ill-used —Jane Austen⟩ ⟨his troubles were really little ones. He had nothing to ~ about —Lenard Kaufman⟩ **b** (1) *archaic* **:** to be ailing (2) **:** to speak of one's illness or symptoms **3 :** to make a formal accusation, charge, or complaint ⟨the French consulate and the English consulate had ~*ed* of him . . . charging him with being high-handed —Louis Bromfield⟩ **4 :** to groan, creak, or make an otherwise mournful sound as though protesting or lamenting ⟨the overloaded wagon ~*ing* at each turn⟩ ~ *vt* **1** *obs* **:** LAMENT **:** weep at **:** BEWAIL **2 :** to say or relate with dissatisfaction, protest, or regret as though expecting sympathy or redress ⟨Cotton Mather ~*ed*, "'Tis dreadful cold, my ink glass . . . is froze" —*Amer. Guide Series: Mass.*⟩ ⟨if we ~ that so vague a term fails to do justice —Edward Sapir⟩

syn REPINE, GRUMBLE, GROUSE, BEEF, GRIPE, CROAK, SQUAWK, BELLYACHE: COMPLAIN, which orig. meant lamenting or bewailing, is now a general term for uttering unhappiness or discontent; it may indicate that a sympathetic reaction is expected or feasible ⟨a voice *complaining* . . . a venomous and senile whimper —Jean Stafford⟩ ⟨he had heard Ed *complaining* of his lot in life and crying out for new times —Sherwood Anderson⟩ ⟨when the people *complain*, said Mirabeau, the people are always right —J.A.Froude⟩ REPINE, now always bookish or literary, may suggest querulous plaintiveness ⟨his old age may have been monotonous, but there was no *repining* about it —Brand Blanshard⟩ In contrast, the following words range from the echoic suggestion of GRUMBLE to the slang form BELLYACHE. GRUMBLE suggests discontented muttering, often from a personality hard to satisfy and given to ill-natured complaint ⟨the way people *grumble* about their rates and taxes —G.B.Shaw⟩ ⟨reluctant laughter and *grumbling* thanks —Kenneth Roberts⟩ GROUSE may be applied to sustained forceful grumbling at annoyances ⟨soldiers *grousing* about their food⟩ ⟨never once have I heard him *grouse* about how tough things are —*Saturday Rev.*⟩ BEEF may suggest angry or emphatic complaint ⟨the *beefing* and clamoring by certain groups for a change —*New Republic*⟩ ⟨a few who have drilled . . . *beef* about being kept in uniform —Dixon Wecter⟩ GRIPE may suggest continued strong grumbling or criticizing, as though motivated by being griped ⟨after two or three days in the Army, he *gripes* like a veteran at the brass, the shavetails, the chow —*Christian Science Monitor*⟩ CROAK, SQUAWK, and BELLYACHE may imply lack of sympathy with the complainer. CROAK may suggest pessimistic, doleful, dismal complaining, SQUAWK a loud raucous outcry, as of a fowl, perhaps ineffective, and BELLYACHE a peevish or disgruntled whining ⟨the little old lady in black . . . tells you how just last fall her husband died in Ohio, and damp mists her glasses; she blinks and *croaks* —R.P.Warren⟩ ⟨the first industries to be hit by the credit curbs have *squawked* —*Atlantic*⟩ ⟨*bellyaching* about rationing, curtailment of civilian goods, administrative confusion, and various other annoyances —*Harper's*⟩

²complain \\"\\ *n* -s [ME *compleyn*, fr. *compleynen*, v.] *archaic* **:** COMPLAINT

¹com·plain·ant \\-nənt\\ *adj* [ME *compleynant*, fr. MF *complaignant*, pres. part. of *complaindre*] **:** COMPLAINING

²complainant \\"\\ *n* -s [ME *compleynant*, fr. MF *complaignant*, fr. *complaignant*, adj.] **1 :** the party who makes the complaint in a legal action or proceeding; *esp* **:** the party filing the bill in equity pleading — compare PLAINTIFF **2** *archaic* **:** one that complains

com·plain·er \\-ānə(r)\\ *n* -s **:** one that complains ⟨a chronic ~⟩; *specif, Scot* **:** COMPLAINANT 1

com·plain·ing·ly *adv* **:** in a complaining manner

com·plain·ing·ness *n* -ES **:** DISCONTENT

com·plaint \\kəmˈplānt\\ *n* -s [ME *compleynte*, fr. MF *complainte*, fr. OF, fr. fem. of *complaint*, past part. of *complaindre*] **1 a** *obs* **:** a cry or loud utterance or series of utterances of pain, rage, or sorrow **:** grieved or sorrowful outcry **b :** a formerly popular poem that laments or protests unrequited love or tells of personal misfortune, misery, or injustice **c :** the act or action of expressing protest, censure, or resentment **:** expression of injustice ⟨a ~ about poor housing⟩ ⟨on ~ of neighbors action was taken⟩ **d :** formal allegation or charge against a party made or presented to the appropriate court or officer (as for a wrong done or a crime committed) and variously applied (as to the initial bill in proceedings in equity, the declaration in a common-law pleading, the statement of claim under the English practice acts, and the initial pleading under the code practice in various states of the U.S.) **2 a :** something that is the cause or subject of protest or grieved outcry ⟨lack of efficiency is the ~ of all who wish to better government⟩ **b :** an ailment or disease of the body ⟨given to taking all sorts of medicine for vague ~s —Morris Fishbein⟩

com·plaint·ive \\-ntiv\\ *adj* **:** prone to complain ⟨a ~ patient⟩

com·plai·sance \\kəmˈplāsᵊn|(t)s *also* kəmˈplāzᵊn|(t)s *or* ˈkämpləˌzan|(t)s *or* -plə̇ˌz- *or* -ˌzaa(ə)n- *or* -ˌzän- *or* -ˌzán- *or* ˌ≈≈ˈ≈\\ *n* -s [F, fr. MF, fr. ML *complacentia* satisfaction, good will, pleasure — more at COMPLACENCE] **:** ready disposition to please (as by acceding to another's wishes) **:** pleasing ingratiating deportment ⟨with that ~ from which a stranger generally infers that he is welcome —William Cowper⟩

com·plai·sant \\|t\\ *adj* [F, fr. MF, pres. part. of *complaire* to acquiesce as a favor, gratify, fr. L *complacēre* to please greatly — more at COMPLACENT] **1 :** marked by an inclination to please or oblige or by courteous agreeability ⟨amid very ~ smiles and general encouragement —*Jane Austen*⟩ **2 :** marked by a willingness to please or serve others, to consent to their wishes, or to lend oneself compliantly to their purposes ⟨boss-ridden conventions turned him down for more ~ candidates —Allan Nevins & H.S.Commager⟩ **syn** see AMIABLE

com·plai·sant·ly *adv* **:** in a complaisant manner

com·pla·nate \\ˈkämpləˌnāt\\ *adj* [L *complanatus*, past part. of *complanare* to make even, make level, fr. *com-* + *-planare* (fr. *planus* level, flat) — more at FLOOR] **:** made level **:** in one plane ⟨~ leaves⟩ **:** FLATTENED

com·pla·na·tion \\ˌkämpləˈnāshən\\ *n* -s [L *complanare* + E *-ation*] **:** a leveling off **:** flattening out

compleat *archaic var of* COMPLETE

complect *vt* -ED/-ING/-S [L *complecti* — more at COMPLEX] *obs* **:** INTERTWINE, EMBRACE; *esp* **:** to plait together **:** INTERWEAVE

com·plect·ed \\kəmˈplektəd\\ *adj* [*complect-* (irreg. fr. *complexion*) + *-ed*] **:** COMPLEXIONED — usu. used in combination ⟨dark-*complected*⟩; not often in formal use

complection *var of* COMPLEXION

¹com·ple·ment \\ˈkämpləmənt\\ *n* -s [ME, fr. L *complementum*, fr. *complēre* to fill up, complete + *-mentum* -ment — more at COMPLETE] **1 :** something that fills up or completes: as **a :** something that fills out and makes perfect **:** a completing or consummating part, integral, or component **:** COMPLETION ⟨a European tour was then the necessary ~ of a gentle upbringing and a liberal education⟩ ⟨although Bergson often represented intuition as a ~ to reason, he as often separated and opposed them —H.J.Muller⟩ **b :** the quantity or number required to fill a thing or make it complete **:** full allowance ⟨a farm with a full ~ of stock⟩ ⟨a platoon with its normal ~ of weapons⟩ ⟨the usual ~ of office personnel⟩ **c :** the necessary and completing opposing item **:** one of two mutually completing parts **:** COUNTERPART ⟨he had found someone whose . . . masculinity was the very ~ of his own fragile graces —H.V.Gregory⟩ ⟨some kind of school was the ~ of each meetinghouse —*Amer. Guide Series: N. C.*⟩ **2** *obs* **a :** the act or action of fulfilling or making up **b :** the quality or state of being complete **3 a :** the amount of angle or arc by which a given angle or arc falls short of 90° **b :** ¹MINOR 4 **c :** the numerical amount that must be added to a number to give the least number containing one more digit ⟨the ~ of 4 is 6 and that of 45 is 55⟩ **4** *obs* **a :** something added for equipping or ornamentation esp. of the person **:** ACCESSORY **b :** a social quality or accomplishment **c :** a ceremonial or courteous observance that rounds off a service or action or the deportment of an individual **5 :** the whole force or personnel of a ship; *specif* **:** the entire force of officers and crew allowed to a naval vessel for wartime operations **6** *heraldry* **:** fullness of the moon **7 :** the interval in music required with a given interval to complete the octave **8 :** an added word by which a predication is made complete (as *president* in "they elected him president" or *white* in "he painted the house white") **9 :** a complementary color **10 :** the thermolabile substance in normal blood serum and plasma that in combination with antibodies causes the destruction of bacteria, foreign blood corpuscles, and other antigens **11** *logic* **:** the negate of a given class *a* or statement *p*

A D C B

complement 3a: *ACB* right angle; *ACD* complement of *DCB* (and vice versa); *AD* complement of *DB* (and vice versa)

²com·ple·ment \\-ˌment,-mənt — *see* ²-MENT\\ *vb* -ED/-ING/-S *vt* **1 :** to fill in or make up (what is lacking) **:** round off ⟨the museum is ~*ed* by a spacious garden —*Amer. Guide Series: Mich.*⟩ ⟨your chosen perfume ~*s* your personality —D.S.Lyle⟩ **2** *obs* **:** COMPLIMENT ~ *vi, obs* **:** COMPLIMENT

com·ple·men·tal \\ˌkämpləˈmentᵊl\\ *adj* **:** that has to do with a complement: as **a :** SUPPLEMENTAL, COMPLETING ⟨should the primary king or queen termite die, there are ~ ones to take their place —*Nature Mag.*⟩ **b** *obs* **:** ACCOMPLISHED **c** *obs* **:** CEREMONIOUS, COMPLIMENTARY

complemental air *n* **:** the quantity of air (about 3000 cubic centimeters) that can be inhaled in addition to one's tidal air

complementally *adv, obs* **:** in a ceremonious manner

complemental male *n* **:** a minute modified male barnacle that lives attached to certain hermaphroditic barnacles

com·ple·men·ta·ri·ness \\ˌkämpləˈmentərēnə̇s, -en·trē-, -rin-\\ *n* -ES **:** the quality or state of being complementary

com·ple·men·tar·i·ty \\ˌkämplə(ˌ)men·ˈtarəd·ē, -ləmən-\\ *n* -ES [*complementary* + *-ity*] **1 :** the interrelationship or the completion or perfection brought about by the interrelationship of one or more units supplementing, being dependent upon, or standing in polar position to another unit or other units ⟨the ~ of the sexes⟩ ⟨the ~ of nature and art⟩ **2 :** the complementary relationship of the electromagnetic wave and corpuscular theories in explaining the dual character of light and other quantized radiation **3 :** correspondence in reverse of part of one molecule to part of another; *esp* **:** the complementary arrangement of chemical groups and electric charges that enables a combining group of an antibody to combine with a specific determinant group of an antigen or hapten

¹com·ple·men·ta·ry \\ˌkämpləˈmentərē, -n·trē, -ri\\ *adj* [F *complémentaire*, fr. *complément* complement (fr. L *complementum*) + *-aire* -ary] **1 :** of, relating to, or suggestive of complementing, completing, or perfecting ⟨their economies are more ~ than competitive —William Petersen⟩ ⟨participation . . . as ~ to observation —Lewis Mumford⟩ **2 :** mutually dependent **:** supplementing and being supplemented in return ⟨farmer and townsman represent ~ interests —*Farmer's Weekly (So. Africa)*⟩ **3 :** being one of a pair of chromatic stimuli that produce an achromatic mixture when combined in suitable proportions ⟨a ~ color⟩ **4 a :** serving as a grammatical complement ⟨a ~ infinitive⟩ **5 :** of or relating to sets of small bodies of igneous rock varying in composition that accompany large masses from which they were derived by differentiation ⟨aplites and other ~ dikes⟩ **6 :** related in relatively fixed proportions ⟨some pairs of commodities are ~ so that the consumer uses more of one the more he uses of the other —G.J. Stigler⟩ **7 :** of or relating to the negate of a given class or statement ⟨the ~ property to blue . . . is not blue —A.J.Ayer⟩ or to two classes or statements each of which is the negation of the other

²complementary \\"\\ *n* -ES **:** something that stands in a complementary relationship; *esp* **:** a complementary color

complementary afterimage *n* **:** a chromatic afterimage having a hue approximately the hue complementary to that of the sensation produced by the original stimulus — called also *negative afterimage*

complementary air *n* **:** COMPLEMENTAL AIR

complementary angles *n pl* **:** two angles whose sum is a right angle

complementary cell *n* **:** any of the loosely arranged cells in a lenticel — compare CLOSING LAYER

complementary distribution *n* **:** a distribution of a pair of speech sounds or a pair of linguistic forms such that the one is found only in environments where the other is not (as the unaspirated *t* of English *stone* and the aspirated *t* of English *tone* or English *your* occurring before a noun, *yours* in all other environments), esp. when used as a basic prerequisite for the classification of nonidentical sounds as allophones of the same phoneme or for the classification of nonidentical linguistic forms as allomorphs of the same morpheme

complementary function *n* **:** the general solution of the auxiliary equation of a linear differential equation

complementary gene *or* **complementary factor** *n* **:** one of two or more genes that when present together produce effects qualitatively distinct from the separate effect of any one of them

complementary male *n* **:** COMPLEMENTAL MALE

complementary pit *n* **:** a pit in one cell of many higher vascular plants complementary to another in an adjacent cell — compare PIT-PAIR

complementary wavelength *n* **:** wavelength of the portion of the visible spectrum required to produce achromatic color by additive mixture with a sample color — see COLOR 1c

com·ple·men·ta·tion \\ˌkämpləmənˈtāshən, -lə(ˌ)men-\\ *n* -s **1 :** the formation of neutral colors from complementaries **2 :** COMPLEMENTARY DISTRIBUTION **3** *logic* **:** the forming of a complement or negate specif. of a class

complemented *past of* COMPLEMENT

complement fixation *n* **:** the absorption of complement to the compound formed by the union of an antibody and the antigen for which it is specific occurring when complement is added to a mixture (in proper proportion) of such an antibody and antigen

complement–fixation test *n* **:** a test for the presence of a particular antibody made by addition of complement and an indicator system to a mixture of known antigen and a serum suspected to contain the specific antibody for this antigen and used esp. in the diagnosis of syphilis — see WASSERMANN TEST

complementing *pres part of* COMPLEMENT

complements *pl of* COMPLEMENT, *pres 3d sing of* COMPLEMENT

¹com·plete \kəm'plēt, *usu* -ēd.+V\ *adj, often* -ER/-EST [ME *complet*, fr. MF, fr. L *completus*, past part. of *complēre* to fill up, fr. *com-* + *plēre* to fill; akin to L *plenus* full — more at FULL] **1 a :** possessing all necessary parts, items, components, or elements **:** not lacking anything necessary **:** ENTIRE, PERFECT ⟨few households would regard breakfast ~ without a plate of porridge —L.D.Stamp⟩ ⟨this man . . . ~ with wings and four stripes on his uniform sleeve —E.K.Gann⟩ ⟨neither one of these publications gives the ~ poems of Smart —A.R.Benham⟩ **b :** having all four sets of floral organs — compare INCOMPLETE, MONOCLINOUS **c** (1) *of a subject or predicate* **:** including modifiers, complements, or objects if any ⟨in the sentence "the little boy hit the ball hard" *the little boy* is the ~ subject and *hit the ball hard* is the ~ predicate⟩ — compare SIMPLE (2) *of a verb* **:** filling out a predication without any object or complement ⟨*moved* in "the train moved" is a ~ verb⟩ **d** *of a diet or ration* **:** BALANCED **2 :** brought to an end or to a final or intended condition ⟨a ~ period of time⟩ ⟨a ~ act⟩ **:** CONCLUDED, COMPLETED ⟨five ~ days⟩ ⟨a ~ revolution⟩ **3** *of a person* **:** possessed of all necessary, usual, or typical qualities, habits, or accomplishments ⟨a ~ man⟩ ⟨a ~ gentleman⟩ ⟨a ~ Englishman⟩; *specif* **:** highly proficient (as in an art or skill) ⟨a ~ landscape artist⟩ ⟨a ~ horseman⟩ **4 :** fully realized **:** carried to the ultimate **:** THOROUGH, TOTAL ⟨in ~ sympathy with his views⟩ ⟨~ surrender⟩ ⟨his ~ inability to understand⟩

²complete \"\ *vt* -ED/-ING/-S **1 :** to bring to an end often into or as if into a finished or perfected state ⟨foolish to put his hand to a task which he could not ~ —John Buchan⟩; *specif* **:** to execute (a forward pass) successfully ⟨State *completed* 10 of 19 passes while Rutgers made good 4 of 10 —*N.Y. Times*⟩ **2 a :** to make whole, entire, or perfect **:** end after satisfying all demands or requirements ⟨art partly ~*s* what nature is herself sometimes unable to bring to perfection —Havelock Ellis⟩ **b :** to mark the end of **:** show attainment to the total or totality of ⟨small mammals, birds, and tropical fish . . . ~ the zoo exhibits —*Amer. Guide Series: N.Y.City*⟩ **c :** ACCOMPLISH, EXECUTE, FULFILL ⟨~ a contract⟩ ⟨a vow *completed*⟩ **d :** CONSUMMATE ⟨allowed the lovers to ~ their marriage —G.M.Trevelyan⟩ **syn** see CLOSE

com·plet·ed·ness *n* -ES **:** COMPLETENESS

complete fertilizer *n* **:** a fertilizer that contains the three primary plant nutrients (nitrogen, phosphoric acid, and potash)

complete integral *n* **:** a solution of a partial differential equation of the first order that contains as many arbitrary constants as there are independent variables

com·plete·ly *adv* **1 :** so as to be complete **:** FULLY ⟨a ~ furnished apartment⟩ **2 :** to a complete degree **:** ENTIRELY ⟨the horse rolled ~ over⟩ ⟨~ at fault⟩

com·plete·ment \-tmənt\ *n* -S **:** COMPLETION ⟨together we have all the elements of ~ —Betty Smith⟩

com·plete·ness \-tnəs\ *n* -ES **1 :** the quality or state of being complete **2** *of an axiomatized system of logic* **:** the state of being so constituted that a contradiction arises through the addition of any formula not previously deducible from the axioms of the system

complete pair *n* **:** CLOSED PAIR

complete primitive *n* **:** the complete integral regarded as the basis of the differential equation

complete quadrilateral *n* **:** a figure that is determined by four coplanar lines, and has four sides and three diagonal axes, each two of which cut the other harmonically in three centers of which one or even two may be at infinity

complete quadrilateral: *AB, BC, CD, DA* sides; *AC, BD, EF* axes

complete solution *n* **:** GENERAL SOLUTION

complete stop *n* **:** a set of organ pipes extending throughout the compass of the manual

com·ple·tion \kəm'plēshən\ *n* -S [L *completion-, completio* filling, fr. *completus* (past part. of *complēre* to complete) + *-ion-, -io* -ion — more at ¹COMPLETE] **1 :** the act or action of completing, becoming complete, or making complete ⟨his ~ of the late artist's unfinished masterpiece⟩; *specif* **:** a forward pass caught by the receiver ⟨out of 10 attempted passes, there were 5 ~*s*⟩ **2 :** the quality or state of being complete **:** FULFILLMENT ⟨his desires having reached ~⟩

completion test *n* **:** an intelligence test requiring that the one to be tested complete a whole (as a sentence or picture) from which certain parts have been omitted

com·ple·tive \kəm'plēd·iv\ *adj* [LL *completivus*, fr. L *completus* + *-ivus* -ive] **:** serving or tending to complete ⟨annotations ~ of the test⟩; *specif, of a verbal aspect* **:** expressing completion of an action — **com·ple·tive·ly** \-d·əvlē\ *adv*

¹com·ple·to·ry \-d·ərē\ *n* -ES [ME *completorie*, fr. LL *completorium*, fr. L *completus* + *-orium*] **:** COMPLINE

²completory \"\ *adj* [²*complete* + *-ory*] **:** COMPLETIVE

¹com·plex \(')käm¦pleks, kəm'p-\ *vt* -ED/-ING/-ES [L *complexus*, past part. of *complecti*] **1 :** to make complex or into a complex ⟨a ~*ing* problem⟩ **2 :** ²CHELATE

²complex \"\ *adj, sometimes* -ER/-EST [L *complexus*, past part. of *complecti* to entwine around, embrace, fr. *com-* + *plectere* to braid — more at PLY] **1 a :** composed of two or more separable or analyzable items, parts, constituents, or symbols **:** COMPOSITE — opposed to *simple* ⟨the ~ sign "2 × 5=10" —A.J.Ayer⟩ ⟨the sea is a ~ mixture of chemicals —W.H. Dowdeswell⟩ **b** (1) *of a word* **:** having a bound form as one or both of its immediate constituents ⟨*unmanly* is a ~ word⟩ — contrasted with *compound, simple* (2) *of a sentence* **:** consisting of a main clause and one or more subordinate clauses ⟨*make hay while the sun shines* is a ~ sentence⟩ — contrasted with *compound, simple* **2 a :** having many varied interrelated parts, patterns, or elements and consequently hard to understand fully ⟨a ~ camera with many attachments⟩ ⟨a ~ industrial process⟩ ⟨~ tissue⟩ **b :** marked by an involvement of many parts, aspects, details, notions, and necessitating earnest study or examination to understand or cope with ⟨an extremely ~ industrial and commercial enterprise far removed from the simplicities of farming —*Amer. Guide Series: Calif.*⟩ ⟨movements as vast and ~ as the migration of peoples —Lewis Mumford⟩ ⟨a ~ mass of diverse laws and customs, written and unwritten —H.O.Taylor⟩ **3 :** formed by union of simpler substances (as compounds or ions) — used of salts, ions, and other chemical combinations ⟨a ~ protein⟩

syn COMPLICATED, INTRICATE, KNOTTY, INVOLVED: COMPLEX stresses the fact of combining or folding together various parts and suggests that considerable study, knowledge, or experience is needed for comprehension or operation ⟨all legal definitions are highly *complex* —C.K.Ogden & I.A.Richards⟩ ⟨the *complex* details of naval, ground, and air activities —F.D.Roosevelt⟩ ⟨a *complex* apparatus of washers, scales, slicers, diffusion tanks, purifiers, filter presses, evaporators, vacuum pans, centrifugal machines, and driers —*Amer. Guide Series: Calif.*⟩ COMPLICATED may heighten notions of difficulty in understanding ⟨business so big and *complicated* that neither the propertied class nor the working class could understand it —G.B.Shaw⟩ INTRICATE suggests difficulty of understanding or appreciating quickly because of perplexing interconnecting, interweaving, or interacting of parts ⟨the economic situation is so complex, so *intricate* in the interdependence of delicately balanced factors —John Dewey⟩ ⟨complex in themselves, and *intricate* in their interaction —H.O.Taylor⟩ KNOTTY suggests so much perplexity, difficulty, or entanglement that solution or understanding is improbable ⟨many *knotty* problems . . . that it will require the combined resources of the linguist, the logician, the psychologist, and the critical philosopher to clear up for us —Edward Sapir⟩ ⟨your question . . . is a *knotty* one, and such as, had I the wisdom of Solomon, I should be puzzled to answer —William Cowper⟩ INVOLVED indicates an intertwining such that some parts return or seem to return upon themselves, as in certain difficult knots, making unraveling or understanding very hard ⟨public issues are so large and so *involved* that it is only a few who can hope to have any adequate comprehension of them —G.L.Dickinson⟩

³com·plex \'käm,pleks *also* 'ₑ'ₑ *sometimes* ₑ'ₑ\ *n* -ES [L *complexus* surrounding, embrace, fr. *complexus*, past part. of *complecti*] **1 :** an association of related things often in intricate combination: as **a :** a group of culture traits relating to a single activity (as hunting, maize growing, pottery making), process (as the use of flint, construction of megalithic monuments), or unit of culture (as Folsom, neo-Eskimo) **:** an aggregate of artifacts — called also *culture complex, trait-complex* **b** [G *komplex*, fr. L *complexus*] **:** a system of repressed or suppressed desires and memories that exerts a dominating influence upon the personality; *broadly* **:** exaggerated reaction (as of fear or sensitiveness) to some subject or situation ⟨she has always had a ~ about bugs⟩ **c :** a group of obviously related units (as of species) of which the degree and nature of the relationship is imperfectly known **d** (1) **:** a haploid chromosome set containing a specified set of genes arranged in a particular order (2) **:** a group of chromosomes that always pass together in meiosis to one daughter cell — compare GENOME **e :** a group of kinds of organisms (as clones, strains, or varieties) showing common adaptation of a particular kind, usu. to a specialized environment **2 :** a conjunction of varied contributing or interacting factors, elements, or qualities: as **a :** a complex substance (as a coordination compound, an ion containing several atoms, or an adsorption compound) ⟨molecular ~*es*⟩ ⟨enzyme-substrate ~⟩ — usu. distinguished from *mixture* **b :** an assemblage of different rocks having structural relations intricately involved ⟨the Archean ~⟩ **c :** a complex word — contrasted with *compound, simplex* **d :** the sum of factors (as symptoms and lesions) characteristic of a disease ⟨symptom ~⟩ ⟨primary tuberculous ~⟩ **syn** see SYSTEM

complexed *past of* COMPLEX

com·plexed·ness \kəm'pleksədnəs, -ks(t)nəs\ *n* -ES **:** COMPLEXITY

complexer *comparative of* COMPLEX

complexes *pres 3d sing of* COMPLEX, *pl of* COMPLEX

complexest *superlative of* COMPLEX

complex fraction *n* **:** a fraction having a fraction or mixed number in the numerator or denominator or in each — called also *compound fraction*

complex function *n* **:** a function of the complex variable

complex idea *n* **:** an idea formed by the mind out of simple ideas known by sensation and reflection

com·plex·i·fy \käm'pleksə,fī, kəm-\ *vt* -ED/-ING/-ES **:** to make complex ⟨problems needlessly *complexified*⟩

complexing *pres part of* COMPLEX

complex integration *n* **:** the integration of a function of a complex variable along an open or closed curve in the plane of the complex variable

¹com·plex·ion *also* **com·plec·tion** \kəm'plekshən\ *n* -S [ME *complexion* temperament, humor, combination of the humors, bodily constitution, fr. MF *complexion*, fr. ML *complexion-, complexio*, fr. L, combination, connection, complication, fr. *complexus* (past part of *complecti*) + *-ion-, -io* -ion] **1 a** *obs* **:** a humor (sense 1b(1)) or combination of humors **b** *in medieval physiology and natural philosophy* **:** the combination in a certain proportion of the hot, cold, moist, and dry qualities that determine the nature or quality of a body or plant **2 a** *obs* **:** bodily constitution or mental makeup ⟨if his ~ incline him to melancholy —John Milton⟩ **b :** a cast of mind **:** an individual complex of attitudes, inclinations, or ways of thinking or feeling ⟨being of more sensitive ~ of mind than myself they were made ill by the suspense —J.H.Newman⟩ **c :** a complex of attitudes, inclinations, orientations, or ways of thought ⟨all the armed partisan groups . . . of whatever political ~ immediately joined in the fighting —*Atlantic*⟩ **3 a :** the hue or appearance of the skin esp. of the face ⟨a fair ~⟩ **b :** the skin of the face ⟨creams for ~ cleaning⟩ **4 :** the appearance or impression of a person or thing ⟨weathering has changed the ~ of the town hall from bright newness to solid conformity with neighboring structures⟩ ⟨the warlike ~ of the news⟩ **5** [L *complexion-, complexio*] *archaic* **:** COMBINATION, AGGREGATE **syn** see DISPOSITION

²complexion \"\ *vt* -ED/-ING/-S [ME *complexiounen* to compose, fr. *complexioun*, n.] **:** to give a color or particular slant to **:** TINGE ⟨the early sun ~*ing* the mountains⟩ ⟨propaganda ~*ed* his views⟩

com·plex·ion·al \-shən°l,-shnəl\ *adj* [ME, fr. ML *complexionalis*, fr. *complexion-, complexio* + L *-alis* -al] **:** of or relating to physical constitution or mental temperament ⟨his ~ hue⟩ ⟨~ political views⟩ — **com·plex·ion·al·ly** \-°lē,-əlē, -li\ *adv*

com·plex·ioned \kəm¦plekshənd\ *adj* [ME *complexiouned* having a (specified) bodily constitution, fr. *complexioun* + *-ed*] **:** having a (specified) facial complexion — used chiefly in combination ⟨a dark-*complexioned* girl⟩ ⟨a muddy-*complexioned* man⟩

com·plex·ion·less \-nləs\ *adj* **:** lacking color **:** PALE

com·plex·i·ty \käm'pleksəd·ē, kəm-, -ətē, -i\ *n* -ES **1 :** the quality or state of being complex **:** COMPOSITENESS, INTRICACY ⟨the ~ of modern society⟩ ⟨the ~ of an adding machine's mechanism⟩ **2 :** something complex **:** an intricacy or complication ⟨the political *complexities* of his office⟩

com·plex·ly \(')käm¦pleksl ē, kəm'-, -li\ *adv* **:** in a complex manner

complex mode *n* **:** a mode that according to the philosophy of the 17th century English philosopher John Locke results from the combination of simple ideas of several kinds (as beauty, gratitude) — contrasted with *simple mode;* compare ¹MODE 6

com·plex·ness \-snəs\ *n* -ES **:** COMPLEXITY

complex number *or* **complex quantity** *n* **:** a number or expression of the form $a+bi$, where a and b are real numbers and $i=\sqrt{-1}$

complex plane *n* **:** a plane whose points are identified by means of complex numbers

complex unit *n* **:** a complex number $a+ib$ whose absolute value $\sqrt{a^2+b^2}$ is 1

com·plex·us \käm'pleksəs, kəm-\ *n, pl* **complexus** [L, surrounding, embrace — more at COMPLEX] **:** an interwoven complicated aggregate of parts **:** COMPLEX ⟨the entire cultural ~ —James Collins⟩ ⟨a baffling ~ of her own imaginings —John Farrelly⟩

complex variable *n* **:** a number or expression of the form $x+iy$ where $i=\sqrt{-1}$ and x and y are in general variables

com·pli·a·ble \kəm'plīəbəl\ *adj* [*comply* + *-able*] **1** *archaic* **:** disposed or apt to agree or yield **:** COMPLIANT **2** *obs* **:** that may be reconciled — **com·pli·a·bly** \-blē\ *adv*

com·pli·ance \kəm'plīən(t)s\ *n* -S [*comply* + *-ance*] **1** *obs* **a :** CIVILITY **b :** friendly or happy agreement **:** HARMONY, CONCORD ⟨~ between man and wife⟩ **2 a :** the act or action of yielding to pressure, demand, or coercion **:** CONFORMANCE ⟨the Counter Reformation was not a ~ with Reform but a defiance of it —H.R.Trevor-Roper⟩ **b :** inclination or readiness to yield to the demands of others often in a servile or spineless fashion ⟨worthy men may be rejected because of their very virtues and unworthy men selected because of their ~ —P.H.Douglas⟩ **3 :** the quality or state of yielding to bending under stresses within the elastic limit; *also* **:** the amount of displacement per unit of applied force **4 a :** conformity in fulfilling formal or official requirements ⟨a letter written in ~ with U.S. Army style⟩ ⟨the . . . provision was designed to tighten ~ with acreage allotments —*Wall Street Jour.*⟩ **b :** cooperation promoted by official or legal authority or conforming to official or legal norms ⟨cheerful, spontaneous cooperation and ~ to orders are results of proper discipline under a respected leader —A.A.Ageton⟩ ⟨an official oath of ~ with the statute —Florence Mishnun⟩ ⟨insure the ~ of all . . . nations —*U. N. Disarmament Commission Resolution*⟩

com·pli·an·cy \-nsē, -si\ *n* -ES [*comply* + *-ancy*] **:** COMPLIANCE

com·pli·ant \-nt\ *adj* [*comply* + *-ant*] **1 :** ready, disposed, or likely to yield (as to pressure or the wishes of another) **:** COMPLAISANT, SUBMISSIVE ⟨above all things ~ and anxious to suit his opinions to those whom he encounters —H.J.Laski⟩ **2** *obs* **:** PLIANT — **com·pli·ant·ly** *adv*

com·pli·ca·cy \'kämpləkəsē, -lēk-, -si\ *n* -ES [fr. *complicate*, adj., after such pairs as E *confederate: confederacy*] **1 :** the quality or state of being complicated ⟨the ~ of his subject matter⟩ **2 :** something that is complicated ⟨the ~ of a watch⟩

com·pli·cant \-kənt\ *adj* [L *complicant-, complicans*, pres. part. of *complicare* to fold together] **:** OVERLAPPING — used of the elytra of certain beetles

¹com·pli·cate \'kämplə,kāt, *usu* -ād.+V\ *vb* -ED/-ING/-S [L *complicatus*] *vt* **1** *obs* **a :** to unite intimately by or as if by intertwining **b :** to fold or twist up together into or as if into a confused or overly involved mass **2 :** to combine esp. in an involved or inextricable manner ⟨his ideals were somehow *complicated* with selfish interest⟩ **3** *obs* **:** to create esp. by joining two or more elements **:** COMPOUND **4 :** to make complex, involved, or difficult ⟨this ~*s* matters⟩ ⟨snobbery *complicated* their social contacts⟩ **5** *med* **:** INVOLVE; *esp* **:** to cause to be more complex or severe ⟨bacterial secondary invaders ~ many virus infections⟩ ~ *vi* **:** to become complicated ⟨the problems grew, multiplied, and *complicated* beyond all reason⟩

²com·pli·cate \-lәkәt, -lēk-, *usu* -kәd.+V\ *adj* [L *complicatus*, past part. of *complicare* to fold together, fr. *com-* + *plicare* to fold — more at PLY] **1 :** made up of intimately united parts **:** COMPLEX ⟨a machine ~ of handmade gears⟩ **2 :** DIFFICULT, INVOLVED ⟨a ~ problem⟩ **3 a :** CONDUPLICATE **b :** folded longitudinally one or more times — used of insects' wings

com·pli·cat·ed \-lə,kād·əd, -ātəd\ *adj* [fr. past part. of *complicate*] **1 :** marked by an interrelation of diverse and often numerous parts, elements, notions, phases, or influences difficult of analysis, solution, or understanding ⟨Virgil compares their ~ evolutions to the windings of the Cretan labyrinth —J.G.Frazer⟩ ⟨when life is so ~ as to lose all homogeneity and unity of purpose —Norman Douglas⟩ ⟨~ machinery⟩ **2 :** having many interconnected parts **:** not simple or easy to fabricate or comprehend ⟨the whole organization of modern industry is a ~ one, dependent upon a host of professionalized skills that link —Lewis Mumford⟩ **syn** see COMPLEX

com·pli·cat·ed·ly *adv* **:** in a complicated manner

com·pli·cat·ed·ness *n* -ES **:** COMPLICACY

com·pli·cate·ness *n* -ES **:** COMPLICACY

com·pli·ca·tion \,kämplə'kāshən\ *n* -S [LL *complication-, complicatio* fr. L *complicatus* + *-ion-, -io* -ion] **1** *obs* **:** a folding together **:** the quality or state of being folded together **2 a** *obs* **:** an intimate combining **:** the quality or state of being intimately combined **b** *psychol* **:** the combination of sense data (as from different senses) into a unitary impression **3 a :** a complicated relationship of parts ⟨because of its ~ no mechanic would touch the engine⟩ **b :** a making difficult, involved, or intricate ⟨his ~ of our plans by not showing up on time⟩ **c :** a complex or intricate feature or element ⟨the ~*s* of jet aircraft⟩ or one that makes complex or intricate ⟨omitted Canada because of the ~*s* of the bilingual culture of sections of that country —J.B.Conant⟩ **d :** a difficult factor or issue often appearing suddenly and unexpectedly and changing existing plans, methods, or attitudes ⟨another ~ . . . was the excess of imports over exports —*Collier's Yr. Bk.*⟩ ⟨~*s* arose on all sides⟩ **e :** a situation or a detail of a character entering into and complicating the main thread of a plot **4** [F, fr. ML *complication-, complicatio*, fr. LL] **:** a secondary disease or condition developing in the course of a primary disease either as a result of the primary disease or arising from independent causes

com·plice \'kämpləs, 'kәm-\ *n* -S [ME, fr. MF, fr. LL *complic-, complex* partner, confederate, fr. L *com-* + LL *-plic-, -plex* (akin to L *plicare* to fold)] *archaic* **:** an associate or accomplice esp. in crime

com·plic·i·ty \kəm'plisəd·ē, -ətē, -i\ *n* -ES [F *complicité*, fr. *complice* + *-ité* -ity] **:** association or participation in or as if in guilt ⟨two men acting in ~⟩ ⟨~ in election abuses —J.G. Randall⟩ ⟨mischievous ~ between brothers⟩

complied *past of* COMPLY

com·pli·er \kəm'plīə(r)\ *n* -S [*comply* + *-er*] **1 :** one that complies **2** *obs* **:** CONFORMIST

complies *pres 3d sing of* COMPLY

¹com·pli·ment \'kämpləmənt\ *n* -S [F, fr. It *complimento*, fr. Sp *cumplimiento*, fr. *cumplir* to complete, accomplish, perform what is due, be courteous (fr. L *complēre* to fill up) + *-miento* -ment — more at COMPLETE] **1 a :** a formal expression (as by speech, gesture, or ceremony) of esteem, respect, affection, or admiration ⟨each candidate was introduced with the usual ~*s*⟩ ⟨a party given in ~ to the bride by her mother⟩ ⟨change the name to Fort Knox, in ~ to the Secretary of War —T.R. Hay⟩; *specif* **:** a remark intended to praise or please ⟨paying his best girl all sorts of ~*s*⟩ **b :** formal recognition **:** respectful consideration ⟨he came only in ~ to the rank of his host⟩ ⟨it behooves us . . . to pay the craftsmen the ~ of making a study of their language —Kenneth Ullyett⟩ **2 compliments** *pl* **:** best wishes **:** REGARDS ⟨to send her ~*s* to a friend⟩ ⟨a free sample is enclosed with the ~*s* of the manufacturer⟩ **3** *now dial* **:** a complimentary gift **:** GRATUITY ⟨to make a ~ of a book⟩

²com·pli·ment \-,ment,-,mənt — *see* ²-MENT\ *vb* -ED/-ING/-S [F *complimenter*, fr. *compliment*, n.] *vt* **1 a** *obs* **:** to greet ceremoniously or flatteringly **b :** to pay a compliment to ⟨~*ing* his friend on the steadfastness of his interest in science —Benjamin Farrington⟩ ⟨she was again ~*ed* at a bridal shower given in her home —*Springfield (Mass.) Union*⟩ **2 :** to present (a person) with a token of esteem, respect, affection, or admiration ⟨~*ed* with an honorary degree⟩ **3 :** CONGRATULATE ⟨~*ed* his men on their conduct⟩ ~ *vi* **:** to pay compliments ⟨refuse to ~ with one another⟩

com·pli·men·tal \,kämplə¦ment°l\ *adj* **1 :** COMPLIMENTARY 1a ⟨his pleasing ~ remarks⟩ **2** *archaic* **:** prone to pay compliments — **com·pli·men·tal·ly** \-°lē,-°li\ *adv, obs*

com·pli·men·tar·i·ly \¦kämplə(,)men¦terəlē, -ləmən-, -rəli; -¦men·trəl-, -ntərəl-\ *adv* **:** in a complimentary manner

com·pli·men·ta·ri·ness \,kämplə'mentərēnəs, -n·trē-, -rin-\ *n* -ES **:** the quality or state of being complimentary

com·pli·men·ta·ry \¦kämplə¦mentərē, -n·trē, -ri\ *adj* **1 a :** expressing regard or praise ⟨the book received ~ reviews —*Current Biog.*⟩ **:** of the nature of or containing a compliment ⟨references to his colleagues were ever ~⟩ **b :** given to or using compliments ⟨a person of a ~ nature⟩ **2 :** presented or given free esp. as a courtesy or favor ⟨a ~ ticket⟩ ⟨~ meals given all who donate over a certain sum⟩

complimentary close *or* **complimentary closing** *n* **:** the word or words that conventionally come immediately before the signature of a letter and express the sender's regard for the receiver (as *very truly yours, sincerely yours, cordially*)

com·pline \'kämplən, -,plīn\ *also* **com·plin** \-,plən\ *n* -S *often cap* [ME *compline, compelin, cumplie*, fr. OF *complie*, modif. (influenced by *complir* to accomplish, finish, fr. L *complēre* to fill up) of LL *completa*, fr. L, fem. of *completus* complete — more at COMPLETE] *Christian relig* **:** the seventh and last of the canonical hours **:** the last liturgical prayer of the day said after nightfall or just before retiring — called also *night song*

¹com·plot \'käm,plät\ *n* -S [MF *complot, complote* crowd, throng, plot] *archaic* **:** PLOT, CONSPIRACY

²com·plot \kəm'plät, kәm-\ *vb* **complotted; complotted; complotting; complots** [MF *comploter*, fr. *complot*, n.] *archaic* **:** to plot together **:** CONSPIRE

complt *abbr* complainant

com·plu·ten·sian \¦kämplü¦tenchən\ *adj, usu cap* [L *complutensis* (fr. *Complutum*, city in Spain — now *Alcalá de Henares*) + E *-ian*] **:** of or relating to the polyglot bible published in Alcalá de Henares, Spain, in 1513–17 and containing the Old Testament in Hebrew, the Targum of Onkelos on the Pentateuch, the Septuagint, the Vulgate, and the Greek New Testament ⟨the *Complutensian* Polyglot⟩

com·plu·vi·um \kəm'plüvēəm, (')käm¦p-\ *n, pl* **complu·via** \-ēə\ [L, fr. *compluere* to flow together, fr. *com-* + *pluere* to rain — more at FLOW] **:** a square opening in the roof of the ancient Roman atrium toward which the roof sloped and through which the rain fell into the impluvium

¹com·ply \kəm'plī\ *vb* -ED/-ING/-ES [It *complire*, fr. Sp *cumplir* to complete, accomplish, perform what is due, be courteous, fr. L *complēre* to fill up — more at COMPLETE] *vi* **1** *obs* **a :** to be ceremoniously courteous **:** execute all formalities **b :** to be complaisant, accommodating, or obsequious **c :** to suit or conform oneself (as to a situation) **2 :** to accord or assent : conform or adapt one's actions (as to another's wishes) ⟨she would not be able to refuse, since all her instinct at this moment was to ~ —Rebecca West⟩ — usu. used with *with* ⟨he usually *complies* with her wishes⟩ ⟨these regulations have been *complied* with⟩ ~ *vt* **1** *obs* : FULFILL, ACCOMPLISH **2** *obs* : to bring into accord or conformity **syn** see OBEY

²**comply** *vt* -ED/-ING/-ES [*com-* around (influenced by L *complecti* to embrace) + *ply* — more at COMPLEX] *obs* : ENFOLD, EMBRACE

¹**com·po** \'käm(,)pō\ *n* -s [short for *composition*] **1** : a mortar made of sand and cement **2** : a carver's mixture of resin, whiting, and glue used on walls and cornices **3** : a mixture of paper, fiber, and a binder that is molded to make ornamental details for furniture

²**compo** \"\ *n* -s [*comp-* (fr. *compensation*) + *-o*] *slang Austral* : worker's compensation for injuries received on the job

com·po·nen·cy \kəm'pōnənsē, 'käm,p-, käm'p-\ *n* -ES [*component* + *-cy*] : component quality

¹**com·po·nent** \kəm'pōnənt, 'käm,p-, käm'p-\ *n* -s [L *component-, componens*] **1** : a constituent part : INGREDIENT ⟨the various ~s of an electric motor⟩ ⟨the essential ~s of Kantian philosophy⟩ **2** *physics* : any one of the vector terms added to form a given vector sum or resultant **3** : an ingredient of a chemical system the concentration of which in the different phases is capable of independent variation ⟨copper and zinc are the ~s of brass⟩ — see PHASE RULE **4** : either of the sequences defining an alphabet in cryptography — see ALPHABET 1j **5** : the smallest unit of classification in the Midwestern system for American archaeology constituting a single complex of traits found in one site or level — see FOCUS; compare ASPECT, PATTERN, PHASE **syn** see ELEMENT

²**component** \"\ *adj* [L *component-, componens*, pres. part. of *componere* to put together — more at COMPOUND] : serving or helping to constitute : CONSTITUENT ⟨~ parts⟩ ⟨~ elements⟩ ⟨two ~ republics of the Union of Soviet Socialist Republics —Vera M. Dean⟩

com·po·nen·tial \¦kämpə¦nenchəl\ *also* **com·po·nen·tal** \-ent³l\ *adj* : of or relating to a component : having components ⟨~ relations⟩ ⟨~ analysis⟩ ⟨~ structure⟩

com·po·ny \kəm'pōnē\ *also* **com·po·né** *or* **com·po·née** \kəm'pōnē, -(,)nā; ¦kämpə¦nā\ *adj* [MF *componé*, alter. (influenced by L *componere* to compose) of *coponné, couponné*, fr. *copon, coupon* piece — more at COUPON] **1** : composed of two alternate tinctures in a single row — used of a heraldic bearing **2** : divided into segments of alternate tinctures following the curve — used of a heraldic bearing having curved lines

¹**com·port** \kəm'pō(ə)rt, -ó(ə)rt,-ōət,-ó(ə)t; *usu* -d·+V\ *vb* -ED/-ING/-S [MF *comporter*, fr. L *comportare* to bring together, fr. *com-* + *portare* to carry — more at PORT] *vi* **1** a *archaic* : BEAR, ENDURE **b** *obs* : BEHAVE, ACT **2** : AGREE, ACCORD, SUIT — used with *with* ⟨the emphasis on the beautiful . . . that ~s with the conventional conception of culture as a life of traditionally molded refinement —Edward Sapir⟩ ~ *vt* **1** *archaic* : to put up with : BEAR, TOLERATE **2** : CONDUCT, BEHAVE ⟨the probationer who ~s himself blamelessly remains obscure, while the one who reverts to crime is likely to hit the headlines —Telford Taylor⟩ **3** : carry or bring esp. together ⟨positivism . . . tried to make of philosophy . . . a technique of existence ~*ing* an inventory of behavior, a description of conduct —*Times Lit. Supp.*⟩ **syn** see BEHAVE

²**comport** *n* -s *obs* : BEHAVIOR, DEPORTMENT

³**com·port** \'käm,pō(ə)rt, -ó(ə)rt,-ōət,-ó(ə)t\ *n* -s [prob. by folk etymology fr. *compotier*] : a bowl-shaped dish with a stem and foot and sometimes with a cover for holding fruit or sweets : COMPOTE

com·port·a·ble \kəm'pōr|d·əbəl, -ó(r)|, -ōə|, |tə-\ *adj* **1** *obs* : ENDURABLE, TOLERABLE **2** : SUITABLE, CONSISTENT ⟨privileges ~ with our position as prisoners —C.B.Nordhoff & J.N. Hall⟩

comportance *n* -s *obs* : BEHAVIOR, COMPORT

com·port·ment \kəm'pōrtmənt, -órt-,-ōət-,-ó(ə)t-\ *n* -s [MF *comportement*, fr. *comporter* + *-ment*] : manner of bearing: as **a** : DEPORTMENT, DEMEANOR ⟨the ~ of a gentleman⟩ **b** **comportments** *pl, obs* : CONDUCT, ACTIONS **c** : HABITS, BEHAVIOR ⟨the ~ of adult insects —*Biol. Abstracts*⟩

compos *pl of* COMPO

com·pose \kəm'pōz\ *vb* -ED/-ING/-S [MF *composer*, modif. (influenced by *poser* to put, place) of L *componere* to put together, arrange (perfect stem *compos-*), fr. *com-* + *ponere* to put, place — more at POSITION, POSE] *vt* **1** a : to form by putting together two or more things, elements, or parts : put together : FASHION — now usu. in passive ⟨a well-*composed* body⟩ ⟨the assembly was *composed* of delegates from every state in the union⟩ **b** : to form the substance of : CONSTITUTE ⟨for the most part avarice and envy *composed* his personality⟩ — now used chiefly in passive ⟨a soup *composed* of many ingredients⟩ **c** (1) : to put (type) together piece by piece (2) : to assemble (as text to be printed) character by character and line by line (3) : to arrange (as input text) into galleys or pages ⟨the computer ~s a galley and produces an output tape for a photocomposer⟩ **2** : to create by mental or artistic labor : design and execute or put together (as by adapting forms of expression to ideas or to laws of harmony or proportion) : CREATE: as **a** : WRITE ⟨~ a book of poems⟩ : PRODUCE ⟨~ a ballad⟩ ⟨~ a history of English law⟩ **b** (1) : to formulate and write (a piece of music) ⟨*composed* a number of stirring marches⟩ (2) : to formulate music for ⟨*composed* several charming songs⟩ **3** : to treat, deal with, or act on so as to reduce (as points at issue) to an innocuous minimum ⟨~ disputes⟩ ⟨when labor and management cannot ~ their differences—H.S.Truman⟩ **4** : to arrange in a fitting, proper, or orderly way : free from an appearance of agitation or disturbance ⟨~ her clothing⟩ ⟨the two men had laid him on the bed and *composed* his limbs —Sheridan Le Fanu⟩ **5** : CALM, SETTLE, TRANQUILIZE ⟨~ a patient⟩ ⟨~ his passions⟩ : adjust (as oneself or one's feelings) esp. by suppressing or overcoming agitation and achieving calm ⟨life moves on . . . and one must ~ oneself to meet it —Rose Macaulay⟩ ~ *vi* **1** : to practice composition (as of literary, musical, or typographical work) : CREATE ⟨at the age of 10 he was *composing* at the piano⟩ **2** *obs* : to come to terms **syn** see CALM

com·posed \-zd\ *adj* [fr. past part. of *compose*] **1** a *archaic* : formed of or made up of parts : COMPOSITE, COMPOUND **b** *obs* : put together well or artistically ⟨a ~ design⟩ **2** : free from indications of agitation or excitement : calm and self-possessed in reality or appearance ⟨cool, ~, mistress of herself and her destiny —Ellen Glasgow⟩ **syn** see COOL

com·pos·ed·ly \-zədlē, -li\ *adv* : in a composed manner

com·posed·ness \-zədnəs, -z(d)n-\ *n* -ES : COMPOSURE

composed throughout *adj* [trans. of G *durchkomponiert*] : THROUGH-COMPOSED

com·pos·er \-zə(r)\ *n* -s : one that composes: as **a** : AUTHOR, WRITER ⟨the various ~s of the Old Testament⟩ **b** : a person who writes music ⟨a ~ of popular songs⟩ **c** : a person who settles, adjusts, or tranquilizes ⟨a determined ~ of differences —C.G.Bolte⟩

composing machine *n* : TYPESETTING MACHINE

composing room *n* : the department in a printing office where typesetting and related operations are performed

composing rule *n* : a thin strip of steel or brass usu. type-high and having an ear at each upper corner against which type is set in and removed from a composing stick

composing stick *n* : a shallow tray formerly of wood but now usu. of metal that has an adjustable slide and is held in one hand by a compositor as he sets type into it with the other hand; *also* : a device of comparable function (as for hand-setting matrices for a slug-casting machine or letters for photocomposition) — called also *stick*

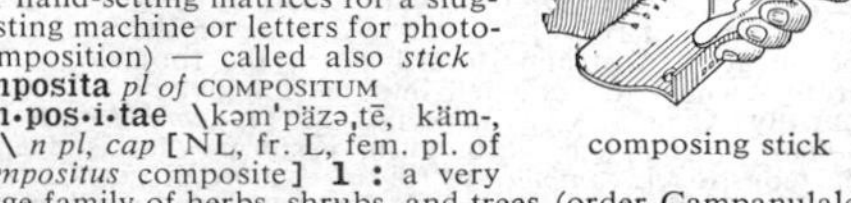

composing stick

composita *pl of* COMPOSITUM

com·pos·i·tae \kəm'päzə,tē, käm-, -tī\ *n pl, cap* [NL, fr. L, fem. pl. of *compositus* composite] **1** : a very large family of herbs, shrubs, and trees (order Campanulales) considered to constitute the most highly evolved plants and characterized by florets arranged in dense heads that resemble single flowers, each floret having a gamopetalous, ligulate, or tubular corolla and a calyx modified into a pappus (as in the dandelion, sunflower, aster, and ragweed) **2** *in some classifications* **a** : a superfamilial group that is coextensive with the family Compositae and is divided into the families Carduaceae, Cichoriaceae, and Ambrosiaceae **b** : CARDUACEAE

¹**com·pos·ite** \(')käm¦päzət, kəm'p-, *usu* -əd·+V; *Brit usu* 'kämpəz-\ *adj* [L *compositus*, past part. of *componere* to put together, fr. *com-* + *ponere* to put, place — more at POSITION] : made up of distinct parts : COMPOUNDED ⟨a ~ racial type⟩ ⟨~ material⟩ ⟨the knight was a ~ portrait of men whom Chaucer personally knew —J.L.Lowes⟩: **a** *usu cap* : belonging to or being a modification of the Corinthian order introduced in Roman imperial times by combining angular Ionic volutes with the acanthus-circled bell of the Corinthian **b** : belonging to, having the characteristics of, or being a member of the family Compositae ⟨a ~ inflorescence⟩ **c** *of a number or an algebraic expression* : made up of two or more integral or real rational prime factors (as in $12 = 2 \times 2 \times 3$; $a^3 - b^3 = (a-b)(a^2 + ab + b^2)$) — compare PRIME **d** *of a ship* : built with a metal framework and wooden keel, planking, and deck — **com·pos·ite·ly** *adv*

²**composite** \"\ *n* -s **1** : something that is made up of diverse elements: as **a** : COMPOUND 1a, 1b **b** : a fingerprint in which elements of varied types (as the arch, loop, and whorl) are combined **c** : a pictorial composition in which two or more images are combined or worked together; *specif* : a composition that fuses different images so that only selected parts of each are revealed in one harmonious formal relationship **d** *or* **composite can** : a container having a fiber body and one or more commonly both ends of metal **2** : a plant of the family Compositae

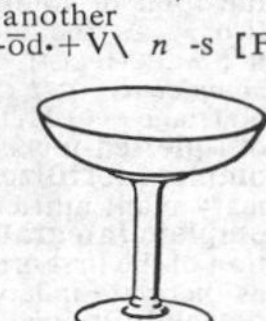

composite 2: section of a composite flower head, *1* disk floret, *2* ray flower, *3* bracts

³**composite** \"\ *vt* -ED/-ING/-S : to make composite or into something composite

composite cone *n* : a volcanic cone composed of intermingled masses or alternate layers of lava and fragmental material

composite dike *also* **composite sill** *n* : a dike or sill composed of two or more varieties of igneous rock presumably resulting from successive injections

composite engine *n* : COMPOUND ENGINE 2

com·pos·ite·ness *n* -ES : the quality or state of being composite

composite photograph *n* : a photograph made by combining several distinct photographs either made one over another on the same plate or made on one print from a number of negatives

composite print *n* **1** : a photographic print made from more than one negative **2** : a motion-picture print bearing both picture and sound-track images

composite sailing *n* : a combination of great circle and parallel sailing in navigation

com·po·si·tion \,kämpə'zishən\ *n* -s [ME *composicioun*, fr. MF *composition*, fr. L *composition-, compositio*, fr. *compositus* (past part. of *componere* to put together, fr. *com-* + *ponere* to put, place) + *-ion-, -io* -ion — more at POSITION] **1** a : the act or action of composing : the formation of a whole esp. by different things being put together ⟨his ~ of long novels⟩ ⟨the slow ~ of a glacier⟩; *specif* : the ordering or arranging of something into proper proportion or relation ⟨force a ~ of overwrought thoughts⟩ **b** (1) : combination of words to form a compound (2) : combination of words, of combining forms, of a word and a combining form, of a word and an affix, or of a combining form and an affix to form a compound **c** : the construction of a literary work esp. with reference to its degree of success in meeting criteria of correctness, order, or proportion **d** *obs* : the reasoning from general principles or causes to particulars : synthetic reasoning **e** : the disposition of the parts of a work of art : FORM, PATTERN ⟨a triangular ~⟩ **f** *logic* (1) : the adjunction of two terms to form a compound term or the adjunction of two propositions or assertions to form a compound assertion (2) : the passage from a concept or assertion about individuals taken separately to a concept or assertion about the class which they compose — see FALLACY OF COMPOSITION **g** : the nature of a chemical compound or mixture as regards the kind and amounts of its constituents being usu. expressed for a chemical compound in numbers of atoms of each element in the molecule or in percentages of each element by weight **h** (1) : the arrangement of type for printing ⟨hand ~⟩ (2) : the production of type or typographic characters arranged for printing ⟨electronic ~⟩ **i** : the kinds and relative numbers of different organisms that make up a population **2** : the manner in which something is composed or compounded: as **a** : the particular arrangement or combination of parts of a unit or whole ⟨the ~ of ingredients in a recipe⟩ ⟨the industrial ~ of a European country⟩ **b** : personal constitution (as of mind and body together) : general makeup ⟨a man with a touch of genius in his ~⟩ **c** : the particular mode or style in the combination of parts in a work of art that produces a harmonious whole ⟨a painting masterful in ~⟩ **d** *obs* : consistency esp. among the items of a report : CONGRUITY **e** : the combination of tones forming a compound organ stop **3** : mutual settlement or agreement: as **a** *archaic* : an agreement esp. between one person and another : SETTLEMENT **b** : an agreement or settlement whereby differences (as between factions) are resolved : TREATY, COMPROMISE ⟨the countries were joined by an ancient ~⟩ ⟨the ~ that was reached in Korea is not satisfactory to America, but it is far better than to continue the bloody, dreary sacrifice —D.D. Eisenhower⟩ **c** : the satisfaction of a wrong or injury by money payment or the money so paid **d** : the adjustment of a debt or avoidance of an obligation or liability by some form of compensation agreed upon between the parties or the sum of money agreed upon in the adjustment; *specif* : settlement of debts by agreement through partial payments of the sums due debtors to avoid bankruptcy **e** *Scots law* : the fine due a superior on the actual or implied entry of a singular successor **4** a : an aggregate, mixture, mass, or body formed by combining two or more elements or ingredients ⟨a ~ of rubber and cork⟩ **b** : a material prepared from or composed of various ingredients and often taking the place of a more expensive or uncompounded material ⟨a facade made of ~ that looks like marble⟩ ⟨~ leather⟩ ⟨~ shingles⟩ **5** : an intellectual creation: as **a** : a piece of writing; *esp* : a written exercise done for a course in writing in school and usu. intended to show study and care in arrangement **b** : a written piece of music; *esp* : an original work of some magnitude and to whose formal structure appropriate attention has been given **c** : a work of art (as a drawing or painting) whose various elements are combined artistically **6** : the quality or state of being compound or composite ⟨the simplicity and absence of ~ in his arguments⟩ **7** : a course in colleges and secondary schools designed to train students to write esp. exposition

com·po·si·tion·al \¦kämpə¦zishən³l, -shnəl\ *adj* : of or having to do with composition ⟨~ laws⟩ ⟨the ~ arrangement with horizontals, verticals, diagonals —Eva M. Neumeyer⟩ — **com·po·si·tion·al·ly** \-³lē,-əlē, -li\ *adv*

composition metal *n* : a cast copper alloy containing usu. more than 80 percent copper together with tin, lead, and zinc

composition of forces *physics* : the finding of a single force if such exists that shall be equal in effect to two or more given forces

composition roller *n* : a printer's inking roller consisting of a metal core covered with a flexible mixture of glue, molasses, and glycerin

com·pos·i·tive \kəm'päzəd·iv\ *adj* [LL *compositivus* suitable for uniting, fr. L *compositus* + *-ivus* -ive] : using or involving composition : SYNTHETIC

com·pos·i·tor \kəm'päzəd·ə(r), -z(ə)tə(r)\ *n* -s [ME *compositour* one that settles a disagreement, fr. MF *compositeur*, fr. ML *compositor*, fr. L, arranger, disposer, fr. *compositus* (past part. of *componere* to put together, fr. *com-* + *ponere* to put, place) + *-or* — more at POSITION] : one that composes; *specif* : one (as a craftsman or a firm) that produces composed matter for printing — **com·pos·i·to·ri·al** \kəm¦päzə¦tōrēəl\ *adj*

compositor's alley *n* : ALLEY 4b

com·pos·i·tum \kəm'päzətəm\ *n, pl* **compositums** \-təmz\ *or* **composi·ta** \-tə\ [LL, fr. L, agreement, fr. neut. of *compositus*] *archaic* : COMPOUND, COMPOSITION

com·pos men·tis \¦kämpə'smentəs\ *adj* [L, lit., having mastery of one's mind] : sane in mind : being of sound mind, memory, and understanding — usu. used predicatively ⟨he was judged *compos mentis*⟩ see NON COMPOS MENTIS

com·po·so·graph \kəm'pōzə,graf\ *n* -s [*compose* + *-o-* + *-graph*] : a synthetic photograph; *esp* : a photograph made up usu. of parts of other photographs and designed to show a scene that never existed

com·pos·si·bil·i·ty \(,)käm,päsə'biləd·ē, kəm-\ *n* -ES [ML *compossibilis* + E *-ity*] : ability or possibility of coexisting ⟨the real ~ of individuals —Grace De Laguna⟩

com·pos·si·ble \(')käm¦päsəbəl, kəm'p-\ *adj* [ML *compossibilis*, fr. L *com-* + *possibilis* possible] : able or possible to coexist with another ⟨a theory ~ with other theories⟩ ⟨contradictory but ~ statements⟩

¹**com·post** \'käm,pōst, *Brit usu* -päst\ *n* -s *often attrib* [ME, stew, compote, fr. MF *composte* compote, *compost* compost; MF *composte* fr. L *composita*, fem. of *compositus*; MF *compost* fr. L *compositus*] **1** a : a mixture consisting usu. largely of decayed organic matter and used for fertilizing and conditioning land; *esp* : such a mixture produced by decomposition in a compost pile **b** : a complex potting soil that is usu. rich in organic matter **2** : MIXTURE, COMPOSITION, COMPOUND ⟨that strange ~ of contradictions, the Scottish character —John Buchan⟩ ⟨sheer melodrama, a ~ of sex and crime —Milton Rugoff⟩ ⟨a ~ of newspaper sensations and prejudice —T.S.Eliot⟩

²**compost** \"\ *vt* -ED/-ING/-S [ME *composten*, fr. MF *composter*, fr. *compost*, n.] **1** : to treat (as land) with compost : MANURE **2** : to cause (as plant debris) to be converted into compost usu. by mixing with suitable adjuncts and piling in a way that encourages decay and decomposition

compost pile *also* **compost heap** *n* : a stack of alternating layers of plant debris and soil often with an admixture of animal manure or chemical fertilizer arranged so as to encourage the rapid conversion of the constituents into compost

com·po·sure \kəm'pōzhə(r)\ *n* -s [*compose* + *-ure*] **1** *obs* : COMPOSITION **2** : calmness or repose esp. in frame of mind or in bearing or appearance : SELF-POSSESSION ⟨Hamlet's ~ in this last part of the play is of supreme beauty —Karl Polanyi⟩ ⟨gazing upon it all with a serene ~ in which one may detect a mild amusement —C.B.Tinker⟩ **syn** see EQUANIMITY

com·po·ta·tion \,kämpō'tāshən\ *n* -s [L *compotation-, compotatio* (trans. of Gk *symposion* drinking party), fr. *com-* + *potatio* potation] : a drinking or tippling together : CAROUSE

com·po·ta·tor \'kämpō,tād·ə(r)\ *n* -s [LL, fr. L *com-* + *potator* drinker, fr. *potatus*, (past part. of *potare* to drink) + *-or* — more at POTABLE] : one who drinks with another

com·pote *also* **com·pot** \'käm,pōt, *usu* -ōd·+V\ *n* -s [F *compote*, fr. OF *composte*] **1** : fruits cooked in syrup in such a way as to keep their form ⟨a ~ of pears⟩ **2** a : a bowl-shaped dish of glass, porcelain, or metal usu. with a base and stem, and sometimes with a cover from which compotes, fruits, nuts, or sweets are served **b** : a small dish of similar form used for individual servings

compote 2a

com·po·tier \¦kämpō¦tyā\ *n* -s [F, fr. *compote* + *-ier* -er] : COMPOTE 2a

compotus *var of* COMPUTUS

¹**com·pound** \(')käm¦paund, kəm'p-\ *vb* -ED/-ING/-S [alter. of ME *compounen*, fr. MF *compon-*, stem of *compondre* to put together, arrange, fr. L *componere*, fr. *com-* + *ponere* to put, place — more at POSITION] *vt* **1** : to put together (as elements, ingredients, or parts) to form a whole : COMBINE, UNITE **2** a : to form or make up (as a composite product) by combining different elements, ingredients, or parts ⟨~ a medicine⟩ ⟨a philosophy ~*ed* of affirmation, action, compassion, and universalism—Norman Cousins⟩ **b** *obs* : COMPOSE, CREATE ⟨~*ed* many hymns and psalms —Richard Montagu⟩ **3** : to settle amicably : adjust by agreement : discharge (an obligation) upon terms different from those which were stipulated, claimed, or demanded (as when a smaller sum is accepted than was asked) : COMPROMISE **4** a : to increase by geometric progression or by an increment that itself increases ⟨interest is ~*ed* quarterly⟩ **b** : to cause to multiply at a faster and faster rate **c** : to add to : AUGMENT ⟨we ~*ed* our error in later policy —Robert Lekachman⟩ ⟨express roads and parkways . . . have ~*ed* . . . parking problems immensely —Hal Burton⟩ **5** : to forbear prosecution of (an offense) for a consideration ⟨~ a felony⟩ **6** : to wind the field magnets of (a dynamo) so as to make excitable by both a shunt and a series current **7** : to combine (as forces and velocities) into a single resultant ~ *vi* **1** : to unite into or as if into a compound ⟨his virtues and vices ~*ed* into a contradictory personality no one could understand⟩ **2** : to come to terms of agreement or payment : settle by a compromise : AGREE ⟨~ with the enemy for peace⟩ ⟨no attempt to ~ with God, to offer future good behavior in exchange for forgiveness —C.S.Forester⟩

²**com·pound** \(')käm¦paund *also* kəm'p-\ *adj* [ME *compouned*, fr. past part. of *compounen*] **1** a : composed of or produced by the union of several elements, ingredients, parts, or things ⟨a ~ substance⟩ **b** : involving combination : COMPOSITE ⟨~ management⟩ **c** *logic* : consisting of several elements; *specif* : having more than one proposition **d** : having or consisting of two, three, or four groups of simple time units to the musical measure (6/8 and 9/8 are ~ rhythms) ⟨~ time⟩ **e** *bot* : composed of two or more similar parts forming a common whole ⟨a ~ ovary⟩ **f** : composed of several joined individuals or elements **2** *of an electrical machine* : compound-wound **3** a *of a word* (1) : being a compound (sense 1a) — compare COMPLEX (2) : being a compound (sense 1b) **b** *of a sentence* : having more than one main clause ⟨*I told him to leave and he left* is a ~ sentence⟩ — compare COMPLEX **c** *of a tense* : formed by the use of an auxiliary verb ⟨*is going, are written, has seen, will arrive* are ~ tenses⟩ — opposed to *simple* **4** *of a fabric* : having one or more extra warps or wefts or both

³**com·pound** \'käm,paund\ *n* -s **1** a : a word consisting of components that are words (as *rowboat, fireman, high school, devil-may-care, airtight, outrun, thereby, whereas, into*) — compare COMPLEX **b** : a word consisting of components that are words, are a word and a combining form (as *centimeter*), are a word and a noninflectional affix (as *builder, reenter*), are combining forms (as *biology*), or are a combining form and a noninflectional affix (as *cephalad, chlorate*) **c** *printing* : a hyphened term **2** : something (as a substance, idea, creation) that is formed by a union of elements, ingredients, or parts ⟨a poisonous ~⟩ ⟨a ~ of Christian mysticism and Greek philosophy⟩ ⟨a ~ of contradictions⟩: **a** : a chemically distinct substance formed by union of two or more ingredients (as elements) in definite proportion by weight and with definite structural arrangement ⟨water is a ~ of oxygen and hydrogen⟩ ⟨the benzene ring is characteristic of numerous complex organic ~s⟩ — see ADDITION COMPOUND, ADSORPTION COMPOUND **b** : a plastering base coat to which sand is added later on the job **c** : a compound engine or compound locomotive **d** : a system of gears on roving and spinning frames to keep yarn speed constant as bobbin circumference increases with the winding of added layers **e** : a mental process (as a blend or pattern) in which different components can be distinguished **3** : COMPOSITION ⟨the peculiar ~ of such material⟩

⁴**compound** \"\ *n* -s [by folk etymology (influence of ³*compound*) fr. Malay *kampung, kampong* group, gathering, cluster of buildings, village] **1** a : a well-demarcated complex of European residences and commercial buildings (as warehouses and factories) esp. in the East Indies, India, and China **b** : an enclosure within which the laborers at So. African gold or diamond mines are confined **c** : a large fenced or walled-in area (as in a prison, detention camp, or cattle yard) **2** *Africa* : inferior beef

com·pound·able \(')käm¦paundəbəl, kəm'p-\ *adj* : capable of being compounded

compound animal *n* : an animal composed of a number of individuals each performing independently some or most of the vital functions yet organically connected so as to form a united colony of zooids ⟨most corals and bryozoans are *compound animals*⟩

compound attack *n* : a fencing attack combining two or more successive movements in order to deceive parries

compound benzoin tincture *n* : FRIAR'S BALSAM

compound-complex *adj, of a sentence* **:** having more than one main clause and at least one subordinate clause (as *he told me to leave and I left as soon as I could*)

compound curve *n* **:** a curve made up of two or more circular arcs of successively shorter or longer radii, joined tangentially without reversal of curvature, and used on some railroad tracks and highways as an easement curve to provide a less abrupt transition from tangent to full curve or vice versa

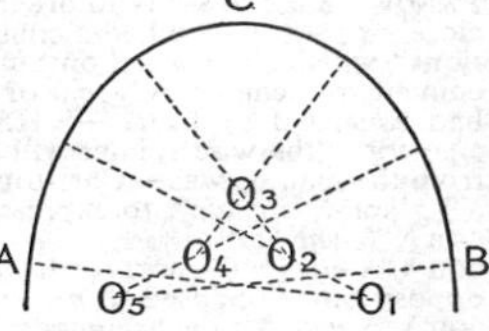

compound curve, *ACB:* successive centers, O_1, O_2, O_3, O_4, O_5

compound discount *n* **:** CHAIN DISCOUNT

compound duties *n pl* **:** a combination of specific and ad valorem customs duties on the same article

compounded *past of* COMPOUND

compound engine *n* **1 :** an engine (as a steam engine) in which the working fluid is expanded successively in two distinct phases so as to minimize losses (as from cylinder condensation) and so allow a high ratio of expansion to be used, the working fluid (as steam) after expanding in the high-pressure cylinder being exhausted into a low-pressure cylinder and then exhausted usu. into a condenser **2** *aeronautics* **:** a propulsive system consisting essentially of a reciprocating engine, a steady-flow gas turbine, and a compressor so arranged that (1) the exhaust from the reciprocating engine drives the turbine, the exhaust from the turbine being directed rearward for jet propulsion, (2) the turbine drives the compressor, the excess turbine power being delivered to the engine shaft through gearing, and (3) the net shaft power of the system is converted to propulsive power by means of a propeller

com·pound·er \(ˈ)kämˌpau̇ndə(r), kəmˈp-\ *n* -s **1** *obs* **:** one that compounds (as a debt, crime, or strife) by agreement or compromise **2 a :** one that compounds products (as drugs) from raw materials or ingredients **b :** one that mixes ingredients to produce specified qualities or quantities in the manufacture of a product; *specif* **:** a refinery worker who blends different grades of oils to meet customer or laboratory specifications **3** *usu cap* **:** a Jacobite favoring the restoration of James II on condition of a general amnesty and of guarantees for the security of the constitution

compound ether *n, archaic* **:** ESTER

compound eye *n* **:** an eye typical of the arthropods found esp. in insects and crustaceans and consisting essentially of a great number (sometimes thousands) of minute simple eyes closely crowded together but optically separated by dark pigment cells, arranged on a convex basal membrane, and covered externally by a chitinous cornea — see OMMATIDIUM; INSECT illustration

compound fold *n, geol* **:** a fold having minor folds imposed upon the main fold, the axes of all being approximately parallel

compound fraction *n* **:** COMPLEX FRACTION

compound fracture *n* **:** a bone fracture associated with lacerated soft tissues through which bone fragments usu. protrude

compound householder *n, Brit* **:** a householder whose taxes are included in his rent

compound infusion of senna : BLACK DRAFT

compounding *pres part of* COMPOUND

compound interest *n* **:** interest paid or computed on the combined sum of the original principal of a loan and interest accrued and payable at the end of each agreed period (as monthly, quarterly, semiannually, or annually) — compare ACCUMULATION FACTOR, SIMPLE INTEREST

compound-interest method *n* **:** a method of determining (as a provision for annual depreciation of an asset) a constant amount made up of an amount periodically set aside that with compound interest will equal the original cost plus interest on the declining investment in the asset — compare STRAIGHT-LINE METHOD

compound interval *n* **:** a musical interval greater than an octave — compare SIMPLE INTERVAL

compound jellyfish *n* **:** SIPHONOPHORE; *esp* **:** a siphonophore with more than one swimming bell

compound leaf *n* **:** a leaf in which the blade is divided to the midrib, forming two or more distinct blades or leaflets on a common axis, the leaflets themselves occas. being compound — compare PALMATE, PINNATE; SIMPLE LEAF

compound lens *n* **:** a lens made of simple lenses mounted on a common axis usu. in close juxtaposition and often cemented together — see ACHROMATIC LENS

compound lever *n* **:** a system (as in various testing machines and weighing scales) of two or more levers arranged to transmit motion or force by linking an arm of each lever to an arm of the next lever in the train

compound locomotive *n* **:** a steam locomotive having two or more cylinders in which the exhaust steam passes from one to another to do additional work before being released

compound magnet *n* **:** a set of magnets placed with like poles together so as to act as a single magnet

compound microscope *n* **:** a microscope consisting of an objective and an eyepiece mounted in a drawtube and focused by means of screw arrangements

compound middle lamella *n* **:** the middle lamella considered as comprising the intercellular cementing layer and the primary walls on both sides of it

compound nucleus *n* **:** an unstable nucleus formed by the coalescence of an atomic nucleus with a captured particle

compound number *n* **:** a number involving different denominations or more than one unit (as 2 ft. 5 in.)

compound ovary *n* **:** an ovary formed by the union of two or more carpels

compound pendulum *n* **:** PHYSICAL PENDULUM

compound perforation *n* **:** a stamp perforation having two perforation numbers, one for the top and bottom of the stamp and one for the sides

compound pier *n* **:** a clustered pier

compound pistil *n* **:** a pistil formed by the union of two or more carpels

compound raceme *n* **:** PANICLE

compound radical *n, archaic* **:** RADICAL 5c

compound ray *n* **:** AGGREGATE RAY

compound relative *n* **1 :** a relative pronoun, adjective, or adverb used without an antecedent (as *what* in "what he says is true", *where* in "this is where he was born") **2 :** a compound formed by adding *so, ever,* or *soever* to a relative pronoun (*whoso, whichever, whatsoever*)

compound rest *n* **:** a tool rest for a lathe having two slides, one mounted on the other

compounds *pres 3d sing of* COMPOUND, *pl of* COMPOUND

compound screw *n* **1 :** DIFFERENTIAL SCREW **2 :** a right-and-left screw

compound sieve plate *n, bot* **:** a sieve plate having the sieve areas in groups separated by a network or bar of cell-wall material

compound spirit of ether : an anodyne mixture of alcohol, ether, and a small quantity of ethereal oil — called also *Hoffmann's anodyne*

compound spirit of myrcia [*Myrcia* (genus of trees and shrubs); prob. fr. confusion between the bayberry (*Pimenta racemosa*) and a tree of the related genus *Myrcia*] **:** BAY RUM

compound stop *n* **:** an organ stop having more than one pipe or reed to each key

compound tincture of benzoin : FRIAR'S BALSAM

compound vault *n* **:** a vault of any form other than the simplest (as a groined vault, ribbed vault, or fan vault)

compound vein *n* **:** a lode composed of two or more nearly parallel veins

compound winding *n* **:** a combination of series winding and shunt winding on the field magnet of a direct-current machine

com·pra·dor \ˌkämprəˈdō(ə)r\ *or* **com·pra·dore** \-dō(ə)r, -dō(ə)r\ *n* -s [Pg *comprador,* lit., buyer, fr. LL *comperator,* fr. (assumed) VL *comperatus* (past part. of assumed VL *comperare* to acquire, buy, fr. L *com-* + *-perare,* fr. *parare* to prepare) + L *-or* — more at PARE] **1 :** a Chinese agent, adviser, or factotum employed by a foreign establishment (as a consulate) in China to have charge of its Chinese employees or to act as an intermediary in business affairs **2 :** one held to be an agent of foreign domination or exploitation

com·pre·ca·tion \ˌkämprəˈkāshən\ *n* -s [L *comprecation-, comprecatio,* fr. *comprecatus* (past part. of *comprecari* to pray to, fr. *com-* + *precari* to pray) + *-ion-, -io* -ion — more at PRAY] *archaic* **:** a praying together

com·preg \ˈkämˌpreg\ *n* -s [back-formation fr. *compregnate*] **:** wood impregnated with a resin and compressed under great heat before the resin sets and similar to impreg in its properties

com·preg·nate \kämˈpregˌnāt, kəm-\ *vt* -ED/-ING/-S [blend of *compress* + *impregnate*] **:** to compress with heat (thin sheets of wood impregnated with a solution of phenol and formaldehyde) into a dense hard homogeneous substance — compare COMPREG

com·pre·hend \ˌkämprəˈhend, -rēˈ-\ *vt* -ED/-ING/-S [ME *comprehenden,* fr. L *comprehendere,* fr. *com-* + *prehendere* to grasp, seize — more at PREHENSILE] **1 :** to see the nature, significance, or meaning of **:** grasp mentally **:** attain to the knowledge of ⟨~ where her duties lie⟩ ⟨stumbled through the brown book, not . . . *~ing* what it meant —Rudyard Kipling⟩ **2 :** to contain or hold within a total scope, significance, or amount often as a part, item, concomitant, or factor **:** EMBRACE ⟨a magnificent view *~ing* all the upper half of the floor of the valley —John Muir †1914⟩ ⟨for philosophy's scope *~s* the truth of everything which man may understand —H.O.Taylor⟩ **3 :** to take in or include by construction or implication **:** COMPRISE, IMPLY ⟨and if there be any other commandment, it is briefly *~ed* in this saying, namely, Thou shalt love thy neighbor as thyself —Rom 13:9 (AV)⟩ **4** *obs* **:** GRASP, SEIZE, ATTAIN **syn** see INCLUDE, UNDERSTAND

com·pre·hend·ible \-dəbəl\ *adj* **:** COMPREHENSIBLE

com·pre·hend·ing·ly *adv* **:** KNOWINGLY

com·pre·hen·si·bil·i·ty \ˌ==ˌhen(t)səˈbilәd·ē, -ətē, -i\ *n* -ES **:** the quality or state of being comprehensible

com·pre·hen·si·ble \ˌ==ˈhen(t)səbəl\ *adj* [L *comprehensibilis,* fr. *comprehensus* (past part. of *comprehendere*) + *-ibilis* -ible] **1** *archaic* **:** capable of being included, contained, or comprised ⟨God . . . is not ~ nor circumscribed —Thomas More⟩ **2 :** capable of being understood **:** INTELLIGIBLE, CONCEIVABLE ⟨an idea ~ to the average mind⟩ — **com·pre·hen·si·ble·ness** *n* -ES — **com·pre·hen·si·bly** \-blē, -li\ *adv*

com·pre·hen·sion \ˌ==ˈhenchən\ *n* -s [MF & L; MF *compréhension,* fr. L *comprehension-, comprehensio,* fr. *comprehensus* (past part. of *comprehendere*) + *-ion-, -io* -ion] **1 a :** the act or action of comprehending or comprising or the fact of being comprehended or comprised **:** INCLUSION ⟨the ~ of many items within a single book⟩ **b :** the faculty or capability of including **:** COMPREHENSIVENESS ⟨a concept whose ~ is so broad as to cover all other concepts⟩ **2 a :** the act or action of grasping (as an idea or process) with the intellect **:** UNDERSTANDING ⟨a real ~ of all difficulties⟩ **b :** the resultant of comprehending mentally **:** apperceptive knowledge or knowing ⟨he has not the slightest ~ of the subject⟩ **c :** the capacity or power of the mind for understanding fully ⟨some readers are dull of ~ —W.M.Thackeray⟩ **3** *obs* **:** SUMMARY, EPITOME **4** *obs* **:** a physical grasping (of something) **:** COMPRESSION **5** *logic* **:** the totality of attributes that make up the notion signified by a general term **:** the sum of the characteristics distinguishing a class **:** INTENSION, CONNOTATION **6 :** inclusion of nonconformists in the Church of England by widening the terms of communion (as by legal enactment during the 17th century)

[1]**com·pre·hen·sive** \ˌ==ˈhen(t)siv, -sēv *also* -səv\ *adj* [L *comprehensivus,* fr. *comprehensus* + *-ivus* -ive] **1 a :** covering a matter under consideration completely or nearly completely **:** accounting for or comprehending all or virtually all pertinent considerations **:** INCLUSIVE ⟨a ~ question⟩ ⟨a ~ plan⟩ ⟨a ~ list⟩ ⟨a ~ index to rare coins⟩ ⟨a ~ whole⟩ **b** *of insurance* **:** covering all hazards of a given type with the exception of individual hazards specif. excluded ⟨a ~ insurance policy⟩ ⟨~ automobile liability⟩ ⟨~ coverage⟩ **2 :** having the power to understand or grasp **:** of wide mental grasp ⟨a ~ head for financial problems⟩ ⟨a ~ student of racial affairs⟩ ⟨a ~ knowledge of physics⟩ **3 a** *of a school* **:** CONSOLIDATED **b** *of a secondary school* **:** offering a full set of curricula (as college preparatory, commercial, and vocational courses together with extracurricular activities) ⟨a ~ high school⟩ **4** *logic* **:** relating to comprehension **:** CONNOTATIVE, INTENSIVE — **com·pre·hen·sive·ly** \-səvlē, -li\ *adv*

[2]**comprehensive** \"\ *n* -s **1 :** a finished or highly detailed layout (as of a proposed advertisement) intended to show how a printed version would appear **2** *or* **comprehensive examination :** an examination designed to test general mastery of a broad academic field (as one taken at the end of the sophomore college year to test a student's readiness to specialize or at the end of the senior college year to test a student's mastery of his field of concentration) — often used in pl.

com·pre·hen·sive·ness *n* -ES **:** the quality or state of being comprehensive

com·presence \(ˈ)käm+\ *n* [*com-* + *presence*] **:** the quality or state of being present together ⟨the ~ of diverse ideas in a single concept⟩

com·present \"+\ *adj* [*com-* + *present*] **:** present together **:** associated in the same complex or grouping **:** related as factors in the same process — used esp. of elements or factors in the same state of consciousness

[1]**com·press** \kəmˈpres\ *vb* -ED/-ING/-ES [ME *compressen,* fr. LL *compressare,* fr. L *compressus,* past part. of *comprimere* to compress, fr. *com-* + *-primere* (fr. *premere* to press) — more at PRESS] *vt* **:** to reduce the volume, size, duration, density, or degree of concentration of by or as if by pressure: as **a :** to make (an opening or the inner capacity of) smaller **:** CONSTRICT, CLOSE ⟨~ a severed artery⟩ **b** (1) **:** to press together **:** SQUEEZE ⟨~ a bundle under one's arm⟩ ⟨his lips were . . . *~ed* by thought —Thomas Hardy⟩ (2) *obs* **:** EMBRACE **c :** to make hard or solid ⟨the lint is then blown into the press and *~ed* into bales —*Amer. Guide Series: Tenn.*⟩ **d :** REPRESS, RESTRAIN ⟨~ an angry mob⟩ ⟨the culprit . . . sat *~ing* hysterics before him —George Meredith⟩ **e :** to reduce the volume of by pressure ⟨~ air⟩ **f :** CONDENSE ⟨~ much thought into few words⟩ ⟨the government . . . *~ed* into less than five years . . . what might have otherwise taken a generation —F.L.Allen⟩ **g :** to make smaller in size ⟨when the bird drops it immediately squats and *~es* its plumage —W.F.Brown b.1903⟩ ⟨the gunman *~ed* his body against the shadowy wall⟩ **h :** to subject (a workman) to compression in an air lock **~** *vi* **:** to undergo compression ⟨if plates are mounted on wood blocks, these blocks may ~ a great deal under pressure —*Theory & Practice of Presswork*⟩ **syn** see CONTRACT

[2]**com·press** \ˈkämˌpres\ *n* -ES [MF *compresse,* fr. *compresser* to compress, fr. LL *compressare*] **1 a :** a covering consisting usu. of a folded cloth that is applied and held firmly by the aid of a bandage over a wound dressing to prevent oozing **b :** a folded wet or dry cloth applied firmly to a part (as to allay inflammation) **2 :** a machine for compressing cotton bales as they come from the gin

com·pressed \kəmˈprest *sometimes* ˈkämˌp-\ *adj* [ME, fr. past part. of *compressen*] **1 :** pressed together **:** COMPACTED **:** reduced in volume by pressure **:** CONDENSED **2 :** flattened as though subjected to compression: **a** *of plant parts* **:** flattened laterally — often used postpositively ⟨petioles ~⟩ **b** *of animals and animal parts* **:** narrow from side to side and correspondingly deep in a dorsoventral direction ⟨the flounders have strongly ~ bodies⟩ — compare DEPRESSED — **com·pressed·ly** \kəmˈprestlē, -sədlē\ *adv*

compressed air *n* **:** air under pressure greater than that of the atmosphere — compare COMPRESS *vt* e

compressed-air illness *also* **compressed-air sickness** *or* **compressed-air disease** *n* **:** CAISSON DISEASE

compressed score *n* **:** SHORT SCORE

compressed tablet *n* **:** a pharmaceutical tablet formed by subjecting dry granular powders to sufficient pressure to make the particles cohere

compressed yeast *n* **:** a cake yeast made by filtering the cells from the liquid in which they are grown, subjecting them to heavy pressure, and mixing them with starch or flour

com·press·ibil·i·ty \kəmˌpresəˈbilәd·ē, -ətē, -i\ *n* -ES **1 :** capability of compression ⟨the ~ of a fluid⟩ **2** *also* **compressibility coefficient** *or* **compressibility modulus :** a number expressing the change in volume of a gas, liquid, or solid per unit pressure and being the reciprocal of the bulk modulus

compressibility burble *n* **:** a burble that occurs in the flow about an airplane at speeds approaching the speed of sound

compressibility coefficient *n* **:** COEFFICIENT OF COMPRESSIBILITY

compressibility effect *n* **:** any of the effects (as abrupt changes in control characteristics) that result from changes in the flow field about an airplane when the velocity at some point in the field reaches the local speed of sound and the air ceases to behave as an incompressible fluid

com·press·ible \kəmˈpresəbəl\ *adj* **:** capable of being compressed — **com·press·ible·ness** *n* -ES — **com·press·ibly** \-blē\ *adv*

com·press·ing·ly *adv* **:** in a compressing manner

com·pres·sion \kəmˈpreshən\ *n* -s *often attrib* [ME *compressioun,* fr. L *compression-, compressio,* fr. *compressus* (past part. of *comprimere* to compress) + *-ion-, -io* -ion] **1 :** the act or action of compressing: **a :** RESTRAINING, REPRESSING ⟨a stern ~ of all emotion⟩ **b :** CONDENSING, CONCENTRATING ⟨the poet's ~ of form and content⟩ **c** (1) **:** the process of compressing the working substance in a heat engine (as the fuel mixture in a cylinder of an internal-combustion engine prior to the explosion) (2) **:** COMPRESSION RATIO **d :** passage of larval stages within the egg whether due to accelerated development or to prolongation of the period preceding hatching **e :** subjection of a workman to compressed air in an air lock before he goes into a caisson to work **2 :** the quality or state of being compressed, pressed in, together, or upon or of being concentrated or condensed ⟨the *~s* of tyranny⟩ ⟨a novel showing admirable ~ of phrase and idea⟩ **3 :** the result of being compressed: as **a :** INDENTATION, HOLLOW, DENT; *esp* **:** the effect of a compressive force upon a body part ⟨~ of an artery by forceps⟩ ⟨~ of the brain by the bones in a depressed fracture⟩ **b :** fossil plant remains that have been somewhat flattened by the vertical pressure of overlying strata **c** (1) **:** the shortening produced in a body by a longitudinal compressive force (as a load applied to a short column) (2) **:** this shortening per unit of length (3) **:** fractional decrease of volume due to pressure (4) **:** COMPRESSIVE STRESS **d :** the reduction of the volume range of an incoming radio signal whether purposely in order to counteract signal fading or distortion or because of some defect in the circuit

com·pres·sion·al \-shənᵊl,-shnəl\ *adj* **:** consisting of, having to do with, or producing compression ⟨a ~ force⟩

compressional wave *also* **compression wave** *n* **:** a longitudinal wave (as a sound wave) propagated by the elastic compression of the medium

compression cup *n* **:** an oil cup or grease cup in which the grease or oil is forced to the bearing surface by compression (as by screwing down the top)

compression dressing *n* **:** PRESSURE DRESSING

compression failure *n* **:** a collapse or buckling of wood fibers resulting from compression along the grain (as that caused by bending or strain)

compression faucet *n* **:** a faucet closed by a valve that is forced against its seat

compression ignition *n* **:** ignition in an internal-combustion engine in which the necessary high temperature is produced by compressing air in the cylinder before admission of the fuel (as in a diesel engine) ⟨*compression-ignition* engine⟩

compression member *n* **:** a structural member (as of a building or an airplane) that is subjected to compressive stresses

compression molding *n* **:** a molding process used esp. for plastics in which heat and pressure are brought to bear on the material in the mold

compression ratio *n* **:** the ratio of the maximum to the minimum volume of the space enclosed by the piston of an internal-combustion engine during a full stroke — called also *compression*

compression ring *n* **:** PISTON RING; *esp* **:** one placed nearest the working face of the piston

compression spring *n* **:** a spring usu. of coil type that is used to offer resistance to a force tending to compress the spring

compression stroke *n* **:** the stroke in the cycle of an internal-combustion engine in which the gases are compressed before firing

compression wood *n* **:** reaction wood formed on the lower sides of branches and leaning trunks and characterized by darker color, glassy appearance, relatively wide and eccentric annual rings, shorter vascular elements, and excessive and uneven shrinkage — compare TENSION WOOD

com·pres·sive \kəmˈpresiv\ *adj* [[1]*compress* + *-ive*] **1 :** of or relating to compression **:** tending to compress ⟨a ~ force⟩ **2 :** characterized by dysphoria and exaggerated feelings of personal inadequacy — **com·pres·sive·ly** \-sə̇vlē\ *adv*

compressive strength *n* **:** the maximum compressive stress that under gradually applied load a given solid material will sustain without fracture — compare TENSILE STRENGTH

compressive stress *n* **:** the stress that results from the shortening in one dimension of an elastic body due to oppositely directed collinear forces tending to crush it

com·pres·som·e·ter \ˌkämˌpreˈsämәd·ә(r), kəmˈpresəˌmēd·ə(r)\ *n* -s [*compression* + *-o-* + *-meter*] **:** an instrument for measuring compression in an elastic solid

com·pres·sor \kəmˈpresə(r)\ *n* -s [L, fr. *compressus* (past part. of *comprimere* to compress) + *-or*] **:** one that compresses: as **a :** a muscle that compresses a part or parts **b :** a machine (as a pump or an engine part) that compresses air, fuel-air mixtures, or other gases — see JET ENGINE illustration **c** *naut* **:** a device for checking a line or cable **d :** a device that introduces intentional compression into a communications signal

com·pres·sure \kəmˈpreshə(r)\ *n* -s [[1]*compress* + *-ure*] **:** COMPRESSION

com·priest \ˈkämˌprēst\ *n* [*com-* + *priest*] **:** a fellow priest

com·pri·mar·io \ˌkämprəˈma(a)rēˌō, -mär-\ *n* -s [It, fr. *com-* (fr. L) + *primario* primary, principal, fr. L *primarius* principal — more at PRIMARY] **:** a singer or dancer esp. in an operatic organization who is ranked usu. just below the primary singers and dancers ⟨a ~ part⟩

comprisal *also* **comprizal** *n* -s [*comprise* + *-al,* n. suffix] *obs* **:** COMPENDIUM, EPITOME

com·prise *also* **com·prize** \kəmˈprīz\ *vb* -ED/-ING/-S [ME *comprisen,* fr. MF *compris* (past part. of *comprendre* to comprehend), fr. L *comprehensus,* past part. of *comprehendere* — more at COMPREHEND] *vt* **1 :** to include esp. within a particular scope **:** sum up **:** COVER, CONTAIN ⟨a whole religion *comprised* within one book⟩ ⟨his program was *comprised* in the party slogan⟩ **2** *obs* **:** UNDERSTAND **3** *obs* **:** to lay hold of **:** SEIZE **4** *obs* **:** ENCLOSE, HOLD **5 a :** to consist of **:** be made up of ⟨the fortress *~s* many miles of entrenchment and well-hidden artillery positions⟩ ⟨the thirty-five essays it *~s* . . . are mostly reprinted from previous collections —Harry Levin⟩ **b :** to make up **:** CONSTITUTE ⟨the receipts . . . *comprised* the fifth-largest gate in boxing history —John Lardner⟩ **~** *vi* **:** to be made up **:** CONSIST — used with *of* ⟨the funds of the association shall ~ of members' subscriptions —*Education*⟩

com·pro·mis \ˌkämprəˈmē\ *n* -ES [F, lit., compromise] **1 :** a formal agreement between nations submitting a dispute to arbitration and defining the terms of the submission, the powers of the tribunal to serve as arbitrator, and the procedure to be followed **2 :** an agreement in Roman civil law between private persons referring a dispute between them to a designated third person for decision

[1]**com·pro·mise** \ˈkämprəˌmīz\ *n* -s [ME, fr. MF *compromis,* fr. L *compromissum,* fr. neut. of *compromissus,* past part. of *compromittere* to promise mutually to abide by the decision of an arbiter, fr. *com-* + *promittere* to promise — more at PROMISE] **1** *obs* **:** an agreement to refer matters in dispute to arbitrators **2 a** (1) *obs* **:** settlement of a dispute by means of an arbiter (2) **:** the delegation to one or more responsible persons of the right to elect — used esp. of papal elections **b :** a settlement by arbitration or by consent reached by mutual concessions **:** a reciprocal abatement of extreme demands or rights resulting in an agreement **:** COMPOSITION **3 :** a committal to something derogatory, hazardous, or objectionable **:** a prejudicial concession **:** SURRENDER ⟨a ~ of character⟩ **4 :** the result or embodiment of concession or adjustment

⟨hand down a ~⟩; *esp* **:** a thing intermediate between or blending qualities of two different things ⟨a ~ solution⟩

2**compromise** \"\ *vb* -ED/-ING/-S *vt* **1** *obs* **a** *of an arbiter* **:** to adjust or settle (a difference) between parties **b :** to bind by mutual agreement **2** *of factions* **:** to adjust or settle by partial mutual relinquishment of principles, position, or claims **:** settle by coming to terms ⟨husband and wife *compromised* their differences⟩ **3 a :** to put in jeopardy **:** endanger (as life, reputation, or dignity) by some act that cannot be recalled **:** expose to suspicion, discredit, or mischief ⟨~ one's conscience⟩ ⟨~ national security⟩ **b :** to cause (a person) embarrassment, humiliation, or shame by improper erotic advances or by allowing the suspicion of such to arise ⟨in those days a girl was *compromised* if she danced more than twice with the same man⟩ **c :** to reveal or expose to unauthorized persons and esp. to an enemy (the nature, details, or workings of classified matter or a classified device) ⟨capture of a number of unenciphered messages will ~ the cryptographic system⟩ ~ *vi* **1 :** to come to a settlement or agreement by mutual concession ⟨union and employer agreed to ~⟩ **2 :** to make a shameful or disreputable concession ⟨rather die than ~⟩ — often used with *with* ⟨gave up a lucrative editorial position . . . rather than ~ with his principles —H.L.Smith b.1906⟩

compromise formation *n* **:** a psychic product, symptom, symbol, or dream form that expresses simultaneously and partially satisfies both the unconscious impulse and the defense against it

compromise joint *n* **:** a step joint used for joining two rails of different sizes or shapes

com·pro·mis·sion \ˌkämprəˈmishən\ *n* -S [ME *compromissioun*, fr. ML *compromission-, compromissio*, fr. L *compromissus* (past part. of *compromittere*) + *-ion-, -io* -ion] **1 a :** delegation of a dispute to arbiters **b :** delegation of the right to elect to one or more persons **2 :** the act or action of jeopardizing (as one's moral or ethical principles)

compromit *vt* **compromitted; compromitted; compromitting; compromits** [ME *compromitten*, fr. L *compromittere* to promise mutually to abide by the decision of an arbiter — more at COMPROMISE] *obs* **:** COMPROMISE

1**com·provincial** \ˈ|käm+\ *adj* [ML *comprovincialis*, fr. L *com-* + *provincialis* provincial] **:** of the same archiepiscopal province ⟨a ~ bishop⟩

2**comprovincial** \"\ *n* -S **:** one of the bishops of a particular archiepiscopal province ⟨a primate's control over his ~*s*⟩

comps *pl of* COMP, *pres 3d sing of* COMP

comp·si·lu·ra \ˌkämpsəˈlu̇rə\ *n, cap* [NL] **:** a genus of tachinid flies including one (*C. concinnata*) that is important in the biological control of several destructive phytophagous moths (as the gypsy, brown-tail, and satin moths)

comp·sog·na·thus \kämpˈsägnəthəs\ *n, cap* [NL, fr. Gk *kompsos-* (fr. *kompsos* elegant) + NL *-gnathus* -gnathous; prob. akin to Lith *švankus* proper] **:** a genus of very small carnivorous saurischian dinosaurs (suborder Theropoda) from the Upper Jurassic of Bavaria with long hind limbs and three-toed feet much like those of a bird

comp·so·thlyp·i·dae \ˌkämpsəthˈlipəˌdē\ [NL, fr. *Compsothlypis*, genus of passerine birds + *-idae*] *syn of* PARULIDAE

1**compt** \ˈkau̇nt, ˈkam(p)t\ *archaic var of* COUNT

2**compt** *adj* [L *comptus*, past part. of *comere* to arrange, adorn, fr. *co-* + *emere* to buy (in preliterary Latin, to take) — more at REDEEM] *obs* **:** NEAT, SPRUCE, POLISHED

compt *abbr* **1** compartment **2** comptroller

compt·er \ˈkau̇ntə(r), ˈkam(p)t-\ *n* -S [alter. (influenced by F *compter* to calculate, count) of *counter* — more at COUNT] *archaic Brit* **:** a prison used esp. for debtors

comptible *adj* [alter. (influenced by *-ible*) of earlier *comptable*, alter. (influenced by MF *comptable* responsible) of *countable* — more at COUNTABLE (responsible)] **1** *obs* **:** RESPONSIBLE, ANSWERABLE **2** *obs* **:** SENSITIVE

comptie *var of* COONTIE

comp·ton effect \ˈkäm(p)tən-\ *also* **compton scattering** *n, usu cap C* [after Arthur H. *Compton* †1962 Am. physicist who first observed it] **:** the scattering of an X-ray or gamma-ray photon upon impact with an electron within an atom accompanied by transfer of a part of the photon's energy to the electron with consequent loss of frequency — compare COMPTON SHIFT

compton electron *n, usu cap C* **:** an electron ejected from an atom by the impact of incident radiation in the Compton effect

compton shift *n, usu cap C* **:** the increase in X-ray or gamma-ray wavelength resulting from the transfer of energy that accompanies the scattering of photons in the Compton effect

comp·trol·ler \kənˈtrōlə(r), ˈkäm(p)ˌt-, kəm(p)ˈt-, ˈkänˌt-, känˈt-\ *n* -S [ME, alter. (influenced by MF *compte* account, count) of *conterroller* controller — more at CONTROLLER, COUNT] **1 :** a controller esp. of accounts or finances **2 :** a public officer whose duty it is to supervise accounts and determine the propriety of expenditures ⟨Army *Comptroller* in the office of the chief of staff at Washington—*Current Biog.*⟩

comptroller general *n, pl* **comptrollers general :** an officer in the U.S. federal government charged with the adjustment of all claims for or against the government and with the investigation of all matters related to the receipt, disbursement, and application of public funds

comptroller of the currency *usu cap both Cs* **:** an official of the Treasury Department of the U.S. government who exercises general control over all national banks and over the issue of federal reserve notes

comp·trol·ler·ship \-ˌship\ *n* -S **:** CONTROLLERSHIP

com·pul·sa·tive \kəmˈpəlsəd·iv\ *adj* [obs. *compulse* to compel (fr. ME *compulsen*, fr. L *compulsus*, past part. of *compellere*) + *-ative*] *obs* **:** COMPULSORY

com·pul·sa·to·ry \kəmˈpəlsəˌtōrē\ *adj* [obs. *compulse* + *-ate* + *-ory*] **:** COMPULSORY ⟨~ taxes⟩

com·pul·sion \kəmˈpəlshən\ *n* -S [ME *compulsioun*, fr. MF or LL; MF *compulsion*, fr. LL *compulsion-, compulsio*, fr. L *compulsus* (past part. of *compellere* to compel) + *-ion-, -io* -ion — more at COMPEL] **1 a :** an act of compelling **:** a driving by force, power, pressure, or necessity ⟨I do not assert that rational reform can wholly dispense with physical ~ —J.A. Hobson⟩ ⟨by ~ of the swirling currents —Mark Twain⟩ ⟨acting under ~, not on his own free will⟩ **b :** a force or agency that compels ⟨it is a shapeless book and it lacks the ~ of the best narrative —John Buchan⟩ **c :** a condition marked by compelling, by forced action or assent ⟨peonage is service to a private master at which a man is kept by bodily ~ against his will —O.W.Holmes †1935⟩ **2 :** an irresistible impulse to perform an irrational act the performance of which tends to disturb a neurotic doer but not a psychotic — compare OBSESSION **syn** see FORCE

compulsion neurosis *n* **:** OBSESSIVE-COMPULSIVE NEUROSIS

com·pul·si·tor \kəmˈpəlsətər\ *n* -S [*compulsit-* (irreg. fr. *compulsatory*) + *-or*] *Scots law* **:** a compulsory agent or means (as a mandate)

1**com·pul·sive** \kəmˈpəlsiv, -sēv *also* -səv\ *adj* [obs. *compulse* + *-ive*] **1 :** having power to compel ⟨admonishing the people in a strangely ~, resonant voice, to be orderly —L.C.Douglas⟩ **:** exercising or applying compulsion ⟨forced to adopt ~ measures to collect taxes⟩ **2** *archaic* **:** produced or caused by compulsion **:** FORCED **3 :** of, having to do with, caused by, or suggestive of psychological compulsion or obsession ⟨mechanical lovemaking, ~ drinking, and considerations of suicide —J.W. Aldridge⟩ — **com·pul·sive·ly** \-sōvlē, -li\ *adv* — **com·pul·sive·ness** *n* -ES

2**compulsive** \"\ *n* -S **1 :** a compelling force ⟨cultural ~*s*⟩ **2 :** one who is subject to a psychological compulsion ⟨the excessive cleanliness of the ~, who is struggling against instinctual demands for dirt and disorder —G.S.Blum⟩

com·pul·so·ri·ly \-s(ə)rəlē, -li\ *adv* **:** in a compulsory manner ⟨candidates . . . must be ~ examined —Barbara Wootton⟩

com·pul·so·ri·ness \-rēnəs, -rin-\ *n* -ES **:** the quality or state of being compulsory

1**com·pul·so·ry** \kəmˈpəls(ə)rē, -ri\ *adj* [ML *compulsorius* coercive, fr. L *compulsus* (past part. of *compellere*) + *-orius* -ory] **1 :** demanded, directed, or designated by authority **:** ENFORCED, MANDATORY ⟨~ retirement⟩ ⟨~ vaccination⟩ ⟨fees ~ for all applicants⟩ **2 :** having the power of compulsion **:** COERCIVE, COMPELLING ⟨~ measures⟩ **3 a** *of education* **:** requiring or insuring under law a minimum literary level and usu. promoted in the case of minors by attendance of an authorized school up to a specified age limit **b :** obligatory esp. for the fulfillment of degree or graduation requirements ⟨for science majors biology and astronomy are ~⟩

2**compulsory** \"\ *n* -ES [ML *compulsorium*, fr. neut. of *compulsorius*, adj.] *archaic* **:** a measure or means (as a legal injunction) compelling obedience

compulsory jurisdiction *n* **1 :** a jurisdiction existing by force of law over a person **2 :** a mandatory jurisdiction that a state has agreed to accept in certain prescribed matters

compulsory listing *n* **:** MULTIPLE LISTING

com·punc·tion \kəmˈpəŋ(k)shən\ *n* -S [ME *compunctioun*, fr. MF *componction*, fr. LL *compunction-, compunctio*, fr. L *compunctus* (past part. of *compungere* to prick hard, sting fr. *com-* + *pungere* to prick, sting) + *-ion-, -io* -ion — more at PUNGENT] **1 a :** anxiety of spirit arising from consciousness of sin **:** deep unease caused by knowledge of guilt ⟨~*s* of conscience⟩ **b :** normal human regret, pity, or anxiety **:** REMORSE ⟨he showed no ~ in planning devilish engines of military destruction —Havelock Ellis⟩ **c :** a twinge of uneasiness **:** SCRUPLE ⟨cheating without ~⟩ **2** *archaic* **:** compassionate sorrow **:** PITY **syn** see PENITENCE, SCRUPLE

com·punc·tion·less \-ləs\ *adj* **:** lacking compunction

com·punc·tious \-shəs\ *adj* [*compunction* + *-ous*] **1 :** arising from remorse or regret ⟨~ feelings⟩ **2 :** feeling remorse or regret ⟨deeply ~ for his outburst⟩ — **com·punc·tious·ly** *adv*

com·pur·ga·tion \ˌkäm(ˌ)pərˈgāshən\ *n* -S [LL *compurgation-, compurgatio*, fr. L *compurgatus* (past part. of *compurgare* to purify wholly, fr. *com-* + *purgare* to purify) + *-ion-, -io* -ion — more at PURGE] **:** vindication (as from a charge) or testimony or evidence that vindicates; *esp* **:** the clearing of a defendant or accused person by oaths of persons who swear to his veracity or innocence — often used of the mode of vindication of ecclesiastical courts or of the similar procedure in old Germanic courts; compare WAGER OF LAW

com·pur·ga·tor \ˈkäm(ˌ)pərˌgād·ər\ *n* -S [ML, fr. L *compurgatus* + *-or*] **:** one that defends or supports another ⟨spoke most kindly as my ~*s* —H.J.Laski⟩; *specif* **:** one that under oath vouches for the blameless character or conduct of an accused person attempting thereby to vindicate him

com·pur·ga·to·ri·al \kəmˌpərgəˈtōrēəl, kəmˌp-, ˈkämˌp-\ *adj* [*compurgatory* + *-al*] **:** COMPURGATORY

com·pur·ga·to·ry \kəmˈpərgəˌtōrē, (ˈ)kämˈp-\ *adj* [*compurgator* + *-ory*] **:** of or relating to a compurgator or compurgation

com·put·abil·i·ty \kəmˌpyüd·əˈbiləd·ē, ˌtəˈb-, -lətē, -i *also* ˌkämpyə\ *n* -ES **:** the quality or state of being computable

com·put·able \kəmˈpyüd·əbəl, ˌtəbəl *also* ˈkämpyə\ *adj* [L *computabilis*, fr. *computare* + *-abilis* -able] **:** capable of being computed — **com·put·ably** \-blē\ *adv*

com·pu·ta·tion \ˌkämpyəˈtāshən\ *n* -S [ME *computacion*, fr. L *computation-, computatio*, fr. *computatus* (past part. of *computare* to compute) + *-ion-, -io* -ion] **1 :** the act or action of computing **:** CALCULATION, RECKONING ⟨there had come many from the north — seven, by the squire's ~ —R.L. Stevenson⟩ **2 :** a way or system of reckoning ⟨conformity with Roman practice in regard to . . . the ~ of Easter —F.M. Stenton⟩ **3 :** the result of computation **:** amount computed

com·pu·ta·tion·al \ˌkämpyəˈtāshənᵊl, -shnəl\ *adj* **:** having to do with computation ⟨~ errors⟩ ⟨~ aids⟩

com·pu·ta·tive \kəmˈpyüd·əd·iv *also* ˈkämpyəˌtād·iv\ *adj* [*compute* + *-ative*] **:** given to or employing computation

com·pu·ta·tor \ˈkämpyəˌtād·ə(r)\ *n* -S [L, fr. *computatus* + *-or*] **:** COMPUTER

1**com·pute** \kəmˈpyüt, *usu* -üd·+V\ *n* -S [LL *computus*, fr. L *computare*] **:** COMPUTATION — used chiefly with *beyond* ⟨future wars will be complex beyond ~ —*U.S. Air Services*⟩

2**compute** \"\ *vb* -ED/-ING/-S [L *computare* — more at COUNT] *vt* **1 :** to determine or ascertain esp. by mathematical means **:** arrive at an answer to or sum for ⟨~ a bank balance⟩ ⟨~ the area of a field⟩ ⟨~ the diameter of the sun⟩ **2** *obs* **:** to make up (as a period of time) ~ *vi* **:** to make calculation **:** RECKON ⟨they ~ by weight in selling grain⟩ **syn** see CALCULATE

com·put·er *also* **com·pu·tor** \-üd·ə(r), -ütə-\ *n* -S **:** one that computes: as **a :** a calculator esp. designed for the solution of complex mathematical problems; *specif* **:** a programmable electronic device that can store, retrieve, and process data **b :** any of several devices for making rapid calculations in navigation or gunnery (as the computing of an air position or the range of fire of a gun) **c :** a person who calculates (as latitudes, longitudes, and areas) for map making from notes made by engineering survey parties

computing machine *n* **:** COMPUTER a

computing scale *n* **:** a weighing machine that indicates both weight and the proper selling price for that weight

com·put·ist \kəmˈpyüd·əst, -ütə-; ˈkämpyətə-\ *n* -S [alter. (influenced by *compute*) of earlier *compotist*, fr. ME *compotiste*, fr. MF, fr. ML *computista, compotista*, fr. LL *computus, compotus* + L *-ista* -ist] **:** one skilled in computing (as dates of the calendar, business accounts, astronomical problems)

com·pu·tus \ˈkämpyətəs\ *n* -ES [ML, fr. LL, computation] **1 :** a medieval set of tables for calculating astronomical events and movable dates in the calendar **2** *also* **com·po·tus** \-pət-\ [LL] **:** COMPUTATION, RECKONING

compy *abbr* company

com·quat *var of* KUMQUAT

comr *abbr* commissioner

1**com·rade** \ˈkämˌrad, -ˌrəd, -ˌraa(ə)d, *Brit sometimes* ˈkəm- *or* -ˌrād\ *n* -S [MF *camarade* group of soldiers sleeping in one room, roommate, companion, fr. OSp *camarada*, fr. *cámara* room, fr. LL *camera* — more at CHAMBER] **1 a** *obs* **:** one that shares the same sleeping quarters as another **b :** one that shares the same fortunes or experiences as another **:** intimate friend **:** COMPANION ⟨an old ~ of fishing and hunting days⟩ — used as a form of address among members of the British Labor party and trade unions and among certain American organizations of a nonpolitical nature **c :** COMRADE-IN-ARMS ⟨his fallen ~*s*⟩ **2 a :** COMMUNIST ⟨the party had forbidden all ~*s* to go to court —Paul Hofmann⟩ — used as a form of address ⟨a speech by *Comrade* Jones⟩ **b :** a person with or suspected of communist or leftist tendencies

2**comrade** \"\ *vi* -ED/-ING/-S **:** to associate in comradeship ⟨the gentlemen *comraded* it with the yeomen —Adrian Bell⟩

comrade-in-arms \ˈ=(ˌ)=ˈ=\ *n, pl* **comrades-in-arms :** a friend made in military service **:** a fellow soldier

com·rade·li·ness \ˈ=(ˌ)lēnəs, -lin-\ *n* -ES **:** CAMARADERIE

com·rade·ly \ˈ=(ˌ)lē, -li\ *adj* **:** of or like a comrade or partner **:** suitable to the relation of comrades ⟨a ~ handshake⟩

com·rade·ry \-drē, -ri\ *n* -ES [trans. of F *camaraderie*] **:** CAMARADERIE

com·rade·ship \-ˌship\ *n* **:** association as comrades ⟨could offer each other mutual aid and ~ —Oscar Handlin⟩

coms *pl of* COM

comsomol *usu cap, var of* KOMSOMOL

com·stock \ˈkämzˌtäk, -mˌst- *sometimes* ˈkəm-\ *also* **com·stock·er** \-kə(r)\ *n* -S [after Anthony *Comstock* †1915 Am. reformer] **:** a ludicrous prude esp. in matters relating to morality in art

com·stock·ery \-k(ə)rē, -ri\ *n* -ES **:** PRUDERY; *specif* **:** prudish concern in hunting down immorality esp. in books, papers, and pictures

comstock mealybug *or* **comstock's mealybug** *n, usu cap C* [after John H. *Comstock* †1931 Am. entomologist] **:** an Asiatic mealybug (*Pseudococcus comstocki*) introduced accidentally into No. America where it is a pest of various cultivated trees (as citrus and apples)

comte \kōⁿt\ *n* -S [F, fr. LL *comit-, comes* — more at COUNT] **:** 3COUNT

com·tesse \kōⁿtes\ *n* -S [F, fr. OF *comtesse, contesse*, fr. *comte, conte* + *-esse* -ess] **:** COUNTESS

comt·ian *also* **comt·ean** \ˈkäm(p)tēən, ˈkōnt-, ˈkōⁿt-\ *adj, usu cap* [Auguste *Comte* †1857 Fr. mathematician and philosopher + E *-ian* or *-an*] **:** of or relating to Auguste Comte or his writings or doctrines — compare POSITIVISM

comt·ism \-ˌtizəm\ *n* -S *often cap* [Auguste *Comte* + E *-ism*] **:** POSITIVISM 1a

comt·ist \-ˌtəst\ *adj or n* [Auguste *Comte* + E *-ist*] **:** POSITIVIST

co·mu·ni·dad \kōˌmünəˈthä(th)\ *n, pl* **comunida·des** \=ˌ==ˈthä(ˌ)thās\ [Sp, *community*, fr. L *communitat-, communitas* — more at COMMUNITY] **:** a relatively independent Peruvian Indian community that developed out of the ayllu, constituted a collective social and economic unit, and also formed an intermediate administrative unit

1**con** \ˈkän\ *vt* **conned; conned; conning; cons** [ME *connen*, alter. (influenced by *con*, 1st & 3d sing. pres. indic., fr. OE, var. of *can*) of *cunnen* — more at CAN] **1** *obs* **:** to have knowledge of **:** KNOW **2 a :** to study in order to know **:** regard or examine closely **:** PERUSE ⟨she had a complete set of "Standard Recitations" which she *conned* on Sundays —Willa Cather⟩ **b :** to commit to memory by vocal or mental repetition ⟨the orator had *conned* it by heart —S.H.Adams⟩ **c :** to reflect upon **:** PONDER ⟨the wise soldier will ~ himself, note his difference from the man he was —Christopher La Farge⟩ — **con thanks** \"-, ˈkən-\ *archaic* **:** to express gratitude **:** ACKNOWLEDGE

2**con** \"\ *var of* CONN

3**con** \"\ *adv* [ME, short for 1*contra*] **:** on the negative side **:** in opposition — opposed to *pro* ⟨much was written pro and ~⟩

4**con** \"\ *n* -S **1 :** the arguments or evidence in opposition to a statement, proposition, or position **2 :** the negative position or one holding it **:** OPPOSITION — opposed to *pro* ⟨an appraisal of the pros and ~*s*⟩

5**con** \"\ *adj* **:** taking the opposing side **:** OPPOSITIONAL, NEGATIVE — opposed to *pro* ⟨pro and ~ arguments⟩

6**con** \"\ *prep* **:** in opposition to **:** on the negative side of **:** AGAINST — opposed to *pro* ⟨forces pro and ~ the issue⟩

7**con** \"\ *n* -S [prob. fr. F *cogner* to beat, fr. OF, fr. L *cuneus* wedge — more at COIN] *now dial Eng* **:** a rap with the knuckles

8**con** \"\ *adj* [by shortening] **:** 2CONFIDENCE

9**con** \"\ *vt* **conned; conned; conning; cons 1 :** to swindle esp. by the confidence game **:** DECEIVE, CHEAT ⟨she *conned* a victim out of his savings⟩ **2 :** to persuade or lure (a person) to the advantage of the persuader **:** TRICK, FOOL ⟨he *conned* her into buying an inferior product⟩ **3 :** CAJOLE, BLARNEY, SOFT-SOAP ⟨a mealymouthed football coach *conning* a boy with a broken knee into playing —A.J.Liebling⟩

10**con** \"\ *n* -S **:** fraudulent appropriation of money ⟨knew too much about ~ to fall for that one —Herbert Gold⟩

11**con** \"\ *n* -S [by shortening] *slang* **:** CONVICT

12**con** \"\ *n* -S [by shortening] *slang* **:** CONDUCTOR 2c

13**con** \"\ *n* -S [short for *consumption*] *slang* **:** a destructive disease of the lungs: **a :** TUBERCULOSIS **b :** silicosis with superimposed tuberculous infection

1**con-** — see COM-

2**con-** *or* **cono-** *comb form* [Gk *kōn-, kōno-*, fr. *kōnos* — more at HONE] **:** cone ⟨*conodont*⟩ ⟨*conoplain*⟩ ⟨*conoscope*⟩

con *abbr* **1** concerto **2** conclusion **3** conic **4** connecting; connection **5** consol; consolidated **6** [L *conjux*] consort **7** consul **8** continued **9** contra

con ab·ban·do·no \ˈkäˌnabənˈdō(ˌ)nō, ˈkō,-; ˈkōˌnä,bän-\ *adv* [It, lit., with abandon] **:** UNRESTRAINEDLY **:** BRILLIANTLY — used as a direction in music

con·a·cas·te \ˌkänəˈkastē\ *n* -S [Sp *conacaste, guanacaste*, fr. Nahuatl *cuauhnacaztli*, lit., ear tree, fr. *cuahuitl* tree + *nacaztli* ear; fr. the shape of the fruit] **:** a tropical American timber tree (*Enterolobium cyclocarpum*) that has coiled ear-shaped fruits and produces a valuable wood

1**con·acre** \ˈkäˌnākə(r)\ *n* -S [alter. of earlier *corn-acre*, lit., field of grain] *in a former Irish land system* **:** the subletting for a single season of small portions of a farm previously prepared for sowing or planting; *also* **:** a single parcel or tenancy so held

2**conacre** \"\ *vt* -ED/-ING/-S **:** to sublet (land) in conacre

con af·fet·to \ˌkänəˈfed·(ˌ)ō, ˌkōn-\ *adv* [It] **:** with feeling and tenderness — used as a direction in music

con agi·li·ta \-nəˈjiləˈtä\ *adv* [It *con agilità*, lit., with agility] **:** with liveliness — used as a direction in music

con agi·ta·zio·ne \ˈkäˌnajəˌtätsēˈōnē, ˈkō,-\ *adv* [It, lit., with agitation] **:** AGITATEDLY — used as a direction in music

con·a·kry *or* **kon·a·kri** *or* **kon·a·kry** \ˈkänəkrē\ *adj, usu cap* [fr. *Conakry, Konakri, Konakry*, seaport on Tombo Island, Guinea] **:** of or from Conakry, the capital of Guinea **:** of the kind or style prevalent in Conakry

co·nal \ˈkōnᵊl\ *adj* [NL *conus* (*arteriosus*) + E *-al*] **:** of or relating to the conus arteriosus

con·albumin \ˈ|kän+\ *n* -S [*com-* + *albumin*] **:** a protein of the white of an egg that is obtained from the filtrate from the crystallization of ovalbumin and that combines with iron salts to form a red iron-protein complex

con al·cu·na li·cen·za \ˌkäˌnalˈkünəlēˈchen(t)(ˌ)sä, ˌkō,-, -(t)sə\ *adv* [It] **:** with some freedom — used as a direction in music

con amo·re \ˌkänəˈmōrē, ˌkōn-, -ōr(ˌ)ā\ *adv* [It] **1 :** with love or devotion **:** with zest or delight ⟨a translation made *con amore* from an obscure early writing⟩ **2 :** TENDERLY — used as a direction in music

con ani·ma \käˈnanəˌmä, kōˈnänē,-\ *or* **con ani·mo** \-mō\ *adv* [It] **:** with spirit — used as a direction in music

co·nar·i·al \kōˈna(a)rēəl\ *adj* [NL *conarium* + E *-al*] **:** PINEAL

conarite *var of* CONNARITE

co·nar·i·um \kōˈna(a)rēəm\ *n, pl* **conar·ia** \-ēə\ [NL, fr. Gk *kōnarion*, lit., small cone, dim. of *kōnos* cone — more at HONE] **:** PINEAL BODY

co·na·tion \kōˈnāshən\ *n* -S [L *conation-, conatio* attempt, fr. *conatus* (past part. of *conari* to attempt) + *-ion-, -io* -ion — more at DEACON] **1 :** the conscious drive to perform apparently volitional acts with or without knowledge of the origin of the drive — distinguished from *affection* and *cognition* **2 :** an instinctually motivated biological striving that may appear in consciousness as volition or desire or in behavior as action tendencies

1**co·na·tion·al** \-shənᵊl, -shnəl\ *adj* [*conation* + *-al*] **:** CONATIVE 1

2**co·na·tion·al** \(ˈ)kōˈnashənᵊl, -naash-, -naish-, -shnəl\ *n* [*co-* + *national*] **:** a fellow national; *esp* **:** a fellow member of a minority national group in a state

3**conational** \"\ *adj* **:** of, relating to, or being a conational — **co·na·tion·al·ist** \"+əst\ *n*

co·na·tive \ˈkōnəd·iv, ˈkän-\ *adj* [*conation* + *-ive*] **1 :** having the characteristics of or involving conation ⟨literature and art appeal as much to the affective and ~ as to the merely cognitive side of man's being —Aldous Huxley⟩ **2 :** denoting an attempt to perform an action — used of verb forms or affixes in certain languages

2**conative** \"\ *n* -S **:** a conative verb form, set of verb forms, or affix

co·na·tus \kōˈnād·əs, -nad-\ *n, pl* **conatus** [NL, fr. L, effort, fr. *conatus*, past part. of *conari* to attempt — more at DEACON] **:** a natural tendency, impulse, or striving **:** CONATION — used in Spinozism with reference to the inclination of a thing to persist in its own being

con bra·vu·ra \ˌkänbrəˈv(y)u̇rə, ˌkōn-\ *adv* [It, lit., with boldness] **:** BOLDLY, BRILLIANTLY — used as a direction in music

con brio \känˈbrē(ˌ)ō, kōn-\ *adv* [It, lit., with vigor] **:** VIGOROUSLY, ENERGETICALLY ⟨a critic who voices his dislikes *con brio* —C.J.Rolo⟩ — often used as a direction in music

conc *abbr* **1** concentrated; concentration **2** concentric **3** concerning **4** concrete **5** [L *concilium*] council

con·cam·er·at·ed \(ˈ)känˈkaməˌrād·əd, kənˈk-\ *adj* [L *concameratus* (past part. of *concamerare* to arch over, fr. *com-* + *camerare* to arch, fr. *camera* arch) + E *-ed* — more at CHAMBER] *archaic* **:** ARCHED, VAULTED

con·cam·er·a·tion \(ˌ)känˌkaməˈrāshən, kən-\ *n* -S [L *concameration-, concameratio*, fr. *concameratus* + *-ion-, -io* -ion] **1 :** a vaulted construction (as a roof or ceiling) **2 :** VAULT 5

con·canavalin \ˈkän+\ *n* -S [*com-* + *canavalin*] *biochem* **:** either of two crystalline globulins occurring with canavalin in the jack bean; *esp* **:** one that is a potent hemagglutinin

1**con·cat·e·nate** \(ˈ)känˈkad·ənət, kənˈk-, -atən-, -atᵊn-, *usu* -əd·+V\ *adj* [ME *concatenat*, fr. LL *concatenatus*] **:** linked together

2**con·cat·e·nate** \känˈkad·əˌnāt, kən-, -atəˌnāt, -atᵊnāt, *usu* -ād·+V\ *vt* -ED/-ING/-S [LL *concatenatus*, past part. of *concatenare*, fr. L *com-* + *catenare* to chain, fr. *catena* chain — more at CHAIN] **:** to link together **:** unite in a series or chain ⟨the present work comprises five essays nicely *concatenated* —Richard Hocking⟩

con·cat·e·na·tion \(ˌ)känˌkad·əˈnāshən, kən-, -atəˈnā-, -atᵊnˈā-\ *n* -S [LL *concatenation-, concatenatio*, fr. *concatenatus* + *-ion-, -io* -ion] **1 a :** the act of concatenating **b :** the state of being concatenated **:** union in a linked series **2 :** a series of links united : a series or order of things depending on each other as if linked together : CHAIN ⟨a complicated ~ of circumstances —Frederick Johnson⟩

con·cat·e·na·tor \kän'kad·ə,nād·ə(r), kən-, -atə,nā-,-at°n,ā-, -ātə-\ *n* -S : one that concatenates

con·caus·al \(')kän¦kȯzəl\ *adj* : operating as a concause

con·cause \'kän,kȯz\ *n* -S [ML *concausa*, fr. L *com-* + *causa* cause — more at CAUSE] : one of several causes acting together

¹con·cave \'kän,kāv, *esp Brit sometimes* -äŋ,-\ *n* -S [MF, fr. *concave*, adj.] **1 a** : a hollow within a mass or in a surface ⟨Vulcan . . . splits the cliff and discloses a ~ fashioned by his art —E.K.Chambers⟩ **b** : a curved recess : a depression resembling a bowl **c** *obs* : the bore of a gun **2 a** : the inner face of a bowl-shaped structure **b** : the vault of the sky **3** *obs* : a concave lens or mirror **4** : a set of bars bearing teeth, rasps, or rubber facing curved partly around a rotating threshing cylinder as an aid in shelling grain or seeds in a thresher

²concave \(')=¦=\ *adj* [MF, fr. L *concavus*, fr. *com-* + *cavus* hollow — more at CAVE] **1** *obs* : having a hollow interior ⟨~ . . . as a worm-eaten nut —Shak.⟩ **2 a** : hollowed or rounded inward like the inside of a bowl **b** : having a shape that is thought of as curving inward — opposed to *convex* **3** : arched in : curving in — used of the side of a curve or surface on which neighboring normals to the curve or surface converge and on which lies the chord joining two neighboring points of the curve or surface; opposed to *convex* — **con·cave·ly** *adv* — **con·cave·ness** *n* -ES

³concave \"\ *vb* -ED/-ING/-S *vt* : to make concave ~ *vi* : to curve concavely

concave grating *n* : a reflection grating ruled on a concave mirror

concave polygon *n* : a polygon with one angle larger than a straight angle

con·cav·er \(')kän¦kāvə(r)\ *n* -S : one that shapes or forms a concave surface or edge

con·cav·i·ty \kän'kavəd·ē, -ətē, -i *sometimes* kən-\ *n* -ES [MF *concavité*, fr. LL *concavitat-*, *concavitas*, fr. L *concavus* + *-itat-*, *-itas* -ity] **1 a** : a concave line or surface or the space included by it : a hollow esp. of a vault or a hemisphere **b** : a depression resembling a bowl **2** : CONCAVE 1 **3** : the quality or state of being concave

con·ca·vo-con·cave \kän¦kā(,)vō¦kän,kāv\ *adj* [*concavo-* (fr. L *concavus*) + E *concave*] : concave on both sides — used esp. of a lens

con·ca·vo-convex \kän¦kā(,)vō+\ *adj* [*concavo-* + *convex*] **1** : concave on one side and convex on the other **2** *of a lens* : having the concave side of greater curvature than the convex side

con·ceal \kən'sēl, *esp bef pause or cons* -ēəl\ *vt* -ED/-ING/-S [ME *concelen*, fr. MF *conceler*, fr. L *concelare*, fr. *com-* + *celare* to hide — more at HELL] **1** : to prevent disclosure or recognition of : avoid revelation of : refrain from revealing : withhold knowledge of : draw attention from : treat so as to be unnoticed ⟨confessing . . . things a woman ought to ~ —Thomas Hardy⟩ **2** : to place out of sight : withdraw from being observed : shield from vision or notice ⟨it grew so thickly as to ~ the roof —Richard Jefferies⟩

syn HIDE, BURY, SECRETE, CACHE, SCREEN, ENSCONCE: CONCEAL and HIDE are general terms often interchangeable. CONCEAL may be applied freely to persons and animals, objects, attributes, conditions, facts, or ideas ⟨Sophia had held the telegram *concealed* in her hand and its information *concealed* in her heart —Arnold Bennett⟩ ⟨Elizabeth was forced to *conceal* her lover from her father —Virginia Woolf⟩ ⟨politeness may *conceal* a legitimate wish that dare not put itself in bald speech —R.P.Blackmur⟩ CONCEAL may indicate any hiding or masking of any motive, from reprehensible secrecy to aesthetic improvement ⟨*conceal* a murder⟩ ⟨*conceal* a scar⟩ ⟨*concealing* a scratch on a piece of furniture⟩ ⟨*conceal* a bad odor⟩ It need not suggest covering. It often implies a certain design or artfulness. HIDE may differ from CONCEAL in suggesting less conscious intent and artfulness, and hence less effectiveness, but occas. more urgency ⟨*hidden* things that had never been concealed, that had merely been dropped away into forgotten corners and out-of-the-way places —Elizabeth M. Roberts⟩ ⟨with these consoling words he tried to *hide* from her the doubt that had entered his mind —Morley Callaghan⟩ It is less applicable than CONCEAL to senses other than sight. BURY suggests concealment in a low place by covering, esp. by heaping something amorphous ⟨loot *buried* under the ground⟩ or, in more figurative senses, it suggests relegation to obscurity ⟨I would myself be half *buried* in shadows and in darkness —Sherwood Anderson⟩ SECRETE is likely to have an increased suggestion of highly purposive, secretive, stealthy concealment ⟨she could scarcely . . . overcome the suspicion of there being many chambers *secreted* —Jane Austen⟩ ⟨and in mere sound *secretes* his inmost sense —Walter de la Mare⟩ CACHE suggests use of storage places affording security or protection as well as concealment, sometimes in the ground. SCREEN suggests protection or concealment from observation or danger by that which screens from a viewer's eyes ⟨*screened* himself under a bush and waited —Thomas Hardy⟩ ⟨the idea of a woman's appealing to her family to *screen* her husband's business dishonor —Edith Wharton⟩ ENSCONCE, in this sense, implies the security of concealment in a raised or walled area ⟨bounded into the vehicle and sat on a stool, *ensconced* from view —Thomas Hardy⟩ ⟨he *ensconced* the boy in a cubbyhole —Peggy Bacon⟩

con·ceal·able \-ēləbəl\ *adj* : capable of being concealed

concealed *adj*, *of a hand in canasta and certain forms of rummy* : fully matched and enabling one to go out without previously having melded

concealed asset *n* : a tangible or intangible asset that is not reflected on the balance sheet in accounting or finance or that is carried at nominal value (as stock of a subsidiary or a valuable patent)

concealed bed *n* : DISAPPEARING BED

concealed damage *n* **1** : damage to the contents of a package that is not apparent until the package is opened **2** : a seed rot of peanuts that is not visible until the seed is broken open and that is caused by invasion of the space between the seed halves by various fungi esp. of the genus *Diplodia*

con·cealed·ly \-ēlədlē, -ēl(d)lē, -li\ *adv* : in a concealed manner

concealed loss *n* : loss of goods from a container not apparent from the condition of the container

con·cealed·ness \-ēlədnəs, -ēl(d)n-\ *n* -ES : the quality or state of being concealed

concealed weapon *n* : a dangerous weapon so carried on the person as to be knowingly or willfully concealed from sight usu. in violation of statute

con·ceal·er \kən'sēlə(r)\ *n* -S : one that conceals

con·ceal·ment \-ē(ə)lmənt\ *n* -S [ME *concelement*, fr. MF, fr. *conceler* + *-ment*] **1 a** : the act or practice of concealing : the state of being concealed ⟨process . . . could not be served by reason of her absence from or ~ within the state —*Detroit Law Jour.*⟩ **b** : the practice or fact of concealing what ought to be revealed : improper secrecy ⟨his secrecy had the character of prudent reserve, not of cunning or ~ —George Bancroft⟩ **2** *obs* : out-of-the-way knowledge : secret information : MYSTERY **3 a** : a means of concealing : a hiding place **b concealments** *pl* : conditions or facilities for concealing

concealment cipher *n* : a method of hiding a message in a cover text (as the trellis cipher)

con·cede \kən'sēd\ *vb* -ED/-ING/-S [F or L; F *concéder*, fr. L *concedere*, fr. *com-* + *cedere* to go along, give way, yield — more at CEDE] *vt* **1** : to grant as a right or privilege : ALLOW, SURRENDER, PERMIT ⟨Britain *conceded* the independence of the colonies⟩ ⟨we cannot ~ an increase in wages now⟩ ⟨he is willing to ~ his share to his sister⟩ **2** : ADMIT, ACKNOWLEDGE ⟨the right of the state to tax is generally *conceded*⟩: **a** : to accept as true or accurate (as something discussed or debated) ⟨still less does he ~ that the British have any claim to the gratitude of the inhabitants —Michael Clark⟩ ⟨we have no choice but to ~ their figures⟩ **b** : to acknowledge grudgingly or hesitantly ⟨*conceded* that it might be a good idea⟩ ⟨they *conceded* that their decision had been unwise⟩ **c** : to acknowledge as won by an opponent without formal determination of the result ⟨South trumped the return and the opponents *conceded* the rest of the tricks⟩ ⟨the senator *conceded* the election shortly after midnight⟩ **d** : to acknowledge a person to have ⟨even his enemies ~ him courage⟩ ~ *vi* : to make concession : YIELD **syn** see GRANT

con·ced·ed·ly *adv* : INDISPUTABLY, ADMITTEDLY ⟨~ honest expressions of opinion —*Time*⟩ ⟨probably not more than one out of ten and ~ not more than one out of four . . . are actually rented —Charles Abrams⟩

¹con·ceit \kən'sēt, *usu.* -ēd·+V\ *n* -S [ME *conceite*, fr. *conceiven* to conceive, after such pairs as ME *deceiven* to deceive: *deceite* deceit] **1 a** (1) : something that results from mental activity : THOUGHT, CONCEPT, CONCEPTION, IDEA (2) *obs* : mental activity : thinking or the capacity to think (3) : individual or personal opinion : JUDGMENT, VIEW **b** : high estimation : favorable opinion : ESTEEM, ADMIRATION; *esp* : excessive appreciation of one's own worth or virtue **2** [trans. of It *concetto* — more at CONCETTO] **a** : a whimsical or fancifully ingenious idea **b** : an elaborate, startling, extravagant, or strained metaphor **c** : the use or the presence of such conceits as an element of poetry **3** : a fancy article : attractive trifle; *esp* : an ingenious decorative item ⟨with new techniques of designing artificial flowers . . . some of the resulting ~*s* are quite fetching —*New Yorker*⟩ **4** *archaic* : capacity for imagination or fancifulness : active fancy **5** *obs* : a seizure of physical or mental illness

syn SELF-LOVE, EGOTISM, EGOISM, SELF-ESTEEM, AMOUR PROPRE: CONCEIT indicates a conviction or assumption of one's own superiority in one or more lines of achievement or a general overall highly favorable notion of oneself usu. accompanied by lack of evaluation and irritating offensiveness ⟨*conceit*, being a false estimate of one's abilities or an overestimate of those that are least important, is both a moral and an intellectual failing —C.W.H.Johnson⟩ ⟨Aristotle's "Poetics" was so hard that nobody could understand it and therefore he was fearful lest he should be thought guilty of presumption and *conceit* in trying to explain it at all —Irving Babbitt⟩ SELF-LOVE in nonphilosophic usages may suggest abnormal concentration on one's own wishes and considerations to the exclusion of others ⟨when I am led by *self-love* to keep my seat whilst ladies stand —James Ford⟩ ⟨but the proper meaning of *self-love* is regard to self in distinction from others or regard to some private interest —G.P.Fisher⟩ EGOTISM may indicate a tendency to attract attention to and center interest on oneself and one's achievements ⟨she had the simplest *egotism*, the most open desire to be thought first always —Virginia Woolf⟩ ⟨*egotism* resides more in a kind of proud isolation, in a species of contempt for the opinions and aims of others —A.C.Benson⟩ EGOISM implies a self-centered concentration on one's own desires and aspirations to the exclusion of interest in others ⟨it's not so much selfishness as a sort of—is *egoism* the word? When she wants to do a thing, she doesn't take into account the wants of others at all —B.A.Williams⟩ ⟨the essence of a self-reliant and autonomous culture is an unshakable *egoism*. It must not only regard itself as the peer of any other culture; it must regard itself as the superior of any other —H.L.Mencken⟩ SELF-ESTEEM may indicate either natural well-based commendable pride in self or more shaky and somewhat vain attempts at self-pride and self-adjustment ⟨I do some things very well; but my *self-esteem* is crushed by the multitude of things at which I am a hopeless duffer —G.B.Shaw⟩ ⟨Hollywood propping up the *self-esteem* of celluloid royalty —Gladys B. Stern⟩ AMOUR PROPRE indicates a pride in oneself, often commendable or pardonable but often delicate and susceptible to being wounded ⟨I should doubt the judgment of anyone who told me that the people of Egypt have no *amour propre* or that there does not exist in Egypt today a legitimate feeling of pride for the nation —*Manchester Guardian Weekly*⟩ ⟨our *amour propre* is concerned in believing the war in which we fought a righteous one and the victory in which we participated an unsullied one —*New Republic*⟩

²conceit \"\ *vb* -ED/-ING/-S *vt* **1** *obs* : to form a conception of : APPREHEND, UNDERSTAND ⟨our great need of him you have right well ~*ed* —Shak.⟩ **2** *now dial* : IMAGINE, SUPPOSE, THINK ⟨I did ~ a most delicious feast —George Herbert⟩ **3** : to fill with fancies **4** *now dial Brit* : to take a fancy to : LIKE **5** : to hold a favorable opinion of (oneself) : ESTEEM ⟨began to ~ himself already a poet —Robert Southey⟩ ~ *vi*, *now dial* : to form an idea : THINK

con·ceit·ed \-ēd·əd,-ētəd\ *adj* [¹*conceit* + *-ed*] **1 a** *obs* (1) : endowed with intelligence or imagination : CLEVER (2) : disposed in opinion or attitude : MINDED; *esp* : favorably disposed or favorably minded — usu. used with *to* or *of* **b** : ingeniously contrived or designed: as (1) : having or exhibiting a literary style marked by conceits (2) : consisting of or constructed upon or around a conceit (3) : containing conceits **2** : entertaining an excessively or unjustifiably high opinion of oneself — **con·ceit·ed·ly** *adv* — **con·ceit·ed·ness** *n* -ES

conceitless *adj*, *obs* : lacking understanding or thought : IGNORANT

con·ceity \kən'sēd·ē, -sād·ē\ *adj* [¹*conceit* + *-y*] **1** *chiefly dial* : CONCEITED, VAIN **2** *chiefly dial* : hard to please

con·ceiv·abil·i·ty \kən,sēvə'biləd·ē, -ətē, -i\ *n* -ES : the quality or state of being conceivable

con·ceiv·able \kən'sēvəbəl\ *adj* **1** : capable of being conceived, imagined, or understood **2** : logically possible — **con·ceiv·able·ness** *n* -ES

con·ceiv·ably \-blē, -li\ *adv* : in a conceivable manner : POSSIBLY

con·ceive \kən'sēv\ *vb* -ED/-ING/-S [ME *conceiven*, fr. OF *conceivre*, *concevoir*, fr. L *concipere* to take, receive, conceive, proclaim, fr. *com-* + *-cipere* (fr. *capere* to seize, take) — more at HEAVE] *vt* **1 a** *of a mammal, esp. a human being* (1) : to become pregnant with : be with (child or young) (2) : BEGET ⟨he *conceived* their child deliberately —Norman Mailer⟩ (3) *obs* : to make pregnant : IMPREGNATE (4) : to be engendered in the womb — used passively ⟨before he was *conceived* —Lk 2:21 (AV)⟩ **b** : to cause to begin : originate or start (something thought of as capable of subsequent growth and development) ⟨Texas was *conceived* in debt and nourished on depleted paper —R.A.Billington⟩ — usu. used figuratively **2 a** : to take into one's mind : be affected by ⟨I have *conceived* a profound prejudice against such methods⟩ **b** : to form in the mind (as a concept or idea) : evolve mentally (as a plan or stratagem) : form a conception of : IMAGINE, VISUALIZE, IMAGE ⟨a building badly *conceived* and carelessly constructed⟩ **3 a** *archaic* : to apprehend (something) by reason or imagination **b** : COMPREHEND ⟨~ the man⟩ : UNDERSTAND, GRASP **4** : to be of the opinion : THINK, SUPPOSE ⟨we cannot ~ that this course is expedient now⟩ **5** *archaic* : to give forth : EXHIBIT, PRODUCE **6** : to give expression to : COUCH, FRAME, PHRASE ~ *vi* **1** : to become pregnant **2** : to have a conception, idea, or opinion : THINK — usu. used with *of* **syn** see THINK

con·celebrant \kən, (')kän +\ *n* -S [L *concelebrant-*, *concelebrans*, pres. part. of *concelebrare*] : one of two or more members of the clergy celebrating the Eucharist or Mass together

con·celebrate \"+\ *vb* -ED/-ING/-S [L *concelebratus*, past part. of *concelebrare* to celebrate in great numbers, fr. *com-* + *celebrare* to celebrate — more at CELEBRATE] *vt* : to celebrate (as Mass) together ~ *vi* : to celebrate the Eucharist or Mass together

con·celebration \(;)kän, kən +\ *n* -S : a celebration of the Eucharist or Mass in which two or more of the clergy unite in saying the words of the liturgy

con·cent \kən'sent\ *n* -S [L *concentus* harmony, fr. past part. of *concinere* to sing together, fr. *com-* + *-cinere* (fr. *canere* to sing) — more at CHANT] **1** *archaic* : a state of accordance : CONSISTENCY **2** *archaic* : concert of voices : concord of sounds

con·cen·ter \kən, (')kän-+\ *vb* -ED/-ING/-S [MF *concentrer*, fr. *com-* + *centre* center — more at CENTER] *vt* : to draw or direct to a common center : bring together at a focus or point (as lines, ideas, or emotions) : CONCENTRATE ~ *vi* : to come to one point : meet in, converge toward, or have a common center ⟨then begins to ~ the . . . nexus of . . . habits of reaction to experience —*Survey Graphic*⟩

con·cen·to \kən'chen(,)tō, -'sen-\ *n* -S [It, fr. L *concentus* harmony — more at CONCENT] : the simultaneous sounding of the tones of a chord — compare *arpeggio*

con·central \kən, (')kän+\ *adj* [*com-* + *central*] : CONCENTRIC — **con·centrally** \"+\ *adv*

¹con·cen·trate \'kän(t)sən‚trāt *also* -än,sen-; *usu* -ād·+V\ *vb* -ED/-ING/-S [*com-* + L *centrum* center + E *-ate* (v. suffix) — more at CENTER] *vt* **1** : to bring or direct toward a common center or objective : FOCUS ⟨*concentrating* all their efforts on reaching shore⟩ : gather into one body, mass, or force ⟨there are times when power must be *concentrated* in a few able hands⟩ **2** : to render less dilute or diffuse: **a** (1) : to remove water from ⟨in making maple syrup one ~*s* the sap by boiling⟩ (2) : to separate dross from ⟨repeated *concentrating* of the ore is necessary⟩ (3) : to free from impurities ⟨copper may be *concentrated* electrolytically⟩ **b** : to express the essence of ⟨the message of the New Testament is *concentrated* in the Sermon on the Mount⟩ : render more condensed ⟨the essence of her sex was *concentrated* in her charming obstinacy⟩ ~ *vi* **1** : to draw toward or meet in a common center **2** : to settle closely : GATHER, COLLECT ⟨recent immigrants tend to ~ in port cities⟩ ⟨social and racial tensions ~ in industrial centers⟩ **3 a** : to bring all one's powers, faculties, or activities to bear (as upon a course of action, a thought, or an object) ⟨~ on a problem⟩ ⟨farmers are *concentrating* on wheat this year⟩ ⟨to be able to ~ on the same matter for a considerable time is essential to difficult achievement —Bertrand Russell⟩ **b** : MAJOR **syn** see UNIFY

²concentrate \"\ *adj* [*com-* + L *centrum* + E *-ate* (adj. suffix)] : CONCENTRATED

³concentrate \"\ *n* -S : something obtained by concentration : a concentration or concentrated substance: as **a** : the remainder of dressed ore that contains the mineral sought **b** : a feedstuff rich in digestible nutrients in comparison to its bulk (as grains, oil meals, or tankage) — opposed to *roughage* **c** : a food reduced in bulk by elimination of watery fluid ⟨orange juice ~⟩

concentrated *adj* **1** : rich in respect to a particular or essential element : STRONG, UNDILUTED ⟨~ sulfuric acid⟩ ⟨a narrow thread of ~ ore seaming the rocky canyon⟩ **2** : INTENSE ⟨her ~ passion held them at bay⟩ : INTENSIVE ⟨only through ~ study can he hope to qualify for the award⟩ — **con·cen·trat·ed·ly** *adv*

concentrated alum *n* : ALUMINUM SULFATE

concentrated feed *n* : any animal feed rich in concentrates and low in roughage

concentrated milk *n* : milk concentrated by removal of water; *esp* : PLAIN CONDENSED MILK

concentrate sprayer *n* : a power sprayer used to apply a highly concentrated pesticide in highly dispersed form usu. by delivering it into a strong air blast generated by fans or blowers — called also *low gallonage sprayer*, *mist concentrate sprayer*, *speed sprayer*

con·cen·tra·tion \,kän(t)sən'trāshən *also* -än,sen-\ *n* -S [*com-* + L *centrum* + E *-ation*] **1** : the act or action of concentrating: as **a** : the bringing to a common center; *esp* : the assembling of troops in an area often as a prelude to military action **b** : a directing of the attention or of the mental faculties toward a single object **c** : an increasing of strength (as of a solute or a gas in a mixture) or a purifying (as of a mineral in ore) by partial or total removal of diluents, solvents, admixed gases, extraneous material, or waste (as by evaporation, diffusion, or selective flotation) **d** : the centering of a student's program of study in one department or field of learning in which he does work of advanced grade — compare DISTRIBUTION 1c **2** : a result of concentrating : a concentrated mass or thing: as **a** *pharmacy* : a crude active principle of a vegetable usu. in the form of a powder or resin **b** : a group of artillery shells fired on a particular area within a limited time — compare BARRAGE **3** *of a solution, mixture, or dispersion* : the relative content of a component (as dissolved or dispersed material) that may be expressed in percentage by weight or by volume, in parts per million, or in grams per liter : STRENGTH **4** : DENSITY 1 **5** : a card game for two or more players in which a pack of cards is laid out card by card face down and at random, the skill of the game consisting of remembering the position of such cards as are briefly turned up in play — called also *memory*

concentration camp *n* : a camp where persons (as prisoners of war, political prisoners, refugees, or foreign nationals) are detained or confined and sometimes subjected to physical and mental abuse and indignity

concentration point *n* : a place at which less than carload shipments on common carriers are assembled to be forwarded in carload lots

con·cen·tra·tive \'kän(t)sən,trād·iv *also* -än,sen-'\ *adj* : serving or tending to concentrate : characterized by concentration

con·cen·tra·tor \-ād·ə(r)\ *n* -S : one that concentrates: as **a** : an apparatus by which something (as an ore or a solution) is concentrated; *sometimes* : an industrial plant specializing in concentration (as of ore) **b** : a worker who tends concentrating apparatus **c** : a student who concentrates (in a particular field of study)

¹con·cen·tric \kən'sen·trik, (')kän¦s-, -rēk\ *also* **con·cen·tri·cal** \-rəkəl, -rēk-\ *adj* [ML *concentricus*, fr. L *com-* + *centrum* center + *-icus* -ic — more at CENTER] **1 a** : having a common center (as circles one within another) — opposed to *eccentric* **b** : having a common axis (as of two or more cones or moraines) : formed about the same axis : COAXIAL **2** *geol* : marked by the loosening and falling away of successive rounded or spherical shells (~ weathering) (~ exfoliation) — **con·cen·tri·cal·ly** \-rək(ə)lē, -rēk-, -li\ *adv*

²concentric \"\ *n* -S : something (as one of two concentric circles) that has a common center with something else

concentric bundle *n* : a plant vascular bundle in which (1) phloem surrounds xylem or (2) xylem surrounds phloem — called also respectively (1) *amphicribral bundle*, (2) *amphivasal bundle*

concentric cable *n* : COAXIAL CABLE

concentric corpuscle *n* : CORPUSCLE OF HASSALL

concentric groove *n* : the single continuous silent groove at the end of a disc recording, cut there to prevent the pickup from traveling further toward the center of the record

con·cen·tric·i·ty \,kän,sen·'trisəd·ē\ *n* -ES : the quality or state of being concentric

concents *pl of* CONCENT

con·cen·tus \kən'sentəs, kän-\ *n*, *pl* **concentus** [L, harmony — more at CONCENT] : the part of a church service (as that in which hymns or psalms are sung) that is sung by the whole choir — contrasted with *accentus*

con·cep·ci·ón *or* **con·cep·ci·on** \kən¦sepsē¦ōn, (;)kän-, -ē¦än, -ē¦ōn, kən'sepshən\ *adj*, *usu cap* [fr. *Concepción*, Chile] : of or from the city of Concepción, Chile : of the kind or style prevalent in Concepción

con·cept \'kän,sept\ *n* -S [LL *conceptus* thought, fr. L, collection, gathering, fetus, fr. *conceptus*, past part. of *concipere* to conceive — more at CONCEIVE] : something conceived in the mind : THOUGHT, IDEA, NOTION: as **a** *philos* : a general or abstract idea : a universal notion: (1) : the resultant of a generalizing mental operation : a generic mental image abstracted from percepts; *also* : a directly intuited object of thought (2) : a theoretical construct ⟨the ~ of the atom⟩ **b** *logic* (1) : an idea comprehending the essential attributes of a class or logical species : a universal term or expression or its meaning (2) : a propositional function, logical relation, or property **c** : an idea that includes all that is characteristically associated with or suggested by a term : CONCEPTION **syn** see IDEA

con·cep·ta·cle \kən'septəkəl\ *n* -S [F, fr. L *conceptaculum*, fr. *conceptus*, past part. of *concipere* to receive, conceive] **1** *obs* : a hollow vessel : RECEPTACLE **2** *bot* **a** *obs* : FOLLICLE **b** : an enclosing cavity just beneath the surface of the plant body that contains reproductive structures in members of the genus *Fucus* and certain other algae — **con·cep·tac·u·lar** \¦känsep¦takyələ(r)\ *adj*

con·cep·tac·u·lum \,kän,sep'takyələm\ *n*, *pl* **conceptacula** \-lə\ [NL, fr. L] : CONCEPTACLE 2

con·cep·ti·ble \kən'septəbəl\ *adj* [ML *conceptibilis*, fr. L *conceptus* + *-ibilis* -ible] : CONCEIVABLE

con·cep·tion \kən'sepshən\ *n* -S [ME *concepcioun*, fr. OF *conception*, fr. L *conception-*, *conceptio*, fr. *conceptus* (past part. of *concipere* to conceive, receive) + *-ion-*, *-io* -ion — more at CONCEIVE] **1 a** : act of becoming pregnant : formation of a viable zygote ⟨fertilization results in the ~ of a new entity capable of developing into a being like its parent⟩ : state of being conceived; *also* : that which is conceived : EMBRYO, FETUS **b** *archaic* : BEGINNING **2** : the capacity, function, or process of forming ideas or abstractions or of grasping the meaning of symbols representing such ideas or abstractions ⟨the essential character of ~ is that in it the universal is thought of as such —G.F.Stout⟩ **3 :** an idea or general notion **:** CONCEPT: **a :** a product of abstract or reflective thinking (as an interpretation or design) **:** an ideal scheme or plan of action ⟨his ~ was on the grand scale but he lacked skill and determination needed to make it real⟩ **b :** the abstract, intellectual, or universal element in cognition as distinguished from the apprehension of concrete particulars in sense perception **c** *obs* **:** CONCEIT **4 :** the originating of something (as an idea or plan) in the mind **syn** see IDEA

con·cep·tion·al \-shənᵊl, -shnəl\ *adj* **:** of, relating to, or being a conception ⟨a plan abstruse and ~⟩

conception control *n* **:** CONTRACEPTION

con·cep·tion·ist \-sh(ə)nəst\ *n* -s **1 :** CONCEPTUALIST **2** *cap* [(*Immaculate*) *Conception* + *-ist*] *Roman Catholicism* **:** a member of any of the various orders or congregations dedicated to and named in honor of the Immaculate Conception

con·cept·ism \'kän,sep,tizəm\ *n* -s [Sp *conceptismo*, fr. *concepto* concept, conceit, ingenious expression (fr. LL *conceptus* thought — influenced in meaning by It *concetto*) + *-ismo* -ism — more at CONCEPT] **:** an obscurely allusive style characterized by ambiguous metaphors and puns that was developed chiefly by Spanish mystics of the 17th century

con·cep·tive \kən'septiv\ *adj* [LL *conceptivus*, fr. L, formally proclaimed. fr. *conceptus* (past part. of *concipere* to conceive, proclaim formally) + *-ivus* -ive — more at CONCEIVE] **:** capable of or relating to conceiving — **con·cep·tive·ly** \-tәvlē\ *adv*

con·cep·tu·al \kən'sepchə(wə)l\, (ˌ)kän¦s-, -psh-\ *adj* [ML *conceptualis*, fr. LL *conceptus* thought + L *-alis* -al — more at CONCEPT] **:** of or relating to concepts ⟨the schizophrenic shows a loss in the ability to abstract or do ~ thinking —Louise Heathers⟩ — **con·cep·tu·al·ly** \-)lē, -li\ *adv*

con·cep·tu·al·ism \-,lizəm\ *n* -s [F *conceptualisme*, fr. ML *conceptualis* + F *-isme* -ism] *philos* **:** a theory that is intermediate between nominalism and realism and holds that universals exist in the mind as subjects of discourse or as predicates which may be properly affirmed of reality

con·cep·tu·al·ist \-ləst\ *n* -s **:** an advocate of conceptualism

con·cep·tu·al·is·tic \kən¦sepchə(wə)¦listik, (ˌ)kän-, -psh-\ *adj* **1 :** typical of or involving conceptualism **2 :** employing or based on concepts

con·cep·tu·al·i·za·tion \kən,sepchə(wə)lə'zāshən, (ˌ)kän-, -psh-, -,lī'z-\ *n* -s **:** the act or process of conceptualizing ⟨~ of field data is an essential prelude to formulation of a working hypothesis⟩

con·cep·tu·al·ize \⸗'⸗⸗(⸗),līz\ *vt* -ED/-ING/-S *see -ize in Explan Notes* **:** to form a concept of; *esp* **:** to interpret conceptually ⟨primitive peoples tend to ~ both groups and relations in terms of personalities⟩

con·cep·tus \kən'septəs, kän-\ *n, pl* **conceptus·es** \-təsəz\ *also* **concep·ti** \-,tī\ [L — more at CONCEPT] **:** a product of conception **:** CONCEPT, FETUS

¹con·cern \kən'sərn, -sən, -səin\ *vb* -ED/-ING/-S [ME *concernen*, fr. MF & ML; MF *concerner*, fr. ML *concernere*, fr. LL, to mix or mingle together, fr. L *com-* + *cernere* to separate, sift — more at SHEAR] *vt* **1 a :** to relate or refer to **:** be about ⟨this story ~s the beginnings of the modern age⟩ **b :** to bear on ⟨another rather serious drawback associated with nucellar seedlings ~*ed* the fact that they were . . . slower in developing flower parts —*Farmer's Weekly (So. Africa)*⟩ **2 :** to have an influence on **:** AFFECT, INVOLVE ⟨racial unrest ~s us all⟩; *also* **:** to be the business or affair of **:** matter to ⟨quarrels between husband and wife ~ the whole family⟩ **3 :** to be a care, trouble, or distress to ⟨his failing health ~s me⟩ **4 :** ENGAGE, OCCUPY, INTEREST ⟨he ~s himself with trivia⟩ ~ *vi, obs* **:** to be of importance **:** MATTER

²concern \"\ *n* -s **1 a :** a connecting relation **:** an active or real part (as of interest or sharing) ⟨he has no ~ in the matter⟩ ⟨their ~ was chiefly to protect their sister's interests⟩ **b :** something that relates or belongs to one **:** BUSINESS, AFFAIR — often used in pl. ⟨let them mind their own ~s⟩ **2 :** matter for consideration **:** OCCUPATION, INTEREST ⟨a problem likely to be a major ~ of the new administration⟩ ⟨describing his ~s with satisfaction⟩ **3 a :** marked interest or regard usu. arising through a personal tie or relationship to the matter under consideration ⟨interest . . . ran . . . all the way from a determination to make war down to no ~ whatsoever —H.S.Canby⟩ **b :** an uneasy state of blended interest, regard, uncertainty and apprehension about a present condition or future development — usu. used without *a* or *the* ⟨an adult who falls on the street is the object of ~ and commiseration —Agnes Repplier⟩ **4 :** an organization or establishment for business or manufacture **:** a firm and its business ⟨a banking ~⟩ **5 :** CONTRIVANCE, GADGET, CONTRAPTION **6** *in Quaker terminology* **:** a strong conviction based on religious insight **syn** see CARE

concernancy *n* -ES [¹*concern* + *-ancy*] *obs* **:** CONCERNMENT

concerned *adj* **1 a :** INTERESTED, SOLICITOUS ⟨greatly ~ not to disappoint a small child's expectations⟩ ⟨we are not ~ to decide which one of the different schools of social theory is correct —John Dewey⟩ **b :** TROUBLED, DISTURBED, BOTHERED, ANXIOUS ⟨a hard man not greatly ~ that his acts lead to misery and indigence for others⟩ ⟨reason . . . to be ~ by the confusions surrounding the old categories of American political thought —August Heckscher⟩ **2 a :** interestedly engaged **:** INVOLVED ⟨a business enterprise in which three men were ~⟩ ⟨too many people are ~ with the bare mechanics of life⟩ ⟨~ with books and music⟩ **b :** culpably involved **:** IMPLICATED ⟨intrigues that important men were ~ in⟩ ⟨everyone ~ in the bribery case has been identified⟩ **3** *dial Eng* **:** INTOXICATED — used esp. in the phrase *concerned in liquor* or *concerned with liquor* — **con·cern·ed·ly** \-nədlē, -li\ *adv* — **con·cerned·ness** \-nədnəs, -n(d)nəs\ *n* -ES

con·cern·ful \-nfəl\ *adj* **:** of concern ⟨an eyesight for ~ reality —Paul Goodman⟩

¹con·cern·ing \-niŋ,-nēŋ\ *prep* [ME, fr. pres. part. of *concernen* to concern] **:** relating to **:** REGARDING, RESPECTING, ABOUT ⟨information ~ drug addiction⟩ ⟨skepticism ~ the effectiveness of controls and subsidies⟩

²concerning \"\ *n* -s [fr. gerund of ¹*concern*] *obs* **:** an affair that concerns one **:** CONCERN

³concerning \"\ *adj* [fr. pres. part. of *concern*] *archaic* **:** giving concern **:** IMPORTANT — **con·cern·ing·ly** *adv, archaic* — **con·cern·ing·ness** *n* -ES *archaic*

con·cern·ment \-nmənt\ *n* -s [*concern* + *-ment*] **1 :** something in which one is concerned or interested **:** CONCERN, BUSINESS ⟨occupied strictly with his own ~s⟩ **2 :** RELATION, BEARING, IMPORTANCE, MOMENT, CONSEQUENCE ⟨a matter of general ~⟩ **3** *archaic* **:** INVOLVEMENT, PARTICIPATION **4 :** special interest **:** SOLICITUDE, ANXIETY

concerns *pres 3d sing of* CONCERN, *pl of* CONCERN

¹con·cert \kən'sərt, -sət,-səit *also* (')kän¦s-; *usu* -d·+V\ *vb* -ED/-ING/-S [MF *concerter*, fr. OIt *concertare*, fr. LL, to collaborate, fr. L, to contend, dispute, debate, fr. *com-* + *certare* to strive, fr. *certus* determined, decided — more at CERTAIN] *vt* **1 :** to plan together **:** settle or adjust by conference, agreement, or consultation ⟨the states involved ~*ed* their differences⟩ **2 :** to make a plan for **:** DEVISE, ARRANGE ⟨representatives . . . met . . . to ~ measures for a united offensive —A.C.Flick⟩ ~ *vi* **:** to act in harmony or conjunction **:** form combined plans — usu. used with *with* ⟨he refused to consult his partners or to ~ with them —*New Republic*⟩

²con·cert \'kän(t)sə(r)t, -n,sərt, -,sət, -,səit, *usu* -d·+V\ *n* -s [F, fr. It *concerto*, fr. *concertare*] **1 a :** agreement in a design or plan **:** union formed by mutual communication of opinions and views **:** accordance in a scheme **b :** a concerted action ⟨the sacrifice was hailed with a ~ of praise⟩ **2 a :** musical accordance or harmony **:** CONCORD **b** *obs* **:** CONCERTO 1 **c :** a group of musicians performing concerted music **d :** a group (as of individuals or nations) acting in harmony **3 a :** a musical performance of some length by several voices or instruments or both — distinguished from *recital* **b :** a public entertainment (as of music or dancing) made up of a number of short compositions or episodes not joined in an integrated whole — compare BALLET, OPERA, VAUDEVILLE — **in concert :** TOGETHER ⟨our enemies working *in concert* could easily cause our downfall⟩ ⟨he acted *in concert* with the others⟩

³concert \"\ *adj* **:** adapted to or capable of performance in concerts ⟨~ hall⟩ ⟨~ pianist⟩

¹con·cer·tante \,kän(t)sə(r)'täntē, ,känchə-, -tän·,tā; ¦kän(t)sə(r)¦tänt\ *also* **con·cer·ta·to** \,kän(t)sə(r)'täd·(,)ō, -nchə-\ *n* -s [*concertante* fr. It, n. & adj., fr. pres. part. of *concertare* to form or perform a concert, fr. *concerto* concert; *concertato* fr. It, n. & adj., fr. past part. of *concertare*] **1 :** a 17th or 18th century musical composition for orchestra with parts for solo instruments or for several solo instruments without orchestra — compare CONCERTO GROSSO **2 :** CONCERTINO 1

²concertante \"\ *also* **concertato** \"\ *adj* [It] **:** displaying or affording opportunity to display brilliancy in a solo part in an instrumental composition ⟨a ~ passage for violin⟩

concert band *n* **:** a band that is made capable of playing symphonic music by the addition of instruments (as the string bass and harp) not adapted to marching — called also *symphony band*

concert border *n* **:** FIRST BORDER

concert dance *n* **:** ballet characterized by seriousness and a minimum of theatrical effects

con·cert·ed \kən'⸗⸗ *also* (')kän¦-\ *adj* **1 a :** mutually contrived or planned **:** agreed on ⟨carefully ~ signals⟩ **b :** performed in unison **:** done together ⟨a ~ sigh that should have been heard in Australia —Bill Alcine⟩ **2 :** arranged in parts for several voices, musical instruments, or dancers (as a trio, string ensemble, or ballet)

con·cert·ed·ly *adv* **:** in concert

concert étude *n* **:** a particularly brilliant instrumental composition evolved from a single technical motive

concertgoer \'⸗(,)⸗,⸗⸗\ *n* -s **:** one that attends concerts esp. habitually

concert grand *n* **:** a grand piano of the largest size and adapted in volume, timbre, and brilliancy of tone to concert use

concerti *pl of* CONCERTO

¹con·cer·ti·na \,kän(t)sə(r)'tēnə\ *n* -s [²*concert* + *-ina*] **1 :** a musical instrument resembling the accordion and differing from it chiefly in being hexagonal in shape, in having finger buttons for keys, and in having melody keys on both ends **2** *or* **concertina wire :** an entanglement of coiled usu. barbed wire that can be pushed together into a compact mass for transporting and extended for use as an obstacle

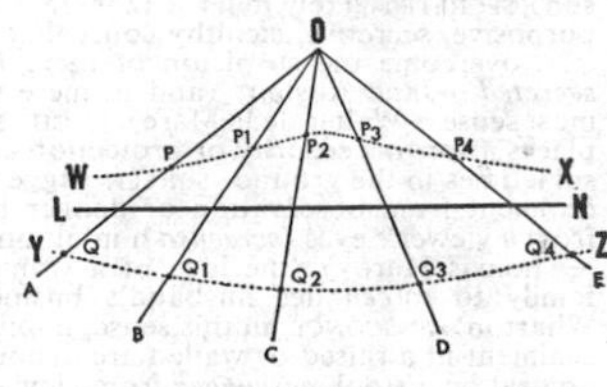
concertina 1

²concertina \"\ *vb* -ED/-ING/-S *vi* **:** to fold up like the bellows of a concertina **:** WRINKLE ⟨her stockings ~*ed* about her ankles⟩ ~ *vt* **:** to cause to fold up like the bellows of a concertina **:** crush together ⟨he dropped to a seat ~*ing* the preacher's hat beneath him⟩

³concertina \"\ *adj* **:** like or suggesting a concertina **:** ACCORDION ⟨a ~ chin⟩; *specif* **:** being or employing a hinged usu. folding mechanism to make enlargement possible ⟨a ~ card table⟩ ⟨a table with ~ extension⟩ ⟨a ~ gate⟩

concerting *pres part of* CONCERT

con·cer·ti·no \,känchər'tē(,)nō, -,cher-\ *n* -s [It, dim. of *concerto* concert, concerto — more at CONCERT] **1 :** the solo instruments in a concerto grosso — distinguished from *ripieno* and *tutti* **2 :** a short concerto typically in free form

con·cert·ize \'kän(t)sə(r),tīz, -ə(r)d·,īz\ *vi* -ED/-ING/-S [²*concert* + *-ize*] **:** to perform in concerts or recitals esp. professionally ⟨only 20 years old, yet he has been *concertizing* . . . for about a half a dozen years —*Consumer Reports*⟩

concertmaster \'⸗⸗ *also* '⸗,⸗ *pronunc at* ²CONCERT +,-\ *or* **con·cert·meis·ter** \+,mīstə(r); *G* kón·'tsert-,mīstər\ *n* [*concertmaster* trans. of G *konzertmeister*; *concertmeister* fr. G *konzertmeister*, fr. *konzert* concert (fr. It *concerto*) + *meister* master, fr. OHG *meistar*, fr. L *magister* — more at CONCERT, MASTER] **:** the leader of the first violins in an orchestra and by custom the subleader of the orchestra

concertmistress *pronunc at* ²CONCERT +,-\ *n* **:** a female concertmaster

con·cer·to \kən'cher|d·(,)ō, -eə|, |(,)tō *sometimes* -chər| *or* -chə| *or* -chəi|\ *n, pl* **concer·ti** \|d·(,)ē, |(,)tē, |d·,i, |,ti\ *or* **concertos** [It — more at CONCERT] **1 :** a composition characteristic of the 16th and 17th centuries for one or more solo voices or instruments with organ or orchestral accompaniment — called also *church concerto* **2 :** CONCERTO GROSSO **3 :** a virtuoso piece for solo instrument or voice and orchestra that is usu. in symphonic form with three contrasting movements, the themes stated alternately by soloist and orchestra, and that is characterized by a bravura solo cadenza

concerto flute *n* **:** FLAUTO TRAVERSO 2

concerto gros·so \⸗¦⸗⸗'grō(,)sō *also* -rō-\ *n, pl* **concerti gros·si** \-(,)sē, -,si\ [It, lit., big concerto] **:** an orchestral composition of the Baroque period with a small group of solo instruments contrasting with the full orchestra

concert overture *n* **:** an orchestral composition that resembles an operatic overture in form or character and is intended for concert performance

concert pitch *n* **1 a :** PHILHARMONIC PITCH **b** INTERNATIONAL PITCH **2 :** an unusually high state or degree of fitness, training, or tension (as in preparation for a concert or athletic contest) ⟨an intensive bit of work done at *concert pitch* —Ngaio Marsh⟩ ⟨a man with energy enough to bring up my plays to *concert pitch* —G.B.Shaw⟩ ⟨it's not easy to keep a filly at *concert pitch* from May to November —G.F.T.Ryall⟩

concerts *pres 3d sing of* CONCERT, *pl of* CONCERT

con·cert·stück *pronunc at* ²CONCERT +,shtik; G kón·'tsert-,shtiek\ *n* -s [G *konzertstück*, fr. *konzert* + *stück* piece, fr. OHG *stucki* — more at STOCK] **:** CONCERTINO 2

con·ces·si·ble \kən'sesəbəl\ *adj* [*concession* + *-ible*] **:** capable of being conceded

con·ces·sion \kən'seshən\ *n* -s [F or L; F *concession*, fr. L *concession-*, *concessio*, fr. *concessus* (past part. of *concedere* to concede) + *-ion-*, *-io* -ion — more at CONCEDE] **1 a :** an act or instance of conceding or yielding esp. to an implied or expressed pressure, claim, demand, or request ⟨at my age I'll make no ~ to style⟩ ⟨the union will seek further ~s before accepting a long-term contract⟩ **b :** the admitting of a point claimed in argument; *esp* **:** the voluntary yielding of a disputable contention **2 :** something granted or conceded **:** a thing yielded **:** ACKNOWLEDGMENT, ADMISSION **:** BOON, GRANT: as **a :** a grant of land or other property esp. from a government in return for services rendered or proposed or for a particular use; *specif* **:** a tract granted to a foreign power in a Chinese treaty port or other trading center and permitted rights of extraterritoriality and local self-government **b :** a usu. exclusive right to undertake and profit by a specified activity ⟨a ~ to build a canal⟩ ⟨conflicting ~s in the oil fields⟩ **c :** a lease of premises or a portion of premises for a particular purpose, esp. for some purpose supplementary to another activity (as the storing of wraps of patrons of a theater) or for providing entertainment); *often* **:** the premises covered by such a concession or the activities for which it is granted ⟨it was reported that some of the ~s at the fair were not honest⟩ **d :** a reduction in price from the current price of a commodity — called also *price concession*

con·ces·sion·aire *also* **con·ces·sion·naire** \kən¦seshə¦na(a)(ə)r, -ne(ə)r,-na(a)ə,-neə\ *n* -s [F *concessionnaire*, fr. *concession* + *-aire* -ary] **:** a person or firm that is the beneficiary of a concession: as **a :** one that owns or operates a stand or booth to sell refreshments or opportunities for entertainment to patrons of a recreational center (as a beach, park, or fair) **b :** one that holds the right to sell a particular type of product or service in a given location **c :** one that provides food service in a factory, school, or other establishment

con·ces·sion·al \kən'seshənᵊl, -shnəl\ *adj* **:** of or relating to concession

¹con·ces·sion·ary \-shə,nerē, -ri\ *adj* [*concession* + *-ary*] **:** of or relating to a concession

²concessionary \"\ *n* -ES [by alter.] **:** CONCESSIONAIRE

con·ces·sion·er \-sh(ə)nə(r)\ *n* -s [by alter.] **:** CONCESSIONAIRE

con·ces·sive \-'sesiv, -esēv *also* -esəv\ *adj* [LL *concessivus*, fr. L *concessus* (past part. of *concedere* to concede) + *-ivus* -ive — more at CONCEDE] **1 :** making for concession **:** being a concession **2 :** denoting concession ⟨the ~ conjunction *though*⟩ ⟨a ~ clause introduced by *although*⟩ — **con·ces·sive·ly** \-səvlē, -li\ *adv*

con·cet·tism \kən'ched·,izəm\ *n* -s [It *concettismo*, fr. *concetto* + *-ismo* -ism] **:** employment of or liking for concetti

con·cet·to \kən'ched·(,)ō\ *n, pl* **concet·ti** \-d·'(,)ē\ [It, fr. LL *conceptus* thought — more at CONCEPT] **:** a conceit esp. in literary style ⟨a work full of orotund phrases and pompous *concetti*⟩

conch \'käŋk, 'känch *also* 'kôŋk— -ŋk *is usual near waters where the conch occurs and hence in sense 3*\ *n, pl* **conchs** \-ŋks\ *or* **conch·es** \-nchəz\ [L *concha*, fr. Gk *konchē*; akin to Skt *śaṅkha* conch] **1 a** (1) **:** any of various large spiral-shelled marine gastropod mollusks; *esp* **:** any member of the genera *Strombus* and *Cassis* of the south Atlantic coast of No. America and the West Indies — see HORSE CONCH, KING CONCH, QUEEN CONCH (2) **:** the shell of a conch often used for cutting cameos and formerly made into horns (3) **:** the animal body of a conch as distinguished from its inanimate shelly parts; *esp* **:** the body as an article of food ⟨fried ~ is a tasty dish⟩ **b :** something resembling a conch (as a shell-shaped ornament) or made from a conch (as a horn) **2 :** the portion of the shell of a tetrabranch cephalopod mollusk that is developed after the embryonic shell **3** *often cap* **a :** a resident native of the Bahamas **b :** any of various persons resident in the Florida keys and nearby parts of the mainland; *esp* **:** one of Bahaman ancestry — often used disparagingly; compare CRACKER 5 **4 :** CONCHA 2b(1) **5 :** BRACKET 3c

conch

conch- *or* **concho-** *comb form* [Gk *konch-*, *koncho-*, fr. *konchē*] **1 :** shell ⟨*conchology*⟩ **2 :** concha ⟨*conchitis*⟩ ⟨*conchotome*⟩

¹con·cha \'käŋkə *also* 'kôŋ-\ *n, pl* **con·chae** \-ŋ,kē, -ŋ,kī\ [in sense 1, fr. It *conca*, fr. LL *concha* apse, fr. L, conch, shell-shaped object or cavity; in sense 2, fr. L] **1 a :** the plain semidome of an apse; *sometimes* **:** APSE **b :** the plain surface of a pendentive **2 :** something suggesting or shaped like a shell: as **a :** a shell-shaped vessel **b** (1) **:** the largest and deepest concavity of the external ear (2) **:** any of the turbinated bones esp. in man — **con·chal** \-ŋkəl\ *adj*

²con·cha \'känchə\ *also* **con·cho** \-n(,)chō\ *n* -s [AmerSp *concha*, fr. Sp, shell, fr. LL *conchula*, dim. of L *concha*] *West* **:** a metal usu. shell-shaped and silver disk that is used as decoration on clothing and harness

con·chate \'käŋ,kāt *also* 'kôŋ-\ *adj* [*conch-* + *-ate*] **1 :** CONCHED **2 :** CONCHIFORM

¹conche \'känch\ *n* -s [F, fr. F dial., trough, fr. OF, shell, fr. L *concha* — more at CONCH] **:** a machine in which chocolate is worked in the preparation of fine grades

²conche \"\ *vt* -ED/-ING/-S **:** to work (chocolate) in a conche

conched \'käŋ(k)t, 'käncht, 'kôŋ(k)t — *see* CONCH\ *adj* [*conch* + *-ed*] **:** having a conch

conch·er \'känchə(r)\ *n* -s [*conche* + *-er*] **:** a tender of a conche

conch hat *n* [*conch* (native of the Bahamas)] **:** a wide-brimmed hat of plaited palmetto leaf worn in the Bahamas

con·chie *also* **con·chy** *or* **con·shy** \'känchē, -chi\ *n, pl* **conchies** [by shortening and alter.] *slang* **:** CONSCIENTIOUS OBJECTOR

conch·if·er·ous \(')käŋ¦kif(ə)rəs, (')kän¦chi-, (')kôŋ¦ki- — *see* CONCH\ *adj* [ISV *conch-* + *-i-* + *-ferous*] **:** producing or having shells

conch·i·form \'käŋkə,fôrm, 'känchə-,'kôŋkə- — *see* CONCH\ *adj* [ISV *conch* + *-iform*] **:** shaped like one half of a bivalve shell **:** shell-shaped

con·chi·o·lin *also* **con·chy·o·lin** \käŋ'kīələn *also* kôŋ-\ *n* -s [*conchiolin* fr. *conch-* + *-i-* + *-ol* + *-in*; *conchyolin* alter. of *conchiolin*] **:** a scleroprotein forming the organic basis of mollusk shells (as mother-of-pearl) — see NACRE 2

con·chit·ic \(')käŋ¦kid·ik *also* (')kôŋ-\ *adj* [Gk *konchitēs* shelly (fr. *konch-* conch- + *-itēs* -ite) + E *-ic*] *of certain rocks* **:** composed of shells **:** containing many shells

¹concho *var of* CONCHA

²con·cho \'kän(,)chō\ *n, pl* **concho** *or* **conchos** *usu cap* [Sp] **1 :** a group of Taracahitian peoples of the state of Chihuahua, Mexico, comprising two major subdivisions, the Chinarra and Chizo, and 29 minor groups **2 :** a member of the Concho peoples

concho- — see CONCH-

con·cho grass \'kän(,)chō-\ *n* [prob. fr. the *Concho* river, Texas] **:** TEXAS MILLET

con·choid \'käŋ,kóid, 'kän,- *also* 'kôŋ,-\ *n* -s [Gk *konchoeidēs*, lit., conchlike, fr. *konch-* conch- + *-oeidēs* -oid] **1 :** a plane curve determined as the collection of pairs of points located on converging rays crossing a fixed line or curve from which each point of the pair is equidistant, measured along a ray **2 :** BULB OF PERCUSSION

conchoid: *AO, BO, CO, DO, EO* rays converging at *O; LN* fixed line; *P*, P^1, P^2, P^3, P^4 points equidistant from *LN; Q*, Q^1, Q^2, Q^3, Q^4 points equidistant from *LN; WX, YZ* branches of conchoid

con·choi·dal \(')⸗¦kóidᵊl\ *adj* [Gk *konchoeidēs* conchoid + E *-al*] **1 :** of, relating to, or having the form or characteristics of a conchoid ⟨a ~ mechanism⟩ **2** *mineralogy* **:** having elevations or depressions shaped somewhat like the inside surface of a bivalve shell — used esp. of a surface produced by fracture — **con·choi·dal·ly** \-dᵊlē\ *adv*

con·cho·log·i·cal \¦käŋkə¦läjəkəl *also* ¦kôŋ-\ *adj* **:** of or relating to conchology — **con·cho·log·i·cal·ly** \-jək(ə)lē\ *adv*

con·chol·o·gist \käŋ'käləjəst *also* kôŋ-\ *n* -s **:** one specializing in conchology

con·chol·o·gize \-,jīz\ *vi* -ED/-ING/-S [*conchology* + *-ize*] **:** to collect and study mollusk shells esp. as a hobby or avocation ⟨*conchologizing* among some new discoveries⟩

con·chol·o·gy \-jē\ *n* -ES [*conch-* + *-logy*] **1 :** the branch of zoology that deals with shells — now usu. distinguished from *malacology* **2 :** a treatise on shells

con·chos·tra·ca \-ŋ'kästrəkə *also* -'kôs-\ *n pl, cap* [NL, fr. *conch-* + *-ostraca*] **:** a small order of freshwater crustaceans (subclass Branchiopoda) entirely enclosed in a bivalve carapace — **con·chos·tra·can** \-rəkən\ *n* -s

conchs *pl of* CONCH

con·chu·cu \kən'chü(,)kü\ *n, pl* **conchucu** *or* **conchucus** *usu cap* [Sp, of AmerInd origin] **1 :** a division of the Chinchaisuyu people of Peru **2 :** a member of the Conchucu people

con·chu·e·la \,känchə'wālə\ *n* -s [MexSp, fr. Sp, small shell, dim. of *concha* shell — more at CONCHA] **:** a flat bright green bug (*Chlorochroa ligata*) that damages wheat, potatoes, and garden crops in the western U. S.

conchy *var of* CONCHIE

con·chyl·i·at·ed \käŋ'kilē,ād·əd, kən-\ *adj* [NL *conchylium* + E *-ate* + *-ed*] *of a dye* **:** derived from mollusks

con·chyl·i·um \-lēəm\ *n, pl* **conchyl·ia** \-ēə\ [NL, fr. L, shellfish, fr. Gk *konchylion* mollusk, shell, fr. *konchē* conch — more at CONCH] **:** the shell of a mollusk

conchyolin *var of* CONCHIOLIN

con·cierge \(')kōⁿ¦syerzh\ *n, pl* **con·cierges** \-zh(əz)\ [F, fr. OF *cumcerges*, fr. (assumed) VL *conservius*, for L *conservus* fellow slave, fr. *com-* + *servus* slave — more at SERVE] **1** *archaic* **:** one in charge of a property **:** a custodian or warden esp. of a castle or prison **2 :** an attendant at the entrance of a building **:** DOORKEEPER; *esp* **:** a resident attendant in a French building who oversees ingress and egress, handles mail, and performs various functions of a janitor or porter ⟨the harassment of a tourist season⟩

con·cier·ge·rie \kōⁿsyerzhərē\ *n* -s [F, fr. *concierge* + *-erie* -ery] **:** the lodging or office of a concierge

con·cil·i·a·ble \kən'silēəbəl, -lyə-\ *adj* [L *conciliare* to bring together + E *-able* — more at CONCILIATE] **:** capable of being conciliated or reconciled

con·cil·i·a·bule \-lē,byül\ *n* -s [F, fr. MF, fr. LL *conciliabulum*, fr. L, place of assembly, fr. *concilium* assembly, council] **:** a clandestine meeting esp. of conspirators or rebels against constituted authority in church or state

con·cil·i·ar \kən'silēər, -ē,är\ *adj* [L *concilium* council + E *-ar* — more at COUNCIL] **1 :** of, relating to, or issued by a council **2 :** of, based on, or relating to conciliarism — **con·cil·i·ar·ly** *adv*

con·cil·i·a·rism \-ēə,rizəm\ *n* -s **:** the theory of church government that places final ecclesiastical authority in representative church councils instead of in a papacy

con·cil·i·a·rist \-,rəst\ *n* -s **:** an advocate of conciliarism ⟨15th century ~s opened the first great modern debate of constitutionalism against absolutism⟩

con·cil·i·ar·i·ty \kən,silē'arəd·ē\ *n* -ES **:** the principle of government found in Eastern Orthodox churches that places final authority in representative councils — compare SOBORNOST

con·cil·i·ate \kən'silē,āt *usu* -ād·+V\ *vb* -ED/-ING/-S [L *conciliatus*, past part. of *conciliare* to bring together, unite, gain, fr. *concilium* assembly, council — more at COUNCIL] *vt* **1 :** to gain (as goodwill or favor) by pleasing acts **2** *obs* **:** ACQUIRE, WIN, GET **3 :** to make compatible **:** cause to be in accord ⟨it is hard to ~ the views of labor and management on this point⟩ **4 :** to win over from a state of hostility or distrust **:** gain the goodwill or favor of **:** MOLLIFY, PROPITIATE, APPEASE ⟨he *conciliated* her mother with shy signs of good blood and breeding⟩ ~ *vi* **:** to become or try to become friendly **:** make friends **syn** see PACIFY

conciliating *adj* **:** CONCILIATORY — **con·cil·i·at·ing·ly** *adv*

con·cil·i·a·tion \kən,silē'āshən\ *n* -s *often attrib* [L *conciliation-, conciliatio*, fr. *conciliatus* + *-ion-, -io* -ion] **1 a :** the act or process of conciliating **:** the effort to establish harmony and goodwill **b :** the intervention in a dispute by an outsider who seeks to achieve agreement between the disputing parties; *specif* **:** the mediation of a labor dispute by a third party, governmental or private, having no power to compel settlement of the dispute but relying only on persuasion and suggestion **2 :** the state of being conciliated **:** the manifesting of goodwill and cooperation ⟨a period of ~ between church and state⟩

con·cil·i·a·tion·ism \-shə,nizəm\ *n* -s **:** belief in or resort to conciliation; *esp* **:** use of a policy of conciliation esp. as contrasted with firmer measures ⟨those favoring open war violently opposed the ~ of their leaders⟩

con·cil·i·a·tion·ist \-sh(ə)nəst\ *n* -s **:** one who advocates conciliation

con·cil·i·a·tive \kən'silē,ād·iv; -lēəd·-,-lyəd·-\ *adj* **:** CONCILIATORY

con·cil·i·a·tor \-ē,ād·ə(r), -ātə-\ *n* -s [L, fr. *conciliatus* + *-or*] **:** one who conciliates **:** PEACEMAKER; *specif* **:** one employed by a labor union to negotiate disputes between the union and management — called also *arbitrator*

con·cil·ia·to·ri·ly \kən¦silyə¦tōrəlē, -lēə-, ÷ -lə-, -tòr-, -li\ *adv* **:** in a conciliatory way

con·cil·ia·to·ri·ness \ᵊ¦ᵊ(ᵊ)ᵊ,tōrēnəs, -,tòr-, -ri-\ *n* -ES **:** the quality or state of being conciliatory

con·cil·ia·to·ry \kən'silyə,tōrē, -lēə-, ÷ -lə-, -tòr-, -ri\ *adj* **:** tending to conciliate **:** PACIFIC, MOLLIFYING, PROPITIATING

con·cil·i·um \kən'silēəm\ *n, pl* **concil·ia** \-ēə\ [L — more at COUNCIL] **:** COUNCIL

¹con·cin·nate \kən'sinət\ *adj* [L *concinnatus*] *of speech or writing* **:** put together with neat propriety **:** of elegant style

²con·cin·nate \'kän(t)sə,nāt\ *vt* -ED/-ING/-S [L *concinnatus*, past part. of *concinnare*, fr. *com-* + *-cinnare* (fr. *cinnus*, a kind of mixed drink)] **:** to place fitly together **:** arrange in good order **:** ADJUST, TRIM

con·cin·ni·ty \kən'sinəd·ē\ *n* -ES [L *concinnitas*, fr. *concinnus* skillfully put together (back-formation fr. *concinnare*) + *-itas* -ity] **1 :** harmony or fitness in the adaptation of parts to a whole or to each other; *often* **:** studied elegance of design or arrangement — used esp. of literary style **2 :** an instance of concinnity

con·cin·nous \-nəs\ *adj* [L *concinnus*] **:** characterized by concinnity **:** NEAT, ELEGANT

concion *n* -s [L *contion-, contio*, fr. *co-* + *vention-, ventio* coming, fr. *ventus* (past part. of *venire* to come) + *-ion-, -io* -ion — more at COME] **1** *obs* **:** ASSEMBLY **2** *obs* **:** a public oration — **concional** *adj, obs*

concionate *vi* -ED/-ING/-S [L *contionatus*, past part. of *contionari*, fr. *contion-, contio* assembly, oration] *obs* **:** HARANGUE, PREACH — **concionatory** *adj, obs*

con·cip·i·ent \kən'sipēənt\ *adj* [L *concipient-, concipiens*, pres. part. of *concipere* to conceive — more at CONCEIVE] **:** CONCEPTIVE, CONCEIVING

con·cise \kən'sīs\ *adj, sometimes* -ER/-EST [L *concisus*, past part. of *concidere* to cut up, fr. *com-* + *-cidere* (fr. *caedere* to cut, hew, strike, kill); akin to MHG *heie* mallet, club, Arm *xait'* to prick] **1 :** marked by brevity in expression or by compact statement without elaboration or superfluous detail **2 :** accomplished in little time **:** brief and curtailed **:** cut short ⟨the effect is a ~ panorama of the city's character —*Amer. Guide Series: Texas*⟩

syn TERSE, SUCCINCT, LACONIC, SUMMARY, PITHY, COMPENDIOUS: CONCISE indicates the cutting out of all superfluities and avoidance of elaboration ⟨Carruthers took a telegram from his pocket . . . It was short and *concise:* "The old man is dead" —A. Conan Doyle⟩ ⟨he [Gladstone] asked whether he should be . . . *concise*, and Peel told him to be long and diffuse —*Times Lit. Supp.*⟩ TERSE may imply finish and pointedness in addition to brevity ⟨as a lecturer his command of *terse* English enabled him to give a maximum of instruction with a minimum of words —J.M.Phalen⟩ ⟨*terse* headlines are another part of the Tribune's campaign to save newsprint —*New Yorker*⟩ SUCCINCT implies extreme compactness and compression ⟨a book must have a title and today it must have a *succinct* title; therefore this book appears as *Richelieu* —Hilaire Belloc⟩ LACONIC indicates shortness to the point of seeming brusque, unconcerned, or mysterious ⟨again he paused longer, and raised his eyebrows still more. "It is sold, sir," was again his *laconic* reply —Bram Stoker⟩ ⟨the *laconic* announcement was made . . . that the sentences of death had been carried out —*Manchester Guardian Weekly*⟩ SUMMARY suggests the treatment of main points with no elaboration or additional explanation; it may apply to treatments and actions done with much promptness or even brusqueness ⟨a presentation as *summary* as is compatible with an adequate statement of the available information —*Internat'l Labor Office Recent Publications*⟩ ⟨a *summary* redress . . . was . . . provided by the crown in a royal proclamation —J.R.Green⟩ ⟨she seemed surprised, and offended . . . and waved us out of the house. *Summary* as the dismissal was, court etiquet no doubt required our compliance —Herman Melville⟩ PITHY suggests a wealth of forcible or telling material briefly presented ⟨a brief, *pithy*, and, as it then appeared to him, unanswerable argument against the immortality of the human soul —Nathaniel Hawthorne⟩ COMPENDIOUS applies to treatments at once full and comprehensive and brief and concise ⟨it would reduce all the feet and combinations of feet to *compendious* and intelligible formulas —R.W.Chapman⟩

con·cise·ly *adv* **:** in a concise manner

con·cise·ness *n* -ES **:** the quality or state of being concise

con·ci·sion \kən'sizhən\ *n* -s [ME *concisioun*, fr. L *concision-, concisio*, fr. *concisus* + *-ion-, -io* -ion] **1** *archaic* **a :** a cutting up or off **:** MUTILATION; *esp* **:** circumcision regarded purely as mutilation **b :** a rending esp. of the church **:** DIVISION, SCHISM **2 :** the quality or state of being concise — used esp. of literary style

con·ci·ta·tion \,kän(t)sə'tāshən\ *n* -s [L *concitation-, concitatio*, fr. *concitatus* (past part. of *concitare* to stir up, rouse, fr. *com-* + *citare* to set in motion) + *-ion-, -io* -ion — more at CITE] **:** the act of stirring up, exciting, or agitating

con·ci·ta·to \,känchə'täd·(,)ō\ *adv (or adj)* [It, lit., stirred up, fr. past part. of *concitare* to stir up, excite, fr. L] **:** in an excited or agitated style — used as a direction in music

concl *abbr* conclusion

con·cla·mant \(')kän¦klāmənt, -lam-\ *adj* [L *conclamant-, conclamans*, pres. part. of *conclamare*] **:** crying out together ⟨the ~ voices of common sense and decency⟩

con·cla·ma·tion \,känklə'māshən, -ŋk-\ *n* -s [L *conclamation-, conclamatio*, fr. *conclamatus* (past part. of *conclamare* to cry out together, fr. *com-* + *clamare* to cry out) + *-ion-, -io* -ion — more at CLAIM] **:** an outcry of many together **:** SHOUT

con·clave \'kän,klāv, *esp Brit sometimes* -äŋ,-\ *n* -s [ME, fr. MF or ML; MF, fr. ML, fr. L, room or apartment that can be locked up, fr. *com-* + *clavis* key — more at CLAVICLE] **1** *obs* **:** a private chamber **:** CLOSET **2 a :** a private meeting **:** a closed or secret assembly; *esp* **:** a meeting of Roman Catholic cardinals secluded continuously in a set of apartments while engaged in choosing a pope **b :** a meeting esp. of a group with shared or specialized interests (as a fraternal society) **:** CONFERENCE, CONVENTION, GATHERING **3 a :** the body of cardinals esp. when considered in respect to their electoral function **b :** any authoritative group exercising wide discretionary powers ⟨secret party ~s that pick the candidates behind the scenes⟩

con·clav·ist \-vəst\ *n* -s [It *conclavista*, fr. *conclave* (fr. ML) + *-ista* -ist] **:** an individual (as an ecclesiastical secretary or a lay servant) who attends a cardinal in a conclave ⟨cardinals who are ill or infirm may have two ~s —Arnaldo Cortesi⟩

con·clud·able *also* **con·clud·ible** \kən'klüdəbəl\ *adj* **:** capable of being inferred or concluded

con·clude \kən'klüd\ *vb* -ED/-ING/-S [ME *concluden*, fr. L *concludere*, fr. *com-* + *-cludere* (fr. *claudere* to shut) — more at CLOSE] *vt* **1 :** to shut up or off **:** ENCLOSE, CONFINE, CONSTRAIN: **a** *archaic* **:** to overcome in argument **:** CONVINCE, CONFUTE **b** *obs* **:** to bar from a course of action **:** PRECLUDE **c** *archaic* **:** to sum up **:** INCLUDE, COMPREHEND **d :** to constrain to a course of action **:** BIND, OBLIGE — now chiefly in legal use **2 :** to reach a final determination or judgment about **:** make a decision about **:** JUDGE, DECIDE — now usu. followed by a clause as object ⟨he *concluded* that he would wait⟩ **3 a :** to bring to an end **:** TERMINATE ⟨they often ~ their meetings with song⟩ ⟨*concluded* his speech with an appeal for unity⟩ **b :** COMPLETE ⟨unable to ~ any sales —*Farmer's Weekly (So. Africa)*⟩ **4 :** to reach an agreement on **:** bring into effect **:** EFFECT ⟨*concluded* an economic agreement⟩ ⟨having *concluded* the bargain they went their separate ways⟩ **5 :** to reach (as an end) by reasoning **:** infer esp. from premises ⟨no one should ~ another's evil deed from surface signs⟩ ~ *vi* **1 :** to come to a decision **:** reach a final judgment or agreement ⟨we *concluded* to wait for fair weather⟩ **2 :** to come to a close ⟨the meeting will probably ~ without any solution of this problem⟩ **:** END **3** *obs* **:** to be conclusive **syn** see CLOSE, INFER

concludent *adj* [L *concludent-, concludens*, pres. part. of *concludere*] *obs* **:** bringing to a close **:** DECISIVE

concluding *adj* **1** *obs* **:** CONCLUSIVE **2 :** FINAL **syn** see LAST

concluding line *n* **:** a line running down the middle of a rope ladder and made fast to each step

con·clud·ing·ly *adv* **:** in a concluding manner

con·clu·sion \kən'klüzhən\ *n* -s [ME *conclusioun*, fr. MF *conclusion*, fr. L *conclusion-, conclusio*, fr. *conclusus* (past part. of *concludere*) + *-ion-, -io* -ion] **1 a :** a reasoned judgment or an expression of one **:** INFERENCE ⟨haphazard thoughts occupy the place of rational ~s —Herbert Spencer⟩ **b** *logic* **:** the necessary consequence of two or more related propositions taken as premises; *esp* **:** the inferred proposition of a syllogism or other form of argument **2** *obs* **:** PURPOSE, AIM **3 :** the last part of anything **:** CLOSE, TERMINATION, END ⟨at the ~ of the contest⟩: as **a :** a final decision or settlement **:** RESULT, OUTCOME ⟨17th century attempts to solve the longitude problem came to no practical ~ —S.F.Mason⟩ **b conclusions** *pl* **:** trial of strength or skill — usu. in the phrase *try conclusions with* **c :** a final summing up (as of a discourse or writing) **d :** the final decision in a law case **e** *Scots law* **:** the final clause of a summons revealing the purpose of an action; *also* **:** the action itself **f :** the final speech of counsel to the court or the jury in a law case **g :** the final part of a pleading in law expressing willingness to offer proof or to submit the case to the court or the jury **4** *obs* **a :** PROPOSITION, PROBLEM, RIDDLE **b :** EXPERIMENT **5 :** ESTOPPEL **6 :** an act or instance of concluding: as **a :** SETTLEMENT **:** arrangement esp. of an armistice **b** *obs* **:** the drawing of an inference **7 :** the main clause of a conditional sentence — contrasted with *condition* **8 :** a pleader's allegation not sufficient in law because the basic facts warranting the statement are not set forth in the pleading — **in conclusion 1 :** FINALLY **2 :** in short

con·clu·sion·al \-zhənᵊl,-zhnəl\ *adj* [ME, fr. *conclusioun* + *-al*] **:** of, relating to, or constituting a conclusion — **con·clu·sion·al·ly** \-ᵊlē, -əlē, -li\ *adv*

conclusion of fact *law* **:** a fact inferred to exist from other facts actually proved by evidence

conclusion of law : the court's statement of the law applicable to a case in view of certain facts found to be true or assumed by the jury to be true **:** the final judgment or decree which the law requires in view of the facts found or the verdict brought in

con·clu·sive \kən'klüs¦iv, ¦ēv *also* -üz¦ *or* ¦əv\ *adj* [LL *conclusivus*, fr. L *conclusus* + *-ivus* -ive] **:** belonging to a close or termination: as **a :** forming an end or termination **b :** putting an end to debate or question esp. by reason of irrefutability **:** involving a conclusion or decision **:** DECISIVE, FINAL ⟨~ evidence⟩ ⟨a ~ presumption⟩

syn DECISIVE, DETERMINATIVE, DEFINITIVE: applied most frequently to evidence or reasoning, CONCLUSIVE means so irrefutable as to end all uncertainty or question ⟨a very persuasive if not a *conclusive* argument —John Marshall⟩ ⟨the wisdom of the new rule was so manifest that it was accepted as a *conclusive* precedent —Frederick Pollock⟩ ⟨the evidence in the two poems which makes it *conclusive* that one is derived from the other —Amy Lowell⟩ Applied to events or influences, DECISIVE indicates that which settles controversy or ends uncertainty ⟨my words had been *decisive*. At least they had put an end to the discussion —Jack London⟩ ⟨he acted that brief period as commander-in-chief, but took no *decisive* steps towards settling the various problems confronting him —Stanley Pargellis⟩ DETERMINATIVE applies to decisions, causes, or influences serving to establish a fixed character or definite goal ⟨an appeal covering similar merchandise is pending . . . which will be *determinative* of this issue —*U.S. Treasury Decisions*⟩ DEFINITIVE, opposed to *tentative* or *provisional*, applies to something final, something obviating further dispute, investigation, or doubt ⟨it is not my purpose to try to offer any *definitive* answers to the questions involved . . . Publishing is now in a very problematical state —J.T.Farrell⟩ ⟨he is ineffably happy over the triumph of his principles and the *definitive* acceptance of his political philosophy —C.G.Bowers⟩

con·clu·sive·ly \¦əvlē, -li\ *adv* **:** in a conclusive manner

con·clu·sive·ness \¦ivnəs, ¦ēv- *also* ¦əv-\ *n* -ES **:** the quality or state of being conclusive

con·coct \kən'käkt, (')kän¦k-\ *vt* -ED/-ING/-S [L *concoctus*, past part. of *concoquere* to boil together, digest, mature, fr. *com-* + *coquere* to cook — more at COOK] **1** *obs* **:** to convert into nourishment by the organs of nutrition **:** DIGEST **2** *obs* **:** to prepare, perfect, or refine chemically by the action of heat **3** *archaic* **:** MATURE ⟨~ fruits⟩ **:** RIPEN ⟨~ a boil⟩ **4 a :** to prepare from crude materials (as food) **:** invent or prepare by combining different ingredients ⟨cleverly ~*ing* delicacies to tempt a flagging appetite⟩ **b :** to put together **:** COMPOSE, DEVISE, FABRICATE — usu. used disparagingly of the agent, the product, or both ⟨continued to ~ and publicize their unsavory views⟩ ⟨they ~*ed* an alibi for the missing man⟩ **syn** see CONTRIVE

con·coct·er *also* **con·coc·tor** \-tə(r)\ *n* -s **:** one that concocts **:** MAKER, FABRICATOR; *also* **:** one that aids in concoction

con·coc·tion \kən'käkshən, kän'k-, 'kän,k-\ *n* -s [L *concoction-, concoctio*, fr. *concoctus* + *-ion-, -io* -ion] **1** *obs* **:** digestion and assimilation of food **2** *obs* **:** a process of ripening or maturation **3 :** something that is concocted (as a food or scheme); *also* **:** something that suggests origin by concoction (as by mingling of diverse elements) **4 a :** the act of preparing (as a made dish or a remedy) by combining different ingredients **b :** an act of composing, fabricating, or making up (as a story or scheme)

con·coc·tive \-ktiv\ *adj* [*concoction* + *-ive*] **:** of or relating to concoction

con·col·or·ous \(')kän¦kələrəs, kən'k-\ *also* **con·col·or·ate** \-rət\ *or* **con·col·or** \'kän,kələ(r)\ *adj* [*concolorous*, fr. *concolor* + E *-ous* or *-ate; concolor* fr. L *concolor*, fr. *com-* + *color*] **1 :** of the same color as a specified article — used esp. to describe one part of an insect by comparison with another ⟨thorax ~ with abdomen⟩ **2 :** of uniform color

con·com·i·tance \kən'kämədən(t)s, kän'k-, -mətən\ *also* -mətᵊn\ *also* **con·com·i·tan·cy** \ ¦sē,¦si\ *n* -s [ML *concomitantia*, fr. L *concomitant-, concomitans* + *-ia* -y] **1 :** a state of accompanying **:** ACCOMPANIMENT; *esp* **:** regular and precise conjunction implying correlative variation of the concomitants **2 :** the doctrine in Roman Catholicism of the existence of both the body and blood of Christ in each element of the Eucharist so that both are received by communicating in one kind only **3 :** an instance of being concomitant **:** a concomitant thing or act ⟨the ~s of a marriage ceremony⟩

¹con·com·i·tant \kən'kämədənt, (')kän¦k-, -mətənt *also* -mətᵊnt\ *adj* [L *concomitant-, concomitans*, pres. part. of *concomitari* to accompany, fr. *com-* + *comitari*, fr. *comit-, comes* companion — more at COUNT] **:** accompanying or attending esp. in a subordinate or incidental way **:** occurring along with or at the same time as and with or without causal relationship ⟨the scholastic belief that man is a child of God and . . . the ~ belief that all men are brothers —Hardin Craig⟩ **syn** see CONTEMPORARY

²concomitant \"\ *n* -s **1 :** something that accompanies or is collaterally connected with another **:** ACCOMPANIMENT ⟨tuberculosis, hookworm, and infant mortality — the pathological ~s of pauperism —Oscar Handlin⟩ **2** *archaic* **:** ASSOCIATE, COMPANION

con·com·i·tant·ly *adv* **:** in a concomitant manner

¹con·cord \'käŋ,kȯrd, -än,-, -ȯ(ə)d\ *n* -s [ME, fr. OF *concorde*, fr. L *concordia*, fr. *concord-, concors* of the same mind, agreeing, fr. *com-* + *cord-, cor* heart — more at HEART] **1 a :** a state of agreement **:** harmony esp. between persons **b :** an agreeable harmonious combination of tones simultaneously heard; *specif* **:** a chord satisfying in harmonic effect and not requiring resolution — contrasted with *discord* **2 :** agreement by stipulation, compact, or covenant **:** TREATY; *esp* **:** one establishing or reestablishing peaceful and amicable relationships between peoples or nations **3 :** AGREEMENT 4

²con·cord \kən'kȯ(ə)rd, -ȯ(ə)d\ *vi* -ED/-ING/-S [ME *concorden*, fr. MF *concorder*, fr. L *concordare*, fr. *concord-, concors*] **:** to act together **:** HARMONIZE, AGREE

³con·cord \'käŋkə(r)d\ *adj, usu cap* [fr. *Concord*, N.H.] **1 :** of or from Concord, the capital of New Hampshire ⟨*Concord* industries⟩ **:** of the kind or style prevalent in Concord **2** *of horse-drawn vehicles* **:** made in a variety of models originated in Concord and used widely throughout the U.S. in the 19th century ⟨*Concord* wagons⟩

⁴concord \"\ *n* -s *usu cap* [by shortening] **:** CONCORD COACH

con·cor·dance \kən'kȯrdᵊn(t)s, kän-, -ȯ(ə)d-\ *n* -s [ME *concordaunce*, fr. MF *concordance*, fr. ML *concordantia*, fr. L *concordant-, concordans* + *-ia* -y] **1 :** an alphabetical verbal index showing the places in the text of a book or in the works of an author where each principal word may be found often with its immediate context; *also* **:** a similar index showing subjects **2 :** CONCORD, AGREEMENT

con·cor·dan·cy \-ᵊnsē, -si\ *n* -ES [ML *concordantia*] **:** AGREEMENT

con·cor·dant \kən'kȯrdᵊnt, (')kän¦k-, -ȯ(ə)d-\ *adj* [ME *concordaunt*, fr. MF *concordant*, fr. L *concordant-, concordans*, pres. part. of *concordare*] **1 :** AGREEING, CORRESPONDENT, HARMONIOUS, CONSONANT ⟨results ~ with the experimental data⟩ ⟨expressed views ~ with his background and training⟩ **2** *geol* **:** manifesting conformity or parallelism in bedding or structure — used of strata **3** *of twins* **:** similar in respect to one or more particular characters — compare DISCORDANT — **con·cor·dant·ly** *adv*

con·cor·dan·tial \¦kän,kȯ(r)¦danchəl, ¦käŋ,-\ *adj* [ML *concordantia* + E *-al*] **:** of or relating to a concordance **:** like a concordance (as in completeness of detail)

con·cor·dat \kən'kȯr,dat, -ȯə¦, ¦,dət, +V *usu* -ad· *or* -əd·\ *n* -s [F, fr. ML *concordatum*, fr. L, neut. of *concordatus*, past part. of *concordare*] **1 a :** a compact between a national government and a religious group establishing terms of agreement concerning matters of mutual interest **b :** a formal agreement between two religious groups establishing the bases of union or common action ⟨a proposed ~ to unite Episcopalian and Presbyterian churches⟩ **2 :** a compact, covenant, or agreement concerning something

con·cor·da·to·ry \kən'kȯrdə,tōrē, kän'-\ *adj* [*concordat* + *-ory*] **:** of, relating to, or established or maintained by means of a concordat

con·cord buggy \'käŋkə(r)d-\ *n, usu cap C* [fr. *Concord*, N.H., where it was first made] **:** a buggy having a body with side-spring suspension

Concord buggy

concord coach \"-\ *n, usu cap 1st C* [fr. *Concord*, N.H., where it was first made] **:** a large closed horse-drawn coach having the body swung on thorough braces, a driver's seat outside in front, and a covered baggage compartment at the rear

con·cor·di·al \(')käŋ¦kȯ(r)dēəl, -än¦-\ *adj* [LL *concordialis*, fr. L *concordia* harmony + *-alis* -al — more at CONCORD] **:** of or belonging to grammatical agreement

concords *pl of* CONCORD, *pres 3d sing of* CONCORD

¹con·corporate \(')kän, kən+\ *adj* [ME *concorporat*, fr. L *concorporatus*, past part. of *concorporare* to unite in one body, fr. *com-* + *corporare* to make into a body — more at CORPORATE] *archaic* **:** united in one body

²con·corporate \(')kän, kən+\ *vb* -ED/-ING/-S [L *concorporatus*] *vt, archaic* **:** to unite (diverse elements) into a single unit **:** make part of a whole ~ *vi, obs* **:** to coalesce into one mass or body

con·cours \kōⁿ'kü(ə)r\ *n, pl* **concours** \-r(z)\ [F, fr. MF, concourse] **:** a public competition **:** CONTEST

con·cours d'e·le·gance \-r,dālā'gäⁿs\ *n* [F *concours d'élégance*, lit., contest of elegance] **:** a show or contest of vehicles or equipages in which the contestants are judged chiefly on excellence of appearance and turnout rather than roadworthiness

con·course \'kän,kōrs, -,kȯrs, -ōəs,-ȯ(ə)s *also* -äŋ,-\ *n* -s [ME *concurs, concourse*, fr. MF & L; MF *concours*, fr. L *concursus*, fr. past part. of *concurrere* to run together — more at CONCUR] **1 :** an act or action of flocking, moving, or flowing together (as of persons or streams) **:** an approaching and merging **2 a :** a meeting produced by voluntary or spontaneous moving and coming together at one place **:** CONFLUENCE, GATHERING, MEETING, CROWD, THRONG **b** *obs* **:** an encounter of hostile forces **c :** CONJUNCTION 5 **3 :** a place or point of meeting: as **a :** an open space where several roads or paths meet **b :** an open space or hall where crowds may gather esp. by chance coming together (as in a large railroad terminal) **4** *law* **a :** the arising of two or more actions that are founded upon the same state of facts and may be pursued simultaneously or consecutively **b** *Scots law* **:** the arising of a criminal and a civil action on the same grounds **5** *archaic* **:** COOPERATION

con·cre·ate \¦känkrē¦āt, ᵊ¦ᵊ¦ᵊ\ *vt* -ED/-ING/-S [LL *concreatus*, past part. of *concreare*, fr. L *com-* + *creare* to create — more at CREATE] *archaic* **:** to create together — **con·cre·a·tion** \,känkrē'āshən\ *n* -s

concredit *vt* -ED/-ING/-S [L *concreditus*, past part. of *concredere*, fr. *com-* + *credere* to entrust, believe — more at CREED] *obs* **:** COMMIT, ENTRUST

con·cremation \(¦)kän+\ *n* -s [LL *concremation-, concrematio*, fr. L *concrematus* (past part. of *concremare* to burn up, fr. *com-* + *cremare* to burn) + *-ion-, -io* -ion — more at CREMATE] **:** BURNING, CREMATION; *specif* **:** SUTTEE

con·cre·ment \'käŋkrəmənt, -änk-\ *n* -s [L *concrementum*, fr. *concrescere*] **:** CONCRETION 3a

con·cresce \kən'kres, (')kän¦k-\ *vi* -ED/-ING/-S [L *concrescere* — more at CONCRETE] **:** to grow together **:** COALESCE

con·cres·cence \-sᵊn(t)s\ *n* -s [L *concrescentia*, fr. *concrescent-, concrescens* (pres. part. of *concrescere*) + *-ia* -y] **1 a :** coalescence esp. of particles **b :** increase by the addition of particles — compare ASSIMILATION, INTUSSUSCEPTION 2 **2** *biol* **:** a union or coalescence of parts originally separate; *specif* **:** convergence and fusion of the lateral lips of the blastopore to form the primordium of an embryo

con·cres·cent \-s°nt\ *adj* [back-formation fr. *concrescence*] **:** exhibiting concrescence **:** grown or growing together ⟨a flower with ~ petals⟩

concreta *pl of* CONCRETUM

[1]**con·crete** \(ˈ)kän¦krēt *sometimes* (ˈ)käŋ¦k- *or* (*except sense 4*) kənˈk-; *in sense 4* ˈ=,= *also* (ˈ)=ˈ=; *usu* -ēd·+V\ *adj* [ME *concret*, fr. L *concretus*, past part. of *concrescere* to grow together, fr. *com-* + *crescere* to grow — more at CRESCENT] **1 :** united in growth: **a** *archaic* **:** compounded of different ingredients **:** COMPOSITE **b :** formed by coalition of separate particles into one mass **:** united in a solid form **2 a :** naming a thing or class of things — opposed to *abstract* ⟨the word *poem* is ~, *poetry* is abstract⟩ **b** *of a unit or number* **:** associated with or applied to particular objects or magnitudes ⟨three men, to give a ~ figure⟩ — opposed to *abstract* **3 a :** characterized by immediate experience of realities whether physical things, sensations, or emotions **:** belonging to or standing for actual things or events **:** not abstract or ideal **:** SPECIFIC, PARTICULAR ⟨a rainbow is ~ color⟩ ⟨they presented ~ proposals for improvement⟩ **b :** REAL, ACTUAL, TANGIBLE ⟨his suspicions had nothing very ~ to go on⟩ ⟨~ proof of the man's guilt⟩ **4 :** relating to or made of concrete

[2]**con·crete** *in sense 1* (ˈ)kän¦k- *sometimes* (ˈ)käŋ¦k- *or* kənˈk-; *in other senses* ˈkän|,k- *also* (ˈ)kän|ˈk- *sometimes* -äŋ|\ *n* -s **1 :** a concrete form or object; *also* **:** something that is concrete — used with *the* **2 :** a compound or mass formed by concretion, spontaneous union, or coalescence of separate particles of matter in one body ⟨a ~ of combustible materials⟩ **3 a :** a hard strong building material made by mixing a cementing material (commonly portland cement) and a mineral aggregate (as washed sand and gravel or broken rock) with sufficient water to cause the cement to set and bind used in the construction of bridges, buildings, dams, pavements, tunnels, and smaller products — compare CINDER CONCRETE, CYCLOPEAN CONCRETE **b :** a surface (as a path or roadway) paved with such artificial stone ⟨since the road was a throughway motorists were asked not to park on the ~⟩ **4 :** crude sugar obtained in compact masses by boiling down cane juice or maple sap **5 :** a waxy essence esp. of flowers prepared by extraction (as with petroleum ether) and removal of the solvent by vacuum distillation and used in perfumery ⟨~ of rose⟩ — compare ABSOLUTE 3 — **in the concrete :** in concrete manifestations, features, or detail **:** in particulars — opposed to *in the abstract*

[3]**con·crete** *in vt sense 3 and vi sense 2* ˈkän|,k- *also* (ˈ)kän|ˈk- *sometimes* -äŋ|; *in other senses* (ˈ)kän|ˈk- *sometimes* (ˈ)käŋ|k- *or* kənˈk-\ *vb* -ED/-ING/-S *vt* **1 a :** to form into a solid mass (as by cooling, evaporation, coagulation, or cementation) **:** SOLIDIFY, CONGEAL **b :** COMBINE, BLEND, FUSE, UNITE ⟨art *concreted* with nature to produce a gracious whole⟩ **2 :** to make actual or real **:** cause to take on the qualities of reality **:** make concrete ⟨the basic *concreting* relation is a symmetrical relation of togetherness —Nelson Goodman⟩ **3 :** to cover with, form of, line with, or set or embed in concrete ~ *vi* **1** *of separate particles* **:** to unite or coalesce into a mass **:** SOLIDIFY, HARDEN, CONGEAL, COAGULATE **2 :** to pour or apply concrete

concrete block *n* **:** a hollow building unit of concrete — called also *cement block*

con·crete·ly *adv* **:** in a concrete manner

concrete masonry *n* **:** block, brick, or tile building units of molded concrete laid by masons in a wall

concrete mixer *n* **:** a machine for mixing the materials of which concrete is made — called also *cement mixer*

concrete nail *n* **:** a nail usu. of hardened steel for use in masonry

con·crete·ness *n* -ES **:** the quality or state of being concrete

concrete paint *n* **:** a paint especially adapted to use on concrete because of its resistance to the free lime in concrete

con·cret·er *or* **con·cre·tor** \-ēd·ə(r), -ētə-\ *n* -s **1 :** one that concretes; *specif* **:** one who builds or works with concrete **2 :** *usu concretor* **:** an apparatus for boiling down crude sugar solutions

concrete saw *n* **:** a saw used to cut grooves in the surface of green concrete pavement slabs to control cracking

concrete universal *n* **1 :** a universal whose connotation is so particularized that it denotes one concrete reality esp. an organized unity as distinguished from a universal that denotes any one of a class — used by Hegelians to contrast terms such as *man, book, church* with those that denote a totality, as *mankind, literature, the church* **2 :** something denoted by a concrete universal

concreting *n* -s **:** the operation involving the mixing, handling, placing, finishing, and curing of concrete

con·cre·tion \kän'krēshən, kən-\ *n* -s [L *concretion-, concretio*, fr. *concretus* (past part. of *concrescere* to grow together) + *-ion-, -io* -ion — more at CONCRETE] **1 a :** the act or process of making or becoming solid, substantial, or real ⟨unity must be achieved in defiance of the unique and particularistic forces of historical ~ —Reinhold Niebuhr⟩ ⟨when it falls back upon the accepted ~ of traditional knowledge —G.K.Anderson⟩ **b :** the action of growing together or being formed into a whole ⟨the ~ of ideas into a working hypothesis⟩ **2 :** the state of being concrete or concreted ⟨the ~ of the mass increases through the years⟩ **3 :** something that is or is made concrete ⟨the language of an art is a ~ of its symbols —*Dance Observer*⟩ **:** a concrete mass **:** a solid body formed by concreting particles: as **a :** a hard usu. inorganic mass (as a bezoar or tophus) formed in a natural body cavity or in the tissues **b :** a mass of mineral matter that is found generally in rock of a composition different from its own and that is produced by deposition from aqueous solution in the rock

con·cre·tion·ary \-shə,nerē\ *adj* **:** relating to or formed by concretion or aggregation **:** producing or containing concretions

con·cret·ism \(ˈ)kän¦krēd·,izəm, -ē,tiz- *sometimes* -äŋ¦k- *or* kənˈk-\ *n* -s [ˈ*concrete* + *-ism*] **:** the representation of abstract things as concrete

concretive *adj* [³*concrete* + *-ive*] *obs* **:** promoting or tending toward concretion

con·cret·i·za·tion \(,)kän,krēd·ə'zāshən *sometimes* -äŋ,k- *or* kən,k-\ *n* -s **:** the act of concretizing or the state of being concrete ⟨~ of ideas⟩

con·cret·ize \(ˈ)kän¦krēd·,īz *sometimes* -äŋ¦k- *or* kənˈk-\ *vb* -ED/-ING/-S [ˈ*concrete* + *-ize*] *vt* **:** to make concrete, specific, or definite ⟨an agent *concretizing* abstractions—Alexis Carrel⟩ ~ *vi* **:** to become concrete ⟨the mental representation . . . ~*s* externally —Heinrich Zimmer⟩

con·cre·tum \kän'krēd·əm *sometimes* -äŋ'- *or* kən'-\ *n, pl* **concre·ta** \-d·ə\ [NL, fr. neut. of L *concretus* concrete — more at CONCRETE] **:** something that is concrete, particular, or directly given — contrasted with *abstractum*

con·cu·bi·nage \kän'kyübənij, kən-\ *n* -s [ME, fr. MF, fr. *concubine* + *-age*] **1 a :** cohabitation of persons not legally married; *esp* **:** a continued association between a man and a woman for such purpose, being under certain primitive systems a socially acceptable relation the offspring of which are neither bastards nor heirs of the male partner **b** *Roman law* **:** the permanent cohabitation of a man and woman that was not recognized in addition to a formal marriage and that was commonly considered an inferior form of marriage the offspring of which were entitled to support but did not come under the potestas of the father but might under the laws of Justinian be legitimated by a subsequent formal marriage **2 :** the state of being or having a concubine **3 :** a state of mental subserviency or bondage

concubinal *adj* [LL *concubinalis*, fr. L *concubina* + *-alis* -al] *obs* **:** CONCUBINARY

[1]**con·cu·bi·nary** \kän'kyübə,nerē, kən-\ *also* **con·cu·bi·nar·i·an** \¦kän,kyübə¦na(a)rēən, kən¦k-\ *adj* [*concubinary* fr. ML *concubinarius*, fr. L *concubina* concubine + *-arius* -ary; *concubinarian* fr. *concubinary* + *-ian*] **:** relating to, living in, or sprung from concubinage

[2]**concubinary** \"\ *n* -ES **:** one living in concubinage

con·cu·bi·nate \kän'kyübənət, kən-, -,nāt\ *n* -s [L *concubinatus*, fr. *concubina* concubine + *-atus* -ate] **:** CONCUBINAGE

[1]**con·cu·bine** \ˈkäŋkyə,bīn, -ānk-\ *n* -s [ME, fr. OF, fr. L *concubina*, fr. *com-* + *-cubina* (fr. *cubare* to lie down) — more at HIP] **1 a :** a woman living in a socially recognized state of concubinage ⟨Hagar and Keturah were the ~*s* of Abraham⟩ **b :** a woman who cohabits with a man without being his wife **:** MISTRESS **2 :** a man living in a state of concubinage to another man or a woman

[2]**concubine** \"\ *vt* -ED/-ING/-S **1** *obs* **:** to make a concubine of **2 :** to provide with a concubine

conculcate *vt* -ED/-ING/-S [L *conculcatus*, past part. of *conculcare*, fr. *com-* + *calcare* to trample, fr. *calc-, calx* heel — more at CALK] *obs* **:** to tread or trample underfoot

con·cu·pis·cence \kän'kyüpəsən(t)s, kən'k- *also* ,känkyüˈpis°n-\ *n* -s [ME, fr. MF, fr. LL *concupiscentia*, fr. L *concupiscent-, concupiscens* + *-ia* -y] **:** strong or ardent desire: **a :** a longing of the soul for what will give it delight or for what is agreeable esp. to the senses — used chiefly by Scholastic philosophers **b :** sexual desire **:** LUST **syn** see DESIRE

con·cu·pis·cent \-nt\ *adj* [L *concupiscent-, concupiscens*, pres. part. of *concupiscere* to desire ardently, fr. *com-* + *-cupiscere* (fr. *cupere* to desire) — more at COVET] **:** LUSTFUL

con·cu·pis·cent·ly *adv* **:** with concupiscence

con·cu·pis·ci·ble \-səbəl\ *adj* [ME, fr. MF or LL; MF, fr. LL *concupiscibilis*, fr. L *concupiscere* + *-ibilis* -ible] **1 :** motivated by a desire for good under the aspect of the agreeable esp. the sensuously agreeable — used chiefly by Scholastic philosophers of the appetite and the passions; opposed to *irascible* **2 :** moved by concupiscence ⟨his ~ intemperate lust —Shak.⟩ **3** *archaic* **:** that merits desire **:** suitable to be longed for or lusted after **:** greatly desirable

con·cur \kən'kər, kän-, +V -ər-; -ˈkə̄, +V -ˈkər- *also* -ˈkə̄r\ *vi* **concurred**; **concurred**; **concurring**; **concurs** [ME *concurren*, fr. L *concurrere*, fr. *com-* + *currere* to run — more at CURRENT] **1** *obs* **:** to come or flow together esp. with force or violence **:** reach a common point or situation **:** CONVERGE, MEET **2 :** to happen together **:** COINCIDE ⟨leisure and opportunity do not always ~⟩ **3 :** to act together to a common end or to produce a single effect ⟨rival political parties ~ in this action⟩ ⟨physical and moral causes had *concurred* to prevent civilization from spreading to that region —T.B.Macaulay⟩ **4** *archaic* **:** to correspond esp. in quality or character ⟨this ~*s* directly with the letter —Shak.⟩ **5 a :** APPROVE — usu. followed by *in* ⟨do you ~ in his statement —J.G.Cozzens⟩ **b :** AGREE ⟨~ with an opinion⟩ **6 :** to join with other claimants in asserting claim against the estate of an insolvent **7 :** to fall on successive days so that celebration of one begins before that of the other ends — used esp. of Christian festivals; compare OCCUR **syn** see AGREE, UNITE

con·cur·rence \kən'kər·ən(t)s, kän'k-, -ˈkə·rə- *also* ˈkän,k-\ *also* **con·cur·ren·cy** \-ənsē, -si\ *n, pl* **concurrences** *also* **concurrencies** [ML *concurrentia*, fr. L *concurrent-, concurrens* + *-ia* -y] **1 a :** agreement or union in action **:** combination of power or influence **:** COOPERATION ⟨~ in doing good⟩ **b :** a meeting of minds **:** agreement in opinion **:** union in design; *also* **:** CONSENT **2 :** competition or rivalry **3 :** the act of concurring **:** a meeting or coming together **:** UNION, CONJUNCTION, COINCIDENCE, CONCOURSE **4** *law* **:** a coincidence of equal powers ⟨a ~ of jurisdiction in two different courts⟩ **5 :** the concurring of Christian festivals

[1]**con·cur·rent** \kən'kər·ənt, (ˈ)kän¦k-, -kə·rə-\ *adj* [ME *concurrant*, fr. MF & L; MF *concurrent*, fr. L *concurrent-, concurrens*, pres. part. of *concurrere*] **1 a :** converging, meeting, intersecting, running together at a point ⟨in both heads the brow ridges are absent, and the eyebrows ~ —C.S.Coon⟩; *specif, math* **:** meeting in a point **b :** running parallel ⟨~ lines of force⟩ **2 :** occurring, arising, or operating at the same time often in relationship, conjunction, association, or cooperation ⟨the power of taxation in the general and state governments is acknowledged to be ~ —John Marshall⟩ ⟨the Germans launched a well-prepared full-scale invasion of southern Norway with the ~ occupation of Trondheim and Narvik —*Times Lit. Supp.*⟩ **3 a :** acting in conjunction **:** marked by accord, agreement, harmony, or similarity in effect or tendency ⟨the ~ testimony of all visitors to the spot⟩ **b :** *of insurance policies* **:** insuring the same property to the same extent or under identical clauses **4** *law* **:** joint and equal in authority **:** taking cognizance of or having authority over the same subject matters **:** operating on the same objects ⟨~ jurisdiction of courts⟩; *also* **:** operating simultaneously ⟨sentenced to serve three ~ life terms⟩ **syn** see CONTEMPORARY

[2]**concurrent** \"\ *n* -s **1 :** one that concurs **:** a joint or contributory cause ⟨to all affairs of importance there are three necessary ~*s* . . . time, industry, and faculties —Henry More⟩ **2** *archaic* **:** RIVAL, OPPONENT

con·cur·rent·ly *adv* **:** in a concurrent manner

concurrent majority *n* **:** a political majority created out of divergent interest groups and temporarily united by general agreement esp. in protecting a minority right

concurrent power *n* **:** a political power exercised independently in the same field of legislation by both federal and state governments

concurrent resolution *n* **:** a resolution passed by both branches of a legislative body; *esp* **:** such a resolution passed by the U.S. Congress expressing the general attitude or intention of Congress but not having the force of law or requiring the signature of the president — compare JOINT RESOLUTION

concurring *pres part of* CONCUR

con·cur·ring·ly *adv* **:** in a concurring manner

concurs *pres 3d sing of* CONCUR

con·cur·sion \kən'kərzhən, kən'-, -rshən\ *n* -s [L *concursion-, concursio*, fr. *concursus* (past part. of *concurrere* to run together) + *-ion-, -io* -ion — more at CONCUR] **:** the act of running together **:** CONCOURSE

con·cur·so \kən'kər(,)sō, kän'-, -ˈkůr-\ *n* -s [Sp, fr. L *concursus* running together, concourse] *civil law* **:** a proceeding by which all creditors may equally establish their respective rights in a single fund

con·cur·sus \-ˈkərsəs\ *n, pl* **concursus** [ML, fr. L, concourse — more at CONCOURSE] *Christian relig* **:** the influx of divine causation upon secondary causes; *esp* **:** the doctrine that before the fall man was preserved from sin by the aid of God

con·cuss \kən'kəs\ *vt* -ED/-ING/-ES [L *concussus*, past part. of *concutere*] **1 :** SHAKE, AGITATE, JAR; *often* **:** to affect with concussion — usu. used as a participle ⟨suffered a ~*ing* blow⟩ ⟨unconscious Charlie who was clearly ~*ed* —C.S.Forester⟩ **2 :** to force or influence by intimidation **:** COERCE

con·cus·sion \kən'kəshən\ *n* -s [MF or L; MF, fr. L *concussion-, concussio*, fr. *concussus* (past part. of *concutere* to shake violently, fr. *com-* + *-cutere*, fr. *quatere* to shake) + *-ion-, -io* -ion — more at QUASH] **1 a :** JOLTING, SHAKING, AGITATING **b :** a smart or hard knock, blow, or collision; *also* **:** the shock of such a blow **:** a stunning, damaging, or shattering effect from such a blow ⟨wood, which responds to ~ with living vibration —Willa Cather⟩ ⟨it is the constant ~ of the cream in the churn which causes the butterfat to gather —*Westralian Farmers Co-op. Gazette*⟩ **2** *civil law, obs* **:** a forcing by threats **3 :** a jarring injury of the brain resulting in disturbance of cerebral function and sometimes marked by permanent damage; *also* **:** the condition of having been so injured **4 :** an inflammatory condition of the feet of horses caused by repeated violent contacts with hard roads **syn** see IMPACT

concussion bellows *n* **:** a small spring-controlled auxiliary bellows for an organ for compensating slight variations in wind pressure

concussion grenade *n* **:** a grenade that relies for its effect on the blast of its detonation rather than the fragmentation of its case and is often designed to stun rather than kill

con·cus·sive \kən'kəsiv\ *adj* [*concussion* + *-ive*] **:** having the power of or being by nature shaking, agitating, or jarring

con·cyclic \(ˈ)kän, kən+\ *adj* [*con-* + *cyclic*] **1 :** lying on one and the same circle — used of a system of points **2 :** cut in circles by the same parallel planes — used of certain systems of quadrics — **con·cyclically** \"\ *adv*

cond \ˈkänd\ *or* **cund** \ˈkənd\ *vt* -ED/-ING/-S [ME *conden* to conduct, alter. of *condien*, fr. MF *conduire*, fr. L *conducere* — more at CONDUCE] **:** CONN

cond *abbr* **1** condensed; condenser **2** condition; conditional **3** conduct; conducted; conductor

con·da·lia \kän'dālyə\ *n, cap* [NL, fr. Antonio *Condal*, 18th cent. Span. explorer + NL *-ia*] **:** a genus of spiny tropical American shrubs or trees (family Rhamnaceae) with small alternate leathery mostly 3-ribbed leaves and small apetalous flowers in sessile umbels

con·demn \kən'dem\ *vt* -ED/-ING/-S [ME *condempnen*, fr. OF *condemner, condempner*, fr. L *condemnare*, fr. *com-* + *-demnare* (fr. *damnare* to condemn) — more at DAMN] **1 :** to pronounce as ill-advised, reprehensible, wrong, or evil typically after definitive judgment and without reservation or mitigation ⟨no conceivable human action which custom has not at one time justified and at another ~*ed* —J.W.Krutch⟩ ⟨~ poetry equally with sex as something at best flippant and at worst immoral —C.D.Lewis⟩ **2 :** to declare the guilt of **:** make manifest the faults of **:** attest to the guilt of ⟨his words ~ him⟩ **3 a :** to pronounce a judicial sentence against **:** sentence to punishment or to suffering or loss **:** DOOM — often used with *to* ⟨driven out from bliss, ~*ed* in this abhorred deep to utter woe —John Milton⟩ **b :** to force, compel, or limit to an action or state ⟨the logic of his being a scientist ~*s* him to abstraction⟩ **4 :** to consign to perdition **:** DAMN — often used imperatively as a mild oath **5** *archaic* **:** to pronounce or find guilty **:** CONVICT — used with *of* ⟨till forging Nature be *condemn'd* of treason —Shak.⟩ **6 :** to adjudge or pronounce to be unfit for use or service **:** adjudge or pronounce to be forfeited ⟨jurisdiction to ~ the ship and her cargo⟩ **7 :** to block up (as a door) **:** close permanently **8 :** to pronounce to be taken for public use under the right of eminent domain **syn** see CRITICIZE

con·demna·ble \-m(n)əbəl\ *adj* **:** liable to be condemned **:** REPREHENSIBLE, BLAMABLE — **con·demna·bly** \-blē, -li\ *adv*

con·dem·na·tion \,kän,dem'nāshən, -,dam-\ *n* -s [ME *condempnacioun*, fr. L *condemnation-, condemnatio*, fr. *condemnatus* (past part. of *condemnare* to condemn) + *-ion-, -io* -ion] **1 :** the act of pronouncing to be wrong or morally culpable **:** CENSURE, BLAME, REPROBATION ⟨the Quakers, in their uncompromising ~ of war —W.R.Inge⟩ **2 :** the act of judicially condemning (as land for public uses) or adjudging unfit for use or forfeited (as a food product) **3 :** the state of being condemned ⟨the hopeless hour of ~ —Washington Irving⟩ **4 :** the ground or reason of condemning ⟨his conduct was sufficient ~⟩ **5** *Roman law* **:** one of the four principal parts of a formula by a praetor to a judex giving him authority to determine the facts of a lawsuit and specific instructions as to what disposition to make of the case if either the plaintiff's claims or the defendant's defenses were found to be true

con·dem·na·to·ry \kən'demnə,tōrē, -tȯrē, -ri\ *adj* [*condemnation* + *-ory*] **:** containing or imposing condemnation or censure **:** CONDEMNING ⟨a ~ sentence⟩ ⟨a ~ decree⟩

condemned *adj* **1 :** pronounced to be wrong, guilty, worthless, or forfeited **:** sentenced to punishment, destruction, or confiscation **2 :** used for condemned persons or things ⟨the ~ cell⟩

con·demn·er *or* **con·demn·or** \kən'dəmə(r)\ *n* -s **:** one that condemns

condemning *adj* **:** CONDEMNATORY — **con·demn·ing·ly** *adv*

con·dens·able *also* **con·dens·ible** \kən'den(t)səbəl\ *adj* **:** capable of being condensed

con·den·sa·ry \-s(ə)rē, -ri\ *n* -ES [by alter.] **:** CONDENSERY

con·den·sate \kən'den,sāt; ˈkändən-, -,den-\ *n* -s [L *condensatus*, past part.] **:** a product of condensation; *esp* **:** a liquid obtained by condensation of a gas or vapor ⟨steam ~⟩

con·den·sa·tion \,kän,den'sāshən, -,dən-\ *n* -s [LL *condensation-, condensatio*, fr. L *condensatus* (past part. of *condensare*) + *-ion-, -io* -ion — more at CONDENSE] **1 a :** the act or process of condensing **b :** the state of being condensed or compressed **c :** a product of condensing **:** a condensed mass **2 a :** reduction of written or spoken expression to more compact form ⟨a prolix lecture greatly in need of ~⟩ **b :** conciseness or compactness of expression ⟨a literary style marked by great ~⟩ **c :** abridgment and usu. compression of a literary work ⟨a staff employed in the ~ of magazine articles⟩ **d :** the work produced by such condensation ⟨a ~ of a popular novel⟩ **3 :** a chemical reaction involving union between atoms (as of carbon in organic compounds) in the same or different molecules often with elimination of a simple molecule (as of water, alcohol, ammonia, or hydrogen chloride) to form a new compound of greater complexity and frequently greater molecular weight ⟨~ of oxygen to ozone⟩ ⟨~ of acetone with benzaldehyde⟩ — compare POLYMERIZATION **4 a :** transition of a substance from the vapor to the liquid phase (as steam to water) **b :** a state or region of maximum pressure and density in a medium traversed by compression waves (as sound waves) — compare RAREFACTION **5** *psychol* **:** representation of several apparently discrete ideas by a single symbol esp. in dreams

con·den·sa·tion·al \¦=(,)=¦=shən°l, -shnəl\ *adj* **:** of or relating to condensation ⟨~ energy⟩

condensation nucleus *n* **:** a small particle (as of dust) upon which water vapor condenses in the atmosphere

condensation polymerization *n* **:** polymerization in which a single molecule is eliminated — distinguished from *addition polymerization*

condensation pump *n* **:** DIFFUSION PUMP

condensation trail *n* **:** CONTRAIL

con·den·sa·tive \kən'den(t)səd·iv\ *adj* [*condensation* + *-ive*] **:** exhibiting, inducing, or tending to condensation

[1]**con·dense** \kən'den(t)s\ *vb* -ED/-ING/-S [ME *condensen*, fr. MF *condenser*, fr. L *condensare*, fr. *com-* + *densare* to make thick or dense, fr. *densus* thick, dense — more at DENSE] *vt* **1 a :** to make more dense or compact **:** compress or concentrate into a smaller compass or volume ⟨the Senate *condensed* the five-year plan into three years —F.L. Paxson⟩ **b :** to reduce (sentences, paragraphs, or larger literary units) to compact form **:** ABRIDGE, COMPRESS ⟨~ a literary work⟩ **2 :** to subject (as atoms) to condensation ~ *vi* **1 a :** to become denser, more compact, or more intense **:** CONTRACT ⟨his anger did not evaporate in words but *condensed* and sank deeper —George Meredith⟩ **b :** to reduce what one says or writes to a concise form **2** *of a chemical substance* **:** to undergo condensation **syn** see CONTRACT

[2]**condense** *adj* [L *condensus*, back-formation fr. *condensare*] *obs* **:** CONDENSED, DENSE

condensed *adj* **1 :** reduced to a dense or denser form; *specif* **:** reduced from gaseous to liquid state **2 a :** concentrated esp. by evaporation or distillation **:** THICKENED, COMPACT **b :** CURT 1a **3** *of a letter or typeface* **:** having a face that is narrower than that of a typeface not so characterized — often used postpositively ⟨Futura Medium ~⟩ ⟨News Gothic Extra ~⟩; compare EXPANDED, EXTENDED

con·densed·ly \-en(t)sədlē, -en(t)s(t)lē\ *adv* **:** in a condensed manner

condensed milk *n* **:** evaporated milk with sugar added

con·densed·ness \-en(t)sədnəs, -en(t)s(t)nəs\ *n* -ES **:** the quality or state of being condensed

condensed system *n* **:** a physical or chemical system in which there is no gaseous phase

con·dens·er \-sə(r)\ *n* -s **1 :** a person that condenses: as **a :** one that prepares short versions of literary material ⟨a ~ who prepared juvenile versions of many classic tales⟩ **b :** an operator of a condensing machine or device **2 :** a machine, instrument, or device that condenses: as **a :** COMPRESSOR b **b :** CAPACITOR **c :** a lens or mirror usu. of short focal length used to concentrate light upon an object **d :** a device that doffs the web from the carding machine and separates and condenses it into slivers or rovings **e :** an apparatus in which steam or water vapor is condensed to water esp. for the purpose of reducing the back pressure in a steam engine or steam turbine, which renders it possible to obtain a greater amount of useful work per pound of steam used **f (1) :** any of various pieces of apparatus for condensing gases or vapors to a liquid or solid state (as a tube surrounded by cold water in a still) — see STILL illustration **(2) :** a body that accepts heat rejected (as in a refrigerating system or a heat engine)

condenser antenna *n* **:** an antenna that consists of a lower conductor constituting a ground or a counterpoise and an upper conductor forming an aerial

condenser microphone *n* **:** a microphone in which the sound waves cause a variation in capacitance, the vibrating diaphragm acting as one plate of a condenser

condenser paper *n* **:** a very thin paper free from electrically conducting particles that is used as an insulator in electrical condensers

con·den·sery \-s(ə)rē, -ri\ *n* -ES [ˈ*condense* + *-ery*] **:** a plant where milk is concentrated by evaporating some of its water

condensible *var of* CONDENSABLE
condensing engine *n* **:** a steam engine in which the steam after exhausting from the cylinder is condensed in a separate condenser
condensing lens *n* **:** CONDENSER 2 c
con·den·sive load \kən'den(t)siv-\ *n* **:** a reactive load in which the current leads the voltage — called also *leading load*
con·de·scend \¦kändə¦send, -dē¦-\ *vb* -ED/-ING/-S [ME *condescenden*, fr. MF *condescendre*, fr. LL *condescendere*, fr. L *com-* + *descendere* to descend — more at DESCEND] *vi* **1** *obs* **:** to go or come down **:** DESCEND **2 :** to stoop or bend to action or speech less formal or dignified than is customary in one's social rank or importance **:** come down to the level of one socially inferior **:** UNBEND ⟨why, if he so dislikes and despises these people, does he ~ to mix with them —F.A. Swinnerton⟩ **3 :** to assume an air of superiority (as to one inferior or less fortunate) **:** act patronizingly ⟨well-fed tourists on their ~*ing* way through less happy lands⟩ — often used in irony ⟨if you will ~ to talk to a simple girl in intelligible terms —T.L.Peacock⟩ **4** *obs* **:** ACQUIESCE, CONSENT **5** *now chiefly Scot* **:** to make a settlement or specification — usu. used with *on* or *upon* ⟨the declaration was made to ~ upon particulars⟩ **~** *vt*, *obs* **:** to agree upon **:** settle upon **:** CONCEDE
con·de·scend·ence \,==ˈ=dən(t)s\ *n* -S [F *condescendance*, fr. *condescendant*, pres. part. of *condescendre*] **1 :** CONDESCENSION, COMPLIANCE, CONCESSION **2** *Scots law* **:** the pleading of the pursuer in a criminal action in which the facts material to the action are set forth
condescendency *n* -ES [modif. of F *condescendance* + E *-y*] *obs* **:** CONDESCENSION
con·de·scend·ent \-dənt\ *n* -S **:** one that condescends
condescending *adj* **:** showing or prompted by condescension
condescendingly *adv* **:** in a condescending manner
con·de·scend·ing·ness *n* -ES **:** CONDESCENSION
con·de·scen·sion \,kändə'senchən, -dē'-\ *n* -S [LL *condescension-*, *condescensio*, fr. *condescensus* (past part. of *condescendere*) + L *-ion-*, *-io* -ion — more at CONDESCEND] **1 :** an act or instance of condescending: **a :** voluntary descent from one's rank or dignity in relations with an inferior **:** affability or informality toward inferiors **b :** disdain veiled by obvious indulgence or patience **2** *obs* **:** CONCESSION, ACQUIESCENCE
con·dic·tio \kən'dikshē,ō, -ktē,ō\ *n, pl* **condicti·o·nes** \kən,dikshē'ō(,)nēz, -ktē'ō,nās\ [L, fr. *condictus* (past part. of *condicere* to make a formal claim, fr. *com-* + *dicere* to say) + *-io* -ion — more at DICTION] *Roman law* **:** a formal claim for a thing **:** an action against a person orig. for a certain sum of money but later also for specific things and still later also for damages of uncertain extent; *also, under Justinian* **:** any claim for restitution or to prevent unjust enrichment
condictio ex le·ge \-ō,ek'slē,jē, -lā,gā\ *n* [LL, lit., formal claim according to law] *Roman law* **:** an action to enforce a statutory right or duty for which no specific remedy was provided
condictio fur·ti·va \-,ō,fər'tīvə, -fůr'tēvə\ *n* [NL, fr. L *condictio rei furtivae* formal claim for a stolen thing] *Roman law* **:** an action in quasi contract for the recovery of a specific stolen thing from the thief or his heirs or recovery of its value if it is not available — called also *condictio ex causa furtiva, condictio rei furtivae*
condictio in·de·bi·ti \-ōin'debə,tī, -,tē\ *n* [L, lit., formal claim for something not owed] *Roman law* **:** an action in quasi contract to recover money paid under a mistake usu. of fact rather than law
con·dic·tion \kən'dikshən\ *n* -S [L *condiction-*, *condictio*] **:** CONDICTIO — **con·dic·tious** \-shəs\ *adj*
condictio tri·ti·ca·ria \-,trid·ə'ka(a)rēə, -kär-\ *n* [NL, fr. LL *condictio triticiaria* formal claim relating to wheat] *Roman law* **:** an action for recovery of the same quality and quantity of fungible property (as wheat) previously loaned by plaintiff to defendant
con·did·dle \kən'did°l\ *vt* -ED/-ING/-S [prob. fr. *com-* + *diddle*] *dial Brit* **:** to make away with secretly **:** STEAL, WASTE
con·dign \kən'dīn, (')kän¦d-\ *adj* [ME *condigne*, fr MF, fr. L *condignus* very worthy, fr. *com-* + *dignus* worthy — more at DECENT] **1** *obs* **:** of equal worth or dignity **b :** WORTHY **2 :** entirely in accordance with what is deserved or merited **:** neither exceeding nor falling below one's deserts — used only of punishments since the end of the 17th century ⟨when an adequate system for control of atomic energy . . . has been agreed upon . . . and ~ punishments set up for violations of the rules —B.M.Baruch⟩ **syn** see DUE
con·dig·ni·ty \kən'dignəd·ē, kän-\ *n* -ES [ML *condignitas*, fr. L *condignus* very worthy + *-itas* -ity] **1** *obs* **:** MERIT, WORTHINESS **2 :** merit described in scholastic theology as earned in distinction from that which is given **:** merit acquired by works performed in a state of grace — distinguished from *congruity*
con·dign·ly *adv* [ME *condignely*, fr. *condigne* + *-ly*] **:** in a condign manner **:** APPROPRIATELY, FITTINGLY — usu. applied to the action of punishing or meting out retribution ⟨~ sentenced to 10 years in jail⟩
con·di·ment \'kändəmənt\ *n* -S [ME, fr. MF, fr. L *condimentum*, fr. *condire* to pickle, season + *-mentum* -ment — more at CONDITE] **:** something usu. pungent, acid, salty, or spicy added to or served with food to enhance its flavor or to give added flavor **:** SEASONING: **a :** an appetizing and usu. pungent substance of natural origin (as pepper, vinegar, or mustard) **b :** any of various complex compositions having similar qualities (as curry or chili powder, pickles, or catsup) — **con·di·men·tal** \¦kändə¦ment°l\ *adj*
condiment set *n* **:** a matched group of containers usu. with tray or rack, including containers for pepper, salt, and mustard and often stoppered cruets for oil and vinegar
con·disciple \¦kän+\ *n* -S [L *condiscipulus*, fr. *com-* + *discipulus* disciple — more at DISCIPLE] **:** a fellow disciple or student **:** SCHOOLFELLOW
condite *vt* -ED/-ING/-S [ME *conditen*, fr. L *conditus*, past part. of *condire*, fr. *condere* to found, build, compose, store up, fr. *com-* + *-dere* to put — more at DO] **1** *obs* **:** PICKLE, PRESERVE **2** *obs* **:** EMBALM
¹con·di·tion \kən'dishən\ *n* -S [ME *condicioun*, fr. MF *condicion*, fr. L *condition-*, *conditio*, alter. of *condicion-*, *condicio* agreement, compact, condition, fr. *com-* + *-dicion-*, *-dicio* (fr. *dicere* to say, determine, proclaim) — more at DICTION] **1 a :** something established or agreed upon as a requisite to the doing or taking effect of something else **:** STIPULATION, PROVISION ⟨many are apt to believe remission of sins but they believe it without the ~ of repentance —Jeremy Taylor⟩ **b** *obs* **:** an agreement determining one or more such prerequisites **:** COVENANT ⟨such sum or sums as are expressed in the ~ —Shak.⟩ **2 :** something that exists as an occasion of something else **:** a circumstance that is essential to the appearance or occurrence of something else **:** PREREQUISITE: as **a** (1) **:** the antecedent of a hypothetical proposition (2) **:** the subordinate clause of a conditional sentence — contrasted with *conclusion* (3) **:** a proposition having a relation to the validity of another such that (1) validity of the first is sufficient evidence that the second is valid or (2) the second can only be valid if the first is also valid — called also respectively (1) *sufficient condition*, (2) *necessary condition* **b :** a provision in a contract, conveyance, grant, or will providing that the beginning, vesting, rescission, or a modification of an estate or interest in property or of a personal obligation must depend upon an uncertain event which may or may not exist or happen; *also* **:** the event itself **c :** a grade usu. designated by the letter E, given at many colleges and universities for work that does not meet the minimum standard required for passing but is not rated an absolute failure, and intended to serve notice on the student that he has a chance to raise his standing to passing level by doing additional work or passing a special examination **d :** a meld in the game panguingue for which a player immediately receives payment from other players **3 a :** something that limits or modifies the existence or character of something else **:** a restriction or qualification ⟨presence of oxygen is a ~ of animal life⟩ **b conditions** *pl* **:** attendant circumstances **:** existing state of affairs ⟨living ~*s*⟩ ⟨playing ~*s*⟩ ⟨adverse weather ~*s*⟩ **c :** something needing remedy **:** unfavorable circumstance ⟨trains were late because of ~*s* west of the city⟩ **4 :** a mode or state of being ⟨matter in a gaseous ~⟩: **a :** social estate **:** RANK, POSITION ⟨all sorts and ~*s* of men —*Bk. of Common Prayer*⟩ **b** *obs* **:** state with reference to moral or natural nature, temperament, character, or disposition **c :** proper or good condition (as for work or sports competition) **:** the state of being fit **:** SHAPE ⟨the crew is out of ~⟩ ⟨getting in ~ for the big game⟩ **d** *of a domestic animal* **:** fat or the state of being fat **:** FINISH **e :** the physical status of the body as a whole ⟨good ~⟩ ⟨poor ~⟩ or of one of its parts — usu. used to indicate abnormality ⟨a serious heart ~⟩ ⟨a disturbed mental ~⟩ **f :** the financial position or state of a person or company **5 a** *obs* **:** QUALITY, ATTRIBUTE, TRAIT ⟨here is the catalog of her ~*s* —Shak.⟩ **b conditions** *pl, archaic* **:** personal nature **:** MANNERS, WAYS ⟨a woman of the most excellent ~*s* —Sir Walter Scott⟩ **6 :** LUPULIN

syn STIPULATION, TERM, PROVISION, PROVISO, RESERVATION, STRING: CONDITION indicates a requisite action, circumstance, or quality on which rests the validity or effectiveness of an agreement, a plan, promise, attribution ⟨to have some job in sight for the boy as a *condition* of his release at the end of his term —R.M.Lovett⟩ ⟨just had to keep writing — writing was a profession, a way of life, a *condition* of his survival —Sherwood Anderson⟩ ⟨respect for human life is undoubtedly, as we are never tired of preaching to some of our own communities, the first *condition* of civilization —W.C.Brownell⟩ STIPULATION may suggest formal, explicit, definite statement binding a party to a contract or agreement to a specified course ⟨the estate deeded the house to Clatsop County in 1936 with the *stipulation* that it be used for philanthropic purposes —*Amer. Guide Series: Oregon*⟩ ⟨a *stipulation* is a statement of conditions that are agreed to in the conduct of some affair —Felix Kaufmann⟩ TERM, used in the plural in this sense, indicates conditions offered or agreed to in a contract, deal, or agreement ⟨the *terms* of the lease are not harsh —C.E.Montague⟩ ⟨under the *terms* of the peace treaty, Bulgaria's armed forces are limited —*Americana Annual*⟩ ⟨to allow reunification on *terms* that meant alliance with the West —F.H.Hartmann⟩ PROVISION in this sense may specif. designate a written formal statement of a condition, directive, or right ⟨the admission of Arkansas with a *provision* in its constitution forbidding the abolition of slavery without the consent of the slaveowners —L.B.Evans⟩ ⟨Murray warned that even if the union were granted its wage increase, the dispute would not be settled until a union shop *provision* was inserted in the new contract —Mary K. Hammond⟩ ⟨this assumes that the framers of a law or constitution can foresee all possible future contingencies and make definite *provisions* for meeting them so that the judge can be merely a logical automaton —M.R.Cohen⟩ PROVISO is likely to indicate a definite binding stipulation ⟨passionate feeling is desirable, provided it is not destructive; intellect is desirable, with the same *proviso* —Bertrand Russell⟩ ⟨Field's company accepted with the *proviso* that it had the right to reject the job as substandard —James Dugan⟩ RESERVATION indicates a qualification or modification of the terms of an agreement or statement, often one to cover contingencies ⟨a blanket financial *reservation* was added that "any future claims and demands of the Allies and the United States of America remain unaffected". The armistice was for one month and was renewed from time to time until peace was signed —B.E.Schmitt⟩ STRING implies a reserving proviso, sometimes one unnoticed or unexpected and quite likely to modify drastically or annul agreements ⟨it is one thing to get a child to admit that he has money, and quite another to get him to part with it. For he will point out that the money was given to him without *strings* or conditions and that in strict commutative justice he may do what he likes with it —J.D.Sheridan⟩ **syn** see in addition STATE
— on condition that *or* **upon condition that :** with the provision that **:** IF
²condition \"\ *vb* **conditioned; conditioned; conditioning** \-sh(ə)niŋ\ **conditions** *vi* **1** *archaic* **:** to make conditions **:** set terms **:** STIPULATE **2 :** to attain proper or fit condition (as of beer in aging) **3 :** to limit and make definite an object of thought **~** *vt* **1 :** to agree by stipulating **:** CONTRACT — followed by an object clause or phrase ⟨~ that they marry⟩ ⟨~ to obey⟩ **2 :** to invest with, limit by, or subject to conditions **:** burden with a condition **:** make conditional ⟨freedom is ~*ed* by our opportunities⟩ ⟨his tenure was ~*ed* on good behavior⟩ **:** restrict or determine as a condition: as **a** *logic* **:** to limit or restrict in thought or conception **b** *law* **:** to charge with a condition **3 :** to put into proper or the desired condition: as **a :** to moisten (wheat) before grinding **b :** to trim (meat) of excess fat and other unsalable portions **c :** to restore the desired amount of moisture to (as fiber, yarn, or paper that has become dry during processing) **d** (1) **:** to purify and humidify (air) (2) **:** AIR-CONDITION **e :** to bring (as an athlete or a team) through a course of training to a state of fitness for contest **f :** FATTEN ⟨~ livestock⟩ **4 :** to test (textile fibers) for foreign inclusions (as of moisture or oil) **5 :** to require (a student) to pass a new examination or show a certain degree of proficiency in a specified study as a condition of remaining in a class or institution **6 a :** to adapt, modify, or mold (as by example, teaching, or training) to the basic patterns and standards of behavior existing in an environing culture ⟨traditional beliefs ~*ing* a child's attitude⟩ **b :** to modify (as an experimental organism) in such a way that an act or response previously associated with a given stimulus or class of stimuli becomes associated with a formerly unrelated stimulus or class of stimuli **syn** see PREPARE
¹con·di·tion·al \-shən°l,-shnəl\ *adj* [ME *condicionel*, fr. MF, fr. LL *condicionalis*, fr. *condicion-*, *condicio* + *-alis* -al] **1 :** containing, implying, subject to, or depending on a condition ⟨~ diplomatic recognition⟩ ⟨a ~ promise⟩ **:** not absolute **:** not certain **:** not full or unreserved — often used with *on* or *upon* ⟨my visit is ~ on his plans⟩ **2 :** expressing a condition or supposition **:** of or belonging to the expression of a condition **:** introducing, containing, or implying a supposition ⟨the ~ conjunctions *if, unless,* and *though*⟩ ⟨the ~ phrases *provided that* and *supposing that*⟩ ⟨the ~ clause *if he speaks*⟩ ⟨the ~ sentence *if he speaks you must listen*⟩ **3 :** true only for certain values of the variables or symbols involved ⟨~ equations⟩ **4 :** CONDITIONED ⟨a ~ stimulus⟩ ⟨a ~ response⟩
²conditional \"\ *n* -S **1 a :** a conditional word, clause, or verb form; *specif* **:** a verb form in the conditional mood **b :** the conditional mood **2 :** IMPLICATION 2b
conditional baptism *n* **:** Christian baptism administered when there is doubt whether a person was ever baptized or whether a former baptism is valid
conditional complex *n* **:** a conditional sentence
conditional fee *n, law* **:** any fee limited upon a condition; *specif* **:** FEE SIMPLE CONDITIONAL
con·di·tion·al·ism \-,lizəm\ *n* -S **:** the doctrine that divine grace and immortality are conditional — **con·di·tion·al·ist** \-ləst\ *n* -S
con·di·tion·al·i·ty \kən,dishə'naləd·ē, -ətē, -i\ *n* -ES **:** the quality or state of being conditional
con·di·tion·al·ly \kən'dishən°lē, -shnəlē, -li\ *adv* [ME *condicionely*, fr. *condicionel* conditional + *-ly*] **:** in a conditional manner **:** subject to a condition **:** not absolutely ⟨~ canceled nine tenths of the obligations still surviving —S.F.Bemis⟩
conditional receipt *n* **:** BINDING RECEIPT
conditional sale *n* **:** a sale in which the vesting of title in the purchaser notwithstanding delivery to him is made to depend upon the due performance of conditions (as payment in full) made a part of the terms of sale — compare HIRE PURCHASE
conditionate *vt* -ED/-ING/-S [ML *conditionatus*, past part. of *conditionare*, fr. L *condition-*, *conditio* condition — more at CONDITION] *obs* **:** CONDITION **:** make conditional
conditioned *adj* [ME *condicioued*, fr. *condicioun* condition + *-ed*] **1 :** subjected to a condition ⟨a ~ student⟩: as **a** *of changes or variations of speech sounds* **:** occurring in a particular environment and predictable in terms of other sounds in the environment ⟨the ~ sound change of Proto-Germanic *k* to English *ch* before *e* or *i*⟩ **b :** brought into a fit condition ⟨a well-*conditioned* steer⟩ **c** *of cut flowers* **:** stood at just above freezing temperature in moistureproof but gas-permeable containers to enhance marketability and keeping qualities **2 :** determined or established by a condition or by conditioning ⟨a ~ reflex⟩
con·di·tion·er \kən'dish(ə)nə(r)\ *n* -S **:** one that conditions: as **a :** a worker who conditions a product (as yarns) **b :** a substance added to a material or a product to improve its physical state ⟨soil ~⟩ ⟨dough ~⟩ **c :** a trainer (as of athletes or show animals) **d :** an apparatus for air-conditioning
conditioning *pres part of* CONDITION
condition powder *n* **:** a veterinary nostrum supposed to improve the general health and well-being of an animal
condition precedent *n* **:** a condition whose fulfillment must precede the vesting of an estate, the taking effect of a contract, or the accruing of a right
conditions *pl of* CONDITION, *pres 3d sing of* CONDITION
condition subsequent *n* **:** a condition whose fulfillment invalidates or modifies an estate, right, or contract previously vested or in effect (as when a horse is bought on condition that he prove sound)
con·di·tio sine qua non \kən'dishē,ō, -did·ē,ō +\ *n* [L] **:** an indispensable condition
con·division \¦kän +\ *n* -S [*com-* + *division*] *logic* **:** reciprocal or coordinate division or one of its resulting divisions
con·do·la·to·ry \kən'dōlə,tōrē\ *adj* [*condole* + *-atory* (as in *consolatory*)] **:** expressing or conveying condolence
con·dole \kən'dōl\ *vb* -ED/-ING/-S [LL *condolēre*, fr. L *com-* + *dolēre* to feel pain, grieve; akin to L *dolare* to hew, Gk *daidalos* ingeniously formed, Skt *dālayati* he splits, causes to burst; basic meaning: to split, carve] *vi* **1** *obs* **:** to sorrow much **:** GRIEVE **2 :** to express sympathetic sorrow **:** grieve in sympathy — usu. used with *with* ⟨~ with her distress of mind —W.S. Gilbert⟩ ⟨we ~ with you in your misfortune⟩ **~** *vt, archaic* **:** to lament or grieve over **:** express one's sympathetic sorrow at (another's misfortune) ⟨came . . . to ~ the death of the late king —John Evelyn⟩; *often* **:** to express formal regrets over
con·do·lence \kən'dōlən(t)s, 'kändəl-\ *n* -S [MF, fr. *condoloir* to condole (fr. L *condolēre*) + *-ence*] **1** *obs* **:** sympathetic sorrow **2 a :** expression of sympathy with another in sorrow or grief ⟨a letter of ~⟩ **b condolences** *pl* **:** a formal avowal of such sympathy ⟨the bereaved parents received more than a hundred ~*s*⟩ **syn** see SYMPATHY
con·do·lent \-lənt\ *adj* [LL *condolent-*, *condolens*, pres. part. of *condolēre*] **:** feeling or expressing condolence ⟨put on ~ faces, and asked him what sorrow it was —Isak Dinesen⟩
con·dol·ing \kən'dōliŋ, -lēŋ\ *adj* **:** CONDOLENT — **con·dol·ing·ly** *adv*
con·dom \'kändəm *also* 'kən-; ÷ 'kəndrəm\ *n* -S [origin unknown] **:** a very thin sheath commonly of rubber placed over the penis (as to prevent conception or venereal infection during coitus)
con·dom·i·nate \(')kän¦dämənət, kən'd-\ *adj* [NL *condominium* + E *-ate*] **:** enjoying or relating to joint rule
con·do·min·i·um \,kändə'minēəm\ *n* -S [NL, fr. L *com-* + *dominium*] **:** joint dominion or sovereignty: **a** *Roman law* **:** common ownership by two or more persons holding undivided fractional shares in the same property and having the right to alienate their shares resembling tenancy in common in Anglo-American law rather than joint tenancy with its rights of survivorship **b :** joint sovereignty or rule by two or more states over a colony or politically dependent territory ⟨the former Anglo-Egyptian ~ over Sudan⟩; *also* **:** the territory so ruled **c** (1) **:** individual ownership of a unit in a multi-unit structure (as an apartment building) (2) **:** a unit so owned (3) **:** a building containing condominiums
con·don·able \kən'dōnəbəl\ *adj* [*condone* + *-able*] **:** EXCUSABLE, FORGIVABLE
con·don·ance \-ōnən(t)s\ *n* -S [*condone* + *-ance*] **:** CONDONATION
con·do·na·tion \,kändō'nāshən, -də'-\ *n* -S [NL *condonation-*, *condonatio*, fr. L, giving away, fr. *condonatus* (past part. of *condonare*) + *-ion-*, *-io* -ion] **1 :** pardon of an offense **:** voluntary overlooking or implied forgiveness of an offense by treating the offender as if it had not been committed **2** *law* **:** expressed or implied forgiveness by a husband or a wife of a breach of marital duty (as adultery) by the other with an implied condition that the offense shall not be repeated
con·done \kən'dōn\ *vt* -ED/-ING/-S [L *condonare* to give, remit, forgive, fr. *com-* + *donare* to donate — more at DONATE] **:** to pardon or forgive (an offense or fault) **:** permit the continuance of (as vice, gambling) **:** cause or justify the condonation of **syn** see EXCUSE
con·done·ment \-nmənt\ *n* -S **:** cancellation in certain card games of a penalty normally due for a misplay or other irregularity if the next opponent makes a play before the irregularity is noticed or sometimes at the option of opposing players
con·dor \'kändə(r), -,dō(ə)r, -,dō(ə); *in sense 2* " *or* 'kōn-,dō(ə)r, -,dōə\ *n* -S [Sp *cóndor*, fr. Quechua *kúntur*] **1 :** a very large American vulture (*Vultur gryphus*) found in elevated parts of the Andes, having the head and neck bare and the plumage dull black with a downy white neck ruff and white patches on the wings, and being one of the largest and most powerful of flying birds though feeding preferably on carrion — see CALIFORNIA CONDOR **2** *pl* **condors** \-rz\ *or* **condo·res** \kən'dōr,ās, kōn'-\ **:** a coin bearing the picture of a condor: **a :** a gold coin formerly issued in Ecuador worth 25 sucres; *also* **:** a corresponding unit of value ⟨a 2-*condor* gold coin was issued⟩ **b :** a Chilean coin, orig. of gold, of silver in 1948 and later of copper and nickel, worth 10 pesos; *also* **:** a corresponding unit of value **c :** a 19th century Colombian gold coin worth 10 pesos; *also* **:** a unit of value equivalent to 10 pesos **3 :** TIFFIN 2

condor 1

con·dot·tiere \,kändə'tye(,)rā, ,kän-,kōn-, -dō't-, ,kōndōtē-'e(,)rā\ *also* **con·dot·tiero** \-(,)rō\ *n, pl* **condottieri** \-(,)rē\ [It *condottiere*, fr. *condotta* act of hiring, troop of mercenaries (fr. fem. of *condotto* — past part. of *condurre* to conduct, hire—, fr. L *conductus*, past part. of *conducere*) + *-iere* -er] **1 :** a leader of a band of mercenary professional soldiers common in Europe from the 14th to the 16th centuries **2 :** a member of the band of a condottiere; *broadly* **:** a professional mercenary soldier **:** FREE LANCE
condr *abbr* conductor
condrodite *var of* CHONDRODITE
con·duce \kən'd(y)üs\ *vb* -ED/-ING/-S [ME *conducen*, fr. L *conducere* to bring together, conduce, hire, fr. *com-* + *ducere* to lead — more at TOW] *vt* **1** *obs* **:** CONDUCT, GUIDE, BRING **2** *obs* **:** to bring about **:** EFFECT **~** *vi* **:** to lead or tend esp. with reference to a desirable result **:** CONTRIBUTE — used with *to* or *toward* ⟨the qualities that ~ to worldly success⟩
con·duce·ment \-smənt\ *n* -S **:** the act of conducing
conducible *adj* [L *conducibilis*, fr. *conducere* + *-ibilis* -ible] *obs* **:** CONDUCIVE, BENEFICIAL
con·du·cive \-siv, -ēv *also* -əv\ *adj* **:** of conducing nature or quality **:** tending to promote ⟨a dry season is ~ to forest fires⟩
con·du·cive·ness *n* -ES **:** the quality or state of being conducive
¹con·duct \'kän(,)dəkt\ *n* -S [alter. (influenced by L *conductus*) of earlier *conduit*, *condit*, fr. ME, fr. OF *conduit*, *conduite* action of leading, commanding, guiding, escorting, fr. ML *conductus* (masc.), *conducta* (fem.), past part. of *conducere* to escort, safeguard on the road, fr. L, to bring together — more at CONDUCE] **1 a** *obs* **:** a company of attendants or guards to guide and protect (as a traveler or caravan) on a journey **b** *obs* **:** a document granting permission to pass in safety **:** a formal permission to pass over, through, or to a particular place **:** SAFE-CONDUCT **c** *archaic* **:** GUIDE, LEADER **2 a :** the act, manner, or process of carrying out (as a task) or carrying forward (as a business, government, or war) **:** MANAGEMENT, DIRECTION ⟨the ~ of the examination should take less than an hour⟩ ⟨the ~ of foreign affairs⟩ **b :** a manner of arrangement or treatment (as of parts in a painting) **:** RENDITION ⟨~ of details⟩ **3 a** *obs* **:** leadership (as of an army) **b** *obs* **:** capability in leadership or management **:** aptitude in command **:** ADDRESS **c :** a mode or standard of personal behavior esp. as based on moral principles — sometimes distinguished from *behavior*

⟨animals . . . do not rise from behavior to ~ —J.S.Clarke⟩ **d :** behavior in a particular situation or relation or on a specified occasion ⟨~ unbecoming to a gentleman⟩ ⟨his disgusting ~ at the party⟩ **4 :** the act or process of leading or guiding **:** GUIDANCE ⟨moving at random under the ~ of chance⟩ ⟨known for his editorial ~ of the local newspaper⟩

²con·duct \kən'dəkt\ *vb* -ED/-ING/-S [alter. (influenced by L *conductus*) of earlier *conduit, condit*, fr. ME *conduiten, conditen*, fr. *conduit, condit*, n. — more at CONDUCT] *vt* **1 :** to bring by or as if by leading **:** LEAD, GUIDE, ESCORT ⟨I made a bridge to a rock whence I can reach the other side, so I shall ~ the lambs that way —Rachel Henning⟩ ⟨I never should have ~*ed* this chronicle to the stage it has now reached —F.M.Ford⟩ **2 a :** to lead as a commander ⟨~ a siege⟩ **b :** to have the direction of **:** RUN, MANAGE, DIRECT ⟨~ a scientific experiment⟩ ⟨~ a daily newspaper column⟩ ⟨~ a small business enterprise⟩ **c :** TREAT, HANDLE, EXECUTE ⟨~ a detail in a painting⟩ ⟨~ an episode in a poem⟩ **d :** to direct as leader the performance or execution of (as a musical work or a group of musicians) **3 a :** to convey in or as if in a channel ⟨phrases which once started on ~ us . . . along a well-worn channel to an inevitable end —J.L.Lowes⟩ **b :** to act as a medium for conveying (as heat or electricity) **:** TRANSMIT **4 :** to behave or comport (oneself) **:** ACQUIT ~ *vi* **1** *of a road or passage* **:** to show the way **:** LEAD **2 a :** to act as leader or director ⟨one could always count on a superb performance from the orchestra when Charles ~*ed*⟩ **b :** to transmit or have the quality of transmitting light, heat, sound, or electricity

syn MANAGE, CONTROL, DIRECT: CONDUCT may imply a leader's supervision, his responsible guidance in a course which he determines ⟨the men who actually *conduct* and order the industry of the country —G.B.Shaw⟩ ⟨Douglas *conducted* conferences and studies which led to a reorganization of the Stock Exchange —*Current Biog.*⟩ ⟨missionaries of the Holy Family *conduct* a training school and home for students and missionaries —*Amer. Guide Series: Texas*⟩ MANAGE may imply handling or maneuvering, or guiding along a desired course or to a desired result; it often indicates a general overseeing, with authority to handle details, cope with problems, and make routine decisions ⟨my young wife who could *manage* a horse better than most men could —Rex Ingamells⟩ ⟨our purpose is to *manage* the government's finances so as to help and not hinder each family in balancing its own budget —D.D.Eisenhower⟩ ⟨now do you leave this affair in my hands. Only tell me which woman it is and I will *manage* the affair —Pearl Buck⟩ ⟨the delight she would take in *managing* a real house, not in any sense as its drudge, but magnificently as its mistress —Floyd Dell⟩ ⟨*manage* a silk mill⟩ ⟨*manage* a baseball team⟩ CONTROL stresses notions of authoritative guiding and, when necessary, checking deviation, excess, or error; it may imply complete subordination or subjection to authoritative or autocratic power ⟨"Come, come, Byron", said the master, *controlling* him with a broad, strong hand; "none of your nonsense, sir." —G.B.Shaw⟩ ⟨it was apparently regarded as impossible to root out bad desires; all we could do was to *control* them —Bertrand Russell⟩ ⟨pirates at one time practically *controlled* the coasts of Florida —*Amer. Guide Series: Fla.*⟩ DIRECT may imply constant guiding, regulating, and administering of activities in the interests of smooth operation ⟨*directing* a research program⟩ ⟨*directing* a manufacturing company⟩ ⟨*directing* Red Cross activities⟩ ⟨a physicist is not interfering with Nature, any more than an architect is interfering with Nature when he *directs* the building of a house —K.K.Darrow⟩ **syn** see in addition BEHAVE

con·duc·ta \kən'dùktə\ *n* -S [Sp, fr. ML *conducta*, fem. of *conductus*, past part. of *conducere* to escort, safeguard on the road — more at CONDUCT] *Southwest* **:** a guarded pack train or caravan; *esp* **:** one carrying bullion prior to the establishment of modern transport

con·duct·ance \kən'dəktən(t)s\ *n* -S **1 :** the act of conducting **:** TRANSMISSION, CONVEYANCE **2 a :** capacity or fitness for conducting ⟨neural ~⟩ **b :** conducting power **:** measure of the readiness with which a given conductor allows an electric current to flow through it **:** the reciprocal of resistance measured by a unit *mho* that is the reciprocal of the ohm

conducting transportation *n* **:** an accounting heading designed to cover those items of expense that arise in the daily service of trains and terminals as distinct from repairs or capital charges

con·duc·tio \kən'dəkshē(,)ō\ *n, pl* **conduc·ti·o·nes** \kən-dəkshē'ō(,)nēz\ [L] **:** HIRING — compare LOCATIO CONDUCTIO

con·duc·tion \kən'dəkshən\ *n* -S [MF, conducting, hiring, fr. L *conduction-, conductio* bringing together, hiring, fr. *conductus* (past part. of *conducere* to bring together, hire) + *-ion-, -io* -ion — more at CONDUCE] **1** *archaic* **:** CONDUCT, MANAGEMENT, SKILL **2 :** the act of conveying (as water through a pipe) **3 :** the transfer of soluble foods, water, and other substances from one part of a plant to another — called also *translocation* **4 :** HIRING **5 a :** transfer of heat through matter by communication of kinetic energy from particle to particle rather than by a flow of heated material — compare CONVECTION **b :** the maintenance of an electric current through metals by a general movement of conduction electrons, through electrolytes by a movement of both positive and negative ions, or through gases by the passage of cathode rays, ionized molecules, or anode rays **6 :** the transmission of excitation through living tissue esp. in a nerve ⟨~ of impulses to the brain⟩

conduction anesthesia *n* **:** BLOCK ANESTHESIA

conduction current *n* **:** a movement of electricity in an electric conductor — compare DISPLACEMENT CURRENT

conductitious *adj* [L *conducticius, conductitius* hired, fr. *conductus* (past part. of *conducere* to hire) + *-icius, -itius* -itious] *obs* **:** HIRED; *also* **:** open to or kept for hire

con·duc·tive \kən'dəktiv, -tēv *also* -təv\ *adj* **:** having the quality or power of conducting **:** possessing conductivity **:** relating to or concerned with conduction (as of electricity) — **con·duc·tive·ly** \-tə̇vlē, -li\ *adv*

con·duc·tiv·i·ty \,kän,dək'tivəd-ē, -ətē, -i\ *n* -ES **:** the quality or power of conducting or transmitting (as heat or electricity): as **a** *physics* **:** the reciprocal of resistivity — compare THERMAL CONDUCTIVITY **b :** the quality of living matter responsible for the transmission of and progressive reaction to stimuli within the living system — compare IRRITABILITY

con·duct·ment \kən'dəktmənt\ *n* -S *archaic* **:** COMMAND, LEADERSHIP

conduct money *n* **:** money paid or to pay for conveyance or for traveling expenses (as of a witness or a man newly enlisted); *esp* **:** a tax levied by Charles I to defray expenses of transporting men to the point of mobilization of the king's army — compare COAT MONEY

con·duc·tom·e·ter \,kän,dək'tämə̇d-ə(r), -ətə(r)\ *or* **con·duc·tim·e·ter** \-'tim-\ *n* -S [²*conduct* + *-o-* or *-i-* + *-meter*] **:** any instrument for measuring conductivity; *specif* **:** one for comparing the rates at which rods of different materials transmit heat

con·duc·to·met·ric *or* **con·duc·ti·met·ric** \kən¦dəktə¦me-trik\ *adj* **:** of, relating to, or involving the measurement of conductivity **:** relating to or by means of conductometry ⟨~ titration⟩

con·duc·tom·e·try \,kän,dək'tämə·trē, -ri\ *n* -ES [²*conduct* + *-o-* + *-metry*] **:** determination of the quantity of a material (as an element or salt) present in a mixture by measurement of its effect on the electrical conductivity of the mixture

con·duc·tor \kən'dəktə(r)\ *n* -S [alter. (influenced by L *conductor* lessee) of earlier *conduitour, conditour* commander, guide, fr. ME, commander, fr. MF *conduiteur* one that conducts, fr. ML *conductor* escorter, manorial manager, commander, fr. L, lessee, fr. *conductus* (past part. of *conducere* to bring together, hire) + *-or* — more at CONDUCE] **1 :** one that conducts (as a person that leads or escorts) **:** GUIDE, ESCORT **2 a** *obs* **:** a commander or leader (as of an army or a ship) **b :** one in charge of a public conveyance (as a streetcar) **c :** a railroad employee who supervises the train crew and collects fares from passengers **3 a :** DOWNSPOUT **b :** LIGHTNING ROD **4** [L, lessee] **:** HIRER; *esp* **:** BAILEE, LESSEE **5 :** a substance or body capable of transmitting electricity, heat, or sound **6 :** a person that conducts an orchestra, chorus, or other group of musical performers **7 :** a bodily part that transmits excitation (as a nerve fiber)

conductor head *n* **:** LEADER HEAD

con·duc·to·ri·al \¦kän¦dək¦tōrēəl, -¦tȯr-\ *adj* **:** of or relating to a conductor esp. of an orchestra — **con·duc·to·ri·al·ly** \-əlē\ *adv*

con·duc·tor·less \kən'dəktə(r)lə̇s\ *adj* **:** having no conductor

con·duc·tress \kən'dək·trə̇s\ *n* -ES [*conductor* + *-ess*] **:** a female conductor; *esp, Brit* **:** a female bus or tram conductor

conducts *pl of* CONDUCT, *pres 3d sing of* CONDUCT

con·duc·tus \kən'dəktəs\ *n, pl* **conductus** \"\ [ML, fr. L *conductus*, past part. of *conducere* to bring together — more at CONDUCE] **:** a medieval vocal composition consisting of one to four voice parts the lowest of which is composed of a Latin text set to an invented melody and accompanied homophonically by the other voices

con·duit \'kän(,)dü̇ət, -,dwit, -,dəwə̇t, -dət, *usu* -d· +V\ *n* -S [ME *condut, condit, conduit*, fr. MF *conduit*, lit., action of leading, commanding — more at CONDUCT] **1 :** a natural or artificial channel through which water or other fluid passes or is conveyed **:** AQUEDUCT, PIPE ⟨the ~ of a volcano⟩ ⟨all the ~*s* of my blood froze up —Shak.⟩ **2** *archaic* **:** FOUNTAIN ⟨the ~*s* round the garden sing —D.G.Rossetti⟩ **3 a** *obs* **:** a passage within or between parts of a building **b :** a narrow often underground passage for private communication **4 :** pipe, tube, or tile for receiving and protecting electric wires or cables (as for telephones or power lines) **5 :** a means of conveying or distributing money ⟨the doctrine that corporations are a ~ for profits —J.T.Norman⟩

conduit box *n* **:** an electric outlet box to which a rigid or flexible conduit runs — compare JUNCTION BOX, SERVICE BOX

conduit system *n* **:** a system for supplying electric power to a car or locomotive by means of one or more underground contact rails

Con·du·let \'kändə,let, -dəlėt\ *trademark* — used for a fitting resembling a pipe or box with a removable cover for access to electric conduits

con·duplicate \(')kän, kən +\ *adj* [L *conduplicatus*, past part. of *conduplicare* to double, fr. *com-* + *duplicare* to double — more at DUPLICATE] **:** folded lengthwise along the midrib so that the halves are applied together by their upper faces — used of leaves or petals in the bud — **con·duplication** \¦kän, kən +\ *n* -S

con·du·ran·gin \,kändə'raŋ(g)ə̇n, -'ranjə̇n\ *n* -S [ISV *condurango* + *-in*] **:** a bitter poisonous yellowish glucoside obtained from condurango

con·du·ran·go \-aŋ(,)gō\ *n* -S [AmerSp *condurango, cundurango*, fr. Quechua *kunturánku*, lit., condor vine] **:** the dried bark of a So. American vine (*Marsdenia cundurango*) used as an alterative and stomachic — see CONDURANGIN

condyl- *or* **condylo-** *comb form* [NL, fr. Gk *kondyl-, kondylo-*, fr. *kondylos* — more at CONDYLE] **:** joint **:** knob **:** condyle ⟨*condyl*oid⟩ ⟨*Condylo*poda⟩

con·dy·lar \'kändələ(r)\ *adj* [*condyl-* + *-ar*] **:** of, relating to, or associated with a condyle

con·dy·larth \'kändə,lärth\ *n* -S [NL *Condylarthra*] **:** an individual or fossil of the order Condylarthra

con·dy·lar·thra \,kändə'lärthrə\ *n pl, cap* [NL, fr. *condyl-* + *-arthra* (neut. pl. of *-arthrus* jointed, fr. Gk *-arthros*, fr. *arthron* joint) — more at ARTHR-] **:** an order or suborder of extinct Eocene ungulate mammals having many primitive characters some of which connect them with the Creodonta and being more or less plantigrade with five-toed limbs and a third trochanter — **con·dy·lar·throus** \¦=¦=¦thrəs\ *adj*

con·dy·lar·thro·sis \,kändə,lär'thrōsə̇s\ *n, pl* **condylar·thro·ses** \-,sēz\ [NL, fr. *condyl-* + *arthrosis*] *anat* **:** articulation by means of a condyle (as that between the head and vertebral column involving the occipital condyles and the atlas)

con·dyle \'kän,dīl, -dᵊl\ *n* -S [F & L; F, fr. L *condylus* knuckle, joint, fr. Gk *kondylos* knuckle, joint, fist; akin to Lith *kánduolas* core, and perh. to Skt *kanda* bulbous root] **1 :** an articular prominence on a bone — used chiefly of such as occur in pairs likened to a pair of knuckles (as those of the occipital bone for articulation with the atlas, those at the distal end of the humerus and femur, and those of the lower jaw) **2 :** a rounded process of the hard integument in the articulations of the limbs of arthropods; *also* **:** a similar process on the mandible of some insects

con·dyl·i·on \kən'dilēən, kän'-, -lē,än\ *n* -S [NL, fr. Gk *kondylion*, dim. of *kondylos* knuckle] **1 :** the lateral tip of the condyle of the lower jaw — see CRANIOMETRY illustration **2 :** the posteriormost point of the articular surface of either occipital condyle of a mammal

con·dy·loid \'kändə,lȯid\ *adj* [*condyl-* + *-oid*] **:** shaped like or situated near a condyle **:** relating to a condyle

condyloid foramen *n* **:** a foramen in front of each condyle of the occipital bone

condyloid joint *n* **:** an articulation in which an ovoid head is received into an elliptical cavity permitting all movements except axial rotation

condyloid process *n* **:** the rounded process by which the ramus of the mandible articulates with the temporal bone

con·dy·lo·ma \,kändə'lōmə\ *n, pl* **condylomas** \-ōməz\ *or* **condyloma·ta** \-ōməd-ə\ [NL, fr. Gk *kondylōma*, fr. *kondylos* knuckle, knob — more at CONDYLE] **:** a new growth like a wart on the outer skin or adjoining mucous membrane usu. near the anus and genital organs — **con·dy·lom·a·tous** \¦=¦=¦läməd-əs, -¦lōm-\ *adj*

con·dy·lo·sto·ma \,kändələ'stōmə\ *n, cap* [NL, fr. *condyl-* + *-stoma*] **:** a genus of large heterotrichous ciliated protozoans having the form of a somewhat flattened ellipsoid with a truncated anterior end and being common and free-living in fresh and salt water

con·dy·lu·ra \,kändə'lürə\ *n, cap* [NL, fr. *condyl-* + *-ura*] **:** a genus of moles having 44 small teeth and a muzzle like a snout that terminates in a fringe of cartilaginous or fleshy processes and comprising the star-nosed moles

con·dy's fluid \'kändēz-, -diz-\ *also* **condy** *n, often cap C* [after Henry Bollman *Condy*, 19th cent. Eng. manufacturing chemist] *chiefly Brit* **:** a common household disinfectant consisting essentially of an aqueous solution of a permanganate

¹cone \'kōn\ *n* -S [MF or L; MF *cone*, fr. L *conus*, fr. Gk *kōnos* — more at HONE] **1 a :** a mass of ovule-bearing or pollen-bearing scales or bracts in trees of the pine family and in cycads arranged usu. on a somewhat elongated axis **:** a carpellate or staminate strobilus; *esp* **:** the carpellate strobilus of pine and related trees — see CONIFERALES **b :** any of several flower or fruit clusters suggesting a cone (as of the hop or certain magnolias) **2 a :** a solid generated by the rotation of a right triangle about one of its legs as axis, the length of this leg being the altitude of the cone and the length of the hypotenuse of the right triangle its slant height — called also *right circular cone* **b :** a solid bounded by a circular or other closed plane base and the surface formed by line segments joining every point of the boundary of the base to a common vertex **c :** a conical surface **:** any surface traced by a moving straight line passing through a fixed vertex **3 :** an object, part, or structure felt to resemble a geometric cone: as **a :** a natural formation built up around the crater of a volcano or the outlet of a geyser ⟨basalt ~⟩ ⟨spatter ~⟩ **b :** a steep alluvial or detrital fan ⟨talus ~⟩ ⟨gravity ~⟩ **c :** one of the short sensory end organs of the vertebrate retina that are the sole receptors present in the fovea and are scattered among the rods over most of the rest of the retina and that function chiefly or wholly in the light-adapted eye and are usu. regarded as the only visual receptors concerned in color vision **d :** any of numerous somewhat conical tropical gastropod mollusks constituting the family Conidae — see CONUS **e :** any of certain conical or conoidal parts: as (1) **:** CONE PULLEY (2) **:** an inner race for ball bearings (3) **:** the portion of the bore of a shotgun that lies immediately forward of the chamber (4) **:** a bobbin upon which yarn is wound preparatory to weaving or knitting it into a fabric; *also* **:** the entire package of yarn and bobbin **f :** PYROMETRIC CONE; *often* **:** the temperature or refractory range indicated by a particular combination of pyrometric cones **g :** an unblocked hat **h :** a cusp of a tooth esp. of the upper jaw **i :** ICE-CREAM CONE **j :** CONE SPEAKER **k :** the cone-shaped part of a gas flame that is immediately adjacent to the source of gas **l :** a cone-shaped area of illumination (as from a searchlight)

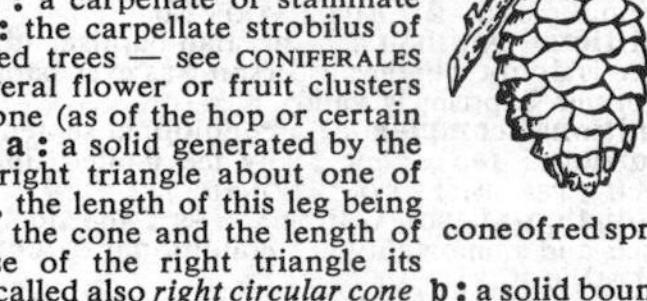
cone of red spruce

²cone \"\ *vb* -ED/-ING/-S *vt* **1 :** to render cone-shaped **:** bevel like the slanting surface of a cone ⟨~ the tires of car wheels⟩ **2 :** to wind on a cone ⟨~ a textile yarn⟩ ~ *vi* **1 :** to form or bear cones (as of a pine tree) **2 :** to form a cone (as of a whirling liquid)

cone adaptation *n* **:** the relatively rapid adaptation of the central portion of the retina of the eye occurring in high light intensities — compare PHOTOPIA

cone anchor *n* **:** a sea anchor shaped like a cone

cone-bearing \'=,==\ *adj* **:** bearing cones **:** belonging to the Pinaceae or Cycadaceae

cone bearing *n, mech engin* **:** a journal bearing containing a taper sleeve capable of endwise movement for taking up wear

cone beetle *n* **:** any of numerous small beetles constituting the genus *Conophthorus* and having larvae that develop in and destroy the growing cones of conifers, esp. pines

cone bit *n* **:** a conical bit for boring

cone brake *n* **:** a friction brake in which the frictional surfaces are cone-shaped

cone clutch *n* **:** a friction clutch in which the frictional surfaces are cone-shaped

cone crusher *or* **cone mill** *n* **:** a mill for crushing ore into sizes suitable for grinding

cone-cut \'=¦=\ *adj* **:** cut from the tapered end of a log much as a pencil is sharpened ⟨certain veneers are *cone-cut*⟩

coned \'kōnd\ *adj* [¹*cone* + *-ed*] **1 :** shaped like a cone or segment of a cone; *also* **:** having a cone **2** *of an airplane* **:** caught by converging searchlight beams and so a target for gunfire

coneflower \'=,==\ *n* **:** any of several composite plants having cone-shaped flower disks: as **a :** a plant of the genus *Rudbeckia* (esp. *R. hirta*) **b :** a plant of the genus *Ratibida* **c :** a plant of the genus *Echinacea*

cone gamba *n* **:** a labial organ stop with conical pipes ending in a bell

conehead \'=,=\ *n* **:** a plant of the genus *Strobilanthes* of the family Acanthaceae

conehead rivet *n* **:** a rivet having a head in the form of a truncated cylindrical cone

cone-in-cone \¦=¦=\ *n* **:** a small-scale geologic structure resembling a set of concentric cones piled one above another developed in sedimentary rocks under pressure with or without solution of adjacent materials

cone joint *n* **:** a joint made by inserting a double cone of iron into the ends of pipes and tightening by screw bolts

cone key *n* **:** any of usu. three taper saddle keys fitting all round a shaft to key on it a piece (as a pulley) the hole in which is too large for the shaft

cone·let \'kōnlə̇t\ *n* -S [¹*cone* + *-let*] **:** a little cone

con·el·rad \'känᵊl,rad, -,raa(ə)d\ *n* -S [*con*trol of *el*ectro-magnetic *rad*iation] **:** a system for preventing an enemy from using radio signals from any particular AM station as a guide for aircraft or missiles by shifting all AM stations to either of the frequencies 640 or 1240 and having them broadcast in a group in random order for short intervals on only these frequencies

cone mandrel *n* **1 :** an expanding mandrel whose diameter is varied by the shifting of conical sleeves **2 :** a blacksmith's conical swage block

cone-nose \'=,=\ *also* **cone-nose bug** *or* **cone-nosed bug** \'=¦=-\ *n* **:** any of certain large bloodsucking bugs of *Triatoma* or closely related genera of the family Reduviidae including insects capable of inflicting extremely painful bites and at least one So. American form (*Panstrongylus megistus* or *Triatoma megista*) that is a vector of Chagas' disease — called also *assassin bug, big bedbug, kissing bug*

cone number *n* **:** a number indicating the fusing point of a particular Seger cone

cone of origin : a clear area of cytoplasm where the axon of a neuron leaves the cell body

cone of silence : a cone-shaped region directly above a radio signal beacon in which signals from the beacon are not received by aircraft

co·ne·pa·te \,kōnə'päd-ā\ *also* **co·ne·patl** \-'äd-ᵊl\ *n* -S [MexSp, fr. Nahuatl *conepatl*, fr. *conetl* small + *epatl* fox] **:** HOG-NOSED SKUNK

co·ne·pa·tus \,kōnə'päd-əs\ *n, cap* [NL, fr. MexSp *conepate*] **:** a genus of mammals (family Mustelidae) comprising the hog-nosed skunks

cone pepper *n* **1 :** a hot pepper (*Capsicum frutescens conoides*) with erect pungent conical fruits that is sometimes considered to be a variety of the cherry pepper **2 :** the fruit of a cone pepper

cone-plant \'=,=\ *n* **:** any of certain small succulent plants constituting a genus (*Conophytum*) of the family Aizoaceae and consisting of inverted cone-shaped bodies each made up of two joined leaves with a small opening through which a stemless flower emerges

cone pulley *n* **:** a pulley in the form of a truncated cone **:** a series of pulleys forming a stepped cone or conoid that are used in pairs (as for varying the velocity ratios of shafts)

stepped cone pulley

con·er \'kōnə(r)\ *n* -S **1 :** a machine operator who mats fur fibers for hat felt **2 :** one that winds yarn on cones or spools (as a workman or a machine)

cones *pl of* CONE, *pres 3d sing of* CONE

cone sheet *n* **:** a tabular body of intruded igneous rock having the form of a segment of a downward-pointing cone **:** one of a group of centrally inclined sheets of igneous rock

cone shell *n* **:** CONE 3d; *also* **:** its shell

cone speaker *n* **:** a loudspeaker in which the vibrating diaphragm is large and conical and usu. made of paper, no horn being used

con es·pres·si·o·ne \,kōnė,sprese'ō(,)nā, ,kōn-\ *adv (or adj)* [It, lit., with expression] **:** with feeling — used as a direction in music

co·nes·si bark \kə'nesē-\ *n* [origin unknown] **:** TELLICHERRY BARK

co·nes·sine \kə'ne(,)sēn, -nesən\ *n* -S [ISV *conessi* (*bark*) + *-ine*] **:** a very bitter poisonous crystalline alkaloid $C_{24}H_{40}N_2$ obtained from certain tropical trees of the family Apocynaceae (esp. *Holarrhena antidysenterica* and *Wrightia zeylandica*)

¹con·es·to·ga \,känə̇'stōgə, '==,==\ *n, pl* **conestoga** *usu cap* [Conestoga *Kanastóge*, lit., at the place of the immersed pole] **1 :** SUSQUEHANNA **2 :** the language of the Susquehanna people

²conestoga \"\ *also* **conestoga wagon** *n, usu cap C* [fr. *Conestoga*, Pa., where it originated] **:** a broad-wheeled covered wagon having a body curving upward toward the ends and suggesting the shape of a boat, usu. drawn by six horses, and used esp. for transporting freight

Conestoga wagon

³conestoga \"\ *n* -S [fr. *Conestoga*, Pa.] **:** BROGAN — compare STOGIE

cone tree *n* **:** a coniferous tree

cone valve *n* **:** a valve with a conical seat

cone wheat *n* [so called fr. its cone-shaped spikes] **:** POULARD WHEAT

co·ney *or* **co·ny** \'kōnē, -ni\ *n, pl* **coneys** *or* **conies** [ME *cony, conig, coning*, back-formation fr. *conies*, pl., fr. OF *connis, conis*, pl. of *connil, conil*, fr. L *cuniculus* rabbit, underground passage, prob. of Iberian origin; akin to Basque *untxi* rabbit, prob. fr. (assumed) *kuntxi* (whence perh. Ar dial. — Spain — *conchair* hound, dog)] **1 a** (1) **:** RABBIT;

esp **:** the European rabbit (*Oryctolagus cuniculus*) (2) **:** LITTLE CHIEF HARE **b :** HYRAX **2 :** rabbit skin or fur; *also* **:** a coat made of rabbit fur clipped and usu. dyed to resemble other furs **3** *obs* **:** DUPE, GULL, SIMPLETON **4** *heraldry* **:** a rabbit borne as a charge **5 :** any of several fishes: as **a :** a dusky black-spotted reddish-finned grouper (*Cephalopholis fulvus*) of the tropical Atlantic **b :** GRAYSBY **c :** INCONNU 2

coney island *n, usu cap C&I* [fr. *Coney Island*, a resort in Brooklyn, N.Y.] **:** a place felt to resemble the resort Coney Island esp. in blatantly entertaining quality or garish attraction

conf *abbr* **1** confederation **2** [L *confer*] compare **3** conference **4** confessor **5** confidential

¹con·fab \ˈkänˌfab, kənˈf-\ *n* -s [by shortening] **:** CONFABULATION ⟨careful ~*s*, handshakings and organization building —*N.Y. Herald Tribune*⟩

²con·fab \kənˈfab, ˈkänˌf-\ *vi* **confabbed; confabbed; confabbing; confabs :** CONFABULATE ⟨I would see them *confabbing* in the shed —Saul Bellow⟩

con·fab·u·lar \kənˈfabyələ(r)\ *adj* [*confabulate* + *-ar*] **:** CONFABULATORY

con·fab·u·late \-ˌlāt\ *vi* -ED/-ING/-S [L *confabulatus*, past part. of *confabulari*, fr. *com-* + *fabulari* to talk, fr. *fabula* narration, account — more at FABLE] **1 :** to talk familiarly together **:** CHAT, PRATTLE **2 :** to hold discussion **:** CONFER, POWWOW — **con·fab·u·la·tor** \-ˌād·ə(r)\ *n* -s

con·fab·u·la·tion \kənˌfabyəˈlāshən, ˌkän-\ *n* -s [ME *confabulacion*, fr. LL *confabulation-, confabulatio*, fr. L *confabulatus* + *-ion-, -io* -ion] **1 a :** familiar talk **:** CONVERSATION ⟨drew closer in whispered ~ —Elinor Wylie⟩; *also* **:** CHAT ⟨the staple of feminine ~*s* —George Santayana⟩ **b :** CONFERENCE, DISCUSSION ⟨plans and intrigues and whispered ~*s* —Max Lerner⟩ **2 :** a filling in of gaps in memory by free fabrication (as in Korsakoff's syndrome) — **con·fab·u·la·to·ry** \kənˈfabyələˌtōrē\ *adj*

con·far·re·a·tion \kənˌfarēˈāshən, ˌkän-\ *n* -s [L *confarreation-, confarreatio*, fr. *confarreatus* (past part. of *confarreare* to unite in marriage by a ceremony prob. including sacrifice of a spelt cake, fr. *com-* + *-farreare* — fr. *farreum* spelt cake, fr. neut. of *farreus* of spelt, fr. *farr-, far* spelt) + *-ion-, -io* -ion — more at BARLEY] **:** a ceremony of Roman patrician marriage that gave special sanctity to the marriage bond and until after the time of Tiberius conferred upon the husband the right of absolute control of the wife as of a daughter — see DIFFARREATION, MANUS; compare COEMPTIO

¹con·fect \kənˈfekt\ *vt* -ED/-ING/-S [L *confectus*, past part. of *conficere* to prepare — more at COMFIT] **1 :** to put together (as ingredients in compounding a medicine) ⟨home-*confected* medicaments —S.H.Adams⟩ **2 a :** PREPARE ⟨hard sauce ~*ed* for the pudding —Silas Spitzer⟩ **:** PICKLE, PRESERVE **b :** to put together (as a novel) from varied and often incongruous material **:** CONSTRUCT ⟨writers busy ~*ing* best sellers⟩ ⟨the majority of attempts to ~ a poetic drama —T.S.Eliot⟩

²con·fect \ˈkänˌfekt\ *n* -s [ML *confectum*, fr. L, neut. of *confectus*, past part. of *conficere*] **:** COMFIT, CONFECTION ⟨a ~ of leafy faces in a tree —Wallace Stevens⟩

con·fec·tio \kənˈfekshēˌō, -ktē,ō\ *n, pl* **confecti·o·nes** \-kshēˈōˌnēz, -ktēˈōˌnās\ **:** CONFECTION 1b

¹con·fec·tion \kənˈfekshən\ *n* -s [ME *confeccioun*, fr. MF *confection*, fr. LL *confection-, confectio*, fr. L, preparation, making, fr. *confectus* + *-ion-, -io* -ion] **1 :** MIXTURE **:** a preparation esp. for human consumption made by mixing diverse ingredients: as **a :** DELICACY; *usu* **:** a preparation of fruits, nuts, roots, or other morsels with sugar **:** SWEETMEAT, PRESERVE, CANDY **b** *pharmacy* (1) *obs* **:** a medicinal preparation made up of diverse drugs or ingredients (2) **:** a soft mass consisting of a vegetable drug or drugs incorporated with sugar, syrup, or honey — compare ELECTUARY **c** *obs* **:** a draft compounded with poison **:** a preparation of poison **2 :** a making or preparing by combining ingredients **:** PREPARATION, MANUFACTURE ⟨the ~ of comedies⟩ **3 :** something elaborate, complex, or ornate in makeup or form: as **a :** an artistic or literary work marked by artificiality or lack of sincerity or made up of unsuitable or incongruous elements combined without real unification or feeling of purpose ⟨an amusing ~ with several charming melodies but no real substance⟩ **b :** an elaborate architectural work; *esp* **:** one combining elements of style or materials that might be expected to give an incongruous effect ⟨a ~ in metal and glass, similar to the original Quai d' Orsay Station in Paris —*Architectural Rev.*⟩ **c :** any of various fancy decorative articles of women's dress or household ornament — often used in advertisements

²confection \"\ *vt* **confectioned; confectioned; confectioning** \-sh(ə)niŋ\ **confections** *archaic* **:** to mix or prepare as a confection

¹con·fec·tion·ary \-shəˌnerē, -ri\ *n* -ES [ML *confectionarius* apothecary, fr. LL *confection-, confectio* + L *-arius* -ary] **1** *archaic* **:** CONFECTIONER **2 a :** a place (as a preserve closet) where confections are kept **b :** CONFECTIONERY 3 **3 :** CONFECTIONERY 1 **4 :** the making of confections

²confectionary \"\ *adj* [*confection* + *-ary*] **1 :** prepared as or being a confection **2 :** of or relating to confections or their making or selling

con·fec·tion·er \-sh(ə)nə(r)\ *n* -s **1** *obs* **:** a compounder esp. of drugs, poisons **2 :** one that deals in confections, candies, and often cakes and ice cream **3 :** a candymaker or cake decorator

confectioners' sugar *n* **:** a highly refined finely powdered sugar

con·fec·tion·ery \-shəˌnerē, -ri\ *n* -ES [¹*confection* + *-ery*] **1 :** sweet edibles (as candy, cake, pastry, candied fruits, ice cream) **:** things prepared and sold by a confectioner **2 :** the confectioner's art or business **3 :** a shop where confectionery is made, sold, or served

con·fed·er·a·cy \kənˈfed(ə)rəsē, -si, *rap.* -dərs-\ *n* -ES [ME *confederacie*, fr. AF, fr. LL *confoederation-, confoederatio* agreement, compact — more at CONFEDERATION] **1 :** a league or compact between two or more persons, bodies of men, or states for mutual support or common action **:** ALLIANCE **2 :** a combination of persons to do an unlawful act or to do a lawful act by unlawful means — see CONSPIRACY **3 :** the body formed by persons, bodies, states, or nations united by a league; *esp* **:** a union of states ⟨the U.S. was orig. a ~⟩ ⟨the Southern *Confederacy*⟩ — now usu. used to imply a looser union than *federation*

con·fed·er·al \-d(ə)rəl\ *adj* [*confederation* + *-al*] **:** of or relating to a confederation (as that of the U.S. under the Articles of Confederation)

con·fed·er·al·ist \-ləst\ *n* -s **:** a member or advocate of a confederation

¹con·fed·er·ate \kənˈfed(ə)rət, *rap.* -dərt; *usu* -əd· *or* -rd· +V\ *adj* [ME *confederat*, fr. LL *confoederatus*, past part. of *confoederare* to unite by a league, fr. *com-* + *foederare* to establish by treaty, fr. L *foeder-, foedus* treaty, league — more at FEDERAL] **1 a :** united in a league **:** allied by treaty **:** engaged in a confederacy or confederation **:** CONFEDERATED ⟨~ governments⟩ **b** *of a person* (1) **:** ASSISTING, ABETTING (2) **:** CONSPIRATORIAL ⟨~ look between father and child —Elizabeth Bowen⟩ **2** *usu cap* **:** of or relating to the Confederate States of America ⟨the *Confederate* army⟩

²confederate \"\ *n* -s [ME *confederat*, fr. LL *confoederatus*, fr. *confoederatus*, past part. of *confoederare*] **1 a :** one united with others in a confederacy or confederation **:** a person or a nation in a confederacy **:** ALLY **b :** a member of a gang **:** ACCOMPLICE 1 **2** *usu cap* **:** an adherent of the Confederate States of America or their cause

³con·fed·er·ate \kənˈfedəˌrāt, *usu* -ād·+V\ *vb* -ED/-ING/-S [¹*confederate*] *vt* **:** to unite (as nations) in a league, confederacy, or conspiracy **:** ALLY ⟨the enemy is just the enemy, regardless of how many nations he has been able to ~ —R.M. Weaver⟩ ~ *vi* **:** to unite in a league **:** join in a mutual contract or covenant **:** band together

confederate heroes day *n, usu cap C&H&D* **:** January 19 observed as a legal holiday in Texas to commemorate Jefferson Davis, Robert E. Lee, and other Confederate heroes

confederate jasmine *n* [so called fr. its cultivation in the southern U.S.] **:** either of two vines of the genus *Trachelospermum:* **a :** STAR JASMINE **b :** a similar vine (*T. asiaticum*) having smaller but broader leathery leaves with blunt tips

confederate memorial day *n, cap C&M&D* **:** any of several days appointed in southern states for the commemoration of servicemen of the Confederacy: **a :** April 26 in Alabama, Florida, Georgia, and Mississippi **b :** May 10 in No. and So. Carolina **c :** June 3 in Kentucky and Louisiana **d :** May 30 in Virginia

confederate rose *n, often cap C* [so called fr. its naturalization in the southern U.S.] **:** a Chinese mallow (*Hibiscus mutabilis*) with showy white or pink flowers that become deep red at night — called also *cotton rose*

confederate violet *n, often cap C* [prob. so called fr. the grayish appearance of the flowers, suggesting the gray uniform of the Confederate army] **:** a violet (*Viola papilionacea priceana*) having white flowers heavily veined with bluish violet

con·fed·er·a·tion \kənˌfedəˈrāshən\ *n* -s [ME *confederacioun*, fr. MF or LL; MF *confederation*, fr. LL *confoederation-, confoederatio* agreement, compact, fr. *confoederatus* + L *-ion-, -io* -ion] **1 a :** an act of confederating or a state of being confederated **:** a compact for mutual support **:** an alliance (as of nations or states) **:** LEAGUE **b** *archaic* **:** CONSPIRACY **2 :** a group of independent nations, states, or tribes more or less permanently united by a treaty or alliance for joint action (as for defense against a common enemy)

con·fed·er·a·tion·ist \-sh(ə)nəst\ *n* -s **:** a supporter or adherent of a confederation or of a policy of confederating

con·fed·er·a·tism \kənˈfed(ə)rəˌtizəm\ *n* -s **:** the system and practice of a confederacy or confederates

con·fed·er·a·tive \kənˈfed(ə)rə|d·iv, -dəˌrā|, |tiv\ *adj* **:** of, relating to, or characteristic of a confederation or confederates

confederator *n* -s *obs* **:** CONFEDERATE, CONSPIRATOR

con·fer \kənˈfər, +V -ər-; -fō, +V -ər- *also* -ōr\ *vb* **conferred; conferred; conferring; confers** [L *conferre* to bring together, contribute, consult, fr. *com-* + *ferre* to carry — more at BEAR] *vt* **1** *obs* **a :** to bring or add together **:** COLLECT **b :** CONTRIBUTE **2** *obs* **:** COMPARE, COLLATE **3 a :** to grant or bestow esp. at a public ceremony (as a title of nobility or an academic degree) **b :** to give or yield (a characteristic or quality, esp. an advantageous one) ⟨carbon ~*s* hardness upon steel⟩ ⟨the mastery of physical nature which this science has *conferred* on its practitioners —A.J.Toynbee⟩ ~ *vi* **1** *obs* **:** CONTRIBUTE **2** *obs* **:** AGREE, CONFORM **3 :** to hold conversation or conference now typically on important, difficult, or complex matters **:** compare views **:** take counsel **:** CONSULT, DELIBERATE

con·fer·ee \ˌkänfəˈrē\ *n* -s [*confer* + *-ee*] **1 :** one conferred with **:** one taking part in a conference **2 :** one upon whom something is conferred

con·fer·ence \ˈkänf(ə)rən(t)s, -fərn-; *in sense 4* " *or* kənˈfər-ən- *also* kənˈfōrən-\ *n* -s [MF or ML; MF *conference*, fr. ML *conferentia*, fr. L *conferent-, conferens* (pres. part. of *conferre*) + *-ia* -y] **1** *obs* **:** comparison of texts **:** COLLATION **2 :** the act of consulting together usu. formally **:** interchange of views **:** DISCUSSION, DELIBERATION ⟨~ maketh a ready man —Francis Bacon⟩ ⟨the president in ~ with his advisers⟩ **3 :** a meeting for consultation, discussion, or an interchange of opinions whether of individuals or groups: **a :** a meeting of the representatives of different nations to discuss international problems or determine general policy ⟨a ~ of foreign ministers⟩ ⟨a summit ~⟩ **b :** a meeting of members of the two branches of a legislature; *specif* **:** one to adjust differences in the provisions of a bill passed in different forms by the House of Representatives and the Senate **c :** a meeting of those members of a legislative body who belong to the same party in order to plan party policy but without binding its members to a certain course of action — compare CAUCUS **4** *also* **con·fer·rence** \kənˈfər-ən- *also* -fərən-\ **:** conferment (as of an academic degree) **5 a** (1) **:** a church court of the early English Presbyterians corresponding roughly to the modern presbytery **:** CLASSIS (2) **:** a stated meeting of preachers and others in the Methodist and Mennonite churches invested with authority to act on or take cognizance of ecclesiastical matters (3) **:** a voluntary association of Congregational churches of a district; *also* **:** a district containing such churches (4) **:** a subdivision of a district in the United Lutheran Church (5) **:** a semiannual general meeting of the Church of Jesus Christ of Latter-day Saints **b :** a league or association of athletic teams esp. representing educational institutions ⟨a football ~⟩ **c :** an association of firms in the same business for carrying out a common policy — compare TRUST **6 a :** an informal meeting for purposes of intensive instruction between a teacher and a student or small group of students **b :** a brief and intensive course often held during a vacation emphasizing practical experience and demonstration and usu. attended by adults

con·fé·ren·cier \kōⁿfārāⁿsyā\ *n* -s [F, fr. *conférence* lecture (fr. MF *conference* comparison, discussion) + *-ier* -er] **1 a :** LECTURER **b :** a master of ceremonies of a revue **2 :** one taking part in a diplomatic conference **:** CONFEREE

con·fer·en·tial \ˌkänfəˈrenchəl\ *adj* [fr. *conference*, after such pairs as E *penitence: penitential*] **:** relating to conference or a conference

con·fer·ment \kənˈfərmənt, -fōm-\ *n* -s **:** a conferring esp. of a title

con·fer·ra·ble \-fər·əbəl *also* -fōrə-\ *adj* [*confer* + *-able*] **:** that may be conferred

con·fer·ral \-fər·əl *also* -fōrəl\ *n* -s **:** the act of conferring **:** CONFERMENT

con·fer·rer *R* -fər·ər, -*R* -fər·ə(r *also* -fōrə(r\ *n* -s **:** BESTOWER, GIVER

con·fer·ru·mi·nate \ˌkänfəˈrümənət\ *also* **con·fer·ru·mi·nat·ed** \-ˌnād·əd\ *adj* [*conferruminate* fr. L *conferruminatus*, past part. of *conferruminare* to solder, glue, fr. *com-* + *ferruminare* to solder, join, fr. *ferrumin-, ferrumen* solder, glue; *conferruminated* fr. L *conferruminatus* + E *-ed* — more at FERRUMINATE] **:** closely adherent — used chiefly of the cotyledons of some sprouting plants

con·fert·ed \kənˈfərd·əd\ *adj* [L *confertus* (past part. of *confercire* to press or cram together, fr. *com-* + *-fercire*, fr. *farcire* to stuff) + *-ed* — more at FARCE] *of plant parts* **:** closely crowded together ⟨the ~ gills of some mushrooms⟩

con·fer·va \kənˈfərvə\ *n* [NL, fr. L, a water plant, fr. *confervēre* to boil together, grow together, heal, fr. *com-* + *fervēre*, *fervere* to boil; fr. its supposed healing power — more at BURN] **1** *cap, in some esp former classifications* **:** a genus of filamentous green algae containing a number of species of doubtful relationship many of which are now usu. placed in the genus *Tribonema* **2** *pl* **confer·vae** \-(ˌ)vē\ **:** an alga of the genus *Tribonema; broadly* **:** any of various filamentous algae that form scums in still or sluggish fresh water

con·fer·va·ce·ae \ˌkänfə(r)ˈvāsēˌē\ [NL, fr. *Conferva*, type genus + *-aceae*] *syn of* ULOTRICHACEAE

con·fer·va·les \-ā(ˌ)lēz\ *n pl, cap* [NL, fr. *Conferva* + *-ales*] *in old classifications* **:** CONFERVOIDEAE

con·fer·void \kənˈfərˌvȯid\ *adj* [ISV *conferv-* (fr. NL *Conferva*) + *-oid*] **:** resembling confervae esp. in being made up of branching filaments — used chiefly of algae

con·fer·voi·de·ae \ˌkänfə(r)ˈvȯidēˌē\ *n pl, cap* [NL, fr. *Conferva* + *-oideae*] *in some esp former classifications* **:** a group comprising filamentous or mosslike green algae (as those of the genera *Chaetophora, Ulothrix,* and *Ulva*) that are now more commonly placed in Ulotrichales

¹con·fess \kənˈfes\ *vb* -ED/-ING/-ES [ME *confessen*, fr. MF *confesser*, fr. OF, fr. *confes* having confessed, fr. L *confessus*, past part. of *confitēri* to confess, fr. *com-* + *-fitēri* (fr. *fatēri* to acknowledge, confess); akin to L *fari* to speak — more at BAN] *vt* **1 :** to tell of or make known (something private, hidden, or damaging to oneself) **:** ADMIT, ACKNOWLEDGE ⟨~ an error⟩ ⟨he ~*ed* his debt⟩ ⟨I ~ myself a traditionalist —R.W. Chapman⟩ **2 a :** to make known or acknowledge (one's sins) esp. to God or to a priest in order to receive absolution **b :** to relieve (oneself) of the burden of sin by confessing (as to God or a priest) **c** *of a priest* **:** to receive the confession of (a penitent) **:** administer confession to **3 :** to admit as true **:** assent to **:** acknowledge esp. after a previous doubt, denial, or concealment **:** CONCEDE ⟨you know perfectly well you've got a stomach ache, if you'd only ~ it —W.F.de Morgan⟩ **4 :** to acknowledge one's faith in **:** acknowledge as one's belief **:** AVOW ⟨many of the churchgoers and ~*ed* Christians are grossly ignorant of the chief doctrines of their faith —*Humanist*⟩ **5 :** to disclose or reveal as an effect discloses its cause **:** PROVE, ATTEST, MANIFEST ⟨and let our ordered lives ~ the beauty of Thy peace —J.G.Whittier⟩ ~ *vi* **1 a :** to disclose one's sins or faults or the state of one's conscience esp. to God or to a priest **b** *of a priest* **:** to hear confession **:** SHRIVE **2 :** ADMIT, OWN ⟨~ to a crime⟩ **syn** see ACKNOWLEDGE — **confess judgment :** to acknowledge that a claim is or is about to become due to another and consent that legal judgment may be entered for the amount when due and unpaid

²confess \"\ *n* -ES [prob. fr. ¹*confess*] **:** an English country-dance for six persons

con·fes·sant \-sᵊnt\ *n* -s [F or ML; F *confessant*, fr. ML *confessant-, confessans*, pres. part. of *confessare* to confess, fr. MF *confesser*] **:** one who confesses esp. to a priest

con·fes·sar·i·us \ˌkänˌfeˈsa(a)rēəs\ *n, pl* **confessar·ii** \-rēˌī, -rēˌē\ [ML, fr. L *confessus* + *-arius*] **:** one who receives confessions; *esp* **:** FATHER CONFESSOR

con·fess·ed·ly \kənˈfesədlē, -li\ *adv* [*confessed* (past part. of *confess*) + *-ly*] **:** by confession or acknowledgment **:** ADMITTEDLY, AVOWEDLY

con·fess·ing·ly *adv* **:** in the manner of one confessing ⟨testimony ~ intimate in tone⟩

con·fes·sio \kənˈfes(h)ēˌō\ *n, pl* **confessi·o·nes** \kənˌfeshēˈō(ˌ)nēz, -sēˈōˌnās\ [ML, fr. LL, tomb of a martyr, fr. L, confession] **:** CONFESSION 8a(3)

con·fes·sion \kənˈfeshən\ *n* -s [ME *confessioun*, fr. MF *confession*, fr. L *confession-, confessio*, fr. *confessus* + *-ion-, -io* -ion] **1 :** the act of confessing **:** ADMISSION **:** a statement of guilt or obligation in a matter pertaining to oneself; *also* **:** the contents of such a statement **2 confessions** *pl* **:** a usu. written statement in which hidden or intimate matters are disclosed ⟨the *Confessions* of St. Augustine⟩; *broadly* **:** intimately autobiographical writing or fiction intended to give the illusion of such writing **3 :** acknowledgment of sins or sinfulness; *specif* **:** the act of disclosing sins or faults to a priest to obtain sacramental absolution or to a minister to obtain pastoral counseling **4 a :** acknowledgment of belief or profession of faith; *specif* **:** a personal declaration of religious faith **b :** a formal statement of doctrinal belief (as a creed or a catechism) ordinarily intended for public avowal by an individual, a group, a congregation, a synod, or a church **5 :** an acknowledgment of guilt by a party accused of an offense (1) made before a judge or court in due course of legal proceedings or (2) made before an officer or other person, no confession being admissible as evidence that is not entirely voluntary and made without being induced by threats, promises, or hope of escape or favor extended by a person in authority — called also (1) *judicial confession,* (2) *extrajudicial confession;* compare ADMISSION **6 :** a form (as for use in public worship) for the general acknowledgment of sinfulness ⟨a general ~⟩ **7 :** a church or body of Christians having a particular confession of faith **:** COMMUNION **8 a** (1) [LL *confession-, confessio*, fr. L] **:** the tomb of a martyr (2) **:** an altar built over the tomb (3) **:** the crypt or shrine or the part of the altar or occas. a large subterranean chapel in which the relics are placed — called also *confessio* **b :** the high altar in a basilica that stands directly over the altar on a martyr's tomb **c :** the entire building enclosing these two altars

¹con·fes·sion·al \-shənᵊl, -shnəl\ *n* -s [F *confessionnal*, fr. NL *confessionale*, fr. neut. of (assumed) NL *confessionalis* of confession, fr. L *confession-, confessio* confession + *-alis* -al] **1 a :** the recess, seat, or enclosed place where a priest sits to hear confessions **b :** the act or practice of confessing to a priest **2** [F *confessionnal*, modif. (prob. influenced by F *confessionnal* place where a priest sits to hear confessions) of LL *confession-, confessio* tomb of a martyr] **:** CONFESSION 8 **3** [²*confessional*] *usu cap* **:** a member of a confessional church

confessional 1a

²confessional \"\ *adj* [*confession* + *-al*] **1 :** of, relating to, or being a confession esp. of faith ⟨a ~ statement⟩ **2 :** adhering to, established on, or defined by a confession of faith ⟨creedal or ~ orthodoxy⟩ ⟨~ boundaries⟩ **:** associated with a confession **:** DENOMINATIONAL ⟨~ schools⟩ ⟨a ~ political party⟩

con·fes·sion·al·ism \-ˌlizəm\ *n* -s **:** the principle that a church should have a confession of faith **:** devotion or adherence to a confession of faith

confession and avoidance *n* **:** an admission of or failure to deny an allegation coupled with the allegation of new matter that avoids or nullifies the effect of the original allegation — used in legal pleas

¹con·fes·sion·ary \-shəˌnerē\ *adj* [prob. fr. (assumed) NL *confessionarius*, fr. L *confession-, confessio* + *-arius* -ary] **:** of or relating to confession ⟨a ~ litany⟩

²confessionary \"\ *n* -ES [NL *confessionarium*, fr. L *confession-, confessio* + *-arium* -ary] *archaic* **:** CONFESSIONAL

con·fes·sion·ist \-sh(ə)nəst\ *n* -s [NL *confessionista*, fr. L *confession-, confessio* + *-ista* -ist] **:** an adherent of a particular confession of faith

confession of faith : CONFESSION 4b

con·fes·sor \kənˈfesə(r)\ *sometimes* ˈkänˌfe-, *archaic* ˈkänfəsə(r) *or* ˈkänfəˌsȯ(ə)r *or* ˈkänfəˌsȯ(ə)\ *n* -s [ME *confessor*, *confessour*, fr. OF & LL; OF *confessour*, fr. LL *confessor*, fr. L *confessus* (past part. of *confitēri* to confess) + *-or* — more at CONFESS] **1 :** one who confesses **:** one who avows belief in someone or something esp. in a religious faith or leader **2 :** a giver of heroic evidence of faith; *specif* **:** a Christian saint who has lived heroically for his faith esp. through a persecution without being martyred ⟨Edward the *Confessor*, King of England 1042–1066⟩ **3 :** one (as a priest) who hears the confessions of others

con·fet·ti \kənˈfed·|ē, -et|, |i *or in sense 1 as It* kōnˈfettē\ *n pl but sing in constr* [It, pl. of *confetto*, fr. ML *confectum* sweetmeat, confection — more at CONFECT] **1 :** bonbons or other candies; *also* **:** their plaster or paper substitutes **2 :** tiny colored paper disks or paper streamers so made as to scatter readily when thrown (as at carnivals, parties, weddings) **3 :** a deep pink to moderate red that is yellower and stronger than laurel pink and yellower than watermelon

con·fi·dant \ˈkänfəˌdant, -daa(ə)nt, ˌ==ˈ= *also* -dänt *or* -dänt; ˈ==dənt *also* -dᵊnt *or* -ˌdent\ *also* **con·fi·dent** \ˈ==dənt *also* -dᵊnt *or* -ˌdent\ *n* -s [F *confident*, fr. It *confidente* confident, trustworthy, fr. L *confident-, confidens* confident] **:** a trusted friend or associate ⟨the nearest thing to a ~ that the lonely man had —*Newsweek*⟩; *esp* **:** one to whom secrets (as of love affairs or political matters) are confided or entrusted **syn** see FRIEND

con·fi·dante *like* CONFIDANT\ *n* -s [F *confidente*, fem. of *confident*] **1 :** a female confidant **2 :** a sofa divided by arms into separate seats: as **a :** one at either end of which a small seat extends beyond the arm **b :** one in the shape of the letter S

confidante 2a

con·fide \kənˈfīd\ *vb* -ED/-ING/-S [ME *confiden*, fr. MF or L; MF *confider*, fr. L *confidere*, fr. *com-* + *fidere* to trust — more at BIDE] *vi* **1 :** to place or have faith **:** have confidence **:** TRUST ⟨we cannot ~ wholly in our own powers⟩ **2 :** to share or impart secrets or intimate matters ⟨a *confiding* letter⟩ — usu. used with *in* ⟨patients too awed by the doctor to ~ in him —Leonard Gross⟩ ~ *vt* **1 :** to tell confidentially ⟨he dared not ~ the secret to his family —George Meredith⟩ **2 :** to give into the care or protection of someone or something **:** ENTRUST, COMMIT ⟨the defense of our island was still *confided* to the militia —T.B.Macaulay⟩ ⟨do not ~ your children to strangers —Mavis Gallant⟩ **syn** see COMMIT

¹con·fi·dence \ˈkänfədən(t)s *also* -dᵊn- *or* -ˌden-\ *n* -s [ME, fr. MF, fr. L *confidentia*, fr. *confident-, confidens* (pres. part. of *confidere* to confide) + *-ia* -y] **1 :** the state of one that confides **:** TRUST, RELIANCE, BELIEF ⟨a cheerful ~ in the mercy of God —T.B.Macaulay⟩ **2 :** feeling or consciousness of reliance on oneself or one's circumstances **:** SELF-CONFIDENCE ⟨a doctor's increasing ~ and skill⟩ ⟨painters who had . . . lost their ~ —W.B.Yeats⟩ **3 :** the state of feeling sure **:** CERTITUDE — usu. used with *of* ⟨great ~ of success⟩ ⟨the level of ~ accepted for a given set of statistical data⟩ **4 :** BRASHNESS, PRESUMPTION, IMPUDENCE ⟨he had that ~ which the first thinker of anything never has, for all thinkers . . . approach the truth full of hesitation and doubt. *Confidence* comes from repetition, from the breath of many mouths —W.B.Yeats⟩ **5** *obs* **:** an object of faith or reliance ⟨for the Lord shall be thy ~ —Prov 3:26

(AV)〉 **6 a :** a relation or state of trust or intimacy between persons who confide in each other 〈take a friend into one's ~ concerning a private affair〉 **b** *obs* **:** TRUSTWORTHINESS **c :** a communication made in confidence 〈the ~*s* between lawyer and client〉 **d :** trust in or support of the policy or action of a prime minister and his cabinet expressed by a formal vote of the legislature in a parliamentary system of government **syn** see TRUST

²**confidence** \"\ *adj* **:** having to do with the appropriation by a swindler of funds entrusted to him usu. by a dupe promised large and easy profits from a type of investment not generally considered ethical 〈~ game〉 〈~ man〉

³**confidence** \"\ *vt* -ED/-ING/-S **:** to swindle esp. by exploiting confidence or desire for quick gain

confidence course *n* **:** OBSTACLE COURSE

confidence interval *n, statistics* **:** an interval which is based on a random sample and for which there is a given probability that it contains a given population parameter (as the mean)

confidence limit *n, statistics* **:** either end point of a confidence interval

confidency *n* -ES [L *confidentia*] *obs* **:** CONFIDENCE

¹**con·fi·dent** \ˈkänfədənt *also* -dᵊnt *or* -ˌdent\ *adj* [MF, fr. L *confident-, confidens*, pres. part. of *confidere* to confide] **1** *obs* **a :** TRUSTFUL, CONFIDING **b :** giving occasion for confidence **:** TRUSTWORTHY **2 :** characterized by confidence, by a strong, reliant, and bold belief in oneself, and by freedom from fear, doubt, and worry 〈advancing from triumph to triumph with clear eye and ~ step —W.R.Inge〉 **3 :** strongly disposed to believe in the merit or truth of something or to accept it as reliable or certain without doubt or reservation — usu. used with *of* or a dependent clause 〈he felt ~ that he could live to see the day —O.E.Rölvaag〉 **4 a :** characterized by an excessive belief in one's rightness, strength, or security and therefore rash or bold 〈I have no cocksure answer . . . Of course ~ answers are common enough —C.E.Montague〉 **b :** DOGMATIC, CONTENTIOUS, PRESUMPTUOUS **5 :** CONFIDENTIAL — obs. except as applied in Scots law to a person standing in such intimate and confidential relations as to be likely to know the state of one's business affairs

syn ASSURED, SANGUINE, SURE, SELF-CONFIDENT, SELF-ASSURED, PRESUMPTUOUS: usu. complimentary, CONFIDENT may imply an undemonstrative firm feeling of certain success 〈a *confident* feeling of immense reserves in strength and endurance —T.E. Lawrence〉 Sometimes it may imply ill-grounded optimism or overbearing presumption 〈we have not realized the hopes of the eighteenth century 'illumination', when *confident* philosophers believed that humanity was shaking off its ancient chains —J.H.Robinson〉 〈he swaggered up the path as if the place belonged to him and we heard his loud, *confident* peal at the bell —A. Conan Doyle〉 ASSURED, sometimes uncomplimentary, indicates utter absence of doubt in one's ability, success, or correctness 〈"All the boys in my class are older, but I keep at the head." Sometimes he was almost too *assured* —Ellen Glasgow〉 〈[he] has *assured* carriage, walking boldly into good hotels and mixing with patrons on terms of equality —Don Marquis〉 SANGUINE, usu. complimentary, stresses extreme optimism 〈a surgeon's commission for the doctor, and a lieutenancy for myself, were certainly counted upon in our *sanguine* expectations —Herman Melville〉 〈his *sanguine* spirit kindled with an enthusiasm which overleaped every obstacle —W.H.Prescott〉 SURE usu. indicates a reasonable, well-grounded confidence 〈individual members may be ill-bred; the House itself has a fine taste and breeding, and a *sure* instinct in matters of conduct —John Buchan〉 〈she tempted the young man into kissing her, and later lay in his arms for two hours, entirely *sure* of herself —Sherwood Anderson〉 SELF-CONFIDENT and SELF-ASSURED intensify suggestions of CONFIDENT and ASSURED and are often not complimentary 〈their claim to superiority is just as stubborn as though it were well-founded, just as *self-assured* as in case of our own really superior nation —Bertrand Russell〉 PRESUMPTUOUS always implies overconfidence and usu. suggests boldness and insolence 〈Arheetoo had known me but two hours and as he made the proposition very coolly, I thought it rather *presumptuous* —Herman Melville〉 〈to write in this way of men like Dante and Shakespeare is really less *presumptuous* than to write of smaller men —T.S.Eliot〉

²**confident** *var of* CONFIDANT

con·fi·den·tial \ˌkänfəˈdenchəl\ *adj* [fr. *confidence*, after such pairs as E *penitence: penitential*] **1 :** communicated, conveyed, acted on, or practiced in confidence **:** known only to a limited few **:** not publicly disseminated **:** PRIVATE, SECRET 〈chary of committing anything of a ~ nature to any more concrete medium than speech —William Faulkner〉 〈~ remarks〉 **2 a :** showing confidence in another **:** disposed to relate or confide private or secret matters 〈growing still more ~ . . . said that I would soon be a most important personage among them —W.H.Hudson〉 **b :** marked by or indicative of confiding or confidence **:** indicative of intimacy, mutual trust, or willingness to confide 〈he slipped his arm through his father's with a ~ pressure —Edith Wharton〉 **c :** receiving confidences **:** treated with confidence **:** adjudged trustworthy 〈he had been his ~ servant and was intimate with all his habits —Anthony Trollope〉 **3 a :** SECRET, HIDDEN, ESOTERIC **b :** characterized by or relating to information unauthorized disclosure of which could be prejudicial to a country's interests — compare CLASSIFIED 2 **syn** see FAMILIAR

confidential communication *n* **:** PRIVILEGED COMMUNICATION 1

confidential employee *n* **:** an employee having access in the course of his duties to confidential information on the employer's labor relations and consequently excludable from union membership

con·fi·den·tial·i·ty \ˌkänfəˌdenchēˈaləd·ē, -ˌden'shal-\ *n* -ES **:** the quality or state of being confidential, private, or secret 〈federal law establishes the ~ of clinical records concerning voluntary patients —D.W.Maurer & V.H.Vogel〉

con·fi·den·tial·ly \ˌkänfəˈdench(ə)lē, -li\ *adv* **:** in a confidential manner 〈addressing him intimately and ~〉 〈leaning ~ across the table —Gerald Beaumont〉

con·fi·den·tial·ness \-chəlnəs\ *n* -ES **:** the quality or state of being confidential **:** CONFIDENTIALITY

con·fi·dent·ly *adv* **:** with confidence **:** with strong assurance **:** POSITIVELY, BOLDLY, UNHESITATINGLY

con·fi·dent·ness *n* -ES **:** CONFIDENCE

confides *pres 3d sing of* CONFIDE

confiding *adj* [fr. pres. part. of *confide*] **:** that confides **:** TRUSTFUL — **con·fid·ing·ly** *adv* — **con·fid·ing·ness** *n* -ES

con·fig·u·ral \kənˈfigyərəl, ÷ -gər-\ *adj* [*configuration* + *-al*] **:** of or relating to a configuration

con·fig·u·rate \-ˌrāt, *usu* -ād·+V\ *vt* -ED/-ING/-S [L *configuratus*, past part. of *configurare* to form from or after, fr. *com-* + *figurare* to form, fr. *figura* figure — more at FIGURE] **:** to give or assign a form to **:** FASHION, SHAPE, FORM

configurated *adj* [fr. past part. of *configurate*] **1** *astrol* **:** associated in a configuration **2** *of glass* **:** having an irregularly patterned surface

con·fig·u·ra·tion \ˌ=ˌ=ˈrāshən *also* ˌkän-\ *n* -S [LL *configuration-, configuratio* comparison, shaping, fr. L *configuratus* + *-ion-, -io* -ion] **1 a** *astrol* **:** relative position or aspect of the planets **b** *astron* **:** any of several limiting apparent positions of a celestial body with respect to another (as conjunction, quadrature, opposition, and elongation) **2 a :** relative disposition or arrangement of parts **:** interrelationships of constituent elements **b :** the contour, pattern, or figure produced by such disposition 〈a network of roads following the ~ of the country —John Buchan〉 **3 :** a geometrical figure usu. consisting of points and lines and the points, lines, and planes which may be derived from them

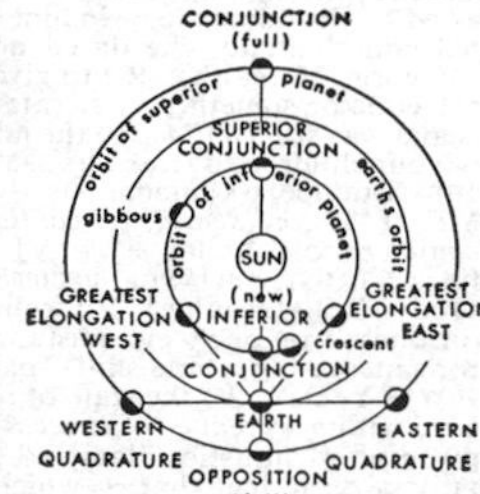

planetary configurations

4 : the structure of chemical compounds esp. with reference to the space relations of the atoms in molecules **5** [G *konfiguration*, fr. LL *configuration-, configuratio*] **:** GESTALT **syn** see FORM

con·fig·u·ra·tion·al \kənˌ=ˌ=ˈrāshənᵊl, ˌkänˌ=ˌ=ˈrā-, -shnəl\ *adj* **:** relating to or based on a configuration — **con·fig·u·ra·tion·al·ly** \-ᵊlē, -əlē\ *adv*

con·fig·u·ra·tion·ism \kənˌ=ˌ=ˈrāshəˌnizəm, ˌkän-\ *n* -S **:** GESTALT PSYCHOLOGY — **con·fig·u·ra·tion·ist** \-sh(ə)nəst\ *n* -S

configurative \kən +\ *adj* [*configuration* + *-ive*] **:** CONFIGURATIONAL

con·figure \kən +\ *vt* -ED/-ING/-S [ME *configuren*, fr. L *configurare*] **1 :** to shape according to some model **:** cause to conform 〈man's nature is *configured* to the divine〉 **2 :** to arrange in a certain form, figure, or shape **:** give a configuration to **:** SHAPE 〈a magnet is surrounded by a *configured* field〉

¹**con·fine** \kənˈfīn\ *vb* -ED/-ING/-S [MF *confiner* to lie contiguous, restrain within limits, fr. *confin*, n., confine] *vi, archaic* **:** to have a common boundary **:** lie contiguous ~ *vt* **:** to hold within bounds **:** restrain from exceeding boundaries: **a :** to keep in narrow quarters **:** IMPRISON **b :** to prevent free outward passage or motion of **:** SECURE, ENCLOSE, FASTEN 〈the loose cloud of hair was *confined* in two plaits —W.H.Hudson〉 〈dikes *confined* the flood waters〉 **c :** to keep from leaving accustomed quarters (as one's room or bed) under pressure of infirmity, childbirth, detention, business reasons 〈now that he was able to employ an assistant, he was not closely *confined* to the store —Ellen Glasgow〉 **d :** to narrow down (range of possible interest, participation, expression) and exclude from embracing various matters possible **:** make applicable only to a limited group 〈for what reason was the Greek tragic poet *confined* to so limited a range of subjects —Matthew Arnold〉 〈a rare luxury *confined* to princes and ministers —T.B. Macaulay〉 **e :** to keep to a certain place or to a limited area **:** prevent unlimited incidence of 〈in *confining* the disease to Memphis —W.F.Willcox〉 〈the buffalo was not *confined* to the open grassland —C.D.Forde〉 **syn** see LIMIT

²**con·fine** \ˈkänˌfīn, *in sense 5a usu* kən'f-\ *n* -S [MF or L; MF *confin*, fr. L *confine*, fr. neut. of *confinis* having the same boundary, adjacent, fr. *com-* + *finis* end, border — more at FINAL] **1** *usu pl* **:** BOUNDS, BORDERS; *esp* **:** the mutual boundary with adjacent regions 〈betwixt the ~*s* of night and day —John Dryden〉 **2** *usu pl* **:** regions along or near a border **:** outlying parts 〈the Newtonian scheme does not banish God from the universe, but it pushes him to the ~*s* —*Times Lit. Supp.*〉 **3** *usu pl* **:** constricting limits (as of an area of activity or operation) **:** SCOPE 〈Darwin had not moved entirely within the ~*s* of the thought of his generation —S.F.Mason〉 〈lifts the story beyond a conventional ~ —*Times Lit. Supp.*〉 **4** *usu pl* **:** enclosed or otherwise limited space or area **:** TERRITORY 〈the future of the city lies in the eastern corner of its ~*s* —*Springfield (Mass.) Daily News*〉 **5 a** *archaic* **:** RESTRICTION, CONFINEMENT 〈the dungeon's grim ~ —Robert Burns〉 **b** *obs* **:** PRISON, DUNGEON 〈many ~*s*, wards, and dungeons —Shak.〉

³**confine** *adj* [MF or L; MF *confin*, fr. L *confinis* adjacent] *obs* **:** NEIGHBORING

con·fined \kənˈfīnd\ *adj* [fr. past part. of *confine*] **:** kept in confines; *often* **:** in childbed **:** in the course of childbirth

con·fined·ly \-īn(ə)dlē\ *adv* **:** in a confined manner

con·fined·ness \-īnədnəs, -īn(d)nəs\ *n* -ES **:** the quality or state of being confined

confineless *adj* [²*confine* + *-less*] *obs* **:** BOUNDLESS, LIMITLESS

con·fine·ment \kənˈfīnmənt\ *n* -S [F, fr. MF, fr. *confiner* + *-ment*] **1 :** the act of confining or state of being confined **:** restraint within limits 〈the mind hates restraint and is apt to fancy itself under ~ when the sight is pent up —Joseph Addison〉 **2 a :** restraint within doors by sickness 〈after several weeks of ~ he was eager to cooperate with his doctor〉 **b :** LYING-IN, ACCOUCHEMENT 〈the ~ took place at home〉

confinement system *n* **:** any system of raising poultry or other livestock in which the animals are kept from contact with the ground primarily as a sanitary measure

confiner *n* -S *obs* **:** one that lives on or within the confines **:** NEIGHBOR, INHABITANT

confining *adj* [fr. pres. part. of *confine*] **:** that confines **:** RESTRAINING, RESTRICTIVE 〈bookkeeping is a ~ occupation〉 〈glaciers flowing . . . between rugged ~ peaks —W.E.Rudolph〉

confining bed *n, geol* **:** a comparatively impervious stratum directly above or below one bearing water or petroleum

con·fin·i·ty \kənˈfinəd·ē\ *n* -ES [MF *confinité*, fr. *confin* adjacent, neighboring + *-ité* -ity] *archaic* **:** community of limits **:** CONTIGUITY, ADJACENCY

con·firm \kənˈfərm, -fəm, -fəim\ *vt* -ED/-ING/-S [ME *confermen, confirmen*, fr. OF *confermer, confirmer*, fr. L *confirmare*, fr. *com-* + *firmare* to make firm, fr. *firmus* firm — more at FIRM] **1 :** to make firm **:** strengthen (as a person) in resolution, conviction, loyalty, position 〈America would once again as a nation confound its critics and . . . ~ its friends —Barbara Ward〉 **2 a :** to make valid by formal assent **:** complete by a necessary approval 〈the Senate ~*s* a treaty〉; *often* **:** to vote approval of (the appointment of a person to an office) 〈the Senate ~*ed* his appointment to the Supreme Court〉 **b :** to give formal acknowledgment of receipt of 〈an order ~*ed* by a stockbroker〉 **3 :** to administer the rite of confirmation to **4 :** to give new assurance of the truth or validity of **:** CORROBORATE 〈~ a rumor〉 〈~ a hypothesis or diagnosis〉 〈~ a plane reservation〉 **5 :** to make firmer or more settled in a conviction, purpose, or habit 〈the experience ~*ed* him in his dislike of foreign cooking〉 **6 :** to state or imply the truth of (as a rumor or forecast) **:** ASSERT, MAINTAIN — usu. used with *that* **7** *Scots law* **:** to ratify the right of (a person) to take and administer property of a deceased person as executor or administrator

syn CORROBORATE, SUBSTANTIATE, VERIFY, AUTHENTICATE, VALIDATE: these may be compared in that they signify to attest or establish usu. beyond a reasonable doubt the truth, accuracy, validity, or genuineness of something. CONFIRM and CORROBORATE both imply an attesting to something already formulated or recognized but not yet made certain. CONFIRM usu. implies the making unquestionable of something in question by means of authoritative statement or indisputable fact 〈they are asked to *confirm* or correct facts —Evelyn Lohr〉 〈there is a rumor — which cannot of course be *confirmed* —Frank Gorrell〉 〈*confirm* the persistent suspicion that eggs are carriers of fowl typhoid —*Collier's Yr. Bk.*〉 CORROBORATE suggests the buttressing or strengthening by authority or fact of something already pretty well established 〈in general, the material illustrates and *corroborates* what has already become known from other sources —G.F.Kennan〉 〈no matter how many *corroborating* tests we may adduce as proof . . . the skeptic still is not convinced —Arthur Pap〉 〈these were the earliest professional sodalities in Spain, though *corroborating* documentation is lacking —G.M.Foster〉 SUBSTANTIATE implies the presenting of evidence adequate to demonstrate or make certain 〈individual differences within one race and culture are well *substantiated* . . . by psychological and practical tests —A.L.Kroeber〉 〈reference material to support, *substantiate*, or enlarge upon the text —Frank Mortimer〉 〈no proof had to be brought forward to *substantiate* the claims they made —Sherwood Anderson〉 VERIFY implies the seeking of a close correspondence between a statement and the facts it involves or an attestation to the correctness of its logic, or, as applied to suspicions or predictions, the actualization in fact of the thing suspected 〈he has explored most of Trans-Jordan, *verified* Biblical accounts by his findings and excavations —*Current Biog.*〉 〈discouraging predictions that have not been *verified* by events —*Times Lit. Supp.*〉 AUTHENTICATE and VALIDATE presuppose a question about genuineness or validity. AUTHENTICATE signifies to establish genuineness by or as if by expert opinion or official or legal document 〈the painting was finally *authenticated* by experts in Barcelona and Madrid —*Time*〉 〈each citizen ought to be *authenticated* as the son of his proper father —H.M.Parshley〉 〈an *authenticated* copy of the Declaration —Dumas Malone〉 VALIDATE generally involves establishing of validity, as of a document by reference to legal or official act or record or as of an opinion or policy by justifying facts or events 〈what directors do . . . by law must be *validated* by formal board action —G.B.Hurff〉 〈the sort of evidence by which one *validates* a scientific hypothesis —*Life*〉 〈the expansion of demand which alone can *validate* the policy —J.A.Hobson〉 〈the two performances more than *validated* the words of praise —Irving Kolodin〉

con·firm·abil·i·ty \=ˌ=əˈbiləd·ē, -ətē, -i\ *n* -ES **:** the quality or state of being confirmable

confirmability theory *n* [*confirmability* fr. *confirmable* + *-ity*] **:** a modification of the verifiability principle according to which a requirement or criterion for the meaningfulness of a factual statement is its susceptibility to the possibility of being either theoretically or actually supported by reference to empirical facts

con·firm·able \=ˈ=əbəl\ *adj* **1 :** capable of being confirmed **2 :** susceptible to the possibility of being either theoretically or actually supported or weakened by reference to empirical facts

con·fir·mand \ˈkänfə(r)ˌmand\ *n* -S [L *confirmandus* fit to be confirmed, fr. *confirmare* to confirm] **:** a candidate for religious confirmation

con·fir·ma·tion \ˌkänfə(r)ˈmāshən\ *n* -S [ME *confirmacioun*, fr. MF *confirmation*, fr. L *confirmation-, confirmatio*, fr. *confirmatus* (past part. of *confirmare*) + *-ion-, -io* -ion] **1 :** the act of confirming or strengthening **:** the act of establishing, assuring, or upholding: **a** (1) **:** a rite of various Christian churches regarded as supplemental to the rite of baptism, held by some churches to be a sacrament, and viewed generally as confirming a person in his religious faith (2) **:** the act or ceremony of confirming or sanctioning 14 to 16 year-old boys and girls in the Jewish faith following their study of the faith and history of Judaism and their declaration of devotion to its principles; *also* **:** the synagogue service now usu. held on Shabuoth in which this religious ceremony occurs **b :** the ratification of an executive act (as a treaty or an appointment) by a legislative body **2 :** CORROBORATION, SUBSTANTIATION 〈the report lacked ~〉: as **a :** something that confirms **:** PROOF, SUPPORT 〈find ~ of a theory〉 **b :** the procedure of supporting a factual statement by means of empirical evidence **c** (1) **:** a written order or agreement that verifies or substantiates an agreement previously concluded orally (2) *in auditing* **:** written substantiation of the existence or value esp. of claims against assets, assets held by others, or assets and liabilities **3 a :** a conveyance by which a voidable estate is made sure and not voidable or by which a particular estate is increased **:** an express or implied contract by which a person makes that firm and binding which was before voidable **b** *Scots law* **:** a sentence empowering an executor upon making inventory of the movables pertaining to the deceased to recover, possess, and administer them

confirmation class *n* **:** a course of study in the fundamentals of religion designed to prepare young people for confirmation and usu. conducted by a pastor, priest, or rabbi; *also* **:** the group of young persons participating in such a class

con·fir·ma·tive \kənˈfərməd·|iv, -fəm-, -fəim-, -mət| *also* |əv\ *adj* [LL *confirmativus*, fr. L *confirmatus* + *-ivus* -ive] **:** tending to confirm or establish — **con·fir·ma·tive·ly** \|əvlē, -li\ *adv*

con·fir·ma·to·ry \-məˌtōrē, -tȯr-, -ri\ *adj* [ML *confirmatorius*, fr. L *confirmatus* + *-orius* -ory] **1 :** serving to confirm **:** CORROBORATIVE **2 :** relating to the rite of confirmation

con·firmed \-md\ *adj* [ME *confermed* chronic, inveterate, fr. past part. of *confermen* to confirm] **:** made firm or established (as by stengthening, accustoming, or settling by long continuance, habitual usage, or determined or expressed preference): **a :** made resolute **:** ENCOURAGED, FORTIFIED 〈southern zealots ~ by early successes at Bull Run〉 **b :** given to habit so long-continued or to a way of acting or thinking so resolutely adhered to that change is unlikely 〈~ pedestrians like my father and me —George Santayana〉 **c :** marked by long continuance **:** deeply ingrained **:** constantly practiced 〈like all other ~ habits . . . easier to obey than to break —Ellen Glasgow〉 **d :** having received the rite of confirmation **syn** see INVETERATE

confirmed credit *n* **:** LETTER OF CREDIT

con·firm·ed·ly \-mədlē, -li\ *adv* [ME *confermedly*, fr. *confermed* + *-ly*] **:** in the manner of one convinced **:** UNALTERABLY 〈~ pro-American . . . on foreign policy —F.H.Gervasi〉

con·firmed·ness \-mədnəs, -m(d)n-\ *n* -ES **:** the quality or state of being confirmed

confirming *pres part of* CONFIRM

con·fir·mor \ˈkänfərˌmȯ(ə)r, kənˈfərmər\ *n* -S **:** one that makes a confirmation of title to another

confirms *pres 3d sing of* CONFIRM

con·fis·ca·ble \kənˈfiskəbəl, (ˈ)känˈf-\ *adj* [prob. fr. F, fr. MF, fr. *confisquer* to confiscate (fr. L *confiscare*) + *-able*] **:** liable to confiscation

con·fis·cat·able \ˈkänfəˌskād·əbəl, -ātə-\ *adj* **:** CONFISCABLE

¹**con·fis·cate** \ˈkänfəˌskāt, kənˈfiskət, *usu* -d·+V\ *adj* [L *confiscatus*, past part. of *confiscare* to confiscate, fr. *com-* + *-fiscare* (fr. *fiscus* basket, purse, treasury) — more at FISCAL] **1** *archaic* **:** appropriated by the government to public use **:** FORFEITED **2 :** deprived of property by confiscation

²**con·fis·cate** \ˈkänfəˌskāt, *archaic* kənˈfi,-, *usu* -ād·+V\ *vt* -ED/-ING/-S [L *confiscatus*] **1 :** to seize as forfeited to the public treasury **:** APPROPRIATE 〈~ an estate〉 〈a capital gains tax that *confiscated* most of the wealth accumulated since 1940 —*Current Biog.*〉 **2 :** to seize by or as if by public authority 〈police *confiscated* the liquor〉 〈the teacher *confiscated* the notes〉 **syn** see APPROPRIATE

con·fis·ca·tion \ˌkänfəˈskāshən, -nˌfi'-\ *n* -S [MF or L; MF, fr. L *confiscation-, confiscatio*, fr. *confiscatus* + *-ion-, -io* -ion] **:** the act of confiscating or state of being confiscated **:** the taking of private property to the public use as being forfeited

con·fis·ca·tor \ˈkänfəˌskād·ə(r), -ātə-, *archaic* kənˈfi,-\ *n* -S [²*confiscate* + *-or*] **:** one that confiscates

con·fis·ca·to·ry \kənˈfiskəˌtōrē, -tȯr-, -ri *sometimes* ˈkänfəs-\ *adj* **:** effecting or constituting confiscation **:** characterized by confiscations 〈~ taxation〉

con·fi·se·rie \kōⁿfēzrē\ *n* -S [F, fr. *confis-* (stem of *confire* to preserve) + *-erie* -ery — more at COMFIT] **:** CONFECTIONERY

con·fi·tent \ˈkänfətənt\ *n* -S [L *confitent-, confitens*, pres. part. of *confitēri* to confess — more at CONFESS] **:** CONFESSANT

con·fi·te·or \kənˈfēd·ē,ō(ə)r, -ētē-, -ēər\ *n* [ME, fr. L, I confess, fr. *confitēri* to confess — more at CONFESS] **:** a liturgical form in which sinfulness is acknowledged and intercession for God's mercy requested

con·fi·te·ria \ˌkänˌfēd·əˈrēə, ˌkänfətə-\ *n* -S [Sp *confiteria*, fr. *confite* comfit (fr. Catal *confit*, fr. ML *confectum*) + *-eria* -ery — more at CONFECT] **:** a Latin-American establishment devoted to the sale of tea, coffee, chocolate, and other beverages and sometimes other refreshments (as pastry and sandwiches)

con·fi·ture \ˈkänfəˌchů(ə)r\ *n* -S [F — more at COMFITURE] **1** *obs* **:** CONFECTION 1b **2 :** preserved or candied fruit **:** JAM

con·flab \ˈkänˌflab, kənˈf-\ *dial var of* CONFAB

con·fla·grant \kənˈflāgrənt\ *adj* [L *conflagrant-, conflagrans*, pres. part. of *conflagrare* to burn, be consumed by fire, fr. *com-* + *flagrare* to burn, blaze — more at BLACK] **:** BURNING, BLAZING

con·fla·grate \ˈkänfləˌgrāt\ *vb* -ED/-ING/-S [L *conflagratus*, past part. of *conflagrare*] *vi* **:** to catch fire ~ *vt* **:** to set on fire

con·fla·gra·tion \ˌkänfləˈgrāshən\ *n* -S [L *conflagration-, conflagratio*, fr. *conflagratus* + *-ion-, -io* -ion] **1** *obs* **a :** consumption by fire **b :** INFLAMMATION, FEVER **2 :** FIRE; *esp* **:** a large disastrous fire involving numerous buildings

con·fla·gra·tor \ˈkänfləˌgrād·ə(r)\ *n* -S [L *conflagratus* + E *-or*] **:** INCENDIARY

con·flag·ra·to·ry \kənˈflagrəˌtōrē\ *adj* [*conflagrate* + *-ory*] **:** INFLAMMATORY

¹**con·flate** \ˈkänˌflāt, kənˈf-\ *adj* [L *conflatus*, past part. of *conflare* to blow together, fr. *com-* + *flare* to blow — more at BLOW] **:** brought together **:** assembled, blended, or consolidated into one 〈~ readings of a text〉

²**con·flate** \kənˈflāt, ˈkänˌf-\ *vt* -ED/-ING/-S [L *conflatus*] **1 :** to bring together **:** COLLECT, MERGE, FUSE **2 a :** to combine (two readings of a text) into a composite whole **b :** to produce (a composite reading or text) by conflation

con·fla·tion \kənˈflāshən\ *n* -S [LL *conflation-, conflatio*, fr. L *conflatus* + *-ion-, -io* -ion] **:** the process or result of conflating **:** BLEND, FUSION; *esp* **:** a composite reading or text

¹**con·flict** \ˈkänˌflikt\ *n* -S [ME, fr. L *conflictus* act of striking together, fr. *conflictus*, past part. of *confligere* to strike together, fight, fr. *com-* + *fligere* to strike — more at PROFLIGATE] **1 a :** clash, competition, or mutual interference of opposing or incompatible forces or qualities (as ideas, interests,

wills) : ANTAGONISM ⟨the convulsions of a soul storm-driven amid unreconcilable spiritual ~s —H.O.Taylor⟩ b : an emotional state characterized by indecision, restlessness, uncertainty, and tension resulting from incompatible inner needs or drives of comparable intensity 2 a : an engagement between men under arms : STRUGGLE, CONTEST, FIGHT b : prolonged fighting esp. with weapons : WARFARE, STRIFE c : the opposition of persons or forces upon which the dramatic action depends in drama or fiction d : CONFLICT OF LAWS 3 : a striking or clashing together of material bodies or substances (as air currents, parts of a mechanism) : COLLISION syn see CONTEST, DISCORD

2**con·flict** \kən'flikt, 'kän,f-\ vi -ED/-ING/-S [ME conflicten, fr. L conflictus, past part. of confligere to fight] 1 : to contend with or against another in strife or warfare ⟨France ~ed with England⟩ ⟨the ~ing nations of Greece and Turkey⟩ 2 : to show variance, incompatibility, irreconcilability, or opposition : evidence variance or disharmony calling for adjustment, harmonizing, bringing into accord ⟨the two versions of the story ~⟩ ⟨nor does the French revolutionary spirit ~ with what we ordinarily mean by respect for law —W.C.Brownell⟩ syn see BUMP, CONTEST

conflicting adj [fr. pres. part. of conflict] : being in conflict, collision, or opposition : CONTENDING, INCOMPATIBLE — **con·flict·ing·ly** adv

con·flic·tion \kən'flikshən\ n -S [L confliction-, conflictio, fr. conflictus + -ion-, -io -ion] : the process of conflicting or state of being in conflict

con·flic·tive \kən'fliktiv, 'kän,f-\ adj : tending to conflict

conflict of interest : a conflict between the private interests and the official responsibilities of a person in a position of trust (as a government official)

conflict of laws : opposition or conflict between the laws of different states or jurisdictions as respects the rights of the same individual; also : a branch of law that deals with the adjustment of such opposition or defines the law applicable to situations or transactions asserted to be governed by divergent local laws

con·flic·tu·al \(')kän¦flikchəwəl, kən'f-, -ksh-\ adj ['conflict + -ual (as in actual)] : marked by, involving, or containing conflict

con·flow \kən'flō, kän-\ vi [com- + flow] : to flow together

confluction n -S [modif. of ML confluxion-, confluxio, fr. LL, abundant flow, fr. L confluxus (past part. of confluere) + -ion-, -io -ion] obs : CONFLUENCE

con·flu·ence \'kän,flüən(t)s\ n -S [LL confluentia act of flowing together, fr. L confluent-, confluens, pres. part. of confluere + -ia -y] 1 a : a coming or flocking together, meeting, or gathering at one place : CONCOURSE ⟨you see this ~, this great flood of visitors —Shak.⟩ b : large assemblage : CROWD 2 a : the flowing together of two or more streams ⟨an island formed by the ~ of two rivers⟩ b : the place of meeting of two streams ⟨Koblenz stands at the ~ of the Rhine and the Moselle⟩ c : the stream or body formed by the junction of two or more streams : a combined flood 3 : CONCRESCENCE 2

1**con·flu·ent** \(')kän¦flüənt, kən'f-\ adj [L confluent-, confluens, pres. part. of confluere to flow together, fr. com- + fluere to flow — more at FLUENT] 1 : flowing together : meeting or coming together : combining to form one ⟨~ streams⟩ ⟨~ glaciers⟩ ⟨~ veins⟩ — opposed to diffluent 2 med a : running or run together : UNITED ⟨~ pustules⟩ b : characterized by confluent lesions ⟨~ smallpox⟩ — compare DISCRETE 1b 3 : coming together smoothly without a notch at the point of junction ⟨~ dorsal fins of certain fishes⟩

2**confluent** \"\ n -S : a confluent stream; broadly : AFFLUENT, TRIBUTARY

con·flux \'kän,fləks\ n -ES [ML confluxus, fr. LL, abundant flow, fr. L confluxus, past part. of confluere] : CONFLUENCE

con·focal \(')kän+\ adj [com- + focal] math : having the same real or imaginary foci — used of conic sections and of conicoids whose principal sections are confocal conics

1**con·form** \kən'fó(ə)rm, -ó(ə)m\ vb -ED/-ING/-S [ME conformen, fr. MF conformer, fr. L conformare to form, conform, fr. com- + formare to form, fr. forma form — more at FORM] vt : to make like : shape to fit : ADAPT ⟨~s the belt to the contour⟩ : bring into harmony or agreement ⟨~ this regulation to existing business practices —M.V.DiSalle⟩ ~ vi 1 : to have the same shape, outline, or contour ⟨the areas of greater rainfall ~ roughly with these forested areas —Amer. Guide Series: Minn.⟩ : be in agreement or harmony ⟨his way of life ~s to his income⟩ — used with to or with 2 a : to be obedient : COMPLY — usu. used with to ⟨men are bound to obey the law of society and ~ to its harmless orders —W.M.Thackeray⟩ : act in accordance with prevailing standard or custom ⟨even without racial and religious segregation the pressure to ~ is intense and stultifying —Sidonie M. Gruenberg⟩ b : to comply with the usages of an established church; esp : to comply with the usages of the Church of England 3 geol : to follow in unbroken sequence of deposition syn see ADAPT, AGREE

2**conform** \"\ adj [ME conforme, fr. MF or LL; MF conforme, fr. LL conformis, fr. L com- + -formis (fr. forma)] archaic : CONFORMABLE — usu. used with to

3**conform** \"\ adv, Scot : CONFORMABLY — used with to

con·form·abil·i·ty \kən,fó(r)mə'biləd·ē, -ətē, -i\ n -ES [conformable + -ity] : the quality of conforming — used esp. of geological strata

con·form·able \-'ə·məbəl\ adj 1 : corresponding in form, character, opinions, social conventions : SIMILAR, HARMONIOUS, ADAPTED — usu. used with to 2 : giving compliance or obedience : SUBMISSIVE, COMPLIANT ⟨I have been to you a true and humble wife, at all times to your will ~ —Shak.⟩ 3 Brit : conforming to the usages of the Church of England esp. as prescribed by the Acts of Uniformity 4 : following in unbroken sequence — used of geologic strata formed by uninterrupted deposition under the same general conditions — **con·form·ably** \-blē, -li\ adv

con·formal \kən, (')kän+\ adj [LL conformalis having the same shape, fr. L com- + formalis having a set form, formal — more at FORMAL] 1 math : conserving the size of all angles and therefore the shape of every elementary triangle — used of a depiction of one surface on another 2 of a map : having the same scale along both the meridian and the parallel at any point and having meridians and parallels at right angles so that the shapes of small areas around that point are true to the shape of the corresponding areas on the earth ⟨Mercator's is the best known of ~ projections⟩ — **con·formality** \,kän,(,)fó(r)'maləd·ē\ n -ES

con·form·ance \kən'fórmən(t)s, -ó(ə)m-\ n -S : the act of conforming : CONFORMITY

conformant adj, obs : CONFORMING, CONFORMABLE

con·for·ma·tion \,kän(,)fó(r)'māshən, -,fə(r)-\ n -S [L conformation-, conformatio symmetrical forming, fr. conformatus (past part. of conformare) + -ion-, -io -ion — more at CONFORM] 1 : the act of conforming or producing conformity : ADAPTATION ⟨~ of lives to duties⟩ 2 : formation of something by appropriate arrangement of parts or elements : an assembling into a whole 3 a : agreement esp. with a model or plan b : STRUCTURE, FORM ⟨~ of the ocean bed⟩ c : the form or outline esp. of an animal or of a dressed carcass : SHAPE d : any of the spatial arrangements of a molecule that can be obtained by rotating the atoms or groups around one or more single bonds syn see FORM

con·for·ma·tor \'känfər,mād·ər\ or **con·for·ma·teur** \,kän,fórmə'tər\ n -S [F conformateur, fr. conformer to conform (fr. L conformare) + -ateur -ator] : an apparatus for taking the conformation of a thing (as of the head for fitting a hat)

conformed past of CONFORM

con·form·er \kən'fórmər, -ó(ə)mə(r\ n -S : one that conforms

conforming pres part of CONFORM

con·form·ism \kən'fór,mizəm, -ó(ə),m-\ n -S [prob. fr. F conformisme, fr. conformiste person inclined to conventional thoughts and actions, English person that conforms to the established Church of England (after such pairs as F déiste deist: déisme deism), fr. E conformist English person that conforms to the established Church of England] : the act, practice, or principle of conforming ⟨unimaginative timid ~ in key positions —K.S.Davis⟩

1**con·form·ist** \-,məst\ n -S : one who conforms esp. to an established church; specif : a person who conforms to the established Church of England

2**conformist** \"\ adj 1 : following prevailing standards or customs ⟨the rest of the law-abiding, ~ family —C.K.Aldrich⟩ 2 a : conforming to a standard ⟨~ guidelines for license renewal —Robert Goralski⟩ b : STANDARDIZING ⟨a ~ culture⟩

con·form·i·ty \kən'fó(r)məd·ē, -ətē, -i\ n -ES [ME conformyte, fr. MF conformite, fr. LL conformitat-, conformitas, fr. conformis conformable + -itat-, -itas -ity — more at CONFORM] 1 a : correspondence in form, manner, or character : a point of resemblance (as of tastes) — usu. used with to b : HARMONY, AGREEMENT, CONGRUITY — usu. used with with ⟨his behavior was in ~ with his ideals⟩ 2 : the action or an act of conforming to something established (as law or fashion) : COMPLIANCE, ACQUIESCENCE 3 a : religious or ecclesiastical compliance; esp : compliance with usages of the Church of England b : action in accordance with some specified standard or authority : OBEDIENCE, SUBMISSION — used with to ⟨~ to duty⟩ 4 : uninterrupted depositional sequence (as of beds or strata of rock) — compare UNCONFORMITY

conformly adv [ME conformely, fr. conforme conformable + -ly — more at CONFORM] obs : CONFORMABLY

conforms pres 3d sing of CONFORM

con·for·ta·ble \kōⁿfórtabl(ᵊ), -b(lə)\ n, pl **confortables** \"\ [F, fr. confortable comfortable, fr. E comfortable] : an all-upholstered chair of the early 19th century

con for·za \kän'fórt(,)sä, kōn-, -,sə\ adv [It] : with force — used as a direction in music

con·found \in senses other than 4 kən'faund also (')kän¦f-; in sense 4 (')kän¦f- sometimes kən'f-\ vt -ED/-ING/-S [ME confounden, fr. OF confondre, fr. L confundere to pour together, confuse, fr. com- + fundere to pour — more at FOUND] 1 archaic : to bring to ruin : DESTROY a : to inflict defeat on (as an army or adversary) b : to cause to fail : BAFFLE ⟨~ their politics, frustrate their knavish tricks —Henry Carey⟩ 2 a : SPOIL, CORRUPT ⟨their native speech was not ~ed with a vulgarized spoken Latin —M.W.Baldwin⟩ b obs : CONSUME, WASTE ⟨he did ~ the best part of an hour in changing hardiment with great Glendower —Shak.⟩ 3 a : to put to shame : DISCOMFIT, ABASH ⟨the influence of . . . El Greco . . . lay dormant for centuries and rose to ~ the critics of later times —Bernard Smith⟩ b : to refute esp. by argument or demonstration : OVERTHROW ⟨this new arm of science may corroborate or ~ the theories of the universe —David England⟩ 4 : to send to perdition : DAMN — used as a mild imprecation ⟨~ it⟩ 5 : to throw (a person) into confusion : strike with amazement : STUPEFY, PERPLEX, CONFUSE ⟨attacks which ~ed opponents with bewildering reverses [of direction] —Springfield (Mass.) Union⟩ 6 : to ignore, overlook, or fail to discern a difference between (two or more things) : mistake (one thing) for another : CONFUSE, MINGLE ⟨they implored Charles not to ~ the innocent with the guilty —T.B.Macaulay⟩ 7 : to cause or to increase disorder in (an existing situation) ⟨ruin upon ruin, rout on rout, confusion worse ~ed —John Milton⟩ ⟨to divide Europe as the politicians have done is to invite confusion and to divide the frontier as the Europeans did is to ~ the confusion —W.P.Webb⟩ syn see PUZZLE

1**confounded** adj [ME, fr. past part. of confounden] 1 : CONFUSED, PERPLEXED ⟨a cloudy and ~ philosopher⟩ 2 : DAMNED, CURSED, BLASTED — used as a mild imprecation ⟨this ~ weather⟩ or as an intensive ⟨close that ~ window⟩

2**confounded** adv : CONFOUNDEDLY

con·found·ed·ly adv : VERY, EXTREMELY, ANNOYINGLY ⟨so ~ without a clear moral purpose —Alfred Kazin⟩

con·found·ed·ness n -ES : the quality or state of being confounded

confounding adj [fr. pres. part. of confound] : that confounds : CONFUSING, PUZZLING — **con·found·ing·ly** adv

confraction n -S [MF & LL; MF confraction, fr. LL confraction-, confractio, fr. L confractus (past part. of confringere to break in pieces, fr. com- + -fringere, fr. frangere to break) + -ion-, -io -ion — more at BREAK] obs : a breaking in pieces

confrairy n -ES [MF confrarie, fr. ML confratria, fr. confratr-, confrater + L -ia -y] obs : CONFRATERNITY

con·fra·ter \kən'fräd·ə(r), (')kän¦f-\ n, pl **confraters** \-ə(r)z\ or **con·fra·tres** \-ä·,trez, -es\ [ML, fr. L com- + frater brother — more at BROTHER] 1 : a member of a confraternity 2 : an associate of a monastery or monastic group who received certain privileges (as a share in prayers) without corresponding responsibilities (as rigorous life or restrictive vows)

con·fraternity \¦kän+\ n -ES [ME confraternite, fr. MF confraternité, fr. ML confraternitat-, confraternitas, fr. confrater, after L frater brother: fraternitat-, fraternitas brotherhood, fraternity] 1 : a society or body of men or of men and women united for a religious, charitable or other purpose or in a profession 2 : fraternal union or communion

con·fraternization \(¦)kän+\ n -S [com- + fraternization] : fraternization together : recognition as a brother

con·frere \(')kōⁿ¦fre(ə)r, -fra(ə)r, 'kän,f-, 'kōn,f-\ n -S [ME, colleague, fellow member esp. of a confraternity, fr. MF, fr. OF (trans. of ML confrater), fr. com- + frere brother, fr. L frater] : COLLEAGUE : a fellow worker (as in a profession or in a field of study); broadly : FELLOW, COMRADE

con·fre·rie \kōⁿfrārē\ n, pl **confreries** \-ē(z)\ [F confrérie, fr. OF confrerie, alter. (influenced by frere) of confrarie] : BROTHERHOOD, ASSOCIATION; often : those sharing a common interest or quality

con·fri·ca·tion \,känfrə'kāshən\ n -S [ME confricacioun, fr. LL confrication-, confricatio, fr. L confricatus (past part. of confricare to rub vigorously, fr. com- + fricare to rub) + -ion-, -io -ion — more at FRICTION] archaic : a rubbing together : FRICTION

1**con·front** \kən'frənt\ vt -ED/-ING/-S [MF confronter to confront, border on, fr. ML confrontare to bound, fr. L com- + ML -frontare (fr. L front-, frons forehead, front) — more at BRINK] 1 a : to stand facing or opposing esp. in challenge, defiance, or accusation : FACE : stand up to ⟨enemies ~ing one another⟩ ⟨~ an accuser in court⟩ b : to face (something dangerous or dreaded) without flinching or avoiding ⟨the test of a free society is its capacity to ~, rather than evade, the vital questions of choice —J.M.Burns⟩ 2 : to put or bring face to face : compel (a person) to face, take account of, or endure — usu. used with by or with ⟨~ a reader with statistics⟩ ⟨~ed by . . . novels . . . frank to the point of immodesty —M.D.Geismar⟩ ⟨poor culprits . . . ~ed with law Latin —R.M.Weaver⟩ 3 a : MEET, ENCOUNTER ⟨recurrent phenomena . . . can always . . . be ~ed experimentally —A.C.Danto⟩ b : to stand before or in the way of ⟨the hardships and problems ~ing the pioneers⟩ 4 : to set in opposition for comparison : COMPARE ⟨conclusions which can be ~ed with experience —Alfred Einstein⟩ syn see MEET

2**confront** n -S obs : CONFRONTING, FACING, AFFRONT

con·front·al \kən'frəntᵊl\ n -S : CONFRONTATION

con·fron·ta·tion \,kän(,)frən-'tāshən\ n -S [F, fr. ML confrontation-, confrontatio comparison, boundary, fr. confrontatus (past part. of confrontare to bound) + L -ion-, -io -ion] : the act of confronting : the state of being confronted: as a : MEETING; specif : the bringing face to face of an accused person and his accusing witnesses — used esp. in the phrase right of confrontation b : the clashing of forces or ideas : CONFLICT c : COMPARISON

con·front·ment \kən'frəntmənt\ n -S 1 : CONFRONTATION 2 obs a : FACE, ASPECT b : AFFRONT

1**con·fu·cian** \kən'fyüshən\ n -S usu cap [Confucius †ab479 B.C. Chin. philosopher + E -an, n. suffix] : a follower of the Chinese philosopher Confucius : an adherent of Confucianism

2**confucian** \"\ adj, usu cap [Confucius + E -an, adj. suffix] : of or relating to Confucius or his teaching or followers

con·fu·cian·ism \-,nizəm\ n -S usu cap : the system of teachings of Confucius and his disciples characterized by central emphasis on the practice and cultivation of the cardinal virtues of filial piety, kindness, righteousness, propriety, intelligence, and faithfulness that historically has formed the basis of much of Chinese ethics, education, statecraft, and religion

con·fu·cian·ist \-,nəst\ adj, usu cap : CONFUCIAN

con fuo·co \kän'fwó(,)kō, kōn-, ,=,fü'ō-\ adv [It, with fire] : FIERILY, IMPETUOUSLY — used as a direction in music

con·fus·able \kən'fyüzəbəl\ adj : capable of being confused — **con·fus·a·bly** \-blē\ adv

1**confuse** adj [ME confus, fr. MF] obs : CONFUSED

2**con·fuse** \kən'fyüz\ vb -ED/-ING/-S [back-formation fr. confused] vt 1 archaic : to bring to ruin : ROUT 2 a : to make ashamed or embarrassed : ABASH, DISCONCERT, FLUSTER b : to make unclear in mind or purpose : MISLEAD, BEWILDER, PERPLEX : throw off 3 a : to dull or make indistinct the outlines or separate elements of (as a picture, pattern, or narrative) : BLUR ⟨~ the issue in a debate⟩ b : to throw into disorder : jumble together ⟨a . . . wind confused the waters —Virginia Woolf⟩ ⟨~ accounts⟩ c : to mistake (one person or thing) for another : fail to distinguish between (two or more separate entities) : CONFOUND ⟨expression may be too easily confused with communication —Havelock Ellis⟩ ~ vi : to fail to discriminate ⟨I always ~ between him and Orion —W.F. de Morgan⟩

con·fused \-zd\ adj [ME, fr. MF confus confused (fr. L confusus, past part. of confundere to pour together, confuse) + ME -ed — more at CONFOUND] 1 : PERPLEXED, DISCONCERTED 2 : mingled so as to be indistinguishable ⟨a ~ shouting⟩ : DISORDERED, MUDDLED ⟨a ~ sea⟩ — **con·fus·ed·ly** \-zədlē, -li\ adv — **con·fused·ness** \-zədnəs, -z(d)n-\ n -S

confused flour beetle n [so called fr. its being confused with the red flour beetle (Tribolium castaneum)] : a cosmopolitan beetle (Tribolium confusum) that feeds both as larva and adult chiefly on damaged grain — called also bran bug

con·fus·ing·ly adv [confusing, adj. (fr. pres. part. of confuse) + -ly] : in a confusing way

con·fu·sio bo·no·rum \kən¦fyüz(h)ē,ōbə'nōrəm\ n [NL, confusion of goods] : COMMIXTURE 3

con·fu·sion \kən'fyüzhən\ n -S [ME, fr. OF, fr. L confusion-, confusio, fr. confusus + -ion-, -io -ion] 1 : OVERTHROW, DEFEAT, RUIN, DESTRUCTION ⟨the defeat and ~ of Carthage in the war with Rome⟩ ⟨~ to such a tyrant king⟩ 2 a : a state of being discomfited, disconcerted, chagrined, or embarrassed esp. at some blunder or check ⟨his sister [was] overcome with ~ and unable to lift up her eyes —Jane Austen⟩ b : state of being confused mentally : lack of certainty, orderly thought, or power to distinguish, choose, or act decisively : PERPLEXITY ⟨slowly emerging from the mental ~ which followed the fall —Havelock Ellis⟩ ⟨present intellectual ~ and moral chaos of the world —John Dewey⟩ 3 a : an act of confusing, of mixing, pouring, blending, or heaping together in disorder with identities and distinctions blended ⟨the ~ of tongues at the tower of Babel⟩ ⟨a ~ of history and poetry in his work⟩ b : an act of mistaking one thing for another, of failing to note distinctions, and of falsely identifying ⟨a formal ~ of poetry and painting —Irving Babbitt⟩ ⟨~ between public and private morality —D.W.Brogan⟩ 4 : a situation or condition marked by lack of order, system, arrangement : an unclear welter or muddle : an utter disorder ⟨a luxuriant crop of very long hair which . . . got itself into great ~ —W.H.Hudson⟩ ⟨the ~ of hills typical of glacial regions —Amer. Guide Series: Minn.⟩ ⟨the dark ~ of German history —A.L.Guérard⟩ ⟨the long uncertainty and bloody ~ that attended the breakdown of the Roman Empire —Lewis Mumford⟩ 5 law a : a merging of two rights in one or of two apparently or really antagonistic interests in one b : COMMIXTURE 3 c Roman & civil law : extinction of an obligation by a person acquiring the right from which the obligation arose

syn DISARRAY, DISORDER, CLUTTER, JUMBLE, PI, SNARL, MUDDLE, CHAOS: CONFUSION is a rather general term suggesting any mixing, blending, adding together that blurs identities and distinctions or any result of such mixing. DISARRAY suggests a disarranging — a breaking away from order, sequence, form, or discipline ⟨the disarray in which the Germans found themselves . . . following on the capitulation of their Italian ally —Times Lit. Supp.⟩ DISORDER indicates a want of order through wonted neglect of it or through some break or interruption in orderly processes or arrangements ⟨our last chance to substitute order for disorder, government for anarchy —E.B.White⟩ ⟨standing between the older America and the new, with the foundations disintegrating under his feet, he confused the disorder in his own mind with the disorder in the external world —V.L.Parrington⟩ CLUTTER implies a confused litter of the miscellaneous and adventitious, impeding free activity or clear perception ⟨what a mess this set is in! if there's one thing I hate . . . it's clutter —Edna St. V. Millay⟩ ⟨this essay clears one irrelevant topic from the clutter of symbolist criticism —Times Lit. Supp.⟩ JUMBLE suggests a heaping together of many incongruous things so that free use, enjoyment, or perception of any individual item is made difficult ⟨the ruptured ambulance convoy . . . a jumble of overturned wagons, spilled pungent powders —Irwin Shaw⟩ ⟨a vast jumble of incoherent erudition on which he drew for purely poetic effects —T.S.Eliot⟩ PI, in this sense from printing, sometimes designates a confusion or disarrangement of small items hard to classify or order like miscellaneous type. SNARL is likely to suggest a knotted entanglement hard to unravel, resolve, or sort out ⟨parachute cords in a snarl⟩ ⟨a snarl of traffic at the bridge entrance⟩ MUDDLE suggests a litter or welter so extreme that making order is impossible and hence a situation marked by bungling, uncertainty, and feeble, dubious, ill-directed expediency ⟨as . . . they all had to live in one small room and the kitchen, the place usually looked a muddle —Nigel Balchin⟩ ⟨the effort to make a distinction . . . produced such a muddle that it was dropped —G.B.Shaw⟩ CHAOS suggests uttermost confusion, with no order, arrangement, regularity, sequence, or predictability; it may suggest primordial formlessness or complete disintegration ⟨disorder to the point of chaos —B.N.Cardozo⟩ ⟨back not merely to the dark ages but from cosmos to chaos —B.M.Baruch⟩ ⟨such social chaos . . . as to make civilization impossible —Blanton Fortson⟩ syn see in addition COMMOTION

con·fu·sion·al \-zhənᵊl, -zhnəl\ adj : characterized by mental confusion

con·fut·able \kən'fyüd·əbəl\ adj [confute + -able] : capable of being confuted

con·fu·ta·tion \,kän(,)fyü'tāshən, -,fyə'-\ n -S [L confutation-, confutatio, fr. confutatus (past part. of confutare) + -ion-, -io -ion] 1 : the act or process of confuting : REFUTATION 2 : something that confutes (as an argument)

con·fu·ta·tive \kən'fyüd·əd·iv\ adj [L confutatus + E -ive] : adapted, designed, or tending to confute

con·fu·ta·tor \'känfyü,tād·ə(r)\ n -S [LL, fr. L confutatus + -or] : one that confutes

1**con·fute** \kən'fyüt, usu -üd·+V\ vt -ED/-ING/-S [L confutare, fr. com- + -futare to beat — more at BEAT] 1 : to overwhelm by argument : refute conclusively : OVERCOME, SILENCE ⟨rugged individualism . . . is confuted in our social legislation and social habits —N. Y. Times⟩ 2 obs : to bring to naught : CONFOUND syn see DISPROVE

2**confute** also **confutement** n -S obs : CONFUTATION

cong abbr 1 congius 2 congregation 3 congress; congressional

con·ga \'käŋgə\ n -S [AmerSp, fr. Sp, fem. of congo of the Congo, fr. Congo, region in Africa] 1 : a Cuban dance of African origin involving three steps followed by a kick and performed by a group usu. in single file following a leader 2 : a tall narrow-headed bass drum beaten with the hands and used to provide the rhythm for the conga dance

con·ga·ree \'käŋgə¦rē\ n, pl **congaree** or **congarees** usu cap [native name] 1 : a Siouan people in the Congaree river valley, So. Carolina 2 : a member of the Congaree people

con·gé \kōⁿzhā, 'kän,jā\ n -S [F, fr. OF congié — more at CONGEE] 1 a : a formal permission to depart (as from one in authority) ⟨you've got your ~, and my blessing on ye —George Meredith⟩ b [F, fr. OF congié] : DISMISSAL ⟨she was given her ~ with a good deal less in the way of salary than she was entitled to —Susan Ertz⟩ ⟨to get by way of ~ a punch in the nose⟩ 2 : a ceremonious bow made as a sign of recognition or at taking one's leave ⟨shuffling forward with a hundred apish ~s —Sir Walter Scott⟩ 3 : LEAVE-TAKING, FAREWELL ⟨we may as well make our ~s here . . . as under the porter's nose —A.T.Quiller-Couch⟩ ⟨the departing spirit saying his ~ dimmer and fainter as he leaves our stupidities behind —Christopher Morley⟩ 4 [F, fr. OF congié] archit : a molding of concave quarter-round profile tangent to a vertical surface and followed by a fillet parallel to that surface — see MOLDING illustration

con·geal \kən'jēl, esp bef pause or cons -ēəl\ vb -ED/-ING/-S [ME congelen, fr. MF congeler, fr. L congelare, fr. com- + gelare to freeze — more at COLD] vt 1 : to change from a fluid to a solid state by or as if by cold ⟨~*ed* the water into ice⟩ **:** FREEZE ⟨tundra ~*ed* forever by the arctic cold⟩ **2 a :** to make (a liquid) viscid or of a consistency like jelly **:** CURDLE, COAGULATE **b** *obs* **:** to make (a liquid) solid or crystalline **3 :** to make rigid or inflexible **:** freeze into a pattern or system ⟨~*ing* the speculations of Aristotle into authoritarian dogma⟩ **:** make immobile **:** PARALYZE ⟨a density of two hundred people to the acre would even further ~ traffic —Lewis Mumford⟩ **~** *vi* **1 :** to grow hard, stiff, or thick from cold or other causes **:** FREEZE, COAGULATE ⟨oil ~*s* in cold weather⟩ **2 a** *of a sentiment* **:** to lose all warmth ⟨his passion for the ballerina soon ~*ed*⟩ **b :** to assume a fixed, rigid, or unchanging form or character ⟨saw . . . factions cleaving classes and classes ~*ing* into castes —Will Durant⟩ ⟨thought lost its vivacity, ~*ing* into a closed system⟩

con·geal·ment \-lmənt\ *n* -S **1 :** the act or action of congealing ⟨the rapid ~ of lava⟩ ⟨a tendency toward ~ of ideas —J.B.Oakes⟩ **2 :** matter that has congealed ⟨a crusty ~ of frost⟩

1con·gee \'kän(,)jē, kən'jē\ *vb* **congeed; congeed; congeeing; congees** [ME *congien*, fr. MF *congier*, fr. *congié*] *vt*, *obs* **:** to grant permission to depart **:** DISMISS **~** *vi* [²*congee*] **1** *now dial* **:** to take one's leave ceremoniously ⟨I have *congeed* with the magistrates⟩ **2 :** to make a ceremonious bow ⟨rubbing servile hands and ~*ing*⟩

2con·gee \"\ *n* -S [ME *congie*, fr. MF *congié*, fr. L *commeatus* going back and forth, leave of absence, furlough, fr. *commeatus*, past part. of *commeare* to go back and forth, frequent, fr. *com-* + *meare* to go — more at PERMEATE] **:** CONGÉ

3con·gee \'kän,jē\ *n* -S [Tamil *kañci*] **1 :** the water in which rice has been boiled and which is used esp. in India for starching clothes or for invalids' diet **2** *China* **:** rice or millet gruel

con·ge·la·tion \,känjə'lāshən\ *n* -S [ME, fr. MF or L; MF *congelation*, fr. L *congelation-*, *congelatio*, fr. *congelatus* (past part. of *congelare* to freeze) + *-ion-*, *-io* -ion] **1 :** the action or process of alteration (as by freezing) from a fluid to a solid or semisolid state; *also* **:** the product of such alteration **2 :** the act, process, or an instance of making numb, hard, or dead by freezing

con·ge·la·tive \'känjə,lād·iv, kən'jelәd·iv\ *adj* [MF *congelatif*, fr. *congeler* to congeal + *-atif* -ative] **:** tending to congeal **:** CONGEALING

con·gel·i·fract \kən'jelə,frakt\ *n* -S [*congeli-* (fr. L *congelare* to freeze) + *-fract* (fr. L *fractus*, past part. of *frangere* to break) — more at BREAK] **:** a rock fragment split off by frost action

con·gel·i·frac·tion \kən¦jelə¦frakshən\ *n* -S [*congeli-* (fr. L *congelare*) + *fraction* (breaking)] **:** splitting of the soil by freezing and thawing — compare CONGELITURBATION

con·gel·i·tur·bate \kən'jelə'tərbət, -,bāt\ *n* -S [*congeli-* (fr. L *congelare*) + *-turbate* (fr. L *turbatus*, past part. of *turbare* to disturb) — more at TURBID] **:** earth material disturbed by frost action and usu. appearing as a rubble coarser than the underlying material

con·gel·i·tur·ba·tion \-(,)tər'bāshən\ *n* -S [*congeli-* (fr. L *congelare*) + *-turbation* (fr. L *turbation-*, *turbatio* disturbance, fr. *turbatus* + *-ion-*, *-io* -ion)] **:** the churning or heaving of the soil by freezing and thawing — compare CONGELIFRACTION

con·ge·na·tor \'känjə,nād·ə(r), kən'jenəd·-\ *n* -S [by alter. (influence of L *-ator*, suffix denoting an agent) — more at -OR] **:** CONGENER

1con·ge·ner \'känjənə(r), kən'jēn-, (')kän¦jēn-\ *also* **co·ge·ner** \'kōjən-, (')kō¦jēn-\ *n* -S [L, of the same race or kind, fr. *com-* + *gener-*, *genus* birth, kind, race — more at KIN] **:** one that bears relationship to another: as **a :** a member of the same genus as another plant or animal ⟨the lion and its smaller ~*s*, the lynx and domestic cat⟩ **b :** a person or thing resembling or suggesting another in nature, character, or action ⟨the living townspeople and their ~*s* in the churchyard⟩ ⟨the New England private schools and their ~*s* west of the Alleghenies —Oliver La Farge⟩ **c :** a chemical substance related to another (as a derivative or an element in the same group of the periodic table as another element) **d :** a secondary product (as an aldehyde or ester) retained in an alcoholic beverage (as whiskey) and significant in the determination of the final characteristics of the beverage — called also *congeneric* **e :** ²COGNATE b

2congener \"\ *adj* [L] **:** CONGENERIC

1con·generic \¦kän+\ *adj* [*com-* + L *gener-*, *genus* + E *-ic*] **1 :** having to do with **:** RELATED ⟨war and its ~ industrial problems⟩ **2 :** belonging to the same genus ⟨~ species⟩ **3 :** belonging to the congeners of an alcoholic beverage ⟨~ substances⟩

2congeneric \"\ *n* -S **:** ¹CONGENER d

con·ge·ner·ous \kən'jēnərəs, -jen-, (')kän¦j-\ *adj* [L *congener* + E *-ous*] **:** akin in nature, origin, or character **:** RELATED, CONGENERIC

con·ge·nial \kən'jēnyəl, -ēnēəl\ *adj* [*com-* + *genius* (person's disposition or inclination) + *-al*] **1 :** having the same nature, disposition, or tastes **:** suited to one another **:** KINDRED ⟨two ~ spirits, united . . . by mutual confidence and reciprocal virtues —T.L.Peacock⟩ **2** *obs* **a :** CONGENITAL **b :** of the same genus or kind **:** having the same origin **3 a :** appropriate and agreeable **:** existing or associated together harmoniously ⟨the free system of government . . . is . . . ~ with reason, with common sense —James Madison⟩ ⟨group of ~ buildings —Lewis Mumford⟩ **b :** PLEASANT, ATTRACTIVE ⟨very ~ music, without affectation or pretense —Irving Kolodin⟩; *often* **:** agreeably suited (as to one's nature, tastes, or outlook) ⟨found the atmosphere of the village ~ and settled down there⟩ **c :** characterized by friendly sociability **:** GENIAL ⟨found in the master of the inn a most ~ host⟩ **4 :** COMPATIBLE 2c(1), 2c(2) **syn** see CONSONANT

con·ge·ni·al·i·ty \kən,jēnē'aləd·ē, -,jēn'ya-, -ətē, -i\ *n* -ES **:** the quality or state of being congenial **:** affinity of spirit or temperament ⟨the ~ of Stoicism to the Roman mind —T.S.Eliot⟩ **:** mutual agreeableness ⟨an easy ~ between officers and men⟩

con·ge·nial·ly \kən'jēnyəlē, -ēnēə-, -li\ *adv* **:** in a congenial manner

con·ge·nial·ness *n* -ES **:** CONGENIALITY

con·gen·i·tal \kən'jenəd·ᵊl, -ətᵊl\ *adj* [L *congenitus* congenital (fr. *com-* + *genitus*, past part. of *gignere* to beget, bring forth) + E *-al* — more at KIN] **1 :** existing at or dating from birth ⟨~ idiocy⟩ ⟨~ malformations⟩ **:** belonging to or associated with from birth **:** INNATE ⟨~ good health⟩ **:** constituting an essential characteristic **:** INHERENT ⟨the ~ State Department fear of newsmen —A.H.Vandenberg †1951⟩ **:** from birth or by nature ⟨a ~ liar⟩ **2 :** acquired during development in the uterus and not through heredity — compare ACQUIRED, FAMILIAL, HEREDITARY **syn** see INNATE

congenital amputation *n* **:** the prenatal loss or nondevelopment of a projecting body part (as a foot or arm) esp. through constriction of the developing structure

con·gen·i·tal·ly \-ᵊlē, -ᵊli\ *adv* **:** in a congenital manner **:** from birth ⟨~ deaf⟩ **:** by nature or disposition ⟨~ incapable of telling the truth⟩ ⟨~ skeptical⟩

congenite *adj* [L *congenitus*] *obs* **:** CONGENITAL

con·ger \'käŋgə(r)\ *n* [ME *congre*, *cunger*, fr. OF *congre*, fr. L *congr-*, *conger*, fr. Gk *gongros*; akin to ON *kökkr* ball, L *gingiva* gum of the mouth, Gk *gongros* excrescence on trees, *gongylos* round, Lith *gunga* hump, lump, ball, and perh. to MLG *kinke* kink; basic meaning: lump] **1** -S **:** CONGER EEL **2** *cap* [NL *Congr-*, *Conger*, fr. L] **:** a genus consisting of the typical conger eels — compare LEPTOCEPHALUS

con·ger·ee \¦käŋgə¦rē\ *n* -S [by alter.] **:** CONGER EEL

conger eel *n* **1 a :** a large strictly marine entirely scaleless eel (*Conger conger*) of a length sometimes as great as eight feet that is an important food fish of Europe and is found on the Atlantic coast of America and on the coasts of Asia and Africa **b :** any other member of the family Congridae some of which (as *Conger caudilimbata*) occur in the West Indies and other warm regions **2 :** a California moray (*Gymnothorax mordax*)

con·ge·ries \'känjə,(,)rēz, -,riz *sometimes* kən'ji(,)rēz *or* -'jiriz *or* -'jirē,ēz *or* -'jerē,ēz\ *also* **con·ge·rie** \'känjə(,)rē, -,ri\ *or* **con·ge·ry** \'känjə,rē, -ri\ *n*, *pl* **congeries** *like sing.* CONGERIES\ [*congeries* fr. L, fr. *congerere* to bring together; *congery* back-formation fr. *congeries*, pl.] **:** a collection or mass of entities (as objects, forces, individuals, ideas) **:** AGGREGATION, AGGLOMERATION ⟨a small ~ of ranches —Bernard De Voto⟩ ⟨society is not a system but a ~ of impermanent groupings —N.N.Foote⟩

conger pike *n* **:** a fierce large silvery scaleless eel (*Muraenesox cinereus*) with a pikelike head and numerous strong canines that is widespread and abundant in the tropical Indian and Pacific oceans and esteemed as food in adjacent lands

1con·gest \kən'jest\ *vb* -ED/-ING/-S [L *congestus*, past part. of *congerere* to bring together, fr. *com-* + *gerere* to bear, carry — more at CAST] *vt* **1** *obs* **:** to gather into a mass **:** COLLECT, AMASS **2 :** to overcrowd, overburden, or fill to excess so as to obstruct (as movement) or hinder (as the functioning of an organ) **:** CLOG, CHOKE ⟨convoys ~*ed* all arterial highways⟩ ⟨the illness ~*ed* his lungs⟩ **:** concentrate esp. by constricting or crowding in a small or narrow space ⟨motor transportation . . . has succeeded the railroad as the most powerful tool for either distributing or ~*ing* the population —Lewis Mumford⟩ **~** *vi* **:** to crowd or mass together (as in a small or narrow space) ⟨clutched each other and ~*ed* in hard knots —Robert Hazel⟩

2con·gest \'kän,jest\ *n* -S *Irish* **:** an inhabitant of a congested district

con·gest·ed \kən'jestəd\ *adj* [fr. past part. of *congest*] **1 :** containing an overaccumulation of blood **:** HYPEREMIC ⟨a ~ mucous membrane⟩ **2 a :** OVERCROWDED ⟨~ slums⟩ ⟨the road was crowded, but as yet far from ~ —H.G.Wells⟩ **b :** encumbered or made turgid or difficult by an excess (as of words or ideas) ⟨a ~ prose⟩ ⟨~ reasoning⟩ **3 :** set close together ⟨~ stamens⟩ ⟨~ spores⟩

con·ges·tion \kən'jes(h)chən\ *n* -S [MF or L; MF, fr. L *congestion-*, *congestio* fr. *congestus* + *-ion-*, *-io* -ion] **1** *obs* **:** ACCUMULATION, GATHERING, HEAP **2 :** a condition of overcrowding ⟨traffic ~⟩ or overburdening ⟨the result was complete mental ~ and overwork —Herbert Read⟩ **:** an excessive accumulation ⟨his face went purple with the ~ of language which couldn't get out —R.P.Warren⟩; *specif* **:** an overaccumulation of blood in the blood vessels of an organ or part whether natural or artificially induced (as for therapeutic purposes)

con·ges·tive \-estiv\ *adj* **:** having to do with congestion

congestive heart failure *n* **:** heart failure in which the heart is unable to maintain an adequate circulation of blood in the tissues of the body or to pump out the venous blood returned to it by the venous circulation — compare CORONARY FAILURE

con·gi·ary \'känjē,erē\ *n* -ES [L *congiarium*, fr. *congius* + *-arium* -ary] **:** a present or largess (as of corn, wine, or oil) made in ancient Rome to the soldiers or the people

con·gi·o·pod·i·dae \,känjē(,)ō'pädə,dē\ *n pl*, *cap* [NL, fr. *Congiopodus*, type genus (prob. irreg. fr. NL *Conger* + Gk *pod-*, *pous* foot) + *-idae* — more at CONGER, FOOT] **:** a small family (type genus *Congiopodus*) of marine fishes (order Scleroparei) of the tropical southern hemisphere having a compressed elongated body, a pronounced snout, a small protractile mouth, and a head partly covered with bony plates

con·gi·us \'känjēəs\ *n*, *pl* **con·gii** \-jē,ī\ [ME, fr. L, prob. modif. of Gk *konchos* conch (also, a liquid measure); akin to Gk *konchē* conch — more at CONCH] **1 :** an ancient Roman unit of liquid capacity equal to ⅛ amphora or 0.84 U.S. gallon **2** *pharmacy* **:** GALLON — abbr. *cong* or *C*

conglaciate *vb* -ED/-ING/-S [L *conglaciatus*, past part. of *conglaciare*, fr. *com-* + *glaciare* to turn into ice, fr. *glacies* ice — more at GLACIER] *obs* **:** to turn into ice **:** CONGEAL

1con·glo·bate \kən'glō,bāt, 'käŋ,g-, 'käŋ,g-\ *vb* -ED/-ING/-S [L *conglobatus*, past part. of *conglobare*, fr. *com-* + *globare* to conglobe, fr. *globus* globe — more at CLIP] **:** to form in a round mass **:** CONGLOBE

2con·glo·bate \kən'glōbət, kän-, -,bāt; 'känglō,bāt, 'käŋg-\ *adj* [L *conglobatus*] **:** collected into or forming a rounded mass or ball

con·glo·ba·tion \,känglō'bāshən, -äŋg-\ *n* -S [L *conglobation-*, *conglobatio*, fr. *conglobatus* + *-ion-*, *-io* -ion] **1 :** the act or action of forming into a round mass **2 :** a rounded mass

con·globe \kən'glōb, kän-\ *vb* -ED/-ING/-S [L *conglobare*] **:** to form into a ball ⟨*conglobed* clouds⟩

1con·glom·er·ate \kən'gläm(ə)rət, *usu* -əd·+V\ *adj* [L *conglomeratus*, past part. of *conglomerare* to roll together, fr. *com-* + *glomerare* to wind into a ball, fr. *glomer-*, *glomus* ball — more at CLAM] **1 :** made up of parts from various sources or composed of various kinds ⟨as ~ a language as English⟩ ⟨the ~ peoples of New England⟩ **2 :** densely clustered ⟨~ flowers⟩ **3** *zool* **:** irregularly grouped in spots ⟨~ eyes⟩

2con·glom·er·ate \-mə,rāt, *usu* -ād·+V\ *vb* -ED/-ING/-S [L *conglomeratus*] *vt* **:** to gather or collect into a mass or coherent whole **:** AMASS, ACCUMULATE **~** *vi* **:** to form into a mass or coherent whole **:** GATHER ⟨numbers of dull people *conglomerated* round her —Virginia Woolf⟩

3conglomerate *like* ¹CONGLOMERATE\ *n* -S [¹*conglomerate*] **:** a mixture gathered from various sources **:** a composite mass ⟨a ~ of houses⟩ ⟨a shoddy ~ of people⟩; *specif* **:** clastic sedimentary rock composed of rounded fragments varying from small pebbles to large boulders in a cement of calcareous material, iron oxide, silica, or hardened clay — compare AGGLOMERATE, BRECCIA

conglomerate

con·glom·er·at·ic \kən¦glämə¦rad·ik, ¦käŋ,g-\ *also* **con·glom·er·it·ic** \-rid·ik\ *adj* [*conglomeratic* fr. ³*conglomerate* + *-ic*; *conglomeritic* irreg. fr. ³*conglomerate* + *-ic*] **:** of or relating to a conglomerate

con·glom·er·a·tion \kən,glämə'rāshən, ,kän,g-\ *n* -S [LL *conglomeration-*, *conglomeratio*, fr. L *conglomeratus* + *-ion-*, *-io* -ion] **:** a conglomerating or state of being conglomerated **:** COLLECTION ⟨the slow ~ of detail⟩ **:** something that is conglomerated ⟨a showy ~ of flowers⟩ **:** a mixed coherent mass ⟨a ~ of antique cars⟩

con·glu·tin \kən, (')kän+\ *n* -S [ISV *com-* + *glutin*; orig. formed as G *konglutin*] *biochem* **:** a legumin from almonds and lupines

con·glu·ti·nant \kən'glüt°nənt, (')kän¦g-\ *adj* [L *conglutinant-*, *conglutinans*, pres. part. of *conglutinare*] **:** causing to adhere **:** promoting adhesion (as between the lips of a wound)

con·glutinate \kən, kän+\ *vb* -ED/-ING/-S [L *conglutinatus*, past part. of *conglutinare* to glue together, fr. *com-* + *glutinare* to glue, fr. *glutin-*, *gluten* glue — more at GLUTEN] *vt* **:** to cause to cohere **~** *vi* **:** COHERE

con·glutination \kən, (,)kän+\ *n* -S [MF, fr. L *conglutination-*, *conglutinatio*, fr. *conglutinatus* + *-ion-*, *-io* -ion] **:** the act or action of conglutinating or the consequent quality or state of being conglutinated: as **a** *med* **:** the union or establishment of continuity of parts — now used only of abnormal adhesion of contiguous surfaces **b :** a mass esp. of things glued together **:** AGGLUTINATION **c** *immunol* (1) **:** a reaction of agglutination and lysis brought about by addition of bovine serum to antibody-treated cells (2) **:** agglutination brought about by serum albumin or plasma proteins when added to cells coated with blocking antibody

con·glutinin \kən, (')kän+\ *n* -S [ISV *com-* + *glutinin*, fr. *glutin* + *-in*; orig. formed as G *konglutinin*] **1 :** a heat-stable component of bovine serum that combines with red blood cells which have been treated with antibody and that causes rapid strong agglutination followed by lysis **2 :** a substance or substances in blood plasma possibly identical with x-protein or perhaps merely a mixture of albumin and globulin that causes clumping when added to red blood cells that are combined with blocking antibody

1congo \'käŋ(,)gō\ *adj*, *usu cap* [fr. *Congo*, territory surrounding the Congo river, West Africa] **:** CONGOLESE

2congo \"\ *n* -ES [fr. *Congo*, territory surrounding the Congo river, West Africa] **1** [AmerF, prob. fr. *Congo* (territory)] **:** a ballroom dance of Haitian origin **2** *South* **a :** WATER MOCCASIN **b :** CONGO SNAKE **3** *usu cap* **:** CONGO COPAL **4** *or* **congo brown** *often cap C* **:** a dark grayish yellowish brown that is stronger and slightly yellower and darker than seal and slightly redder and darker than sepia brown — called also *Antwerp brown*, *asphaltum*, *bitumen*

3congo \"\ *usu cap*, *var of* KONGO

congo buffalo *n*, *usu cap C* [*Congo*, territory surrounding the Congo river, West Africa] **:** a rather small reddish Cape buffalo (*Syncerus caffer nanus*) from equatorial central and west Africa sometimes regarded as a distinct species (*S. nanus*)

congo copal *or* **congo gum** *n*, *usu cap Congo* **:** a hard insoluble colorless to amber copal derived esp. from certain trees of the genus *Copaifera* but found chiefly as a fossil resin in the Congo and used in making varnish

congo dye *n*, *usu cap C* **:** any of a group of direct azo dyes most of which are derivatives of benzidine — see DYE table I

congo eel *n* **1 :** CONGO SNAKE **2 :** WRYMOUTH **3 :** MUD EEL

congo floor fly *n*, *usu cap C* **:** a large yellowish brown fly (*Auchmeromyia luteola*) of tropical Africa related to the blowflies and having spiny nocturnal larvae that live in the earthen floors of native huts and come out at night to suck the blood of the occupants

congo floor maggot *n*, *usu cap C* **:** the larva of the Congo floor fly

congo jute *n*, *usu cap C*, *chiefly in the Belgian Congo* **:** ARAMINA

1con·go·lese \¦käŋgō¦lēz, -ēs\ *also* **con·go·ese** \-ŋ(,)gō¦ē-\ *adj*, *usu cap* [*congolese* modif. (influenced by *-ese*) of F *congolais*, irreg. fr. *Congo*; *congoese* fr. *Congo* + E *-ese*] **1 :** of, relating to, or characteristic of the Congo region or either of the Congo republics in Africa **2 :** of, relating to, or characteristic of the Congolese

2congolese \"\ *also* **congoese** \"\ *n*, *pl* **congolese** *also* **congoese** *usu cap* **1 :** a native or inhabitant of the Congo region or of either of the Congo republics **2 :** a language native to the Congo region

congo mahoe *n*, *usu cap C* **:** KENAF

congoni *var of* KONGONI

congo pea *n*, *usu cap C* [*Congo*, territory in West Africa] **:** PIGEON PEA

congo peacock *n*, *usu cap C* **:** AFROPAVO 2

congo pink *n*, *often cap C* **:** a grayish reddish orange that is redder, lighter, and stronger than Etruscan red or hyacinth red and deeper than Persian melon

congo red *n*, *usu cap C* [trans. of G *kongorot*] **:** an azo dye that is red in alkaline solution and blue in acid solution and is used chiefly as an indicator and as a biological stain — see DYE table I (under *Direct Red 28*)

congo root *n*, *usu cap C* **:** SAMPSON SNAKEROOT

congo rubber *n*, *usu cap C* **:** an African rubber derived from any of several woody vines of the genus *Landolphia*

congo rubine *or* **congo rubin** *n*, *usu cap C* **:** a direct azo dye used esp. for dyeing cotton, wool, and silk bluish red — see DYE table I (under *Direct Red 17*)

congo snake *n* **:** an elongated bluish black amphibian (*Amphiuma means*) of the southeastern U.S. that has two pairs of very short limbs each with two or three toes and attains a length of three feet — called also *blind eel*, *congo eel*, *lamper eel*

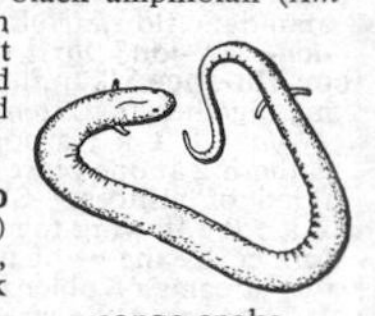
congo snake

congo tobacco *n*, *usu cap C* **:** HEMP 1

con·gou \'käŋ(,)gō,-gü\ *also* **con·go** \-gō\ *n* -S [prob. fr. Chin (Amoy) *kong-hu* expenditure of time and effort, pains taken (Pek *kung¹-fu¹*)] **:** black tea from China

con·grat·u·lant \kən'grachələnt, *chiefly in substand speech* -ajə-\ *adj* [L *congratulant-*, *congratulans*, pres. part. of *congratulari*] **:** expressive of congratulation

con·grat·u·late \=ˈ==,lāt, *usu* -ād·+V\ *vb* -ED/-ING/-S [L *congratulatus*, past part. of *congratulari* to wish joy, fr. *com-* + *gratulari* to wish joy, fr. *gratus* pleasing — more at GRACE] *vt* **1 :** to express sympathetic pleasure to on account of success or good fortune **:** wish joy to **:** FELICITATE ⟨~ herself on finding a job⟩ ⟨~ the boy for keeping a cool head⟩ ⟨~ his son upon his graduation⟩ **2** *archaic* **:** to express sympathetic pleasure or satisfaction at **3** *obs* **:** SALUTE, GREET **~** *vi* **1** *archaic* **:** to rejoice together **:** express or feel sympathetic joy **2 :** to present one's expressions of sympathetic pleasure at another's good fortune

con·grat·u·la·tion \=,==ˈlāshən\ *n* -S [MF or L; MF, fr. L *congratulation-*, *congratulatio*, fr. *congratulatus* + *-ion-*, *-io* -ion] **1 :** the act of congratulating a person or body **2 :** an expression of sympathetic pleasure **:** FELICITATION — used chiefly in pl. ⟨~*s* on our safe arrival⟩ **3** *obs* **:** a grateful expression of one's joy (as at his own good fortune) **:** REJOICING

con·grat·u·la·tor \=ˈ==,lād·ə(r), -ātə-\ *n* -S **:** one that congratulates

con·grat·u·la·to·ry \=ˈ==lə,tōrē, -tȯr-, -ri\ *adj* [ML *congratulatorius*, fr. L *congratulatus* + *-orius* -ory] **:** expressing or conveying congratulations ⟨~ handshake⟩ ⟨~ telegram⟩

con gra·zia \kän'grätsēə, kōn-\ *adv* [It, with grace] **:** with grace **:** GRACEFULLY — used as a direction in music

congree *vi* **congreed; congreed; congreeing; congrees** [prob. fr. *com-* + *gree* (agree)] *obs* **:** AGREE

con·greet \kən'grēt\ *vi* -ED/-ING/-S [*com-* + *greet*] *obs* **:** to greet mutually

con·gre·gant \'käŋgrəgənt, -rēg-\ *n* -S [L *congregant-*, *congregans*, pres. part. of *congregare*] **:** one that congregates with others; *specif* **:** a member of a congregation

1con·gre·gate \-,gāt, *usu* -ād·+V\ *vb* -ED/-ING/-S [ME *congregaten*, fr. L *congregatus*, past part. of *congregare*, fr. *com-* + *gregare* to collect, fr. *greg-*, *grex* flock — more at GREGARIOUS] *vt* **:** to collect together into a group, crowd, or assembly ⟨the captains *congregated* their men⟩ **~** *vi* **:** to come together, collect, or concentrate in a particular locality or group ⟨would not have been practical to ~ in cities unless the annual food supply was well assured —Owen & Eleanor Lattimore⟩ ⟨the young men *congregated* uneasily in impermanent groups —Irwin Shaw⟩ **:** become situated together or in proximity to each other ⟨on Schermerhorn Street ~ many charitable institutions —*Amer. Guide Series: N. Y. City*⟩ **syn** see GATHER

2con·gre·gate \-gət *also* -,gāt, *usu* -d·+V\ *adj* [ME *congregat*, fr. L *congregatus*] **1 :** COLLECTED, ASSEMBLED ⟨a host of ~ angels⟩ **2 :** designed for, devoted to, or housing an undifferentiated group of persons, esp. one whose institutional treatment, care, or custody is provided for through mass facilities ⟨~ prison⟩ ⟨~ methods of care⟩

con·gre·ga·tion \,==ˈgāshən\ *n* -S [ME *congregacioun*, fr. MF *congregation*, fr. L *congregation-*, *congregatio*, fr. *congregatus* + *-ion-*, *-io* -ion] **1 a :** an assembly of persons **:** GATHERING; *esp* **:** an assembly of persons met for the worship of God and for religious instruction **:** a body of people who habitually so meet **b** (1) *obs* **:** the whole number or body (2) **:** the whole body of Christians or an organized body of believers in a particular locality; *also* **:** SECT, DENOMINATION **c :** a collection or gathering of animals or things ⟨a foul and pestilent ~ of vapors —Shak.⟩ ⟨a great ~ of birds flew overhead⟩ **2 :** the act or an instance of congregating or bringing together **:** the state of being congregated **3** [LL *congregation-*, *congregatio*, trans. of Heb *gāhāl*] **:** the sacred community or whole body of the Jewish people **4** *sometimes cap*, *Roman Catholicism* **a :** a company or order of religious persons under a common rule either with or without vows **b :** a permanent body or committee of cardinals to which is entrusted some department of the church business **c :** a group of monasteries forming a subdivision of an order which agree to unite in closer ties of discipline and doctrine **5 :** a deliberative meeting of the governing body of an English university **6** *cap* **:** the Protestant party in Scotland at the time of the Reformation; *also* **:** a local body of this party **7 :** the whole body of people of a settlement, town, or parish in those No. American colonies in which the Congregational Church was established

1con·gre·ga·tion·al \¦==¦=shənᵊl, -shnəl\ *adj* **1 :** of or relating to or like a congregation **:** conducted or participated in by a congregation **:** connected with a particular congregation of worshipers ⟨~ singing⟩ **2** *usu cap* **:** belonging to Congregationalism or to Congregationalists **:** INDEPENDENT ⟨a *Congregational* church⟩ **3 :** of or relating to congregationalism (sense 1) — **con·gre·ga·tion·al·ly** \-ᵊl¦ē, -əl¦ē, ¦i\ *adv*

2congregational \"\ *n* -S **:** CONGREGATIONALIST

congregational christian *adj*, *usu cap both Cs* **:** of or relating to a denominational union of churches effected in 1931 between the Congregational Church and the Christian Church

con·gre·ga·tion·al·ism \,==ˈgāshənᵊl,izəm, -shnə,li-\ *n* -S **1 :** a system of church government in which the local congregation has full control and final authority over church matters within its own area **2** *cap* **:** the faith and government of those evangelical and trinitarian churches that recognize the congregation of each local church as independent of all dictation in church matters within its own area and that trace their formal beginning to England

[1]**con·gre·ga·tion·al·ist** \-shən°ləst, -shnəl-\ *n* -s **1** *usu cap* **:** one who belongs to a Congregational church **:** one who adheres to Congregationalism — compare INDEPENDENT **2 :** an adherent to or proponent of congregationalism (sense 1)

[2]**congregationalist** \⸗⸗¦⸗⸗(⸗)⸗\ *adj, usu cap* **:** of, sponsored by, characteristic of, or resembling a Congregational church or Congregationalism

congregationist *n* -s *usu cap, obs* **:** CONGREGATIONALIST 1

con·gre·ga·tive \'⸗⸗,gād·iv\ *adj* [LL *congregativus*, fr. L *congregatus* + *-ivus* -ive — more at CONGREGATE] **:** tending to gather into or appeal to a group ⟨~ salesmen⟩ ⟨~ piety⟩

con·gre·ga·tor \-d·ə(r)\ *n* -s [LL, fr. L *congregatus* + *-or*] **:** one that congregates

[1]**con·gress** \'käŋgrəs *also* 'kȯŋ-, *chiefly in substand speech* -ŋr-\ *n* -ES [L *congressus*, fr. *congressus*, past part. of *congredi* to go or come together, fr. *com-* + *gradi* to step, go — more at GRADE] **1 a :** the act or action of coming together **:** a meeting esp. of persons or minds ⟨he was generally to be found in intellectual ~ with Keyserling —*Newsweek*⟩ **b :** SEXUAL INTERCOURSE, COITION **2 :** a meeting of heads of states or their foreign ministers, ambassadors, or envoys for discussion and adjustment of international problems or affairs ⟨the *Congress* of Vienna⟩ ⟨parliament is not a ~ of ambassadors from different and hostile interests —Edmund Burke⟩ **3 :** the supreme legislative body of a nation and esp. of a republic ⟨in form at least the ~es of So. American nations resemble our own⟩ ⟨the *Congress* of the U.S.⟩ **4 :** an organization designed to promote some object of common interest to its membership and usu. made up of delegates from a group of constituent organizations **:** ASSOCIATION ⟨the Massachusetts *Congress* of Parents and Teachers, Incorporated⟩ ⟨the *Congress* for Cultural Freedom⟩ ⟨the Canada Trades and Labor *Congress*⟩ **5 :** a particular meeting of a group (as a national legislature or cultural association) **:** a session or single sitting of an organization ⟨the Seventy-first *Congress* was dominantly Republican —H. R.Penniman⟩ ⟨his committee . . . has over 3000 bills per *Congress* referred to it —*Publishers' Weekly*⟩ ⟨the Social Democratic party's ~ was held in June⟩ **6 :** a coming together or meeting of persons ⟨the rupture of the disciplined silence sent an uneasy stir among the exhausted ~ of soldiers —Jack Belden⟩ ⟨a ~ of goons and thugs —S.H.Holbrook⟩ **7 :** a seasonal assemblage of amphibians (as certain toads and frogs) for breeding purposes

[2]**con·gress** \kən'gres\ *vi* -ED/-ING/-ES **:** to come together **:** ASSEMBLE

congress cap *n, usu cap 1st C* **:** a small white cloth cap worn by members of the Congress party of India

congress gaiter *or* **congress shoe** *n, often cap C* [[1]*congress*; fr. its former popularity among members of the U.S. Congress] **:** a flexible ankle-high shoe having deep elastic gussets in the sides of the upper — compare ROMEO

con·gres·sion \kən'greshən\ *n* -s [L *congression-*, *congressio*, fr. *congressus* (past part. of *congredi*) + *-ion-*, *-io* -ion — more at CONGRESS] **:** the act or action of coming together (as into assembly, combat, coition); *specif* **:** the coming together of the chromosomes of a dividing cell to form the metaphase plate

con·gres·sio·nal \kən'greshən°l, -shnəl\ *adj* **:** of or relating to a legislative congress ⟨the *Congressional* Register of the U.S.⟩ ⟨~ permission to . . . check names and fingerprints —R.S.Brown⟩ — **con·gres·sio·nal·ly** \-°l|ē, -əl|, |i\ *adv*

congressional district *n* **:** one of the territorial divisions of each state of the U.S. from which a member of the House of Representatives is elected — compare APPORTIONMENT

con·gress·ist *pronunc at* [1]CONGRESS + əst\ *also* **con·gres·sio·nal·ist** \kən'greshən°ləst, -shnəl-\ *or* **con·gres·sio·nist** \-sh(ə)nəst\ *n* -s **:** a member or adherent of a congress

con·gress·ite \'käŋgrə,sīt\ *n* -s *usu cap* **:** a member of the Indian Congress Party

con·gress·man *pronunc at* [1]CONGRESS + mən\ *n, pl* **congressmen :** a member of a congress; *esp* **:** a member of the House of Representatives of the U.S. Congress ⟨*Congressman* and Mrs. Smith were present⟩ ⟨*congressmen* quoted "The White Man's Burden" in Washington —Thomas Beer⟩

congressman-at-large \¦⸗⸗⸗⸗¦⸗\ *n, pl* **congressmen-at-large :** a member of the U. S. House of Representatives elected by the voters of an entire state rather than by those of a single congressional district

congress money *n* **:** paper money (as that issued by the Continental Congress or by the U.S. Congress during and after the panic of 1837)

con·gress·wom·an \'käŋgrə,swu̇mən\ *n, pl* **congresswom·en** \-wimən\ **:** a woman who is a member of a congress (as of the House of Representatives of the U.S. Congress)

con·gri·dae \'käŋgrə,dē\ *n pl, cap* [NL, fr. *Congr-*, *Conger*, type genus + *-idae*] **:** the family of fishes (order Apodes) comprising the conger eels and extinct related forms — **con·groid** \-,grȯid\ *adj or n*

con·grio \'käŋgrē,ō\ *n* -s [Sp, fr. L *congr-*, *conger* — more at CONGER] **:** a large Chilean cusk eel esteemed as food

congrue *vi; pres part* **congruing** [L *congruere*] *obs* **:** to be in harmony **:** AGREE

con·gru·ence \kən'grüən|(t)s, kän'g-, 'kän,g-, 'käŋ,g-; 'käŋgrəwən|\ *n* -s [ME, fr. L *congruentia*, fr. *congruent-*, *congruens* + *-ia*] **1 :** the quality or state of according or coinciding **:** CONGRUITY, HARMONY **2 :** AGREEMENT 4

con·gru·en·cy \|sē,|si\ *n* -ES [ME, fr. L *congruentia*] **:** the quality or state of according or coinciding **:** CONGRUITY, CONGRUENCE ⟨the ~ of ends and means⟩; *specif* **:** the relation of congruent propositions in logic

con·gru·ent \|t\ *adj* [L *congruent-*, *congruens*, pres. part. of *congruere* to come together, coincide, agree] **1 a :** in agreement **:** COINCIDING, CORRESPONDING ⟨to keep imaginary characters ~ with actual models —Bernard De Voto⟩ ⟨hypotheses ~ with our experiences⟩ **b** *logic* **:** relating to or predicable of the same subject **:** differing from each other but predicable as true of the same state of things ⟨~ propositions⟩ **2** *geom* **:** superposable so as to be coincident throughout **3 :** relating to the melting point at which there coexist for a molecular compound both liquid and solid phases having the same composition — **con·gru·ent·ly** *adv*

con·gru·en·tial \¦kän,grü¦enchəl, ¦käŋ,-\ *adj* [fr. *congruence*, after such pairs as E *penitence: penitential*] **:** having to do with congruence; *specif* **:** characterized by agreement (sense 4)

con·gru·ism \'kän(,)grü,izəm, 'käŋ(-; 'käŋgrə,wi-\ *n* -s [F *congruisme*, fr. *congru* suitable (fr. L *congruus*) + *-isme* -ism] **:** a theory advanced by the Molinists according to which divine grace is efficacious because it is given by God in circumstances which he foreknows to be congruous and favorable to its operation

con·gru·ist \-rüəst, -rəwəst\ *n* -s [F *congruiste*, fr. *congru* + *-iste* -ist] **:** an adherent of congruism

con·gru·i·ty \kən'grüəd·ē, kän'-,kän'-\ *n* -ES [ME *congruite*, fr. MF *congruité*, fr. LL *congruitat-*, *congruitas*, fr. L *congruus* + *itat-*, *-itas* -ity] **1 :** the quality or state of agreeing or coinciding (as one with another or with something referred to) **:** CONFORMITY, CORRESPONDENCE ⟨~ of thought and action⟩ ⟨the ~ of God's law with natural law⟩ **2 a :** SUITABILITY, APPROPRIATENESS **:** inner harmony **:** agreement or accordance of the parts of a whole ⟨we can . . . judge the coherence and ~ of its language —C.D.Lewis⟩ ⟨a spot which returned upon the memory of those who loved it with an aspect of peculiar and kindly ~ —Thomas Hardy⟩ **b** *obs* **:** natural aptitude or fitness (as for one's work) **3 :** merit described in scholastic theology as granted through divine generosity **:** merit given rather than earned or given in excess of that which is earned — distinguished from *condignity* **4 :** an instance or point of agreement or correspondence ⟨the occasional *congruities* between fact and prophecy⟩ **5** *obs* **:** correspondence in physical structure or substance tending to promote union or mixture

con·gru·ous \'käŋgrəwəs\ *adj* [L *congruus*, fr. *congruere* to come together, coincide, agree, fr. *com-* + *-gruere* (as in *ingruere* to fall upon, attack); akin to Gk *zachreēs* attacking violently, Lith *griūti* to collapse, fall in ruins, Russ *grukhnut'sya* to fall down with a clatter] **1 a :** in agreement, harmony, or correspondence ⟨did not choose to wear the tailored clothes that would be ~ with . . . her alert, military bearing —Tennessee Williams⟩ ⟨the new psychology was ~ with the conception of man as part of an unseen and infinite spiritual universe —Sherwood Eddy⟩ **b :** conforming to the circumstances or requirements of a situation **:** REASONABLE, SUITABLE, APPROPRIATE ⟨the Old Cemetery . . . , a fenced-in burying ground on a knoll above the highway is unusually ~ here —*Amer. Guide Series: Vt.*⟩ ⟨a ~ room to work in —G.B. Shaw⟩ **2 :** marked by inner harmony, coherence, or agreement of its parts ⟨a ~, plausible story, consistent in all its details⟩ ⟨proud of appearing in such incongruous attires — proud of the fact that he always made them look ~ —G.K. Chesterton⟩ **syn** see CONSONANT

con·gru·ous·ly *adv* **:** in a congruous manner **:** AGREEABLY, FITTINGLY, APPROPRIATELY

con·gru·ous·ness *n* -ES **:** the state or quality of being congruous

con gu·sto \kän'gü(,)stō, kōn-, -'gə(-\ *adv* [It] **:** with taste — used as a direction in music

con·hy·drine \kän'hīdrən, -,drēn\ *n* -s [ISV *coniine* + *hydrate* + *-ine*] **:** a poisonous crystalline alkaloid $C_8H_{17}NO$ occurring in poison hemlock; 2-(α-hydroxy-propyl)-piperidine

coni *pl of* CONUS

[1]**coni-** *comb form* [L *coni-*, fr. *conus* — more at CONE] **:** cone ⟨*Coni*rostres⟩

[2]**coni-** *or* **conio-** *comb form* [G & NL; G *koni-* & NL *coni-*, *conio-*, fr. Gk *koni-* dust & MGk *konio-*, fr. Gk *konia*, *konis* — more at INCINERATE] **:** dust ⟨*coni*osis⟩ **:** spores ⟨*Conio*phora⟩

co·ni·bo \kə'nē(,)bō\ *n, pl* **conibo** *or* **conibos** *usu cap* [Sp, fr. Conibo] **1 a :** a Panoan people of the lower Ucayali river valley in Peru **b :** a member of such people **2 :** the language of the Conibo people

[1]**con·ic** \'känik, -nēk *sometimes* 'kōn-\ *adj* [Gk *kōnikos*, fr. *kōnos* cone + *-ikos* -ic — more at HONE] **1 :** CONICAL **2 :** of or relating to a cone **3** *of a hand* **:** of medium size with a slightly tapering palm and fingers full at the base and slightly pointed at the tip usu. held by palmists to indicate qualities of impulse and instinct and usu. an artistic nature

[2]**conic** \"\ *n* -s **:** CONIC SECTION

con·i·cal \-nəkəl, -nēk-\ *adj* [Gk *kōnikos* + E *-al*] **:** resembling a cone **:** having the shape of a cone ⟨~ roots⟩ — see ROOT illustration — **con·i·cal·ly** \-k(ə)lē, -li\ *adv* — **con·i·cal·ness** \-kəlnəs\ *n* -ES

con·i·cal·i·ty \,⸗⸗'kaləd·ē\ *n* -ES **:** CONICITY

conical surface *n, math* **:** the surface generated by a moving straight line which always passes through a fixed point and intersects a fixed curve

conical vault *n, archit* **:** a vault of which the curved elements, usu. arcs of circles, are larger at one extremity than at the other and whose soffit is therefore conical in form

co·ni·ca·ri \,kōnə'kärē, ,kän-, -'karē\ *n, pl* **conicari** *or* **conicaris** *usu cap* [Sp, fr. a native name] **1 :** a Taracahitian people of Sonora, Mexico **2 :** a member of the Conicari people

co·nic·e·ine \kə'nisēən; ,kōnə'sēən, ,kän-\ *n* -s [G *conicein*, modif. of ISV *conicine* coniine, modif. of G *koniin* — more at CONIINE] **:** any of several poisonous bases $C_8H_{15}N$ prepared from the alkaloids of poison hemlock

con·i·chal·cite \,känə'kal,sīt\ *n* -s [G *konichalzit*, fr. Gk *konia* plaster, ash, dust + *chalkos* copper + G *-it* -ite; akin to Gk *konis* dust — more at CHALC-] **:** a mineral $CaCu(AsO_4)(OH)$ consisting of basic copper calcium arsenate occurring in green masses

co·nic·i·ty \kō'nisəd·ē\ *n* -ES **:** the quality or state of being conical **:** CONICALNESS

con·i·cle \'känəkəl, 'kōn-\ *n* -s [*cone* + *-icle* (as in *particle*)] **:** a small cone

con·i·coid \-nə,kȯid\ *n* -s [*conic* + *-oid*] **:** a surface of second degree **:** QUADRIC

co·ni·cop·o·ly \,känə'käpəlē\ *n* -ES [Tamil *kaṇakkappiḷḷai*, fr. *kaṇakkan* accountant (fr. Skt *gaṇaka* mathematician, astrologer, fr. *gaṇayati* he reckons, fr. *gaṇa* series, multitude) + *piḷḷai* child (respectful title of certain castes)] *in the Madras area* **:** a native accountant or clerk

conic projection *n, mapping* **:** a projection based on the principle of a hollow cone placed over a sphere so that when the cone is unrolled the line of tangency becomes the central or standard parallel of the region mapped, all parallels being arcs of concentric circles and the meridians being straight lines drawn from the cone's vertex to the divisions of the standard parallel

conic section *n* **1 :** a plane curve, line, or point that is the intersection of a plane and a right circular conical surface **2 :** a curve generated by a point which always moves so that the ratio of its distance from a fixed point to its distance from a fixed line is constant

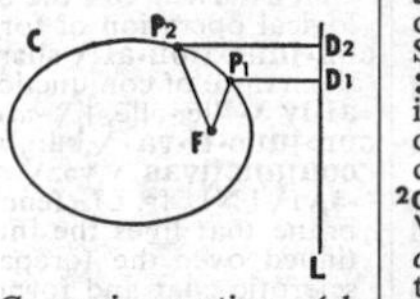

C, P_2, P_1, D_2, D_1, F, L

C conic section (ellipse); *F* fixed point; *L* fixed line; P_1, P_2 points on conic section; FP_1, $P_1D_1 = FP_2$, P_2D_2

co·ni·dae \'kōnə,dē\ *n pl, cap* [NL, fr. *Conus*, type genus + *-idae*] **:** a family of mollusks (group Toxoglossa) comprising the cones

co·i·den·drin \,känə'dendrən, ,kōn-\ *n* -s [*conifer* + *dendr-* + *-in*] **:** a crystalline hydroxy lactone $C_{20}H_{20}O_6$ found esp. in waste sulfite pulp liquor — called also *tsugaresinol*

conidi- *or* **conidio-** *comb form* [*conidium*] **:** conidia ⟨*conidi*iferous⟩

conidia *pl of* CONIDIUM

co·nid·i·al \kə'nidēəl\ *also* **co·nid·i·an** \-ēən\ *adj* [NL *conidium* + E *-al* or *-an*] **:** relating to, resembling, of the nature of, or producing conidia

co·nid·i·oid \-ē,ȯid\ *adj* [*conidi-* + *-oid*] **:** CONIDIAL

co·nid·i·o·phore \-ēə,fō(ə)r\ *n* -s [ISV *conidi-* + *-phore*] **:** a structure that bears conidia; *specif, in certain fungi* **:** a specialized typically erect and aerial hyphal branch that produces successive conidia by abstriction — **co·nid·i·oph·o·rous** \kə¦nidē¦äf(ə)rəs\ *adj*

co·nid·io·spore \kə'nidēə,spō(ə)r\ *n* -s [*conidi-* + *spore*] **:** CONIDIUM

co·nid·i·um \kə'nidēəm\ *n, pl* **conid·ia** \-ēə\ [NL, fr. *con-* (fr. Gk *konis* dust) + *-idium* — more at INCINERATE] *biol* **:** an asexual spore produced by abstriction, budding, or septation from the tip of a conidiophore; *broadly* **:** any asexual spore not borne within an enclosing structure — compare ENDOSPORE

conies *pl of* CONY

co·ni·fer \'känəfə(r) *also* 'kōn-\ *n* -s [NL *Coniferae*] **:** a plant of the order Coniferales

co·nif·er·ae \kō'nifə,rē, kə'-\ *n pl, cap* [NL, fr. L, pl. fem. of *conifer* cone-bearing, fr. *coni-* + *-fer*] *in some classifications* **:** a category of trees and shrubs treated variously as a family, order, or class coextensive with the order Coniferales

co·nif·er·a·les \⸗,⸗⸗'rā(,)lēz; ,känəfə-, ,kōn-\ *n pl, cap* [NL, fr. L *conifer* + NL *-ales*] **:** an order of chiefly evergreen gymnospermous trees and shrubs having acicular to linear or lanceolate leaves and the ovulate strobilus a woody cone or fleshy aril and comprising a variable number of families of which Taxaceae, Pinaceae, and Taxodiaceae are most generally recognized

co·nif·er·in \kō'nifərən, kə'-\ *n* -s [ISV *conifer* + *-in*; orig. formed as G *koniferin*] **:** a crystalline glucoside $C_{16}H_{22}O_8$ found esp. in the cambium of coniferous trees

co·nif·er·oph·y·tae \-fə,tē\ *n pl, cap* [NL, fr. L *conifer* + NL *-o-* + *-phytae* (pl. fem. equivalent of *-phyta*)] **:** a subclass of Gymnospermae comprising profusely branched plants with simple leaves, small pith, abundant xylem, and little cortex and including the surviving orders Ginkgoales, Coniferales, and Gnetales and the extinct order Cordaitales — compare CYCADOPHYTAE — **co·nif·er·o·phyte** \kō'nifərō,fīt, kə'-\ *n* -s — **co·nif·er·o·phyt·ic** \⸗¦⸗⸗⸗¦fid·ik\ *adj*

co·nif·er·ous \kō'nif(ə)rəs, kə'-\ *adj* [L *conifer* + E *-ous*] **1 :** bearing cones ⟨~ pine⟩ ⟨~ trees⟩ **2 :** of or relating to conifers ⟨~ wood⟩ **:** characterized by the predominance of coniferous trees ⟨the ~ forest belt⟩

co·nif·er·yl alcohol \⸗'⸗fərəl-\ *n* [ISV *coniferyl* (fr. *coniferin* + *-yl*) + *alcohol*] **:** a white crystalline alcohol $C_{10}H_{12}O_3$ obtained by hydrolysis of coniferin with emulsin or found as an ester in benzoin and held to be involved in the formation of lignin; 4-hydroxy-3-methoxy-cinnamyl alcohol

con·i·fi·ca·tion \,känəfə'kāshən, ,kōn-\ *n* -s [fr. [1]*cone*, after such pairs as E *code: codification*] **:** the act or process of tapering toward the top ⟨~ of the social structure⟩

co·ni·form \'kōnə,fȯrm, 'kän-\ *adj* **:** shaped like a cone

co·ni·ine \'kōnēən, -ē,ēn\ *also* **co·nine** \-nən, -,nēn\ *n* -s [*coniine* fr. G *koniin*, fr. LL *conium* hemlock + G *-in* -ine; *conine* ISV, modif. of *coniine* — more at CONIUM] **:** a liquid alkaloid $C_8H_{17}N$ with a penetrating odor and burning taste that is found in the poison hemlock and is a powerful poison that paralyzes the motor nerves; 2-propyl-piperidine

con·i·lu·rus \,kän°l'(y)u̇rəs\ *n, cap* [NL, fr. *conil-* (fr. *konilos*, erroneous reading of Gk *koniklos* rabbit, fr. L *cuniculus*) + *-urus* — more at CONEY] **:** a genus of rodents consisting of the Australian jerboa rats

coning *pres part of* CONE

conio- — see [2]CONI-

co·ni·o·gram·me \,kōnēō'gra(,)mē\ *n, cap* [NL, fr. *conio-* (fr. Gk *kōnion*, dim. of *kōnos* cone) + Gk *grammē* line; akin to Gk *graphein* to write — more at HONE, CARVE] **:** a small genus of ferns (family Polypodiaceae) of the Pacific islands and Japan often grown for ornament and characterized by large entire or pinnate fronds and elongate sori lacking indusia and reaching from midrib to leaf margin — see BAMBOO FERN

coniology *var of* KONIOLOGY

coniometer *var of* KONIMETER

co·ni·oph·o·ra \,kōnē'äfərə\ *n, cap* [NL, fr. [2]*coni-* + *-phora*] **:** a genus of fungi (family Thelephoraceae) of which one species (*C. cerebella* syn. *C. puteana*) often causes dry rot in the timbers of buildings

co·ni·op·ter·y·gid \,kōnē(,)äp'terəjəd, -ē,äptə'rij-\ *n* -s [NL *Coniopterygidae*] **:** an insect of the family Coniopterygidae — called also *dusty wing*

co·ni·op·te·ryg·i·dae \,kōnē,äptə'rijə,dē\ *n pl, cap* [NL, fr. *Coniopteryg-*, *Coniopteryx*, type genus (fr. [2]*coni-* + *-pteryx*) + *-idae*] **:** a family of small humpbacked insects (order Neuroptera) that have pollinose wings resembling those of moths and predatory larvae which feed esp. on mites and scales

co·ni·o·se·li·num \,kōnē(,)ōsə'līnəm\ *n, cap* [NL, fr. *conio-* (fr. *Conium*) + *Selinum* (genus name formerly used for what is now called *Conioselinum*), fr. LL *selinon* celery — more at CELERY] **:** a genus of aromatic herbs (family Umbelliferae) having much-dissected leaves and compound umbels of minute white flowers — see HEMLOCK PARSLEY

co·ni·o·thyr·i·um \,kōnēō'thirēəm\ *n, cap* [NL, fr. [2]*coni-* + *thyr-* (fr. Gk *thyreos* oblong shield, fr. *thyra* door) + *-ium* — more at DOOR] **:** a form genus of imperfect fungi (family Sphaeropsidaceae) with dark olivaceous spores that includes a species (*C. diplodiella*) that causes white rot of grapes

co·ni·ros·tres \,kōnə'rä(,)strēz, ,kän-\ *n pl, cap* [NL, fr. [1]*coni-* + *-rostres* (fr. L *rostrum* beak) — more at ROSTRUM] *in former classifications* **:** an artificial group of birds including the finches and weaverbirds and often the tanagers

co·ni·um \kō'nīəm, 'kōnēəm\ *n* [NL, fr. LL, hemlock, fr. Gk *kōneion*, perh. fr. *kōnos* cone — more at HONE] **1 a** *cap* **:** a genus of poisonous herbs (family Umbelliferae) having spotted stems, large decompound leaves with lanceolate pinnatifid leaflets, and white flowers **b** -s **:** any plant of the genus *Conium* **2** -s **:** the dried full-grown but unripe fruit of the poison hemlock containing the alkaloids coniine and methyl coniine and used as a narcotic and sedative

con·i·za·tion \,kōnə'zāshən, ,kän-, -,nī'z-\ *n* -s [[1]*cone* + *-ization*] **:** the electrosurgical excision of a cone of tissue from a diseased uterine cervix

conj *abbr* **1** conjugation **2** conjunction; conjunctive

conject *vb* -ED/-ING/-S [ME *conjecten*, fr. L *conjectare* to throw together, conjecture, fr. *com-* + *-jectare* (fr. *jactare* to throw) — more at JET] **1** *obs* **:** CONJECTURE **2** *obs* **:** PLAN, PLOT

conjector *n* -s [alter. (influenced by L *conjector*) of ME *conjectere*, modif. (influenced by ME *-ere* -er) of L *conjector* diviner, soothsayer, fr. *conjectus* (past part. of *conjicere*) + *-or*] *obs* **:** CONJECTURER

con·jec·tur·al \kən'jekchərəl, -ksh(ə)rəl\ *adj* [L *conjecturalis*, fr. *conjectura* + *-alis* -al] **1 :** of the nature of or involving or based on conjecture ⟨~ emendations⟩ **2 :** given to conjectures ⟨a ~ critic —Samuel Johnson⟩ — **con·jec·tur·al·ly** \-lē,-li\ *adv*

[1]**con·jec·ture** \kən'jekchə(r), -ksh-\ *n* -s [ME, fr. MF or L; MF *conjecture*, fr. L *conjectura*, fr. *conjectus* (past part. of *conjicere* to throw together, conjecture, divine, fr. *com-* + *-jicere*, fr. *jacere* to throw) + *-ura* -ure — more at JET] **1** *obs* **a :** interpretation of signs or omens; *also* **:** a conclusion so drawn **b :** SUPPOSITION ⟨now entertain ~ of a time when —Shak.⟩ **2 :** inference from defective or presumptive evidence **:** the act of making or stating of being absorbed in making such inference ⟨lost in ~⟩ **3 :** an inference or conclusion drawn or deduced by surmise or guesswork ⟨a mistaken ~⟩; *specif* **:** a conjectural emendation of a text

[2]**conjecture** \"\ *vb* **conjectured; conjectured; conjecturing** \-kchəriŋ, -ksh(ə)r-\ **conjectures** [ME *conjecturen*, fr. MF *conjecturer*, fr. *conjecture*, n.] *vt* **:** to arrive at by conjecture or to make conjectures as to **:** infer by way of surmise **:** form opinions concerning on grounds confessedly insufficient to certain conclusion ~ *vi* **:** to make or form conjectures; *esp* **:** to indulge in surmise

syn CONJECTURE, SURMISE, and GUESS may be compared in that they can all signify the forming of an opinion or the arriving at a conclusion on insufficient evidence or without evidence or signify the opinion or conclusion arrived at in this way. Of the three, CONJECTURE usu., though not always, suggests some evidence although insufficient; it usu. implies a strong awareness that what evidence there may be is not really sufficient ⟨it is easy to dismiss the false Cleopatra but the true one can only be *conjectured*, for the material for a reasoned verdict is lost —John Buchan⟩ ⟨Washington *conjectured* that at least 300 of the enemy were killed —*Amer. Guide Series: Pa.*⟩ SURMISE may be used in the same way as CONJECTURE although it usu. strongly implies the flimsiness of the evidence ⟨the rest of them were on holiday supposedly attending to their religious duties, though Simon *surmised* that they would be strolling idly about —L.C.Douglas⟩ ⟨as to how they came there he could only *surmise* that they had entered through the stable yard, as otherwise he must have observed their approach —Rafael Sabatini⟩ ⟨we are not told what their business was but we may *surmise* it was the fur trade —G.F.Hudson⟩ GUESS usu. implies a complete or almost complete absence of evidence; it suggests rather the use of intuition or suspicion and a reliance upon chance for verification ⟨you would never *guess* from meeting them that anyone would pay them for their ideas —Rose Macaulay⟩ ⟨Tristram *guessed* what was passing in his friend's mind —T.B.Costain⟩ ⟨he expected this eighteen-year-old girl to *guess* his love and understand its esoteric quality, without being told —H.S.Canby⟩

con·jec·tur·er \-kchərər, -ksh-; -ksh(ə)rə(r)\ *n* -s **:** one that conjectures

con·join \kən'jȯin, (')kän¦j-\ *vb* -ED/-ING/-S [ME *conjoynen*, fr. MF *conjoindre*, fr. L *conjungere*, fr. *com-* + *jungere* to join — more at YOKE] *vt* **:** to join together (as separate entities) for a common purpose or a common end ⟨the two are historically ~*ed* but not connected in a causal way at all —*Times Lit. Supp.*⟩ ⟨belief in a transcendent God ~*ed* with belief in an afterlife —A.J.Ayer⟩ ~ *vi* **:** to join together for a common purpose or a common end ⟨a certain complex of conditions ~ to create the boom —D.M.Friedenberg⟩ **:** be in conjunction (as of celestial bodies) **syn** see JOIN, UNITE

conjoined \-nd\ *adj* [fr. past part. of *conjoin*] **1 :** being, coming, or brought together so as to meet, touch, or overlap ⟨~ heads on a coin⟩ **2** *of heavenly bodies* **:** in conjunction — **con·join·ed·ly** \-nədlē\ *adv*

conjoined in lure *heraldry* **:** joined together with their tips downward — used of two wings

[1]**con·joint** \-ȯint\ *adj* [ME, fr. MF, past part. of *conjoindre*] **1 :** UNITED, CONJOINED **2 :** related to, made up of, or carried on by two or more in combination **:** JOINT, COMBINED, SIMULTANEOUS — **con·joint·ly** *adv*

[2]**conjoint** \"\ *n* -s **1 :** an associate in interest or obligation **2 conjoints** *pl* **:** husband and wife taken collectively (as in cases of community property)

con·joint·ment \kən'jȯintmənt\ *n* -s [[1]*conjoint* + *-ment*] **:** CONJUNCTION, COMBINATION

conjoint tendon *also* **conjoined tendon** *n* **:** the common tendon of the transverse and internal oblique muscles of the abdomen extending from the linea alba to the pubic bone

con·jubilant \kən, (')kän+\ *adj* [ML *conjubilant-*, *conjubilans*, pres. part. of *conjubilare*, fr. L *com-* + *jubilare* to shout for joy — more at JUBILATE] **:** shouting together with joy

con·ju·ga·ble \ˈkänjəgəbəl\ *adj* [*conjugate* + *-able*] **:** that is capable of conjugation

con·ju·ga·cy \-gəsē\ *n* -ES [*conjugate* + *-cy*] **:** conjugate state **:** relation of conjugates

con·ju·gal \ˈkänjəgəl, -jēg-; kənˈjüg-\ *adj* [MF or L; MF, fr. L *conjugalis,* fr. *conjug-, conjux* husband, wife, consort, fr. *conjungere* to join together, unite in marriage] **1 :** of or relating to marriage, the married state, or married persons in their mutual relations **:** MATRIMONIAL, CONNUBIAL ⟨~ worries⟩ ⟨~ politeness⟩ **2 :** consisting of or based on the husband, wife, and their offspring as constituting the functional familial unit in a society ⟨the modern American family is of the ~ type⟩ — contrasted with *consanguine;* compare FAMILY — **con·ju·gal·i·ty** \ˌkänjəˈgaləd-ē, -jēˈ-\ *n* -ES — **con·ju·gal·ly** *pronunc at* CONJUGAL + ē *or* i\ *adv*

con·ju·ga·les \ˌkänjəˈgā(ˌ)lēz\ *n pl, cap* [NL, fr. L, pl. of *conjugalis* of marriage] *in some classifications* **:** an order equivalent to Zygnematales

conjugal rights *n pl* **:** the sexual rights or privileges implied by and involved in the marriage relationship **:** the right of coitus between husband and wife

con·ju·gant \ˈkänjəgənt\ *n* -S [L *conjugant-, conjugans,* pres. part. of *conjugare* to unite] **:** one of a pair of conjugating gametes or organisms

con·ju·gase \-ˌgās, -āz\ *n* -S [ISV *conjug-* (fr. *conjugate,* n.) + *-ase*] **:** any of a group of enzymes found in blood or in certain organs (as kidney and pancreas) and in some vegetables (as potatoes) that bring about the breakdown of conjugates of pteroylglutamic acid (as pteroyl-hepta-glutamic acid)

con·ju·ga·ta \ˌkänjəˈgād-ə\ *n, pl* **conjuga·tae** \-ˌā,tē\ [NL, fr. L, fem. of *conjugatus*] **:** the dorsoventral diameter of the human pelvis measured from the sacral promontory to the pubic symphysis

con·ju·ga·tae \-ˌā,tē\ *n pl, cap* [NL, fr. L, nom. pl. fem. of *conjugatus*] *in some classifications* **:** a subclass equivalent to the order Zygnematales

¹con·ju·gate \ˈkänjəgət, -jēg-, -jə,gāt; *usu* -d.+V\ *adj* [ME *conjugat,* fr. L *conjugatus,* past part. of *conjugare* to unite, fr *com-* + *jugare* to join, marry, fr. *jugum* yoke — more at YOKE] **1 :** yoked or joined together esp. in pairs **:** MATED, COUPLED ⟨~ relationship⟩ **:** acting or operating as if joined ⟨~ foci⟩ **:** SIMULTANEOUS ⟨~ deviation of the eyes⟩ ⟨~ effect of two forces⟩ **2 :** bearing to each other a relation characterized by having certain features in common but by being opposite or inverse in some particular ⟨~ complex numbers⟩ ⟨~ axes of a pendulum⟩ ⟨~ foci of a lens⟩ **3 a :** BIJUGATE **b :** of or relating to algae that reproduce sexually by conjugation **4** *of words in the same language* **:** having the same derivation and therefore usu. some likeness in meaning ⟨*just, justice, justly* are ~⟩ **5 a :** CONJUGATED 2 **b** *of acids and bases in pairs* **:** related by the difference of a proton ⟨the acid NH_4^+ and the base NH_3 are ~ to each other⟩ **c :** relating to layers of immiscible solutions that can exist side by side at equilibrium **6** *of two leaves of a book* **:** forming a single piece **7 :** so formed that one gear will drive the other with constant relative angular speed — used of a pair of gear teeth or of gear teeth profiles; *also* **:** relating to such gear teeth or profiles — **con·ju·gate·ly** *adv* — **con·ju·gate·ness** *n* -ES

²con·ju·gate \-jə,gāt, *usu* -ād.+V\ *vb* -ED/-ING/-S [L *conjugatus*] *vt* **1 :** to give in some prescribed order the various inflectional forms of **:** INFLECT — used esp. of a verb, rarely of a preposition ⟨~ the Latin verb *amare*⟩ **2 :** to join together **:** YOKE, COUPLE **3** *of a chemical compound* **:** to unite (as with the elimination of water) so that the product is easily broken down (as by hydrolysis) into the original compounds ⟨benzoic acid is *conjugated* with glycine to hippuric acid in the body⟩ ~ *vi* **1 :** to join together; *specif* **:** to unite in marriage **2** *biol* **:** to unite in pairs: **a :** to fuse esp. in conjugation **b :** to pair in synapsis

³conjugate *like* ¹CONJUGATE\ *n* -S [in sense 1, fr. L *conjugatus* etymologically related, past part. of *conjugare* to unite; in senses 2 & 4, fr. ¹*conjugate;* in sense 3, fr. NL *Conjugatae*] **1 :** a word that has the same derivation as another in the same language and that therefore usu. resembles it in meaning **2 a :** CONJUGATE AXIS **b :** CONJUGATE DIAMETER **3 :** an alga of the order Zygnematales **4** *chem* **:** a substance that is conjugated (sense 2a)

conjugate alphabet *n* **:** one of a pair of alphabets in cryptography consisting of an enciphering alphabet and its equivalent deciphering alphabet

conjugate axis *n* **:** the line through the center of an ellipse or a hyperbola and perpendicular to the line through the two foci

conjugate complex number *n* **:** one of two complex numbers differing only in the sign of the imaginary part (as *a+bi* and *a−bi*)

conjugate conductor *n* **:** either of two branches of an electrical network such that a change in the impressed electromotive force of one does not produce a change in the current of the other

conjugated *adj* [fr. past part. of *conjugate*] **1 :** CONJUGATE 1 **2** *chem* **a :** formed by the union of two compounds or united with another compound ⟨some enzymes are ~⟩ ⟨~ bile acids⟩ **b** (1) **:** having or characterized by a special mutual influence due to proximity in the molecule — used of certain groups or bonds or of compounds or systems containing them (2) *organic chem* **:** relating to or containing a system of two double bonds separated by a single bond (as in $CH_2{=}CH{-}CH{=}CH_2$ or $CH_2{=}CH{-}CH{=}O$) — often distinguished from *allenic* and *isolated* ⟨~ double bonds⟩ ⟨~ drying oils⟩ ⟨~ fatty acids⟩ ⟨a ~ system of alternating single and double bonds⟩

conjugate diameter *n* **1 :** CONJUGATA **2 a :** one of two diameters of a central conic section each of which bisects all chords parallel to the other **b :** one of three diameters of a central quadric having as its conjugate diametral plane the plane of the other two

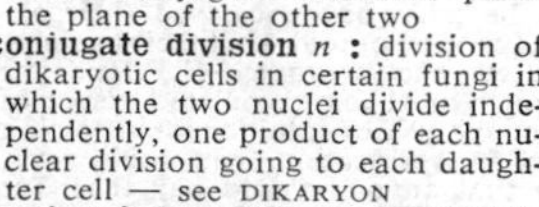

AB, CD conjugate diameters 2a

conjugate division *n* **:** division of dikaryotic cells in certain fungi in which the two nuclei divide independently, one product of each nuclear division going to each daughter cell — see DIKARYON

conjugated protein *also* **conjugate protein** *n* **:** a compound (as hemoglobin) of a protein (as globin) with a nonprotein substance (as heme) — distinguished from *simple protein;* compare CHROMOPROTEIN, GLYCOPROTEIN, LIPOPROTEIN, NUCLEOPROTEIN, PHOSPHOPROTEIN

conjugate hyperbola *n* **:** either of two hyperbolas having the same asymptotes, the conjugate axis of each being the transverse axis of the other

conjugate lines *n pl* **1** *of a conic section* **:** two lines each of which passes through the pole of the other **2** *of a quadric* **:** two lines so arranged that each intersects the polar line of the other

conjugate planes *n pl, of a quadric* **:** two planes so arranged that each contains the pole of the other with respect to the quadric

conjugate point *n* **1 :** either of two points lying with respect to a conic each on the polar of the other **2 a :** one of two points in reference to a rigid body such that if an impulse is applied at either the body will start to rotate about an instantaneous axis through the other, one point becoming the center of suspension of the body considered as a pendulum and the other becoming the center of oscillation **b :** one of two points in an optical system either of which is the real or virtual focus of the other

conjugate roots *n pl* **:** roots of an algebraic equation that are conjugate complex numbers

conjugate triangles *n pl* **:** two triangles in which the vertices of each are the poles with respect to a given curve of the sides of the other

conjugating tube *n* [*conjugating* fr. gerund of *conjugate*] **:** a tube in various algae (as members of the genus *Spirogyra*) formed by the fusion of a process of one cell with a like process of another sexually opposite cell into a canal and used by one or both gametes in coming together for conjugation

con·ju·ga·tion \ˌkänjəˈgāshən\ *n* -S [LL & L; LL *conjugation-, conjugatio* class of verbs having same type of inflectional forms, fr. L, combining, mixture, fr. *conjugatus* (past part. of *conjugare* to unite) + *-ion-, -io* -ion — more at CONJUGATE] **1 :** the act of joining together, uniting, or combining **:** the state of being joined together **:** UNION ⟨~ of the sexes⟩ **2** *obs* **:** something joined together or combined **3 a :** a presentation in some prescribed order of the inflectional forms of a verb **b :** verb inflection **c :** a class of verbs having the same type of inflectional forms ⟨the strong and the weak ~⟩ ⟨the Latin second ~ with its infinitive ending in *-ēre*⟩ **d :** any of several sets of inflectional forms belonging to a verb esp. in Sanskrit and the Semitic languages including the forms of the simple verb and various derivative sets of forms that typically add to the meaning of the simple verb a passive, reflexive, causative, intensive, frequentative, or desiderative meaning **4 a :** fusion of two gametes with ultimate union of their nuclei which is the common sexual process among the lower thallophytes resulting typically in formation of a thick-walled zygote, being comparable to fertilization in higher forms though male and female are not usu. recognizable, and similarly producing a genetically distinct new generation **b :** temporary cytoplasmic union in pairs of ciliated protozoa accompanied by complex nuclear phenomena comparable to meiosis and fertilization and resulting in two individuals with new genetic constitutions **5** *chem* **:** the state of being conjugated (sense 2b)

con·ju·ga·tion·al \ˌ¦känjəˈ¦gāshənᵊl, -shnəl\ *adj* **:** of or relating to conjugation — **con·ju·ga·tion·al·ly** \-ᵊl¦ē, -əl¦ē, ¦i\ *adv*

conjugation canal *n* **:** CONJUGATING TUBE

conjugation cell *n* **:** GAMETE

con·ju·ga·tive \ˈkänjə,gād-iv\ *adj* **:** relating to, tending to, or characterized by conjugation

con·ju·gi·al \kənˈjügēəl\ *adj* [L *conjugialis,* fr. *conjugium* marriage (fr. *conjug-, conjux* husband, wife) + *-ialis* -ial — more at CONJUGAL] **:** MATRIMONIAL — used to distinguish the Swedenborgian conception of marriage as a spiritual union

¹con·junct \kənˈjəŋ(k)t, (ˈ)kän¦j-\ *adj* [ME, fr. L *conjunctus,* past part. of *conjungere* to join together — more at CONJOIN] **1 :** JOINED, UNITED **:** bound together ⟨folk tunes and texts independent or ~⟩ ⟨man . . . feels himself to be ~ with a social group —Rufus Jones⟩ **2 :** belonging to, made up of, or effected by combined elements or persons **:** JOINT ⟨Sicily was reduced in . . . 1806 by a brilliant ~ operation —P.G. Mackesy⟩ **3 :** being so related to a person (as an insolvent) as to be legally incompetent to act as witness or judge in matters affecting him **4** *in Irish and Welsh verb inflection* **:** belonging to or characteristic of a verb that is preceded by any of several particles or compounded with a preverb ⟨the ~ form⟩ ⟨a ~ ending⟩ — opposed to *absolute* **5** *music* **:** relating to diatonic motion — contrasted with *disjunct*

²con·junct \ˈkän,j-\ *n* -S **1 :** a person or thing joined or associated with another **2 a :** CONJUNCTURE 2 **b** *logic* (1) **:** a component of a conjunction (2) **:** CONJUNCTION 7

conjunct degrees *n pl* **:** adjacent successive tones of the musical scale

con·junc·tion \kənˈjəŋ(k)shən\ *n* -S [ME *conjunctioun,* fr. MF *conjonction,* fr. L *conjunction-, conjunctio,* fr. *conjunctus* + *-ion-, -io* -ion] **1 :** the act of conjoining or state of being conjoined **:** UNION, ASSOCIATION, COMBINATION ⟨things not normally seen in ~⟩ ⟨the view that cause is constant ~ —E.H. Madden⟩ **2 :** an instance of conjoining or coming together **:** UNION, ASSOCIATION ⟨quartering . . . was the normal way of indicating a ~ of lordships —A.R.Wagner⟩ **3 :** occurrence together **:** concurrence esp. of events or routes ⟨from the state line route 17 proceeds in ~ with route 6 for a few miles⟩ **4** *obs* **:** sexual union **:** union in wedlock **5 a :** the apparent meeting or passing of two or more celestial bodies in the same degree of the zodiac **b :** a configuration in which two celestial bodies have their least apparent separation ⟨a ~ of Mars and Jupiter⟩ — compare OPPOSITION; see CONFIGURATION illustration **6 :** a linguistic form (as an uninflected word) that joins together words or word groups such as sentences (as *but* in "He tried. But he failed"), clauses (as *if* in "I'll go if you will"), phrases (as *and* in "over the river and through the woods"), words (as *or* in "first or last"), or a word and a phrase (as *and* in "my brother and I") **7** *logic* **a :** a statement that is true only if both its components are true — called also *joint assertion* **b :** the binary connective used in logic **c :** the logical operation of forming a conjunction

con·junc·tion·al \-shənᵊl, -shnəl\ *adj* **:** of or relating to or of the nature of conjunction or a conjunction — **con·junc·tion·al·ly** \-ᵊl¦ē, -əl¦ē, ¦i\ *adv*

con·junc·ti·va \ˌkän,jəŋkˈtīvə, -tēvə; kənˈjəŋ(k)təvə\ *n, pl* **conjunctivas** \-vəz\ *or* **conjuncti·vae** \-ˌī,vē, -ē,vī, -ə,vē, -ə,vī\ [NL, fr. LL, fem. of *conjunctivus*] **1 :** the mucous membrane that lines the inner surface of the eyelids and is continued over the forepart of the eyeball covering part of the sclerotic coat and forming epithelium over the cornea — see EYE illustration **2 :** the flexible usu. infolded and membranous suture between adjoining segments of an insect's body or appendages — **con·junc·ti·val** \ˌ¦kän,jəŋ¦kˈtīvəl, -tēv-; kənˈjəŋ(k)təv-\ *adj*

¹con·junc·tive \kənˈjəŋ(k)tiv, -tēv *also* -təv\ *adj* [LL *conjunctivus,* fr. L *conjunctus* + *-ivus* -ive — more at CONJUNCT] **1 :** CONJOINING, CONNECTING, CONNECTIVE ⟨~ forces in society⟩ **2 :** CONJOINED, CONJUNCT **:** done or existing in conjunction ⟨the ~ operation of several independent factors⟩ **3 a :** being a conjunction (sense 6) ⟨a ~ particle⟩ **b :** functioning like a conjunction; *specif* **:** connecting the sentence or main clause in which it occurs with the preceding one and qualifying the whole sentence or clause in which it occurs rather than any single word or phrase in it ⟨~ adverbs such as *hence, yet, so, consequently, however*⟩ **4** *of the mood of a verb* **:** SUBJUNCTIVE **5** *of a conjunction* **:** COPULATIVE 1a **6** *of a pronoun form* **:** unstressed and closely attached to the verb as an enclitic or proclitic ⟨French *me, le, te, se* are ~⟩ — contrasted with *disjunctive* — **con·junc·tive·ly** \-tīvlē, -li\ *adv*

²conjunctive \"\ *n* -S **:** something conjunctive: as **a** (1) **:** CONJUNCTION 7 (2) **:** the connective in a conjunction **b** (1) **:** CONJUNCTION 6 **:** a word (as *moreover* in "I don't know, moreover I don't care") or word group (as the phrase *in case* in "take your umbrella in case it should rain") functioning like a conjunction (2) **:** a copulative conjunction (3) **:** the conjunctive mood of a language or a form in it

conjunctive legacy *n* **:** a legacy awarding under Roman law the same thing to two or more persons in one dispositive clause and giving each colegatee the right of increasing his share proportionately to his interest if the share of any other colegatee lapses or becomes vacant before it vests — distinguished from *disjunctive legacy*

conjunctive tissue *n* **:** sometimes lignified parenchymatous ground tissue in which the vascular bundles are embedded in certain dicotyledons (as the beet) and in those monocotyledons in which secondary thickening occurs

con·junc·ti·vi·tis \kən,jəŋ(k)təˈvīd-əs, -ītəs\ *n* -ES [NL, fr. *conjunctiva* + *-itis*] **:** inflammation of the conjunctiva

conjunct motion *or* **conjunct progression** *n* **:** melodic movement by scale intervals

conjuncts *pl of* CONJUNCT

conjunct system *n* **:** a diatonic series of tones in Greek music comprising three conjunct tetrachords

conjunct tetrachords *n pl* **:** two adjacent tetrachords in which the highest note of one is the same as the lowest note of the other

con·junc·ture \kənˈjəŋ(k)chə(r), -)sh-\ *n* -S [F *conjoncture,* fr. ML *conjunctura,* fr. L *conjunctus* + *-ura* -ure] **1 :** CONJUNCTION, UNION, COMBINATION ⟨the ~ of realism with idealism —Frank Swinnerton⟩ **2 :** a combination or complication (as of circumstances or events) esp. producing a crisis or critical point **:** JUNCTURE ⟨~s that arise out of the circumstances of the industrial system at large —Thorstein Veblen⟩

con·ju·ra·tion \ˌkänjəˈrāshən\ *n* -S [ME *conjuracioun,* fr. MF & L; MF *conjuration* constraining of spirits or devils, fr. L *conjuration-, conjuratio* conspiracy, fr. *conjuratus* (past part. of *conjurare*) + *-ion-, -io* -ion] **1** *archaic* **a :** a swearing together **:** a league by a common oath (as for a criminal purpose) **b :** CONSPIRACY **2 :** a constraining of spirits or devils by invocation of a sacred name or by a spell **:** INCANTATION **3 a :** a magic expression used in conjuring **:** CHARM, SPELL **b :** a conjuring trick **4 :** the act of charging or calling upon in a sacred name or in a solemn manner usu. by appealing to something binding (as an oath) **:** a solemn appeal **:** ADJURATION

¹con·jure *in senses vt 2 & vi 2* ˈkänjə(r) *also* ˈkən-; *in other senses* kənˈjü(ə)r *or* -ùə\ *vb* **conjured; conjured; conjuring** \ˈkänj(ə)riŋ, ˈkən-; kənˈjùr-\ **conjures** [ME *conjuren,* fr. OF *conjurer,* fr. L *conjurare* to swear together, conspire, fr. *com-* + *jurare* to swear — more at JURY] *vt* **1 a** *obs* **:** to call on or charge in a solemn manner (as by invoking a sacred name) **b :** to entreat earnestly or solemnly **:** IMPLORE, BESEECH ⟨I ~ you . . . to weigh my case well —Sheridan Le Fanu⟩ **2 a :** to summon or constrain (as a spirit or a devil) to appear or to obey one by invoking a spell or a sacred name **b** (1) **:** to affect or effect by or as if by magic **:** call forth or send away by magic arts **:** excite, bring about, get, or convey as if by magic **:** create in reality or to the imagination as if by magic — often used with *up* ⟨~ up an image⟩ (2) **:** INVENT, CONTRIVE ⟨you've *conjured* up some scheme to get us safely away —T.B.Costain⟩ ~ *vi* **1** *obs* **:** to swear together **:** CONSPIRE ⟨when those gainst states and kingdoms do ~ —Edmund Spenser⟩ **2 a :** to summon a devil or spirit to appear or obey one by invoking a sacred name or by some spell **b :** to practice magical arts **:** CHARM ⟨prayed and *conjured,* but all was useless —Herman Melville⟩ **c :** to use a conjurer's tricks **:** JUGGLE

²con·jure \ˈkänjə(r) *also* ˈkən-\ *adj* **1** *of a person* **:** practicing magic, esp. voodoo **2** *of a thing* **:** used in the practice of magic, esp. voodoo ⟨~ ball⟩ ⟨~ bag⟩

con·jur·er *or* **con·ju·ror** \ˈkänjərə(r), -j(ə)rə *also* ˈkən-\ *n* -S [*conjurer* fr. ME *conjurere,* fr. *conjuren* to conjure + *-ere* -er; *conjuror* fr. ME *conjerour,* fr. *conjeren, conjuren* + *-our* -or] **1 :** one that practices magic arts **:** one that pretends to act by the aid of supernatural power **:** WIZARD **2 :** one that performs feats of legerdemain and illusion **:** MAGICIAN, JUGGLER

con·jury \ˈkänj(ə)rē, -ri *also* ˈkən-\ *n* -ES [*conjure* + *-y*] **:** the practice of magic **:** CONJURING

¹conk \ˈkäŋk, ˈkȯŋk\ *n* -S [prob. alter. of *conch*] **1** *slang* **:** NOSE **2** *slang* **:** HEAD

²conk \"\ *vt* -ED/-ING/-S *slang* **:** to hit esp. on the head **:** knock out

³conk \"\ *n* -S [by alter.] **:** CONCH 3

⁴conk \"\ *n* -S [prob. alter. of *conch*] **1 :** the visible fruiting body of a tree fungus **:** BRACKET 3c **2 :** the decay in the wood of living trees caused by a fungus — **conky** \-kē, -ki\ *adj*

⁵conk \"\ *vi* -ED/-ING/-S [prob. imit.] **1 :** to break down **:** STALL, FAIL — used esp. of an engine or motor and usu. with *out* **2 a :** to lose consciousness **:** FAINT — usu. used with *out* ⟨~*ed* out from hunger and lack of sleep⟩ **b :** to go to sleep — usu. used with *off* or *out* ⟨go upstairs and ~ off⟩ **c :** DIE — often used with *out* ⟨caught pneumonia and almost ~*ed* out⟩

conk·a·nee hemp \ˈkäŋkənē-\ *n* [prob. irreg. fr. *Konkan,* coast region of Bombay state, India] **:** SUNN

¹conk·er \ˈkäŋkə(r), ˈkȯŋ-\ *n* -S [*conch* + *-er* (influenced by *conquer*)] **1 conkers** *pl* **:** a game popular in England in which each player swings a horse chestnut or orig. a snail shell threaded on a string to try to break one held by his opponent **2 :** a horse chestnut or snail shell esp. when used in conkers

²conker *var of* KUNKUR

conky \-kē\ *n* -ES [¹*conk* + *-y*] *slang* **:** a person having a large or prominent nose

con mae·stà \ˌk¦än,mīˈstä, ¦k¦än,mä,eˈstä, ¦ōn-\ *adv* [It] **:** with majesty — used as a direction in music

con man \ˈkän,man, -maa(ə)n\ *n* [by shortening] **:** a confidence man

con mo·to \känˈmō,tō, kōn-\ *adv* [It, with movement] **:** with movement **:** SPIRITEDLY — used as a direction in music

¹conn *also* **con** \ˈkän\ *vt* -ED/-ING/-S [alter. of *cond,* prob. taken as past tense] **:** to conduct or superintend the steering of (a ship or airplane) **:** watch the course of (a ship) and direct the helmsman how to steer

²conn \"\ *n* -S **:** the control exercised by one who guides or directs the movements of a ship

conn *abbr* **1** connected; connection **2** connotation; connotative

con·nach \ˈkänəḵ\ *vt* -ED/-ING/-S [ScGael *conach* murrain; akin to IrGael, murrain, rabies, rage] *Scot* **:** SPOIL, WASTE

con·nacht *also* **con·naught** \ˈkä(ˌ)nȯt\ *adj, usu cap* [fr. *Connacht* or *Connaught,* Ireland] **:** of or from the province of Connacht, Ireland **:** of the kind or style prevalent in Connacht

con·na·ra·ce·ae \ˌkänəˈrāsē,ē\ *n pl, cap* [NL, fr. *Connarus,* type genus + *-aceae*] **:** a family of mostly tropical climbing shrubs or small trees (order Rosales) closely related to the Leguminosae but lacking stipules — **con·na·ra·ceous** \¦==ˈrāshəs\ *adj*

con·na·rite *also* **con·a·rite** \ˈkänə,rīt\ *n* -S [ISV *connar-, conar-* (fr. Gk *konnaros*) + *-ite;* orig. formed as G *konarit*] **:** a mineral consisting of hydrous nickel silicate occurring as small green crystals or grains

con·na·rus \ˈkänərəs\ *n, cap* [NL, fr. Gk *konnaros,* a kind of prickly evergreen (perh. the Christ's-thorn *Paliurus spina-christi*)] **:** a large genus (the type of the family Connaraceae) of tropical shrubs or trees bearing indehiscent one-seeded pods — see ZEBRAWOOD

con·na·tal \(ˈ)kä¦nād-ᵊl, kəˈn-, -ātᵊl\ *adj* [*connate* + *-al*] **:** CONGENITAL — **con·na·tal·ly** \-ād-ᵊlē, -ātᵊlē\ *adv*

con·nate \(ˈ)kä¦nāt, kəˈnāt, *usu* -ād.+V\ *adj* [L *connatus,* past part. of *connasci* to be born together, fr. L *com-* + *nasci* to be born — more at NATION] **1 :** CONGENITAL, INNATE, INBORN ⟨~ ideas⟩ **2 :** agreeing in nature **:** AKIN, ALLIED, COGNATE, CONGENIAL ⟨~ spirits⟩ **3 :** born, produced, or originated together ⟨~ qualities⟩ **4** *biol* **a :** congenitally united ⟨~ leaves⟩ **b :** firmly united **:** FUSED ⟨~ bones⟩ — distinguished from *connivent;* compare ADNATE **5** *geol* **:** entrapped in sediments at the time of their deposition **:** originating at the same time as adjacent or intermingled materials ⟨~ water⟩ — **con·nate·ly** *adv*

con·na·tion \(ˈ)kä¦nāshən, kəˈn-\ *n* -S **:** congenital union

con·na·tive \(ˈ)kä¦nād-iv, kəˈn-, -ātiv\ *adj, obs* **:** CONNATE 1

con·natural \(ˈ)kä, kə+\ *adj* [ML *connaturalis,* fr. L *com-* + *naturalis* natural — more at NATURAL] **1 :** connected by nature **:** INBORN, INHERENT, NATURAL ⟨man's ~ sense of the good⟩ **2 :** of the same nature **:** ALLIED, COGNATE ⟨and mix with our ~ dust —John Milton⟩ **3** *obs* **:** SUITABLE, CONGENIAL — **con·naturality** \"+\ *n* -ES — **con·naturally** \"+\ *adv*

con·nect \kəˈnekt\ *vb* -ED/-ING/-S [L *connectere, conectere,* fr. *com-, co-* + *nectere* to bind — more at ANNEX] *vt* **1 :** to join, fasten, or link together usu. by means of something intervening ⟨a bus line ~*s* the two towns⟩ ⟨~ a garden hose to the faucet⟩ ⟨the ties that ~*ed* new Europe to old —Stringfellow Barr⟩ **2 :** to place or establish in any of various intangible relationships (as association in thought or logic, the relationship of follower, official, or employee, or a relationship of things similar in purpose, motivation, configuration, or substance) ⟨~ his success with hard work and study⟩ ⟨~ himself with a radical school of painters⟩ ⟨she could not ~ her mother's meanness with the magnitude of what had happened —Louis Auchincloss⟩ ⟨the emphasis on the subjective expression of the art of the mentally ill which ~*s* it with certain tendencies of modern art —H.S.Langfeld⟩ ⟨the marriage of the children ~*ed* the two families⟩ ~ *vi* **1 a :** JOIN, UNITE ⟨one room ~*s* with the other by means of a hallway⟩; *also* **:** ADJOIN **b :** to have a relationship ⟨his character seems at first not to ~ with his painting —A.M.Daintrey⟩ **2 a** *of a means of transportation* **:** to meet for the transference of passengers ⟨the New York and Boston trains ~ at Albany⟩ **b** *of a passenger* **:** to transfer esp. from one train or bus to another that covers a different part of one's route — used with *with* ⟨to ~ with the Chicago train in St. Louis⟩ **3 :** to hit solidly or successfully ⟨~ for a double⟩ ⟨~ with a knockout punch⟩; *esp* **:** to hit a home run **syn** see JOIN

connected *adj* **1 :** joined or linked together ⟨a ~ series⟩ **2 :** having the parts or elements logically related ⟨a ~ view of the problem⟩ or continuous ⟨~ reading from the great authors⟩ **3 :** related by blood or marriage ⟨a well-*connected* Edinburgh family —Rosemary Benét⟩ ⟨a well-*connected* Marylander — it was supposed that his grandfather was the younger brother of the Earl of Wemyss —Van Wyck Brooks⟩ **4** *chess* **a** *of pawns* **:** on adjacent squares **b** *of rooks* **:** mutually supported (as on an empty rank) — **con·nect·ed·ly** *adv* — **con·nect·ed·ness** *n* -ES

connected load *n* **:** the total electric power-consuming rating of all devices (as lamps or motors) connected to a distribution system

connected surface *n, math* **:** a surface from any point of which a continuous path can be drawn to any other point of it without crossing its boundary

connecter *var of* CONNECTOR

con·nect·i·cut \kə'ned·ə̇kət, -netə-, *usu* -kəd·+V\ *adj, usu cap* [fr. *Connecticut,* state in the northeastern U.S., fr. *Connecticut* river, prob. fr. Mohican *quinnitukq-ut* at the long tidal river] **:** of or from the state of Connecticut ⟨*Connecticut* flora⟩ **:** of the kind or style prevalent in Connecticut

connecticut chest *n, usu cap 1st C* **:** an early American framed chest with the front panels decorated usu. with split spindles and tulip and sunflower patterns carved in flat relief — called also *sunflower chest*

con·nect·i·cut·er \-,kəd·ə(r), -,kətə-, -,kəd·ə-\ *n* -s *cap* **:** a native or resident of the state of Connecticut

connecticut warbler *n, usu cap C* **:** a large wood warbler (*Oporornis agilis*) gray to greenish above and yellow below that breeds in north-central No. America and winters in Brazil

connecting filament *n* **:** OOBLAST

connecting note *or* **connecting tone** *n* **:** a note common to two successive chords

connecting rod *n* **:** a rigid rod that transmits power from one rotating part of a machine to another in reciprocating motion (as from a crankpin to a piston) — see CROSSHEAD illustration

con·nec·tion \kə'nekshən\ *n* -s [L *connexion-, connexio,* fr. *connexus* (past part. of *connectere* to connect) + *-ion-, -io* -ion — more at CONNECT] **1 a :** the act of connecting **:** a coming into or being put in contact ⟨~ with the island was made by a causeway⟩ **b :** sexual relation or intercourse ⟨had had no ~ with any other woman —John Abernethy⟩ **2 :** the state of being connected or linked **:** ALLIANCE, UNION ⟨Canada's political ~ with England⟩ ⟨~ between church and state⟩ **3 a :** relationship or association in thought (as of cause and effect, logical sequence, mutual dependence or involvement) ⟨the ~ of intelligence and success⟩ **b :** CONTEXT, REFERENCE, OCCASION ⟨in this ~ the word has a different meaning⟩ **c :** COHERENCE, CONTINUITY ⟨a confused multitude without order or ~ —John Locke⟩ **4 :** CONNECTIVE b, d **5 a :** something that connects **:** COUPLING, LINK ⟨plumbing ~*s*⟩ **b :** a means of communication ⟨telephone ~⟩ or transport ⟨the train makes ~ with the steamer⟩ ⟨to miss a ~⟩ **6 :** a person connected with others by marriage, remote blood relationship, or such a tie as a common interest ⟨he has powerful ~*s* in high places⟩ **7 :** a social, professional, or commercial relationship in a practical or active way: as **a :** POSITION, JOB **b :** a permanent or continuing arrangement to execute orders or advance interests esp. at a distance ⟨a firm's foreign ~*s*⟩ **c** *slang* **:** a source of contraband (as a narcotic drug) **8 :** a set or group of persons connected or associated together in a common interest: **a :** DENOMINATION, SECT **b :** a political faction **c** *Brit* **:** the owner of a racehorse and his associates **d :** a large family **:** CLAN **e :** a clientele esp. of a doctor or lawyer **9 :** a religious association practicing connexionalism — **con·nec·tion·al** \-kshənᵊl, -kshnəl\ *adj*

con·nec·tion·ism \-shə,nizəm\ *n* -s **:** a theory that learning takes place through the formation of connections or associative bonds between contiguous stimulus and response

¹con·nec·tive \kə'nektiv, -tēv *also* -təv\ *adj* [L *connectere* to connect + E *-ive*] **:** tending to connect **:** CONNECTING — **con·nec·tive·ly** *adv*

²connective \"\ *n* -s **:** something that connects: **a :** the tissue connecting the pollen sacs of an anther **b :** a linguistic form that connects words or word groups; *esp* **:** a relative pronoun **:** CONJUNCTION, PREPOSITION **c :** a nerve that connects two ganglia esp. of the same side of the body **d** *logic* **:** a constant (as *or, if-then, and, not*) linking two statements or attaching to a single statement so that the truth-value of the composite is determined by the truth-value of the components

connective tissue *n* **1 :** any of various tissues of mesodermal origin having abundant intercellular substance or interlacing processes and showing little tendency for the constituent cells to aggregate in sheets or masses — compare EPITHELIUM **2 :** connective tissue made up of stellate or spindle-shaped cells with interlacing processes that pervades, supports, and binds together other tissues and organs and forms ligaments, tendons, and aponeuroses — compare ADIPOSE TISSUE, AREOLAR TISSUE, ELASTIC TISSUE, WHITE FIBROUS TISSUE

con·nec·tiv·i·ty \,kä,nek'tivəd·ē, -ətē, -i\ *n* -ES **:** the quality or state of being connective

con·nec·tor *also* **con·nec·ter** \kə'nektə(r)\ *n* -s **1 :** one who connects: **a :** a worker who couples railroad coaches **b :** a construction worker who guides and bolts structural steel members as they are hoisted into position in the framework of a building or bridge **2 :** something that connects: as **a :** a flexible tube for connecting the ends of tubes **b :** a railroad coupling **c** (1) **:** a device for detachably connecting flexible electrical conductors together (2) **:** a fitting for joining wires without splicing **d :** the part of the firing mechanism of small arms that transmits the motion of the trigger to the sear **e :** a metallic fitting for joining timbers

connector, 2 c (1)

connector neuron *n* **:** an internuncial neuron

conned *past of* CON *or of* CONN

con·nell·ite \'kän ᵊl,īt\ *n* -s [Arthur *Connell fl*1857 Brit. chemist + E *-ite*] **:** a mineral $Cu_{19}(SO_4)Cl_4(OH)_{32}.3H_2O$(?) consisting of hydrous copper sulfate chloride commonly in slender prisms

con·ne·ma·ra pony \,känə'märə-\ *n, usu cap C* [fr. *Connemara,* district in Connacht province, Ireland] **:** a small hardy horse of an Irish breed of uncertain origin noted for its intelligence and stamina

¹con·ner \'kənə(r), 'kän-\ *n* -s [ME, fr. OE *cunnere* examiner, tempter, fr. *cunnian* to examine; akin to OE *cunnan* to be able — more at CAN] *archaic* **:** one that tests or examines ⟨election of four ale ~*s* for the City of London —*Scotsman*⟩

²conner *var of* CUNNER

¹connex *n* -ES [MF *connexe* connected property, fr. *connexe,* adj., connected, related, fr. L *connexus,* past part. of *connectere* — more at CONNECT] **1** *obs* **a :** BOND, TIE **b :** a connected incident or property **2** *obs* **:** a conditional proposition in logic

²con·nex \kə'neks\ *vb* -ED/-ING/-ES [MF *connexer,* fr. *connexe* connected] **:** CONNECT

³connex \'kä(,)neks, -,niks\ *adj* [L *connexus*] **1 :** CONNECTED: as **a :** closely connected **:** linked in meaning (as *father-son, left-right*) —opposed to *disparate* **b** *of a dyadic relation* **:** connecting every two distinct members of its field ⟨in the field of positive integers, the relation *less than or equal to* is ~ for either a ≤ b or b ≤ a⟩ **2 :** belonging to or constituting one syntactical unit ⟨in *the dog barked,* the complete sentence or either or both of its constituents are ~⟩

con·nex·ion \kə'nekshən\ *chiefly Brit var of* CONNECTION

con·nex·ion·al \kə'nekshənəl, -kshnəl\ *chiefly Brit var of* CONNECTIONAL

con·nex·ion·al·ism \kə'nekshənə,lizəm\ *n* -s **:** a form of church organization esp. in mission areas where scattered churches are held together by itinerant evangelists

con·nex·i·ty \kə'neksəd·ē, -ətē, -i\ *n* -ES [F *connexité,* fr. *connexe* + *-ité* -ity] **1 :** the character of being connex **2 :** something that is connex **3 :** the state of being syntactically connex

connexive *adj* [L *connexivus,* fr. *connexus* (past part. of *connectere*) + *-ivus* -ive — more at CONNECT] **1** *obs* **:** CONDITIONAL **2** *obs* **:** CONJUNCTIVE, CONNECTIVE

con·nex·i·vum \,kä,nek'sēvəm\ *n, pl* **connexi·va** \-və\ [NL, fr. L, neut. of *connexivus*] **:** the flattened often much dilated lateral border of the abdomen of hemipterous insects

con·nie \'känē\ *n* -s [prob. by shortening & alter.] **:** INCONNU

¹conning *pres part of* CON

²conning *n* -s [fr. gerund of ¹*conn*] **:** the giving of directions (as of course and speed) for steering or guiding a ship or aircraft

conning tower *n* **:** an armored pilothouse (as on a submarine) usu. having narrow horizontal slits for observation and housing the means of communication with all parts of the ship

con·nip·tion \kə'nipshən\ *or* **conniption fit** *n* -s [origin unknown] **:** a fit of rage, hysteria, or alarm ⟨to throw a ~⟩

conniption bug *n* **:** HELLGRAMMITE

con·niv·ance *also* **con·niv·ence** \kə'nīvən(t)s\ *n* -s [F or L; F *connivence,* fr. L *conniventia,* fr. *connivent-, connivens* (pres. part. of *connivēre*) + *-ia*] **1 :** the act of conniving **:** intentional failure to notice or discover a wrongdoing **:** passive consent or cooperation **2 :** corrupt or guilty assent to wrongdoing that involves knowledge of and failure to prevent or oppose it but no actual participation in it — compare ACCOMPLICE

connivancy *n* -ES [L *conniventia*] *obs* **:** CONNIVANCE

con·nive \kə'nīv\ *vb* -ED/-ING/-S [F or L; F *conniver,* fr. L *conivēre, connivēre* to close the eyes, wink, be indulgent, connive, fr. *com-* + *-nivēre* (akin to *nictare* to wink); akin to OE & OHG *hnīgan* to bow, bend, Goth *hneiwan* to bow, ON *hnīga* to bow, L *nicere* to beckon, and perh. to Lith *knibti* to break by bending] *vi* **1 :** to pretend ignorance or unawareness of something one ought morally or officially or legally to oppose **:** fail to take action against a known wrongdoing or misbehavior — usu. used with *at* ⟨~ at the violation of a law⟩ **2 a :** to be indulgent, tolerant, or secretly in favor or sympathy **:** WINK — usu. used with *at* ⟨~ at youthful follies⟩ **b :** to cooperate secretly **:** have a secret understanding — usu. used with *with* ⟨officials who were not above *conniving* with him in importing goods —J.A.Krout⟩ **3 :** CONSPIRE, INTRIGUE ⟨she loved to ~ with her friends in their amours —Helen Howe⟩ ⟨he had declared that no candidate was ever chosen without *conniving* —*Time*⟩ ~ *vt, obs* **:** to shut the eyes to **:** wink at

con·niv·ent \-vənt\ *adj* [L *connivent-, connivens,* pres. part. of *connivēre*] **1** *obs* **:** CONNIVING **2 :** converging but not fused into a single part ⟨an insect with ~ wings⟩ ⟨~ stamens⟩ — distinguished from *connate*

con·niv·er \-və(r)\ *n* -s **:** one that connives

con·niv·ery \-v(ə)rē, -ri\ *n* -ES [*connive* + *-ry*] **:** the practice of conniving

con·no·chae·tes \,känə'kēd·ēz\ *n, cap* [NL, fr. Gk *konnos* beard + NL *-chaetes*] **:** the genus of ruminants (family *Bovidae*) comprising the gnus

con·nois·seur \¦känə'sər, -sō *also* -sü(ə)r, -süə *sometimes* -syü-, '==,=\ *n* -s [obs. F (now *connaisseur*), fr. OF *connoisseor,* fr. *conoiss-* (stem of *conoistre* to know, fr. L *cognoscere*) + *-eor* -or — more at COGNITION] **1 :** one who is expert in a subject; *esp* **:** one who understands the details, technique, or principles of an art and is competent to act as a critical judge **2 :** a discriminating judge or critic of something **:** one who enjoys with discrimination and appreciation of subtleties ⟨a ~ of his own responses⟩ ⟨a ~ of rare tobaccos⟩

con·nois·seur·ship \,==¦=,ship\ *n* -s **:** expertness in a matter of taste or discrimination **:** knowledgeability esp. in aesthetic or recondite matters ⟨none of that pedantic affectation of ~ which makes a premature fuss over trifles —Irvin Stock⟩ ⟨esthetic ~ has generally displaced a creative conception of art —Walter Gropius⟩

con·no·ta·tion \,känə'tāshən, -nō't-\ *n* -s [ML *connotation-, connotatio,* fr. *connotatus* (past part. of *connotare* to connote) + *-ion-, -io* -ion] **1 a :** the conveying or suggesting a meaning by a word along with or apart from the thing it explicitly names or describes ⟨the value of ~ in poetry⟩ ⟨it was quite wrong to call it mind, the ~ was false —Willa Cather⟩ — compare DENOTATION 2 **b :** something implied or suggested by a word or sometimes by a thing **:** IMPLICATION ⟨using a literary language in which the ~*s* of words tend to overwhelm their precise significance —Walter Lippmann⟩ ⟨stayed in one place long enough for it to assume familiar ~*s* —Norman Mailer⟩ **2 :** the meaning of a word (as a word representing an emotion, a feeling, quality, a moral idea) **:** SIGNIFICATION ⟨that abuse of logic which consists in moving counters about as if they were known entities with a fixed ~ —W.R.Inge⟩ **3 :** the property or group of properties connoted by a term in logic and signified by or comprised in a concept or essential to the thing named **:** COMPREHENSION, SIGNIFICATION — contrasted with *denotation* — **con·no·ta·tion·al** \¦==¦=shənᵊl, -shnəl\ *adj*

con·no·ta·tive \'känə,tād·|iv, -tāt|, |ēv *also* |əv; *sometimes* kə'nōd·əd·iv\ *adj* [ML *connotativus,* fr. *connotatus* + L *-ivus* -ive] **1 :** connoting or tending to connote **:** relating to connotation **:** bearing implication **2** *logic* **:** having connotation **:** denoting a subject and implying an attribute — **con·no·ta·tive·ly** \'känə,tād·əvlē, -tātəv-, -li\ *adv*

connotative definition *n* **:** a statement of the equivalence of connotation between the defined term and another expression

con·note \kə'nōt, (')kä¦nōt, *usu* -ōd·+V\ *vt* -ED/-ING/-S [ML *connotare,* fr. L *com-* + *notare* to mark, note — more at NOTE] **1** *of a word or phrase* **a :** to signify in addition to its exact explicit meaning ⟨the word *home* usu. ~*s* comfort and security⟩ **b :** to have as the sum of meanings **:** MEAN, SIGNIFY ⟨to some *Bohemian* ~*s* a slovenly crank⟩ ⟨*anabolism* is a word used to ~ building up or assimilative processes —C.H.Best & N.B.Taylor⟩ **2 a :** to arouse as an inseparably associated idea or feeling **:** IMPLY, SUGGEST ⟨unless a few desiccated potted palms ~ the Orient —Truman Capote⟩ **b :** to be associated with or inseparable from as a consequence or concomitant ⟨guilt usu. ~*s* suffering⟩ **3** *logic* **:** to imply, indicate, or involve as an attribute **:** bear as connotation — contrasted with *denote* ⟨the word *white* denotes all white things, as snow, paper, the foam of the sea, etc., and implies, or, as it was termed by the schoolmen, ~*s,* the attribute *whiteness* —J.S.Mill⟩

conns *pres 3d sing of* CONN, *pl of* CONN

con·nu·bi·al \kə'n(y)übēəl\ *adj* [L *connubialis,* fr. *connubium, conubium* marriage (fr. *com-, co-* + *-nubium,* fr. *nubere* to marry) + *-alis* -al — more at NUPTIAL] **:** of or relating to marriage or the marriage state **:** CONJUGAL ⟨I never could imagine ~ bliss till after tea —W.S.Maugham⟩ — **con·nu·bi·al·ly** \-ēəlē, -li\ *adv*

con·nu·bi·al·i·ty \=,=bē'aləd·ē, -ətē, -i\ *n* -ES **:** the married state; *also* **:** something characteristic of it

con·nu·bi·um *also* **co·nu·bi·um** \kə'n(y)übēəm\ *n, pl* **connu·bia** *also* **conu·bia** \-bēə\ [L] **1** *Roman law* **:** lawful marriage **2** *Roman law* **:** the right to intermarry — called also *jus conubii*

con·ny \'känē, -ni\ *dial Eng var of* CANNY

conny boy \"-\ *n* [origin unknown] **:** a worker who removes sludge and incrustations from refining pans and vats

cono- — see ²CON-

con·ob \(')kä¦nōb\ *n, pl* **conob** *or* **conobs** *usu cap* **:** KANHOBAL

co·no·car·pus \¦kōnə¦kärpəs, ¦kän-\ *n, cap* [NL, fr. ²*con-* + *-carpus*] **:** a monotypic genus of tropical American trees or shrubs (family Terminaliaceae) with dense flower heads resembling buttons — see BUTTON TREE 1

co·no·ceph·a·lum \-¦sefələm\ *n, cap* [NL, fr. ²*con-* + *-cephalum* (irreg. fr. Gk *-kephalos* -cephalous)] **:** a small genus of liverworts (family Marchantiaceae) having conical long-stalked female receptacles

co·no·dont \'kōnə,dänt, 'kän-\ *n* -s [ISV ²*con-* + *-odont;* orig. formed as G *konodont*] **:** a Palaeozoic fossil sometimes considered to be teeth of extinct cyclostomes but more probably the remains of an unknown invertebrate form of life

¹co·noid \'kō,nȯid, 'kä,n-\ *n* -s [Gk *kōnoeides* small cone, fr. neut. of *kōnoeidēs,* adj.] **1** *math* **:** a surface generated by a straight line that is perpendicular to and intersects a fixed straight line *l,* is revolved about *l,* and at the same time is translated along *l* **2 :** something that has a conoidal form (as a rifle bullet)

²conoid \"\ *adj* [Gk *kōnoeidēs* conical, fr. *kōn-* ²con- + *-oeidēs* -oid] **:** shaped like or nearly like a cone **:** CONOIDAL

co·noi·dal \(')kō¦nȯidᵊl, kə'n-, (')kä¦n-\ *adj* [Gk *kōnoeidēs* + E *-al*] **:** like a conoid **:** resembling or approaching a cone in shape — **co·noi·dal·ly** \-dᵊlē, -li\ *adv*

conoid ligament *n* **:** the posterior fasciculus of the coracoclavicular ligament connecting the conoid tubercle and the base of the coracoid

conoid tubercle *n* **:** a prominence on the underside of the clavicle that forms one attachment of the conoid ligament

co·nol·o·phus \kə'näləfəs, kō'n-\ *n, cap* [NL, fr. ²*con-* + Gk *lophos* crest] **:** a genus of iguanid lizards including a single large burrowing form (*C. subcristatus*) of the Galápagos islands

co·noph·o·lis \-'näfələs\ *n, cap* [NL, fr. ²*con-* + *-pholis*] **:** a small genus of parasitic scaly herbs (family Orobanchaceae) with flowers in a thick spike — see SQUAWROOT

co·no·phor oil \'kōnəfə(r)-, 'kän-\ *n* [NL *conophorum* (specific epithet of *Tetracarpidium conophorum*), fr. Gk *kōnophoron,* neut. of *kōnophoros,* fr. *kōno-* ²con- + *-phoros* -phorous] **:** a drying oil resembling perilla oil in properties that is obtained from the fruit of a western African vine (*Tetracarpidium conophorum*) of the family Euphorbiaceae

¹co·no·pid \'kōnə,pid, 'kän-\ *adj* [NL *Conopidae*] **:** of or relating to the Conopidae

²conopid \"\ *n* -s **:** a fly of the family Conopidae

co·nop·i·dae \kə'näpə,dē, kō'n-\ *n pl, cap* [NL, fr. *Conop-, Conops,* type genus (fr. Gk *kōnōps* gnat, mosquito) + *-idae*] **:** a family of broadheaded flies (order Diptera) comprising the thickheaded flies or wasp flies

co·no·po·phag·i·dae \,kōnə(,)pō'fajə,dē, ,kän-\ *n pl, cap* [NL, fr. *Conopophaga,* type genus (fr. Gk *kōnōp-, kōnōps* gnat, mosquito + NL *-o-* + *-phaga*) + *-idae*] **:** a small family of birds (order Passeriformes) that are related to the ovenbirds and have a large head and in some cases a very short tail

co·no·rhi·nus \,kōnə'rīnəs, ,kän-\ [NL, fr. ²*con-* + *-rhinus*] *syn of* TRIATOMA

co·no·scen·te \,kōnə'shentē, ,kän-\ *var of* COGNOSCENTE

co·no·scope \'kōnə,skōp, 'kän-\ *n* -s [²*con-* + *-scope*] **:** a polariscope for examining the interference figures produced by crystals in convergent polarized light — **co·no·scop·ic** \¦==¦skäpik\ *adj*

co·no·tra·che·lus \,kōnə·'trākələs, -trak-, -ə·trə'kēləs\ *n, cap* [NL, fr. ²*con-* + Gk *trachēlos* neck, throat] **:** a large genus of small, dark-colored American weevils (family Curculionidae) the larvae of which develop in fruits and seeds — see PLUM CURCULIO

con ot·ta·va \¦känə¦tävə, ¦kōn-\ *adv* (*or adj*) [It] **:** COLL' OTTAVA

co·noy \kə'nȯi\ *n, pl* **conoy** *or* **conoys** *usu cap* [prob. fr. Algonquian *Kanawha*] **1 a :** an Indian people that dwelt between the Potomac river and Chesapeake Bay, Maryland **b :** a member of such people **2 :** a dialect of Nanticoke

conquassation *n* -s [L *conquassation-, conquassatio,* fr. *conquassatus* (past part. of *conquassare* to shake severely, fr. *com-* + *quassare* to shake) + *-ion-, -io* -ion —more at QUASH] *obs* **:** a severe shaking

con·quer \'käŋkə(r) *sometimes* 'kōŋkə(r)\ *vb* **conquered; conquered; conquering** \-k(ə)riŋ\ **conquers** [ME *conqueren,* fr. OF *conquerre,* fr. (assumed) VL *conquaerere,* alter. (influenced by L *quaerere* to ask, search) of L *conquirere* to search for, bring together, fr. *com-* + *-quirere* (fr. *quaerere*)] *vt* **1** *obs* **:** to procure by effort; ACQUIRE, GET, GAIN **2 :** to gain or acquire by force of arms **:** take possession of by violent means **:** gain dominion over **:** SUBJUGATE **3 :** to overcome by force of arms **:** VANQUISH ⟨if we be *conquer'd* let men ~ us —Shak.⟩ **4 :** to gain or win by overcoming obstacles or opposition **:** gain mastery over (as by exploration, penetration, or surmounting) ⟨the mountain was ~*ed*⟩ **5 :** to subdue or overcome by mental or moral power **:** SURMOUNT ⟨~ difficulties⟩ ⟨~ her fear⟩ ~ *vi* **:** to gain the victory **:** make conquests **:** be victorious ⟨resolved to ~ or to die⟩ ⟨hail the ~*ing* hero⟩

syn DEFEAT, VANQUISH, OVERCOME, SURMOUNT, SUBDUE, SUBJUGATE, REDUCE, OVERTHROW, ROUT, BEAT, LICK: these verbs are all of a kind in signifying to get the better of or bring to subjection. CONQUER and DEFEAT are perhaps the most general. DEFEAT usu. signifies merely the fact of getting the better of or winning against ⟨the enemy were successfully *defeated*⟩ ⟨he *defeated* the older man in the tennis tournament⟩ ⟨a distortion of the news picture which *defeats* the whole purpose to which our system is committed —F.L.Mott⟩ CONQUER, however, usu. implies a large and significant action as of a large force in war or an action involving an all-inclusive effort and a more or less permanent result ⟨Caesar *conquered* most of Gaul⟩ ⟨culture *conquers* more surely than the sword —A.M.Young⟩ ⟨science has *conquered* yellow fever —*Amer. Guide Series: La.*⟩ ⟨the 21-year-old Englishman who *conquered* the most dangerous river in the world —*N. Y. Times Book Rev.*⟩ VANQUISH suggests a significant action of a certain dignity usu. in the defeat of a person rather than a thing and usu. carrying the suggestion of complete defeat ⟨to overthrow the enemy solely by his own strength — to *vanquish* him solely by his own effort —Lafcadio Hearn⟩ ⟨to *vanquish* an opponent in a championship match at tennis⟩ OVERCOME usu. implies an opposing, more or less fixed obstacle to be dealt with ⟨to *overcome* the enemy's shore fortifications⟩ ⟨*overcoming* difficult legal obstacles —*Americana Annual*⟩ ⟨using the airlift to *overcome* the blockade —*Collier's Yr. Bk.*⟩ ⟨to *overcome* a speech defect⟩ SURMOUNT, like OVERCOME, implies an opposing, more or less fixed obstacle but carries the idea of surpassing or exceeding rather than overcoming in face-to-face conflict ⟨the technical problems to be *surmounted* —K.F.Mather⟩ ⟨many petty faults which he is apparently unable to *surmount* —*New Republic*⟩ ⟨Simon . . . has an inner force that is capable of *surmounting* conditions —Malcolm Cowley⟩ SUBDUE, SUBJUGATE, and REDUCE all throw emphasis upon the condition of subjection resulting from defeat. SUBDUE signifies to bring under control by or as if by overpowering ⟨in 1803 Commodore Edward Preble *subdued* the Barbary Coast pirates —*Amer. Guide Series: Maine*⟩ ⟨in their last century of conquest they almost succeeded in *subduing* the whole island —Paul Blanshard⟩ ⟨all violence or recklessness of feeling has been finally *subdued* —Willa Cather⟩ ⟨the wilderness had been almost completely *subdued* by cutting down the forests and building roads and cities⟩ SUBJUGATE signifies to bring into and keep in subjection, often as a slave is in subjection ⟨authoritarian reaction which overwhelmed Italy and *subjugated* it for two centuries —R.A.Hall b.1911⟩ ⟨the heart and imagination *subjugating* the senses and understanding —Matthew Arnold⟩ REDUCE signifies surrender and submission but usu. of a town or fortress under attack or siege ⟨the town and finally the province were *reduced* by the invaders⟩ OVERTHROW is much like OVERCOME but carries the strong idea of disaster to the overthrown ⟨to *overthrow* the established government by violence⟩ ⟨to get swiftly through the field of fire and pierce and *overthrow* the enemy lines —Tom Wintringham⟩ ⟨a huge body of evidence . . . completely *overthrows* the older view —*Meanjin*⟩ ROUT always suggests a defeat so complete as to cause flight or the complete dispersion of the opposition ⟨twelve hundred French and a large force of Indians . . . were intercepted . . . and utterly *routed,* only 200 of the French escaping capture or death —R.W.Bingham⟩ ⟨Weaver with the assistance of two other gunboats *routed* a large force of Texas cavalry when they attacked Fort Butler —L.H.Bolander⟩ BEAT and LICK are mainly characteristic of a different style of expression or level of usage than the preceding verbs. BEAT means the same as and is as comprehensive as DEFEAT but usu. applies to smaller, less significant actions than, say, CONQUER or VANQUISH ⟨the local ball team won the state championship by *beating* all comers⟩ LICK, a more informal word for DEFEAT, usu. implies the complete humbling or humiliation of the person defeated ⟨the fighter must be confirmed in the belief that he can *lick* anybody in the world —A.J. Liebling⟩ ⟨with the problem growing, the railroads have redoubled their efforts to *lick* it —William Faulkner⟩

con·quer·ing·ly *adv* **:** in a conquering manner

con·quer·or \-k(ə)rə(r)\ *n* -s [ME *conquerour,* fr. OF *conquereor,* fr. *conquerre* + *-eor* -or] **1 :** one that conquers **:** one that wins a country in war, subdues or subjugates a people, or overcomes an adversary **:** WINNER, VICTOR — compare CONQUISTADOR **2** *obs* **:** deciding game **:** RUBBER

¹con·quest \'kä|n,kwest, |ŋ,k- *also* -,kwəst *sometimes* 'kō|\ *n* -s [ME *conquest, conqueste,* fr. OF *conquest, conqueste,* fr. (assumed) VL *conquaesitus, conquaesita,* alter. of L *conquisitus* (masc.) *conquisita* (fem.), past part. of *conquirere* to search for, bring together — more at CONQUER] **1 :** the act or process of conquering or acquiring by force **:** the act of overcoming ⟨three years sufficed for the ~ of the country —W.H.Prescott⟩ **2 :** the act of gaining by or as if by struggle ⟨the ~ of liberty⟩ ⟨she came dressed for ~⟩ ⟨an army bent on ~⟩ **3** *obs* **:** the state of being conquered **4 a :** something that is conquered **:** a possession gained by physical or moral force; *esp* **:** territory definitely appropriated in war **b :** a person whose favor, heart, or hand has been won ⟨what ~ brings he home —Shak.⟩ **5** *feudal law* **:** acquisition of property by purchase or means other than inheritance **:** ACQUISITION; *also* **:** the property so acquired **syn** see VICTORY

²conquest \", kən'kwest\ *vt* -ED/-ING/-S [ME *conquesten,* fr. MF *conquester,* fr. *conquest, conqueste,* n.] **1** *archaic* **:** ACQUIRE, GAIN **2** *archaic* **:** CONQUER, VANQUISH

conquest state *n* **:** a state formed by or based upon the subjugation of the original inhabitants

con·qui·an \'käŋkēən\ *n* -s [MexSp *con quien,* fr. Sp *¿con quién?* with whom?] **:** a card game for two played with 40 cards in which each player tries to form three or four of a kind or sequences and from which all games of rummy developed

con·quin·a·mine \(ˈ)känˈkwinə,mēn, kənˈk-, -,mə̇n\ *n* -s [ISV *com-* + *quinamine;* orig. formed as G *konquinamin*] **:** a crystalline alkaloid $C_{19}H_{24}N_2O_2$ found with quinamine in cinchona barks

con·qui·nine \ˈkäŋkwə̇,nēn, -ink-, -,nə̇n\ *n* -s [ISV *com-* + *quinine;* orig. formed as G *konquinin*] **:** QUINIDINE

con·quis·ta·dor \kə̇nˈk(w)istə,dȯ(ə)r, (ˈ)kä\|, (ˈ)kȯ\|, (ˈ)kō\|, \|ŋˈk(w)-, -k(w)ēs-, -ˈdō(ə)r, -ˈdȯ(ə), -dōə\ *n, pl* **conquistadores** \-ˈdȯ(ə)rz,-dō(ə)-, -ˈdȯ(ə)z,-dōəz; -ˈdȯ(,)rēz, -dō(,)-, -(,)rās\ *or* **conquistadors** \-ˈdȯ(ə)rz,-dō(ə)rz, -ˈdȯ(ə)z,-dōəz\ [Sp, fr. *conquistado* (past part. of *conquistar* to conquer, fr. *conquista* conquest, fr. fem. of *conquisto*, past part. of *conquerir* to conquer, fr. L *conquirere* to search for, bring together) + *-or* — more at CONQUER] **:** CONQUEROR; *specif* **:** any one of the leaders in the Spanish conquest of America, esp. of Mexico and Peru, in the 16th century

con·rad·son carbon test \ˈkänrədsən-\ *n, usu cap 1st C* [after Dr. Pontus H. *Conradson*, 20th cent. scientist, its inventor] **:** a determination of the weight of carbon residue of an oil (as a lubricating oil) obtained on evaporation to dryness in a closed vessel

con·ring·ia \känˈriŋ(g)ēə, -rinjēə\ *n, cap* [NL, fr. Herman *Conring* †1681 Ger. scholar + NL *-ia*] **:** a genus of Eurasian herbs (family Cruciferae) with entire clasping leaves, small yellow flowers in racemes, and long slender pods — see HARE'S-EAR 2

cons *pl of* CON, *pres 3d sing of* CON

cons *abbr* **1** consecrated **2** conservative **3** consigned; consignment **4** consol; consolidated **5** consonant **6** constable **7** constitution **8** construction **9** consul **10** consulting

con·san·guine \(ˈ)kän\|saŋgwə̇n *also* -\|sangw-\ *adj* [F *consanguin*, fr. L *consanguineus*, fr. *com-* + *sanguineus* of blood — more at SANGUINE] **:** CONSANGUINEOUS; *specif* **:** based on an extended group of blood relations esp. of unilinear descent and constituting the functional familial unit in a society ⟨the ~ family type of the matriarchal Hopi⟩ — contrasted with *conjugal;* compare FAMILY

con·san·guin·eal \ˈkänsaŋˈgwinēəl, -sanˈgw-\ *adj* [L *consanguineus* + E *-al*] **:** CONSANGUINE ⟨~ ties are the normal basis for the transmission of land rights —W.H.Goodenough⟩

con·san·guin·ean \-ˈgwinēən\ *adj* [L *consanguineus* + E *-an*] *Roman law* **:** having the same father

con·san·guin·eous \-nēəs\ *adj* [L *consanguineus*] **1 :** of the same blood ⟨a ~ mating⟩ **:** descended from the same person (as a father) or the same ancestor ⟨~ brothers⟩; *also* **:** of or relating to persons so related ⟨a ~ community⟩ — distinguished from *affinal;* compare CONSANGUINE **2 :** of the same origin ⟨~ igneous rocks⟩ — **con·san·guin·eous·ly** *adv*

con·san·guin·i·ty \ˈkänsaŋˈgwinəd·ē, -sanˈgw- -ətē, -i\ *n* -ES [ME *consanguinyte*, fr. MF *consanguinité*, fr. L *consanguinitat-, consanguinitas*, fr. *consanguineus* + *-itat-, -itas* -ity] **1 :** the quality or state of being related by blood or descended from a common ancestor **:** BLOOD RELATIONSHIP — distinguished from *affinity* and commonly expressed in degrees of consanguinity ⟨according to one scheme a person has ~ of the second degree with his grandfather, grandson, uncle, cousin-german, and nephew or with corresponding female relations⟩; compare AGNATE, COGNATE **2 :** genetic relationship; *specif* **:** the spatial, chronological, and compositional relationship existing between the various rocks in a single petrographic province **3 :** a close relation or connection **:** AFFINITY ⟨the ~ of all religions⟩

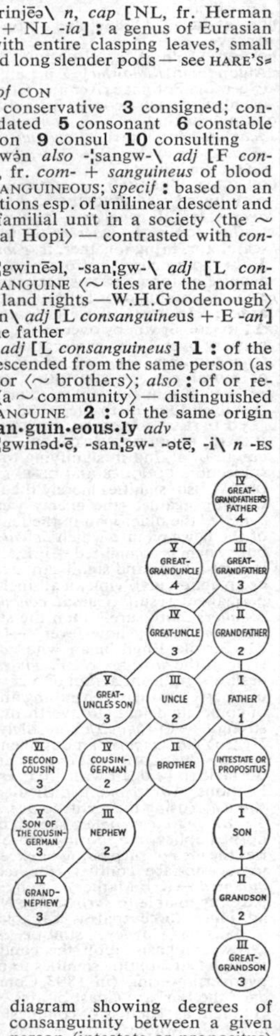

diagram showing degrees of consanguinity between a given person (intestate or propositus) and lineal and collateral relations according to the common-law and canon-law computation (Arabic numerals) and the civil-law computation (Roman numerals), lineal relations being represented by the disks vertically connected, collateral relations by those at the side

consarcinate *vt* -ED/-ING/-S [L *consarcinatus*, past part. of *consarcinare*, fr. *com-* + *-sarcinare* (fr. *sarcire* to mend, patch)] *obs* **:** to patch together — **consarcination** *n* -S *archaic*

con·sarn \(ˈ)kənˈsärn, kən-ˈs-, -sän\ *vt* -ED/-ING/-S [alter. of ¹*concern;* prob. euphemism for *confound*] *dial* **:** DAMN — a mild imprecation

¹**con·sarned** \(ˈ)kənˈsärnd, kənˈs-, -sänd\ *also* **consarn** \-särn, -sän\ *adj, dial* **:** DAMNED, CONFOUNDED — a mild imprecation ⟨that ~ old thief —Kate D. Wiggin⟩

²**consarned** \"\ *also* **consarn** \"\ *adv* [¹*consarned, consarn*] *dial* **:** TERRIBLY, AWFULLY — a mild imprecation ⟨he was always ~ lucky⟩

con·science \ˈkänchən(t)s *sometimes* ˈkȯn-\ *n* -S [ME, fr. OF, fr. L *conscientia*, fr. *conscient-, consciens* (pres. part. of *conscire* to know, be conscious, fr. *com-* + *scire* to know) + *-ia* -y — more at SCIENCE] **1 a :** the sense of right or wrong within the individual ⟨decide a matter according to your own ~⟩ **:** the awareness of the moral goodness or blameworthiness of one's own conduct, intentions, or character together with a feeling of obligation to do or be that which is recognized as good often felt to be instrumental in producing feelings of guilt or remorse for ill-doing; *specif* **:** the part of the superego in psychoanalysis of which the ego is conscious and through which the commands and admonitions of the superego are communicated to the ego **b :** the faculty, power, or principle (as in an individual, nation, or group) that guides toward the right and away from the wrong ⟨~ rather than professional loyalty was his spiritual leader⟩ ⟨the still small voice of his ~⟩ **2** *obs* **:** inmost thought or sense **:** knowledge of inner self **:** CONSCIOUSNESS ⟨a ~ of having done his duty⟩ **3 a** *obs* **:** conscientious observance **:** REVERENCE, REGARD — used with *of* or *to* ⟨mere ~ of royal rank⟩ **b :** observance of or loyalty to the dictates of the moral or ethical sense **:** CONSCIENTIOUSNESS ⟨forbidden by ~ and by law⟩ ⟨they blunder along badly enough in all ~ —Walter Lippmann⟩ **4 :** sensitive regard for fairness or justice **:** SCRUPLE, COMPUNCTION ⟨a legal advisor with no ~ for his client's feeling⟩ ⟨a profiteer with no ~⟩ — **in all conscience** *or* **in conscience** *adv* **1 :** in all reasonableness and fairness **2 :** beyond a doubt

conscience clause *n* **:** a clause in a general law exempting persons whose religious scruples forbid compliance therewith (as from taking judicial oaths)

con·science·less \-ləs\ *adj* **:** lacking a conscience **:** not guided by conscience **:** UNSCRUPULOUS

conscience money *n* **:** money paid to relieve the conscience by rendering or restoring usu. anonymously what has been wrongfully acquired or withheld (as a tax payment)

con·scient \-chənt\ *adj* [L *conscient-, consciens*, pres. part. of *conscire* to be conscious] **:** CONSCIOUS

con·sci·en·tious \ˈkänchēˈenchəs *also* -änsē\|- *sometimes* ˈkȯn-\ *adj* [F *conscientieux*, fr. ML *conscientiosus*, fr. L *conscientia* conscience + *-osus* -ous — more at CONSCIENCE] **1 :** governed by or made in accordance with the dictates of conscience **:** HONEST, SCRUPULOUS ⟨a ~ public servant⟩ ⟨~ judgments⟩ ⟨too ~ to cultivate political arts that were repulsive to him —S.E.Morison & H.S.Commager⟩ **2 :** marked by or done with exact or thoughtful attention **:** METICULOUS, CAREFUL ⟨a very ~ description of every feature —R.P.Warren⟩ ⟨~ about justifying every phrase —Leslie Rees⟩ ⟨a ~ reader of newspapers —Willa Cather⟩ **syn** see UPRIGHT

con·sci·en·tious·ly *adv* **:** in a conscientious manner

con·sci·en·tious·ness \ˌ==ˈ==nəs\ *n* -ES **:** the quality or state of being conscientious

conscientious objection *n* **:** objection on moral or religious grounds (as to service in the armed forces or to bearing arms)

conscientious objector *n* **:** one who refuses or is exempted from service in the armed forces as contrary to his moral or religious principles; *also* **:** one who although serving in the armed forces is exempted for like reasons from bearing arms

conscionable *adj* [*conscion-* (back-formation fr. *conscience*, taken as pl.) + *-able*] **:** CONSCIENTIOUS

¹**con·scious** \ˈkänchəs *sometimes* ˈkȯn-\ *adj* [L *conscius*, fr. *com-* + *-scius* (fr. *scire* to know) — more at SCIENCE] **1 :** knowing secret human thoughts **:** noting human actions — used of inanimate things as if capable of human perception ⟨cries that fell upon the ~ air⟩ **2 :** perceiving, apprehending, or noticing with a degree of controlled thought or observation **:** recognizing as existent, factual, or true: **a :** knowing or perceiving something within oneself or a fact about oneself ⟨~ of his own deficiencies⟩ ⟨~ of having succeeded⟩ ⟨the careful tread of one ~ of his alcoholic load —Thomas Hardy⟩ — formerly used with *to* and a reflexive pronoun ⟨~ to himself of being remiss⟩ **b :** recognizing as factual or existent something external ⟨Rose was ~ that she was steadily bringing the tiller over —C.S.Forester⟩ ⟨I suddenly became ~ that some one was looking at me —Oscar Wilde⟩ — formerly used with *to* ⟨~ to a crime⟩ **3** *obs* **:** inwardly aware of guilt **:** having knowledge of wrongdoing **:** GUILTY **4 a :** present esp. to the senses **:** VISIBLE ⟨the ~ grace of a thoroughbred horse⟩ **b :** subjectively perceived **:** personally felt ⟨~ guilt⟩ **5 a :** having rational power **:** capable of thought, will, design, or perception ⟨not a mindless force but a ~ one, bent upon our destruction —C.B.Nordhoff & J.N.Hall⟩ **b :** involving rational power, perception, and awareness **:** embodying consideration and decision ⟨our ~ actions⟩ ⟨all ~ experience has of necessity some degree of imaginative quality —John Dewey⟩ **6 :** marked by self-consciousness **:** aware of the scrutiny of others to a point of not appearing natural or spontaneous **:** AFFECTED, MANNERED ⟨she is artificial . . . one can feel always the heavily ~ performer —G.J.Nathan⟩ **7 :** mentally active **:** fully possessed of one's mental faculties **:** having emerged from sleep, faint, or stupor **:** AWAKE ⟨the patient becoming ~ as the anesthesia wears off⟩ **8 a :** marked by full recognition, candid acceptance, or frank espousal of a given role and often by pervasive conviction in filling it ⟨a deliberate and ~ artist with an abiding care for craftsmanship —*Times Lit. Supp.*⟩ ⟨a restrained . . . altogether ~ comedian, an artful creature of merriment —*Time*⟩ **b :** assumed, determined, treated, or executed with awareness, care, purpose, or consideration ⟨a half-*conscious* effort, like our self-deceptive pretence of jollity at a threadbare joke —Nathaniel Hawthorne⟩ ⟨the settlers in Minnesota . . . had neither leisure nor impulse for a ~ art —*Amer. Guide Series: Minn.*⟩ **9 a :** likely to notice, consider, or appraise ⟨a style-*conscious* buyer⟩ **b :** concerned with, interested in, realizing, or pondering significance or potentialities ⟨modern air-*conscious* businessmen⟩ **c :** marked by a strong or compulsive complex of feelings or notions ⟨an extremely class-*conscious* appeal⟩ **syn** see AWARE

²**conscious** \"\ *n* -ES **:** CONSCIOUSNESS 5

con·scious·ly *adv* **:** in a conscious manner

con·scious·ness \-nə̇s\ *n* -ES **1 a :** awareness or perception of an inward psychological or spiritual fact **:** intuitively perceived knowledge of something in one's inner self **b :** inward awareness of an external object, state, or fact ⟨a ~ . . . of what really is at stake in modern philosophy —Hannah Arendt⟩ **c :** concerned awareness **:** INTEREST, CONCERN — often used with an attributive noun ⟨tax ~⟩ ⟨class ~⟩ ⟨rank ~⟩ **2 :** the state or activity that is characterized by sensation, emotion, volition, or thought **:** mind in the broadest possible sense **:** something in nature that is distinguished from the physical **3 :** the totality in psychology of sensations, perceptions, ideas, attitudes, and feelings of which an individual or a group is aware at any given time or within a particular time span — compare STREAM OF CONSCIOUSNESS **4 :** waking life (as that to which one returns after sleep, trance, fever) wherein all one's mental powers have returned ⟨the ether wore off and the patient regained ~⟩ **5 :** the part of mental life or psychic content in psychoanalysis that is immediately available to the ego — compare PRECONSCIOUS, UNCONSCIOUS 2

con·scribe \kənˈskrīb\ *vt* -ED/-ING/-S [L *conscribere* to enroll, fr. *com-* + *scribere* to write — more at SCRIBE] **1 :** LIMIT, CIRCUMSCRIBE ⟨ill-health . . . *conscribed* the force of his intentions —*Times Lit. Supp.*⟩ **2 :** to enlist forcibly **:** CONSCRIPT, IMPRESS ⟨the power to ~ everybody and everything in the case of war —Aldous Huxley⟩

¹**con·script** \ˈkän,skript\ *adj* [MF & L; MF *conscript, conscrit*, fr. L *conscriptus*, past part. of *conscribere* to write together, enroll, fr. *com-* + *scribere* to write — more at SCRIBE] **1 :** enrolled into service by compulsion **:** CONSCRIPTED, DRAFTED ⟨~ soldiers⟩ ⟨a hospital served by ~ nurses⟩ **2 :** made up of impressed or drafted persons ⟨~ armies⟩ ⟨a ~ labor camp⟩

²**conscript** \"\ *n* -S [trans. of F *conscrit*] **:** one that has been enrolled into service (as by arbitrary compulsion or by the dictates of law); *esp* **:** a recruit secured by conscription

³**conscript** \kənˈskript\ *vt* -ED/-ING/-S [²*conscript*] **:** to enroll into service by compulsion ⟨~ soldiers⟩ ⟨a labor battalion ~*ed* from the ranks of political outcasts⟩ ⟨though I could ~ my body I could not ~ my mind —M.R.Cohen⟩

con·scrip·tion \kənˈskripshən\ *n* -S [F, fr. L *conscription-, conscriptio* written composition, conscription, fr. *conscriptus* (past part. of *conscribere* to write together, enroll) + *-ion-, -io* -ion — more at CONSCRIPT] **:** the enlisting or procurement of services, money, property, or profits by an authority ⟨the ~ of government workers from private business⟩; *esp* **:** a compulsory enrollment of men for service in the armed forces

con·scrip·tion·ist \-nə̇st\ *n* -S **:** a person who favors or advocates military conscription ⟨a ~ point of view⟩

¹**con·se·crate** \ˈkänsə̇,krāt, *usu* -ād.+V\ *adj* [ME *consecrat*, fr. L *consecratus*, past part. of *consecrare* to consecrate, fr. *com-* + *sacrare* to consecrate, fr. *sacr-, sacer* sacred — more at SACRED] **:** CONSECRATED, HALLOWED

²**consecrate** \ˈkänsə̇,krāt, *usu* -ād.+V\ *vb* -ED/-ING/-S [ME *consecraten*, fr. L *consecratus*, past part.] *vt* **1 a :** to induct (a person) into a permanent office with a religious rite — usu. used with a double object ⟨~ the young prince king⟩; used in the Anglican Communion only of the induction of a bishop; compare ORDAIN **b :** to confirm officially (a rank, dignity, or office) by religious or civil ceremonies or rites ⟨the place where kings were *consecrated*⟩ **2 a :** to make or declare sacred or holy **:** effect the consecration of **:** set apart, dedicate, devote to the service or worship of God ⟨~ a church⟩ **b :** to effect the liturgical transubstantiation of **c :** to deliver up or give over often with or as if with deep solemnity, dedication, or devotion — used with *to* ⟨a gang leader who *consecrated* his fortune to charity⟩ ⟨a pupil who ~*s* himself to study⟩ **d** *obs* **:** DOOM, CONDEMN — used with *to* **3 :** to render inviolate or venerable ⟨rules or principles *consecrated* by time —Edmund Burke⟩ **:** make memorable, significant, or consequential ⟨a slogan *consecrated* by the party⟩ ⟨a document *consecrated* by the presence of the national emblem⟩ ~ *vi* **:** to perform consecration (as of the elements in the Eucharist)

con·se·crat·ed·ness \ˈ==,==, ,==ˈ==\ *n* -ES **:** CONSECRATION 1d

con·se·cra·tion \,känsə̇ˈkrāshən\ *n* -S [ME *consecracioun*, fr. L *consecration-, consecratio*, fr. *consecratus* + *-ion-, -io* -ion] **1 :** the solemn dedication (as of a person, thing, ideal) with or as if with religious rites and usu. to some high purpose, office, or function: as **a :** ordination or elevation to a sacred or high office ⟨~ of a bishop⟩ ⟨the . . . ~ of an English king —F.M. Stenton⟩ **b :** apotheosis esp. of a Roman emperor or hero of classic literature **c :** the solemn dedication in perpetuity of a church or of vessels used in the Eucharist esp. in the Roman Catholic Church **d :** devotion or appropriation to any special purpose ⟨the ~ of money to a hobby⟩ ⟨their ~ of all ingenuity to ridding the land of foreign troops⟩ ⟨complete moral ~ which is at the base of Willa Cather's work —M.D.Geismar⟩ **2** *often cap* **:** the part of a Christian liturgy in which the bread and wine are consecrated — compare TRANSUBSTANTIATION

con·se·cra·tive \ˈkänsə̇,krād·iv\ *adj* **:** solemnly dedicational

con·se·cra·tor \ˈkänsə̇,krād·ə(r), -ātə-\ *n* -S [LL, fr. L *consecratus* + *-or*] **:** one that consecrates

con·se·cra·to·ry \ˈkänsə̇krə,tōrē, -tȯrē, -ri; *chiefly Brit* ˈ== ,krātərē, -ri\ *adj* **:** serving to consecrate ⟨a ~ prayer⟩

¹**con·sec·ta·ry** \kənˈsektərē\ *n* -ES [L *consectarium*, fr. neut. of *consectarius* logically following, fr. *consectari* to follow after, fr. *com-* + *sectari* to follow, accompany, fr. *secta* sect — more at SECT] **:** CONSEQUENCE, COROLLARY ⟨a ~ drawn from careful observations⟩

²**consectary** *adj* [L *consectarius*] *obs* **:** following by consequence **:** CONSEQUENT

con·se·cu·tion \,känsə̇ˈkyüshən\ *n* -S [L *consecution-, consecutio*, fr. *consecutus* (past part. of *consequi* to follow) + *-ion-, -io* -ion — more at CONSEQUENT] **1 :** advance in argument from antecedent to consequent **:** logical sequence **:** chain of reasoning ⟨reading each . . . chapter separately abandoning any search for ~ of argument —*Times Lit. Supp.*⟩; *specif, obs* **:** the inferred part of an argument **:** the necessary sequence **2 :** sequence esp. of events, similar harmonic intervals in music, or tenses in grammar ⟨~ of octaves⟩ **:** SUCCESSION ⟨~ of sins⟩

con·sec·u·tive \kənˈsek(y)əd·iv, -ətiv, -əv\ *adj* [F *consécutif*, fr. L *consecutus* + F *-if* -ive] **1 a :** following esp. in a series **:** one right after the other often with small intervening intervals **:** SUCCESSIVE, SEQUENT ⟨four ~ terms in office⟩ ⟨the coastal battery scored several ~ hits⟩ **b :** having no interval or break **:** CONTINUOUS ⟨the most important cause . . . has run throughout post-Conquest history like a ~ thread —G.G.Coulton⟩ ⟨a ~ conversation⟩ **2 :** proceeding by successive interrelated stages of thought **:** marked by logical sequence ⟨~ premises⟩ ⟨a ~ thinker⟩ **3 a :** expressing result ⟨a ~ conjunction⟩ — often used of a clause (as *that he ran away* in "he was so frightened that he ran away") **b** *Semitic grammar* **:** characterized by attachment to an imperfect verb form of a sense that otherwise would belong to the perfect or to a perfect verb form of a sense that otherwise would belong to the imperfect — used of the conjunction meaning "and" that is prefixed to such a verb form or of the verb itself — **con·sec·u·tive·ly** *adv* — **con·sec·u·tive·ness** *n* -ES

consecutive intervals *n pl* **:** a recurrence in music of the same interval between two parts or voices in successive chord progressions

con·sec·u·tives \kənˈsek(y)əd·ivz, -ətivz\ *n pl* **:** CONSECUTIVE INTERVALS; *esp* **:** consecutive fifths and octaves

con·se·nes·cence \,kän(t)sə̇ˈnesən(t)s\ *n* -S [L *consenescere* to grow old together, to grow old in a profession, to become weak (fr. *com-* + *senescere*, incho. of *senere* to be old, fr. *senex* old) + E *-ence* — more at SENIOR] **:** general decay esp. from old age

con·sen·sion \kənˈsenchən\ *n* -S [L *consension-, consensio*, fr. *consensus* (past part. of *consentire*) + *-ion-, -io* -ion] **:** unanimity of opinion or attitude

con·sen·su·al \kənˈsenchəwəl\ *adj* [L *consensus* + E *-al*] **1 :** existing or made by mutual consent without the intervention of any act of writing ⟨a ~ contract⟩ ⟨the powers of the United Nations are ~ in nature —*Jour. of Internat'l Affairs*⟩ **2 :** involving or caused by involuntary action or movement accompanying or correlative with voluntary action or movement ⟨~ reactions⟩ — **con·sen·su·al·ly** \-wəlē, -li\ *adv*

con·sen·sus \kənˈsen(t)səs\ *n* -ES [L, fr. *consensus*, past part. of *consentire* to feel together, agree — more at CONSENT] **1 a :** harmony, cooperation, or sympathy esp. in different parts of an organism **b :** group solidarity in sentiment and belief ⟨a kind of unspoken ~ . . . appeared —Henry Dicks⟩ ⟨broad group ~, as manifested in the folkways, mores, and other institutional usages —H.A.Bloch⟩ **2 a :** general agreement **:** UNANIMITY, ACCORD ⟨the ~ of their opinion, based on reports that had drifted back from the border —John Hersey⟩ **b :** collective opinion **:** the judgment arrived at by most of those concerned ⟨in the ~ of a number of critics —*Current Biog.*⟩ **3 :** a formal statement of religious belief **:** CONFESSION

¹**con·sent** \kənˈsent\ *vi* -ED/-ING/-S [ME *consenten*, fr. OF *consentir*, fr. L *consentire* to feel together, agree, consent, fr. *com-* + *sentire* to feel — more at SENSE] **1** *archaic* **:** to be in harmony or concord esp. in opinion, statement, or sentiment **2 :** to express a willingness (as to accept a proposition or carry out a particular action) **:** give assent or approval **:** AGREE — usu. used with *to* ⟨~ to shoulder a debt⟩ ⟨~ to cross-examination⟩ **syn** see ASSENT

²**consent** \"\ *n* -S [ME, fr. OF *consent, consente*, fr. *consentir*, v.] **1 a :** compliance or approval esp. of what is done or proposed by another **:** ACQUIESCENCE, PERMISSION ⟨to do something without ~⟩ ⟨to find general ~ to his opinion⟩ ⟨the passionless ~ of the human mind —W.L.Sperry⟩ **b :** capable, deliberate, and voluntary agreement to or concurrence in some act or purpose implying physical and mental power and free action — distinguished from *assent;* see AGE OF CONSENT **2** *archaic* **:** correspondence in parts, activities, operations **:** HARMONY, COHERENCE **3 :** agreement among persons usu. as to a course of action or concerning a particular point of view or opinion ⟨by common ~ the host drank first⟩ ⟨by the ~ of scholars . . . it is by far the greatest —*Choice & Interesting Books*⟩; *specif* **:** voluntary agreement in political theory by a people to organize a civil society and give authority to the government ⟨the ~ theory meant that the people as a whole were sovereign —Russell Davenport⟩ **4** *archaic* **:** the being of one mind **:** ACCORD, UNANIMITY **5** *obs* **:** OPINION, FEELING — **of consent** *obs* **:** ACCESSORY ⟨some villains of my court are *of consent* . . . in this —Shak.⟩

con·sen·ta·ne·ous \ˈkänsənˈtānēəs, -sen-\ *adj* [L *consentaneus*, fr. *consentire* — more at CONSENT] **1 :** AGREEING, SUITED ⟨perfectly ~ to scientific truth —T. L. Peacock⟩ **2 :** done or made by the consent of all **:** UNANIMOUS ⟨~ profession of loyalty —G.P.Fisher⟩ — **con·sen·ta·ne·ous·ly** *adv*

consent decree *n* **:** a consent judgment by a court exercising equity jurisdiction or invoking equitable remedies

consent dividend *n* **:** an arrangement by which stockholders agree to report as income a portion of the corporation's retained profits and to pay taxes thereon

consent election *n* **:** an election to determine a bargaining agent held at the request of both union and employer

con·sen·tience \kənˈsen(t)shəns\ *n* -S **:** unity of consciousness felt as arising from sensation without regard to intellect

con·sen·tient \kənˈsen(t)shənt\ *adj* [L *consentient-, consentiens*, pres. part. of *consentire* — more at CONSENT] **1 :** united in opinion, judgment, view **:** UNANIMOUS ⟨such ~ reports⟩ **2 :** disposed to agree with or conform to ⟨~ to adverse criticism⟩ — **con·sen·tient·ly** *adv*

con sen·ti·men·to \ˈkän,sentə̇ˈmen(,)tō, ˈkȯn-\ *adv* [It] **:** with feeling — used as a direction in music

con·sent·ing·ly *adv* **:** with consent or aquiescence

con·sent·ing·ness *n* -ES **:** CONSENT

consent judgment *n* **:** a judgment by a court exercising common-law jurisdiction entered by consent of the parties upon stipulation or agreement

con·sent·ment \kənˈsentmənt\ *n* -S [ME *consentement*, fr. MF, fr. *consentir* to consent + *-ment* — more at CONSENT] *archaic* **:** CONSENT

¹**con·se·quence** \ˈkän(t)sə̇,kwen(t)s, -sēk,k-, -,kwən- *sometimes* ˈkȯn-\ *n* -S [ME, fr. MF, fr. L *consequentia*, fr. *consequent-, consequens* + *-ia*] **1 :** something that is produced by a cause or follows from a form of necessary connection or from a set of conditions **:** a natural or necessary result ⟨this refined taste is the ~ of education and habit —Joshua Reynolds⟩ ⟨his training had been poor and in combat he suffered the ~*s*⟩ ⟨she was always quick and as a ~ received high grades⟩ **2 a :** a conclusion that results from reason or argument **:** an inference or proposition inferred from previous propositions ⟨we can deduce . . . many ~*s* each of which can be tested by experiment —J.B.Conant⟩; *specif* **:** a statement derivable from other statements in accordance with the transformation rules of the language system they belong to **3** *obs* **a :** the act or action of following in succession **:** SEQUENCE **b :** the rational process by which effect follows cause **:** logical sequence **4 a :** importance often with respect to what comes after or in power to produce an effect **:** VALUE, MOMENT ⟨a mistake of no ~⟩ ⟨a problem of grave international ~⟩ **b :** social importance or distinction ⟨a person of some ~⟩ ⟨she had managed to bring with her a certain urban ~ —Margery Sharp⟩ **5 :** the appearance of importance esp. in demeanor **:** DIGNITY ⟨his voice had authority and his bearing ~⟩; *esp* **:** SELF-IMPORTANCE ⟨with all the ~ of a peacock⟩ **6 consequences** *pl but sing in constr* **:** a game in which a brief and humorous story descriptive of two people, their meeting, and its consequences is made up as the

players in turn write answers to a series of questions, each one concealing what he has written before passing the paper to his neighbor for the next answer **syn** see EFFECT, IMPORTANCE — **in consequence** *adv* **:** as a result **:** CONSEQUENTLY, HENCE — **in consequence of** *prep* **:** by reason of **:** as a result of ⟨*in consequence of* their efforts a report was handed down⟩

²consequence *vi* -ED/-ING/-S *obs* **:** INFER

consequency *n* -ES [L *consequentia*] *obs* **:** CONSEQUENCE

¹con·se·quent \ˈkän(t)sə̇ˌkwent, -sēˌk-, -ˌkwənt *sometimes* ˈkōn-\ *n* -S [ME, fr. L *consequent-, consequens*] **1 a :** something that is deduced from reasoning or argumentation or follows from propositions by rational deduction **:** INFERENCE, CONCLUSION; *specif* **:** the clause in a hypothetical proposition that states what the hypothesis entails or implies (as the conclusion of a conditional sentence) **b** *obs* **:** something that results from a cause **:** CONSEQUENCE, OUTCOME **2 :** a thing or circumstance (as an event or phenomenon) that follows another in time or order without being a result or without any causal connection being implied; *specif* **:** the second term of a ratio **3 a** *in canon and fugue* **:** the musical restatement of the subject **:** COMES **b :** an answering phrase or section of a musical sentence or section — compare ANTECEDENT 6 **4 :** a stream or valley that has developed in harmony with the general slope of an existing land surface

²consequent \"\ *adj* [MF, fr. L *consequent-, consequens*, pres. part. of *consequi* to follow, fr. *com-* + *sequi* to follow — more at SUE] **1** *obs* **:** following in time or order **:** SUBSEQUENT ⟨in ~ years⟩ **2 a :** following esp. as a result or effect **:** RESULTANT ⟨the period of tension and the ~ need for military preparedness —D.W.Mitchell⟩ — often used with *on* or *upon* ⟨the decline in . . . trade ~ upon the growth of economic nationalism —*Encyc. Americana*⟩ **b :** following by necessary inference or rational deduction ⟨a proposition ~ to other propositions⟩ **3 :** observing the just order of cause and effect **:** logically consistent **:** RATIONAL ⟨not one could give a clear and ~ account —J.F. Brown⟩ **4 :** constituting the conclusion of a conditional sentence ⟨a ~ clause⟩ **5 :** developed in harmony with the general slope of an existing land surface ⟨a ~ stream⟩ ⟨a ~ valley⟩ — compare ANTECEDENT, OBSEQUENT, RESEQUENT, SUBSEQUENT, SUPERIMPOSED

con·se·quen·tial \ˌkän(t)sə̇ˈkwenchəl, -sēˈk- *sometimes* ˌkōn-\ *adj* [L *consequentia* + E *-al*] **1 :** of the nature of or following as a consequence, result, or logical inference **:** involving logical sequence ⟨with the procedure in Committee of Supply and the ~ proceedings in Committee of Ways and Means —T.E.May⟩ **2 :** of the nature of a secondary result **:** INDIRECT ⟨more important is the ~ loss that can flow from destruction of records —*Financial Times (London)*⟩ **3 a :** following in due course **:** falling in consequence — often used with *on* or *upon* ⟨a result ~ upon bankruptcy⟩ **b :** governed or guided by logical sequence **:** RATIONAL ⟨any system of ~ conduct that in their most reasonable moments they might have been capable of forming —Earl of Chesterfield⟩ **4 :** of importance **:** of consequence **:** bringing about or responsible for significant changes or results ⟨reports of a ~ nature⟩ ⟨the only ~ immigrant group at first were the French —Oscar Handlin⟩ ⟨many errors have been made but hardly one as grave and ~ as this failure —E.J.Simmons⟩ **5 :** having or displaying importance or assuming distinction to a point of being pompous **:** SELF-IMPORTANT ⟨~ deportment⟩ ⟨a loud ~ voice⟩ — **con·se·quen·tial·ly** \-shəlē, -li\ *adv*

consequential contempt *n* **:** CONSTRUCTIVE CONTEMPT

consequential damages *n pl* **:** the damages that do not arise as an immediate or natural and probable result of the act of the party but are an incidental result of it and are generally not recoverable because remote except in case of special damages or special statutory provision

con·se·quen·ti·al·i·ty \ˌkän(t)sə̇ˌkwen(t)shēˈaləd·ē, -sēˌk-, -ətē, -i\ *n* -ES **:** air of importance **:** SELF-IMPORTANCE ⟨his intolerable ~⟩

consequential loss *n* **:** an indirect or secondary loss occasioned by direct property loss (as that caused by a fire) and often provided for by special provisions in insurance policies or by special policies (as rent insurance or business interruption insurance)

con·se·quent·ly \ˈkän(t)sə̇ˌkwentlē, -sēˌk- -ˌkwən-, -li\ *adv* [ME, fr. MF *consequent* + ME *-ly* — more at CONSEQUENT] **1** *obs* **a :** in order **:** SUBSEQUENTLY **b :** in succession **2 :** as a result **:** in view of the foregoing **:** ACCORDINGLY ⟨taxes were lowered and ~ complaints were fewer⟩ **3** *archaic* **:** in a logical manner

consequent pole *n* **:** any one of the magnetic poles that appear in a nonuniformly magnetized body excepting those poles near its ends

con·ser·tal \kənˈsərd·ᵊl\ *adj* [L *consertus* (past part. of *conserere* to connect, fr. *com-* + *serere* to bind together) + E *-al* — more at SERIES] *of an igneous rock* **:** of a texture in which the irregularly shaped crystals interlock **:** SUTURED

conservacy *n* -ES [AF *conservacie*, fr. ML *conservatia*, fr. L *conservatus* + *-ia* -y] *obs* **:** CONSERVATION 2

con·serv·an·cy \kənˈsərvən(t)sē, -sə̄v-, -si\ *n* -ES [alter. of *conservacy*] **1** *Brit* **:** a board that has jurisdiction over a river or port esp. for the regulation of fisheries and navigation ⟨the Thames *Conservancy*⟩ **2 :** conservation esp. of natural resources ⟨~ work being done on the . . . rivers to control floods —*Americana Annual*⟩; *specif* **:** an organization designed and often government-sponsored to conserve and protect natural resources (as trees or wildlife)

conservant *adj* [L *conservant-, conservans*, pres. part. of *conservare* to preserve] *obs* **:** CONSERVING, PRESERVING ⟨the procreant and ~ cause —Abraham Fraunce⟩

con·ser·va·tion \ˌkän(t)sə(r)ˈvāshən\ *n* -S [ME *conservacioun*, fr. MF *conservation*, fr. L *conservation-, conservatio*, fr. *conservatus* (past part. of *conservare* to conserve) + *-ion-, -io* -ion — more at CONSERVE] **1 :** deliberate, planned, or thoughtful preserving, guarding, or protecting **:** a keeping in a safe or entire state **:** PRESERVATION ⟨the ~ of the ideal of liberty⟩ ⟨the ~ of religious shrines⟩ ⟨the ~ of the individual's nervous energy —Ralph Linton⟩; *specif* **:** the repair and preservation of works of art **2 :** care or keeping and supervision of something by a governmental authority or by a private association or business: as **a :** planned management of a natural resource to prevent exploitation, destruction, or neglect ⟨wild-life ~⟩ ⟨~ of the Northwest⟩ **b :** the wise utilization of a natural product esp. by a manufacturer so as to prevent waste and insure future use of resources that have been depleted **3 :** a field of knowledge concerned with coordination and plans for the practical application of data from ecology, limnology, pedology, and other sciences that are significant to preservation of natural resources ⟨offering graduate degrees in ~⟩

con·ser·va·tion·al \ˌ==ˈvāshənᵊl, -shnəl\ *adj* **:** tending to conserve **:** PRESERVATIVE ⟨~ measures to protect wildlife⟩

con·ser·va·tion·ist \ˌkän(t)sə(r)ˈvāsh(ə)nə̇st\ *n* -S **:** one that advocates conservation esp. of natural resources (as forests)

conservation of charge *or* **conservation of electricity :** a principle in physics: if two or more charges combine to form one or conversely if one charge breaks up into two or more or if charged elementary particles are created or annihilated, the algebraic sum of the charges equals the single charge

conservation of energy : a principle in physics: the total energy of an isolated system remains constant irrespective of whatever internal changes may take place, energy disappearing in one form reappearing in another — compare DEGRADATION OF ENERGY, DISSIPATION OF ENERGY, MASS-ENERGY EQUATION

conservation of mass : a principle in classical physics: the total mass of any material system is neither increased nor diminished by reactions between the parts — compare MASS-ENERGY EQUATION

conservation of momentum : a principle in physics: the total linear momentum of a system of particles not acted upon by external forces is constant in magnitude and direction irrespective of any reactions among the parts of the system

con·serv·a·tism \kənˈsərvəd·ˌizəm, -sə̄v-,-səiv-, -vəˌtiz-\ *n* -S [*conservative* + *-ism*] **1 a :** the disposition in politics to preserve what is established ⟨twentieth century politics of New Jersey has continued to be dominated . . . by the natural ~ of the industrial and business interests —*Amer. Guide Series: N.J.*⟩ **b :** a political philosophy based on a strong sense of tradition and social stability, stressing the importance of established institutions (as religion, property, the family, and class structure), and preferring gradual development with preservation of the best elements of the past to abrupt change ⟨political ~ in the United States . . . has become identified with the business interests —Francis Biddle⟩ **2** *usu cap* **a :** the principles and policies of the Conservative party in the United Kingdom ⟨the fundamental and distinct tenets of *Conservatism* —R.A.Butler⟩ **b :** the Conservative party or its members ⟨whether *Conservatism* enjoys a long tenure of office —L.D.Epstein⟩ **3 a :** the tendency to accept an existing fact, order, situation, or phenomenon and to be cautious toward or suspicious of change **:** extreme wariness and caution in outlook ⟨acquired ~ which normally increases with increasing age and sagacity —H.G.Armstrong⟩ ⟨~ in banking practices⟩ ⟨~ in interpreting data⟩ **b :** strong resistance to innovation **:** relative freedom from change ⟨the ~ of the area . . . has helped to preserve the evidences of its past —R.W. Southern⟩; *specif* **:** the tendency of certain plants or animal groups (as the brachiopods) to remain narrowly adapted to a particular environment and undergo minimal evolutionary change or differentiation **4 :** CONSERVATIVE JUDAISM

con·serv·a·tist \-vəd·ə̇st, -vətə̇st\ *n* -S [*conservatism* + *-ist*] **:** one who supports conservative forces, principles, or ideas

¹con·serv·a·tive \kənˈsərvəd·|iv, -sə̄v-,-səiv-, -vət|iv *also* |əv\ *adj* [ME, fr. MF & LL; MF *conservatif*, fr. LL *conservativus*, fr. L *conservatus* (past part of *conservare* to conserve) + *-ivus* -ive — more at CONSERVE] **1 :** having the power or tendency to preserve in a safe and entire state **:** PRESERVATIVE ⟨the ~ powers of the Egyptian climate have given us priceless relics in near-perfect condition⟩ ⟨~ of all good things⟩; *specif* **:** designed to preserve parts or restore function ⟨~ surgery⟩ — compare RADICAL **2 a :** of or relating to a political party, point of view, or philosophy that advocates preservation of the established order and views proposals for change critically and usu. with distrust ⟨~ elements opposed to . . . further steps toward socialization or nationalization —*Collier's Yr. Bk.*⟩ **b :** of, relating to, or constituting a political party professing the principles of conservatism: as (1) *usu cap* **:** of or constituting one of the two major parties in the United Kingdom evolving from the 18th century Tories and in modern times associated with policies advocating support of established institutions, a close relationship with the Commonwealth and Empire, and a positive although limited role by the government in social and economic affairs ⟨the parliamentary *Conservative* party is preeminently recruited from the upper and upper-middle classes —J.F.S.Ross⟩ ⟨a handsome *Conservative* majority . . . emerged from the general election —J.A.Hawgood⟩ — compare LABOR, LIBERAL, TORY, UNIONIST, WHIG (2) *usu cap* **:** Progressive Conservative **3 a :** tending or disposed to maintain existing views, habits, conditions, or institutions **:** opposed to radical or basic changes **:** exhibiting minimal change **:** TRADITIONAL ⟨~ policies⟩ ⟨a ~ administration⟩ ⟨a ~ genus⟩ **b :** not in excess ⟨~ action⟩ **:** CAUTIOUS ⟨a ~ point of view⟩ ⟨a ~ utterance⟩ **:** MODERATE ⟨a ~ estimate of 200⟩ **:** unwilling to overreach **:** involving little or fearful of risk ⟨a ~ banker⟩ ⟨~ investments⟩ **c :** tending to avoid dissonance, showiness, or effects that would attract undue or immediate attention **:** cleaving to traditional norms of taste, elegance, or manners ⟨a ~ suit⟩ ⟨a rich but ~ architectural style⟩ **4 :** of or relating to Conservative Judaism

syn REACTIONARY, DIE-HARD, TORY: CONSERVATIVE suggests desire to retain and maintain existing institutions, procedures, and ways and to resist and suspect proposals for change ⟨although he was naturally *conservative* and did not disturb the predominance of Latin and Greek, he somewhat modified the curriculum —C.M.Fuess⟩ REACTIONARY applies to wishes to return to an older outworn order or to influences making for such a return; unlike CONSERVATIVE, it is almost always derogatory ⟨both the Reformation and the Counter Reformation were *reactionary;* they thought they brought the Middle Ages to an end, they themselves were medieval in spirit and method —W.R.Inge⟩ DIE-HARD implies a stubborn, truculent retention of older procedures and resistance to new ⟨some *die-hard* individual may insist on driving a horse and buggy after all the rest of his society have automobiles —Ralph Linton⟩ ⟨while the Progressive Conservative platform reflected the party's *die-hard* conservatism on most issues, it came out, in striking contrast to previous policies, for the principle of expanding international trade —*Collier's Yr. Bk.*⟩ TORY may suggest a sometimes reactionary allegiance to long-established principles and social customs ⟨to a slow-moving and *Tory* society they were radical changes shocking to men's minds —C.W.de Kiewiet⟩

²conservative \"\ *n* -S [ME, fr. *conservative*, adj.] **1** *archaic* **:** a preservative agent or principle **:** PRESERVER, CONSERVER ⟨the Holy Spirit is the great ~ of the new life —Jeremy Taylor⟩ **2 a :** an adherent or advocate of political conservatism ⟨it is the task of the ~ not to defeat but to forestall revolutions —H.A.Kissinger⟩ **b** *usu cap* **:** a member or supporter of a conservative political party; *esp* **:** a member of the Conservative party of the United Kingdom ⟨both *Conservatives* and Labour competed for the middle-class vote —Roy Lewis & Angus Maude⟩ **3 :** one who adheres to traditional, time-tested, long-standing methods, procedures, or views **:** a moderate, cautious, or discreet person ⟨a ~ in his choice of clothes⟩ ⟨the firm was always the ~ in marine architecture⟩

conservative baptist *n, usu cap C&B* **:** a member of one of the independent Baptist churches belonging to the Conservative Baptist Association of America which took its present name in 1946 and withdrew from the American Baptist Convention in 1951

conservative jew *n, usu cap C&J* **:** an adherent of Conservative Judaism

conservative judaism *n, cap C&J* **:** a middle-of-the-road development in Judaism that began in the 19th century in western Europe and attained a large following in the U.S. and that accepts limited modifications in liturgy and in ritual practice but stresses the historic laws of the Bible and the Talmud and also the authority and sanctity of the religious traditions of the Jewish people — compare ORTHODOX JUDAISM

con·serv·a·tive·ly *adv* **:** in a conservative manner

con·serv·a·tive·ness *n* -ES **:** CONSERVATISM

con·serv·a·tize \kənˈsərvəˌtīz\ *vb* -ED/-ING/-S [*conservative* + *-ize*] *vi* **:** to grow conservative ~ *vt* **:** to make conservative ⟨unions are being *conservatized* —Theodore Levitt⟩

con·ser·va·toire \kənˌsərvəˈtwär, ₌ˈ₌₌ˌ₌\ *n* -S [F, fr. It *conservatorio* — more at CONSERVATORY] **:** CONSERVATORY

con·ser·va·tor \ˈkän(t)sə(r)ˌvād·ə(r), -ˌvātə- ; *esp in senses 2 and 3* kənˈsərvəd·ər, -sə̄vəd·ə,-səivəd·ə, -vətə-\ *n* -S [ME *conservatour*, fr. MF or L; MF *conservateur*, fr. L *conservator*, fr. *conservatus* (past part. of *conservare* to keep, protect) + *-or* — more at CONSERVE] **1 :** one that preserves from injury or violation **:** PROTECTOR, PRESERVER ⟨a fine art ~⟩ **2 :** a person, official, or institution designated (as by a court) to take over and protect the interests of an incompetent (as a minor child, an insane person, a convict) **3 :** an official charged with the protection of any of various things concerned with public welfare and interests ⟨~ of a river⟩ ⟨~ of fisheries⟩; *also* **:** a person placed by the secretary of the treasury in charge of a national bank whose affairs are not in a satisfactory condition **4 :** an overflow reservoir to permit expansion of a liquid (as oil in a transformer or water in a heating system)

con·ser·va·to·ri·um \kənˌsərvəˈtōrēəm, -tȯr-\ *n* -S [G *konservatorium*, modif. of It *conservatorio*] **:** ¹CONSERVATORY 3

conservator of the peace [trans. of ML *custos pacis* or AF *gardein de la pees*] **:** an officer charged with maintaining the public peace or one having this power as an adjunct of another office

con·ser·va·tor·ship *pronunc at* CONSERVATOR +ˌship\ *n* -S **:** the office of conservator

¹con·serv·a·to·ry \kənˈsərvəˌtōrē, -sə̄v-,-səiv-, -ˌtȯr-, -ri\ *n* -ES [L *conservatus* + E *-ory*] **1** *archaic* **:** a place for the preservation or safekeeping of things **2 :** a greenhouse sometimes attached to a dwelling for growing or displaying plants **3** [It *conservatorio*, fr. *conservato* (past part. of *conservare* to keep, preserve, maintain) (fr. L *conservatus*) + *-orio* -ory (fr. L *-orium*)] **:** a school of advanced standing specializing in one of the fine arts (as music, drama, or dance) and emphasizing technical instruction and practical performance ⟨the Wilkes-Barre Municipal *Conservatory*⟩

²conservatory \"\ *adj* [LL *conservatorius*, fr. L *conservatus* + *-orius* -ory] **:** having the quality or power of conserving or preserving **:** PRESERVATIVE ⟨the ~ legal protection of wildlife⟩

¹con·serve \kənˈsərv, -sə̄v, -səiv; *in sense 2 also* ˈkänˌs-\ *vt* -ED/-ING/-S [ME *conserven*, fr. MF *conserver*, fr. L *conservare*, fr. *com-* + *servare* to keep, guard, protect, preserve, observe; akin to OE *searu* weapons, armor, skill, ON *sörvi* pearl necklace, *sörvar* armed men, Goth *sarwa* weapons, armor, Gk *horminos* salvia, Av *haraiti, haurvaiti* he guards] **1 :** to keep in a safe or sound state (as by deliberate, planned, or intelligent care) **:** preserve from change or destruction **:** SAVE ⟨~ national forests⟩ ⟨~ moral standards⟩ **2 :** to preserve (as fruits) with sugar **:** make a conserve of — **con·serv·er** *n*

²conserve \ˈkänˌsərv, -sə̄v, -səiv; *Brit usu* kənˈs-\ *n* -S [ME, fr. *conserven*, v.] **1** *archaic* **:** a conserving agent **:** PRESERVATIVE ⟨his passion for Eustacia had been a sort of ~ of his whole life —Thomas Hardy⟩ **2 a :** SWEETMEAT; *esp* **:** a candied fruit **:** CONFECTION **b :** PRESERVE 2b; *specif* **:** one prepared from a mixture of fruits (as rhubarb, raisins, and oranges) sometimes with the addition of nuts **3 :** an obsolete medicinal preparation made by mixing undried vegetable drugs with sufficient powdered sugar to form a soft mass — see ¹CONFECTION 1b

consgt *abbr* consignment

con·shy \ˈkänchē, -chi\ *var of* CONCHIE

con·sid·er \kənˈsidə(r)\ *vb* **considered; considered; considering** \-d(ə)riŋ\ **considers** [ME *consideren*, fr. MF *considerer*, fr. L *considerare*, lit., to observe the stars, fr. *com-* + *-siderare* (fr. *sider-, sidus* star, constellation) — more at SIDEREAL] *vt* **1 :** to reflect on **:** think about with a degree of care or caution ⟨before she could ~ what to do, her husband came in —Thomas Hardy⟩ ⟨~ how serious your position is⟩ **2 :** to think of, regard, or treat in an attentive, solicitous, or kindly way ⟨he ~*ed* her every wish⟩ **3 :** to look at or gaze on steadily or with earnest reflection ⟨the old gentleman ~*ed* him attentively —Edith Wharton⟩ **4 :** to think of **:** come to view, judge, or classify ⟨~ thrift essential⟩ ⟨~ a leader to be unwise⟩ **5** *obs* **:** REQUITE, REMUNERATE **6 :** to regard highly **:** RESPECT, ESTEEM ⟨he is more ~*ed* abroad than here⟩ **7 :** to be of the opinion **:** SUPPOSE ⟨I ~ it's best that he left when he did⟩ **8 :** to give thought to with a view to purchasing, accepting, or adopting ⟨~ an apartment⟩ ⟨~ a trade-in on a car⟩ ~ *vi* **1** *obs* **:** to look attentively ⟨then the priest shall ~: and, behold, if the leprosy have covered all his flesh, he shall pronounce him clean that hath the plague —Lev 13:13 (AV)⟩ **2 :** REFLECT, DELIBERATE, PONDER ⟨paused a moment to ~⟩

syn CONTEMPLATE, STUDY, WEIGH, REVOLVE, EXCOGITATE: CONSIDER often indicates little more than *think about.* It may occasionally suggest somewhat more conscious direction of thought, somewhat greater depth and scope, and somewhat greater purposefulness ⟨glancing at that, as at something she would take up presently and *consider* —Mary Austin⟩ ⟨love she *considered*, and hate, the enduringness and the moral and spiritual consequences of each —Rose Macaulay⟩ ⟨when I came to *consider* his conduct, I realized that he was guilty of a confusion —T.S.Eliot⟩ CONTEMPLATE stresses the steady calm focussing of one's attentive thought but implies nothing about the aims, methods, or results of that thinking ⟨fine gentlemen and fine ladies are charming to *contemplate* in history —Bertrand Russell⟩ ⟨the poet "has an idea", and in the course of *contemplating* it he draws from his subconscious a string of associated ideas and images —C.D.Lewis⟩ STUDY implies sustained, purposeful effort, care for both details and significance and ramifications, and full knowledge as an end ⟨I like very naturally to think that I am being read, but the idea that I am being *studied* fills me . . . with a deepening gloom —Aldous Huxley⟩ ⟨Bryce, who had *studied* the matter so thoroughly, was wont to insist it is the smallest democracies which today stand highest in the scale —Havelock Ellis⟩ WEIGH suggests thoughtful arrival at an evaluation or decision in which evidence leading to opposite conclusions has been examined and evaluated ⟨the problem is to get them [the young] to *weigh* evidence, draw accurate inferences, make fair comparisons, invent solutions, and form judgments —C.W. Eliot⟩ ⟨the fine balance with which Johnson *weighed* and sustained his judgments of human flaws and virtues —H.V. Gregory⟩ In this sense REVOLVE suggests turning over the matter under consideration so that all facets of it may be viewed and thought about ⟨should he write to his son? For a time he *revolved* a long, tactful letter in his mind —H.G.Wells⟩ ⟨she was desperately *revolving* the risk of taking him into the front room to have out of him what his distrait presence half declared —Mary Austin⟩ EXCOGITATE suggests deep thought and is likely to connote the fact of a notion or concept having been evolved or contrived as well as the fact of the occurrence of thought ⟨the more sophisticated views on mental structure which Freud himself *excogitated* —*Times Lit. Supp.*⟩

syn REGARD, ACCOUNT, RECKON, DEEM: of this series REGARD is probably the least rich in suggestion. It may, but does not necessarily, connote viewing without reflection and, consequently, quick judgment based on appearances alone from a purely personal point of view ⟨a church . . . which *regarded* all dissentients as rebels and traitors —W.R.Inge⟩ ⟨to *regard* her passion . . . and its tragic sequel as a romantic episode of girlhood —Rose Macaulay⟩ Although often interchangeable with REGARD, CONSIDER may suggest a degree of reflection and hence a more soundly based judgment ⟨it seems, however, best to *consider* as literature only works in which the aesthetic function is dominant —René Wellek & Austin Warren⟩ ACCOUNT probably more common with plural than with singular subjects and certainly more common in passive than in active uses, most often suggests a consensus, a generality of opinion or judgment ⟨the pier . . . was *accounted* a most excellent piece of stonework —William Cowper⟩ ⟨*accounted* the best jockey of the lot —Agnes M. Cleaveland⟩ RECKON, often informal in its tone, may suggest counting or computation underlying a judgment or indicating a point of view ⟨not to be *reckoned* one character . . . but to *reckon* in the gross, in the hundred or thousand of the party —R.W.Emerson⟩ It may on the other hand suggest casual judgment or supposition or guess ⟨another field where the dominance of the method of sociology may be *reckoned* as assured —B.N.Cardozo⟩ DEEM has a wide aura of suggestion. It often sounds archaic or literary; it is likely to sound formal or pompous or, by irony therefore, modest or whimsical. It may suggest considered, judicious judgment ⟨investigation of all the facts which it *deems* relevant —H.S.Truman⟩ It also may apply to unreflective, intuitive choice ⟨*deeming* a figure of speech to be worth frequent use —C.E.Montague⟩

¹con·sid·er·a·ble \kənˈsidər(ə)bəl, -drəb-, *rapid -R* -dəb-\ *adj, sometimes* -ER/-EST [ME, fr. ML *considerabilis*, fr. L *considerare* to consider + *-abilis* -able] **1** *obs* **a :** capable of being perceived or understood **:** PERCEPTIBLE, COGNIZABLE ⟨a ~ truth⟩ **b :** calling for consideration **:** requiring to be observed, borne in mind, or attended to **:** NOTABLE ⟨a ~ testimony⟩ **2 :** worthy of consideration **:** of consequence or distinction **:** IMPORTANT, SIGNIFICANT ⟨a series of rather ~ observations on human behavior⟩ ⟨William Faulkner is . . . the most ~ 20th-century American writer of short fiction —William Peden⟩ **3 a :** rather large in extent or degree ⟨a ~ distance⟩ ⟨a ~ number⟩ ⟨he got in ~ trouble⟩ **b :** great in size **:** LARGE ⟨a house with a ~ barn in back⟩ ⟨fingers, with a ~ diamond on one, a star sapphire on another —Glenway Wescott⟩

²considerable \"\ *n* -S **1** *obs* **:** a thing to be considered **2 :** a considerable amount, degree, or extent ⟨learned ~ of his life⟩ ⟨anything else the proprietor can get together and the public will stand for, which is ~ —W.L.Gresham⟩

³considerable \"\ *adv, now dial* **:** CONSIDERABLY

con·sid·er·a·bly \-blə, -bli\ *adv* **1** *obs* **:** in a way demanding or warranting consideration **:** NOTABLY **2 :** to a notable extent or degree **:** MARKEDLY, MUCH ⟨fallen ~ in price⟩

considerance *n* -S [ME *consideraunce*, fr. MF *considerance*, fr. L *considerantia*, fr. *considerant-, considerans* (pres. part. of *considerare*) + *-ia* -y] *obs* **:** CONSIDERATION

con·sid·er·ate \kənˈsid(ə)rə̇t, *usu* -d·+V\ *adj* [L *consideratus*, past part. of *considerare* — more at CONSIDER] **1 :** marked by or given to consideration or sober reflection **:** regardful of consequences or circumstances **:** CIRCUMSPECT, CAREFUL ⟨a cold and ~ temperament⟩ **2 :** observant of the rights and feelings of others **:** showing thoughtful kindness ⟨too courteous and ~ to make stubborn subordinates bend properly to his will —Allan Nevins & H. S. Commager〉 — **con·sid·er·ate·ly** \-dər(ə)tlē, -drət-, -li\ *adv* — **con·sid·er·ate·ness** \-d(ə)rətnəs\ *n* -ES

con·sid·er·a·tion \kən,sidə'rāshən\ *n* -S [ME *consideracioun*, fr. MF *consideration*, fr. L *consideration-, consideratio*, fr. *consideratus* + *-ion-, -io* -ion] **1** *obs* : OBSERVATION, CONTEMPLATION 〈his careful ~ of each object〉 **2** : continuous and careful thought : DELIBERATION, ATTENTION 〈to read a book with ~〉 〈to take a matter into ~〉 〈his request was under ~〉 **3 a** : something that is considered as a ground of opinion or action : MOTIVE, REASON 〈weighing several ~*s*〉 **b** : a taking into account 〈in ~ of the enormous difficulties involved〉 **4** : thoughtful regard : sympathetic notice 〈his ~ of the needs of others〉; *specif* : attentive or formal respect 〈diplomats used to the punctilious ~ of foreign officials〉 **5** : a result of reflecting or pondering : mature opinion 〈his ~*s* favoring one profession over another〉 **6** : the act of regarding or weighing carefully 〈during his ~ of the problem〉 **7** : ESTEEM, REGARD, ESTIMATION 〈a person of ~ in his own field〉 **8** : something given as recompense: as **a** : PAYMENT, REWARD 〈a ~ paid for legal services〉 **b** (1) : something that is legally regarded as the equivalent or return given or suffered by one for the act or promise of another — an act or forbearance or the promise of it done or given by one party in return for the act or promise of another — see GOOD CONSIDERATION, VALUABLE CONSIDERATION (2) : a judgment of a court — **in consideration of** *prep* : as payment or recompense for 〈a small fee *in consideration of* many kind services〉

con·sid·er·a·tive \kən'sid(ə)rəd·iv\ *adj* [ME, fr. MF *consideratif*, fr. *consideration* + *-if* -ive] : CONSIDERATE 1

considered *adj* [fr. past part. of *consider*] **1** : matured by extended deliberative thought **2** : regarded with respect or esteem **syn** see DELIBERATE

¹**con·sid·er·ing** \kən'sid(ə)riŋ\ *prep* [ME, fr. pres. part. of *consideren* to consider] : in view of : taking into account 〈he did well ~ his limitations〉

²**considering** \"\ *conj* : inasmuch as 〈~ he was new at the game, he did very well〉

³**considering** \"\ *adv* : taking all circumstances into account 〈the boy does well, ~〉

con·sid·er·ing·ly *adv* : in a considering manner

considers *pres 3d sing of* CONSIDER

con·sign \kən'sīn\ *vb* -ED/-ING/-S [MF *consigner*, fr. L *consignare* to seal, vouch for, sign, fr. *com-* + *signare* to mark, seal, fr. *signum* mark, sign — more at SIGN] *vt* **1** *obs* **a** : to place a seal or sign upon **b** [MF or LL; MF *consigner*, fr. LL *consignare*, fr. L] : to make the sign of the cross on or for (as at baptism or confirmation) : CONFIRM **2** *archaic* : to attest or confirm (as a truth, fact, promise) by some sign or token 〈a pact ~*ed* by holy oaths〉 **3** : to give over to another's charge, custody, or care : COMMISSION, ENTRUST 〈~ her single daughters to the care of their sister —Jane Austen〉 〈in spite of the thankless tasks ~*ed* to him —*Times Lit. Supp.*〉 **4** : to give, transfer, or deliver over by or as if by signing over esp. into the possession of another or into a lasting state : commit in a formal or solemn manner 〈~ a body to the grave〉 〈after a death they ~*ed* the name of the deceased to oblivion, and never mentioned it again —J.G.Frazer〉 〈~ a letter to the flames〉 **5** : to make a legal consignation or deposit of (as money) in making a tender of payment or in surrendering money to abide the determination of the rights of competing claimants **6** : to send or address to an agent in another place to be cared for or sold or for the use of such agent 〈~ a ship〉 〈~ goods〉 ~ *vi, obs* : SUBSCRIBE, AGREE, SUBMIT 〈heaven ~*ing* to my good intents —Shak.〉 **syn** see COMMIT

con·sig·na·tary \kən'signə,terē, -ri\ *n* -ES [*consignation* + *-ary*] : CONSIGNEE; *specif* : one who in Roman and civil law has received money on deposit (as by consignation)

con·sig·na·tion \,känsig'nāshən\ *n* -S [ML *consignation-, consignatio* sealing, marking, branding, fr. L, written proof, document, fr. *consignatus* (past part. of *consignare*) + *-ion-, -io* -ion] **1** : the act of marking with the sign of the cross **2** : a deposit of something a person owes tendered under judicial sanction by a debtor or a surrender of money by one claiming no interest therein to abide the determination of the rights of competing claimants **3** *archaic* : confirmatory indication by or as if by a sign or token 〈the Scriptures having their ~ from God〉 **4** *obs* : the act of consigning (as to another person or to a state) : COMMITTING, ENTRUSTING

con·sign·ee \¦kän,sī¦nē, ¦kän(t)sə¦nē, kən,sī¦nē\ *n* -S [*consign* + *-ee*] : one to whom something is consigned or shipped

con·significant \¦kän+\ *adj* [ML *consignificant-, consignificans*, pres. part. of *consignificare* to consignify] : SYNCATEGOREMATIC

con·signification \¦kän+\ *n* -S [ML *consignification-, consignificatio*, fr. *consignificatus* (past part. of *consignificare*) + *-ion-, -io* -ion] : connotative or contextual meaning : joint signification — **con·significa·tive** \¦kän+\ *adj*

con·signify \(')kän, kən+\ *vt* -ED/-ING/-ES [ML *consignificare*, fr. L *com-* + *significare* to signify — more at SIGNIFY] *archaic* : to signify in combination with something else

¹**con·sign·ment** \kən'sīnmənt\ *n* -S [*consign* + *-ment*] **1** : the act of consigning something 〈the ~ of finished products to a wholesaler〉 **2** : something that is consigned esp. in a single shipment 〈the first ~ of new cars to reach the city〉 — **on consignment** *adj (or adv)* : shipped to a dealer who acts as agent (as for a manufacturer) to sell, auction, or exhibit with the agreement that he may take title to and pay for what he sells, that he must remit the proceeds of sales less commission to the shipper, and that he may return anything left unsold 〈goods shipped *on consignment*〉

²**consignment** \"\ *adj* : of, relating to, or received as goods on consignment 〈a ~ account〉 〈~ marketing〉 〈a ~ sale〉 〈~ merchandise〉 〈selling on a ~ basis〉

consignment note *n* : AIRWAYBILL

con·sign·or \kən'sīnə(r), ¦kän,sī¦nó(ə)r, ¦kän(t)sə¦nó(ə)r, kən,sī¦nó(ə)r, -nó(ə)\ *also* **con·sign·er** \kən'sīnə(r)\ *n* -S : one that consigns something (as the goods of an individual shipment)

con·sil·ience \kən'silyən(t)s, -lēən-\ *n* -S [*com-* + *-silience* (as in *resilience*)] : the concurrence of generalizations from separate classes of facts in logical inductions so that one set of inductive laws is found to be in accord with another set of distinct derivation — **con·sil·ient** \-lyənt, -lēənt\ *adj*

con·similar \(')kän, kən+\ *adj* [obs. E *consimile* (fr. ME, fr. L *consimilis* entirely similar, fr. *com-* + *similis* similar) + *-ar* — more at SIMILAR] : sharing in similarity or being entirely similar; *specif* : having both valves alike 〈~ diatoms〉 — **con·similarity** \¦kän, kən+\ *n* -ES

¹**con·sist** \kən'sist\ *vi* -ED/-ING/-S [MF & L; MF *consister*, fr. L *consistere* to stand still or firm, be steadfast, exist, fr. *com-* + *sistere* to stand, cause to stand; akin to L *stare* to stand — more at STAND] **1** : to become comprised : LIE, RESIDE, INHERE — used with *in* 〈national strength ~*s* not alone in national armies〉 **2** *obs* : to become founded, based, or upheld — used with *on* or *upon* **3** *obs* : to have place or station : STAND, LIE — used chiefly with *in, within, between* **4** *archaic* : to exist in a fixed or permanent state (as of a body made up of parts in union) : hold together : BE **5** : to become composed or made up — used with *of* 〈coal ~*s* mainly of carbon〉 **6** *obs* : INSIST, URGE, DEMAND — used with *on* or *upon* **7** : to be consistent, harmonious, or in accordance — used with *with* 〈the testimony ~*ed* with all known facts〉 **8** *archaic* : to exist or be capable of existing — used with *with* 〈refined tastes do not long ~ with abject poverty〉

²**consist** \", 'kän,sist\ *n* -S : makeup or composition (as of coal sizes or a railroad train) by classes, types, or grades and arrangement

con·sist·ence \kən'sistən(t)s\ *n* -S [MF *consistance*, fr. *consistant*, pres. part. of *consister*] : CONSISTENCY

con·sist·en·cy \kən'sistənsē, -si\ *n* -ES **1 a** *archaic* : the condition (as of a material) of standing together or remaining fixed in union : FIRMNESS 〈to boil a substance into a ~〉 **b** : persistence of firmness (as in following a single or predetermined plan, method, or procedure) : singleness of purpose : PERSISTENCY 〈Haydn's twenty sonatas are distinguished by the ~ with which their cheerful mood is maintained —A.E. Wier〉 **2 a** : a degree of firmness, density, viscosity, or resistance to movement or separation of constituent particles 〈the ~ of syrup〉 **b** : the manifestation of mutual attraction of particles at different moisture contents 〈~ of soil〉 **c** : the percentage by weight of dry fibrous matter in a stock suspension about to be made into paper **3 a** : agreement or harmony of parts, traits, or features : uniformity among a number of things : CORRESPONDENCE 〈a ~ of style in the furnishings and decorations of all the rooms〉; *specif* : the characteristic of two or more propositions and derivatively of properties and propositional functions in logic that appertains if their conjunction does not result in a contradiction **b** : harmony of conduct or practice with profession : persistent adherence to moral or ethical standards in thought or action 〈the ~ with which the foremost philosophic apostle of practicing what one preaches followed his own advice —*Americana Annual*〉

con·sist·ent \kən'sistənt\ *adj* [L *consistent-, consistens*, pres. part. of *consistere*] **1** *archaic* : marked by unchanging position or by firmness, stiffness, solidity, or coherence 〈organs made ~ by cartilage〉 : stationary, changeless, and enduring 〈the ~ pines on the ledge〉 **2 a** : marked by harmony, regularity, or steady continuity throughout : showing no significant change, unevenness, or contradiction 〈in art all styles are good provided . . . they are ~ and harmonious within themselves —J.W.Krutch〉 〈the influence of America should be ~ in seeking for humanity a final peace —F.D.Roosevelt〉 **b** : marked by agreement and concord 〈opinions ~ with each other〉 : coexisting and showing no noteworthy opposing, conflicting, inharmonious, or contradictory qualities or trends : COMPATIBLE — usu. used with *with* 〈drinking more hollands and water than is ~ with decorum —George Borrow〉 〈is your aunt's romanticism always ~ with accuracy —Edith Wharton〉 **c** : showing steady regular conformity to character, profession, belief, or custom 〈a ~ advocate of a high protective tariff and was for many years president of the Protective Tariff League —A.L.Churchill〉 **d** : jointly assertable so as to be true or not contradictory : COMPOSSIBLE **syn** see CONSONANT

consistent equations *n pl* : a set of equations possessing a common solution

consistently *adv* : in a consistent manner: as **a** : COMPATIBLY 〈~ with standards〉 : CONGRUOUSLY 〈one cannot ~ defend such dishonesty〉 **b** : in harmony with 〈~ with our intentions〉 **c** : in a persistent or even manner : UNIFORMLY 〈a ~ ironic tone throughout the whole novel〉

con·sist·om·e·ter \,känsə'stäməd·ə(r)\ *n* -S [*consistency* + *-o-* + *-meter*] : a device for measuring consistency or flow characteristics of a viscous or plastic substance (as a lubricating grease or a starch suspension)

con·sis·to·ri·al \¦känsə¦stōrēəl, -stȯr-\ *adj* [ME, fr. ML *consistorialis*, fr. LL & ML *consistorium* + L *-alis* -al] : of or having to do with a consistory

consistorian *adj* [LL & ML *consistorianus*, fr. *consistorium* + L *-anus* -an] *obs* : CONSISTORIAL

con·sis·to·ry \kən'sist(ə)rē, -ri *Brit also* 'känsist(ə)ri\ *n* -ES [ME *consistorie*, fr. MF, fr. ML & LL; ML *consistorium* church tribunal, fr. LL, place of assembly, imperial council, fr. L *consistere* to stand still or firm + *-orium* -ory — more at CONSIST] **1 a** *obs* : a place of assembly (as a council chamber) **b** : a solemn assembly : COUNCIL **2** : a church tribunal or governing body: as **a** *also* **consistory court** : a diocesan court with jurisdiction in matters (as of marriage and titles) relating to general ecclesiastical and moral discipline; *specif* : a similar court in the Church of England presided over by the bishop's chancellor or commissary and dealing only with spiritual and ecclesiastical matters **b** : a solemn meeting of Roman Catholic cardinals convoked and presided over by the pope **c** : an advisory body in the Eastern Orthodox Church assisting the ecumenical patriarch of Constantinople in the affairs of his diocese **d** : a church council in certain churches with a presbyterian polity (as the Dutch and other Reformed churches) charged with managing the general affairs of a church and composed of the ministers, the elders, and sometimes (as in the Evangelical and Reformed church) the deacons of the congregation **e** : an administrative body of clerical and lay officers appointed by civil authority to administer ecclesiastical affairs in Lutheran state churches **3 a** : the organization or a branch of the organization that confers the degrees of the Ancient and Accepted Scottish Rite of Freemasonry usu. from the 19th to the 32d inclusive; *also* : a meeting of such an organization or branch **b** : a building serving as headquarters for a Masonic consistory

¹**con·so·ciate** \kən'sōs(h)ēət, (')kän¦-, -shət, -shē,āt, -sē,āt, *usu* -əd·+V\ *adj* [ME *consociat*, fr. L *consociatus*, past part. of *consociare* to associate, unite, fr. *com-* + *sociare* to join, unite, fr. *socius* associate, ally — more at SOCIAL] : united in fellowship : intimately associated 〈a ~ family〉

²**con·so·ci·ate** \kən'sōs(h)ē,āt, (')kän¦-, *usu* -ād·+V\ *vb* -ED/-ING/-S [L *consociatus*] *vt* : to unite or bring into association 〈Swedenborg's best of angels . . . did not live *consociated* —Van Wyck Brooks〉 〈the *consociated* Congregational churches of New England〉 ~ *vi* : to associate esp. in fellowship or partnership : enter into intimate or close association 〈*consociating* with the best of men〉 〈the churches *consociated* to fight against their dissolution〉

³**con·so·ciate** *see adj*\ *n* -S [¹*consociate*] : one who is united with another : ASSOCIATE, CONFEDERATE 〈~*s* in a plot〉

con·so·ci·a·tion \kən,sōsē'āshən, (')kän¦==¦==, -ōshē-\ *n* -S [L *consociation-, consociatio*, fr. *consociatus* + *-ion-, -io* -ion] **1 a** : the act of uniting in fellowship or association 〈the possibility of friendly ~ with the countess —Carl Van Vechten〉 **b** *archaic* : intimate or close association : ALLIANCE, CONFEDERATION 〈~ with God〉 〈to enter into a ~ with friendly countries〉 **2** : an association or confederation of churches or religious societies: as **a** (1) : a voluntary council or union of neighboring Congregational churches for cooperation in ecclesiastical matters (2) : a standing council with disciplinary authority composed of the ministers and representative laymen in a district in Connecticut Congregationalism **b** : the union of churches on a Presbyterian basis among English Puritans **3 a** : a community within an ecological association having a single dominant which is usu. one of the dominants of the association 〈a sugar-maple ~ in a beech-maple association〉 — compare FACIATION **b** : an association having a single dominant

con·so·ci·a·tion·al \kən¦==¦āshən^{ə}l, (')kän-, -āshnəl\ *adj* : of or having to do with a consociation

con·so·ci·a·tion·ism \kən,==ə'āshə,nizəm, (')kän-\ *n* -S : the theory or practice of church consociation

con·so·cia·tive \kən'sōs(h)ē,ād·iv, (')kän¦-, -ōshəd·iv, -ōs(h)ēəd·iv\ *adj* : promoting, exhibiting, or having to do with association or fellowship 〈~ behavior〉 〈the headmaster who knew little about games, though . . . approving of their ~ virtues —V.V.Nabokov〉

con·so·ci·es \kən'sōs(h)ē,ēz, (')kän¦-\ *n, pl* **consocies** [*consociation* + *-ies* (as in *species*)] : a consociation of plants in a developmental stage

con·sol \'kän,säl, kən'-\ *n* -S *sometimes cap, often attrib* [*consolidated* annuity] : a bond issue having no maturity date although the issuer may have the right to call for redemption; *esp* : a perpetual interest-bearing obligation first issued by the British government in 1751 〈the ~ market〉 — usu. used in pl. 〈an old dowager countess whose money was all in *Consols* —Samuel Butler †1902〉

con·sol·a·ble \kən'sōləbəl\ *adj* : that can be consoled — **con·sol·able·ness** \-nəs\ *n* -ES — **con·sol·ably** \-blē, -bli\ *adv*

con·so·la·men·tum \kən'sōləmentəm\ *n, pl* **consolamen·ta** \-tə\ [ML, fr. L *consolari* + *-mentum* -ment] : the Cathari rite of spiritual baptism usu. administered just before death making the candidate one of the perfecti

¹**consolate** *vt* -ED/-ING/-S [L *consolatus*] *obs* : CONSOLE

²**consolate** *adj* [L *consolatus*] *obs* : CONSOLED, COMFORTED

con·so·la·tion \,kän(t)sə'lāshən\ *n* -S [ME *consolacioun*, fr. MF or L; MF *consolation*, fr. L *consolation-, consolatio*, fr. *consolatus* (past part. of *consolari* to console) + *-ion-, -io* -ion] **1 a** : alleviation of distress or misery (as by sympathetic care or attention or by the soothing or mitigating effects of natural or psychological phenomena) : COMFORT, SOLACE 〈nothing brings me so much ~ as music —Havelock Ellis〉 〈he had sought the ~ of the twilight —Elinor Wylie〉 **b** : an instance or act of comforting or being comforted 〈~*s* to offset the inevitable physical decay that befalls most of us —Elmer Davis〉 **2 a** : a fine paid by the loser in some card games (as ombre) **b** : a contest (as a game, match, or race) held for those who have lost in the early stages of a tournament 〈~ match〉 〈~ race〉 **c** *or* **consolation prize** : a prize of relatively little value given to a runner-up or a loser **3** : CONSOLAMENTUM

consolator *n* -S [L, fr. *consolatus* + *-or*] *obs* : one that consoles

¹**con·sol·a·to·ry** \kən'sōlə,tōrē, -tȯrē, -ri; *chiefly Brit* -'sälət(ə)rē, -ri\ *adj* [ME, fr. L *consolatorius*, fr. *consolatus* + *-orius* -ory] : designed or tending to bring consolation 〈~ words〉 〈a gesture ~ to his injured pride〉

²**consolatory** *n* -S *obs* : a consolatory communication

¹**con·sole** \kən'sōl\ *vb* -ED/-ING/-S [F *consoler*, fr. L *consolari*, fr. *com-* + *solari* to console, comfort — more at SILLY] *vt* : to soothe in distress or depression : alleviate the grief and raise the spirits of : COMFORT 〈*consoling* advice〉 〈~ herself with music〉 ~ *vi* : to alleviate grief or disappointment : SOOTHE **syn** see COMFORT

²**console** \'kän,sōl\ *n* -S [F, short for MF *consolateur* consoler, carved human figure used as a bracket to support cornices, fr. L *consolator*] **1 a** : an architectural member usu. in Roman and neoclassic style having its sides nearly plane and more or less parallel and a profile of scroll shape (as an ogee curve) and projecting from a wall to form a bracket or corbel (as for the support of a cornice, window head, or bust) or from a keystone (as for ornament) — see ANCON **b** : a similar member reversed and depending upon the horizontal rather than the vertical surface and used to finish a parapet or gallery with an ornament shaped like a scroll **2** : CONSOLE TABLE **3 a** : the desk from which an organ is played and which contains the keyboards, pedal board, and other controlling mechanisms **b** : a panel or cabinet on which are mounted dials, switches, and other apparatus used in centrally controlling electrical or mechanical devices **4** : a cabinet (as for a radio or television set) often decorated and designed to rest directly on the floor and usu. against a wall

console supporting a cornice

console table *n* [²*console*] : a table fixed to a wall with its top supported by one or more consoles, front legs, or an eagle or other carved motive; *broadly* : any table to be placed against a wall (as a side or pier table)

18th cent. console table

con·so·lette \,känsə'let, '==,=\ *n* -S [²*console* + *-ette*] : a small cabinet containing a radio, television, or record player designed to be placed against a wall

¹**con·sol·i·date** \kən'sälə,dāt, *usu* -ād·+V\ *vb* -ED/-ING/-S [L *consolidatus*, past part. of *consolidare* to make firm, fr. *com-* + *solidare* to make firm, fr. *solidus* solid — more at SAFE] *vt* **1 a** : to join together (as two or more items into one unit, or whole) : UNITE 〈~ various ideas〉 〈~ several colleges into a university〉 **b** *law* (1) : to cause to become united and extinguished in a superior right or estate by both becoming vested in the same person (2) : to join in or cause to proceed as a single action — used of causes of action or of actions started separately **2 a** : to make firm or secure : STRENGTHEN, CONFIRM 〈~ their hold on first place〉 〈~ the economic power of an empire with great merchant fleets〉; *specif* : to organize and strengthen by military means (as a position or ground recently captured) **b** : to make stronger or more secure 〈condemnation of Italy . . . *consolidated* Italian-American support for Il Duce —Oscar Handlin〉 〈~ his reputation〉 : make more tangible or effective 〈five years . . . have only *consolidated* the paradoxes —James Cameron〉 **3** : to make or form into a solid or hardened mass 〈the press ~*s* fibers into board under pressures which vary from 300 to 1000 pounds a square inch —*Monsanto Mag.*〉 ~ *vi* **1** : to become firm or hard (as by solidifying, freezing, uniting, adhering) : grow solid 〈the mud of the roads *consolidated* in the freezing night〉 **2** : to unite or grow into a coherent whole 〈his ideas *consolidated* into a plan〉; *specif* : to undergo merger (as for mutual advantage) **syn** see UNIFY

²**consolidate** \-,dāt, -,dət\ *adj* [L *consolidatus*] : made solid, firm, or coherent : CONSOLIDATED 〈one of Montague's earliest ~ memories —Peggy Bennett〉

consolidated *adj* **1** : that has become firm or solid; *specif* : SOLIDIFIED 〈a ~ lung in pneumonia〉 — compare CONSOLIDATION 1b(1) **2** : joined together into a coherent, compact, or unified whole 〈a ~ balance sheet〉 〈a ~ European army〉

consolidated annuities *n pl* : CONSOLS

consolidated school *n* : a school formed by merging two or more public schools usu. of the elementary level and often located in a rural district — compare UNION SCHOOL

consolidated statement *n* : a balance sheet or profit and loss statement of two or more affiliated enterprises (as a parent company and its wholly owned subsidiary companies)

consolidated stock *n* : CONSOLS

con·sol·i·da·tion \kən,sälə'dāshən\ *n* -S [ME *consolidacion*, fr. LL *consolidation-, consolidatio*, fr. L *consolidatus* + *-ion-, -io* -ion — more at CONSOLIDATE] **1 a** : the process of becoming firm or solid 〈the ~ of fibrous matter under pressure〉 **b** (1) : the process by which an infected lung passes from an aerated collapsible condition to one of airless solid consistency through the accumulation of exudate in the alveoli and adjoining ducts 〈pneumonic ~〉 (2) : tissue that has undergone consolidation 〈areas of ~〉 — compare RESOLUTION **c** : the passage from a loosely aggregated or liquid condition to firm rock through the effect of pressure, chemical action, or crystallization : LITHIFICATION **2** : the process of becoming or making stronger or more secure 〈the ~ of gains〉 〈his ~ of political power〉 〈the year 1952 was one of ~ in physics —*Americana Annual*〉 〈her more recent fiction suggests nothing more than a ~ of her previous achievement —W.S.Graham〉 **3** : the process of uniting or the quality or state of being united : COMBINATION, UNIFICATION 〈the ~ of several works into one volume〉 〈the present ~ of rural schools〉 〈the twin Communist goals of ~ of the Communist world and disintegration of the rest —J.P.Lash〉; *specif* : the unification of two or more corporations by dissolution of existing ones and creation of a single new corporation

con·sol·i·da·tion·ist \-nəst\ *n* -S : one who advocates consolidation; *esp* : an advocate of a strong federal government

con·sol·i·da·tor \-'sälə,dād·ə(r)\ *n* -S : one that consolidates

con·sol·ing·ly *adv* : in a consoling manner

consols *pl of* CONSOL

con·so·lute \'kän(t)sə,lüt\ *adj* [LL *consolutus* dissolved together, fr. L *com-* + *solutus*, past part. of *solvere* to set free, loosen, dissolve — more at SOLVE] **1 a** : miscible in all proportions : mutually soluble — used of two or more liquids **b** : soluble in each of two nonmiscible liquids in contact with each other **2** : of or relating to liquids perfectly miscible under certain conditions

consolute temperature *n* : CRITICAL SOLUTION TEMPERATURE

con·som·mé *also* **con·som·me** \'känsə,mā, ¦==¦=; *Brit* kən'sämā *or* kō^{n}sómā\ *n* -S [F *consommé*, fr. past part. of *consommer* to accomplish, consume, boil down, fr. L *consummare* to complete, finish — more at CONSUMMATE] : a soup made usu. of meat stock often in combination and condensed by boiling, highly seasoned, cleared, and strained

consomol *usu cap, var of* KOMSOMOL

con·so·nance \'kän(t)s(ə)nən(t)s\ *n* -S [ME, fr. MF, fr. L *consonantia*, fr. *consonant-, consonans* + *-ia* -y] **1** : harmony of parts : pleasing, desired, or logical agreement among components 〈~ of thought and expression〉 〈the literary conceptions which prevailed were in ~ with the social structure —V.F.Calverton〉 〈she spoke with an angry . . . vehemence that was strangely out of ~ with her ordinary serenity of demeanor —William Black〉 **2 a** : correspondence of sounds : recurrence of like or similar sounds : ACCORD 〈a pleasing ~ among final syllables〉 — compare ASSONANCE **b** : a combination of musical tones felt as satisfying and restful; *specif* : an interval included in a major or minor triad and its inversions — compare DISSONANCE **c** : sympathetic vibration : RESONANCE — used by some to distinguish the sympathetic vibration of independent things (as two musical strings or two electric circuits) from *resonance* **d :** recurrence or repetition of identical or similar consonants; *specif* **:** correspondence of consonants alone unaccompanied by like correspondence of vowels at the ends of two or more syllables, words, or other units of composition — called also *consonant-rhyme;* compare ALLITERATION, ASSONANCE

con·so·nan·cy \ˈkän(t)s(ə)nənsē, -si\ *n* -ES [ME *consonancie,* fr. MF & L; MF, fr. L *consonantia*] **:** the quality or state of being harmonious or congruent ⟨~ of sounds⟩ ⟨~ of related parts⟩

¹con·so·nant \ˈkän(t)s(ə)nənt\ *n* -S [ME, fr. L *consonant-, consonans,* fr. pres. part. of *consonare* to sound at the same time] **1 :** one of a class of speech sounds (as *p, g, n, l, s, r, w*) characterized by constriction or closure at one or more points in the breath channel; *broadly* **:** any sound in a syllable other than the one most prominent sound (as the second element of a falling diphthong) — compare CONSONANTAL VOWEL, SEMIVOWEL, VOWEL **2 :** a letter representing a consonant — usu. used in English of all letters in the alphabet except *a, e, i, o,* and *u*

²consonant \"\ *adj* [MF, fr. L *consonant-, consonans,* pres. part. of *consonare* to sound at the same time, agree, fr. *com-* + *sonare* to sound — more at SOUND] **1 :** suiting or according with a circumstance or situation or conforming to a standard or pattern without discord or difficulty ⟨Fijians possessed a physical endurance ~ with their great stature —V.G. Heiser⟩ ⟨it is . . . more ~ with the Puritan temper to abolish a practice than to elevate it —A.T.Quiller-Couch⟩ **2 :** agreeable in sound; *specif* **:** harmonically satisfying — contrasted with *dissonant* **3 :** having like sounds ⟨~ words⟩ **4 :** CONSONANTAL **5 :** relating to or exhibiting consonance **:** RESONANT **syn** CONSISTENT, COMPATIBLE, CONGRUOUS, CONGENIAL, SYMPATHETIC: CONSONANT implies general harmony and stresses lack of factors making for discord or difficulty ⟨the book presented meditations which were so *consonant* with Christian views that its Christian readers from Alfred to Dante mistook them for Christian sentiments —H.O.Taylor⟩ ⟨even the man's start and suspicious stare as the priest went by were *consonant* enough with the vigilance and jealousy of such a type —G.K.Chesterton⟩ The implications of CONSISTENT are much the same, although it may tend to suggest accord on small details in addition to main matters ⟨Father John did not think it to be *consistent* with his dignity to answer this sally —Anthony Trollope⟩ ⟨I have decided that the course of conduct which I am following is *consistent* with my sense of responsibility as president in time of war —F.D.Roosevelt⟩ COMPATIBLE indicates capacity for existing together without discord or conflict, although not necessarily in positive agreement or harmony ⟨all systems of economy that are to be *compatible* with man's continual adaptation to a changing world must employ both the principle of order and that of freedom —M.R.Cohen⟩ ⟨in ordinary society it is notoriously difficult for people of very unequal fortune to be friends in the true sense; that beautiful relationship is not *compatible* with patronage and dependence —H.J.Mackinder⟩ CONGRUOUS suggests a more positive harmony, a suitability of things likely to make for a pleasant impression ⟨thoughts *congruous* to the nature of their subject —William Cowper⟩ ⟨the doctrine is not always quite *congruous* with itself —Havelock Ellis⟩ CONGENIAL is likely to imply pleasing concord or satisfying harmony ⟨I was brought up in the freer, less conventional atmosphere of South Australia, and this English life, with its proprieties and its primness, is not *congenial* to me —A. Conan Doyle⟩ ⟨the ideal of a Greek democracy was vastly *congenial* to his aristocratic temperament —V.L.Parrington⟩ SYMPATHETIC may apply to a milder appeal or to a less hearty acceptance, but it always indicates a strong tendency toward concord ⟨a semimystical, *sympathetic* harmony between husband and wife —Norman Cameron⟩ ⟨thus a tête-à-tête with a man of similar tastes, who is just and yet *sympathetic,* critical yet appreciative . . . this is a high intellectual pleasure —A.C. Benson⟩

con·so·nan·tal \ˌkän(t)səˌnantᵊl, -naan-\ *adj* **1 :** being or functioning as a consonant **:** of or relating to a consonant **2 :** marked by or consisting of consonants ⟨a ~ diphthong⟩ ⟨a ~ Hebrew text⟩ — **con·so·nan·tal·ly** \-tᵊlē, -li\ *adv*

con·so·nan·tal·i·za·tion \ˌkän(t)səˌnantᵊlə̇ˈzāshən\ *also* **con·so·nant·i·za·tion** \ˌkän(t)sənəntə̇ˈz-, -ˌnant-\ *n* -S **:** the act or action of consonantalizing

con·so·nan·tal·ize \ˌkän(t)səˈnantᵊlˌīz\ *also* **con·so·nant·ize** \ˈkän(t)sənənˌtīz\ *vb* -ED/-ING/-S *vt* **:** to change into or articulate as a consonant (as when the ē in *piteous* is pronounced \y\ rather than \ē\ ~ *vi* **:** to change a vowel to a consonant ⟨the tendency to ~⟩

consonantal stem *n* **:** CONSONANT STEM

consonantal vowel *n* **:** the unstressed less prominent part of a diphthong (as the \i\ of \ȯi\ in \ˈbȯi\ *boy*)

consonant declension *n* **:** a declension characterized by the addition of case endings to a stem that ends in a consonant

con·so·nan·tic \ˌkän(t)səˈnantik\ *adj* **:** CONSONANTAL

con·so·nant·ism \ˈkän(t)sənənˌtizəm\ *n* -S **1 :** the consonant system (as of a language or dialect) **2 :** the consonants, sequence of consonants, or quality peculiar to the consonants of a word or group of related words ⟨the ~ of the 4 words hardly seems . . . to point to Scandinavian origin —Stephen Ullmann⟩

con·so·nan·tize \ˈkän(t)s(ə)nənˌtīz\ *vt* -ED/-ING/-S **:** to change into or articulate as a consonant

con·so·nant·ly *adv* **:** in a consonant manner

con·so·nant·ness *n* -ES **:** the quality or state of being consonant

consonant-rhyme \ˈ≈(≈)≈ˌ≈\ *n* **:** CONSONANCE 2 d

consonants *pl of* CONSONANT

consonant shift *n* **1 :** the set of regular changes in consonant articulation which distinguish the Germanic languages from the other Indo-European languages and through which Indo-European voiceless stops become Germanic voiceless fricatives (as in Greek *pyr, treis, kardia* compared with English *fire, three, heart*), Indo-European voiced stops become Germanic voiceless stops (as in Old Slavic *jablŭko,* Greek *dyo, genos* compared with English *apple, two, kin*), and Indo-European voiced aspirated stops become Germanic voiced fricatives (as in Sanskrit *nābhi, madhya* "mid", Latin *helvus* compared with English *navel,* Old Norse *mithr* "mid", English *yellow*) — called also *first consonant shift, Germanic consonant shift* **2 :** the set of regular changes in consonant articulation which distinguish High German from the other Germanic languages and through which Germanic voiceless stops become High German affricates or voiceless fricatives (as in English *pound, open, ten, eat, corn, make* compared with German *pfund, offen, zehn, essen,* Upper German *kchorn,* German *machen*) and Germanic voiced stops become High German voiceless stops (as in English *rib, middle,* Dutch *egge* "edge", compared with German *rippe, mittel* "means", *ecke* "corner") — called also *second consonant shift, High German consonant shift* **3 :** the Germanic and High German consonant shifts together **4 :** any set of regular changes in consonant articulation in the history of a language or dialect ⟨the Armenian *consonant shift*⟩

consonant stem *n* **:** a word or stem belonging to a consonant declension

consopite *vt* -ED/-ING/-S [L *consopitus,* past part. of *consopire* to put to sleep, fr. *com-* + *sopire* to put to sleep — more at SOPITE] *obs* **:** to lull to sleep **:** QUIET

consopition *n* -S [L *consopitus* + E *-ion*] *obs* **:** a lulling to sleep

con sor·di·no \ˌkän(t)sȯ(r)ˈdē(ˌ)nō, -kōn-\ *adv* [It] **:** with the mute — used as a direction in music

¹con·sort \ˈkänˌsȯrt, -sȯ(ə)t, *usu* -d·+V\ *n* -S [ME, fr. MF, fr. L *consort-, consors,* fr. *com-* + *sort-, sors* lot, fate, share — more at SORT] **:** one that shares the company of or is associated with another: as **a** *obs* **:** a colleague of one's profession or official office **b :** COMPANION ⟨the criminal and his semirespectable ~*s*⟩ ⟨the second volume is in every respect a splendid ~ of the first⟩; *specif* **:** a ship accompanying another ⟨far astern . . . he could see the brown sail and the red sail of their ~*s* —C.S.Forester⟩ **c :** a wife or husband **:** SPOUSE, MATE ⟨the queen attended the opening of the exhibition with her ~⟩ — compare PRINCE CONSORT

²consort \"\ *n* -S [MF *consorte* company, fr. *consort*] **1** *obs* **:** ASSEMBLY, COMPANY, GROUP ⟨in one ~ there sat cruel revenge and rancorous despite —Edmund Spenser⟩ **2 :** concurrence or accord **:** CONJUNCTION, ASSOCIATION ⟨I can claim that poetry . . . had ~ with me through life —A.T. Quiller-Couch⟩ — often used with *in* ⟨he ruled in ~ with his father⟩ **3** [prob. by folk etymology fr. MF *concert* — more at CONCERT] **a :** a group of musicians entertaining by voice or instrument or the entertainment they afford **b** *obs* **:** harmony of sounds **c :** a set of 16th and 17th century musical instruments of the same family (as viols) played in concert

³consort \kənˈsȯ(ə)rt, -sȯ(ə)t *sometimes* ˈkänˌsȯrt, -ˌsȯ(ə)t, *usu* -d·+V\ *vb* -ED/-ING/-S [¹*consort*] *vt* **1 :** to unite esp. in affection, harmony, company, marriage **:** ASSOCIATE ⟨the ideals that naturally ~ themselves with the word civilization —Isaac Taylor⟩ **2** [²*consort* (harmony of sounds)] *obs* **:** to sound in harmony **:** HARMONIZE **3** *obs* **:** ESCORT, ATTEND, ACCOMPANY ~ *vi* **1 :** to keep company ⟨a unit's soldiery . . . ~*ing* with women —Fred Majdalany⟩ ⟨from this time on he ~*ed* more and more with Methodists —Allen Johnson⟩ **2** [²*consort* (harmony of sounds)] *obs* **:** to make harmony **:** PLAY **3** [²*consort* (accord)] **:** to be or come into accord **:** HARMONIZE ⟨except in matters of doctrine Pilgrim and Puritan ~*ed* ill together —V.L.Parrington⟩ ⟨the statement of faith . . . is so inane that . . . an apostate . . . can easily ~ to it —H.H.Savage⟩ ⟨the illustrations ~ admirably with the text —*Times Lit. Supp.*⟩

con·sor·tion \kənˈsȯrshən\ *n* -S [L *consortion-, consortio,* fr. *consort-, consors* partner + *-ion-, -io* -ion — more at CONSORT] **:** ASSOCIATION, ALLIANCE

con·sort·ism \ˈkänˌsȯrd·ˌizəm\ *n* -S [¹*consort* + *-ism*] **:** SYMBIOSIS

con·sor·ti·um \kənˈsȯrsh(ē)əm, -ȯrd·ēəm\ *n, pl* **consor·tia** \-rsh(ē)ə, -rd·ēə\ *also* **consortiums** \-mz\ [L, fellowship, fr. *consort-, consors* + *-ium*] **1 :** an international business or banking agreement or combination (as for the financial assistance of another nation or for the control of a particular industry in a country or countries) — compare CARTEL, TRUST **2 :** ASSOCIATION, FELLOWSHIP, CLUB, SOCIETY ⟨speaking of distinguished *consortia,* a new one called the Renaissance Society of America is announced —*N.Y. Herald Tribune Bk. Rev.*⟩ **3 a :** marital association — used chiefly in a legal action for damages for injury to a spouse or for alienation of a spouse's affections ⟨loss of ~⟩ **b :** persistent intimate association of different kinds of organisms usu. with close physical contact (as in the symbiosis of certain algae)

con·species \(ˈ)kän, kən+\ *n, pl* **conspecies** [*com-* + *species*] **:** a congeneric species

con·specific \ˌkän+\ *adj* [fr. *conspecies,* after such pairs as *species: specific*] **:** of the same species

con·spec·tus \kənzˈpektəs, -nˈsp-\ *n* -ES [L, fr. *conspectus,* past part. of *conspicere* to perceive — more at CONSPICUOUS] **1 :** a survey (as of a comprehensive subject) usu. in brief compass or rapid topical summary and often providing an overall view or perspective ⟨a ~ of the history of human thought⟩ **2 :** OUTLINE, LIST, SYNOPSIS ⟨a brief ~ on rose diseases and their control —*Experiment Station Record*⟩ **syn** see ABRIDGMENT

con·sper·gent \kənzˈpərjənt, -nˈsp-\ *n* -S [L *conspergent-, conspergens,* pres. part. of *conspergere* to sprinkle, fr. *com-* + *-spergere* (fr. *spargere* to scatter, strew) — more at SPARK] **:** a dusting powder (as lycopodium) used to coat the surface of handmade pills to prevent them from adhering to one another

con·sperse \kənzˈpərs, (ˈ)känzˌ-, kənˈsp-, (ˈ)känˌs-\ *adj* [L *conspersus,* past part. of *conspergere*] **:** thickly and irregularly strewn (as with fine spots or punctures)

con·spi·cu·i·ty \ˌkänzpə̇ˈkyüəd·ē, -än(t)sp-, -ə̇tē, -i\ *n* -ES [*conspicuous* + *-ity*] **:** CONSPICUOUSNESS

con·spic·u·ous \kənˈspikyəwəs, -nˈsp-\ *adj* [L *conspicuus,* fr. *conspicere* to get sight of, perceive, fr. *com-* + *-spicere* (fr. *specere* to look) — more at SPY] **1 :** obvious to the eye or mind **:** plainly visible **:** MANIFEST ⟨~ at a great distance⟩ ⟨an intention ~ only to his friends⟩ **2 :** attracting or tending to attract attention by reason of size, brilliance, contrast, station **:** STRIKING, EMINENT ⟨a ~ tower⟩ ⟨~ statesmen⟩ **3 :** undesirably noticeable by reason of violation of good taste or sense ⟨a ~ necktie⟩ ⟨against spending money for cement sidewalks, which he considered ~ waste —E.W.Smith⟩ **syn** see NOTICEABLE

conspicuous consumption *n* **:** lavish or wasteful spending regarded as establishing or enhancing social prestige

con·spic·u·ous·ly *adv* **:** in a conspicuous manner

con·spic·u·ous·ness \-nə̇s\ *n* -ES **:** the quality or state of being conspicuous

con·spir·a·cy \kənzˈpirəsē, -nˈsp-, -si\ *n* -ES [ME *conspiracie,* alter. (influenced by *-cie* -cy) of *conspiracioun* — more at CONSPIRATION] **1 a :** an illegal, treasonable, or treacherous plan to harm or destroy another person, group, or entity ⟨the ~ to murder Caesar⟩ ⟨his theory of the trade-union movement as a ~ against the unorganized worker —L.A. Fiedler⟩ **b :** an agreement manifesting itself in words or deeds and made by two or more persons confederating to do an unlawful act or use unlawful means to do an act which is lawful **:** CONFEDERACY **2 :** a combination of persons banded secretly together and resolved to accomplish an evil or unlawful end ⟨a ~ made up of storm troopers and disgruntled aristocrats⟩ **3 :** a striking concurrence of tendencies, circumstances, or phenomena as though in planned accord ⟨the portentous ~ of night and solitude and silence —Ambrose Bierce⟩ **syn** see PLOT

conspiracy of silence : a secret agreement to keep silent about an occurrence, situation, or subject esp. to promote or protect selfish interests ⟨local manufacturers were accused of a *conspiracy of silence* on the child-labor situation⟩

con·spir·ant \kənzˈspīrənt, -nˈsp-\ *adj* [F, fr. L *conspirant-, conspirans,* pres. part. of *conspirare*] *archaic* **:** CONSPIRING

con·spi·ra·tion \ˌkänzpəˈrāshən, -än(t)sp-\ *n* -S [ME *conspiracioun,* fr. OF *conspiration,* fr. L *conspiration-, conspiratio,* fr. *conspiratus* (past part. of *conspirare*) + *-ion-, -io* -ion] **1 :** the act or action of plotting or secretly combining ⟨an everlasting ~ against authority⟩ **2** *obs* **:** CONSPIRACY, PLOT **3 :** joint effort toward a particular end ⟨a ~ to give evidence of faith by good works⟩ — **con·spi·ra·tion·al** \ˌ≈≈ˈ≈shənᵊl, -shnəl\ *adj*

con·spir·a·tive \kənzˈpirəd·iv, -nˈsp-\ *adj* [*conspiration* + *-ive*] **:** of or having to do with conspiracy or a conspiracy ⟨the discovery of possible ~ codes and ciphers —Joseph Barnes⟩

con·spir·a·tor \kənzˈpirəd·ə(r), -nˈsp-, -ətə-\ *n* -S [ME *conspiratour,* fr. MF *conspirateor,* fr. L *conspirator,* fr. *conspiratus* (past part. of *conspirare*) + *-or*] **:** one that conspires esp. treasonably **:** PLOTTER

con·spir·a·to·ri·al \kənˌzpirəˈtōrēəl, -nˌsp-, -tȯr-\ *adj* **:** of, having to do with, or suggestive of conspiracy or a conspiracy ⟨~ propaganda⟩ ⟨~ funds⟩ ⟨~ glances⟩ — **con·spir·a·to·ri·al·ly** \-rēəlē, -li\ *adv*

con·spire \kənzˈpī(ə)r, -nˈsp-, -īə\ *vb* -ED/-ING/-S [ME *conspiren,* fr. MF *conspirer,* fr. L *conspirare* to blow together, harmonize, agree, plot, fr. *com-* + *spirare* to breathe, blow — more at SPIRIT] *vt* **1 :** PLOT, PLAN, CONTRIVE ⟨your fall and mine do they alike ~ —Robert Southey⟩ **2** *obs* **:** to unite in producing or contributing to ~ *vi* **1 :** to make an agreement with a group and in secret to do some act (as to commit treason or a crime or carry out a treacherous deed) **:** plot together ⟨~ against the state⟩ ⟨lamented that the English workers . . . had never learned to ~ —*Time*⟩ **2 :** to concur or work to one end **:** act in harmony ⟨circumstances of life have *conspired* . . . to render any fixed and authoritative belief incredible —Walter Lippmann⟩

con·spir·ing·ly *adv* **:** in a conspiring manner

con spir·i·to \känˈspirəd·(ˌ)ō, -änˈsp-, kōn-\ *adv* [It] **:** with spirit or animation — used as a direction in music

con·spue \kənˈspyü, -nˈsp-\ *vt* -ED/-ING/-S [F *conspuer,* fr. L *conspuere,* fr. *com-* + *spuere* to spit — more at SPEW] **:** to spurn with contempt as if by spitting upon

const *abbr* **1** constable **2** constant **3** constituent **4** constitution **5** construction

con·sta·ble \ˈkänztəbəl, -än(t)st-; *chiefly Brit* ˈkən-\ *n* -S [ME *conestable,* fr. OF, fr. LL *comes stabuli* officer of the stable, chief equerry, marshal, fr. *comes* officer, count + *stabuli,* gen. of *stabulum* stable — more at COUNT, STABLE] **1 :** the chief officer of the household, court, or army of a nobleman or king during the middle ages who often acted as commander in chief of the army next to the king and as supreme judge of the military courts and courts of chivalry ⟨*constable* of Scotland⟩ ⟨lord high *constable* of England⟩ **2 :** the warden or governor of a royal castle or fortress or of a fortified town **3 :** a military officer esp. of the middle ages **4 a :** a public officer responsible for keeping the public peace and for certain petty judicial duties **b** *Brit* **:** a policeman of the lowest rank

constablery *n* -ES [ME *conestablerie,* fr. MF, fr. *conestable* + *-erie* -ery] *obs* **:** the office of or district under a constable

con·sta·ble·wick \-ˌwik\ *n* -S [*constable* + *wick* (village)] **:** the jurisdiction or district of a constable

¹con·stab·u·lary \kənzˈtabyəˌlerē, -nˈst-, -ri\ *n* -ES [ME *constabularie,* fr. ML *constabularia,* fr. *constabularius, conestabulus* constable (fr. LL *comes stabuli*) + L *-aria* -ary, n. suffix — more at CONSTABLE] **1 :** CONSTABLEWICK **2 :** a body of constables or policemen (as of a particular town, district, country) **3 :** an armed police force organized on military lines but distinct from the regular army ⟨the Royal Irish *Constabulary*⟩

²constabulary \"\ *adj* [ML *constabularius,* fr. *constabulus* constable + L *-arius* -ary, adj. suffix] **:** of, relating to, or suggestive of a constable or constabulary ⟨~ duties⟩ ⟨possessed of a ~ power before which barbaric . . . forces will stand in awe —Sir Winston Churchill⟩

con·stance \ˈkänztən(t)s, -änst-\ *n* -S [ME *constaunce,* fr. MF *constance,* fr. L *constantia*] **1** *obs* **:** CONSTANCY 1, 3 **2 :** the relative occurrence of a kind of organism (as a species) in several examples of a particular type of ecological community based on counts of sample plots of uniform size in each example and commonly expressed as a percentage of the whole population of the sample plot

con·stan·cy \ˈkänztənsē, -än(t)st-, -si\ *n* -ES [L *constantia,* fr. *constant-, constans* (pres. part. of *constare*) + *-ia* -y] **1 a :** steadfastness or firmness of mind (as under duress, hardship, suffering) **:** FORTITUDE, ENDURANCE ⟨resolute ~ in the face of odds⟩ **b :** steadiness in attachments **:** FIDELITY, LOYALTY ⟨the Pony Express was served by the best of its men with ~ and devotion —S.H.Adams⟩ **2** *obs* **:** CERTAINTY **3 :** freedom from change **:** STABILITY, UNIFORMITY ⟨it was shown that among the characteristics of the words of science were their ~ of meaning —T.H.Savory⟩ **4 :** CONSTANCE 2 — **for a constancy** *adv* **:** as something permanent ⟨such a job would be bad *for a constancy*⟩

¹con·stant \ˈkänztənt, -n(t)st-\ *adj* [ME, fr. MF, fr. L *constant-, constans,* pres. part. of *constare* to stand firm, be consistent, fr. *com-* + *stare* to stand — more at STAND] **1 :** marked by firmness, steadfastness, resolution, or faithfulness **:** not weak, yielding, vacillating, or disloyal ⟨a man ~ in adherence to his ideals⟩ ⟨a ~ friend⟩ **2 :** fixed and invariable ⟨the content of constitutional immunities is not ~ but varies from age to age —B.N.Cardozo⟩ **:** remaining unchanged **:** STEADY, UNIFORM ⟨a *constant*-flow calorimeter⟩ **3 :** marked by continual recurring or by regular occurrence, operation, or manifestation ⟨their aims and their methods have been subject to ~ scrutiny, not only by professionals, but also by parents and citizens —J.B.Conant⟩ ⟨the children running in and out of the house were a ~ annoyance⟩ **4** *obs* **:** firm and steady **:** IMMOVABLE, SOLID **5** *obs* **:** confident in opinion **:** POSITIVE, CERTAIN **syn** see CONTINUAL, FAITHFUL, STEADY

²constant \"\ *n* -S **1 :** something that does not vary or change in its relationship or in an essential relationship with other things ⟨the one ~ in all this is that each page is indelibly marked with personality —E.A.Weeks⟩ ⟨the environment should be the ~; the individual, the variable —W.H.Whyte⟩: as **a :** an abstract number or a physically dimensional quantity having a fixed or approximately fixed value (as in a situation or throughout the operation concerned) and being sometimes universal and permanent (as the circular ratio π or the constant of gravitation) or sometimes characteristic of some substance or instrument (as the refractive index of an optical glass or the sensitivity of a galvanometer) **b :** a magnitude in mathematics that is assumed not to change its value in a certain discussion, process, or stage of investigation — opposed to *variable* **c :** a term in logic with an invariant denotation **:** a symbol with fixed designation (as a connective, quantifier, or parenthesis) — contrasted with *variable* **d :** a kind of plant or animal (as a species or variety) that is regularly present in a particular ecological community (as an association) **2 :** a secondary-school subject considered of such basic importance that it is required of all pupils

con·stant·an \ˈkänztənˌtan, -n(t)st-\ *n* -S [ISV ¹*constant* + *-an*] **:** an alloy of about 55 percent copper and 45 percent nickel that is used for electrical resistors and in thermocouples

con·stan·tia \kənzˈtanch(ē)ə, kȯnˈtän(t)sēə, -nˈst-\ *n* -S *often cap* [prob. fr. Afrik *constantia-* (in *constantiawyn* Constantia wine), fr. *Constantia,* former estate near Cape Town, Union of So. Africa] **:** a white or red dessert wine produced on vineyards near Wynberg, a suburb of Cape Town, Union of So. Africa

con·stan·tine \ˈkänztənˌtēn, -än(t)st-, -ˌtīn\ *adj, usu cap* [fr. *Constantine,* Algeria] **:** of or from the city of Constantine, Algeria **:** of the kind or style prevalent in Constantine

con·stan·tin·i·an \ˌkänztənˈtinēən, -än(t)st-, -ˈtēn-, -nyən\ *adj, usu cap* [*Constantine* I †A.D.337 Roman emperor + E *-ian*] **:** of, derived from, or resembling the Roman emperor Constantine the Great or his reign (A.D. 306–337)

constantinian monogram *n, usu cap C* **:** CHI-RHO

con·stan·ti·no·ple \ˌkänzˌtantᵊnˈōpəl, -änˌsta-, -antəˈnō- *sometimes* ≈ˈ≈≈ˌ≈≈ *or* kən-\ *adj, usu cap* [fr. *Constantinople* (now Istanbul, Turkey)] **:** CONSTANTINOPOLITAN

con·stan·ti·no·pol·i·tan \(ˈ)känzˌtantᵊnōˈpälətᵊn, kən-, -nˌsta-, -antə(ˌ)nō- *also* -lətən *or* -ləd·ən\ *adj, usu cap* [LL *constantinopolitanus,* fr. *Constantinopolis* Constantinople (now Istanbul, Turkey), capital of the Byzantine Empire until 1453 and of Turkey from 1453–1922 (after LL *metropolis: metropolitanus* metropolitan), fr. LGk *Kōnstantinoupolis,* fr. *Kōnstantinou* (gen. of *Kōnstantinos* Constantine I) + Gk *polis* city — more at POLICE] **:** of, relating to, or connected with Constantinople

constant-level watering \ˌ≈≈ˈ≈≈-\ *n* **:** a system of watering plants in greenhouse beds or benches in which the water is maintained at a desired constant level usu. automatically

con·stant·ly *adv* **1** *archaic* **:** with loyalty **:** FAITHFULLY **2** *obs* **:** with confidence **:** FIRMLY **3 :** without variation, deviation, or change **:** EVER, ALWAYS ⟨to be ~ on the alert⟩ **4 :** with regular occurrence **:** INCESSANTLY ⟨write letters ~⟩

con·stant·ness *n* -ES **:** the quality or state of being constant **:** CONSTANCY

constant of aberration : the maximum apparent displacement of a star from its mean position due to the aberration of light corresponding to the earth's orbital motion and having a value of about 20.5 seconds of angle

constant of gravitation : the acceleration produced by the attraction of a unit of mass at unit distance and having a value of about 6.670×10^{-8} in cgs units

constant of nutation : the amplitude of the celestial-latitude component of the precessional nutation of the earth's axis that is equal to about 9.2 seconds of arc — compare NUTATION 2

constant of precession : the average annual rate of the precession of the equinoxes along the ecliptic amounting to about 50.26 seconds of arc

constant white *n* **:** BLANC FIXE

con·stat \ˈkänˌstat, -nˌst-\ *n* -S [L, it is certain, 3d pers. sing. pres. indic. of *constare* to be certain, stand firm — more at CONSTANT] **:** a legal certificate showing what appears upon record touching a matter in question

con·sta·ta·tion \ˌkänztəˈtāshən, -n(t)stə-\ *n* -S [F, fr. *constater* + *-ation*] **:** basic assumption **:** ASSERTION ⟨the mere ~ that a century and a half ago the family counted for much more than it does now —F.R.Leavis⟩

con·state \kənzˈtāt, -nˈst-, *usu* -ād·+V\ *vt* -ED/-ING/-S [F *constater,* fr. L *constat* it is certain] **:** to assert positively

¹con·stel·late \ˈkänztəˌlāt, -än(t)st-, *usu* -ād·+V\ *vb* -ED/-ING/-S [LL *constellatus* studded with stars, fr. L *com-* + *stellatus* set with stars, fr. *stella* star + *-atus* -ate — more at STAR] *vt* **1 a** *obs* **:** to affect with stellar influence **b** *astrology* **:** to fashion or predestine esp. by an especial conjunction of planets ⟨an individual *constellated* to be great⟩ **2 :** to unite in a cluster esp. with a radiance or display suggestive of a constellation ⟨manifestations . . . *constellated* around a single motif —A.L.Kroeber⟩ ⟨it is not strange that the 19th century is *constellated* with demonic figures —Henry Miller⟩ **3 :** to set or adorn with or as if with stars or constellations **:** STUD ⟨hills . . . *constellated* and twinkling with street lamps —J.B. Priestley⟩ **~** *vi* **:** to cluster like stars in a constellation ⟨all writers of note ~ there in the summer⟩ ⟨the tendency of symbolisms to ~ in accordance with an unconscious or intuitive logic —Edward Sapir⟩

²constellate \-,lāt, -lət\ *adj* [LL *constellatus*] **:** CONSTELLATED

con·stel·la·tion \,känztə'lāshən, -än(t)st-\ *n* -s [ME *constellacioun*, fr. MF *constellation*, fr. LL *constellation-, constellatio*, fr. *constellatus* + L *-ion-, -io* -ion] **1 a :** the configuration of stars esp. at one's birth that in astrology determines one's fate or status in life ⟨to be born under the ~ that makes a man rich⟩ — compare HOROSCOPE **b** *obs* **:** character or constitution as determined by or as if by the stars ⟨a person of whatever profession or ~⟩ **2 :** any one of 88 arbitrary configurations of stars or an area of the celestial sphere covering one of these configurations and numbering 48 according to the 2d century A.D. catalogue of Ptolemy, each named after a mythological personage, animal, or inanimate object, the remaining 40 having been added later to fill in areas of the sky left vacant by the ancients (as in the region around the south celestial pole invisible to the Mediterranean world) **3 :** an assemblage, collection, or gathering esp. of a splendid, radiant, or excellent sort ⟨a ~ of atomic scientists⟩ ⟨the carpet was scattered with a ~ of gardenias —P.L.Fermor⟩ **4 a :** PATTERN, ARRANGEMENT ⟨the state's interpretation of welfare is set in the ~ of security, order, justice, and freedom —Asher Achinstein⟩ **b :** a determining, differentiating, or individualizing pattern or grouping ⟨the unique and flavorful ~ of qualities, the emphases and shadings of the universal human that make a Frenchman —Robert Redfield⟩ **c** (1) **:** a group of consciously related esp. emotionally significant ideas (2) **:** an assemblage or configuration of stimulus conditions or factors affecting behavior and personality development ⟨the way in which family ~ and handling of punishment influenced this particular boy —S.B.Sarason⟩ (3) **:** an assemblage or configuration of behavioral or personality traits or characteristics

con·stel·la·tion·al \¦≈≈¦lāshən³l, -shnəl\ *adj* **:** of or having to do with a constellation

con·stel·la·to·ry \kənz'telə,tōrē, (')känz¦t-, kən'st-, (')kän¦st-, -tȯr-, -ri\ *adj* [*constellation* + *-ory*] **:** of, having to do with, or suggestive of a constellation ⟨~ magnitude⟩ ⟨~ brilliance⟩

con·ster \'kän(t)stə(r)\ *vb* -ED/-ING/-S [by alter.] *archaic* **:** ¹CONSTRUE

con·ster·nate \'känztə(r),nāt, -än(t)st-, *usu* -ād·+V\ *vt* -ED/-ING/-S [L *consternatus*, past part. of *consternare*] **:** to fill with dismay or astonishment ⟨the colonel was not only embarrassed, he was *consternated* —Hervey Allen⟩

con·ster·na·tion \,känztə(r)'nāshən, -än(t)st-\ *n* -s [F or L; F, fr. L *consternation-, consternatio*, fr. *consternatus* (past part. of *consternare* to overcome, confuse, perplex, fr. *com-* + *-sternare*, akin to ON *stara* to stare) + *-ion-, -io* -ion — more at STARE] **:** amazement or dismay that hinders or throws into confusion **:** confused and distressing excitement **:** grievous exasperation or distraction ⟨to flee in ~⟩ ⟨the two, father and son, stared at each other in ~, and neither knew what to do —Pearl Buck⟩ **syn** see FEAR

con·sti·pate \'känztə,pāt, -än(t)st-, *usu* -ād·+V\ *vb* -ED/-ING/-S [L *constipatus*, past part. of *constipare*, fr. *com-* + *stipare* to press together — more at STIFF] *vt* **1** *obs* **:** to make firm or hard (as by thickening, pressing together, condensing) **2** [ML *constipatus*, fr. L] **:** to make costive **:** cause constipation in **3 :** to make immobile, inactive, or dull **:** STULTIFY ⟨Paris quickens the mind, New York energizes the character, London ~s the soul —Cyril Connolly⟩ **~** *vi* **:** to make evacuation of the feces difficult or infrequent

con·sti·pa·tion \,känztə'pāshən, -än(t)st-\ *n* -s [LL *constipation-, constipatio*, fr. L *constipatus* + *-ion-, -io* -ion] **1** *obs* **a :** COMPRESSION, CONDENSATION **b :** CONTRACTION, CONSTRICTION **2** [MF or ML; MF, fr. ML *constipation-, constipatio*, fr. LL] **a :** abnormally delayed or infrequent passage of dry hardened feces associated with varying degrees of stasis of the lower bowel **b :** STULTIFICATION ⟨~ of intellectual freedom⟩

con·stit·u·en·cy \kənz'tichəwənsē, -n'st-, -si\ *n* -ES **1 a :** a body of citizens or voters that is entitled to elect a representative to a legislative or other public body **b :** the residents in an electoral district **c :** an electoral district **2 :** a group or body that patronizes, supports, or offers representation **:** body of supporters ⟨there was no ~ of millionaires to back him⟩ **3 :** the constituents of a linguistic construction or a compound

TABLE OF CONSTELLATIONS

NAME AND PRONUNCIATION	[3]GENITIVE AND PRONUNCIATION	MEANING	DECLINATION
[1]Andromeda \an'drämədə\	Andromedae \-,dē\	*Andromeda, the Chained Lady*	40° N
Antlia (Antlia Pneumatica) \'antlēən(y)ü'mad·ikə\	Antliae \-ē,ē\	*Pump (Air Pump)*	35° S
Apus \'āpəs\	Apodis \'apədəs\	*Bird of Paradise*	75° S
[1]Aquarius \ə'kwa(a)rēəs\	Aquarii \-rē,ī\	*Water Carrier*	10° S
[1]Aquila \'akwələ\	Aquilae \-,lē\	*Eagle*	5° N
[1]Ara \'a(a)rə\	Arae \'a(a),rē\	*Altar*	55° S
[1]Aries \'a(a)rē,ēz, 'er-,'ār, -rēz\	Arietis \ə'rīəd·əs\	*Ram*	20° N
[1]Auriga \ȯ'rīgə\	Aurigae \-ī,jē\	*Charioteer*	40° N
[1]Boötes \bō'ōd·ēz\	Boötis \-'ōd·əs\	*Herdsman*	30° N
Caelum (Caela Sculptoris) \'sēləm (-lə ,skəlp'tōrəs)\	Caeli \-,lī\	*Graving Tool*	40° S
Camelopardalis \kə,melə'pärd³ləs, ,kamə(,)lō'-\	Camelopardalis \"\	*Giraffe*	70° N
[1]Cancer \'kan(t)sər\	Cancri \'kaŋ,krī\	*Crab*	20° N
Canes Venatici \'kā,nēzvə'nad·ə,sī\	Canum Venaticorum \'kānəmvə,nad·ə-'kōrəm\	*Hunting Dogs*	40° N
[1]Canis Major \¦kānə'smājər, -¦a-\	Canis Majoris \-,smə'jōrəs\	*Larger Dog*	20° S
[1]Canis Minor \-'smīnər\	Canis Minoris \-,smī'nōrəs\	*Lesser Dog*	5° N
[1]Capricornus \¦kaprə¦kȯrnəs\	Capricorni \,≈≈'≈,nī\	*Horned Goat*	20° S
[2]Carina \kə'rīnə\	Carinae \-,nē\	*Keel*	60° S
[1]Cassiopeia \,kasēə'pē(y)ə\	Cassiopeiae \-pē,(y)ē, -,(y)ī\	*Cassiopeia, the Lady in the Chair*	60° N
[1]Centaurus \sen'tȯrəs\	Centauri \-,rī\	*Centaur*	45° S
[1]Cepheus \'sē,fyüs, -,fēəs\	Cephei \-,fē,ī\	*Cepheus, the Monarch*	70° N
[1]Cetus \'sēd·əs\	Ceti \-ē,tī\	*Whale*	5° S
Chamaeleon \kə'mēlyən, -lēən\	Chamaeleontis \-,mēlē'äntəs\	*Chameleon*	80° S
Circinus \'sərs³nəs\	Circini \-n,ī\	*Pair of Compasses*	65° S
Columba (Columba Noae) \kə'ləmbə'nō,ē\	Columbae \-m,bē\	*Dove (Noah's Dove)*	35° S
Coma Berenices \'kōmə,berə'nī(,)sēz\	Comae Berenices \-(,)mē,b-\	*Berenice's Hair*	25° N
[1]Corona Australis \kə'rōnə,ȯ'strāləs, -al-\	Coronae Australis \-(,)nē,ȯ-\	*Southern Crown*	40° S
[1]Corona Borealis \-,bōrē'aləs, -'ā-\	Coronae Borealis \-(,)nē,b-\	*Northern Crown*	30° N
[1]Corvus \'kȯrvəs\	Corvi \-,vī\	*Crow*	20° S
[1]Crater \'krād·ər\	Crateris \krā'ti(ə)rəs\	*Cup*	15° S
Crux \'krəks\	Crucis \'krüsəs\	*Southern Cross*	60° S
[1]Cygnus \'signəs\	Cygni \-,nī\	*Swan*	40° N
[1]Delphinus \del'fīnəs\	Delphini \-,nī\	*Dolphin*	15° N
Dorado \də'rä(,)dō\	Doradus \-,dəs\	*Dorado [a fish]*	60° S
[1]Draco \'drā,kō\	Draconis \drā'kōnəs\	*Dragon*	65° N
[1]Equuleus \e'kwülēəs\	Equulei \-lē,ī\	*Colt*	5° N
[1]Eridanus \ə'rid³nəs\	Eridani \-n,ī\	*Eridanus, the River Po*	20° S
Fornax \'fȯr,naks\	Fornacis \fȯr'nasəs, -'ā-\	*Furnace*	30° S
[1]Gemini \'jemə,nī\	Geminorum \,jemə'nōrəm\	*Twins*	25° N
Grus \'grəs, -üs\	Gruis \'grüəs\	*Crane*	45° S
[1]Hercules \'hərkyə,lēz\	Herculis \-yələs\	*Hercules*	30° N
Horologium \,hȯrə'lōjēəm\	Horologii \-ōjē,ī\	*Clock*	50° S
[1]Hydra \'hīdrə\	Hydrae \-,drē\	*Water Monster*	10° S
Hydrus \'hīdrəs\	Hydri \-,drī\	*Water Snake*	70° S
Indus \'indəs\	Indi \-,dī\	*Indian*	55° S
Lacerta \lə'sərd·ə\	Lacertae \-r,tē\	*Lizard*	45° N
[1]Leo \'lē(,)ō\	Leonis \lē'ōnəs\	*Lion*	15° N
Leo Minor \-'mīnər\	Leonis Minoris \-nə,smī'nōrəs\	*Smaller Lion*	25° N
[1]Lepus \'lēpəs, -'e-\	Leporis \'lepərəs\	*Hare*	20° S
[1]Libra \'lībrə\	Librae \-,brē\	*Balance*	15° S
[1]Lupus \'lüpəs\	Lupi \-,pī\	*Wolf*	40° S
Lynx \'liŋks\	Lyncis \'linsəs\	*Lynx*	45° N
[1]Lyra \'līrə\	Lyrae \-,rē\	*Lyre*	35° N
Mensa (Mons Mensae) \'men(t)sə ('mänz'men,sē)\	Mensae \'men,sē\	*Table (Table Mountain)*	75° S
Microscopium \,mīkrə'skōpēəm\	Microscopii \-pē,ī\	*Microscope*	35° S
Monoceros \mə'näsərəs\	Monocerotis \-,näsə'rōd·əs\	*Unicorn*	5° S
Musca \'məskə\	Muscae \'mə,sē\	*Fly*	70° S
Norma \'nȯrmə\	Normae \-,mē\	*Square (and Rule)*	50° S
Octans \'äk,tanz\	Octantis \äk'tantəs\	*Octant*	85° S
[1]Ophiuchus \,äfē'(y)ükəs\	Ophiuchi \-ü,kī\	*Serpent Holder*	0°
[1]Orion \ə'rīən\	Orionis \ə'rīənəs, ,ȯrē'ōnəs\	*Orion, the Hunter*	0°
Pavo \'pā(,)vō, -'ä-\	Pavonis \pə'vōnəs\	*Peacock*	65° S
[1]Pegasus \'pegəsəs\	Pegasi \-ə,sī\	*Pegasus, the Winged Horse*	20° N
[1]Perseus \'pər,süs\	Persei \-rsē,ī\	*Perseus, the Rescuer or Champion*	45° N
Phoenix \'fēniks\	Phoenicis \fē'nīsəs\	*Phoenix*	50° S
Pictor \'piktər\	Pictoris \pik'tōrəs\	*Painter's Easel*	55° S
[1]Pisces \'pi,sēz\	Piscium \'pis(h)ēəm\	*Fishes*	10° N
[1]Piscis Austrinus \'pisə,sȯ'strīnəs\	Piscis Austrini \-,nī\	*Southern Fish*	30° S
[2]Puppis \'pəpəs\	Puppis \"\	*Stern*	30° S
[2]Pyxis \'piksəs\	Pyxidis \-ksədəs\	*Mariner's Compass*	30° S
Reticulum \rə'tikyələm\	Reticuli \-,lī\	*Net*	60° S
[1]Sagitta \sə'jid·ə\	Sagittae \-i,tē\	*Arrow*	20° N
[1]Sagittarius \,sajə'terēəs\	Sagittarii \-rē,ī\	*Archer*	30° S
[1]Scorpius \'skȯrpēəs\	Scorpii \-pē,ī\	*Scorpion*	30° S
Sculptor \'skəlptər\	Sculptoris \,skəlp'tōrəs\	*Sculptor's Workshop*	30° S
Scutum \'sk(y)üd·əm\	Scuti \-ü,tī\	*Shield*	10° S
[1]Serpens \'sərpənz, -,penz\	Serpentis \(,)sər'pentəs\	*Serpent*	0°
Sextans \'sek,stanz\	Sextantis \sek'stantəs\	*Sextant*	5° S
[1]Taurus \'tȯrəs\	Tauri \-,rī\	*Bull*	20° N
Telescopium \,telə'skōpēəm\	Telescopii \-pē,ī\	*Telescope*	50° S
[1]Triangulum \trī'aŋgyələm\	Trianguli \-,lī\	*Triangle*	30° N
Triangulum Australe \-,ȯ'strā(,)lē\	Trianguli Australis \-,lī,ȯ'strāləs\	*Southern Triangle*	65° S
Tucana \tü'kanə, -'ä-\	Tucanae \-,nē\	*Toucan*	65° S
[1]Ursa Major \'ərsə'mājər\	Ursae Majoris \'ər,sēmə'jōrəs\	*Larger Bear*	50° N
[1]Ursa Minor \'ərsə'mīnər\	Ursae Minoris \'ər,sē,mī'nōrəs\	*Smaller Bear*	80° N
[2]Vela \'vēlə\	Velorum \vē'lōrəm\	*Sails*	45° S
[1]Virgo \'vər,gō\	Virginis \-rjənəs\	*Virgin*	0°
Volans (Piscis Volans) \'pisəs'vō,lanz\	Volantis \vō'lantəs\	*Flying Fish*	70° S
Vulpecula \,vəl'pekyələ\	Vulpeculae \-,lē\	*Little Fox*	25° N

[1]One of the 48 constellations of Ptolemy. [2]One of the subdivisions of the Ptolemaic constellation Argo or Argo Navis \¦är(,)gō-'nāvəs\ the Ship Argo, which included Carina, Puppis, Pyxis, and Vela. [3]The genitive is used in referring to the individual stars of a constellation (as α Aurigae for the star Capella).

¹con·stit·u·ent \kənz'tichəwənt, -n'st-\ *n* -s [F *constituant*, fr. *constituant*, adj.] **1 :** a person who appoints another to act for him as attorney-in-fact **:** PRINCIPAL **2 a :** one of a group who elects another to represent him in a legislative assembly or to a public office **b :** a citizen or resident of a district represented by one so elected **3 a :** a thing, person, or organism that along with others serves in making up a complete whole or unit **:** an essential part **:** COMPONENT ⟨matter and radiation, the two ~s of the physical universe —James Jeans⟩ ⟨society is held together by the mutual needs of its ~s —Abram Kardiner⟩ **b** (1) **:** an element or radical that is part of a chemical compound (as hydrogen or oxygen in water) (2) **:** a phase of a chemical system — compare COMPONENT 3 **c :** a part of an alloy or metallic mixture that can be distinguished microscopically **d :** one of two or more linguistic forms that enter into a construction or a compound and are either immediate and normally two in number (as *he* and *writes for the stage* in the construction "he writes for the stage") or ultimate and of any number (as *he, write, -s, for, the,* and *stage* in the same construction) **syn** see ELEMENT

²constituent \"\ *adj* [F or L; F *constituant*, fr. L *constituent-, constituens*, pres. part. of *constituere* to constitute — more at CONSTITUTE] **1 :** serving to form, compose, or make up a unit or whole **:** COMPONENT ⟨molecules and their ~ atoms —A.C.Morrison⟩ ⟨within the broad confines of science there are many ~ sciences —T.H.Savory⟩ **2 a :** having power to elect or appoint ⟨a ~ body⟩ **b :** having the right or power to create a government or frame or amend a constitution ⟨a ~ group⟩ ⟨a ~ assembly⟩ — **con·stit·u·ent·ly** *adv*

constituta *pl of* CONSTITUTUM

con·sti·tu·ta pe·cu·nia \¦känztə¦tüd·əpə¦k(y)ünēə, -än(t)stə¦-\ *n* [LL, lit., money agreed upon] **:** PACTUM DE CONSTITUTO

¹con·sti·tute \'känztə,t(y)üt, -än(t)stə,t(y)-, *rapid* -än(t)sə-,t(y)- *or* -än(t),st(y)-, *usu* -üd·+V\ *vt* -ED/-ING/-S [L *constitutus*, past part. of *constituere* to constitute, fr. *com-* + *-stituere* (fr. *statuere* to set, place) — more at STATUTE] **1 a :** to appoint to an office, function, or dignity ⟨legal authority ~s all magistrates⟩ ⟨*constituted* authorities⟩ **b :** to make (a person or thing) something ⟨he *constituted* himself their guide⟩ ⟨I shall ~ you skipper and pilot of the craft —William Black⟩ **2** *archaic* **:** to set or station in a situation, state, character **:** PLACE ⟨the fiery star of Mars *constituted* in the midst of heaven —John Gaule⟩ **3 :** to set up **:** ESTABLISH: as **a :** to put into force (as a law) **:** ENACT ⟨such regulations as are *constituted* by the government⟩ **b :** FOUND ⟨~ a social club for immigrants⟩ **:** formally establish ⟨~ a provisional government⟩ ⟨in 1833 Ceylon had been *constituted* a British crown colony —*Current Biog.*⟩ **c :** to give due or lawful form to (as a proceeding or document) **:** legally process ⟨an agreement *constituted* by writing⟩ **d :** to cause (as a trait) to become fixed **:** DETERMINE **4 :** to make up (the element or elements of which a thing, person, or idea is made up) **:** FORM, COMPOSE ⟨52 cards ~ a pack⟩ ⟨vivacity ~s her greatest charm⟩

²constitute \"\ *adj* [L *constitutus*] **1** *archaic* **:** CONSTITUTED, ESTABLISHED **2** *archaic* **:** FORMED

³constitute \"\ *n* -s [¹*constitute*] **:** a linguistic form with more than one immediate constituent **:** CONSTRUCTION, COMPOUND

con·sti·tu·tion \,känztə't(y)üshən, -än(t)stə't(y)-, *rapid* -än(t)sə't(y)- *or* -än(t)'st(y)-; '≈≈'≈≈\ *n* -s [ME *constitucioun*, fr. MF *constitution*, fr. L *constitution-, constitutio*, fr. *constitutus* + *-ion-, -io* -ion] **1 a** (1) **:** an authoritative ordinance or enactment (2) **:** an enactment of a Roman emperor **b :** an established law or settled custom **:** ORDINANCE ⟨the sacred ~s of the church⟩ **2 :** the act of establishing, making, or setting up ⟨before the ~ of civil laws⟩ **3 a :** the whole physical makeup of the individual comprising the inherited qualities as modified by the environment **:** PHYSIQUE — compare DIATHESIS **b** *archaic* **:** the aggregate of an individual's mental powers or qualities **:** TEMPERAMENT, DISPOSITION **4 :** the mode or manner in which something is constituted, constructed, or organized **:** the structure, composition, physical makeup, or nature of anything specif. as determined by the interrelation of its atoms, elements, or parts ⟨the ~ of the sun⟩ ⟨the ~ of society⟩; *specif* **:** the structure of a compound as determined by the kind, number, and arrangement of atoms in its molecule **5 :** the mode in which a state or society is organized; *esp* **:** the manner in which sovereign power is distributed ⟨democratic ~⟩ **6 a :** the system or body of fundamental rules and principles of a nation, state, or body politic that determines the powers and duties of the government and guarantees certain rights to the people — see FLEXIBLE CONSTITUTION, RIGID CONSTITUTION, UNWRITTEN CONSTITUTION **b :** the written instrument embodying these fundamental rules and constituting the organic law of the land **c :** the basic rules governing a social or professional organization **syn** see PHYSIQUE

¹con·sti·tu·tion·al \¦känztə¦t(y)üshən³l, -än(t)stə¦t(y)-, *rapid* -än(t)sə¦t(y)- *or* -än(t)¦st(y)-; -shnəl\ *adj* [*constitution* + *-al*] **1 a :** having to do with, inherent in, or affecting the constitution or structure of body or mind ⟨~ symptoms⟩ ⟨~ strength⟩ **b :** of benefit to or intended to benefit one's physical or mental makeup ⟨a ~ stroll⟩ **2 :** having to do with, belonging to, or forming the composition or makeup of something **:** ESSENTIAL ⟨the very ~ part of a system⟩ **3 :** in accordance with or authorized by the constitution of a state or a society ⟨~ reforms⟩ ⟨~ limitations⟩ ⟨~ rights⟩ **4 :** regulated by, dependent on, or ruling according to a constitution or constitutional forms limiting arbitrary or absolute power ⟨~ monarchy⟩ ⟨~ government⟩ ⟨~ democracy⟩ **5 :** of, relating to, or dealing with a constitution ⟨~ crisis⟩ ⟨~ theory⟩ or its interpretation, formulation, or amendment ⟨~ assembly⟩ ⟨~ court⟩ **6 :** loyal to or supporting the existing constitution or established form of government ⟨they organized a ~ fact on⟩

²constitutional \"\ *n* -s **:** a walk or other exercise taken for one's health

constitutional formula *n* **:** STRUCTURAL FORMULA

con·sti·tu·tion·al·ism \-n³l,izəm, -nə,liz·m\ *n* -s **1 :** the doctrine or system of government in which the governing power is limited by enforceable rules of law and concentration of power is prevented by various checks and balances so that the basic rights of individuals and groups are protected **2 :** adherence to the principles of constitutionalism

con·sti·tu·tion·al·ist \-,ləst\ *n* -s **1 :** one who studies or writes on constitutionalism **2 :** an adherent or advocate of constitutionalism or of some particular constitution; *specif, usu cap* **:** an advocate of the U.S. Constitution about the time of its adoption

con·sti·tu·tion·al·i·ty \¦känztə,t(y)üshə'naləd·ē, -än(t)stə-,t(y)-, *rapid* -än(t)sə,t(y)- *or* -än(t),st(y)-; -ətē, -i\ *n* -ES **1 :** the quality or state of being constitutional ⟨with the restoration of ~, a distinguished lawyer . . . came to power —Rodrigo Niró⟩ **2 :** the quality or state of being consistent with the provisions of a constitution (as the U.S. Constitution)

con·sti·tu·tion·al·ize \,≈(≈)'≈shən³l,īz, -shnə,līz\ *vt* -ED/-ING/-S **:** to provide with a constitution or organize along constitutional principles ⟨~ the government of the church on the lines of a medieval system of representation —G.H. Sabine⟩ ⟨attempts to ~ Spain —John Gunther⟩

constitutional law *n* **:** the area of law that has to do with the subject matter and with the interpretation and construction of constitutions or that deals with the nature and organization of government, its sovereign powers and their distribution and mode of exercise, and the relation of the sovereign to the subjects or citizens; *specif* **:** the constitution of a particular state with the judicial constructions and interpretations that it has received

con·sti·tu·tion·al·ly \¦≈(≈)¦≈shən³lē, -shnəlē, -li\ *adv* **1 a :** with respect to mental or spiritual makeup ⟨~ unable to grasp subtleties⟩ **b :** with respect to bodily makeup ⟨~ a weakling⟩ **2 :** in basic or essential structure or composition **:** FUNDAMENTALLY ⟨despite repeated heatings the material remained ~ the same⟩ **3 :** in accordance with the constitution or fundamental law **:** LEGALLY ⟨was not ~ eligible to fill an office⟩

constitutional psychology *n* **:** the systematic attempt to

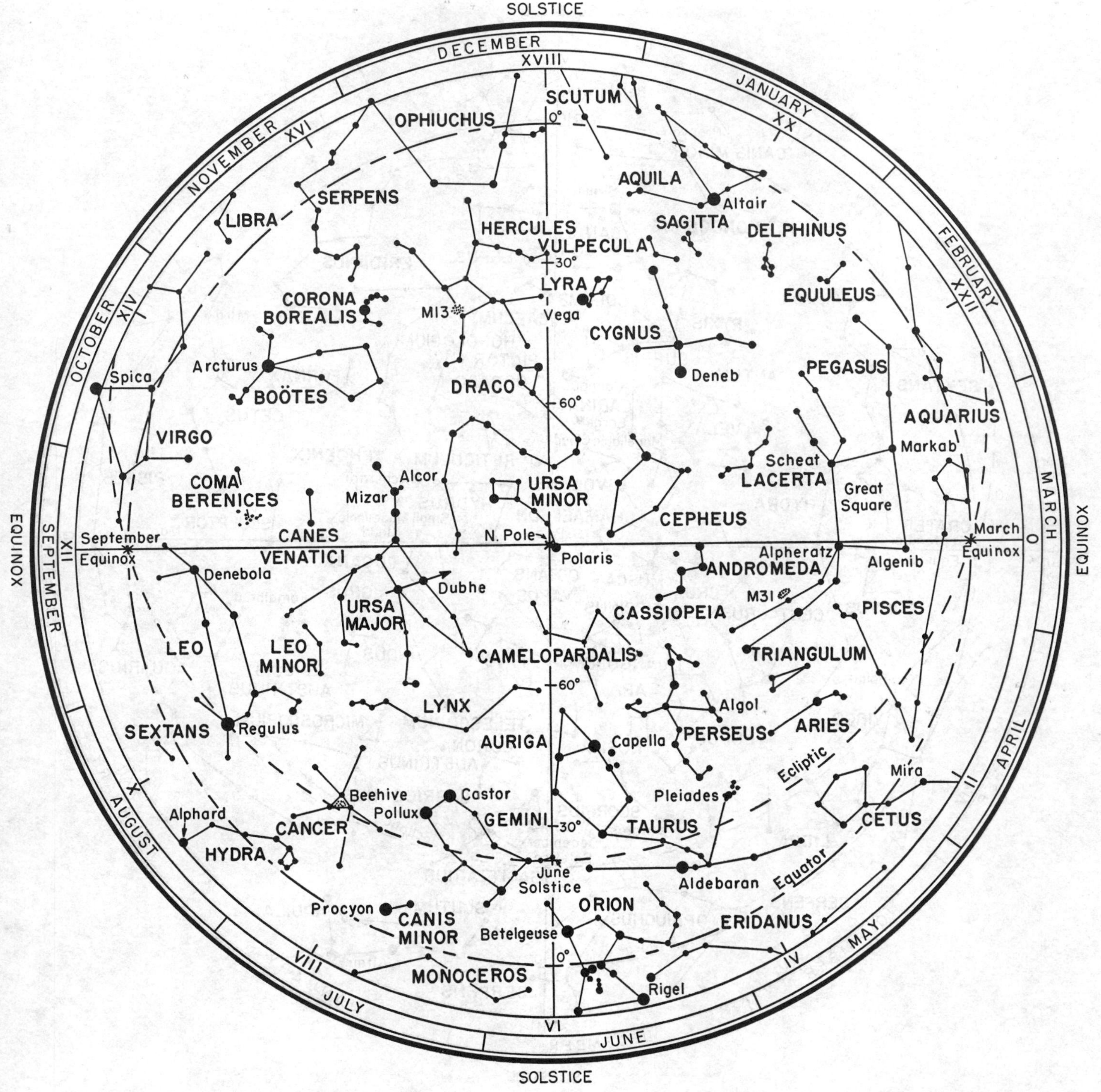
SOLSTICE
DECEMBER
JANUARY
FEBRUARY
MARCH
APRIL
MAY
JUNE
JULY
AUGUST
SEPTEMBER
OCTOBER
NOVEMBER
EQUINOX
EQUINOX
SOLSTICE
XVIII
XX
XXII
0
II
IV
VI
VIII
X
XII
XIV
XVI
SCUTUM
OPHIUCHUS
SERPENS
LIBRA
AQUILA
Altair
SAGITTA
DELPHINUS
HERCULES
VULPECULA
LYRA
Vega
M13
CORONA BOREALIS
EQUULEUS
CYGNUS
Deneb
Arcturus
BOÖTES
Spica
DRACO
PEGASUS
AQUARIUS
VIRGO
Markab
Scheat
LACERTA
Great Square
COMA BERENICES
Alcor
Mizar
URSA MINOR
CEPHEUS
September Equinox
CANES VENATICI
N. Pole
Polaris
Alpheratz
Algenib
March Equinox
Denebola
Dubhe
ANDROMEDA
URSA MAJOR
M31
CASSIOPEIA
PISCES
LEO
LEO MINOR
CAMELOPARDALIS
TRIANGULUM
LYNX
Algol
SEXTANS
Regulus
AURIGA
Capella
PERSEUS
ARIES
Ecliptic
Mira
Beehive
Castor
Pleiades
Alphard
CANCER
Pollux
GEMINI
TAURUS
CETUS
HYDRA
June Solstice
Aldebaran
Equator
Procyon
CANIS MINOR
ORION
Betelgeuse
ERIDANUS
MONOCEROS
Rigel
0°
30°
60°
60°
30°
0°

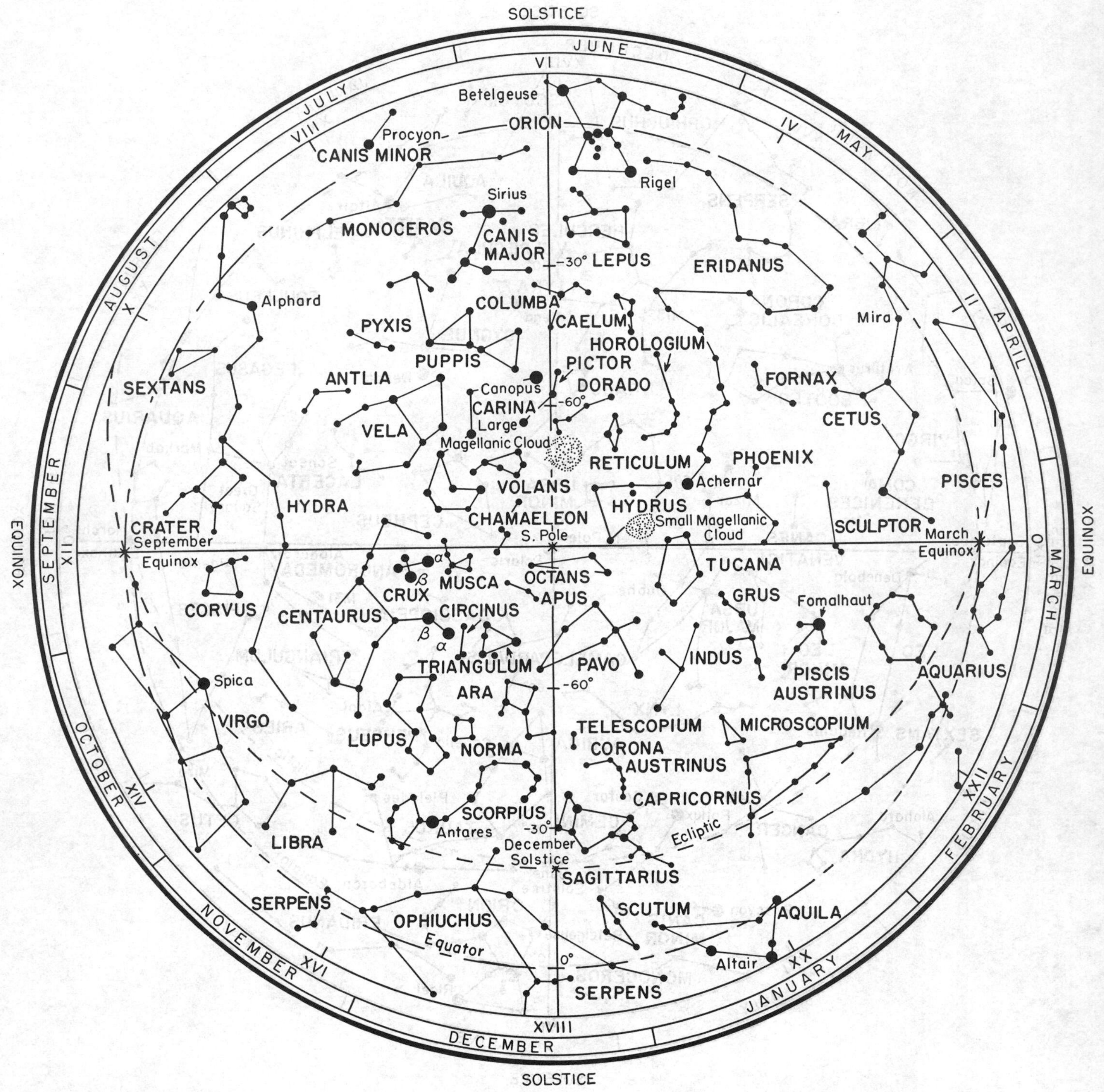
SOLSTICE
EQUINOX
EQUINOX
SOLSTICE
JUNE
MAY
APRIL
MARCH
FEBRUARY
JANUARY
DECEMBER
NOVEMBER
OCTOBER
SEPTEMBER
AUGUST
JULY
Betelgeuse
ORION
Procyon
CANIS MINOR
Rigel
Sirius
MONOCEROS
CANIS MAJOR
LEPUS
ERIDANUS
Alphard
COLUMBA
CAELUM
PYXIS
HOROLOGIUM
Mira
PUPPIS
PICTOR
SEXTANS
ANTLIA
Canopus
DORADO
FORNAX
CARINA
CETUS
Large Magellanic Cloud
VELA
RETICULUM
PHOENIX
VOLANS
Achernar
PISCES
HYDRA
HYDRUS
CHAMAELEON
Small Magellanic Cloud
CRATER
September Equinox
S. Pole
SCULPTOR
March Equinox
TUCANA
MUSCA
CRUX
OCTANS
CORVUS
APUS
GRUS
CENTAURUS
CIRCINUS
Fomalhaut
TRIANGULUM
INDUS
PAVO
Spica
ARA
PISCIS AUSTRINUS
AQUARIUS
VIRGO
TELESCOPIUM
MICROSCOPIUM
LUPUS
NORMA
CORONA AUSTRINUS
CAPRICORNUS
SCORPIUS
Antares
LIBRA
December Solstice
Ecliptic
SAGITTARIUS
SERPENS
SCUTUM
AQUILA
OPHIUCHUS
Equator
Altair
SERPENS
-30°
-60°
0°

account for such psychological variables as temperament and character in terms of bodily shape and organic function
constitutional type *n* **:** bodily habitus or makeup — used esp. in coordinating bodily proportions with factors concerned in normal or abnormal physiologic or psychologic functions; compare ECTOMORPHIC, ENDOMORPHIC, MESOMORPHIC
constitutional water *n* **:** the water contained in a mineral after its temperature has been raised to 110° C and its hygrometric water driven off
con·sti·tu·tion·er \ˌ=(=)ˈ=sh(ə)nə(r)\ *n* -s **:** a framer or supporter of a constitution
con·sti·tu·tion·ist \-nəst\ *n* -s **:** CONSTITUTIONALIST
constitution mirror *n, often cap C* **:** a mirror of Sheraton design usu. having a row of balls under the top cornice, side pilasters, and a painted panel above the looking glass — called also *tabernacle mirror*
con·sti·tu·tive \ˈkänztəˌt(y)üd·iv, -än(t)stəˌt(y)-; kənzˈtichəd·iv, -ənˈsti-\ *adj* **1 a :** having the power to enact or establish **:** CONSTRUCTIVE **b :** having the character of stating a condition of the possibility of experience and hence of natural phenomena — used in Kantianism of the categories (as those of quantity and quality); contrasted with *regulative* **2 a :** that gives the essential quality or nature **:** ESSENTIAL ⟨a truly ~ ingredient⟩ **b :** tending or assisting to constitute **:** COESSENTIAL, COMPONENT ⟨reason as a ~ factor of faith —W.R.Inge⟩ ⟨for the part evidently is ~ of the whole —A.N.Whitehead⟩ **3 :** relating to or dependent on constitution (as the arrangement of atoms in a molecule) ⟨a ~ property⟩ — compare ADDITIVE 3, COLLIGATIVE — **con·sti·tu·tive·ly** \-d·əvlē\ *adv*
con·sti·tu·tum \ˌkänztəˈtüd·əm, -än(t)stəˈt-\ *n, pl* **consti·tu·ta** \-üd·ə\ [L, neut. of *constitutus*] *Roman law* **:** an agreement not made by formal stipulation whereby one promises to discharge on a given day at a fixed place an existing obligation of himself or another or to give security for its fulfillment
constitutum deb·i·ti \-ˈdebədˌī\ *n* [L, agreement concerning a debt] *Roman law* **:** a promise not founded on formal stipulation by one to pay an existing debt of himself or of another at a fixed time and place
constitutum pos·ses·so·ri·um \-ˌpōzəˈsōrēəm, -sȯr-\ *n* [L, agreement of possessors] *Roman law* **:** the change in intention of one having legal possession of real or personal property whereby he remains in control but transfers the legal possession to another
constl *abbr* constitutional
constr *abbr* construction
con·strain \kənˈstrān, kənˈstr-\ *vb* -ED/-ING/-S [ME *constrainen*, fr. MF *constraindre, constreindre*, fr. L *constringere*, fr. *com-* + *stringere* to draw tight — more at STRAIN] *vt* **1 a :** to force by stricture, restriction, or limitation imposed by nature, oneself, or circumstances and exigencies ⟨no one shall ~ me against my conscience to reveal my beliefs —Alexander Laing⟩ ⟨fate was ~*ing* him to follow Cleopatra —John Buchan⟩ **b :** to bring about by force or necessity ⟨the evidence ~*ing* belief in his guilt⟩ **c :** to restrict the motion of (a mechanical body) along a curve or surface to a particular mode ⟨a wheel is ~*ed* to rotate on its axle⟩ **2 a :** to force or force out in an artificial or unnatural way ⟨a ~*ed* polite laugh at his attempt at humor⟩ **b :** to check esp. from free or easy indication or expression **:** stifle the spontaneity of ⟨tensions ~*ed* their friendship because of the difference in station —*New Republic*⟩ **3 a :** to make fast by or as if by bonds or fetters **:** IMPRISON ⟨~*ed* to a dungeon⟩ ⟨the winds ~*ed* by magic⟩ **b :** to compress tightly **:** bind narrowly **:** SQUEEZE ⟨his clothes . . . ~ him so much that he seems rather their prisoner than their proprietor —Earl of Chesterfield⟩ **c** *obs* **:** CONSTRICT, CONSTRINGE **d :** to withhold or restrain by force **:** subject to restraint or repression ⟨~*ing* my mind not to wander from the task —Charles Dickens⟩ **e :** to cause to suffer from duress or affliction **:** DISTRESS, OPPRESS ⟨poverty constantly ~*ing* him⟩ ~ *vi* **:** to force or oblige one **:** COMPEL ⟨doctrine that enlightens but does not ~⟩ **syn** see FORCE
con·strained·ly \-n(ə)dlē\ *adv* **:** in a constrained manner
con·strained·ness \-nədnəs, -n(d)nəs\ *n* -ES **:** the quality or state of being constrained
con·strain·ing·ly *adv* **:** in a constraining manner
con·strain·ment \-nmənt\ *n* -s **:** CONSTRAINT
con·straint \kənˈstrānt, kənˈstr-\ *n* -s [ME, fr. MF *constreinte, constrainte*, fr. fem. of *constreint, constraint*, past part. of *constreindre, constraindre*] **1 a :** the act or action of using force or threat of force to prevent or condition an action **b :** the quality or state of being checked, restricted, or compelled to avoid or perform some action ⟨the individual spirit anxious for freedom from ~ —W.C.Brownell⟩ ⟨the ~ and monotony of a monastic life —Matthew Arnold⟩ **c :** a constraining agency **:** a constricting, regulating, or restricting force **:** CHECK ⟨a government works only by means of external ~*s*, generally by the fear of punishment —M.R.Cohen⟩ **d :** a restriction or limitation that contains a motion or other process (as the action of a cam in machinery) **2 :** compulsion by circumstances **:** the force of necessity **:** EXIGENCY ⟨obligation is felt by the good man, whereas the bad one feels ~ —Samuel Alexander⟩ **3 a :** control over one's own feelings, behavior, or actions that is exercised either to feign or repress ⟨a youth ill brought up, without the training which teaches us that we must put some ~ upon our feelings —Matthew Arnold⟩ **b :** the sense of being constrained, checked, or inhibited **:** EMBARRASSMENT ⟨a ~ between us as if we were strangers —J.P.Marquand⟩ **4 :** the restoring force on an ion in a crystal per unit displacement constituting a measure of the forces acting between ions in a lattice **syn** see FORCE
con·strict \kənˈstrikt, kənˈstr-\ *vb* -ED/-ING/-S [L *constrictus*, past part. of *constringere* — more at CONSTRAIN] *vt* **1 a :** to subject (as a body part) to compression **:** SQUEEZE **b :** to draw together or render narrower (as a mouth, orifice, channel, passage) **:** CONSTRINGE ⟨a hard rock obstruction which ~*ed* the valley's width from five miles to one —*Amer. Guide Series: Texas*⟩ **2 :** to stultify, stop, or cause to falter esp. under emotional or psychological duress or pressure of circumstances **:** CRAMP, INHIBIT ⟨personal stresses ~*ed* his poetry —A.C.Ward⟩ ⟨~ our generous impulses as a people —F.L. Allen⟩ ~ *vi* **1 :** to become constricted **2 :** to engage in constricting something **syn** see CONTRACT
constricted *adj* **1 a :** drawn together **:** NARROWED, CONTRACTED ⟨a ~ passageway⟩ **b** *bot* **:** contracted or compressed at regular intervals **:** MONILIFORM ⟨a ~ pod⟩ ⟨a ~ legume⟩ **2 :** CRAMPED, INHIBITED, NARROW ⟨a ~ view of life⟩
con·stric·tion \kənˈstrikshən, kənˈstr-\ *n* -s [F or L; F *constriction*, fr. L *constriction-, constrictio*, fr. *constrictus* + *-ion-, -io* -ion] **1 a :** the act of constricting **:** COMPRESSING ⟨the slow ~ of a snake coiled around its prey⟩ **b :** temporary or permanent contraction resulting in the narrowing of a channel (as a blood vessel or ureter) and impeding passage through it **c :** a bringing of one organ of speech close enough to another so that audible friction is produced when breath of sufficient intensity passes between **2 :** the quality or state of being constricted or contracted ⟨the ~ of international trade brought on by war⟩ **3 a :** something that blocks, impedes inhibits, or hinders ⟨the swollen river piled up refuse against every ~ along the bank⟩ **b :** narrowness, repression, or inhibition esp. in emotional or intellectual activity ⟨the excessive ~ of Puritanism —E.A.Mowrer⟩ ⟨the lifelong fighter against cruelty, bigotry, and ~ —C.H.Driver⟩ **4 :** a feeling or sensation of tightness, narrowness, or compression ⟨a ~ in the throat brought on by emotion⟩ **5 :** a part that is narrowed down, compressed, or contracted ⟨a ~ in a waterway⟩
constriction disease *n* **:** a disease of peach trees caused by a fungus of the genus *Phomopsis* and having symptoms similar to those of dieback (sense 1)
¹con·stric·tive \kənˈstriktiv, (ˈ)känz¦tr-, kənˈstr-, (ˈ)kän¦str-, -tēv *also* -təv\ *adj* [LL *constrictivus*, fr. L *constrictus* + *-ivus* -ive] **:** of, having to do with, or marked by constriction **:** tending to constrict **:** CONSTRINGENT
²constrictive \"\ *n* -s **:** FRICATIVE
con·stric·tor \kənˈstriktə(r), kənˈstr-\ *n* -s [NL, fr. L *constrictus* + *-or* — more at CONSTRICT] **:** one that constricts: as **a :** a muscle that contracts a cavity or orifice or compresses an organ **b :** a snake that kills its prey by rhythmically compressing it in coils of the body until the heartbeat and respiration are checked; *esp* **:** a member of the Boidae (as the boa constrictor or the anaconda)
constrictor knot *n* **:** a knot that consists of a half-knot under a single turn and is used to bind a cylindrical object and keep it from expanding

constrictor knot

con·stringe \kənˈztrinj, kənˈstr-\ *vt* -ED/-ING/-S [L *constringere* — more at CONSTRAIN] **1 :** to draw or press together **:** COMPRESS, CONSTRICT ⟨*constringed* between two forces⟩ **2 :** to cause to shrink ⟨cold ~*s* the pores⟩
con·strin·gent \kənˈztrinjənt, kənˈstr-\ *adj* [L *constringent-, constringens*, pres. part. of *constringere*] **:** causing constriction
constrn *abbr* construction
con·stru·a·ble \kənˈztrüəbəl, (ˈ)känz¦tr-, kənˈstr-, (ˈ)kän¦str-\ *adj* **:** that may be construed ⟨he made speeches ~ as promises that he would stay by the governorship —*Economist*⟩
con·stru·al \kənˈztrüəl, kənˈstr-\ *n* -s [*construe* + *-al*] **:** an interpreting (as of facts, data, a statement) **:** INTERPRETATION ⟨in this case genealogy and taxonomy rest partly on admitted facts but partly also on ~ of fact —A.L.Kroeber⟩
¹con·struct \kənˈztrəkt, (ˈ)känz¦tr-, kənˈstr-, (ˈ)kän¦str-\ *adj* [ME, fr. L *constructus*, past part. of *construere*] *archaic* **:** CONSTRUCTED
²construct \kənˈztrəkt, kənˈstr-\ *vt* -ED/-ING/-S [L *constructus*, past part. of *construere* to pile up, construct, fr. *com-* + *struere* to pile up, arrange, build — more at STRUCTURE] **1** *obs* **:** to construe or interpret (as a document, statement, expression) **2 :** to form, make, or create by combining parts or elements **:** BUILD, FABRICATE ⟨in ~*ing* the new freeway⟩ ⟨~ a new dormitory⟩ ⟨a well-*constructed* blend of unimpeachable teas —*New Yorker*⟩ ⟨an elegantly ~*ed* pair of dark green trousers —Mollie Panter-Downes⟩ **3 a :** to create by organizing ideas or concepts logically, coherently, or palpably ⟨a well-*constructed* argument⟩ ⟨Proust ~*s* a moral scheme out of phenomena whose moral values are always shifting —Edmund Wilson⟩ **b** (1) **:** to arrange (words or morphemes) in a meaningful combination (2) **:** to produce (as a sentence) by such arrangement of words or morphemes **4 a :** to draw (a geometrical figure) with suitable instruments so as to fulfill certain specified conditions ⟨~ a regular octagon with sides of given length⟩ **b :** to assemble separate and often disparate elements into (an abstract or nonrepresentational sculptural creation) **5 a :** to fabricate out of heterogeneous or discordant elements ⟨by India, they mean the political unit ~*ed* by English rule —D.W.Brogan⟩ ⟨a ~*ed* international language —Edward Sapir⟩ **b** (1) **:** FEIGN ⟨~*ed* dignity —John Buchan⟩ (2) **:** to infer in law **syn** see BUILD
³construct \ˈkänzˌtrəkt, ˈkänˌstr-\ *n* -s **1 :** something that is constructed esp. by a process of mental synthesis: as **a :** an object of thought constituted by the ordering or systematic uniting of experiential elements (as percepts and sense data) and of terms and relations **b :** an intellectual or logical construction **:** an operational concept; *also* **:** the result of such a construction or concept ⟨the ~*s* of science⟩ **2 a :** CONSTRUCT STATE **b :** a noun in the construct state
construct form *n* **:** CONSTRUCT STATE
con·struct·ible \kənˈztrəktəbəl, kənˈstr-\ *adj* [²*construct* + *-ible*] **:** capable of being constructed
con·struc·tion \kənˈztrəkshən, kənˈstr-\ *n* -s [ME *construccioun*, fr. MF *construction*, fr. L *construction-, constructio*, fr. *constructus* + *-ion-, -io* -ion] **1 a** *obs* **:** the act of construing (as in translating) **b :** the syntactical relation of a word, phrase, or clause to another **c :** the arrangement and connection of words in a sentence **:** syntactical arrangement **d :** any meaningful combination of linguistic forms — see MORPHOLOGICAL CONSTRUCTION, SYNTACTIC CONSTRUCTION **2 a :** the act of putting parts together to form a complete integrated object **:** FABRICATION ⟨during the ~ of the bridge⟩ **b** (1) **:** the form or manner in which something has been put together **:** DESIGN ⟨several ships of similar ~⟩ ⟨an analysis of the ~ of a time bomb⟩ (2) **:** the science or study of building or erection ⟨two years in college mastering ship ~⟩ **c :** something built or erected **:** STRUCTURE ⟨raw new ~*s* along a highway⟩ **3 a** (1) **:** the act of construing, interpreting, or explaining a declaration or fact **:** INTERPRETATION ⟨putting the worst ~ on things innocent —Rudyard Kipling⟩; *also* **:** the result of such an act (2) **:** the discovery and application of the meaning and intention of a statement or fact to a particular state of affairs ⟨the ~ put on a statute by a lawyer⟩ **b** (1) **:** the process of mentally uniting ideas or conceptions so as to form an organic or congruous object of thought (2) **:** a procedure in logic that utilizes contextual definition to construct or analyze an actual entity (as a table) or an inferred entity (as a subatomic particle) by translating statements containing the name of the entity into synonymous statements that eliminate it in favor of names of experientially more fundamental elements (as sense data); *also* **:** the resultant conception or mental or logical entity formed through such a procedure **4 a :** the act of constructing a geometrical figure; *also* **:** its result **b :** an abstract or nonrepresentational sculptural creation composed of separate and often disparate elements
con·struc·tion·al \kənˈztrəkshənᵊl, (ˈ)känz¦tr-, kənˈstr-, (ˈ)kän¦str-, -shnəl\ *adj* **1 :** deduced by or dependent on interpretation **2 :** STRUCTURAL ⟨~ details⟩ ⟨~ drawings⟩ **3 :** of or having to do with construction ⟨great ~ activity in the new nation's shipyards⟩ **4 :** of, resulting from, or being constructive geological processes (as those involving deposition and volcanic eruption) ⟨half of the area . . . is made up of ~ plains, as yet mostly undissected by erosion —*Amer. Guide Series: Nebr.*⟩ — **con·struc·tion·al·ly** \-nᵊlē, -nəlē, -li\ *adv*
construction bond *n* **:** a bond furnished by a contractor for the completion of his contract for construction work
con·struc·tion·ism \kənˈztrəkshəˌnizəm, kənˈstr-\ *n* -s **1 a :** advocacy of, reliance on, or employment of construction or constructive methods or processes **b :** a doctrine or theory based on construction **2 :** CONSTRUCTIVISM
con·struc·tion·ist \-sh(ə)nəst\ *n* -s **:** one who construes an instrument (as the U.S. Constitution) in a specific way ⟨the Soviet Union, abandoning its usual strict ~ position, urged a broad interpretation of what constitutes "states directly concerned" —C.D.Fuller⟩ ⟨the loose, or broad, ~*s* . . . contended that the national government had all powers which could by any reasonable interpretation be regarded as implied in the letter of the granted powers —F.A.Ogg & P.O.Ray⟩ — compare IMPLIED POWER
construction loan *n* **:** a loan secured by lien on property to finance a building project until completion and issuance of the long-term mortgage
construction paper *n* **:** colored paper suitable for crayon or ink drawings and watercolors and for making cutouts — compare ART PAPER
construction wrench *n* **:** an open-end wrench used by steel construction workers and having a long handle tapering to a blunt point that is used to hold matching holes (as for bolts or rivets) in alignment
con·struc·tive \kənˈztrəktiv, (ˈ)känz¦tr-, kənˈstr-, (ˈ)kän¦str-, -tēv *also* -təv\ *adj* [ML *constructivus*, fr. L *constructus* + *-ivus* -ive — more at CONSTRUCT] **1 :** derived from or depending on construction or interpretation **:** not directly expressed **:** INFERRED — often used in law of an act or condition assumed from other acts or conditions which are considered by inference or by public policy as amounting to or involving the act or condition assumed **2 :** of, having to do with, or promoting construction or creation ⟨~ philosophy⟩ ⟨~ work⟩ ⟨~ fingers⟩ **3 :** helpful toward further development **:** promoting improvement or advance ⟨~ criticism⟩ ⟨a ~ attitude⟩ ⟨a ~ program⟩ **4 :** CONSTRUCTIVIST
constructive catabolism *n* **:** catabolic activity that results in the production of new substances other than excretions (as nectar in flowering plants)
constructive contempt *n* **:** a contempt that is committed outside the presence of a court in session or of a judge acting in a judicial capacity and is either civil in character when in willful disobedience to a lawful order or decree made for the benefit of a party or criminal in character when tending to belittle or insult the court or judge or to interfere with or degrade or obstruct justice **:** an indirect or consequential contempt — compare CRIMINAL CONTEMPT, DIRECT CONTEMPT
constructive delivery *n* **:** a delivery not accompanied by an actual transfer of possession of the property delivered yet recognized as having been intended by the parties and as sufficient in law (as where one sells to another and agrees to hold the goods as agent for the buyer or where one delivers the documentary evidence of title to another)
constructive escape *n* **:** the obtaining by a prisoner of more liberty than the law allows
constructive eviction *n* **:** any act or acts legally equivalent to or producing the same result as an actual eviction
constructive fraud *n* **:** conduct that is based on acts, omissions, or concealments considered fraudulent and that gives one an advantage against another because such conduct though not actually fraudulent, dishonest, or deceitful demands redress for reasons of public policy (as because of some private or public trust or confidence or fiduciary relationship or because of undue influence) — see FRAUD, MISREPRESENTATION; compare DECEIT
con·struc·tive·ly *adv* **:** in a constructive manner
constructive malice *n* **:** IMPLIED MALICE
constructive mileage *n* **:** mileage that is in excess of actual distance covered by freight shipments or passengers and is used in the computation of rates and in giving allowance for expenses
con·struc·tive·ness *n* -ES **:** the quality or state of being constructive
constructive total loss *n* **:** a loss to insured property that is not total but is so great that repair would cost more than the value of the property
constructive trust *n* **:** a trust set up by a court to deal with property that has been acquired by fraud or by inequitable means; *specif* **:** a trust so formed to distribute property where distribution and enjoyment under the original transaction was against the principles of equity — compare EXPRESS TRUST, RESULTING TRUST
con·struc·tiv·ism \kənˈztrəktəˌvizəm, kənˈstr-\ *n* -s **:** attachment to or employment of construction or constructive methods or principles: as **a :** an anti-illusionistic style of stage setting that employs practical but nonrealistic arrangements of steps, platforms, and scaffolding for acting areas and that is held to form a mise en scène appropriate to an age of technological progress **b :** nonfigurative art (as that produced by the school founded in Moscow in 1920 as a secession from suprematism) concerned with formal organization of planes and expression of volume in terms of modern industrial materials (as glass and plastic)
¹con·struc·tiv·ist \kənˈztrəktəvəst, (ˈ)känz¦tr-, kənˈstr-, (ˈ)kän¦str-\ *adj* [*constructive* + *-ist*] **:** of or belonging to constructivism **:** adhering to or following a theory, method, or practice of constructivism
²constructivist \"\ *n* -s **:** an adherent or follower of a theory, method, or practice of constructivism
con·struc·tor \kənˈztrəktə(r), kənˈstr-\ *n* -s [²*construct* + *-or*] **1 :** one that constructs ⟨the company was a ~ of automatic elevators⟩ **2 :** a naval officer supervising the construction and repair of ships — called also *naval constructor* **3 :** one that creates a constructivist work of art
constructs *pres 3d sing of* CONSTRUCT, *pl of* CONSTRUCT
construct state \ˈkänzˌtrəkt-, ˈkänˌstr-\ *n* **:** a noun inflectional form typically designating what is possessed and accompanied by another noun designating the possessor (as Hebrew *ben* "son" in *ben Yishay* "son of Jesse") **:** the relation expressed by such a form — called also *construct form*; compare ABSOLUTE STATE, EMPHATIC STATE
con·struc·ture \kənˈztrəkchə(r), kənˈstr-, -kshə(r)\ *n* -s [²*construct* + *-ure*] *archaic* **:** STRUCTURE, CONSTRUCTION
¹con·strue \kənˈztrü, kənˈstrü *also* ˈkänzˌtrü *or* ˈkänˌstrü\ *vb* -ED/-ING/-S [ME *construen*, fr. LL *construere*, fr. L, to construct — more at CONSTRUCT] *vt* **1 a :** to analyze the arrangement and connection of words in (a sentence or part of a sentence) **:** translate piecemeal in such an order as to show the syntactical relation of the parts **b :** to combine idiomatically ⟨the verb *trust* is sometimes *construed* with *in*⟩ **2 a :** to put a construction on **:** discover and apply the meaning and intention of with reference to a particular state of affairs ⟨freedom of the press, literally *construed*, is the freedom to publish anything at all —F.L.Mott⟩ ⟨is it within judicial power, in *construing* the amendment, to abolish segregation —*N.Y. Times*⟩ **b :** to understand usu. in a particular way **:** explain the sense or intention of often to one's own satisfaction or according to or in conformity with a given set of circumstances ⟨~ an action as one pleases⟩ ⟨energy could be *construed* as something subsidiary to matter —A.N.Whitehead⟩ **3** *obs* **:** CONSTRUCT ~ *vi* **1 a :** to construe a sentence or part of a sentence esp. in connection with translating **b** *of a sentence or part of a sentence* **:** to be construable **2** *obs* **:** INFER — used with *of*
²construe \ˈkänzˌtrü, ˈkänˌstrü *sometimes* kənzˈtrü *or* kənˈstrü\ *n* -s **:** an act of construing esp. by piecemeal translation; *also* **:** the translated version resulting from such an act
constuprate *vt* -ED/-ING/-S [L *constupratus*, past part. of *constuprare*, fr. *com-* + *stuprare* to ravish] *obs* **:** RAVISH
con·substantial \ˌ¦kän+\ *adj* [LL *consubstantialis*, fr. L *com-* + *substantia* substance + *-alis* -al — more at SUBSTANCE] **:** of the same kind or nature **:** having the same substance or essence **:** COESSENTIAL ⟨Three Persons in one ~ Godhead —R.M.Benson⟩ — **con·substantially** \ˌ¦kän+\ *adv*
con·substantialism \ˌ¦kän+\ *n* -s **:** the doctrine of consubstantiality or of consubstantiation
con·substantiality \ˌ¦kän+\ *n* -ES [LL *consubstantialitas*, fr. *consubstantialis* consubstantial + L *-itas* -ity] **:** the quality or state of being consubstantial ⟨the ~ of the persons of the Trinity⟩
¹con·substantiate \ˌ¦kän+\ *vt* -ED/-ING/-S [NL *consubstantiatus*, past part. of *consubstantiare*, fr. L *com-* + NL *-substantiare* (fr. L *substantia* substance)] **:** to regard as or make to be united in one common substance or nature ⟨language *consubstantiated* with thought⟩
²con·sub·stan·ti·ate \ˌ¦kän(t)səbzˈtanch(ē)ət, -səbˈstan-, -ēˌāt\ *adj* [NL *consubstantiatus*] **:** CONSUBSTANTIAL
con·substantiation \ˌ¦kän+\ *n* -s [NL *consubstantiation-, consubstantiatio*, fr. *consubstantiatus* + L *-ion-, -io* -ion] **:** the theological doctrine of the actual substantial presence and combination of the body of Christ with the bread and wine of the sacrament of the Lord's Supper — distinguished from *transubstantiation*
con·sue·tude \ˈkän(t)swəˌt(y)üd\ *n* -s [ME, fr. L *consuetudo* — more at CUSTOM] **1 :** social usage **:** CUSTOM, HABIT ⟨the stain hath become engrained by . . . ~ —Sir Walter Scott⟩ **2 :** custom or a custom imbued with legal force ⟨a right depending upon ~⟩ ⟨the laws and ~*s* of a clan⟩
con·sue·tu·di·nal \ˌ¦==¦t(y)üdᵊnəl\ *adj* [L *consuetudin-, consuetudo* custom + E *-al*] **1 :** CONSUETUDINARY **2** *of a verb form or aspect* **:** denoting customary action (as in French *il vendait* "he used to sell")
¹con·sue·tu·di·nary \ˌkän(t)swəˈt(y)üdᵊnˌerē, -ri\ *n* -ES [ML *consuetudinarius*, fr. LL *consuetudinarius*, adj.] **:** a manual embodying the customs or usages of a particular body; *esp* **:** one containing ritualistic and ceremonial observances of monastic discipline
²consuetudinary \ˌ¦==¦==¦==\ *adj* [LL *consuetudinarius*, fr. L *consuetudin-, consuetudo* custom + *-arius* -ary] **:** derived from or depending on habit or custom ⟨~ law⟩
con·sue·tu·do \ˌkän(t)swəˈt(y)üdō\ *n, pl* **consuetudi·nes** \-dᵊnˌēz\ [L, custom] **:** a custom or usage; *esp* **:** one having essentially the force of law
¹con·sul \ˈkän(t)səl\ *n* -s [ME, fr. L, fr. *consulere* to consult — more at CONSULT] **1 a** (1) **:** either of the two joint chief magistrates of the Roman republic (2) **:** a high honorary official of the Roman empire **b :** a municipal magistrate (as in Italy) during the middle ages **c :** one of the chief magistrates of the French republic from 1799 to 1804 or of one of the Italian republics established upon the French pattern **2** *obs* **:** a member of a council esp. of a trading company **3 :** an official appointed by or with the authority of a government to reside in a foreign country to represent the interests of citizens of the appointing country (as in commerce)
²consul \"\ *vt* -ED/-ING/-S **:** to submit (as an invoice) to a consul for inspection and approval
con·sul·age \-lij\ *n* -s [¹*consul* + *-age*] **:** a duty or tax paid for consular protection
con·sul·ar \ˈkän(t)s(ə)lə(r) *also* -syəl-\ *adj* [L *consularis*, fr.

consul + -aris -ar] : of, having to do with, or of the nature of a consul, his office, or his duties ⟨both Polybius and Cicero speak of the ~ power as monarchical —C.H.McIlwain⟩
consular agent *n* : an official assuming consular duties at a place where a full consular post is not maintained
consular court *n* : one of the courts presided over by a minister or consul established by treaty in certain foreign countries and assigned criminal and civil jurisdiction over actions involving nationals of the country having extraterritorial rights
consular document *n* : a document (as a bill of lading, consular invoice, or certificate of origin) bearing the visa of a consul of the country of destination
consular invoice *n* : an invoice visaed by a consular officer of the country of destination
con·sul·ary \'kän(t)sə,lerē, -ri *also* -syə,l-\ *adj* [LL *consularius*, fr. L *consul* + *-arius* -ary] : CONSULAR
[1]**con·sul·ate** \'kän(t)s(ə)lət *also* -syəl- *sometimes* ,lāt, *usu* -d.+V\ *n* -s [ME *consulat*, fr. L *consulatus*, fr. *consul* + *-atus* -ate — more at CONSUL] **1** : government by consuls ⟨at that time Rome was still under the ~⟩ **2 a** : the office of consul ⟨while Caesar held the ~⟩ **b** : the term of office of a consul ⟨during his ~⟩ **3** : the jurisdiction of a consul : consular territory ⟨attended to matters within his ~⟩ **4** : the premises or the residence of a consul ⟨a ~ of the U.S. . . . is a fairly safe place in times of disturbances —F.A.Magruder⟩
[2]**consulate** \-,lāt, *usu* -ād.+V\ *vt* -ED/-ING/-S **1** : to conduct a consular inspection of (as an invoice) **2** : to submit (papers or records) for consular inspection and visa
consulate general \-lət- *sometimes* -,lāt-\ *n, pl* **consulates general** : the residence, office, or jurisdiction of a consul general
consul general *n, pl* **consuls general** : a consul of the first rank stationed in an important place or having jurisdiction in several places or over several consuls
con·sul·ship \'kän(t)səl,ship\ *n* : the office or term of office of a consul : CONSULATE 2
[1]**con·sult** \kən'səlt\ *vb* -ED/-ING/-S [MF or L; MF *consulter*, fr. L *consultare*, freq. of *consulere* to consult, fr. *com-* + *-sulere* (perh. akin to Gk *helein* to take) — more at SELL] *vt* **1** *obs* **a** : to deliberate on : DISCUSS **b** : to take counsel to bring about : DEVISE, CONTRIVE **2 a** : to ask advice of : seek the opinion of : apply to for information or instruction ⟨~ a doctor about an ailment⟩ **b** : to refer to esp. for information ⟨~ a dictionary⟩ **3** : to have prudent regard to : have an eye to : CONSIDER ⟨~ one's pocketbook before buying⟩ ~ *vi* : to take counsel : deliberate together : CONFER ⟨after ~*ing* with a lawyer⟩ ⟨the three powers would ~ on how to ameliorate the internal political conflict —W.S.Vucinich⟩
[2]**consult** \'kän,səlt *sometimes* kən's-\ *n* -s [MF *consulte*, fr. *consulter*, v.] **1** *archaic* : the act of consulting or deliberating **2 a** : CONSULTATION ⟨their ~*s* produced resolutions of violence —Thomas Carte⟩ **b** *archaic* : a secret meeting for devising treasonable or seditious actions : CABAL
con·sul·tant \kən'səlt³nt, -tənt\ *n* -s [F, fr. L *consultant-, consultans*, pres. part. of *consultare*] **1** : one who consults another **2** : one who gives professional advice or services regarding matters in the field of his special knowledge or training (as a consulting physician or engineer) : EXPERT
con·sul·ta·ry response \kən'səlt(ə)rē-, 'kän(t)səl,terē-\ *n* : the opinion of a court of law on a special case
con·sul·ta·tion \,kän(t)səl'tāshən\ *n* -s [ME *consultacioun*, fr. MF *consultation*, fr. L *consultation-, consultatio*, fr. *consultatus* + *-ion-, -io* -ion] **1** : a council or conference (as between two or more persons) usu. to consider a special matter ⟨holding frequent ~*s* with his lawyer to discuss the case⟩; *specif* : a formal deliberation between two or more physicians on the diagnosis of a disease or its treatment in a patient **2** : the act of consulting or conferring : deliberation of two or more persons on some matter ⟨the two firms were in ~ over the construction of the new airplane⟩
con·sul·ta·tive \kən'səltəd·|iv, -tət|iv *also* |əv; 'kän(t)səl-,tād·|iv, -tāt|iv *also* |əv\ *adj* [*consultation* + *-ive*] : of or having to do with consultation : having the privilege or right of conference : ADVISORY ⟨employed in a ~ capacity only⟩
con·sul·ta·to·ry \kən'səltə,tōrē, -tōrē, -ri\ *adj* [L *consultatorius*, fr. *consultatus* + *-orius* -ory] : of or having to do with consultation : ADVISORY, CONSULTATIVE
con·sult·er \kən'səltə(r)\ *n* -s : one that consults
consulting *adj* **1** : that advises : that aids esp. by providing professional or expert advice ⟨a ~ architect⟩ ⟨a ~ psychologist⟩ **2** : of or having to do with consultation or a consultant ⟨the ~ room of a psychiatrist⟩ ⟨the ~ services of a law firm⟩
con·sul·tive \kən'səltiv, -tēv *also* -təv\ *adj* : CONSULTATIVE
con·sul·tor \kən'səltə(r)\ *n* -s [L, fr. *consultus*, past part. of *consulere* + *-or* — more at CONSULT] : one that consults or advises; *esp* : a person expert in a particular field of knowledge who is chosen by the Roman Catholic Church esp. for assisting and advising a bishop
con·sul·to·ry \kən'səlt(ə)rē; (')kän(t)səl,tōrē, -tōrē, -ri\ *adj*, *archaic* : CONSULTATORY
con·sum·able \kən'sümәbəl\ *adj* : capable of being consumed ⟨~ goods⟩
con·sume \kən'süm\ *vb* -ED/-ING/-S [ME *consumen*, fr. MF or L; MF *consumer*, fr. L *consumere* to take completely, consume, fr. *com-* + *sumere* to take, fr. *sub-* + *emere* to buy, obtain — more at REDEEM] *vt* **1** : to destroy or do away with completely (as by fire, disease, famine, decomposition) ⟨the blaze *consumed* several blocks⟩ : cause to waste away utterly ⟨plague *consumed* an entire generation⟩ **2 a** : to spend wastefully : SQUANDER ⟨~ the family income on luxuries⟩ **b** (1) : to use up : EXPEND ⟨an iron furnace *consumed* thousands of cords for fuel —*Amer. Guide Series: Mich.*⟩ (2) : to use up (as time) ⟨hours *consumed* in reading⟩ ⟨visitors who wish to spend a brief vacation . . . and to ~ as little of it as possible in transit —*Amer. Guide Series: Vt.*⟩ **c** : to utilize (an economic good) in the satisfaction of wants or the process of production ⟨the production of nuclear energy . . . soon to ~ 10 percent of all the electricity we produce —*New Republic*⟩ **3** : to eat or drink esp. without measure ⟨the banqueters *consumed* several kegs of beer⟩ **4** : to engage or absorb fully the attention, interest, or energy of : ENGROSS ⟨when the rage and the hatred that ~ one are more than one can bear —Kay Boyle⟩ ~ *vi* : to waste or burn away : PERISH ⟨as quickly as blossoms ~ away⟩ ⟨leaves, which were quietly *consuming* in bonfires —Sylvia T. Warner⟩ **syn** see EAT, MONOPOLIZE, WASTE
con·sum·ed·ly \kən'sümədlē, -li\ *adv* : EXCESSIVELY ⟨I shall miss him ~ —O.W.Holmes †1935⟩
con·sum·er \kən'sümə(r)\ *n* -s *often attrib* : one that consumes ⟨the ship's boilers were great ~*s* of cordwood —*Amer. Guide Series: Minn.*⟩ ⟨~*s* of political propaganda —Louis Simpson⟩; *specif* : one that utilizes economic goods ⟨~ commodity⟩ ⟨~ demand⟩ ⟨~ price⟩ ⟨~ cooperative⟩ — compare PRODUCER
consumer credit *n* : credit (as a charge account or installment loan) that is granted to an individual esp. to finance the purchase of consumer goods or defray personal or family expenses and is usu. repaid in installments
consumer goods *also* **consumer items** *n pl* : economic goods that directly satisfy human wants or desires — compare PRODUCER GOODS
consumer price index *n* : an index measuring the change in the cost of typical wage-earner purchases of goods and services expressed as a percentage of the cost of these same goods and services in some base period — called also *cost-of-living index*
consumer sovereignty *n* : the economic power exercised by the preferences of consumers in a free market
consumer's surplus *also* **consumer's rent** *n* : the amount above the actual price of a commodity a purchaser would pay in order not to go without the commodity
con·sum·ing·ly *adv* : INTENSELY, DEVOTEDLY ⟨~ earnest⟩
con·sum·ing·ness *n* -ES : the quality or state of being consuming
[1]**con·sum·mate** \kən'səmət, 'kän(t)səm-, *usu* -əd.+V\ *adj* [ME *consummat*, fr. L *consummatus*, past part. of *consummare* to sum up, finish, fr. *com-* + *-summare* (fr. *summa* sum) — more at SUM] **1** *archaic* : brought to completion : FINISHED **2** : complete in every detail : PERFECT ⟨a ~ little model of a clipper ship⟩ **3** : extremely skilled and accomplished : supremely capable or proficient ⟨a ~ actor⟩ ⟨a ~ politician⟩ ⟨a ~ liar⟩ **4 a** : of the very highest or finest : supremely excellent ⟨a ~ wisdom⟩ ⟨a ~ performance⟩ **b** : greatest possible : EXTREME ⟨~ treachery⟩ ⟨~ cruelty⟩ — **con·sum·mate·ly** *adv*
[2]**con·sum·mate** \'kän(t)sə,māt, *usu* -ād.+V; "*consummated*" *in the passage "It is consummated" in some versions of the Bible is often pronounced* kən'səməd·əd *or* -mətəd\ *vb* -ED/-ING/-S [L *consummatus*] *vt* **1 a** : to bring to completion : FINISH, COMPLETE ⟨~ a business merger⟩ ⟨~ a military alliance⟩ **b** : to bring to the highest point or degree : make perfect ⟨their happiness was *consummated* when they bought their house⟩ **c** : to bring about : ACHIEVE ⟨the opportunity to ~ such a desire⟩ ⟨annexation was *consummated* by a joint resolution —Oscar Handlin⟩ **2** : to complete (marital union) by the first act of sexual intercourse after marriage **3** *obs* : to put an end to ~ *vi* : to come to fulfillment or perfection; *specif* : to engage in the first act of sexual intercourse after marriage
con·sum·ma·tion \,kän(t)sə'māshən\ *n* -s [ME *consummacioun*, fr. MF *consommation*, fr. L *consummation-, consummatio*, fr. *consummatus* + *-ion-, -io* -ion] **1** : the act of completing, achieving, or bringing to perfection ⟨the ~ of a contract by mutual signature⟩ ⟨production of the new model marks the ~ of this particular design⟩; *specif* : the consummating of a marriage **2** : the finish or ultimate end ⟨death is the ~ of life⟩; *specif* : the supreme or highest goal ⟨the universal loving-kindness of Deity as the ~ of existence —W.L.Sullivan⟩
con·sum·ma·tive \'kän(t)sə,mād·iv, kən'səməd·iv\ *adj* : serving or tending to consummate : COMPLETING, FINAL — **con·sum·ma·tive·ly** \-d·əvlē\ *adv*
con·sum·ma·tor \'kän(t)sə,mād·ə(r)\ *n* -s [LL, fr. L *consummatus* + *-or*] : one that consummates
con·sum·ma·to·ry \kən'səmə,tōrē, -tōrē, -ri\ *adj* : of or having to do with consummation : CONCLUDING, COMPLETING, FINISHING ⟨a ~ act⟩ ⟨art as appreciation, as ~ experience —J.L.Blau⟩ ⟨in proper sequence of preparatory, intermediate, and ~ situations —*Psychiatry*⟩
con·sumpt \kən'səmpt, -səm-\ *n* -s [by shortening] *chiefly Scot* : CONSUMPTION
con·sumpt·ed \-təd\ *adj* [*consumption* + *-ed*] *dial* : affected with consumption
con·sump·ti·ble \kən'səmptəbəl\ *n* -s [*consumption* + *-ible*] : an object (as an economic good) that in use is consumed (as by wear, decay, attrition)
con·sump·tion \kən'səmpshən\ *n* -s [ME *consumpcioun*, fr. L *consumption-, consumptio*, fr. *consumptus* (past part. of *consumere* to consume) + *-ion-, -io* -ion — more at CONSUME] **1 a** : the act or action of consuming or destroying ⟨the ~ of organic matter by fire⟩ ⟨the ~ of an entire generation of young men in a war⟩ **b** : the wasting, using up, or wearing away of something ⟨the slow ~ of a person's vitality⟩ ⟨the ~ of a fortune⟩ **2** : the utilization of economic goods in the satisfaction of wants or in the process of production resulting in immediate destruction (as in the eating of foods), gradual wear and deterioration (as in the habitation of dwellings), no change aside from natural decay (as in the enjoyment of art objects), or transformation into other goods (as in manufacturing) — see CONSPICUOUS CONSUMPTION **3 a** : a progressive wasting away of the body; *esp* : the disabling wasting stage of pulmonary tuberculosis characterized by great destruction of lung tissue and systemic toxemia **b** : TUBERCULOSIS — not used technically
consumption function *n* : a function relating the level of consumer expenditures to national income orig. believed to be a constant but subsequently held to fluctuate under various conditions
consumption goods *n pl* : CONSUMER GOODS
consumption weed *n* : FALSE WINTERGREEN
[1]**con·sump·tive** \kən'səmptiv, -tēv *also* -təv\ *adj* [*consumption* + *-ive*] **1 a** : tending to consume or be consumed : DESTRUCTIVE, WASTEFUL ⟨~ fires⟩ ⟨duties ~ of time and money⟩ **b** : of or having to do with the consumption of economic goods ⟨that milk which is in excess of ~ requirement . . . is termed "surplus" —A.L.Anderson⟩ **2 a** : wasted or reduced by or as if by a sickness **b** (1) : affected with consumption ⟨a ~ boy⟩ (2) : of, having to do with, or suggestive of consumption ⟨a ~ cough⟩ — **con·sump·tive·ly** \-tə̇vlē, -li\ *adv*
[2]**consumptive** \"\ *n* -s : a person affected with consumption
consumptive's weed *n* [so called fr. its use in the relief of bronchial disorders] : YERBA SANTA
consumptive use *n* : the total seasonal water loss from an area of land due to plant growth and evaporation usu. being expressed in acre-feet
cont *abbr* **1** containing **2** contemporary **3** contents **4** continent; continental **5** continued; continuous **6** contract **7** contrary **8** control
con·ta·bes·cence \,käntə'bes³n(t)s\ *n* -s [ISV *contabesc-* (fr. L *contabescere* to waste away, fr. *com-* + *tabescere* to melt gradually, to decay) + *-ence* — more at THAW] : abortion of an anther — **con·ta·bes·cent** \¦==¦bes³nt\ *adj*
[1]**con·tact** \'kän,takt\ *n* -s [F or L; F, fr. L *contactus*, fr. *contactus*, past part. of *contingere* to touch on all sides — more at CONTINGENT] **1 a** : union or junction of body surfaces : a touching or meeting ⟨cooled by ~ with the air⟩ ⟨sexual ~⟩ : IMPACT ⟨body ~ in football and hockey⟩ **b** *geom* : the meeting of curves or surfaces so as to have tangents or tangent planes in common **c** : the apparent touching or mutual tangency of the limbs of any two celestial bodies or of the disk of one body with the shadow of another during an eclipse, transit, or occultation **d** (1) : the junction or touching surface of two electrical conductors through which a current passes (2) : a special part (as a platinum stud) made for such a junction for temporary or momentary connection **2 a** : association or relationship (as in physical or mental or business or social meeting or communication) ⟨students and teachers in daily ~⟩ ⟨Japan's new ~*s* with Europe⟩ : direct experience through the senses ⟨a mental patient's infrequent ~*s* with reality⟩ **b** : a condition or an instance of meeting, connecting, or communicating ⟨ordinary men were made to feel a direct ~ with their God —H.S.Canby⟩ ⟨keep in ~ with the other members⟩ ⟨neither party had made any ~ with the other⟩ ⟨made ~ with the enemy⟩ **c** : ACCULTURATION **d** : direct visual observation of the surface of the ground or water made from an airplane esp. as an aid to judging position and properly guiding the airplane ⟨flying by ~ rather than flying by instruments⟩ **e** : an instance of establishing communication with someone ⟨a radio ~⟩ or of observing or receiving a significant signal from a person or object (as by radar or sonar) ⟨got three ~*s* on the radarscope⟩; *also* : a person or object with which such contact is made **3 a** : a person serving as go-between, messenger, agent, or source of special information esp. in a secret activity ⟨the ~ for the syndicate⟩ ⟨a newspaperman's ~*s* are often cabdrivers or bartenders⟩ **b** : any person or animal that has been in contact with a person or animal affected with a contagious disease **4** : the often irregular surface that constitutes the junction of two bodies of rock different in kind, age, or origin **5** : CONTACT LENS
[2]**con·tact** \", kən't-, kän't-\ *vb* -ED/-ING/-S *vt* : to bring into contact : enter or be in contact with : **a** : to press against : MEET, TOUCH ⟨brake shoes ~ the inside diameter of the drum⟩ : JOIN ⟨where the line of ordinary low water . . . directly ~*ed* the open sea —*U.S.Code*⟩ **b** : to make connection with : get in communication with : REACH — used often where the means is not precisely specified ⟨~ your local dealer⟩ ⟨the salesman ~*ed* a few prospects⟩ **c** : to talk or confer with : INTERVIEW : apply to : APPROACH ⟨the first company you ~ may not . . . use your services —W.J.Reilly⟩ ⟨the department . . . was ~*ed* to learn of availability and costs —R.C.Emery⟩ ~ *vi* : to make contact ⟨the point at which the two surfaces ~⟩
[3]**contact** \'kän,takt\ *adj* **1** : of, maintaining, or establishing contact ⟨a ~ man⟩ ⟨~ area⟩ : involving, permitting, or activated by contact ⟨~ weather⟩ ⟨~ fuse⟩ **2** *geol* : lying along or near or genetically connected with a contact ⟨a ~ deposit⟩ **3** : characterized by or normally involving body contact between players ⟨football and hockey are ~ sports⟩ **4** : caused or transmitted by direct or indirect contact (as with an allergen or a contagious disease) ⟨~ allergy⟩ ⟨~ transmission⟩
[4]**contact** \"\ *adv* : by direct visual observation of the earth ⟨the ceiling was so low that the patrol was flown ~ —J.L.Foley⟩
contact acid *n* : sulfuric acid produced by contact catalysis
con·tac·tant \kən'taktənt, (')kän¦-\ *n* -s [[1]*contact* + *-ant*] : any allergen that produces manifestations of hypersensitivity at the site of contact with the skin or the mucosa
contact bed *n* : a watertight bed filled with coke or other coarse material and used for purifying sewage which after being run into the bed and left for some hours in contact with the material to promote bacterial action is filtered off and the bed aerated
contact block *n* : a block of conducting material forming one of the two surfaces of an electric contact
contact catalysis *n* : catalysis in which the catalyst is a solid in contact with gaseous or liquid reactants
contact clip *n* : the clip into which the blade of an electrical switch enters or which it embraces
contact electricity *n* : electricity arising on two dissimilar bodies at their surface of contact
contact flying *n* : navigation of an airplane by means of direct observation of landmarks — contrasted with *instrument flying*
contact lens *n* : a thin lens of glass or plastic designed to fit over the cornea for the correction of refractive errors; *also* : a similar lens or a prism employed by the ophthalmologist in eye examinations with a gonioscope
contact light *n* : one of a series of white marker lights placed in parallel rows on either side of an airfield runway to provide a visual aid to the pilot in landing
contact maker *n* : a device for making or for making and breaking an electric contact
contact metamorphic *adj* : formed by or associated with contact metamorphism
contact metamorphism *or* **contact metasomatism** *n* : metamorphosis found in the region of contact of a rock mass with an igneous intrusion
contact microphone *n* : a microphone designed to be used in contact with the source of sound or with a resonating or conducting surface
contact mineral *n* : a mineral whose origin is due to contact metamorphism
con·tac·tor \'kän,taktə(r), kən't-, kän't-\ *n* -s : a device for repeatedly establishing and interrupting an electric power circuit under normal conditions
contact potential *n* **1** : VOLTA EFFECT **2** : grid bias in a vacuum tube due to the lodging of space-charge electrons upon the grid wires
contact print *n* : a photographic print made by passing light through the negative while it is held in contact with the sensitized paper, plate, or film — compare PROJECTION PRINT
contact receptor *n* : a receptor for a stimulus (as taste) produced by an object touching it — compare DISTANCE RECEPTOR
contact rock *n* : rock associated with a contact metamorphic zone — compare CONTACT METAMORPHISM
contacts *pl of* CONTACT, *pres 3d sing of* CONTACT
contact series *n* : an arrangement of metals so that each is positively electrified by contact with the next
contact twin *n* : a twin crystal in which the two individuals are joined along a plane
con·tac·tu·al \kən'takchəwəl, (')kän¦-\ *adj* [fr. [1]*contact*, after such pairs as E *fact: factual*] : of, relating to, or involving contact — **con·tac·tu·al·ly** \-wəlē, -li\ *adv*
contact vein *n* : a vein formed along the common boundary of two different rock formations : a contact deposit of tabular form
contact zone *n* : a zone surrounding or adjacent to an igneous intrusion in which rocks have been affected by heat or magmatic solutions and gases
contagia *pl of* CONTAGIUM
con·ta·gion \kən'tājən\ *n* -s [ME *contagioun*, fr. MF & L; MF *contagion*, fr. L *contagion-, contagio*, fr. *contag-* (fr. *contingere* to touch, to pollute) + *-ion-, -io* -ion — more at CONTINGENT] **1 a** : the process by which disease is transmitted from one person to another by direct or indirect means **b** : a contagious disease **c** : something that serves as a medium to transmit disease : a virus or other infective agent that may produce disease **2 a** : POISON ⟨I'll touch my point with this ~ —Shak.⟩ **b** : contagious influence, quality, or nature ⟨to dare the vile ~ of the night —Shak.⟩ **c** : evil or corrupting influence or contact ⟨war . . . had become . . . a ~ attacking neutrals as well as belligerents —*Saturday Rev.*⟩ **3 a** : the spread or communication or the tendency to be communicated of any influence, doctrine, emotion, or emotional state ⟨the ~ of love obeys no human logic —John Erskine †1951⟩ ⟨the ~ of mob enthusiasm —H.L.Mencken⟩ **b** : an influence, doctrine, or emotion that spreads rapidly ⟨when people began to run the ~ spread and soon the whole mob was running⟩
con·ta·gion·ist \-nəst\ *n* -s : one who believes in the contagiousness of certain diseases before proof is available
con·ta·gi·os·i·ty \kən,tājē'äsəd·ē\ *n* -ES [F *contagiosité*, fr. L *contagiosus* + F *-ité* -ity] : the state of being contagious or the degree of contagiousness
con·ta·gious \kən'tājəs\ *adj* [ME, fr. MF *contagieus*, fr. LL *contagiosus*, fr. L *contagio* + *-osus* -ous] **1 a** : communicable by contact : CATCHING ⟨~ diseases⟩ — compare INFECTIOUS **b** : bearing contagion ⟨many persons . . . are ~ long before they are aware of the presence of their disease —*Jour. Amer. Med. Assoc.*⟩ **c** : for contagious diseases ⟨a ~ ward⟩ **2** *obs* : causing disease : NOXIOUS **3** : spreading or communicable from one to another : exciting similar emotions or conduct in others ⟨a ~ grin⟩ ⟨~ enthusiasm⟩ : exciting enthusiasm : exciting response ⟨~ music⟩ — **con·ta·gious·ly** *adv*
contagious abortion *n* **1** : brucellosis in domestic animals characterized by abortion: **a** : bovine brucellosis caused by a brucella (*Brucella abortus*), contracted by ingestion, by copulation, or possibly by wound infection, and characterized by proliferation of the organism in the fetal membranes inducing abortion, subsequent invasion of the regional lymph nodes and udder with the formation of chronic foci of infection, and sometimes reinvasion of the uterus when pregnancy is reestablished, though a degree of local immunity usu. appears after one or more abortions, an affected cow carrying her calf to term even though retaining a chronic brucella infection outside the uterus **b** : any brucellosis of swine or goats having a somewhat similar course to bovine brucellosis but usu. caused by different brucellae **2** : any of several contagious or infectious diseases of domestic animals marked by abortion (as vibrionic abortion of sheep or an acute salmonellosis of the mare)
contagious bovine pleuropneumonia *n* : pleuropneumonia of cattle
contagious disease *n* : a disease communicable by contact with one suffering from it, with a bodily discharge of such a patient, or with an object touched by such a patient or his bodily discharges — compare INFECTIOUS DISEASE; GERM THEORY
contagious distribution *n*, *statistics* : a distribution for which the number of variates in some classes is influenced by a tendency of the variates to occur in aggregates
contagious ecthyma *n* : SORE MOUTH
contagious epithelioma *n* : FOWL POX
contagious indigestion *n* : BLUE COMB
contagious magic *n* : magic based on the assumption that things once associated are able to affect one another when separated so that anything done to an object (as a garment or a hair) will affect its former owner
con·ta·gious·ness \kən'tājəsnəs\ *n* -ES : the quality or state of being contagious
contagious pleuropneumonia *n* : pleuropneumonia of cattle
con·ta·gium \kən'tāj(ē)əm\ *n, pl* **conta·gia** \-j(ē)ə\ [L, fr. *contingere* to touch, pollute — more at CONTINGENT] : a virus or living organism capable of causing a communicable disease
con·tain \kən'tān\ *vb* -ED/-ING/-S [ME *conteinen, contenen*, fr. OF *contenir*, fr. L *continēre*, fr. *com-* + *-tinēre* (fr. *tenēre* to hold) — more at THIN] *vt* **1** : to keep within limits : hold back or hold down: as **a** : RESTRAIN, CONTROL ⟨tried to ~ his tendency to argue⟩ : SUPPRESS ⟨unable to ~ his laughter⟩ ⟨all the appearance of ~*ed* rage⟩ ⟨able to ~ himself⟩ **b** : CHECK, HALT, WITHSTAND, STEM ⟨~ an advancing flood⟩ ⟨economic inflation has so far been ~*ed*⟩ ⟨~*ed* the enemy's attack⟩ **c** : to confine (the enemy) to the immediate terrain or to a limited area : prevent (the enemy) from making a breakthrough **d** : to follow successfully a policy of containment

toward (a hostile power) : hold in check **2 a :** to have within : HOLD ⟨the box ~*ed* only some old papers and a few odds and ends⟩ **b :** to consist of wholly or in part : COMPRISE, INCLUDE ⟨the bill ~*s* several new clauses⟩ **c :** ENCLOSE ⟨the building ~*s* classrooms and an auditorium⟩ **3 a :** to have capacity for : be able to hold : be equivalent to ⟨a bushel ~*s* four pecks⟩ **b :** to extend over : MEASURE, OCCUPY ⟨the farm ~*s* more than 10,000 acres⟩ **c** (1) : to be a multiple of or to be divisible by usu. without a remainder (2) : ENCLOSE, INCLUDE, BOUND **4 :** IMPLY, ENTAIL ⟨the conclusions are ~*ed* in the premises⟩ **5 a** *archaic* : to keep or retain under or as if under control ⟨impossible that he could at once ~ . . . every part of his wide-extended dominions —Edward Gibbon⟩ **b** *obs* : RETAIN, KEEP ~ *vi* **1** *obs* : to conduct oneself : BEHAVE **2 a :** to restrain oneself (as from laughter) **b** *obs* : to live in continence

syn HOLD, ACCOMMODATE: to CONTAIN is usu. to have within ⟨the top compartment *contains* tools most often used⟩ ⟨old river valleys . . . are still visible and usually *contain* lakes or chains of lakes —*Amer. Guide Series: Minn.*⟩ ⟨animal protein and animal fat *contained* in an ordinary mixed diet —N.C. Wright⟩ ⟨the picture *contains* strange figures⟩ To HOLD is usu. to have the capacity to contain or retain ⟨the jug, which *holds* over a gallon, contained only a pint⟩ Often, however, the two words are used interchangeably, esp. in the past tenses ⟨the compartments of the cash register *contained* the various denominations of coins but were often empty⟩ ⟨the box *held* his clothes and some small valueless trinkets⟩ To ACCOMMODATE is to hold conveniently or without crowding ⟨the bus *accommodates* about 60 passengers and the driver⟩

con·tained \kən'tānd\ *adj* [ME *conteined*, fr. past part. of *conteinen*] **1 :** RESTRAINED, CONTROLLED ⟨striking with ~ ferocity at my head —R.L.Stevenson⟩ : COMPOSED, CALM ⟨the ~ peace of the village⟩ — see SELF-CONTAINED **2 :** SUSTAINED, SUPPORTED — now used chiefly in compounds ⟨the Tsarist Russian land-*contained* expansion —Owen Lattimore⟩ — **con·tain·ed·ly** \-'tānədlē, -li\ *adv*

con·tain·er \kən'tānə(r)\ *n* -s : one that contains: as **a :** a receptacle (as a box or jar) or a formed or flexible covering for the packing or shipment of articles, goods, or commodities **b :** a portable usu. metal compartment in which freight is placed for convenience of movement esp. on railroad container cars

container board *n* : any of the various paperboards (as corrugated board, fiberboard) from which containers are made

container car *n* : an open-top railroad freight car specially fitted for the accommodation of containers

containing *pres part of* CONTAIN

con·tain·ment \kən'tānmənt\ *n* -s **1 :** the act of containing : RESTRAINT, CONSTRAINT, CONTROL **2 a :** the policy or the process of preventing the expansion beyond prescribed limits of a hostile power or ideology or inimical forces esp. by employing political, economic, and propaganda pressure and by strengthening friendly powers **b :** the result to be attained by such a policy or process

contains *pres 3d sing of* CONTAIN

contakion *var of* KONTAKION

con·tam·i·nant \kən'tamənənt\ *n* -s [L *contaminant-, contaminans*, pres. part. of *contaminare*] : something that contaminates

¹**con·tam·i·nate** \kən'tamə,nāt, *usu* -ād·+V\ *vt* -ED/-ING/-S [L *contaminatus*, past part. of *contaminare* to bring into contact, contaminate; akin to L *contingere* to touch, pollute — more at CONTINGENT] **1 :** to soil, stain, corrupt, or infect by contact or association ⟨a surgical wound *contaminated* by bacteria⟩ ⟨believers *contaminated* by the presence of infidels⟩ : make inferior or impure by mixture : POLLUTE ⟨iron *contaminated* by phosphorus⟩ **2 :** to render unfit for use by the introduction of unwholesome or undesirable elements ⟨water *contaminated* by sewage⟩ ⟨~ a state the size of Maryland with radioactivity —R.E.Lapp⟩

syn TAINT, ATTAINT, POLLUTE, DEFILE: these all mean to make impure or unclean. CONTAMINATE implies an action by something external to an object which by entering into or coming in contact with the object destroys its purity ⟨the surgical wound became *contaminated*⟩ ⟨the incoming air will not be *contaminated* with exhaust or oil fumes —H.G.Armstrong⟩ ⟨you allowed your fine magazine to be *contaminated* with such a vicious, foul, and absurd writing —*Fortune*⟩ TAINT usu. suggests a less complete debasing than CONTAMINATE, often suggesting only a partial contamination, but stresses more strongly the sullied or stained quality of the thing acted upon ⟨water . . . becomes *tainted* easily through smells and impurities in the air —Henry Wynmalen⟩ ⟨the poison of greed, ambition, and vulgarity had not *tainted* the Italian air —Ann Bridge⟩ ATTAINT, less frequently used than TAINT, has come, because of etymological similarity, to be used as synonymous with TAINT though it suggests the idea of infection or of inevitable corruption following from an original sullying contact ⟨our writers have been *attainted* by the disease they must help to cure —Waldo Frank⟩ ⟨the slightest contact with them *attaints* and works corruption of the blood —G.W.Johnson⟩ POLLUTE carries strongly the idea of a completed process of contamination, esp. and usu. an offensive contamination ⟨water *polluted* by garbage and other filth⟩ DEFILE implies a willful befouling of what ought to be kept clean, clear, or bright, frequently, therefore, suggesting violation, profanation or desecration ⟨wheat which the mice ate or *defiled* —F.E.Garlough⟩ ⟨cruelty is not only the worst accusation that can be brought against a man, *defiling* the whole character —Hilaire Belloc⟩ ⟨the Sabbath must not be *defiled* —William McFee⟩

²**contaminate** *adj* [L *contaminatus*] *obs* : CONTAMINATED

con·tam·i·na·tion \kən,tamə'nāshən\ *n* -s [LL *contamination-, contaminatio*, fr. L *contaminatus* + *-ion-, -io* -ion] **1 a :** the act or process of contaminating or the state of being contaminated **b :** something that contaminates : IMPURITY **2 a :** a blending in manuscript tradition whereby a single manuscript contains readings belonging to different groups **b :** a blending of legends or stories resulting in new combinations of incident or in modifications of plot **3** [G *kontamination*, fr. LL *contamination-, contaminatio*] : the blending of two linguistic forms (as words or word groups) into a single new one (as *irregardless*, prob. from *irrespective* and *regardless*, *different than*, prob. from *different from* and *other than*) — compare ³BLEND d **4 :** corruption of relatively inexperienced offenders by hardened criminals within a prison population

con·tam·i·na·tive \kən'tamə,nād·iv, -āt|iv *also* |əv; -'taməˌnəd·|iv, -nət|iv *also* |əv\ *adj* : tending to contaminate

con·tam·i·na·tor \kən'tamə,nād·ə(r), -ātə-\ *n* -s : one that contaminates

¹**con·tango** \kən'taŋ(,)gō\ *n, pl* **contangos** *or* **contangoes** [perh. alter. of *continue*] : premium or interest paid on a fixed day on the London stock exchange by a buyer to the seller to be allowed to defer payment until a future settlement — compare BACKWARDATION

²**contango** \"\ *vi* -ED/-ING/-ES : to allow deferment of payment of the purchase price of stocks in consideration of a contango

con·ta·rin·ia \,käntə'rinēə\ *n, cap* [NL] : a large genus of gall midges (family Cecidomyiidae) including several that invade buds and flowers of economically important plants

contbd *abbr* contraband

contbg *abbr* contributing

contbn *abbr* contribution

contbr *abbr* contributor

contd *abbr* continued

conte \'kōnt, -ō"t\ *n, pl* **contes** \-t(s)\ [F, fr. *conter* to relate — more at COUNT] **1 :** a short tale esp. of adventure ⟨a ~ in the old-fashioned sense, a tale of temptation and adventure, innocence and world-wickedness —Parker Tyler⟩ — compare SHORT STORY **2 :** a narrative somewhat shorter than the average novel but longer than a short story ⟨a ~ rather than a full-length novel —*John O'London's Weekly*⟩

Conté \(')kōn¦tā, -ō"¦-\ *trademark* — used for crayons and stationery

con·temn \kən'tem\ *vt* **contemned; contemned** \-temd\ **contemning** \-temiŋ *sometimes* -temniŋ\ **contemns** [ME *contempnen*, fr. MF *contempner, contemner*, fr. L *contemnere*, fr. *com-* + *temnere* to slight, despise — more at STAMP] : to view or treat with contempt as mean and despicable : reject with disdain : DESPISE, SCORN ⟨those who have ~*ed* its visual art —David Sylvester⟩ **syn** see DESPISE

con·temner *also* **con·temnor** \kən'temə(r), -mnə-\ *n* -s [MF *contemneur*, fr. *contemner* + *-eur* -or] **1 :** one that contemns ⟨the agrarian, the ~ of cities —*Times Lit. Supp.*⟩ ⟨the ~ of democracy who outstrips the aristocrats —C.C.Abbott⟩ **2** *usu* **contemnor** : one that is held to be in contempt of court

con·tem·per \kən'tempə(r)\ *vt* -ED/-ING/-S [L *contemperare*, fr. *com-* + *temperare* to temper — more at TEMPER] *archaic* : to moderate by mixing : BLEND, QUALIFY, ADAPT

contemperament *n* -s [LL *contemperamentum*, fr. L *contemperare* + *-mentum* -ment] *obs* : CONTEMPERATION

contemperation *n* -s [MF, fr. LL *contemperation-, contemperatio*, fr. L *contemperatus* (past part. of *contemperare*) + *-ion-, -io* -ion] *obs* : the act of contempering or state of being contempered : ACCOMMODATION; *also* : something that contempers : COMPROMISE

contemperature *n* -s [MF, fr. L *contemperatus* + MF *-ure* -ure] *obs* : harmonious or proportionate mixture

con·tem·pla·ble \kən'templəbəl\ *adj* [L *contemplabilis*, fr. *contemplari* contemplate + *-abilis* -able] : capable of being contemplated ⟨she found the nearer past . . . framed and ~ like the pictures on the wall —Dorothy M. Richardson⟩

con·tem·plant \-plənt\ *adj* [L *contemplant-, contemplans*, pres. part. of *contemplari*] : CONTEMPLATING

con·tem·plate \'käntəm,plāt, -(,)tem-; *rap. often* 'kānəm,-; *sporadically and old-fash* kən'tem,-; *usu* -ād·+V\ *vb* -ED/-ING/-S [L *contemplatus*, past part. of *contemplari, contemplare*, fr. *com-* + *-templari, -templare* (fr. *templum* space for observation marked out by the augur) — more at TEMPLE] *vt* **1 :** to view with sustained attention : gaze at thoughtfully for a noticeable time : observe with ostensibly steady reflection ⟨a way of looking her over from beneath lowered lids while he affected to be . . . *contemplating* the tip of his shining boot —Edith Wharton⟩ **2 :** to view mentally with continued thoughtfulness, attention, or reflection : muse or ponder about ⟨while in your pride ye ~ your talents, power, or wisdom —William Wordsworth⟩ **3 :** to view mentally in a stated or implied way with thoughtfulness and reflection: **a :** to think about or regard from a certain viewpoint or in a certain light or respect ⟨the opinion . . . that while science, by a deliberate abstraction, ~*s* a world of facts without values, religion ~*s* values apart from facts —W.R.Inge⟩ **b :** to have in view as a purpose : anticipate doing or performing : plan on : INTEND, PLAN ⟨absent-mindedly feeling in their pockets as men do when *contemplating* a purchase —Kenneth Roberts⟩ **c :** to dream of as a cherished aim : ENVISION ⟨the moment and the act he had *contemplated* for weeks with a thrill of pleasure —Thomas Hardy⟩ **d :** to presume or imply as a concomitant or result : POSTULATE, PRESUPPOSE ⟨the law would seem to ~ that it should be made to the secretary of state —John Marshall⟩ **4 :** to view or regard (as an object or an objective fact) with detachment ⟨since contemplation is an intellectual exercise it cannot allow itself to be identified with the thing *contemplated* —Leon Livingstone⟩ — compare ENJOY ~ *vi* : PONDER, MUSE, MEDITATE ⟨to sit still and ~ — to remember the faces of women without desire —R.L.Stevenson⟩ **syn** see CONSIDER

con·tem·plat·ing·ly *adv* : CONTEMPLATIVELY

con·tem·pla·tion \,käntəm'plāshən, -(,)tem'-\ *n* -s [ME *contemplacioun*, fr. OF *contemplation*, fr. L *contemplation-, contemplatio*, fr. *contemplatus* + *-ion-, -io* -ion] **1 a :** meditation on spiritual things as a form of private devotion **b :** a state of mystical awareness of God's being or presence : an ecstatic perception of God ⟨a state of rapture . . . in which the soul is freed from its senses and organs and lost in pure ~ —Frank Thilly⟩ **2 :** an act of the mind in considering with attention : continued attention to a particular subject : MEDITATION, MUSING, STUDY **3** *obs* : REGARD, CONSIDERATION; *also* : something for which such consideration is asked : PETITION, PRAYER, REQUEST **4 :** the act of viewing steadfastly and attentively : the viewing of something (as a picture or a scene) for its own sake **5 :** the act of looking forward to an event : the act of intending or considering a future event : EXPECTATION ⟨a shooting match . . . and other sports were in ~ —S.E.White⟩

¹**con·tem·pla·tive** \kən'templəd·|iv, -ət|iv, *also* |əv; 'käntəm,plād·|iv, -(,)tem-, -āt|iv *also* |əv\ *adj* [ME, fr. MF *contemplatif*, fr. L *contemplativus*, fr. *contemplatus* + *-ivus* -ive] **1 :** marked by or accompanied by contemplation : addicted to contemplation : suggesting or suited to contemplation : MEDITATIVE **2** *usu* kən'templə-\ : practicing or devoted to meditation (as religious meditation and prayer) ⟨the ~ life⟩ ⟨merely a ~ thinker, withdrawn from active life —Theodore Spencer⟩ **3** *obs* **a :** THEORETICAL **b :** THEORIZING — **con·tem·pla·tive·ly** \-əvlē, -li\ *adv* — **con·tem·pla·tive·ness** \-ivnəs, -ēv- *also* -əv-\ *n* -ES

²**contemplative** \kən'tem-\ *n* -s [ME, fr. MF *contemplatif*, fr. *contemplatif*, adj.] : one who practices contemplation

con·tem·pla·tor \'käntəm,plād·ə(r), -(,)tem-, -ātə-\ *n* -s [L, fr. *contemplatus* + *-or*] **1 :** a person who contemplates or is contemplative **2** *obs* : THEORIZER, SPECULATOR

¹**con·tem·po·ra·ne·an** \kən¦tempə¦rānēən, (')kän-, -nyən\ *adj* [L *contemporaneus* + E *-an*] : CONTEMPORANEOUS

²**contemporanean** \"\ *n* -s : CONTEMPORARY

con·tem·po·ra·ne·i·ty \kən,tempərə'nēəd·ē, (')kän-, -ətē, -i\ *n* -ES [fr. *contemporaneous*, after such pairs as E *spontaneous: spontaneity*] : the quality or state of being contemporaneous

con·tem·po·ra·ne·ous \kən¦tempə¦rānēəs, (')kän¦-, -nyəs\ *adj* [L *contemporaneus*, fr. *com-* + *tempor-*, *tempus* time + *-aneus* (as in *subterraneus* subterranean) — more at TEMPORAL] **1 :** existing or occurring during the same time (as during a year, decade, or longer span of time) ⟨the Classical Revival or Federal style, which was virtually ~ with the Regency in England —*Amer. Guide Series: Pa.*⟩ ⟨love of school is not ~ with residence therein; it is an after product —C.H.Grandgent⟩ **2 :** originating, arising, or being formed or made at the same time : marked by characteristics compatible with such origin ⟨the portions of the reef that are surrounded by ~, pure, fragmentary limestone —*Jour. of Geol.*⟩ **syn** see CONTEMPORARY

con·tem·po·ra·ne·ous·ly *adv* : at or near the same time

con·tem·po·ra·ne·ous·ness *n* -ES : CONTEMPORANEITY

con·tem·po·rar·i·ly \kən¦tempə¦rerəlē, (')kän¦-, -li\ *adv* : CONTEMPORANEOUSLY

con·tem·po·rariness \=ˈ==,=rēnəs, -rin-, =,==ˈ===\ *n* -ES : the quality or state of being contemporary

¹**con·tem·po·rary** \kən'tempə,rerē, -ri\ *adj* [*com-* + L *temporarius* of time, temporary — more at TEMPORARY] **1 :** happening, existing, living, or coming into being during the same time, sometimes during the same year, decade, century, or period as something else mentioned ⟨Dante had put some ~ popes in Hell —M.R.Cohen⟩ ⟨Renaissance painting, which was ~ with the great age of exploration —Lewis Mumford⟩ **2 :** marked by characteristics of the present period : MODERN ⟨~ shooting and sometimes during the present ⟨we are not without ~ talent; but for works of genius we must still look to the past —Edith Wharton⟩ ⟨the avenging on the ~ woman of resentments inculcated by an earlier woman —Philip Wylie⟩ **2 a :** occurring at the same moment : SIMULTANEOUS ⟨~ turns of two wheels⟩ **b :** having existed through the same period : originating at the same time ⟨~ rock strata⟩ **3 :** of or as though of the present period : marked by characteristics compatible with being of the present period; *sometimes* : ADVANCED, MODERN, UP-TO-DATE : au courant ⟨peculiarly ~ in his anxiety, his longing for a faith —Alfred Kazin⟩

syn CONTEMPORANEOUS, SIMULTANEOUS, SYNCHRONOUS, COEVAL, COETANEOUS, COINCIDENT, CONCOMITANT, CONCURRENT: CONTEMPORARY, indicating, like the others, existence or incidence at the same time, is likely to be used in reference to years, decades, lifetimes, and similar time spans ⟨Faraday's work on electricity coupled with Joseph Henry's exactly *contemporary* research on the electromagnet —Lewis Mumford⟩ ⟨*contemporary* with those intermediaries, or following hard upon them, were the great missionaries or converters —H.O.Taylor⟩ There is little difference between CONTEMPORARY and the less common CONTEMPORANEOUS ⟨the A. F. of L. was closer to *contemporaneous* British labor organizations than to the American Knights of Labor —Allan Nevins & H.S.Commager⟩ SIMULTANEOUS is likely to describe occurrence of two things at precisely the same minute or within the same limited period of time ⟨the three men, deftly timing the roll, made a *simultaneous* leap aboard the schooner —Jack London⟩ ⟨control of the air involves the *simultaneous* use of two types of planes — first, the long-range heavy bomber; second, light bombers, dive bombers, torpedo planes —F.D.Roosevelt⟩ SYNCHRONOUS may describe continuing action taking place over somewhat longer periods ⟨French speech has run a similar and almost *synchronous* course with English —Havelock Ellis⟩ COEVAL may be used in reference to periods, ages, eras, eons ⟨if the meteorites represent fragments of the solar system, we may conclude that the system is *coeval* with the Earth —F.L.Whipple⟩ COETANEOUS, a close synonym of COEVAL, may suggest origination at the same time ⟨the Alleghenies and other *coetaneous* mountain chains⟩ COINCIDENT refers to occurrences, events, incidents, developments taking place at the same time but may minimize ideas of causal relationship ⟨the growth of the mine union movement was *coincident* with the growth of business and manufacturing —T.R.Hay⟩ CONCOMITANT describes a development taking place at the same time but one of subordinate incidental character ⟨a bite from any carnivorous animal is likely to lead to some measure of *concomitant* poisoning —*Discovery*⟩ ⟨*concomitant* with the creation of these new rhythms came . . . "the dance craze" —Oscar Hammerstein *b*1895⟩ CONCURRENT may add to the idea of occurrence at the same time the notion of accord, agreement, fitness between the things involved ⟨great cultural achievements have not been inevitably, or even generally, *concurrent* with great material power —Lyman Bryson⟩

²**contemporary** \"\ *n* -ES **1 :** one that is contemporary with another ⟨Petrarch and Chaucer were *contemporaries*⟩ **2 :** one of the same or nearly the same age as another **3 :** a newspaper or periodical contemporary with another

con·tem·po·rize \kən'tempə,rīz\ *vb* -ED/-ING/-S [LL *contemporare* (fr. L *com-* + *-temporare*, fr. *tempor-*, *tempus* time) + E *-ize* — more at TEMPORAL] *vt* : to make contemporary ~ *vi* : to be contemporary : SYNCHRONIZE

¹**con·tempt** \kən'tem(p)t\ *n* -s [ME, fr. L *contemptus*, fr. *contemptus*, past part. of *contemnere* to despise — more at CONTEMN] **1 a :** the act of despising or the state of mind of one who despises : the feeling with which one regards something that is esteemed low, vile, or worthless : DISDAIN, SCORN **b :** the condition of having no respect, concern, or regard for something ⟨and, in ~ of heaven and hell, dies rather than bear some yoke of priests or kings —John Masefield⟩ **2 :** the state of being despised : DISGRACE, SHAME ⟨bring his nation into ~⟩ **3** *obs* : an object of contempt **4 a :** willful disobedience to or open disrespect of the valid rules, orders, or process or the dignity or authority of a court or a judge acting in a judicial capacity whether by contumacious or insolent language, by disturbing or obstructive conduct, or by mere failure to obey the orders of the court **b :** willful disobedience to a lawful order of or willful obstruction of a legislative body in the actual course of exercising its lawful legislative powers **c :** an act or expression denoting such contempt of judicial or legislative authority

²**contempt** \"\ *vt* -ED/-ING/-S *archaic* : CONTEMN

con·tempt·ibil·i·ty \kən,tem(p)tə'biləd·ē, -ətē, -i\ *n* -ES [LL *contemptibilitas*, fr. *contemptibilis* + L *-itas* -ity] : the quality or state of being contemptible; *also* : an instance of this

con·tempt·ible \kən'tem(p)təbəl\ *adj* [ME, fr. LL *contemptibilis*, fr. L *contemptus* (past part. of *contemnere* to despise) + *-ibilis* -ible — more at CONTEMN] **1 :** worthy of contempt : meriting scorn and condemnation as paltry, mean, base, or vile : held in contempt ⟨the Christianity which these emperors aimed at suppressing was . . . philosophically ~, politically subversive, and morally abominable —Matthew Arnold⟩ **2 :** worthy of being scorned, rejected, or ignored esp. for poverty or penury : unworthy of consideration ⟨with that property he will never be a ~ man —Jane Austen⟩ **3** *obs* : SCORNFUL, CONTEMPTUOUS ⟨'tis very possible he'll scorn it, for the man . . . hath a ~ spirit —Shak.⟩

syn DESPICABLE, PITIABLE, SORRY, SCURVY, CHEAP, BEGGARLY, SHABBY: CONTEMPTIBLE means deserving of contempt for any reason ⟨a curse may, like rags and dirt, be supposed to benefit a man by making him appear vile and *contemptible* —J.G.Frazer⟩ ⟨the one disgraceful, unpardonable, and to all time *contemptible* action of my life was to allow myself to appeal to society for help and protection —Oscar Wilde⟩ DESPICABLE, a more scornful term, may indicate utter worthlessness or suggest bitterness and indignation ⟨all things are sold . . . the smallest and most *despicable* —P.B.Shelley⟩ ⟨even excellent science could and did often make *despicable* morality —Christian Gauss⟩ PITIABLE applies to that which inspires mixed contempt and pity ⟨the resorting to epithets . . . is a *pitiable* display of intellectual impotence —M.R. Cohen⟩ ⟨that *pitiable* husk of a man . . . a shadow of his former insolence and splendor —E.V.Lucas⟩ SORRY is close to PITIABLE and suggests inadequacy, wretchedness, or sordidness ⟨I am a *sorry* physician and do but aggravate a disorder which I am seeking to cure —Benjamin Jowett⟩ ⟨one bids the poor pretender take his *sorry* self, a trouble and disgrace, from out the sacred presence —Robert Browning⟩ SCURVY implies the mean and vile inspiring disgust and contempt ⟨the *scurvy* mutilation of a portrait by a noble lord who had sat for it and then did not like it —C.E.Montague⟩ ⟨since some villain robbed his mates of their pork, we'll put it out of his power to play that *scurvy* trick again —C.B.Nordhoff & J.N.Hall⟩ CHEAP and BEGGARLY imply the petty, mean, and paltry ⟨any *cheap* and facile gibes about the duplicity and dissimulation of that church —T.S.Eliot⟩ ⟨the South in 1800 was a land of contrasts, of opulence and squalor . . . fine mansions, *beggarly* taverns —Van Wyck Brooks⟩ CHEAP may also indicate meretricious availability ⟨the wide insatiable mouth, painted as red as a wound, and the flaunting bare knees . . . *cheap*, that was the trouble —Ellen Glasgow⟩ SHABBY connotes the tawdry, worn-out, or ignoble ⟨a *shabby* electric sign that had said *Cedar Hill* before it lost its globes —Dashiell Hammett⟩ ⟨the old story, ever *shabby*, ever pitiful, of a man for whom intrigue was a substitute for creativeness —Max Lerner⟩

con·tempt·ible·ness *n* -ES \-nəs\ : the quality or state of being contemptible

con·tempt·ibly \kən'tem(p)təblē, -li\ *adv* **1 :** in a contemptible manner **2** *obs* : CONTEMPTUOUSLY

contempt of court : CONTEMPT 4a

con·temp·tu·ous \kən'tem(p)chəwəs\ *adj* [L *contemptus* contempt + E *-ous*] **1 :** manifesting, feeling, or expressing contempt or disdain ⟨the crowd were actively against him, and he was utterly ~ and indifferent —Ernest Hemingway⟩ ⟨the gambler smiled a thin, ~ smile —Dashiell Hammett⟩ **2** *archaic* : contemptible or exciting contempt : DESPICABLE — **con·temp·tu·ous·ly** *adv* — **con·temp·tu·ous·ness** *n* -ES

con·tend \kən'tend\ *vb* -ED/-ING/-S [MF or L; MF *contendre*, fr. L *contendere* to stretch vigorously, to strive, contend, fr. *com-* + *tendere* to stretch — more at TEND] *vi* **1 :** to strive or vie esp. with determination and exertion in contest or rivalry or against difficulties, exigencies, or failings ⟨the Manichean theory of a good and an evil spirit ~*ing* on nearly equal terms —W.R.Inge⟩ ⟨the *African Queen* might soon be ~*ing* with difficulties of refueling —C.S.Forester⟩ **2 :** to strive in debate : engage in discussion : ARGUE ⟨stubbornly ~*ed* for what he believed to be the truth —H.E.Starr⟩ ~ *vt* **1 :** MAINTAIN, ASSERT, ARGUE ⟨~*ing* that literature must serve a moral function —C.I.Glicksberg⟩ **2 :** to struggle for : CONTEST ⟨she ~*ed* every point, objected to every request —Margaret Mead⟩

syn COPE, FIGHT, BATTLE, WAR: CONTEND is a general term indicating endeavoring or striving to vanquish an opponent or to overcome difficulties or adversities ⟨the lusty wrestlers shall *contend* —William Wordsworth⟩ ⟨ladies *contended* for the honor of being taken down to dinner by the brilliant French journalist —W.C.Brownell⟩ ⟨since they had left the Espanola country behind them, they had *contended* first with wind and sandstorms, and now with cold —Willa Cather⟩ COPE may imply contending with an adversary on even or better than even terms and defeating or parrying his efforts, or facing adversity, difficulty, exigency and finding expedients ⟨a boy of barely sixteen cannot stand against the moral pressure of a father and mother who have always oppressed him any more than he can *cope* physically with a powerful full-grown man —Samuel Butler †1902⟩ ⟨the National Government had to *cope* with . . . provincial separatism —Owen & Eleanor Lattimore⟩ ⟨the inadequate medical staff, without drugs, could not *cope* with the situation —W.B.Hesseltine⟩ FIGHT is likely to involve notions of more strenuous activity or even violence than CONTEND or COPE; it suggests constant vigorous effort ⟨while Spaniards *fought* back with gun and Gospel to retain control of territories painfully won —R.A. Billington⟩ ⟨the advocates of the old classical education have been gallantly *fighting* a losing battle for over half a century —W.R.Inge⟩ ⟨he had *fought* like a demon every inch of the way against poverty and discouragement —A.W.Long⟩ BATTLE and WAR are more figurative; the first suggests contending as under battle conditions, with fierce fighting, resolute attack and defense, and changing fortunes ⟨grimy rescue teams working in shifts *battled* gas and smoke tonight attempting to reach an estimated sixty men still entombed by a Christmastide mine explosion —*N. Y. Times*⟩ ⟨thou wouldst have nobly stirred thyself and *battled* for the right —William Wordsworth⟩; the second suggests sustained struggle as under war conditions ⟨to *war* against my people and my knights —Alfred Tennyson⟩ ⟨spent his life *warring* against war, and disease, and poverty —V.L.Parrington⟩ ⟨housewife that is forever *warring* with the dust —Edith Sitwell⟩ **syn** see in addition COMPETE

con·tend·er \-də(r)\ *n* -S : CONTESTANT; *esp* : a contestant for a championship or high honor ⟨the leading ~ in his class⟩

[1]**con·tent** \kən'tent\ *adj* [ME *contente, content,* fr. MF *content,* fr. L *contentus,* fr. past part. of *continēre* to contain, hold together, restrain — more at CONTAIN] **1 a :** having the desires limited to whatever one has : not disposed to complain or grumble : SATISFIED, CONTENTED ⟨~ with any food that God doth send —Edmund Spenser⟩ **b :** inclined by wish, ambition, or design to no greater state or further act or advance than that specified ⟨presidents who have been ~ to leave the active leadership . . . to . . . Congress —A.N.Holcombe⟩ ⟨~ to wait his turn⟩ **2 a :** GRATIFIED, PLEASED — archaic except in the phrase *well content* **b** *archaic* : WILLING, CONSENTING **3 :** ASSENTING, AGREEING — used specif. in the British House of Lords as an affirmative response in voting

[2]**content** \"\ *vt* -ED/-ING/-S [ME *contenten,* fr. MF *contenter,* fr. *content,* adj.] **1 :** to make content : appease the desires of : SATISFY ⟨my own garden must ~ me this year —A.T.Quiller-Couch⟩ **2 :** to limit (oneself) in requirements for satisfaction or in immediate desires or actions — used with *with* ⟨he ~*ed* himself with threats⟩ **3** *obs* **a :** to satisfy the expectations or claims of : PAY **b :** GRATIFY, PLEASE ⟨his painted skin ~*s* the eye —Shak.⟩ **syn** see SATISFY

[3]**content** \"\ *n* -S [[1]*content*] **1 :** the state of being content : SATISFACTION, CONTENTMENT; *esp* : freedom from dissatisfaction, anxiety, or agitation ⟨cuddles down . . . with a grunt of sleepy ~ —Stephen Crane⟩ ⟨ate to his heart's ~⟩ — formerly also used in pl. **2** *obs* : acquiescence without examination ⟨the sense they humbly take upon ~ —Alexander Pope⟩ **3** *obs* : something that contents : a means of contentment **4 a :** an expression of assent to a bill or motion in the British House of Lords **b :** a member of the House of Lords who votes assent

[4]**content** \'kän,tent *sometimes* kən't-\ *n* -S [ME, fr. *content,* adj., contained, fr. L *contentus,* past part. of *continēre* to contain — more at CONTAIN] **1** *usu pl* **a :** something that is contained : the thing, things, or substance in a receptacle or an enclosed space ⟨he emptied his pocket of its ~*s*⟩ ⟨the ~*s* of the room⟩ **b :** the topics, ideas, facts, or statements in a book, document, or letter ⟨a table of ~*s*⟩ ⟨summarize the ~*s* of a will⟩ **2 a :** the matter esp. of a book or discourse : SUBJECT MATTER, SUBSTANCE ⟨when a man has nothing to say . . . sonority without ~ is the smartest effect he can achieve —G.W.Johnson⟩ **b :** essential meaning or significance ⟨if Zionism is to have ~ and vitality, it must impose obligation —Rose L. Halprin⟩ ⟨trying to translate these words "human values" . . . into . . . technical terminology and to put some ~ into them —F.S.C.Northrop⟩ **c :** the sum of events, physical detail, and information embodied in a work of art esp. as it gives rise to ideas and emotions — often contrasted with *form* **3** *archaic* **a :** CAPACITY, SIZE ⟨the ~ of a cask⟩ **b :** quantity of space, area, or length contained in certain limits : VOLUME ⟨the solid ~ of a tree⟩ **4 a :** the matter dealt with in a field of study : the subject matter of a discipline or an educational course ⟨the ~ of a national culture⟩ ⟨the ~ of sociology is inexhaustible —F.H.Giddings⟩ **b :** something that constitutes a part or element or a series of parts considered abstractly or without precise determination ⟨~ of consciousness⟩ **5 :** the amount of specified material contained, present, or yielded : PROPORTION ⟨the sulfur ~ of a sample of coal⟩ ⟨to reduce the soda ~ and increase the silica in glass⟩

content analysis *n* [[4]*content*] : a detailed study and analysis of the manifest and latent content of various types of communication (as newspapers, radio programs, and propaganda films) through a classification, tabulation, and evaluation of their key symbols and themes in order to ascertain their meaning and probable effect

contentation *n* -S [ME *contentacioun* payment, fr. ML *contentation-, contentatio,* fr. *contentatus* (past part. of *contentare* to pay, satisfy, fr. L *contentus*) + *-ion-, -io* -ion] **1** *obs* : a making or being contented; *also* : whatever makes one content **2** *obs* : state of contentment

con·tent·ed \kən'tentəd\ *adj* **1 :** CONTENT : easy in mind : satisfied esp. with one's lot in life : characterized by or suggesting contentment ⟨leading ~ lives⟩ ⟨a ~ little sigh⟩ **2** *obs* : WILLING — **con·tent·ed·ly** *adv*

con·tent·ed·ness \-nəs\ *n* -ES : CONTENTMENT

con·ten·tion \kən'tenchən\ *n* -S [ME *contencioun,* fr. MF, fr. L *contention-, contentio,* fr. *contentus* (past part. of *contendere* to contend) + *-ion-, -io* -ion — more at CONTEND] **1 :** an act or instance of contending : violent effort or struggle to obtain, resist, or compete : CONFLICT, STRIFE ⟨in spite of the violent ~*s* of the great . . . many of the cities of Italy were advancing in prosperity —C.E.Norton⟩ **2 :** strife in words : ALTERCATION, CONTROVERSY, SQUABBLING ⟨to escape the theological ~*s* in the Congregational parish —S.E.Morison⟩ — often used in the phrase *bone of contention* **3 :** a point advanced or maintained in a debate or argument : the subject matter of debate or strife : CLAIM, CHARGE, THESIS ⟨supporting his ~ with biblical and mythological evidence —*Amer. Guide Series: Pa.*⟩ ⟨the ~ that the growers . . . concurred with the pricing and grading —*Farmer's Weekly (So. Africa)*⟩ **4** *archaic* : strong effort : earnest striving ⟨a study that requires effort and ~ of mind —William Whewell⟩ **5 :** RIVALRY, COMPETITION ⟨too slow to keep him in ~ with even the cheapest of company —D.M.Mankiewicz⟩ **syn** see DISCORD

con·ten·tion·al \-chən°l\ *adj* : characterized by contention : CONTENTIOUS

con·ten·tious \kən'tenchəs\ *adj* [ME *contenciose,* fr. L *contentiosus,* fr. *contentio* contention + *-osus* -ose, -ous] **1 a :** given to contention : marked by an often perverse and wearisome tendency to quarrels and disputes ⟨a ~ nature⟩ **b :** engaged in, employed in, or serving to carry on contention ⟨~ language⟩ ⟨~ objection⟩ ⟨the most ~, quarrelsome, disagreeing crew —George Berkeley⟩ **2 :** likely to cause contention : apt to arouse argument, conflict, or marked difference of opinion ⟨a ~ argument⟩ ⟨a ~ issue⟩ **3 :** relating to or involving the litigation of differences between contending parties **syn** see BELLIGERENT

contentious jurisdiction *n* : jurisdiction over matters in controversy — compare VOLUNTARY JURISDICTION

con·ten·tious·ly *adv* : in a contentious manner

con·ten·tious·ness *n* -ES : QUARRELSOMENESS

[1]**con·tent·less** \kən'tentləs\ *adj* : DISSATISFIED

[2]**con·tent·less** \'kän,tentləs *sometimes* kən't-\ *adj* : lacking content or meaning

con·tent·ment \kən'tentmənt\ *n* -S [ME *contentement,* fr. MF, fr. *contenter* to content + *-ment* — more at CONTENT] **1** *archaic* : the act or process of making content : SATISFYING ⟨~ of avarice is impossible⟩ **2 :** the quality or state of being contented **3 :** something that affords content or pleasure ⟨an old man's small ~*s*⟩ **4** *archaic* : GRATIFICATION, PLEASURE

content psychology \'=,=-\ *n* [[4]*content*] : the study of the components and constituents of consciousness specif. by introspective methods — contrasted with *act psychology*

contents *pres 3d sing of* CONTENT, *pl of* CONTENT

content subject *n* [[4]*content*] : a subject (as history, geography, science) studied in order to acquire a certain body of information rather than to achieve competence in a skill (as penmanship, typing, or composition)

con·terminal \kən, (')kän+\ *adj* [ML *conterminalis,* fr. L *com-* + *terminalis* terminal — more at TERMINAL] : CONTERMINOUS

con·terminate \kən, (')kän+\ *adj* [LL *conterminatus,* past part. of *conterminare* to border on, fr. L *com-* + *terminare* to terminate — more at TERMINATE] : CONTERMINOUS

contermine *vb* -ED/-ING/-S [F *conterminer,* fr. LL *conterminare*] *vt, obs* : to make conterminous ~ *vi, obs* : to be conterminous

con·ter·mi·nous \kən'tərm(ə)nəs, (')kän¦-, -tōm-\ *adj* [L *conterminus,* fr. *com-* + *terminus* boundary — more at TERM] **1 a :** having a common boundary (as with another section or country) : BORDERING, ADJACENT ⟨the side of Germany ~ with France⟩ ⟨Colorado and Utah are ~⟩ **b** *of a boundary* : COMMON, COINCIDENT ⟨states with a ~ boundary⟩ **2 :** COTERMINOUS **3 :** enclosed within one common boundary ⟨the 48 ~ states of the U.S.⟩ **syn** see ADJACENT

con·ter·mi·nous·ly *adv* : in a conterminous manner or position : so as to be conterminous

contes *pl of* CONTE

con·tes·sa \kən'tesə\ *n* -S [It, fem. of *conte* count, fr. L *comit-, comes* associate, companion — more at COUNT] : COUNTESS

contesseration *n* -S [LL *contesseration-, contesseratio,* fr. *contesseratus* (past part. of *contesserare* to contract friendship by means of tesserae, fr. L *com-* + *tessera* die, square tablet, token of friendship) + L *-ion-, -io* -ion — more at TESSERA] *obs* : the act of contracting friendship or union

[1]**con·test** \kən'test *also* 'kän,t-\ *vb* -ED/-ING/-S [MF *contester,* fr. L *contestari* to call to witness & *contestari (litem)* to introduce (a lawsuit) by calling witnesses, bring an action, fr. *com-* + *testari* to be a witness, fr. *testis* witness — more at TESTIS] *vt* **1 :** to make the subject of dispute, contention, or battle ⟨~ a seat in congress⟩ ⟨~ an issue⟩ ⟨~ a prize⟩ ⟨~ every inch of land in their retreat⟩ **2 :** to make a subject of litigation : dispute or resist by course of law : DEFEND ⟨~ a suit⟩ : CONTROVERT ~ *vi* : STRIVE, VIE ⟨~ with an opponent in argument⟩ ⟨~ against too strict regulations⟩

syn RESIST, WITHSTAND, OPPOSE, FIGHT, COMBAT, CONFLICT, ANTAGONIZE: these terms indicate a setting of one person or thing against another in a hostile or competing way and may be roughly distinguished according to the degree to which one of the things or forces takes the initiative against the other. RESIST and WITHSTAND suggest generally that the initiative lies wholly with the person or force competed against. RESIST implies an overt recognition of a hostile or threatening force and a positive effort to counteract it, repel it, or ward it off ⟨the criminal *resisted* captivity⟩ ⟨*resist* the pressure of political orthodoxy⟩ ⟨*resist* the enemy attacks⟩ WITHSTAND suggests a successful resistance so that if nothing is gained, at least nothing is lost ⟨most plants cannot *withstand* frost⟩ ⟨*withstand* the impact of humiliation and disease⟩ ⟨*withstand* the attacks by air⟩ CONTEST and OPPOSE suggest a more positive action against a threatening or objectionable force. CONTEST suggests the raising of the issue, the bringing into open question of the matter over which there is conflict ⟨the board's power to inspect private welfare agencies was later *contested* and restricted —*Amer. Guide Series: N. Y.*⟩ ⟨it is impossible to *contest* your principle —George Meredith⟩ ⟨attempt to reconcile *contesting* parties⟩ OPPOSE, perhaps the most general of the terms, can indicate almost any degree of attitude from mild objection to positive belligerence, and can suggest any action from a mere contrastive setting of one thing against another to open violence against an opposing force, although in all instances positive action is implied ⟨the chronic objector, who *opposes* every popular measure —S.M.Crothers⟩ ⟨he had been much *opposed* by women, crossed, balked, wronged, misled —Francis Hackett⟩ ⟨Whipple was said to be the only man in public life who dared *oppose* wholesale executions of the Sioux captives —*Amer. Guide Series: Minn.*⟩ ⟨human art, as *opposed* to mere tools and mechanical contrivances —Edward Clodd⟩ FIGHT and COMBAT suggest strong action. FIGHT puts the initiative clearly in the hands of the subject of the verb and stresses the forthrightness or belligerence of the action ⟨*fight* the enemy on all fronts⟩ ⟨*fight* the forces of evil⟩ ⟨*fight* extradition⟩ COMBAT stresses more the force or impact, though it says nothing about the success, of counteraction ⟨*combat* pollution in streams⟩ ⟨*combat* aggression⟩ ⟨*combat* business depressions⟩ CONFLICT and ANTAGONIZE do not fit easily into the scale. CONFLICT, never used transitively, indicates merely the fact of competition, friction, or hostility between two forces ⟨the two men *conflict* on all major principles⟩ ⟨one nation can *conflict* with another in territorial claims⟩ ⟨two logical principles often *conflict*⟩ ANTAGONIZE once carried the idea of placing oneself in opposition or in the position of antagonist but in current general use carries only the idea of arousing antagonism or making antagonistic ⟨to *antagonize* the other students in the class⟩ **syn** see in addition COMPETE

[2]**contest** \'kän,test\ *n* -S [MF *conteste,* fr. *contester,* v.] **1 :** earnest struggle for superiority or victory : COMPETITION, EMULATION, STRIFE, ARGUMENT; *also* : an encounter of such nature (as in arms) ⟨what mighty ~*s* rise from trivial things —Alexander Pope⟩ ⟨reelected almost without a ~⟩ **2 :** a competition in which each contestant performs without direct contact with or interference from his competitors — sometimes distinguished from *game* ⟨an oratorical ~⟩

syn CONFLICT, COMBAT, FIGHT, AFFRAY, FRAY: CONTEST is a general term applying orig. to arguments but now also to any competition or struggle ⟨boundary controversies or other *contests* between states (as, for instance, the litigation arising out of Chicago's attempted use of the waters of the Great Lakes) —Felix Frankfurter⟩ ⟨an athletic *contest*⟩ ⟨prominent among the great events which the 18th century witnessed was the *contest* between England and France for the control of the Mississippi valley —G.M.Capers⟩ CONFLICT implies a jarring clash ranging from discordant argument through any sustained active opposition up to warfare ⟨he then returned to Massachusetts with authority to enlist troops, which led to a *conflict* with the state authorities —C.R.Fish⟩ ⟨primitive competition was a *conflict* as to which should murder the other man and his wife and children; modern competition in the shape of war still takes this form —Bertrand Russell⟩ COMBAT implies an encounter, often an armed one ⟨these progressive leaders in both parties rose only after bitter struggle. They were the product of more than a lively contest. Sometimes the contests were *combats* —W.A.White⟩ ⟨he [Alexander the Great] had mastered, in defiance of fatigue, hardship, and *combat* . . . unknown Indian regions —George Grote⟩ FIGHT implies a rigorous strenuous struggle, sustained at high pitch for a time at least, and resolute and determined ⟨the *fight* at the rampart⟩ ⟨the *fight* for world peace⟩ ⟨mental *fight* means thinking against the current, not with it. That current flows fast and furious —Virginia Woolf⟩ AFFRAY, now somewhat literary in suggestion, may indicate a wild, confused, sharp fight ⟨the suppressing of riots and *affrays* —Edmund Burke⟩ ⟨*affray.* — Fighting together of two or more persons in a public place to the terror of the persons lawfully there —*General Laws of the Commonwealth of Mass.*⟩ FRAY, also somewhat literary, may apply to any fight or combat marked by quick individual action against a background of noisy confusion ⟨a *fray* is a fight in a public place to the terror of the people, in which acts of violence occur or dangerous weapons are exhibited or threatened to be used —*U.S. Manual for Courts-Martial*⟩

con·test·able \kən'testəbəl, 'kän,te-\ *adj* [F, fr. *contester* to contest + *-able* — more at CONTEST] : capable of being contested — **con·test·ably** \-blē\ *adv*

[1]**con·tes·tant** \kən'testənt *also* 'kän,-\ *n* -S [F, fr. pres. part. of *contester*] : one that participates in a contest; *specif* : one that contests or challenges an award or decision (as in election returns or in legal proceedings)

[2]**contestant** \"\ *adj* [F, pres. part.] : CONTESTING, DISPUTING ⟨the ~ parties in a court action⟩

con·tes·ta·tion \,kän,tə'stāshən, -(,)te's-\ *n* -S [MF & L; MF, fr. L *contestation-, contestatio,* fr. *contestatus* (past part. of *contestari* to call to witness) + *-ion-, -io* -ion — more at CONTEST] **1 :** an act or instance of contesting : CONTROVERSY, COMPETITION **2 :** a position assumed or a point made in controversy : CONTENTION **3 :** the preface of the Mass — used in the old Gallican liturgy

contested *past of* CONTEST

contested election *n* : an election of which the legality or validity of the result is challenged by the losing candidate

con·test·ee \¦kän¦tə¦stē, -(,)te¦s-; kən¦te¦s-\ *n* -S [[1]*contest* + *-ee*] : one whose election is contested

contesting *pres part of* CONTEST

contests *pres 3d sing of* CONTEST, *pl of* CONTEST

con·teur \kōn'tər, kō^{n}'t-\ *n, pl* **conteurs** \-r(z)\ [F, fr. *conter* to relate, count + *-eur* -or — more at COUNT] : a reciter or composer of contes : STORYTELLER

con·text \'kän,tekst\ *n* -S [ME, fr. L *contextus* connection, coherence, fr. *contextus,* past part. of *contexere* to weave, join together, fr. *com-* + *texere* to weave — more at TECHNICAL] **1** *obs* : the weaving together of words in language; *also* : the discourse or writing so produced **2 :** the part or parts of a written or spoken passage preceding or following a particular word or group of words and so intimately associated with them as to throw light upon their meaning **3 :** the interrelated conditions in which something exists or occurs : ENVIRONMENT ⟨historical ~⟩ ⟨within the general ~ of world disarmament —M.W.Straight⟩ ⟨that each man have an understanding of himself and of his job in its ~ —Oscar Handlin⟩ **4** *obs* **a :** coherence in discourse **b :** CONTEXTURE **5 :** things or conditions that serve to date or characterize an article (as a primitive artifact) : SURROUNDINGS **6 :** the fleshy part of the pileus of a mushroom or other pileate fungus as distinguished from the hymenium

con·tex·tu·al \kən'tekschəwəl, (')kän¦-\ *adj* [*context* + *-ual* (as in *textual*)] : in, relating to, determined by, or conforming to a context — **con·tex·tu·al·ly** \-wəlē, -li\ *adv*

contextual definition *n* : a definition in which the meaning of a word, expression, or symbol is partly or wholly determined by defining the meaning of a larger expression containing the definiendum (as a definition of *legal right* by the statement "X has a *legal right* to *y* = X has a claim upon somebody for possession of *y* which the courts will sustain") — contrasted with *explicit definition;* compare RECURSIVE DEFINITION

con·tex·tu·al·ism \kən'tekschəwə,lizəm\ *n* -S : PRAGMATISM, OPERATIONALISM

con·tex·tu·al·ist \-ləst\ *n* -S : PRAGMATIST, OPERATIONALIST

con·tex·tu·al·is·tic \kən¦tekschəwə¦listik, (')kän¦-\ *adj* : of, relating to, or having the characteristics of contextualism

con·tex·tur·al \kən'tekschərəl\ *adj* : relating to or producing contexture

con·tex·ture \kən'tekschə(r)\ *n* -S [F, fr. L *contextus* + F *-ure*] **1 :** the act or process of weaving or of assembling and putting together parts into a connected structure **2 :** the arrangement and union of the constituent parts of a thing ⟨myriads of flies . . . rose up momentarily; then, keeping their ~ like a veil, fell into place again —Hugh McCrae⟩ : structural character of a thing ⟨a critic with no perception of the ~ of the narrative⟩ : physical constitution : TEXTURE **3 :** a body or structure made by the interweaving or putting together of parts ⟨this sweet shady arbor . . . a ~ of woodbines, sweetbriar, jessamine, and myrtle —Izaak Walton⟩ : FABRIC ⟨a ~ of lies⟩ **4 :** CONTEXT ⟨setting him clearly in the ~ of his time as none of the biographies has done it —*New Republic*⟩

contg *abbr* containing

con·ti·cent \'käntəsənt\ *adj* [L *conticent-, conticens,* pres. part. of *conticēre* to be silent, fr. *com-* + *tacēre* to be silent — more at TACIT] : SILENT

con·tig·na·tion \,käntəg'nāshən\ *n* -S [L *contignation-, contignatio,* fr. *contignatus* (past part. of *contignare* to join with beams, fr. *com-* + *-tignare,* fr. *tignum* beam) + *-ion-, -io* -ion — more at STAKE] **1** *archaic* : a framing together of timbers : a joining esp. of beams and boards **2** *archaic* **a :** FRAMEWORK, STRUCTURE **b :** FLOOR, STORY

con·ti·gu·i·ty \,käntə'gyüəd·ē, -ətē, -i\ *n* -ES [F or L; F *contiguité,* fr. ML *contiguitat-, contiguitas,* fr. L *contiguus* + *-itat-, -itas* -ity] **1 :** the state of being contiguous : intimate association or relation : close proximity **2** *obs* : a continuous mass or series

con·tig·u·ous \kən'tigyəwəs\ *adj* [L *contiguus,* fr. *contingere* to touch on all sides — more at CONTINGENT] **1 a** (1) **:** touching along boundaries often for considerable distances ⟨Kentucky and Tennessee are ~⟩ ⟨a lot ~ to a road⟩ (2) *of angles* : ADJACENT 2 **b :** next or adjoining with nothing similar intervening ⟨the ~ bedroom —W.M.Thackeray⟩ ⟨two ~ benches —Jane Austen⟩ **c :** NEARBY, CLOSE : not distant ⟨while the dwelling vibrates to the din of the ~ torrent —William Wordsworth⟩ **d :** CONTINUOUS, UNBROKEN, UNINTERRUPTED : touching or connected throughout ⟨the houses . . . ~ all along from end to end of the town —Nathaniel Hawthorne⟩ **2 a :** immediately preceding or following in time or sequence : without intervening interval or item; *also* : involving items so occurring or arranged **b :** near in time or sequence **syn** see ADJACENT

con·tig·u·ous·ly *adv* : in a position or way that is contiguous

con·tig·u·ous·ness *n* -ES : CONTIGUITY

con·ti·nence \'känt(°)nən(t)s, -tənən-\ *also* **con·ti·nen·cy** \-t(°)nənsē, -tənən-, -si\ *n, pl* **continences** *also* **continencies** [*continence* fr. ME, fr. MF, fr. L *continentia,* fr. *continent-, continens* + *-ia* -y; *continency* fr. L *continentia*] **1 :** self-restraint from yielding to impulse or desire ⟨he knew what to say, so he knows also when to leave off, a ~ which is practiced by few writers —John Dryden⟩ **2 :** self-restraint in refraining from sexual intercourse **3 :** the ability to retain a bodily discharge voluntarily ⟨fecal ~⟩

[1]**con·ti·nent** \'känt(°)nənt, -tənənt\ *adj* [ME, fr. MF, fr. L *continent-, continens,* fr. pres. part. of *continēre* to hold together, repress, contain — more at CONTAIN] **1 :** exercising continence, specif. sexual continence : TEMPERATE, MODERATE, CHASTE **2** *obs* **a :** serving to restrain or limit : RESTRICTIVE **b :** CONNECTED, CONTINUOUS ⟨~ islands⟩ **3 :** containing or able to contain or retain **syn** see SOBER

[2]**continent** \" *sometimes* -t°n,ent *or* -tə,ne-\ *n* -S [in senses 1, 2, & 3, fr. L *continent-, continens,* pres. part. of *continēre* to contain, hold together, be continuous; in other senses, fr. L *continent-, continens* continuous mass of land, fr. *continent-, continens,* pres. part.] **1** *archaic* **a :** whatever contains something : RECEPTACLE **b :** whatever restrains or bounds something **2** *archaic* : whatever is the seat or the external representative of something or represents the totality of a complex being **3** *obs* : CAPACITY, CONTENT **4 a :** a continuous extent or mass of land : MAINLAND **b** *obs* : the land, the earth, or the world **5 a :** one of the great divisions of land on the globe; *specif* : a large body of land differing from an island or a peninsula in its size and in its structure, which is that of a large basin bordered by mountain chains (as No. America, So. America, Europe, Asia, Africa, Australia, and Antarctica) **b** *usu cap* : the continent of Europe — used with *the* ⟨traveling on the *Continent*⟩ **6 :** a large segment of the earth's outer shell including a terrestrial continent and the adjacent continental shelf

[1]**con·ti·nen·tal** \¦känt°n¦ent°l, -tə¦ne-, -təl *also rap. attrib* 'känt,ne-\ *adj* [[2]*continent* + *-al*] **1 a :** of or relating to the continent of Europe or the countries of the continent of Europe as distinguished from the British Isles **b :** of or relating to the continent of No. America **c** (1) *often cap* : of, relating to, or concerning the colonies or states later forming the U.S. ⟨*Continental* Congress⟩ (2) : WORTHLESS, CONFOUNDED — used in imprecation in negative expressions such as *not worth a continental damn* **d :** of, relating to, or concerning the continental U.S. **2 a :** of, relating to, or characteristic of a continent ⟨~ waters⟩ **b :** having large daily and annual ranges of temperature (as in the interior of a continent) **c :** NONMARINE — **con·ti·nen·tal·ly** \-t°lē, -təlē, -li\ *adv*

[2]**continental** \"\ *n* -S **1 a** *often cap* : an American soldier of the Revolution in the Continental army **b :** a piece of the Continental paper currency **c :** an inhabitant of a continent (as the continent of Europe) **2 :** the least bit : DAMN ⟨not worth a ~⟩ ⟨don't care a ~⟩

continental block *or* **continental mass** *n* : CONTINENT 6

continental breakfast *n, often cap C* : a light breakfast (as rolls or toast with coffee)

continental celtic *n, usu cap both Cs* : a division of the Celtic languages including Gaulish

continental code *n, sometimes cap 1st C* **:** the international Morse code — see MORSE CODE table

continental currency *n, usu cap 1st C* **1 :** the paper money issued by the Continental Congress during the American Revolution **2 :** a series of early American pattern dollar-size coins, struck in England in pewter, silver, and brass and bearing on the obverse the legend "Continental Currency" and the date 1776

continental divide *n* **:** a divide separating streams which flow to opposite sides of a continent

continental dollar *n, usu cap C* **1 :** a one-dollar note of Continental paper currency **2 :** a Continental currency coin

continental drift *n* **:** a hypothetical slow movement of the continents on a supposed deep-seated viscous or plastic zone within the earth — compare WEGENER HYPOTHESIS

continental glacier *n* **:** an ice sheet covering a considerable part of a continent — compare OCEANITY

continental heel *n* **:** a high slender shoe heel having a slightly curved back line and a slightly curved or straight breast line

continental island *n* **:** an island (as Great Britain) that is near and geologically related to a continent — compare OCEANIC ISLAND

con·ti·nen·tal·ism \ˌkäntᵊnˈentᵊlˌizəm, -təˈne-, -təˌli-\ *n* -s **1 :** a thing (as an expression, trait, opinion) characteristic of a continent or the residents of a continent, esp. the continent of Europe **2 :** a policy favoring the restricting of relations (as political and economic) to countries of the same continent ⟨warned against a narrow nationalism or even a ~ —*New Republic*⟩

con·ti·nen·tal·ist \-tᵊləst, -təl-\ *n* -s **:** a supporter or advocate of continentalism

con·ti·nen·tal·i·ty \ˌkäntᵊnᵊnˈtaləd·ē, -təˌne-, -ətē, -i\ *n* -ES **1 :** the quality or state of being continental **2 :** the degree to which a climate has continental qualities — compare OCEANITY

con·ti·nen·tal·ize \ˌkäntᵊnˈentᵊlˌīz, -təˈne-, -təˌlīz\ *vt* -ED/-ING/-S [prob. fr. F *continentaliser,* fr. *continental* (fr. E) + *-iser* -ize] **1 :** to make continental in scope, character, culture, or ideas ⟨~ American literature as a protest against local color —Carl Van Doren⟩ **2** *sometimes cap* **:** to affect with the ways or ideas of European culture ⟨the gradual *continentalizing* of American habits of recreation —*Nation*⟩

continental morse code *n, usu cap M* **:** the international Morse code — see MORSE CODE table

continental plateau *or* **continental platform** *n* **:** a broad protuberance of the surface of the lithosphere coinciding approximately with a continent but including also the continental shelf

continental pronunciation *n, sometimes cap C* **:** a method of pronouncing Latin and Greek in which the vowel values approximate those of the languages spoken on the European continent (as \ē\ for the letter *ī* and \ā\ for the letter *ē*) and the consonants are pronounced approximately as in English

continental rummy *or* **continental rum** *n, usu cap C* **:** a game of rummy for several players in which only sequences or the entire hand but no lesser part of it may be melded

continental shelf *n* **:** a comparatively shallow submarine plain of a width varying from several to several hundred miles forming a border to a continent and typically ending in a continental slope

continental slope *n* **:** the usu. steep slope from a continental shelf to the oceanic abyss

continental sunday *n, often cap C&S* **:** Sunday as observed on the continent of Europe commonly without special restrictions on public behavior and activities as distinguished from common British and American practice

continental system *n* **:** FRENCH SYSTEM

continental tea *n* [so called fr. its alleged use as tea during the Revolution] **:** LABRADOR TEA a

continental terrace *n* **:** the submerged margin of a continent (sense 6) including both the continental shelf and the continental slope

con·ti·nent·ly *adv* [¹*continent* + *-ly*] **:** in a continent or temperate manner **:** CHASTELY

con·tin·gence \kənˈtinjən(t)s\ *n* -s [in sense 1, fr. L *contingere* + E *-ence,* in sense 2, fr. MF] **1 :** CONTACT, TOUCHING ⟨angle of ~⟩ **2 :** CONTINGENCY

con·tin·gen·cy \kənˈtinjənsē, -si\ *n* -ES [MF or ML; MF *contingence,* fr. ML *contingentia,* fr. LL, possibility, fr. L *contingent-, contingens* (pres. part. of *contingere* to touch on all sides, to happen) + *-ia*] **1 :** the quality or state of being contingent: as **a** (1) **:** the condition that something may or may not occur **:** the condition of being subject to chance (2) **:** the happening of anything by chance **:** FORTUITOUSNESS **b** (1) **:** close connection or relationship esp. of a causal nature (2) *obs* **:** CONTACT, CONTINGENCE **2** [*contingence* + *-y*] **a :** something that is contingent **:** an event or condition occurring by chance and without intent, viewed as possible or eventually probable, or depending on uncertain occurrences or coincidences ⟨the remarkable position of the queen rendering her death a most important ~ —Henry Hallam⟩ **b :** a possible future event or condition or an unforeseen occurrence that may necessitate special measures ⟨a reserve fund for *contingencies*⟩ **c :** something liable to happen as a chance feature or accompaniment of something else ⟨*contingencies* of marriage⟩ **syn** see JUNCTURE

contingency coefficient *n* **:** COEFFICIENT OF CONTINGENCY

contingency fund *n* **:** assets segregated as a fund for the purpose of meeting a specific or general contingency and usu. accompanied by a contingency reserve

contingency method *n* **:** a statistical method for computing the probability of the joint occurrence of attributes (as blue eyes and blond hair) which do not admit of refined measurement but can be roughly grouped

contingency reserve *n* **:** an appropriation of surplus or retained earnings that may or may not be funded, indicating a reservation against a specific or general contingency

contingency table *n, math* **:** a table in which the rows tabulate the frequency distribution of one variable and the columns that of another, serving therefore to indicate the existence of a contingency or correlation between the variables — compare CONTINGENCY METHOD

¹**con·tin·gent** \kənˈtinjənt\ *adj* [ME, fr. MF, fr. L *contingent-, contingens,* pres. part. of *contingere* to touch on all sides, happen, fr. *com-* + *-tingere* (fr. *tangere* to touch) — more at TANGENT] **1** *obs* **:** in contact **:** TOUCHING **2 :** of possible occurrence **:** likely but not certain to happen ⟨a bogey's alarum of ~ grave results —George Meredith⟩ **3 a :** happening by chance **:** affected by unforeseen causes or conditions **:** not patently necessary **:** unpredictable in occurrence or outcome ⟨a ~ event⟩ ⟨floods ~ and unexpected⟩ **b :** intended for use in exigent circumstances not completely foreseen **c :** unpredictable in outcome or effect because happening by chance and modified by unseen causes and unforeseen conditions ⟨speaks so scornfully of the ~ and tentative character of scientific knowledge —Sidney Hook⟩ **4 a :** dependent on, associated with, or conditioned by something else, sometimes indirectly or remotely ⟨the continuance of the latter is wholly ~ on the presence of the former —C.H. Grandgent⟩ **b :** dependent for effect on or liable to modification by something that may or may not occur ⟨a ~ estate⟩ ⟨a ~ legacy⟩ **5** *logic* **a :** not necessary **:** not true a priori **b** *of a proposition* **:** capable of being proved true or false only by experience **:** EMPIRICAL, FACTUAL **6 :** not necessitated **:** FREE — used of human volition, action, or existence **syn** see ACCIDENTAL

²**contingent** \"\ *n* -s [in sense 1, fr. ¹*contingent;* in other senses fr. F, fr. *contingent,* adj.] **1 a :** something that is contingent **:** CONTINGENCY **b :** a chance occurrence **:** ACCIDENT **c :** an extra salesperson who is available on call **2 :** a quota (as one's part in a general contribution): as **a :** a number of personnel supplied to the armed forces from a section ⟨the Ohio ~ in the army⟩ **b :** the military forces supplied by one combatant in an allied effort ⟨the British ~ in the Low Countries campaign⟩ **3 a :** a representational group ⟨the French ~ of Olympic athletes⟩ **b :** any group distinguished from the other members of an assemblage or organization ⟨the Democratic ~ at the conference⟩

contingent annuity *n* **:** an annuity terminable upon the happening of a future event uncertain either as to the date or the possibility of occurrence

contingent beneficiary *n* **:** a secondary beneficiary under a life-insurance policy whose rights mature if the primary beneficiary predeceases the insured or dies before payment of proceeds is completed

contingent fee *n* **:** a fee for services (as of a lawyer or agent) to be paid in the event of success in a particular transaction usu. as a specified percentage of the sum realized for the client or principal

contingent fund *n* **:** CONTINGENCY FUND

contingent liability *n* **:** an amount that may or may not be owed dependent on the outcome of a contingency (as a discounted note receivable)

con·tin·gent·ly *adv* [ME, fr. ¹*contingent* + *-ly*] **:** in a contingent way or manner **:** PROVISIONALLY, ACCIDENTALLY

contingent symbiosis *n* **:** HELOTISM 2

contingent truth *n* **:** EMPIRICAL TRUTH

contingent use *n, law* **:** a use to come into operation on a future uncertain event

continua *pl of* CONTINUUM

con·tin·u·al \kənˈtinyəwəl, -yəl\ *adj* [ME, fr. MF *continuel,* fr. L *continuus* continuous + MF *-el* -al — more at CONTINUOUS] **1 :** continuing in time **:** proceeding without stopping, interruption, or intermission **:** going on indefinitely — now used only of things ⟨the ~ dread of falling into poverty which haunts us all at present —G.B.Shaw⟩ **2 :** recurring in steady and rapid succession **:** repeated at intervals with brief perhaps regular intermissions in time ⟨~ storm . . . with frequent showers of snow —William Wordsworth⟩ **3** *obs* **a :** continuously acting or engaged **:** CONSTANT **b** *of disease* **:** CHRONIC **c :** forming a continuous series or whole **:** UNBROKEN

syn CONTINUOUS, CONSTANT, INCESSANT, UNREMITTING, PERPETUAL, PERENNIAL: CONTINUAL and CONTINUOUS indicate lasting occurrence or presence over long periods ⟨we live in a country where his Majesty's Cabinet governs subject to the *continual* superintendence, correction, and authority of Parliament —Sir Winston Churchill⟩ ⟨the new struggle was *continuous,* the old had been sporadic —Lewis Mumford⟩ CONTINUAL is somewhat more common than CONTINUOUS in describing intermittent action, but both words are well-established and satisfactory in this sense ⟨the century and a half that followed the gathering of the estates at Westminster was a time of almost *continual* war —J.R.Green⟩ ⟨*continual* and regular impulses of pleasurable surprise from the metrical arrangement —William Wordsworth⟩ ⟨*continuous* landslides raised the cost of maintenance so high that a loss was sustained each year —*Amer. Guide Series: Conn.*⟩ Unlike CONTINUAL in this respect, CONTINUOUS may apply to space as well as time ⟨the *continuous* plains of the Great Lowland overlap from the Continental and Arctic drainage of the Heartland into the east of the European peninsula —H.J.Mackinder⟩ CONSTANT strongly implies lasting steadiness, lack of change, or uniformity ⟨unfortunately, perhaps, experience does not grow at a *constant,* but at an accelerated, rate —J.W.Krutch⟩ ⟨personal goodness . . . of a very fitful cast — an occasional almost oppressive generosity rather than a mild and *constant* kindness —Thomas Hardy⟩ INCESSANT suggests virtually ceaseless uninterrupted activity ⟨his *incessant* talking and shouting and bellowing of orders had been too much —Jack London⟩ ⟨over that which we call the meaning of the words a poet uses, there goes on an *incessant* play of suggestion, caught from each user's own adventures among words —J.L.Lowes⟩ UNREMITTING indicates unceasing activity without slackening or halting ⟨sporadic outbursts are converted by the rationalization into purposive and *unremitting* activity —Aldous Huxley⟩ ⟨the men fifteen or twenty paces apart, all in concealment and under injunction of strict silence and *unremitting* vigilance —Ambrose Bierce⟩ PERPETUAL indicates lasting duration or unfailing repetition ⟨sins unatoned for and uncondoned bring purgatorial or *perpetual* torment after death, even as holiness brings eternal bliss —H.O.Taylor⟩ ⟨their heroic defense will be recorded for all time. It will be *perpetual* proof that democracy . . . can show the stuff of which it was made —F.D. Roosevelt⟩ ⟨weary . . . of *perpetual* state business and perpetual honors; he wanted a rest —Robert Graves⟩ PERENNIAL connotes either existence over a long period or certain recurrence ⟨those who have lived before such terms as "highbrow fiction", "thrillers", and "detective fiction" were invented realize that melodrama is *perennial* —T.S.Eliot⟩ ⟨to all who profess faith in the democratic ideal Jefferson is a *perennial* inspiration —V.L.Parrington⟩

con·tin·u·al·ly \-yəlē, -yəwəlē, -li\ *adv* [ME *continuelly,* fr. *continuel* + *-ly*] **1 :** in a continual way **:** UNCEASINGLY **2 :** continuously in time **:** without intermission **3 :** in regular or repeated succession **:** very often

con·tin·u·ance \kənˈtinyəwən(t)s\ *n* -s [ME, fr. MF, fr. *continuant*] **1 :** a holding on or remaining in a particular state or course of action **:** permanence esp. of action, condition, habits, or abode **:** PERSEVERANCE: **a :** PROLONGATION, DURATION ⟨great plagues, and of long ~ —Deut 28:59 (AV)⟩ **b :** a continuing or remaining in some place or condition **:** ABIDING, STAY ⟨~ in office⟩ **2 :** uninterrupted succession **:** continuation esp. of a species **3** *obs* **a :** CONTINUITY **b :** DURABILITY, PERMANENCE ⟨you call in question the ~ of his love —Shak.⟩ **4 :** a continuation or sequel esp. to a novel **5 :** the adjournment of the court proceedings in a case to a future day; *also* **:** the entry of such adjournment and the grounds thereof on the record

con·tin·u·an·cy \-wənsē, -si\ *n* -ES **:** CONTINUANCE

¹**con·tin·u·ant** \kənˈtinyəwənt\ *adj* [F or L; F *continuant,* fr. L *continuant-, continuans,* pres. part. of *continuare* to continue — more at CONTINUE] **1 :** CONTINUING **2** *phonetics* **:** of, being, or having the character of a continuant

²**continuant** \"\ *n* -s **:** one that continues **:** something that serves for continuation: as **a :** a consonant that may be continued or prolonged without alteration for the duration of an emission of breath **:** an open consonant: (1) *in some classifications* **:** any consonant except a stop or an affricate (2) *in some classifications* **:** any consonant except a stop, an affricate, a nasal, or a semivowel — compare SPIRANT **b** *math* **:** a determinant of which all the elements are zero except those of a principal diagonal and the two adjacent minor diagonals, one of the latter being made up of −1's **c** *philos* **:** something that continues to exist throughout some limited or unlimited period of time during which its inner states or its outer connections with other continuing existences may be changing or remaining unchanged — contrasted with *occurrent* **d :** a linguistic form descending without change or with only regular phonetic change from a form in an ancestral language or an earlier stage of the same language (as *bed* from Old English *bed, home* from Old English *hām,* Latin *unus* "one" from assumed Indo-European *oinos*) — compare REFLEX

¹**continuate** *adj* [L *continuatus,* past part. of *continuare* to continue] **1** *obs* **:** continuous without break or interruption in substance **2** *obs* **:** CONTINUOUS, UNINTERRUPTED, CHRONIC — **continuately** *adv, obs*

²**con·tin·u·ate** \kənˈtinyəˌwāt\ *vt* -ED/-ING/-S [L *continuatus*] *archaic* **:** to make continuous or give continuity to

con·tin·u·a·tion \kənˌtinyəˈwāshən\ *n* -s [ME *continuacioun,* fr. MF *continuation,* fr. L *continuation-, continuatio,* fr. *continuatus* + *-ion-, -io* -ion] **1 :** continuance in a state, existence, or activity **:** uninterrupted extension or succession **:** PROLONGATION ⟨~ of the war into next year⟩ **:** the causing of something to continue ⟨payments made in ~ of his obligated support⟩ **2 :** the action of carrying on or resuming after an interruption or break ⟨~ of the meeting was delayed until the next day⟩ **3 a :** something that continues, extends, increases, or supplements ⟨the border is a ~ of the central design⟩ **b continuations** *pl, obs slang* **:** TROUSERS, GAITERS **c :** a work (as a periodical or numbered monograph) issued in successive parts; *also* **:** one of the parts **4 :** CONTANGO

continuation school *n* **1 :** a school above the elementary level enabling young people in trade or industry to continue their schooling in their spare time **2 :** a small secondary school in Canada usu. in a remote rural area

¹**con·tin·u·a·tive** \kənˈtinyəˌwād·iv, -yəwəd·iv\ *adj* [LL *continuativus,* fr. L *continuatus* (past part. of *continuare* to continue) + *-ivus* -ive] **1 :** causing continuance or tending to continue **2 a** *of a modifier* **:** NONRESTRICTIVE **b** *of a verb form or aspect* **:** expressing continuation of an action — **con·tin·u·a·tive·ly** \-d·əvlē\ *adv*

²**continuative** \"\ *n* -s [LL *continuativus,* adj.] **:** something continuative: as **a :** a logical statement denoting continuance **b :** a continuative verb form **:** the continuative aspect **c** *phonetics* **:** CONTINUANT

con·tin·u·a·tor \kənˈtinyəˌwād·ə(r)\ *n* -s [F *continuateur,* fr. L *continuatus* + F *-eur* -or] **:** one that continues (as a work, a style, a tradition)

con·tin·ue \kənˈti(ˌ)nyü, -tinyə (*this pronunc bef a vowel or pause is esp S*); *often* -ˌnyəw+V\ *vb* -ED/-ING/-S [ME *continuen,* fr. MF *continuer,* fr. L *continuare* to connect, continue, fr. *continuus* continuous — more at CONTINUOUS] *vi* **1 a :** to be steadfast or constant in a course or activity **:** keep up or maintain esp. without interruption a particular condition, course, or series of actions **:** PERSEVERE, ENDURE, PERSIST ⟨~ to go to church each Sunday⟩ **b :** to keep going **:** maintain a course, direction, or progress ⟨the boat *continued* downstream after discharging the passengers⟩ ⟨the broad beach ~s all the way along the promenade⟩ — often used with *on* ⟨they *continued* on for a quarter of a mile —Norman Mailer⟩ **2 :** to be permanent or durable **:** remain in existence **:** ENDURE, LAST ⟨but now thy kingdom shall not ~ —1 Sam 13:14 (AV)⟩ **3 :** to remain in a place or condition ⟨if the patient ~s unconscious⟩ **:** ABIDE, STAY ⟨he cannot long ~ here⟩ **4 :** to proceed to discourse esp. after intermission ~ *vt* **1 :** to carry onward or extend **:** keep up or maintain (as an activity) ⟨*continued* walking all day⟩ **:** PROLONG **:** add to or draw out in length, duration, or development ⟨~ the battle⟩; *specif* **:** to resume (as a discourse) esp. after intermission **2 :** to cause to last, endure, or keep on ⟨*continued* my subscription for another year⟩ **3 :** to allow or cause to remain (in a place or condition) **:** RETAIN ⟨the trustees were *continued*⟩ **4 :** to keep on the court calendar **:** subject to further consideration **:** postpone by a continuance — used of a legal proceeding

syn LAST, ENDURE, ABIDE, PERSIST: CONTINUE indicates a remaining or going on, often in an uninterrupted way, without ceasing or ending ⟨in *continuing* cancer research lies the ultimate hope of providing the clinician with solutions to his many diagnostic and therapeutic dilemmas —*Americana Annual*⟩ ⟨the illusion *continues* that civilization can somehow be reconciled with atomic war —D.F.Fleming⟩ LAST may focus attention on a length of existence greater than the normal or expected ⟨the work that Michelangelo did complete has *lasted* well —Stringfellow Barr⟩ ENDURE often calls attention to resistances to destructive and disintegrative forces ⟨it is only the exceptional skeleton, protected by favorable circumstances, of which the bones will *endure* for thousands of years —A.L.Kroeber⟩ ⟨the government thus established *endured* till Oregon became a Territory —Joseph Schafer⟩ ABIDE, often poetic or archaic, may suggest unchanging constancy and stability ⟨O Thou who changest not, *abide* with me —Henry Lyte⟩ ⟨notwithstanding the countless features of . . . living which were *abiding,* the changes made themselves felt —John Mason Brown⟩ PERSIST may imply continuing or recurring with or as if with resolution, doggedness, or stubbornness ⟨the idea that there exists a universal remedy which is sovereign over all diseases has *persisted* through the centuries —G.W.Gray b.1886⟩ ⟨this tribal structure, though simplified to some extent by past reforms, still *persists* —Patrick Smith⟩ ⟨these forests have reigned supreme for countless millenia, probably having *persisted* more or less unchanged for a longer period than any other contemporary forest type —W.H. Hodge⟩

continued *adj* [ME, fr. past part. of *continuen*] **1 :** stretching out in time or space esp. without interruption **:** CONSTANT, CONTINUOUS ⟨cold weather, and ~ rain —John Dryden⟩ **2 :** resumed after interruption ⟨a ~ story⟩ — **con·tin·ued·ly** *adv* — **con·tin·ued·ness** *n* -ES

continued bass *n* **:** CONTINUO

continued bond *n* **:** a bond that need not be presented for payment at maturity but may be held for a further period usu. upon specified terms

continued fraction *n* **:** an expression in the form of a fraction whose numerator is an integer and whose denominator is an integer plus a fraction whose numerator is an integer and whose denominator is an integer plus a fraction, and so on; thus: $\cfrac{a}{a'+\cfrac{b}{b'+\cfrac{c}{c'+\ldots}}}$

continued product *n* **:** a finite or infinite product of the form $(1 + a_1)\ (1 + a_2)\ (1 + a_3) \ldots (1 + a_n) \ldots$ none of whose factors are zero

continued proportion *n, math* **:** a proportion in which the consequent of each ratio is the antecedent of the next (as $4:8=8:16=16:32$)

continued voyage *n* **:** CONTINUOUS VOYAGE

continues *pres 3d sing of* CONTINUE

continuing *adj* [ME, fr. pres. part. of *continuen*] **1 :** CONTINUOUS, CONSTANT **2 :** needing no renewal **:** LASTING, ENDURING ⟨a ~ contract⟩ — **con·tin·u·ing·ly** *adv*

continuing agreement *n* **:** an agreement made by a regular borrower with his lender, giving to the latter continued rights (as of collateral) for repeated transactions

con·ti·nu·is·mo \kənˌtinəˈwiz(ˌ)mō\ *n* -s [AmerSp, fr. Sp *continuar* to continue (fr. L *continuare*) + *-ismo* -ism — more at CONTINUE] **:** the practice in some Latin-American countries of maintaining a chief executive in power beyond the legal term of his office by such methods as amending the constitution or drafting a new one exempting the incumbent from the usual prohibition against reelection

con·ti·nu·i·ty \ˌkäntᵊnˈ(y)üəd·ē, -ntᵊnˈ(y)ü-, -ətē, -i\ *n* -ES [MF or L; MF *continuité,* fr. L *continuitat-, continuitas,* fr. *continuus* + *-itat-, -itas* -ity] **1 a :** the quality or state of being continuous **:** uninterrupted connection or succession **:** close union of parts **:** COHESION, COHERENCE ⟨the highest percentage of cures with the least disturbance in the ~ of tissue —E.D. Osborne⟩ ⟨~ of management⟩ **b :** the quality or state of continuing without essential change **:** uninterrupted persistence of a particular quality or essential with reference to conjoint changing qualities ⟨the life of ancient Rome, its unbroken ~ through the centuries, and its connection with the life of the modern world —H.N.Fowler⟩ **c :** continuousness in time **:** duration without intermission; *specif* **:** uninterruptedness of existence (as of germ plasm) **2 :** something that shows continuity **:** a connected or unbroken course or series: as **a :** the narrative line or the thematic development of an idea in a motion picture **b :** a detailed scenario or shooting script showing dialogue, shots, and transitions **c :** the script for a radio or television program (as of the introductory and transitional material used by an announcer or master of ceremonies of a musical or variety program); *also* **:** the lines read from such a script **d :** the story and dialogue of a comic strip; *also* **:** a daily comic strip or picture strip that sustains a narrative **3 :** an individual feature, element, or unit of a connected series ⟨number of *continuities* that can be discovered in the play —R.A.Brower⟩ **4** *math* **:** the property characteristic of a continuous function; *also* **:** an example of such property — compare DISCONTINUITY 3

continuity acceptance *n* **:** a department of a broadcasting company in which program material and commercials are examined and if necessary edited to assure conformity with government regulations and company policy

continuity girl *or* **continuity clerk** *n* **:** a member of a motion-picture crew that is responsible for recording the details of a take in order to avoid discrepancies and to facilitate editing

continuity title *n* **:** a legend or subtitle inserted into a motion picture to introduce a change of time or place or supply a necessary circumstance to the narrative

con·tin·uo \kənˈtinə(ˌ)wō *also* -inyə-\ *n* -s [It, lit., continuous, fr. L *continuus*] **:** an instrumental part usu. for keyboard instrument accompanying solo or choral or concerted instrumental voices and consisting of a succession of bass notes with numerals and other marks placed under each note according to a system that indicates the chords that are required at each step but leaves to the player's discretion the actual arrangement of the notes constituting each successive chord — called also *figured bass, thorough bass*

con·tin·u·ous \kənˈtinyəwəs\ *adj* [L *continuus,* fr. *continēre* to hold together — more at CONTINENT] **1 a :** characterized by uninterrupted extension in space : stretching on without break or interruption ⟨a ~ and rather spacious channel —C.H.Grandgent⟩ **b** : characterized by uninterrupted extension in time or sequence : continuing without intermission or recurring regularly after minute interruptions ⟨humanism has been sporadic, but Christianity ~ —T.S.Eliot⟩ ⟨a ~ rearrangement of electrons in the solar atoms results in the emission of light —James Jeans⟩ **2** : operated without interruption ⟨a ~ furnace⟩ ⟨a ~ retort⟩ **3** *of sculpture* : having one depicted scene following another without an obvious break **4** *of a beam, span, truss* : having three or more supports or extending over two or more panels — see BRIDGE illustration **5** *of plant spores* **a** : lacking septa **b** : merging or in protoplasmic continuity with the tissue of the cap or peridium (as in certain fungi) **6** : PROGRESSIVE 7 **7** : of the nature of a continuum **8** *of a function* : having an arbitrarily small numerical difference between the value at a point and the value at any point in a sufficiently small neighborhood of the point **syn** see CONTINUAL

continuous brake *n* : a train-brake system consisting of a series of brakes attached one to each car and operated on all the cars from one point

continuous current *n* : DIRECT CURRENT

continuous easement *or* **continuous servitude** *n, law* : an easement that does not require the act of man for its enjoyment (as an easement of drainage by a natural watercourse or a right of light or air) — compare DISCONTINUOUS EASEMENT

continuous girder *or* **continuous beam** *n* : a girder or beam having more than two supports

continuous hinge *n* : PIANO HINGE

continuous industry *n* : an industry in which most of the material is received at one point from which successive operations turn it into a finished product (as yarn spinning and paper manufacture)

continuous kiln *n* **1** : a series of connected kilns or one continuous chamber through which a fire travels, green brick being set ahead of the fire **2** : a long narrow kiln which is hottest in its middle portion and through which ware travels on cars or conveyor — called also *tunnel kiln*

con·tin·u·ous·ly *adv* : in a continuous manner ⟨a double feature alternates ~ throughout the day⟩

continuous mill *n* : a mill consisting of a series of consecutive rolls or dies; *specif* : one used in wire drawing through which a rod is passed from one set of rolls or dies to the next until finished

continuous miner *n* : a machine that cuts and loads coal in one continuous operation

continuous mixer *n* : a mixer (as of asphalt) into which the ingredients of the mix are introduced continuously, are mixed as they pass through the mixer, and are then discharged in a continuous operation — opposed to *batch mixer*

con·tin·u·ous·ness \-nəs\ *n* -ES : the quality or state of being continuous

continuous performance *n* : a performance (as of a motion-picture program) that is repeated continuously till closing so customers need not come at the beginning to see a complete showing

continuous phase *n* : DISPERSION MEDIUM

continuous pool *n* : fifteen-ball pool in which whenever 14 balls have been pocketed the frame is set up anew to be broken while or after pocketing the 15th ball

continuous spectrum *n* : a spectrum (as of light emitted by a white-hot lamp filament) having no apparent breaks or gaps throughout its wavelength range

continuous spinning *n* : rayon spinning in which extrusion, coagulation, washing, and winding are accomplished continuously on one machine

continuous variation *n, biol* : variation in which a series of intermediate types connects the extremes — compare QUANTITATIVE INHERITANCE

continuous voyage *n* : a voyage which in view of its purposes is regarded in international law as one single voyage though interrupted (as in transshipment of contraband of war) — see ULTIMATE DESTINATION

continuous watermark *n* : a watermark on stamps consisting of letters, words, or a phrase repeated continuously, only part of the mark appearing on each stamp

continuous waves *n pl* **1** : radio waves that continue with unchanging intensity or amplitude without modulation and that are used in telegraphy in which the wave is turned on and off with a key to form the dots and dashes of a code ⟨*continuous-wave* telegraphy⟩ — abbr. *CW* **2** : radio waves of which the intensity continues unchanged except for modulation — called also *modulated continuous waves;* see INTERRUPTED CONTINUOUS WAVES

con·tin·u·um \kən'tin(y)əwəm\ *n, pl* **contin·ua** \-wə\ *also* **continuums** [L, neut. of *continuus* — more at CONTINUOUS] **1** : something that is absolutely continuous and selfsame: as **a** : something of which no distinction of content can be affirmed except by reference to something else (as duration and extension which are capable of supporting distinctions only by reference to numbers or to such relations as those of *now* to *then, here* to *there, before* to *after*) **b** : something of which the only assertable variation is variation in time or space **2 a** : something in which a fundamental common character is discernible amid a series of insensible or indefinite variations ⟨a sensation ~⟩ **b** : an identity of substance uniting discrete parts; *broadly* : CONTINUITY **3** : a set that has the same transfinite cardinal number as the set of real numbers or the set of all the points of a straight line used as a number scale **4 a** : an ideal substance or medium containing no vacant spaces and devoid of discrete structure **b** : a continuous portion of a spectrum

contl *abbr* **1** continental **2** control

cont·line \'känt,līn, -lən\ *or* **cant·line** \'kant-\ *or* **cunt·line** \'kənt-\ *n* -S [*contline* fr. alter. of ²*cant* + *line; cantline* fr. ²*cant* + *line; cuntline* by folk etymology (influence of *cunt*) fr. *contline*] **1** : the space between the strands on the outside of a rope **2** : the space between the bilges of two casks stowed side by side

contn *abbr* continuation

con·to \'kän(,)tō\ *n* -S [Pg, lit., number, fr. LL *computus* computation — more at COUNT] *in Portugal and Brazil* : a monetary unit equal to 1,000,000 reis or to 1000 Portuguese escudos or 1000 Brazilian cruzeiros

con·to·ise \,käntə'wēz\ *n* -S [by alter.] : COINTISE

¹**con·tor·ni·ate** \kən'tȯ(r)nēət, -ē,āt\ *adj* [It *contorniato,* fr. past part. of *contorniare* to make a circuit or outline, fr. *com-* + *torniare* to surround, measure in circuit, fr. *tornio, torno* turning lathe, circuit, fr. L *tornus* lathe — more at TURN] : encircled by a groove just inside the edge ⟨a ~ medal⟩

²**contorniate** \"\ *also* **con·tor·ni·a·to** \=,=nē'äd·ō\ *n, pl* **contorniates** \-ts\ *also* **contornia·ti** \-'äd·ē\ [*contorniate* fr. F, fr. It *contorniato; contorniato* fr. It, fr. *contorniato,* adj.] : a thin bronze contorniate medallion of the Roman Empire first used about the time of Constantine the Great supposedly in connection with a game like chess

con·tort \kən'tȯ(ə)rt, -ȯ(ə)t, *usu* -d·+V\ *vb* -ED/-ING/-S [L *contortus,* past part. of *contorquēre* to twist, fr. *com-* + *torquēre* to twist — more at TORTURE] *vt* : to twist or twist together esp. in a strained or violent manner : turn awry : BEND, DISTORT ⟨branches that had been ~*ed* and gnarled by years of struggle to survive —*New Yorker*⟩ ⟨~ spelling and grammar⟩ ~ *vi* : to twist into a strained shape or expression (as from pain or violent feeling) ⟨his face would ~ in a grimace at the heat —D.C.Jenkins⟩ ⟨fine features hardened and ~*ed* with rage⟩ **syn** see DEFORM

con·tor·tae \kən'tȯrd·ē\ [NL, fr. fem. pl. of L *contortus*] *syn of* GENTIANALES

contorted *adj* **1** : twisted together : TWISTED ⟨a ~ coastline⟩ ⟨tears streaked her ~ face⟩ **2** : CONVOLUTE ⟨~ leaves in the bud⟩ — **con·tort·ed·ly** *adv*

con·tor·tion \kən'tȯrshən, -tȯ(ə)shən\ *n* -S [F & L; F *contorsion,* fr. L *contortion-, contortio,* fr. *contortus* + *-ion-, -io* -ion] : the act or result of contorting or the state of being contorted : a twisting into abnormal or grotesque shape : a needlessly or unduly complicated action or posture ⟨goes through tremendous ~*s* in an effort to link together her two separate plots—James Yaffe⟩ — **con·tor·tion·al** \-shənᵊl, -shnəl\ *adj*

con·tor·tion·ate \kən'tȯ(r)sh(ə)nət, -,nāt\ *adj* : CONTORTIVE

con·tor·tion·ist \kən'tȯ(r)sh(ə)nəst\ *n* -S : one who contorts or resorts to or practices contortions; *specif* : an acrobat who specializes in throwing his body into unnatural or extraordinary postures — **con·tor·tion·is·tic** \=,=shə¦nistik\ *adj*

con·tor·tive \kən'tȯrd·iv, -tȯ(ə)d·-\ *adj* : causing or characterized by or tending to contortions or twisting

¹**con·tour** \'kän,tu̇(ə)r, -tu̇ə\ *n* -S [F, modif. of It *contorno,* fr. *contornare* to surround, sketch in outline, round off, fr. L *com-* + *tornare* to turn in a lathe, fr. *tornus* lathe — more at TURN] **1** : the delimitations of a figure: **a** : the drawn or painted outline of a two-dimensional figure **b** : the periphery of a form seen two-dimensionally ⟨the ~ of a mountain silhouetted against the sky⟩ **c** : SHAPE, FORM ⟨the ~*s* of a statue⟩ ⟨the ominous ~*s* of a ravine⟩ — usu. used in pl.; used of any irregularly shaped body or uneven surface or curving line ⟨the ~*s* of the shoreline⟩ **2** : the individual features or the order or arrangement of features of anything having discernible and usu. complex structure — usu. used in pl. ⟨the ~*s* of a melody⟩ ⟨the ~*s* of the plan are beginning to emerge⟩ ⟨poetry is a discovery of ~*s* and connections —C.S.Kilby⟩ **3 a** *math* : a plotted curve : GRAPH **b** : a line or surface at all points of which a certain quantity, otherwise variable, has the same value (as lines of equal elevation on the ground or isothermal surfaces in a heat-conducting solid) : CONTOUR LINE **4** : a sequence of levels of pitch or stress typically extending over several successive words in an utterance **syn** see OUTLINE

²**contour** \"\ *vb* -ED/-ING/-S *vt* **1 a** : to draw or shape the contours of **b** : to shape (a thing) to fit the contours of something else ⟨~ the waist of a jacket⟩ **2 a** : to construct (as a road) in conformity to a contour **b** : to cultivate (land) along lines connecting points of equal elevation **c** : to provide (as a map) with contour lines ~ *vi* : to draw or plot a contour

³**contour** \"\ *adj* **1** : following the contour lines or running furrows or ridges along the contour lines to retard erosion of sloping land by runoff rainwater ⟨~ plowing⟩ **2** : made to fit the contour of something enclosed or contained ⟨~ sheet⟩

contour chair *n* [fr. *Contour,* a trademark] : a chair esp. designed to fit the form of the human body

contour feather *n* : one of the medium-sized feathers that form the general covering of a bird and determine the external contour — compare DOWN, FLIGHT FEATHER

contour interval *n* : the vertical distance between the elevations represented by adjacent contour lines on a map

contour line *n* : an imaginary line connecting the points on a land surface that have the same elevation; *also* : the line representing this on a map or chart

contour map *n* : a map showing the configuration of a surface by means of contour lines drawn at regular intervals of elevation (as one for every 20 feet)

contour map

con·tour·né \,käntu̇r¦nā\ *adj* [F, past part. of *contourner* to round off, twist, fr. It *contornare* to round off] *heraldry* : turned about — used of a figure facing to the sinister

contr *abbr* **1** contract; contraction; contractor **2** contralto **3** contrary **4** control; controller

¹**con·tra** \'käntrə\ *prep* [ME, fr. L, adv. & prep. — more at COUNTER] : AGAINST — used chiefly in the phrase *pro and contra*

²**contra** \"\ *adv* [ME, fr. L] : to the contrary : CONTRARIWISE

³**contra** \"\ *n* -S **1** : CONTRARY : a thing opposite or against another **2** : OFFSET : an item on the opposite side of an account or statement — compare PER CONTRA

⁴**contra** \'käntrə, 'kōn-\ *n* -S [by shortening and alter.] : CONTREDANSE 1

contra- *prefix* [ME, fr. L *contra-, contra* against — more at COUNTER] **1** : against : contrary : contrasting : in opposition ⟨*contra*-acting⟩ ⟨*contra*indicative⟩ ⟨*contra*tenor⟩ **2** : pitched below normal bass ⟨*contra*bassoon⟩ ⟨*contra*octave⟩ ⟨*contra*posaune⟩

¹**con·tra·band** \'käntrə,band, -baa(ə)nd\ *n* -S [It *contrabbando,* fr. ML *contrabannum,* fr. L *contra-* + ML *bannus, bannum* decree, of Gmc origin; akin to OHG *ban* command — more at BANNER] **1** : illegal or prohibited traffic : SMUGGLING ⟨persons the most bound in duty to prevent ~ —Edmund Burke⟩ **2** : goods or merchandise the importation, exportation, or sometimes possession of which is forbidden; *also* : smuggled goods **3** : a Negro slave who during the Civil War escaped to or was brought within the Union lines **4** : CONTRABAND OF WAR

²**contraband** \"\ *adj* : prohibited or excluded by law or treaty : FORBIDDEN ⟨~ liquor⟩ ⟨~ cargo⟩

³**contraband** \"\ *vt* -ED/-ING/-S **1** : to import illegally (as prohibited goods) : SMUGGLE **2** : to declare prohibited : FORBID

con·tra·band·age \-dij\ *n* -S : traffic in contraband

con·tra·band·ist \-dəst\ *n* -S [Sp *contrabandista,* fr. *contrabando* contraband (fr. obs. It) + *-ista* -ist] : one engaged in contraband trade : SMUGGLER

contraband of war : something that according to international law cannot be supplied to one belligerent except at the risk of seizure and condemnation by the other

¹**con·tra·bass** \'käntrə,bās\ *n* -ES [obs. It *contrabasso* (now *contrabbasso*), fr. *contra-* + *basso* — more at BASSO] : the largest instrument of the viol family having usu. four strings tuned in fourths and a range of about three octaves — called also *bass, bass fiddle, bull fiddle, double bass, string bass*

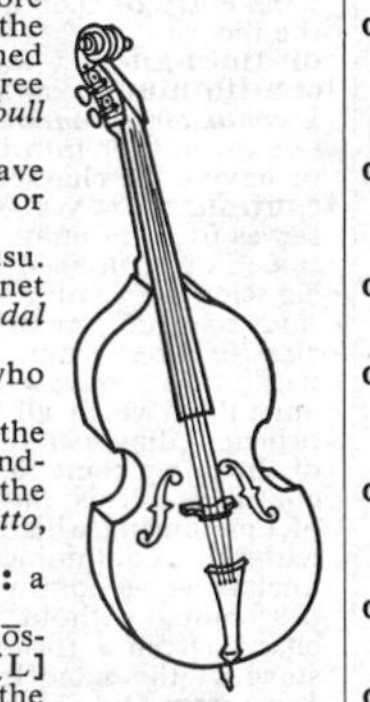

contrabass

²**contrabass** \"\ *adj* : pitched an octave below the normal bass instrumental or vocal range

contrabass clarinet *n* : a clarinet usu. pitched an octave below the bass clarinet — called also *double-bass clarinet, pedal clarinet*

con·tra·bass·ist \-səst\ *n* -S : one who plays a contrabass instrument

con·tra·bassoon \¦käntrə +\ *n* : the largest member of the oboe family sounding an octave lower in pitch than the bassoon — called also *contrafagotto, double bassoon*

con·tra·bassoonist \¦käntrə +\ *n* -S : a contrabassoon player

con·tra bo·nos mo·res \¦kōntrə¦bōnōs¦mō(,)rās, ¦kän-, -(,)rāz,-rez,-rēz\ *adj* [L] : against good morals : harmful to the moral welfare of society — used of contracts, which are then void by public policy

con·tra·cep·tion \¦käntrə¦sepshən\ *n* -S [*contra-* + *conception*] : the prevention of conception or impregnation by voluntary and artificial means — compare RHYTHM METHOD

¹**con·tra·cep·tive** \¦käntrə¦septiv *also* -təv\ *adj* [*contra-* + *conceptive*] : used for or relating to contraception

²**contraceptive** \"\ *n* -S : a contraceptive agent or device

con·tra·clockwise \¦käntrə + \ *adj (or adv)* [*contra-* + *clockwise*] : COUNTERCLOCKWISE

¹**con·tract** \'kän,trakt\ *n* -S [ME, fr. L *contractus,* fr. *contractus,* past part. of *contrahere* to draw together, collect, cause, make a bargain, make a contract, fr. *com-* + *trahere* to draw — more at DRAW] **1 a** : an agreement between two or more persons or parties to do or not to do something : BARGAIN, COMPACT, COVENANT; *esp* : an agreement that is legally enforceable — see QUASI CONTRACT; compare CONSIDERATION 8b, DEED, NUDUM PACTUM, PACTUM, PAROL CONTRACT, SPECIALTY CONTRACT **b** : the act by which two persons enter into the marriage relation; *also* : the agreement so to do : BETROTHAL **c** *archaic* : a legal transaction (as a grant between private parties or a grant, charter, or franchise from the state) ⟨no State shall . . . pass any bill of attainder . . . or law impairing the obligation of ~*s* — *U.S. Constitution*⟩ **d** : a collective agreement (as between an employer and a union) **2** *obs* : a drawing together : mutual attraction **3** : a writing made by the parties to evidence the terms and conditions of a contract **4** : the department or principles of law having to do with contracts **5** *card games* **a** : an undertaking usu. by the player or side that makes the highest bid to win a specified number of tricks or points; *also* : the number of tricks or points so undertaken **b** *contract bridge* : the final bid **c** : CONTRACT BRIDGE **6** [²*contract*] : a word or form undergoing contraction or resulting from contraction **7** : the customary unit of trading in produce exchanges ⟨one ~ in wheat is 5,000 bushels⟩ **8** : one of the installments in a course of schoolwork which a student undertakes to complete within a given time working at his own speed and under individual instruction according to a system originated in the public high school of Dalton, Mass.

²**contract** \(')kän¦trakt', kən-'-\ *adj* [ME, fr. MF *contracte,* fr. L *contractus,* past part.] : CONTRACTED ⟨a ~ noun⟩ : SHRUNKEN, NARROWED

³**contract** *in sense 1 usu* 'kän,trakt; *in other senses usu* kən'trakt\ *vb* -ED/-ING/-S [MF *contracter* to agree upon, enter into, fr. L *contractus* contract (agreement)] *vt* **1 a** : to enter into with mutual obligations : establish or undertake by contract ⟨~*ed* an engagement with a neighboring . . . farmer —Rose Macaulay⟩ : place under contract **b** : BETROTH, AFFIANCE ⟨~*ed* his daughter with the son of an old friend⟩ **2 a** : to bring on oneself : acquire usu. involuntarily (as a habit) : CATCH ⟨~ a disease⟩ ⟨~*ed* pneumonia⟩ **b** : INCUR ⟨~ an obligation⟩ ⟨~*ed* numerous debts⟩ **3 a** : LIMIT, RESTRICT ⟨the town's limits had not been ~*ed*⟩ **b** *obs* : ABRIDGE **c** : to draw together so as to wrinkle : KNIT ⟨a frown ~*ed* his brow⟩ **d** : to draw together or nearer : CONCENTRATE ⟨~ his armies into one force⟩ **4** [L *contractus,* past part.] : to reduce to less compass or smaller size : squeeze or force together : SHORTEN, NARROW, LESSEN ⟨~ a muscle⟩ : cause to shrink ⟨reexpand the world which Bacon had so effectively ~*ed* —J.W.Krutch⟩ **5** : to shorten (as a word) by omitting one or more sounds or letters or by reducing two or more vowels or syllables to one ~ *vi* **1** : to make a contract : COVENANT, BARGAIN ⟨responsible for ~*ing* with local institutions for the confinement . . . of Federal offenders —*Current Biog.*⟩ ⟨~ for the supply of meat to the barracks⟩ **2** : to draw together so as to diminish in size or extent : SHRINK ⟨iron ~*s* in cooling⟩ : become reduced in compass, duration, or length ⟨years ~*ing* to a moment —William Wordsworth⟩; *specif, of a muscle or muscle fiber* : to shorten and broaden

syn CONDENSE, COMPRESS, CONSTRICT, DEFLATE, SHRINK: CONTRACT is a general antonym for *expand* and indicates any drawing in and limiting of area or scope ⟨the range of classical reading might extend, or from time to time *contract* —H.O.Taylor⟩ ⟨since World War II gold mining has expanded considerably while supplies of Negro labor have been *contracting* —*N.Y. Times*⟩ ⟨he sank back into his chair, seeming to *contract,* to wither before their shocked eyes —Angus Mowat⟩ CONDENSE indicates a reduction of space occupied with resulting greater compactness of original material ⟨*condense* gas into a liquid⟩ ⟨in so far as we can *condense* Langland's message into a few words, we must sum it up as a long search for three degrees of excellence in life — Do Well, Do Better, and Do Best —G.G. Coulton⟩ COMPRESS indicates a pressing, often against resistance, into smaller compass and definite shape ⟨great depths of snow are accumulated, and this weight causes lower layers to *compress* and form ice —Patricia Spring⟩ ⟨one of those tiny handkerchiefs, *compressed* into the shape of a small puffball by being clutched in the palm of a feverish hand —J.C.Powys⟩ ⟨I shall make no attempt to *compress* a history of modern philosophy within the limits of one lecture —A.N.Whitehead⟩ CONSTRICT indicates a binding, squeezing, or gripping contracting, often forced, onerous, or painful ⟨the education of this promising young aristocrat *constricted* by the anti-intellectual traditions of his class excluded him from "the two great conceptions of our day . . . artistic integrity . . . and . . . social justice" —Harry Levin⟩ ⟨from the health point of view garments should in general never be so tight as to *constrict* the tissues —Morris Fishbein⟩ DEFLATE indicates contracting brought about by the exhausting of air or gas that fills or inflates it ⟨*deflate* a balloon⟩ ⟨in his lecture on temperance he *deflated* those who felt too superior to associate with a reformed drunkard —Ruth P. Randall⟩ SHRINK indicates a contracting of length, scope, or volume but may suggest the contracting of wet fabrics ⟨as colonial empires *shrink,* Europe's horizons will too —A.E.Stevenson †1965⟩ ⟨in 1906 he met his first sharp reverse in losses incurred by the San Francisco earthquake, but it was not until some seven years later that his modest fortune began to *shrink* —G.C.Knight⟩ **syn** see in addition PROMISE

con·tract·able \kən-'traktəbəl, (')kän-¦-\ *adj* : capable of being contracted ⟨~ diseases⟩

con·tract·ant \kən-'traktᵊnt, (')kän-¦-\ *n* -S [F *contractant,* fr. pres. part. of *contracter*] : one that contracts

contract bond \'kän,trakt-\ *n* : a bond or other form of indemnity agreement to indemnify one against loss or damage by reason of the breach of a contract (as for building, construction, or supply)

contract bridge \'=,=-\ *n* : a card game for four players in two partnerships identical with auction bridge except that odd tricks do not count toward making game or scoring slam bonuses unless they are undertaken in the contract — see BRIDGE, DUPLICATE BRIDGE

contract carrier \'=,=-\ *n* : a transport line that carries persons or property under contract to one or a limited number of shippers — compare COMMON CARRIER

contracted *adj* **1 a** : agreed upon : BARGAINED ⟨a ~ peace⟩ **b** : BETROTHED **2** : ABRIDGED, CONCISE **3** : ILLIBERAL, SELFISH, NARROW ⟨a ~ mind⟩ **4** : drawn together : SHRUNKEN, WRINKLED ⟨~ brow⟩ : NARROW, SHORTENED ⟨a ~ rest period⟩ — **con·tract·ed·ly** *adv* — **con·tract·ed·ness** *n* -ES

contracted foot *or* **contracted heel** *n* : a horse's foot exhibiting a shrinking or contraction of the lateral hoof walls preventing the proper expansion of the parts and producing pressure on the soft structures causing pain and lameness

contracted pelvis *n* : a pelvis that is abnormally small in one or more principal diameters and that consequently interferes with normal parturition

contract grade \'kän,trakt-\ *n* : a certain grade of a product (as wheat or cotton) defined and established by an exchange dealing in this product and assumed to be understood in every transaction between floor traders

con·tract·ile \kən-'traktᵊl, (')kän-¦-\ *also* **con·tract·ible** \-təbəl\ *adj* [³*contract* + *-ile* or *-ible*] : tending to contract : having the power or property of contracting : displaying or producing contraction

contractile cell *n* : one of the wall cells whose hygroscopic contraction causes the rupture of a sporangium or anther — see DEHISCENCE a (1)

contractile vacuole *n* : a vacuole in many unicellular organisms that gradually enlarges and suddenly collapses, dispersing its watery content often in regular pulsations, and that is thought to maintain the normal hydrostatic relation of the organism with its environment — see AMOEBA illustration

con·trac·til·i·ty \,kän-(,)trak'tiləd·ē, -ətē, -i\ *also* **con·tract·ibil·i·ty** \kən-,traktə'bil-, ,kän-\ *n* -ES : the capability or quality of shrinking or contracting; *esp* : the power of shortening or drawing into a more compact form possessed by living muscle fibers and to a less extent by many forms of living matter

contract in \'kän,trakt-\ *vi, Brit* : to consent in writing to pay to a trade union a levy for political use — compare CONTRACT OUT

contracting *pres part of* CONTRACT

con·trac·tion \kən-'trakshən\ *n* -S [L *contraction-, contractio,* fr. *contractus* (past part. of *contrahere* to draw together) + *-ion-, -io* -ion — more at CONTRACT] **1** [³*contract* (enter into) + *-ion*] : the making of a contract, agreement, or covenant ⟨the ~ of peace and friendship⟩ ⟨~ of marriage⟩ **2 a** : the action or process of becoming smaller, shorter, or pressed together ⟨the ~ of a gas on cooling⟩ : decrease of size or scope ⟨the ~ at the end of a discharge nozzle⟩ : the quality or state of being contracted : NARROWNESS ⟨complaining of monotony and the ~ of his life⟩ **b** (1) : the shortening and thickening of a muscle or muscle fiber (2) : a percussive tightening of the muscles usu. beginning in the pelvic region, affecting the whole body, and followed by release, the series constituting one of the basic movements of the modern dance **c** : a reduction in the volume of credit outstanding **d** : a reduction in business activity **3** : the act of acquiring or incurring (as a debt) or catching (as an infection) **4 a** (1) : a shortening of a word, syllable, or word group by omission of one or more sounds or letters or by the reduction of two or more vowels or syllables to one — used esp. of shortening in the interior of a word (as *e'er* for *ever*) and of shortening of enclitics (as *'ll* for *will* in *they'll*) and proclitics (as *'t* for *it* in *'t is*) — compare SYNCOPE 2a (2) **:** a form produced by such a shortening **b** (1) **:** representation of a word or part of a word by a nonalphabetic shorthand symbol (as the Latin genitive plural ending *-orum* by *4* or the *m* in Latin *cum* by a mark over the preceding letters, *cū*) — compare SUSPENSION (2) **:** a shorthand sign made up of two or more strokes and representing a word (3) **:** a conventional abbreviation; *esp* **:** one that uses the initial and final letters of a word, sometimes with one or more medial letters (as *Dr.* for *Doctor* or, in Late Latin manuscripts, *ds* for *deus, dns* for *dominus*) (4) **:** a braille sign representing a word of several letters (as *and*) or part of a word (as *com*) by means of a 1-cell or 2-cell character or representing a word by means of its chief consonants (as *rcv* for *receive*) **c** *classical prosody* **:** the substitution of one long syllable for two short ones — contrasted with *resolution*

con·trac·tion·al \kən·'trakshən°l, (')kän·¦-, -shnəl\ *adj* **:** of, relating to, or caused by contraction

con·trac·tion·ist \-shənəst\ *n* -s **:** an advocate of contraction esp. of the U.S. paper currency — opposed to *expansionist*

contraction joint *n* **:** EXPANSION JOINT

contraction rule *n* **:** a patternmaker's rule in which the divisions are made larger (1/96 for iron, 1/64 for brass) than standard measures to allow for contraction during cooling of the metal being cast

con·trac·tive \kən·'traktiv, (')kän·¦-, -tēv *also* -təv\ *adj* [³*contract* + *-ive*] **:** tending to produce contraction **:** CONTRACTILE — **con·trac·tive·ly** \-tə̇vlē, -li\ *adv*

contract labor \'kän·,trakt-\ *n* **1 :** labor based on a free but legally enforceable contract **2 :** labor imported from a foreign country under agreement to work for a particular employer

con·tract·less \'ˌ=,=ləs\ *adj* **:** lacking a contract

contract note \'=,=-\ *n* **:** a brief written announcement given by a factor or broker to his principal that he has bought or sold for his principal a certain amount of merchandise or securities at the terms specified

contract of affreightment \'¦=,=-\ **:** a charter party in which the vessel leased remains in the management of the owner

con·tract·om·e·ter \,kän·(,)trak'täməd·ə(r)\ *n* -s [³*contract* + *-o-* + *-meter*] **:** an instrument that measures stresses developed in electrolytically deposited metals

contract on \kən·'trakt-\ *vt* **:** to shrink on (as a steel tire to a wheel)

con·trac·tor \'kän,traktə(r), kən·'-\ *n* -s [LL, fr. L *contractus* (past part. of *contrahere* to contract + *-or* — more at CONTRACT] **1 a :** one that contracts **:** a party to a bargain **:** one that formally undertakes to do something for another **b :** one that performs work (as a printing job) or provides supplies on a large scale (as to troops) according to a contractual agreement at a price predetermined by his own calculations **c :** one who contracts on predetermined terms to provide labor and materials and to be responsible for the performance of a construction job in accordance with established specifications or plans — called also *building contractor* **2 :** something (as a muscle) that contracts or shortens

contract out \'kän·,trakt-\ *vi, chiefly Brit* **:** to remove oneself by contract from an incurred obligation ⟨believed that France could *contract out* of the war⟩; *specif* **:** to make formal refusal as a union member to contribute to a political levy — compare CONTRACT IN ~ *vt* **:** to send or assign outside on contract (as a part or process in manufacturing)

contract pinochle \'=,=-\ *n* **:** any of various partnership pinochle games in which a player may pass and later reenter the auction

contract practice \'=,=-\ *n* **:** medical service furnished by a physician or group of physicians to a group or class of individuals under an agreement (as with an industrial plant or a fraternal organization) that specifies the scope of the services to be rendered and the amount and form of the compensation — compare GROUP PRACTICE

contract quasi \'¦=,=ˈ=,=\ *or* **contract uti** \-'yü,tī, -'ü,tē\ *n* **:** QUASI CONTRACT

contract rummy \'=,=-\ *n* **:** any of several rummy games in which restriction is placed on what a player must meld in order to go out

contracts *pl of* CONTRACT, *pres 3d sing of* CONTRACT

contract shop \'=,=-\ *n* **1 :** a shop operating under a contract system **2 :** CLOSED SHOP **3 :** a shop in which conditions of employment are covered by a collective agreement

contract station \'=,=-\ *n* **:** a postal station operated under contract by private employees and usu. located in a private establishment (as a drugstore) — compare CLASSIFIED STATION

contract system \'=,=-\ *n* **1 :** an arrangement whereby industrial activities are carried out by a contractor intermediary between the manufacturer or entrepreneur and the workers **2 :** the system of selling to a contractor at a fixed sum per unit of time the labor of convicts to be performed within a prison under prison discipline with the contractor supervising the work and furnishing the materials — compare CONVICT LABOR SYSTEM, LEASE SYSTEM

contract tablet \'=,=-\ *n* **:** an ancient Babylonian or Assyrian clay tablet on which a contract was inscribed

contract theory \'=,=-\ *n* **:** a theory or the group of theories holding that society originated in a contract — compare SOCIAL CONTRACT

con·trac·tu·al \kən·'trakchəwəl, (')kän·¦-, -kshə-\ *adj* [L *contractus* contract + E *-al* — more at CONTRACT] **:** of, relating to, or implying a contract **:** bound or secured by a contract ⟨~ obligations⟩ ⟨a ~ salary increase⟩ — **con·trac·tu·al·ly** \-wəlē, -li\ *adv*

contractual liability insurance *n* **:** insurance against loss due to liability assumed under a contract

con·trac·ture \kən·'trakchə(r), -kshə-\ *n* -s [L *contractura* drawing together, fr. *contractus* (past part. of *contrahere* to draw together) + *-ura* -ure — more at CONTRACT] **1** *archit* **:** a narrowing of the girth of a column (as at the top) — compare ENTASIS **2 a :** a permanent shortening of muscle, tendon, fascia, or scar tissue producing deformity or distortion — see DUPUYTREN'S CONTRACTURE, ISCHEMIC CONTRACTURE **b :** an atypical contraction of skeletal muscle differing from the twitch and from tetanus in the slowness of its development and relaxation, in the absence of summation, and in anomalies of the associated electrical phenomena

con·trac·tus fi·du·ci·ae \kən·'traktəsfī'dükē,ī, -,fī'd(y)üshē,ē\ *n* [L, lit., contract of trust] **:** FIDUCIA

contract verb \'=,=-\ *n* [²*contract*] **:** a verb characterized by contraction (sense 4a) — used esp. in Greek grammar

contract whist \'=,=-\ *n* **:** a card game in which the deal, auction, and scoring are as in contract bridge but the play is as in whist with no dummy hand exposed

contra dance *var of* CONTREDANSE

con·tra·dict \,kän·trə'dikt\ *vb* -ED/-ING/-S [L *contradictus*, past part. of *contradicere* to speak against, fr. *contra-* + *dicere* to speak — more at DICTION] *vt* **1** *obs* **:** to resist or oppose in argument (as the claim or proposal of another) **2 :** to assert the contrary of **:** take issue with **:** GAINSAY, IMPUGN ⟨deny the truth of ⟨please ~ anything you hear said about . . . me —Sheila Kaye-Smith⟩ **3 a** *logic* **:** to be the contradictory of **b :** to be contrary or opposed to **:** go counter to ⟨no truth can ~ another truth —Richard Hooker⟩ **:** act in a manner contrary to ⟨his practice ~*s* his principles⟩ ~ *vi* **:** to deny, dispute, or assert the contrary of something ⟨he thought it outrageous to dispute and ~ —H.G.Wells⟩ **syn** see DENY

con·tra·dict·ed·ness \,==ˈ==əd·nəs\ *n* **:** the quality or state of being contradicted

con·tra·dict·er *or* **con·tra·dic·tor** \,==ˈ=tə(r)\ *n* -s **:** one who contradicts

con·tra·dic·tio in ad·jec·to \,kän·trə'diktē(,)ō,inad'yek(,)tō, -'dikshē(,)ō,ina'jek-\ *n, pl* **contradicti·o·nes in adjecto** \,==,==ō,nēz-\ [NL, lit., contradiction in what is added] **:** contradiction in terms

con·tra·dic·tion \,kän·trə'dikshən\ *n* -s [ME *contradiccioun*, fr. L *contradiction-, contradictio*, fr. *contradictus* + *-ion-, -io* -ion] **1 a :** the act of opposing in speech **:** GAINSAYING **b :** assertion of the contrary to what has been said or affirmed **:** denial of the truth of a statement **2 a :** a statement or proposition containing contradictory parts ⟨both parts of a ~ cannot possibly be true —Thomas Hobbes⟩ **b :** a self-contradictory phrase or expression ⟨a round square is a ~ in terms⟩ **3 a :** logical incongruity **:** INCOMPATIBILITY ⟨many patriots found no ~ in devoting their energies to the cause . . . and . . . making a little profit on the side —Sidney Warren⟩ **b :** opposition of facts, forces, tendencies, qualities, or events ⟨the inner ~*s* of an economic system⟩ **4 a :** direct opposition of logical contradictories **b :** an instance that violates the law of contradiction

con·tra·dic·tious \¦==¦=shəs\ *adj* [*contradiction* + *-ous*] **1 a** *obs* **:** CONTRADICTORY; *also* **:** ADVERSE **b** *archaic* **:** SELF-CONTRADICTORY **2 :** inclined to contradict or cavil **:** CONTRARY ⟨when a man won't even agree with you that times are bad you know he is of an independent and ~ nature —A.J. Liebling⟩ — **con·tra·dic·tious·ly** *adv*

con·tra·dic·tive \¦==¦diktiv, -tēv *also* -təv\ *adj* **:** CONTRADICTORY — **con·tra·dic·tive·ly** \-tə̇vlē, -li\ *adv*

con·tra·dic·to·ri·ly \,kän·trə¦diktərəlē, -k·trəlē, -li\ *adv* **:** in a contradictory manner **:** OPPOSINGLY, CONTRASTINGLY

con·tra·dic·to·ri·ness \-dikt(ə)rēnəs, -ri-\ *n* -ES **:** the quality or state of being contradictory

¹**con·tra·dic·to·ry** \,kän·trə'diktərē, -k·trē, -ri\ *n* -ES [ME, fr. LL *contradictorius*, adj.] **1 a :** a word, proposition, or principle that contradicts another **b :** OPPOSITE, CONTRARY ⟨it is common with princes to will *contradictories* —Francis Bacon⟩ **2** *logic* **a :** a proposition so related to another that if either of the two is true the other must be false and if either is false the other must be true **:** a proposition having the same terms as another proposition but opposite in quality and quantity ⟨"all *a* is *b*" is the ~ of "some *a* is not *b*"⟩ **b :** a term that is the exact negative of another ⟨"white" and "not white" are *contradictories*⟩ — distinguished from *contrary*

²**contradictory** \¦==¦=(ə)=\ *adj* [LL *contradictorius*, fr. L *contradictus* + *-orius* -ory] **1 :** tending to contradict **:** having the character or qualities of contradiction ⟨schemes . . . ~ to common sense —Joseph Addison⟩ **:** given to contradiction **:** CONTRADICTIOUS ⟨an irritable ~ nature⟩ **:** involving or causing contradiction ⟨uncoordinated often ~, agricultural programs⟩ **2** *logic* **:** being or having the character of a contradictory **syn** see OPPOSITE

contradicts *pres 3d sing of* CONTRADICT

con·tra·distinct \¦kän·trə +\ *adj* [*contra-* + *distinct*] **:** distinct by way of or by reason of contrast — **con·tra·distinctly** *adv*

con·tra·distinction \¦kän·trə +\ *n* [*contra-* + *distinction*] **1 :** the act of contradistinguishing **2 :** distinction by contrast **:** OPPOSITION ⟨to use that term art in ~ to science —J.W. Krutch⟩

con·tra·distinctive \¦kän·trə +\ *adj* [*contra-* + *distinctive*] **:** having the quality of contradistinction **:** serving to contradistinguish — **con·tra·distinctively** *adv*

con·tra·distinguish \¦kän·trə+\ *vt* [*contra-* + *distinguish*] **:** to distinguish by a contrast of opposite qualities ⟨man's earlier discoveries in mathematics were made by observation of his physical surroundings, as ~*ed* from abstract reason —A.N.Whitehead⟩

con·tra·fact \'kän·trə,fakt\ *or* **con·tra·fac·tum** \'==,=təm, ,==ˈ=\ *n, pl* **contrafacts** \-ts\ *or* **contrafac·ta** \-tə\ [NL *contrafactum*, fr. ML, neut. of *contrafactus*, past part. of *contrafacere* to counterfeit (trans. of MF contrefaire), fr. L *contra-* + *facere* to do — more at DO] **:** a 16th century musical setting of the mass or a chorale or hymn produced by replacing the text of a secular song with religious poetry — compare PARODY MASS

con·tra·fagotto \,kän·trə+\ *n, pl* **contrafagotti** [It, fr. *contra-* (fr. L) + *fagotto* bassoon — more at FAGOTTO] **1 :** CONTRABASSOON **2 :** a reed organ stop of 16-foot pitch

con·tra·flexure \¦kän·trə+\ *n* [*contra-* + *flexure*] **:** a bending in opposite directions like the curve of an ogee; *also* **:** the point where this occurs **:** a point of contrary flexure or inflexion that in a fixed beam is a point of zero bending moment

con·tra·flow \'kän·trə + ,-\ *n* [*contra-* + *flow*] **:** COUNTERFLOW

con·tra·hent \'kän·trəhənt\ *adj* [L *contrahent-, contrahens*, pres. part. of *contrahere* — more at CONTRACT] **:** entering into covenant **:** CONTRACTING ⟨one of the parties ~⟩

contrahierba *var of* CONTRAYERVA

con·tra·ion \¦kän·trə+\ *n* [*contra-* + *ion*] **:** COUNTERION

¹**con·trail** \'kän,trāl\ *n* -s [*condensation trail*] **:** streaks of condensed water vapor created in the air by an airplane or rocket esp. at high altitudes — called also *vapor trail*

con·tra·indicate \¦kän·trə+\ *vt* [prob. back-formation fr. *contraindication*] **:** to make (a treatment or procedure) inadvisable ⟨the ugly side of cortisone does not . . . completely ~ its use —Berton Roueché⟩ — **con·tra·indicative** \¦kän·trə+\ *adj*

con·tra·indication \¦kän·trə+\ *n* [*contra-* + *indication*] **:** an indication, symptom, or condition that makes inadvisable a particular treatment or procedure

con·tra·ion \¦kän·trə+\ *n* [*contra-* + *ion*] **:** COUNTERION

¹**con·trair** \kən·'trār, 'kän·trər\ *adv* (*or adj*) [ME *contrare*, *contrair*, fr. MF *contraire*, — more at CONTRARY] *Scot* **:** CONTRARY

²**contrair** \"\ *vt* -ED/-ING/-S [ME *contraren*, fr. *contrare*, adj.] *Scot* **:** OPPOSE, THWART

con·tra·lateral \¦kän·trə+\ *adj* [ISV *contra-* + *lateral*] **:** located or occurring on or acting in conjunction with similar parts on an opposite side of the body ⟨the brain cortex controls ~ muscles⟩ — compare IPSILATERAL

con·tral·to \kən·'tral(,)tō *also* -räl-\ *n* -s *often attrib* [It, fr. *contra-* (fr. L) + *alto* — more at ALTO] **1 :** the higher of the two countertenor voices or voice parts sung or to be sung in early 4-part church music by the highest adult male voice **:** ALTO 1 **2 a :** the lowest female singing voice or a singer possessing such a voice **:** ALTO 2; *specif* **:** a woman's voice rich and powerful in the lower range with a compass of about two octaves from f upward **b :** the part sung or to be sung by such a singer

con·tra mun·dum \¦kän·trə¦mündəm, -mən-\ *adv* (*or adj*) [NL] **:** against the world **:** in defiance of all general opinion

con·tra·octave \¦kän·trə+\ *n* [*contra-* + *octave*] **:** the musical octave that begins on the third C below middle C — see PITCH illustration

con·tra pa·cem \¦kän·trə¦pä(,)kem, -pāsəm\ *adv* (*or adj*) [ML] **:** against the peace — used of a legal allegation once material in prosecution for trespass but now purely formal

con·tra·pás \,kōn·trə'päs\ *n, pl* **contrapa·ses** \-ä(,)säs\ [Sp, fr. Catal *contrapàs*, fr. *contra-* (fr. L) + *pas* step, dance step, fr. L *passus* step — more at PACE] **:** a Catalan chain dance of ceremonial origin with grapevine steps varied in rhythm and direction according to the province

con·tra·ple·tal \¦kän·trə¦plēd·°l\ *adj* **:** polar and complementary

con·tra·plete \'kän·trə,plēt\ *n* -s [*contra-* + *-plete* (as in *complete*)] **:** one of the complementary relata of a polar relationship

con·tra·plex \'kän·trə,pleks\ *adj* [*contra-* + *-plex* (as in *duplex*)] **:** relating to or capable of sending two messages by telegraph in opposite directions at the same time — compare DIPLEX

con·tra·polarization \¦kän·trə+\ *n* [*contra-* + *polarization*] **:** the dilating influence of strongly polarizing atoms (as Li^+) on closed groups (as ClO_4 or CO_3) that may even cause the group to break up

con·tra·pone \'kän·trə,pōn\ *vt* -ED/-ING/-S [L *contraponere* — more at CONTRAPOSITION] **:** CONTRAPOSE

con·tra·po·nend \'kän·trəpə,nend, -pō,-\ *n* -s [L *contraponendum* thing that is to be contraposed, neut. of *contraponendus*, gerundive of *contraponere*] *logic* **:** a proposition upon which the operation of contraposition is performed

con·tra·posaune \¦kän·trə+\ *n* -s [G *kontraposaune*, fr. *kontra-* contra- (fr. L *contra-*) + *posaune* trombone — more at POSAUNE] **:** a powerful reed organ stop sounding an octave or sometimes two octaves lower than the ordinary posaune

con·tra·pose \'kän·trə,pōz\ *vt* -ED/-ING/-S [L *contrapositus*, past part. of *contraponere* to place opposite — more at CONTRAPOSITION] **1 :** to set over against (as the thumb to the fingers) **2** *logic* **:** to convert (a proposition) by contraposition

contraposed shoreline *n* **:** a shoreline along which wave action has removed a cover of marine sediments and exposed a previously buried land surface

con·tra·pos·it \'kän·trə,päzət\ *vt* -ED/-ING/-S [L *contrapositus*, past part.] **:** CONTRAPOSE 2

con·tra·pos·i·ta \,kän·trə'päzəd·ə\ *n pl* [L, pl. of *contrapositum* antithesis, fr. neut. of *contrapositus*] *logic* **:** the two propositions appearing in a process of contraposition

con·tra·position \¦kän·trə+\ *n* [LL *contraposition-, contrapositio*, fr. L *contrapositus* (past part. of *contraponere* to place opposite, fr. *contra-* + *ponere* to put, place) + *-ion-, -io* -ion — more at POSITION] **1 :** a placing over against **:** OPPOSITION, ANTITHESIS **2** *logic* **:** an operation of immediate inference in which the terms of a given proposition are permutated and negated (as given the contraponend "all S is P", there follows the contrapositive "all not-P is not-S" and vice versa)

¹**con·tra·pos·i·tive** \¦kän·trə¦päzəd·iv\ *adj* [*contraposition* + *-ive*] **:** of, relating to, or characterized by contraposition

²**contrapositive** \"\ *n, logic* **:** a proposition resulting from the operation of contraposition

con·trap·pos·to \,kōntrə'pä(,)stō\ *n* -s [It, contraposition, fr. *contrapposto* (past part. of *contrapporre* to oppose), fr. L *contrapositus*, past part. of *contraponere* to place opposite — more at CONTRAPOSITION] **:** a position of the depicted human body (as in late Renaissance painting and sculpture) in which twisting of the vertical axis results in hips, shoulders, and head turned in different directions

con·tra·prop \'kän·trə,präp\ *n* -s [*contra-* + *prop*] **:** CONTRA-ROTATING PROPELLER

con·trap·tion \kən·'trapshən\ *n* -s [perh. blend of *contrivance*, *trap*, and *invention*] **:** CONTRIVANCE **:** a newfangled or complicated device — usu. used in mild scorn or indulgence

con·tra·pun·tal \¦kän·trə¦pənt°l\ *adj* [It *contrappunto* counterpoint + E *-al*] **1 :** of, relating to, or according to the rules of counterpoint **2 :** POLYPHONIC **3 :** presenting a contrast of or interweaving of component elements — **con·tra·pun·tal·ly** \-t°lē, -li\ *adv*

con·tra·pun·tal·ist \-ləst\ *n* -s **:** CONTRAPUNTIST

con·tra·pun·tist \'kän·trə,pəntəst, ,==ˈ==\ *n* -s [It *contrappuntista*, fr. *contrappunto* + *-ista* -ist] **:** one skilled in counterpoint or one who writes or uses counterpoint

con·tra·pun·to \,kän·trə'pən(,)tō\ *n* -s [It *contrappunto*] **:** COUNTERPOINT

con·tra·remonstrance \¦kän·trə+\ *n* [NL *contraremonstrantia*, fr. L *contra-* + NL *remonstrantia* — more at REMONSTRANCE] **:** a remonstrance to a remonstrance

con·tra·remonstrant \¦kän·trə+\ *n* [NL *contraremonstrant-*, *contraremonstrans*, fr. L *contra-* + NL *remonstrant-*, *remonstrans* — more at REMONSTRANT] **:** one who makes a contraremonstrance

con·trar·i·ant \kən·'trerēənt, (')kän·¦t-\ *adj* [ME *contrariaunt*, fr. MF *contrariant*, fr. LL *contrariant-*, *contrarians*, pres. part. of *contrariare* to oppose, fr. L *contrarius*] **:** OPPOSED, ANTAGONISTIC, CONTRARY ⟨~ factions⟩ — **con·trar·i·ant·ly** *adv*

contraried *past of* CONTRARY

contraries *pl of* CONTRARY, *pres 3d sing of* CONTRARY

con·tra·ri·e·ty \,kän·trə'rīəd·ē, -ətē, -i\ *n* -ES [ME *contrariete*, fr. MF *contrarieté*, fr. LL *contrarietat-*, *contrarietas*, fr. L *contrarius* + *-tat-, -tas* -ty] **1 :** the quality or state of being contrary **:** OPPOSITION, DISAGREEMENT **2 :** something that is contrary to something else ⟨how can these *contrarieties* agree? —Shak.⟩: **a :** ANTAGONISM **b :** INCONSISTENCY, DISCREPANCY **c :** ADVERSITY **3** *logic* **:** the relation of contraries — see OPPOSITION

con·trar·i·ly \(')kän¦trerəlē, kən·'t- — *see* ²CONTRARY\ *adv* **:** in a contrary way **:** CONTRARIWISE, OTHERWISE

con·trar·i·ness *pronunc at* ²CONTRARY + nəs\ *n* -ES [ME *contrarinesse*, fr. *contrarie*¹ + *-nesse* -ness] **:** the quality or state of being contrary **:** OPPOSITION, PERVERSENESS

con·trar·i·ous \kən·'trerēəs, (')kän·¦t-\ *adj* [ME, fr. OF *contrarious*, fr. ML *contrariosus*, fr. L *contrarius* contrary + *-osus* -ous — more at CONTRARY] **1** *obs* **:** contrary in tendency or character **:** OPPOSED, HOSTILE **2 a :** PERVERSE, REFRACTORY, ANTAGONISTIC ⟨~ moods⟩ **:** VEXATIOUS ⟨~ weather⟩ **b** *archaic* **:** PREJUDICIAL, HARMFUL — **con·trar·i·ous·ly** *adv*

¹**con·trari·wise** *pronunc at* ²CONTRARY + ,wīz\ *adv* [ME *contrarie wise*, fr. *contrarie* + *wise*, n.] **1 :** on the contrary **:** OPPOSITELY **:** on the other hand ⟨not rendering evil for evil, or railing for railing; but ~, blessing —1 Pet 3:9 (AV)⟩ **2 a :** in contrary order **:** in a contrary manner **:** vice versa **:** CONVERSELY ⟨everything that acts upon the fluids must at the same time act upon the solids and ~ —John Arbuthnot⟩ **b :** on opposite sides or in opposite directions ⟨facing ~⟩ ⟨moving ~⟩ **3 :** PERVERSELY, CONTRARILY

²**contrariwise** \"\ *adj* **:** CONTRARY, PERVERSE ⟨her unexpected and ~ conversation —C.E.Craddock⟩

con·tra·rotating propeller \¦kän·trə+...-\ *n* [*contra-* + *rotating*] **:** one of a pair of propellers (as on a ship or airplane) mounted on concentric shafts, having a common drive, and turning in opposite directions to reduce the torque reaction

con·tra·rotation \¦kän·trə+\ *n* [*contra-* + *rotation*] **:** rotation contrary to another rotation (as of a propeller)

¹**con·trary** \'kän,trer|ē, *Brit usu & US sometimes* -trər|ē; *sometimes* 'kän·tr|ē *or* kən·'trer|ē; |i\ *n* -ES [ME *contrarie*, modif. (influenced by L *contrarius*) of OF *contraire*, fr. *contraire*, adj.] **1 :** the opposite **:** a proposition, fact, or condition incompatible with another **2 :** one of a pair of opposites (as objects, facts, qualities) ⟨thinking well of oneself . . . is the exact ~ of self-importance —F.A.Swinnerton⟩ ⟨pleasure and pain, wetness and dryness are *contraries*⟩ **3** *logic* **a :** a proposition so related to another that though both may be false they cannot both be true **:** a universal proposition affirming what another universal proposition denies or denying what another affirms (as "every vine is a tree" and "no vine is a tree") — distinguished from *converse;* compare OPPOSITION, SUBCONTRARY **b contrar·ies** *pl* **:** CONTRARY TERMS **4 contrar·ies** *pl, Brit* **:** foreign matter (as buttons and pins in rags or wax and bitumen in waste papers) that is removed in papermaking before pulping — **by contraries** *adv* **:** in a manner opposite to what is logical or expected ⟨in dreams things often go *by contraries*⟩ — **on the contrary** *adv* **1 :** on the other hand **2 :** just the opposite **:** NO ⟨"you look tired". "*On the contrary*, I feel fine"⟩ — **to the contrary** *adv* **:** to the opposite effect **:** NOTWITHSTANDING ⟨I know she's unhappy, all her brave talk *to the contrary*⟩

²**contrary** \", *but* kən·'trer|ē *or* |i *is as frequent as any other pronunc for sense 4*\ *adj* [ME *contrarie*, modif. (influenced by L *contrarius* contrary) of MF *contraire*, fr. L *contrarius*, fr. *contra* against + *-arius* -ary — more at CONTRA-] **1 a :** diametrically different **:** OPPOSED ⟨a move ~ to government policy⟩ ⟨facts which point to a ~ conclusion⟩ **b :** opposite in character or nature ⟨firm in the ~ intention⟩ **:** tending to an opposite or opposing course esp. of thought or development ⟨confirmatory or ~ evidence⟩ **c :** mutually opposed **:** ANTAGONISTIC ⟨holding ~ opinions⟩ **2 :** that is the other or opposite ⟨belonging to the ~ sex⟩ **:** opposite in position or direction **:** on the other side **:** in the other way ⟨moving the ~ way⟩ **3 :** opposed to one's interests or desires **:** UNFAVORABLE, PREJUDICIAL ⟨~ to the work which ye intend —Edmund Spenser⟩ — now used only of wind or weather ⟨prevented by ~ winds from reaching port⟩ **4 a :** disposed temperamentally to oppose, contemn, or disregard the wishes or suggestions of others **:** obstinately self-willed in refusing to concur ⟨they've been in your way all these years and you've always complained of them, so don't be ~ —Willa Cather⟩ **b :** expressive of or characteristic of such a temperament **:** PERVERSE ⟨a ~ word⟩ ⟨~ act⟩

syn PERVERSE, RESTIVE, BALKY, FROWARD, WAYWARD, CANTANKEROUS, CROSS-GRAINED, ORNERY: CONTRARY indicates a self-willed opposition to others' wishes, suggestions, and advice ⟨a very *contrary* child⟩ ⟨if you was to take it into your head . . . to marry a man like that . . . you wouldn't hear a single *contrary* word out of me or your ma —Erskine Caldwell⟩ PERVERSE, sometimes a stronger word, may imply wrongheaded, determined, or cranky opposition to the right, correct, established, or normal ⟨a malicious and *perverse* refusal to be convinced by the "greatest and highest evidences" which God has condescended to give to men —Leslie Stephen⟩ ⟨Rimbaud was the rebel incarnate . . . he was *perverse*, untractable, adamant until the very last hour —Henry Miller⟩ ⟨usually the most affectionate and docile of wives, Maimiti was now in one of the *perverse* humors which accompany her condition —C.B.Nordhoff & J.N.Hall⟩ RESTIVE may imply an obstinate disinclination to follow orders or act in accordance with established custom ⟨the common man . . . is increasingly *restive* under the state of "things as they are" —Thorstein Veblen⟩ Increasingly in today's English it suggests a disinclination arising from restlessness or impatience ⟨the freemen of the Massachusetts towns were *restive* under the strict rule of the magistrates —V.L.Parrington⟩ BALKY, often applied to animals, connotes a tendency to refuse to follow certain orders or to act or function as expected ⟨examination of witnesses mostly reluctant if not downright *balky* —*Nation*⟩ FROWARD implies habitual disobedience and refusal to comply with requests ⟨Russell had always been *froward*, arrogant, and mutinous —T.B.Macaulay⟩ ⟨*froward* beyond control, the insurgent young physician refused to submit the validity of his opinions to the decision of the clergy —John Bennett⟩ WAYWARD suggests extreme self-will and preference for one's own way and often implies an almost ungovernable wantonness ⟨one of the brightest intellects of the university, but he is *wayward*, dissipated, and unprincipled. He was nearly expelled over a card scandal in his first year —A. Conan Doyle⟩ ⟨conceived . . . by a *wayward* mulatto girl in a tryst —Worth T. Hedden⟩ CANTANKEROUS suggests truculent irritability ⟨Giddy felt *cantankerous* and wanted to get a rise out of Kennedy —Willa Cather⟩ ⟨a group of people . . . who are, almost by definition, *cantankerous*, jealous, and uncooperative —James Laughlin⟩ CROSS-GRAINED stresses irascibility and perhaps moroseness ⟨*cross-grained* as a hickory knot, he even resented persuasion from Emerson to convictions he already held —Isabel Paterson⟩ ORNERY suggests crusty disagreeableness ⟨you might find that bear and try to throw him, if you feel so *ornery* —Hervey Allen⟩ ⟨he's *ornery*, hardheaded, the damnedest . . . hotheaded man you ever saw —M.W.Straus⟩ **syn** see in addition OPPOSITE

³contrary *like* ²CONTRARY\ *vt* -ED/-ING/-ES [ME *contrarien*, fr. MF *contrarier*, fr. LL *contrariare* — more at CONTRARIANT] *now dial* : to act contrary to : OPPOSE, CONTRADICT ⟨try to do as they tell you and don't ~ them —H.L.Davis⟩

⁴contrary *like* ²CONTRARY\ *adv* [ME *contrarie*, fr. *contrarie*, adj.] : in a contrary way or manner : CONTRARILY, CONTRARIWISE, COUNTER

contrary-minded *pronunc at* ²CONTRARY + ¦mīndəd\ *adj* : of a contrary opinion

contrary motion *n* : melodic progression of two voices moving in opposite directions

contrary terms *n* : terms that cannot both be affirmed in the same sense of the same subject (as *white* and *black*, *good* and *bad*)

contras *pl of* CONTRA

con·tra·seasonal \¦kän·trə +\ *adj* [*contra-* + *seasonal*] : contrary or opposite to the normal seasonal trend ⟨a ~ rise in unemployment⟩ — **con·tra·seasonally** *adv*

¹con·trast \ˈkän‚trast, -raa(ə)st,-raist *also* -rȧst\ *n* -s [F *contraste*, fr. *contraster*] **1** [MF *contrast*, alter. (influenced by OIt *contrasto*, fr. *contrastare*) of *contrest*, fr. *contrester*] *obs* : STRIFE, OPPOSITION **2 a** : diversity of adjacent elements in a work of art — opposed to *gradation*, *transition* **b** : juxtaposition of dissimilar elements in a work of art (as complementary colors or lines of different weight) **3 a** : divergence between objects belonging to or having qualities belonging to the same category or associated in an actual or assumed relationship ⟨the ~ between the British and American forms of democracy⟩ ⟨blue eyes form a striking ~ to dark hair⟩ ⟨many authors develop their characters by ~⟩ **b** : comparison of like objects by means of which dissimilar qualities are made prominent ⟨a child of average ability may appear dull by ~ with a brilliant brother⟩ **4** : a person or thing exhibiting difference upon comparison with another ⟨as a ~ to the Queen, Ophelia brings a note of tenderness into the violent tragedy of *Hamlet*⟩ **5 a** : the quality of a photograph determined by the magnitude of the brightness differences between adjacent parts **b** : the ratio of the maximum and minimum illuminances in a scene ⟨a scene-lighting ~ of three to one⟩ **6** : a relationship accentuating the differences rather than the similarities between simultaneously or sequentially presented stimuli ⟨a color ~⟩ **syn** see COMPARISON

²contrast \kən·ˈt-, ˈkän‚t- *also* ˈkän·ˈt-\ *vb* -ED/-ING/-S [F *contraster*, fr. MF, to battle, resist, alter. (influenced by OIt *contrastare*) of *contrester*, fr. (assumed) VL *contrastare*, fr. *contra-* + *stare* to stand — more at STAND] *vi* : to form a contrast : exhibit somewhat marked or noticeable difference or opposition ⟨his fine words ~*ed* with his unscrupulous behavior⟩ ~ *vt* **1** : to put in contrast : set off by contrast or form a contrast to **2** : to compare in respect of differences : exhibit esp. antithetically the differences and relative worth of ⟨compare and ~ the two eras⟩ **syn** see COMPARE

con·trast·able \kən·ˈt...stəbəl, (ˈ)kän¦t-\ *adj* : capable of being contrasted

contrast bath \ˈkän‚t...-\ *n* : a therapeutic immersion of a bodily part (as a leg) alternately in hot and cold water

con·trast·ed·ly *adv* : in a contrasted manner

con·trast·ing·ly *adv* : in a way that makes a contrast ⟨demonstrating ~ and startlingly the infinitely greater worth of practices that derive from a spiritual view of the nature of man —J.F.Dulles⟩

con·tras·tive \kən·ˈtrastiv, -raas-,-rais- *also* -rȧs-; (ˈ)kän¦-; -tēv *also* -təv\ *adj* : forming or consisting of a contrast : CONTRASTING — **con·tras·tive·ly** \-təvlē, -li\ *adv*

contrastive linguistics *n* : a branch of linguistics concerned with showing the differences and similarities in the structure of at least two languages or dialects

contrast medium \ˈkän‚trast-,-raa(ə)st-,-raist- *also* -rȧst-\ *n* : a material comparatively opaque to X rays that is injected into a hollow organ to provide contrast with the surrounding tissue and make possible radiographic and fluoroscopic examination

con·trasty \ˈ=¦=stē, -ti\ *adj*, *usu* -ER/-EST : displaying marked contrast of visual tone; *esp* : having or producing in photography a great difference in brightness between highlights and shadows — compare CHALKY

con·tra·suggestible \¦kän·trə +\ *adj* [*contra-* + *suggestible*] : likely to respond to a suggestion by doing or believing the contrary

con·tra·tab·u·lar \¦kän·trə¦tabyələ(r)\ *adj* [*contra-* + L *tabula* board, tablet, will + E *-ar* — more at TABLE] *Roman law* : contrary to the terms of a written instrument, usu. a will

contratabular possession *n*, *Roman law* : possession of a decedent's estate granted contrary to the terms of his will (as where an emancipated son is neither instituted as heir nor expressly disinherited but is given possession by the praetor)

con·trate \ˈkän‚trāt\ *adj* [prob. fr. *contra-* + *-ate*] : having gear teeth set on the face of the wheel and perpendicular to its plane : relating to such an arrangement — used of a wheel in timepieces having verge or platform escapements

con·tra·tempo \¦kän·trə +\ *n* -s [It *contrattempo*, fr. *contra-* (fr. L) + *tempo*] : SYNCOPATION 2

con·tra·tenor \¦kän·trə +\ *n* -s [It *contratenore*, fr. *contra-* + *tenore* tenor — more at TENOR] : COUNTERTENOR

contra trombone *n* [*contra-*] : a reed organ stop of 16-foot pitch in the manual organ and 32-foot pitch in the pedal organ and similar to the contraposaune but less powerful

con·tra·valid \¦kän·trə +\ *adj* [*contra-* + *valid*] **1** : having no validity : FALSE, INDEFENSIBLE **2** *logic, of a sentence or class of sentences* : having every sentence in the system as a consequence : SELF-CONTRADICTORY — **con·tra·validity** \¦kän·trə +\ *n* -ES

con·tra·vallation \¦kän·trə +\ *n* -s [modif. (influenced by L *contra-*) of F *contrevallation*, fr. *contre-* (fr. L *contra-*) + LL *vallation-*, *vallatio* rampart, entrenchment — more at VALLATION] : a series of works confronting the walls of an invested place to isolate the defenders and safeguard the besiegers against sallies; *also* : construction of such works

con·tra·vene \‚kän·trə¦vēn, ˈ==‚=\ *vb* -ED/-ING/-S [MF or LL; MF *contrevenir*, fr. LL *contravenire*, fr. L *contra-* + *venire* to come — more at COME] *vt* **1** : to go or act contrary to : obstruct the operation of : INFRINGE, DISREGARD ⟨~ a law⟩ **2** : to oppose in argument : CONTRADICT, DISPUTE ⟨a proposition . . . not likely to be *contravened* —Robert Southey⟩ ~ *vi* : to make a contravention **syn** see DENY

con·tra·ven·tion \‚kän·trə¦venchən, ˈ==¦==\ *n* -s [MF, fr. LL *contraventus* (past part. of *contravenire*) + MF *-ion*] **1** : the act of contravening : VIOLATION, INFRINGEMENT ⟨warrants in ~ of the acts of Parliament —T.B.Macaulay⟩ **2 a** : the lowest class of offenses in the law codes of many European countries constituted by those punishable in police courts **b** *Scots law* : an act in violation of the provisions of a deed resulting in a forfeiture of an estate **c** *Scots law* : an act in violation of a legal obligation to keep the peace **syn** see BREACH

con·tra·version \¦kän·trə +\ *n* -s [*contra-* + L *-version-*, *-versio* (fr. *versus* — past part. of *vertere* to turn — + *-ion-*, *-io* -ion) — more at WORTH] : a turning toward the opposite side

con·tra·vindicate \¦kän·trə +\ *vi* [L *contra vindicatus*, past part. of *contra vindicare*, fr. *contra* + *vindicare* to claim — more at VENGEANCE] : to make a defense or a counterclaim in a Roman legal action to recover possession of property

con·tra·wise \ˈkän·trə‚wīz\ *adv* [alter. (influenced by *contra-*) of *contrariwise*] **1** : CONTRARIWISE **2** : CONTRA

con·tra·yer·va \‚kän·trə¦yərvə, ‚kōn-, -yer-\ *or* **con·tra·hier·ba** \-trə¦yerbə, -yervə\ *n* -s [Sp *contrayerba*, *contrahierba*, fr. *contra-* + *yerba*, *hierba* herb, grass, poison, fr. L *herba* herb; fr. the belief that it was a poison antidote — more at HERB] : a tropical American herb (*Dorstenia contrayerva*) the aromatic root of which was formerly used as a stimulant, tonic, and diaphoretic; *also* : any West Indian species of *Aristolochia* similarly used

con·tre basse \kōⁿ·trəbäs, ˈkän·trə‚bās\ *n* [F *contrebasse*, lit., contrabass, fr. MF, fr. OIt *contrabasso* — more at CONTRABASS] : a wood or metal organ stop of 16-foot pitch with a string tone — called also *violone*

con·tre·coup \ˈkōn·trə‚kü, ˈkän-‚, ‚==ˈ=\ *n* -s [F *contre-coup*, fr. *contre-*, counter- + *coup* blow — more at COUP] : injury of one part of an organ (as the brain) as a result of the transmitted shock from a blow on the opposite side

con·trec·ta·tion \‚kän‚trekˈtāshən\ *n* -s [L *contrectation-*, *contrectatio* act of touching, feeling, fr. *contrectatus* (past part. of *contrectare* to touch, feel, fr. *com-* + *-trectare*, fr. *tractare* to handle) + *-ion-*, *-io* -ion — more at TREAT] : the initial stage of the sexual act concerned with manual contact and tumescence

con·tre·danse \kōⁿ·trədäⁿs, ˈkän·trə‚dan(t)s\ *or* **con·tra dance** \ˈkän·trə‚dan(t)s\ *n* -s [F *contredanse*, by folk etymology (influence of *contre-* counter-) fr. E *country-dance*] **1** *usu contra dance* : a folk dance in which couples face each other in two lines or in a square — compare COUNTRY-DANCE, LONGWAYS **2** *usu contredanse* : a piece of music for a contra dance characterized by strongly marked duple rhythm in repeating 8-measure units

con·tre·fort \kōⁿ·trəfȯr, ˈkän·trə‚fōrt\ *n* -s [F, fr. MF — more at COUNTERFORT] : COUNTERFORT

con·tre gambe \kōⁿ·trəgäⁿb, ˈkän·trə‚gam(b)\ *n* -s [F *contre-gambe*, fr. *contre-* counter- + *gambe* viola da gamba, short for *viole de gambe*, part trans., part alter. of It *viola da gamba* — more at VIOLA DA GAMBA] : an organ flue stop of 16-foot pitch with a string tone

con·tre-jour \¦kōn·trə¦zhü(ə)r\ *adj* [F, lit., counter-daylight] *of a photograph* : taken with the camera pointed toward or nearly toward the chief source of light

con·tre·temps \kōⁿ·trətäⁿ, ˈkän·trə‚täⁿ\ *n*, *pl* **contretemps** \", -täⁿz\ [F, fr. *contre-* counter- + *temps* time, fr. L *tempus* — more at TEMPORAL] **1** : an inopportune embarrassing occurrence : MISHAP, MISCHANCE ⟨he moves steadily from one blunder to the next ~ to the next embarrassment —H.A. Smith⟩ **2** : SYNCOPATION

con·tre viole \kōⁿ·trəvyȯl, ˈkän·trəvē‚ōl\ *n* [F *contre-viole*, lit., counter viol] : a 16-foot organ stop with a string tone

contributary *var of* CONTRIBUTORY

con·trib·ute \kən·ˈtribyət, -i(‚)byüt, *chiefly in substand speech* -‚bət; *usu* -d·+V\ *vb* **contributed** \-yəd·əd, -yətəd\ **contributed** \" \ **contributing** \-yəd·iŋ, -yətiŋ\ **contributes** \-yəts, -yüts\ [L *contributus*, past part. of *contribuere* to bring together, fr. *com-* + *tribuere* to grant, impart — more at TRIBUTE] *vt* **1 a** : to give or grant in common with others (as to a common fund or for a common purpose) : give (money or other aid) for a specified object ⟨~ $10 to the project⟩ **b** : to furnish or supply (as a share or part to the advance of a project or development) ⟨primitive living conditions . . . have *contributed* a lot to the drift away from these Kimberley stations —F.J.R.Rodd⟩ : add (as knowledge or effort) to a common interest or activity ⟨these explorers *contributed* much to our knowledge of the Arctic⟩ **2** : to supply (as an article) for a publication ~ *vi* **1** *obs* : to pay tribute **2** : to give a part to a common fund or store : lend assistance or aid to a common purpose : have a share in any act or effect ⟨they . . . *contributed* to obstruct the progress of wisdom —Oliver Goldsmith⟩ **3** : to write and submit articles to a publication ⟨has written novels and *contributed* to magazines⟩

contributing *adj* : that contributes a share in anything or has a part in producing an effect : making a contribution to ⟨the seaport was a ~ factor in the growth of the city⟩ : that contributes regularly ⟨a ~ editor⟩ ⟨~ members pay the regular two-dollar dues⟩

con·tri·bu·tion \‚kän·trə¦byüshən\ *n* -s [ME *contribucioun*, fr. MF *contribution*, fr. LL *contribution-*, *contributio*, dividing, distributing, assigning, fr. L *contributus* + *-ion-*, *-io* -ion] **1** : a payment imposed upon a body of persons or on the population of a territory by civil, military, or ecclesiastical authority : IMPOST; *esp* : a tax or imposition levied on the people of a country by an army of occupation orig. as a payment for exemption from pillage but later to meet military necessity **2** : act of contributing ⟨the ~ of funds to a campaign⟩ **3 a** : something that is contributed : a sum or thing voluntarily contributed ⟨a five-dollar ~ to charity⟩ : the portion or share that an individual contributes to the common store ⟨a great ~ to our knowledge of the stars⟩ : a share contributed to any act or effect ⟨a ~ to the progress of the war⟩ **b** : something written or prepared for publication esp. in a periodical **c** : the whole that is formed by the gifts of individuals ⟨the total ~ amounted to $500⟩ **4 a** : a pro rata apportionment of loss among all the insurance policies covering a property as provided for by a clause in some policies **b** : a distribution of surplus by allocating to each life-insurance policy the excess of premiums and interest earned thereon over the expenses of management, cost of insurance, and the policy value at the date of computation; *also* : the excess so distributed **c** : a sum paid by an employer to an unemployment or group-insurance fund or for retirement benefits for employees; *also* : a sum paid by employees under such a plan **5** : a payment of an individual's share in a loss for which several are jointly liable; *also* : the amount so paid by one of them

con·trib·u·tive \kən·ˈtribyəd·iv, -yətiv\ *adj* [MF *contributif*, fr. L *contributus* + MF *-if* -ive] : contributing or tending to contribute — **con·trib·u·tive·ly** \-əvlē\ *adv*

con·trib·u·tor \-yəd·ə(r), -ətə-\ *n* -s [AF *contributour*, fr. L *contributus* + AF *-our* -or] **1** : one that contributes; *specif* : one that contributes articles to a publication (as a periodical) ⟨a prolific ~ to magazines⟩ **2** *obs* : one that pays tribute

con·trib·u·to·ri·al \kən·¦tribyə¦tōrēəl\ *adj* : of or relating to contributing or to a contributor — **con·trib·u·to·ri·al·ly** \-əlē\ *adv*

¹con·trib·u·to·ry \kən·ˈtribyə‚tōrē, -ȯr-, -ri\ *also* **con·trib·u·tary** \-ter-\ *adj* [ME *contributorie*, *contributarie*, fr. L *contributus* (past part. of *contribuere* to bring together) + ME *-orie* -ory *or -arie* -ary — more at CONTRIBUTE] **1** : subject to or contributing to a common fund or enterprise : subject to levy or furnishing a share or contingent ⟨~ allies⟩ **2** : of the nature of or forming a contribution : entering, given, occurring, or acting as a contribution, share, or aid toward effecting an end or result ⟨~ factors in a crisis⟩ **3** *obs* : TRIBUTARY **4** *of an insurance or pension plan* : contributed to both by employers and employees

²contributory \"\ *n* -ES [ME *contributorie*, fr. *contributorie*, adj.] **1** : one that contributes or is bound to contribute; *also* : a contributing factor **2** *Eng law* : one (as a past or present member) who is liable to contribute to the payment of the debts of a corporation on its being wound up

contributory mortgage *n*, *Brit* : PARTICIPATING MORTGAGE

contributory negligence *n*, *law* : negligence by an injured party that combines with the negligence of the injurer as a proximate and efficient cause in producing the injury and that bars recovery by the injured party at common law but may only diminish his damages in admiralty and under many statutes — compare WORKMEN'S COMPENSATION INSURANCE

con·trist \kən·ˈtrist\ *vt* -ED/-ING/-S [MF *contrister*, fr. L *contristare*, fr. *com-* + *tristare* to sadden, fr. *tristis* sad — more at TRISTE] : SADDEN

contristate *vb* -ED/-ING/-S [L *contristatus*, past part. of *contristare*] *obs* : SADDEN

con·trite \(ˈ)kän¦trīt, kən·ˈt-, *usu* -īd·+V\ *adj* [ME *contrit*, fr. MF, fr. ML *contritus*, fr. L, bruised, fr. past part. of *conterere* to grind, bruise, fr. *com-* + *terere* to rub, grind — more at THROW] **1** : broken down in spirit with grief and penitence for sin or shortcoming : REMORSEFUL : humbly and thoroughly penitent ⟨a ~ heart, O God, thou wilt not despise —Ps 51:17 (AV)⟩ **2** : proceeding from contrition ⟨~ sighs⟩ **3** *obs* : crushed or worn from rubbing — **con·trite·ly** *adv* — **con·trite·ness** *n* -ES

con·trit·ed \kən·ˈtrīd·əd\ *adj* [L *contritus* + E *-ed*] *archaic* : CONTRITE

con·tri·tion \kən·ˈtrishən\ *n* -s [ME *contricioun*, fr. OF *contricion*, fr. LL *contrition-*, *contritio*, fr. L *contritus* + *-ion-*, *-io* -ion] **1** : state of being contrite : consciousness of guilt or sin giving rise to humility and sorrow ⟨the tears of my ~ . . . repentance for things past —Edmund Spenser⟩ ⟨tears of ~ for her negligence⟩ **2** *obs* : the act of grinding : FRICTION **syn** see PENITENCE

con·trit·u·rate \kən·ˈtrichə‚rāt\ *vt* -ED/-ING/-S [*com-* + *triturate*] : TRITURATE, PULVERIZE

con·triv·able \kən·ˈtrīvəbəl\ *adj* : capable of being contrived

con·triv·ance \kən·ˈtrīvən(t)s\ *n* -s **1** : the act or faculty of contriving ⟨a ready and lively ~ of certain ideal solutions —J.P.Anton⟩ : inventive ability : skill at devising : INGENUITY ⟨the writer's expert ~ often becomes mere trickery⟩ **2** : the quality or state of being contrived : artificial arrangement or mechanical assembling as opposed to natural or logical development ⟨at times in the story ~ is obvious and so are coming events —L.T.Bulman⟩ ⟨the lack of emotional impact which is the effect of a too careful ~ —*Times Lit. Supp.*⟩ **3** : a thing contrived: **a** : ARTIFICE, SCHEME, PLAN ⟨telling a story honestly without dramatic ~*s*⟩ ⟨government is a ~ of human wisdom —Edmund Burke⟩ **b** : a mechanical device : INVENTION, APPLIANCE ⟨how prosaic the modern . . . ~*s* compared to the old boilers [fire-engines] —Elmer Rice⟩

con·triv·an·cy \-vənsē\ *n* -ES : the faculty or means of contriving

¹con·trive \kən·ˈtrīv\ *vb* -ED/-ING/-S [alter. of ME *contreven*, *controven*, fr. MF *controver*, fr. LL *contropare* to compare, fr. L *com-* + LL *-tropare* (perh. fr. L *tropus* metaphor, trope, figure of speech) — more at TROPE] *vt* **1 a** : DEVISE, PLAN, PLOT ⟨~ means of meeting⟩ **b** : to fabricate as a work of art or ingenuity : DESIGN, INVENT ⟨from stone, wood, shell, and bone the Indians *contrived* . . . household utensils —*Amer. Guide Series: Tenn.*⟩ **2** *now dial* : to find out : UNDERSTAND **3** *obs* : to form, shape, lay out, or adapt by contrivance ⟨the whole shire *contrived* into 33 hundreds —John Speed⟩ **4** : to bring about by stratagem or with difficulty : EFFECT, MANAGE — often followed by the infinitive ⟨he *contrived* to win the cooperation . . . of Voltaire, Buffon —*Times Lit. Supp.*⟩ ~ *vi* : to make devices : form plans, schemes, or designs : PLAN, SCHEME, PLOT ⟨if we were perfectly satisfied with the present we should cease to ~, to labor, and to save for the future —T.B.Macaulay⟩

syn DEVISE, INVENT, FRAME, CONCOCT: CONTRIVE may suggest ingenuity and cleverness in planning or effecting ⟨a couple of neighboring farmers in a village will *contrive* and practice as many tricks to overreach each other at the next market —Earl of Chesterfield⟩ ⟨the little dress that Maman had so cleverly *contrived* out of two Empire scarves —Anne D. Sedgwick⟩ ⟨you have come here to cast me off and artfully *contrive* that it should appear to be my doing —T.L.Peacock⟩ Sometimes it applies to a deliberate cleverness in factitious works ⟨the *contrived* simplicity of the novel —C.C.Walcutt⟩ DEVISE may suggest reflection, analysis, and experimentation continued over a considerable period ⟨Paterson gradually shifted from cotton to silk manufacture after 1840, when John Ryle *devised* a way of winding silk on a spool —*Amer. Guide Series: N.J.*⟩ ⟨a real science — as well as a real philosophy — of human nature could not be born until there were *devised* techniques of accurate observation and verified experiment —H.A.Overstreet⟩ ⟨within a year they had *devised* the "Pond alphabet" of the Sioux language —*Amer. Guide Series: Minn.*⟩ INVENT may connote more of finding, discovering, making, or making up than of ingenuity or reflection ⟨Newton *invented* the differential and the integral calculus and discovered the laws of motion —K.K.Darrow⟩ ⟨1856, when simultaneously Bessemer *invented* his converter and Siemens introduced the open-hearth process —S.F.Mason⟩ ⟨his pains to *invent* a complete, generally unlovely terminology of his own —H.J.Muller⟩ ⟨he did not know the schoolteacher's name but *invented* one for her —Sherwood Anderson⟩ ⟨I *invented* a monster called Hormuz, who lived in the woods behind the town and devoured little children —John Reed⟩ FRAME in this sense suggests a careful devising and constructing to fit a situation ⟨*framing* legislation which may make valuable contributions to a badly needed national water policy —K.S.Davis⟩ ⟨absorbed in *framing* a question that he was intent on persuading a friend, who was a member of Parliament, to ask in the House of Commons —Osbert Sitwell⟩ CONCOCT may suggest devising by ingenious or inventive combining of ingredients ⟨the most loathsome and noisome abominations that his fervid imagination could *concoct* out of his own bitter experiences and the manners and customs of his cruel times —C.W.Eliot⟩

²contrive *vt* -ED/-ING/-S [L *contriv-*, perf. stem of *conterere* to bruise, grind, consume, exhaust — more at CONTRITE] *obs* : to wear away : CONSUME : PASS ⟨~ time⟩

con·trived \-vd\ *adj* [fr. past part. of ¹*contrive*] : showing the effects of planning or devising : ARTIFICIAL, LABORED, UNNATURAL ⟨the layman writhes at the ~ coyness of the dialect —Bernard De Voto⟩ ⟨music — always one of the most ~ of all the arts —Winthrop Sargeant⟩ — **con·triv·ed·ly** \-vədlē, -li\ *adv*

con·triv·er \-və(r)\ *n* -s [¹*contrive* + *-er*] : one that contrives ⟨hasty ~ of popular fiction —A.C.Ward⟩ ⟨~*s* of leisure-time activities —Mary McCarthy⟩ ⟨an excellent ~ in housekeeping —Oliver Goldsmith⟩

¹con·trol \kən·ˈtrōl\ *vt* **controlled**; **controlled**; **controlling**; **controls** [ME *controllen*, fr. MF *conteroller*, *contreroller*, fr. *contrerolle*, n.] **1** *obs* : to check by a duplicate register or account : REGULATE ⟨~ accounts⟩ **2 a** *archaic* : to check, test, or verify by counter or parallel evidence : verify by comparison **b** : to incorporate suitable controls in (as an experiment) or provide (as an experimental procedure) with suitable controls (devise *controlled* tests of the efficacy of a drug) **3** *obs* : to call to account : CENSURE **4 a (1)** : to exercise restraining or directing influence over : REGULATE, CURB ⟨~ one's anger⟩ ⟨*controlling* her interest in the enterprise⟩ (2) : to have power over : RULE ⟨a single company ~*s* the industry⟩ **b** *obs* : OVERPOWER **c** : to reduce the incidence or severity of esp. to innocuous levels ⟨~ an insect population⟩ ⟨~ a disease⟩ **syn** see CONDUCT

²control \"\ *n* -s *often attrib* [MF *contrerolle* copy of an account, counter-register, verification, scrutiny, fr. *contre-* counter- + *rolle* roll, catalog, account — more at ROLL] **1 a** : the act or fact of controlling ⟨man's increasing ~ over nature⟩ : power or authority to guide or manage : directing or restraining domination ⟨under parental ~⟩ ⟨the car went out of ~ on a curve⟩ **b** : effective and reliable skill in the use of a tool, instrument, technique or artistic medium ⟨have ~ of several languages⟩ ⟨the singer's ~ of her voice was perfect⟩ ⟨a poet's ~ of a variety of metrical forms⟩ ⟨a baseball pitcher needs ~ as well as speed⟩ **c** : regulation or direction in the use or application of an artistic medium resulting in proportion and appropriate emphasis **d** : reduction or regulation of wildlife population of an area by killing **e** : the regulation of economic activity esp. by government directive ⟨price ~*s*⟩ ⟨wage ~*s*⟩ ⟨rent ~⟩ — usu. used in pl. **f** : application of policies and procedures for directing, regulating, and coordinating production, administration, and other business activities in a way to achieve the objectives of the enterprise **2** : RESTRAINT, RESERVE ⟨~ of the passions⟩ : SELF-RESTRAINT : possession and command of one's faculties ⟨her hands wrung pale in effort at ~ —Amy Lowell⟩ **3** : a means or method of controlling : one that controls or determines: as **a** : something that affords a standard of comparison or means of verification (as an organism, culture, or group in a control experiment) : CONTROL EXPERIMENT ⟨half the dogs were injected, the others reserved as a ~⟩ ⟨a ~ group⟩ **b** : a hand-operated or automatic mechanism used to regulate or guide the operation of a machine or an apparatus or system (as a steam shovel, a radio, a heating system) — usu. used in pl. **c** : a system of relatively precise field measurements (as a traverse or a triangulation system) with which local secondary surveys may be tied in to ensure their essential accuracy **d** : a personality or spirit believed to actuate the utterances or performances of a spiritualist medium **e** : any of the physical factors (as latitude, altitude, ocean currents) determining the climate of a place **f** : any of the factors determining the nature of geological formations at a given place **g** : a recording device in the form of a letter or number or combination of letters and numbers in the margin of a sheet of British stamps printed between 1887 and 1948 **h** : a control mark on a stamp **syn** see POWER

control account *n* : a financial account that summarizes detailed subsidiary accounts or records — called also *controlling account*

control assay *n* : an exact assay (as of ore or metal); *esp* : one made of a sample from a shipment

control board *n* : a panel at which circuit changes are made (as for theater lighting)

control center *n* : an installation or activity from which a series of operations is directed ⟨civil defense *control center*⟩

control clock *n* : MASTER CLOCK

control column *n* : an airplane lever that operates the elevators by a fore-and-aft motion and the ailerons by turning a wheel mounted at the upper end of the lever — compare CONTROL STICK

control electrode *n* : the electrode in an electron tube whose voltage with respect to the voltage of the cathode determines the electron flow to the anode

control experiment *n* : an experiment for checking the results of other experiments by maintaining the same conditions except in some one particular and thus inferring the causal significance of this varied factor — compare BLANK DETERMINATION, CONTROLLED EXPERIMENT

control grid *n* : a grid usu. placed between the cathode and plate of an electron or vacuum tube to modulate the flow of electrons

control head *n* : a casinghead for controlling unexpected flows of oil or gas from a well which is being drilled

con·trol·la·bil·i·ty \kən-ˌtrōlə'biləd-ē, -ətē, -i\ *n* -ES : the quality or state of being controllable ⟨the ~ of forest fires⟩

con·trol·la·ble \kən'trōləbəl\ *adj* : capable of being controlled — **con·trol·la·bly** \-blē, -li\ *adv*

controlled *adj* [fr. past part. of *control*] : restrained, managed, or kept within bounds (as of decorum or good taste) ⟨with ~ half-conscious desperation —John Hurkan⟩ : conducted or maintained in accordance with fixed rules, restraints, or procedures ⟨study disease under ~ conditions —V.G.Heiser⟩

controlled experiment *n* : a complex experiment including one or more control experiments or blank determinations along with the actual experimental tests

controlled hypotension *n* : low blood pressure induced and maintained to reduce blood loss or to provide a bloodless field during surgery

controlled school *n* : a British voluntary usu. denominational school receiving more than half of its maintenance costs from public funds and in return giving up its control over staff appointments — compare AIDED SCHOOL

con·trol·ler \kən'trōlə(r), 'kän‚t-\ *n* -S [ME *conterroller*, fr. MF *contrerolleur*, fr. *contrerolle* copy of an account, counter-register + *-eur* -or — more at CONTROL] **1 a** : one that keeps a duplicate record in order to control accounts **b** : an officer appointed to check expenditure (as a steward) **c** : the chief accounting officer of a business enterprise whose duties usu. include responsibility for all accounting, budgeting, costing, and internal auditing functions, the measuring of performance against previously approved plans and standards, and the interpreting and reporting thereon to other members of the management responsible for policy or executive action **d** : COMPTROLLER 2 **2 a** : one that controls or has power or authority to control **b** : an iron block usu. bolted to a ship's deck into the hollows of which the links of the cable drop as it comes aboard and thus hold fast until disengaged **c** : CONTROL 3b **d** : an electric device for governing in some predetermined way the power delivered to the apparatus (as a motor) to which it is connected **e** : an administrator of a control law (as of price controls or crop controls) **f** : one that controls the use or flight pattern of aircraft or guided missiles by means of electronic or radio communication

con·trol·ler·ship \-(r)‚ship\ *n* -S **1** : the office of controller **2** : the position and functions of a controller

con·trol·less \kən'trōlləs\ *adj* : lacking control

controlling *pres part of* CONTROL

controlling account *n* : CONTROL ACCOUNT

controlling interest *n* : sufficient stock ownership in a corporation to exert control over policy; *also* : a person or group that possesses such an interest

con·trol·ling·ly *adv* : in a controlling manner

control mark *n* : a mark (as a numeral or a device) on a stamp usu. overprinted for checking on its use

con·trol·ment \kən'trōlmənt\ *n* -S [ME, fr. *controllen* to control + *-ment*] *archaic* : the act of controlling : CHECK

control number *n* **1** : a control on a sheet of British stamps **2** : a numerical control mark on a stamp; *also* : a serial or catalog number of a precanceled stamp

control panel *n* : PANELBOARD 3

control room *n* : the room (as in a broadcasting station) in which the control instruments are located

controls *pres 3d sing of* CONTROL, *pl of* CONTROL

control species *n* : a species of animal predator or parasite introduced into a region to prey on another kind of animal or plant that is considered undesirable

control stick *n* : an airplane lever that operates the elevators by a fore-and-aft motion and the ailerons by a side-to-side motion — compare CONTROL COLUMN

control surface *n* : a movable airfoil designed to change the attitude of an aircraft

control tower *n* : an elevated glass-enclosed structure which has an unobstructed view of a landing field and from which air traffic may be controlled usu. by radio

control track *n* : an auxiliary sound track for a motion picture usu. placed on the same film with the program material and used to control additional features of sound reproduction (as variation in amplification and use of additional speakers)

controversal *adj* [L *controversus*, turned in the opposite direction, disputed (fr. *contro-* — akin to *contra-* — + *versus*, past part. of *vertere* to turn) + E *-al* — more at WORTH] **1** *obs* : CONTROVERSIAL **2** *obs* : turning or looking opposite ways

controverse *n* -S [MF, fr. L *controversia*] *obs* : CONTROVERSY

con·tro·ver·sial \‚käntrə'vərshəl, -vōi‚ -vəi\, |sēəl *also* |shēəl\ *adj* [LL *controversialis*, fr. L *controversia* controversy + *-ialis* -ial] **1** : subject to controversy : relating to or arousing controversy : being an object of controversy ⟨a ~ figure in public life⟩ ⟨the matter is . . . highly ~ and calculated to provoke violent dissent in many quarters —*Times Lit. Supp.*⟩ **2** : given to controversy : engaging in controversy : DISPUTATIOUS, POLEMIC ⟨dogmatic treatises commonly were ~ . . . , directed against pagans or Jews, or Gnostics or Manicheans —H.O.Taylor⟩ — **con·tro·ver·sial·ism** \-ə‚lizəm\ *n* -S — **con·tro·ver·sial·ly** \-əlē, -li\ *adv*

con·tro·ver·sial·ist \-ələst\ *n* -S : one who engages in controversy : DISPUTANT ⟨in his novels the ~ often takes precedence of the artist —B.R.Redman⟩

con·tro·ver·sion \'käntrə‚vərzhən *also* -rsh-\ *n* -S [ML *controversion-*, *controversio*, alter. of L *controversia* controversy] **1** *obs* : CONTROVERSY **2** : the act of controverting ⟨an argument in ~ of an assertion⟩ **3** [L *controversus* + E *-ion*] : a turning in the opposite direction ⟨a general ~ in ethics⟩

con·tro·ver·sy \'käntrə‚vərsē, -vōs-‚-vəis-, -si, *Brit also* kən'trävə(r)si\ *n* -ES [ME *controversie*, fr. L *controversia*, fr. *contro-* (akin to L *contra-*) + *-versia* (fr. *versus*, past part. of *vertere* to turn) — more at WORTH] **1 a** : the act of disputing or contending **b** (1) : a cause, occasion, or instance of disagreement or contention : a difference marked esp. by the expression of opposing views : DISCUSSION, DISPUTE, DEBATE ⟨engaged in a long ~ with university officials and had denounced evolutionary teachings —*Amer. Guide Series: Minn.*⟩ (2) : QUARREL, STRIFE **2** : a suit in law or equity — distinguished from *case* as not including criminal actions or proceedings ⟨the judicial power shall extend . . . to *controversies* to which the U.S. shall be a party; to *controversies* between two or more States —*U.S. Constitution*⟩ — **in controversy** : to be decided by factual evidence rather than by legal decision

con·tro·vert \'käntrə‚vərt, -vōt,-vəit, ¦==¦=, *usu* -d· +V\ *vb* -ED/-ING/-S [fr. *controversy*, after such pairs as E *conversion*: *convert*] *vt* **1** *obs* : to oppose or contest by action or argument (as possession of a property) **2** : to dispute or oppose by reasoning : DENY, CONTRADICT ⟨~ a point in a discussion⟩ ~ *vi* : to engage in controversy **syn** see DISPROVE

controverted election *n*, *Brit* : CONTESTED ELECTION

con·tro·vert·ible \¦==¦təbəl\ *adj* : capable of being controverted — **con·tro·vert·ibly** \-blē, -i\ *adv*

con·tro·vert·ist \-təst\ *n* -S : CONTROVERSIALIST

con·tu·ber·nal \kən't(y)übə(r)nᵊl\ *adj* [L *contubernalis* tentmate, fr. *com-* + *-tubernalis* (fr. *taberna* hut, booth + *-alis* -al) — more at TAVERN] : living together : INTIMATE

con·tu·ma·cious \¦käntə¦māshəs, -n‚tyə¦-‚-n‚tyü¦-‚-nchə¦-\ *adj* [*contumacy* + *-ous*] : perverse in resisting authority : stubbornly disobedient : REBELLIOUS, IRRECONCILABLE ⟨to refer the case of a ~ witness to the court for punishment —H.A. Schweinhaut⟩ **syn** see INSUBORDINATE

con·tu·ma·cious·ly *adv* : PERVERSELY, REBELLIOUSLY, STUBBORNLY

con·tu·ma·cy \kən't(y)üməsē, (')kän¦t-, -si; 'käntəm-, -n‚tyə-‚-nchə-\ *n* -ES [ME *contumacie*, fr. L *contumacia*, fr. *contumac-*, *contumax* insubordinate (fr. *com-* + *-tumax*, fr. *tumēre* to swell, be proud) + *-ia* -y — more at THUMB] **1** : stubborn resistance to authority; *specif* : willful contempt of court **2** : refusal to comply ⟨the ~ of Frenchmen in stolidly remaining French —G.W.Johnson⟩

con·tu·me·li·ous \¦käntə¦mēlēəs, -n‚tyə¦-‚-n‚tyü¦-‚-nchə¦-\ *adj* [MF *contumelieus*, fr. L *contumeliosus*, fr. *contumelia* + *-osus* -ous] : exhibiting contumely : insolently abusive and humiliating : DESPITEFUL, DISDAINFUL ⟨~ taunts⟩ ⟨a ~ critic⟩ — **con·tu·me·li·ous·ly** *adv*

con·tu·me·ly \kən't(y)üməlē, (')kän¦t-, -li; 'käntə‚mēlē, -n‚tyə-‚-nchə-, -‚məl-; *in the Hamlet soliloquy often* 'känchəml- *or* -n‚tyəml- *or* -n‚tyüml-\ *n* -ES [ME *contumelie*, fr. MF, fr. L *contumelia*, perh. fr. *com-* + *-tumelia* (akin to *tumēre* to swell); fr. its assumed earlier meaning of "puffed-up, arrogant speech" — more at THUMB] **1** : rude language or treatment arising from haughtiness and contempt ⟨the book bristles with ~ and wrath —*New Yorker*⟩ **2** : an instance or exhibition of contumely : INSULT ⟨their tracts got burnt or treated with even worse ~ —Samuel Butler †1902⟩ **3** : the suffering of contumely : HUMILIATION ⟨a capacity for bearing ~ —Herman Wouk⟩

con·tund \kən'tənd\ *vt* -ED/-ING/-S [L *contundere* — more at CONTUSE] *archaic* : POUND, BRUISE

con·tur·ba·tion \‚käntə(r)'bāshən\ *n* -S [ME, fr. L *conturbation-*, *conturbatio*, fr. *conturbatus* (past part. of *conturbare* to disturb, fr. *com-* + *turbare* to disturb, fr. *turba* disorder) + *-ion-*, *-io* -ion — more at TURBID] *archaic* : DISTURBANCE

con·tuse \kən't(y)üz\ *vt* -ED/-ING/-S [MF *contuser*, fr. L *contusus*, past part. of *contundere* to beat, crush, fr. *com-* + *tundere* to beat — more at STUTTER] **1** : to beat or pound together (as in a mortar) **2** : to injure or disorganize (superficial or deeper tissues) with or without breaking the skin : BRUISE

con·tu·sion \kən't(y)üzhən\ *n* -S [ME *conteschown*, fr. MF *contusion*, fr. L *contusion-*, *contusio*, fr. *contusus* + *-ion-*, *-io* -ion] **1** : the act of contusing or the state of being contused **2** : a bruise caused by external violence and characterized by hemorrhage into and swelling of the superficial or deeper-lying tissues with or without a break in the covering skin or membrane **syn** see WOUND

con·tu·sioned \-zhənd\ *adj* : CONTUSED, BRUISED

conubium *var of* CONNUBIUM

con·u·lar·ia \‚känᵊl'a(a)rēə, -nyə'la-\ *n*, *cap* [NL, fr. *conulus* small cone (dim. of L *conus* cone) + *-aria* — more at CONE] : a genus of Paleozoic and Mesozoic tapering shells possibly of worms of uncertain relationships

con·u·lar·i·id \-ēəd\ *n* -S [NL *Conulariida*] : a fossil or individual of the group Conulariida

con·u·la·ri·i·da \‚känᵊlə'rīədə, -nyələ'-\ *n pl*, *cap* [NL, fr. *Conularia* + *-ida*] : a phylum or other group of extinct invertebrate animals of uncertain relationships known from pyramidal usu. 4-sided chitinophosphatic tests widely distributed in Devonian, Pennsylvanian, and Permian rocks

restoration of an individual conulariid

con·ule \'känᵊl, -nyəl\ *n* -S [NL *conulus*, dim. of L *conus* cone] : one of the somewhat conical void elevations of the body surface of certain sponges — **con·u·lose** \-nᵊl‚ōs, -nyə‚lōs\ *adj*

co·nun·drum \kə'nəndrəm\ *n* -S [origin unknown] **1** *obs* **a** : CONCEIT, WHIM, FANCY **b** : PUN, QUIBBLE **2** : a riddle based on some fanciful or fantastic resemblance between things quite unlike and forming a puzzling question whose answer is or involves a pun (as in "Why didn't the children of Israel starve in the desert? Because of the *sand which is* there") **3 a** : a question or problem to which only a conjectural answer can be made ⟨the political ~s, particularly the problem of how the richer areas . . . can be made to subsidize the poorer —Douglass Cater⟩ **b** : a puzzle or problem that is usu. intricate and difficult of solution ⟨it's been a chronic ~ where they were to pay taxes and vote: some have paid taxes to both states, some to neither —*N.Y. Times*⟩ **syn** see MYSTERY

con·ur·ba·tion \‚känə(r)'bāshən\ *n* -S [*com-* + L *urb-*, *urbs* town + E *-ation* — more at URBAN] : a great aggregation or continuous network of urban communities ⟨the Paris ~ covers the whole of the Department of the Seine and also parts of Seine-et-Oise and Seine-et-Marne —Brian Chapman⟩

con·ure \'känyə(r)\ *n* -S [NL *Conurus* (in some classifications, a genus of parrots), fr. ²*con-* + *-urus*] : any of several tropical American parrots (of *Aratinga* and related genera) closely related to and resembling in their brilliant coloration the macaws

con·u·rop·sis \‚kän(y)ə'räpsəs\ *n*, *cap* [NL, fr. *Conurus* + *-opsis*] : a genus of small American parrots including among recent forms only the extinct Carolina parakeet

co·nus \'kōnəs\ *n* [NL, fr. L, cone — more at CONE] **1** *cap* : a very large genus (the type of the family Conidae) of pectinibranchiate tropical marine snails comprising the cones and including many beautiful and harmless forms and a few chiefly in the southwest Pacific that are highly dangerous by biting with the radula and injecting a paralytic venom that has been known to cause death in man — see GEOGRAPHER CONE, TEXTILE CONE **2** *pl* **co·ni** \-‚nī,-(‚)nē\ [NL, by shortening] : CONUS ARTERIOSUS

con·u·sa·ble \'kän(y)əzəbəl\ *adj* [AF, fr. OF *conissable*, fr. *coniss-*, *conoiss-* (stem of *conoistre* to know) + *-able* — more at COGNIZANCE] *law* : capable of being judicially examined : subject to legal jurisdiction ⟨the matter was particularly reserved for Parliament as being ~ by them alone —T.E.May⟩

conus ar·te·ri·o·sus \-är‚tirē'ōsəs\ *n*, *pl* **coni arte·rio·si** \-‚sī, -(‚)sē\ [NL, lit., arterial cone] **1** : a prolongation of the ventricle of amphibians and certain fishes that is equipped with a spiral valve by which venous blood going to the pulmocutaneous arteries is separated from arterial blood going to the aorta and systemic arteries **2** : a conical prolongation of the right ventricle in man and mammals from which the pulmonary arteries emerge

conv *abbr* **1** convalescent **2** convenient **3** convent **4** convention **5** conversation **6** converted; converter; convertible **7** convict **8** convocation

con·va·lesce \‚känvə'les\ *vi* -ED/-ING/-S [L *convalescere*, fr. *com-* + *valescere* to grow strong, fr. *valēre* to be strong, be well — more at WIELD] : to gather strength : recover health and strength gradually after sickness or weakness : RECOVER

con·va·les·cence \-sᵊn(t)s\ *n* -S [MF, fr. LL *convalescentia*, fr. L *convalescent-*, *convalescens* (pres. part. of *convalescere*) + *-ia*] **1** : gradual recovery of health and strength after disease ⟨a patient well advanced in ~⟩ **2** : the time between the subsidence of a disease and complete restoration to health ⟨quiet and rest during ~⟩

con·va·les·cen·cy \-ənsē\ *n* -ES [LL *convalescentia*] *archaic* : CONVALESCENCE

¹**con·va·les·cent** \¦känvə¦lesᵊnt\ *adj* [L *convalescent-*, *convalescens*, pres. part. of *convalescere*] **1** : recovering from sickness or debility : partially restored to health or strength ⟨~ children nearly ready to leave the hospital⟩ **2** : of, for, or relating to convalescence or convalescents ⟨a patient in a ~ ward⟩ — **con·va·les·cent·ly** *adv*

²**convalescent** \"\ *n* -S : one recovering from sickness

convalescent home *n* : an institution for the care of convalescing patients

convalescent serum *n* : serum obtained from one who has recovered from an infectious disease and considered to be esp. rich in antibodies against the infectious agent of the disease

con·val·la·mar·in \kən‚valə'ma(a)rən, ‚känvə'lamər-\ *n* -S [ISV *convall-* (fr. NL *Convallaria*) + *amar-* (fr. L *amarus* bitter) + *-in* — more at AMAROID] : a bitter poisonous glycoside extracted from the lily of the valley

con·val·lar·ia \‚känvə'la(a)rēə\ *n* -S [NL *Convallaria*, genus of plants having as its only species the lily of the valley, fr. L *convallis* enclosed valley (fr. *com-* + *vallis* valley) + NL *-aria* — more at VALE] : the dried rhizome and roots of the lily of the valley

con·val·lar·in \‚känvə'la(a)rən, kən'valər-\ *n* -S [ISV *convallar-* (fr. NL *Convallaria*) + *-in*; orig. formed as G *konvallarin*] : a poisonous glycoside extracted from the lily of the valley

con·val·la·tox·in \¦kän‚valə¦täksən, -nvələ¦-\ *n* -S [NL *Convallaria* + E *toxin*] : a crystalline glycoside $C_{29}H_{42}O_{10}$ obtained from the flowers of the lily of the valley that acts on the heart and that on hydrolysis yields strophanthidin and rhamnose

con va·ri·a·zio·ni \¦kän‚värē‚ätsē¦ō(‚)nē, ¦kōn-\ *adv* [It] : with variations — used as a direction in music

con·variety \¦kän+\ *n* -ES [*com-* + *variety*] : a group of cultivated varieties within a species or an interspecific hybrid ⟨the Darwin tulips constitute a ~⟩

con·vect \kən'vekt\ *vb* -ED/-ING/-S [back-formation fr. *convection*] *vi* : to transfer heat by convection ~ *vt* : to circulate (warm air) by convection : transfer (heat) by convection

con·vec·tion \-kshən\ *n* -S [LL *convection-*, *convectio*, fr. L *convectus* (past part. of *convehere* to bring together, fr. *com-* + *vehere* to carry) + *-ion-*, *-io* -ion — more at WAY] **1** : the action or process of conveying or transmitting **2** : a mechanically or thermally produced upward or downward movement of a limited part of the atmosphere that is essential to the formation of many clouds (as cumulus clouds) and is used in certain heating systems **3 a** : the circulatory motion that occurs in a fluid at a nonuniform temperature owing to the variation of its density and the action of gravity **b** : the transfer of heat by this automatic circulation of a fluid — compare CONDUCTION 5a **c** : the transfer of electricity in the form of a surface charge on a moving body (as an electrostatic-generator belt)

con·vec·tion·al \-shənᵊl, -shnəl\ *adj* : of, relating to, or produced by convection

convection current *n* **1 a** : a stream of fluid propelled by thermal convection **b** : thermally produced vertical air flow **2** : a surface charge of electricity on a moving body — compare CONVECTION 3c

con·vec·tive \kən'vektiv\ *adj* [*convection* + *-ive*] **1** : having the property or power of conveying : TRANSPORTING ⟨the ~ force of water⟩ **2** : of or relating to convection

con·vec·tor \-tə(r)\ *n* -S : something that convects; *specif* : a room-heating unit in which air heated by contact with a heating device (as a radiator or finned tube) in a casing having openings at top and bottom circulates by convection

¹**convenable** *adj* [ME, fr. MF, fr. *convenir* to be suitable, convenient + *-able*] *archaic* : in accord with circumstances : PROPER

²**con·ven·able** \kən'vēnəbəl\ *adj* [*convene* + *-able*] : capable of being convened or assembled

con·ve·nance \kōⁿv(ə)näⁿs; 'känvənən(t)s\ *n*, *pl* **convenances** \kōⁿv(ə)näⁿs; 'känvənən(t)səz, -‚nän(t)-\ [F, fr. *convenant*, pres. part. of *convenir* to be suitable] **1** : conventional usage **2** *convenances pl* : the things established by custom as proper to social intercourse : CONVENTIONS ⟨a forthright man with little regard for the ~s⟩ **syn** see FORM

con·vene \kən'vēn\ *vb* -ED/-ING/-S [ME *convenen*, fr. MF *convenir* to agree, be suitable, meet, fr. L *convenire*, fr. *com-* + *venire* to come — more at COME] *vi* **1** *of persons* : to come together, meet, or assemble in a group or body (as in a formal meeting for some specific purpose) ⟨the executive directors *convened* once a week⟩ **2** *of things* : to come, be brought, or occur together at one place or time ⟨large stars *convening* for nativity eve —Genevieve Taggard⟩ **3** *of a body of persons* : to meet in formal session ⟨the Seventy-Fifth Congress *convened* in January⟩ ⟨a special committee of jurists *convened* in Washington —Vera M. Dean⟩ ~ *vt* **1** : to summon to appear before a tribunal or authority ⟨Tom was . . . *convened* before Mr. Allworthy —Henry Fielding⟩ **2** : to cause (persons) to assemble in a group or body : call or gather together ⟨Mlle. Boulanger, who *convened* her bright young composers . . . in Paris —H.W. Wind⟩ : CONVOKE ⟨*convened* the assembly⟩ ⟨the court-martial . . . was never *convened* —Anthony Powell⟩ ⟨a world conference was *convened* in Paris⟩

con·ven·er \-nə(r)\ *or* **con·ve·nor** \"‚ -‚nō(ə)r,-‚nó(ə)\ *n* -S *chiefly Brit* : one that convenes; *esp* : the chairman of a committee or other organized body of persons

con·ven·er·ship \-(r)‚ship\ *n* -S *chiefly Brit* : the office of official convener

¹**con·ve·nience** \kən'vēnyən(t)s, -nēən-\ *n* -S [ME, fr. MF, fr. L *convenientia*, fr. *convenient-*, *conveniens* + *-ia*] **1** *obs* : AGREEMENT, HARMONY, CONGRUITY, APTITUDE **2** : fitness or suitability for performing some action or fulfilling some requirement ⟨the ~ of the new alphabet for transcribing spoken English⟩ **3** : a favorable or advantageous condition, state, or circumstance : ADVANTAGE ⟨it becomes something of a virtue as well as a ~ to be domesticated —Walter de la Mare⟩ **4** : something that provides comfort or advantage : something suited to one's material wants: **a** : an arrangement, appliance, device, material, or service conducive to personal ease or comfort ⟨a landscaped corner lot, handy to all ~s⟩ ⟨carry camping ~s and . . . supplies on packhorses —H.E.Scudder⟩ **b** : TOILET 5 **5** : a convenient condition or time : OPPORTUNITY ⟨answer at your earliest ~⟩ **6** : freedom from difficulty, discomfort, or trouble ⟨chairs arranged for his own ~⟩ : EASE, COMFORT, EFFICIENCY ⟨impressed by the greater ~ and cheapness of canal transportation⟩ ⟨buildings are not grouped like that by pure accident, though ~ probably had much to do with it —Willa Cather⟩

²**convenience** \"\ *vt* -ED/-ING/-S : to afford convenience to : ACCOMMODATE ⟨the new system of collection *convenienced* the taxpayer⟩

convenience goods *n pl* : articles that are purchased frequently for immediate use in readily accessible stores and with a minimum of effort (as tobacco, magazines, gum, or candy) — contrasted with *shopping goods*

convenience outlet *n* : a receptacle in a wall or baseboard for connection to lamps or other electrical appliances

con·ve·nien·cy \-ənsē\ *n* -ES [ME *conveniencie*, fr. L *convenientia*] *archaic* : CONVENIENCE

con·ve·nient \kən'vēnyənt, -nēənt\ *adj* [ME, fr. L *convenient-*, *conveniens* suitable, pres. part. of *convenire* to come together, be suitable — more at CONVENE] **1** *obs* **a** : FIT, ADAPTED, SUITABLE, CONGRUOUS ⟨feed me with food ~ for me —Prov 30:8 (AV)⟩ **b** : APPROPRIATE, BECOMING, PROPER **2 a** : suited to personal ease or comfort or to easy performance of some act or function ⟨programs broadcast at hours that are more ~ for the housewife⟩ **b** : suited to the needs or the circumstances of a particular situation ⟨he had . . . the ~ habit of discounting the sufferings of the victims of civilization on the score of their presumed insensibility —Benjamin Farrington⟩ **c :** affording accommodation or advantage ⟨Europe is so divided from Asia by deserts and mountains . . . that it is very ~ to call it a continent —Samuel Van Valkenburg & Ellsworth Huntington⟩ **:** well adapted to ready use ⟨there is no ~ experimental animal for investigating the cold virus —C.H.Andrewes⟩ **3 :** near at hand **:** easily accessible **:** HANDY ⟨the crossroads church, set . . . at a point ~ to a group of plantations —*Amer. Guide Series: Va.*⟩ — **con·ve·nient·ly** *adv*

1con·vent \'känvənt, -,vent\ *n* -s [alter. (influenced by ML & L *conventus*) of earlier *covent*, fr. ME, fr. OF, fr. ML *conventus* community of monks or nuns, fr. L, assembly, fr. *conventus*, past part. of *convenire* to come together — more at CONVENE] **1 :** an association or community of recluses devoted to a religious life under a superior **:** a body of monks, friars, or nuns constituting one local community — now usu. restricted to a convent of nuns **2** *obs* **:** ASSEMBLY, MEETING ⟨these . . . witches beginning to dance (which is an usual ceremony at their ~s or meetings) —Ben Jonson⟩ **3 :** a house or set of buildings occupied by a community of religious recluses **:** a monastery or nunnery — now usu. restricted to a nunnery

2convent *vb* -ED/-ING/-S [L *conventus*, past part. of *convenire*] *vt, obs* **:** to cause to come together **:** summon to meet **:** CONVENE, CITE ⟨command him to ~ his whole host —George Chapman⟩ ~ *vi, obs* **:** to meet together

con·ven·ti·cal \kən'ventəkəl\ *adj* [in sense 1, fr. 1*convent* + *-ical*; in sense 2, fr. 1*conventicle*] **1 :** of or relating to a convent **2 :** of or relating to a conventicle — **con·ven·ti·cal·ly** \-tək(ə)lē\ *adv*

1con·ven·ti·cle \-kəl\ *n* -s [ME *conventicle, conventicule*, fr. L *conventiculum*, dim. of *conventus* assembly — more at CONVENT] **1 :** an assembly, meeting, or convention esp. of a society or body of persons **2 :** an assembly or meeting of an irregular or unlawful character or regarded as having a sinister or evil purpose or tendency **3 :** an assembly for religious worship; *esp* **:** a secret meeting for worship by a group not sanctioned by civil law (as one formerly held by nonconformists in England) **4 :** a meetinghouse or meeting place of a religious group esp. of nonconformists

2conventicle \"\ *vi* -ED/-ING/-S **:** to assemble in a conventicle **:** frequent conventicles

con·ven·ti·cler \-k(ə)lə(r)\ *n* -s **1 :** one who supports or frequents conventicles **2 :** SEPARATIST — used disparagingly

con·ven·tic·u·lar \,kän,ven'tikyələ(r)\ *adj* [L *conventiculum* + E *-ar*] **:** of, relating to, or resembling a conventicle

con·ven·tion \kən'venchən\ *n* -s [ME *convencioun*, fr. MF or L; MF *convention*, fr. L *convention-, conventio*, fr. *conventus* (past part. of *convenire* to come together, be suitable, agree) + *-ion-, -io* -ion — more at CONVENE] **1 a :** an agreement between persons or parties **b :** an agreement between two or more states arranging for the regulation of matters affecting all of them (as postage, copyright, or the conduct of war) **c :** an agreement enforceable in law **:** CONTRACT, COVENANT **d :** a compact between commanders of opposing armies esp. concerning the exchange of prisoners or the suspension of hostilities **e :** an agreement or decision about basic concepts or principles (as geometric axioms) voluntarily but not altogether arbitrarily arrived at though based neither on physical experiments nor on a priori judgments **f :** an axiom or principle regarded as true by convention **2 a** (1) *obs* **:** a meeting or coming together by chance or plan of two or more persons (2) *obs* **:** the gathering together or union of things (3) *obs* **:** the act of summoning before a court or other authority (4) **:** the summoning or convening of an assembly ⟨forced his ~ of the council⟩ **b** (1) **:** a body or assembly of persons met for some common purpose; *esp* **:** a formal and special or regular assembly of delegates or members of a party or association met to accomplish some specific civil, social, political, or ecclesiastical object or for the exchange of ideas, views, and information of common interest to the group ⟨an annual sales ~⟩ ⟨the American Legion ~⟩ (2) **:** a special assembly of representatives or delegates convened for the purpose of framing or amending a constitution (3) **:** a meeting of the local members of an American political party or of delegates on the county, state, or national level for the purpose of formulating the party platform or of selecting candidates for office ⟨the Democratic national ~⟩ ⟨aldermanic district ~⟩ **c :** a state or national organization of one of several Protestant denominations ⟨the American Baptist *Convention*⟩ ⟨the North Carolina state ~⟩ **d :** an Episcopal diocesan or general legislative assembly **3 a :** usage, custom, or practice generally agreed on and followed esp. in social usage or moral matters ⟨words express whatever meaning ~ has attached to them —O.W.Holmes †1935⟩ ⟨rigid ~ prescribes that such meetings open with prayer —D.L.Cohn⟩ ⟨the child is trained to fit into his world, both of fact and ~ —H.A.Overstreet⟩ **b :** a rule, custom, or belief widely accepted and established by long usage ⟨this . . . is not a rule of law; it is a usage or ~ of the Commonwealth which is accepted as binding in practice by all the members —K.C.Wheare⟩ **:** a rule of conduct or behavior **:** a customary pattern of conduct ⟨a rebel against the ~s of education —Allen Johnson⟩ **:** a rule, mode, or principle of conduct accepted by society ⟨Henry the Fifth, who asserted that the great made their ~s and lesser people followed them —J.F.Wharton⟩ **c :** a practice in bidding or playing that by agreement between partners in certain card games (as bridge) conveys some information not necessarily deducible by logic **d** (1) **:** a practice, device, or mode of performance established by custom and widely recognized and accepted ⟨the ~ of the first-person narrator who observes all but is not implicated in the action⟩ ⟨singing ~s such as the use of falsetto and nasality⟩ ⟨putting a front-view eye into a profile face, a ~ found in all primitive art —Herbert Read⟩ **:** a representation or mode of performance recognized as a substitute for a natural form or mode ⟨the ~s of Renaissance iconography⟩ (2) **:** a representation (as in art or design) that simplifies, symbolizes, or substitutes for a natural form ⟨the ~ of representing vegetation by circles and slabs⟩ **syn** see FORM

con·ven·tion·al \-chən°l, -chnəl\ *adj* [LL *conventionalis*, fr. L *convention-, conventio* convention + *-alis* -al] **1 a :** based on, settled by, or formed by agreement or compact **:** STIPULATED, CONTRACTUAL — compare JUDICIAL, LEGAL ⟨~ services reserved by tenures upon grants, made out of the crown or knights' service —Matthew Hale⟩ **b :** CONVENTIONARY **2 a :** according with, sanctioned by, conforming to, or based on convention, custom, or traditional usages or attitudes ⟨a skillful . . . journalist, ~ and conformist except in a strong bent toward liberal humanitarianism —H.S.Canby⟩ **:** established and sanctioned by general agreement and usage **:** TRADITIONAL ⟨it has been ~ to regard the Horites as a legendary race of cave dwellers —E.W.K.Mould⟩ **b** (1) **:** lacking spontaneity, originality, or individuality **:** TRITE ⟨to distinguish . . . that which is organic, animated, expressive, from that which is only ~, derivative, inexpressive —Walter Pater⟩ ⟨a politician of small vision and ~ mind —*New Republic*⟩ (2) **:** commonly encountered, observed, or performed **:** COMMONPLACE, ORDINARY, USUAL ⟨dead-alive, hackneyed people . . . scarcely conscious of living except in the exercise of some ~ occupation —R.L.Stevenson⟩ **c** (1) **:** in accordance with a mode of artistic representation that simplifies or provides symbols or substitutes for natural forms **:** ABSTRACT (2) **:** based on a convention and depending for effectiveness or understanding on recognition of the convention ⟨a ~ bid in bridge indicating extraordinary strength in one suit⟩ (3) **:** of traditional design ⟨silver having a ~ pattern⟩ (4) *of a playing card back* **:** bearing a symmetrical nonpictorial design **3 :** of, like, or relating to a convention, assembly, or public meeting **syn** see CEREMONIAL

conventional heir *n* **:** one entitled by contract to be heir

con·ven·tion·al·ism \kən'venchən°l,izəm, -chnə,li-\ *n* -s **1 :** observance of or tendency to observe conventions ⟨such social compulsives as fear of ridicule, desire for public esteem, prestige, social habits — all that J. S. Mill included in "the authority of *Conventionalism*" —Jerome Frank⟩ **2 :** a conventional practice, usage, or principle ⟨he thanked his soldiers after a victory, but he did not order Te Deums to be sung for it; and in the absence of these ~s he perhaps showed more real reverence —J.A.Froude⟩ **3 :** a theory that regards the principles of logic, mathematics, or science as conventions (sense 1e) or as true by convention

con·ven·tion·al·ist \-n°ləst, -nəl-\ *n* -s **1 :** a member or supporter of a convention (as a constitutional convention) **2 :** an observer of conventions **:** a conventional person **3 :** an adherent of philosophical conventionalism — **con·ven·tion·al·ist·ic** \kən,venchən°l'istik, -chnə'li-\ *adj*

con·ven·tion·al·i·ty \kən,venchə'naləd·ē, -ətē, -i\ *n* -ES **1 :** the quality or state of being conventional; *specif* **:** adherence to established or traditional social, intellectual, or artistic conventions **2 :** something that is established by conventional use **:** a conventional usage, practice, or thing ⟨the tired *conventionalities* of sex and violence in this melodrama —Anthony Boucher⟩

con·ven·tion·al·i·za·tion \kən,venchən°lə'zāshən, -chnəl-\ *n* -s **:** the act, practice, or product of conventionalizing

con·ven·tion·al·ize \kən'venchən°l,īz, -nchnə,līz\ *vb* -ED/-ING/-S *see -ize in Explan Notes, vt* **1 :** to make conventional **:** cause to conform to conventional rules, patterns, attitudes ⟨*conventionalized* behavior⟩ **2** *in art and design* **a :** to treat in a conventional or nonnaturalistic manner ⟨flowers are *conventionalized* to serve as a motif⟩ **b :** to establish as a readily interpreted mode of representation ⟨an alphabet developing out of *conventionalized* pictographs⟩ ~ *vi* **:** to follow conventional principles

con·ven·tion·al·ly \-n°lē, -nəlē, -li\ *adv* **:** in a conventional manner **:** in accordance with convention

conventional mortgage *n* **:** a real-estate mortgage not underwritten by a government agency

conventional person *n* **:** JURISTIC PERSON

con·ven·tion·ary \kən'venchə,nerē\ *adj* [ML *conventionarius*, fr. L *convention-, conventio* + *-arius* -ary] **:** acting under convention or contract **:** settled by express agreement — used now chiefly of a form of tenure existing in Cornwall and parts of Devonshire, England

convention blank *n* **:** a report form required to be filed by insurance companies with state insurance departments

con·ven·tio·neer \kən,venchə'ni(ə)r, -iə\ *n* -s **:** a person attending a convention

con·ven·tion·er \=ˈ==nə(r)\ *n* -s **1 :** a person attending a convention **2 :** a member of a convention

con·ven·tion·ist \-nəst\ *n* -s **1 :** a member of a convention **2** *obs* **:** a party to a convention or contract

conventions *pl of* CONVENTION

con·ven·to \kōn'ven(,)tō, kən'-\ *n* -s [PhilSp, fr. Sp, convent, fr. ML *conventus* — more at CONVENT] **:** the residence of a parish priest in the Philippines or in Spanish America

convents *pl of* CONVENT, *pres 3d sing of* CONVENT

1con·ven·tu·al \kən'venchəwəl\ *adj* [ME, fr. MF or ML; MF, fr. ML *conventualis*, fr. *conventus* convent + L *-alis* -al — more at CONVENT] **1 :** of, relating to, or befitting a convent or the monastic life **:** MONASTIC ⟨in a ~ cell⟩ ⟨various ~ groups⟩ **2** *usu cap* **:** of or relating to the Friars Minor Conventual

2conventual \"\ *n* -s **:** a member of a conventual community; *specif, usu cap* **:** FRIAR MINOR CONVENTUAL

con·ven·tu·al·ly \-wəlē, -li\ *adv* **:** in a manner belonging to or befitting a convent or the monastic life **:** MONASTICALLY

conventual mass *n, usu cap C&M* **:** a daily mass celebrated for and usu. in the presence of the members of a monastic community

con·verge \kən'vərj, -vōj, -vəij\ *vb* -ED/-ING/-S [ML *convergere*, fr. L *com-* + *vergere* to bend, incline — more at WRENCH] *vi* **1 :** to tend toward one point **:** approach nearer together ⟨the radii of a circle ~ toward the center⟩ **:** move toward a single point **:** come together **:** MEET ⟨in the Forum . . . where all the ways of the world *converged* —John Buchan⟩ ⟨she and her husband both *converged* upon the caller —H.G.Wells⟩ **2 :** to come together, meet, or join so as to form a single product or come to bear on or conclude in a single thing or place ⟨the real social forces which *converged* to bring the Nazis and Fascists to power —W.G.Carleton⟩ ⟨the demand necessarily *converged* upon banks situated in the financial centers —G.L.Harrison⟩ **3** *biol* **:** to develop or possess similar characters — compare CONVERGENCE 3 **4** *of a sequence, series, or integral* **:** to be convergent **:** approach a limit ~ *vt* **:** to cause to tend to one point **:** cause to approach nearer together **:** cause to come together

con·ver·gence \-jən(t)s\ *n* -s **1 a :** the act or condition of converging ⟨~ of two valleys⟩ **:** tendency or movement toward union or uniformity ⟨~ of the earnings of skilled and unskilled workers⟩ **:** coming together or joining so as to bear on a single object or conclude in a single product ⟨~ of kindred qualities in two otherwise alien tongues —J.L.Lowes⟩ **b :** an embryonic movement that involves streaming of material from the dorsal and lateral surfaces of the gastrula toward the blastopore and concurrent shifting of lateral materials toward the mid-dorsal line and that is a process fundamental to the establishment of the germ layers **2 :** the state or property of being convergent **3 :** the development or possession of similar characters by animals or plants of different groups due to similarity in habits or environment (as the resemblance in form of body of the whales and fishes) — compare PARALLELISM, RADIATION **4** *anthrop* **:** the independent apparently accidental development of similarities between separate cultures — compare DIFFUSION, PARALLELISM **5 :** movement of the two eyes so coordinated that the images of a single point fall on corresponding points of the two retinas **6 :** overlapping synaptic innervation of a single cell by more than one nerve fiber — compare FACILITATION **7 :** the accumulation of air in a layer or region due to inflowing winds

con·ver·gen·cy \-ənsē, -si\ *n* -ES **:** the quality or state of converging **:** CONVERGENCE

con·ver·gent \-jənt\ *adj* [ML *convergent-, convergens*, pres. part. of *convergere* — more at CONVERGE] **1 :** tending to move toward one point or to approach each other **:** CONVERGING ⟨~ lines⟩ **:** coming together **:** JOINING ⟨great ~ movement of the nations to make a world peace —H.G.Wells⟩ **2 a :** exhibiting convergence in form, function, or development **b :** of or relating to the process of convergent evolution by which genetically distinct organisms sharing a common environment come to mimic one another — compare RADIATION **3 a** *of an improper integral* **:** having a value that is a real number **b :** characterized by having the *n*th term or the sum of the first *n* terms approach a finite limit ⟨a ~ sequence⟩ ⟨a ~ series⟩ — see ABSOLUTELY CONVERGENT — **con·ver·gent·ly** *adv*

converging lens *n* **:** a lens whose focus for parallel rays is real — compare DIVERGING LENS

converging meniscus *n* **:** a meniscus lens of true crescent-shaped section — see LENS illustration

con·vers·able *also* **con·vers·ible** \kən'vərsəbəl, -vōs-, -vəis-\ *adj* [MF *conversable*, fr. *converser* to converse + *-able* — more at CONVERSE] **1 :** capable of being readily conversed with **:** pleasant and easy to converse with ⟨a friendly ~ man⟩ **2** *archaic* **:** of, concerning, or suitable for social intercourse ⟨the evening was quiet and ~ —Jane Austen⟩

con·ver·sance \kən'vərs°n(t)s, -vōs-,-vəis-; 'känvə(r)sən-\ *or* **con·ver·san·cy** \kən'vərsənsē, -si; 'känv-\ *n, pl* **conversances** *or* **conversancies :** the quality or state of being conversant ⟨~ with a particular subject⟩

1con·ver·sant \kən'vərs°nt, -vōs-,-vəis-; 'känvə(r)sənt\ *adj* [ME *conversaunt*, fr. MF *conversant*, fr. L *conversant-, conversans*, pres. part. of L *conversari* to associate with — more at CONVERSE] **1** *archaic* **:** accustomed to dwell or stay **:** abiding for a considerable amount of time ⟨they who have been ~ abroad —Joseph Addison⟩ **2** *archaic* **:** having an interest or concern **:** OCCUPIED — used with *in, about, with, among* ⟨long ~ in this horrid practice —Oliver Goldsmith⟩ ⟨the passions which are ~ about the preservation of the individual —Edmund Burke⟩ **3** *archaic* **:** having frequent, customary, or familiar association **:** intimately acquainted ⟨I have been ~ with the first persons of the age —John Dryden⟩ — used with *with, in, among* ⟨to be ~ in great men's families—Robert Boyle⟩ **4 :** having knowledge or experience ⟨British officers . . . must be ~ with the ways of a dozen or more castes —Christopher Rand⟩ ⟨anyone ~ with other parts of England found our neighborhood very depressing —Joyce Warren⟩ **:** familiar or acquainted by use or study **:** well-informed — used with *with*, formerly often with *in* ⟨~ with business trends⟩ ⟨deeply ~ in the Platonic philosophy —John Dryden⟩ **5** *archaic* **:** inclined to conversation

2conversant \"\ *n* -s **:** one who converses ⟨conversation recorded without the knowledge of the ~s —R.C.Pooley⟩

con·ver·sant·ly *adv* **:** in the manner of one who has knowledge or experience (as of a subject or a thing)

con·ver·sa·tion \,känvə(r)'sāshən\ *n* -s [ME *conversacioun*, fr. MF *conversation*, fr. L *conversation-, conversatio* frequent abode in a place, intercourse, manner of life, fr. *conversatus* (past part. of *conversari* to associate with) + *-ion-, -io* -ion — more at CONVERSE] **1** *obs* **a :** the action of living or dwelling in a place ⟨for our ~ is in heaven —Phil 3:20 (AV)⟩ **b :** the action of living, associating, or having dealings with others ⟨my long . . . ~ with him, that continued to his death for twenty-three years —Gilbert Burnet⟩ **c :** manner of living **:** conduct or behavior ⟨be ye holy in all manner of ~ —1 Pet 1:15 (AV)⟩ **d :** those with whom one associates **:** social circle **:** COMPANY ⟨you may know the man by the ~ he keeps —Thomas Shelton⟩ **e :** occupation or association esp. with an object of study or a subject **:** close acquaintance or intimacy ⟨experience in business and ~ in books —Francis Bacon⟩ **2 :** SEXUAL INTERCOURSE — used esp. in the phrase *criminal conversation* **3 a** (1) **:** oral exchange of sentiments, observations, opinions, ideas **:** colloquial discourse ⟨in casual ~ on the street corner⟩ ⟨we had talk enough but no ~; there was nothing discussed —Samuel Johnson⟩ (2) **:** an instance of conversational exchange **:** TALK, COLLOQUY ⟨had a long ~ with his friend⟩ **b** *archaic* **:** a meeting or assembly for conversing or discussing: (1) **:** a public conference or debate (2) **:** an at home or reception **:** CONVERSAZIONE **c :** an informal exploratory discussion of an issue by diplomats of two or more governments or by officials or representatives of any institutions or groups ⟨diplomatic ~s⟩ ⟨~s among representatives of the colleges, business, and industry —H.D. Gideonse⟩ **4 :** CONVERSATION PIECE — **make conversation :** to talk or converse for the sake of conversing, with no particular purpose, and usu. under some social compulsion ⟨he was only *making conversation* while they waited for the train⟩

con·ver·sa·tion·al \,==ˈsāshən°l, -shnəl\ *adj* **1 :** inclined to converse **:** fond of or given to conversation **2 :** of, for, characteristic of, or suited to conversation or oral communication ⟨written in an easy informal ~ style⟩ ⟨a ~ method of teaching by question and answer⟩ ⟨~ talent⟩ — **con·ver·sa·tion·al·ly** \-°lē, -əlē, -li\ *adv*

con·ver·sa·tion·al·ist \-ləst\ *or* **con·ver·sa·tion·ist** \-sh(ə)nəst\ *n* -s **:** one who converses much or who excels in conversation

conversation chair *n* **1 :** a small upright chair with a padded top rail on the back orig. designed in the 18th century for a man to sit in facing backwards astride the seat with his arms resting on the top rail **2 :** a double chair designed so that two people can sit side by side but facing in opposite directions **:** TÊTE-À-TÊTE 2

conversation piece *n* **1** *or* **conversation picture** *also* **conversation :** a painting of a group of figures (as members of a family) shown in their customary indoor or outdoor surroundings **2 :** a piece of writing (as a play) that depends for its effect chiefly upon the wit or excellent quality of its dialogue **3 :** something that furnishes a subject of conversation (as by reason of its novel, striking, or amusing appearance) ⟨pink elephant beer mugs and Diamond Jim apron waistcoats are *conversation pieces*—Sylvia Wright⟩ ⟨set off . . . with *conversation piece* gloves trailing sweeping panels of white satin lined in champagne tulle —*Time*⟩

conversative *adj* [*conversation* + *-ive*] *obs* **:** CONVERSATIONAL

con·ver·sa·zi·o·ne \,känvə(r)sätsē'ō(,)nē, ,kōn-, -,sat-, -(,)nā\ *n, pl* **conversaziones** \-,nēz, -,näz\ *or* **conversazio·ni** \-(,)nē\ [It, lit., conversation, fr. L *conversation-, conversatio*] **:** a meeting, reception, or assembly for conversation and social recreation or for discussion of art, literature, or science

1con·verse \kən'vərs, -vōs, -vəis\ *vb* -ED/-ING/-S [ME *conversen*, fr. MF *converser*, fr. L *conversari* to associate with, fr. *conversare* to turn often, freq. of *convertere* to turn around — more at CONVERT] *vi* **1** *obs* **:** to move about, live, or dwell esp. in a place ⟨impurities . . . contracted by *conversing* to and fro in a defiling world —Robert Boyle⟩ **2** *obs* **:** to have sexual intercourse **3** *archaic* **:** to become occupied or engaged (as with a subject) **:** have acquaintance or familiarity from long intercourse or study ⟨he had . . . *conversed* so much with money —Henry Fielding⟩ **4** *obs* **:** to have dealings **:** ASSOCIATE (as with another) ⟨to seek the distant hills and there ~ with nature —James Thomson †1748⟩ ⟨Indians . . . *conversed* with the islands near them —Daniel Defoe⟩ **5 :** to engage in conversation **:** exchange thoughts and opinions in speech **:** TALK ⟨they *conversed* like gentlemen, about the racing season, the hunting, the new roads —Stark Young⟩ ~ *vt, obs* **:** to associate or hold conversation with **syn** see SPEAK

2con·verse \'kän,v-\ *n* -s **1** *obs* **a :** intimate association **:** social intercourse **b :** CONVERSATION 1e **c :** CONVERSATION 1c **2 :** familiar discourse **:** free exchange of thoughts or views **:** TALK ⟨a freedom to resolve difference by ~ —Julian Huxley⟩ ⟨some perception of the . . . intimate ~ between instructor and student —Allen Johnson⟩ **3** *obs* **:** sexual intercourse **:** CONVERSATION 2

3con·verse \kən'v-, (')kän'v-\ *adj* [L *conversus*, past part. of *convertere*] **:** turned about **:** reversed in order or relation **:** acting oppositely or contrarily ⟨deduction . . . runs not from the indubitable data to one's theoretical conclusions, but in the ~ direction, from the theory back to the facts —F.S.C. Northrop⟩ **:** that is the converse of something **:** with the principal terms transposed ⟨Socrates, while he said that the true tragic writer was also an artist in comedy, did not lay down the ~ proposition that the true comic writer is also an artist in tragedy —Samuel Alexander⟩ — **con·verse·ly** *adv*

4con·verse \'kän,v-\ *n* -s **1 :** something related to something else in a way that is turned about in order, its statement being derived from that of the other by transposing two principal or antithetical terms ("a rainy day and a clear night" is the ~ of "a clear day and a rainy night"): as **a :** a theorem formed by the interchange of hypothesis and conclusion in a given theorem **b :** a proposition in logic obtained by conversion ⟨the ~ of "no *S* is *P*" is "no *P* is *S*" and of "some *S* is *P*" is "some *P* is *S*"⟩ — distinguished from *contrary* **2 :** a thing that is the opposite or reverse of another ⟨proclaim him moral, as well as wise, and the pleasing ~ every-way of his disgraced cousin —George Meredith⟩

syn OBVERSE, REVERSE: these three nouns mean in common that which is the opposite in some way of another thing. Although in its chief application, that is, to statements, CONVERSE implies an interchange or transposition of the significant terms of a given proposition, in popular use it often signifies a proposition or fact that is merely antithetical or opposing in some way ⟨the relation of wife to husband is called the *converse* of the relation of husband to wife—Bertrand Russell⟩ ⟨the words "I need you" are as potent as ever, and Anthony Gilfillan had made a slip in psychology when he imagined that the *converse* "You need me" would weigh much —William McFee⟩ ⟨if the man stood to profit he would offer his services; if the *converse* were true he would avoid any involvement⟩ Applied to the two faces of a coin or medal, OBVERSE refers to the face containing the head and the principal inscription, REVERSE to the other. In strict transfer of this use, OBVERSE may signify the more apparent and intentionally conspicuous side or face of anything, REVERSE the less apparent or less conspicuous side; in common use, however, OBVERSE and REVERSE are used alike to refer to the other side or face of anything or to the opposite of anything ⟨good and evil are but the *obverse* and *reverse* sides of the same shield —M.J. Herskovits⟩ ⟨love means discrimination and preference, and the *obverse* of that is natural aversion —M.R.Cohen⟩ ⟨their rise was merely the *obverse* of the Empire's fall—A.J.Toynbee⟩ ⟨on one side of the sheet was the title; on the *reverse*, the dedication⟩

conversed *past of* CONVERSE

converses *pres 3d sing of* CONVERSE, *pl of* CONVERSE

conversi *pl of* CONVERSUS

1con·ver·si·ble \kən'vərsəbəl, -vōs-,-vəis-\ *adj* [L *conversibilis*, fr. *conversus* + *-ibilis* -ible] **:** capable of being converted or transposed

2conversible *var of* CONVERSABLE

conversing *pres part of* CONVERSE

con·ver·sion \kən'vərzhən, -vəzh-,-vəizh-, *Brit usu & US also* -shən\ *n* -s [ME *conversioun*, fr. MF *conversion*, fr. L *conversion-, conversio*, fr. *conversus* (past part. of *convertere* to turn round, convert) + *-ion-, -io* -ion — more at CONVERT] **1 a** (1) **:** change from one belief, view, course, party, or principle to another **:** the bringing over or persuasion of a person to a particular belief, party, or principle ⟨his ~ to, and disillusionment with, the Communist party —Sidney Hook⟩; *specif* **:** the bringing over or persuasion of a person to the Christian faith ⟨in order to help forward ~*s* among her people —I.B. Richman⟩ (2) **:** a change of one's feelings or one's point of view from a state marked by indifference or opposition to one of zealous acceptance, liking, or devotion ⟨Melville's sudden passionate ~ to Shakespeare —K.S.Davis⟩; *specif* **:** such a change in one's religious orientation marked also by a concomitant change in belief **b** (1) **:** change from one form, state, or character into another ⟨turtles . . . await ~ into canned meat and soup —*Amer. Guide Series: Fla.*⟩ ⟨the company's ~ to war production⟩ (2) **:** translation (as of a literary text) from one language into another (3) **:** structural change or remodeling usu. to increase efficiency or usefulness ⟨~ of the aircraft carrier will include strengthening of the flight deck and increasing the fuel capacity⟩ (4) **:** the transformation of an unconscious mental conflict into a symbolically equivalent bodily symptom (5) **:** a change in type of forest management (as from coppice forest system to seedling forest system) (6) **:** the making of a score on a try for point after touchdown in football or a free throw in basketball **c :** an appropriation of and dealing with the property of another as if it were one's own without right ⟨the ~ of a horse⟩ **d :** change from one use or purpose to another ⟨~ of the electronic eye, then used mainly to open doors . . . into an anticrime device —Alan Hynd⟩; *also* **:** the thing so converted (as a hunting rifle converted from a military rifle) **2** *obs* **:** the action of revolving (as on an axis) or turning (as from one position or direction to another) ⟨the ~ of the needle to the north —Sir Thomas Browne⟩ **3 a :** the act of interchanging the terms of a proposition (as by putting the subject in place of the predicate or the contrary) — see CONVERSION PER ACCIDENS, SIMPLE CONVERSION **b :** a change or reduction of the form of a mathematical proposition or expression ⟨the ~ of equations⟩ ⟨the ~ of proportions⟩; *esp* **:** reduction by clearing of fractions **c :** change from one thing to another by substitution **:** EXCHANGE ⟨~ on the railroad from steam to diesel locomotives⟩ **d :** the exchange of property of one nature to property of another nature (as of real to personal, heritable to movable, or the reverse) sometimes considered for legal purposes as having taken place although no actual exchange has been made (as where a trustee has been directed to sell real estate and buy bonds but fails to do so) **e** (1) **:** the exchange of outstanding currency for a new monetary unit as part of the reconstruction of a currency system (2) **:** the change of one or more security issues into a single new issue (3) **:** the exchange of one kind of security for another **f :** the act of converting an insurance policy **4** *in compounding interest* **:** the creation at each interest period of a new principle sum by adding the accrued interest to the principal of the preceding period **5 :** the amount (as of a hydrocarbon oil) converted in a chemical reaction or decomposition **6 :** the transferring of information from one code to another usu. with a simultaneous transfer from one recording medium to another

con·ver·sion·ary \-nerē\ *adj* **:** of or relating to conversion (sense 1c) ⟨commit a ~ act⟩

conversion cost *n* **:** the combined total of direct labor cost and burden incurred in processing raw materials to a finished state

conversion hysteria *or* **conversion reaction** *n* **:** a psychoneurosis manifested by somatic conversion symptoms

con·ver·sion·ist \-nəst\ *n* -s **:** one devoting himself to converting others (as to a belief in Christianity)

conversion per accidens *n, logic* **:** the transposing of the subject and predicate of a proposition involving the limitation of quantity from universal to particular, valid of universal affirmatives ⟨"some *P* is *S*" is the *conversion per accidens* of "all *S* is *P*"⟩

conversion privilege *n* **:** the contractual right to exchange one security for another at the owner's option (as the right to exchange bonds to common stock of the issuer at a fixed ratio)

conversion table *n* **:** a table of equivalents for changing units of measure or weight into other units

con·ver·sive \kən'vərsiv, -vəs-,-vəis-\ *adj* [F *conversif*, fr. *conversion* + *-if* -ive] **:** CONSECUTIVE 3b

con·ver·so \kən'ver(,)sō, kōn-\ *n* -s [Sp, convert, fr. *converso* converted, fr. ML *conversus*] **:** a Jew who publicly recanted his faith and adopted Christianity under the pressure of the Spanish Inquisition

con·ver·sus \kən'vərsəs, -vəs-, -vəis-; -ver-\ *n, pl* **conver·si** \-,sī, -(,)sē\ [ML, fr. L, past part. of *convertere*] **1 :** a lay brother **2 :** an administrator of episcopal or monastic property

¹con·vert \kən'vərt, -vət, -vəit, *usu* -d·+V\ *vb* -ED/-ING/-S [ME *converten*, fr. OF *convertir*, fr. ML *convertere*, fr. L, to turn around, employ, transform, fr. *com-* + *vertere* to turn — more at WORTH] *vt* **1 a** (1) **:** to bring over or persuade (a person or group) to a particular belief, view, course, party, or principle often from a previously held position ⟨he was ~*ed* to the Copernican theory by . . . the professor of astronomy —S.F.Mason⟩ ⟨~ young people to the pleasures of reading⟩ ⟨an ex-Tory who . . . had gone to give a Socialist editor a good piece of her mind and come away ~*ed* —N.F.Busch⟩; *specif* **:** to bring over or persuade to the Christian faith ⟨no attempt was made to ~ the Moslems —W.H.Prescott⟩ (2) **:** to bring about a spiritual conversion in (as a religious conversion in a person or group) **b** (1) **:** to change or turn from one state to another **:** alter in form, substance, or quality **:** TRANSFORM, TRANSMUTE ⟨sheepskins are ~*ed* into parchment⟩ ⟨ideas . . . ~*ed* into deeds —John Mason Brown⟩ (2) **:** to turn (iron) into steel by the Bessemer process **:** turn (matte) into copper **:** make (Bessemer steel) from iron **:** make (copper) from matte (3) **:** to change the chemical nature of (as by changing starch into dextrose) (4) **:** to finish (gray goods) by dyeing, bleaching, or printing (5) **:** to score on (a try for point after touchdown in football or a free throw in basketball) (6) **:** to process (paper) as by gumming or waxing; *also* **:** to fabricate (paper) into finished products ⟨~ paper into envelopes or paperboard into cartons⟩ **c** (1) **:** to change or turn from one use, purpose, or function to another ⟨~*ing* some newly unpacked article . . . into a missile against the head of some unfortunate servant —T.L.Peacock⟩ ⟨every possible industry was ~*ed* to produce war goods —Morris Sayre⟩ (2) **:** to remodel in order to accommodate to a new manner of operation or change from one type to another ⟨~ a coal furnace to oil⟩ ⟨a trawler ~*ed* into a minesweeper⟩ (3) **:** to appropriate dishonestly or illegally ⟨~*ing* to its own . . . use 80,000 bushels of corn stored for the Commodity Credit Corp. —*Time*⟩ **2 a** *obs* **:** to cause to turn **:** TURN, DIRECT ⟨which way shall I first ~ myself —Ben Jonson⟩ **b** *obs* **:** to turn back **:** cause to return **:** turn in the opposite direction **3** [ME *converten*, fr. OF *convertir*, fr. LL *convertere* to convert, fr. L, to turn around, transform] **a** *obs* **:** to translate into another language ⟨which story . . . Catullus more elegantly ~*ed* —Ben Jonson⟩ **b** *logic* **:** to make a conversion of (a proposition) **c :** to exchange for a specified equivalent ⟨~ stock holdings into cash⟩ **d :** to create a situation that causes (property of one nature) to be deemed in equity changed into property of another nature — compare CONVERSION 3d **e :** to exchange (one security) for another under a conversion privilege or an offer made by the issuer **f :** to turn (one type of money) into another in the market or merely for purposes of calculation ⟨~ francs into dollars⟩ **g :** to exchange (an insurance policy) for one of a different type ~ *vi* **1 :** to make or undergo a conversion **:** undergo physical, moral, or functional change ⟨let grief ~ to anger —Shak.⟩ ⟨factories were ~*ing* to war production⟩ ⟨a sofa that ~*s* into a bed⟩ **2 :** to make a score on a try for point or a free throw **syn** see TRANSFORM

²con·vert \'kän,v-\ *n* -s **:** a person or group that is converted to a religious faith or to a particular belief, attitude of mind or feeling, course, party, or principle ⟨a ~ and disciple of Saint Paul⟩ ⟨the first American novelist to become a . . . ~ to naturalism —Malcolm Cowley⟩; *esp* **:** one who has experienced conversion

converted *past of* CONVERT

converted rice *n* [fr. *Converted*, a trademark] **:** rice that has been processed to retain its natural mineral and vitamin content and to have improved keeping qualities

con·ver·tend \'känvə(r),tend\ *n* -s [L *convertendum* thing that is to be converted, neut. of *convertendus*, gerundive of *convertere* — more at CONVERT] **:** a proposition in logic subjected to the process of conversion

con·vert·er \kən'vər|d·ə(r), -və|,-vəi|, |tə-\ *n* -s **:** one that converts a thing, person, or group ⟨is the steer that eats eight pounds of wheat, corn, and soybeans to give us one pound of meat an efficient food ~ —George Poindexter⟩: as **a :** a workman or machine that performs a step or series of steps in the transformation of materials into a manufactured product (as a furnace in which air is blown through crude metal or matte to refine it or the operator of such a furnace) **b** *or* **conver·tor** \"\ **:** a device for changing energy from one form to another (as formerly a transformer or now a machine employing mechanical rotation) — see MOTOR CONVERTER, SYNCHRONOUS CONVERTER **c :** a businessman or firm that buys unfinished goods for finishing; *specif* **:** one that buys gray goods and finishes them by dyeing, bleaching, or printing **d :** a radio device usu. consisting of an oscillator and mixing tube that is used in superheterodyne receivers or other equipment where a change of signal frequency is desired **e** (1) **:** a cipher machine; *esp* **:** an electric one adaptable to automatic operation (2) **:** a machine that transfers information from one code to another and usu. from one recording medium to another **f :** an auxiliary device for adapting a television receiver to receive channels for which it was not orig. designed

converter plant *n* **:** an indicator plant capable of absorption of selenium or copper and sometimes leaving a residue of it in upper layers of the soil

con·vert·ibil·ity \kən,vər|d·ə'biləd·ē, -və|,-vəi|, |tə'-, -ətē, -i\ *n* -ES **1 :** the quality of being convertible; *specif* **:** the ability of currency to be exchanged for gold or other currencies without restriction ⟨a bilateral ~ of the currencies of the two friendly countries⟩ **2 :** the ability, the freedom, or the right to exchange a currency for gold or other currencies without restriction ⟨the two countries adopted a mutual ~⟩

¹con·vert·ible \kən'vər|d·əbəl, -və|,-vəi|, |təb-\ *adj* [ME, fr. MF, fr. ML *convertibilis*, fr. L, changeable, fr. *convertere* to turn round, transform + *-ibilis* -ible — more at CONVERT] **:** capable of being converted: as **a :** interchangeable in meaning ⟨*synonymous* and *equivalent* are ~ terms⟩ **b :** capable of being changed in form, properties, type, or use **:** capable of being adapted to more than one use ⟨heat ~ into electricity⟩ ⟨an afternoon dress ~ for evening wear⟩: as (1) **:** capable of being worn in more than one way ⟨a ~ collar worn open or closed⟩ (2) *of an automobile* **:** having a top that may be folded back, lowered, or removed ⟨a ~ coupe⟩ ⟨a ~ sedan⟩ **c** *logic* **:** capable of being transposed by conversion **d :** capable of being converted to a belief, opinion, or principle ⟨a man not easily ~ to strange manners and morals⟩ **e** (1) **:** capable of being exchanged for a specified equivalent (as property, value, or obligation of another kind) ⟨preferred stock ~ at an agreed ratio into common⟩ (2) *of currency* **:** capable of being exchanged without restriction for currency of another kind ⟨francs ~ into dollars⟩ — **con·vert·ible·ness** *n* -ES

²convertible \"\ *n* -s **:** something that is convertible: as **a :** a convertible term in a logical proposition **b :** a convertible automobile — compare HARDTOP CONVERTIBLE

con·vert·ibly \-blē,-bli\ *adv* **:** INTERCHANGEABLY

converting *pres part of* CONVERT

con·vert·i·plane *or* **con·vert·a·plane** \kən'vərd·ə,plān\ *n* [¹*convert* + connective *-i-* or *-a-* + *-plane*] **:** an aircraft combining the vertical takeoff of the helicopter with the greater forward speed of the airplane, having a rotating airfoil for vertical lift, and capable of conversion to a fixed-wing configuration for forward flight

con·ver·tive \kən'vərd·iv\ *adj* **:** tending to convert **:** CONVERTING

converts *pres 3d sing of* CONVERT, *pl of* CONVERT

con·veth \'kän,veth\ *n* -s [ML *conveth, cuneveth*, of Celt origin; akin to MIr *connmedh* quarterage, billeting — more at COYNYE] **:** a burden upon land under the Scottish tribal chiefs orig. of a night's entertainment of the chief and his followers

¹con·vex \(')kän¦veks, kən'v-\ *adj* [MF or L; MF *convexe*, fr. L *convexus* vaulted, arched, convex, concave, fr. *com-* + *-vexus* (akin to *vacillare* to sway, stagger) — more at VACILLATE] **1 :** curved or rounded as the exterior or a section of a spherical or circular form — used of a spherical surface or curved line viewed from without; opposed to *concave* **2 :** arched up **:** bulging out — used of that side of a curve or surface on which the tangent line or plane lies or on which normals at neighboring points diverge; opposed to *concave* — **con·vex·ly** *adv* — **con·vex·ness** *n* -ES

²con·vex \(')kän¦v-\ *n* -ES *archaic* **:** a convex body, surface, or part (as a vault or arch seen from without); *specif* **:** the vault of the sky ⟨half heaven's ~ glitters with the flame —Thomas Tickell⟩

³con·vex \'kän,v-, kən'v-\ *vb* -ED/-ING/-ES **:** to bend convexly **:** bow outward in a convex curve

con·vex·i·ty \kən'veksəd·ē, kän-, -ətē, -i\ *n* -ES [MF or L; MF *convexité*, fr. L *convexitat-, convexitas*, fr. *convexus* convex + *-itat-, -itas* -ity] **1 :** the quality or state of being convex ⟨a degree of ~⟩ **2 :** a convex surface, curve, part, or body ⟨a man . . . with a ripe ~ under his waistcoat —Leslie Charteris⟩

con·vexo–concave \kən¦veksō +\ *adj* [¹*convex* + *-o-* + *concave*] **1 :** convex on one side and concave on the other **2 :** having the convex side of greater curvature than the concave

con·vexo–convex \kən¦veksō +\ *adj* [¹*convex* + *-o-* + *convex*] **:** BICONVEX

convex polygon *n* **:** a polygon each of whose angles is less than a straight angle

¹con·vey \kən'vā\ *vb* -ED/-ING/-S [ME *conveyen*, fr. OF *conveier*, fr. (assumed) VL *conviare*, fr. L *com-* + *-viare* (fr. *via* way) — more at VIA] *vt* **1** *obs* **:** to accompany as a guide or escort **:** LEAD, CONDUCT ⟨~ him to the tower —Shak.⟩ **2 a :** to bear from one place to another **:** CARRY, TRANSPORT ⟨the Irish mail was ~*ed* by coach to Holyhead —O.S.Nock⟩ **b :** to impart or communicate either directly by clear statement or indirectly by suggestion, implication, gesture, attitude, behavior, or appearance ⟨words will not ~ what is in my heart —H.S.Truman⟩ ⟨something . . . which ~*ed* the idea that he could say more if he chose—Samuel Butler †1902⟩ **c** (1) *archaic* **:** STEAL (2) *obs* **:** to carry or take away or remove usu. secretly **d :** to transfer or deliver (as property) to another; *specif* **:** to transfer (as real estate) or pass (a title, as to real estate) by a sealed writing **e :** to serve as a channel or medium for in carrying or in aiding passage from one place or person to another **:** cause to pass from one place or person to another **:** TRANSMIT ⟨an infection ~*ed* by food⟩ ⟨a pipe for ~*ing* water⟩ ⟨~ this message to your brother⟩ **3** *obs* **:** to derive by succession or descent **4** *obs* **:** to manage or conduct (as affairs) esp. with privacy or craft ⟨~ the business as I shall find means —Shak.⟩ ~ *vi, law* **:** to make conveyance **syn** see CARRY

²convey *n* -s *obs* **:** a convoy or protective escort

con·vey·al \-āəl\ *n* -s **:** CONVEYING, CONVEYANCE

con·vey·ance \-āən(t)s\ *n* -s **1 :** the action of conveying: as **a :** the communication or transmission of thought, idea, or meaning ⟨~ of the meaning . . . through speech —A.T. Davison⟩ **b :** CARRYING, TRANSPORTING, TRANSPORTATION ⟨the railways are . . . suited to the ~ of heavy loads at high speed —O.S.Nock⟩ **:** a serving as a means of transportation ⟨~ of irrigation water⟩ **c :** the act by which the title to property (as real estate) is transferred **:** the transfer of ownership — compare CONVEYANCING 2 **d** *archaic* **:** a carrying off or removal (as feloniously or by stealth) **:** THEFT **e** *obs* (1) **:** the act or manner of conducting or managing (2) **:** crafty or dishonest management **:** underhanded work or practice **:** TRICK, ARTIFICE **2 :** a means or way of conveying: as **a** *obs* **:** a way or means of communicating (as thought or meaning) or passing (as from place to place) **b :** an instrument in writing (as a deed or mortgage) by which the title to property is conveyed from one person to another **c** *obs* **:** a channel or passage for conduction or transmission (as of fluids or electricity) ⟨these pipes and these ~*s* of our blood —Shak.⟩ **d :** a means of carrying or transporting something (as persons as passengers) **:** VEHICLE ⟨all . . . who had horses and ~*s* of any sort —Kenneth Roberts⟩

con·vey·anc·er \-ənsə(r)\ *n* -s **1 :** one that conveys something **2 :** one whose business is conveyancing; *esp* **:** a lawyer who specializes in the conveyancing of properties

con·vey·anc·ing \-ənsiŋ\ *n* -s **1** *obs* **:** crafty management or practice **2 :** the act or business of drawing deeds, leases, or other writings for transferring the title to property **:** the branch of law having to do with titles and their transference

con·vey·er *or* **con·vey·or** \kən'vāə(r)\ *n* -s **1 :** one that conveys: as **a :** one that carries or transmits ⟨a ~ of bold new ideas⟩ **b** *obs* **:** THIEF **c :** a person who transfers property **2 a** *usu conveyor* **:** a mechanical apparatus for carrying packages or bulk material from place to place: as (1) *or* **conveyor belt :** an endless moving belt (as of canvas, rubber, metal) on which items, packages, or material to be moved may be placed and which operates over terminal pulleys or rollers together with receiving and delivery appliances — called also *band conveyor, belt conveyor* (2) **:** a set of arms or trays for carrying that travel on an endless chain (3) **:** two or more slow-moving chains on which bulky parts of work in process are placed so that smaller parts may be added as the work passes — called also *chain conveyor* (4) **:** containers (as baskets or carriages) or hooks attached to a moving chain or cable suspended by rollers from overhead supports (5) **:** a series of horizontal rollers spaced close together and turned by power in the same direction (6) **:** buckets attached to or forming a continuous moving chain — called also *bucket conveyor* (7) **:** wooden or steel plates attached to endless chains and running in a trough through which material to be moved is dragged (8) **:** an enclosed single-plate or double-plate helix formed about a turning shaft that moves material along a trough or tube — called also *auger conveyor, screw conveyor* (9) **:** air pumps or blowers arranged to draw or force material to be moved and air through a hose or pipe usu. to a separator where the solid material falls to the bottom — called also *pneumatic conveyor, wind conveyor* **b :** one that operates a conveyor

conveying *pres part of* CONVEY

conveyor belt *n* **:** CONVEYER 2a (1)

conveyor–belt \'≈,≈,≈\ *adj* [*conveyor belt*] **:** of, relating to, or characteristic of mass production ⟨*conveyor-belt* uniformity⟩ ⟨*conveyor-belt* shoddiness —Roy Lewis & Angus Maude⟩

con·vey·or·ize \kən'vāə,rīz\ *vt* -ED/-ING/-S **1 :** to equip with a conveyor ⟨*conveyorized* assembly lines⟩ ⟨~ an industrial plant⟩ **2 :** to do, achieve, or effect by means of a conveyor ⟨*conveyorized* . . . heat-treatment of gears —*Chem. Abstracts*⟩ ⟨the *conveyorized* assembly of radios⟩

conveys *pres 3d sing of* CONVEY, *pl of* CONVEY

¹con·vict \kən'vikt\ *adj* [ME, fr. L *convictus*] *archaic* **:** CONVICTED

²convict \"\ *vt* -ED/-ING/-S [ME *convicten*, fr. L *convictus*, past part. of *convincere* to convict, prove — more at CONVINCE] **1 a :** to find or declare guilty of an offense or crime by the verdict or decision of a court or other authority ⟨he was tried, ~*ed*, and fined $50⟩ **b :** to show or prove to be guilty of something blamable (as wrong or error) ⟨their writings ~ them of an ignorance of history⟩ **2 a** *obs* **:** to demonstrate by proof or evidence **:** PROVE **b :** to convince of error or sinfulness ⟨~ us of sin⟩ **c** *archaic* **:** to prove to be false or in the wrong **:** REFUTE

³con·vict \'kän,v-\ *n* -s [¹*convict*] **1 :** a person pronounced guilty by a competent tribunal of a criminal offense; *esp* **:** a person convicted of and under sentence for a felony or serious crime ⟨~*s* transported to the colonies for life⟩ **2 :** a person serving a prison sentence usu. for a long term ⟨~ labor⟩ ⟨~ uniforms⟩ **3** *or* **convict fish** [so called fr. the resemblance of their striped skin to the traditionally striped garb of convicts] **:** any of various striped or barred fishes **syn** see CRIMINAL

con·vict·ed \-təd\ *adj* [*conviction* + *-ed*] **:** conscious of and repentant for one's sin **:** CONVERTED

convict goods \'≈,≈-\ *n pl* [³*convict*] **:** goods produced by convict labor

con·vic·tion \kən'vikshən\ *n* -s [ME *conviccioun*, fr. LL *conviction-, convictio* proof, fr. L *convictus* + *-ion-, -io* -ion — more at CONVICT] **1 :** the act of proving, finding, or adjudging a person guilty of an offense or crime ⟨~ of the prisoner for burglary⟩; *specif* **:** the proceeding of record by which a person is legally found guilty of any crime esp. by a jury and on which the judgment is based **2** *obs* **:** demonstration or proof; *esp* **:** the proof or exposure of error **3 a :** the act of convincing a person of error or of compelling the admission of a truth **b** (1) **:** the state of being convinced of error or compelled to admit the truth ⟨all his tedious talk is but vain boast, or subtle shifts ~ to evade —John Milton⟩ (2) **:** the state of being convinced of and repentant for one's sin — often used with *under* ⟨making them think in order to bring them to ~ of sin —G.B.Shaw⟩ ⟨unaware that for a month he had been under ~⟩ **4 a :** a strong persuasion or belief ⟨the ~ that the next man he would meet . . . would be his father —E.J.Simmons⟩ ⟨~ that learning was essential for godliness —K.B.Murdock⟩ **b :** the state of being convinced (as of the truth or rightness of one's belief or acts) ⟨he was an internationalist by ~⟩ **:** a feeling or awareness of the rightness, truth, or certainty of what is thought, spoken, or done ⟨the actors played with great ~⟩ ⟨not enough ambition to shape his thought, nor enough ~ to give rhythm to his style —W.B. Yeats⟩ **c convictions** *pl* **:** strongly held beliefs or views ⟨certain thoughts sustain us in defeat . . . and it is these thoughts . . . that we call ~*s* —W.B.Yeats⟩ **syn** see OPINION

con·vic·tion·al \-shən°l, -shnəl\ *adj* **:** of or concerning conviction

con·vict·ism \'kän(,)vik,tizəm\ *n* -s [³*convict* + *-ism*] **:** the policy or practice of transporting convicts to colonial penal settlements

con·vic·tive \kən'viktiv\ *adj* [L *convictus* + E *-ive*] **:** producing or tending to produce conviction **:** CONVINCING ⟨a ~ answer⟩ — **con·vic·tive·ly** \-təvlē\ *adv*

convict labor system *n* **:** a plan or system for utilizing convict labor often authorized by law — compare CONTRACT SYSTEM, LEASE SYSTEM, PIECE PRICE SYSTEM, PUBLIC ACCOUNT SYSTEM, PUBLIC WORKS AND WAYS SYSTEM, STATE USE SYSTEM

con·vic·tor \-tə(r)\ *n* -s [L, fr. *convictus* (past part. of *convivere* to live with, feast together, fr. *com-* + *vivere* to live) + *-or* — more at QUICK] *archaic* **:** a table companion **:** COMMONER

con·vince \kən'vin(t)s\ *vt* -ED/-ING/-S [L *convincere* to refute, convict, prove, fr. *com-* + *vincere* to conquer — more at VICTOR] **1 a** *obs* **:** to overcome by argument **:** CONFUTE ⟨Satan stood . . . confuted and *convinced* —John Milton⟩ **:** prove to be wrong or in error **:** demonstrate the fallacy of ⟨God never wrought miracle to ~ atheism because his ordinary works ~ it —Francis Bacon⟩ **b** *obs* **:** OVERPOWER, OVERCOME, SUBDUE **2 a** *obs* **:** to prove guilty **:** CONVICT ⟨which of you *convinceth* me of sin —Jn 8:46 (AV)⟩ **b** *obs* **:** DEMONSTRATE, PROVE ⟨to ~ the honor of my mistress —Shak.⟩ **3 :** to bring to or cause to have belief, acceptance, or conviction ⟨this ruse succeeded in *convincing* his pursuers that he was drowned —S.P.B.Mais⟩ **:** bring by argument to give assent or have belief ⟨it is difficult to ~ people that . . . we would also gain something —Vera M. Dean⟩

convinced *adj* **:** having or feeling strong belief or conviction ⟨he was a ~ and fanatical pacifist —W.A.White⟩ **:** CERTAIN, SURE ⟨~ that it would be to their advantage to join —A.P. Ryan⟩ — **con·vinced·ly** \-sədlē, -stlē, -li\ *adv* — **con·vinced·ness** \-sədnəs, -s(t)n-\ *n* -ES

con·vince·ment \-smənt\ *n* -s **:** the action of convincing or the state of being convinced; *esp* **:** religious conviction or conversion ⟨many of the first ~*s* by Quaker missionaries —*Times Lit. Supp.*⟩

con·vinc·er \-sə(r)\ *n* -s **:** one that convinces; *specif* **:** a particular act or argument that brings conviction ⟨the offer of $15 was the ~⟩

convincing *adj* **1 :** satisfying or assuring by argument or proof ⟨one very ~ test which so strongly supports the tradition that it seems conclusive —Hilaire Belloc⟩ **2 :** having the power to convince one of the truth, rightness, or reality of what is done or stated **:** PLAUSIBLE ⟨the dialogue is most ~ —G.C. Sellery⟩ ⟨more ~ than most spy novels —Anthony Boucher⟩ **syn** see VALID

con·vinc·ing·ly *adv* : in a convincing manner

con·vive \kōⁿvēv, 'kän,vīv\ *n, pl* **convives** \kōⁿvēv, 'kän-,vīvz\ [F, fr. L *conviva* one who lives with another, eats with another, fr. *com-* + *-viva* (fr. *vivere* to live) — more at QUICK] : a fellow banqueter or feaster : a comrade at table

con·viv·i·al \kən'vivēəl, -vyəl\ *adj* [LL *convivialis*, fr. L *convivium* banquet (fr. *com-* + *-vivium*, fr. *vivere* to live) + *-alis* -al — more at QUICK] : of, relating to, or occupied with feasting, drinking, and good company ⟨the lighthearted cup and the ~ jest for them —W.S.Gilbert⟩ : fond of good company and of festivity ⟨Virginians of the ~ sort, sportsmen, lovers of scenery, lovers of horses —Van Wyck Brooks⟩ **syn** see SOCIAL

con·viv·i·al·i·ty \kən,vivē'aləd·ē, -ətē, -i\ *n* -ES **1** : convivial quality esp. of spirit or humor ⟨his ~, warmth, and good nature were irresistible⟩ **2** : convivial activities or behavior ⟨evenings spent in ~⟩

con·viv·i·al·ly \kən'vivēəlē, -vyəl-, -li\ *adv* : in a convivial manner

con·viv·i·um \-vēəm\ *n, pl* **conviv·ia** \-vēə\ [L] **1** : a convivial gathering : BANQUET **2** [NL, fr. L] : a subdivision of a commiscuum comprising a group of organisms that are set apart by characters other than interfertility and are maintained by some isolating mechanism other than intersterility and usu. equivalent in scope to a taxonomic subspecies or variety

con·vo·cate \'känvə,kāt\ *vt* -ED/-ING/-S [L *convocatus*, past part. of *convocare*] *archaic* : to call together : CONVOKE

con·vo·ca·tion \,känvə'kāshən, -nvō'-\ *n* -S [ME *convocacioun*, fr. MF *convocation*, fr. L *convocation-, convocatio*, fr. *convocatus* (past part. of *convocare* to convoke) + *-ion-, -io* -ion — more at CONVOKE] **1 a** : an assembly or meeting of persons convoked ⟨the Accession Council, the oldest governmental ~ in England —*Time*⟩; *also* : the people so assembled **b** (1) : an assembly of representatives of Church of England clergy that is constituted by statute to consult on ecclesiastical affairs (2) : a meeting of an organization in the Protestant Episcopal Church that is composed of the clergy and some of the laity of a territorial division of a diocese to promote interest in such matters as diocesan missions; *also* : the organization itself which is a purely voluntary one with no legislative functions or the territorial division (3) : the annual meeting in the Protestant Episcopal Church of the bishop, clergy, and lay delegates of a missionary jurisdiction which not being a diocese cannot hold a diocesan convention **c** *at some British universities* (1) : a deliberative, advisory, or elective body composed usu. of graduates or of those with the degree of M.A.; *also* : an assembly of this body (2) : a purely social group open to all graduates who pay a membership fee **d** (1) : an assembly of the members of a college or university to observe a particular ceremony (as the opening of the academic year or the announcing of prizes, awards, and honors) (2) *at some Canadian universities* : COMMENCEMENT 2 **e** : a meeting of a chapter of Royal Arch Masons or a reunion of Scottish Rite for the conferring of degrees **2** : the act of calling or assembling by summons ⟨at the time of the ~ of the parliament⟩

con·vo·ca·tion·al \¦=¦=¦shənᵊl, -shnəl\ *adj* : of or relating to a convocation — **con·vo·ca·tion·al·ly** \-ᵊlē, -əlē\ *adv*

con·voke \kən'vōk\ *vt* -ED/-ING/-S [MF *convoquer*, fr. L *convocare*, fr. *com-* + *vocare* to call — more at VOICE] : to call together : summon to meet : assemble by summons (as a parliament, council, or other official body) ⟨the government *convoked* a congress of physicists⟩

con·vo·lu·ta \,känvə'lüd·ə\ *n, cap* [NL, fr. L, fem. of *convolutus*] : a genus of marine acoelous flatworms (the type of the family Convolutidae) including a number of forms having symbiotic algae in the parenchyma

¹**con·vo·lute** \'känvə,lüt *also* -əl,yüt, *usu* -üd.+V\ *vb* -ED/-ING/-S [L *convolutus*, past part. of *convolvere* to enfold, enwrap — more at CONVOLVE] *vt* **1** : to twist or coil around (an object) **2** : to make convolute : TWIST ⟨*convoluting* and entangling his phrases —George Saintsbury⟩ ~ *vi* : TWIST, COIL : assume twisted or tangled form ⟨grief had *convoluted* into monomania —Edgar Saltus⟩

²**convolute** \"\ *adj* [L *convolutus*] : rolled or wound together one part upon another : COILED — used esp. of cotyledons, of flowers or leaves in the bud, or of discoid shells having the inner whorls somewhat concealed by the outer — **con·vo·lute·ly** *adv*

convoluted *adj* **1** : folded in curved or tortuous windings : having convolutions : COILED ⟨a highly ~ brain —*No. Amer. Rev.*⟩ ⟨beaks recurved and ~ like a ram's horn —Thomas Pennant⟩ **2** : complicated and involved ⟨~ form⟩ ⟨his ~ later stories have more layers of meaning . . . than Henry James' —DeLancey Ferguson⟩ : having intricate and complexly related detail ⟨a ~ process of reasoning⟩

convoluted tubule *n* **1** : PROXIMAL CONVOLUTED TUBULE **2** : DISTAL CONVOLUTED TUBULE

con·vo·lu·tion \,känvə'lüshən\ *n* -S [L *convolutus* + E *-ion*] **1 a** : a tortuous or sinuous winding, fold or design (as of something rolled or folded upon itself) : COIL, WHORL, FOLD, SINUOSITY ⟨the ~s of the intestines⟩ **b** : one of the irregular ridges upon the surface of the brain, esp. of the cerebrum, of some animals : GYRUS **c** : TWISTING, WINDING : a complication or intricacy of form, design, or structure ⟨as a lover, as a writer, as a soldier, as an aesthete, and as a public official his life was of an almost inconceivable ~ —*Times Lit. Supp.*⟩ **2** : the act or action of convoluting or of following a convoluted course ⟨o'er the sea in ~s swift, the feathered eddy floats —James Thomson †1748⟩

con·vo·lu·tion·al \¦=¦=¦shənᵊl, -shnəl\ *adj* : of, relating to, or resembling a convolution

convolution of bro·ca \-(')brō¦kä, -'brōkə\ *usu cap B* [trans. of F *circonvolution de Broca*, after Paul *Broca* †1880 Fr. surgeon] : a brain center associated with the motor control of speech usu. in the left but sometimes in the right inferior frontal convolution

con·volve \kən'välv\ *vb* -ED/-ING/-S [L *convolvere*, fr. *com-* + *volvere* to roll — more at VOLUBLE] *vt* **1** *obs* : ENFOLD, ENWRAP, ENCLOSE **2** : to roll together : roll or twist (one part) on another : WRITHE ⟨*convolving* his chin and cheek in a rapid series of pursed lips and horrible squints —Thomas Wolfe⟩ ~ *vi* : to roll together or circulate involvedly ⟨the sweeping brushstrokes ~ like thunderclouds —R.C.Peace⟩

con·vol·vu·la·ce·ae \kən,välv(y)ə'lāsē,ē\ *n pl, cap* [NL, fr. *Convolvulus*, type genus + *-aceae*] : a family of twining vines, erect herbs, shrubs, or trees (order Polemoniales) comprising the morning-glory family and having alternate leaves and regular pentamerous flowers with plaited corollas — **con·vol·vu·la·ceous** \¦=¦=¦=¦shəs\ *adj*

con·vol·vu·lin \=¦=¦lən\ *n* -S [G *konvolvulin*, fr. NL *Convolvulus* (genus name of *Convolvulus schiedanus*) + G *-in*] : an ether-insoluble glucosidic constituent of true jalap resin

con·vol·vu·lus \-ləs\ *n* [NL, fr. L, bindweed, fr. *convolvere* to enfold, enwrap — more at CONVOLVE] **1** *cap* : a genus of erect trailing or twining herbs and shrubs (family Convolvulaceae) having the style undivided or merely cleft at its apex and with two linear stigmas — see BINDWEED, MORNING GLORY **2** *pl* **convolvuluses** \-ləsəz\ *or* **convolvu·li** \-,lī, -,lē\ : a plant of the genus *Convolvulus*

¹**con·voy** \'kän,vȯi, kən'v-\ *vt* -ED/-ING/-S [ME *convoyen*, fr. MF *convoier*, *conveier* — more at CONVEY] **1 a** : ACCOMPANY, ESCORT ⟨~ him out across the terrace —D.C.Peattie⟩ : GUIDE, CONDUCT **b** : to accompany or escort for protection ⟨he is . . . ~*ed* by Secret Service agents —*Newsweek*⟩; *specif* : to provide protective escort for (as a group of merchant ships) ⟨tankers ~*ed* by destroyers and aircraft⟩ **2** *obs* : CARRY, CONVEY

²**con·voy** \'kän,vȯi\ *n* -S *often attrib* [MF *convoi*, fr. *convoier*] **1** : one that convoys, escorts, or accompanies: as **a** : a funeral train **b** : a protective force (as of troops or warships) escorting ships, persons, or goods moving by sea or land : ESCORT ⟨a Dutch man-of-war of forty guns, which was ~ to the . . . fleet —Richard Steele⟩ **c** : CONDUCTOR, GUIDE ⟨Oh be some god his ~ to our shore —Alexander Pope⟩ **2** : the act of convoying, accompanying, or escorting esp. for protection ⟨they vanished quietly upstairs in ~ of the manager's wife —Arnold Bennett⟩ ⟨to obtain the ~ of a man-of-war —T.B.Macaulay⟩ **3** : an individual or group that is convoyed or a group organized for convenience or protection in moving: as **a** : a train of vehicles transporting goods under armed escort : a group of persons or vehicles traveling under escort **b** : a body of merchant ships sailing under the protection of an armed escort ⟨each ~ escorted by seven warships⟩ **c** : a body of persons or vehicles organized into a unit for the purpose of orderly or efficient movement ⟨a storm was raging . . . and cars had to fight their way through in ~ —G.R.Stewart⟩

¹**con·vul·sant** \kən'vəlsᵊnt\ *adj* [¹*convulse* + *-ant*] : causing convulsions : CONVULSIVE

²**convulsant** \"\ *n* -S : an agent that produces convulsions

con·vulse \kən'vəls\ *vb* -ED/-ING/-S [L *convulsus*, past part. of *convellere* to tear loose, dislocate, fr. *com-* + *vellere* to pluck, pull — more at VULNERABLE] *vt* **1** : to shake violently : agitate greatly : throw into confusion ⟨the world is *convulsed* by the agonies of great nations —T.B.Macaulay⟩ ⟨the ferment of change that has *convulsed* . . . our twentieth-century world —A.E.Stevenson †1965⟩ **2** : to affect with violent and irregular contractions of the muscles : shake with irregular spasms (as in agony from grief or pain) ⟨she writh'd about, *convuls'd* with scarlet pain —John Keats⟩ **3** : to cause to laugh violently ⟨he . . . *convulsed* the country with the famous kitten-and-coat saga —Scott Fitzgerald⟩ ~ *vi* : to become affected with convulsions ⟨some will ~ as a result of high fever⟩ **syn** see SHAKE

con·vul·sed·ly \-sədlē, -li\ *adv* : with spasmodic shaking

con·vul·sion \kən'vəlshən\ *n* -S [MF or L; MF *convulsion*, fr. L *convulsion-, convulsio*, fr. *convulsus* + *-ion-, -io* -ion] **1 a** *obs* : spasmodic contraction of the muscles : CRAMP **b** : an abnormal, violent, and involuntary contraction or series of contractions of the muscles — often used in pl. ⟨a patient suffering from ~s⟩ **2** *obs* : WRENCHING, TEARING **3 a** : a forceful wrenching, distorting, or upheaving seismic action ⟨the ~s which physical nature has always in reserve . . ., earthquakes of Lisbon, eruptions of Mount Pelée —Samuel Alexander⟩ **b** : a period of violent social or political stress, strain, surging action, and confusion ⟨the vast social ~s of a continent in travail —Reinhold Niebuhr⟩ **c** : an uncontrolled fit : a powerful emotional upheaval ⟨a ~ of grief and anger⟩ : PAROXYSM ⟨~s of sobbing —Joseph Conrad⟩ ⟨literally throwing themselves down on the ground in ~s of unholy mirth —Rudyard Kipling⟩ **syn** see COMMOTION

¹**con·vul·sion·ary** \-,nerē\ *n* -ES [F *convulsionnaire*, fr. *convulsion* + *-aire* -ary] **1** : one who has convulsions esp. as a result of religious mania or ecstasy **2** *usu cap* : one of a body of Jansenist fanatics in France in the early 18th century who exhibited convulsions esp. at the tomb of the Jansenist François de Paris in the cemetery of St-Médard at Paris

²**convulsionary** \"\ *adj* [*convulsion* + *-ary*] **1** : of, relating to, or resembling a convulsion ⟨~ struggles —Sir Walter Scott⟩ **2** *usu cap* : of or relating to the Convulsionaries

con·vul·sion·ist \-,nəst\ *n* -S *sometimes cap* [F *convulsionniste*, fr. *convulsion* + *-iste* -ist] : CONVULSIONARY

convulsion root *or* **convulsion weed** *n* : INDIAN PIPE

con·vul·sive \kən'vəlsiv, -sēv *also* -səv\ *adj* [F *convulsif*, fr. *convulsion* + *-if* -ive] **1** : producing or accompanied by convulsion ⟨~ disorders⟩ : affected by or having convulsions ⟨~ children⟩ : accompanying or resembling convulsion ⟨~ motions⟩ **2** : resembling convulsion in being violent, sudden, frantic, or spasmodic ⟨the nation . . . made a ~ effort to free itself from military domination —T.B.Macaulay⟩ ⟨he had a ~ drive, a boundless and explosive fervor —S.N.Behrman⟩ ⟨a ~ little hug —Agnes S. Turnbull⟩ — **con·vul·sive·ly** \-səvlē, -li\ *adv* — **con·vul·sive·ness** \-sivnəs, -sēv- *also* -səv-\ *n* -ES

convulsive therapy *n* : SHOCK THERAPY

cony *var of* CONEY

cony-catch *vb* [back-formation fr. *conycatcher*] *obs* : DECEIVE, CHEAT, TRICK

conycatcher *n* [*cony* + *catcher*] *obs* : CHEAT, SHARPER, SWINDLER

con·y·rine \'känə,rēn, -,rən\ *n* -S [ISV, alter. (influenced by *pyridine*) of *coniine*; orig. formed as G *konyrin*; fr. the fact that conyrine stands in the same chemical relationship to coniine as does pyridine to piperidine] : an oily base $C_8H_{11}N$ obtained as a decomposition product of coniine; 2-propyl-pyridine

¹**coo** \'kü\ *vi* **cooed; cooed; cooing; coos** [imit.] **1 a** : to make the low soft cry of a dove or pigeon ⟨in the coconut palms overhead doves were gloomily ~*ing* —John Dos Passos⟩ ⟨~*ing* like a dove to summon a great peace conference —A.L.Guérard⟩ **b** : to make a similar sound sometimes fatuously often in showing affection or pleasure or in seeking to placate **2** : to talk fondly or amorously ⟨such ~*ing* and kissing among us that indeed it is scandalous —John Dryden⟩

²**coo** \"\ *n* -S **1** : a soft low cry; *typically* : the call of a dove or pigeon ⟨the grave ~ of a dove —Sidney Lanier⟩ **2** : a sound or expression similar to a coo often in indication of or implying affection, fondness, or peaceful intent

³**coo** \"\ *interj* [origin unknown] *Brit* — used to express surprise, surprised pleasure, or wonder ⟨~, what an evening that was —Clemence Dane⟩

coob \'küb\ *n* -S [by alter.] *South* : ¹COOP 1

coo·ba *or* **coo·bah** \'kübə, -(,)bä\ *n* -S [native name in Australia] : an Australian wattle (*Acacia salicina*) with foliage resembling willow — called also *native willow*

cooch *or* **cootch** \'küch\ *n* -ES [by shortening & alter. fr. earlier *hootchy-kootchy*] : a pseudo-Oriental female dance common in carnivals and fairs and marked by a sinuous and often suggestive twisting and shaking of the torso and limbs ⟨a roving carnival ~ dancer —Frank Barton⟩ ⟨a circus ~ show⟩

¹**coo·ee** *also* **coo·ey** \'kü,ē\ *n* -S [origin unknown] *chiefly Austral* : a cry to attract attention or give warning — **within cooee** : within hailing distance : not unapproachable

²**cooee** *also* **cooey** \"\ *vi, chiefly Austral* : to call cooee

coo·ee bird \'küē,-\ *n* [native name in Australia, prob. of imit. origin] : an Australian koel (*Eudynamys scolopacea*)

coof \'küf\ *n* -S [perh. alter. of *goff*] *chiefly Scot* : a stupid fellow : DOLT, LOUT

coohee *cap, var of* COHEE

cooing *adj* : uttering coos ⟨~ voice⟩ ⟨~ baby⟩ : fondly amorous — **coo·ing·ly** *adv*

¹**cook** \'ku̇k\ *n* -S *often attrib* [ME *cooke, coke*, fr. OE *cōc*; akin to OHG *koch*, OS *kok*; all fr. a prehistoric WGmc word borrowed fr. L *cocus, coquus*, fr. *coquere* to cook; akin to OE *āfigen* fried, Gk *pessein* to cook, digest, W *pobi* to bake, Serb *peći*, Lith *kepti*, Skt *pacati* he cooks] **1 a** : one who prepares food for the table (as in a private home, public eating place, or institution) **b** : one who prepares a particular kind of food ⟨a pastry ~⟩ **2 a** : one who cooks meats, fruits, fish, vegetables, or other foods for commercial canning **b** : a packing-house worker who cooks meats to prepare them for smoking, molding, or packing **3 a** : an often technical or industrial process comparable to cooking food ⟨a 20-minute ~⟩; *specif* : the cooking of cellulosic raw materials in papermaking **b** : substance or material so treated : a product thus obtained **c** : one who conducts such a cook **4 a** : a previously unrecognized or unrecorded series of moves in a chess or checkers game prepared as a surprise for an opponent esp. in tournament play **b** : a solution to a chess or checkers problem unforeseen by the composer

²**cook** \"\ *vb* -ED/-ING/-S [ME *coken*, fr. *coke*, n.] *vi* **1** : to do the work of a cook : prepare food for the table by a heating process **2 a** : to undergo the action of being cooked ⟨the rice is ~*ing* now⟩ **b** : to suffer through the effects of noticeable or great heat ⟨~*ing* in the heat of the city⟩ **3** : DEVELOP, OCCUR, HAPPEN ⟨find out what was ~*ing* in the committee⟩ ~ *vt* **1** : to make up : fabricate often factitiously as an expedient : CONCOCT, IMPROVISE — usu. used with *up* ⟨if she hadn't any problems, I said, she could ~ up some —J.B.Benefield⟩ ⟨we ~*ed* up a scheme to buy some desert land —W.A.White⟩ **2** : to prepare for eating by a heating process (as boiling, roasting, or baking) **3** : to alter to convey an untrue impression : FALSIFY, DOCTOR, ANGLE, MANIPULATE ⟨an old hand at company manipulation, he prepares to ~ the books —*Punch*⟩ **4 a** : to bring decisively to a bad end : UNDO, RUIN, KILL ⟨my chances were ~*ed* by this decision⟩ **b** *Brit* : to wear out : EXHAUST, FATIGUE ⟨too ~*ed* to leave camp again —J.H. Williams⟩ **5 a** : to expose to fire, heat, or some agency felt to be similar in a technical process ⟨a coke brazier was ~*ing* rivets —George Farwell⟩ ⟨~*ing* TNT —Stanley Frank⟩ **b** : to make radioactive ⟨put into a nuclear reactor and ~*ed*⟩ **6** : to enervate, make suffer, or parch with excessive heat ⟨the sun ~*ing* the dry plains⟩ — **cook one's goose** : to settle, undo, or ruin (a person) irretrievably — **cook with gas** *slang* : to perform excellently : do very well; *also* : to be on the right track

³**cook** \"\ *vi* -ED/-ING/-S [perh. of Scand origin; akin to Icel *kūka* to defecate, Sw & Norw dial. *kukka* to defecate, Shetland Norse *kuk* dried excrement; perh. akin to G *kauchen* to crouch] *Scot* : to crouch down in hiding : take cover

cook·able \-kəbəl\ *n* -S : foodstuff to be cooked

cookbook \'=,=\ *n* [perh. trans. of G *kochbuch* or D *kookboek*] : a book of directions and recipes for cooking

cook cheese *n* : a cheese made of skim milk with the curd cured a few days, heated to honey consistency, and poured into hot containers — see CUP CHEESE

cook·ee \'ku̇kē, =¦=\ *n* -S [¹*cook* + *-ee*] : a cook's helper esp. in a logging camp

cooke·ite \'ku̇,kīt\ *n* -S [Josiah P. *Cooke* †1894 Am. chemist + E *-ite*] : a micaceous mineral related to lepidolite

cook·er \'ku̇kə(r)\ *n* -S **1** : a utensil, device, or apparatus for cooking **2** : an eatable for cooking as opposed to being served or eaten raw ⟨we had better grade those apples as ~s⟩ **3** : one that cooks or attends the cooking process of foods or of ingredients of commercial products: as **a** : one that cooks grain meal to prepare a mash that will be distilled into high wine for use in gin, whiskey, and commercial alcohol **b** : one that cooks veneer by steam pressure to harden the glue **c** : a worker who uses mixing, cooking, and cooling equipment to process cereals **d** : a worker who cooks ground cottonseed or linseed meal in steam kettles prior to its being formed into cakes and pressed **4** *Brit* : COOKSTOVE

cook·ery \'ku̇k(ə)rē, -ri\ *n* -ES [ME *cokerie*, fr. *coken* to cook + *-erie* -ery] **1** : the art, science, process, or practice of cooking **2** : an establishment or apparatus for cooking : a place for cooking

cookery-book \'=(=)=,=\ *n, chiefly Brit* : COOKBOOK

cook-general \'=¦=-\ *n, pl* **cooks-general** *Brit* : a servant who does both cooking and general housework

cookhouse \'=,=\ *n* **1 a** : a compartment or building for cooking **b** : a circus tent for cooking **2** : a ship's galley

¹**cook·ie** *or* **cooky** *also* **cook·ey** \'ku̇kē, -ki\ *n, pl* **cookies** *also* **cookeys** *often attrib* [D *koekje, koekie*, dim. of *koek* cake, fr. MD *coeke*; akin to OHG *kuocho* cake — more at CAKE] **1** : any of various small sweet cakes either flat or slightly raised, cut from rolled dough, dropped from a spoon, or cut into pieces after baking **2** : a moderate brown that is yellower, lighter, and stronger than bay or auburn and lighter, stronger, and slightly redder than chestnut brown **3** : an appliance or strip of material (as of leather or metal) inserted in a shoe over the insole from heel to shank to support the arch **4 a** : a little girl : CHILD, SWEETHEART — used usu. as an affectionate term of address **b** *slang* : PERSON, GUY ⟨tough ~⟩ ⟨smart ~⟩ **5 cookies** *pl, slang* : the contents of one's stomach : what one has recently eaten ⟨she got sick and tossed her *cookies*⟩

²**cookie** *var of* COOKY

cookie cutter *n* : a sharp-bladed device for cutting cookies in particular shapes from rolled dough

cookie press *n* : an implement consisting of a hollow barrel to hold cookie dough, a plunger, and interchangeable plates of various designs through which the dough is pressed onto a sheet for baking

cookie pusher *n* : a careerist (as a diplomat) attentive to form and protocol but generally pliant and without force; *broadly* : a vacuous person without force who is given to an active but innocuous social life

cookie sheet *n* : a flat rectangle of metal with a rolled edge on one, two, or three sides designed for the baking of cookies or biscuits

cooking *adj* [fr. gerund of ²*cook*] **1** : fit for being cooked : useful in cooking ⟨~ apples⟩ ⟨~ salt⟩ ⟨~ sherry⟩ **2** : used in cooking : designed to serve in cooking ⟨~ utensils⟩

cook·less \'ku̇kləs\ *adj* **1** : not having a cook **2** : not being cooked

cook off *vi, of a cartridge* : to fire as a result of being allowed to rest in the chamber of an overheated weapon

cook·out \'ku̇,kau̇t\ *n* -S [fr. *cook out*, v.] : an outing at which a meal is cooked and served in the open; *also* : the meal cooked at such an outing

cookroom \'=,=\ *n* : KITCHEN, GALLEY

cooks *pl of* COOK, *pres 3d sing of* COOK

cookshack \'=,=\ *n* : a shack used for cooking; *sometimes* : a portable kitchen

cookshop \'=,=\ *n* : a shop supplying or serving cooked food : EATING HOUSE

cook's tour \'ku̇ks-\ *n, usu cap C* [after Thomas *Cook* †1892 Eng. tourist agent] : a quick tour in which attractions are viewed very briefly and cursorily : a quick cursory scanning ⟨a 15-hour *Cook's tour* of the Philippines —*Newsweek*⟩

cookstove \'=,=\ *n* : a stove for cooking

cookware \'=,=\ *n* : utensils used in cooking

cook wrasse *n* : a wrasse (*Crenilabrus mixtus*) of English waters

¹**cooky** *var of* COOKIE

²**cooky** *or* **cookie** \'ku̇kē, =¦=\ *n, pl* **cookies** [¹*cook* + *-y*, *-ie*] : a cook esp. on a ranch, at a camp, or on a ship; *sometimes* : a female cook

¹**cool** \'kül\ *adj* -ER/-EST [ME *cole*, fr. OE *cōl*; akin to OHG *kuoli* cool, OE *calan* to get cold, *cald, ceald* cold — more at COLD] **1 a** : moderately cold : between tepid and chill : lacking in warmth ⟨a ~ wind⟩ ⟨water a little too ~ for swimming⟩ ⟨preferred to drink coffee when it was ~ rather than hot⟩ **b** : CHILLY ⟨shivering in the ~ air of the evening⟩ **c** : having refrigeration facilities : under refrigeration **2 a** : unaffected by passion, agitation, alarm, perturbation, unsteadying tension : showing calmness, steadiness, impassiveness, resolution, or control ⟨"never shoot in a passion", the excellent advice went on; "only a ~ hand is steady" —Joseph Hergesheimer⟩ ⟨he was very ~ outwardly, but was nervous all the same —Bram Stoker⟩ **b** : free from excitement, strong feeling, passion, or confusion : marked by deliberate judgment and temperate moderation ⟨the heated personal disputes . . . gave way to ~ negotiations —G.B.Shaw⟩ **c** : EXPERIENCED, SOPHISTICATED **3** : lacking ardor, enthusiasm, warmth, friendliness, or affability : unresponsive and apathetic or unfriendly and antagonistic ⟨he received a very ~ reception⟩ ⟨"a pity you take on so . . .", the young lady said, with a ~, slightly sarcastic air —W.M.Thackeray⟩ **4** *of a scent* : WEAK, FAINT ⟨the trail of the fox is ~⟩ **5 a** : as indicated : CERTAIN, POSITIVE : not scant or bare : WHOLE, FULL ⟨a ~ million in gambling debts⟩ **b** : gained, lost, executed, or reckoned calmly or deliberately without excitement or fuss ⟨he made a ~ $100,000 by his investment schemes⟩ **6** : marked by deliberate unabashed effrontery, presumption, or lack of due deference, respect, or discretion ⟨a ~ reply⟩ ⟨a ~ pleasure in stripping the Indians of their horses or silver or blankets —Willa Cather⟩ **7 a** : facilitating or suggesting pleasurable sensations of comfort or ease at relief from heat ⟨a ~ dress⟩ ⟨a ~ air-conditioned room⟩ ⟨the ~ beauty of freshwater lakes —*Amer. Guide Series: Mich.*⟩ **b** : marked by lack of fervor, dash, or excitement : RESTFUL, UNEMOTIONAL, STUDIED ⟨simple ~ clear prose⟩ ⟨~ jazz⟩ ⟨sweet ~ paintings that are more refreshing than stimulating —*Time*⟩ **c** *of a color* : producing an impression of coolness; *specif* : of a hue in the range violet through blue to green **d** *of a musical tone* : relatively lacking in timbre or resonance **8** *slang* : GREAT, EXCELLENT; *esp* : showing a mastery of the latest in approved technique and style ⟨as an actor he's real ~⟩ ⟨a ~ performance⟩

syn COMPOSED, COLLECTED, UNRUFFLED, IMPERTURBABLE, NONCHALANT: COOL implies general self-control uninfluenced by excitement or emotion ⟨my work, I am often told, is *cool* and serene, entirely reasonable and free of passion —Havelock Ellis⟩ ⟨this wonder, that when near her he should be *cool* and composed, and when away from her wrapped in a tempest of desires —George Meredith⟩ It may also imply calm courage, deliberateness, effrontery, or indifference ⟨*cool* and deliberate, he gave his orders in a voice devoid of alarm —J.J.Floherty⟩ ⟨the sudden change in her voice, from *cool* imperial arrogance to terrified pleading —Robert Graves⟩ COMPOSED refers to absence of indications of agitation or tension ⟨she was *composed* without bravado —Agnes Repplier⟩ ⟨did he appear . . . *composed*, or was he agitated and alarmed —C.B.Nordhoff & J.N.Hall⟩ COLLECTED implies a concentration of faculties to avoid or overcome distraction ⟨they did not look very unhappy, though Mrs. Hawthorne wore her *collected* Sunday expression —Archibald Marshall⟩ UNRUFFLED implies an accustomed calmness even in exciting situations ⟨on the one hand, feeling at its keenest edge and highest tension; on the other the low, placid, *unruffled* level of our normal moods —J.L.Lowes⟩ ⟨the familiar estate of marriage was preserved in the *unruffled* calm of their bedroom as in an embalming fluid —Ellen Glasgow⟩ IMPERTURBABLE implies extreme and accustomed calm, rendering one unlikely to be disconcerted, disturbed, or alarmed ⟨Irving, the pleasure-loving, genial, *imperturbable* traveler and gentle hedonist —Saxe Commins⟩ ⟨at her side sat a rosy-cheeked *imperturbable* nurse in a stiff white uniform —W.H.Wright⟩ NONCHALANT suggests easy casualness and an appearance of detached indifference or carefreeness ⟨at the back [of the ambulance], haughty in white uniform, *nonchalant* on a narrow seat was The Doctor —Sinclair Lewis⟩

²**cool** \"\ *vb* -ED/-ING/-S [ME *colen*, fr. OE *cōlian* to become cool, fr. *cōl* cool] *vi* **1 :** to become cool : lose heat or warmth : lose some characteristic likened to heat (as force or activity) ⟨the summer ~*ed* into autumn —Arnold Bennett⟩ ⟨the material exposed to radiation was left alone to ~ for a long time⟩ — sometimes used with *off* or *down* ⟨~*ing* off in the evening breezes⟩ **2 a :** to lose ardor or passion : become less fervent, zealous, impassioned, angry, or affectionate : lose intensity : MODERATE ⟨his anger ~*ed*⟩ — often used with *off* or *down* ⟨give those hotheads a chance to ~ off —L.C.Douglas⟩ **b :** to lose enthusiasm or interest and to become tepid, indifferent, suspicious, or inimical — used with *on, to,* or *toward* ⟨its main backers have ~*ed* on the project⟩ **c :** to become less hot : allow enough time to pass for a lessening of the police's efforts to capture one — usu. used with *off* ⟨hiding out to ~ off⟩ ~ *vt* **1 a :** to impart a feeling of coolness or cold to; *often* : to refresh by countering the effects of heat ⟨the breeze ~*ed* them⟩ — often used with *off* or *down* ⟨a swim ~*ed* us off a little⟩ **b :** to make less hot or warm : cause loss of heat in : reduce in temperature often to a satisfactory or pleasurable point ⟨~ the milk before storing it⟩ ⟨~ the vegetables with refrigeration⟩ ⟨an engine ~*ed* with water⟩ ⟨~ the room with a fan⟩ ⟨~ the emotions and restore peace —*N.Y. Times*⟩ — sometimes used with *off* or *down* ⟨the agitation was ~*ed* down —J.A.Froude⟩ **2 :** to moderate the heat or excitement of : ALLAY ⟨~ her growing anger⟩ : MODERATE, CALM **3 a :** to check decisively : rob of force or effectiveness : STOP **b :** to knock out; *also* : KILL ⟨the gangsters ~*ed* him for squealing⟩ — **cool one's heels :** to wait esp. for a long time : be kept waiting from or as if from disdain or discourtesy ⟨forced to *cool his heels* outside for 40 minutes —*Newsweek*⟩

³**cool** \"\ *n* -S [ME *cole*, fr. *cole*, adj.] **1 :** a cool time, place, occasion, or situation ⟨the ~ of evening⟩ **2 :** COOLNESS

⁴**cool** \"\ *adv* [¹*cool*] : in a cool manner : COOLLY ⟨play it ~⟩

coo·la·bah *or* **coo·li·bah** \'külə,bä\ *n* -S [native name in Australia] : any of several Australian gum trees (as *Eucalyptus coolabah, E. microtheca,* or *E. largiflorens*)

coo·la·mon \'külə,män, -mən\ *also* **coo·la·man** *or* **coo·li·man** \-,man, -mən\ *n* -S [native name in Australia] : an Australian vessel of bark or wood that resembles a basin and is used for carrying and holding water

cool·ant \'külənt\ *n* -S [²*cool* + *-ant*] : a cooling usu. fluid agent (as a liquid applied to the edge of a cutting tool to carry off frictional heat or a circulating fluid for cooling an engine)

cool bath *n* : a bath in which the temperature of the water is between 65° and 80° F

¹**cooler** *comparative of* COOL

²**cool·er** \'külə(r)\ *n* -S **1 :** one that cools : one that either brings about loss of heat or protects from heat: as **a :** a vessel or container in which water, milk, or other liquids are cooled or kept cool **b :** a device, implement, or machine by means of which food is cooled or kept cool **c :** a refrigerated room or box kept at a moderately cold temperature for the storing of perishables (as meat) **d :** AIR-CONDITIONER **2 a :** one that abates or damps excitement, passion, fervor, optimism, or happiness ⟨putting a ~ on his hopes⟩ **b :** LOCKUP, JAIL; *esp* : a prison cell for the confinement of violent or refractory prisoners **3 a :** a cooling drug or agent : REFRIGERANT — compare SURFACE COOLER **b :** a tall chilled nonalcoholic drink (as lemonade) **c :** a thirst-quenching drink consisting of gin, rum, whiskey, or wine to which are added grenadine or other flavoring ingredients and sugar and served iced with the spirally cut rind of a lemon or other citrus fruit in a tall glass **4 a :** one that operates a cooling device or machine **b :** a worker who stacks hot bread on racks or conveyors for removal to a cooling room **c :** one that cools charges of artificial graphite electrodes by gradual removal of insulating material from the electrothermal furnace **5 :** COOLER NAIL **6 :** a light blanket or wrap used to protect a horse while cooling out

coolerman \'==,man\ *n, pl* **coolermen 1 :** one who tends refrigeration equipment or a refrigerated storage room **2 :** an operator of equipment for cooling molasses in a sugar refinery

cooler nail *n* : a wire nail similar in shape to a common nail but slenderer and usu. cement-coated to increase its holding power

coolest *superlative of* COOL

cooley *var of* ¹COULEE 1

coo·ley's anemia *also* **cooley's disease** \'külēz-\ *n, usu cap C* [after Thomas B. *Cooley* †1945 Am. pediatrician] : THALASSEMIA

coolhouse \'=,=\ *n* : a greenhouse maintained at a cool temperature for the forcing of hardy plants or the winter storage of dormant plants

coo·lidg·e·an \(')kü¦lijēən\ *adj, usu cap* [Calvin *Coolidge* †1933 30th president of the U.S. + E *-an*] : of, relating to, or reminiscent of Calvin Coolidge or his times or policies

coo·lidge tube \'külij-\ *n, usu cap C* [after William D. *Coolidge* †1975 Am. physicist] : a vacuum tube for the generation of X rays in which the cathode consists of a spiral filament of incandescent tungsten and the target which also serves as anode is of massive tungsten, the temperature of the cathode determining the intensity of the X rays while the applied voltage determines wavelength

¹**coo·lie** *also* **coo·ly** \'külē, -li\ *n, pl* **coolies** [Hindi *kulī, qulī*, prob. of Dravidian origin; akin to Tamil *kūli* wages] **1 :** an unskilled laborer, carrier, or porter or a semiskilled menial usu. in or from the Far East hired for low or subsistence wages **2** *Africa* : a person of Indian origin or descent

²**coolie** *var of* ¹COULEE 1

coo·lie·ism \'külē,izəm\ *n* -S [¹*coolie* + *-ism*] : exploitation of imported coolies at substandard wages; *also* : any similarly exploitative system

cooliman *var of* COOLAMON

cooling *pres part of* COOL

cooling board *n, chiefly South* : a board on which a corpse is laid during preparation for burial

cool·ing·ly *adv* : in a cooling manner

cooling-off *adj* : designed to allow intemperate feeling to abate and to permit negotiation between contestants (as between a call to strike and its taking effect or as between the start of a dispute between nations and their resorting to force) ⟨a *cooling-off* period⟩ ⟨a *cooling-off* agreement⟩ ⟨*cooling-off* legislation⟩

cooling time *n* : a lapse of time that under all the circumstances of a case ought to produce a subsiding of passion previously provoked so that the provocation cannot then be set up as a defense for subsequent acts

cooling tower *n* : a structure over which circulated water that is to be reused as a coolant is trickled to reduce its temperature by partial evaporation

cool·ish \'külish, -lēsh\ *adj* : somewhat cool ⟨gray fog and ~ to cold weather —John Steinbeck⟩

cool·ly \'kül(l)ē, -i\ *or* **cooly** \-lē, -li\ *adv* [¹*cool* + *-ly*] **1 :** in a cool manner : without heat or excessive cold **2 a :** without passion or ardor : CALMLY, DELIBERATELY **b :** with indifference : IMPUDENTLY

cool·ness \'külnəs\ *n* -ES : the quality or state of being cool: as **a :** CHILLINESS ⟨the ~ of the night⟩ **b :** CALMNESS, SELF-POSSESSION ⟨showed great ~ and courage in a desperate conflict —L.C.Hatch⟩ **c :** lack of ardor, enthusiasm, or friendly warmth ⟨a long-standing ~ between the two families⟩ **d :** SELF-ASSURANCE ⟨takes possession of the territory with all the ~ of a usurper —Mary Cowden-Clarke⟩

cool-off \'=,=\ *n* -S [fr. *cool off*, v.] : a cooling-off period

cool out *vt* : to cause (a horse) to move about quietly after heavy exercise until sweating has ceased and relaxation is attained

cools *pres 3d sing of* COOL, *pl of* COOL

coolth \'külth\ *n* -S [*cool* + *-th* (as in *warmth*)] : the state or occasion of being cool

coolweed \'=,=\ *n* [¹*cool* + *weed*; fr. its habit of growing in cool places] : RICHWEED 1

coolwort \'=,=\ *n* **1 :** FALSE MITERWORT **2 :** TOOTHWORT 2 **3 :** FAIRY CUP 3

¹**cooly** *var of* COOLIE

²**cooly** *var of* COOLLY

cooly sore *n* [¹*cooly*] : TROPICAL ULCER 2

¹**coom** *or* **coomb** \'küm\ *n* -S [ME *culme* — more at CULM] **1** *dial Brit* **a :** SOOT, SMUT **b :** coal dust or coal slack **2 :** grease exuding from axle boxes or bearings

²**coom** *or* **coomb** \"\ *n* -S [origin unknown] *Scot* : the wooden centering or frame on which a masonry arch is built

¹**coomb** *or* **coombe** \'küm, 'kōm\ *var of* COMBE

²**coomb** *or* **coom** \'küm\ *n* -S [ME *combe*, fr. OE *cumb*, a liquid measure; akin to MLG *kump* bowl, vessel, MHG *kumpf* bowl, Pers *gumbed* arch, dome, drinking vessel, OE *cofa* room — more at COVE] : an English unit of capacity equal to 4 imperial bushels or 4.13 U.S. bushels

coombe *or* **coom** \'küm\ *dial var of* ⁴CULM 2

¹**coon** \'kün\ *n* -S [short for *raccoon*] **1 :** RACCOON **2 :** a rustic, eccentric, or undignified person **3 :** a supporter or member of the American Whig party **4 :** NEGRO — usu. taken to be offensive

²**coon** \"\ *vb* -ED/-ING/-S *vt* **1** *dial* : to crawl or creep along (a place of insecure footing) ⟨he ~*ed* a log that spanned the stream⟩ **2** *slang* : STEAL ⟨every man that had ~*ed* a horse in the county was in cahoots with them —Howard Troyer⟩ ~ *vi, dial* : to crawl or creep in a place of insecure footing

coon bear *n* : GIANT PANDA

coon bug *n* : a black-and-white Australian bug (*Oxycarenus luctuosus*) having the immature stages bright red and feeding on the foliage of native and cultivated plants often causing serious defoliation

coon·can \'kün,kan\ *or* **coon king** *n* -S [by folk etymology fr. MexSp *conquián*, fr. Sp *¿con quién?* with whom?] : a game of rummy derived from conquian and played by two or more with two packs including two jokers — called also *double rum*

coon cat *n* **1** *chiefly NewEng* : ANGORA CAT **2 :** CACOMISTLE **3 :** COATI

coon dog *n* : a sporting dog trained to hunt raccoons

coon·er \'künə(r)\ *n* -S : COON DOG

coon grape *n* **1 :** a woody vine (*Ampelopsis cordata*) of the southeastern U. S. with inedible bluish fruit and foliage like that of the grape **2 :** a fox grape (*Vitis labrusca*)

coonhound \'=,=\ *n* : COON DOG; *specif* : a large black-and-tan hound with a short dense coat of a breed developed esp. for use as coon dogs

coonier *comparative of* COONY

cooniest *superlative of* COONY

coon·i·ly \'kün^əlē, -nəlē\ *adv* : in a coony manner

coon·i·ness \-nēnəs\ *n* -ES : CAGEYNESS, CANNINESS ⟨a sort of slang that . . . will impart to the user an appearance of savviness, ~, and general know-how —W.H.Whyte⟩

¹**coon·jine** \'kün,jīn\ *vb* -ED/-ING/-S [origin unknown] : to walk, dance, or carry with a sidling waddling shuffle

²**coonjine** \"\ *n* -S **1 :** a step or dance suggestive of the rhythmic shuffle of riverboat loaders **2 :** a song accompanying the coonjine

coon oyster *n* **1 :** MANGROVE OYSTER **2 :** an oyster undersized and inferior because of growth in a crowded situation

coonroot \'=,=\ *n* [short for *puccoonroot*, fr. *puccoon* + *root*] : BLOODROOT 1

coon's age *n* : a long while ⟨been sick for a *coon's age*⟩

coon shouter *n* [¹*coon* (Negro)] : one that sings in the manner of a blackface minstrel — compare COON SONG, SHOUT SONG

coonskin \'=,=\ *n* **1 :** the skin or pelt of the raccoon **2 :** a coat, cap, or other article made of coonskin

coon song *n* [¹*coon* (Negro)] : a typically ragtime and usu. sentimental popular song of the 19th century derived from or related to the songs of the southern Negro

coonskin cap

coon-striped shrimp \'=;=-\ *n* : a large edible shrimp (*Pandalus danae*) common in moderately deep water from San Francisco to Alaska

coontail \'=,=\ *n* : HORNWORT

coon·tie \'küntē\ *or* **comp·tie** \'kämptē\ *n* -S [Seminole *kunti* coontie flour] : any of several tough woody plants of the genus *Zamia* of Florida and tropical America whose roots and half-buried stems yield an arrowroot

coony \'künē\ *adj* -ER/-EST [¹*coon* + *-y*] : showing astute and clever closeness : CAGEY, CANNY ⟨a ~ candidate remaining mum⟩

¹**coop** \'küp *also and S usu* 'kůp\ *n* -S [ME *cupe*, akin to OE *cȳpa, cȳpe* basket — more at KIPE] **1 a :** a cage or small enclosure for poultry or other small animals : PEN; *also* : a small building for housing poultry **b :** a poorly made or ramshackle structure with holes or cracks in the walls **2 :** a confined area : a narrow constricted space: as **a :** JAIL **b :** quarters in which voters were cooped **c :** a small booth or gallery ⟨reporters in the press ~⟩

coop 1a

²**coop** \"\ *vt* -ED/-ING/-S **1 :** to confine in a narrow restricted often crowded area : deprive of free motion by cramped quarters — often used with *up* ⟨poor emigrants, ~*ed* up in their steerage quarters —Ruth Park⟩ **2 :** to place or keep in a coop : PEN — often used with *up* ⟨rabbits ~*ed* up in their hutches⟩ **3 :** OBSTRUCT, RESTRAIN, INHIBIT — often used with *up* ⟨~*ing* up the mind in dogma⟩ **4** *slang* : to hold (voters that are often unqualified or bribed) in seclusion under guard until election day **syn** see ENCLOSE

³**coop** \'küp, 'kůp, 'kōp, 'käp\ *v imper* [contr. of *come up*] *dial* : COME — a call to domestic animals

⁴**coop** \'küp\ *n* -S [by alter.] *substand* : COUPÉ

co-op *also* **coop** \'kō,äp, =ˈ=\ *n* -S [by shortening] : COOPERATIVE

¹**coop·er** \'küpə(r), 'kůp-\ *n* -S [ME *couper, cowper*, fr. MD *cūper* fr. *cūpe* cask + *-er*) or MLG *kūper* (fr. *kūpe* cask + *-er*); MD *cūpe* and MLG *kūpe*, fr. ML *copa*, alter. of L *cupa* — more at HIVE] **1 a :** one that makes or repairs wooden casks or tubs — called also *cooperer* **b :** a shipboard artisan who repairs casks and other vessels **2 :** an English tradesman who samples, bottles, or retails wine **3** [so called fr. the daily allotment of stout and porter to coopers at breweries] : porter and stout in equal parts

²**cooper** \"\ *vb* **coopered; coopered; coopering** \-p(ə)riŋ\ **coopers** *vt* **1 a :** to do the work of a cooper on : engage in the manufacture or repair of (barrels or casks) : secure with hoops **b :** to put into proper or presentable shape or form — used with *up* or *out* **2 :** to pack or stow in casks or barrels **3 :** SPOIL, RUIN ⟨the dodge was ~*ed* by the police⟩ **4 :** to cover holes and cracks inside (a freight car) to prevent leakage of bulk grain ~ *vi* : to work at or do coopering

³**cooper** \", 'kōp-\ *or* **cop·er** \'kōp-\ *n* -S [prob. modif. of D *koper* buyer, fr. *kopen* to buy (fr. MD *cōpen*) + *-er*; akin to OHG *koufōn* to buy — more at CHEAP] : a ship equipped to supply liquor and tobacco to fishing fleets in the North sea in the 19th century

coop·er·age \'küp(ə)rij, 'kůp-\ *n* -S [¹*cooper* + *-age*] **1 :** a cooper's place of business **2 a :** a cooper's work **b :** the products of a cooper's work : casks and tubs **3 :** pay for cooperage **4 :** casks for draft beer or bulk wine

co·op·er·ant \(')kō¦äp(ə)rənt\ *adj* [LL *cooperant-, cooperans*, pres. part. of *cooperari*] : working in cooperation ⟨man and nature intimately ~ —John Collier b.1884⟩

¹**co·op·er·ate** \kō'äpə,rāt, '=¦==,=, *usu* -ād·+V\ *vi* -ED/-ING/-S [LL *cooperatus*, past part. of *cooperari*, fr. L *co-* + *operari* to work — more at OPERATE] **1 :** to act or work with another or others to a common end : operate jointly ⟨marines and navy men *cooperated* in the attack⟩ ⟨the police force always ~*s* with the fire department⟩ **2 :** to act together : produce an effect jointly ⟨heavy rains and rapid thaws *cooperated* to bring disastrous floods⟩ **3 :** to associate with another or others for mutual often economic benefit ⟨many nations *cooperated* in the trade agreement⟩ **syn** see UNITE

²**cooperate** \(')kō¦äp(ə)rət *also* (')kō¦äpə,rāt, *usu* -d·+V\ *adj* : made cooperative : brought into working together ⟨~ forces⟩

co·op·er·a·tion \kō,äpə'rāshən, (')=,==¦==\ *n* -S [ME *cooperacioun*, fr. L *cooperation-, cooperatio*, fr. *co-* + *operation-, operatio* work, operation — more at OPERATION] **1 :** the act of cooperating : a condition marked by cooperating : joint operation : common effort or labor ⟨the river was dredged by the two states acting in ~⟩ **2 :** association of persons for their common often economic benefit : association in a venture (as an industry, credit group, consumer group) the profits or benefits of which are shared : collective action for common well-being or progress **3** *biol* : a dynamic social process associated with organisms living in some degree of aggregation (as in communities or colonies) and characterized by sufficient mutual benefit to outweigh disadvantages (as competition) associated with crowding; *esp* : PROTOCOOPERATION

co·op·er·a·tion·ist \-nəst\ *n* -S : one who advocates or practices cooperation

¹**co·op·er·a·tive** \(')kō¦äp(ə)rəd·iv, -rətiv: (')kō¦äpə,rād·iv, -ātiv, -ēv *also* -əv\ *adj* [LL *cooperativus*, fr. *cooperatus* + L *-ivus* -ive] **1 a :** marked by cooperation : marked by working together or by joint effort toward a common end ⟨the work demanded ~ organization⟩ ⟨wherever there was a prospect of a steady return to ~ agriculture, ceorls tended to live together —F.M.Stenton⟩ **b :** given to or marked by willingness and ability to work with others in a common effort : not motivated entirely by selfish individual aims : refraining from malingering, lowering morale, or obstructing accomplishment ⟨the professor was not promoted because he was not ~⟩ ⟨the historians are more ~ than they used to be; they engage in joint projects and have common standards —*Times Lit. Supp.*⟩ **2 a :** of, relating to, or organized as a cooperative ⟨a ~ business enterprise⟩ **b :** belonging to or undertaken by a cooperative ⟨~ producers⟩ ⟨~ farming⟩ ⟨~ marketing⟩ **c :** favoring the organization of cooperatives ⟨the ~ movement⟩ **3 :** showing organized diversification of student activities to include practical work (as in industry, agriculture, social welfare, or in college maintenance activities and domestic chores like cooking and cleaning) ⟨the ~ plan at various universities⟩ ⟨~ courses requiring outside work in industry —*Mass. Inst. of Technology Bull.*⟩ ⟨a ~ dormitory⟩ **syn** see SOCIAL

²**cooperative** \"\ *n* -S : an enterprise or organization owned by and operated for the benefit of those using its services ⟨marketing ~*s*⟩ ⟨a consumers' ~⟩

cooperative bank *n* : SAVINGS AND LOAN ASSOCIATION

co·op·er·a·tive·ly \-əvlē, -li\ *adv* : in a cooperative manner ⟨other groups acted ~⟩ : according to a cooperative plan or arrangement ⟨farmers selling milk ~⟩

co·op·er·a·tive·ness \-əvnəs\ *n* -ES : the quality or state of being cooperative

co·op·er·a·tor \kō'äpə,rād·ə(r), -ātə- *also* (')kō¦ä-\ *n* -S [LL, fr. *cooperatus* + *-or* — more at COOPERATE] **1 :** one that cooperates: **a :** COWORKER, COLLEAGUE, COLLABORATOR ⟨the ~*s* with whom he worked⟩ **b :** one who follows with thoroughness the directions or suggestions of a government, governmental agency, or political party ⟨soil conservation programs gaining more ~*s*⟩ **2 :** a member of a cooperative : an advocate of cooperative principles and practices

co·oper·cu·lum \,kōō'perk(y)ələm, -pər-\ *n, pl* **coopercu·la** \-lə\ [L, cover, lid, fr. *cooperire* to cover — more at COVER] : the cover of a pyx

coopered joint *n* : a joint in a curved part of a wooden object (as a piece of furniture) made to resemble a joint made in a barrel

coop·er·er \'küp(ə)rə(r), 'kůp-\ *n* -S : COOPER

coop·er-hew·itt lamp \¦küpə(r)¦hyüət-\ *n, usu cap C&H* [fr. *Cooper Hewitt*, a trademark] : a commercial mercury-vapor lamp

¹**coo·pe·ria** \kü'pirēə\ *n, cap* [NL, fr. Daniel *Cooper* †1842 Eng. botanist + NL *-ia*] : a small genus of bulbous herbs (family Amaryllidaceae) having solitary fragrant white flowers with erect anthers — see RAIN LILY

²**cooperia** \"\ *n, cap* [NL, fr. *Cooper* Curtice †1939 Am. veterinarian + NL *-ia*] : a genus of small reddish brown nematode worms (family Trichostrongylidae) including several species infesting the small intestine of sheep, goats, and cattle and sometimes held responsible for marked catarrhal inflammation, anemia, and diarrhea — **coop·er·id** \'küp(ə)rəd\ *n* -S

coopering *n* -S : the work or trade of a cooper

coop·er·ite \'küpə,rīt\ *n* -S [R. A. *Cooper fl ab*1920, who first described it + E *-ite*] : a steel-gray mineral PtS of metallic luster consisting of a sulfide of platinum belonging to the tetragonal system and occurring usu. in irregular grains

coopers *pl of* COOPER, *pres 3d sing of* COOPER

cooper's flag *or* **cooper's reed** *n* [¹*cooper*] : the cattail whose long leaves are sometimes used between barrel staves to make the barrel watertight

cooper's hawk *also* **cooper hawk** *n, usu cap C* [after William *Cooper* †1864 Am. naturalist] : an American hawk (*Accipiter cooperii*) that is larger than the similarly colored sharp-shinned hawk and has a more rounded tail

cooper's ligament *n, usu cap C* [after Sir Astley P. *Cooper* †1841 Eng. surgeon] : a strong ligamentous band extending upward and backward from the base of Gimbernat's ligament along the iliopectineal line to which it is attached

coop·ery \'küp(ə)rē, 'kůp-, -ri\ *n* -ES [¹*cooper* + *-y*] : COOPERAGE

cooping *pres part of* COOP

coops *pl of* COOP, *pres 3d sing of* COOP

co-ops *pl of* CO-OP

co-opt \kō'äpt, '=,=\ *vt* -ED/-ING/-S [L *cooptare*, fr. *co-* + *optare* to choose — more at OPINE] **1 :** to choose or elect into a body or group as a fellow member ⟨outside persons may be *co-opted* to committees —W.A.Robson⟩ **2 a :** to appoint usu. as a colleague **b :** to appoint or deputize summarily; *sometimes* : PREEMPT, COMMANDEER

co-op·tate \kō'äp,tāt, '=¦=,=\ *vt* -ED/-ING/-S [L *cooptatus*, past part. of *cooptare*] : CO-OPT, CHOOSE

co-op·ta·tion \,kō(,)äp'tāshən, '=(,)=¦==\ *n* -S [L *cooptation-, cooptatio*, fr. *cooptatus* + *-ion-, -io* -ion] : election or selection usu. to a body or group by vote of its own members

co-optative \(')kō + \ *adj* : practicing or chosen by co-optation : of or relating to co-optation

co-option \(')kō + \ *n* -S [*co-opt* + *-ion*] : CO-OPTATION

co-op·tive \(')kō¦äptiv\ *adj* : CO-OPTATIVE

¹**co·or·di·nate** \(')kō¦ȯrd(^ə)nət, -ōd^ən-, -ȯ(ə)dn-, -d^ən,āt, -d,nāt, *usu* -d· +V\ *adj* [back-formation fr. *coordination*] **1 a :** equal in rank, quality, or significance : similar in order or nature : not subordinate ⟨keeping the branches of government ~⟩ **b :** being of equal rank in a compound sentence ⟨~ clauses⟩ : standing in the same rank or relation in a sentence ⟨*by sea* and *by land* are ~ in "they travel by sea and by land"⟩ **2 a :** of or marked by coordination : marked by related actions or processes cooperating : composed of things of equal rank or order : COORDINATED **b** *chem* : relating to or formed by coordination ⟨6-*coordinate* complexes⟩ **c :** COORDINATING **3 a** *of a university* : giving degrees to both men and women taught by the same faculty but in separate classes and sometimes on separate campuses **b** *of a college* : being one of the colleges of a coordinate university, esp. the women's branch — **co·or·di·nate·ly** *adv* — **co·or·di·nate·ness** *n* -ES

²**coordinate** \-d^ən,āt, *usu* -ād· +V\ *vb* -ED/-ING/-S [back-formation fr. *coordination*] *vt* **1 :** to make coordinate : put in the same order or rank ⟨~ the two groups in classification⟩ **2 :** to bring into a common action, movement, or condition : regulate and combine in harmonious action : HARMONIZE ⟨~ the work of various bureaus⟩ ⟨~ the divergent Gospel stories

—*America*⟩ ⟨~ muscular movements⟩ **3 a :** to attach so as to form a coordination complex ⟨a *coordinated* group⟩ ⟨a *coordinated* molecule⟩ **b :** to constitute by such attachment ⟨*coordinated* salts⟩ ~ *vi* **1 :** to be or become coordinate **:** act together in a smooth concerted way ⟨muscles of spastics do not ~⟩ **2** *chem* **:** to combine by means of a coordinate bond

³coordinate *as at adj*\ *n* -s [¹*coordinate*] **1 :** one who is of equal rank, authority, or importance with another ⟨in the federal system each of the ~s has equal power⟩ **2 a :** any one of a set of numbers used in specifying the location of a point on a line, in space, or on a given plane or other surface ⟨latitude and longitude are ~s of a point on the earth's surface⟩ **b :** any one of a set of variables or parameters used in specifying the state of a substance (as temperature, pressure, or entropy) or the motion of a particle (as position, velocity, or momentum)

coordinate bond *or* **coordinate covalence** *n* **:** a covalent bond typical of coordination complexes that is held to consist of a pair of electrons donated by only one of the two atoms it joins [as in the compound $(C_2H_5)_3N{:}BF_3$ formed from triethylamine $(C_2H_5)_3N$: and boron fluoride BF_3] — called also *dative bond, semipolar bond*

coordinated *adj* **:** dexterous in the use of more than one set of muscle movements to a single end ⟨she was usually good with her hands and well ~ —Mary McCarthy⟩

coordinate geometry *n* **:** ANALYTIC GEOMETRY

coordinate paper *n* **:** GRAPH PAPER

coordinate space *n* **:** space in the usual sense of three-dimensional geometry as distinguished from various symbolic phase spaces

coordinate system *n, math* **:** a system of coordinates

coordinating conjunction *n* **:** a conjunction that joins together words or word groups of equal grammatical rank as sentences (as *and* in "He tried. And he succeeded"), clauses (as *but* in "he speaks French but I don't"), phrases (as *or* in "by night or by day"), words (as *and* in "comes and goes"), or a word and a phrase (as *or* in "now or in the future")

co·or·di·na·tion \kō,ȯ(r)dᵊnʹāshən, (ˌ)⸗,⸗⸗ʹ⸗⸗\ *n* -s [F or LL; F *coordination*, fr. LL *coordination-, coordinatio*, fr. L *co-* + *ordination-, ordinatio* arranging, ordination — more at ORDINATION] **1 :** a making or being coordinate **:** arrangement in the same order, class, rank, or dignity **:** coordinate relation ⟨~ of the executive, legislative, and judicial authority⟩ **2 :** combination in suitable relation for most effective or harmonious results **:** the functioning of parts in cooperation and normal sequence ⟨demand a single national military policy, proper ~ of our armed services —D.D.Eisenhower⟩

coordination complex *n* **:** a compound or ion that contains a central usu. metallic atom or ion combined by coordinate bonds with a definite number of surrounding ions, groups, or molecules, that retains its identity more or less even in solution, and that may be nonionic {as tri-ammine-trinitro-cobalt $[Co(NH_3)_3(NO_2)_3]^0$}, cationic {as hex-ammine-cobalt-(III) $[Co(NH_3)_6]^{+++}$}, or anionic {as hexachloroplatinate-$[PtCl_6]^{--}$} — see ¹CHELATE

coordination compound *n* **:** a compound in which atoms are combined with each other by coordinate bonds; *esp* **:** a coordination-complex compound

coordination number *n* **1 :** the number of attachments being usu. four or six to the central atom in a coordination complex **2 :** a number used in classifying various arrangements in space of constituent groups of crystals, the number being a function of the relative sizes and polarization properties of oppositely charged ions forming the solid crystal lattice

co·or·di·na·tive \(ˈ)kō¦ȯ(r)d(ᵊ)nəd·iv, -ətiv; -dᵊn,ād·iv, -ātiv\ *adj* [*coordination* + *-ive*] **1** *of a conjunction* **:** COORDINATING **2 :** that coordinates ⟨a ~ mechanism⟩ **:** having reference to coordination ⟨~ duties⟩ **3** *linguistics* **:** having two or more heads — used of an endocentric construction (as *books and papers*); opposed to *subordinative*

co·or·di·na·tor \kōʹȯ(r)dᵊn,ād·ə(r), -ātə- *also* (ˈ)kō¦ȯ-\ *n* -s **1 :** one that coordinates; *esp* **:** one that expedites by recommending although often not supervising measures which eliminate confusion **2 :** an educator who is responsible for coordinating academic instruction with the on-the-job activities of employed students and the vocational requirements encountered by recent graduates **3 :** a coordinating conjunction

coorg \ˈku̇(ə)rg\ *n* -s *usu cap* [fr. *Coorg*, region of India] **:** one of a Dravidian people in southwest India — called also *Kadaga*

coo·rie \ˈküri\ *vi* -ED/-ING/-S [freq. of *coor*, var. of *cower*] *chiefly Scot* **:** CROUCH, COWER, STOOP

¹coos *pres 3d sing of* COO, *pl of* COO

²coos \ˈküs\, *n, pl* **coos** *usu cap* **1 a :** a Kusan people of Oregon **b :** a member of such people **2 :** the language of the Coos people

coos·er \ˈküsər, ˈkəs-\ *n* -s [alter. of ¹*courser*] *chiefly Scot* **:** STALLION

co·ossification \(ˈ)kō + \ *n* -s [*co-* + *ossification*] **:** the process of coossifying

co·ossify \(ˈ)kō + \ *vi* -ED/-ING/-ES [*co-* + *ossify*] **:** to grow together by ossification (as of bones or parts of a bone) **:** ANKYLOSE

coost \ˈküst\ *Scot past of* CAST

¹coot \ˈküt, *usu* -üd·+V\ *n* -s [ME *coote*; akin to D *koet* coot] **1 :** any of certain sluggish slow-flying slaty-black birds that somewhat resemble ducks, have lobed toes and the upper mandible prolonged on the forehead as a horny frontal shield, and constitute a genus (*Fulica*) of the family Rallidae, the No. American representative (*F. americana*) being distinguished from the common one of the Old World (*F. atra*) by a white wing patch **2 :** any No. American scoter; *sometimes* **:** any of several other American ducks — often used with a qualifying word ⟨mud ~⟩ **3 :** a person often old and harmless and sometimes not bright ⟨poor old ~ with no one to look after him —Ruth Park⟩ ⟨crazy as a ~⟩ **4 :** a large purplish blue rail (*Porphyrio porphyrio*) widely distributed in Australia and the islands of the southwestern Pacific esp. in marshland and about forest margins — called also *bald coot, swamphen*

²coot \ˈkēt\ *n* -s [MLG *kote* hoof, fetlock; akin to MD *cote* knuckle, knucklebone, OFris *kāte* knuckle, MLG *kūt* entrails, calf of the leg — more at KYTE] *Scot* **:** the ankle joint; *also* **:** ¹FOOT 1

coo·ta·mun·dra wattle \,küd·əʹmandrə-\ *also* **cootamundra** *n, usu cap C* [fr. *Cootamundra*, N. S. W., Australia] **:** a small Australian tree (*Acacia baileyana*) with delicate feathery foliage and golden-yellow flowers

cootch *var of* COOCH

¹coo·ter \ˈküt·ə(r)\ *dial Eng var of* COLTER

²coo·ter \ˈküd·ə(r), ˈku̇-\ *n* -s [of African origin; akin to Bambara and Malinke *kuta* turtle] *chiefly South & Midland* **:** any of several turtles or tortoises of the southern and eastern U.S.; *esp* **:** the slider turtle (*Pseudemys concinna*) and certain closely related forms

³cooter \ˈ"\ *vi* -ED/-ING/-S *chiefly South* **:** LOITER, IDLE

cooter grass *n* [²*cooter*] **:** WATER SHIELD 2

¹coot·ie \ˈkütē\ *n* -s [alter. of Sc *coodie*, dim. of *cood* tub, fr. ScGael *cùdainn* large tub, prob. fr. ON *kūtr* cask; akin to ON *kot* cottage — more at COT] *Scot* **:** a wooden bowl or vessel

²cootie *or* **cooty** \ˈküd·ē, -ütē\ *adj* -ER/-EST [²*coot* + *-ie, -y*] *Scot, of fowls* **:** FEATHER-LEGGED

³cootie \ˈ"\ *n* -s [perh. modif. of Malay *kutu* louse] **1 :** BODY LOUSE **2 :** a game in which players compete to finish the pictorial and stylized representation of a cootie, the markings on a die representing its parts and the representation being added to according to throws of the die

¹cop \ˈkäp\ *n* -s [ME, fr. OE *copp* top, summit; perh. akin to Norw dial. *kup* humpback, Sw dial. *kupa* beehive, OE *cȳpa* basket — more at KIPE] **1** *chiefly dial Eng* **:** TOP, HEAD, CREST **2 :** a cylindrical, conical, or conical-ended mass of thread, yarn, or roving wound upon a quill or tube **3 :** a tube or quill upon which thread, yarn, or roving is wound **4 :** a heap or pile: **a** *dial Eng* **:** a bank of earth (as earth thrown up from digging a ditch and left as a hedge bank) **b :** the bank of a golf bunker

²cop \ˈ"\ *vt* **copped; copped; copping; cops :** to wind on a cop

³cop \ˈ"\ *vt* **copped; copped; copping; cops** [alter. of *cob* (to strike)] *dial Eng* **:** to strike (a person) esp. on the head

⁴cop \ˈ"\ *vb* **copped; copped; copping; cops** [perh. fr. D *kapen* to steal, plunder, fr. Fris *kāpia* to take away, buy, fr. OFris, to buy; akin to OHG *koufōn* — more at CHEAP] *vt* **1** *slang* **:** CATCH, CAPTURE ⟨~ a prize⟩ **:** get hold of ⟨they *copped* the best seats⟩ **:** TAKE **2** *slang* **:** to steal esp. on the spur of the moment **:** SWIPE ⟨somebody *copped* my watch⟩ ~ *vi, slang* **:** WIN ⟨there's 20 bucks extra in it for you if you ~⟩ **syn** see STEAL — **cop a plea** *slang* **:** to plead guilty to a lesser charge in order to avoid standing trial for a more serious one — compare BARGAIN PLEA — **cop it** *slang* **:** to get beaten, scolded, punished **:** catch it; *sometimes* **:** get killed

⁵cop \ˈ"\ *n* -s *slang Brit* **:** CAPTURE, ARREST ⟨it's a fair ~. I'll go quiet —Arthur Morrison⟩

⁶cop \ˈ"\ *n* -s [short for ³*copper*] **:** POLICEMAN

cop *abbr* **1** copper **2** copulative **3** copy **4** copyright

co·pa \ˈkōpə, -(ˌ)pä\ *n* -s [AmerSp (Panama) *copá*] *in Panama* **:** YAYA a

co·pa·cet·ic *or* **co·pe·set·ic** \ˌ¦kōpə¦sed·ik\ *adj* [origin unknown] *slang* **:** very satisfactory **:** fine and dandy ⟨his smile told him that everything was ~ —Robert Bloch⟩

co·pa de oro \,kōpədäʹō(,)rō, -dēʹ-\ *n* [AmerSp, lit., cup of gold] **:** CUPFLOWER 3

co·pa·ene \kōʹpä,ēn, ʹ⸗⸗,⸗\ *n* -s [*copaiba* + *-ene*] *chem* **:** an oily tricyclic sesquiterpene $C_{15}H_{24}$ occurring in certain essential oils (as oil of supa)

¹co·pai·ba \kōʹpībə, -pābə\ *n* -s [Sp & Pg; Sp, fr. Pg *copaiba*, of Tupian origin; akin to Guarani *cupaiba* copaiba, Tupi *copaiba, copaiiva*] **1** *also* **copaiba balsam :** the oleoresin obtained from several So. American trees of the genus *Copaifera* as a viscid transparent pale yellow or brown liquid of aromatic odor that has a stimulant action on mucous membranes **2 a :** a tree of the genus *Copaifera* **b :** the wood of one of these trees or sometimes of certain related trees

²copaiba \ˈ"\ [NL, fr. Sp & Pg] *syn of* COPAIFERA

copaiba oil *n* **:** a colorless or pale yellow essential oil obtained from copaiba and used chiefly as an odor fixative in soaps and perfumes

copaiba resin *n* **:** the resin that remains after distilling off the essential oil from copaiba

co·pa·if·era \,kōpäʹif(ə)rə\ *n* [NL, fr. *copai-* (fr. ISV *copaiba*) + *-fera* (fem. of *-fer* -ferous)] **1** *cap* **:** a genus of tropical American and African trees (family Leguminosae) with pinnate leaves, racemose apetalous flowers, strong durable wood of moderate weight and density, and an oily liquid of commercial importance — see ¹COPAIBA **2** -s **:** ¹COPAIBA 1

co·pain \kōpaⁿ\ *n* -s [F, alter. of OF *compain*, fr. LL *companio* — more at COMPANION] **:** COMRADE, PAL

co·pai·va \kōʹpīvə, -pävə\ [NL, fr. Sp *copaiba* or Pg *copaiba*] *syn of* COPAIFERA

co·pai·yé family \kōʹpī(,)yā-, -pä(,)-\ *n* [AmerSp *copaiyé* (*Vochysia guianensis*), fr. Macusi *kopai-ye*] **:** VOCHYSIACEAE

copaiyé wood *n* [AmerSp *copaiyé*] **:** the compact wood of a So. American tree (*Vochysia guianensis*)

co·pal \ˈkōpəl, -,pal\ *n* -s [Sp, fr. Nahuatl *copalli* resin] **:** a resinous exudation from various tropical trees that is collected from living trees or dug from the ground as a fossil, that when hard must be rendered soluble in alcohol and other organic solvents by heating, and that is used chiefly in making varnishes and printing ink — see CONGO COPAL, KAURI 3, MANILA COPAL

co·pal·che \,kōpəlʹchā, ʹ⸗⸗,⸗, kəʹpal(,)chā\ *or* **co·pal·chi** \,kōpəlʹchē, ʹ⸗⸗,⸗, kəʹpal(,)chē\ *n* -s [AmerSp *copalché, copalchi*] **1 :** either of two So. American trees (*Strychnos pseudo-quina* and *Croton niveus*) having bitter medicinal bark used locally as a febrifuge **2 :** a Mexican shrub or small tree (*Coutarea latiflora*) of the family Rubiaceae having fragrant white flowers and bark that is used locally as a febrifuge

co·pal·co·co·te \,kōpəlkəʹkōd·(,)ā\ *also* **co·pal·jo·co·te** \-pəlhə-\ *n* -s [MexSp, fr. Nahuatl *copalxocotl*, fr. *copalli* gum, resin + *xocotl* acid fruit] **:** a Mexican tree (*Cyrtocarpa procera*) of the family Anacardiaceae with yellow fruits that resemble plums and are used locally as a remedy for leprosy

co·pal·if·er·ous \ˌ¦kōpə¦lif(ə)rəs\ *adj* [*copal* + *-i-* + *-ferous*] **:** yielding or producing copal

co·pal·ite \ˈkōpə,līt\ *also* **co·pal·ine** \-,lēn, -,lən\ *n* -s [*copalite* fr. *copal* + *-ite*; *copaline*, ISV *copal* + *-ine*] **:** a resinous substance that is apparently a vegetable resin and that is partly mineralized by remaining in the earth

co·palm \ˈkō,päm\ *n* -s [LaF *copalm*, *copal*, fr. MexSp *copalme*] **1 :** STORAX 2b **2 :** SWEET GUM 1

copal tree *n* **:** any of several trees (as of the genus *Copaifera*) that yield fragrant resins

co·parcenary \(ˈ)kō + \ *n* -ES [*co-* + *parcenary*] **1 :** partnership in inheritance **:** joint heirship **2 :** joint ownership

co·parcener \(ˈ)kō + \ *n* -s [*co-* + *parcener*] **:** a joint heir

co·part \ˈkō +,-\ *n* -s [*co-* + *part*] **:** a joint or coordinate part

copartment *obs var of* COMPARTMENT

co·partner \(ˈ)kō + \ *n* [*co-* + *partner*] **1 :** PARTNER **:** fellow partner ⟨the authority of a partner to bind his ~s —*Encyc. Britannica*⟩ **2** *obs* **:** COPARCENER

co·partnership \(ˈ)kō + \ *n* -s **1 :** the state or right of a copartner ⟨extend ~ to employees⟩ **2 :** a company of copartners **:** PARTNERSHIP

co·part·nery \(ˈ)kō¦pärtnərē, -pät-, -ri\ *n* -ES **:** COPARTNERSHIP

copatain *var of* COPINTANK

¹cope \ˈkōp\ *n* -s [ME, fr. OE *-cāp*, fr. ML *capa*, fr. LL *cappa* — more at CAP] **1 a** *archaic* **:** a long cape or cloak esp. for outdoor wear **b :** an orig. hooded ecclesiastical vestment in the form of a long semicircular cloak open in front except at the top where it is united by a band or clasp **2 :** something felt to resemble a cope (as by concealing or covering over) **:** a vault or canopy (as the vault, arch, or expanse of heaven) ⟨the dark sky's starry ~ —P.B.Shelley⟩ **3 :** COPING **4 :** a muzzle for a ferret **5 a :** the top part of a flask, mold, or pattern; *also* **:** the brick structure in which the outer surface of a loam mold is formed **b :** the outer case in bell founding

3 2 1

bishop with *1* cope, *2* crosier, *3* miter

²cope \ˈ"\ *vb* -ED/-ING/-S [ME *copen*, fr. *cope*, n.] *vt* **:** to dress, cover, or furnish with a cope **:** cover as if with a cope or a coping ~ *vi* **:** to form a cope or arch **:** BEND, ARCH

³cope \ˈ"\ *vb* -ED/-ING/-S [ME *copen, coupen*, fr. MF *couper* to strike, cut off, cut, fr. OF, fr. *coup* blow, fr. LL *colpus*, fr. L *colaphus* blow with the fist, fr. Gk *kolaphos* buffet; akin to Gk *klan* to break — more at HALT] *vi* **1** *obs* **:** STRIKE, FIGHT **2 a :** to maintain a contest or combat usu. on even terms or with success — used with *with* ⟨how effectively he can ~ with local law-enforcement agencies —D.W.Maurer⟩ **b :** to face or encounter and to find necessary expedients to overcome problems and difficulties ⟨he died before the war. He couldn't have *coped* now —Rose Thurburn⟩ — often used with *with* ⟨~ intelligently with weighty problems of public policy —C.H.Grandgent⟩ **3** *archaic* **:** MEET, ENCOUNTER ~ *vt* **1** *obs* **:** to meet in combat ⟨the yesterday *coped* Hector in the battle —Shak.⟩ **2** *obs* **:** come in contact with **:** MEET **3** *obs* **:** MATCH ⟨three thousand ducats due unto the Jew we freely ~ your courteous pains withal —Shak.⟩ **syn** see CONTEND

⁴cope \ˈ"\ *vb* -ED/-ING/-S [ME *copen* to buy, fr. MD; akin to OHG *koufōn* to buy — more at CHEAP] *dial Eng* **:** EXCHANGE, BARTER

⁵cope \ˈ"\ *vt* -ED/-ING/-S [prob. fr. F *couper* to cut] **1 :** to notch or cut away a part of (as a timber or a structural-steel flange) to fit or give clearance for some other member **2 :** to cut or shape (the end of a structural member or a molding) to fit a coping or conform to the shape of another member; *also* **:** to make (a joint) by so shaping a joining part

copeck *var of* KOPECK

cope cutter *n* [¹*cope* (coping)] **:** a cutter for undercutting the shoulder of a tenon

co·pe·han \kōʹpä(h)ən\ *n, pl* **copehan** *or* **copehans** *usu cap* **1 :** a language family of the Penutian stock in California comprising Patwin and Wintun **2 :** WINTUN 2

co·pei \kōʹpāē\ *n* -s [AmerSp *copey*, fr. Taino] **:** PITCH APPLE

co·pe·la·ta \,kōpəʹläd·ə\ *or* **co·pe·la·tae** \-d·(,)ē\ [NL, fr. Gk *kōpelatēs* rower, fr. *kōpē* oar + *-latēs* (fr. *elaunein* to drive) — more at COPEPODA, ELASTIC] *syn of* LARVACEA

co·pel·li·dine \kōʹpelə,dēn, kəʹ-, -,dən\ *n* -s [fr. ISV *collidine*, after such pairs as ISV *pyridine*: *piperidine*; orig. formed as G *kopellidin*] **:** any of several liquid bases $C_8H_{17}N$; hexahydro-collidine

cope·man \ˈkōpmən\ *n, pl* **copemen** [D *koopman*, fr. *koop* trade (fr. MD *coop*) + *man*, fr. MD; akin to OHG *kouf* trade and to OHG *man* — more at CHEAP, MAN] *archaic* **:** CHAPMAN

cope·mate \ˈkōp,māt\ *or* **copes·mate** \-p,sm-\ *n* -s [*copemate*, fr. ³*cope* + *-mate*; *copesmate*, alter. (influenced by obs. E *copesman, copeman* merchant) of *copemate*] **1** *obs* **:** ANTAGONIST **2** *obs* **:** PARTNER, COMRADE, ASSOCIATE ⟨misshapen Time, *copesmate* of ugly Night —Shak.⟩

co·pen \ˈkōpən\ *or* **copen blue** *n* -s [*copen*, short for ²*copenhagen*; *copen blue* fr. *copenhagen blue*] **:** a variable color averaging a moderate blue that is redder, lighter, and stronger than pompadour, bluebird, azurite blue, or Dresden blue and greener, lighter, and stronger than luster blue

co·pe·na \kəʹpēnə\ *adj, usu cap* [conical *piles* + *-ena* (as in *Adena*)] **:** of or belonging to an ancient culture in northern Alabama characterized by conical burial mounds

¹co·pen·ha·gen \ˌ¦kōpən¦hāgən, -hāg-\ *adj, usu cap* [fr. *Copenhagen*, Denmark] **:** of or from Copenhagen, the capital of Denmark **:** of the kind or style prevalent in Copenhagen

²copenhagen \ˈ"\ *or* **copenhagen blue** *n* -s **:** a grayish blue that is redder and paler than electric, redder, stronger, and slightly lighter than Gobelin, stronger and slightly greener than old china, and redder, lighter, and stronger than average shadow blue

co·pen·ha·gen·er \,⸗⸗ʹ⸗gənə(r)\ *n* -s *cap* [*Copenhagen*, Denmark + E *-er*] **:** a native or resident of Copenhagen

co·pe·og·na·tha \,kōpēʹägnəthə\ [NL, fr. *copeo-* (fr. Gk *kopeus* chisel) + *-gnatha*; akin to Gk *koptein* to smite, cut off — more at CAPON] *syn of* CORRODENTIA

¹co·pe·pod \ˈkōpə,päd\ *adj* [NL *Copepoda*] **:** of or belonging to the Copepoda

²copepod \ˈ"\ *n* -s **:** one of the Copepoda

co·pep·o·da \kōʹpepədə\ *n pl, cap* [NL, fr. Gk *kōpē* oar + NL *-poda*; akin to L *capere* to take, seize — more at HEAVE] **:** a subclass of Crustacea comprising minute aquatic forms abundant in both fresh and salt waters and including the order Eucopepoda of which the members are chiefly free-living and important as fish food and the order Branchiura which is parasitic on the skin and gills of fish — **co·pep·o·dan** \(ˈ)kō¦pepədən\ *adj or n* — **co·pep·o·dous** \-dəs\ *adj*

co·pep·o·did \kōʹpepədəd\ *n* -s [²*copepod* + *-id*] **:** a free-swimming larval stage of certain parasitic copepods

¹cop·er \ˈkōpə(r)\ *n* -s [⁴*cope* + *-er*] *Brit* **:** a dealer or bargainer; *specif* **:** a horse dealer esp. if dishonest

²coper \ˈ"\ *var of* COOPER

³coper \ˈ"\ *n* -s [⁵*cope* + *-er*] **:** one that copes **:** a machine for coping or notching girders **:** a coping machine

¹co·per·ni·can \kōʹpərnəkən, kəʹ-, -pə̄n-\ *adj, usu cap* [Nicolaus *Copernicus* (Kopernik) †1543 Pol. astronomer + E *-an*] **1 :** of, relating to, or being the astronomic system of Copernicus in which the sun is taken as the center of the planets **2 :** of radical or major importance or degree ⟨a ~ revolution in psychologic theory⟩ — **co·per·ni·can·ism** \-kə,nizəm\ *n* -s *usu cap*

²copernican \ˈ"\ *n* -s *usu cap* **:** a believer in the Copernican system of astronomy usu. as opposed to the Ptolemaic

copernican system *n, usu cap C* **:** the system of planetary motions maintained by Copernicus according to which the earth rotates on an axis once each day and revolves around the sun once each year while the other planets have orbits also centered near the sun

co·per·ni·cia \,kōpə(r)ʹnish(ē)ə\ *n* [NL, fr. Nicolaus *Copernicus* + NL *-ia*] **1** *cap* **:** a small genus of lofty tropical American fan palms having cup-shaped flowers followed by a one-seeded drupe — see CARNAUBA **2** -s **:** a palm of the genus *Copernicia*

coperose *obs var of* COPPERAS

copes *pl of* COPE, *pres 3d sing of* COPE

copesetic *var of* COPACETIC

copesmate *var of* COPEMATE

cope·stone \ˈ⸗,⸗\ *n* [¹*cope* (coping) + *stone*] **1 :** COPING STONE **2 :** a finishing touch **:** CROWN

co·pey oak \kōʹpā(ē)-\ *n, usu cap C* [AmerSp *copey* copei — more at COPEI] **:** a large Central American white oak (*Quercus copeyensis*) that reaches a height of 125 feet or more and a diameter of 8 feet

coph *var of* QOPH

co·phasal \(ˈ)kō + \ *adj* [*co-* + *phasal*] **:** having the same phase — **co·phasally** \(ˈ)kō + \ *adv*

co·pi·a·pite \,kōpēə,pīt\ *n* -s [G *copiapit*, fr. *Copiapó*, Chile, its locality + G *-it* -ite] **:** a mineral composed of a basic iron sulfate $(Fe,Mg)Fe_4(SO_4)_6(OH)_2.20\,H_2O$, of yellow color and metallic taste (hardness 2.5, sp. gr. 2.10)

copied *past of* COPY

cop·i·er \ˈkäpē(ə)r\ *n* -s **1 :** one that copies **:** TRANSCRIBER, COPYIST **2 :** one that imitates an example **:** IMITATOR

copies *pl of* COPY, *pres 3d sing of* COPY

co·pigment \(ˈ)kō + \ *n* [*co-* + *pigment*] **:** one of a group of colorless or pale substances (as certain tannins and anthoxanthins) that affect the color of flowers by combining with anthocyanins thereby increasing the blue tone of these pigments

co·pi·hue \kəʹpē(,)wā\ *n* -s [AmerSp, fr. Araucan *copiu*] **:** CHILE-BELLS

co·pilot \(ˈ)kō + \ *n* [*co-* + *pilot*] **:** a qualified airplane pilot who assists or relieves the pilot but is not in command of the airplane

¹cop·ing \ˈkōpiŋ\ *n* -s [fr. gerund of ²*cope* (bend)] **:** the highest or covering course of a wall often of tile and usu. with a sloping top to carry off water and commonly cut with a drip

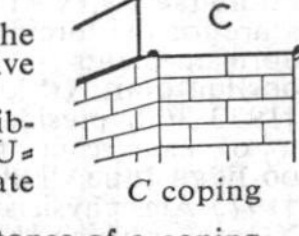

C coping

²coping \ˈ"\ *n* -s [fr. gerund of ⁵*cope*] **:** the operation of sawing stone with an abrasive wheel

coping saw *n* [¹*coping*] **:** a small blade of ribbon shape held under tension in a U-shaped frame and used for cutting intricate patterns in wood

coping stone *n* [¹*coping*] **:** one of the stones of a coping

copintank *or* **copertank** *n* -s [origin unknown] *obs* **:** a sugar-loaf hat

co·pi·os·i·ty \,kōpēʹäsəd·ē, -ətē, -i\ *n* -ES [MF *copiosité*, fr. LL *copiositat-, copiositas*, fr. L *copiosus* + *-itat-, -itas* -ity] **:** COPIOUSNESS

co·pi·ous \ˈkōpēəs\ *adj* [ME, fr. L *copiosus*, fr. *copia* abundance, fr. *co-* + *-opia* (fr. *ops* power, wealth) — more at OPULENT] **1 a :** having or yielding an abundance or plenty **:** ABOUNDING ⟨~ springs⟩ **b :** plentiful in number **2 a :** full of thought, information, matter ⟨Shakespeare whose soul was so ~ —Gilbert Highet⟩ **b :** profuse or exuberant in words, expression, or style **3 :** present in large quantity **:** PLENTIFUL, ABUNDANT, LAVISH ⟨~ footnotes⟩ ⟨the ~ matter of my song —John Milton⟩ ⟨~ amounts of beer and sandwiches consumed —Robert Shaplen⟩ **syn** see PLENTIFUL

co·pi·ous·ly *adv* **:** in a copious manner **:** ABUNDANTLY, RICHLY, AMPLY ⟨he dined slowly and ~⟩

co·pi·ous·ness \-nəs\ *n* -ES **:** PLENTY, RICHNESS, FULLNESS

copist *n* -s [MF *copiste* — more at COPYIST] *obs* **:** COPIER 1

co·planar \(ˈ)kō + \ *adj* [*co-* + *planar*] **:** lying or acting in the same plane — **co·planarity** \ˌ¦kō + \ *n* -ES

cop·lin jar \ˈkäplən-, ˈkōp-\ *or* **coplin staining jar** *n, cap C* [after William M. L. *Coplin* †1928 Am. physician] **:** a covered glass vessel that is rectangular in cross section and grooved inside for holding microscope slides vertical during processing

co·plowing \(ˈ)kō + \ *n* [*co-* + *plowing*] **:** cooperative plowing

co·polymer \(ˈ)kō + \ *n* [*co-* + *polymer*] **:** a product of copolymerization ⟨GR-S is a ~ of butadiene and styrene⟩

co·polymeride \(ˈ)kō + \ *n* [*co-* + *polymeride*] **:** COPOLYMER

co·polymerization \(ˌ)kō + \ *n* **:** the act or process of copolymerizing

co·polymerize \(ˈ)kō + \ *vb* [*co-* + *polymerize*] **:** to polymerize together — used of two or more polymerizing substances that together form complex molecules usu. of high molecular weight (as plastics and synthetic rubber)

cop out *vi* [⁴*cop*] **1** *slang* **:** to meet failure or death **2** *slang* **:** to cop a plea

cop·pa \'käpə\ *n* -s [It, lit., cup, fr. LL *cuppa*; fr. its shape — more at CUP] : an Italian sausage made chiefly of pork butts and seasoned with cayenne pepper

copped \'käpt\ *adj* [ME, fr. [1]*cop* + *-ed*] : rising to a top or head : CONICAL, PEAKED ⟨~ hills —Shak.⟩

[1]**cop·per** \'käpə(r)\ *n* -s [ME *coper*, fr. OE; akin to MD *koper*, OHG *kupfar*, ON *koparr*; all fr. a prehistoric WGmc-NGmc word borrowed fr. LL *cuprum* copper, fr. L *cyprum*, fr. *(aes) Cyprium*, lit., metal of Cyprus, fr. *aes* metal + *Cyprium*, neut. of *Cyprius* of Cyprus, fr. Gk *Kyprios*, fr. *Kypros* Cyprus (island in the Mediterranean)] **1** : a common reddish chiefly univalent and bivalent metallic element that is ductile and malleable and one of the best conductors of heat and electricity, that is the only metal that occurs native abundantly in large masses, being found also in various ores (as chalcopyrite, chalcocite, bornite, cuprite, and malachite), that is used in industry, engineering, and the arts both in the pure state and in brass, bronze, and other alloys, and that is an important trace element in animal and plant nutrition — symbol *Cu*; see ELEMENT table **2 a** : a coin or token made of copper **b** : a minor coin made of bronze (as a U.S. cent or a British halfpenny, penny, or farthing) **3** : copper sheathing of a vessel **4 a** *chiefly Brit* : a large boiler (as for cooking or laundering) now often of iron ⟨a soap ~⟩ **b coppers** *pl* : the boilers and cooking vessels in a ship's galley **5 a** *or* **copper red** : a grayish reddish orange that is redder and darker than Etruscan red or hyacinth red and yellower and darker than Persian melon — called also *carnelian*, *wax red* **b** : a moderate reddish orange to brownish orange **6** : SOLDERING IRON **7** : the mouth and throat — used esp. in *hot coppers*, *cool one's coppers*, implying a parched condition due to excessive drinking **8** : any of various small butterflies of the family Lycaenidae with copper-colored wings; *esp* : AMERICAN COPPER **9** : the token used in coppering in the game of faro **10** : a copper sheet like a shield with a T-shaped ridge across it that was used as a symbol of wealth or distinction in ceremonial exchange among the Indians of the northwest coast of No. America

[2]**copper** \"\ *adj* **1** : of copper ⟨~ wire⟩ **2** : relating to copper, copper mining, or copper smelting **3** : having the characteristic color of copper ⟨a hot and ~ sky —S.T.Coleridge⟩ **4** : of the color copper or copper brown

[3]**copper** \"\ *vt* **coppered; coppered; coppering** \-p(ə)riŋ\ **coppers 1** : to cover, coat, or sheathe with or as if with copper **2** : to treat with copper or a copper compound **3 a** : to lay a copper cent or token upon or against (a card or bet) in the game of faro to indicate that the player bets against its winning **b** : HEDGE

[4]**copper** \"\ *n* -s [[2]*cop* + *-er*] : one that cops : an operator of a copping machine

[5]**copper** \"\ *n* -s [[4]*cop* + *-er*] *slang* : POLICEMAN

copper acetate *n* : an acetate of copper: as **a** : the normal salt $Cu(C_2H_3O_2)_2$ forming dark green crystals — called also *cupric acetate* **b** : any of several basic salts derived from this — see VERDIGRIS 2

copper age *n*, *usu cap C&A* : the aeneolithic age

cop·per·as \'käp(ə)rəs\ *n* -ES [alter. of ME *coperose*, fr. MF *coperose*, *couperose*, fr. (assumed) VL *cuprirosa*, fr. LL *cupri-* (fr. *cuprum* copper) + L *rosa* rose — more at ROSE] **1** *obs* : VITRIOL 1a **2** : green ferrous sulfate heptahydrate **3** *archaic* : a green obtained by use of copperas in dyeing — used attributively esp. of trousers

copperas black *n* : a black obtained by the use of logwood with copperas as a mordant in dyeing cloth

copper barilla *n* : a native copper concentrate

copper beech *n* : a beech that is a variety (*Fagus sylvatica atropunicea*) of the European beech with copper-colored shining leaves — called also *purple beech*

copper-belly \'⸗⸗,⸗⸗\ *n* **1** : COPPERHEAD 1 **2** : the common American water snake (*Natrix sipedon*)

copper bit *n* : the copper head of a soldering iron to which an iron shank is attached; *also* : SOLDERING IRON

copper blight *n* [so called fr. the coppery sheen of the diseased leaves] : a leaf-spot disease of tea caused by a fungus (*Guignardia camelliae*)

copper blue *n* : AZURITE BLUE

copperbottom \'⸗⸗,⸗⸗\ *vt* : to make copper-bottomed

copper-bottomed \¦⸗⸗¦⸗⸗\ *adj* : having a bottom of copper ⟨a *copper-bottomed* boiler⟩ or sheathed with copper ⟨a *copper-bottomed* ship⟩

copper brown *n* : a variable color averaging a strong brown that is stronger and slightly yellower and darker than average russet, duller and slightly yellower than rust, and deeper and slightly redder than gold brown

copper butterfly *n* : COPPER 8

copper cent *n* **1** : a large U.S. cent of the series coined 1793–1857 and made of copper **2** : MITE, WHIT, TRIFLE, PARTICLE **3** : a bronze cent

copper chloride *n* : a chloride of copper: **a** : a white poisonous powder CuCl made by reducing cupric chloride and used chiefly as a catalyst and as an absorbent of carbon monoxide — called also *copper(I) chloride*, *cuprous chloride* **b** : a yellowish brown deliquescent anhydrous powder $CuCl_2$ made by heating copper in chlorine or a green crystalline dihydrate $CuCl_2.2H_2O$ made by evaporating cupric oxide in hydrochloric acid, both being used chiefly as a mordant in dyeing and printing and in some metallurgical processes — called also *copper(II) chloride*, *cupric chloride* **c** : any of various basic chlorides (as a brown powder $CuCl_2.3CuO$) or mixtures formed on exposure of cupric chloride to air used as pigments and fungicides — called also *copper oxychloride*

copper chromite catalyst *n* : a catalyst composed essentially of oxides of copper and chromium and used in the hydrogenation of organic compounds

copper citrate *n* : a green or bluish green crystalline powder used as an astringent and antiseptic — called also *cupric citrate*

copper cyanide *n* : a cyanide of copper; *specif* : a white crystalline poisonous powder CuCN made by reaction of cuprous chloride with sodium cyanide and used chiefly in electroplating because of its ability to form complex cyanides

coppered *past of* COPPER

copper-faced \'⸗¦⸗\ *adj* **1** : faced or covered with copper ⟨*copper-faced* type⟩ **2** : having a face like copper : BRAZEN

copper finch *n* : CHAFFINCH

copper glance *n* : CHALCOCITE

copper green *n* **1** : MALACHITE GREEN 1a **2** : MALACHITE GREEN 2

copperhead \'⸗⸗,⸗\ *n* **1 a** : a pit viper (*Agkistrodon contortrix* syn. *A. mokasen*) widely distributed in upland areas of the eastern U.S. that attains a length of three feet, is coppery brown above with dark transverse blotches that render it inconspicuous among fallen leaves, and is usu. regarded as much less dangerous than a rattler of comparable size **b** : a very venomous but sluggish Australian elapid snake (*Denisonia superba*) **c** : a harmless Indian colubrid snake (*Elaphe radiata*) **2 a** : a person in the northern states who sympathized with the South during the Civil War **b** : one whose loyalty is questioned **3** : a ground squirrel (*Citellus lateralis*) of the western U.S. having a yellowish head and shoulders and conspicuously striped body **4 a** : AMERICAN GOLDENEYE **b** : YELLOW-HEADED BLACKBIRD **5** *or* **copperhead bream** : BLUEGILL

cop·per·head·ism \"+,izəm\ *n* -s : sympathy for the Confederate cause in the Civil War : disloyalty to the Union

copper hydroxide *n* : a hydroxide or hydrated oxide of copper; *specif* : the hydroxide $Cu(OH)_2$ obtained as a blue precipitate by the action of alkali on cupric salt solutions or as blue crystals and used chiefly as a mordant and in preparing cuprammonium solution

copper indian *n*, *cap I* : YELLOWKNIFE

coppering *pres part of* COPPER

copper iris *n* : an herb (*Iris fulva*) of the southern U.S. with a reddish brown flower

cop·per·ish \'käpərish\ *adj* : resembling or suggesting copper : somewhat coppery

cop·per·ize \-,rīz\ *vt* -ED/-ING/-S : to impregnate or plate with copper : treat with copper or a copper compound

copperleaf \'⸗⸗,⸗\ *n* [so called fr. the color of the matured plant] : a plant of the genus *Acalypha* (esp. *A. virginica*)

copper loss *n* : electrical energy wasted as heat in a copper conductor

copper luster *n* : a metallic luster on pottery obtained by firing a copper-salt glaze applied to the pottery surface

copper naphthenate *n* : a green cupric salt of a commercial naphthenic acid used on textiles and in paints to prevent growth of fungi and barnacles

copper nickel *n* : NICCOLITE

coppernose \'⸗⸗,⸗\ *n* [prob. by folk etymology fr. F *couperose* coppernose, copperas — more at COPPERAS] **1** : an inflamed nose such as that of acne rosacea or that sometimes produced by habitual drunkenness **2 a** : AMERICAN SCOTER **b** : BLUEGILL

coppernosed bream \'⸗⸗¦⸗-\ *also* **coppernosed sunfish** *n* : BLUEGILL

copper number *n* : a number that expresses the amount of copper reduced from the cupric to the cuprous state (as in Fehling solution) by a given amount of cellulose material and that is useful as a measure of purity esp. in relation to strength and resistance to chemical deterioration of paper and other cellulose products

copper oxide *n* : any oxide of copper: as **a** : the oxide Cu_2O that occurs naturally as cuprite and is obtained as red or yellow crystals or powder by oxidation of copper in a furnace or by electrolysis and that is used chiefly as a pigment (as in ceramics and in antifouling paints) and as a seed disinfectant and fungicide — called also *copper(I) oxide*, *cuprous oxide*, *red copper oxide* **b** : the monoxide CuO that occurs naturally as paramelaconite and tenorite, is obtained usu. in black amorphous form by oxidizing copper, and is used chiefly in preparing cuprammonium solution, as a pigment in ceramics, as a catalyst for hydrogenations, and in chemical analysis — called also *black copper oxide*, *copper(II) oxide*, *cupric oxide*

copper oxychloride *n* : COPPER CHLORIDE c

[1]**copperplate** \'⸗⸗¦⸗\ *n* [[1]*copper* + *plate*] **1 a** : a plate of polished copper on which a design or writing is engraved or etched **b** : a printed impression taken from such a plate **c** : a print or printing made by an intaglio process from a copperplate **d** : copperplate engraving or printing **2** : a handwriting based on models engraved in copper with a burin and characterized by lines of sharply contrasting thickness achieved through the use of a very fine pen applied with varying pressure

[2]**copperplate** \"\ *vt* -ED/-ING/-S **1** : to engrave on a copperplate **2** : to print from a copperplate

copperplate press *n* : a manually operated printing press used for making prints from intaglio metal plates

copper pyrites *n* : CHALCOPYRITE

copper red *n* : [1]COPPER 5a

copper-rose \'⸗⸗,⸗\ *var of* COPROSE

copper rust *n* : VERDIGRIS 3

coppers *pl of* COPPER, *pres 3d sing of* COPPER

copper-skin \'⸗⸗,⸗\ *n* : AMERICAN INDIAN

coppersmith \'⸗⸗,⸗\ *n* [ME *copresmyth*, fr. *copre*, *coper* copper + *smyth* smith] **1** : one who makes objects (as kettles, coils, tubing, and fittings) from sheet copper and brass : a worker in copper **2** : a barbet (*Megalaima haemacephala*) of India, southeast Asia, and islands of the southwest Pacific having a characteristic ringing note

coppersmithing \'⸗⸗,⸗⸗\ *n* -s : the work or occupation of a coppersmith

copper snake *n* : any of certain somewhat copper-colored snakes: as **a** : a coppery brown Australian venomous snake (*Pseudechis cupreus*) related to the Australian black snake **b** : a small harmless colubrid snake (*Storeria occipitomaculata*) of eastern No. America

copper spot *n* : a disease of lawn and golf-green grasses caused by a fungus (*Gloeocercospora sorghi*) and producing dead areas of a coppery red color

copper sulfate *n* : any sulfate of copper; *specif* : the normal sulfate $CuSO_4$, white when anhydrous but best known as the blue crystalline pentahydrate $CuSO_4.5H_2O$, that is made by roasting copper sulfide ores and by the action of sulfuric acid on copper or copper oxide and that is used chiefly as a fungicide and algicide, in dyeing and printing, in making pigments and other compounds, and in electric batteries — see BORDEAUX MIXTURE

copper sulfide *n* : any sulfide of copper: as **a** : the black crystalline sulfide Cu_2S occurring naturally as chalcocite — called also *cuprous sulfide* **b** : the black, bluish black, or brownish black crystalline sulfide CuS occurring naturally as covellite and precipitated by hydrogen sulfide from a solution of a cupric salt — called also *cupric sulfide*

copper tan *n* : a light reddish brown that is duller and slightly yellower than peach tan and duller and yellower than monkey skin

coppertip \'⸗⸗,⸗\ *n* : a bulbous African herb (*Crocosma aurea*) of the family Iridaceae of branching habit that is often cultivated for its bright yellow panicled flowers

copper vitriol *n* : COPPER SULFATE

copperweed \'⸗⸗,⸗\ *n* [so called fr. the copper-colored flowers] : a tall shrubby herb (*Oxytenia acerosa*) of the family Compositae that is troublesome esp. in the Western U.S. as a plant poisonous to stock

cop·pery \'käp(ə)rē, -ri\ *adj* : mixed with copper : containing copper : like copper (as in color or taste)

copper yellow *n* : QUINCE YELLOW

coppery snake *n* : a small harmless colubrid snake (*Prosymna sundevallii*) occurring in southern Africa

[1]**cop·pice** \'käpəs\ *n* -s [MF *copeiz*, *coupeiz*, fr. *couper* to cut — more at COPE] **1** : a thicket, grove, or growth of small trees that are cut on a short rotation : COPSE **2 a** : wood cut from coppice growth **b** : UNDERWOOD, BRUSHWOOD **3** : a forest originating mainly from sprouts or root suckers as opposed to one derived from seed

[2]**coppice** \"\ *vb* -ED/-ING/-S *vt* : to cause to grow in the form of a coppice : cut back so as to produce shoots from old stumps ~ *vi* : to form a coppice : sprout freely from the base

coppice oak *n* : bark from roots of the kermes oak

coppice shoot *n* : a young tree that has grown from a sucker and not from seed

cop·ping \'käpiŋ\ *n* -s [[1]*cop* (thread wound on a spindle) + *-ing*] : the forming of the cop in spinning

coppled *adj* [obs. E *copple* crest on a bird's head (fr. AF *copel* top of the head, top of a plant, dim. of OF *cope* drinking vessel, fr. LL *cuppa*) + *-ed* — more at CUP] **1** *obs* : CONICAL, COPPED **2** *obs* : CRESTED

[1]**cop·py** \'käpi\ *n* -ES [by shortening & alter.] *dial Eng* : COPPICE

[2]**coppy** \"\ *n* -ES [prob. fr. [1] *coppy*] *dial Eng* : a low stool

copr- *or* **copro-** *comb form* [NL, fr. Gk *kopr-*, *kopro-*, fr. *kopros*; akin to Lith *šikti* to void excrement, Skt *śakṛt* dung] **1** : dung : feces ⟨*copremia*⟩ ⟨*coprolite*⟩ **2** : filth : obscenity ⟨*coprolalia*⟩ **3** *usu copro-* : related to coprostanol

copr *abbr* copyright

co·pra \'kōprə, 'käp-\ *n* -s [Pg, fr. Malayalam *koppara*, prob. fr. Hindi *khoprā*] : coconut meat dried esp. for export before the coconut oil is pressed out

copra beetle *also* **copra bug** *n* : RED-LEGGED HAM BEETLE

copra cake *n* : COCONUT CAKE

copra itch *n* : GROCER'S ITCH

copra meal *n* : COCONUT MEAL

copra oil *n* : coconut oil pressed out from copra

co·precipitate \¦kō+\ *vb* [*co-* + *precipitate*] : to precipitate together

co·precipitation \¦kō+\ *n* : the process of coprecipitating

co·presence \(')kō+\ *n* [*co-* + *presence*] : occurrence of two or more things together in the same place and time

cop·ri·nus \'käprənəs, kə'prīnəs\ *n*, *cap* [NL, fr. Gk *koprinos* of dung, fr. *kopros* dung; fr. the habitat of some species — more at COPR-] : a genus of black-spored agarics of the family Agaricaceae in which the pileus breaks down at maturity into an inky fluid — see SHAGGYMANE

cop·ro·culture \¦käprə+\ *n* [ISV *copr-* + *culture*] : culture of feces (as for detection of pathogenic microorganisms)

cop·ro·dae·al *or* **cop·ro·de·al** \¦käprə¦dēəl\ *adj* [NL *coprodaeum*, *coprodeum* + E *-al*] : relating or belonging to the coprodaeum

cop·ro·dae·um *or* **cop·ro·deum** \,käprə'dēəm, '⸗⸗,⸗⸗\ *n* -s [NL, fr. *copr-* + *-odaeum*, *-odeum* (fr. Gk *hodaion*, neut. of *hodaios* on the way, fr. *hodos* way) — more at CEDE] : the innermost division of the cloaca of birds or reptiles

co·product \(')kō+\ *n* [*co-* + *product*] : BY-PRODUCT 1

cop·ro·lag·nia \,käprə'lagnēə, '⸗⸗,⸗⸗⸗\ *n* -s [NL, fr. *copr-* + *-lagnia*] : sexual excitement produced by contact with feces — **cop·ro·lag·nist** \-nəst\ *n* -s

cop·ro·la·lia \-lālēə\ *n* -s [NL, fr. *copr-* + *-lalia*] **1** : obsessive or uncontrollable use of obscene language **2** : the use of obscene (as scatological) language as sexual gratification

cop·ro·lite \'käprə,līt\ *n* -s [*copr-* + *-lite*] : fossil excrement being often a valuable source of information about the food and habits of extinct animals — **cop·ro·lit·ic** \¦⸗⸗¦lid·ik\ *adj*

cop·ro·lith \'käprə,lith\ *n* -s [NL *coprolithus*, fr. *copr-* + *-lithus* -lith] : a mass of hard fecal matter in the intestine

co·prol·o·gy \kə'präləjē\ *n* -ES [ISV *copr-* + *-logy*] **1** : SCATOLOGY **2** : PORNOGRAPHY

co·proph·a·gan \kə'präfəgən\ *n* -s [NL *Coprophaga* (former subfamily of beetles containing the dung beetle, fr. *copr-* + *-phaga*, neut. pl. of *-phagus* -phagous) + E *-an*] : one that feeds on excrement; *specif* : DUNG BEETLE

cop·ro·pha·gia \,käprə'fāj(ē)ə, '⸗⸗,⸗(⸗)⸗\ *n* -s [NL, fr. *copr-* + *-phagia*] : COPROPHAGY — **cop·ro·phag·ic** \¦⸗⸗¦fajik\ *adj* — **co·proph·a·gous** \kə'präfəgəs\ *adj*

co·proph·a·gist \kə'präfəjəst\ *n* -s : one that practices coprophagy

co·proph·a·gy \-jē\ *n* -ES [ISV *copr-* + *-phagy*] : the feeding on or eating of dung or excrement that is normal behavior among many insects, birds, and other animals but in man is a symptom of some forms of insanity

cop·ro·phil·ia \,käprə'filēə, '⸗⸗,⸗⸗⸗\ *n* -s [NL, fr. *copr-* + *-philia*] : marked interest in excrement; *esp* : use of feces or filth for sexual excitement — **cop·ro·phil·i·ac** \¦⸗⸗¦filē,ak\ *n* -s

cop·ro·phil·ic \¦käprə¦filik\ *adj* [in sense 1, fr. NL *coprophilia* + E *-ic*; in sense 2, fr. *copr-* + *-philic*] **1** : relating to coprophilia **2** : COPROPHILOUS

co·proph·i·lous \kə'präfələs\ *adj* [*copr-* + *-philous*] **1** : growing or living on dung ⟨~ fungi⟩ ⟨~ beetles⟩ **2** : fond of pornography

cop·ro·porphyrin \¦käprə +\ *n* -s [ISV *copr-* + *porphyrin*] : any of four isomeric porphyrins $C_{20}H_6N_4(CH_3)_4(CH_2CH_2COOH)_4$ of which types I and III are found in feces and urine esp. in certain pathological conditions and also in yeast

cop·ro·porphyrinuria \¦käprə +\ *n* -s [NL, fr. ISV *coproporphyrin* + NL *-uria*] : excretion of coproporphyrin in the urine

co·proprietor \¦kō +\ *n* [*co-* + *proprietor*] : a joint owner — **co·proprietorship** \¦kō +\ *n*

cop·rose \'kä,prōz\ *n* -s [perh. modif. of D *klaproos*, fr. *klappen* to clap, chat (fr. MD *clappen*) + *roos* rose, fr. MD *rôse*, *rōse*, fr. L *rosa* — more at CLAP, ROSE] *dial Brit* : CORN POPPY

co·pros·ma \kə'präzmə\ *n* [NL, fr. *copr-* + *-osma*] **1** *cap* : a genus of shrubs or small trees of the family Rubiaceae found in New Zealand, Australia, and Hawaii and having shining often variegated leaves and small flowers with revolute corolla lobes **2** -s : a plant of the genus *Coprosma*

cop·ro·stane \'käprə,stān\ *n* -s [ISV *copr-* + *-stane* (as in *cholestane*)] : a crystalline steroid hydrocarbon $C_{27}H_{48}$ stereoisomeric with cholestane

co·pros·ta·nol \kə'prästə,nōl, -nȯl\ *n* -s [*coprostane* + *-ol*] : a crystalline sterol $C_{27}H_{47}OH$ formed by bacterial reduction of cholesterol in the intestines and present in feces — called also *3-coprostanol*, *coprosterol*

co·pros·ter·ol \-tə,rōl, -rȯl\ *n* -s [*copr-* + *sterol*] : COPROSTANOL

cop·ro·zo·ic \¦käprə¦zōik\ *adj* [*copr-* + *-zoic*] *of an animal* : COPROPHILOUS — **cop·ro·zo·on** \,⸗⸗'zō,än, '⸗⸗,(⸗)⸗\ *n*, *pl* **copro·zoa** \-zōə\

[1]**cops** *or* **copse** \'käps\ *n*, *pl* **copses** [ME *cops*, *copse*, *cospe* shackle, hasp, fr. OE *cops*, *cosp* shackle; akin to OS *-cosp* shackle] *dial Eng* : a hasp, clevis, or similar coupling device

[2]**cops** *pl of* COP, *pres 3d sing of* COP

cops and robbers *n* : children's play in which the players imitate the chasing, shooting, and capturing of criminals by police

[1]**copse** \'käps\ *n* -s [by alter.] : COPPICE ⟨near yonder ~ where once the garden smiled —Oliver Goldsmith⟩

[2]**copse** \"\ *vb* -ED/-ING/-S : COPPICE

copse laurel *n* : SPURGE LAUREL

copsewood \'⸗,⸗\ *n* **1** : COPSE **2** : the underwood of a copse

cops·ing \'käpsiŋ\ *n* -s [[1]*copse* + *-ing*] : COPSEWOOD, COPPICE

copsy \'käpsē, -si\ *adj* [[1]*copse* + *-y*] : abounding in copses

copt \'käpt\ *n* -s *cap* [Ar *qubṭ*, *qibṭ*, *qubṭ*, *qibṭ* Copts, *qubṭī*, *qibṭī*, *qubṭī*, *qibṭī* Coptic, fr. Copt *gyptios*, *kyptaios* Egyptian, fr. Gk *aigyptios*, fr. *Aigyptos* Egypt] : an Egyptian of the native race descended from the ancient Egyptians; *esp* : a member of the Coptic church

cop·ter \'käptə(r)\ *n* -s [by shortening] : HELICOPTER

[1]**cop·tic** \'käptik, -tēk\ *adj*, *usu cap* [*Copt* + *-ic*] **1** : relating or belonging to the Copts, to Coptic, or to the Egyptian Christian church **2** *fine art* : produced in Egypt during the Christian period; *specif* : having to do with the distinctive art of Christian Egypt which reached its apex in the 6th century

[2]**coptic** \"\ *n* **1** *cap* : an Afro-Asiatic language descended from ancient Egyptian and used by the Egyptians from about the 3d century A.D. to about 1500 when it was superseded by Arabic and became a dead language except for continued liturgical use in the Coptic church **2** -s : OXBLOOD

cop·tis \'käptəs\ *n*, *cap* [NL, irreg. fr. Gk *koptein* to cut off; fr. the divided leaves — more at CAPON] : a genus of small herbs of the family Ranunculaceae that are found in the north temperate zone and have basal divided or compound leaves, a slender rootstock, and white flowers on a scape — see GOLDTHREAD

cop·u·la \'käpyələ\ *n*, *pl* **copulas** \-ləz\ *also* **copu·lae** \-,lē\ [L, bond — more at COUPLE] **1** : something that connects : LINK: as **a** : the connecting link or relation between the subject and predicate of a strictly formulated proposition; *esp* : such a link when it is a form of the verb *to be* (as in "he is a shoemaker" instead of "he makes shoes") — see BE, PREDICABLE **b** : a linguistic form that links a subject with its predicate and sometimes has some additional meaning of its own (as *looks* in "that looks good," *got* in "he got sleepy") and sometimes not (as *is* in "that is right") **c** : any of certain connecting structures; *specif* : a basibranchial or basihyal bone or cartilage **2** : sexual union : COPULATION — used chiefly in law **3** : COUPLER 1c **4** : a descant having a florid cadential passage usu. in the plainsong tenor **5** *obs* : a chemical compound that joins itself to another

cop·u·la·ble \-ləbəl\ *adj* [[2]*copulate* + *-able*] *chem* : able to couple or be coupled

cop·u·lar \-lə(r)\ *adj* [*copula* + *-ar*] : relating to or of the nature of a copula

[1]**cop·u·late** \-lət, -,lāt\ *adj* [ME *copulat*, fr. L *copulatus*, past part. of *copulare* to bind, fr. *copula*] : JOINED, COUPLED

[2]**copulate** \'käpyə,lāt, *usu* -ād·+V\ *vi* -ED/-ING/-S [L *copulatus*] **1** : to join or unite **2 a** : to unite in sexual intercourse : engage in coitus **b** *of gametes* : to fuse permanently — compare CONJUGATE

cop·u·la·tion \,käpyə'lāshən\ *n* -s [ME *copulacioun*, fr. MF *copulation*, fr. L *copulation-*, *copulatio*, fr. *copulatus* + *-ion-*, *-io* -ion] **1** : the act of coupling or joining : the state of being coupled or joined : UNION, CONJUNCTION ⟨wit, you know, is the unexpected ~ of ideas —Samuel Johnson⟩ **2 a** : sexual union : COITUS **b** : permanent fusion of gametes — compare CONJUGATION **3** : the joining of subject and predicate by a copula **4** : COUPLING — compare COUPLE *vi* 2b

copulation path *n* : the intracytoplasmic course followed by the male pronucleus in approaching the female pronucleus during fertilization and often delineating the direction of the first cleavage furrow

[1]**cop·u·la·tive** \'käpyə,lād·iv, -lət̬-, -,lāt|, -lət|, |ēv\ *adj* [ME *copulatif*, fr. MF or LL; MF, fr. LL *copulativus*, fr. L *copulatus* + *-ivus* -ive] **1 a** *of a conjunction* : joining together coordinate words or word groups and expressing addition of their meanings ⟨*and* in "bread and meat" is ~⟩ — contrasted with *disjunctive* **b** : containing words or word groups joined by a copulative conjunction ⟨~ sentences⟩ **c** *of a verb* : being a copula (sense 1b) **d** *of a compound* : belonging to the dvandva class **2** : relating to or serving for copulation ⟨~ organs⟩ **3** : of or relating to coupling of chemical compounds or radicals — **cop·u·la·tive·ly** \|əvlē, -li\ *adv*

²**copulative** \"\ *n* -s **1** : a copulative conjunction **2** : a compound belonging to the dvandva class

cop·u·la·to·ry \'käpyələ,tōrē, -tȯrē, -ri\ *adj* : relating to or used in copulation ⟨~ organs⟩ : tending or serving to unite : COPULATIVE

co·punctal \(')kō+\ *adj* [*co-* + *punctal*] *geom* : having a point in common : relating to a point at which lines or planes meet : ¹CONCURRENT 1

¹**copy** \'käpē, -pi\ *n* -ES [ME *copie*, fr. MF, fr. ML & L; ML *copia* imitation, transcript, fr. L, abundance, number, ability, power — more at COPIOUS] **1** *obs* : PLENTY, COPIOUSNESS **2** : an imitation, transcript, or reproduction of an original work (as of a letter, an engraving, a painting, a statue, a piece of furniture, a dress) **3** *English law* **a** : the transcript of the roll of the manorial court containing the entries made by the steward of the admissions of tenants to land according to custom under the tenure thence called copyhold **b** : a holding or estate by copyhold **4** : one of a series of esp. mechanical reproductions of the same original text, engraving, or photograph : an individual example of a series of identical impressions (as of type, a printing plate) ⟨a book printed in 500 *copies*⟩ ⟨a rag-paper ~ of a newspaper⟩ ⟨a presentation ~⟩ **5 a** *archaic* : something that is or is to be imitated or transcribed : an example (as of penmanship) : MODEL, PATTERN **b** : a picture that is to be photographically reproduced **6 a** : matter to be set up for printing or photoengraving (as a draft of a news story, an author's manuscript, or a picture) ⟨this is dirty ~⟩ **b** : something considered printable or newsworthy — used in the singular and without an article ⟨crime makes good ~⟩ **c** : the text of an advertisement — **by copy** *English law* : by copy of the manorial court roll

²**copy** \"\ *vb* -ED/-ING/-ES [ME *copien*, fr. MF *copier*, fr. ML *copiare*, fr. *copia*] *vt* **1** : to make a copy of : print, engrave, or paint after an original : DUPLICATE, REPRODUCE, TRANSCRIBE; *specif* : to duplicate (a document) by pressing in a copying press **2** : to attempt to resemble : follow esp. in manners or course of life ⟨when art *copies* nature⟩ ~ *vi* **1** : to make a copy ⟨he *copies* from Rembrandt⟩ **2** : to undergo copying ⟨the document did not ~ well⟩

syn IMITATE, MIMIC, APE, MOCK, BURLESQUE: COPY applies to the making of duplications of originals with resemblances as close as circumstances will permit ⟨you gave natives bits to *copy* under all possible threats against lapses of accuracy —Mary Austin⟩ ⟨later examples of the Greek revival travestied the classic style rather than *copied* it —*Amer. Guide Series: Mass.*⟩ IMITATE suggests following a pattern or model in overall qualities or in some specific characteristics, without precluding considerable variation ⟨she slept for hours in the daytime, *imitating* the cats —Jean Stafford⟩ ⟨plaster was originally painted to *imitate* marble —*Amer. Guide Series: Minn.*⟩ ⟨their pots seem to *imitate* leather vessels —V.G.Childe⟩ MIMIC may suggest a copying either exact in emulation of or fidelity to the original or heightened for making sport of or satirizing ⟨he learned to call wild turkeys with a piece of bone through which he was able to *mimic* the notes of the bird —Van Wyck Brooks⟩ ⟨he attends even to their air, dress, and motions, and imitates them liberally and not servilely; he copies but does not *mimic* —Earl of Chesterfield⟩ APE likewise may apply to close copying in emulation; often it suggests inept, presumptuous, or servile copying of a better or more worthy original ⟨the pride that *apes* humility —F.M.Ford⟩ ⟨feudal principalities each *aping* sovereignty —Will Durant⟩ ⟨the lower classes *aped* the rigid decorum of their "betters" with laughable results —Harrison Smith⟩ MOCK usu. applies to imitation or repetition with scornful derisive intent ⟨she contended every point, objected to every request, shirked her work, fought with her sisters, *mocked* her mother —Margaret Mead⟩ ⟨half a dozen jackals went through the compound singing and a hyena stood afar off and *mocked* them —Rudyard Kipling⟩ BURLESQUE applies to imitation designed to ridicule by grotesque exaggeration ⟨she read these letters aloud, *burlesquing* them in spite of protests —Katherine Mansfield⟩ ⟨most of the local humor is corny, but it's shrewd, earthy, and droll, *burlesquing* in its extravagance the pompousness of our national self-esteem —Bergen Evans⟩

copyboard \'==,=\ *n* : the backing on which the original to be reproduced is positioned in front of the camera in photoengraving

¹**copybook** \'==,=\ *n* **1** : a book containing copies (as of accounts) **2** : a book formerly used in elementary schools containing samples of penmanship (as in the form of proverbs or moral precepts) for the learner to imitate

²**copybook** \"\ *adj* : characterized by conventionality or triteness ⟨old-fashioned standards of morality and ~ virtues —Lucius Garvin⟩ ⟨~ maxims⟩

copyboy \'==,=\ *n* : one who carries copy and runs errands (as in a newspaper office or publishing house)

¹**copycat** \'==,=\ *n* [²*copy* + *cat*] : one who slavishly imitates or adopts the behavior or practice of another

²**copycat** \"\ *vb* **copycatted**; **copycatted**; **copycatting**; **copycats** *vi* : to act as a copycat ~ *vt* : IMITATE

copy cutter *n* : a newspaper employee who divides copy into takes and apportions them to compositors

copydesk \'==,=\ *n* : the desk in a newspaper editorial office at which copyreaders edit copy and write headlines

copy editor *n* **1** : COPYREADER **2 a** : an editor who prepares copy for the printer **b** : an editor in charge of a copydesk and copyreaders on a newspaper

copyfit \'==,=\ *vt* : to fit (printer's copy) to the required space (as by cutting or expanding the copy or the space and by the use of different-size typefaces, measures, and leading) — **copyfitter** \'==,==\ *n*

copy·graph \'käpē,graf\ *n* -s [¹*copy* (manuscript) + *-graph*] : HECTOGRAPH — **copy·graphed** \-ft\ *adj*

copyhold \'==,=\ *n* [ME, fr. *copy*, *copie* copy (transcript) + *hold*] **1** : a tenure of land in England and Ireland until largely abolished by the Copyhold Act of 1894 by copy of court roll, at the will of the lord, and according to the custom of the manor of which the land was a part **2** : an estate held by copyhold

¹**copyholder** \'==,==\ *n* [*copyhold* + *-er*] : one holding land in copyhold

²**copyholder** \"\ *n* [¹*copy* + *holder*] **1** : a device for holding copy that is being typed, typeset, or photographically reproduced **2** : one who assists a proofreader by reading copy aloud or following copy as the proofreader reads aloud

copyholding \'==,==\ *n* : the work of a copyholder (sense 2)

copying *pres part of* COPY

copying ink *n* : ink suitable for writing or typing that is to be copied by direct transfer (as in a copying press)

copying paper *n* : thin unsized paper used for taking copies by direct transfer (as in a copying press)

copying press *n* : an obsolescent device in which an original (as a letter) in copying ink is transferred in reverse by being pressed against an absorbent translucent sheet which is read from the reverse side — called also *letterpress*

copy·ism \'käpē,izəm\ *n* -s : the act or practice of copying esp. mechanically or unthinkingly

copy·ist \-ēəst\ *n* -s [alter. of earlier *copist*, fr. MF *copiste*, fr. *copier* to copy + *-iste* -ist — more at COPY] **1** : one who is employed to make copies (as of instrumental scores) : COPIER, TRANSCRIBER **2** : IMITATOR, PLAGIARIST, COPYCAT **3 a** : one who makes paper novelties according to pattern **b** : a hand sewer who copies hats **c** : one who copies or adapts clothing designs by sketching or making models

copy·man \-ē,man, -maa(ə)n\ *n*, *pl* **copymen** : COPYCUTTER

copy number *n* : a numeral placed on a book to distinguish it from other copies of the same title

copy paper *n* : COPYING PAPER

copy·read \'käpē,rēd\ *vt* : to edit (as manuscript or copy) for printing

copy·reader \-də(r)\ *n* **1** : a publishing-house editor who reads and corrects manuscript copy and sometimes specifies size and style of type and the positioning of illustrations; *also* : one who edits copy and adds headlines for a newspaper **2** : one who reads and evaluates usu. unsolicited manuscripts for publication

¹**copyright** \'==,=\ *n* [¹*copy* + *right*] : the exclusive, legally secured right to reproduce (as by writing or printing), publish, and sell the matter and form of a literary, musical, or artistic work (as by dramatizing, novelizing, performing or reciting in public, or filming) for a period in the U. S. of 28 years with a right of renewal for another 28 years — see LITERARY PROPERTY; compare PATENT, TRADEMARK

²**copyright** \"\ *adj* : secured by copyright : COPYRIGHTED

³**copyright** \"\ *vt* -ED/-ING/-s : to secure a copyright on

copy·right·able \'==,rīd·əbəl, -ītə-\ *adj* : capable of being copyrighted

copywriter \'==,==\ *n* : a writer of advertising or publicity copy

coq *or* **coque** \'kȯk\ *n* -s [F *coq*, fr. OF *coc* — more at COCKEREL] : ¹COCK; *specif* : a trimming of cock feathers on a woman's hat

coque \"\ *n* -s [F, lit., shell, fr. L *coccum* excrescence on a tree; fr. their original shell-like appearance — more at COAK] : a loop of ribbon or feathers used in trimming hats

coque·ci·grue \'käksə,grü, ,==\'=\ *n* -s [F, fr. MF] : an imaginary creature regarded as an embodiment of absolute absurdity

co·quei·ro \kü'kārü; kə'ka(a)rü, -rō, -rə\ *n* -s [Pg, fr. *côco* coconut — more at COCO] : OURICURY

coque·li·cot \'käklə,kō, 'kōk-\ *n* -s [F, cry of a cock, cock, poppy, of imit. origin; fr. a comparison of the flower to the comb of a cock] **1 a** : any of several poppies of the genus *Papaver*; *esp* : CORN POPPY **b** : a mallow (*Callirhoë papaver*) of the southern U. S. that resembles a poppy **2** : PONCEAU

¹**co·quet** \kō'ket\ *n* -s [F, dim. of *coq* cock — more at COQ] **1** *obs* : a man who indulges in coquetry **2** : COQUETTE

²**coquet** \(')=¦=\ *adj* [F, fr. *coquet*, n.] **1** *obs* : boldly amorous in manner **2** : COQUETTISH

³**co·quet** *or* **co·quette** \kō'ket, *usu* -ed· +V\ *vb* **coquetted**; **coquetted**; **coquetting**; **coquets** *or* **coquettes** [partly fr. ¹*coquet*, partly fr. *coquette*, n.] *vt*, *obs* : to treat coquettishly : flirt with ⟨you are *coquetting* a maid of honor —Jonathan Swift⟩ ~ *vi* **1** : to trifle in love : play the coquette ⟨she *coquetted* with the solid husbands of her friends —Dorothy Parker⟩ ⟨the courtiers stood around . . . *coquetting* and making their pretty speeches —Francis Hackett⟩ **2** : deal playfully instead of seriously : PLAY, DALLY — used with *with* ⟨we have *coquetted* with a serious matter⟩

coque·toon \'käka,tün, ,==\'=\ *n* -s [native name in western Africa] : GRIMME

co·quet·ry \'kōkətrē, -ri *sometimes* kō'ket-\ *n* -ES [F *coquetterie*, fr. *coquette* + *-erie* -ery] **1** : the conduct or art of a coquette : effort or action intended to attract admiration, gallantry, or affection without responsive feeling : a trifling in love **2** : a dallying or trifling attention or consideration (as to a cause) without serious espousal **3** : delicate charm of a type distinctive of coquettes ⟨lack of ~ — in the sense of a lighthearted desire to please — is a lack of charity, of natural kindness —*English Digest*⟩

co·quette \kō'ket, *usu* -ed· +V\ *n* -s [F, fem. of *coquet*] **1** : a woman who endeavors without affection to attract men's amorous attention : FLIRT ⟨instruct the eyes of young ~*s* to roll —Alexander Pope⟩ — sometimes, with *male*, used of a man **2** : any of several tropical hummingbirds (of *Lophornis* and related genera) with crested head and metallic-tinted neck feathers **3** : a moderate to strong yellowish pink that is yellower and paler than coral blush

co·quett·ish \(')kō¦ked·ish, -eti-, -ēsh\ *adj* : having the air or nature of a coquette or coquetry : practicing or exhibiting coquetry ⟨heartless, ~ women, who put self first and played with fire —Margaret A. Barnes⟩ — **co·quett·ish·ly** *adv* — **co·quett·ish·ness** *n* -ES

co·qui \'kōkwē\ *or* **coqui partridge** *n* -s [Sechuana, quail] : a small francolin (*Francolinus coqui*) widely distributed in African grasslands

co·quil·lage \,kōkə'läzh, '==,=\ *n* -s [F, shellfish, shellfish used as decorations, fr. *coquille* + *-age*] : decoration imitating shells

co·quil·la nut \kə'kilə,-, kō'kē(l)yə,-\ *n* [modif. of Pg *coquilho*, dim. of *côco* coconut — more at COCO] : the nut of a piassava palm (*Attalea funifera*) of Brazil having a hard hazel-brown shell much used like vegetable ivory by turners

co·quille \kō'kil, kə'-, -kēl; *F* kôkēʸ\ *n* -s [F, lit., shell — more at COCKLE] **1** : SHELL: as **a** : a shell-like dish in which food is served : SCALLOP **b** : the expansion of the guard of a sword or dagger **c** : a ruching or edging gathered and fulled in a shell-like design and used for clothing or millinery trimming **2 a** *or* **coquille board** : an artist's white drawing board with stippled texture that produces a dotted drawing that looks like a half tone but may be reproduced as a line cut **b** : a drawing technique involving the use of coquille board

coquille lens *n* [*coquille*] : an oval glass of curved surface and uniform thickness used in eyeglasses

co·quim·bite \kō'kim,bīt, kə'-\ *n* -s [G *coquimbit*, fr. *Coquimbo* province in Chile (where it was discovered) + G *-it* -ite] : a mineral consisting of a hydrous ferric sulfate $Fe_2(SO_4)_3 \cdot 9H_2O$ occurring in white or slightly colored masses

co·qui·na \kō'kēnə, kə'-\ *n* -s [Sp, prob. irreg. dim. of *concha* shell — more at CONCHA] **1** : a small marine clam of the genus *Donax* (esp. *D. variabilis*) used for broth or chowder **2** : a soft whitish limestone formed of broken shells and corals cemented together that is found in the southern U. S. and used for roads and for building

co·qui·ta \-'kēd·ə\ *n* -s [AmerSp, fr. Sp *coquito*] : the strong cordage fiber of the coquito palm

co·qui·to \-d·ō\ *also* **coquito palm** *n* -s [Sp *coquito*, dim. of *coco* coco palm, fr. Pg *côco* — more at COCO] : a pinnate-leaved palm (*Jubaea spectabilis*) of Chile whose sap is used in making palm honey, seeds for sweetmeats, and fiber for cordage

¹**cor** *var of* KOR

²**cor** *n* -s [origin unknown] *obs* : salt fish; *esp* : COD

³**cor** \'kȯ(ə)r\ *n*, *pl* **cordia** \-rdēə\ [L — more at HEART] : HEART

cor- — see COM-

¹**cor** *abbr* **1** corner **2** cornet **3** coroner **4** coronet **5** corpus

²**cor** *or* **corr** *abbr* **1** correct; corrected; correction **2** correlative **3** correspondence; correspondent; corresponding **4** corrigendum **5** corrugated **6** corrupt; corruption

¹**co·ra** \'kōrə, 'kȯrə\ *n* -s [origin unknown] : a gazelle (*Gazella arabica*) found from Persia to No. Africa

²**cora** \"\ *n*, *cap* [NL, perh. fr. Gk *korē* girl, doll, pupil of the eye; fr. its circular shape; akin to L *crescere* to grow — more at CRESCENT] : a genus of basidiolichens superficially resembling the bracket fungi and widely distributed on soil and trees in Central and So. America

³**cora** \"\ *n*, *pl* **cora** *or* **coras** *usu cap* [Sp, of AmerInd origin] **1 a** : a Taracahitian people of the states of Jalisco and Nayarit, Mexico including the Cora proper and the Coano, **b** : a member of such people **2** : the language of the Cora people

co·ra·be·ca \,kōrə'bēkə, ,kȯr-, -'bākə\ *or* **co·ra·ve·ca** \-'vē-, -'vä-\ *n*, *pl* **corabeca** *or* **corabecas** *or* **coraveca** *or* **coravecas** *usu cap* [AmerSp *corabeca*, of AmerInd origin] **1 a** : an extinct people of Bolivia **b** : a member of such people **2** : the language of the Corabeca people considered by some Americanists as an independent linguistic family and by others as Otoquian or uncertain — **co·ra·be·can** *or* **co·ra·ve·can** \¦==¦=kən\ *adj*, *usu cap*

co·ra·ci·ae \kō'rāsē,ē, kə'-\ [NL, pl. of *Coracias*] *syn of* CORACII

co·ra·ci·as \kō'rāsēəs, kə'-\ *n*, *cap* [NL, fr. Gk *korakias*, a kind of chough; akin to Gk *korax* raven — more at RAVEN] : a genus of vigorous active brightly colored birds related to and somewhat resembling the kingfishers and being the type of a widespread Old World family Coraciidae

cor·a·cid·i·um \,kȯrə'sidēəm\ *n*, *pl* **coracid·ia** \-dēə\ [NL, fr. Gk *korak-*, *korax* raven, anything hooked like a raven's beak + NL *-idium*] : the onchosphere of a tapeworm at about the time of hatching while still surrounded by the embryophore which in Pseudophyllidea is ciliated

co·ra·cii \kō'rāsē,ī, kə'-\ *n pl*, *cap* [NL, pl. of *Coracius* (syn. of *Coracias*, fr. Gk *korakias*)] : the suborder of Coraciiformes that includes the rollers, hoopoes, wood hoopoes, and related birds

cor·a·ci·idae \,kȯrə'sīə,dē\ *n pl*, *cap* [NL, fr. *Coracias*, type genus + *-idae*] : a family (order Coraciiformes) of Old World birds including the common roller and certain related birds

co·ra·ci·i·form \kə'rāsēə,fȯrm, ¦kȯrə¦sīə-,\ *adj* [NL *Coraciiformes*] : of or relating to the Coraciiformes

co·ra·ci·i·for·mes \kə,rāsēə'fȯr,mēz, ,kȯrə,sīə'f-\ *n pl*, *cap* [NL, fr. *Coracii* + *-formes*] : an order of chiefly arboreal birds comprising the rollers, kingfishers, hornbills, hoopoes, motmots, and related forms and formerly containing also the hummingbirds, woodpeckers, swifts, and owls

cor·a·cite \'kȯrə,sīt\ *n* -s [Gk *korak-*, *korax* raven + E *-ite*; fr. its black color] : URANINITE

cor·a·cle \'kȯrəkəl, 'kär-\ *n* -s [alter. of earlier *corougle*, fr. W *corwgl*, *cwrwgl*, fr. *corwg*, *cwrwg*, fr. MW *corwc*; akin to MIr *curach* boat, L *corium* leather — more at CUIRASS] **1** : a small boat made by covering a wicker frame with hide or leather and used by the ancient Britons **2** : a boat made of broad hoops covered with horsehide or tarpaulin and used in parts of the British Isles

coracles

coraco- *comb form* [NL, fr. *coracoides* coracoid] : coracoid and ⟨*coraco*costal⟩

cor·a·co·bra·chi·a·lis \,kȯrə(,)kō,brākē'āləs, -brak-\ *n*, *pl* **coracobra·chia·les** \-,lēz\ [NL, fr. *coraco-* + L *brachialis* brachial] : a muscle extending between the coracoid process and the middle of the shaft of the humerus

¹**cor·a·coid** \'kȯrə,kȯid\ *adj* [NL *coracoides*, fr. Gk *korakoeidēs*, lit., like a raven, fr. *korak-*, *korax* raven + *-oeidēs* -oid — more at RAVEN] : relating to the coracoid bone or process

²**coracoid** \"\ *n* -s : a cartilage bone of the shoulder girdle of many vertebrates that extends from the scapula to or toward the sternum and is well-developed in most reptiles, in the birds and monotremes, but in the higher mammals including man is rudimentary and represented by the coracoid process of the scapula

cor·a·coid·al \¦kȯrə¦kȯidᵊl\ *adj* : CORACOID

coracoid ligament *n* : the transverse ligament of the scapula which bridges over the suprascapular notch

coracoid process *n* : the rudimentary coracoid bone of most mammals ankylosed with and forming a process of the scapula and in man extending upward and inward from the scapula and then curving forward and finally outward

cor·a·co·ra·di·a·lis \,kȯrə(,)kō,rādē'āləs\ *n*, *pl* **coracora·dia·les** \-,lēz\ [NL, fr. *coraco-* + ML *radialis* radial — more at RADIAL] : the short head of the biceps muscle

co·rail \kə'rā(ə)l, kō'-\ *n* -s [F (*bois de*) *corail*, (*bois*) *corail*, lit., coral wood; *corail* coral, fr. MF *coral*] : AFRICAN PADAUK

¹**cor·al** \'kȯrəl, 'kär- *sometimes* 'kȯr-\ *n* -s [ME, fr. MF, fr. L *corallum*, *corallium*, fr. Gk *korallion*] **1 a** : a skeletal deposit produced esp. by certain anthozoan polyps: (1) : the richly red precious coral secreted by a gorgonian (*Corallium nobile*) (2) : any marine deposit like coral resulting from vital activities of various organisms (as hydrocorals, stony corals, certain algae, or bryozoans and worms) **b** : a polyp or polyp colony together with its membranes and skeleton, the majority being compound animals resembling small sea anemones united into branching, encrusting, or more or less solid colonies by a continuous sheet of tissue that together with the basal epidermis of the individual polyps secretes the largely calcareous skeletal framework, the colony enlarging by asexual reproduction of the individual polyps and new colonies being established by motile planulae produced by sexual reproduction — often used with a qualifying term ⟨rose ~⟩ ⟨mushroom ~⟩ ⟨brain ~⟩ **2** : a piece of coral; *esp* : a piece of coral or other material often fitted with small bells and given to infants as a plaything or teething ring **3** : something bright red in color: as **a** : a bright-reddish ovary (as that of a lobster or scallop); *also* : the cooked roe of a lobster **b** : a variable color averaging a deep pink that is yellower and duller than fiesta or begonia and yellower and darker than sweet William **c** *of textiles* : a strong pink that is yellower and stronger than carnation rose, bluer, stronger, and slightly lighter than rose d'Althaea, and lighter, stronger, and slightly yellower than sea pink

coral 1b: portion of a colony of red coral with polyps expanded

²**coral** \"\ *adj* **1** : of coral **2** : of the color coral red or coral

³**coral** \"\ *vt* -ED/-ING/-s [²*coral*] : to make coral red or coral in color

coral bead *n* **1** : JEQUIRITY BEAN **2** : the red fruit of the Carolina moonseed; *also* : CAROLINA MOONSEED

coral bean *n* **1** : MESCAL BEAN 2a **2** *or* **coral bean tree** : either of two tropical American coral trees: **a** : a small chiefly West Indian tree (*Erythrina corallodendron*) with deep scarlet flowers and black-spotted red seeds **b** : CEIBO 1

coralbells \'==,=\ *n pl but sing or pl in constr* : a perennial herb (*Heuchera sanguinea*) of the western U.S. that has flowers in feathery spikes and is used as an ornamental

coralberry \'==- — *see* BERRY\ *n* **1** : an American dwarf shrub (*Symphoricarpos orbiculatus*) bearing clusters of small white flowers succeeded by red berries **2** : any of certain plants of the genus *Ardisia* (esp. *A. crenulata*)

coral blow *n* : CORAL PLANT 2c

coral blush *n* : a moderate to strong yellowish pink

coralbush \'==,=\ *n* : an Australian shrub (*Templetonia retusa*) with brilliant scarlet flowers

coral cod *n* : a brilliant red-and-blue percoid food fish (*Plectropomus leopardus*) of Australian coral reefs

coral crab *n* **1** : either of two large yellow or reddish spider crabs (*Mithrax cornutus* and *M. hispidus*) widely distributed in shallow water from the Carolinas to southern Brazil **2** : the queen crab and related forms

coral creeper *n* : CORAL PEA

coral drops *n pl but sing or pl in constr* : a half-hardy Mexican bulbous herb (*Bessera elegans*) of the family Liliaceae that is often cultivated for its showy red and white flowers

coral evergreen *n* : a ground pine (*Lycopodium clavatum*)

coral fish *n* : any of numerous bright-colored fishes living among coral reefs (as members of the families Chaetodontidae, Apogonidae, and Pomacentridae)

coralflower \'==,==\ *n* **1** : CORAL PEA **2** : CHRIST'S-THORN

coral fungus *n* [so called fr. its growing in masses like coral] : any fungus of the family Clavariaceae

coral gem *n* : a small much-branched shrub (*Lotus bertheletii*) of the Canary islands

coral greenbrier *n* : a vine (*Smilax walteri*) of the southern U.S. with smooth branches and coral-red berries

coral head *n* : a rounded often knobby protuberance of coral-line material on the submerged portion of a coral reef or in close proximity to it

coral honeysuckle *n* : TRUMPET HONEYSUCKLE

coral insect *n* : a coral polyp

corall- *or* **coralli-** *or* **corallo-** *comb form* [NL, fr. L *corallium* — more at CORAL] : coral ⟨*coralli*form⟩ ⟨*corall*oid⟩ ⟨*Corall*orhiza⟩

coralla *pl of* CORALLUM

co·ral·lic \kə'ralik\ *adj* [L *corallum*, *corallium* coral + E *-ic*] : of or like coral

co·ral·li·dae \kə'ralə,dē\ [NL, fr. *Corallium*, type genus + *-idae*] *syn of* CORALLIIDAE

cor·al·lig·e·na \-'lijənə\ *n pl*, *cap* [NL, fr. *corall-* + *-gena* (neut. pl. of *-genus* -genous)] : a formerly recognized group more or less equivalent to Anthozoa and comprising coral-forming coelenterates

cor·al·li·idae \,kȯrə'līə,dē\ *n pl*, *cap* [NL, fr. *Corallium*, type genus + *-idae*] : a family of erect branching corals (order Gorgonacea) having a dense skeletal axis free or nearly free from horny material — see CORALLIUM

coral lily *n* : an Asiatic bulbous lily (*Lilium pumilum*) having scarlet showy flowers

coral limestone *n* : a rock consisting of the calcareous skeletons of coral polyps often cemented by calcium carbonate

cor·al·li·na \,kȯrə'līnə\ *n*, *cap* [NL, fr. LL, fem. of *corallinus* coral-red] : a genus of red algae typifying the family Corallinaceae

cor·al·li·na·ce·ae \ˌ==lə'nāsēˌē\ *n pl, cap* [NL, fr. *Corallina,* type genus + *-aceae*] **:** a family of red algae (order Cryptonemiales) of which the thallus becomes hard and brittle from the deposition of calcium carbonate which sometimes forms beautifully colored deposits like coral and contributes to reef formation — **cor·al·li·na·ceous** \ˌ==lə¦nāshəs\ *adj*

¹cor·al·line \'kȯrəˌlīn, 'kär-, -lən\ *adj* [F *corallin,* fr. MF, fr. LL *corallinus,* fr. L *corallium* coral + *-inus* -ine — more at CORAL] **1 :** like coral in color or form **:** of the color coral red or coral **2 :** composed of coral or corallines **3** [NL *Corallina*] **:** belonging to or resembling the genus *Corallina* or the family Corallinaceae

²coralline \"\; *in sense 3 usu* -ˌlēn, -lən\ *n* -s [F, fr. MF, fr. fem. of *corallin,* adj.] **1 :** a calcareous alga of the family Corallinaceae **2 :** any animal that resembles a coral; *esp* **:** a bryozoan or hydroid that forms delicate somewhat branching or frondose growths **3** *also* **cor·al·lin** \-ələn\ -s **a :** a poisonous yellow dye consisting of the sodium salt of aurin — called also *yellow coralline* **b :** AURIN **c :** ROSOLIC ACID **a d :** a red dye derived from aurin — called also *red coralline*

coralline limestone *n* **:** CORAL LIMESTONE

cor·al·li·ta *or* **cor·al·i·ta** \ˌkȯrə'lēd·ə\ *n* -s [modif. of AmerSp *coralito, coralillo,* dim. of Sp *coral,* fr. L *corallum* — more at CORAL] **:** CORALVINE

cor·al·lite \'kȯrəˌlīt\ *n* -s [ISV *corall-* + *-ite*] **:** the skeleton of a single coral polyp consisting of a septate investing wall or theca and an underlying basal plate and being imbedded in the general structure of the corallum

co·ral·li·um \kə'ralēəm\ *n, cap* [NL, fr. L, coral — more at CORAL] **:** a genus (the type of the family Coralliidae) of corals having the skeletal axis very hard and red or pink and including the red coral of commerce

cor·al·loid \'kȯrəˌlȯid, 'kär-\ *or* **cor·al·loid·al** \¦==¦lȯidᵊl\ *adj* [ISV *corall-* + *-oid, -oidal*] **:** having the form or appearance of coral **:** branching like coral ⟨a ~ root⟩

cor·al·lo·rhi·za \ˌkȯrə(ˌ)lō'rīzə\ *n, cap* [NL, fr. *corall-* + *-rhiza*] **:** a genus of leafless root-parasitic or saprophytic orchids of wide distribution in temperate regions having small purplish or yellowish racemose flowers with an entire or lobed lip

co·ral·lum \kə'raləm\ *n, pl* **coral·la** \-lə\ [L *corallum, corallium* coral — more at CORAL] **:** the entire skeleton of a compound coral — compare CORALLITE

co·ral·lus \-ləs\ [NL, prob. fr. L *corallum* coral] *syn of* BOA

coral orchid *n* **:** a plant of the genus *Corallorhiza*

coral pea *n* **:** an Australian plant of the genus *Kennedya* having scarlet flowers (esp. *K. prostrata*)

coral pink *n* **:** a moderate yellowish pink that is redder, lighter, and stronger than dusty pink, redder and darker than peach pink, and redder and deeper than average peach

coral plant *n* **1** *obs* **:** a coral like a plant **2 a :** a much-cultivated East Indian plant (*Jatropha multifida*) with showy scarlet flowers and deeply incised leaves **b :** any plant of the genus *Erythrina* (esp. *E. corallodendron*) **c :** an essentially leafless Mexican shrub (*Russelia equisetiformis*) like a rush with bright-red flowers — called also *coral blow*

coral rag *n* **:** a calcareous rock composed largely of coral-reef deposits and used locally in Britain as a building stone

coral red *n* **:** a variable color averaging a strong reddish orange that is redder and deeper than fire red and yellower and paler than paprika or poppy — compare CORAL 3b

coral reef *n* **:** a reef often of great extent made up chiefly of fragments of corals, coral sands, algal and other organic deposits, and the solid limestone resulting from their consolidation — see ATOLL

coral-reef limestone \'==¦=-\ *n* **:** a limestone composed of reef-forming coral **:** a fossil coral reef

coralroot \'==ˌ=\ *n* **:** a plant of the genus *Corallorhiza*

coral rose *n* **:** a variable color averaging a deep yellowish pink to moderate reddish orange

corals *pl of* CORAL, *pres 3d sing of* CORAL

coral shrub *n* **:** a low New Zealand shrub (*Helichrysum coralloides*) with stout tubercled white-woolly stems

coral snake *n* **1 :** any of a number of venomous elapid snakes with some red in their pattern: as **a :** any of several brilliantly banded in red, black, and yellow or white and extremely venomous but sluggish and retiring New World snakes (genus *Micrurus*) widely distributed in So. and Central America with two species (*M. fulvius* and *M.,* or *Micruroides, euryxanthus*) extending into the southern U.S. — called also *harlequin snake* **b :** any snake of an Indian genus (*Callophis*) that is reddish beneath with variously patterned dorsal surface **c :** a small venomous but harmless Australian snake (*Rhynchoelaps australis*) brilliantly marked with black and white on a red ground **d :** a small widely distributed arboreal snake (*Aspidelaps lubricus*) of southern Africa handsomely banded with black and orange bars **2 :** any of several nonvenomous snakes resembling those of the genus *Micrurus:* as **a :** KING SNAKE **b :** a common So. American aniliid (*Anilius scytale*)

coral spot *n* **:** a disease of trees and shrubs caused by a fungus (*Nectria cinnabarina*) which produces cankers on the twigs and branches

coral sumac *n* **:** POISONWOOD 1

coral tree *n* **:** any of numerous trees and shrubs constituting the genus *Erythrina,* having scarlet to coral red flowers and often bright red seeds, and being cultivated in warm regions as an ornamental: as **a :** a small thorny tree (*E. indica*) of tropical Asia and northern Australia **b :** CORAL BEAN 2a **c :** KAFFIR BOOM

coralvine \'==ˌ=\ *n* **:** a West Indian climbing plant (*Antigonon leptopus*) grown widely as an ornamental, in some areas being evergreen, and having cordate leaves and clusters of pinkish flowers succeeded by brightly colored veiny fruit

coralwood \'==ˌ=\ *n* **:** RED SANDALWOOD 2

coralwort \'==ˌ=\ *n* **1 :** any plant of the genus *Dentaria* having a knotted white rootstock; *esp* **:** a common European toothwort (*D. bulbifera*) **2 :** CORALROOT

Cor·a·mine \'kȯrəˌmēn, 'kōr-, -mən\ *trademark* — used for nikethamide

co·ram ju·di·ce \ˌkō(ˌ)ram¦yüdəˌkā, -ōrəm-, -¦jüdəˌsē\ *adv (or adj)* [L, lit., before a judge] **:** before a judge having jurisdiction

¹coram no·bis \-¦nōbəs\ *adj (or adv)* [NL, lit., before us] **1** *obs, of a writ of error* **:** for the review in the King's Bench of its own judgments as to errors of fact **2 :** based upon an alleged error of fact — used of a writ of review in some jurisdictions

²coram nobis \"\ *n* **:** a writ of error or a writ of review coram nobis ⟨some doubt as to the continued availability of *coram nobis* in the federal courts —*Harvard Law Rev.*⟩

coram non judice \-¦nōn¦-, -nän-\ *adv (or adj)* [ML, lit., before one not a judge] **:** before a judge not competent or without jurisdiction

coram pa·ri·bus \-¦pärēbus, -pa(a)r-, -bəs\ *adv (or adj)* [ML] **:** before one's peers

coram po·pu·lo \-¦pōpüˌlō, -päp-, -p(y)ə,-\ *or* **coram pu·bli·co** \-¦püblēˌkō, -pəb-, -lə,-\ *adv (or adj)* [L] **:** in public ⟨I did not . . . tear my hair *coram populo* over my loss —Joseph Conrad⟩

cor an·glais \ˌkȯrō|n'glā, -räl, |ŋ'-\ *n* [F] **1 :** ENGLISH HORN **2 :** an organ stop with tone quality similar to that of the English horn

cor·a·nine \'kȯrəˌnīn, -nən, -ˌnēn\ *n, pl* **coranine** *or* **cor·anines** *usu cap* **:** COREE

¹co·ran·to \kə'ran(ˌ)tō, kō'-, -rän-\ *n, pl* **corantos** *or* **corantoes** [modif. of F *courante*] **:** COURANTE

²coranto *n, pl* **corantos** *or* **corantoes** [modif. of F *courant* — more at COURANT] *obs* **:** ¹COURANT

coras *pl of* CORA

coraveca *usu cap, var of* CORABECA

-co·rax \kōˌraks, kəˌr-\ *n comb form* [NL, fr. Gk *korax* — more at RAVEN] **:** crow **:** raven ⟨Phalacrocorax⟩

cor·ban *or* **kor·ban** \'kȯrˌban, -bän, ='=\ *n* -s [Heb *qorbān* offering] *among the ancient Hebrews* **:** any sacrifice or oblation; *specif* **:** an offering devoted to God particularly in fulfillment of a vow and therefore not to be appropriated to any other purpose

cor·beau \(')kȯ(r)¦bō\ *n* -s [F, crow, raven, fr. OF *corbel*] **:** a greenish black

cor·beil *or* **cor·beille** \'kȯ(r)bəl, *F* kȯrbeʸ\ *n* -s [F *corbeille,* lit., basket, fr. LL *corbicula,* dim. of L *corbis* basket; perh. akin to Gk *karphos* dry stalk — more at HARP] **1 :** a sculptured basket of flowers or fruit as an architectural decoration **2** *usu corbeille* **:** a basket of flowers or fruit

¹cor·bel \'kȯ(r)bəl\ *n* -s [ME, fr. MF, dim. of *corp* raven, fr. L *corvus* — more at RAVEN] **:** an architectural member which projects from within a wall and supports a superincumbent weight; *esp* **:** one that is stepped upward and outward from a vertical surface

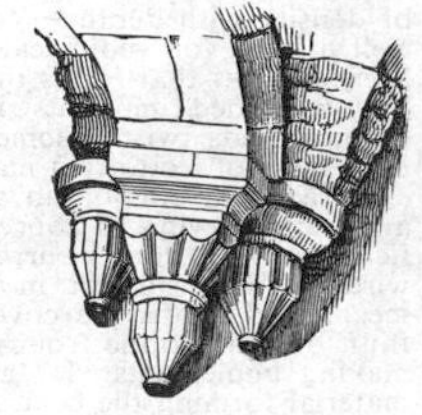
corbels

²corbel \"\ *vb* **corbeled** *or* **corbelled; corbeled** *or* **corbelled; corbeling** *or* **corbelling** \-b(ə)liŋ\ **corbels** *vt* **:** to furnish with or make into a corbel for decoration or as a support — often used with *out* ⟨resting on two rows of ~*ed* brick courses —*Amer. Guide Series: Minn.*⟩ ⟨with oak posts ~*ed* to form bold brackets —*Antiques*⟩ ~ *vi* **:** to project from a vertical surface on corbels or upward and outward in the manner of a stepped corbel ⟨a pulpit ~*ing* out over our heads⟩

corbel arch *or* **corbeled arch** *n* **:** a structure which spans an opening like an arch by having successive courses of masonry project farther inward as they rise on each side of the gap

corbeling *or* **corbelling** *n* -s **1 a :** a member that serves as a corbel; *esp* **:** continuous corbeled masonry **b :** ornamental molding having steps like a corbel **2 a :** the use of the corbel as a supporting member **b :** the act of constructing a stepped corbel

corbel-step \'==ˌ=\ *n* [by alter.] **:** CORBIESTEP

corbel table *n* **:** a projecting course (as of masonry) resting on a horizontal row of corbels

corbel vault *n* **:** a corbeled covering like a vault

¹cor·bic·u·la \kȯ(r)'bik(y)ələ\ *n, pl* **corbicu·lae** \-ˌlē, -ˌlī\ [NL, fr. LL, little basket — more at CORBEIL] **:** POLLEN BASKET

²corbicula \"\ *n, cap* [NL, fr. LL, little basket] **:** a genus (the type of the family Corbiculidae of the suborder Submytilacea) of small edible mussels native to fresh or brackish waters of eastern Asia but also introduced in parts of California

cor·bic·u·late \(')kȯ(r)¦bik(y)ələt, -ˌlāt\ *adj* [NL ¹*corbicula* + E *-ate*] **:** having corbiculae

¹cor·bie \'kȯrbī\ *n* -ES [ME, modif. (influenced by *-ie*) of OF *corbin,* fr. L *corvinus* of a raven — more at CORVINE] *chiefly Scot* **:** RAVEN, CARRION CROW

²corbie \'kȯ(r)bē\ *n* -s [prob. native name in Tasmania] **:** the subterranean larva of a Tasmanian ghost moth (*Oncopera intricata*) that feeds on the roots of grasses and is a destructive pest of pastureland

corbie gable *n* [*corbiestep* + *gable*] **:** a gable having corbiesteps

cor·bie·step \'kȯ(r)bēˌ-\ *n* [¹*corbie* + *step*] **:** one of a series of steps which rise toward the ridgepole of a building and terminate the upper part of a gable wall

gable with corbiesteps

cor·bi·na \kȯ(r)'bēnə\ *or* **cor·vi·na** \-'vē-\ *n* -s [MexSp, fr. Sp, an acanthopterygian fish, fr. fem. of *corvino* of a raven, ravenlike, fr. L *corvinus;* fr. the color — more at CORVINE] **1 :** a bluish gray dark-spotted whiting (*Menticirrhus undulatus*) that is favored by surf casters along the California coast **2 :** any of several weakfishes **3 :** a croaker (*Micropogon undulatus*) popular as a food and game fish on the Atlantic coast of No. America

cor·bin bone \'kȯ(r)bənˌ-\ *n* [OF *corbin* raven] **:** the caudal segment of the sternum of a deer

cor bo·vi·num \ˌkȯrbō'vīnəm\ *n* [NL, lit., ox heart] **:** a greatly enlarged heart

cor·bu·li·dae \kȯ(r)'byüləˌdē\ *n pl, cap* [NL, fr. *Corbula,* type genus (fr. L *corbula* little basket, dim. of *corbis* basket) + *-idae* — more at CORBEIL] **:** a family of bivalve mollusks (suborder Myacea) comprising the basket shells

cor·cass \'kȯrkəs\ *n* -ES [modif. of IrGael *corcach,* fr. MIr; akin to Gk *koryza* nasal mucus — more at CORYZA] *Ireland* **:** a marsh or mud flat along the bank of a tidal river

cor·cho·rus \'kȯ(r)kərəs\ *n, cap* [NL, fr. L, a kind of pulse, fr. Gk *korchoros,* a kind of pimpernel (*Anagallis*)] **:** a widely distributed genus of tropical herbs or undershrubs (family Tiliaceae) having large leaves and yellow flowers in cymose clusters

cor·cir \'kȯ(r)kə(r)\ *or* **corke** \'kȯ(ə)rk, -ō(ə)k\ *or* **cor·ker** \'kȯ(r)kə(r)\ *n* -s [ScGael *corcur* purple, fr. L *purpura* — more at PURPLE] **:** ARCHIL 3

¹cord \'kȯ(ə)rd, -ō(ə)d\ *n* -s [ME, fr. OF *corde,* fr. L *chorda* catgut, chord, cord, fr. Gk *chordē* — more at YARN] **1 a :** a long slender flexible roughly cylindrical construction usu. of several threads or yarns twisted or woven together and used for tying, binding, or connecting **:** a small rope **:** STRING **b :** the hangman's rope ⟨O, the charity of a penny ~ —Shak.⟩ **c** (1) **:** any of various strings for communicating motion in a pattern-weaving or a Jacquard loom (2) **:** a space on a design paper representing a warp thread **d :** a heavy string used as a material (as in braid or cordonnet) **e :** any of the heavy strings or small hemp ropes usu. four to six in number which extend across the backbone of a book, which are usu. attached to the board of the cover, and to which the sections are handsewn — called also *band* **f :** a heavy thread or firm yarn made by tightly twisting together two or more threads or plied yarns and used often in the manufacture of heavy-duty fabrics **g :** one of the round plies forming a multistrand thread ⟨sewing thread is usually *3-cord* or *6-cord*⟩ **2 :** a moral, spiritual, or emotional bond or influence by which one is held, drawn, or sustained as if by a cord ⟨the interwoven ~*s* of affection and confidence that wind between her and her husband —Roger Angell⟩ **3 a :** an anatomical structure resembling a cord; *esp* **:** TENDON, NERVE — see SPERMATIC CORD, SPINAL CORD, UMBILICAL CORD, VOCAL CORDS **b :** a small flexible insulated electrical cable usu. consisting of a pair of insulated stranded wires twisted together and having a plug at one or both ends used to connect a lamp, electric iron, toaster, or other appliance with a receptacle **c :** STRIA 3 **4 a :** any of various units of quantity for wood cut for fuel or pulp; *esp* **:** a unit equal to a stack 4x4x8 foot or 128 cubic feet **b :** a unit for rough building stone equal to 128 cubic feet **5 a :** a rib like a cord on a textile **b** (1) **:** a fabric made with such ribs or a garment made of such a fabric — compare CORDUROY, WHIPCORD (2) **cords** *pl* **:** trousers made of such fabric **c :** CORD TIRE **d :** a composition and fabric material used in the outsole of a work shoe or sport shoe

²cord \"\ *vt* -ED/-ING/-S [ME *corden,* fr. *cord,* n.] **1 :** to tie, bind, fasten, or connect with a cord ⟨package already . . . ~*ed* lengthwise —R.V.Morse⟩ **2 :** to pile up (as wood) in cords; *also* **:** to pile deeply ⟨rooms ~*ed* nine feet deep with gold and emeralds —Bernard DeVoto⟩ **3 :** to ornament or finish with cord **4 :** to connect the treadles of (a hand loom) by cords with the leaves of the heddles so as to produce the pattern

cord·age \-dij, -dēj\ *n* -s [MF, fr. *corde* + *-age*] **1 :** ropes or cords; *esp* **:** the ropes in the rigging of a ship **2 :** the number of cords (as of wood) on a given area

cordage tree *n* **:** an Australasian tree (*Plagianthus pulchellus*) the bark of which was formerly used esp. for tying fence posts and rafters

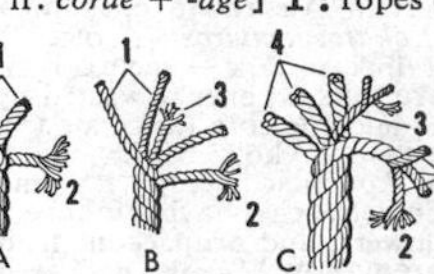

cordage 1: hawser-laid rope, *A;* shroud-laid rope, *B;* typical three-strand four-hawser cable, *C;* *1* strands; *2* yarns; *3* core; *4* ropes

cor·dai·ta·ce·ae \ˌkȯ(r)-dāˌī'tāsēˌē, -ˌdī't-\ *n pl, cap* [NL, fr. *Cordaites,* type genus + *-aceae*] **:** a family of chiefly Paleozoic plants (order Cordaitales) of which *Cordaites* is the chief and typical genus — **cor·dai·ta·ceous** \ˌkȯ(r)dāˌī¦tāshəs, -ˌdī¦t-\ *adj*

cor·dai·ta·les \ˌkȯ(r)dāˌī'tāˌlēz, -ˌdī't-\ *n pl, cap* [NL, fr. *Cordaites* + *-ales*] **:** an order of extinct gymnospermous plants first known from the Pennsylvanian and probably extinct since the Mesozoic that had tall arborescent trunks structurally comparable to or more advanced than those of cycads and branched in the upper part, long simple parallel-veined leaves spirally arranged, and separate male and female strobili — see CORDAITACEAE — **cor·dai·ta·le·an** \¦=(=)ˌ=¦tālēən\ *adj*

cor·dai·te·an \¦kȯ(r)dā¦īd·ēən, (')kȯ(r)¦dīd·-\ *adj* [NL *Cordaites* + E *-an*] **:** of, relating to, or characteristic of the genus *Cordaites*

cor·dai·tes \ˌkȯ(r)dā'īd·ˌēz, kȯ(r)'dīd·-\ *n, cap* [NL, fr. August K.J.*Corda* †1849 Bohemian botanist + L *-ites* -ite] **:** the type genus of Cordaitaceae comprising tall Paleozoic forest trees that superficially resembled the modern screw pines but structurally were intermediate in some respects between the cycadophytes and the more advanced coniferophytes

cor·date \'kȯ(r)dət, -ˌdāt\ *adj* [NL *cordatus,* fr. L *cord-, cor* heart + *-atus* -ate — more at HEART] **1 :** shaped like a heart ⟨a ~ shell⟩ **2 :** having a rounded base with a notch at the point of attachment ⟨a ~ leaf⟩ — see LEAF illustration — **cor·date·ly** *adv*

cor·dax \'kȯ(r)ˌdaks\ *var of* KORDAX

cord connector *n* **:** CONNECTOR 2c(1)

corde \kȯ(r)'dā\ *n* -s [F *cordé,* past part. of *corder* to cord, fr. *corde,* n., cord — more at CORD] **:** cord that is usu. covered with silk or rayon and used esp. for crocheting handbags

cord·ed \'kȯ(r)dəd\ *adj* [ME, fr. past part. of *corden*] **1 a :** made of or provided with cords or ridges or markings ⟨a ~ ladder —Shak.⟩; *specif* **:** having muscles or tendons standing up in ridges like cords ⟨face . . . drawn and pallid, with a ~ neck —Ellen Glasgow⟩ **b** *of muscles* **:** tense or taut ⟨the ~ muscles relaxed⟩ **c** *of ply cordage* **:** with the plies given an extra amount of twist **2 :** bound, fastened, or wound about with cords **3 a :** striped, ribbed, or otherwise decorated with cord or lines like cords **:** TWILLED ⟨a ~ cloth⟩ **:** finished with cord ⟨a ~ seam⟩ ⟨~ lace⟩ **b** *of pottery* **:** having a decoration made by pressing cords into the clay before firing

cor·de·lière \ˌkȯ(r)dᵊl'ye(ə)r\ *n* -s [F, fr. MF, knotted rope worn by Cordeliers, fr. *Cordelier,* a kind of Franciscan friar, fr. *cordel,* dim. of *corde* cord, rope — more at CORD] *heraldry* **:** a knotted cord (as around the escutcheon of a widow)

¹cor·delle \'kȯ(r)ˌdel, '=ˌ=, '=dᵊl\ *n* -s [F, dim. of *corde*] **:** a towline esp. as used on keelboats on U.S. and Canadian rivers

²cordelle \"\ *vb* -ED/-ING/-S **:** to tow by a cordelle

cor·de·nuit \ˌkȯ(r)dən'wē, -dᵊn-\ *n* -s [F, lit., night horn] **:** a soft-toned labial organ stop of metal or wood usu. of 8= foot pitch

cord·er \'kȯ(r)də(r)\ *n* -s **1 :** one that cords; *specif* **:** one that stitches cord or braid on fabric **2 :** TUCKER 1a(2)

cord foot *n* **:** a quantity of wood equal to a stack 4x4x1 foot or 16 cubic feet

cord glottis *n* **:** the opening between the vocal cords proper as distinguished from the whisper glottis — called also *voice glottis*

cordgrass \'=ˌ=\ *n* **:** a grass of the genus *Spartina*

¹cordia *pl of* COR

²cor·dia \'kȯ(r)dēə\ *n, cap* [NL, fr. Euricius *Cordus* †1535 and his son Valerius *Cordus* †1544 Ger. scholars + NL *-ia*] **:** a large genus of chiefly tropical shrubs and trees (family Boraginaceae) that have fleshy often edible fruits and wood varying from dense, heavy, and dark to spongy, light, and pale, that are often pleasantly scented, and that have considerable use in cabinetmaking and general construction

¹cor·dial \'kȯ(r)jəl; *US sometimes and Brit usu* 'kȯ(r)dyəl *or* -dēəl\ *adj* [ME, fr. ML *cordialis,* fr. L *cord-, cor* heart + *-ialis* -ial — more at HEART] **1 :** of, belonging to, or proceeding from the heart **:** VITAL ⟨opened my left side and took from thence a rib with ~ spirits warm and life-blood streaming fresh —John Milton⟩ **2 :** tending to revive, cheer, or invigorate ⟨a ~ medicine or drink⟩ ⟨drink this ~ wine —S.T.Coleridge⟩ **:** invigorating or cheering ⟨for fainting age what ~ drop remains —Alexander Pope⟩ **3 a :** sincerely or deeply felt **:** HEARTFELT, HEARTY ⟨showed a ~ regard for his visitor's comfort⟩ ⟨a ~ and active dislike for both his parents —Samuel Butler †1902⟩ **b :** showing warm and often hearty friendliness, favor, or approval ⟨they gave us a ~ reception, and a hearty supper, and we sat up talking until a late hour —Herman Melville⟩ ⟨relations between white and black . . . are not merely good: they are ~ —*Economist*⟩ ⟨his argument had ~ support from the experts⟩ **syn** see GRACIOUS

²cordial \"\ *n* -s **1 a :** an invigorating and stimulating medicine, food, or drink ⟨the peppermint water and other ~*s* —Thomas DeQuincey⟩ **b :** something that comforts, gladdens, and exhilarates ⟨charms to my sight, and ~*s* to my mind —John Dryden⟩ **2 :** LIQUEUR; *sometimes* **:** a somewhat sharp and spicy drink or one made by infusion of fruit juice or wine with spirits

cor·di·al·i·ty \ˌkȯ(r)jē'aləd·ē, kȯ(r)'jal-, -ətē, -i; *US sometimes and Brit usu* ˌkȯ(r)dē'al- *or* -d'yal-\ *n* -ES [F *cordialité,* fr. MF, fr. *cordial* (fr. ML *cordialis*) + *-ité* -ity] **:** cordial quality **:** sincere affection and kindness **:** warmth of regard ⟨the ~ of his greeting was pleasant to his guests⟩ **:** good will or good feeling **:** FAVOR ⟨the city's ~ to new industry⟩

cor·dial·ly \'kȯ(r)jəlē, -li; *US sometimes and Brit usu* 'kȯ(r)dyə- *or* -dēə-\ *adv* **1 :** in a cordial manner **:** with sincere good will ⟨welcomed his friends ~⟩ ⟨~ yours⟩ **2 :** with zeal **:** vigorously and sincerely **:** EMPHATICALLY ⟨Jefferson and Hamilton ~ disliked each other —H.E.Scudder⟩

cor·dial·ness \-əlnəs\ *n* -ES **:** the quality or state of being cordial **:** CORDIALITY

cordier *comparative of* CORDY

cor·di·er·ite \'kȯ(r)dēəˌrīt\ *n* -s [F, fr. Pierre L. A. *Cordier* †1861 Fr. geologist, who first described it + F *-ite*] **:** an orthorhombic mineral of various shades of blue with vitreous luster and strong dichroism consisting of a silicate of aluminum, iron, and magnesium $(Mg,Fe)_2Al_4Si_5O_{18}$ easily altered by exposure (hardness 7–7.5, sp. gr. 2.60–2.66)

cordiest *superlative of* CORDY

cor·di·form \'kȯrdəˌfȯrm\ *adj* [F *cordiforme,* fr. L *cord-, cors* heart + F *-iforme* -iform — more at HEART] **:** shaped like a heart

cordiform tendon *n* **:** the central tendon of the diaphragm

cor·dil·le·ra \ˌkȯ(r)dᵊl'erə, -l'ye- *also* kȯ(r)'dilərə\ *n* -s [Sp, fr. *cordilla,* dim. of *cuerda* rope, string, line of mountain peaks, fr. L *chorda* cord — more at CORD] **:** a group of mountain ranges forming a mountain system of great linear extent often consisting of a number of more or less parallel chains ⟨the No. American ~ includes all the mountains from the eastern face of the Rocky mountains to the Pacific ocean —W.J.Miller⟩ — **cor·dil·le·ran** \¦kȯ(r)dᵊl¦erən, -l¦ye-, (')=¦dilər-\ *adj*

cording *n* -s **1 :** cord often covered with fabric for decorative effects **2 :** the act or result of ornamenting with cord

cording quires *n* **:** the two outside quires of a ream of paper

cord·ite \'kȯrˌdīt\ *n* -s [¹*cord* + *-ite*] **:** a smokeless powder composed of nitroglycerin, guncotton, and mineral jelly usu. gelatinized by the addition of acetone and pressed out into cords resembling brown twine

cordleaf \'=ˌ=\ *n* **:** any plant of the family Restionaceae; *esp* **:** a plant of the genus *Restio*

cord moss *n* **:** any moss of the genus *Funaria; esp* **:** the common moss (*F. hygrometrica*) that is particularly frequent on recently burned-over soil and that has a twisted hygroscopic seta which uncoils when moist

¹cór·do·ba *or* **cor·do·ba** \'kȯ(r)dəbə, -əvə; -(ˌ)bä, -(ˌ)vä\ *adj, usu cap* [fr. *Córdoba,* Spain & *Córdoba,* Argentina] **1** *or* **cor·do·va** \"\ **:** of or from the city of Córdoba, Spain **:** of the kind or style prevalent in Córdoba, Spain **:** CORDOVAN **2 :** of or from the city of Córdoba, Argentina **:** of the kind or style prevalent in Córdoba, Argentina

²cordoba \"\ *n, pl* **cordobas** [Sp *córdoba,* after Francisco Fernández de *Córdoba* †1526 Sp. explorer] **1 :** the basic monetary unit of Nicaragua — see MONEY table **2 :** a silver coin struck in 1912 representing one cordoba but later withdrawn from circulation **3 :** a currency note representing one cordoba

[1]**cor·do·bán** \ˌkȯ(r)dəˈbän; ˈ⸗⸗(ˌ)bän, -(ˌ)vän, -bən, -vən\ *n* -s [Sp — more at CORDOVAN] : cordovan leather

[2]**cordoban** \"\ *adj, usu cap* [Sp *cordobán*, fr. *Córdoba*, Argentina + *-án* (as in *cordobán* of Córdoba, Spain)] : of or belonging to Córdoba, Argentina

[1]**cor·don** \ˈkȯrdᵊn, -ȯ(ə)d-, -ˌdän; *in senses 2a–c usu* -dᵊn\ *n* -s [MF, dim. of *corde* string, rope — more at CORD] **1 a** : an ornamental cord, braid, lace, or string used esp. on costumes: as (1) : an ornamental cord encircling a heraldic shield esp. of an ecclesiastical dignitary (2) : a cord or ribbon worn as a badge of honor or as a decoration of an order of knighthood — see GRAND CORDON **b** : STRINGCOURSE **2 a** : a line or series of troops or of military posts placed at intervals and enclosing an area to prevent passage **b** : a barrier of any kind operating to close off, restrict, or control access or communication ⟨a traffic ~ around the business center of a city⟩ ⟨protected from the mainland by a ~ of seven hills —Horace Sutton⟩ **c** : a line or circle of persons or objects around any person or place ⟨a ~ of police kept back the crowd⟩ ⟨a ~ of ramshackle market stalls was thrown around the circular facade to accommodate the provision merchants —Lewis Mumford⟩ **d** : CORDON SANITAIRE **3** : an espalier trained to a single horizontal shoot or to two opposed shoots so as to form one line

[2]**cordon** \-dᵊn, -ˌdän; *in sense 2 usu* -dᵊn\ *vt* -ED/-ING/-S [MF *cordonner*, fr. *cordon*, n.] **1** : to ornament with a cordon **2** : to form a protective or restrictive cordon around (an area) : close to communication with the outside by a cordon — often used with *off* ⟨were not allowed inside the front yard, which was ~*ed off* by the police —Marcia Davenport⟩

cor·do·na·zo \ˌkȯ(r)dᵊnˈä(ˌ)sō\ *n* -s [MexSp, short for Sp *cordonazo de San Francisco* autumnal storm, lit., lash of St. Francis (around whose birthday — Oct. 4 — such storms occur); *cordonazo* fr. *cordón* rope worn by friars (fr. OSp, fr. OF *cordon*) + *-azo* (suffix denoting a blow) — more at CORDON] : a southerly hurricane wind that occurs along the west coast of Mexico when a tropical cyclone passes northward offshore

cor·don bleu \ˌkȯrdōⁿˈblœ; *esp in senses 2 and 3* ˌkȯrdᵊnˈblü *or* -(ˌ)dänˈ-\ *n, pl* **cordon bleus** \-œ(z), -üz\ *also* **cordons bleus** \"\ [F, lit., blue cordon] **1** : the blue ribbon worn as a decoration by members of the old order of the Holy Ghost **2 a** : a person eminent for his rank or authority; *specif* : a cook of great skill **3** *also* **cordon bleu finch** : any of several African waxbills (genus *Uraeginthus*) that have a clear bright blue breast and tail and drab back and underparts and that are often kept as cage birds

cor·don·net \ˌkȯ(r)dᵊnˈet, -nˈā, ˈ⸗⸗ˌ⸗\ *n* -s [F, dim. of *cordon*] : a thread or small cord used to edge braid, to make tassels and fringes, or to outline the design of lace and embroidery

cor·don sa·ni·taire \kȯrdōⁿsänēter\ *n, pl* **cordon sanitaires** *also* **cordons sanitaires** \"\ [F, lit., sanitary cordon (quarantine line)] : a chain of nations designed as a protection or buffer against a nation considered potentially aggressive or ideologically dangerous

cordotomy *var of* CHORDOTOMY

cordova *usu cap, var of* CORDOBA

[1]**cor·do·van** \ˈkȯ(r)dəvən\ *adj* [OSp *cordovān* (now *cordobán*), Mozarabic alter. of OSp *cordovano*, fr. *Córdova* (now *Córdoba*), Spain + Sp *-ano* -an] **1** *usu cap* : of or belonging to Córdoba, esp. Córdoba, Spain **2** : made of cordovan leather

[2]**cordovan** \"\ *n* -s [Sp *cordobán*, fr. *cordobán*, adj.] **1** *cap* : a native or resident of Córdoba, esp. Córdoba, Spain **2 a** : a soft fine-grained colored leather manufactured of split horsehides, goatskins, or pigskins **b** : leather tanned from the inner layer of horsehide from the rump area and distinguished for its nonporosity, density, and long-wearing qualities — called also *shell cordovan* **3 a** : a dark grayish brown that is yellower than average chocolate brown and yellower and slightly less strong than African brown **b** : a variable color averaging a dark grayish red that is darker and slightly yellower than average rose brown

cords *pl of* CORD, *pres 3d sing of* CORD

cord switch *n* : a snap switch mounted at the end of a cord suspended from a ceiling fixture — called also *pendant switch*

cord tire *n* : a pneumatic tire having a carcass constructed of cords running parallel to each other and crossed by small threads

cor·du·la \kȯ(r)ˈd(y)üla; ˈkȯ(r)d(y)ələ, -(r)jələ\ *n, cap* [NL, prob. irreg. fr. LGk *kordylē* club, fr. Gk, bump, swelling; prob. fr. the shape of the column — more at CARDINAL] : a large genus of tropical Old World terrestrial orchids resembling the common lady's-slippers

[1]**cor·du·roy** \ˈkȯ(r)dəˌrȯi *sometimes* -(r)dyə,- *or* -(r)jə,-\ *n* -s *often attrib* [earlier *corderoy*, perh. fr. the name *Corderoy*] **1 a** : a cut-pile fabric with vertical ribs or wales usu. made of cotton in plain or twill weave in various weights with up to 22 wales per inch and used for clothing and interior decoration ⟨a ~ jacket⟩ **b corduroys** *pl* : trousers of corduroy **2 a** : CORDUROY ROAD **b** : the material or structure of such a road **c** : a road surface ribbed transversely

[2]**corduroy** \"\ *vt* -ED/-ING/-S **1** : to build (a road) of logs laid side by side transversely **2** : to build a corduroy road across (as a swamp)

corduroy road *n* : a road built of logs laid side by side transversely and usu. used in low or swampy places

cord·wain \ˈkȯrdˌwān\ *n* -s [ME *cordwane*, fr. MF *cordoan*, fr. OSp *cordován* (now *cordobán*) — more at CORDOVAN] *archaic* : cordovan leather

cord·wain·er \-nər\ *n* -s [ME *cordewaner*, fr. OF *cordoanier*, fr. *cordoan*] **1** *archaic* : a worker in cordovan leather **2** : SHOEMAKER

cord·wain·ery \-nərē\ *n* -ES : SHOEMAKING

cord·wind·er \ˈkȯrdˌwīndər\ *n* -s [by folk etymology] : CORDWAINER

cordwood \ˈ⸗ˌ⸗\ *n* [[1]*cord* (measure) + *wood*] : wood piled up or sold in cords : wood for fuel cut to the length of four feet so as to be readily measurable in cords; *also* : standing timber of such size and quality as to be fit only for burning as fuel

cordy \ˈkȯrdē, -ȯ(ə)dē, -di\ *adj* -ER/-EST **1** : of or like cord : having cords or parts resembling cords **2** : of a thready or striated appearance

cor·dy·ceps \ˈkȯ(r)dəˌseps\ *n, cap* [NL, irreg. fr. LGk *kordylē* club (fr. Gk, bump, swelling) + L *-ceps* (fr. *caput* head) — more at CARDINAL, HEAD] : a genus of ascomycetous fungi (family Hypocreaceae) parasitic in insect larvae and ultimately converting the whole body into a sclerotium — see AWETO

cor·dyl·i·dae \kȯ(r)ˈdiləˌdē\ *n pl, cap* [NL, fr. *Cordylus*, type genus (fr. Gk *kordylos* water newt) + *-idae*; prob. akin to Gk *kordylē* bump, swelling — more at CARDINAL] : a small family of spiny ovoviviparous African lizards somewhat resembling tiny crocodiles

cor·dy·li·ne \ˌkȯ(r)dᵊlˈī(ˌ)nē\ *n* [NL, irreg. fr. LGk *kordylē* club, fr. Gk, bump, swelling; fr. the stout caudex] **1** *cap* : a genus of tropical Old World plants (family Liliaceae) having a creeping rhizome and often included in the genus *Dracaena* but distinguished by the single ovule in each cell of the ovary and by the solitary pedicles — see TI; compare DRACAENA **2** -s : any tree of the genus *Cordyline*

cor·dyl·ite \ˈkȯ(r)dᵊlˌīt\ *n* -s [ISV *cordyl-* (fr. LGk *kordylē* club) + *-ite*; orig. formed as G *kordylit*] : a mineral (Ce,La)$_2$Ba(CO$_3$)$_3$F$_2$ consisting of a carbonate and fluoride of cerium, lanthanum, and barium

cor·dy·lo·bia \ˌkȯ(r)dᵊlˈōbēə\ *n, cap* [NL] : a genus of true flies (family Calliphoridae) including the African tumbu fly

cor·dy·lu·ri·dae \ˌkȯ(r)dᵊlˈ(y)u̇rəˌdē\ [NL, fr. *Cordylura*, type genus (fr. LGk *kordylē* club + Gk *oura* tail) + *-idae* — more at -UROUS] *syn of* SCATOPHAGIDAE

[1]**core** \ˈkō(ə)r, -ȯ(ə)r,-ōə,-ȯ(ə)\ *n* -s [ME] **1** : the central and often foundational part of a body, mass, or construction usu. distinct from the enveloping part by a difference in nature or by being cut out or separated ⟨the ~ of a storm⟩ ⟨~ of a city⟩ ⟨~ of a flame⟩: as **a** : the central portion in certain fruits (as the hard central section of a pineapple); *esp* : the papery or leathery carpels composing the ripened ovary in fruits of the apple family **b** : a hard unburned central part of a piece of coal or limestone; *also* : an unburned or overburned piece of limestone found in hydrated lime **c** : the necrotic slough in the central part of a boil **d** : the central or axial interior part of a structure (as a column or wall) often made of inferior material **e** : a separate portion of a foundry mold which shapes the interior of a hollow casting or which makes a hole in or through a casting; *also* : a part of the mold made separately and inserted for shaping some part of the casting **f** : a portion removed from the interior of a mass usu. to determine the interior composition or hidden condition ⟨the holes bored in the ice provided ~s for determination of the variation of density with depth —Valter Schytt⟩ ⟨took a ~ from the well drilling for geological and chemical analysis⟩ **g** : the bony process that forms the central axis of the horns of the hollow-horned ruminants **h** : the central strand around which other strands twist in some kinds of rope — called also *heart* **i** : a mass of iron often made up of thin plates or wires and enclosed in a coil (as in an electromagnet, transformer, or armature) serving to concentrate and intensify the magnetic field resulting from a current in the coil **j** : the conducting wire with its insulation in an electric cable but not including mechanical protective covering **k** : a nodule of obsidian, flint, or other stone from which flakes have been struck for making implements **l** : a wall or structure of impervious material forming the central part of an embankment or dike (as a dam) the outer parts of which are pervious **m** : a hollow space in the body of a large metal type or in the metal base of a stereotype or electrotype; *also* : a hollow stereotype mount **n** : the unaffected interior of a carburized or case-hardened piece of metal **o** : the central part of the earth having a radius of about 2100 miles and displaying notably different physical properties from the surrounding mantle and crust **p** : the cylindrical portion of a lock which rotates when the key is turned **q** : a stiff tube on which paper or other material may be wound ⟨paper toweling wound on a paperboard ~⟩ **r** (1) : the central layer of wood on which veneers are glued in making plywood or veneered wood for cabinetwork (2) : the center ply of a piece of plywood **s** : CENTRUM **t** : the remainder of an atom after the removal of the valency electrons — called also *rumpf* **u** : an arrangement of a course of studies that combines under certain basic topics material from subjects conventionally separated and aims to provide a common background for all students, to integrate the individual student's program, and to relate the work of the school to experience and to society ⟨~ curriculum⟩ ⟨~ program⟩ **v** : the shield of a continent **w** : the plug or neck of a volcano **x** : the central part of an anticlinal or domal structure or of mountains having a folded or completely crumpled structure **y** : the part of an automobile radiator in which most of the cooling of the water takes place **z** : the center or base portion of a clad product **aa** : the place in a nuclear reactor where fission occurs **2** : the part (as of an individual, a class, an entity) that is basic, essential, vital, or enduring as distinct from the incidental or transient ⟨a hard ~ of perhaps 10 percent who have been in the party for 15 years —A.M.Schlesinger b.1917⟩ ⟨carrier task forces are the ~ of the Navy —T.K. Finletter⟩ : the essential meaning or gist ⟨the ~ of the book is thus an attempt to comprehend the nature of total war —*Times Lit. Supp.*⟩ : the inmost or most intimate part ⟨their theory of life had its ~ of soundness —George Eliot⟩ ⟨his wife was Victorian to the ~ —Robert Payne⟩ **syn** see CENTER

[2]**core** \"\ *vt* -ED/-ING/-S **1** : to take out the core of ⟨~ an apple⟩ **2** : to drill through the core of : remove the axial portion of ⟨~ the barrel after casting it⟩ **3** : to take a core from as a sample of interior composition ⟨~ an oil well⟩ ⟨~ a salt formation⟩ **4** : to form (as a hole in a casting) by means of a core

[3]**core** \ˈkō(ə)r, -ōə\ *n* -s [alter. of ME *chore* chorus, choir, company, fr. L *chorus* — more at CHORUS] **1** *chiefly Scot* : a company (as of players in a curling match) **2** *dial Eng* **a** : a gang of miners in one shift **b** : underground working time or shift esp. in a mine

[4]**core** *var of* KOR

corean *usu cap, var of* KOREAN

core barrel *n* **1** : a tube inside a drill pipe and supported by a bit to receive the core in core boring **2** : a tube usu. of iron on which a foundry loam core is formed

core bit *n* : a hollow cylindrical bit that is the cutting part of a core drill

corebox \ˈ⸗ˌ⸗\ *n* : an open box in which a foundry core is formed

co·recreation \(ˈ)kō+\ *n* [*co-* + *recreation*] : recreation engaged in jointly by both sexes

cored *adj* **1** : having the core removed ⟨~ apples⟩ **2** : cast or made with a hollow core ⟨metal type with a ~ base⟩ **3** : having a core composed of a specified material or character and esp. differing from that of the outer part ⟨carbon arcs ~ with various salts⟩ ⟨black-*cored* pottery⟩

cored carbon *n* : a carbon for arc lights that has a small core of softer material to keep the crater central

co·redeem \ˌ¦kō+\ *vt* [*co-* + *redeem*] : to share in the process or function of redeeming

co·redemption \ˌ¦kō+\ *n* [*co-* + *redemption*] : participation in the act or process of redemption

co–redemptrix \ˌ¦kō+\ *n, often cap C&R* [NL, fr. *co-* + *redemptrix*, fem. of L *redemptor* redeemer — more at REDEMPTOR] : a female sharer in the redemption of the human race (as the Virgin Mary among some Roman Catholics)

core diameter *n* : MINOR DIAMETER

core drill *n* : a drill that removes a cylindrical core from the drill hole — compare DIAMOND DRILL, SHOT DRILL — **core drilling** *n*

co·ree \ˈkō(ˌ)rē\ *n, pl* **coree** *or* **corees** *usu cap* **1** : an extinct Indian people of the coast of No. Carolina of uncertain linguistic affinities **2** : a member of the Coree people

cor·e·go·nid \ˌkȯrəˈgōnəd\ *n* -s [NL *Coregonidae*] : WHITEFISH 1a

cor·e·go·ni·dae \ˌ⸗⸗ˈgōnəˌdē\ *n pl, cap* [NL, fr. *Coregonus*, type genus + *-idae*] *in some classifications* : a family of fishes (order Isospondyli) comprising the freshwater whitefishes and now usu. included among the Salmonidae

cor·e·go·nine \ˈkȯrə¦gōˌnīn, -ˌnən\ *adj* [NL *Coregonus* + E *-ine*] : of or belonging to the genus *Coregonus* or to freshwater whitefishes

cor·e·go·nus \ˌ⸗⸗ˈgōnəs\ *n, cap* [NL, fr. Gk *korē* pupil of the eye + NL *-gonus* (fr. Gk *gōnia* angle) — more at CRESCENT, DIAGONAL] : a genus of plainly colored salmonid fishes comprising the typical whitefishes of the lakes of Europe, Asia, and No. America — see WHITEFISH

[1]**cor·e·id** \ˈkȯrēəd\ *adj* [NL *Coreidae*] : of or relating to the Coreidae

[2]**coreid** \"\ *n* -s : any true bug of the family Coreidae

co·re·i·dae \kəˈrēəˌdē\ *n pl, cap* [NL, fr. *Coreus*, type genus (fr. Gk *koris* bedbug) + *-idae*; akin to Gk *keirein* to cut — more at SHEAR] : a large family of true bugs (order Hemiptera) comprising the squash bugs and leaf-footed bugs and including many that are injurious to cultivated plants

co·relate \ˌ¦kō+\ *vt* [back-formation fr. *corelation*] *now chiefly Brit* : to relate to each other : CORRELATE

co·relation \ˌ¦kō+\ *n* [*co-* + *relation*] *now chiefly Brit* : CORRELATION

core·less *pronunc at* [1]CORE + ləs\ *adj* : not having a core

co·religionist *also* **co·religionary** \ˌ¦kō+\ *n, pl* **coreligionists** *also* **coreligionaries** [*co-* + *religion* + *-ist* or *-ary*] : one having the same religion ⟨Mohammedans did not like to hold their ~s in slavery —C.S.Forester⟩

co·rel·la \kəˈrelə\ *n* -s [native name in Australia] : any of certain Australian cockatoos; *esp* : a long-billed cockatoo (*Kakatoe tenuirostris*) often kept as a cage bird and readily trained to talk — see BARE-EYED COCKATOO

core loss *n* : energy wasted by hysteresis and eddy currents in a magnetic core (as of an armature or transformer)

co·re·ma \kōˈrēmə, kəˈ-\ *n, cap* [NL, fr. Gk *korēma* broom, fr. *korein* to sweep] : a small genus of low shrubs (family Empetraceae) having foliage resembling heath, small apetalous flowers, and drupaceous fruits — see BROOM CROWBERRY

coremaker \ˈ⸗ˌ⸗⸗\ *n* **1** : one that makes sand cores for metal castings or clay cores for iron pipe or metal cores for building tile **2** : an operator of a machine that winds tubular paperboard cores for rolls of paper

co·re·mi·um \kōˈrēmēəm, kəˈ-\ *n, pl* **core·mia** \-mēə\ [NL, fr. Gk *korēma* broom + NL *-ium*] : a fruiting body characteristic of certain imperfect fungi (as the Stilbellaceae) and consisting of a sterile stalk of parallel or fascicled hyphae and a terminal head of fertile or spore-bearing branches — compare SYNNEMA

core oil *n* : oil used to bind sand for foundry cores

co·re·op·sis \ˌkōrēˈäpsəs, ˌkȯr-\ *n* [NL, fr. *core-* (fr. Gk *koris* bedbug) + *-opsis*; fr. the shape of the achene — more at COREIDAE] **1** *cap* : a genus of herbs (family Compositae) many of which are used in cultivation and which have showy flower heads with involucral bracts in two distinct series of eight each, the outer being commonly connate at the base **2** *pl* **coreopsis** : a plant of the genus *Coreopsis* — called also *tickseed*; compare CALLIOPSIS

core oven *n* : an oven in which foundry cores are baked

core print *n* : the part of a foundry pattern which makes an opening in a mold to receive a core and to support it while the metal is being poured

co·requisite \(ˈ)kō+\ *n* [*co-* + *requisite*] : a formal course of study required to be taken simultaneously with another

cor·er \ˈkōrə(r), ˈkȯr-\ *n* -s **1** : an instrument for taking out cores ⟨an apple ~⟩ ⟨a ~ for taking geological samples⟩ **2** : a tube or cylinder impelled into the sea bottom to obtain samples of its composition and the animal life inhabiting it

cores *pl of* CORE, *pres 3d sing of* CORE

co·respondent \ˌ¦kō+\ *n* [*co-* + *respondent*] : a joint respondent; *specif* : a person charged with adultery in a divorce suit and proceeded against together with the respondent

core tool *n* : a stone age tool made by striking flakes from a nodule — compare FLAKE TOOL

core wall *n* : CORE 1*l*

corf \ˈkȯ(ə)rf, ˈkȯ(ə)f\ *n, pl* **corves** \-vz\ [ME, basket, fr. MD *corf* or MLG *korf*, prob. fr. L *corbis* — more at CORBEIL] **1** *Brit* : a basket, tub, or truck used in a mine for conveying ore or coal to the pit mouth **2** *Brit* : a cage like a basket used by fishermen for keeping live lobsters or other catch

cor·fi·ote \ˈkȯ(r)fēˌōt\ *n* -s *cap* [F, fr. *Corfou* Corfu (Greek island in the Ionian sea) + F *-i-* + *-ote*] : a native or resident of the island of Corfu, off the coast of southwest Albania

corge \ˈkȯ(ə)rj, -ȯ(ə)j\ *n* -s [Pg *corja*, prob. fr. Malayalam *kōṭi*] *India* : a unit of 20 : SCORE

corgi *n* -s [W, fr. *cor* dwarf + *-gi* (fr. *ci* dog); akin to Corn & Bret *ki* dog, OIr *cū*, OE *hund* — more at HOUND] : WELSH CORGI

coria *pl of* CORIUM

co·ri·a·ceous \ˌ¦kōrē¦āshəs, ¦kȯr-\ *adj* [LL *coriaceus* — more at CUIRASS] : like leather in appearance, texture, or quality : TOUGH ⟨a ~ leaf⟩

co·ri·al \ˌkōrēˈäl, ˈ⸗⸗ˌ⸗\ *n* -s [AmerSp, of Arawakan or Cariban origin; akin to Arawak *kuljara* corial, Macusi *kulial*] : a Guianan native dugout canoe

co·ri·a·myr·tin \ˌkōrēəˈmərtᵊn, ˌkȯr-, ˈ⸗⸗⸗ˌ⸗⸗\ *n* -s [ISV *coriamyrt-* (fr. NL *Coriaria myrtifolia*, a species of shrubs) + *-in*; orig. formed as F *coriamyrtine*] : a bitter poisonous crystalline compound $C_{15}H_{18}O_5$ found in an Old World dye plant (*Coriaria myrtifolia*)

co·ri·an·der \ˈkōrēˌandə(r), ˌkȯr-, -aand-\ *n* -s [ME *coriandre*, fr. OF, fr. L *coriandrum*, fr. Gk *koriandron*, *koriannon*, fr. *koris* bedbug; fr. its odor — more at COREIDAE] **1** : an Old World herb (*Coriandrum sativum*) with aromatic fruits **2** *or* **coriander seed** : the ripened dried fruit of coriander used for flavoring esp. of pickles, curries, confectioneries, and liquors

coriander oil *n* : a colorless or pale-yellow essential oil obtained from the dried ripe fruit of coriander and used chiefly as a flavoring agent

co·ri·an·drol \ˌkōrēˈanˌdrōl, ˌkȯr-, -ˌdrōl\ *n* -s [ISV *coriandr-* (fr. L *coriandrum*) + *-ol*; orig. formed as G *koriandrol*] : dextrorotatory linalool

co·ri·an·drum \-ˈandrəm\ *n, cap* [NL, fr. L] : a genus of slender annual herbs (family Umbelliferae) with pinnately dissected leaves and white flowers in compound umbels and with the petals of the outer flowers in each umbel enlarged and like rays

co·ri·ar·ia \ˌkōrēˈa(a)rēə, ˌkȯr-\ *n, cap* [NL, fr. L, fem. of *coriarius* useful for tanning leather, fr. *corium* leather + *-arius* -ary; fr. the use of the leaves in tanning — more at CUIRASS] : a small widely distributed genus (coextensive with the family Coriariaceae of the order Sapindales) of shrubs or subshrubs having small opposite leaves, terminal racemes of very small flowers, and purplish fruit — see TUTU — **co·ri·ar·i·a·ceous** \¦⸗⸗¦⸗rē¦āshəs\ *adj*

co·ri ester \ˈkōrē-\ *n, usu cap C* [after Carl F. *Cori* b1896 and his wife Gerty T. *Cori* †1957 Am. biochemists] : GLUCOSE PHOSPHATE a

cor·i·me·lae·na \ˌkȯrəməˈlēnə\ *n, cap* [NL, fr. *cori-* (fr. Gk *koris* bedbug) + *melaena* (fr. Gk *melaina*, fem. of *melas* black) — more at COREIDAE, MULLET] : a genus of small black bugs comprising the negro bugs

co·rin·don \kəˈrindən\ *n* -s [F, fr. Tamil *kurundam*] : CORUNDUM

co·rinne \kəˈrin\ *n* -s [origin unknown] : the common gazelle (*Gazella dorcas*)

cor·inth \ˈkȯrən(t)th, ˈkär-\ *n* -s [obs. E *corinth* currant, alter. (influenced by Greek city name *Corinth*) of *currant*] : any of certain usu. red dyes (as Congo corinth G)

[1]**co·rin·thi·an** \kəˈrin(t)thēən\ *n* -s *cap* [L *Corinthiensis*] **1** : a native or resident of Corinth, Greece **2 a** : a gay profligate licentious man **b** : a fashionable man-about-town : SPORTSMAN **c** : an amateur yachtsman or sailor

[2]**corinthian** \"\ *adj, usu cap* [L *Corinthiensis*, adj. & n., fr. *Corinthus* Corinth, city in ancient Greece, fr. Gk *Korinthos*] **1 a** : of, relating to, or characteristic of Corinth **b** : of, relating to, or characteristic of Corinthians **2** : of or belonging to the lightest and most ornate of the three Greek orders that is characterized esp. by its bell-shaped capital enveloped with acanthuses — see CAPITAL illustration **3** : of or belonging to the type of decorative painting on vases practiced in Corinth in the 7th century B.C. and characterized by ornamentation with figures in black and purple and many details rendered by incision (as the engraving of fine lines in the dark silhouette) **4** : elegant and ornate in style or manner, esp. in literary style

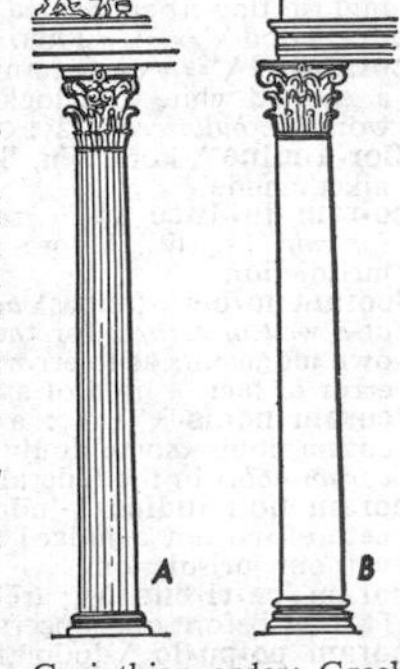

Corinthian order: Greek Corinthian order, *A*; Roman Corinthian order, *B*

corinthian atrium *n, usu cap C* : an atrium having a peristyle

co·rin·thi·an·ism \-ˌnizəm\ *n* -s *usu cap* **1** : Corinthian profligacy or elegance **2** : amateur yachting

corinthian pink *n, often cap C* : a moderate pink to light grayish red that is very slightly darker than lilac (sense 3b)

corinthian purple *n, often cap C* : a grayish purplish red that is redder and deeper than average rose plum, redder and slightly less strong than Aztec maroon, and redder and duller than tourmaline pink

corinthian red *n, often cap C* : a grayish red that is bluer and duller than bois de rose or Pompeian red, yellower and duller than appleblossom, and deeper than livid brown

co·ri·o·lis acceleration \(ˈ)kōrē¦ōləs-\ *n, usu cap C* [after Gaspard G. *Coriolis* †1843 Fr. civil engineer] : a quantity that must be added vectorially to the acceleration of a body with respect to another accelerated body to get the true acceleration of the former ⟨*Coriolis acceleration* applies to the motion of a long-range projectile with respect to the rotating earth⟩

coriolis force *n, usu cap C* [after G. G. *Coriolis*] : the force corresponding to the Coriolis acceleration of a body equal to the product of the mass by the Coriolis acceleration and responsible as a result of the earth's rotation for the deflection of projectiles and the motion of the winds to the right in the northern hemisphere and to the left in the southern hemisphere

co·ri·ta \kə'rēd·ə\ *n* -s [MexSp] **:** a small boat resembling a coracle used by the Indians of southern California

co·ri·um \'kōrēəm, 'kȯr-\ *n, pl* **co·ria** \-rēə\ [NL, fr. L, leather — more at CUIRASS] **1 :** DERMIS 1 **2 :** the layer of the mucous membranes corresponding to the dermis **3 :** the chief or middle division of the thickened portion of the hemelytra of true bugs (order Hemiptera)

corival *var of* CORRIVAL

co·rixa \kə'riksə\ *n, cap* [NL, irreg. fr. Gk *koris* bedbug — more at COREIDAE] **:** a genus (the type of the family Corixidae) of carnivorous aquatic bugs comprising the boat bugs and having the hind pair of legs modified into elongated swimming organs which resemble oars — **co·rix·id** \-səd\ *n or adj*

co·riz·i·dae \kə'rizə,dē\ [NL, fr. *Corizus*, type genus (fr. Gk *koris* bedbug) + *-idae*] *syn of* COREIDAE

¹cork \'kȯ(ə)rk, 'kō(ə)k\ *n* -s [ME *corke* cork (bark), cork sandal, prob. fr. Ar *qurq*, fr. L *cortic-*, *cortex* bark, cork — more at CUIRASS] **1 a :** the outer tissues of the stem of the cork oak that in young stems consists of epidermis, cortical tissue, and periderm and in older stems of secondary phloem and periderm, that attains great thickness, and that is used commercially for cork stoppers and insulation — see VIRGIN CORK **b :** PHELLEM **2 :** a piece of cork **:** something made from a piece of cork: as **a :** a usu. tapering or cylindrical stopper cut out of cork for a bottle, jug, or other container; *also* **:** a similar stopper of other material ⟨a rubber ~⟩ **b :** a float for a fishing line **3** *Scot* **:** a small employer **:** OVERSEER **4 :** a light brown that is yellower and darker than blush, yellower and deeper than alesan, and yellower and slightly lighter than French beige **5 :** a disease of apples and related plants (as pear and quinces) caused by boron deficiency and characterized by internal brown, dry, spongy or corky, bitter-tasting flecks in the fruits — called also *corky core*

²cork \"\ *vb* -ED/-ING/-S *vt* **1 :** to furnish or fit with cork ⟨fishermen ~ their nets⟩ **2 :** to stop up with a cork ⟨~ the bottle⟩ **:** seal (the contents) in a container by means of a cork ⟨~ the wine securely⟩ **3 :** to close up or seal off (as a passage) ⟨for Charleston's ~*ed* with a Northern fleet —S.V. Benét⟩ **:** seal against escape **:** press down ⟨keeping his emotions ~*ed* up inside him⟩ **4 :** to blacken (as one's face) with burnt cork ⟨minstrels with ~*ed* faces⟩ **5 :** to develop corky tissue over (wounds or cuts) — used of a plant or tuber **~** *vi, of a plant or tuber* **:** to develop corky tissue over wounds or cuts

³cork \"\ *vb* -ED/-ING/-S [by folk etymology] **:** CALK, CAULK

⁴cork \"\ *n* -s [by folk etymology] **:** CALK

⁵cork \"\ *adj, usu cap* [fr. *Cork*, county in Ireland] **1 :** of or from the city of Cork, Ireland **:** of the kind or style prevalent in Cork **2 :** of or from County Cork, Ireland **:** of the kind or style prevalent in County Cork

cork·age \'kȯrkij, -ō(ə)k-, -kēj\ *n* -s **1 :** the corking or uncorking of bottles **2 a :** a charge made by a hotel or restaurant for serving bottles of wine or other liquor bought elsewhere **b :** a charge made by a restaurant for every bottle of liquor served

cork-bark elm *n* **:** ROCK ELM 1a

cork black *n* **:** a black pigment made by charring cork

corkboard \'⸗,⸗\ *n* **:** a heat-insulating material made of granulated cork compressed in sheets or blocks and baked

cork cambium *n* [¹*cork*] **:** PHELLOGEN

cork carpet *n* **:** a floor covering similar to linoleum and made of ground cork, rubber, and linseed oil

corke *or* **corker** *var of* CORCIR

corked *adj* [fr. past part. of ²*cork*] *of wine or brandy* **:** having the unpleasant odor and taste resulting from corking

cork elm *n* **1 :** ROCK ELM 1a **2 :** WINGED ELM

cork·er \'kȯrkər, 'kō(ə)kə(r\ *n* -s **1 :** one that corks bottles or other containers **2** *slang* **:** a person or thing of excellent or remarkable quality ⟨the story is amazingly good — a ~⟩ **3 :** CAPPER 5 **4** *or* **corker nail :** COOLER NAIL

cork fir \'⸗,⸗\ *also* **corkbar fir** \'⸗,⸗'⸗\ *n* **:** an evergreen tree (*Abies arizonica*) of Arizona and New Mexico with yellowish white thick corky bark

corkier *comparative of* CORKY

corkiest *superlative of* CORKY

¹corking *adj* [fr. pres. part. of ²*cork* (influenced in meaning by CORKER)] **:** extremely fine **:** extraordinarily good ⟨a ~ satire . . . which I conjure you to read —H.J.Laski⟩ ⟨a pitcher with a ~ fast ball⟩

²corking \"\ *n* -s [fr. gerund of ²*cork*] **:** impairment of the quality of wine or brandy usu. by the action of an injurious microorganism and perhaps resulting from a tainted cork or a seal that is not airtight

corking pin *n* [*corking* perh. alter. of *calkin*] *dial* **:** a large pin

cork·ite \'kȯr,kīt\ *n* -s [F, fr. *Cork*, county in Ireland, its locality + F *-ite*] **:** a phosphate-sulfate-hydroxide of lead and iron $PbFe_3(PO_4)(SO_4)(OH)_6$ that is isomorphous with beudantite

cork jacket *n* **:** a sleeveless canvas jacket with slabs of cork sewn into pockets on the front and back and used as a life preserver

cork leg *n* [¹*cork*] **:** an artificial leg

corkline \'⸗,⸗\ *n* **:** the upper line of a gill net having cork or other floats at intervals to give the net buoyancy — compare LEAD LINE 1b

cork oak *n* **:** an oak (*Quercus suber*) of southern Europe and northern Africa and esp. abundant in Spain and Portugal, attaining a height of 40 feet and furnishing the cork of commerce which is cut off in large plates at intervals of from 12 to 15 years

cork·o·ni·an \(')kȯ(r)'kōnēən, -nyən\ *n* -s *cap* [*Cork*, county & city in Ireland + E *-onian* (as in *Oxonian*)] **:** a native or resident of Cork, Ireland

cork paint *n* **:** a coating of fine cork embedded in the base coat of paint on steel parts of ships to prevent sweating

cork paper *n* **:** a heavy wrapping paper surfaced with powdered cork and used to protect fragile articles

cork pine *n* [¹*cork*] **:** lumber sawed from mature specimens of a common white pine (*Pinus strobus*)

corks *pl of* CORK, *pres 3d sing of* CORK

¹cork·screw \'⸗,⸗\ *n* **1 :** a pointed spiral piece of metal having a handle and used for drawing corks from bottles **2 a :** an imperfection in silk filament **b :** a defect in unevenly twisted yarns resembling the spiral of a corkscrew

corkscrew

²corkscrew \"\ *adj* **:** having the shape or taking the course of a corkscrew **:** SPIRAL ⟨a ~ curl⟩ ⟨the ~ motion of the ship over the heavy swell⟩

³corkscrew \"\ *vt* **1 :** to cause to proceed in a spiral or winding course **:** WIND ⟨the road ~*ed* its way in and out of a gully —Ngaio Marsh⟩ **2 :** to elicit (as information) with difficulty or by roundabout questioning ⟨every word had to be ~*ed* out of him⟩ **3 :** to twist into a spiral ⟨~ copper tubing⟩ **~** *vi* **:** to move spirally or in a twisting or winding course ⟨the plane ~*ed* down toward the earth⟩ **:** take a winding or spiraling course ⟨the road ~*s* up the steep valley⟩

corkscrew flower *n* **:** SNAILFLOWER 1

corkscrew grass *n* **:** an Australian grass (*Stipa setacea*) that is like a corkscrew in the lower part of its fruiting awn

cork tan *n* **:** a light brown that is yellower and darker than blush and darker and slightly redder than cork

cork tile *n* **:** an elastic noiseless flooring tile made of cork shavings compressed and baked

cork tree *n* **1 :** CORK OAK **2** *Austral* **:** a prickly Australian coral tree (*Erythrina vespertilio*) with soft spongy wood **3 :** an Asiatic tree (*Phellodendron amurense*) with compound leaves, a turpentine odor when bruised, and deeply fissured corky bark **4** *West Indies* **:** PORTIA TREE

corkwing \'⸗,⸗\ *or* **corkwing wrasse** *n* **:** a small variably colored European wrasse (*Cremilabrus melops*)

corkwood \'⸗,⸗\ *or* **corkwood tree** *n* **:** any of various chiefly tropical American or Australian trees and shrubs having lightweight or corky wood; *esp* **:** a small tree or coarse shrub (*Leitneria floridana*) of the southeastern U.S. that has a swollen base, pale fissured bark, somewhat lanceolate and hairy leaves, and extremely soft light wood weighing about 12½ pounds to the cubic foot

corkwood elm *n* **:** ROCK ELM 1a

corkwood family *n* **:** LEITNERIACEAE

corky \'kȯrkē, 'kō(ə)k-, -ki\ *adj* -ER/-EST [¹*cork* + *-y*] **1 :** resembling cork: as **a :** shriveled up **:** DRY, WITHERED ⟨bind fast his ~ arms —Shak.⟩ **b :** light or buoyant in spirits **:** LIVELY, SKITTISH ⟨a jovial ~ fellow⟩ **c** *of cheese* **:** firm, hard, without plasticity, and tending to break up under pressure **2 a** *of wine or brandy* **:** CORKED **b :** peculiar to or suggestive of a beverage spoiled by corking ⟨~ taste or odor⟩ **3** *of dogs* **:** compactly built and lively

corky core *also* **corky pit** *n* **:** ¹CORK 5

corky ring spot *n* **:** INTERNAL BROWN SPOT

corky scab *n* **:** POTATO SCAB

corm \'kȯ(ə)rm, 'kō(ə)m\ *n* -s [NL *cormus*] **:** a rounded thick modified underground stem base bearing membranous or scaly leaves and buds and acting as a vegetative reproductive structure in certain monocotyledonous plants (as gladiolus and crocus) — distinguished from *bulb;* compare TUBER

corm of crocus

corm- *or* **cormo-** *comb form* [NL, fr. Gk *korm-*, *kormo-* tree trunk, fr. *kormos* — more at CORMUS] **:** tree trunk **:** stem ⟨*Cormophyta*⟩

C or M *abbr* cost or market

cor·ma·tose \'kȯrmə,tōs\ *adj* [*corm* + *-atose* (as in *comatose*)] **:** having or producing corms

corm·el \'kȯrməl, kȯr'mel\ *n* -s [*corm* + *-el*] **:** one of the small or secondary corms produced annually by an old corm — called also *bulblet*

cor·mid·i·um \kȯr'midēəm\ *n, pl* **cormid·ia** \-ēə\ [NL, fr. Gk *kormos* tree trunk + NL *-idium*] **:** the entire body or colony of a compound animal; *sometimes* **:** one of the clusters of zooids usu. consisting of a helmet-shaped bract, a gastrozooid, and one or more gonophores often functioning as swimming bells and arising from the main stem of a calycophoran — used chiefly of the Siphonophora

cor·moid \'kȯr,mȯid\ *adj* **:** like a corm

cor·moph·y·ta \kȯr'mäfəd·ə\ *n pl, cap* [NL, fr. *corm-* + *-phyta*] *in older classifications* **:** a division comprising all plants that have a stem and root

cor·mo·phyte \'kȯrmə,fīt\ *n* -s [NL *Cormophyta*] **:** a plant of the division Cormophyta

cor·mo·phyt·ic \,kȯrmə¦fid·ik\ *adj* [NL *Cormophyta* + E *-ic*] **:** of, relating to, or characteristic of the Cormophyta

cor·mo·rant \'kȯrm(ə)rənt, 'kō(ə)m-; -mə,rant, -raa(ə)nt\ *n* -s [ME *cormeraunt*, fr. MF *cormorant*, *cormaran*, fr. OF *cormareng*, fr. *corp* raven (fr. L *corvus*) + *marenc* of the sea, fr. L *marinus* — more at RAVEN, MARINE] **1 :** any of various dark-colored web-footed seabirds (family Phalacrocoracidae) that have a long neck, stiff wedge-shaped tail, slender hooked beak, and a patch of bare often brightly colored distensible skin under the mouth, that occur on most tropical and temperate seacoasts of the world but more abundantly in the southern hemisphere, that are used in parts of eastern Asia for catching fish by having a band placed about the throat to prevent them from swallowing their catch, and that are such voracious eaters of fish that they have become an emblem of gluttony **2 :** a gluttonous, greedy, or rapacious person ⟨the bead-eyed ~*s* of lost estates, who love to rummage into fusty rooms —Howard Griffin⟩ ⟨[a place seeker's] ~ appetite for office —John Quincy Adams⟩

cor·mose \'kȯr,mōs\ *or* **cor·mous** \'kȯrməs\ *adj* **:** bearing or producing corms

cor·mus \'kȯrməs\ *n, pl* **cor·mi** \-,mī, -,mē\ [NL, corm, cormus, fr. Gk *kormos* tree trunk, fr. *keirein* to shear — more at SHEAR] **:** the entire body or colony of a compound animal

¹corn \'kȯ(ə)rn, 'kō(ə)n\ *n* -s *often attrib* [ME, fr. OE; akin to OHG & ON *korn* grain, Goth *kaurn*, L *granum*, Gk *gēras* old age, Skt *jīrṇa* worn out, frail, old; basic meaning: ripening] **1** *now chiefly dial* **:** a small hard particle **:** GRAIN ⟨a ~ of salt⟩ ⟨a ~ of gunpowder⟩ **2 :** a small hard seed (as of an apple, a pepper, or a coffee cherry) **3 a :** the seeds of any of the cereal grasses used for food; *esp* **:** the seeds of the important cereal crop (as wheat, oats, or Indian corn) of a particular region **b** *Brit* **:** WHEAT **c** *Scot & Irish* **:** OATS **d :** INDIAN CORN **4 :** the kernels of sweet corn or maize served as a vegetable while still soft and milky ⟨a dish of ~⟩ — see CORN ON THE COB **5 a :** a plant that produces corn — now used of the grain crop, the stalks and ears after reaping, or the ears ready for threshing **b corns** *pl, obs* **:** kinds or crops of grain **:** CEREALS **c** *obs* **:** the stalk of a cereal plant ⟨playing on pipes of ~ —Shak.⟩ **6 :** CORN WHISKEY **7 :** a moderate yellow that is redder and deeper than colonial yellow, greener, lighter, and stronger than brass, and redder, lighter, and stronger than mustard yellow **8 :** something (as writing, music, or acting) that is corny ⟨plot dealing with . . . Greek gods, nymphs, and shepherds, and a score . . . that has become dreadfully familiar as dinner music. . . . One false move and it would degenerate into intolerable ~ —Winthrop Sargeant⟩ ⟨it's corny, but ~ is the staff of entertainment life —Yasha Frank⟩ **9 :** CORN SNOW — **acknowledge the corn :** to admit or confess a charge, fault, error, or failure ⟨when his error was proved he had to *acknowledge the corn*⟩

²corn \"\ *vb* -ED/-ING/-S *vt* **1 :** to form into grains **:** GRANULATE ⟨~ gunpowder⟩ **2 a :** to preserve or season with salt in grains **:** cure by salting **:** sprinkle with salt **b :** to salt lightly in brine containing preservatives, sweetening, and sometimes spices ⟨you can ~ beef in a few weeks⟩ ⟨~ a tongue⟩ **3 :** to plant (land) with corn ⟨~*ing* my land to death —Russell Lord⟩ **4 :** to feed with corn or grain ⟨~ horses⟩ **~** *vi* **1** *obs* **:** to become granular **2 :** to form or fill with the corn or seed — used of cereals or pulse or their ears or pods

³corn \"\ *n* -s [ME *coorne*, fr. MF *corne* horn, fr. L *cornu* — more at HORN] **1 :** a horny hardening and thickening of the epidermis at some point (as on a toe) produced by friction or pressure and formed into a central conical mass extending into the dermis — called also *clavus;* compare CALLOSITY **2 :** a reddish painful discoloration of the sole of the fore hoof of a horse usu. caused by pressure resulting from improper shoeing and resultant bruises of the velvety tissue overlying the horn which diffuse blood into it **3 :** the abnormal growth on the feet of poultry affected with bumblefoot

¹-corn \,kȯrn, -,kō(ə)n\ *n comb form* -s [L *-cornis* -horned, fr. *cornu* horn] **:** one having (such or so many) horns ⟨unicorn⟩

²-corn \"\ *adj comb form* [L *-cornis*] **:** having (such or so many) horns **:** horned

cor·na·ce·ae \kȯr'nāsē,ē\ *n pl, cap* [NL, fr. *Cornus*, type genus + *-aceae*] **:** a family of mainly temperate-region trees, shrubs, or herbs (order Umbellales) comprising the dogwoods and related plants and having small clustered flowers, an inferior ovary, and drupaceous fruit — **cor·na·ceous** \(')kȯr¦nāshəs\ *adj*

cor·na·da \kȯr'nädə, *or as Sp*\ *n* -s [Sp, fr. *corn-* (fr. *cuerno* horn, fr. L *cornu*) + *-ada* (fr. L *-ata*) — more at -ADE] **:** a wound inflicted by a bull's horn in formal bullfighting

corn aphid *or* **corn aphis** *n* **:** CORN LEAF APHID

cornball \'⸗,⸗\ *n, often attrib* [*corn ball* "ball of popped corn and molasses" (influenced in meaning by ¹*corn* "something corny" & *screwball*, *meatball*)] *slang* **:** an unsophisticated person **:** RUBE, HICK; *also* **:** something corny ⟨such ~ phrasing as "on the boards" —Walter Kerr⟩

corn beef *n* **:** corned beef

corn belt *n* **:** an area in which more land is used for the cultivation of corn than for any other single crop (as the central portion of the U.S. from western Ohio into Nebraska and Kansas including northern Missouri, eastern So. Dakota, and southwestern Minnesota)

corn billbug *n* **:** any of several billbugs that feed on maize

cornbind \'⸗,⸗\ *n, Brit* **:** CORN BINDWEED

corn binder *n* **:** an implement for harvesting standing corn or other tall crops grown in rows comprising a cutter and a device for packing and tying the stalks into bundles — called also *corn harvester, row binder*

corn bindweed *n* **:** a bindweed of grainfields (as black bindweed and field bindweed)

corn borer *n* **:** any of several insects that bore in maize: as **a :** the larva of an Old World moth (*Ostrinia nubilalis*) of the family Pyraustidae introduced into and now widespread in eastern No. America where it is a major pest in the stems and crowns of maize, dahlias, potatoes, and many other plants — called also *European corn borer* **b :** a larval pyralidid moth (*Diatraea grandiosella*) of similar habits native to Mexico but now widespread in the southwestern U.S. — called also *southwestern corn borer* **c :** SOUTHERN CORNSTALK BORER **d :** GRANARY WEEVIL

cornbottle \'⸗,⸗⸗\ *n* [¹*corn* + blue*bottle*] **:** CORNFLOWER 1b

corn bran *n* **:** the hull of the grain of Indian corn separated during milling and used as livestock feed

corn bread *n* **:** bread made with cornmeal: as **a :** cornmeal mixed with shortening and water and baked or fried **b :** cornmeal mixed with wheat flour, eggs, milk, and leavening and baked

corn broom *n* **:** a broom made from the panicles of broomcorn

corn bunting *n* **:** a grayish brown streaked bird (*Emberiza calandra*) of marshy fields or brushland of Europe

corn buttercup *n* **:** CORN CROWFOOT

corn cake *n* [¹*corn* (maize) + *cake*] **:** corn bread baked in a pan in an oven or as small cakes on a griddle

corn catchfly *n* **:** a European annual herb (*Silene armeria*) adventive as a garden escape in No. America

corn centaury *n* **:** CORNFLOWER 1b

corn chamomile *n* **:** FIELD CHAMOMILE

corn chandler *n, Brit* **:** a retailer of grain and allied products

corn chop *n* **:** coarse feed consisting of bran, husk, and germ fragments removed from corn which is being ground into meal — often used in pl.

corn chrysanthemum *n* **:** CORN MARIGOLD

corncob \'⸗,⸗\ *n* **1 :** the axis on which the kernels of Indian corn are arranged **2 :** an ear of Indian corn

corncob pipe *also* **corncob** *n* **:** a tobacco pipe with a bowl made from a corncob or made to resemble a corncob

corn cockle *or* **corn campion** *n* **:** an annual hairy weed (*Agrostemma githago*) common in grainfields and having purplish red flowers — called also *crown-of-the-field*

corncracker \'⸗,⸗⸗\ *n* **1 a :** KENTUCKIAN — used as a nickname **b :** CRACKER 5 **2 :** a mill, machine, or device for the coarse grinding of corn

corncrake \'⸗,⸗\ *n* [ME, fr. *corn* + *crake*] **:** a common Eurasian short-billed rail (*Crex crex*) that frequents grainfields — called also *land rail*

corncrib \'⸗,⸗\ *n* **:** a crib for holding or storing ears of Indian corn

corn crowfoot *n* **:** a common European crowfoot (*Ranunculus arvensis*) with pale yellow flowers and spiny achenes

corncrusher \'⸗,⸗⸗\ *n* **:** a machine or device for crushing grain

corncutter \'⸗,⸗⸗\ *n* [³*corn*] **:** CHIROPODIST

corn cutter *n* [¹*corn*] **1 :** a machine for cutting up stalks of Indian corn as food for cattle **2 :** a knife (as a sickle) or a machine for cutting down the stalks of Indian corn

corn dance *n* **:** a No. American Indian ceremonial dance expressing supplication or thanksgiving for the maize crop and held at such stages as the planting, ripening, or harvesting of the grain — called also *green corn dance;* compare ⁴BUSK, RAIN DANCE

corn dodger *n* [¹*corn* (maize) + *dodger* (cake)] *chiefly South & Midland* **:** a cake of corn bread often shaped by hand and fried on a griddle, baked in an oven, or boiled as a dumpling with ham and cabbage or with greens

corn drake *n, dial Eng* **:** CORNCRAKE

corn dumpling *n* **:** a boiled corn dodger

corne- *or* **corneo-** *comb form* [F *corné-*, *cornéo-*, fr. *corné* corneous (fr. L *corneus*), *cornée* cornea (fr. ML *cornea*)] **1 :** corneous **:** corneous and ⟨*corneo*calcareous⟩ **2 :** cornea ⟨*corne*itis⟩ **:** corneal and ⟨*corneo*sclerotic⟩

¹cor·nea \'kȯ(r)nēə\ *n* -s [ML, fr. L, fem. of *corneus* horny — more at CORNEOUS] **1 :** the transparent part of the coat of the eyeball which covers the iris and pupil and admits light to the interior, which is of mesodermic origin and is covered externally by the ectodermic conjunctival epithelium, and which is composed of layers of interlacing fibers continuous with those of the sclerotic coat and united by a cementing substance — see EYE illustration **2 :** the outer transparent covering of the compound eyes of arthropods which is divided into small facets, each acting as a lens

²cornea *pl of* CORNEUM

cor·nea·gen \'kȯ(r)nēə,jen\ *or* **cor·ne·ag·e·nous** \¦kȯ(r)nē¦ajənəs\ *adj* [*cornea* + *-gen*, n. suffix (here in attributive use) or *-genous*] **:** secreting cornea — used of the hypodermal cells that underlie the ocelli and ommatidia in insects

cor·ne·al \'kȯ(r)nēəl\ *adj* **:** of or related to the cornea

corneal transplant *n* **:** the transplanting of a piece of transparent cornea from a donor eye into the space made by excision of a piece of a patient's opaque cornea to provide a clear window for vision; *also* **:** the piece transplanted

corn earworm *n* **:** the large smooth longitudinally striped yellow-headed destructive larva of a noctuid moth (*Heliothis zea*) that is worldwide in distribution but esp. destructive in warm regions and that feeds on many cultivated plants usu. (as on maize) by entering at the tip of the ear, feeding on the developing kernels, and befouling the area in which it lodges with frass and debris — called also *bollworm, tobacco budworm, tomato fruitworm, vetchworm*

corned *past of* CORN

cor·ne·in \'kȯ(r)nēən\ *n* -s [ISV *corne-* (fr. L *corneus* horny) + *-in;* orig. formed as G *kornein*] **:** an iodized nitrogenous substance showing some protein reactions and constituting the organic basis of corals

cor·ne·itis \,kȯ(r)nē'īd·əs\ *n* -ES [NL, fr. *corne-* + *-itis*] **:** KERATITIS

cor·nel \'kȯrnᵊl, -,nel\ *n* -s [prob. fr. (assumed) obs. LG *kornelle*, fr. MLG *kornelle*, fr. OF *cornelle*, *cornolle*, fr. (assumed) VL *cornulla*, dim. of (assumed) VL *corna*, alter. of L *cornum* cornel cherry, fr. *cornus* cornel tree; akin to Gk *kranos* cornel tree, Lith *Kirnis*, god of cherries, Gk *kerasos* cherry tree] **:** a plant of *Cornus* or a related genus: as **a :** CORNELIAN CHERRY **b :** RED DOGWOOD 1 **c :** DWARF CORNEL **d :** FLOWERING DOGWOOD

cor·ne·lian \kȯ(r)'nēlyən\ *n* -s [alter. of ME *cornceline*, fr. MF, perh. fr. *cornelle* cornel cherry + *-ine;* fr. its color] **:** CARNELIAN

cornelian cherry \"-\ *n* [*cornel* + *-ian*] **1 :** a European shrub or small tree (*Cornus mas*) **2 :** the berry borne on the cornelian cherry tree

cornelian red *n* **:** COPPER 5a

cor·ne·muse \'kȯ(r)nə,myüz *or as F*\ *n* -s [ME, fr. MF, back-formation fr. *cornemuser* to play the cornemuse, fr. *corne* horn (fr. L *cornu*) + *muser* to play the bagpipe — more at HORN, MUSETTE] **:** a French bagpipe

corneo- — see CORNE-

cor·ne·ous \'kȯ(r)nēəs\ *adj* [L *corneus* horny, fr. *cornu* horn — more at HORN] **:** of a texture resembling horn **:** HORNY

¹cor·ner *R* 'kȯrnər *sometimes* 'kōnər; *–R* 'kȯ(ə)nə(r\ *n* -s [ME, fr. OF *cornere*, *corniere*, fr. *corne* corner, horn, fr. L *cornu* horn, end, point] **1 a :** the point or place where converging lines, edges, or sides meet **:** ANGLE ⟨the ~ of a square⟩ ⟨~ of a box⟩ ⟨the ~*s* of his eyes and mouth⟩ **b :** an angular part at the meeting point of two of the sides or edges of something ⟨lift up the ~*s* of the tablecloth⟩; *also* **:** a small piece separated (as by tearing off) or separate from something but including such an angular part **c :** the place of intersection of two streets or roads **d :** a stake, tree, or other mark designating the point of intersection of two boundary lines of a piece of land **e :** a piece designed to form, occupy, mark, protect, or ornament a corner of something (as a leather or metal cap for the corner of a book); *also* **:** a design for a corner ornament or a device (as type or a stamp) for impressing it **f :** a corner kick in soccer or a free hit from an opponent's defensive corner in field hockey **g :** the area or edge of home plate nearest or farthest from the batter ⟨the inside ~ is that closest to the batter, the outside ~ is that farthest from him⟩ **h :** one of the two pairs of opponents in a 4-hand card game ⟨play for 10 cents a ~⟩ — distinguished from *side* **2 a :** the space between meeting lines, walls, or borders close to the vertex of the angle ⟨the southwest ~ of the state is hilly⟩ **b (1) :** a secret place or place of secrecy ⟨dark deeds done in ~*s*⟩

: an out-of-the-way place remote from ordinary life or affairs ⟨a quiet ~ of a small New England town⟩ : a small part or area (as of one's mind); *esp* : one that is secret, private, or little known ⟨kept a ~ of their minds free from the strict rule of logic —G.G.Coulton⟩ ⟨every ~ of his inoffensive life was open to the day —Dorothy Sayers⟩ ⟨he had a soft ~ in his heart for Valentine —F.M.Ford⟩ (2) : any place or part (as of the world) whether far or near ⟨starlings are found in every ~ of England⟩ : the remotest extremity (as of the earth) : a far place ⟨the power of England extended to all ~s of the world⟩ : a part or area esp. of a field of activity ⟨establishing frequency modulation in every ~ of the . . . electronics industry —C.B.Fisher⟩ (3) : a point of view : an observer or critic of the scene ⟨this ~ believes that the music should be of prime interest to the collector —Howard Taubman⟩ : a place of observation; *specif* : a regular column in a periodical devoted to a particular interest or activity ⟨verses from his pen had appeared in the poet's ~ of the . . . *Journal* —W.B.Parker⟩ **c** : a position from which escape or retreat is difficult or impossible : a position of danger, difficulty, or embarrassment ⟨he was daring but not imprudent and never got himself into such a tight ~ that he could not escape⟩ **d** (1) : the angle of the ring in which a boxer rests and is worked on by his seconds during the periods between rounds (2) : the party of supporters, well-wishers, or adherents associated with a contestant or with one engaged in some effort, struggle, or controversy ⟨he will have most of the businessmen in his ~ in his fight for the nomination⟩ **3** *obs* : a direction from which the wind blows ⟨sits the wind in that ~—Shak.⟩ **4 corners** *pl* : CHARACTERISTICS, TRAITS, MANNERS; *esp* : rough, rude, or uncultivated manners or ways ⟨a year or two at a good school will round off some of his rough ~s⟩ **5 a** : the critical moment in any series of events; *esp* : the moment marking a turning point from failure to success — used esp. in the phrase *turn the corner* ⟨the business has turned the ~ after three years of losses⟩ **b** : the halfway point toward game on a cribbage board **6 a** : control or ownership by an individual or group of enough of the available supply of a commodity or a security to permit manipulation of the selling price ⟨made a fortune from a ~ in cotton⟩ — compare TRUST **b** : possession of the whole amount or supply of something ⟨a ~ on vigor and virtue —H.J.Muller⟩ : the unique possession of a privilege or ability ⟨a ~ on sales of out-of-town papers —H.H.Martin⟩ **7** : the adjacent dancer standing at a right angle in a square dance ⟨the man's ~ is the woman to his left; his partner is on his right⟩ **8** : CORNER TOOTH — **around the corner** : about to be met, to occur, or to be realized : IMMINENT : at hand ⟨promised that better times were just *around the corner*⟩

²**corner** \"\ *vb* **cornered; cornered; cornering** \-n(ə)riŋ\ **corners** [ME *corneren*, fr. *corner*, n.] *vt* **1 a** : to drive into a corner or into a position where escape is difficult or impossible : bring to bay ⟨largest known eel . . . not usually aggressive, but dangerous when ~*ed* —J.L.B.Smith⟩ **b** : to force into a position of difficulty or embarrassment ⟨the prosecutor ~*ed* the witness and forced out the truth⟩ : catch and hold the attention of (a person) esp. so as to force an interview ⟨he ~*s* the secretary on his way to lunch . . . and says what he has to say right in his ear —Clarence Woodbury⟩ **2** : to get command of a large part of the supply of (as a stock or a commodity) so as to be able to dictate one's own price ⟨~ the common stock of a railroad⟩ ⟨~ the rye market⟩ : get a corner on ⟨you have not ~*ed* all the good ideas —Beatrice S. Rossell⟩ — compare ENGROSS **3** : to cut with an ax a wide chip from each half or each corner of (a box) in turpentine orcharding ~ *vi* **1** : to meet or converge at a corner or angle ⟨the spot where three states ~⟩ **2** *of an automobile* : to turn to one side or the other ⟨a car that ~*s* at high speed without skidding, swerving, or excessive leaning⟩

³**corner** \"\ *adj* [¹*corner*] **1** : situated at a corner; *specif* : situated at a street corner or an intersection ⟨the ~ grocer, druggist or other small merchant —*Time*⟩ **2** : used or fitted by shape or design for use in or on a corner ⟨a ~ brace⟩ ⟨a triangular ~ table⟩

cornerball \'⸗⸗,⸗\ *n* : a game in which each team occupying half of a court with one man stationed in each far corner of the opponents' side tries to seize the ball when it is thrown up at the center line and throw it over the opponents' heads to one of its corner men

corner bead *n* **1** : a bead having a quirk on each side and worked on or fixed to the angle of any architectural work esp. for protecting an angle of a wall **2** : STAFF ANGLE

cornerbind \'⸗⸗,⸗\ *n* : a hook or chain used in binding logs, timber, or lumber on vehicles

corner bit brace *or* **corner brace** *n* : ANGLE BRACE 2

corner boy *n, chiefly Irish* : one who loafs at street corners

corner card *n* : RETURN CARD 2

corner chair *n* : a chair whose curved or angular back is set around one corner of its seat and extends on each side to another corner — called also *roundabout chair, writing chair*

corner chisel *n* : a chisel having two cutting edges at right angles to each other for cutting mortise corners or angles

corner clump *n, Brit* : CORNER QUAD

corner cupboard *n* : a cupboard fitting into a corner of a room

cornered *adj* [ME, fr. ¹*corner* + -*ed*] **1** : having corners of a specified number or type ⟨three-*cornered* hat⟩ ⟨sharp-*cornered*⟩ **2** : involving a specified number of participants ⟨a three-*cornered* contest for mayor⟩ **3** : brought to bay : TRAPPED ⟨savage as a ~ rat⟩ : in a position of difficulty ⟨he answered reluctantly, feeling ~⟩

corner chair

corner influence *n* : the additional value to land resulting from its location at or near a street intersection

cornering *n* -s [¹*corner* + -*ing*] : the construction of a corner in building; *also* : CORNER ⟨dovetailed or square ~s⟩

cornering tool *n* : a tool with a curved cutting edge used by woodworkers for rounding sharp corners and edges

corner kick *n* : a free kick in soccer from close to the point of intersection of the goal line and a touchline allowed to the opposite side when a player has sent the ball behind his own goal line

corner lady *n* : the woman at a man's left in a square-dance set — called also *left-hand lady;* compare OPPOSITE LADY, PARTNER, RIGHT-HAND LADY

cornerpiece \'⸗⸗,⸗\ *n* : CORNER 1e

corner quad *n, printing* : an L-shaped quad commonly used as an inside support for a mitered corner

corners *pl of* CORNER, *pres 3d sing of* CORNER

cornerstone \'⸗⸗,⸗\ *n* [ME *cornerston*, fr. *corner* + *ston* stone] **1** : a stone forming a part of a corner or angle in a wall and esp. lying at the foundation of a principal angle; *specif* : such a stone laid at the formal inauguration of the erection of a building, usu. inscribed with the date or other matters, and often hollowed out to receive records, documents, or relics **2** : the event, fact, or thing that forms the principal foundation or support upon which an achievement is based or from which a development makes its beginning ⟨this first bill is the ~ of the administration's economic policy⟩ : the principal or fundamental element, feature, or part of something ⟨natural selection remains the ~ of evolutionary theory —E.W.Sinnott⟩

corner tooth *n* : one of the third or outer pair of incisor teeth of each jaw of a horse

corner tree *n* : a tree marking a surveyor's corner

cornerwise \'⸗⸗,⸗\ *or* **cor·ner·ways** \'⸗⸗,wāz\ *adv* : with the corner set in front : DIAGONALLY

¹**cor·net** \(')kȯr¦net, -ó(ə)¦-, *usu* -ed.+V; *Brit usu* 'kó(ə)nit\ *n* -s [ME *cornette*, fr. MF *cornet*, fr. OF, dim. of *corn* horn, fr. L *cornu* — more at HORN] **1 a** *often* **cor·nett** \"\ : a Renaissance woodwind with a cup mouthpiece and tapered wooden or ivory body with no flare, six finger holes, and one thumb hole used esp. with church choral music — called also *zinke;* compare SERPENT **b** : a valved brass instrument primarily used in bands that resembles the trumpet in shape and pitch range but has a less brilliant quality — called also *cornopean* **c** (1) : a cornet player (2) : the part played by or written for a cornet player **d** : one of several organ stops **2** : something rolled or formed in the shape of a cone: as **a** : a piece of paper rolled into a cone shape and twisted at the end for use as a container **b** *also* **cor·nette** \"\ : a metallic bead flattened out and made into a roll for treatment with acid in assaying **c** : a cone-shaped pastry shell that is often filled with whipped cream **d** *Brit* : ICE-CREAM CONE **e** : a thin slice (as of meat or smoked salmon) rolled into a cone shape

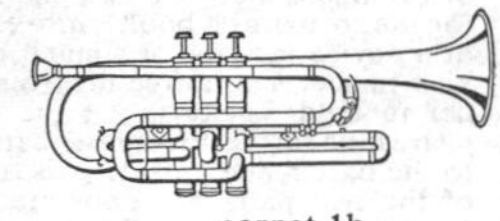

cornet 1b

²**cornet** \"\ *n* -s [MF *cornette*, fr. *corne* horn (fr. L *cornu*) + -*ette*] **1** *also* **cornette a** : a woman's cap or headdress varying in style from the 15th through the 18th centuries and usu. made of delicate materials with lappets of lace or ribbon **b** : a lappet of such a headdress **2 a** : the standard of a troop of cavalry **b** : a troop of cavalry **c** (1) : the onetime fifth grade of commissioned officer in a British cavalry troop who carried the standard (2) : the onetime lowest commissioned rank in the U. S. cavalry

cor·net-à-pis·tons \-,a'pistənz, -,ä|, -,ə|, |(,)pē'stōⁿ *or as F*\ *n, pl* **cornets-à-pistons** \", -nets- *or as F*\ [F, lit., cornet with valves] : ¹CORNET 1b

cor·net·cy \'kó(r)nətsē, -si\ *n* -ES [²*cornet* (officer) + -*cy*] : the office, rank, or commission of a cornet

cornetfish \(')⸗¦⸗,⸗\ *n* [so called fr. the long snout] : any of several slender elongated fishes (family Fistulariidae) of tropical seas having an elongated tubular snout and the scales replaced by bony plates — called also *flutemouth*

cor·net·ist *or* **cor·net·tist** \(')kó(r)¦ned·əst, -etə-\ *n* -s : a performer on the cornet

cor·ne·tite \'kó(r)nə,tīt\ *n* -s [F, fr. Jules *Cornet* †1929 Belgian geologist + F -*ite*] : a mineral consisting of basic copper phosphate $Cu(PO_4)(OH)_3$

cor·net·ti·no \,kó(r)nə'tē(,)nō\ *n* -s [It, lit., small cornet, dim. of *cornetto*] : a 2-foot reed organ stop

cor·net·to \kó(r)'ned·(,)ō\ *n, pl* **cornet·ti** \-d·(,)ē\ [It, dim. of *corno* horn, fr. L *cornu*] : ¹CORNET 1a

cor·ne·um \'kó(r)nēəm\ *n, pl* **cor·nea** \-ēə\ [NL, fr. L, neut. of *corneus* horny, fr. *cornu* horn — more at HORN] : STRATUM CORNEUM

corn-fed \'⸗,⸗\ *adj* **1** : fed or fattened on corn or other grain ⟨*corn-fed* hogs⟩ **2** : well fed : PLUMP, HEALTHY ⟨a husky, *corn-fed* youth of twenty-eight . . . addicted to thick, rare beefsteaks —W.A.White⟩

cornfield \'⸗,⸗\ *n* : a field in which corn is grown

cornfield ant *n* : a dark brown No. American ant (*Lasius alienus*) that colonizes the corn-root aphid on maize and cotton

cornfield meet *n, slang* : a head-on collision of railroad trains

cornfield pea *n, South* : COWPEA

corn flag *n* **1** : a plant of the genus *Gladiolus* (esp. *G. segetum*) **2** : a yellow iris (*Iris pseudacorus*) of Europe naturalized in the eastern U. S.

cornflakes *n pl* : a breakfast cereal made from the coarse meal of hulled corn by moistening, heating, and rolling it into flakes that are subsequently dried and usu. toasted

corn flea beetle *n* : a common flea beetle (*Chaetocnema pulicaria*) destructive to maize foliage in the eastern U. S.

corn flour *n* **1** : white, finely ground, and bolted cornmeal **2** *Brit* : CORNSTARCH

cornflower \'⸗,⸗\ *n* [so called fr. its growth in grainfields] **1 a** : CORN COCKLE **b** : a European plant (*Centaurea cyanus*) having flower heads with blue, pink, or white rays that is often cultivated in No. America — called also *bluebottle* **c** : a dogtooth violet (*Erythronium americanum*) **2** *or* **cornflower blue** : a variable color averaging a moderate purplish blue that is redder, lighter, and stronger than marine blue, redder, stronger, and slightly lighter than gentian blue, and lighter and stronger than old glory blue

cornflower aster *n* : STOKES' ASTER

corn fodder *n* : the entire Indian-corn plant cut and used either fresh or dry-cured for forage; *also* : the leaves and tops dry-cured for use as a stock feed — compare STOVER

corn fodder disease *n* : CORNSTALK DISEASE

corn gallon *n* : an old unit of capacity equal to 272¼ cubic inches or 4.46 liters

corn gluten *n* : a protein-rich product separated from starch in the wet-milling process

corn gluten feed *n* : a by-product of the wet-milling process consisting of corn gluten meal and other fractions (as bran)

corn gluten meal *n* : a high-protein feed consisting chiefly of corn gluten

corn god *n* : any one of a class of deities believed to promote crop growth and to share the annual growth, decay, and rebirth of vegetable life

corn grass *n* **1** : SILKY BENT GRASS **2** : a panic grass (*Panicum clandestinum*)

corn grits *n pl* : HOMINY — compare ¹GRITS 2

corn gromwell *n* : an annual or biennial herb (*Lithospermum arvense*) with inconspicuous white flowers growing as a weed in fields — called also *field gromwell*

corn harvester *n* : CORN BINDER

corn-hog ratio *n* : a measure of the relative profitability of producing market pork at different times expressed as the number of bushels of maize equal in market value to 100 pounds of live hogs ⟨a profitable *corn-hog ratio* is 11: 1 or higher⟩

cornhouse \'⸗,⸗\ *n, New Eng & South* : CORNCRIB

cornhusking \'⸗,⸗⸗\ *n* : the husking of corn; *specif* : HUSKING BEE

corni *pl of* CORNO

¹**cor·nice** \'kȯrnəs, 'kó(ə)n-, *esp by builders* ÷-nish *or* ÷-nesh\ *n* -s [MF *corniche, cornice*, fr. It *cornice*, perh. modif. (influenced by *cornice* crow, fr. L *cornic-, cornix*) of L *coronis* curved line, fr. Gk *korōnis*, fr. *korōnē* anything curved — more at CROWN, RAVEN] **1 a** : the typically molded and projecting horizontal member that crowns an architectural composition; *specif* : the uppermost of the three members of a classic entablature — see ENTABLATURE illustration **b** : the top course of the wall when treated as a finish or crowning member **c** : a member in a piece of furniture resembling a cornice **2** : a decorative band of metal or wood used to conceal curtain fixtures — compare VALANCE 1 **3** : an overhanging mass of snow, ice, or rock usu. on a ridge or at the top of a couloir

C cornice 1a

²**cornice** \"\ *vt* -ED/-ING/-S : to furnish or crown with or as if with a cornice

cornice brake *n* : ⁴BRAKE 5

cor·niche \'kȯr|nish, |nēsh, kȯr|'nēsh, -ó(ə)|\ *or* **corniche road** *n* -s [*corniche* fr. F, lit., cornice; *corniche road* part trans. of F *route en corniche*] : a road built along the edge of an overhanging precipice or along the face of a cliff

cor·ni·cle \'kó(r)nəkəl\ *n* -s [L *corniculum*, dim. of *cornu* horn — more at HORN] : a little horn or horn-shaped process; *specif* : either of two protruding dorsal tubes in aphids that secrete a waxy fluid and were formerly believed to discharge honeydew

cor·nic·u·late \kó(r)'nikyələt\ *adj* [L *corniculatus*, fr. *corniculum* + -*atus* -ate] : having horns or small horn-shaped processes

corniculate cartilage *n* : a small nodule of yellow elastic cartilage articulating with the apex of the arytenoid

cor·nic·u·lum \-ləm\ *n, pl* **cornicu·la** \-lə\ [L, little horn] : a small horn-shaped part or process

cor·nic·u·lus \-ləs\ *n, pl* **cornicu·li** \-,lī, -,lē\ [NL, alter. of L *corniculum*] : one of the horny tips of the ovipositor of an orthopterous insect

corni di bassetto *pl of* CORNO DI BASSETTO

corni di caccia *pl of* CORNO DI CACCIA

cornier *comparative of* CORNY

corniest *superlative of* CORNY

cor·nif·ic \(')kó(r)¦nifik\ *adj* [L *cornu* horn + E -*i-* + -*fic*] : producing horns : forming horn

cor·ni·fi·ca·tion \,kó(r)nəfə'kāshən\ *n* -s [L *cornu* horn + E -*i-* + -*fication*] **1** : conversion into horn or a horny substance or tissue **2** : the conversion of the vaginal epithelium from the columnar to the squamous type

cor·ni·form \'kȯrnə,fȯrm\ *adj* [L *cornu* horn + E -*iform*] : shaped like a horn

cor·ni·fy \-,fī\ *vi* -ED/-ING/-ES [L *cornu* horn + E -*i-* + -*fy*] : to become converted or changed into horn or horny tissue

cor·nig·er·ous \(')kȯr¦nijərəs\ *adj* [L *corniger* horn-bearing (fr. *cornu* horn + -*i-* + -*ger*, fr. *gerere* to bear) + E -*ous* — more at JEST] : having horns

corni inglesi *pl of* CORNO INGLESE

corn·i·ly \'kó(r)nᵊlē, -nəl|, |i\ *adv* [*corny* + -*ly*] : in a corny manner

cor·nin \'kȯrnən\ *n* -s [L *cornus* cornel + E -*in* — more at CORNEL] **1** : VERBENALIN **2** : CORNUS 2

corn·i·ness \'kó(r)nēnəs, -nin-\ *n* -ES [*corny* + -*ness*] : the quality or state of being corny ⟨a musical revue marked by banality and ~⟩

corning *pres part of* CORN

¹**cor·nish** \'kȯrnish, -ó(ə)n-, -nēsh\ *adj, usu cap* [*Cornwall*, county in southwest England + E -*ish*] **1 a** : of, relating to, or characteristic of Cornwall, England **b** : of, relating to, or characteristic of Cornishmen **2** : of, relating to, or characteristic of the Cornish language

²**cornish** \"\ *n* -ES *usu cap* **1** : a Celtic language of Cornwall, England, extinct since the late 18th century — see INDO-EUROPEAN LANGUAGES table **2 a** : an English breed of domestic fowls with pea combs, very close feathering, and compact sturdy bodies **b** : a bird of the Cornish breed now much used in cross-breeding for meat production

³**cornish** \"\ *dial var of* CORNICE

cornish chough *n, usu cap 1st C* [¹*cornish*] **1** : a red-billed chough (*Pyrrhocorax pyrrhocorax*) now rare in England but found in mountainous parts of Europe and northern Africa **2** : the heraldic representation of a Cornish chough with black feathers and red legs and beak

cornish diamond *n, usu cap C* : a quartz crystal from Cornwall

cornish elm *n, usu cap C* : a narrow-pyramidal tree (*Ulmus stricta*) long cultivated for its graceful habit and ascending branches

cornish heath *n, usu cap C* : a low bushy shrub (*Erica vagans*) common on the moors of Cornwall and in southwestern Europe and often cultivated elsewhere

cor·nish·man \-mən\ *n, pl* **cornishmen** *cap* : a native or resident of Cornwall, England

cornish pasty *n, usu cap C* : cooked meat and vegetables encased in pastry and baked

cornish stone *n, usu cap C* : china stone found in extensive beds in Cornwall and Devonshire, England, and much used in English ceramics

corn juice *n* : WHISKEY; *esp* : CORN WHISKEY

corn kale *n* [so called fr. its frequent occurrence as a weed in fields of grain] : CHARLOCK

corn knife *n* : a long heavy knife used in chopping down Indian cornstalks in harvesting by hand

corn·land \'kȯrn,land\ *n* [ME, fr. ¹*corn* + *land*] : land used for or suitable for the growing of corn

corn law *n* : a law regulating trade in grain; *specif, usu cap C&L* : one of a series of laws in force in Great Britain before 1846 that prohibited or laid heavy duties upon the importation of foreign grain for home consumption except when the price rose above a certain rate

corn leaf aphid *n* : a dusky greenish or brownish aphid (*Rhopalosiphum maidis*) that feeds on the foliage and flowers of maize and other commercially important grasses

corn lily *n* **1** : HEDGE BINDWEED **2** : FIELD BINDWEED **3** : WANDFLOWER 1 **4** : a plant of the genus *Ixia* **5** : a tall white hellebore (*Veratrum californicum*) with broad plaited leaves and panicles of greenish flowers that is a characteristic floral element of moist upland meadows of the Sierra Nevada of California

corn liquor *n* : CORN WHISKEY

cornloft \'⸗,⸗\ *n* : GRANARY

corn maggot *n* **1** : SEED-CORN MAGGOT **2** : the larva of the gout fly

corn marigold *n* : a European herb (*Chrysanthemum segetum*) with bright yellow rays that is common in grainfields — called also *field marigold*

corn mayweed *n* **1** : FIELD CHAMOMILE **2** : a European weed (*Matricaria inodora*) with white flowers and finely divided leaves that is naturalized and sometimes cultivated in eastern No. America

cornmeal \'⸗¦⸗\ *n* : meal made from white or yellow corn

corn mill *n* **1** *Brit* : a flour mill **2** : a mill for grinding corn

corn mint *n* : a European mint (*Mentha arvensis*) naturalized in No. America with a pubescent stem and flowers in subglobose axillary clusters — called also *field mint*

cornmonger \'⸗,⸗⸗\ *n, archaic* : a grain dealer

corn mustard *n* : CHARLOCK

cor·no \'kȯr(,)nō\ *n, pl* **cor·ni** \-nē\ [It, horn, fr. L *cornu* — more at HORN] : FRENCH HORN

corno di bas·set·to \¦⸗(,)⸗(,)dēbə'se,tō\ *n, pl* **corni di bassetto** \¦⸗(,)⸗-\ [It] **1** : BASSET HORN **2** : an 8-foot reed organ stop of clarinet quality

corno di cac·cia \-,dē'kä(,)chä\ *n, pl* **corni di caccia** [It, lit., hunting horn] : NATURAL HORN

corno flute *n* [It *corno* horn + E *flute*] : a soft 8-foot organ stop

corn oil *n* : a yellow semidrying fatty oil obtained from the germs of corn kernels and used chiefly as a salad oil and in soft soaps — called also *maize oil*

cor·no in·gle·se \¦kȯr(,)nō|iŋ'glāsē, -in'g-, -ā(,)sā,-āsē\ *n, pl* **cor·ni in·gle·si** \-r(,)nē|...ā(,)sē, -āzē\ [It] : ENGLISH HORN

corn on the cob : corn cooked and eaten on the cob

cor·no·pe·an \,kȯrnə'pēən, kȯr'nōpē-\ *n* -s [perh. fr. It *corno* horn + *pean* paean, fr. L *paean*] **1** *Brit* : ¹CORNET 1b **2** : a powerful 8-foot reed organ stop

corn oyster *n* : a fritter containing young corn cut from the cob and cooked on a griddle

corn parsley *n* : a wild parsley (*Petroselinum segetum*) found as a weed in European grainfields

corn picker *n* : a machine for gathering the ears and removing the husks from standing Indian corn

corn pink *n* : CORN COCKLE

corn plant *n* : any of several plants of the genus *Dracaena* with broad leaves either green or variously striped (esp. *D. fragrans* and *D. deremensis*)

corn planter *n* : any of various mechanical devices for planting Indian corn in furrows or hills

corn plow *n, chiefly Midland* : a machine for cultivating corn

corn pone *n, South & Midland* : corn bread often made without milk or eggs, shaped in irregular ovals by the palm of the hand, and baked or fried on a griddle

corn popper *n* : any of various utensils used in popping corn

corn poppy *n* : an annual red-flowered poppy (*Papaver rhoeas*) common in European grainfields and cultivated in several varieties — called also *field poppy*

corn pudding *n* : a pudding made with sweet corn canned or cut from the cob, eggs, milk, and other ingredients

corn-root aphid *n* : a destructive aphid (*Anuraphis maidiradicis*) that feeds on the roots esp. of maize or cotton and is dependent on the cornfield ant for distribution and care

corn rootworm *n* : the root-eating larva of any of several cucumber beetles of the genus *Diabrotica* — used esp. when the larvae are found on the roots of maize

corn rose *n* **1** : CORN POPPY **2** : CORN COCKLE

corns *pl of* CORN, *pres 3d sing of* CORN

-corns *pl of* -CORN

cornsack \'⸗,⸗\ *n, chiefly Austral* : a burlap bag : GUNNYSACK

corn salad *n* [so called fr. its occurrence as a weed in fields of grain] : a plant of the genus *Valerianella; esp* : a low European herb (*V. olitoria*) that is widely cultivated as a salad plant and potherb

corn sap beetle *n* : a small brown beetle (*Carpophilus dimidiatus*) with truncate wing covers that is related to the dried-fruit beetle, that is sometimes a destructive pest of sweet corn, and that feeds on decaying fruits and vegetation and sometimes swarms in rice mills

corn sheller *n* **1** : a machine or device that separates the kernels of corn from the cob **2** *slang* : a repeating firearm ⟨defending himself with a *corn sheller*⟩

corn shucking *n* : CORNHUSKING

corn silk *n* : the silky styles on an ear of Indian corn

corn smut *n* : a smut attacking Indian corn — compare BOIL SMUT, HEAD SMUT

corn snake *n* [so called fr. its being found in corncribs and cornfields] **:** a large harmless No. American snake (*Elaphe guttata*) brightly blotched with scarlet on a grayish ground — called also *red rat snake*

corn snakeroot *n* **:** BUTTON SNAKEROOT

corn snapdragon *n* **:** a European wild snapdragon (*Antirrhinum orontium*)

corn snapper *n* **:** a machine that snaps the ear of corn from the stalk but does not husk it

corn snow *n* **:** granular snow formed by alternate thawing and freezing — called also *spring corn, spring snow*

corn speedwell *n* **:** a small annual or winter annual speedwell (*Veronica arvensis*) of Europe and America found in fields and waste places and having median and upper leaves entire or toothed

corn spurry *or* **corn spurrey** *n* **:** a small European weed (*Spergula arvensis*) with whorled leaves and white flowers

cornstalk \ˈ=,=\ *n* **1 :** a stalk of Indian corn **2** *slang Austral* **:** AUSTRALIAN; *specif* **:** a native of New So. Wales

cornstalk disease *also* **cornstalk poisoning** *n* **1 :** a severe frequently fatal intoxication of cattle fed on corn fodder that resembles pasteurellosis but is usu. considered due to abnormalities in the nitrogen content of the fodder **2 :** an acute encephalitic disease of horses fed on moldy corn fodder

cornstalk pine *n* **:** LOBLOLLY PINE 1

cornstalk weed *or* **cornstalk pondweed** *n* **:** a river weed (*Potamogeton lucens*) with shining elongated leaves

cornstarch \ˈ=,=\ *n* **:** starch resembling a fine white flour made from corn and used chiefly in foods as a thickening agent (as in puddings and gravies), in making corn syrup and sugars, and in the manufacture of adhesives and sizes for paper and textiles

corn stick *n* **:** a corn bread baked in a special muffin pan having cups shaped like ears of corn

cornstock \ˈ=,=\ *n* **:** CORNSTALK

corn sugar *n* **:** DEXTROSE; *esp* **:** dextrose made by complete hydrolysis of cornstarch

corn syrup *n* **:** a transparent thick syrup containing dextrins, maltose, and dextrose that is obtained by partial hydrolysis of cornstarch and is used chiefly in foods (as in bakery products and candy) and in the brewing industry — called also *glucose, starch syrup*

corn thistle *n* **:** CANADA THISTLE

cor·nu \ˈkȯr(,)n(y)ü\ *n, pl* **cor·nua** \-_n(y)əwə\ [L, horn — more at HORN] **:** something shaped like or resembling a horn; *esp* **:** a bodily structure suggesting a horn in form (as either of the lateral divisions of a bicornuate uterus, one of the lateral processes of the hyoid bone, or one of the gray columns of the spinal cord) — **cor·nu·al** \-_nyəwəl\ *adj*

cor·nu·co·pia \,kȯ(r)n(y)əˈkōpēə *sometimes* -nēˈk- *or* -niˈk-\ *n* -s [LL, fr. L *cornu copiae* horn of plenty, fr. *cornu* horn + *copiae*, gen. of *copia* abundance, plenty — more at COPIOUS] **1 :** a curved goat's horn from the mouth of which fruit and ears of grain overflow used as a decorative motif in art, architecture, and design (as on furniture, porcelain, and silverwork), emblematic of abundance, and representing the horn of the Greek nymph Amalthea that was endowed with the virtue of becoming filled with whatever its possessor wished — called also *horn of plenty* **2 :** something that produces an overflowing and inexhaustible supply esp. of desirable things ⟨American consumption . . . allows mass production to continue with safety its outpouring of goods from its miraculous ~ —P.M.Mazur⟩ **:** an inexhaustible store **:** ABUNDANCE ⟨a pair of books that . . . add up to a 550-page ~ of humor —Bernard Kalb⟩ **3 :** a receptacle shaped like a horn or cone (as a paper horn filled with candy or a pastry filled with whipped cream) **4 :** a protrusion of the choroid plexus into each lateral recess of the fourth ventricle of the brain

cornucopia 1

cor·nu·co·pi·an \¦==¦=pēən\ *adj* **:** resembling a cornucopia **:** existing in or producing abundance ⟨~ industry⟩ **:** marked by abundance ⟨~ markets⟩

cornucopia sofa *n* **:** an early 19th century sofa with arms carved in the form of cornucopias

cor·nu·da \kȯrˈnüdə\ *n* -s [AmerSp, fr. Sp, fem. of *cornudo* horned, fr. L *cornutus*] **:** HAMMERHEAD 3a

cor·nule \ˈkȯr(,)nyül\ *n* -s [LL *cornulum* small horn, dim. of L *cornu* horn] **:** a small horny plate or process; *specif* **:** one of those that serve as teeth in the lower jaw of the duckbill

cor·nu·li·tes \,kȯrnyəˈlīd·ēz\ *n, cap* [NL, fr. LL *cornulum* + NL *-ites* -ite] **:** a genus of extinct tubicolous annelids known from trumpet-shaped tubes with annulations and longitudinal striations found in Ordovician and Silurian strata

corn up *vt, slang* **:** to make corny **:** introduce corny elements into ⟨*corn up* a story⟩

cor·nu·pete \ˈkȯrnyə,pēt\ *adj* [LL *cornupeta*, fr. L *cornu* horn + LL *-peta* (fr. L *petere* to go to, head for, attack) — more at FEATHER] **:** goring or attacking with the horns — used of a bull represented in sculpture or painting

cor·nus \ˈkȯrnəs\ *n* [NL, fr. L, cornel — more at CORNEL] **1** *cap* **:** a genus of shrubs and small trees of the family Cornaceae usu. having very hard wood and perfect flowers with a 2-celled ovary — see CORNEL, DOGWOOD; compare KINNIKINNICK **2** -ES **:** the dried bark of the root of the flowering dogwood containing a bitter principle sometimes used as a mild astringent and stomachic

cor·nu spiral \(ˈ)kȯrˌn(y)ü-\ *n, usu cap C* [after Marie Alfred *Cornu* †1902 Fr. physicist] **:** a spiral of two oppositely coiled branches obtained by plotting as abscissas and ordinates respectively the corresponding values of a certain two integrals and used to afford graphical solution of various problems in diffraction of light

¹**cor·nute** \(ˈ)kȯrˌn(y)üt\ *vt* -ED/-ING/-S [L *cornutus* horned, fr. *cornu* horn] *archaic* **:** to bestow horns upon **:** make a cuckold of **:** CUCKOLD

²**cornute** \"\ *n* -s [L *cornutus* horned] **:** something forked or having horns: as **a :** ¹CUCKOLD 1 — compare HORN 4b **b** [LL *cornutus*, fr. L] **:** DILEMMA; *esp* **:** a sophistical dilemma

³**cornute** \"\ *adj* [L *cornutus*] *bot* **:** CORNUTED

cor·nut·ed \-üdəd\ *adj* [fr. past part. of *cornute*] **:** bearing or having horns or shaped like a horn

cor·nu·to \kȯrˈnü,tō\ *n* -s [It, fr. L *cornutus* horned] **:** CUCKOLD — compare HORN 4b

corn violet *n* **:** a European herb (*Specularia speculum-veneris*) with purple flowers

corn·wall \ˈkȯrn,wȯl, -,wəl\ *adj, usu cap* [fr. *Cornwall*, former county in England] **:** of or from Cornwall, England **:** of the kind or style prevalent in Cornwall **:** CORNISH

corn·wal·lis \kȯrnˈwälə̇s, -wȯl-\ *n* -ES [after Charles, 1st Marquis *Cornwallis* †1805 Eng. soldier] **:** a muster in masquerade formerly held in New England and believed to commemorate the surrender of Lord Cornwallis at Yorktown

corn·wall·ite \ˈkȯrn,wȯ,līt, -,wə,l-\ *n* -s [G *cornwallit*, fr. *Cornwall*, former county in southwest England, its locality + G *-it* -ite] **:** a mineral consisting of a basic copper arsenate $Cu_5(AsO_4)_2(OH)_4.H_2O$ resembling malachite

cornwall stone *n, usu cap C* **:** CORNISH STONE

corn weevil *n* **1 :** GRANARY WEEVIL **2 :** a billbug attacking maize

corn whiskey *n* **:** whiskey distilled from corn mash; *specif* **:** whiskey distilled from a mash made up of not less than 80 percent corn and aged in uncharred or used charred oak containers — compare BOURBON 4

corn wil·lie \(ˈ)kȯrnˌwilē\ *n* [*corn* (as in *corn beef*) + *Willie*, nickname for *William*] *slang* **:** canned corned beef esp. as an army ration

corn woundwort *n* [so called fr. its growth in cultivated areas] **:** a European weed (*Stachys arvensis*) naturalized in No. America and in Australia — called also *shiverweed*

¹**corny** \ˈkȯrnē, ˈkō(ə)n-, -ni\ *adj, usu* -ER/-EST [ME, fr. ¹*corn* + *-y*] **1** *archaic* **:** tasting strongly of malt **2 :** of or relating to corn **:** producing, abounding in, or full of corn ⟨the ~ ear —Matthew Prior⟩ **3 :** using familiar and stereotyped formulas believed to appeal to the unsophisticated **:** TRITE ⟨the American satirizing the Englishman and the Englishman satirizing the American reach their corniest and most obvious depths —Stephen Potter⟩ ⟨a play full of ~ music and ~ jokes⟩ **:** mawkishly sentimental ⟨fantasy about a blue kitten . . . in less talented hands . . . could have been painfully ~ —*Atlantic*⟩ **:** OLD-FASHIONED ⟨TV sets are selling poorly because their styling is a little backward, sort of ~ —*Time*⟩ **:** characterized by threadbare moralizing, exaggerated theatricality, or grandiose but commonplace sentiments ⟨especially eloquent in a slightly ~ way, with the wide gestures and grandiloquent intonations of a U. S. senator —F.L.Allen⟩

²**corny** \"\ *adj, usu* -ER/-EST [³*corn* + *-y*] **1 :** relating to corns **2 :** having corns on the feet

co·ro·a·do \,kȯrəˈwä(,)dō\ *n, pl* **coroado** *or* **coroados** *usu cap* [Pg, lit., crowned one, fr. *coroado* (past part. of *coroar* to crown), fr. L *coronatus*, past part. of *coronare* to crown; fr. their crown-shaped hairdress — more at CROWN] **1 :** BORORO **2 :** the Caingang people of São Paulo, southeastern Brazil

co·ro·di·ary *or* **cor·ro·di·ary** \kəˈrōdē,erē\ *n* -ES [ML *corrodiarius*, fr. *corrodium* + L *-arius* -ary] **:** the recipient of a corody

cor·o·dy *or* **cor·ro·dy** \ˈkȯrədē\ *n* -ES [ME *corodie*, fr. ML *corrodium, corredium, conredium*, irreg. fr. OF *corroi, conroi, conrei* order, arrangement, fr. *corroyer, correer, conreer* to prepare, arrange, furnish — more at CURRY] **1 a :** the right of free quarters due a lord on circuit from his vassals **b :** an allowance of food, clothing, or other commodities due from a religious house to the crown and assigned to one of its subjects **2 :** an allowance of provisions for maintenance (as food or clothing) that is dispensed as a charity

corojo *var of* COROZO

co·rol·la \kəˈrälə\ *n* -s [NL, fr. L, small garland, dim. of *corona* — more at CROWN] **:** the inner set of floral leaves that immediately surround the sporophylls, consist of separate or fused petals, and are often highly colored in contrast to the calyx but sometimes inconspicuous or even absent

open flower of the cinnamon rose showing corolla

cor·ol·la·ceous \¦kȯrə¦lāshəs, ¦kär-\ *adj* [*corolla* + *-aceous*] **:** of or resembling a corolla

¹**cor·ol·lary** \ˈkȯrə,lerē, ˈkär-, -eri, *Brit usu* kəˈrälərī\ *n* -ES [ME *corolarie*, fr. LL *corollarium*, fr. L, gratuity, garland, fr. *corolla* small garland + *-arium* -ary — more at COROLLA] **1 a :** a proposition that follows upon one just demonstrated and that requires no additional proof **b :** a deduction, consequence, or additional inference more or less immediate from a proved proposition **2** *obs* **a :** something appended to a speech or writing **:** APPENDIX, CONCLUSION **b :** something beyond what is due **:** something added or superfluous **3 a :** something that naturally follows **:** a practical consequence **:** RESULT ⟨the war has . . . paved the way for an economic and, as a ~, a semipolitical internationalism —Edward Sapir⟩ ⟨love was a stormy passion, and jealousy its normal ~ —Ida Treat⟩ **b :** something that incidentally or naturally attends or accompanies **:** ACCOMPANIMENT ⟨only after the physical impossibility of the revolutionary goals had been demonstrated did its political ~ find acceptance —H.A.Kissinger⟩ ⟨a ~ to the problem of the number of vessels to be built was that of the types of vessels to be constructed —Daniel Marx⟩

²**corollary** \"\ *adj* **:** constituting a corollary: **a :** derived from a proposition **:** CONSEQUENTIAL **b :** that follows from or derives naturally from a circumstance or phenomenon **:** RESULTING ⟨a sound economy and the ~ prosperity⟩ **c :** occurring together with or accompanying another phenomenon **:** ASSOCIATED, SUPPLEMENTARY ⟨five years after the Emancipation Proclamation the Fourteenth Amendment was established as a ~ measure⟩ ⟨expansion of the knowledge of atomic energy leading to ~ experimentation . . . in power generation —*Americana Annual*⟩

co·rol·late \kəˈräl,lāt, ˈkȯrəl, ¦_lət\ *or* **co·rol·lat·ed** \|,lād·əd\ *adj* [*corollate*, ISV *coroll-* (fr. NL *corolla*) + *-ate; corollated* fr. *coroliate* + *-ed*] **:** having a corolla

corolla tube *n* **:** TUBE 1b(2)

cor·ol·lif·er·ous \¦kȯrə¦lif(ə)rəs\ *adj* [ISV *coroll-* (fr. NL *corolla*) + *-i-* + *-ferous*; prob. orig. formed as F *corollifère*] **:** bearing or having a corolla

co·rol·li·form \kəˈrälə,fȯrm\ *adj* [ISV *coroll-* (fr. NL *corolla*) + *-iform*; prob. orig. formed as F *corolliforme*] **:** having the form of a corolla

co·rol·line \kəˈräl,līn, ˈkȯrə,-\ *adj* [*corolla* + *-ine*] **1 :** relating to or resembling a corolla **2 :** borne on a corolla

cor·o·man·del \,kȯrəˈmand³l\ *n* -s *often cap* [*Coromandel* coast, southeast India] **:** COLCOTHAR 2

coromandel ebony \¦==¦==-\ *also* **coromandel** \,==ˈ==\ *n, usu cap C* **:** an East Indian timber tree (*Diospyros melanoxylon*) with a hard dark-colored wood

coromandel gooseberry *n, usu cap C* **:** CARAMBOLA

coromandel screen *n, often cap C* [so called fr. its being formerly brought to Europe by way of the Coromandel coast] **:** a Chinese lacquered folding screen

coromandel wood *n* **:** CALAMANDER

¹**co·ro·na** \kəˈrōnə\ *n* -s [L, garland, crown, cornice — more at CROWN] **1 :** the projecting part of a classic cornice the underside of which is often cut with a drip **2 :** something suggesting a crown: as **a** (1) **:** a usu. colored circle often seen around and close to a luminous body (as the sun or moon) caused by diffraction produced by suspended droplets or occas. particles of dust — see HALO 1 (2) **:** the tenuous outermost part of the atmosphere of the sun extending for millions of miles from its surface, containing very highly ionized atoms of iron, nickel, and other gases that indicate a temperature of millions of degrees, and appearing to the naked eye as a pearly gray halo around the moon's black disk during a total eclipse of the sun but observable at other times with a coronagraph; *also* **:** a similar portion of the atmosphere of a star (3) **:** a circle of light made by the apparent convergence of the streamers of the aurora borealis about a spot in the heavens toward which the dipping needle points **b** [NL, fr. L] **:** the upper portion of a body part (as of a tooth or of the skull) **c** [NL, fr. L] **:** CROWN 12a **d** [ML, fr. L] **:** a crown or circlet suspended from the roof or vaulting of churches to hold tapers lighted on solemn occasions **e** [NL, fr. L] **:** an appendage or series of united appendages borne on the inner side of the corolla in certain flowers (as in the daffodil, jonquil, and milkweed) and often resembling an additional whorl of the perianth **f** [ML, fr. L] (1) **:** a circlet (as of gold) on an ecclesiastical vestment for the head (2) **:** the tonsure of a cleric **g :** a faint glow adjacent to the surface of an electrical conductor at sufficiently high voltage that results from electrical discharge and indicates an early stage of electric breakdown in the surrounding air or gas **h :** a usu. radial zone of minerals surrounding another mineral or occurring at the contact between certain minerals (as olivine and feldspar) **i** [NL, fr. L] **:** the group of cells at the apex of the oogonium in stoneworts **j** [NL, fr. L] **:** the ciliated trochal disk of rotifers and some other organisms **3** [NL, fr. L] **:** MEDULLARY SHEATH **2 4** [It, lit., crown, fr. L] **:** a mark ⌒ used in musical notation to indicate a hold or a pause **:** FERMATA **5 :** ¹KRONE **6 :** ROSARY **7** [fr. *La Corona*, a trademark] **:** a long cigar having the sides straight to the unsealed end and roundly blunt at the sealed end **8** [NL, fr. L] **:** the main part of the calcareous test of a sea urchin excluding the apical system of plates **9** [Sp, lit., crown, fr. L] **:** a saddle blanket shaped to the saddle and bound at the margin with a fold of different color

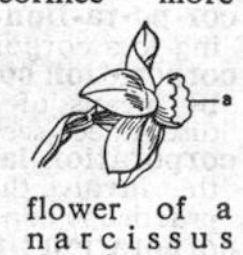

flower of a narcissus showing a corona

²**corona** \"\ [NL, fr. L, garland, crown — more at CROWN] *syn of* CORONATAE

cor·o·nach \ˈkȯrənək, -nəḵ\ *n* -s [ScGael *corranach* & IrGael *coránach*, fr. MIr *com-* together + (assumed) MIr *rānach* outcry, weeping — more at CO-] **:** a lamentation for the dead as sung or played on the bagpipes in Scotland and Ireland **:** DIRGE

corona discharge *n* [¹*corona*] **:** the discharge of electricity causing a corona (sense 2g)

cor·o·na·dite \,kȯrəˈnä,dīt\ *n* -s [Francisco Vásquez *Coronado* †1554 Sp. explorer + E *-ite*; fr. its occurrence in the Coronado vein, Greenlee county, southeast Arizona] **:** a lead and manganese oxide $MnPbMn_6O_{14}$ that is an important constituent of manganese ore, occurs in black massive form with fibrous structure, and is isostructural with hollandite

¹**cor·o·na·do** \-ä(,)dō\ *n* -s [AmerSp, fr. Sp (past part. of *coronar* to crown), fr. L *coronatus*, past part. of *coronare* to crown; fr. the yellow band on its side — more at CROWN] **:** AMBERJACK

²**coronado** \"\ *n, pl* **coronado** *or* **coronados** *usu cap* [AmerSp, fr. Sp, past part. of *coronar* to crown; fr. their crown-shaped hairdress] **1 :** CAINGANG **2 :** ²MATACO **3 :** ABIPÓN

co·ro·na·graph *or* **co·ro·no·graph** \kəˈrōnə,graf\ *n* -s [*coronagraph* alter. of *coronograph*, fr. ¹*corona* + *-o-* + *-graph*] **:** a telescope designed to facilitate observations of the sun's corona without benefit of a total solar eclipse, usu. containing a monochromatic objective lens and a series of diaphragms to eliminate scattered light, and used with a monochromatic filter matching one of the wavelength regions of the bright emission lines of the corona — **co·ro·na·graph·ic** *or* **co·ro·no·graph·ic** \kə¦rōnə¦grafik\ *adj*

¹**cor·o·nal** *also* **cor·o·nel** \ˈkȯrən³l, ˈkär-\ *n* -s [ME *coronal*, *coronell*, fr. AF *coronal*, fr. L *coronalis* of a crown, fr. *corona* crown + *-alis* -al] **1 :** a circlet for the head esp. implying rank or dignity **:** CROWN, CORONET; *also* **:** such a circlet around a helmet **2 :** a garland of flowers or leaves for the head

²**cor·o·nal** \ˈkȯrən³l, ˈkär- *or, with reference to something familiarly known as "corona"*, kəˈrōn-\ *adj* [MF or L; MF *coronal*, fr. L *coronalis*] **1 :** of or relating to a corona or crown (as a king's crown, the corona of a flower, the sun's corona, the crown of a tooth) ⟨the law and his ~ oath require his . . . assent to what laws the Parliament agree upon —John Milton⟩ **2** *anat* **:** lying in the direction of the coronal suture **:** of or relating to the frontal plane which passes through the long axis of the body **3** *phonetics* **:** RETROFLEX

cor·o·nale \,kȯrəˈna(,)lē, -nā-, -nä-\ *n* -s [NL, fr. L, neut. of *coronalis* coronal] **:** the point of the coronal suture marking the greatest diameter of the frontal bone

coronal root *n* **:** an adventitious root that springs from the stem just above the surface of the ground (as in wheat) — compare SEMINAL ROOT

coronal suture *n* **:** a suture extending across the skull between the parietal and frontal bones

co·ro·na ra·di·a·ta \kə¦rōnə,rādēˈād·ə\ *n, pl* **coro·nae radia·tae** \-,nē, . . . ˈā,tē\ [NL, lit., rayed crown] **1 :** the zone of small follicular cells immediately surrounding the ovum in the Graafian follicle and accompanying the ovum on its discharge from the follicle **2 :** a large mass of medullated nerve fibers radiating from the internal capsule to the cerebral cortex

¹**cor·o·nary** \ˈkȯrə,nerē, ˈkär-, -ri\ *adj* [L *coronarius*, fr. *corona* garland, crown + *-arius* -ary] **1 :** of, relating to, or being a crown or coronal **:** forming or designed to form a crown or coronal **2** *anat* **a :** resembling a crown or circlet **:** encircling another part **b :** relating to or involving the coronary vessels of the heart; *broadly* **:** of or relating to the heart

²**coronary** \"\ *n* -ES **1 :** CORONARY ARTERY **2 a :** CORONARY OCCLUSION **b :** CORONARY THROMBOSIS

coronary artery *n* **1 :** either of the two arteries, right and left, which arise from the aorta immediately above the semilunar valves and supply the tissues of the heart itself **2 :** one of various arteries encircling the lips **3 :** the artery passing along the lesser curvature of the stomach

coronary bone *n* **:** the small pastern bone of the horse and related animals

coronary cushion *also* **coronary band** *or* **coronary ring** *n* **:** a thickened band of extremely vascular tissue that lies at the upper border of the wall of the hoof of the horse and related animals and that plays an important part in the secretion of the horny walls

coronary disease *also* **coronary artery disease** *or* **coronary heart disease** *n* **:** a condition (as sclerosis or thrombosis) that reduces the blood flow through the coronary arteries to the heart muscle

coronary failure *n* **:** heart failure in which the heart muscle is deprived of the blood necessary to meet its functional needs as a result of narrowing or blocking of one or more of the coronary arteries

coronary insufficiency *n* **:** cardiac insufficiency of relatively mild degree

coronary ligament *n* **1 :** the folds of peritoneum connecting the posterior surface of the liver and the diaphragm **2 :** a part of the capsular ligament of the knee connecting each semilunar fibrocartilage with the margin of the head of the tibia

coronary occlusion *n* **:** the partial or complete blocking of a coronary artery (as by a thrombus or by spasm or sclerosis of the artery)

coronary sclerosis *n* **:** sclerosis of the coronary arteries of the heart

coronary sinus *n* **:** a venous channel that is derived from the sinus venosus, is continuous with the largest of the cardiac veins, receives most of the blood from the walls of the heart, and opens into the right atrium

coronary sulcus *n* **:** a depression surrounding the heart at the atrioventricular junction and giving passage to coronary arteries, veins, and sinus

coronary thrombosis *n* **:** the formation of a thrombus in a coronary artery of the heart

coronary valve *n* **:** the fold of endocardium at the opening of the coronary sinus into the right atrium

coronary vein *n* **1 a :** any of several veins that drain the tissues of the heart and empty into the coronary sinus **b :** CARDIAC VEIN — not used technically **2 :** a vein draining the lesser curvature of the stomach and emptying into the portal vein

coronas *pl of* CORONA

cor·o·na·ta \,kȯrəˈnād·ə, -ād·ə\ [NL, fr. L, neut. pl. of *coronatus*] *syn of* CORONATAE

cor·o·na·tae \-d·(,)ē\ *n pl, cap* [NL, fr. L, fem. pl. of *coronatus*] **:** an order of Scyphomedusae comprising rather large pelagic or deep-sea jellyfishes that have marginal tentacles and the bell margin divided into lappets

¹**cor·o·nate** \ˈkȯrə,nāt, ˈkär-\ *vt* -ED/-ING/-S [L *coronatus*, past part. of *coronare* to crown, fr. *corona* garland, crown] **:** CROWN

²**coronate** \"\ *adj* [L *coronatus*] **:** CROWNED, CORONATED

cor·o·nat·ed \-ād·əd\ *adj* [fr. past part. of ¹*coronate*] **:** CROWNED; *specif* **:** having a crown, crest, corona, or some similar structure — used esp. of univalve shells when the spire is surrounded by a row of spines or tubercles

cor·o·na·tion \,kȯrəˈnāshən, ,kär-\ *n* -s *often attrib* [ME *coronacioun*, fr. MF *coronation*, fr. *coroner* to crown + *-ation* — more at CROWN] **1 :** the act or occasion of crowning: as **a :** the ceremony of investing a sovereign or his consort with the royal crown **b :** the ceremony of enthroning or of celebrating the official accession of a sovereign ⟨~ festivities of the present emperor of Japan —Edwin Strawbridge⟩ **c :** the crowning or ceremonious installation of a person that is chosen as the principal in a celebration or other function or that is the winner of a contest (as a beauty contest) ⟨the ~ of the queen of the lilac festival⟩ ⟨the ~ of this year's Miss America⟩ **2 :** a culminating act or event **:** an act or event that brings to completion ⟨the victory is a ~ of all our efforts⟩ **3 :** the official accession to the highest office among a group or the ceremony marking such an accession ⟨the anniversary of the pope's ~ —*Springfield (Mass.) Daily News*⟩ ⟨the Iowan tribe . . . council put off scheduling a ~ —*Life*⟩

coronation oath *n* **:** an oath taken by a sovereign at coronation

coronel *var of* CORONAL

cor·o·nene \ˈkȯr-ə-,nēn\ *n* -s [L *corona* crown + E *-ene*] **:** a pale yellow very high-melting fluorescent hydrocarbon $C_{24}H_{12}$ having a molecular structure like a crown with six benzene rings fused together

cor·o·ner \ˈkȯrənə(r), ˈkär-\ *n* -s [ME *coroner, corowner*, fr. AF *corouner*, fr. OF *corone, coroune* crown (fr. L *corona*) + AF *-er* (fr. L *-arius*) — more at -ER] **1 :** an officer of an earlier time in England whose duty was to keep a record of the pleas of the crown in a county and guard the royal revenues arising from them **2 :** a public officer whose principal duty is to inquire by an inquest held in the presence of a jury into the cause of any death which there is reason to suppose is not due to natural causes — compare MEDICAL EXAMINER **3 :** a chief constable of a sheading in the Isle of Man

[1]**cor·o·net** \ˌkȯrəˈnet, ˌkär-, *usu* -ed·+V; *esp Brit* ˈ≈≈ˌnət\ *n* -s [MF *coronette,* fr. OF *coronete,* fr. *corone* crown + *-ete* -ette] **1 a :** a small or lesser crown usu. signifying a high rank below that of a sovereign **b :** CROWN **2 :** something resembling or suggesting a coronet: as **a :** an ornamental wreath, circlet, or band for the head usu. for wear by women on formal occasions **b :** a small structure resembling a crown: (1) **:** the lower part of a horse's pastern where the horn terminates in skin (2) **:** the burr of an antler (3) **:** a terminal circle of small spines or hairs (as on the genitalia of certain arthropods) **3 :** a card sequence in some card games (as vint) consisting of three or more cards in any suit or three or four aces held in one hand **4 :** a white band in the habit of certain Catholic sisterhoods that encircles the face and to which a black veil is pinned

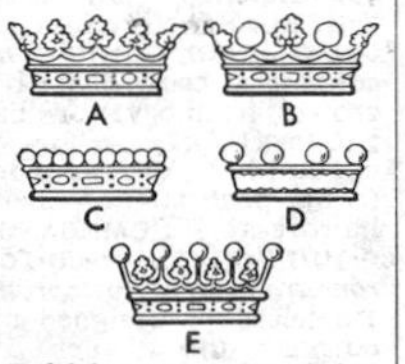

A B C D E

British coronets: duke, *A;* marquess, *B;* viscount, *C;* baron, *D;* earl, *E*

[2]**coronet** \"\ *vt* **coroneted** *or* **coronetted; coroneted** *or* **coronetted; coroneting** *or* **coronetting; coronets :** to provide with a coronet: **a :** to raise to a rank or position that warrants the wearing of a coronet; *esp* **:** to raise to such a rank in an official ceremony ⟨the ~*ing* of a May queen⟩ **b :** to decorate or adorn with a coronet ⟨a heraldic shield bearing a ~*ed* miter⟩ ⟨plain and ~*ed* designs —Charles Hasler⟩

coronet boot *n* **:** a shield of heavy leather or rubber placed over the hoof wall and coronet of the rear hooves of a racehorse to prevent injury from blows by the front shoes

coroneted *or* **coronetted** *adj* [[1]*coronet* + *-ed*] **:** of noble birth or rank ⟨the princess and her ~ companions⟩

cor·o·nilla *in sense 1* ˌkȯrəˈnilə, *in sense 2* -nē(y)ə\ *n* [NL, irreg. fr. L *corona* crown; fr. the flower clusters — more at CROWN] **1 a** *cap* **:** a genus of Old World often woody herbs (family Leguminosae) having purple, pink, or yellow flowers in long-stalked axillary heads or umbels — see AXSEED, SCORPION SENNA **b** -s **:** any plant of the genus *Coronilla* **2** *also* **co·ro·ni·llo** \-nē(ˌ)(y)ō\ -s [AmerSp *coronilla, coronillo,* fr. Sp *coronilla* crown of the head, dim. of *corona* crown, fr. L] **:** a valuable timber tree (*Gleditsia amorphoides*) of Argentina the bark of which yields a saponin

cor·o·nil·lin \-nilən\ *n* -s [ISV *coronill-* (fr. NL *Coronilla*) + *-in*] **:** a poisonous yellow glucoside from seeds of plants of the genus *Coronilla* that affects the heart like digitalis

co·ro·ni·on \kəˈrōnēˌän, -ēən\ *n, pl* **coro·nia** \-ēə\ [NL, irreg. fr. Gk *korōnē* crow; akin to Gk *korax* raven — more at RAVEN] **:** the tip of the coronoid process of the mandible — see CRANIOMETRY illustration

co·ro·nis \kəˈrōnəs\ *n* -ES [L, fr. Gk *korōnis,* fr. *korōnē* anything curved — more at CROWN] **:** a mark ʼ used in Greek over a vowel to indicate contraction

cor·o·ni·tis \ˌkȯrəˈnīd·əs\ *n* -ES [NL, fr. *coron-* (fr. E *coronary cushion*) + *-itis*] **:** inflammation of the coronary cushion of animals

co·ro·ni·um \kəˈrōnēəm\ *n* -s [NL, fr. L *corona* + NL *-ium*] **:** a hypothetical chemical element thought to have been detected in the solar corona whose spectrum showed a number of lines later identified as belonging to iron, nickel, and other elements highly ionized at the extreme solar temperatures

co·ro·no- *comb form* [prob. fr. F, fr. *coronal,* adj.] *anat* **:** coronal and ⟨ *corono*basilar⟩ ⟨*corono*facial⟩

cor·o·no·frontal \ˌkȯrəˌnō, kəˌrō(ˌ)nō +\ *adj* **:** of or relating to the forehead and crown of the head

coronograph *var of* CORONAGRAPH

cor·o·noid \ˈkȯrəˌnȯid\ *adj* [ISV *coron-* (fr. Gk *korōnē* coronoid process, anything curved) + *-oid*] **:** of, relating to, or indicating the coronoid process or coronoid fossa ⟨~ teeth⟩

coronoid fossa *n* **:** a depression of the humerus into which the coronoid process fits when the arm is flexed

coronoid process *n* **1 :** the anterior process of the superior border of the ramus of the mandible **2 :** a flared process of the lower anterior part of the upper articular surface of the ulna fitting into the coronoid fossa when the arm is flexed

co·ron·o·pus \kəˈränəpəs, -rōn-\ *n, cap* [NL, fr. Gk *korōnopous* hartshorn plantain, fr. *korōno-* (fr. *korōnē* crow) + *pous* foot — more at FOOT] **:** a small genus of widely distributed ill-smelling herbs (family Cruciferae) with pinnately divided leaves and compact racemes of minute whitish flowers along the depressed stems — see SWINE CRESS

cor·o·nule \ˈkȯrəˌnyül, kəˈrō-\ *n* -s [NL *coronula,* fr. ML, fr. L *corona* crown + *-ula* -ule] **:** the peripheral ring of spines on the shells of some diatoms (as members of the genus *Stephanodiscus*)

cor·o·plast \ˈkȯrəˌplast\ *n* -s [Gk *koroplastēs,* fr. *koro-* (fr. *koros* boy, puppet) + *plastēs* molder, modeler (fr. *plassein* to form, mold) — more at CRESCENT, PLASTIC] **:** a modeler of wax or terra-cotta figurines (as of young women) of ancient Greece

co·ro·zo \kəˈrō(ˌ)sō\ *or* **co·ro·jo** \-rōˌhō\ *also* **co·ro·so** \-rō(ˌ)sō\ *n* -s [AmerSp, fr. Sp *corozo, corojo* fruit pit, fr. (assumed) VL *carudium,* fr. Gk *karydion* small nut, dim. of *karyon* nut — more at CAREEN] **1** *also* **corozo palm :** any of several tropical American palms: as **a :** IVORY PALM **b :** COHUNE PALM **c :** COYOL 1 **d :** any of several palms of the genus *Cocos* **2** *also* **corozo nut :** the seed of the ivory palm **3** *also* **corozo fiber :** a strong leaf fiber obtained from a coyol (*Acrocomia lasiospatha*) and used for making ropes

corp \ˈkȯrp\ *dial var of* CORPSE

corp *abbr* **1** corporal **2** corporation

corpora *pl of* CORPUS

[1]**cor·po·ral** \ˈkȯrp(ə)rəl, ˈkȯ(ə)p-\ *n* -s [ME *corporale,* fr. MF *corporal,* fr. ML *corporale,* fr. L, neut. of *corporalis* of the body; fr. the doctrine that the bread of the Eucharist becomes or represents the body of Christ] **:** a linen cloth on which the sacred elements are consecrated in the Eucharist or with which they are covered — called also *communion cloth*

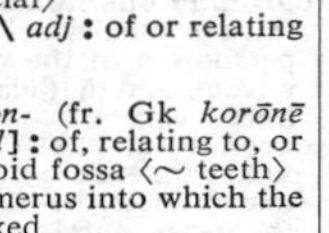

corporal

[2]**corporal** \"\ *adj* [ME *corporel, corporal,* fr. MF, fr. L *corporalis,* fr. *corpor-, corpus* body + *-alis* -al — more at MIDRIFF] **1 a :** affecting, relating to, or belonging to the body ⟨whipping and other ~ punishments⟩ ⟨spiritual and ~ needs⟩ ⟨~ works of mercy⟩ **b** *obs* **:** existing in bodily form discernible to the senses **:** MATERIAL, CORPOREAL ⟨what seemed ~ melted as breath into the wind —Shak.⟩ **c** *archaic* **:** performed, or enjoyed with the body **:** PHYSICAL **2 :** of or relating to the body as distinguished from the head and limbs **syn** see BODILY

[3]**corporal** \"\ *n* -s [MF, lowest noncommissioned officer, alter. (prob. influenced by *corps* body) of *caporal,* fr. It *caporale,* fr. *capo* head, chief (after such pairs as It *tempo* time: *temporale* temporal), fr. L *caput* head — more at HEAD] **1 a :** a noncommissioned army officer just below a sergeant and above a private first class **b :** a noncommissioned marine officer just below a sergeant and above a lance corporal **2 :** a fallfish (*Semotilus corporalis*) **3 :** an assistant to a precinct police sergeant

corporal forbes \-ˈfȯrbz, -rbəs\ *n, usu cap C&F* [prob. by folk etymology] *India* **:** CHOLERA MORBUS

cor·po·ral·i·ty \ˌkȯ(r)pəˈraləd·ē\ *n* -ES [ME *corporalite,* fr. LL *corporalitas,* fr. L *corporalis* + *-itat-, -itas* -ity] **:** the quality or state of being or having a body or a material or physical existence

cor·po·ral·ly \ˈkȯ(r)p(ə)rəlē, -li\ *adv* **:** in a corporal manner

corporal major *n* [[3]*corporal*] **:** the highest noncommissioned officer in the British household cavalry; *also* **:** his office or rank

corporal oath *n* [[2]*corporal*] **:** an oath solemnized by actually touching a sacred object (as the Bible)

corporal punishment *n* [[2]*corporal*] **1 :** punishment applied to the body of an offender including the death penalty, whipping, and imprisonment **2 :** punishment administered by an adult (as a parent or a teacher) to the body of a child ranging in severity from a slap to a spanking

corporal's guard *n* [[3]*corporal*] **:** a small group of persons (as of followers or adherents) ⟨scarcely more than a *corporal's guard* of these talented men are left —S.H.Holbrook⟩

cor·po·ral·ship \ˈkȯ(r)p(ə)rəlˌship\ *n* -s [[3]*corporal* + *-ship*] **1** *obs* **:** a body of soldiers under a corporal's command **2** *or* **corporalcy** -ES [*corporalcy* fr. [3]*corporal* + *-cy*] **:** a corporal's office or position **:** the rank of corporal

corpora lutea *pl of* CORPUS LUTEUM

cor·po·ra pe·dun·cu·la·ta \ˌkȯrp(ə)rəpəˌdəŋkyəˈläd·ə, -lä-\ *n pl* [NL, lit., pedunculate bodies] **:** a pair of stalked bodies on the dorsal part of the insect forebrain believed to function as association centers

corpora quad·ri·gem·i·na \-ˌkwädrəˈjemənə\ *n pl* [NL, lit., fourfold bodies] **:** two pairs of colliculi on the dorsal surface of the midbrain composed of white matter externally and gray matter within, the superior pair containing correlation centers for optic reflexes and the inferior pair containing correlation centers for auditory reflexes

corpora striata *pl of* CORPUS STRIATUM

[1]**cor·po·rate** \ˈkȯrp(ə)rət, ˈkȯ(ə)p-, *usu* -ȧd·+V\ *adj* [L *corporatus,* past part. of *corporare* to make into a body, fr. *corpor-, corpus* body — more at MIDRIFF] **1 a :** formed into or forming a body by legal enactment **:** united in an association and endowed by law with the rights and liabilities of an individual **:** INCORPORATED ⟨a ~ town⟩ ⟨a new federal agency, set up in ~ form to insure state school . . . bonds —Edgar Fuller⟩ **b :** of or relating to a corporation or to corporations in general ⟨a plan to reorganize the ~ structure⟩ ⟨whether the tax should be applied to business (particularly ~ business) as such —H.M.Groves⟩ **:** of or relating to an incorporated body ⟨the ~ powers of the municipality⟩ **2** *obs* **:** having a body **:** MATERIAL **3 a :** of or relating to a unified body made up of individuals or particulars **:** AGGREGATE ⟨the student experiences as part of his training the ~ life of the college⟩ **:** made or performed as a body or in a body rather than individually ⟨human law arises by the ~ action of a people —G.H.Sabine⟩ **b :** combined, united, or grouped together into one usu. cohesive body ⟨the yeomen . . . were a ~ society like the country gentry —Adrian Bell⟩ ⟨the immunities and good fellowship with which the Senate, as a ~ group, cushions conflicts within its own circle —Charles McKinley⟩ **c :** of or relating to the whole group as distinguished from the individual members ⟨sacrifice their individual rights for . . . the ~ good —Rebecca West⟩ **d :** consisting of two or more persons jointly responsible (as for the authoring of a novel) ⟨a ~ author⟩ **:** consisting of a group or corporation ⟨a ~ defendant⟩ ⟨a ~ person⟩ **4 :** CORPORATIVE 2 — **cor·po·rate·ly** *adv*

[2]**cor·po·rate** \ˈkȯrpəˌrāt, *usu* -ād·+V\ *vt* -ED/-ING/-S [L *corporatus*] **:** INCORPORATE

corporate colony *n* **:** a charter colony (as Connecticut or Rhode Island) having a royal charter granted to the inhabitants as a corporate body

corporate county *n* **:** COUNTY 3a

corporate member *n* **:** an actual or voting member of a corporation as distinct from an associate or honorary member

corporate name *n* **:** the legal name of a corporation

cor·po·rate·ness *n* -ES **:** the quality or state of being a corporate body

corporate stock *n* **1 :** stock issued by a corporate business enterprise **2** *chiefly Brit* **:** MUNICIPAL SECURITY

corporate suretyship *or* **corporate bonding** *n* **:** the business of issuing fidelity and surety bonds engaged in by a corporation (as a casualty insurance company)

corporate trust *n* **:** a trust in which the cestui que trust is a corporation — opposed to *personal trust*

cor·po·ra·tion \ˌkȯ(r)pəˈrāshən\ *n* -s *often attrib* [ME, fr. ML *corporation-, corporatio,* fr. L *corporatus* + *-ion-, -io* -ion] **1 :** a body of persons associated for some purpose (as standardization of conditions): as **a** *obs* **:** a group of merchants or traders united in an association **:** a trade guild **b :** the body of municipal authorities of a town or city ⟨the *Corporation* of the City of London⟩ **2** *Roman & civil law* **a :** a group of persons or objects treated by the law as an individual or unity having rights or liabilities distinct from those of the persons or objects composing it **:** UNIVERSITY — called also *body corporate* **b :** a single person or object treated by the law as having a legal individuality or entity other than that of a natural person **:** ARTIFICIAL PERSON **3** *or* **corporation aggregate** *English & US common & statute law* **:** a body formed and authorized by law to act as a single person and endowed by law with the capacity of succession **:** an entity recognized by law as constituted by one or more persons and as having various rights and duties together with the capacity of succession ⟨a ~ is an artificial being, invisible, intangible, and existing only in contemplation of law —John Marshall⟩ — see COMPANY 3, ECCLESIASTICAL CORPORATION, MUNICIPAL CORPORATION, PRIVATE CORPORATION, PUBLIC CORPORATION, PUBLIC SERVICE CORPORATION, QUASI CORPORATION **4 :** the area governed by a municipal corporation ⟨within the ~ limits of Chicago⟩ **5 :** an association of employers and employees in a basic industry or of members of a profession organized as an organ of political representation in a corporative state and responsible for supervision and control of production, wages, working conditions, and all matters pertaining to that industry or profession — see CORPORATISM **6 :** a fat or protuberant belly **:** POTBELLY

cor·po·ra·tion·al \ˌkȯ(r)pəˈrāshənᵊl, -shnəl\ *adj* **:** of or relating to a corporation

corporation cock *or* **corporation stop** *n* **:** a water or gas cock by means of which utility-company employees connect or disconnect service lines to a consumer

corporation lawyer *n* **:** an attorney who specializes in cases that involve the law as it pertains to corporations **:** one whose practice is confined to the legal affairs of a corporation

corporation life insurance *n* **:** life insurance purchased by a corporation on the lives of officers, employees, or principal stockholders and of which the corporation is the beneficiary

corporation sole *n* **:** a corporation consisting of only one person; *esp* **:** ECCLESIASTICAL CORPORATION

corporation stock *n, chiefly Brit* **:** MUNICIPAL SECURITY

cor·po·rat·ism *or* **cor·po·ra·tiv·ism** *pronunciations at* [1]CORPORATE & CORPORATIVE + ˌizəm\ *n* -s **:** a system or principle in which a whole society is organized into industrial and professional corporations serving as organs of political representation and controlling to a large extent the persons and activities within their jurisdiction with emphasis on labor-management cooperation ⟨the *corporativism* of Fascist Italy —A.J.Bruwer⟩

cor·po·rat·ist *pronunc at* [1]CORPORATE + ȯst\ *adj* **:** based upon or favoring corporatism ⟨~ doctrines⟩

cor·po·ra·tive \ˈkȯ(r)pəˌrād·iv, ˈkȯ(r)p(ə)rəd·|, -ət|,-ət|, |ēv *also* |əv\ *adj* [[1]*corporate* + *-ive*] **1 :** of, relating to, or consisting of a corporation **2 :** based on, organized according to, or favoring the principles of corporatism **:** CORPORATE ⟨a ~ state⟩ ⟨a ~ government⟩ ⟨a ~ parliament⟩

cor·po·ra·tor \ˈkȯ(r)pəˌrād·ə(r), -ātə-\ *n* -s [[2]*corporate* + *-or*] **1 :** a corporation member (as an official of a municipal corporation) **:** a corporation stockholder **2 :** INCORPORATOR a

corpora vilia *pl of* CORPUS VILE

cor·po·re·al \(ˈ)kȯ(r)ˈpōrēəl, -pȯr-\ *adj* [L *corporeus* of the body (fr. *corpor-, corpus* body) + E *-al* — more at MIDRIFF] **1 :** having, consisting of, or relating to a physical material body: as **a :** not spiritual ⟨some few traces of a diviner nature which look out through his ~ baseness —Robert Browning⟩ **b :** not immaterial or intangible **:** SUBSTANTIAL ⟨that which is created is of necessity ~ and visible and tangible —Benjamin Jowett⟩ **2** *archaic* **:** of, relating to, or affecting the human body **:** CORPORAL **3 :** tangible and palpable **:** not insubstantial **:** MATERIAL ⟨~ property⟩ ⟨~ hereditaments, mainly land and large savings⟩ **syn** see BODILY, MATERIAL

cor·po·re·al·ist \≈ˈ≈≈ȯst\ *n* -s **:** MATERIALIST

cor·po·re·al·i·ty \(ˌ)≈ˌ≈≈ˈaləd·ē\ *n* -ES **:** the quality or state of being corporeal **:** corporeal existence

cor·po·re·al·ize \≈ˈ≈≈ˌəˌlīz\ *vt* -ED/-ING/-S **:** to make corporeal

cor·po·re·al·ly \(ˈ)kȯ(r)ˈpōrēəlē, -pȯr-, -li\ *adv* **:** in a corporeal manner **:** in the body

cor·po·re·als \≈ˈ≈≈əlz\ *n pl* **1 :** material things **2** *law* **:** corporeal property

cor·po·re·i·ty \ˌkȯ(r)pəˈrēəd·ē\ *n* -ES [ML *corporeitat-, corporeitas,* fr. L *corporeus* corporeal + *-itat-, -itas* -ity] **:** the quality or state of having or being a body **:** the state of being corporeal **:** physical nature **:** MATERIALITY

cor·por·i·fy \kȯ(r)ˈpȯrəˌfī\ *vt* -ED/-ING/-ES [L *corpor-, corpus* body + E *-ify*] **:** to form into a body **:** EMBODY, INCORPORATE, SOLIDIFY

cor·po·sant \ˈkȯ(r)pəˌsant *also* -ˌza-\ *n* -s [Pg *corpo-santo,* lit., holy body, fr. *corpo* body (fr. L *corpus*) + *santo* holy, fr. L *sanctus* — more at SAINT] **:** SAINT ELMO'S FIRE

corps \ˈkō(ə)r|, -ō(ə)r|,-ōə|,-ō(ə)|\ *n, pl* **corps** \|z\ [F, fr. L *corpus* body] **1 a :** an organized subdivision of the military establishment ⟨the Marine *Corps*⟩ ⟨the Ordnance *Corps*⟩ **b :** a tactical unit usu. consisting of two or more divisions and auxiliary arms and services **c** (1) **:** a local unit of the Salvation Army that administers a Salvation Army center (2) **:** such a center established for the propagation of the Gospel and the administration of welfare services **2 a :** a body of persons associated together or acting under common direction ⟨his ~ of laborers⟩ **b :** a body of persons having a common activity or occupation ⟨a ~ of trained lifeguards⟩ ⟨the press ~⟩ ⟨the English . . . succeeded in building up a remarkable public service ~ —C.J.Friedrich⟩ **c :** an association of German university students binding its members to strict adherence to certain customs and a fixed code of honor **3 :** CORPS DE BALLET

corps area *n* **:** a territorial division of the U.S. for purposes of administration and training of the army

corps·bru·der \ˈkōrˌbrüdər, ˈkȯr-\ *n, pl* **corpsbruders** \-ərz\ *or* **corps·brü·der** \-ˌbrüedər\ [G *korpsbruder,* fr. *korps* corps (fr. F *corps*) + *bruder* brother, fr. OHG *bruoder* — more at BROTHER] **1 :** a comrade in a German student corps **2 :** a close comrade

corps de bal·let \ˌkōrdə(ˌ)baˈlā, ˌkȯr-\ *n, pl* **corps de ballet** \"\ [F] **:** the ensemble or chorus of a ballet company as distinguished from soloists and principals

corps d'elite \-dāˈlēt\ *n, pl* **corps d'elite** \"\ [F *corps d'élite*] **1 :** a body of picked troops **2 :** a group of the best men of any category ⟨thirteen reporters — the *corps d'elite* of a great newspaper —*N.Y. Herald Tribune*⟩

corps di·plo·ma·tique \ˌ≈ˌdipləˌmaˈtēk\ *n, pl* **corps diplomatique** \"\ [F] **:** the body of diplomatic officers accredited to a government

[1]**corpse** \ˈkȯ(ə)rps, -ō(ə)ps\ *n* -s [ME *corps,* fr. MF, fr. L *corpus* — more at MIDRIFF] **1** *obs* **:** a human or animal body whether living or dead **2 a :** a dead body esp. of a human being **b :** something that has been forgotten or discarded or that is no longer active, vital, or effective ⟨it was an awful thing to look at the ~ of a city . . . that once had been so beautiful and gay —*Nat'l Geographic*⟩ **3** *obs* **:** the main portion or substance **:** the collective whole **:** BODY ⟨one . . . uniform ~ of law —Francis Bacon⟩ **4 :** an endowment belonging to a prebend or other ecclesiastical office

[2]**corpse** \"\ *vt* -ED/-ING/-S **1** *dial Brit* **:** KILL **2 :** to confuse (an actor) in performance **:** spoil (an actor's speech or a scene) by cutting in or by blundering

corpse candle *n* **:** a luminous appearance resembling the flame of a candle sometimes seen in churchyards and thought to presage someone's death

corpse plant *also* **corpse light** *n* **:** INDIAN PIPE

corps·man \ˈkōr(z)mən, ˈkȯr-\ *n, pl* **corpsmen :** HOSPITAL CORPSMAN

corps of cadets : a body of cadets under instruction and military discipline and control at a school, college, or service academy

corps troops *n pl* **:** troops assigned or attached to a corps but not part of one of the divisions in the corps

corpsy \ˈkȯrpsē\ *adj* -ER/-EST [[1]*corpse* + *-y*] **:** like or suggesting a corpse ⟨a cool ~ smell —Christopher Morley⟩ ⟨looking a bit ~⟩

cor·pu·lence \ˈkȯ(r)pyələn(t)s\ *n* -s [MF *corpulence,* fr. L *corpulentia,* fr. *corpulentus* + *-ia*] **:** bulkiness of body; *usu* **:** excessive fatness **:** FLESHINESS, OBESITY

cor·pu·len·cy \-nsē, -si\ *n* -ES [L *corpulentia*] **:** CORPULENCE

cor·pu·lent \-nt\ *adj* [ME, fr. L *corpulentus,* fr. *corpus* body + *-ulentus* -ulent] **1 :** having a large bulky body **:** fat and heavy **:** OBESE ⟨a ~ giant, over six feet in height, and . . . as big round as a hogshead —Herman Melville⟩ **:** LARGE, MASSIVE ⟨his money belt was . . . ~ —Elinor Wylie⟩ **2** *archaic* **:** CORPOREAL, MATERIAL **syn** see FAT

cor·pu·lent·ly *adv* **:** in a corpulent manner ⟨a ~ constructed man⟩

cor·pu·lent·ness *n* -ES **:** CORPULENCE

cor pul·mo·na·le \ˌkȯrˌpu̇lməˈna|(ˌ)lē, -ˌpəl-, -nā-, -nä-\ *n, pl* **cor·dia pulmona·lia** \ˈkȯrdēə,p...|ˈlēə\ [NL, lit., pulmonary heart] **:** heart disease secondary to disease of the lungs or their blood vessels **:** pulmonary heart disease

cor·pus \ˈkȯrpəs, -ōəp-\ *n, pl* **corpo·ra** \-p(ə)rə\ [ME, fr. L] **1 :** the body of a man or animal esp. when dead **2 a :** the main part or body of a structure or organ ⟨the ~ of the jaw⟩ ⟨the ~ of the uterus⟩ **b :** the main body or corporeal substance of a thing; *specif* **:** the principal of a fund or estate as distinct from income or interest **c :** the main body, the substance, or the essential element of a thing ⟨a ferocious metaphysical dispute. The ~ of the dispute was a squirrel —William James⟩ **3 a :** the whole body or total amount of writings of a particular kind or on a particular subject (as the total production of a writer or the whole literature of a subject) ⟨the Dickens ~⟩ ⟨judging the ~ of American literature in the light of these standards —C.I.Glicksberg⟩ **b :** a collection or body esp. of knowledge or evidence ⟨a sizable ~ of opinion⟩; *specif* **:** the collection of recorded utterances that is used as a basis for the descriptive analysis of a language or dialect **4** *in the tunica-corpus theory* **:** the inner of the two growth regions into which the apical meristem is considered divisible consisting of a core of cells which divide at various angles and provide for increase in bulk

corpus al·bi·cans \-ˈalbəˌkanz\ *n, pl* **corpora albican·tia** \-ˌalbəˈkanchēə\ [NL, lit., whitish body] **1 :** MAMMILLARY BODY **2 :** the white fibrous scar remaining in the ovary after resorption of the corpus luteum that replaces a discharged Graafian follicle

corpus cal·lo·sum \-(ˌ)kaˈlōsəm, -ˌkəˈl-\ *n, pl* **corpora callo·sa** \-sə\ [NL, lit., callous body] **:** the great band of commissural fibers uniting the cerebral hemispheres in man and in the higher mammals — see BRAIN illustration

corpus ca·ver·no·sum \-ˌkavərˈnōsəm\ *n, pl* **corpora caverno·sa** \-sə\ [NL, cavernous body] **:** a mass of erectile tissue with large interspaces capable of being distended with blood; *esp* **:** one of those that form the bulk of the body of the penis or of the clitoris

[1]**corpus christi** \ˌkȯrpəˈskristē\ *n, pl* **corpus christis** *usu cap both Cs* [ME. fr. ML, lit., body of Christ] **:** a Roman Catholic festival in honor of the Eucharist observed on the Thursday after Trinity Sunday

[2]**corpus christi** \"\ *adj, usu cap both Cs* [fr. *Corpus Christi,* city of Texas] **:** of or from the city of Corpus Christi, Texas ⟨*Corpus Christi* refineries⟩ **:** of the kind or style prevalent in Corpus Christi

cor·pus·cle \ˈkȯ(r)ˌpəsəl *also* -ˌp-\ *n* -s [L *corpusculum,* dim. of *corpus* body] **1 :** a minute or elementary particle; *specif* **:** ELECTRON **2 a :** a living cell; *usu* **:** one that is somewhat isolated and not aggregated into continuous tissues (as red and white blood cells or cells isolated in the matrix of cartilage or bone) — compare BLOOD, LYMPH **b :** any of various small circumscribed bodies composed of many cells — usu. used with a qualifying term ⟨the tactile ~*s*⟩ ⟨Malpighian ~*s*⟩

corpuscle of has·sall *or* **corpuscle of has·sal** \-ˈhasəl\ *usu cap H* [after Arthur H. Hassall †1894 Eng. physician] **:** one of the small usu. concentrically striated bodies in the thymus body representing remains of the epithelial tissue found in early stages of development

corpuscle of herbst \-ˈhe(ə)rpst\ *usu cap H* [trans. of G *herbstsches körperchen,* after Ernst F. *Herbst* †1893 Ger. physician] **:** any of certain tactile organs found in birds related to Pacinian corpuscles

corpuscle of krause *usu cap K* **:** KRAUSE'S CORPUSCLE

corpuscle of meissner *usu cap M* **:** MEISSNER'S CORPUSCLE

corpuscle of the spleen : MALPIGHIAN CORPUSCLE 2

corpuscle of va·ter \-ˈfätər\ *usu cap V* [trans. of G *vatersches körperchen,* after Abraham *Vater* †1751 Ger. anatomist] **:** PACINIAN CORPUSCLE

cor·pus·cu·lar \(ˈ)kȯ(r)ˈpəskyələ(r)\ *adj* [L *corpusculum* + E *-ar*] **:** relating to, dealing with, or composed of corpuscles

corpuscular philosophy *n* **:** the philosophy that attempts to account for the phenomena of nature by the characteristics (as motion, figure, rest, position) of minute particles of matter

corpuscular theory *n* **:** a theory in physics: light consists of material particles sent off in all directions from luminous bodies

cor·pus·cu·lat·ed \-,lād·əd\ *adj* [L *corpusculum* + E *-ate* + *-ed*] **:** furnished with or containing corpuscles

cor·pus·cule \kó(r)'pə,skyül\ *n* -s [F *corpuscule*, fr. L *corpusculum*] **:** CORPUSCLE

cor·pus·cu·lum \kó(r)'pəskyələm\ *n, pl* **corpuscu·la** \-lə\ [L] **:** CORPUSCLE

corpus de·lic·ti \-də'lik,tī, -k(,)tē\ *n, pl* **corpora delicti** [NL, lit., body of the crime] **1 :** the substantial and fundamental fact or facts (as, in murder, actual death and its occurrence as a result of criminal agency) necessary to prove the commission of a crime **2 :** the material substance (as the body of the victim of a murder) upon which a crime has been committed

corpus ju·ris \-'jürəs\ *n, pl* **corpora juris** [LL] **:** a body of law **:** a comprehensive collection of the law of a country or jurisdiction

corpus lu·te·um \-'lüd·ēəm\ *n, pl* **corpora lu·tea** \-ēə\ [NL, lit., yellowish body] **1 :** a reddish yellow endocrine body consisting of pale secretory cells derived from granulosa cells and filling the cavity of a Graafian follicle following discharge of the ovum and regressing rather quickly if the ovum is not fertilized but persisting throughout the ensuing pregnancy if it is fertilized **2 :** the fresh substance of the corpora lutea of the hog or cow dried and powdered and used in the treatment of conditions due to ovarian dysfunction

corpus stri·a·tum \-,strī'ād·əm\ *n, pl* **corpora stria·ta** \-d·ə\ [NL, lit., striated body] **:** either of a pair of masses of nervous tissue beneath and external to the anterior cornua of the lateral ventricles of the brain and forming part of their floor, each mass containing two large nuclei of gray matter that are separated by sheets of white matter to give the mass a striated appearance in section

corpus vi·le \-'vī(,)lē\ *n, pl* **corpora vil·ia** \-'vilēə\ [NL, lit., worthless body] **:** something felt to be of so little value that it may be experimented with or upon without concern for loss or damage ⟨literature may come to be used as a *corpus vile* for acute dons to sharpen their wits upon —*Times Lit. Supp.*⟩

corr *abbr* — see COR

cor·rade \kə'rād, kó'-\ *vb* -ED/-ING/-S [L *corradere* to scrape together, fr. *com-* + *radere* to scrape — more at RASE] *vt* **:** to wear away by abrasion ⟨a stream ~s its banks⟩ ~ *vi* **:** to crumble away through abrasion

¹cor·ral \kə'ral, kó'-\ *n* -s [Sp, fr. (assumed) VL *currale* enclosure for vehicles, fr. L *currus* cart, fr. *currere* to run — more at CURRENT] **1 a :** a pen or enclosure for confining or capturing livestock **b :** an enclosure that resembles a corral ⟨spectators were held in a roped-off ~ until they could be seated⟩ **c :** a fish trap resembling a corral in shape **2 :** an enclosure made with wagons as a place of defense for an encampment

²corral \"\ *vb* **corralled; corralled; corralling; corrals** *vt* **1 :** to enclose in a corral or similar pen or yard **:** round up (as cattle) and drive into a corral **2 :** to arrange (wagons) so as to form a corral **3 a :** to get hold of, get control over, catch, or gather up (something wandering or elusive) **:** get possession of ⟨~ a new desk for his secretary⟩ ⟨taxi drivers *corralling* customers for a hotel⟩ ⟨the winning candidate is the man who can ~ the most votes⟩ **b :** to bring together in one place ⟨~ all the passengers in the lounge⟩ **:** restrict to a particular place ⟨reporters *corralled* the congressman in a corner of the lobby⟩ **:** restrict the movement of ⟨boys quickly *corralled* a small brush fire and put it out⟩ ~ *vi* **:** to form a protective corral around an encampment ⟨the train probably would ~ by alternate wagons, the first wagon turning right, the second left . . . until the circle was formed —W.F.Harris⟩ **syn** see ENCLOSE

cor·ra·sion \kə'rāzhən, kó'-\ *n* -s [ISV *corras-* (fr. L *corrasus*, past part. of *corradere*) + *-ion*] **:** the wearing away of rocks and soil by the abrasive action of material moved along by wind, waves, streams, or glaciers **:** one of the several processes of erosion

cor·ra·sive \-āsiv, -āziv\ *adj* [ISV *corras-* (fr. L *corrasus*) + *-ive*] **:** producing or tending to produce corrasion

cor·rea \kə'rēə, -rāə\ *n* [NL, after José F. *Correa* da Serra †1823 Port. statesman and botanist] **1** *cap* **:** a small genus of Australian shrubs (family Rutaceae) most of which have tubular scarlet, yellow, or white flowers **2** -s **:** any plant of the genus *Correa* — called also *native fuchsia*

cor·re·al \(')kó¦rē(ə)l, 'kōrē-\ *adj* [LL *correus* joint criminal (fr. L *com-* + *reus* accused person, prob. fr. *res* lawsuit, thing) + E *-al* — more at REAL] *civil law* **:** having or constituting a joint obligation or right that may be enforced in full against any one of several joint debtors or by any one of several joint creditors against a single debtor

cor·re·al·i·ty \,kōrē'aləd·ē\ *n* -ES **:** the quality or state of being correal

¹cor·rect \kə'rekt, *rap.* 'kre-\ *vb* -ED/-ING/-S [ME *correcten*, fr. L *correctus*, past part. of *corrigere* to make straight, correct, fr. *com-* + *-rigere* (fr. *regere* to lead straight, guide, rule) — more at RIGHT] *vt* **1 a :** to make or set right **:** remove the faults or errors from **:** AMEND ⟨~ some of the mistaken ideas about farming —C.R.Hope⟩ ⟨his answer was wrong and he at once ~*ed* himself⟩ ⟨legislative action designed to ~ existing difficulties —*U.S. Code*⟩ ⟨~ abuses in the city prison⟩ **b :** to counteract or neutralize by means of opposite qualities or tendencies — used esp. of what is undesirable ⟨the good philosopher was leaning a little in the other direction to ~ the excess of my hellenizing zeal —A.N.Whitehead⟩ **c :** to alter or adjust so as to bring to some standard or required condition ⟨~ a reading of a gas volume for temperature and pressure⟩ ⟨~ a lens for spherical aberration⟩ ⟨~ the timing in a motor⟩ **2 a :** to rebuke or to punish or discipline for some fault or lapse (as from propriety) ⟨the older woman ~*ed* the man for taking liberties⟩ **b :** to point out for amendment the errors or faults of ⟨the student had to be ~*ed* several times during her recitation⟩ ⟨~ proof by indicating the changes to be made in type⟩ ⟨a teacher ~*s* examination papers⟩ **3** *obs* **:** to bring order to **:** TAME ~ *vi* **:** to make corrections

syn RECTIFY, EMEND, REMEDY, REDRESS, AMEND, REFORM, REVISE: these verbs mean, in common, to right what is wrong. One CORRECTS something by altering what is inaccurate, untrue, or imperfect in it or about it so that it is accurate, true, or perfect, or by putting against it or substituting for it what is accurate, true, or perfect ⟨to *correct* a false accusation⟩ ⟨to *correct* a wrong address on a package⟩ ⟨to *correct* a serious fault of character⟩ ⟨to *correct* spelling errors⟩ One RECTIFIES a mistake or an injustice or a deviation from a standard by the elimination or nullification of the mistake or injustice or by making the deviation conform to the standard ⟨an incredible, disgraceful blunder, which should be *rectified* at the earliest possible moment —*New Republic*⟩ ⟨to have exploited, rather than tried to *rectify* . . . misunderstandings —*Times Lit. Supp.*⟩ ⟨set himself to *rectify* the spiritual and physical poverty of his people — Green Peyton⟩ One EMENDS by freeing from error or defect, esp. a statement that misrepresents a speaker's intention or a piece of writing that contains doubtful readings ⟨to *emend* a financial report hastily and inaccurately compiled⟩ ⟨to *emend* a transcription of an ancient religious scroll⟩ One REMEDIES a cause of trouble, harm, or evil by rendering it innocuous or substituting for it what is good, right, or helpful ⟨the crime can never be *remedied*, it can only be expiated —C.D.Lewis⟩ ⟨done much to *remedy* the confusion —*Amer. Guide Series: Vt.*⟩ ⟨must *remedy* their deficiencies —*Loyola Univ. Bull.*⟩ One REDRESSES an unfairness, injustice, or imbalance sometimes by elimination of it but usu. by making a reparation or providing compensation ⟨trying to *redress* the serious dislocations resulting from . . . bad policies —E.B. George⟩ ⟨to *redress* the imbalance in American politics —M.W.Straight⟩ ⟨the wrongs that were to be righted, the grievances to be *redressed*, the abuses to be done away with —Malcolm Muggeridge⟩ ⟨the *redress* of certain social inequities —W.R.Inge⟩ One AMENDS something by making such corrections or alterations as will better it ⟨to *amend* her life⟩ ⟨the work once done he could not or would not *amend* it —W.B.Yeats⟩ ⟨to *amend* local traffic regulations⟩ One REFORMS something by making drastic alterations for the better, usu. so that it acquires a new form or character ⟨to *reform* an inefficient administrative system⟩ ⟨*reformed* the rules of procedure of the mayor's court —M.L.Bonham⟩ ⟨to *reform* sloppy habits of study⟩ One REVISES something when he makes changes that presumably improve it without drastically altering the character of the whole, usu. after looking it over carefully ⟨to *revise* a manuscript story⟩ ⟨to *revise* his opinions⟩ ⟨to *revise* a business organization⟩ **syn** see in addition PUNISH

²correct \"\ *adj, sometimes* -ER/-EST [ME, corrected, fr. L *correctus*] **1 :** adhering or conforming to an approved or conventional standard: as **a** *of literary or artistic style* **:** conforming to recognized conventions or an established mode ⟨a ~ Palladian portico⟩ **b :** suiting or conforming to conventionally recognized principles of thought, behavior, or taste ⟨the ~ tip is sixpence —Richard Joseph⟩ ⟨Soviet criticism . . . tried to rule on the attitude of the author as ~ or incorrect —Edmund Wilson⟩ **c :** scrupulously in accord with social proprieties ⟨rebuffed or evaded with dry ~ civilities —John Hurkan⟩ **:** placing high value on propriety ⟨a careful and ~ young man⟩ **d** *of speech or writing* **:** conforming to the generally accepted rules of grammar or to what is regarded as the best usage **2 a :** conforming to or agreeing with fact **:** ACCURATE ⟨have a ~ answer to the problem⟩ **:** conforming to logical or proven principles or agreeing with known truth ⟨it would be ~ to call it the best possible treaty⟩ ⟨the ~ way to hold the tool⟩ **b** *of a copy or reproduction* **:** free from errors **:** identical in relevant characteristics **:** EXACT **3 :** conforming to or agreeing with a set figure (as the price established for an article of merchandise) ⟨sent the ~ return postage⟩

syn ACCURATE, EXACT, PRECISE, NICE, RIGHT: CORRECT means hardly more than freedom from fault or error, often as judged by some conventional or acknowledged standard ⟨it is our custom at Shangri-La to be moderately truthful, and I can assure you that my statements about the porters were almost *correct* —James Hilton⟩ ⟨the more *correct* social circles of Boston and Cambridge —Florence H. Bullock⟩ ACCURATE implies positive and careful fidelity to fact or truth ⟨the phrases are good enough for statesmen, who identify order with orders and creation with regulations, but the poet-writer must be more *accurate* than that —E.M.Forster⟩ ⟨a solecism of this kind . . . would have seemed a shocking thing to . . . so *accurate* a scholar —L.P.Smith⟩ EXACT, sometimes interchangeable with PRECISE, generally emphasizes the strictness of the agreement or conformity with fact, standard, or truth ⟨not less than a hundred and thirty feet surely . . . a hundred and twenty-eight, to be *exact* —Dorothy Sayers⟩ ⟨sciences are not vague. On the contrary they are *exact*. They are based on fact, proven fact —T.B.Costain⟩ PRECISE carries the idea of sharpness of definition or delimitation or scrupulous exactness ⟨I saw the outside of the note, addressed in straggling, irregular characters, very unlike Holmes' usual *precise* hand —A. C. Doyle⟩ ⟨only an endlessly patient, careful, laborious, *precise* investigator could set up the new revolutionary conceptions needed to replace these traditions and preconceptions —Havelock Ellis⟩ NICE, in the sense pertinent here, implies great, sometimes excessive, precision or delicacy as in discrimination of terms or the adjustment of interrelated parts ⟨the small provincial gentry of the West, as drawn by Miss Austen . . . are *nice* in their gentility almost to a fault —G.M.Trevelyan⟩ ⟨it was a time of revolution, when *nice* legal distinctions are meaningless —John Buchan⟩ ⟨the detail of the cornices, the delicate fanlight and *nice* disposition of carved ornament on the white exterior —*Amer. Guide Series: Vt.*⟩ RIGHT, very close in meaning to CORRECT, has a more positive suggestion, often implying more than mere avoidance of error ⟨the *right* practice of "art for art's sake" was the devotion of Flaubert or Henry James —T.S.Eliot⟩ ⟨where water from wells has just that *right* degree of permanent hardness to favor brewing —L.D.Stamp⟩

—correct in the mouth *Brit, of sheep* **:** having the full adult complement of permanent teeth

cor·rect·able \-təbəl\ *adj* **:** capable of being corrected

cor·rec·tant \kə'rektənt\ *n* -s [¹*correct* + *-ant*] **:** CORRECTIVE

corrected *past of* CORRECT

corrected establishment *n* [*corrected* fr. past part. of *correct*] **:** the mean of all high-water lunitidal intervals for at least a month used in navigation to find the approximate time of high water by adding it to the time of the moon's upper transit as shown in the nautical almanac

corrected grain *n* **:** leather that has been lightly buffed or skived to remove grain defects

corrected time *n* **:** a ship's elapsed time less her time allowance in yacht racing

correcting *pres part of* CORRECT

cor·rect·ing·ly *adv* **:** in a correcting manner

cor·rec·tion \kə'rekshən, *rapid* 'kre-\ *n* -s [ME *correccion*, fr. MF *correction*, fr. L *correction-, correctio*, fr. *correctus* (past part. of *corrigere* to make straight, correct) + *-ion-, -io* -ion — more at CORRECT] **1 :** the action or an instance of correcting: as **a :** the action or an instance of remedying or removing error or defect **:** AMENDMENT, RECTIFICATION ⟨the ~ of stream pollution by the treatment of sewage⟩ ⟨~ of inaccuracies in accounting⟩ **b :** the act or an instance of calling attention to, reproving, or punishing faults or deviations from propriety or rectitude **:** REBUKE ⟨kept an iron potlid by him as a projectile for the ~ of Mrs. Cruncher in case he should observe any symptoms of her saying grace —Charles Dickens⟩ **c :** the action or an instance of making that right which was wrong or of bringing into conformity with a standard ⟨the ~ of injustice⟩ ⟨small frontier ~*s* were made by the conference of nations⟩ **d :** the action or an instance of counteracting or neutralizing something harmful or undesirable ⟨~ of acidity⟩ ⟨~ of visual defects with eyeglasses⟩ **e :** the action or an instance of adjusting or altering so as to produce a particular condition or result ⟨~ of photographic lenses⟩ **f :** a reversal of an exaggerated trend in a market or industry; *esp* **:** a decline in market price or in business activity following a protracted sharp rise **2 a :** something that is or should be substituted in place of what is wrong ⟨mark ~*s* on an examination paper⟩; *specif* **:** an indication on a proof of a change to be made by the printer **b :** a quantity applied by way of correcting (as for inaccuracy in an instrument or of its adjustment); *specif* **:** the quantity that must be algebraically added to the result of a measurement to obtain the correct value — compare ERROR 5 **3 :** the treatment of offenders through a program involving penal custody, parole, and probation ⟨disabilities from which the field of ~ has suffered —*Yale Law Jour.*⟩ ⟨two prison wards under the *Correction* Department —*N.Y. Times*⟩ — often used in pl. ⟨training in the techniques of casework, probation and parole, and the general field of ~*s* —L.J. Sharp⟩ ⟨the ~*s* worker who has the interest and courage to look at his own work objectively —C.C.Scott⟩ **— under correction :** subject to correction ⟨I am speaking *under correction*, for only the editors know . . . how much . . . were usable —H.L.Savage⟩

cor·rec·tion·al \-shən³l, -shnəl\ *adj* **:** of or relating to correction; *esp* **:** dealing with or charged with the administration of corrections **:** concerned with or providing corrections ⟨a ~ court⟩ ⟨a ~ institution⟩ ⟨a ~ probation service was instituted⟩

correction line *n* **:** one of a set of parallels of latitude 24 miles apart that is used for laying out nominally square sections and townships in the public land survey

cor·rec·ti·tude \-tə,tüd,-tə-,tyüd\ *n* -s [blend of ²*correct* and *rectitude*] **:** correctness or propriety of conduct

¹cor·rec·tive \kə'rektiv, -tēv *also* -təv; *rapid* 'kre-\ *adj* [MF *correctif*, fr. ML *correctivus*, fr. L *correctus* + *-ivus* -ive] **:** tending to correct ⟨~ lenses⟩ ⟨~ punishment⟩ **:** having the power or property of correcting, counteracting, or restoring to a normal condition ⟨~ exercises⟩ **:** CORRECTIONAL — **cor·rec·tive·ly** \-təvlē, -li\ *adv* — **cor·rec·tive·ness** \-tivnəs, -tēv- *also* -təv-\ *n* -ES

²corrective \"\ *n* -s **1 :** something that corrects **:** a corrective agent ⟨uses criticism as a ~ of abuses⟩ ⟨phenobarbital is a ~ of ephedrine⟩ **:** REMEDY ⟨his speech was a timely ~ for national complacency⟩ **2** *obs* **:** a change that corrects

corrective justice *n* **:** RETRIBUTIVE JUSTICE

cor·rect·ly *adv* **:** in a correct manner

cor·rect·ness *n* -ES **:** the quality or state of being correct

cor·rec·tor \-tə(r)\ *n* -s [ME *correctour*, fr. MF *correcteur*, fr. L *corrector*, fr. *correctus* + *-or*] **1 :** one that corrects ⟨a ~ of abuses⟩ ⟨time is a great ~ of taste⟩ ⟨hire someone to be a ~ of incoming manuscripts⟩ **2** *or* **corrector of the press** *Brit* **:** PROOFREADER

corrects *pres 3d sing of* CORRECT

cor·reg·i·dor \kə'regə,dó(ə)r, *or as Sp*\ *n, pl* **corregidors** \-rz\ *or* **corregido·res** \kə,regə'dōrēz, *or as Sp*\ [Sp, corrector, magistrate, fr. *corregir* to correct, fr. L *corrigere*] **:** a Spanish magistrate; *esp* **:** the chief magistrate or governor of a town in Spain or the Spanish colonies

¹cor·re·late \'kórə,lāt, 'kär-, *usu* -ād+V\ *n* -s [back-formation fr. *correlative* & *correlation*] **1 :** either of two things so related that one directly implies or is complementary to the other (as husband and wife) **2 :** one of two related things viewed in terms of its relationship to the other **:** CORRELATIVE ⟨expressing himself in . . . works of art that are the objective ~ of his inner emotional tensions —Herbert Read⟩ **3 :** a phenomenon that accompanies another, usu. also paralleling it (as in form, type, development, or distribution) and being related in some way to it ⟨the tribal division coincides with geographic features and has a linguistic ~⟩

²correlate \" *sometimes* ,==ˈ=\ *vb* -ED/-ING/-S *vi* **:** to bear reciprocal or mutual relations ⟨doctrine and worship ~ as theory and practice —E.B.Tylor⟩ ~ *vt* **1 :** to establish a definite stratigraphic relationship between ⟨~ the faunas or formations of two areas⟩ **2 a :** to establish a mutual or reciprocal relation of ⟨non-science and nonsense are nearly synonymous to many who highly ~ science and sense —Harlow Shapley⟩ **:** relate as necessary or invariable accompaniments with or without the implication of causality ⟨~ emotional states with physiological changes⟩ **b :** to determine, establish, or show a usu. causal relationship between ⟨~ their environment with the health of the children —*Times Lit. Supp.*⟩ **3 :** to establish a one-to-one correspondence of (two sets or series of things) **:** relate so that to each member of one set or series a corresponding member of another is assigned ⟨the scores made by high school juniors . . . on seven standard . . . tests were *correlated* with teachers' ratings of those pupils on dramatic talent —*Quarterly Jour. of Speech*⟩ **4 a :** to put in relation with each other **:** connect systematically **:** present or set forth so as to show relationship ⟨he ~*s* the findings of the scientists, the psychologists, and the mystics —Eugene Exman⟩ **b :** to bring into complementary relationship with each other **:** organize so as to advance effectively a common program ⟨~ the activities of the college and the . . . organizations for rural improvement —*Amer. Guide Series: Mich.*⟩

³correlate \'==,=\ *adj* **1 :** CORRELATED **2** *geol* **:** belonging to the same stratigraphic horizon ⟨~ strata⟩

correlated *adj* [fr. past part. of *correlate*] **1 :** closely, systematically, or reciprocally related ⟨human faculties form a ~ whole; and this composite human nature seeks to act, to function —H.O.Taylor⟩ **2 :** related as a universal accompaniment whether causally connected or not ⟨nest building is ~ with a precise physiological state —E.A.Armstrong⟩ **3 :** relating to or indicating the relationship between the attributes in a mathematical correlation

cor·re·la·tion \,==ˈlāshən\ *n* -s [ML *correlation-, correlatio*, fr. L *com-* + *relation-, relatio* relation — more at RELATION] **1 :** the act or process of correlating **:** the condition or fact of being correlated ⟨the exact ~ of tempo, emphasis, and climax —Parker Tyler⟩; *specif* **:** the relation of phenomena as invariable accompaniments of each other whether causally connected or not ⟨the assumption is that there is a positive ~ between performance and pay —Kermit Eby⟩ **2 :** reciprocal or mutual relation in the occurrence (as of deafness in blue-eyed white cats or the expression of apical dominance in plants) of different structures, characteristics, or processes in organisms **3 :** an interdependence between mathematical variables esp. in statistics **4 :** determination of synchrony, of homotaxis, or of relation to the scale of geologic time — usu. used in the comparison of geologic formations or of fossil faunas or floras belonging to different districts

cor·re·la·tion·al \¦==¦=shən³l, -shnəl\ *adj* **:** of or concerning correlation **:** employing correlation ⟨metaphysics is a basic and ~ discipline —V.C.Aldrich⟩

correlation coefficient *n* **:** a number that serves to measure the degree of correlation between two mathematical variables, being the quotient of the arithmetic mean of the products of the corresponding deviations (from their means) of the values of the variables in question divided by the product of the corresponding standard deviations of the two variables

correlation curve *n* **:** CORRELOGRAM

correlation ratio *n* **:** a number other than the correlation coefficient that measures the degree of correlation between two mathematical variables

¹cor·rel·a·tive \kə'reləd·|iv, -lət|, |ēv *also* kó'- *or* |əv\ *adj* [ML *correlativus*, fr. L *com-* + LL *relativus* relative — more at RELATIVE] **1 :** naturally related (as by occurring in conjunction) **:** CORRESPONDING ⟨points of view toward the contemporary world always imply ~ points of view toward . . . a dozen crucial issues in past centuries —Paul Farmer⟩ **2 :** having, indicating, or involving a reciprocal relation **:** being a correlate ⟨linked the continuing progress of our system to a ~ development in the economies of all democratic peoples —N.A.Rockefeller⟩ **:** reciprocally related esp. so that each directly implies the existence of the other ⟨the ~ rights and duties between shareholders, directors, and executives —G.B. Hurff⟩ **3** *of paired words or expressions* **:** regularly used together but typically not adjacent to each other ⟨the ~ conjunctions *either* . . . *or*⟩ ⟨the ~ demonstratives *the former* . . . *the latter*⟩ **4** *biol* **:** exhibiting correlation — **cor·rel·a·tive·ly** \|əvlē, -li\ *adv*

²correlative \"\ *n* -s **:** CORRELATE: as **a :** either of two correlative words or expressions **b :** a word denoting a correlate (sense 1)

cor·rel·a·tiv·i·ty \kə,relə'tivəd·ē, (,)kó,-\ *n* -ES **:** the quality or state of being correlative

cor·rel·o·gram \kə'relə,gram\ *n* -s [*correlation* + *-o-* + *-gram*] **:** a curve plotted to exhibit the assumed correlation between two mathematical variables — called also *correlation curve*

cor·ren·te \kə'rentē, kó'- *or as It*\ *n* -s [It, modif. of MF *courante* — more at COURANTE] **:** COURANTE

cor·re·spond \¦kórə¦spänd, ¦kär-\ *vi* -ED/-ING/-S [MF or ML; MF *correspondre*, fr. ML *correspondēre*, fr. L *com-* + *respondēre* — more at RESPOND] **1 a :** to be in conformity or agreement **:** SUIT, AGREE ⟨incomes do not always ~ with the efforts or skill that appear to be involved —J.A.Hobson⟩ **:** match or compare closely ⟨the man whose consciousness does not ~ to that of the majority is a madman —G.B.Shaw⟩ ⟨the numbers of the paragraphs ~ with numbers on the map⟩ **b :** to be equivalent ⟨government budgets, in their final form . . . ~ to "intention surveys" of expenditure —G.W. Mitchell⟩ **:** be parallel **:** be the counterpart ⟨the English parish may be said to ~ closely to the French rural commune —G.M.Harris⟩ **2 a** *obs* **:** to have communication, commune, or intercourse with persons or affairs **b :** to communicate with a person by exchange of letters ⟨~*ed* regularly with friends⟩ **3** *archaic* **:** to make a return **:** RESPOND ⟨Matilda might not ~ to his passion —Horace Walpole⟩ **4 :** to be connected by means of a geometrical transformation or by means of a functional relation (as of the values $x = 2$ and $y = \frac{1}{2}$ in the relation $y = \frac{1}{x}$) **syn** see AGREE

cor·re·spon·dence \,==ˈ=dən(t)s\ *n* -s [ME, fr. MF or ML; MF *correspondence, correspondance*, fr. ML *correspondentia*, fr. *correspondent-, correspondens* + L *-ia*] **1 a :** the state or condition of agreement of things or of one thing with another **:** relation of congruity **:** resemblance or similarity of detail ⟨Joyce elaborates a point-to-point ~ between the spiritual movements of a little Dublin city-dweller and the mythical wanderings of Ulysses —Francis Fergusson⟩ **b :** an instance or point of agreement, similarity, or analogy ⟨many ~*s* between the two plays⟩ **c** *math* **:** definite association of certain members of one aggregate with each member of a second and of certain members of the second with each member of the first **2 a** *archaic* **:** relations between persons or groups **:** social or business relations or communication **b :** the communication between persons by an exchange of letters ⟨a long ~ between the two friends⟩; *also* **:** any communication by letter ⟨application should be made by ~ or in person at our offices⟩ **c :** the letters exchanged by correspondents ⟨publication of the Holmes-Laski ~⟩ **d :** the news, information, or opinion contributed by a correspondent to a newspaper or periodical **e :** study or instruction carried on by written communication between student and a correspondence school

correspondence principle *n* **:** a principle of spectroscopy: the characteristics of spectral series are in approximate agreement with both the classical electromagnetic theory and the quantum theory of electron transitions, the correspondence becoming closer as the quantum numbers involved become greater

correspondence school *n* **:** a school often connected with a university extension that teaches nonresident students by mailing to them lessons and exercises which upon completion are returned to the school for grading

correspondence theory *n* **:** a theory holding that truth consists in agreement between judgments or propositions and an independently existing reality — contrasted with *coherence theory*

cor·re·spon·den·cy \-dənsē, -si\ *n* -ES [ML *correspondentia*] **1 :** CORRESPONDENCE 1 **2** *obs* **:** CORRESPONDENCE 2

¹**cor·re·spon·dent** \¦==¦=dənt\ *adj* [ME, fr. MF or ML; MF *correspondent, correspondant,* fr. ML *correspondent-, correspondens,* pres. part. of *correspondēre* — more at CORRESPOND] **1 :** having a relation of likeness **:** being similar or analogous to something ⟨you tell of . . . preparing books — I have nothing ~. I am fooling around . . . dabbling in philosophy —O.W.Holmes †1935⟩ **:** CORRESPONDING ⟨each advantage having ~ disadvantages⟩ **2 :** being in agreement **:** SUITING, FITTING — used with *with* or *to* ⟨the outcome was entirely ~ with my wishes⟩ **3** *obs* **:** OBEDIENT, SUBMISSIVE

²**correspondent** \"\ *n* -S **1 :** something that corresponds **:** something equivalent or similar ⟨this fish, the Oriental ~ of the celebrated tarpon of the western Atlantic —H.M. Smith⟩ **2 a :** one who communicates with another by letter esp. as part of a regular exchange **b** *archaic* **:** one who communicates with another esp. secretly **:** ACCOMPLICE **c :** one who has regular commercial relations with another esp. with a concern at a distance ⟨the New York ~ of a San Francisco brokerage house⟩ **d :** one who communicates information or comment to a newspaper by letter ⟨no letter to the editor will be printed unless it bears the ~'s name and address⟩ **e :** one employed by a newspaper or broadcasting company to contribute regular news reports or interpretations from a location distant from the home office **f :** a clerk who handles correspondence for a business concern

cor·re·spon·dent·ly *adv* **:** in a correspondent manner

corresponding *adj* [fr. pres. part. of *correspond*] **1 a :** agreeing in kind, degree, position, function, or other respects ⟨the figures are large but the ~ totals next year will be larger⟩ **b :** RELATED, DERIVED, ACCOMPANYING ⟨all rights carry with them ~ responsibilities —W.P.Paepcke⟩ **2 :** charged with the duty of writing letters ⟨~ secretary⟩ **:** participating or serving at a distance and by mail ⟨~ member of the society⟩

cor·re·spond·ing·ly *adv* **:** in a corresponding manner ⟨is less than one inch long and is ~ small in its other dimensions —Morris Fishbein⟩

corresponding points *n pl* **:** points on the retinas of the two eyes which when simultaneously stimulated normally produce a single visual impression

corresponding states *n pl, physical chem* **:** the states of two or more substances in which their pressures are proportional to their critical pressures, their temperatures to their critical temperatures, and their volumes to their critical volumes

corresponds *pres 3d sing of* CORRESPOND

cor·re·spon·sive \¦==¦spän(t)siv\ *adj* [fr. *correspond,* after E *respond: responsive*] **:** mutually responsive **:** CORRESPONDING

co·rri·da \kō'rrēthä\ *n* -S [Sp (often in the combination *corrida de toros* bullfight), lit., act of running, fr. fem. of *corrido,* past part. of *correr* to run, fr. L *currere* — more at CURRENT] **:** BULLFIGHT

co·rri·do \-(,)thō\ *n* -S [Sp, prob. fr. past part. of *correr* to run] **:** a Mexican narrative folk ballad usu. on a topical subject

cor·ri·dor \'kōrədə(r), 'kär- *also* -,dō(ə)r *or* -d(ə)\ *n* -S [MF, fr. OIt *corridore,* fr. *correre* to run, fr. L *currere*] **1 a :** a usu. covered passageway; *esp* **:** one into which compartments or rooms open (as in a hotel or on certain types of trains) **b :** a gallery or passageway connecting several apartments of a building **c :** a place of gossip or intrigue outside a meeting hall ⟨it was assumed around legislative ~s that the bill would be defeated⟩ **2 a :** a usu. narrow passageway or route ⟨the Rhineland . . . has been the usual ~ of German attack —A.H. Vandenberg †1951⟩ **b :** a narrow strip of land through foreign-held territory providing access to a place ⟨Vienna, . . . ninety miles behind the Iron Curtain, is connected with the western world by two official ~s, each one containing a railroad line and a highway —Joseph Wechsberg⟩ or joining a country to its seaport ⟨the Polish ~ across Germany to Danzig⟩ **c :** an open or cleared strip ⟨fire hazard is reduced by frequent ~s cut through the forest —*Amer. Guide Series: Ark.*⟩ **d :** a restricted lane for air traffic **e :** a pair of parallel ridges and the valley between them esp. when the longer axis of the valley is parallel to and in line with the route of advance of an attacking force **3 :** a densely populated strip of land including two or more major cities ⟨the Northeast ~ stretching from Washington into New England —S.D.Browne⟩

cor·rie *also* **cor·ry** \'kōrē\ *n, pl* **corries** [ScGael *coire,* lit., kettle; akin to OIr *coire* kettle; akin to OE & OHG *hwer* kettle, ON *hverr,* Skt *caru*] **:** CIRQUE

cor·rie·dale \-,dā(ə)l\ *n* -S *usu cap* [*Corriedale,* ranch in New Zealand where the breed was developed] **:** a member of a dual-purpose breed of rather large usu. hornless sheep developed in New Zealand from the Lincoln, Leicester, and Merino breeds

cor·ri·gan pulse \'kōrəgən-\ *n, usu cap* [after Sir Dominic J. *Corrigan* †1880 Irish physician, who described it] **:** a pulse characterized by a sharp rise to full expansion followed by immediate collapse that is seen in aortic insufficiency — called also *water-hammer pulse*

cor·ri·gen·dum \,kōrə'jendəm, ,kär-\ *n, pl* **corrigen·da** \-də\ [L, neut. of *corrigendus,* gerundive of *corrigere*] **1 :** an error to be corrected; *esp* **:** an error in a printed work discovered after printing and shown with its correction on a separate sheet bound with the original **2 :** a list of errors in a printed work, with corrections — sometimes pl. but sing. in constr.

cor·ri·gent \'=rəjənt\ *n* -S [L *corrigent-, corrigens,* pres. part. of *corrigere*] **:** a substance added to a medicine to modify its action or counteract a disagreeable effect

cor·ri·gi·bil·i·ty \,kōrəjə'bilәd·ē, ,kär-, -rej-, -ətē, -i *sometimes* kə,rij-\ *n* -ES **:** the quality or state of being corrigible

cor·ri·gi·ble \'kōrəjəbəl, 'kär-, -rej- *sometimes* kə'rij-\ *adj* [ME *corrigabill,* fr. MF *corrigible,* fr. ML *corrigibilis,* fr. L *corrigere* to correct + *-ibilis* -ible — more at CORRECT] **1 a :** capable of being set right, amended, or reformed **:** CORRECTABLE ⟨a ~ defect⟩ **b :** capable of being modified or corrected as a result of empirical or experimental observation ⟨the ~ nature of the findings of experimental science⟩ **2** *obs* **:** deserving chastisement **:** PUNISHABLE **3** *obs* **:** having the power to correct **:** CORRECTIVE ⟨~ authority —Shak.⟩ — **cor·ri·gi·bly** \-blē, -li\ *adv*

cor·rig·i·o·la \kə,rijē'ōlə\ *n, cap* [NL, fr. LL, a plant (perh. *Polygonum aviculare*), dim. of L *corrigia* shoelace, prob. of Celt origin; akin to OIr *cuimrech* fetter, fr. a prehistoric compound whose first and second constituents respectively are akin to L *com-* and to MHG *ric* bond, fetter, knot, W *rhwym* bond, obligation, OE *rāw* row — more at COM-, ROW] **:** a genus of low herbs having alternate entire stipulate leaves and small white or greenish flowers succeeded by one-seeded utricles that is placed in the family Caryophyllaceae or sometimes in the Illecebraceae or is made the type of a separate family

cor·rig·i·o·la·ce·ae \kə,rijēə'lāsē,ē\ *n pl, cap* [NL *Corrigiola,* type genus + *-aceae*] *in some classifications* **:** a family of plants typified by the genus *Corrigiola*

¹**cor·ri·val** \kə'rīvəl, kō'-,kō'-\ *n* -S [MF *corrival,* fr. L *corrivalis,* fr. *com-* + *rivalis* rival — more at RIVAL] **:** RIVAL, COMPETITOR

²**corrival** \"\ *adj* **:** having rivaling claims **:** RIVAL

¹**cor·rob·o·rant** \kə'räb(ə)rənt\ *adj* [L *corroborant-, corroborans,* pres. part. of *corroborare*] *of a medicine, archaic* **:** STRENGTHENING, INVIGORATING

²**corroborant** \"\ *n* -S *archaic* **:** an invigorating medicine **:** TONIC

¹**cor·rob·o·rate** \kə'räbə,rāt, *usu* -ād·+V\ *vb* -ED/-ING/-S [L *corroboratus,* past part. of *corroborare,* fr. *com-* + *roborare* to strengthen, fr. *robor-, robur* strength — more at ROBUST] *vt* **1** *obs* **:** to make strong or strengthen in body or construction **2 :** to establish or make firm ⟨~ his authority⟩ **:** establish legally or by law **3 :** to provide evidence of the truth of **:** make more certain **:** CONFIRM ⟨the authority of religion and science did not ~ Bellamy's high view of man —Joseph Schiffman⟩ **~** *vi* **:** to give evidence or confirmation **syn** see CONFIRM

²**cor·rob·o·rate** \-b(ə)rət\ *adj* [L *corroboratus*] *archaic* **:** CORROBORATED

cor·rob·o·ra·tion \kə,räbə'rāshən\ *n* -S [MF or LL; MF *corroboration,* fr. LL *corroboration-, corroboratio,* fr. L *corroboratus* + *-ion-, -io* -ion] **1 :** the act of corroborating **:** a strengthening or confirming ⟨sought ~ for his views⟩ **2 :** something that corroborates

¹**cor·rob·o·ra·tive** \kə'räbə,rād·|iv, -āt|, -b(ə)rəd·|,-b(ə)rət|, |ēv *also* |əv\ *adj* [MF *corroboratif,* fr. *corroborer* to strengthen (fr. L *corroborare*) + *-atif* -ative] **:** serving or tending to corroborate **:** CONFIRMATORY ⟨~ details⟩ — **cor·rob·o·ra·tive·ly** \|əvlē, -li\ *adv*

²**corroborative** \"\ *n* -S *archaic* **:** CORROBORANT

cor·rob·o·ra·tor \-bə,rād·ə(r), -ātə-\ *n* -S **:** one that corroborates

cor·rob·o·ra·to·ry \-b(ə)rə,tōrē, -tȯr-, -ri\ *adj* [¹*corroborate* + *-ory*] **:** CORROBORATIVE

¹**cor·rob·o·ree** \kə'räbərē\ *n* -S [native name in New South Wales, Australia] **1 a :** a nocturnal festivity with songs and symbolic dances by which the Australian aborigines celebrate events of importance **b :** a song or chant made for such a festivity **2** *Austral* **a :** a festivity or social gathering; *esp* **:** a gathering of noisy or uproarious character **b :** TUMULT, UPROAR

²**corroboree** \"\ *vi* **corroboreed; corroboreed; corroboreeing** \-(,)rēiŋ\ **corroborees :** to hold or take part in a corroboree

cor·rode \kə'rōd\ *vb* -ED/-ING/-S [ME *corroden,* fr. L *corrodere* to gnaw to pieces, fr. *com-* + *rodere* to gnaw — more at RAT] *vt* **1 :** to eat away by degrees as if by gnawing ⟨*corroded* by consumption and indigence⟩ **:** wear away or diminish by gradually separating or destroying small particles or converting into an easily disintegrated substance; *esp* **:** to eat away or diminish by acid or alkali reaction or by chemical alteration ⟨the metal was *corroded* beyond repair by exposure⟩ ⟨the caustic substance *corroded* the material so that it fell apart in the hands⟩ **2** *obs* **:** to eat or gnaw away **3 :** to weaken or destroy (as spirit, strength, or force) by a gradual process of impairment ⟨manners and miserliness that ~ the human spirit —Bernard DeVoto⟩ **~** *vi* **1 :** to act corrosively ⟨certain chemicals will ~ if left on bare metal⟩ **2 :** to undergo corrosion ⟨the bare metal began to ~ after a few weeks of exposure to the weather⟩

cor·ro·dent \kə'rōdᵊnt\ *adj or n* [L *corrodent-, corrodens,* pres. part. of *corrodere*] **:** CORROSIVE

cor·ro·den·tia \,kōrə'denchēə\ *n pl, cap* [NL, fr. L neut. pl. of *corrodent-, corrodens*] **:** an order of small soft-bodied insects having chewing mouthparts and either two pairs of wings held over the back like a roof or no wings at all, the best= known members of the order being the book lice

corrodiary *var of* CORODIARY

cor·rod·ibil·i·ty \kə,rōdə'bilәd·ē\ *n* -ES **:** capability of being corroded ⟨the relative ~ of different kinds of atmospheres —*Mill & Factory*⟩

cor·rod·i·ble \kə'rōdəbəl\ *adj* **:** capable of being corroded

corroding lead \-¦led\ *n* [*corroding* fr. gerund of *corrode*] **:** lead sufficiently pure to be used in making white lead by a process of corroding

corrody *var of* CORODY

cor·ro·si·ble \kə'rōsəbəl, -ōzə-\ *adj* [*corros-* (as in *corrosive*) + *-ible*] **:** CORRODIBLE

cor·ro·sion \kə'rōzhən\ *n* -S [ME *corosion,* fr. LL *corrosion-, corrosio* act of gnawing, fr. L *corrosus* (past part. of *corrodere*) + *-ion-, -io* -ion] **1 :** the action, process, or effect of corroding: as **a :** the action or process of corrosive chemical change not necessarily accompanied by loss of form or compactness; *typically* **:** a gradual wearing away or alteration by a chemical or electrochemical essentially oxidizing process (as in the atmospheric rusting of iron) **b :** a gradual weakening, loss, or destruction (as of spirit or force) ⟨the ~ of faith and the corruption of moral standards —*Times Lit. Supp.*⟩ **c :** erosion of land or rock; *specif* **:** the removal of soil or rock by the solvent or chemical action of running water — compare CORRASION **2 a :** a product of corrosion ⟨a hard ~ of white lead⟩ **b :** a study specimen of an organ or other structure prepared by injection of hollow parts (as blood vessels) with a plastic and subsequent removal of the surrounding tissue by corrosion

cor·ro·sion·al \-nᵊl\ *adj* **:** resulting from corrosion ⟨~ grooving in a steam boiler⟩

corrosion border *or* **corrosion zone** *n* **:** RESORPTION BORDER

corrosion fatigue *n* **:** the fatigue of a material that is accompanied and aggravated by corrosion and that may cause fracture of the material much below the ordinary fatigue limit

¹**cor·ro·sive** \kə'rōs|iv, |ēv *also* -ōz| *or* |əv; *archaic* 'kōrə-\ *adj* [ME *corosif,* fr. MF or ML; MF *corrosif,* fr. ML *corrosivus,* fr. L *corrosus* + *-ivus* -ive] **:** having the power to corrode **:** CORRODING: as **a :** bringing about or causing chemical corrosion ⟨a ~ alkali⟩ ⟨a ~ dampness⟩ **b :** weakening and destroying by a gradual process of breaking down or wearing away ⟨that most ~ instrument of disintegration the European world has yet known: class warfare —Sir Thomas Beecham⟩ **c :** having the power to wound the feelings **:** SARCASTIC ⟨~ satire⟩ **:** tending to cut deeply or affect powerfully and usu. unfavorably **:** BITING ⟨Veblen's ~ and coruscating observations on society —C.E.Lindblom⟩

²**corrosive** \"\ *n* -S [ME *corosif,* prob. fr. *corosif,* adj.] **1 :** a substance that corrodes **:** CAUSTIC **2 :** something that weakens or destroys ⟨criminal ~s against . . . society —Marjorie Grene⟩

cor·ro·sive·ly \|əvlē, -li\ *adv* **:** in a corrosive manner ⟨dialogue that is ~ revealing —*Time*⟩

cor·ro·sive·ness *n* -ES **:** the quality or state of being corrosive **:** the tendency to corrode

corrosive sublimate *n* **:** MERCURY CHLORIDE b

cor·ro·siv·i·ty \,kō(,)rō'sivəd·ē\ *n* -ES **:** the quality of being corrosive

¹**cor·ru·gate** \'kōrə,gāt, 'kär- *sometimes* -ryə-; *usu* -ād·+V\ *vb* -ED/-ING/-S [L *corrugatus,* past part. of *corrugare,* fr. *com-* + *rugare* to wrinkle, fr. *ruga* wrinkle — more at ROUGH] *vt* **:** to form or contract into wrinkles or folds ⟨*corrugated* his brows in thought —John Buchan⟩ **:** shape into alternating ridges and grooves **:** FURROW ⟨the wind ~s the surface of the sea⟩ ⟨the roots *corrugated* the path⟩; *specif* **:** to shape (sheet metal or other material) into straight, parallel, regular, and equally curved ridges and hollows **~** *vi* **:** to become corrugated ⟨surfaces speedily rutted and *corrugated* — N.C.Rockwood⟩

²**cor·ru·gate** \-gət\ *adj* [L *corrugatus*] *archaic* **:** CORRUGATED

corrugated *adj* [fr. past part. of ¹*corrugate*] **1 :** formed into folds or furrows **:** having a ridged or furrowed surface ⟨angry face and ~ brow⟩ ⟨~ waves of the dunes⟩ **:** having even parallel ridges and furrows ⟨~ fabric⟩ ⟨~ steel rollers⟩ **2 :** made of material (as metal or paper) with corrugations ⟨~ hut⟩ ⟨~ boxes⟩

corrugated bar *n* **:** a steel bar for reinforcing concrete having spiral or transverse ridges or nubs at short intervals on each face to provide a bond with the concrete

corrugated board *n* **:** a paperboard having permanent corrugations; *also* **:** such a sheet with an adherent flat board on one or both sides

corrugated fastener *n* **:** a small corrugated strip of steel sharp on one of the long edges and hammered in as a fastener across wood joints in rough carpentry

corrugated iron *n* **:** usu. galvanized sheet iron or sheet steel shaped into straight parallel regular and equally curved ridges and hollows

corrugated lens *n* **:** a lens in which concentric portions are cut out from the surface so as to lessen the weight without affecting the focal power

corrugated paper *n* **:** a thick coarse paper corrugated to give it elasticity and used as a protective wrapper

corrugated pottery *n* **:** coil pottery usu. with indentations on the surface of the coils typical of modified Basket Maker culture and common in later stages of the Anasazi culture

cor·ru·ga·tion \,==' gāshən\ *n* -S [ML *corrugation-, corrugatio,* fr. L *corrugatus* + *-ion-, -io* -ion] **1 :** the act of corrugating or state of being corrugated **2 :** a ridge or groove of a corrugated surface ⟨gravel roads with ~s and potholes⟩ **3 :** a small furrow used for the distribution of irrigation water

1 2

corrugated lens: *1* inner face cut away; *2* outer face cut away

cor·ru·ga·tor \'==,gād·ə(r), -ātə-\ *n* -S [NL, fr. L *corrugatus* + *-or*] **:** one that corrugates: as **a :** a muscle that contracts the skin into wrinkles **b :** an implement for furrowing land for irrigation **c :** a machine or a workman that makes corrugations in material (as paperboard)

¹**cor·rupt** \kə'rəpt\ *vb* -ED/-ING/-S [ME *corrupten,* fr. L *corruptus,* past part. of *corrumpere,* fr. *com-* + *rumpere* to break — more at REAVE] *vt* **1 a :** to change from good to bad in morals, manners, or actions **:** make base **:** PERVERT ⟨there is an opposite error . . . and that is the belief that children are naturally virtuous, and are only ~*ed* by . . . their elders' vices —Bertrand Russell⟩ **b :** BRIBE ⟨large corporations made an unsuccessful effort to ~ federal auditors⟩ **c :** to degrade with unsound principles or moral values ⟨enslave America with machines . . . and ~ it with materialism —Brooks Atkinson⟩ **:** WEAKEN, PERVERT ⟨such behavior ~*s* party discipline⟩ **:** SPOIL, RUIN ⟨that fevered imagination which ~*ed* everything that touched me —W.H.Hudson⟩ **2 :** to spoil or make putrid by decomposition or rotting **:** taint or infect with infectious or putrefying matter ⟨a city ~*ed* with the plague⟩ **3 :** to subject (a person) to corruption of blood **4 a :** to change (a language) in such a way that standard forms become different from earlier forms regarded as better or purer — not used technically **b :** to change (as a word) often by substitution of the familiar for the unfamiliar or by adaptation to the sound system of a language ⟨Dutch *koolsla* was ~*ed* to English *coldslaw*⟩ — not used technically **5 :** to alter from the original or correct form or version (as by error, omission, or addition) ⟨the text was ~*ed* by careless copyists⟩ **~** *vi* **1 a :** to become tainted, rotten, or putrid ⟨leaving the bodies to ~ on the field⟩ **b :** to become morally debased, perverted from right principles, weakened, or unsound ⟨power tends to ~ and absolute power ~*s* absolutely —J.E.E.Dalberg-Acton⟩ **2 :** to cause disintegration, spoiling, or ruin ⟨lay not up for yourselves treasures upon earth, where moth and rust doth ~ —Mt 6:19 (AV)⟩ **syn** see DEBASE

²**corrupt** \"\ *adj, sometimes* -ER/-EST [ME, fr. MF or L; MF, fr. L *corruptus*] **1 a :** DEPRAVED, EVIL **:** perverted into a state of moral weakness or wickedness ⟨humanity they knew to be ~ and incompetent from the day of Adam's creation —Henry Adams⟩ **b :** of debased political morality **:** characterized by bribery, the selling of political favors, or other improper political or legal transactions or arrangements ⟨~ judges⟩ ⟨~ and incompetent city government⟩ **2** *archaic* **:** tainted by decomposition or rotting **:** PUTRID **3 a :** adulterated or debased by change from an original condition of purity or excellence **:** debased or contaminated by the addition of undesirable elements ⟨forsook classic . . . plays for . . . melodramas that culminated in the ~ . . . imitations known as thrillers and tearjerkers —*Amer. Guide Series: N.J.*⟩; *specif* **:** altered from the original or correct condition (as by error) ⟨many of the original Scarlatti . . . notations have been deleted . . . by editors . . . simply because they were copying an edition already ~ —D.D. Boyden⟩ **b** *of a language* **:** changed from an earlier form regarded as better or purer — not used technically **c** *of a word or other linguistic form* **:** characterized by having undergone linguistic change — not used technically **4 :** affected by corruption of blood **syn** see VICIOUS

cor·rupt·ed·ly *adv* **:** in a corrupt manner

cor·rupt·ed·ness *n* -ES **:** the quality or state of being corrupted

cor·rupt·er \-tə(r) *or* **cor·rup·tor** \" *also* -,tȯ(ə)r *or* -ō(ə)\ *n* -S **:** one that corrupts

cor·rupt·ibil·i·ty \kə,rəptə'biləd·ē, -ətē, -i\ *n* -ES [F or LL; F *corruptibilité,* fr. LL *corruptibilitat-, corruptibilitas,* fr. *corruptibilis* + L *-itat-, -itas* -ity] **:** capability of being corrupted **:** liability to corruption

cor·rupt·ible \kə'rəptəbəl\ *adj* [ME, fr. MF or LL; MF, fr. LL *corruptibilis,* fr. L *corruptus* + *-ibilis* -ible] **1 :** capable of being corrupted **2 :** subject to corruption **:** PERISHABLE — **cor·rupt·ible·ness** *n* -ES — **cor·rupt·ibly** \-blē, -bli\ *adv*

cor·rupt·ing·ly *adv* **:** in a corrupting manner

cor·rup·tion \kə'rəpshən\ *n* -S [ME *corrupcioun,* fr. MF *corruption,* fr. L *corruption-, corruptio,* fr. *corruptus* + *-ion-, -io* -ion] **1 a :** impairment of integrity, virtue, or moral principle **:** DEPRAVITY ⟨the luxury and ~ . . . among the upper classes —W.N.Ewer⟩ **b** (1) **:** decay or decomposition of matter (as by rotting or by oxidation) ⟨~ of the bone⟩ ⟨~ of metal⟩ (2) **:** decay of the body after death ⟨death had apparently devoted the body to ~ —Mary W. Shelley⟩ **c :** inducement (as of a political official) by means of improper considerations (as bribery) to commit a violation of duty ⟨the ~ of officials by gambling bosses⟩ ⟨exposing ~ in city politics⟩ **d :** the changing or state of being changed for the worse **:** a departure from what is pure or correct or from the original ⟨the ~ of every art form⟩ ⟨the ~ of the text introduced by copyists⟩ **2** *archaic* **:** an agency or influence that corrupts ⟨the love of money is the ~ of states —Benjamin Jowett⟩ **3** *now dial* **:** a product of decomposition or putrefaction **:** putrid matter **:** PUS **4 a :** an instance of making or becoming corrupt **:** a result of perversion ⟨modern ~s of religious faith —Reinhold Niebuhr⟩; *specif* **:** an erroneous reading in a text ⟨a manuscript full of ~s⟩ **b** (1) *of a word or other linguistic form* **:** change in form often consisting of substitution of the familiar for the unfamiliar or adaptation to the sound system of a language — not used technically (2) **:** a word or form resulting from such a change — not used technically **c** (1) *of a language* **:** change from an earlier form regarded as better or purer — not used technically (2) **:** a language or dialect resulting from such a change — not used technically **5** *dial Brit* **:** evil or irascible nature **:** TEMPER

cor·rup·tion·ist \-sh(ə)nəst\ *n* -S **:** one who practices or defends corruption esp. in a position of public trust

corruption of blood : a legal taint that was one of the results of a conviction by attainder, that barred the attainted person from inheriting, retaining, or transmitting any estate, rank, or title, and that was abolished in England in 1870 and never was recognized in the U.S. ⟨the Congress shall have power to declare the punishment of treason, but no attainder of treason shall work *corruption of blood* or forfeiture except during the life of the person attainted —*U.S. Constitution*⟩

cor·rup·tive \-ptiv, -tēv *also* -təv\ *adj* [MF or LL; MF *corruptif,* fr. LL *corruptivus,* fr. L *corruptus* + *-ivus* -ive] **:** producing or tending to produce corruption — **cor·rup·tive·ly** \-təvlē, -li\ *adv*

cor·rupt·less \kə'rəptləs, *rapid* -pl-\ *adj* **:** INCORRUPTIBLE

cor·rupt·ly \-ptlē, -li, *rapid* -pl-\ *adv* **:** in a corrupt manner **:** by corruption

cor·rupt·ness \-p(t)nəs\ *n* -ES **:** the quality or state of being corrupt

corruptor *var of* CORRUPTER

corrupt practices act *n* **:** any of various statutes in the U.S. limiting the amount and source of political campaign contributions and requiring detailed reports of expenditures

corrupts *pres 3d sing of* CORRUPT

corry *var of* CORRIE

cors *pl of* COR

cor·sac *or* **cor·sak** \'kōr,sak, =ˈ=\ *n* -S [Russ *korsak,* fr. Kirghiz *karsak*] **:** a small yellowish brown bushy-tailed fox (*Vulpes corsac*) of central Asia — called also *Afghan fox*

cor·sage \kōr'säzh, kō(ə)'-, -säj, '=,= *also* |j *or* kə(r)'s-\ *n* -S [F, upper part of the body, bust, bodice, fr. OF, upper part of the body, fr. *cors* body (fr. L *corpus*) + *-age* — more at

MIDRIFF] **1 :** the waist or bodice of a woman's dress **2 :** an arrangement of flowers to be worn as a costume accessory (as on the bodice or at the waist)

cor·sair \R 'kȯr,sa(a)(ə)r, -se(ə)r; –R 'kȯ(ə),sa(a)lə, -selə, +V " *or* \|(ə)r\ *n* -s [MF & OIt; MF *corsaire* pirate, fr. OProv *corsari,* fr. OIt *corsaro, corsare, corsale,* fr. ML *cursarius,* fr. L *cursus* course + *-arius* -ary — more at COURSE] **1 :** a privateer of the coast of the Barbary States authorized by his government to prey upon the commerce and harry the shores of Christian nations **2 :** a pirate of any kind or period **3 :** a California rockfish (*Sebastomus rosaceus*) **4 :** any of several large nocturnal reduviid bugs not normally bloodsuckers but capable of inflicting an extremely painful bite

¹corse \'kȯ(ə)rs\ *n* -s [ME *cors,* fr. OF, body] *archaic* **:** a dead body **:** CORPSE ⟨that thou, dead ∼, again in complete steel, revisits thus the glimpses of the moon —Shak.⟩

²corse \"\ *vt* -ED/-ING/-S [ME *corsen*] *archaic* **:** BARTER

³corse *Scot var of* CROSS

¹corse·let *also* **cors·let** \'kȯrslət\ *n* -s [MF *corselet,* dim. of *cors* waist of a garment, body] **1 a :** a usu. tight-fitting garment covering the trunk but usu. not the arms or legs **b** *usu corslet* (1) **:** a piece of armor for the trunk usu. consisting of a breastplate and backpiece (2) **:** a pikeman's armor including helmet (3) *usu corslet* **:** a soldier wearing a corslet **c :** a sash or close-fitting midriff section of a woman's dress **2** [F, fr. MF] **a :** the hard prothorax of a beetle **b :** an area of enlarged scales surrounding the body immediately behind the head in certain mackerels and related fishes **c :** the bony exoskeleton of a turtle

²cor·se·let *or* **cor·se·lette** \¦kȯrsə¦let\ *n* -s [fr. *Corselette,* a trademark] **:** a foundation garment combining girdle and brassiere

corse·pres·ent \'≈,≈≈\ *n* [ME *corspresent,* fr. *cors* corpse + *present*] **:** a gift made to the clergy from the goods of the deceased at the time of a funeral

¹cor·set \'kȯrsət, 'kȯ(ə)s-, *usu* -ėd·+V\ *n* -s [ME, fr. OF, dim. of *cors*] **1 :** a medieval jacket usu. close-fitting and often laced **2 a :** a woman's close-fitting boned supporting undergarment often hooked and laced, extending from above or beneath the bust or from the waist to below the hips, and having garters attached — sometimes used in pl. **b :** a support for injured bones or muscles or for correcting deformities of the spine or thorax

²corset \"\ *vt* -ED/-ING/-S **1 :** to dress in or fit with a corset **2 :** to restrict closely or control rigidly ⟨most governments ∼*ed* their countries in trade controls —*Wall Street Jour.*⟩

corset cover *n* **:** a woman's undergarment that is worn over a corset

cor·se·tiere \¦kȯ(r)sə¦ti(ə)r, -sə·¦tye(ə)r\ *also* **cor·se·tier** \-sə¦ti(ə)r, -sə·¦tyā\ *n* -s [*corsetiere* fr. F *corsetière,* fem. of *corsetier; corsetier* fr. F, fr. *corset* + *-ier* -er] **:** one who makes, fits, or sells corsets, girdles, or brassieres

cor·set·less \'kȯ(r)sətləs\ *adj* **:** not having a corset

cor·set·ry \'kȯ(r)sətrē\ *n* -ES **1 :** the art of making or fitting corsets, girdles, and brassieres **2 :** corsets, girdles, and brassieres

¹cor·si·can \'kȯ(r)səkən, -sēk-\ *adj, usu cap* [*Corsica,* French island in the Mediterranean + E *-an*] **1 :** of, relating to, or characteristic of the island of Corsica in the Mediterranean sea **2 :** of, relating to, or characteristic of Corsicans

²corsican \"\ *n* -s *cap* **1 :** a native or inhabitant of Corsica **2 :** the dialect of Italian spoken in Corsica

corsican mint *n, usu cap C* **:** a minute low creeping mint (*Mentha requienii*) with tiny pale purple flowers

corsican moss *n, usu cap C* **:** a small red alga (*Alsidium helminthocorton*) of the Mediterranean formerly much used as an anthelminthic — called also *wormmoss*

corsican pine *or* **corsican fir** *or* **corsican larch** *n, usu cap C* **:** a European pine (*Pinus laricio*) of symmetrical growth that is closely related to the Austrian pine and is the source of a large quantity of resin from which turpentine and Burgundy pitch are made

corsing *pres part of* CORSE

corsive *obs var of* CORROSIVE

corslet *var of* CORSELET

cor·so \'kȯr(,)sō\ *n* -s [It, lit., course, fr. L *cursus* — more at COURSE] **:** STRUT

cor·ta·de·ria \,kȯrd·ə'dirēə\ *n, cap* [NL, fr. AmerSp *cortadera* plant with sharp-edged leaves (fr. Sp, hot chisel, fr. *cortar* to cut, fr. L *curtare* to shorten, fr. *curtus* short) + NL *-ia* — more at CURT] **:** a genus of So. American grasses with tall stems and large silky panicles — see PAMPAS GRASS

cor·te \'kȯr,tā\ *n* -s [AmerSp (Argentina), gracefulness, good breeding, corte, fr. Sp, court] **:** a dip or backward step in ballroom dancing with knee bend by the man or the corresponding forward step by the woman

cor·tege *also* **cor·tège** \'kȯr,tezh, -ō(ə)-, ≈'≈\ *n* -s [F *cortège,* fr. It *corteggio,* fr. *corteggiare* to court, fr. *corte* court, fr. L *cohort-, cohors* enclosure, court — more at COURT] **1 :** a train of attendants **:** RETINUE **2 :** a procession of mourners at a funeral

cor·tex \'kȯr\|,teks, -ō(ə)\|\ *n, pl* **corti·ces** \\|_d·ə,sēz\ *or* **cortex·es** \\|,teksəz\ [L, bark — more at CUIRASS] **1 a :** the bark of various plants used medicinally (as cinchona bark or cotton-root bark) **b :** the peel of any of several fruits — used esp. in the writing of medical prescriptions **2 a :** the outer or superficial part of an organ or structure (as the kidney, adrenal gland, or a hair); *esp* **:** the outer layer of gray matter of the cerebrum and cerebellum that contains most of the higher nervous centers (as those concerned with the interpretation and correlation of sensory impressions) **b :** the outer part of certain organisms (as some protozoans) — compare MEDULLA **3 a :** the cylinder of primary tissue surrounding the stele of a vascular plant, extending from endodermis, pericycle, or vascular tissue on the inside to the epidermis or into the bark on the outside, and consisting in its simplest form of thin-walled parenchyma cells which function in photosynthesis and food storage but often esp. in herbaceous plants consisting at least in part of collenchyma or sclerenchyma cells or both which function in support and sometimes where much secondary growth occurs consisting of crowded and crushed cells that eventually slough off partially or wholly; *broadly* **:** all tissues outside the xylem — see SECONDARY CORTEX **b :** the layer of nearly cubical cells surrounding the central core of certain brown algae immediately beneath the superficial layer **c :** a layer of compacted and often somewhat fused fungal hyphae on either or both surfaces of many lichens that is often limited externally by an outer dermal layer — called also *pseudocortex* **d :** the peridium of a fungus

cor·tex·one \'kȯ(r),tek,sōn\ *n* -s [*cortex* + *-one*] **:** DEOXYCORTICOSTERONE

cor·tez \kȯr'tez, -es\ *n* -ES [AmerSp] **1** *in Panama* **:** TIBOURBOU **2 :** any of several Central American timber trees of the genus *Tabebuia* (esp. *T. chrysantha*)

corti apparatus *n, usu cap C* [after Alfonso *Corti* — more at ARCH OF CORTI] **:** ORGAN OF CORTI

cor·ti·cal \'kȯ(r)d·\|əkəl, -)t\|, \|ēk-\ *adj* [NL *corticalis,* fr. L *cortic-, cortex* + *-alis* -al] **1 a :** of, relating to, or located in or on the outer part of something ⟨∼ secretion⟩ ⟨∼ cells of a fruit⟩ **b :** of, relating to, or consisting of cortex **2 a :** involving or resulting from the action or condition of the cerebral cortex as distinguished from the more peripheral parts (as sense organs) ⟨∼ blindness⟩ ⟨∼ deafness⟩ **b :** mental as opposed to sensory — **cor·ti·cal·ly** \\|ək(ə)lē, \|ēk-, -li\ *adv*

cortical rhythm *n* **:** the apparently inherent rhythmic electrical oscillations taking place in the brain in the absence of evident external stimulation

cor·ti·cate \'kȯ(r)d·ə,kāt, -,kət\ *adj* [L *corticatus,* fr. *cortic-, cortex* + *-atus* -ate] **:** covered with bark or with a cortex or specially developed external investment

cor·ti·cat·ed \-,kād·əd\ *adj* [L *corticatus* + E *-ed*] **:** CORTICATE

cor·ti·cif·u·gal \¦kȯ(r)d·ə¦sifyəgəl\ *adj* [L *cortic-, cortex* bark, cortex + E *-i-* + *-fugal*] **:** originating within and passing away from the cortex ⟨a ∼ nerve fiber⟩

cor·ti·cip·e·tal \-¦sipəd·ᵊl\ *adj* [L *cortic-, cortex* + E *-i-* + *-petal*] **:** originating without and passing to or toward the cerebral cortex ⟨a ∼ nerve fiber⟩

cor·ti·ci·um \kȯ(r)'tis(h)ēəm\ *n, cap* [NL, fr. L *cortic-, cortex* bark + NL *-ium* — more at CUIRASS] **:** a genus of basidiomycetous fungi (family Thelephoraceae) that are distinguished by a simple smooth-surfaced prostrate or resupinate sporophore and that include a number of forms parasitic on wood or on economic crops — see BOTTOM ROT 1, PINK DISEASE, RHIZOCTONIA

cortico- *comb form* [L *cortic-, cortex* bark] **1 :** cortex; *esp* **:** cerebral cortex ⟨*cortico*efferent⟩ **2 :** cortical and ⟨*cortico*spinal⟩

cor·ti·co·adrenal \¦kȯrtə,kō+\ *adj* **:** of or relating to the adrenal cortex — compare ADRENAL GLAND

cor·ti·co·ad·re·nal·o·trop·ic \¦kȯrd·ə,kō¦drēnᵊlō¦träpik\ *or* **cor·ti·co·ad·re·no·trop·ic** \-rēnō¦t, -ren-\ *adj* [*corticoadrenal* or *corticoadrenal* + *-o-* + *-tropic*] **:** ADRENOCORTICOTROPIC

cor·ti·co·afferent \¦kȯrd·ə,kō+\ *adj* **:** CORTICIPETAL

cor·ti·co·efferent \"+\ *adj* **:** CORTICIFUGAL

¹cor·ti·coid \'kȯrd·ə,kȯid\ *adj* [L *cortic-, cortex* bark, cortex + E *-oid*] **:** relating to or similar (as in activity) to a corticoid

²corticoid \"\ *n* -s **:** any of various steroids several of which are hormones (as corticosterone, cortisone, and aldosterone) extracted from the adrenal cortex

cor·ti·co·line \kȯr'tikə,līn\ *or* **cor·ti·co·lous** \-¦ləs\ *also* **cor·ti·cole** \'kȯrd·ə,kōl\ *adj* [*corticoline* fr. *corticole* + *-ine; corticolous* irreg. fr. F *corticicole* corticoline + E *-ous; corticole* irreg. fr. F *corticicole,* fr. L *cortic-, cortex* bark + F *-i-* + *-cole* -colous] **:** growing on bark ⟨∼ lichens⟩ ⟨∼ fungi⟩

cor·ti·co·peduncular \¦kȯrd·ə,kō+\ *adj* **:** of or relating to the cerebral cortex and peduncles

cor·ti·co·pontocerebellar \"+\ *adj* [*cortico-* + *pontocerebellar*] **:** of or indicating a tract of nerve fibers or a path for nervous impulses that passes from the cerebral cortex through the internal capsule to the pons to the white matter and cortex of the cerebellum

cor·ti·co·ru·bral tract \"+¦rübrəl-\ *n* [*cortico-* + L *rubr-, ruber* red + E *-al* — more at RED] **:** a conducting path of the brain extending from the cortex of the frontal lobe to the red nucleus

cor·ti·co·spinal \¦kȯrd·ə,kō+\ *adj* **:** of or relating to cerebral cortex and spinal cord or to the pyramidal tract

corticospinal tract *n* **:** PYRAMIDAL TRACT

cor·ti·co·steroid \"+\ *n* -s [ISV *cortico-* + *steroid*] **:** CORTICOID

cor·ti·cos·ter·one \,kȯrd·ə'kästə,rōn, -ə,kō'sti,rōn\ *n* -s [*cortico-* + *sterol* + *-one*] **:** a colorless crystalline steroid hormone $C_{21}H_{30}O_4$ extracted from the adrenal cortex or made synthetically; 11,21-dihydroxy-progesterone

cor·ti·co·striate \¦kȯrd·ə,kō+\ *adj* [*cortico-* + *-striate* (fr. *corpus striatum*)] **:** relating to or connecting the corpus striatum and the cerebral cortex

cor·ti·cothalamic \"+\ *adj* **:** of or relating to the cerebral cortex and the thalamus

cor·ti·co·troph·ic \¦kȯrd·ə,kō¦träfik\ *or* **cor·ti·co·trop·ic** \-träpik\ *adj* **:** influencing a cortex; *specif* **:** influencing or stimulating the adrenal cortex ⟨∼ pituitary fractions⟩

cor·ti·co·troph·in \,≈≈'≈fən\ *or* **cor·ti·co·trop·in** \-trōpən\ *n* -s [*cortico-* + *-trophin, -tropin* (fr. *-trophic, -tropic* + *-in*)] **:** a preparation of the adrenocorticotropic hormone extracted from the anterior pituitary of certain domesticated animals and used esp. in the treatment of rheumatoid arthritis and rheumatic fever

cor·ti·le \kȯr'tē,lā\ *n, pl* **corti·li** \-(,)lē\ [It, fr. (assumed) VL *cohortile,* fr. L *cohort-, cohors* enclosure, court — more at COURT] **:** an open courtyard enclosed by the walls of a building or buildings (as a cloister garth)

cor·tin \'kȯrtᵊn\ *n* -s [*cortex* + *-in*] **1 :** the active principle of the adrenal cortex now known to consist of several hormones **2 :** an aqueous hormone-containing extract of the adrenal cortex — compare CORTICOID

cor·ti·na \kȯr'tīnə, -tēnə\ *n, pl* **corti·nae** \-ī,nē, -ē,nī\ [NL, fr. LL, curtain — more at CURTAIN] **:** the cobwebby remnants of the veil which in mature specimens of certain fungi (order Agaricales) hang from the border of the pileus

cor·ti·nar·i·ous \¦kȯrtᵊn¦a(a)rēəs, -ȯrd·ə¦na-\ *adj* [NL *cortina* + E *-arious* (fr. L *-arius*) — more at -ARY] **:** CORTINATE

cor·ti·nar·i·us \,≈≈'≈rēəs\ *n, cap* [NL, fr. *cortina* + L *-arius* -ary; fr. the prominent cortina] **:** a large genus of rusty-spored agarics having a pileus of various colors, powdery gills, and a prominent cortina

cor·ti·nate \'kȯrtᵊn,āt, -rd·ə,nāt\ *adj* [NL *cortina* + E *-ate*] **:** characterized by a cortina

cortine *obs var of* CURTAIN

cor·ti's ganglion \'kȯrd·ēz-, -r,tēz-\ *n, usu cap C* [after Alfonso *Corti* — more at ARCH OF CORTI] **:** a mass of bipolar nerve cells occupying the spiral canal in the modiolus of the cochlea and containing the axons that comprise the cochlear division of the eighth cranial nerve

cor·ti·sol \'kȯrd·ə,sȯl, -sōl\ *n* -s [*cortisone* + *-ol*] **:** HYDROCORTISONE

cor·ti·sone \'kȯ(r)d·ə,sōn, -)tə-, -,zōn\ *n* -s [alter. of *corticosterone*] **:** a colorless crystalline steroid hormone $C_{21}H_{28}O_5$ of the adrenal cortex prepared from the adrenal glands of certain domesticated animals or made synthetically that acts chiefly on carbohydrate metabolism, is usu. administered in the form of its 21-acetate in the treatment esp. of rheumatoid arthritis, rheumatic fever, and certain allergic diseases, and is also used locally in certain inflammatory diseases of the eye; 17-hydroxy-11-dehydrocorticosterone

corti's organ *n, usu cap C* [after Alfonso *Corti*] **:** ORGAN OF CORTI

cort·landt·ite \'kȯ(r)tlən,dīt, -n,tīt\ *n* -s [*Cortlandt* township, Westchester county, N.Y. + E *-ite*] **:** a variety of peridotite consisting essentially of hornblende and olivine

co·ru·co \kə'rü(,)kō\ *n* -s [MexSp] **:** ADOBE BUG

coru·mi·na·ca \kə,rümə'näkə\ *n, pl* **coruminaca** *or* **coruminacas** *usu cap* [native name] **1 a :** an Otuke people **b :** a member of such people **2 :** the language of the Coruminaca people formerly considered to constitute the Coruminacan language family

co·ru·mi·na·can \kə¦rümə¦näkən\ *adj, usu cap* [*Coruminaca* + E *-an*] **:** of, relating to, or characteristic of the Coruminaca people

co·ru·na \kə'rün(y)ə\ *or* **co·ru·ña** \-ünyə\ *or* **co·run·na** \-'rənə\ *adj, usu cap* **:** LA CORUNA

co·run·deph·i·lite \kə,rən'däfə,līt, ,kō(,)rə-\ *n* -s [*corundum* + *-o-* + *-phil* + *-ite;* fr. its occurrence together with corundum in one locality] **:** a chlorite $(Mg,Fe)_3(Al,Fe)_3(Si,Al)_4O_{10}(OH)_8$ consisting of magnesium, iron, aluminum hydroxyl silicate

co·run·dum \kə'rəndəm\ *n* -s [Tamil *kuruntam,* fr. Skt *kuruvinda* ruby] **:** aluminum oxide Al_2O_3 occurring in nature in massive form and as variously colored rhombohedral crystals including the gems ruby, sapphire, oriental amethyst, oriental emerald, and oriental topaz, synthesized both in gem and industrial quality, extremely tough and with a hardness exceeded only by a few substances (as silicon carbide and diamond), and used industrially as an abrasive (hardness 9, sp. gr. 3.95–4.10)

co·rus·cant \kə'reskənt; 'kȯrə-, 'kär-\ *adj* [ME, fr. L *coruscant-, coruscans,* pres. part. of *coruscare*] **:** GLITTERING, GLEAMING, CORUSCATING

cor·us·cate \'kȯrə,skāt, 'kär-, *usu* -ād·+V\ *vi* -ED/-ING/-S [L *coruscatus,* past part. of *coruscare* to flash, vibrate; perh. akin to Gk *skairein* to gambol — more at CARDINAL] **1 :** to gleam with intermittent flashes **:** GLITTER, SPARKLE ⟨polished brass, *coruscating* helmets and horses shining like table silver —Edith Wharton⟩ **2 :** to be brilliant or showy in technique or style ⟨an ornate style that *coruscated* with verbal epigrams —Aldous Huxley⟩ **:** be brilliant or keen in intelligence or wit ⟨far-darting, restlessly *coruscating* soul —Thomas Carlyle⟩

cor·us·cat·ing·ly *adv* [*coruscating,* adj. (fr. pres. part. of *coruscate*) + *-ly*] **:** in a flashing, brilliant, or keen manner

cor·us·ca·tion \,≈≈'skāshən\ *n* -s [MF or LL; MF *coruscation,* fr. LL *coruscation-, coruscatio,* fr. L *coruscatus* + *-ion-, -io* -ion] **1 :** the act of coruscating or the light so produced **:** GLITTER, SPARKLE ⟨a ∼ of lights burned like . . . rubies set in the silver shield of the night —H.G.Wells⟩ **2 :** a brilliant flash of wit **:** the play of intellectual brilliance ⟨continuous verbal ∼ sometimes makes attention difficult, so that the line of the play . . . is obscured —*New Republic*⟩

cor·vée \'kȯr,vā, ≈'≈\ *n* -s [ME *corvee,* fr. MF, fr. ML *corrogata,* fr. LL, contribution, collection, fr. L, fem. of *corrogatus,* past part. of *corrogare* to bring together by entreaty, fr. *com-* + *rogare* to ask, request — more at RIGHT] **1 :** unpaid labor (as on roads) for a day or longer period due from a vassal to his lord **2 :** unpaid or partially paid labor exacted usu. in lieu of taxes by public authorities (as for the construction or repair of highways, bridges, or canals) **3 :** an onerous or unpleasant and unavoidable task ⟨the daily ∼ of bringing . . . the women in to shop —A.J.Liebling⟩

corves *pl of* CORF

cor·vette \(')kȯr¦vet\ *n* -s [F, fr. MF, prob. fr. MD *corf* basket (or, a ship) — more at CORF] **1 :** a warship with flush deck ranking in the old sailing navies next below a frigate and having usu. only one tier of guns **2 :** a highly maneuverable orig. British and Canadian escort ship that is smaller than a destroyer, armed with antisubmarine and antiaircraft guns and depth charges, and equipped with detection devices

cor·vi·dae \'kȯrvə,dē\ *n pl, cap* [NL, fr. *Corvus,* type genus + *-idae*] **:** a large and widely distributed family of typical passerine birds having a stout moderately long cultrate bill and including the ravens, crows, choughs, magpies, and jays

cor·vi·form \'kȯrvə,fȯrm\ *adj* [L *corvus* + E *-iform*] **:** like a crow in form **:** CORVINE

corvina *var of* CORBINA

cor·vine \'kȯr,vīn\ *adj* [L *corvinus,* fr. *corvus* + *-inus* -ine] **:** of or relating to the crow **:** resembling a crow

cor·void \-vȯid\ *adj* [L *corvus* + E *-oid*] **:** resembling a crow or other member of the Corvidae

cor·vus \-vəs\ *n, cap* [NL, fr. L, raven — more at RAVEN] **:** a widely distributed genus (the type of the family Corvidae) of large active harsh-voiced usu. dark-colored birds including the common crows and ravens

cor·vus·ite \-və,sīt\ *n* -s [L *corvus* + E *-ite;* fr. its color] **:** a hydrous vanadium oxide $V_7O_{17}.nH_2O$ of blue-black to brown color

cor·y·bant \'kȯrə,bant, 'kär-, -rē,-, -baa(ə)nt\ *n, pl* **corybants** \-ts\ *or* **cor·y·ban·tes** \,≈≈'ban(,)tēz, -baan-\ *usu cap* [L *Corybant-, Corybas,* fr. Gk *Korybant-, Korybas,* prob. alter. of *Kyrbant-, Kyrbas*] **1 :** one of the attendants of the Greek nature goddess Cybele who were supposed to accompany her with wild dances and music **2 :** one of the priests of Cybele who act as Corybants with orgiastic processions and rites

cor·y·ban·tic \¦≈≈¦≈tik, -tēk\ *adj* [Gk *Korybantikos,* fr. *Korybant-, Korybas* + *-ikos* -ic] **:** like or in the spirit of a Corybant; *specif* **:** WILD, FRENZIED ⟨excited by the ∼ mood of the gathering⟩

cor·y·bul·bine \,kȯrə'bəl,bēn, -bən\ *n* -s [ISV *cory-* (fr. NL *Corydalis*) + *bulb-* (fr. NL *bulbosa* — former specific epithet of *Corydalis cava* — fr. L, fem. of *bulbosus* bulbous) + *-ine* — more at BULBOUS] **:** a crystalline alkaloid $C_{21}H_{25}NO_4$ obtained from the roots of species of *Corydalis*

co·ry·ci·um \kə'ris(h)ēəm\ *n* -s *often cap* [NL] **:** a globular object from Finnish Precambrian rocks thought to be the fossil remains of an unknown life-form

co·ryd·a·line \kə'ridᵊl,ēn, -ᵊlən\ *n* -s [G *korydalin,* fr. NL *Corydalis* + G *-in* -ine] **:** a bitter crystalline alkaloid $C_{22}H_{27}NO_4$ obtained from the root of species of *Corydalis*

¹co·ryd·a·lis \-ᵊləs\ *n* [NL, fr. Gk *korydallis* crested lark; fr. the shape of the flowers; akin to L *cornu* horn — more at HORN] **1 a** *cap* **:** a large genus of herbs (family Fumariaceae) that are native to north temperate regions and southern Africa and have decompound leaves, racemose irregular flowers, and a several-seeded capsular fruit **b** -ES **:** any plant of this genus **2** -ES **:** the dried tubers of squirrel corn and Dutchman's-breeches containing the alkaloid corydaline and formerly used as a tonic

²corydalis \"\ [NL, alter. (influenced by Gk *korydallis*) of *Corydalus*] *syn of* CORYDALUS

corydalis green *n* **:** a grayish yellow green that is yellower and paler than average sage green, greener, lighter, and stronger than mermaid, and yellower, lighter, and stronger than palmetto

co·ryd·a·lus \-ᵊləs\ *n, cap* [NL, fr. L, crested lark, fr. Gk *korydalos;* akin to L *cornu* horn — more at HORN] **:** a genus (the type of the family Corydalidae) of large megalopterous insects that includes the dobsons and in some classifications is placed in the family Sialidae

cor·y·dine \'kȯrə,dēn, -dən\ *n* -s [ISV *coryd-* (fr. NL *Corydalis*) + *-ine*] **:** a crystalline alkaloid $C_{20}H_{23}NO_4$ obtained esp. from the roots of plants of the genus *Corydalis*

co·ryd·o·ra \kə'ridərə\ *n* -s [back-formation fr. *Corydoras,* taken as a plural] **:** any of various small catfishes often kept as scavengers in the tropical aquarium

co·ryd·o·ras \-dərəs\ *n, cap* [NL] **:** a genus (family Callichthyidae) comprising small often brightly colored tropical catfishes often less than an inch in adult length

cor·y·la·ce·ae \,kȯrə'lāsē,ē\ *n pl, cap* [NL, fr. *Corylus,* type genus + *-aceae*] *in some classifications* **:** a family coextensive with the Betulaceae

cor·y·la·ceous \¦kȯrə¦lāshəs\ *adj* [NL *Corylaceae* + E *-ous*] **:** of or relating to the genus *Corylus* **:** BETULACEOUS

cor·y·lop·sis \-läpsəs\ *n, cap* [NL, fr. *Corylus* + *-opsis*] **:** a small genus of shrubs (family Hamamelidaceae) of the temperate regions of Asia having racemose flowers — compare HAMAMELIS

cor·y·lus \'kȯrələs\ *n, cap* [NL, fr. L *corylus, corulus* hazel or filbert shrub — more at HAZEL] **:** a genus of shrubs or small trees (family Betulaceae) comprising the hazels and having the nut enclosed in a leafy involucre — see FILBERT

cor·ymb \'kȯ,rim(b), 'kä,-, -,rəm(b)\ *n, pl* **corymbs** \-mz\ [F *corymbe,* fr. L *corymbus* cluster of fruits, cluster of flowers, fr. Gk *korymbos* summit, cluster of fruits or flowers; prob. akin to L *cornu* horn — more at HORN] **:** a flat-topped inflorescence; *specif* **:** a flower cluster or inflorescence in which the flower stalks arise at different levels on the main axis and reach about the same height so that there results a somewhat flat-topped cluster in which the outer flowers open first, the inflorescence being indeterminate — compare CYME

corymb

cor·ymbed \-md\ *adj* **:** having corymbs

cor·ym·bif·er·ous \¦kȯrəm¦bif(ə)rəs, ¦kär-, -,rim-\ *adj* [NL *corymbifer* (fr. L *corymbus* + *-fer*) + E *-ous*] **:** bearing clusters of berries, fr. *corymbi-* — fr. *corymbus* — + *-fer*) + E *-ous*] **:** bearing corymbs

cor·ym·bose \'≈(,)≈,bōs, kə'rim-\ *adj* [NL *corymbosus,* fr. L *corymbus* corymb + *-osus* -ose] **:** resembling a corymb **:** borne in a corymb — **cor·ym·bose·ly** *adv*

co·rym·bous \kə'rimbəs, kō'-\ *adj* [*corymb* + *-ous*] **:** CORYMBOSE

cor·y·ne·bacteriaceae \¦kȯrə,nē+\ *n pl, cap* [NL, fr. *Corynebacterium,* type genus + *-aceae*] **:** a family (order Eubacteriales) of chiefly gram-positive and nonmotile pleomorphic rod-shaped bacteria that include important parasites as well as saprophytes of soil and dairy products — see CORYNEBACTERIUM, ERYSIPELOTHRIX, LISTERIA

cor·y·ne·bacterial \"+\ *adj* [NL *Corynebacterium* + E *-al*] **:** of, relating to, or caused by bacteria of the genus *Corynebacterium*

cor·y·ne·bacterium \"+\ *n* [NL, fr. Gk *korynē* club + NL *bacterium;* akin to L *cornu* horn — more at HORN] **1** *cap* **:** a large genus (the type of the family Corynebacteriaceae) of usu. gram-positive aerobic to microaerophilic nonmotile bacteria that occur as irregular or branching rods often banded with metachromatic granules and include a number of important parasites of man, lower animals, and plants — see DIPHTHERIA, RING ROT **2** *pl* **corynebacteria :** any bacterium of the genus *Corynebacterium*

co·ryn·e·form \kə'rinə,fȯrm\ *adj* [*coryne-* (fr. NL *Corynebacterium*) + *-form*] **:** resembling bacteria of the genus *Corynebacterium*

cor·y·ne·um \,kȯrə'nēəm, kə'rinē-\ *n, cap* [NL, fr. Gk *korynē* club] **:** a large form genus of imperfect fungi of the family Melanconiaceae having dark-colored fusiform sometimes dry spores with long stalks and several septa — see CALIFORNIA BLIGHT

cor·y·no·car·pus \ˌkȯrənō'kärpəs\ *n, cap* [NL, fr. *coryno-* (fr. Gk *korynē* club) + *-carpus*] **:** a genus (coextensive with a family Corynocarpaceae of the order Sapindales) comprising trees of New Zealand and Polynesia with smooth entire leaves and small white flowers having glandular scales alternating with the petals

cor·y·no·mor·pha \-ō'mȯrfə\ *n, cap* [NL, fr. *coryno-* (fr. Gk *korynē*) + *-morpha*] **:** a genus of solitary marine hydrozoans

cor·y·pha \'kȯrəfə\ *n, cap* [NL, fr. Gk *koryphē* top, summit] **:** a small genus of very large East Indian and Australian fan palms that have a spineless trunk and that die after once fruiting — see BOOK PALM, GEBANG PALM, TALIPOT

cor·y·phae·ni·dae \ˌkȯrə'fēnəˌdē\ *n pl, cap* [NL, fr. *Coryphaena*, type genus (fr. Gk *koryphaina* dolphin, prob. fr. *koryphē*) + *-idae*] **:** a family (coextensive with the genus *Coryphaena*) of large active pelagic percoid fishes comprising the dolphins (sense 2) — **cor·y·phae·noid** \-ˌnȯid\ *adj*

cor·y·phae·noi·di·dae \-ˌfə'nȯidəˌdē\ [NL, fr. *Coryphaenoides*, type genus (fr. *Coryphaena* + *-oides* -oid) + *-idae*] *syn of* MACRURIDAE

cor·y·phae·us \ˌkȯrə'fēəs\ *n, pl* **cory·phaei** \-ēˌī\ [L, leader, fr. Gk *koryphaios* leader, leader of the chorus, fr. *koryphē* top, summit; akin to L *cornu* horn — more at HORN] **1 :** the leader of a chorus — see CHORAGUS 2 **2 :** the leader of a party, school of thought, or other group of persons

cor·y·phée \ˌkȯrə¦fā, ¦kär-, -rē¦-\ *n* -S [F, fr. L *coryphaeus*] **:** a ballet dancer who dances in a small group instead of in the corps de ballet or as a soloist; *broadly* **:** a dancer in the chorus **:** CHORUS GIRL

cor·y·phene \'kȯrəˌfēn\ *n* -S [F *coryphène*, fr. NL *Coryphaena*] **:** a fish of the genus *Coryphaena* — compare DOLPHIN 2

co·ryph·o·don \kə'rifəˌdän\ *n* [NL, fr. Gk *koryphē* point, top + NL *-odon*] **1** *cap* **:** a genus of extinct mammals (order Pantodonta) from the Lower Eocene of Europe and America varying in size between the tapir and rhinoceros and having short plantigrade 5-toed feet like the elephant and sometimes small or rudimentary horns **2** -S **:** any animal or fossil of the genus *Coryphodon* — **co·ryph·o·dont** \-nt\ *adj or n*

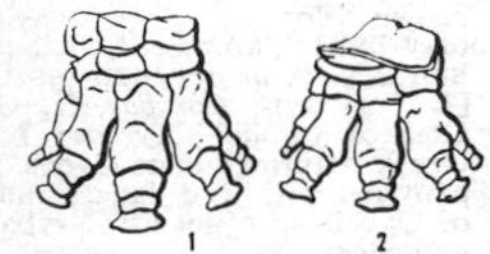

coryphodon: *1* forefoot, *2* hind foot

co·ryth·o·sau·rus \kəˌrithə'sȯrəs\ *n, cap* [NL, fr. *corytho-* (fr. LGk *korythos* crested, fr. Gk *koryth-*, *korys* helmet) + *-saurus*; akin to L *cornu* horn — more at HORN] **:** a genus of duck-billed dinosaurs (suborder Ornithopoda) having a thin domed bony crest capping the skull and found in Upper Cretaceous formations of western No. America

cor·y·tu·ber·ine \ˌkȯrə'tübəˌrēn, -ə'tyü-, -bərən\ *n* -S [ISV *cory-* (fr. NL *Corydalis*) + *tuber-* (fr. NL *tuberosa* — former specific epithet of *Corydalis cava* — fr. L, fem. of *tuberosus* tuberous) + *-ine* — more at CORYDALIS, TUBEROUS] **:** a crystalline alkaloid $C_{19}H_{21}NO_4$ obtained from the roots of certain fumeworts (as members of the genus *Corydalis*)

co·ry·za \kə'rīzə\ *n* -S [LL, fr. Gk *koryza* nasal mucus; akin to OE *hrot* thick fluid, OHG *hroz* nasal mucus, ON *horr* nasal mucus, Skt *kardama* mud, dirt] **:** an acute inflammatory contagious disease involving the upper respiratory tract: **a :** COMMON COLD **b :** such a disease in domestic animals characterized by inflammation of and discharge from the mucous membranes of the upper respiratory tract, sinuses, and eyes; *esp* **:** such a disease in chickens usu. caused by a bacterium (*Hemophilus gallinarum*) — called also *roup* — **co·ry·zal** \-zəl\ *adj*

cos *n* **:** COS LETTUCE

cos *abbr* **1** cosine **2** consul; consulship

COs *pl of* CO

COS *abbr* **1** cash on shipment **2** chief of section **3** chief of staff **4** condemned or suppressed

co sa *abbr* [It *come sopra*] as above

co·sa·lite \'kōzəˌlīt, -ōsə-\ *n* -S [fr. *Cosalá*, Sinaloa, Mexico + E *-ite*] **:** a lead-gray or steel-gray mineral $Pb_2Bi_2S_5$ composed of lead, bismuth, and sulfur (sp. gr. 6.39–6.75)

co·saque \kō'zäk, kə'-, -zak\ *n* -S [F, lit., Cossack, fr. Russ *kazak* & Ukrainian *kozak* — more at COSSACK] **:** CRACKER 2c

co·set \'käsət\ *n* -S [prob. alter. of OE *cotsæta* cottager, fr. *cot* cottage + *-sæta* resident (fr. the stem of *sittan* to sit) — more at COT, SIT] **:** a class of medieval English peasant landholders — see ¹COTTER 2

cos·ci·no·dis·ca·ce·ae \ˌkäs(ˌ)nōdi'skāsēˌē\ *n pl, cap* [NL, fr. *Coscinodiscus*, type genus + *-aceae*] **:** a family of diatoms (order Centrales) having the characteristics of *Coscinodiscus*

cos·ci·no·dis·cus \-'diskəs\ *n, cap* [NL, fr. Gk *koskinon* sieve + NL *-discus*] **:** a large genus (the type of the family Coscinodiscaceae) of chiefly marine disk-shaped diatoms that are often abundant in the plankton — see CYCLOTELLA

cos·ci·no·man·cy \'käsənōˌmansē\ *n* -ES [LL *coscinomantia*, fr. Gk *koskinomanteia*, fr. *koskinon* sieve + *-manteia* -mancy] **:** divination by the mode of sieve and shears

cos·co·ro·ba \ˌkäskə'rōbə\ *n* -S [Sp] **:** a large white So. American bird (*Coscoroba coscoroba*) of the family Anatidae that is intermediate in several respects between the ducks and swans

cose \'kōz\ *vi* -ED/-ING/-S [back-formation fr. *cosy*] **:** to make oneself cozy **:** be cozy

co·secant \(ˈ)kō+\ *n* -S [NL *cosecant-*, *cosecans*, fr. L *co-* + *secant-*, *secans*, pres. part. of *secare* to cut — more at SAW] **:** the distance between the vertex of an angle and any other point on its terminal side divided by the nonzero ordinate of this point, the vertex coinciding with the origin of a plane rectangular coordinate system and the initial side of the angle coinciding with the positive x-axis — abbr. *cosec* or *csc*

co·seism \(ˈ)kō +\ *n* -S [*co-* + *seism*] **:** a line drawn about an epicenter through all the coseismal points — called also *coseismal line*

¹**co·seismal** *or* **co·seismic** \(ˈ)kō +\ *adj* [*co-* + *seismal*, *seismic*] **:** simultaneously affected by the same phase of any particular seismic shock **:** relating to or being such simultaneous affection

²**coseismal** \"\ *n* -S **:** COSEISM

co·session \(ˈ)kō +\ *n* -S [*co-* + *session* (Christ's sitting)] **:** the theological doctrine of the enthronement of the ascended Christ at the right hand of the Father

¹**co·sey** *or* **co·sie** \'kōzē, -zi\ *archaic var of* ¹COZY

²**cosey** *var of* ²COZY

¹**cosh** \'käsh, 'kōsh\ *adj* [origin unknown] **1** *chiefly Scot* **:** COMFORTABLE, SNUG **2** *chiefly Scot* **:** TIDY, NEAT **3** *chiefly Scot* **:** STILL, QUIET

²**cosh** \'käsh\ *n* -ES [perh. fr. Romany *kosh*, *koshter* stick, skewer] *chiefly Brit* **:** a weighted weapon usu. similar to a blackjack; *also* **:** an attack with a cosh

³**cosh** \"\ *vt* -ED/-ING/-ES *chiefly Brit* **:** to strike or assault with or as if with a cosh

cosh *abbr* [*cosine* + *hyperbolic*] hyperbolic cosine

cosh·er \'käshə(r), 'kōsh-\ *vb* **coshered; coshered; coshering** \-sh(ə)riŋ\ **coshers** [IrGael *cōisir* feast, banquet] *vi* **1** *Irish* **:** to lodge and eat at the expense of dependents or tenants **2** *Irish* **:** to live at another's expense **:** SPONGE **3** *Irish* **:** to make a visit **:** have a friendly chat ~ *vt* **:** PET, PAMPER

cosh·er·er \-sh(ə)rə(r)\ *n* -S **:** one that coshers

cosh·ery \-sh(ə)rē, -ri\ *n* -ES **:** coshering or entertainment so exacted

cosier *comparative of* COSY

cosiest *superlative of* COSY

co·signatory \(ˈ)kō +\ *n* -ES [*co-* + *signatory*] **:** one of the joint signers of a document (as a treaty)

cosily *var of* COZILY

cos·in·age \'kəzᵊnij\ *n* -S [ME — more at COUSINAGE] **:** COUSINHOOD — see WRIT OF COSINAGE

co·sine \'kō +ˌ-\ *n* -S [NL *cosinus*, fr. ML *sinus* sine] **:** the abscissa of any point, except the vertex, on the terminal side of an angle, divided by the distance between the vertex and the point, the vertex coinciding with the origin of a plane rectangular coordinate system and the initial side of the angle coinciding with the positive x-axis — abbr. *cos*

cosine curve *n* **:** a curve whose equation in Cartesian coordinates is of the form $y = a \cos x$

cosine law *n* **:** either of two laws of radiation: **a :** the radiant flux emitted in a given direction from a given small area of a perfectly diffusing surface varies as the cosine of the angle of emission **b :** the irradiation by parallel rays falling on a surface varies as the cosine of the angle of incidence

cosiness *var of* COZINESS

cosing *pres part of* COSE

cos lettuce \'käs-\ *n, sometimes cap C* [fr. *Cos*, *Kos*, Greek island of the Dodecanese in the Aegean sea] **:** a variety (*Lactuca sativa longifolia*) of lettuce having long spoon-shaped leaves with large midribs and columnar heads — called also *romaine lettuce*

cosm- *or* **cosmo-** *comb form* [ME (in *cosmographie* cosmography), fr. L *cosm-*, LL *cosmo-*, fr. Gk *kosm-*, *kosmo-*, fr. *kosmos*] **:** world **:** universe ⟨*cosmorama*⟩ ⟨*cosmogenesis*⟩

-cosm \ˌkäzəm\ *n comb form* -S [ME *-cosme*, fr. MF, fr. ML *-cosmus*, fr. Gk *kosmos*] **:** world ⟨*microcosm*⟩ ⟨*loxocosm*⟩

cos·ma·tesque \¦käzmə¦tesk\ *adj, sometimes cap* [It *cosmatesco*, fr. *Cosmati* + *-esco* -esque] **:** of, relating to, or resembling Cosmati work

cos·ma·ti work \(ˈ)käz¦mäd·ē-, (ˈ)kōz¦-\ *n, usu cap C* [after *Cosmati*, a group of It. artists active in Rome and vicinity from *ab*1150–1320, pl. of the name *Cosmas*; fr. the fact that many members of the group had the given name *Cosmos* (*Cosimo*)] **:** a style of fine mosaic inlay in geometric patterns made of colored marbles, glass paste, and gold leaf developed during the 12th and 13th centuries

cos·me·col·o·gy \ˌkäzmə'käləjē\ *n* -ES [*cosm-* + *ecology*] **:** the science that considers the earth in its relation to cosmic phenomena

¹**cos·met·ic** \käz'med·ik, -etik, -ēk\ *n* -S [in sense 1, fr. Gk *kosmētikē*, fr. fem. of *kosmētikos*, adj.; in sense 2, fr. Gk *kosmētikos*, adj.] **1** *archaic* **:** the art of beautifying the body — sometimes used in pl. **2 :** a preparation (except soap) to be applied to the human body for beautifying, preserving, or altering the appearance of a person (as for theatricals) or for cleansing, coloring, conditioning, or protecting the skin, hair, nails, lips, eyes, or teeth

²**cosmetic** \(ˈ)ˌ¦ˌˌ\ *adj* [Gk *kosmētikos* skilled in arrangement or adornment, fr. *kosmētos* well-arranged (fr. *kosmein* to arrange, adorn, fr. *kosmos* order, ornament) + *-ikos* -ic] **:** relating to or making for beauty esp. of the complexion **:** BEAUTIFYING ⟨~ salves⟩; *also* **:** correcting defects esp. of the face ⟨~ surgery⟩

cos·met·i·cal \(ˈ)käz¦med·əkəl, -etə-\ *adj* [Gk *kosmētikos* + E *-al*] **:** relating to cosmetics or to physical appearance — **cos·met·i·cal·ly** \-ək(ə)lē, -li\ *adv*

cos·me·ti·cian \ˌkäzmə'tishən\ *n* -S [¹*cosmetic* + *-ician* (as in *physician*)] **:** one who is expert in the use of cosmetics **:** a makeup artist

cos·me·tol·o·gist \-'täləjəst\ *n* -S **:** one who gives beauty treatments (as to skin and hair) — called also *beautician*

cos·me·tol·o·gy \-'täləjē\ *n* -ES [F *cosmétologie*, fr. *cosmétique* cosmetic (fr. E *cosmetic*) + *-o-* + *-logie* -logy] **:** the art or practice of cosmetic treatment of the skin, hair, and nails and professional application of cosmetics

cos·mic \'käzmik, -mēk\ *adj* [Gk *kosmikos* of the universe, fr. *kosmos* order, universe + *-ikos* -ic] **1 :** of, from, or relating to the cosmos, the extraterrestrial vastness, or the universe in contrast to the earth alone; *sometimes* **:** of, from, or relating to the cosmos as an ordered system or the cosmos outside the solar system ⟨in addition to these general ~ theories there were particular problems, above all that of the diurnal rotation of the earth —Douglas Bush⟩ ⟨the misty radiance of a setting sun, whose streamers are like the spokes of some gigantic ~ wheel —J.L.Lowes⟩ **2 :** characteristic of the cosmos **:** of a magnitude universally transcending or subsuming **:** VAST, UNFATHOMED, INFINITE, GRAND, GRANDIOSE ⟨anthropomorphism . . . making man the central aim or goal of the whole ~ process —M.R.Cohen⟩ ⟨an abiding illness of the 20th century democratic man — a ~ boredom —Albert Hubbell⟩ **3 :** relating to cosmism **syn** see UNIVERSAL

cos·mi·cal \'käzməkəl\ *adj* [Gk *kosmikos* + E *-al*] **1** *obs* **:** relating to the terrestrial world **2 :** COSMIC — **cos·mi·cal·ly** \-k(ə)lē, -li\ *adv*

cos·mi·cal·i·ty \ˌkäzmə'kaləd·ē\ *n* -ES **:** the quality or state of being cosmic

cosmic dust *n* **:** very fine particles of solid matter in any part of the universe including meteoric dust and zodiacal light particles in the solar system, interstellar matter that absorbs starlight and forms the vast dark nebulae of the Milky Way galaxy, and lanes of dark matter in other galaxies

cosmic noise *n* **:** unidentified celestial radio-frequency radiation; *esp* **:** such radiation originating outside the Milky Way

cosmic philosophy *n* **:** COSMISM

cosmic radiation *n* **:** radiation made up of cosmic rays

cosmic ray *n* **:** a stream of atomic nuclei of heterogeneous extremely penetrating character that enter the earth's atmosphere from outer space at speeds approaching that of light and with energies ranging from a few billion to at least 10^7 billion electron volts and that bombard atmospheric atoms to produce mesons as well as secondary particles possessing some of the original energy

cosmic-ray shower \'ˌˌ¦ˌ-\ *n* **:** a shower of ionizing particles originating in several respects by a single cosmic ray that reveals itself by leaving tracks in a cloud chamber or by actuating a counting tube

cosmic-ray telescope *n* **:** a set of counting tubes so arranged as to register by simultaneous ionic discharge only those cosmic rays coming from a selected direction in space

cosmic year *n* **:** the estimated time required for a star at the sun's distance from the center of the Milky Way galaxy to make one trip around it in a circular orbit, about 200 million years

cos·mine \'käzˌmēn, -mən\ *n* -S [Gk *kosmos* order, arrangement + E *-ine*] **:** a bony material infiltrated by vascular channels that resembles dentin and underlies the ganoin in certain primitive ganoid scales

cos·mism \'käzˌmizəm\ *n* -S [*cosm-* + *-ism*] **:** a philosophy of the cosmos or of cosmic evolution esp. as interpreted teleologically by John Fiske — **cos·mist** \-məst\ *n* -S

cosmo- — see COSM-

cos·mo·chemistry \¦käzmō, ¦käzmə +\ *n* [*cosm-* + *chemistry*] **:** the study of the chemical composition of and changes in the universe

cos·mo·genesis \" +\ *n, pl* **cosmogeneses** [NL, fr. *cosm-* + *-genesis*] **:** COSMOGONY — **cos·mo·genetic** \" +\ *adj*

cos·mog·e·ny \käz'mäjənē, -ni\ *n* -ES [Gk *kosmogeneia*, fr. *kosm-* cosm- + *-geneia* -geny] **:** COSMOGONY

cos·mo·gon·ic \¦käzmə¦gänik, -nēk\ *or* **cos·mo·gon·i·cal** \-nəkəl\ *also* **cos·mog·o·nal** \(ˈ)käz¦mägənəl\ *adj* [*cosmogony* + *-ic*, *-ical* or *-al*] **:** relating to or dealing with cosmogony

cos·mog·o·nist \käz'mägənəst\ *n* -S [NL *cosmogonia* + E *-ist*] **:** one specializing in or occupied with cosmogony

cos·mog·o·ny \-'mägənē, -ni\ *n* -ES [NL *cosmogonia*, fr. Gk *kosmogonia*, fr. *kosm-* cosm- + *-gonia* -gony] **1 :** the creation, origination, or manner of coming into being of the world or universe **2 :** a theory or account of the origination of the universe ⟨a primitive ~⟩ **3 :** a part of the science of astronomy that deals with the origin and development of the universe and its components

cos·mog·ra·pher \-'mägrəfə(r)\ *n* -S [*cosmography* + *-er*] **1 :** one skilled or occupied in cosmography **2** *obs* **:** GEOGRAPHER

cos·mo·graph·ic \¦käzmə¦grafik\ *or* **cos·mo·graph·i·cal** \-fəkəl\ *adj* [F *cosmographique*, fr. *cosmographie* (fr. LL *cosmographia*) + *-ique* -ic, *-ical*] **:** concerned with or relating to cosmography — **cos·mo·graph·i·cal·ly** \-fək(ə)lē\ *adv*

cos·mog·ra·phist \käz'mägrəfəst\ *n* -S [*cosmography* + *-ist*] **:** COSMOGRAPHER

cos·mog·ra·phy \-fē, -fi\ *n* -ES [ME *cosmographie*, fr. LL *cosmographia*, fr. Gk *kosmographia*, fr. *kosm-* cosm- + *-graphia* -graphy] **1 :** a general description of the world or of the universe **:** a recital of cosmic principles or speculations **2 :** the science that deals with the constitution of the whole order of nature or the figure, disposition, and relation of all of its various parts

cos·moid \'käzˌmȯid\ *adj* [*cosmine* + *-oid*] **:** relating to or being a ganoid scale that contains a cosmine layer

cos·mo·labe \'käzməˌlāb\ *n* -S [MF, fr. *cosm-* + *-labe*] **:** an instrument resembling the astrolabe formerly used for measuring angular distances between heavenly bodies

cos·mo·line \'käzməˌlēn, -ˌlən\ *vt* -ED/-ING/-S **:** to smear with Cosmoline grease (as for storage) ⟨Tokyo fell and the guns were *cosmolined* —John Scarne⟩

Cosmoline \"\ *trademark* — used for petrolatum

cos·mo·log·ic \¦käzmə¦läjik, -jēk\ *or* **cos·mo·log·i·cal** \-jəkəl\ *adj* [*cosmology* + *-ic* or *-ical*] **:** of or relating to cosmology — **cos·mo·log·i·cal·ly** \-jək(ə)lē, -li\ *adv*

cos·mol·o·gist \käz'mäləjəst\ *n* -S [*cosmology* + *-ist*] **:** one skilled in, occupied with, or propounding a cosmology

cos·mol·o·gy \-'mäləjē, -ji\ *n* -ES [NL *cosmologia*, fr. *cosm-* + *-logia* -logy] **1 :** a branch of systematic philosophy that deals with the character of the universe as a cosmos by combining speculative metaphysics and scientific knowledge; *esp* **:** a branch of philosophy that deals with the processes of nature and the relation of its parts — compare ONTOLOGY **2 :** a particular theory or body of doctrine relating to the natural order **3 :** astronomy dealing with the origin, structure, and space-time relationships of the universe

cos·mo·naut \'käzməˌnȯt, -ˌnät\ *n* -S [part trans. of Russ *kosmonavt*, fr. Gk *kosmos* + Russ *-navt* (as in *aeronavt* aeronaut)] **:** a traveler beyond the earth's atmosphere **:** ASTRONAUT

cos·mo·plastic \¦käzmə +\ *adj* [Gk *kosmoplastēs* molder of the world (fr. *kosm-* cosm- + *plastēs* molder, fr. *plassein* to mold) + E *-ic* — more at PLASTIC] **:** of a molding force regarded as operative in the formation of the world independently of God **:** world-forming ⟨~ and hylozoic atheisms —Ralph Cudworth⟩

cos·mo·poi·et·ic \¦käzmōˌpȯi¦ed·ik, -məˌ-\ *adj* [Gk *kosmopoiētikos*, fr. *kosm-* cosm- + *poiētikos* capable of making, creative, poetical — more at POETIC] **:** cosmos-producing **:** world-creating

cos·mop·o·lis \käz'mäpələs\ *n* -ES [NL, fr. F *cosmopolitain* & E *cosmopolitan*, after F *métropolitain* & E *metropolitan*: LL *metropolis*] **1 :** a community of citizens of the world bound by juridical or moral principles **2 :** a city of world importance or inhabited by many nationalities

¹**cos·mo·pol·i·tan** \¦käzmə¦pälətᵊn *also* -ətən *or* -əd·ən\ *adj* [F *cosmopolitain*, fr. MF, fr. *cosmopolite* + *-ain* (as in MF *métropolitain* metropolitan)] **1 :** marked by interest in, familiarity with, or knowledge and appreciation of many parts of the world **:** not provincial, local, limited, or restricted by the attitudes, interests, or loyalties of a single region, section, or sphere of activity **:** worldwide rather than regional, parochial, or narrow ⟨the softened ~ teaching of the prophets of the captivity and the rigid national teaching of the instructors of Israel's youth —Matthew Arnold⟩ ⟨his ~ benevolence, impartially extended to all races and to all creeds —T.B.Macaulay⟩ **2 :** marked by sophistication and savoir faire arising from urban life and wide travel ⟨the instructor began to put on the airs of the city. He wanted to appear ~ —Sherwood Anderson⟩ **3 :** composed of persons, constituents, or elements from all parts of the world or from many different places or levels ⟨that queer, ~, rather sinister crowd that is to be found around the Marseilles docks —Rose Macaulay⟩ **4 :** widely distributed and common **:** found in most parts of the world and in varied ecological conditions — used of kinds of organisms ⟨coccidia are ~ parasites⟩ **syn** see UNIVERSAL

²**cosmopolitan** \"\ *n* -S **:** one that is cosmopolitan

cos·mo·pol·i·tan·ism \-ˌizəm\ *n* -S **1 :** the quality or state of being cosmopolitan **:** cosmopolitan character **2 a** (1) **:** the theory or advocacy of the formation of a world society or cosmopolis (sense 1) ⟨advocates of internationalism who decry the sovereignty or need of state organization . . . are called proponents of ~ —F.L.Burdette⟩ (2) **:** a climate of opinion distinguished by the absence of narrow national loyalties or parochial prejudices and by a readiness to borrow from other lands or regions in the formation of cultural or artistic patterns ⟨a genial ~ was the hallmark of that enlightened age⟩ ⟨the literary ~ was followed by an artistic ~ which transcended all frontiers —Paul Wescher⟩ **b :** excessive admiration and imitation of the cultural traits or achievements of others at the expense of the cultural identity or integrity of one's own land or region ⟨a "divine provincialism" . . . is but ill replaced by a ~ lacking in virtue and distinction —Agnes Repplier⟩

cos·mo·pol·i·tan·ize \-ˌīz\ *vt* -ED/-ING/-S **:** to make cosmopolitan

cosmopolitan justice *n* **:** a theory of criminal jurisdiction whereby any state having before it a criminal who has committed a grave offense anywhere in the world may punish him without regard to his citizenship or where he acted or what state was injured

cos·mo·pol·i·tan·ly *adv* **:** in a cosmopolitan manner

¹**cos·mop·o·lite** \käz'mäpəˌlīt\ *n* -S [NL *cosmopolites*, fr. Gk *kosmopolitēs*, fr. *kosm-* cosm- + *politēs* citizen — more at POLICE] **1 :** one that is at home in every country **:** a citizen of the world **:** one without national prejudices or attachments **2 a :** a cosmopolitan organism **b :** a literary form (as a tale, proverb, or maxim) occurring in many different languages or areas **3 :** PAINTED LADY

²**cosmopolite** \(ˈ)ˌ¦ˌˌ\ *adj* **:** COSMOPOLITAN

cos·mo·political \¦käzmō, ¦käzmə +\ *adj* **:** of the nature of universal polities or interests

cos·mo·po·lit·ism \käz'mäpəˌlīd·ˌizəm, -ˌləˌtiz-, ˌkäzmə'pälə-\ *n* -S **:** COSMOPOLITANISM

cos·mo·ra·ma \ˌkäzmə'ramə, -rämə, 'ˌˌ¦ˌ\ *n* -S [*cosm-* + *panorama*] **:** an exhibition of views of various parts of the world made to appear realistic by mirrors, lenses, and illumination — **cos·mo·ram·ic** \¦ˌ¦ramik\ *adj*

cos·mor·gan·ic \¦käzˌmȯ(r)¦ganik\ *adj* [*cosm-* + *organic*] **:** relating to or implying an organic cosmos ⟨a ~ evolution⟩

cos·mos \'käzməs\ *in senses 1 & 2 also* -ˌmōs *or* -ˌmäs\ *n* [Gk *kosmos*, fr. Gk, order, ornament, universe] **1** -ES **a :** the universe conceived as an orderly and harmonious system — contrasted with *chaos* **b :** ORDER, HARMONY **2** -ES **:** a self-inclusive system characterized by order and harmony amid complexity of detail **3** *cap* [NL, fr. Gk *kosmos*] **:** a genus of tropical American herbs (family Compositae) having opposite leaves, flowers solitary in loose corymbose panicles, and flower heads with prominent rays most cultivated varieties of which are derived from a Mexican species (*C. bipinnatus*) and are popular fall-blooming annuals **4** *pl* **cosmos** \-məs, -məz\ *also* **cosmoses :** any plant or flower of the genus *Cosmos*

cos·mos·o·phy \käz'mäsəfē\ *n* -ES [ISV *cosm-* + *-sophy*] **:** a body of belief or theory about the cosmos

cos·mo·sphere \'käzmə+ˌ-\ *n* -S [*cosm-* + *-sphere*] **1 :** the material universe **2 :** an apparatus for showing the position of the earth at any given time with respect to the fixed stars that consists of a hollow glass globe on which are depicted the stars and constellations and within which is a terrestrial globe

cos·mo·tellurian \¦käz(ˌ)mō, ¦käzmə+\ *adj* [*cosm-* + *tellurian*] **:** relating to or affecting both heavens and earth

cos·mo·the·ism \'käzmə(ˌ)thēˌizəm, ˌˌ'th-\ *n* -S [*cosm-* + *-theism*] **:** ascription of divinity to the cosmos **:** identification of God with the world **:** PANTHEISM — **cos·mo·the·ist** \¦käzmə¦thēəst, -ˌthēˌist, -ˌˌ'thēəst\ *n* -S — **cos·mo·the·is·tic** \ˌˌˌthē¦istik\ *adj*

cos·mo·thet·ic \¦käzmə¦thed·ik\ *adj* [*cosm-* + Gk *thetikos* positive, fr. *thet-* (stem of *tithenai* to set, place, assume) + *-ikos* -ic — more at DO] *philos* **:** positing the external world — compare COSMOTHETIC IDEALISM

cosmothetic idealism *n* **:** a theory that posits a real external world but denies that mind has immediate cognizance of matter — compare REPRESENTATIONALISM

cos·mo·zo·ic \¦käzmə¦zōik\ *adj* [*cosm-* + *-zoic*] **:** of or relating to the hypothetical origination of life in or from outer space ⟨~ theories⟩

cos·mo·zo·ism \ˌkäzmə'zōˌizəm, 'ˌˌ¦ˌˌ\ *n* -S [*cosm-* + *zoism*] **:** the theory or conception of the cosmos as animate

-cosms *pl of* -COSM

co·solvent \(ˈ)kō+\ *n* [*co-* + *solvent*] **:** a solvent that in conjunction with another solvent can dissolve a solute ⟨ether and alcohol are ~s for pyroxylin⟩

co·sovereignty \(ˈ)kō+\ *n* [*co-* + *sovereignty*] **:** joint sovereignty

co·specific \¦kō+\ *adj* [*co-* + *specific*] **:** of the same species

co·sponsor \(ˈ)kō+\ *n* [*co-* + *sponsor*] **:** a joint sponsor

cos·sack \ˈkäˌsak *also* -ˌsək\ *n* -s *sometimes cap* [Russ *kazak* & Ukrainian *kozak*, fr. Turk *kazak* free, independent person, adventurer, vagabond] **1 :** a member of a favored military caste of Russian frontiersmen and border guards in Czarist Russia, esp. in the Ukraine, who played an important part in Russian expansion in the Ukraine and eastward into southeastern Russia, the Caucasus, and Siberia **2 :** a member of an armed contingent (as company police) using force to suppress or break up some activity (as a strike or demonstration)

cossack green *n* **:** a dark yellowish green that is yellower and duller than holly green (sense 1), lighter and stronger than deep chrome green, and yellower and paler than average hunter green

cossack post *n, sometimes cap C* **:** a onetime 4-man outguard that posted a single sentinel

cos·sae·an \kəˈsēən\ *n* -s *cap* [L *Cossaeus* (fr. Gk *Kossaios*, fr. *Kossaia*, land of the Kassites) + E *-an*] **:** KASSITE 1

cosse green \ˈkäs-\ *n* [F *cosse* pod, fr. (assumed) VL *coccia*, alter. (influenced by L *coccum* kermes berry, excrescence on a plant) of L *cochlea* snail — more at COCHLEA, COCC-] **:** a strong yellow green that is yellower and slightly duller than viridine yellow and yellower, lighter, and stronger than parrot green

¹**cos·set** \ˈkäsət, *usu* -d·+V\ *n* -s [origin unknown] **:** a lamb reared without the aid of the dam **:** a pet lamb **:** PET

²**cosset** \"\ *vt* -ED/-ING/-s **:** to treat as a pet **:** FONDLE, PAMPER, CODDLE ⟨my complaint is that my life is too ~*ed* and padded —John Buchan⟩ ⟨one who ~*ed* his health —Joyce Cary⟩

cos·sette \käˈset, kə'-, ˈkäsət\ *n* -s [F, dim. of *cosse* pod — more at COSSE GREEN] **:** a strip or slice (as of sugar beet or potato) **:** CHIP

¹**cos·sid** \ˈkäsəd\ *n* -s [Hindi *qāṣid*, fr. Ar] *India* **:** a mounted messenger

²**cossid** \"\ *adj* [NL *Cossidae*] **:** of or belonging to the family Cossidae

cos·si·dae \ˈkäsəˌdē\ *n pl, cap* [NL, fr. *Cossus*, type genus + *-idae*] **:** a family of nocturnal moths with heavy spindle-shaped bodies and strong narrow wings including the goat moths, carpenter moths, and related forms and having larvae that bore in the wood of living trees

cos·sus \ˈkäsəs\ *n, cap* [NL, fr. L, a kind of larva under the bark of trees; perh. akin to Gk *skedannynai* to scatter — more at SHATTER] **:** the type genus of Cossidae including a number of moths the larvae of which were once highly esteemed as food and are still eaten by Australian aborigines — see WITCHETTY GRUB

cos·sy·rite \ˈkäsəˌrīt\ *n* -s [G *cossyrit*, fr. *Cossyra*, island near Sicily (now *Pantelleria*) + G *-it* -ite] **:** a variety of aenigmatite occurring in minute crystals in lava

¹**cost** \ˈkȯst *also* ˈkäst\ *n* -s [ME, fr. OF, fr. *coster*, v.] **1 a :** the amount or equivalent paid or given or charged or engaged to be paid or given for anything bought or taken in barter or for service rendered **:** CHARGE, PRICE **b :** whatever must be given, sacrificed, suffered, or forgone to secure a benefit or accomplish a result ⟨to retain life at the ~ of honor⟩ **2 :** loss, deprivation, or suffering as the necessary price of something gained or as the unavoidable result or penalty of an action ⟨knowledge is gained at the ~ of innocence⟩ ⟨he found him, to his ~, a dangerous enemy⟩ **3 :** the expenditure or outlay of money, time, or labor ⟨to spare no ~ in furnishing a house⟩ ⟨to live *cost*-free⟩ **4 costs** *pl* **:** expenses incurred in litigation: as **a :** those payable to the attorney or counsel by his client esp. when fixed by law **b :** those given by the law or the court to the prevailing against the losing party in equity and frequently by statute — called also *bill of costs* **5 :** an item of outlay incurred in the operation of a business enterprise (as for the purchase of raw materials, labor, services, supplies) including depreciation and amortization of capital assets — see ACTUAL COST, CONVERSION COST, DIRECT COST, DISTRIBUTION COST, HISTORICAL COST, INDIRECT COST, PREDETERMINED COST, PRIME COST, PRODUCTION COST, STANDARD COST **6 :** something that is sacrificed to obtain something else — see ALTERNATIVE COST, REAL COST

²**cost** \"\ *vb* **cost; cost; costing; costs** [ME *costen*, fr. MF *coster*, fr. L *constare* to stand with or at, cost, agree — more at CONSTANT] *vi* **1 :** to require expenditure or payment **2 :** to require effort, suffering, or loss ~ *vt* **1 a :** to have a price of ⟨the book ~*s* five dollars⟩ **b :** to cause or require the expenditure or loss of ⟨riots between natives and foreigners ~ some lives —*Encyc. Americana*⟩ ⟨to prepare oneself for this ~*s* some trouble —I.A.Richards⟩ **2 :** to cause to pay, suffer, or lose something ⟨it will ~ you about $10 each way —Richard Joseph⟩ ⟨long wait had ~ him his dinner —T.B.Costain⟩ ⟨rear guard action that ~ the British dearly —F.V.W.Mason⟩

³**cost** \"\ *vb* -ED/-ING/-s [prob. fr. ¹*cost*] *vt* **:** to estimate or figure on the cost of ⟨some colleges try to ~ menus before they use them —*College and Univ. Business*⟩ ~ *vi* **:** to estimate or figure on costs ⟨standardize ~*ing* in an industry⟩

⁴**cost** \"\ *n* -s [MF *coste*, lit., rib — more at COAST] **:** RIBBON 2a

cost- *or* **costi-** *or* **costo-** *comb form* [F, fr. L *costa*] **:** rib **:** costa ⟨*costectomy*⟩ ⟨*costiform*⟩ **:** costal and ⟨*costoradial*⟩ ⟨*costosternal*⟩

cos·ta \ˈkästə\ *n, pl* **cos·tae** \-(ˌ)stē, -ˌstī\ [L, rib — more at COAST] **:** a rib or a bodily structure resembling a rib: as **a** *anat* **:** the side or border of a part **b** *bot* **:** a leaf vein; *esp* **:** MIDRIB **c** *zool* **:** any of various ridged or thickened linear parts; *specif* **:** the anterior vein of an insect's wing

cost accountant *n* **:** one skilled in the technique of cost accounting **:** one whose business or vocation is accounting for costs

cost accounting *n* **1 :** the branch of accounting that deals with systematically classifying, recording, analyzing, and summarizing in those books of account constituting a cost system the cost elements of material, labor, and burden incident to production or to the rendering of a service **2 :** the art of devising and installing cost systems

¹**cos·tal** \ˈkästᵊl\ *adj* [F, fr. MF, fr. *coste* side, rib + *-al* — more at COAST] **:** of or relating to a costa or rib; *also* **:** relating to or situated near ribs ⟨a ~ scale or plate⟩ ⟨a *costal*-veined leaf⟩

²**costal** \"\ *n* -s **:** a costal element (as a plate or nerve)

costal cartilage *n* **:** any of the cartilages that connect the distal ends of the ribs with the sternum and by their elasticity permit of the movements of the walls of the chest in respiration — see THORAX

cos·tal·ly \ˈkästəlē\ *adv* **:** in a costal position or direction; *specif* **:** toward or at the costal vein or adjoining margin of an insect's wing

costal-nerved \ˈ==ˌ=\ *adj, bot* **:** costal-veined — see ¹COSTAL

costal process *n* **1 :** the ventral or anterior root of the transverse process of a cervical vertebra **2 :** a process of the sternum of many birds with which the ribs articulate

costal respiration *n* **:** inspiration and expiration produced chiefly by movements of the ribs — distinguished from *diaphragmatic respiration*

cost analysis *n* **1 :** the act of breaking down a cost summary into its constituents and studying and reporting on each factor **2 :** the comparison of costs (as of standard with actual or for a given period with another) for the purpose of disclosing and reporting on conditions subject to improvement

cost and freight *n* **:** a charge or quotation made in waterborne export trade by a seller to a buyer that includes the price of the goods and all transportation costs to a designated destination — abbr. *C and F*

co·sta·no·an \kəˈstänəwən, kō'-\ *n, pl* **costanoan** *or* **costanoans** *usu cap* [*Costano*, a division of the Costanoan (fr. Sp *costeño*, lit., coastman, fr. *costa* coast, fr. L *costa* rib, side) + E *-an* — more at COAST] **1 a :** an Indian people of coastal California from San Francisco Bay to Monterey **b :** a member of such people **2 :** a language of the Costanoan people **3 :** a language family of the Penutian stock comprising only the Costanoan language or languages

¹**co·star** \ˈkō+\ *n* [*co-* + *star*] **:** a star whose role in a motion picture or a play is equal in importance to that of another leading player

²**costar** \(ˈ)kō+\ *vi* **:** to appear with another star in a motion picture or a play ~ *vt* **:** to employ or present (a player) as one of two or more leading players in a motion picture or play

cos·tard \ˈkästə(r)d, ˈkȯs-; *Brit usu* ˈkəs-\ *n* -s [ME, perh. fr. OF *coste* rib + ME *-ard*; fr. its ribbed appearance — more at COAST] **1 :** any of several large oval strongly ribbed English cooking apples — compare CODLING, PIPPIN **2** *archaic* **:** PATE ⟨whether your ~ or my ballow be the harder —Shak.⟩

costardmonger *archaic var of* COSTERMONGER

cos·ta ri·ca \ˌkästəˈrēkə, ˌkȯs-, ˌkōs-\ *adj, usu cap C&R* [fr. *Costa Rica*, country in Central America] **:** of or from Costa Rica **:** of the kind or style prevalent in Costa Rica **:** COSTA RICAN

¹**cos·ta ri·can** \-kən\ *adj, usu cap C&R* [*Costa Rica*, the country + E *-an*] **1 :** of, relating to, or characteristic of Costa Rica **2 :** of, relating to, or characteristic of Costa Ricans

²**costa rican** *n, pl* **costa ricans** *cap C&R* **:** a native or inhabitant of Costa Rica

cos·ta·ta \käˈstād·ə\ *n pl, cap* [NL, fr. L, neut. pl. of *costatus*] *in certain classifications* **:** a suborder of Salientia comprising the frogs and toads with ribs that is nearly coextensive with the family Discoglossidae — compare PHANEROGLOSSA

cos·tate \ˈkäˌstāt, -ˌstət\ *adj* [L *costatus*, fr. *costa* rib + *-atus* -ate — more at COAST] **:** having ribs: as **a :** having one or more longitudinal ribs or nerves ⟨a ~ leaf⟩ **b :** having ridges on the surface ⟨a ~ shell⟩

cos·tated \-ˌstād·əd\ *adj* [L *costatus* + E *-ed*] **:** COSTATE

cost bond *n* **:** a bond filed by plaintiff guaranteeing payment of court costs

cost book *n, Brit* **:** a book made up every 16 weeks containing the names of the shareholders and the number of shares held by each partner and particulars of all transactions in a partnership formed for working a mine

cost card *n* **:** COST SHEET

cost center *n* **:** the most appropriate production unit (as a single machine, a group of machines or workers, or a department) into which manufacturing operations may be divided to facilitate the allocation and application of cost factors

cost clerk *n* **1 :** one who computes the cost of producing or selling goods or of any phase of business operations **2 :** a clerk who checks the cost of each item purchased against the seller's price list

cost control *n* **:** use by management of cost analyses and their interpretation in corrective measures toward increasing efficiency and economy of operation

cos·tean *or* **cos·teen** \käˈstēn, ˈ=ˌ=\ *vi* -ED/-ING/-s [fr. (assumed) Corn *costēn*, prob. fr. *codha* to fall, happen + *stēn* tin; akin to ON *hitta* to hit, find — more at HIT, STANNUM] *Brit* **:** to dig trenches or small pits through the surface soil or debris to the underlying rock in place for the purpose of exposing the outcrop of a mineral deposit and determining its course

cos·ter \ˈkästə(r)\ *n* -s [by shortening] *Brit* **:** COSTERMONGER

costermonger \ˈkästə(r)+ˌ-\ *n* [*coster* (alter. of *costard*) + *monger*] **1** *archaic Brit* **:** a street seller of fruit **2** *Brit* **:** a hawker of fruit or vegetables from a street stand, barrow, or cart

cost factor *n* **:** an element or condition related to a unit of product or to an activity or to a service for which money must be spent (as raw material, direct labor, and burden)

cost finding *n* **:** COST ACCOUNTING

cost·ful \ˈkȯstfəl\ *adj* [ME, fr. ¹*cost* + *-ful*] *archaic* **:** COSTLY

costi- — see COST-

cos·ti·a·sis \käˈstīəsəs\ *n, pl* **costia·ses** \-ˌsēz\ [NL, fr. *Costia* (genus name of *Costia necatrix*) + *-iasis*] **:** a frequently fatal disease of freshwater fishes due to invasion of the skin by a flagellated protozoan (*Costia necatrix*)

costing *n* -s [fr. gerund of ³*cost* (estimate cost)] **1** *chiefly Brit* **:** COST ACCOUNTING **2 :** the calculating, recording, and allocating of current costs and determining of prospective costs for the guidance of management in regulating operations

cost, insurance, and freight *adj* **:** subject to agreement that cost of transportation and insurance be paid by the seller of goods to the named point of destination — abbr. *CIF*

cos·tive \ˈkästiv, ˈkȯs-\ *adj* [ME *costif*, modif. of MF *costivé*, past part. of *costiver* to bind, constipate, fr. L *constipare* — more at CONSTIPATE] **1 a :** CONSTIPATED **b :** causing constipation **2 a :** slow or stiff in action or expression **:** SLUGGISH ⟨the system . . . was so ~ that no new design could ever be expected —*Economist*⟩ ⟨readers now wearied by the ~ pronouncements —*Times Lit. Supp.*⟩ **b :** NIGGARDLY — **cos·tive·ly** \-stəvlē\ *adv*

cos·tive·ness \-nəs\ *n* -ES [ME *costyfnes*, fr. *costyf*, *costif* costive + *-nes* -ness] **:** CONSTIPATION

cost keeper *n* **:** COST ACCOUNTANT

cost ledger *n* **:** one of the books of account in a cost system to which entries are posted from books of original entry, the various accounts therein showing the accumulated costs classified as to order, process, type of expense, and department

cost·less \ˈkȯstləs *also* ˈkäs-, *rap.* -s(t)l-\ *adj* **:** costing nothing

cost·li·ness \ˈkȯstlēnəs, -lin- *also* ˈkäs-, *rap.* -s(t)l-\ *n* -ES **:** the quality or state of being costly **:** high price or value **:** EXPENSIVENESS

cost·ly \ˈkȯstlē, -li *also* ˈkäs-, *rap.* -s(t)l-\ *adj* -ER/-EST [ME, fr. ¹*cost* + *-ly*] **1 :** of great cost or value **:** FINE, RICH, SPLENDID ⟨they are clad in very ~ robes of silk; they are girdled like queens —Lafcadio Hearn⟩ **2 :** involving excessive expenditure **:** necessitating considerable loss or sacrifice ⟨to encourage me in litigation and to make it as protracted and ~ as he can —G.B.Shaw⟩ **3 :** EXTRAVAGANT, PRODIGAL, LAVISH ⟨~ entertainment⟩ ⟨~ habits⟩

syn COSTLY, EXPENSIVE, DEAR, VALUABLE, PRECIOUS, INVALUABLE, PRICELESS: COSTLY stresses high price and may suggest elegance, sumptuousness, or luxury ⟨the curtains and upholstery of the chairs and sofas and the hangings of my bed are of the *costliest* and most beautiful fabrics, and must have been of fabulous value when they were made —Bram Stoker⟩ ⟨walls, columns, and arches seem a quarry of precious stones, so beautiful and *costly* are the marbles with which they are inlaid —Nathaniel Hawthorne⟩ EXPENSIVE may imply a cost above a purchaser's means or above intrinsic valuation ⟨the father was unable to give the child as *expensive* an education as he had desired —J.A.Froude⟩ DEAR indicates a high cost, often one greatly increased because of scarcities ⟨the lively affection seamen have for strong drink is well known; but in the South Seas, where it is so seldom to be had, a thoroughbred sailor deems scarcely any price too *dear* which will purchase his darling "tot" —Herman Melville⟩ VALUABLE may suggest hope or chance of great gain or usefulness or of high price in sale or exchange ⟨how *valuable* these lands were to become Congress could hardly guess, nor did it suspect that the grants in the northern part of the state were to be worth millions in timber and iron —*Amer. Guide Series: Minn.*⟩ PRECIOUS may stress extremely great value, often value brought about by rareness or scarcity ⟨a *precious* thing, a treasure beyond diamonds or rubies —Jack London⟩ ⟨we of the Bounty's launch had been so accustomed to thinking of wine and spirits as the most *precious* of commodities, to be taken only a spoonful at a time —C.B.Nordhoff & J.N.Hall⟩ In other than monetary matters, these words keep more or less the same connotations. COSTLY, DEAR, and EXPENSIVE may describe great expenditure of resources, materials, or effort ⟨in order to finance the ever more *costly* equipment and maintenance of the new paid soldiery, the rulers of Europe had recourse to the financier —Lewis Mumford⟩ ⟨their stout resistance was destined to cost them *dear* . . . many thousand citizens were ruined, many millions of property confiscated —J.L.Motley⟩ DEAR and PRECIOUS are often used in matters of emotion ⟨and measureless sweet I deem her, and *dear* she is to mine eyes —William Morris⟩ ⟨his child, his *precious* possession —W.F. de Morgan⟩ ⟨*precious* Savior, still our refuge —Joseph Scriven⟩ VALUABLE often describes things or conditions quite advantageous or useful ⟨that the release of the information at the time it is received will not prove *valuable* to the enemy —F.D. Roosevelt⟩ INVALUABLE and PRICELESS may describe any thing or condition of such great worth that evaluation is practically impossible ⟨this *invaluable* liquor was of a pale golden hue, like other of the rarest Italian wines —Nathaniel Hawthorne⟩ ⟨control of the sea was a *priceless* asset to the Union, the navy maintained communications with Europe, cut off those of the South, captured important coastal cities —S.E.Morison & H.S.Commager⟩

cost·mary \ˈkȯstˌmerē, -ˌma(a)rē, -ˌmārē, -ri *also* ˈkäst-\ *n* -ES [ME *costmarie*, fr. *coste* costmary (fr. OE *cost*, fr. L *costum*, fr. Gk *kostos* costusroot) + *Marie* Mary (the Virgin *Mary*)] **1 :** a tansy-scented herb (*Chrysanthemum balsamita*) that has yellow flowers shaped like buttons and is used as a potherb and salad plant and now less commonly in flavoring ale and beer — called also *alecost*, *bible leaf* **2 :** the common tansy (*Tanacetum vulgare*)

costo- — see COST-

cos·to·central \ˌkästə, ˌkästō+\ *adj* [*cost-* + *central*] **:** relating to or joining a rib and a vertebral centrum

cos·to·chondral \"+\ *adj* [*cost-* + *chondral*] **:** relating to or joining a rib and costal cartilage

cos·to·clavicular \"+\ *adj* [*cost-* + *clavicular*] **:** of or relating to a ligament connecting the costal cartilage of the first rib with the clavicle

cos·to·coracoid \"+\ *adj* [*cost-* + *coracoid*] **:** relating to or joining the ribs and coracoid process or bone

costocoracoid membrane *n* **:** a strong fascia that ensheathes and extends between the subclavius and pectoralis minor muscles and that protects the axillary vessels and nerves

cost of living : the cost of purchasing those goods and services which are included in an accepted standard level of consumption

cost-of-living index \ˌ==ˌ==-\ *n* **:** CONSUMER PRICE INDEX

cost of money : rate of interest or dividend payment on borrowed capital

cost of sales 1 *in retailing* **:** the purchase cost or inventory value of merchandise sold during a stated period plus the cost of direct work thereon (as alterations or workroom charges) **2** *in manufacturing* **:** the production cost or inventory value of goods sold during a stated period

cos·ton light \ˈkȯstən-, ˈkäs-\ *n, usu cap C* [after B. F. *Coston* *fl*1840, its inventor] **:** a signal made by burning lights of different colors that is used by ships at sea and in the life-saving service

cos·to·transverse \ˌkästə, ˌkästō+\ *adj* [*cost-* + *transverse*] **:** relating to or connecting a rib and the transverse process of a vertebra

cos·to·xiphoid \"+\ *adj* [*cost-* + *xiphoid*] **:** relating to or connecting a costal cartilage and the xiphoid process

cost-plus *adj* **:** providing for calculation of payment for work done under contract by adding to actual cost either a fixed fee or a percentage of the cost as profit

cos·trel \ˈkästrəl\ *n* -s [ME, fr. MF *costerel*, fr. *costier* at the side (fr. *coste* rib, side) + *-el* (dim. suffix) — more at COAST] *now dial Eng* **:** a leather, earthenware, or wooden container for liquids having ears by which it may be hung up; *specif* **:** a small wooden keg

costs *pl of* COST, *pres 3d sing of* COST

cost sheet *n* **:** a sheet on which detailed cost elements relating to a specific production order or process are assembled — called also *cost card*

cost system *n* **:** books of account specif. designed for purposes of cost accounting **:** a cost-accounting system

cos·tu·la \ˈkäschələ, -styə-\ *or* **cos·tule** \-schəl, -styəl\ *n, pl* **costu·lae** \-ˌlē, -ˌlī\ *or* **costules** [NL *costula*, fr. L *costa* rib + NL *-ula* — more at COAST] *zool* **:** a small ridge (as one of those that make up the sculpture of a mollusk shell) — **cos·tu·la·tion** \ˌ==ˈlāshən\ *n* -s

¹**cos·tum·bris·ta** \ˌkōstəmˈbristə, ˌkäs-, -rēs-\ *n* -s [Sp, fr. *costumbre* custom (fr. L *consuetudin-*, *consuetudo*) + *-ista* -ist — more at CUSTOM] **:** a Spanish or Latin-American writer whose work is marked by usu. realistic depiction of local or regional customs and types

²**costumbrista** \ˌ==ˈ==\ *adj* **:** depicting local or regional customs, scenes, or types in literature or art ⟨a ~ novel⟩ ⟨a ~ picture⟩

¹**cos·tume** \ˈkäˌst(y)üm, *sometimes* ˈ=ˈ= *or* =ˈ= *or* ˈkästəm *or* *sporadically* ˈkäschəm\ *n* -s [F, fr. It *costume* custom, dress, fr. L *consuetudin-*, *consuetudo* custom — more at CUSTOM] **1** *archaic* **:** custom or style with respect to manners, dress, arms, and other surroundings of a place or period depicted in a painting **2 :** the distinctive style and prevailing fashion of personal adornment including the style of wearing the hair, jewelry, and apparel of all kinds characteristic of any period, country, class, occupation, or occasion **3 :** the distinctive dress of a particular period, locality, or occupation worn in the drama, at fancy-dress balls, or for festivals or carnivals **4 :** the chiefly outer garments worn by a person at any one time; *esp* **:** a woman's ensemble of dress with coat or jacket

²**costume** \"\ *vt* -ED/-ING/-s **:** to provide with a costume ⟨*costumed* in medieval armor⟩ **:** design costumes for ⟨~ a play⟩

³**costume** \"\ *adj* **1 a :** characterized by the use of costume (sense 3) ⟨a ~ ball⟩ **b :** depicting or portraying a subject taken from a bygone age or set in an exotic locale and usu. marked by the display or depiction of colorful costumes or pageantry ⟨a ~ movie⟩ ⟨a ~ novel⟩ **2 :** suitable for or enhancing the effect of a particular costume ⟨a ~ handbag⟩

costume jewelry *n* **:** jewelry for wear with current fashions usu. made of inexpensive materials (as metal, shells, plastics, wood) often set with imitation or semiprecious stones

cos·tum·er \-mə(r)\ *n* -s [¹*costume* + *-er*] **1 :** one that makes or deals in costumes (as for stage or fancy-dress events) **2 :** CLOTHES TREE

cos·tum·ery \-m(ə)rē, -ri\ *n* -ES [¹*costume* + *-ery*] **1 :** articles of costume **:** a quantity of costumes **2 :** the art of costuming

cos·tum·ier \ˌkästəmˈyā, ˈ==ˌ=, (ˈ)käˌst(y)ümē(r), ˈkästəmə(r)\ *n* -s [F, fr. *costume* costume + *-ier* -er — more at COSTUME] **:** one that makes, sells, or rents costumes

cost unit *n* **:** a unit of a commodity or service selected as the appropriate unit for cost purposes

cos·tus oil \ˈkȯstəs-, ˈkäs-\ *n* [*costus*root + oil] **:** a light yellow essential oil obtained from costusroot

cos·tus·root \ˈkȯstəs, ˈkästəs+\ *n* [Gk *kostos* costusroot + E *root*] **:** the fragrant root of an annual herb (*Saussurea lappa*) native to Kashmir that yields a volatile oil used in perfumery, in sachets, and for preserving furs

co·surety \(ˈ)kō+\ *n* [*co-* + *surety*] **:** a person who is a surety with another

co·suretyship \(ˈ)kō+\ *n* [*co-* + *suretyship*] **:** joint liability with another as surety on the same obligation

co·swearer \(ˈ)kō+\ *n* [*co-* + *swearer*] **:** one bound by a common oath with another; *specif* **:** COMPURGATOR

cosy *var of* COZY

¹**cot** \ˈkät, *usu* -ˈd·+V\ *n* -s [ME, fr. OE; akin to MHG *kūz* pit as a place of execution, ON *kot* small hut, Goth *qithus* stomach, L *guttur* throat, Gk (Maced. dial.) *goda* intestines, Skt *guda* bowel, rectum; basic meaning: round, curved] **1 :** a small house **:** a cottage or hut **2 :** COTE 3 **3 :** a cover or sheath: as **a :** the cloth covering of a drawing roller in a spinning frame **b :** a protective cover for a finger

²**cot** \"\ *vt* **cotted; cotted; cotting; cots :** to provide shelter for **:** put in a cot

³**cot** *or* **cott** \"\ *n* -s [ME *cot*, fr. AF, perh. fr. ML *cottum* quilt] **:** a matted or felted lock of wool or hair (as in the fleece of a sheep or the fur of a cat) **:** refuse wool

⁴**cot** \"\ *vi* **cotted; cotted; cotting; cots :** to form cots **:** MAT

⁵**cot** \ˈkät, ˈkōt\ *n* -s [IrGael *coite*] *Irish* **:** a small boat

⁶**cot** \ˈkät, *usu* -ˈd·+V\ *n* -s [Hindi *khāṭ* bedstead, bier, fr. Skt *khaṭvā*, of Dravidian origin; akin to Tamil-Malayalam *kaṭṭil* bedstead, bier] **1** *India* **:** a light bedstead **:** CHARPOY **2 :** a small bed that is often collapsible and that is used typically for camping or by a child

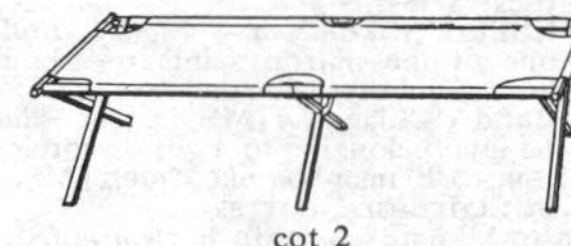
cot 2

3 : a bed made of canvas stretched on a frame, suspended like a hammock, and formerly used on shipboard esp. by officers and sick persons **4 :** a wheeled stretcher for hospital, mortuary, or ambulance service

⁷**cot** \"\ *n* -s [by shortening] **:** APRICOT

cot *abbr* cotangent

co·ta *or* **cot·ta** \ˈkōd·ə, -ōˌtä\ *n* -s [Tag, Bisayan & Taw-Sug *kutā* fort, of Dravidian origin; akin to Tamil *koṭṭai* fort] **:** a fort formerly common in parts of the Philippines

co·tangent \(ˈ)kō+\ *n* [NL *cotangent-*, *cotangens*, fr. *co-* + *tangent-*, *tangens* tangent] **:** the abscissa of any point except the vertex on the terminal side of an angle divided by the nonzero ordinate of the point, the vertex coinciding with the origin of a plane rectangular coordinate system and the initial side of the angle coinciding with the positive x-axis — abbr. *cot* or *ctn*

co·tar·i·us \kə'ta(a)rēəs, kō'-\ *n, pl* **cotarii** \-rē,ī\ [ML — more at COTTER] **:** ¹COTTER 2

co·tar·nine \kō'tär,nēn, -,nən\ *n* -s [ISV, anagram of *narcotine;* prob. orig. formed as G *kotarnin*] **:** a crystalline alkaloid $C_{12}H_{15}NO_4$ obtained by the oxidation of narcotine and used chiefly in the form of its chloride in checking bleeding esp. from small blood vessels

cot bed *n* [⁶*cot*] **:** a light narrow single bed

¹**cotch** \'käch\ *vb* -ED/-ING/-ES [by alter.] *dial* **:** ¹CATCH

²**cotch** \"\ *n* -ES [Malay *kachu* — more at CATECHU] **:** CATECHU

¹**cote** \'kōt, *usu* -ōd·+V; *sometimes esp in senses 3 & 4* 'kät\ *n* -s [ME, fr. OE; akin to OE *cot* cottage — more at COT] **1** *now dial Eng* **:** ¹COT 1 **2 :** the ancient holding of a cotter consisting typically of a house or hut and five acres of land **3 :** a shed or coop for small domestic animals; *specif* **:** a structure for pigeons **4 :** a sheltering structure ⟨a bell ~⟩

²**cote** *vt* -ED/-ING/-S [prob. fr. MF *cotoyer,* fr. OF *costoier,* fr. *coste* side, coast — more at COAST] *obs* **:** to pass by

³**côte** \'kōt\ *n* -s [F, slope, side, rib, fr. OF *coste* — more at COAST] **:** a French hillside vineyard or series of hillside vineyards — often used prepositively in compounds (as *Côte Rotie*) naming such vineyards and their wines — compare CHÂTEAU 3, CLOS

cote–armour *n, pl* **cotes–armours** [ME *cote armure,* fr. MF *cote a armeure,* coat with (heraldic) arms] *obs* **:** COAT OF ARMS

co·teau \kō'tō, kō'-\ *n, pl* **co·teaux** \-'tō(z)\ [CanF, fr. F, slope of a hill, small hill, fr. OF *costel* slope, dim. of *coste* slope, side, rib] **1 :** a hilly upland including the divide between two valleys **:** DIVIDE **2 :** the side of a valley

co·teen \kō'tēn, kō't-, '⸗,⸗\ *n* -s [¹*cot* + *-een*] *Irish* **:** ¹COT

cote·har·die \(')kōd;ärdē, -ōt;ä-, -ōt;hä-\ *n* -s [MF *cote hardie,* lit., bold tunic] **:** a long-sleeved medieval garment that was usu. thigh-length and belted for men and full-length for women and that was made to fit closely often by buttoning or lacing

cô·te·lé \;kōd·ᵊ;lā\ *adj* [F, lit., ribbed, fr. MF *costelé,* fr. *costel* small rib (dim. of *coste* rib) + *-é* (fr. L *-atus* -ate) — more at COAST] *in decorative art* **:** having a broken outline of straight or curved portions

côte·lette \kōt'let\ *n* -s [F — more at CUTLET] **:** CUTLET

co·tenancy \(')kō+\ *n* [*co-* + *tenancy*] **:** JOINT TENANCY

co·tenant \(')kō+\ *n* [*co-* + *tenant*] **:** JOINT TENANT

co·ten·tion \(')kō;tenchən\ *n* -s [*co-* + *attention*] **:** a mode of attention or sustained interest undisturbed by the intrusion of affect — compare DITENTION

cotehardie

co·ten·tive \-entiv\ *adj* [fr. *cotention,* after E *attention: attentive*] **:** of, relating to, or marked by cotention

co·tenure \(')kō+\ *n* [*co-* + *tenure*] **:** joint tenure

cot·er·ell \'käd·ərəl\ *n* -s [ME *coterel,* fr. OF & ML; OF *coterel,* fr. ML *coterellus,* dim. of *cotarius* cotter] **:** ¹COTTER 2

co·te·rie \'kōd·ə·rē, |tərē, -ri; ,⸗⸗'rē; *esp archaic* |kä|\ *n* -s *often attrib* [F, fr. MF, association of peasant tenants, fr. (assumed) *cotier* cottager (fr. ML *cotarius*) + MF *-ie* -y — more at COTTER] **:** an intimate often exclusive group of persons having a binding common interest or purpose **:** CLIQUE ⟨the aristocratic ~ finally got the upper hand —Edith Hamilton⟩

co·ter·mi·nous \(')kō;tərmənəs, -;tōm-\ *adj* [alter. of *conterminous*] **1 :** having the same or coincident boundaries **:** covering or involving the same area ⟨the city of Washington and the District of Columbia are ~⟩ **2 :** coincident or coextensive in range, scope, limit, time, or duration ⟨the 35 year period . . . ~ with the career of the hardy Champlain —Allan Nevins & H.S.Commager⟩ **:** identical with ⟨since folk culture has always existed, a study of its origins is ~ with the study of the origins of culture itself —S.W.Mintz⟩ **syn** see ADJACENT

co·ter·mi·nous·ly *adv* **:** in a coterminous manner **:** so as to be coterminous

¹**cotes** *pl of* COTE, *pres 3d sing of* COTE

²**côtes** *pl of* CÔTE

coth *abbr* [*co*tangent + *hyperbolic*] hyperbolic cotangent

coth·a·more \'kōt(h)ə,mōr\ *n* -s [IrGael *cōta mōr,* lit., big coat] **:** a frieze overcoat made in Ireland

coth·er·stone \'kaṯhə(r)stən\ *n* -s *usu cap* [fr. *Cotherstone,* Yorkshire, England] **:** a rennet cheese of cow's milk resembling Stilton

cothouse \'⸗,⸗\ *n* [¹*cot* + *house*] *chiefly Scot* **:** COT, COTTAGE

co·thurn \'kō,thərn, ⸗'⸗\ *n* -s [F & L; F *cothurne,* fr. L *cothurnus*] **:** COTHURNUS

co·thur·nal \(')kō;thərnəl\ *adj* [L *cothurnus* + E *-al*] **1 :** of or relating to the cothurnus **2 :** of, relating to, or characteristic of tragedy

co·thur·nus \kō'thərnəs, kə'-\ *n, pl* **cothur·ni** \-,nī\ [L, fr. Gk *kothornos*] **1 :** a thick-soled laced boot reaching halfway to the knees worn by actors in the Greek and Roman tragic drama — called also *buskin* **2 :** the dignified and somewhat stilted spirit of ancient tragedy

co·tidal \(')kō+\ *adj* [*co-* + *tidal*] **:** marking or indicating an equality in the tides or a coincidence in the time of high or low tide ⟨~ lines on a chart⟩

co·til·lion \kō'tilyən, kə'-\ *also* **co·til·lon** \", kōtēyōⁿ\ *n* -s [F *cotillon,* lit., petticoat, fr. OF, fr. *cote* coat — more at COAT] **1 :** a ballroom dance for couples that resembles the quadrille and is possibly based on French peasant dances **2 :** an elaborate dance executed under the leadership of one couple at formal balls and marked by the giving of favors and frequent changing of partners **:** GERMAN **3 :** a formal ball (as one at which debutantes are presented to society)

co·tin·ga \kō'tiŋgə, kə'-\ *n* [NL, fr. F *cotinga,* of Tupian origin; akin to Tupi *coting* to wash, *tinga* white] **1** *cap* **:** the type genus of Cotingidae **2** -s **:** a bird of the genus *Cotinga* or family Cotingidae

cotinga purple *n, often cap C* **:** IMPERIAL 10

co·tin·gi·dae \kō'tinjə,dē, kə'-\ *n pl, cap* [NL, fr. *Cotinga,* type genus + *-idae*] **:** a family of birds (suborder Tyranni) of tropical America related to the manakins

cot·i·nus \'kätᵊnəs\ *n, cap* [NL, fr. L *cotinus,* a kind of shrub furnishing a purple color] **:** a genus of shrubs or small trees (family Anacardiaceae) that are sometimes included in *Rhus* but distinguished by plumose sterile pedicels in the fruiting panicles — see SMOKE TREE

¹**cot·ise** *also* **cot·ice** *or* **cot·tise** *or* **cot·tice** \'käd·əs\ *n* -s [MF *cotice, costice,* fr. *coste* rib + *-ice* — more at COAST] *heraldry* **:** one of a pair of narrow stripes borne one along each side of but slightly separated from a bend, fess, bar, pale, or chevron

²**cotise** \"\ *vt* -ED/-ING/-S *heraldry* **:** to put cotises along the sides of

cotised *adj, heraldry* **:** borne between cotises ⟨a fess ~⟩

co·titular \(')kō+\ *n* -s [*co-* + *titular*] **:** one of the patron saints to whom a church is jointly dedicated

cotised bend

cot·land \'kätlənd\ *n* [ME, fr. ¹*cot* + *land*] **:** the land belonging to a cot or cotter

cot·man \'kätmən\ *n, pl* **cotmen** [ME, fr. ¹*cot* + *man*] *chiefly Scot* **:** COTTAGER, COTTER

¹**co·to** \'kōd·ō\ *or* **coto bark** *n* -s [Sp *cotocoto,* fr. Quechua *kkhotokkhoto*] **:** the bark of an unidentified tree of northern Bolivia formerly used as an astringent and stomachic

²**coto** \"\ *n, pl* **coto** *or* **cotos** *usu cap* [Sp, of AmerInd origin] **1 a :** a Tucano people of eastern Ecuador **b :** a member of such people **2 :** the Tucano language of the Coto people

³**coto** \" *also* **coc·to** \'kōk(,)tō, 'käk-\ *n, pl* **coto** *or* **cotos** *also* **cocto** *or* **coctos** *usu cap* [Sp, of AmerInd origin] **1 a :** a Chibchan people of Costa Rica **b :** a member of such people **2 :** the Chibchan language of the Coto people

co·to·in \'kōd·əwən\ *n* -s [ISV ¹*coto* + *-in;* orig. formed as G *kotoin*] **:** a crystalline ketone $C_{14}H_{12}O_4$ occurring in true coto bark and formerly used in intestinal disorders; 2,6-dihydroxy-4-methoxy-benzophenone

co·to·na·me \,kōd·ə'nä(,)mā\ *or* **co·to·nam** \'⸗⸗,näm, -,nam\ *n, pl* **cotoname** *or* **cotonames** *or* **cotonam** *or* **cotonams** *usu cap* [Sp *cotoname,* of AmerInd origin] **1 a :** an Indian people of northeastern Mexico **b :** a member of such people **2 :** the Coahuiltecan language of the Cotoname people

co·to·ne·as·ter \kə,tōnē'astə(r), ⸗'⸗⸗,⸗⸗ *also* 'kätᵊn,ēst-\ *n* [NL, fr. L *cotoneum, cydoneum* quince + NL *-aster* — more at QUINCE] **1** *cap* **:** a genus of Old World shrubs (family Rosaceae) with small, numerous, and mostly entire leaves and fruit a pome containing two to five nutlets **2** -s **:** any shrub of the genus *Cotoneaster*

co·ton·er·ol A \kə;tänə,rō'lā, -rō'-\ *n, usu cap C* [origin unknown] **:** a direct dye — see DYE table I (under *Direct Black 22*)

co·to·nier \,kōtən'yā, ,kōt-, '⸗⸗,⸗\ *n* -s [LaF *cotonnier,* fr. F, cotton plant, fr. *coton* cotton + *-ier* -er — more at COTTON] *dial* **:** a sycamore (*Platanus occidentalis*)

cot·quean \'kät,kwēn\ *n* -s [¹*cot* + *quean* (woman)] **1** *obs* **:** the wife of a cotter **2** *archaic* **a :** a coarse masculine woman **b :** a man who busies himself with affairs properly feminine

co–tradition \;kō +\ *n* [*co-* + *tradition*] **:** the entire cultural history of an area in which a number of cultures have been interrelated over a period of time

cot·rine \'kä·trən, -·,trēn\ *n* -s [origin unknown] **:** a dark orange yellow to light yellowish brown that is very slightly redder than spruce yellow

co·trustee \(;)kō +\ *n* [*co-* + *trustee*] **:** a joint trustee

cots *pl of* COT, *pres 3d sing of* COT

cots·wold \'kät,swōld, -,swəld\ *n* -s *usu cap* [fr. *Cotswold* hills, Gloucestershire, England, where the breed developed] **:** a sheep of an English breed of large long-wooled sheep

cott *var of* COT

¹**cot·ta** \'käd·ə, -ätə\ *n* -s [ML, of Gmc origin; akin to OHG *kozza* coarse mantle — more at COAT] **:** a short white ecclesiastical vestment worn by various clerics, altar boys, and choristers — compare SURPLICE

cotta

²**cot·ta** *var of* COTA

cot·tage \'käd·ij, -ätij, -ēj\ *n* -s [ME *cotage,* fr. (assumed) AF, fr. ME ¹*cot* + OF *-age*] **1 :** the dwelling of a rural laborer, small farmer, or miner **:** COT **2 :** a small structure built as a temporary or occasional shelter typically for shepherds or hunters **:** HUT, SHACK **3 :** a detached one-family house; *esp* **:** a frame house of no more than one or two stories **4 a :** one of several detached dwelling units forming part of a resort hotel, sanatorium, hospital, or school **:** GUESTHOUSE; *specif* **:** one of several small detached dwelling units that house neglected or delinquent children and are designed to reproduce a noninstitutional familial environment **b :** a small house designed typically for summer use

cottage bonnet *n* **:** a woman's bonnet of a shape fashionable in England in the first half of the 19th century

cottage cheese *n* **:** a soft uncured cheese made from soured skim milk — called also *Dutch cheese, pot cheese, smearcase*

cottage curtains *n pl* **:** a double set of straight-hanging window curtains, one for each sash, the upper set often made with ruffles and tiebacks and usu. overlapping the lower set

cottage fried potatoes *n pl* **:** raw or cooked potatoes sliced and fried in a heavy skillet — called also *home fried potatoes*

cottage hospital *n* **1** *Brit* **:** a small hospital that is served by local general practitioners **2 :** a hospital consisting of or including several detached or semidetached cottages

cottage industry *n* **:** an industry based upon the family unit as a labor force in which workers using their own equipment at home process goods usu. belonging to a merchant employer and supplement their income from small agricultural holdings

cottage lily *n* **:** MADONNA LILY

cottage loaf *n, Brit* **:** a loaf of bread consisting of a smaller round part on top of a larger round part

cottage nail *n* **:** a small cut nail similar to a shingle nail and available in lengths ¾ in. to 1½ in.

cottage organ *n* **:** a small reed organ

cottage or·né \-(')ȯr;nā\ *n, pl* **cottages ornés** \-"\ [F, lit., ornate cottage] **:** a picturesquely designed small country house of 19th century England

cottage period *n* **:** a period in a country's economic development when its industry is primarily cottage industry

cottage piano *n* **:** a small upright piano of the 19th century

cottage pie *n* **:** SHEPHERD'S PIE

cottage pink *n* **:** a very fragrant tufted pink (*Dianthus plumarius*) with solitary flowers having petals deeply cleft and rose or pink-colored with a striate or darker center

cottage pudding *n* **:** plain cake covered with a hot sweet sauce

cot·tag·er \'käd·ijə(r), -ätı-, -ēj-\ *n* -s **1 :** ¹COTTER 2 **2** *Brit* **:** a rural laborer **3 :** one who resides in a cottage at a resort

cottage rose *n* **:** a European rose (*Rosa alba*) or any of several forms derived from it having broad serrate nonglandular leaves and flowers with a smooth hypanthium

cottage style *n* **:** a book cover design made of panels with sides resembling gables developed by the 17th century English binder Samuel Mearne

cottage tulip *n* **:** any of various tall-growing tulips that flower in May as distinguished from the very early-flowering and the late-flowering tulips — compare DARWIN TULIP

cot·tagey \-jē\ *adj* **:** resembling or suggesting a cottage

cot·ta grass \'käd·ə-\ *n* [modif. of NL *Cottea,* genus name of *Cottea pappophoroides*] **:** an erect branching perennial grass (*Cottea pappophoroides*) of the southwestern U.S. with narrow attenuate leaves

cotte \'kät, 'kȯt\ *n* -s [F, fr. OF *cote, cotte* — more at COAT] **:** a tight-fitting garment resembling the cotehardie

cotted *past of* COT

¹**cot·ter** *or* **cot·tar** \'käd·ə(r), -ätə-\ *n* -s [ME *cottar, cotar,* fr. ML *cottarius, cotarius,* fr. ME ¹*cot* + L *-arius* -ary — more at COT] **1 a :** COTTIER 2 **b :** COTTIER 3 **2 :** a peasant of a class of medieval English villeins ranking next above the slaves and below the bordars and usu. including the coscets **3** *in Scotland* **a :** a peasant occupying a small holding orig. in return for services **b :** a peasant tenant similar to the Irish cottier

²**cotter** \"\ *vb* -ED/-ING/-S [prob. freq. of ⁴*cot*] **1** *dial Brit* **a :** MAT, ENTANGLE **b :** CLOT, CONGEAL, COAGULATE **2** *dial Eng* **:** SHRIVEL, SHRINK, PUCKER, WITHER — often used with *up*

³**cotter** *also* **cottar** \"\ *n* -s [short for *cotterel*] **1 a :** a wedge-shaped or tapered piece used to fasten together parts of a machine or structure by being driven into a tapered opening through one or all the parts — called also *key* **b :** COTTER PIN **2 :** TOGGLE

⁴**cotter** \"\ *vt* -ED/-ING/-S **:** to fasten with a cotter

cotter drill *n* [³*cotter*] **:** TRAVERSE DRILL

cot·ter·el \'kätər(ə)l, -·trōl\ *n* -s [origin unknown] **1** *dial Eng* **:** ³COTTER **2** *dial Eng* **:** a bar, crane, or pothook for a fireplace

b a c b

a cotter fastening parts *b* and *c*

cotter mill *n* [³*cotter*] **:** a milling cutter for forming grooves, slots, or keyways

cotter pin *n* [³*cotter*] **:** a half-round metal strip bent into a pin whose ends can be flared after insertion through a slot or hole

cotterway \'⸗⸗,⸗\ *n* [³*cotter* + *way*] **:** a slot or hole that receives a cotter **:** KEYWAY

cot·tid \'käd·əd\ *n* -s **:** a fish of the family Cottidae

cot·ti·dae \'käd·ə,dē\ *n pl, cap* [NL, fr. *Cottus,* type genus + *-idae*] **:** a family of fishes (order Scleroparei) comprising the sculpins and related forms all of which have a tapering body, wide mouth, and large head and occur in fresh and salt water in the cold and temperate parts of the northern hemisphere

¹**cot·ti·er** \'käd·ēə(r), -ätē-\ *n* -s [fr. (assumed) MF *cotier* — more at COTERIE] **1 :** ¹COTTER 2 **2 :** a tenant in Ireland formerly renting a small farm under the rack-rent system, the land being let to the highest bidder **3 :** a peasant farmer

²**cottier** *comparative of* COTTY

cottiest *superlative of* COTTY

cotting *pres part of* COT

cottise *or* **cottice** *var of* COTISE

cot·tle \'käd·ᵊl, -ätᵊl\ *n* -s [origin unknown] **1 :** a band or wall typically of clay that encircles an object to be molded and determines the outer extremity of the completed mold **2 :** a cylinder usu. of waterproof paper used for retaining plaster-of-paris slurry around a mold or form

¹**cot·ton** \'kätᵊn\ *n* -s *often attrib* [ME *coton,* fr. MF, fr. Ar dial. *quṭun,* fr. Ar *quṭn*] **1 :** a soft fibrous usu. white substance that clothes the seeds of various plants esp. of the genus *Gossypium,* is composed of unicellular hairs forming fine twisted fibers from ½ inch to over 2 inches long when mature, and is used extensively in the making of threads, yarns, and fabrics **2 :** any plant of the genus *Gossypium* characterized by an erect and freely branching habit, alternate lobed leaves, and large creamy white or yellow flowers that soon turn red and are subtended by a cup-shaped involucre and produce a capsular fruit that bursts open when ripe thereby exposing the seeds and attached hairs — see SEA ISLAND COTTON, UPLAND COTTON **3 a :** a fabric made of cotton **b :** a garment made of cotton **4 a :** any of the various yarns spun from the short carded fiber and the long combed fiber of cotton **b :** any of the various hard-twisted or loose-twisted threads of cotton used for sewing, embroidery, and crocheting **5 :** any downy substance resembling cotton produced by such plants as the silk-cotton tree and cottonwood **6 :** a woolen fabric resembling frieze and made in England in the 16th and 17th centuries **7 :** CELLULOSE NITRATE 2

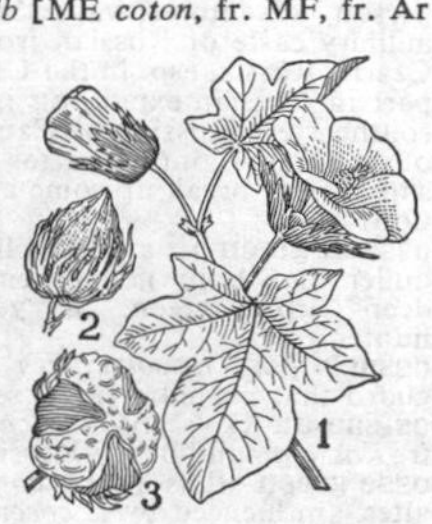

cotton: *1* flowering branch; *2* unopened fruit; *3* fruit partly open

²**cotton** \"\ *vb* **cottoned; cottoned; cottoning** \-t(ᵊ)niŋ\ **cottons** [ME *cotonen,* fr. *coton,* n.] *vt* **1** *obs* **:** to furnish with a down or nap **2 :** to wrap as if in cotton **:** CODDLE ~ *vi* **1** *obs* **a :** to rise with a nap **b :** to go on prosperously **:** develop well **:** SUCCEED **2 a :** to harmonize in action or association **:** AGREE **b :** to make friends **:** FRATERNIZE ⟨a quarrel will end in one of you being turned off, in which case it will not be easy to ~ with another —Jonathan Swift⟩ **3 :** to become attached by or as if by personal liking **:** TAKE — used with *to* ⟨he rather ~*s* to the idea —John Galsworthy⟩ **4 :** UNDERSTAND, PERCEIVE, TUMBLE — used with *to* or *on to* ⟨could ~ on to the fact that it was my car —Nigel Balchin⟩ **5 :** to curry favor **:** TOADY

cot·ton·ade \,kätᵊn'ād, '⸗⸗,⸗\ *n* -s [F *cotonnade,* fr. *coton* cotton (fr. MF) + *-ade*] **:** a heavy coarse twilled cotton fabric made to resemble woolen fabric and used for work clothes

cotton anthracnose *n* **:** a destructive disease of cotton caused by an ascomycete (*Glomerella gossypii*) that produces reddish brown to light-colored or necrotic spots on seedling parts and on leaves, stems, and bolls

cotton aphid *n* **:** a small widely distributed and variably colored aphid (*Aphis gossypii*) that attacks the leaves of various plants and is esp. injurious to cotton, cucurbits to which it transmits certain mosaic diseases, and citrus

cotton ball *n* **:** a disease of the cranberry caused by a fungus (*Sclerotinia oxycocci*) that forms a cottony mass of mycelium in the center of affected berries

cotton–boll weevil \'⸗⸗;⸗-\ *n* **:** BOLL WEEVIL

cotton bollworm *n* **:** CORN EARWORM — used of the worm when feeding in cotton bolls

cotton bur *n* **:** the dried cotton boll and attached pedicel of snapped or stripped cotton after the lint and seed are removed

cottonbush \'⸗⸗,⸗\ *n, Austral* **:** either of two low Australian forage shrubs (*Kochia villosa* and *Bassia bicornis*)

cotton cake *n* **:** COTTONSEED CAKE

cotton candy *n* **:** a candy made in a special machine by spinning sugar that has been boiled to a high temperature

cotton dauber *n* **:** either of two lygus bugs (*Lygus elesius* and *L. oblineatus*) that attack cotton plants in the southwestern U.S.

cotton dye *n* **:** any of various direct dyes — see DYE table I (under *Direct Brown 57, Direct Blue 41, Direct Yellow 26*)

cottoned out *adj* **:** deprived of its crop-producing capacity by continuous cropping with cotton

cotton fern *n* **:** a Californian fern (*Notholaena newberryi*) characterized by a hairy covering on the fronds

cottonfish \'⸗⸗,⸗\ *n* [so called fr. the sticky threads it exudes] **1 :** BOWFIN **2** *Austral* **:** COTTON SPINNER

cotton fleahopper *n* **:** a small green No. American mirid bug (*Psallus seriatus*) that feeds on the young squares and new growth of cotton and on many other cultivated and wild plants

cotton gin *n* **:** a machine that separates the seeds, hulls, and foreign material from cotton

cotton grass *or* **cotton rush** *n* [so called fr. the tufted heads] **:** any sedge of the genus *Eriophorum*

cotton gum *n* [so called fr. the tufts of cottony hairs on the seeds] **:** TUPELO GUM

cot·ton·ize \'kätᵊn,īz\ *vt* -ED/-ING/-S **:** to make like cotton; *specif* **:** to reduce (flax, hemp) to short cottony fiber

cotton leafworm *n* **:** the slender greenish black-and-white-marked larva of a tropical American noctuid moth (*Alabama argillacea*) that migrates northward as far as southeastern Canada in the spring and deposits its eggs on cotton leaves on which the larvae feed often thereby defoliating the plants — called also *cotton leaf caterpillar*

cot·ton·less \-ləs\ *adj* **:** being without cotton

cotton moth *n* **:** any moth whose larva feeds on cotton; *esp* **:** the adult of the cotton leafworm

cotton mouse *n* **:** a rather large dark field mouse (*Peromyscus gossypinus*) widely distributed in the southeastern U. S.

cottonmouth \'⸗⸗,⸗\ *also* **cottonmouth moccasin** *n* [so called fr. the white interior of the mouth] **:** WATER MOCCASIN

cotton mule *n* **:** a small mule suitable for the cultivation of cotton — distinguished from *sugar mule*

cotton picker *n* **:** a machine for gathering the ripe lint and seed of cotton from the standing stalk

cotton–picking \;⸗⸗,⸗⸗\ *adj* **:** DAMNED — often used as a generalized expression of disapproval

cotton powder *n* **:** an explosive (as tonite) in which guncotton is a prominent ingredient

cotton press *n* **1 :** a press for baling ginned cotton **2 :** a building where cotton is baled

cotton rat *n* **:** a destructive long-haired burrowing rat (*Sigmodon hispidus*) native to the southern U.S. and Central America that in a typical subspecies (*S. h. hispidus*) has recently proved valuable in poliomyelitis research

cotton rock *n* **1 :** decomposed chert **2 :** a magnesian limestone

cotton–root bark \'⸗⸗;⸗-\ *n* **:** the recently gathered air-dried bark of the roots of various cultivated cottons (esp. *Gossypium herbaceum*) formerly used as an emmenagogue

cotton root rot *n* **:** a destructive wilting and browning disease of cotton and other plants in the Southwest caused by a fungus (*Phymatotrichum omnivorum*)

cotton rose *n* **1 :** CONFEDERATE ROSE **2 :** FILAGO 2; *esp* **:** an annual herb (*Filago germanica*) with capitate clusters of woolly heads — called also *herba impia*

cotton rust *n* **1 :** a disease of cotton caused by a rust fungus (*Puccinia stakmanii*) that produces slightly elevated greenish yellow or orange aecia chiefly on the undersurface of the leaves **2 :** a potash-deficiency disease of cotton that produces a rusty brown color in the leaves

cottons *pl of* COTTON, *pres 3d sing of* COTTON

cottonseed \'⸗⸗,⸗\ *n* **:** the seed of the cotton plant

cottonseed cake *n* **:** the solid mass remaining after the oil has been expressed from cottonseeds — called also *cotton cake*

cottonseed feed *n* **:** a mixture of cottonseed hulls and cottonseed meal containing less than 36 percent protein

cottonseed foots *n pl* **:** residue from cottonseed-oil refining

cottonseed hulls *n pl* **:** the outer covering of cottonseeds used as a roughage for feeding cattle

cottonseed meal *n* **:** a meal high in protein obtained in the production of cottonseed oil usu. by grinding cottonseed cake and used as a feed for livestock and as a fertilizer

cottonseed oil *n* **:** a semidrying fatty oil that is obtained from cottonseed by expression or solvent extraction, is pale yellow after refining, contains principally glycerides of linoleic, oleic, and palmitic acids, and is used chiefly in salad and cooking oils and after hydrogenation in shortenings and margarine

cotton shrimp *n* **:** a condition of shrimp in which the animal appears bluish and the flesh soft, white, and cottony
cotton shrub *n* **1 :** ¹COTTON 2 **2 :** a half-buried low Australian shrub (*Dryandra nivea*) of the family Proteaceae
cotton–sick \ˈ=,=\ *adj* **:** unable to produce cotton because infested with cotton pests — used of land
cotton sled *n* **:** a box-shaped machine with a V-shaped opening that when drawn over cotton plants pulls off the bolls and directs them into the box
cotton spinner *n* **:** a sea cucumber (esp. *Holothuria forskali*) that ejects a mass of white Cuvierian organs when disturbed
cotton spirits *n* **:** a solution of a stannic salt; *esp* **:** the chloride used as a mordant for cotton
cotton stainer *n* **:** any of several red and black or dark brown bugs (genus *Dysdercus*) that are economic pests of cotton and oranges and other fruits in warmer areas; *specif* **:** a red and dark brown bug (*D. suturellus*) that injures cotton in the southern U.S. by puncturing the developing bolls thereby causing an exudation that stains the lint
cotton stripper *n* **:** STRIPPER 3b
cotton sweep *n* **:** a small wide-bladed tool used for the surface cultivation of soils growing cotton
cottontail \ˈ==,=\ *n* **1** *or* **cottontail rabbit :** any of several rather small No. American rabbits (genus *Sylvilagus*) sandy brown in color with a white-tufted underside of the tail **2 :** the tail of a cottontail rabbit
cotton teal *n* [prob. so called fr. the white cottony patches on the wings of the male] **:** the Indian pygmy goose (*Nettapus coromandelianus*)

cottontail

cotton thistle *n* **:** a biennial white-tomentose prickly Eurasian herb (*Onopordon acanthium*) with pale purple flowers that is naturalized in No. America — called also *Scotch thistle*
cotton tie *n* **:** a band of steel used to encircle a bale of cotton and thus hold it together
cottontop \ˈ==,=\ *n* **:** COTTON GRASS
cotton tree *n* **1 :** any of various trees belonging to the genera *Bombax* and *Ceiba; esp* **:** CEIBA 2a **2 :** WAYFARING TREE 1 **3 :** either of two cottonwoods (*Populus balsamifera* and *P. heterophylla*) **4 :** BLACK POPLAR 1 **5** *Austral* **:** MAJAGUA a
cotton waste *n* **:** WASTE 4a(1)
cotton wax *n* **:** a wax occurring as a coating on raw cotton fibers
cottonweed \ˈ==,=\ *n* **1 :** CUDWEED a **2 :** a common milkweed (*Asclepias syriaca*) with dull purplish flowers **3 :** a plant of the genus *Diotis* (family Compositae) having cottony foliage **4 :** INDIAN MALLOW 1 **5 :** PEARLY EVERLASTING
cotton whig *n, usu cap C&W* **:** member of the northern Whig party about 1850 esp. in Massachusetts who favored a conciliatory policy toward the South
cotton wilt *n* **1 :** a disease of cotton caused by the growth of a fungus (*Fusarium vasinfectum*) in the water-conducting vessels and characterized by wilting, yellowing, blighting, and death **2 :** a blight of cotton caused by a fungus (*Verticillium alboatrum*) and characterized by pale yellow mottled areas on the leaves
cottonwood \ˈ==,=\ *n* **1 :** any of several American trees of the genus *Populus* having a tuft of cottony hairs on the seed; *esp* **:** a common poplar (*P. deltoides*) of the eastern and central U. S. that is often cultivated for its rapid growth and luxuriant foliage or in Europe as a timber tree — see TREE illustration **2 :** WHITE BASSWOOD **3 :** an Australian tree (*Bedfordia salicina*) of the family Compositae having abundant down on its leaves **4 :** PAULOWNIA 2
cottonwood leaf beetle *n* **:** an oval yellowish or reddish black-marked beetle (*Chrysomela scripta*) having a dusky blackish larva that feeds on and defoliates cottonwood
cotton wool *n* **1 a :** raw cotton; *esp* **:** cotton batting **b :** excessive protection or comfort ⟨a *cotton wool* existence⟩ **2** *Brit* **:** ABSORBENT COTTON
cotton worm *n* **:** COTTON LEAFWORM
cot·tony \ˈkät(ᵊ)nē, -ni\ *adj* **1 :** covered with hairs or pubescence **:** DOWNY, NAPPY, WOOLLY **2 :** resembling cotton in appearance or character; *esp* **:** SOFT
cottony–cushion scale \ˈ=(=)=ˈ==-\ *n* **:** a scale (*Icerya purchasi*) introduced into the U.S. from Australia that infests citrus and other plants — see VEDALIA
cottony houseleek *n* **:** COBWEB HOUSELEEK
cottony leak *n* **:** a soft watery rot of cucumbers caused by a phycomycete (*Pythium aphanidermatum*)
cottony maple scale *n* **:** a brown oval soft scale (*Pulvinaria innumerabilis*) that in summer becomes covered with a white cottony secretion beneath which its eggs are laid, that is widespread in No. America, and that attacks and often kills various native and cultivated trees and shrubs
cottony rot *also* **cottony mold** *n* [so called fr. the fluffy white masses appearing on the rotted tissue] **:** a fungous disease of various plants caused by a fungus (*Sclerotinia sclerotiorum*) that produces wilt and rot of the stem and often of other parts
cot·trel \ˈkätərl, -trəl\ *var of* COTTEREL
cot·trell process \ˈkä·trəl-, kä·ˈtrel-\ *n, usu cap C* [after Frederick G. *Cottrell* †1948 Am. chemist, its inventor] **:** electrostatic precipitation in which both the charging and precipitation are carried out in a single piece of equipment
cotts *pl of* COTT
cot·tus \ˈkäd·əs\ *n, cap* [NL, fr. Gk *kottos*, a kind of river fish] **:** the type genus of the family Cottidae
cot·ty \ˈkäd·ē\ *adj, usu* -ER/-EST [³*cot* + *-y*] **:** ENTANGLED, MATTED
cot·u·la \ˈkächələ, -äd·ᵊlə,-ätᵊlə, -ätyələ\ *n* -s [NL, fr. L, small vessel, fr. Gk *kotylē* cup, small vessel, anything hollow — more at KETTLE] **:** MAYWEED
co·tun·nite \kəˈtə,nīt\ *n* -s [G *cotunnit*, fr. *Cotunnius* (latinization of Domenico *Cotugno* †1822 Ital. anatomist) + G *-it* -ite] **:** a mineral consisting of lead chloride $PbCl_2$ that is soft and of white to yellowish color (sp. gr. 5.24)
co·tur·nix \kəˈtərniks\ *n, cap* [NL, fr. L, quail] **:** a genus of birds (family Phasianidae) containing the common European and Old World quails
cotwal *var of* KOTWAL
co–twin \(ˈ)kō+\ *n* -s **:** the birth partner of a twin
cotyl– *or* **cotyli–** *or* **cotylo–** *comb form* [Gk *kotyl-, kotylo-*, fr. *kotylē*] **:** cup **:** organ or part like a cup ⟨*cotyl*oid⟩ ⟨*cotyli*form⟩ ⟨*Cotylo*sauria⟩ **:** acetabular and ⟨*cotylo*sacral⟩
–cot·yl \ˌkäd·ᵊl, -ätᵊl\ *n comb form* -s [*cotyledon*] **:** cotyledon ⟨*dicotyl*⟩ ⟨*epicotyl*⟩
cot·y·la \ˈkäd·ᵊlə\ *or* **cot·y·le** \-l(,)ē\ *n* -s [NL *cotyla*, fr. L *cotyla, cotula* small vessel — more at COTULA] **:** COTULA
cot·y·lar \-l(ə(r)\ *adj* [NL *cotyla* + E *-ar*] **:** of or relating to a cotyla
cot·y·le·don \ˌkäd·ᵊlˈēdᵊn, -ätᵊlˈ-, ˈ==,==\ *n* [NL, fr. L, navelwort, fr. Gk *kotylēdōn* cup-shaped hollow, navelwort, fr. *kotylē* cup, anything hollow — more at KETTLE] **1** -s **:** a placental lobule with its included and complexly branched villous tree — used esp. of the discrete placental lobules typical of ruminants **2** -s **:** the first leaf or one of the first pair or whorl of leaves developed by the embryo in seed plants and in ferns and related plants that functions primarily to make stored food in the endosperm available to the developing young plant but in some cases acts as a storage or photosynthetic organ — called also *seed leaf;* see SCUTELLUM 1b **3 a** *cap* **:** a large genus of herbaceous succulent southern African plants (family Crassulaceae) having a gamopetalous corolla of five petals and usu. twice as many stamens as petals **b** -s **:** any plant of this genus
cot·y·le·don·al \ˌ==ˈēdᵊnᵊl, -ˈed-\ *or* **cot·y·le·don·ar** \-nə(r)\ *adj* [NL *cotyledon* + E *-al* or *-ar*] **:** belonging to or resembling a cotyledon
cot·y·le·don·ary \-n,erē\ *or* **cot·y·le·don·ous** \-nəs\ *adj* [NL *cotyledon* + E *-ary* or *-ous*] **:** consisting of, having, or resembling cotyledons
co·tyl·i·form *or* **ko·tyl·i·form** \kəˈtilə,fȯrm, ˈkäd·ᵊlə,-\ *adj* [*cotyl-* or Gk *kotyl-* + E *-iform*] **:** ACETABULAR
cot·y·lig·er·ous \ˌkäd·ᵊlˈijərəs\ *adj* [*cotyl-* + *-gerous*] **:** having cuplike cavities or cotyledons
cot·y·loid \ˈkäd·ᵊl,ȯid\ *adj* [Gk *kotyloeidēs* cup-shaped, fr. *kotyl-* cotyl- + *-oeidēs* -oid] **:** ACETABULAR
cotyloid bone *n* **:** a small bone forming part of the acetabulum of some mammals
cotyloid cavity *n* **:** ACETABULUM 2a
cotyloid notch *n* **:** ACETABULAR NOTCH
cot·y·loph·o·ra \ˌkäd·ᵊlˈäf(ə)rə\ [NL, fr. *cotyl-* + *-phora*] *syn of* PECORA
cot·y·loph·o·rous \ˌ==ˈäf(ə)rəs\ *adj* [*cotyl-* + *-phorous*] **:** having a cotyledonary placenta
cot·y·lo·saur \ˈkäd·ᵊlə,sȯ(ə)r\ *n* -s [NL *Cotylosauria*] **:** a reptile of the order Cotylosauria
cot·y·lo·sau·ria \ˌkäd·ᵊləˈsȯrēə\ *n pl, cap* [NL, fr. *cotyl-* + *-sauria*] **:** an order of Anapsida comprising extremely primitive late Paleozoic and early Triassic reptiles with short legs and massive bodies — **cot·y·lo·sau·rian** \-rēən\ *adj or n*
co·type \ˈkō+\ *n* [*co-* + *type*] **1 :** SYNTYPE 1 **2 :** PARATYPE 1 **:** ISOTYPE 1b (1) — compare HOLOTYPE
couac \ˈkwak, ˈkwäk\ *n* -s [F, of imit. origin] **:** the strident tone sometimes produced by a reed instrument when the reed is out of order or when the instrument is blown incorrectly
cou·cal \ˈkükəl\ *n* -s [F, perh. fr. *coucou* cuckoo (of imit. origin) + *alouette* lark, fr. OF *aloete*, dim. of *aloe*, fr. L *alauda*, fr. Gaulish] **:** any of various large long-tailed, brown-and-black cuckoos (genus *Centropus*) of Africa, southern Asia, and Australia that resemble pheasants esp. in plumage pattern and habits — see CROW PHEASANT
¹couch \ˈkau̇ch; *in sense 9 usu* ˈküch\ *vb* -ED/-ING/-ES [ME *couchen*, fr. MF *couchier, coucher* to lay down, put to bed, fr. L *collocare* to lay, put, place, fr. *com-* + *locare* to place — more at LOCATE] *vt* **1 a** *obs* **:** to set over **:** OVERLAY, INLAY **b :** to embroider by laying an outlining thread along the surface and fastening it with small stitches at regular intervals **2 a :** to compose, settle, or recline for sleep or rest ⟨at the end of the day's journey the camels needed no urging to be ~*ed* —John Sköllе⟩ — used of an animal usu. reflexively or passively ⟨a lion ~*ing* himself by the tree⟩ **b :** to compose for sleep **:** cause to lie down **:** BED — used of a person usu. reflexively or passively ⟨~*ed* on the ground⟩ **c :** to place, locate, or settle esp. in a position suggesting security, protection, or repose **:** place in a particular setting or background ⟨~*ed* in the magnificence of gorgeous and elaborate costumes —Faubion Bowers⟩ **3** *archaic* **:** to lay or deposit in a bed or layer (as in building or gardening) **:** BED **4 :** to place or hold in a position level and pointed forward ready or as if ready for use ⟨advancing with spears ~*ed*⟩ ⟨~*ing* his lance, he seated himself firmly in his saddle —W.S.Maugham⟩ **5 :** EXPRESS **: a :** to place or compose in a specified kind of language **:** WORD, PHRASE ⟨prayer, ~*ed* in the idiom of the Bible —Edna Ferber⟩ **b :** to include or imply obscurely or so as to make comprehension difficult ⟨all this and more . . . lies naturally ~*ed* under this allegory —Roger L'Estrange⟩ **6** *archaic* **:** to place in hiding or ambush **:** set in hiding or lurking — usu. used reflexively or in the passive **7 :** to treat (a cataract or a person having a cataract) by an operation intended to restore partial vision by displacing the lens of the eye into the vitreous **8 :** to bring down **:** LOWER, DEPRESS, CONTRACT ⟨some of the quills ~*ed*, some still erect⟩ **9 a :** to press (a wet sheet of new handmade paper still on the mold) onto a felt **b :** to press (a sheet of paper stock) on the wire of a cylinder machine and transfer onto a felt for further pressing and drying **c :** to press water from (a sheet) on a couch roll of a fourdrinier machine or extract it by a suction couch preparatory to transferring to a felt ~ *vi* **1 :** to lie down for or as if for sleep or rest **a** *of a person* **:** to recline on or as if on a bed; *sometimes* **:** to couple in sexual intercourse ⟨a goddess ~*ing* with a mortal —Andrew Lang⟩ **b** *of an animal* **:** to lie down, recline, or kneel for or as if for rest ⟨boars ~*ing*⟩ ⟨the odd way a camel ~*es*⟩ **c :** to lie or be situated ⟨the deep that ~*es* beneath —Deut 33:13 (RSV)⟩ **2 :** to bend down low: **a :** to kneel, stoop, or bow esp. in obeisance, subserviency, or submission **b :** to lie or lurk in concealment or ambush ⟨~*ing* in the wood to waylay the traveler⟩ **3** *of leaves* **:** to lie in a heap or mass while decomposition or fermentation proceeds **syn** see LURK
²couch \ˈkau̇ch; *in sense 3 often and in sense 4 usu* ˈküch\ *n* -ES *often attrib* [ME *couche*, fr. MF, fr. OF *culche, couche*, fr. *couchier*] **1 a** *archaic* **:** BED **b** *archaic* **:** a piece of furniture or other arrangement on which one sleeps **c :** an article of furniture for sitting or reclining; *specif* **:** a piece of upholstered furniture that is long enough to lie down on or that can seat several persons and that has sometimes a headrest at one end or sometimes a raised back and arms at both ends **:** SOFA **d :** a psychiatrist's or psychoanalyst's couch on which patients recline **2 a :** the den of an animal **b :** the burrow of an otter **3 :** a layer or stratum that is preliminary in some fine arts processes to later layers **4 :** a board covered with felt or flannel on which the sheets of pulp for handmade paper are pressed — compare COUCH ROLL
³couch *var of* COUCH GRASS
couch·an·cy \ˈkau̇chənsē\ *n* -ES **:** a lying down for repose esp. by an animal
couch·ant \ˈkau̇chənt, *sometimes* küshäⁿ\ *adj* [ME, fr. MF, fr. pres. part. of *coucher*] **1 :** COUCHING ⟨an animal lying ~⟩ **2 :** lying down with the head up — used of a heraldic lion or other beast; distinguished from *dormant* **syn** see PRONE
couchant and levant *adj* [ME — more at LEVANT AND COUCHANT] **:** LEVANT AND COUCHANT
cou·ché \(ˈ)küˈshā\ *adj* [F, fr. past part. of *coucher* to lay down — more at COUCH] *heraldry* **:** INCLINED **:** not erect ⟨a ~ shield with its sinister angle uppermost⟩
couched *adj* [fr. past part. of ¹*couch*] **:** COUCHÉ
couched harp *n* **:** SPINET
cou·chee \küˈshā, ˈ=,=\ *n* -s [F *couchée*, fr. fem. of *couché*, past part. of *coucher*] **:** a reception given late in the evening esp. by royalty or nobility
couch·er \ˈküchər; *in sense 2 sometimes* ˈkau̇ch-\ *n* -s [¹*couch* + *-er*] **1** *Scot* **:** COWARD **2 :** one that couches handmade paper
couches *pres 3d sing of* COUCH, *pl of* COUCH
couch grass \ˈkau̇ch-, ˈküch-\ *also* **couch** *n* -ES [alter. of *quitch* (*grass*)] **1 :** any of various grasses having creeping rhizomes by which they spread rapidly: as **a :** a European grass (*Agropyron repens*) naturalized throughout No. America as a weed — called also *quack grass, quick grass, quitch grass, scutch grass, twitch grass, witchgrass* **b :** a redtop (*Agrostis alba*) **c :** SLENDER FOXTAIL **2** *Austral* **:** BERMUDA GRASS
¹couching *pres part of* COUCH
²couch·ing \ˈkau̇chiŋ\ *n* -s [ME, fr. gerund of *couchen*] **:** a style of embroidery in which a flat or raised design is made by laid threads or cords fastened down by small stitches at regular intervals

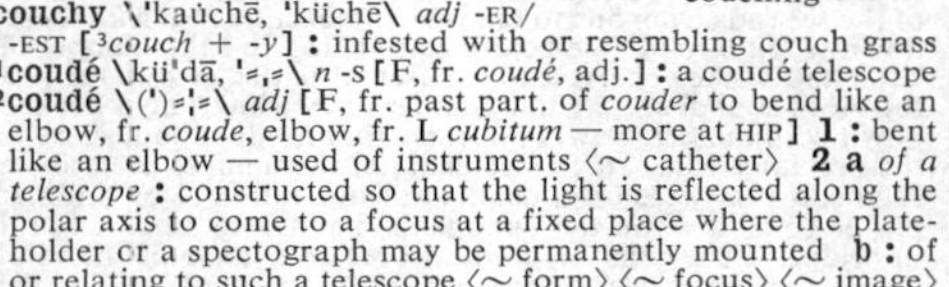

couching

couch roll \ˈküch- *sometimes* ˈkau̇ch-\ *n* [¹*couch*] *papermaking* **:** a large roll that removes water from the wet web as it leaves the wire and is guided onto the felt
couchy \ˈkau̇chē, ˈküchē\ *adj* -ER/-EST [³*couch* + *-y*] **:** infested with or resembling couch grass
¹coudé \küˈdā, ˈ=,=\ *n* -s [F, fr. *coudé*, adj.] **:** a coudé telescope
²coudé \(ˈ)=ˈ=\ *adj* [F, fr. past part. of *couder* to bend like an elbow, fr. *coude*, elbow, fr. L *cubitum* — more at HIP] **1 :** bent like an elbow — used of instruments ⟨~ catheter⟩ **2 a** *of a telescope* **:** constructed so that the light is reflected along the polar axis to come to a focus at a fixed place where the plateholder or a spectrograph may be permanently mounted **b :** of or relating to such a telescope ⟨~ form⟩ ⟨~ focus⟩ ⟨~ image⟩ ⟨~ spectrograph⟩
cou·dière \küdˈye(ə)r, ˈ=,=\ *n* -s [F, fr. *coude* elbow] **:** CUBITIERE
coué·ism \küˈā,izəm, ˈ==,==\ *n* -s *cap* [F *couéisme*, fr. Émile *Coué* †1926 Fr. pharmacist & psychotherapist, its originator + F *-isme* -ism] **:** a system of psychotherapy based upon autosuggestion of health and general well-being and improvement
cou·ette flow \küˈet-\ *n, usu cap C* [F *couette* machine bearing, lit., feather bed, fr. OF *coute, cuilte* quilt, mattress — more at QUILT] **:** the shearing flow of a fluid between two parallel surfaces in relative motion (as of the oil in a cylindrical bearing)
cou·gar \ˈkügə(r), -,gär,-,gȧ(r\ *also* **cou·guar** \", -,gwär,-,gwȧ(r\ *n, pl* **cougars** *also* **cougar** [F *couguar*, modif. (influenced by *jaguar*) of NL *cuguacuarana*, modif. of Tupi *suasuarana, çuçuarana*, lit., false deer, fr. *suasú, suusú* deer + *rana* false; fr. its color] **:** a large powerful tawny brown unspotted cat (*Felis concolor*) longer limbed and less bulky than the jaguar and formerly widespread over most of the Americas but now extinct in much of the U. S. and eastern Canada — called also *American lion, catamount, mountain lion, panther, puma*
¹cough \ˈkȯf *also* ˈkäf\ *vb* -ED/-ING/-S [ME *coughen*, fr. (assumed) OE *cohhian* (of which *cohhettan* is a freq.); akin to MD *cochen* to cough, MHG *küchen* to breathe heavily, prob. of imit. origin] *vi* **1 :** to expel air from the lungs suddenly with an explosive noise usu. in a series of efforts **2 :** to make a noise like that of coughing: as **a :** to fire in a single short burst or series of separate bursts ⟨the machine gun ~*ed* once⟩ **b** *of an engine* **:** to go through an operation cycle without continuous firing ⟨the engine began to ~ on the hill⟩ ~ *vt* **1 :** to expel by coughing — used with *up* or *out* ⟨~ up mucus⟩ **2 :** DISCLOSE — used with *up* or *out* ⟨~ up all he knows⟩
²cough \"\ *n* -s *often attrib* [ME *coughe*, fr. *coughen*, v.] **1 :** a condition marked by repeated coughing **:** an ailment manifesting itself by frequent coughing ⟨he has a bad ~⟩ **2 :** an explosive expulsion of air from the lungs acting as a protective mechanism to clear the air passages or as a symptom of pulmonary disturbance **3 :** a single burst of firing **:** a single firing or irregular bursts of firing in the cylinders of a motor
cough drop *n* **:** a lozenge or troche used to relieve coughing
coughroot \ˈ=,=\ *n* [so called fr. its use as a remedy for coughs] **:** a wake-robin (*Trillium cernuum*) of north eastern No. America having nodding flowers almost hidden by the leaves
cough syrup *n* **:** any sweet usu. medicated liquid used as a remedy for cough
cough up *vt* **:** to hand over **:** give up **:** DELIVER, PAY, CONTRIBUTE ⟨*cough up* the money for the tickets⟩
coughweed \ˈ=,=\ *n* **:** GOLDEN RAGWORT
coughwort \ˈ=,=\ *n* [so called fr. its use as a remedy for coughs] **:** COLTSFOOT a
cou·gnar \ˈkün,yär, ˈku̇n,-\ *n* -s [Malay *chunya*] **:** a three-masted square-rigged Malay ship
couhage *var of* COWAGE
coul \ˈkōl, ˈkül, ˈkau̇(ə)l\ *dial var of* COWL
coul *abbr* coulomb
could *or archaic 2d sing* **couldst** [alter. (influenced by *should* and *would*) of ME *coude, couthe*, fr. OE *cūthe;* akin to OHG *konda* could, ON *kunna*, Goth *kuntha* — more at CAN] *past of* CAN — used in auxiliary function in the past tense ⟨he found he ~ go⟩, in the past conditional ⟨he said he would go if he ~⟩, and as an alternative to *can* suggesting less force or certainty or as a polite form in the present ⟨~ you do this for me⟩ and the present conditional ⟨if you ~ come we would be pleased⟩
could·est \ˈku̇dəst\ *archaic past 2d sing of* CAN
couldn't **:** could not
cou·lé \küˈlā, ˈ=,=\ *n* -s [F, fr. *coulé*, past part. of *couler*] **1 a :** a slur in music **b :** one of several graces usu. of two or three sliding notes indicated by a dash **c :** a sliding from one note or one string to another (as on a banjo) **2 :** a gliding dance step
¹cou·lee \ˈkülē, -li *sometimes* küˈlā *or* ˈ=,=\ *n* -s [CanF *coulée*, fr. F, flowing, flow of lava, fr. fem. of *coulé*, past part. of *couler* to flow, glide, fr. L *colare* to strain, purify, fr. *colum* sieve — more at HEDGE] **1** *also* **cou·lie** \ˈkülē, -li\ *chiefly West* **a :** a small often intermittent stream **:** a dry creek bed sometimes running in a wet season **b :** a steep-walled valley or ravine varying widely in size and often having a stream at the bottom **c :** a small valley or low-lying area **2** [F] **:** a thick sheet or stream of lava esp. when solidified
²cou·lée \küˈlā, ˈ=,=\ *n* -s [F, short for *écriture coulée*, lit., flowing writing, fr. *écriture* writing + *coulée*, fem. of *coulé*, past part. of *couler* to flow] **:** a French commercial and official hand based partly on bâtarde
cou·lee cricket \ˈkülē-\ *n* [¹*coulee* (valley) + *cricket*] **:** a large wingless cricket (*Peranabrus scabricollis*) of the northwestern U. S. sometimes destructive to crops
cou·leur \küˈlər, -ˈlœ\ *n* -s [F, fr. L *color* — more at COLOR] **1 :** ¹COLOR 1 **2 :** the color of the first card dealt in the winning row in the game of rouge et noir — compare INVERSE
¹couleur de rose \(ˈ)=ˈ=də ˈrōz\ *n* [F] **:** ROSE **:** rose color
²couleur de rose \(ˈ)=ˈ=ˈ=\ *adj* **:** ROSY, ROSEATE
cou·lier \ˈkülyə(r)\ *n* -s [prob. fr. F *coulière*, lit., sliding, gliding, fr. *couler* to slide, glide, flow — more at COULEE] **:** the cam motion that controls delivery of yarn over needles on a full-fashioned knitting machine
cou·lisse \küˈlēs\ *n* -s [F (also, groove, door, window, or partition that slides in a groove), fr. OF *couleice* portcullis, short for *porte couleïce*, lit., sliding door, fr. *porte* door + *couleïce*, fem. of *couleïz* slidable, penetrating, fr. *couler* to slide, flow — more at COULEE] **1 a :** a side scene of the stage in a theater or the space between the side scenes **b :** a place behind the scenes **c :** a lobby, corridor, or other place where informal discussion is likely **2 :** a piece of timber having a groove in which something glides (as an upright of a sluice)
cou·loir \külˈwär\ *n* -s [F, lit., colander, fr. LL *colatorium* sieve, fr. L *colatus* (past part. of *colare* to strain) + *-orium* -ory — more at COULEE] **1 :** a deep gorge **:** a gully on a mountainside esp. in the Swiss Alps **2 :** PASSAGE, GANGWAY, CORRIDOR
cou·lomb \ˈkü,läm, -,lōm, =ˈ=\ *n* -s *sometimes cap* [after Charles A. de *Coulomb* †1806 Fr. physicist] **1 :** the practical mks unit of electric charge equal to the quantity of electricity transferred by a current of one ampere in one second and now taken as the standard in the U.S. **2 :** a unit of electric charge equal to 0.999835 coulomb and formerly taken as the standard — called also *international coulomb*
coulomb field *n, sometimes cap C* **:** a field of coulomb force (as due to an electric charge)
coulomb force *n, sometimes cap C* **:** any of the forces of attraction or repulsion that obey the inverse-square law and are derived from a Newtonian potential — compare NEWTONIAN FORCE
cou·lom·bi·an \(ˈ)küˈlämbēən, -ˈlōm-\ *also* **cou·lom·bic** \-bik\ *adj, often cap* [C. A. de *Coulomb* + E *-ian* or *-ic*] **:** of or relating to the discoveries or laws of C. A. de Coulomb
cou·lomb·me·ter \ˈkü(,)läm,mēd·ə(r), -(,)lōm,-, =ˈ=,-\ *n* [ISV *coulomb* + *-meter*] **:** COULOMETER
coulomb's law *n, cap C* [after C. A. de *Coulomb*] **:** a statement in physics: the force of attraction or repulsion acting along a straight line between two electric charges or two magnetic poles is directly proportional to the product of the charges or pole strengths and inversely to the square of the distance between them
cou·lom·e·ter \küˈlämәd·ə(r), kəˈ-\ *n* [alter. of *coulombmeter*] **:** VOLTAMETER; *sometimes* **:** one in which a metal other than silver is deposited or gas is evolved
cou·lo·met·ric \ˌküləˈme·trik\ *adj* **:** of or relating to coulometry — **cou·lo·met·ri·cal·ly** \-trək(ə)lē\ *adv*
coulometric titration *n* **:** a method of titration in which the titrating agent is produced in a solution by electrolysis and the required amount of the agent is determined by measuring the number of coulombs used in preparing it
cou·lom·e·try \küˈlämə·trē, kəˈ-\ *n* -ES [*coulomb* + *-metry*] **:** chemical analysis performed by determining the amount of a substance released in an electrolysis by measuring the number of coulombs used
cou·lom·mi·ers \kə,ləmˈēˈā\ *n, usu cap* [F, fr. *Coulommiers*, town in central France where it is produced] **:** a small mold-ripened fresh or cured Brie cheese
coul·son·ite \ˈkōlsə,nīt\ *n* -s [Arthur L. *Coulson b* 1898 geologist in India + E *-ite*] **:** vanadoan magnetite
coulter *var of* COLTER
coul·ter·neb \ˈkōltə(r),neb\ *n* -s [*coulter* + *neb;* fr. the shape of the bill] *dial Brit* **:** PUFFIN
coul·ter pine \ˈkōltə(r)-\ *or* **coulter's pine** *n, usu cap C* [after Thomas *Coulter* †1843 Irish botanist] **:** a tall pine (*Pinus coulteri*) of the southwestern U. S. with cones 9 to 15 inches long and consisting of stout sharp-pointed scales — called also *big-cone pine*
cou·ma \ˈkümə\ *n* -s [NL, genus to which the couma belongs, fr. F, fr. Tupi *cumá*] **1 :** a tropical So. American tree (*Couma utilis*) of the family Apocynaceae — see COW TREE, SORVA **2 :** the edible sweet fruit of the couma

cou·mal·ic acid \(ˈ)kü¦malik-, -mā-\ *also* **cu·mal·ic acid** \(ˈ)kyü-\ *n* [ISV *coumalic*, blend of *coumarin* and *malic*] **:** a white crystalline acid $C_6H_4O_4$ formed by heating malic acid with sulfuric acid or zinc chloride; 5-coumalin-carboxylic acid

cou·ma·lin *also* **cu·ma·lin** \ˈk(y)ümələn\ *n* -s [ISV *coumalic* + *-in*] **:** pyrone (sense 1a) or any of its derivatives

cou·ma·ran \ˈk(y)ümə,ran\ *n* -s [ISV *coumarin* + *-an;* prob. orig. formed as G *kumaran*] **:** a colorless oil C_8H_8O formed by reducing coumarone of which it is the dihydride

cou·ma·ra nut \ˈkümərə-\ *n* [alter. of *coumarou*] **:** TONKA BEAN

cou·ma·rin *also* **cu·ma·rin** \ˈk(y)ümərən, -,rēn\ *n* -s [F *coumarine*, fr. *coumarou* + *-ine*] **:** a toxic white crystalline lactone $C_9H_6O_2$ with an odor of new-mown hay that is found in many plants (as the tonka bean and clover), is made synthetically, and is used in perfumery and soap, in the synthesis of dicoumarol, and formerly in flavoring; 1,2-benzopyrone; *also* **:** any derivative (as umbelliferone) of this compound

cou·ma·rone *or* **cu·ma·rone** \-,rōn\ *n* -s [ISV *coumar*in + *-one;* prob. orig. formed as G *kumaron*] **:** a heavy oily compound C_8H_6O present in solvent naphtha and made synthetically; *also* **:** any derivative of this compound — called also *benzofuran*

coumarone–indene resin *also* **coumarone resin** *n* **:** any of a group of thermoplastic resins obtained by polymerization of mixtures of coumarone and indene (as those obtained from solvent naphtha) and used chiefly in coatings, paints, printing ink, and asphalt tile — called also *paracoumarone-indene resin*

cou·ma·rou \ˌk(y)ümə¦rü\ *or* **cu·ma·ra** \ˈ⸗mərə\ *or* **cu·ma·ru** \⸗mə¦rü\ *n* -s [F, fr. Sp or Pg; Sp *cumarú*, fr. Pg, fr. Tupi *cumarú, cumarú*] **1 :** the tonka-bean tree **2 :** the seeds of the tonka-bean tree

coumbite *var of* COMBITE

coun *abbr* **1** council **2** counsel

¹coun·cil \ˈkau̇n(t)səl *also* ˈkän-\ *n* -s [ME *counceil, conceil* (influenced in meaning by ME *counseil, conseil* counsel, council), fr. OF *concile* assembly, ecclesiastical assembly, fr. LL & L; LL *concilium* ecclesiastical assembly, fr. L, assembly, fr. *com-* + *-cilium* (fr. *calare* to call) — more at COUNSEL, LOW] **1 a :** an assembly of ecclesiastics or church representatives convened to consider matters of doctrine, discipline, law, morals, or the relation of the Christian church to world problems ⟨seven widely recognized ecumenical (or general) ~*s* of the Christian church are those held at Nicaea, 325; Constantinople, 381; Ephesus, 431; Chalcedon, 451; Constantinople, 553; Constantinople, 680; Nicaea, 787⟩ **b :** a meeting of the Sanhedrin or of a similar minor assembly with limited jurisdiction ⟨the Pharisees went out and held a ~ against him —Mt 12:14 (AV)⟩ **2 :** a deliberative assembly ⟨the department is under a prefect and an elected general ~ of 36 members —*Statesman's Yr. Bk.*⟩ **:** an assembly or meeting held for consultation, advice, or discussion ⟨a ~ among the leaders⟩ **:** a meeting for discussion **3 :** a somewhat permanent group elected or appointed to constitute an advisory body or a body with a degree of legislative power ⟨a privy ~⟩ ⟨a ~ of state⟩ ⟨a governor's ~⟩ **4 :** an administrative body: as **a :** a local governing instrumentality (as of a town, borough, city, or county) ⟨county ~*s* in England⟩ ⟨borough ~*s* in the U.S.⟩ **b :** a collegial executive body ⟨the Federal *Council* of Switzerland⟩ **c :** one of three governing bodies of a British university composed chiefly of persons not otherwise connected with the institution and charged with administrative functions — compare COURT 4c, SENATE **d :** SOVIET **e :** a governing body consisting of voting delegates from local labor unions united in a federation **5 :** the deliberation carried on in a council or council chamber **:** CONSULTATION ⟨summoned to ~⟩; *sometimes* **:** COUNSEL **6 a :** a federation of or a central body uniting a group of organizations **b :** a local chapter of an organization **c :** CLUB, SOCIETY, ASSOCIATION

²council \ˈ"\ *vi* **counciled** *or* **councilled; counciled** *or* **councilled; counciling** *or* **councilling** \-s(ə)liŋ\ **councils :** to hold a council **:** meet and deliberate in council — used esp. of the councils of American Indians

³council \ˈ"\ *adj* **1 :** used for councils esp. by or with No. American Indians ⟨a ~ ground⟩ **2** *Brit* **:** built, maintained, or operated by a local governing agency ⟨a ~ house⟩ ⟨~ flats⟩

council board *or* **council table** *n* **:** the table around which a council holds consultation; *also* **:** the council itself in deliberation

council fire *n* **:** the ceremonial fire kept burning during a council of No. American Indians; *also* **:** the council itself — compare LONG HOUSE 2

council–general \¦⸗⸗¦⸗(⸗)⸗\ *n, pl* **councils–general** [trans. of F *conseil général*] **:** a deliberative body of a French administrative department

coun·cil·lor *or* **coun·cil·or** \ˈkau̇n(t)s(ə)lə(r) *also* ˈkän-\ *n* -s [alter. (influenced by *council*) of *counsellor, counselor*] **:** a member of a council **:** one appointed or elected to advise or supervise

coun·cil·lor·ship \-,ship\ *n* -s **:** the position or function of a councillor

coun·cil·man \ˈkau̇n(t)səlmən *also* ˈkän-\ *n, pl* **councilmen :** a member of a council, and esp. of a city council

council–manager plan *n* **:** a method of municipal government in which legislative and policy-determining powers are held by an elected council that employs a city manager who is responsible to the council for city administration — compare COMMISSION PLAN

coun·cil·man·ic \¦kau̇n(t)səl¦manik *also* ¦kän-\ *adj* [irreg., fr. *councilman* + *-ic*] **:** of, by, or for a council or councilman

council of ministers *often cap C&M* [trans. of F *conseil des ministres*] **:** CABINET 4b ⟨the French *Council of Ministers*⟩

council of state : an administrative or deliberative body for state matters **:** a governmental council considering high policy matters

council of war 1 : an assembly of officers usu. of high rank called to consult with the commander on questions of importance or emergency **2 :** a deliberation to concert measures

council school *n, Brit* **:** a nondenominational elementary or secondary school provided and maintained by a local education authority — called also *county school;* compare PUBLIC SCHOOL, VOLUNTARY SCHOOL

council tool *n* **:** a long-handled combination hoe and rake of which the blade consists of mowing-machine blade sections attached to a piece of angle iron

councilwoman \ˈ⸗⸗,⸗⸗\ *n, pl* **councilwomen :** a female member of a council

¹coun·sel \ˈkau̇n(t)səl *also* ˈkän-\ *n* -s *see sense 6a* [ME *counseil, conseil*, fr. OF *conseil*, fr. L *consilium*, fr. *com-* + *-silium* (perh. akin to Gk *helein* to take) — more at SELL] **1 a :** instruction or recommendation esp. when given as a result of consultation **:** OPINION, ADVICE, DIRECTION ⟨his own more wary followers took heed to his ~ —W.H.Prescott⟩ **b :** a policy or plan of action or behavior ⟨observe the sixth commandment, not as a precept of divine law but as a ~ of profitable prudence —W.L.Sullivan⟩ **2 :** interchange of opinion esp. on possible procedure **:** DISCUSSION, DELIBERATION, CONSULTATION **3** *obs* **:** faculty or exercise of deliberate judgment **:** PRUDENCE, THOUGHTFULNESS **4** *archaic* **:** a plan arrived at through deliberation **:** INTENTION, PURPOSE ⟨the ~ of the Lord stands forever —Ps 33:11 (RSV)⟩ **5 a** *archaic* **:** secret purpose or opinion **:** private confidence **:** SECRET ⟨did you ne'er hear say, two may keep ~, putting one away —Shak.⟩ **b :** reflection, thought, intent, or plan discreetly and carefully guarded from being known — used in the phrase *keep one's own counsel* ⟨chary and given to keeping his own ~⟩ **6 :** ADVISER: **a** *pl* **counsel** (1) **:** a lawyer engaged in the trial or management of a cause in court **:** BARRISTER ⟨his ~ is able⟩ ⟨the arguments of ~⟩ ⟨to have the assistance of ~ for his defense —*U.S. Constitution*⟩ ⟨if ~ are familiar with the rules of this court⟩ ⟨~ for Johnson argued brilliantly in behalf of their client — Marshall Smelser & H.W.Kirwin⟩ (2) **:** a lawyer appointed or engaged to advise and represent a particular client, public officer, or public body in legal matters (as before a government agency) — called also *legal counsel* **b :** CONSULTANT 2

²counsel \ˈ"\ *vb* **counseled** *or* **counselled; counseled** *or* **counselled; counseling** \-s(ə)liŋ\ *or* **counselling; counsels** [ME *counseilen, conseillen*, fr. OF *conseiller*, fr. L *consiliari*, fr. *consilium*] *vt* **1 :** to advise esp. seriously and formally after consultation ⟨~*ed* them to avoid rash actions —George Orwell⟩; *esp* **:** to advise (students) on personal or vocational problems **2 :** to recommend esp. as the best or most expedient act, course, or policy ⟨~ great caution⟩ ⟨he wrote to his father ~*ing* further delay —T.E.Lawrence⟩ ~ *vi* **:** CONSULT, DELIBERATE ⟨~*ing* about the problem⟩

coun·sel·able *or* **coun·sel·la·ble** \ˈkau̇n(t)s(ə)ləbəl *also* ˈkän-\ *adj* **:** willing to receive advice; *also* **:** ADVISABLE

coun·sel·ee \¦kau̇n(t)sə¦lē, -)¦slē *also* ¦kän-\ *n* -s **:** one who is being counseled

counseling *n* -s [ME *counseilling, conseilling* advising, fr. gerund of *counseilen, conseilen* to counsel] **:** a practice or professional service designed to guide an individual to a better understanding of his problems and potentialities by utilizing modern psychological principles and methods esp. in collecting case history data, using various techniques of the personal interview, and testing interests and aptitudes ⟨vocational ~⟩

counsellor seal *n* [so called fr. the long whitish hair of the head that suggests a lawyer's wig] **:** a large So. Pacific hair seal (*Arctocephalus cinereus*)

counsel of despair : an expression of hopelessness or resignation

counsel of perfection 1 : instruction given for the attainment of perfection **2 :** an unrealizable ideal

coun·sel·or *or* **coun·sel·lor** \ˈkau̇n(t)s(ə)lə(r) *also* ˈkän-\ *n* -s [ME *conseiler, counseilour*, fr. OF *conseilleor*, fr. L *consiliator*, fr. *consiliatus* (past part. of *consiliari* to counsel) + *-or* — more at COUNSEL] **1 :** one that counsels **:** ADVISER **2 :** one that gives advice in law and manages cases for clients in court **:** COUNSEL 6 **3 :** COUNCILLOR **4 :** one of the two aids to a president of any unit in the Mormon Church **5 a :** a faculty member assigned to advise students on personal, academic, and vocational matters **b :** one who engages in or whose profession is counseling **c :** an official who directs a group of camp members in some recreational activity (as swimming, dramatics, handicrafts) **6 :** a diplomatic official at an embassy or legation ranking just below an ambassador or minister

counselor–at–law \¦⸗(⸗)⸗(,)⸗¦⸗\ *n, pl* **counselors–at–law :** COUNSELOR 2

counsels *pl of* COUNSEL, *pres 3d sing of* COUNSEL

¹count \ˈkau̇nt\ *vb* -ED/-ING/-S [ME *counten*, fr. MF *conter, compter*, fr. L *computare* to reckon, compute, fr. *com-* + *putare* to consider, think — more at PAVE] *vt* **1 a :** to indicate, name, or separate (units out of a body of units) one by one or group after group to find the total number of units involved or concerned **:** NUMBER, TALLY, RECKON ⟨~ the pages of a manuscript⟩ — sometimes used with *up* or *over* ⟨~ up the money in the register⟩ **b :** to tell over or name the numbers in regular order up to and including (a specified number) ⟨~ ten before answering⟩ **c :** to include in a tallying and reckoning ⟨about 100 people present, ~*ing* women and children⟩ **d :** to compute or tally mechanically and record a total ⟨a machine that ~*s* cars crossing the bridge⟩ **e :** to call aloud (beats or time units) esp. in the practicing of a musical composition ⟨~ eighth notes⟩ **f** (1) **:** to recollect or keep track of the number of cards that have been played in (a specified suit) ⟨~ trumps⟩ (2) **:** to estimate or mentally reconstruct the distribution of cards in (another player's hand) (3) **:** to count the points in (a hand of cards) — compare POINT COUNT **2 a :** CONSIDER, ACCOUNT, REGARD, JUDGE ⟨~ oneself lucky⟩ ⟨the true dignity of man . . . is ~*ed* folly —W.E.Channing⟩ **b :** ESTIMATE, ESTEEM ⟨he ~*ed* it nothing that his follower had sacrificed his life⟩ **c :** to record as of a particular opinion or persuasion ⟨~ me as uncommitted⟩ ⟨stand and be ~*ed*⟩ **d** *dial* **:** SUPPOSE, GUESS, RECKON ⟨I ~ there's three of them coming⟩ **3 :** to amount to **:** have a total of ⟨they ~*ed* 30 —Lord Byron⟩ ~ *vi* **1** *archaic* **:** to think much of something **:** care about something **:** take account ⟨no man ~*s* of her beauty —Shak.⟩ **2 a :** to recite or indicate the numbers in order ⟨a little child who could not ~⟩ ⟨~ by fives⟩ **:** count the units in a group ⟨interrupted while he was ~*ing*⟩ **b :** to mark the time by counting aloud the beats in a musical composition **3 a :** to rely or depend on someone or something in plans or calculations — used with *on* or *upon* ⟨the man they ~*ed* on in this crisis —Stuart Cloete⟩ **:** look forward to, expect, or plan on something with assured confidence ⟨~ on clear weather⟩ ⟨~*ing* on his car to get him there on time⟩ **b :** to expect, predict, or take something into consideration — usu. used with *on* ⟨they ~ on winning⟩ ⟨he had not ~*ed* on paying and had brought no money⟩ **4** *English law, obs* **:** to plead in court **:** state a complaint in court **5 :** to add up **:** amount in number **:** TOTAL — sometimes used with *up* ⟨it ~*s* up to a sizable sum⟩ **6 a :** to have value, meaning, weight, significance, or importance ⟨landscape ~*s* in the character of a place, but people ~ more —H.L.Davis⟩ **:** merit consideration **:** be of consequence or account ⟨these are the men who really ~⟩ **b :** to be of account **:** have status or rank **:** become classed or regarded ⟨achievements such as the TVA have ~*ed* for far more . . . than our military power —M.W.Straight⟩ ⟨the things that ~*ed* so much with us when we were young —Louis Bromfield⟩ **7 :** to make a score ⟨~*ed* twice in the third inning⟩

syn TELL, ENUMERATE, NUMBER: COUNT is likely to call attention to the finding of a total without minimizing the notion of numbering units or groups in the process of attaining to that total ⟨as many as 30 bonfires could be *counted* within the whole bounds of the district —Thomas Hardy⟩ TELL, now archaic in suggestion, may center attention on the fact of units being counted ⟨*telling* one's beads⟩ ⟨a shepherd *telling* his sheep⟩ ENUMERATE may suggest counting up or totaling with specific and clear treatment of each item ⟨Pliny *enumerates* among the trees of Syria the date, pistachio, fig, cedar, juniper, terebinth, and sumac —P.K.Hitti⟩ ⟨among the *enumerated* powers, we do not find that of establishing a bank or creating a corporation —John Marshall⟩ NUMBER may suggest either limited allotting or precise ordering in sequence ⟨the days of every man are *numbered*⟩ ⟨to *number* the volumes on the shelf⟩ **syn** see in addition RELY

—**count coup** *of an American Indian* **:** to make a coup; *also* **:** to relate the story of one's coups — **count heads** *or* **count noses :** to count the number (as of persons) present

²count \ˈ"\ *n* -s [ME *counte*, fr. MF *conte, compte*, fr. LL *computus* computation, fr. L *computare* to reckon, compute] **1 :** the action or process of numbering, counting, or reckoning ⟨completing the ~ of the ballots⟩ **2 a** *archaic* **:** a reckoning of money, goods, or conduct ⟨call to ~ —Edmund Spenser⟩ **:** ACCOUNT; *specif* **:** a statement of stewardship or managing **b :** formulation of a total arrived at by examination of a sample ⟨a ~ of white corpuscles⟩ **c :** population enumeration **:** CENSUS **3** *archaic* **:** consideration as important **:** ESTIMATION, REGARD **4 :** number or sum total obtained by counting **:** ENUMERATION, TALLY ⟨the official ~ came to over a hundred⟩ **5 a :** ALLEGATION, CHARGE; *specif* **:** a particular allegation or charge separately stating the cause of action or prosecution in a legal declaration or indictment ⟨the jury found him innocent on the first ~, guilty on the second and third⟩ ⟨guilty on all ~*s*⟩ **b :** the declaration in common-law pleading when the plaintiff has but one cause of action and makes but one statement of it **c :** a specific point under consideration **:** ISSUE ⟨disagreeing on this ~⟩ **6 a :** the calling off of the seconds from one to ten when a boxer has been knocked down ⟨took a ~ of nine before getting up⟩ **b :** the number of balls and strikes charged to a baseball batter at one turn ⟨a full ~ of 3 and 2⟩ **c :** the number of bowling pins knocked down with the first bowl of a frame that is added to a spare in the previous frame **d :** an estimate of the number of cards in each suit that were orig. dealt to or are still held by another player ⟨take a ~ on the opponents' hands⟩ **e :** point count in bridge **f :** a point or points scored in a game or the total points that have been scored up to any particular time ⟨the ~ now stands at 15-30⟩ **7 a :** an oyster, terrapin, or food fish of a size reckoned as standard or above a specified minimum size — used chiefly in selling by the number **b :** a stem bearing nine or more hands of bananas **c :** the number of sheets of paper or board that make up a given weight or unit **8 a :** a system of measuring yarns by the number of hanks or yards per pound and indicating size or fineness **b :** the number of warp yarns and weft yarns per inch in a textile fabric — compare ⁵PICK 2b **9 :** an indication by an enumerating device of an ionizing event (as the arrival of a cosmic-ray particle) or of the total number of such events in a given period; *also* **:** a single ionizing event — compare COUNTING TUBE

³count \ˈ"\ *n* -s [MF *conte, comte*, fr. LL *comit-, comes*, fr. L, associate, companion, one of the imperial court or train, lit., one who goes with another, fr. *com-* + *-it-, -es* (fr. *ire* to go) — more at ISSUE] **:** a European nobleman whose rank corresponds to that of a British earl

¹count·able \ˈkau̇ntəbəl\ *adj* [ME, fr. MF *contable, comptable*, fr. *conter, compter* to count + *-able* — more at COUNT] **1** *archaic* **:** liable for an account **:** ACCOUNTABLE, RESPONSIBLE **2 :** capable of being counted **:** DENUMERABLE ⟨a ~ set⟩

²countable \ˈ"\ *n* -s **1 :** something that is countable **2 :** COUNT NOUN

countdown \ˈ⸗¦⸗\ *n* -s [*count down*, v.] **:** an audible backward counting off in fixed units (as seconds) from an arbitrary starting number (as 10) to mark the diminishing time remaining before the execution of an operation ⟨the ~ concluded, "four, three, two, one," and then the firing button was pushed⟩; *also* **:** the length of time marked by such a counting or required by the entire sequence of steps in readying a missile for flight — compare ZERO HOUR

¹coun·te·nance \ˈkau̇nt(ᵊ)nən(t)s, -tən-\ *n* -s [ME *countenaunce*, fr. MF *contenance* behavior, demeanor, fr. ML *continentia*, fr. L, continence, restraint, fr. *continent-, continens* (pres. part. of *continēre* to hold together, restrain, contain) + *-ia* -y — more at CONTAIN] **1** *obs* **a :** BEARING, DEMEANOR **b :** BEHAVIOR, COMPORTMENT **c :** bearing or behavior as indicative of goodwill or ill will **2 a :** calm expression **:** facial expression indicating composure ⟨he kept his ~ so well that he had the air of having made a finished speech —G.B.Shaw⟩; *also* **:** mental composure ⟨startled and also somewhat out of ~ —Arnold Bennett⟩ **b :** the expressive appearance of one's face **:** LOOK, EXPRESSION ⟨a ~ which expressed both good humor and intelligence —Sir Walter Scott⟩ **3** *archaic* **a :** ASPECT, SEMBLANCE **b** (1) **:** a mere appearance or show (2) **:** a feigned or assumed appearance **:** PRETENSE **4 :** FACE, VISAGE; *esp* **:** the face as an indication of mood, emotion, or character ⟨good-looking and gentlemanlike, he had a pleasant ~ —Jane Austen⟩ **5** *archaic* **:** the appearances that one maintains **:** STANDING, DIGNITY **6 a** *obs* **:** CREDIT, ESTEEM **b :** appearance of favor **:** bearing or expression appearing or calculated to approve or encourage **:** SANCTION **:** moral support **:** GOODWILL ⟨his having had no support or ~ in accepted tradition —F.R.Leavis⟩ ⟨give the hussy no ~ —S.E.Morison & H.S. Commager⟩ **c** *obs* **:** confidence arising from favor and encouragement **:** TRUST **syn** see FACE

²countenance \ˈ"\ *vt* -ED/-ING/-S [MF *contenancer*, fr. *contenance*, n.] **:** to give countenance to **:** extend approval or toleration to **:** ENCOURAGE, SANCTION, SUPPORT, FAVOR, CONDONE ⟨asked his family to ~ her⟩ ⟨although militant, he never *countenanced* violence⟩ **syn** see FAVOR

coun·te·nanc·er \-sə(r)\ *n* -s **:** one that countenances **:** ENCOURAGER

¹count·er \ˈkau̇ntə(r)\ *n* -s [ME *countour*, fr. MF *comptouer, comptoir*, fr. ML *computatorium* computing place, place of accounts, fr. L *computatus* (past part. of *computare* to compute) + *-orium* -ory — more at COUNT] **1 a :** an article used in reckoning; *esp* **:** a piece (as of metal, ivory, wood, bone) used in keeping accounts and in playing games of chance **b :** one of a set of small objects (as disks or squares of wood, plastic, bone) with which a game (as a board game) is played **2** *obs* **:** a prison esp. for debtors that is attached to a city court **3 a :** an imitation often in base metal of a coin **b :** TOKEN **c :** money in general or a particular coin **d :** a possession or attribute of value in bargaining ⟨the Guam fortifications were intended as a bargaining ~ in possible future negotiations —*New Republic*⟩ ⟨to use sex as a ~ rather than value it as either a means of self-expression or communication —Margaret Mead⟩ **:** ASSET **4 a :** a table, shelf, or other level surface usu. of a height convenient for a person standing before it and over which transactions may be conducted **:** a table, case, or shelf on which goods are displayed and over which payment for purchases is made **:** any article of business, store, or institutional furniture that separates clientele from personnel and over which transactions are made **b :** a long and somewhat narrow serving area flanked by a row of stools ⟨eating at the ~ rather than taking a table⟩ **:** flat working space on the top of kitchen equipment or furnishings **5 :** COUNTERWORD ⟨a cliché, a worn ~ of a word, with its original meaning all effaced —Havelock Ellis⟩ — **over the counter** *adv* **:** in or through a broker's office rather than through a stock exchange ⟨bought stock *over the counter*⟩ — **under the counter** *adv* **:** in a stealthy or surreptitious manner **:** illicitly and privately **:** according to an arrangement that does not apply to a total clientele

²count·er \ˈ"\ *n* -s [ME *countere, countour*, fr. MF *conteor*, fr. *conter* to count + *-eor* -or — more at COUNT] **:** one that counts: as **a :** a worker who counts units of materials in process or finished products for purposes of inspection, record keeping, or distribution **b :** one that counts votes **c :** SPEED COUNTER **d** (1) **:** an instrument for recording the number of repetitions of an operation (as the revolution of a shaft) or of things produced (as copies printed on a printing press) (2) **:** a device, unit, or circuit in a business machine (as a cash register or bookkeeping machine) that automatically performs certain mathematical operations and records the results (as the automatic totaling of certain classes of figures entered in the machine or the counting of certain classes of operations performed on the machine) **e :** a device for detecting the passage of ionizing particles whose presence is recorded in the form of electrical impulses **f :** CLASSIFIER 2

³coun·ter \ˈ"\ *vb* -ED/-ING/-S [ME *countren*, partly short for *encountren* to encounter, partly fr. MF *contre* against, contrary — more at ENCOUNTER] *vt* **1 a :** to act or operate in opposition to **:** argue against **:** contend with or against **:** OPPOSE, COMBAT ⟨~*ing* the claim for damages⟩ **b :** CHECK, OFFSET, NULLIFY ⟨~*ing* the trend towards decentralization⟩ ⟨means to ~ or neutralize an enemy's sea mines and torpedoes —*N. Y. Times*⟩ **2 a :** to fight against **:** encounter in opposition **:** meet in combat ⟨~*ing* the foe valiantly⟩ **b :** to adduce in answer to another's contention ⟨he ~*ed* that his warnings had been ignored⟩ **3** *obs* **:** to perform variations upon (a song or instrumental composition) ~ *vi* **1 :** to meet attacks or arguments step by step with appropriate defensive or retaliatory steps ⟨~*ing* with surprise sallies against the besiegers⟩ ⟨~*ing* with appeals to other authorities⟩ **2 :** to deliver a blow while receiving or parrying one (as in boxing) ⟨he ~*ed* with his left⟩ **3 :** to sing a counter or accompanying voice part to a principal melody

⁴coun·ter \ˈ"\ *adv* [ME *countre*, fr. MF *contre*, fr. L *contra* against, fr. OL *com* with (whence L *cum*) + *-tra* (comparative suffix) — more at COM-] **1 :** in a direction contrary to the true or indicated course; *esp, of hounds* **:** so as to follow a trail in the wrong direction **2 :** in a contrary or opposite trend or direction **:** to a different and esp. a contrary or antagonistic result or effect — often used with *go* or *run* ⟨moral obligations or interests which persistently go ~ to our general pleasure-seeking tendencies —Joseph Margolis⟩

⁵coun·ter \ˈ"\ *n* -s [⁴,⁶*counter*] **1 :** the direction opposite to that taken by the game in hunting ⟨the hounds taking the ~⟩ **2 :** the after portion of a boat from the waterline to the extreme outward swell or stern overhang — see SHIP illustration **3 :** the breast of a horse **4** [It *contro*, fr. *contro*, prep., against, var. of *contra*, fr. L] **a :** a circular parry in fencing in which the blade follows that of the opponent and meets it again where the former engagement was, diverting the point **b :** the act of giving a blow when receiving or parrying one (as in boxing); *also* **:** the blow so given **c :** a second diagonal tension member commonly having a turnbuckle and provided in certain panels of a truss where the stress in the main diagonal is subject to reversal under change of load **5** [short for *counterfort*] **:** a stiffener of leather, fiber, or other material shaped and skived to a soft edge and intended to give permanent form to a boot or shoe upper around the heel

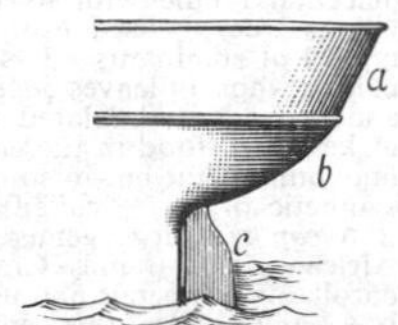

a stern, *b* counter, *c* rudder

6 [by shortening] : COUNTERTENOR **7** : CONTRARY, OPPOSITE ⟨promising the ~⟩ ⟨believing the ~ of what was said⟩ **8** : an agency, move, or force that offsets, checks, neutralizes, or otherwise acts in opposition : ANSWER, REJOINDER, PARRY, CHECK, DEFENSE ⟨this salutary ~ to the baleful influence of our philosophical extremists —J.A.Mourant⟩ ⟨the dramatic ~ to an unexpected thrust —E.M.Lustgarten⟩ ⟨a football formation used as a ~ to an overshifted defense⟩ **9 a** : CROSS LODE **b** [by shortening] : COUNTERSHAFT **c** [by shortening] : COUNTERSEAL **10 a** : any of the areas in the faces of printing type that are less than type high and enclosed by the strokes of the letter — see TYPE illustration **b** : the matching counterpart of a die (sense 6h(1)), usu. of softer and less permanent material — called also *force* **11** : a 3-lobed school skating figure performed on either edge and either forward or backward in which the skater executes a turn at each junction of the three lobes against the natural rotation of the curve being skated and remains on the same edge throughout — compare ROCKER

6coun·ter \"\ *adj* [4*counter*] **1** : marked by or tending toward an opposite direction, motion, or effect : OPPOSED, CONTRARY: **a** : moving in an opposite direction ⟨a ship slowed down by ~ tides⟩ **b** : serving to answer, check, offset, or challenge the action of another (as an opponent) : RETALIATORY ⟨a sally of the tongue may invite a ~ sally of the fists —V.L.Parrington⟩ ⟨the westward expansion of the southern slave power in search of unexhausted land, or the ~ expansion of the free-soil movement —Ellen Semple⟩ **c** : given to or marked by opposition, hostility, or antipathy ⟨from being current with his times and his fellow men he seemed to become ~ —H.S. Canby⟩ **d** : situated opposite : lying opposite ⟨and clambered halfway up the ~ side —Alfred Tennyson⟩ **e** : NULLIFYING, COUNTERMANDING ⟨~ orders from the colonel⟩ **2** : duplicate and serving as a tally or check ⟨a ~ list⟩ **syn** see ADVERSE

7coun·ter \"\ *vt* -ED/-ING/-S [5*counter*] : to furnish with a counter ⟨~*ing* a shoe⟩

counter- *prefix* [ME *countre-*, fr. MF *contre-*, *contre* — more at COUNTER (adv.)] **1 a** : contrary : opposite : adverse ⟨*counter*current⟩ ⟨*counter*order⟩ **b** : opposing : retaliatory : answering ⟨*counter*blow⟩ ⟨*counter*weapon⟩ **2** : complementary : corresponding : alternate ⟨*counter*weight⟩ ⟨*counter*part⟩ ⟨*counter*theme⟩ **3** : duplicate : substitute ⟨*counter*foil⟩

coun·ter·act \ˌkau̇ntəˈrakt\ *vt* -ED/-ING/-S [*counter-* + *act*] : to act in opposition to : make ineffective by opposite force : mitigate ill effects of : CHECK, OFFSET, NEUTRALIZE, NULLIFY ⟨the spontaneous physiological processes which ~ disease before medical science comes into play —Havelock Ellis⟩ **syn** see NEUTRALIZE

coun·ter·ac·tant \-tənt, -tᵊnt\ *adj* : COUNTERACTING

coun·ter·act·ing·ly *adv* : in a counteracting manner

coun·ter·action \ˈkau̇ntər+\ *n* -S **1** : contrary action : OPPOSITION, RESISTANCE ⟨scheming ~⟩ **2** : act or action of counteracting : a counteracting agency ⟨the ~ of centripetal forces on centrifugal tendencies⟩

1coun·ter·active \"+\ *adj* [*counteract* + *-ive*] : tending to counteract **syn** see ADVERSE

2counteractive \"\ *n* -S : a counteractive agency

coun·ter·agent \ˈkau̇ntər+,-\ *n* [*counter-* + *agent*] : one that counteracts

coun·ter·approach \"+\ *n* [trans. of F *contre-approches*] : approaches (sense 4b) advanced from defensive works to meet hostile approaches

1coun·ter·arch \"+\ *n* [*counter-* + *arch*] : an opposite and strengthening arch

2counterarch \ˌkau̇ntər+\ *vt* : to supply with a counterarch

counterargument \"+\ *n* [*counter-* + *argument*] : an opposing or answering argument

1coun·ter·attack \ˈkau̇ntər+\ *n* [*counter-* + *attack*] **1** : an attack against an enemy attacking force usu. with limited tactical objectives (as to regain a key position) — compare COUNTEROFFENSIVE **2** : an aggressive action in defense : an attack on one attacking ⟨a ~ on his detractors⟩

2counterattack \ˌ==+\ *vi* : to make a counterattack : attack in reprisal or retaliation ⟨the defenders have ~*ed* with the charges that the critics themselves are fascist —Paul Woodring⟩ ~ *vt* : to make a counterattack against

1coun·ter·balance \ˈkau̇ntə(r)+\ *n* [*counter-* + *balance*] **1** : a weight that balances another : COUNTERPOISE **2** : an agency, force, or power that balances, offsets, checks, or neutralizes an opposing force ⟨his chary caution serving as a ~ to her impetuousness⟩

A counterbalance of locomotive driving wheel

2counterbalance \ˌ==+\ *vt* **1** : to serve as a counterbalance to : oppose with an equal weight : BALANCE, COUNTERPOISE, COUNTERVAIL ⟨the inward thrust is *counterbalanced* by the outer⟩ **2** : to oppose with equal force or significance : CHECK, OFFSET, NEUTRALIZE, BALANCE, COMPENSATE ⟨those two opposite causes seem to ~ one another —Adam Smith⟩ **3** : to equip with counterbalances ⟨two *counterbalanced* cable cars⟩

counterbalanced window *n* : a double-hung window in which the upper and lower sashes are so connected that they balance

coun·ter·battery \ˈkau̇ntə(r)+\ *n* [trans. of MF *contre-batterie*] : artillery fire directed against enemy artillery ⟨guns assigned to a ~ mission⟩

coun·ter·blast \"+\ *n* [*counter-* + *blast*] : a check, offset, balance, or counteraction marked by strength, vigor, explosiveness, and lack of restraint ⟨the secretary's tirade drew a ~ from the opposition leader⟩

coun·ter·blow \"+\ *n* [*counter-* + *blow*] : a return blow : a reprisal measure : RETALIATION ⟨the ~ delivered against the aggressor —*Soviet Russia Today*⟩

1coun·ter·bore \ˌkau̇ntə(r)+\ *vt* [*counter-* + *bore*] : to form a counterbore in : enlarge (part of a hole) by means of a counterbore

2counterbore \ˈ==+,-\ *n* **1** : a flat-bottomed enlargement of the mouth of a cylindrical bore **2** : a drill for making a counterbore — compare COUNTERSINK

count·er·boy \ˈkau̇ntə(r)+,-\ *n* [1*counter* + *boy*] : a boy who does the work of a counterman

1coun·ter·brace \ˈkau̇ntə(r)+,-\ *n* [*counter-* + *brace*] : a brace counteracting the strain of another brace: **a** : the brace of the fore-topsail on the leeward side of a ship **b** : 5COUNTER 4c

2counterbrace \ˌ==+\ *vb* [*counter-* + *brace*] : to brace in opposite directions ⟨~ a ship's yards⟩; *also* : to brace so that opposite stresses are resisted

coun·ter·brand \ˈkau̇ntə(r)+,-\ *n* [*counter-* + *brand*] : a brand put on cattle to supersede a previous brand

1counterbuff *n* [*counter-* + *buff*] *obs* : COUNTERBLOW, REBUFF

2counterbuff *vt*, *archaic* : to strike back at : REBUFF

counter card *n* [1*counter*] : an advertising placard for use on or in a store counter

countercast *n* -S [*counter-* + *cast*] *obs* : an antagonistic trick or artifice

countercaster *n* -S [1*counter* (piece used in keeping account) + *caster*] *obs* : a reckoner of accounts : BOOKKEEPER

coun·ter·cathexis \ˌkau̇ntə(r)+\ *n*, *pl* **countercathexes** [*counter-* + *cathexis*] : the act by the ego of blocking from consciousness objectionable notions and impulses of the id

1coun·ter·change \ˈ==+,-\ *n* [part trans. of MF *contrechange*, fr. *contre-* counter- + *change* exchange change — more at CHANGE] **1** *obs* : EXCHANGE, RECIPROCATION, ALTERNATION **2** : the contrast of a dark area against a light ground with a light area against a dark ground in a painting

2counterchange \ˌ==+\ *vt* [part trans. of MF *contrechanger*, fr. *contrechange*, n.] **1** : to cause to change places or characteristics : SHIFT, TRANSPOSE **2** : to make checkered (as with contrasting colors) ⟨elms that ~ the floor of this flat lawn with dusk and bright —Alfred Tennyson⟩ **3** *heraldry* **a** : to depict (charges or a charge borne on a party or varied field) in the tincture of the opposite part of the field from that on which each charge or each part of a charge lies **b** : to reverse the two tinctures of (a varied field) on the opposite sides of a line of partition

counterchanged *adj* **1** *heraldry* : each one or each part having the tincture of the opposite portion of the field — used of charges or a charge borne so as to lie on both tinctures of a party or varied field **2** *heraldry* : having the two tinctures reversed on the opposite sides of a line of partition — used of a varied field

1coun·ter·charge \ˌkau̇ntə(r)+\ *vt* [*counter-* + *charge*] : to charge in opposition, contradiction, or reply

2countercharge \ˈ==+,-\ *n* : an opposing or retaliatory charge

1coun·ter·check \ˈkau̇ntə(r)+,-\ *n* [*counter-* + *check* (n.)] **1** *obs* : a rebuke in answer to another **2** : a check or restraint often operating against something that itself exercises a restraining force

2countercheck \ˌ==+\ *vt* [*counter-* + *check* (v.)] **1** : CHECK, COUNTERACT **2** : to check a second time for verification

counter check *n* [1*counter*] : a blank check obtainable at a bank esp. to be cashed only at the bank by the drawer

1coun·ter·claim \ˈkau̇ntə(r)+\ *n* [*counter-* + *claim* (n.)] : an opposing claim; *esp* : a law claim of matter constituting a distinct cause of action made by a defendant in an action as an offset to a claim made on him and distinct from his defense, being in effect a distinct action that is sometimes allowed to be brought in order to reduce amount and cost of litigation

2counterclaim \ˌ==+\ *vb* [*counter-* + *claim* (v.)] *vi* : to enter or plead a counterclaim ~ *vt* : to ask in a counterclaim

1coun·ter·clockwise \ˌkau̇ntə(r)+\ *adv* [*counter-* + *clockwise*] : in a direction opposite to that in which the hands of a clock rotate : from horizontal left down or nearer and then upwards to horizontal right — opposed to *clockwise*

2counterclockwise \"\ *adj* : moving or directed counterclockwise : LEFTHANDED, LEVOROTATORY

coun·ter·colored \ˌkau̇ntə(r)+\ *adj* [*counter-* + *colored*] *heraldry* : COUNTERCHANGED

coun·ter·com·po·ny \ˌkau̇ntə(r)kəmˌpōnē\ *adj* [trans. of F *contre-componé*] *heraldry* : composed of a double row of small squares of alternating tinctures

coun·ter·couchant \"+\ *adj* [*counter-* + *couchant*] *heraldry* : couchant with heads in opposite directions

coun·ter·courant \"+\ *adj* [*counter-* + *courant*] *heraldry* : running in opposite directions ⟨two stags ~⟩

coun·ter·cry \ˈkau̇ntə(r) +,-\ *n* [*counter-* + *cry*] : an answering cry ⟨cries of "Espionage" and *countercries* of "Nonsense" —*Time*⟩

1coun·ter·current \ˈkau̇ntə(r) +,-\ *n* [*counter-* + *current* (n.)] : a current flowing in a direction opposite to that of another one ⟨an oceanic ~⟩

2countercurrent \ˌ==+\ *adj* [*counter-* + *current* (adj.)] **1** : flowing in an opposite direction **2** : involving flow of materials in opposite directions ⟨acetylene dissolved by ~ treatment with water⟩

3countercurrent \ˌ==+\ *or* **coun·ter·currently** \"+\ *adv* : in a direction opposite to that in which something else is flowing ⟨a gas passed ~ to a fluid running through a tube⟩

coun·ter·cyclical \ˌkau̇ntə(r)+\ *adj* [*counter-* + *cyclical*] : calculated to check excessive developments in a business cycle : COMPENSATORY ⟨~ budget policies of the government⟩

coun·ter·dike \ˈ==+,-\ *n* [*counter-* + *dike*] : a second or reserve dike

1coun·ter·disengage \ˌ==+\ *vi* [*counter-* + *disengage*] *fencing* : to disengage into the previous line and at the moment when one's adversary disengages — **coun·ter·disengagement** \"+\ *n* -S

2coun·ter·disengage \ˈkau̇ntə(r)+\ *n* : the act of counter-disengaging

coun·ter·earth \ˈkau̇ntər+,-\ *n* [*counter-* + *earth;* trans. of Gk *antichthōn*] : a planet supposed in Pythagoreanism to accompany the earth in its revolutions and to shield it from the fire at the center of the universe

countered *past of* COUNTER

counter electromotive force *n* [6*counter*] : the electromotive force that develops in some circuits from chemical or magnetic effects of the current and that opposes the impressed electromotive force producing the current — called also *back electromotive force*

coun·ter·embattled \ˌkau̇ntər+\ *adj* [*counter-* + *embattled*] *heraldry* : embattled on opposite sides with the battlement or merlon on one side opposed to the embrasure on the other

coun·ter·embowed \"+\ *adj* [*counter-* + *embowed*] *heraldry* : bent or curved one to the dexter and the other to the sinister

1coun·ter·enamel \ˈkau̇ntər+\ *n* [*counter-* + *enamel* (n.); trans. of F *contre-émail*] : enamel on the reverse side of an enameled plate, plaque, or shield

2counterenamel \ˌ==+\ *vt* [*counter-* + *enamel* (v.); trans. of F *contre-émailler*] : to enamel on the reverse side

coun·ter·espionage \ˌkau̇ntər+\ *n* [*counter-* + *espionage;* part trans. of F *contre-espionnage*] : the activity concerned with the discovery and defeat of enemy espionage

1coun·ter·etch \ˌkau̇ntər+\ *vt* [*counter-* + *etch*] : to clean (a lithographic plate) with dilute acid solution

2counteretch \ˈ==+,-\ *n* : the cleaning (as of a lithographic plate) by counteretching; *also* : the solution used for such cleaning

coun·ter·exposition \ˌkau̇ntər+\ *n* [*counter-* + *exposition*] : a secondary exposition of a musical fugue with the subject and answer usu. in reverse order

1coun·ter·factual \ˌkau̇ntə(r)+\ *adj* [*counter-* + *factual*] : contrary to fact — **coun·ter·factually** \"+\ *adv*

2counterfactual \"+\ *n* -S : a logical conditional whose antecedent is or is presumed to be contrary to fact (as *if he had come*)

coun·ter·faller \ˈkau̇ntə(r)+,-\ *n* -S [*counter-* + *faller*] : a wire in a spinning mule that lifts the yarn when it is not depressed by a faller so as to keep tension uniform

counterfeisance *n* -S [part trans. of MF *contrefaisance*, fr. *contrefaisant*, pres. part. of *contrefaire* to imitate — more at COUNTERFEIT] *obs* : COUNTERFEITING, IMPOSTURE

1coun·ter·feit \ˈkau̇ntə(r)ˌfit, *usu* -id·+V; *Brit also* -ˌfēt\ *vb* -ED/-ING/-S [ME *countrefeten*, fr. MF *contrefait*, past part.] *vt* **1** *obs* : IMPERSONATE **2** : to put on the false appearance of : FEIGN, SIMULATE ⟨~ sorrow and mask inward glee⟩ **3 a** : to endeavor or succeed in having the appearance or characteristics of without attempt to deceive or delude : IMITATE, COPY ⟨fiction that seeks to ~ reality —Bernard De Voto⟩ **b** : to imitate fraudulently : copy with intent to deceive : make a fraudulent copy or replica of (something of value, as a coin, bill, note, or signature) ⟨a gang ~*ing* $50 bills⟩ **4 a** *archaic* : to use as a model : seek to imitate : EMULATE **b** *obs* : to cause to have a false or misleading appearance : DISGUISE ~ *vi* **1** : to try to deceive by pretending or dissembling : SIMULATE, FEIGN **2** : to practice counterfeiting of valuables ⟨held on charges of ~*ing*⟩ **syn** see ASSUME

2counterfeit \"\ *adj* [ME *countrefet*, fr. MF *contrefait*, past part. of *contrefaire* to imitate, draw, paint, fr. *contre-* counter- + *faire* to make, fr. L *facere* — more at DO] **1 a** : SPURIOUS : not genuine or authentic; *esp* : not composed by the author indicated or under the circumstances ascribed ⟨a ~ gospel rejected as apocryphal⟩ **b** : made in fraudulent imitation : produced with intent to deceive : FORGED ⟨a ~ diamond made of paste⟩; *esp* : made fraudulently in imitation of a government issue ⟨a ~ stamp⟩ ⟨a ~ bill⟩ **2 a** : FEIGNED : assumed with calculation to mislead ⟨a ~ joy at her friend's engagement⟩ **b** : marked by false pretense : SHAM, PRETENDED ⟨an impostor, a ~ prince⟩ **3** *archaic* : represented in a picture or by means of a picture : PORTRAYED ⟨look here upon this picture and on this, the ~ presentment of two brothers —Shak.⟩

syn SPURIOUS, BOGUS, FAKE, SHAM, PSEUDO, PINCHBECK, PHONY: COUNTERFEIT applies to something made or fabricated in quite close imitation of something else, esp. to something genuine or original and with intent to deceive ⟨a *counterfeit* coin⟩ ⟨a *counterfeit* passport⟩ ⟨the austere word of genuine religion is: save your soul! The degenerate counsel of a *counterfeit* religion is: salve your soul! —W.L.Sullivan⟩ SPURIOUS applies to what is not genuine, authentic, or true without necessarily implying fraudulent purpose or deceiving imitation ⟨the French look on us English monk-made knights as *spurious* and adulterine, unworthy of the name of knight —Charles Kingsley⟩ ⟨it is certain that the letter, attributed to him, directing that no Christian should be punished for being a Christian, is *spurious* —Matthew Arnold⟩ BOGUS is likely to imply fraud, imposture, or deception, sometimes self-deception ⟨in red cambric and *bogus* ermine, as some kind of king —Mark Twain⟩ ⟨*bogus* naturalization of immigrants and repeating at elections were now carried to hitherto unknown lengths —A.F.Harlow⟩ ⟨nostalgia can be the trickiest of maladies. It invests the past with *bogus* glamour —W.C. Richards⟩ FAKE implies a false fabrication or fraudulent manipulation ⟨a *fake* ruby⟩ ⟨a *fake* cure-all⟩ ⟨another source of quick money was selling life memberships in *fake* yacht clubs —Alva Johnston⟩ ⟨any Americans who cling to illusions about communism and its *fake* Utopia—A.E.Stevenson b.1900⟩ SHAM may suggest thinness and obviousness of the disguise, naiveté of the deception, or lack of intent to imitate exactly ⟨a garden adorned with *sham* ruins and statues —L.P.Smith⟩ ⟨he [Euripides] looked at war and he saw through all the *sham* glory to the awful evil beneath —Edith Hamilton⟩ ⟨not one officer among them whose experience of war extended beyond a drill on muster day and the *sham* fight that closed the performance —Francis Parkman⟩ PSEUDO (often appearing as a combining form) may apply to either pretentious, spurious imitation or to imitation to deceive ⟨the cottage seemed very small and horribly 'arty-crafty'. 'Everything looks so *pseudo*,' said Lucy —Frances Towers⟩ ⟨those democrats who wholeheartedly are democrats and not *pseudo*-democrats —*Fortnightly*⟩ ⟨these *pseudo*-evangelists pretended to inspiration —Thomas Jefferson⟩ PINCHBECK may apply to a cheap imitation, often to a poor copy of something costly or grand ⟨*pinchbeck* imitations of the glory of ancient Rome —*Manchester Guardian Weekly*⟩ ⟨greater numbers could afford the *pinchbeck* splendor of organizations like the Colonial Order of the Crown —J.D.Hart⟩ PHONY, more forceful than most in this group, stigmatizes anything spurious ⟨the *phony* aura of romance which travel bureaus are wont to attach to the West Indies —Gladwin Hill⟩ ⟨the Germans were deceiving us at that very moment with a *phony* show of strength —F.E.Fox⟩

3counterfeit \"\ *n* -S [ME *countrefet*, fr. *countrefet*, adj.] **1 a** : an imitation or replica markedly close or faithful to an original and typically made to deceive for gain ⟨the $10 bill turned out to be a ~⟩ **b** : a close approximation likely to be confused with reality or with the genuine ⟨that temporary ~ of fame which is publicity —Irwin Edman⟩ **2** *archaic* : a representation, counterpart, or picture : an art work closely similar to its subject ⟨fair Portia's ~ —Shak.⟩ **3** *archaic* : PRETENDER, IMPOSTOR **syn** see IMPOSTURE

coun·ter·feit·er \-ˌfid·ə(r), -fitə-, -fētə-\ *n* -S [ME *countrefetere*, fr. *countrefeten* + *-ere* -er] : one that forges or makes fraudulent imitations of current money; *also* : one that copies or imitates with either good or bad intent

coun·ter·feit·ly *adv* : in a counterfeit manner : by use of counterfeits

coun·ter·feit·ness *n* -ES : the quality or state of being counterfeit

coun·ter·flashing \ˈkau̇ntə(r) +,-\ *n* [*counter-* + *flashing* (metal strips)] : a strip of sheet metal in the form of an inverted L built into a vertical wall of masonry and bent down over the flashing to make it watertight

coun·ter·flood \ˌ== +\ *vt* [*counter-* + *flood*] : to flood compartments in (a ship) to counterbalance listing and loss of trim resulting esp. from already flooded compartments

coun·ter·flory *also* **coun·ter·fleury** \ˈ== +\ *adj* [part trans. of MF *contrefleuri*, fr. *contre-* counter- + *fleuri* fleury — more at FLEURY] *heraldry* : flory on opposite sides so that the middles of the flowers are apparently covered by a part of the charge — used of an ordinary

coun·ter·flow \" +,-\ *n* [*counter-* + *flow*] : flow in opposite directions or the opposite direction — used esp. of fluids in adjacent parts of an apparatus (as a heat exchanger)

coun·ter·foil \ˈkau̇ntə(r) +,-\ *n* -S [*counter-* + *foil*] : a form giving main particulars of something treated in more detail on another and detachable form : a detachable stub usu. serving as a record or receipt (as on a check or ticket)

coun·ter·force \" +,-\ *n* [*counter-* + *force*] : a force, power, activity, or trend that opposes or counters another

coun·ter·fort \" +,-\ *n* -S [part trans. of MF *contrefort*, fr. *contre-* counter- + *fort* strength, force, fr. *fort*, adj., strong — more at FORT] : a buttress built against or integral with a wall (as a retaining wall or dam) but on the back or thrust-receiving side

coun·ter·fugue \" +,-\ *n* [trans. of F *contre-fugue*] : a fugue in which the answer is an inverted imitation of the subject

coun·ter·gambit \"+,-\ *n* [*counter-* + *gambit*] : a chess gambit offered by the second player

counter game *n* [1*counter*] : any of various games usu. played with dice on a store counter in which a customer attempts to win a prize

coun·ter·gauge *or* **coun·ter·gage** \ˈkau̇ntə(r)+,-\ *n* [*counter-* + *gauge*, *gage*] : an adjustable gauge with double points for transferring measurements from one piece of lumber to another

count·er·girl \"+,-\ *n* [1*counter-* + *girl*] : a girl counterman

coun·ter·glow \"+,-\ *n* [*counter-* + *glow;* trans. of G *gegenschein*] : GEGENSCHEIN

coun·ter·guard \"+,-\ *n* [part trans. of MF *contre-garde*, fr. *contre-* counter- + *garde* guard, fr. OF *guarde* — more at GUARD] : an outwork protecting from a breaching fire the faces of a bastion, ravelin, or similar work

counter hoop *n* [6*counter*] : the outer hoop that clamps and tightens a drumhead

countering *pres part of* COUNTER

coun·ter·intelligence \ˌkau̇ntər+\ *n* [*counter-* + *intelligence*] : organized activity of an intelligence service designed to block an enemy's sources of information by concealment, camouflage, censorship, and other measures, to deceive the enemy by ruses and misinformation, to prevent sabotage, and to gather political and military information

coun·ter·ion \ˈ==+,-\ *n* [*counter-* + *ion*] : an ion having a charge opposite to that of the substance with which it is associated (as in an electric double layer)

1coun·ter·irritant \ˈ==+,-\ *n* [*counter-* + *irritant*] : an agent applied locally to produce superficial inflammation with the object of reducing inflammation in deeper adjacent structures (as a mustard plaster applied to the chest in bronchitis); *broadly* : an additional irritation or discomfort that diverts attention from another

2counterirritant \"\ *adj* : having the properties of a counterirritant : dealing with or marked by counterirritants

coun·ter·irritate \ˈkau̇ntər +,-\ *vt* [*counter-* + *irritate*] : to irritate as an offset to adjacent inflammation : treat with counterirritants — **coun·ter·irritation** \"+,-\ *n*

count·er·jumper \ˈkau̇ntə(r) +,-\ *n* [1*counter* + *jumper*] : a store clerk

1coun·ter·lath \"+,-\ *n* [*counter-* + *lath*] **1** : a batten laid lengthwise between two rafters to afford a bearing for laths laid crosswise **2** : any lath laid without actual measurement between two gauged laths **3** : any of a series of laths nailed to the timbers to raise the sheet lathing above their surface to afford a key for plastering **4** : one of many laths used in preparing one side of a partition or framed wall when the other side has been covered in and finished

2counterlath \"\ *vt* : to furnish with counterlaths

coun·ter·lode \ˈkau̇ntə(r) +,-\ *n* [*counter-* + *lode*] : CROSS LODE

count·er·man \ˈkau̇ntə(r)ˌman, -ˌmaa(ə)n *also* -mən\ *n*, *pl* **countermen** [1*counter* + *man*] **1** : one that tends a counter; *specif* : one that serves food over the counter of a cafeteria or lunchroom **2** : a marker in a laundry or cleaning and dyeing establishment **3** : one that sells or directs the sale of automobile parts; *sometimes* : a manufacturer's representative **4** : a clerk in charge of stockroom supplies

1coun·ter·mand \ˈkau̇ntə(r)ˌmand, -ˌmaa(ə)nd, -ˌmänd, ˌ==ˈ=\ *vt* -ED/-ING/-S [ME *countermaunden*, fr. MF *contremander*, fr. *contre-* counter- + *mander* to command, fr. L *mandare* — more at MANDATE] **1** : to revoke (a former command) : cancel or rescind (an order) by giving a contrary order ⟨~ an order for goods⟩ **2** : to recall or order back by a superseding contrary order ⟨~ reinforcements⟩ **3** : to stop or prohibit by revoking an order or issuing a contrary order ⟨~ a payment⟩ **4** *obs* **a** : to oppose or go counter to a command of **b** : FRUSTRATE, COUNTERACT

²**countermand** \"\ *n* -s [part trans. of MF *contremand*, fr. *contremander*] : a contrary order : revocation of an order or command; *specif* : a legal revoking order or act ⟨halting and retreating according to the ~ of the first orders⟩

¹**coun·ter·march** \ˈkau̇ntə(r)+ˌ-\ *n* [*counter-* + *march* (n.)] : a marching back; *specif* : a march by troops back over ground recently passed over : an evolution by which a unit reverses direction while marching but keeps the same order

²**countermarch** \ˌ==+\ *vi* [*counter-* + *march* (v.)] : to march back; *specif* : execute a countermarch

¹**coun·ter·mark** \ˈ==+ˌ-\ *n* [trans. of MF *contremarque*] **1** : an added mark designed to secure greater safety or more complete identification: **a** : a mark put on a package of goods belonging to several persons to show that it may not be opened except in the presence of all **b** : a hallmark added to that of the artificier of gold or silver work **2** : an artificial cavity formerly made in the teeth of horses to disguise their age — compare ³BISHOP **3 a** : a mark on a coin that is not part of the original design but that has been added as indication of a change in the coin's value, in its issuing authority, or in its country of circulation **b** : a mark on a coin added as attestation of purity or standard value : CHOP MARK

²**countermark** \ˌ==+\ *vt* [trans. of F *contremarquer*] : to apply a countermark to ⟨~ silverware⟩

coun·ter·measure \ˈ==+ˌ-\ *n* [*counter-* + *measure*] : a measure, means, or expedient calculated to counter, check, or offset another

coun·ter·melody \"+ˌ-\ *n* [*counter-* + *melody*] : a secondary melody sounded or to be sounded simultaneously with the principal one

coun·ter–memorial \ˌkau̇ntə(r)+\ *n* [*counter-* + *memorial*] : an answer admitting, denying, or commenting on charges in a memorial in international law

¹**coun·ter·mine** \ˈ==+ˌ-\ *n* [*counter-* + *mine* (subterranean passage)] **1** : a tunnel for intercepting an enemy mine **2** : a stratagem for defeating an attack : COUNTERPLOT

²**countermine** \ˌ==+\ *vt* **1** : to frustrate or combat by secret measures ⟨know exactly the play of another in order to ~ him —Henry Fielding⟩ **2** : to oppose by means of a countermine : intercept with a countermine : destroy (a laid mine or a minefield) with an explosion ~ *vi* : to make or lay down countermines

coun·ter·mortar \"+\ *adj* [*counter-* + *mortar*] : directed against enemy mortars ⟨~ fire⟩

coun·ter·move \ˈkau̇ntə(r)+ˌ-\ *n* [*counter-* + *move*] : an action designed to check, offset, or counter another

coun·ter·movement \"+ˌ-\ *n* [*counter-* + *movement*] : a movement in an opposite direction

¹**coun·ter·mure** \ˈkau̇ntə(r)+ˌ-\ *n* [alter. of earlier *contremeur*, fr. MF *contremur*, fr. *contre-* counter- + *mur* wall — more at MURE] **1** : a second or supplementary wall : a wall raised behind another that might be breached **2** : a wall raised by besiegers confronting a besieged place

²**countermure** \ˌ==+\ *vt* -ED/-ING/-S : to protect or fortify with a countermure

coun·ter·naiant \"+\ *adj* [*counter-* + *naiant*] *heraldry* : swimming in opposite directions

coun·ter·offensive \ˈkau̇ntər+\ *n* [*counter-* + *offensive*] : a military offensive operation that is undertaken by a defending force on a large scale and usu. embodies a general shift from defense to attack with important objectives (as the destruction of the enemy's forces) — compare COUNTERATTACK

coun·ter·opening \" + ˌ-\ *n* [*counter-* + *opening*] : an aperture on the opposite side or in a different place; *specif* : a surgical opening made opposite another to facilitate drainage (as of an abscess)

coun·ter·order \" + ˌ-\ *n* [*counter-* + *order*] : a contradicting or countermanding order

counterpace *n* [*counter-* + *pace*] *obs* : COUNTERMOVEMENT

¹**counterpane** *n* -s [ME *contrepane*, fr. *contre-* counter- + *pane, pan* piece, part, piece of cloth, coverlet — more at PANE] *obs* : COUNTERPART

²**coun·ter·pane** \ˈkau̇ntə(r),pān *also chiefly Brit* -ˌpin\ *n* -s [by folk etymology (influence of *pane* coverlet) fr. obs. E *counterpoint*, fr. ME *countrepointe*, by folk etymology (influence of *countre-* counter-) fr. MF *coute pointe*, fr. OF, fr. *coute* quilt + *pointe* (fem. of *point*, past part. of *poindre* to prick, stitch), fr. L *puncta*, fem. of *punctus*, past part. of *pungere* to prick — more at QUILT, PUNGENT] : BEDSPREAD

¹**coun·ter·part** \ˈkau̇ntə(r) + ˌ-\ *n* [*counter-* + *part*] **1** : one of two corresponding copies of a legal instrument (as an indenture) : DUPLICATE **2 a** : a thing that may be applied to another thing so as to fit perfectly (as a seal to its impression) **b** : something that serves to complete or complement : COMPLEMENT ⟨retain export controls . . . only where needed as a ~ of domestic distribution controls —*U.S.Code*⟩ **c** : one playing opposite in a play ⟨Miss Doe as heroine served as an adequate ~ to the lead role⟩ **3 a** : one remarkably similar to another : a person or thing so like another that it seems a duplicate ⟨mistook a feverish flush as the ~ of healthy color⟩ **b** : EQUIVALENT : something or someone having the same use, role, or characteristics often in a different sphere or period ⟨metal knives and axes came into use promptly, replacing their stone ~*s* —E.H.Spicer⟩ ⟨such laws in psychology he thought to be the ~ of the laws of mechanics in physics —S.F.Mason⟩

²**counterpart** \"\ *adj* : of or relating to a fund set up by a nation receiving economic aid from another, the fund being in the currency of the former and its amount being equal to the value of the goods and services received ⟨~ funds⟩ ⟨~ francs⟩

coun·ter·passant \ˌkau̇ntə(r)+\ *adj* [part trans. of F *contre-passant*, fr. *contre-* counter- + *passant* — more at PASSANT] *heraldry* : passant in opposite directions ⟨two lions ~⟩

coun·ter·plan \ˈ== + ˌ-\ *n* [*counter-* + *plan*] : a plan countering another : an alternate or substitute plan

coun·ter·plea \" + ˌ-\ *n* [*counter-* + *plea*] : a replication to a legal plea : an answering plea

¹**coun·ter·plot** \" + ˌ-\ *vb* [*counter-* + *plot* (v.)] *vi* : to plot against one that has given himself to plotting : INTRIGUE ~ *vt* : to intrigue against (a plotter) : contend against or foil with plots ⟨~ the wily courtiers⟩

²**counterplot** \"\ *n* [*counter-* + *plot* (n.)] : a plot or artifice opposed to another

¹**coun·ter·point** \ˈkau̇ntə(r) + ˌ-\ *n, often attrib* [earlier *conterpoint*, fr. MF *contrepoint*, fr. *contre-* counter- + *point* dot, musical note — more at POINT] **1 a** : one or more independent melodies added as accompaniment to a primary melody (as the cantus firmus) **b** : the combination of two or more related but independent melodies into a single harmonic texture in which each retains its linear or horizontal character **c** : melodic part writing : POLYPHONY — see DOUBLE COUNTERPOINT, QUADRUPLE COUNTERPOINT, SINGLE COUNTERPOINT, TRIPLE COUNTERPOINT **2 a** : a foil or contrasting element : a matching, complementing, or contrasting item : OPPOSITE, ANTITHESIS ⟨this subtle novelist employs another symbolic situation to serve as ~ to the basic one —Robert Humphrey⟩ **b** : any artistic arrangement or device using significant contrast or interplay of distinguishable elements ⟨the ~ of two interwoven dramatic plots⟩; *specif* : motions in dance juxtaposed rhythmically and visually against the music or against other motions by parts of the body or groups of dancers

²**counterpoint** \"\ *vt* **1 a** : to compose or arrange in counterpoint **b** : to compose in counterpoint rhythm **2** : to set off, emphasize, or enliven by contrast or juxtaposition (as in fiction, film cutting, painting) : set in contrast ⟨a deep streak of conventionality that is ~*ed* by an intense sensuality —C.J. Rolo⟩

counterpoint rhythm *n* : rhythm including so much metrical inversion that the prevailing cadence ceases at times to prevail and so that a complex rhythm results from the concomitance of the basic cadence with its inversion ⟨if . . . reversal is repeated in two feet running . . . it is . . . the superinducing . . . of a new rhythm upon the old . . . [so that] two rhythms are in some measure running at once . . . and this is *counterpoint rhythm* —G.M.Hopkins⟩

¹**coun·ter·poise** \ˌkau̇ntə(r) + \ *vt* [alter. (influenced by *poise*) of ME *countrepesen, counterpeisen*, fr. MF *contrepeser*, fr. *contre-* counter- + *peser* to weigh — more at POISE] **1** : to counteract equally : equal in weight, effect, or power : COMPENSATE, OFFSET ⟨sorrow *counterpoising* happiness at the event⟩ **2 a** : to bring into a condition of equilibrium or stability ⟨all parts of the sphere were nicely *counterpoised*⟩ **b** : to bring into balance by or as if by addition of weight on an opposite side : COUNTERBALANCE ⟨scales in which the weight on one side must be *counterpoised* by a weight in the other —Richard Jefferies⟩ **3** *archaic* : CONSIDER, PONDER; *esp* : to weigh (one consideration) against another — used with *with*

²**counterpoise** \ˈ== +\ *n* [alter. (influenced by *poise*) of ME *countrepeis*, fr. MF *contrepeis, contrepois*, fr. *contre-* counter- + *peis, pois* weight — more at POISE] **1** : a weight acting against another : COUNTERWEIGHT: as **a** : that part of the mechanism in some scales that is suspended from the end of a beam upon which weights are placed to counterbalance load on a platform **b** : any weight used to counterbalance some other part of a scale **2** : an equivalent power : an equal force acting in opposition : COUNTERBALANCE, CHECK ⟨his robust strength was a ~ to the disease⟩ **3** : a state of balance : EQUILIBRIUM ⟨the ~ of day and night⟩ **4** : balance of a horseman in his saddle **5** : a system of wires or other conductors except the ground forming the lower plate of a radio condenser antenna **6** : an earth conductor usu. buried below a transmission line for protection of the line against lightning

coun·ter·poison \" + ˌ-\ *n* [part trans. of MF *contrepoison*, fr. *contre-* counter- + *poison*] **1** *obs* : ANTIDOTE **2** : a poison that counteracts another poison

coun·ter·pole \" + ˌ-\ *n* [*counter-* + *pole*] : an exact opposite

coun·ter·pose \ˌkau̇ntə(r) +\ *vt* [*counter-* + *-pose* (as in *compose*); trans. of L *contraponere*] : to place counter to : juxtapose in opposition, for contrast, or in equilibrium ⟨the view that *counterposed* "formal democracy" to "real democracy" —Sidney Hook⟩ — **coun·ter·position** \" +\ *n*

coun·ter·potent \ˌkau̇ntə(r) +\ *n* [*counter-* + *potent*] : a variety of the heraldic fur potent in which each pane stands head to head or foot to foot with one of the same tincture above or below it

coun·ter·preparation \" +\ *n* [*counter-* + *preparation*] : preparation to meet something being prepared; *specif* : prearranged fire against an enemy that is preparing for attack

coun·ter·pressure \ˈ== + ˌ-\ *n* [*counter-* + *pressure*] : pressure countering that exerted : force in a contrary or reverse direction

coun·ter·proof \" + ˌ-\ *n* [*counter-* + *proof*] : a reversed print taken from an ordinary fresh proof by contact impression and used to study the state of the engraved plate

coun·ter·proposal \ˈkau̇ntə(r) + \ *n* [*counter-* + *proposal*] : a countering proposal : a rejoinder to something proposed

coun·ter·prove \ˌ== +\ *vt* [*counter-* + *prove*] : to take a counterproof of

counter·pull \ˈ== + ˌ-\ *n* [*counter-* + *pull*] : a countering attraction or force

coun·ter·punch \" + ˌ-\ *n* [*counter-* + *punch*] **1** : a support beneath metal being hammered or punched from above **2** : a punch in boxing thrown after an opponent's lead; *broadly* : any countering blow or attack ⟨the enemy air forces seeking to deliver a ~⟩

coun·ter·puncher \" + ˌ-\ *n* : a boxer who uses the counterpunch as his characteristic style : one that counterattacks

coun·ter·puncture \ˈkau̇ntə(r) + ˌ-\ *n* [*counter-* + *puncture*] : a surgical counteropening

coun·ter·quartered \ˌ== +\ *adj* [*counter-* + *quartered*] *heraldry, of a grand quarter* : divided again into quarters

coun·ter–rampant \" +\ *adj* [*counter-* + *rampant*] *heraldry* : rampant and facing each other — used of two animals ⟨two lions *counter-rampant*, supporting a dexter hand gules⟩; compare COMBATANT

counter rate *n* [¹*counter* + *rate*] : the rate at which a bank makes loans to its regular customers

coun·ter·reaction \ˌkau̇ntə(r) + \ *n* [*counter-* + *reaction*] : a reaction opposing the main action

coun·ter·recoil \" +\ *n* [*counter-* + *recoil*] : the return of an artillery piece to the firing position after recoil

coun·ter·reconnaissance \ˈkau̇ntə(r) +\ *n* [*counter-* + *reconnaissance*] : measures taken to prevent an enemy's reconnaissance

coun·ter·reformation \" +\ *n* [*counter-* + *reformation*; trans. of G *gegenreformation*] : a reformation countering or counteracting another ⟨the *Counter-Reformation* regained much . . . for Roman Catholicism —J.S.Roucek⟩

coun·ter·remonstrant \" +\ *n* [*counter-* + *remonstrant*; trans. of D *contra-remonstrant*] : a remonstrant of an opposing party or movement

coun·ter·revolution \" +\ *n* [*counter-* + *revolution*; trans. of F *contre-révolution*] : a revolution in opposition to a current or earlier revolution

¹**coun·ter·revolutionary** \ˌkau̇ntə(r) +\ *adj* [*counter-* + *revolutionary*] : marked by opposition or antipathy to a current or earlier revolution ⟨arrested for ~ tendencies⟩

²**counterrevolutionary** \"\ *n* : one that abets, encourages, sympathizes with, or takes part in a counterrevolution

coun·ter·revolutionist \ˌkau̇ntə(r) +\ *n* [*counter-* + *revolutionist*] : COUNTERREVOLUTIONARY

coun·ter·riposte \ˈkau̇ntə(r) + ˌ-\ *n* [*counter-* + *riposte*; part trans. of F *contre-riposte*] : a riposte delivered after parrying the adversary's riposte

coun·ter·rotating propeller \ˌ== + . . . -\ *n* [*counter-* + *rotating*] : CONTRAROTATING PROPELLER

coun·ter·rotation \"+\ *n* [*counter-* + *rotation*] : counterclockwise rotation

counters *pl of* COUNTER, *pres 3d sing of* COUNTER

coun·ter·salient \" +\ *adj* [*counter-* + *salient*; trans. of F *contre-saillant*] *heraldry* : leaping in opposite directions

coun·ter·scarp \ˈkau̇ntə(r) + ˌ-\ *n* [part trans. of MF *contrescarpe*, fr. *contre-* counter- + *escarpe* scarp — more at SCARP] : the exterior slope or wall of the ditch in a work of fortification

coun·ter·sea \" + ˌ-\ *n* [*counter-* + *sea*] : a sea running counter to the wind or to another sea

coun·ter·seal \" + ˌ-\ *n* [*counter-* + *seal*] **1** : a seal that is imposed upon the reverse of a main or usu. larger seal **2** : the reverse die of a double seal

coun·ter·secure \ˌkau̇ntə(r) +\ *vt* [*counter-* + *secure*] **1** *of a borrower* : to give a security to (one who has become a bond for the borrower) to protect against default by the borrower **2** : to give additional security to or for

coun·ter·selection \" +\ *n* [*counter-* + *selection*] : selection opposed in its effects to natural selection: as **a** : preservation of the unfit : dysgenic selection (as forced on man by social customs) **b** : selection in plant or animal breeding against a quality undesirable from the point of view of the breeder though likely to be retained in a state of nature ⟨~ against low milk production in cattle⟩

coun·ter·sense \ˈkau̇ntə(r) + ˌ-\ *n* [*counter-* + *sense*; trans. of F *contresens*] : a meaning or interpretation opposed to the original or intended meaning

coun·ter·shading \ˌkau̇ntə(r) +\ *n* [*counter-* + *shading*] : coloration (as of an animal) with parts normally in shadow being light or parts normally illuminated being dark — compare PROTECTIVE COLORATION

coun·ter·shaft \ˈ== + ˌ-\ *n* [*counter-* + *shaft*] **1** : a mechanism used to transmit motion and power from a main driving shaft to an individual machine, typically mounted by hangers on a ceiling, and driven by one belt from the main shaft and in turn driving the machine by another belt **2** : a short shaft in a machine (as an automobile) carrying intermediate gears to transmit motion usu. with change of speed or direction or both from one set of gears to another — **coun·ter·shaft·ing** *n*

¹**coun·ter·sign** \ˈ== + ˌ-\ *n* [*counter-* + *sign* (n.); trans. of F *contresigne*] **1 a** : a special mark for identifying or authenticating : COUNTERMARK **b** : the signature of a secretary or other person to attest authenticity of a paper of writing already signed by another **2** : a sign used in reply to another; *specif* : a military secret signal (as a word or phrase) that must be given by anyone wishing to pass

²**coun·ter·sign** \ˈ== +ˌ\ *vt* [*counter-* + *sign* (v.); trans. of F *contresigner*] **1** : to add one's signature to (a document) after another's to attest authenticity **2** : CONFIRM, CORROBORATE, SANCTION

coun·ter·signature \" +\ *n* [fr. ²*countersign*, after such pairs as E *sign: signature*] : the signature of one that countersigns

¹**coun·ter·sink** \ˈ== +\ *vt* **countersunk** \"+ˌsəŋk\ **countersunk; countersinking; countersinks** [*counter-* + *sink*] **1** : to make a countersink on (a hole) **2** : to set the head of (as a screw) at or below the surface esp. by means of a countersink

²**countersink** \ˈ== + ˌ-\ *n* **1** : a funnel-shaped enlargement at the outer end of a drilled hole usu. for the reception of a screw, bolt, or rivet head **2** : a bit or drill for making such an enlargement — compare COUNTERBORE

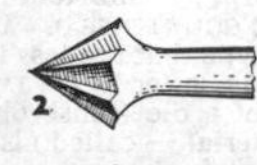

countersinks : *1* flat, *2* rose, *3* snail

coun·ter·sinker \" + ˌ-\ *n* : a worker that countersinks drilled holes

coun·ter·slope \" + ˌ-\ *n* [*counter-* + *slope*] : a slope in an opposite direction

coun·ter·spy \" + ˌ-\ *n* [*counter-* + *spy*] : one who spies against spies : one who investigates and seeks to check the activities of spies, espionage agents, and subversives

¹**coun·ter·stain** \ˈkau̇ntə(r) + ˌ-\ *n* [*counter-* + *stain* (n.)] : a stain used to color parts of a microscopy specimen not affected by another stain; *esp* : a cytoplasmic stain used to contrast with or enhance a nuclear stain

²**counterstain** \ˌ== +\ *vt* [*counter-* + *stain* (v.)] : to stain (a tissue or microscopy specimen) with an additional usu. contrasting color

¹**coun·ter·stamp** \ˌkau̇ntə(r) +\ *vt* [*counter-* + *stamp* (v.)] **1** : to stamp or impress (something already stamped or signed) — compare COUNTERSIGN **2 a** : to countermark (a coin) **b** : to stamp (a different coin design or a countermark) onto a coin ⟨~ a coin of Heraclius on a coin of Justinian⟩ ⟨~ a Texan 8-real piece on a Mexican 5-real piece⟩

²**counterstamp** \ˈ== + ˌ-\ *n* [*counter-* + *stamp* (n.)] **1** : a stamp or impression put upon something (as a check or paper) that has already been stamped **2** : a numismatic countermark

coun·ter·statement \" + ˌ-\ *n* [*counter-* + *statement*] : a statement opposing or denying another statement : REJOINDER

coun·ter·stroke \" + ˌ-\ *n* [*counter-* + *stroke*] : a stroke in return : COUNTERBLOW

coun·ter·subject \" + ˌ-\ *n* [*counter-* + *subject*] : a contrasting or secondary melody in contrapuntal music

coun·ter·sun \" + ˌ-\ *n* [*counter-* + *sun*] : ANTHELION

coun·ter·sunk \ˈkau̇ntə(r)+ˌ-\ *adj* [fr. past part. of ¹*countersink*] **1** : having a countersink at the top ⟨a ~ hole⟩ **2** : having the head set in a countersink ⟨a ~ screw⟩

countersway *n* [*counter-* + *sway*] *obs* : force in an opposite direction

coun·ter·tenor \ˈkau̇ntə(r)+\ *n* [ME *cowntu rtenur*, fr. MF *contreteneur*, fr. *contre-* counter- + *teneur, tenour* tenor — more at TENOR] **1** : one of the middle parts in music between the tenor and the soprano **2 a** : a tenor with an unusually high range and tessitura **b** : a man's countertenor voice

countertenor clef *n* : ALTO CLEF

coun·ter·theme \"+ˌ-\ *n* [*counter-* + *theme*] **1** : COUNTERSUBJECT **2** : a theme or thesis controverting another theme or thesis

coun·ter·thrust \"+ˌ-\ *n* [*counter-* + *thrust*] : a thrust offsetting or opposing another force

counter timber *n* [⁵*counter*] : one of the short vertical timbers between the stern timbers in the counter of a square-stern wooden boat

coun·ter·tonic \ˌkau̇ntə(r) +\ *adj* [*counter-* + *tonic*] *of a syllable or vowel* : between tonic and atonic in stress : bearing secondary stress

coun·ter·trades \ˈ==+ˌ-\ *n pl* [*counter-* + *trades*, pl. of ¹*trade* (wind)] : the westerly winds above the trade winds

coun·ter·transference \ˌ==+\ *n* [*counter-* + *transference*] **1** : transference evidenced by the psychoanalyst during the course of treatment; *esp* : the psychoanalyst's reactions to his patient's transference **2** : the complex of feelings of a therapist toward his patient

counter tube *n* [²*counter*] : COUNTING TUBE

coun·ter·turn \ˈ==+ˌ-\ *n* [*counter-* + *turn*] **1** [trans. of Gk *antistrophē*] : an unexpected turn or development in the action of a play esp. at the climax **2** : a turn in the opposite direction ⟨amid the turns and ~*s*, the strife and various trials of our complex being —William Wordsworth⟩

coun·ter·type \"+ˌ-\ *n* [*counter-* + *type*] : a corresponding type : EQUIVALENT

¹**coun·ter·vail** \ˈkau̇ntə(r),vāl, ˌ==ˈ=, *esp before pause or cons* -āəl\ *vb* -ED/-ING/-S [ME *countrevailen*, fr. MF *contrevaloir*, fr. *contre-* counter- + *valoir* to be worth, fr. L *valēre* to be strong, healthy, to be worth — more at WIELD] *vt* **1** : to compensate for : make up for : furnish or serve as an equivalent to **2** *archaic* : EQUAL, MATCH **3** : to oppose or exert force against : COUNTERACT, OFFSET ⟨the absence of fuss . . . ~*ed* any tendency to self-importance —Sylvia T. Warner⟩ ~ *vi* : to exert force against an opposing side ⟨~*ing* military power —D.D.Eisenhower⟩

²**countervail** *n* [ME *countervaille*, fr. *countrevailen*, v.] *archaic* : a countervailing power or value : EQUIVALENT

countervailing duty *n* **1** : a duty or surtax imposed on imports to offset an excise or inland revenue tax put upon articles of the same class manufactured at home **2** : a duty imposed to offset the advantage to foreign producers derived from a subsidy that their government offers for the production or export of the article taxed

coun·ter·vair \ˈkau̇ntə(r)+ˌ-\ *n* [part trans. of F *contrevair*, fr. *contre-* counter- + *vair* — more at VAIR] : a heraldic vair in which each pane stands broad edge to broad edge or point to point with one of the same tincture above or below it

coun·ter·view \"+ˌ-\ *n* [*counter-* + *view*] **1** *archaic* : view from opposite viewpoints : confrontation or juxtaposition for the sake of contrast **2** : an opposite view : an opposing opinion

counter voltage *n* [⁶*counter*] : COUNTER ELECTROMOTIVE FORCE

coun·ter·weigh \ˌkau̇ntə(r)+\ *vb* [ME *countreweyen*, fr. *countre-* counter- + *weyen* to weigh — more at WEIGH] *vt* : COUNTERBALANCE ~ *vi* : to act as a counterpoise

¹**coun·ter·weight** \ˈ==+ˌ-\ *n* [*counter-* + *weight*] : an equivalent weight : COUNTERPOISE, COUNTERBALANCE; *specif* : a weight that is placed on a mechanism that is out of balance at a place opposite to the heaviest point and that is just sufficiently heavy to restore the balance of the mechanism

²**counterweight** \ˌ==+\ *vt* : to equip with a counterweight : balance by means of a counterweight : COUNTERBALANCE

counterweighted window *n* : a window with vertical sliding sashes whose weights are balanced by sash weights

counterweight system *n* : a system for flying stage scenery by means of adjustable counterweights that are connected by cables running over loft blocks to battens which support the scenery

count·er·word \ˈkau̇ntə(r)+ˌ-\ *n* [¹*counter* (object used in reckoning) + *word*] : a word that has a broad and vague range of meaning through widespread use in many markedly different situations (as *case, awfully, fix, job, payoff*)

¹**coun·ter·work** \ˈ==+ˌ-\ *n* [*counter-* + *work* (n.)] **1** : any work done counter to another work **2 counterworks** *pl* : fortifications constructed to counteract the effect of fortifications of the enemy

²**coun·ter·work** \ˌ==+\ *vb* [*counter-* + *work* (v.)] *vi* : to work in opposition ~ *vt* : to work against : have a contrary effect on : COUNTERACT ⟨~*ing* his rival's designs⟩

count·ess \ˈkau̇ntəs\ *n* -ES [ME *cuntesse, contesse*, fr. OF *contesse*, fem. of *conte* count — more at COUNT] **1 a** : the wife or widow of an earl in the British peerage **b** : the wife or widow of a count in the Continental nobility **2** : a woman who holds in her own right the rank of earl or count

countfish \ˈ=ˌ=\ *n* [¹*count*; fr. its use as a gauge to determine what fish shall count as being large enough to be sold at a certain price per dozen] : SNAPPER

coun·ti·an \ˈkau̇ntēən\ *n* -s [¹*county* + *-an*] : a native or resident of a particular usu. specified county

counties *pl of* COUNTY

count in *vt* [¹*count*] : INCLUDE; *specif* : to consider as a participant ⟨if there is going to be a game *count me in*⟩

counting *pres part of* COUNT

counting cell *or* **counting chamber** *n* : an accurately sized chamber in a microslide designed to accommodate a definite volume of fluid and usu. ruled into divisions to facilitate the counting under the microscope of contained cells or bacteria

counting frame *also* **counting rail** *n* **:** a frame strung with movable beads on wires and used in teaching elementary number concepts **:** ABACUS

counting glass *n* **:** a magnifying glass used in counting threads per inch in fabrics

countinghouse \'=,=\ *n* [ME *counting hous*] **:** a building, room, or office in which a banker, merchant, trader, or manufacturer keeps books and transacts business

counting–out rhyme \'=¦=-\ *n* **:** one of the meaningless rhymes (as "eeny, meeny, miny, mo") traditionally used to count out a player in a child's game

counting room *n* **:** COUNTINGHOUSE

counting scales *n* **:** weighing scales calibrated to count the units in a quantity being weighed

counting tube *n* **:** an ionization chamber designed to respond to passage through it of fast-moving ionizing particles and usu. connected to some device (as a Geiger counter) for counting the particles

count·less \'kaůntlәs\ *adj* [²*count* + *-less*] **:** of such great number as to defy counting or recalling **:** INNUMERABLE, MYRIAD, MANY ⟨the ~ halls in some palace of the Arabian Nights —Nathaniel Hawthorne⟩ ⟨for ~ centuries Mars has been the star of war —H.G.Wells⟩

count noun *n* [²*count*] **:** a noun that forms a plural and is used with a numeral, with words such as *many* or *few*, or in English with the indefinite article *a* or *an* (as *bean, stick, sheet, beer* in "a dark beer") — contrasted with *mass noun*

count off *vi* **:** to call in turn from right to left or front to rear numbers determining individual positions in a military or similar formation usu. at command by the persons in the formation ~ *vt* **:** to separate into parts or divisions by or as if by counting **:** select or designate as members of a group by or as if by counting ⟨*counted off* three men to help with the job⟩

coun·tour *or* **coun·tor** \'kaůntә(r)\ *n* -s [ME *countour* (also, accountant), fr. OF *conteor* — more at COUNTER (one that counts)] **:** a pleader in an English court; *specif* **:** SERGEANT-AT-LAW

count out *vt* **1 :** to consider or list as nonparticipating **:** omit from consideration as unimportant, insignificant, or impracticable **:** EXCLUDE ⟨*count* one *out* of a poker hand⟩ ⟨help from such sources can be *counted out*⟩ **2 :** to indicate (a player) for a special role in or for exclusion from a child's game by pointing on recitation of the last syllable of a rhyme **3 :** to bring about or declare adjournment of (the House of Commons) by ascertaining that a quorum is not present **4 :** to signalize the knockout of (a boxer who is down) by completing an audible count of 10 seconds before the boxer rises **5 :** to clarify the rhythmical ordering of (the musical notes of a piece) by counting orally the beats in each bar **6 a :** to defraud (a winning candidate) of office by a false return or count of votes **b :** to reject (certain votes) from an official election count ~ *vi* **:** to announce before the completion of play in certain card games that one has already achieved a score sufficient to win the game

count palatine *n, pl* **counts palatine** [³*count*] **1 a :** a count having supreme judicial authority in the later Roman Empire **b :** a count granted the right to exercise certain imperial powers in his own domain under the German Emperors **2 :** the earl or proprietor of a county palatine in England or Ireland

coun·tree *or* **coun·trie** \'kәntrē, =¦=\ *archaic var of* COUNTRY

coun·tri·fied *also* **coun·try·fied** \'kәntrә,fīd, -trē,-\ *adj* [¹*country* + *-fy*] **1 :** marked by country rather than city ways and fashions **:** PROVINCIAL, RUSTIC, UNSOPHISTICATED ⟨so very rural and silly as I always have been . . . you yourself notice my ~ ways — Thomas Hardy⟩ **2 :** like or suggestive of the country **:** RURAL, BUCOLIC, NATURAL ⟨how ~ the sparrows and the leaves are —Charles Dickens⟩

¹**coun·try** \'kәn-trē, -ri\ *n* -ES [ME *cuntree, contree*, fr. OF *contrée*, fr. ML *contrata* landscape, country, lit., that which is situated opposite the beholder, fr. L *contra* against, on the opposite side + *-ata* (fem. of *-atus* -ate) — more at COUNTER] **1 a :** an expanse of land of undefined but usu. considerable extent **:** REGION, DISTRICT ⟨the North ~⟩ **b :** a district or area marked by some distinguishing feature ⟨hill ~⟩ ⟨Indian ~⟩ ⟨tobacco ~⟩ ⟨bad ~ for walking⟩ **c :** LAND ⟨much ~ sown to grass⟩ **2 a :** the land of a person's origin, birth, residence, or citizenship **:** motherland or home region ⟨in my own ~⟩ **b :** a political state or nation **:** the territory of a usu. independent nation that is distinct as to name and the characteristics or attributes of its people ⟨the ~ of Mexico⟩ **c :** area of interest or affiliation **:** SPHERE ⟨the borderline ~ between aesthetics and psychology —Kathleen Raine⟩ **3 a :** the people of a state or district **:** POPULACE, CITIZENRY ⟨the Hunt Fête . . . drew the entire ~ —Elizabeth Bowen⟩ **b :** the jury by which a defendant is tried — used esp. in legal phrases ⟨the litigant puts himself upon his ~⟩ ⟨tried by God and his ~⟩ **c :** the electorate regarded as the authority to which political controversy may be appealed ⟨the government will go to the ~ with this issue⟩ **4 :** rural regions as distinguished from city, town, or other thickly inhabited and built-up areas ⟨walk out in the ~⟩ **5 a :** a region of the ocean **b :** the part of a ship esp. in the U. S. Navy near officers' cabins ⟨wardroom ~⟩ ⟨admiral's ~⟩ **6** *cricket* **:** OUTFIELD **7** *or* **country rock :** the rock in which a mineral deposit or intrusion is enclosed — **across country** *adv* **:** ³CROSS-COUNTRY

²**country** \"\ *adj* [ME *cuntree, contree*, fr. *cuntree, contree*, n.] **1 a** *obs* **:** of one's own country **:** NATIVE **b** *India* **:** of or belonging to India or an adjacent land ⟨three European ships and a ~ ship⟩ **2 a :** living, located, or operating in the country **:** of, belonging, or appropriate to rural regions **:** suitable to or suggestive of the country rather than the city ⟨a ~ school⟩ ⟨one big rawboned ~ preacher —Eudora Welty⟩ ⟨expensive and decorative ~ clothes —Susan Ertz⟩ **b :** prepared, processed, or preserved with farmhouse supplies and procedures rather than those employed in industrial plants ⟨~ butter⟩ ⟨~ sugar⟩ ⟨~ ham⟩

country almond *n* **:** MALABAR ALMOND

country bank *n* **:** a commercial bank not in a reserve or central reserve city

country beam *n* **:** a setting of the headlights of an automobile to illuminate the road far ahead — compare DIMMER

country bishop *n* **:** CHOREPISCOPUS

country borage *n* **:** an aromatic fleshy herb (*Coleus aromaticus*) of India and Ceylon

country–bred \'=¦=,=\ *adj* **:** bred or reared in the country

country club *n* **:** an upper-class suburban or outlying club or clubhouse for social life, golf, and other recreation

country cousin *n* **:** a country visitor ingenuously unfamiliar with city ways and sights

country damage *n* **:** depreciation of cotton or other commodities by weather, excessive or careless handling, or transit

country–dance \'=,=\ *n* **1 :** any native English social dance in which dancers form square or circular figures or partners in rows face each other and which usu. has its origin in gatherings of rural folk — compare CONTREDANSE **2 :** a piece of music written or customarily played for a country-dance

country desk *n* **:** a state department subbranch dealing with a particular country

country fever *n, South & Midland* **:** MALARIA

countryfied *var of* COUNTRIFIED

country fig *n* **1 :** a western African tree (*Nauclea esculentus*) of the family Rubiaceae with bark formerly reputed to have astringent and febrifugal properties **2 :** CLUSTER FIG

countryfolk \'=,=\ *n pl* **1 :** fellow countrymen **2 :** country dwellers **:** RUSTICS

country gentleman *n* **1 :** a well-to-do country resident **:** an owner of a country estate **2 :** one of the English landed gentry

country hide *n* **:** a hide usu. of inferior quality removed by a farmer, ranchman, or local butcher — compare PACKER HIDE

country house *n* **:** a house or mansion in the country; *specif* **:** COUNTRYSEAT — compare TOWN HOUSE

country jake *n* **:** RUSTIC, YOKEL

coun·try·man \'kәntrēmәn, -trәm-; *in sense 3 often* -,man, -,maa(ә)n\ *n, pl* **countrymen** [ME *contreeman*, fr. *contree* country + *man*] **1 :** an inhabitant or native of a specified country ⟨a north ~⟩ **2 :** one born, residing, or holding citizenship in the same country as another **:** COMPATRIOT ⟨liked abroad but hated by his *countrymen*⟩ **3 :** one living in the country **:** HUSBANDMAN, FARMER; *also* **:** one marked by country ways **:** RUSTIC ⟨some great gawk of a ~ —Donagh MacDonagh⟩

country mile *n* **:** a long distance ⟨loud enough to be heard a *country mile*⟩

country music *n* **:** HILLBILLY MUSIC

country pay *n* **:** rural commodities used in lieu of money in transactions

countrypeople \'=,=\ *n, pl in constr* **:** COUNTRYFOLK

country road *n* **:** a usu. unpaved rural road off the main highway

country rock *n* **1 :** COUNTRY 7 **2 :** the common rock of a region

country sausage *n* **:** fresh pork sausage orig. prepared on the farm and usu. sold in bulk to be made into patties but also available in links both fresh and smoked

country school *n* **:** a school in a rural district; *specif* **:** a one-room rural school in which all elementary grades are taught by one teacher

country·seat \'=,=\ *n* **:** a country mansion or estate; *esp* **:** the country residence of an English person of rank or of a country gentleman

country·side \'=,=\ *n* **1 :** a particular rural district **:** a country neighborhood **:** country as contrasted with city ⟨he returned to his native ~ —I.M.Price⟩ ⟨the ~ bright with wild flowers⟩ **2 :** citizenry or inhabitants of a countryside ⟨the whole ~ had risen solid against the invader —E.H.Stuart-Jones⟩

country store *n* **:** a retail store carrying widely diversified goods, supplies, and equipment orig. for serving a sparsely populated region

country town *n* **:** a town usu. small and concerned primarily with serving the surrounding rural area

coun·try·ward \'kәntrē,wәrd, -trә,-, -,wōd\ *adv* [ME *contreewarde*, fr. *contree* country + *-warde* -ward] **:** toward the country

coun·try·wide \'=¦wīd\ *adj* **:** extended throughout the whole country

countrywoman \'=,=\ *n, pl* **countrywomen** [ME *contreewoman*, fr. *contree* country + *woman* woman] **1 :** a woman compatriot **2 :** a woman resident of the country

counts *pl of* COUNT, *pres 3d sing of* COUNT

count·ship \'kaůnt,ship\ *n* [³*count* + *-ship*] **1 :** the rank or office of a count **2 :** the domain or territory of a count

count wheel *n* [²*count*] **:** the notched wheel that in some clocks regulates the number of strokes in sounding the hour

¹**coun·ty** \'kaůntē, -ti\ *n* -ES [ME *counté, counte*, fr. AF *counté*, fr. OF *cunté, conté* domain of a count, fr. ML *comitatus*, fr. LL, office of a count, fr. *comit-, comes* count + L *-atus* -ate — more at COUNT] **1** *obs* **:** COUNTY COURT **2 :** the domain of a European count or earl **3 :** one of the territorial divisions of Great Britain and Ireland constituting the chief units for administrative, judicial, and political purposes and comprising the districts that were formerly Anglo-Saxon shires and other areas which never were shires: as **a** *or* **county corporate :** one of certain districts consisting of cities and towns with neighboring territories separated out of the older shires and given the status of county — called also *corporate county* **b :** the largest administrative unit for local government in Great Britain and Northern Ireland — called also in England and Wales *administrative county* and in Scotland *civil county* **c** *or* **county borough :** a borough of at least 100,000 inhabitants that has been given the status of an administrative county **4 a :** the people of a county **b** *Brit* **:** the gentry of an English county ⟨never happier than when they were entertaining the ~ —W.S. Maugham⟩ **5 a :** the largest division for local government within a state of the U. S. with administrative functions differing from state to state — compare MUNICIPAL CORPORATION, PARISH, QUASI CORPORATION, TOWN, TOWNSHIP **b** *in Rhode Island* **:** a judicial district **c :** the county government regarded as a source of poor relief or other services esp. for the destitute ⟨throwing his money away and if we don't get a guardian for him he'll be on the ~ —Willard Robertson⟩ **6 :** the largest local administrative unit in various countries esp. in the British Commonwealth

²**county** \"\ *adj* **1 :** of, for, or relating to a county ⟨a ~ treasurer⟩ **:** concerned in county affairs **:** administered by a county **2** *chiefly Brit* **:** of, belonging to, or appropriate to the county gentry ⟨her mother's clothes being excessively ~ —Michael Arlen⟩ ⟨a ~ family⟩

³**county** *n* -ES [modif. of MF *conte* count — more at COUNT] *obs* **:** ³COUNT

county agent *n* **:** a consultant and advisor employed jointly by the federal and state governments to provide information concerning proper methods in agriculture and home economics by means of lectures, demonstrations, and discussions in rural areas and to assist in the solution of problems related thereto — called also *agricultural agent, extension agent*

county attorney *n* **:** a district attorney for a county

county board *n* **:** the elected administrative body of a U.S. county

county clerk *n* **:** an elected county official whose duties vary widely but are likely to include serving as secretary to the county board, issuing licenses, keeping records, and acting as county auditor or comptroller

county college *n* **:** a British continuation school for persons under 18 not receiving full-time education elsewhere

county commissioner *n* **:** a county administrator **:** a member of a county board

county court *n* **1 :** the court formerly assembled for an English county that was presided over by the sheriff and attended by suitors who represented all the lands in the county or shire and were the doomsmen of the court and that had jurisdiction as a court of first instance in both civil and criminal cases and as a court of appeal from the minor courts and had also certain administrative and legislative powers **2 :** any of various English judicial courts for civil actions established by the County Courts Act of 1846 mainly for the recovery of small debts **3 :** a court having a designated jurisdiction usu. both civil and criminal within the limits of a U. S. or British colonial county

county fair *n* **:** a fair usu. held annually at a set location in a county esp. to exhibit local agricultural products

county farm *n* **:** the poor farm of a county

county home *or* **county house** *n* **:** the poorhouse of a county

county library *n* **:** a library unit supported by public taxation for the use of all or part of a county

county manager *n* **:** the chief executive of a county having a system of government similar to the council-manager plan

county palatine *n* **:** the dominion or territory of a count palatine **:** a county in England of which the earl or lord orig. had royal powers with exclusive civil and criminal jurisdiction

county rate *n, Brit* **:** a tax levied upon the county and collected by county officers

county road *n* **:** a highway maintained by a county

county school *n, Brit* **:** COUNCIL SCHOOL

county seat *or* **county site** *n* **:** a town which is the seat of county administration and in which the county offices, courthouse, and jail are located

county sessions *n, Brit* **:** the general quarter sessions of the peace for each county held four times a year

county solicitor *n* **:** DISTRICT ATTORNEY

county town *n, now chiefly Brit* **:** COUNTY SEAT

county unit system *n* **:** a system of voting in a primary election in Georgia whereby each county is allotted a certain number of unit votes so that the candidate winning the highest popular vote in the county receives all that county's unit votes and the one who receives a majority of the state's unit votes is nominated

coun·ty·wide \'kaůntē¦wīd, -tә¦-\ *adj* **:** extending over the whole county **:** present throughout the county

¹**coup** \'kaůp, 'kōp, 'kәůp\ *vt* -ED/-ING/-S [ME *coupen* to pay for, fr. ON *kaupa* to buy — more at CHEAP] *dial Brit* **:** EXCHANGE, BARTER

²**coup** \'kaůp\ *n* -S [ME *caupe* blow, fr. MF *coup* — more at COPE] *chiefly Scot* **:** FALL, TUMBLE, UPSET

³**coup** \"\ *vb* -ED/-ING/-S [ME *cowpen* to strike, fr. MF *couper* — more at COPE] *vt* **1** *chiefly Scot* **:** OVERTURN, UPSET **2** *chiefly Scot* **:** to drink off **:** DRAIN ~ *vi, chiefly Scot* **:** UPSET, CAPSIZE

⁴**coup** \'kü\ *n, pl* **coups** \-üz\ [F — more at COPE] **1 a :** BLOW, STROKE **b :** the act practiced by some American Indians (as the Plains Indians) of striking or touching an enemy in warfare in such a manner as is by custom considered a deed of bravery **c :** any of various acts recognized by custom as laudatory **2 a** *English billiards* **:** the pocketing of the cue ball without its touching another ball **b :** a roll of a roulette wheel, cast of dice, deal of cards, or similar event after which bets are settled **c :** an end play in bridge in which declarer trumps to reduce his trump holdings to avoid being forced to lead from his own hand at an inopportune later time **d :** a particularly brilliant or skilled play in a board game or card game **3 a :** a highly successful stroke, action, plan, or stratagem **:** a clever device ⟨a clever fraud which, like many other ~s of history, used religion as its chief vehicle —R.W.Murray⟩ **b :** COUP D'ETAT

⁵**coup** \"\ *vt* **couped** \-üd\ **couped** \"\ **couping** \-üiŋ\ **coups** \-üz\ **:** to execute a bridge coup in playing (a hand)

cou·page \(')kü¦päzh\ *n* -S [F, act of cutting, fr. MF, fr. *couper* to cut + *-age* — more at COPE] **:** the process of unhairing skins

coup–cart \'=,=\ *n* [³*coup* + *cart*] *chiefly Scot* **:** DUMPCART

coup d'ar·chet \¦kü,där¦shā\ *n, pl* **coups d'archet** \"\ [F] **:** a stroke of the bow in violin playing

coup de fou·dre \¦küdә¦füdr(ᵊ), -d(rә)\ *n, pl* **coups de foudre** \"\ [F, lit., clap of thunder] **:** an astonishing occurrence; *esp* **:** overwhelming love at first sight

coup de glotte \-¦glät\ *n, pl* **coups de glotte** \"\ [F] **:** the glottal stop esp. in singing and elocution as a prefixion to words that in ordinary pronunciation begin with a vowel sound

coup de grace \-¦gräs\ *n, pl* **coups de grace** \"\ [F *coup de grâce*] **1 :** a death blow or shot administered in mercy to end the suffering of a person or animal mortally wounded **2 :** a decisive finishing blow **:** an act or event that puts an end to something ⟨an incident that gave the *coup de grace* to Harriet's Calvinist faith —Edmund Wilson⟩

coup de main \-¦maⁿ\ *n, pl* **coups de main** \"\ [F, lit., hand stroke] **:** a sudden attack in force **:** vigorous attack **:** sudden forceful development

coup de poing \-¦pwaⁿ\ *n, pl* **coups de poing** \"\ [F, lit., blow with the fist] **:** a biface stone hand ax typical of the Abbevillian epoch

coup de re·pos _rә¦pō\ *n, pl* **coups de repos** \"\ [F, lit., stroke of rest] **:** a chess move leaving the main features of a position unchanged when the adversary can change these only to his disadvantage

coup d'e·tat \¦kü(,)dā¦tä, -tȧ *also* -üdә¦-\ *n, pl* **coups d'etat** \"\ *also* **coup d'etats** \-äz,-äz\ [F *coup d'état*, lit., stroke of state] **1 :** a sudden decisive exercise of localized or concentrated force unseating the personnel of a government **2 :** a coup violently and unexpectedly reformulating state policy **:** an unexpected or sudden measure of state often involving force or threat of force

coup de the·atre \¦küdә(,)tā¦ä·tr(ᵊ), -t(rә)\ *n, pl* **coups de theatre** \"\ [F *coup de théâtre*, lit., stroke of theater] **:** a sudden and sensational turn in a play; *also* **:** a sudden dramatic and unexpected turn or stroke of events

coup d'oeil \kü'dәry, -'dәy\ *n, pl* **coups d'oeil** \"\ [F, lit., stroke of the eye] **:** a glance embracing a wide view **:** a survey accomplished with a glance ⟨his penetrating *coup d'oeil* which makes him a master at rapid chess —A.J.Liebling⟩

¹**coupe** *obs var of* COOP

²**cou·pé** *or* **coupe** \(')kü¦pā, *in sense 2b often* 'küp\ *n* -S [F *coupé*, fr. past part. of *couper* to cut, cut off; in senses 2 & 3, fr. F *coupé*, prob. fr. *carrosse coupé*, lit., cut-off coach, fr. *carrosse* coach + *coupé*, past part. of *couper*] **1** *ballet dancing* **:** a quick sharp cut finishing with an extension **2 a :** a 4-wheeled closed horse-drawn carriage for two persons inside with an outside seat for the driver in front **b** *usu* **coupe :** a closed 2-door automobile with one seat compartment and a separate luggage compartment — see CLUB COUPE **3 a :** the front or after compartment of a Continental stagecoach **b** *Brit* **:** an end compartment of a railway carriage often with a seat on one side only **4 :** CUTOVER 2

coupé 2a

³**coupe** \'küp\ *n* -S [F, cup, fr. LL *cuppa* — more at CUP] **1 a :** a dessert commonly served in a glass and consisting of ice cream or an ice topped with mixed fruit, whipped cream, or other garnish **b :** the glass for serving this dessert; *esp* **:** a footed glass having a deep lower cup and a wide shallow upper cup **2 :** a rimless plate or wide shallow rimless bowl

¹**couped** *past of* COUP

²**couped** \'küpt\ *adj* [F *coupé* (fr. past part. of *couper*) + E *-ed*] **1** *heraldry* **:** cut off smoothly — used esp. of the head or limb of an animal; compare ERASED **2** *heraldry* **:** cut off short at the ends so as not to extend to the edges of the field

coupe de ville \(')kü¦pādә¦vil, ¦küpdә-\ *n, pl* **coupes de ville** \-pāzdә¦vil, -psd-; -pādә¦vilz, -pd-\ [F *coupé de ville* town coupé] **:** a convertible coupe in which the top may be adjusted to cover either both seats or the back seat alone

¹**coup·er** \'kaůpәr, 'küp-\ *n* -S [¹*coup* + *-er*] *chiefly Scot* **:** a dealer esp. in horses and cattle

²**couper** \'kaůpә(r), 'kōp-\ *n* -S [prob. fr. ³*coup* (overturn) + *-er*] **:** a lever in a loom for lifting the harness

coup·ette \(')kü¦pet\ *n* -S [³*coupe* (glass) + *-ette*] **:** a small coupe used in serving cold seafood appetizers, fruit, or ices

coupette

couping *pres part of* COUP

coup·ist \'küәst\ *n* -S [⁴*coup* + *-ist*] **:** one that attempts or supports a coup d'etat

¹**cou·ple** \'kәpәl\ *vb* **coupled; coupled; coupling** \'kәp(ә)liŋ, -lēŋ\ **couples** [ME *couplen* to join, connect, fr. OF *copler, coupler*, fr. L *copulare*, fr. *copula* bond] *vt* **1 :** to connect for consideration together **:** join together for combined effect or consideration ⟨supported the bill . . . and *coupled* it with a demand for national reclamation —P.C. Phillips⟩ **:** unite or link esp. abstract or immaterial things ⟨individuality of expression *coupled* with the spice of novelty —J.L.Lowes⟩ ⟨trade-union pressure *coupled* with unemployment —H.B.Parkes⟩ **2 :** to fasten together **:** JOIN, LINK ⟨*coupling* his holdings and his deceased brother's⟩: as **a :** to fasten with a leash ⟨*coupling* the hounds⟩ **b :** to connect with a coupling ⟨*coupling* the freight cars⟩ **c :** to connect (as two or more keys or keyboards of an organ) by a coupler **d** (1) **:** to bring (two physical systems) into such relation that the performance of one influences the performance of the other (as in suspending two pendulums from different points on the same horizontal rope) (2) **:** to bring (two electric circuits) into such close proximity as to permit mutual influence (3) **:** to join (electric circuits or devices) into a single circuit **e :** to cause (as an aromatic diazonium compound) to unite with another compound usu. with the elimination of a simple molecule (as hydrochloric acid in the formation of an azo dye) — compare CONJUGATE 3 **f :** to record on opposite sides of a phonograph record or in the same series of records ⟨his first symphony being *coupled* with his third⟩ **3 a :** to join in marriage or sexual union **b :** to bring into association (as friendship, companionship, partnership, opposition, or rivalry) **c :** to cause (domestic animals) to breed or copulate ~ *vi* **1 :** to unite in sexual union — often used with *with* **2 a :** to come together **:** JOIN **b** *of chemical compounds or radicals* **:** to unite usu. with elimination of a simple molecule (as of hydrochloric acid)

²**couple** \"; *"a couple of" is often* ә'kәplә(v)\ *n, pl* **couples** *also* **couple** [ME, pair, bond, fr. OF *cople, couple*, fr. L *copula* bond, band, fr. (assumed) L *co-apula*, fr. L *co-* + (assumed) L *-apula* (fr. L *apere* to fasten, tie) — more at APT] **1 a :** a man and his wife **:** a man and woman married or engaged ⟨she and Jon would make a lovely ~ —John Galsworthy⟩ **b :** a man and woman paired as partners in any work, recreation, or other activity **c :** a man and wife employed together to perform usu. related jobs in a single establishment (as butler and cook in a household) **d :** any two persons

paired together in some work, enterprise, or activity **2 :** MATING, COPULATION ⟨birds in ~⟩ **3 a :** a pair of animals often of different sexes **b :** a pair of hounds **c :** a ewe and lamb **4 :** something that joins or links two things together: as **a** *couples pl* **:** a pair of collars joined by a chain for coupling two hounds together **b :** COUPLER 1c **5 a :** two of the same kind considered together **:** PAIR **b** COUPLE-CLOSE 2 **c :** two equal and opposite forces that act along parallel lines **d :** VOLTAIC COUPLE **e :** BINARY STAR — **a couple of :** two or an indefinite small number of **:** FEW ⟨*a couple of* days ago⟩ ⟨for *a couple of* centuries — the fourth to the sixth —I.M.Price⟩ ⟨I only had *a couple of* drinks⟩

³couple \"\ *adj* **:** TWO — used with *a* ⟨a ~ more oaths⟩ ⟨a ~ nights ago⟩

couple-beggar *n* [¹*couple* + *beggar*] *obs* **:** a marrier of beggars **:** a performer of clandestine or irregular marriages

couple-close \ˌ=ˌ=ˈklōs\ *n* -s [²*couple* + *close*] **1** *heraldry* **:** a cotise paralleling a chevron **2 :** a pair of rafters framed together with a tie fixed at their feet or with a collar beam

coupled *adj* [ME, joined, fr. past part. of *couplen* to couple, join — more at COUPLE] **1** *of a quadrupedal mammal* **:** having a coupling of a specified sort — usu. used in combination ⟨long-*coupled*⟩ ⟨well-*coupled*⟩ **2 :** entered in a horse race as a single entry ⟨two of that stable's horses ~ in the third race⟩ **3** *of a fighting cock* **:** crippled specif. by a back wound paralyzing the legs **4 a :** mechanically or electrically connected **b** *of a photographic range finder* **:** connected to the focusing mechanism so that operation of the finder focuses the lens

coupled column *n, archit* **:** one of a pair of columns set nearer together than others of the same order or forming one of many groups of two used esp. in the neoclassic art of the 17th century and later

coupled engine *n* **:** a locomotive engine having two or more driving wheels on either side joined by a coupling rod

cou·ple·ment \ˈkəpəlmənt\ *n* -s [MF, fr. *coupler* to couple, join + *-ment* — more at COUPLE] *archaic* **:** the act or result of coupling

cou·pler \ˈkəplə(r)\ *n* -s **1 a :** one that couples (as a link, ring, or shackle that connects cars or the ends of a chain belt) **b :** COUPLING **c :** a contrivance on a keyboard instrument by which any two or more of the manuals or a manual and the pedal keyboard or keys of the same keyboard an octave apart are connected so as to act together when one is played **d :** a radio device coupling two electric circuits **e :** an agent (as a mutual solvent) that renders two nonmiscible liquids miscible or aids in the formation of emulsions (as of oils in soap solutions) — called also *coupling agent* **2 :** a compound in a color-photography emulsion or developer solution that combines with the oxidized developer to form a dye — compare COLOR DEVELOPER

coupler developer *n* **1 :** COUPLER 2 **2 :** a photographic developer solution having a coupler as one of its constituents

cou·pler·ess \ˈkəplərə̇s\ *n* -ES **:** PROCURESS

couples *pres 3d sing of* COUPLE, *pl of* COUPLE

cou·plet \ˈkəplə̇t\ *n* -s [MF, dim. of *couple* pair — more at COUPLE] **1 :** two successive lines of verse usu. having some unity greater than that of mere contiguity (as that provided by rhythmic correspondence, rhyme, or the complete inclusion of a grammatically or rhetorically independent utterance) **:** DISTICH — see CLOSED COUPLET, OPEN COUPLET **2 a :** PAIR, COUPLE **:** a pair born together **:** TWINS **b :** a pair of items of the same kind occurring together **3 :** a window of two lights **4 :** one of the musical episodes alternating with the main theme (as in the early French rondos)

cou·pling \ˈkəpliŋ, -lēŋ\ *n* -s [ME, fr. gerund of *couplen* to couple, join] **1 :** the act of bringing together **:** PAIRING **:** a coming together; *specif* **:** sexual union **2 :** a device that serves to couple or connect the ends of adjacent parts or objects ⟨a belt ~⟩ ⟨a car ~⟩ ⟨a shaft ~⟩ ⟨a pipe ~⟩ — see FLUID COUPLING **3 :** the joint together with its supporting structures between the last lumbar vertebra and the sacrum that joins the hindquarters to the trunk; *broadly* **:** the part of the body or the conformation and proportionate length of the part of the body that joins the hindquarters to the forequarters — used of a horse, dog, or other mammalian quadruped **4 a :** an arrangement of two electric circuits by means of which the electromotive force and current in one circuit are influenced by the electromotive force and current in the other **b :** an interaction between two systems or parts of the same system, esp. between parts of atomic or molecular systems (as the mutual magnetic influence of two spinning electrons) **5 :** the tendency of certain genetic characters to be inherited together presumably because of linkage of the dominant genes that control their expression — compare REPULSION

coupling box *n* **:** JUNCTION BOX

coupling coefficient *n, physics* **:** an abstract number representing the degree in which the performance of either of two coupled systems influences that of the other

coupling rein *n* **:** the short rein that runs from the inner side of the bridle of one horse of a pair to the draft rein of the other horse

coupling rod *n* **:** a link connecting two or more cranks or their equivalents (as the side rod of a locomotive)

cou·pon \ˈk(y)üˌpän\ *n* -s [F, fr. OF *coupon*, *copon* piece, fr. *couper*, *coper* to cut — more at COPE] **1 :** a statement of due interest to be cut from a bearer bond when payable and presented for payment **2 :** a form, slip, or section of a paper resembling a bond coupon in that it may be surrendered in order to obtain some article, service, or accommodation: as **a :** one of a series of attached tickets or certificates often for accommodations or services to be detached and presented as needed ⟨a railroad ticket with many ~*s*⟩ **b :** a ticket or form authorizing purchases of rationed commodities as indicated ⟨a clothing ~⟩ ⟨the three ~*s* required for the gasoline⟩ **c :** a token or certificate given with a purchase and redeemable in merchandise or cash — compare TRADING STAMP **d :** a trademark, wrapper, box top, or similar evidence of a purchase for which premium articles are given **e :** a part of a printed advertisement designed to be cut or torn off for use as an order blank or as a form for inquiry **f :** a leaf of a credit account booklet to be removed to accompany installment payments and identify the customer **g :** a form or check indicating a credit against future purchases or expenditures **h** *Brit* **:** a blank for entering one's choices in a sports pool ⟨filling out his football ~⟩ **3 :** a test sample ⟨taking off a ~ of the steel plate⟩ **4 :** a party recommendation given to a candidate for parliament in acknowledgment of his pledge to the party leader

coupon bond *n* **:** a bond on which interest is paid by coupons

coupon clipper *n* **:** a wealthy and idle person whose chief labor is clipping and cashing bond coupons

cou·pon·less \-lə̇s\ *adj* **:** not having a coupon

coups *pres 3d sing of* COUP, *pl of* COUP

coupstick *n* [⁴*coup* + *stick*] **:** a stick or switch used in counting a coup in warfare or symbolically on ceremonial occasions

cour *chiefly Scot var of* COWER

cour·age \ˈkər·ij, ˈkə·r|, |ēj\ *n* -s [ME *corage*, fr. OF *corage*, *curage*, fr. *cuer* heart (fr. L *cor*) + *-age* — more at HEART] **1** *obs* **:** the heart as the seat of intelligence or feeling ⟨this soft ~ makes your followers faint —Shak.⟩ **2** *obs* **:** INCLINATION, INTENTION ⟨I'd such a ~ to do him good —Shak.⟩ **3** *obs* **:** a proud and angry temper **:** high spirit **4 :** mental or moral strength enabling one to venture, persevere, and withstand danger, fear, or difficulty firmly and resolutely ⟨I would define true ~ to be a perfect sensibility of the measure of danger and a mental willingness to endure it —W.T.Sherman⟩ **5 :** confidence that encourages and sustains ⟨a ~ resting on God —Daniel Defoe⟩ ⟨the ~ of his convictions⟩

syn METTLE, SPIRIT, RESOLUTION, TENACITY: COURAGE is the firmness of spirit that faces danger or extreme difficulty without flinching or retreating ⟨*courage* to fight for our ideals although we are certain they shall never be realized —Paul Eldridge⟩ ⟨*courage* to act on limited knowledge, *courage* to make the best of what is here and not whine for more —Robert Frost⟩ METTLE suggests an ingrained capacity for meeting strain or difficulty without fear or with fortitude and resilience of spirit or mind ⟨difficulties calculated to test the *mettle* of even the bravest men⟩ ⟨showed his *mettle* in two strenuous European campaigns⟩ SPIRIT, like METTLE in suggesting a quality of temperament, implies an ability to hold one's own, fight for one's principles, or keep up one's morale when opposed, interfered with, or checked ⟨to show his *spirit* by fighting to the last ditch⟩ ⟨a man of considerable *spirit* standing virtually alone in defense of his rights as a citizen⟩ RESOLUTION, like COURAGE, implies firmness of spirit but puts stress upon determination to achieve one's end rather than upon the facing of danger without flinching ⟨she sat for twenty minutes or more ere she could summon *resolution* to go down to the door, her courage being lowered to zero by her physical lassitude —Thomas Hardy⟩ ⟨a man of a strong *resolution* and a set purpose; a man not desirable to be met rushing down a narrow pass with a gulf on either side, for nothing would turn the man —Charles Dickens⟩ TENACITY adds to RESOLUTION the idea of stubborn persistence or unwillingness to recognize defeat ⟨all his convictions were strong and he held them with an unswerving *tenacity* —F.T.Persons⟩ ⟨the roots insinuate themselves into the rocks with such demoniac *tenacity* that only dynamite will dislodge them permanently —Norman Douglas⟩

cou·ra·geous \kəˈrājəs\ *adj* [ME *corageous*, fr. OF *corageus*, fr. *corage* courage + *-eus* -ous] **:** having or characterized by courage **:** marked by bold resolution in withstanding the dangerous, alarming, or difficult **:** BRAVE ⟨a frank ~ heart and buoyant spirit triumphed over pain —William Wordsworth⟩ ⟨a ~ rescue⟩ ⟨a ~ example⟩ **syn** see BRAVE

cou·ra·geous·ly *adv* **:** in a courageous manner

cou·ra·geous·ness *n* -ES **:** the quality or state of being courageous

¹cou·rant \ˈkər·ənt, ˈkə·rənt *sometimes* ˈku̇rənt *or* k(y)üˈrant *or* -üˈränt\ *n* -s [prob. fr. F *courante*, fr. fem. of *courant* current, running, fr. pres. part. of *courir* to run] **:** NEWSPAPER — obs. except in names of newspapers

²cou·rant \ˈku̇rənt; küˈrant, -änt\ *adj* [F, fr. pres. part. of *courir* to run, fr. L *currere* — more at CURRENT] *heraldry* **:** RUNNING ⟨a stag ~⟩

³cou·rant \kəˈrant\ *vi* -ED/-ING/-S [*courante*] **1** *dial Eng* **:** ROMP, CAPER **2** *dial Eng* **:** to go about gossiping

cou·rante *also* **cou·rant** \küˈränt, -ant\ *n* -s [MF *courante*, fr. fem. of *courant*, pres. part. of *courir* to run] **1 a :** a dance of Italian origin marked by quick running steps **b :** a similar but graver and more formal dance developed in France in the 17th century **2 :** music for a courante or having the rhythm of a courante that is in rather quick ³⁄₂ measure and is characterized by dotted notes and shifts to ⁶⁄₄ measure **3** *dial Eng* **:** a running about **:** ROMP, CAROUSE

cou·ra·ta·ri \ˌku̇rəˈtärē\ *n* -s [NL, fr. Galibi *couratary* couratari tree] **1 :** a tropical So. American tree (*Couratari tauari*) of the family Lecythidaceae **2 :** the laminated inner bark of the couratari that occurs in the form of thin whitish sheets and is used for rough clothing, wrapping, and cordage

courb \ˈkü(ə)rb\ *vb* -ED/-ING/-S [ME *courben*, fr. MF *courber* — more at CURB] *archaic* **:** BEND, BOW

cour·ba·ril \ˈku̇rbəˌril, ¦ku̇rbə¦ril\ *n* -s [F, fr. Island Carib *kurbaril*] **1 :** a West Indian locust tree (*Hymenaea courbaril*) with a very hard tough wood **2** *or* **courbaril copal :** the resin from the courbaril tree

courbash *var of* KURBASH

courbe *adj* [ME, fr. MF — more at CURB] *obs* **:** BENT

cour·bette \(ˈ)ku̇r¦bet\ *n* -s [F, fr. MF, fr. *courber* to bend + *-ette*] **:** CURVET

cour d'hon·neur \ˌku̇r,dȯ¦nər\ *n, pl* **cours d'honneur** \"\ [F, lit., court of honor] **:** a monumental forecourt to a building

cou·reur de bois \kü¦rərdəb¦wä\ *n, pl* **coureurs de bois** \"\ [CanF, lit., woods runner] **:** a French or French and Indian half-breed trapper, woodsman, or hunter of No. America and esp. of Canada

courge \ˈkü(ə)rzh\ *n* -s [F, lit., gourd, fr. MF dial., fr. L *cucurbita* — more at GOURD] **:** an elongated basket for holding sand eels and other live bait in sea fishing

courge green *n* [F *courge* gourd] **:** a moderate yellow green that is yellower, lighter, and slightly stronger than average moss green, yellower and duller than average pea green, and yellower and lighter than spinach green

cou·ri·da \küˈrēdə\ *n* -s [native name in Brit. Guiana] **:** BLACK MANGROVE 1

courie *var of* COWRIE

cou·ri·er \ˈku̇rēə(r), ˈkər·ē-, ˈkə·rē-, ˈkürē- *sometimes* ˈkōrē-\ *n* -s *often attrib* [MF *courrier*, fr. OIt *corriere*, fr. *correre* to run (fr. L *currere*) + *-iere* -er (fr. OF *-ier*) — more at CURRENT] **1 :** one that carries messages, news, or information either with urgent haste or in accordance with a regular schedule **:** MESSENGER ⟨a ~ who will carry the tidings of distress —B.N.Cardozo⟩ ⟨~ communication nearly equivalent to postal service —F.B Warren⟩: as **a :** a member of a diplomatic service entrusted with bearing messages ⟨~*s* who carry official despatches possess the right of inviolability —G.H.Stuart⟩ **b :** an espionage agent transferring secret information; *sometimes* **:** a runner of contraband or illicit materials **:** an underworld liaison man **c :** a member of the armed services whose duties include carrying mail, information, or supplies **2 :** a traveler's paid attendant **:** a servant who facilitates travel arrangements; *often* **:** a tourists' guide employed by a travel agency **3** *Canad* **:** MAIL CARRIER **4 :** a plane or other conveyance used in courier duties

cour·lan \ˈku̇rlən, (ˈ)ku̇r¦län\ *n* -s [F, alter. of *courliri*, fr. Galibi *kurliri*] **:** a long-billed bird (*Aramus guarana*) intermediate in some respects between the cranes and the rails that occurs in much of So. and Central America and is represented in Florida, Cuba, and Jamaica by the limpkin

cou·ronne \küˈrȯn\ *n* -s [F, lit., crown, fr. L *corona* — more at CROWN] **:** a loop added to the cordonnet on the edge of point lace or in the body of the pattern

¹course \ˈkō(ə)rs, -ō(ə)rs,-ōəs,-ȯ(ə)s\ *n* -s [ME *cours*, *course*, fr. OF *cors*, *cours*, *corse*, *course*, fr. L *cursus*, fr. *cursus*, past part. of L *currere* to run] **1 a :** the act or action of moving in a particular path from point to point ⟨the planets in their ~*s*⟩ **b** *obs* **:** RUN, GALLOP **c** *archaic* **:** a charge by opposing knights **:** ONSET **:** passage at arms **:** BOUT **d :** a life regarded as a race **:** LIFE HISTORY **:** CAREER ⟨ending his ~ with fame and wealth⟩ **e :** the pursuit of game by hounds — usu. used with *of* or *at* ⟨the ~ at the deer⟩ **f :** RACE ⟨a prize for winning the ~⟩ **g :** a progressing or proceeding along a straight line without change of direction ⟨the ship made many ~*s* sailing through the islands⟩ **2 :** the path over which something moves or the way which something extends **:** the line or way described by some motion, progression, or series **:** the direction taken or the ground traversed **:** TRACK, WAY ⟨the ~ of an ocean current⟩ ⟨the ~ of a mountain range⟩ ⟨his ~ was straight east⟩: as **a :** RACECOURSE **b** (1) **:** the track or way taken by a ship or the direction of flight of an airplane **:** the way projected and assigned usu. measured as a clockwise angle from north — see COMPASS COURSE, MAGNETIC COURSE, TRUE COURSE (2) **:** a point of the compass **c** *obs* **:** a fashionable place or way for riding or driving **d :** a channel through which water flows **:** WATERCOURSE **e :** GOLF COURSE **f :** horizontal direction of a geological structure **:** STRIKE **3 a :** accustomed procedure **:** customary action **:** usual method of proceeding ⟨the law taking its ~⟩ ⟨to die according to the ~ of nature⟩ **b :** policy chosen **:** manner of conducting oneself **:** conduct esp. when reprehensible **:** way of acting **:** BEHAVIOR ⟨persisting in his evil ~*s*⟩ ⟨our wisest ~ is to retreat⟩ **c :** progress or progression through a series (as of acts or events) or through a development or a period ⟨watching man's hesitant ~ through . . . this time of trouble —Herrymon Maurer⟩ ⟨a highway in ~ of construction⟩ ⟨in the ~ of his service he rose to the rank of colonel⟩ **4 :** an ordered continuing process, succession, sequence, or series ⟨following the ~ of the argument⟩ ⟨the ~ of history⟩ ⟨the ~ of the hearings⟩: as **a :** the series of prayers used in the daily canonical hours **b courses** *pl* **:** MENSTRUATION **c** (1) **:** an educational unit usu. at the high school, college, or university level consisting of a series of instruction periods (as lectures, recitations, and laboratory sessions) dealing with a particular subject ⟨an English ~⟩ ⟨a ~ in trigonometry⟩ (2) **:** a series of such courses coordinated to constitute a curriculum and leading typically to a degree ⟨a premedical ~⟩ ⟨a commercial ~⟩ **d :** a series of doses or medicaments usu. administered over a designated period of time ⟨a ~ of three doses daily for five days⟩ **e :** the series of changes or the shifting path through a series of changes that a single bell makes in change ringing **f :** a sequence of different crops in crop rotation **g :** a series of rounds fired at a target or at a series of targets under specified conditions **5 :** a single member of a sequence **:** one item in a series: as **a :** a division of a meal **:** the part of a meal served at one time with its accompaniments ⟨a seven-*course* meal⟩ ⟨the main ~ was roast beef⟩ **b :** ROW, LAYER: as (1) **:** a horizontal layer forming one of a series (as of concrete in road making, of lumber in a lumber pile, or of shingles on a roof) (2) **:** a continuous level range of brick or masonry throughout a wall (3) **:** a lode of ore (4) **:** a horizontal row of loops or stitches in knitted fabrics formed by one passage of the yarn or thread — compare WALE (5) **:** a strake of plating on a ship's hull **c** (1) **:** the lowest sail on any square-rigged mast of a ship ⟨the fore ~⟩ (2) **:** a length esp. of a rope or cable **d** *obs* **:** a time or occasion coming to each individual **:** TURN **e :** a set of persons appointed to hold some office or perform some duty ⟨the ~ of priests then performing the rites⟩ **f** *archaic* **:** each one of several attacks in series **g :** a set of things made or used together ⟨a ~ of candles⟩ **h :** a single string or two or more strings (as of a lute) tuned in unison or octaves and played together for increased volume **6 :** faculty or opportunity of moving, flowing, or circulating ⟨that the word of the Lord may have free ~ —2 Thess 3:1 (AV)⟩ **syn** see WAY — **as of course** *law* **:** as a thing to be granted upon a mere showing of the usual grounds and as not within the discretion of the judge to withhold — **in course** *adv* **1 a** *obs* **:** in turn **b :** in regular succession **:** in the usual or natural order **2 :** as a result of study and examination ⟨a degree taken *in course*, not an honorary one⟩ **3** *now dial* **:** of course **:** as might be expected — **in due course** *adv* **:** after natural passage of time **:** without modification of usual procedure **:** REGULARLY — **in full course :** moving or operating rapidly, at maximum speed, or without check or restraint — **in short course** *adv* **:** after a short period **:** BRIEFLY — **of course 1 :** of or following the ordinary way or procedure **:** NATURAL ⟨a thing *of course*⟩ ⟨a matter *of course*⟩ **2 :** as might be expected **:** without question **:** NATURALLY, CERTAINLY ⟨*of course* we will go⟩ **3 :** on the other hand **:** BUT

²course \"\ *vb* -ED/-ING/-S [ME *coursen*, fr. *cours*, *course*, n. — more at ¹COURSE] *vt* **1 a :** to hunt or pursue (game) with hounds ⟨*coursing* the stag⟩ **b :** to chase (game) with dogs by sight rather than scent ⟨~ a hare⟩ **c :** to cause (dogs) to chase after game **2 :** to follow close upon **:** PURSUE, RUN, CHASE ⟨we *coursed* him at the heels —Shak.⟩ **3** *obs* **:** to drive with blows **:** BLUDGEON, TROUNCE **4 a :** to run or move swiftly through or over **:** take one's course through **:** TRAVERSE ⟨jets *coursed* the area daily⟩ **b :** to cause (dogs) to run in a race **:** RACE **5 a :** to follow the course of (a stream) ⟨*coursing* the river⟩ **b :** to trace (a bee) by observing flight direction ⟨*coursing* the bee to its hive⟩ **6 :** to lay or form in courses ⟨~ bricks⟩ ⟨*coursing* the lumber⟩ **7 :** to divert and direct (an air current) along a certain route through a mine ~ *vi* **1 a :** to run or gallop esp. in a tournament or race or in hunting **b :** to take a course **:** pursue a certain course ⟨*coursing* along the coast⟩ **c :** to run or drive rapidly and steadily often over a set course or through a certain channel ⟨two Zuni runners . . . *coursed* over the sand with the fleetness of young antelope —Willa Cather⟩ **d :** to traverse or flow strongly or rapidly esp. on or as if on a certain path **:** PULSATE, SURGE ⟨blood *coursing* through his veins⟩ ⟨sap *coursing* through the young trees⟩ **2** *of a bell* **:** to move in change ringing steadily up or down in the striking order through a series of changes ⟨the biggest bell *coursing*⟩ **syn** see RUN

³course *obs var of* COARSE

coursed *adj* [fr. past part. of ²COURSE] **1 :** hunted with dogs ⟨a ~ hare⟩ **2 :** arranged in courses ⟨~ masonry⟩

coursed ashlar *n* **:** ashlar masonry in which the stones in a course are of the same height

coursed rubble *n* **:** masonry composed of roughly shaped stones fitting approximately on level beds

course of sprouts [prob. so called fr. the use of sprouts as switches in flogging] **:** a course of instruction marked by corporal punishment, hazing, rigorous discipline, or grueling tests or by thoroughness or difficulty

course of study 1 : the total number of courses offered by a school or college or by one of its branches **:** CURRICULUM **2 :** COURSE 4c

course protractor *n* **:** a navigation instrument for measuring bearings and comparing them against chart courses

¹cours·er \ˈkōrsər, ˈkȯr-, -ōəsə(r, -ō(ə)sə(r\ *n* -s [ME, fr. OF *coursier*, fr. *cours* course, run + *-ier* -er — more at COURSE] **:** a swift or spirited horse **:** WAR-HORSE, CHARGER

²courser \"\ *n* -s [*course* + *-er*] **1 :** a dog for coursing **2 :** one that courses **:** HUNTSMAN **3 :** any of a small group of birds that are related to the plovers and that inhabit Africa and southern Asia and are remarkable for their speed in running

courses *pl of* COURSE, *pres 3d sing of* COURSE

coursing *n* -s [fr. gerund of ²*course*] **:** conduction of the air current of a mine in different directions by means of doors and stoppings

coursing joint *n* **:** the mortar joint between two courses of bricks or stones

¹court \ˈkō(ə)r|t, -ȯ(ə)r|t,-ōə|t,-ȯ(ə)|t, *usu* |d·+V\ *n* -s [ME, fr. OF, fr. L *cohort-*, *cohors* enclosure, court, thing enclosed, crowd, fr. *co-* + *-hort-*, *-hors* (akin to L *hortus* garden) — more at YARD] **1 a :** the residence or establishment of a sovereign or similar dignitary and his retinue **:** the meeting place of a sovereign and his retinue, officers, or councillors ⟨riding to the king's ~⟩ **b :** a sovereign's formal assembly of his councillors and officers for administrative deliberation ⟨faced with these difficulties the king held a general ~⟩ **c :** the sovereign and his officers and advisers as constituting the governing power ⟨the ~ has decided against the alliance⟩ **d :** the family, officers, councillors, attendants, and retinue of a sovereign ⟨the ~ were enjoying the tournaments⟩ **:** the structure of social life revolving around a sovereign ⟨the gaiety of the ~⟩ **e :** an assembly held by a sovereign for diplomatic or social purposes **:** a state reception ⟨the ~ was held on Thursday⟩ ⟨being presented at ~ was the culmination of her social career⟩ **f** (1) **:** an assembly of one given the title of sovereign and his or her attendants ⟨the May queen and her ~⟩ (2) **:** a session in which one honored or prominent receives, is visited by, or talks freely with those seeking him out ⟨the old coach holding ~ in the locker room after the game⟩ **2 a :** a manor house, castle, or large building or group of buildings surrounded by its usu. enclosed grounds — now usu. used in the names of buildings or manors ⟨Hampton *Court*⟩ **b :** a group of cottages or cabins often in a formal arrangement **:** MOTEL **c :** an open space enclosed wholly or partly by buildings, walls, or fences **:** YARD; *sometimes* **:** an open area circumscribed on all sides by a single building ⟨the ~ at the center of the palace⟩ **d :** a quadrangular space either walled or marked off for playing one of various games with a ball (as lawn tennis, racquets, handball, or basketball); *also* **:** a division marked off in such a court ⟨a service ~⟩ ⟨the back ~⟩ **e :** an open area about a Jewish tabernacle or sanctuary **f :** an often paved yard opening off a street and built around with houses **:** a wide alley with only one opening onto a street **g :** a section of an exhibition or museum devoted to a particular exhibit or group of exhibits **h :** a place on or within a plant that provides circumstances suitable for some biological process (as infection or decay) to get a start **3 a :** the persons duly assembled under authority of law for the administration of justice **:** an official assembly legally met together for the transaction of judicial business **:** a judge or judges sitting for the hearing or trial of cases **b :** a session of such a court ⟨~ is now adjourned⟩ **c :** a chamber, hall, building, or other place for the administration of justice ⟨not enough seats in the ~ to accommodate the crowd⟩ **d :** a judge or judges in session viewed as individual persons ⟨restoratives were applied and the ~ was able to gasp "twenty dollars" —D.D.Martin⟩ ⟨the ~ was inconsistent in his rulings⟩ **e :** a faculty or agency whereby judgment or evaluation is made ⟨condemned in the ~ of human reason —M.R.Cohen⟩ **f :** a body of citizens convened to try a case ⟨condemned by the Athenian ~⟩ **g :** a body exercising the self-assigned role of judging and imposing punishments ⟨an investigating committee becoming a de facto ~⟩ **4 a :** an assembly or board vested with legislative or administrative as well as judicial powers ⟨many county governing boards are called ~*s* —J.E.Pate⟩ **b :** PARLIAMENT, LEGISLATURE ⟨the laws enacted by the high ~ of the land⟩

⟨the Great and General *Court* of Massachusetts⟩ **c :** a body of directors, managers, or delegates qualified to superintend the general affairs of an organization ⟨~ of a university⟩ **:** a body exercising judicial powers over its members or the members of a body represented by it ⟨commissioner's ~⟩ ⟨an ecclesiastical ~⟩; *also* **:** the assembly of such a body **5 :** ATTENTIONS: **a :** respectful deference **:** conduct or address calculated to win favor or dispel hostility **:** HOMAGE ⟨pay ~ to the king⟩ **b :** attentions intended to attract affection **:** wooing devices and techniques ⟨to pay ~ to a wealthy widow⟩ **6 :** a local chapter or lodge of any of various organizations **7** [short for *court shoe*] *Brit* **:** ³PUMP — **in open court :** with opportunity for public knowledge **:** not covertly or privately **:** OPENLY ⟨a judgment read *in open court*⟩ — **out of court 1 :** without a court hearing **:** by private arrangement ⟨settling the dispute *out of court*⟩ **2 :** out of consideration **:** extraneous to a discussion **:** too ill-advised or ridiculous to be considered ⟨the nationalists . . . have put themselves *out of court* as desirable rulers of African communities —A.P.Ryan⟩

²**court** \"\ *vb* -ED/-ING/-S *vt* **1 a :** to seek to win, gain, or achieve ⟨~ opportunity⟩ ⟨~ the favor of her professional associates —Tennessee Williams⟩ **b** (1) **:** to allure with attractions **:** INVITE, TEMPT, ATTRACT ⟨mountain streams ~*ing* the fishermen⟩ (2) **:** to act so as to invite, induce, call forth, or provoke ⟨~*ing* a disastrous defeat⟩ ⟨one ~*s* derision by imitating a classic without improving it —D.S.Berkeley⟩ **2 a :** to seek the affections of **:** make love to **:** WOO; *specif* **:** to seek to marry **b** *of an animal* **:** to perform actions to attract for mating ⟨a male bird ~*ing* a female⟩ **3 a :** to seek to attract by paying court **:** serve with attentions and courtesies **:** treat with blandishments and flatteries ⟨young nobles ~*ing* the dowager queen⟩ **b :** to seek the goodwill of **:** offer advantages and rewards to for support or alliance ⟨both candidates ~*ing* the independent voter⟩ ~ *vi* **1 :** to engage in social activities leading to engagement and marriage ⟨how the two met, how they ~*ed*, how they married —Quentin Reynolds⟩ **2** *of an animal* **:** to engage in play, display, and similar activity leading to mating ⟨a pair of robins ~*ing* in the trees⟩

³**court** \"\ *adj* **:** of, relating to, or appropriate to a court: as **a :** of, relating to, appropriate to, or frequenting a royal court; *sometimes* **:** FORMAL ⟨a ~ ball⟩ **b :** of or appropriate to a legal court; *sometimes* **:** LEGALISTIC, FORMALISTIC **c :** of a court game (as basketball or tennis) ⟨a ~ star⟩

court art *n* **:** art forms that exemplify or illustrate the elegant tastes or customs of a royal court — often opposed to *folk art*

court baron \ˈ=ˌ=ˈ=\ *n, pl* **courts baron** *or* **court barons** [AF *court baron*, lit., baron's court] **:** an inferior manorial court presided over by its lord or his steward that had jurisdiction over certain cases (as petty offenses) arising on the manor and affecting its tenants and that was abolished in England in 1867 after having fallen into disuse and was early abolished in New York, Pennsylvania, and Maryland where it existed briefly

court bond *n* **:** a surety bond required of litigants to insure payment of costs or the meeting of other obligations

court bouillon \(ˌ)kůr, (ˌ)kōr, (ˌ)kȯr+; *South often* ˌkübeˈän *or* -ˌōn *or* -ˌōⁿ\ *n* [F *court-bouillon*, fr. *court* short (fr. L *curtus* shortened) + *bouillon* — more at SHEAR] **:** a fish stock usu. containing seasoning, vegetables, and wine

court card *pronunc at* ¹COURT + ,-\ *n* [by folk etymology (influence of ¹*court*) fr. *coat card*] **:** FACE CARD

court christian *n, often cap both Cs* [trans. of AF *court cristiene*] **:** ECCLESIASTICAL COURT

court circular *n, usu cap both Cs* **:** the bulletin issued daily by the court of Great Britain to the press containing news of the court and the royal family

court clinic *n* **:** a clinic making psychiatric diagnosis of legal offenders in order to provide the judge with information and advice

courtcraft \ˈ=ˌ=\ *n* **:** the art or craft of conducting the affairs of a court **:** skill at improvising and implementing policy

court cupboard *n* [prob. fr. ¹*court*] **:** a cupboard of the 16th and 17th centuries in two sections the upper of which is closed with a door or doors and the lower open — compare PRESS CUPBOARD

court cupboard

court dance *n* **:** a grave and stately dance suitable for court functions — distinguished from *folk dance*

court day *n* [ME *corte day*, fr. *corte, court* court + *day*] **:** a day on which a court is in session

court dress *n* **:** formal dress prescribed for those appearing at a royal court

courted *past of* COURT

courte-échelle \ˌkůrd·(ˌ)āˈshel\ *n, pl* **courte-échelles** \-l(z)\ [F *courte échelle*, lit., short ladder] **:** a mountaineering maneuver in which a climber clambers on the body or head of another in order to reach a hold

cour·te·ous \ˈkərd·ēəs, ˈkȯ|, ˈkəi|, |tēəs, *esp Brit* ˈkȯ| *or* |·tyəs\ *adj* [alter. (influenced by *-eous*) of earlier *curtes, curtayse*, fr. ME *curteis, corteis*, fr. OF, fr. *court, cort* court — more at COURT] **1 :** marked by polished manners, gallantry, or ceremonial usage of a court **:** befitting a chevalier, courtier, or cosmopolitan ⟨presentation at St. James's had made him ~ —Jane Austen⟩ ⟨this love was ~, delicately ceremonial, precise —H.O.Taylor⟩ **2 :** marked by respect for and consideration of others **:** observing gentle or polished forms of social conduct often with inner sincerity **:** WELL-MANNERED ⟨too ~ and considerate to make stubborn subordinates yield —Allan Nevins & H.S.Commager⟩ ⟨most ~ and helpful in assisting me —Huntington Library⟩ **syn** see CIVIL

cour·te·ous·ly *adv* [alter. (influenced by *courteous*) of earlier *curtysely*, fr. ME *curteisly*, fr. *curteis* + *-ly*] **:** in a courteous manner

cour·te·ous·ness *n* -ES [ME *curteisnesse*, fr. *curteis* courteous + *-nesse* -ness] **:** the quality or state of being courteous **:** gracious civility **:** POLITENESS, COURTESY

cour·te·san *also* **cour·te·zan** \ˈkōrd·əzən, ˈkərˌ|ˈkōəˌ|ˈkȯ|, ˈkə|ˌˈkəi|, |tə-, -əsən *also* -ˌzan *or* -ˌsan *or* -aa(ə)n, *esp Brit* ˌ==ˈzan\ *n* -S [MF *courtisane*, fr. OIt *cortigiana* woman courtier, fem. of *cortigiano* courtier, fr. *corte* court (fr. L *cohort-, cohors*) + *-igiano* (suffix denoting origin, fr. *-ese* — fr. L *-ensis* — + *-ano* -an) — more at COURT] **:** a prostitute or kept woman often with a clientele drawn from a court or from the wealthy or the upper class

¹**cour·te·sy** \ˈkərd·əsē, ˈkə|, ˈkəi|, |tə-, *esp Brit* ˈkȯ|; *sense 4 and* ³COURTESY *are* " *or like* CURTSY\ *n* -ES [ME *curteisie, corteisie*, fr. OF, fr. *curteis, corteis* courteous + *-ie* -y] **1 a :** courteous behavior **:** well-mannered conduct indicative of respect for or consideration of others ⟨here was true ~ — the civil deed that shows the good heart —E.M.Forster⟩ **b :** a courteous act or expression **:** a favor courteously performed ⟨rising to receive him with every refinement of manner known to the time and with all the engaging graces and *courtesies* —Charles Dickens⟩ **c** *archaic* **:** a conventional expression of respect (as a bow) **2 a :** the sanction of general allowance or acceptance with goodwill despite facts or official regulation **:** INDULGENCE ⟨mountains they are called . . . but they are such by ~ only, for . . . the largest rises little more than 1300 feet —Hodding Carter⟩ **b :** consideration, cooperation, and generosity in providing or according (as a gift, loan, or privilege) **:** GRATUITY, GIFT ⟨the flowers were placed in the church through the ~ of the florist⟩ ⟨the player's costumes are by ~ of the department store⟩; *also* **:** AGENCY, MEANS ⟨all . . . swung obligingly into place . . . by ~ of a revolving stage —Robert Lawrence⟩ **3 :** CURTESY **4 :** ¹CURTSY

²**courtesy** \"\ *adj* **1 :** granted or performed as a courtesy or by way of courtesy ⟨a ~ letter⟩ ⟨~ visit⟩ **:** acting as or performing a courtesy **2 :** popularly conceded but not legally valid ⟨a ~ rank⟩ **:** done or performed as a ceremony usu. without official significance ⟨~ inspections⟩ **3 :** enjoying privileges of membership without officially belonging ⟨a hospital's ~ staff of doctors⟩ **:** conveying or granting privileges of membership to nonmembers

³**courtesy** \"\ *vb* -ED/-ING/-ES **:** ²CURTSY

courtesy book *n* **1 :** a medieval or Renaissance book designed to prepare the young nobleman for the proper pursuit of his courtly duties and pleasures **2 :** a book designed to prepare a young gentleman for public duties and conduct **:** a book of advice about social conduct

courtesy call *n* **:** a social call made for reasons of general courtesy and without a more specific purpose

courtesy card *n* **:** a card entitling its holder to some special privilege (as purchasing on credit or enjoying guest privileges)

courtesy literature *n* **:** literature comprising courtesy books and similar pieces

courtesy of the port : the extension to a passenger returning from a foreign port of the privilege of immediate customs examination of his baggage

courtesy title *n* **1 :** a title granted by usage and in some cases royal permission to certain lineal relatives of British peers: as **a :** a title in the style of a peerage borne by an heir in the direct line of a duke or marquess and by the eldest son of an earl and consisting in the case of the eldest son of the father's secondary title and in the case of the eldest son of the eldest son of another minor title attached to the peerage (as of the eldest son of the duke of Devonshire titled Marquess of Hartington and the eldest son of the marquess titled Earl of Burlington) **b :** a title consisting of the prefix "Lord", "Lady", or "the Honourable" added to the Christian name of other children of British peers **2 :** a title taken by the user and commonly accepted without consideration of official right (as *professor* for any teacher or *colonel* for any notable citizen)

court game *n* **:** an athletic game played on a court

court gray *n* **:** a very pale green that is yellower and paler than tourmaline and bluer and duller than emerald tint — called also *starling's-egg green*

court guide *n* **:** a directory of persons (as those received at court) who have status in British society

court hand *n* [¹*court* (of law) + *hand*] **:** the hand formerly used in charters, deeds, and other legal documents

court holy water *n* [¹*court*] *obs* **:** empty or insincere fair words **:** FLATTERY

courthouse \ˈ=ˌ=\ *n* [ME, fr. ¹*court* + *hous* house] **1 :** a building in which established courts are held **:** the principal building in which county offices are housed and in which county administrative affairs are conducted and which often contains also the county jail **2 :** COUNTY SEAT — used chiefly in place names in Virginia and some nearby states ⟨Appomattox *Courthouse*⟩; abbr. *C. H.*

cour·tier \ˈkōr|d·ēər, ˈkȯr-; ˈkōə|d·ēə(r, ˈkȯ(ə)|; |tēə-,|tyə- *also* |chə(r) *sometimes* ˈkůr| *or* ˈkůə|, or |ˌchi(ə)r *or* |ˌchiə *or* ˌ=ˈti(ə)r *or* ˌ=ˈtiə\ *n* -S [ME *courteour*, fr. (assumed) AF *courteour*, fr. OF *corteier* to be at the court of a prince (fr. *cort, court* court + *-our* -or) — more at COURT] **1 :** a gentleman attendant or habitué of a sovereign's court; *sometimes* **:** a ruler's satellite esp. given to flattery, soliciting favor, and connivance **2** *archaic* **:** one that courts or woos

cour·tier·ly *adj* **:** like a courtier **:** having the characteristics of a courtier

courting *pres part of* COURT

courting chair *n* **:** LOVE SEAT

courting mirror *n* **:** a usu. small mirror having a narrow wooden frame with insets of painted glass

court lands *n pl, English law* **:** land kept in demesne

court leet *n, pl* **courts leet** *also* **court leets :** a court formerly held in England and the colonies with jurisdiction over civil matters and petty offenses and surviving in England only for ceremonial purposes

courtlike \ˈ=ˌ=\ *adj* **:** ELEGANT, COURTLY

court·li·ness \ˈkōrtlēnəs, ˈkōət-,ˈkȯ(ə)t-, -lin-\ *n* -ES **:** the quality of being courtly **:** ELEGANCE, DIGNITY

court·ling \ˈkōrtliŋ, ˈkȯrt-,ˈkōət-,ˈkȯ(ə)t-, -lēŋ\ *n* -S [¹*court* + *-ling*] **:** a courtier esp. when young or insignificant

¹**court·ly** \-lē,-li\ *adj* -ER/-EST [ME, fr. ¹*court* + *-ly*] **1 a :** marked by highbred polish, stateliness, and ceremony **:** characteristic of court usage or of courtiers ⟨and the stately Spanish men . . . with their ~ foreign grace —Alfred Tennyson⟩ **b :** marked by elegance, richness, wit, or refinement befitting a court ⟨luxury and all manner of conceits are part and parcel of such a ~ civilization —George Santayana⟩ ⟨the ~ wit of the Cavalier —V.L.Parrington⟩ **2 a :** belonging to a court **:** appropriate to or suggestive of a court ⟨a ~ manor⟩ **:** participating in or serving at court functions ⟨the ~ guard⟩ **b :** favoring a court party or faction or its policies ⟨the plans of the ~ adherents⟩ **3 a :** strongly marked by formality and ceremony ⟨~ addresses⟩ **b :** utterly lacking in sincerity **:** FLATTERING, UNCTUOUS, OBSEQUIOUS ⟨~ protestations⟩ **syn** see CIVIL

²**courtly** \"\ *adv* **:** in a courtly manner **:** POLITELY

courtly love *n* **:** a late medieval highly conventionalized code prescribing conduct and emotions of ladies and their lovers and providing the theme of an extensive medieval courtly literature

court·man \ˈ=mən, -ˌman\ *n, pl* **courtmen** [ME, fr. ¹*court* + *man*] **:** COURTIER

¹**court-martial** \ˈ=ˌ==\ *n, pl* **courts-martial** *also* **court-martials** [alter. of earlier *martial court*] **1 :** a court consisting of commissioned officers and in the U. S. in some instances other personnel of the armed forces for the trial of offenders who are members of the armed forces or are within the jurisdiction of the armed forces and for the trial of offenses against military law **2 :** a session of a court-martial **:** a trial by court-martial

²**court-martial** \"\ *vt* **court-martialed** *also* **court-martialled; court-martialed** *also* **court-martialled; court-martialing** *also* **court-martialling** \-sh(ə)liŋ\ **court-martials :** to subject to trial by court-martial

court-noué \ˌkůr,nüˈā, -rnəˈwā\ *n* -S [F, fr. *court* short (fr. L *curtus* shortened) + *noué* knotted, past part. of *nouer* to tie, knot, fr. OF *noer* — more at SHEAR, DENOUEMENT] **:** a disease of the grape characterized by shortening of internodes, by small leaves, and by decline of vigor — called also *roncet*

court of admiralty : ADMIRALTY 3

court of appeal 1 *or* **court of appeals :** a court hearing appeals from the decisions of lower courts — compare APPELLATE, COURT OF FIRST INSTANCE **2** *usu cap C&A* **:** an appellate court usu. exercising final jurisdiction over civil cases in England and Wales from which appeal may be taken only to the House of Lords — compare HIGH COURT OF JUSTICE

court of cassation *often cap both Cs* [trans. of F *cour de cassation*] **:** the highest court of appeal esp. in various European countries

court of chivalry 1 *often cap both Cs* **:** an English court orig. dealing with military discipline but at various times trying cases concerning prisoners of war, high treason and rebellion, peerage claims, offenses against the honor of other persons, and usurpation or unlawful assumption of honors and still retaining jurisdiction in cases involving the right to armorial bearings — see COURT OF HONOR 1b, COURT OF THE CONSTABLE AND MARSHAL, EARL MARSHAL'S COURT **2 :** COURT OF HONOR

court of claims : a court having jurisdiction over claims (as against a government) ⟨the U.S. *Court of Claims*⟩

court of common pleas *often cap both Cs&P* **1 :** a former superior court of English common law at Westminster having jurisdiction over the ordinary civil suits between subject and subject and now forming part of the Court of King's Bench **2 :** a court of intermediate rank in some American states usu. having civil and criminal jurisdiction

court of criminal appeal *usu cap both Cs&A* **:** an appellate court usu. exercising final jurisdiction over criminal cases in England and Wales and from which appeal may be taken only to the House of Lords

court of delegates *often cap C&D* **:** a former English high court of appeal composed of commissioners appointed by the Crown and having jurisdiction over ecclesiastical cases now heard by the Judicial Committee of the Privy Council

court of domestic relations : a court having jurisdiction of family disputes that involve the rights and duties of husband and wife and parent and child esp. in matters affecting support, custody, and welfare of children and often having advisory and investigative powers and the assistance of psychiatrists, physicians, and other experts — called also *family court*; compare JUVENILE COURT

court of dustyfoot \-ˈ=ˌ=\ **:** COURT OF PIEPOUDRE

court of equity *also* **court of conscience :** a court having jurisdiction over suits in equity and administering justice and providing remedies according to the rules and principles of equity

court of errors : a court having jurisdiction to hear appeals on error

court of exchequer *usu cap C&E* **:** EXCHEQUER 2

court of first instance : the court first taking jurisdiction of a case — compare COURT OF APPEAL

court of honor 1 a : a tribunal to investigate questions of personal honor (as a military court investigating questionable acts) **b :** a court of chivalry (sense 1) in the exercise of its function esp. in the 17th century as a tribunal for trial of slanders against people of honor and for usurpation or unlawful assumption of armorial ensigns or of privileges of rank or office **2 a :** a troop committee in the British boy scout and girl guide movements that is composed of the troop leader or the guider and the patrol leaders and that deals with internal matters of discipline, expenditure, and general administration **b** (1) **:** a local or national group of authorized officials of the Boy Scouts of America that grants to scouts certificates of promotion and honor medals (2) **:** a meeting of or a ceremony conducted by this group **c :** the planning body of a girl scout troop composed of troop officers and adult leader **3 :** a group of outstanding usu. noncompeting exhibits in a stamp exhibit

court of inquiry : a military court to inquire into and report on some military matter (as the conduct of an officer)

court of king's bench *or* **court of queen's bench** *usu cap C&K&B&Q* **:** a former superior court presided over by the sovereign of England and following his person and now forming the King's Bench or Queen's Bench Division of the High Court of Justice entertaining as a superior court of record criminal cases on its crown side and civil cases on its plea side and embracing the jurisdiction of the former Court of Common Pleas and Court of Exchequer

court of last resort : a court of final appeal

court of law : a court that hears cases and decides them on the basis of statutes or the common law — compare EQUITY 2

court of love : a court of ladies supposed to have been held in medieval times to pass on questions of courtesy and courtly love

court of pie·pou·dre *or* **court of pie·pow·der** \-ˈpī,paůdə(r)\ [alter. of earlier *court of pipowders*, fr. ME *court of pepowders*, fr. ¹*court* + *of* + *pepowders, pipoudres*, pl. of *pipoudre* itinerant trader, fr. AF *piepoudrous*, fr. OF *pied, pié* foot (fr. L *ped-, pes*) + AF *poudrous* dusty, fr. OF *poudre* dust + *-ous, -eus* -ous — more at FOOT, POWDER] **1 :** an English summary court of record incident by the common law to every fair or market to administer justice for commercial injuries at that fair or market **2 :** a U.S. small-debts court

court of record [ME, fr. ¹*court* + *of* + *record*] **:** a court whose acts and judicial proceedings are written down for a perpetual memorial and hence are established and proved by the record

court of requests : an English court for the recovery of small debts

court of review : an appellate court

court of session *usu cap C&S* **:** the supreme civil court of Scotland

court of sessions : a court with power to hold sessions of the peace; *specif* **:** any of various U.S. state criminal courts of record

court of the constable and marshal *usu cap both Cs & M* **:** the English court of chivalry at the period when both the lord high constable and the earl marshal presided in it — compare EARL MARSHAL'S COURT

court of the lord lyon *usu cap C & both Ls* **:** LYON COURT

court of wards *or* **court of wards and liveries** *usu cap C&W &L* **:** an English court of record under the feudal system having jurisdiction over matters dealing with estates held of the Crown including their transfer from a deceased tenant to his heir and the payment of taxes and rents due the Crown from such estates

cour·toi·sie \ˌkůr·ˌtwäˈzē\ *n* -S [F, fr. MF *corteisie* — more at COURTESY] **:** COURTLINESS; *esp* **:** the code of courtly love

court order *n* **:** an order issuing from a competent court requiring a person to do or abstain from doing a certain act

court painter *n* **:** an artist holding the official position of painter to a royal court

court party *n* **:** a faction or party supporting the royal court esp. in political matters

court plaster *n* [so called fr. its cosmetic use by ladies at royal courts] **:** an adhesive plaster usu. of silk coated with a mixture of isinglass and glycerin that was formerly used for medical and cosmetic purposes — see ¹PATCH 2

court reporter *n* **:** a stenographer who records and transcribes a verbatim report of all proceedings in a law court

court roll *n* [ME *corte rolle*, fr. *corte, court* court + *rolle* roll] **:** a roll used in the records of a court

courtroom \ˈ=ˌ=\ *n* **:** a room in which a court of law is held

courts *pl of* COURT, *pres 3d sing of* COURT

courts baron *pl of* COURT BARON

court·ship \ˈkōr|t,ship, ˈkȯr|,ˈkōə|,ˈkȯ(ə)|, |ˌchip\ *n* **1** *obs* **:** conduct appropriate to a court or courtier **:** COURTLINESS, COURTESY **:** a courtier's state or condition ⟨gallants full of ~ and of state —Shak.⟩ **2 a** *obs* **:** the act of paying court **:** performance of ceremonial or complimentary courtesies ⟨his ~ to the common people —Shak.⟩ **b** *obs* **:** practice of a courtier's arts **:** use of diplomacy, flattery, finesse, and connivance **3 a :** the process of paying court to or showing attention to and affection for another person with intentions that involve marriage or other intimacy **b :** the relationship between a couple from awakening of deep interest to formal engagement **:** the period of such relationship **4 :** the act of trying to gain support or goodwill **:** solicitation and enticement **:** the endeavor to win, gain, or attain ⟨the duke's ~ of factions as yet uncommitted⟩ **5 :** the somewhat stereotyped and often complicated behavior culminating in copulation in many animals

court shoe *n* [so called fr. its use as a part of court dress] *Brit* **:** ³PUMP

courts leet *pl of* COURT LEET

courts-martial *pl of* COURT-MARTIAL

court tennis *n* **:** an ancient and complicated game played with a ball and rackets in an enclosed court that is usu. a covered building of peculiar construction, there being used in play besides a specially marked-out floor with a net crossing it the main walls, lower inner walls with sloping roof, various openings (as the dedans, grille, and winning gallery), and a projection in the main wall — see HAZARD SIDE, SERVICE SIDE, TAMBOUR; RACKET illustration

courtyard \ˈ=ˌ=\ *n* **:** a court or enclosure adjacent to or attached to a house, castle, palace, or other building; *specif* **:** a service area adjoining an apartment building, hotel, or commercial structure

cous \ˈkaů(ə)s\ *also* **cow·ish** \ˈkaůish\ *n* -ES [perh. fr. Nez Percé *kowish*] **:** an herb (*Lomatium cous*) of the northwestern U.S. having edible roots

cous·cous \ˈkü,sküs\ *or* **cous·cou·sou** *or* **cus·cu·su** \ˌküskəˈsü\ *or* **cus·cus** \ˈkü,sküs\ *n, pl* **couscouses** *or* **couscousous** *or* **cuscusus** *or* **cuscuses** [F *couscous, couscoussou*, fr. Ar *kuskus*, fr. *kaskasa* to pound, pulverize] **:** a No. African dish consisting variously of cracked wheat steamed and eaten as a cereal or with meat and vegetables as a main dish or with fruits and nuts as a dessert

cousen *obs var of* COZEN

¹**cous·in** \ˈkəzᵊn\ *n* -S [ME *cosin*, fr. OF *cosin, cousin*, fr. L *consobrinus* child of a mother's sister, cousin, fr. *com-* + *sobrinus* cousin on the mother's side, fr. *soror* sister — more at SISTER] **1 a** *obs* (1) **:** someone collaterally related more remotely than a brother or sister (as a nephew) (2) **:** one that is legally next of kin whether collaterally or lineally related except parent or child **b :** a child of one's uncle or aunt — called also *first cousin, full cousin, own cousin*; see CROSS-COUSIN, PARALLEL COUSIN **c :** a relative descended from one's grandparent or from a more remote ancestor by two or more steps and in a different line, a distinction often being made between (1) those descended an equal number of steps and (2) those descended an unequal number of steps from a common ancestor ⟨the children of first ~*s* are second ~*s* to each other, the children of second ~*s* are third ~*s*, etc.⟩ ⟨the child of one's first ~ is one's first ~ once removed, the latter's child is one's first ~ twice removed, etc., though these are often called also second and third ~*s* respectively⟩ **d :** a kinsman having some distant

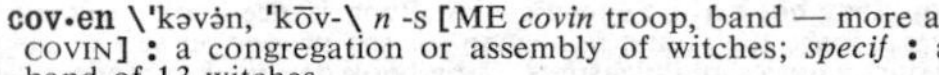

relationship usu. by blood **2 :** one marked by relationship, resemblance, or similar position or status **:** one readily associated with or thought of in connection with another **:** EQUIVALENT, COMPLEMENT, COUNTERPART, OPPOSITE NUMBER ⟨rural children deserve as good an education as their city ~s get —Benjamin Fine⟩ ⟨the sonic barrier and its higher-speed ~, the thermal barrier —B.K.Thorne⟩ **3** — used as a title by a sovereign in addressing or formally naming a nobleman of his own country or another sovereign and in English writs and commissions issued by the crown to refer to earls and peers of higher rank ⟨my noble lords and ~s all, good morrow —Shak.⟩ **4 a :** FRIEND, COMRADE, ASSOCIATE **b** *obs* **:** FOOL, GULL, DUPE **c :** a competitor who is frequently and easily defeated or thwarted by an opponent not clearly superior ⟨a pitcher who is a ~ to a certain batter⟩ **d :** an acquaintance of long, intimate, or informal standing **5 :** a person of a race or people ethnically or culturally related or similar ⟨our English ~s⟩ ⟨today's islanders resemble their mainland ~s —*Nat'l Geographic*⟩

²cousin \"\ *vi* **cousined**; **cousined**; **cousining** \ˈkəz(ə)niŋ\ **cousins** *NewEng* **:** to visit relatives esp. when distant

cous·in·age \ˈkəz(ə)nij\ *n* -s [ME *cosinage,* fr. MF *cosinage, cousinage,* fr. OF, fr. *cosin, cousin* + *-age*] **1 :** relationship of cousins **:** KINSHIP **2 :** a collection of cousins **:** KINSFOLK

cous·in·ess \-zᵊnəs\ *n* -ES [ME *cosiness,* fr. *cosin* + *-ess, -esse* -ess] **:** a female cousin **:** KINSWOMAN

cousin–german \ˌ=ˈ=ˌ=\ *n, pl* **cousins–german** [ME *cosin germain,* fr. MF, fr. OF, fr. *cosin* + *germain* related by descent from a common ancestor, having the same parents — more at GERMAN] **:** COUSIN 1b

cous·in·hood \ˈkəzᵊn,hu̇d\ *n* -s **1 :** KINSFOLK, KINSMEN **2 :** the relationship of cousins **:** the condition of being a cousin

cousin–in–law \ˈ===,=\ *n, pl* **cousins–in–law 1 :** a wife or husband of one's cousin **2 :** a cousin of one's wife or one's husband

cousin jack \ˌ==ˈjak\ *n, pl* **cousin jacks** *usu cap C&J* [¹*cousin* + *Jack* (the name)] **:** CORNISHMAN; *esp* **:** a Cornish miner

cous·in·ly *adj* **:** like or becoming a cousin ⟨shyly gave her a ~ kiss⟩

cous·in·ry \ˈkəzᵊnrē\ *n* -ES **:** a body of cousins or kinsfolk

cous·in·ship \-ᵊn,ship\ *n* -s **:** relationship of cousins **:** the fact of being a cousin **:** KINSHIP

cous·si·net \ˌküsᵊnˈā, -ᵊnˈet\ *n* -s [F, fr. OF, small cushion, dim. of *coussin* cushion — more at CUSHION] **1 :** a stone placed on the impost of a pier for receiving the first stone of an arch **2 :** the bolster or cushion of an Ionic capital

cou·tel \(ˈ)küˈtel\ *n* -s [MF, knife, fr. L *cultellus,* dim. of *culter* knife, plowshare — more at COLTER] **:** a medieval short knife or dagger

¹couth \ˈküth\ *adj* -ER/-EST [ME, pleasant, familiar, known, fr. OE *cūth* familiar, known; akin to OHG *kund* known, ON *kunnr,* Goth *kunths;* all fr. past part. of a prehistoric Gmc verb represented by OE *cunnan* to know, be able — more at CAN] *Scot* **:** COUTHIE

²couth \"\ *adj* -ER/-EST [back-formation fr. *uncouth*] **:** marked by finesse, polish, grooming, breeding, or sophistication **:** SMOOTH

couth·ie \-thē\ *adj* -ER/-EST [¹*couth* + Sc *-ie* -y (adj. suffix)] **1** *chiefly Scot* **:** PLEASANT, KINDLY, FRIENDLY **2** *chiefly Scot* **:** COMFORTABLE, SNUG

cou·til \küˈtē(ə)l, -til\ *n* -s [F, fr. OF, smooth tightly woven cloth used for covering mattresses, fr. *coute* quilt, mattress — more at QUILT] **:** a firm durable cotton or cotton and rayon fabric that is usu. woven in herringbone twill and is used esp. for foundation garments and suitings

cou·ture \küˈtu̇(ə)r *or as F*\ *n* -s [F, sewing, dressmaking, fr. OF *cousture* sewing, seam, fr. (assumed) VL *consutura,* fr. L *consutus* (past part. of *consuere* to sew together, fr. *com-* + *suere* to sew) + *-ura* -ure — more at SEW] **:** the business of designing, making, and selling fashionable expensive custom-made women's clothing; *collectively* **:** the designers and establishments engaged in this business

cou·tu·rier \küˈtu̇rēər; küˈtu̇rē,ā, (,)=,==ˈ=; küˈtu̇r,yā, ,=,=ˈ=\ *n* -s [F, dressmaker, fr. OF *cousturier* tailor's assistant, fr. *cousture* + *-ier* -er] **:** an establishment engaged in the business of couture; *also* **:** the proprietor of or designer for such an establishment

cou·tu·riere \küˈtu̇rēˌe(ə)r; küˈtu̇rē,e(ə)r, (,)=,==ˈ=; küˈtu̇r,ye(ə)r, ,=,=ˈ=\ *n* -s [F *couturière,* fr. OF *cousturiere* seamstress, fem. of *cousturier*] **:** a female couturier

cou·vade \küˈväd\ *n* -s [F, fr. MF, cowardly inactivity, fr. *couver, cover* to sit on (as a female bird on eggs), brood over + *-ade* — more at COVEY] **:** a custom among primitive peoples in many parts of the world in accordance with which when a child is born the father takes to his bed as if he himself had suffered the pains of childbirth, cares for the child, and submits himself to fasting, purification, or various taboos

cou·vert \(ˈ)küˈve(ə)r\ *n* -s [F, fr. MF, fr. OF *covert, couvert* covered, past part. of *covrir, couvrir* to cover — more at COVERT] **1 :** a table cover **2 :** COVER CHARGE

cou·verte \(ˈ)küˈve(ə)rt\ *n* -s [F, fr. fem. of *couvert* covered (past part. of *couvrir* to cover), fr. OF *covert, couvert*] **:** hard porcelain glaze

cou·xia \ˈküshēə\ *or* **cou·xio** \ˌküshēˈü, -ēˈō\ *n* -s [Tupi *cuchiu, cuxiu*] **:** SAKI

co·valence *or* **co·valency** \(ˈ)kō+\ *n* [*co-* + *valence, valency*] **:** nonionic valence characterized by the sharing of electrons usu. in pairs by two atoms in a chemical compound; *also* **:** the number of pairs of electrons an atom can share with its neighbors — distinguished from *electrovalence*

co·valent \"+\ *adj* **:** of relating to, or characterized by covalence — **co·va·lent·ly** *adv*

covalent bond *n* **:** a nonionic chemical bond formed by shared electrons, usu. a pair belonging orig. each to a different atom or both to one atom — distinguished from *electrovalent bond;* see COORDINATE BOND

co·va·re·ca \ˌkōvəˈrākə\ *n, pl* **covareca** *or* **covarecas** *usu cap* [AmerSp, prob. fr. Covareca] **1 a :** an extinct Otukian people of Paraguay **b :** a member of such people **2 :** the language of the Covareca people formerly considered to constitute a language family

co·variance \(ˌ)kō+\ *n* [*co-* + *variance*] **:** the arithmetic mean or the expected value of the product of the deviations of corresponding values of two variables from their respective mean values

co·variant \"+\ *adj* [ISV *co-* + *variant*] **:** changing along with something else so as to preserve certain mathematical interrelations unchanged

co·variation \"+\ *n* [*co-* + *variation*] **:** coincident variation

¹cove \ˈkōv\ *n* -s [ME, den, cave, fr. OE *cofa* den, small room; akin to OHG *chubisi* hut, ON *kūfr* heap, Gk *gypē* cave, Skt *guda* rectum — more at COT] **1** *Scot* **:** a hollow in a rock formation **:** CAVERN **2 :** a concavity or recessed place in a structure: as **a :** a member (as a molding) with a concave cross section **b :** a hollow slot in a spar into which the boltrope on a sail slides as a means of securing the sail to the spar **c :** a recess or trough for concealed lighting at the upper part of a wall **3 a :** a small sheltered inlet or bay ⟨an irregular shoreline broken by many ~s —*Amer. Guide Series: Mich.*⟩ **b :** a shallow tidal stream or arm of the sea **:** a backwater near the mouth of a tidal stream **4 :** a deep recess or small valley in the side of a mountain **:** a level area sheltered by hills or mountains **5 :** a basin or hollow where the surface of the land has caved in (as from solution of underlying rock)

²cove \"\ *vt* -ED/-ING/-S **1 :** to make or build in a hollow concave form **2 :** to provide (as a ceiling) with a cove

³cove \"\ *n* -s [Romany *kova* thing, person] *slang Brit* **:** MAN, CHAP, FELLOW, BLOKE

cove ceiling *n* **:** a ceiling the part of which next the wall is constructed in a cove

coved vault *n* **:** CLOISTER VAULT

cove lighting *n* **:** indirect interior lighting from incandescent or fluorescent lamps concealed in a reflecting trough near the ceiling

cove ceiling

co·vel·lite \kōˈve,līt, ˈkōvə,-\ *also* **co·vel·line** \-,lēn\ *n* -s [*covellite* fr. *covelline* + *-ite; covelline* fr. F, fr. Niccolò *Covelli* †1829 Ital. chemist who discovered it + F *-ine*] **:** a native copper sulfide CuS — called also *indigo copper*

co·ven \ˈkəvən, ˈkōv-\ *n* -s [ME *covin* troop, band — more at COVIN] **:** a congregation or assembly of witches; *specif* **:** a band of 13 witches

¹cov·e·nant \ˈkəvənənt *sometimes* -vnə-\ *n* -s *often attrib* [ME, fr. OF, fr. pres. part. of *covenir* to agree, be suitable, meet, fr. L *convenire* — more at CONVENE] **1 a :** an agreement that is usu. formal, solemn, and intended as binding **:** COMPACT ⟨international law, which depends upon the sanctity of ~s between rulers —G.H.Sabine⟩ ⟨the ~ among the people to defend their religion⟩ **b :** a particular stipulation in a covenant — obs. except in law **2** *obs* **:** SECURITY, PLEDGE **3 a :** an undertaking or promise of legal validity: as (1) **:** a contract under seal distinguished from other specialties by the promise or undertaking contained in it (2) **:** a particular agreement contained in a specialty or deed incidental to its main purpose — see USUAL COVENANTS (3) **:** the document or writing containing the terms of the agreement or promise **b :** the common-law form of action to recover damages for breach of such a contract **4 :** a solemn compact between members of a church to maintain its faith and discipline; *also* **:** the document recording such a compact **5 :** the promises of God as revealed in the Scriptures conditioned on certain terms on the part of man (as obedience, repentance, and faith); *specif* **:** an agreement regarded as having been made between God and his people Israel (as represented by Abraham, David, and others) whereby Israel was to be faithful to God and God was to protect and bless his faithful people

²covenant \", *before a syllable-increasing inflectional suffix usu* -və,nant *or* -və,naa(ə)nt\ *vb* -ED/-ING/-S [ME *covenanten,* fr. *covenant,* n.] *vt* **1 :** to promise solemnly by or as if by a covenant **:** pledge in formal agreement ⟨~*ing* that their hostages would be present⟩ ⟨~*ing* to sell only to certain buyers⟩ **2 :** to lay down as a condition **:** STIPULATE ⟨before signing, he ~*ed* that he would remain in possession⟩ **~** *vi* **:** to enter into a covenant **:** to come to formal agreement **:** CONTRACT ⟨his retainers ~*ing* in loyalty to the king⟩ **syn** see PROMISE

cov·e·nan·tal \ˌkəvəˈnantᵊl, -naan-\ *adj* **:** of or relating to a covenant ⟨the . . . purposes of a ~ God —N.H.Snaith⟩ — **cov·e·nan·tal·ly** \-ᵊlē,-ᵊli\ *adv*

covenanted *adj* [fr. past part. of *covenant*] **1 :** bound by a covenant: **a** *of an official of the Indian Civil Service* **:** bound by a covenant with the East India Company or later with the British government to observe certain regulations and assume certain obligations **b :** having subscribed to a covenant ⟨a ~ king⟩ **2 :** established by a covenant

cov·e·nan·tee \ˌkəvə,nanˈtē, -naan-; ˌkəv(ə)nən-\ *n* -s **:** the person to whom a promise in the form of a covenant is made

¹cov·e·nan·ter \ˈkəvə,nantə(r), -naan-, *in sense 2 often* ˌ==ˈ==; ˈkəv(ə)nən-\ *n* -s **1 :** one that makes a covenant **2** *usu cap* **a :** a signer or adherent of the Scottish National Covenant of 1638; *esp* **:** one of those who steadfastly held to the principles of this Covenant during the persecution under Charles II and James II (1661–1687) **b :** CAMERONIAN **c :** a member of a Reformed Presbyterian church

²covenanter \"\ *adj, usu cap* **:** of or relating to the Covenanters ⟨with their Scotch-Irish fire and *Covenanter* background —F.S.Mead⟩

covenanting *adj* [fr. pres. part. of *covenant*] **1 :** belonging to a covenant **2 :** entering into a covenant

covenant of salt [so called fr. its being ratified by eating a meal, the preservative quality of the salt perh. symbolizing a long-lasting agreement] **:** an inviolable covenant

cov·e·nan·tor \like COVENANTER, *or* ,==(,)=ˈtȯ(ə)r *or* ,==ˈtȯ(ə)r *or* -ˈtō(ə)r\ *n* -s **:** the party to a covenant who is bound to perform the obligation expressed in it

covenant theology *n* **:** FEDERAL THEOLOGY

covens *pl of* COVEN

¹cov·en·try \ˈkävəntrē, -ri, *more often in US than Brit speech* ˈkəv-\ *adj, usu cap* [fr. *Coventry,* city and county borough, Warwickshire, England] **:** of or from the city of Coventry, England **:** of the kind or style prevalent in Coventry

²coventry \"\ *n* -ES *usu cap* **:** a state of ostracism or exclusion from the society of one's fellows (as for objectionable conduct) ⟨sent to *Coventry*⟩

coventry bell *n, usu cap C* **1 :** a Eurasian perennial herb (*Campanula trachelium*) **2 :** CANTERBURY BELL **3 :** EUROPEAN PASQUEFLOWER

coventry blue *n, usu cap C* [fr. *Coventry,* England, where it was first made] **:** a blue embroidery thread

co–venture \(ˈ)kō+\ *n* -s **:** a cooperative that terminates after a certain project has been completed

¹cov·er \ˈkəvə(r)\ *vb* **covered**; **covered**; **covering** \ˈkəv(ə)riŋ, -rēŋ\ **covers** [ME *coveren, covren,* fr. OF *covrir,* fr. L *cooperire,* fr. *co-* + *operire* to cover, fr. (assumed) L *opverire,* fr. L *op-* (akin to L *ob* to, before, against) + (assumed) L *verire* to cover — more at EPI-, WEIR] *vt* **1 a :** to guard from attack **:** protect by interposition as a defending element **:** guard the safety and further the success of by aggressive action precluding attack ⟨units ~*ing* the retreat of the main army⟩ ⟨ships ~*ing* approaches to the harbor⟩ ⟨~*ing* the landing with a naval bombardment⟩ **b** (1) **:** to serve as a defense unit or center for **:** have within the range of one's guns **:** COMMAND ⟨forts ~*ing* the city⟩ ⟨artillery ~*ing* the channel⟩ (2) **:** to have within direct range of an aimed or drawn firearm ⟨the deputy ~*ed* the wounded gangster⟩ (3) **:** to protect by being in position and readiness to fire at a possible attacker ⟨the others in the patrol were ~*ing* the leader⟩ **c** (1) **:** to afford protection or security to typically by means of some stated provision **:** insure against a specified risk **:** guarantee indemnification to ⟨a policy ~*ing* the traveler in all kinds of accidents⟩ ⟨~ teachers by the retirement plan⟩ (2) **:** to afford protection against or compensation or indemnification for ⟨~ any storm losses⟩ ⟨~ loss of time due to illness⟩ (3) **:** to protect (oneself) against the consequences of possible loss or incrimination ⟨they felt themselves to be exposed to unnecessary risk, and they started to ~ themselves —Roy Lewis & Angus Maude⟩ ⟨~ himself with an alibi⟩ **d** (1) **:** to guard (as an opponent) in order to obstruct a play ⟨~*ing* the ends on a forward pass⟩ ⟨keeping the wings ~*ed* in hockey⟩ (2) **:** to station oneself so as to be able to receive a throw to (a base in baseball) ⟨the pitcher ~*ed* first on the bunt⟩ **e** (1) **:** to guard against or make provision for (a demand or charge) by means of a reserve stock or deposit ⟨a balance to ~ the check⟩ ⟨money to ~ his debts⟩ (2) **:** to maintain a check on by patrolling or watching ⟨motorcycle police ~*ing* the roads⟩ (3) **:** to protect by contrivance or expedient ⟨otherwise slavers could ~ themselves by that flag with impunity —S.F. Bemis⟩ **2 a** (1) **:** to hide from sight or knowledge **:** prevent observation or knowledge of **:** divert attention from **:** conceal the impression of by a device for masking **:** CONCEAL ⟨a show of his old arrogance to ~ his embarrassment —Agnes S. Turnbull⟩ ⟨the shrewd purpose, ~*ed* over with pretentious rhetoric —V.L.Parrington⟩ (2) **:** to conceal or mask as blameworthy or illicit ⟨fanaticism ~*s* a weakness of moral position —Weston La Barre⟩ — often used with *up* or *over* ⟨~ up a scandal⟩ ⟨~*ing* up his own lack of trust⟩ (3) **:** to divert attention from (another who is engaged in something criminal or unethical) (4) **:** to obliterate from knowledge or remembrance (as through complete forgiveness) ⟨blessed is he . . . whose sin is ~*ed* —Ps 32:1 (AV)⟩ (5) **:** to block (an actor or a stage property) from being seen by an audience or photographed by a camera (6) **:** MAKE *vt* 13b (7) **:** ²BLANKET 3d **b :** to envelop or lie over or around so as to present an ornamental, disguising, or protecting exterior ⟨all that beauty that doth ~ thee —Shak.⟩ **3 :** to put, lay, or spread something over, on, or before (as for protecting, enclosing, or masking) **:** OVERLAY ⟨~*ing* the seed bed with straw⟩ ⟨~*ing* the bruise with salve⟩ **4 a :** to lie over **:** spread over **:** be placed on or often over the whole surface of **:** ENVELOP, FILM, COAT ⟨snow ~*ing* the highways⟩ ⟨new paint ~*ing* the old⟩ ⟨~*ed* with oil⟩ ⟨a badly wounded man ~*ed* with blood⟩ **b :** to extend thickly over conspicuously or dominatingly **:** abound over **:** occupy the whole surface of ⟨locusts ~*ing* the plains⟩ ⟨armadas ~*ing* the sea⟩ ⟨invaders ~*ing* the land⟩ **c :** to appear here and there on the surface of **:** DOT, DAPPLE — usu. used with *with* ⟨a resort area ~*ed* with lakes⟩; often in Brit. use with *in* ⟨the backs of his huge hands were ~*ed* in thick black hair —George Bellairs⟩ **5 :** to protect or conceal (one's body or a part of it) from view typically with an article of clothing or bedding ⟨~ her nakedness⟩ ⟨~ your head⟩ ⟨~ your mouth while coughing⟩ **6 :** to equip with a cover **:** place or set a cover over permanently or temporarily ⟨~ a book with leather⟩ ⟨~ a couch with mohair⟩ ⟨~ a pan with a lid⟩ **7 :** to put a surface layer over usu. completely ⟨a tent ~*ed* with skins⟩ ⟨~*ing* the old roof with new shingles⟩ ⟨~*ing* the page with ink⟩ **8 a :** to fill (a blank surface) completely ⟨~*ing* the sheet of paper with marks⟩ ⟨~*ing* the silk with embroidery⟩ **b :** to spread a cloth over in preparing to serve a meal **9 :** to rise above and immerse ⟨floodwaters ~*ing* the town⟩ ⟨enough water to ~ the vegetables⟩ **10 a :** to copulate with (a female) **:** SERVE — usu. used of an animal (as a horse) ⟨a horse ~*s* a mare⟩ **b :** to sit on and incubate (eggs) **:** BROOD **11 :** to bring upon or earn for (a person) a large or excessive amount of something usu. immaterial ⟨~*ed* with shame at his failure⟩ ⟨~*s* himself with glory in the battle⟩ **12 a :** to play a higher-ranking card immediately after or on (a previously played card) ⟨North ~*ed* West's jack with the queen⟩ **b :** to be higher in rank than (the previously played card) ⟨the king from the dummy ~*ed* the queen led by East⟩ **13 a :** to have width or scope enough to include or embrace ⟨an examination ~*ing* the year's work⟩ ⟨we must remember that no laws can be provided to ~ every contingency —F.D.Roosevelt⟩ **b :** to comprise, include, or embrace in an effective scope of treatment or operation ⟨policy clauses ~*ing* the situation⟩ ⟨plans ~*ing* unexpected enemy attacks⟩ **14 :** to subsume in an overall class, significance, or meaning ⟨people are so intensely for anything ~*ed* by the word *democratic* —M.R.Cohen⟩ ⟨a formula which should ~ everything I wished to include —T.S.Eliot⟩ **15 :** to treat or deal with; *often* **:** DISCUSS ⟨material ~*ed* in the first chapter⟩ ⟨a talk ~*ing* an important question⟩ **16 a :** to serve often with scope or inclusiveness in an indicated or expected way ⟨bus lines ~*ing* the area⟩ **:** operate in **b :** to have (a locality or a group of persons) as one's territory or field of activity (as in selling the merchandise or promoting the interests of a company or in rendering social or business service) ⟨one salesman ~*s* the whole state⟩ **17 a :** to pass over at an indicated speed **:** journey through while executing one's mission **:** TRAVEL, TRAVERSE ⟨~*ing* 10 miles that day⟩ ⟨~*ing* the distance to the city in two hours⟩ ⟨prospectors who ~*ed* this range⟩ **b :** to be found over or in **:** INHABIT ⟨tribes that ~ these areas⟩ **c :** to travel to or through as a sightseer **:** visit as a sightseer ⟨~*ing* three states in two days⟩ ⟨the trip ~*ed* the museum that afternoon⟩ **18 :** to be adequate to defray or compensate **:** defray the cost of **:** pay for **:** BALANCE ⟨a reserve fund to ~ unexpected expenses⟩ ⟨a special grant to ~ the research program⟩ **19 :** to place one's money or stake upon or in equal jeopardy with (the money or stake of one's opponent) in a bet **:** answer to (a similar offer or challenge) **:** accept an offered bet by (a person) **20 :** to extend a treatment over **:** range in treatment through or over ⟨a series of medical examinations ~*ing* three weeks⟩ ⟨a novel ~*ing* three generations⟩ **21 :** to buy securities or commodities for delivery against (an earlier short sale) ⟨~*ing* his shorts⟩ ⟨~ his sales⟩ **22 :** to report news about **:** investigate, watch, and check on for newsworthy material **:** be responsible for information about **:** take news pictures of ⟨reporters and radio commentators ~*ing* the campaign⟩ **23 :** to extend over (an indicated area) ⟨a park ~*ing* 50 acres⟩ **~** *vi* **1 a** *obs* **:** to spread a table for a meal **b :** to put one's hat back on after having stood bareheaded **2 :** to spread over a surface ⟨this paint ~*s* well⟩ **3 :** to buy stocks or commodities for delivery on a date fixed by a previously contracted sale ⟨~*ing* at a loss⟩ **4 a :** to guard a player, play, or position (as in basketball) **b :** to play a higher-ranking card on a lower-ranking one **5** *of a bird or mammal* **:** to become covered with feathers or hair (as after a molt) **6 a :** to conceal something illicit, blameworthy, or embarrassing from notice **:** prevent one from being censured for error, laxity, or omission — usu. used with *up* ⟨~ up for a careless friend⟩ **b :** to act as a substitute or replacement to prevent loss or disaster during an absence ⟨a fire company ~*ing* for another answering a call⟩ ⟨a stand-in ~*ing* for an injured star⟩ **c :** to assume a defensive position (as in boxing) that protects the face and midriff — often used with *up* ⟨the challenger ~*ed* up⟩ — **cover one's tracks** *or* **cover up one's tracks :** to conceal traces to elude pursuit **:** hide or mask evidences of usu. blameworthy or illicit activity ⟨he was guilty but he had *covered his tracks* too well to be convicted⟩ — **cover the ground** *or* **cover ground 1 :** to traverse a course or distance with satisfying speed ⟨that new outfielder can really *cover the ground*⟩ ⟨a bulldozer that *covers the ground* well⟩ **2 :** to embrace or treat a subject or to perform or execute an assignment esp. with thoroughness and efficiency ⟨the lecturer *covered the ground* well⟩ ⟨the book *covers* a lot of *ground*⟩

²cover \"\ *n* -s *often attrib* [ME, fr. *coveren* to cover] **1 :** something that protects, shelters, or guards ⟨run for ~ when the fight starts⟩: as **a** (1) **:** a place of natural shelter for an animal or bird esp. when sought as game ⟨foxes in a ~⟩ (2) **:** the factors that provide natural shelter and protection for wild animals (as suitable arrangements of vegetation, denning sites, or rock formations) (3) **:** plants and their residues covering the ground and retarding runoff and erosion of soil **b** (1) **:** a position or situation affording protection from enemy fire ⟨as the gunners ducked behind ~ —C.S.Forester⟩ ⟨the platoon sergeant crawls and slithers from ~ to ~ —Burtt Evans⟩ ⟨~ and concealment⟩ (2) **:** the protection offered by aircraft in tactical support of a military operation ⟨landing on the beach under heavy air ~⟩ **c** (1) **:** a deposit or sum of money sufficient to secure against loss or to meet an obligation (2) **:** insurance coverage **d** (1) **:** COVER POINT (2) **covers** *pl* **:** cover point and extra cover point ⟨a drive through the ~s⟩ **2 :** something that is placed over or about another thing **:** something that covers: **a :** LID, TOP ⟨a box ~⟩ **b** (1) **:** a binding or case for a book or the comparable outer part of a pamphlet or magazine; *also* **:** either rectangular portion of this cover extending from the backbone and forming the front or the back ⟨front ~⟩ (2) **:** JACKET 3f (1) **c :** an overlay or outer layer esp. for protection ⟨a mattress ~⟩ **d** (1) [trans. of F *couvert*] **:** a tablecloth and the other table fittings; *esp* **:** the table fittings for use of one person at a meal ⟨~*s* were laid for 50 guests⟩ (2) **:** COVER CHARGE **e :** COPULATION **:** an act of covering — usu. used of animals (as horses) **f :** ROOF ⟨exhibits under ~⟩ **g** (1) **:** a cloth used on a bed for warmth or for decoration (as a quilt, blanket, bedspread, or coverlet) (2) **:** bedclothes for covering a person in bed — usu. used in pl. **h** *Brit* **:** an automobile tire tread **i :** something that covers the ground: (1) **:** VEGETATION ⟨a thick forest ~ in these areas⟩ (2) **:** snow esp. for skiing ⟨the lodge area had a good ~⟩ **j :** a large shallow salt pan with a movable roof used for making salt from brine by evaporation in the sun **k :** COVER STONE **l :** the overburden or cap rock above a deposit (as of ore, oil, or coal) **m :** full obscuration of the sky by clouds **:** the extent to which clouds obscure the sky ⟨clear weather with only $\frac{1}{10}$ ~⟩ **3 :** something that conceals or obscures **:** CONCEALMENT: as **a :** the total factors making for hiding or obscuring ⟨a crime committed under ~ of darkness⟩ **b :** a masking device or pretext **:** SCREEN, GUISE ⟨the club was a ~ for a subversive group⟩ ⟨we may admit that our conventional morality often serves as a ~ for hypocrisy and selfishness —Lucius Garvin⟩ ⟨under ~ of altruism he took greedy advantage of the wartime misfortunes —Ann F. Wolfe⟩ ⟨a spy with a ~ name⟩ **c** (1) **:** an envelope or wrapper that contains or has contained mail matter (2) **:** an envelope, wrapper, letter sheet, or postal card bearing stamp and postmark or other markings showing that it has passed through the mails — see FLOWN COVER, STAMPLESS **4 a :** the uniform appearance of plain closely woven goods with threads evenly spaced **b :** the nap on fabric **5 :** the whole width of a horseshoe ⟨a shoe with a ~ of 6 inches⟩ — **from cover to cover** *of a book* **:** from the front cover through to the back cover **:** COMPLETELY, THOROUGHLY ⟨read *from cover to cover*⟩ — **off cover** *of a stamp* **:** having been removed from the cover (sense 3c(2)) — **on cover** *of a stamp* **:** remaining on the cover (sense 3c(2)) — **under cover 1 :** in an envelope or wrapper **2 :** enclosed within a missive addressed to a person other than the intended recipient **3 :** under concealment **:** in secret

cover address *n* **:** an address to which mail can be sent for forwarding to the real addressee and which is used to conceal the name or address of the addressee or in the case of illicit correspondence to avoid arousing the suspicion of the postal authorities

cov·er·age \ˈkəv(ə)rij, -rēj\ *n* -s [¹*cover* + *-age*] **1 :** the act or fact of including or treating **:** a thing that covers **:** COVER: as **a :** INSURANCE **:** protection by insurance policy **:** inclusion within the scope of a protective or beneficial plan ⟨~ against liability claims⟩ ⟨~ for librarians in the teachers' retirement system⟩ **b :** the amount (as of gold) available to meet liabilities ⟨a 40 percent gold ~ of outstanding bank notes⟩ **c :** treatment to publicize or make known ⟨the ~ of the subject in his botany text⟩: (1) **:** news reporting and comment ⟨~ of the state department involves certain technical problems⟩ (2) **:** amount of news reporting ⟨the revolution was given scant ~ abroad⟩ ⟨the dictator demanded better ~ for his domestic program⟩ **d :** provision of cover by aircraft **e :** vegetation covering the ground **:** GROUND COVER **2 :** whatever is covered **:** scope or extent of covering **:** aggregate of items covered: as **a :** the area that may be covered with a gallon of paint, varnish, or other surface cover — distinguished from *hiding power* **b :** extent of covering by plant sprays **c :** the aggregate of risks covered by the terms of a contract of insurance ⟨a policy with extensive ~⟩ **d** (1) **:** the number of persons or the population area reached or served by a communication or a medium of communication **:** percentage of potential customers covered ⟨an advertisement with wide ~⟩ ⟨a radio station with more power and greater ~⟩ (2) **:** the circulation of a newspaper or periodical in a given area or throughout a class of people **e :** the area of the subject that is or can be included clearly in a photographic image **f :** percentage of ground area occupied by buildings

cov·er·all \ˈ==,=\ *n* -s [¹*cover* + *all*] **:** an outer garment worn to protect other garments; *esp* **:** a one-piece combination of overalls and shirt — usu. used in pl.

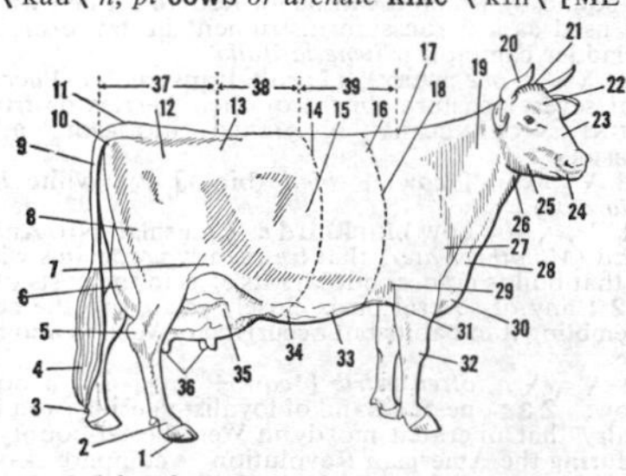

coveralls

cover–all \"\ *adj* [¹*cover* + *all*] **:** COMPREHENSIVE ⟨*cover-all* provisions⟩

cover charge *n* **:** a charge made by a restaurant or nightclub for service or entertainment in addition to the charge for food and drink ⟨a 2-dollar *cover charge* per person⟩

cov·er·chief \ˈkəvə(r)-; *last syll like that of* HANDKERCHIEF\ *n* [ME *coverchief, keverchief* — more at KERCHIEF] **:** a covering for the head; *also* **:** HANDKERCHIEF

cover crop *n* **:** a crop (as rye or clover) planted in orchards or in otherwise bare fields to prevent soil erosion and to help soil improvement

covered *adj* [ME, having a cover, fr. past part. of *coveren* to cover] **1 :** with contracted throat **:** not open **:** CLOSED, THIN — used esp. of a tone in the upper register **2 :** included in the group with respect to which a particular contract or agreement is in force ⟨domestic service is now a ~ job under the social-security law⟩

covered bridge *n* **:** a bridge that has its roadway protected by a roof and enclosing sides

covered dish *n* **:** CASSEROLE

covered–dish supper *n* **:** a community meal to which each guest brings one dish, all dishes being shared by all

covered fifth *n* **:** HIDDEN FIFTH

covered octave *n* **:** HIDDEN OCTAVE

covered smut *n* **:** a smut disease of grains in which the spore masses are covered or held together for some time by the persistent grain membrane and glumes — compare LOOSE SMUT

covered wagon *n* **1 :** a broad-wheeled wagon with a canvas top supported by bows ⟨the *covered wagon* of the pioneers⟩ — see ²CONESTOGA, PRAIRIE SCHOONER **2** *Brit* **:** BOXCAR

covered way *n* **:** a corridor running along the top of a counterscarp and protected by an embankment whose outer slope forms the glacis

cov·er·er \ˈkəvərə(r)\ *n* -s [ME, fr. *coveren* to cover + *-er, -ere* -er] **:** a factory workman who puts a cover or wrapping on manufactured articles

cover girl *n* **:** a usu. beautiful girl whose picture appears on a magazine cover

cover glass *n* **1 :** a piece of very thin glass used to cover microscopic preparations mounted on glass slides **2 :** a sheet of plain glass used to protect the surface of a transparency to which it is bound

cover in *vt* **1 :** to finish the covering over of; *esp* **:** complete a roof over **2 :** to cover (into)

¹cov·er·ing \ˈkəv(ə)riŋ, -rēŋ\ *n* -s [ME *coveringe,* fr. *coveren* to cover + *-inge, -ing* -ing (n. suffix)] **:** something that covers or conceals: as **a :** COVER 2g **b :** purchases by short sellers in security and commodity markets to close out their commitments

²covering \"\ *adj* [fr. pres. part. of *cover*] **:** that covers: as **a :** protecting or supporting a position or a force ⟨~ fire for the platoon that was moving up⟩ **b :** containing explanation, additional information, and often recommendation of an accompanying communication ⟨a ~ letter⟩ ⟨a ~ note⟩

covering disease *n* **:** DOURINE

covering power *n* **:** the extent of the field over which a photographic lens can give a sharp image often expressed as an angle

cover into *vt* **1 :** to transfer to **:** enter into the receipt records of **:** assign to the control of ⟨funds *covered into* the treasury by the bill⟩ **2 :** to cause to be included or embraced within or under a particular system or category ⟨the power to *cover into* the civil service any minor government office⟩

cov·er·less \ˈkəvə(r)ləs\ *adj* **:** not having a cover

cov·er·let \ˈkəvə(r)lə̇t *also* -,le|t *or* -,li|t; *usu* |d·+V\ *n* -s [ME, by folk etymology (influence of ME *-let*) fr. *coverlite,* fr. AF *coverelyth,* fr. *covere-* (fr. OF *covrir* to cover) + *lyth, lit* bed, fr. L *lectus* — more at COVER, LIE] **1 :** a bedspread sometimes quilted or of heavy material **2** *archaic* **:** COVER

cov·er·lid \-,lid, -lə̇d\ *n* -s [ME, by folk etymology (influence of ME *lid*) fr. *coverlite* coverlet] *dial* **:** BEDSPREAD

cover memory *n* **:** SCREEN MEMORY

cover note *n, Brit* **:** a preliminary memorandum or binder for insurance

cover paper *n* **:** a strong durable printable paper of a type suitable for booklet or magazine covers

cover plate *n* **1 :** a cover, hood, or head used to close in or cover over the end or top of a receptacle, chamber, or section of a structure **2 :** a plate riveted to the flange of a steel beam, girder, or column to increase its strength — called also *flange plate*

cover point *n* [¹*cover* + *point*] **1 a :** a cricket fielding position between point and mid off **b :** a player in this position **2 a :** a lacrosse position between point and first defense **b :** a player in this position

covers *pres 3d sing of* COVER, *pl of* COVER

cover–shame \ˈ==,=\ *n* [¹*cover* + *shame*] **1** *obs* **:** a device for masking something shameful ⟨put on holy garments for a *cover-shame* of lewdness —John Dryden⟩ **2** [so called fr. its use to induce abortion] **:** SAVIN

cover shot *n* **:** a wide-angle photographic shot including a whole scene

cover slip *n* **:** COVER GLASS 1

coverslut \ˈ==,=\ *n* [¹*cover* + *slut*] **:** an outer garment worn to conceal untidy clothes

cover spray *n* **:** a pesticidal spray applied esp. to fruit trees at intervals after the petals fall in order to provide a protective coverage for the foliage

cover stone *n* **:** the coarse mineral aggregate strewn over the surface of a bituminous bound or treated pavement

cover story *n* **:** a story accompanying a magazine-cover illustration

cover symbol *n* **:** a symbol standing for two or more related phonemes (as *V* or *C* in *VCV,* meaning vowel + consonant + vowel)

¹cov·ert \ˈkəvə(r)|t, ˈkōvə(r)|t, -ō,vər|t, -ō,və̄|t, -ō,vəi|t, *usu* |d·+V\ *adj* [ME, fr. OF (past part. of *covrir* to cover), fr. L *coopertus,* past part. of *cooperire* to cover — more at COVER] **1 a :** marked by or as if by concealment **:** kept private **:** not open, overt, or avowed **:** HIDDEN, VEILED ⟨ostensibly in sympathy but with ~ malice⟩ **b :** of hidden or doubtful meaning ⟨the ~ wording of the message⟩ **c :** performed or expressed surreptitiously, with reluctance to admit or avow, or with attempt at concealment ⟨listening to the long story with ~ yawns⟩ ⟨at first in ~ conversation and now more openly in published works —W.H.Camp⟩ **2** *obs* **:** SECRETIVE, DECEITFUL **3 :** covered over, sheltered, and secluded esp. in sylvan surroundings ⟨starting from some ~ place, saluted the chance comer on the road —William Wordsworth⟩ **4** *of a woman* **:** married and under cover, authority, or protection of the husband — see FEME COVERT **5 a :** subconsciously motivated **:** implicit rather than explicit **:** UNDERLYING ⟨~ behavior⟩ ⟨~ needs⟩ **b :** not sanctioned or allowed open social expression ⟨~ cultural configurations and values⟩ **syn** see SECRET

²cov·ert \ˈkəvə(r)|t, *usu* |d·+V; *Brit often* ˈkəvə(r\ *n* -s [ME, fr. MF, fr. *covert,* adj.] **1 a :** hiding place **:** SHELTER, REFUGE ⟨soldiers firing from ~*s*⟩ **b :** a coppice affording cover for game **:** a hiding place in such a coppice ⟨the king shot a stag as it broke from ~ —S.P.B.Mais⟩ **c :** a masking or concealing device ⟨deliberation as a ~ for their inactivity⟩ **2** *archaic* **:** something that covers **:** COVERING ⟨the thick ~ on a walnut⟩ ⟨a bed without ~*s*⟩ **3 :** a feather covering the bases of the quills of the wings and tail of a bird — called also *tectrix;* see BIRD illustration **4** *or* **covert cloth :** a firm durable twilled sometimes waterproofed coating and suiting usu. made of mixed-color yarns that give a flecked effect; *also* **:** a similar cotton or rayon fabric for sportswear

¹covert–baron \¦=(,)=¦==\ *adj* [AF *couverte baroun,* alter. of *coverte de baron,* lit., covered by a husband] **:** ¹COVERT 4

²covert–baron \"\ *n, pl* **coverts–baron :** the status of one married, usu. a woman

covert brown *n* [²*covert* + *brown*] **:** a variable color averaging a grayish olive that is redder and duller than average olive drab and redder and lighter than bronzesheen

cover text *n* **:** a text in clear language within which a ciphertext is concealed (as by a grille)

covert gray *n* [²*covert* + *gray*] **:** a variable color averaging a light olive gray that is deeper and slightly greener than piping rock and paler and slightly greener than slate tan

cover title *n* **:** the title lettered on the cover (as of a book, magazine, or catalog)

co·vert·ly *adv* [ME, fr. ¹*covert* + *-ly*] **1 :** in a covert manner ⟨glancing ~ over his shoulder⟩ **2 :** with suggestive implication rather than direct expression

co·vert·ness *n* -ES **:** the quality or state of being covert

covert tan *n* [²*covert* + *tan*] **:** a light grayish olive color that is redder and stronger than Quaker gray, lighter and slightly redder and less strong than hemp, and redder, lighter, and stronger than twine

cov·er·ture \ˈkəvər,chu̇(ə)r, -,chər\ *n* -s [ME, fr. OF, fr. *covert* (past part. of *covrir* to cover) + *-ure*] **1 a :** a decorative or protective covering **b :** SHELTER, PROTECTION, DISGUISE **2 :** the legal status of a woman during marriage and under the cover, authority, and protection of her husband

cover type *n* **:** the plant growth characteristic of an area

cover–up \ˈ==,=\ *n* -s [fr. *cover up,* v.] **:** a device or stratagem for masking, concealing, or preventing investigation, incrimination, or discovery ⟨a *cover-up* for incompetence and wishful thinking —Herbert Elliston⟩ ⟨using a contrived accident as a *cover-up* for murder⟩

coves *pl of* COVE, *pres 3d sing of* COVE

cov·et \ˈkəvə̇t, *usu* ·ə̇d·+V\ *vb* -ED/-ING/-S [ME *coveiten,* fr. OF *coveitier,* fr. *coveitié* covetousness, desire, fr. (assumed) VL *cupidictat-, cupidictas,* alter. of L *cupiditat-, cupiditas,* fr. *cupidus* desirous (fr. *cupere* to desire) + *-itat-, -itas* -ity; akin to MHG *verwepfen* to become moldy, Icel *hvap* dropsical flesh, Goth *afhwapjan* to choke, extinguish, L *vapor* steam, vapor, Gk *kapnos* smoke, Skt *kupyati* he swells with rage, is angry; basic meaning: smoking, boiling] *vt* **1 :** to wish for earnestly **:** crave possession or enjoyment of **:** long for ⟨winning ~*ed* honors⟩ ⟨her invitations came to be ~*ed* by people who were desirous of moving in good society —G.B.Shaw⟩ **2 :** to desire (another's possession or attribute) inordinately or culpably ⟨neither shalt thou ~ thy neighbor's house, his field, or his manservant —Deut 5:21 (AV)⟩ ⟨this region originally belonged to the Sioux but was ~*ed* for its rich resources by the Chippewa —*Amer. Guide Series: Minn.*⟩ **~** *vi* **:** to feel or cherish inordinate desire or craving for another's possession or attributes ⟨you should be content with what you have . . . it is a sin to ~ —Edna S. V. Millay⟩ — formerly used with *for* or *after* ⟨the wealth that many had ~*ed* after was willed to various charities⟩ **syn** see DESIRE

cov·et·able \ˈkəvə̇d·əbəl\ *adj* [ME *covaytabill,* modif. (influenced by ME *coveiten* to covet) of MF *covoitable,* fr. OF *coveitable,* fr. *coveitier* to covet + *-able*] **:** DESIRABLE

cov·et·ing·ly *adv* **:** in a coveting manner

covetise *n* -s [ME *coveitise,* fr. OF, alter. (influenced by *-ise* as in *marcheandise* merchandise) of *coveitié*] *obs* **:** inordinate desire **:** COVETOUSNESS

cov·e·tive·ness \ˈkəvə̇d·ivnə̇s\ *n* -ES [*covet* + *-ive* + *-ness*] **:** an inclination or desire to acquire and possess esp. as indicated phrenologically

cov·e·tous \ˈkəvə̇d·əs, -ə̇təs, *Brit also* ÷ -vəchəs\ *adj* [ME *coveitous,* fr. OF, fr. *coveitié* + *-ous*] **:** given to, marked by, or arising from coveting: **a :** marked by craving and deep desire to own wealth or possessions ⟨it's on your account that he's been so particular about money of late, he was never ~ before —G.B.Shaw⟩ **b :** having a craving for possession — used with *of,* formerly with *for* ⟨a man ~ of honors⟩ **c :** marked by inordinate, culpable, or envious desire for another's possessions ⟨throwing ~ eyes out of their forests on the fields and vineyards of their neighbors —J.A.Froude⟩

syn GREEDY, ACQUISITIVE, GRASPING, AVARICIOUS: COVETOUS stresses strength of desire, usu. for what is rightfully another's and generally with envy ⟨France, jealous as it was of his greatness and *covetous* of his Gascon possessions —J.R.Green⟩ ⟨first settlers brought fine hunting dogs . . . of which the Indians were so *covetous* that a day was set each year when settlers traded dogs —*Amer. Guide Series: Va.*⟩ GREEDY stresses lack of restraint ⟨a child *greedy* for candy⟩ ⟨with eyes by the gold lust blinded, with the *greedy* griping hand —William Morris⟩ ⟨he loved learning; he was *greedy* of all writings and sciences —G.G.Coulton⟩ ACQUISITIVE implies not only eagerness to possess but aptitude for acquiring and retaining ⟨one of those strenuous, *acquisitive* women —E.A.Weeks⟩ ⟨our present *acquisitive* society, in which our craving for material things seems never to be satisfied —R.E.Baber⟩ GRASPING always implies an unashamed selfishness in acquiring, usu. by any quick means ⟨a *grasping* old miser⟩ ⟨*grasping* commercialism —George Nobbe⟩ AVARICIOUS implies eagerness and the capacity for indiscriminate acquisition befitting a grasping person and strongly suggests stinginess ⟨an *avaricious* black-market profiteer⟩ ⟨dust and ashes, and fiery lava are sufficient to satisfy the most *avaricious* thrill seeker —E.B. Branson & W.A.Tarr⟩ ⟨the *avaricious* old man lived in squalor, keeping his money hidden in odd places around his house⟩

cov·e·tous·ly *adv* [ME *coveitously,* fr. *coveitous* + *-ly*] **:** in a covetous manner

cov·e·tous·ness *n* -ES [ME *coveitousnesse,* fr. *coveitous* + *-nesse* -ness] **:** the state of being covetous **:** AVARICE

¹cov·ey \ˈkəvē, -vi\ *n* -s [ME, fr. MF *couvee, covee,* fr. OF *covee,* fr. fem. of *cové,* past part. of *cover* to sit on (as a female bird on eggs), brood over, fr. L *cubare* to lie down — more at HIP] **1 :** a brood of birds **:** a mature bird or pair of birds with a brood of young **:** a small flock or number of birds of the same kind — used typically of partridges and certain related birds; compare BEVY **2 a :** COMPANY, CROWD, BAND, CREW ⟨a ~ of friends —John Buchan⟩ ⟨a ~ of schoolgirls —H.V.Morton⟩ ⟨a ~ of suspicious nuns —Earle Birney⟩ **b :** a number of things of the same kind **:** GROUP ⟨barricades and a ~ of tanks —Virginia A. Oakes⟩ ⟨a ~ of queries answered for about-to-be brides —*Mademoiselle*⟩ ⟨a ~ of conferences —*Economist*⟩

²cov·ey \ˈkōvi\ *n* -s [³*cove* + *-y*] *slang Brit* **:** a young fellow

cov·in *also* **cov·ine** \ˈkəvə̇n, ˈkōv-\ *n* -s [ME *covin, covine,* fr. MF *covin* band, affair, *covine* affair, fr. ML *convenium* agreement, arrangement, fr. L *convenire* to agree — more at CONVENE] **1** *archaic* **:** CREW, BAND, CONFEDERACY **2 a :** collusive agreement between two or more persons to the detriment of a third **:** CONSPIRACY **b :** *archaic* **:** FRAUD, TRICKERY **3 :** COVEN

coving *n* -s [¹*cove* (molding) + *-ing*] **:** COVE; *specif* **:** the molding or members that form a cove

cov·i·nous \ˈkəvə̇nəs, ˈkōv-\ *adj* [*covin* + *-ous*] **:** marked by covin **:** COLLUSIVE, FRAUDULENT — **cov·i·nous·ly** *adv*

covin–tree \ˈ==,=\ *n* [¹*covin* + *tree*] **:** a tree in front of a Scottish mansion beneath which a laird or owner formerly met his visitors or his retainers

¹cow \ˈkau̇\ *n, pl* **cows** *or archaic* **kine** \ˈkīn\ [ME *cou* (pl.

cow: *1* hoof, *2* pastern, *3* dewclaw, *4* switch, *5* hock, *6* rear udder, *7* flank, *8* thigh, *9* tail, *10* pinbone, *11* tail head, *12* thurl, *13* hip, *14* barrel, *15* ribs, *16* crops, *17* withers, *18* heart girth, *19* neck, *20* horn, *21* poll, *22* forehead, *23* bridge of nose, *24* muzzle, *25* jaw, *26* throat, *27* point of shoulder, *28* dewlap, *29* point of elbow, *30* brisket, *31* chest floor, *32* knee, *33* milk well, *34* milk vein, *35* fore udder, *36* teats, *37* rump, *38* loin, *39* chine

ky, kyn), fr. OE *cū* (pl. *cȳ, cȳe,* gen. *cūna, cȳna*); akin to OHG *kuo* cow, ON *kȳr,* L *bos* ox, cow, Gk *bous* head of cattle, cow, Skt *go* bull, cow] **1 a :** the mature female of wild or domestic cattle of the genus *Bos* or of any of the various animals the male of which is called *bull* (as the moose, certain seals, or the alligator) — see HEIFER **b :** a domestic bovine animal regardless of its sex or age ⟨bring home the ~*s*⟩ **2 :** a person clumsy, obese, coarse, or otherwise unpleasant; *sometimes* **:** PROSTITUTE **3** *slang Austral* **:** a troublesome or unpleasant person or thing ⟨shot by some silly ~ with a gun⟩ — compare FAIR COW **4** *slang* **:** MILK

²cow \"\ *n* -s [origin unknown] *Scot* **:** GOBLIN, BUGBEAR

³cow \"\ *vt* -ED/-ING/-S [alter. of ²*coll*] **1** *chiefly Scot* **:** to cut short **:** POLL, CROP **2** *Scot* **:** OVERTOP, EXCEED

⁴cow \"\ *n* -s [origin unknown] **1** *chiefly Scot* **:** a bare twig of heather or broom **2** *chiefly Scot* **:** a brush of twigs **:** BESOM

⁵cow \"\ *vt* -ED/-ING/-S [prob. of Scand origin; akin to Dan *kue* to subdue, Sw & Norw *kuva,* obs. Sw & Norw *kuv* hump] **:** DAUNT, AWE **:** intimidate with threats, show of strength, or impressiveness **:** dispirit into inactivity or submission ⟨he flung them back, commanded them, ~*ed* them with his hard, intelligent eyes, like a tamer among beasts —Arthur Morrison⟩ ⟨frightfulness inaugurated by the military chiefs to ~ the inhabitants —A.D.H.Smith⟩ **syn** see INTIMIDATE

⁶cow \"\ *n* -s *Scot* **:** FRIGHT, SCARE, ALARM

⁷cow \"\ *n* -s [alter. of ¹*cowl* (chimney pot)] *dial Eng* **:** a chimney cowl

cow·age *also* **cow·hage** *or* **cou·hage** \ˈkau̇ij\ *n* -s [Hindi *kavāc, kāvāc,* prob. fr. Skt *kapikacchu,* fr. *kapi* monkey (of Hamitic origin; akin to Egypt *gif,* an eastern African ape) + *kacchu* itch, of Dravidian origin; akin to Kanarese *kajji* itch] **1 :** a tropical woody vine (*Mucuna pruritum*) having crooked pods covered with barbed brittle hairs that cause severe itching **2 :** the hairs of the cowage mixed with honey or other vehicle used as a vermifuge **3 :** TRUMPET CREEPER

cow·an \ˈkau̇ən\ *n* -s [Sc, fr. *cowan* unskilled worker at masonry, of unknown origin] **:** one who is not a Freemason; *esp* **:** one who would pretend to Freemasonry or intrude upon its secrets

cow·an·young \ˈkau̇ən,yəŋ\ *n* -s [prob. native name in Australia] **:** a horse mackerel (*Trachurus novaezelandiae*) of Australia and New Zealand often canned for food

¹cow·ard \ˈkau̇(ə)rd, |əd\ *n* -s [ME *coward, cuard,* fr. OF *coart, cuart,* adj & n., fr. *coe, coue* tail (fr. L *cauda*) + *-art* -ard; fr. the idea of a coward retreating to the tail end of an army, or fr. the idea of a frightened animal with its tail between its legs] **:** one who shows ignoble fear **:** a basely timid, easily frightened, and easily daunted person ⟨a ~, irresolute, impulsive in any crisis —Walter de la Mare⟩ ⟨is an arrant ~ and shows the white feather at the slightest display of pluck in his antagonist —John Burroughs⟩

²coward \"\ *adj* [ME *coward, cuard,* fr. OF *coart, cuart,* adj. & n.] **1 a :** having or arising from a coward's nature **:** TIMID, FAINTHEARTED, COWARDLY ⟨that craven ~ knight —Edmund Spenser⟩ ⟨neither altogether ~ nor brave —John Reed⟩ **b :** of or characteristic of a coward or cowardice ⟨~ cries⟩ ⟨~ deceit⟩ **2** *heraldry* **:** borne in the escutcheon with his tail doubled between his legs ⟨a lion ~⟩ **syn** see COWARDLY

³coward *vt* -ED/-ING/-S [ME *cowarden,* fr. ¹*coward*] *obs* **:** to make timorous **:** FRIGHTEN **:** cause to show cowardice

cow·ard·ice \-də̇s *sometimes* -,dīs\ *n* -s [ME *cowardise,* fr. OF *coardise, cuardise,* fr. *coart, cuart* coward + *-ise* -ice] **:** the quality of a coward **:** ignoble timidity **:** fainthearted lack of courage; *also* **:** lack of resolution in the face of hostile sentiments of others ⟨the mean between foolhardiness and ~ —G.L.Dickinson⟩ ⟨to abandon that logic was to abandon clearness of mind: it was mental ~ —F.M.Ford⟩

cow·ard·li·ness \-dlēnə̇s, -lin-\ *n* -ES **:** the quality or state of being cowardly

¹cow·ard·ly \-dlē, -li\ *adv* [ME, fr. ²*coward* + *-ly*] **:** in a cowardly manner

²cowardly \"\ *adj* [¹*coward* + *-ly*] **:** like or befitting a coward **:** showing a coward's nature **:** marked by or arising from utter lack of courage **:** ignobly timid and faint-hearted ⟨~ dogs, ye will not aid me then —P.B.Shelley⟩ ⟨if you want to make charges, make them openly. I will not listen to ~ hints —Sinclair Lewis⟩

syn COWARD, PUSILLANIMOUS, POLTROON, CRAVEN, DASTARDLY, RECREANT: COWARDLY, the most general term of this group, and COWARD indicate weak and ignoble timidity ⟨a timid and *cowardly* man, who, according to one account, now surrendered Lothian to King Malcolm for fear that he might avenge the victories won over him by his brother —E.A.Freeman⟩ ⟨you are an incompetent *cowardly* rascal, sir! damn me if you're not! are you afraid of a crowd of bloody savages whilst you have arms in your hands—C.B.Nordhoff & J.M.Hall⟩ ⟨you laughed in my face as you are trying to laugh now, only your *coward* heart cannot keep your lips from twitching —A. Conan Doyle⟩ PUSILLANIMOUS connotes abjectness and contemptibility ⟨I lived in a continual indefinite pining fear; tremulous, *pusillanimous,* apprehensive of I knew not what —Thomas Carlyle⟩ POLTROON, uncommon as an adjective, suggests complete cowardice ⟨we had to make a show of impotence, which gave them to understand that the Arabs were too *poltroon* to cut the line near Maan and keep it cut —T.E.Lawrence⟩ CRAVEN implies extreme defeatism and complete lack of resistance ⟨your prayers will do more for me . . . than the swords of the *craven* sycophants would have done had they remained true —Alfred Tennyson⟩ ⟨a man whom a *craven* fear had made insensible to shame —T.B.Macaulay⟩ DASTARDLY is used in references to situations and personalities blending utter cowardice with the treacherous or outrageous ⟨since the unprovoked and *dastardly* attack by Japan on Sunday, December 7th —F.D.Roosevelt⟩ ⟨they'll spare the women; but my man tells me they have taken an oath to give no quarter to the men —the *dastardly* cowards —W.M.Thackeray⟩ RECREANT, currently more common in the meaning of *apostate,* implies abject lack of resistance ⟨when I was bewildered and *recreant* and was inclined to go back upon all my fiercest convictions —Victoria Sackville-West⟩

cow·ard·ness *n* -ES [ME *cowardnesse,* fr. *coward* + *-nesse* -ness] **:** the quality or state of being coward **:** COWARDICE

cowbane \ˈ=,=\ *n* [¹*cow* + *bane*] **:** any of several poisonous plants of the family Umbelliferae: as **a** (1) **:** the European water hemlock (2) **:** an American water hemlock; *esp* **:** SPOTTED COWBANE **b :** a hog fennel (*Oxypolis rigidior*) that is widespread in wet lowlands in the eastern and central U.S.

cow bean *n* **:** COWPEA

cow beet *n* **:** MANGEL-WURZEL

cowbell \ˈ=,=\ *n* **1 a :** a bell hung about the neck of a cow to make a sound by which it can be located **b :** a bell without a clapper used as a percussion instrument in dance orchestras **2 :** a bladder campion (*Silene latifolia*)

cowberry \ˈ=,=- — *see* BERRY\ *n* [prob. trans. of NL *Vaccinium*] **:** any of several pasture shrubs or their berries or fruits: as **a :** MOUNTAIN CRANBERRY **b :** MARSH CINQUEFOIL **c :** PARTRIDGEBERRY 1

cowbind \ˈ=,=\ *n* [ˡ*cow* + *bind* (bine)] **:** a white bryony (*Bryonia alba*)

cowbird \ˈ=,=\ *also* **cow blackbird** *n* **1 :** a small No. American blackbird (*Molothrus ater*) that frequently associates with cattle and that builds no nest but lays its eggs in the nests of other birds **2 :** any of several birds closely related to the cowbird and resembling it in habits but occurring in Mexico and further south

ˡ**cowboy** \ˈ=,=\ *n, often attrib* [ˡ*cow* + *boy*] **1 :** a boy that tends cows **2 a :** one of a band of loyalist guerillas and irregular cavalry that operated mostly in Westchester county, New York, during the American Revolution — compare SKINNER 2 **b :** an outlaw or gangster in the early days of the U.S. West **3 a :** one who tends and drives herds of cattle particularly in western U.S. and Canada; *typically* **:** a distinctively accoutered horseman tending large herds of beef cattle — called also *cowpuncher, puncher* **b :** a usu. mounted cattle ranch hand **c** (1) **:** a rodeo rider **:** a performer who gives exhibitions of roping, riding, bulldogging (2) **:** an actor whose usual role is that of a cowboy, a gunman, or adventurer in a western **4 :** NEW BRONZE **5 :** one given to display or to recklessness; *esp* **:** an automobile driver who violates rules of safety and law ⟨a cautious highway cyclist, though; no ~ stuff —W.L.Gresham⟩

²**cowboy** \"\ *vi* -ED/-ING/-S **:** to drive an automobile recklessly

cowboy boot *n* **:** a boot made with a high arch, a high Cuban heel, and usu. fancy stitching and worn esp. by American cowboys

cowboy hat *n* **:** a wide-brimmed hat with a large soft crown of the type worn by western ranch hands

cowboy pool *n* **:** pool played with a cue ball and three object balls numbered 1, 3, and 5, the object being to score exactly 90 points by caroms and by pocketing the object balls, 10 points more by caroms only, and finally a single point by pocketing the cue ball after contact with the number one ball

cowboys and indians *n, usu cap I* **:** a children's game involving mock pursuits, gunfights, and killings as though between cowboys and Indians

cowboy suit *n* **:** a child's outfit typically with colored shirt, wide belt, and chaps simulating the dress of a cowboy

cowbrute \ˈ=,=\ *n, chiefly Midland* **:** a cow or steer esp. when range-bred and wild

cow calf *n* **:** HEIFER

cow camp *n* **:** a cowboy camp **:** a roundup headquarters

cow cane *n, Austral* **:** a sugarcane grown for silage

cowcatcher \ˈ=,==\ *n* **1 :** PILOT 4a **2 :** a brief radio and television commercial given just before a program and advertising a secondary product of the program's sponsor

cow clover *n* **:** ZIGZAG CLOVER

cow cockle *n* **:** COWHERB

cow cocky *n, chiefly Austral* **:** a small dairy farmer

cow college *n* **1 :** a college devoted to agriculture **:** a university school of agriculture **2 :** a freshwater or provincial college or university that lacks culture, sophistication, and tradition

cow corn *n* **:** POD CORN

cow cress *n* **:** FIELD CRESS

cow·cum·ber \ˈkau̇,kəm(b)ə(r)\ *dial var of* CUCUMBER

cow·die \ˈkau̇dē\ *n* -S [modif. of Maori *kawri*] **:** KAURI

cow·dria \ˈkau̇drēə\ *n, cap* [NL, fr. Edmund V. *Cowdry* b1888 Am. scientist + NL *-ia*] **:** a genus of small pleomorphic intracellular rickettsias known chiefly from ticks but including the causative organism (*C. ruminantium*) of heartwater disease of ruminants

cowed *past of* COW

co·ween \kəˈwēn, kōˈ-\ *n* -S [of Algonquian origin; akin to Malecite *ku-wēs* mallard, Pequot *ungwáums* old squaw duck, Narragansett *queequeekum* duck] **:** OLD-SQUAW

cow·er \ˈkau̇(ə)r\ *vb* **cowered; cowered; cowering** \-au̇(ə)riŋ\ **cowers** [ME *couren*, of Scand origin; akin to Norw *kura* to cower, OSw *kūra* to sit still, Dan *kure* to sit or lie still; akin to MHG & MLG *kūren* to lie in wait, lurk, ON *kārr* curly hair, Gk *gyros* round, MIr *gūaire* hair, Lith *gauras* body hair, and perh. to ON *kot* small hut — more at COT] *vi* **1** *now dial Eng* **:** to crouch down **:** SQUAT **2 :** to shrink away or cringe usu. in abject fear of something menacing or domineering and sometimes from cold ⟨they all ~*ed* silently in their places, seeming to know in advance that some terrible thing was about to happen —George Orwell⟩ ⟨~*ing* in their huts like so many rabbits in their burrows, listening in fear —Charles Kingsley⟩ ~ *vt, chiefly Scot* **:** to bend down

cowfish \ˈ=,=\ *n* **1 a :** any of various small cetaceans (as the grampus and species of porpoises and dolphins) **b :** SIRENIAN **2 :** any of various boxfishes having projections resembling horns over the eyes

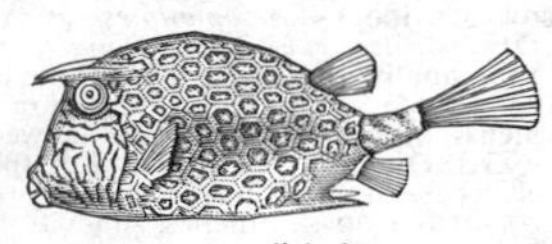
cowfish 2

cow fulani *n, pl* **cow fulani** *or* **cow fulanis** *usu cap C&F* [ˡ*cow*] **:** one of a nomadic group of the Fulani people of West Africa

cowgate \ˈ=,=\ *n* -S [back-formation fr. earlier *kynegates*, fr. *kine* (*archaic* pl. of ˡ*cow*) + *gates*, pl. of *gate* (way)] **:** a right to pasture one cow on common land ⟨a cottager having two ~*s* on the common⟩

cowgirl \ˈ=,=\ *n* **1 :** a girl who tends cows **2 :** a girl or woman working, performing, or acting as a cowboy

cowgram \ˈ=,=\ *n* -S [ˡ*cow* + *gram* (chick-pea)] **:** CHICK-PEA

cowgrass \ˈ=,=\ *n, Austral* **:** RED CLOVER

cowhage *var of* COWAGE

cowhand \ˈ=,=\ *n* [ˡ*cow* + *hand* (laborer)] **:** a man engaged to assist with ranch work and the care of range cattle **:** COWBOY

cow·heart·ed \ˈkau̇ˌhärd·əd\ *adj* -ER/-EST [influenced in meaning by *coward*] **:** COWARDLY

cow·heel \ˈ=,=\ *n* **:** the foot of a cow or ox stewed into a jelly

cow·heifer \ˈ=,==\ *n, Brit* **:** a young cow up to the time of attaining a full set of adult teeth

cow·herb \ˈ=,=\ *n* **:** a European soapwort (*Saponaria vaccaria* or *Vaccaria pyramidata*) with pale rose-colored flowers

cowherd \ˈ=,=\ *n* [ME *cowherde*, fr. OE *cūhyrde*, fr. *cū* cow + *hyrde* herder — more at COW, HERD] **:** one who tends cows

ˡ**cowhide** \ˈ=,=\ *n* [ˡ*cow* + *hide*] **1 :** the hide of a cow **2 :** leather made of the hide of a cow or other adult bovine animal **3 a :** a coarse whip made of rawhide or of braided leather **b :** a shoe or boot of cowhide

²**cowhide** \"\ *vt* -ED/-ING/-S **:** to flog with a cowhide whip

cow hitch *n, naut* **:** a clumsy or slippery hitch

cow hock *n* **:** a hock of a horse or dog that turns or bends inward like that of a cow so that the shanks of the hind legs are very close

cow-hocked \ˈkau̇ˌhäkt\ *adj* **:** having cow hocks

cow horse *n* **:** COW PONY

cowhouse \ˈ=,=\ *n* **:** a barn for cows

cow hunt *n* **:** ROUNDUP 2

cow·i·chan \ˈkau̇əchən\ *n, pl* **cowichan** *or* **cowichans** *usu cap* **1 :** a Salishan people of Vancouver Island **2 :** a member of the Cowichan people

cowier *comparative of* COWY

cowiest *superlative of* COWY

cowing *pres part of* COW

ˡ**cowish** *var of* COUS

²**cowish** \ˈkau̇ish\ *adj* **1 :** like a cow **:** BOVINE **2** *obs* **:** FEARFUL, COWARDLY

cow·itch \ˈkau̇ich\ *n* -ES [by folk etymology] **:** COWAGE

cow keeper *n* **1 :** one that keeps cows **2** *obs* **:** one appointed by a town or village to superintend pasturing of cows and sometimes distributing milk

cow killer *n* **:** the wingless female of certain wasps of the family Mutillidae; *esp* **:** the large red and black velvet ant (*Dasymutilla occidentalis*) that has a severe sting

ˡ**cowl** \ˈkau̇l, *esp before pause or consonant* -au̇əl\ *n* -S [ME *cowle*, fr. OE *cugele*, fr. LL *cuculla* monk's hood, fr. L *cucullus* hood, perh. of Celt origin; akin to OIr *cūl* hiding place; akin to Gk *keuthein* to conceal — more at HIDE] **1 a :** a usu. sleeveless garment composed of a hood attached to a gown or robe and worn as the typical garb of a monk **b :** a hood esp. of a monk **c :** the symbol of a monk or of things monastic **:** the condition of a monk or fact of being a monk ⟨abandoning the ~ to assume a layman's life⟩; *sometimes* **:** MONK **d :** a part of a garment modeled after some part of the monk's cowl; *esp* **:** a draped neckline on a woman's garment **2 a** *Scot* **:** a cap worn in the house **:** NIGHTCAP **b** *dial Eng* **:** a swelling on the head **:** BOIL **3 :** something resembling a cowl in shape **:** HOOD: as **a :** a chimney covering designed to improve the draft by directing the smoke out horizontally often by use of a revolving metal hood **b :** a curved hood or a cap on a ventilator pipe to improve the draft **:** a covered air exhaust **c :** the top portion of the front part of an automobile body forward of the two front doors to which are attached the windshield and instrument board **d :** COWLING

C cowl 1b

²**cowl** \"\ *vt* -ED/-ING/-S **1 a :** to garb with a cowl; *specif* **:** to make a monk of **b :** to cover as if with a cowl ⟨peaks ~*ed* in clouds⟩ **2 :** to equip or cover with a cowl ⟨an airplane engine ~*ed* in⟩

³**cowl** \ˈkōl, ˈkül, ˈkau̇(ə)l\ *n* -S [ME *cowle, cuvel*, fr. OE *cȳfel, cūfel*, fr. ONF *cuvele* small vat, fr. LL *cupella*, dim. of L *cupa* tub, cask — more at HIVE] *now dial Eng* **:** a large tub or vessel; *esp* **:** a vessel with two handles to facilitate carrying

cowle \ˈkau̇(ə)l\ *n* -S [Hindi *qawl*, fr. Ar *qawl* saying] *India* **:** a grant or engagement in writing esp. of safe-conduct or amnesty

cowled *adj, biol* **:** shaped like a hood **:** HOODED, CUCULLATE

cowled seal *n* **:** COUNSELLOR SEAL

cow·ley father \ˈkau̇lē, -li *also* ˈkül-\ *n, cap C&F* [fr. *Cowley*, suburb of Oxford, England] **:** a member of the Society of Mission Priests of St. John the Evangelist, an Anglican religious community founded at Oxford in 1865 by the Rev. R. M. Benson (1824–1915)

cowlick \ˈ=,=\ *n* **:** a lock or tuft of hair growing in a different direction from the rest of the hair and usu. turned up or awry as if licked by a cow

cowlicks \ˈ=,=\ *n pl but sing or pl in constr* **:** SILVER BELL

cow·like \ˈkau̇ˌlīk\ *adj* **:** resembling, suggestive of, or having the characteristics of a cow

cow lily *n* **1 :** a marsh marigold (*Caltha palustris*) **2 :** SPATTERDOCK

cowl·ing \ˈkau̇liŋ\ *n* -S [ˡ*cowl* + *-ing*] **:** a removable metal covering that houses the engine and sometimes also a portion of the fuselage or nacelle of an aircraft; *broadly* **:** a metallic cover over or around any engine

cow·litz \ˈkau̇ləts\ *n, pl* **cowlitz** *or* **cowlitzes** *usu cap* [fr. the *Cowlitz* river in southwestern Wash.] **1 a :** a Salishan people of the Cowlitz river valley in southwestern Washington **b :** a member of such people **2 :** the language of the Cowlitz people

cowlstaff *as at* ³COWL + ,-\ *n* [ME *cuvelstaf*, fr. *cuvel* vessel + *staf* staff — more at COWL, STAFF] *now dial Eng* **:** a staff from which a vessel is suspended by its handles and carried between two persons

cow·man \ˈkau̇mən *also* -,man\ *n, pl* **cowmen** **1 :** one who tends cows **2 :** a cattle owner **:** cattle rancher

cow-nosed ray *or* **cow-nose ray** \ˈ=,=-\ *n* **:** a large sting ray of the genus *Rhinoptera* (esp. *R. bonasus* of the eastern coast of America)

cow oak *n* [so called fr. the fact that its acorns are relished by cows] **:** BASKET OAK

co-worker \(ˈ)kō+\ *n* [*co-* + *worker*] **:** one who works with another **:** a fellow worker

co·worship \(ˈ)kō+\ *n* [*co-* + *worship*] **:** worship within two distinctive religious faiths at the same time

cow parsley *n* **:** WILD CHERVIL 1

cow parsnip *n* **:** a plant of the genus *Heracleum* (esp. the English *H. sphondylium* or the No. American *H. lanatum*)

cow pat *n* **:** a dropping of cow dung

cow·pea \ˈ=,=\ *n* **1 a :** a sprawling herb (*Vigna sinensis*) found throughout the tropics of the Old World, more nearly related to the bean than to the pea, and cultivated in the southern U.S. for forage and green manure **b :** the seed of this plant used for food esp. in the southern U.S. — called also *blackeye, blackeye bean, black-eyed pea* **2 :** MEADOW PEA

cowpea aphid *n* **:** a widely distributed shiny black aphid (*Aphis craccivora*) feeding esp. on cowpeas and other legumes

cowpea weevil *n* **:** a small nearly cosmopolitan weevil (*Callosobruchus maculatus*) having larvae that eat the interior of cowpeas, common peas, and beans

cow pen *n* **:** a pen for cows; *specif* **:** the enclosed area adjoining or surrounding a cow shed or cow barn

cow·pen \ˈ=,=\ *vt* **:** to pen cows upon (ground) for fertilization

cow·per·i·tis \,kau̇pəˈrīd·əs, ,küp-, -ītəs\ *n* -ES [NL, fr. William *Cowper* + NL *-itis*] **:** inflammation of Cowper's glands

cow·per's gland \ˈkau̇pə(r)z-, ˈküp-\ *n, usu cap C* [after William *Cowper* †1709 Eng. surgeon, its discoverer] **:** either of two small glands discharging into the male urethra — called also *bulbourethral gland*

cow pilot *n* **:** SERGEANT MAJOR 4

cow poison *n* **:** a tall mountain larkspur (*Delphinium trollifolium*) of the American Pacific coast that is poisonous to stock

cowpoke \ˈ=,=\ *n* [prob. alter. (influenced by *poke*, "to punch") of *cowpuncher*] **:** COWBOY 3a

cow pony *n* **:** a light saddle horse trained and used for herding cattle

cowpox \ˈ=,=\ *n* -ES **1 :** a mild eruptive disease of cattle (as cows) that when communicated to man (as by vaccination or natural inoculation) protects against smallpox **:** VACCINIA **2 :** an eruptive disease in cows that when communicated to man (as during milking) causes nodules on the hands — called also *false cowpox;* compare MILKER'S NODULES

cowpuncher \ˈ=,==\ *n* **:** COWBOY 3a

ˡ**cow·rie** *or* **cow·ry** *also* **cou·rie** \ˈkau̇rē\ *n, pl* **cowries** *also* **couries** [Hindi *kaurī*, fr. Skt *kaparda*, of Dravidian origin; akin to Tamil-Malayalam *kavaṭi* cowrie] **:** any of numerous marine gastropod mollusks of a family (Cypraeidae) widely distributed in warm seas with shells that are beautifully polished, often brightly colored, and much used for ornament or as money; *also* **:** a cowrie's shell

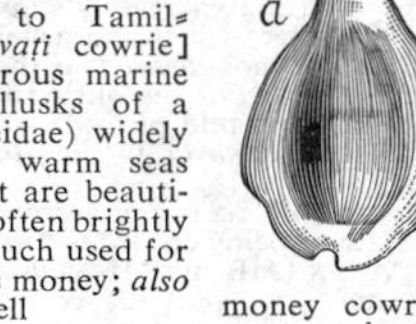
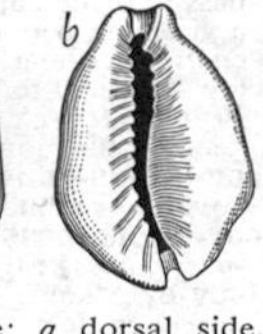

money cowrie: *a* dorsal side, *b* ventral side

²**cowrie** *var of* KAURI

cow·roid \ˈkau̇,rȯid\ *n* -S [ˡ*cowrie* + *-oid*] **:** an inscribed Egyptian seal in the shape of a cowrie

cows *pl of* COW, *pres 3d sing of* COW

cow·shard \ˈ=,=\ *n* -S *now dial Eng* **:** a dropping of cow dung

cow shark *n* **:** a shark of the family Hexanchidae; *esp* **:** a large shark (*Hexanchus griseus*) having six gill openings on each side and being widely distributed in warm and temperate seas

cow·sharn \ˈ=,=\ *n* -S *now dial Eng* **:** cow dung

ˡ**cowskin** \ˈ=,=\ *n* [ˡ*cow* + *skin*] **1 :** cow leather **:** COWHIDE **2 :** a cowhide whip

²**cowskin** \"\ *vt* **:** COWHIDE

cow·slip \ˈ=,=\ *n* -S *often attrib* [ME *cowslyppe*, fr. OE *cūslyppe*, lit., cow dung, fr. *cū* cow + *slyppe, slypa* pulp, paste — more at COW, SLIP] **1 a :** a primrose (*Primula veris*) that is common in the British isles and has umbels of fragrant yellow or sometimes purplish flowers that appear in early spring **b :** a marsh marigold (*Caltha palustris*) **c :** SHOOTING STAR **d :** VIRGINIA COWSLIP **2 :** ZINC ORANGE

cow·son \ˈkau̇(z)(,)sən\ *n* -S *Brit* **:** BASTARD — a generalized term of abuse

cow sorrel *n* **:** SHEEP SORREL

cow's-tail \ˈ=,=\ *or* **cow tail** *n* **:** a frayed end of a line where the strands have come unlaid

cowsucker \ˈ=,==\ *n* [so called fr. the belief that they milk cows] **:** any of various No. American harmless colubrid snakes

cow·tail \ˈ=,=\ *n* **:** a wool of the coarsest grade sheared from the hind legs of the sheep

cowth·wort \ˈkü,thwərt\ *n* [origin unknown] **:** MOTHERWORT 1

cowtongue \ˈ=,=\ *n* **:** YELLOW CLINTONIA

cow town *n* **:** a small cattle center that is typically provincial or unruly ⟨wide-open *cow towns* —Ross Santee⟩ ⟨a typical small *cow town*, with the usual single crooked street —P.E.Lehman⟩

cow tree *n* **1** [trans. of AmerSp *árbol de vaca*] **a :** a So. American tree (*Brosimum galactodendron*) yielding a rich milky juice sometimes used as food **b :** any of several other trees (as the balata and the couma) yielding a similar juice **c :** a Guatemalan tree (*Couma guatemalensis*) related to the cow tree **2** [so called fr. the use of its leaves as food for cattle] **:** KARAKA

cow vetch *n* **:** TUFTED VETCH

cow waddy *n* **:** COWBOY 3a

cowwheat \ˈ=,=\ *n* **:** an herb of the genus *Melampyrum* (esp. *M. arvense*) found as a weed in European wheat fields

cowy \ˈkau̇ē\ *adj* -ER/-EST [ˡ*cow* + *-y*] **1 :** suggestive of a cow **2 :** marked with a taste or flavor strongly suggestive of a cow ⟨fresh warm ~ milk⟩

cow yard *n, dial* **:** COW PEN, BARNYARD

ˡ**cox** *obs var of* COKES

²**cox** \ˈkäks\ *n* -ES [euphemism for *God*] **:** ⁵COCK

³**cox** \"\ *n* -ES [by shortening] **:** COXSWAIN

⁴**cox** \"\ *vb* -ED/-ING/-ES **:** to steer or direct as coxswain

coxa \ˈkäksə\ *n, pl* **cox·ae** \-,sē, -,sī\ [L, hip; akin to OHG *hāhsina* hock, OIr *coss* foot, Skt *kakṣa* armpit] **1 :** the hip joint **:** HIP **2** [NL, fr. L] **:** the first segment of the leg of an insect or other arthropod by which the leg articulates with the body

cox·al \ˈkäksəl\ *adj* [prob. fr. F, fr. L *coxa* + F *-al*] **:** of, relating to, or near a coxa

coxal cavity *n* **:** one of the cavities on the lower surface of the body of arthropods in which the coxae of the limbs articulate

cox·al·gia \käkˈsalj(ē)ə\ *also* **cox·al·gy** \ˈ=,=jē\ *n, pl* **coxalgias** *also* **coxalgies** [NL *coxalgia*, fr. L *coxa* + NL *-algia*] **1 :** pain in the hip **2 :** hip-joint disease — **cox·al·gic** \(ˈ)=ˈ=jik\ *adj*

coxal gland *n* **:** one of certain paired glands with ducts opening in the coxal region of arthropods and in some forms (as spiders) functioning as excretory organs

cox and box *usu cap C&B, var of* BOX AND COX

cox·bones \ˈkäks+,-\ *n pl* [ME *cokkes bones*, euphemism for *Goddes bones* God's bones] **:** ⁵COCK

cox·comb \ˈkäks+,-\ *n* -S [ME *cokkes comb* cock's comb — more at COCKSCOMB] **1 a** *obs* **:** a jester's cap adorned with a strip of red **b** *archaic* **:** PATE, HEAD **2 a** *obs* **:** FOOL **b :** a vain conceited foolish usu. male person that is falsely proud of his achievements and foppish or finical about his dress **3 :** a cleat near the end of a yardarm to afford a lead in hauling out reef earings **4 :** a hinge with the scrolled ends of each half resembling a cock's comb made in the 17th century

cox·comb·i·cal \(ˈ)käkˈskōməkəl, -ˈkäm-\ *also* **cox·comb·ic** \-mik\ *adj* **:** marked by a coxcomb's characteristics **:** FOPPISH, VAIN, DANDYISH

cox·comb·ly \ˈ=,skōmlē\ *adj, archaic* **:** resembling a coxcomb esp. in manner or dress

cox·comb·ry \-mrē\ *n* -ES **1 :** the behavior or manners of a coxcomb **:** FOPPERY **2 :** a trait or characteristic of a coxcomb ⟨a ~ of his to affect the modish⟩

cox·i·el·la \,käksēˈelə\ *n, cap* [NL, fr. Herald R. *Cox* b1907 Am. scientist + NL *-i-* + *-ella*] **:** a genus of small pleomorphic rickettsias occurring intercellularly in ticks and intracellularly in the cytoplasm of vertebrates and including the causative organism (*C. burnetii*) of Q fever

cox·ite \ˈkäk,sīt\ *n* -S [NL *coxa* + E *-ite*] **:** one of a pair of lamellate structures on the underside of each abdominal segment in insects of the order Thysanura

cox·i·tis \käkˈsīd·əs\ *n, pl* **cox·it·i·des** \-sid·ə,dēz\ [NL, fr. L *coxa* hip + NL *-itis* — more at COXA] **:** inflammation of the hip joint

cox·o·femoral \,käksə+\ *adj* [*coxo-* (fr. L *coxa*) + *femoral*] **:** of or relating to the hip and thigh

coxon *n* [by alter.] *obs* **:** COXSWAIN

cox·op·o·dite \käkˈsäpə,dīt\ *n* -S [*coxo-* (fr. NL *coxa*) + *-podite*] **:** the basal or first joint of a crustacean limb

cox·sack·ie virus \(,)ku̇k,säkē-, -sak-; (,)käk,sa-\ *n, usu cap C* [fr. *Coxsackie*, N.Y., home of the patient in whom the virus was first found] **:** any of several related but serologically distinct viruses apparently related to the virus of poliomyelitis and associated with certain diseases of man — compare EPIDEMIC PLEURODYNIA, HERPANGINA

ˡ**cox·swain** *also* **cock·swain** \ˈkäksᵊn *also* -,swān\ *n* -S [ME *cokswayne*, fr. *cok*, a kind of boat + *swayne* servant — more at COCK, SWAIN] **1 :** a sailor who has charge of a ship's boat and its crew and who usu. steers **2 :** a steersman of a racing shell who usu. directs the crew

²**coxswain** \"\ *vb* -ED/-ING/-S *vt* **:** to steer or direct as coxswain ~ *vi* **:** to act as coxswain

coxwell chair *often cap 1st C, var of* COGSWELL CHAIR

ˡ**coxy** \ˈkäksi\ *adj* -ER/-EST [alter. of *cocks*, pl. of ˡ*cock* (in the phrase *cocks of the game* fighting cocks) + *-y*] *Brit* **:** CONCEITED, IMPUDENT, ARROGANT

²**coxy** *also* **cox·ey** \ˈkäksē\ *n, pl* **coxies** *also* **coxeys** [modif. of NL *coccidiosis*] **:** avian coccidiosis

ˡ**coy** \ˈkȯi\ *adj* -ER/-EST [ME, fr. MF *coi* calm, tranquil, fr. L *quietus* quiet, calm — more at QUIET] **1** *obs* **:** QUIET, STILL ⟨the court became ~⟩ **2 a :** shrinking bashfully from familiarity **:** SHY **:** modestly or warily rejecting approaches or overtures ⟨like a lot of wild young colts, very inquisitive, but very ~ and not to be cajoled easily —Samuel Butler †1902⟩ ⟨the moon was a ~ or a wanton maiden, who either fled from or pursued the sun —J.G.Frazer⟩ **b** *archaic* **:** INACCESSIBLE, SECLUDED ⟨a sequestered ~ retreat⟩ **c :** archly affecting shy or demure reserve **:** marked by cute, coquettish, or artful playfulness ⟨using ~ tricks to awaken interest⟩ ⟨the combination of the adult and childish in the style will seem a bit too ~ —Louise S. Bechtel⟩ **d :** showing marked often playful or irritating reluctance to make a definite or committing statement ⟨a politician ~ about his intentions⟩ **syn** see SHY

²**coy** \"\ *vb* -ED/-ING/-S [ME *coyen* to calm, caress, coax, fr. *coy*, adj.] *vt, obs* **:** CARESS ~ *vi* **1** *archaic* **:** to act coyly — sometimes used with *it* ⟨a shy maiden ~*ing* it⟩ **2 :** DEMUR, WITHDRAW

coy *abbr* company

coy·dog \ˈkī, ˈkȯi+,-\ *n* [*coyote* + *dog*] **:** a hybrid between a coyote and a feral dog found in parts of the northeastern U.S.

coy·ly *adv* **:** in a coy manner

coy·ness *n* -ES **:** the quality or state of being coy

coy·nye \ˈkȯin(y)ē\ *or* **coyne** \-n\ *or* **coi·gny** \-n(y)ē\ *n* -S [ME *coynee*, fr. MIr *coinnemh;* akin to MIr *connmedh* quarterage, billeting] **:** an Irish chieftain's exaction of food and drink from his tenants for his soldiers — compare BONAGHT

co·yo \ˈkō(,)yō\ *n* -S [AmerSp *coyó*, fr. Maya] **1 :** a Mexican and Central American avocado (*Persea schiedeana*) **2 :** the fruit of the coyo

co·yol \(ˈ)kōˈyōl, kəˈy-\ *also* **coyol palm** *n* -S [MexSp *coyol*, fr. Nahuatl *coyolli*, lit., bell; fr. the shape of the fruit and the rattle made by the dried fruit when shaken] **1 :** any of several tropical American palms of the genus *Acrocomia* (esp. *A. vinifera*) **2 :** the fiber of a coyol

ˡ**coy·ote** \ˈkī,ōt *also* -,yōt *sometimes* ˈkȯi,-, *usu* -ōd-+V; kīˈōd·(,)ē, -ō(,)tē *also* -ˈyō- *sometimes* kȯiˈ- *or* kəˈ- *or* kēˈ-\ *n, pl* **coyotes** *or* **coyote** [MexSp, fr. Nahuatl *coyotl*] **1 :** a small wolf (*Canis latrans*) native to the western part of No. America and well established northward in Alaska and eastward at least as far as New York state — called also *prairie wolf* **2 :** an objectionable person **:** CHISELER

²**coyote** \"\ *vi* **coyoteed** \-d·(,)ēd\ *or* **coyoted** \-d·əd, -d·(,)ēd\ **coyoteed** *or* **coyoteing** *or* **coyoting** \-d·iŋ\ **coyotes** \-ts, -d·(,)ēz\ *West* **:** to mine by sinking small shallow shafts with drifts running in several directions — compare GOPHER

³**coyote** \"\ *adj* **:** marked by shallow excavation or digging suggestive of a coyote's hole ⟨a ~ shaft⟩ ⟨a ~ cellar⟩

coyote blast *n* **:** blasting in a coyote hole

coyote brush *also* **coyote bush** *n* **:** a prostrate spreading or erect smooth evergreen shrub (*Baccharis pilularis*) of the southwestern U.S. having ovoid flower heads in a leafy panicle made up of sessile clusters — called also *kidneywort*

coyote dance *n* **:** a dance mimetic of the coyote; *esp* **:** a Yaqui Indian prowling dance by three members of the warriors' society

coyote getter *n* **:** a device used to kill coyotes by shooting cyanide into the mouth when the animal disturbs the bait

coyote hole *n* **:** a short T-shaped blasthole — compare ²COYOTE

co·yo·te·ro \ˌkōyəˈte(ˌ)rō\ *n* -s *usu cap* [MexSp, fr. *coyote* + *-ero* -er; fr. their reputation for eating coyote meat] **:** an Indian of an Apache division comprising the Pinal White Mountain and Tonto groups

coyote willow *n* **:** SANDBAR WILLOW b

co·yo·til·lo \ˌkōyəˈtilō, -tē(ˌ)lō, -tēl(ˌ)yō\ *n* -s [MexSp, dim. of *coyote*] **:** a low poisonous shrub (*Karwinskia humboldtiana*) of the southwestern U.S. and Mexico

coy·pu *also* **coy·pou** \ˈkȯi(ˌ)pü, ·ˈ·\ *n* -s [AmerSp *coipú*, fr. Araucan *coypu*] **1 :** a So. American aquatic rodent (*Myocastor coypus*) with webbed feet and dorsally located mammae that has been introduced into other regions for the sake of its fur and is now thoroughly naturalized on the U.S. Gulf Coast and Pacific Northwest and is a pest in parts of England because of its destruction of marsh vegetation **2 :** NUTRIA 1b

coystrill *var of* COISTREL

coz \ˈkəz\ *n, pl* **cozes** *or* **coz·zes** \-əzəz\ [by shortening & alter.] **:** COUSIN

¹**coze** \ˈkōz\ *n* -s [prob. fr. F *causer* to chat] **:** CHAT

²**coze** \"\ *vi* -ED/-ING/-s [F *causer*, fr. OF, to plead a case, fr. L *causari*, fr. *causa* cause — more at CAUSE] **:** CHAT, GOSSIP

coz·en \ˈkəzᵊn\ *vb* **cozened; cozened; cozening** \-z(ᵊ)niŋ\ **cozens** [obs. It *cozzonare* to act like a horse trader or knave, to cheat, fr. *cozzone* horse trader, matchmaker, fr. L *coction-, coctio, cocion-, cocio* horse trader] *vt* **1 :** to deceive by artful wheedling or tricky dishonesty **:** CHEAT, DEFRAUD ⟨~*ing* his unsuspecting and unsophisticated brother⟩ **2 :** to beguile craftily **:** victimize by chicanery **:** DELUDE, DECEIVE ⟨he had ~*ed* the world by fine phrases —T.B.Macaulay⟩ **3 :** to bring about, induce, or obtain by artful wheedling or tricky dishonesty ⟨~*ing* the old man into signing the paper⟩ ⟨with a conscious knowledge of their art, ~*ed* their supper out of Mrs. Torrelli —John Steinbeck⟩ ~ *vi* **:** to act with artful deceit **:** CHISEL ⟨cheated and plundered by gentlemen who prospered in ~*ing* —V.L.Parrington⟩ **syn** see CHEAT

coz·en·age *also* **coz·in·age** \-z(ᵊ)nij\ *n* -s **1 :** the art or practice of cozening **:** ARTIFICE, FRAUD ⟨a thievish rogue expert at ~⟩ **2 :** an act of cozening **:** an instance of deception ⟨his frauds and ~*s*⟩

co·zey *or* **co·zie** \ˈkōzē, -zi\ *archaic var of* COZY

cozier *n* [MF *couseor* seamster, tailor, fr. (assumed) VL *consutor*, fr. L *consuere* to sew together (fr. *com-* + *suere* to sew) + *-ator* — more at SEW] *obs* **:** SHOEMAKER, COBBLER

co·zi·ly *or* **co·si·ly** \ˈkōz(ə)lē, -li\ *adv* **:** in a cozy manner **:** SNUGLY, INTIMATELY

co·zi·ness *or* **co·si·ness** \ˈkōzēnəs, -zin-\ *n* -ES **:** the quality or state of being cozy **:** SNUGNESS

co·zonal \(ˈ)kō+\ *adj* [*co-* + *zonal*] **:** TAUTOZONAL

¹**co·zy** *or* **co·sy** \ˈkōzē, -zi\ *adj* -ER/-EST [prob. of Scand origin; akin to Norw *kose* (*sig*) to be snug, *koselig* snug, cozy] **1 :** enjoying, affording, or suggesting warmth, homey ease, and freedom from care and inconvenience often within smallish or compact quarters ⟨he felt ~ watching the hearth fire⟩ ⟨~ blankets⟩ ⟨a ~ lakeside cabin⟩ ⟨the happy life that pair had led in the ~ studio in Montmartre —W.S.Maugham⟩ **2 a :** marked by or suggestive of the warm and understanding intimacy of the family or the friendly familiarity of a close group **:** lacking restraint or cold formality ⟨desirous of living on the ~ footing of a father-in-law —Herman Melville⟩ ⟨the *coziest* picture of Johnson working, no longer "in the gloom of solitude" but surrounded by friends —J.W.Krutch⟩ ⟨a ~, first-person, family kind of democracy —Ruth Gruber⟩ **b :** showing or suggesting close association often for devious connivance ⟨the ~ prewar cartel which was profitable to them and their fellow industrialists —*America*⟩ **3 :** marked by or suggestive of a discreet and cautious attitude or procedure that avoids anything forthright, novel, or extreme ⟨a ~ waiting game⟩ ⟨instead of acting ~, the scheduled airlines have fought . . . at every turn —*Air Transportation*⟩ **syn** see COMFORTABLE

²**cozy** *adv* **:** in a cautious manner — often used in the phrase *play it cozy* ⟨play it ~ and wait for the other team to make a mistake —Bobby Dodd⟩

³**cozy** *or* **cosy** *also* **co·sey** \"\ *n* -ES [prob. fr. ¹*cozy*] **:** a covering or holder for food; *esp* **:** a holder for keeping tea, eggs, or muffins warm

co·zymase \(ˈ)kō+\ *n* [*co-* + *zymase*] **:** DIPHOSPHOPYRIDINE NUCLEOTIDE

cozy up *vi* [¹*cozy*] **:** to attain or try to attain to familiarity, friendship, or intimacy **:** ingratiate oneself — usu. used with *to* ⟨*cozying up to* the party leaders⟩ ⟨trying to *cozy up to* the boss's secretary⟩

cp *abbr* **1** centipoise **2** compare **3** coupon

CP *abbr* **1** candlepower **2** carriage paid **3** cerebral palsy **4** charter party **5** chemically pure **6** civil procedure **7** code of procedure **8** [It *colla parte*] with the solo part **9** command post **10** common pleas **11** common prayer **12** communist party **13** court of probate **14** custom of port

CPA *abbr or n* -s certified public accountant

CPC *abbr* **1** chronic passive congestion **2** crafts, protective, custodial

CPC and N *abbr* certificate of public convenience and necessity

CPCU *abbr* chartered property casualty underwriter

cpd *abbr* compound

CPD *abbr* **1** charterers pay dues **2** contact potential difference

CPFF *abbr* cost plus fixed fee

CPI *abbr* constitutional psychopathic inferior

cpl *abbr* **1** complete **2** corporal

CPM *abbr* **1** common particular meter **2** cycles per minute

CPO *abbr* chief petty officer

c power supply \ˈsē-\ *n, usu cap C* **:** a battery or voltage-divider section supplying direct voltage in the grid circuit of an electron tube — compare A POWER SUPPLY, B POWER SUPPLY; C BATTERY

cpr *abbr* copper

CPS *abbr* **1** constitutional psychopathic state **2** cycles per second

cpt *abbr* **1** captain **2** counterpoint

cptr *abbr* carpenter

CQ \(ˈ)sē¦kyü\ [abbr. for *call to quarters*] — communication code letters used at the beginning of radiograms of general information or safety notices or by shortwave amateurs as an invitation to talk to other shortwave amateurs

CQ *abbr* **1** charge of quarters **2** commercial quality **3** conceptual quotient

cr *abbr* **1** center **2** circular **3** commander **4** councillor **5** crate **6** created **7** credit; creditor **8** creed **9** creek **10** crescendo **11** crew **12** crochet **13** crown **14** cruiser **15** cruzeiro

CR *abbr* **1** carrier's risk **2** change of rating **3** class rate **4** commodity rate **5** company's risk **6** conditioned reflex; conditioned response **7** creditable record **8** critical ratio **9** crossroad **10** currency regulation **11** current rate

Cr *symbol* chromium

¹**crab** \ˈkrab, -aa(ə)b\ *n* -s [ME *crabbe*, fr. OE *crabba;* akin to OHG *krebiz* crab, ON *krabbi*, OE *ceorfan* to cut — more at CARVE] **1 a :** any of a number of chiefly marine largely carnivorous rather stocky and broadly built crustaceans: (1) **:** any member of the tribe Brachyura distinguished by a short broad and usu. flattened carapace, a small abdomen that curls forward beneath the body and fits into a groove in the thorax, short antennae, and the anterior pair of limbs modified as pincers or grasping organs (2) **:** any of various members of the tribe Anomura resembling the brachyurans in having the abdomen reduced and permanently flexed — see HERMIT CRAB, PURSE CRAB **b :** KING CRAB **2 :** any of various machines or apparatus esp. for raising or hauling heavy weights: as **a :** a winch mounted (as on skids) so that it can be moved **b :** the part of an overhead traveling crane that rolls along the track and carries the load **c :** a claw for anchoring a portable machine **d :** a machine for textile crabbing **3 crabs** *pl* **:** a losing throw of two or three in the game of hazard — compare CRAP 1 **4 a** (1) [so called fr. the hooked feet resembling those of a crab] **:** CRAB LOUSE (2) **crabs** *pl* **:** PEDICULOSIS — usu. used with *the* **b :** the larva of a stone fly **5 :** apparent sideways motion esp. of an airplane headed into a crosswind

²**crab** \"\ *vb* **crabbed; crabbed; crabbing; crabs** *vt* **1 :** to cause to move sideways or in an indirect or diagonal manner ⟨on the upstream trip broadside winds *crabbed* the boat close to the riverbank⟩; *specif* **:** to head (an airplane or glider) by means of the rudder into a crosswind to counteract drift and thus give the aircraft apparent sidewise motion with respect to the ground **2 :** to subject to crabbing ~ *vi* **1 a** (1) **:** to move sideways, indirectly, or diagonally ⟨at high speed the car would ~ around corners⟩ (2) *of a pilot* **:** to crab an airplane or glider **b :** to scuttle or scurry sideways like a crab ⟨jumping aboard and *crabbing* along the gunwale to the controls —K.M.Dodson⟩ **2 :** to fish for or catch crabs

³**crab** \"\ *adj, music* **:** moving backwards

⁴**crab** \"\ *n* -s [ME *crabbe*, perh. fr. *crabbe* crab (the crustacean) — more at ¹CRAB] **1 :** CRAB APPLE **2 :** a cudgel of crab-tree wood **:** CRABSTICK

⁵**crab** \"\ *vb* **crabbed; crabbed; crabbing; crabs** [ME *craben, crabben*, prob. back-formation fr. *crabbed*] *vt* **1** *archaic Brit* **:** ANGER, IRRITATE **2 :** to make sullen **:** SOUR ⟨old age had *crabbed* his nature⟩ ⟨then what's *crabbing* you? —S.H.Adams⟩ **3 :** to complain about **:** criticize peevishly or petulantly **:** pull to pieces ⟨~ the conduct of a neighbor⟩ ⟨each side tended to ~ the weapon of the other —Bernard Brodie⟩ **4 :** SPOIL, RUIN ⟨~ a deal⟩ ⟨an unknown . . . might have *crabbed* his own act if he had started clobbering a war hero —James Marlow⟩ ⟨the author's writing . . . is not so much *crabbed* by technical jargon as by a pedantic style —*Infantry Jour.*⟩ ~ *vi* **1 :** to be ill-tempered **:** GROUSE ⟨she'd always be *crabbing* without cause⟩ **2 :** to criticize in a petty, peevish, or petulant manner **:** COMPLAIN ⟨~ at a person⟩ ⟨his boss *crabbed* about him⟩

⁶**crab** \"\ *n* -s **1 :** a sour ill-tempered person **:** CROSSPATCH **2 :** an instance of critical carping **:** testy objection

⁷**crab** \"\ *vb* **crabbed; crabbed; crabbing; crabs** [D *krabben* to scratch, claw, fr. MD *crabben;* akin to OE *crabba* crab — more at ¹CRAB] *of hawks* **:** SCRATCH, FIGHT

⁸**crab** \"\ *var of* CARAPA

crab apple *n* [⁴*crab*] **1 a :** a wild apple typically with small sour fruits: as (1) **:** a rather small round-headed Eurasiatic tree (*Malus sylvestris*) that is the chief ancestor of cultivated apples (2) **:** any of several American wild apples — usu. used in combination; see AMERICAN CRAB APPLE, IOWA CRAB, OREGON CRAB APPLE, SOUTHERN CRABAPPLE (3) **:** SIBERIAN CRAB **b :** a cultivated apple with small usu. brightly colored fruits: as (1) **:** any of various apples having usu. acid fruits used esp. for preserving and being derived in whole or in part from the Siberian crab (2) **:** a cultivated flowering crab **2 :** the fruit of a crab apple **3 :** a moderate reddish orange that is lighter, stronger, and slightly yellower than flamingo, redder, lighter, and stronger than coral red, and redder, lighter, and stronger than burnt ocher

crab·bed \ˈkrabəd\ *adj* [ME, partly fr. *crabbe* (crustacean), partly fr. *crabbe* (crab apple) + *-ed*] **1 a :** perversely obstinate **:** INTRACTABLE, CONTRARY ⟨he sets out his theory with such ingenuity . . . that it would be a ~ mind indeed that didn't respond —R.J.Cruikshank⟩ **b :** out of humor **:** CROSS, PETULANT ⟨the only audible response in this country should be a ~ and jaundiced bickering —*Economist*⟩ **2 :** characterized by harshness or roughness **:** BITTER ⟨a ~ satirist⟩ ⟨~ wit⟩ **3** *obs* **:** CROOKED, GNARLED, ROUGH **4 :** difficult to understand **:** INTRICATE, OBSCURE ⟨~ style⟩ ⟨the ~ complexities of fine automotive machinery —*Newsweek*⟩ ⟨his mature compositions are generally considered the more cerebral and ~ —Sarah R. Watson⟩ **5** *of handwriting* **:** difficult to read ⟨wrote laboriously in his old man's ~ hand —Verne Athanas⟩ **syn** see SULLEN

crab·bed·ly *adv* [ME, fr. *crabbed* + *-ly*] **:** in a crabbed manner

crab·bed·ness *n* -ES [ME *crabbydnesse*, fr. *crabbyd, crabbed* + *-nesse* -ness] **:** the quality or state of being crabbed

¹**crab·ber** \ˈkrabə(r)\ *n* -s [¹*crab* + *-er*] **1 a :** one that fishes for or catches crabs **b :** a boat used in crab fishing **2 :** WINCHMAN **3** [²*crab* + *-er*] **:** an operator of a machine for crabbing

²**crabber** \"\ *n* -s [⁵*crab* + *-er*] **:** one that carps or complains

crab·bery \-b(ə)rē, -ri\ *n* -ES [¹*crab* + *-ery*] **:** a place where crabs abound or are fished for

crabbing *n* -s [fr. gerund of ²*crab*] **:** a finishing process for setting the warp and weft threads of woolen and worsted fabrics by winding the cloth under tension on rollers and subjecting it to boiling water or steam which is followed by a cooling process

crab·bit \ˈkrabət\ *chiefly Scot var of* CRABBED

¹**crab·by** \ˈkrabē, -bi\ *adj* -ER/-EST [in sense 1, fr. ⁴*crab* + *-y;* in sense 2, fr. ⁶*crab* + *-y*] **1** *obs* **:** CROOKED, ROUGH, PERPLEXING **2 :** CROSS, CHURLISH, ILL-NATURED

²**crabby** \"\ *adj* -ER/-EST [¹*crab* + *-y*] **1 :** resembling a crab **2 :** abounding in crabs

crab cactus *n* **:** a So. American cactus (*Zygocactus truncatus*) with red flowers — called also *Christmas cactus*

crab canon *n* [³*crab*] **:** a canon with a theme that is repeated backward — called also *canon cancrizans*

crab claw *n* **1 :** a claw or clutch for grappling or fastening **:** PAWL **2 :** an Oceanian lateen sail

crab-eater \ˈ·,··\ *n* **1 :** any of several fishes and birds reputed to eat crabs (as the sergeant fish and various herons) **2 :** CRABEATER SEAL **3 :** CRAB-EATING RACCOON **4 :** COBIA

crabeater seal \ˈ-\ *or* **crab-eating seal** \ˈ·,··\ *n* **:** a silvery gray antarctic seal (*Lobodon carcinophaga*) subsisting largely on crustaceans

crab-eating fox *or* **crab-eating dog** *n* **:** a wild dog (*Dusicyon cancrivorus*) of northern So. America

crab-eating macaque *n* **:** a macaque (*Macaca irus*) of southeastern Asia, Borneo, and the Philippines — called also *croo monkey*

crab-eating opossum *n* **:** a So. American opossum (*Didelphis marsupialis*)

crab-eating raccoon *n* **:** a So. American raccoon (*Procyon cancrivorus*)

crab float *n* **:** a live-box in which crabs are kept

crab form *n* [³*crab*] **:** the placing of the notes of a musical theme, voice part, or twelve-tone row in reverse order in either direct or inverted imitation

crabgrass \ˈ·,·\ *n* **1 :** any of several grasses that have creeping or decumbent stems which root freely at the nodes and that are often pests in turf or cultivated lands: as **a :** any of several grasses of the genus *Digitaria; esp* **:** LARGE CRABGRASS **b :** YARD GRASS **c :** EGYPTIAN GRASS **2 :** KNOTGRASS 1 **3 :** a glasswort (*Salicornia europaea*) supposed to be a food for crabs

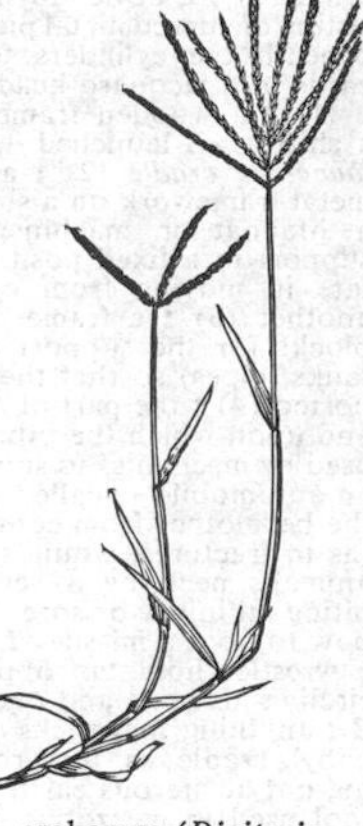
crabgrass (*Digitaria sanguinalis*)

crabhole \ˈ·,·\ *n* **:** the hole in which a crab (as a land crab) lives

cra·bier \ˌkrab(ē)ˈyā, ˈ·(·),·\ *n* -s [F, fr. *crabe* crab (fr. MF, fr. MD *crabbe*) + *-ier* -er; akin to OE *crabba* crab — more at CRAB] **:** any of several crab-eating birds of the Caribbean area

crab line *n* **:** a soft-laid rope of ¼-inch diameter or less used as net mending and trawl twine and as bait line (as by inserting bait between strands in the crab-fishing industry)

crab locomotive *n* **:** a small mine locomotive on which is mounted a power-driven winch

crab louse *n* [¹*crab*] **:** a sucking louse (*Phthirus pubis*) infesting the human body in the pubic region

crab·man \ˈkrab,man, -ˌmən\ *n, pl* **crabmen :** a seller of crabs

crab nut *n* [⁸*crab*] **:** the seed of the carapa

crab plover *n* **:** a bird (*Dromas ardeola*) like a plover widely distributed along the east coast of Africa and the southern shores of Asia where it feeds chiefly on crabs and burrows into sandbanks to deposit its single white egg

crab pot *n* **:** a pot for trapping crabs

crab reel locomotive *n* **:** CRAB LOCOMOTIVE

crabs *pl of* CRAB, *pres 3d sing of* CRAB

crab's claw *n* **:** WATER SOLDIER

crab's-eye \ˈ·,·\ *n* **1 :** a hard calcareous mass found in the stomach of certain crustaceans (as the European crayfish) that was formerly used in medicine — compare GASTROLITH **2 :** JEQUIRITY

crab's-eye vine *n* **:** INDIAN LICORICE

crab spider *n* **:** any of the numerous spiders that make up the family Thomisidae and resemble crabs in attitude and in ability to run sideways

crab·stick \ˈ·,·\ *n* [⁴*crab* + *stick*] **1 :** a stick, cane, or cudgel of crab-tree wood **2 :** a crabbed ill-natured person

crab stock *n* **:** a seedling of the common apple that is used as a stock

¹**crab tree** *n* [⁴*crab*] **1 :** a crab-apple tree **2** *Austral* **:** NATIVE QUINCE

²**crab tree** *n* [⁸*crab*] **:** CARAPA

crabwise \ˈ·,·\ *adv* [¹*crab* + *-wise*] **1 :** SIDEWAYS ⟨the battleship was pushed several feet ~ by its nine-gun broadside⟩ **2 :** in a sidling or cautiously indirect manner ⟨Canada has moved ~ toward socialism —W.G.Hardy⟩

¹**crabwood** \ˈ·,·\ *n* [⁸*crab* + *wood*] **:** a timber tree (*Carapa guianensis*) of tropical So. America

²**crabwood** \"\ *n* [prob. fr. ⁴*crab* + *wood*] **:** a tree (*Gymnanthes lucida*) of the West Indies and southern Florida that contains a poisonous juice

crab yaws *n pl* **:** secondary lesions of yaws characterized by thickening of the skin on the soles of the feet and formation of fissures and ulcers which causes a waddling gait

crac·ca \ˈkrakə\ [NL, fr. L, a kind of leguminous plant, perh. vetch] *syn of* TEPHROSIA

crac·i·dae \ˈkrasəˌdē\ *n pl, cap* [NL, fr. *Crac-, Crax*, type genus + *-idae*] **:** a family of gallinaceous birds of the warmer parts of America that comprises the curassows, guans, and chachalacas and is related to the megapodes

-cracies *pl of* -CRACY

¹**crack** \ˈkrak\ *vb* -ED/-ING/-s [ME *crakken*, alter. (influenced by *crak*, n.) of *craken*, fr. OE *cracian;* akin to OE *cearcian* to creak, gnash, OHG *krahhōn* to crack, Skt *garjati* he roars, OE *cran* crane — more at CRANE] *vi* **1 :** to make a loud sharp sudden sound or series of such sounds (as the snap of a whip, a rifle shot) **:** give forth a report ⟨wood ~*ing* in a fire⟩ ⟨his high yell of laughter ~*ed* out when he thought of something funny —Virginia D. Dawson & Betty D. Wilson⟩ **2 :** to snap asunder ⟨the ropes ~*ed* under pressure⟩ **:** open in chinks **3 a** *chiefly Scot* **:** TALK, CHAT, GOSSIP **b** *now dial* **:** to speak pompously **:** BRAG, BOAST **4 :** to become ruined or impaired **:** FAIL: as **a :** to lose control or effectiveness esp. when working or competing under pressure ⟨his reserve ~*ed*⟩ ⟨any pitcher is liable to ~ during a tight game⟩ — often used with *up* ⟨if he doesn't rest he'll ~ up completely⟩ **b :** to fail in tone production **:** become discordant or harsh ⟨his voice ~*ed*⟩ **c :** to smash up a vehicle esp. by losing control — used with *up* ⟨he ~*ed* up taking a curve⟩ **5 a** (1) **:** to go or travel at good speed (2) *archaic* **:** to proceed under or as if under full sail or steam — used with *on* **b :** to move toward an objective **:** PROGRESS ⟨get ~*ing*⟩ **6 a** *of chemical compounds* **:** to break up into simpler compounds usu. as a result of heating **:** undergo pyrolysis **b** *of an emulsion* **:** BREAK *vi* 7 f (2) **7** *of hot syrup* **:** to break when dropped into cold water and subjected to moderate pressure ~ *vt* **1 :** to break or burst: as **a :** to break (something brittle or hollow) with a sharp or explosive sound ⟨~ a nut⟩ **b :** to break (anything hard or brittle) so that clefts, chinks, or fissures appear on the surface ⟨the fall ~*ed* the cup across the bottom⟩ ⟨the storm broke a dozen windowpanes and ~*ed* many others⟩ **2 a :** to utter esp. suddenly and sententiously **:** tell strikingly ⟨~ a jest⟩ ⟨~ a joke⟩ **b :** to cry up **:** EXTOL, PRAISE — used with *up* ⟨the car wasn't all the dealer ~*ed* it up to be⟩ ⟨he ~*ed* up Whitehead to the stars —H.J.Laski⟩ **3 :** to strike with a sharp noise **:** SLAP, BANG ⟨~ a person over the head⟩ **4 :** to put on (as full sail, steam, speed) **:** clap on — used with *on* ⟨he liked everything about this convoy: he liked its air of purpose as it ~*ed* on speed —Nicholas Monsarrat⟩ **5 :** to break open or into: as **a :** to open (as a bottle) and usu. drink ⟨~ a fifth⟩ **b :** to puzzle out and solve, expose, or reveal the mystery of ⟨~ an enemy code⟩ ⟨~ a garbled message⟩ ⟨~ a crime syndicate wide open⟩ ⟨~ the logic of an argument⟩ **c :** to break into ⟨~ a safe⟩; *specif, Brit* **:** to break into (a house) — often used in the phrase *crack a crib* **d :** to open slightly ⟨~ a door⟩ ⟨~ a window⟩ ⟨~ a throttle⟩ ⟨~ a valve⟩ **e :** to enter or win recognition by (an exclusive profession, coterie, society) ⟨it has been extremely difficult . . . for foreign artists . . . to ~ the Parisian art front without going there to live —J.T.Soby⟩ **f :** to open (a book) for the purpose of study ⟨~ a physics text⟩ ⟨several students were up . . . ~*ing* the books beyond midnight —Jack Edison⟩ **6 :** VIOLATE, DAMAGE, DESTROY: as **a :** to impair often irreparably **:** WRECK, RUIN ⟨~ a bank⟩ ⟨~ an opponent's courage⟩ — often used with *up* ⟨~ a new car up⟩ **b :** to make (the voice) discordant or harsh **:** destroy the tone of **c :** DISORDER, CRAZE ⟨worry had ~*ed* his otherwise expansive personality⟩ **d :** to interrupt (as a settled usage, condition, continuity, tradition) sharply or abruptly ⟨his criticism ~*ed* our complacency⟩ **7 :** to cause to make a sharp noise ⟨~ one's knuckles⟩ **8 a** (1) **:** to subject (hydrocarbon oils or gases) to cracking (2) **:** to produce by cracking — usu. used in past participle ⟨~*ed* gasoline⟩ **b :** to break up (chemical compounds) into simpler compounds usu. by means of heat **:** subject to pyrolysis **9 a** *in contract bridge* **:** DOUBLE **b** *in poker* **:** OPEN ⟨~ the pot⟩ **syn** see BREAK — **crack a smile :** SMILE — **crack the whip :** to adopt sometimes suddenly or unexpectedly an authoritative, tyrannical, or threatening pose or policy ⟨he has made great industrial corporations jump . . . when he *cracks the whip* —*Time*⟩ — **crack wise** [by analysis fr. ¹*wisecrack*] *slang* **:** to make a smart remark

²**crack** \"\ *n* -s [ME *crak;* akin to OHG *krach* loud noise, OE *cracian*, v.] **1 a :** a loud earsplitting roar or peal ⟨a ~ of thunder⟩ ⟨the ~ of trumpets⟩ ⟨the ~ of a cannon⟩ — often used interjectionally **b :** a sudden sharp noise **:** a brief intense report **:** BANG ⟨the jug hit the floor with a terrible ~⟩ ⟨the chair went over with a ~⟩ ⟨the ~ of a rifle⟩ — often used interjectionally ⟨~! went the whip⟩ **c :** the breaking or broken tone of the voice (as when changed at puberty) **2 a** *now dial* **:** boasting or an instance of boasting **b** *chiefly dial Brit* (1) **:** TALK, CONVERSATION, GOSSIP (2) **:** TALE, STORY, JOKE (3) **cracks** *pl* **:** NEWS **c :** a sharp, cutting, or sarcastically witty remark **:** QUIP ⟨Washington was not famous for saying funny things but sometimes he got off a ~ that was widely appreciated —Roger Butterfield⟩ **3 a :** a narrow break or thin slit (as in or across a surface) sometimes caused by incomplete joining, drying, or setting, by strain or decay, or by a blow or fall not sufficiently violent to cause a complete break **:** FISSURE ⟨a windowpane full of ~*s*⟩ ⟨trip over a ~ in the ice⟩ **b :** a narrow opening ⟨you can leave the outer door open a ~ so you can hear if anyone comes —John Steinbeck⟩ **c :** an open crosswise streak in woven fabrics **4 a :** a weakness or flaw caused by decay, age, or deficiency **:** UNSOUNDNESS ⟨a ~ in a person's mind⟩ ⟨little rifts and ~*s* . . . in the whole bland, ecclesiastical facade of Victorian England —C.D.Lewis⟩ **b :** a crazy or erratic person **:** CRACKPOT ⟨the ~*s* who . . . interest themselves . . . in every sensational murder case —D.L. Champion⟩ **5** *obs* **:** a roguish boy **:** WAG **6** *slang Brit* **:** a thing or person of superior excellence or ability ⟨Australia sent a couple of ~*s* to defend the trophy⟩ **7** *archaic* **:** PROSTITUTE **8 :** MOMENT, INSTANT ⟨I'll be there in a ~⟩ ⟨at the ~ of dawn⟩ **9 a** *archaic* **:** BURGLAR **b :** HOUSEBREAKING, BURGLARY ⟨a successful ~⟩ **10 :** a sharp resounding blow ⟨a ~ on the head⟩ **11 :** a single effort or attempt ⟨get rid of a job at one ~⟩ ⟨he said he didn't know how to swim but would take a ~ at it⟩ **12 :** the stage at which syrup from boiling sugar breaks with a snap when chilled by being dripped from a spoon or dropped into water **13 :** a poultry egg with a

noticeably cracked shell but with unbroken membrane — contrasted with *check*
syn FISSURE, CREVICE, CHINK, CLEFT, CRANNY: CRACK is likely to indicate a line of breaking or splitting in a continuing surface with or without perceptible separation into an opening that resembles a slit ⟨a *crack* in a pane of glass⟩ ⟨*cracks* in the parched mud⟩ FISSURE usu. indicates a narrow opening of some depth as a result of some rending or breaking force ⟨a *fissure* in the stone floor, like a *crack* in china, which was plastered up with clay —Willa Cather⟩ CREVICE indicates an opening like a fissure but less strongly suggests forceful recent cleavage and may lend itself to use in situations involving accumulation, deposit, growth, or concealment within ⟨the cross formed by snow in the *crevices* of the rock⟩ ⟨intolerance can always find some *crevice* in the administration of the law —Zechariah Chafee⟩ CHINK suggests a space or hole, often a slit, permitting one to see through or to utilize in escape, evasion, or deft attack ⟨I felt as if I had slipped through some *chink* in the veil of the past and become a medieval student —John Buchan⟩ ⟨Republicans . . . had independently been studying the Truman armor for new *chinks* —*Atlantic*⟩ CLEFT suggests a V-shaped indention, as though made with a splitting wedge, in some formation ⟨Dover, an English seaport . . . occupies a wide *cleft* in the chalk hills formed by the valley of the river Don —*Chambers's Encyc.*⟩ CRANNY suggests a slit, niche, or recess, often one in a wall or enclosed structure and often small and easy to overlook ⟨they explored every nook and *cranny* of the West, seeking out passes through mountain barriers —R.A.Billington⟩ **syn** see in addition JOKE
³crack \"\ *adj* [²*crack* (something excellent)] **:** of superior excellence or ability ⟨a ~ ship⟩ ⟨a ~ tennis player⟩ ⟨a ~ regiment⟩ ⟨~ maintenance and cargo specialists —B.M. Bowie⟩
crackajack *var of* CRACKERJACK
crackaloo *var of* CRACK-LOO
crack arrester *n* **1 :** a plate on a ship riveted over a crack in another plate or over a stressed area where a crack might start **2 :** a hole drilled or a slot cut at the apex of a crack in the plate of a ship to stop the crack from spreading or at a point of stress to stop a crack from starting
crackbrain \'ˌ=ˌ=\ *n* **:** a person of unbalanced or erratic tendencies or ideas **:** CRACKPOT
crackbrained \'ˌ=¦=\ *adj* **:** ERRATIC, UNREASONABLE, CRAZY ⟨a ~ genius⟩ ⟨a ~ feminist⟩ ⟨a ~ scheme⟩
crack down *vi* **:** to take punitive action **:** enforce strict conformance with or increase the severity of regulations or restrictions — usu. used with *on* ⟨the government *cracked down* on violators⟩
crackdown \'ˌ=ˌ=\ *n* -s [*crack down*] **:** an act or instance of cracking down
cracked *adj* [ME *crackyd*, fr. past part. of *crakken* to crack] **1 a :** broken (as by a sharp blow) so that the surface is fissured ⟨~ china⟩ **b :** broken into coarse particles ⟨~ wheat⟩ ⟨~ ice⟩ **c :** marked by harsh or discordant notes or by failure to sustain tones ⟨a ~ voice⟩ ⟨a ~ laugh⟩ **2 a :** DAMAGED, FLAWED ⟨a ~ reputation⟩ **b** *obs* **:** BANKRUPT **c :** mentally disturbed **:** CRAZY; *also* **:** intensely preoccupied **:** having a fixed idea **:** ENTHUSIASTIC — **cracked·ness** \'krak(t)nəs\ *n* -ES
cracked cocoa *n* **:** CACAO NIBS
cracked heels *n* **:** grease heel of the horse
cracked plate *n* **:** a postage stamp showing a mark or line not part of the original design and due to a crack or flaw in the printing plate
cracked stem *n* **:** a boron-deficiency disease of celery characterized by brownish leaf mottling and brittleness and crosswise cracking of the leafstalks
crack·er \'krakə(r)\ *n* -s **1** *chiefly dial* **a :** bragging liar **:** BOASTER **b :** LIE **c :** one that quips or relates wittily ⟨a ~ of jokes⟩ **2 :** anything that makes a cracking or snapping noise: as **a :** FIRECRACKER **b :** the cracking or snapping part at the end of a whiplash **:** SNAPPER **c :** a paper cylinder-shaped holder for a party favor containing an explosive that discharges when the ends are pulled sharply **3 :** one that cracks esp. into pieces: **a crackers** *pl* **:** NUTCRACKER **b :** one that softens and breaks down slabs of milled rubber so that they can be more easily cut for feeding into the tubing machine **4 :** a small dry bakery product made of flour and water with or without leavening and shortening and salted, semisweet, or plain **5** [prob. fr. *cracker* "boaster"] **a** *South* **:** POOR WHITE — usu. used disparagingly **b :** GEORGIAN — used as a nickname **c :** FLORIDIAN — used as a nickname **6** *Brit* **:** a rapid pace **7 :** a light yellowish brown that is redder and slightly lighter and stronger than khaki, duller than walnut brown, less strong and slightly yellower and lighter than cinnamon, and duller and slightly redder than manila **8 :** the equipment in which cracking is carried out
cracker-barrel \'ˌ=ˌ=ˌ=\ *adj* [fr. *cracker barrel;* fr. its being formerly a popular feature of the country store where discussions on any and all subjects are carried on] **:** suggestive of the intimate homespun nature of a country store ⟨the *cracker-barrel* democracy of the rural life —W.R.Goldschmidt⟩
crackerberry \'ˌ=ˌ— *see* BERRY\ *n* [so called fr. the noise produced when it is eaten] **:** DWARF CORNEL
¹crack·er·jack \'krakə(r),jak\ *also* **crack·a·jack** \-kə,j-\ *n* -s [prob. fr. ¹*crack* (to go fast) + *-er* + *jack* (fellow)] **1 :** an exceptionally skilled person ⟨a good student and a ~ on the football field⟩ ⟨the humor she was a ~ at —Saul Bellow⟩ **2 :** a thing of highest excellence ⟨a ~ of a book —Fitzhugh Green⟩
²crackerjack *also* **crackajack** \"\ *adj* **:** of striking ability or excellence ⟨a ~ revolver shot⟩ ⟨a ~ bicycle⟩
Cracker Jack *trademark* — used for a confection of popcorn and sometimes shelled peanuts coated with syrup
cracker mill *n* **:** a mill made of large disks covered with projecting teeth set face to face and rotating in opposite directions and used to crush previously softened grain
cracker-off \'ˌ=ˌ=¦=\ *n, pl* **crackers-off** [fr. *crack off*, v.] **:** a glassworker that trims glass chemical ware with a flame and diamond or removes the blowpipe from the neck of a glass object **:** WETTER-OFF
¹crack·ers \'krakə(r)z\ *n pl but sing or pl in constr* [so called fr. the cracking noise produced by the seeds when the berries are eaten] **:** BLACK HUCKLEBERRY
²crackers \"\ *adj* [fr. pl. of *cracker* (influenced in meaning by *cracked, crackbrain*)] *slang Brit* **:** CRAZY ⟨I'm here to tell you that you're driving me ~ —Noel Coward⟩; *also* **:** intensely enthusiastic **:** CRACKED ⟨we went ~ about them —Clarence Woodbury⟩
crack·et \'krakət\ *dial Brit var of* CRICKET
crackhalter *n* [¹*crack* + *halter*] *obs* **:** GALLOWS BIRD
crackhemp *n* [¹*crack* + *hemp*] *obs* **:** GALLOWS BIRD
crackier *comparative of* CRACKY
crackiest *superlative of* CRACKY
¹crack·ing \'krakiŋ, -kēŋ\ *adj* [fr. pres. part. of ¹*crack*] **:** GREAT, SMASHING ⟨his dying was ~ relief —Elizabeth Bowen⟩ ⟨a ~ regimental salute —Geoffrey Household⟩
²cracking \"\ *adv* **:** SUPERLATIVELY — usu. used with *good* ⟨a ~ good show⟩
³cracking \"\ *n* -s [fr. gerund of ¹*crack*] **:** a process in which relatively heavy hydrocarbons (as fuel oils and naphthas from petroleum) are broken up into lighter products (as gasoline and ethylene) by means of heat and usu. pressure and sometimes catalysts — see CATALYTIC CRACKING, THERMAL CRACKING
crackjaw \'ˌ=ˌ=\ *adj* [¹*crack* + *jaw*] **:** hard to pronounce **:** JAWBREAKING ⟨a ~ name⟩
¹crack·le \'krakəl\ *vb* **crackled; crackled; crackling** \-k(ə)liŋ\ **crackles** [freq. of ¹*crack*] *vi* **1 a :** to make small sharp sudden repeated noises ⟨a fire *crackling* in the hearth⟩ ⟨the dry leaves *crackled* along the walk⟩ **b :** to be alive (as with animation, enthusiasm, excitement, suspense) **:** SPARKLE ⟨an anthology that ~*s* with wit and wisdom —Bennett Cerf⟩ ⟨the very air, charged by an invisible generator, ~*s* with new business —Clifton Fadiman⟩ **2 :** to develop a surface network of fine cracks ⟨varnish applied over wet paint is likely to ~⟩ **:** become crackled ⟨his face was so dry and grimy that he thought he could feel his skin ~ —Stephen Crane⟩ ~ *vt* **1 :** to crush or crack with a series of sharp snapping noises ⟨thrust her hand between a sheaf of loosened papers and *crackled* them —Rosamond Langbridge⟩ **2 :** to detach or curtail (a note or chord) in lute music

²crackle \"\ *n* -s **1 a :** the noise of slight and frequent cracks or reports ⟨the ~ of small arms⟩ ⟨the ~ of laughter⟩ ⟨the ~ as he folded his newspaper⟩ **b :** SPARKLE, EFFERVESCENCE ⟨the dry ~ of Yankee wit —Clifton Fadiman⟩ **2 a :** a network of fine cracks on an otherwise smooth surface (as on pottery and glassware) — compare CRAZE **b :** a painted surface in which numerous fine cracks have been caused by superimposition of layers which contract differently in the process of drying **3 :** CRACKLING 2b
crack·led \'krakəld\ *adj* **1 :** having the rind crisp and brittle ⟨~ roast pork⟩ **2 :** covered with or as if with minute cracks ⟨pottery with a ~ finish⟩
crack·less \'krakləs\ *adj* **:** not having a crack
crack·le·ware \'ˌ=ˌ=ˌ=\ *n* [²*crackle* + *ware*] **:** glazed ceramic ware with a crazed finish
¹crack·ling \'krak(ə)liŋ\ *adj* **1 :** that crackles ⟨~ sounds⟩ ⟨~ wit⟩ **2** *of wine* **:** mildly sparkling **:** PÉTILLANT
²crackling \"; *in sense 2 & 3 often* -lən\ *n* -s **1 :** a series of small sharp cracks or reports (as from frozen snow being walked over or rifle fire at a distance) **2 a :** refuse of tallow melting used as food for dogs — usu. used in pl. **b :** the crisp residue left after the fat has been separated from the fibrous tissue in rendering lard or frying or roasting the skin of pork, turkey, duck, or goose — usu. used in pl.; compare CRACKLING BREAD **3** *dial Eng* **:** CRACKNEL 1 — usu. used in pl.
crackling bread \'krakliŋ-, -klən-\ *or* **crack·lin bread** \-lən-\ *n, chiefly South* **:** corn bread made with cracklings
crack-loo \'kra,klü\ *also* **crack·a·loo** \-akə,lü\ *n* -s [*crack-loo* fr. ²*crack* + *loo; crackaloo* fr. ²*crack* + connective *-a-* + *loo*] **:** a gambling game in which players toss up coins and consider the winner the one whose coin falls and rests nearest to a crack in the floor
crack·ly \'krak(ə)lē, -li\ *adj* -ER/-EST **:** inclined to crackle **:** crisp and brittle
crack·nel \'kraknəl\ *n* -s [ME *krakenelle*, perh. modif. of MF *craquelin*, fr. MD *crākelinc*, fr. *crāken* to crack; akin to OE *cracian* to crack — more at CRACK] **1 :** a hard brittle biscuit **2 :** CRACKLING 2 — usu. used in pl.
crackowe *var of* CRAKOW
crack·pot \'ˌ=ˌ=\ *n, often attrib* [¹*crack* + *pot* "head"] **:** one given to erratic, impractical, or lunatic ideas or notions ⟨a new crop of ~*s* determined to lead the country into chaos —Bill Mauldin⟩ ⟨~ ideas⟩ — **crack·pot·ism** \"+,izəm\ *n* -s
crackrope \'ˌ=ˌ=\ *n* [ME *crakraip*, fr. *craken, cracken* to crack + *raip*, var. of *rope*] **1** *archaic* **:** GALLOWS BIRD **2 :** ROGUE, WAG
cracks *pl of* CRACK, *pres 3d sing of* CRACK
crackskull \'ˌ=ˌ=\ *n* [¹*crack* + *skull*] *archaic* **:** CRACKBRAIN
cracks·man \'kraksmən\ *n, pl* **cracksmen** [*cracks* (pl. or gen. sing. of ²*crack* "burglary") + *man*] **:** BURGLAR, HOUSEBREAKER; *also* **:** SAFECRACKER
crack-the-whip \ˌ=ˌ='=\ *n* **:** a game in which players join hands in a line and rush forward together until the leader's sudden turn causes the line to swing around rapidly often throwing off players at the opposite end
crack-up \'ˌ=ˌ=\ *n* -s [fr. *crack up*, v.] **:** an instance of cracking up: as **a :** NERVOUS BREAKDOWN **b :** a wrecking or smashing esp. of a vehicle; *specif* **:** an accident involving serious but repairable structural damage to an aircraft **c :** COLLAPSE, BREAKDOWN ⟨the *crack-up* of a political coalition⟩
crack willow *n* **1 :** a common and widely cultivated Old World willow (*Salix fragilis*) — called also *brittle willow, snap willow* **2 :** any of several willows closely related to the crack willow
¹cracky \krakē, -ki\ *adj* -ER/-EST [²*crack* + *-y*] **1 a :** having cracks **b :** inclined to crack **2** *chiefly dial Eng* **:** CRACKBRAINED
²cracky \"\ *interj* [alter. of *crickey, crikey*] — a mild oath; used in the phrase *by cracky*
cracky wagon *n* [prob. fr. ²*crack* (noise) + *-y*] **:** a light wagon without springs drawn by one horse
cra·co·vi·enne \krə,kōvē'en, ˌ=ˌ=ˌ=\ *n* -s [F, fr. fem. of *cracovien* of Cracow, fr. *Cracovie* (Cracow), Poland + F *-ien* -ian] **:** KRAKOWIAK
cra·cow *or* **kra·kow** \'krā,kau̇, -raˌ-, -rāˌ-, -(,)kō; 'krä,küf, -,kòf\ *adj, usu cap* [fr. *Cracow* (*Kraków*), Poland] **:** of or from the city of Cracow, Poland **:** of the kind or style prevalent in Cracow
cracowe *var of* CRAKOW
crac·tic·i·dae \krak'tisə,dē\ *n pl, cap* [NL, fr. *Cracticus*, type genus (fr. Gk *kraktikos* noisy, fr. assumed Gk *kraktos*, verbal of Gk *krazein* to croak) — + Gk *-ikos* -ic + *-idae* — more at ROOK] **:** a small family of Australasian oscine birds that were formerly included in the family Laniidae — see STREPERA
-cra·cy \krəsē, -si\ *or* **-oc·ra·cy** \ˈäkrəsē, -si\ *n comb form* -ES [MF & LL; MF *-cratie*, fr. LL *-cratia*, fr. Gk *-kratia*, fr. *kratos* strength, power — more at HARD] **1 :** form of government; *also* **:** state having such a form ⟨*democracy*⟩ ⟨mob*ocracy*⟩ ⟨squir*ocracy*⟩ **2 :** social or political class (as of powerful persons) ⟨pluto*cracy*⟩ ⟨snob*ocracy*⟩ **3 :** theory of government or of social organization ⟨techno*cracy*⟩
¹cra·dle \'krād^əl\ *n* -s [ME *cradel*, fr. OE *cradol* cradle, cot; akin to OHG *kratto* basket, Skt *grantha* knot, ON *karmr* breastwork, L *grumus* pile of earth scratched together, Gk *grypos* bent, Skt *guṇa* rope, string; basic meaning: turning, twisting] **1 a :** a bed or cot for a baby usu. oscillating on rockers or swinging on pivots ⟨rock a ~⟩ **b :** the earliest period of life **:** INFANCY ⟨from the ~ to the grave⟩ **c :** a place where something began to develop **:** region of origin ⟨the Nile valley conceived of as the ~ of civilization⟩

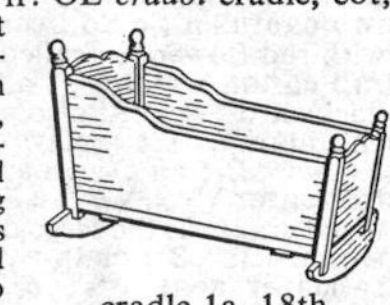
cradle 1a, 18th century

2 : a resting place, framework, container, or grip felt to resemble the restraining or supporting nature of a baby's cradle or of its shape: as **a** (1) **:** a framework of bars and rods joined by crosspieces (as a workman's suspended scaffold or the ribbing of a vaulted ceiling to be covered with plaster) (2) **:** a supporting foundation usu. of concrete for maintaining the proper gradient of a pipe drain located on a subgrade not capable of supporting it (3) **:** a frame in which the treads and risers of stairs are glued together (4) **:** a framework of ribs often joined by crosspieces and attached to the back of a painted panel to prevent warping or splitting (5) **:** the support for a telephone receiver or handset **b** (1) **:** an implement with rods like fingers attached to a scythe and used formerly esp. for harvesting grain (2) **:** a device in weaving consisting of curved metal pieces fastened beneath the cylinders to catch the cards of a jacquard head as they fall **c** (1) **:** a wooden frame supporting a ship when launched — called also *launching cradle* (2) **:** a wooden or metal framework on a ship (as under a lifeboat or machinery) used to support in a fixed position or facilitate in moving from one place to another (3) **:** a frame of timber or blocks for the support of large rounded objects (as boats, tanks, pipes) so that they do not roll esp. while being transported (4) **:** the part of a gun carriage that supports the tube and upon which the tube recoils (5) **:** a low frame on casters used by mechanics to support themselves while working under an automobile — called also *creeper* **d** (1) **:** a frame to keep the bedclothes from contact with an injured part of the body (as in fractures, wounds, burns) (2) **:** a frame placed on an animal's neck by a veterinarian to keep the animal from biting an injury or sore **e :** a device on the string of a stonebow to hold a missile **f :** CAT'S CRADLE **g :** a grip by which a wrestler holds an opponent in a doubled-up position by circling his head and one leg and interlocking his own hands **3 :** anything that rocks or may be rocked in the manner of a baby's cradle: as **a :** a rocking device used by miners in washing out auriferous earth by hand — called also *rocker* **b :** a tool used in mezzotint engraving that by a rocking motion raises burrs on the surface of the plate

cradle 2b(1)

²cradle \"\ *vb* **cradled; cradled; cradling** \-d(^ə)liŋ\ **cradles** *vt* **1 a :** to place or keep (a baby) in or as if in a cradle ⟨they *cradled* their youngest on the sun porch⟩ ⟨an occasional Paiute woman with baby *cradled* on her back —*Amer. Guide Series: Nev.*⟩ **b :** SHELTER, REAR ⟨while Italy was *cradling* the strange Etruscan culture —Jacquetta & Christopher Hawkes⟩ **c :** to support protectively or intimately **:** hold closely ⟨*cradled* his head on his folded arms —MacKinlay Kantor⟩ ⟨*cradling* a cup of coffee in his hand —Luke Short⟩ **2 :** to cut (as grain) with a cradle scythe **3 a :** to place in or provide with a special or suitable form or container ⟨~ a boat⟩ ⟨~ the receiver of a telephone⟩ ⟨~ machinery for shipment⟩ **b :** to furnish or reinforce with a ribbed framework ⟨~ a painting⟩ ⟨~ a panel⟩ **4 :** to wash in a miner's cradle ⟨~ out a few grains of gold⟩ **5 :** to keep (a lacrosse ball) in the pocket of the crosse with rotating motions ~ *vi* **1** *obs* **:** to rest in or as if in a cradle **2 :** to wash out ore in a cradle **3 :** to cut grain with a cradle scythe
cradleboard \'ˌ=ˌ=ˌ=\ *n* **:** a board or flat framework to which American Indians traditionally and often today bind a child during the infant stage of growth
cradle cannon *n* **:** a cannon in billiards made when the balls are close beside a pocket
cradle cap *n* **:** eczema of the crown of the head in infants marked by greasy, gray, or dark brown adherent scaly crusts that often coalesce to form a coating resembling a cap
cradle knoll *n* **:** a small knoll (as on a logging road) that requires grading
cradleland \'ˌ=ˌ=ˌ=\ *n* **:** the land or region of origin
cra·dler \'krād(ə)lə(r)\ *n* -s [²*cradle* (to mow) + *-er*] **:** one that cradles (as in reaping wheat)
cradle roll *n* **:** a listing kept by a church of the names of very young children esp. those of members
cradle roof *n* **:** a timber roof much used in the middle ages with the rafters, collar beams, and braces of each truss combined into a form approaching that of an arch and thus giving the effect of a series of arches or when ceiled of a barrel vault — compare COMPASS ROOF
cradles *pl of* CRADLE, *pres 3d sing of* CRADLE
cradle scythe *n* **:** a scythe equipped with a cradle
cradle snatcher *n* **:** one that weds or associates with one of the opposite sex who is comparatively very young
cradlesong \'ˌ=ˌ=\ *n* [ME *cradyl songe*, fr. *cradyl* cradle + *songe* song] **:** LULLABY, BERCEUSE
cradle vault *n* **:** BARREL VAULT
cradlewalk *n, obs* **:** a walk covered by arching trees
cradling *n* -s **1 :** the act of using a cradle **2 :** the placing of the cables of a suspension bridge closer together at the center of span than at the supporting towers **3 :** a wooden or iron framework **:** structural work in the form of a cradle or cradles; *specif* **:** a framework in arched or coved ceilings to which the laths are nailed
¹craft \'kraft, -raa(ə)ft, -raift, -rȧft\ *n* -s *see sense 6* [ME, fr. OE *cræft* strength, skill — more at CRAVE] **1** *obs* **:** STRENGTH, FORCE **2 :** skillfulness in planning, making, or executing **:** artistic dexterity ⟨great ~ in catching fish⟩ ⟨manual ~⟩ — often used in combination ⟨stage*craft*⟩ ⟨siege*craft*⟩ ⟨wine*craft*⟩ ⟨campaign*craft*⟩ **3 a :** an occupation, trade, or pursuit requiring manual dexterity or the application of artistic skill ⟨the carpenter's ~⟩ ⟨the ~ of playwriting⟩ ⟨learn a ~ from the ground up⟩ **b :** any one of the seven divisions of Camp Fire Girl activities **4 a** *obs* **:** EXPEDIENT, TRICK, ARTIFICE **b :** skill in deceiving for the promotion of one's own ends **:** CUNNING, GUILE ⟨an enemy of great ~ and subtlety⟩ ⟨Henry, out of a lifetime of political ~, coached Cranmer how to turn the tables on his accusers —Francis Hackett⟩ **5 a :** the members of a particular trade or an association of these **:** GUILD ⟨the ~ of ironmongers⟩ **b** *often cap* **:** the brotherhood of Freemasons **6** *pl usu* **craft a :** a boat esp. of small size ⟨a seaworthy ~⟩ ⟨these fascinating ~ that floated downstream —*Amer. Guide Series: Ind.*⟩ ⟨storm warnings put up for small ~⟩ **b :** AIRCRAFT ⟨helicopter delivery service . . . using four ~ —*Tide*⟩ **7** [origin unknown] **:** the equipment for catching and killing fish **syn** see ART
²craft \"\ *vt* -ED/-ING/-S **:** to make or construct esp. by or as if by hand ⟨scale models he has ~*ed* —*Newsweek*⟩
³craft \'kraft\ *chiefly Scot var of* ¹CROFT
craft·i·ly \'kraftəlē, -raaf-,-raif-,-rȧf-, -li\ *adv* [ME, fr. OE *cræftiglice*, fr. *cræftig* + *-lice* -ly] **1** *archaic* **:** SKILLFULLY **2 :** SLYLY, ARTFULLY ⟨a ~ devised trap⟩
craft·i·ness \-tēnəs, -tin-\ *n* -ES **:** the quality or state of being crafty
craft·less \-tləs\ *adj* **:** not having a craft
crafts·man \-f(t)smən\ *n, pl* **craftsmen** [ME *craftes man*, fr. *craftes* (gen. sing. of ¹*craft*) + *man*] **1 :** one who practices some trade or handicraft (as a bricklayer, woodcarver, plumber) **:** ARTISAN **2 :** one who creates or performs with skill or dexterity esp. in the manual arts ⟨jewelry made by Old World *craftsmen*⟩ **3 :** one who does work of consistently high quality ⟨as a novelist he was a consummate ~⟩ — **crafts·man·ship** \-,ship\ *n*
craftsmaster *n* [*crafts* (gen. of ¹*craft*) + *master*] *obs* **:** a skilled craftsman
craftswoman \'ˌ=ˌ=\ *n, pl* **craftswomen :** a female craftsman
craft union *n* **:** a labor union whose membership is limited to workmen following the same craft — compare INDUSTRIAL UNION
craftwork \'ˌ=ˌ=\ *n* **:** work usu. done by hand that exhibits artistry and individuality ⟨~ in metal⟩; *also* **:** a product of such work ⟨pottery and other imported ~⟩
crafty \-ftē, -ti\ *adj, usu* -ER/-EST [ME, fr. OE *cræftig* strong, skillful, fr. *cræft* + *-ig* -y] **1** *dial chiefly Brit* **:** SKILLFUL, CLEVER, INGENIOUS **2** *obs* **:** showing skill **:** skillfully made **3 :** adept at deceiving others **:** CUNNING, WILY **syn** see SLY
¹crag \ krag, -raa(ə)g,-raig\ *n* -s [ME, of Celt origin; akin to OIr *crec* crag, OW *creik* rock; perh. akin to OE *heard* hard — more at HARD] **1 :** a steep rugged rocky eminence **:** a rough broken cliff or projecting point of rock **2 a** *archaic* **:** a sharp detached fragment of rock **b :** a sedimentary rock found in Norfolk, Suffolk, and Essex, England, and composed of fragments of shells mingled with sand
²crag \"\ *n* -s [ME *crag, crage*, fr. MD *crāghe*; akin to ME *crawe* craw — more at CRAW] **1** *chiefly Scot* **:** NECK **2** *chiefly Scot* **:** THROAT
crag and tail *n* **:** an elongate hill having at one end a steep face of ice-smoothed rock and at the other a gentle slope of rock or glacial drift
crag-fast \'ˌ=ˌ=\ *adj* **:** stranded on or as if on a crag and unable to ascend or descend ⟨~ sheep⟩
crag·gan \'kragən\ *n* -s [ScGael *cragan*, akin to MIr *crocān* pot, prob. fr. OE *crocca* — more at CROCK] **:** a rude earthenware vessel for domestic use made in the Hebrides
crag·ged \'kragəd, -raag-,-raig-\ *adj* **:** CRAGGY
crag·ged·ness *n* -ES **:** CRAGGINESS
crag·gi·ly \-gəlē, -li\ *adv* **:** in a craggy manner
crag·gi·ness \-gēnəs, -gin-\ *n* -ES **:** the quality or state of being craggy
crag·gy \-gē,-gi\ *adj, usu* -ER/-EST [ME, fr. ¹*crag* + *-y*] **1 :** full of or abounding in crags ⟨~ slopes⟩ **2 :** ROUGH, RUGGED ⟨~ facial features⟩ ⟨a ~ personality⟩
crag martin *n* **:** ROCK SWALLOW
cra·go \'krāgō\ *n, cap* [NL, alter. of *Crangon*] **:** a genus (the type of the family Crangonidae) of large shrimps including the black-tailed shrimp (*C. nigricauda*) of the Pacific coast of No. America
crags·man \'kragzmən\ *n, pl* **cragsmen :** one expert in climbing crags or cliffs
craich \'krāk\ *var of* CREAGH
crai·chy \'krāchi\ *adj* [origin unknown] **1** *dial Eng* **:** DILAPIDATED **2** *dial Eng* **:** INFIRM, AILING
¹craig \'krāg\ *n* -s [ME *crag* — more at CRAG (rock)] *Scot* **:** ¹CRAG
²craig \"\ *also* **craig·ie** *or* **craigy** \-gi\ *n, pl* **craigs** *also* **craigies** [*craig* fr. ME *crag, crage; craigie, craigy*, dim. of *craig* — more at CRAG (neck)] *Scot* **:** ²CRAG
craik \'krāk\ *Scot var of* CRAKE
crai·sey \'krāzi\ *var of* ³CRAZY
¹crake \'krāk\ *n* -s [ME, prob. fr. ON *krāka* crow or *krākr* raven — more at CROW] **1** *dial Brit* **:** CROW, ROOK **2 :** any of various rails; *esp* **:** the corncrake and other short-billed kinds **3 :** the corncrake's cry

²crake \"\ *vi* -ED/-ING/-S [ME *craken*, prob. of imit. origin] **1 :** to cry out harshly and loudly ⟨crows *craking* in a field⟩ **2** *dial Brit* **:** COMPLAIN, FRET

³crake \"\ *vi* -ED/-ING/-S [ME *craken* — more at CRACK] *dial Brit* **:** ¹CRACK *vi* 3

crakeberry \ˈ≈- — *see* BERRY\ *n* [¹*crake* + *berry*] **:** CROWBERRY 1a

cra·kow *also* **cra·kowe** *or* **crac·kowe** *or* **cra·cowe** \ˈkrä,kaů, -ra,-, -rā,-, -(,)kō\ *n* -S [ME *crakowe*, fr. *Cracow* (*Kraków*) Poland whence they came] **:** a shoe, boot, or slipper made with an extremely long pointed toe and worn in Europe in the 14th and 15th centuries

¹**cram** \ˈkram, -raa(ə)m\ *vb* **crammed; crammed; cramming; crams** [ME *crammen*, fr. OE *crammian;* akin to OHG *krimman* to press, ON *kremja* to squeeze, L *gremium* lap, Skt *grāma* multitude, pile, village, L *grex* herd — more at GREGARIOUS] *vt* **1 :** to fill esp. forcibly with more than is necessary or appropriate **:** pack tight **:** load to overflowing **:** JAM ⟨~ a suitcase with clothes⟩ ⟨a *crammed* schedule⟩ ⟨a novel *crammed* with surprises⟩ **2 a :** to fill with food to satiety **:** OVERFEED, STUFF; *esp* **:** to feed forcibly in order to fatten (poultry) either through a tube inserted into the crop or by thrusting long strips of dough down the gullet by hand **b :** to eat voraciously or clumsily **:** BOLT ⟨rebuke a child for *cramming* his food⟩ **3 :** to thrust, jam, or drive in or as if in a rough, clumsy, willful, or unsuitable manner ⟨he *crammed* the letters in his pocket⟩ ⟨~ lies down another's throat⟩ **4 a :** to put (a person) hastily through a course of memorizing esp. in preparation for an examination **b :** to study (a subject) under pressure ⟨~ physics for the final examination⟩ ~ *vi* **1 :** to eat greedily or to satiety **:** STUFF **2 :** to study intensively or under pressure esp. for an examination — often used with *up* ⟨~ up on mathematics⟩ **syn** see PACK

²**cram** \"\ *n* -S **1 :** a compressed multitude or crowd **:** CRUSH ⟨there was such a ~ in the church that the procession had almost to fight its way to the high altar —Bruce Marshall⟩ **2 :** studying or instructing under pressure or limitations of time esp. for a coming examination ⟨he got through his senior year finally by sheer ~⟩ ⟨students attending ~ courses before their exams⟩

³**cram** \"\ *n* -S [G, Sw, Dan & Norw *kram* trifles, small wares, rubbish; G, fr. MHG *krām* stretched out cloth, tent covering, merchandise booth, fr. OHG *crām* market booth; Sw, Dan & Norw, fr. MLG *krām* market booth, tent covering, small wares; akin to MD *crāme*, *craem* tent flap, market booth, small wares] *dial* **:** anything unwanted or in the way **:** JUNK

cram·a·sie *or* **cram·a·sy** \ˈkraməzē\ *archaic var of* CRAMOISIE

¹**cram·be** \ˈkrambē\ *n, cap* [NL, fr. L, cabbage, fr. Gk *krambē;* akin to LGk *krambos* dry, withered — more at RUMPLE] **:** a genus of chiefly Old World mostly annual herbs (family Cruciferae) having coarse lyrate leaves and panicled white flowers — see SEA KALE

²**crambe** *vi* -ED/-ING/-S [obs. E *crambe* crambo — more at CRAMBO] *obs* **:** to play crambo

cram·ber·ry \ˈkram,berē, -₋b(ə)rē, -ri — *see* BERRY\ *now dial var of* CRANBERRY

¹**cram·bid** \ˈkrambəd\ *adj* [NL *Crambidae*] **:** of or relating to the Crambidae

²**crambid** \"\ *n* -S **:** any moth of the family Crambidae

cram·bi·dae \ˈkrambə,dē\ *n pl, cap* [NL, fr. *Crambus*, type genus + *-idae*] *in some esp former classifications* **:** a family that comprises small moths which wrap the wings about the body when at rest and that is now usu. made a subfamily of Pyralididae — compare CHILO, CORN BORER, GRASS MOTH

cram·ble *or* **cram·mel** \ˈkraməl\ *vi* -ED/-ING/-S [fr. obs. E, to crawl, of unknown origin] *dial Eng* **:** to walk or move stiffly or with difficulty **:** HOBBLE

cram·bling rocket \ˈkramb(ə)liŋ-\ *n* [prob. fr. pres. part. of obs. E *cramble* to crawl] **:** a European herb (*Reseda lutea*) resembling the common garden mignonette

cram·bo \ˈkram(,)bō\ *n* -ES [alter. of earlier *crambe*, fr. L, cabbage — more at CRAMBE] **1 :** a game in which one player gives a word or line of verse that is to be matched in rhyme by other players **2 :** ineffectual, fatuous, or second-rate rhyme or rhyming ⟨this was nothing but ~⟩

crambo clink *or* **crambo jingle** *n, Scot* **:** DOGGEREL, CRAMBO

cram·bus \ˈkrambəs\ *n, cap* [NL, fr. LGk *krambos* dry, withered — more at RUMPLE] **:** a genus of small moths (family Pyralididae) that have fringed hindwings and include several economic pests with larvae that are webworms

crame \ˈkrām\ *n* -S [ME, fr. MD *crāme* or MLG *krāme;* akin to OHG *crām* market booth] *Scot* **:** a booth, stall, or tent where goods are sold (as at a fair)

cram–full \ˈ≈¦≈\ *adj* [²*cram*] **:** as full as can be **:** OVERFLOWING ⟨a novel *cram-full* of suspense⟩

cra·mi·gnon \kråmēnyōⁿ\ *n* -S [F] **:** a festive dance of southern France in which the dancers are in chain formation

cram·mer \ˈkramə(r)\ *n* -S **:** one that crams: as **a :** an apparatus for cramming poultry **b** *Brit* **:** a school or instructor that crams students (as for college, a branch of the armed forces, a profession, a civil-service examination)

¹**cram·oi·sie** *or* **cram·oi·sy** \ˈkraməzē, krəˈmȯi-, ˈkra,mȯi-\ *n, pl* **cramoisies** [ME *cremesye*, *crammasy*, fr. MF *cremosi*, *cramoisi*, adj.] **:** crimson cloth

²**cramoisie** *or* **cramoisy** \"\ *adj* [ME *crymysy*, *cramysse*, fr. MF *cremosi*, *cramoisi*, fr. Ar *qirmizī* red of the kermes — more at CRIMSON] **:** CRIMSON

¹**cramp** \ˈkramp, -raa(ə)mp, -raimp\ *n* -S [ME *crampe*, fr. MF, of Gmc origin; akin to MD *crampe* cramp, hook] **1 a** (1) **:** a spasmodic painful involuntary contraction of a muscle ⟨a ~ in the leg⟩ (2) **:** a case or instance of such a contraction ⟨suffering from the ~⟩ **b :** a temporary paralysis of certain muscles from overuse — see WRITER'S CRAMP **c** (1) **:** a sharp abdominal pain — used usu. in pl. (2) **cramps** *pl* **:** painful menstruation **2 cramps** *pl* **a :** a partial paralysis of the hindquarters occasionally seen in pregnant animals **b :** the condition of birds unable to fly as a result of narrow confinement

²**cramp** \"\ *n* -S [obs. D *krampe* hook (fr. MD *crampe*) or LG, fr. MLG; akin to OHG *kramph* bent, ON *kreppa* to clench, Latvian *grumbt* to become wrinkled, OE *cradol* cradle — more at CRADLE] **1 a :** a device usu. of iron bent at the ends or of dovetail form used to hold together blocks (as of stone or timbers) **b :** ¹CLAMP 1 **c :** a piece of wood used in the manufacture of shoes and having a curve corresponding to that of the upper part of the instep on which the upper leather of a boot is stretched — called also *crimp* **2 a :** something that confines or contracts **:** RESTRAINT, SHACKLE ⟨authoritarian ~s on free thinking⟩ **b :** the quality or state of being confined or compressed **:** CONSTRAINT ⟨the ~ and pettiness of bourgeois life⟩

cramp 1a

³**cramp** \"\ *vb* -ED/-ING/-S [partly fr. ¹*cramp*, partly fr. ²*cramp*] *vt* **1 :** to cause to have a cramp **:** affect with or as if with cramp ⟨gout ~*ing* his limbs⟩ ⟨his hands were ~*ed* for lack of movement⟩ **2 :** COMPRESS, RESTRAIN, CONFINE ⟨prisoners ~*ed* in fetters⟩ ⟨a spirit ~*ed* with dogma⟩ ⟨they ~*ed* the livestock in ancient barns⟩; *also* **:** to restrain from free expression of one's tastes or skill **:** dampen the spirits of — used esp. in the phrase *cramp one's style* **3 :** to turn (the front wheels of a vehicle) to right or left ⟨~ the wheels into the curb . . . when parked —C.P.Taylor⟩ **4 a :** to fasten or hold with a cramp **b :** to form on a cramp ⟨~ bootlegs⟩ ~ *vi* **:** to suffer from or as if from cramps

⁴**cramp** \"\ *adj* [prob. fr. ³*cramp*] **1 :** KNOTTY, DIFFICULT ⟨not to add any of the ~ reasons for this opinion —S.T. Coleridge⟩ **2 :** CONTRACTED, NARROW, CONFINED ⟨a ~ corner⟩

cramp bark *n* [¹*cramp*] **1 :** CRANBERRY BUSH 2 **2 :** the dried bark of the cranberry tree used as an antispasmodic

cramp bone *n* [¹*cramp*] **:** the patella of a sheep formerly used as a charm for the cramp

cramp colic *n* [¹*cramp*] *South & Midland* **:** APPENDICITIS

cramped odds *n pl* **:** odds in court tennis that place a limitation on play instead of on the score only

cramp·er \-pə(r)\ *n* -S **1 :** one that cramps **2** *obs* **:** CRAMP IRON

cramp·ette *also* **cramp·et** \ˈkrampət\ *n* -S [ME *crampette*, fr. MD *crampe* hook + ME *-ette* — more at CRAMP] **1 :** the chape of a sword scabbard; *specif* **:** a conventionalized representation of such a chape used as a charge in heraldry **2** *usu* **crampet a** *obs* **:** FERRULE **b :** CRAMPIT

crampfish \ˈ≈,≈\ *n* [¹*cramp* + *fish;* fr. its ability to give electric shocks] **:** ELECTRIC RAY

cramp·ing·ly *adv* **:** in a cramping manner

cramp iron *n* **1 :** ²CRAMP 1a **2 :** a metal piece attached at each side of a horse-drawn vehicle where a front wheel may rub when cramped

cramp·it \ˈkrampət\ *n* -S [alter. of *crampette*] **:** a sheet of iron on which a player stands to deliver his stone in curling

cram·pon \ˈkram,pän; *US also & Brit usu* -₋pən\ *also* **cram·poon** \-,pün, ≈ˈ≈\ *n* -S [MF, *crampon*, of Gmc origin; akin to MD *crampe* hook — more at CRAMP **1 :** a form of hooked clutch or dog for raising heavy objects (as stones, lumber, blocks of ice) **:** GRAPPLING IRON — used usu. in pl. **2 :** a steel frame provided with spikes and attached to a boot with straps for use as a climbing iron on ice and snow

crampon 1

cram·pon·née *also* **cram·po·née** \¦krampəˈnā, -nē\ *adj* [F *cramponné*, past part. of *cramponner* to fasten with cramps, fr. *crampon*] *of a cross* **:** having a short squared projection from the end of each arm at a right angle, all the projections being turned in the same rotary direction

cramp ring *n* [¹*cramp*] **1 :** a ring supposed to avert or cure sickness (as cramp or epilepsy); *specif* **:** one formerly consecrated for this purpose by one of the sovereigns of England on Good Friday **2** *obs* **:** FETTER, SHACKLE

cramps *pl of* CRAMP, *pres 3d sing of* CRAMP

crampy \ˈkrampē, -raim-, -pi\ *adj* -ER/-EST [¹*cramp* + *-y*] **:** affected with, resembling, or marked by a cramp **:** productive of cramps; *specif* **:** STRINGHALTED ⟨a ~ horse⟩

crams *pres 3 sing of* CRAM, *pl of* CRAM

¹**cran** \ˈkran\ *n* -S [ME, crane — more at CRANE] *Scot* **:** a common swift (*Apus apus*)

²**cran** \"\ *n* -S [ScGael *crann* tree, lot, measure of herring; akin to OIr *crann* tree — more at HURST] **:** British unit of capacity for fresh herrings equal to 37½ imperial gallons

cran·age \ˈkrānij, -nēj\ *n* -S [ME, fr. *cran* crane + *-age*] **1 :** the use of a crane (as for loading and unloading ships) **2 :** the price paid for the use of a crane

¹**cran·ber·ry** \ˈkran,berē, -raan-, -₋b(ə)rē, -ri *also* ÷ -am(,)- — *see* BERRY\ *n* -ES [part modif., part trans. of LG *kraanbere*, *kroonbere*, fr. *kraan*, *kroon* crane (fr. MLG *krān*, *krāne*) + *bere* berry; akin to OE *cran* crane — more at CRANE] **1 :** the bright red acid berry produced by any of several plants of the genus *Vaccinium* (as *V. oxycoccus* and *V. macrocarpon*) — see AMERICAN CRANBERRY, EUROPEAN CRANBERRY **2 :** any plant that produces cranberries — see OXYCOCCUS **3 :** any of numerous plants having fruit resembling a cranberry — see AUSTRALIAN CRANBERRY **4 a :** BOG BILBERRY **b :** MOUNTAIN CRANBERRY **5 :** a dark red that is bluer, lighter, and stronger than average garnet, bluer and slightly lighter and stronger than pomegranate, and bluer, lighter, and stronger than average wine

²**cranberry** \"\ *vi* **:** to gather or seek cranberries

cranberry bog *or* **cranberry marsh** *n* **:** a low periodically flooded area in which cranberries are grown

cranberry bush *n* **1 :** any plant bearing cranberries **2** *or* **cranberry tree :** a shrub or tree (*Viburnum trilobum*) of No. America and Europe with prominently 3-lobed leaves and red fruit — called also *highbush cranberry;* see GUELDER ROSE

cranberry fruitworm *n* **:** the larva of a small snout moth (*Acrobasis vaccinii*) that feeds in and destroys the growing fruits of cranberry and blueberry

cranberry gall *n* **:** a disease of the cranberry and related species caused by a fungus (*Synchytrium vaccinii*) and producing reddish galls on stem, leaves, flowers, and fruits

cranberry gourd *n* **1 :** a So. American tuberous-rooted herbaceous vine (*Abobra tenuifolia*) with 5-lobed or much divided leaves and small greenish fragrant flowers **2 :** the small fruit of the cranberry gourd at first white and later carmine used for ornament

cranberry rake *or* **cranberry scoop** *n* **:** a scoop with teeth on the front edge for harvesting cranberries

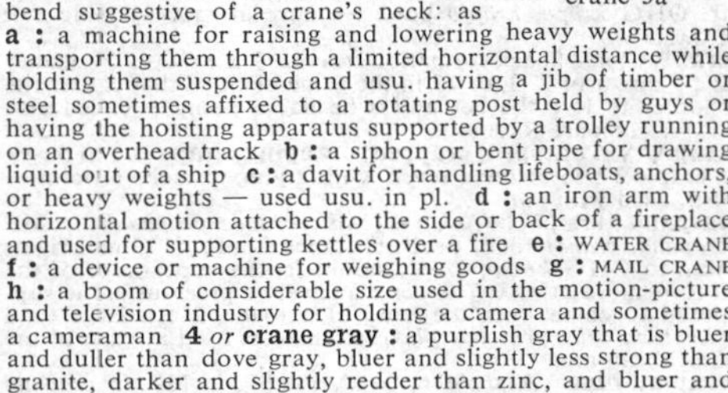

cranberry rake

cranberry scald *or* **cranberry blast** *n* **:** a disease of the cranberry caused by a fungus (*Guignardia vaccinii*) producing a blasting of the flowers and scalding and rotting of the fruit

cranberry spanworm *n* **:** any of several loopers attacking chiefly cranberries

crance \ˈkran(t)s\ *or* **crance iron** *also* **cranse** *n* -S [D *krans*, lit., wreath, fr. MD *crans*, fr. MHG *kranz*, fr. OHG] **:** a band on the outer end of a bowsprit to which the bobstays and bowsprit shrouds are fastened

cranch *var of* CRAUNCH

cran·dall·ite \ˈkrandəl,īt\ *n* -S [M. L. *Crandall*, 20th cent. Am. mining engineer + E *-ite*] **:** a mineral consisting of hydrous calcium-aluminum phosphate $CaAl_3(PO_4)_2(OH)_5H_2O$ occurring in white to grayish fine-fibrous masses

¹**crane** \ˈkrān\ *n, pl* **cranes** *or* **crane** [ME *cran*, fr. OE; akin to OHG *krano* crane, ON *trani*, Gk *geranos*, L *grus* crane, Skt *jarate* he cries, it sounds; basic meaning: croaking] **1 :** any bird of the family Gruidae (order Gruiformes) consisting of a small group of tall wading birds superficially resembling the herons but structurally more nearly related to the rails and being usu. larger than the herons and differing from them in having a schizognathous skull, plumage more compact, partly naked head, obtuse bill with large nostrils near the middle, and elevated hind toe **2 a** *Midland* **:** GREAT BLUE HERON **b** (1) **:** the common heron (2) **:** CORMORANT **3** *pl* **cranes :** a projection often horizontal swinging about a vertical axis or having at one end a bend suggestive of a crane's neck: as **a :** a machine for raising and lowering heavy weights and transporting them through a limited horizontal distance while holding them suspended and usu. having a jib of timber or steel sometimes affixed to a rotating post held by guys or having the hoisting apparatus supported by a trolley running on an overhead track **b :** a siphon or bent pipe for drawing liquid out of a ship **c :** a davit for handling lifeboats, anchors, or heavy weights — used usu. in pl. **d :** an iron arm with horizontal motion attached to the side or back of a fireplace and used for supporting kettles over a fire **e :** WATER CRANE **f :** a device or machine for weighing goods **g :** MAIL CRANE **h :** a boom of considerable size used in the motion-picture and television industry for holding a camera and sometimes a cameraman **4** *or* **crane gray :** a purplish gray that is bluer and duller than dove gray, bluer and slightly less strong than granite, darker and slightly redder than zinc, and bluer and darker than cinder gray — called also *Prince gray*

crane 3a

²**crane** \"\ *vb* -ED/-ING/-S *vt* **1 :** to raise or lift by or as if by a crane ⟨~ up building material⟩ **2 :** to stretch (the neck) forward ⟨~ one's neck to get a better view⟩ ⟨~ one's neck out a window⟩ ~ *vi* **1 :** to stretch out one's neck **:** bend forward with head and neck in order to see better ⟨*craning* for a look⟩ **2 a :** to stop at an obstacle in hunting and look over before leaping **b :** to look before one leaps **:** HESITATE

³**crane** \"\ *n* -S [MF *crâne*, fr. ML *cranium* — more at CRANIUM] *archaic* **:** CRANIUM

crane·ber·ry \"- — *see* BERRY\ *archaic var of* CRANBERRY

crane fly *n* **1 :** any of numerous long-legged slender two-winged flies (family Tipulidae) that resemble large mosquitoes but do not bite, that produce larvae which usu. live in the ground or sometimes in water, and that are destructive to the roots of native and cereal grasses — see RANGE CRANE FLY **2 :** any of various flies somewhat similar in form to the crane fly

crane–fly orchid \ˈ≈¦≈-\ *n* **:** a small orchid (*Tipularia discolor*) of the eastern U.S.

crane follower *n* **:** a worker who assists with the grappling of a load by a crane and who follows it to help with its deposition — called also *burdenman*, *groundsman*, *slingman*, *spotter*

crane line *n* **1 :** one of the lines running from the spritsail topmast of a sailing ship to the middle of the forestay to steady the former or one of the small lines for preventing the lee backstays from chafing against the yards **2 :** a small line joining the backstays on a sailing ship — used usu. in pl.

crane·man \ˈkrān,man, -₋mən\ *n, pl* **cranemen 1 :** a crane operator **2 :** a worker who assists a drop-hammer operator to reduce the size of hot steel blooms by hoisting them into position

cranes·bill \ˈkrānz,bil\ *n* **:** a plant of the genus *Geranium* (as *G. dissectum*, *G. maculatum*, *G. robertianum*)

crane ship *n* **:** a ship equipped with cranes for handling heavy weights

crane shot *n* **:** BOOM SHOT

cranet *n* -S [modif. of MF *crinete* mane — more at CRINET] *obs* **:** CRINET

crane·way \ˈ≈,≈\ *n* **1 a :** the part of an area served by a crane **b :** the beams on which a crane trolley travels **2 :** the opening in the end of an industrial building which allows cranes to pass from the interior to the yard

crane willow *n* **:** BUTTONBUSH

crang *var of* KRENG

cranging hook *var of* KRENGING HOOK

cran·gon \ˈkran,gän, -₋gōn\ [NL, fr. Gk *krangōn* shrimp, prawn; perh. akin to Gk *keras* horn — more at HORN] *syn of* CRAGO

cran·gon·i·dae \kranˈgänə,dē, -ˈgōn-\ *n pl, cap* [NL, fr. *Crangon*, type genus + *-idae*] **:** a large family of shrimps that have the first two pairs of legs chelate and the first pair enlarged and usu. unsymmetrical — see SNAPPING SHRIMP

crani- *or* **cranio-** *comb form* [*cranium*] **:** cranium ⟨*crani*ostosis⟩ ⟨*cranio*metry⟩ **:** cranial and ⟨*cranio*spinal⟩

¹**crania** *pl of* CRANIUM

²**cra·nia** \ˈkrānēə\ *n, cap* [NL, fr. ML *cranium* + NL *-ia*] **:** a genus of inarticulate brachiopods attached by the surface of the ventral valve

-cra·nia \¦krānēə, -nyə\ *n comb form* -S [NL, fr. ML *cranium* + L *-ia* -y] **:** -skulledness ⟨platy*crania*⟩ **:** condition of the skull or head ⟨amphi*crania*⟩

cra·ni·acromial \¦krānē+\ *adj* [*crani-* + *acromial*] **:** having to do with the cranium and acromion

cra·ni·ad \ˈkrānē,ad\ *adv* [*crani-* + *-ad*] **:** toward the head or anterior end ⟨dissected out the growth as far ~ as the base of the hyoid⟩

cra·ni·al \ˈkrānēəl, -nyəl\ *adj* [*cranium* + *-al*] **1 :** of or belonging to the skull **2 :** of or belonging to the cranium proper **3 :** CEPHALIC 1 ⟨the ~ end of the spinal column⟩

cranial bones *n pl* **:** those bones of the skull that enclose the brain — compare CRANIAL SEGMENT

cranial capacity *n* **:** the cubic capacity of the braincase estimated for the living by a formula based on head measurements and determined for the skull by filling the cranial cavity with particulate material (as mustard seed or small shot) and measuring the volume of the latter

cranial flexure *n* **:** the middle of the three anterior flexures of a vertebrate embryo

cranial fossa *n* **:** one of the three large depressions in the posterior, middle, and anterior aspects of the floor of the cranial cavity which lodge respectively the cerebellum and the temporal and frontal lobes of the two hemispheres of the cerebrum

cra·ni·al·gia \,krānēˈalj(ē)ə\ *n* -S [NL, fr. *crani-* + *-algia*] **:** pain occurring within the skull **:** HEADACHE

cranial index *n* **:** the ratio multiplied by 100 of the maximum breadth of the skull to its maximum height — compare CEPHALIC INDEX

cra·ni·al·ly \ˈkrānēəlē, -nyəl-, -əli\ *adv* **:** in a cranial position or relation ⟨a duct opening ~ into the nasopharynx⟩

cranial module *n* **:** a measure of the external size of the skull obtained by averaging its length, breadth, and auricular height

cranial nerve *n* **:** any of the nerves that arise from the vertebrate brain, pass through openings in the skull to the periphery of the body (as the head), comprise 12 pairs in reptiles, birds, and mammals and usu. 10 in fishes and amphibians, and are sensory, motor, or mixed in constitution — see ABDUCENS NERVE, ACCESSORY NERVE, AUDITORY NERVE, FACIAL NERVE, GLOSSOPHARYNGEAL NERVE, HYPOGLOSSAL NERVE, OCULOMOTOR NERVE, OLFACTORY NERVE, OPTIC NERVE, TRIGEMINAL NERVE, TROCHLEAR NERVE, VAGUS NERVE

cranial segment *n* **:** any of three annular segments into which the bones of the cranium proper may be grouped: **a :** an occipital segment consisting of the basioccipital, exoccipital, and supraoccipital bones **b :** a parietal segment consisting of the basisphenoid, alisphenoid, and parietal bones **c :** a frontal segment consisting of the presphenoid, orbitosphenoid, and frontal bones

cra·ni·a·ta \,krānēˈād·ə\ [NL, fr. *crani-* + *-ata*] *syn of* VERTEBRATA

¹**cra·ni·ate** \ˈkrānēət, -ē,āt\ *adj* [in sense 1, fr. NL *Craniata;* in sense 2, fr. *crani-* + *-ate*] **1 :** of or relating to the Vertebrata **:** VERTEBRATE ⟨the lowest ~ fishes⟩ **2 :** having a skull or cranium

²**craniate** \"\ *n* -S **:** a craniate animal

cra·nic \ˈkrānik\ *adj* [prob. fr. F *crânique*, fr. *crâne* cranium + *-ique* -ic — more at CRANE] **:** CRANIAL

cra·nid·i·um \krəˈnidēəm\ *n, pl* **cranid·ia** \-dēə\ [NL, fr. LGk *kranidion* small skull, dim. of *kranion* skull — more at CRANIUM] **:** the central part of the cephalon of a trilobite bounded by the facial sutures

cra·ni·ec·to·mize \,krānēˈektə,mīz\ *vt* -ED/-ING/-S **:** to perform a craniectomy on

cra·ni·ec·to·my \,krānēˈektəmē\ *n* -ES [ISV *crani-* + *-ectomy;* prob. orig. formed as F *craniectomie*] **:** the surgical removal of a portion of the skull

cranies *pl of* CRANY

craning *pres part of* CRANE

cranio- — see CRANI-

cra·ni·o·cele \ˈkrānēə,sēl\ *n* -S [*crani-* + *-cele*] **:** ENCEPHALOCELE

cra·ni·o·cerebral \¦krānēō, -nēə+\ *adj* [*crani-* + *cerebral*] **:** involving both cranium and brain ⟨a ~ wound⟩

cra·ni·o·cla·sis \,krānēˈōklāsəs, -nēˈäkləsəs-\ *n, pl* **cranioclases** \-,sēz\ [NL, fr. *crani-* + *-clasis*] **:** the crushing of the fetal head in difficult delivery

cra·ni·o·facial \¦krānēō, -nēə+\ *adj* [*crani-* + *facial*] **:** of, relating to, or involving both the cranium and the face ⟨~ morphology⟩ ⟨~ studies⟩

craniofacial index *n* **:** the ratio of the breadth of the cranium to the breadth of the face

cra·ni·o·graph \ˈkrānēə,graf, -råf\ *n* [ISV *crani-* + *-graph*] **:** an instrument used for the accurate depiction of a skull in outline

cra·ni·og·ra·pher \,krānēˈägrəfə(r)\ *n* -S [*crani-* + *-grapher*] **:** a specialist in descriptive craniology

cra·ni·o·log·i·cal \¦krānēə¦läjəkəl\ *adj* **:** of or belonging to craniology — **cra·ni·o·log·i·cal·ly** \-jək(ə)lē\ *adv*

cra·ni·ol·o·gist \,krānēˈäləjəst\ *n* -S **:** a specialist in craniology

cra·ni·ol·o·gy \-jē\ *n* -ES [prob. fr. G *kraniologie*, fr. *kranio-* crani- + *-logie* -logy] **1** *obs* **:** PHRENOLOGY **2 :** a science dealing with variations in size, shape, and proportions of skulls esp. as characterizing the different races of men — compare CRANIOMETRY

cra·ni·om·e·ter \,krānēˈäməd·ə(r)\ *n* [ISV *crani-* + *-meter;* prob. orig. formed as F *craniometre*] **:** an instrument for measuring skulls

cra·ni·o·met·ric \¦krānēə¦me·trik, -nēō-\ *also* **cra·ni·o·met·ri·cal** \-·trəkəl\ *adj* **:** of or belonging to craniometry — **cra·ni·o·met·ri·cal·ly** \-rək(ə)lē\ *adv*

craniometric point *n* **:** LANDMARK 2c (2)

cra·ni·om·e·trist \,krānēˈämə·trəst\ *n* -S **:** a student or practitioner of craniometry

cra·ni·om·e·try \-rē\ *n* -s [ISV *crani-* + *-metry*] : a science dealing with measuring the skull esp. for determining the dimensions and proportions characteristic of a particular race, sex, developmental stage, or somatotype — distinguished from *cephalometry*

points and planes in craniometry: *A* auriculo-infraorbital plane; *B* alveolocondylean plane; *1* metopion; *2* ophryon; *3* glabella; *4* nasion; *5* rhinion; *6* dacryon; *7* orbital point; *8* malar point; *9* acanthion; *10* alveolar point or prosthion; *11* symphysion; *12* pogonion; *13* gnathion; *14* coronion; *15* condylion; *16* gonion; *17* mastoidale; *18* auricular point; *19* supra-auricular point; *20* entomion, at arrow, left; asterion at junction of sutures, right; *21* inion; *22* lambda; *23* obelion; *24* bregma; *25* stephanion; *26* sphenion; *27* pterion; *28* crotaphion; *29* jugal point

cra·ni·op·a·gus \,krānē'äpəgəs\ *n, pl* **cra·niopa·gi** \-ə,jē, -,jī\ [NL, fr. *crani-* + *-pagus*] : a pair of twins joined at the heads

cra·ni·o·phore \'krānēə,fō(ə)r\ *n* -s [ISV *crani-* + *-phore;* orig. formed in F] : a device for holding skulls in position (as for taking measurements)

cra·ni·o·plas·ty \-,plastē\ *n* -ES [ISV *crani-* + *-plasty*] : the surgical correction of skull defects

cra·ni·o·ra·chis·chi·sis \,krānē(,)ōrə'kiskəsəs\ *n, pl* **cranio·rachischi·ses** \-,sēz\ [NL, fr. *crani-* + *rachi-* + *-schisis*] : a congenital fissure of the skull and spine

cra·ni·o·sacral \¦krānēō, -nēə+\ *adj* [*crani-* + *sacral*] **1 a** : of or belonging to the cranium and the sacrum **b** : supplied with nerves from these areas **2** : PARASYMPATHETIC

cra·ni·os·chi·sis \,krānē'äskəsəs\ *n, pl* **cranioschi·ses** \-,sēz\ [NL, fr. *crani-* + *-schisis*] : a congenital fissure of the skull

cra·ni·o·scop·ic \¦krānēō¦skäpik, -nēə¦-\ *also* **cra·ni·o·scop·i·cal** \-pəkəl\ *adj* : of or belonging to cranioscopy

cra·ni·os·co·pist \,krānē'äskə,pist\ *n* -s : a specialist in cranioscopy

cra·ni·os·co·py \-kəpē\ *n* -ES [*crani-* + *-scopy*] : observations on or examination of the human skull

cra·ni·o·ta \,krānē'ōd·ə\ [NL, alter. of *Craniata*] *syn of* VERTEBRATA

cra·ni·o·tabes \¦krānēə, -nēō+\ *n* [NL, fr. *crani-* + *tabes*] : a thinning and softening of the infantile skull in spots usu. due to rickets or syphilis

cra·ni·o·tome \'krānēə,tōm\ *n* -s [ISV *crani-* + *-tome*] : an instrument used in performing craniotomy

cra·ni·ot·o·my \,krānē'äd·əmē\ *n* -ES [ISV *crani-* + *-tomy*] **1** : the operation of cutting or crushing the fetal head to effect delivery **2** : surgical opening of the skull

cra·ni·o·topography \¦krānē(,)ō, -nēə+\ *n* [*crani-* + *topography*] : a science that deals with the relations of the skull surface to the parts of the brain

cra·ni·um \'krānēəm\ *n, pl* **craniums** \-mz\ *or* **cra·nia** \-nēə\ [ML, fr. Gk *kranion;* akin to Gk *kara* head — more at CEREBRAL] **1** : SKULL; *specif* : the part of the skull that encloses the brain and is composed of continuous cartilage in the embryos of all craniate vertebrates and in certain lower vertebrates or of distinct bones more or less fused together in adult higher vertebrates : CALVARIUM, BRAINCASE — see CHONDROCRANIUM **2** [NL, fr. ML] : EPICRANIUM 1

[1]**crank** \'kraŋk, -raiŋk\ *n* -s [ME *cranke,* fr. OE *cranc-* (as in *crancstæf,* a weaving instrument); akin to OHG *krankolōn* to stumble, become weak, MHG *kranc* weak, OE *crincan* to fall in battle, OE *cradol* cradle — more at CRADLE] **1** : a part of an axis bent at right angles: as **a** (1) : a bent part of an axle or shaft or an arm keyed at right angles to the end of a shaft by which circular motion is imparted to or received from it or by which reciprocating motion is changed into circular motion or vice versa — see BELL CRANK (2) : DISK CRANK **b** : an elbow-shaped brace, bracket, or support **c** : a machine consisting of a disk that can be revolved by hand with some effort and that was formerly used as a means of disciplinary exercise in prisons **d** : a fireclay stand (as in glost firing) **2** : something crooked or out of line: as **a** *archaic* : a bend, turn, or winding (as in a road, channel, path) **b** : a twist or turn of speech : a conceit consisting of a fantastic change of the form or meaning of a word — used esp. in the phrase *quips and cranks* **c** (1) : a fantastic, fanciful, or impractical turn of mind or action : WHIM ⟨a man subject to unpredictable ~*s*⟩ (2) : a person with a fanciful, impractical, or crackbrained obsession or project : one overenthusiastic or overly active and attentive in some particular field or activity ⟨~ adherents of a lost cause⟩ ⟨a gun ~⟩ ⟨~ letters⟩ ⟨a ~ on the subject of tax reform⟩ **d** : a bad-tempered often quarrelsome person : GROUCH, CROSSPATCH

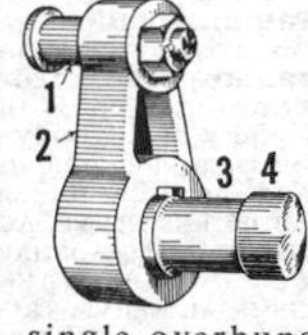

single overhung crank: *1* crankpin, *2* web, *3* journal, *4* crankshaft

[2]**crank** \"\ *vb* -ED/-ING/-S *vi* **1** : to run or move with a winding course : wind and turn : ZIGZAG ⟨the river comes ~*ing* into the town⟩ ⟨the hare ~*ed* and doubled⟩ **2** : to turn a crank (as in starting an automobile engine) ~ *vt* **1** : to bend into the shape of a crank : bend back or down **2** : to furnish or fasten with a crank **3** : to move or operate by a crank : start or attempt to start (an engine) by use of a crank — often used with *up*

[3]**crank** \"\ *adj* -ER/-EST [prob. fr. [1]*crank*] **1** *now chiefly Scot* **a** : DISTORTED, BENT ⟨a ~ tree trunk⟩ **b** : AWKWARD, DIFFICULT ⟨a ~ word to pronounce⟩ **2** : out of kilter : working with difficulty : LOOSE ⟨~ machinery⟩

[4]**crank** \"\ *n* -s [perh. fr. [1]*crank;* fr. the creaking sound made by a windlass] : a grating or creaking sound

[5]**crank** \"\ *vi* -ED/-ING/-S : to make a creaking or raucous sound

[6]**crank** \"\ *adj* -ER/-EST [ME *cranke*] **1** *obs* : LUSTY, VIGOROUS **2** *now dial* **a** : MERRY, HIGH-SPIRITED **b** : inclined to exult : COCKY, CONFIDENT

[7]**crank** \"\ *adv, obs* : LUSTILY, VIGOROUSLY, BOLDLY

[8]**crank** \"\ *n* -s [D or LG *kranke* sick person, fr. *krank* sick, fr. MD *cranc* and MLG *krank* sick, weak; akin to MHG *kranc* weak — more at [1]CRANK] *obs* : a person who pretends to have epilepsy in order to get sympathy and money

[9]**crank** \"\ *adj* -ER/-EST [short for *crank-sided*] : very easily tipped by any external force (as that of the wind on the sails) — used of a boat; compare STEADY, STIFF

crank arm *n* : CRANK WEB; *specif* : the offset portion of a crankshaft to which connecting rod and piston are attached

crank axle *n* **1** : a driving axle formed with a crank or cranks **2** : a carriage axle bent twice at a right angle near the ends to allow a low body with large wheels

crank brace *n* : a brace having a shank bent in the form of a crank by which it is rotated

crankcase \'=,=\ *n* : the housing of the crankshaft of an engine (as in an automobile)

cranked \'kraŋkt, -raiŋ-\ *adj* [[1]*crank* + *-ed*] : formed with or having a bend or crank : provided with a crank ⟨a ~*ed* axle⟩

crank·er \-kə(r)\ *n* -s [[2]*crank* + *-er*] : one that cranks; *specif* : one who arranges ceramic flatware on cranks

crank·ery \-k(ə)rē\ *n* -ES [[1]*crank* (crotchety person) + *-ery*] : the practices or ideas of a crank or crackpot

crank hanger *n* **1** : a support for a bell crank **2** : BRACKET 2b

crank·i·ly \-kəlē, -li\ *adv* [[1]*cranky* + *-ly*] : in a cranky manner ⟨~ individualistic artists⟩

crank·i·ness \-kēnəs, -kin-\ *n* -ES [[1]*cranky* + *-ness*] : the quality or state of being cranky: as **a** : irritable or unreasonable temper ⟨the fussy ~ of the dyspeptic⟩ **b** : emotional or intellectual perversity or idiosyncrasy ⟨the reader can sometimes glimpse a sort of perverse . . . ~ at work —*Canadian Forum*⟩

crank·ish \-kish\ *adj* [[1]*crank* + *-ish*] : FREAKISH, CRACKPOT, PERVERSE ⟨the word . . . occurs with a ~ and verbally impoverished tastelessness about 200 times —Mary McCarthy⟩

crank·ism \-,kizəm\ *n* -s [[1]*crank* + *-ism*] : the attitude or activity of a crank or crackpot

[1]**cran·kle** \'kraŋkəl\ *vb* -ED/-ING/-S [freq. of [2]*crank*] *vt, obs* : to break into turns, bends, or angles : CRINKLE ~ *vi, archaic* : BEND, TURN, WIND, ZIGZAG

[2]**crankle** \"\ *n* -s : BEND, TURN, TWIST, CRINKLE ⟨the ~*s* of a brook⟩

crank·less \'kraŋkləs, -raiŋ-\ *adj* : not having a crank

crank·ous \'kraŋkəs\ *adj* [[1]*crank* + *-ous*] *Scot* : FRETFUL, PEEVISH

crank out *vt* [[2]*crank*] : to produce esp. in a mechanical or unfeeling manner ⟨he *cranked out* two novels per year⟩

crankpin \'=,=\ *n* : the cylindrical piece that projects from a crank web or disk and serves as a revolving journal for the bearing at the end of a connecting or coupling rod

crank plane *or* **crank planer** *n* : a planer whose bed is crank-driven

crank press *n* : a punch press in which power is applied to the slide through a crank

cranks *pl of* CRANK, *pres 3d sing of* CRANK

crankshaft \'=,=\ *n* : a shaft driven by or driving a crank

crank-sided \'=¦==\ *adj* [*crank-* perh. irreg. fr. D *krengen* to careen, fr. MD *crenghen* to cause to turn, causative fr. the root of *cringhen* to turn; akin to MHG *krinc* ring — more at CRINGE] **1** : [9]CRANK **2** : on one side : ASKEW, LOPSIDED ⟨knocked *crank-sided* off its foundation⟩

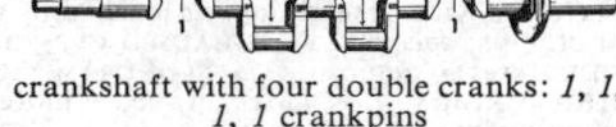

crankshaft with four double cranks: *1, 1, 1, 1* crankpins

crank tail *n* : a short crooked tail (as that of a bulldog) resembling a crank handle

crank throw *n* **1** : CRANK ARM, CRANK WEB **2** : the radial displacement from crankshaft center to crankpin center

crank·um \'kraŋkəm\ *n* -s [[1]*crank* (whim) + L *-um* (neut. n. ending]] : an eccentric turn : CROTCHET, VAGARY

crank web *n* : the portion of a crank between the crankpin and the shaft or between adjacent crankpins — called also *crank arm, crank throw*

[1]**cranky** \'kraŋkē, -raiŋ-, -ki\ *adj* -ER/-EST [D or LG *krank* sick + E *-y* — more at CRANK (person pretending epilepsy)] *dial* : SICKLY, AILING, INFIRM

[2]**cranky** \'kraŋki\ *adj* -ER/-EST [[6]*crank* + *-y*] *dial chiefly Eng* : [6]CRANK 2

[3]**cranky** \'kraŋkē, -raiŋ-, -ki\ *adj* -ER/-EST [[1]*crank* + *-y*] **1** *dial* : SILLY, IMBECILE, CRAZY, INSANE **2 a** : out of working order : in bad condition ⟨a ~ old wagon⟩ **b** : uncertain in operation : likely to miscarry, operate peculiarly, or break down : needing especial attention or ingenuity to operate : UNPREDICTABLE, ERRATIC ⟨a rickety sled pulled by a ~ tractor —*Nat'l Geographic*⟩ **3 a** : marked by capricious eccentricity or wrongheadedness ⟨fighting for a European and ripened and wise philosophy against an insular and immature and ~ one —*Times Lit. Supp.*⟩ **b** : given to fretful fussiness : CROTCHETY, IRRITABLE ⟨a ~ old man⟩ **4** : full of twists and turns : CROOKED, TORTUOUS ⟨a ~ road⟩ **syn** see IRASCIBLE

[4]**cranky** \"\ *adj* -ER/-EST [[9]*crank* + *-y*] *of a boat* : liable to heel or tip : CRANK

cranky fan *n* [[3]*cranky;* fr. its erratic flight] : a grayish Australian fantail (*Rhipidura flabellifera*)

cran·nage \'kranij\ *n* -s [[2]*cran* + *-age*] : amount of herrings in crans

cran·nied \'kranēd, -nəd\ *adj* [ME *cranyyd,* fr. *crany* cranny + *-ed*] **1** : having crannies, chinks, or fissures ⟨~ earth⟩ **2** *obs* : of the form of a cranny

cran·nock \'kranək\ *n* -s [ML *crannoca, crannocus,* of Celt origin; akin to W *crynog* crannock] : an old unit of capacity once used in the west of England and in Wales and Ireland and equal to two, four, or more bushels

cran·nog \'kranəg\ *n* -s [ScGael *crannag* & IrGael *crannōg,* fr. MIr *crannōc* wooden structure, fr. OIr *crann* tree — more at HURST] : an artificial fortified island constructed in a lake or marsh orig. in prehistoric Ireland and Scotland

[1]**cran·ny** \'kranē, -ni\ *n* -ES [ME *cranie, crany,* fr. MF *cran, cren* notch + ME *-y* — more at CRENEL] **1** : a small break or slit (as in a rock wall or cliff) : NICHE, CREVICE ⟨flowers growing in *crannies*⟩ **2** : a small obscure cleft, corner, or closed space that is easy to overlook and is a likely place for concealing something or for hiding : RECESS ⟨pursuing their subtleties into the last refuge and ~ of logic —V.L.Parrington⟩ **syn** see CRACK

[2]**cranny** \"\ *vi* -ED/-ING/-ES **1** : to become full of crannies : form crannies ⟨earth ~*ing* in the hot sun⟩ **2** : to enter or penetrate by or as if by crannies ⟨the rain *crannied* into the old house⟩

cran·reuch \'kran(,)ru̇k\ *n* -s [alter. of earlier *cranra, crainroch,* prob. modif. of ScGael *crannreotha, crannreothadh,* perh. fr. *crann* to wither + *reotha, reodhadh* frost; perh. akin to OIr *crann* tree and to OE *frēosan* to freeze — more at HURST, FREEZE] *Scot* : HOARFROST, RIME

crans *pl of* CRAN

cranse *var of* CRANCE

crants *n* -ES [D *krans* — more at CRANCE] *obs* : GARLAND, WREATH

crany *n* -ES [ML *cranium*] *obs* : CRANIUM

[1]**crap** \'krap\ *n* -s [ME, fr. MD *crap, crappe* pork chop, greaves, grain in chaff, fr. *crappen* to tear or break off] **1** *dial Eng* : residue from rendered fat — used usu. in pl. **2** *archaic slang* : MONEY **3 a** : EXCREMENT — usu. considered vulgar **b** : DEFECATION — usu. considered vulgar **4** *slang* : something deceitful, useless, or empty : NONSENSE, RUBBISH

[2]**crap** \"\ *vb* **crapped**; **crapped**; **crapping**; **craps** *vi* **1** : DEFECATE — usu. considered vulgar **2** *slang* : to behave or act in a foolish, deceiving, or useless manner ⟨don't ~ around like that⟩ ~ *vt, slang* : DECEIVE, BEFOOL

[3]**crap** \'krap, -räp\ *dial var of* CROP

[4]**crap** \'krap\ *n* -s [prob. fr. G dial *krape* clamp for torturing, fr. OHG *krāpo, krāpfo* hook — more at CRAVE] *slang Brit* : GALLOWS

[5]**crap** \"\ *n* -s [back-formation fr. *craps*] **1** : CRAPS ⟨~ game⟩ **2** : a throw of 2, 3, or 12 in the game of craps that causes the shooter to lose the bet unless he has a point — called also *craps;* compare NATURAL

[6]**crap** \"\ *vi* **crapped**; **crapped**; **crapping**; **craps** **1** : to throw a crap **2** : to throw a seven while trying to make a point — usu. used with *out*

cra·paud \kra'pō, '=(,)=\ *n* -s [ME *crepaude, crapaulde,* fr. MF *crapaud, crapot* toad, prob. fr. *crape* hook, of Gmc origin; akin to OHG *krāpo, krāpfo* hook; fr. the appearance of the feet — more at CRAP] **1** *obs* : a jewel or precious stone supposed to come from the head of a toad **2** : a large toad (*Leptodactylus pentadactylus*) esteemed as food in parts of the Caribbean area

[1]**crap·au·dine** \,krapə'dēn, '==,=\ *n* -s [F, fr. MF, fr. *crapaud* toad + *-ine*] : an ulcer on the coronet of a horse

[2]**crapaudine** \¦==¦=\ *adj* [F (*à la*) *crapaudine,* lit., in a toadlike manner, fr. *crapaud* toad + *-ine*] *cookery, of small birds* : prepared by splitting down the back and flattening the breast — often used postpositively ⟨pigeon ~⟩

[1]**crape** \'krāp\ *n* -s [alter. of earlier *crespe,* fr. obs. F (now *crêpe*), fr. MF, fr. *crespe,* adj., curly, fr. OF, fr. L *crispus* — more at CRISP] **1** : CREPE **2** *archaic* : a thin worsted stuff formerly used for the gowns of clergymen and sometimes considered to be a symbol of the clergy **3** : a piece of black crepe used for a specific purpose: as **a** : a band of crepe worn on a hat or sleeve as a sign of mourning **b** : a piece of crepe worn over the face as a disguise

[2]**crape** \"\ *vt* -ED/-ING/-S : to drape, cover, or shroud with or as if with crape ⟨dark clouds *craping* the sun⟩ ⟨a widow *craped* in the latest fashion⟩

[3]**crape** \"\ *vt* -ED/-ING/-S [F *crêper,* fr. MF *cresper,* fr. *crespe,* adj.] : to make (the hair) curly

crape fern *n* : a New Zealand fern (*Todea superba*) of the family Osmundaceae with a short trunk, pinnate fronds, and densely woolly stalks

crapehanger *var of* CREPEHANGER

crape jasmine *n* : a cultivated shrub (*Ervatamia coronaria*) of the family Apocynaceae having crimped or wavy corollas — called also *Adam's apple*

crape moss *n* : SPANISH MOSS

crape myrtle *also* **crepe myrtle** *or* **crêpe myrtle** *n* : an ornamental East Indian shrub (*Lagerstroemia indica*) commonly planted in the southern U.S. for its white, pink, red, or purplish flowers

crape needle *n* : LADY'S-COMB

cra·pette \kra'pet, krə'-\ *n* -s [F] : RUSSIAN BANK

crap out *vi* [[2]*crap*] **1** *slang* **a** : to pass out (as from an injury) **b** : to fall asleep (as from exhaustion) **2** *slang* : to avoid assigned duty or obligations

crap·per \'krapə(r)\ *n* -s [[2]*crap* + *-er*] : TOILET, PRIVY — usu. considered vulgar

crap·pie \'kräpē, -pi *sometimes* -rap-\ *also* **crop·pie** \-räp-\ *n* -s [CanF *crapet*] : either of two No. American sunfishes most abundant in the Great Lakes region and Mississippi valley and introduced elsewhere — see BLACK CRAPPIE, WHITE CRAPPIE

crap·pin \'krapən\ *n* -s [Sc [3]*crap* (crop of a bird) + *-in* (alter. of E *-ing*)] *chiefly Scot* : CROP, STOMACH

crap·pit head \'krapət-\ *n* [*crappit* prob. fr. past part. of Sc *crap* to cram, fr. [3]*crap* (top)] *Scot* : stuffed haddock head

crap·po \'krapō\ *n* -ES [by alter.] : CARAPA 2

crap·py \'krapē, -pi\ *adj* -ER/-EST [[1]*crap* + *-y*] *slang* : markedly inferior in quality : LOUSY

craps \'kraps\ *n pl but usu sing in constr* [LaF, fr. F *crabs, craps,* fr. E *crabs* lowest throw at hazard, fr. pl. of [1]*crab*] **1** : a gambling game in which a player rolls two dice and wins his bet if the throw is 7 or 11, loses it if the throw is 2, 3, or 12, or gets a point if the throw is 4, 5, 6, 8, 9, or 10, in which case he continues to throw until he wins by throwing his point again or loses both bet and dice by throwing 7 **2** : [5]CRAP 2

crapshooter \'=,==\ *n* [[5]*crap* + *shooter*] : one that plays craps

crap shooting *n* [[5]*crap*] : the game or playing of craps

crap table *n* [[5]*crap*] : a high table that is used for playing craps and that has a raised rim against which the dice must be thrown

crap·u·lence \'krapyələn(t)s\ *n* -s **1** *archaic* : sickness occasioned by intemperance (as in food or drink) **2** : great intemperance esp. in drinking

crap·u·lent \-lənt\ *adj* [LL *crapulentus,* fr. L *crapula* intoxication] *archaic* : suffering from excessive eating or drinking

crap·u·lous \'krapyələs\ *adj* [LL *crapulosus,* fr. L *crapula* intoxication (fr. Gk *kraipalē* intoxication, drunken headache) + *-osus* -ous; prob. akin to Gk *kara* head, and to Gk *pallein* to shake, quiver — more at CEREBRAL, POLEMIC] **1** : intemperate esp. in drink ⟨a ~ old reprobate⟩ **2** : suffering the effects of, derived from, or suggestive of intemperance esp. in drink ⟨a ~ stomach⟩ ⟨~ slumber⟩ ⟨~ stupidities⟩ — **crap·u·lous·ly** *adv*

crapy \'krāpē, -pi\ *adj* -ER/-EST [[1]*crape* + *-y*] : of, resembling, or draped in crape ⟨a ~ fabric⟩ ⟨a ~ procession⟩

cra·que·lé \(')kra¦klā\ *adj* [F, fr. past part. of *craqueler* to crack, crackle, fr. *craquer* to crack, crackle, of imit. origin] : CRACKLED ⟨a ~ glaze⟩

cra·que·lure \kra'klu̇(ə)r, '=,=\ *n* -s [F, fr. *craqueler* + *-ure*] : a cracking (as of varnish, color, or enamel) on a work of plastic art

crare *obs var of* CRAYER

[1]**crash** \'krash, -raa(ə)sh, -raish\ *vb* -ED/-ING/-ES [ME *crasschen,* perh. alter. of *crasen* to break — more at CRAZE] *vt* **1 a** : to break into pieces violently and noisily : SMASH, SHATTER ⟨~ a glass against a wall⟩ **b** : to bring (an airplane) down in such a manner that damage is sustained in landing **2 a** : to cause to make a loud noise : make a loud shattering or clattering noise with **b** : to force (as one's way) with loud crashing noises ⟨~ one's way through brush⟩ **3** *obs* : to snap (the teeth) together : GNASH **4 a** : to enter or attend without invitation or credentials or without paying ⟨~ a dance⟩ ⟨~ an executive's office⟩ **b** : to gain acceptance, position, or recognition in usu. suddenly and spectacularly ⟨the murder ~*ed* the headlines⟩ ⟨when television ~*ed* the retail market⟩ ~ *vi* **1 a** : to break or go to pieces esp. with or as if with violence and noise ⟨the national economy ~*ed*⟩ **b** : to crash an airplane **2** : to make a loud smashing or shattering noise ⟨~*ing* thunder⟩ **3 a** : to move with or as if with a crashing noise ⟨the doors ~*ed* open⟩ ⟨he ~*ed* into the room⟩ **b** : to force one's way with or as if with a crash ⟨he ~*ed* through the line for a touchdown⟩ — **crash the gate** : to enter without paying or without authority or permission ⟨all the kids used to sneak in . . . they had a million ways of *crashing the gate* —J.T. Farrell⟩ : enter successfully : make the grade ⟨he was the boy who made good, the outsider who *crashed* all *the gates* of Philadelphia —H.S.Commager⟩

[2]**crash** \"\ *n* -ES **1** : a loud sound (as of many hard things smashing or shattering) : SMASH ⟨a ~ of thunder⟩ ⟨the ~ of a military band⟩ ⟨a ~ of applause⟩ ⟨a ~ of static⟩ — often used interjectionally ⟨~ went the lamp against the floor⟩ **2** : a breaking to pieces esp. by or as if by collision : a smashing esp. of or as if of heavy bodies; *also* : an instance of crashing ⟨an airplane ~⟩ ⟨the ~ of a falling tree⟩ **3 a** : a sudden failure esp. of a business : a sudden widespread business collapse ⟨stock market ~⟩ **b** : the period of heavy mortality and sharp decline in numbers of an animal with strongly developed population cycles; *also* : the decline in population during such a period **4** *archaic* : SPELL, BOUT, TURN — used esp. in the phrase *have a crash at* **5** : a basket of glass or pottery fragments used in the theater to imitate the sound of breaking glass

[3]**crash** \"\ *adj* : designed to meet emergency conditions esp. in the shortest possible time by maximum utilization of resources ⟨a ~ program⟩ ⟨~ priority⟩ ⟨do a ~ job of making the most needed changes —G.C.Smith⟩

[4]**crash** \"\ *n* -ES [prob. modif. of Russ *krashenina* colored linen, fr. *krashenie* dyeing, fr. *krasit'* to color, beautify, fr. *krasa* beauty; prob. akin to Skt *carkṛti* praise — more at CADUCEUS] **1 a** : a coarse fabric made in plain weave of uneven linen, rayon, cotton, or jute and cotton yarns and used for draperies, toweling, and table linen and often in smooth-finished form for clothing **b** : a fabric covering for a carpeted floor (as for use during a dance) **2** : a grayish yellow that is greener and duller than chamois, slightly greener and less strong than old ivory, and greener and duller than flax

crash boat *n* : a fast motorboat used to rescue survivors of a plane crash at sea

crash cover *n* : an airmail cover that has been in an airplane crash

crash cymbal *n* : a single cymbal suspended by a cord and struck with a drumstick

crash dive *n* : a dive made by a submarine (as in avoiding attack) in the least possible time

crash-dive \'=¦=\ *vi, of a submarine* : to submerge in the shortest possible time ~ *vt* : to dive into ⟨hit by flak, the plane . . . rolled over . . . in an attempt to *crash-dive* the escort carrier —*Time*⟩

crash finish *n* [[4]*crash*] : a finish esp. of paper resembling coarse linen

crash helmet *n* : a usu. plastic or leather helmet that is worn (as by auto racers, bobsledders, motorcycle policemen) as protection for the head in an accident

crashing *adj* [fr. pres. part. of [1]*crash*] **1** : OUT-AND-OUT, UTTER ⟨a ~ bore⟩ ⟨a ~ cliché⟩ **2** : SUPERLATIVE, STUNNING ⟨a ~ virtuoso⟩ ⟨a ~ effect⟩

crash-land \'=¦=\ *vt* : to land (an airplane) under conditions (as damaged landing gear or the absence of an adequate landing area) that result in structural damage usu. extensive enough to prevent takeoff ~ *vi* : to crash-land an airplane — **crash landing** *n*

crash pad *n* : padding (as on the inside of a tank or car) to protect the occupants from injury in the event of an accident or sudden jolt

crash truck *or* **crash wagon** *n* **:** a specially equipped truck designed to rescue survivors of an airplane crash

cra·sis \'krāsəs\ *n, pl* **cra·ses** \-,sēz\ [NL, fr. Gk *krasis* mixing, combination, fr. *kerannynai* to mix — more at CRATER] **1 a** *obs* **:** a blend or combination of constituents **b** *archaic* **:** CONSTITUTION **2 :** a contraction of two vowels or diphthongs esp. in Latin and Greek at the end of one word and the beginning of an immediately following word into one long vowel or diphthong (as in Latin *cogo* for *coago* and in Greek *kan* for *kai an*)

cras·pe·da·cus·ta \,kraspədə'küstə, -'kəs-\ *n, cap* [NL, irreg. fr. *craspedon* velum + Gk *kystis* bladder — more at CYST] **:** a cosmopolitan genus of small freshwater hydrozoan medusae — see MICROHYDRA

cras·pe·do·ta \,==='dōd·ə\ *n pl, cap* [NL, irreg. fr. *craspedon* velum, fr. Gk *kraspedon* edge, border, fr. *kras-* head + *pedon* ground; akin to Gk *kara* head and to Gk *pod-, pous* foot — more at CEREBRAL, FOOT] **:** the velate medusae regarded as a natural group more or less equivalent to Hydrozoa — **cras·pe·do·tal** \¦==¦dōd·ᵊl\ *adj*

cras·pe·dote \'kraspə,dōt\ *adj* [NL *Craspedota*] **:** VELATE — used chiefly of hydrozoan medusae

crass \'kras, -raa(ə)s, -rais\ *adj* -ER/-EST [L *crassus* thick, fat, gross — more at HURDLE] **1** *archaic, of the texture or makeup of a substance* **:** THICK, DENSE, COARSE **2 :** lacking delicacy **:** devoid of refined sensitivity **:** GROSS, UNFEELING, STUPID ⟨~ butchery⟩ ⟨~ avarice⟩ ⟨a ~ misreading of a statement⟩ **syn** see STUPID

cras·sa·men·tum \,krasə'mentəm\ *n, pl* **crassamentums** \-mz\ *or* **crassamen·ta** \-tə\ [NL, fr. L, sediment, dregs, fr. *crassare* to make thick (fr. *crassus*) + *-mentum* -ment] **:** the clot formed in coagulation of blood **:** COAGULUM

cras·sa ne·gli·gen·tia \¦krasə,neglə'jenchēə\ *n* [LL] **:** GROSS NEGLIGENCE

cras·si·so·ma \,krasə'sōmə\ *n, cap* [NL, fr. L *crassi-* (fr. *crassus* thick, fat) + NL *-soma*] **:** a genus of hookworms including the only worm (*C. urosubulatum*) commonly infesting swine in No. America

cras·si·tude \'krasə,t(y)üd\ *n* -S [ME, fr. L *crassitudo*, fr. *crassus* + *-i-* + *-tudo* -tude] **1** *obs* **:** thickness (as of a solid body) **2 :** crass quality or state **:** GROSSNESS; *also* **:** an instance of grossness

crass·ly *adv* **:** in a crass manner

crass negligence *n* **:** GROSS NEGLIGENCE

crass·ness \'krasnəs, -raas-, -rais-\ *n* -ES **:** the quality or state of being crass ⟨the arrogance and ~ of the industrial millionaires —Edmund Wilson⟩

cras·sos·trea \krə'sästrēə\ *n, cap* [NL, fr. L *crassus* thick, fat + *ostrea* oyster — more at OYSTER] **:** a genus of bivalve mollusks comprising those oysters that discharge their reproductive products directly into the water and have no larval development in the gills of the parent, and now usu. including the Virginia oyster — compare GRYPHAEA 1, OSTREA

cras·su·la \'kras(y)ələ\ *n* [NL, fr. ML, stonecrop, orpine, fr. L *crassus* + *-ula* (dim. suffix)] **1** *cap* **:** a genus of chiefly So. African succulent herbs (family Crassulaceae) having opposite leaves and flowers with petals separate or connate only at the base **2** *pl* **crassu·lae** \-,lē, -,lī\ *also* **crassulas :** a plant of the genus *Crassula* **3** *pl* **crassulae :** a thickening of the middle lamella and primary wall between or around bordered pits or pit fields esp. prominent on the radial walls of tracheids in gymnosperm wood — called also *bar of Sanio, rim of Sanio, Sanio's beam*

cras·su·la·ce·ae \,==='lāsē,ē\ *n pl, cap* [NL, fr. *Crassula*, type genus + *-aceae*] **:** a family of mostly fleshy herbs and subshrubs (order Rosales) having a scalelike gland at the base of each of the three or more connate pistils — compare SEDUM, STONECROP — **cras·su·la·ceous** \¦==¦lāshəs\ *adj*

-crat \,krat, *usu* -ad·+V\ *or* **-ocrat** \ə,krat, ō,-, *usu* -ad·+V\ *n comb form* -S [F *-crate*, back-formation fr. *-cratie* -cracy & *-cratique* -cratic] **1 :** advocate or partisan of a theory of government ⟨demo*crat*⟩ ⟨physio*crat*⟩ ⟨theo*crat*⟩ **2 :** member of a (specified) dominant class ⟨bureau*crat*⟩ ⟨pluto*crat*⟩ **3 :** member or supporter of a political party or faction ⟨Dixie*crat*⟩ — **-crat·ic** \¦krad·|ik, -at|ik, |ēk\ *adj comb form* [MF *-cratique*, fr. ML *-craticus*, fr. Gk *-kratikos*, fr. *kratos* strength, power + *-ikos* -ic — more at HARD]

cra·tae·gus \krə'tēgəs\ *n, cap* [NL, fr. Gk *krataigos*, prob. fr. *kratos* strength + *-aigos* (akin to Gk *aigilōps* Turkey oak) — more at HARD, OAK] **:** a genus of usu. thorny shrubs and small trees (family Rosaceae) having usu. stipulate leaves, an inferior ovary, and mature carpels that are hard and bony with a pulpy fruit — see HAWTHORN

cra·tae·va \-ēvə\ *n, cap* [NL, irreg. after *Cratevas* (Gk *Krateuas*), 1st cent. B.C. Gk. herbalist] **:** a small genus of tropical shrubs (family Capparidaceae) having trifoliolate leaves, flowers with stalked petals, and striped berries — see GARLIC PEAR

cratch \'krach\ *n* -ES [ME *cracche, crecche*, fr. OF *creche* manger, of Gmc origin; akin to OHG *krippa* manger — more at CRIB] *dial Brit* **:** a crib or rack esp. for fodder **:** MANGER; *also* **:** GRATING, FRAME

¹crate \'krāt, *usu* -ād·+V\ *n* -S [L *cratis* wickerwork, hurdle — more at HURDLE] **1 :** a container used to transport wares: as **a :** a rigid shipping structure that consists usu. of a wood frame of which the size and shape are usu. determined by the article to be shipped, the structure often being built around the article, and which is often not completely enclosed but is often reinforced with sheathing **b :** a similar structure used esp. for agricultural products and having a frame covered by thin boards with openings left between for ventilation ⟨an orange ~⟩ **2 :** a lead grating used in making white lead **3 :** an obsolete, patched-up, or badly used vehicle ⟨his car was an old ~⟩ ⟨to replace plane losses they built spare-parts ~*s* from wrecked machines —*Time*⟩

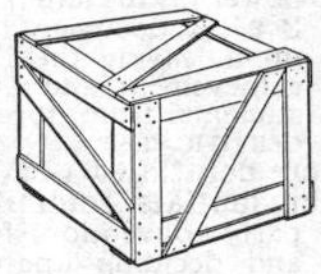

crate 1a

²crate \"\ *vt* -ED/-ING/-S **:** to pack in a crate or case esp. for transportation

¹cra·ter \'krād·ə(r), -ātə-\ *n* -S [L, mixing bowl, mouth of a volcano, fr. Gk *kratēr*, fr. *kerannynai* to mix; akin to Skt *śrīta* mixed, and prob. to OE *hrēran* to stir, OHG *hruoren*, ON *hrœra*] **1 :** a hole at the top of a cone-shaped object: as **a** (1) **:** the depression above or around the orifice of a volcano that often appears as a funnel-shaped pit maintained by successive explosions at the top of a built-up cone (2) **:** the flaring or bowl-shaped opening of a geyser (3) **:** a depression formed by the impact of a meteorite (4) **:** any of thousands of formations on the lunar surface ranging in size from small pocks less than a mile in diameter to walled plains nearly 150 miles across and thought by many astronomers to be caused by the impact of huge meteorites and by others to be of igneous origin **b :** a hole in the ground made by the explosion of a projectile, bomb, or charge **c :** the cup-shaped cavity formed at the end of the positive carbon of a direct-current arc lamp **d :** an eroded crateriform lesion of a wall or surface (as the site of an ulcer of the stomach or duodenal wall) **2 :** KRATER

²crater \"\ *vb* -ED/-ING/-S *vi* **:** to form a crater ⟨the surface ~*ed* with the constant dropping of water⟩ ~ *vt* **:** to form or make a crater in ⟨artillery ~*ed* the roads⟩

³crat·er \"\ *n* -S [²*crate* + *-er*] **:** one that packs articles into crates for shipment **:** one that builds crates around large objects (as pianos)

cra·ter·al \'krād·ərəl\ *or* **cra·ter·ine** \-ə,rīn\ *or* **cra·ter·ous** \-ərəs\ *adj* [¹*crater* + *-al* or *-ine* or *-ous*] **:** of, belonging to, or resembling a crater

cra·tered \-ə(r)d\ *adj* [¹*crater-* + *-ed*] **:** having a crater or craters **:** full of craters ⟨the ~ moon⟩

cra·ter·el·lus \,krād·ə'reləs\ *n, cap* [NL, irreg. fr. L *crater*] **:** a genus of fleshy or membranous white-spored mushrooms (family Thelephoraceae) having the shape of a club, shelf, or funnel and resembling *Cantharellus* but having the hymenium at most only rugose and not in prominent gills

cra·ter·i·form \'krād·ərə,fȯrm, krə'terə,-\ *adj* [ISV ¹*crater* + *-iform*] **:** having the form of a crater; *specif* **:** of the form of a bowl or saucer ⟨a flower with a ~ corolla⟩

cra·ter·less \'krād·ə(r)ləs, -ātə-\ *adj* **:** not having a crater

cra·ter·let \'krād·ə(r)lət, -ātə-\ *n* -S **:** a little crater

-cratic — see -CRAT

cra·tic·u·lar \krə'tikyələ(r)\ *adj* [L *craticula* fine hurdlework, gridiron (dim. of *cratis* hurdle) + E *-ar* — more at HURDLE] *bot* **:** having to do with a resting stage in diatoms during which new valves are formed within the old ones

c ration \'sē-\ *n, usu cap C* **:** a canned field ration of the U.S. Army

cra·ton \'krā,tän\ *n* -S [G *kraton*, modif. of Gk *kratos* strength, power — more at HARD] **:** a stable relatively immobile area of the earth's crust that forms the nuclear mass of a continent or the central basin of an ocean — compare SHIELD — **cra·ton·al** \(')krā¦tänᵊl\ *or* **cra·ton·ic** \-nik\ *adj*

-crats *pl of* -CRAT

cra·tur \'krātər\ *Scot & Irish var of* CREATURE

¹craunch \'krȯnch, -rän-\ *also* **cranch** \-rän-\ *vb* -ED/-ING/-ES [prob. of imit. origin] **:** CRUNCH

²craunch \"\ *also* **cranch** \"\ *n* -ES **1 :** act or action of craunching **:** CRUNCH **2 :** anything that is craunched **:** material to craunch

¹cra·vat \krə'vat, *usu* -ad·+V\ *n* -S [F *cravate* cravat, linen scarf worn in 17th cent. by Croatian mercenaries, fr. *Cravate* Croatian, fr. G (dial.) or Serbo-Croatian; G (dial.) *Krawat*, fr. Serbo-Croatian *Hrvat;* akin to OSlav *Chŭrvatinŭ* Croatian] **1 a :** a band or scarf of fine cloth often trimmed with lace and worn around the neck tied in a bow or knotted in such a way that the ends hung down in front **b :** NECKTIE **2 :** a wrinkle of flesh on the neck esp. of a dog **3 :** a bandage made by folding the point of a triangular piece of material toward the base, folding the base over the point, and folding the whole again

²cravat \"\ *vt* **cravatted; cravatted; cravatting; cravats :** to dress with or as if with a cravat ⟨a handsomely *cravatted* young man⟩

crave \'krāv\ *vb* -ED/-ING/-S [ME *craven*, fr. OE *crafian;* akin to ON *krefja* to crave, OE *cræft* strength, skill, OHG *kraft* strength, skill, *krāpo, krāpfo* hook, ON *kraptr* strength, skill, OE *cradol* cradle — more at CRADLE] *vt* **1 a :** to ask authoritatively **:** DEMAND ⟨~ a hearing before a court⟩ **b** *chiefly Scot* **:** DUN ⟨~ a debtor⟩ **2 a :** to ask earnestly **:** BEG, BESEECH, IMPLORE ⟨~ a person's pardon⟩ ⟨~ the indulgence of an audience⟩ **b** *obs* **:** to ask to know **3 a :** to want greatly **:** NEED ⟨~ sweets⟩ ⟨~ fresh air⟩ **b :** to yearn for **:** REQUIRE ⟨an ego *craving* flattery⟩ **4 :** to demand as necessary or expedient **:** REQUIRE ⟨orders *craving* immediate attention⟩ ~ *vi* **:** to have a strong or inward desire ⟨~ after inspiration⟩ ⟨~ for good food⟩ **syn** see DESIRE

¹cra·ven \'krāvən\ *adj* [alter. of ME *cravant*, perh. fr. OF *crevant*, pres. part. of *crever* to burst, cause to burst, fr. L *crepare* to crack, creak, break — more at RAVEN] **1 :** DEFEATED, VANQUISHED — used in the phrase *to cry craven* acknowledging defeat **2 :** lacking even the rudiments of courage **:** characterized by abject defeatism **:** contemptibly fainthearted ⟨a ~ proposal for putting up the white flag —F.L.Allen⟩ **syn** see COWARDLY

²craven \"\ *n* -S **1 :** an avowed coward **:** a weakhearted person **2 :** a cock that lacks courage or shows little or no inclination to fight

³craven \"\ *vt* -ED/-ING/-S *archaic* **:** to make cowardly or timid

cra·ven·ette \,krāvə'net, '==,= *also* -rav-\ *vt* -ED/-ING/-S [fr. *Cravenette*, a trademark] **:** to make (a textile) water-repellent ⟨*cravenetted* khaki⟩

cravenhearted \¦==¦==\ *adj* **:** COWARDLY, CRAVEN

cra·ven·ly *adv* **:** in a craven manner

cra·ven·ness \-ən(n)əs\ *n* -ES **:** the quality of being craven **:** feebleness of courage **:** COWARDICE

crav·er \'krāvə(r)\ *n* -S [ME, fr. *craven* to crave + *-er*] **:** one that craves

¹craving *n* -S [ME, fr. gerund of *craven* to crave] **1** *obs* **:** urgent asking **:** ENTREATING **2 a :** an urgent need for gratification ⟨a ~ for tobacco⟩ **b :** the desire to satisfy a vague inner need **:** LONGING, YEARNING ⟨a ~ to be understood⟩ ⟨the deepest ~*s* of his being — to create and, as Byron says, in creating live —C.S.Kilby⟩

²craving *adj* [fr. pres. part. of *crave*] **1** *obs* **:** urgently entreating **:** BEGGING **2 :** desiring deeply or inwardly ⟨~ passion⟩ — **crav·ing·ly** *adv* — **crav·ing·ness** *n* -ES

cra·vo \'krävō\ *n* -ES [origin unknown] **:** OPAH

¹craw *Scot var of* CROW

²craw \'krȯ\ *n* -S [ME *crawe*, fr. (assumed) OE *crawa;* akin to MHG *krage* neck, throat, ON *kragi* collar, OIr *brāgae* neck, Gk *bronchos* trachea, L *vorare* to devour — more at VORACIOUS] **1 :** the crop of a bird or insect **2 :** the stomach esp. of a lower animal

craw–craw \'krȯ,krȯ\ *n* -S [prob. modif. & redupl. of D *krauwen* to scratch, fr. MD; akin to OHG *krouwōn* to scratch — more at CRUMB] **:** an itching skin disease produced by the young of a filarial worm (*Onchocerca volvulus*) migrating in the subcutaneous tissues — compare ONCHOCERCIASIS

craw·dad \'krȯ,dad\ *also* **craw·dab** \-,dab\ *n* -S [alter. of *crawfish*] *chiefly Midland* **:** CRAYFISH

¹craw·fish \'krȯ+,-\ *n* [by folk etymology fr. ME *crevis* — more at CRAYFISH] **1 :** CRAYFISH **2 :** SPINY LOBSTER **3** *in California* **:** GHOST SHRIMP

²crawfish \"\ *vi* **:** to retreat from a position **:** back out — usu. used with *out* ⟨we'll just have to ~ out of shaking hands with them —Sally Benson⟩

¹crawk \'krȯk\ *vi* -ED/-ING/-S [imit.] **:** to utter a harsh squawk ⟨the crows ~*ing* overhead⟩

²crawk \"\ *n* -S **:** a sound-effects man who imitates animals (as for radio programs)

¹crawl \'krȯl\ *vb* -ED/-ING/-S [ME *crawlen*, fr. ON *krafla* to crawl, creep; akin to ON *krabbi* crab — more at CRAB] *vi* **1 :** to move or go slowly (as an insect, snake, turtle) with the body close to the ground **:** CREEP **2 :** to move, progress, or advance slowly or laboriously **:** drag along ⟨hardly able to ~⟩ ⟨the hours ~*ed* by⟩ ⟨tanks and amphibian tractors were ~*ing* up on the beach —H.L.Merillat⟩ **3 :** to advance servilely, abjectly, or furtively ⟨~ into favor⟩ **4** *of plants* **:** to spread by extending stems, branches, or tendrils **:** CREEP, TRAIL **5 a :** to be alive or swarming with or as if with a great number of creeping things ⟨a kitchen ~*ing* with ants⟩ ⟨a living room ~*ing* with bric-a-brac⟩ **b :** to have an unpleasant sensation as if insects were creeping over one **:** become unnaturally upset, perturbed, or anguished ⟨his flesh was ~*ing* with the need of alcohol —Eddie Doherty⟩ **6 :** to swim a crawl ⟨~ across the pool in record time⟩ **7 :** to fail to stay evenly spread **:** draw into puddles or dense areas — used of paint, varnish, glaze ~ *vt* **1 :** to move upon in or as if in a creeping manner ⟨the meanest person who ever ~*ed* the earth⟩ **2** *slang* **:** to reprove with severity ⟨they got no good right to ~ me for what I wrote —Marjorie K. Rawlings⟩

²crawl \"\ *n* -S **1 a :** the act or action of crawling ⟨a dangerous ~ up a roof⟩ **b :** slow or laborious motion or progress ⟨will speed up the gluey ~ of the Sunday driver —Lewis Mumford⟩ **c** *chiefly Brit* **:** a leisurely progress from one bar to another — used usu. in combination ⟨beer ~⟩ **2 :** a prone speed swimming stroke consisting of a double overarm stroke combined with a flutter kick usu. in a ratio of six leg kicks to two arm strokes — called also *American crawl;* see AUSTRALIAN CRAWL, TRUDGEN CRAWL **3 a** *or* **crawl box :** a revolving drum on which lettering can be affixed in producing creeper titles in motion pictures and television **b :** a group of titles rolled on a crawl **4 :** a pulley block that has sheaves that roll laterally along a rope and is used for transporting a suspended load

³crawl \"\ *n* -S [D *kraal* — more at KRAAL] **:** an enclosure (as one used in shallow waters to confine lobsters or turtles)

crawl·er \'krȯlə(r)\ *n* -S **1 :** one that crawls: as **a** (1) **:** a newly hatched or first-stage insect that has not lost the ability to crawl about **:** TRIUNGULIN (2) **:** HELLGRAMMITE **b** *Austral* **:** a servile person **c** (1) *Brit* **:** a cruising taxi (2) **:** a Caterpillar tractor **d** (1) **:** either of the treads of a crawler tractor (2) **:** CREEPER TITLE **2 :** a garment similar to overalls and suitable for wear by children while crawling — usu. used in pl. ⟨gabardine ~*s*⟩; compare CREEPER

crawler crane *n* **:** a crane mounted on and operating from a crawler tractor

crawler wheel *n* **:** either of a pair of wheels carrying and running on an endless metal belt (as on a crawler tractor)

craw·ley root \'krȯlē-\ *n* [by folk etymology] **:** a coralroot (*Corallorrhiza odontorhiza*) of dry woodlands in eastern and central No. America that produces a scape of small white to purple crimson-spotted flowers and has an irregular perennial rootstock which is sometimes collected for use as a diaphoretic

craw·lie \'krȯlē\ *n* -S [prob. fr. ¹*crawl* + *-ie*] **:** YABBY

crawling *n* -S [fr. gerund of ¹*crawl*] **:** an undesirable drawing together or lumping of a surface finish (as of paint, enamel, glaze)

crawl·ing·ly *adv* **:** in a crawling manner

crawl·ing·ness *n* -ES **:** the quality or state of being crawling

crawls *pl of* CRAWL, *pres 3d sing of* CRAWL

crawl space *n* **:** a space about two feet high provided in a building in order to enable workmen to gain access to plumbing, wiring, and other equipment

crawly \'krȯlē, -li\ *adj* -ER/-EST [¹*crawl* + *-y*] *adj* **:** CREEPY

craws *pl of* CRAW

craw·thump·er \'krȯ,thəmpə(r)\ *n, usu cap* [fr. *Crawthumper*, a nickname for Roman Catholics] **:** MARYLANDER — used as a nickname

crax \'kraks\ *n, cap* [NL, modif. of Gk *krex*, a kind of long-legged bird — more at CREX] **:** the type genus of Cracidae

cray \'krā\ *n* -S [short for *crayfish*] **:** a spiny lobster (*Jasus lalandii*) of Australia

crayer \'kra(a)(ə)r\ *n* -S [ME *crayer*, fr. MF *crayer, croyer*, fr. OF *croier*] **:** a former small sailing cargo boat

cray·fish \'krā+,-\ *n* [by folk etymology fr. ME *crevis*, fr. MF *crevice*, of Gmc origin; akin to OHG *krebiz* crab — more at CRAB] **1 :** any of numerous freshwater crustaceans of the tribe Astacura resembling the lobster but usu. much smaller in size, all those of the northern hemisphere belonging to a single family (Astacidae) which includes the genera *Astacus* with species in Europe, Asia, and western No. America, and *Cambarus* to which most No. American forms belong **2 :** SPINY LOBSTER

cray·let \'krālət\ *n* -S [*cray* + *-let*] **:** any of several small anomuran crustaceans of Australia belonging to the genus *Galathea* and resembling lobsters

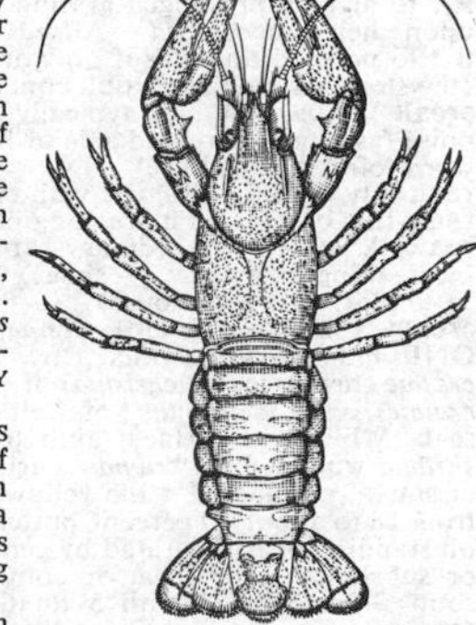

crayfish

¹cray·on \'krā,än, -āən *also* 'kran *or* -rän\ *n* -S [F, crayon, pencil, dim. of *craie* chalk, fr. L *creta*] **1 a :** a stick of white or colored chalk or clay and graphite used for drawing **b :** a stick of colored wax composition used for drawing and coloring **c :** LITHOGRAPHIC CRAYON **d :** a cosmetic in stick or pencil form used esp. for coloring eyebrows **2 :** a crayon drawing

²crayon \"\ *vt* -ED/-ING/-S [F *crayonner*, fr. *crayon*] **1 :** to draw or color with a crayon ⟨~ a portrait⟩ **:** cover or decorate with crayon work ⟨a wall ~*ed* with colorful designs⟩ **2 :** to sketch out **:** draw up ⟨a plan carefully ~*ed* out⟩

crayon board *n* **:** cardboard with a surface for crayon drawing

crayon green *n* **:** a light yellowish green that is yellower and paler than apple green (sense 2), greener, lighter, and stronger than pistachio, and greener and deeper than ocean green

cray·on·ist \-nəst\ *n* -S **:** a specialist in the use of crayons

crayon manner *n* **:** a manner of etching in which the ground is perforated with various needles, roulettes, or mattoirs to produce the effect of crayon or chalk drawing on the print — called also *chalk manner*

crayon sauce *n* **:** powdered crayon used for retouching in photography

crayonstone \'=(,)=, '=(=)+,-\ *n* **:** a lithographic drawing made directly upon the stone

cray·thur \'krāthər\ *Irish var of* CREATURE

¹craze \'krāz\ *vb* -ED/-ING/-S [ME *crasen*, of Scand origin; akin to OSw *krasa* to crush, smash, Norw, to crush, smash, crunch, prob. of imit. origin] *vt* **1** *obs* **:** to break to pieces **:** CRUSH, SMASH **2 a** *now dial Brit* **:** to break without separation of parts **:** CRACK ⟨*crazing* the jug⟩ **b :** to produce minute cracks on the surface or glaze of — compare ²CRACKLE 2 **3** *archaic* **:** to weaken or injure physically **:** make infirm **4 :** to derange the intellect of **:** make insane or as if insane ⟨*crazed* by drink⟩ ⟨they were *crazed* by the famine and pestilence of that last bitter winter —*Amer. Guide Series: Wash.*⟩ ~ *vi* **1** *archaic* **:** SHATTER, BREAK **2 :** to become crazed **:** go mad **3 :** to develop a mesh of fine cracks — used of solid plastics, surface coating (as pottery glazing), and adhesives

²craze \"\ *n* -S **1** *obs* **a :** BREAK, FLAW, DEFECT **b :** physical weakness **:** INFIRMITY **2 :** a transient infatuation **:** FAD, MANIA ⟨his ~ for easy money⟩ ⟨the cocktail ~⟩ ⟨a ~ for internal improvements spread over the country —Isaac Lippincott⟩ **3 a :** a crazy condition ⟨in a ~ with pain⟩ **b :** CRAZINESS, INSANITY ⟨the aristocracy and intricacy of their ~ —Frederic Morton⟩ **4 a :** cracking of ceramic glaze due to unequal contraction of body and glaze — compare ²CRACKLE 2 **b :** hairline cracks on the surface (as of paint) **syn** see FASHION

craz·ed·ly \'krāzədlē, -li\ *adv* **:** in a crazed manner **:** CRAZILY

craz·ed·ness \-zədnəs\ *n* -ES **:** the quality or state of being crazed

cra·zi·ly \'krāz(ə)lē, -li\ *adv* **:** in a crazy manner

cra·zi·ness \-zēnəs, -zin-\ *n* -ES **:** the quality or state of being crazy

crazing *n* -S [fr. gerund of ¹*craze*] **:** the formation of minute cracks (as on glaze, enamel, varnish) usu. attributed to shrinkage or sometimes to moisture

¹cra·zy \'krāzē, -zi\ *adj* -ER/-EST [²*craze* + *-y*] **1 a :** full of cracks or flaws **:** DAMAGED, UNSOUND ⟨a ~ old building⟩ ⟨embarked in a ~ dugout canoe —*Nat'l Geographic*⟩ **b :** not straight or upright **:** CROOKED, ASKEW ⟨a ~ tower⟩ ⟨~ little cow paths —T.H.Fielding⟩ **c :** not in order **:** JUMBLED DISORDERED ⟨a ~ pile of equipment⟩ **d** *of livestock brands* **:** UPSIDE-DOWN — see BRAND illustration **2** *archaic* **:** broken down in health **:** AILING, INFIRM, FRAIL **3 a :** broken or as if broken in mind **:** INSANE ⟨yelling like a ~ man⟩ ⟨~ with hatred⟩ ⟨go ~ with drink⟩ **b :** arising from, produced by, or suggestive of insanity ⟨a ~ leer and giggle⟩ ⟨~ turmoil⟩ **c :** devoid of common sense: as (1) **:** IMPRACTICAL ⟨a ~ plan⟩ ⟨a ~ idealist⟩ (2) **:** ERRATIC ⟨a ~ driver⟩ **d :** out of the ordinary **:** ODD, UNUSUAL ⟨a ~ taste in hats⟩ ⟨a cart pushed by a ~ little old man⟩ **4 a :** distracted with desire or excitement **b :** absurdly fond **:** INFATUATED ⟨~ over a girl⟩ ⟨a thrill-*crazy* mob⟩ **c :** passionately preoccupied **:** OBSESSED ⟨~ about new cars⟩ **d :** wildly or intensely eager ⟨~ to try out a new boat⟩ **5 :** WILD 8 — often used in the names of card games similar to those in which a card of a specified rank is wild ⟨~ jacks⟩

²crazy \"\ *adv* **:** to a crazy degree or extent ⟨~ mean neighbors drove him to violence —G.S.Perry⟩; *esp* **:** VIOLENTLY ⟨a ~ mad policeman⟩ ⟨~ drunk⟩

³crazy *also* **cra·zey** \"\ *n, pl* **crazies** *also* **crazeys** [origin unknown] *dial Eng* **:** any of several plants of the family Ranunculaceae: as **a :** BUTTERCUP 1 **b :** a marsh marigold (*Caltha palustris*)

crazy ant *n* **:** a very active ant (*Paratrechina longicornis*) native to the tropics and now found in buildings and protected areas in many temperate regions

crazy bone *n* **:** FUNNY BONE

crazy chick disease *also* **crazy chick** *n* **:** a nervous disease of young chickens caused by inadequate intake of vitamin E and marked by severe muscular incoordination and tremors followed by paralysis and by renal congestion and failure — called also *nutritional encephalomalacia*

crazy eights *n pl but sing in constr* **:** EIGHT 8

crazy house *n* **1 :** an insane asylum **2 :** a building in an amusement park containing fun-provoking devices (as distortion mirrors, compressed-air jets, chute-the-chutes)

crazy quilt *n* **1 :** a patchwork quilt made without a design or pattern **2 :** an incoherently pieced-together entity **:** JUMBLE PATCHWORK ⟨our *crazy quilt* divorce laws⟩ ⟨his body a *crazy quilt* of cuts and bruises —*Newsweek*⟩
crazy top *n* **:** any of several plant diseases in which the top growth undergoes characteristic alteration: as **a :** a disease of citrus that occurs on alkaline soils, that is marked by loss of mature leaves, stiff brushy terminal growth, and abnormal fruits, and that may be related to or a form of stubborn disease **b :** a disease of corn that is prob. due to a virus and that is characterized by the appearance of vegetative shoots often in bunches in place of floral organs **c :** a disease of almonds that is probably caused by a virus and is characterized by growth failure of many flower and leaf buds resulting in a sparse open tree with little fruit
crazyweed \ˈ⸗,⸗\ *n* [so called fr. its toxic effect upon horses and cattle] **1 :** LOCOWEED **2 :** WHITE LOCOWEED
cre- *or* **creo-** *also* **kreo-** *comb form* [G *kreo-*, fr. Gk *kre-, kreo-*, fr. *kreas* — more at RAW] **:** flesh ⟨*creo*dont⟩ ⟨*creo*phagous⟩ ⟨*kreo*toxism⟩
crea·chy \ˈkrēchi\ *var of* CRAICHY
creagh \ˈkrāk\ *n* -s [ScGael *creach;* akin to MIr *crech* raid] **1** *chiefly Scot* **:** a plundering raid **2** *chiefly Scot* **:** PLUNDER, BOOTY
creaght \ˈkrā(k)t\ *n* -s [IrGael *caoraidheacht*, fr. MIr *caeraigheacht*, fr. OIr *caera* sheep; prob. akin to L *caper* goat — more at CAPRIOLE] **1** *Irish* **:** a herd of cattle driven about for pasture or with a warring band **2** *Irish* **:** RAPPAREE
¹creak \ˈkrēk\ *vi* -ED/-ING/-S [ME *creken* to utter a harsh cry, of imit. origin] **1** *obs* **a :** CROAK **b :** to speak querulously **2 :** to make a prolonged grating or squeaking sound ⟨doors upon their hinges ~*ed* —Alfred Tennyson⟩ ⟨~*ing* saddles⟩ **3 :** to proceed on or as if on worn wheels, springs, or joints ⟨the story ~*s* along to a dull conclusion⟩
²creak \ˈ"\ *n* -s **:** a high typically subdued rasping or grating noise (as of an ungreased axle or hinge or of the movement of worn joints of furniture)
creak·i·ly \-kəlē, -li\ *adv* **:** with creaks **:** with creaking
creak·ing·ly *adv* **:** in a creaking manner
creaky \ˈkrēkē, -ēki\ *adj* -ER/-EST **1 :** apt to creak **:** marked by creaking **:** SQUEAKY ⟨~ shoes⟩ **2 :** DILAPIDATED, DECREPIT ⟨a ~ plot⟩ ⟨a ~ old house⟩
¹cream \ˈkrēm\ *n* -s [ME *creme, creime*, fr. MF *cresme* & ONF *craime;* MF *cresme*, fr. OF, alter. (influenced by *cresme* chrism, fr. LL *chrisma*) of (assumed) OF *craime* (ONF *craime*), fr. LL *cramum*, of Celt origin; akin to W *cramen* scab, MIr *screm* surface; akin to MHG *schram* gash, ON *skrāma* wound, Lith *kramas* scurf, Gk *keirein* to cut — more at SHEAR, CHRISM] **1 :** the yellowish part of milk containing from 18 to about 40 percent butterfat that rises to the surface on standing or is separated by centrifugal force **2 a :** a food or substance made from or containing cream ⟨~ of celery soup⟩ — usu. used with a qualifying word ⟨Bavarian ~⟩ ⟨tapioca ~⟩ **b :** a solid or liquid substance resembling or suggesting cream in appearance or consistency: as (1) **:** any of a class of cosmetic preparations used esp. for cleansing, softening, smoothing, and protecting the skin ⟨emollient ~⟩ ⟨finishing ~⟩ — see COLD CREAM, SHAVING CREAM, VANISHING CREAM (2) **:** any of various medicinal preparations usu. classed as ointments (3) **:** a sweet or candy of a consistency suggesting cream ⟨a box of chocolate ~*s*⟩ (4) **:** ICE CREAM ⟨bring along a quart of vanilla ~⟩ (5) **:** the part of an emulsion or suspension that rises and collects on the surface **3 :** the best, most desirable, or choicest part of something ⟨the ~ of society⟩ ⟨the ~ of the crop⟩ **:** QUINTESSENCE ⟨the ~ of the jest⟩ **4 :** CREAMER 2 **5 :** a pale yellow that is lighter, slightly greener, and very slightly stronger than ivory, paler than straw, and greener and paler than leghorn **6 :** a cream-colored animal (as a horse or rabbit)
²cream \ˈ"\ *vb* -ED/-ING/-S [ME *cremen*, fr. *creme*, n.] *vi* **1 a :** to form cream ⟨let the milk stand till it ~*s*⟩ **b :** to become covered with cream ⟨beer ~*ing* in a glass⟩ **c :** to become like cream **:** FOAM, FROTH ⟨waves ~*ing* on the rocks⟩ **d :** to undergo creaming **2 :** to proceed with foamy spray and wake (as of a ship) ~ *vt* **1 a :** to draw off by skimming **:** take the cream off (milk) **b :** to take or remove (the choicest part) — often used with *off* ⟨~ off the best of a country's production by export⟩ **2 a :** to furnish with or as if with cream **:** prepare with cream or a cream sauce **b :** to rub, stir, or beat (as butter) until of a light creamy consistency **c :** to blend (as butter and sugar) by stirring or beating **d** *slang* **:** BEAT, LAMBASTE **3 a :** to cause or allow cream to form on (milk) **b :** to cause to froth or foam ⟨the ship's wake ~*ed* the waves⟩ **c :** to bring about creaming of ⟨rubber latex is ~*ed* by salts of alginic acid⟩ **4 :** to apply a cosmetic cream to ⟨~*ing* her face daily⟩
³cream \ˈ"\ *adj* [¹*cream*] **1 a :** having the consistency and appearance of cream ⟨~ soup⟩ **b :** having cream added **2 :** of the color cream
cream·able \-məbəl\ *adj* **:** having the quality necessary for creaming ⟨~ lard⟩
cream beige *n* **:** SANDSTONE 2
cream buff *n* **:** a pale to grayish yellow that is slightly greener than Naples yellow and redder and stronger than wine yellow
cream bun *n, Brit* **:** a bun filled with cream **:** CREAM PUFF
creambush \ˈ⸗,⸗\ *n* [so called fr. the white flowers] **:** OCEAN SPRAY
cream cheese *n* **1 :** an unripened cheese made from whole sweet milk enriched with cream or by working cream into a skimmed-milk curd and often containing as high as 50 percent fat **2** *dial* **:** CHEDDAR CHEESE; *esp* **:** one that is made from whole milk
creamcups \ˈ⸗,⸗\ *n pl but sing or pl in constr* [so called fr. the appearance of the flower] **1 :** any of several Californian annuals of the family Papaveraceae (esp. *Platystemon californicus*) **2 :** OCEAN SPRAY
cream·er \ˈkrēmə(r)\ *n* -s **1 :** a can or pan in which milk is set to form cream **:** a cream separator **2 :** a small pitcher or jug for serving cream
cream·ery \ˈkrēm(ə)rē, -ri\ *n* -ES [¹*cream* + -*ery*] **1 :** an establishment where butter and cheese are made or where milk and cream are sold or processed; *also* **:** the work of such an establishment **2 :** a building where milk and other dairy products are stored **:** DAIRY
cream–faced \ˈ⸗;⸗\ *adj* **:** PALE ⟨*cream-faced* from fear⟩
cream ice *n, Brit* **:** ICE CREAM
cream·i·ly \ˈkrēməlē, -li\ *adv* [*creamy* + -*ly*] **1 :** in the manner of or with the appearance of cream ⟨swift waters dashing ~ over the falls⟩ **2 :** SOFTLY, SUAVELY, BLANDLY ⟨~ venomous politeness —*Time*⟩
cream·i·ness \ˈkrēmēnəs, -min-\ *n* -ES **:** the quality or state of being creamy in texture or color
creaming *n* -s [fr. gerund of ²*cream*] **:** reversible separation of an emulsion or suspension by rising or settling of the dispersed particles (as oil droplets or suspended solids) ⟨~ of rubber latex⟩
cream laid *n* -s *chiefly Brit* **:** a cream-colored laid writing paper
cream·less \-mləs\ *adj* **:** not having cream
cream line *n* **:** the place where the risen cream meets the milk, esp. as seen in a transparent milk bottle
cream nut *n* [prob. so called fr. the rich flavor] **1 :** BRAZIL NUT **2 :** the nut of the cauchillo
cream of lime 1 : a scum of calcium carbonate formed on a solution of milk of lime by combination with the carbon dioxide of the air **2 :** a mixture of slaked lime and water
cream of tartar [prob. so called fr. its being the choicest or most essential ingredient in tartar] **:** a white crystalline salt $KHC_4H_4O_6$ with a pleasant acid taste found in grapes and in tartars from wine making, prepared esp. from argols and also synthetically from tartaric acid, and used chiefly in foods (as baking powder and hard candy) and in certain treatments of metals (as in the electrolytic tinning of iron and steel); potassium hydrogen tartrate — called also *potassium acid tartrate, potassium bitartrate*
cream–of–tartar tree *n* [so called fr. the taste of the fruit] **:** a desert tree (*Adansonia gregorii*) of northern Australia that produces an agreeably acid fruit — called also *Australian baobab, sour gourd*
cream puff *n* **1 :** a round shell of light pastry filled with whipped cream or a cream filling **2** *slang* **a :** a timid, weak, ineffectual, or oversensitive person ⟨no namby-pamby, *cream puff* fighter —*Sporting Life*⟩ **b :** something trifling or inconsiderable ⟨the play is a diverting *cream puff*⟩
creams *pl of* CREAM, *pres 3d sing of* CREAM
cream sauce *n* **:** WHITE SAUCE
cream soda *n* **:** a carbonated soft drink flavored with vanilla and sweetened with sugar
cream soup *also* **cream–soup bowl** *n* **:** a two-handled soup bowl
cream–soup spoon *n* **:** a round-bowled spoon slightly shorter than a standard soup spoon
creamware \ˈ⸗,⸗\ *n* **:** cream-colored pottery
cream wove *n* -s *chiefly Brit* **:** a cream-colored wove writing paper
creamy \ˈkrēmē, -mi\ *adj* -ER/-EST [¹*cream* + -*y*] **1 :** full of or containing cream **2 :** resembling cream in nature, appearance, color, or taste **:** soft and smooth **:** LUSCIOUS
cre·ance \ˈkrēən(t)s\ *n* -s [ME *creaunce* trust, confidence, leash for a hawk, fr. MF *creance*, fr. (assumed) VL *credentia* trust, belief (whence ML *credentia* promise, security given, credit, belief) — more at CREDENCE] **:** a fine line used to leash a hawk during training
¹crease \ˈkrēs\ *n* -s [prob. alter. of earlier *creaste*, fr. ME *creste* crest] **1 a :** a line, groove, or ridge that is made by or as if by folding a pliable substance and is generally larger or longer than a wrinkle and not so deep as a fold **b :** a similar mark on the skin esp. about the face or neck ⟨a ~ between the eyes⟩ — usu. used in pl. ⟨many ~*s* about her mouth —Eve Langley⟩ **c :** the front or back edge of a man's trouser leg esp. when pressed — often used in pl. **2 a :** the diagonal ventral fold marking the anterior and medial margin of junction of either leg and the trunk in man **b :** the medial cleft between the buttocks **3 :** a specially marked area in various field sports: **a** (1) **:** POPPING CREASE (2) **:** BOWLING CREASE (3) **:** RETURN CREASE (4) **:** GROUND 5h(2) **b :** an area surrounding the goal (as in lacrosse and hockey) forbidden to attacking players unless the ball or puck is in it — called also *goal crease;* see ICE HOCKEY illustration **4 :** the longitudinal groove on the ventral surface of certain grains (as of wheat)
²crease \ˈ"\ *vb* -ED/-ING/-S *vt* **1 :** to make a crease in or on **:** WRINKLE ⟨a frown *creased* his forehead⟩ **2 a :** to stun (as a wild horse wanted alive) by placing a grazing shot that does not cause permanent injury **b :** to wound slightly esp. by grazing ⟨the bullet *creased* him⟩ **:** GRAZE ⟨*creased* his head⟩ ~ *vi* **:** to become creased or wrinkled ⟨this dress material will not ~ easily⟩
³crease *var of* KRIS
crease·less \-ləs\ *adj* **:** not having a crease
creas·er \ˈkrēsə(r)\ *n* -s **:** one that creases: as **a :** a tool or a sewing-machine attachment for making lines or creases on leather or cloth as guides to sew by **b :** a tool for making creases or beads (as in sheet iron) **c :** a tool for making the band impression distinct on the backbones of books or for making blind lines or creases on the cases of books
creashaks *n, pl* **creashaks** [origin unknown] **:** BEARBERRY 1
crea·sing \ˈkrēsiŋ\ *n* -s [prob. fr. E dial. *crease* ridge tile (prob. alter. of earlier E *creast* crest, fr. ME *creste*) + E -*ing* (n. suffix)] **:** one or more courses of bricks or tiles, each course projecting slightly, crowning a wall or chimney
creasol *var of* CREOSOL
creasote *var of* CREOSOTE
creasy \ˈkrēsē, -si\ *adj* -ER/-EST [¹*crease* + -*y*] **:** having or forming creases
cre·at \(ˈ)krēˌat\ *n* -s [Hindi *kariyāt, kiryāt*] **:** an East Indian herb (*Andrographis paniculata*) having a juice that is a strong bitter tonic variously used in local medicine
creat- *or* **creato-** *comb form* [F *créat-*, fr. Gk *kreas* — more at RAW] **:** flesh ⟨*creat*ine⟩ ⟨*creato*phagous⟩
¹cre·ate \krēˈāt\ *adj* [ME *creat*, fr. L *creatus*, past part. of *creare* to create — more at CRESCENT] *archaic* **:** CREATED
²cre·ate \(ˈ)krēˌāt, *usu* -ād·+V\ *vb* -ED/-ING/-S [ME *createn*, fr. L *creatus*] *vt* **1 :** to bring into existence **:** make out of nothing and for the first time ⟨God *created* the heaven and the earth —Gen 1:1 (AV)⟩ **2 :** to cause to be or to produce by fiat or by mental, moral, or legal action: as **a :** to invest with a new form, office, or rank **:** constitute by an act of law or sovereignty ⟨~ one a peer⟩ ⟨~ a new administrative post⟩ **:** APPOINT ⟨~ one a judge⟩ **b :** to produce or effect as an act of grace ⟨~ in me a clean heart —Ps 51:10 (AV)⟩ **c :** to bring about by a course of action or behavior ⟨~ an impression of invincibility⟩ ⟨~ an opportunity to talk to someone⟩ ⟨~ a demand for a product by advertising⟩ ⟨~ a disturbance⟩ **3 :** to cause or occasion — used of natural or physical causes and esp. of social and evolutionary or emergent forces ⟨a famine ~*s* high food prices⟩ ⟨modern science, which *created* this dilemma, is also capable of solving it —Bruce Bliven b. 1889⟩ **4 a :** to produce (as a work of art or of dramatic interpretation) along new or unconventional lines ⟨*created* a new Hamlet⟩ **b :** to design (as a costume or a dress) ~ *vi* **1 :** to make or bring into existence something new (as something of an imaginative or artistic character) **:** INVENT ⟨quick to imitate but powerless to ~⟩ **2** *slang Brit* **:** to complain loudly **:** carry on **:** GRIPE ⟨don't go near him while he's *creating*⟩
cre·at·ed·ness \krēˈādədnəs, -ātə-\ *n* -ES **:** the quality or state of being created
cre·at·ic \(ˈ)krēˌad·ik\ *adj* [*creat-* + -*ic*] **:** relating to or caused by flesh or animal food ⟨~ nausea⟩
cre·atine \ˈkrēəˌtēn, -tən\ *n* -s [ISV *creat-* + -*ine;* orig. formed as F *créatine*] **:** a white crystalline compound $NH_2C(=NH)N(CH_3)CH_2COOH$ found esp. in the muscles of vertebrates both as phosphocreatine and as the free form and also in the blood and obtained from meat extracts; 1-methylguanidine-acetic acid
creatine phosphate *or* **creatine phosphoric acid** \ˈ"+\ *n* **:** PHOSPHOCREATINE
cre·at·i·nine \krēˈatᵊnˌēn, -tᵊnən\ *n* -s [G *kreatinin*, fr. *kreatin* creatine + -*in* -ine] **:** a white crystalline strongly basic compound $C_4H_7N_3O$ formed from creatine by dehydration and found esp. in muscle, blood, and urine
cre·atin·uria \ˌkrēətəˈn(y)u̇rēə\ *n* -s [NL, fr. ISV *creatine* + NL -*uria*] **:** the presence of creatine in urine; *esp* **:** an increased or abnormal amount of it therein ⟨marked ~ may accompany some endocrine disorders⟩
cre·ation \krēˈāshən\ *n* -s [ME *creacioun*, fr. MF or L; MF *creation*, fr. L *creation-, creatio*, fr. *creatus* (past part. of *creare* to create) + -*ion-, -io* -ion] **1 :** the act of creating; *esp* **:** the act of bringing into existence from nothing the universe or the world or the living and nonliving things in it **2 :** the act or practice of making, inventing, devising, fashioning, or producing: as **a :** the act of investing with a new rank or office ⟨a baron of recent ~⟩ ⟨the ~ of a special committee⟩ **b :** the presentation of a new conception in an artistic embodiment; *esp* **:** the first dramatic representation of a role ⟨Jefferson's ~ of Rip Van Winkle⟩ **3 :** something that is created: as **a :** WORLD **b :** creatures singly or as an aggregate ⟨throughout all ~⟩ **c :** an original work of art or of the imagination ⟨the question of whether folk songs are the ~*s* of groups or individuals⟩ **d :** an article of attire of new and striking design
cre·ation·al \(ˈ)krēˈāshənᵊl, -shnəl\ *adj* **:** of or relating to creation
cre·ation·ary \krēˈāshəˌnerē\ *adj* **:** of the nature of or relating to creation
cre·ation·ism \-ˌnizəm\ *n* -s **1 :** a doctrine or theory of creation holding that matter, the various forms of life, and the world were created by a transcendent God out of nothing — compare EVOLUTIONISM **2 :** the theological doctrine that the human soul is separately created in each individual born — compare INFUSIONISM, TRADUCIANISM
cre·ation·ist \-sh(ə)nəst\ *n* -s **:** a believer in creationism — **cre·ation·is·tic** \krēˌāshəˈnistik, ˌkrēˌā⸗ˈ⸗⸗\ *adj*
cre·ative \(ˈ)krēˈād·|iv, -āt|, |ēv *also* |əv *sometimes* ˈkrēəd·| *or* -ēət|\ *adj* **1 :** having the power or quality of creating **:** given to creation **2 :** PRODUCTIVE — used with *of* ⟨events ~ of alarm⟩ **3 :** having the quality of something created rather than imitated or assembled **:** expressive of the maker **:** IMAGINATIVE ⟨~ art⟩ ⟨~ writing⟩ — **cre·ative·ly** *adv*
creative evolution *n* **:** evolution conceived as a creative rather than a mechanically explicable process — see BERGSONISM; compare ÉLAN VITAL, EMERGENT EVOLUTION
cre·ative·ness *n* -ES **:** CREATIVITY
creative play *n* **:** children's play (as modeling or painting) that tends to satisfy the need for self-expression as well as to develop manual skills
cre·ativ·i·ty \ˌkrēˌāˈtivəd·ē, -rēə'-, -ətē, -i\ *n* -ES **:** the quality of being creative **:** ability to create ⟨the ~ of generations of immigrants —D.D.McKean⟩
creato- — see CREAT-
cre·ator \(ˈ)krēˈād·ə(r), -ātə-; krēˈāˌtȯ(ə)r, -tȯ(ə)\ *n* -s [ME *creatour*, fr. OF, fr. L *creator*, fr. *creatus* (past part. of *creare* to create) + -*or*] **:** one that creates, produces, or constitutes **:** MAKER, AUTHOR, INVENTOR
cre·atress \(ˈ)krēˈā·trəs\ *n* -ES [*creator* + -*ess*] **:** a woman that creates (as a dramatic role)
cre·atrix \-triks\ *n, pl* **cre·atri·ces** \krēˈā·trəˌsēz, ˌkrēə·ˈtrī-(ˌ)sēz\ [L, fem. of *creator*] **:** CREATRESS
creats *pl of* CREAT
crea·tur·al \ˈkrēch(ə)rəl\ *adj* **:** belonging to or of the nature of a creature ⟨~ sensibilities⟩
crea·ture \ˈkrēchə(r), *dial* ˈkrid·ə(r) *or* ˈkrēd·- *or* ˈkrād·-\ *n* -s [ME, fr. OF, fr. LL *creatura*, fr. L *creatus* + -*ura* -ure] **1 :** something whether animate or inanimate regarded as created: as **a** *obs* **:** WORLD, CREATION, UNIVERSE **b** *archaic* **:** something (as food or drink) that serves man's material comfort ⟨were put to it to reconcile the phrase good ~*s* . . . with the fare set before us —Charles Lamb⟩ **c** *chiefly dial* **:** SPIRITS; *esp* **:** WHISKEY — usu. used with *the* ⟨a drop o' the ~⟩ **2 a :** one of the lower animals ⟨visited in their haunts the wild ~*s* of the woods⟩; *esp* **:** a farm animal — compare CRITTER **b :** a human being ⟨fellow ~*s*⟩ **:** PERSON ⟨the dearest ~ in the world⟩ ⟨the poor ~ has had a hard life⟩ — often used in disparagement ⟨I'll never speak to that ~ again⟩ **c :** a being of anomalous, unspecified, or uncertain aspect or nature ⟨strange fearsome ~*s*, neither man nor beast⟩ ⟨a world of fancy peopled by ~*s* unknown to man⟩ **3 a :** one that owes existence or position to another and is therefore subject to control or undue influence **:** a servile dependent **:** INSTRUMENT, MINION ⟨the Governor was a mere ~ of the Senator's⟩ ⟨the bank is a ~ of Congress⟩ **b :** one whose will is not free ⟨a ~ of habit⟩ ⟨the individual who is simultaneously the creator, the carrier, and the ~ of all institutions —Abram Kardiner⟩
creature comfort *n* **:** something (as food or warmth) that gives bodily comfort
crea·ture·li·ness \ˈkrēchə(r)lēnəs, -lin-\ *n* -ES **:** the quality or state of being a creature esp. in sharing kinship with the animals
crea·ture·ly \-lē, -li\ *adj* **:** characteristic of a creature **:** CREATURAL
creb·ri·ty \ˈkrebrəd·ē\ *n* -ES [L *crebritat-, crebritas*, fr. *crebr-, creber* frequent + -*itat-, -itas* -ity; akin to L *crescere* to grow — more at CRESCENT] **:** FREQUENCY
crèche \ˈkresh, -rāsh\ *n* -s [F, fr. OF *creche* manger, crib — more at CRATCH] **1 :** a day nursery **2 :** a foundling hospital **3 :** a representation of the stable at Bethlehem with the infant Jesus surrounded by Mary, Joseph, the oxen and asses, and adoring shepherds and magi
cré·cy \ˈkrāsē, krāˈsē, ˈkresē\ *adj, usu cap* [F *Crécy* carrot of a choice variety, fr. *Crécy*, commune in northern France where it is grown] **:** prepared with carrots — used esp. of soups, eggs, entrees
credal *var of* CREEDAL
cre·dence \ˈkrēdᵊn(t)s\ *n* -s [ME, fr. MF or ML; MF *credence* trust, confidence, fr. ML *credentia* promise, security given, credit, belief, fr. (assumed) VL *credentia* trust, belief, fr. L *credent-, credens* (pres. part. of *credere* to trust, believe) + -*ia* -y — more at CREED] **1 :** acceptance (as of a story or statement) as true **:** BELIEF ⟨to give ~ to gossip⟩ ⟨to withhold ~ from the miracles of Scripture⟩ **2 :** TRUSTWORTHINESS, RELIABILITY ⟨the words of a man of ~⟩ ⟨the ~ of the senses⟩ **3 :** CREDENTIALS — now used only in the phrase *letters of credence* **4** [MF, fr. OIt *credenza*] **:** a sideboard, elaborate cupboard, or buffet of the Renaissance period used chiefly for valuable plate and vessels — see CREDENZA **5** *or* **credence table** [F *crédence* table for bread and wine beside the communion table, sideboard or buffet of the Renaissance period, fr. MF *credence* sideboard or buffet of the Renaissance period] **:** a small table, shelf, or niche beside the communion table where the bread and wine rest before consecration **syn** see BELIEF
cre·den·da \krəˈdendə, krēˈ-\ *n pl* [L, neut. pl. of *credendus*, gerundive of *credere* to believe] **:** doctrines to be believed **:** articles of faith — distinguished from *agenda*
cre·den·dum \-dəm\ *sing of* CREDENDA
cre·dent \ˈkrēdᵊnt\ *adj* [L *credent-, credens*, pres. part. of *credere*] **1** *archaic* **:** giving credence **:** CONFIDING ⟨if with too ~ ear you list his songs —Shak.⟩ **2** *obs* **:** CREDIBLE
¹cre·den·tial \krəˈdenchəl, krēˈ-\ *adj* [ML *credentialis*, fr. *credentia* + L -*alis* -al] **:** giving a title or claim to credit or confidence **:** ACCREDITING — used chiefly in the phrase *credential letters*
²credential \ˈ"\ *n* -s **1 :** something that gives a title to credit or confidence **2 credentials** *pl* **:** testimonials showing that a person is entitled to credit or has a right to exercise official power (as the letters given by a government to an ambassador) **3 a :** a document, issued to a college or university student upon leaving the institution, that testifies to his academic achievement and his personal character ⟨evaluating ~*s* of students from foreign countries⟩ **b :** DEGREE, DIPLOMA, CERTIFICATE
cre·den·tialed \-ld\ *adj* **:** having or furnished with credentials
credentials committee *n* **:** a committee (as at a national party convention) for examining the credentials of delegates and deciding upon contested claims to represent certain groups of the membership
cre·den·za \krəˈdenzə, krēˈ-\ *n* -s [It, lit., belief, confidence, fr. ML *credentia* security given, belief; fr. the practice of placing a lord's food and drink on a sideboard or buffet to be tasted by a servant before being put on the lord's table in order to make sure that it contained no poison] **1 :** CREDENCE 4 **2 :** a sideboard, buffet, or bookcase patterned after the credence of the Renaissance period; *esp* **:** one without legs whose base rests flat on the floor

20th century credenza

cre·dé's method \krəˈdāz-\ *n, cap C* [trans. of G *credésche methode*, after Karl S.F. Credé †1892 Ger. gynecologist] **1 :** the prevention of gonorrheal ophthalmia in the eyes of newborn infants by instillation of silver nitrate solution into the eyes **2** *also* **credé's maneuver :** expression of the placenta after birth by manual compression of the uterus through the abdominal wall
cred·i·bil·i·ty \ˌkredəˈbiləd·ē, -ətē, -i\ *n* -ES [ML *credibilitat-, credibilitas*, fr. L *credibilis* + -*itat-, -itas* -ity] **:** the quality or power of inspiring belief ⟨an account lacking in ~⟩ **:** worthiness of belief ⟨doubts the ~ of the story⟩ **:** capacity for belief ⟨strains her reader's ~ —*Times Lit. Sup.*⟩
cred·i·ble \ˈkredəbəl\ *adj* [ME, fr. L *credibilis*, fr. *credere* + -*ibilis* -ible] **1 :** capable of being credited or believed **:** worthy of belief ⟨~ information⟩ **:** entitled to confidence **:** TRUSTWORTHY ⟨a ~ witness⟩ **2** *obs* **:** CREDULOUS **3** *obs* **:** CREDITABLE, REPUTABLE — **cred·i·bly** \-blē, -li\ *adv*
cred·i·ble·ness \-nəs\ *n* -ES **:** the quality of being credible
¹cred·it \ˈkredət, *usu* -əd·+V\ *n* -s [MF, reputation, commercial credit, fr. OIt *credito*, fr. L *creditum* loan, fr. neut. of *creditus*, past part. of *credere*] **1 a :** the balance in a person's favor in an account; *also* **:** an amount or limit to the extent of which a person may receive goods or money for payment in the future **b :** an amount or sum placed at a person's disposal by a bank **:** a loan of money **c :** time given for payment for goods or services sold for future payment ⟨long-term ~⟩ **d** (1) **:** an entry on the right-hand side of an account constituting an addition to a revenue, net worth, or liability account (2) **:** a deduction from an expense or asset account **e :** any one of or the sum of the items entered on the right-hand side of an account — abbr. *cr;* opposed to *debit* **f :** a sum of money (as to meet unexpected demands) voted by the British parliament for use during the fiscal year by the administration

⟨votes of ~⟩ **g :** a deduction from an amount otherwise due ⟨a tax ~ for dividends received⟩ ⟨a ~ for returned goods⟩ **2 a :** reliance on the truth or reality of something **:** BELIEF, FAITH, TRUST ⟨give no ~ to these idle rumors⟩ **b** *obs* **:** something believed **:** a believed report **3 a :** influence or power derived from enjoying the confidence of another or others **:** STANDING ⟨I will use my ~ with her to persuade her to go⟩ **b :** reputation esp. when favorable **:** good name **:** ESTEEM ⟨he lived with ~ in the village⟩; *also* **:** financial or commercial trustworthiness **:** reputation entitling one to be trusted with money or goods advanced **4** *archaic* **:** the quality of being believed or of being worthy of belief **:** authority causing belief **:** CREDIBILITY **5 :** a source of honor ⟨he was a ~ to his family⟩ **6 a :** something that gains or adds to reputation or esteem **:** HONOR ⟨he took no ~ for his generous act⟩ ⟨it is to his ~ that he acknowledged his error⟩ **b :** RECOGNITION, ACKNOWLEDGMENT, ASCRIPTION ⟨he did not actually write the book, but he got ~ for it⟩ **c :** a printed or spoken acknowledgment of the authorship, source, or ownership of material used in a publication or in a play, motion picture, or radio or television program **d :** a recognition by name of a person contributing to a performance (as the author, director, or producer of a broadcast, telecast, or stage play) **e :** recognition by a school or college typically measured in credit hours that a student has fulfilled a requirement leading to a degree (as by completing a course) **syn** see BELIEF, INFLUENCE

²credit \"\ *vt* -ED/-ING/-S [partly fr. L *creditus* (past part. of *credere*); partly fr. ¹*credit*] **1 a :** to supply goods on credit to **b** *obs* **:** ENTRUST **2 :** to trust in the truth of **:** BELIEVE ⟨if we can ~ ancient reports⟩ **3** *archaic* **:** to bring credit or honor upon **4 :** to enter upon the credit side of an account **:** give credit for **:** place to the credit of — opposed to *debit* **5 :** to give credit to: as **a :** to consider usu. favorably as the source, author, motivating agent, or performer of an action or as possessor of a trait — usu. used with *with* ⟨Rivera, who is ~*ed* with introducing the spermaceti industry to the colonies —*Amer. Guide Series: R.I.*⟩ ⟨we are ~*ed* with hospitality, good nature, and high sexual morality —H.L.Carter⟩ **b :** to attribute (as an act or a trait) to some person — usu. used with *to* ⟨they ~ the invention to him⟩ **syn** see ASCRIBE

cred·it·abil·i·ty \ˌkredəd·əˈbiləd·ē, -edətə-, -lətē, -i\ *n* -ES **:** the quality or state of being worthy of belief or acceptance; *also* **:** a believable thing

cred·it·able \ˈkredəd·əbəl, -ətəbəl\ *adj* [partly fr. L *creditus* (past part. of *credere*) + E *-able;* partly fr. ²*credit* + *-able*] **1 :** worthy of belief **2 a :** sufficiently good to bring reputation or esteem **:** deserving of judicious praise **:** REPUTABLE ⟨a ~ performance⟩ **b :** SUITABLE, RESPECTABLE ⟨born of ~ parents⟩ **3 :** worthy of having commercial credit **4 :** capable of being credited or ascribed ⟨victory was directly ~ to his efforts⟩ ⟨5 years of ~ service toward a retirement eligibility⟩ — **cred·it·ably** \-blē, -li\ *adv*

cred·it·able·ness \-nəs\ *n* -ES **:** the quality of being creditable

credit card *n* **1 :** a small card (as one issued by hotels, restaurants, stores, or petroleum companies) authorizing the person or company named or its agent to charge goods or services **2 :** a record in a mercantile credit department of a credit customer's purchases and payments used to check credits on orders received from him

credit hour *n* **:** the unit of measuring educational credit usu. consisting of one weekly period lasting approximately one hour of classroom work or a given number of periods of laboratory work throughout one semester or term

credit instrument *n* **:** a document (as a check, letter of credit, or bond) other than paper money that evidences a debt

credit insurance *n* **:** insurance against excessive loss due to default of debtors

cred·it·less \ˈkredətləs\ *adj* **:** having no credit

credit life insurance *n* **:** insurance on the life of a debtor under an installment purchase contract relieving the debtor's estate of further payments in event of his death

credit line *n* **1 :** a line, note, or name that accompanies and acknowledges the source of an item (as a news dispatch, a published article, or a television program) **2 :** the amount fixed as the limit of the credit to be extended to a customer

credit man *n* **:** one who investigates the financial standing of an individual or a firm to determine what credit should be extended

credit manager *n* **:** one in charge of the credit department of a business organization; *also* **:** CREDIT MAN

credit memorandum *n* **:** a document issued by a seller as confirmation to a customer that a credit adjustment has been made to his account (as for merchandise returned or for errors)

credit money *or* **credit currency** *n* **:** money accepted because of the credit of the issuer rather than for its intrinsic commodity value

cred·i·tor \ˈkredəd·ə(r), -ətə-\ *n* -S [ME *creditour*, fr. MF *crediteur*, fr. L *creditor*, fr. *creditus* (past part. of *credere* to trust) + *-or*] **1 :** one who gives credit in business matters **:** one to whom money is due — opposed to *debtor* **2** *Roman law* **:** any person to whom a debt is owed, who has a civil cause of action for anything due him, or who has a right to enforce a duty owed to him under any obligation arising out of a contract, quasi contract, delict or quasi delict

creditor nation *n* **:** a nation whose investments abroad exceed in value the investments made in it by foreign countries — compare DEBTOR NATION

creditor's bill *n* **:** a bill in equity filed by one or more creditors, usu. in behalf of all who may become parties to the action, to collect or protect debts where an execution at law would not be available for the purpose

cred·i·tor·ship \-ə(r),ship\ *n* -S **:** the state or fact of being a creditor ⟨assets of ~⟩

credit rating *n* **:** an estimate of the amount of credit that can safely be extended to a person or company as determined usu. by a mercantile agency or a credit man on the basis of financial resources, ability to repay advances, and record in paying debts

credits *pl of* CREDIT, *pres 3d sing of* CREDIT

credit slip *n* **1 :** DEPOSIT SLIP **2 :** a slip issued as evidence of a credit given for the value of merchandise returned

credit union *n* **:** a cooperative association that makes small loans to its members at low interest rates

cred·ner·ite \ˈkrednə,rīt\ *n* -S [G *crednerit*, fr. K. F. Heinrich *Credner* †1876 Ger. geologist + G *-it* -ite] **:** a grayish to black foliated mineral $CuMn_2O_4$ consisting of copper, manganese, and oxygen

cre·do \ˈkrē(ˌ)dō, ˈkrā(-\ *n* -S [ME, fr. L, I believe, 1st pers. sing. pres. indic. of *credere*] **1** *often cap* **a :** a confession of faith said or sung in Christian liturgies **b :** a choral setting of the Apostles' Creed or the Nicene Creed **2 :** a strongly held or frequently affirmed belief or conviction; *esp* **:** a generality or system adopted as a guide to action or achievement **:** TENET, DOCTRINE ⟨an artist's ~⟩ ⟨a ~ of usefulness to society⟩

credo play *n, usu cap C* **:** a medieval play based on the Apostles' Creed acted at York, England, at Lammastide

cre·du·li·ty \krəˈd(y)üləd·ē, krēˈ-,kre'-, -ətē, -i *sometimes* -ˈjü-\ *n* -ES [ME *credulite*, fr. MF or L; MF *credulité*, fr. L *credulitat-, credulitas*, fr. *credulus* + *-itat-, -itas* -ity] **:** belief or readiness of belief esp. on slight or uncertain evidence **:** GULLIBILITY ⟨ready ~ in the face of repeated assertions is one of the curses of the modern world —Bertrand Russell⟩ ⟨to strain ~ to the breaking point —T.S.Eliot⟩

cred·u·lous \ˈkrejələs\ *adj* [L *credulus*, fr. *credere*] **1 :** ready or inclined to believe esp. on slight or uncertain evidence; easily imposed upon ⟨a boy very ~ of life —Sinclair Lewis⟩ **2 :** based upon or proceeding from credulity ⟨~ superstition⟩ — **cred·u·lous·ly** *adv* — **cred·u·lous·ness** *n* -ES

¹cree \ˈkrē\ *vt* **creed; creed; creeing; crees** [F *crever* to cause to burst — more at CRAVEN] *dial Eng* **:** to soften (grain) into a pulpy mass by boiling

²cree \"\ *n, pl* **cree** *or* **crees** *usu cap* [short for earlier *Christenaux, Christeno*, fr. CanF *Christianaux, Christino*, prob. fr. Ojibwa *Kenistenoag*] **1 a :** an Indian people ranging from James Bay in Ontario to the Saskatchewan river in Saskatchewan and south into Montana **b :** a member of such people **2 :** an Algonquian language of the Cree, Montagnais, and Naskapi peoples **3 :** a syllabic writing system used in writing Cree and other languages

¹creed \ˈkrēd\ *n* -S [ME *crede*, fr. OE *crēda*, fr. L *credo* (first word of the Apostles' and Nicene Creeds), 1st pers. sing. pres. indic. of *credere* to believe; akin to OIr *cretim* I believe, Av *zrazdā-* to believe, Skt *śrad-dadhāti* he believes, *śraddhā* belief, confidence; all fr. a prehistoric IE combination whose first constituent means "magic power" and is akin to OIr *cretar* holy relic and whose second constituent is the verb represented by Skt *dadhāti* he puts, places — more at DO] **1 :** a brief authoritative doctrinal formula beginning with such words as "Credo", "Credimus", "I believe", "We believe", intended to define what is held by a Christian congregation, synod, or church to be true and essential and exclude what is held to be false belief **2** *cap* **:** that portion of a Christian liturgy in which a profession of faith is corporately recited ⟨the sermon follows the ~⟩ **3 a :** a formulation or system of religious faith ⟨a religion of usage and sentiment rather than of ~ —John Buchan⟩; *esp* **:** one definitively stated (as for affirmation or confession) ⟨drew up a ~ whose acceptance was required of all believers⟩ **b :** a religion or religious sect ⟨men of all races and ~s⟩ **c :** a formulation or epitome of principles, rules, opinions, and precepts formally expressed and seriously adhered to and maintained **:** a notion or complex of notions viewed as so expressed or adhered to ⟨that general distrust of logic and dethroning of reason . . . formulated into a ~ by D. H. Lawrence —C.D.Lewis⟩ ⟨the devotion to work . . . became a ~ and the principal article of economic faith —W.P. Webb⟩ **syn** see RELIGION

²creed *vb* -ED/-S [L *credere* to believe] *obs* **:** BELIEVE

creed·al *also* **cre·dal** \ˈkrēdᵊl\ *adj* [*creedal* fr. ¹*creed* + *-al; credal* prob. fr. *credo* + *-al*] **:** of or relating to a creed

creed·al·ism \-ᵊl,izəm\ *n* -S **:** undue insistence upon traditional statements of belief

creed·ed \-dəd\ *adj* [¹*creed* + *-ed*] **:** having a creed

creed·ite \ˈkrē,dīt\ *n* -S [*Creede* quadrangle (U.S. Geol. Survey), southwest Colorado, its locality + E *-ite*] **:** a mineral $Ca_3Al_2F_4(OH, F)_6(SO_4).2H_2O$ consisting of hydrous calcium aluminum fluoride with calcium sulfate, occurring in white to colorless grains, and radiating crystalline masses (hardness 2, sp. gr. 2.7)

creed·less \ˈkrēdləs\ *adj* **:** not having a creed

creed·more \ˈkrēd,mō(ə)r\ *n* -S [fr. *Creedmoor*, a trademark] **:** a man's heavy blucher shoe with gusset and laces

creeds·man \ˈkrēdzmən\ *n, pl* **creedsmen :** one who follows a creed

¹creek \ˈkrēk, ˈkrik — ˈkrik *is less frequent in the South than in the rest of the US and less frequent in urban than in rural areas*\ *n* -S [ME *creke, crike*, fr. ON *-kriki* bend, concavity; akin to ON *krīkr* bend, bay, *krōkr* hook — more at CROOK] **1 a** *chiefly Brit* **:** a small inlet or bay narrower and extending farther into the land than a cove **:** a narrow recess in the shore of the sea, a river, or a lake ⟨each ~ and cavern of the dangerous shore —William Cowper⟩ — used in the U.S. only in names given during the earliest period of English colonization **b :** a saltwater estuary of a small river or stream emptying on a low coast or into the lower reaches of a wide river **2 :** a natural stream of water normally smaller than and often tributary to a river — compare BRANCH, BROOK, RUN **3** *archaic* **:** a narrow commonly winding strip of comparatively flat land between hills or mountains **4** *dial chiefly Brit* **:** a narrow or winding passage **:** a concealed or secret corner ⟨each ~ and cranny of his chamber —Thomas Gray⟩ — **up the creek** *adv* **:** in a difficult or perplexing position

²creek \ˈkrēk\ *n, pl* **creek** *or* **creeks** *usu cap* [prob. so called fr. the numerous streams in the territory of the Creek Confederacy] **1 a :** CREEK CONFEDERACY **b :** a member of any of the peoples of the Creek Confederacy **2 :** MUSKOGEE 2

creek broadbill *n* [¹*creek*] **:** LESSER SCAUP

creek chub *n* **:** a common chub (*Semotilus atromaculatus*) of small streams of eastern No. America

creek confederacy *n, usu cap both Cs* [²*creek*] **:** an American Indian confederacy organized around the Muskogee and including the Hitchiti, Alabama, and Koasati that dominated most of Georgia, Alabama, and northwestern Florida before their removal to Oklahoma

creek duck *n* [¹*creek*] **:** GADWALL

creek fern *n* [¹*creek*] **:** a stout New Zealand fern (*Lomaria fluviatilis*) with a large crown of numerous pinnate fronds

creekfish \ˈ=,=\ *n* **:** CHUB SUCKER

creek grass *n* **:** a No. American pondweed (*Potamogeton epihydrus*) with linear submerged and elliptical floating leaves

creek gum *n* **:** any of several Australian eucalypts (as *Eucalyptus gunnii* and *E. rostrata*)

creek nettle *n* **:** a tall nettle (*Urtica holosericea*) growing along streams on the Pacific coast of the U. S.

creek·ol·o·gy \krēˈkäləjē, kri'-\ *n* -ES [¹*creek* + *-o-* + *-logy*] **:** any method of searching for oil based on a limited knowledge of geology and practiced esp. by wildcat prospectors

creek sedge *n* **:** a salt-marsh grass (*Spartina alterniflora glabra*) common along the Atlantic coast of No. America

creekstuff \ˈ=,=\ *n* **:** a grass (*Spartina cynosuroides*) growing along creeks and in salt marshes

creek thatch *n* [¹*creek*] **:** any grass of the genus *Spartina*

¹creel \ˈkrēl, *esp before pause or consonant* -ēəl\ *n* -S [ME *crele, crelle, creille*, prob. fr. (assumed) MF *creille* small gridiron (OF & MF *greille*), fr. L *craticula*, dim. of *cratis* wickerwork — more at HURDLE] **1 :** a wickerwork receptacle: as **a :** a basket for carrying fish or peat on the back **b :** an angler's basket **c :** a trap for fish or lobsters **2** *dial Eng* **:** a framework of varying form (as a rack for plates or a frame on which to slaughter pigs or shear sheep) **3** *textile manuf* **:** a bar or set of bars with skewers for holding paying-off bobbins (as in the roving machine or mule); *also* **:** any frame for holding the bobbins or spools — **in a creel** *adv, Scot* **:** in a state of temporary confusion

creel 1b

²creel \"\ *vt* -ED/-ING/-S **1 :** to put (fish) in a creel **:** CATCH, TAKE ⟨the number of trout ~*ed* per angler⟩ **2 :** to set up the creel on (a textile machine)

creel census *n* **:** the collection of data concerning the number of fish caught by sport fishermen (as on a particular stream or in a particular area) used esp. in determining effects of stocking and in planning future limits for various species

creel·er \ˈkrēl(ə)r\ *n* -S [¹*creel* + *-er*] **:** a textile worker who replaces empty spools in the creel of a warping machine

creeling *n* -S [¹*creel* + *-ing* (n. suffix)] *Scot* **:** a hazing ceremony in which a newly married man is made to carry a creel of stones until released by his wife

creem \ˈkrēm\ *vt* -ED/-ING/-S [perh. irreg. fr. OE *crimman* to cram; akin to OHG *krimman* to scratch, press, OE *crammian* to cram — more at CRAM] *dial Eng* **:** to squeeze or hug (as in wrestling) **:** CRUSH, MASH

¹creep \ˈkrēp\ *vb* **crept** \-krept\ **crept; creeping; creeps** [ME *crepen*, fr. OE *crēopan;* akin to ON *krjūpa* to creep, MLG *kruppen* to bend, Lith *grubinėti* to stumble, Gk *grypos* bent — more at CRADLE] *vi* **1 :** to move along with the body prone and close to or touching the ground **:** move slowly on all fours **:** CRAWL ⟨watched the foxes ~ into their den⟩ **2 a :** to go very slowly ⟨the hours *crept* by⟩ ⟨~*ing* like snail, unwillingly to school —Shak.⟩ **:** to go timidly or cautiously or so as to escape notice or attention ⟨~ away into retirement⟩ **b :** to go or enter stealthily and secretly **:** STEAL ⟨~ and intrude into the fold —John Milton⟩ **:** to advance or enter unnoticed little by little **:** insinuate itself or oneself ⟨age ~*s* upon us⟩ ⟨a note of irritation had *crept* into his voice⟩ **c :** to move or behave with servility or exaggerated humility **:** CRINGE ⟨you'll come ~*ing* back when your money is gone⟩ **3 a** *of a liquid* **:** to spread slowly and steadily over a surface **b** *of sand or loose soil* **:** to shift or advance slowly ⟨sand dunes ~*ing* inland year by year⟩ **c** *of a plant* **:** to spread or grow over the ground or other surface by rooting at intervals or clinging with tendrils, stems, or aerial roots **4 a :** to move or stir slightly by swelling or shrinking (as the skin of the body) ⟨the thought makes my flesh ~⟩ **b :** to slip, slide, or gradually shift position (as a belt on a pulley, a bearing on an axle, a steel rail on a supporting surface) because of strain or vibration **c** *of a film of paint or emulsion* **:** to slide or sag on drying **d :** to change shape permanently from prolonged stress or exposure to high temperatures or both (as turbine blades or flooring material) **5** *Brit* **:** to drag in deep water with creepers (as to recover a cable) — used with *for* **6 a :** to slip or become slightly displaced **b** *of railroad rails* **:** to shift longitudinally **7 :** to rise above the surface of a solution upon the walls of a vessel ⟨salt crystals ~ in a voltaic cell⟩ **8** *of an arrow* **:** to edge forward just before release **9 a** *of a belt* **:** to slip or slide backwards on a pulley by reason of the extension or contraction of the belt as the tension is changed in passing from the tight side to the slack side or vice versa **b** *of metal* **:** to undergo creep ~ *vt, archaic* **:** to creep along or over

²creep \"\ *n* -S **1 :** the act of creeping **:** a movement of or like creeping **:** a very slow pace ⟨traffic moving at a ~⟩ ⟨the ~ of the centuries⟩ **2 a :** a tightening of the skin of the body caused by horror, disgust, or fear esp. of the strange or supernatural **:** SHIVER, SHUDDER — usu. used in pl. ⟨snakes give me the cold ~*s*⟩ **b :** a strong sensation (as of unease, revulsion, or fear) induced in a person by some other person or thing — usu. used in pl. ⟨he's crazy . . . he gives me the ~*s* —Carson McCullers⟩ **3 :** a pen or other enclosure so fenced that young animals can enter while adults are excluded and used esp. to supply special or supplementary feed **4 :** GRAPNEL, DRAG, CREEPER **5 a :** a slow longitudinal movement of the rails of a track under traffic **b :** gradual retrograde movement (as of a belt on a pulley or a tire on a wheel) **c :** the drawing together of the edges of two metal parts as a result of expansion from the heat due to welding; *also* **:** the amount the edges are drawn together **d :** the play or slack in the trigger mechanism of a firearm before it releases the hammer or firing pin **6 :** a gradual usu. downhill movement (as of loose rock, soil, sand, or shale) that is due mainly to gravity together with freezing and thawing or wetting and drying **7 a :** a slow rising of the floor of a mining gallery occasioned by the pressure of incumbent strata upon the pillars or sides; a gradual movement of mining ground **b :** a slight sometimes audible movement of rock along a fault without producing a perceptible earthquake **8 :** the slow change of dimensions of an object (as of wood, rubber, plastics) due to prolonged exposure to high temperature or stress: as **a :** deformation of a concrete structure or a casting under sustained stress **b :** progressive plastic flow of a metal under constant or nearly constant stress — usu. used of slow deformation of hot metal under a long-sustained load of magnitude less than would deform it in a brief time **9 creeps** *pl* **:** a deficiency disease esp. of sheep and cattle associated with abnormal calcium-phosphorus ratio in the diet and characterized by progressive anemia, painful softening of the bones, and a stiff slow gait **10** *slang* **a :** a sneak thief that works in or in connivance with a cheap hotel or flophouse ⟨he was rolled by a ~⟩; *also* **:** a stealthy snooper (as for facts useful for blackmail) **b :** an unpleasant, unattractive, obnoxious, or insignificant person **11 :** RELAXATION 6

creep·age \ˈkrēpij\ *n* -S **:** gradual movement **:** CREEP: as **a :** leakage of electricity over a surface of a dielectric **b :** the creeping of an electrolyte up the sides and parts of a cell **c :** the slow spreading or movement of a substance (as oil along a shaft or rust over a surface)

creep·er \-pə(r)\ *n* -S [ME *crepere*, fr. OE *crēopere*, fr. *crēopan* to creep + *-ere* -er — more at CREEP] **1 :** one that creeps; *esp* **:** an animal (as an insect or reptile) having a creeping gait or locomotion **2 a** *archaic* **:** a servile opportunist **b** *obs* **:** a reporter of odd bits for newspapers **:** a free-lance hack writer **3 :** any plant that creeps: as **a :** HEDGE BINDWEED **b :** WILD CUCUMBER **c :** TRUMPET CREEPER **d :** VIRGINIA CREEPER **4 :** any of various rather small birds that creep or clamber over trees and bushes searching for insects: as **a :** any member of the family Certhiidae **b :** any of several American warblers — see HONEYCREEPER, TREE CREEPER, WALL CREEPER **5 :** any of various tools or implements designed to assist a man, animal, or machine to advance or climb: as **a :** a fixture with iron points worn on the shoe to prevent slipping (as on ice) — usu. used in pl. **b :** CLIMBING IRON — usu. used in pl. **c :** CLIMBER 2b **6 :** GRAPNEL **7 :** a device for supplying or moving material in a steady flow: as **a :** an endless belt or chain conveyor **b :** a spiral or screw conveyor (as for grain) **8 creepers** *pl* **:** CROCKETS **9 a :** a genetic anomaly of the domestic fowl marked by shortening and thickening of the long bones in the heterozygote and completely lethal when homozygous — compare ACHONDROPLASIA **b** *or* **creeper fowl :** an individual exhibiting this anomaly **10 :** a garment similar to a romper and suitable for wear by children while creeping — usu. used in pl.; compare CRAWLER **11 :** a small frame or platform mounted on casters, used for supporting the knees when scrubbing floors or the body when working under an automobile **12** *cricket* **:** a bowled ball that rolls along the ground after pitching

creeper 5a

creep·ered \-ə(r)d\ *adj* **:** overgrown with creeping plants

creeper lane *n* **:** an extra lane provided on an uphill grade for the use of slow-moving vehicles on a superhighway

creep·er·less \-ə(r)ləs\ *adj* **:** having no creeper **:** being without a creeper

creeper title *or* **creeping title** *n* **:** a long title on a movie or television screen that moves continuously into view from below while it is being read

creep–feed \ˈ=,=\ *vt* **:** to feed (young animals) in a creep

creep feeder *n* **:** CREEP 3

creephole \ˈ=,=\ *n* **1 :** a retreat through or into which an animal creeps (as to escape notice) **2 :** SUBTERFUGE, EXCUSE

creep·ie \ˈkrēpē\ *n* -S [¹*creep* + *-ie*] *dial Brit* **:** a low three-legged stool **:** CUTTY STOOL

creepier *comparative of* CREEPY

creepiest *superlative of* CREEPY

creep·i·ly \ˈkrēpəlē, -li\ *adv* **:** in a creepy manner ⟨footsteps sounding ~ in a lonely house⟩

creep·i·ness \ˈkrēpēnəs, -pin-\ *n* -ES **:** the quality or state of being creepy **:** EERINESS

¹creeping *n* -S [ME *crepinge*, gerund of *crepen* to creep] **1 a :** the action of one that creeps **b :** an instance of such action **2 :** a running together of the lines in a photoengraving causing a distorted image

²creeping *adj* [ME *crepinge*, pres. part. of *crepen* to creep] *of a plant* **:** tending to spread over the ground or other substrate: as **a :** PROSTRATE, PROCUMBENT, TRAILING **b :** spreading by rhizomes or stolons

creeping barrage *n* **:** ROLLING BARRAGE

creeping bellflower *n* **:** an erect European herb (*Campanula rapunculoides*) with creeping rootstocks

creeping bent *also* **creeping bentgrass** *n* **:** a common pasture or lawn grass (*Agrostis palustris*) that spreads by long stolons

creeping bur *n* **1 :** BUR CLOVER **2 :** GROUND PINE 2

creeping buttercup *n* **:** CREEPING CROWFOOT

creeping char·lie \-ˈchärlē\ *n, cap 2d C* **1 :** a stonecrop (*Sedum acre*) **2 :** MALLOW **3 :** MONEYWORT **4 :** GROUND IVY

creeping crowfoot *n* **:** a perennial European crowfoot (*Ranunculus repens*) with long creeping stolons

creeping cucumber *n* **:** a small herbaceous vine (*Melothria pendula*) bearing oblong green fruits

creeping devil cactus *n* **:** a prostrate much-branched very spiny cylindrical cactus (*Machaerocereus eruca*)

creeping disk *n, zool* **:** the smooth adhesive lower surface of the foot or sometimes of the entire body of mollusks and some other invertebrates on which they creep along

creeping eruption *n* **:** a human skin disorder that is characterized by a red line of eruption which fades at one end as it progresses at the other and that is usu. caused by insect or worm larvae and esp. those of the dog hookworm burrowing in the subdermal tissue

creeping fern *n* **:** CLIMBING FERN

creeping fescue *n* **:** RED FESCUE

creeping fig *n* **:** a prostrate or climbing Asiatic fig (*Ficus pumila*) commonly cultivated in greenhouses

creeping forget-me-not *n* **:** a low perennial European herb (*Omphalodes verna*) of the family Boraginaceae

creeping greenhead *n* **:** CLUSTERED BLUET

creeping hemlock *n* **:** GROUND HEMLOCK

creeping indigo *n* **:** a suberect or prostrate herb (*Indigofera endecaphylla*) that is woody at the base and has red flowers in dense axillary racemes

creeping jen·nie \-ˈjenē\ *n, usu cap J* **1 :** MONEYWORT **2 :** WILD CUCUMBER c **3 :** GROUND PINE **4 :** FIELD BINDWEED
creeping juniper *n* **1 :** SAVIN 1 **2 :** an American juniper (*Juniperus horizontalis*) with prostrate or procumbent rooting stems
creeping lawyer *n* **:** a small half-buried prickly New Zealand blackberry (*Rubus parvus*) with large juicy fruit
creeping loosestrife *n* **:** MONEYWORT
creep·ing·ly *adv* **:** in a creeping manner
creeping oxeye *n* **:** a West Indian maritime semiprostrate herb (*Wedelia triobata*) of the family Compositae with bright yellow flowers
creeping paralysis *or* **creeping palsy** *n* **1 :** a disease (as locomotor ataxia) characterized by gradual and spreading loss of muscular function **2 :** any gradual loss of effectiveness or vigor ⟨a *creeping paralysis* in a nation's intellectual life⟩
creeping phlox *n* **:** a perennial phlox (*Phlox stolonifera*) with long creeping leafy runners
creeping pine *n* **1** *in Europe* **:** MUGHO PINE **2** *West* **:** WHITE-BARK PINE
creeping sailor *n* **1 :** STRAWBERRY GERANIUM **2 :** a stonecrop (*Sedum acre*)
creeping sal·ly \-ˈsalē\ *n, usu cap S* **:** MONEYWORT
creeping snowberry *n* **:** an American prostrate woody vine (*Gaultheria hispidula*) with white berries
creeping sow thistle *n* **:** PERENNIAL EUROPEAN SOW THISTLE
creeping spear grass *n* **:** WIRE GRASS a
creeping spike rush *n* **:** a cylindrical-stemmed sedge (*Eleocharis palustris*)
creeping strawberry *n* **:** DEWDROP 2
creeping thistle *n* **:** CANADA THISTLE
creeping thyme *n* **:** WILD THYME
creeping wheat grass *n* **:** COUCH GRASS 1 a
creeping willow *n* **:** a small Eurasian trailing or straggling bush (*Salix repens*) of which several varieties are cultivated
creeping wintergreen *n* **:** any prostrate plant of the genus *Gaultheria* (esp. *G. procumbens* in eastern No. America and *G. humifusa* in the Rocky mountains)
creeping zinnia *n* **:** a low branching leafy annual (*Sanvitalia procumbens*) with heads of flowers resembling zinnias
creep joint *n* **1 :** a gambling establishment that changes its location each night **2 :** a brothel in which a patron's clothes are rifled **3 :** any place of unsavory reputation (as one frequented by homosexuals)
creepmouse \ˈ=,=\ *n* **:** a creeping mouse; *also* **:** a motion or tickling suggestive of a creepmouse
cree potato *or* **cree turnip** *n, usu cap C* **:** BREADROOT
creeps *pres 3d sing of* CREEP, *pl of* CREEP
creepy \ˈkrēpē, -pi\ *adj* -ER/-EST **1 :** marked by creeping or slow motion ⟨man had to pass through a ~, slimy, slithery, finny, furry past —Waldemar Kaempffert⟩ **2 :** having or producing a sensation as if insects are creeping on the skin **:** inducing a nervous, shivering apprehension **:** CRAWLY, EERIE ⟨~ dark things crawled over them —C.E.W.Bean⟩ **3 :** causing horror esp. by suggestion ⟨a ~ tale⟩ **:** UNNATURAL, WEIRD, UNCANNY ⟨there is something ~ about him⟩
crees *pres 3d sing of* CREE, *pl of* CREE
creese *var of* KRIS
creesh \ˈkrēsh\ *n* -ES [ME *cresche*, fr. MF *creisse, cresse, craisse*, fr. (assumed) VL *crassia* — more at GREASE] *chiefly Scot* **:** GREASE
creesh·ie *or* **creeshy** \-shi\ *adj, chiefly Scot* **:** GREASY
cree·tur \ˈkrēd·ə(r)\ *dial var of* CREATURE
creish \ˈkrēsh, ˈkrāsh\ *var of* CREESH
cré·mant \krāmäⁿ, ˈkremənt\ *adj* [F, fr. pres. part. of *crémer* to become covered with cream or foam, fr. MF *cremer*, fr. *creme, cresme* cream — more at CREAM] *of wine* **:** mildly sparkling **:** CRACKLING — see PÉTILLANT
cre·mas·ter \krəˈmastə(r), krēˈ-\ *n* -S [NL, fr. Gk *kremastēr*, fr. *kremannynai* to hang; prob. akin to Lith *karti* to hang with a rope] **1 :** a thin muscle consisting of loops of fibers derived from the internal oblique muscle and descending upon the spermatic cord to surround and suspend the testicle **2 :** a usu. hooked process of the posterior end of the lepidopterous pupa that serves to suspend the pupa — **crem·as·te·ri·al** \¦kreməˈstirēəl\ *adj* — **crem·as·ter·ic** \-ˈsterik\ *adj or n*
cre·mate \ˈkrē,māt *also* krēˈ- *or* krəˈ-; *usu* -ād·+V\ *vt* -ED/-ING/-S [L *crematus*, past part. of *cremare* — more at HEARTH] **:** to reduce (a dead body) to ashes by the action of fire either directly or in an oven or retort ⟨ritual pits whose contents included charcoal and *cremated* human bones —*Notes & Queries*⟩
cre·ma·tion \krēˈmāshən, krəˈ-\ *n* -S [L *cremation-, crematio*, fr. *crematus* + *-ion-, -io* -ion] **1 :** the act or practice of cremating the dead **2 :** the destruction of records or documents (as expired bonds or coupons) by fire ⟨watch the ~ of a batch of canceled securities —*New Yorker*⟩
cre·ma·tion·ism \-,nizəm\ *n* -S **:** the advocacy or practice of cremation
cre·ma·tion·ist \-,nəst\ *n* -S **:** one advocating or practicing cremation
cre·ma·tor \ˈkrē,mād·ə(r), -ātə-; krēˈ-, krəˈ-\ *n* -S [LL, fr. L *crematus* + *-or*] **1 :** one that cremates corpses **2 :** CREMATORY
cre·ma·to·ri·um \,krēməˈtōrēəm, ,krem-, -tȯr-\ *n, pl* **crema·to·ria** \-rēə\ *or* **crematoriums** [NL] **:** CREMATORY
¹**cre·ma·to·ry** \ˈ==,=rē, -ri\ *n* -ES [NL *crematorium*, fr. L *crematus* + *-orium* -ory] **1 a :** a furnace for cremating the bodies of the dead **b :** a building containing such a furnace **2 :** INCINERATOR
²**crematory** \ˈ"\ *adj* [*cremate* + *-ory* (adj. suffix)] **:** of or relating to cremation
crème \ˈkrem, ˈkrām, ˈkrēm\ *n, pl* **crèmes** \-m(z)\ [F, fr. OF *cresme* — more at CREAM] **1 :** cream or cream sauce as used in cookery **2 :** a sweet liqueur — usu. used with the flavor specified **3 :** CREAM 2 b
crème d'a·na·nas \¦kremˌdȧnäˈnä, ¦krām-, ¦krēm-, -nəˈ-\ *n, pl* **crèmes d'ananas** [F, lit., cream of pineapples] **:** a liqueur flavored with pineapple
crème de ba·nanes \¦=dəbäˈnän, -bəˈ-\ *n, pl* **crèmes de bananes** [F, lit., cream of bananas] **:** a liqueur flavored with bananas
crème de ca·cao \¦kremdəˈkō(,)kō; ¦kremdə,kākäˈō, ¦krām-, -kəˈō\ *n, pl* **crèmes de cacao** [F, lit., cream of cacao] **:** a relatively sweet liqueur flavored with cacao beans and vanilla used as an after-dinner cordial and as a cocktail ingredient esp. in an Alexander or pousse-café
crème de café \-dəkäˈfā, -kəˈfā\ *n, pl* **crèmes de café** [F, lit., cream of coffee] **:** a coffee-flavored liqueur
crème de cas·sis \-dəkäˈsē(s), -kəˈ-\ *n, pl* **crèmes de cassis** [F, lit., cream of black currants] **:** a black-currant liqueur
crème de la crème \¦kremdəlä¦krem, -ləˈ-; ¦krām . . . ¦krām\ *n* [F, lit., cream of the cream] **:** the very best **:** the highest elite ⟨these dinings and winings, mostly among the *crème de la crème* of the literati —E.F.Payne⟩
crème de menthe \¦kremdəˈmenth, -mint; ¦kremdəˈmäⁿt, ¦krām-\ *n, pl* **crèmes de menthe** [F, lit., cream of mint] **:** a relatively sweet green or white liqueur flavored with various mints, principally peppermint
crème de mo·ka \¦kremdəmōˈkä, ¦krām-; ¦kremdə¦mōkä\ *n, pl* **crèmes de moka** [F, lit., cream of mocha] **:** a liqueur flavored with coffee essence and other aromatic substances
crème de no·yau \¦kremdə,nwäˈyō, ¦krām-; ¦kremdən¦wīˈō\ *n, pl* **crèmes de noyau** [F, lit., cream of kernel] **:** a liqueur with a brandy base flavored primarily with essential oils derived from the kernels of peaches, plums, and cherries or from almonds, the predominant flavor being that of bitter almonds
crème de vio·lette \¦kremdə¦vyōˈlet, ¦krām-; ¦kremdəˈvī(ə)lət\ *n, pl* **crèmes de violette** [F, lit., cream of violet] **:** a sweet violet-flavored liqueur — compare CREME YVETTE
cré·me·rie \ˈkrem(ə)(,)rē; ˈkrem-, ˈkrām-, ,=(=)ˈ=\ *n* -S [F, fr. *crème* cream + *-erie* -ery] **:** a small shop for dairy products **:** DAIRY LUNCH
Crème Yvette \,kremēˈvet, -rām-, -rēm-\ *trademark* — used for a bluish violet-flavored liqueur
cremnitz white *usu cap C, var of* KREMNITZ WHITE
crem·o·carp \ˈkremə,kärp, -rēm-\ *n* -S [ISV *cremo-* (fr. Gk *kremannynai* to hang) + *-carp*; prob. orig. formed as F *crémocarpe*] **:** a dry dehiscent fruit characteristic of plants of the family Umbelliferae that consists of two indehiscent one-seeded mericarps which split apart at maturity and remain pendent from the summit of the carpophore

cremona *var of* CROMORNA
cre·mone bolt \krəˈmōn-, krāˈ-\ *n* [F *crémone*, prob. fr. *Crémone* (Cremona), city in northern Italy] **:** a fastening used on double doors and casement windows that has vertical rods moved up and down so that the ends of the bolts engage the top and bottom of the frame

cremone bolt

cre·morne bolt \-ˈmȯ(ə)rn-\ *n* [*cremorne* modif. of F *crémone*] **:** CREMONE BOLT
crems white *usu cap C, var of* KREMS WHITE
cren- *or* **creno-** *comb form* [Gk *krēn-, krēno-*, fr. *krēnē* spring; perh. akin to OE *hærn, hræn* sea, ON *hrǫnn* wave] **1 :** spring **:** mineral spring ⟨*crenic*⟩ ⟨*crenotherapy*⟩ **2 :** crenic acid ⟨*crenite*⟩
cre·na \ˈkrēnə, -renə\ *n, pl* **cre·nae** \-(,)nē, -,nī\ [ML, fr. *crenare* to split] **:** NOTCH, INDENTATION, CLEFT, SCALLOP
cre·nate \ˈkrē,nāt, -re,-, -,nət\ *adj* [NL *crenatus*, fr. ML, past part. of *crenare* to split — more at CRENEL] **:** having the margin cut into rounded scallops — used esp. in botany of foliar structures ⟨a bi*crenate* leaf⟩ and in physiology of shrunken red blood corpuscles; see CRENATION — **cre·nate·ly** *adv*
cre·nat·ed \-,nād·əd\ *adj* [NL *crenatus* + E *-ed*] **:** CRENATE
cre·na·tion \krēˈnāshən, -reˈ-, -rəˈ-\ *n* -S [*crenate* + *-ion*] **1 a :** one of a series of rounded projections forming an edge (as of a leaf or a coin) **b :** the quality or state of being crenate **2 :** shrinkage or the shrunken condition of red blood cells exposed to hypertonic solutions in which the cell margins become crenate
cren·a·ture \ˈkrenəchə(r), -rēn-\ *n* -S [*crenate* + *-ure*] **:** CRENATION; *also* **:** a notch or indentation (as between crenations)
¹**cren·el** \ˈkrenᵊl\ *also* **cre·nelle** \krəˈnel\ *n* -S [MF *crenel*, fr. OF, dim. of *cren* notch, fr. *crener* to notch, fr. ML *crenare*, fr. (assumed) VL *crinare* to split, perh. of Celt origin; akin to OIr *criathar* sieve; akin to Gk *krinein* to separate — more at CERTAIN] **:** one of the embrasures alternating with merlons in a battlement — see BATTLEMENT illustration
²**crenel** \ˈ"\ *vt* **creneled** *or* **crenelled**; **creneled** *or* **crenelled**; **creneling** *or* **crenelling** \ˈkren(ᵊ)liŋ\ **crenels** [F *créneler*, fr. OF *creneler*, fr. *crenel*] **:** CRENELLATE
cré·ne·lé *or* **cre·nel·lé** *also* **cre·ne·lee** \¦krānᵊl¦ā, -ren-\ *adj* [MF *crenelé*, fr. past part. of *creneler* to crenellate] *heraldry* **:** having the upper edge crenellated **:** EMBATTLED
cren·el·et \ˈkrenᵊlət, -ᵊl,et\ *n* -S [¹*crenel* + *-et*] **:** a small crenel or an imitation of one (as in a design)
¹**cren·el·late** *also* **cren·el·ate** \ˈkrenᵊl,āt, *usu* -ād·+V\ *vt* -ED/-ING/-S [¹*crenel* + *-ate* (vb. suffix)] **:** to furnish (as a wall or a manor house) with battlements **:** CASTELLATE
²**crenellate** *or* **crenelate** \ˈ", -lət\ *adj* [¹*crenel* + *-ate* (adj. suffix)] **:** CRENELLATED
cren·el·lat·ed *or* **cren·el·at·ed** \ˈkrenᵊl,ād·əd\ *adj* [fr. past part. of *crenellate*] **1 :** having battlements **:** CASTELLATED **2 :** embattled or having repeated indentations like those in a battlement ⟨a ~ pattern⟩ **3** *bot* **:** minutely crenate **4 :** having crenations; *esp, of a coin* **:** having crenations on the edge of the hole made by cutting out the center
crenellated molding *n* **:** a molding of embattled or indented pattern common in medieval buildings
cren·el·la·tion *or* **cren·el·a·tion** \,krenᵊlˈāshən\ *n* -S **1 :** the act of crenellating **2 :** BATTLEMENT **3 :** CRENEL

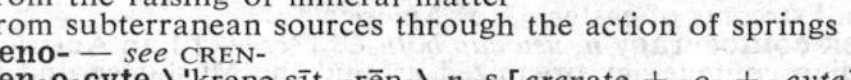
crenellated molding

cre·nit·ic \krəˈnid·ik\ *adj* [*cren-* + *-ite* + *-ic*] **:** relating to or resulting from the raising of mineral matter from subterranean sources through the action of springs
creno- — *see* CREN-
cren·o·cyte \ˈkrenə,sīt, -rēn-\ *n* -S [*crenate* + *-o-* + *-cyte*] **:** a red blood cell with notched serrated edges (as that resulting from crenation)
cren·o·thrix \-,thriks\ *n, cap* [NL, fr. *cren-* + *-thrix*] **:** a genus (the type of the family Crenotrichaceae) usu. regarded as including a single species (*C. polypora*) of attached sheathed unbranched chlamydobacteria that are a frequent nuisance in water pipes and iron-containing springs and that have cylindrical or spherical cells which divide in three planes to form nonmotile spherical conidia
cren·u·la \ˈkrenyələ, -nᵊlə\ *n, pl* **crenu·lae** \-nyə,lē, -nᵊl,ē, -nyə,lī\ [NL, dim. of ML *crena*] **:** CRENULATION
cren·u·late \-nyələt, -nᵊlət, -nyə,lāt, -nᵊl,āt\ *adj* [NL *crenulatus*, fr. *crenula* + L *-atus* -ate] **:** minutely crenate ⟨~ leaf edge⟩ ⟨a ~ shoreline⟩
cren·u·lat·ed \-nyə,lād·əd, -nᵊl,ā-\ *adj* [*crenulate* + *-ed*] **:** minutely crenate
cren·u·la·tion \,krenyəˈlāshən, -nᵊlˈā-\ *n* -S [*crenulate* + *-ion*] **1 :** a minute crenation **2 :** the state of being minutely crenate
creo- — see CRE-
¹**cre·o·dont** \ˈkrēə,dänt\ *adj* [NL *Creodonta*] **:** of or relating to the Creodonta
²**creodont** \ˈ"\ *n* -S [NL *Creodonta*] **:** any mammal of the suborder Creodonta
cre·o·don·ta \,krēəˈdäntə\ *n pl, cap* [NL, fr. *cre-* + *-odonta*] **:** a suborder of extinct primitive mammals (order Carnivora) showing relationship to the early ungulates and known from fossil remains in Eocene and Oligocene formations — compare HYAENODON
¹**cre·ole** \ˈkrē,ōl\ *n* -S [F *créole*, fr. Sp *criollo*, fr. Pg *crioulo* slave born in his master's house, Negro born in the colonies, white person born in the colonies, prob. dim. of *cria* slave brought up in his master's house, fr. *criar* to bring up, fr. L *creare* to create, beget — more at CRESCENT] **1** *usu cap* **:** one of native birth but of European descent — used in the West Indies, in Spanish America, and formerly in French settlements of No. America **2** *usu cap* **:** a white person descended from early French or sometimes Spanish settlers of the southern U.S. esp. in the Gulf states and preserving a characteristic form of French speech and culture **3** *usu cap* **a :** a person of mixed French and Negro or Spanish and Negro descent speaking a dialect of French or Spanish — used esp. in Mississippi, Alabama, and Florida **b** *Alaska* **:** a person of mixed Russian and Eskimo or Indian descent **4** *usu cap* **:** any of several creolized languages: as **a :** the creolized French spoken by many Negroes in southern Louisiana **b :** the creolized French spoken by the great majority of the inhabitants of Haiti — called also *Haitian Creole* **5** *or* **creolefish :** a serranoid market fish (*Paranthias furcifer*) from tropical America **syn** see DIALECT
²**creole** \ˈ"\ *adj* **1** *usu cap* **:** being a Creole **:** of or belonging to the Creole group or culture ⟨~ landowners⟩ **2** *sometimes cap, in Louisiana & the West Indies* **:** of native origin or production or of the local variety ⟨~ cattle⟩ ⟨~ vegetables⟩ **3** *often cap* **:** being or having the characteristics of a creolized language ⟨a ~ dialect⟩ ⟨the ~ French of Saint Lucia⟩ **4** *sometimes cap* **:** of, belonging to, or characteristic of native-born people of European (as Spanish) descent resident esp. in Spanish America ⟨a ~ culture neither Indian nor Iberian —G.M. Foster⟩ **5** *of food* **:** prepared in a style characterized by the use of rice, okra, tomatoes, peppers, and high seasonings ⟨~ sauce⟩ ⟨lobster ~⟩
creole lily *n, usu cap C* **:** an Easter lily that has rather short foliage giving it a columnar habit, that has flowers shorter than those of the Croft lily, and that is much used for forcing
cre·o·lite \ˈkrēə,līt\ *n* -S [perh. fr. ¹*creole* + *-ite*] **:** a jasper with red and white bands found in California
cre·ol·i·za·tion \,krēələˈzāshən, -ē(,)ōl-\ *n* -S **:** the act or process of creolizing
cre·ol·ize \ˈkrēə,līz, -ēō,-\ *vt* -ED/-ING/-S **1 :** to make Creole **:** cause to adopt Creole qualities or customs ⟨*creolized* immigrants⟩ **2 :** to cause to become a creolized language ⟨pidgin which has existed over several centuries without becoming *creolized* —C.F.Hockett⟩
creolized language *also* **creole language** *n* **:** a language resulting from the acquisition by a subordinate group of the language of a dominant group, with phonological changes, simplification of grammar, and an admixture of the subordinate group's vocabulary, and serving as the mother tongue of its speakers, not solely for communication between people of different languages — compare PIDGIN

cre·oph·a·gous \(ˈ)krē¦äfəgəs\ *adj* [Gk *kreophagos*, fr. *kre-* cre- + *-phagos* -phagous] **:** CARNIVOROUS
cre·oph·a·gy \-ˈ=fəjē\ *n* -ES [Gk *kreophagia*, fr. *kre-* cre- + *-phagia* -phagy] **:** the use of flesh as food
cre·o·sol *also* **cre·a·sol** \ˈkrēə,sōl, -,sȯl\ *n* -S [ISV *creosote* + *-ol*; prob. orig. formed as G *kreosol*] **:** a colorless aromatic phenol $CH_3O(CH_3)C_6H_3OH$ obtained from beechwood tar and guaiacum resin; 2-methoxy-*para*-cresol
cre·o·so·tate \ˈkrēə,sōd·,āt, -ə,sō,tāt, -əsə,tāt\ *n* -S [*creosote* + *-ate*] **:** a mixture or compound with creosote
¹**cre·o·sote** \ˈkrēə,sōt, *usu* -ōd·+V\ *n* -S [G *kreosot*, fr. *kre-* cre- + Gk *sōtēr* preserver, fr. *sōzein* to preserve; akin to L *tumēre* to swell — more at THUMB] **1** *also* **creasote** \ˈ"\ **:** a colorless or yellowish oily liquid that has a burning smoky taste, contains a mixture of phenolic compounds (as guaiacol), is obtained by the distillation of wood tar, esp. that of beechwood, and is used chiefly as an expectorant in chronic bronchitis and as a collector and frother in ore flotation — called also *wood creosote* **2 :** CREOSOTE OIL 2
²**creosote** \ˈ"\ *vt* -ED/-ING/-S **:** to impregnate (wood) with creosote oil
creosote bush *n* [so called fr. the odor of its foliage] **:** a desert shrub (*Larrea tridentata*) of the southwestern U.S. and adjacent Mexico having persistent resinous aromatic foliage and small bright-yellow flowers — see SONORA GUM
creosote carbonate *n* **:** a yellow oily liquid consisting of a mixture of the carbonates of the constituents of creosote used esp. as an expectorant in chronic bronchitis
creosote oil *n* **1 :** the part of the wood-tar distillate from which creosote is obtained by refining **2 :** a yellowish to dark-colored heavy oil that consists chiefly of liquid and solid aromatic hydrocarbons, tar acids, and tar bases, is obtained by distillation of coal tar, and is used as a preservative for wood, as an insecticide, and in ore flotation — called also *coal-tar creosote*
cre·o·sot·ic \¦krēə¦säd·ik, -sōd-\ *adj* **:** of or relating to creosote
crep·ance \ˈkrepən(t)s, -rēp-\ *n* -S [modif. of It *crepaccio*, aug. of *crepa* crack, fr. *crepare* to crack, burst, fr. L, to crack, creak, break — more at CRAVEN] **:** an injury to a horse's leg caused by interference
¹**crepe** *or* **crêpe** \ˈkrāp; *in sense 3 also* -rep\ *n* -S [F *crêpe* — more at CRAPE] **1 :** a lightweight fabric of various fibers (as silk or cotton) with a crinkled surface obtained by using hard-twisted yarns, by printing with caustic soda, by weaving with varied tensions, or by embossing **2 :** CRAPE 3 **3 :** a small very thin pancake **4 :** CREPE RUBBER
²**crepe** *or* **crêpe** \ˈkrāp\ *vt* -ED/-ING/-S **:** to make (as paper) crinkly like crepe **:** CRINKLE
³**crepe** \ˈ"\ *adj* **1 :** of highly twisted yarns used for dullness and durability in hosiery and for crinkled effects in woven fabrics **2 :** of fancy weaves producing a pebbly or rough grainy surface on fabrics **3 :** made of crepe rubber
crepe-back \ˈ=,=\ *adj, of reversible satins* **:** having a crepe surface on the back and a satin surface on the front
crepe de chine \¦krāpdəˈshēn\ *n, pl* **crepes de chine** \-p(s)də-\ *or* **crepe de chines** \-nz\ *often cap 2d C* [F *crêpe de Chine*, lit., China crepe] **1 :** a silk fabric woven in the gum **2 :** a soft fine clothing crepe with a smoother face than other crepes that is woven of silk, rayon, cotton, or wool in plain weave
crepe hair *n* **:** artificial hair used as stage makeup
crepehanger *also* **crape·hanger** \ˈkrāp+,-\ *n* [¹*crepe* or ¹*crape* + *hanger*] **:** one who takes a pessimistic view of things **:** KILLJOY ⟨man is doomed, say the ~*s*, to overpopulate his planet —*Time*⟩
crepe marocain *n* [F *crêpe marocain*, lit., Moroccan crepe] **:** MAROCAIN
crepe myrtle *or* **crêpe myrtle** *var of* CRAPE MYRTLE
crepe paper *n* **:** paper with a crinkled or puckered texture
crepe rubber *n* **:** crude rubber in the form of nearly white to brown crinkled sheets prepared by passing coagulated latex through grooved rollers and used esp. for shoe soles
crepe su·zette \¦krāp(,)süˈzet, -rep-, -(,)sœˈ-\ *n, pl* **crepes suzette** \-p(s)(,)s-\ *or* **crepe suzettes** \-ts\ [F *crêpe Suzette*, fr. *crêpe* (pancake) + *Suzette* (dim. of the name *Suzanne* Susan)] **:** a small thin pancake folded in quarters or rolled, heated in a sauce of butter, sugar, orange or lemon juice, grated rind, and a liqueur (as curaçao) to which is added a pony or two of cognac and cointreau, and usu. set ablaze before serving
crep·ey *or* **crepy** \ˈkrāpē, -pi\ *adj* -ER/-EST [¹*crepe* + *-y*] **:** like crepe **:** CRINKLY
cre·pid·u·la \krəˈpijələ, -idyələ, -idᵊlə\ *n, cap* [NL, fr. L, small sandal, dim. of *crepida* sandal, fr. Gk *krēpid-, krēpis* boot; akin to OIr *cairem* shoemaker, Lith *kurpe* shoe, and prob. Gk *keirein* to cut — more at SHEAR] **:** a genus of marine gastropods (suborder Taenioglossa) comprising the typical slipper limpets
crep·i·ness \ˈkrāpēnəs, -pin-\ *n* -ES **:** the quality or state of being crepey
cre·pip·o·da \¦krəˈpipədə\ [NL, fr. *crepi-* (perh. fr. Gk *krēpis* boot) + *-poda*] *syn of* AMPHINEURA
cre·pis \ˈkrēpəs\ *n* [NL, fr. L, a plant, fr. Gk *krēpis*, lit., boot] **1** *cap* **:** a genus of herbs (family Compositae) with alternate or basal chiefly pinnatifid leaves and heads of yellow or orange colored flowers — see HAWK'S-BEARD **2 crepis** *pl* **:** a plant of the genus *Crepis*
crep·i·tant \ˈkrepəd·ənt, -ətənt *also* -ətᵊnt\ *adj* [L *crepitant-, crepitans*, pres. part. of *crepitare*] **:** having or making a crackling sound **:** CRACKLING, RATTLING ⟨~ dead leaves⟩ ⟨~ radio static⟩ ⟨a ~ joint⟩
crepitant rale *n* **:** a peculiar crackling sound audible with inspiration in pneumonia and other lung diseases
crep·i·tate \ˈkrepə,tāt, *usu* -ād·+V\ *vi* -ED/-ING/-S [L *crepitatus*, past part. of *crepitare* to rattle, crackle, fr. *crepitus*, past part. of *crepare* to crack — more at RAVEN] **:** to make a series of small sharp rapidly repeated explosions or sounds **:** CRACKLE
crep·i·ta·tion \,==ˈtāshən\ *n* -S [LL *crepitation-, crepitatio*, fr. L *crepitatus* + *-ion-, -io* -ion] **1 :** the act or an instance of crepitating **:** a crackling noise **:** CRACKLING **2** *med* **:** a grating or crackling sound or sensation (as that produced by the fractured ends of a bone moving against each other or as that in tissues affected with gas gangrene) ⟨~ in the arthritic knee⟩ **:** CREPITANT RALE
crep·i·tus \ˈkrepəd·əs, -ətəs\ *n, pl* **crepitus** [L, fr. *crepitus*, past part. of *crepare*] *med* **:** CREPITATION
creplich *var of* KREPLACH
cre·pon \ˈkrā(,)pän, -re(,)-\ *n* -S [F, fr. *crêpe* crepe — more at CRAPE] **:** a heavy crepe fabric characterized by a crinkled puckered face
crept *past of* CREEP
cre·pus·cu·lar \krəˈpəsk(y)ələ(r)\ *adj* [L *crepusculum* + E *-ar*] **1 :** of, relating to, or like twilight **:** GLIMMERING **:** imperfectly luminous **:** DIM ⟨~ depths of personality —William James⟩ **2 :** active in the twilight ⟨~ insects⟩
crepuscular light *n* **:** a faint light (as of a slightly illuminated sky)
crepuscular ray *n* **:** a streak of light that seems to radiate from the sun shortly before or after sunset when sunlight shines through a break in the clouds or a notch in the horizon line and illuminates atmospheric haze or dust particles
cre·pus·cule \krəˈpə,sk(y)ü(ə)l, ˈkrep-\ *or* **cre·pus·cle** \krəˈpəsəl\ *n* -S [L *crepusculum*, fr. *creper* dusky, dark] **:** a time of half-light; *specif* **:** TWILIGHT
crepy *var of* CREPEY
¹**cre·scen·do** \krəˈshen(,)dō, -ˈse-; krāˈsh-, kreˈsh-\ *n, pl* **crescendos** *or* **crescendoes** [It, fr. *crescendo* (verbal of *crescere* to grow), fr. L *crescendum*] **1 a :** a swelling in volume of sound esp. in playing or singing music **b :** a passage so performed **2 a :** any gradual increase (as in physical or emotional force or intensity) ⟨a ~ of irritation⟩ ⟨a ~ of attacks upon the town⟩ ⟨a ~ of color spread over the sky⟩ **b :** the peak of such an increase ⟨the gale reached its ~ in the evening⟩
²**crescendo** \ˈ"\ *adj (or adv)* [It, lit., growing, fr. L *crescendum*, gerund of *crescere* to grow] **:** with an increase in volume — used as a direction in music and often indicated by the abbr. *cresc* or the symbol —
³**crescendo** \ˈ"\ *vi* -ED/-ING/-ES **:** to grow esp. in volume of

sound or in emotional intensity ⟨chants that . . . had ~*ed* to a wild frenzy —Hendrik de Leeuw⟩
crescendo pedal *n* **:** an organ pedal by which most of the stops comprising the organ may be gradually thrown on or off in proper order as to quality and volume
¹cres·cent \ˈkresᵊnt *sometimes* ˈkrezᵊnt\ *n* -s [ME *cressant, cressent,* fr. MF *creissant, croissant* crescent, time between the new and full moon, fr. pres. part. of *creistre, croistre* to increase, grow, fr. L *crescere;* akin to OE *herseweæstm* millet grain, OS *hirsi* millet, OHG *hirsi, hirso* millet, L *creare* to create, produce, beget, bring forth, Gk *koros* boy, puppet, *korē* girl, virgin, pupil of the eye, Lith *šerti* to feed, Alb *thjer* acorn; basic meaning: growing, feeding] **1 a** (1) **:** the aspect presented by the moon at any stage between new moon and first quarter and between last quarter and the succeeding new moon (2) **:** any of the similar aspects of Venus and Mercury when less than half of the illuminated hemisphere is visible **b :** the shape or figure defined by a convex and a concave edge **2 a :** a representation of the crescent moon used as an ornament, emblem, or badge **b :** a heraldic charge that consists of the figure of the crescent moon with the horns directed upward and is often used as a cadency mark to distinguish a second son and his descendants **3 :** an object shaped like a crescent: as **a :** ROLL, BUN, COOKIE **b :** a raised cordonnet used in needlepoint laces for separating or outlining a portion of the design **c :** an anatomical structure or section **d :** the concave in the edge of a roller in a lever escapement to allow passage of the guard pin — called also *passing hollow* **e :** PAVILLON CHINOIS **4 a :** an area shaped like a crescent ⟨the industrial ~ along the Gulf coast⟩ **b :** a semicircular row of houses or the street serving such a row ⟨the bedlam of roads, ~*s*, drives . . . that form the suburbs of Dublin —*Irish Digest*⟩ **5 :** the gametocyte of the falciparum malaria parasite that is shaped like a crescent and constitutes a distinguishing character of malignant tertian malaria

crescent 1b

²crescent \"\ *adj* [L *crescent-, crescens,* pres. part. of *crescere*] **1 :** INCREASING, GROWING ⟨there was a ~ humming on the rails —Thomas Wolfe⟩ **2 :** having the shape or outline of a crescent **:** MENISCOID ⟨New Orleans . . . built on a ~ sweep of the Mississippi —Allan Nevins & H. S. Commager⟩
³crescent \"\ *or* **crescent spot** *or* **crescent spot butterfly** *n* -s [¹*crescent*] **:** any of numerous small butterflies (genera *Phyciodes* and *Melitaea*) having white spots on the wings
cre·scen·tia \krəˈsensh(ē)ə\ *n, cap* [NL, fr. Pietro Crescenzi (Petrus de *Crescentiis*) †1310? Ital. writer on agriculture + NL *-ia*] **:** a genus of tropical American trees (family Bignoniaceae) distinguished chiefly by short trunk, crooked limbs, often drooping branches, purplish blotched flowers, and large globose fruits — see CALABASH
cres·cen·tic \krəˈsentik\ *adj* **:** resembling or suggesting a crescent ⟨~ patterns of meandering channels —P.E.James⟩
crescentic lobe *n* **:** SEMILUNAR LOBE
crescent of gia·nuz·zi \-jəˈnütsē\ *usu cap G* [after Giuseppe *Giannuzzi* †1876 Ital. physiologist] **:** DEMILUNE
cres·cent·oid \ˈkresᵊn‚tȯid\ *adj* **:** CRESCENTIC
crescent stretcher *n* **:** a curved stretcher peculiar to American Windsor chairs of the 18th and early 19th centuries
crescent terrapin *n* **:** a common No. American turtle (*Graptemys pseudogeographica*) olive with black blotches and a yellow crescent behind each eye
cres·cive \ˈkresiv\ *adj* [L *crescere* + E *-ive*] **:** INCREASING, GROWING **:** capable of growth ⟨the emergence of a ~ American culture —Louis Wirth⟩ — **cres·cive·ly** \-sə̇vlē\ *adv*
cres·co·graph \ˈkreskə‚graf\ *n* -s [L *crescere* + E *-o-* + *-graph*] **:** an instrument for making perceptible the growth of plants — **cres·co·graph·ic** \¦==¦grafik\ *adj*
cre·sol \ˈkrē‚sōl, -‚sȯl\ *n* -s [ISV *cres-* (irreg. fr. *creosote*) + *-ol;* prob. orig. formed as G *kresol*] **1 :** any of three poisonous colorless crystalline or liquid isomeric phenols $CH_3C_6H_4OH$ distinguished as *ortho*-cresol, *meta*-cresol, and *para*-cresol, obtained usu. from coal tar, and used chiefly as disinfectants, in making phenolic resins and plasticizers, and in organic synthesis; methyl-phenol **2 :** a mixture of isomeric cresols obtained from coal tar
cresol red *n* **:** a dye $C_{21}H_{18}O_5S$ of the sulfonephthalein series derived from *ortho*-cresol that is obtained as a reddish brown crystalline powder and is used as an acid-base indicator
cre·sor·ci·nol \‚krēsȯrˈsᵊn‚ōl, -‚ōl\ *n* -s [ISV *cresol* + *orcinol*] **:** crystalline phenol $CH_3C_6H_3(OH)_2$ isomeric with orcinol; 4-methyl-resorcinol
cre·so·tate \ˈkrēsə‚tāt, -res-\ *also* **cre·sot·i·nate** \krəˈsätᵊn‚āt\ *n* -s [ISV *cresotic* (in *cresotic acid*) + *-ate*] **:** a salt of cresotic acid
cre·sot·ic acid \krəˈsäd·ik-\ *n* [ISV *cresotic* (fr. *cresot-* — prob. irreg. fr. *creosote* — + *-ic*) + *acid*] **:** any of 10 isomeric acids $CH_3C_6H_3(OH)COOH$ derived from the cresols; hydroxy-toluic acid
cres·o·tine yellow G \‚kresə‚tēn-\ *n, usu cap C&Y* [*cresotine,* fr. *cresotic* + *-ine*] **:** a direct dye — see DYE table I (under *Direct Yellow 20*)
cres·o·tin·ic acid \¦kresə¦tinik-, -rēs-\ *n* [ISV *cresotinic* (fr. *cresot-* + *-in* + *-ic*) + *acid*; prob. orig. formed as G *kresotinsäure*] **:** CRESOTIC ACID
cres·oxide \krəs, kres+\ *n* [*cresol* + *oxide*] **:** a salt of cresol
cresoxy- *comb form* [ISV *cresol* + *oxy-*] **:** TOLOXY-
cress \ˈkres\ *n* -ES [ME *cresse,* fr. OE *cressa, cresse, cærse;* akin to MD *kersse* cress, OHG *kresso, kressa,* and perh. to L *gramen* grass, Gk *grastis* green fodder, *gran* to gnaw, Skt *grasati* he eats, devours; basic meaning: eating, nibbling] **1 :** any of numerous plants of the family Cruciferae whose moderately pungent leaves are used in salads and garnishes: as **a :** WATERCRESS **b :** GARDEN CRESS **2 :** any plant that resembles a true cress — usu. used with a qualifying word ⟨Peter's ~⟩
cres·set \ˈkresə̇t\ *also* **cris·set** \ˈris-\ *n* -s [ME, fr. MF *cresset, craisset,* fr. OF *craisset,* fr. *craisse* grease, fr. (assumed) VL *crassia* — more at GREASE] **1 :** an iron vessel or basket used for holding burning oil, pitchy wood, or other illuminant and mounted as a torch or suspended as a lantern **:** a fire basket ⟨blazing ~*s*, fed with naphtha and asphaltus —John Milton⟩ **2** *or* **cres·et** \-res-\ **:** a small furnace or iron fire cage used in coopering to heat and so bend staves to shape
cress green *n* **:** a moderate yellow green that is greener and deeper than average moss green, yellower and darker than average pea green, and yellower and duller than apple green (sense 1) — called also *cresson, watercress*
cres·son \kreˈsäⁿ, kresōⁿ\ *n* -s [F, cress, of Gmc origin; akin to OHG *kresso* cress] **:** CRESS GREEN

cresset

cress rocket *n* **:** a yellow-flowered Spanish herb (*Vella pseudocytisus*) of the family Cruciferae
cressweed \ˈ=‚=\ *n* **:** SAND ROCKET
cresswort \ˈ=‚=\ *n* **:** a plant of the family Cruciferae
cres·sy \ˈkresē\ *adj* -ER/-EST **:** abounding in cresses
¹crest \ˈkrest\ *n* -s [ME, fr. MF *creste,* fr. L *crista;* akin to OE *hrisian* to shake, OHG *hris* twig, ON *hrista* to shake, Goth *afhrisjan* to shake off, MIr *cressaim* I shake, OPruss *craysi* blade of grass, straw, L *curvus* curved — more at CROWN] **1 a :** a usu. ornamental tuft or process on the head of a bird or animal; *specif* **:** COCKSCOMB — see BIRD illustration **b** (1) **:** the plume of feathers, painted metal fan, modeled emblem, or other decoration worn on a knight's helmet; *esp* **:** one indicating the identity of the wearer (2) **:** the apex of a helmet ⟨on his ~ sat horror plumed —John Milton⟩ (3) **:** a heraldic device that represents the crest formerly borne upon the helmet of a knight, is depicted in a full achievement of arms upon the helmet, and is also used separately as an ornament or cognizance (as for plate or liveries) (4) **:** a heraldic device depicted above the escutcheon but not upon a helmet — used esp. in the official heraldry of the New World (5) **:** an escutcheon of arms (6) **:** a complete coat of arms — not used technically (7) **:** an emblem, badge, device, or other object regularly used as a symbol (as of a family, tribe, or nation) — usu. used only of emblems employed among peoples who do not practice the European system of heraldry ⟨the Indians . . . mark off the hunting ground selected by them by blazing the trees with their ~*s* —*Amer. Anthrop. Assoc. Memoir*⟩ (8) **:** an identifying mark usu. consisting of painted rings placed near the vanes of an arrow (9) **:** high spirits or self-confidence **:** PRIDE, COURAGE, TEMPER **c :** a process or prominence on any part of the body of an animal: as (1) **:** the upper curve or ridge of the neck of a horse or other quadruped (2) **:** the mane borne by such a crest (3) **:** a ridge esp. when longitudinal and median or serrated or tuberculated (as that on the back of certain lizards) — compare BASILISK (4) **:** a ridge esp. on a bone ⟨the ~ of the tibia⟩ ⟨the ~ of the ilium⟩ — see FRONTAL CREST, OCCIPITAL CREST **2 :** the top of a structure or natural formation: as **a :** the highest point of a mountain **:** SUMMIT **:** the highest line of a range of mountains or hills or fold of rock ⟨the ~ of a watershed⟩ ⟨the ~ of an anticline⟩ **b :** the top edge of a dam or weir **c :** the ridge of a roof **3 a** *physics* (1) **:** the highest part of the oscillating surface in a gravity wave or a ripple on a liquid at any instant — contrasted with *trough* (2) **:** the maximum attained by a wave variable during the passage of a complete cycle **:** PEAK ⟨~ voltage⟩ **b :** the highest stage of a river in flood **4 a :** one of the high points of an action or process marked by a periodic alternation of rise and fall ⟨at the ~ of each breath, weeping threatened her —Elizabeth Taylor⟩ **b :** the culmination of an action or process **:** CLIMAX ⟨the ~ of a civilization⟩ ⟨at the ~ of his fame⟩ ⟨the ~ of the evening's excitement⟩ **5 :** a structure terminating or crowning an organ (as the persistent style forming a partial aril in plants of the genus *Sanguinaria*) **6 :** the outermost part of a screw thread often in the form of a rounded or flat-surfaced helical ridge
²crest \"\ *vb* -ED/-ING/-S [ME *cresten,* fr. *crest,* n.] *vt* **1 :** to furnish with a crest **:** serve as a crest for **:** TOP, CROWN **2 :** to reach the crest of (as a mountain or wave) ~ *vi* **1** *obs* **:** to bear oneself proudly or erectly **2 :** to form or rise to a crest ⟨the river is expected to ~ at noon⟩
crest·al \ˈkrestəl\ *adj* **:** at, near, on, or relating to a crest
crest clearance *n* **:** the radial clearance between the crest of a screw thread and the root of the thread mating with it
crest coronet *n* **1 :** a coronet supporting the crest in some coats of arms either instead of the wreath or additional to and resting upon it **2 :** DUCAL CREST CORONET
crest·ed \ˈkrestə̇d\ *adj* [ME, fr. ¹*crest* + *-ed*] **1 :** having a crest ⟨a ~ bird⟩ — often used in combination ⟨fan-*crested*⟩ ⟨golden-*crested*⟩ **2 :** emblazoned with a crest **:** COMBED ⟨a cock argent ~ gules⟩
crested auklet *or* **crested auk** *n* **:** an auklet (*Aethia cristatella*) with a recurved frontal crest
crested barbet *n* **:** a large barbet (*Trachyphonus raillantii*) of southern and eastern Africa that is brightly marked with red and yellow and has a small crest of dusky feathers
crested cariama *n* **:** a cariama (*Cariama cristata*) of the campos of southern Brazil that is yellowish gray mottled with dark brown on the back and somewhat striped below and has a large frontal crest of stiff filamentous feathers
crested coralroot *n* **:** a leafless scaly-stemmed orchid (*Hexalectris spicata*) with a spike of brownish purple striped flowers
crested dogstail *n* **:** a European grass (*Cynosurus cristatus*) used for pasture and forage and also in lawns and bearing flowers in stiff panicles resembling spikes
crested duck *n* **:** a long-legged short-necked So. American duck (*Lophonelta specularoides*) related to the sheldrakes
crested fern *n* **:** CREST FERN
crested flycatcher *n* **:** any of various flycatchers having a prominent crest; *esp* **:** an eastern No. American flycatcher (*Myiarchus crinitus*) that is olive brown above with gray chest, yellow belly, and reddish brown tail and is nearly as large as the robin — called also *great crested flycatcher*
crested guinea fowl *n* **:** a game bird (*Guttera edouardi*) of northern West Africa
crested hair grass *n* **:** JUNE GRASS 2
crested hamster *n* **:** a cat-sized nocturnal arboreal African rodent (*Lophiomys imhassi*) having a bushy tail and a crest of erectile hair on the back
crested hen *n, usu cap C&H* **:** a Danish hopping dance for two women and a man
crested iris *also* **crested dwarf iris** *n* **:** a low-growing herb (*Iris cristata*) that spreads by rhizomes and rootless stolons and has pale lilac flowers with an orange-tipped white crest
crested lark *n* **:** a common stout-bodied lark (*Galerida cristata*) of Europe sometimes kept as a cage bird
crested leaf monkey *n* **:** a Malaysian leaf monkey (*Presbytis mitratus*) having a black crest and pale abdomen
crested oriole *n* **:** a So. American cacique (*Xanthornus decumanus*)
crested penguin *n* **:** ROCK HOPPER
crested pig *n* **:** a wild swine (*Sus cristata*) of eastern Asia that is blackish brown and has a crest of stiff black bristles
crested screamer *n* **1 :** a screamer (genus *Chauna*) distinguished from the horned screamer by a feathery crest on the back of the head; *esp* **:** CHAJA **2 :** CARIAMA
crested shield fern *n* **:** CREST FERN
crested shrimp *n* **:** a large shrimp (genus *Eusicyonia*) of the tropical Atlantic ocean
crested titmouse *or* **crested tit** *n* **:** a European titmouse (*Parus cristatus*) with a speckled black and whitish crest
crested wheat grass *n* **:** a European grass (*Agropyron cristatum*) grown in the U.S. for forage and erosion control and having flowers in a short spike resembling a comb
crested wren *n* **:** KINGLET
crestfallen \ˈ=¦=\ *adj* **1 :** with drooping crest or hanging head **:** DISPIRITED, DEJECTED, COWED ⟨let it make thee ~ —Shak.⟩ **2** *of a horse* **:** having the upper part of the neck hanging to one side — **crest·fall·en·ly** *adv* — **crest·fall·en·ness** \ˈ=¦fȯlən(n)ə̇s\ *n* -ES
crest fern *or* **crested fern** *n* **:** a tall woodland fern (*Dryopteris cristata*) of No. America, Europe, and Asia
crest·ing \ˈkrestiŋ\ *n* -s [¹*crest* + *-ing*] **1 :** an ornamental crest (as on the ridge of a roof or at the top of a clock) **2 a :** the members that form the crest **b :** the ornamentation (as carving or fretwork) on a top member (as on the crest rail of a chair)
crest·less \ˈkres(t)lə̇s\ *adj* **:** without a crest; *specif* **:** of low birth ⟨the ~ churls of England —Sir Walter Scott⟩
crest line *n* **:** an elongate crest or a linear series of crests ⟨a wave with a long *crest line*⟩ ⟨the *crest line* of the mountains⟩
crest·more·ite \ˈkres(t)mō‚rīt, -mȯ‚-\ *n* -s [*Crestmore,* Calif. + E *-ite*] **:** a mineral consisting of hydrated calcium silicate occurring in compact snow-white masses
crest rail *n* **:** the top rail of a chair back esp. when distinctively carved or shaped
crests *pl of* CREST, *pres 3d sing of* CREST
crest table *n* **:** a crested or saddleback coping used for the top of a wall
crest tile *n* **:** one of the tiles made to cover the ridge of a roof by fitting upon it like a saddle
crest voltmeter *n* **:** PEAK VOLTMETER
cres·well·i·an \(ˈ)krezˈwelēən\ *adj, usu cap* [*Creswell* Crags, northeast Derbyshire, England + E *-ian*] **:** of or relating to a Mesolithic development of the Aurignacian in Great Britain
cres·yl \ˈkresəl, -rēs-\ *n* -s [ISV *cresol* + *-yl*] **:** TOLYL
cres·yl·ate \ˈkresə‚lāt, -lət\ *n* -s [*cresyl* + *-ate*] **:** a salt of cresol or cresylic acid — used chiefly commercially
cre·syl·ic \krəˈsilik\ *adj* [ISV *cresyl* + *-ic*] **:** relating to, containing, or derived from cresol or creosote
cresylic acid *n* **1 :** CRESOL; *esp* **:** a crude mixture of the three cresols **2 :** a mixture of phenols (as cresols and xylenols) obtained from coal tar or cracked petroleum oils
cres·yl·ite \ˈkresə‚līt\ *n* -s [ISV *cresyl* + *-ite*; orig. formed as F *crésylite*] **:** an explosive consisting of trinitrocresol or of trinitrocresol and picric acid
cre·ta \ˈkrēd·ə\ *n* -s [L] **1 :** CHALK **2 :** FULLER'S EARTH
¹cre·ta·ceous \krəˈtāshəs\ *adj* [L *cretaceus,* fr. *creta* chalk] **1 :** relating to, having the characteristics of, or abounding in chalk **:** CHALKY ⟨~ formations⟩ **2** *usu cap* **:** of or relating to the last period of the Mesozoic era and the corresponding system of rocks, the deposits of the period including the larger part of the known chalk beds, greensand marl, and most of the coal of the U.S. west of the Great Plains, the vegetation of the period having approached the modern temperate and subtropical flora in general aspect, and the reptiles of the period having remained dominant on the land and in the sea, ganoid fishes for the first time having become subordinate to teleosts — see GEOLOGIC TIME table — **cre·ta·ceous·ly** *adv*
²cretaceous \"\ *n* -ES *usu cap* **:** the Cretaceous period or system of rocks
cre·tac·ic \krəˈtasik\ *adj, usu cap* [ISV *cretaceous* + *-ic*] **:** CRETACEOUS
¹cre·tan \ˈkrētᵊn\ *adj, usu cap* [L *cretanus,* fr. *Creta* Crete (fr. Gk *Krētē*) + *-anus* -an] **1 :** of, relating to, or characteristic of Crete, an island in the eastern part of the Mediterranean sea **2 :** of, relating to, or characteristic of Cretans
²cretan \"\ *n* -s *cap* [L *cretanus,* fr. *cretanus,* adj.] **:** a native or inhabitant of Crete
cretan bear's-tail *n, usu cap C* **:** a tall European herb (*Celsia arcturus*) with elongate clusters of long-stalked flowers
cretan dittany *also* **crete dittany** *n, usu cap C* **:** an herb (*Origanum dictamnus*) native to Crete having drooping spikes of pink flowers and a once-believed power to expel arrows from the body
cretan hemp *n, usu cap C* **:** BASTARD HEMP 1
cretan mullein *n, usu cap C* **:** an erect herb (*Celsia cretica*) with broad oblong leaves and irregular short-stalked flowers in loose elongate clusters found along the Mediterranean
cretan rockrose *n, usu cap C* **:** a southern European rockrose (*Cistus creticus*) that is one of the sources of labdanum
cretan spikenard *n, usu cap C* **:** an Asiatic valerian (*Valeriana phu*) sometimes cultivated as a substitute for the true spikenard
cre·te·fac·tion \¦krēd·ə¦fakshən\ *n* -s [*crete-* (fr. L *creta* chalk) + *-faction*] **:** CRETIFICATION
cre·tic \ˈkrēd·ik\ *n* -s [LL *creticus* constituting an amphimacer, fr. Gk *krētikos* amphimacer, fr. *krētikos* (adj.) Cretan, fr. *Krētē* + *-ikos* -ic] **:** AMPHIMACER
cre·ti·fi·ca·tion \‚krēd·əfəˈkāshən, ˈ===‚==\ *n* -s [L *creta* chalk + E *-i-* + *-fication*] **:** the process or an instance of cretifying
cre·ti·fy \ˈkrēd·ə‚fī\ *vt* -ED/-ING/-ES [L *creta* chalk + E *-i-* + *-fy*] **:** to convert into chalk **:** infiltrate with calcium salts **:** CALCIFY
cre·tin \ˈkrētᵊn; *Brit usu* -ret-\ *n* -s [F *crétin,* fr. F dial. *cretin* Christian, human being, kind of deformed idiot found in the Alps, fr. L *christianus* Christian; fr. the desire to indicate that such idiots were after all human — more at CHRISTIAN] **:** one afflicted with cretinism; *broadly* **:** a person showing marked mental deficiency
cre·tin·ism \-ᵊn‚izəm\ *n* -s [F *crétinisme,* fr. *crétin* + *-isme* -ism] **:** a condition originating during fetal life or early infancy characterized by stunted physical and mental development and caused by severe thyroid deficiency — called also *infantile myxedema;* compare MONGOLISM, MYXEDEMA
cre·tin·ize \-ᵊn‚īz\ *vt* -ED/-ING/-S [F *crétiniser,* fr. *crétin* + *-iser* -ize] **:** to reduce to the condition of a cretin
cre·tin·oid \-ᵊn‚ȯid\ *adj* [ISV *cretin* + *-oid*] **:** like a cretin **:** resembling cretinism
cre·tin·ous \-ᵊnəs\ *adj* [ISV *cretin* + *-ous*] **1 :** relating to a cretin **2 :** being a cretin or affected with cretinism
cre·tion \ˈkrēshən\ *n* -s [L *cretion-, cretio,* fr. *cretus* (past part. of *cernere* to cern, discern) + *-ion-, -io* -ion — more at CERTAIN] **1** *Roman law* **:** an act before a magistrate by which an outside heir declares his acceptance of the succession **2** *Roman law* **:** the time allowed an heir to make his declaration of cretion — compare JUS DELIBERANDI — **cre·tion·ary** \-ə‚nerē\ *adj*
cre·to-mycenaean \¦krēd·ō+\ *adj, usu cap C&M* [*Crete* + E *-o-* + *mycenaean*] **:** characterizing the civilization prob. originating in Crete but first widely known through discoveries at Mycenae — compare MYCENAEAN
cre·tonne \ˈkrē‚tän, krəˈ-; *Brit usu* kreˈ- *or* ˈkre‚-\ *n* -s [F, fr. *Creton,* village in Normandy where it was made] **:** a strong unglazed cotton or linen fabric similar to chintz but usu. printed with larger floral designs, woven in plain or fancy weaves, and used esp. for curtains and upholstery
creutzer *var of* KREUZER
cre·val·le \krəˈvalē, -lə, -lā\ *also* **cre·val·ly** \-lē\ *n, pl* **crevalles** *also* **crevallies** [alter. of *cavalla*] **:** CAVALLA; *esp* **:** a carangid fish (*Caranx hippos*) important as a food fish along the west coast of Florida, widely but sparsely distributed elsewhere in the western Atlantic, and represented in the Pacific by the same or a closely related species
cre·vasse *also* **cre·vass** \krəˈvas, -aa(ə)s *sometimes* -väs *or* -vȧs *or* ˈkrevə̇s\ *n, pl* **crevasses** [F, fr. OF *crevace*] **:** a break, opening, or chasm of some width and considerable depth: as **a :** a split or cleavage through massed ice, glacier, snow field, or earth after earthquakes **b** [AmerF, fr. F] **:** a breach in the levee of a river
creve·coeur \ˈkrev‚kər, =ˈ=\ *n* -s *often cap* [F *crèvecœur,* prob. fr. *Crèvecœur,* Calvados dept., France] **:** a domestic fowl of a French breed that is black and crested and has a V-shaped comb
cre·vette \krəˈvet\ *n* -s [F, shrimp, fr. MF, lit., little goat, prob. irreg. fr. (assumed) MF dial. (northern) *kevre* she-goat (fr. L *capra,* fem. of *capr-, caper* goat) + MF *-ette;* fr. its habit of leaping — more at CAPRIOLE] **:** a strong yellowish pink that is redder and very slightly darker than average salmon, redder and darker than salmon pink, and deeper than melon — called also *prawn*
crev·ice \ˈkrevə̇s\ *n* -s [ME *crevice, crevace,* fr. MF *crevace,* fr. OF, fr. *crever* to break, burst, fr. L *crepare* to crack, break — more at CRAVEN] **:** a narrow opening of some depth caused esp. by a split or cleavage **:** a narrow recess like a slit ⟨hidden in a ~ under a cliff⟩ **syn** see CRACK
crev·iced \-st\ *adj* [*crevice* + *-ed*] **:** having a crevice
cre·vic·u·lar \krəˈvikyələ(r)\ *adj* [irreg. fr. *crevice* + *-ular*] *anat* **:** of, relating to, or involving a crevice, esp. the gingival crevice
¹crew *chiefly Brit past of* CROW *vi* 1
²crew \ˈkrü\ *n* -s [ME *crue* reinforcement, body of soldiers, fr. MF *creue* increase, fr. OF, fem. of *creu,* past part. of *creistre* to grow — more at CRESCENT] **1** *archaic* **:** a band or force of armed men ⟨that fair ~ of knights —Edmund Spenser⟩ **2 :** a company of people temporarily associated together **:** ASSEMBLAGE, THRONG, RETINUE ⟨mirth, admit me of thy ~ —John Milton⟩ **3 a :** a group of people regarded as associated by common traits, interests, or purpose **:** SET, GANG, MOB ⟨that crooked politician and his ~ of heelers⟩ **b :** a company or squad of men working on one job or under one foreman **:** GANG ⟨lumbering ~⟩ ⟨wrecking ~⟩ ⟨stage ~⟩ **c :** a group of men organized to serve or operate a machine, vehicle, or other apparatus (as a fieldpiece, railroad train, or tank) ⟨mortar ~⟩ **4 a :** the company of seamen who man a ship **:** the whole company belonging to a ship sometimes including the officers and master **b :** a small body or gang of men on a ship who work under the direction of some petty officer or who are assigned to some particular duty ⟨the galley ~⟩ **c :** the body of men manning a racing shell ⟨a college ~⟩ ⟨~ practice⟩; *also* **:** ROWING ⟨his chief activities were wrestling and ~⟩ **d :** the persons who man an aircraft in flight — called also *flight crew* **5 :** a subdivision of an explorer unit of the Boy Scouts of America made up of two or more explorers and corresponding to a boy scout patrol
³crew \"\ *vb* -ED/-ING/-S *vi* **:** to act as a member of a crew ⟨~ on the winning sailboat⟩ ~ *vt* **:** to serve on (a ship or aircraft) as a crew member ⟨any man who has ~*ed* both conventional fighters and jets —*Aero Digest*⟩
⁴crew \"\ *n* -s [partly fr. ME, fish trap, fr. ScGael *crō* pen for animals, hut; partly fr. W *crau* pigpen & Corn *crow;* akin to OIr *crāu* stable, hut — more at CRYPT] *dial Brit* **:** a pen for cattle, swine, or sheep
crew chief *n* **:** a noncommissioned officer (as in the U.S. Air Force) who supervises a ground crew of airplane mechanics
crew cut *or* **crew haircut** *n* **:** a very short hair style copied from a style worn by oarsmen with the hair more or less resembling the bristle surface of a brush
crewe *n* -s [MF *crue, cruie* — more at CRUET] *obs* **:** CRUSE, POT
crew·el \ˈkrüəl, *Brit usu* -ü‚il\ *n* -s [ME *crule*] **1 :** worsted slackly twisted yarn used for embroidery **2 :** CREWELWORK
crewel needle *n* **:** a long-eyed needle used esp. for embroidery
crewel stitch *n* **:** STEM STITCH
crewelwork \ˈ==‚=\ *n* **:** embroidery consisting of simple

stitches (as stem stitch, chain stitch, buttonhole stitch) worked with crewel in floral and scroll patterns on plain material often of linen or cotton and used for interior decoration

crew·er \ˈkrüə(r)\ *n* -s [origin unknown] **:** one that curves tongues for spring clips and harness buckles

crewet *var of* CRUET

crew·less \ˈkrülə̇s\ *adj* **:** being without a crew

crew·man \ˈkrümən\ *n, pl* **crewmen :** a member of a crew

crew neck *or* **crew neckline** *n* [²crew] **:** a straight neckline like a slit that runs from shoulder to shoulder adapted from the pullovers worn by oarsmen

crew–served \ˈ=ˌ=\ *adj* [²crew] *of a weapon* **:** operated by two or more men

crex \ˈkreks\ *n, cap* [NL, fr. Gk *krex,* a long-legged bird; akin to Gk *kirkos* hawk — more at CIRCAETUS] **:** a genus of birds (family Rallidae) including the corncrake

cri·ant \ˈkrīənt, krēäⁿ\ *adj* [F, fr. pres. part. of *crier* to cry out, fr. OF — more at CRY] **:** attracting attention by gaudiness **:** GARISH, LOUD ⟨~ wallpaper⟩

¹crib \ˈkrib\ *n* -s [ME, manger, stall, fr. OE *cribb* manger; akin to OHG *krippa* manger, MHG *krebe* basket, ON *kjarf* bundle, sheaf, Gk *griphos* reed basket, Skt *grapsa* bunch, tuft, OE *cradol* cradle — more at CRADLE] **1 a :** MANGER; *esp* **:** a barred or slatted manger for the feeding of hay or other bulky fodder **b** *obs* **:** an osier or wickerwork basket **c :** BIN, CRATE, BOX **d** *archery* **:** a box topped with netting or perforated board in which to stand arrows **e** *slang* **:** SAFE 1 b **2 :** an enclosure esp. of framework: as **a :** a stall for an ox or other stabled animal **b :** a small bedstead with high enclosing usu. slatted sides for a child; *also* **:** CRADLE 1a **c :** a heavy supporting or strengthening framework (as for a roof or a house being moved or a shaft) **d :** a frame of logs or beams to be filled with heavy material (as stones or rubble) and sunk as a foundation or retaining wall in the building of docks, piers, dams, and similar structures **e :** a wooden framework with upright rods used as a drying rack **f** *archaic* **:** JAIL **g :** an enclosure in a workshop or factory where tools or supplies are issued to workers **h :** a structure enclosing a water intake and filter offshore in a lake (as one of the Great Lakes) **i :** an enclosure in shallow water (as at the edge of a lake) where small children may play in safety **3 a :** HUT, HOVEL; *sometimes* **:** a small narrow room **b** *slang* **:** a building (as a house or store) considered with a view to unlawful entry — used chiefly in the phrase *crack a crib* **c :** a house of prostitution; *esp* **:** a room or shack where a prostitute plies her trade as contrasted with a more extensive establishment **d :** a building usu. of open or slat construction for the storing of grain (as corn) **e :** CABOOSE 3 **4 a :** the cards discarded for the dealer to use in scoring in cribbage **b** *slang* **:** CRIBBAGE **5 a :** a small theft **:** something stolen **b :** PLAGIARISM **c** (1) **:** PONY 4 (2) **:** a key to an understanding of a literary work; *esp* **:** an explication that follows a text line by line or page by page (3) **:** a phrase of probable words determining some of a cipher key **d :** a device or object used for cheating in an examination **6 :** CRÈCHE 3 **7** *chiefly Brit* **:** LUNCH — used esp. of the meal that a workman carries with him to eat at his place of employment **8 :** something forming a barrier: as **a :** WEIR **b :** a barrier for reducing the flow of water downstream but extending only part way from shore and thence upstream so as to form a sheltered area (as for storing logs) **c :** a retaining wall of logs used to protect road cuts **9 :** the space between two adjacent railroad ties

crib 2b

²crib \"\ *vb* **cribbed; cribbed; cribbing; cribs** *vt* **1 :** to confine to a small area or within narrow limits **:** CAGE, CRAMP, RESTRAIN ⟨now am I cabin'd, *cribbed,* confined —Shak.⟩ **2 a :** to provide with a crib; *esp* **:** to line or support with a framework of timber **b :** to put (as grain) into a crib **3 :** to surround (floating logs) with a boom and draw on to a raft **4 :** PILFER, PURLOIN, STEAL ⟨put together a jet fighter with parts *cribbed* from all over Europe —*Time*⟩; *esp* **:** to appropriate (as a passage or idea) and use as one's own **:** PLAGIARIZE ⟨the screen writers were able to ~ a few useful lines from Christopher Marlowe —*Newsweek*⟩ ~ *vi* **1 a :** STEAL, PILFER, PLAGIARIZE **b :** to use a crib in preparing a lesson or taking an examination **:** CHEAT ⟨pupils charged that *cribbing* had been going on at the school for years⟩ **2 :** CRIB-BITE **3** *slang Brit* **:** COMPLAIN, GRIPE

crib·bage \ˈkribij, -bēj\ *n* -s [*crib* (discarded cards) + *-age*] **:** a card game for two and sometimes three or four players each of whom is dealt six cards one or two of which are discarded before play to form an extra hand counting for the dealer, the object of the game being to form various counting combinations in the hand and in the cards played

cribbage board *n* **:** a cribbage scoring board usu. in the form of a narrow rectangle having holes by which each player can count with pegs up to 121 usu. twice around

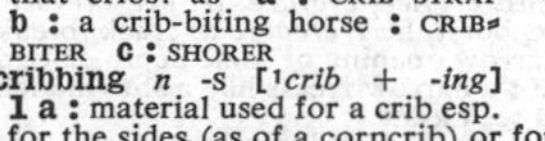
cribbage board

crib·ber \ˈkribə(r)\ *n* -s **:** one that cribs: as **a :** CRIB STRAP **b :** a crib-biting horse **:** CRIB-BITER **c :** SHORER

cribbing *n* -s [¹*crib* + *-ing*] **1 a :** material used for a crib esp. for the sides (as of a corncrib) or for the lining (as of a shaft) **b :** CRIB 2 c **2 :** CRIB-BITING

crib–bite \ˈ=ˌ=\ *vi* [back-formation fr. *crib-biter* & *crib-biting*] **:** to be addicted to crib-biting — **crib–biter** \ˈ=ˌ==\ *n*

crib–biting \ˈ=ˌ==\ *n* -s **:** the habit of some horses of making peculiar movements with the head, gnawing at the manger or other object with the teeth, and slobbering and salivating while so doing — called also *cribbing;* compare WIND SUCKING

¹crib·ble \ˈkribəl\ *n* -s [MF *crible,* fr. LL *criblum,* alter. of L *cribrum* — more at CRIBELLUM] **1 :** SIEVE, STRAINER **2** *obs* **:** coarse flour or meal

²cribble \"\ *vt* **cribbled; cribbled; cribbling** \-b(ə)liŋ\ **cribbles** [F *criblé,* adj.] **:** to cover (a surface) with small round holes or dots; *specif* **:** to make a pattern of small round punctures in (a block or plate) in engraving

cribbled *adj* **:** having a surface pattern composed of small round holes or dots; *specif* **:** CRIBLÉ

crib·el·la·tae \ˌkribəˈlād·(ˌ)ē, -lād-\ *n pl, cap* [NL, fr. *cribellum* + L *-atae* (fem. pl. of *-atus* -ate)] *in some classifications* **:** a division of arachnomorph spiders comprising those that have a cribellum

crib·el·late \ˈkribələt, lāt\ *also* **crib·el·lat·ed** \ˈ==ˌlād·əd\ *or* **cri·bel·lar** \krə̇ˈbelə(r)\ *adj* [NL *cribellum* + E *-ate, -ated* or *-ar*] **1 :** of, having, or relating to a cribellum **2** [NL *Cribellatae*] **:** of or relating to the Cribellatae

cri·bel·lum \krə̇ˈbeləm\ *n, pl* **cribel·la** \-lə\ [NL, fr. LL, small sieve, dim. of L *cribrum* sieve; akin to L *cernere* to sift, discern — more at CERTAIN] **1 :** a special spinning organ having numerous fine perforations and situated in front of the ordinary spinning organs that is found only in spiders of certain families **2 :** a chitinous plate with perforations which constitute the openings of minute ducts leading from certain glands of insects

cri·blé *also* **cri·blée** \(ˈ)krēˈblā\ *adj* [F *criblé,* masc., & *criblée,* fem., fr. *crible* sieve — more at CRIBBLE] *of an engraving* **:** having a background pattern composed of small white dots produced by cribbling the plate — see MANIÈRE CRIBLÉE

cri·bo \ˈkrē(ˌ)bō\ *n* -s [origin unknown] **:** a large harmless snake (*Drymarchon corais corais*) that is closely related to the No. American indigo snake and widely distributed in the West Indies and tropical America where it is of some importance as a destroyer of venomous snakes

crib·ral \ˈkribrəl\ *adj* [L *cribrum* + E *-al*] **:** of or relating to a sieve or structure like a sieve **:** CRIBROSE

crib·rate \ˈkribˌbrāt, -brə̇t\ *adj* [L *cribrum* sieve + E *-ate* — more at *cribellum*] **:** like a sieve — **crib·rate·ly** *adv*

cri·bra·tion \krə̇ˈbrāshən\ *n* -s [L *cribratus* (past part. of *cribrare* to sift, fr. *cribrum* sieve) + E *-ion*] **:** the act or an instance of sifting (as drugs)

crib·ri·form \ˈkribrə̇ˌfȯrm\ *adj* [L *cribrum* sieve + E *-iform*] **:** pierced with small holes like a sieve ⟨a ~ bone⟩

cribriform fascia *n* **:** the perforated fascia covering the saphenous opening in the fascia lata of the thigh and giving passage to various blood and lymph vessels

cribriform plate *n* **:** the horizontal plate of the ethmoid bone perforated with numerous foramina for the passage of the olfactory nerve filaments from the nasal cavity

crib·rose \ˈkriˌbrōs\ *adj* [ISV *cribr-* (fr. L *cribrum* sieve) + *-ose*] **:** CRIBRIFORM, PERFORATED

cribs *pl of* CRIB, *pres 3d sing of* CRIB

crib strap *n* **:** a strap fitted closely about the throat of a horse to prevent crib-biting or wind sucking

cribwork \ˈ=ˌ=\ *n* -s **1 :** a framework formed by or as if by logs arranged as in a crib **:** a structure made with cribs **2 :** CRIB 2c, 2d

¹cri·ce·tid \krə̇ˈsēd·ə̇d, -sed-\ *adj* [NL *Cricetidae*] **:** of or relating to the family Cricetidae

²cricetid \"\ *n* -s **:** a rodent of the family Cricetidae

cri·cet·i·dae \krə̇ˈsed·əˌdē\ *n pl, cap* [NL, fr. *Cricetus,* type genus + *-idae*] **:** a family of myomorph rodents comprising the New World mice, the lemmings, voles, hamsters, and related forms that are mostly small, resemble mice or rats, and have three molar teeth on each side whose cusps in the upper series are arranged in transverse pairs

cric·e·tine \ˈkrisəˌtīn\ *n* -s [NL *Cricetinae,* subfamily of rodents, fr. *Cricetus,* type genus + *-inae*] **:** a rodent of the Cricetidae

cri·ce·tu·lus \krə̇ˈsēd·ələs, -sed-\ *n, cap* [NL, dim. of *Cricetus*] **:** a large genus of small short-tailed Asiatic hamsters that resemble the New World white-footed mice

cri·ce·tus \-ˈsēd·əs, -ˈsed-\ *n, cap* [NL, of Slav origin; akin to Czech *křeček* hamster, Pol *skrzeczek*] **:** the type genus of Cricetidae comprising Old World hamsters of moderate to large size and including the golden hamster

¹crick \ˈkrik\ *n* -s [ME *cryk, crykke*] **:** a painful spasmodic condition of a muscle (as of the neck or back)

²crick \"\ *vt* -ED/-ING/-S **1 :** to cause a crick in (as the neck) **:** WRENCH **2 :** to turn or twist (as the head) esp. into a strained position ⟨~*ing* her head sideways —Elizabeth Bowen⟩

³crick \"\ *n* -s [ME *crike* — more at CREEK] *dial* **:** CREEK 2

⁴crick \"\ *vi* -ED/-ING/-S [imit.] **:** to make a slight abrupt sound

⁵crick \"\ *n* -s [F *cric* jackscrew, fr. MF, fr. MHG *kriec*] **:** a small jackscrew

¹crick·et \ˈkrikə̇t, *usu* -ə̇d·+V\ *n* -s [ME *criket,* fr. MF *criquet,* of imit. origin] **1 :** any of certain saltatorial insects that constitute a family Gryllidae, that are noted for the chirping notes of the males produced by rubbing together specially modified parts of the fore wings, and that include the European house cricket (*Acheta domestica*) which is naturalized in parts of America and lives in human dwellings and the common large black American field cricket (*A. assimilis*) which also enters houses — see MOLE CRICKET, TREE CRICKET **2 :** any of various insects other than crickets; *esp* **:** GRASSHOPPER — usu. used with a qualifying word; see MORMON CRICKET, SAND CRICKET **3 :** something making a sound like the chirp of a cricket: as **a :** a roller in the bit of a horse **b :** a small metal toy or signaling device that makes a sharp click or snap when pressed **4 :** a person regarded as like a cricket (as in smallness and briskness or in rusticity) **5 :** a small false roof or a canted part of a roof to throw off water from behind an obstacle (as a chimney) **6 :** a low wooden footstool

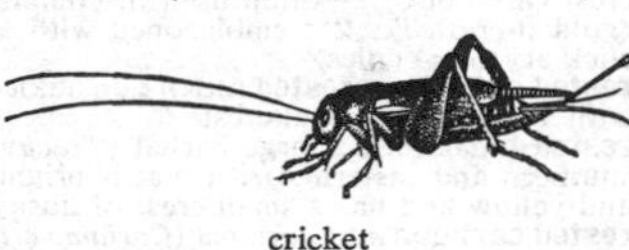
cricket

²cricket \"\ *n* -s [MF *criquet* goal stake in old games of bowls, perh. fr. *criquer* to crack, of imit. origin; fr. the sound of the balls striking the stakes] **1 :** a game played with a ball and bat by two sides of usu. 11 players each on a large field centering upon two wickets pitched 22 yards apart and defended each by a batsman for one over against a bowler, a run being scored each time the two batsmen exchange their wicket positions on hit or passed balls without either being out — see INNING **2 :** fair and honorable behavior like that of a sportsman **:** proper and gentlemanly conduct

typical positions of cricket players in the field: *1* bowler, *2* wicketkeeper, *3* first slip, *4* second slip, *4A* third man, *5* point, *6* cover point, *6A* extra cover, *7* mid off, *8* long off, *9* long on, *10* mid on, *11* short leg, *11A* square leg, *11B* long leg; *B* batsman, *U* umpire

³cricket \"\ *vi* -ED/-ING/-S **:** to play cricket

cricket ball *n* [²*cricket*] **:** the ball with a dark hard leather cover about 9 inches in circumference used in cricket

cricket bat *n* [²*cricket*] **:** the bat usu. made of willow with a long rectangular blade shaped like a paddle and a short handle used in cricket

cricket–bat willow \ˈ==ˌ=-\ *n* **:** a Eurasian tree (*Salix alba caerulea*) having ascending branches and smooth foliage

cricket bird *n* **:** GRASSHOPPER WARBLER

cricket chair *n* **:** a small armchair or rocker usu. of maple with turned legs and posts, a padded seat and a back cushion, and usu. a cloth skirt dropping down from the seat cushion

crick·et·er \ˈkrikəd·ə(r)\ *n* -s [²*cricket* + *-er*] **:** one that plays cricket

cricket frog *n* [¹*cricket;* from its chirping] **:** a small American tree frog (*Acris gryllus*)

crick·ety \ˈkrikəd·ē\ *adj* **:** like a cricket esp. in liveliness or sound

cricks *pl of* CRICK, *pres 3d sing of* CRICK

crico- *comb form* [NL, fr. *cricoides* cricoid] **:** cricoid ⟨*cricot*omy⟩ **:** cricoid and ⟨*crico*thyroid⟩

¹cri·coid \ˈkrīˌkȯid\ *n* -s [NL *cricoides,* fr. Gk *krikoeidēs* ring-shaped, fr. *krikos* ring + *-oeidēs* -oid — more at CIRCLE] **:** a cartilage of the larynx which articulates with the lower cornua of the thyroid cartilage and with which the arytenoid cartilages articulate

²cricoid \"\ *adj* **:** being or relating to the cricoid

cri·co·ne·ma \ˌkrīkəˈnēmə\ *n, cap* [NL, fr. *crico-* + Gk *nēma* thread — more at NEEDLE] **:** the type genus of Criconematidae including short stout strongly annulated nematode worms with the annular cuticle prolonged into posteriorly directed scales or spines

cri·co·ne·mat·i·dae \ˌkrī(ˌ)kōnəˈmad·əˌdē\ *n pl, cap* [NL, fr. *Criconemat-, Criconema,* type genus + *-idae*] **:** a family of nematode worms (suborder Tylenchina) that includes a number of saprophagous and rhizophagous forms and a few plant parasites

cri de coeur *or* **cri du coeur** \ˌkrēdəˈkər\ *n, pl* **cris de coeur** *or* **cris du coeur** \ˌkrē(z)d-\ [F, lit., cry from the heart] **:** passionate protest, appeal, or complaint

cried *past of* CRY

cri·er *or* **cry·er** \ˈkrī(ə)r, -īə\ *n* -s [ME *criere,* fr. MF *crieor,* fr. *crier* to cry, shout + *-eor* -or — more at CRY] **:** one that cries: **a :** an officer who proclaims the orders or directions of a court **b :** a person appointed to make public proclamations in a loud voice **:** TOWN CRIER **c :** a person who cries goods for sale **:** HAWKER, AUCTIONEER

cries *pres 3d sing of* CRY, *pl of* CRY

crig \ˈkrig\ *n* -s [IrGael *criogān* bruise, sore] **:** ⁵BLOW 1a

cri·key \ˈkrīkē\ *or* **crick·ey** \ˈkrikē\ *or* **crick·ety** \-kəd·ē\ *or* **cricky** \-kē\ *interj* [euphemism for *Christ*] — a mild oath, often in the phrase *by crikey*

crile \ˈkrīl\ *n* -s [obs. D *kriel* hunchback, dwarf, collection of small items; akin to MD *crauwel, crouwel* hook, OHG *krouwōn* to scratch — more at CRUMB] *chiefly Scot* **:** a short deformed person **:** DWARF

¹crime \ˈkrīm\ *n* -s [ME, fr. MF, fr. L *crimen* accusation, fault, crime; perh. akin to OHG *scrīan* to cry out — more at SCREAM] **1 a :** an act or the commission of an act that is forbidden or the omission of a duty that is commanded by a public law of a sovereign state to the injury of the public welfare and that makes the offender liable to punishment by that law in a proceeding brought against him by the state by indictment, information, complaint, or similar criminal procedure **:** an offense against public law (as a misdemeanor, felony, or act of treason) providing a penalty against the offender but not including a petty violation of municipal regulation — compare DELICT, MALICE, MALUM IN SE, MALUM PROHIBITUM, TORT, WRONG **b :** an offense against the social order or a violation of the mores that is dealt with by community action rather than by an individual or kinship group **2** *obs* **a :** CHARGE, ACCUSATION **b :** cause for accusation or reproach **3 a :** a gross violation of law — distinguished from *misdemeanor, trespass* **b :** a grave or aggravated offense against or departure from moral rectitude **4 :** criminal activity **:** conduct in violation of the law **5 a :** an evil act **:** SIN **:** a violation of divine law; *esp* **:** a grievous sin **b :** sinful conduct **:** WRONGDOING **6 :** something reprehensible, foolish, indiscreet, or disgraceful ⟨it's a ~ to waste good food⟩ ⟨the bishop's ~ was that he dogmatized —Walter Moberly⟩

²crime \"\ *vt* -ED/-ING/-S *slang Brit* **:** to indict and punish (a soldier) for a minor infraction of military rules

crime against humanity : atrocity (as extermination, enslavement, or deportation under inhuman conditions) that is directed esp. against an entire population or segment of a population on specious grounds and without regard to individual guilt or responsibility even on such grounds

crime against nature : a sexual act that is regarded by the law as abnormal **:** SODOMY, BUGGERY

cri·me·an \(ˈ)krīˈmēən, krə̇ˈ-\ *adj, usu cap* [*Crimea,* peninsula in southern Russia + E *-an*] **:** of, relating to, or originating in Crimea

crimean gothic *n, usu cap C&G* **:** a dialect of the Gothic language known only from a list of words in use in the Crimea in the 16th cent.

crimean pine *n, usu cap C* **:** an evergreen tree (*Pinus nigra caramanica*) of Asia Minor with esp. the lower branches sharply ascending and rigid twisted glossy leaves

crimean snowdrop *n, usu cap C* **:** a bulbous herb (*Galanthus plicatus*) of the Crimea with bluish green foliage

crimean wheat *n, usu cap C* **:** any of several wheats introduced from the Crimean region of Russia and grown extensively in the Great Plains area and in Canada

crime·ful \ˈkrīmfəl\ *adj* **:** marked by crime or notable for crimes **:** CRIMINAL ⟨feats so ~ and so capital in nature —Shak.⟩

crime·less \-lə̇s\ *adj* **:** INNOCENT; *esp* **:** free of crime ⟨I am loyal, true, and ~ —Shak.⟩

cri·men \ˈkrīmən, -(ˌ)men\ *n, pl* **crim·i·na** \ˈkrimənə\ [L — more at CRIME] **:** CRIME

crimen ex·tra·or·di·nar·i·um \-ˌekstrəˌō(r)də̇ˈna(a)rēəm\ *n, pl* **crimina extraordinaria** [LL, lit., extraordinary crime] **:** a crime in Roman law that was considered extraordinary in that punishment was not fixed by earlier written law but was left to the discretion of the judge

crimen fal·si \-ˈfȯl(t)ˌsī\ *n* [LL, crime of falsifying] **:** FALSI CRIMEN

crime of passion 1 : a crime committed in the heat of passion **2 :** CRIME PASSIONEL

crime pas·si·o·nel *also* **crime pas·si·on·nel** \ˌkrēm‚päsēəˈnel\ *n, pl* **crimes passionels** \"\ [F, lit., crime of passion] **:** a crime due to sexual motives

crime wave *n* **:** a transitory but marked and relatively widespread increase in crime

¹crim·i·nal \ˈkrimənᵊl, -mnəl\ *adj* [ME *cryminall,* fr. MF or LL; MF *criminel,* fr. LL *criminalis,* fr. L *crimin-, crimen* crime + *-alis* -al — more at CRIME] **1 :** involving or being a crime ⟨~ carelessness⟩ **2 :** relating to crime or its punishment ⟨a ~ action⟩ — distinguished from *civil* **3 :** guilty of crime or serious offense ⟨he created a government that was frankly ~ —Eric Linklater⟩ ⟨~ in the sight of God and man⟩ **4 a :** REPREHENSIBLE, BLAMEWORTHY, DISGRACEFUL ⟨she was a ~ idiot to marry a man with his record⟩ ⟨it was one of those ~ adventures that marked the road of the Communist International during the twenties —D.J.Dallin⟩ **b :** EXCESSIVE, EXTORTIONATE ⟨saddle horses to be had not too far from the campus, but the rates were absolutely ~ —Edward Newhouse⟩ **5 :** of or suitable to a criminal ⟨the twists of the ~ mind⟩ **6 :** concerned with crime or criminal law

²criminal \"\ *n* -s [F *criminel,* fr. *criminel,* adj.] **1 :** one that has committed a crime **:** MALEFACTOR **2 :** a person who has been convicted of one or more crimes ⟨habitual ~*s*⟩

syn FELON, CONVICT, MALEFACTOR, CULPRIT, DELINQUENT: these words mean, in common, one guilty of a transgression or an offense, esp. against the law. CRIMINAL designates one who commits some serious violation of the law, of public trust, or common decency, as vicious unwarranted attack, embezzlement, or murder. FELON, the legal term for one popularly called a criminal, designates one guilty of a felony, which usu. with legal exactness covers all lawbreaking punishable by death or prolonged confinement (as in a state penitentiary) and is distinguished from a misdemeanor ⟨men were transported with the worst *felons* for poaching a few hares or pheasants —G.B.Shaw⟩ ⟨the casual or accidental *felon* who is impelled into a misdeed by force of circumstances —R.S.Banay⟩ CONVICT designates one convicted of a crime or felony but has come more generally to signify any person serving a long prison term ⟨the stranger turned out to be a *convict* who had escaped on the way to prison⟩ ⟨a riot among *convicts* in a state penitentiary⟩ MALEFACTOR signifies one who has committed an evil deed or serious offense but suggests little or no relation to courts or punishment ⟨most of our *malefactors,* from statesmen to thieves —T.S.Eliot⟩ ⟨a *malefactor* robbing small stores at night and setting fire to them⟩ CULPRIT often carries the weakened sense of one guilty of a crime ⟨after the series of crimes, the police tried for several weeks to find the *culprit*⟩ but more generally either suggests a trivial fault or offense, esp. of a child ⟨the *culprits* were two boys, one about 12 years old, the other about 10 —Green Peyton⟩ or applies to a person or thing that causes some undesirable condition or situation ⟨another group of supposed *culprits* who are being blamed for the present inflationary situation —T.O.Waage⟩ ⟨the *culprit* holding up world peace and understanding —W. A. Lydgate⟩ DELINQUENT applies to an offender against duty or the law esp. in a degree not constituting crime; in its present semilegal use, in application to juvenile offenders against civil or moral law, it usu. implies a habitual tendency to commit certain offenses and contrasts with CRIMINAL in implying a sociological or psychological rather than judicial attitude toward the offender ⟨whether a customer who has missed a payment is . . . a habitual *delinquent* —C.W.Phelps⟩ ⟨we label as *delinquents* those who do not conform to the legal and moral codes of society—*Federal Probation*⟩

criminal abortion *n* **:** ILLEGAL ABORTION

criminal anthropology *n* **:** CRIMINOLOGY; *specif* **:** Lombrosian doctrines

criminal assault *n* **:** a violent physical attack upon a person esp. with sexual contact or attempt at sexual contact **:** RAPE

criminal conspiracy *n* **:** CONSPIRACY 1b

criminal contempt *n* **1 :** contempt that is committed in the presence of a court in session or a judge acting in a judicial capacity or so near to either of these as to interfere with the proceedings and that tends to belittle or insult the judge or to degrade or obstruct justice **:** a direct contempt not affecting a civil remedy of a party — compare CONSTRUCTIVE CONTEMPT **2 :** contempt that tends to interfere directly with a legislature or one of its committees exercising its lawful powers or that constitutes disrespect for its authority in the course of its lawful proceedings

criminal conversation *n* **:** unlawful intercourse with a married woman **:** adultery considered as a tort — abbr. *crim. con.*

criminal court *n* **:** a court established with jurisdiction to try and punish offenders against the criminal laws

crim·i·nal·ism \'krimən°l,izəm, -mnə,li-\ *n* -s [prob. fr. F *criminalisme*, fr. LL *criminalis* criminal + F *-isme* -ism] : the tendency to criminality; *also* : habitual criminality
crim·i·nal·ist \-mən°ləst, -mnəl-\ *n* -s [F *criminaliste* or G *kriminalist*, fr. NL *criminalista*, fr. L *criminalis* + *-ista* -ist] **1** : a specialist in criminal law **2** : a specialist in criminology
crim·i·nal·is·tic \¦krimən°l¦istik, -mnə¦li-\ *adj* : tending to criminality
crim·i·nal·is·tics \-ks\ *n pl but sing in constr* [G *kriminalistik*, fr. *kriminalist* criminalist + *-ik* -ics] : scientific crime detection : the application of techniques from the physical sciences and psychology to the problems of criminal identification and apprehension
crim·i·nal·i·ty \,krimə'naləd·ē, -ətē, -i\ *n* -ES [F or ML; F *criminalité*, fr. ML *criminalitat-*, *criminalitas*, fr. LL *criminalis* criminal + L *-itat-*, *-itas* -ity — more at CRIMINAL] **1** : the quality or state of being guilty of crime or of being criminal **2** : an act or practice that constitutes a crime **3** : the criminal class ⟨prohibition opened up a world of profits to organized ~ —*Newsweek*⟩
criminal law *n* : a branch of jurisprudence that relates to crimes — distinguished from *civil law*
criminal lawyer *n* : a lawyer who specializes in cases that involve the law as it relates to crime
crim·i·nal·ly \'krimən°lē, -mnəlē, -i\ *adv* [¹*criminal* + *-ly*] **1** : according to criminal law ⟨to proceed against him ~⟩ **2** : in a criminal manner : in violation of law : WICKEDLY ⟨~ involved with gamblers⟩ **3** : REPREHENSIVELY, DISGRACEFULLY, SHAMEFULLY ⟨the lawns were ~ kept —J.T.Jackson⟩ ⟨he calls our schools ~ superficial and ill-disciplined⟩
crim·i·nal·ness \-mən°lnəs, -mnəl-\ *n* -ES : CRIMINALITY
crim·i·nal·oid \-mən°l,ȯid, -mnə,lȯid\ *n* -s [²*criminal* + *-oid*] : a person with some criminal characteristics : an occasional criminal
criminals *pl of* CRIMINAL
criminal syndicalism *n* : a statutory crime in many states of the U.S. consisting of acts of violence or of advocating violence or other illicit means of bringing about political change or alterations in government
crim·i·nate \'krimə,nāt, *usu* -ād·+V\ *vt* -ED/-ING/-S [L *criminatus*, past part. of *criminari* to accuse, fr. *crimin-*, *crimen* crime — more at CRIME] **1 a** : to accuse of or charge with a crime **b** : INCRIMINATE **2** : to accuse or represent as criminal : censure by charging or implying something criminal **syn** see ACCUSE
crim·i·na·tion \,krimə'nāshən\ *n* -s [L *crimination-*, *criminatio*, fr. *criminatus* + *-ion-*, *-io* -ion] : the act of criminating : ACCUSATION ⟨an attitude of cold determined ~⟩
crim·i·na·tive \'krimə,nād·iv, -mənəd·-\ *adj* : leading to or involving crimination : charging with crime
crim·i·na·tor \-,nād·ə(r)\ *n* -s [L, fr. *criminatus* + *-or*] : one that criminates
crim·i·na·to·ry \'krimənə,tōrē, -,tȯr-, -ri\ *adj* : relating to or involving crimination : ACCUSING ⟨a ~ conscience⟩
crim·i·ne *or* **crim·i·ni** *or* **crim·i·ny** \'krimənē, -rīm-\ *interj* [prob. euphemism for Christ] — used chiefly to express surprise
criming *pres part of* CRIME
crim·i·no·genesis \¦krimə(,)nō+\ *or* **cri·mo·genesis** \¦krīmə+\ *n* [*criminogenesis*, NL, fr. L *crimin-*, *crimen* crime + NL *-o-* + *-genesis*; *crimogenesis*, NL, alter. of *criminogenesis*] : the origin of crime
crim·i·no·gen·ic \¦krimə(,)nō¦jenik\ *or* **cri·mo·gen·ic** \¦krīmə¦-\ *adj* [*criminogenic* fr. L *crimin-*, *crimen* + E *-o-* + *-genic*; *crimogenic* alter. of *criminogenic*] : producing or leading to crime or criminality
crim·i·no·log·i·cal \¦krimənə¦läjəkəl\ *also* **crim·i·no·log·ic** \-¦läjik\ *adj* : of or relating to criminology — **crim·i·no·log·i·cal·ly** \-jək(ə)lē\ *adv*
crim·i·nol·o·gist \¦==¦näləjəst\ *n* -s : one that specializes in criminology
crim·i·nol·o·gy \-jē, -ji\ *n* -ES [It *criminologia*, fr. L *crimin-*, *crimen* crime + It *-o-* + *-logia* -logy] : the scientific study of crime as a social phenomenon, of criminal investigation, of criminals, and of penal treatment
crim·i·no·sis \,krimə'nōsəs\ *n*, *pl* **crimino·ses** \-,sēz\ [NL, fr. L *crimin-*, *crimen* crime + NL *-osis*] : psychoneurotic behavior taking the form of criminal or antisocial acts; *also* : a tendency toward such behavior
crim·i·not·ic \¦==¦näd·ik\ *adj* [fr. NL *criminosis*, after such pairs as NL *hypnosis*: E *hypnotic*] : suffering from criminosis ⟨a ~ individual⟩ : marked by criminosis ⟨~ behavior⟩
crim·i·nous \'krimənəs\ *adj* [MF *crimineux*, fr. ML *criminosus*, fr. L, reproachful, slanderous, fr. *crimin-*, *crimen* crime + *-osus* -ous] **1 a** *obs* : deserving punishment : CRIMINAL **b** : guilty of crime ⟨~ clerks⟩ **2** : concerned with crime ⟨an hysterical ~ tale⟩ ⟨the author's ~ reputation —Anthony Boucher⟩
crimmer *var of* KRIMMER
crim·my \'krimē, -mi\ *adj* [prob. alter. of E dial. *creemy*, fr. ¹*creem* + *-y*] *NewEng* : COLD, CHILLY
¹**crimp** \'krimp\ *vb* -ED/-ING/-S [D or LG *krimpen* to shrink, shrivel; akin to ON *kreppa* to clench — more at CRAMP] *vi* : to acquire, assume, or exhibit a creased or wavy appearance : WRINKLE ⟨hair that ~s easily⟩ ~ *vt* **1** : to cause to become wavy, crinkled, bent, or warped ⟨lumber ~*ed* by exposure to weather⟩: as **a** : to wave or curl (hair) usu. with a hot iron **b** : to cause the muscles of (a fresh fish) to contract by gashing or slashing; *also* : GASH, CUT **c** : to fix (cloth) in small pleats or folds **d** : to form (leather) into a desired shape (as in making boot uppers or saddles) **e** : to give (synthetic fibers) a curl like that of natural fibers **f** : to draw or pinch in or together in glass manufacturing to form a neck, produce fluting, or set off a base (as in the making of a vase) **g** : to roll or curl the edge of (as a steel panel) **h** : CORRUGATE ⟨~*ing* sheet iron⟩ **2** : to close, unite, or make continuous by crimping, pinching together, or folding: as **a** : to fold inward (as the edge of a tin can or a shotgun shell) to retain a head or other cover **b** : to pinch or press together (as the margins of a pie crust) in order to seal **3** : to press in in order to contract (as the end of a pipe) **4** : to put a crimp in : CRAMP, INHIBIT ⟨~*ing* sales by credit controls⟩ ⟨stern knights ~*ed* by their armor⟩
²**crimp** \"\ *n* -s **1** : something produced by or as if by crimping: as **a** : a section of hair artificially waved or curled — usu. used in pl. ⟨her head covered with ~*s*⟩ **b** : the succession of waves in wool fiber ⟨a fine ~ is typical of the best wools⟩; *also* : induced waviness of a synthetic fiber (as nylon) **c** : disordering of fibers in wood (as by too rapid drying) **d** : ²CRAMP 1c **e** : the fold formed by crimping esp. on a can or cartridge **f** : an offset in a structural steel member (as a web stiffener) that adapts it to fit over another member **g** : a slight bend or crease put in a playing card in order to identify it **2** : an interfering element : something that cramps or inhibits : OBSTACLE, CURB — used chiefly in the phrase *put a crimp in* ⟨strikes last year put a serious ~ in production —*Time*⟩
³**crimp** \"\ *adj* [perh. fr. LG *krimp* crooked, shrunken; akin to LG & D *krimpen* to shrink, shrivel] **1** *archaic* : easily crumbled : FRIABLE **2** : CRIMPED, CRINKLED — **crimp·ness** *n* -ES
⁴**crimp** \"\ *n* -s [D or LG *krimp*, perh. fr. *krimpen* to shrink, shrivel] : an old game of cards
⁵**crimp** \"\ *n* -s [perh. fr. ¹*crimp*] : a person who entraps or forces men into shipping as sailors or enlisting in an army or navy against their will or while insensible — compare PRESS GANG
⁶**crimp** \"\ *vt* -ED/-ING/-S : to trap into military or sea service : IMPRESS
crimp·age \-pij\ *n* -s [⁵*crimp* + *-age*] *archaic* : money paid to a crimp for his services
crimped *adj* [fr. past part. of ¹*crimp*] : marked or affected by crimping; *esp* : CRAMPED, HANDICAPPED, STRAITENED ⟨cash-*crimped* savings banks —*Newsweek*⟩ ⟨exposing briefly their ~ personalities and petty goals —*Time*⟩
¹**crimp·er** \'krimpə(r)\ *n* -s [¹*crimp* + *-er*] : one that crimps (as bottle tops)
²**crimper** \"\ *n* -s [⁶*crimp* + *-er*] : ⁵CRIMP
crimping iron *n* [fr. pres. part. of ¹*crimp*] : a fluted block or die for crimping
crim·ple \'krimpəl\ *n* -s [²*crimp* + *-le*] : ²CRIMP; *esp* : CURL, WAVE
crimpy \'krimpē, -pi\ *adj* -ER/-EST [¹*crimp* + *-y*] **1** : having a crimped appearance : FRIZZY ⟨~ hair⟩ **2** *of weather* : UNPLEASANT : raw and cold
¹**crim·son** \'krimzən *also* -m(p)sən\ *n* -s [ME *cremesin*, *crimisin*, fr. OSp *cremesin*, fr. Ar *qirmizī* red of the kermes, fr. *qirmiz* kermes, perh. of Indic origin; akin to Skt *krmi* worm; akin to Lith *kirmis* worm, OIr *cruim*] **1 a** : any of several deep or vivid reds or purplish reds of rather indefinite range **b** : a pigment or dye that colors crimson **2** : something crimson ⟨a coat of fine-woven ~⟩
²**crimson** \"\ *adj* [ME *cremesin*, *crimisin*, fr. *cremesin*, *crimisin*, n.] **1** : of the color crimson **2** : resembling the color crimson; *esp* : BLOODY **3** : flushed from embarrassment or anger **4** : VIOLENT, LURID ⟨writes of ~ deeds and barbaric days —Andrea Parke⟩ ⟨circulating ~ rumors⟩ — **crim·son·ly** *adv* — **crim·son·ness** \-°n(n)əs\ *n* -ES
³**crimson** \"\ *vb* -ED/-ING/-S *vt* : to make crimson : dye with crimson ~ *vi* : to become crimson: **a** : BLUSH, FLUSH **b** : RIPEN ⟨apples ~*ing* in the fall⟩
crimson antimony *n* : ANTIMONY VERMILION
crimson climbing rata *n* : a New Zealand woody vine (*Metrosideros diffusa*) that produces a profusion of brilliant red flowers
crimson clover *n* : a European annual clover (*Trifolium incarnatum*) that has cylindrical spiky heads of crimson flowers and that is extensively cultivated in the U.S. as a forage plant
crimson flag *n* : a South African herb (*Schizostylis coccinea*) of the family Iridaceae with clustered fleshy roots, narrow leaves, and a slender stalk bearing a number of crimson flowers shaped like a bell
crimson–fronted bullfinch \¦==¦==-\ *n* : HOUSE FINCH
crimson glory vine *n* : a Japanese grape (*Vitis kaempferi*) with very colorful autumnal foliage
crimson haw *n* : SCARLET HAW
crimson lake *n* **1 a** : a lake that is made from cochineal and that is similar to carmine — called also *Florentine lake* **b** : lake that is made from redwood **2** : a moderate red that is yellower than cerise, yellower and slightly darker than claret (sense 3a), and bluer and very slightly lighter than Turkey red — called also *sultan*
crimson madder *n* : MADDER CRIMSON
crimson manuka *n* : a usu. shrubby red-flowered New Zealand tea tree (*Leptospermum scoparium*)
crimson rambler *n* : a well-known hardy climbing rose (*Rosa barbierana*) originating as a hybrid between *R. wichuraiana* and *R. cathayensis*
crimson sage *n* : a coarse herb (*Ramona grandiflora*) of the western U.S. with showy crimson flowers
crimson tragopan *n* : a crimson Indian tragopan (*Tragopan satyra*) that has the feathers ocellated with white and that is a favorite game bird
crim·sony \'krimzənē *also* -m(p)sənē\ *adj* : tinged with or resembling crimson
crin \'krin\ *n* -s [by shortening] : CRINOLINE 1
cri·nal \'krīn°l\ *adj* [L *crinalis*, fr. *crinis* hair + *-alis* -al; akin to L *crista* crest — more at CREST] : of or relating to the hair
crine \'krīn\ *vb* -ED/-ING/-S [ScGael *crìon* to wither; akin to OIr *crín* withered, L *caries* decay — more at CARIES] *vi*, *Scot* : SHRINK, SHRIVEL ~ *vt*, *Scot* : to cause to dry up, shrink, or shrivel
crined \'krīnd\ *adj* [MF *crin* hair (fr. L *crinis*) + E *-ed* — more at CRINAL] : emblazoned with hair ⟨a unicorn argent ~ or⟩
crin·et \'krinət\ *n* -s [MF *crinete*, *crignete* mane, fr. OF *crignete*, dim. of *crin* hair, horsehair, mane] : articulated armor protecting the upper surface of the neck of a medieval war horse
¹**cringe** \'krinj\ *vb* -ED/-ING/-S [ME *crengen*, causative fr. the root of OE *cringan* to fall, yield; akin to MHG *krinc* ring, circle, ON *kringr* circle, OE *cradol* cradle — more at CRADLE] *vi* **1** : to draw in or contract one's muscles involuntarily : SHRINK, HUDDLE, CROUCH ⟨we ~ under the blasting wind —C.S.Houston⟩ **2** : to shrink in fear or servility : bend or crouch with base humility **3** : to make court in a degrading or servile manner : to approach with fawning and self-abasement ~ *vt* **1** *obs* : to draw in or together : cause to shrink or wrinkle : CONTRACT, CONTORT **2** *archaic* : to meet, greet, or escort with cringes ⟨hence, and bow and ~ him here —Lord Byron⟩
²**cringe** \"\ *n* -s **1** : excessive deference : SERVILITY, FAWNING ⟨the provincial tends to suffer a cultural ~ toward urban centers⟩ **2** : a cringing act; *specif* : an excessive or servile bow ⟨performing ~*s* and congees like a court chamberlain —W.M.Thackeray⟩
cringe·ling \-jliŋ\ *n* -s : CRINGER
cring·er \-jə(r)\ *n* -s : one that cringes
cringing *adj* **1** : that shrinks in fear or servility ⟨a ~ rascal⟩ **2** : ABJECT, SERVILE ⟨~ caution⟩ — **cring·ing·ly** *adv* — **cring·ing·ness** *n* -ES
crin·gle \'kriŋgəl\ *n* -s [LG *kringel*, dim. of *kring* ring, circle, fr. MLG *kring*, *krink*; akin to MHG *krinc* ring, circle] : a ring or loop for holding or fastening something: as **a** : TERRET **b** : a thimble, grommet, eyelet, or rope loop worked into or attached to the edge of a sail and used for making fast various ropes and lines

cringle b

crin·gle–cran·gle \¦kriŋgəl¦kraŋgəl\ *adv (or adj)* [prob. alter. of *crinkle-crankle*] : in a zigzag manner
crini- *comb form* [L, fr. *crinis*] : hair ⟨*crini*culture⟩ ⟨*crini*parous⟩
cri·nière \krēn'ya(a)(ə)r\ *n* -s [F, fr. MF, fr. *crin* hair, horsehair, mane — more at CRINED] : CRINET
crin·i·ger \'krinəjə(r)\ *n*, *cap* [NL, fr. L *criniger* long-haired, fr. *crini-* + *-ger* -gerous; fr. the hairlike filaments on some of the feathers] : a genus of thick-billed harsh-voiced Asiatic and African bulbuls
crin·i·on \'krinē,än\ *n* -s [NL, fr. L *crinis* hair + Gk *-ion* (dim. suffix) — more at CRINOL] : TRICHION
¹**cri·nite** \'krī,nīt, -ri,-\ *adj* [L *crinitus*, past part. of *crinire* to provide with hair, fr. *crinis* hair] : covered or provided with hairy growths : like hair or a hair
²**crinite** \"\ *n* -s [ISV *crinoid* + *-ite*] : a fossil crinoid
¹**crink** \'kriŋk\ *n* -s [LG *krink* circle, ring; akin to MHG *krinc* circle, ring — more at CRINGE] *dial Eng* : BEND, TWIST
²**crink** \"\ *vt* -ED/-ING/-S *dial Eng* : BEND, TWIST, WRENCH
³**crink** \"\ *vi* -ED/-ING/-S [imit.] : to make or emit a thin abrupt metallic or crackling sound ⟨cicadas ~*ing* in the heat⟩
¹**crin·kle** \'kriŋkəl\ *vb* **crinkled**; **crinkled**; **crinkling** \-k(ə)liŋ\ **crinkles** [ME *crynkelen*, *crenklen*, *crounkilen*; akin to MD *crinkelen* to crinkle, OE *cringan* to fall, yield — more at CRINGE] *vi* **1 a** : to form many short bends or turns : TURN, WIND **b** : to move in waves : WRINKLE, RIPPLE **2** *now dial Eng* : CRINGE; *also* : to turn aside or draw back from a purpose or promise **3** : to give forth a thin metallic or crackling sound : RUSTLE ⟨stiff silk *crinkling* and swishing about her ankles⟩ ~ *vt* : to cause to crinkle ⟨the damp air *crinkled* her hair about her face⟩ : WRINKLE, RIPPLE, CURL ⟨a breeze barely *crinkling* the ripening wheat⟩
²**crinkle** \"\ *n* -s **1** : WINDING, TURN, WRINKLE, CORRUGATION, FOLD **2 a** : cork (sense 5) when marked by internal necrotic regions **b** : potato mosaic in which puckered crinkly-edged downward-curved leaves occur **c** : any of several diseases characterized by crinkling of leaf margins (as strawberry crinkle)
crinkle·awn \'kriŋkəl,ȯn\ *n* -s : a grass (*Trachypogon montufari*) of the southwestern U.S. having spiky racemes and long awns
crinkle–bush \'==,=\ *n* : the dyed sprays of an Australian shrub (*Lomatia silaifolia*) used by decorators and florists for ornament
crin·kle–cran·kle \¦kriŋkəl¦kraŋkəl\ *n* -s [*crinkle* + *crankle*] : a winding in and out : SINUOSITY, ZIGZAG
crinkled *also* **crinkle** *adj* : having crinkles: as **a** *of a fabric* : woven or processed so as to produce a wholly or partially puckered surface — compare SEERSUCKER **b** *of a finish* : having a roughened surface thrown into fine wrinkles ⟨finished in ~ black enamel⟩
crinkle·root \'==,=\ *n* : an American plant of the genus *Dentaria* (esp. *D. diphylla*)
crin·kly *also* **crin·kley** \'kriŋk(ə)lē, -li\ *adj* -ER/-EST **1** : full of crinkles : WAVY, WRINKLY **2** : CRACKLY, RUSTLING
crin·kum–cran·kum \¦kriŋkəm¦kraŋkəm\ *n* -s [alter. (influenced by L nouns ending in *-um*) of *crinkle-crankle*] *archaic* : something full of twists and turns : a thing fancifully or excessively intricate and elaborate
¹**cri·noid** \'krī,nȯid, -ri,-\ *adj* [NL *Crinoidea*] : of or relating to the Crinoidea : CRINOIDAL
²**crinoid** \"\ *n* -s : one of the Crinoidea : SEA LILY
cri·noi·dal \(')krī¦nȯid°l, krə'-\ *adj* : of or relating to crinoids : consisting of or containing crinoids ⟨~ limestone⟩
cri·noi·dea \krə'nȯidēə, -rī'-\ *n pl*, *cap* [NL, fr. Gk *krinon* lily + NL *-oidea*] : a large class of chiefly tropical or fossil echinoderms that have a more or less cup-shaped body provided with five or more feathery arms commonly bifurcated or many-branched and bearing pinnules, a mouth lying between the arms on the concave upper surface, and opposite the mouth usu. a long jointed stalk fixed to the base of the body and having its opposite end divided into rhizoid processes that anchor the animal to the sea bottom — compare COMATULID, SEA LILY — **cri·noi·de·an** \krə'nȯidēən, (')krī¦-\ *adj or n*
¹**crin·o·line** \'krin°lən, -°l,ēn *also* ,=°l'ēn *sometimes* '=°l,īn\ *n* -s [F, fr. It *crinolino*, fr. *crino* horsehair (fr. L *crinis* hair) + *lino* flax, linen, fr. L *linum* — more at CRINAL, LINEN] **1** : a stiffened open-weave fabric of horsehair or cotton used for interlinings and millinery and for underskirts to expand the overskirts; *also* : this fabric without stiffening used for surgical purposes (as in bandages impregnated with plaster of paris) **2 a** : HOOPSKIRT **b** : a full stiff skirt or underskirt
²**crinoline** \"\ *adj* **1** : of or relating to crinoline ⟨~ bandage⟩ **2** : suggesting, typified by, or having a crinoline : belonging to the crinoline era; *esp* : OUTDATED, OLD-FASHIONED
crin·o·lined \-nd\ *adj* **1** : wearing a crinoline ⟨a pretty ~ miss⟩ **2** : stiffened with crinoline ⟨a ~ petticoat⟩
cri·nos·i·ty \krī'näsəd·ē, krə'-\ *n* -ES [L *crinis* hair + E *-osity*] : HAIRINESS
crins *pl of* CRIN
cri·num \'krīnəm\ *n* [NL, fr. L *crinum*, *crinon* lily, fr. Gk *krinon*] **1** *cap* : a large genus of chiefly tropical bulbous herbs (family Amaryllidaceae) that are often cultivated for their umbels of showy and often fragrant white flowers which are frequently tinged or banded with red **2** -s : any plant of the genus *Crinum*
-cri·nus \¦krīnəs\ *n comb form* [NL, fr. Gk *krinon* lily] : a crinoid — in generic names of Crinoidea ⟨Actino*crinus*⟩ ⟨Pentacrinus⟩
crin ve·ge·tal \,kraⁿ,vāzhā'täl\ *n*, *pl* **crins vegetal** *or* **crin vegetals** \"\ [F *crin végétal*, lit., vegetable hair] : the fiber of the European hemp palm
cri·o·bo·li·um \,krīə'bōlēəm\ *also* **cri·ob·o·ly** \krī'äbəlē\ *n*, *pl* **criobo·lia** \-lēə\ *also* **criobolies** [LL *criobolium*, fr. LGk *kriobolion*, fr. Gk *krios* ram + *-bolion* (fr. Gk *ballein* to throw); akin to L *cornu* horn — more at HORN, DEVIL] : a ceremony in the cult of certain Mediterranean deities (as Cybele and Attis) in which a ram was sacrificed so that the blood fell on the devotee — compare TAUROBOLIUM
cri·oc·er·as \krī'äsərəs\ *n*, *cap* [NL, fr. Gk *krios* ram + NL *-ceras*] : a genus of Cretaceous ammonites with complexly plicated septa — **cri·o·cer·a·tite** \,krīə'serə,tīt\ *n* -s — **cri·o·cer·a·tit·ic** \¦==¦==¦tid·ik\ *adj*
cri·oc·er·is \krī'äsərəs\ *n*, *cap* [NL, fr. Gk *krios* ram + NL *-ceris* (alter. of *-ceras*)] : a large cosmopolitan genus of beetles (family Chrysomelidae) including the asparagus beetle
cri·ol·la \krē'ōl(y)ə\ *n* -s *sometimes cap* [Sp, fem. of *criollo*] : a female criollo
cri·ol·lis·mo \,krēə'liz(,)mō\ *n* -s [Sp, fr. *criollo* + *-ismo* -ism] : preoccupation in the arts and esp. the literature of Latin America with native scenes and types; *esp* : nationalistic preoccupation with such matter
¹**cri·ol·lo** \krē'ōl(y)ō\ *n* -s *sometimes cap* [Sp — more at CREOLE] **1 a** : a person of pure Spanish descent born in Spanish America — compare CREOLE **b** : any person born and usu. raised in a Spanish-American country; *esp* : one of Spanish descent **2** [AmerSp, fr. Sp] : an animal of any of various breeds or strains of domestic animals developed in Latin America: as **a** : a small vigorous usu. dun or light brown So. American horse developed by judicious interbreeding of native and Arab stock **b** : a long-wooled sheep of Spanish origin now restricted to the Andes and adjacent Argentina **c** : any of several local strains of cattle some of predominantly dairy type, others of beef **3** : any of various cacaos with very rough but thin-shelled pods and white seeds of superior quality — compare FORASTERO
²**criollo** \"\ *adj*, *sometimes cap* [Sp, fr. *criollo*, n.] **1** : of, relating to, or being a criollo **2** : native to a Spanish-American country as opposed to European : not alien to Spanish America
cri·o·phore \'krīə,fō(ə)r\ *n* -s [F, carrying a ram, fr. Gk *kriophoros*, fr. *krios* ram + *-phoros* -phorous] : a statue, figurine, or other representation in ancient art of a man carrying a ram
¹**crip** \'krip\ *n* -s [by shortening] : CRIPPLE — often taken to be offensive
²**crip** \"\ *adj* : such as a cripple could perform : EASY ⟨a ~ course⟩ ⟨a ~ shot in basketball⟩
cripes \'krīps\ *also* **cripe** \-p\ *interj* [euphemism for *Christ*] — a mild oath
¹**crip·ple** \'kripəl\ *n* -s [ME *cripel*, fr. OE *crypel*; akin to MLG *kropel*, *krepel*, cripple, ON *kryppill*, OE *cryppan* to bend, *crēopan* to creep — more at CREEP] **1 a** : one that has lost or never has had the use of a limb or limbs or has lost a greater part of such use : a lame person or animal : one that creeps, halts, or limps **b** : a person disabled, deficient, or ineffective in a specified manner or fashion ⟨a heart ~⟩ ⟨social and mental ~*s*⟩ **c** : a game bird or mammal injured but not recovered by the hunter **2** : SUPPORT; *esp* : a temporary staging used in washing or painting windows **3 a** : something flawed or imperfect (as a badly done job, a damaged railway car, or a cake marred in the baking) **b** *dial* : swampy or low wet ground usu. covered with brush or thickets **4** : a baseball pitch delivered without much stuff on it esp. when the count favors the batter (as at three balls and no strikes) ⟨hit the ~ for a double⟩ **5** : a unit in a building frame that is shorter than is usual for such a unit (as a stud reaching only from a window opening to a ceiling beam)
²**cripple** \"\ *adj* [ME *cripel*, fr. *cripel*, n.] : being a cripple : LAME; *also* : worn out : INFERIOR
³**cripple** \"\ *vb* **crippled**; **crippled**; **crippling** \-p(ə)liŋ\ **cripples** [ME *criplen*, fr. *cripel*, n.] *vt* : to make a cripple of: as **a** : to deprive of the use of a limb (as a leg or foot) ⟨those sorry thousands *crippled* by arthritis⟩ **b** : to deprive of strength, efficiency, wholeness, or capability for service ⟨strikes are *crippling* our basic industries⟩ ⟨such a sea would ~ any boat⟩ ~ *vi* : to be, become, or act like a cripple: **a** : to walk lamely : HOBBLE, HALT **b** : to become disabled, incapacitated, or weakened **syn** see MAIM, WEAKEN
crip·ple·dom \-(,)dəm\ *n* -s : CRIPPLEMENT
crip·ple·ment \-mənt\ *n* -s : crippled condition : LAMENESS
crip·pler \-p(ə)lə(r)\ *n* -s **1** : one that cripples; *esp* : a disease that results in crippling ⟨polio is still a major ~ of children⟩ **2** : a wooden tool used in graining leather
¹**crippling** *adj* [fr. pres. part. of ³*cripple*] **1** : that cripples ⟨a ~ sense of personal inferiority⟩ **2** : caused by crippling ⟨~ losses of game by careless hunters⟩ — **crip·pling·ly** *adv*
²**crippling** *n* -s [fr. gerund of ³*cripple*] : the state of being or process of becoming crippled; *specif* : the failure of the webs of steel beams or girders by buckling due to excessive loading **2** : shoring for the side of a building
crips \'krips\ *adj* -ER/-EST [ME — more at CRISP] *dial* : CRISP
crise \'krēz\ *n* -s [F, fr. L *crisis*] : a moment of risk or stress : CRISIS; *also* : a state of perturbation
cri·sic \'krīsik\ *adj* [*crisis* + *-ic*] : of or relating to a crisis
cri·sis \'krīsəs\ *n*, *pl* **cri·ses** \-,sēz\ *also* **crisises** \-səsəz\ [L, fr. Gk *krisis*, fr. *krinein* to separate — more at CERTAIN] **1 a** : the turning point for better or worse in an acute disease or fever; *esp* : a sudden turn for the better (as sudden abatement in severity of symptoms or abrupt drop in temperature)

— compare LYSIS **b** : a paroxysmal attack of pain, distress, or disordered function ⟨tabetic ~⟩ ⟨cardiac ~⟩ **c** : an emotionally significant event or radical change of status in a person's life **2 a** : the point of time when it is decided whether an affair or course of action shall proceed, be modified, or terminate : decisive moment : turning point **b** : such a point in the course of the action of a play or other work of fiction — compare CLIMAX, RESOLUTION **c** : the immediate sequel to the culminating point of a period of prosperity and rising markets at which the business organism is severely strained and forced liquidation occurs — see BUSINESS CYCLE **3 a** : an unstable state of affairs in which a decisive change is impending ⟨recurrent cabinet *crises* trouble France⟩ **b** : a psychological or social condition characterized by unusual instability caused by excessive stress and either endangering or felt to endanger the continuity of the individual or his group; *esp* : such a social condition requiring the transformation of existing cultural patterns and values **syn** see JUNCTURE

crisis theologian *n* : an adherent of crisis theology

crisis theology *n* : neoorthodoxy esp. in its pessimistic view of human nature that holds that man and all human institutions are inevitably confounded by their own inner contradictions and that the resultant crisis forces man to despair of his own efforts and possibly to turn to divine revelation and grace in faith

¹crisp \ˈkrisp\ *adj* -ER/-EST [ME *crisp, crips* curly, fretted, fr. OE *crisp* curly, fr. L *crispus;* akin to MHG *rispen* to curl, OHG *hrispahi* bush, thicket, ON *rispa* to scratch, W *crych* curly, L *curvus* curved — more at CROWN] **1 a (1)** : CURLY, WAVY; *also* : having close stiff curls or waves or being somewhat wiry and stiff ⟨the short ~ hair of the natives⟩ **(2)** : having or made up of crisp hair ⟨a ~ hairdo⟩ ⟨the bull is commonly ~*er* about the forehead than his cows⟩ **b** : having the surface roughened into small folds or curling wrinkles ⟨~ whitecaps blown up by the wind⟩ **c** : CURLED **2 a** : having such a texture as to break apart easily and with a clear-cut fracture : BRITTLE, FRIABLE ⟨~ snow crackling underfoot⟩ **b** *of pastry* : SHORT **c** : firm and fresh : not flabby and wilted ⟨~ lettuces with the dew still on them⟩ **3** : exhibiting or suggesting some combination of qualities characteristic of or attributable to that which is crisp: **a** : sharp, clean-cut, and clear ⟨a ~ illustration⟩ : concise and orderly to the point of terseness ⟨~ military reports⟩ ⟨a ~ reply⟩ **b** : noticeably neat and spruce in appearance or deportment : well-groomed **c** : SPRIGHTLY, BRISK, VIVACIOUS ⟨a ~ manner⟩ : lively and sparkling ⟨~ repartee⟩ ⟨dialogue as ~ as Shaw at his best⟩ **d** : COLD, FROSTY, SNAPPY ⟨~ winter weather⟩; *also* : fresh and invigorating ⟨a ~ odor of pines⟩ ⟨a ~ autumn breeze⟩ **e** *of a trigger* : releasing the firing mechanism smoothly and easily — compare ²CREEP 5d **syn** see INCISIVE

²crisp \"\ *vb* -ED/-ING/-S [ME *crispen,* fr. *crisp,* adj.] *vt* **1 a** : CURL, CRIMP ⟨~ her hair⟩ ⟨~ the nap of cloth⟩ **b** : to cause to ripple or undulate irregularly : WRINKLE ⟨a lake ~*ed* by the west wind⟩ **c** : to make crisp ⟨~*ing* celery in ice water⟩ **2** : to cause to crackle ⟨the wheels ~ the gravel⟩ **3** : to fold (cloth) into lengths ~ *vi* **1** : CURL, RIPPLE ⟨her fingers ~*ed* on the tablecloth —Rebecca West⟩ ⟨leaves ~*ing* and fluttering in the sunlight⟩ **2** : to become crisp ⟨bread ~*ing* in the oven⟩ ⟨the ground ~*ed* with frost⟩

³crisp \"\ *n* -S [¹*crisp*] : something crisp or brittle ⟨dinner burned to a ~⟩: as **a** *slang* : BANK NOTE **b** *chiefly Brit* : POTATO CHIP — usu. used in pl.

cris·pate \ˈkriˌspāt, -spət\ *or* **cris·pat·ed** \-ˌspād·əd\ *adj* [*crispate* fr. L *crispatus,* past part. of *crispare* to curl, fr. *crispus* curly; *crispated* fr. L *crispatus* + E *-ed*] : having a crisped appearance : irregularly curled or crinkled : CRISPED

cris·pa·tion \kriˈspāshən\ *n* -S [L *crispatus* + E *-ion*] **1** : the act or process of curling : the state of being curled : UNDULATION **2** : a slight shrinking or spasmodic contraction ⟨few men can look down from a great height without creepings and ~*s* —O.W.Holmes †1894⟩

crisped *adj* [ME, curled, fr. past part. of *crispen* to curl — more at CRISP] **1** : made crisp : curled esp. in ringlets : RIPPLED **2** : contorted or twisted ⟨the ~ leaves of the cabbage⟩

crisp·en \ˈkrispən\ *vb* -ED/-ING/-S [¹*crisp* + *-en*] *vt* : to make crisp ⟨celery ~*ed* by frost⟩ ~ *vi* : to become crisp ⟨a pasty ~*ing* in the oven⟩

crisp·er \ˈkrispə(r)\ *n* -S : one that crisps; *specif* : a closed container intended to prevent loss of moisture from fresh produce stored in a mechanical refrigerator

cris·pin \ˈkrispən\ *n* -S [after St. *Crispin* †*ab*287 patron saint of shoemakers] : SHOEMAKER, COBBLER

crisp·i·ness \ˈkrispēnəs, -pin-\ *n* -ES : CRISPNESS, BRITTLENESS, FLAKINESS

crisply *adv* : in a crisp manner ⟨never spoke or wrote except ~ —R.H.Rovere⟩

crisp·ness \ˈkrispnəs\ *n* -ES [ME *cryspeness,* fr. *cryspe, crisp* + *-ness*] : the quality or state of being crisp

crispy \ˈkrispē, -pi\ *adj* -ER/-EST [ME, curly, fr. ¹*crisp* + *-y*] : CRISP

criss \ˈkris\ *n* -ES [alter. of ¹*crest*] : a wooden stand with a curved top on which crest tiles are shaped

cris·sal \ˈkrisəl\ *adj* [NL *crissalis,* fr. *crissum* + L *-alis* -al] : relating to or having a crissum — used chiefly in vernacular names of birds ⟨a ~ bunting⟩

crissal thrasher *n* : a thrasher (*Toxostoma crissalis*) occurring in the southwestern U.S. and distinguished by colored crissal feathers

¹criss·cross \ˈkriˌskrȯs *also* -räs\ *n* -ES [alter. of *christcross*] **1** : CHRISTCROSS; *esp* : MARK 2b(1) **2** *archaic* : TICKTACKTOE **3** : a crisscross pattern or something made up of one : NETWORK ⟨a ~ of greenery overhead —*New Yorker*⟩ **4** : something disordered or at cross purposes : confused state ⟨the fallacy which leads to this ~ of interpretations and opinions is the familiar one of confusing what the poet creates with what he represents —Susanne K. Langer⟩ ⟨a depressing ~ of figures⟩ **5** : a play in football in which the paths of two offensive players cross; *also* : a pass pattern in which two receivers cross to opposite sides of the field

²crisscross \"\ *vb* -ED/-ING/-ES *vt* **1** : to mark or score with intersecting lines ⟨~ the fat with a sharp knife⟩ **2** : to pass back and forth through or over ⟨British ships ~*ed* the seas⟩ ~ *vi* **1** : to go or pass back and forth ⟨birds ~*ing* in the blue⟩ **2** : to run toward opposite sides of the football field (as on a pass pattern) ⟨had the ends ~ downfield to confuse the pass defenders⟩

³crisscross \"\ *also* **criss·crossed** \ˈ≈;≈\ *adj* : marked or characterized by crisscrossing ⟨his ~ course⟩ : so arranged that constituent parts cross ⟨a ~ bodice⟩ ⟨~ fires⟩ : disposed in or made up of crossing lines ⟨~ threads⟩ ⟨a ~ pattern⟩

⁴crisscross \"\ *adv* **1** : in opposite directions : in a way to cross something else : by crossing one another **2** : with opposition or hindrance : at cross-purposes : AWRY, ASKEW, CONTRARILY ⟨things go ~⟩

criss·crossing \ˈ≈,≈≈\ *also* **crisscross breeding** *n* : a system of breeding domestic animals involving the use of purebred sires of two breeds alternately or crossbred females of the same breeds in such an order that the females are always bred to the males with which they have least blood in common — compare ROTATION CROSSING

crisscross inheritance *n* : inheritance of sex-linked characters transmitted from fathers to daughters or from mothers to sons

crisscross-row \ˈ≈;≈-\ *n* [alter. of *christcross-row*] : ALPHABET

crisset *var of* CRESSET

cris·sum \ˈkrisəm\ *n, pl* **cris·sa** \-sə\ [NL, fr. L *crissare, crisare* to wiggle the backside while having sexual intercourse (said of a woman); akin to OE *hrith* fever, *scrīthan* to go, move around, OHG *hritto* fever, *scrītan* to go, step, ON *hrīth* storm, attack, *skrītha* to creep, glide, W *cryd* fever, *ysgryd* shiver, Lith *skrytis* felly of a wheel, and prob. to L *curvus* curved — more at CROWN] : the part of a bird surrounding the cloacal opening; *also* : the feathers covering that region : the under tail coverts

cris·ta \ˈkristə\ *n, pl* **cris·tae** \-ˌstē, -ˌstī\ [L — more at CREST] : CREST, RIDGE: as **a** : the keel of a carinate sternum **b** : CRISTA ACUSTICA **c** : a membranous spiral fold running the length of the body of certain spirochetes **d** : an elevation of the surface of a bone for the attachment of a muscle or tendon

crista acus·ti·ca \-əˈküstəkə\ *n, pl* **cristae acusti·cae** \-təˌkē, -ˌsē, -ī\ [NL, lit., acoustic crest] **1** : one of the areas of specialized sensory epithelium in the ampullae of the semicircular canals of the ear serving as end organs for the labyrinthine sense **2** : an auditory organ on the fore tibia of certain insects (as most grasshoppers)

cris·tate \ˈkriˌstāt, -stət\ *also* **cris·tated** \-ˌstād·əd\ *adj* [L *cristatus,* fr. *crista* crest + *-atus* -ate] : having a crista or crest : CRESTED

cris·ta·tel·la \ˌkristəˈtelə\ *n, cap* [NL, fr. L *cristatus* + NL *-ella*] : a genus (class Phylactolaemata) comprising freshwater bryozoans that form elongated creeping gelatinous colonies with the zooids restricted to the upper surface

cris·ti·spi·ra \-ˈspīrə\ *n, cap* [NL, fr. *cristi-* (fr. L *crista* crest) + L *spira* coil, twist — more at CREST, SPIRE] : a genus of large flexuous coarsely spiral bacteria (family Spirochaetaceae) parasitic in mollusks and having a crista along one side of the body

cris·ti·vomer \ˌkristə +\ *n, cap* [NL, fr. *cristi-* + *vomer*] : the genus (family Salmonidae) to which the lake trout belongs

cris·to·bal·ite \kriˈstōbəˌlīt\ *n* -S [G *cristobalit,* fr. Cerro San *Cristóbal,* Pachuca, Mexico + G *-it* -ite] : silica occurring in white octahedra stable at high temperature — compare QUARTZ, TRIDYMITE

cristy \ˈkristē\ *n* -ES *often cap* [by shortening and alter.] : CHRISTIANIA

crit *abbr* critical; criticism; criticized

critch \ˈkrich\ *n* -ES [origin unknown] *dial Eng* : an earthenware dish : CROCK

cri·te·ri·ol·o·gy \krīˌtirēˈäləjē\ *n* -ES [*criterion* + *-logy*] : the part of logic dealing with the establishment of criteria

cri·te·ri·on \krīˈtirēən *sometimes* krəˈ-\ *n, pl* **crite·ria** \-rēə\ *also* **criterions** [Gk *kritērion,* fr. *kritēs* judge, fr. *krinein* to separate, decide — more at CERTAIN] **1** : a characterizing mark or trait ⟨increased speed, climb, and ceiling, three of the four basic *criteria* of air combat —*Science News Letter*⟩ ⟨a special constitutional ~ of that person —*Jour. Amer. Med. Assoc.*⟩ **2** : a standard on which a decision or judgment may be based ⟨the accepted *criteria* of adequate diet⟩ : a standard of reference : YARDSTICK : an identifying indication ⟨what then are the *criteria* of a desirable organization of utilities —*Harper's*⟩ : a basis for discrimination : GROUND **3** : an expression by whose value varieties of a mathematical form may be distinguished ⟨~ of a conic⟩ **syn** see STANDARD

cri·te·ri·um \-rēəm\ *n, pl* **crite·ria** \-rēə\ [LL, fr. Gk *kritērion*] : CRITERION

crith \ˈkrith\ *n* -S [Gk *krithē* barleycorn (or, a small weight); akin to Gk *kri* barley — more at HORDEUM] : the weight of a liter of hydrogen at 0° C and 760 millimeter pressure (0.08987 gram)

cri·thid·ia \krəˈthidēə\ *n* [NL, fr. Gk *krithidion,* dim. of *krithē* barleycorn] **1** *cap* : a genus of flagellates (family Trypanosomatidae) that are exclusively parasites of invertebrates esp. in the digestive tract of insects and that occur typically as elongated forms morphologically like trypanosomes but pass through developmental stages all in a single host in which they are indistinguishable from typical leptomonads and leishmanias **2** -S **a** : any flagellate of the genus *Crithidia* **b** : any flagellate of the family Trypanosomatidae when exhibiting a typical crithidial form

cri·thid·i·al \-dēəl\ *adj* [NL *Crithidia* + E *-al*] : of, like, or relating to crithidias : CRITHIDIFORM

cri·thid·i·form \-dəˌfȯrm\ *adj* [NL *Crithidia* + E *-form*] : resembling a crithidia in structure

crith·mene \ˈkrithˌmēn\ *n* -S [ISV *crithm-* (fr. NL *Crithmum* — genus name of the samphire *Crithmum maritimum* — fr. Gk *krēthmon* samphire) + *-ene;* orig. formed as It *critmene*] : TERPINENE b

¹crit·ic \ˈkrid·ik, -itik, -ēk\ *n* -S [MF & L; MF *critique,* fr. L *criticus,* fr. Gk *kritikos,* fr. *kritikos,* adj., able to discern or judge, fr. *kritos* (verbal of *krinein* to judge, discern) + *-ikos* -ic — more at CERTAIN] **1 a** : one who expresses a reasoned opinion on any matter (as a work of art or a course of conduct) involving a judgment of its value, truth, or righteousness, an appreciation of its beauty or technique, or an interpretation **b** : one who engages often professionally in the analysis, artistic evaluation, or appreciation of works of art (as literary or dramatic works) **2** : one given to harsh or captious judgment : CARPER, CAVILER ⟨~*s* using hindsight in the best tradition of Monday morning quarterbacks⟩

²critic \"\ *adj* [MF & L; MF *critique,* fr. L *criticus,* fr. Gk *kritikos*] : CRITICAL

³critic \"\ *vb* **criticked; criticked; criticking; critics** [¹*critic*] *vi* : to act as a critic ~ *vt, obs* : to pass judgment on : CRITICIZE

⁴critic \"\ *n* -S [partly fr. ¹*critic;* partly fr. Gk *kritikē,* fr. fem. of *kritikos*] **1** *archaic* : CRITICISM **2** *archaic* : CRITIQUE

crit·i·cal \ˈkrid·əkəl, -itək-, -ēk-\ *adj* [¹*critic* + *-al*] **1 a** : inclined to criticize severely and unfavorably : given to noticing faults and imperfections ⟨cooler and more ~ in temper; hard to please —Willa Cather⟩ **b** : consisting of, marked by, being, or involving criticism ⟨the ~ writings of Swinburne⟩ ⟨a ~ biography⟩ ⟨his ~ insight⟩; *also* : of or in the judgment of critics ⟨the book won wide ~ praise⟩ ⟨the play was a ~ success⟩ **c** : exercising or involving careful judgment or judicious evaluation : DISCRIMINATING, CAREFUL, EXACT ⟨a ~ weighing of all the factors leaves no doubt that the countryman labors under real disadvantages⟩ ⟨a cautious ~ mind⟩ **d** : including variant readings and scholarly emendations ⟨a ~ edition⟩ — compare VARIORUM **2** : of, relating to, or being a turning point or specially important juncture: **a** : indicating or being the stage of a disease at which an abrupt change for better or worse may be anticipated with reasonable certainty ⟨the ~ phase of a fever⟩ **b** : relating to, indicating, or being a state in which or a measurement or point at which some quality, property, or phenomenon suffers a finite change or undergoes drastic alteration ⟨the parabola is a ~ curve through which a conic section passes from an ellipse into a hyperbola⟩ **c** : CRUCIAL, DECISIVE ⟨a ~ analogy between sound and light⟩ ⟨this will be the ~ test in the series⟩ **d** : indispensable for the weathering, the solution, or the overcoming of a crisis; *specif* : essential for the conduct of war but available only in short supply ⟨~ materials⟩ **e** : in or approaching a crisis esp. through economic disorders or by virtue of a disaster ⟨a ~ area⟩ **3 a** : of doubtful issue : attended by risk or uncertainty ⟨our situation became ~ with the early freeze⟩ **b** *of kinds of organisms* **(1)** : so nearly related as to be distinguished with difficulty ⟨two ~ species⟩ **(2)** : rare and diminishing in numbers ⟨a ~ element in the local flora⟩ **4** : of sufficient size to sustain or to be capable of sustaining a chain reaction — used of a mass of fissionable material

syn HYPERCRITICAL, CENSORIOUS, FAULTFINDING, CARPING, CAPTIOUS, CAVILING: CRITICAL may describe a disposition to find and to stress faults ⟨the attitude of Euripides . . . is so . . . frankly *critical* that a recent writer has even gone so far as to maintain that his main object . . . was to discredit the myths —G.L.Dickinson⟩ Unlike the other words in this list, CRITICAL may describe fair, judicious evaluation ⟨the exemplars of . . . the *critical* spirit, discriminators between the false and the true —P.E.More⟩ The other words in the list are all close in suggestion and are often interchangeable. HYPERCRITICAL and CENSORIOUS indicate a tendency to discover and stress errors and imperfections ⟨exceedingly difficult to please, not . . . because he was *hypercritical* and exacting, but because he was indifferent —Arnold Bennett⟩ ⟨"do you mean that you heard a fellow doubt my wife . . .?" "The world's very *censorious,* old boy" —W.M.Thackeray⟩ FAULTFINDING, sometimes implying lack of background and discrimination, describes a temperament that is exacting and almost impossible to satisfy. CARPING and CAPTIOUS may imply perverse ill-natured faultfinding ⟨these criticisms of a book that is a labor of love may seem ungracious or even *carping* —M.R.Cohen⟩ ⟨after reading a work of such amplitude it seems *captious* to protest that the motivating forces . . . are inadequately analyzed —Geoffrey Bruun⟩ CAVILING suggests frequent petty objections ⟨those *caviling* critics who snipe from the musty back rooms of libraries —Charles Ramsdell⟩ **syn** see in addition ACUTE

critical angle *n* **1** : the least angle of incidence at which total reflection takes place when a ray of light or other electromagnetic radiation passes through one medium toward another that is less refracting **2** *or* **critical angle of attack** *aeronautics* : the angle of attack at which the flow about an airfoil changes abruptly with corresponding abrupt changes in the lift and drag, an airfoil possibly having two or more critical angles one of which usu. corresponds to the angle of maximum lift

C O″ O′ O C″ B″ B′ B A

critical angle: *AOB, AO′B′, AO″B″* angles of incidence; *AOC* refracted ray, *AO″C″* totally reflected ray; *AO′B′* critical angle

critical apparatus *n* : APPARATUS CRITICUS

critical coefficient *n* : the ratio of the critical temperature to the critical pressure

critical constant *n* : the critical temperature, critical pressure, or critical density of any one substance — usu. used in pl.

critical density *n* : the density of a substance in its critical state

critical flicker frequency *or* **critical fusion frequency** *n* : the threshold at which light from an intermittent source is seen half the time as flickering and half the time as fused or continuous

critical idealism *n* : TRANSCENDENTAL IDEALISM

crit·i·cal·i·ty \ˌ≈≈ˈkaləd·ē, -ətē, -i\ *n* -ES : a critical quality or condition — used esp. of fissionable material

crit·i·cal·ly \ˈ≈≈k(ə)lē, -li\ *adv* : in a critical manner : with criticism

crit·i·cal·ness \-kəlnəs\ *n* -ES : the quality or state of being critical ⟨the ~ of the situation called for quick action⟩

critical philosophy *n* : Kantianism esp. with reference to the critical establishment of necessary presuppositions for knowledge

critical point *n* **1** *math* : a point on the graph of a function where the derivative of the function is zero or infinite **2** : TRANSFORMATION TEMPERATURE **3 a** : the point on a phase diagram of a pure substance that corresponds to its critical state **b** : CRITICAL STATE

critical potential *n* : either the radiation potential or the ionization potential of an atom

critical pressure *n* : the pressure exerted by a substance in its critical state

critical ratio *n* : the ratio of any one deviation from the mean in a set of observed values of the same statistical variable to the standard deviation of the set or to the corresponding probable error

critical realism *n* : a system of philosophical realism that incorporates features approximating to the Kantian theory of knowledge (as that of a group of American realists in 1920)

critical realist *n* : one who adheres to or advocates critical realism

critical size *n* : the size corresponding to the critical mass

critical solution temperature *n* : the temperature at which complete miscibility is reached as the temperature is raised or in some cases lowered — used of two liquids that are partially miscible under ordinary conditions; called also *consolute temperature*

critical state *n* : a state attainable by every chemically stable pure substance in which the liquid and the vapor phases have the same density

critical temperature *n* **1 a** : the temperature of a substance in its critical state : the highest temperature at which it is possible to separate substances into two fluid phases (vapor and liquid) **b** : the transition temperature of a solid from one allotropic form to another (as the Curie point of a metal) **2** : TRANSFORMATION TEMPERATURE

critical value *n, math* : the value of the argument or independent variable corresponding to a critical point of a function

critical velocity *n* : the greatest velocity with which a fluid can flow through a given conduit without becoming turbulent

critical volume *n* : the specific volume of a substance in its critical state : the reciprocal of the critical density

crit·ic·as·ter \ˈ≈≈ˌkastə(r), ˌ≈≈ˈ≈≈\ *n* -S [¹*critic* + *-aster*] : an inferior or contemptible critic ⟨should make real critics proud of their vocation and the ~*s* ashamed of their presumption —W.H.Gardner⟩

crit·i·cism \ˈkrid·əˌsizəm, -itə-,-ēt-\ *n* -S [¹*critic* + *-ism*] **1 a** : the act of criticizing usu. unfavorably : faultfinding disapproval and objection **b** : CRITIQUE **2** *obs* : a subtle point or fine distinction : NICETY, SUBTLETY **3** : the art of evaluating or analyzing with knowledge and propriety works of art or literature ⟨the first principle of ~, which is, to consider the nature of the piece, and the intent of its author —Alexander Pope⟩; *broadly* : similar consideration of other than literary matters (as moral values or the soundness of scientific hypotheses and procedures) **4** : the scientific investigation of literary documents (as the Bible) in regard to such matters as origin, text, composition, character, or history **5** : CRITICAL PHILOSOPHY

crit·i·ciz·able \ˌ≈≈ˈsīzəbəl\ *adj* : that may be criticized : subject to criticism

crit·i·cize \ˈ≈≈ˌsīz\ *vb* -ED/-ING/-S *see -ize in Explan Notes* [¹*critic* + *-ize*] *vi* **1** : to act as a critic : consider and estimate worth or value ⟨the man who did not ~ or reflect —G.L. Dickinson⟩ **2** : to find fault : stress faults, errors, or demerits ⟨an unpleasant person, always *criticizing*⟩ ~ *vt* **1** : to consider the merits and demerits of and judge accordingly : EVALUATE ⟨Dr. Burney *criticized* the manuscript very favorably —Elizabeth Lee⟩ **2** : to stress the faults and demerits of : cavil at ⟨we are trying to get away from the word "management" because it has been lambasted, ridiculed, *criticized,* and blasted —*Personnel Jour.*⟩

syn REPREHEND, REPROBATE, BLAME, CENSURE, CONDEMN, DENOUNCE: CRITICIZE, among more erudite persons, is likely to indicate measured judgment or evaluation ⟨he does not *criticize,* he denounces —*Times Lit. Supp.*⟩ Often it means focusing attention on weak points, demerits, failings, and delighting in pointing them out ⟨newspaper policy is attacked, display advertising is *criticized,* features are ridiculed —*Public Relations Jour.*⟩ REPREHEND, now more commonly used with grammatical objects designating things, actions, or qualities than persons, may imply a severe rebuke decided on after deliberate judgment ⟨being to advise or *reprehend* any one, consider whether it ought to be in public or in private . . and in reproving show no signs of choler —George Washington⟩ ⟨the thing to be *reprehended* is the confusing misuse of the word "verse" —C.H.Grandgent⟩ REPROBATE may suggest strong disapproval and firm rejection or final refusal to tolerate or sanction ⟨those peaceful and friendly conferences between capitalists and trade-union leaders which are so *reprobated* by Marxist critics —H.B.Parkes⟩ ⟨he *reprobated* the "paltry jealousy" manifested toward Congress —H.R. Warfel⟩ BLAME is now likely to indicate the placing of responsibility for something bad or unfortunate on a person or thing although it is still sometimes used as a general antonym of *praise* ⟨the general was *blamed* for the defeat⟩ ⟨Heine . . . cared . . . whether people praised his verses or *blamed* them —Matthew Arnold⟩ CENSURE indicates disapproval delivered sternly, often as a reprimand from someone in an authoritative or competent position ⟨the *Times* published an article . . . in which . . . all contemporary literature was *censured* —E. M.Forster⟩ CONDEMN may suggest a severe, unmitigated, final, or definitive judgment which is wholly unfavorable ⟨vice, on this view, is *condemned* because it is a frustration of nature —G.L.Dickinson⟩ ⟨the entire week before election was a holiday and was *condemned* by ministers as a time "to meet, to smoke, to drink, carouse, and raise the devil" —*Amer. Guide Series: N.H.*⟩ DENOUNCE suggests stigmatizing publicly with force, vehemence, or conviction ⟨members of the owning classes, who *denounce* alike the encroachment of the state and of organized labor upon the wealth which they have "made" —J.A.Hobson⟩ ⟨in all ages, priests and monks have *denounced* the growing vices of society —Henry Adams⟩

crit·i·ciz·er \-zə(r)\ *n* -S : CRITIC

criticked *past of* CRITIC

criticking *pres part of* CRITIC

critics *pl of* CRITIC, *pres 3d sing of* CRITIC

critic teacher *n* : a secondary or elementary schoolteacher who supervises the practice teaching of a student teacher

1cri·tique \kri'tēk *also* krē'- *or* krə'-\ *n* -s [alter. (influenced by F *critique*) of 4*critic*] : an act of criticizing; *esp* : a critical examination or estimate of a thing or situation (as a work of art or literature) with a view to determining its nature and limitations or its conformity to standards

2critique \"\ *vt* -ED/-ING/-S : CRITICIZE, REVIEW

critize *vt* -ED/-ING/-S [1*critic* + *-ize*] *obs* : CRITICIZE

crit·ter *or* **crit·tur** \'krid·ə(r), -itə-\ *n* -s [alter. of *creature*] **1** *dial* : CREATURE **2 a** *dial* : ANIMAL **b** *dial* : a domestic animal; *esp* : a horse or a cow **c** *chiefly South* : HORSE **d** *North* : BULL

1criz·zle \'krizəl\ *vb* -ED/-ING/-S [origin unknown] *vi, dial* : to become rough or crumpled (as of the surface of freezing water) ~ *vt, chiefly dial* : to roughen or crumple the surface of

2crizzle \"\ *n* -s *now dial* : a roughened surface (as of the skin when exposed to sun and wind)

criz·zling \'kriz(ə)liŋ\ *n* -s : the blemish on a surface (as of glass) due to crumpling or roughening

cro \'krō\ *n* -ES [ME *cro, croy*, fr. ScGael *crō*, lit., blood; akin to MIr *crū, crō* blood, L *cruor* — more at RAW] : satisfaction in an amount suitable to the rank of the parties involved made in early Scottish law for the killing of a man

1croak \'krōk\ *vb* -ED/-ING/-S [ME *croken*, of imit. origin] *vi* **1 a** : to make a deep harsh sound ⟨the frogs ~*ed*⟩ **b** : to speak in a hoarse throaty raucous voice ⟨I tried to ask . . . but my voice just ~*ed* indistinguishably —Kenneth Roberts⟩ **2 a** : to protest dismally or dolefully : grumble dourly : COMPLAIN ⟨a querulous patient always ~*ing* about the hospital⟩ **b** : to predict evil : talk dismally ⟨misanthropists always ~*ing* about man's demerits⟩ **3** *slang* : DIE ~ *vt* **1** : to forebode, announce, or utter in a hoarse raucous voice ⟨the raven . . . that ~*s* the fatal entrance of Duncan —Shak.⟩ **2** *slang* : to kill esp. with brutal violence **syn** see COMPLAIN

2croak \"\ *n* -s **1** : the hoarse harsh cry of a frog or raven or a similar sound ⟨the ~ of an old woman⟩ ⟨a strange ~ of a laugh⟩; *esp* : an expiring gasp ⟨his last ~⟩ **2** : an asthmatic disease affecting the hawk — usu. used in pl.

croak·er \-kə(r)\ *n* -s **1** : an animal that croaks (as a frog) **2** : any of various fishes esp. of the family Sciaenidae that produce croaking or grunting noises (as certain grunts and surf fishes): as **a** : ATLANTIC CROAKER **b** : FRESHWATER DRUM **c** : QUEENFISH **3** : one that murmurs, grumbles, or complains unreasonably; *esp* : one that habitually forbodes evil ⟨it didn't turn out as bad as the ~*s* thought⟩ **4** [1*croak* (to kill) + *-er*] *slang* : DOCTOR

croaker family *n* : SCIAENIDAE

croaking gourami *n* : a rare East Indian green and gold freshwater labyrinth fish (*Ctenops vittatus*) sometimes kept in the tropical aquarium and noted for its ability to make croaking sounds when removed from the water

croaking lizard *n* : a gecko (*Thecadactylus rapicadus*) occurring in the West Indies and Central and So. America

croaking sac *n* : VOCAL SAC

croaky \'krōkē, -ōki\ *adj* -ER/-EST : deeply hoarse : CROAKING ⟨a ~ voice⟩

croat \'krō,a\|t, -,ät, 'krō(ə)\|t, *usu* \|d·+V\ *n* -s *cap* [NL *Croata*, fr. Serbo-Croatian *Hrvat*] **1** : CROATIAN **2** : a member of a former French light cavalry regiment made up largely of Croatians

cro·atan \,krōə¦tan\ *also* **croatan indian** *n* -s *usu cap C&I* [fr. *Croatan*, island, off the coast of No. Carolina] : one of a group of people of mixed Indian, white, and Negro ancestry in southern No. Carolina and adjoining sections of So. Carolina — sometimes used disparagingly

1cro·atian \krō'āshən\ *n* -s *cap* [*Croatia*, region of southeastern Europe and federated republic of Yugoslavia + E *-ian*] **1** : a native or inhabitant of the former Austrian province of Croatia or of the federal republic of Croatia in Yugoslavia **2 a** (1) : a south Slavic people that settled in Croatia in the 7th century and who are closely akin to the Serbs (2) : a member of such people — compare SERB, SERBO-CROATIAN, YUGOSLAV **b** : a south Slavic language spoken by the Croatian people and distinct from Serbian only in its use of the Latin alphabet and in certain minor dialect differences

2croatian \(')=¦==\ *adj, usu cap* **1 a** : of, relating to, or characteristic of Croatia **b** : of, relating to, or characteristic of Croatians **2** : of, relating to, or characteristic of the Croatian language

croc \'kräk\ *n* -s [by shortening] : CROCODILE

croc·ard *also* **crock·ard** \'kräkərd, krō'kärd\ *n* -s [ME *crocarde*, fr. MF *crocard*, perh. fr. *croc* hook (of Scand origin; akin to ON *krōkr* hook) + *-ard* — more at CROOK] : a coin of base metal that circulated in England at two to the penny during the 13th century and until its circulation was prohibited in 1310 — compare POLLARD 1

cro·ce·an *also* **cro·ci·an** \'krōchēən\ *adj, usu cap* [Benedetto *Croce* †1952 Ital. philosopher & statesman + E *-an*] : of, having to do with, or suggesting Croce or his idealist philosophy of the spirit or his liberalism

cro·ce·ic acid \(')krō¦sēik-\ *n* [*crocein* + *-ic*] : CROCEIN ACID

cro·ce·in \'krōsēən\ *or* **cro·ce·ine** \", -ē,ēn\ *n* -s *usu cap* [ISV *croce-* (fr. L *croceus* of saffron) + *-in, -ine*] : any of several red or orange acid azo dyes — see DYE table I (under *Acid Orange 12, Acid Red 25*)

crocein acid *or* **croceine acid** *n* : a crystalline acid $HOC_{10}H_6SO_3H$ used as an intermediate in making azo dyes; 2-naphthol-8-sulfonic acid — called also *Bayer's acid*

croceine scarlet MOO \-,e,mō'ō, -,em,dəbə'lō\ *n, usu cap C&S* : BRILLIANT CROCEIN

cro·ce·tin \'krōsət°n\ *n* -s [ISV *croc-* (fr. *crocin*) + *-et-* + *-in*; prob. orig. formed as G *krozetin*] : red crystalline dicarboxylic carotenoid acid $C_{20}H_{24}O_4$ obtained by hydrolysis of crocin — called also *alpha-crocetin*

cro·ce·us \'krōsēəs\ *n* -ES [L, adj., of saffron, saffron-colored, fr. *crocus* saffron — more at CROCUS] : SAFFRON 3

croche \'krōsh\ *n* -s [MF *croche*, lit., hook] : a little knob at the top of a deer's antler

1cro·chet \(')krō¦shā\ *n* -s [F, hook, crochet work, fr. MF, dim. of *croche* hook, of Scand origin; akin to ON *krōkr* hook — more at CROOK] **1 a** : needlework consisting of the interlocking of looped stitches formed with a single thread and a hooked needle ⟨~ work⟩ ⟨~ hook⟩ ⟨she looked up from her ~ —Alma Stone⟩ **b** : a stitch used in crochet **2** : a hook or hooked process: as **a** : one of a series of minute hooks on the apical surface of the proleg of a caterpillar **b** : CROTCHET 2c(1)

position of thread and needle in crochet work

2crochet \"\ *vb* -ED/-ING/-S *vt* : to make of crochet ⟨Meggie . . . returned to the counterpane she was ~*ing* — Ellen Glasgow⟩ ~ *vi* : to work with crochet

cro·chet·er \-āə(r)\ *n* -s : one that crochets; *specif* : one that crochets trimmings by machine on knitted garments

crochet file *n* : a thin flat file rounded on the edges and tapering to a point

crocheting *n* -s **1** : the act or action of one that crochets **2** : crochet work

croci *pl of* 1CROCUS

cro·cid·o·lite \krō'sid°l,īt\ *n* -s [G *krokydolith*, fr. Gk *krokyd-, krokys* nap on cloth + G *-o-* + *-lith* -lite] : a lavender-blue or leek-green mineral of the amphibole group that is a variety of riebeckite and occurs in silky fibers and in massive and earthy form — called also *blue asbestos*; see TIGEREYE

croc·i·du·ra \,kräsə'd(y)urə, ,krōs-\ *n* [NL, fr. *crocid-* (fr. Gk *krokyd-, krokys* nap on cloth) + *-ura*; akin to Gk *krekein* to weave — more at REEL] **1** *cap* : a genus including the Old World house shrew and musk shrew **2** *pl* **crociduras** \-əz\ *or* **crocidu·rae** \-ü,rē\ : any member of the genus *Crocidura*

cro·cin \'krōs°n, -sən\ *n* -s [ISV *croc-* (fr. L *crocus* saffron) + *-in*; prob. orig. formed in G — more at CROCUS] : a yellow glycoside $C_{44}H_{64}O_{24}$ of crocetin occurring in species of crocus (as saffron) and gardenia that is active in inducing sexual change in certain algae

1crock \'kräk\ *n* -s [ME *crocke*, fr. OE *crocc*; akin to OS *krūka* pot, ON *krukka*, OE *crūce* pot, pitcher, MHG *krūche* crock, pitcher, and perh. to OHG *kriochan* to creep — more at CRUTCH] **1** : a thick earthenware pot or jar **2** *dial Eng* : a cooking pot usu. of iron **3** : a broken piece of earthenware : a potsherd used esp. to cover the hole in a flowerpot **4** *dial* : loose black particles collected from combustion (as on cooking utensils or in a chimney) : SOOT, SMUT **5** : coloring matter that rubs off from cloth or dyed leather

2crock \"\ *vb* -ED/-ING/-S *vt* **1** : to put in a crock ⟨~ butter⟩ **2** : to provide drainage in (a flowerpot) by means of a crock **3** *dial* : to soil with crock : SMUDGE ~ *vi, of dye or dyed fabric or leather* : to transfer color under rubbing : rub off ⟨a suede that will not ~⟩

3crock \"\ *n* -s [ME *crok*, prob. of Scand origin; akin to Norw dial. *krokje* broken-down horse or person, Icel *kraki* delicate boy, LG *krakke* broken-down horse, D *kraak* broken-down cow or person, and perh. to ON *krōkr* hook, corner — more at CROOK] **1** *dial Brit* : an old or barren ewe **2** : an old or broken-down animal; *esp* : an old or broken-down horse **3** : one that is broken down, disabled, or impaired ⟨over three quarters of all the ships were ~*s* —*Yale Rev.*⟩ ⟨an old ~ of 104 who does nothing but sit by the fire —Richard Joseph⟩ ⟨the poor old ~ who feels tired every afternoon at three, from a complicated set of physical and psychological causes —Martin Mayer⟩

4crock \"\ *vb* -ED/-ING/-S *vt* : to cause to become impaired : put out of commission : DISABLE ⟨~ his thumb⟩ — often used with *up* ⟨a *crocked*-up athlete⟩ ~ *vi* : to become impaired : break down ⟨his physical vigor ~*ed*⟩ ⟨the mare soon ~*ed*⟩

crockard *var of* CROCARD

crocked *adj* [prob. fr. past part. of 4*crock*] *slang* : DRUNK

crock·ery \'kräk(ə)rē, -ri\ *n* -ES : vessels formed of fired clay esp. for domestic use : EARTHENWARE

crock·et \'kräkət\ *n* -s [ME *croket*, fr. ONF *croquet* shepherd's crook, dim. of *croc* hook, of Scand origin; akin to ON *krōkr* hook — more at CROOK] **1** : an ornament usu. in the form of curved and bent foliage used on the edge of a gable or spire **2** : CROCHE

crocket

crock·et·ed *also* **crock·et·ted** \-əd·əd\ *adj* : furnished with crockets ⟨a ~ spire⟩

crock·et·ing *also* **crock·et·ting** \-əd·iŋ\ *n* -s : ornamentation with crockets

crocking *n* -s [fr. gerund of 2*crock*] **1** : the transfer or rubbing off of leather-finishing materials or color onto materials coming into contact with the leather **2** : the tendency of a painted surface to show color irregularity on rubbing

crock tile *n* : a hard-burned glazed clay drain tile with or without bell-shaped ends

crocky \'kräkē\ *adj* -ER/-EST [3*crock* + *-y*] : impaired in one's powers : physically frail

1croc·o·dile \'kräkə,dīl\ *n* -s *see sense 1* [alter. (influenced by L *crocodilus*) of ME *cocodrille*, fr. OF, fr. ML *cocodrillus*, alter. of L *crocodilus, corcodillus*, fr. Gk *krokodeilos, krokodilos*, alter. of (assumed) *krokodrilos*, fr. *krokē* pebble + *drilos* worm; akin to Skt *śarkara* pebble — more at SUGAR] **1** *pl sometimes* **crocodile a** : any of several large thick-skinned long-bodied aquatic reptiles of tropical and subtropical waters constituting *Crocodylus* and one or two closely related genera and including certain voracious forms (as the Nile crocodile [*C. niloticus*] or the very large estuarine crocodile [*C. porosus*] of eastern Asia and the Pacific islands) that do not hesitate to attack man **b** : a reptile of the order Loricata — see ALLIGATOR **c** : crocodiles' skin tanned for use in manufacturing (as of handbags, shoes, luggage, and belts) **2** *archaic* : one who hypocritically affects sorrow — compare CROCODILE TEARS **3** *chiefly Brit* : a number of persons moving in a long file; *esp* : the file formed by the members of a school out for a walk

2crocodile \"\ *vi* -ED/-ING/-S *of paints* : ALLIGATOR

crocodile bird *n* : an African plover (*Pluvianus aegyptius*) that alights upon the crocodile and devours its insect parasites and reputedly even enters its open mouth in pursuit of flies

crocodile clip *n* : ALLIGATOR CLIP

crocodile shears *n pl* : LEVER SHEARS

crocodile squeezer *n* : a squeezer consisting of a lever device with powerful jaws between which metal is placed for shingling

crocodile tears *n pl* [so called fr. the ancient belief that crocodiles shed tears over their victims and make moaning sounds to attract prey] **1** : false or affected tears : hypocritical sorrow **2** : a disorder characterized by a profuse flow of tears initiated by chewing or the taste of food and occurring in facial paralysis

croc·o·dil·ia \,kräkə'dilēə\ [NL, fr. *Crocodilus* + *-ia*] *syn of* 2LORICATA

1croc·o·dil·ian \,kräkə¦dilēən, -lyən\ *adj* [1*crocodile* + *-ian*] **1** : FALSE, INSINCERE ⟨~ grief⟩ ⟨a ~ lament⟩ **2 a** : of, relating to, or characteristic of a crocodile ⟨a ~ walk⟩ **b** : LORICATE

2crocodilian \"\ *n* -s [NL *Crocodilia* + E *-an*] : any of an order (Loricata) of reptiles including the crocodiles, alligators, and related extinct forms

croc·o·dil·i·dae \,kräkə'dilə,dē\ [NL, fr. *Crocodilus* + *-idae*] *syn of* CROCODYLIDAE

croc·o·dil·oid \,kräkə'di,lȯid, 'kräkə,dī,-\ *adj* : like a crocodile

croc·o·di·lus \,kräkə'dīləs\ [NL, fr. L, crocodile] *syn of* CROCODYLUS

croc·o·dyl·i·dae \-'dilə,dē\ *n pl, cap* [NL, fr. *Crocodylus*, type genus + *-idae*] : a family of the order Loricata variously construed as including all recent and some fossil crocodilians or as comprising only the true crocodiles, the alligators, caimans, and gavials being excluded

croc·o·dy·loi·dea \-,də'lȯidēə\ *n pl, cap* [NL, fr. *Crocodylus* + *-oidea*] *in some classifications* : a suborder of Loricata containing recent crocodiles and related forms

croc·o·dy·lus \-'dīləs\ *n, cap* [NL, alter. of L *crocodilus* crocodile] : the type genus of Crocodylidae

croc·o·ite \'kräkə,wīt\ *or* **croc·oi·site** \'kräkwə,zīt\ *n* -s [*crocoite* fr. G *krokoit*, alter. of *krokoisit*; *crocoisite* fr. G *krokoisit*, fr. F *crocoise* (fr. Gk *krokoeis* saffron-colored, fr. *krokos* saffron) + G *-it* -ite — more at CROCUS] : a mineral $PbCrO_4$ consisting of native lead chromate in monoclinic crystals — called also *red lead ore*

cro·con·ic acid \krə'känik-\ *n* [part trans. of G *krokonsäure*, fr. *krokon-* (irreg. fr. Gk *krokos* crocus, saffron) + *säure* acid] : a yellow crystalline hydroxy ketone $C_5O_3(OH)_2$ obtained from rhodizonic acid and various other oxygen derivatives of benzene and that forms yellow or orange-colored salts

crocs *pl of* CROC

1cro·cus \'krōkəs\ *n* [NL, fr. L, fr. Gk *krokos*, of Sem origin; akin to Assyr-Bab *kurkanū* saffron, crocus, Heb *karkōm*, Aram *kurkĕmā*, Ar *kurkum*] **1 a** *cap* : a large genus of perennial herbs (family Iridaceae) native chiefly to the Mediterranean region but widely cultivated for their solitary long-tubed flowers that arise with the slender linear leaves from a fibrous-coated corm **b** *pl* **crocuses** \-səz\ *also* **cro·ci** \-ō,sī, ō,kī\ *or* **crocus** : a bulb, plant, or flower of the genus *Crocus* **2** *pl* **crocuses a** : a deep yellow or red powder that is usu. the oxide of some metal; *esp* : a dark red ferric oxide obtained similarly to colcothar and used for polishing metals — called also *crocus mar·tis* \¦krōkə'smärd·əs\, *crocus of Mars* \-ōkəsəv'märz\ **b** : SAFFRON 2 **3** *pl* **crocuses a** : a pale to grayish reddish purple that is less strong than Argyle purple **b** : a light reddish purple that is redder, lighter, and stronger than rose purple

2cro·cus \'krōkəs\ *n* -ES [origin unknown] *chiefly South* : coarse sacking (as gunny or burlap) ⟨~ bag⟩ ⟨a bushel of potatoes in a ~ sack⟩

3crocus \"\ *n* -ES [alter. of *croaker* (doctor)] : a quack doctor

4crocus \"\ *n* -ES [by alter.] **1** : ATLANTIC CROAKER **2** : FRESHWATER DRUM

crocus cloth *n* [1*crocus* (powder)] : cloth that has finely divided ferric oxide glued to one side and is used for fine abrading or polishing

crocus of antimony : a brownish yellow product mainly sodium thioantimonite Na_3SbS_3 or potassium thioantimonite K_3SbS_3 obtained as a slag in refining antimony

cro·cu·ta \krō'kyüd·ə\ *n, cap* [NL, fr. L *crocuta, corocottas*, a kind of wild animal, perh. the hyena, fr. Gk *krokottas, korokottas*] : the genus consisting of the African spotted hyena

croes *pl of* CRO

croe·sus \'krēsəs\ *n, pl* **croesuses** \-ēsəsəz\ *also* **croe·si** \-ē,sī\ *usu cap* [after *Croesus* †546B.C. wealthy king of ancient Lydia, fr. L, fr. Gk *Kroisos*] : a very rich man ⟨the arrogant *Croesus* of the neighborhood who was brought down to size . . . by the parish drunk —*N.Y. Times Book Rev.*⟩

1croft \'krȯft, *Brit usu & US also* -ä-\ *n* -s [ME, fr. OE; akin to MD *krocht* hill, field of dunes, OE *crēopan* to creep — more at CREEP] **1** *chiefly Brit* : a small enclosed field usu. adjoining a house **2** *chiefly Brit* : a small farmhold usu. of 5 to 10 acres that is worked by a tenant

2croft \"\ *vb* -ED/-ING/-S *vt, Brit* : to expose (as linen) on the grass for bleaching in the sun ~ *vi, Brit* : to live as a crofter

3croft \"\ *n* -s [ME *crofte*, fr. MD *crofte, crochte*, fr. ML *crupta*, fr. L *crypta* — more at CRYPT] : CRYPT, VAULT, CAVERN

croft·er \-tə(r)\ *n* -s [1*croft* + *-er*] *chiefly Brit* : one that rents and works a croft

croft·ing \-tiŋ\ *n* -s [1*croft* + *-ing*] **1** *chiefly Brit* **a** : the quality or state of being successively cropped **b** : the land so cropped **2** *chiefly Brit* : the system of tenancy of crofters ⟨~ townships⟩ ⟨the ~ problem⟩

croft lily \'krȯft- *also* -ä-\ *n, usu cap C* [after Sydney *Croft*, †*ab* 1940 Am. horticulturist] : an Easter lily characterized by short stems, long leaves, and pure white flowers with strongly recurved perianth tips

crof·ton weed \'krȯftən- *also* -räf-\ *n, often cap C* [origin unknown] : an herb (*Eupatorium riparium*) native to the New World but now common in Australia that is a troublesome weed on rangelands

crohn's disease \'krōnz-\ *n, usu cap C* [after Burill B. *Crohn* *b*1884 Am. physician] : REGIONAL ILEITIS

croisade [MF — more at CRUSADE] *obs var of* CRUSADE

1croise *vt* -ED/-ING/-S [ME *croisen*, fr. OF *croisier*, fr. *crois* cross, fr. L *cruc-, crux* — more at RIDGE] *obs* : to make the sign of the cross on or over (a person) esp. in sanctification of a vow to fight the foes of Christianity

2croi·sé \krə¦wä¦zā, (')krwä-\ *adj* [F, fr. past part. of *croiser* to cross, fr. OF *croisier*] : with the legs crossed and the body at an oblique angle to the audience — used of a ballet pose

crois·es \'krȯizəz\ *n pl* [F *croisés*, pl. of *croisé*, fr. OF *croisié*, fr. past part. of *croisier*] *archaic* : persons croised as crusaders

crois·sant \krə¦wä¦sä^n, (')krwä-\ *n, pl* **croissants** \-ä^n(z)\ [F, lit., crescent — more at CRESCENT] : a rich crescent-shaped roll ⟨reading the newspaper with my coffee and ~ —Noel Barber⟩

croix·an \'krȯiən\ *adj, usu cap* [fr. *Croixan*, subdivision of the American Cambrian, fr. Saint *Croix*, county & river in Wisconsin + E *-an*] : of or relating to a subdivision of the American Cambrian — see GEOLOGIC TIME table

cro·jack \'kräjik\ *n* -s [by alter.] : CROSSJACK

cro·ker sack \'krōkə(r)-\ *n* [alter. of 2*crocus*] *chiefly South* : a sack made of crocus : a burlap bag

cro·ki·nole \'krōkə,nōl\ *n* -s [F *croquignole* fillip, fr. MF, irreg. fr. *croquer* to crunch] : a game resembling squails ⟨a ~ board⟩ ⟨a ~ party⟩

cro-magnon \krō'magnən, -maig- *also* -g,nän *or* -manyən *or* -mäny- *or* -n,yän; *or as* F\ *n* -s *usu cap C&M* [fr. *Cro-Magnon*, a cave near Les Eyzies, Dordogne dept., France, where type specimens were found] **1** : a tall erect race of men having large faces and deep-set eyes known from skeletal remains found with Aurignacian artifacts chiefly in southern France and regarded by some anthropologists as the substratum of the modern European population or even as surviving in comparative purity in local areas ⟨*Cro-Magnon* race⟩ ⟨*Cro-Magnon* skeletons⟩ **2** : an Upper Paleolithic European man including such diverse forms as the Brünn and Grimaldi races

crom·bec \'kräm,bek\ *n* -s [F, fr. Afrik *krombek*, fr. *krom* crooked (fr. MD *crom*) + *bek* beak, fr. MD *bec*, fr. OF; akin to OHG *krump, krumpf* crooked — more at CRUMP, BEAK] : any of numerous small short-tailed African warblers constituting a genus (*Sylvietta*) of the family Sylviidae and widely distributed in dry open country

crome \'krōm\ *n* -s [ME *crome, crombe, cromp*, prob. fr. MD *crampe* hook, cramp — more at CRAMP] *now dial Eng* : HOOK; *also* : a long stick with a hook at the end

cromeski *or* **cromesqui** *var of* KROMESKI

crom·lech \'kräm,lek, -ek\ *n* -s [W, fr. *crom* (fem. of *crwm* bent) + *llech* slate, flat stone; akin to LGk *krambos* dry, withered and to OIr *lie* stone, Bret *lia* — more at RUMPLE] **1** : DOLMEN **2** : a circle of monoliths usu. enclosing a dolmen or mound

cro·mor·na \krō'mȯrnə, krə'-\ *also* **cre·mo·na** \krə'mōnə\ *n* -s [modif. of F *cromorne*] : a reed stop in the organ usu. of 8-foot pitch

cro·morne \krō'mȯrn, krə'-\ *n* -s [F, fr. G *krummhorn*, fr. *krumm* crooked (fr. OHG *krump*) + *horn*, fr. OHG — more at CRUMP, HORN] **1** : CROMORNA **2** : KRUMMHORN

crom·wel·li·an \(')kräm¦welēən\ *adj, usu cap* [Oliver *Cromwell* †1658 "lord protector" of England + E *-ian*] **1** : of, relating to, or suggestive of Cromwell or the period of Puritan ascendancy in England or to its politics or methods **2** : of or relating to a style of furniture in vogue under the Protectorate and early Restoration characterized by straight lines, refined moldings, and simplicity of ornament

cromwellian chair *n, usu cap 1st C* : a square low-backed chair of simple design having turned legs and usu. covered with leather fastened by metal nails

Cromwellian chair

cro·nar·ti·um \krō'närshēəm, -rd·ēəm\ *n, cap* [NL] : a genus of rust fungi (family Melampsoraceae) having aecia produced in raised or swollen sori and teliospores borne in waxy pillars or columns — see WHITE PINE BLISTER RUST

crone \'krōn\ *n* -s [ME, fr. ONF *carogne* carrion, hag, fr. (assumed) VL *caronia* — more at CARRION] **1** : a withered old woman esp. in humble circumstances ⟨an old half-witted ~ whom peasants called a witch —Ernest Poole⟩ **2** : an old man useless or womanish from senility **3** [prob. fr. obs D *karonje, kronje* old ewe, hag (now "hussy"), fr. MD *cronghe* hag, fr. ONF *carogne*] : an old ewe

1cronk \'kräŋk, 'krȯŋk\ *n* -s [imit.] : a hoarse croak (as of a raven) or honk (as of a wild goose)

2cronk \"\ *vi* -ED/-ING/-S : to make a croaking or honking noise ⟨the wild-goose wedge . . . ~*s* harsh —W.P.Johnston⟩

3cronk \"\ *adj* [Yiddish or G *krank*, fr. MHG *kranc* weak — more at CRANK] **1** *slang Austral* **a** : SICK, AILING **b** : INFIRM, UNSOUND **2** *slang Austral* : FRAUDULENT, DISHONEST

cron·stedt·ite \'krän,sted·,īt\ *n* -s [G *cronstedit*, fr. Baron Axel F. *Cronstedt* †1765 Sw. mineralogist + G *-it* -ite] : a mineral consisting of a black hydrous iron silicate of the chlorite group, crystallizing in hexagonal prisms with perfect basal cleavage, and showing a dark green streak (sp. gr. 3.34–3.35)

1cro·ny \'krōnē, -ni\ *n* -ES [fr. earlier *chrony* (university slang), perh. fr. Gk *chronios* long-lasting, fr. *chronos* time] : an intimate companion esp. of long standing : a familiar friend : an old chum

2crony \"\ *vi* -ED/-ING/-ES : to associate intimately ⟨~ with a person⟩

cro·ny·ism \-nē,izəm, -ni,iz-\ *n* -s : partiality to cronies esp. as evidenced in the appointing of political hangers-on to office without due regard being taken of their qualifications

1crooch \'krüch\ *vb* -ED/-ING/-ES [ME *crouchen* — more at CROUCH] *dial* : 1CROUCH

2crooch \"\ *n* -ES *dial* : 2CROUCH

crood \'krüd\ *vi* -ED/-ING/-S [imit.] *Scot* : COO

1croo·dle \'krüd°l\ *vi* -ED/-ING/-S [freq. of *crood*] *dial Brit* : to make a low murmuring sound

2croodle \"\ *vi* -ED/-ING/-S [prob. freq. of Sc *crood* to crowd, fr. ME *crouden* — more at CROWD] **1** *dial Brit* : to huddle together (as from cold); *also* : CUDDLE, SNUGGLE **2** *dial Brit* : COWER, CROUCH

1crook \ˈkru̇k\ *n* -s [ME *crok*, fr. ON *krōkr* hook; akin to OHG *krācho* hook-shaped tool, ON *kraki* pole with a hook, Gk *gyrgathos* wicker basket, Latvian *gredzens* ring, OE *cradol* cradle — more at CRADLE] **1 :** any implement having a bent or hooked form: as **a** *obs* **:** SICKLE **b :** hook (as a pothook) **c :** the hinge of a gate or door **d** *archaic* **:** (1) the staff used by a shepherd (2) CROSIER 2 **2 a** *obs* **:** a piece of trickery **:** ARTIFICE, SUBTERFUGE **b :** a person given to crooked or fraudulent practices **:** SWINDLER, THIEF ⟨what the insurance ~ does is always the same act: fakes an accident and claims . . . damages —Henry La Cossitt⟩ **3 a** *obs* **:** a bending of the knee or body in reverence **b :** the act or action of bending **4 a :** a portion of something that is hook-shaped, curved, or bent ⟨the ~*s* of a river⟩ ⟨the ~ of an umbrella handle⟩ **b** (1) **:** a small tube inserted in the tube of a trumpet or horn to change its pitch or key (2) **:** the curved tube carrying the mouthpiece of a bassoon **c :** a longitudinal warp in a piece of lumber determined by its deviation from a straight line drawn from one edge at one end to the corresponding edge at the opposite end **5 :** an angular or odd-shaped bit of land **6** *usu pl, obs* **:** BRACKET 4b

crook 1d (1)

2crook \"\ *vb* **crooked** \-kt\ **crooked** \"\ **crooking; crooks** [ME *croken*, fr. *crok*, n.] *vt* **1 :** to turn from a straight line **:** BEND ⟨*crooked* his neck in order to get a better view —Hamilton Basso⟩ **2** *obs* **:** to twist perversely **:** MISAPPLY **3** *slang* **a :** to make dishonest or ineffective **:** cause to go wrong ⟨~ a deal⟩ **b :** CHEAT ⟨you wouldn't ~ a friend, would you?⟩ **c :** to obtain or manipulate dishonestly or by fraud ⟨he was living pretty much from supplies ~*ed* from the army⟩ ~ *vi* **1 :** BEND, CURVE, WIND ⟨a river ~*ing* through a valley⟩ ⟨sunflowers, ~*ing* over in the sun —William Goyen⟩ **2** *archaic* **:** to bow (as in obeisance) **3** *obs* **:** to turn from a straight or direct course

3crook \"\ *adj* [perh. alter. of *3cronk*] **1** *Austral* **a :** physically unwell **:** SICK ⟨~ with the flu⟩ **b :** out of sorts **:** ANGRY, ILL-HUMORED, IRRITABLE — often used with *go* ⟨he's going ~ at the men for not working⟩ **2** *Austral* **a :** out of order **:** not in proper working condition ⟨something ~ with the car⟩ **b :** poorly suited **:** UNSATISFACTORY ⟨a ~ place for a dance — not enough girls —Nevil Shute⟩

crookback \ˈ=,=\ *n* **1** *obs* **:** a crooked back **2** *obs* **:** HUNCHBACK

crookbacked \ˈ=,=\ *adj* **:** HUMPBACKED ⟨those poor babes their ~ uncle murdered —H.H.Milman⟩

crookbill \ˈ=,=\ *n* **:** WRYBILL

crook·ed \ˈkru̇kəd\ *adj, sometimes* -ER/-EST [ME *croked*, partly fr. *crok*, n. + *-ed*, partly fr. past part. of *croken* to crook] **1 :** having or distinguished by a crook or curve **:** not straight **:** BENT, TWISTED ⟨a ~ road⟩ ⟨the pictures on a wall are ~⟩ ⟨an aged man with a ~ frame⟩ **2 :** not straightforward **:** deviating from rectitude ⟨~ dealings⟩; *esp* **:** FRAUDULENT, DISHONEST ⟨~ politicians⟩ ⟨a ~ business⟩ ⟨~ profits⟩ — **crook·ed·ly** *adv*

crooked-foot \ˈ==,=\ *n* **:** a deformity of a horse's hoof due to irregular growth induced by improper trimming and shoeing

crook·ed·ness \-kədnəs\ *n* -ES [ME *crokednesse*, fr. *croked* + *-nesse* -ness] **1 :** the quality or state of being crooked **2 :** DISHONESTY

crooked stick \ˈ==ˈ=\ *n, dial* **:** a worthless or idle man; *esp* **:** one not fitting into society ⟨she picked up a *crooked stick* for a husband⟩

crooked-wood \ˈ==,=\ *n* **:** BUTTONBUSH

crook·en \ˈkru̇kən\ *vb* -ED/-ING/-S [*1crook* + *-en*] *dial Brit* **:** BEND, CROOK ⟨a . . . *crookened*-limbed speck of a dwarf —*Irish Statesman*⟩

crook·ery \ˈkru̇kərē, -ri\ *n* -ES [*1crook* (swindler) + *-ery*] **:** crooked dealings or practices ⟨all the ~ exposed in the Internal Revenue Bureau —*New Orleans States*⟩ ⟨unmasks the ~ of a fellow journalist —*Time*⟩

crookes dark space \ˈkru̇ks-\ *n, usu cap C* [after Sir William *Crookes* †1919 Eng. physicist] *physics* **:** a dark space between the cathode glow and the negative glow — called also *cathode dark space*

crookes glass *n, usu cap C* [after Sir Wm. *Crookes*] **:** one of several types of glass designed to diminish the transmission of ultraviolet rays

crookes·ite \ˈkru̇k,sīt\ *n* -s [F, fr. Sir Wm. *Crookes* + F *-ite*] **:** a mineral $(Cu,Tl,Ag)_2Se$ consisting of selenide of copper, thallium, and silver occurring in lead-gray metallic-looking masses (sp. gr. 6.9)

crookes tube *n, usu cap C* [after Sir Wm. *Crookes*] **:** a vacuum tube evacuated to a pressure of about .04 mm of mercury for demonstrating the properties of cathode rays

crookneck \ˈ=,=\ *n* [*1crook* + *neck*] **1 :** any of numerous bush or vining squashes that are characterized by elongated tapering recurved necks: **a :** SUMMER CROOKNECK **b :** WINTER CROOKNECK **2 a :** a disease of tobacco producing one-sided development of the midribs of the leaves **b :** a copper and zinc deficiency disease of pineapples

crooks *pl of* CROOK, *pres 3d sing of* CROOK

crool \ˈkrül\ *vi* -ED/-ING/-S [imit.] **:** to make a repeated low, liquid, or gurgling sound ⟨a ~*ing* dove⟩

croo·mia \ˈkrümēə\ *n* [NL, fr. H. B. *Croom* †1837 Amer. botanist + NL *-ia*] **1** *cap* **:** a genus of herbs (family Stemonaceae) of the southern U.S. having horizontal rootstocks, leaves near the top of the stem, and nodding flowers **2** -s **:** a plant of the genus *Croomia*

croo monkey \ˈkrü-\ *n* [origin unknown] **:** CRAB-EATING MACAQUE

1croon \ˈkrün\ *vb* -ED/-ING/-S [ME *croynen* to bellow, fr. MD *cronen*; akin to OHG *krōnen* to chatter, beat, L *gingrire* to honk (of geese), Gk *gingras* Phoenician flute, MIr *grith* cry, Skt *jarate* he cries — more at CRANE] *vi* **1** *chiefly Scot* **a :** to make a continuous hollow sound **:** low (as of cattle) **:** boom (as of a bell) **b :** LAMENT, WAIL, MOAN ⟨~*ing* for her lost child⟩ **2 a :** to make a continued moaning sound ⟨with the doctor's fiddle ~*ing* away down the corridor —Hervey Allen⟩ ⟨the wind ~*ing* in the trees⟩; *specif* **:** to sing in a gentle murmuring manner and often wordlessly ⟨~ over a baby⟩ **b :** to sing in half voice esp. into a closely held microphone ~ *vt* **1 :** to sing (as a lullaby, song, or lament) in a crooning manner ⟨~ a hit song⟩ **2 :** to sing to in a soft composing manner **:** LULL ⟨~ a child to sleep⟩

2croon \"\ *n* -s **1 :** the sound made in crooning (as low murmuring, humming, or singing) **:** LAMENT **2 :** a song that is crooned or adapted to crooning

croon·er \-nə(r)\ *n* -s **:** one that croons; *specif* **:** a singer of popular songs who uses a soft-voice technique adapted to amplifying systems

croose *var of* CROUSE

1crop \ˈkräp\ *n* -s [ME, fr. OE *cropp* craw, cluster, head of a plant; akin to OHG *kropf* goiter, craw, ON *kroppr* torso, body, OE *crēopan* to creep — more at CREEP] **1 a** *now Scot* **:** the top, head, or highest part orig. of an herb, flower, or tree **b :** FINIAL **c :** the upper part of a whip **:** the stock or handle of a whip; *specif* **:** a riding whip with a short straight stock and a loop **d :** OUTCROP **2 a :** an enlargement of the gullet of many birds that forms a pouch which serves as a receptacle for the food and for its preliminary maceration **b** *dial, of a human* **:** STOMACH; *also* **:** THROAT **c :** an enlargement of the gullet of some animals (as insects) **3 :** something that has been cut or trimmed or that is the result of cutting and trimming: as **a :** the part of the chine of a quadruped (as a domestic cow) lying immediately behind the withers — usu. used in pl.; see cow illustration **b** *dial* **:** a cut of meat from this region **:** short ribs or spareribs **c :** the portion of tanned hide resulting from cutting in half along backbone and then trimming off the belly **4 a :** an earmark on an animal; *esp* **:** one made by a straight cut squarely removing the upper part of the ear **b** [*2crop*] **:** a close cut of the hair; *also* **:** a style of wearing the hair cut short **5 :** the end or ends of an ingot, billet, slab, bar, or other semifinished metallic mill product cut off and discarded because of defects **6 a** (1) **:** a plant or animal or plant or animal product that can be grown and harvested extensively for profit or subsistence ⟨an apple ~⟩ ⟨a maple-sugar ~⟩ ⟨a ~ of foals⟩ (2) *in turpentine orcharding* **:** the working unit generally equal to 10,000 boxes and usu. coming from a tract of timber of some 250 acres comprising about 5000 trees **b :** the product or yield of anything formed together ⟨a ~ of garnets⟩ ⟨the ice ~⟩ **c :** a batch or lot (as of something produced during a particular cycle) **:** COLLECTION ⟨a ~ of lies⟩ ⟨a ~ of war babies⟩ ⟨it was there the more unscrupulous whaling captains got their bumper ~ of hands —H.A.Chippendale⟩ ⟨a bumper ~ of best stories —Bennett Cerf⟩ **7 :** the total yearly production from a specified area ⟨the local grange reported that the county corn ~ had never been better⟩

2crop \"\ *vb* **cropped; cropped; cropping; crops** [ME *croppen*, fr. *crop*, n. (top)] *vt* **1 a :** to cut off (as the top or upper or outer parts of a tree or plant) **:** lop off ⟨~ branches⟩; *specif* **:** to trim esp. by the cutting off of grass, leaves, buds, or twigs ⟨~ a hedge⟩ ⟨*cropped* lawns⟩ **b** (1) **:** to clip off the tops of (the ears) as a means of identifying animals or formerly as a punishment for criminals (2) **:** to trim (the wattles of a bird) — compare DUB **c :** to shear (cloth) **d :** to cut (the hair) close ⟨these Indians *cropped* their hair above the eyebrows and along the nape of the neck —Alfred Métraux & Curt Nimuendajú⟩ **e** (1) **:** to trim (as a book) too close to the printed matter (2) **:** to cut off or mask out unwanted parts of (as a photograph that is to be engraved or an overlarge halftone cut) (3) **:** to trim down arbitrarily **:** excise to suit one's purposes ⟨he relied on *cropped* passages from the Old Testament —*Time*⟩ **2 a** *now dial Brit* **:** to gather (as flowers) **:** PLUCK **b :** to gather by or as if by cutting **:** REAP, HARVEST ⟨a continuous *cropping* of forest lands —E.S.Mason⟩ ⟨the number of trout *cropped* each year⟩ **3 :** to feed or graze on esp. by biting off the tenderer shoots **:** BROWSE ⟨sheep *cropping* a meadow⟩ **4 a :** to cause (land) to bear produce **:** PLANT, CULTIVATE ⟨after the land has been *cropped* for about three years it is allowed to revert to bush —Madeline Manoukian⟩ **b :** to grow as a crop ⟨potatoes are *cropped* in the valley⟩ ~ *vi* **1 :** to feed on grass **:** GRAZE ⟨it was so quiet that I could hear the sheep *cropping* —Mary Webb⟩ **2 a :** to yield a crop ⟨the berry bushes were in their first season but *cropped* well⟩ **b :** FARM, CULTIVATE ⟨he ~*s* far more heavily than in the North —*McGill News*⟩; *specif* **:** to farm as a sharecropper ⟨I tried to get hold of Tom . . . and found he was *cropping* at a Mr. Bannerman's —Caroline Gordon⟩ **3 a :** to appear at the surface **:** OUTCROP ⟨the rocks which ~ out on the Allegheny plateau —*Jour. of Geol.*⟩ **b :** to turn up or appear unexpectedly or casually ⟨problems kept *cropping* up⟩ ⟨the naïveté that ~*s* out in his work⟩

1crop-bound \ˈ=,=\ *adj, of poultry* **:** having the crop distended and paralyzed from overeating or from swallowing coarse fibrous matter

2crop-bound \"\ *n* **:** the condition of crop-bound poultry

crop duster *n* **:** one that sprays crops with fungicidal or insecticidal dust from a low-flying airplane ⟨ex-Air Force pilot who has become a *crop duster* —Henry Cavendish⟩

crop-dusting \ˈ=,==\ *n* **:** the application of fungicidal or insecticidal dusts to crops esp. from an airplane

crop-ear \ˈ=,=\ *n* **:** a person or animal whose ears have been cropped

crop-eared \ˈ=ˈ=\ *adj* **1 :** having the ears cropped ⟨a *crop-eared* horse⟩ **2 :** having the hair cropped so that the ears are conspicuous — used esp. of the English Puritans

crop-full \ˈ=ˈ=\ *adj* **:** having a full crop or stomach **:** OVERFULL ⟨a person *crop-full* of news —Scott Fitzgerald⟩

crop grass *n* **1 :** YARD GRASS **2 :** a crab grass (*Digitaria sanguinalis*) ⟨struggled all summer to rid the lawn of *crop grass*⟩

crophead \ˈ=,=\ *n* **:** the top of an ingot

crop-headed \ˈ=ˈ==\ *adj* **:** having the hair of the head cut close

crop index *n* **:** the number that expresses the relative yield of the crops on a particular area with the average yield over an entire region being taken as 100

crop insurance *n* **:** insurance available to farmers against loss or damage to growing crops as a result of natural hazards (as hail, drought, flood, insects)

cropland \ˈ=,land, -aa(ə)nd\ *n* **:** land that is suited to or used for crops

crop·man \-,man, -,mən\ *n, pl* **cropmen :** a scrap remover in a rolling mill

crop mark *n* **:** any of the marks used to indicate places where a drawing or photograph is to be cropped

crop meter *n* **:** an instrument connected to an automobile speedometer and used to register mileage of fields of each crop growing adjacent to a road

crop-milk \ˈ=,=\ *n* **:** a secretion resembling milk that is produced in the crop of certain pigeons and doves and used to feed the young

crop pasture *n* **:** a field on which a crop (as corn, soybeans, or peanuts) is allowed to become fairly mature before animals are grazed on it

cropped *past of* CROP

1crop·per \ˈkräpə(r)\ *n* -s [ME, fr. *croppen* to crop + *-er*] one that crops: as **a** (1) **:** one that raises produce; *specif* **:** SHARECROPPER ⟨returned to the soil as ~*s* and later as tenants —*Amer. Guide Series: Tenn.*⟩ (2) **:** a market gardener who raises special crops out of season **b :** a plant that yields a crop ⟨this raspberry is a good ~⟩ **c :** a worker who cuts hides into crops and butt bends — called also *carver* **d** (1) **:** any of various workers who shear textiles, metals, or leather (2) **:** a machine for doing this work

2cropper \"\ *n* -s [*1crop* (gullet) + *-er*] **:** a pigeon resembling the pouter

3cropper \"\ *n* -s [perh. fr. *1crop* (neck) + *-er*] **1 :** a severe fall ⟨first time in the saddle he got an awful ~⟩ **2 :** a sudden or violent failure or collapse ⟨his delusions and the ~*s* they cost him —Edmund Wilson⟩ — often used with *come* ⟨to see their betters come a ~ —Tyrone Guthrie⟩

croppie *var of* CRAPPIE

cropping *pres part of* CROP

crop·py \ˈkräpē\ *n* -ES [*2crop* + *-y*] **:** one of the Irish rebels of 1798 who wore their hair cut close to the head as a token of sympathy with the French Revolution

crop rotation *n* **:** the practice of growing different crops in succession on the same land chiefly to preserve the productive power of the soil

crops *pl of* CROP, *pres 3d sing of* CROP

crop seed *n* **:** small sweet potatoes culled from the regular crop for use as seed stock — compare SLIP SEED

cropsick \ˈ=,=\ *adj* [*1crop* (stomach) + *sick*] *now dial Eng* **:** sick from excess in eating or drinking

cropweed \ˈ=,=\ *n* **:** KNAPWEED

crop worm *n* **:** any of several nematode worms (as members of the genus *Capillaria*) that invade the mucosa of the crop of domestic poultry

1cro·quet \(ˈ)krōˈkā\ *n* -s [F dial., hockey stick, fr. ONF, shepherd's crook — more at CROCKET] **1 :** a game in which players drive wooden balls with mallets through a series of wickets set out on a lawn in a particular order — compare ROQUE **2 :** the driving away of another's ball in the game of croquet by striking one's own placed in contact with it

2croquet \"\ *vb* -ED/-ING/-S *vt* **:** to drive away (another's ball) in the game of croquet by striking one's own ball placed against the other ball ~ *vi* **:** to croquet another's ball

croquet set

cro·quette \(ˈ)krōˈket, *usu* -ed·+V\ *n* -s [F, fr. *croquer* to crunch (of imit. origin) + *-ette*] **:** a small cone-shaped or rounded mass consisting usu. of minced fowl, meat, or vegetable coated with egg and bread crumbs and fried in deep fat ⟨sweet potato ~*s*⟩ ⟨chicken ~*s*⟩

cro·qui·gnole \ˈkrōkə,nōl *also* -kən,yōl\ *n* -s [F, a kind of biscuit, irreg. fr. *croquer* to crunch] **:** a method used in waving the hair by winding it on curlers from the ends of the hair toward the scalp

cro·quill \ˈkrō,kwil\ *n* -s [by alter.] **:** CROW QUILL

cro·quis \(ˈ)krōˈkē\ *n, pl* **croquis** \-ē(z)\ [F, fr. *croquer* to crunch, know a person slightly, sketch] **:** a sketch or study; *esp* **:** a preparatory drawing or design for a projected work of art ⟨the design and layout started with ~ or thumbnail sketches —Fred Freeman⟩

crore \ˈkrō(ə)r\ *n, pl* **crores** *also* **crore** [Hindi *karor*] **:** ten million ⟨100 ~ of rupees⟩; *specif* **:** a unit of value equal to ten million rupees or 100 lakhs

cro·sier *or* **cro·zier** \ˈkrōzhə(r)\ *n* -s [ME *croser*, fr. MF *crossier* staff bearer, fr. *crosse* pastoral staff (fr. OF *croce*, of Gmc. origin; akin to OHG *krucka* crutch) + *-ier* -er — more at CRUTCH] **1** *obs* **a :** the bearer of the pastoral staff of a bishop **b :** the bearer of a cross before an archbishop **2 :** the pastoral staff of a bishop, abbot, or abbess resembling a shepherd's crook and borne as a symbol of the pastoral office; *also* **:** the processional cross or cross-staff of an archbishop in the Church of England **3 :** any botanical structure with a curled, coiled, or circinate end (as the young frond of a fern)

cro·siered \ˈkrōzhə(r)d\ *adj* **:** bearing or having a crosier

crosnes *also* **crosne** \ˈkrōn\ *n, pl* **crosnes** \-nz\ [F, fr. *Crosnes*, town near Corbeil, France, where it was first cultivated] **:** CHINESE ARTICHOKE

crosier 2

1cross \ˈkrȯs *also* ˈkräs\ *n* -ES [ME *cros, crosse*, fr. OE *cros*, fr.

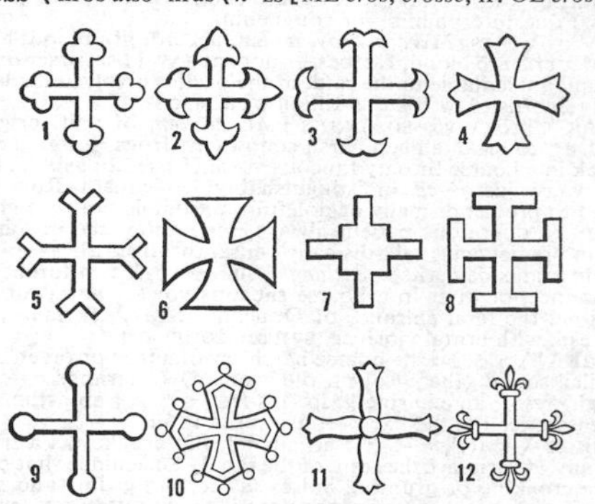

crosses 5a: *1* botonée, *2* fleury, *3* moline, *4* patonce, *5* fourchée, *6* formée, *7* quadrate, *8* potent, *9* pommée, *10* clechée, *11* avellan, *12* fleurettée

ON or OIr; ON *kross*, fr. (assumed) OIr *cross* (whence MIr), fr. L *crux* — more at RIDGE] **1 a :** a structure usu. consisting of an upright with a transverse beam used esp. by the ancient Romans as a means of execution ⟨the slave who revolted was fastened to a ~⟩ — see CRUCIFY, CRUX COMMISSA, CRUX DECUSSATA, CRUX IMMISSA **b** *often cap* **:** the cross on which Jesus Christ was crucified ⟨the day when Jesus died on the *Cross*⟩ **2 a :** CRUCIFIXION ⟨the penalty of the ~⟩; *specif* **:** the crucifixion and death of Jesus Christ regarded as the culmination of his mission of redemption ⟨by thy *Cross* and Passion . . . Good Lord, deliver us —Litany in *Bk. of Com. Prayer*⟩ **b :** the gospel of redemption through the death of Jesus Christ ⟨the doctrine of the ~, as the one great rule and hope of the world —G.A. Poole⟩ **3 :** an affliction or trial regarded as a test of Christian steadfastness, patience, or virtue — often used in the phrase *bear one's cross, take one's cross*, or *take up one's cross* with allusion to such biblical passages as Mt 10: 38, 16: 24, 27: 32; *broadly* **:** any affliction, trial, or trouble ⟨it was Ian's ~ to be a social coward —Hamilton Basso⟩ **4 :** SIGN OF THE CROSS **5 a :** a device or emblem composed essentially of an upright bar traversed by or joined at the top to a horizontal one but found in many varying types and used by people of various cultures as a symbol having any of various meanings, or as an amulet, and adopted by Christians because of its resemblance to the instrument of Jesus' crucifixion as a symbol of the culmination of his mission of redemption through his death or as a symbol of the Christian faith, a Christian people, or Christendom, and also widely used without specific religious symbolism in countries having a predominantly Christian background — see CALVARY CROSS, CELTIC CROSS, CROSS-CROSSLET, CROSS OF LORRAINE, GREEK CROSS, LATIN CROSS, MALTESE CROSS, PAPAL CROSS, PATRIARCHAL CROSS, SAINT ANDREW'S CROSS, TAU CROSS **b :** something that this device or emblem symbolizes (as Christianity or Christendom) ⟨to fight for the ~⟩ **6 a :** a cross-shaped badge, ornament, or article of ecclesiastical furniture used as a religious emblem **b :** a staff surmounted by a cross or crucifix borne in religious processions; *specif* **:** CROSS-STAFF 1 **7 a :** a monument or other structure in the form of a cross or surmounted by a cross ⟨a boundary ~⟩ ⟨a ~ over a grave⟩; *esp* **:** a cross set up in the center or market place of a town **b** *now Scot* **:** MARKET **8 :** a figure or mark formed by two intersecting lines or bars usu. of equal or approximately equal length and crossing at or about their midpoints (as + or ×) ⟨written in warm terms with plenty of ~*es* indicating kisses —L.A.Norris⟩ ⟨the morning star, represented by a ~ —L.H.Appleton⟩ ⟨a single ~ placed opposite one of the party names and counted as a vote —F.A.Ogg & P.O.Ray⟩; *specif* **:** such a cross (as in ink or pencil) used as a signature — see CHRISTCROSS **9 a :** a badge or emblem of an order of chivalry or a decoration of honor having the form of a cross or of a number of rays, often more or less than four, radiating from a common center — compare CROSS OF FOURTEEN POINTS **b :** one entitled to wear such a badge or emblem ⟨he is a Victoria *Cross*⟩ **10** *archaic* **a :** a cross-shaped impression on a coin **b :** a coin having such an impression **11** *heraldry* **:** an ordinary having the form of a pale and a fess combined intersecting in the center of the field **12 :** a pipe fitting with four branches the axes of which usu. form right angles **13 :** a piece of fur made of sections or of whole skins sewed in the form of a cross **14 :** any device or emblem of an extensive category that includes not only the cross (sense 5a) in all of its varieties but also various other devices of which a cross forms a part (as the swastika) or which are analogous to the cross ⟨as early as 317 B.C., the coins of Sicily bear the three-armed ~ as a symbol —E.S.Holden⟩ — see ANKH; compare TRISKELION **15** *obs* **:** a transverse part of an object (as the cross guard of a sword or dagger, the stock of an anchor, or the cross stroke on a letter *t*) **16** *obs* **:** a position wherein one thing rests over another in the form of a cross — used with *in* or *on* **17** *archaic* **:** the intersection of two ways or lines **:** CROSSING **18 :** an accidental contact between two electrical conductors **19 :** THWARTING, VEXATION, ANNOYANCE ⟨a ~ in love⟩ **20 a :** an act of crossing (as between breeds, races, or kinds of individuals) ⟨his first ~ of radish and cabbage was unsuccessful⟩ **b :** a crossbred individual or kind **:** a product of crossing ⟨the blue-gray ~ resulting from breeding a Galloway cow to a white Shorthorn bull exhibits outstanding beef conformation⟩ **c :** one that combines characteristics of two different types or individuals ⟨a ~ between a hiss and a spit —H.J.Laski⟩ **21 a :** something that is not honest or fair (as a contest) **:** something fraudulent or predeterminedly dishonest ⟨I never fought a ~ or struck a foul blow in my life —G.B.Shaw⟩ **b :** dishonest or illegal practices — used esp. in the phrase *on the cross* ⟨he earned money mostly on the ~⟩; see DOUBLE CROSS **22 :** a motion that intersects or goes across: as **a :** a movement from one part of the stage of a theater to another or from one side to the other **b :** a hook crossed over the opponent's lead in boxing — usu. used with *right* or *left* ⟨I caught him off guard with . . . a lucky right ~ —G.A.Hamid⟩ **syn** see TRIAL — **in cross 1** *of four heraldic bearings* **:** two in upright and two in horizontal position so as to approach or join at a common center ⟨four lozenges conjoined *in cross*⟩ **2** *of four or more heraldic bearings* **:** arranged as if along the arms of a cross ⟨four mullets *in cross*⟩ — **per cross** *heraldry* **:** divided into four parts by an upright and a horizontal line crossing each other **:** QUARTERLY

2cross \"\ *vb* **crossed** *also* **crost; crossed** *also* **crost; crossing; crosses** [ME *crossen*, fr. *cros*, n.] *vt* **1 a :** to lie or be situated across ⟨the bandoliers ~*ed* his chest⟩ ⟨the point where the two braces ~ each other⟩ **b :** INTERSECT ⟨the two lines ~ each other at right angles⟩; *specif* **:** to cross (one another) as pairs so that each member of one pair meets each member of the other — used in mathematics of two pairs of lines in space **2 :** to fasten (a sail or yard) across a mast ⟨the sails were ~*ed* and the voyage begun⟩ **3 a :** to make the sign of the cross upon or over **:** BLESS ⟨pilgrims ~*ed* by a bishop⟩ ⟨the communicants ~*ed* themselves devoutly and knelt in prayer⟩ **b :** to place a coin in (the hand of a gypsy fortune-teller) when paying for a consultation **c :** to place (one's fingers) in a crossed position (as the middle finger over the index finger) as a gesture intended to bring good luck, to free one from responsibility while telling a lie, or to indicate private reservations when making a statement **d :** to draw a cross over (one's heart) with one's finger as a gesture intended to indicate the absolute truthfulness of a statement **4 a :** to cancel by or as if by marking a cross on or drawing a line through **:** strike out **:** ERADICATE — usu. used with *off* or *out* ⟨~ out a bad debt⟩ ⟨~ names off a list⟩ ⟨~ out portions of a text⟩ **b** *obs* **:** to cut off **:** DEBAR **5 a :** to lay or place crosswise usu. with one above and almost parallel to the other ⟨~ the arms⟩ — often used with *over* ⟨he sat down and ~*ed* one leg over the other⟩ **b :** to arrange in a crisscross pattern ⟨to start a fire first ~ some dry twigs⟩ **c :** to place one's leg over (as a horse or saddle) **:** sit astride **:** RIDE ⟨the best pony that was ever ~*ed*⟩ **6 a** (1) **:** to run counter to **:** OPPOSE ⟨he was ugly if ~*ed*⟩ **:** THWART ⟨~*ed* in love⟩ (2) **:** to deny the validity of **:** CONTRADICT ⟨~ a person's statement⟩ **b** (1) *obs* **:** to encounter hostilely **:** engage in combat with (2) **:** to confront in a troublesome or bothersome manner **:** OBSTRUCT ⟨the ship was ~*ed* by contrary winds⟩ **c** (1) **:** to spoil completely **:** DISRUPT — used with *up* ⟨his not appearing ~*ed* up the whole program⟩ (2) **:** to deceive, betray, or turn against — used with *up* ⟨~ someone up on a deal⟩ **7 a :** to extend from one edge or corner of to the other **:** TRAVERSE ⟨a highway ~*ing* the entire state⟩ ⟨a forest that ~*es* the length of a valley⟩ **b :** to reach or attain ⟨only two runners ~*ed* the finish line⟩ ⟨the number of accidents ~*ed* the 1000 mark in July⟩ **c** (1) **:** to go from one side of to the opposing side ⟨~ a street⟩ ⟨~ a mine field⟩ (2) **:** to pass over on (as an elevated structure) from one side to the other ⟨~ a bridge⟩ ⟨~ a trestle⟩ **8 a :** to draw a line across or on (as something already drawn) ⟨~ one's *t's*⟩ ⟨~ line A at right angles with a second line B⟩ **b :** to mark or figure with or as if with lines **:** STREAK ⟨a mineral ~*ed* with irregular yellow lines⟩ **c** *Brit* **:** to draw two parallel lines across the face of (a check) often with *& Co* written between them in order to indicate that payment is to be made only through a bank ⟨if a check is sent it should be ~*ed* and made nonnegotiable —*Australian Home Beautiful*⟩ or to write or print between two parallel lines drawn across the face of (a check) the name of the particular bank through which payment is to be made ⟨checks . . . should be made payable to "The Times Publishing Co., Ltd.," and ~*ed* "Barclays Bank Ltd." —*Times Lit. Supp.*⟩ **9 :** to cause (an animal or plant) to interbreed with another animal or plant of a different race or kind **:** HYBRIDIZE, CROSS-POLLINATE ⟨improvements were made by ~*ing* mongrel sows with imported boars —E.D.Ross⟩ **10 :** to occur to ⟨an idea ~*ed* me once that he might be an actor —G.B.Shaw⟩ — often used with *mind* ⟨misgivings of every sort ~*ed* my mind⟩ **11 a :** to come upon **:** MEET ⟨~ an acquaintance on the street⟩ **b :** to meet and pass on the way because of setting out or being sent out at approximately the same time ⟨our letters must have ~*ed* each other⟩ **12 a :** CROSS-PLOW **b** (1) **:** to intersect the path in front of (the bows) of another ship ⟨a destroyer ~*ed* the bows of the transport⟩ (2) **:** to ride across the course of (another horse) in horse racing or polo **13 a :** to carry, transport, or take across ⟨a man bold enough to take his chances could ~ livestock to the Texas side of the river —F.B.Gipson⟩ **b :** to transfer (as from one side to another) — usu. used with *under* or *over* ⟨to tie the knot ~ the right hand under the left⟩ **14 :** to name as trump (a suit) of a different color from the card turned in the game of euchre ~ *vi* **1 a** *obs* **:** to run counter **:** be at odds — used with *upon* or *with* **b :** to ride across the course of another horse ⟨the jockey claimed there was too much bumping and ~*ing* in the race⟩ **2 :** to move, pass, or extend across something ⟨a path that ~*es* through the garden⟩ ⟨a throw that ~*ed* from left field to first base⟩ ⟨the ship ~*ed* over the equator⟩; *specif* **:** to pass from one side of the theater stage to another — used with *over* **3 :** to lie or be athwart each other ⟨the two highways ~ nearby⟩ **4 :** to meet in passing esp. from opposite directions ⟨our letters ~*ed* in the mail⟩ **5 :** to interbreed (as of two races) **:** HYBRIDIZE; *specif, of a gene* **:** to pass from one homologous chromosome to another — used with *over;* see CROSSING-OVER — **cross a person's palm** *or* **cross a person's hand** *slang* **:** BRIBE ⟨his palm had been amply ~*ed*⟩ — **cross swords :** to come to grips **:** be drawn into combat or altercation ⟨*cross swords* with one's landlady over the rent⟩ — **cross the floor** *Brit* **:** to vote with the opposing party on a legislative measure proposed by one's own party — **cross the line** *also* **cross over the line :** to take up status as a white ⟨the place where hundreds of light-skinned persons with a modicum of colored blood *crossed over the line* —Hamilton Basso⟩ — **cross the T :** to maneuver warships in a surface battle so that one's line of ships passes across the bow of the enemy's line of ships and that all of one's own broadsides can be concentrated on the leading ship of the enemy

³cross \"\ *adj* -ER/-EST [¹*cross*] **1 a :** lying across or athwart ⟨the crazy tangle of ~ wires —H.J.Muller⟩ **:** extending from one side to the other ⟨~ members should be all steel or metal or equivalent strength —*Bookmobile Specifications*⟩ **b :** moving across **:** traversing from one side to the other ⟨~ ventilation⟩ ⟨~ traffic⟩ **2** *archaic* **:** not accordant with what is wished or expected **:** THWARTING, PERVERSE, UNFAVORABLE ⟨bowed down by a ~ fortune⟩ ⟨~ weather⟩ **3 :** running counter **:** OPPOSING, OPPOSITE ⟨a ~ wind⟩ ⟨tugging on some issues in ~ directions —*N.Y.Times*⟩ ⟨ideas ~ to those of most other people⟩; *specif* **:** mutually opposed ⟨working at ~ purposes⟩ **4 :** involving mutual interchange **:** RECIPROCAL ⟨a system of ~ payments was worked out by the two governments⟩ **5 a** *archaic* **:** CONTENTIOUS, FRACTIOUS, PERVERSE, CONTRARIOUS **b :** marked by bad temper and irritable disposition **:** easily vexed **:** SNAPPISH, GRUMPY, PEEVISH ⟨a woman who feels that her future is uncertain . . . can be . . . ~ with her husband and children —Harrison Smith⟩ ⟨a ~ answer⟩ **6 :** extending over, covering, or treating several categories, groups, conditions, or classes — used chiefly in adjective-noun compounds ⟨a *cross*-cultural perspective⟩ ⟨~ sample records of . . . 1800 children —*Amer. Child*⟩ **7 :** CROSSBRED, HYBRID; *specif* **:** heterozygous for a recessive character **syn** see IRASCIBLE

⁴cross \"\ *prep* [by shortening] **:** ACROSS ⟨the daily flight of an eagle back and forth ~ the river to its nest —*Amer. Guide Series: Texas*⟩

⁵cross \"\ *adv* [in sense 1, short for *across;* in other senses, partly fr. ¹*cross*, partly, fr. ³*cross*] **1** *archaic* **:** from side to side **:** ACROSS, ATHWART **2** *archaic* **:** CONTRARIWISE, UNFAVORABLY **3 :** not parallel **:** CROSSWISE, CRISSCROSS — used chiefly with verbs ⟨to *cross*-wind wire on a spool⟩

cross- *or* **crosso-** *comb form* [NL, fr. Gk *krossoi* tassels, fringe; akin to OE *oferhrǣgan* to tower above, MHG *ragen* to tower up, stick up, MD *raghen*, Gk *krossai* coping of a parapet, OIr *crích* end, furrow, Russ *krokva* pole, rafter; basic meaning: jutting out, sticking up] **:** fringe ⟨*Cross*aster⟩ ⟨*crosso*pterygian⟩ ⟨*Crosso*soma⟩

cross·abil·i·ty \ˌkrȯsəˈbiləd-ē *also* ˌkräs-\ *n* **:** the ability of different species or varieties to cross with each other

cross·able \ˈ=səbəl\ *adj* **:** capable of being crossed ⟨a river ~ at several points⟩; *specif* **:** capable of crossing **:** admitting of being crossed ⟨a plant ~ with other varieties⟩

cross action *n* **:** a legal action by a party sued made against the person who has sued him and upon the same subject matter

cross agglutination *n* **:** agglutination of cells of one species by serum of an animal immunized against another usu. closely related species — called also *group agglutination*

cross aisle *n, obs* **:** TRANSEPT

cross and english bond *n, usu cap E* **:** a bond formed by laying the inner part of a wall in one way and the outer part in another

cross and pile *n* [ME; *pile* reverse of a coin, fr. MF, pillar, pier of a bridge, device for stamping coins, reverse of a coin — more at PILE] **1** *archaic* **:** HEADS OR TAILS **2** *archaic* **:** MONEY

crossarm \ˈ=ˌ=\ *n* **:** an arm fastened at right angles to an upright (as the horizontal member of a cross or a traverse on a telephone pole)

cros·sas·ter \krōˈsastə(r)\ *n, cap* [NL, fr. *cross-* + *-aster*] **:** a widely distributed genus (family Solasteridae) of brightly colored starfishes including the circumpolar rose star (*C. papposa*)

cross axle *n* **1 :** a shaft, windlass, or roller worked by levers at opposite ends (as in the copperplate printing press) **2 :** a driving axle with cranks set at an angle of 90 degrees

cross-back \"\ *n* [fr. *cross back*, v.] **1 :** the act or action of breeding back a crossbred individual to one of the parent breeds **2 :** the offspring of such breeding

crossband \"\ *adj* **:** *of a twist in textile manufacture* **:** left-hand or S-shaped — compare OPENBAND

crossbanded \ˈ=ˌ==\ *adj* **1 :** having or utilizing a crossband ⟨~ construction⟩ **2 :** having crossbanding ⟨a ~ and inlaid table⟩

crossbanding \ˈ=ˌ==\ *n* **1** *also* **crossband** \ˈ=ˌ=\ **:** a piece of veneer (as in a 5-ply panel) glued between the core and an outer ply and having the grain at right angles to that of the core **2 :** a veneer border (as on furniture) with its grain at right angles to the grain of the adjacent wood

crossbar \ˈ=ˌ=\ *n* **:** a traverse bar: as **a :** the horizontal member of a cross **b :** a horizontal brace **:** RUNG, ROUND **c :** a traverse bar or stripe esp. on fabrics ⟨a ~ design⟩ **d** (1) **:** a bar within a printer's chase running from top to bottom or from side to side and used to strengthen the chase and facilitate locking (2) **:** a horizontal stroke in a letter (as that joining the upright strokes in A and H) — see TYPE illustration **e** (1) **:** the horizontal bar across the goalposts in football and soccer (2) **:** a loose horizontal bar on uprights used in high jumping (3) **:** HORIZONTAL BAR **f :** the top bar of a bicycle frame **g :** a bar of insulating material to which the blades of a multipole knife switch are attached

cross-barred shell \ˈ=ˌ=-\ *n* **:** any mollusk of the genus *Cancellaria* or family Cancellariidae — called also *crossbar*

crossbar shot *n* **1 :** a round shot with two projections so that it appears to have a bar running through its center **2 :** an obsolete projectile that folds into a sphere for loading but that on leaving the gun opens into a cross with a quarter ball at the end of each arm

crossbeak \ˈ=ˌ=\ *n* **:** CROSSBILL

crossbeam \ˈ=ˌ=\ *n* **:** a traverse beam (as a structural girder or the horizontal member of a cross)

crossbearer \ˈ=ˌ==\ *n* **:** one that bears a cross: as **a :** an attendant who carries a cross in a religious procession or ceremony **:** CRUCIFER **b :** a device of transverse bars for supporting the grate bars of a furnace or the planking or roadway of a bridge

cross bearings *n pl* [³*cross*] **:** compass bearings of two or more points taken simultaneously to fix a position (as of a ship)

cross-bedded \ˈ=ˈ==\ *adj* [⁵*cross*] **:** having minor beds or laminae lying oblique to the main beds of stratified rock ⟨*cross-bedded* sandstone⟩

cross-bedding \ˈ=ˈ==\ *n* **1 :** the quality or state of being cross-bedded **2 :** a cross-bedded structure

crossbelt \ˈ=ˌ=\ *n* [³*cross* + *belt*] **:** a double belt passing over both shoulders and crossing at the breast or a single belt passing obliquely across the breast ⟨sergeants wearing ~*s* and sidearms⟩

crossbench \ˈ=ˌ=\ *n, often attrib* [³*cross* + *bench*] **:** one of the benches in the House of Lords of the British parliament which is set at right angles to other benches and on which neutral or independent members sit ⟨a ~ mind⟩ — **crossbencher** \ˈ=ˌ==\ *n*

cross-bill \ˈ=ˌ=\ *n* [³*cross*] **1 :** a bill in equity by a defendant against a plaintiff respecting the matter in question in a suit **2 :** a bill of exchange given in return for another

crossbill \"\ *n* **:** any of several finches constituting a genus (*Loxia*), having a bill adapted to the extraction of seeds from fruits and tree cones by means of strongly curved and overlapping mandibles, and inhabiting coniferous forests of the northern hemisphere — see RED CROSSBILL, WHITE-WINGED CROSSBILL

crossbill

cross-bind \ˈ=ˌ=\ *vt* [⁵*cross*] **1 :** to bind or grip (a creeping railroad rail) by placing the outside spikes in advance of inside ones in the direction of creep so that any movement in the tie end caused by the creeping rail will cramp both the inside and outside spikes against the rail **2 :** to arrange (spikes) in such a way as to cross-bind a railroad rail

cross bit *n* **:** a rock drill made with cruciform cutting edges and used in mining

crossbite \ˈ=ˌ=\ *vt* [⁵*cross* + *bite*] *archaic* **:** to cheat in return **:** OUTWIT, COZEN

cross-blocking \ˈ=ˈ==\ *n* [³*cross*] **:** mechanical thinning of sugar beets or other crops with an implement carrying knives or sweeps driven across the rows

cross-body ride *n* [³*cross*] **:** a wrestling position in which a contestant has a scissors hold on the opponent's near leg and underhooks or overhooks the opponent's far arm

crossbolt \ˈ=ˌ=\ *n* [³*cross* + *bolt*] **:** a double bolt in a lock having two parts that can be shot simultaneously in opposite directions

crossbolt safety *n* **:** a safety device on certain firearms that utilizes a metal bar which can be positioned to act as a positive block to trigger movement

cross bond *n* [³*cross*] **1 :** a masonry bond in which courses of Flemish bond alternate with courses of stretchers **2 :** an electrical connection between the ground feeder or conductor and the rails of an electric railway or between rails of one or more tracks for equalizing the return current flowing in the rails and for bridging around possible open joint bonds

cross-bond \ˈ=ˌ=\ *vt* [*cross bond*] **:** to provide with a cross bond

crossbones \ˈ=ˌ=\ *n pl* **:** two leg or arm bones placed or depicted crosswise — see SKULL AND CROSSBONES

crossbow \ˈ=ˌ=\ *n* [ME *crosbowe*, fr. *cros* cross + *bowe* bow (weapon)] **:** a weapon having a short bow mounted crosswise near the end of a wooden stock that resembles the stock of a modern rifle and that is often provided with a mechanical device by which the string is drawn back and fixed and being usu. shot from the shoulder by means of a trigger that releases the string and discharges a quarrel lying in a groove in the stock — see ARBALEST

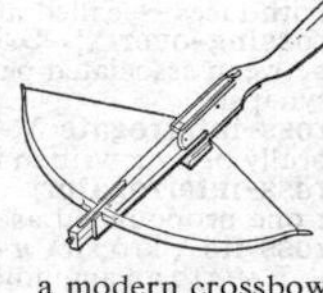

a modern crossbow

crossbowman \ˈ=ˌ=mən\ *n, pl* **crossbowmen :** a man (as a soldier or hunter) whose weapon is a crossbow

cross brace *n* **:** a crosspiece that transmits, diverts, or resists weight or pressure

cross bracing *n* **1 :** any system of bracing by means of cross struts or ties; *specif* **:** CROSS BRIDGING **2 :** bracing consisting of two diagonal members which intersect or cross each other

cross break *n* [³*cross*] **:** a separation of wood cells across the grain

¹crossbred \ˈ=ˌ=\ *adj* [⁵*cross* + *bred*] **1 :** produced by crossing **:** HYBRID; *specif* **:** produced by interbreeding two pure but different breeds, strains, or varieties **2 :** subjected to cross-breeding

²crossbred \ˈ=ˌ=\ *n* -s **1 :** a crossbred individual **2 :** CROSSBRED WOOL

crossbred wool *n* **:** wool from crossbred sheep

¹crossbreed \ˈ=ˈ=\ *vb* [⁵*cross* + *breed* (v.)] **:** HYBRIDIZE, CROSS; *esp* **:** to breed between two varieties or breeds of the same species — compare INBREED, INTERBREED, INTERCROSS, LINEBREED, OUTBREED, OUTCROSS

²crossbreed \ˈ=ˌ=\ *n* **:** a strain or an individual produced by crossbreeding **:** HYBRID

cross bridging *n* [³*cross*] **:** traverse rows of small diagonal braces or struts set in pairs and crossing each other between the timbers (as of a floor)

crossbuck \ˈ=ˌ=\ *n* [³*cross* + *buck* (as in *sawbuck*)] **:** an X-shaped highway warning sign at a highway-railroad intersection

cross buck *n* [³*cross*] **:** an offensive play in football in which a back faking to receive the ball charges into the line of scrimmage diagonally across the path of the ball carrier

cross-buttock \ˈ=ˈ==\ *n* [³*cross*] **:** a throw in wrestling in which a wrestler turns his side to his opponent, places his leg across both legs of his opponent, and pulls him forward over his hip

cross calvary *n, usu cap 2d C* **:** CALVARY CROSS

cross cell *n* [³*cross*] **:** any of certain cells found just below the hypodermis of the wheat grain having long axes at right angles to the pericarp and thin walls with transverse pits and in young grains containing chlorophyll

¹cross-check \ˈ=ˈ=\ *vt* [⁵*cross*] **1 :** to obstruct in ice hockey by holding or thrusting one's stick held in both hands across an opponent's face or body **2 :** to check (as data, reports, statements) from various angles or sources to determine accuracy or validity

²cross-check \"\ *n* **1 a :** an illegal cross-checking of an opposing player **b :** an illegal stopping of an opponent by holding the handle of the stick across his body or face in the game of lacrosse **2 a :** an act or action of cross-checking ⟨a *cross-check* made by comparing foreign and domestic news accounts⟩ **b :** a means of cross-checking ⟨lists used as *cross-checks*⟩

cross claim *n* [³*cross*] **:** a claim made by the defendant against the plaintiff and raised in the defendant's answer

cross cleavers *n pl but sing in constr* [so called fr. the fact that its leaves are arranged in sets of four that resemble crosses] **:** a wild licorice (*Galium circaezans*)

cross code *n* **:** a method of communication with the deaf-blind in which taps and strokes in various numbers, combinations, and positions on an imaginary cross usu. on the back of the hand stand for the letters of the alphabet

cross complaint *n* [³*cross*] **:** a complaint used in code pleading whereby a defendant by his answer or separate pleading sets up a claim against a codefendant or a third person arising out of the same subject matter of the original complaint

cross-compound \(ˈ)=+ *pronunc at* COMPOUND *adj* \ *adj* [⁵*cross*] *of a compound engine* **:** having cylinders side by side

cross-connection \ˈ=ˈ==\ *n* [³*cross*] **:** a connection in a plumbing installation through which water may possibly pass to or come in contact with another part (as a water inlet in a bathtub that may at times be below the water level of the tub)

cross correspondence *n* [³*cross*] **:** agreement or coherence of messages reputed to have been received by two spiritualist mediums as if fragments from the same control

cross counter *n* [³*cross*] **:** ¹CROSS 22b

¹cross-country \ˈ=ˈ==\ *adj* [⁴*cross*] **1 :** extending or moving across a country ⟨a *cross-country* railroad⟩ ⟨a *cross-country* concert tour⟩ **2 a :** proceeding over countryside (as across fields and through woods) and not by roads or paths ⟨a *cross-country* race⟩ **b :** having to do with cross-country sports ⟨a *cross-country* champion⟩

²cross-country \"\ *n* **:** cross-country sports ⟨interest in *cross-country* is growing in eastern colleges⟩; *specif* **:** a cross-country event (as in skiing, horse racing, distance running) — compare LANGLAUF

³cross-country \"\ *adv* **:** across the countryside ⟨a river meandering *cross-country*⟩ **:** by a course going directly over the countryside ⟨a group of tanks moving *cross-country*⟩

cross-cousin \ˈ=ˈ==\ *n* [³*cross*] **:** one of two cousins esp. of different sex who are respectively the children of a brother and of a sister ⟨the institution of *cross-cousin* marriage⟩ — compare PARALLEL COUSIN

cross-crosslet \ˈ=ˈ==\ *n, pl* **cross-crosslets** *or* **crosses crosslet** [ME *cros croslette*, fr. *cros* cross + *croslette* crosslet] **1 :** CROSSLET 1a **2** *heraldry* **:** a cross with a crossbar near the end of each arm

cross-crosslet 2

cross-cultural \ˈ=ˈ(=)=\ *adj* [⁵*cross*] **:** dealing with or offering comparison between two or more different cultures or cultural areas ⟨assembling data for a *cross-cultural* survey⟩ ⟨a *cross-cultural* investigation of the psychological significance of drama in war among primitive peoples —Lucile H. Charles⟩

crosscurrent \ˈ=ˈ==\ *n* [³*cross* + *current*] **1 :** a current traverse to the general forward direction (as of water in a river) **2 :** a conflicting tendency — usu. used in pl. ⟨the political ~*s* that disrupt the business of government⟩

¹crosscut \ˈ=ˌ=\ *vt* [⁵*cross* + *cut* (v.)] **:** to cut (something) traversely: as **a :** to cut (as wood) with a crosscut saw **b :** to go or move across ⟨a stream which ~*s* the country from north to south —*Harper's*⟩ **c** (1) **:** INTERSECT ⟨dimensions ~ one another, levels imply parallelism —A.L.Kroeber⟩ (2) **:** to enter into (as a different category) **:** impinge on ⟨a legal document that ~*s* medical knowledge⟩ **d :** to break up (as an association) **:** DIVIDE ⟨dissension and jealousy *crosscutting* a political party⟩ **e :** to subject (a film or the lines of action of a film) to crosscutting ⟨the scenario and the technical feat of *crosscutting* the stories are things ingeniously accomplished —Parker Tyler⟩

²crosscut \"\ *adj* **1 :** made or used for crosscutting ⟨a saw with ~ teeth⟩ **2 :** cut across or traversely ⟨a ~ incision⟩

³crosscut \ˈ=ˌ=\ *n* **1 :** something that cuts through traversely (as a path cutting across countryside or a cut sawed through a log) ⟨a ~ through the park⟩; *specif* **:** a mine working driven horizontally and at right angles to an adit, drift, or level or across or toward a vein or ore body or across the general trend of the rock formation **2 :** CROSS SECTION ⟨a novel that gives a ~ of American business activity⟩ **3 :** an instance of crosscutting in the editing of motion-picture film **4 :** a gemstone cut so that the arrangement of the facets produces an effect resembling that of a cross **5** [¹*crosscut*] **:** a tool that cross-cuts; *esp* **:** CROSSCUT SAW

crosscut file *n* **:** a file of uniform width that has a blunt rounded edge on one side tapering to a thin edge on the other and that is used for sharpening saw teeth having straight sides and round gullets

crosscut saw *n* **:** a saw designed chiefly to cut across the grain of wood — compare RIPSAW

crosscut shank *n* **:** a retail cut from the fore shank of a beef — see BEEF illustration

crosscutter \ˈ=ˌ==\ *n* **1 :** one that cuts stock lumber into lengths, cuts out imperfections, or squares the ends **2 :** BUCKER b

crosscutting \ˈ=ˌ==\ *n* **:** a technique of motion-picture film editing in which fragments of two or more lines of action are intermingled so as to appear alternately in the finished picture

cross-date \ˈ=ˌ=\ *vb* [⁵*cross*] *vi* **:** to show by close similarity of spacing, cell structure, and related criteria that certain of the annual rings of two or more different trees or pieces of wood were produced in the same year ~ *vt* **:** to establish (trees or pieces of wood) as cross-dating with each other — compare DENDROCHRONOLOGY

cross dating *n* **:** the correlation of distinctive traits between two or more sites or levels in different localities for purposes of chronology; *specif* **:** the establishment of the date of an archaeological site or level by comparing its distinctive traits with those of another site or level of known date that is assumed to be of similar age

cross direction *n* [³*cross*] **:** the dimension at right angles to the machine direction of a sheet of paper

¹cross-dye \ˈ=ˌ=\ *vt* [⁵*cross* + *dye* (v.)] **:** to dye by the process of cross-dyeing

²cross-dye \"\ *n* **1 :** the dye used in cross-dyeing **2 :** a fabric that has been cross-dyed

³cross-dye \ˈ=ˌ=\ *adj* **:** treated by or resulting from cross-dyeing ⟨~ rayon⟩ ⟨~ effects⟩

cross dye black RX \-ˌärˈeks\ *n, usu cap C&D&B* **:** a sulfur dye — see DYE table I (under *Sulfur Black 2*)

cross-dyeing \ˈ=ˌ==\ *n* **:** the production by either of two methods of multicolored effects on fabrics woven of more than one kind of fiber (as animal and vegetable fibers) having different affinities for dyes: **a :** the dyeing of a fabric by dyeing one or more kinds of fiber in the fabric with or without subsequent dyeing of the other fibers present **b :** the dyeing of one kind of fiber (as wool) after it has been woven with other fiber (as cotton) already dyed in the form of yarn

crosse \ˈkrȯs *also* ˈkräs\ *n* -s [F, lit., crosier (pastoral staff) — more at CROSIER] **:** the stick used in lacrosse

crossed *past of* CROSS

crossed belt *n* **:** a pulley belt whose sides cross each other so that the direction of rotation is reversed

crossed nicols *n pl, often cap N* **:** two nicol prisms placed one in front of the other and so oriented that their transmission planes for plane-polarized light are at right angles with the result that light transmitted by one is stopped by the other unless modified by some intervening body

crossed paralysis *or* **crossed palsy** *n* **:** paralysis affecting the extremities of one side and the face on the opposite side or the arm on one side and the leg on the other

crossed pyramidal tract *n* **:** a tract of motor nerve fibers in the lateral column of the spinal cord

crossed specially *adj, Brit* **:** bearing the name of the bank by which payment of a check is to be made — compare ²CROSS 8c

cross education *n* [³*cross*] **:** improvement of one side of the body in a performance which is practiced by the other

¹**cross·er** \-sə(r)\ *comparative of* CROSS

²**crosser** \"\ *n* -s [²*cross* + -*er*] **:** one that crosses; *specif* **:** ²STICKER 2

crosses *pl of* CROSS *or of* CROSSE, *pres 3d sing of* CROSS

crossest *superlative of* CROSS

cross·ette \(ˈ)krȯˈset\ *n* -s [F *crossette*, dim. of *crosse* crosier (pastoral staff) — more at CROSIER] **1 :** a projection at a corner of the architrave of a door or window — called also *ancon, ear, elbow* **2 :** a projection in a voussoir (as of a flat arch) fitting into a corresponding recess in the adjacent voussoir

cross-examination \ˌ=ˌ==ˈ==\ *n* **:** a careful examination ⟨a little *cross-examination* seldom fails to reveal that he desires art to reproduce only certain aspects of the natural world —Hunter Mead⟩; *specif* **:** a questioning designed esp. to check the accuracy of answers to prior questions ⟨under *cross-examination* the witness admitted his information was all secondhand⟩

cross-examine \ˌ=ˌ=ˈ=\ *vt* [⁵*cross*] **:** to examine by a series of questions designed to check the accuracy of answers to previous questions **:** examine closely or repeatedly; *specif* **:** to examine (a witness who has testified for the other side in a legal action) esp. in order to disprove testimony already given

cross-examiner \"+ə(r)\ *n* **:** one that cross-examines

cross-eye \ˈ=ˌ=\ *n* [³*cross*] **1 :** squint in which the eye turns inward toward the nose — called also *esotropia;* compare WALLEYE **2 cross-eyes** \ˈ=ˌ=\ *pl* **:** eyes affected with cross-eye ⟨the use of muscle exercises in the treatment of *cross-eyes*⟩

cross-eyed \ˈ=ˌ=\ *adj* [³*cross*] **1 :** affected with cross-eye **:** having cross-eyes ⟨a *cross-eyed* child⟩ **2 :** COCKEYED 2b ⟨to attempt to investigate both at the same time (to say nothing of all six) would be a *cross-eyed* procedure —Anna G. Hatcher⟩

cross facet *n* **:** SKEW FACET

¹**cross-fade** \ˈ=ˌ=\ *vt* [⁵*cross* + *fade*] **:** to fade in (a sound or image) in a motion picture or a radio or television program while fading out another sound or image ⟨the scream of the charlady . . . was *cross-faded* into the shriek of a nearby train —Lewis Herman⟩; *also* **:** to fade in (a camera or piece of sound equipment) while fading out another camera or piece of sound equipment — compare DISSOLVE

²**cross-fade** \ˈ=ˌ=\ *n* **1 :** an act or instance of cross-fading **2 :** the technique of cross-fading

crossfall \ˈ=ˌ=\ *n* [³*cross* + *fall*] **:** the transverse sloping of a roadway toward the shoulder or gutter on either side

cross fault *n* [³*cross*] **:** a dip fault or oblique fault

¹**cross-feed** \ˈ=ˌ=\ *n* [³*cross* + *feed* (n.)] **:** a feeding mechanism that acts transversely to the longitudinal axis of the machine bed — see ²FEED 5

²**cross-feed** \ˈ=ˌ=\ *vb* **:** to feed into a machine transversely

cross-fertile \ˈ=ˈ=(ˌ)=\ *adj* **:** fertile in a cross ⟨the true pumpkins and the summer squashes are generally *cross-fertile*⟩

cross-fertilizable \ˈ=ˈ==ˌ===\ *adj* **:** capable of cross-fertilization

cross-fertilization \ˈ=ˌ=ˈ=(ˌ)=ˈ==\ *n* **1** *in seed plants* **a :** fertilization between gametes produced by separate individual plants **b :** fertilization between different kinds of individuals (as species or varieties) resulting in the production of hybrids **2 :** CROSS-POLLINATION — not used technically **3 :** the fertilization of the eggs of an animal by spermatozoa of another individual esp. in potentially hermaphroditic forms **4 :** interchange or interplay (as between different ideas, cultures, or categories) esp. of a vitalizing, broadening, or productive nature ⟨the best work in the field of the novel came from the *cross-fertilization* of realism with the movement of regionalism —R.A.Hall b.1911⟩

cross-fertilize \ˈ=ˈ==ˌ=\ *vb* [⁵*cross* + *fertilize*] *vt* **:** to accomplish cross-fertilization of ~ *vi* **:** to undergo cross-fertilization

cross file *n* [³*cross* + *file* (tool)] **:** CROSSING FILE

¹**cross-file** \ˈ=ˌ=\ *vb* [⁵*cross* + *file* (to rub)] **:** to file by applying pressure against the work with no pressure on the return

²**cross-file** \"\ *vb* [⁵*cross* + *file* (to arrange)] *vi* **:** to register as a candidate in the primary elections of more than one political party ~ *vt* **:** to register (a person) as a candidate for more than one party ⟨is nominally *cross-filed* as a Republican —Gladwin Hill⟩

cross-fingering \ˈ=ˈ=(=)=\ *n* [³*cross*] **:** fingering out of serial order (as in producing certain chromatic tones) in the playing of certain wind instruments

cross fire *n* [³*cross*] **1 a :** firing in combat from two or more points so that the lines of fire cross ⟨gaps in the barrier of artillery . . . filled by the *cross fires* of . . . machine guns —M.H.Armor⟩ **b** (1) **:** a position or situation wherein the forces of opposing factions meet or cross ⟨a son caught in the emotional *cross fire* of his parents⟩ (2) **:** rapid or heated interchange ⟨the *cross fire* of question and answer⟩ **2 :** noise or interfering current set up in a telephone or telegraph circuit by the operation of a neighboring circuit — compare CROSS TALK **3 :** a sidearm pitch in baseball that cuts across the plate at an angle **4** *or* **cross figure :** a pattern in the figure of certain woods caused by distortion of the wood fibers and characterized usu. by parallel mottled bands at right angles to the grain

cross-fire \ˈ=ˌ=\ *vb* [*cross fire*] *vi* **1 :** to set up or cause cross fire **2 :** to overreach by striking the opposite forefoot — used of horses (as pacers) **3 a :** to aim over the left or the right barrel of a double-barreled shotgun instead of over the center rib ⟨he overcame a tendency to *cross-fire*⟩ **b :** to fire upon an adjacent target rather than on one's own ~ *vt* **:** to burn (the leg of a horse) with a firing iron in a checkerboard pattern for therapeutic purposes

cross-firing \ˈ=ˌ==\ *n* **:** a method of radiation therapy in which the rays are directed from different points to meet at the same point in the patient

cross flute *n* **:** TRANSVERSE FLUTE

cross flux *or* **cross field** *n* [³*cross*] **:** a component of flux at right angles to that produced by field magnets (as in a dynamo)

cross-fold \ˈ=ˌ=\ *n* [³*cross*] **:** a secondary geological fold at right or nearly right angles to a primary fold

crossfoot \ˈ=ˌ=\ *vt* [⁵*cross* + *foot* (to sum up)] **:** to add (figures) across instead of up or down

crossfooter \"+ə(r)\ *n* **:** any device on a bookkeeping or other office machine that crossfoots; *specif* **:** the key that actuates this operation on the machine or the device that registers or makes visible the result

cross fox *n* [³*cross*] **:** a melanistic color phase of the red fox or sometimes of the common European fox characterized by a somewhat definite dark cross-shaped mark on the back and shoulders; *also* **:** fox fur or a fox pelt in such a color phase

cross-fur \ˈ=ˌ=\ *vt* [⁵*cross*] **:** to apply traverse furring to (as ceiling joists)

cross-garnet \ˈ=ˌ==\ *n, archaic* **:** a T-shaped hinge

cross-gartered \ˈ=ˈ==\ *adj* [⁵*cross*] **:** wearing garters crossed along the leg (as in some ancient or medieval costumes)

cross grain *n* [³*cross*] **1 :** a grain running transversely to the regular grain or not parallel to the long axis of the piece (as in certain wood) **2 :** interweaving grain in lumber

cross-grained \ˈ=ˈ=\ *adj* **1 :** having the grain or fibers running diagonally, transversely, or irregularly **2 a :** difficult to deal with, handle, or master ⟨a *cross-grained* problem⟩ ⟨the story . . . *cross-grained* in its structure —D.L.Morgan⟩ **b :** morosely irascible **:** grumpy and intractable **:** perversely contrary ⟨a spiteful *cross-grained* old woman⟩ **syn** see CONTRARY

cross-grain·ed·ness \(ˈ)=ˈ=nədnəs\ *n* -ES **:** the quality or state of being cross-grained **:** PERVERSITY

cross guard *n* **:** a sword or bayonet guard consisting of a short bar which crosses the blade at its junction with the hilt

crosshackle \ˈ=ˌ==\ *vt* [⁵*cross* + *hackle*] **:** to cross-question esp. annoyingly

cross hair *n* **:** one of the fine wires or spider lines mounted as a reticle in the focus of the eyepiece of optical instruments and used as a reference line in the field or for marking the instrumental axis

¹**cross-handed** \ˈ=ˈ==\ *adj* [⁵*cross*] **:** with the hands crossed or in reverse of the usual position ⟨a *cross-handed* grip on a ball bat⟩

²**cross-handed** \"\ *adv* **:** in a cross-handed manner ⟨using a canoe paddle *cross-handed*⟩

¹**crosshatch** \ˈ=ˌ=\ *vb* [⁵*cross* + *hatch*] **:** to mark with or as if with crosshatch ⟨a slum ~*ed* with dismal streets⟩; *esp* **:** to shade with crosshatch ⟨a drawing with shadows ~*ed* in⟩ — compare HACHURE

²**crosshatch** \ˈ=ˌ=\ *n* **:** a pattern made up of one series of parallel lines crossing (as at right angles or obliquely) another series of parallel lines with the space between the lines in one series usu. being identical to the space between the lines in the other series ⟨abrupt gradients on these maps are indicated by ~⟩ ⟨a ~ of branches⟩

cross-hatching \ˈ=ˌ==\ *n* **1 a :** the process of marking with crosshatch **b :** the effect produced by such a process **2 :** a pottery design that consists of two series of parallel lines intersecting each other usu. at an oblique angle and is typical of Hopewell pottery

¹**crosshaul** \ˈ=ˌ=\ *n* [³*cross* + *haul*] **1 a :** a loading device consisting of a chain having each end fastened to opposing sides of a vehicle (as a sled or wagon) and the resulting loop passed under the object to be loaded (as a log) and back to a source of power that rolls the object usu. up a ramp onto the vehicle **b** *also* **crosshauling** \ˈ=ˌ==\ **:** the method of loading employing this device **2 :** an instance where the transportation of goods promotes or creates crosshauling ⟨millions of railroad car miles . . . saved by the elimination of ~*s* —K.A.Solmssen⟩

²**crosshaul** \"\ *vb* **:** to transport under conditions that promote or create crosshauling

crosshauling \ˈ=ˌ==\ *n* **:** the regular transportation (as by railroad) of goods away from a locality while similar or corresponding goods are transported into the locality ⟨efforts to eliminate ~ of farm produce⟩

crosshead \ˈ=ˌ=\ *n* [³*cross* + *head*] **1 :** a beam or bar across the head or end of a rod or a block attached to it and carrying a knuckle pin; *esp* **:** a block guided so as to move in a straight line and serving as a connection between the piston rod and the connecting rod of a steam engine **2 :** a heavy rectangular guide frame attached to the hoisting cable just above the bucket in a mine **3 :** *also* **crossheading** \ˈ=ˌ==\ **:** a heading centered in a column and preceding text or (as in a long newspaper article) between portions of text

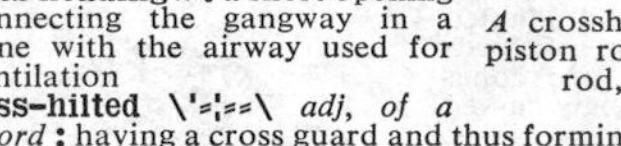

A crosshead, *B* guide, *C* piston rod, *D* connecting rod, *E* wrist pin

cross heading *n* **:** a short opening connecting the gangway in a mine with the airway used for ventilation

cross-hilted \ˈ=ˈ==\ *adj, of a sword* **:** having a cross guard and thus forming with the blade a Latin cross

cross-immunity \ˌ==ˈ===\ *n* [³*cross*] **:** immunity toward one of a pair of antigens following immunization toward the other that is used to assess the relationship between certain antigens

cross-immunization \ˌ=+\ *n* [³*cross*] **:** the act or action of effecting cross-immunity

¹**cross-index** \ˈ=ˈ=ˌ=\ *vb* [⁵*cross* + *index* (v.)] *vt* **1 a :** to refer by means of a note at one place to matter at another place ⟨all items in the biology file are *cross-indexed* to related material in the zoology file⟩ **b :** to refer from (a variant or subordinate entry) to a main entry ⟨"public sanitation" should be *cross-indexed* to "public health"⟩ **2 :** to provide (as the body of a text, an index, or a file) with cross-references ⟨a *cross-indexed* report⟩ ~ *vi* **:** to function as or become provided with a cross-referring note or index ⟨most variants *cross-index* to main entries⟩ ⟨all annotations for the most part *cross-index*⟩

²**cross-index** \"\ *n* **:** a note, series of notes, or index that cross-indexes ⟨each *cross-index* is written on a blue slip⟩ ⟨a text with a *cross-index* in footnotes as well as a general index in the back⟩

cross infection *n* [³*cross*] **:** infection esp. between the newborn

crossing *n* -s **1 :** the act or action of crossing: as **a** *archaic* **:** the making of the sign of the cross **b :** a traversing or going across ⟨a channel ~⟩ ⟨a ~ made without incident⟩ ⟨the troops effected a ~ under fire⟩ **c** (1) **:** a drawing of lines across esp. in canceling — often used with *out* or *off* ⟨a letter full of misspellings and ~*s out*⟩ (2) *Brit* **:** the crossing of a check ⟨fraudulent ~*s*⟩ **d :** an opposing, blocking, or thwarting esp. in an unfair or dishonest manner ⟨a jockey fined for ~ and bumping⟩ **e :** INTERBREEDING, HYBRIDIZING, CROSS-POLLINATING **2 a :** a place or structure that crosses or is crossed: as **a** (1) **:** a place or structure (as on a street or over a river) on which pedestrians or vehicles cross ⟨the right to build additional Hudson river ~*s* —*N.Y. Times*⟩; *esp* **:** CROSSWALK (2) **:** INTERSECTION ⟨at the ~ of Main street and State⟩ **b :** the place in a church where the transept crosses the nave **c** (1) **:** the point at which a railroad track crosses another track or a highway at grade (2) **:** a structure consisting of four connected frogs used where two railroad tracks intersect at grade to permit traffic to move along either track

crossing file *n* **:** a file similar to a half-round file but convex on both faces — called also *cross file*

crossing-over \ˌ==ˈ==\ *n* **:** interchange of genes or segments between associated parts of homologous chromosomes during synapsis

cross-interrogate \ˌ==ˈ=ˌ=\ *vt* [⁵*cross*] **:** to cross-question orally or by a written interrogatory

cross-interrogatory \ˌ=ˌ==ˈ==\ *n* **:** CROSS-QUESTION; *esp* **:** one propounded as an interrogatory in taking a deposition

cross·ite \ˈkrȯˌsīt\ *n* -s [Whitman *Cross* †1949 Am. geologist + E -*ite*] **:** an amphibole intermediate in composition between glaucophane and riebeckite

cross·jack \ˈkräjik, ˈkrȯsˌjak\ *n* [³*cross* + *jack* (flag)] **:** a now rarely used square sail set on the lower yard of the mizzenmast — see SAIL illustration, SHIP illustration

cross keys *n pl but sing in constr* [³*cross*] **:** a heraldic representation of two keys laid crosswise in saltire

cross kick *n* [³*cross*] **:** a lateral kick in rugby; *esp* **:** one from a wing toward the center of the field

cross-laminated \ˈ=ˌ==\ *adj* [⁵*cross*] **:** CROSS-BEDDED

cross-lamination \ˌ=ˌ==ˈ=\ *n* [³*cross*] **:** CROSS-BEDDING

cross-leaved heath *also* **cross-leaf heath** \ˈ=ˌ=\ *n* **:** a low perennial European shrub (*Erica tetralix*) of bogs and marshy ground that is often used for ornament

cross-legged *esp US* ˈ=ˌlegəd, *esp Brit* -gd\ *adj* (*or adv*) [⁵*cross*] **1 :** with the legs crossed and the knees spread wide ⟨beside her sitting *cross-legged* on the ground there was a child —Olive H. Prouty⟩ **2 :** with one leg placed over and across the other ⟨sat *cross-legged* beating time in the air with his free foot⟩

crosslegs \ˈ=ˌ=\ *adv* [³*cross* + *legs*] **:** in a cross-legged position

¹**crosslet** *n* -s [ME *crosselette*, fr. OF *croisol* lamp (fr. — assumed — VL *croceolus*, dim. of a word of Gmc origin) + ME -*ette;* akin to ON *krōkr* hook — more at CROOK] *obs* **:** CRUCIBLE

²**cross·let** \ˈkrȯslət *also* -räs-\ *n* -s [ME *croslette*, fr. *cros* cross + -*lette* -let] **1 a** *heraldry* **:** a small cross orig. of no fixed shape but in the late medieval period usu. botonée as also in the 20th century in the work of some artists but since the 16th century usu. in the form of a Greek cross with a crossbar near the end of each arm — called also *cross-crosslet* **b :** a Greek cross with a crossbar near the end of each arm used in architecture or design or as an ornament **2 :** a small cross used as an ornament **3 :** a small cross sometimes found attached to a letter or figure (as the right end of the horizontal stroke of the figure 4 in the date) on any of various issues of coins

cross-level \ˈ=ˈ==\ *vt* [⁵*cross*] **:** to level (as a surveyor's transit) at right angles to the principal line of sight

cross liability *n* [³*cross*] **:** liability of each of the two or more vessels involved in a collision when both or all are to blame

cross license *n* [*cross license*] **:** a license that is granted by a patent holder to another (as a competitor) who reciprocates with a similar license and that is designed to control the marketing of the products involved or to further their development

cross-license \ˈ=ˈ==\ *vb* [⁵*cross* + *license* (v.)] *vt* **:** to give a license to another to use (a patent or invention) in return for a similar license ~ *vi* **:** to practice cross-licensing

cross-lift \ˈ=ˈ=\ *vt* [⁵*cross*] **:** to raise (a gun or other object) by crossing handspikes under from opposite sides

crosslight \ˈ=ˌ=\ *n* [³*cross* + *light*] **1 :** a light that crosses the path of another light and illuminates what the other leaves dark **2 :** something that indirectly casts light on or aids in comprehension ⟨new material . . . throws a *crosslight* on Chinese history —Owen & Eleanor Lattimore⟩ — **crosslighted** \ˈ=ˌ==\ *adj*

crosslighting \ˈ=ˌ==\ *n* **:** the lighting of an object from the side

¹**crossline** \ˈ=ˌ=\ *n* [³*cross* + *line*] **:** a line that crosses something: as **a :** a trotline set across a stream **b :** a subhead (as between banks) in a newspaper

²**crossline** \"\ *adj* [³*cross* + *line* (n.)] **:** of, relating to, or being the offspring resulting from the crossbreeding of two pure lines ⟨~ pigs⟩

¹**cross-link** \ˈ=ˌ=\ *n* [³*cross* + *link* (n.)] **:** a comparatively short connecting unit (as a chemical bond or a chemically bonded atom or group) between neighboring chains of atoms in a complex chemical molecule (as a polymer) — used esp. in relation to thermosetting plastics, vulcanized rubber, and proteins

²**cross-link** \ˈ=ˌ=\ *vt* **:** to join by cross-links ⟨*cross-linked* polymers⟩ ~ *vi* **:** to form cross-links

cross-linkage \ˈ=ˈ==\ *n* [³*cross*] **1 :** CROSS-LINK **2 :** the process of cross-linking

cross lode *n* [³*cross*] **:** a geological vein that intersects a principal lode — called also *counterlode*

cross-lots \ˈ=ˌ=\ *adv* [⁴*cross*] **:** by a short cut (as across the fields or vacant lots instead of by the road or sidewalk) — often used with *cut* ⟨going home they cut *cross-lots*⟩

cross-lot strut *n* **:** a bracing timber or steel strut extending across an excavation

cross·ly *adv* **:** in a cross manner

cross-magnetizing field *n* [⁵*cross*] **:** CROSS FLUX

cross matching *n* [³*cross*] **:** the testing of the compatibility of the bloods of transfusion donor and recipient by mixing the serum of each with the red cells of the other to determine the absence of agglutinative reactions

cross-mate \ˈ=ˈ=\ *vb* [⁵*cross*] **:** CROSSBREED

cross modulation *n* [³*cross*] **:** electrical intermodulation in which there are produced frequencies equal to the sums and differences of a desired and an undesired frequency or of their harmonics

cross moline *n, pl* **crosses moline :** a cross with the end of each arm forked and recurved and often used in heraldry as a cadency mark for the eighth son

cross multiplication *n* [³*cross*] **:** the multiplying of a numerator of one fraction by the denominator of another (as in clearing an equation of fractions)

cross·ness *n* -ES **:** the quality or state of being cross **:** PEEVISHNESS ⟨some breeds of bees are notorious for their ~, especially when there is thunder in the air —Robert Lynd⟩

crosso- — see CROSS-

cross of calvary *usu cap 2d C* **:** CALVARY CROSS

cross of con·stan·tine \-ˈkänztənˌtēn, -ən(t)stə-, -ˌtīn\ *usu cap 2d C* [after *Constantine* I (the Great) A.D. †337 Roman emperor] **:** CHI-RHO

cross of eight points : MALTESE CROSS 1b

cross of fourteen points : an emblem consisting of seven bars radiating from a center, broadening toward the end, and having each end indented in the form of a V

cross of lor·raine \-ləˈrān, -lōˈ-, -lȯˈ-\ *usu cap L* [fr. *Lorraine*, region in western Europe] **1 :** a cross with two crossbars having the upper one intersecting the upright above its middle and the lower one which is longer than the upper one intersecting the upright below its middle **2 :** a patriarchal cross sometimes depicted botonée

cross of Lorraine 1

cross of mal·ta \-ˈmȯltə\ *usu cap C & M* **:** MALTESE CROSS 1b

cross of st. andrew *usu cap S&A* **:** SAINT ANDREW'S CROSS

cross of st. anthony *usu cap S&A* **:** SAINT ANTHONY'S CROSS

cross of the resurrection *usu cap R* **:** a slender cross with a pennant at the junction of the bars

cros·so·po·dia \ˌkräsəˈpōdēə, -rȯs-\ *n pl* [NL, fr. *cross-* + *-podia*, pl. of *-podium*] **:** sinuous markings on certain sedimentary rocks that are supposed to be trails left by creeping marine animals

cros·sopt \ˈkräˌsäpt, -rȯ,-\ *adj or n* [by shortening] **:** CROSSOPTERYGIAN

cros·sop·te·ryg·ia \(ˌ)kräˌsäptəˈrijēə, -rȯ,-\ [NL] *syn of* CROSSOPTERYGII

¹**cros·sop·te·ryg·ian** \ˈ=ˌ=təˈrij(ē)ən\ *adj* [NL *Crossopterygii* + E -*an*] **:** of or relating to the Crossopterygii

²**crossopterygian** \"\ *n* -s **:** a fish of the superorder Crossopterygii

cros·sop·te·ryg·ii \(ˌ)=ˌ=təˈrijēˌī\ *n pl, cap* [NL, fr. *cross-* + *-pterygii*] **1 :** a superorder of Choanichthyes comprising the lobe-finned fishes that have existed since the Devonian but are now largely extinct, that have paired fins somewhat resembling limbs with a scaly axis fringed on one or both sides by dermal rays, and that are generalized fishes in some respects resembling elasmobranchs and in others foreshadowing terrestrial vertebrates which may have evolved from unknown early members of the group — compare LATIMERIA **2** *in some classifications* **:** a division of fishes coextensive with Choanichthyes or comprising Choanichthyes together with Cladistia — compare ACTINISTIA, RHIPIDISTIA

cross order *n* [³*cross*] **:** an order in a stock exchange to buy matched with an order to sell at the same price so that execution on the open market is unnecessary

cross or pile *n, archaic* **:** CROSS AND PILE

cros·so·so·ma \ˌkräsəˈsōmə, -rȯs-\ *n, cap* [NL, fr. *cross-* + *-soma*] **:** a small genus of shrubs (constituting the family Crossosomataceae) restricted to the southwestern U.S. and Mexico and having small simple leathery leaves that are often clustered on short branches and solitary terminal flowers — **cros·so·so·ma·ta·ceous** \ˌ==ˌsōməˈtāshəs\ *adj*

cros·so·the·ca \ˌ=ˈthēkə\ *n, cap* [NL, fr. *cross-* + *-theca*] **:** a form genus of fossil plants that are known from fructifications bearing pendulous sporangia in epaulet-shaped clusters and occurring on pecopteroid plant remains and that are usu. considered to be seed ferns

cross-out test \ˈ=ˌ=-\ *n* [fr. *cross out*, v.] **:** a mental test in which the task is to cancel items that are superfluous or incongruous

¹**crossover** \ˈ=ˌ==\ *n* [fr. *cross over*, v.] **1 a :** CROSSING 2a (1) **b :** a diagonal railroad track affording passage between two parallel lines **c :** the duct leading from one stage to the adjoining stage (as in a pump or turbine) **2 a :** an instance of the process of crossing-over **b :** a character or an individual having characters inherited by crossing-over **3 a** (1) **:** an exchange of dance places by partners esp. when face to face in open position (2) **:** a dance movement in which the man

transfers the woman from one arm across in front of him to the other **b** : a ball bowled by a right-hander that hits to the left of the kingpin

[2]**crossover** \"\ *adj* : having two pieces that cross esp. one over the other ⟨a ~ shawl⟩ ⟨a ~ collar⟩

crossover network *n* : a circuit that separates the range of frequencies in an audio signal into two or more parts so that each part may be delivered to a different speaker

crosspatch \ˈ-ˌ-\ *n* [[3]*cross* (ill-humored) + *patch* (fool)] : an ill-natured person ⟨an old ~⟩

cross peen *n* [[3]*cross*] : the wedge-shaped edge of a hammer-head running crosswise to the direction of the handle — see PEEN illustration

crosspiece \ˈ-ˌ-\ *n* [[3]*cross* + *piece*] : a horizontal member of a figure or structure (as the crossbar of the letter H, the arm of a cross, or the bar connecting two bits or knightheads on a boat)

cross-plow *or* **cross-plough** \ˈ-ˌ-\ *vb* [[5]*cross*] *vi* : to plow across an earlier plowing ~ *vt* : to plow (a field) so that the furrows cross those of an earlier plowing

cross-point \ˈ-ˌ-\ *vt* [[5]*cross* + *point*] : to point (a rope) by plaiting the nettles or seizing crosswise

cross-pollinate *or* **cross-pollinize** \ˈ-ˈ--ˌ-\ *vt* [[5]*cross*] : to subject to the operation of cross-pollination

cross-pollination \ˌ-ˌ--ˈ--\ *n* : the transfer of pollen from one flower to the stigma of another by various devices in the structure of the plant, by the agency of wind or insects, or artificially; *often* : the artificial transfer of pollen from one flower to another of a different variety in order to induce hybridization

cross product *n* [[3]*cross*] : the vector product of two vectors

cross-purpose \ˈ-ˈ--\ *n* [[3]*cross*] **1** *usu pl* **a** : a purpose usu. unintentionally or innocently contrary to another purpose of oneself or of someone else ⟨the terrible *cross-purposes* at work in modern society —Nicolás Monjo⟩ — often used with *at* ⟨the two men were always working at *cross-purposes*⟩ **b** : a subject different from and often ludicrously mistaken for the intended subject — used with *at* ⟨to talk at *cross-purposes*⟩ **2** *pl but sing in constr* : a game in which questions and answers are made so as to involve ludicrous combinations of ideas

cross quarters *n pl but sing in constr* : an architectural ornament consisting of a cruciform flower in tracery

[1]**cross-question** \ˈ-ˈ--\ *n* : a question that is put in cross-examination

[2]**cross-question** \"\ *vt* [[5]*cross* + *question* (v.)] : to subject to close questioning; *specif* : CROSS-EXAMINE

crossrail \ˈ-ˌ-\ *n* [[3]*cross* + *rail*] **1** : the horizontal member (as of a planer) supporting the toolheads and on which the toolheads traverse **2** : a horizontal structural member in a chair back or piece of case furniture

cross rate *n* [[3]*cross*] : the rate of exchange of two foreign currencies based on their quotation in a third market ⟨the sterling-dollar *cross rate* in francs in Paris⟩

cross ratio *n* [[3]*cross*] : an anharmonic ratio in mathematics

cross-reaction \ˌ-ˌ-ˈ--\ *n* [[3]*cross*] : the immunological phenomenon wherein one antigen reacts toward antibodies developed against another and which has been used to study relationships between viruses

cross-refer \ˌ-ˌ-ˈ-\ *vb* [[5]*cross*] *vt* : to refer (a reader) from one place to another (as in a book, list, or catalog) ~ *vi* : to make a cross-reference

[1]**cross-reference** \ˈ-ˈ-(-)-\ *n* [[3]*cross*] **1** : a notation or direction at one part of a work referring to pertinent information at another part of the work ⟨a file system complete with *cross-references* and bibliographies⟩ **2** : a grammatical agreement consisting of the use of a substantive and an equivalent pronoun or other substitute in the same construction (as *Marie* and *elle* in French *Marie où est-elle?* "where is Mary"? and as *John* and *he* in substandard English "John he went home")

[2]**cross-reference** \"\ *vt* **1** : to supply with cross-references ⟨*cross-reference* a catalog⟩ **2** : to refer from (as one subject) to a related subject ⟨a book given coherence by *cross-referenced* paragraphs⟩ ~ *vi* : CROSS-REFER

cross-reference code *n* : TWO-PART CODE

cross relation *n* [[3]*cross*] : FALSE RELATION

cross remainder *n* [[3]*cross*] : either of two or more remainders left by law to two or more persons so that upon failure of one his share goes to the other or others

cross-rhythm \ˈ-ˈ--\ *n* [[3]*cross*] : the simultaneous use of contrasting rhythmic patterns

cross-rib \ˈ-ˌ-\ *n* [[3]*cross*] : an arch supporting and strengthening a vault

crossroad \ˈ-ˌ- *also* ˈ-ˈ-\ *n, often attrib* [[3]*cross* + *road*] **1** : a road that crosses a main road or runs across country between main roads ⟨he came by way of a ~⟩ **2** *often pl but sing or pl in constr* : the place of intersection of two or more roads ⟨traffic stalled at a ~⟩ ⟨a remote ~*s* hamlet⟩ ⟨the . . . travelers reached a ~*s* marked by a signpost —F.V.W.Mason⟩ **3** *usu pl but sing or pl in constr* **a** : a small community located at a crossroads and often serving as the meeting place of the inhabitants of the surrounding countryside ⟨the small general store at any ~*s* —J.M.Mogey⟩ ⟨physicians then were to be found . . . even at some of the ~*s* —*Jour. Amer. Med. Assoc.*⟩ **b** : a central meeting place : FOCAL POINT ⟨like Broadway for showmen or Wall Street for financiers, it is a ~*s* for army men —Green Peyton⟩ ⟨England will be uncomfortable while confusion lasts in Europe for a world ~*s* community —Griffin Barry⟩ **4** *usu pl but sing or pl in constr* : a crucial or critical point or place esp. where a decision or choice must be made ⟨it is generally realized that defense policy is at the ~*s* —Lewis Hastings⟩

cross roll *n* : a figure-skating movement made by crossing the free foot onto the outside edge behind the outside edge of the skating foot — called also *Dutch roll*

crossrow *n* [[1]*cross* + *row*; fr. its formerly being printed with a cross preceding it] *obs* : ALPHABET

[1]**crossruff** \ˈ-ˌ-\ *n* [[3]*cross* + *ruff*] : a series of plays in some card games in which partners alternately trump different suits and lead to each other for that purpose

[2]**crossruff** \"\ *vt* : to effect a crossruff by leading (two specified suits) alternately ⟨~ spades and hearts⟩ ~ *vi* : to effect a crossruff

cross saltire *n* : SALTIRE

cross sea *n* [[3]*cross*] : a choppy sea in which the waves run in different directions (as from a change in the wind or to a certain extent from a change in tide)

cross section *n* [[3]*cross*] **1 a** : a cutting or section across : a section at right angles to esp. the longer axis of anything **b** : a piece of something cut off in a direction at right angles to an axis **c** : a view, diagram, or drawing representing such a cutting **2** : a measure of the probability of an encounter between particles such as will result in a specified effect (as ionization or capture) and commonly expressed as the effective area that one particle presents to the other as a possible target for such encounter — compare BARN **3** : a composite representation typifying the constituents of a thing in their relations ⟨a *cross section* of the people⟩ — **cross-sectional** \ˈ-ˈ-(-)-\ *adj*

cross-section \ˈ-ˈ--\ *vt* [*cross section*] **1** : to represent in cross section : make a cross section of ⟨*cross-section* a ship⟩ **2** : to cut or divide into cross sections ⟨a city *cross-sectioned* by canals⟩ ⟨*cross-section* a heart to show its chambers⟩ **3** : to take at regular intervals levelings across (as a railroad or highway embankment) for the purpose of plotting transverse contours in the estimation of earthwork

cross-section paper *n* : paper ruled vertically and horizontally in squares (as for drawings or plans)

cross signal *n* [[3]*cross*] : a signal blast usu. forbidden because of the danger of collision that is made by one ship approaching another in the opposite direction and indicates a desire to pass on the side opposite to that orig. signaled by the other ship

cross skip *n* [[3]*cross*] : a skip with the free foot crossed in front

cross slide *n* [[3]*cross*] : a member of a machine (as of a lathe) on which the tool carriage moves at right angles to its principal direction of travel

cross-spale *also* **cross-spall** \ˈ-ˌ-\ *n* [[3]*cross*] : a temporary wooden brace used in shipbuilding secured horizontally across a frame to hold it in position until the deck beams are in place

cross spider *n* : the common European garden spider (*Araneida diadema*) that has a cross-shaped mark on its abdomen

cross springer *n* [[3]*cross*] : DIAGONAL RIB

cross-staff \ˈ-ˌ-\ *n* **1 a** : a processional staff usu. with a cross or crucifix borne before an archbishop in his own province **b** : CROSIER **2** : an instrument once used at sea for taking the altitudes of celestial bodies, esp. of the sun **3** : a surveying instrument for laying off offsets perpendicular to the main course and consisting of two pairs of sights at right angles to each other on a staff sharp at the end

cross-sterile \ˈ-ˈ(ˌ)-\ *adj* : sterile in a particular cross ⟨plants of widely different geographic origin are often *cross-sterile* even though closely related⟩ — **cross-sterility** \ˌ-ˌ-ˈ---\ *n*

[1]**cross-stitch** \ˈ-ˌ-\ *n* [[3]*cross*] **1** : any needlework stitch that forms an X **2** : work having cross-stitch

[2]**cross-stitch** \"\ *vt* : to sew cross-stitch on ~ *vi* : to work with cross-stitch

cross-stitch

cross-stone \ˈ-ˌ-\ *n* **1** : CHIASTOLITE **2** : STAUROLITE

cross street *n* [[2]*cross*] : a street intersecting a main thoroughfare esp. at right angles and continuous on both sides of it — compare SIDE STREET

cross string *n* [[3]*cross*] : one of the horizontal strings running across the head of a racket

cross suit *n* [[3]*cross*] : a suit of different color from the trump suit

cross tag *n* [[2]*cross*] : a game of tag in which the player who is it must chase any player who passes between him and the one he is pursuing

cross talk *n* [[3]*cross*] **1 a** : voice sounds heard in a telephone receiver which are induced in the receiver circuit by a neighboring telephone circuit **b** : interference in radiotelephony caused by received waves of frequency other than that to which the receiving set is tuned **c** : the transfer of a recorded signal from one layer of a magnetic tape to another while the tape is wound on a reel **2 a** : CONVERSATION ⟨the one-color groups form, but *cross talk* between them is not uncommon —Walter Goodman⟩ **b** *Brit* : REPARTEE ⟨snatches of *cross talk*, lifted wholesale from a current . . . show —Nicholas Monsarrat⟩

cross tau *n* : TAU CROSS — used esp. in blazoning heraldic arms

cross·tie \ˈ-ˌtī\ *n* [[3]*cross* + *tie*] : a tie placed across something for support; *specif* : a railroad tie — **cross·tied** \-ˌtīd\ *adj*

cross timber *n* [[3]*cross*] : a strip of woodland chiefly of oaks stretching across grassland esp. in Texas

cross-tolerance \ˈ-ˈ-(-)-\ *n* [[3]*cross*] : a tolerance or resistance to the action of a drug brought about by the development of a tolerance to another drug of similar pharmacologic action that has been in continued use

cross tongue *n* [[3]*cross*] : a cross-grained tongue of wood used to give additional strength to a tenoned frame

[1]**crosstown** \ˈ-ˈ-\ *adv* [[4]*cross* + *town*] : in a direction extending or running across town ⟨taxis cruising ~⟩

[2]**crosstown** \ˈ-ˌ-\ *adj* **1** : situated at opposite points of a town ⟨~ neighbors⟩ **2** : extending across a town ⟨a ~ street⟩ **3** : running across a town esp. traverse to main thoroughfares ⟨a ~ bus⟩

crosstree \ˈ-(ˌ)-\ *n* [[3]*cross* + *tree*] : two horizontal crosspieces of timber or metal supported by trestletrees at a masthead that spread the upper shrouds in order to support the mast — usu. used in pl.; see SHIP illustration

cross turret *n* [[3]*cross*] : a lathe turret whose motion is horizontal and at right angles to the ways of the lathe

cross vault *or* **cross vaulting** *n* [[3]*cross*] : a vault formed by the intersection of two or more simple vaults — see VAULT illustration

crossvein \ˈ-ˌ-\ *n* [[3]*cross* + *vein*] **1** : a vein (as in a mine) that crosses or intersects an older, larger, or more productive vein **2** : any vein in an insect's wing extending transversely to the longitudinal veins

cross vine *n* **1** : a woody vine (*Bignonia capreolata*) of the southern U. S. with stems that often show a conspicuous cross in a transverse section **2** : TRUMPET CREEPER **3** : PEPPER VINE **2**

cross-voting \ˈ-ˈ--\ *n* [[3]*cross*] **1** : voting in which individuals of one party vote with another **2** : a list system permitting a voter to select names from more than one party list — compare PANACHAGE

crosswalk \ˈ-ˌ-\ *n* [[3]*cross* + *walk*] : a specially paved or marked path for pedestrians crossing a street or road

crossway \ˈ-ˌ-\ *n* [ME *cros waye*, fr. *cros* cross + *waye* way] : CROSSROAD ⟨the aerial ~ of the southern Caribbean area —*Americana Annual*⟩ — often used in pl. ⟨at that point came definite ~*s*, and a call for final choice —G.G.Coulton⟩

cross·ways \ˈ-ˌ-\ *adv* [[1]*cross* + *-ways*] : CROSSWISE, DIAGONALLY ⟨two boards nailed over a door ~⟩ ⟨parallel and not ~⟩

crossweed \ˈ-ˌ-\ *n* [so called fr. the cruciate flowers] : either of two plants of the genus *Diplotaxis* (*D. tenuifolia* or *D. muralis*) that are related to and resemble mustards

crosswind \ˈ-ˌ-\ *n* [[3]*cross* + *wind*] : a wind blowing in any direction not parallel to a course (as of an airplane or projectile) ⟨~ landing⟩ ⟨~ takeoff⟩

crosswind force *n* : the component perpendicular to the lift and to the drag of the total air force on an airplane or any part thereof

cross wire *n* : CROSS HAIR

[1]**crosswise** \ˈ-ˌ-\ *adv* [ME *croswise*, fr. *cros* cross + *-wise*] **1** *archaic* : in the form or figure of a cross ⟨a chapel built ~⟩ **2** : so as to cross something : ACROSS ⟨placed ~⟩ **3** : in a way contrary to what is right or purposed ⟨things are going ~⟩

[2]**crosswise** \"\ *adj* **1** : TRAVERSE, CROSSING ⟨a ~ street⟩ **2** : DIAGONAL ⟨a ~ brace⟩

crossword \ˈ-ˌ-\ *or* **crossword puzzle** *n* [[3]*cross* + *word*] : a puzzle in which words are filled into a pattern of numbered squares in answer to correspondingly numbered clues and in such a way that they read across and down and so that usu. most letters appear as part of two words

cross·word·er \ˈ-ˌwərdər\ *n* : one who solves crossword puzzles

crosswort \ˈ-ˌ-\ *n* : any of several plants having leaves in whorls of four or opposite and 2-ranked: as **a** : BONESET **1** **b** : LOOSESTRIFE **c** : a weedy yellow-flowered European bedstraw (*Galium cruciatum*) that is occas. cultivated

crost *past of* CROSS

crostarie *n* -S [ScGael *crois-tàra*, prob. fr. *crois* cross + *tàir* contempt, reproach; akin to MIr *cross* and to MIr *tār* contempt — more at CROSS] : FIERY CROSS **1**

[1]**cro·tal** \ˈkrōtˌtal, -ōd-ᵊl\ *n* -S [L *crotalum* rattle, castanet, fr. Gk *krotalon*, fr. *krotein* to clap; akin to OE *hrindan* to thrust, ON *hrinda* to push] **1** : CROTALUM **2** : a small spherical metal rattle (as on a harness)

[2]**crotal** *var of* CROTTLE

[3]**crot·al** \ˈkrădᵊl\ *adj* [[2]*crotal*] **1** : reddish brown ⟨a suit of ~ tweed⟩ **2** : of or relating to crottle ⟨a ~ dye⟩

cro·ta·lar·ia \ˌkrōd-ᵊlˈa(a)rēə, -rād-\ *n* [NL, fr. L *crotalum* + NL *-aria*, fr. the rattling of the ripe seeds in the pod when shaken] **1** *cap* : a very large genus of mainly tropical herbs (family Leguminosae) with chiefly simple leaves and showy yellow flowers in racemes — see SUNN **2** -S : any plant of the genus *Crotalaria*; *specif* : any of several plants of this genus used for pasture and green-manure crops

cro·ta·lar·i·o·sis \ˌ---ˌrēˈōsəs\ *n, pl* **crotalario·ses** \-ˌsēz\ [NL, fr. *Crotalaria* (genus name of *Crotalaria dura*, which ingested causes the disease) + *-osis*] : CROTALISM

cro·tale \ˈkrōˌtal, -ōd-ᵊl\ *n* -S [F, fr. L *crotalum*] : CROTALUM

cro·tal·ic \(ˈ)krōˈtalik\ *adj* [NL *Crotalus* + E *-ic*] : of or relating to rattlesnakes

[1]**cro·ta·lid** \ˈkrōd-ᵊləd\ *adj* [NL *Crotalidae*] **1** : of or belonging to the family Crotalidae ⟨~ snakes⟩ **2** : typical of a pit viper ⟨~ venom⟩

[2]**crotalid** \"\ *n* -S : a crotalid snake

cro·tal·i·dae \krōˈtaləˌdē\ *n pl, cap* [NL, fr. *Crotalus*, type genus + *-idae*] : a family of venomous snakes sometimes regarded as a viperid subfamily (Crotalinae) comprising the pit vipers

cro·tal·i·form \(ˈ)-ˈ-ləˌfȯrm\ *adj* [NL *Crotalus* + E *-iform*] : resembling a rattlesnake

cro·ta·lin \ˈkrōd-ᵊlən, -răd-\ *n* -S [NL *Crotalus* + E *-in*] : rattlesnake venom

cro·ta·line \-ᵊlˌīn, -ᵊlən\ *adj* [NL *Crotalus* + E *-ine*] : CROTALID

cro·ta·lism \ˈkrōd-ᵊlˌizəm, -răd-\ *n* -S [NL *Crotalaria* (genus name of *Crotalaria sagittalis*) + E *-ism*] : the poisoning or poisoned condition of animals caused from eating rattlebox (*Crotalaria sagittalis*) or other crotalarias in the field or as hay — called also *crotalariosis*

cro·ta·lo \-ᵊl(ˌ)ō\ *n* -ES [It, fr. L *crotalum*] : CROTAL

cro·ta·loid \-ᵊlˌȯid\ *adj* [ISV *crotal-* (fr. NL *Crotalus*) + *-oid*] : resembling the Crotalidae, esp. the rattlesnakes

cro·ta·lum \-ᵊləm\ *n, pl* **crota·la** \-ᵊlə\ [L — more at CROTAL] : one of a pair of small cymbals or rods used like castanets by dancers in antiquity

cro·ta·lus \-ᵊləs\ *n, cap* [NL, alter. of L *crotalum* rattle, castanet] : the type genus of the Crotalidae — see RATTLESNAKE

cro·taph·i·on \krōˈtafēˌän\ *n* -S [NL, fr. Gk *krotaphion*, neut. of *krotaphios* of the temples, fr. *krotaphos* temple] *anthrop* : a point at the tip of the greater wing of the sphenoid — see CRANIOMETRY illustration

cro·ta·phy·tus \ˌkrōd-əˈfīd-əs, ˌkrăd-\ *n, cap* [NL, modif. of Gk *krotaphitēs* of the temples, fr. *krotaphos* temple + *-itēs* -ite; akin to Gk *krotein* to clap — more at CROTAL] : a genus of lizards (family Iguanidae) of the southern and western U.S. including the collared lizard

[1]**crotch** \ˈkräch\ *n* -ES [prob. alter. of [1]*crutch*] **1 a** : a pole having a fork on one end and used esp. as a prop **b** : a stanchion on a ship with two arms or a hollowed top (as for supporting a boom or spare yards) : CRUTCH **c** : ALLIGATOR 6b **2 a** : something in the form of an angle usu. less than a right angle formed by the parting (as from a trunk or body) of two legs, branches, or members ⟨the ~ of a human being⟩ ⟨the ~ of a tree⟩ ⟨the ~ of the letter Y⟩ **b** : something from, between, or at the intersection of an object in the form of a crotch: as (1) : wood taken from the section just below the fork of a tree and used chiefly for its swirl-figured grain in the manufacture of furniture ⟨~ veneer⟩ ⟨~ mahogany⟩ (2) : the section of a garment where the leg seams meet ⟨the ~ of a pair of pants⟩; *specif* : a detachable piece of cloth forming the crotch section of a garment (3) : a 4½-inch square at each corner of a billiard table **3 a** : a wrestling hold in or near an opponent's crotch **b** : the situation in billiards when both object balls lie within the same crotch and allow only three counts unless one of the balls is forced out

[2]**crotch** \"\ *vb* -ED/-ING/-ES *vt* **1** : to provide with a crotch ⟨a ~*ed* stick⟩ : give the form of a crotch to; *esp* : to notch (a log) on opposite sides to provide a grip for the dogs in hauling **2** : MARRY, SPLICE ⟨~ two rope ends that have been opened in the form of a crotch⟩ **3** : to play (an object ball) into a crotch in billiards ~ *vi* **1** : to play on balls lying in the crotch in billiards **2** : to take a position or lie within a crotch — used of the object balls in billiards

crotch-buck \ˈ-ˌ-\ *also* **crotch-horn buck** \ˈ-ˌ-\ *n* : a buck deer with at least one antler forked

crotch chain *n* : a tackle for loading a log sideways on a sled or skidway

[1]**crotch·et** \ˈkrächət, *usu* -əd-+V\ *n* -S [ME *crochet* hook, crocket, quarter note, fr. MF — more at CROCHET] **1** : CROCKET **1** **2** *obs* **a** : a small hook or hooked instrument **b** : BROOCH **c** *zool* (1) : a process or organ shaped like a hook or fork; *specif* : a simple curved seta that is notched at the distal end and that is found in annelids (2) : CROCHET 2a **3 a** : an out-of-the-ordinary attitude or habit : an opinion usu. of little ultimate importance and often serving to mark off a person from others : WHIM, PECULIARITY ⟨his political ~*s*⟩ ⟨~*s*, though plentiful, had not yet snatched away the reins of his judgment —Marvin Lowenthal⟩ **b** : a strange or peculiar trick, dodge, or device ⟨bookkeeping full of unorthodox ~*s*⟩ ⟨fainting was just one of her ~*s*⟩ ⟨a prose style burdened with Victorian ~*s*⟩ **4** *chiefly Brit* : QUARTER NOTE **5** *now Brit* : BRACKET 4a

[2]**crotchet** \"\ *vb* **crotcheted** *also* **crotchetted; crotcheted** *also* **crotchetted; crotcheting** *also* **crochetting; crochets** : to provide or adorn with crockets

[3]**crotchet** \"\ *n* -S [[1]*crotch* + *-et*] *archaic* : CROTCH

crotch·e·teer \ˌkrachəˈti(ə)r\ *n* -S [[1]*crotchet* (whim) + *-eer*] : one who has a crotchet or who thrusts his crotchets on others

crotch·ety \ˈkrächəd-ē, -ətē, -i\ *adj* [[1]*crotchet* + *-y*] **1** : given to crotchets : subject to whims, crankiness, or ill temper ⟨a ~ old man⟩ **2** : full of or arising from crotchets ⟨a ~ style⟩

crotch tongue *n* : a V-shaped part joining the front and rear sleds of a logging sled

crotchy \ˈkrächē, -chi\ *adj* : full of crotches ⟨a ~ tree⟩

crotesco *obs var of* GROTESQUE

-crot·ic \ˈkrädik, -ēk\ *adj comb form* [NL *-crotus* (fr. Gk *-krotos*, fr. *krotos* beat, clapping) + E *-ic*; akin to Gk *krotein* to clap — more at CROTAL] : having (such) a heartbeat or pulse ⟨poly*crotic*⟩

cro·tin \ˈkrōtᵊn\ *n* -S [NL *Croton* (genus name of *Croton tiglium*) + E *-in*] : a mixture of poisonous proteins found in the seeds of a small Asiatic tree (*Croton tiglium*) related to the spurges

-cro·tism \krəˌtizəm, krō,-\ *n comb form* -S [*-crotic* + *-ism*] : condition of having (such) a heartbeat ⟨di*crotism*⟩

cro·ton \ˈkrōtᵊn\ *n* [NL, fr. Gk *krotōn* tick, castor-oil plant] **1** *cap* : a genus of herbs and shrubs of the spurge family with stellate-pubescent foliage and small dioecious flowers — see CASCARILLA, CROTON OIL **2** -S **a** : a plant of the genus *Croton* **b** : a plant of the related genus *Codiaeum* (esp. *C. variegatum*)

cro·ton·aldehyde \ˌkrōtᵊn+\ *n* [ISV *crotonic* + *aldehyde*] : a pungent liquid aldehyde $CH_3CH{=}CHCHO$ obtained by dehydration of aldol and used chiefly as an intermediate in organic synthesis and as a warning agent in fuel gases; β-methyl-acrolein

cro·ton·ate \ˈkrōtᵊnˌāt, -ᵊnət\ *n* -S [ISV *crotonic* + *-ate*] : a salt or ester of crotonic acid

cro·ton bug \ˈkrōtᵊn-\ *n, usu cap C* [fr. *Croton* river, Westchester co., N.Y., used as a water supply by New York City] : a small active winged cockroach (*Blattella germanica*) prob. of African origin but common aboard ships and in urban buildings wherever food and moisture are available — called also *German cockroach, water bug*

cro·ton·ic acid \(ˈ)krōˈtänik-\ *n* [F *crotonique*, fr. NL *Croton* + F *-ique* -ic] : an unsaturated aliphatic acid $CH_3CH{=}CHCOOH$ existing in cis and trans forms; β-methyl-acrylic acid; *esp* : the colorless crystalline trans form obtained in the carbonization of wood, made by oxidation of crotonaldehyde, and used chiefly in making synthetic resins and coatings

crotonic aldehyde *n* : CROTONALDEHYDE

croton oil *n* : a viscid acrid yellow to brown fatty oil obtained from the seeds of a small Asiatic tree (*Croton tiglium*) that acts as a drastic cathartic, vesicant, and pustulant

cro·ton·o·yl \krōˈtänəˌwil, -ˌwēl\ *n* -S [*crotonic* + *-o-* + *-yl*] : the univalent radical $CH_3CH{=}CHCO{-}$ of crotonic acid

cro·to·nyl \ˈkrōtᵊnˌil, -ᵊl\ *n* -S [ISV *crotonic* + *-yl*] **1** : CROTONOYL **2** : CROTYL

cro·toph·a·ga \krōˈtäfəgə\ *n, cap* [NL, fr. Gk *krotōn* tick + NL *-phaga*] : a genus of birds consisting of the anis

cro·toph·a·gine \-ˌjīn, -jən\ *adj* [NL *Crotophaga* + E *-ine*] : of or relating to birds of the genus *Crotophaga*

cro·tox·in \krōˈtäksən\ *n* [blend of NL *Crotalus* (genus name of *Crotalus terrificus*) and E *toxin*] : a crystalline neurotoxin obtained from the venom of the cascabel

crot·tels \ˈkräd-ᵊlz\ *n pl* [pl. of *crottel*, fr. MF *crote* (of Gmc origin; akin to MHG dial. *krotz* spot, obs. D *krotte* spot on clothes) + E *-el* (var. of *-le*)] : excrement esp. of hares

crot·tle *also* **crot·tal** *or* **crot·al** \ˈkräd-ᵊl\ *n* -S [ScGael *crotal*; akin to IrGael *crotal* kernel, rind, crottle] *Scot* : any of several lichens from which dyes are made; *esp* : a member of the genus *Parmelia* that yields reddish brown or purple dye — often used in pl.

cro·tyl \ˈkrōd-ᵊl, -ōˌtil\ *n* -S [ISV *crotonic* + *-yl*] : the butenyl radical $CH_3CH{=}CHCH_2{-}$ — called also *2-butenyl*

[1]**crouch** \ˈkrau̇ch\ *vb* -ED/-ING/-ES [ME *crouchen*, perh. fr. MF *crochir* to become hook-shaped, fr. *croche* hook — more at CROCHET] *vi* **1 a** *obs* : to bend low as a sign of reverence or deference ⟨~ to the crucifix⟩ **b** : to stoop with the limbs close to the body ⟨beside the kitchen fires, old women ~*ed* as they

turned the spit —Van Wyck Brooks⟩ **c :** to lie close to the ground with the legs bent (as of a wildcat) **d :** to lower the body stance esp. by flexing the legs ⟨a tackle ~*ing* at the line of scrimmage⟩ ⟨the sprinter ~*ed* and waited for the gun⟩ **2 :** to bend or bow servilely **:** stoop meanly **:** FAWN, CRINGE ⟨made black Jove to kneel and ~ to me —Christopher Marlowe⟩ ~ *vt* **:** to bow esp. in humility or fear **:** BEND ⟨~ one's head⟩ ⟨~ the knee⟩

²crouch \"\ *n* -ES **1 :** the act or action of crouching **2 :** the position of crouching ⟨a boxer who fights mostly in a ~⟩

crouch·ant \ˈkrau̇chənt\ *adj* [¹*crouch* + *-ant* (as in *couchant*)] **:** CROUCHING

crouchback *n* [ME *crouchbak*, fr. *crouchen* to crouch + *bak* back] *obs* **:** HUNCHBACK

crouch·er \ˈkrau̇chə(r)\ *n* -S **:** one that crouches esp. in a servile or flattering manner

crouch ware \ˈkrau̇ch-\ *n* [origin unknown] **:** an early Staffordshire pottery made of clay and sand and glazed with salt

¹croup \ˈkrüp\ *n* -S [ME *croupe*, fr. OF *crope, croupe*, of Gmc origin; akin to OHG *kropf* craw — more at CROP] **1 a :** the part of the back above the hind limbs of a quadruped (as a horse) **:** RUMP, CRUPPER — see HORSE illustration **b :** the place behind the saddle **2** *obs* **:** BUTTOCKS **3 :** the part of a side horse to the right of the pommels

²croup \"\ *vi* -ED/-ING/-S [prob. of imit. origin] **1** *now dial Brit* **a :** to cry hoarsely ⟨the raven ~*s*⟩ **b :** to speak hoarsely **2 :** to cough with the hoarse ringing cough of croup

³croup \"\ *n* -S **1 :** a spasmodic laryngitis in infants and children characterized by episodes of difficult breathing and hoarse metallic cough that occur esp. at night and may be relieved by steam inhalations **2** *in domestic animals* **:** any of several diseases or inflammatory conditions in which pseudomembranous deposits are formed in hollow organs

crou·pade \krüˈpād, ˈ⸗ˌ⸗\ *n* -S [F (trans. of It *groppata*), fr. *croupe* hindquarters (fr. OF *crope, crupe*) + *-ade* — more at CROUP] **:** a curvet with the hind legs of the horse well under his belly

crou·pi·er \ˈkrüpēə(r), -ē,ā\ *n* -S [F, lit., one who rides behind another on a horse, fr. *croupe* hindquarters + *-ier* -er] **1 :** an assistant and adviser to a person engaged in a gambling game — now used only in connection with certain games (as baccarat and chemin de fer) **2 a :** an employee of a gambling casino who watches, collects, and pays bets and assists the tourneur or dealer in charge of the table **b :** a representative of a gambling house or casino who officiates at a gaming table **3 :** one who at a public dinner party sits at the lower end of the table as assistant chairman

croup kettle *n* [³*croup*] **:** a kettle for the production of steam or medicated vapor for treating croup or bronchitis

crou·pon \ˈkrüpən\ *n* -S [F, aug. of *croupe* hindquarters] **:** untanned cattlehide from which belly and shoulder areas have been trimmed

croup·ous \ˈkrüpəs\ *adj* [³*croup* + *-ous*] **1 :** relating to or resembling croup ⟨pneumonia which . . . was lobar in distribution and ~ in character —*Science*⟩ **2 :** attended with the formation of a deposit or membrane ⟨~ enteritis⟩

croupous pneumonia *n* **1 :** LOBAR PNEUMONIA **2 :** shipping fever of cattle

croup tent *n* [³*croup*] **:** a covering or shelter over the head and shoulders within which a stream of medicated vapor is maintained for the relief of some respiratory conditions

croupy \ˈkrüpē, -pi\ *adj* -ER/-EST [³*croup* + *-y*] **:** of, arising from, like, or indicating croup ⟨a ~ cough⟩

¹crouse \ˈkrüs\ *adj* [ME, prob. fr. MLG *krūse* confused, mixed-up, curly; akin to MHG *krūs* curly, OHG *krol* — more at CURL] **1** *chiefly Scot & Irish* **a :** BOLD, CONFIDENT **b :** COCKY **2** *chiefly Scot & Irish* **:** BRISK, LIVELY, CHEERFUL — **crouse·ly** *adv*

²crouse \"\ *adv, chiefly Scot & Irish* **:** BOLDLY, BRISKLY — often used with *craw* or *crack* ⟨he wouldn't have crawed so ~ if he'd known⟩

crou·stade \krüˈstäd, ˈ⸗ˌ⸗\ *n* -S [F, fr. Prov *croustado* — more at CUSTARD] **:** a crisp shell (as of toasted or fried bread) in which to serve food

croûte \ˈkrüt\ *n* -S [F, lit., crust, fr. OF *crouste* — more at CRUST] **:** a slice of toasted or fried bread cut in fancy shape and used as a foundation in serving food

crouth *var of* CRWTH

crou·ton \ˈkrü,tän, ⸗ˈ⸗\ *n* -S [F *croûton*, dim. of *croûte*] **:** a small cube of bread toasted or fried crisp and used in soups and garnishing

¹crow \ˈkrō\ *n* -S [ME *crowe*, fr. OE *crāwe*; akin to OHG *krāwa, krāja* crow, OS *krāja*, MD *crā, crāie*, OE *crāwan*, v.] **1 :** any of various large usu. entirely glossy black birds of *Corvus* and related genera noted for their alertness and intelligence: as **a :** CARRION CROW **b** *Brit* **:** the rook represented in different regions by distinct subspecies — see EASTERN CROW **c :** the common crow (*C. brachyrhynchos*) of No. America **2 :** any bird of the family Corvidae — used chiefly in combination; see FISH CROW, HOODED CROW, PIPING CROW **3 a :** a bar of iron with a beak, crook, or claw; *esp* **:** CROWBAR **b :** a yoke applied to a street water main to hold the drill for tapping the main **4** *archaic* **:** a grapnel used esp. in siege operations **5** *obs* **:** a door knocker **6 :** a slightly violet black seen on a glossy surface **7 :** NEGRO — usu. taken to be offensive; compare JIM CROW **8** *usu cap* **a** (1) **:** a Siouan people inhabiting the region between the Platte and Yellowstone rivers — called also *Absaroka* (2) **:** a member of such people **b :** the language of the Crow people **9** *slang* **:** the eagle worn on the sleeves of petty officers of the U.S. naval forces — **as the crow flies :** in a straight line **:** by a direct course ⟨by rail today is 80½ miles, whereas it is only 49 miles *as the crow flies* —O.S. Nock⟩ — **crow to pull** *or* **crow to pluck** *or* **crow to pick 1 :** a fault to find ⟨no *crow to pull* with him⟩ **2 :** a disagreeable or embarrassing matter to settle ⟨brothers with a *crow to pluck*⟩

²crow \"\ *vb* **crowed** \ˈkrōd\ *also in vi sense 1 chiefly Brit* **crew** \ˈkrü\ **crowed; crowing; crows** [ME *crowen*, fr. OE *crāwan*; akin to OHG *krāen* to crow, MLG *krēien*, OSlav *grajati* to croak, OE *cran* crane — more at CRANE] *vi* **1 :** to make the loud shrill sound characteristic of a cock ⟨the second time the cock *crew* —Mk 14:72(AV)⟩ ⟨a cockerel *crew* from a blossoming apple bough —W.B.Yeats⟩ **2** *archaic* **:** to utter a sound expressive of joy or pleasure (as of a baby or child) **3 a :** to shout esp. in exultation, exuberance, or defiance ⟨550 people who had crowded into the old New Orleans dance hall . . . stamped and ~*ed* —*Time*⟩ **b :** EXULT ⟨~*ing* over a recent success⟩ **c :** BRAG ⟨~ over one's ancestors⟩ ⟨he had nothing to ~ about⟩ ~ *vt* **:** to greet or wake by crowing — often used with *up* ⟨roosters ~*ing* the sleeping barnyard up⟩ **syn** see BOAST

³crow \"\ *n* -S **1 :** the cry of the cock ⟨an old cock . . . with . . . a faltering ~ —W.M.Thackeray⟩ **2 :** a triumphant cry **:** an exultant outburst ⟨she gave a little ~ of happiness and gaiety —Charles Reade⟩

⁴crow \"\ *n* -S [perh. by folk etymology fr. D *kroos*, fr. MD *croos* intestine; akin to MHG *kræse*, OHG *chrōse*, a kind of fritter, MHG *krūs* curly — more at CROUSE] **:** the mesentery of an animal esp. when used as food

crowbait \ˈ⸗ˌ⸗\ *n* **:** a worn-out emaciated horse **:** a horse of poor quality and conformation

crowbar \ˈ⸗ˌ⸗\ *n* [prob. so called fr. the forked end it sometimes has, likened to a crow's foot] **:** a usu. bent iron or steel bar that is usu. wedge-shaped at the working end and is used esp. as a pry or lever — compare PINCH BAR

crowbells *n pl* **1** *obs* **:** DAFFODIL **2** *obs* **:** BLUEBELL

crowberry \ˈ⸗- — *see* BERRY\ *n* **1 :** any of several heaths or related plants: **a :** an undershrub (*Empetrum nigrum*) of arctic and alpine regions with an insipid black berry **b :** BEARBERRY 1 **c :** AMERICAN CRANBERRY **d :** WHORTLEBERRY 1 **2 a :** the fruit of a crowberry **b :** RED CROWBERRY 2

crowberry family *n* **:** EMPETRACEAE

crowbill \ˈ⸗ˌ⸗\ *n* [¹*crow* + *bill*] **:** a conical arrowhead made of horn — compare ¹PILE 4a

crow corn *n* **:** COLICROOT

¹crowd \ˈkrau̇d\ *vb* -ED/-ING/-S [ME *crouden*, fr. OE *crūdan* to press, hasten, drive; akin to MLG *krūden* to annoy, MHG *kroten* to press, crowd, annoy, OE *crod* multitude, Norw *kryda* to swarm, MIr *gruth* curds] *vi* **1 a :** to press on **:** HURRY ⟨~ on one's way⟩ ⟨the ships ~*ed* northward⟩ **b :** to force a way **:** appear in an oppressive or importunate manner ⟨darkness of evening ~*ed* in⟩ ⟨his heart ~*ed* up into his breast —Pearl S. Buck⟩ **c :** to press close ⟨the players ~*ed* around the coach⟩ ⟨new cheap labor ~*ing* on the heels of earlier comers —*Amer. Guide Series: Minn.*⟩ **2 :** to collect in numbers **:** THRONG ⟨memories ~ in from every stage of the journey —Barbara Ward⟩ ⟨policemen warning people not to ~⟩ ~ *vt* **1 :** ENCUMBER, BURDEN, CRUSH, OPPRESS ⟨~ a person's patience with solicitations⟩ ⟨a person ~*ed* to death with titles and honors⟩ **2 a :** to fill by pressing or thronging together **:** fill or occupy to excess or obstruction ⟨~ a bus with children⟩ ⟨10,000 spectators ~*ing* a stadium⟩ ⟨his mind was ~*ed* with the detail he observed —Nevil Shute⟩ **b :** to press, force, or thrust esp. into a small space or little time **:** COMPRESS, COMPACT, CRAM ⟨~ children into a bus⟩ ⟨the same wish to ~ meaning is responsible for a good many slurred references —John Berryman⟩ ⟨a multitude of things were ~*ed* together⟩ **3** *obs* **:** to confine forcibly **:** IMPRISON — usu. used with *in* **4 :** PUSH, MOVE, FORCE — usu. used with *off* or *out* ⟨~ a person off the sidewalk⟩ ⟨we have allowed a false creed to ~ out the real American tradition —Bradford Smith⟩ **5 a :** to urge on **:** HURRY ⟨we ~*ed* the motor to ten knots —Clifford Gessler⟩ ⟨I ~*ed* him until streams of sweat ran —J.H.Stuart⟩ **b** (1) **:** to put on (sail) in excess of the usual amount so as to attain maximum speed (2) **:** INCREASE ⟨the engineer ~*s* steam in the cylinders —Frederick Way⟩ — often used with *on* ⟨~ on speed⟩ **6 :** to put pressure upon (as by solicitation) **:** dun unreasonably or harshly ⟨I'd never ~*ed* him with questions —J.B.Benefield⟩ **7 :** THRONG, JOSTLE ⟨changes . . . ~ each other in a whirl of confusing images —N.M.Butler⟩ **8 a :** to press close to ⟨one car ~*ing* the car in front⟩ ⟨~*ing* thirty and still not married⟩ **b :** to be a close second to **:** nearly overtake **c :** to stand close to (the plate) when batting in baseball **9 :** to count on or trust to (luck) unreasonably ⟨~*ing* his luck for all it was worth —F.B. Gibson⟩ **syn** see PACK, PRESS

²crowd \"\ *n* -S **1 a :** a large number of persons esp. when collected into a somewhat compact body without order **:** THRONG ⟨a ~ of little children⟩ **b :** an unorganized aggregate of people temporarily united in response to a common stimulus or situation in which the individuality of the participants is submerged — compare MOB **2 :** the great body of the people **:** POPULACE ⟨no man more hated and feared by the ~, the generality of mankind —Edith Sitwell⟩ ⟨all our ideas are ~ ideas —T.H.Ferril⟩ **3 :** a large number of things collected or closely pressed together **:** MULTITUDE ⟨~*s* of fine silver dust —G.H.Johnston⟩ ⟨an exciting ~ of incidents —H.C.Webster⟩ ⟨a ~ of wasps, hornets, flies, and gnats —Ellen Glasgow⟩ **4 :** a group of people with something (as a habit, interest, occupation) in common **:** an exclusive company **:** SET, CLIQUE ⟨the cocktail ~⟩ ⟨the Hollywood ~⟩ ⟨I don't like him or his ~⟩ ⟨in with the wrong ~⟩ **5 a :** the impressed forward movement of the dipper of a power shovel that forces it into the material to be moved **b :** the mechanism that does the forcing

syn THRONG, PRESS, CRUSH, MOB, ROUT, HORDE: CROWD indicates a massed group of persons, often closely pressed and often with subordination of individualities involved ⟨the *crowd* came pouring out with a vehemence that nearly took him off his legs —Charles Dickens⟩ ⟨we get the real sense of a *crowd* of human beings, animated, as a *crowd*, by an instinct and a genius different from that of any of its particular members —Laurence Binyon⟩ THRONG is closely synonymous with CROWD; occas. it may suggest surging motion or bustling confusion ⟨summer tourists come to join the shopping *throngs* on summer evenings —*Amer. Guide Series: N.H.*⟩ ⟨sailors hung from yards and bowsprits to shout the names of vessels to the bewildered, harried *throng* —Kenneth Roberts⟩ PRESS, not now used so much as formerly, may suggest compact concentration in which movement is difficult ⟨they could not come nigh unto him for the *press* —Mk 2:4 (AV)⟩ CRUSH more strongly stresses compact concentration and difficulty of passage through; it is rarely used without connotation of discomfort ⟨the *crush* was terrific for that time of day . . . for the street was blocked —Virginia Woolf⟩ ⟨a *crush* of dancing couples packed the floor —Hamilton Basso⟩ MOB, usu. derogatory, is likely to indicate a rough crowd composed of lower elements, often one disposed to disorder, riot, or other antisocial action and one abrogating any finer feeling ⟨Oliver was burned in effigy, and Hutchinson's town house was gutted by the *mob* —C.L.Becker⟩ ⟨the *mob*, loudly as they clamored for their own rights, cared nothing for the rights of others —J.A.Froude⟩ ROUT is sometimes a close synonym of MOB; it may suggest a concentration of hectic or disorderly activity in a circumscribed space ⟨the busy *rout* of the street could be seen. He loved the changing panorama of the street —Theodore Dreiser⟩ ⟨a kind of jollity and recklessness which was born in the fort, at the old *routs* and balls —Bruce Hutchison⟩ ⟨a flying *rout* of suns and galaxies, rushing away from the solar system and from one another —E.M.Forster⟩ HORDE may apply to a large surging mass or crowd of rough or savage individuals disposed to predatory or destructive action ⟨*hordes* of desperadoes and gunmen who found the river at this point a convenient crossing —*Amer. Guide Series: Texas*⟩ ⟨*hordes* of sturdy rogues and vagrants —G.E.Fussell⟩ ⟨a *horde* of heavily armed buffoons in big boots went stamping round my decks for hours, poking their great stupid faces into everything —*Times Lit. Supp.*⟩

³crowd \", ˈkrüd\ *n* -S [ME *crowde, crouth*, fr. (assumed) MW *crwth* (whence W *crwth* fiddle); akin to MIr *crott* harp, L *curvus* curved — more at CROWN] **1 :** CRWTH **2** *dial Eng* **:** FIDDLE

⁴crowd \"\ *vi* -ED/-ING/-S *dial Eng* **:** FIDDLE

crowded *adj* **1 :** filled with numerous things or people often overly compacted or concentrated ⟨a ~ valley⟩ ⟨a ~ program⟩ ⟨a brilliant, ~, highly colored book —Gerald Bullett⟩ ⟨a ~ theater⟩ **2 :** COMPRESSED, COMPACTED ⟨St.-Étienne, ~ within a series of narrow valleys —James Bird⟩ **:** resting or placed close together ⟨small ~ freckles⟩ **3 :** full of or rich in events or experience ⟨a ~ life⟩ ⟨a ~ career⟩ — **crowd·ed·ly** *adv* — **crowd·ed·ness** *n* -ES

¹crowd·er \ˈkrau̇də(r), -rüd-\ *n* -S [ME *crowdere*, fr. *crowde* fiddle + *-ere* -er] **1 :** one that plays a crowd **2** *dial Eng* **:** FIDDLER

²crowd·er \ˈkrau̇də(r)\ *n* -S [¹*crowd* + *-er*] **1 :** one that crowds ⟨that type of fighter, a ~ with both hands milling at all times —*Ring*⟩ **2** *Brit* **:** a worker who loads handmade bricks on barrows

crowder pea *n* [²*crowder*] **:** any cowpea in which the seeds are produced in long narrow pods and closely crowded during development

crowd grass *n* [¹*crowd*; fr. its tendency to crowd out other plants] **:** CHARLOCK

crowding engine *or* **crowding motor** *n* **:** the engine on a power shovel that forces the dipper into the material

crowds *pres 3d sing of* CROWD, *pl of* CROWD

crowdweed \ˈ⸗ˌ⸗\ *n* [¹*crowd* + *weed*; fr. its tendency to crowd out other plants] **1 :** CHARLOCK **2 :** FIELD CRESS

crow·dy *also* **crow·die** \ˈkrōdē, -üdē, -üdē\ *n, pl* **crowdies** [origin unknown] *chiefly Scot* **:** a thick gruel of oatmeal and water or milk **:** PORRIDGE

crowed *past of* CROW

crow fig *n* **:** NUX VOMICA 1

crowflower \ˈ⸗ˌ⸗\ *n* [¹*crow* + *flower*; fr. the shape of the leaf] **:** RAGGED ROBIN

crowfoot \ˈ⸗ˌ⸗\ *n, pl* **crowfeet** *see sense 1* **1** *pl usu* **crowfoots :** any of numerous plants having leaves pedately lobed; *specif* **:** a plant of the genus *Ranunculus* **2 :** any of several plants with flowers or other structures suggestive of a bird's foot (as the male orchis, the wild hyacinth, and certain club mosses) **3 :** CROW'S-FOOT a — usu. used in pl. ⟨eyes . . . edged with *crowfeet* wrinkles —*Time*⟩ **4** *on a boat* **a :** a number of small lines rove through a long block **b :** an iron stand fastened at one end to a mess table and at the other to a beam above and used to hang articles on **5 :** CALTROP 2a **6 :** a brace end consisting of branching parts: as **a :** a brace end in boilers having each of its branching parts fastened to the shell **b :** the crosspiece that holds a manhole or handhole plate in place **7 :** a mark used on drawings esp. to limit a dimension or indicate a note

crowfooted \ˈ⸗ˌ⸗⸗\ *adj* **:** having corbiesteps — used esp. of a gable

crowfoot family *n* **:** RANUNCULACEAE

crowfoot grass *n* **:** CRABGRASS 1

crowfoot violet *n* **:** BIRD'S-FOOT VIOLET

crow garlic *n* [ME *crawegarlek*, fr. *crawe, crowe* crow + *garlek* garlic] **:** a wild onion (*Allium vineale*) having no bulblets in the flower cluster and with narrow terete leaves that extend one-third way to halfway up the stiff stem — called also *field garlic, wild garlic*

crowhop \ˈ⸗ˌ⸗\ *n* **1 :** a short quick jump (as that of a startled crow) **2 :** a stiff-legged hop made by a horse often with the back arched

crow-hop \"\ *vi* [*crow hop*] **1 :** to hop or jump like a crow **2** *of a horse* **:** to buck without violence and with a series of short stiff-legged jumps

crowing *pres part of* CROW

crowing area *or* **crowing ground** *or* **crowing territory** *n* **:** the mating site selected and defended by a cock pheasant — compare TERRITORIALITY

crowkeeper \ˈ⸗ˌ⸗⸗\ *n, now dial Eng* **:** a person employed to scare off crows

¹crowl \ˈkrōl, -ül\ *n* -S [origin unknown] *Scot & Irish* **:** a dwarfed person

²crowl \"\ *vt* -ED/-ING/-S *Scot & Irish* **:** STUNT, DWARF

¹crown \ˈkrau̇n\ *n* -S [ME *coroune, croun, crowne*, fr. OF *corone, curune*, fr. L *corona* garland, wreath, crown, fr. Gk *korōnē* anything curved, tip of a bow, stem of a ship, kind of crown, fr. *korōnos* curved; akin to L *curvus* curved, Gk *skairein* to dance, MIr *cruind* round, Skt *krīḍati* he dances, plays, OE *hrīth* storm, *hrith* fever, OHG *hrito* fever, ON *hrīth* attack, storm, period of time; basic meaning: turning, bending] **1 :** a reward of victory or mark of honor ⟨the ~ of life everlasting⟩ ⟨a ~ of glory⟩; *esp* **:** the title representing the championship in a sport ⟨to win the heavyweight boxing ~⟩ ⟨contending for the intercollegiate football ~⟩ **2 :** a royal or imperial headdress or cap of sovereignty worn by monarchs and usu. made of precious metals and adorned with precious stones **:** DIADEM — see CORONET **3 :** the highest part of something: as **a** (1) **:** the topmost part of the skull or head (2) **:** HEAD 1 **b :** the summit of a mountain **c** (1) **:** the head of foliage in a tree or shrub (2) **:** CROWN CANOPY **d :** CORONA 1 **e :** the vertex or top part of an arch or arched surface (as a street or deck rounding toward the middle); *specif* **:** the difference in elevation between the center and edges of a rounded roadway **f** (1) **:** the part of a hat or other headgear covering the crown of the head (2) **:** the piece of harness that in a bridle passes over the head — called also *crownpiece* **g :** the branched portion of an antler **h** (1) **:** the part of a tooth external to the gum — see TOOTH illustration (2) **:** an artificial substitute for the natural crown of a tooth **i :** the tuft of leaves at the apex of a pineapple **j :** the portion of a brilliant above the girdle — compare PAVILION **k :** the dome of a furnace, gas retort, or brick kiln **l :** the crest of a bird **4 :** a wreath, band, or circular ornament for the head that is made of flowers, fabric, or metal and worn as a decorative clothing accessory or as a mark of prestige, preeminence, or accomplishment **5 :** something felt to resemble the form or shape of a wreath or crown: as **a :** CORONA 2a(1) **b :** a circlet of tapers **c :** the entire body of a crinoid **d :** the knurled cap on top of the stem for winding a watch **e** (1) **:** CROWN GLASS (2) **:** CROWN LENS **f** *also* **crown cap** *or* **crown cork :** a metal cap usu. lined (as with cork), used as a closure for a narrow-necked container (as a bottle), and locked in place by its fluted rim being crimped down and around the rounded lip of the container **6** *often cap* **a** (1) **:** imperial or regal power or dominion **:** SOVEREIGNTY (2) **:** the government under a constitutional monarchy **b :** one entitled to wear a crown; *esp* **:** the monarch in his official capacity as supreme ruler **7 :** something that imparts beauty, splendor, honor, or finish **:** high point **:** CULMINATION ⟨whatever the beginnings of religion, Jesus is the ~ and climax —J.C.Swaim⟩ ⟨your companionship was the ~ of his life —H.J.Laski⟩ **8 :** something bearing a representation of a crown: as **a** (1) **:** any of several old gold coins with a crown as part of the device (as an English crown of the rose) — compare CROWN GOLD (2) **:** an English coin worth 5 shillings issued since 1551 but now struck only on special occasions and orig. made of silver but since 1946 of cupronickel (3) **:** any dollar-size silver coin **b :** a size of paper orig. watermarked with a crown and now measuring usu. 15 x 20 or 15 x 19 inches **c :** a green or blue symbol resembling a crown that marks the fifth suit in some five-suit packs of playing cards **9 a :** a unit of value equivalent to the value of a crown **b** (1) **:** KORUNA (2) **:** KRONA (3) **:** KRONE (4) **:** KROON **10 :** the highest quality or state of something **11 :** a representation of a crown (as a heraldic bearing, watermark, hallmark) **12 a :** the region of a seed plant usu. at ground level at which stem and root merge **b :** the thick arching end of the shank of an anchor where the arms are joined to it — see ANCHOR illustration **c** *in carding* **:** the crossbar connecting the prongs of card teeth at back of the card clothing **13 :** the bit of a diamond drill **14 a :** COURONNE **b** (1) **:** a knot formed in the strands of a rope to prevent untwisting (2) **:** an interweaving of the strands of a rope to add a finish to a wall knot — see WALL AND CROWN **15 :** the colon esp. of a domestic animal

imperial state crown of England

²crown \"\ *vb* -ED/-ING/-S [ME *corounen, crounen*, fr. OF *coroner*, fr. L *coronare*, fr. *corona* crown] *vt* **1 a :** to place a crown or wreath upon the head of ⟨the May queen ~*ed* each child⟩; *specif* **:** to place a crown upon in order to invest with regal dignity and power — often used with a double object ⟨~ a person king⟩ **b :** to encircle or encompass ⟨perspiration ~*ed* his forehead⟩ — often used with *with* ⟨his head was ~*ed* with thorns⟩ **c :** to recognize officially as ⟨he was ~*ed* heavyweight boxing champion⟩ — often used with a double object ⟨the association ~*ed* him athlete of the year⟩ **2 :** to imbue or endow **:** ENRICH, ADORN — usu. used with *with* ⟨a man ~*ed* with wisdom⟩ ⟨she ~*ed* all about her with beauty⟩ **3 :** to surmount, top, or cap ⟨a sun helmet ~*ing* an impressively big head —Earle Birney⟩ ⟨patches of clay ~ the higher slopes —L.D.Stamp⟩; *esp* **:** to top (a checker) with a checker to make a king **4 a :** to bring to a happy, suitable, or successful conclusion **:** round off **:** finish off **:** CLIMAX ⟨Christmas dinner . . . was ~*ed* . . . by a sleek jet-black plum pudding —Silas Spitzer⟩ ⟨you can ~ your trip to Europe with a wonderful side trip —*Saturday Rev.*⟩ **b :** to form or provide the finishing element of **:** COMPLETE ⟨each stanza is ~*ed* with a couplet⟩ ⟨to ~ all, none of the trucks would start⟩ **5 :** to provide with something like a crown: as **a :** to fill so that the surface forms a crown ⟨he ~*ed* each tankard⟩ **b :** to put an artificial crown upon (a tooth) **c :** to provide (a road) with a crown **d :** to place the cap on (a bottle) **6 :** to inflict a blow or bruise on the crown of **:** hit on the head ⟨getting ~*ed* with a beer bottle by a South African trooper —Hal Lehrman⟩ **7 :** TOP ⟨~ a plant⟩ ~ *vi* **1** *of a checker man* **:** to become a king ⟨a single man ~*s* on reaching the king row —*New Complete Hoyle*⟩ **2** *in childbirth* **:** to appear at the vaginal opening — used of the first portion (as the crown of the head) of the infant to appear ⟨a low spinal anesthetic was given when the head ~*ed* —*Jour. Amer. Med. Assoc.*⟩ **3** *of fire* **:** to sweep to or through the crown canopy of a forest

³crown \ˈkrün, -rau̇n\ *vt* -ED/-ING/-S [back-formation fr. ²*crowner*] *now dial* **:** to hold a coroner's inquest on

crown agent *n, usu cap C&A* **1 :** an agent for the British crown; *specif* **:** a solicitor under the lord advocate in charge of criminal proceedings in Scotland **2 :** an agent in England acting in behalf of the business and financial interests of a British colony

crown·al \ˈkrau̇nᵊl\ *n* -S [alter. (influenced by ¹*crown*) of ¹*coronal*] *archaic* **:** CORONET, CROWN, WREATH

crown aloes *n pl* **:** a commercial variety of aloes

crown and anchor *n* **:** chuck-a-luck played with three dice having faces bearing a crown, an anchor, and the four aces and with a cloth or board marked with similar figures on which the players place their bets

crown antler *n* **:** the topmost branch or tine of an antler

crown·ation \krü'nāshən, -raù'-\ *n* -s [by alter. (influenced by ¹*crown*)] *now dial Eng* **:** CORONATION 1

crownbeard \'ˌ=ˌ=\ *n* [so called fr. the appearance of the flowers] **:** any plant of the genus *Verbesina*

crown bird *n* **:** CROWNED CRANE

crown block *n* **:** a timber or steel pulley support connecting at the top the derrick posts of an oil well

crown bud *n* **:** the first flower bud that is formed normally on an untopped chrysanthemum plant and that is accompanied by vegetative buds

crown canker *n* **:** canker disease of roses caused by an imperfect fungus (*Cylindrocladium scoparium*)

crown canopy *n* **:** the cover formed by the top branches of trees in a forest

crown cap *or* **crown cork** *n* **:** CROWN 5f

crown class *n* **:** any of several classes into which a forest of even age can be classified according to the height and relative density of and amount of light received by its crown canopy

crown colony *n, often cap both Cs* **:** a colony of the British Commonwealth over which the crown (as through an appointed governor) retains some control

crown daisy *n* **:** a shrubby annual composite herb (*Chrysanthemum coronarium*) of the Mediterranean region with dissected foliage and yellowish white flower heads

crown dancers *n pl* [so called fr. the yucca crowns they wear] **:** GAHE

crown debt *n* **:** a debt due under English law to the crown and upon which if on record the crown has the remedy of extent

crown density *n* **:** the relation of the area of the crown canopy of a forest to the land area determined esp. by the distance apart of the trees and the compactness of the crowns of the individual trees

crowned \'kraünd\ *adj* [ME *crouned,* fr. past part. of *crounen* to crown] **1 a :** invested with or as if with the royal crown ⟨a ~ sovereign⟩ ⟨Death the ~ phantom —Thomas De Quincey⟩ **b :** arising from, based on, or peculiar to the royal crown ⟨~ authority⟩ ⟨~ tyranny⟩ **2 :** provided with or as if with a crown ⟨a ~ seal⟩ ⟨a ~ decoration⟩ — often used in combination ⟨a high-*crowned* hat⟩ ⟨an orange-*crowned* bird⟩

crowned crane *n* **:** any crane of an African genus (*Balearica*) distinguished by a stiff bristly yellow crest on the back of the head — called also *crown bird*

crowned eagle *n* **:** a large forest-dwelling African eagle (*Stephanoaetus coronatus*) that has a yellowish-marked crest and the breast feathers yellow tipped with black and that feeds chiefly on monkeys and small antelopes

crowned pigeon *n* **:** any of several pigeons constituting a genus (*Goura*) native to New Guinea and adjacent islands having a high fan-shaped erect crest of lacy feathers and slaty-blue plumage and being occas. as large as geese

crow needle *n, often pl but sing or pl in constr* [so called fr. the long beaks of the fruit] **:** LADY'S-COMB

¹crown·er \'kraünə(r)\ *n* -s [ME *crounere,* fr. *crounen* to crown + *-ere* -er] **1 :** one that crowns: as **a :** a crowning or consummating act ⟨we slipped our cables, as a ~ to our fun ashore —R.H.Dana⟩ **b :** a fall or bruise on the crown of the head **2 :** an inspector of shoes; *esp* **:** one who looks for flaws that may have occurred in the lasting department

²crown·er \'krünə(r), -raün-\ *n* -s [ME, alter. (influenced by *croun, crowne* crown) of *coroner, corowner* — more at CORONER] *chiefly dial* **:** CORONER

crown·et \'kraünət\ *n* -s [ME, alter. (influenced by ME *croun, crowne* crown) of *coronette* — more at CORONET] *archaic* **:** CORONET

crown fire *n* **:** a forest fire that advances often at great speed from crown to crown often well in advance of the fire on the ground

crown flower *n* **:** a large shrub (*Calotropis gigantea*) with white and pale lavender flowers used for leis in Hawaii

crown gall *n* **1 :** a disease of various plants esp. destructive to pome and stone fruits, grapes, and roses caused by a bacterium (*Agrobacterium tumefaciens*) which forms tumorous enlargements mainly just below ground on the stem — see BLACK KNOT 4, HAIRY ROOT **2 :** CROWN WART

crown gate *n* **:** the head gate (as of a lock of a canal)

crown gear *n* **:** a gear whose teeth project parallel to the axis and whose pitch surface is a plane — see CROWN WHEEL

crown girdler *n* **:** STRAWBERRY ROOT WEEVIL

crown glass *n* **1 :** glass blown and whirled into the form of a flat disk having a bull's-eye in the center **2 :** alkali-lime silicate optical glass having relatively low index of refraction and low dispersion value — compare FLINT GLASS **3 :** CROWN LENS

crown gold *n* **:** gold eleven-twelfths fine that was used in the minting of the crown of the rose from 1526 and adopted in 1634 as the standard for other English gold coins

crown graft *n* **1** *Brit* **:** BARK GRAFTING **2 :** a plant graft made at the level of the crown

crown gum *n* **:** a crude coagulated latex taken from certain Central American trees and used as a substitute for chicle

crown head *n* **:** KING ROW

crown imperial *n* **:** a Eurasian spring-blooming herb (*Fritillaria imperialis*) having at the top of the stalk a cluster of pendent bell-shaped flowers surmounted by a whorl of leaves

¹crown·ing \'kraüniŋ, -nēŋ\ *n* -s [ME *coruning, crouning,* fr. gerund of *corunen, crounen* to crown — more at CROWN] **:** the act or action of bestowing or providing with a crown ⟨the ~ of the May queen⟩ ⟨the ~ of a road⟩; *esp* **:** the marriage ceremony in the Eastern Church in which the officiating priest places crowns on the heads of bride and bridegroom

²crowning \"\ *adj* [fr. pres. part. of ²*crown*] **1 :** TOPPING, SURMOUNTING ⟨a . . . pavilion with ~ gable pediment —*Amer. Guide Series: Maine*⟩ **2 :** SUPREME, ULTIMATE ⟨her ~ glory⟩ ⟨the ~ achievement of his life⟩ ⟨and how shall we rate his ~ poem? —J.C.Ransom⟩

crown jewels *n pl* **:** the jewels (as crown, scepter, and other precious objects of symbolic value) appendant to the office of a sovereign; *specif* **:** the jewels belonging to a sovereign's regalia

crown knot *n* **:** a knot tied in the unlaid strands at the end of a rope and used chiefly as part of other knots

crown knot

crown land *n* **1 :** land belonging to the crown and yielding revenues that the reigning sovereign is entitled to **:** the crown's domain or estate ⟨the conqueror inherited from his . . . predecessors a considerable revenue, derived in the main from *crown lands* —F.M.Stenton⟩ **2 :** public land in some British dominions or colonies ⟨*crown lands* of Australia⟩

crownland \'ˌ=ˌland\ *n* [trans. of G *kronland*] **:** one of the provinces of the old Austro-Hungarian Empire

crown law *n* **:** the part of English common law that applies to criminal prosecutions

crown leather *n* **:** a strong leather used esp. for belting, washers, valve cups, and belt laces and tanned usu. by drumming with warm fats and other materials

crown lens *n* **:** the crown glass component of an achromatic lens

crown·less \-ləs\ *adj* **:** being without a crown ⟨crowned and ~ rulers of men —Jane Wilde⟩

crown monkey *n* **:** BONNET MONKEY

crown office *n* **1 :** the office of the Court of King's Bench in English law in which certain procedure formerly took place on the criminal-law side and in matters relating to the prerogative writs of quo warranto, mandamus, and prohibition **2 :** a department for the King's Bench division in the central office of the High Court of Justice in English law **3** *in English law* **a :** the Chancery Office in which the great seal is generally affixed **b :** the former office of the common-law side of the Chancery Court

crown-of-the-field \'ˌ===ˌ=\ *n* **:** CORN COCKLE

crown of the rose [¹*crown* (coin); fr. the rose on its face] **:** an English gold coin first struck by Henry VIII in 1526

crown of thorns 1 [so called fr. the wreath placed on Jesus' head by Roman soldiers who mocked him as "King of the Jews" prior to his crucifixion] **:** a severe infliction **:** unmerited injury **2 a :** a somewhat climbing bushy spurge (*Euphorbia milii*) of Madagascar that has long thick woody stems covered with stout spines, few leaves mostly restricted to the new growth, and flowers subtended by brilliant scarlet bracts and that is sometimes cultivated in the greenhouse **b :** CARAUNDA

crown palm *n* **:** a West Indian pinnate-leaved palm (*Englerophoenix caribaea*) related to the coconut palm

crownpiece \'ˌ=ˌ=\ *n* **:** a piece or part forming the crown or top of something; *specif* **:** CROWN 3f(2)

crown post *n* **:** KING POST

crown prince *n* **1 :** the heir apparent to a crown or throne **2 :** a person esp. prepared or favored to fill a forthcoming vacancy ⟨the former president's handpicked *crown prince* —*Springfield (Mass.) Union*⟩

crown princess *n* **1 :** the wife of a crown prince **2 :** a female heir apparent or heir presumptive to a crown or throne

crown pulley *n* **:** a pulley in the crown block of an oil-well derrick

crown roast *n* **:** a fancy roast of lamb, veal, or pork made from the rib portions of two loins by trimming off the backbone and skewering the ends together in a circle with the bones outside

crown roast

crown rot *n* **:** any rot affecting the part of a plant at or near the ground level and caused in the sugar beet by boron deficiency or in rhubarb by a fungus (*Phytophthora parasitica*) — compare COLLAR ROT

crown-rump length *n* **:** SITTING HEIGHT

crown rust *n* [so called fr. the crown of blunt teeth surmounting the terminal cells of the teliospores of the causal fungus] **:** a leaf rust of oats and other grasses characterized by rounded light-orange uredinia and buried telia

crowns *pl of* CROWN, *pres 3d sing of* CROWN

crown saw *n* **:** a saw for cutting round holes having its teeth at the edge of a hollow cylinder — called also *cylinder saw, hole saw*

crown saw attached to arbor

crown's evidence *n* **:** KING'S EVIDENCE

crownshaft \'ˌ=ˌ=\ *n* **:** the extension that rises above the flower cluster of the shaft of many palms, is composed of the erect sheathing petioles of the crown leaves, and resembles a trunk

crown sheet *n* **1** *also* **crown plate :** the plate that forms the top of the furnace or firebox of an internally fired steam boiler **2 :** one of the upper steel plates in an oil still

crown shell *n* **:** ACORN BARNACLE

crown side *n* **:** the criminal-law side in English law

crown vent *n* **:** a vent for a plumbing fixture in which the vent pipe is connected at the top of the curve in the pipe that forms the trap

crown vetch *n* **:** AXSEED

crown wart *n* **:** a disease of alfalfa caused by a fungus (*Urophlyctis alfalfae*) which produces large dirty-white excrescences at the stem base

crown wheel *n* **:** a crown gear of light construction: as **a :** the crown-shaped horizontal escape wheel of a verge escapement timepiece **b :** a contrate wheel in the winding mechanism of a watch that drives the ratchet wheel and is itself driven by the winding-stem pinion

crownwort \'ˌ=ˌ=\ *n* [so called fr. the arrangement of the petals] **:** a plant of the genus *Malesherbia*

crownwort family *n* **:** MALESHERBIACEAE

crow onion *n* **:** CROW GARLIC

crow pheasant *n* **:** the common coucal (*Centropus sinensis*) of India and China that is a large cuckoo of terrestrial habits

crow poison *n* **1 :** a small American plant (*Nothoscordum bivalve*) poisonous to stock **2 :** FLY POISON

crow quill *n* [¹*crow* + *quill* (of which they were formerly made)] **:** a narrow flexible artist's pen that is usu. circular in section at the holder end and that produces a very fine line which can be thickened by slight pressure

crows *pl of* CROW, *pres 3d sing of* CROW

crow's ash *n* **:** either of two Australian timber trees of the genus *Flindersia:* **a :** FLINDOSA **b :** a closely related tree (*Flindersia bennettiana*)

crow's-bill \'ˌ=ˌ=\ *n, pl* **crow's-bills :** CORACOID PROCESS

crow's-foot \'ˌ=ˌ=\ *n, pl* **crow's-feet :** something felt to resemble a crow's foot or the outline of a crow's footprint: as **a :** a set of wrinkles around the outer corners of the eyes resulting from age, mental distress, or habitual squinting — usu. used in pl. **b :** CROWFOOT 4 **c :** CALTROP 2a **d :** a triangular figure filled with interlacing stitches and used as a finish or decoration on tailored garments **e :** CROWFOOT 7 **f :** CROWFOOT 1 **g** *aeronautics* (1) **:** a system of diverging short ropes for distributing the pull of a single rope (2) **:** an arrangement in which the strands of a cord are opened out so that they can be effectively cemented to a fabric surface **h** (1) **:** BIRD'S-MOUTH (2) **:** the veining in a streaked stone (as marble)

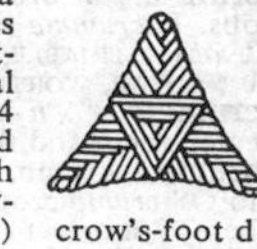
crow's-foot d

crow-shrike \'ˌ=ˌ\ *n* **:** any of several Australian butcher-birds or currawongs (esp. *Cracticus nigrogularis, C. torquatus,* or *Strepera graculina*) — compare PIPING CROW

crow's nest *n* **1 a :** a partly enclosed platform for a lookout on a boat usu. placed well up on the foremast **b :** an elevated platform (as on a traffic-control tower, oil derrick, or coast-guard lookout) **c :** a maneuverable bucket-shaped platform on a crane (as used by workers trimming off high tree branches) **d :** the cupola in a caboose **2 :** WILD CARROT

crow-soap \'ˌ=ˌ\ *n* **:** SOAPWORT

crowstep \'ˌ=ˌ\ *n* **:** CORBIESTEP — **crow-stepped** \'ˌ=ˌstept\ *adj*

crow tit *n* **:** any of various small birds of *Paradoxornis* or related genera of southeastern Asia that resemble tits

crowtoe \'ˌ=ˌ\ *n* **1 :** a toothwort (*Dentaria laciniata*) of the eastern U.S. **2 :** a bird's-foot trefoil (*Lotus corniculatus*) **3** *Brit* **:** WOOD HYACINTH **4** *Brit* **:** MALE ORCHIS **5** *Brit* **:** BUTTERCUP

crow-tread *vt* [¹*tread* (copulate); fr. the belief that crows tread hens against their will] *obs* **:** to treat ignominiously

crow-victuals \'ˌ=ˌ==\ *n pl but sing or pl in constr* **:** GROUND IVY

croy \'krȯi\ *n* -s [ML *croya, croa* fish trap, fr. ScGael *crō* pen for animals, hut — more at CREW] **:** a barrier built out in a stream as a fish shelter or means of allaying bank erosion

croy·don \'krȯid°n\ *adj, usu cap* [fr. *Croydon,* England] **:** of or from the county borough of Croydon, Surrey, England **:** of the kind or style prevalent in Croydon

¹croze \'krōz\ *n* -s [prob. fr. MF *crues* cavity, hole, groove; akin to OProv *croza* hole, cave, It dial. *croso* deep] **1 :** the groove near either end of a barrel stave in which the barrelhead is inserted **2 :** a plane or machine for cutting the croze in staves

²croze \"\ *vt* -ED/-ING/-S **1 :** to make a croze in (a stave) **2 :** to fold and refold (felt hat bodies) during sizing

croz·er \'krōzə(r)\ *n* -s **:** one that crozes; *specif* **:** CHUCKER 2

crozier *var of* CROSIER

crt *abbr* **1** court **2** crate

CRT *abbr* cathode-ray tube

cru \'krü, -rüe\ *n, pl* **crus** \-üz,-üe(z)\ [F, quantity in which something is produced, production, producing field, graded field, fr. *crû* (past part. of *croître* to grow) fr. OF *creüe* — more at CREW] **:** a French vineyard producing wine grapes; *esp* **:** one formally graded as to the quality of its annual production ⟨a claret from one of the better ~*s*⟩

¹crub \'krüb, -rəb\ *dial var of* CRIB

²crub \"\ *dial var of* CURB

cruce *n* -s [by shortening] *obs* **:** CRUCIBLE

cruces *pl of* CRUX

cru·cet·house \'krüsət,haùs\ *n* [OE *crucethūs,* fr. *crucet-* (fr. L *cruciatus* torture, fr. *cruciatus,* past part. of *cruciare* to torture, fr. *cruc-, crux* cross) + *hūs* house — more at RIDGE, HOUSE] **:** a chest used in medieval torture to hold the body of one who was to be pressed with stones

cru·cial \'krüshəl\ *adj* [F, fr. L *cruc-, crux* cross + F *-ial*] **1** *archaic* **:** characteristic of or having the form of a cross **:** CRUCIFORM, CRUCIATE, CROSSED, INTERSECTING ⟨a ~ scar⟩ **2 :** important or essential as decisive or as resolving a crisis **:** marked by final determination of a doubtful issue ⟨a ~ decision⟩ ⟨a ~ operation⟩ ⟨the ~ game of a series⟩; *broadly* **:** SEVERE, TRYING, TESTING ⟨a ~ experience⟩ ⟨a ~ moment⟩

syn see ACUTE

cru·ci·al·i·ty \ˌkrüshē'alədē, krüˌshal-, -ətē, -i\ *n* -ES **:** the quality or state of being crucial ⟨the episodes chosen by Homer have no evident ~ for the course of the war —S.G.F. Brandon⟩

cru·cial·ly \'krüshəl|ē, |i, *rapid* -shl|\ *adv* **:** in a crucial manner **:** to a crucial degree ⟨~ necessary⟩ ⟨~ tested in a laboratory⟩

cru·cian carp \'krüshən-\ *also* **crucian** *n* -s [modif. of LG *karuse, karuske* (fr. MLG *karuske, karusse*) or Fris *krūsken* both fr. Lith *karušis, karōsas;* akin to Russ *karas'* crucian carp, Pol *karaś,* and perh. to Skt *kilāsa* spotted, leprous] **:** a European carp (*Carassius vulgaris* syn. *C. carassius*)

cru·cia·nel·la \ˌkrüshə'nelə\ *n, cap* [NL, irreg. dim. of L *cruci-, crux* cross; fr. the arrangement of the leaves] **:** a genus of herbs or low shrubs (family Rubiaceae) with opposite or whorled leaves and small tubular flowers in close clusters

¹cru·ci·ate \'krüshē,āt\ *adj* [NL *cruciatus,* fr. L *cruci-, crux* cross + *-atus* -ate] **:** cross-shaped or marked with a cross ⟨a ~ bandage⟩: **a :** having leaves or petals in the form of a cross **:** CRUCIFORM **b :** CROSSING — used esp. of the wings of some insects — **cru·ci·ate·ly** *adv*

²cruciate \"\ *vt* -ED/-ING/-S [L *cruci-, crux* cross + E *-ate*] **:** to mark with a cross

cruciate ligament *n* **:** any of several more or less cross-shaped ligaments: as **a :** a V-shaped arrangement of fibers over the extensor tendons of the ankle **b :** either of two ligaments in the knee joint that cross each other from femur to tibia **c :** a complex ligament made up of the transverse ligament of the atlas and vertical fibrocartilage extending from the odontoid process to the border of the foramen magnum

cru·ci·ble \'krüsəbəl\ *n* -s [ME *corusible,* fr. ML *crucibulum, crucibolum* small lamp, earthen pot for melting metals, prob. by folk etymology (influence of L *cruc-, crux* cross, and *turibulum* thurible) fr. OF *croiseul* — more at CRUSIE] **1 :** a vessel or melting pot of some very refractory material (as clay, graphite, porcelain, or a relatively infusible metal) that may vary in size from a small laboratory utensil for chemical analysis to very large industrial equipment and that is used for melting and calcining a substance (as metal and ore) which requires a high degree of heat **2 :** something that tests as if by fire **:** a severe test or trial ⟨~ of affliction⟩ ⟨~ of war⟩

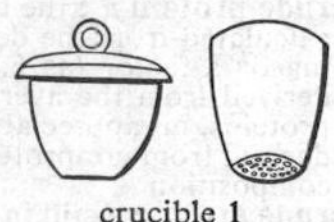
crucible 1

crucible furnace *n* **:** a furnace for heating material contained in crucibles

crucible steel *n* **:** hard cast steel (as for dies and cutting tools) made in pots that are lifted from the furnace before the metal is poured into molds

cru·cib·u·lum \krü'sibyələm\ *n, cap* [NL, fr. ML, earthen pot — more at CRUCIBLE] **:** a genus of bird's-nest fungi (family Nidulariaceae) with the peridium consisting of one layer and opening by a deciduous yellow tomentose membrane

cru·ci·fer \'krüsəfə(r)\ *n* -s [LL, fr. L *cruci-, crux* cross + *-fer* — more at CROSS] **1 :** one that carries a cross (as at the head of an ecclesiastical procession) **2** [NL *Cruciferae*] **:** any plant of the family Cruciferae **:** CRESS

cru·cif·er·ae \krü'sifəˌrē\ *n pl, cap* [NL, fr. L *cruci-, crux* + *-ferae* (fem. pl. of *-fer*)] **:** a family of herbs (order Rhoeadales) characterized by cruciate tetramerous flowers and by the fruit which is a silique or a silicle — see BRASSICA

cru·cif·er·ous \(')krü'sif(ə)rəs\ *adj* [L *cruci-, crux* + E *-ferous*] **1 :** bearing a cross **2** [NL *Cruciferae* + E *-ous*] **:** belonging to or having the characteristics of the mustards or related plants

cru·ci·fi·er \'krüsəˌfī(ə)r, -īə\ *n* -s [ME, fr. *crucifien* + *-er*] **:** one that crucifies

cru·ci·fix \-ˌfiks\ *n* -ES [ME, fr. ML & LL; ML *crucifixus* representation of Christ on the cross, fr. LL, the crucified Christ, fr. *crucifixus,* past part. of *crucifigere* to crucify, fr. L *cruci-, crux* cross + *figere* to fasten — more at RIDGE, DIKE] **1 :** a representation of Christ on the cross usu. painted in the Eastern Church or sculptured or molded and affixed in the Western Church ⟨the cross, too, by degrees became the ~ —H.H.Milman⟩; *also* **:** the cross itself as a Christian emblem **2** *obs* **:** the crucified Christ **3 :** a gymnastic stunt in which a performer supports himself on the rings by his hands with his arms held rigid in a horizontal position

crucifix fish *n* **:** any of several saltwater catfishes (genus *Arius*) of the Caribbean area with the bones of the lower part of the skull arranged in the form of a crucifix

crucifix 1

cru·ci·fix·ion \ˌkrüsə'fikshən\ *n* -s [LL *crucifixion-, crucifixio,* fr. *crucifixus* + *-ion-, -io* -ion] **1 a :** the act of crucifying **b** *usu cap* **:** the crucifying of Christ — usu. used with *the* **2 :** the state of one who is crucified **:** death upon a cross **3 :** extreme and painful punishment **:** intense persecution, affliction, or suffering **:** TORTURE ⟨the daily ~ of the Negro in our midst —Max Lerner⟩; *specif* **:** mental suffering for a principle or cause

crucifixion thorn *n* **:** CHRIST'S-THORN

¹cru·ci·form \'krüsəˌfȯrm\ *adj* [L *cruci-, crux* cross + E *-form* — more at RIDGE] **:** forming or arranged in a cross **:** CRUCIATE ⟨a ~ aircraft wing⟩ — **cru·ci·form·ly** *adv*

²cruciform \"\ *n* -s **:** a figure representing or resembling a cross **:** CROSS ⟨the ground plan is a ~⟩

cruciform ligament *n* **:** CRUCIATE LIGAMENT c

cru·ci·fy \'krüsəˌfī\ *vt* -ED/-ING/-ES [ME *crucifien,* fr. OF *crucifier,* fr. LL *crucifigere* — more at CRUCIFIX] **1 :** to put to death by nailing or binding the hands and feet to a cross **2 :** to destroy the power or ruling influence of **:** subdue completely **:** MORTIFY ⟨they that are Christ's have *crucified* the flesh —Gal 5:24(AV)⟩ **3 a :** to treat cruelly (as in severe punishment) **:** TORMENT, TORTURE **b :** to harry, persecute, or pillory esp. for some cause or principle **:** DENIGRATE ⟨~ a political leader⟩

cruck \'krək\ *n* -s [ME *crokke,* prob. var. of *crok* crook — more at CROOK] **:** one of a pair of curved timbers forming a principal support of a roof in primitive English house construction

¹crud \'krəd, 'krüd\ *n* -s [ME *crudd* — more at CURD] **1** *dial* **:** ¹CURD **2 :** a deposit or incrustation of filth, grease, or refuse **:** an impurity or unwanted foreign substance **3 :** a usu. ill-defined or imperfectly identified bodily disorder ⟨jungle ~⟩ — **crud·dy** \-dē\ *adj*

²crud \"\ *vb* **crudded; crudded; crudding; cruds** [ME *crudden* — more at CURD] *dial* **:** ²CURD

crud·dle \'krəd°l, -rüd-\ *vb* -ED/-ING/-S [freq. of ²*crud*] *dial* **:** CURDLE

¹crude \'krüd\ *adj* -ER/-EST [ME, fr. L *crudus* raw — more at RAW] **1 :** in a natural state **:** not cooked or prepared by fire or heat **:** not altered or prepared for use by any process **:** RAW ⟨~ flesh⟩ **:** not refined ⟨~ sugar⟩ ⟨~ rubber⟩ **2** *obs* **:** UNDIGESTED **:** not digestible **:** not brought into a form to give nourishment **3** *obs* **:** UNRIPE **:** not mature or perfect **:** IMMATURE, UNDEVELOPED ⟨I come to pluck your berries harsh and ~ —John Milton⟩ **4 :** marked by the primitive, gross, or elemental or by the most readily apprehended **:** wanting subtlety, nuance, or complexity **:** low in perception, analysis, or appreciation ⟨a ~ notion⟩ ⟨a ~ theory⟩ ⟨it was there that the ~ dogmatism of New England was refined and humanized —H.L.Mencken⟩ **5 :** marked by uncultivated simplicity **:** wanting in elegance, discrimination, or polish esp. in choice of words or figures ⟨*cruder,* because less capable of expressing complicated, subtle, and surprising emotions —T.S.Eliot⟩ **:** noticeable or offensive for vulgarity ⟨~ barracks conversations⟩ **:** harshly loud **:** GRATING **:** unpleasant through lack of modulation or relief ⟨the China asters smear their ~ colors —Amy Lowell⟩ **6 :** quite oblivious or contemptuous of the refined or elevated ⟨the ~ masses of Teutondom which poured into Provincia to be leavened by its culture —H.O.Taylor⟩ **7 :** rough or inexpert in plan or execution **:** wanting advanced technical skill in contrivance and elegance in effect ⟨the *cruder* means of transportation, by wooden ships propelled by the wind . . . by oxcart —A.C.Morrison⟩ **8 :** lacking any covering, glossing, concealing, or masking **:** lacking mitigation, alleviation, or reservation **:** OBVIOUS, SHEER, UTTER, BALD, STARK ⟨~ facts⟩ ⟨~ necessity⟩ ⟨~ sensation⟩ ⟨not the ~ beauty of the eye. It was not beauty pure and simple —Virginia Woolf⟩ **9** *archaic* **:** constituting the part of a word that remains constant or nearly constant throughout a paradigm **:** being the base to which inflectional affixes are attached ⟨the stem or ~ form of a word⟩ **10** *of statistics* **:** tabulated without breaking down into classes ⟨~ death rate⟩ **11** *of animal feedstuffs* **:** reacting like members of a particular class of nutrients to certain identifying tests though not necessarily chemically a member of such class ⟨~ protein includes all the nitrogenous compounds of a feed⟩ ⟨~ fat is high in this analysis but digestible fats are low⟩ **syn** see RUDE

²**crude** \"\ *n* -s **:** a substance in its natural unprocessed state: as **a :** CRUDE OIL **b :** initial products of distillation of crude oil without cracking or other treatment **c :** a crude substance (as benzene, toluene, xylene, cresol, naphthalene, anthracene, or carbazole) distilled from coal tar

crude drug *n* **:** a plant or animal drug occurring in either the fresh or dried condition and either whole or reduced in particle size by cutting or grinding

crude fiber *n* **:** the chiefly cellulose material obtained as a residue in the chemical analysis of vegetable substances (as foods and animal feeds)

crude·ly *adv* **:** in a crude manner **:** ROUGHLY, SIMPLY, APPROXIMATELY, BLUNTLY

crude·ness *n* -ES **:** the quality or state of being crude

crude oil *or* **crude petroleum** *n* **:** petroleum as it occurs naturally, as it comes from an oil well, or after extraneous substances (as entrained water, gas, and minerals) have been removed

crude protein *n* **:** the approximate amount of protein in foods calculated from the determined nitrogen content by multiplying by a factor (as 6.25 for many foods and 5.7 for wheat) derived from the average percentage of nitrogen in the food proteins, an appreciable error thus resulting if the nitrogen is derived from nonprotein material or from a protein of unusual composition

crude still *n* **:** a still in which crude oil is first distilled — compare TAR STILL

cru·di·ty \ˈkrüdəd-ē, -ətē, -i\ *n* -ES [MF or L; MF *crudité*, fr. L *cruditat-, cruditas*, fr. *crudus* raw + *-itat-, -itas* -ity — more at RAW] **1 :** the quality or state of being crude **:** lack of polish, refinement, or subtlety **:** RAWNESS, ROUGHNESS, HARSHNESS **2 :** something (as undigested matter) that is crude **:** something that is unfinished or undeveloped or offensive to refined taste **:** IMPOLITENESS, IMPERFECTION ⟨*crudities* of speech and behavior⟩

cru·dle \ˈkrədᵊl, -rüd-\ *vb* -ED/-ING/-S [freq. of ²*crud*] *dial* **:** CURDLE

cruds *pl of* CRUD, *pres 3d sing of* CRUD

¹**cru·el** \ˈkrü|əl, -ü|əl *also* -ü|l, *esp Brit* |(,)il\ *adj* **crueler** *or* **crueller; cruelest** *or* **cruellest** [ME, fr. OF, fr. L *crudelis*, irreg. fr. *crudus* raw — more at RAW] **1 a :** disposed to inflict pain esp. in a wanton, insensate, or vindictive manner **:** pleased by hurting others **:** SADISTIC **:** devoid of kindness **b :** RAPACIOUS, RAVENING **:** given to killing and mangling or to tormenting prey **c :** arising from or indicative of an inclination to enjoy another's pain or misfortune ⟨~ epigrams⟩ ⟨~ slanders⟩ **2 a :** bitterly conducted **:** devoid of mildness **:** causing or conducive to injury, grief, or pain ⟨a ~ struggle for existence⟩ **b :** stern, rigorous, and grim **:** unrelieved by leniency or softness ⟨a monastic regula stern and ~⟩ **c :** bitterly ironical **3 :** SEVERE, DISTRESSING **:** extremely painful **:** EXTREME **syn** see FIERCE

²**cruel** \"\ *adv, now dial* **:** CRUELLY, EXTREMELY ⟨a ~ hard job⟩

³**cruel** \"\ *vt* -ED/-ING/-S *slang Austral* **:** to destroy all chance of success **:** SPOIL ⟨that ~*ed* the experiment⟩

cruel and unusual punishment *n* **:** punishment to include torture, barbarous punishments, degrading punishments not known to the common law, and punishments so disproportionate to the offense as to shock the general moral sense ⟨excessive bail shall not be required, nor excessive fines imposed, nor *cruel and unusual punishments* inflicted —*U.S. Constitution*⟩

cruelhearted \ˌ=ˈ=ˌ=, ˈ=ˌ=ˌ=\ *adj* **:** having a cruel heart

cru·el·ly *pronunc at* CRUEL + ē *or* i\ *adv* [ME, fr. ¹*cruel* + *-ly*] **1 :** so as to pain **:** MERCILESSLY **:** so as to cause pain or hurt ⟨~ done to death⟩ **2 :** EXTREMELY, SEVERELY ⟨the rooms are ~ overcrowded with furniture —F.A.Swinnerton⟩

cru·el·ness *n* -ES [ME *cruelnes*, fr. *cruel* + *-nes* -ness] **:** CRUELTY

cruel plant *n* [so called fr. the fact that insects become entangled in the flowers] **:** any of several plants of the genera *Araujia*, *Schubertia*, or *Cynanchum* (family Asclepiadaceae)

cru·els \ˈkrüəlz\ *n pl* [MF *escroele, escroielle*, fr. OF, fr. (assumed) VL *scrofellae*, fr. LL *scrofulae* — more at SCROFULA] *chiefly Scot* **:** SCROFULA

cru·el·ty *pronunc at* CRUEL + tē *or* ti\ *n* -ES [ME *cruelte*, fr. OF *crueltė*, fr. L *crudelitat-, crudelitas*, fr. *crudelis* cruel + *-itat-, -itas* -ity — more at CRUEL] **1 :** the quality or state of being cruel **:** disposition to inflict pain or suffering or to enjoy its being inflicted **:** INHUMANITY **2 :** a cruel action **:** inhuman treatment ⟨the *cruelties* of racial discrimination⟩ **3** *obs* **a :** severity of pain **b :** harshness of discipline **4 :** conduct of either party in a divorce action that endangers the life or health of the other; *also* **:** acts that cause mental suffering or fear

cru·en·ta·tion \ˌkrü,enˈtāshən, -üən-\ *n* -S [LL *cruentation-, cruentatio* staining with blood, fr. L *cruentatus* (past part. of *cruentare* to make bloody, fr. *cruentus* bloody) + *-ion-, -io* -ion; akin to L *cruor* blood — more at RAW] **:** the oozing of blood from a corpse after incision or according to superstitious belief in the presence of the murderer

cruentous *adj* [L *cruentus*, fr. *cruor* blood] *obs* **:** BLOODY

cru·et *also* **crew·et** \ˈkrüət\ *n* -S [ME *cruette*, fr. AF *cruet*, dim. of OF *crue, cruie*, of Gmc origin; akin to OS *krūka* pot — more at CROCK] **:** a usu. glass bottle or vessel used to hold vinegar, oil, or other condiments for table use or to hold wine or water for altar service

cruet

¹**cruise** \ˈkrüz\ *vb* -ED/-ING/-S [D *kruisen* to make a cross, move crosswise, cruise, fr. MD *crucen*, fr. *crūce* cross, fr. L *cruc-, crux* — more at RIDGE] *vi* **1 :** to sail about touching at a series of ports as distinguished from voyaging to a set destination **2** *slang* **:** to be on one's way **:** GO ⟨you ~ right along and cheer her up —J.C.Lincoln⟩ **3 :** to travel for the sake of traveling without destination or other definite purpose **4 :** to go about at random but on the lookout for possible developments (as of a taxicab or a police car) **5 a** *of an airplane* **:** to fly at the most efficient operating speed of the engine **b** *of an automobile* **:** to travel at a speed suitable for maintaining steadily for long distance; *sometimes* **:** to go at or near the highest speed that can be safely and steadily maintained **~** *vt* **1 :** to cruise over or about ⟨*cruising* the Mediterranean in a yacht⟩ **2 :** to explore with reference to the possible lumber yield ⟨~ a section of land⟩ ⟨~ the timber in a holding⟩ **3 :** to fly (an airplane) or drive (a car or truck) at cruising speed ⟨the car can be *cruised* at 70 mph⟩

²**cruise** \"\ *n* -S **1 :** the act of cruising **:** a journeying from or as if from port to port ⟨the ~ of a trapper for game⟩ **2 a :** the trip of a cruising ship **b :** any casual trip

cruise car *n* **:** SQUAD CAR

cruis·er \-zə(r)\ *n* -S [D *kruiser*, fr. *kruisen* to cruise + *-er*] **1 :** a boat or vehicle (as a taxicab or police car) that cruises **2 :** any of certain warships: **a :** an 18th century privateer **b :** a large fast moderately armored and gunned warship usu. of 6000 to 15,000 tons displacement — see GUIDED MISSILE CRUISER, HEAVY CRUISER, LIGHT CRUISER **3 :** a powerboat equipped with cabin, permanent berths, fixed plumbing, and other arrangements necessary for cooking and living aboard — called also *cabin cruiser* **4 :** a person who cruises: **a :** one who estimates the volume and value of marketable timber on a tract of land and maps it out for logging **b** *slang* **:** PROSTITUTE **c :** TRAVELER **5 :** a high-topped laced boot used by lumbermen in cruising timber **6 :** FASHION GRAY **7** [by shortening] **:** CRUISERWEIGHT

cruiser stern *n* **:** a stern on high-speed naval vessels designed without overhang to give maximum immersed length

cruiserweight \ˈ=ˌ=ˌ=\ *n* [so called fr. the comparison of the second-heaviest boxing class (light-heavyweight) to the traditionally second heaviest warship (cruiser)] *chiefly Brit* **:** a light-heavyweight boxer or class

crui·sie *var of* CRUSIE

cruising radius *n* **1 :** the maximum distance that the fuel capacity of a naval vessel or an airplane will allow it to go and return from at cruising speed **2 :** the distance an animal may move from an initial point (as a den) in the course of a day

cruis·keen \(ˈ)krüshˌkēn\ *or* **cruis·ken** \ˈkrüskən\ *n* -S [IrGael *crūiscín* & ScGael *crūisgean*, both fr. (assumed) MD *croeskijn*, dim. of MD *croese, crose* jug, pitcher — more at CRUSE] *Irish & Scot* **:** a small pitcher or jug for holding liquor

cruive \ˈkrēv\ *n* -S [ME (Sc dial) *crufe, crove*, prob. fr. ScGael *crō* pen for animals, hut — more at CREW] *Scot* **:** a small rude enclosure (as a hovel or a pen for animals)

crul·ler \ˈkrələ(r)\ *n* -S [D *krulle*, a kind of twisted cake, fr. *krul* curly, fr. MD *crulle*; akin to MHG *krol, krul* curly — more at CURL] **1 :** a small sweet cake made of a rich egg batter formed into twisted strips and fried brown in deep fat **2** *North & Midland* **:** an unraised doughnut **:** FRIEDCAKE

crum *archaic var of* CRUMB

¹**crumb** \ˈkrəm\ *n* -S [ME *crumme*, fr. OE *cruma*; akin to MHG *krume* crumb, MD *crume*, Icel *krumur* soft inside, OHG *krouwōn* to scratch, L *grumus* pile of dirt, Gk *grymea* bag, trash, fish remnants, Alb *grime* crumb; basic meaning: something scratched together; akin to OE *cradol* cradle — more at CRADLE] **1 :** a small fragment or piece; *esp* **:** a very small piece of bread or other food broken or rubbed off **2 :** a little **:** BIT ⟨a ~ of comfort⟩ **3 :** the soft part of bread — opposed to *crust* ⟨if you can't get ~, you'd best eat crust⟩ **4 :** any material resembling bread crumb: as **a :** loose friable soil **b :** shredded alkali cellulose **5 a :** BODY LOUSE **b** *slang* **:** a worthless person **6 crumbs** *pl* **:** a mixture of sugar, butter, and flour used as a topping on pastry (as coffee cake) — **to a crumb :** to the last detail

²**crumb** \"\ *vt* -ED/-ING/-S [ME *crummen*, fr. *crumme*, n.] **1 :** to break into crumbs ⟨~ bread⟩ **2 :** to cover, thicken, or dress with crumbs **3 :** to remove crumbs from ⟨~ the table⟩

crumbcloth \ˈ=ˌ=\ *n* **1 :** a cloth often of damask formerly laid under a dining table to receive falling fragments **2 :** a heavy damask suitable for embroidery

crumb·i·ness \ˈkrəmēnəs, -in-\ *n* -ES **:** the quality or state of being crumby

¹**crum·ble** \ˈkrəmbəl\ *vb* **crumbled; crumbled; crumbling** \-b(ə)liŋ\ **crumbles** [alter. (influenced by ¹*crumb*) of earlier *crimble*, fr. ME *kremelen*, freq. of OE *gecrymian* to crumble, fr. *cruma* crumb — more at CRUMB] *vt* **:** to break into small pieces **~** *vi* **:** to fall into small pieces ⟨stone that ~*s* quickly⟩ **:** fall to decay or ruin **:** DISINTEGRATE, COLLAPSE ⟨*crumbling* walls⟩ **syn** see DECAY

²**crumble** \"\ *n* -S **1** *dial* **:** CRUMB **2 :** crumbling substance **:** fine debris

crum·bli·ness \ˈkrəmb(ə)lēnəs, -lin-\ *n* -ES **:** the quality or state of being crumbly

crum·bling·ness \-b(ə)liŋnəs\ *n* -ES **:** the quality or state of being crumbling

crum·blings \ˈkrəmbliŋz\ *n pl* **:** crumbled particles **:** CRUMBS

crum·bly \-b(ə)lē, -bli\ *adj* **:** easily crumbled **:** FRIABLE ⟨~ soil⟩

crumb-of-bread sponge *n* **:** a common encrusting sponge (*Halichondria panicea*) lacking microscleres and having the megascleres irregularly arranged

cru·men \ˈkrümən, -ˌmen\ *or* **cru·me·na** \krüˈmēnə, -ˈmānə\ *n, pl* **crumens** \-ənz,-enz\ *or* **crumenas** \-ēnəz,-ānəz\ *or* **crume·nae** \-ē,nē, -ā,nī\ [L *crumena, crumina* purse, bag, modif. of Gk *grymea* bag, trash — more at CRUMB] *zool* **:** POUCH: as **a :** the suborbital gland that secretes a waxy substance and is present in many deer and antelopes **b :** one into which the mouthparts of certain bugs can be retracted

crum·mie *or* **crum·my** \ˈkrəmi\ *n, pl* **crummies** [Sc *crum, crumb* crooked (fr. ME *crumb*, fr. OE) + *-ie, -y*; akin to OE *crump* crooked — more at CRUMP] *chiefly Scot* **:** COW; *esp* **:** one with crumpled horns

crum·mock \ˈkrəmək\ *n* -S [ScGael *cromag* anything bent, fr. *crom* crooked; akin to OIr *cromm*, OE *gehrumpen* wrinkled — more at RUMPLE] *chiefly Scot* **:** a staff with a crooked head

¹**crum·my** *or* **crumby** \ˈkrəmē, -mi\ *adj* -ER/-EST [*crummy* fr. obs. E *crumme* crumb (fr. ME) + E *-y* — more at CRUMB] **1** *obs* **:** FRIABLE, CRUMBLY **2** *slang* **a :** MISERABLE, FILTHY **b :** CHEAP, WORTHLESS **3** *Brit* **:** PLUMP, BUXOM

²**crummy** \"\ *n* -ES [prob. fr. ¹*crummy*; fr. the fact that food is eaten there and that it is traditionally untidy] *slang* **:** CABOOSE

¹**crump** \ˈkrůmp, ˈkrəmp\ *adj* [ME *crumb, crump*, fr. OE; akin to OS *crumb* crooked, OHG *krump, krumpf* crooked, *kramph* bent — more at CRAMP] *chiefly dial Brit* **:** CROOKED, BENT

²**crump** \"\ *vb* -ED/-ING/-S [ME *crumpen*, fr. *crump*, adj.] *now dial Eng* **:** CROOK, CURVE **:** curl up

³**crump** *n* -S [¹*crump*] *obs* **:** HUMPBACK

⁴**crump** \ˈkrəmp\ *vi* -ED/-ING/-S [imit.] **1 :** to make a crunching sound (as in eating) **:** CRUNCH **2 :** to explode heavily (as of a bomb) **:** THUMP, THWACK ⟨the shells ~*ed* in the road behind us⟩

⁵**crump** \"\ *n* -S **1 :** a crunching sound **2** *Brit* **:** BLOW, THUMP **3 a :** the explosion of a heavy shell or bomb **b :** SHELL, BOMB

⁶**crump** \"\ *adj* [perh. alter. (influenced by ⁴*crump*) of ³*crimp*] *chiefly Scot* **:** BRITTLE, FRIABLE, CRISP

crum·pet \ˈkrəmpət\ *n* -S [perh. fr. ME *crompid (cake)* wafer (lit., curled-up cake), fr. *crompid, crumped*, past part. of *crumpen* to curve, curl up — more at CRUMP] **:** a small round cake made of rich unsweetened batter cooked on a griddle and usu. served split and toasted

crump hole *n* [⁵*crump*] **:** a bomb crater

¹**crum·ple** \ˈkrəmpəl\ *vb* **crumpled; crumpled; crumpling** \-p(ə)liŋ\ **crumples** [fr. (assumed) ME *crumplen*, freq. of *crumpen* to crump — more at CRUMP (to crook)] *vt* **1 :** to press or twist into folds or wrinkles ⟨~ a paper⟩ **:** RUMPLE **:** make creases in ⟨a smile *crumpled* his face⟩ **:** bend and crush out of shape ⟨the crash *crumpled* both fenders badly⟩ **2 :** to cause to collapse **:** break the resistance of ⟨swearing always *crumpled* her⟩ **~** *vi* **1 :** to show wrinkles after crushing ⟨tinfoil ~*s* readily⟩ **2 :** to collapse as if crumpled ⟨at the sound of the shot the figure suddenly *crumpled*⟩ — often used with *up* ⟨he lay there all *crumpled* up⟩

²**crumple** \"\ *n* -S **:** a wrinkle, fold, or crease made by crumpling or squeezing **:** a crumpled part of something

crumpled *adj* [ME *crumpled, crompled*, past part. of (assumed) *crumplen*] **1 :** wrinkled, creased, or bent out of shape by or as if by pressing, folding, or crushing ⟨a ~ pack of cigarettes⟩ **2 :** bent spirally **:** CURVED ⟨the cow with the ~ horn⟩

crum·pler \-p(ə)lə(r)\ *n* -S **:** one that crumples

crump·ling \ˈkrůmpliŋ, -rəm-\ *n* -S [¹*crump* + *-ling*] *dial Eng* **:** something stunted or shriveled (as an apple or cucumber)

crum·ply \ˈkrəmp(ə)lē, -li\ *adj* **:** full of crumples **:** having a tendency to crumple

crump·sall yellow \ˈkrəm(p)səl-\ *n, usu cap C* [fr. *Crumpsall*, suburb of Manchester, England, where chemicals are manufactured] **:** a mordant dye — see DYE table I (under *Mordant Yellow 20*)

¹**crunch** \ˈkrənch\ *vb* ED/-ING/-ES [alter. of ¹*craunch*] *vi* **1 :** to chew with a crushing or grinding noise **2 :** to grind or press with a noise of crushing **3 :** to move or proceed with a crunching sound **~** *vt* **1 :** to bite with a crushing noise **2 :** to crush or grind (as under a foot or wheel) with a noise ⟨~*ed* the crisp snow⟩

²**crunch** \"\ *n* -ES **1 :** the act of crunching **2 :** a sound made by crunching ⟨hear the ~ of his saddle shoes on the gravel lane —A.W.Turnbull⟩ **3 :** a piece made or separated by crunching

crunch·er \-chə(r)\ *n* -S *slang* **:** a finishing blow

crunch·i·ness \ˈkrənchēnəs, -chin-\ *n* -ES **:** the quality or state of being crunchy **:** CRISPNESS

crunch·ing·ly *adv* **:** in a crunching manner

crunch·ing·ness *n* -ES **:** the quality or state of being crunching

crunchweed \ˈ=ˌ=\ *n* **:** CHARLOCK

crunchy \ˈkrənchē, -chi\ *adj* -ER/-EST **:** that crunches **:** CRUNCHING, CRISP

crun·kle \ˈkrůŋkəl, -əŋk-\ *vt* -ED/-ING/-S [ME *crounkilen* — more at CRINKLE] *dial Brit* **:** CRUMPLE, WRINKLE

cruor *n* -S [L, blood — more at RAW] *obs* **:** the clotted portion of coagulated blood

crup·per \ˈkrəpə(r), -rüp-,-růp-\ *n* -S [ME *croper, cruper*, fr. OF *cropiere, crupiere*, fr. *crope, crupe* hindquarters + *-iere* -er — more at CROUP] **1 :** a leather loop passing under a horse's tail and buckled to the saddle to keep it from slipping forward — see HARNESS illustration **2 :** the rump of a horse **:** CROUP; *broadly* **:** HINDQUARTERS, BUTTOCKS

crura *pl of* CRUS

cru·ral \ˈkrůrəl\ *adj* [MF or L; MF *crural*, fr. L *cruralis*, fr. *crur-, crus* leg + *-alis* -al] **:** relating to the thigh or leg or any of the crura; *specif* **:** FEMORAL ⟨~ artery⟩ ⟨~ nerve⟩

crural arch *n* **:** POUPART'S LIGAMENT

crural septum *n* **:** a thin fascia that normally closes the femoral ring and prevents descent of abdominal viscera into the femoral canal

cruro- *comb form* [NL, fr. L *crur-, crus* leg] **:** crural and ⟨*cruro*inguinal, *cruro*tarsal⟩

¹**crus** \ˈkrüs, ˈkrəs\ *n, pl* **cru·ra** \ˈkrůrə\ [L; akin to Arm *srunk* shinbones, calves of the legs] **1 :** the part of the hind limb between the femur or thigh and the ankle or tarsus **:** SHANK **2 :** any of various parts likened to a leg or to a pair of legs: as **a :** either of the diverging proximal ends of the corpora cavernosa **b :** the tendinous attachments of the diaphragm to the bodies of the lumbar vertebrae forming the sides of the aortic opening — often used in pl. **c** *crura, pl* **:** the peduncles of the cerebrum — called also *crura ce·re·bri* \-ˈserə,brī, -ˈkerə,brē\ **d** *crura, pl* **:** the peduncles of the cerebellum **e** *crura, pl* **:** the posterior pillars of the fornix — called also *crura for·ni·cis* \-ˈfȯrnə,sis, -ə,kis\ **f :** either of a pair of basal processes on the brachidia of certain brachiopods — see BRACHIOPOD illustration

²**crus** *pl of* CRU

¹**cru·sade** \(ˈ)krüˈsād\ *n* -S [blend of earlier *croisade* & *crusado*; *croisade* fr. MF, modif. (influenced by OProv *crozada*) of OF *croisée*, fr. fem. of past part. of *croiser* to take up the cross, fr. *crois* cross; *crusado* modif. of Sp *cruzada* (after Prov *crozada*), fr. fem. of past part. of *cruzar* to take up the cross, fr. *cruz* cross; OF *crois* and Sp *cruz* fr. L *cruc-, crux* — more at RIDGE] **1** *usu cap* **:** an expedition undertaken for a declared religious purpose (as recovering Jerusalem from the Muslims in the middle ages) **:** a campaign or war sanctioned by the church against unbelievers or heretics **2 :** any remedial activity pursued with zeal and enthusiasm ⟨a ~ against drinking⟩

THE CHIEF CRUSADES

NAME	DATE	OUTCOME
First	1096–99	Took Jerusalem
Second	1147–49	Unsuccessful
Third	1189–92 (or 91)	Conquest of Acre
Fourth	1202–04	Established Latin Empire in East
Fifth	1228–29	Jerusalem taken, but lost, finally, 1244
Sixth	1248–54	Unsuccessful
Seventh	1270	Unsuccessful

²**crusade** \"\ *vi* -ED/-ING/-S **:** to engage in a crusade **:** attack zealously **:** strive to further a cause ⟨a newspaper *crusading* against corruption⟩

cru·sad·er \-də(r)\ *n* -S **:** one engaged in a crusade

¹**cru·sa·do** \krüˈzä(,)dō, -)thü, -ˈsä(,)dō, -ˈsā(,)dō\ *also* **cru·za·do** \-ˈzä(,)dō, -)thü\ *n, pl* **crusadoes** *or* **crusados** [Pg *cruzado*, lit., marked with a cross, fr. past part. of *cruzar* to mark with a cross, fr. *cruz* cross, fr. L *cruc-, crux* — more at RIDGE] **:** an old gold coin of Portugal orig. issued by Alfonso V (1438-81) having a cross on the reverse in commemoration of the king's crusading struggle against the Muslims of No. Africa; *also* **:** a similar Portuguese coin in silver first issued by John IV (1640-56)

²**cru·sa·do** \-ˈsā(,)dō\ *n, pl* **crusados** *or* **crusadoes** [modif. of Sp *cruzada* — more at CRUSADE] *archaic* **:** CRUSADE

cruse \ˈkrüz, -üs\ *n* -S [ME *cruse, crowse*, prob. fr. MD *croese* jug, pitcher; akin to MHG *krūse* pitcher, OE *crūse*] **:** a small vessel (as a jar, pot) for holding a liquid (as water, oil, honey)

¹**crush** \ˈkrəsh\ *vb* -ED/-ING/-ES [ME *crusshen*, fr. MF *cruisir, croissir*, of Gmc origin; akin to MLG *krossen* to crush, OSw *krusa, krosa* to crush, *krysta* to gnash, Goth *kriustan* and perh. to Sk *brychein* to gnash, Lith *grūti* to collapse] *vt* **1 :** to press between two hard bodies ⟨~ grapes⟩ **:** squeeze or force by pressure so as to damage or destroy the structure of **:** force together into a mass ⟨~ clothes into a box⟩ ⟨~ out a cigarette⟩ ⟨~*ed* under the wheels of a truck⟩ **2 :** to press or cause to press closely **:** embrace strongly **:** HUG, SQUEEZE ⟨~*ed* her child to her breast⟩ **3 :** to reduce to particles by pounding or grinding **:** COMMINUTE, BRAY ⟨~ rock⟩ **4 a :** to suppress or overwhelm as if by pressure or weight ⟨truth, ~*ed* to earth, shall rise again —W.C.Bryant⟩ **b :** to oppress or burden grievously ⟨a ~*ing* burden of debt⟩ **c :** to subdue completely **:** EXTINGUISH, STIFLE ⟨the rebellion was ~*ed*⟩ ⟨poverty ~*ed* his spirit⟩ ⟨a ~*ing* retort⟩ **5 :** CROWD, PUSH ⟨~*ed* into the elevator⟩ **6** *archaic* **:** to drink up **:** finish off ⟨come and ~ a cup of wine —Shak.⟩ **7 a :** to subject (paper in process) to greater than usual roller pressure accidentally or deliberately ⟨the mottled appearance of a ~*ed* finish⟩ **b :** to flatten out the grain of (as leather) by ironing or pressing **8** *also* **crush-dress** \ˈ=ˌ=\ **:** to form or dress (an abrasive wheel) by forcing to revolve against a hardened steel roll **~** *vi* **1** *obs* **:** CRASH **2 :** to become crushed ⟨an eggshell ~*es* easily⟩ **3 :** to advance with or as if with crushing ⟨several men ~*ed* ruthlessly toward the door⟩

syn QUELL, EXTINGUISH, SUPPRESS, QUENCH, QUASH: CRUSH indicates the utter destruction of effectiveness by heavy ruthless pressure and force smashing resistance and strangling growth ⟨the sternest of those iron proconsuls who were employed by the House of Austria to *crush* the lingering public spirit of Austria —T.B.Macaulay⟩ ⟨to *crush* the individual by its demand for unwavering obedience, total loyalty, and absolute uniformity —Oscar Handlin⟩ QUELL now indicates overwhelming completely and reducing to inactivity or passivity ⟨the nation obeyed the call, rallied round the sovereign, and enabled him to *quell* the disaffected minority —T.B. Macaulay⟩ ⟨police *quelling* the disturbance⟩ ⟨peace depends on the existence of organized power to *quell* transgressors of the peace —Bruce Bliven b.1889⟩ EXTINGUISH suggests a total ending as sudden, thorough, and decisive as putting out a fire with water ⟨lives that were to be *extinguished* in Hitler's gas chambers —Isaac Deutscher⟩ ⟨the Black Death itself had *extinguished* many painfully acquired patrimonies —Roy Lewis & Angus Maude⟩ ⟨we must not let such embers of freedom as existed in Eastern Europe and the Balkans be *extinguished* in the hour of liberation —Vera M. Dean⟩ SUPPRESS may suggest rendering ineffective or nonexistent by the power of governmental, legal or legalistic, or social pressure ⟨to provide for calling forth the militia to execute the laws of the Union, *suppress* insurrections, and repel invasions —*U. S. Constitution*⟩ ⟨President Lincoln authorized searches and arrests without warrants, caused newspapers to be *suppressed*, declared martial law even in regions where the regular courts were open —F.A.Ogg & P.O.Ray⟩ ⟨*suppressing* gambling and prostitution⟩ QUENCH suggests a checking of force, impetus, effectiveness, or ardor by or as if by drenching, dampening, cooling, or slaking ⟨his misfortunes never *quenched* his sprightly spirit —R.M.Lovett⟩ ⟨the rising of the Speaker of the House *quenches* all voices and decides all quarrels —J.P. Martin⟩ ⟨nothing could be farther from me than a desire to *quench* the imagination, on the contrary I would preserve it —George Santayana⟩ QUASH indicates summary and decisive extinction or subduing ⟨the poverty-stricken Hitler, whom the death of his mother deprived of a home and whose hope to study architecture had been *quashed* —G.N.Shuster⟩ ⟨he foresaw that the dreadful woman . . . would *quash* his last chance of life —Charles Dickens⟩

²**crush** \"\ *n* -ES **1** *obs* **:** clashing noise **:** CRASH **2 :** the act of crushing **:** violent compression **:** DESTRUCTION, RUIN ⟨the ~ of worlds —Joseph Addison⟩ **3 :** the amount of material crushed or prepared as if crushed (as for further treatment in a manufacturing process); *specif* **:** the quantity of cottonseed crushed for the extraction of oil in a given period **4** *obs* **:** BRUISE **5 a :** a violent crowding (as of people or animals)

: a crowd that produces uncomfortable pressure ⟨a ~ in the subway⟩ **b** : a large reception or party **6** : an intense and usu. passing attachment or infatuation ⟨have a ~ on someone⟩ ⟨her schoolgirl ~*es*⟩; *also* : the object of one's attachment **7** : a fenced passage narrow at one end that is used in Australia esp. in handling cattle (as for branding or vaccination) **syn** see CROWD

crush·able \-shəbəl\ *adj* : that can be crushed; *esp* : that can be crushed without harm ⟨a ~ dress material⟩

crush breccia *n* : a breccia of cataclastic texture formed by mechanical crushing in earth-crust movements

crush conglomerate *n* : an altered crush breccia whose fragments have been rounded by attrition

crushed *past of* CRUSH

crushed leather *n* : leather that has had its grain pattern accentuated by boarding, plating, or other process

crushed levant *or* **crushed morocco** *n* : a smooth-surfaced strong flexible leather obtained by crushing a coarse-grained goatskin

crushed steel *n* : an abrasive made by suddenly cooling steel and then reducing it to powder

crushed strawberry *n* : a deep to strong yellowish pink

crush·er \-shə(r)\ *n* -s **1** : one that crushes: as **a** : a machine for crushing rock, oilseeds, grapes, or other material **b** : a worker tending a crushing machine **2 a** : a crushing blow : KNOCKOUT **b** : a conclusive or overwhelming fact, realization, or retort

crushes *pres 3d sing of* CRUSH, *pl of* CRUSH

crush hat *n* : a hat that may be crushed, bent, or folded without injury (as a soft felt hat); *specif* : OPERA HAT

crushing *adj* [fr. pres. part. of *crush*] : OVERWHELMING, DEVASTATING ⟨a ~ retort⟩ : DECISIVE, FINISHING ⟨a ~ blow⟩

crush·ing·ly *adv* : in a crushing manner : OVERWHELMINGLY, WITHERINGLY

crushing strength *n* : the greatest compressive stress that a brittle solid (as stone or concrete) can sustain without fracture

crush-out \ˈ=,=\ *n* [fr. *crush out*, v.] *slang* : a prison break

crush-room \ˈ=,=\ *n, chiefly Brit* : the foyer of a theater or opera house

crush syndrome *n* : the physical responses to severe crushing injury of muscle tissue involving esp. shock and partial or complete renal failure; *also* : the renal failure associated with such responses

crush zone *also* **crush plane** *n, geol* : the zone of crushing along a fault characterized by the presence of fault breccia, gouge, mylonite

cru·sie \ˈkrüzē, -ēzē\ *n* -s [modif. of MF *creuset*, alter. of *croiseul*, fr. OF *crosel, cruisel*] *Scot* : a rude iron lamp or candlestick

cru·si·ly *or* **cru·sil·ly** \ˈkrüsəlē, -üzə-\ *adj* [MF *crusillié, croisillé*, fr. *croisille*, dim. of *crois* cross, fr. L *cruc-, crux* — more at RIDGE] *heraldry* : sprinkled with cross-crosslets

cru·soe \ˈkrü(,)sō *sometimes* -)zō\ *n* -s *usu cap* [after Robinson *Crusoe*, shipwrecked hero of the novel *Robinson Crusoe* (1719) by Daniel Defoe †1731 Eng. journalist & novelist] : a solitary castaway : one that lives or survives by his own unaided effort and ingenuity — called also *Robinson Crusoe* — **cru·so·ni·an** \(ˈ)krüˈsōnēən, -ˈzō\ *adj, usu cap*

¹crust \ˈkrəst\ *n* -s [ME *crouste, cruste*, fr. MF & L; MF *croste, crouste*, fr. L *crusta* shell, crust, inlaid work; akin to OE *hrūse* earth, ground, OHG *hrosa, hroso* ice, crust, ON *hrjōsa* to shudder, Gk *kryos, krymos* icy cold, frost, *krystallos* ice, crystal, Latvian *kruvesis* frozen mud, L *cruor* blood — more at RAW] **1 a** : the hardened exterior or surface part of bread — opposed to *crumb* **b** : a piece of this or of any bread grown dry or hard : a remnant of food : a bare living ⟨what does he do to earn his ~⟩ **2** : the pastry portion of a pie **3** : a hard or brittle external coat or covering of something : a hard exterior surface : outer shell : INCRUSTATION: as **a** : the hard surface layer formed on many soils esp. when dry or on snow, mud, or lava **b** : the outer part of the earth composed essentially of crystalline rocks and varying in thickness from place to place but prob. nowhere more than a few score miles thick as distinguished from the underlying zones composed of denser but less rigid matter **c** : the horny outer wall of a hoof (as of the horse) **d** : a deposit built up on the interior surfaces of a wine bottle during a long period of aging **e** (1) : a wound covering composed primarily of serum and blood dried into a hardened mass — called also *scab* (2) : an encrusting deposit of serum, cellular debris, and bacteria present over or about lesions of certain skin diseases (as impetigo or eczema) **4 a** : a defensive simulation or covering or hardness in behavior ⟨a ~ of indifference⟩ **b** *slang* : aggressiveness obtuse to the feelings of others : NERVE ⟨he had the immortal ~ to ask me for a loan⟩ **5** *archaic* : a crusty or surly person **6** : the state of rough-tanned hides or skins before they are dyed; *also* : a skin in this state

²crust \"\ *vb* -ED/-ING/-S [ME *crousten*, fr. MF *crouster, croster*, fr. *crouste, croste*] *vi* : to form a crust : become encrusted ⟨~*ing* had begun over the wound⟩ ⟨lava ~*s* as it cools⟩ ~ *vt* : to form a crust on : cover (a surface) with incrustation ⟨ice ~*ed* the pond⟩

¹crus·ta \ˈkrəstə\ *n, pl* **crus·tae** \-,stē, -tī\ [L, shell, crust, inlaid work] **1** : something prepared (as an engraved gem or a plate embossed in low relief) for inlaying or applying (as to a vase) **2** *anat* : the lower or ventral of the two parts into which the substantia nigra divides the cerebral peduncles

²crusta \"\ *n* -s [irreg. fr. ¹*crust*] : a cocktail containing an alcoholic liquor, flavored variously with bitters, curaçao, and lemon juice, and served in a glass lined with lemon or orange peel and frosted with powdered sugar ⟨rum ~⟩ ⟨gin ~⟩

crus·ta·cea \,krəˈstāsh(ē)ə\ *n pl* [NL, fr. neut. pl. of *crustaceus* crustaceous] **1** *cap* : a large class of Arthropoda comprising the majority of the marine or freshwater arthropods (as lobsters, shrimps, crabs, water fleas, and barnacles) and some terrestrial forms (as the wood lice) all having a body that is divided into segments of head, thorax, and abdomen of which the first two often consolidate into a cephalothorax and that is enclosed in a chitinous integument often hardened with calcareous matter into a firm exoskeleton, having a pair of appendages which are variously differentiated into mouthparts, walking legs, and swimmerets each associated with each segment, and having two pairs of antennae — compare BRANCHIOPODA, CIRRIPEDIA, COPEPODA, MALACOSTRACA, TRILOBITA **2** : members of the class Crustacea : CRUSTACEANS

¹crus·ta·cean \,krəˈstāshən\ *also* **crus·ta·ceal** \-sh(ē)əl\ *adj* [NL *Crustacea* + E *-an* or *-al*] : belonging or relating to the Crustacea : CRUSTACEOUS

²crustacean \"\ *n* -s : an animal of the class Crustacea

crus·ta·ce·ol·o·gy \,krə,stāshēˈäləjē\ *n* -ES [ISV *crustaceo-* (fr. NL *Crustacea*) + *-logy*] : a branch of zoology that treats of crustaceans

crus·ta·ceous \,krəˈstāshəs\ *adj* [NL *crustaceus*, fr. L *crusta* shell, crust + *-aceus* -aceous — more at CRUST] **1** : of the nature of, having, or suggesting a crust or shell **2** : ²CRABBY 1, CRUSTY 1a(2) **3** : belonging to the Crustacea : CRUSTACEAN **4** *bot* **a** : having a brittle crust **b** *of a lichen* : having a crusty thallus adhering inseparably to rocks, bark, soil

crust·al \ˈkrəst°l\ *adj* [L *crusta* shell, crust + E *-al*] : relating to a crust esp. of the earth or the moon

crus·ta·tion \,krəˈstāshən\ *n* -s [L *crustatus* (past part. of *crustare* to cover with a shell, fr. *crusta* shell) + E *-ion*] **1** : the act or process of forming a crust ⟨soil ~⟩ **2** : a thin coating or layer : DEPOSIT

crust·ed \ˈkrəstəd\ *adj* [ME, fr. *cruste* crust + *-ed*] **1** : covered with a crust : hardened on the surface (as by freezing or congealing) **2** : having an adhering deposit or layer ⟨~ with salt⟩ : having the accretion of age ⟨~ port⟩ ⟨a ~ conservative⟩

crust fold *n, geol* : a fold of large dimensions perhaps involving much minor folding and faulting such as would produce an entire mountain chain or an oceanic deep

crus·tif·ic \(ˈ)krəˈstifik\ *adj* : forming a crust

crus·ti·fi·ca·tion \,krəstəfəˈkāshən\ *n* -s : INCRUSTATION; *specif* : a mineral deposit formed in successive layers or crust by crust usu. in a cavity or fissure

crus·ti·fied \ˈkrəstə,fīd\ *adj* : formed by or filled with successively deposited layers of minerals

crust·i·ly \-tᵊlē, -li\ *adv* : in a crusty or surly manner

crust·i·ness \ˈkrəstēnəs, -tin-\ *n* -ES : SURLINESS, IRRITABILITY

crusting *pres part of* CRUST

crust·less \-s(t)ləs\ *adj* : being without a crust

crus·tose \ˈkrə,stōs\ *adj* [L *crustosus* crusted, fr. *crusta* crust + *-osus* -ose — more at CRUST] : forming a thin brittle crust; *specif, of a lichen* : having a thin thallus adhering closely to the substratum of rock, bark, or soil

crust roan *n* : a sheepskin tanned with sumac and dried but not dyed or grained

crusts *pl of* CRUST, *pres 3d sing of* CRUST

crusty \ˈkrəstē, -ti\ *adj* -ER/-EST [ME, fr. *cruste* crust + *-y*] **1 a** (1) : having a crust (2) : having or forming a crisp dry outer layer **b** *of wine* : CRUSTED : old and mellow ⟨a flagon ~ —W.M.Thackeray⟩ **2** : genuinely or apparently abrupt, surly, and uncivil in address or disposition and often crude in appearance ⟨a ~ old fellow, as close as a vise —Nathaniel Hawthorne⟩ **3** : FILTHY, VILE ⟨~ jokes⟩ **syn** see BLUFF

crut \ˈkrət\ *n* -s [by alter.] *substand* : ¹CRUD 2,3

¹crutch \ˈkrəch\ *n* -ES [ME *crucche*, fr. OE *crycc*; akin to OS *krukka* crutch, OHG *krucka*, Norw dial. *krykkja* crutch, OHG *kriochan* to creep, OIr *gruc* wrinkle, OE *cradol* cradle — more at CRADLE] **1 a** : a support to aid the disabled in walking made usu. of a split staff long enough to reach to the armpit and fitted at the top with a curved crosspiece and another crosspiece at hand level **b** : any prop, support, or assisting device **2 a** : the raised part at either end of a saddle **b** (1) : the part of a saddletree that supports the pommel (2) : a forked leg rest constituting the pommel of a sidesaddle **3** : the crotch of a human being or of an animal (as a sheep) **4** : something resembling a crutch in shape or use: as **a** : a support made by joining inclined timbers near the top **b** : the depending forked rod by which the pendulum of a clock is moved **c** (1) : a breasthook at the stern of a ship (2) : a forked or 2-legged support for a fore-and-aft boom when its sail is stowed (3) : a forked stanchion to support any spar or rail when not in use **d** *chiefly Brit* : ROWLOCK **e** : a bar with a crosspiece at the end used for stirring (as formerly in making soap)

crutches 1

²crutch \"\ *vb* -ED/-ING/-ES *vt* **1** : to support on or as if on crutches : prop up **2** : to stir or mix with or as if with a crutch; *specif* : to mix (soap) with other substances in a crutcher **3** : to clip (a sheep or wool from a sheep) so as to remove the urine-stained or daggy locks from around the crutch ~ *vi* : to go on crutches

crutched \ˈkrəcht\ *adj* **1** : supported upon or as if upon a crutch ⟨a ~ invalid⟩ **2** : caught or fixed in or as if in a forked crutch ⟨it is there that we see ourselves ~ between love grown old and indifference —George Meredith⟩ **3** : furnished with a crutch or a handle like a crutch ⟨a ~ umbrella⟩

crutch·er \-chə(r)\ *n* -s : a usu. steam-jacketed mixing device for incorporating fillers and perfume into soap

crutching *n* -s [fr. gerund of ²*crutch* (to clip wool)] : removal of wool from the crutch of a sheep; *also* : the wool crutched

crutch strike *n* : blowfly strike in or about the sheep's crutch

cruth *var of* CRWTH

crut·ter \ˈkrəd·ə(r)\ *n* -s [E dial. *crut* passage in a mine cut across strata of rock + E *-er*] : one that drills and prepares a blasting charge in a coal mine; *also* : one who clears away blasted rock

crux \ˈkrəks *also* -rüks\ *n, pl* **cruxes** \-ksəz\ *also* **cru·ces** \ˈkrü,sēz\ [L, cross, torture — more at RIDGE] **1 a** : a puzzling, confusing, or difficult problem : an unsolved question ⟨a scholarly ~ about the meaning of a line in Shakespeare⟩ **b** : a determinative point at issue : a pivotal or essential point requiring resolution or resolving an outcome ⟨the ~ of the problem⟩ **2** : a main or central feature (as of an argument or plan) ⟨he discarded all but the essential ~*es* of his argument —Carl Van Doren⟩

crux an·sa·ta \-,anˈsād·ə, -sä-\ *n, pl* **cruces ansa·tae** \-ā,tē, -ä,tī\ [NL, lit., cross with a handle] : ANKH

crux ca·pi·ta·ta \-,kapəˈtād·ə, -tä-\ *n, pl* **cruces capita·tae** \-ā,tē, -ä,tī\ [NL, lit., cross having a head] : CRUX IMMISSA

crux com·mis·sa \-kəˈmisə, -ˈkä,m-\ *n, pl* **cruces commis·sae** \-,sē, -,sī\ [NL, lit., connected cross] **1** : a cross of crucifixion in which the upright shaft does not extend higher than the transverse beam — compare CRUX DECUSSATA, CRUX IMMISSA **2** : TAU CROSS 1

crux de·cus·sa·ta \-,dekəˈsād·ə, -äd·ə\ *n, pl* **cruces decussa·tae** \-ā,tē, -ä,tī\ [NL, lit., decussate cross] **1** : a supposed variety of the cross of crucifixion consisting of two intersecting beams set up in the form of an X : a decussate cross — compare CRUX COMMISSA, CRUX IMMISSA **2** : SAINT ANDREW'S CROSS

crux gam·ma·ta \-gəˈmād·ə, -äd·ə\ *n, pl* **cruces gamma·tae** \-ā,tē, -ä,tī\ [NL, lit., gamma cross] : GAMMADION

crux im·mis·sa \-iˈmisə, -ˈi,mə-\ *n, pl* **cruces immis·sae** \-,sē, -,sī\ [NL, lit., cross hanging down] **1** : a cross of crucifixion in which the top of the upright shaft extends above the transverse beam — called also *crux capitata*; compare CRUX COMMISSA, CRUX DECUSSATA **2** : LATIN CROSS 1

crux stel·la·ta \-steˈlād·ə, -äd·ə\ *n, pl* **cruces stella·tae** \-ā,tē, -ä,tī\ [NL, lit., starred cross] : a cross with arms that end in stars

cruzado *var of* CRUSADO

cru·zei·ro \krüˈzā(,)rō, -)rü\ *n* -s [Pg, fr. *cruz* cross + *-eiro* -er — more at CRUSADO] **1** : the basic monetary unit of Brazil — see MONEY table **2** : a coin representing one cruzeiro

crwth *also* **cruth** *or* **crouth** \ˈkrüth\ *n* -s [W — more at CROWD] : an ancient Celtic musical instrument with a shallow body and a varying number of strings that were orig. plucked but later played with a short bow — called also *crowd*

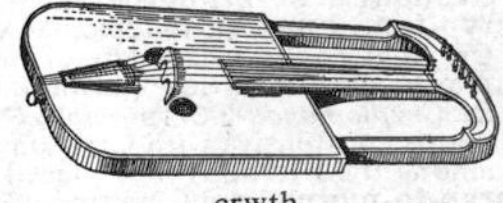

crwth

¹cry \ˈkrī\ *vb* **cried; crying; cries** [ME *crien*, fr. OF *crier*, fr. L *quiritare* to cry out for help (from a citizen), to scream, shriek, fr. *Quirit-, Quiris*, Roman citizen — more at QUIRITARIAN] *vi* **1** : to call loudly : call out (as from pain, anger, or in asking for help or mercy) : SHOUT **2** : to express grief, pain, or distress by sobbing and weeping : WAIL, WEEP, LAMENT ⟨she could not stop ~*ing* and the sobbing had a strangled sound —Carson McCullers⟩ **3 a** *of an animal* : to utter a characteristic sound or call ⟨the blown spume, and the sea gulls ~*ing* —John Masefield⟩ **b** *of a hound* : to yelp in the chase : give tongue **4** *of things* : to require or suggest strongly a given disposition or remedy ⟨the occasion ~*ing* for a new man —Francis Hackett⟩ — often used with *out* ⟨a hundred things which ~ out for planning —Roger Burlingame⟩ ~ *vt* **1** : to ask for earnestly or excitedly : BEG, BESEECH — now used chiefly in the phrase *cry quarter* **2** : to utter loudly : call out : SHOUT ⟨I heard a voice cry "Murder"—Shak.⟩ : declare publicly : PROCLAIM ⟨voice . . . ~*ing* in the wilderness, Prepare ye the way of the Lord —Mk 1:3 (AV)⟩ — often used with *out* **3 a** : to make public proclamation of or about : ADVERTISE, PUBLICIZE ⟨a popular TV performer to ~ their wares —*Atlantic*⟩ **b** *dial* : to publish the banns of marriage of ⟨be *cried* in the kirk on Sunday —D.M.Moir⟩ **4 a** *Scot* : SUMMON **b** *obs* : DEMAND : call for **5** *obs* : PRAISE, EXTOL **syn** see EXCLAIM — **cry halves** : to claim an equal share — **cry harrow** *or* **cry haro** : DENOUNCE ⟨you may *cry haro* upon me for a cynic —G.A.Sala⟩ — **cry havoc** : to sound an alarm : warn of disaster — **cry one's eyes out** : to weep excessively — **cry over spilled milk** : to express vain regrets for what cannot be recovered or undone : complain uselessly — **cry quits** : to call matters even (as in a contest) : propose truce : QUIT : leave off ⟨kept up the applause after the majority had *cried quits* —*N.Y. Times*⟩ — **cry wolf** [so called fr. the fable of the shepherd boy who gave the alarm of "wolf" in fun] : to give alarm without occasion

²cry \"\ *n* -ES [ME, fr. OF *cri*, fr. *crier*, v.] **1 a** : the utterance of the emotion of affliction or distress esp. when inarticulate ⟨the ~ of the children —Elizabeth B. Browning⟩ **b** *obs* : OUTCRY, CLAMOR ⟨confused ~ —Edmund Spenser⟩ **2** : a loud vehement utterance of a sound expressing strong or sudden emotion ⟨*cries* of rage and pain⟩ **3 a** *obs* : a proclamation, summons, or announcement made publicly and usu. orally **b cries** *pl, Scot* : banns of marriage **4** : ENTREATY, APPEAL ⟨deaf to their *cries*⟩ **5** : a loud shout (as expressing excitement or urgency) ⟨there was a ~ of "man overboard"⟩ **6 a** : a word or phrase used as a watchword, a battle cry, or a slogan repeated by a faction or party ⟨"death to the invader" was the ~⟩ **b** : a vendor's habitual words used in announcing his wares **7 a** : common report : RUMOR ⟨the ~ goes that you shall marry her —Shak.⟩ **b** : a general opinion or belief : prevailing fashion ⟨to be in the tradition is now the ~ —F.J.Mather⟩ **8** : the utterance of the general opinion, feeling, or desire : the public voice raised in anger, protest, or approval ⟨repeated droughts brought a ~ for water⟩ **9** : an act of shedding tears : a fit of weeping ⟨a good ~ made her feel better⟩ **10 a** : an inarticulate vocal sound characteristic of an animal ⟨a hawk's ~⟩ **b** : the yelping of hounds in the chase **c** : a pack of hounds **11** : a noise resembling the crying of a man or animal ⟨the ~ in an overloaded loudspeaker⟩ ⟨a brace block's creaking ~ —John Masefield⟩; *specif* : the characteristic noise made by block tin and certain other metals under bending **syn** see FASHION — **a far cry** : a great distance : a long way — **in full cry** : in full pursuit : in full career — **out of all cry** : beyond reckoning : beyond reason : EXCESSIVELY

cry- *or* **cryo-** *also* **kryo-** *comb form* [G *kryo-*, fr. Gk, fr. *kryos* icy cold — more at CRUST] : cold : freezing ⟨*cry*anesthesia⟩ ⟨*cryo*gen⟩ ⟨*kryo*konite⟩

crybaby \ˈ=,==\ *n* : one who cries or complains easily or often

crybaby tree *n* : a Brazilian coral tree (*Erythrina crista-galli*) with small red-orange flowers commonly cultivated esp. under glass in the U.S.

cry back *vi* : to revert to a former type (as after crossbreeding)

cry down *vt* : DISPRAISE, DISPARAGE, DEPRECIATE ⟨I no longer feel obliged to *cry down* Great Britain in order to exalt the U.S. —Hamlin Garland⟩

cryer *var of* CRIER

¹crying *adj* [ME, fr. pres part. of *crien* to cry] **1** : calling for notice : ACUTE ⟨a ~ need⟩ **2** : NOTORIOUS, HEINOUS ⟨a ~ shame⟩ **syn** see PRESSING

²crying *or* **crying out** *n* -s *now chiefly Scot* : CHILDBIRTH, CONFINEMENT

crying bird *n* : LIMPKIN

crying hare *n* : PIKA

crym- *or* **crymo-** *comb form* [NL, fr. Gk *krym-, krymo-*, fr. *krymos* icy cold — more at CRUST] : cold : frost ⟨*crym*odynia⟩ ⟨*crymo*therapy⟩

cry·mo·therapy \ˌkrīmō+\ *or* **cryo·therapy** \ˌkrīō+\ *n* [ISV *crym-* or *cry-* + *therapy*; prob. orig. formed as F *crymothérapie*] : therapeutic use of cold to reduce sensitivity to pain, to check shock or hemorrhage, or to control psychopathic excitement — compare REFRIGERATION

cry·oc·o·nite \krīˈäkə,nīt\ *n* -s [ISV *cry-* + *con-* (fr. Gk *konis* dust) + *-ite*; orig. formed as Sw *krykonit* — more at NIT] : dust that is found on the surface of a glacier (as the Greenland ice cap) esp. on the bottom of small depressions and is formed as a result of differential melting of the ice

cry off *vt* : to call off (as a bargain) ~ *vi, chiefly Brit* : to excuse oneself (as from a promise or agreement) : beg off : obtain release (as from punishment)

cry·o·gen \ˈkrīəjən, -,jen\ *n* -s [*cry-* + *-gen*] : a substance for obtaining low temperatures : REFRIGERANT : freezing mixture

cry·o·gen·ic \ˌkrīōˈjenik\ *adj* [*cry-* + *-genic*] : of or relating to the production of very low temperatures

cry·o·gen·ics \ˌ==ˈ=niks\ *n pl but usu sing in constr* : the branch of physics that relates to the production and effects of very low temperatures — formerly called *cryogeny*

cryo·globulin \ˌkrīō+\ *n* [*cry-* + *globulin*] : any of several proteins similar to gamma globulins (as in molecular weight) that precipitate usu. in the cold from blood serum esp. in pathological conditions (as multiple myeloma) and that redissolve on warming

cryo·hydrate \ˌkrīō+\ *n* [*cry-* + *hydrate*] : a crystalline solid of constant composition and definite freezing point that is obtained by freezing a saturated solution and contains the same ratio of solute and solvent as were present in the saturated solution — compare EUTECTIC

cryo·hy·dric \ˌkrīōˈhīdrik\ *adj* [*cryohydrate* + *-ic*] : of or relating to a cryohydrate or the temperature at which it freezes

cry·o·lite \ˈkrīə,līt\ *n* -s [ISV *cry-* + *-lite*; orig. formed as G *chryolith*] : a mineral consisting of sodium-aluminum fluoride Na_3AlF_6 found in Greenland usu. in white cleavable masses of waxy luster and used in making soda and aluminum (hardness 2.5, sp. gr., 2.95–3.0)

cry·o·lith·i·o·nite \,krīōˈlithēə,nīt, -ləˈthīə-\ *n* -s [alter. of earlier *kryolithionite*, fr. *kryo-* cry- + *lithionite* (obs. syn. of *lepidolite*), fr. G *lithionit*, fr. obs. NL *lithion* (now *lithia*) + G *-it* -ite] : a mineral composed of a fluoaluminate of sodium and lithium $Na_3Li_3(AlF_6)_2$ found in the Ural mountains

cry·ol·o·gy \krīˈäləjē\ *n* -ES [*cry-* + *-logy*] **1** : the study of snow and ice; *sometimes* : GLACIOLOGY **2** : the science of refrigeration

cryo·magnetic \ˌkrīō+\ *adj* [*cry-* + *magnetic*] : relating to or dependent on the production of very low temperatures by the adiabatic demagnetization of certain salts

cry·om·e·ter \krīˈämәd·ə(r)\ *n* [ISV *cry-* + *-meter*] : an instrument for the measurement of low temperatures

cry·om·e·try \-mə·trē\ *n* -ES [ISV *cry-* + *-metry*] : the measurement of low temperatures

cryo·pedologic \ˌkrīō+\ *adj* : caused by or associated with permanently frozen ground or intensive frost action

cryo·pedology \ˌ==+\ *n* [*cry-* + *pedology* (science of soil)] : the study of frozen ground and intensive frost action

cry·o·phile \ˈkrīō,fīl\ *n* -s [*cry-* + *-phile*] : a cryophilic microorganism

cry·o·phil·ic \ˌkrīōˈfilik\ *adj* [*cry-* + *-phile* + *-ic*] *biol* : preferring low temperatures; *specif, of bacteria* : developing best at temperatures below 10° C

cry·o·phor·ic \ˌkrīōˈfōrik\ *adj* [NL *cryophorus* + E *-ic*] : of or relating to the process of freezing water by its own evaporation

cry·oph·o·rus \krīˈäfərəs\ *n* -ES [NL, fr. *cry-* + *-phorus* -phore] : an instrument that illustrates the freezing of water by its own evaporation

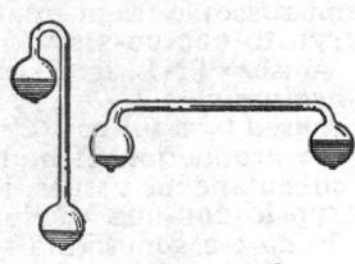

two forms of cryophorus

cry·o·phyl·lite \,krīōˈfi,līt\ *n* -s [*cry-* + Gk *phyllon* leaf + E *-ite* — more at BLADE] : a lithium mica related to zinnwaldite

cryo·planation \ˌkrīō+\ *n* [*cry-* + *planation*] : the modification of a land surface by intensive frost action that generally decreases the steepness of slopes and lowers the tops of hills and mountains

cry·o·scope \ˈkrīə,skōp\ *n* [back-formation fr. *cryoscopy*] : an instrument for determining freezing points (as of milk for detection of added water)

cry·o·scop·ic \ˌkrīəˈskäpik\ *or* **cry·o·scop·i·cal** \-pəkəl\ *adj* [ISV *cryoscopy* + *-ic, -ical*] : of or relating to cryoscopy — **cry·o·scop·i·cal·ly** \-ək(ə)lē\ *adv*

cry·os·co·py \krīˈäskəpē\ *n* -ES [ISV *cry-* + *-scopy*; prob. orig. formed as F *cryoscopie*] : the determination of freezing points produced in liquid by dissolved substances in order to determine molecular weights of solutes and certain properties (as concentration or osmotic pressure) of solutions

cry·o·sel \ˈkrīə,sel\ *n* -s [F, fr. *cry-* + *sel* salt, fr. L *sal* — more at SALT] : CRYOHYDRATE

cry·o·stat \-,stat\ *n* -s [ISV *cry-* + *-stat*] : an apparatus for maintaining a constant low temperature esp. below 0° C (as by means of liquid helium)

cryotherapy *var of* CRYMOTHERAPY

cry·o·tron \ˈkrīə,trän\ *n* -s [*cry-* + *-tron*] : a device performing some of the functions of an electron tube and consisting of a straight wire and another wire wound in a coil around it kept at a temperature near absolute zero, the straight wire being superconducting at the low temperature but becoming nonsuperconducting when a current passes through the coil wire

cry out *vi* : to protest or complain loudly or vigorously ⟨those who *cry out* against federal interference⟩

¹crypt \ˈkript\ *n* -s [L *crypta* vault, cavern, fr. Gk *kryptē*, fr. fem. of *kryptos* hidden, fr. *kryptein* to hide; akin to ON *hreysar* heap of stones, OIr *crāu* stable, hut, Lith *krauti* to pile up] **1** : a vault or other chamber wholly or partly underground; *esp* : a vault under the main floor of a church **2** [NL *crypta*, fr. L] *anat* : PIT, DEPRESSION : a simple gland, glandular cavity, or tube : FOLLICLE

²crypt \'krip(t)\ *n* -s [in sense 1, short for *cryptogram;* in sense 2, short for *cryptography & cryptanalysis*] **1** *slang* : CRYPTOGRAM; *esp* : one favored by puzzlers **2** *slang* : CRYPTOGRAPHY, CRYPTANALYSIS

crypt- *or* **crypto-** *also* **krypt-** *or* **krypto-** *comb form* [NL, fr. Gk *kryptos*] **1** : hidden : covered ⟨*crypto*branch⟩ ⟨*crypto*porticus⟩ **2** : invisible : latent ⟨*crypto*crystalline⟩ ⟨*crypto*mere⟩ **3** : occult ⟨*crypt*esthesia⟩ **4** : secret : private ⟨*crypto*gram⟩ ⟨*crypto*nym⟩ **5** : hidden by dissembling : unavowed ⟨*crypto*fascist⟩ ⟨*crypto*rationalism⟩

crypt·al \'kript³l\ *adj* : of, like, or relating to a crypt

crypt·analysis \¦kript+\ *n* [*crypto*gram + *analysis*] **1** : the solving of cryptograms or cryptographic systems **2** : the theory of solving cryptograms or cryptographic systems : the art of devising methods for this — called also *cryptanalytics*

crypt·analyst \(')kript+\ *n* [fr. *cryptanalysis*, after E *analysis: analyst*] : one who does cryptanalysis esp. as a profession

crypt·analytic \¦kript+\ *adj* [fr. *cryptanalysis*, after E *analysis: analytic*] : of or relating to cryptanalysis ⟨information gained by ~ work⟩

crypt·analytics \¦kript+\ *n pl* : CRYPTANALYSIS 2

crypt·analyze \(')kript+\ *vt* [fr. *cryptanalysis*, after E *analysis: analyze*] : to solve by cryptanalysis

cryp·ta·rithm \'kriptə,rithəm, -thəm\ *n* -s [*crypto*gram + *arithm*etic] : a cryptogram in which letters represent digits and the key is obtained by studying arithmetical operations so written

crypt·ed \'kriptəd\ *adj* : VAULTED

cryp·te·ro·ni·a·ce·ae \,kriptə,rōnē'āsē,ē\ *n pl, cap* [NL, fr. *Crypteronia*, type genus (irreg. fr. *crypt-* + Gk *eros* love) + *-aceae;* akin to Gk *erōs* love — more at EROS] : a family (coextensive with the genus *Crypteronia*) of East Indian trees of uncertain affinities within the order Myrtales that have long finger-shaped clusters of greenish white flowers and capsular fruits

crypt·esthesia *or* **crypt·aesthesia** \¦kript+\ *n* [NL, fr. *crypt-* + *esthesia, aesthesia*] : CLAIRVOYANCE — **crypt·esthetic** \"+\ *adj*

cryp·tic \'kriptik, -tēk\ *also* **cryp·ti·cal** \-tәkəl, -tēk-\ *adj* [LL *crypticus*, fr. Gk *kryptikos*, fr. *kryptos* hidden + *-ikos* -ic, -ical — more at CRYPT] **1** : HIDDEN, SECRET, OCCULT ⟨a ~ language⟩ **2** : ENIGMATIC, MYSTERIOUS ⟨~ prophecies⟩ ⟨a ~ remark⟩ **3** : of the nature of a crypt **4** : serving to conceal — used esp. of the pattern or coloring of an animal **5** *med* : UNRECOGNIZED **6** : BRIEF, CURT, ABBREVIATED ⟨a ~ syllogism⟩ **7** : employing cipher or code **syn** see OBSCURE

cryp·ti·cal·ly \-tәk(ə)lē, -tēk-, -li\ *adv* : in a cryptic way : MYSTERIOUSLY, ENIGMATICALLY

cryptic species *n* : one of two or more morphologically indistinguishable biological groups that are incapable of interbreeding — compare PHYSIOLOGIC RACE

crypt·i·tis \krip'tīdəs\ *n* -ES [NL, fr. *crypta* crypt (gland) + *-itis* — more at CRYPT] : inflammation of a crypt (as an anal crypt)

¹cryp·to \'krip(,)tō\ *n* -s [*crypt-*] : one who adheres or belongs secretly to a party, sect, or other group ⟨fellow travelers and ~s⟩ ⟨the ~ vote⟩

²crypto \"\ *adj* [by shortening] : CRYPTOGRAPHIC ⟨teletype, either ~ or in clear⟩

cryp·to·batholithic \¦krip(,)tō\ *adj* [*crypt-* + *batholithic*] : of or relating to ore deposits formed near a batholith that is not exposed at the surface

cryp·to·biotic \"+\ *adj* [*crypt-* + *-biotic*] : living in concealment — used of insects or other animals that live in secluded situations (as underground or in wood)

cryp·to·blast \'kriptə,blast\ *n* -s [*crypt-* + *-blast*] : a sterile conceptacle (as in plants of the genus *Fucus*)

cryp·to·bran·chia \,kriptə'braŋkēə\ *also* **cryp·to·bran·chi·a·ta** \-,braŋkē'ādə, -ädə\ *n pl, cap* [NL, fr. *crypt-* + *-branchia, -branchiata*] : any of various groups of animals having concealed gills — **cryp·to·bran·chi·ate** \¦kriptə¦braŋkēət, -ē,āt\ *adj*

¹cryp·to·bran·chid \¦kriptə¦braŋkəd\ *adj* [NL *Cryptobranchidae*] : belonging or relating to the Cryptobranchidae

²cryptobranchid \"\ *n* -s : one of the Cryptobranchidae

cryp·to·bran·chi·dae \,kriptə'braŋkə,dē\ *n pl, cap* [NL, fr. *Cryptobranchus*, type genus + *-idae*] : a family of large aquatic salamanders including the American hellbenders and the Asiatic giant salamanders, all distinguished by amphicoelous vertebrae, external fertilization, and the absence of eyelids and of lacrimal and septomaxillary bones and with Hynobiidae forming a suborder of Caudata comprising primitive salamanders with relatively generalized skeletons

cryp·to·bran·chus \-ŋkəs\ *n, cap* [NL, fr. *crypt-* + Gk *branchos* gill; prob. akin to Gk *bronchos* windpipe, throat — more at CRAW] : the type genus of Cryptobranchidae comprising the hellbenders

cryp·to·car·ya \-'ka(a)rēə\ *n, cap* [NL, fr. *crypt-* + *-carya* (fr. Gk *karyon* nut) — more at CAREEN] : a genus of tropical trees (family Lauraceae) having flowers with nine fertile and three sterile stamens and with the ripened ovary embedded in the succulent calyx tube

cryp·to·ceph·a·la \-'sefələ\ *n pl, cap* [NL, fr. *crypt-* + *-cephala*] *in some classifications* : a primary division of Polychaeta in which the peristomium is greatly developed and the prostomium is reduced — compare PHANEROCEPHALA

cryp·to·ce·ra·ta \,kriptōsə'rädə, -ädə\ *n pl, cap* [NL, fr. *crypt-* + *-cerata* (fr. Gk *kerat-*, *keras* horn) — more at HORN] : a division of Heteroptera comprising chiefly aquatic bugs (as the boat bugs) with the antennae shorter than the head and usu. hidden in cavities beneath the eyes — compare GYMNOCERATA — **cryp·toc·er·ous** \(')krip¦täsərəs\ *adj*

cryp·to·clas·tic \¦kriptə¦klastik\ *adj* [ISV *crypt-* + *clastic;* orig. formed as G *kryptoklastisch*] *of a rock* : made up of microscopic fragmental particles

cryp·to·coc·co·sis \,kriptə(,)kä'kōsəs\ *n, pl* **cryptococco·ses** \-ō,sēz\ [NL, fr. *Cryptococcus* (genus name of *Cryptococcus neoformans*) + *-osis*] : a chronic or subacute infectious disease caused by a fungus (*Cryptococcus neoformans*) and marked by the production of nodular lesions or abscesses in the lungs, subcutaneous tissues, joints, and esp. the brain and meninges

cryp·to·coc·cus \,kriptə'käkəs\ *n* [NL, fr. *crypt-* + *-coccus*] **1** *cap* : a genus (the type of the family Cryptococcaceae) of yeastlike budding imperfect fungi that includes a number of saprophytes and a few serious pathogens and is often treated as a synonym of *Torula* or of *Torulopsis* — see CRYPTOCOCCOSIS, EPIZOOTIC LYMPHANGITIS **2** *pl* **cryp·to·coc·ci** \-'käk,kī, -kē, -äk,sī, -äksē\ : any organism of the genus *Cryptococcus; broadly* : TORULA 1a

cryp·to–communist \¦krip(,)tō+\ *n, usu cap 2d C* [*crypt-* + *Communist*] : one who secretly sympathizes with communism or is secretly a member of the Communist party

cryp·to·cor·y·ne \,kriptə'kȯrə,nē\ *n* [NL, fr. *crypt-* + Gk *korynē* club, knobby bud; perh. akin to Gk *kara* head — more at CEREBRAL] **1** *cap* : a genus of aquatic herbs (family Araceae) that have broad leaves and long slender spathes and are often used as aquarium plants **2** -s : any plant of the genus *Cryptocoryne*

cryp·to·crystalline \¦krip(,)tō+\ *adj* [ISV *crypt-* + *crystalline;* orig. formed as G *kryptokrystallinisch*] *of a rock* : indistinctly crystalline : having a structure that, though crystalline, is so fine that no distinct particles are recognizable even under the microscope

cryp·to·di·ra \,kriptə'dīrə\ *n pl, cap* [NL, fr. *crypt-* + *-dira* (fr. Gk *deirē* neck); akin to L *vorare* to devour — more at VORACIOUS] *in some classifications* : a suborder of Thecophora comprising turtles that bend the neck in a vertical plane in order to retract it into the shell — **cryp·to·di·ran** \¦==¦=rən\ *adj or n* — **cryp·to·dire** \'==,dī(ə)r\ *n* -s — **cryp·to·di·rous** \¦==¦dīrəs\ *adj*

cryp·to–fascist \¦krip(,)tō+\ *n* [*crypt-* + *fascist*] : one who has secret fascist sympathies but is not an avowed fascist

crypt of lieberkühn *usu cap L* [trans. of G *Lieberkühnsche krypte*, after Johann N. *Lieberkühn* †1756 Ger. anatomist] : LIEBERKÜHN'S GLAND

crypt of mor·ga·gni \-mȯr'gänyē\ *usu cap M* [trans. of It *critta di Morgagni*, after Giovanni B. *Morgagni* †1771 It. physician] : any of the pouched cavities of the rectal mucosa immediately above the anorectal junction, intervening between vertical folds of the rectal mucosa

cryp·to·gam \'kriptə,gam\ *n* -s [F *cryptogame*, fr. NL *Cryptogamia*] : a plant reproducing by means of spores and not producing flowers or seed (as ferns, mosses, algae, or fungi) — see CRYPTOGAMIA

cryp·to·gam·ia \,kriptə'gamēə, -ām-\ *n, cap* [NL, fr. *crypt-* + *-gamia* (fr. Gk *-gamia* -gamy)] *in former classifications* : a class or subkingdom embracing all cryptogams — compare PHANEROGAMIA

cryp·to·gam·ic \¦kriptə¦gamik\ *also* **cryp·to·gam·i·cal** \-məkəl\ *or* **cryp·tog·a·mous** \(')krip¦tägəməs\ *or* **cryp·to·gam·i·an** \¦kriptə¦gamēən, -ām-\ *adj* [NL *Cryptogamia* + E *-ic*, *-ical* or *-ous* or *-an*] : belonging or relating to the nonflowering plants or to the old group Cryptogamia

cryp·to·genetic \¦kriptō+\ *adj* [ISV *crypt-* + *genetic*] : CRYPTOGENIC

cryp·to·gen·ic \¦kriptə¦jenik\ *adj* [*crypt-* + *-genic*] : of obscure or unknown origin — used chiefly of diseases; opposed to *phanerogenic*

cryp·to·gram \'kriptə,gram, -raa(ə)m\ *n* -s [F *cryptogramme*, fr. *crypt-* + *-gramme* -gram] **1** : a writing in cipher or code **2** : a figure or representation having a hidden significance — **cryp·to·gram·mic** \¦==¦gramik\ *adj*

cryp·to·gram·ma \,kriptə'gramə\ *n, cap* [NL, fr. *crypt-* + Gk *gramma* letter, line of a drawing, fr. *graphein* to scratch, write, draw; prob. fr. the lines of sporangia, sometimes hidden by the reflexed margin of the frond — more at CARVE] : a genus of ferns (family Polypodiaceae) of arctic and north temperate regions having indusia formed by the revolute margins of fertile fronds that are much taller and have narrower divisions than the sterile ones — see ROCK BRAKE

¹cryp·to·graph \'kriptə,graf, -raa(ə)f,-raif,-räf\ *n* -s [back-formation fr. *cryptography*] **1** : CRYPTOGRAM **2** : a device for enciphering and deciphering : a simple cipher machine

²cryptograph \"\ *vt* : to convert (a text) into code or cipher

cryp·tog·ra·pher \krip'tägrəfə(r)\ *n* -s [NL *cryptographia* + E *-er*] : one that practices cryptography: as **a** : a cryptographic clerk **b** : one who devises cryptographic methods or systems **c** : CRYPTANALYST

cryp·to·graph·ic \¦kriptə¦grafik, -fēk\ *adj* : belonging or relating to cryptography ⟨~ methods⟩ : relating to a code or cipher system or to knowledge gained from a decipher or a decode ⟨~ information⟩ : employing cryptography ⟨~ writing⟩ — **cryp·to·graph·i·cal·ly** \-fәk(ə)lē, -fēk-, -li\ *adv*

cryp·tog·ra·phist \krip'tägrəfəst\ *n* -s : one who practices secret writing

cryp·tog·ra·phy \-fē,-fi\ *n* -ES [NL *cryptographia*, fr. *crypt-* + *-graphia* -graphy] **1** : secret writing : cryptic symbolization **2 a** : the art or practice of preparing or reading messages in a form intended to prevent their being read by those not privy to secrets of the form; *also* : the science of devising methods and means for this — compare CIPHER 2, CODE 3 **b** : CRYPTANALYSIS

cryp·to·halite \,kriptō+\ *n* [ISV *crypt-* + *halite;* orig. formed as It *criptoalite*] : a rare mineral consisting of ammonium fluosilicate $(NH_4)_2SiF_6$

cryp·to·lae·mus \,kriptə'lēməs\ *n, cap* [NL, fr. *crypt-* + *-laemus* (fr. Gk *laimos* throat, gullet)] : a genus of small predacious coccinellid beetles including an Australian species (*C. montrouzieri*) that has been widely introduced to control mealybug infestations on citrus

cryp·to·lite \'kriptə,līt\ *n* -s [ISV *crypt-* + *-lite;* orig. formed as G *kryptolith*] : MONAZITE

cryp·tol·o·gist \krip'täləjəst\ *n* -s : CRYPTOGRAPHER b

cryp·tol·o·gy \-jē,-ji\ *n* -ES [NL *cryptologia*, fr. *crypt-* + *-logia* -logy] : the scientific study of cryptography and cryptanalysis

cryp·to·medusoid \¦krip(,)tō+\ *adj* [*crypt-* + *medusoid*] : relating to the final stage in the reduction of the medusa or free-swimming generation of a hydroid to a rudiment bearing the sex cells within the gonophore

cryp·to·melane \,kriptə+\ *n* -s [*crypt-* + *-melane*] : a mineral consisting of an oxide of manganese and potassium, prob. $KMn_8O_{16}.H_2O$, common in manganese ores

cryp·to·mere \'kriptə,mi(ə)r\ *n* -s [*crypt-* + *-mere*] : a gene or factor (as a heterozygous recessive) not detectable by inspection of the individual carrying it but demonstrable by suitable crosses — **cryp·tom·e·rism** \krip'tämə,rizəm\ *n* -s

cryp·to·me·ria \,kriptə'mirēə\ *n* [NL, fr. *crypt-* + Gk *meros* part + NL *-ia;* fr. the concealment of the seeds of the cones within bracts — more at MERIT] **1** *cap* : a monotypic genus of evergreen trees (family Pinaceae) with verticillate branches, subulate leaves, and globose cones — see JAPANESE CEDAR **2** -s : any tree of the genus *Cryptomeria*

cryp·tom·er·ous \(')krip¦tämərəs\ *adj* [*crypt-* + *-merous*] *of a rock* : very finely crystalline

cryp·tom·e·ter \krip'tämәd·ə(r)\ *n* -s [*crypt-* + *-meter*] : an instrument for determining the hiding power of a paint

cryp·to·mitosis \¦krip(,)tō+\ *n, pl* **cryptomitoses** [NL, fr. *crypt-* + *mitosis*] : a type of nuclear division in certain protozoa characterized by formation of a modified achromatic spindle and by absence of differentiated chromosomes

cryp·tom·ne·sia \,krip,täm'nēzhə\ *n* -s [NL, fr. *crypt-* + *-mnesia*] : the appearance in consciousness of memory images which are not recognized as such but which appear as original creations — **cryp·tom·ne·sic** \-ēzik,-ēsik\ *adj*

cryp·tom·o·nad \krip'tämə,nad\ *n* -s [NL, fr. *Cryptomonad-*, *Cryptomonas*] : a flagellate of the order Cryptomonadina

cryp·to·mon·a·da·les \,kriptō,mänə'dā(,)lēz\ *n pl, cap* [NL, fr. *Cryptomonad-*, *Cryptomonas* + *-ales*] : an order of algae that is coextensive with Cryptomonadina and is usu. included among the Pyrrophyta or placed in the class Flagellatae

cryp·to·mo·nad·i·da \,krip(,)tōmə'nadədə\ [NL, fr. *Cryptomonad-*, *Cryptomonas* + *-ida*] *syn of* CRYPTOMONADINA

cryp·to·mo·nad·i·dae \-nadə,dē\ *n pl, cap* [NL, fr. *Cryptomonad-*. *Cryptomonas*, type genus + *-idae*] : a large family (order Cryptomonadina) of chiefly freshwater and holophytic plantlike flagellates with the anterior end truncate and two anterior flagella — see CHILOMONAS

cryp·to·mon·a·di·na \-,mänə'dīnə, -dēnə\ *n pl, cap* [NL, fr. *Cryptomonad-*, *Cryptomonas* + *-ina*] : a small order of plantlike flagellates having one or two flagella and usu. yellow-brown chromatophores — see CRYPTOMONADALES, CRYPTOMONADIDAE

cryp·tom·o·nas \krip'tämənəs, -,nas\ *n, cap* [NL, fr. *crypt-* + *-monas*] : the type genus of Cryptomonadidae comprising small elliptical freshwater protozoans with two chromatophores

cryp·to·mys \'kriptə,mis\ *n, cap* [NL, fr. *crypt-* + *-mys*] : a genus of blind burrowing mole rats of southern Africa

cryp·to·ne·mi·a·les \,kriptə,nēmē'ā(,)lēz\ *n pl, cap* [NL, fr. *crypt-* + Gk *nēma* thread + NL *-i-* + *-ales* — more at NEEDLE] : an order of red algae (class Rhodophyceae) having the auxiliary cells borne on filaments that differ markedly from the vegetative filaments (as in lacking chromatophores and in being filled with dense protoplasm)

cryp·to·neu·rous \¦kriptō¦n(y)ürəs\ *adj* [NL *cryptoneurus*, fr. *crypt-* + *-neurus* (fr. Gk *neuron* nerve) — more at NERVE] : having no distinct or recognizable nervous system

cryp·to·nym \'kriptə,nim\ *n* -s [prob. fr. F *cryptonyme*, fr. *crypt-* + *-onyme* -onym] : a secret name — **cryp·ton·y·mous** \(')krip¦tänəməs\ *adj*

cryp·to·perthite \¦kriptō+\ *n* -s [ISV *crypt-* + *perthite;* orig. formed as G *kryptoperthit*] : a perthite with lamellae of submicroscopic dimensions, such lamellae being observable by X-ray diffraction or by the electron microscope — **cryp·to·perthitic** \¦==+\ *adj*

cryp·to·phy·ce·ae \,kriptə'fīsē,ē, -fis-\ *n pl, cap* [NL, fr. *crypt-* + *-phyceae*] : a class of motile usu. brownish green algae that are sometimes included among the Pyrrophyta and that have asymmetrical compressed cells enclosed in a firm periplast and with the two slightly unequal flagella inserted laterally or terminally

cryp·to·phyte \'kriptə,fīt\ *n* -s [prob. fr. F, fr. *crypt-* + *-phyte*] : a plant that produces its buds underwater or underground on corms, bulbs, or rhizomes — **cryp·to·phyt·ic** \¦==¦fid·ik\ *adj*

cryp·to·pine \'kriptə,pēn, -,pən\ *n* -s [*crypt-* + *opium* + *-ine*] : a colorless crystalline alkaloid $C_{21}H_{23}NO_5$ obtained from opium and plants of the genus *Corydalis*

cryp·to·por·ti·cus \,kriptō'pȯrd·əkəs\ *n, pl* **cryptoporticus** [L, fr. *crypt-* + *porticus* portico — more at PORCH] : a porch, gallery, or ambulatory in ancient Roman architecture that was wholly or partly concealed, had few openings, and served for private communication

cryp·to·pyrrole \¦kriptō+\ *n* -s [ISV *crypt-* + *pyrrole*] : a liquid homologue $C_8H_{13}N$ of pyrrole formed during reduction of hemin or phylloporphyrin with hydriodic acid; 2, 4-dimethyl-3-ethyl-pyrrole

¹cryp·tor·chid \krip'tȯrkəd\ *also* **cryp·tor·chis** \-kəs\ *n, pl* **cryptorchids** *also* **cryptorchises** [NL *cryptorchid-*, *cryptorchis*, fr. *crypt-* + *orchid-*, *orchis* testicle, fr. Gk — more at ORCHIS] : one affected with cryptorchidism

²cryptorchid \(')=¦==\ *adj* : exhibiting or affected with cryptorchidism

cryp·tor·chi·dism \krip'tȯrkə,dizəm\ *also* **cryp·tor·chism** \-,kizəm\ *n* -s [NL *cryptorchidismus*, *cryptorchismus*, fr. *crypt-* + *-orchidismus*, *-orchismus* -orchism] : a condition in which one or both testes fail to descend normally

cryp·to·rhyn·chus \,kriptə'riŋkəs\ *n, cap* [NL, fr. *crypt-* + *-rhynchus*] : a large cosmopolitan genus of weevils including numerous pests of economic plants (as the poplar borer)

cryptos *pl of* CRYPTO

cryp·to·si·pho·nia \,kriptō,sī'fōnēə\ *n, cap* [NL, fr. *crypt-* + *siphon-* + *-ia*] : a genus of marine Pacific red algae (order Cryptonemiales) including one that is common on the coast and has a compressed tubular thallus with few branches and many short branchlets disposed along them

cryp·to·ste·gia \,kriptə'stējēə\ *n, cap* [NL, fr. *crypt-* + Gk *stegē* roof + NL *-ia;* fr. the concealment of the corona within the tube of the corolla; akin to Gk *stegein* to cover — more at THATCH] : a genus of chiefly tropical African woody vines (family Asclepiadaceae) that have large polished leaves and funnel-shaped flowers and are important as a source of rubber — see INDIA-RUBBER VINE

cryp·tos·ter·ol \krip'tästə,rōl, -rōl\ *n* -s [ISV *crypt-* + *sterol*] : LANOSTEROL

cryp·to·sto·ma·ta \,kriptə'stōməd·ə\ *n pl, cap* [NL, fr. *crypt-* + *-stomata*] : a group of Paleozoic bryozoa (class Gymnolaemata) in which the true apertures of the zooecia are concealed at the bottom of vestibular tubes — **cryp·to·stome** \'==,stōm\ *adj or n*

cryp·to·termes \¦krip(,)tō+\ *n, cap* [NL, fr. *crypt-* + *Termes*] : a cosmopolitan genus of dry-wood termites that is sometimes considered a subgenus of *Kalotermes* — see POWDER-POST TERMITE

cryp·to·volcanic \¦krip(,)tō+\ *adj* [*crypt-* + *volcanic*] *of a rock structure* : produced by completely concealed volcanic activity — **cryp·to·volcanism** \"+\ *n* — **cryp·to·volcano** \"+\ *n*

cryp·to·xanthin \,kriptō+\ *n* [ISV *crypt-* + *xanthin*] : a red crystalline carotenoid alcohol $C_{40}H_{55}OH$ that occurs in many plants (as yellow Indian corn and papaya), in blood serum, and in some animal products (as butter and egg yolk) and that is a precursor of vitamin A; 3-hydroxy-β-carotene — called also *cryptoxanthol*

cryp·to·zoa \,kriptə'zōə\ *n pl* [NL, fr. *crypt-* + *-zoa*] **1** : the animals that live a cryptobiotic life among the organic debris of a forest floor **2** : structures in Precambrian rocks thought to be the remains of primitive life — compare CRYPTOZOON

cryp·to·zo·ic \¦kriptə¦zōik\ *adj* [*crypt-* + *-zoic*] **1** : CRYPTOBIOTIC **2** *of a geologic eon* : prior to the beginning of the Cambrian period — compare PHANEROZOIC

cryp·to·zo·ite \,kriptə'zō,īt\ *n* -s [*crypt-* + *-zoite* (as in *sporozoite*)] : a malaria parasite that develops in tissue cells from the sporozoite, ultimately giving rise to the forms that invade the blood cells

cryp·to·zo·nia \-ōnēə\ *n pl, cap* [NL, fr. *crypt-* + Gk *zōnē* girdle + NL *-ia* — more at ZONE] *in some classifications* : a division of starfishes having the marginal plates inconspicuous and being nearly equal to the orders Spinulosa and Forcipulata combined — opposed to *Phanerozonia*

cryp·to·zo·on \-ō,än\ *n, cap* [NL, fr. *crypt-* + *-zoon*] : a form genus of Cambrian and Precambrian reef-forming fossils that are usu. considered to be the remains of mats of filamentous calcareous algae

cryp·to·zy·gous \¦kriptə¦zīgəs, (')krip¦täzəgəs\ *adj* [*crypt-* + *-zygous*] : having a wide skull and a narrow face so that the zygomatic arches are concealed when the skull is viewed from above — **cryp·to·zy·gy** \'kriptə,zīgē, krip'täzə|, |jē\ *n* -ES

crypts *pl of* CRYPT

crysal *var of* CHRYSAL

¹crys·tal \'krist³l\ *n* -s [ME *cristal*, fr. OF, fr. L *crystallum*, fr. Gk *krystallos* — more at CRUST] **1** *obs* : clear ice **2** : quartz that is transparent or nearly so and that is either colorless or only slightly tinged; *also* : a piece of this material (as one cut for personal ornament or for use in magic art) — called also *rock crystal;* compare CAIRNGORM, PEBBLE 2; CRYSTAL GAZING **3** : something (as clear water) resembling crystal in transparency and colorlessness **4 a** : a body formed by the solidification under favorable conditions of a chemical element, a compound, or an isomorphous mixture and having a regularly repeating internal arrangement of its atoms; *esp* : such a body that has natural external plane faces as a result of the internal structure **b** : a substance having certain properties of crystals — see LIQUID CRYSTALS **5 a** : glass of superior quality and often with ornamental cutting : FLINT GLASS; *also* : a piece of this material ⟨a fine dinner set of ~⟩ **b** : a colorless transparent diamond **6** : the glass or transparent plastic that covers the dial of a watch or clock **7 a** : a crystalline material used in a sharply tuned electromechanical transducer often as a frequency-determining element : a quartz plate **b** : a class of detector in a radio receiver

²crystal \"\ *adj* [ME *cristal*, fr. *cristal*, n.] **1** : consisting of or resembling crystal : CRYSTALLINE, CLEAR, TRANSPARENT, LUCID ⟨~ streams⟩ ⟨the ~ clearness of his arguments⟩ **2 a** : relating to or using a crystal ⟨a ~ radio receiver⟩ **b** : utilizing a Rochelle salt or other crystal as the basic conversion mechanism — used esp. of a microphone, phonograph pickup, or cutting head

³crystal \"\ *vt* **crystaled** *or* **crystalled; crystaled** *or* **crystalled; crystaling** *or* **crystalling; crystals** : to make into crystal : cover with crystal ⟨the frost that ~*ed* it over⟩

crystal ball *n* **1** : a sphere esp. of quartz crystal traditionally used by fortune-tellers **2** : a means or method of divining or predicting future events ⟨used history as his *crystal ball*⟩ ⟨in spite of the precise technique now available . . . only the *crystal ball* of guesswork is consulted —L.P.Crespi⟩

crystal clock *n* : QUARTZ-CRYSTAL CLOCK

crystal detector *n, radio* : a detector that depends for its operation on the rectifying action of the surface of contact between certain crystals (as of galena) and a metallic electrode

crystal flower *n* : a low No. American herb (*Mitella nuda*) with basal rounded leaves and greenish flowers

crystal gazer *n* : one that practices crystal gazing

crystal gazing *n* **1** : the art or practice of concentrating upon a glass or crystal globe with the aim of inducing a psychical state in which divination can be performed **2** : the attempt to predict future events or developments or to make difficult judgments esp. without adequate data

crystal glass *n* : a clear glass with a high refractive index; *esp* : such glass containing lead

crystal globe *n* : GAZING GLOBE

crystal grating *n* : a diffraction grating for X rays or gamma rays utilizing the natural spacing of a crystal lattice as the grating space

crystal gray *n* : CINDER 5

crystall- *or* **crystallo-** *comb form* [Gk *krystal-*, *krystallo-*, fr. *krystallos* ice, crystal — more at CRUST] : crystal ⟨*crystal*liferous⟩ ⟨*crystallo*luria⟩ ⟨*crystallo*genic⟩

crystal lattice *n* : the arrangement of atoms, molecules, or ions of a crystal in the form of a space lattice

crys·tal·lic \(')kri¦stalik\ *adj* : relating to crystals or crystallization

crys·tal·lif·er·ous \¦kristə¦lif(ə)rəs\ *adj* [ISV *crystall-* + *-i-* + *-ferous;* prob. orig. formed as F *cristallifère*] : producing or bearing crystals

crys·tal·li·form \kriˈstaləˌfȯrm\ *adj* [*crystall-* + *-iform*] **:** having crystalline form
crys·tal·lig·er·ous \ˌkristəˈlijərəs\ *adj* [*crystall-* + *-i-* + *-gerous*] **:** CRYSTALLIFEROUS
crys·tal·lin \ˈkristələn\ *n* -s [G & Sw; G *kristallin*, fr. Sw, fr. *kristall-* crystall- + *-in*] *biochem* **:** either of two globulins in the crystalline lens
crys·tal·line \ˈkristələn, -ˌlīn *sometimes* -ˌlēn, *archaic* kriˈstal-\ *adj* [ME *cristallin*, fr. MF & L; MF *cristallin*, fr. L *crystallinus*, fr. Gk *krystallinos*, fr. *krystallos* ice, crystal + *-inos* -ine — more at CRUST] **1 :** made of crystal **2 :** resembling crystal: as **a :** TRANSPARENT, PURE, PELLUCID ⟨the ~ sky —John Milton⟩ **b :** CLEAR-CUT ⟨~ sharpness of outline —John Buchan⟩ **3 a :** of the nature of or relating to a crystal **:** formed by crystallization **:** having regular arrangement of the atoms in a space lattice — opposed to *amorphous* **b :** having the internal structure though not necessarily the external form of a crystal ⟨granite is only ~, while quartz crystal is perfectly crystallized⟩ **4** *of rock* **:** composed of crystals or fragments of crystals
crystalline cone *n* **:** a transparent conical refractive body that functions as a lens in each ommatidium of the compound eye of many arthropods
crystalline flake *n* **:** graphite in flaky form either in rock matrix or separated from it
crystalline glaze *n* **:** a pottery glaze that on cooling permits the formation of crystals
crystalline heaven *or* **crystalline sphere** *n* **:** either of two transparent spheres imagined in the Ptolemaic system of astronomy to exist between the region of the fixed stars and the primum mobile in order to explain certain observed movements of the heavenly bodies
crystalline lens *n* **:** the lens of the eye in vertebrates
crystalline solution *n* **:** SOLID SOLUTION
crystalline style *or* **crystalline stylet** *n* **:** a long cylindrical or tapered translucent gelatinous rod in the digestive tract of many bivalve mollusks
crystalline veratrine *n* **:** CEVADINE
crys·tal·lin·i·ty \ˌkristəˈlinəd-ē\ *n* -ES [ISV *crystalline* + *-ity*] **:** the quality or state of being crystalline **:** degree of crystallization
crystal liquid *n* **:** LIQUID CRYSTAL
crys·tal·lite \ˈkristəˌlīt\ *n* -s [G *kristallit*, fr. *kristall-* crystall- + *-it* -ite] **1 a :** a minute mineral form like those common in glassy volcanic rocks and some slags usu. not referable to any mineral species but marking the first step in the crystallization process **b :** a single grain in a polycrystalline medium; *also* **:** a crystallographically homogeneous domain within such a grain **2 a :** any part of a plant-cell wall in which the chain molecules of cellulose lie parallel **b :** MICELLE — used esp. of the structural units of fibers (as cellulose) and other high polymers (as rubber) **c :** an oriented or crystalline region (as of high lateral order in natural and synthetic fibers) — **crys·tal·lit·ic** \ˌ⸗⸗ˈlid·ik\ *adj*
crys·tal·liz·able \ˈ⸗⸗ˌlīzəbəl, ˌ⸗⸗ˈ⸗⸗⸗\ *adj* **:** capable of forming or of being formed into crystals
crys·tal·li·za·tion \ˌkristələˈzāshən, -ˌlīz-\ *n* -s **1 :** the process of crystallizing **2 :** a form of body resulting from crystallizing — compare CRYSTAL SYSTEM
crys·tal·lize *also* **crys·tal·ize** \ˈkristəˌlīz\ *vb* -ED/-ING/-S *see -ize in Explan Notes* [*crystall-* or ¹*crystal* + *-ize*] *vt* **1 :** to cause to form crystals or assume crystalline form; *esp* **:** to cause to assume perfect or large crystals **2 :** to cause to take a fixed and definite form ⟨tried to ~ his thoughts⟩ **3 :** to coat with crystals esp. of sugar ⟨~ cherries⟩ ~ *vi* **1 :** to become converted into crystals **:** assume crystalline form **:** solidify by crystallizing **:** deposit crystals — often used with *out* **2 :** to become fixed and definite in form — often used with *out* ⟨opinion has *crystallized* out into two sharply opposed viewpoints —S.F.Mason⟩
crystallized *adj* **1 :** formed into crystals **2 :** coated with crystals esp. of sugar **:** CANDIED **3 :** definite in form ⟨failure to distinguish between ~ and uncrystallized opinion —*Psychological Abstracts*⟩
crys·tal·liz·er \-zə(r)\ *n* -s **:** one that crystallizes: as **a :** an apparatus for carrying out crystallization (as by cooling, evaporation, or the use of a vacuum) **b :** a reagent that causes or promotes crystallization
crystallo- see CRYSTALL-
crys·tal·lo·blast \ˈkristəlōˌblast, kriˈstalə,-\ *n* -s [back-formation fr. *crystalloblastic*] **:** one of the components of a crystalloblastic rock or rock mass
crys·tal·lo·blas·tic \ˌkristəlōˈblastik\ *adj* [ISV *crystall-* + *-blastic*; orig. formed as G *kristalloblastisch*] **1** *of a rock* **:** of or relating to any crystalline texture resulting from metamorphism **2 :** denoting a structure produced by crystals growing in a solid solution
crys·tal·lo·genesis \ˌkristəlō+\ *n* [NL, fr. *crystall-* + L *genesis*] **:** the production or formation of crystals
crys·tal·lo·gen·ic \ˌ⸗⸗⸗ˈjenik\ *or* **crys·tal·lo·gen·i·cal** \-jenəkəl\ *also* **crys·tal·lo·ge·net·ic** \-jəˈned·ik\ *adj* [ISV *crystall-* + *-genic*, *-genical* (fr. *-genic* + *-al*) or *-genetic*] **:** crystal-producing ⟨~ attraction⟩
crys·tal·log·e·ny \ˌkristəˈläjənē\ *n* -ES [ISV *crystall-* + *-geny*] **:** the formation of crystals as a branch of crystallography
crys·tal·lo·gram \ˈkristəlōˌgram, kriˈstalə,-\ *n* -s [*crystall-* + *-gram*] **:** a photographic record of crystal structure obtained through the use of X rays
crys·tal·log·ra·pher \ˌkristəˈlägrəfə(r)\ *n* -s [*crystallography* + *-er*] **:** a specialist in crystallography
crys·tal·lo·graph·ic \ˌkristəlōˈgrafik\ *or* **crys·tal·lo·graph·i·cal** \-fəkəl\ *adj* **:** relating to or dealing with crystallography or crystals ⟨~ textures⟩ ⟨~ axes⟩ — **crys·tal·lo·graph·i·cal·ly** \-fək(ə)lē\ *adv*
crys·tal·log·ra·phy \ˌkristəˈlägrəfē\ *n* -ES [F or NL; F *cristallographie*, fr. NL *crystallographia*, fr. *crystall-* + *-graphia* -graphy] **:** the science of crystallization dealing with the system of forms among crystals, their structure, and their forms of aggregation
¹**crys·tal·loid** \ˈkristəˌlȯid\ *adj* [ISV *crystall-* + *-oid*; prob. orig. formed as F *cristalloïde*] **:** having some or all of the properties of crystal
²**crystalloid** \"\ *n* -s [ISV, fr. ¹*crystalloid*] **1 :** a substance (as a salt or sugar) that forms a true solution, in solution diffuses readily through a membrane, and is capable of being crystallized — compare COLLOID **2 :** one of the minute particles resembling crystals and consisting of protein that are found in certain cells esp. of oily seeds (as the Brazil nut and castor bean) — called also *protein crystal*
crys·tal·loi·dal \ˌkristəˈlȯidᵊl\ *adj* **:** having the properties of or relating to a crystalloid
crys·tal·lo·luminescence \ˌkristə(ˌ)lō+\ *n* [*crystall-* + *luminescence*] **:** the emission of light by certain substances while crystallizing (as by common salt while precipitating from a hot solution of alcohol) — **crys·tal·lo·luminescent** \"+\ *adj*
crys·tal·lo·magnetic \"+\ *adj* [*crystall-* + *magnetic*] **:** relating to the magnetic properties of crystals and crystal structure
crys·tal·lo·man·cy \ˈkristəlōˌman(t)sē\ *n* -ES [*crystall-* + *-mancy*] **:** divination by crystal gazing **:** CRYSTAL GAZING
crys·tal·lu·ria \ˌkristəˈl(y)u̇rēə\ *n* -s [NL, fr. *crystall-* + *-uria*] **:** the presence of crystals in the urine indicating renal irritation (as that caused by sulfa drugs)
crystal-palace blue *n* **:** a deep blue that is greener and duller than Yale blue and greener and paler than royal (sense 8b)
crystal-palace green *n* **:** STONE GRAY
crystal pickup *n* **:** a phonograph pickup in which stylus movements generate a voltage by bending or twisting a Rochelle salt or other crystal
crystals *pl of* CRYSTAL, *pres 3d sing of* CRYSTAL
crystal sand *n* **:** very minute crystals that are scattered through the tissue of most plants and are of the same nature and origin as raphides but not needle-shaped
crystal set *n* **:** a radio receiver having a crystal detector and no vacuum tubes
crystals of ve·nus \-ˈvēnəs\ *usu cap V* **:** crystallized copper acetate
crystal spectrometer *n* **:** an X-ray spectrometer employing a crystal grating
crystal system *n* **:** any of the six or sometimes seven main

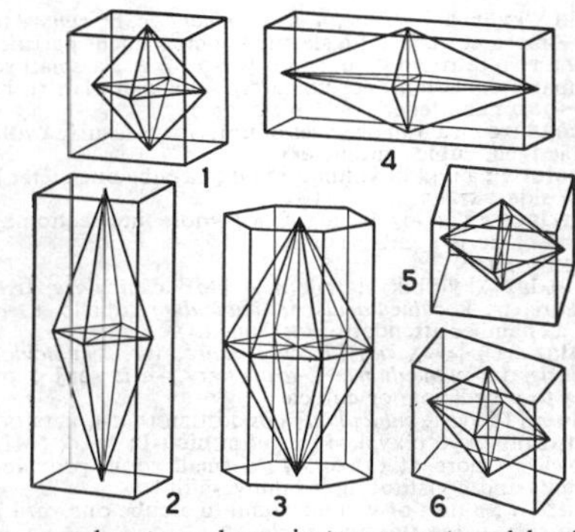

crystal systems shown in transparent models of forms analogous to the cube and the octahedron of the isometric system: *1* isometric, *2* tetragonal, *3* hexagonal, *4* orthorhombic, *5* monoclinic, *6* triclinic

groups into which crystals are commonly classified according to the relative lengths and inclinations of their axes or according to their respective symmetries — see HEXAGONAL SYSTEM, ISOMETRIC SYSTEM, MONOCLINIC SYSTEM, ORTHORHOMBIC SYSTEM, RHOMBOHEDRAL SYSTEM, TETRAGONAL SYSTEM, TRICLINIC SYSTEM, TRIGONAL SYSTEM
crystal tea *n* **1 :** a No. American cinquefoil (*Potentilla tridentata*) with trifoliolate 3-toothed leaflets and small white cymose flowers **2 :** LABRADOR TEA a
crystal vinegar *n* **:** vinegar that has been decolorized by distillation or filtration
crystal violet *n*, *often cap C&V* **:** a basic triphenylmethane dye consisting essentially of hexamethyl-pararosaniline chloride and used similarly to methyl violet and in medicine as an anthelmintic and bactericide and in the treatment of burns — called also *gentian violet*, *methylrosaniline chloride*; see DYE table I (under *Basic Violet 3* and *Solvent Violet 9*)
crystalwort \ˈ⸗⸗ˌ⸗\ *n* **1 :** a plant of the order Ricciales (esp. of the genus *Riccia*) **2 :** a hepatica (*Hepatica americana*) having reniform leaves
crys·to·le·um \kriˈstōlēəm\ *n* -s [*crystal* + L *oleum* oil — more at OIL] **:** an obsolete process in which a photograph was transferred to glass, the paper backing removed, and the image layer colored by the application of colors to the back
crys·to·sphene \ˈkristəˌsfēn\ *n* -s [*cryst-* (irreg. fr. Gk *krystallos* ice) + *-o-* + Gk *sphēn* wedge — more at CRYSTAL, SPOON] **:** a buried sheet of ice under the tundra of northern America formed by the freezing of spring water which rises from the rock beneath alluvial deposits or under swamps and spreads laterally at the zone of freezing
cry up *vt* **:** to enhance the value or reputation of by public praise **:** EXTOL ⟨will hear him generally *cried up* as the most attentive and best of brothers —Jane Austen⟩
cs *abbr* **1** case **2** census **3** centistoke **4** consciousness **5** consul
CS *abbr* **1** capital stock **2** chief of staff **3** civil service **4** [It *colla sinistra*] with the left hand **5** common serjeant **6** conditioned stimulus **7** cooperative society **8** court of sessions **9** current series
Cs *symbol* cesium
c's *or* **cs** *pl of* C
csardas *var of* CZARDAS
csc *abbr* cosecant
csch *abbr* [F *cosécant hyperbolique*] hyperbolic cosecant
c-scroll \ˈ⸗ˌ⸗\ *n*, *cap C* **:** a carved shaped ornamental motive in the form of the letter C that is used decoratively esp. on furniture
CSF *abbr* cerebrospinal fluid
csg *abbr* casing
c-shaped \ˈ⸗ˌ⸗\ *adj*, *cap C* **:** having the shape of a capital C
c sharp \ˈ⸗ˈ⸗\ *n*, *usu cap C* **1 :** the keynote of C-sharp major or C-sharp minor **2 :** the tone a half step above C
c-sharp major \ˈ⸗ˌ⸗ˈ⸗⸗\ *n*, *usu cap C* **:** the major musical key having a signature of seven sharps
c-sharp minor \ˈ⸗ˌ⸗ˈ⸗⸗\ *n*, *usu cap C* **:** the minor musical key having a signature of four sharps
csk *abbr* **1** cask **2** countersink
c spring *n*, *cap C* **:** a leaf spring the ends of which are formed in a large curve roughly resembling the letter C
CSR *abbr* certified shorthand reporter; chartered stenographic reporter
CST *abbr* central standard time
c-stage resin *n*, *usu cap C* **:** RESITE
cstg *abbr* casting
ct *abbr* **1** carat **2** carton **3** caught **4** cent **5** centum **6** circuit **7** count **8** county **9** court **10** current
CT *abbr* **1** cable transfer **2** central time **3** certificated teacher; certified teacher **4** code telegram **5** combat team **6** commercial traveler **7** current transformer
CTA *abbr* [L *cum testamento annexo*] with the will annexed
cten- *or* **cteno-** *comb form* [NL, fr. Gk *kten-*, *kteno-*, fr. *kten-*, *kteis* — more at PECTINATE] **:** comb ⟨*cten*acanthus⟩ ⟨*cteno*phore⟩
cten·acan·thus \ˌtenəˈkan(t)thəs, ˌtēn-\ *n*, *cap* [NL, fr. *cten-* + *-acanthus*] **:** a genus of Upper Devonian and Lower Permian sharks related to *Cladoselache* and known chiefly from its very stout fin spines
cte·nac·o·don \təˈnakəˌdän\ *n*, *cap* [NL, fr. *cten-* + Gk *akē* point + NL *-odon* — more at EDGE] **:** a genus of small primitive mammals (order Multituberculata) from the Upper Jurassic of Europe and No. America
ctene \ˈtēn\ *n* -s [Gk *kten-*, *kteis* comb] **:** COMB 4c
cte·nid·i·al \təˈnidēəl\ *adj* [NL *ctenidium* + E *-al*] **:** relating or belonging to a ctenidium
cte·nid·i·um \-ēəm\ *n*, *pl* **ctenid·ia** \-ēə\ [NL, fr. *cten-* + *-idium*] **1 :** the gill of a mollusk consisting typically of a respiratory structure that resembles a comb or feather, has a main stem with lateral lamellae, and is developed from the inner side of the mantle — distinguished from *ceras* **2 :** a structure consisting of a row of spines resembling the teeth of a comb on the head or thorax, or both, of certain fleas
cten·ii \ˈtenēˌī, ˈtēn-\ *n pl* [NL, fr. Gk *kten-*, *kteis* comb — more at PECTINATE] **:** spinules or teeth on the posterior margin of a ctenoid scale
¹**cten·i·zid** \ˈtenəzəd\ *adj* [NL *Ctenizidae*] **:** of or relating to the family Ctenizidae
²**ctenizid** \"\ *n* -s **:** a spider of the family Ctenizidae
cte·niz·i·dae \təˈnizəˌdē\ *n pl*, *cap* [NL, fr. *Cteniza*, type genus (fr. Gk *ktenizein*, dim. of *kten-*, *kteis* comb) + *-idae* — more at PECTINATE] **:** a family of large burrowing spiders — see TRAP-DOOR SPIDER
cteno·ce·phal·i·des \ˌtenōsəˈfaləˌdēz\ *n*, *cap* [NL, fr. *cten-* + *cephal-* + Gk *-idēs* (patronymic suffix)] **:** a genus of fleas (family Pulicidae) including the dog flea (*C. canis*) and cat flea (*C. felis*)
cteno·ceph·a·lus \-ˈsefələs\ [NL, fr. *cten-* + *-cephalus*] *syn of* CTENOCEPHALIDES — a prior usage invalid as a homonym
cteno·cyst \ˈtenəˌsist\ *n* [*cten-* + *-cyst*] **:** a characteristic sensory or balancing organ of Ctenophora situated at the aboral pole of the body
cteno·dac·tyl·i·dae \ˌtenōˌdakˈtiləˌdē\ *n pl*, *cap* [NL, fr. *Ctenodactylus*, type genus (fr. *cten-* + Gk *daktylos* finger) + *-idae*] **:** a family of African rodents of uncertain systematic relationships that are distinguished by the presence of strong stiff bristles on the hind feet — see GUNDI
cteno·dip·te·ri·ni \ˌtenōˌdiptəˈrīˌnī\ *n pl*, *cap* [NL, fr. *cteno-* (fr. *Ctenodus*) + *Dipterus* + *-ini*] *in some classifications* **:** an order of late Paleozoic dipnoan fishes with small and numerous cranial bones
cten·odus \ˈtenədəs\ *n*, *cap* [NL, fr. *cten-* + *-odus*] **:** a genus of Carboniferous dipnoan fishes whose dental plates have radiating tuberculated ridges
cten·oid \ˈteˌnȯid, ˈtē-,-\ *adj* [ISV, fr. Gk *ktenoeidēs* comblike, fr. *kten-*, *kteis* comb + *-oeidēs* -oid — more at PECTINATE] **1 :** having the margin toothed like a comb ⟨~ scales are characteristic of spiny-rayed fishes⟩ **2 :** consisting of scales with ctenoid margins ⟨~ scalation⟩; *often* **:** having such scales ⟨~ fishes⟩
cte·noi·dei \təˈnȯidēˌī\ *n pl*, *cap* [NL, fr. Gk *ktenoeidēs* comblike] **:** an artificial group formerly regarded as an order that includes fishes with ctenoid scales and is more or less exactly coextensive with Acanthopterygii
cte·noph·o·ra \təˈnäfərə\ *n pl*, *cap* [NL, fr. *cten-* + *-phora*] **:** a small phylum sometimes esp. formerly considered a class of Coelenterata and consisting of widely distributed and at times very abundant marine hermaphroditic solitary animals that superficially resemble jellyfishes, are usu. more or less ellipsoidal with decided biradial symmetry, and swim by means of eight meridional bands of transverse ciliated plates, each plate representing a row of large modified cilia — compare NUDA, TENTACULATA; COMB 4c; VENUS'S-GIRDLE — **cte·noph·o·ral** \-rəl\ *adj* — **cte·noph·o·ran** \-rən\ *n or adj* — **cten·o·phor·ic** \ˌtenəˈfȯrik\ *adj* — **cte·noph·o·rous** \təˈnäfərəs\ *adj*
cte·noph·o·rae \təˈnäfəˌrē\ *syn of* CTENOPHORA
cteno·phore \ˈtenəˌfō(ə)r\ *n* -s [NL *Ctenophora*] **:** one of the Ctenophora
cteno·pla·na \ˌtenəˈplānə\ *n*, *cap* [NL, fr. *cten-* + L *plana*, fem. of *planus* flat, level — more at FLOOR] **:** a genus of ctenophores consisting of a single species of small degenerate bottom-dwelling forms lacking ciliated swimming plates that are widely distributed in the Indian and Pacific oceans
cteno·sto·ma·ta \ˌtenəˈstōməd·ə\ *n pl*, *cap* [NL, fr. *cten-* + *-stomata*] **:** an order of Bryozoa (class Gymnolaemata) having a circle of processes resembling bristles that close the aperture when the tentacles are retracted — **cteno·stom·a·tous** \ˌtenəˈstämәd·əs\ *adj* — **cteno·stome** \ˈtenəˌstōm\ *n* -s
cte·tol·o·gy \təˈtäləjē\ *n* -ES [*cteto-* (fr. Gk *ktētos* that may be acquired, fr. *ktasthai* to acquire) + *-logy* — more at CHECK] **:** a branch of biology that deals with the origin and development of acquired characters
ctf *abbr* certificate
ctge *abbr* cartage
c3 \ˈsēˈthrē\ *adj*, *usu cap C* **1** *Brit* **:** assigned to a classification for recruits of the lowest grade of physical fitness for military service in World War I **2** *Brit* **:** very inferior in quality or state **:** THIRD-RATE

ctenophore: *1* tentacle extended, *2* tentacle partially contracted, *3* tentacle sheath, *4* funnel, *5* pole plate, *6* excretory pores, *7* axial funnel tube, *8* tentacular canal, *9* paragastric canal, *10* stomodaeum, *11* mouth

ctl *abbr* cental
CTL *abbr* constructive total loss
ctmo *abbr* **1** centesimo **2** centimo
ctn *abbr* **1** carton **2** cotangent
cto *abbr* concerto
-c·to·nus \ktənəs\ *n comb form* [NL, fr. Gk *ktonos* murder; akin to Gk *kteinein* to slay, Skt *kṣaṇoti* he wounds, injures, OPer a-*hshata* unhurt] **:** killer — in generic names esp. of insects ⟨Dendro*ctonus*⟩
C to S *abbr* carting to shipside
ctr *abbr* **1** center **2** counter
ctss *abbr* countess
c-tumor \ˈ⸗ˌ⸗⸗\ *n* **:** a swelling or proliferation produced in plant tissue by a c-mitotic agent (as certain insecticides and herbicides)
ctvo *abbr* centavo
cu *abbr* **1** cubic **2** cumulative
CU *abbr* close-up
Cu *symbol* [L *cuprum*] copper
cua·dri·lla \kwäˈdrē(y)ə, -ēlyə\ *n* -s [Sp, division of an army into 4 parts for distribution of booty, group of horsemen at a tourney, bullfighter's retinue, dim. of *cuadra* square, fr. L *quadra*; akin to L *quattuor* four — more at FOUR] **:** the team assisting the matador in the bullring
cua·dri·lle·ro \ˌkwädrə(l)ˈye(ˌ)rō\ *n* -s [Sp, fr. *cuadrilla* + *-ero* -er] **:** a member of the cuadrilla
cua·gua·yo·te \ˌkwägwəˈyōd·ē\ *n* -s [MexSp *cuaguayote*, *cuahuayote*, fr. Nahuatl *cuauhayotli*, lit., tree gourd, fr. *cuauh-* (fr. *cuahuitl* tree) + *ayotli* gourd] **:** a small Mexican tree (*Pileus mexicanus*) of the family Caricaceae having leaves and fruit that yield a proteolytic enzyme
cuamuchil *var of* HUAMUCHIL
cuan·do \ˈkwän(ˌ)dō\ *n* -s [AmerSp, fr. Sp, when, fr. L *quando*; fr. the fact that each strophe of the song originally sung to accompany this dance began with *cuando* — more at QUANTITY] **:** an Argentine dance resembling a minuet
cua·pi·nole \ˌkwäpəˈnōl\ *n* -s [Sp *cuapinol*, *guapinol*, fr. Nahuatl *cuauhpinolli*, lit., flour tree, fr. *cuauh-* (fr. *cuahuitl* tree) + *pinolli* flour] **:** the floury powder found in its pods] **:** COURBARIL
cuar·tel \kwärˈtel\ *n*, *pl* **cuarte·les** \-ˈtāˌlās\ [Sp, fr. MF *quartier* — more at QUARTER] **:** BARRACKS
cuar·te·la·zo \ˌkwärd·ᵊlˈä(ˌ)sō\ *n* -s [AmerSp, fr. Sp *cuartel* + *-azo* (suffix denoting a blow)] **:** a military coup usu. originating in a single barracks **:** seizure of power by an army — used chiefly of Latin-American army revolts
cua·tro-ojos \ˌkwä·trōˈō(ˌ)hōs, -hōz\ *n*, *pl* **cuatro-ojos** \-hōz\ [AmerSp, fr. Sp *cuatro* four (fr. L *quattuor*) + *ojos*, pl. of *ojo* eye, fr. L *oculus* — more at FOUR, EYE] **:** FOUR-EYES
¹**cub** \ˈkəb, ˈkəb\ *vt* **cubbed; cubbed; cubbing; cubs** [fr. obs. E *cub* pen, stall, fr. D *kub*, *kubbe* lean-to for cattle (obs.), thatched roof, fish trap, fish basket, fr. MD *cubbe*; akin to MHG *kobe* pigpen, cage, OE *cofa* room, cave — more at COVE] *now dial Eng* **:** to shut up **:** CONFINE
²**cub** \ˈkəb\ *n* -s *often attrib* [origin unknown] **1 a :** a young carnivorous mammal (as a fox or bear) **b :** a young shark **2 :** a young person; *esp* **:** an awkward or ill-mannered boy ⟨I began to envy those young ~s at the university —Sir Winston Churchill⟩ **3 :** APPRENTICE ⟨a ~ pilot on a steamboat⟩; *esp* **:** a young and inexperienced newspaper reporter **4 :** CUB SCOUT
³**cub** \"\ *vb* **cubbed; cubbed; cubbing; cubs 1 :** to bring forth — used of those animals of which the young are commonly called cubs **2 :** to hunt fox cubs
Cub \"\ *trademark* — used for a light low-horsepower high-wing airplane
cub- *or* **cubi-** *or* **cubo-** *comb form* [NL, fr. Gk *kyb-*, *kybo-*, fr. *kybos* — more at CUBE] **1 a :** cube ⟨*cub*octahedron⟩ ⟨*cubi*form⟩ ⟨*cubo*mancy⟩ **b :** of the third algebraic degree ⟨*cub*invariant⟩ ⟨*cubo*cubic⟩ **2** *cubo-* **:** cuboid and ⟨*cubo*metatarsal⟩
¹**cu·ba** \ˈkyübə\ *adj*, *usu cap* [fr. *Cuba*, island in the West Indies] **:** of or from Cuba **:** of the kind or style prevalent in Cuba **:** CUBAN
²**cuba** \"\ *n* -s *often cap* [fr. *Cuba*, island in the West Indies] **:** WALLFLOWER 4
cuba bark *or* **cuba bast** *n*, *usu cap C* **:** the coarse strong bast fiber found in any of certain plants of the genus *Hibiscus* and esp. in majagua and used in tropical America for making twine and ropes
cub·age \ˈkyübij\ *n* -s [¹*cube* + *-age*] **:** cubic content, volume, or displacement
cuba grass *n*, *usu cap C* **:** JOHNSON GRASS
cu·ba·laya \ˌkyübəˈlāə\ *n* -s *often cap* [blend of *Cuba* and *Malaya*] **:** a fowl of a breed of Cuban origin from oriental ancestry that resembles the Sumatra but is much smaller
cu·ba li·bre \ˌkyübəˈlēbrə\ *n*, *pl* **cuba libres** [AmerSp, lit., free Cuba (originally a drink of water and sugar or honey drunk by insurrectionists during the Cuban War of Independence)] **:** a tall drink made from lime juice, rum, and a cola beverage iced and usu. garnished with lime peel

1cu·ban \'kyübən\ *adj, usu cap* [Sp *cubano*, adj. & n., fr. *Cuba*, island in the West Indies + Sp *-ano* -an] **1 :** of, relating to, or characteristic of Cuba **2 :** of, relating to, or characteristic of Cubans

2cuban \"\ *n* [Sp *cubano*, adj. & n.] **1** *cap* **:** a native or inhabitant of Cuba **2** *also* **cuban tobacco** *usu cap C* **:** a chiefly filler-leaf tobacco derived from seed obtained from Cuba — compare BROADLEAF 2, HAVANA SEED

cuban bast *n, usu cap C* **:** the bast fiber of the mountain mahoe

cuban blindfish *n, usu cap C* **:** either of two blindfishes (*Lucifuga subterranea* and *Stygicola dentata*) of the family Brotulidae found in cave streams in Cuba

cuban cedar *n, usu cap 1st C* **:** SPANISH CEDAR

cuban crocodile *n, usu cap 1st C* **:** a small crocodile (*Crocodylus rhombifer*) found only in the island of Cuba

cuban ebony *n, usu cap C* **:** GRANADILLA TREE

cuban eight *n, usu cap C* **:** an acrobatic maneuver by an airplane consisting of three-quarters of a normal loop, a half roll, three quarters of another normal loop, and another half roll followed by recovery from the dive to straight level flight

cuban heel *n, usu cap C* **:** a broad medium-high heel with a moderately curved back and a straight breast line

Cuban heel

cu·ban·ite \'kyübə,nīt\ *n* -s [G *cuban* cubanite (fr. Sp *cubano* Cuban) + E *-ite*] **:** a bronze-yellow copper-iron sulfide $CuFe_2S_3$

cu·ban·ize \-īz\ *vt* -ED/-ING/-S *often cap* **:** to make Cuban in quality or in interests

cuban lily *n, usu cap C* **:** a bulbous plant (*Scilla peruviana*) of the Mediterranean region

cuban macaw *n, usu cap C* **:** a large macaw (*Ara tricolor*) that formerly inhabited Cuba but is now exterminated

cuban oysterwood *n, usu cap C* **:** a thin cross section of a West Indian tree (*Gymnanthes lucida*) used as a veneer — used esp. in the lumber trade

cuban pine *n, usu cap C* **:** CARIBBEAN PINE

cuban sand *n, often cap C* **:** a light grayish yellowish brown that is yellower and paler than almond brown and less strong than gravel

cuban spinach *n, usu cap C* **:** INDIAN LETTUCE 3

cuban vanilla *n, usu cap C* **:** a West Indian shrub (*Eupatorium dalea*)

cu·ba·rithm slate \'kyübə,rithəm-, -thəm-\ *n* [1*cube* + *arithmetic*] **:** a braille slate consisting of a box divided into square compartments into which cubes bearing on each face a number in braille dots may be placed in the usual pattern for performing arithmetical problems

cu·ba·ture \'kyübə,chü(ə)r\ *n* -s [1*cube* + *-ature* (as in *quadrature*)] **1 :** determination of cubic contents **2 :** CUBIC CONTENT, VOLUME

cubbed *past of* CUB

cub·ber \'kəbə(r)\ *n* -s [*cub (scout)* + *-er*] **:** an adult who is active in the cub-scouting program of the Boy Scouts of America

1cubbing *pres part of* CUB

2cubbing *n* -s [2*cub* + *-ing*] *Brit* **:** the hunting of young foxes esp. as a means of training the hounds

cub·bish \'kəbish\ *adj* **:** resembling a cub **:** AWKWARD, UNCOUTH — **cub·bish·ly** *adv*

cub·by \-bē\ *n* -ES [obs. E *cub* pen, stall + *-y* — more at CUB] **1 :** a snug or confined place (as for hiding) **:** a small room **:** a cramped space ⟨a little ~ of an office⟩ **2 :** a small closet or cupboard for storage **3 :** CUBBY PEN

cubbyhole \'⸗⸗,⸗\ *n* **1 :** CUBBY 1, 2 **2 :** PIGEONHOLE 6

cubbyhouse \'⸗⸗,⸗\ *n* **:** PLAYHOUSE

cubby locker *n, Brit* **:** GLOVE COMPARTMENT

cubby pen *n* **:** a small baited enclosure (as of upright sticks or sometimes stones) with traps so arranged that an animal cannot reach the bait without being caught by a trap

1cube \'kyüb\ *n* -s [MF, fr. L *cubus*, fr. Gk *kybos* cube, cubical die, vertebra, hollow before the hip (in cattle) — more at HIP] **1 a :** the regular solid of six equal square sides — see VOLUME table **b :** the product got by taking a number or quantity three times as a factor ⟨2×2×2=8, the ~ of 2⟩ **c :** CUBAGE **2 :** a block or set for road paving **3 :** one of the geometric forms into which a natural object is resolved in cubist art **4** *slang* **:** DIE — usu. used in pl. ⟨throw the ~s⟩ **5 :** the crystal form in the isometric system that consists of six like, mutually perpendicular faces and differs from the geometrical cube in that the six faces need not be square but must only bear like relations to the internal structure of the crystal **6 :** a cubic portion of morphine

cube 1a

2cube \"\ *vt* -ED/-ING/-S **1 :** to raise to the third power **:** form the cube of **2 :** to measure the cubic content of ⟨~ a house⟩ **3 :** to form into a cube **:** cut into cubes ⟨~ carrots⟩ **4 :** to cut partly through one or both surfaces of (a steak) in a checkered pattern in order to increase tenderness by breaking the fibers

3cu·be *or* **cu·bé** \'kyü,bā, ⸗'⸗\ *n* -s [AmerSp *cubé*] **1 :** any of several tropical American shrubs or climbers used as fish poisons and in the manufacture of insecticides; *esp* **:** any of certain plants of the genus *Lonchocarpus* (esp. *L. utilis* and *L. urucu*) the roots of which contain rotenone **2 :** the material from cube used as a fish poison or also in ground and refined form as an insecticide — called also *barbasco, timbo*

cu·beb \'kyü,beb\ *n* -s [MF *cubebe*, fr. OF, fr. ML *cubeba*, fr. Ar *kubābah, kabābah*] **1 a :** the dried unripe nearly full-grown fruit of the Java pepper which is crushed and smoked in cigarettes for catarrh and from which there is prepared an oleoresin formerly used medicinally **b :** one of these fruits **2** *or* **cubeb cigarette :** a cigarette containing cubeb **3 :** JAVA PEPPER

cubeb oil *n* **:** a colorless or greenish essential oil that is obtained from cubebs, has an odor resembling pepper, and is used in lozenges

cube·let \'kyüblət\ *n* -s **:** a little cube

cub·er \'kyübə(r)\ *n* -s **:** one that cubes; *esp* **:** a device or machine that cuts food into cubes or scores slices of meat to break the tough fibers

cu·be·ra \k(y)ü'berə\ *n* -s [Sp] **:** a large coarse snapper (*Lutjanus cyanopterus*) of the tropical western Atlantic esp. abundant about Cuba

cube root *n* **:** a number or quantity whose cube is the given number or quantity (3 is a *cube root* of 27)

cube spar *n* **:** ANHYDRITE

cube steak *n* **:** a steak that has been made tender by any of several means; *esp* **:** a small thin slice of a tough cut of beef shaped round or square that has been cubed

cube sugar *n* **:** white granulated sugar moistened with white syrup, molded into cubes, and dried

cube–hunting \'⸗,⸗⸗\ *n* **:** CUBBING

cubi- — see CUB-

1cu·bic \'kyübik, -bēk\ *adj* [MF or L; MF *cubique*, fr. L *cubicus*, fr. Gk *kybikos*, fr. *kybos* cube + *-ikos* -ic — more at HIP] **1 :** having the form of a cube **:** CUBICAL **2** *mineralogy* **a :** relating to the cube considered as a crystal form ⟨a ~ face⟩ **b :** ISOMETRIC **3 a :** THREE-DIMENSIONAL **b :** being the volume of a cube whose edge is a specified unit ⟨64 ~ inches⟩ **4** *math* **:** of third degree, order, or power — **cu·bic·ly** \-bəklē, -bēk-, -li\ *adv*

2cubic \"\ *n,* **:** a cubic curve, equation, or polynomial

cu·bi·cal \'kyübəkəl, -bēk-\ *adj* **1 :** CUBIC; *esp* **:** shaped like a cube **2** *physics* **:** relating to volume ⟨~ expansion⟩ — **cu·bi·cal·ly** \-k(ə)lē, -li\ *adv*

cubic centimeter *n* **:** a unit of volume equal to a cube one centimeter long on each side — see METRIC SYSTEM table

cubic content *n* **:** VOLUME 4

cubic coordination *n* **:** HEXAHEDRAL COORDINATION

cubic determinant *n* **:** a mathematical form analogous to a square determinant but with constituents forming a cube

cubic equation *n* **:** a polynomial equation in which the highest sum of exponents of variables in any term is three

cubic foot *n* **:** a unit of volume equal to a cube one foot long on each side — see MEASURE table

cubic foot bottle *n* **:** a metal container having a capacity of one cubic foot for use in the testing of gas-meter provers and precision gas meters

cubic inch *n* **:** a unit of volume equal to a cube one inch long on each side — see MEASURE table

cu·bic·i·ty \kyü'bisəd·ē\ *n* -ES **:** the quality or state of being cubic

cu·bi·cle \'kyübəkəl, -bēk-\ *n* -s [L *cubiculum*, fr. *cubare* to lie down — more at HIP] **1 :** a sleeping compartment partitioned off from a large room ⟨a dormitory ~⟩ **2 a :** a small room or compartment often approximately square in plan ⟨a bathhouse ~⟩ ⟨a bank teller's ~⟩ **b :** CARREL

cubic measure *n* **:** a unit or series of units for measuring volume (as cubic inch, cubic centimeter)

cubic meter *n* **:** a unit of volume equal to a cube one meter long on each side **:** STERE

cubic surface *n* **:** an algebraic surface whose intersection by an arbitrary plane is a cubic curve

cubic ton *n* **:** TON 2c

1cu·bic·u·lar \kyü'bikyələ(r)\ *n* -s [ME *cubiculare*, fr. MF *cubiculaire*, fr. L *cubicularius*, fr. *cubiculum* cubicle + *-arius* -ary] **:** a chamber attendant **:** CHAMBERLAIN

2cubicular \(')⸗¦⸗⸗⸗\ *adj* [F *cubiculaire*, fr. L *cubicularius, cubicularis*, fr. *cubiculum* + *-arius* -ary, *-aris* -ar] **:** of or relating to a bedroom or cubicle

cubiculo *n* [It, fr. L *cubiculum*] *obs* **:** CUBICULUM, BEDROOM

cu·bic·u·lum \kyü'bikyələm\ *n, pl* **cubicu·la** \-lə\ [ML, fr. L, cubicle — more at CUBICLE] **:** a small room provided in catacombs and constituting a family vault

cubic yard *n* **:** a unit of volume equal to a cube one yard long on each side — see MEASURE table

cu·bi·form \'kyübə,fȯrm\ *adj* [*cub-* + *-iform*] **:** of the shape of a cube

cub·ism \'kyü,bizəm\ *n* -s *sometimes cap* [F *cubisme*, fr. *cube* + *-isme* -ism — more at CUBE] **1** *fine art* **a :** the typically monochromatic expression of natural forms in terms of simplified planes and lines and basic geometric shapes sometimes organized to depict the subject simultaneously from several points of view — compare ANALYTICAL **b :** the arbitrary arrangement and interrelation of contours and fragments of contours on a picture surface without necessary reference to natural objects or their structure — compare SYNTHETIC **2 :** a French abstract art movement embracing analytical cubism from about 1906 to 1912 and synthetic cubism from 1913 into the following decade **3 :** a technique of writing that attempts to exploit abstract structural relationships of things by using bizarre associations and dissociations in imagery, the simultaneous evocation of several points of view toward the material, and other devices

1cub·ist \'kyübəst\ *n* -s *often cap* [F *cubiste*, fr. *cube* + *-iste* -ist] **:** an adherent or follower of a theory, method, or practice of cubism

2cubist \"\ *adj* **1 :** relating to or characteristic of cubism **2 :** composed of or decorated with geometric forms or patterns **:** GEOMETRIC, CUBISTIC

cu·bis·tic \(')kyü¦bistik, -tēk\ *adj* **1 :** CUBIST; *esp* **:** of or resembling cubist painting **2 :** of excessively intricate or contrived geometric design ⟨the ~ panels of the thirties —Kay Boyle⟩

cu·bit \'kyübət, *usu* -əd·+V\ *n* -s [ME *cubite*, fr. L *cubitus, cubitum* elbow, cubit — more at HIP] **1 :** any of various ancient units of length based on the length of the forearm from the elbow to the tip of the middle finger and usu. equal to about 18 inches but sometimes to 21 or more **2 :** CUBITUS

1cu·bi·tal \-bəd·ᵊl\ *adj* [ME, fr. L *cubitalis*, fr. *cubitus, cubitum* elbow, cubit + *-alis* -al] **:** of or relating to a cubitus ⟨~ nerve⟩

2cubital \"\ *n* -s **1** *obs* **:** a sleeve covering the forearm **2 a :** CUBITUS **b :** SECONDARY 6a

cu·bi·tale \,kyübə'ta(,)lē, -ā(,)lē, -ä(,)lē\ *n, pl* **cubital·ia** \-lēə\ [NL, fr. L, neut. of *cubitalis* cubital] **:** any of the cuneiform bones

cubital fossa *n* **:** the anterior depression at the elbow

cubit arm *n, heraldry* **:** a hand and arm couped at the elbow

cu·bi·tiere \¦kyübə·¦tye(ə)r\ *n* -s [F *cubitière*, fr. L *cubitum* elbow + F *-ière* -er — more at HIP] **:** an elbow guard in medieval armor

cubito- *comb form* [F, fr. L *cubitus* elbow] **:** cubital and ⟨*cubitocarpal*⟩

cu·bi·tus \'kyübəd·əs\ *n, pl* **cubi·ti** \-bə,tī\ [L, elbow, cubit — more at CUBIT] **1 a :** FOREARM, ANTEBRACHIUM **b :** ULNA **2** [NL, fr. L] **:** one of the primary veins of an insect's wing, located between the media and the anal vein

cubmaster \'⸗,⸗⸗\ *n* [*cub (scout)* + *master*] **:** a male adult leader of a cub-scout pack of the Boy Scouts of America

cubo- — see CUB-

cub·octahedral \(¦)kyü¦b+,-\ *adj* [*cub-* + *octahedral*] **:** of or relating to a cuboctahedron

cub·octahedron \"+\ *also* **cu·bo-octahedron** \¦kyü,bō+\ *n* [*cub-* + *octahedron*] **:** one of the 13 Archimedean solids having as faces six equal squares and eight equal regular triangles and formed by cutting off the corners of a cube

1cu·boid \'kyü,bȯid\ *adj* [NL *cuboides*, fr. Gk *kyboeidēs* cubelike, fr. *kybos* cube + *-oeidēs* -oid — more at CUBE] **:** approximately cubic in shape; *specif* **:** being the outermost of the distal row of tarsal bones of many of the higher vertebrates that supports the fourth and fifth metatarsals and is considered as representing the fused fourth and fifth distal tarsal bones

2cuboid \"\ *n* -s [NL *cuboides*, fr. *cuboides*, adj.] **1 :** a rectangular parallelepiped **2 :** the cuboid bone

cu·boi·dal \(')kyü¦bȯidᵊl\ *adj* **1 :** relating to or like a cuboid **2 :** relating to or being a more or less cubical structure

cuboidal epithelium *n* **:** epithelial tissue made up of small polygonal cells much shorter than columnar cells but not thin and flat like squamous cells

cu·bo·man·cy \'kyübə,man(t)sē\ *n* -ES [F *cubomancie*, fr. *cub-* + *-mancie* -mancy] **:** divination with dice

cu·bo·medusae \¦kyü(,)bō+\ *n pl, cap* [NL, fr. *cub-* + *Medusae*] **:** an order or suborder of Scyphozoa with a 4-sided cup-shaped umbrella and four perradial tentaculocysts — **cu·bo·medusan** \"+\ *adj or n*

cubs *pres 3d sing of* CUB, *pl of* CUB

cub scout *n* **:** a member of the scouting program of the Boy Scouts of America for boys of the age range 8–10 — compare BOY SCOUT, EXPLORER; SEE BEAR, BOBCAT, LION, WEBELOS, WOLF

cub shark *n* **:** a stout sluggish bottom-dwelling shark (*Carcharhinus leucas*) widely distributed along the western Atlantic shores and commonly entering fresh water; *also* **:** the young of various other sharks

cu·ca \'kükə\ *n* -s [Quechua *kúka*] **:** COCA

cu·ca·ra·cha \,kükə'rächə\ *n* -s [fr. (*La*) *Cucaracha* The Cockroach, Mexican popular song to which it is danced] **:** a Mexican ballroom and nightclub dance

cu·chia \'küchēə\ *n* -s [NL, fr. Beng *kūciyā*] **:** a sluggish fish (*Amphipnous cuchia*) resembling an eel, inhabiting swamps in Bengal, and having membranous vascular sacs enabling it to breathe air and most fins absent or vestigial

cuck *vt* -ED/-ING/-S [back-formation fr. *cucking stool*] *obs* **:** to punish by the cucking stool

cuck·hold \'kək,hōld, 'kə,kō-\ *n* -s [perh. fr. E dial. *cuck* muck (alter. of E 2*cack*) + E *hold*, v.] **:** a concave shovel for cutting off the tempered clay coming from the pugmill in brickmaking

cuck·ing stool \'kəkiŋ-\ *n* [ME *cucking stol*, lit., defecating chair, fr. *cucking* (fr. pres. part. of *cukken* to defecate, alter. of *cakken*) + *stol* chair — more at CACK, STOOL] **:** a chair in which such offenders as scolds, prostitutes, or dishonest tradesmen were formerly fastened for punishment by public exposure or ducking in water — compare DUCKING STOOL

cuck·le \'kəkəl\ *dial var of* 1COCKLE

1cuck·old \'kəkəld *sometimes* 'kük-\ *n* -s [ME *cukeweld, cokewold*] **1 :** a man whose wife is unfaithful **:** the husband of an adulteress — see 1HORN 4b **2 a :** COWFISH 2 **b :** COWBIRD

2cuckold \"\ *vt* -ED/-ING/-S **:** to make a cuckold of (a husband)

3cuck·old \'kəkəl(d)\ *also* **cuckold bur** *n* -s [*cuckold* prob. alter. of *cockle; cuckold bur* prob. alter. of *cocklebur*] **1 :** any of several plants of the genus *Bidens; esp* **:** an erect annual No. American beggar-tick (*B. connata*) with small barbed fruits **2 :** COCKLEBUR 1

cuckoldly *also* **cuckoldy** *adj, obs* **:** having the qualities of a cuckold

cuck·ol·dom \-dəm\ *n* -s **1 :** the state of being a cuckold **2 :** ADULTERY, CUCKOLDRY

cuck·old·ry \-drē, -ri\ *n* -ES **:** the practice of making cuckolds

1cuck·oo \'kü(,)kü, 'kü(-\ *n* -s [ME *cuccu, cuckow*, of imit. origin like MLG *kukuk*, MD *coecoec*, OF *cucu*, L *cuculus*, Gk *kokkyx*, Skt *kokila*] **1 a :** a familiar European bird (*Cuculus canorus*) that is grayish brown above and white barred with dusky on the underparts and is noted for its characteristic two-syllabled whistle and for its habit of laying its eggs in the nests of other birds for them to hatch **b :** any member of the large family (Cuculidae) to which this bird belongs — see ANI, BLACK-BILLED CUCKOO, COUCAL, ROADRUNNER **2 a :** the call of the cuckoo **b :** any repeated vapid calling or utterance **3** *music* **:** a whistle that imitates the song of the cuckoo **4 :** a silly or slightly crackbrained person **:** one erratic in behavior

2cuckoo \"\ *vb* -ED/-ING/-S *vt* **:** to repeat monotonously as a cuckoo does its call ~ *vi* **:** to utter the call of the cuckoo or a sound like it

3cuckoo \"\ *adj* **1 a :** of or resembling the cuckoo **b** *of a domestic fowl* **:** barred like the underparts of the cuckoo **2 a :** SILLY, STUPID, CRAZY **b :** dazed or unconscious esp. from a blow ⟨knocked him ~⟩ **3 a :** like a cuckoo in habits **b** *of certain ants* **:** living as social parasites

cuckoo bee *n* **:** any of various apoid bees (as members of the family Nomadidae) that live esp. in the larval stage as inquilines or parasites in the nests of other bees

cuckoo–bread \'⸗(,)⸗,⸗\ *n* **:** WOOD SORREL 1a

cuckoo–buds \'⸗(,)⸗,⸗\ *n pl but sing or pl in constr* **1 :** a common Old World crowfoot (*Ranunculus bulbosus*) **2 :** CUCKOO-PINT

cuckoo–button \'⸗(,)⸗,⸗⸗\ *n* **:** a burdock (*Arctium minus*)

cuckoo clock *n* **:** a wall or shelf clock that announces the hours by sounds resembling a cuckoo's often also with the appearing of an imitation cuckoo

cuckoo clover *n* **:** CUCKOOFLOWER 1

cuckoo dove *n* **:** any of several large chiefly ground-dwelling doves of a genus (*Macropygia*) distinguished by an elongated graduated tail, widely distributed in southeast Asia, the Pacific Islands, and Australia, and feeding chiefly on seeds, small fruits, and grain

cuckoo falcon *n* **:** any of numerous falcons of a genus (*Aviceda*) distinguished by a crested head and doubly notched bill and commonly resembling cuckoos in color and pattern

cuckooflower \'⸗(,)⸗,⸗⸗\ *n* **1 :** a bitter cress (*Cardamine pratensis*) of Europe and America **2 :** RAGGED ROBIN **3 :** WOOD SORREL 1a

cuckoo clock

cuckoo froth *n* [so called fr. the frothy secretion on the stem popularly believed to be cuckoo spittle] **:** CUCKOOFLOWER

cuckoo gillyflower *n* **:** RAGGED ROBIN

cuckoo lamb *n* [so called fr. its being born in the mating season of the cuckoo] **:** a late-born lamb

cuckoo–meat \'⸗(,)⸗,⸗\ *n* **:** WOOD SORREL 1a

cuck·oo·pint \'⸗(,)⸗,pint\ *n, pl* **cuckoopint** [short for *cuckoopintle*, fr. ME *cokkupyntel*, fr. *cokku, cuckow* cuckoo + *pyntel* pintle (penis); fr. the shape of the spadix] **:** a common European arum (*Arum maculatum*) with lanceolate erect spathe and short purple spadix

cuckoo ray *n* **:** a European ray (*Raja noevus*)

cuckoo shrike *n* **:** any of numerous Old World birds somewhat like flycatchers in habits constituting the family Campephagidae but formerly often included in the family Laniidae and differing from the true shrikes esp. in their undulating flight resembling that of the cuckoo

cuckoo's–leader \'⸗(,)⸗¦⸗⸗\ *n, pl* **cuckoo's–leaders** [so called fr. the belief that it arrives in the spring shortly before the cuckoo] *dial Eng* **:** WRYNECK

cuckoo sorrel *n* **:** WOOD SORREL 1a

cuckoo spit *n* **1** *also* **cuckoo spittle a :** a frothy secretion exuded upon plants by the nymphs of spittle insects — called also *frog spit, snake spit, toad spit* **b :** an insect secreting this **:** SPITTLE INSECT **2 a :** CUCKOOFLOWER 1 **b :** CUCKOOPINT **c :** WOOD ANEMONE b

cuckoo's–sandy \'⸗(,)⸗,⸗⸗\ *n, pl* **cuckoo's–sandies** [so called fr. its nest being favored by the cuckoo] **:** MEADOW PIPIT

cuckoo wasp *n* **:** any of certain usu. brilliantly metallic-green or metallic-blue wasps that constitute the family Chrysididae or the superfamily Chrysidoidea and lay their eggs in the provisioned larval cells of other hymenopterous insects

cuckoo wrasse *n* **:** a brilliantly colored European wrasse (*Labrus mixtus*) the male orange or yellow banded with bright blue and the female reddish brown blotched with black

cuckquean *n* -s [*cuckold* + *quean*] *obs* **:** a woman whose husband is unfaithful to her

cucks *pres 3d sing of* CUCK

cuck·stool \'kək,stül\ *n* [ME *cukstol*, lit., defecating chair, fr. *cukken* to defecate (alter. of *cakken*) + *stol* chair — more at CACK, STOOL] **:** CUCKING STOOL

cu·cu·ba·no \kü'kübə,nō\ *n* -s [AmerSp (Puerto Rico) *cucúbano*] **:** a large luminous click beetle (*Pyrophorus luminosus*) of the West Indies having a larva also luminous that is predacious on other insects

1cu·cu·jid \kə'küyəd, kə'k(y)üjəd\ *adj* [NL *Cucujidae*] **:** of or relating to the family Cucujidae

2cucujid \"\ *n* -s **:** a cucujid beetle

cu·cu·ji·dae \-üyə,dē, -üjə-\ *n pl, cap* [NL, fr. *Cucujus*, type genus (prob. fr. Sp *cocuyo, cucuyo* fire beetle) + *-idae*] **:** a family of small flattened elongated beetles (suborder Polyphaga) that live mostly under the bark of trees — compare SAW-TOOTHED GRAIN BEETLE

cu·cu·jo \-ü(,)yō, -ü(,)jō\ *n* -s [modif. of Sp *cocuyo, cucuyo*, fr. Taino, fr. *cuyo* fire] **:** a luminous click beetle (*Pyrophorus noctilucus*) related to the cucubano and having a similar distribution

cu·cu·li \'k(y)üky,lī\ *n pl, cap* [NL, fr. L, pl. of *cuculus* cuckoo — more at CUCKOO] **:** a suborder of Cuculiformes coextensive with the family Cuculidae

cu·cu·li·dae \kə'k(y)ülə,dē\ *n pl, cap* [NL, fr. *Cuculus*, type genus + *-idae*] **:** a family of birds (order Cuculiformes) that comprises the cuckoos, including the anis and roadrunners

cu·cu·li·form \-lə,fȯrm\ *adj* [L *cuculus* cuckoo + E *-iform*] **:** like or belonging to the cuckoos or the Cuculiformes

cu·cu·li·for·mes \⸗,⸗lə'fȯr(,)mēz\ *n pl, cap* [NL, fr. *Cuculus* + *-iformes*] **:** a small order of birds comprising the cuckoos, touracos, various related birds, and formerly the parrots and having 10 primaries and the feet zygodactyl except in the touracos in which the outer toe is reversible

cu·cu·line \'k(y)ük(y)ə,līn\ *adj* [L *cuculus* cuckoo + E *-ine*] **:** of, like, or relating to the cuckoos

cu·cul·la \kə'külə, kyü'kələ\ *n* -s [ML, fr. LL, cowl — more at COWL] **:** a loose sleeveless garment put on over the head and used esp. to protect other garments; *specif* **:** a monk's scapular

cu·cul·lar·is \,kyükə'la(a)rəs\ *n, pl* **cucullar·es** \-(,)rēz\ [NL, fr. L *cucullus* cap + *-aris* -ar] **:** TRAPEZIUS

cu·cul·late \'kyükə,lāt, kyü'kələt\ *also* **cu·cul·lat·ed** \'kyükə,lād·əd\ *adj* [ML *cucullatus*, fr. L *cucullus* cap, hood + *-atus* -ate — more at COWL] **1 :** shaped like a hood ⟨the posterior sepal in the flower of aconite is ~⟩ **:** having the basal edges rolled inward ⟨~ leaves⟩ **2 :** having the prothorax elevated so as to form a sort of hood receiving the head — used of certain insects — **cu·cul·late·ly** *adv*

cu·cul·li·form \kyü'kələ,fȯrm\ *adj* [ISV *cucull-* (fr. L *cucullus* cap, hood) + *-iform* — more at COWL] **:** CUCULLATE

cu·cul·lus \kyü'kələs\ *n, pl* **cucul·li** \-,lī\ [NL, fr. L, cap, hood — more at COWL] **:** the anterior dorsal shield of the cephalothorax in pseudoscorpions and Ricinulei

cu·cu·lus \'k(y)ük(y)ələs\ *n, cap* [NL, fr. L, cuckoo — more at CUCKOO] **:** the type genus of Cuculidae comprising the typical cuckoos

cu·cu·mar·ia \,kyük(y)ə'ma(a)rēə\ *n, cap* [NL, fr. L *cucumis* cucumber + NL *-aria* — more at CUCUMBER] **:** the type genus of Cucumariidae

cu·cu·ma·ri·idae \,kyük(y)əmə'rīə,dē\ *n pl, cap* [NL, fr. *Cucumaria*, type genus + *-idae*] **:** a large family of shallow-water sea cucumbers (order Dendrochirota) having a number of intricately branched oral tentacles, an internal madreporite, and a well-developed respiratory tree

cu·cum·ber \'kyü,kəmbə(r)\ *sometimes* '⸗,⸗⸗ *or* ⸗'⸗⸗; *archaic or humorous* 'kau̇(,)-\ *n* -s [ME *cucumer, cucumber*, fr. MF & L;

MF *cocombre, concombre*, fr. L *cucumer-, cucumis*, prob. (like Gk *sikyos* cucumber) of non-IE origin] **1 a :** the succulent fruit of a vine (*Cucumis sativus*) cultivated from earliest times as a garden vegetable, having a smooth or warty surface, and varying in shape from cylindrical to globular — see GHERKIN **b :** the annual trailing or climbing vine that bears cucumbers — see CUCUMIS **c :** any of several other plants of the genus *Cucumis* or the family Cucurbitaceae — usu. with qualifying word ⟨bitter ~⟩ ⟨snake ~⟩ **2 :** CUCUMBER TREE **3 :** SEA CUCUMBER

cucumber angular leaf spot *n* **:** a leaf spot of cucumber caused by a bacterium (*Pseudomonas lachrymans*)

cucumber beetle *n* **:** any of several leaf beetles that are esp. injurious to cucumbers and squashes, attacking the leaves as adults and the roots and stems as larvae — see SPOTTED CUCUMBER BEETLE, STRIPED CUCUMBER BEETLE; compare CORN ROOTWORM

cucumber family *n* **:** CUCURBITACEAE

cucumber fly *n* **:** MELON FLY

cucumber magnolia *n* **:** CUCUMBER TREE 1

cucumber melon *or* **cucumber apple** *n* **:** MANGO MELON

cucumber mildew *n* **1 :** either of two fungi destructive to cucumbers and melons: **a :** a downy mildew (*Peronoplasmopara cubensis*) **b :** a powdery mildew (*Erysiphe cichoracearum*) **2 :** a disease caused by cucumber mildew

cucumber mosaic *n* **:** a virus disease of cucumbers and related fruits transmitted by the melon aphid and producing characteristic mottling of the foliage and smooth pale fruits often with swellings or warts

cucumber root *n* **:** INDIAN CUCUMBER

cucumber scab *n* **:** a disease of the cucumber caused by a fungus (*Cladosporium cucumerinum*) characterized by spotting and blighting of the leaves and dark sunken cavities on the fruit

cucumber tree *n* **1 :** any of several American magnolias (esp. *Magnolia acuminata*) having fruit like a small cucumber **2 :** TULIP TREE **3** *India* **:** BILIMBI

cu·cu·mis \ˈkyük(y)əməs\ *n, cap* [NL, fr. L, cucumber — more at CUCUMBER] **:** a genus of plants (family Cucurbitaceae) that are native to the warmer parts of the world, that include the cucumbers and muskmelons, and that have small sepals and a corolla with five petals

cu·curb \kyüˈkərb\ *n* -S [by shortening] **:** CUCURBIT 2

cu·cur·bit \kyüˈkərbət, *attrib* (ˈ)=ˈ==\ *n* -S [ME *cucurbite*, fr. MF, fr. L *cucurbita* gourd] **1** [so called fr. its shape] **:** a vessel or flask used in distillation as a part of or in conjunction with an alembic **:** MATRASS — see ALEMBIC illustration **2** [NL *Cucurbita*] **:** any plant of the genus *Cucurbita* or of the family Cucurbitaceae

cu·cur·bi·ta \-bəd·ə\ *n, cap* [NL, fr. L, gourd — more at GOURD] **:** the type genus of Cucurbitaceae comprising tropical herbaceous vines that have a bell-shaped gamopetalous corolla five-lobed to the middle or a little lower, coherent stamens, and a many-seeded fleshy fruit with a hard rind, that include the squashes, pumpkins, vegetable marrows, and certain gourds, and that are now nearly cosmopolitan in cultivation

cu·cur·bi·ta·ce·ae \(ˌ)kyü,kərbəˈtāsēˌē\ *n pl, cap* [NL, fr. *Cucurbita*, type genus + *-aceae*] **:** a family of chiefly herbaceous tendril-bearing vines (order Campanulales) that are characterized by an inferior ovary and anthers usu. united and that include food plants (as the cucumber, melon, squash, and pumpkin), drug plants (as the colocynth), and ornamental plants (as the gourds) — **cu·cur·bi·ta·ceous** \(ˌ)=ˌ==ˈtāshəs\ *adj*

cu·cur·bi·tar·i·a·ce·ae \(ˌ)kyü,kərbə,ta(a)rēˈāsēˌē\ *n pl, cap* [NL, fr. *Cucurbitaria*, type genus (fr. L *cucurbita* gourd + NL *-aria*) + *-aceae*] **:** a family of ascomycetous fungi (order Sphaeriales) having the perithecia in caespitose clusters on the stroma

cucurbit mosaic *n* **:** CUCUMBER MOSAIC

cucurbit wilt *n* **:** a disease of cucumbers and related plants characterized by sudden wilting of affected plants and caused by a motile bacterium (*Erwinia tracheiphila*)

1cud \ˈkəd *also* ˈküd\ *n* -S [ME *cudde*, fr. OE *cwidu, cwudu, cudu* cud, gum mastic; akin to OHG *kuti* glue, ON *kvātha* resin, MIr *bethe, beithe* box (tree), Skt *jatu* lac, gum; basic meaning: resin] **1 :** the portion of food that is brought up into the mouth by ruminating animals from their first stomach to be chewed a second time **2 :** something ruminated ⟨chewing on the ~ of old problems⟩ **3 :** a portion of chewing tobacco or chewing gum

2cud \"\ *vi* **cudded; cudded; cudding; cuds :** to chew the cud

cu·da \ˈküdə\ *n* -S [short for *barracuda*] **:** GREAT BARRACUDA

cud·bear \ˈkəd,ba(a)(ə)r\ *n* -S [irreg. (pron. spelling) after Dr. *Cuthbert* Gordon, 18th cent. Scot. chemist] **:** a coloring matter prepared from lichens similarly to archil and sometimes considered a form of archil, obtained as a red or purple powder, and used in coloring pharmaceutical preparations

cudden *n* -S [origin unknown] *obs* **:** FOOL, DOLT

1cud·dle \ˈkədᵊl\ *vb* **cuddled; cuddled; cuddling** \ˈkəd(ə)liŋ\ **cuddles** [origin unknown] *vt* **:** to hold close for warmth or comfort or in affection **:** FONDLE, HUG ~ *vi* **:** to lie close or snug **:** NESTLE, SNUGGLE

2cuddle \"\ *n* -S **:** a close embrace **:** the act of nestling

3cuddle \"\ *now dial var of* 1CUTTLE

cud·dle·some \ˈkədᵊlsəm\ *adj* **:** fit for or inviting cuddling **:** LOVABLE ⟨a ~ and merry girl —J.B.Cabell⟩

cud·dly \ˈkəd(ᵊ)lē, -li\ *adj* -ER/-EST **:** CUDDLESOME

1cud·dy \ˈkədē\ *n* -ES [origin unknown] **1 :** a small cabin formerly under the poop deck; *also* **:** the galley or pantry of a small ship **2 :** a small room or closet (as a cupboard)

2cud·dy \ˈküdi, ˈkədi\ *or* **cuddie** *n, pl* **cuddies** [perh. fr. *Cuddy*, nickname for *Cuthbert*] **1** *dial Brit* **:** ASS, DONKEY **2** *dial Brit* **:** BLOCKHEAD, LOUT

cuddyhole \ˈ==,=\ *n* **:** 1CUDDY 2

1cud·gel \ˈkəjəl\ *n* -S [ME *kuggel*, fr. OE *cycgel*; akin to MD *cōghele* stick with a rounded end, MHG *kugele* ball, OHG *coccho* rounded ship, Lith *gugà* pommel, hump, hill; basic meaning: ball; akin to OE *cot* cottage, den — more at COT] **1 :** a short heavy stick that is shorter than a quarterstaff and is used as an instrument of punishment or a weapon **2 cudgels** *pl* **:** CUDGEL PLAY

2cudgel \"\ *vt* **cudgeled** *or* **cudgelled; cudgeled** *or* **cudgelled; cudgeling** *or* **cudgelling** \-j(ə)liŋ\ **cudgels :** to beat with or as if with a cudgel **:** BELABOR, THRASH, DRUB, RACK ⟨~*ed* his brains for a rhyme⟩

cudgel play *n* **:** a fighting or sporting contest with cudgels

cud·ger·ie \ˈkəjərē\ *n* -S [native name in Australia] **:** BUNJI-BUNJI

cudweed \ˈ=,=\ *n* **:** any of several composite plants with silky or woolly foliage: as **a :** a European perennial herb (*Gnaphalium sylvaticum*) sometimes cultivated and widely naturalized as an escape in temperate No. America; *broadly* **:** any plant of the genus *Gnaphalium* **b :** LADIES' TOBACCO **c :** COTTON ROSE 2 **d :** WORMWOOD 1

cudweed mugwort *n* **:** PRAIRIE SAGE

1cue \ˈkyü\ *n* -S [ME *cu*] **1 :** the letter *q* **2** *dial Eng* **:** the shoe of an ox

2cue \"\ *n* -S [prob. fr. *q, qu*, abbr. (used as a direction in actors' copies of plays) of L *quando* when — more at QUANTITY] **1 a :** a word, phrase, or bit of stage business in a play serving as a signal to the actor who is to act or speak next that it is time for him to begin **b :** a similar signal to a member of the stage crew to begin a particular operation (as producing a sound effect or lighting change) **c :** a musical passage from another instrumental or voice part inserted usu. in smaller type in an instrumental or accompanying part to signal a place of entrance or to permit substitution or doubling **2 a :** a signal to begin an action **:** STIMULUS **b :** a hint, intimation, or suggestion as to what course of action to take or when to take it ⟨the Cairo press, which takes its ~ carefully from the government in political affairs —R.C.Doty⟩ **c :** an item or feature acting as an indication of the nature of the object or situation perceived ⟨a subliminal hearing ~⟩ ⟨foreshortened lines in a picture are ~*s* to depth perception⟩ **3 :** the part one has to perform in or as if in a play ⟨was it my ~ to fight? —Shak.⟩ **4** *archaic* **:** attitude of mind **:** MOOD, TEMPER, HUMOR ⟨nobody was in the ~ to dance —Nathaniel Hawthorne⟩

3cue \"\ *vt* **cued; cued; cuing** *or* **cueing; cues 1 :** to give a cue to (as in a play) **:** PROMPT **2 :** to insert (a musical passage) as or provide (a musical score) with a cue — usu. used with *in* **3 :** CUE-BID **4 :** to insert or provide for the insertion of into a continuous performance — usu. used with *in* or *into* ⟨~ a duet into the scene⟩ ⟨~ in a sound effect⟩

4cue \"\ *n* -S [F *queue*, lit., tail, fr. OF *cōe, coue* — more at COWARD] **1 :** QUEUE 2 **2 a :** a leather-tipped tapering rod used to strike the ball in billiards and other games **b :** a long-handled instrument with a concave head used to shove the disks in shuffleboard

5cue \"\ *vb* **cued; cued; cuing** *or* **cueing; cues** *vt* **1 :** to form into a queue **:** BRAID, TWIST **2 :** to strike (as a billiard ball) with a cue ~ *vi* **1 :** to line up in a queue — usu. used with *up* **2 :** to use a cue **:** strike with a cue

cue ball *n* [4*cue*] **1 :** the ball that a player strikes with his cue in billiards and pool as distinguished from any of the other balls on the table — compare OBJECT BALL **2 :** either of the two white balls used in ordinary billiards — see SPOT BALL

cue bid *n* [2*cue*] **1 :** a bid in contract bridge in a suit previously bid by an opponent made with the purpose of showing an ace or a void in that suit **2 :** a bid in contract bridge showing the ace or less often a void or a king in the suit

cue-bid \ˈ=ˌ=\ *vb* [*cue bid*] *vi* **:** to make a cue bid ~ *vt* **:** to indicate possession of (an ace, void, or king) by bidding the suit

cue·ca \ˈkwākə\ *n* -S [AmerSp, short for *zamacueca*] **:** a So. American esp. Chilean courtship dance — called also *zamacueca*

cue·ist \ˈkyüəst\ *n* -S [4*cue* + *-ist*] **:** BILLIARDIST

cue·man \ˈkyümən\ *n, pl* **cuemen** [4*cue* + *man*] **:** one who uses a cue **:** a billiard player — **cue·man·ship** \-,ship\ *n* -S

cuena *var of* QUENA

cuer·da \ˈkwerdə, -rthə\ *n* -S [AmerSp, fr. Sp, cord, rope, fr. L *chorda* catgut, chord, cord — more at CORD] **:** a Puerto Rican unit of land measure equal to 0.97 acre

cuerda se·ca \,==ˈsākə, ˈsekə\ *n* [Sp, lit., dry cord] **:** a technique used to simulate mosaic and cloisonné enamel effects in colored ceramic tiles

cue sheet *n* [2*cue*] **:** a detailed outline of a television or radio program giving cues and timing for each item

cues·ta \ˈkwestə, -wās-\ *n* -S [Sp, fr. L *costa* side, rib — more at COAST] **1** *Southwest* **:** a sloping plain esp. with the upper end at the crest of a cliff **:** a hill or ridge with a steep face on one side and gentle slope on the other **2 :** a landform commonly found in regions of gently tilted sedimentary rocks and consisting of an inclined upland the slope of which conforms with the dip of a resistant bed or series of beds and a relatively steep escarpment descending abruptly from its crest

cue·va \ˈkwāvə\ *n, pl* **cueva** *or* **cuevas** *usu cap* [Sp] **1 a :** a Cunan people of Panama **b :** a member of such people **2 :** a Chibchan language of the Cueva people

1cuff \ˈkəf\ *n* -S [ME *coffe, cuffe*, perh. modif. of MF *coife, coiffe* coif — more at COIF] **1 a :** the part of a glove covering the wrist and sometimes the forearm **b :** EPIMANIKION **c :** a covering (as of stiff paper) for the forearm to prevent soiling the sleeves **2 a :** a band used to finish the end of a sleeve either by turning back a part of the sleeve or by attaching a separate piece **b :** the part of a sleeve at the wrist (as a coat sleeve that is finished by a hem) **c :** any of various separate bands worn at the wrist **d :** the turned-back hem of a trouser leg **3 a :** a piece of leather or other material sewn outside on the top of a shoe upper usu. for ornament **:** a wide collar **b :** the top band of a sock or stocking **4 :** HANDCUFF — usu. used in pl. **5 :** something resembling or likened to a cuff for the wrist (as the ferrule on a tool handle) **6 :** an inflatable band that is wrapped about an extremity to control the flow of blood through the part when recording blood pressure with the sphygmomanometer — **off the cuff** *adj (or adv)* **:** SPONTANEOUS, UNPREPARED, AD-LIB, INFORMAL — **on the cuff** *adj (or adv)* **1 :** on credit **2 :** on the house **:** GRATIS

2cuff \"\ *vt* -ED/-ING/-S **1 :** to furnish with a cuff **2 :** HANDCUFF

3cuff \"\ *vb* -ED/-ING/-S [perh. fr. obs. E *cuff* glove, fr. ME *cuffe*] *vt* **:** to strike with the palm of the hand or in a manner suggesting such a blow **:** BUFFET ⟨~ a boy over the ears⟩ ⟨~*ed* by the gale —Alfred Tennyson⟩ ~ *vi* **:** FIGHT, SCUFFLE **syn** see STRIKE

4cuff \"\ *n* -S **:** a blow with the hand esp. when open **:** SLAP ⟨gave him a good ~⟩

5cuff \"\ *n* -S [prob. modif. of Romany *kova* thing, person — more at COVE] **:** an old codger; *esp* **:** an old miser

6cuff \"\ *n* -S [perh. alter. of 1*scuff*] *Scot* **:** 3SCRUFF

1cuff·er \ˈkəfə(r)\ *n* -S [1*cuff* + *-er*] **:** one that stitches cuffs to various articles of clothing or who folds the top of short hose

2cuffer \"\ *n* -S [E dial. *cuff* to talk over, gossip (perh. fr. 5*cuff*) + E *-er*] *Brit* **:** a preposterous story **:** YARN

cuf·fin \ˈkəfən\ *n* -S [prob. modif. of Romany *kova* thing, person] **:** FELLOW, CHAP — see QUEER CUFFIN

cuff link *n* **:** a usu. ornamental device consisting of two pieces like buttons joined by a shank, chain, or bar for passing through buttonholes to fasten a cuff without overlapping the cuff ends — usu. used in pl.

cuff links

cufic *usu cap, var of* KUFIC

cui bo·no \ˈkwēˈbō(ˌ)nō, ˈküē-\ *n* [L, to whose advantage?] **1 :** the principle that probable responsibility for an act or event lies with one who had something to gain by it ⟨a *cui bono* approach to an investigation⟩ **2 :** usefulness or utility as a principle in estimating the value of an act or policy

cui·ca \ˈkwēkə\ *n* -S [Pg, fr. Tupi, cavy, fr. Guarani; fr. its squealing sound] **:** a Brazilian rhythm instrument consisting of a drumhead vibrated by oscillating a rosined string that has been placed through a hole made in it

cui·ca·tec \,kwēkəˈtek, ,==ˈ=\ *or* **cui·ca·te·co** \,kwēkəˈtā(ˌ)kō\ *n, pl* **cuicatec** *or* **cuicatecs** *or* **cuicateco** *or* **cuicatecos** *usu cap* [Sp *cuicateco*, of AmerInd origin] **1 a :** an Indian people of the district of Cuicatlan in the Mexican state of Oaxaca **b :** a member of such people **2 :** the Mixtecan language of the Cuicatec people

cui·chun·chul·li \,kwēchənˈchülē\ *n* -S [modif. of AmerSp *cuichunchulo*, fr. Quechua *quichay* to open + *chunchulo* bowels] **:** the root of a So. American shrub (*Ionidium glutinosum*) of the family Violaceae used locally as an emetic

cu·ie·jo \küˈyā(ˌ)hō\ *n* -S [modif. of AmerSp *cuyeo*] **:** a tropical American nighthawk (*Nyctidromus albicollis*) the dried and ground bones of which are highly esteemed in parts of its range as a love potion — called also *pauraque*

cuif \ˈküf, ˈkēf\ *var of* COOF

cui in vi·ta \,kwē(ˌ)inˈwē,tä\ *n* [ML, lit., to whom in life] **:** a writ of entry by means of which a widow sought to recover lands which had belonged to her but had been transferred by her husband during his lifetime

cuing *pres part of* CUE

cuir \ˈkwi(ə)r\ *n* -S [F, lit., leather, fr. L *corium*] **:** DORADO 2

1cui·rass \kwēˈras, kwiˈ-,kyüˈ-,kyüˈ-, -raa(ə)s, ˈ=,=\ *n* -ES [ME *curas*, fr. MF *curasse, cuirasse*, fr. LL *coriacea*, fem. of *coriaceus* leathern, fr. L *corium* skin, hide + *-aceus* -aceous; akin to OE *heortha* deerskin, OHG *herdo* fleece, sheepskin, ON *hörundr* skin, Goth *hairthra* intestines, MIr *curach* skin boat, L *cortic-, cortex* bark, cork, Skt *kṛtti* hide, Gk *keirein* to cut — more at SHEAR] **1 a :** a piece of armor made orig. of leather and covering the body from neck to girdle; *esp* **:** one consisting of a coupled breastplate and backpiece — usu. used in pl. ⟨a pair of ~*es*⟩ **b :** the breastplate of such a piece **c :** any ancient close-fitting body armor **2 :** protecting armor plate (as of a ship) **3** *zool* **:** an armor of bony plates or other protective structure that is felt to resemble a cuirass **4 a :** a plaster cast for the trunk and neck **b :** a respirator that covers the chest or the chest and abdomen and provides artificial respiration by means of an electric pump

2cuirass \"\ *vt* -ED/-ING/-ES **:** to cover or armor with or as if with a cuirass

cui·ras·sier \,kwirəˈsi(ə)r, ˌkyür-\ *n* -S [F, fr. *cuirasse* + *-ier* -er] **:** a mounted soldier wearing a cuirass; *specif* **:** a soldier of a certain type of heavy cavalry in the French and other European armies

cuir-bouil·li \,kwir(ˌ)büˈyē\ *n* -S [F *cuir bouilli*, lit., boiled leather] **:** leather softened by soaking, pressed, molded, or stamped to shape, and hardened by drying and used for armor in the middle ages and for decorative objects (as book covers)

cuir ci·se·lé \ˌkwir,sēz(ə)ˈlā, -,siz-\ *n, pl* **cuir ciselés** [F, lit., chiseled leather] **:** an ancient style of decoration made on leather book covers by outlining with a knife and stippling the uncut background; *also* **:** an object so decorated

cui·sine \kwəˈzēn, kwēˈ-\ *n* -S [F, lit., kitchen, fr. LL *coquina* — more at KITCHEN] **:** manner of preparing food **:** style of cooking ⟨the inn's ~ is American, not French⟩

cui·si·nier \ˌkwē(ˌ)zənˈyā\ *n* -S [F, fr. *cuisine* + *-ier* -er] **:** COOK, CHEF 2

cui·si·nière \-ˈye(ə)r\ *n* -S [F, fem. of *cuisinier*] **:** a female cuisinier

cuis·sard *or* **cuis·sart** \kwēˈsär\ *n* -S [F, fr. *cuisse* + *-ard*] **:** CUISSE

cuisse \ˈkwis\ *also* **cuish** \-ish\ *n* -S [back-formation fr. ME *cusseis, cushies*, fr. MF *cuissaux*, pl. of *cuissel*, fr. *cuisse* thigh, fr. L *coxa* hip, thigh — more at COXA] **:** defensive plate armor for the thighs esp. in front — see ARMOR illustration

cuit *or* **cute** *n* [ME *cute*, adj., boiled down (of wine), fr. MF *cuit*, fr. past part. of *cuire* to boil, cook, fr. L *coquere* to cook — more at COOK] *obs* **:** new wine boiled down

cuit·la·tec \ˈkwitlə,tek, ˈkwēt-, ,==ˈ=\ *or* **cuit·la·te·co** \,==ˈtā(ˌ)kō\ *n, pl* **cuitlatec** *or* **cuitlatecs** *or* **cuitlateco** *or* **cuitlatecos** *usu cap* [Sp *cuitlateco*, of AmerInd origin] **1 a :** a people of unknown affiliations in Guerrero and Michoacán, Mexico **b :** a member of such people **2 :** the language of the Cuitlatec people

cuit·tle \ˈkütᵊl, ˈkət-\ *vt* -ED/-ING/-S [origin unknown] *Scot* **:** COAX, WHEEDLE

cui·vré \(ˈ)kwēvˈrā\ *adj* [F, fr. past part. of *cuivrer* to play with a brassy tone, fr. *cuivre* copper, fr. OF, fr. (assumed) VL *coprium*, fr. L *cyprium*] **:** OVERBLOWN — used as a direction in music for brass instruments (as the muted horn)

cuke \ˈkyük\ *n* -S [by shortening and alter.] **:** CUCUMBER

-cular — see -CLE

cu·lasse \kyüˈlas\ *n* -S [F, fr. *cul* bottom, backside] **:** CULET 1

cul·bert·son system \ˈkəlbə(r)tsən-\ *n, usu cap C* [after Ely *Culbertson* †1955 Amer. authority on contract bridge] **:** a system of bidding in contract bridge characterized by the use of approach and forcing bids, limited no-trump bids, and ace-showing no-trump bids — called also *approach-forcing system*

culch *var of* CULTCH

cul·dee \ˈkəl,dē\ *n* -S *often cap* [NL *culdei* (pl.), alter. (influenced by NL *cultores Dei* worshipers of God) of ML *keldei, keledei*, fr. OIr *cēle Dē*, lit., companion of God, fr. *cēle* companion + *Dē*, gen. of *Dia* God; akin to L *civis* citizen and to L *deus* god — more at CEMETERY, DEITY] **1** *archaic* **:** one of a class of religious recluses appearing first in Ireland in the 7th century **2** *archaic* **:** an Irish or Scottish monk

cul-de-four \ˌkəldəˈfü(ə)r *also* ˌkül-, *F* kü̅dfüːr\ *n, pl* **culs-de-four** \"\ [F, lit., bottom of an oven] **1 :** a vault shaped like a quarter sphere or like a hemisphere **2 :** VAULT — compare SEMIDOME

cul-de-lampe \ˌkəldəˈlamp *also* ˌkül-, *F* kü̅dlãⁿp\ *n, pl* **culs-de-lampe** \"\ [F, lit., lamp bottom] **1 :** any of various ornaments or parts resembling the conical bottom of ancient lamps (as a pendant from a roof or an isolated corbel supporting an oriel, column, or turret) **2 :** TAILPIECE

cul-de-sac \ˌkəldəˈsak, -dē;- *also* ˌkül- *sometimes* -säk *or* -sȧk, *F* kü̅dsȧk\ *n, pl* **culs-de-sac** \-ks\ *also* **cul-de-sacs** \-ks\ [F, lit., bottom of the bag] **1** *anat* **a :** a blind diverticulum or pouch (as the cecum); *also* **:** the closed end of such a pouch **b** *or* **cul-de-sac of douglas** *usu cap 2d D* [after James *Douglas* †1742 Scot. physician and anatomist] **:** POUCH OF DOUGLAS **2 :** a passage or alley with no exit forward **:** BLIND ALLEY; *esp* **:** a street that is closed at one end but usu. has a circular area for turning around at that end **3 :** a point beyond which further advance or progress is or seems to be impossible ⟨worked himself into a *cul-de-sac* within three or four hundred feet of the top —Andrew Hamilton & Chandler Harris⟩ ⟨his own investigations into the substantiality of matter lead him into a *cul-de-sac* —Leslie Paul⟩

culdo- *comb form* [*cul*-de-sac of Douglas] **:** pouch of Douglas ⟨*culdo*centesis⟩

Cul·do·scope \ˈkəldə,skōp, ˈkül-\ *trademark* — used for a specialized endoscope employed in culdoscopy

cul·do·scop·ic \ˌ=ˈ=ˈskäpik\ *adj* [*culdoscopy* + *-ic*] **:** of, relating to, or involving culdoscopy

cul·dos·co·py \ˌkəlˈdäskəpē, ˌkül-\ *n* -ES [*cul*-de-sac of *Douglas* + *-scopy*] **:** a technique for endoscopic visualization and minor operative procedures on the female pelvic organs in which the instrument is introduced through a puncture in the wall of the pouch of Douglas

cu·let \ˈkyülət\ *n* -S [F, dim. of *cul* bottom, backside, fr. L *culus*; akin to OFris *skūl* hiding place, MLG *schūl*, ON *skjōl* hiding place, refuge, barn, OIr *cūl* hiding place, W *cil*, OE *hȳdan* hide — more at HIDE] **1 :** the small flat facet at the bottom of a brilliant parallel to the table — called also *collet*; see BRILLIANT illustration **2 :** a piece of plate armor covering the buttocks

cu·lex \ˈkyü,leks\ *n, cap* [NL, fr. L, gnat; akin to OIr *cuil* gnat and prob. to Skt *śūla* spit, spear, sharp pain, L *cuneus* wedge] **:** a large cosmopolitan genus of mosquitoes that includes the common house mosquito (*C. pipiens*) of Europe and No. America, a widespread tropical mosquito (*C. quinquefasciatus* or *C. fatigans*) which transmits certain filarial worms parasitic in man, and other mosquitoes which have been implicated as vectors of virus encephalitides and possibly of other diseases of man and animals — compare ANOPHELES

cul·gee \ˈkəlˌgē\ *n* -S [Hindi *kalgī*, fr. Per *kalgī* jeweled plume] **:** a jeweled plume worn in India on the turban

culic- *or* **culici-** *comb form* [NL, fr. L *culic-, culex*] **:** gnat **:** mosquito ⟨*Culic*idae⟩ ⟨*culici*fuge⟩

1cu·li·cid \ˈkyüləsəd, -,sid; kyüˈlisəd\ *adj* [NL *Culicidae*] **:** of or relating to the Culicidae

2culicid \"\ *n* -S **:** one of the Culicidae **:** MOSQUITO

cu·lic·i·dae \kyüˈlisə,dē\ *n pl, cap* [NL, fr. *Culic-, Culex*, type genus + *-idae*] **:** a family of slender long-legged two-winged flies having the body and appendages partly covered with hairs or scales and the mouthparts adapted for piercing and sucking, comprising the mosquitoes, and having active aquatic larvae known as wrigglers

cu·li·cide \ˈkyülə,sīd\ *n* -S [blend of *culic-* and *-cide*] **:** an insecticide that destroys mosquitoes

cu·lic·i·dol·o·gist \kyü,lisəˈdäləjəst\ *n* -S [NL *Culicidae* + E *-ologist* (as in *bacteriologist*)] **:** one specializing in the study of mosquitoes

1cu·li·cine \ˈkyülə,sīn, -,sən\ *adj* [NL *Culic-, Culex* + E *-ine*] **:** of, involving, or affecting mosquitoes of *Culex* or many related genera (as *Aedes*) — compare ANOPHELINE

2culicine \"\ *n* -S **:** a culicine mosquito

cu·li·la·wan \,külēˈläwən\ *or* **culilawan bark** *n* -S [Malay *kulit lawang*, fr. *kulit* bark + *lawang* cinnamon] **:** the aromatic bark of a tree (*Cinnamomum culilawan*) of the Moluccas

cul·i·nar·i·an \,kələˈnerēən, ,kyül-\ *n* -S [*culinary* + *-an*] **:** COOK, CHEF

cul·i·nary \ˈkələ,nerē, ˈkyül-, -ri\ *adj* [L *culinarius*, fr. *culina* kitchen + *-arius* -ary — more at KILN] **:** of or relating to the kitchen or cookery ⟨~ art⟩ **:** suited for cooking ⟨~ herbs⟩

cu·li·no \küˈlē(ˌ)nō, -)nüˌ\ *n, pl* **culino** *or* **culinos** *usu cap* [Pg, of AmerInd origin] **1 :** an Indian people of western Brazil that is closely related to the Arauá **2 :** a member of the Culino people

1cull \ˈkəl\ *vt* -ED/-ING/-S [ME *cullen, colen*, fr. MF *cuillir, coillir* to pick, gather, fr. L *colligere* to gather, collect — more at COLLECT] **1 a :** GATHER, PLUCK ⟨~ flowers⟩ **b :** to pick out and collect **:** CHOOSE ⟨~*ed* the best passages from the poet's works⟩ **2 a :** to subject (as a field) to culling **b :** to identify and remove culls from (a flock or herd) **3 :** to select or separate out as inferior or worthless

2cull \"\ *n* -S **1** *obs* **:** the act of culling **:** SELECTION **2 :** something rejected esp. as being inferior or worthless (as a cow from the herd, diseased plants from healthy ones, or nonlaying hens from a flock) — usu. used in pl. **3 a :** a grade of lumber below the lowest common grade **b :** PECKY CYPRESS

3cull \"\ *adj* [2*cull*] **:** culled out esp. as inferior **:** being a cull; *specif* **:** being a low grade of animal carcass used for processed meat food products

4cull \"\ *vt* -ED/-ING/-S [by alter.] *now dial* **:** 1COLL

5cull \", ˈkül\ *n* -S [perh. short for *cullion*] *dial Brit* **:** DUPE, GULL, SIMPLETON

cull·age \ˈkəlij\ *n* -s [¹*cull* + *-age*] **:** material eliminated in culling

cull board *n* [¹*cull*] **:** a table used for culling (as on an oyster boat)

cullender *var of* COLANDER

cul·len earth \ˈkələn-\ *n* [alter. of *Cologne earth*] **:** VANDYKE BROWN 2

cull·er \ˈkələ(r)\ *n* -s **:** one that culls: as **a :** one who inspects barrel staves **b :** one who examines poultry to detect inferior layers **c :** a scaler of logs **d :** one who picks out imperfect cookies or cakes in a bakery

cul·let \ˈkələt\ *n* -s [perh. fr. F *cueillette* act of gathering, picking, fr. L *collecta* — more at COLLECT] **:** broken or refuse glass that is generally added to a batch of new material to facilitate melting in glass manufacturing

cul·li·bil·i·ty \ˌkələˈbiləd·ē\ *n* -ES [¹*cully* + *-bility*] **:** GULLIBILITY

culling *n* -s **:** something culled out **:** CULL — usu. used in pl.

cul·lion \ˈkəlyən\ *n* -s [ME *coillon, colyoun* testicle, fr. MF *coillon, couillon*, fr. (assumed) VL *coleon-, coleo*, fr. L *coleus* scrotum, perh. fr. *colum* sieve, strainer; fr. the shape of a straining bag — more at HEDGE] **1** *obs* **:** TESTIS **2** *archaic* **:** a mean or base fellow **3 :** ORCHID 1

cul·lion·ly *adj, archaic* **:** MEAN, BASE

¹**cul·lis** \ˈkələs\ *n* -ES [ME *colis, colice*, fr. MF *coleïs*, fr. *coler* to strain, fr. L *colare*, fr. *colum* sieve — more at HEDGE] **:** a strong clear broth of meat (as for invalids)

²**cullis** \ˈ"\ *n* -ES [F *coulisse* groove, gutter — more at COULISSE] **:** a gutter in a roof **:** CHANNEL, GROOVE

¹**cul·ly** \ˈkəlē\ *n* -ES [perh. alter. of *cullion*] **1** *archaic* **:** one easily tricked or imposed on **:** DUPE, GULL **2** *slang* **:** COMPANION, MATE

²**cully** \ˈ"\ *vt* -ED/-ING/-ES **:** to impose on **:** TRICK, CHEAT, DECEIVE

¹**culm** \ˈkəlm, ˈkəu̇m\ *n* -s [ME *culme*; prob. akin to ME *col* coal — more at COAL] **1 :** refuse coal screenings often piled in heaps **:** SLACK **2 a :** a shoal-water deposit of conglomerates, sandstones, and shales in which marine fossil-bearing beds alternate with those containing plant remains **b** *also* **culm measures :** a Lower Carboniferous formation consisting of such deposits that in parts of Europe underlies the productive coal measures and has the stratigraphic position elsewhere occupied by the mountain limestone

²**culm** \ˈ"\ *adj, usu cap* [fr. *Culm*, division of the European Carboniferous, fr. ¹*culm*] **:** of or relating to a division of the Carboniferous of Europe — see GEOLOGIC TIME table

³**culm** \ˈ"\ *n* -s [modif. of L *culmen* — more at HILL] *obs* **:** CULMEN

⁴**culm** \ˈ"\ *n* -s [L *culmus* stalk — more at HAULM] **1 :** the jointed stem of a grass usu. hollow except at the often swollen nodes and usu. herbaceous except in the bamboos and other arborescent grasses; *also* **:** one of the solid stems of sedges, rushes, and similar monocotyledonous plants **2 culms** *pl, Brit* **:** rootlets of brewer's malt often used as fodder

cul·mann's diagram \ˈkülmənz-, -ˌmänz-\ *n, usu cap C* [after Karl *Culmann* †1881 Ger. engineer] **:** FUNICULAR POLYGON 2

culm bank *n* [¹*culm*] **:** a storage dump of culm

cul·men \ˈkəlmən\ *n, pl* **culmens** \-nz\ *or* **culmi·na** \-nə\ [L — more at HILL] **1 :** ACME, CULMINATION **2** [NL, fr. L] **:** the dorsal ridge of a bird's bill

culmi- *comb form* [L *culmus* — more at HAULM] **:** stalk **:** culm ⟨*culmi*colous⟩ ⟨*culmi*genous⟩

culm·ide \ˈkəlˌmīd\ *adj, usu cap* [fr. *Culmide*, mountain-making episode, fr. *Culm*, division of the European Carboniferous + E *-ide*] **:** of or relating to mountain-making movements in the Carboniferous era — see GEOLOGIC TIME table

cul·mi·nant \ˈkəlmənənt\ *adj* [ML *culminant-, culminans*, pres. part. of *culminare* to culminate] **1 :** being at greatest altitude or on the meridian **2 :** fully developed ⟨the blow was not the expression of any ~ rebellion —J.B.Clayton⟩

cul·mi·nate \-ˌnāt, *usu* -ād.+V\ *vb* -ED/-ING/-S [ML *culminatus*, past part. of *culminare*, fr. LL, to crown, fr. L *culmin-, culmen* top — more at HILL] *vi* **1** *of a celestial body* **:** to reach the highest altitude **:** come to the meridian; *also* **:** to be directly overhead **2 a :** to rise to or form a summit (as of a mountain or wave) ⟨a helmet *culminating* in a crest⟩ **b :** to reach the highest point (as of rank or power) ⟨the house of Burgundy was rapidly *culminating* —J.L.Motley⟩ **c :** to reach a climactic or decisive point ⟨the troubles of the year *culminated* in rioting in November⟩ ~ *vt* **:** to bring to a head **:** be the culminating point of **:** CLIMAX, CAP ⟨the agreement *culminated* a long controversy —*Newsweek*⟩

cul·mi·na·tion \ˌkəlməˈnāshən\ *n* -s [ML *culminatus* + E *-ion*] **1 :** the highest point reached by a celestial body in its diurnal revolution; *also* **:** the lowest point reached by a circumpolar celestial body **2 :** that in which something culminates **:** culminating position **:** SUMMIT, ACME, CONSUMMATION, CLIMAX ⟨the ~ of a brilliant career⟩ ⟨the ~ of years of effort⟩

cu·lotte \(ˈ)k(y)üˈlät\ *n* -s [F, lit., breeches, dim. of *cul* bottom, backside — more at CULET] **1 :** hair on the thighs of an animal (as a Pomeranian dog) **:** BREECHING **2 :** a divided skirt; *also* **:** a garment having a divided skirt — often used in pl.

cul·pa \ˈku̇lpə, ˈkəl-\ *n, pl* **cul·pae** \-ülˌpī, -əlˌpē\ [L, guilt, fault; prob. akin to OIr *col* sin, blame, W *cwl*] **1** *Roman & civil law* **:** actionable negligence or fault; *specif* **:** the failure to use the care and diligence demanded by the special relationship between the plaintiff and defendant under the particular circumstances that arises from inattention, careless conduct, or want of care — distinguished from *dolus* **2** *Roman & civil law* **:** all actionable fault or misconduct including both negligence and willful or wanton wrongs arising from malice, fraud, or a desire for wrongful gain **3 :** CULPA LEVIS

cul·pa·bil·i·ty \ˌkəlpəˈbiləd·ē, -ətē, -i\ *n* -ES **:** the quality or state of being culpable **:** BLAMEWORTHINESS

cul·pa·ble \ˈkəlpəbəl\ *adj* [ME *coupable, culpabil*, fr. MF *coupable, culpable*, fr. L *culpabilis*, fr. *culpare* to blame (fr. *culpa*) + *-abilis* -able] **1** *obs* **:** GUILTY, CRIMINAL **2 :** meriting condemnation or censure esp. as criminal ⟨~ plotters⟩ ⟨~ homicides⟩ or as conducive to accident, loss, or disaster ⟨~ negligence⟩ ⟨is it not . . . ~ and unworthy, thus beforehand to slur her honor —P.B.Shelley⟩ **syn** see BLAMEWORTHY

cul·pa·ble·ness *n* -ES [ME *coupablenesse*, fr. *coupable* + *-nesse* -ness] **:** the quality or state of being culpable **:** CULPABILITY

cul·pa·bly \-blē, -li\ *adv* **:** in a manner or to a degree deserving blame or censure **:** REPREHENSIBLY

culpa la·ta \ˌ==ˈläd·ə, -lā-\ *or* **culpa mag·na** \-ˈmägnə, -mag-\ *n* [LL, lit., great negligence] *Roman & civil law* **:** the absence of the degree of care even inattentive or thoughtless persons would exercise under all the circumstances **:** GROSS NEGLIGENCE

culpa le·vis \-ˈlevəs\ *n* [NL *culpa levis*, lit., slight negligence] *Roman & civil law* **:** ordinary or slight negligence arising from failure to exercise such care as a diligent father is accustomed to observe in his own affairs under all the circumstances

culpa levis in ab·strac·to \-ˌinəbzˈtrak(ˌ)tō, -ˌiˌnab-, -bˈst-\ *n* [NL, lit., slight negligence in the abstract] *Roman & civil law* **:** ordinary negligence arising from the failure to exercise the very high degree of care that men of good business or very prudent persons would exercise under all the circumstances

culpa levis in con·cre·to \-ˌinˌkänˈkrēˌtō\ *n* [NL, lit., slight negligence in the concrete] *Roman & civil law* **:** ordinary negligence arising from one's failure to exercise such care in the interest of another as he exercises in his own affairs

culpa le·vis·si·ma \-leˈvisəmə\ *n* [NL, lit., slightest negligence] *Roman & civil law* **:** negligence arising from the slightest fault **:** very slight negligence arising from the failure to exercise the most exact care which a most diligent father would exercise under all the circumstances

cul·pa·to·ry \ˈkəlpəˌtōrē\ *adj* [L *culpatus* (past part. of *culpare* to blame, fr *culpa* fault, blame) + E *-ory* — more at CULPA] **:** CENSORIOUS, ACCUSING

cul·peo \ˈkülˈpā(ˌ)ō\ *n* -s [Sp, fr. Araucan *culpeu*] **:** a So. American mammal (*Dusicyon magellanicus*) that was formerly considered a true dog (genus *Canis*); *also* **:** any of several closely related species

cul·prit \ˈkəlprət *also* -ˌprit; *usu* -d.+V\ *n* -s [AF *cul.* (abbr. of *culpable* guilty) + *prit, prist, prest* ready (i.e., to prove it), fr. L *praestus* — more at PRESTO] **1 a :** one accused of or arraigned for a crime **b :** one accused of a fault **2 a :** one guilty of a crime **b :** one guilty of a fault **syn** see CRIMINAL

culs-de-four *pl of* CUL-DE-FOUR

culs-de-lampe *pl of* CUL-DE-LAMPE

culs-de-sac *pl of* CUL-DE-SAC

cult \ˈkəlt\ *n* -s [F & L; F *culte*, fr. L *cultus* care, cultivation, culture, adoration, fr. *cultus*, past part. of *colere* to till, cultivate, dwell, inhabit, worship — more at WHEEL] **1 :** religious practice **:** WORSHIP **2 :** a system of beliefs and ritual connected with the worship of a deity, a spirit, or a group of deities or spirits ⟨the ~ of Apollo⟩ ⟨the earth ~⟩ **3 a :** the rites, ceremonies, and practices of a religion **:** the formal aspect of religious experience ⟨dissent occurs in all three fields of expression of religious experience, in doctrine, in ~, and organization —Joachim Wach⟩ **b** *Roman Catholicism* **:** reverence and ceremonial veneration paid to God or to the Virgin Mary or to the saints or to objects that symbolize or otherwise represent them (as the crucifix or a statue) — called also *cultus*; compare DULIA, HYPERDULIA, LATRIA **4 :** a religion regarded as unorthodox or spurious ⟨the exuberant growth of fantastic ~*s*⟩; *also* **:** a minority religious group holding beliefs regarded as unorthodox or spurious **:** SECT ⟨provided a haven for persecuted ~*s*⟩ **5 :** a system for the cure of disease based on the dogma, tenets, or principles set forth by its promulgator to the exclusion of scientific experience or demonstration **6 a :** great or excessive devotion or dedication to some person, idea, or thing ⟨the ~ of success⟩; *esp* **:** such devotion regarded as a literary or intellectual fad or fetish ⟨the ~ of art-for-art's sake⟩ **b :** the object of such devotion ⟨square dancing has developed into something of a ~ —R.L.Taylor⟩ **c** (1) **:** a body of persons characterized by such devotion ⟨America's growing ~ of home fixer uppers —*Wall Street Jour.*⟩ (2) **:** a usu. small or narrow circle of persons united by devotion or allegiance to some artistic or intellectual program, tendency, or figure (as one of limited popular appeal) ⟨the exclusive ~ of those that profess to admire his esoteric verse⟩ **syn** see RELIGION

cultch *or* **culch** \ˈkəlch\ *n* -ES [perh. fr. a F dial. form of F *couche* couch, bed, fr. OF *culche, couche* — more at COUCH] **1 a :** material (as oyster shells) laid down on oyster grounds to furnish points of attachment for the spat; *also* **:** similar material provided for any other shellfish **b :** a horny or gelatinous egg mass of a mollusk **2** *chiefly NewEng* **:** TRASH, RUBBISH

cul·tel·la·tion \ˌkəltəˈlāshən\ *n* -s [F, fr. L *cultellus* + F *-ation*] **:** the transferring in surveying of the exact location of a point from a higher level (as an overhanging cliff) to a lower by dropping a sharp-pointed marking pin

cul·tel·lus \kəlˈteləs\ *n, pl* **cultel·li** \-eˌlī, -(ˌ)lē\ [NL, fr. L, small knife, dim. of *culter* knife, plowshare — more at COLTER] **:** one of the sharp pointed cutting organs (as mandibles and maxillae) of many bloodsucking flies

culti *pl of* CULTUS

cul·tic \ˈkəltik\ *adj* **:** of or relating to a cult ⟨a temple that became the ~ center of the entire province⟩

cul·ti·cut·ter \ˈkəltəˌkəd·ə(r)\ *n* [*cultivator* + *cutter*] **:** a cultivator with blades that cut into sod or cover crop

cul·ti·gen \ˈkəltəjən, -ˌjen\ *n* -s [*cultivated* + *-gen*] **1 :** a cultivated organism (as maize) of a variety or species for which a wild ancestor is unknown **2 :** CULTIVAR — not used technically

cul·ti·pack \ˈkəltəˌpak\ *vt* [*cultivate* + *pack*] **:** to firm and pulverize (a seedbed) with a corrugated roller

cul·ti·pack·er \-kə(r)\ *n* [fr. *Cultipacker*, a trademark] **:** a corrugated roller used to break clods and firm a seedbed

cul·ti·ros·tral \ˌkəltəˈrästrəl\ *adj* [NL *Cultirostres* + E *-al*] **:** having a cultrate bill **:** of or relating to the Cultirostres

cul·ti·ros·tres \ˌ==ˈ=(ˌ)strēz\ *n pl, cap* [NL, fr. *culti-* (fr. L *culter* knife, plowshare) + *-rostres* (fr. L *rostrum* beak) — more at COLTER, ROSTRUM] *in old classifications* **:** a group including the storks, herons, cranes, and various other large birds with pointed sharp-edged bills

cult·ish \ˈkəltish\ *adj* **:** of, relating to, or suggesting a cult ⟨a ~ belief that such composers . . . could hardly be represented on the modern grand —Irving Kolodin⟩

cult·ism \ˈkəlˌtizəm\ *n* -s **1 :** devotion to the doctrine or practice of a cult ⟨however foolish the ~ of those who systematized his half-truths —P.T.Homan⟩ **:** a cultish tendency or outlook ⟨to avoid any taint of ~, each issue will have a different editor —*Time*⟩ **:** a tendency to form or embrace a cult ⟨America's intellectual history is rich in ~, faddism, and large-scale self-deception —R.H.Rovere⟩ **2 :** WORSHIP, VENERATION ⟨lived in a world of antiquities and were actuated by . . . ~ of the dead —J.P.Marquand⟩

cult·ist \ˈkəltəst\ *n* -s **:** a devotee or practitioner of a cult **:** SECTARIAN

cul·ti·va·bil·i·ty \ˌkəltəvəˈbiləd·ē\ *n* -ES **:** the quality or state of being cultivable

cul·ti·va·ble \ˈkəltəvəbəl\ *adj* [F, fr. MF, fr. *cultiver, coutiver* to cultivate (fr. OF) + *-able* — more at CULTIVATE] **:** capable of being cultivated

cul·ti·var \ˈkəltəˌvär\ *n* -s [*cultivated variety*] **:** an organism of a kind (as a variety, strain, or race) that has originated and persisted under cultivation

cul·ti·vat·able \ˈkəltəˌvād·əbəl, -ātə-\ *adj* **:** CULTIVABLE

cul·ti·vate \ˈkəltəˌvāt, *usu* -ād.+V\ *vt* -ED/-ING/-S [ML *cultivatus*, past part. of *cultivare*, fr. OF *cultiver, coutiver*, fr. *culti, couti* cultivable, fr. ML *cultivus*, fr. L *cultus* (past part. of *colere* to till, cultivate, dwell, inhabit) + *-ivus* -ive — more at WHEEL] **1 :** to prepare for the raising of crops **:** prepare and use for such a purpose **:** TILL ⟨~ the soil⟩; *specif* **:** to loosen or break up the soil about (growing crops or plants) for the purpose of killing weeds and modifying moisture retention of the soil esp. with a cultivator **2 :** to protect and encourage the growth of: **a :** to till or labor over; *esp* **:** to apply methods of culturing to ⟨~ oysters⟩ ⟨~ yeasts⟩ **b :** to improve by labor, care, or study **:** bring to culture, civilization, or refinement ⟨writers who ~ style⟩ **3 :** to cause to grow by special attention or by studying, advancing, developing, practicing, or publicizing **:** FURTHER, ENCOURAGE ⟨Italy, where law and medicine were *cultivated*, and the North, where theology with logic and metaphysics were supreme —H.O. Taylor⟩ **4 :** to seek the society of **:** make friends with ⟨outraged constantly by the odd assortment of people my father *cultivated* —Elsa Maxwell⟩ **syn** see NURSE

cultivated *adj* **1 a** *of a plant* **:** grown or developed by human care **:** DOMESTICATED ⟨~ varieties of roses⟩ **b** *of a field* **:** under cultivation **:** in crops **2** *of a person, quality, or faculty* **:** socially well-trained **:** CULTURED, REFINED, EDUCATED ⟨~ speech⟩ ⟨~ tastes⟩ ⟨~ voices⟩

cultivated pearl *n* **:** CULTURED PEARL

cul·ti·va·tion \ˌkəltəˈvāshən\ *n* -s **1 :** the act or art of cultivating: as **a :** the art or process of agriculture **:** TILLAGE; *esp* **:** intertillage to destroy weeds and loosen soil ⟨fields brought under ~⟩ **b :** CULTURE 6 **c :** a fostering or practicing esp. of a branch of learning **:** a training and developing (as of taste, mind, manners) **d :** assiduous development of personal relations ⟨~ of new friendships⟩ **2 :** something produced by cultivating **:** CULTURE, REFINEMENT, CIVILIZATION ⟨a man of charm and ~⟩ **3 :** land being cultivated ⟨villagers working on the headman's ~*s*⟩

cul·ti·va·tor \ˈkəltəˌvād·ə(r), -ātə-\ *n* -s **1 :** one that cultivates (as the soil, an art, a discipline) **:** FARMER; *esp* **:** one that cultivates the soil as a mode of life ⟨by contrast with their nomadic neighbors these Indians are ~*s* and skilled craftsmen⟩ **2 :** an implement (as a hand tool or a large wheeled horse-drawn or tractor-drawn vehicle) that consists usu. of a frame upon which are fastened shares, discs, or tines and that is used for breaking up the soil surface esp. among growing crops in order to aerate the soil, conserve moisture, and control weeds — compare GO-DEVIL, SULKY

cultivator 2

cultivator shield *n* **:** an attachment to a cultivator to prevent damage to the crop

cult object *n* **:** an object of religious devotion, veneration, or ritualistic and symbolic value within a system of worship

cult of the dead : ANCESTOR CULT

cul·trate \ˈkəlˌtrāt\ *also* **cul·trat·ed** \-ād·əd\ *adj* [*cultrate* fr. L *cultratus* knife-shaped, fr. *cultr-, culter* knife + *-atus* -ate; *cultrated* fr. L *cultratus* + E *-ed* — more at COLTER] **:** sharp-edged and pointed **:** shaped like a pruning knife ⟨a crow's beak is ~⟩

cults *pl of* CULT

cul·tu·al \ˈkəlch(ə)wəl\ *adj* [F *cultuel*, fr. *culte* cult + *-uel* (as in *mutuel* mutual) — more at CULT] **:** of or relating to cult or worship

cul·tur·able \ˈkəlch(ə)rəbəl\ *adj* [²*culture* + *-able*] **:** capable of culture **:** CULTIVABLE

cul·tur·al \ˈkəlch(ə)rəl, +V *also* -chərl\ *adj* [¹*culture* + *-al*] **1 :** of or relating to the artistic and intellectual aspects or content of human activity ⟨a person of broad ~ interests⟩ ⟨organized ~ activity at the camp includes theatricals and study circles⟩ **2 a :** produced by breeding ⟨a ~ variety⟩ **b :** of or relating to the culture of a plant **:** HORTICULTURAL 2 **3 a :** dealing with culture data ⟨~ anthropology⟩ ⟨Portuguese ~ influences in Brazil⟩ ⟨all humans are strongly influenced by ~ inheritance as well, which is transmitted outside the body, such as language, custom, education, and so on —L.C.Dunn⟩ **b :** of, relating to, or being the complex of institutionalized traits learned and transmitted by man as a member of society **4 :** MAN-MADE ⟨~ features of the landscape⟩

cultural anthropology *n* **:** the division of anthropology that deals with the study of culture in all its aspects and that utilizes the methods, concepts, and data of archaeology, ethnology and ethnography, folklore and linguistics, and sometimes those of the sociological and psychological sciences — distinguished from *physical anthropology*

cultural change *n* **:** modification of a society through innovation, invention, discovery, or contact with other societies

cultural drift *n* **1 :** the spread of culture traits throughout an area **2 :** the tendency of a culture or its institutions to manifest cumulative variation in certain directions

cultural evolution *n* **:** EVOLUTION 6b

cultural history *n* **1 :** the history of a culture or culture area ⟨a *cultural history* of the Southwest⟩; *specif* **:** a history treating one or a number of historic world cultures as an integrated unit for purposes of cross comparison with others and for analysis of the forces presumed to be in operation as regards cultural growth, development, fruition, and decay **2 :** history that esp. by contrast with narrative political history concentrates upon the social, intellectual, and artistic aspects or forces in the life of a people or nation — compare SOCIAL HISTORY

cul·tur·al·ist \-ch(ə)rələst\ *n* -s **1 :** one that emphasizes the importance of culture in determining behavior **2 :** a specialist in the study of culture; *specif* **:** a cultural anthropologist

cul·tur·al·ized \-ch(ə)rəˌlīzd\ *adj* **:** deriving from or imposed or conditioned by culture

cultural lag *n* **:** a relatively slower advance or change of one aspect of a culture; *esp* **:** the slower development of nonmaterial as contrasted with material or technological culture traits

cul·tur·al·ly \ˈkəlch(ə)rəlē, -li\ *adv* **1 :** with regard to culture ⟨~ the period was one of rapid advance⟩ **:** in a cultural manner ⟨will seek every evening to do something that is ~ satisfying and significant —*Current Biog.*⟩ **2 :** according to the prevailing culture ⟨handled and fed, clothed and cared for in ~ approved ways —Grace De Laguna⟩ **3 :** according to the principles of culture for a plant or crop

cultural nature *n* **:** HUMAN NATURE a

cultural sociology *n* [trans. of G *kultursoziologie*] **:** the sociological study of the historical processes involved in cultural phenomena (as art, philosophy, religion)

¹**cul·ture** \ˈkəlchə(r)\ *n* -s [ME, fr. MF, fr L *cultura*, fr. *cultus* (past part. of *colere* to till, cultivate) + *-ura* -ure — more at WHEEL] **1 a :** the art or practice of cultivating **:** the manner or method of cultivating **:** TILLAGE ⟨we ought to blame the ~, not the soil —Alexander Pope⟩ **b** *obs* **:** cultivated land **:** a cultivated area **2 :** the act of developing by education, discipline, social experience **:** the training or refining of the moral and intellectual faculties **3 a :** the cultivation or rearing of a particular product or crop or stock for supply ⟨the ~ of the vine⟩ ⟨bee ~⟩ **b :** steady endeavor at improvement of or in a special line ⟨~ of the sonnet⟩ **c :** professional or expert care and training ⟨voice ~⟩ ⟨beauty ~⟩ **4 a :** the state of being cultivated; *esp* **:** the enlightenment and excellence of taste acquired by intellectual and aesthetic training **:** the intellectual and artistic content of civilization **:** refinement in manners, taste, thought **b :** acquaintance with and taste in fine arts, humanities, and broad aspects of science as distinguished from vocational, technical, or professional skill or knowledge **5 a :** the total pattern of human behavior and its products embodied in thought, speech, action, and artifacts and dependent upon man's capacity for learning and transmitting knowledge to succeeding generations through the use of tools, language, and systems of abstract thought **b :** the body of customary beliefs, social forms, and material traits constituting a distinct complex of tradition of a racial, religious, or social group ⟨a nation with many ~*s*⟩ ⟨Plains Indian ~⟩ ⟨but to many men today the most interesting thing about society is its ~ . . . that complex whole that includes knowledge, belief, morals, law, customs, opinions, religion, superstition, and art —Preserved Smith⟩ **c :** a complex of typical behavior or standardized social characteristics peculiar to a specific group, occupation or profession, sex, age grade, or social class ⟨youth ~⟩ ⟨middle class ~⟩ **d :** a recurring assemblage (as of artifacts, house types, methods of burial, and other evidences of a way of life) that differentiates a group of archaeological sites **6 a :** cultivation of living material (as bacteria or tissues) in prepared nutrient media; *also* **:** an instance of such cultivation or a growth that is the intended product of it **b :** any inoculated nutrient medium whether or not it contains living organisms — see MEDIUM 8; PURE CULTURE **7 :** the details of a map in the aggregate that represent cultural features (as canals, buildings, roads)

²**culture** \ˈ"\ *vt* **cultured; cultured; culturing** \-ch(ə)riŋ\ **cultures** [MF *culturer*, fr. *culture*, n.] **1 :** CULTIVATE **2** *biol* **a :** to grow (as microorganisms or tissues) in a prepared medium **b :** to start a culture from ⟨~ soil⟩; *also* **:** to make a culture of ⟨*cultured* milk⟩

culture and personality *n* **:** an area of investigation within anthropology concentrating upon the psychological orientation of culture and the dynamic structure of personality developed within it

culture area *n* **:** a contiguous geographic area comprising a number of societies that possess the same or similar traits or that share a dominant cultural orientation ⟨the cattle complex serves to delimit the East African *culture area*⟩

culture-bound \ˈ==ˌ=\ *adj* **:** limited by or valid only within a particular culture ⟨intelligence tests are commonly *culture-bound* to some degree⟩

culture center *n* **:** the region of a culture area showing the greatest concentration of traits peculiar to or typical of the area

culture complex *n* **:** ³COMPLEX 1a

culture conflict *n* **:** the conflict of behavior patterns and values that results when different cultures are incompletely assimilated; *esp* **:** the conflict that may find expression in high rates of criminality and delinquency

culture contact *n, chiefly Brit* **:** ACCULTURATION

cultured *adj* **1 :** being under culture **:** CULTIVATED ⟨~ fields⟩ **2 :** well-educated **:** URBANE, POLISHED **:** having refined taste, speech, and manners **3 :** grown or produced under artificial conditions ⟨bacteria ~ for vaccine production⟩

cultured milk *or* **cultured buttermilk** *n* **:** the product resulting from the souring of skimmed or partially skimmed milk by the addition of a culture of lactic acid bacteria

cultured pearl *also* **culture pearl** *n* **:** a natural pearl grown under controlled conditions (as by inserting a seed pearl into the mantle of an oyster and keeping the oyster in a sea bed for some years)

culture feature *n* **:** a man-made feature (as a town, road, bridge, or house) of a region

culture hero *n* **1 :** a legendary figure variously represented as a beast, bird, man, or demigod to whom a people attributes the factors that appear most essential to its existence and culture (as important inventions, the overcoming of major obstacles, the exercise of divine leadership, and the origin of itself, mankind, natural phenomena, or the world) **2 :** one that symbolizes the ideal of a people or a group

culture-historical \ˌ====ˌ===\ *adj* [trans. of G *kulturhistorisch*] **:** being or relating to the theory and methods of the Vienna school of ethnology

culture language *n* **:** a language that is learned by many members of other speech communities for the sake of access to the culture of which it is the vehicle

culture myth *n* **:** a myth accounting for the discovery of arts and sciences

culture trait *n* **:** TRAIT 4

cul·tur·ist \ˈkəlch(ə)rəst\ *n* -s **1 :** one engaged in a culture **2 :** an advocate of culture or of a particular method of cultivating mind or body **3 :** one that breeds or raises animals esp. of kinds not usu. regarded as domesticated (as fishes or game birds)

cul·tur·o·log·i·cal \ˌkəlch(ə)rəˈläjəkəl\ *adj* **:** of or relating to culturology **:** of, relating to, or applying a methodology that regards culture as an autonomous self-determined process and explains human behavior in terms of that process — **cul·tur·o·log·i·cal·ly** \-jək(ə)lē\ *adv*

culturologist *n* -s **:** a specialist in or advocate of culturology

cul·tur·ol·o·gy \-jē\ *n* -ES [¹*culture* + *-o-* + *-logy*] **:** the science of culture; *specif* **:** a methodology esp. associated with the American anthropologist Leslie A. White that treats culture as a self-contained self-determined process and regards cultural traits (as technologies, ideologies, and institutions) as the products of antecedent and concomitant cultural elements and as developing independently of other data (as climatic environment, human physical type, or human wishes and purposes)

¹**cul·tus** \ˈkəltəs\ *n, pl* **cultuses** \-təsəz\ *or* **cul·ti** \-ˌtī, -ˌtē\ [NL, fr. L, adoration — more at CULT] **1 :** organized religious practice or system of worship **:** the practical aspect of a religion embodying the aggregate of its ritual forms, sacred ceremonies, liturgies, rites, and all acts expressive of veneration or worship **2 :** CULT 3b

²**cultus** \"\ *or* **cultus cod** *n* -ES [Chinook *kúltus* worthless] **:** LINGCOD

cultus image *or* **cultus statue** *n* [¹*cultus*] **:** an image or statue that is a direct object of worship

¹**cul·ver** \ˈkəlvə(r), ˈkúl-\ *n* -s [ME, fr. OE *culfre, culufre*, fr. (assumed) VL *columbra*, fr. L *columbula*, dim. of *columba* dove — more at COLUMBA] **:** DOVE, PIGEON; *specif, Brit* **:** WOOD PIGEON

²**cul·ver** \ˈkəlvə(r)\ *n* -s [by shortening] **:** CULVERIN

culverfoot \ˈ==ˌ=\ *n, pl* **culverfoots** [ME *culverfot*, fr. ¹*culver* + *fot* foot; fr. the shape of the leaves] **:** any of several plants of the genus *Geranium*; *esp* **:** the small-flowered European cranesbill (*G. columbinum*) — compare DOVE'S-FOOT

culverhouse \ˈ==ˌ=\ *n* [ME *culverhous*, fr. ¹*culver* + *hous* house] **:** DOVECOTE

cul·ve·rin \ˈkəlvərən\ *also* **cul·ve·ring** \-riŋ\ *n* -s [ME, fr. MF *coulevrine, couleuvrine*, fr. *couleuvre* adder, snake (fr. L *colubra*, fem. of *colubr-, coluber* snake) + *-ine* — more at COLUBER] **:** a firearm that was orig. a rude musket but was in the 16th and 17th centuries a long cannon (as an 18-pounder) with serpent-shaped handles

cul·ver·key \ˈkəlvə(r)ˌkē\ *n* [¹*culver* + *key*] **1** *dial Eng* **:** WOOD HYACINTH **2** *dial Eng* **:** COWSLIP 1a

cul·ver's root \ˈkəlvə(r)z-\ *or* **culver's physic** *also* **culvers** *n, usu cap C* [after a Dr. *Culver* fl before 1716 Am. physician who used it for medicinal purposes] **1 :** a tall perennial herb (*Veronicastrum virginicum*) common in eastern No. America **2 :** the rhizome and roots of Culver's root used as a cathartic

¹**cul·vert** \ˈkəlvə(r)t, *chiefly in dial or substand speech* -lbə-; *usu* |d·+V\ *n* -s [origin unknown] **1 :** a transverse drain or waterway (as under a road, railroad, or canal) **2 :** a conduit for a culvert **3 :** a bridge over a culvert

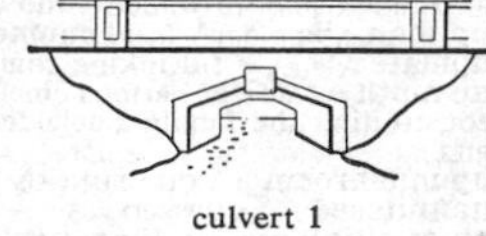
culvert 1

²**culvert** \"\ *vt* -ED/-ING/-S **1 :** to provide (a road) or bridge (a stream) with a culvert **2 :** to channel (a river) underground

cul·vert·age \ˈkəlvə(r)d·ij\ *n* -s [OF, fr. *culvert* serf (fr. L *collibertus* fellow freedman, fr. *com-* + *libertus* one made free, fr. *liber* free) + *-age* — more at LIBERAL] **:** VILLENAGE; *also* **:** reduction to villenage with forfeiture of estate

culverwort \ˈ==ˌ=\ *n* [¹*culver* + *wort*] **:** GARDEN COLUMBINE

¹**cum** \(ˈ)küm, (ˈ)kəm\ *prep* [L; akin to L *com-* — more at CO-] **:** WITH **:** combined with ⟨the entertainment-*cum*-profit motive —*Newsweek*⟩ **:** INCLUDING **:** along with ⟨house-*cum*-farm⟩ ⟨the members of this orchestra-*cum*-ballet —*New Yorker*⟩

²**cum** \ˈ=\ *adj (or adv)* [in sense 1, by shortening; in sense 2, fr. ¹*cum*] **1 :** CUM LAUDE **2 :** including dividend ⟨the ~ price of a stock⟩

cum- *or* **cumo-** *comb form* [*cumin*] **:** cumic **:** cumin ⟨*cum*aldehyde⟩ ⟨*cumo*quinol⟩

cum *abbr* cumulative

cu·ma·cea \kyüˈmāshēə\ *n pl, cap* [NL, fr. *Cuma*, type genus (irreg. fr. Gk *kyma* sprout, wave, anything swollen) + *-acea* — more at CYME] **:** an order of small sessile-eyed malacostracan marine crustaceans (division Peracarida) having a carapace formed by fusion of the first three or four thoracic segments with the head — **cu·ma·cean** \(ˈ)=ˈ=shən\ *adj or n* — **cu·ma·ceous** \-shəs\ *adj*

cu·ma·gloia \ˌkyüməˈglóiə\ *n, cap* [NL, irreg. fr. Gk *kyma* sprout, wave, anything swollen + *gloia*, var. of *glia* glue — more at CLAY] **:** a genus of marine red algae (family Helminthocladiaceae) occurring commonly along the Pacific coast of No. America as a summer annual, the mature thallus consisting of a disk-shaped holdfast and a simple or sparsely branched upper portion with numerous fine cylindrical branches

cu·mal·de·hyde \kyüˈmaldəˌhīd\ *n* [*cum-* + *aldehyde*] **:** an aromatic oily aldehyde $(CH_3)_2CHC_6H_4CHO$ found in cumin oil and other essential oils and used in perfumes and flavors; *para*-isopropyl-benzaldehyde — called also *cuminaldehyde*

cumalic acid *var of* COUMALIC ACID

cumalin *var of* COUMALIN

cu·man \k(y)üˈmän, ˈ=ˌ=\ *or* **co·man** \kōˈ-, ˈ=ˌ-\ *or* **ku·man** \k(y)üˈ-, ˈ=ˌ-\ *n, pl* **cuman** *or* **cumans** *or* **coman** *or* **comans** *or* **kuman** *or* **kumans** *usu cap* [ML *Cumani* (pl.), fr. MGk *Koumanoi*] **1 a :** a Turkic people who occupied parts of southern Russia and the Moldavian and Wallachian steppes during the 9th, 10th and 11th centuries and were driven out by the Tatar and Mongol invasions and some of whom passed into Hungary where they were absorbed **b :** a member of such people **2 :** the Turkic language of the Cuman people

cu·ma·na·go·to \küˌmänəˈgōd·(ˌ)ō\ *n, pl* **cumanagoto** *or* **cumanagotos** *usu cap* [Sp, of AmerInd origin] **1 a :** a Cariban people of Venezuela **b :** a member of such people **2 :** the language of the Cumanagoto people

cu·ma·ni·an \kyüˈmānēən\ *n* -s *usu cap* [*Cuman* + *-ian*] **:** CUMAN

cumara *or* **cumaru** *var of* COUMAROU

cumarin *var of* COUMARIN

cumarone *var of* COUMARONE

cu·mat·o·phyte \kyüˈmad·əˌfīt\ *also* **cu·ma·phyte** \ˈkyüməˌ-\ *n* -s [*cumatophyte* irreg. fr. Gk *kymato-* (fr. *kymat-, kyma* wave) + E *-phyte*; *cumaphyte* irreg. fr. Gk *kyma* wave + E *-phyte* — more at CYME] **:** a plant adapted for growth under surf conditions **:** SURF PLANT — **cu·mat·o·phyt·ic** \(ˈ)kyüˌmad·əˈfid·ik\ *also* **cu·ma·phyt·ic** \ˌkyümə-\ *adj*

cu·may \küˈmī(ˌ)ē, ˌkümaˈē\ *n* -s [Pg *cumai, cumahy*, fr. Tupi *cumá*] **:** a small tree or shrub (*Zschokkea arborescens*) of the family Apocynaceae of the Amazon valley; *also* **:** its gum

cum·bent \ˈkəmbənt\ *adj* [L *-cumbent-, -cumbens*, pres. part. of *-cumbere* to lie (as in *recumbere* to lie down) — more at RECUMBENT] **:** RECUMBENT

¹**cum·ber** \ˈkəmbə(r)\ *vt* **cumbered; cumbered; cumbering** \-b(ə)riŋ\ **cumbers** [ME *cumbren, combren*, perh. fr. OF *combrer* to prevent, hinder, fr. (assumed) OF *combre* abatis — more at ENCUMBER] **1** *obs* **a :** to destroy utterly **:** DEFEAT **b :** TROUBLE, HARASS ⟨Martha was ~*ed* about much serving —Luke 10:40 (AV)⟩ **2 :** to hinder or bother by being in the way ⟨~*ed* with heavy clothing⟩ **3 :** to weigh down needlessly **:** burden uselessly **:** clutter up ⟨~ the memory with trivial facts⟩ ⟨an old walnut tree . . . had perished a long time ago, but still stood and was ~*ing* the earth —A.E.Coppard⟩ **syn** see BURDEN

²**cumber** \"\ *n* -s [ME *cumbre, combre*, fr. *cumbren, combren*, v.] **:** something that cumbers: as **a** *archaic* **:** CARE, WORRY **b** *archaic* **:** TROUBLE, INCONVENIENCE **c :** HINDRANCE, BURDEN, ENCUMBRANCE

cum·ber·land \ˈkəmbə(r)lənd\ *adj, usu cap* [fr. *Cumberland* county, England] **:** of or from the county of Cumberland, England **:** of the kind or style prevalent in Cumberland **:** CUMBRIAN

cum·ber·some \ˈkəmbə(r)səm\ *adj* **1 a** *obs* **:** difficult of passage or access **b** *chiefly dial* **:** BURDENSOME, TROUBLESOME **2 :** awkward, inconvenient, or difficult to handle, carry, or manage **:** of an excessive size, shape, or length ⟨plants wrapped for carrying are sometimes ~⟩ **:** CLUMSY, UNWIELDY ⟨~ technical terms⟩ **3 :** slow-moving **:** PONDEROUS, LUMBERING ⟨~ administrative procedures⟩ ⟨the grizzly bear looked ~ and awkward⟩ **syn** see HEAVY

cum·ber·some·ly \-lē, -li\ *adv* **:** in a cumbersome manner

cum·ber·some·ness \-nəs\ *n* -ES **:** the quality or state of being cumbersome

cumb·ly \ˈkəmlē, -li\ *n* -ES [Hindi *kamlī*, fr. Skt *kambala* woolen blanket] *India* **:** a blanket made of wool or goat's hair; *also* **:** the material of such blankets

cum·brance \ˈkəmbrən(t)s\ *n* -s [ME *cumbraunce, combraunce*, fr. *cumbren, combren* to cumber + *-aunce* -ance] **:** ENCUMBRANCE, TROUBLE

¹**cum·bri·an** \ˈkəmbrēən\ *adj, usu cap* [NL *Cumbria* Cumberland county (fr. ML, ancient Celtic kingdom in northwestern Britain, of Celt origin; akin to W *Cymro* Welshman) + E *-an*] **1 :** CUMBERLAND **2 :** of, relating to, or characteristic of Cumbrians

²**cumbrian** \"\ *n* -s *cap* **:** a native or inhabitant of Cumberland

cum·brous \ˈkəmbrəs\ *adj* [ME, fr. *cumbren* to cumber + *-ous*] **1** *obs* **a :** difficult to pass through or over **:** hard to reach **b :** giving trouble **:** VEXATIOUS **2 :** making action or motion difficult **:** UNWIELDY, CLOGGING, CUMBERSOME **syn** see HEAVY

cum·brous·ly *adv* [ME, fr. *cumbrous* + *-ly*] **:** in a cumbrous way **:** CLUMSILY, PONDEROUSLY

cum·brous·ness *n* -ES **:** the quality or state of being cumbrous

cum·bu \ˈkəm(ˌ)bü\ *n* -s [Kaunada & Telugu *kambu* or Tamil *kampu*] **:** FEARL MILLET 1

cum dividend \ˈküm-, kəm-\ *adv (or adj)* [¹*cum*] **:** with the value of a pending dividend included in the sale price of a security, the buyer being entitled to the dividend when paid — opposed to *ex dividend*

cu·mene \ˈkyü(ˌ)mēn\ *n* -s [ISV *cum-* + *-ene*; orig. formed as F *cumène*] **:** a colorless oily hydrocarbon $(CH_3)_2CHC_6H_5$ obtained by acid-catalyzed alkylation of benzene with propylene and used as an additive for high-octane motor fuel; isopropyl-benzene

cumene hydroperoxide *n* **:** an oily liquid made by oxidation of cumene with air and used as a polymerization catalyst (as in making synthetic rubber) and as a source material for the production of phenol and acetone

cu·men·gite *also* **cu·men·geite** \kyüˈmenˌjīt, -ˌgīt\ *n* -s [G *cumengit*, fr. Édouard *Cumenge* †1902 Fr. mining engineer + G *-it* -ite] **:** a mineral $Pb_4Cu_4Cl_8(OH)_8.H_2O$ consisting of a basic lead-copper chloride occurring in deep blue tetragonal crystals

cu·me·nyl \ˈkyüməˌnil\ *n* -s [*cumene* + *-yl*] **:** any of three univalent radicals $(CH_3)_2CHC_6H_4$— derived from cumene by removal of one hydrogen atom; isopropyl-phenyl

cumfrey *var of* COMFREY

cu·mic acid \ˈkyümik-\ *n* [*cum-* + *-ic*] **:** a white crystalline acid $(CH_3)_2CHC_6H_4COOH$ obtained by oxidation of cumin oil; *p*-isopropyl-benzoic acid

cumic aldehyde *n* **:** CUMALDEHYDE

cu·mi·dine \ˈkyüməˌdēn, -dən\ *n* -s [ISV *cum-* + *-idine*; orig. formed as G *kumidin*] **:** any of three isomeric liquid bases $C_3H_7C_6H_4NH_2$ derived from cumene; isopropyl-aniline; *esp* **:** the para isomer made by nitration of cumene followed by reduction

cum·in *also* **cum·min** \ˈkəmən\ *n* -s [ME *comin, cummin*, fr. OE *cymen*; akin to OHG *kumīn* cumin, MLG *kōmen*, all fr. a prehistoric WGmc word borrowed fr. L *cuminum*, fr. Gk *kyminon*, of Sem origin; akin to Ar *kammūn* cumin, Heb *kammōn*] **:** a dwarf plant (*Cuminum cyminum*) of the family Umbelliferae that is native to Egypt and Syria and has long been cultivated for its aromatic seeds which are used in flavoring

cum·i·nal·de·hyde \ˌkəməˈnaldəˌhīd\ *n* [ISV *cumin* + *aldehyde*] **:** CUMALDEHYDE

cu·min·ic acid \(ˈ)kyüˈminik-\ *n* [ISV *cumin* + *-ic*] **:** CUMIC ACID

cumin oil *also* **cummin oil** *n* **:** a colorless to yellow essential oil obtained from cuminseeds

cu·min·o·in \kyüˈminəwən\ *n* -s [ISV *cumin* + *-oin* (as in *benzoin*); orig. formed as G *kuminoin*] **:** a white crystalline compound $C_{20}H_{24}O_2$ prepared from cumaldehyde and analogous to benzoin

cu·mi·nol \ˈkyüməˌnól, -nōl\ *n* -s [ISV *cumin* + *-ol*] **:** CUMALDEHYDE

cuminseed *or* **cumminseed** \ˈ==ˌ=\ *n* **:** the seed of the cumin plant

cu·mi·nyl \ˈkyüməˌnil\ *n* -s [ISV *cumin* + *-yl*] **:** the univalent radical $(CH_3)_2CHC_6H_4CH_2$— derived from the para isomer of cymene; *para*-isopropyl-benzyl

cum lau·de \kúmˈlaúdə, -dē, -dā; kəmˈlȯd-\ *adv (or adj)* [NL, with praise] **:** with distinction — used as a mark of meritorious achievement in the academic requirements for graduation from school or college; compare MAGNA CUM LAUDE, SUMMA CUM LAUDE

cum·ly \ˈkəmlē, -li\ *var of* CUMBLY

cum·mer \ˈkəmər\ *n* -s [ME *commare* godmother, fr. MF *commere*, fr. LL *commater*, fr. L *com-* + *mater* mother — more at MOTHER] **1** *chiefly Scot* **:** GODMOTHER **2** *chiefly Scot* **:** an intimate female friend **3** *chiefly Scot* **:** a woman or girl; *also* **:** WITCH **4** *chiefly Scot* **:** MIDWIFE

cum·mer·bund \ˈkəmə(r)ˌbənd\ *n* -s [Hindi *kamarband*, fr. Per, fr. *kamar* waist, loins + *band* band, bandage; akin to Av *bandō* band, fetter, Skt *bandha* binding — more at BAND] **:** a broad sash worn as a waistband by men in India; *also* **:** a similar waistband worn in place of a vest with men's dress clothes and adapted in various styles for women's clothes

cummerbund

cum·ming·ton·ite \ˈkəmiŋtəˌnīt\ *n* -s [*Cummington*, Mass. + E *-ite*] **:** a mineral $(Fe,Mg)_7Si_8O_{22}(OH)_2$ consisting of an iron-magnesium amphibole isomorphous with anthophyllite

cum·mock \ˈkəmək\ *var of* CAMMOCK

cumo- — see CUM-

cu·mol \ˈkyüˌmól, -mōl\ *n* -s [ISV *cum-* + *-ol*; prob. orig. formed as G *kumol*] **:** CUMENE

cu·mo·yl \ˈkyüməˌwil\ *n* -s [*cum-* + *-yl*] **:** the radical $(CH_3)_2CHC_6H_4CO$—

cum pri·vi·le·gio \ˌkúmˌprivəˈlāgē(ˌ)ō, ˌkəm-, -lē-, -jē-\ *adv* [NL] **:** with privilege — used esp. in a published book to indicate that the issue is duly licensed or authorized

cumquat *var of* KUMQUAT

¹**cum·shaw** *also* **cum·sha** \ˈkəmˌshȯ\ *n* -s [Chin (Amoy) *kam sia* & (Pek.) *kan³ hsieh⁴* grateful thanks (a phrase used by beggars)] **:** PRESENT, BONUS, GRATUITY, TIP

²**cumshaw** \"\ *vt* -ED/-ING/-S **:** to make a present of ⟨resigned to ~*ing* ten cents an hour to any stevedore foreman who would give them a short job —N.C.McDonald⟩

cumul- *or* **cumuli-** *or* **cumulo-** *comb form* [NL, fr. L *cumulus* heap, mass — more at CUMULATE] **1 :** cumulus and ⟨*cumulo*-cirrus⟩ **2 :** cumulus ⟨*cumul*ous⟩ **3 :** heap **:** mass ⟨*cumul*ose⟩

cu·mu·lant \ˈkyümyələnt, ÷ -mə-\ *n* -s [L *cumulant-, cumulans*, pres. part. of *cumulare* to heap up] **:** any of the statistical coefficients that arise in the series expansion in powers of *x* of the logarithm of the moment-generating function

cu·mu·lar \-lə(r)\ *adj* [L *cumularis*, fr. L. *cumulus* heap + *aris* -ar] **:** CUMULOUS

¹**cu·mu·late** \ˈkyümyəˌlāt, ÷ -mə-, *usu* -ād·+V\ *vb* -ED/-ING/-S [L *cumulatus*, past part. of *cumulare* to pile up, fr. *cumulus* heap, mass; akin to L *cavus* hollow — more at CAVE] *vt* **1 :** to gather or pile up into a heap **:** heap together **:** ACCUMULATE **2 a :** to combine (as votes, law actions, or penalties) into one; *specif* **:** to combine (the entries of preceding issues) in successive issues (as of an index or catalog) **b :** to enlarge (a collection) by addition of new material ⟨~ an index⟩ ~ *vi* **:** to become massed **:** form into a cumulus **:** ACCUMULATE ⟨sets up tensions which ~ —P.M.Gregory⟩

²**cumulate** \-ˌlət, -ˌlāt\ *adj* [L *cumulatus*] **:** heaped up **:** gathered in a heap

cu·mu·lat·ed \-ˌlād·əd\ *adj, of the molecule of an organic compound* **:** characterized by two double bonds on the same atom (as C—C—C) — compare CONJUGATED

cu·mu·la·tion \ˌ==ˈlāshən\ *n* -s **1 :** a heaping together **:** a gradual building up ⟨~ of effect of a drug⟩ ⟨the ~ of a body of jurisprudence⟩ **2 :** the product or result of cumulating ⟨three ~*s* of the index were published yearly⟩

cu·mu·la·tive \ˈ==lə|d·iv, -ˌlā|, |tiv, -ēv\ *adj* **1 :** increasing in size or strength by successive additions without corresponding loss ⟨the ~ effect of small daily doses⟩ ⟨a ~ weight of evidence⟩ **2 a** *of evidence* **:** tending to prove the same point to which other evidence has been offered **b** *of a legacy* **:** given by the same testator to the same legatee **3** *criminal law* **a** *of a sentence* **:** to be carried into effect after the convict has suffered a punishment to which he has already been sentenced **b** *of a penalty* **:** increasing in severity with repetition of the offense **4 a** *of preferred dividends or contingent interest* **:** to be added if not paid when due to the next payment or a future payment **b** *of stock* **:** bearing such a dividend **5 :** formed by the addition of new material of the same kind as that already collected ⟨~ record⟩; *specif* **:** having reference to or prepared according to a system whereby additional entries for books or periodical articles are integrated in a later issue of a printed index to maintain the original order of arrangement (as alphabetically by subject) ⟨~ book index in the reference library⟩ **6 :** ¹COPULATIVE 1a — **cu·mu·la·tive·ly** \-əvlē, -li\ *adv*

cumulative error *n* **:** an error whose degree or significance gradually increases in the course of a series of measurements or connected calculations; *specif* **:** an error that is repeated in the same sense or with the same sign

cumulative intercession *n* **:** the assumption of liability for another's debt by the addition of a new debtor or security

cu·mu·la·tive·ness *pronunc at* CUMULATIVE + nəs\ *n* -ES **:** the quality or state of being cumulative

cumulative scoring *n* **:** a scoring of duplicate bridge that ranks contestants by the sum of all points scored by each on all boards played — called also *total-point scoring*; compare MATCH POINT

cumulative temperature *n* **:** the algebraic sum for a week, month, or other considerable period of the daily or other unit interval departures of the average temperature of the air from any arbitrary value, commonly 42° F

cumulative voting *n* **:** proportional representation that allocates to each voter as many votes as there are persons to be voted for and permits him to cast these votes for one person or to distribute them among the candidates as he pleases

cu·mu·lene \ˈkyümyəˌlēn\ *n* -s [*cumulated* + *-ene*] **:** a hydrocarbon containing cumulated double bonds

cumuli- *or* **cumulo-** — see CUMUL-

cu·mu·li·form \ˈkyümyələˌfȯrm\ *adj* [*cumul-* + *-form*] **:** of the form of a cumulus

cu·mu·lo·cirrus \ˌkyümyə(ˌ)lō, ÷ -mə-+\ *n* [NL, fr. *cumul-* + *cirrus*] **:** a small cumulus cloud at a high altitude having the whiteness and delicacy of the cirrus

cu·mu·lo·nimbus \"+\ *n* [NL, fr. *cumul-* + *nimbus*] **:** a mountainous cumulus cloud often spread out in the shape of an anvil extending to great heights and topped with a fibrous veil of ice crystals **:** THUNDERCLOUD — see CLOUD illustration

cu·mu·lose \ˈkyümyəˌlōs, ÷-mə-\ *adj* [*cumul-* + *-ose*] **1 :** full of heaps **2** *of a soil deposit* **:** consisting chiefly of accumulated organic matter

cu·mu·lo·stratus \ˌkyümyə(ˌ)lō, ÷-mə-+\ *n* [NL, fr. *cumul-* + *stratus*] **:** a cumulus whose base extends horizontally as a stratus cloud

cu·mu·lous \ˈkyümyələs, ÷-mə-\ *adj* [*cumul-* + *-ous*] **1 :** resembling cumulus **2 :** CUMULATIVE

cu·mu·lo·volcano \ˌkyümyə(ˌ)lō, ÷-mə-+\ *n* [*cumul-* + *volcano*] **:** a dome-shaped volcano formed by the extrusion of highly viscous lava

cu·mu·lus \ˈkyümyələs, ÷-mə-\ *n, pl* **cumu·li** \-ˌlī, -ˌlē\ [L, heap — more at CUMULATE] **1 :** the acme of an accumulation **:** HEAP, ACCUMULATION ⟨what a tremendous lot of stuff makes up the ~ called "the home" —E.B.White⟩ **2** [NL, fr. L] **:** a massy cloud form usu. occurring in the low or middle cloud regions at elevations between 2,000 and 15,000 feet, having a flat base and rounded outlines often piled up like a mountain, commonly appearing in the early afternoon on warm days, and sometimes affording rain or thunder gusts — see CLOUD illustration **3** *or* **cumulus ooph·o·rus** \-ōˈäf(ə)rəs\ [*cumulus*, NL, fr. L; *cumulus oophorus*, NL, lit., ovarian heap] *anat* **:** the projecting mass of granulosa cells that bears the developing ovum in a Graafian follicle

cumulus con·ges·tus \-kənˈjestəs\ *n, pl* **cumuli conges·ti** \-ˌstī, -(ˌ)stē\ [NL, lit., pressed together, thick cumulus] **:** a swelling cumulus cloud of cauliflower appearance

cumulus hu·mi·lis \-ˈhyüməlә̇s\ *n, pl* **cumuli humi·les** \-ˌlēz\ [NL, lit., low cumulus] **:** a small white cumulus cloud appearing in fine weather

cu·myl \ˈkyüməl\ *n* -s [ISV *cum-* + *-yl*] **1 :** CUMOYL **2 :** CUMINYL **3 :** CUMENYL

cu·na \ˈkünə\ *n, pl* **cuna** *or* **cunas** *usu cap* [Sp, of AmerInd origin] **1 a :** a Cunan people of the Republic of Panama **b :** a member of such people **2 :** the Chibchan language of the Cuna people

cu·nab·u·la \kyüˈnabyələ\ *n pl* [L, fr. *cunae* cradle — more at CEMETERY] **:** INCUNABULA

cu·nan \ˈkünən\ *n, pl* **cunan** *or* **cunans** *usu cap* [*Cuna* + *-an*] **1 :** a language family of the Chibchan stock including Coiba, Cueva, Cuna, and San Blas **2 a :** the peoples speaking Cunan languages **b :** a member of one of such peoples

cunc·ta·tion \kəŋkˈtāshən\ *n* -s [L *cunctation-, cunctatio*, fr. *cunctatus* (past part. of *cunctari* to hesitate) + *-ion-, -io* -ion — more at ¹HANG] **:** DELAY, PROCRASTINATION

cund *var of* COND

cun·de·a·mor \ˌkün(ˌ)dāəˈmō(ə)r\ *n* -s [AmerSp, prob. fr. Sp *cunde* (3d sing. pres. indic. of *cundir* to spread, swell) + *amor* love, fr. L — more at AMOROUS] **:** CYPRESS VINE 1

cun·dy \ˈkəndē\ *n* -ES [by alter.] *chiefly Scot* **:** CONDUIT

cu·ne·al \ˈkyünēəl\ *adj* [NL *cunealis*, fr. L *cuneus* wedge + *-alis* -al — more at COIN] **:** relating to a wedge **:** shaped like a wedge

cu·ne·ate \ˈkyünēˌāt, -ēət\ *also* **cu·ne·at·ed** \-ˌād·əd\ *adj* [L *cuneatus*, fr. *cuneus* wedge + *-atus* -ate, -ated — more at CULEX] **:** shaped like a wedge **:** narrowly triangular with the acute angle toward the base ⟨a ~ leaf⟩ — see LEAF illustration — **cu·ne·ate·ly** *adv*

cuneate lobe *n* **:** CUNEUS 3

cu·ne·at·ic \ˌkyünēˈad·ik\ *adj* [L *cuneatus* + E *-ic*] **:** CUNEIFORM

¹**cu·ne·i·form** \kyüˈnēəˌfȯrm, ˈkyünēə-, ˈkyünə-\ *adj* [prob. fr. F *cunéiforme*, fr. MF, fr. L *cuneus* wedge + MF *-iforme* -iform — more at CULEX] **1 :** of, relating to, or being any of several somewhat wedge-shaped chiefly skeletal elements: as **a :** any of three small bones of the tarsus lying between the navicular and the first three metatarsals **b :** the pyramidal bone of the wrist **c :** either of a pair of rods of yellow elastic cartilage lying in the arytenoepiglottic folds of the larynx **2** *of a human skull* **:** wedge-shaped as viewed from above — used of a head type not uncommon in the Mediterranean subrace **3 a :** composed of strokes having the form of a wedge or arrowhead — used of the characters employed in a system of writing in which the strokes are formed by the impression of a stylus in soft clay or are written in some other medium but with strokes in imitation of ones impressed on clay **b :** written in cuneiform characters — used of a document or of a language **c :** made up of cuneiform characters ⟨tablets . . . were written in an alphabetic ~ script —L.A.Weigle⟩

2cuneiform \"\ *n* **1 :** cuneiform writing **2 :** a cuneiform part; *specif* **:** a cuneiform bone or cartilage

cuneiform

cu·ne·i·form·ist \-məst\ *n* -s **:** a student of or an expert in the deciphering or study of cuneiform

cu·ne·o- \ˈkyünē(ˌ)ō, -ēə\ *comb form* [NL, fr. L *cuneus* wedge] **:** cuneiform and ⟨*cuneo*cuboid⟩

cu·nette \kyüˈnet\ *n* -s [F, fr. It *cunetta,* alter. (resulting from incorrect division, *la-* being taken as *la,* fem. def. art.) of *lacunetta,* dim. of *lacuna* pond, fr. L — more at LAGOON] **1 :** a channel of small cross section dug in the bottom of a much larger channel or conduit to concentrate the flow at low-water stages **2 :** a reinforcement of a canal bank constructed of piles and planking

cu·ne·us \ˈkyünēəs\ *n, pl* **cunei** \-ēˌī\ [L, wedge — more at CULEX] **1 :** WEDGE **:** something shaped like a wedge **2 :** one of the wedge-shaped blocks of seats into which the cavea of the ancient Roman theater was divided by stairways **3** [NL, fr. L] **:** a convolution of the mesial surface of the occipital lobe of the brain above the calcarine fissure that forms a part of the visual cortex

cun·ge·boi \ˈkənjəˌbȯi\ *or* **cun·ge·voi** \-ˌvȯi\ *n* -s [native name in Australia] *Austral* **:** an ascidian of the family Cynthiidae that grows upon rock and is used for bait

cu·nic \ˈkyünik\ *also* **cunic mixture** *n* -s [LL *cu*prum copper + E *nic*otine — more at COPPER] **:** a mixture of copper sulfate and nicotine sulfate administered to livestock as an anthelmintic

cu·nic·u·lus \kyüˈnik(y)ələs\ *n* [L, rabbit, rabbit burrow — more at CONY] **1** *pl* **cunicu·li** \-ˌlī, -ˌlē\ **:** an underground passage (as a burrow or mine); *specif* **:** one of the prehistoric underground drains about ancient Rome **2** *cap* [NL, fr. L] **a :** a genus of pacas **b** *in some classifications* (1) **:** DICROSTONYX (2) **:** ORYCTOLAGUS **3** *pl* **cuniculi** [NL, fr. L] **:** the burrow of an itch mite in the skin

cu·nit \ˈkyünət\ *n* -s [¹*C* (100) + *unit*] **:** a unit of volume that is sometimes used for pulpwood and is equal to 100 cubic feet of solid wood

cun·je·voi \ˈkənjəˌvȯi\ *n* -s [native name in Australia] **:** a large Australian aroid (*Alocasia macrorrhiza*) whose poisonous juice is similar in its action to that of dumb cane

1cun·ner \ˈkənə(r)\ *also* **con·ner** \", ˈkän-\ *n* -s [origin unknown] **:** either of two wrasses: **a :** an English wrasse (*Crenilabrus melops*) **b :** an American wrasse (*Tautogolabrus adspersus*) that is abundant on the rocky shores of New England and is a good though generally small food fish

2cunner \"\ *n* -s [prob. alter. of ¹*canoe*] **:** a sailing canoe made of logs that was formerly common in Chesapeake Bay

cun·ni·lin·gu·ism \ˌkənəˈliŋgəˌwizəm\ *n* -s [NL *cunnilingus* + E *-ism*] **:** the practice or habit of cunnilingus

cun·ni·lin·gus \-ˈliŋgəs\ *or* **cun·ni·linc·tus** \-ŋktəs\ *n* -ES [*cunnilingus,* NL, fr. L, one who licks the vulva, fr. *cunni-* (fr. *cunnus* vulva) + *-lingus* (fr. *lingere* to lick); *cunnilinctus,* NL, fr. L *cunni-* + *linctus* act of licking, fr. *linctus,* past part. of *lingere* to lick — more at LICK] **:** stimulation of the vulva or clitoris with the lips or tongue

1cun·ning \ˈkəniŋ, -nēŋ\ *adj, often* -ER/-EST [ME, fr. pres. part. of *cunnen* to know — more at CAN] **1** *obs* **a :** possessed of or marked by knowledge, learning, or lore **b :** possessing occult or magical knowledge **2 :** marked by dexterous or crafty use of some special skill, knowledge, or other resource ⟨gnomes and the brownies, the ~ little people who know how to use the bellows, the forge, the hammer and the anvil —Lewis Mumford⟩ ⟨the birds . . . were found singularly ~ and repeatedly eluded the aim of these prime shots —George Meredith⟩ **3 :** marked by keen insight, practical analytic intelligence, resourcefulness, or ability to anticipate, escape, elude ⟨the same ~ artist Daedalus who planned the Labyrinth —J.G. Frazer⟩ ⟨his ~ knowledge of the weaknesses of the human heart —T.S.Eliot⟩ **4 :** marked by wiles, craftiness, artfulness, or trickery in attaining ends ⟨the ~ contrivance of traps and pitfalls —Lewis Mumford⟩ ⟨this ~ subterfuge of, Januslike, looking two ways at once —C.C.Furnas⟩ **5 :** appealing (as by reason of smallness, prettiness, quaintness, or archness) **:** FETCHING ⟨a ~ little baby⟩ ⟨a ~ little kitten⟩ **syn** see CLEVER, SLY

2cunning \"\ *n* -s [ME, fr. ger. of *cunnen* to know] **1** *obs* **:** KNOWLEDGE, LEARNING **2** *obs* **:** ART; *esp* **:** magic art **3 :** SKILL, DEXTERITY ⟨let my right hand forget her ~ —Ps 137:5 (AV)⟩ **4 :** skill in deceiving or using indirect or subtle methods **:** ability to mislead, trap, or escape an enemy or opponent **:** SLYNESS, CRAFT **syn** see ART, DECEIT

cun·ning·ham·ia \ˌkəniŋˈhamēə, -ŋˈam-\ *n, cap* [NL, fr. Allan *Cunningham* †1839 or his brother Richard †1835 Eng. botanists + NL *-ia*] **:** a small genus of decorative Asiatic evergreen trees (family Pinaceae) having flat leaves arranged spirally and singly along the whorled branches

cun·ning·ly *adv* [ME, fr. ¹*cunning* + *-ly*] **:** with cunning **:** in a dexterous, subtle, or ingenious way **:** CLEVERLY, ARTFULLY ⟨a trap ~ placed in the trail⟩ ⟨a ~ wrought brass figure⟩

cun·ning·ness *n* -ES [ME *cunningnesse,* fr. *cunning* + *-nesse* -ness] **:** the quality or state of being cunning

cun·nus \ˈkənəs\ *n, pl* **cun·ni** \-ˌnī, -(ˌ)nē\ [L; akin to L *cutis* skin — more at HIDE] **:** the female external genitals **:** VULVA

1cun·ny–thumb \ˈkənē+ˌ\ *adv* [obs. *cunny* woman, rabbit (alter. of *cony*) + *thumb*] *marbles* **:** with the thumb bent in behind the second finger of the closed hand **:** INEXPERTLY

2cunny–thumb \ˈ==+\ *vb, marbles* **:** to shoot inexpertly

cu·no·nia \kyüˈnōnēə\ *n, cap* [NL, fr. John C. *Cuno,* 18th cent. Dutch botanist + NL *-ia*] **:** a genus (the type of the family Cunoniaceae) of shrubs or small trees with pinnate leaves, racemose white flowers, and bark that is used for tanning

cu·no·ni·a·ce·ae \kyüˌnōnēˈāsēˌē\ *n pl, cap* [NL, fr. *Cunonia,* type genus + *-aceae*] **:** a family of trees and shrubs (order Rosales) that are sometimes placed in the family Saxifragaceae but are distinguished by opposite or verticillate leaves and small flowers borne in dense clusters — **cu·no·ni·a·ceous** \ˈ=;=;=ˈāshəs\ *adj*

cunt \ˈkənt\ *n* -s [ME *cunte;* akin to OFris & MLG *kunte* female pudenda, MD *conte,* Norw & Sw dial. *kunta,* MLG *kutte* female pudenda, MHG *kotze* prostitute, and perh. to OE *cot* cottage — more at COT] **:** the female pudenda **:** a woman regarded as a sexual object; *also* **:** COITUS — usu. considered obscene

cuntline *var of* CONTLINE

cun·yie \ˈkünē\ *or* **cun·zie** \-nzē\ *n* -s [ME (Sc dial.) *cunye,* fr. a MF dial. word akin to MF *coing, coin* wedge, stamp corner — more at COIN] *Scot* **:** COIN, MONEY

cu·on \ˈkyüˌän\ *n, cap* [NL, modif. of Gk *kyōn* dog — more at HOUND] **:** a genus of Asiatic wild dogs (family Canidae) characterized by the absence of the usual last lower molar and including the dhole

cu·o·rin \ˈkyü(ə)rən\ *n* -s [ISV *cuor-* (fr. It *cuore* heart, fr. L *cor*) + *-in* — more at HEART] **:** an amorphous phosphatide obtained from heart muscle and soybeans that resembles cephalin and is held to be a mixture

1cup \ˈkəp\ *n* -s [ME *cuppe,* fr. OE; akin to OFris *kopp* head, cup, MLG *kopp* drinking vessel, MD *coppe,* OHG *kopf;* all fr. a prehistoric WGmc word borrowed fr. LL *cuppa* cup, alter. of or akin to L *cupa* vat, tub — more at HIVE] **1 :** a usu. open bowl-shaped drinking vessel often having a handle and a stem and base and sometimes a lid ⟨finely made wine ~*s*⟩ **:** CHALICE; *specif* **:** a handled vessel of china or glass that is set on a saucer and used for hot liquids (as coffee, tea, or soup) **2 a :** the containing part of a drinking vessel that has a stem and a foot **b :** a drinking vessel and its contents **:** the beverage or food contained in a cup ⟨a second ~ of coffee⟩ **c :** the consecrated wine of the Communion **3 :** something (as an experience or sensation) that is to be enjoyed or endured **:** something that falls to one's lot **:** PORTION ⟨his ~ of bitterness is full⟩ **4 cups** *pl* **:** prolonged or convivial drinking ⟨thence from ~*s* to civil broils —John Milton⟩ **5** *sometimes cap* **:** an ornamental cup offered as a prize esp. when symbolic of a championship ⟨the ~ race for large yachts⟩; *often* **:** a prize other than or in addition to money **6 :** something felt to resemble a cup esp. in shape or use: as **a :** a socket or recess in which something turns (as the hipbone or the recess in which a capstan spindle turns) **b :** a metal or earthenware receptacle that is shaped like a flowerpot and that is attached to a tree in turpentine orcharding to collect the resin **c** (1) **:** an athletic supporter reinforced with metal for providing extra protection to the wearer in certain strenuous sports (as boxing, hockey, football) (2) **:** either of the two parts of a brassiere that are shaped like and fit over the breasts **d** *med* **:** a small bell-shaped glass formerly used in cupping **e :** a cap of metal shaped like the femoral head and used in plastic reconstruction of the hip joint **f :** the metal case inside a hole in golf; *also* **:** the hole itself **g :** an annular trough filled with water at the base of each section of a telescopic gas holder into which fits the grip of the section next outside **7 a :** a cup-shaped organ or part of a plant (as an apothecium or peridium, a volva, or in seed plants a cupule, a calyx, or corolla) **b :** a cup-shaped structure; *esp* **:** a cup-shaped external skeleton (as the theca of a coral or the calyx of a crinoid) **8 :** a usu. iced beverage resembling punch in its ingredients but served from a pitcher rather than a bowl ⟨claret ~⟩ ⟨cider ~⟩ ⟨champagne ~⟩ **9 :** a curve across the grain or width of a piece of lumber **10 :** CUPFUL **11 :** a food served in a cup-shaped usu. footed vessel ⟨fruit ~⟩ — **in one's cups :** in a state of intoxication **:** DRUNK ⟨blurted out the story while *in his cups*⟩

2cup \"\ *vb* **cupped; cupped; cupping; cups** *vt* **1** [ME *cuppen,* fr. *cuppe,* n.] *med* **:** to subject to cupping **2 :** to make or curve into a hollow or cup shape ⟨*cupping* his hand to his ear⟩ **3 :** to receive, take, or place in or as if in a cup ⟨~ water from a stream⟩ ⟨*cupping* his chin in his hand⟩ ⟨a town *cupped* by surrounding hills⟩ **4 :** to provide a cup for catching latex or sap from the trunk of (a tree) in rubber and turpentine culture ~ *vi* **1 a :** to grow or become cup-shaped **b** *of a board* **:** to warp crosswise **2 :** to undergo or perform cupping **3 :** to make a depression in the ground with the club when hitting a golf ball

3cup \ˈküp, ˈkəp\ *var of* ³COOP

cu·pa·lo *n* -s [by alter.] **:** CUPOLA

cup and ball *n* **1 :** a bilboquet having a cup; *also* **:** the game of maneuvering the bilboquet so as to catch the ball in the cup **2 :** the cross-parting in columnar igneous rocks in which one face of the parting is concave and the other convex (as in the columnar basalt of the Giant's Causeway on the north coast of Ireland)

cup–and–ball joint *n* **:** BALL-AND-SOCKET JOINT

cup and cone *n* **:** BELL AND HOPPER

cup and ring *n* **:** a cup-shaped pit surrounded by a ring or rings cut in stone found in bronze age cup sculpture

cup–and–saucer \ˈ;==ˈ==\ *n* [so called fr. the shape of the flower] **:** a plant that is a cultivated variety (*Campanula medium calycanthema*) of the Canterbury bell

cup–and–saucer limpet *also* **cup–and–saucer** *n* [so called fr. the shape of the inverted shell, the inner shelf of which resembles a cup sitting on the saucer-shaped outer shell] **:** a mollusk of the family Calyptraeidae

cup–and–saucer vine *n* [so called fr. the shape of the flower] **:** CATHEDRAL BELLS

cu·pa·nia \kyüˈpānēə\ *n, cap* [NL, fr. Francesco *Cupani* †1711 Sicilian botanist + NL *-ia*] **:** a genus of tropical American timber trees (family Sapindaceae) with greenish or white paniculate flowers and capsular fruit — see GUARA

cu·pay \küˈpä, -ˈpī\ *also* **cu·pey** \-ˈpā\ *n* -s [Sp *cupey, copey,* fr. Taino] **:** PITCH APPLE

cup baller *n* **:** ⁵BATTER 2a(1)

cup barometer *n* **:** a barometer consisting of a graduated glass tube about 34 inches long filled with mercury and inverted in a cup containing mercury, the column of mercury in the tube descending until balanced by the pressure of the atmosphere, its rise and fall being a measure of change of atmospheric pressure

cupbearer \ˈ=ˌ==\ *n* [ME *copberer,* fr. *cop* cup (var. of *cuppe*) + *berer* bearer] **:** one whose office it is to fill and hand the cups in which wine is served

1cup·board \ˈkəbə(r)d\ *n* [ME *cupbord,* fr. *cuppe* cup + *bord* board, table — more at BOARD] **1 a :** a board or shelf for cups and dishes **b :** ³BUFFET 2 **2** *obs* **:** a set of dishes as kept on a sideboard **3 :** a closet with shelves to receive cups, dishes, or food; *also* **:** any small closet

2cupboard \"\ *vt* -ED/-ING/-S **:** to put away or collect in or as if in a cupboard

cupboard love *n* **:** insincere love professed for the sake of gain — **cupboard lover** *n*

cupcake \ˈ=ˌ=\ *n* **:** a small cake baked in any cup-shaped container or utensil (as a paper cup or a muffin pan)

cup cheese *n* **:** cook cheese that is poured into china cups

cup coral *n* **:** a cup-shaped coral formed by a single polyp

cup custard *n* **:** custard baked in and usu. served in cup-shaped ceramic or glass cookware

cup drill *n* **:** a grain drill having a cup-shaped attachment by which grasses and legumes can be seeded with the grain

1cu·pel \kyüˈpel, ˈ=ˌpel, ˈ=pəl\ *n* -s [F *coupelle,* dim. of *coupe* cup, fr. LL *cuppa* — more at CUP] **1 :** a small shallow porous refractory cup esp. of bone ash used in assaying to separate precious metals from lead **2 :** the hearth of a small furnace used in commercial separation of precious metals from lead

2cupel \"\ *vt* **cupeled** *or* **cupelled; cupeled** *or* **cupelled; cupeling** *or* **cupelling; cupels** [F *coupeller,* fr. *coupelle,* n.] **:** to refine by means of a cupel — **cu·pel·er** *or* **cu·pel·ler** \-lə(r)\ *n* -s

cu·pel·la·tion \ˌkyüpəˈlāshən\ *n* -s [²*cupel* + *-ation*] **:** refinement (as of gold or silver) in a cupel by melting the metallic charge and then exposing it to a blast of air, the lead, copper, tin, and other unwanted metals being oxidized and partly sinking into the porous cupel and partly being swept away by the blast

cu·pe·ño \kəˈpān(ˌ)yō\ *n, pl* **cupeño** *or* **cupeños** *usu cap* [Sp, fr. *Kupa,* a Cupeño town] **1 :** a Shoshonean people of California **2 :** a member of the Cupeño people

cup fern *n* [so called fr. its cup-shaped indusium] **:** HAY-SCENTED FERN

cup·fer·ron \ˈkəpfəˌrän, ˈk(y)üp-\ *n* -s [ISV *cup*ric + *fer*ric + *-on*] **:** a colorless crystalline salt $C_6H_5N(NO)ONH_4$ that is a precipitant for copper and iron from solutions and is used also in the analysis of other metals esp. of the uranium group **:** the ammonium salt of *N*-nitroso-*N*-phenyl-hydroxylamine

cupflower \ˈ=ˌ==\ *n* **1 :** NIEREMBERGIA 2 **2 :** a Chilean plant (*Scyphanthus elegans*) of the family Loasaceae with yellow flowers **3 :** a Mexican shrub (*Solandra guttata*) of the family Solanaceae

cup·ful \ˈkəpˌfu̇l\ *n, pl* **cupfuls** *also* **cupsful** \-pˌfu̇lz, -psˌfu̇l\ **1 :** as much as a cup will hold **2** *cookery* **:** a half pint **:** eight ounces

cup fungus *n* [so called fr. the cup-shaped ascoma] **:** a fungus of the order Pezizales — compare DISCOMYCETES

cup grass *n* [so called fr. the shape of the callus] **:** any of several grasses constituting a genus (*Erichloa*) of annual and perennial grasses chiefly of warm or tropical regions; *esp* **:** a common weedy annual grass (*E. contracta*) of the eastern and central U.S. that has villous spikelets and the second glume acuminate

cup grease *n* **:** a grease used in grease cups; *esp* **:** a mixture of a mineral oil and lime or soda soap with or without other ingredients (as rosin, oil, graphite, mica)

cu·phea \ˈkyüfēə\ *n, cap* [NL, irreg. fr. Gk *kyphos* hump; fr. the protuberance on the calyx tube; akin to OE *hūfe* hood, Gk *kyptein* to bend forward, stoop, Skt *kakubha* high, eminent, OE *hēah* high — more at HIGH] **:** a large genus of American plants (family Lythraceae) with opposite leaves and solitary slightly irregular flowers — see CIGAR FLOWER, WAXWEED

cupholder \ˈ=ˌ==\ *n* **:** a sports contestant successful in the latest trial for a cup

cup hook *n* **:** a screw hook that usu. has a collar at the base of the thread and that is used esp. for hanging up cups by their handles

cu·pid \ˈkyüpəd\ *n* -s [after *Cupid,* Roman god of love, fr. ME *Cupide,* fr. L *Cupido*] **:** a naked usu. winged infantile figure representing the god of love and often holding a bow and arrow **:** CHERUB 3

cu·pid·i·ty \kyüˈpidəd·ē, -ətē, -i\ *n* -ES [ME *cupidite,* fr. MF *cupidité,* fr. L *cupiditat-, cupiditas,* fr. *cupidus* desirous + *-itat-, -itas* -ity — more at COVET] **1** *archaic* **:** strong desire **:** ardent longing **:** LUST **2 :** inordinate desire for wealth **:** AVARICE, GREED ⟨these reports . . . inflamed . . . curiosity and ~ all the more —R.W.Murray⟩

syn CUPIDITY, GREED, RAPACITY, AVARICE can signify in common an inordinate desire for wealth or possessions. CUPIDITY stresses the intensity of the desire, strongly suggesting covetousness ⟨the vast *cupidity* of business in preempting the virgin resources of California —V.L.Parrington⟩ ⟨the poverty-stricken man gazed at the silverware and jewels with *cupidity* shining intensely in his face⟩ GREED implies inordinate desire as a controlling passion and usu. connotes both meanness and covetousness ⟨[his] face and green-gray eyes mirrored a low, incessant, gnawing *greed* . . . for power, for money, for destruction —W.A.White⟩ ⟨the craving for more than she needs is a symptom of neurotic *greed* —Leo Gurko⟩ ⟨their whole being made over to desire for an iced cake or a caramel. It was an honest *greed* —Audrey Barker⟩ RAPACITY implies not only cupidity but the actual seizing of the thing desired or of anything that will satisfy greed, often suggesting extortion, plunder, or oppressive exactions ⟨the *rapacity* of the tax collectors was nothing to the greed of the landlords⟩ ⟨the *rapacity* of the first foreign conquest on this continent —Russell Lord⟩ ⟨the *rapacity* of the warlords —Nathaniel Peffer⟩ AVARICE stresses both greed and miserliness ⟨life . . . was a sort of furnace in which all the elements of human nature were transmuted into a single white flame, an incandescence of the passion of *avarice* —Van Wyck Brooks⟩ ⟨economy approached the border of *avarice* —Ellen Glasgow⟩

cu·pi·don \ˈkyüpəˌdän, -dᵊn\ *n* -s [F, fr. *Cupidon,* Roman god of love, fr. L *Cupido*] **:** CUPID

cupid's bow *n, usu cap C* **:** the classical form of bow; *also* **:** a line like it esp. as seen in shapely lips

cupid's–dart \ˈ==ˌ=\ *n, pl* **cupid's–darts** *usu cap C* [so called fr. the belief that it is efficacious as a love philter] **:** BLUE SUCCORY

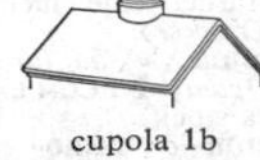
Cupid's bow

cupid's darts *n pl but usu sing in constr, usu cap C* [so called fr. the red shafts in the crystals] **:** ONEGITE

cupid's–delight \ˈ===ˌ=\ *n,pl* **cupid's–delights** *usu cap C* **:** WILD PANSY

cu·pis·ni·que \ˌküpēzˈnē(ˌ)kā, -ēˈsn-\ *adj, usu cap* [fr. *Cupisnique,* valley on the northern coast of Peru, where the remains were found] **:** of or relating to the coastal section of the Chavin culture of ancient Peru

cu·pi·u·ba \ˌküpēˈübə\ *n, pl* **cupiuba** [Pg *cupiúba*] **:** a tropical American tree (*Goupia glabra*) of the family Celastraceae with hard heavy reddish brown wood that is used for furniture, railroad ties, and general construction — called also *kabukalli*

cup joint *n* **:** BELL-AND-SPIGOT JOINT

cup jolly *n* **:** a jollier that makes cups

cup leather *n* **:** a packing (as in hydraulic cylinders and pumps) that consists of a ring of leather of a U-shaped or cup-shaped cross section and that is made tight by the pressure of the fluid on the hollow side

cup·less \ˈkəpləs\ *adj* **:** being without a cup

cup lichen *also* **cup moss** *n* **:** a lichen having cup-shaped fruiting bodies or stalks (as *Lecanora tartarea* and various species of *Cladonia*)

cuplike \ˈ=ˌ=\ *adj* **:** resembling a cup esp. in having or forming a rounded smooth-walled hollow

cup·man \ˈkəpmən\ *n, pl* **cupmen :** TOPER

cupmate \ˈ=ˌ=\ *n* **:** drinking companion

cup moth *n* **:** any of various chiefly tropical New World moths constituting the family Eucleidae — see SADDLEBACK CATERPILLAR

cup mushroom *n* **:** CUP FUNGUS

cup nutseed *n* **:** CUPSEED

cup of elijah *usu cap E* **:** ELIJAH'S CUP

cup of flame : CALIFORNIA POPPY

cup of gold : CUPFLOWER 3

cup of tea 1 : something one likes or excels in **:** something or someone suited to one's taste ⟨mathematics is not my *cup of tea*⟩ **2 :** a thing to be reckoned with **:** MATTER, AFFAIR

1cu·po·la \ˈkyüpələ, ÷-pəˌlō *sometimes* ÷ˈkü- *or* ÷-pyə-\ *n* -s [It, fr. L *cupula* little tub, small burying vault, dim. of *cupa* tub — more at HIVE] **1 a :** a rounded vault raised on a circular or other base and forming a roof or a ceiling — compare DOME **b :** a small structure built on top of a roof to provide interior lighting, to serve as a lookout, or for ornamental purposes **:** LANTERN **2 :** a vertical cylindrical furnace for melting iron in the foundry having tuyeres and tapping spouts near the bottom **3 :** CUPULA **4 :** DOME 4f **5 :** BEEHIVE KILN **6 :** a geological dome projecting from a batholith **7 a :** a revolving armored turret of a tank or pillbox for fire or observation **b :** BLISTER 8b **8 :** an observation post in the roof of a railroad caboose used by brakemen to keep watch over a train while it is in motion

cupola 1b

2cupola \"\ *vt* -ED/-ING/-S **:** to furnish with a cupola

cu·po·lat·ed \-ˌlād·əd\ *adj* **:** having a cupola

cu·po·lo *n* -s [by alter.] **:** CUPOLA

cupped *adj* **1 :** formed like a cup **:** cup-shaped ⟨calling through ~ hands⟩ **2 :** having cup-shaped depressions (as those worn in stairs by use) **3** *of a golf ball* **:** lying in a small depression

cup·pen *or* **cup·pin** \ˈkəpən\ *n* -s [by alter.] *dial* **:** COWPEN

cupping *n* -s [fr. gerund of ²*cup*] **1 :** a technique formerly employed for drawing blood to the surface of the body for producing counterirritation or for bloodletting by application of a glass vessel from which air had been evacuated by heat, forming a partial vacuum **2 :** vibration of a band saw causing it to cut lumber of uneven thickness **3 :** a concave depression in a body organ; *also* **:** the formation of such a depression

cupping glass *n* **:** a small glass cup in which a partial vacuum is produced for cupping

cup plant *n* **:** a tall yellow-flowered herb (*Silphium perfoliatum*) of the U.S. whose upper leaves are connate at the base and form a cup around the stem

cup plate *n* **:** a small usu. glass ornamental plate, formerly used to hold a cup after the hot beverage had been poured into a deep saucer for cooling and drinking

cup·py \ˈkəpē, -pi\ *adj* -ER/-EST **1 :** HOLLOW **:** like a cup **2 :** full of small depressions ⟨a ~ lie for a golf ball⟩ ⟨a ~ racetrack⟩ **3** *of timber* **:** marred by ring shakes

cupr- *or* **cupro-** *comb form* [LL *cupr-,* fr. *cuprum* — more at COPPER] **1 a :** copper ⟨*cupr*ite⟩ **b :** copper and ⟨*cupro*nickel⟩ **2** *cupro-* **:** containing univalent copper **:** cuprous ⟨*cupro*cyanide⟩

cu·pram·mo·ni·um \ˌk(y)üprəˈmōnēəm, -nyəm\ *n* -s [*cupr-* + *ammonium*] **1 :** any of certain complex ammino radicals or cations containing copper and ammonia; *esp* **:** the bivalent tetrammine-copper cation $Cu(NH_3)_4$ compounds of which are formed by the action of ammonia on ordinary cupric compounds **2 :** CUPRAMMONIUM SOLUTION **3 :** CUPRAMMONIUM RAYON

cuprammonium rayon *n* **:** a rayon made from cellulose dissolved in cuprammonium solution

cuprammonium solution *n* **:** a deep blue solution of cupric hydroxide or cupric oxide in aqueous ammonia used as a solvent for cellulose (as in making cuprammonium rayon) — called also *Schweizer's reagent*

cu·prea bark \ˈk(y)üprēə-\ *n* [AmerSp *cuprea,* any of several rubiaceous plants (including *Remijia purdieana*), fr. LL, fem. of *cupreus* cupreous] **:** the coppery-red bark of either of two So. American trees (*Remijia pedunculata* and *R. purdieana*) that yields quinine

cu·pre·ine \ˈk(y)üprēˌēn, -ēən\ *n* -s [*cuprea* (*bark*) + *-ine*] **:** a crystalline alkaloid $C_{19}H_{22}N_2O_2$ that occurs in cuprea bark and cinchona bark closely related to quinine

cu·prene \ˈk(y)üˌprēn\ *n* -s [ISV *cupr-* + *-ene;* prob. orig. formed as F *cuprène*] **:** a light yellow to dark brown inert

insoluble solid obtained by polymerization of acetylene (as by heating in the presence of copper or copper oxides)
cu·pre·ous \ˈk(y)üprēəs\ *adj* [LL *cupreus*, fr. *cuprum* copper — more at COPPER] **:** containing or resembling copper **:** COPPERY
cu·pres·sa·ce·ae \ˌk(y)üprəˈsāsēˌē\ *n pl, cap* [NL, fr. *Cupressus*, type genus + *-aceae*] *in some classifications* **:** a family of coniferous trees and shrubs comprising the cedars and junipers and including all members of Pinaceae with leaves decussate or in three ranks and usu. resembling flat scales
cu·pres·sin·e·ous \ˌ⸗⸗ˈsinēəs\ *adj* [NL *Cupressineae*, tribe including the cypress (fr. *Cupressus* + *-ineae*) + E *-ous*] **:** relating to or resembling the cypress or family Cupressaceae
cu·pres·si·nox·y·lon \k(y)üˌpresəˈnäksəˌlän\ *n* [NL, fr. *cupressino-* (fr. L *cupressinus* of cypress, fr. *cupressus* cypress + *-inus* -ine) + *-xylon*] **1** *cap* **:** a genus of fossil plants having an internal structure similar to that of present-day *Cupressus* and related genera **2** -s **:** any fossil wood having this structure
cu·pres·sus \k(y)üˈpresəs\ *n* [NL, fr. L, cypress — more at CYPRESS] **1** *cap* **:** a genus of evergreen trees (family Pinaceae) having small scaly appressed leaves similar to those of the juniper and globose cones composed of peltate scales — see MONTEREY CYPRESS **2** -ES **:** any tree of the genus *Cupressus* — see CYPRESS 1
cupri- *comb form* [*cupr-* + *-i-*] **1 :** copper ⟨*cupri*ferous⟩ **2** [ISV, fr. *cupric*] **:** containing bivalent copper **:** cupric ⟨*cupri*tartrate⟩
cu·pric \ˈk(y)üprik\ *adj* [LL *cupr*um copper + E *-ic* — more at COPPER] **:** of, relating to, or containing copper in the bivalent state
cupric acetate *n* **:** COPPER ACETATE a
cupric ammonia complex *n* **:** the cuprammonium cation $Cu(NH_3)_4$
cupric chloride *n* **:** COPPER CHLORIDE b
cupric citrate *n* **:** COPPER CITRATE
cupric hydroxide *n* **:** the copper hydroxide $Cu(OH)_2$
cupric oxide *n* **:** COPPER OXIDE b
cupric sulfate *n* **:** the copper sulfate $CuSO_4$
cupric sulfide *n* **:** COPPER SULFIDE b
cu·prif·er·ous \(ˈ)k(y)üˈprif(ə)rəs\ *adj* [*cupri-* + *-ferous*] **:** containing copper
cu·prite \ˈk(y)üˌprīt\ *n* -s [G *kuprit*, fr. *kupr-* cupr- + *-it* -ite] **:** an important ore of copper, cuprous oxide, or red copper oxide Cu_2O occurring massive or in isometric crystals or sometimes in capillary forms — called also *red copper ore, ruby copper ore*
cuprobismutite *n* [*cupr-* + *bismutite*] *obs* **:** a mineral consisting of an intimate mixture of bismuthinite and emplectite
cu·pro·copiapite \ˌk(y)üprō+\ *n* [*cupr-* + *copiapite*] **:** a mineral $CuFe_4(SO_4)_6(OH)_2.20H_2O$ consisting of a hydrous basic sulfate of copper and iron
cu·pro·cyanide \"+\ *n* [*cupr-* + *cyanide*] **:** a compound of copper and cyanogen with another element or other elements
cu·proid \ˈk(y)üˌprȯid\ *n* -s [ISV *cupr-* + *-oid*; orig. formed as G *kuproid*] *crystallog* **:** a solid related to a tetrahedron and having 12 equal triangular faces
cu·pro·nickel \ˌk(y)üprō+\ *n* [*cupr-* + *nickel*] **:** an alloy of copper and nickel; *esp* **:** the alloy containing about 70 percent copper and 30 percent nickel used esp. to make condenser plates and tubes for evaporators and heat exchangers
cu·pro·ri·va·ite \ˌ⸗⸗ˈrēvəˌīt, -ri-, -ˌvīt\ *n* -s [*cupr-* + *rivaite* (syn. of *wollastonite*), fr. Dr. Carlo *Riva* Ital. mineralogist + E *-ite*] **:** a mineral approximately $CaCuSi_4O_{10}.H_2O$ consisting of a hydrous silicate of calcium and copper
cu·pro·sklodowskite \ˌk(y)üprō+\ *n* [*cupr-* + *sklodowskite*] **:** a mineral $Cu(UO_2)_2Si_2O_7.6\text{–}7H_2O$ consisting of hydrous copper uranyl silicate
cu·pro·tungstite \"+\ *n* [*cupr-* + *tungstite*] **:** a mineral $Cu_2(WO_4)(OH)_2$ consisting of cupric tungstate
cu·pro·uranite \"+\ *n* [ISV *cupr-* + *uranite*] **:** TORBERNITE
cu·prous \ˈk(y)üprəs\ *adj* [*cupr-* + *-ous*] **:** of, relating to, or containing copper in the univalent state
cuprous chloride *n* **:** COPPER CHLORIDE a
cuprous cyanide *n* **:** the copper cyanide CuCN
cuprous oxide *n* **:** COPPER OXIDE a
cuprous sulfide *n* **:** COPPER SULFIDE a
cu·prum \ˈk(y)üprəm\ *n* -s [LL — more at COPPER] **:** COPPER — symbol *Cu*
cups *pres 3d sing of* CUP, *pl of* CUP
cup sculpture *n* **:** a bronze age sculpture in stone characterized by pits within circles, concentric circles, and spirals
cupseed \ˈ⸗ˌ⸗\ *n* **:** a woody vine (*Calycocarpum lyoni*) of the family Menispermaceae of the southern U.S. having the stone of the fruit hollowed out on one side like a shallow cup
cupsful *pl of* CUPFUL
cup shake *n* **:** RING SHAKE
cup–shot *or* **cup–shotten** *adj, obs* **:** TIPSY, INTOXICATED
cup sponge *n* **:** a cup-shaped sponge
cup·stone \ˈ⸗ˌ⸗\ *n* **:** a stone or rock surface bearing cup sculpture
cup tie *n* **:** a deciding contest in a competition for a cup
cup towel *n* **:** DISH TOWEL
cu·pu·la \ˈkyüp(y)ələ\ *n, pl* **cupu·lae** \-ˌlē\ [NL] **:** CUPULE, CUP: as **a :** the bony apex of the cochlea **b :** the peak of the pleural sac covering the apex of the lung
cu·pu·late \-ˌlāt, -lət\ *also* **cu·pu·lar** \-lə(r)\ *adj* [NL *cupula* + E *-ate*] **:** shaped like a cupule **:** having or bearing a cupule
cu·pule \ˈkyüˌp(y)ül\ *n* -s [NL *cupula*, fr. LL, small tub, dim. of L *cupa* tub, cask — more at HIVE] **1 a :** a cup-shaped involucre in which the bracts are indurated and coherent and which is esp. characteristic of the oak **b :** the ascoma of a discomycete **c :** a cup-shaped outgrowth of the thallus of certain liverworts (order Marchantiales) **d :** a cup-shaped corolla **2 :** a small cup-shaped depression **3 :** a small sucker (as on the feet of certain male flies)
cu·pu·lif·er·ae \ˌkyüp(y)əˈlifəˌrē\ *n pl, cap* [NL, fr. *cupula* + *-i-* + *-ferae* (fem. pl. of *-fer* -ferous)] *in some classifications* **:** an order or family of catkin-bearing trees including oaks, chestnuts, beeches, birches, and others that are now usu. divided among the families Betulaceae and Fagaceae — **cu·pu·lif·er·ous** \ˌ⸗⸗ˈlif(ə)rəs\ *adj*
cu·pu·li·form \ˈ⸗⸗ləˌfȯrm\ *adj* [ISV *cupuli-* (fr. NL *cupula*) + *-form*] **:** CUPULATE
cu·pu·lo \"\ *n* -s [by alter.] **:** CUPOLA
cup wheel *n* **:** a cup-shaped grinding wheel
¹cur \ˈkər, +V ˈkər·; ˈkə̄, +V ", ˈkər· *also* ˈkə̄\ *n* -s [ME *curre*, short for *kurdogge*, fr. (assumed) ME *curren* to growl + ME *dogge* dog; akin to MLG *kurren* to growl, MHG *kurren* to grunt, ON *kurra* to grumble, OE *cran* crane — more at CRANE] **1 :** DOG: **a** *dial chiefly Brit* **:** SHEEP DOG, WATCHDOG **b** *also* **cur dog :** a mongrel or inferior dog **c :** a dog other than a foxhound — used by fox hunters **2 :** an objectionable often surly, low, or cowardly person **3** *dial chiefly Brit* **:** GOLDENEYE 1a
cur *abbr* **1** currency **2** current
cur·abil·i·ty \ˌkyu̇rəˈbilədē, -ətē, -i\ *n* -ES **:** the quality or state of being curable
cur·able \ˈkyu̇rəbəl\ *adj* [ME, fr. MF or L; MF *curable*, fr. L *curabilis*, fr. *curare* to take care of, heal + *-abilis* -able — more at CURE] **:** capable of being cured **:** susceptible to remedy — **cur·able·ness** *n* -ES — **cur·ably** \-blē, -bli\ *adv*
cu·ra·ca \küˈräkə\ *n* -s [Sp, fr. Quechua] **:** a member of the Inca provincial nobility often acting as administrator or ruler over an ayllu or group of ayllus
cu·ra·çao \ˌk(y)u̇rəˈsau̇, *esp Brit* -sō\ *also* **cu·ra·çoa** \ˌ⸗⸗ˈsōə, ˌ⸗⸗ˈsō\ *n* -s [D *curaçao*, short for *curaçao-oranjeappel* curaçao orange, out of which it was made, fr. *Curaçao*, island in Netherlands Antilles] **1 :** an orange-flavored liqueur that is made from the dried peel of the sour orange and that varies in color from yellow to brown but is sometimes colorless **2** *also* **curaçao orange** *or* **curaçoa orange :** SOUR ORANGE
cu·ra·cy \ˈkyu̇rəsē, -si\ *n* -ES [fr. *curate*, after such pairs as E *legate: legacy*] **:** the office or employment of a curate
cu·ragh *var of* CURRAGH
cu·ra·re \k(y)u̇ˈrärē\ *or* **cu·ra·ra** \-ärə\ *n* -s [Pg & Sp *curare*, fr. Carib *kurari*] **1 :** any of certain complex arrow poisons of So. American Indians that have a paralytic action, include varied plant and animal ingredients, and usu. depend for their effectiveness on aqueous extracts of plants of the genus *Strychnos* (esp. *S. toxifera*) **2 :** a dried aqueous extract of the woody vine (*Strychnos toxifera*) or of certain closely related plants that is rich in alkaloids which act on the neuromuscular junction of skeletal muscle or on cardiac muscle producing paralysis — see CALABASH CURARE **3 :** a purified extract of a So. American menispermaceous vine (*Chondodendron tomentosum*) that is used medicinally to produce muscular relaxation during shock therapy for certain mental diseases and as an adjunct to anesthesia in surgery — called also *tube curare*; see TUBOCURARINE
cu·ra·ri·form \k(y)u̇ˈrärəˌfȯrm, -ˈrar-\ *adj* [*curare* + *-iform*] **:** producing the muscular relaxation characteristic of curare
cu·ra·rine \k(y)u̇ˈrärən, -äˌrēn\ *n* -s [ISV *curare* + *-ine*] **:** any of several alkaloids obtained from curare: as **a :** one of three alkaloids from calabash curare — usu. used with a preceding *C* and a following Roman numeral ⟨*C-curarine* I⟩ ⟨*C-curarine* III⟩ **b :** TUBOCURARINE
cu·ra·ri·za·tion \k(y)u̇ˌrärəˈzāshən\ *n* -s **:** administration of curare or one of its derivatives to induce relaxation of voluntary muscles (as in spastic disorders) or as an adjunct to certain anesthetics; *also* **:** the state resulting from such treatment
cu·ra·rize \k(y)u̇ˈräˌrīz\ *vt* -ED/-ING/-S **:** to bring under the influence of curare; *esp* **:** to induce curarization
cu·ras·sow \ˈkyu̇rəˌsō\ *n* -s [alter. of *Curaçao*, island of Netherlands Antilles] **:** any of several large arboreal birds of So. and Central America that are distantly related to the domestic fowl, that constitute *Crax* and related genera of the family Cracidae, and that are highly esteemed as game and for food
cu·rat·age \ˈkyu̇rədij\ *n* -s [*curate* + *-age*] **:** the residence of a curate
¹cu·rate \ˈkyu̇rət\ *n* -s [ME *curat*, fr. ML *curatus*, fr. *cura* cure of souls (fr. L, care) + L *-atus* -ate — more at CURE] **1 :** one who has the care of souls **:** CLERGYMAN **2 :** an assistant or a deputy of a rector or vicar in the churches of the Anglican communion and in the Roman Catholic Church
²cu·rate \kyəˈrāt, ˈkyu̇ˌr-\ *vt* -ED/-ING/-S [back-formation fr. *curator*] **:** to act as curator of
curate's assistant *n* **:** MUFFIN STAND
cu·rat·ess \ˈkyu̇rədəs\ *n* -ES **:** a curate's wife
cu·ra·tial \kyəˈrāshəl, *attrib* " *or* ˈkyu̇ˌr-\ *adj* **:** of curatic status
cu·rat·ic \kyəˈradik\ *also* **cu·rat·i·cal** \-dəkəl\ *adj* **:** of or relating to a curate
cu·ra·tion \kyəˈrāshən\ *n* -s [ME *curacioun*, fr. MF *curation*, fr. OF, fr. L *curation-, curatio*, fr. *curatus* (past part. of *curare* to take care of, heal) + *-ion-, -io* -ion — more at CURE] **:** CURE
cu·ra·tive \ˈkyu̇rədiv, -ət\ *adj* [MF *curatif*, fr. OF, fr. *curer* to take care of, heal + *-atif* -ative — more at CURE] **:** relating to or used in the cure of diseases **:** tending to cure — **cu·ra·tive·ly** \-ə̇vlē, -li\ *adv*
cu·ra·tor \kyəˈrādə(r), ˈkyu̇ˌrā-, ˈkyu̇rəl, ˈkyüˌrā-, \tə-\ *n* -s [ME *curatour* guardian, curate, fr. MF *curateur*, fr. OF, fr. L *curator* manager, overseer, guardian, fr. *curatus* + *-or*] **1 a** *Roman law* **:** a person corresponding nearly to the guardian of English law and appointed to manage the affairs of a person past the age of puberty while he is a minor or of any such person when legally incompetent (as a spendthrift or a lunatic) **b :** a similar guardian in various modern legal systems (as the Scots law or Roman Dutch law) appointed for minors or others past the age of pupillarity **2** [L] **a :** a person having the care and superintendence of something **:** OVERSEER, MANAGER, STEWARD **b :** one in charge of the exhibits, research activities, and personnel of a museum, zoo, or other place of exhibit **c :** one in charge of a single collection or subject of study in such an institution ⟨~ of manuscripts⟩ ⟨~ of birds⟩ **3 a :** a member of a board of trustees charged with administering the business of a university or a division thereof ⟨~s of the university⟩ ⟨~s of the university library⟩ **b :** a member of a body that elects certain professors at Scottish universities ⟨the patronage of seventeen chairs, previously in the gift of the Town Council, was transferred to seven ~s —*Edinburgh Univ. Cal.*⟩ **c :** the director of an educational fund who is entrusted with selecting and advising holders of fellowships under that fund ⟨~ of fellowships⟩ **4 :** a cricket groundsman
curator bo·nis \-ˈbōnəs\ *n, pl* **curators bonis** [NL, lit., curator for goods] *Scots law* **:** a guardian in charge of the goods, property, or person of a minor or incompetent person
cu·ra·to·ri·al \ˌkyu̇rəˈtōrēəl, -ˈtȯr-\ *adj* [L *curatorius* + E *-al*] **:** of or relating to a curator or his work
cu·ra·tor·ship *pronunc at* CURATOR +ˌship\ *n* -s **:** the office, position, duties, or jurisdiction of a curator ⟨appointed a new man to the ~ of the museum⟩ ⟨fulfilled his ~ with efficiency and care⟩ ⟨the ~ of the international committee extended over the disputed territory⟩
cu·ra·tory \kyəˈrādərē, ˈkyu̇rəˌtōrē\ *n* -ES [ME *curatorie*, fr. LL *curatoria*, fr. L *curator* + *-ia*] **1 :** CURATORSHIP **2 :** a body of curators
cu·ra·trix \kyəˈrāˌtriks\ *n, pl* **curatri·ces** \kyəˈrāˌtrəˌsēz, ˌkyu̇rəˈtrī(ˌ)sēz\ [LL, fem. of L *curator*] **:** a female curator
¹curb \ˈkərb, -əb,-əib\ *vi* -ED/-ING/-S [ME *courben*, fr. MF *courber*, fr. L *curvare*, fr. *curvus* bent, curved — more at CROWN] *archaic* **:** BEND, BOW, CRINGE
²curb \"\ *n* -s *often attrib* [partly fr ¹*curb*; partly fr MF *courbe* curve, curved piece of wood or iron, fr *courbe* crooked, curved, bent, fr L *curvus*] **1 :** a chain or strap attached to the upper part of the branches of a bit and used to restrain a horse — see BIT illustration **2 :** a usu. curved enclosing frame, border, or edging; *specif* **:** the framing round the mouth of a well or of a shaft or at the change of slope in a roof **3 :** a swelling on the back of the hind leg of a horse just behind the lowest part of the hock joint that is due to strain or rupture of the ligament and generally causes lameness **4 :** CHECK, RESTRAINT, CONTROL ⟨a ~ on rising prices⟩ ⟨a ~ on their unruliness⟩ ⟨the ~ of his mother's will had held him —Margaret Deland⟩ **5 :** a raised edge or margin **:** a wall or casing to strengthen or confine **a :** a crib for molding a block of concrete **b :** the casing of a turbine wheel **c :** the curved guide for directing water against the buckets or floats of a breast wheel **d :** a flat ring usu. of wood on which a complete section of brickwork lining for a shaft or well is built **e :** a lead flashing for the curb plate of a curb roof **f :** the lower of the two slopes of a mansard roof **g** *Brit* **:** a massive ornamental fireplace fender without a plane horizontal top **h :** an iron border to the incorporating bed of a gunpowder mill **i :** a timber nosing for a brick step **6 :** a siding (as of stone or concrete) built along the edge of a street to form part of a gutter **7** *or* **curb plate :** a circular frame or plate around an opening to strengthen it (as the casing for a skylight, the wall plate at the springing of a dome, or the race of a windmill) **8 :** the walls of a chamber in which sulfuric acid is manufactured **9 a :** a sidewalk market **:** a street market **b** *also* **curb market** [so called fr. the fact that it orig. transacted its business on the street] **:** a market for trading in securities not listed on the N. Y. Stock Exchange; *also* **:** the personnel, organization, or facilities of such a market
³curb \"\ *vt* -ED/-ING/-S **1 :** to put a curb on (a horse) **:** check (a horse) with a curb **2 a :** to bring to a stop and halt the forward course or progress of usu. sharply ⟨attempts to ~ lynching by legislation have taken various forms —F.W. Coker⟩ **b .** to restrain, abate, or moderate the course or force of **:** GUIDE, CONTROL, MANAGE ⟨the sober scientific method does not stimulate the imagination; it ~s it —S.M.Crothers⟩ **3 a :** to furnish (a street) with a curb **b :** build a curb around ⟨~ a well⟩ **4 :** to make (telegraph signals) shorter and sharper by reducing retardation thus increasing speed **5 :** to lead (a dog) to the gutter or other suitable place for defecation **syn** see RESTRAIN
⁴curb \"\ *adj* [³*curb*] **:** used in or concerned with sending curbed telegraph signals
curbash *var of* KURBASH
curb bit *n* **:** a stiff bit having branches by which a leverage is obtained upon the jaws of a horse — see BRIDLE illustration
curb box *n* **:** a vertical cast-iron pipe extending from curb or sidewalk level down to the shutoff at the water-main connection
curb chain *n* **1 :** a flat chain hooked into the eyes of a curb bit and passed under the chin of a horse where it augments the leverage of the bit **2 :** a jewelry chain composed of round links slightly twisted to make them lie flat and close together
curb edger *n* **:** a tool used in cement work for finishing edges (as of cement walks) — compare TROWEL
curb·ing \-biŋ,-bēŋ\ *n* -s [²*curb* (rim) + *-ing*] **1 :** the material of which a curb is made **2 :** CURB
curbline \ˈ⸗ˌ⸗\ *n* **:** the boundary between a roadway and a sidewalk area
curb pin *n* **:** REGULATOR PIN
curb roof *n* **:** a roof with a ridge at the center and a double slope on each of its two sides — compare GAMBREL ROOF, MANSARD ROOF
curbs *pres 3d sing of* CURB, *pl of* CURB
curb service *n* **1 :** service extended to persons sitting in parked automobiles esp. at a street curb ⟨the store offered *curb service*⟩ **2 :** any special service or favor

curb roof

curbside \ˈ⸗ˌ⸗\ *n* **1 :** the side of a pavement bordered by a curb ⟨trees set at intervals along the ~ —Kay Boyle⟩ **2 :** SIDEWALK ⟨~ interview⟩
¹curbstone \ˈ⸗ˌ⸗\ *n* [²*curb* (rim) + *stone*] **:** a stone set along a margin as a limit and protection — called also *edgestone*
²curbstone \"\ *adj* **1 :** operating in a curb market or on the street without maintaining an office ⟨a ~ broker⟩ **2 :** based on chance impression, random observation, or hunches ⟨~ advice⟩ ⟨~ opinion⟩ **:** not having the benefit of training or experience **:** AMATEURISH ⟨a ~ commentator⟩
curb·ston·er \"+ə(r)\ *n* **:** a curbstone broker or vendor
curby \-bē\ *adj* -ER/-EST [²*curb* (swelling) + *-y*] *of an equine hock* **:** affected with curb; *also* **:** liable to become affected with curb by reason of being thick, coarse, or overbent
cur·cas oil \ˈkərkəs-\ *n* [NL *curcas* (specific epithet of *Jatropha curcas*), fr. Sp *curcaso*] **:** a colorless to yellowish cathartic fatty oil that contains a toxic principle, is obtained from physic nuts, and is used chiefly in medicine and soap-making
curch \ˈkərch\ *n* -ES [ME *curch, courche*, prob. back-formation fr. *courcheis*, pl., fr. MF *couvrechiés*, pl. of *couvrechef* kerchief — more at KERCHIEF] *Scot* **:** KERCHIEF 1
cur·chie *or* **cur·chy** \ˈkərchē\ *dial var of* CURTSY
cur·cu·lio \(ˌ)kərˈkyülēˌō\ *n* [NL, fr. L, grain weevil; prob. akin to L *curvus* curved — more at CROWN] **1** *cap* **:** the type genus of Curculionidae including a number of typical weevils most of which feed in nuts **2** -s **:** any of various weevils; *esp* **:** one that injures fruit (as the plum curculio)
¹cur·cu·li·on·id \(ˌ)kərˈkyülēˈänəd, ˌkərˌk-\ *adj* [NL *Curculionidae*] **:** of or relating to the Curculionidae
²curculionid \"\ *n* -s **:** a beetle of the family Curculionidae
cur·cu·li·on·i·dae \(ˌ)kərˌkyülēˈänəˌdē\ *n pl, cap* [NL, fr. *Curculion-, Curculio*, type genus + *-idae*] **:** a family of snout beetles (suborder Rhynchophora) consisting of the typical weevils and including many that injure fruits and crops
cur·cu·ma \ˈkərkyəmə\ *n* [NL, fr. Ar *kurkum* saffron, crocus] **1 a** *cap* **:** a genus of Old World tropical herbs (family Zingiberaceae) having tuberous roots and spicate flowers, some members having roots that yield starch — see TURMERIC, ZEDOARY **b** -s **:** any plant of the genus *Curcuma* **2** -s **a :** an arrowroot obtained from a curcuma **b :** TURMERIC 1a(2)
curcuma paper *n* **:** TURMERIC PAPER
curcuma starch *n* **:** TIKOR
cur·cu·min \ˈkərkyəmən\ *n* -s [G, fr. NL *Curcuma* (genus name of *Curcuma longa*) + G *-in*] **:** an orange-yellow crystalline compound $C_{21}H_{20}O_6$ constituting the coloring principle of turmeric and used chiefly in coloring foods
curcumin S *n, usu cap C* [ISV *Curcum-* (fr. NL *Curcuma*, genus that produces it) + *-in*] **:** a direct yellow dye — see DYE table I (under *Direct Yellow 11*)
¹curd \ˈkərd, -əd,-əid\ *n* -s *often attrib* [ME *curd, crudd*; prob. akin to OE *crūdan* to press — more at CROWD] **1 a :** the part of milk coagulated by souring or being treated with certain enzymes, consisting mainly of casein, and used as food either as produced or as made into cheese — distinguished from *whey*; often used in pl. ⟨~s and cream⟩ ⟨~s and whey⟩ **b :** a food resembling milk curd in form or appearance ⟨soybean ~⟩ **c :** a gray or whitish coagulant; *specif* **:** the precipitate formed when soap is used in hard water **2 :** the granular mass of soap that separates from the lye and rises when salt is added to the boiled mixture of lye and fat in soapmaking **3 :** the undeveloped or partially developed flower head or aggregation of flower heads that forms the edible part of certain brassicas (as cauliflower and broccoli)
²curd \"\ *vb* -ED/-ING/-S [ME *curden, crudden*, fr. *curd, crudd*, n.] *vt* **1 :** to cause to thicken or congeal **:** COAGULATE, CURDLE ~ *vi* **:** to become coagulated or thickened **:** separate into curds and whey
curd cheese *n* **:** COTTAGE CHEESE
curd knife *n* **:** a device consisting of fine wires or blades stretched in a steel frame and used to cut soft curd into cubes to facilitate drainage of whey
cur·dle \ˈkərdᵊl, -ədᵊl,-əidᵊl\ *vb* **curdled; curdled; curdling** \-d(ᵊ)liŋ\ **curdles** [freq. of ²*curd*] *vt* **1 :** to change (milk) into curds **:** cause curds to form in (milk) ⟨the milk is *curdled*⟩ **2 :** to cause to coagulate **:** CONGEAL, FREEZE ⟨~ the whites of eggs⟩ **3 :** SPOIL, ADDLE, SOUR, EMBITTER ⟨disappointments *curdling* his previously gay disposition⟩ ~ *vi* **1 :** to form curds **:** change into curd **:** COAGULATE ⟨the milk has *curdled*⟩ **2 :** to appear as though covered with curds **:** accumulate scurf **3 :** CONGEAL, FREEZE ⟨the latex ~s in small lumps⟩ **4 :** to become bitter **:** go bad or wrong **:** SPOIL, SOUR ⟨envy soon ~s into hate —J.A.Froude⟩ ⟨how ambition frustrated will ~ —Robert Hatch⟩ — **curdle the blood :** to fill with horror ⟨his account fairly *curdled my blood*⟩
curd·ly \-d(ᵊ)lē\ *adj* **:** CURDLED **:** having a curdled appearance
curd mill *n* **:** a machine that cuts slabs of cheddared curd into pieces of uniform size
cur dog *n* **:** CUR b
curd soap *n* **:** soap separated as curds by addition of salt during saponification; *also* **:** a solidified neat soap of open finish
curdwort \ˈ⸗ˌ⸗\ *n* **:** YELLOW BEDSTRAW
curdy \-dē\ *adj* -ER/-EST **:** resembling curds in consistency and appearance **:** coagulating into curds
¹cure \ˈkyu̇(ə)r, -u̇ə\ *n* -s [ME (also, care), fr. OF, fr. ML & L; ML *cura* cure of souls, fr. L, care, medical attendance, healing; akin to OL *coiraveront* they cared for, Paelignian *coisatens*, and perh. to Goth us*haista* needy] **1 a :** spiritual charge of a parish **:** the office of a parish priest or of a curate **b :** CURACY, PARISH **2 a** *obs* **:** a medical course of treatment for a bodily ailment — used without implication of success **b :** recovery from a disease ⟨his ~ was complete⟩; *also* **:** remission of signs or symptoms of a disease ⟨clinical ~⟩ esp. during a prolonged period of observation ⟨5-year ~ of cancer⟩ **:** return to freedom from an infecting agent ⟨biologic ~ of typhoid⟩ — compare ARREST, QUIESCENCE, REMISSION **c :** a drug, treatment, regimen, or other agency that cures a disease ⟨water ~⟩ ⟨quinine is a ~ for malaria⟩ **d :** a course or period of treatment; *esp* **:** one designed to interrupt an addiction or compulsive habit ⟨take a ~ for alcoholism⟩ or to improve general health ⟨an annual ~ at a spa⟩ **e :** SPA ⟨one of the fashionable ~s⟩ **3 :** REMEDY **:** a procedure or agency that heals or permanently alleviates a troublesome or harmful situation ⟨the attractively plausible idea that the ~ for negative attitudes and misinformation is information —W.H.Whyte⟩ **4 :** a process or method involving aging, seasoning, washing, drying, heating, smoking, or otherwise treating whereby a product is preserved, perfected, or readied for use **5** *maritime law* **:** the medical care awarded a merchant seaman injured or taken sick in the course of his duties **syn** see REMEDY
²cure \"\ *vb* -ED/-ING/-S [ME *curen* to take care of, heal, fr. MF *curer* to take care of, heal, cleanse, fr. L *curare* to take care of, heal, fr. *cura*, n.] *vt* **1 :** HEAL **a :** to restore to health, soundness, or normality ⟨~ him of his illness⟩ ⟨*curing* his patients rapidly by new procedures⟩ ⟨a child *cured* of lisping⟩ **b :** to bring about recovery from **:** REMEDY ⟨any physician can ~ a clean wound⟩ ⟨antibiotics ~ many formerly intractable infections⟩ **2 a :** to treat so as to remove, eliminate, or rectify ⟨every fact you learn ~s ignorance or confusion —J.M. Barzun⟩ ⟨no amount of sweeping and clean mats could ~ the bedbugs⟩ **b :** to free or relieve (a person) from an objectionable or harmful condition or inclination ⟨the loss *cured* him of his gambling⟩ ⟨a rebuff that *cured* him of his brash aggressiveness⟩ **3 :** to subject to a preservative process ⟨~ meat by salting⟩ ⟨drying the hay to ~ it⟩ ⟨*curing* tobacco by aging it⟩ **:** perfect by chemical change (as rubber by vulcanizing, plastics by treating with heat or chemicals to make them infusible and insoluble, or green concrete by maintaining proper condi-

tions of moisture and temperature) **4 :** to clear (land) for cultivation or other use **5 :** to make acceptable in legal procedure (the appearance of objectionable evidence, the omission of relevant matter, or supposed error in charging the jury) by admission of certain evidence giving charges considered under the law to nullify any effect prejudicial to the appellant that any defective evidence or charges might have ~ *vi* **1 :** *of a product* **:** to undergo a preservative process **2 a :** to effect a cure ⟨careful living ~s more often than it kills⟩ **b :** to take a cure (as in a sanatorium or at a spa)

syn HEAL, REMEDY: CURE and HEAL may apply, literally and often interchangeably, to wounds or diseases ⟨mind and will are so powerful they can *heal* the sick —C.A.Dial⟩ CURE, however, more commonly applies to restoration of a healthy or normal condition of body or organism ⟨*cure* a headache⟩ ⟨*cure* a cold⟩ HEAL commonly applies to restoration to soundness of an affected part after a wound or lesion ⟨*heal* an open sore⟩ ⟨*heal* a cut in the hand⟩ Figuratively, one *cures* a bad condition of things, but *heals* a breach as in human relations ⟨*cure* him of his faults —Douglas Stewart⟩ ⟨went far toward *curing* the cynicism of youth —Dixon Wecter⟩ ⟨half a century's estrangement between the farmers and the townsmen may yet be *healed* —Roy Lewis & Angus Maude⟩ ⟨*heal* a split in his own Liberal Party —*Time*⟩ REMEDY applies to the use of any means of correction or relief of a morbid or evil condition ⟨*remedy* the common cold⟩ ⟨anxieties would be *remedied* —J.A. Pike⟩ ⟨*remedy* the breakdown of international prestige —Max Ascoli⟩ ⟨the theory that better religion, better houses, or larger prisons can *remedy* the badly functioning brain —*Atlantic*⟩

³**cu·ré** \kyəˈrā, ˈkyu̇ˌrā, *F* kᵫrā\ *n* -S [F, fr. OF, fr. *cure* cure of souls (after ML *curatus* parish priest)] **:** a parish priest

cure–all \ˈ⸗,⸗\ *n, pl* **cure–alls 1 :** a remedy for all diseases or ills **:** PANACEA **2 :** any of several plants of reputed medicinal value: as **a :** a balm (*Melissa officinalis*) **b :** WATER AVENS **c :** HEAL-ALL 2

cure·less \ˈ⸗ləs\ *adj* **:** being without a cure

cur·er \ˈkyu̇rə(r)\ *n* -S **1 :** HEALER, SHAMAN **2 :** one that cures (as fish, meat, leather, rubber)

cures *pl of* CURE, *pres 3d sing of* CURE

cu·rete \kyəˈrēt\ *n* -S *usu cap* [L *Curetes* (pl.), fr. Gk *Kourētes*] **:** a priest of the Cretan goddess Rhea

cu·rett·age \kyəˈred·ij, ˌkyu̇rəˈtäzh\ *n* -S [F, fr. *curette* + *-age*] **:** scraping of a bodily cavity by means of a curette to clean its surface, to obtain material for diagnostic purposes, or to remove a lesion or foreign body

¹**cu·rette** *or* **cu·ret** \kyəˈret, *usu* -ed·+V\ *n* -S [F *curette*, fr. *curer* to cure, cleanse + *-ette* — more at CURE] **:** a scoop, loop, or ring used as a scraper in performing curettage

²**curette** *or* **curet** \ˈ"\ *vt* **curetted; curetted; curetting; curettes** *or* **curets :** to scrape with a curette

cu·rette·ment *also* **cu·ret·ment** \kyəˈretmənt\ *n* -S **:** CURETTAGE

¹**cur·few** \ˈkər(ˌ)fyü, -ə(-,-əi(-\ *n* -S *often attrib* [ME *corfeu, curfew*, fr. MF *cuevrefeu, covrefeu*, signal given in the evening to put out or bank the fire in the hearth, curfew, fr. *covrir* to cover + *feu* fire, fr. L *focus* fireplace, hearth — more at COVER, FOCUS] **1 a :** an order or regulation enjoining withdrawal of persons (as juveniles, military personnel, or other specified classes) from the streets or the closing of business establishments or places of assembly at a stated hour usu. of the evening **b :** the sounding of a bell or other signal to announce the beginning of a time of curfew **c :** the bell or other signal so used **d :** the hour at which curfew becomes effective **e :** the period of time during which a curfew is in effect **2** *obs* **:** a morning signal bell **3 :** a utensil for covering a hearth fire esp. to permit its burning safely overnight

²**curfew** \ˈ"\ *vt* -ED/-ING/-S **:** to impose a curfew upon ⟨the only . . . nightclub that remains open in an otherwise ~*ed* town —Herbert Kubly⟩

cur·fuf·fle \kərˈfəfəl\ *var of* CARFUFFLE

cu·ria \ˈkyu̇rēə\ *n, pl* **curi·ae** \-ē,ē, ˈku̇rē,ī\ [L, fr. (assumed) OL *covīria*, fr. L *co-* + (assumed) OL *-viria* (fr. L *vir* man) — more at VIRILE] **1 a :** a political subdivision comprising several gentes of the tribe in early Rome — compare GENS **b :** the place of assembly of one of these subdivisions **c :** a division of the people or the senate in Italian cities under Roman rule **2** [ML, fr. L] **:** a feudal assembly or court of justice; *esp* **:** a court held in the king's name **3** *often cap* [ML, fr. L] **:** the full body of organized congregations, tribunals, and offices that aid the pope in the administration and government of the Roman Catholic Church

¹**cu·ri·al** \-ēəl\ *adj* [ME, fr. MF or ML & L; MF *curial*, fr. ML *curialis* of a feudal or ecclesiastic curia, fr. L, of a Roman curia, fr. *curia* + *-alis* -al] **:** of or relating to a curia

²**curial** \ˈ"\ *n* -S [L *curialis*, fr. *curialis*, adj.] **:** a member of an ancient curia

cu·ri·al·ism \-ˌlizəm\ *n* -S **:** the view or doctrine of the ultramontane party in the Latin church **:** the system or policy of the Roman curia **:** VATICANISM, ULTRAMONTANISM

cu·ri·al·ist \-ˌləst\ *n* -S **:** a supporter of curialism

cu·ri·al·is·tic \ˌkyu̇rēəˈlistik\ *adj* **:** of or relating to curialism or curialists

cu·ri·al·i·ty \ˌkyu̇rēˈaləd·ē\ *n* -ES *Scots law* **:** CURTESY

cu·ria·ra \ˌk(y)u̇rēˈärə\ *n* -S [AmerSp, of Cariban origin; akin to Carib *culiala* dugout canoe] **:** a So. American dugout canoe

curia re·gis \ˌ⸗⸗⸗ˈrējəs\ *n, pl* **curiae regis** *usu cap C&R* [ML, lit., king's curia] **:** a small permanent council in medieval England composed of those members of the great council serving as officers of the royal household

cu·ri·bo·ca \ˌk(y)u̇rəˈbōkə\ *n* -S [Pg *cariboca, curiboca*, fr. Tupi] **:** a dark-complexioned Brazilian of mixed white and Indian or Indian and Negro blood

cu·rie \ˈkyu̇rē, -u̇,rē, kyəˈrē; *in the open compounds that follow, the last two pronunciations are more frequent than for the measure*\ *n* -S [after Mme. Marie *Curie* (Marja Sklodowska) †1934 Pol.-Fr. chemist] **1 :** a unit quantity of radon that in radioactive equilibrium contains one gram of radium **2 :** a unit quantity of any radioactive nuclide in which exactly 3.7×10^{10} disintegrations occur per second **3 :** a unit of radioactivity equal to 3.7×10^{10} disintegrations per second

curie point *or* **curie temperature** *n, usu cap C* [after Pierre *Curie* †1906 Fr. chemist] **1 :** a temperature at which there is a transition in a substance from one phase to another of markedly different magnetic properties; *specif* **:** the temperature at which there is a transition between the ferromagnetic and paramagnetic phases — compare CURIE-WEISS LAW **2 :** a temperature at which the anomalies that characterize a ferroelectric substance disappear **:** either the upper or the lower temperature limit of the ferroelectric state

curie's law *n, usu cap C* [after P. *Curie*] **:** a law of magnetism now replaced by the Curie-Weiss law: the susceptibility of a paramagnetic substance is inversely proportional to the absolute temperature

cu·rie·therapy \ˌkyu̇rē+\ *n* -ES [F *curiethérapie*, fr. Pierre & Marie *Curie* + *-thérapie* -therapy] **:** RADIOTHERAPY

curie–weiss law \-ˈwīs-,-ˈvīs-\ *n, usu cap C&W* [after Pierre *Curie* & Pierre-Ernest *Weiss* †1940 Fr. physicists] **:** a law of magnetism: the susceptibility of a paramagnetic substance is inversely proportional to the excess of its temperature above the Curie point, below which it ceases to be paramagnetic

cu·rine \ˈkyu̇ˌrēn\ *n* -S [ISV *curare* + *-ine*; orig. formed as G *kurin*] **:** a crystalline alkaloid $C_{36}H_{38}N_2O_6$ obtained from tube curare **:** levorotatory bebeerine

curing *pres part of* CURE

cu·rio \ˈkyu̇rē,ō\ *n* -S [short for *curiosity*] **:** something arousing interest as being novel, rare, or bizarre **:** CURIOSITY ⟨the priceless paintings, the tapestries, and the ~s that adorn the rooms —A.B.Osborne⟩ ⟨as an unmarried woman traveling alone, she was distrusted as a ~ —Galbraith Welch⟩

cu·ri·o·log·ic \ˌkyu̇rēəˈläjik\ *or* **cu·ri·o·log·i·cal** \-jəkəl\ *adj* [*curiologic* fr. LGk *kyriologikos* in an obvious sense, fr. *kyriologia* obvious language (fr. Gk *kyrios* ruling, literal — fr. *kyros* power, might — + *-logia* -logy) + Gk *-ikos* -ic; akin to Skt *śūra* powerful, L *cavus* hollow; *curiological* fr. *curiologic* + *-al* — more at CAVE] **:** representing things by their pictures instead of by symbols — used of hieroglyphic writing — **cu·ri·o·log·i·cal·ly** \-jək(ə)lē\ *adv*

cu·ri·o·log·ics \ˌ⸗⸗⸗ˈ⸗jiks\ *n pl but sing in constr* **:** curiologic writing

cu·ri·o·sa \ˌkyu̇rēˈōsə, -ōzə\ *n pl* [NL (influenced in meaning by E *curio* and *curious*), fr. L, neut. pl. of *curiosus* careful, inquisitive — more at CURIOUS] **1 :** CURIOSITIES, RARITIES **2 :** books strange or unusual in subject or treatment; *specif* **:** FACETIAE, PORNOGRAPHY, EROTICA

curiosa fe·li·ci·tas \-fəˈlisə,tas\ *n, pl* **curio·sae felicita·tes** \-ō,sēfə,lisəˈtād·ēz, -ō,zē-\ [L, careful felicity] **:** a studied felicity of expression

cu·ri·os·i·ty \ˌkyu̇rēˈäsəd·ē, -ür-, -s(ə)tē, -i\ *n* -ES [ME *curiosite*, fr. MF *curiosité*, fr. L *curiositat-, curiositas*, fr. *curiosus* + *-itat-, -itas* -ity] **1 :** desire to know: **a** *archaic* **:** a blamable tendency or desire to inquire into or seek knowledge (as of sacred matters) or to inquire too minutely into any subject **b :** NOSINESS **:** inquisitiveness about others' concerns ⟨to escape the ~ of prying neighbors⟩ **c :** desire to investigate **:** interest leading to inquiry ⟨intellectual ~⟩ ⟨his own ~ to know what really happened long ago —G.M.Trevelyan⟩ **d** *archaic* **:** scientific or artistic interest **:** desire to evaluate and appreciate **2** *archaic* **a :** careful workmanship **:** accuracy or perfection in construction **b :** undue nicety, subtlety, or fastidiousness **c :** proficiency acquired by careful practice **:** INGENUITY **3 a** *obs* **:** a matter (as a question, argument, theory, or experiment) that is curious and ingenious **b :** one that arouses curiosity **:** one that arouses attention or awakes interest esp. for strange, uncommon, or exotic characteristics ⟨an architectural ~⟩ ⟨his uncommon illness was a medical ~⟩ ⟨exploiting the poet as a ~⟩ **c :** an unusual knickknack (as a travel souvenir) **d :** ability to arouse curiosity esp. through novelty **:** INTEREST, PIQUANCY ⟨the ~ of the operation⟩ **e :** curious trait or aspect ⟨another ~ observable in these verbs with separable suffixes —Charlton Laird⟩

cu·ri·o·so \ˈē'ō(ˌ)sō, -)zō\ *n* -S [It, curious or inquisitive person, fr. *curioso*, adj., curious, fr. L *curiosus*] **:** one that makes a practice of inquiring into esoteric matters; *specif* **:** a collector of curios or objets d'art

cu·ri·ous \ˈkyu̇rēəs, -ür-\ *adj, sometimes* -ER/-EST [ME, fr. MF *curios*, fr. L *curiosus* careful, inquisitive, fr. *curi-* (fr. *cura* care) + *-osus* -ous — more at CURE] **1 a** *archaic* **:** made or prepared with careful skill **:** elaborately or exquisitely executed **:** DAINTY, ELABORATE, RECHERCHÉ **b** *obs* **:** minutely searching **:** ABSTRUSE, RECONDITE **c** *archaic* **:** marked by precise accuracy or careful ingenuity **d** *now dial* **:** CHOICE, EXCELLENT, SUPERLATIVE **2 a :** marked by desire to investigate and learn **:** showing interest in finding or searching out information **:** INQUISITIVE ⟨a rationalist who was ~ and had a sort of scientific interest in life —D.H.Lawrence⟩ ⟨a man, like a cat, is ~ about his environment and keeps investigating it —Stuart Chase⟩ **b :** given to investigating concerns other than one's own ⟨an apprentice ~ of his master's secrets⟩; *often* **:** marked by inquisitiveness about others' concerns **:** PRYING, NOSY ⟨~ about the neighbors' doings⟩ **c** *archaic* **:** having a connoisseur's or virtuoso's interests **3 a** *now dial* **:** difficult to please **:** FASTIDIOUS **b** *archaic* **:** CAREFUL, SOLICITOUS, CHARY, CAUTIOUS **4 a** *archaic* **:** accompanied by feelings of interest **:** INTERESTING **b :** exciting attention, inquiry, speculation, or surprise as strange, hard to explain, unusual, or novel **:** awakening inquisitiveness **:** EXTRAORDINARY ⟨whatever we're thoroughly unfamiliar with is apt to seem to us odd . . . or ~ —J.L.Lowes⟩ **c** *of a book* **:** EROTIC, PORNOGRAPHIC

syn INQUISITIVE, PRYING, SNOOPY, NOSY: CURIOUS always suggests an eager desire to learn and may or may not imply such objectionable qualities as intrusiveness or impertinence ⟨a *curious* person, who searches into things under the earth and in heaven —Benjamin Jowett⟩ ⟨anyone who is prematurely *curious* to see the difference in treatment between different centuries —Henry Adams⟩ ⟨it was as if listening to her I had taken advantage of having seen her poor, bewildered, scared soul without its veils. But I was *curious* too . . . I was anxious, anxious to know a little more —Joseph Conrad⟩ INQUISITIVE implies habitual and perhaps impertinent search for information, sometimes about matters secret and unrevealed ⟨we were in plain sight of everybody passing; and therefore we had no lack of visitors among such an idle, *inquisitive* set as the Tahitians —Herman Melville⟩ ⟨well, this Elsie, she was a bit *inquisitive*, as girls are, and one day . . . she managed to take a peep through a keyhole or something of that kind, and caught the old lady just in the act of putting the stuff away —Dorothy Sayers⟩ PRYING implies officious meddling ⟨in Texas the fearful, thirsty citizen may be afraid to have a drink on his front porch because of the *prying* eyes of his bluenosed neighbor across the hedge —Stanley Walker⟩ ⟨and down in one corner of the chest, safe from the *prying* eyes of my messmates, was a velvet-lined box from Maiden Lane. It contained a bracelet and necklace —C.B.Nordhoff & J.N.Hall⟩ To this SNOOPY adds the suggestion of slyness or sneaking ⟨the businessman sufficiently *snoopy* to discover what Jones has saved —*Atlantic*⟩ NOSY, suggesting a dog's procedure, implies desire for full information about any new situation ⟨doesn't want *nosy* state officials or city slickers prying into its manners and morals —*Fortnight*⟩ **syn** see in addition STRANGE

cu·ri·ous·ly *adv* [ME, fr. *curious* + *-ly*] **:** in a curious manner; *esp* **:** in a way or to a degree inspiring curiosity

cu·ri·ous·ness *n* -ES [ME, fr. *curious* + *-ness*] **:** the quality of being curious: as **a** *obs* **:** CAREFULNESS, PAINSTAKING **b :** curious workmanship **:** ingenuity of contrivance **c :** INQUISITIVENESS, CURIOSITY **d :** NOVELTY, ODDITY

cu·rite \ˈkyu̇ˌrīt\ *n* -S [F, fr. Pierre *Curie* †1906 Fr. chemist + F *-ite*] **:** a radioactive mineral $2PbO.5UO_3.4H_2O$ occurring in orange acicular crystals and supposed to be a hydrous lead uranyl uranate

cu·ri·ti·ba \ˌk(y)u̇rəˈtēbə\ *adj, usu cap* [fr. *Curitiba*, Brazil] **:** of or from the city of Curitiba, Brazil **:** of the kind or style prevalent in Curitiba

cu·ri·um \ˈkyu̇rēəm\ *n* -S [NL, fr. Marie & Pierre *Curie* + NL *-ium* — more at CURIE] **:** a metallic radioactive trivalent element artificially produced (as by bombardment of plutonium with high-energy helium nuclei) — symbol *Cm;* see ELEMENT table

¹**curl** \ˈkərl, *esp before pause or consonant* ˈkər-əl; ˈkəl, ˈkəil\ *vb* -ED/-ING/-S [ME *curlen, crullen*, fr. *crolle, crulle* curly, prob. fr. MD; akin to OHG *krol* curly, Norw *krull*, MHG *krūs*, OE *crēas* fine, elegant, *cradol* cradle — more at CRADLE] *vt* **1 :** to twist or form into coils or ringlets (as the hair) **2 :** to form into a curved shape **:** make a curve or curves in or on **:** TWIST ⟨~*ed* one leg about the other⟩ **3 :** to furnish with or as if with curls ⟨a head ~*ed* with graceful locks⟩ **4 :** to contort in a grimace or similar expression of feeling ⟨~*ing* his lips in a sneer⟩ ⟨she looked at him contemptuously and then ~*ed* her mouth up in anger —Liam O'Flaherty⟩ **5 :** to cut so thinly as to create a twisted or ringed effect ⟨~*ed* bacon⟩ ⟨~*ed* celery stalks⟩ ~ *vi* **1 :** to grow in coils or spirals ⟨her hair ~*s* naturally⟩ ⟨a ~*ing* vine⟩ **:** form ripples, crinkles, or ringlets ⟨her hair ~*s* only in damp weather⟩ ⟨bacon ~*s* when fried⟩ ⟨the crisp white edge of a ~*ing* wave —F.J.Mather⟩ **2 :** to move or progress in curves or spirals ⟨the lanes ~ and wind into a . . . sort of labyrinth —Faubion Bowers⟩ **:** form into rings or curves ⟨the snake lashed and ~*ed* —William Beebe⟩ **:** roll or move in ripples ⟨his laughter ~*ed* round his sentences —Virginia Woolf⟩ **3 :** to twist or contort (as in a grimace) ⟨his lip ~*ed* in scorn⟩ **4 :** to play the game of curling **syn** see WIND — **curl the hair :** FRIGHTEN, STUN, NONPLUS, AMAZE ⟨it's enough to *curl your hair* to watch his acrobatic stunts⟩

²**curl** \ˈ"\ *n* -S **1 :** a lock of hair that coils **:** RINGLET **2 :** something having a curling or coiling shape (as a shaving of wood) **:** COIL, SPIRAL **3 :** the action or fact of curling **:** the state of being curled ⟨keep the hair in ~⟩ **4 a :** an eddy in a stream **b** *South* **:** a bend in a stream **5 :** an abnormal rolling or curling of leaves; *also* **:** a malformation caused by the feeding of aphids or other sucking insects — compare LEAF CURL, LEAF ROLL **6 a** *archery* **:** a sudden turn in the grain of a bow **b :** a curved or spiral marking in the grain of wood **7 :** TENDRIL **8** *math* **:** the vector product of the operator *del* and the vector **9 :** the degree to which a sheet of paper departs from a plane when freely exposed to the atmosphere

curl cloud *n* **:** a cirrus cloud

curled \-ld\ *adj* [ME *curled, crulled*, past part. of *curlen, crullen* to curl — more at CURL] *bot* **:** having crisped leaves ⟨~ lettuce⟩

curled cress *n* **:** WINTER CRESS

curled dock *n* **:** a European dock (*Rumex crispus*) with curled leaves that has become naturalized as a weed in the U.S.

curled hair *n* **:** hair of the manes and tails of horses prepared for upholstery and cushioning purposes

curled mallow *n* **:** a European mallow (*Malva verticillata crispa*) with curled and twisted leaves

curled mustard *n* **:** an Asiatic herb (*Brassica juncea crispifolia*) whose crispy curled foliage is used for greens

curled·ness \ˈkərlədnəs, ˈkəl-,ˈkəil-, -l(d)nəs\ *n* -ES **:** the quality or state of being curled

curled–toe paralysis *n* **:** ariboflavinosis of young chickens and turkeys marked by retarded growth, weakness of the legs with a squatting shuffle, and the turning inward of the toes

curl·er \ˈkərlər; ˈkələ(r, ˈkəil-\ *n* -S **1 :** one that curls: **a :** a worker who curves the brims of felt hats **b :** a worker who shapes feathers into curls **c :** a metal or plastic pin on which hair is wound for curling **2 :** a player of the game of curling

cur·lew \ˈkər(ˌ)lü *also* -rl(ˌ)yü\ *n, pl* **curlews** *or* **curlew** [ME *corlewe, curlewe*, fr. MF *corlieu, courlis*, of imit. origin] **:** any of a number of wide-ranging chiefly migratory birds (family Scolopacidae) esp. of the genus *Numenius* having long legs, a long slender bill that curves downward, and plumage variegated with brown and buff

curlewberry \ˈ⸗(,)⸗— *see* BERRY\ *n* **1 :** CROWBERRY 1a **2 :** the fruit of the curlewberry

curlew bug *n* **:** CORN BILLBUG

curlew jack *n* **:** WHIMBREL

curlew sandpiper *n* **:** a sandpiper (*Calidris ferruginea*) that is widely distributed in the Old World and has a curved bill like that of a curlew

¹**cur·li·cue** *also* **cur·ly·cue** *or* **cur·ley·cue** *or* **cur·le·cue** \ˈkərlē,kyü, -əl-,-əil-, -lə,-\ *or* **car·la·cue** \ˈkärl-, -äl-\ *n* -S [*curly* + *cue* (queue)] **:** a fancifully curved or spiral figure (as a flourish in writing)

²**curlicue** \ˈ"\ *vb* -ED/-ING/-S *vi* **:** to form curlicues ⟨the words *curlicued* almost illegibly across the brown-edged paper —Nancy Cardozo⟩ ~ *vt* **:** to decorate with curlicues ⟨houses *curlicued* in exuberant outburst of Tyrolean design —Claudia Cassidy⟩

cur·lie·wur·ly \ˌkərlēˈwərlē\ *n, pl* **curliewurlies** [redupl. of *curly*] **:** something fantastically circular or curly

curl·i·ly \ˈkərləlē, ˈkəl-,ˈkəil, -əli\ *adv* **:** in a curly manner

curl·i·ness \-lēnəs, -lin-\ *n* -ES **:** the quality or state of being curly

curl·ing \ˈkərliŋ, -əl-,-əil-, -lēŋ\ *n* -S [ME, act of curling, fr. gerund of *curlen* to curl] **:** a game developed in Scotland in which two teams of four men each send stones spinning over a stretch of ice about 42 yards long toward a target circle in an attempt to place a stone nearest the center

2 3 5 6 7 4 1 8 4 YDS. 7 YDS.

diagram of either end of a curling rink: *1* foot score, *2* back score, *3* sweeping score, *4* hog score, *5* tee, *6* 2-ft. circle, *7* 4-ft. circle, *8* 6-ft. circle (outer limit of parish)

curling dies *n pl* **:** a set of shaping tools consisting of a die and a punch that bends the edges or ends of the work into a form having a circular cross section

curling iron *n* **:** a rod-shaped usu. metal instrument which is heated by direct flame or electricity and around which a lock of hair to be curled or waved is wound

curling machine *n* **:** a machine made with one or more sets of curling dies and used to curl or crimp the ends of cans

curling stone *n* **:** a stone or sometimes iron ellipsoid with a gooseneck handle for delivery in the game of curling

curlpaper \ˈ⸗,⸗⸗\ *n* **:** a strip or piece of paper around which a lock of hair is wound for curling — usu. used in pl.

curls *pres 3d sing of* CURL, *pl of* CURL

curl up *vi* **1 :** to roll oneself into the shape of a ball, a coil, or a curl ⟨*curl up* in a chair⟩ **2 :** to give up **:** COLLAPSE, SLUMP ⟨on the battlefield they would surely lie down and *curl up* —Dorothy C. Fisher⟩

curling stone

curly \ˈkərlē, -əl-,-əil-, -li\ *adj* -ER/-EST [²*curl* + *-y*] **1 :** curling or tending to curl **:** having curls **:** full of ripples **:** CRINKLED **2 a** *of the grain of wood* **:** having fibers that curve in and out without crossing and often form alternating light and dark lines ⟨~ maple⟩ **b :** having such grain **3 :** having a tilde

curly birch *n* **:** YELLOW BIRCH

curly clematis *n* **:** a shrubby climber (*Clematis crispa*) having nodding urn-shaped flowers with open flaring top and with recurved crisped sepals

curly–coated retriever \ˈ⸗⸗,⸗⸗-\ *n* **1** *usu cap both Cs&R* **:** a breed of sporting dogs having a long head, dark eyes, deep chest and shoulders, and a black or liver coat of short crisp curly hair **2 :** a dog of the Curly-Coated Retriever breed

curly dock *n* **:** CURLED DOCK

curly dwarf *n* **:** a phase of rugose mosaic involving dwarfing and leaf curling often without mottled symptoms

curly grass *n* **:** a rare small fern (*Schizaea pusilla*) with slender spiraling fronds

curlyhead \ˈ⸗⸗,⸗\ *n* **1 :** a person with curly hair **2 curlyheads** *pl but sing or pl in constr* \ˈ⸗⸗,⸗\ **:** something suggestive of curly hair; *specif* **:** a clematis (*Clematis ochroleuca*) of the eastern U.S.

curly indigo *n* **:** SENSITIVE JOINT VETCH

curly leaf *n* **:** a plant disease characterized by curling of the leaves: as **a :** curly top of the beet **b :** RASPBERRY MOSAIC

curlylocks \ˈ⸗⸗,⸗\ *n pl but sing in constr* **:** one having curly hair

curly mesquite *also* **curly mesquite grass** *n* **:** a valuable creeping pasture grass (*Hilaria belangeri*) of the southwestern U.S.

curly n *n* **:** the letter *n* with tilde (as *ñ*)

curly–pate \ˈ⸗⸗,⸗\ *n* **:** a curly-headed person

curly–toe \ˈ⸗⸗,⸗\ *n* **:** CURLED-TOE PARALYSIS

curly top *n* **:** a destructive virus disease esp. of beets and particularly the sugar beet but also of other plants (as tomato, bean, or squash) that is transmitted in the western U.S. by the beet leafhopper and causes prompt death in plants affected when young and a curling and puckering of the leaves in plants affected when half grown or older and some necrosis of the phloem in all parts

curly wolf *n, slang* **:** a tough objectionable character

cur·mud·geon \(ˌ)kərˈməjən, ˈkər,m-\ *n* -S [origin unknown] **1** *archaic* **:** a grasping avaricious man **:** MISER **2 :** a crusty, ill-tempered, or difficult and often elderly person **:** CHURL ⟨grew up into something of a top brass ~ —*Time*⟩ ⟨a cantankerous old ~⟩

cur·mud·geon·ish \-nish\ *adj* **:** somewhat curmudgeonly ⟨made him feel mean and small and ~ —Cora Jarrett⟩

cur·mud·geon·ly \-nlē\ *adj* **:** like or characteristic of a curmudgeon esp. in being crotchety, surly, or cantankerous **:** CHURLISH ⟨whose temper was not so ~ as that of his famous friend —Edith Sitwell⟩ **syn** see STINGY

cur·mur·ring \kərˈmərin\ *n* -S [fr. pres. part. of *curmurr* to rumble, fr. Sc *cur-* (intensive prefix) + *murr* to purr] *Scot* **:** rumbling esp. in the bowels

curn *or* **curran** \ˈkərn\ *n* -S [ME *curn;* akin to ME *corn* grain — more at CORN] **1** *Scot* **:** GRAIN, CORN **2** *Scot* **:** a small number **:** FEW

cur·ney *or* **cur·nie** \ˈkərnē\ *n, pl* **curneys** *or* **curnies** [*curn* + *-ey -ie* (dim. suffix)] *Scot* **:** a company esp. of persons

cur·nock \ˈkərnək\ *n* -S [ME *carnok*, of Celt origin; akin to W *crynog* crannock] **:** CRANNOCK

cur·pin \ˈkərpən\ *n* -S [alter. of *croupon*, fr. ME, fr. OF, aug. of *croupe* rump — more at CROUP] *chiefly Scot* **:** RUMP, BUTTOCKS; *also* **:** CRUPPER

cur·ple \ˈkərpəl\ *n* -S [ME (Sc dial.) *courpale*, alter. of *croper, crupere* crupper — more at CRUPPER] *Scot* **:** CRUPPER; *also* **:** BUTTOCKS

curr \ˈkər(·)\ *vi* -ED/-ING/-S [imit.] **:** to make a murmuring sound (as of doves) ⟨the owlets ~ —William Wordsworth⟩

cur·rack *or* **cur·rach** \ˈkərək, -rəḵ\ *n* -S [modif. of ScGael *curran*] *Scot* **:** a wicker pannier

cur·ragh *or* **cur·rach** \'kərə(k)\ *n* -s [partly fr. ME *currok,* fr. ScGael *curach;* partly fr. IrGael *currach;* akin to MIr *curach* coracle — more at CORACLE] **1** *Irish* **:** marshy wasteland **2** *Irish & Scot* **:** CORACLE
currajong *var of* KURRAJONG
currance *n* -s [L *curr*ere to run + E *-ance* — more at CURRENT] *obs* **:** CURRENT, FLOW
cur·rant \'kər·ənt, 'kə·rə-\ *n* -s *often attrib* [ME *rayson of Coraunte,* a variety of small raisin principally grown in Greece, lit., raisin of Corinth, fr. AF *raisin de Corauntz,* fr. *Corauntz* Corinth, Greece, fr. L *Corinthus,* fr. Gk *Korinthos*] **1 :** a small seedless raisin grown chiefly in the Levant and used extensively in cookery and confectionery **2 :** the acid edible fruit of several plants of the genus *Ribes* used chiefly for jams and jellies — see BLACK CURRANT, RED CURRANT, WHITE CURRANT **3 :** a plant of the genus *Ribes* that bears currants **4** *or* **currant red :** GOYA
currant aphid *n* **:** an aphid (*Cryptomyzus ribis*) that is very destructive to the new leaves of currants in spring
currant borer *n* **:** the larva of a small yellow clearwing moth (*Ramosia tipuliformis*) that bores longitudinal tunnels in the canes of currants and gooseberries and often kills them
currant bush *n* **1 :** CURRANT 3 **2** *in Australia* **:** a shrub (*Apophyllum anomalum*) of the family Capparidaceae that bears small berries and serves as a browse plant
currant-leaf \'=,=\ *n* **:** MITERWORT
currant leaf spot *n* **:** any of three fungous diseases of the currant: **a :** an angular leaf spot caused by an imperfect fungus (*Cercospora angulata*) **b :** an anthracnose characterized by small brownish or black spots and caused by a discomycete (*Pseudopeziza ribis*) **c :** a grayish-centered leaf spot caused by an ascomycetous fungus (*Mycosphaerella grossulariae*)
currant rust *n* **:** any of several rusts affecting currants; *esp* **:** WHITE PINE BLISTER RUST
currant spanworm *n* **:** a larval moth (*Itame ribearia*) that is extremely injurious to the leaves or fruit of the currant
currant stem girdler *n* **:** the larva of a sawfly (*Janus integer*) that feeds in and frequently girdles the shoots of the currant and gooseberry
currant tomato *n* **1 :** a Peruvian plant (*Lycopersicon pimpinellifolium*) bearing its spherical small scarlet fruits in long racemes **2 :** the fruit borne on the currant tomato
currantworm \'==,=\ *n* **:** any of various insect larvae that feed on the leaves or the developing fruit of the currant: as **a :** any of several sawfly larvae that feed on currant leaves **b :** CURRANT SPANWORM **c :** a maggot (*Epochra ribearia*) that feeds in the fruit **d :** a caterpillar (*Zophodia convolutella*) that attacks the fruit of currants and gooseberries — see IMPORTED CURRANTWORM
cur·ra·wong \'kərə,wȯŋ, -wäŋ\ *n* -s [native name in Australia] **:** any of several loud-voiced fruit-eating Australian birds constituting the genus *Strepera* of the family Cracticidae — called also *bell magpie*
cur·ren·cy \'kər·ənsē, 'kə·rə-, -si\ *n* -ES *often attrib* [ML *currentia* flowing, fr. L *current-, currens* (pres. part. of *currere* to run) + *-ia*] **1 a :** circulation as a medium of exchange ⟨the ~ of these coins⟩ **b :** CIRCULATION **:** general use **:** general acceptance **:** the fact of being commonly accepted, used, and repeated **:** PREVALENCE ⟨a story that enjoyed wide ~⟩ ⟨a version that gained ~⟩ — used chiefly of reports, sayings, and ideas **c :** the time of such currency **:** the time during which something is current ⟨a test to ensure that he can do a satisfactory weld . . . throughout the ~ of the work —S.C.Robertson⟩ **2 a :** something that is in circulation as a medium of exchange including coin, government notes, and bank notes ⟨the silver ~⟩ ⟨the note ~⟩ ⟨the use of beads as minor ~ in Africa —*advt*⟩ **b :** paper money in circulation ⟨the gift purse contained both coin and ~⟩ **c (1) :** the amount of paper and metallic money in circulation **(2) :** the amount of paper money in circulation **d :** a common article for bartering ⟨tobacco being the ~ of the colony⟩ ⟨furs as ~ in dealing with the natives⟩ **e :** a medium of intellectual exchange or expression ⟨ideas are the ~ of the few —Roy Lewis & Angus Maude⟩ ⟨neither side possessed any ~ but clichés —Jan Struther⟩ ⟨sadism is the ~ in which every activity is expressed when its organized forms are . . . frustrated —Abram Kardiner⟩ **f :** a set of values and designations used in certain British colonies instead of the legal values and proper designations of the English coinage system ⟨six pence in ~ equals three pence in sterling⟩ **3 :** a native-born Australian ⟨his ~ sons and daughters⟩
currency bond *n* **:** a bond payable as to both interest and principal in any form of money that is legal tender within the country of issue — compare GOLD BOND
currency declaration *n* **:** a statement of currency ownership made by a traveler on entering or by a shipper on sending parcels to a country (as one having foreign-exchange control)
currency doctrine *or* **currency principle** *n* **:** the principle that banks should issue notes only against coin or bullion — compare BANKING DOCTRINE
currency dollar *n* **:** CONTINENTAL DOLLAR
currency unit *n* **:** MONETARY UNIT
¹cur·rent \'kər·ənt, 'kə·rə-\ *adj* [ME *curraunt, coraunt,* fr. OF *corant, curant,* pres. part. of *corre, courre* to run, fr. L *currere;* akin to MHG *hurren* to hurry, OIr & MW *carr* vehicle, Gk *epikouros* hastening to aid, and perh. to OE & OHG *horsc* wise, quick, ON *horskr*] **1 a** *archaic* **:** RUNNING, FLOWING, MOVING **b** *archaic* **:** FLUENT **:** flowing easily and smoothly **c (1) :** presently elapsing ⟨the ~ fiscal year⟩ ⟨the ~ month⟩ **(2) :** occurring in or belonging to the present time **:** in evidence or in operation at the time actually elapsing ⟨the ~ crisis⟩ ⟨~ excitement over elections⟩ ⟨~ services⟩ **(3)** *of a serial publication* **:** most recent ⟨the ~ number of a quarterly magazine⟩ **2 a :** being in use as a medium of exchange **:** circulating as money ⟨the ~ coin of the realm⟩ **b** *obs* **:** not counterfeit or spurious **:** GENUINE **3 a :** in general knowledge, acceptance, use, or practice **:** PREVALENT, ACCUSTOMED, GENERAL **:** commonly accepted, engaged in, followed, used, or practiced **:** in vogue **:** CONTEMPORARY ⟨~ fashions⟩ ⟨~ customs⟩ ⟨~ beliefs⟩ ⟨~ theories of education⟩ **b** *math* **:** varying from point to point **:** GENERAL **syn** see PREVAILING
²current \"\ *n* -s [ME *curraunt,* fr. MF *curant,* fr. *curant,* adj.] **1 a :** the part of a fluid body (as air or water) moving continuously in a certain direction **:** STREAM **b :** the swiftest part of a stream **c :** a tidal or nontidal movement often horizontal of lake or ocean water **:** DRIFT **d :** condition of flowing **:** flow marked by force or strength **:** FLOW, FLUX ⟨the violent ~ of the mountain stream⟩ **e :** the velocity of flow of a fluid in a stream ⟨measured the ~ and temperature in the sea just off the ice shelf —Valter Schytt⟩ **2 :** inclination given a channel or a surface shedding water **:** PITCH, TILT ⟨the ~ of the gutter⟩ **3 :** course of events **:** TENOR, TREND, TENDENCY **:** flux of forces ⟨in the deep emotional and creative ~s that produced the Renaissance —G.C.Sellery⟩ ⟨strong ~s of public opinion⟩ ⟨an adventure that changed the whole ~ of his life —Sherwood Anderson⟩ **4 a :** ELECTRIC CURRENT **b :** the intensity of an electric current **syn** see FLOW, TENDENCY
current account *n* **1 a :** an account between two parties having a series of transactions not covered by evidences of indebtedness (as notes or certificates) and usu. subject to settlements at stated intervals (as monthly or quarterly) — called also *account current, book account, open account, running account* **b :** a statement or transcript of such an account **2 :** an open account with a balance not yet due **3 :** CHECKING ACCOUNT — distinguished from *deposit account*
current assets *n pl* **:** assets of a short-term nature (as cash, accounts receivable, or merchandise) — contrasted with *capital assets*
current balance *n* **:** an instrument for measuring electric currents by weighing the mechanical force exerted
current-bedded \'=;=\ *adj* **:** relating to or exhibiting stratification features produced by currents
current bedding *n* **:** cross-bedding produced by water currents or air currents
current cost *n* **:** a cost whose factors are valued at present-day acquisition and production costs
current density *n* **:** the current per unit area of cross section perpendicular to flow in a region through which an electric current is flowing

PRINCIPAL OCEAN CURRENTS, DRIFTS, STREAMS

NAME	OCEAN	DESCRIPTION
Agulhas current	Indian	warm; partly a continuation of Mozambique current; flows SW along SE coast of Africa, turns E at about 40° S
Alaska current	Pacific	cold; a branch of Aleutian current; flows N from about 45° N and counterclockwise in Gulf of Alaska
Aleutian current	Pacific	cold; flows E at about 45° N; branches into Alaska and California currents
Antarctic West Wind drift	Atlantic-Indian-Pacific	cold; encircles Antarctica S of about 50° S
Antilles current	Atlantic	warm; flows NW along N coast of Greater Antilles; joins Florida current
Arctic current *or* Arctic stream: Labrador current		
Australia current: East Australian current; West Australian current		
Benguela current	Atlantic	cold; flows N along W coast of southern Africa
Black current *or* Black stream: Kuroshio current		
Brazil current	Atlantic	warm; flows S along E coast of So. America to about 40° S, then turns E into So. Atlantic current
California current	Pacific	cold; a branch of Aleutian current; flows SE along coast of No. America from about 45° N to about 20° N; joins No. Equatorial current
Canaries current *or* Canaries drift	Atlantic	cold; flows SW from about 40° N along coast of west Africa to about 20° N; joins No. Equatorial current
Cape Horn current	Pacific-Atlantic	cold; flows E off S tip of So. America
Caribbean current	Atlantic	warm; formed by joining of part of No. Equatorial current and a branch of So. Equatorial current; flows NW along N coast of So. America into Caribbean sea
Chilean current: Peru current		
East Australian current	Pacific	warm; flows S along E coast of Australia, then counterclockwise in Tasman sea and E from New Zealand
East Greenland current	Arctic-Atlantic	cold; flows SW along E coast of Greenland
El Niño	Pacific	warm; periodic; flows S from Colombia along coast of So. America between Peru current and the shorelines
Equatorial countercurrent	Pacific-Indian	warm; flows E along equator; affected by monsoons
Falkland current	Atlantic	cold; flows NE along coast of Argentina; joins Brazil current turning E into So. Atlantic current
Florida current	Atlantic	warm; a part of the Gulf stream from Straits of Florida to Cape Hatteras
Guinea current	Atlantic	warm; flows E in Gulf of Guinea along S coast of west Africa
Gulf drift: No. Atlantic drift		
Gulf stream	Atlantic	(1) the warm current flowing along coast of No. America from Cape Hatteras to the Grand Banks, formed by merging of Florida and Antillean currents; (2) the entire stream from the Straits of Florida to the NW coast of Europe, including the Florida current and No. Atlantic drift
Gulf Stream drift: No. Atlantic drift		
Humboldt current: Peru current		
Japan current *or* Japan stream *also* Japanese current: Kuroshio current		
Kurile current: Oyashio current		
Kuroshio current	Pacific	warm; flows NE from E coast of Philippines along E coast of Japan; turns E at about 40° N, becomes part of No. Pacific drift
Labrador current	Atlantic	cold; flows S from Baffin Bay through Davis strait to Newfoundland; E branch joins No. Atlantic drift flowing E; W branch flows into Gulf of St. Lawrence
Monsoon current *or* Monsoon drift	Indian	warm; N of equator; direction of flow dependent on monsoons
Mozambique current *also* Natal current	Indian	warm; flows SW along SE coast of Africa through Mozambique channel; see Agulhas current
No. Atlantic drift *or* No. Atlantic current	Atlantic	warm; continuation of Gulf stream joined by E branch of Labrador current in region of Grand Banks; flows NE to NW coast of Europe
No. Equatorial current	Atlantic-Pacific	warm; flows W, N of equator
No. Pacific drift *or* No. Pacific current	Pacific	warm; formed by merging of Japan and Oyashio currents; flows E to W coast of No. America at about 40° N; branches into Alaska and California currents
Norwegian current	Atlantic	warm; continuation of No. Atlantic drift; flows NE along coast of Norway into Arctic ocean
Oyashio current *or* Oya Siwo current *also* Okhotsk current	Pacific	cold; flows SW from Bering sea along Kurile islands and E coast of Japan; meets Kuroshio current at about 40° N
Peru current *also* Peruvian current	Pacific	cold; flows N and NW along coast of N Chile, Peru, and Ecuador; turns W to join So. Equatorial current
So. Atlantic current	Atlantic	cool; flows E from So. America toward southern tip of So. Africa, between latitude 35° S and 45° S, as part of the Antarctic West Wind drift
So. Equatorial current	Atlantic-Pacific-Indian	warm; flows W just S of the equator; in the Atlantic it branches, forming the Brazil and Caribbean currents
So. Indian drift *or* So. Indian current: Antarctic West Wind drift		
So. Pacific current *or* So. Pacific drift: Antarctic West Wind drift		
Subarctic current: Aleutian current		
Tsushima current: Kuroshio current		
West Australian current	Indian	cold; flows N along W coast of Australia; one branch turns W to join the So. Equatorial current, the other continues NE along N coast of Australia
West Greenland current	Atlantic	cold; continuation of East Greenland current; flows NW along SW coast of Greenland
West Wind drift: Antarctic West Wind drift		

cur·ren·te ca·la·mo \kə,rentē'kalə,mō\ *adv* [L, lit., with running pen] **:** OFFHAND **:** without deep reflection ⟨written *currente calamo*⟩
current events *n pl but sing or pl in constr* **:** contemporary developments in local, national, or world affairs; *also* **:** the organized study of such developments
current intensity *or* **current strength** *n* **:** the magnitude of an electric current as measured by the quantity of electricity crossing a specified area of equipotential surface per unit time
current liability *n* **:** a liability that arises in the ordinary course of business and must be met in a comparatively short time (as an account payable or an accrual of interest not yet due)
current limiter *n* **:** a fuse to break a circuit when a predetermined current is exceeded
current-limiting reactor \'==,===\ *n* **:** an electrical inductance made up of a number of turns of wire of low ohmic resistance and inserted in series with a line to limit the current that can flow under short circuit
cur·rent·ly *adv* **1 :** FLUENTLY, READILY ⟨reading 16th century writing as ~ . . . as we read our own is an illusion —Virginia Woolf⟩ **2 :** at present ⟨~ engaged in scientific research⟩ ⟨~ running at the local theater⟩
currently insured *adj* **:** entitled to retirement payments under federal old-age and survivors insurance or at death having at least 6 quarters of coverage within the 3 years immediately preceding
current meter *n* **:** an instrument for measuring the velocity of flow of a fluid (as water) in a stream
current money *n* **:** lawful or universally acceptable money
cur·rent·ness *n* -ES **:** the state of being current **:** CURRENCY
current of action : ACTION CURRENT
current of rest : an electric current that is due to a difference of potential between two inactive parts of an organism (as between two regions on an unstimulated nerve) and that is modified when excitation occurs
current ratio : the ratio between current assets and liabilities used in appraising credit worthiness of a business
current ripple *or* **current mark** *n* **:** an asymmetrical ripple mark formed by currents of water on the surface of sediments (as river bars, tidal flats, beaches, or sand dunes) — compare OSCILLATION RIPPLE
current tap *n* **:** a device permitting the attachment of a branch electrical circuit to a main circuit by means of an attachment plug or cap
current transformer *n* **:** a transformer whose primary carries the whole of an alternating current to be measured or controlled and whose secondary is connected to a measuring or control device
current yield *n* **:** the rate of return given by a bond on its current price without allowance for the fact that it will be paid at par at maturity

cur·ri·cle \'kərəkəl\ *n* -s [L *curriculum* running, racecourse, chariot] **:** a 2-wheeled chaise usu. drawn by two horses
cur·ric·u·lar \kə'rikyələ(r)\ *adj* [*curriculum* + *-ar*] **:** of or relating to the curriculum **:** of or relating to academic courses of study
cur·ric·u·lum \-ləm\ *n, pl* **curricu·la** \-lə\ *also* **curriculums** [NL, fr. LL, course of a year, fr. L, running, racecourse, chariot, fr. *currere* to run — more at CURRENT] **1 :** the whole body of courses offered by an educational institution or one of its branches ⟨widening the college ~⟩ **2 :** any particular body of courses set for various majors ⟨the ~ in engineering⟩ ⟨the premedical ~⟩ **3 :** all planned school activities including besides courses of study organized play, athletics, dramatics, clubs, and home-room program **4 a :** general education and breeding ⟨people who had not learned courtesy in the course of an elaborate ~⟩ **b :** a work schedule
cur·ric·u·lum vi·tae \kə,rikələm'wē,tī, -kyələm'vī,tē\ *n, pl* **curricu·la vitae** \-lə'-\ [L, course of (one's) life] **:** a brief account of one's life **:** a brief statement including biographical data ⟨applications should include a *curriculum vitae* —*Science*⟩
cur·ri·er \'kər·ēə(r), 'kə·rē-\ *n* -s [alter. (influenced by ¹*curry*) of ME *corier,* fr. MF, fr. L *coriarius,* fr. *corium* leather + *-arius* -ary — more at CUIRASS] **:** one that curries: as **a :** a worker who performs any of the operations (as oiling, softening, or rolling) necessary to bring tanned hides or skins to salable form **b :** one that curries a horse
²currier *n* -s [origin unknown] **:** a 16th century firearm resembling the harquebus
cur·ri·ery \'kər·ēərē, 'kə·rē-, -əri\ *n* -ES [¹*curry* + *-ery*] **1 :** the trade of a currier of leather **2 :** a place where currying is done
curring *pres part of* CURR
cur·rish \'kər·ish, \ēsh –R *also* 'kər\ *adj* [ME, fr. *curre* cur + *-ish*] **:** like a cur **:** MONGREL; *also* **:** BASE, MEANSPIRITED, IGNOBLE — **cur·rish·ly** *adv*
currs *pres 3d sing of* CURR
¹cur·ry \'kər·ē, 'kə·r|, |i\ *vb* -ED/-ING/-ES [ME *curraven, corien,* fr. OF *correer, conreer* to prepare, arrange, furnish, curry, fr. (assumed) VL *conredare,* fr. L *com-* + (assumed) VL *redare* to provide — more at ARRAY] *vt* **1 :** to comb the hair or coat of (as a horse) with a currycomb **2 :** to incorporate oils and greases into (heavy leathers) in order to increase strength, water repellency, and pliability **3 :** BEAT, DRUB, THRASH **4 :** to make presentable **:** DRESS, ARRANGE, COMB, GROOM ⟨a courtier well *curried*⟩ ~ *vi, archaic* **:** to engage in flattery, blandishment, and cajolery — **curry fa·vor** \-'fāvə(r)\ [alter. (influenced by *favor,* n.) of ME *curraven favel* to curry a chestnut horse, trans. of MF *estriller fauvel*] **:** to seek to gain favor by flattery or attentions
²curry \"\ *also* **cur·rie** \"\ *n* -ES [Tamil-Malayalam *kari*] **1 :** CURRY POWDER **2 :** a food seasoned with curry powder ⟨vegetable ~⟩ ⟨lamb ~⟩ ⟨shrimp ~⟩

³**curry** \"\ *vt* -ED/-ING/-ES **:** to flavor or cook (a food) with curry

⁴**curry** *vi* -ED/-ING/-ES [perh. back-formation fr. *currier*, obs. var. of *courier*] *obs* **:** COURSE, SCURRY

¹**currycomb** \ˈ==,=\ *n* [¹*curry* + *comb*] **:** a comb made of rows of metallic teeth or serrated ridges and used esp. in currying a horse

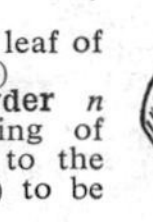
currycomb

²**currycomb** \"\ *vt* **:** to comb (as a horse) with a currycomb **:** CURRY

curry leaf *n* [²*curry*] **:** the pungent leaf of an Asiatic shrub (*Murraya koenigii*)

curry powder *also* **currie powder** *n* [²*curry*] **:** a condiment consisting of ground spices blended according to the type of food (as egg or vegetable) to be curried

curs *pl of* CUR

¹**curse** \ˈkərs, -əs, -əis\ *n* -S [ME *curs*, fr. OE] **1 a :** a calling to a deity to visit evil on one **:** a solemn pronouncement or invoking of doom or great evil on one **:** an imprecation for harm **b :** any utterance marked by malediction or execration **:** OATH **c :** evil effects brought about by a curse or by or as if by something cursed ⟨a witch putting a ~ on them⟩ ⟨an ancient house and family on which a ~ had long rested⟩ **2 :** excommunication or anathema **:** formal and extreme church censure **3 :** something that is cursed or worthy of being cursed **:** an evil, misfortune, or source of harm **:** SCOURGE ⟨intolerance is the greatest ~ of every land —Kenneth Roberts⟩ ⟨such ~s as yaws and malaria —Robert Trumbull⟩ **4 :** MENSTRUATION — used with *the*

²**curse** \" *or, as a vi & in vt sense 2c,* ˈkəs\ *vb* -ED/-ING/-S [ME *cursen*, fr. OE *cursian*, fr. *curs*, n.] *vt* **1 :** to rail at typically impiously and profanely **:** BLASPHEME ⟨*cursing* his god⟩ ⟨*cursing* his wretched fate⟩ **2 a :** to utter words calculated to consign to great evil **:** assign to an evil fate **:** DAMN, DOOM ⟨a blasphemer *cursed* by his gods⟩ **b :** to pronounce a formal curse on **:** ANATHEMATIZE, EXCOMMUNICATE ⟨an act *cursed* by the high church council⟩ **c :** to swear at **:** call on fate to visit with dire misfortune and evil **:** invoke divine vengeance or anger against — sometimes used with *out* ⟨he *cursed* out his treacherous ally⟩ ⟨*cursing* his servant for his stupidity⟩ **3 :** to bring evil on **:** visit with retribution **:** punish with wrath sometimes divine **:** endow to one's detriment **:** AFFLICT, HARASS ⟨*cursed* with misfortunes⟩ ⟨*cursed* by society as always outcast⟩ ⟨*cursed* by misplaced loyalties⟩ ~ *vi* **:** to utter curses, oaths, and imprecations **:** SWEAR ⟨rebuked for his *cursing*⟩ ⟨he ~s too much⟩ **syn** see EXECRATE

cursed \ˈkərsəd, -əs-, -əis-, -st — *in sense 1 -st is rare except in poetry; in sense 2, either -səd or -st but -st is usual nonattributively; in sense 3 -st is usual*\ *also* **curst** \-st\ *adj, sometimes* -ER/-EST [ME *cursd, cursed, curste*, fr. past part. of *cursen*] **1 :** worthy of being cursed **:** execrable, wicked, hateful, or obnoxious ⟨his ~ stupidity⟩ **2 :** under a curse ⟨villagers shun the place believing it to be ~⟩ **3** *now chiefly dial* **:** of a vicious or irritable disposition **:** CANTANKEROUS, SHREWISH

cursed crowfoot *n* **:** an annual or short-lived perennial herb (*Ranunculus sceleratus*) growing in marshy places and having stems hollow and basal leaves reniform with the upper ones smaller and marked with three linear segments

curs·ed·ly \-sədlē, -li\ *adv* [ME, fr. *cursed* + *-ly*] **:** INTENSELY, DAMNABLY, BITTERLY ⟨~ hard job⟩ ⟨~ cold weather⟩

curs·ed·ness \-sədnəs\ *n* -ES [ME *cursednes*, fr. *cursed* + *-nes* -ness] **:** the quality or state of being hateful, vicious, or perverse **:** bad temper **:** bad disposition

cursed thistle *n* **1 :** BLESSED THISTLE **2 :** CANADA THISTLE

curse of scot·land \-əvˈskätlənd, -əvˈsk-\ *cap S* [so called fr. its similarity to the coat of arms of Sir John Dalrymple, 1st Earl of Stair †1707 Scot. lawyer, as lord advocate partly responsible for the massacre of the MacDonald clan at Glencoe, Scotland, in 1692] **:** the nine of diamonds in playing cards

cursitor *n* -S [AF & ML; AF *coursetour*, fr. ML *cursitor* runner, alter. of L *cursor* — more at CURSOR] *obs* **:** COURIER

¹**cur·sive** \ˈkərsiv\ *adj* [F or ML; F *cursif*, fr. ML *cursivus*, lit., running, fr. L *cursus* (past part. of *currere* to run) + *-ivus* -ive] **:** RUNNING, COURSING: as **a** *of writing* **:** flowing often with the strokes of successive characters joined and the angles rounded ⟨children are still taught ~ writing —Marcia Winn⟩ **b :** having a flowing, easy, impromptu character ⟨the ~ quality of a rapid sketch —Tatiana Proskouriakoff⟩ **:** done in an offhand or casual manner without great attention to detail ⟨a somewhat free and ~ rendering of Horace —Cyril Connolly⟩

²**cursive** \"\ *n* -S **1 :** a manuscript written in cursive writing **2 :** a style of printed letter imitating handwriting — sometimes used of letters that do not join each other and thereby distinguished from *script*

Italian cursive
cursive 2

cur·sive·ly *adv* **:** in a cursive style or manner

cur·sive·ness *n* -ES **:** the quality of being cursive

cur·sor \-sə(r), -,sȯ(ə)r, -ȯ(ə)\ *n* -S [obs. E, runner, fr. ME, fr. L, fr. *cursus* (past part. of *currere* to run) + *-or* — more at CURRENT] **:** a part of a mathematical instrument that moves back and forth upon another part

cursorary *adj* [obs. E *cursor* + *-ary*] *obs* **:** CURSORY

cur·so·res \,kərˈsȯr(,)ēz\ *n pl, cap* [NL, fr. L, pl. of *cursor* runner] **1** *in some esp former classifications* **:** any of certain groups of long-legged birds **2** *in some esp former classifications* **:** a group consisting of the wolf spiders and other forms that make no web but pursue their prey

cur·so·ria \-ōrēə\ *n pl, cap* [NL, fr. LL, neut. pl. of *cursorius* of running, fr. L *cursus* running, course (fr. *cursus*, past part.) + *-orius* -ory] *in some classifications* **:** a suborder of Orthoptera including cockroaches, mantes, and stick insects comprising those that progress by running and not leaping — compare SALTATORIA

cur·so·ri·al \,kərˈsōrēəl\ *adj* [LL *cursorius* of running + E *-al*] **1 :** adapted to running ⟨~ insects⟩ **:** having limbs adapted to running and not to prehension ⟨a ~ horse⟩ — opposed to *fossorial* **2 a** [NL *Cursores* + E *-ial*] **:** of or relating to the Cursores **b** [NL *Cursoria* + E *-al*] **:** of or relating to the Cursoria

cur·so·ri·ly \ˈkərs(ə)rəlē, -əl, -əi, -li *sometimes* |z(-\ *adv* **:** in a cursory manner

cur·so·ri·ness \-)rēnəs, -rin-\ *n* -ES **:** the quality of being cursory

cur·so·ri·us \,kərˈsōrēəs\ *n, cap* [NL, fr. LL *cursorius* of running] **:** a genus of birds (family Glareolidae) comprising the typical coursers — compare GLAREOLA

cur·so·ry \ˈkərs(ə)rē, -əl, -əi, -ri *sometimes* |z(-\ *adj* [LL *cursorius* of running] **:** rapidly often superficially performed with scant attention to detail **:** marked by hurried passing over or through something that invites exhaustive treatment **:** HASTY ⟨investigations were ~ to the point of being slapdash —Norman Moss⟩ ⟨studied three months in a ~ fashion —C.G. Bowers⟩ ⟨issued either no reports at all or only extremely ~ ones —John Brooks⟩

curst *var of* CURSED

cur·sus \ˈkərsəs\ *n, pl* **cursus** [ML, fr. L, course — more at COURSE] **:** movement or flow of style; *specif* **:** a pattern of cadence at the end of a sentence or phrase in medieval Latin prose which aimed by varying rhythm to avoid stressing the ultimate syllable

curt \ˈkərt, -əl, -əi, *usu* |d·+V\ *adj* -ER/-EST [L *curtus* shortened — more at SHEAR] **1 a** *of speech or writing* **:** brief or concise **:** sparing of words **:** CONDENSED, TERSE ⟨wrote with ~ realistic precision —Carl Van Doren⟩ ⟨a ~, clean, and complete account⟩ **b :** marked by such shortness of speech, writing, or manner as to suggest discourtesy, displeasure, or peremptoriness **:** LACONIC, TERSE ⟨a ~ message . . . bade her return at once to Rome —John Buchan⟩ **:** BRUSQUE, ABRUPT ⟨a ~ nod⟩ **2 :** short in linear extent **:** SHORTENED **syn** see BLUFF

curt *abbr* current

¹**cur·tail** \,kərˈtāl, ˈkə̄-, ˈkəi-, kə(r)ˈt-, *esp before pause or consonant* -āəl\ *vt* -ED/-ING/-S [by folk etymology fr. earlier *curtal* to make a curtal of, fr. *curtal*, n.] **1 a :** to cut off the end or any part of **:** shorten in linear extent **:** reduce in area or amount ⟨whether the hair is ~*ed* or long and upswept —*New Yorker*⟩ ⟨its area — it had extended . . . southward to the Ohio and westward to the Mississippi — was greatly ~*ed* —B.K. Sandwell⟩ **b :** to diminish (intangible objects or values) **:** shorten in duration or scope **:** ABRIDGE, REDUCE ⟨~ the power of feudal militarists —Vera M. Dean⟩ ⟨~ the working day⟩ **2 :** to deprive, dock, or rob (a person) of a right, privilege, or possession as indicated — used with *of* ⟨~*ed* of his heritage⟩ ⟨~*ed* of one's citizenship⟩ **syn** see SHORTEN

²**curtail** \ˈ=,=\ *n* -S [prob. by folk etymology fr. *curtal*, n.] **:** the scroll end of any architectural member (as a step at the foot of a flight)

cur·tailed·ness \(,)=ˈtāləd nəs, -l(d)n-\ *n* -ES **:** the quality or state of being curtailed

cur·tail·ment \(,)=ˈ= mənt\ *n* -S **:** the act of curtailing **:** the fact of being curtailed

¹**cur·tain** \ˈkərtᵊn, -əl, -əi| *sometimes* |tən *or* |d·ən\ *n* -S *often attrib* [ME *curtine, cortine, curteyne*, fr. OF *curtine, cortine*, fr. LL *cortina* (trans. of Gk *aulaia*, fr. *aulē* court, hall), fr. L *cort-* (*cohort-*), *cors* (*cohors*) enclosure, court + *-ina* -ine — more at AULA, COURT] **1 a :** a piece of material finished with hems, ruffles, pleats, or casings and hung usu. by the top edge on rods or poles at windows or sometimes on beds for decoration, privacy, and control of light and drafts **b :** any similar material that serves to screen, divide, protect, conceal, or decorate ⟨a plastic shower ~⟩ ⟨isinglass side ~s on a car⟩ **2 a :** SCREEN **:** a device that hides or masks **:** an agency that conceals **:** a check to clear perception, understanding, or communication ⟨the rebel fort, less than a mile away, was wholly lost behind ~s of rain —Kenneth Roberts⟩ ⟨a ~ of reserve which she meant to draw again across her features —Marcia Davenport⟩ **b :** an arrangement of moving items or particles serving to screen or protect ⟨a ~ of bullets around the outpost⟩; *specif* **:** a protective sheet or spray of water thrown by a fire hose or sprinkler **c :** a barrier to free communication or exchange of information typically implemented by rigid censorship and restriction on travel and trade **:** a line demarcating the operation of such a barrier ⟨an iron ~⟩ ⟨a security ~⟩ **3 a :** the part of a bastioned front that connects two neighboring bastions — see BASTION illustration **b :** a similar stretch of plain wall **c :** a geological formation similar in effect **4 a :** the screen separating the stage from the auditorium of a theater **b :** the ascent of the curtain at the beginning of a play ⟨~ is at 8:30⟩ **c :** the descent of the curtain at the end of a scene or act of a play **d :** a theatrical effect just prior to the descent of the curtain **e :** the final situation or line of an act; *esp* **:** the closing scene of a play **f :** music used to signal the end of a scene or act of a radio or television program **g curtains** *pl* **:** END **:** definitive conclusion; *esp* **:** DEATH — used as a predicate noun ⟨it was ~s for him when his treason was discovered⟩ **5 a :** the part of a wall of a building that is between two pavilions or towers **b :** an exterior wall that serves to enclose rather than to support **6 :** a floating boom to protect a riverbank **7** *chiefly dial* **:** SHADE 7g

²**curtain** \"\ *vb* **curtained; curtained; curtaining** \-t(ᵊ)niŋ, -tən-, -d·ən-\ **curtains** [ME *curtinen, cortinen, curteynen*, fr. *curtine, cortine, curteyne*, n.] *vt* **1 :** to enclose with or as if with curtains **:** furnish with curtains **2 :** to veil with or as if with a curtain ⟨an area ~*ed* off from the rest of the world⟩ ⟨Father had never ~*ed* his eyes —Isa Glenn⟩ ~ *vi, of paint* **:** to sag or droop because of too heavy application

curtain board *n* **:** a partition of noncombustible material fitting tightly against a ceiling and intended to prevent or retard the spread of fire and heat

curtain call *n* **:** an appearance by a performer (as at the final curtain of a play) in response to the applause of the audience

curtainfall \ˈ==,=\ *n* **:** the fall of a curtain at the end of a play **:** CONCLUSION

cur·tain·ing \-t(ᵊ)niŋ, -tən-, -d·ən-\ *n* -S **:** material for curtains

curtain lecture *n* **:** a censorious lecture by a wife to her husband in privacy, often in bed

cur·tain·less *pronunc at* ¹CURTAIN +ləs\ *adj* **:** being without a curtain

curtain line *n* **:** the final line of an act or play

curtain raiser *also* **curtain lifter** *n* **1 :** a short play usu. of one scene with few characters used to open a performance **2 :** a usu. short and unimportant preliminary to a main or significant event

curtain shutter *n* **:** a focal-plane photographic shutter

curtain speech *n* **1 :** the last speech of an act or play **2 :** any speech in front of the curtains by author, actor, or manager

curtain stretcher *n* **:** an adjustable rigid frame to which curtains are attached for drying after laundering in order to restore their original dimensions and smoothness

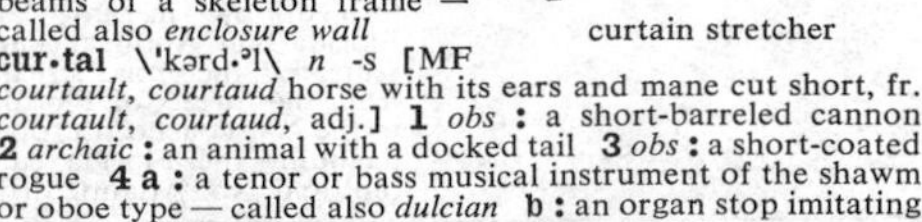
curtain stretcher

curtain wall *n* **1 :** CURTAIN 5 **2 :** a nonbearing wall between columns or piers that is not supported by the girders or beams of a skeleton frame — called also *enclosure wall*

¹**cur·tal** \ˈkərd·ᵊl\ *n* -S [MF *courtault, courtaud* horse with its ears and mane cut short, fr. *courtault, courtaud*, adj.] **1** *obs* **:** a short-barreled cannon **2** *archaic* **:** an animal with a docked tail **3** *obs* **:** a short-coated rogue **4 a :** a tenor or bass musical instrument of the shawm or oboe type — called also *dulcian* **b :** an organ stop imitating the tone of this instrument — compare DULCIANA

²**curtal** \"\ *adj* [MF *courtault, courtaud*, fr. *court* short, fr. L *curtus* shortened — more at SHEAR] **1** *obs* **:** having a docked tail **2** *obs* **:** made or being short **:** CURTAILED, CURT, BRIEF **3** *archaic* **:** wearing a short frock

curtal ax \ˈkərd·ᵊl,aks\ *or* **cur·tle ax** \"\ *n* [by folk etymology fr. MF *coutelas* — more at CUTLASS] **:** CUTLASS

curtal sonnet *n* **:** a curtailed or contracted sonnet; *specif* **:** a sonnet of eleven lines rhyming *abcabc dcbdc* or *abcabc dbcdc* with the last line a tail

cur·tate \ˈkər,tāt\ *adj* [L *curtatus*, past part. of *curtare* to shorten, fr. *curtus* shortened — more at SHEAR] **:** comparatively short or shortened ⟨~ expectation of life⟩; *specif, of an annuity* **:** payable to the end of each complete year survived but not for part of a year

curtate distance *n* **:** the distance of a planet or comet from the sun or earth as measured in the plane of the ecliptic or the distance from the sun or earth to that point where a perpendicular let fall from the planet upon the plane of the ecliptic meets that plane

curted *adj* [L *curtus* + E *-ed*] *obs* **:** SHORTENED **:** made curt

curter *comparative of* CURT

curtest *superlative of* CURT

cur·te·sy \ˈkərd·əsē\ *or* **curtesy initiate** *n, pl* **curtesies** *or* **curtesies initiate** [ME *curtasy, curteisie, corteisie* curtesy, courteous behavior — more at COURTESY] **:** the future potential interest that a husband has in all real estate in which his wife has an estate of inheritance arising upon the birth to them of a child alive and capable for an instant of inheriting from her the interest at common law and that is as often defined by statute, a life estate for his life or sometimes a one-third interest in fee which becomes consummate upon his surviving his wife and thereby having the right of enjoyment

cur·ti·lage \ˈkərd·ᵊlij\ *n* -S [ME, fr. OF *cortillage*, fr. *cortil* court, courtyard (fr. *cort* court, yard) + *-age* — more at COURT] **:** a yard, courtyard, or other piece of ground included within a fence surrounding a dwelling house

cur·tis·ite \ˈkərd·ə,sīt\ *n* -S [P. L. *Curtis*, 20th cent. American who discovered it + E *-ite*] **:** a mineral consisting of a hydrocarbon compound $C_{24}H_{18}$ found at Skaggs Springs, California

cur·tis stage \ˈkərd·əs-\ *n, usu cap C* [after Charles Gordon *Curtis* †1953 Amer. inventor] **:** a stage in the high-pressure section of a turbine consisting of two rows of impulse blades with intermediate reversing buckets

cur·ti·us rearrangement \ˈkürtsēəs-\ *n, usu cap C* [after Theodor *Curtius* †1928 Ger. chemist] **:** the conversion by heat of an acid azide $RCON_3$ into nitrogen and an isocyanate RNCO

curt·ly *adv* **:** in a curt manner

curt·ness *n* -ES **:** the quality of being curt **:** shortness of speech or manner ⟨offended by the ~ of the refusal⟩

¹**curt·sy** *or* **curt·sey** \ˈkərtsē, -ət-, -əit-, -si\ *n, pl* **curtsies** *or* **curtseys** [alter. of *courtesy*] **:** an act of civility, respect, or reverence made mainly by women and consisting of a slight dropping of the body with bending of the knees ⟨*curtsies* from all the . . . ladies of the train —Sir Walter Scott⟩ **:** a gesture of courteous recognition

²**curtsy** *or* **curtsey** \"\ *vb* **curtsied** *or* **curtseyed; curtsied** *or* **curtseyed; curtsying** *or* **curtseying; curtsies** *or* **curtseys** *vi* **:** to make a curtsy — often used with *to* ⟨~*ing* to the queen⟩ ~ *vt* **1** *obs* **:** to make a curtsy to **2** *archaic* **:** to express by curtsying

cu·ru·ba \kəˈrübə\ *n* -S [Pg, fr. Tupi] **1 :** SWEET CALABASH **2 :** CASSABANANA

cu·ru·cu·cu \ˌsürəkəˌkü, ˌkür-, -rəküˌkü\ *n* -S [modif. of Pg *çurucucú, surucucú*, fr. Tupi *surucucú*] **:** BUSHMASTER

cu·rule \ˈkyü,rül, -ür,yül, ˈkyü,rül\ *adj* [L *curulis, currulis* of a chariot (as in *sella curulis* curule chair), fr. *currus* chariot, fr. *currere* to run — more at CURRENT] **1 :** of or relating to a style of seat reserved in ancient Rome for the use of the highest dignitaries and usu. made like a campstool with curved legs **:** having or consisting of tangent semicircular segments forming legs, backs, or other structural members ⟨a ~ chair⟩ **:** having or consisting of one such segment ⟨a ~ leg⟩ **2 :** privileged to sit in a curule chair because of high rank or dignity ⟨a ~ magistrate⟩

curule seat

cu·ru·pay \ˌkürəˈpī\ *n* -S [AmerSp, fr. Guarani] **1 :** ANGICO **2 :** the hard heavy reddish brown wood of the angico

cu·ru·ro \kəˈrü(,)rō\ *n* -S [Sp, modif. of Araucan *curi*] **:** a small burrowing hystricomorph rodent (*Spalacopus poeppigi*) of Chile

cur·va·ceous *also* **cur·va·cious** \ˌkərˈvāshəs, ˌkə̄-, ˌkəi-\ *adj* [³*curve* + *-aceous, -acious*] **:** having a well-proportioned feminine figure marked by pronounced curves **:** marked by sex appeal — **cur·va·ceous·ness** *n*

cur·va·tion \ˌkərˈvāshən\ *n* -S [L *curvation-, curvatio*, fr. *curvatus* (past part. of *curvare* to bend, curve, fr. *curvus* curved) + *-ion-, -io* -ion — more at CROWN] **:** CURVATURE

cur·va·ture \ˈkərvə,chü(ə)r, -əv-, -əiv-, -üə *sometimes* -və-, ,tyü-\ *n* -S [L *curvatura*, fr. *curvatus* + *-ura* -ure] **1 a :** CURVE **:** curved part **b :** the act of curving or the state of being curved **2** *of a plane curve* **:** the rate of change per unit of arc length of the angle through which the tangent turns in rolling round from point to point of the curve **3 a :** an abnormal curving ⟨~ of the spine⟩ — see KYPHOSIS, SCOLIOSIS **b :** a curved surface of an organ ⟨the lesser ~ of the stomach⟩

curvature of field : a defect in an optical system that results in points on an object plane perpendicular to the axis being imaged on a curved surface rather than on a plane

¹**curve** \ˈkərv, -əv, -əiv\ *adj* [L *curvus* bent, curved — more at CROWN] *archaic* **:** CURVED

²**curve** \"\ *vb* -ED/-ING/-S [L *curvare*, fr. *curvus*] *vi* **:** to have or take a turn, change, or deviation from a straight line or course or from a level surface typically with a rounded gradual effect and without sharp breaks or angularity ⟨the road ~s around the town⟩ ~ *vt* **1 :** to cause to curve **:** form into a curving surface **:** BEND ⟨*curving* the line gracefully⟩ ⟨*curving* the strips slightly⟩ **2 a :** to throw or propel (as a ball) so that a course follows curves or appears to curve ⟨*curving* the next pitch⟩ **b :** to throw a curve ball to (a batter)

syn BEND, TWIST: CURVE describes any deviation or swerving from the straight or level that suggests an arc of a circle or an ellipse ⟨his lips were *curved* in a smile —Kenneth Roberts⟩ ⟨over the roof a few swallows were *curving* —Ellen Glasgow⟩ BEND is likely to refer to an angular turning or curving at a certain point under a degree of force or pressure ⟨*bend* the steel strips as required⟩ ⟨*bend* the glass tube at the point indicated⟩ Figuratively BEND may imply some forcing or distortion of materials or of facts, or some pressure on or persuasion of people ⟨was somewhat prone to *bend* logic to meet the demands of argument —E.S.Bates⟩ ⟨not all prescriptive speech aims purely and typically at *bending* the hearer's attitudes to those of the speaker —W.D.Falk⟩ TWIST is likely to suggest a force having a spiraling effect throughout the object involved rather than an effect at one point ⟨the light steel rods *twisted* together by the explosion⟩ Figuratively TWIST suggests a more extreme distortion than BEND ⟨an unconquerable confidence . . . which understates or *twists* into a wry joke the fatal moment of war —*Times Lit. Supp.*⟩

³**curve** \"\ *n* -S [¹*curve*] **1 :** a line or surface that curves **:** a bending without angles **:** BEND, FLEXURE ⟨a train going around a ~⟩ ⟨the stream describing many ~s through the valley⟩ **2 :** something curved: as **a :** a curving line of the human body; *esp* **:** a curving line characteristic of an attractive feminine figure — usu. used in pl. **b :** FRENCH CURVE **c curves** *pl* **:** PARENTHESES **3 a** *or* **curve ball :** a baseball pitch in which the ball swerves or appears to swerve from its normal or expected course of flight because of a spin put on it in delivery — compare INSHOOT, OUTSHOOT **b :** a ball bowled by a right-handed bowler that starts to the right and then veers to the left — compare HOOK **c :** TRICK, DECEPTION **:** the act of deluding or breaking a promise **4 :** GRAPH: as **a :** a usu. curved line representing graphically a variable element as affected by one or more conditions ⟨the price ~ mounts to a peak in summer⟩ **b :** an indication of development or progress **:** COURSE, RATE, TREND **5 a :** a line that may be precisely defined by an equation in such a way that the coordinates of its points are functions of a single independent variable or parameter **b** (1) **:** the intersection of two geometrical surfaces (2) **:** the path of a moving point **6 :** a teacher's arrangement of grades purporting to represent the distribution of excellent, medium, and poor performances that may be expected in a certain assignment or over a certain period ⟨a teacher marking on a ~ will give more C's than A's or D's⟩ **7 :** CHARACTERISTIC CURVE a

curve-billed thrasher \ˈ=,=-\ *n* **:** a light brownish gray thrasher (*Toxostoma curvirostre curvirostre*) of southwestern No. America having white wing bars and black tail tipped with white

curved bar *n, usu cap C&B* **:** the highest rank in the Girl Scout intermediate program symbolized by a red, green, and gold pin bearing the Girl Scout trefoil and motto and surmounting a curved bar

curved knife-tooth harrow *n* **:** ACME HARROW

curved·ly \-vədlē, -vd-\ *adv* **:** in a curved manner

curved·ness \-vədnəs, -v(d)n-\ *n* -ES **:** the quality or state of being curved

curve-drawing meter \ˈ=,==-\ *n* **:** RECORDING METER

curved runner *n* **:** a furrow opener for a corn or cotton planter adapted to soil free from trash

curve fitting *n* **:** the determination of a curve of assigned character (as an exponential curve) that approaches most closely or fits best a number of points in a plane

curve of areas : a curve that is composed in its forward half of a curve of versed sines and in its after half of a trochoid and is used in distributing the displacement in the design of a ship

curve of pursuit : a curve described by a point moving always directly toward or from a second point that is itself moving according to a given law

curves *pres 3d sing of* CURVE, *pl of* CURVE

curve·some \ˈkərvsəm\ *adj* **:** CURVACEOUS

¹**cur·vet** \ˌkərˈvet, ˌkərˈvet *also* ˈkərvə|t; *usu* |d·+V\ *n* -S [modif. of It *corvetta*, fr. OIt, fr. MF *courbette*, fr. *courber* to bend, curve (fr. L *curvare*) + *-ette* — more at CURVE] **:** a leap of a horse in which he raises both forelegs at once equally advanced and as they are falling raises his hind legs so that for an instant all four legs are in the air at the same time

²**curvet** \"\ *vi* **curvetted** *or* **curveted; curvetted** *or* **curveted; curvetting** *or* **curveting; curvets** [It *corvettare*, fr. *corvetta*] **1 :** to make a curvet **:** LEAP, BOUND **2 :** PRANCE, CAPER, GYRATE

curvi- *comb form* [MF or LL; MF, fr. LL, fr. L *curvus*] **:** curved; bent ⟨*curviform*⟩ ⟨*curvifoliate*⟩ ⟨*curvirostral*⟩

cur·vi·linear *or* **cur·vi·lineal** \ˌkərvə+\ *adj* [*curvi-* + *linear* or *lineal*] **1 :** consisting of or bounded by curved lines ⟨a ~ angle⟩ **:** following a curve ⟨~ motion⟩ **:** represented by a curved line **2 :** marked by flowing tracery and showing relationships to French flamboyant styles ⟨~ Gothic⟩ **3 :** CURVACEOUS — **curvilinearity** \"+\ *n* -ES — **curvilinearly** \"+\ *adv*

curvilinear coordinates *n pl* **:** a system of geometrical coordinates in which if only one of the coordinates is allowed to vary the locus may be a plane or twisted curve
curvilinear motion *n* **:** motion in which the direction of the velocity of a body is variable and the path of the body is a curved line
curving *pres part of* CURVE
cur·vi·ty \'kərvəd·ē\ *n* -ES [MF or LL; MF *curvité*, fr. LL *curvitat-, curvitas*, fr. L *curvus* curved + *-itat-, -itas* -ity — more at CROWN] *archaic* **:** CURVATURE, CURVE
cur·vom·e·ter \,kər'vämәd·ər\ *n* -S [*curve* + *-o-* + *-meter*] **:** an instrument for measuring the length of a curve, the simplest form consisting essentially of a wheel that is rolled tangentially along the curve and a recording dial
curvy *also* **curv·ey** \'kərvē\ *adj* -ER/-EST **:** CURVED; *esp* **:** CURVACEOUS
cur·wil·let \,kər'wilət\ *n* -S [imit.] *dial Eng* **:** SANDERLING
cus·co bark *or* **cuz·co bark** \'kü(,)skō-\ *n* [fr. *Cuzco*, Peru] **:** cinchona bark from a common cinchona (*C. pubescens*)
cus·co·hygrine *or* **cus·ko·hygrine** \;kü(,)skō+\ *n* -S [G *cuskohygrin*, fr. *cusko* cusco bark + *hygrin* hygrine] **:** an oily base $C_{13}H_{24}N_2O$ occurring with hygrine in the leaves of the cusco-bark tree and in coca leaves
cus·co·nine \'küskə,nēn, -,nən\ *n* -S [ISV *cusco* (*bark*) + connective *-n-* + *-ine*, *-in*; prob. orig. formed as G *cuskonin*] **:** a crystalline alkaloid $C_{23}H_{26}N_2O_4$ found in cusco bark
cuscousou *or* **cuscusu** *var of* COUSCOUS
¹**cus·cus** \'kəskəs\ *n* -ES [NL, fr. a native name in New Guinea] **:** any of several bright-colored woolly-haired arboreal marsupials (genus *Phalanger*) that superficially resemble monkeys and are common in New Guinea and tropical northern Australia
²**cuscus** *var of* KHUSKHUS
³**cuscus** *var of* COUSCOUS
cus·cu·ta \(,)kə'sk(y)üd·ə\ *n, cap* [NL, fr. ML, dodder, fr. Ar *kushūth, kashūta, kashūtha*] **:** a large and widely distributed genus of twining leafless parasitic herbs (family Convolvulaceae) comprising the dodders and having whitish or yellow filamentous stems
cu·sec \'kyü,sek\ *n* -S [*cubic foot per second*] **:** a volumetric unit of flow equal to a cubic foot per second
¹**cush** \'kush, 'küsh\ *n* -ES [of African origin; akin to Hausa *ku³sha¹* thin cake made of peanuts, Efik *kus³kus¹* couscous, both fr. Ar *kuskus* couscous] *South* **:** a dish of seasoned corn meal dough fried, baked with meat, or boiled in pot liquor
²**cush** \'kush\ *also* **cusha** \-shə\ *n, pl* **cushes** *also* **cushas** [prob. fr. E dial., a call to cows; akin to ON *kussi* calf, G dial. *küse*] *dial Eng* **:** COW
³**cush** \'kush\ *n* -ES [origin unknown] *slang* **:** MONEY
⁴**cush** \'kush\ *n* -ES [Hindi *kuś*, love grass (*Eragrostis cynosuroides*), fr. Skt *kuśa* grass, sacred grass; perh. akin to ORuss *kustŭ* bush, Lith *kuokštas*] *India* **:** SORGHUM
cush·ag \'kü,shag, -,shəg\ *n* -S [modif. of Manx *cuishag vooar*, lit., big stalk] *Isle of Man* **:** TANSY RAGWORT
cush·at \'kəshət, 'kush-,'küsh-\ *also* **cush·ie** \-shē\ *n* -S [ME *cowscott, cowschote*, fr. OE *cūscote, cūcsceote*] *chiefly Scot* **:** RINGDOVE 1
cushat lily *n* **:** INDIAN CUCUMBER
cu·shaw \kə'shó, kü'-, 'kü,shó, 'ku,shó\ *also* **ca·shaw** \kə-'shó\ *n* -S [perh. of Algonquian origin; akin to *escushaw* it is green (in some Algonquian language of Virginia)] **:** WINTER CROOKNECK; *esp* **:** one (as a butternut squash) having the body of the fruit much enlarged
cush-cush \'kush,kush\ *n* -ES [origin unknown] **:** a tropical American yam (*Dioscorea trifida*) with small yellow-skinned edible tubers
cushier *comparative of* CUSHY
cushiest *superlative of* CUSHY
cush·i·ly \'kushəlē, -li\ *adv* **:** in a cushy manner
cush·ing's disease \'kushiŋz-\ *n, usu cap C* [after Harvey *Cushing* †1939 Amer. surgeon] **:** Cushing's syndrome esp. when caused by excessive production of ACTH by the pituitary gland
cushing's syndrome *n, usu cap C* **:** an abnormal bodily condition characterized by obesity and muscular weakness associated with the excessive production of hydrocortisone due to adrenal or pituitary dysfunction
¹**cush·ion** \'kushən *sometimes* -shin\ *n* -S *often attrib* [ME *cuisshin, cusshin*, fr. MF *coissin, cussin, coussin*, fr. (assumed) VL *coxinus*, fr. L *coxa* hip + *-inus* -ine — more at COXA] **1 a :** a bag or case made typically of cloth, upholstery, or matting that is stuffed with a soft or resilient material and used for sitting, reclining, or kneeling **:** PILLOW, PAD **b :** the cushion on the seat of a ruler or judge often regarded as a symbol of his office **c :** the cushion on which a Bible or other book rests on a lectern **d :** a cushion regarded as a symbol of ease and luxury **2 :** a part resembling a pad: as **a :** the fleshy part of the rump of the horse or pig **b** (1) **:** the frog of a horse's hoof (2) **:** the pad just above the hoof **c :** the fleshy forefate or top lips of certain animals (as the bulldog) **d :** PULVILLUS **e :** the ball of the thumb **f :** the soft feathers about the base of the tail of a hen esp. when present in excess **g :** STRAWBERRY COMB **h :** a boned shoulder of pork or lamb with a pocket for stuffing **3 :** something resembling a cushion in properties or use: as **a :** PILLOW 3 **b :** PINCUSHION **c :** RAT 3 **d :** BUSTLE **e :** the pad of springy rubber affixed along the upper part of the inside of the rim of a billiard table or pool table — called also *bank* **f :** the head of a drill brace **g :** a padded insole **:** a padded insert in a shoe at the ball or heel **h :** a strip of soft resilient rubber between the breaker and carcass of a pneumatic tire to secure the adhesion of carcass to tread and assist in protecting the former **i** (1) **:** an architectural part (as a frieze) that projects convexly — compare CUSHION CAPITAL (2) **:** the top stone of a pier supporting an arch **j :** an artificial pool provided to absorb the kinetic energy of falling water and so prevent erosion **k :** an elastic body (as of air or steam) for reducing shock; *esp* **:** the steam allowed to remain in an engine cylinder after exhaust in order to avoid shock by reducing the momentum of the reciprocating parts **l :** a layer of fine material (as sand, granulated slag, bituminous mastic, or stone screenings) placed on top of a foundation for a block pavement **m** *or* **cush·ion·ing** \-sh(ə)niŋ, -shin-\ **:** a structure or material used to separate and protect goods in transit from shock and damage **n :** a felt mat laid under a large rug to ease the effect of wear **o :** a pad on which gold leaf is placed to be cut **4** *obs* **:** a swelling like that of pregnancy **5 a :** something serving to mitigate the effects of economic disturbances ⟨public works to provide jobs as a ~ against unemployment⟩ **:** a factor that lessens adverse developments in the economy and limits price declines in markets; *esp* **:** a monetary reserve for use in special circumstances ⟨a thickened ~ of liquid assets for protection —*N.Y. Herald Tribune*⟩ **b :** MARGIN **:** reserve supply ⟨a ~ of resources⟩ **6 :** a medical method, procedure, or drug that eases a patient's discomfort without necessarily affecting his basic condition **7 :** program material that can be lengthened, shortened, or omitted entirely to make a radio or television program end exactly on time
²**cushion** \"\ *vt* **cushioned; cushioned; cushioning** \-sh(ə)niŋ, -shin-\ **cushions 1 :** to seat (a person) on a cushion **:** prop up or make comfortable with cushions ⟨nurses ~*ing* his injured shoulder⟩ **2 a :** to suppress by ignoring ⟨~*ing* the scandalous occurrence⟩ **b :** to mitigate the effects of **:** PALLIATE **:** protect by absorbing or checking harmful force or shock **:** keep from harm or shock as if with a cushion ⟨~*ing* the blow⟩ ⟨~*ing* the public from disappointment⟩ **3 :** to provide or equip with a cushion or cushions **:** PAD ⟨~ the wooden seats⟩ **:** protect from jarring effects with or as if with a cushion ⟨soft tires that ~ the ride⟩ **4 :** to check gradually so as to minimize shock due to the inertia of moving parts ⟨~ a piston by leaving some steam in the cylinder after exhaust⟩
cushion aloe *n* **:** a plant of the genus *Haworthia*
cushion capital *n* **1 :** an architectural capital so sculptured as to look like a cushion pressed down by the weight of its entablature **2 :** a capital esp. in the Romanesque style modeled like a bowl whose upper part is cut away on four sides
cushion carom *also* **cushion shot** *n* **1 :** a billiard carom in which the cue ball goes to a cushion before touching the second object ball **2 cushion caroms** *pl but sing in constr* **:** any of the billiard games in which one or more cushions must be touched before completion of a carom
cushion comb *n* **:** STRAWBERRY COMB
cushion cut *n* **:** STEP CUT
cushion dance *n* **:** an old English round dance in which a dancer and the partner of his choice knelt and kissed on a cushion that he placed before her
cushionflower \'==,=\ *n* **:** an Australian shrub (*Hakea laurina*) with large globose crimson-yellow flowers
cushion head *n* **:** a lined paper pad used for protecting the facing layer of apples in a barrel
cush·ion·less \-ləs\ *adj* **:** being without a cushion
cushion pink *n* **:** MOSS CAMPION
cushion plant *n* **:** any plant that grows in a dense cushiony tuft (as many xerophilous and alpine plants) thereby preventing excessive transpiration
cushions *pl of* CUSHION, *pres 3d sing of* CUSHION
cushion sole *n* **:** a special shoe insole having a padded surface facing the foot
cushion star *n* **:** any of numerous thickened more or less globose pentamerous starfishes belonging to *Goniaster* and related genera
cush·iony \'kushənē, -shinē, -ni\ *adj* **:** like a cushion **:** SOFT, CUSHY **:** serving as a cushion **:** equipped with cushions
¹**cush·ite** \'kə,shīt\ *n* -S *cap* [*Cush* (Kush), ancient country in the Nile valley adjoining Egypt + E *-ite*] **:** a native or inhabitant of ancient Cush
²**cushite** \"\ *adj, usu cap* **:** of or relating to ancient Cush
¹**cush·it·ic** \,kə'shid·ik\ *n* -S *cap* [¹*Cushite* + *-ic*] **:** a subfamily of the Afro-Asiatic language family comprising a number of languages spoken in East Africa and esp. in Ethiopia and Somaliland — see AFRO-ASIATIC LANGUAGES table
²**cushitic** \;=;==\ *adj, usu cap* **1 :** of, relating to, or characteristic of the Cushites **2 :** of, relating to, or characteristic of the Cushitic languages
cush·la·mo·chree *or* **cush·la·ma·chree** \,kushləmə'krē, -'krē\ *n* -S [IrGael *cuisle mo chroidhe*, lit., vein of my heart] *chiefly Irish* **:** DARLING
cushy \'kushē, -shi\ *adj* -ER/-EST [modif. of Hindi *khush* pleasant, fr. Per *khūsh*] **:** SOFT, PLEASANT, COZY, COMFORTABLE **:** entailing little hardship or difficulty ⟨a ~ job with a high salary in the home office⟩
cusk \'kəsk\ *n, pl* **cusk** *or* **cusks** [prob. alter. of *tusk*] **1 :** a

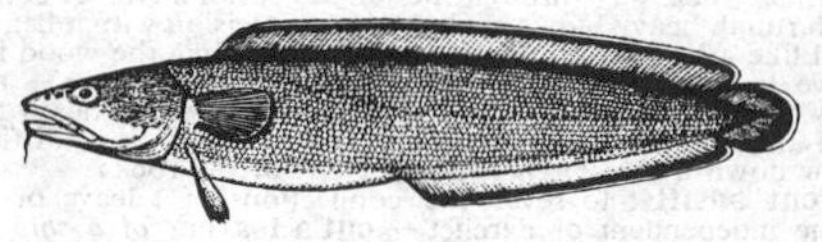

cusk

large edible marine fish (*Brosme brosme*) related to the cod — called also *tusk* **2 :** the New World burbot
cusk eel *n* **:** a fish of the family Ophidiidae
cuskohygrine *var of* CUSCOHYGRINE
cusp \'kəsp\ *n* -S [L *cuspis* point] **1 :** the beginning or first entrance of any house in astrological nativity calculations **2 :** POINT, APEX ⟨the ~ of a cone⟩ ⟨the ~ of a peak⟩: as **a :** either horn of the crescent moon or other crescent-shaped luminary **b :** a fixed point on a mathematical curve at which a point tracing the curve would exactly reverse its direction of motion, the tangents to the two parts of a cusp coinciding at the cusp **c :** an ornamental pointed projection (as from the intrados of a Gothic arch) formed by or arising from the intersection of two arcs or foils **d** (1) **:** a point or projection on the occlusal surface of a tooth (2) **:** one of various folds or flaps forming a cardiac valve **e** *bot* **:** a sharp and rigid point **3 :** a landform characterized by a projection with indentations of crescent shape on either side (as along a shoreline or in a mountain front) **4 :** a skate mark left on the ice in executing a half-turn from edge to edge — **cusped** \'kəspt\ *adj*

cusp 2c: *1* cusp

cus·par·ia bark \,kə'spa(a)rēə-\ *n* [AmerSp *cusparia, cuspare*, of Cariban origin; akin to Galibi *cuspare*, the tree from which it is obtained] **:** ANGOSTURA BARK
cus·pa·rine \'kəspə,rēn, -,rən\ *n* -S [F, fr. NL *Cusparia* genus of So. Amer. trees (fr. AmerSp) + *-ine*] **:** a crystalline alkaloid $C_{19}H_{17}NO_3$ found in angostura bark
cus·pate \'kə,spā|t, -,spə|t, *usu* |d·+V\ *also* **cus·pat·ed** \-,spād·əd\ *adj* [*cusp* + *-ate*] **:** having a cusp; *also* **:** shaped like a cusp ⟨a ~ shoreline⟩
cus·pid \'kəspəd\ *n* -S [back-formation fr. *bicuspid*] **:** CANINE TOOTH
cus·pi·dal \'kəspəd^əl\ *adj* [L *cuspid-, cuspis* point + E *-al*] **:** constituting or resembling a cusp **:** having or relating to a cusp
cuspidal cubic *n* **:** a plane cubic of the third class with one cusp, one point of inflexion, and no node
cuspidal curve *n* **:** a mathematical curve marking a sharp ridge on a surface corresponding to a cusp on a plane curve
cuspidal locus *n, math* **:** the locus of the cusps of a family of curves
cuspidal point *n, math* **1 :** CUSP 2b **2 :** a point on a ruled surface where a generator or ruling intersects a consecutive ruling
cus·pi·date \-,dāt, *usu* -ād·+V\ *or* **cus·pi·dat·ed** \-,dād·əd\ *adj* [*cuspidate* fr. L *cuspidatus*, past part. of *cuspidare* to make pointed, fr. *cuspid-, cuspis* point; *cuspidated* fr. L *cuspidatus* + E *-ed*] **:** having a cusp **:** terminating in a point ⟨a ~ leaf⟩ — see LEAF illustration
cus·pi·da·tion \,kəspə'dāshən\ *n* -S **:** decoration with cusps ⟨the ~ of an arch⟩
cus·pi·dine \'kəspə,dēn, -dīn\ *n* -S [It *cuspidina*, fr. L *cuspid-, cuspis* point + It *-ina* -ine] **:** a mineral $Ca_4Si_2O_7(F,OH)_2$ consisting of a basic silicate of calcium
cus·pi·dor *also* **cus·pa·dore** \'kəspə,dō(ə)r, -ó(ə)r,-ōə,-ó(ə)\ *n* -S [Pg *cuspidouro* place for spitting, fr. *cuspir* to spit, fr. L *conspuere* — more at CONSPUE] **:** SPITTOON
cusp·ing \'kəspiŋ\ *n* -S [*cusp* + *-ing*] **:** cuspate ornamentation
cus·pule \'kə,spyül\ *n* -S [*cusp* + *-ule*] **:** a small tubercle on the occlusal surface of a tooth
¹**cuss** \'kəs\ *n* -ES [alter. of ¹*curse*] **1 :** CURSE, OATH, SWEARWORD ⟨has yet to . . . utter his first ~ —*Atlantic*⟩ **2 :** FELLOW ⟨poor little ~⟩ ⟨an independent ~, but he's awful good —Bill Mauldin⟩ ⟨a crotchety, antic, and lovable old ~ —*New Yorker*⟩
²**cuss** \"\ *vb* -ED/-ING/-ES [by alter.] *vt* **:** CURSE — often used with *out* ⟨~*ing* out the driver ahead⟩ ~ *vi* **:** CURSE ⟨in the habit of ~*ing*⟩
cuss·ed \'kəsəd\ *adj* [fr. past part. of ²*cuss*] **1 :** CURSED **2 :** PERVERSE, OBSTINATE, CANTANKEROUS — **cuss·ed·ly** *adv*
cuss·ed·ness *n* -ES **:** disposition to willful perversity **:** CANTANKEROUSNESS, OBSTINACY
cus·ser \'küsər, 'kəs-\ *Scot var of* ¹COURSER
cus·so \'kü\|(,)sō, 'kü\|,'kə\|\ *n* -S [Amharic *kussu*] **:** BRAYERA
cussword \'=,=\ *n* **1 :** CUSS 1 **2 :** a term of abuse **:** a derogatory term ⟨in its lexicon, "academic" and "bookish" are sort of ~s —W.L.Miller⟩
cus·tard \'kəstə(r)d\ *n* -S *often attrib* [ME *custarde, crustade*, a kind of pie, prob. modif. of OProv *croustado*, fr. *crosta* crust (fr. L *crusta*) + *-ado* -ate — more at CRUST] **1 :** a sweetened mixture of milk and eggs that is baked, boiled, or frozen **2 :** a dish prepared with a custard base ⟨corn ~⟩
custard apple *n* **1 a :** any of various fruits of trees of the genus *Annona*; *esp* **:** BULLOCK'S-HEART **b :** a tree of this genus (as a bullock's-heart or sweetsop) **2 :** PAPAW 2
custard-apple family *n* **:** ANNONACEAE
custard cheeses *n pl* **:** CHEESE 4
custard cup *n* **:** a heat-resistant cup of porcelain or glass in which an individual custard is baked
custard-pie \';=;=\ *adj* [so called fr. the frequent pie-throwing battles waged in early motion-picture comedies] **:** SLAPSTICK **:** relating to or marked by broadest comedy ⟨~ antics⟩
cus·te·nau \kü'stā,naù\ *n, pl* **custenau** *or* **custenaus** *usu cap* [Sp, of AmerInd origin] **1 a :** an Arawakan people of the Xingú river valley, Brazil **b :** a member of such people **2 :** the language of the Custenau people
cus·ter·ite \'kəstə,rīt\ *n* -S [*Custer* co., Idaho + E *-ite*] **:** CUSPIDINE
cus·tock \'kəstək\ *var of* CASTOCK
cu·sto·de \kü'stōdē, -,dā\ *n, pl* **custodes** \-ēz,-āz\ *or* **custo·di** \-(,)dē\ [It, fr. L *custod-, custos* — more at CUSTODY] **:** CUSTODIAN
cus·to·dee \,kəstə'dē\ *n* -S **:** one to whom custody is given
custodes *pl of* CUSTOS
cus·to·dia \(,)kə'stōdēə\ *n, pl* **custodi·ae** \-dē,ē, -dē,ī\ [ML, fr. L, guarding, keeping — more at CUSTODY] **:** CUSTODIAL
¹**cus·to·di·al** \;kə;stōdēəl, ,kə's-\ *adj* [L *custodia* + E *-al*] **:** relating to or marked by guardianship or maintaining safely; *specif* **:** marked by or given to watching and protecting rather than seeking to cure ⟨~ care rather than a therapeutic program⟩
²**custodial** \"\ *n* -S [ML *custodia* + E *-al*] **:** a receptacle for sacred objects (as the Host)
cus·to·di·am \(,)kə'stōdēəm, -ē,am\ *n* -S [L, acc. of *custodia*] **:** a grant of land in possession of the English crown to a person who acts as custodee or lessee
cus·to·di·an \(,)kə'stōdēən\ *n* -S [*custody* + *-an*] **1 a :** one that guards and protects or maintains **:** one entrusted officially with guarding and keeping (as property, artifacts, or records) or with custody or guardianship (as of a prisoner, inmate, or ward) ⟨the ~ of the manor and the park⟩ ⟨the ~ in charge of a prison camp⟩ **b :** a monitor preserving a cherished intangible often with or as if with a vested proprietary right ⟨I trust we acquit ourselves worthily as ~s of this sacred mystery —Elinor Wylie⟩ ⟨~s of very glorious traditions and the trustees of a spiritual wealth —W.R.Inge⟩ **2 a :** BUILDING SUPERINTENDENT **b :** one who takes charge of the recording, safekeeping, and release of all valuables that come into the hands of the police department **3 :** an agency that takes care of securities including collection of income but without authority to buy and sell
cus·to·di·an·ship \-,ship\ *n* **:** the office or duty of a custodian ⟨the sense of ~ of a faith received —R.M.French⟩
cus·to·di·er \-dēər\ *n* -S [ME, fr. L *custodia* custody + ME *-er*] *now chiefly Scot* **:** CUSTODIAN
cus·to·dy \'kəstədē, -di\ *n* -ES [ME *custodie*, fr. L *custodia* guarding, keeping fr. *custod-, custos* guardian, keeper + *-ia*; perh. akin to Gk *keuthein* to hide — more at HIDE] **1 a :** the act or duty of guarding and preserving (as by a duly authorized person or agency) **:** SAFEKEEPING ⟨the Serials Division has ~ of newspapers, unbound periodicals, and government and other serials —L.H.Evans⟩ **b :** protection, care, maintenance, and tuition **:** GUARDIANSHIP ⟨orphans in the ~ of their uncle⟩ **2 :** judicial or penal safekeeping **:** control of a thing or person with such actual or constructive possession as fulfills the purpose of the law or duty requiring it **:** imprisonment or durance of persons or charge of things ⟨a man held in police ~⟩ ⟨a suspect in protective ~⟩ **3 :** a territorial division of the Franciscan order smaller than a province
¹**cus·tom** \'kəstəm\ *n* -S [ME *custume, custom, costome*, fr. OF *custume, costume*, fr. L *consuetudin-, consuetudo*, fr. *consuetus*, past part. of *consuescere* to accustom, fr. *com-* + *suescere* to become accustomed, accustom; akin to L *suus* one's own — more at SUICIDE] **1 a :** a form or course of action characteristically repeated under like circumstances **:** a usage or practice that is common to many or to a particular place or class or is habitual with an individual ⟨one of the many gracious ~s of the late Queen —G.W.Talbot⟩ **b** (1) **:** long-established, continued, peaceable, reasonable, certain, and constant practice considered as unwritten law and resting for authority on long consent **:** a usage that has by long continuance acquired a legally binding force (2) **:** the usage of a country or particular locality having the force of law in that country or locality ⟨the ~ of London⟩ **c :** repeated practice ⟨~ makes all things easy —Jean Ingelow⟩ **d :** the whole body of usages, practices, or conventions that regulate social life **:** usual manner and method of living and doing **:** social habit ⟨the icy chains of ~ —P.B.Shelley⟩ — compare FOLKWAY **2** *obs* **:** a due or rent in money, in kind, or in services that a feudal tenant was bound to render to his lord **:** the obligation to render or right to receive such due or rent **3 customs** *pl* **a :** duties, tolls, or imposts imposed by the sovereign law of a country on commodities imported into or exported from the country — compare RATE **b** *usu sing in constr* **:** the agency, establishment, or procedure for collecting such customs **4 a :** business patronage **:** personal and often habitual patronage of an establishment **:** habit of purchasing or buying services **:** amount of business ⟨the town shopkeepers sought his ~ —Adrian Bell⟩ ⟨paying personal calls on likely firms to try to obtain their ~ —F.W.Crofts⟩ **b :** CUSTOMERS ⟨the ~ liked the new line⟩ **5 :** CELEBRATION; *esp* **:** a celebration formerly held by the Dahomeans and Ashanti and attended with much human sacrifice **6 :** a custom-built automobile
syn see HABIT
²**custom** \"\ *vt* -ED/-ING/-S [ME *customen*, fr. MF *costumer*, fr. *costume* custom] **1** *archaic* **:** ACCUSTOM **2** *obs* **:** to deal with as a customer
³**custom** \"\ *adj* [¹*custom*] **1 a :** made or performed according to personal order usu. to individual specifications ⟨preferred ~ suits and luxurious cars⟩ ⟨a ~ set of silver⟩ **b :** performed or effected by an owner of machinery or facilities according to special personal order ⟨the ~ work I did for the neighbors with the tractor plowing and with the cornpicker picking corn —John Dos Passos⟩ ⟨doing ~ smelting for small companies⟩ ⟨began the ~ manufacture of agricultural chemicals⟩ **2 :** specializing in custom work or operation ⟨a ~ tailor⟩ ⟨a ~ cabinetmaker⟩ ⟨a ~ sawmill⟩
cus·tom·able \-məbəl\ *adj* [ME, fr. MF *costumable*, fr. *costumer* to accustom + *-able*] *archaic* **:** subject to the payment of customs **:** DUTIABLE
customal *var of* CUSTUMAL
cus·tom·ar·i·ly \;kəstə;merəlē, -li\ *adv* **:** by custom **:** in a customary manner
cus·tom·ar·i·ness \-rēnəs, -rin-\ *n* -ES **:** the quality or state of being customary
¹**cus·tom·ary** \'kəstə,merē, -ri\ *adj* [ML *customarius*, fr. OF *costumier*, fr. LL *consuetudinarius*, fr. L *consuetudin-, consuetudo* habit + *-arius* -ary — more at CUSTOM] **1** *law* **a :** liable or subject to, or holding by payment of, customs or dues ⟨~ tenure⟩ ⟨~ lands⟩ **:** fixed by custom ⟨~ rent⟩ **b :** holding or held by or owing validity as law to custom ⟨~ tenants⟩ ⟨~ services⟩ **2 :** agreeing with custom **:** established by custom **:** commonly practiced, used, or observed **:** familiar through long use or acquaintance ⟨events that are familiar and ~ are those we are least likely to reflect upon —John Dewey⟩ ⟨incensed at a refusal of ~ marks of courtesy —W.R. Inge⟩ **3** *of a verb form or aspect* **:** expressing habitual action
syn see USUAL
²**customary** \"\ *n* -ES [ML *customarium*, fr. neut. of *customarius*, adj.] **1 :** a book or body of customary laws (as of a manor or district) **2 :** CONSUETUDINARY **3 :** the customary aspect of a verb **:** a customary form of a verb
customary court *n* **:** a court that was formerly a part of a court baron and that exercised jurisdiction over the transfer, surrender, admittance, incidents, and tenures of copyhold estates
custom-built \;=;=\ *adj* **:** built to individual specifications rather than as part of a mass-production plan **:** MADE-TO-ORDER, TAILOR-MADE
cus·tom·er \'kəstəmə(r)\ *n* -S [ME *custumer, costomer*, partly fr. MF *costumier, custumier* tax collector, fr. OF, fr. *costume, custume* custom + *-ier* -er; partly fr. ME *custume, custom, costome* custom + *-er* — more at CUSTOM] **1** *obs* **:** a customs collector **:** a customhouse official **2 a :** one that purchases some commodity or service ⟨she had never seen that ~ before⟩; *esp* **:** one that purchases systematically or frequently ⟨these countries are the largest ~s of U.S. products⟩ ⟨lost most of her ~s through neglect and rudeness⟩ **b :** one that patronizes or uses the services (as of a library, restaurant, or theater) **:** CLIENT **3** *obs* **:** PROSTITUTE **4 :** an individual usu. having some specified distinctive trait or traits that one has or may have some dealing, encounter, or relationship with ⟨what sort of a ~ is he?⟩ ⟨compact of bone and gristle and grim insensitiveness, dangerous ~s every one —Dorothy C. Fisher⟩ ⟨the mule deer buck is an ugly ~ —D.C.Peattie⟩ ⟨a smooth ~, could look after himself —Rex Ingamells⟩ **5 :** a fox that affords good sport in a hunt

customer agent *n* **:** a foreign purchaser who buys goods outright for resale to his trade

customer ownership *n* **:** the partial or complete ownership of a concern (as a public utility) by those who buy or use its output or merchandise

customer's broker *or* **customer's man** *n* **:** a broker's employee who takes buying and selling orders and seeks to induce trading by advising customers and maintaining friendly relations with them

customhouse *also* **customshouse** \ˈ⸗⸗,⸗\ *n* [ME *custom-hous,* fr. ¹*custom* + *hous* house] **:** a building where customs and duties are paid or collected and where vessels are entered and cleared

customhouse broker *n* **:** an agent who acts for merchants in entering and clearing goods and vessels

cus·tom·ize \ˈkəstə,mīz\ *vt* -ED/-ING/-S [³*custom* + *-ize*] **:** to build, fit, or alter according to individual specifications ⟨*customizing* an automobile⟩ ⟨*customized* hair styling⟩

custom–made \ˌkəstə(m)ˈmād\ *adj* **:** CUSTOM-BUILT, TAILOR-MADE, MADE-TO-ORDER

custom of kent \-ˈkent\ *usu cap K* [fr. *Kent* county, England] **:** GAVELKIND

custom of merchants : LAW MERCHANT

customs *pl of* CUSTOM, *pres 3d sing of* CUSTOM

customs bond *n* **:** a bond given by an importer for payment of damage resulting from failure to comply with the customs laws and regulations

customs union *n* **:** a union between two or more states that have abolished tariffs and other restrictions on their interstate trade and have adopted a common commercial policy toward other states

custom–tailor \ˌ⸗⸗ˈ⸗⸗\ *vt* **:** to treat, alter, plan, or build according to individual specifications or needs ⟨new tenants . . . find that they live in a model city, *custom-tailored* to their needs —*Dupont Mag.*⟩

cus·tos \ˈkə,stäs, -tōs; ˈkü,stōs, ˈkü,-\ *n, pl* **cus·to·des** \(,)kəˈstō(,)dēz; küˈstō,dās, kü-\ [ME, guardian, fr. L — more at CUSTODY] **1 :** KEEPER, CUSTODIAN, GUARD **2 :** DIRECT 1 **3** [ML, fr. L] **:** a superior of a Franciscan province or custody

custos ro·tu·lo·rum \-,rächə'lōrəm, - läd-ᵊlˈō-,-ˈōd-ᵊlˈō-\ *n, pl* **custodes rotulorum** [NL, keeper of the rolls] **:** the principal justice of the peace in an English county who is also keeper of the rolls and records of the sessions of the peace

custrel *n* -S [ME *custrell,* prob. modif. of MF *coustillier* soldier carrying a short sword, squire of a knight — more at COISTREL] *obs* **:** an armor-bearer to a knight

cus·tu·mal \ˈkəstəməl, -schəm-\ *or* **cus·tom·al** \-stəm-\ *n* -S [ML (*liber*) *custumalis,* fr. L *liber* book + ML *custumalis* of customs, fr. OF *costumal,* fr. *costume* custom + *-al* — more at CUSTOM] **:** a written collection of the customs of a monastery, a manor, or a locality

¹**cut** \ˈkət, *usu* -əd·+V\ *vb* **cut; cut; cutting; cuts** [ME *cutten, kitten;* perh. akin to Sw dial. *kata* to cut] *vt* **1 a :** to penetrate with or as if with an edged instrument **:** CLEAVE, PIERCE **:** make an incision in **:** GASH, SLASH ⟨~ one's hand with a knife⟩ **b** (1) **:** to operate on **:** castrate (as a domestic animal) (2) **:** to perform lithotomy upon **c :** to hurt the feelings of ⟨sarcasm ~s him to the quick⟩ **d :** to strike sharply with a cutting effect ⟨~ him across the legs with a whip⟩ **e :** to slice or enter into with an effect like that of an edged instrument ⟨icy blasts that ~ one to the marrow⟩ **f :** to score the surface of (a cylinder or bearing) by moving other parts over it usu. without sufficient lubrication **g :** to experience the growth of (a tooth) through the gum **2 :** to reduce by or as if by severing a part: as **a :** TRIM, PARE ⟨~ one's nails⟩ **b :** to shorten (as for reading or presentation) by omissions ⟨~ a manuscript⟩ **c :** to reduce the intensity of: (1) **:** to cause to be less thick, viscous, or tenacious **:** DISSOLVE, DILUTE ⟨alcohol ~s shellac⟩ (2) **:** to dilute or adulterate (liquor) by adding water or other nonalcoholic liquid **:** reduce the concentration or strength of **d :** to reduce in amount **:** LOWER, DIMINISH ⟨~ prices⟩ **e :** to trim (book edges) slightly in order to loosen leaves for reading, produce pleasing margins, or bring the book to the size desired **f :** to remove (excess metal) with an edged tool or an oxidizing flame **g :** to trim and join (motion-picture shots or sound tracks) **:** edit (a film) by rearrangements and omissions **h :** to take away show points from (an animal being shown) for a fault (as of conformation or color) **3 a** (1) **:** MOW, REAP ⟨~ hay⟩ (2) **:** to sever from the growing plant ⟨~ flowers⟩ (3) **:** to yield as a crop ⟨that field ~s several tons of hay⟩ **b** (1) **:** to divide into parts or to sever a part from by an edged tool ⟨~ bread⟩ (2) **:** to separate or remove by an edged tool ⟨~ a slice of bread⟩ (3) **:** to divide for distribution or apportionment **:** CARVE ⟨~ meat⟩ **c :** FELL, HEW ⟨~ timber⟩ **d :** to slit (folded but untrimmed pages of a book) **e :** to separate (a person) from an organization ⟨a coach who ~ two men from his football squad⟩ **:** DETACH **:** single out and remove, extract, or isolate — often used with *out* ⟨*cutting* these steers out from the herd⟩ **f :** to uncouple (two railroad cars or a car and locomotive) **g** (1) **:** to hit (a ball) with a glancing blow so as to deflect it and put a spin on it ⟨~ a tennis ball with an inclined racket⟩ (2) *cricket* **:** to deflect (a bowled ball) to the off with a chopping stroke (3) **:** to hit and propel (an object ball in pool or billiards) at a marked angle by a very fine contact **h :** to cause to move along (as a timber, roller, or gun) by prying or driving each end alternately sideways **i :** to change the direction of **:** TURN ⟨the driver ~ the wheels sharply⟩ **j :** to proceed with a very near approach to **:** SKIRT **4 a :** to divide into segments **:** separate into parts with an action or result suggestive of that of an edged instrument **:** divide off or up **b :** INTERSECT, CROSS ⟨the lines ~ one another⟩ **c :** to describe (an intersecting line) ⟨*cutting* a diagonal across the state⟩ **d :** BREAK, INTERRUPT, SEVER **:** make the use of for travel, transportation, or communication impossible **:** break the continuity of ⟨the enemy had ~ our communication lines⟩ **e** (1) **:** to divide or separate (a deck of cards) esp. into two portions by removing cards from the top (2) **:** to draw (a card) from the deck esp. for the purpose of deciding the deal **f :** to salt out (as soap) **g :** to cut apart (full printed sheets of text, maps, or illustrations) in preparation for binding **h :** to divide (as spoils or profits) into shares **:** SPLIT **i** *of a pitched baseball* **:** to pass over (a part of the plate) ⟨a fast ball that ~ the inside corner⟩ **5 a :** STOP, CEASE **:** desist from ⟨~ the nonsense⟩ **b :** to break off an acquaintance with **:** OSTRACIZE ⟨friends ~ him as news of the scandal spread⟩ **:** refuse to recognize (an acquaintance) ⟨~ him dead in the street⟩ **c :** to absent oneself usu. without excuse from (a lecture, recitation, or other academic function or an engagement) **d :** to stop (a motor or engine) by opening a switch or closing a throttle valve **:** turn off **:** adjust to a lesser or minimal speed or intensity **e :** to terminate the photographing of (a motion-picture scene) **f :** to terminate the transmission of (part of a radio or television program) **g :** to ignore an admonition or direction of and proceed ⟨~ a red light⟩ **6 a :** to make by or as if by cutting **:** give form or shape to by cutting: as (1) **:** to carve (as a statue) (2) **:** to shape (as by grinding facets) ⟨~ a diamond⟩ (3) **:** to engrave (as a woodcut) (4) **:** to shear out (5) **:** to hollow out (as by erosion), bore, or excavate ⟨floodwaters ~ new channels⟩ ⟨~ a tunnel⟩ (6) **:** to pierce (as by excavation) ⟨~ a dike⟩ **b :** to record a speech, musical selection, or other sound on (a phonograph record) **c :** to type (a stencil) **:** type on a stencil ⟨army orders being ~⟩ **7 a :** to engage in (a grotesque, frolicsome, or mischievous action) — used esp. in the phrases *cut a caper* and *cut didoes* **b :** to give the appearance or impression of **:** MAKE — usu. used with *figure* as object ⟨tall and stately, he ~ a fine figure as a senator⟩ ~ *vi* **1 a :** to do the work of or as if of an edged tool **:** serve in or as if in dividing or gashing ⟨a knife that ~s well⟩ **b :** to permit of being cut **:** admit of incision or severance ⟨cheese ~s easily⟩ **c :** to perform the operation of dividing, severing, incising, or intersecting **:** use a cutting instrument ⟨a tailor busy *cutting*⟩ **d :** to pierce through incisively **e** *of a horse* **:** to interfere slightly esp. by brushing the inner aspect of the corona of a hoof **f :** to make a stroke with a whip, sword, or other weapon ⟨a duelist *cutting* at his adversary⟩ **:** inflict a sharp painful stroke ⟨a heavy whip that ~s deep⟩ **g :** to wound feelings or sensibilities ⟨remarks that ~⟩ **h :** to cut in surgery **:** OPERATE **i :** to have constricting and chafing effects ⟨a coat that ~s at the armpits⟩ **j :** to be of effect, influence, or significance ⟨an analysis that ~s deep⟩ **2 a** (1) **:** to divide a pack of cards into two or more portions in order to decide the deal or trump, change the order of the cards, or settle a bet as to who will have the highest (2) **:** to draw a card from the pack in order to decide the deal or choice of seats or partners **b :** to divide spoils **:** SPLIT **3 a :** to go, pass, or proceed esp. with dispatch ⟨~ along a side road⟩ ⟨a launch *cutting* across the harbor⟩ **b :** to go across rather than around **:** make a short cut **:** proceed obliquely from a straight course ⟨~ across the campus⟩ ⟨~ down the alley⟩ **c :** to move away quickly **:** leave hurriedly **d :** to execute a dancing coupé **e :** to move swiftly as if passing through — usu. with *through* ⟨a yacht *cutting* through the water⟩ **f :** to describe an often oblique or diagonal line ⟨a road that ~s through the swamp⟩ **g :** to change in direction **:** VEER, SWERVE, TURN ⟨the carriage ~ to the right⟩; *esp* **:** to swerve sharply from one's original direction so as to elude an opponent ⟨an end who ~s in to receive a pass⟩ ⟨a wing who must ~ in order to get around the defense⟩ **h :** to make an abrupt transition from one sound or image to another in motion pictures, radio, or television **i :** to stop a dancing couple and take the place of one of the partners — usu. used with *in* **4** *of a color in a painting* **:** to stand out prominently **5 a :** to absent oneself from an appointment or academic session **b :** to cease photographing motion pictures **c** *of an engine or machine* **:** to fail or cease operation

syn CARVE, SLIT, SLASH, CHOP, HEW: CUT is a general term without much connotational force and is generally interchangeable with the others in this group. CARVE, in earlier English likewise general in meaning, is likely now to suggest purposive, deft, and careful cutting with a sharp knife or chisel to achieve a desired form or shape ⟨*carve* a figure from wood⟩ ⟨a statue *carved* from granite⟩ SLIT indicates a narrow lengthwise cutting with a sharp instrument, often with some skill or dexterity ⟨the surgeon *slit* the abdominal wall above the appendix⟩ ⟨*slit* a sealed envelope⟩ CARVE and SLIT may indicate care, skill, deftness, and restraint; SLASH, CHOP, and HEW are likely to suggest violent forceful action. SLASH may suggest swinging sweeping strokes made forcefully or fiercely without precision in direction and inflicting gashes with a long blade as of a sword, machete, or straight razor ⟨his face was *slashed* with dueling scars⟩ ⟨*slashing* their way through the jungle⟩ CHOP involves cutting with rough heavy blows made without precision with a heavier tool like a hatchet or chopping knife ⟨*chopping* the wood into stove lengths⟩ ⟨the workmen *chopped* down the tree⟩ HEW may suggest sustained great energy in cutting with a heavy tool like an ax or large chisel through something large or difficult ⟨*hew* down a forest⟩ ⟨*hew* a crypt out of the rock⟩

— **cut adrift :** to sever the connections of **:** leave or become independent or derelict — **cut a feather** *of a ship* **:** to cause the water to rise in a feathery foam or spray on each side of the stem when under way — **cut and run 1 :** to cut mooring cables and sail before the wind **2 :** to hurry off abruptly ⟨hearing the alarm, the gang *cut and ran*⟩ — **cut a rug** *slang* **:** DANCE; *esp* **:** JITTERBUG — **cut a rusty :** to be clever or otherwise noticeable — **cut a swathe :** to make an impression **:** have an effect **:** attract attention — **cut both ways** *or* **cut two ways :** to have a mixed effect **:** have both favorable and unfavorable results or implications **:** avail for either of two counterarguments or implications ⟨a fact that *cuts both ways* in the case⟩ — **cut corners** *also* **cut a corner :** to perform some action in the quickest, easiest, or cheapest way **:** cut out inessentials **:** neglect strict requirements for the sake of expediency ⟨the factory has increased profits 10 per cent by *cutting corners* wherever possible⟩ ⟨*cut a corner* in simplifying the inspection⟩ — **cut fine :** to be precise or meticulous in treating **:** allow no leeway concerning **:** proceed in by finical consideration ⟨to allow only 90 seconds for this operation is *cutting it fine*⟩ — **cut flush :** to trim the edges and covers of (a book) to the same size — **cut ice :** to have weight or influence **:** be of importance — usu. used in negative constructions ⟨his opinion *cuts* no *ice* with them⟩ ⟨a speech that did not *cut* much *ice*⟩ — **cut into 1 :** DIMINISH, DECREASE ⟨late votes for Doe were *cutting into* Roe's early lead⟩ ⟨the decline of the neighborhood *cut into* the value of his house⟩ ⟨new competitors would *cut into* existing markets⟩ **2 :** to join (a card game) by cutting in — **cut loose 1 :** to free from custody, contact, restraint, or check **2 :** to free oneself from domination, control, restraint, inhibition, or influence ⟨he *cut loose* from his domineering father⟩ **3 :** to act, proceed, or perform with abandon or wildness ⟨the rattled pitcher *cut loose* with a wild pitch⟩ **:** celebrate or enjoy oneself with carefree abandon and lack of restraint ⟨convention delegates *cutting loose* at night⟩ — **cut one's eye :** to glance obliquely — **cut one's eyeteeth** *or* **cut one's wisdom teeth :** to acquire wisdom or sophistication — **cut one's teeth on** *or* **cut one's eyeteeth on :** to learn, do, or perform as a beginning or at the start of one's career **:** start with **:** do while young and inexperienced ⟨he *cut his eyeteeth on* algebra at the age of eight⟩ — **cut one's throat :** to injure irreparably **:** DESTROY, RUIN — **cut short 1 :** to arrest or check abruptly **:** INTERRUPT ⟨his words being *cut short* by the disturbance in the audience⟩ **2 :** to terminate usu. in an untimely or premature manner **:** END ⟨illness *cutting short* his career⟩ — **cut square :** to cut (a postage stamp) from a cover with margins forming a square or rectangle — **cut stick** *or* **cut one's stick** *dial* **:** to run away **:** ESCAPE — **cut the buck :** to act efficiently or rapidly **:** do well what is expected of one — **cut the ground from under :** to deprive of foundation or basis **:** destroy claims or appearances of the validity of **:** destroy the effectiveness or cogency of ⟨a fact that *cuts the ground from under* his argument⟩ — **cut the gun :** to close the throttle of an airplane engine — **cut the knot :** to resolve a difficulty by prompt arbitrary action — see GORDIAN KNOT — **cut the muster** *or* **cut the mustard** *slang* **:** to achieve the standard of performance necessary for success ⟨in our work . . . those of our fellow workers who can't or won't *cut the mustard* must of necessity be shoved out —*Atlantic*⟩ — compare PASS MUSTER — **cut the pan :** to salt out (soap) — **cut to pieces :** to impose crushing defeat and loss upon **:** DECIMATE ⟨a unit *cut to pieces* by the enemy fire⟩ — **cut to shape :** to cut (a stamp) from a cover leaving no margins at all — **cut to the bone :** to reduce to the barest minimum **:** divest of anything that could be regarded as nonessential, extra, or extrinsic — **cut up touches :** to exchange comments **:** CHAT

²**cut** \"\ *n* -S **1 :** something that is cut or cut off **:** a severed

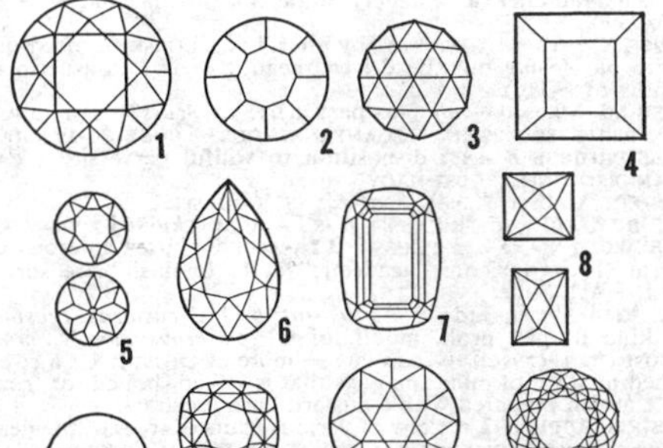

cut 5c: *1* brilliant; *2* single; *3* rose; *4* table; *5* Swiss, top and back; *6* pendeloque; *7* emerald; *8* French; *9* cabochon; *10* Lisbon; *11* star; *12* Portuguese

part or portion **:** DIVISION, SEGMENT, PIECE: as **a** [ME *cut, cutte,* fr. *cutten,* v.] **:** one of a number of straws or sticks cut in uneven lengths and used to draw lots **b :** a slice of food (as of meat or bread) **c :** a unit indicating yarn size based on the number of fixed-length hanks per pound ⟨a 1-*cut* asbestos or glass yarn has one 100-yard hank to the pound; a 4-*cut* has four 100-yard hanks per pound⟩ ⟨a 1-*cut* woolen yarn has 300 yards per pound; a 6-*cut* has 1800 yards per pound⟩ **d** (1) **:** a length of cloth as cut from a loom or packaged for selling varying from 40 to 100 yards in length (2) **:** a section cut from such a length of cloth ⟨he sold 5-yard ~s for dresses⟩ **e :** a field under cultivation **:** a specified part of such a field **f :** LUNCH, SNACK **g :** a part of a tree bough from which rails and board may be split **h :** the yield of products that are cut (as grain, timber, or lumber) during a specified period or operation **i :** a segment or section of a meat animal carcass **:** a piece from such a segment ⟨a rib ~⟩ **j cuts** *pl* **:** persons who have cut each other socially **:** former friends now not speaking **k :** a part of a band of animals that has been separated from a main herd **l :** a fraction separated in the course of a process (as distilling) ⟨the lighter ~s of petroleum⟩ **m :** SHARE **:** portion of gain, profit, or loot **:** allotment from some often illicit venture **n cuts** *pl* **:** hard candies broken into irregular shapes and sizes **o :** a dispersion of a certain number of pounds of shellac or resin per gallon of volatile liquid paint **p :** a part of salable size cut off from a sponge too large to be marketable **q :** the material removed by a cutting tool **:** the thickness of the chip removed ⟨a ~ of ⅛ inch⟩ **r :** needles per inch in latch-needle circular or flat knitting machines **:** the relative fineness of fabric therefrom **s :** one or more scoring points taken from a show animal for a fault **t :** two or more cars coupled together or to a locomotive but not conforming to specifications for a train **u :** a compass bearing line or a set of intersecting bearing lines that indicate a ship's position **2 a** [ME, fr. *cutten,* v.] *now dial* **:** a man or woman who is disliked; *specif* **:** TROLLOP **b** *obs* **:** PLOW HORSE, CART HORSE **3 :** the effect produced by cutting: as **a :** a notch, creek, channel, or inlet made by excavation or worn by natural action (as of water) ⟨a ~ or canal⟩ **b :** an opening made with an edged instrument **:** CLEFT, GASH, SLASH **:** a wound made by cutting ⟨a ~ in the thigh⟩ **c** *obs* **:** an ornamental slash in a garment **d :** a natural cleft resembling a cut ⟨the ~s of a maple leaf⟩ **e :** a surface or outline left by cutting ⟨a clean or smooth ~⟩ **f :** a passage cut as a roadway ⟨a railway ~⟩ **g :** a grade or step (as in a social or economic scale) ⟨be a ~ above one's neighbor⟩ ⟨a few lads several ~s above the ordinary —J.F.Powers⟩; *also* **:** a social stratum **h :** a narrow opening in the floor of a theater stage for the passage of scenery **i** *also* **cut point** (1) **:** a mathematical division **:** something that divides into two classes (2) *in the aggregate of rational numbers* **:** a partition or border constituted by an irrational number **j :** the notchings made in a key **k** (1) **:** a printing surface used for a pictorial illustration or matter not readily reproducible in type (as a line or halftone engraving or an electrotype or stereotype molded therefrom) — called also *block* (2) **:** a print or impression from a cut; *also* **:** any printed illustration **4 :** the act or an instance of cutting: as **a :** a gesture or expression that wounds the feelings (as a harsh criticism or sarcastic remark); *esp* **:** personal discourtesy in neglecting to recognize an acquaintance **b :** a straight or easy passage or course ⟨took a ~ through the woods⟩ **c** (1) **:** a stroke with the edge of a fencing weapon — distinguished from *thrust* (2) **:** the motion of giving a cut **d :** a stroke or blow with the edge of a knife or other edged tool **:** the lash of a whip **e :** the act of removing a part (as of a composition) or reducing or dividing as if by use of a knife ⟨make ~s in a drama⟩ ⟨a ~ in prices⟩ ⟨salary ~s and other retrenchments⟩ **f :** a quick replacement of one foot by the other in dancing — compare COUPÉ **g** *of a horse* **:** the action of cutting **:** INTERFERING **h :** act or turn of cutting cards; *also* **:** the result of cutting **:** a card so obtained **i** (1) **:** a student's voluntary absence from a regular academic class or function at which attendance is expected (2) **:** an instructor's or other official's absenting himself from class or other academic function and thereby canceling its meeting ⟨giving his class a ~ when he was out of town⟩ **j** (1) **:** a stroke that cuts a ball; *also* **:** the spin imparted by such a stroke (2) **:** such a cricket stroke on the off side between point and the wicket; *also* **:** a cricketer who plays this stroke — see LATE CUT (3) **:** a swing by a batter at a pitched baseball **k :** an exchange of captures in checkers **l :** an abrupt transition from one sound or image to another in motion pictures, radio, or television **5 a :** the shape and style in which a thing is cut, formed, or made; *esp* **:** the distribution of material or the design characterizing a garment ⟨clothes of the latest ~⟩ **b :** PATTERN, TYPE, APPEARANCE ⟨an odd ~ of a dog⟩ ⟨others of her ~⟩ **c :** style of cutting a gem **d** [by shortening] **:** HAIRCUT — **cut of one's jib :** the appearance of one's face **:** COUNTENANCE ⟨I like the *cut of your jib,* or you wouldn't be sitting there opposite me —G.N.Boothby⟩

³**cut** \"\ *adj* [ME *cutt, kitt,* fr. past part. of *cutten, kitten* to cut] **1 :** subjected to cutting **:** formed or fashioned by cutting: **a :** detached by cutting; *specif* **:** cut from a growing plant ⟨~ flowers⟩ **b :** sliced, chopped, or shredded; *specif* **:** shredded for use in smoking ⟨~ tobacco⟩ **c** *archaic* **:** showing ornamental cuts or slashes ⟨a ~ doublet⟩ **d** [ME, fr. *cutt* cut (castrated)] **:** CASTRATED ⟨a ~ horse⟩ **e :** cut from a coin of larger denomination — used esp. of metallic money (as pieces of eight) circulated in the West Indies and in parts of the American mainland in the 18th and early 19th centuries **2 :** INCISED, LOBED ⟨a flower with ~ leaves⟩ **3 :** DRUNK ⟨~ last night and unable to remember⟩

cut- *or* **cuti-** *comb form* [NL, fr. L *cuti-,* fr. *cutis* skin — more at HIDE] **:** skin ⟨*cutin*⟩ ⟨*cuticolor*⟩ ⟨*cutigeral*⟩ **:** cuticle ⟨*cutification*⟩

cut across *vt* **1 :** to avoid following or being subsumed, defined, or determined by or in accordance with **:** COUNTER, TRANSCEND ⟨an issue that *cuts across* party lines⟩ **2 :** to include within the scope of effect or significance ⟨a development that *cuts across* all strata of society⟩

cut-and-come-again \ˌ⸗⸗ˈ⸗⸗ˈ⸗\ *n* -S **:** TEN-WEEK STOCK

cut-and-cover \ˌ⸗⸗ˈ⸗⸗\ *adj* **:** constructed in a cut or trench and after completion covered as with some of the excavated material or paving ⟨a *cut-and-cover* conduit⟩

cut-and-dried *also* **cut-and-dry** \ˌ⸗⸗ˈ⸗\ *adj* **:** in accordance with a plan, set procedure, or formula **:** without spontaneity, freshness, interest, or novel development **:** ROUTINE ⟨their plans were *cut-and-dried,* down to the smallest detail —E.A. Peers⟩ ⟨a *cut-and-dried* committee meeting⟩

cut and fill *n* **1 :** the leveling or gradational process whereby waves, currents, streams, or winds erode material from one place and deposit it near by until the surfaces of erosion and deposition become continuous and uniform in grade; *esp* **:** the action of a meandering stream in cutting from its concave banks and depositing within its loops **2 :** the excavating of material in one place and the depositing of it nearby (as in building a road or canal) ⟨wholly obscured by the construction of two later highways, demanding a considerable amount of *cut and fill* —G.R.Stewart⟩

cut and thrust *n* **1 :** cutting and thrusting with a sword **2 :** the interplay of a sharp struggle ⟨the inevitability of war between the two . . . powers was implicit . . . in the *cut and thrust* necessarily concealed at the time —*Times Lit. Supp.*⟩

cut-and-try \ˌ⸗⸗ˈ⸗\ *adj* **:** marked by experimental procedure **:** EMPIRICAL ⟨there were no analytical procedures to help him, but although he had to work by *cut-and-try* methods, he tried —C.E.Waters⟩

cu·ta·ne·al \kyüˈtānēəl\ *adj* [NL *cutaneus* + E *-al*] **:** CUTANEOUS

cutaneo- *comb form* [F *cutanéo-,* fr. *cutané* cutaneous, fr. NL *cutaneus*] **:** skin and ⟨*cutaneo*visceral⟩

cu·ta·ne·ous \kyüˈtānēəs\ *adj* [NL *cutaneus,* fr. L *cutis* skin — more at HIDE] **:** of or relating to the skin **:** existing on or affecting the skin ⟨a ~ nerve⟩ ⟨a ~ infection⟩ ⟨~ test⟩ — **cu·ta·ne·ous·ly** *adv*

cutaneous sensation *n* **:** a sensation (as of warmth, cold, contact, or pain) aroused by stimulation of end organs in the skin

¹**cutaway** \ˈ⸗⸗,⸗\ *adj* [fr. past part. of *cut away,* v.] **1 :** having parts cut away **:** made or styled quite trim or scant as if to suggest that some materials have been cut off or away ⟨a dress with ~ shoulders⟩ **2 :** having a cutting action ⟨a ~ harrow⟩ **3 :** illustrating or conforming to a style of pictorial presentation in which an outer surface or cover is not fully shown and in which inner details are made apparent ⟨a ~ picture of the street showing the subway below⟩

²cutaway \"\ *n* -s **1** *also* **cutaway coat** : a coat with skirts cut on a tapering line from the front waistline to form tails at the back — compare TAILCOAT **2** : a disc harrow with notched discs **3 a** : a cutaway picture or representation **b** : a shot that interrupts the main action of a film or television program to take up a related subject or to depict action supposed to be going on at the same time as the main action **4** : a back dive in which the head is lowered toward the board after the takeoff — compare BACKWARD DIVE, GAINER

cutaway coat

cut back *vt* **1** : to shorten by cutting off the end ⟨*cut back* a word⟩ : PRUNE ⟨*cut back* the shoots of a plant⟩ **2** : to return (a distillate) to a still (as in petroleum refining); *also* : to thin (as asphalt) by the addition of lighter oils **3** : REDUCE, DECREASE; *sometimes* : ELIMINATE, ABOLISH ⟨*cut back* military expenditure⟩ ⟨*cut back* reforestation work⟩ ~ *vi* : to interrupt the sequence of a plot by introducing events prior to those last presented ⟨then the script *cut back* to the old man's childhood⟩

cutback \'ˌ=\ *n* -s [*cut back*] **1** : something that is cut back; *specif* : a product (as asphalt) thinned or made less viscous by the addition of lighter oils **2** : a reduction (as in rate, amount, or number) ⟨a ~ in orders or in production⟩ ⟨budget limitation required ~s in personnel allowances⟩ : discontinuance before full quota or fulfilment is achieved **3** : a shift from a chronological order in narration to events earlier than those last presented : a motion picture or television shot in which previously depicted action is reverted to and continued — compare FLASHBACK **4** : a market animal rejected or put in a lower class than its fellows because of inferior condition or size **5** : any football play in which the runner cuts back **6** : a part of a word or pronunciation printed (as in a dictionary) to represent the whole word or pronunciation the missing part of which is given elsewhere

cutbank \'ˌ=\ *n, West* : a steep bare slope formed typically by stream erosion

cut bone *n* : raw bone coarsely ground and used chiefly as a feed for poultry

cut card *n* : a guide or other card of a card series equipped with a tab for use in filing

cut-card work *n* : relief ornament of silverware common in the 12th century consisting of a thin sheet of silver cut into a pattern and soldered onto the surface of the piece usu. around a spout, handle, or finial

¹cutch *also* **kutch** \'kəch\ *n* -ES [modif. of Malay *kachu* — more at CATECHU] **1** : CATECHU **2** : a tanning extract derived from any of several mangrove barks of Borneo and the Philippines

²cutch \"\ *n* -ES [modif. of F *caucher*, fr. *caucher* to press, trample, alter. (influenced by F dial. *cauquer*) of OF *chaucher*, fr. L *calcare* to tread on, trample, fr. *calc-, calx* heel — more at CALK] : a packet of vellum or tough paper leaves in which gold is first beaten into thin sheets

³cutch \"\ *n* -ES [alter. of *quitch*] : COUCH GRASS 1a

⁴cutch *var of* CULTCH

cut·cher·ry *or* **cut·chery** \(ˌ)kə'cherē, 'kəchərē\ *n* -ES [Hindi *kacahrī*, fr. *kaca-* (prob. fr. Prakrit *kacca*, fr. Skt *kṛtya*) + *-hri* (prob. fr. Prakrit *ghara* house, hearth); akin to Skt *kṛtya* act, action, *karman* act, work and to Skt *gharma* heat — more at KARMA, WARM] *India* : a public office for administrative or judicial business : COURTHOUSE; *also* : any administrative office (as of a planter)

cut down *vt* **1 a** : to remodel by removing extras or furnishings and fittings not completely necessary; *specif* : RAZEE **b** : to remake in a smaller size ⟨*cutting down* her older sister's dress⟩ **2** : to strike down and kill, incapacitate, or take out of activity ⟨the swordsman *cut down* his foe⟩ ⟨was *cut down* by the voters of Washington —Murray Kempton⟩ **3** : to diminish the scope, volume, or intensity of : REDUCE, CURTAIL ⟨*cut down* expenses⟩ ⟨*cut down* the accident rate⟩ **4** : to separate into parts in ore dressing ⟨*cut down* a sample of ore⟩ ~ *vi* : to lessen or retard volume or activity ⟨*cut down* on smoking⟩ — **cut down to size** : to reduce from an inflated or exaggerated importance to true or suitable stature ⟨the challenger looks impressive, but stiffer competition will *cut* him *down to size*⟩

cutdown \'ˌ=\ *n* [*cut down*] **1** : DECREASE, REDUCTION ⟨a ~ in production⟩ ⟨a ~ in employment⟩ **2** : incision of a superficial blood vessel (as a vein) to facilitate insertion of a catheter (as for administration of fluids)

¹cute *var of* CUIT

²cute \'kyüt, *usu* -üd·+V\ *adj* -ER/-EST [short for ¹*acute*] **1** : marked by acuteness and shrewdness : INGENIOUS, CLEVER, SHARP ⟨a most particular ~ lawyer —T.C.Haliburton⟩ ⟨the apprehension of the ~ practical man —Francis Hackett⟩ **2** : ATTRACTIVE, PRETTY — a generalized expression of approval sometimes suggesting daintiness, fine features, deftness, or delicacy ⟨a ~ kid with pigtails bound in red ribbons —W.A. White⟩ ⟨young, dark and small, with pretty features as regular as if they had been cut by a die. "He's ~," I said —Dashiell Hammett⟩ ⟨a ~ little bungalow⟩ ⟨a ~ wristwatch⟩ **3** : obviously straining for effect : mawkish through affected archness, prettiness, or contrivance : ARTIFICIAL, MANNERED ⟨~, self-conscious, and elaborate in its use of trick devices —C.M. Smith⟩ ⟨a bad book, shallow, corny, and unmercifully ~ —L.A.Fiedler⟩ — **cute·ly** *adv*

cute·ness *n* -ES : the quality or state of being cute ⟨the delicacy and taste of a fairy story told without ~ —Brooks Atkinson⟩

cu·ter \'kyüd·ə(r)\ *n* -s [alter. of *quarter*] : a 25-cent piece : QUARTER

cu·te·re·bra \ˌkyüd·ə'rēbrə, kyü'terəbrə\ *n, cap* [NL, fr. L *cutis* skin + *terebra* borer — more at HIDE, THROW] : the type genus of Cuterebridae comprising large usu. dark-colored botflies with larvae that form tumors under the skin of rodents, cats, and other small mammals

cu·te·re·brid \-brəd\ *n* -s [NL *Cuterebridae*] : a botfly of the family Cuterebridae

cu·te·reb·ri·dae \ˌkyüd·ə'rebrəˌdē\ *n pl, cap* [NL *Cuterebra*, type genus + *-idae*] : a family of chiefly New World botflies that occur under the skin or sometimes in the throat or nasal sinuses of various mammals and that include a botfly (*Dermatobia hominis*) that normally parasitizes man — see CUTEREBRA

cu·te·re·brine \ˌ;kyüd·ə;rēbrən, (')kyü;terəb-, -ˌbrīn\ *adj* [NL *Cuterebra* + E *-ine*] : of or relating to the genus *Cuterebra* or family Cuterebridae

cutes *pl of* CUTIS

cutey *var of* CUTIE

cut film *n* : SHEET FILM

cut flower *n* : a flower cut from the plant for use in decoration

cut gear *n* : a gear whose teeth have been machined

cut glass *n* : glassware usu. made of flint glass that is ornamented with patterns cut into its surface by an abrasive wheel and polished

cut-grass \'ˌ=\ *n* : a grass having minute hooked bristles along the edges of the leaf blade; *specif* : a species of *Leersia* — see RICE CUT-GRASS

cu·thae·an *or* **cu·the·an** \kyü'thēən\ *n* -s *usu cap* [*Cuthah*, ancient city of Babylonia whence many Cuthaeans were taken according to 2 Kings 17:24 + E *-an*] : a member of a group of people of ancient Babylonia who were sent as colonists to Samaria

cuti- — see CUT-

cu·ti·cle \'kyüd·ə̇kəl, -üt|, |ēk-\ *n* -s [L *cuticula*, dim. of *cutis* skin — more at HIDE] **1** : SKIN, PELLICLE, MEMBRANE, INTEGUMENT: as **a** : an external membranous or hardened noncellular investment secreted by the cells of the epidermis or by the outer surface of the body (as in arthropods) **b** : the epidermis of man or other animals lacking a noncellular integument **c** : the cell wall of a unicellular animal **2** *bot* : a thin continuous noncellular film of fatty substances secreted by epidermal and other cells on the external surface of many leaves, stems, fruits, and other plant organs, functioning in preventing desiccation **3** : dead or cornified epidermis (as that surrounding the base and sides of a fingernail or toenail) **4** : a thin skin formed on the surface of a liquid **5** : an outermost layer (as the bloom on the shell of an egg or the scaly outer layer of a wool fiber)

cu·ti·col·or \'kyüd·əˌkələ(r)\ *adj* [*cut-* + *color*] : having the color of flesh

cu·tic·u·la \kyü'tikyələ\ *n, pl* **cuticu·lae** \-ˌlē\ [L] : CUTICLE 1a; *specif* : the outer body wall of an insect, secreted by the hypodermis

cu·tic·u·lar \(')kyü;tikyələ(r)\ *adj* [L *cuticula* + E *-ar*] : of or relating to a cuticle or cuticula : EPIDERMAL

cu·tic·u·lar·i·za·tion \kyüˌtikyələrə'zāshən\ *n* -s : the state of being or process of becoming cuticularized ⟨heavy root ~⟩ ⟨gradual ~ of the vaginal mucosa⟩

cu·tic·u·lar·ized \=ˈ===ˌrīzd\ *adj* **1** : covered with or altered into cuticle ⟨a ~ surface⟩ ⟨~ cells⟩ **2** : CUTINIZED

cuticular transpiration *n* : the transpiration of gases or vapor directly through the external membranes

cu·tic·u·late \-ˌlət, -ˌlāt\ *adj* [L *cuticula* + E *-ate*] : possessing a cuticle

cu·ti·dure \'kyüd·əˌd(y)u̇(ə)r\ *also* **cu·ti·du·ris** \ˌkyüd·ə'd(y)u̇rə̇s\ *n, pl* **cuti·dures** \-ˌd(y)u̇(ə)rz, -'d(y)u̇(ˌ)rēz\ [*cutidure* fr. F, fr. *cut-* + *dure*, fem. of *dur* hard, fr. L *durus*, *cutiduris*, fr. NL, fr. F *cutidure* — more at DURE] : CORONARY CUSHION

cut·ie *or* **cut·ey** \'kyüd·|ē, -üt|, |i\ *n, pl* **cuties** *or* **cuteys** [*cute* + *-ie, -ey*] **1** : an attractive person; *esp* : a pretty girl **2** : an athlete who attempts to outthink and outmaneuver an opponent

cutie pie *n* **1** *slang* : a cute person : SWEETHEART **2** : a portable gamma-radiation detecting and measuring and beta-radiation detecting instrument that includes an ionization chamber and a direct-reading microammeter with a pointer

cu·ti·fi·ca·tion \ˌkyüd·əfə'kāshən\ *n* -s [*cuticle* + *-fication*] : formation of cuticle

cu·tig·er·al \(')kyü;tijərəl\ *adj* [ISV *cut-* + L *gerere* to bear + ISV *-al* — more at CAST] : bearing skin

cutigeral cavity *n* : the depression on the inner superior border of a horse's hoof

cut in *vi* **1** : to thrust oneself usu. with abruptness or force into a position between others or belonging to another; *specif* : to drive a vehicle rapidly into place in a moving line of vehicles ⟨there was a steady flow of traffic on the avenue, but we managed to *cut in*⟩ **2** : to join a card game previously begun by other persons **3** : to interrupt : interpose sharply : join in anything suddenly — often used with *on* ⟨*cutting in* on the conversation⟩ **4** : to interrupt a dancing couple and take one of them for one's partner — often used with *on* **5** : to become connected or started in operation usu. automatically ⟨when more power is needed, the auxiliary motor *cuts in*⟩ **6** : to cut blubber from a newly killed whale ~ *vt* **1** : to cut up (a whale) to obtain blubber **2** : to mix (as fat and flour for pastry) with cutting motions of a knife, spatula, or blender **3** : to introduce into a number, group, or sequence ⟨*cut in* titles in a motion picture⟩ **4** : to connect (a piece of electrical apparatus) into a circuit : to connect (as a part or an engine) to a mechanical apparatus so as to permit or facilitate its operation ⟨*cut in* a spare fuel tank⟩ ⟨*cut in* a rocket engine⟩ **5** : INCLUDE; *specif* : to include among those benefiting or favored — often used with *on* ⟨*cut* them *in* on the profit⟩

¹cut-in \'ˌ=\ *n, pl* **cut-ins** [*cut in*] : something cut in: as **a** : a shot inserted in a motion picture or television program in interruption of the main action **b** : a radio or television announcement or advertising message originating locally and introduced into a network program **c** : a share in another's royalties or profits ⟨a singer receiving a *cut-in* from publisher and author⟩ : a person receiving such a share **d** : a heading or illustration placed in a space provided by beginning or ending consecutive lines of text short of the column edge

²cut-in \"\ *adj* [*cut in*] **1** : inserted by or as if by cutting **2** : marked by cutting in on dancing partners ⟨a *cut-in* affair⟩ **3** : occupying space left by lines shorter than the full-length lines of a column or paragraph ⟨a *cut-in* heading or illustration⟩

cu·tin \'kyüt°n\ *n* -s [ISV *cut-* + *-in*; orig. formed as F *cutine*] : the insoluble water-impermeable complex aggregate of waxes, fatty acids, soaps, higher alcohols, and resinous material that is found as a continuous external lamella on the outer wall of the epidermis in leaf and stem of plants — compare CUTICLE, SUBERIN

cu·tin·i·za·tion \ˌkyüt°nə̇'zāshən\ *n* -s [ISV *cutinize* + *-ation*] : infiltration of plant cell walls with cutin — compare CUTICULARIZATION, SUBERIZATION

cu·tin·ized \'==ˌīzd\ *adj* [*cutin* + *-ized*] : infiltrated with cutin ⟨~ epidermal cells⟩

cu·tis \'kyüd·ə̇s\ *or* **cutis ve·ra** \ˌ==ˈvirə\ *n, pl* **cu·tes** \'kyüˌtēz\ *or* **cutises** *or* **cutes ve·rae** \ˌkyüˌtēz'viˌrē\ [*cutis* fr. L, skin; *cutis vera* fr. L, lit., true skin — more at HIDE] : the dermis of the skin

cutis an·se·ri·na \ˌ==ˌan(t)sə'rīnə\ *n, pl* **cutes anseri·nae** \-ī,nē\ [NL, lit., goose skin] : GOOSEFLESH

cutis plate *n* : DERMATOME 2a

cut·lash \'kətˌlash\ *n* -ES [by folk etymology] : CUTLASS

cut·lass *also* **cut·las** \'kətləs\ *n* -ES [alter. of earlier *coutelace*, fr. MF *coutelas*, aug. of *coutel* knife, fr. L *cultellus* small knife, dim. of *culter* knife — more at COLTER] **1** : a short heavy curving cutting sword formerly used by sailors on war vessels **2** : MACHETE

cutlass 1

cutlass fish *n* : any fish of the family Trichiuridae; *esp* : a long thin fish (*Trichiurus lepturus*) often occurring on the coasts of the southern U.S. and the West Indies

cut-leaved \'ˌ=\ *also* **cut-leaf** \'ˌ=\ *adj* : having leaves that are more than normally divided ⟨*cut-leaved* maple⟩

cut·ler \'kətlə(r)\ *n* -s [ME, fr. MF *coutelier*, fr. LL *cultellarius*, fr. L *cultellus* small knife + *-arius* -ary — more at CUTLASS] : a person that makes, deals in, or repairs cutlery

cut·le·ria \ˌkət'lirēə\ *n, cap* [NL, fr. Manasseh *Cutler* †1823 Am. clergyman and botanist + NL *-ia*] : a genus (the type of the family Cutleriaceae) of marine brown algae characterized by true alternation of generations, the gametophyte being an upright plant with a broad flat forking thallus and the sporophyte a flat lobed disk — **cut·le·ri·a·ceous** \ˌkət;lirē;āshəs\ *adj*

cut·le·ri·a·ce·ae \ˌ=ˌ==ˈāsēˌē\ *n pl, cap* [NL, fr. *Cutleria*, type genus + *-aceae*] : a family of algae coextensive with the order Cutleriales

cut·le·ri·a·les \-'ā(ˌ)lēz\ *n pl, cap* [NL, fr. *Cutleria* + *-ales*] : an order of marine brown algae (class Phaeophyta) having a flattened blade-shaped or discoid thallus in which growth is partially or entirely trichothallic

cut·ler·ite \'kətləˌrīt\ *n* -s *usu cap* [Alpheus *Cutler*, 19th cent. Am. theologist, its organizer + E *-ite*] : a member of the Church of Jesus Christ organized in 1853

cut·lery \'kətlərē, -ri\ *n* -ES [ME *cutellerie*, fr. MF *coutelerie*, fr. OF, fr. *coutel* knife + *-erie* -ery — more at CUTLASS] **1** : edged or cutting tools (as shears, knives, surgical instruments); *specif* : implements for use in cutting, serving, and eating food — compare FLATWARE **2** : the business of making or selling cutlery

cut·let \'kətlət, *usu* -əd·+V\ *n* -s [F *côtelette*, fr. OF *costelette*, dim. of *coste* rib, side, fr. L *costa* — more at COAST] **1** : VEAL CUTLET **2** : a small slice of meat cooked by broiling or frying ⟨pork ~⟩ **3** : a food mixture shaped to resemble a meat cutlet ⟨cheese ~⟩

cutline \'ˌ=\ *n* [²*cut* (printing block) + *line*] : LEGEND, CAPTION

cut·ling \'kətliŋ, 'kəd·°liŋ\ *n* -s [*cutler* + *-ing*] : the occupation of a cutler

cut·lings \'kütlənz, 'kət-\ *n pl* [¹*cut* + *-lings* (pl. of *-ling*)] *dial Eng* : grits of oatmeal or barley

cutlip minnow \'ˌ=-\ *n, or* **cutlips** \'ˌ=\ *n pl but sing or pl in construction* : an olive-colored cyprinid fish (*Exoglossum maxillingua*) of the northeastern U.S. and adjoining Canada having the lower lip 3-lobed

cut man \'ˌ=\ *n* : a newspaperman in charge of advertising and layout cuts

cutmeter \'kətˌmēd·ə(r)\ *n* : a hand tachometer for determining the cutting speed of machine tools

cut money *n* : a currency circulating in the West Indies and in parts of the American mainland in the 18th and early 19th centuries, obtained by cutting the Spanish American dollar or its fractions into halves, quarters, or eighths to obtain small change — compare³ BIT 2b

cut nail *n* : a nail cut or stamped from sheet metal

cu·to·cellulose \ˌ;kyüd·(ˌ)ō+\ *n* [*cutin* + *-o-* + *cellulose*] : cellulose associated with cutin in the cuticle of certain plants

cut off *vt* **1** : DETACH : strike off : SEVER ⟨*cut off* 20 years of his life⟩ **2** : to cause the death of : end life : bring to an untimely end ⟨suddenly *cut off* by a fever in the plenitude of health, vigor, and aspirations —George Grote⟩ **3** : INTERCEPT, STOP : stop the passage of ⟨*cut off* supplies from a beleaguered town⟩ ⟨*cutting off* communications between the defenders⟩ **4** : to shut off : BAR ⟨the fence *cut off* his view⟩ ⟨the river *cutting off* their retreat⟩ ⟨a scandal *cutting* her *off* from society⟩ ⟨*cut off* from one another by miles of moorland —L.D.Stamp⟩ **5 a** : to end suddenly : break off : terminate abruptly : interrupt and silence ⟨*cutting off* hope of reconciliation⟩ ⟨*cutting off* the prisoner's protests⟩ **b** : to turn off : stop the operation of ⟨*cut off* the engine⟩ **6** : SEPARATE, ISOLATE ⟨*cut* himself *off* entirely⟩ ⟨*cut* herself *off* from her family⟩ **7** : DISINHERIT; *sometimes* : to bequeath to (a person) a ridiculously paltry sum (as to indicate displeasure with the legatee) ⟨*cut off* his scapegrace son with a hundred dollars⟩ **8** : INTERRUPT, STOP : turn off : stop the operation of ⟨*cut off* a motor⟩ ⟨*cut off* a radio program⟩; *specif* : to stop or interfere with (someone speaking on a telephone) by breaking the connection ⟨he had spoken only a dozen words when the operator *cut* him *off*⟩ **9** : to intercept (a baseball thrown from the outfield usu. toward home plate) ~ *vi* : to cease operating ⟨a motor may *cut off* if it is overtaxed⟩

¹cutoff \'ˌ=\ *n* -s [*cut off*] **1** : the action or act of cutting off: **a** : the act of shutting off admission of working fluid to an engine cylinder **b** : CESSATION : suspension of activity, operation, or established trend ⟨a firm ~ in wage boosts had to be made somewhere —*Time*⟩ **c** *music* (1) : GENERAL PAUSE (2) : a conductor's gesture (as an abrupt sweep of the hand) commanding a sharp cessation of playing **d** : interception by an infielder of a baseball thrown from the outfield to home plate **2 a** : the new and relatively short channel formed when a stream cuts through the neck of an oxbow **b** : any route that cuts away from a main or accustomed course in order to shorten passage : SHORTCUT, BYPASS **c** : a channel made to straighten a stream (as for the facilitation of log driving) **3** : a device for cutting off: as **a** : a mechanism for shutting off the admission of a working fluid (as steam) to an engine cylinder — compare VALVE GEAR **b** : a device in the mechanism of magazine rifles that when in active use prevents the feeding of cartridges from the magazine into the chamber with the gun then being used as a single-loader **c** : any device for stopping or changing a current (as of grain in a chute or water in a spout) **d** : FIRE STOP **e** : a wall or similar structure to stop or reduce seepage and percolation of water **f** : a device to stop passage of light : HOOD, SHUTTER **g** : a device for eliminating undesirable sound frequencies **h** *or* **cutoff rule** : a horizontal rule or its imprint separating discontinuous printed matter **4** : something that is cut off; *specif* : the crescent-shaped body of water cut off from a channel when a stream cuts through an oxbow **5** : the point, date, or period for a cutoff: as **a** : the point in a cycle of operations of an engine at which a cutoff occurs **b** : a date marking the end of a period or operation (as for the submission of offers or the filing of applications for tax refunds) **c** : a point or date where an accounting period ends and settlement or closing is made

²cutoff \"\ *adj* [partly fr. *cut off*; partly fr. past part. of *cut off*] **1** : that is cut off or serves to cut off ⟨~ valve⟩ **2** *of a shoe vamp* : cut off at the line at which the toe cap is stitched on

cutoff saw *n* **1** : a circular, band, or power-driven hacksaw for cutting off metal bars, pipes, or lumber : SWING SAW **2** : a carpenter's crosscut handsaw

cut oil *n* : an emulsion of water in petroleum; *esp* : one of natural origin

cut on *vt, chiefly South* : to turn on ⟨*cut on* the light⟩

¹cut out *vt* **1** : to cut so as to remove : remove by cutting ⟨a surgeon *cutting out* diseased tissue⟩ **2** : to form by erosion : EXCAVATE, CARVE ⟨valleys *cut out* by swift rivers⟩ **3** : to form or shape by cutting ⟨a dressmaker *cutting out* a garment⟩ **4 a** : PLAN, PROJECT ⟨tasks *cut out* for the week⟩ **b** : to form or assign through necessity ⟨have one's work *cut out* for one⟩ **5** : to take the place of (as a rival) : SUPPLANT, ELIMINATE ⟨*cutting out* her other boyfriends⟩ **6** : DEBAR, EXCLUDE **7 a** : REMOVE, OMIT ⟨*cutting out* the needless explanation in the speech⟩ **b** (1) : ELIMINATE ⟨wasteful expenditure that must be *cut out*⟩ (2) : to stop or desist from ⟨the children were told to *cut out* the noise⟩ **8** : to capture (a ship) by cutting off possible defenses or means of escape ⟨*cutting out* a sloop of war from the enemy fleet⟩ **9** : DEPRIVE, DEFRAUD ⟨*cutting* him *out* of his share⟩ **10 a** : to separate (an animal) from a herd **b** : to thin out ⟨*cutting out* carrot seedlings⟩ **11** : DISCONNECT : detach and separate : remove from a series or circuit ⟨*cut out* a car from a train⟩ : make inoperative ⟨*cut out* the number 3 motor⟩ ~ *vi* **1** : to clear out : depart in haste ⟨the rest of the gang *cut out* for safety⟩ **2** : to withdraw from a card game as a result of another player's cutting in : cut too low to be one of a card-playing group **3** : to cease operating or operating effectively ⟨one of the airplane's engines *cut out*⟩ **4** : to swerve out of a traffic line

²cut out *adj* [fr. past part. of ¹*cut out*] : naturally fitted : endowed with suitable characteristics ⟨not *cut out* to be a lawyer⟩ ⟨*cut out* for stage work⟩

¹cutout \'ˌ=\ *n* -s [¹*cut out*] **1 a** : something cut out or off from something else: as (1) : a picture or figure (as of a doll, animal, or building) cut from or designed to be cut from paper or cardboard for children to play with — usu. used in pl. (2) : a shape or design (as a printed or lithographed representation of an advertised article) cut out of or designed to be cut out of cardboard, wood, or similar material and used as a holder or background for display of merchandise **b** (1) : a piece of painted scenery from which parts have been cut out so as to form apertures or outlines (2) : an aperture or an object thus formed **c** : a notable break designed in an otherwise continuing line or surface **d** : a flat pictorial presentation done in metal **e** : an animal cut out from a herd **2** : one that cuts out (as by interrupting, closing off, or conducting outward): as **a** : a device (as a switch, circuit breaker, valve, or clutch) for interrupting or closing a connection **b** : a valve in the exhaust pipe of an internal-combustion engine through which the exhaust gases may escape without going through the muffler **c** *also* **cutout block** *or* **cutout base** : a fuse block **3 a** : the act or an instance of cutting out **b** *Austral* : the end of sheep shearing

²cutout \"\ *adj* [partly fr. ¹*cut out*; partly fr. past part. of ¹*cut out*] **1** : having for its function cutting out ⟨a ~ valve⟩ **2** : made by cutting out : prepared for cutting out ⟨~ designs⟩ **3** : having parts cut out ⟨a ~ shoe⟩

cutout box *n* : a fireproof box or cabinet with hinged door or doors that houses the switches and fuses for the various leads of an electrical wiring system

cutout switch *n* : an electric switch that isolates a circuit or piece of equipment after the current has been interrupted by other means

cut over *vt* **1** : to cut most or all of the merchantable timber of (a forest) **2** : to open one set of connections on (a machine) and simultaneously to close another set so as not to interfere with normal functioning

¹cutover \'ˌ=ˌ=\ *n* -s [*cut over*] **1** : land the timber of which has been cut over **2** : a disengage in fencing executed over the adversary's foil followed immediately by a lunge **3** : a change from one procedure or service to another (as from direct to alternating current or from manual to dial telephones) : the period of such change

²cutover \"\ *adj* [fr. past part. of *cut over*] : having been cut over in lumbering ⟨a ~ area⟩

cut plug *n* : a cake of pressed tobacco used for chewing

cut point *n* : ²CUT 3i

cut proud *adj, of animals* : imperfectly castrated

cutpurse \'ˌ=\ *n* [ME *cutpurs*, fr. *cutten* to cut + *purs* purse] **1** : a thief who cuts purses from girdles **2** : PICKPOCKET

cut-rate \'ˌ=\ *adj* : marked by, offering, or making use of a reduced rate or price ⟨a *cut-rate* store⟩ ⟨*cut-rate* commodities⟩ ⟨*cut-rate* passengers⟩; *sometimes* : poor in quality : SECOND=

RATE, CHEAP, IMITATION ⟨a mountebank caesar, a *cut-rate* dictator⟩
cut round *vi* **:** to act demonstratively ⟨she shouted and laughed and *cut round*⟩
cuts *pres 3d sing of* CUT, *pl of* CUT
cut square *n* **:** a usu. nonadhesive postage stamp that has been cut square
cut stone *n* **:** stone dressed smooth with a chisel or saw
cut string *n* **:** OPEN STRING
cut sugar *n* **:** CUBE SUGAR
cut·ta·ble \ˈkəd·əbəl\ *adj* [ME, fr. *cutten* to cut + *-able*] **:** capable of being cut
cut·tage \ˈkəd·ij\ *n* -s **:** the practice or method of propagating plants by means of cuttings — compare GRAFTAGE
cut-tail \ˈ=,=\ *n* -s **:** a tall eucalypt (*Eucalyptus fastigiata*) of Australia
cut·ta·nee \kəˈtänē\ *n* -s [Hindi *kattānī*, fr. Ar *kattān* flax, linen] **:** piece goods of fine linen or of silk and cotton mixed made in India
cut·teau \,kəˈtō\ *n* -s [modif. of F *couteau* knife, fr. OF *coutel* — more at CUTLASS] *archaic* **:** a large knife used in carving or fighting
cut·ted \ˈkəd·əd, -d·ət\ *adj* [ME, fr. past part. of *cutten* to cut] **1** *now dial* **:** cut or cut short; *also* **:** having the skirts cut short **2** *now dial* **:** cut short in expression **:** CONCISE, CURT
¹**cut·ter** \ˈkəd·ə(r), ˈkətə-\ *n* -s *often attrib* [ME, fr. *cutten* to cut + *-er*] **1 :** one that cuts: **a :** one whose work is cutting or involves cutting: as (1) **:** one that castrates animals ⟨a horse ~⟩ (2) **:** one that cuts cloth or fur to measure in making garments (3) **:** one that cuts flat glass or grinds designs on glass (4) **:** an operator of a machine for pulverizing crushed ore samples into powder for chemical analysis (5) **:** a miner who uses hand tools to extract coal in underground areas (6) **:** one that cuts and shapes gems (7) **:** one that cuts or carves building and monumental stone (8) **:** one that edits individual motion-picture shots and assembles them into a finished motion picture **b** (1) **:** an instrument that cuts **:** a machine, machine part, or tool that cuts (2) **:** a rotary cutting tool with many cutting edges (3) **:** a device for vibrating a cutting stylus in exact accord with electrical input in disc recording (4) **:** the cutting stylus **:** the sapphire or diamond point of a stylus **2** *obs* **a :** BRAVO, BULLY **b :** CUTTHROAT, HIGHWAYMAN **3 a :** a cutting comment **b :** one that cuts an acquaintance **4 :** a fore tooth **:** INCISOR — distinguished from *grinder* **5 a :** a boat, usu. broad and square sterned, motor powered or rowed, carried aboard large ships for carrying stores or passengers **b :** a fore-and-aft rigged sailing boat with jib, forestaysail, and mainsail, the single mast now usu. stepped further aft than that of a sloop, the hull formerly being typically of extreme length and depth but now not usu. distinguished from that of a sloop **c :** a small armed boat in the government service, in the U.S. Coast Guard being over 83 feet in length and not classed as an auxiliary **d :** a boat carrying coaches, trainers, and officials at a boat race **6 :** a light sleigh drawn by one or two horses **7 :** a soft brick that can be cut or rubbed to shape **8 :** an inferior grade of carcass beef of which only the ribs and loins are sometimes marketed as cuts, the remainder being boned out for processing into beef products (as sausage) **9 :** a leaf of flue-cured tobacco pulled from the higher portion of the lower half of the stalk **10** *slang* **:** REVOLVER

cutter 5b

²**cut·ter** \ˈkütə(r), ˈkət-\ *vi* -ED/-ING/-S [prob. of imit. origin like MHG *kuteren* to giggle, coo] *dial Brit* **:** to talk confidentially or in a low voice
³**cut·ter** \ˈkəd·ə(r), ˈkətə-\ *vt* -ED/-ING/-S *usu cap* [*Cutter* (*number*)] **:** to assign a Cutter number to
cutter bar *n* [¹*cutter*] **1 :** a bar on a chucking lathe that fits a tool holder at one end and supports a cutting tool at the other **2 :** a bar with pointed guards along which the knife runs in a mowing machine or along which a sickle blade runs in a combine or binder
cutter bounce *n* [¹*cutter*] **:** a tendency of the recording cutter to move up and down continuously during disc recording and produce a groove varying in depth
cutter brig *n* [¹*cutter*] **:** a vessel rigged like a yawl but having square topsails on the mainmast
cutter classification *n, usu cap 1st C* [after Charles A. *Cutter* †1903 Amer. librarian] **:** EXPANSIVE CLASSIFICATION
cutterhead \ˈ==,=\ *n* [¹*cutter* + *head*] **:** any head (as on a lathe) for holding rotating or other cutting tools
cut·ter·man \ˈ==mən, -,man\ *n, pl* **cuttermen** [¹*cutter* + *man*] **1 :** an operator of a machine for cutting rolls of paper or cellophane to length **2 :** an operator of a power-driven press that cuts out envelope blanks from sheets of paper **3 :** an operator of a machine for cutting strands of smokeless powder into grains to produce explosives having uniform ballistic qualities **4 :** CLUTCHMAN
cut·ter number \ˈkəd·ə(r)-, ˈkətə(r)-\ *n, usu cap C* [after Charles A. *Cutter* †1903 Am. librarian] **:** a combination of characters representing an author's surname, composed of the initial letter or the first letters followed by numbers (as M62 = Milne, M64 = Milton), chosen to make the numerical order of the symbols correspond to the alphabetical order of the names, and used to arrange books in the same class alphabetically by authors
cut terrace *n, geol* **:** a bench or platform cut by waves at the base of a cliff — applied esp. after the bench has emerged
cutters *pl of* CUTTER, *pres 3d sing of* CUTTER
cutter yacht *n* [¹*cutter*] **:** a yacht built like a cutter
¹**cutthroat** \ˈ=,=\ *n* [¹*cut* + *throat*] **1 :** one likely to cut throats **:** MURDERER **:** a murderous character **:** a hired killer; *sometimes* **:** one fierce and unprincipled ⟨a band of ~*s* that terrorized the area⟩ **2** *or* **cutthroat finch :** a small African bird (*Amadina fasciata*) resembling a finch and having a deep crimson band about the throat and the rest of the plumage grayish brown marked with white **3** [by shortening] **:** CUTTHROAT TROUT **4 a :** any cutthroat game **b :** CUTTHROAT CONTRACT **5 :** straight razor **6 :** KOSHER HIDE
²**cutthroat** \"\ *adj* **1 :** having the characteristics of a cutthroat **:** MURDEROUS, CRUEL ⟨a ~ rogue⟩ **2 :** marked by fierce and unprincipled practices **:** MERCILESS, RUTHLESS ⟨~ competition⟩ **:** difficult to win, gain from, or compete against ⟨~ stocks⟩ **3 :** characterized by each player playing for himself rather than having a permanent partner — used esp. of partnership games adapted for three players ⟨~ bridge⟩ ⟨~ pinochle⟩
cutthroat contract *n* **1 :** contract bridge in which partnerships are determined by the bidding **2 :** any of various three-hand forms of contract bridge
cutthroat trout *n* **:** a large trout (*Salmo clarki*) native to cold lakes and rivers from northern California to southern Alaska, attaining a maximum weight of 65 pounds, and typically having numerous rounded black spots and a red mark under the jaw, a pattern subject to great variation in local races
cutties *pl of* CUTTY
cut time *n* **:** ²ALLA BREVE
¹**cutting** *n* -s [ME, fr. gerund of *cutten* to cut] **1 :** something cut or cut off, out, or over: as **a :** a section of a plant of stem, root, or leaf origin capable of sending out roots and used for propagation; *specif* **:** a stem cutting **b** (1) **:** a crop (as of indigo, grain, or hay) that has been cut esp. at a single mowing (2) **:** FELLING **c** *chiefly Brit* **:** an excavation or cut (as for a canal, railway, or highway) **d** *chiefly Brit* **:** a clipping (as from a newspaper or magazine) **e cuttings** *pl* **:** rock particles brought to the surface in well drilling **2** *obs* **:** TALLAGE **3 :** something made by cutting; *esp* **:** RECORDING
²**cutting** *adj* [ME, fr. pres. part. of *cutten*] **:** given to or designed for cutting: as **a :** EDGED, SHARP **:** made for cutting, severing, or dividing ⟨a ~ blade⟩ **b :** marked by sharp piercing cold ⟨the ~ winds of January⟩ **c :** marked by or given to penetrating sarcastic asperity wounding the feelings of others ⟨disagreeably arrogant or contemptuous in a ~ way —Edmund Wilson⟩ **d :** grown or cultivated for cutting ⟨flowers from the ~ garden⟩ **e :** SHARP, INTENSE **:** demanding attention ⟨a ~ pain⟩ ⟨a ~ whistle⟩ **syn** *see* INCISIVE
cutting angle *n* **:** the angle between the cutting face of a cutting tool and the surface of the work back of the tool
cutting board *n* **:** a board on which material (as leather or cloth) is laid for cutting
cutting fluid *n* **:** a fluid used esp. for cooling, lubrication, rust prevention, or chip flushing in a machine metal-cutting operation or for other special effects in other metal working operations
cutting grass *n* **1** *Austral* **:** any of several sedges of the genera *Gahnia* and *Cladium*; *esp* **:** a widely distributed sedge (*C. psittacorum*) with sharp-edged triquetrous leaves — called also *cutty grass* **2 :** a sedge of the genus *Scleria*; *esp* **:** a high-climbing tropical American sedge (*S. flagellum-nigrorum*) with cutting stems
cutting head *n* **:** CUTTER 1b(3)
cutting horse *n* **:** a quick light saddle horse trained for use in separating cattle from a herd — compare QUARTER HORSE
cut·ting·ly \-ŋlē, -li\ *adv* **:** in a cutting manner
cutting oil *n* **:** an oil or oily preparation used as a cutting fluid; *esp* **:** a water-insoluble oil (as a mineral oil containing a fatty oil) — compare SOLUBLE OIL 2
cutting pliers *n* **:** pliers that have a cutting blade on the side of the jaws
cutting press *n* -s **:** a device for trimming book edges and boards for covers
cutting rule *n* **:** a sharp steel rule slightly more than type-high to be placed in a form in a printing press or in a cutting and creasing machine for cutting paper or cardboard
cutting shoe *n* **:** a horseshoe having a narrow inner branch with nail holes at the toe only used for shoeing horses that interfere
cutting stage *or* **cutting-in stage** *n* **:** a stage rigged over the side of a whaler to support men engaged in cutting blubber
cutting stick *n* **:** a strip of wood countersunk in the table of a paper-cutting machine to receive the knife edge as it completes cutting the sheets
cutting stylus *n* **:** a cutting tool used in disc recording to engrave grooves in the original record
cutting torch *also* **cutting blowpipe** *n* **:** a blowpipe by which metal is preheated with a flame and then oxidized rapidly and removed by a jet of oxygen issuing centrally through the preheating flame
¹**cut·tle** \ˈkəd·ᵊl, ˈ|tᵊl\ *n* -s [ME *cotul, codull*, fr. OE *cudele*; akin to MHG *kutel* tripe, OHG *kiot* bag, pocket, OE *codd* husk, scrotum — more at COD] **:** CUTTLEFISH
²**cuttle** *n* -s [origin unknown] *obs* **:** BULLY, RUFFIAN
³**cut·tle** \ˈkəd·ᵊl, ˈ|tᵊl\ *vt* -ED/-ING/-S [fr. *cuttle*, n., "folded layer of cloth", of unknown origin] **:** to fold (cloth) in pleats after it has been finished
cuttlebone \ˈ==,=\ *n* [¹*cuttle* + *bone*] **:** the shell or bone of cuttlefishes used for making polishing powder or for hanging in bird cages to supply lime and salts
cuttlefish \ˈ==,=\ *n* [¹*cuttle* + *fish*] **:** a 10-armed marine cephalopod mollusk of the family Sepiidae (order Decapoda) differing from a squid in possessing a calcified internal shell; *broadly* **:** any of various other cephalopods (as the squids and octopuses) — see SEPIA
cut·tler \ˈkəd·ᵊlə(r), |t(ᵊ)l-\ *n* -s **:** one that cuttles
¹**cut·ty** \ˈkəd·ē, ˈkü|, |tē, -i\ *adj* [²*cut* + *-y*] *dial chiefly Brit* **:** SHORT, SHORTENED, STUBBY
²**cutty** \"\ *n* -ES **1** [short for *cutty spoon*] *chiefly Scot & Irish* **:** a short spoon **2** [short for *cutty pipe*] *chiefly Brit* **:** a short tobacco pipe **3** *chiefly Scot* **a :** a small or mischievous girl **b** [perh. fr. ²*cut* (trollop) + *-y*] **:** a woman of loose morals **:** BAGGAGE **4** *dial Brit* **:** WREN **5** *Scot* **:** HARE
cutty grass \"-\ *n* [by alter.] *Austral* **:** a cutting grass (*Cladium psittacorum*)

cuttlefish

cut·ty·hunk \ˈkəd·ē,həŋk\ *n* -s [fr. *Cuttyhunk* Island, Mass.] **:** a handlaid twisted linen fishing line suitable for deep-sea sport fish; *broadly* **:** any twisted linen fishing line
cutty sark *n* [¹*cutty*] **1** *chiefly Scot* **:** a short garment (as a shirt, slip, or skirt); *sometimes* **:** a woman's short undergarment **2** *chiefly Scot* **:** WOMAN, HUSSY
cutty stool *n* [¹*cutty*] **1** *chiefly Scot* **:** a low stool **2 :** a seat in old Scottish churches where offenders esp. against chastity were made to sit for public rebuke
cutty wren *n* [²*cutty*] *dial Brit* **:** WREN
¹**cut-under** \ˈ=ˈ==\ *adj* [fr. past part. of *cut* + *under* (adv.)] **:** so made that front wheels can go under the body in turning — used esp. of a carriage or wagon
²**cut-under** \ˈ=,==\ *n, pl* **cut-unders :** a cut-under vehicle
cut under *vt* **:** UNDERSELL
cut up *vt* **1 a :** to cut into parts or pieces ⟨*cut up* a steer⟩ ⟨*cut up* a log into timbers⟩ **b :** to inflict great loss on **:** cut to pieces ⟨the attackers being *cut up* by the stalwart defense⟩ **c :** to chop into parts **:** destroy the continuity of ⟨his sleep being *cut up* by the noise⟩ **d :** to wound deeply **:** GRIEVE, DISTRESS, HURT, CHAGRIN ⟨*cut up* by the adverse criticism⟩ ⟨*cut up* by her jilting him⟩ **2 :** to damage by or as if by cutting **:** GASH, SLASH ⟨the new lawn was *cut up* by the heavy truck⟩ **3 :** to sever at the bottom or root ⟨*cut up* weeds⟩ **4 :** to shape by cutting esp. after a pattern (as cloth) **5 :** to criticize adversely **:** subject to carping hostile criticism **:** CENSURE ⟨revenged himself by *cutting up* the author's next publication⟩ ⟨an underlying sentiment among lawyers against being *cut up* by outsiders —John Galsworthy⟩ **6 :** PERFORM, EXECUTE ⟨*cutting up* mischief⟩ **~** *vi* **1 :** to admit of being cut up ⟨this wood *cuts up* readily⟩ **2 :** to behave in a comic, boisterous, or unruly manner **:** show off **:** CLOWN **:** demand attention by unsanctioned behavior ⟨the average cowboy was a young fellow and he *cut up* plenty, meaning no harm to anyone —S.E.Fletcher⟩ ⟨she *cut up* with other men and after about a year ran off entirely —Danforth Ross⟩
cutup \ˈ=,=\ *n* -s [*cut up*] **:** one that cuts up and clowns or acts boisterously **:** SHOW-OFF
cut velvet *n* **:** a brocaded fabric with a background of chiffon or voile and a pattern of velvet
cutwater \ˈ=,==\ *n* **1 :** the forepart of a ship's stem — see SHIP illustration **2 :** a structure built around or upstream from a bridge pier with an angle or edge to resist better the action of water, ice, or flotsam **:** the sharpened end of the pier itself **3 :** BLACK SKIMMER
cutweed \ˈ=,=\ *n* **:** any of various marine algae: as **a :** BLADDER WRACK 1 **b :** SEA GIRDLE 2
cutwork \ˈ=,=\ *n* **1 :** an embroidery usu. on linen in which a design is outlined in buttonhole stitch and the intervening material is then cut away **2 :** a method of making lace by supporting it on a fabric foundation
cutworm \ˈ=,=\ *n* **:** any of certain smooth-bodied chiefly nocturnal caterpillars (family Noctuidae) that hide by day in soil and debris and feed at night on plant stems near ground level or climb into trees to feed on flower buds and that mature in midsummer into egg-laying moths
cu·vée *also* **cu·vee** \(ˈ)k(y)üˈvā, *F* küvā\ *n* -s [F *cuvée*, fr. *cuve* tub, vat] **1 :** bulk wine; *esp* **:** wine in casks or vats so blended by the vintner as to ensure uniformity and marketability — usu. used of French wine (as Burgundy) **2 :** a blend of still wines prepared for use in secondary fermentation in the production of champagne
cu·vette \(ˈ)k(y)üˈvet\ *n* -s [F, dim. of *cuve* tub, vat, fr. OF, fr. L *cupa* — more at HIVE] **1 :** a small often transparent vessel (as a tube or basin) that is used in scientific research **2 :** a carved semiprecious or precious stone with raised design (as a figure like a cameo) on the floor of a hollowed-out background
cu·vie·ri·an \(ˈ)k(y)üˈvirēən, ˌk(y)üvēˈir-\ *adj, usu cap* [Georges L. C. *Cuvier* †1832 Fr. naturalist + E *-ian*] **:** of or relating to Cuvier or his classification of animals
cuvierian organ \"-\ *or* **cu·vier's organ** \ˈk(y)üvē,āz-, küvyāz-\ *n, usu cap C* **:** a glandular tubule of uncertain function that can be extruded from the cloaca of certain holothurians
cuvierian vein *n, usu cap C* **:** CARDINAL VEIN
cuy·a·hoga red \(ˈ)kīˈhōgə, ˌkīəˈh|, kəˈh|, |ägə, |ōgə\ *n, often cap C* [prob. fr. *Cuyahoga* river or *Cuyahoga* county, Ohio] **:** OLD ROSELEAF
cuzco bark *var of* CUSCO BARK
cv *or* **cvt** *abbr* convertible
CV *abbr* **1** *often not cap* chief value **2** *often not cap* [It *colla voce*] with the voice **3** common version
c virus *n, cap C* **:** COXSACKIE VIRUS
cw *abbr* clockwise
CW *abbr* **1** chemical warfare **2** child welfare **3** churchwarden **4** cold water **5** commercial weight **6** continuous wave
cwm \ˈküm\ *n* -s [W, valley; akin to Gk *kymbē* drinking cup — more at HUMP] **:** CIRQUE 3
CWO *abbr* **1** cash with order **2** chief warrant officer **3** commissioned officer from warrant rank **4** commissioned warrant officer
cwt *abbr* [L *centum* + E *weight*] hundredweight
cx *abbr* convex
-cy \-sē,-si\ *n suffix* -ES [ME *-cie*, fr. OF, fr. LL *-cia*, fr. L *-tia*, partly fr. L *-t-* (as final stem consonant) + *-ia* -y, partly fr. Gk *-teia, -tia*, fr. *-t-* (as final stem consonant) + *-eia, -ia* -y] **:** act **:** action **:** practice **:** function ⟨pira*cy*⟩ ⟨prophe*cy*⟩ **:** rank **:** office ⟨baronet*cy*⟩ ⟨chaplain*cy*⟩ ⟨general*cy*⟩ **:** body **:** class ⟨aristocra*cy*⟩ **:** state **:** quality ⟨accura*cy*⟩ ⟨bankrupt*cy*⟩ ⟨normal*cy*⟩ — orig. and still often replacing a final *-t* or *-te* of the base noun or adjective
cy *abbr* **1** capacity **2** county **3** currency **4** cycle
cy·am·e·lide \sīˈamə,līd, -,ləd\ *n* -s [ISV *cya-* (fr. *cyan-*) + *mel*am + *-ide*] **:** a white amorphous compound $(CNOH)_x$ formed by the polymerization of cyanic acid
cy·an \ˈsī,an, -īən\ *n* -s [Gk *kyanos*] **:** any of a group of colors of greenish blue hue, medium lightness, and high saturation; *specif* **:** one of the subtractive primaries
cyan- *or* **cyano-** *comb form* [G *cyan-, zyan-*, fr. Gk *kyan-, kyano-*, fr. *kyanos* dark blue enamel, lapis lazuli] **1 :** dark blue **:** blue ⟨*cyano*type⟩ ⟨*cyan*osis⟩ **2 a :** cyanogen (sense 1) ⟨*cyan*amide⟩ ⟨*cyano*phoric⟩ — compare ISOCYAN- **b** *now usu cyano-* **:** containing cyanogen in place of hydrogen — in names of organic compounds ⟨*cyano*benzoic acid⟩ **c** *now usu cyano-* **:** containing cyanogen regarded as replacing hydroxyl or oxygen or as coordinated to a central atom — in names of inorganic acids and salts ⟨*cyano*auric acid⟩ ⟨*cyano*ferrate⟩ **3 :** cyanide ⟨*cyano*genetic⟩
-cy·an \ˈsī,an, -īən\ *n comb form* -s [Gk *kyanos*] **:** blue pigment ⟨algo*cyan*⟩ ⟨leuco*cyan*⟩
cy·an·a·mide \sīˈanəməd, -,mīd\ *also* **cy·an·a·mid** \-məd\ *n* -s [ISV *cyan-* + *amide, amid*; orig. formed as G *cyanamide*] **1 :** a colorless crystalline acidic compound $CNNH_2$ obtained by the action of ammonia gas on cyanogen chloride and by acidification of calcium cyanamide **2 :** CALCIUM CYANAMIDE — used esp. of the commercial products
cyanamide process *n* **:** a nitrogen-fixation process in which calcium cyanamide is formed from calcium carbide and nitrogen at high temperature
Cy·a·nan·throl \,sīəˈnan,thrōl, -rōl\ *trademark* — used for an acid dye; see DYE table I (under *Acid Blue 47*)
cy·a·nas·tra·ce·ae \,sīə,nasˈtrāsē,ē\ *n pl, cap* [NL, fr. *Cyanastrum*, type genus (fr. *cyan-* + L *astrum* star, fr. Gk *astron*) + *-aceae* — more at STAR] **:** a small family (order Xyridales) consisting of a single genus (*Cyanastrum*) of tropical African bog or aquatic herbs with tuberous rootstocks and paniculate or racemose flowers
cy·a·nate \ˈsīə,nāt, -,nət\ *n* -s [ISV *cyan-* + *-ate*; prob. orig. formed as G *zyanat*] **:** a salt or ester of cyanic acid
cyan blue *n* **:** a moderate bluish green to greenish blue that is paler than gendarme and less strong than parrot blue
cy·an·ea \sīˈanēə, -ān-\ *n, cap* [NL, fr. L, fem. of *cyaneus* dark blue, fr. Gk *kyaneos*, fr. *kyanos* dark blue enamel, lapis lazuli] **:** a genus of scyphozoan jellyfishes chiefly of temperate and arctic seas that includes the common red stinging jellyfish (*C. capillata*) of the No. Atlantic coast which reputedly attains a maximum diameter of over seven feet
cy·an·e·ous \-ēəs\ *or* **cy·an·e·an** \-ēən\ *adj* [*cyaneous* fr. L *cyaneus* dark blue; *cyanean* fr. L *cyaneus* + E *-an*] **1 :** CERULEAN **2 :** of a dark blue
cyanhydrin *var of* CYANOHYDRIN
cy·an·ic \(ˈ)sīˈanik, -nēk\ *adj* [ISV *cyan-* + *-ic*] **1 :** relating to or containing the cyanogen radical — used esp. of certain acids and their derivatives **2** [F *cyanique*, fr. *cyan-* + *-ique* -ic] **:** having a blue color; *specif* **:** having blue color in at least part of the flower — compare XANTHIC
cyanic acid *n* [ISV *cyanic* + *acid*; orig. formed as G *zyansäure*] **:** a strong acid HOCN or HNCO obtained by heating cyanuric acid as a mobile and very volatile liquid that is stable below 0° C but at ordinary temperature rapidly polymerizes to cyamelide and cyanuric acid — see ISOCYANIC ACID
cy·a·ni·da·tion \,sīənəˈdāshən, -īə,nīˈd-, (,)sī,anəˈd-\ *n* -s [*cyanide* + *-ation*] **:** the act or process of cyaniding; *esp* **:** CYANIDE PROCESS
¹**cy·a·nide** \ˈsīə,nīd, -,nəd\ *n* -s [ISV *cyan-* + *-ide*] **1 :** a compound of cyanogen usu. with a more electropositive element or radical **:** a salt or ester of hydrocyanic acid — see NITRILE **2 a :** POTASSIUM CYANIDE **b :** SODIUM CYANIDE
²**cy·a·nide** \-,nīd\ *vt* -ED/-ING/-S **:** to treat with a cyanide: as **a :** to subject to the cyanide process **b :** to treat (iron or steel) by immersion in molten cyanide in order to produce a hard surface by causing carbon and nitrogen to be taken up in a thin outer layer — see CASE HARDEN **c :** to fumigate (as greenhouses or flour) with hydrogen cyanide gas
cyanide mill *n* **:** a mill in which the cyanide process is used
cyanide process *n* **:** a method of extracting gold and silver from ores by treatment with a dilute solution of sodium cyanide or calcium cyanide, the dissolved metal being afterwards precipitated from the solution and cast into ingots
cy·an·i·din \sīˈanədən\ *n* -s [ISV *cyan-* + *-idin*] **:** an anthocyanidin occurring widely in the form of glycosides (as cyanin) and usu. obtained as the brown-red crystalline chloride $C_{15}H_{11}ClO_6$ (as by hydrolysis of cyanin or by synthesis from pyrocatechol derivatives)
cy·a·ni flower \ˈsīə,nī-\ *n* [NL *cyani*, fr. *cyanus* (specific epithet of *centaurea cyanus*), fr. Gk *kyanos* dark blue enamel] **:** the blue flower of a bachelor's button (*Centaurea cyanus*) used to color sachet powders
cy·a·nin \ˈsīənən\ *n* -s [*cyan-* + *-in*] **:** a violet crystalline anthocyanin pigment $C_{27}H_{30}O_{16}$ found esp. in the petals of the rose, cornflower, and dahlia; cyanidin 3,5-diglucoside
cy·a·nine \ˈsīə,nēn, -,nən\ *n* -s [ISV *cyan-* + *-ine*] **1** *or* **cyanine dye :** any of a large class of usu. unstable dyes that are important in photography for sensitizing film to light from the green, yellow, red, and infrared regions of the spectrum and that are characterized by a structure containing two heterocyclic rings derived from quinoline or a related base (as benzothiazole) and typically joined by one or more carbon atoms — see CARBOCYANINE **2 :** any of a class of cyanine dyes in which the two heterocyclic rings are joined by only one carbon atom (as in =CH—); *specif* **:** any such dye containing two quinoline rings — called also *monomethine, simple cyanine* **3** *also* **cy·a·nin** \-,nən\ *or* **cyanine blue a :** a blue cyanine dye (sense 2) $C_{29}H_{35}IN_2$ obtained from quinoline, lepidine, and isoamyl iodide; 1,1′-di-isoamyl-4,4′-cyanine iodide — called also *quinoline blue* **b :** a homologue (as the diethyl compound) of this dye — called also *quinoline blue*
cyanine blue *n* **1 a :** a strong blue that is greener and deeper than Sèvres and redder and darker than cerulean blue (sense 1b) — called also *Leitch's blue* **b :** a deep purplish blue that is less strong and very slightly redder than sapphire (sense 2a) and bluer and duller than hyacinth blue or Mazarine blue **2** *also* **cyanine :** a blue pigment consisting of a mixture of cobalt blue and Prussian blue — called also *Leitch's blue* **3 :** CYANINE 3
cy·a·nite \ˈsīə,nīt\ *also* **ky·a·nite** \ˈkī-\ *n* -s [G *zyanit*, fr. *zyan-* cyan- + *-it* -ite] **:** a mineral Al_2SiO_5 consisting of an aluminum silicate occurring commonly in blue thin-bladed triclinic crystals and crystalline aggregates — called also *disthene* — **cy·a·nit·ic** \ˌsīəˈnid·ik\ *adj*

cy·a·nize \'sīə,nīz\ *vt* -ED/-ING/-S [ISV *cyan-* + *-ize*] **:** to convert into cyanide

cyanmethemoglobin *var of* CYANOMETHEMOGLOBIN

cy·a·no \'sīə(,)nō\ *adj* [*cyan-*] **:** relating to or containing the cyanogen group — used esp. of organic compounds; compare CYAN- 2

cyano- — see CYAN-

cy·a·no·acetate \¦sīə(,)nō+\ *n* [*cyan-* + *acetate*] **:** a salt or ester of cyanoacetic acid

cy·a·no·acetic acid \¦sīə,nō+ . . -\ *n* [ISV *cyan-* + *acetic*] **:** a colorless hygroscopic crystalline acid $CNCH_2COOH$ obtained by treating chloroacetic acid with sodium cyanide and used in organic synthesis

cy·a·no·auric acid \¦==(,)=+ . . .-\ *n* [*cyan-* + *auric*] **:** a white crystalline acid $H[Au(CN)_4].3H_2O$ that on heating decomposes into gold, cyanogen, and hydrogen cyanide — called also *tetracyanoauric acid*

cy·a·no·benzene \¦sīə(,)nō+\ *n* [*cyan-* + *benzene*] **:** BENZONITRILE

cy·a·noch·ro·ite \,sīə'näkrə,wīt\ *n* -S [modif. of It *cianocrome* (fr. *ciano-* cyan- + *-crome*, fr. Gk *chrōma* color) + E *-ite* — more at CHROMATIC] **:** a mineral $K_2Cu(SO_4)_2.6H_2O$ consisting of a hydrous sulfate of potassium and copper found rarely at Vesuvius

cy·a·no·cit·ta \,sīə(,)nō'sidə\ *n, cap* [NL, fr. *cyan-* + Gk *kitta, kissa* jay; akin to OE *higora, higore* magpie, jay, MLG *heger* jay, OHG *hehara* jay, Skt *kiki, kikidīvi* blue jay] **:** a genus of American jays largely blue in color — see BLUE JAY 1

cy·a·no·cobalamin \¦sīə(,)nō+\ *n* -S [*cyan-* + *cobalamin*] **:** VITAMIN B_{12} (1)

cy·a·noc·o·rax \,sīə'näkə,raks\ *n, cap* [NL, fr. *cyan-* + LL *corax* raven, fr. Gk *korax* — more at RAVEN] **:** a genus of mostly green and yellow Central and So. American jays — see GREEN JAY

cy·a·no·crystallin \¦sīə(,)nō+\ *n* -S [*cyan-* + *crystallin*] **:** the blue pigment of the shells and eggs of lobsters and crabs turned red by acids or boiling water

cy·a·no·ethylation \"+\ *n* [*cyan-* + *ethylation*] **:** the introduction of the beta-cyano-ethyl group $CNCH_2CH_2-$ into a compound usu. by means of acrylonitrile ⟨~ of cotton⟩

cy·an·o·gen \sī'anəjən, -,jen\ *n* -S [F *cyanogène*, fr. *cyan-* + *-gène* -gen] **1 :** a univalent radical —CN present in hydrogen cyanide and other simple and complex cyanides (as ferricyanides) — called also *cyano group*; compare ISOCYANO **2 :** a colorless flammable poisonous gas $(CN)_2$ having an odor like that of peach leaves, variously formed (as by heating mercuric cyanide), and polymerizing readily — called also *dicyanogen*

cyanogen bromide *n* **:** a colorless crystalline poisonous compound $CNBr$ having a pungent irritating vapor and used in organic synthesis

cyanogen chloride *n* **:** a colorless very pungent poisonous low-boiling liquid compound $CNCl$ obtained by the action of chlorine on hydrocyanic acid or a cyanide and polymerizing on storage to cyanuric chloride

cy·a·no·genet·ic \¦sīə,nō+\ *also* **cy·a·no·gen·ic** \¦sīə,nō¦jenik\ *adj* [*cyan-* + *-genetic* or *-genic*] **:** capable of producing cyanide (as hydrogen cyanide) ⟨~ plants⟩ ⟨~ glycosides⟩

cyano group *n* **:** CYANOGEN 1

cy·a·no·guanidine \¦sīə(,)nō+\ *n* [*cyan-* + *guanidine*] **:** DICYANDIAMIDE

cy·a·no·hy·drin \,sīə(,)nō'hīdrən\ *also* **cy·an·hy·drin** \,sī,an'-, -'ən'-\ *n* -S [ISV *cyan-* + *-hydrin*] **:** any of a class of organic compounds containing both cyano and alcoholic hydroxyl groups usu. made by the addition of hydrogen cyanide to an aldehyde or ketone **:** a hydroxy nitrile; *esp* **:** an alpha-hydroxy nitrile

cy·a·no·maclurin \¦sīə(,)nō+\ *n* -S [*cyan-* + *maclurin*] **:** a colorless crystalline compound $C_{15}H_{12}O_6$ found in jackwood

cy·a·nom·e·ter \,sīə'nämədə(r)\ *n* -S [F *cyanomètre*, fr. *cyan-* + *-mètre* -meter] **1 :** an instrument for measuring degrees of blueness (as of the sky) **2 :** an apparatus for determining cyanogen or a cyanide

cy·a·no·methemoglobin \¦sīə,nō+\ *or* **cy·an·methemo·globin** \¦sī,an, -ən+\ *n* -S [ISV *cyan-* + *methemoglobin*; orig. formed as G *zyanmethämoglobin*] **:** a bright red crystalline compound formed by the action of hydrogen cyanide on methemoglobin in the cold or on oxyhemoglobin at body temperature

cy·a·no·met·ric \¦sīə(,)nō¦me·trik\ *adj* **:** of or relating to cyanometry

cy·a·nom·e·try \,sīə'nämə·trē\ *n* -ES **1 :** measurement of the blueness of light **2 :** determination of or with cyanogen or a cyanide **:** the use of the cyanometer

cy·a·nope \'sīə,nōp\ *n* -S [Gk *kyanōpēs* dark-eyed, fr. *kyan-* cyan- + *-opēs* (fr. *ōp-, ōps* eye, face) — more at EYE] **:** a person with fair hair and brown eyes — compare GLAUCOPE

cy·an·o·phile \sī'anə,fīl\ *also* **cy·an·o·phil** \-,fil\ *n* -S [ISV, back-formation fr. *cyanophilous*] **:** a cyanophilous tissue element

cy·a·noph·i·lous \,sīə¦näfələs\ *also* **cy·a·no·phil·ic** \¦sīanō-¦filik\ *adj* [ISV *cyan-* + *-philous, -philic*; orig. formed as G *zyanophil*] **:** having an affinity for blue or green dyes — used of cells or tissues

cy·a·no·phor·ic \¦sīə,nō¦fȯrik\ *adj* [*cyan-* + *-phore* + *-ic*] **:** CYANOGENETIC

cy·a·no·phy·ce·ae \,sīə,nō'fīsē,ē, -fis-\ [NL, fr. *cyan-* + *-phyceae*] *syn of* MYXOPHYCEAE

[1]cy·a·no·phy·cean \¦sīə,nō¦fishən\ *also* **cy·a·no·phy·ceous** \-shəs\ *adj* [NL *Cyanophyceae* + E *-an* or *-ous*] **:** MYXOPHYCEAN

[2]cyanophycean \"\ *n* -S **:** any member of the Myxophyceae **:** BLUE-GREEN ALGA

cy·a·no·phy·cin \,sīə,nō'fīs°n\ *n* -S [ISV *cyanophyc-* (fr. NL *Cyanophyceae*) + *-in*] **:** granular protein material forming food reserve in the cells of blue-green algae and concentrated esp. in the peripheral region of the cell

cy·a·noph·y·ta \,sīə'näfədə\ *n pl, cap* [NL, fr. *cyan-* + *-phyta*] **:** a division or other category of lower plants coextensive with the class Myxophyceae

cy·a·no·platinite \¦sīə(,)nō+\ *n* -S [*cyan-* + *platinite*] **:** PLATINOCYANIDE

cy·a·nose \'sīə,nōs *also* -ōz\ *also* **cy·an·o·site** \sī'anə,sīt\ *n* -S [*cyanose* fr. F, fr. *cyan-* + *-ose*; *cyanosite* fr. *cyanose* + *-ite*] **:** CHALCANTHITE

cy·a·nosed \'sīə,nōzd, -ōst\ *adj* [NL *cyanosis* + E *-ed*] **:** affected with cyanosis

cy·a·no·sis \,sīə'nōsəs\ *n, pl* **cyano·ses** \-ō,sēz\ [NL, fr. Gk *kyanōsis* dark blue color, fr. *kyan-* cyan- + *-ōsis* -osis] **:** a dusky bluish or purplish discoloration of the skin or mucous membranes due to deficient oxygenation of the blood either locally (as in certain vasomotor disturbances) or systemically (as in some congenital heart defects)

cy·a·no·spi·za \,sīə,nō'spīzə\ [NL, fr. *cyan-* + Gk *spiza* chaffinch] *syn of* PASSERINA

cy·a·not·ic \,sīə¦nädik\ *adj* [fr. NL *cyanosis*, after such pairs as NL *chlorosis*: E *chlorotic*] **:** relating to or associated with cyanosis ⟨~ heart disease⟩ **:** CYANOSED

cy·a·not·ri·chite \,sīə'nä·trə,kīt\ *n* -S [G *zyanotrichit*, fr. *zyan-* cyan- + Gk *trich-, thrix* hair + G *-it* -ite — more at TRICHINA] **:** a mineral $Cu_4Al_2(SO_4)(OH)_{12}.2H_2O$ occurring as a hydrous basic copper aluminum sulfate in bright blue fibrous forms

cy·an·o·type \sī'anə,tīp\ *n* [*cyan-* + *-type*] **:** BLUEPRINT

cyans *pl of* CYAN

-cyans *pl of* -CYAN

cy·a·nu·ra·mide \,sīə'n(y)u̇rəl,mīd, (,)sī,anyə'ral, |,məd\ *n* -S [G *zyanuramid*, fr. *zyanursäure* cyanuric acid + *amid* amide] **:** MELAMINE

cy·a·nu·rate \,sīə'n(y)u̇,rāt, -,rət\ *n* -S [ISV *cyanuric* + *-ate*] **:** a salt or ester of cyanuric acid

cy·an·u·ret \sī'anyə,ret\ *n* -S [*cyan-* + *-uret*] **:** CYANIDE

cy·a·nu·ric \¦sīə¦n(y)u̇rik\ *adj* [ISV *cyan-* + L *urea* + ISV *-ic* — more at UREA] **:** relating to derivatives of symmetrical triazine formed by polymerization of certain cyanogen compounds (as cyanic acid and cyanogen chloride)

cyanuric acid *n* [part trans. of G *zyanursäure*, fr. *zyanur-* (fr. *zyan-* cyan- + NL *urea*) + *säure* acid] **:** a crystalline weak acid $C_3N_3(OH)_3$ usu. made by hydrolysis of cyanuric chloride and yielding cyanic acid when heated; *s*-triazine-2,4,6-triol

cyanuric chloride *n* **:** a crystalline compound $C_3N_3Cl_3$ made by polymerization of cyanogen chloride and used in organic synthesis; 2,4,6-trichloro-*s*-triazine

cy·aph·e·nine \sī'afə,nēn, -,nən\ *n* -S [ISV *cyan-* + *phenine*; orig. formed as G *zyaphenin*] **:** a white crystalline compound $C_{21}H_{15}N_3$ formed esp. by the polymerization of benzonitrile; 2,4,6-triphenyl-*s*-triazine

cyath- *or* **cyatho-** *comb form* [NL, fr. Gk *kyath-, kyatho-*, fr. *kyathos* — more at CYATHUS] **:** cup **:** cup-shaped ⟨*Cyathaspis*⟩ ⟨*cyatholith*⟩

cy·a·thas·pis \,sīə'thaspəs\ *n, cap* [NL, fr. *cyath-* + *-aspis*] **:** a genus of small Upper Silurian ostracoderms having the dorsal shield composed of a median plate and three smaller pieces

cy·ath·ea \sī'athēə\ *n, cap* [NL, irreg. fr. Gk *kyatheion* little cup, dim. of *kyathos* cup — more at CYATHUS] **:** the type genus of the family Cyatheaceae

cy·ath·e·a·ce·ae \(,)sī,athē'āsē,ē\ *n pl, cap* [NL, fr. *Cyathea*, type genus + *-aceae*] **:** a family of tropical tree ferns having the sporangia crowded, stalked, and either naked or more often with a cup-shaped indusium — compare SILVER TREE FERN — **cy·ath·e·a·ceous** \(')sī¦athē¦āshəs\ *adj*

cy·ath·i·form \sī'athə,fȯrm\ *adj* [ISV *cyath-* + *-iform*; prob. orig. formed as F *cyathiforme*] **:** shaped like a cup

cy·ath·i·um \sī'athēəm\ *n, pl* **cyath·ia** \-ēə\ [NL, fr. Gk *kyathion, kyatheion*, dim. of *kyathos* cup] **:** an inflorescence consisting of a cuplike involucre with the flowers arising from its base (as in the poinsettia)

cy·a·tho·phyl·li·dae \,sīə,thō'filə,dē\ *n pl, cap* [NL, fr. *Cyathophyllum*, type genus (fr. *cyath-* + *-phyllum*) + *-idae*] **:** a family of Paleozoic tetracorals esp. abundant in the Devonian — **cy·a·tho·phyl·loid** \¦sīə,thō¦fi,lȯid\ *adj or n*

cy·a·tho·zooid \¦sīə(,)thō+\ *n* [*cyath-* + *zooid*] **:** the imperfect primary zooid of certain compound tunicates (as those of the genus *Pyrosoma*) from which the secondary zooids bud

cy·a·thus \'sīəthəs\ *n* [L & Gk; L *cyathus*, fr. Gk *kyathos*; akin to Gk *koilos* hollow — more at CAVE] **1** *or* **ky·a·thos** \'kīə,thäs\ *pl* **cya·thi** \-,thī\ *or* **kya·thoi** \-,thȯi\ **:** a long-handled cup or earthenware ladle used esp. in ancient Greece for filling drinking cups with wine **2** *pl* **cyathi** [NL, fr. L] **:** any small cup-shaped cavity or organ of a plant; *esp* **:** CUPULE 1c **3** *cap* [NL, fr. L] **:** a genus of bird's-nest fungi having the fruit body narrowed at the base and flaring at the top — compare NIDULARIACEAE

cy·ber·net·ic \,sībə(r)¦ned·ik *sometimes* -nē- — *see* CYBERNETICS\ *adj* [back-formation fr. *cybernetics*] **:** of, relating to, or involving cybernetics — **cy·ber·net·i·cal** \-ikəl\ *adj* — **cy·ber·net·i·cal·ly** \-ik(ə)lē\ *adv*

cy·ber·net·i·cist \,sībə(r)'ned·əsəst *sometimes* -nē-\ *also* **cy·ber·ne·ti·cian** \-)nə'tishən\ *n* -S **:** a specialist in cybernetics

cy·ber·net·ics \,sībə(r)'ned·iks; *sometimes* -nē-, *a pronunc advocated by the introducer of the term*\ *n pl but sing or pl in constr* [Gk *kybernētēs* steersman, governor (fr. *kybernan* to steer) + E *-ics* — more at GOVERN] **:** the comparative study of the automatic control system formed by the nervous system and brain and by mechanical-electrical communication systems and devices (as computers or thermostats)

cy·bis·tax \sə'bi,staks, 'sibə,s-\ *n, cap* [NL] **:** a genus of tropical American trees (family Bignoniaceae) having digitate leaves with five to nine leaflets and greenish or yellow flowers in terminal clusters

cy·bis·ter \sə'bistə(r), 'sibəs-\ *n, cap* [NL, modif. of Gk *kybistētēr* diver, tumbler, fr. *kybistan* to turn a somersault; prob. akin to Gk *kyphos* bent — more at CYPHELLA] **:** a genus of large diving beetles destructive to young fishes in hatcheries

cyb·o·tac·tic \¦sibə¦taktik\ *adj* [fr. NL *cybotaxis*, after such pairs as NL *taxis*: E *tactic*] **:** of or relating to cybotaxis

cyb·o·tax·is \,sibə'taksəs\ *n, pl* **cybotax·es** \-k(,)sēz\ [NL, fr. *cybo-* (fr. Gk *kybos* cube) + *-taxis* — more at CUBE] **:** a transient orientation of molecules in a liquid revealed by X-ray diffraction effects analogous to those produced by crystals — compare LIQUID CRYSTAL

cyc *abbr* **1** cycle; cycling **2** cyclopedia **3** cyclorama

cy·cad \'sīkəd, -,kad\ *n* -S [NL *Cycad-, Cycas* — more at CYCAS] **1 :** any plant of the family Cycadaceae **2 :** a fossil cycadean trunk

cy·ca·da·ce·ae \,sīkə'dāsē,ē, ,sik-\ *n pl, cap* [NL, fr. *Cycad-, Cycas*, type genus + *-aceae*] **:** a family of very ancient tropical gymnospermous plants (order Cycadales) resembling palms but showing a close relationship to ferns and lower groups in that fertilization takes place by means of spermatozoids — **cy·ca·da·ceous** \¦==¦dāshəs\ *adj*

cy·ca·da·les \,=='dā(,)lēz\ *n pl, cap* [NL, fr. *Cycad-, Cycas* + *-ales*] **:** an order of gymnospermous plants abundant in the Mesozoic but now reduced to a few localized and widely scattered tropical forms that have an unbranched trunk which is tall and arborescent or squat and tuberous with a large pith and starchy cortex and that bears a terminal crown of long pinnate leaves together with one or more very large cones — see CYCADACEAE

cy·ca·de·an \¦sīkə¦dēən, ¦sik-\ *adj* [*cycad* + *-ean*] **:** of, relating to, or characteristic of the order Cycadales

cy·cad·e·oid \sī'kadē,ȯid, sə'-\ *adj* [NL *Cycadeoidea*] **:** resembling or related to a cycad or a plant of the fossil genus *Cycadeoidea*

cy·cad·e·oi·dea \=,=ē'ȯidēə\ *n, cap* [NL, fr. *Cycadeae* (subfamily of *Cycadaceae*) (formerly used as syn. of *Cycadaceae*) (fr. *Cycad-, Cycas*, type genus + *-eae*) + *-oidea*] **:** a genus of fossil gymnospermous plants of the Mesozoic era (family Bennettitaceae) having short stout trunks clothed in a dense armor of spirally arranged leaf bases and topped by a crown of fronds

cycad family *or* **cycas family** *n* **:** CYCADACEAE

cycad fern *n* **:** any fossil plant of the order Cycadofilicales

cy·cad·i·form \sī'kadə,fȯrm, sə'-\ *adj* [*cycad* + *-iform*] **:** having the form of a cycad

cy·ca·do·filicales \¦sīkə(,)dō, ¦sik-+\ *n pl, cap* [NL, fr. *cycado-* (fr. *Cycadales*) + *Filicales*] **:** an order of fossil gymnospermous trees or climbing plants first known from the Devonian that had foliage like that of ferns, definite seeds borne on modified leaves rather than in strobili or cones, and secondary wood like the higher gymnosperms but primary wood resembling that of ferns — see SEED FERN

cy·ca·do·filices \"+\ [NL, fr. *cycado-* (fr. *Cycadales*) + *Filices*] *syn of* CYCADOFILICALES

cy·ca·doph·y·ta \sīkə'däfədə, ,sik-\ [NL *cycado-* (fr. *Cycadales*) + *-phyta*] *syn of* CYCADOPHYTAE

cy·ca·doph·y·tae \,=='fə,tē\ *n pl, cap* [NL, fr. *cycado-* (fr. *Cycadales*) + *-phytae* (pl. fem. equivalent of *-phyta*)] **:** a subclass of Gymnospermae comprising unbranched plants with pinnate leaves, large pith, little xylem, and a thick cortex and including the surviving order Cycadales and the extinct orders Bennettitales and Cycadofilicales — compare CONIFEROPHYTAE — **cy·cad·o·phyte** \sī'kadə,fīt, sə'-\ *n* -S — **cy·cad·o·phyt·ic** \(')sī¦kadə¦fid·ik, sə¦-\ *adj*

cy·cas \'sī,kas, -,kəs\ *n, cap* [NL, perh. fr. Gk *kykas*, MS var. of *koïkas*, acc. pl. of *koïx* doom palm (*Hyphaene thebaica*)] **:** a genus (the type of the family Cycadaceae) of widely distributed tropical trees having pinnate leaves and columnar stems covered with the persisting bases of the old leaves — see SAGO PALM

cycl- *or* **cyclo-** *comb form* [NL *cyclo-*, fr. Gk *kykl-, kyklo-*, fr. *kyklos* circle, wheel — more at WHEEL] **1 :** circle **:** ring ⟨*cyclometer*⟩ ⟨*cyclotron*⟩ **2 :** cycle ⟨*cyclographer*⟩ **3 :** cyclic compound ⟨*cycloheptane*⟩ ⟨*cycloolefin*⟩ **4 :** ciliary body (of the eye) ⟨*cyclodialysis*⟩ ⟨*cyclitis*⟩

cy·clad·ic \sə'kladik, (')sī¦k-\ *adj, usu cap* [*Cyclades*, Greek islands in the Aegean sea (fr. L, fr. Gk *Kyklades*) + E *-ic*] **:** of or relating to the Cyclades islands; *specif* **:** of or relating to the pre-Mycenaean culture that prevailed there — compare MINOAN

cyc·la·mate \'siklə,māt, 'sik-\ *n* -S [*cyclohexyl-sulfamate*] **:** an artificially prepared sodium or calcium salt of an acid $C_6H_{11}NHSO_3H$ used esp. formerly as a sweetener but largely discontinued because of the possibly harmful effects of its metabolic breakdown product cyclohexylamine

cy·cla·men \'sīkləmən *also* 'sik-\ *n* [NL, fr. Gk *kyklaminos, kyklamis* (*Cyclamen graecum*), prob. fr. *kyklos* circle, wheel — more at WHEEL] **1** *cap* **:** a small genus of widely cultivated Eurasian plants (family Primulaceae) having centrally depressed rounded tubers, basal leaves, and nodding white, pink, or purplish flowers with reflexed petals **2** -S **a :** a plant or flower of the genus *Cyclamen* **b :** SHOOTING STAR **3** -S **:** a very dark reddish purple

cyclamen aldehyde *n* **:** a colorless liquid aldehyde $C_3H_7C_6H_4CH_2CH(CH_3)CHO$ having a lily-of-the-valley odor, made synthetically, and used in perfumes esp. for soap; *p*-isopropyl-α-methyl-hydrocinnamaldehyde

cyclamen mite *n* **:** a minute translucent greenish mite (*Steneotarsonemus pallidus*) living on the leaves of the cyclamen and other greenhouse plants and in western No. America being a serious pest of strawberries that causes general dwarfing and death of flowers and fruit

cy·cla·min \'==mən\ *n* -S [It *ciclamina*, blend of *ciclamino* cyclamen (fr. NL *cyclamin-, cyclamen*) and *-ina* -in] **:** a white amorphous saponin constituting the active principle of the root of a cyclamen (*Cyclamen europaeum*) and formerly used as an emetic and purgative

cyc·la·mine \'==,mēn, -,mən\ *n* -S [*cycl-* + *-amine*] **:** a cyclic nitrogenous base (as pyrrole)

cyc·lam·mo·ni·um \,siklə'mōnēəm, -nyəm\ *n* [*cycl-* + *ammonium*] **:** the substituted ammonium radical corresponding to a cyclamine

cyc·lane \'si,klān, 'sī,-\ *n* -S [ISV *cycl-* + *-ane*] **:** CYCLOPARAFFIN

cyc·la·nor·bi·dae \,siklə'nȯrbə,dē, ,sīk-\ *n pl, cap* [NL, fr. *Cyclanorbis*, type genus + *-idae*] *in some classifications* **:** a small family of primitive African and Asiatic turtles related to and commonly included in Trionychidae

cyc·lan·tha·ce·ae \,si,klan'thāsē,ē, ,sī-\ *n pl, cap* [NL, fr. *Cyclanthus*, type genus + *-aceae*] **:** a small family of plants (order Cyclanthales) that resemble palms and have monoecious flowers in dense alternating spirals or whorls around a fleshy spadix — **cyc·lan·tha·ceous** \¦=,=¦thāshəs\ *adj*

cyc·lan·tha·les \-ā(,)lēz\ *n pl, cap* [NL, fr. *Cyclanthus* + *-ales*] **:** an order of tropical monocotyledonous plants that is coextensive with the family Cyclanthaceae and is sometimes included in the order Palmales

cy·clan·thus \sə'klan(t)thəs, sī'-\ *n* [NL, fr. *cycl-* + *-anthus*] **1** *cap* **:** a small genus of tropical American acaulescent plants (family Cyclanthaceae) having milky juice, equitant reedlike leaves, and unisexual flowers **2** *pl* **cyclan·thi** \-n,thī\ **:** any plant of the genus *Cyclanthus*

cy·clar \'sīk(ə)lə(r), 'siklə-\ *adj* [[1]*cycle* + *-ar*] **:** CYCLIC

cyc·lar·thro·sis \,si,klär'thrōsəs, ,sī-\ *n, pl* **cyclarthro·ses** \-ō,sēz\ [NL, fr. *cycl-* + *arthrosis*] **:** PIVOT JOINT

[1]cyc·las \'sikləs\ *n, pl* **cyc·lades** \-lə,dēz\ [ML, fr. L, woman's robe with a border around it, fr. Gk *kyklas*, fr. *kyklas*, adj., encircling, fr. *kyklos* circle, wheel — more at WHEEL] **1 :** a sleeveless tunic shorter in front than behind and worn esp. in the 14th century by knights over their armor **2 :** a full-length garment similar to a cyclas but worn by women

[2]cyclas \"\ [NL, fr. L] *syn of* SPHAERIUM

[1]cy·cle \'sīkəl, *in sense 6* " *or* 'sik-\ *n* -S *often attrib* [F or LL; F *cycle*, fr. LL *cyclus*, fr. Gk *kyklos* ring, circle, cycle, wheel — more at WHEEL] **1 :** an interval of time during which one sequence of a regularly recurring succession of events or phenomena is completed: as **a :** a recurrent period of time that is used as a basis of chronology usu. beginning and ending by occurrence of the same natural phenomenon (as the passage of a comet) **b :** a period of time during which something becomes established, reaches a peak, and declines ⟨the early mining ~s of gold and silver in the west⟩ **2 a :** a recurrent sequence of events which occur in such order that the last event of one sequence immediately precedes the recurrence of the first event in a new series — compare LIFE CYCLE **b :** a complete course of operations or events returning upon itself and restoring the original state ⟨the common ~ of birth, growth, senescence, and death —T.C.Schneirla & Gerard Piel⟩ ⟨the sporogonic ~ of the malaria mosquito⟩ **c** (1) **:** one complete performance of a vibration, electric oscillation, current alternation, or other periodic process (2) **:** CYCLES PER SECOND — compare HERTZ **d :** a series of operations at the end of which a working substance is returned to its original state usu. with accompanying conversion of heat into mechanical work or vice versa **e :** the sequence of activities repeated in each performance of an operation or task — used chiefly in connection with time and motion studies **f :** BUSINESS CYCLE **g :** a series of changes usu. but not necessarily leading back to the starting point ⟨the ~ of nitrogen in the living world⟩ ⟨the geochemical ~ of an element passing through various processes which may lead to repetition⟩ **h :** a regular periodic fluctuation in the abundance of certain kinds of animals **3 :** a circular or spiral arrangement: as **a** (1) **:** an imaginary circle or orbit in the heavens (2) **:** CELESTIAL SPHERE **b** (1) *in phyllotaxy* **:** a section or turn of the spiral between one member and the next immediately over or below it (2) **:** a whorl of floral leaves **c :** RING 22 **d :** a set of septa or tentacles of like age in a coral or sea anemone **e :** a set of regularly recurring values of a periodic variable **4 :** a long period of time **:** AGE ⟨better fifty years of Europe than a ~ of Cathay —Alfred Tennyson⟩ **5 a :** a group or series of works (as poems, plays, novels, or songs) treating the same theme ⟨a sonnet ~⟩ **b :** the complete series of poetic or prose narratives dealing typically with the exploits of a legendary hero and his followers ⟨the Arthurian ~⟩ **6** [by shortening] **a :** BICYCLE **b :** TRICYCLE **c :** MOTORCYCLE **7 :** the series of a single, double, triple, and home run hit by one player during one baseball game ⟨hit for the ~⟩

[2]cy·cle \'sīkəl, *in sense 2* " *or* 'sik-\ *vb* **cycled; cycled; cycling** \-k(ə)liŋ\ **cycles** *vi* **1 a :** to pass through a cycle of changes ⟨the machine automatically ~s —*Industrial Equipment News*⟩ **b :** to recur in cycles ⟨prosperity goes *cycling* on from generation to generation⟩ **2 :** to ride a cycle (as a bicycle) ~ *vt* **:** to cause to go through a cycle

cycle billing *n* **:** a system of billing in which a proportionate fraction of the customers of an organization are billed on each working day of the month to equalize the work involved

cy·cle·car \'sīkəl,=, 'sik-\ *n* [*motorcycle* + *car*] **:** a small 3-wheeled or 4-wheeled motor-driven vehicle

cycle form *n* **:** CYCLICAL FORM

cy·clene \'si,klēn, 'si,-\ *n* -S [ISV *cycl-* + *-ene*] **1 :** CYCLOOLEFIN **2 :** TRICYCLENE

cycle of erosion : the sequence of changes in a landscape from the start of its erosion by running water, waves and currents, or glaciers until it has been reduced to the baselevel of erosion which limits the activity of the agents concerned — called also *geomorphic cycle*

cycle of indiction : INDICTION 1a

cycle of the sun *or* **cycle of sundays** *usu cap Sundays* **:** a period of 28 years at the end of which the days of the month according to the Julian calendar return to the same days of the week — called also *solar cycle*

cy·cler \'sīk(ə)lə(r), 'sik-\ *n* -S **:** one that rides or travels on a cycle

cycles *pl of* CYCLE, *pres 3d sing of* CYCLE

cycles per second : the number of recurrences of a periodic vibration or other wave-form activity occurring in the course of a second

cycle time *n* **:** the time required to complete a cycle — used esp. in connection with time and motion studies

cycli *pl of* CYCLUS

cy·cli·ae \'siklē,ē, 'sik-\ *n pl, cap* [NL, fr. Gk *kykliai*, fem. pl. of *kyklios* round, fr. *kyklos* circle, wheel — more at WHEEL] *in some classifications* **:** a subclass of Cyclostomi coextensive with the genus *Palaeospondylus*

cy·li·an \'siklēən\ *adj* [Gk *kyklios* round, cyclic + E *-an*] **:** CYCLIC

[1]cy·clic \'sīklik, -lēk *also* 'sik-\ *adj* [F or L; F *cyclique*, fr. L *cyclicus*, fr. Gk *kyklikos*, fr. *kyklos* cycle, circle + *-ikos* -ic — more at WHEEL] **1 a :** of, relating to, or belonging to a cycle **b :** moving in cycles ⟨~ time⟩ **c :** being a fate of the individual life ⟨the ~ fate of the individual life —H.G.Wells⟩ **2 a :** of, belonging to, or relating to a cycle of writings ⟨a ~ narrative⟩ **b :** being concerned with the production of cyclic writings ⟨a ~ poet⟩ **3** *classical prosody* **:** being of shortened time value in verse analyzed as logaoedic in rhythm — used esp. of a dactylic foot; compare TROCHAIC DACTYL **4** *of a plant* **:** having the floral leaves arranged in cycles **5 a :** recurrent at definite or stated periods ⟨~ phenomena⟩ ⟨~ breathing⟩ **b** *of animals* **:** subject to cycle (sense 2h) — compare IRRUPTIVE **6** : of, relating to, or characterized by a ring of atoms ⟨benzene and pyridine are ~ compounds⟩ — see CARBOCYCLIC, HETEROCYCLIC, ISOCYCLIC

²cyclic \"\ *n* -s : a cyclic chemical compound

cy·cli·cal \'sīklәkәl, 'sik-, -lēk-\ *adj* [F *cyclique* or L *cyclicus* + E *-al*] **1** : CYCLIC **2 a** : related to or caused by a business cycle ⟨~ unemployment⟩ ⟨a period of ~ expansion⟩ **b** : relating to or esp. subject to the influence of recurring economic fluctuations ⟨a ~ industry⟩

cyclical form *n* **1** : musical composition consisting of several movements (as a sonata, suite, or symphony) **2** : musical composition that employs the same theme in several movements

cy·cli·cal·i·ty \,sīklә'kalәd-ē, ,sik-\ *n* -ES : CYCLICITY

cy·cli·cal·ly \'sīklәk(ә)lē, 'sik-, -lēk-, -)li\ *adv* : in a cyclical manner

cyclic chorus *n* : the chorus that sang and danced to the dithyrambic odes round the altar of Dionysus in ancient Greece

cyclic curve *n* **1 a** : the intersection of a sphere and a quadric surface — called also *spherical cyclic curve* **b** : the stereographic projection of such an intersection — called also *plane cyclic curve* **2** : a curve (as a cycloid or epicycloid) generated by any point on a circular disk as it rolls along a given curve

cyclic function *n* : a mathematical function that changes in value by an additive constant whenever its variable arguments pass continuously through a cycle of values

cy·cli·cism \'sīklә,sizәm, 'sik-\ *n* -s : CYCLICITY

cy·clic·i·ty \sī'klisәd-ē, sә'k\ *n* -ES : the quality or state of being cyclic ⟨an absolute ~ with which men go down into extinction every generation, to be replaced by a new crop of germ cell bearing tyros —E.R.Bentley⟩

cy·cli·cize \'sīklә,sīz, 'sik-\ *vt* -ED/-ING/-S : CYCLIZE

cy·cli·cly *adv* : in a cyclic manner

cyclic permutation *n* : a permutation in which a set of symbols is rearranged by putting the first for the last (as in *ABC, BCA, CAB, ABC*) or vice versa

cyclic-pitch control *n* : control of the lateral and longitudinal motion of a helicopter by means of an adjustable device that varies the pitch of the rotor blades during each rotation cycle so that there can be forward, backward, or lateral motion

cyclic poets *n pl* **1** : the poets who followed Homer and composed epics on the Trojan war and its heroes **2** : a series or coterie of poets writing on one subject

cyclic rate *n* : the rate of fire of an automatic weapon usu. expressed as number of rounds fired per minute

cyclics *pl of* CYCLIC

cyclic salt *n* : sodium chloride and other soluble salts carried inland by wind from a body of salt water and ultimately returned to the sea by rivers

cyclic train *n* : a system of gearing in which at least one axis has itself a motion of rotation about a fixed axis (as an epicyclic gear train)

cycling *n* -s **1** : the action or practice of riding a cycle (as a bicycle) **2** : cyclic movement; *esp* : movement through a circular course **3** : the cyclic variation due to the lag behind the action of a device (as a thermostat) that is intended to maintain constant automatic control

cy·clist \'sīk(ә)lәst, 'sik-\ *n* -s : one that rides a cycle ⟨lodging facilities . . . are available to all ~s, as to all other sportsmen who travel under their own steam —*Cycling Handbook*⟩

cy·cli·tis \sә'klīd-әs, sī-\ *n* -ES [NL, fr. *cycl-* + *-itis*] : inflammation of the ciliary body

cy·cli·tol \'sīklә,tōl, 'sik-, -ōl\ *n* -s [*cycl-* + *-itol* (as in *inositol, quebrachitol*)] : an alicyclic polyhydroxy compound (as inositol, quebrachitol)

cy·cli·za·tion \,sīk(ә)lә'zāshәn, ,siklә-\ *n* -s [ISV *cyclize* + *-ation*] : formation of one or more rings ⟨~ of open-chain hydrocarbons gives naphthenes or aromatic hydrocarbons⟩ — compare AROMATIZATION

cy·clize \'sī,klīz, 'sīkә,līz, 'si,klīz\ *vb* -ED/-ING/-S [ISV *cycl-* + *-ize*] *vt* : to subject to cyclization ~ *vi* : to undergo cyclization

cyclized rubber *n* : rubber obtained in the form of a white powder or of chips by cyclization usu. in the presence of a catalyst (as stannic chloride) and used chiefly in making adhesives, coatings for paper, printing ink, and paint — called also *cyclorubber*

cyclo- *in pronunciations below*, ¦==\sī(,)klō *or* \si\ *or* -klә\ — see CYCL-

cy·clo·aliphatic \¦== *at* CYCLO-+\ *adj* [*cycl-* + *aliphatic*] : ALICYCLIC

cy·clo·alkane \"+\ *n* [*cycl-* + *alkane*] : CYCLOPARAFFIN

cy·clo·alkene \"+\ *n* [ISV *cycl-* + *alkene*] : a cycloolefin of the formula C_nH_{2n-2}

cy·clo·alkyl \"+\ *n* [*cycl-* + *alkyl*] : any univalent radical (as cyclohexyl) formed by removal of one hydrogen atom from a cycloalkane

cy·clo·barbital \"+\ *n* [*cycl-* + *barbital*] : a white crystalline compound $C_{12}H_{16}N_2O_3$ used as a sedative and hypnotic; 5-(1-cyclohexen-1-yl)-5-ethyl-barbituric acid

cy·clo·both·ra \,==+'bäthrә\ *n* -s [NL, fr. *cycl-* + Gk *bothros* pit; perh. akin to OE *bedd* bed — more at BED] : a Mexican herb (*Calochortus flavus*) often cultivated for its yellow flower

cy·clo·butane \¦== *at* CYCLO-+\ *n* [ISV *cycl-* + *butane*] : a saturated cyclic hydrocarbon C_4H_8 obtained synthetically as an easily condensable gas — called also *tetramethylene*

cy·clo·chae·ta \,==+'kēd-ә\ *n, cap* [NL, fr. *cycl-* + *-chaeta*] : a genus of peritrichous ciliates that have marginal cirri about a ventral disk armed with chitinous hooks, are commensals or ectoparasites on aquatic animals, and include one (*C. domerguei*) which is sometimes destructive to freshwater fishes in hatcheries or aquariums

cy·clo·coe·li·dae \,==+'sēlә,dē\ *n pl, cap* [NL, fr. *Cyclocoelum*, type genus (fr. *cycl-* + *-coelum*, neut. of *-coelus* -coelous) + *-idae*] : a family of flattened digenetic trematodes that are parasites in the respiratory organs of birds and that have no oral and often no ventral sucker, an anterior mouth, and intestinal ceca fused posteriorly

cy·clo·converter \¦== *at* CYCLO- +\ *n* [*cycl-* + *converter*] : an electronic device for controlling the speed of a synchronous motor by supplying it with alternating current of grid= controlled frequency

cy·clo·dehydration \"+\ *n* [*cycl-* + *dehydration*] : cyclization involving chemical dehydration

cy·clo·dehydrogenation \"+\ *n* [*cycl-* + *dehydrogenation*] : DEHYDROCYCLIZATION

cy·clo·dialysis \"+\ *n* [NL, fr. *cycl-* + *dialysis*] : surgical detachment of the ciliary body from the sclera to reduce tension in the eyeball in some cases of glaucoma

cy·clo·diathermy \"+\ *n* [*cycl-* + *diathermy*] : partial or complete destruction of the ciliary body by diathermy to relieve certain conditions characterized by increased tension within the eyeball

cy·clo·ganoidei \"+\ *n pl, cap* [NL, fr. *cycl-* + *Ganoidei*] *in some classifications* : a group of ganoid fishes having cycloid scales, closely approaching the teleosts in structure, and including the bowfin as the only living example

cy·clo·genesis \"+\ *n* [NL, fr. *cyclo-* (fr. E *cyclone*) + L *genesis*] : the process of development or intensification of a cyclone

cy·clo·gen·ic \¦== *at* CYCLO- + ¦jenik\ *adj* [*cycl-* + *-genic*] : of or relating to life cycles : having phases in the course of development ⟨a ~ bacterium⟩

cy·clog·e·ny \sī'kläjәnē\ *n* -ES [*cycl-* + *-geny*] : LIFE CYCLE

cy·clo·gi·ro *also* **cy·clo·gy·ro** \¦== *at* CYCLO- + ¦jī(,)rō\ *n* -s [*cycl-* + *giro, gyro*] : a rotary-wing aircraft whose support in the air is normally derived from airfoils arranged like the paddles of a paddle wheel, mechanically rotated about horizontal axes perpendicular to the plane of symmetry of the aircraft, and having an angle of attack that is always less than the stalling angle

cy·clo·gram \'==,gram\ *n* -s [*cycl-* + *-gram*] : a photograph made by taking intermittent exposures of a moving object to which a light has been attached and serving to project the motion of that object in dotted curves

cy·clo·heptane \¦== *at* CYCLO-+\ *n* [ISV *cycl-* + *heptane*] : an oily saturated cyclic hydrocarbon C_7H_{14}

cy·clo·heptanone \"+\ *n* [ISV *cycl-* + *heptanone*] : a colorless liquid ketone $C_7H_{12}O$ with a peppermint odor — called also *suberone*

cy·clo·hexane \"+\ *n* [ISV *cycl-* + *hexane*] : a colorless

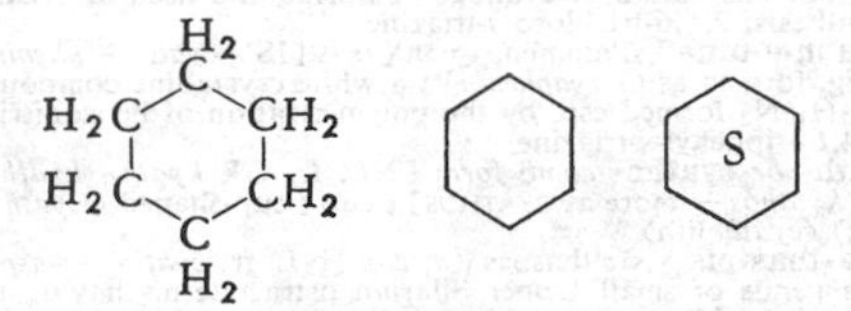

structural formula for cyclohexane (three methods of representation, S denoting saturation)

liquid saturated cyclic hydrocarbon C_6H_{12} having a pungent odor, found in petroleum, made synthetically by hydrogenation of benzene, and used chiefly as a solvent (as for resins and waxes) and in organic synthesis esp. in making adipic acid; hexahydrobenzene — see NAPHTHENE

cy·clo·hex·a·nol \,==+'heksә,nōl, -ōl\ *n* -s [ISV *cyclohexane* + *-ol*] : a colorless oily alcohol $C_6H_{11}OH$ that has an odor like camphor, is made by the catalytic hydrogenation of phenol or oxidation of cyclohexane, and is used chiefly as a solvent, as a stabilizer for emulsions, and in the manufacture of adipic acid; hexahydro-phenol

cy·clo·hex·a·none \-,nōn\ *n* -s [ISV *cyclohexane* + *-one*] : a liquid ketone $C_6H_{10}O$ made by the oxidation of cyclohexanol or cyclohexane and used chiefly as a solvent and in organic synthesis

cy·clo·hexene \¦== *at* CYCLO-+\ *n* [ISV *cycl-* + *hexene*] : a colorless liquid unsaturated cyclic hydrocarbon C_6H_{10} made by dehydrating cyclohexanol — called also *tetrahydrobenzene*

cy·clo·hex·i·mide \,==+'heksә,mīd, -,mәd\ *n* -s [*cyclohexanone* + *imide*] : a colorless crystalline antibiotic $C_{15}H_{23}NO_4$ isolated from streptomycin-producing strains of a soil bacterium (*Streptomyces griseus*) that is effective against several yeasts and harmful fungi

cy·clo·hexyl \,==+\ *n* [ISV *cycl-* + *hexyl*] : a univalent radical C_6H_{11} formed by removal of hydrogen from cyclohexane

cy·clo·hex·yl·a·mine \,==,hek'silә,mēn, -'heksәlә-, -,mәn\ *n* [ISV *cyclohexyl* + *amine*] : a colorless liquid amine C_6H_{11}-NH_2 having a strong fishy odor, made usu. by catalytic hydrogenation of aniline, and used chiefly in organic synthesis

¹cy·cloid \'sī,klȯid\ *n* -s [F *cycloïde*, fr. Gk *kykloeidēs*, adj., circular, fr. *kykl-* cycl- + *-oeidēs* -oid] **1** : a curve traced by any point on the circumference of a circle that rolls without sliding on a straight line **2** : CYCLOTHYME

cycloid: *P* generating point

²cycloid \"\ *adj* [Gk *kykloeidēs*] **1** : arranged or progressing in circles : CIRCULAR ⟨~ protoplasmic movements⟩ **2** : having concentric lines of growth and a smooth margin and surface ⟨~ scales are characteristic of soft-rayed fishes⟩ : consisting of scales of this type ⟨~ scalation⟩ : having scales of this type ⟨~ fishes⟩ — compare CTENOID **3** : CYCLOTHYMIC

cy·cloi·dal \(')sī'klȯid-ᵊl\ *adj* **1** : of, relating to, or resembling a cycloid **2** : ²CYCLOID 2

cycloidal pendulum *n, physics* : a heavy particle constrained to frictionless oscillation under gravity along the arc of a cycloid and having a period that is strictly independent of amplitude

cycloidal propeller *n* : a vertical axis marine propeller sometimes used on shallow draft vessels

cy·cloi·dei \sī'klȯidē,ī\ *n pl, cap* [NL, fr. *cycl-* + *-oidei*] *in former classifications* : a group of fishes including those with cycloid scales (as most teleosts) — **cy·cloi·di·an** \(')sī¦klȯidēәn\ *adj or n*

cy·clo·lith \'== *at* CYCLO- + ,lith\ *n* -s [*cycl-* + *-lith*; trans. of W *cromlech*] : CROMLECH **2**

cy·clol·y·sis \sī'klälәsәs\ *n, pl* **cycloly·ses** \-ә,sēz\ [NL, fr. *cyclo-* (fr. E *cyclone*) + *-lysis*] : the process of decay of a cyclone

cy·clom·e·ter \sī'klämәd-ә(r)\ *n* -s [*cycl-* + *-meter*] **1** : an instrument used to measure arcs of circles **2** : a contrivance for recording the revolutions of a wheel and often used for registering distance traversed by a wheeled vehicle

cy·clo·mor·phic \¦== *at* CYCLO- + ¦mȯrfik\ *adj* [*cycl-* + *-morphic*] : exhibiting cyclomorphosis

cy·clo·mor·pho·sis \,==+'mȯrfәsәs *sometimes* -,mȯr'fōs-\ *n, pl* **cyclomorpho·ses** \-,sēz\ [NL, fr. *cycl-* + *-morphosis*] : cyclically recurrent polymorphism occurring esp. in marine planktonic animals possibly in response to seasonal changes in environmental salinity

cy·clo·my·ar·ia \,==,mī'a(a)rēә\ *n pl, cap* [NL, fr. *cycl-* + *-myaria*] : a suborder of Thaliacea comprising tunicates with a barrel-shaped body — compare DOLIOLUM — **cy·clo·my·ar·i·an** \¦==,==¦rēәn\ *adj*

cy·clone \'sī,klōn\ *n* -s [modif. of Gk *kyklōma* wheel, coil of a snake, fr. *kyklos* wheel, circle — more at WHEEL] **1 a** : a storm or system of winds that rotates about a center of low atmospheric pressure clockwise in the southern hemisphere and counterclockwise in the northern, advances at a speed of 20 to 30 miles an hour, is often violent in the tropics and usu. moderate elsewhere, often brings abundant precipitation, and usu. has a diameter of 50 to 900 miles — see ANTICYCLONE, EXTRATROPICAL CYCLONE, TROPICAL CYCLONE **b** *chiefly Midwest* : TORNADO **2** : something felt to resemble a cyclone esp. in violence or intensity ⟨his story provoked a ~ of laughter⟩ **3** *or* **cyclone collector** *also* **cyclone separator** : any of certain centrifugal devices for separating solid material from gases or liquids (as dust particles from air or skins and seeds from fruit juice) **syn** see WIND

Cyclone \"\ *trademark* — used for a chain link fence

cyclone burner *n* : a swirling combustion device for utilizing low-grade pulverized coal as fuel and producing the ash as fluid slag

cyclone cellar *n* : a cellar or covered excavation for refuge from a cyclone or other dangerous windstorm

cyclone center *n* : the region of lowest barometric pressure about which cyclonic winds are blowing

cyclone plant *n* : WINGED PIGWEED

cy·clon·ic \(')sī¦klänik, -nēk\ *also* **cy·clon·i·cal** \-nәkәl, -nēk-\ *adj* **1** : of, relating to, or having the characteristics of a cyclone **2** : resembling a cyclone esp. in violence and vigor ⟨a man given to ~ rages⟩ ⟨a voluble, ~, half-mad painter —Roland Gelatt⟩

cy·clon·i·cal·ly \-nәk(ә)lē, -nēk-, -li\ *adv* : in the manner of a cyclone

cyclonic region *n* : the area covered by a cyclone

cyclonic storm *n* : CYCLONE 1a

cy·clo·nite \'sīklә,nīt, 'sik-\ *n* -s [*cyclo*-trimethylene-tri-*nitramine*] : a powerful high explosive consisting of colorless crystals of symmetrical hexahydro-trinitro-triazine used esp. in detonators, bombs, and shells — called also *RDX*

cy·clo·octa·tet·ra·ene \¦== *at* CYCLO- + ,äktә'te-trә,ēn\ *n* -s [ISV *cycl-* + *octa-* + *tetra-* + *-ene*] : a liquid unsaturated cyclic hydrocarbon C_8H_8 that resembles benzene in its cyclic completely conjugated structure but is much more reactive than benzene and is usu. made by catalytic polymerization of acetylene under pressure

cy·clo·olefin \¦==+\ *n* [ISV *cycl-* + *olefin*] : an alicyclic hydrocarbon containing an unsaturated ring; *esp* : any cyclic hydrocarbon of the formula C_nH_{2n-2} containing only one double bond in the ring

cy·clo·paraffin \"+\ *n* [*cycl-* + *paraffin*] : a saturated cyclic hydrocarbon of the formula C_nH_{2n} : a member of the series starting with cyclopropane and cyclobutane or an alkyl derivative of one of these — called also *cycloalkane;* compare NAPHTHENE

cy·clo·pe·an \¦sīklә¦pēәn, (')sī¦klōp-\ *also* **cy·clo·pi·an** \(')sī¦klōp-\ *adj* [*cyclopean* fr. LL *Cyclopeus* (fr. Gk *Kyklōpeios*, fr. *Kyklōps* Cyclops) + E *-an; cyclopian* fr. L *Cyclopius* (fr. Gk *Kyklōpios*, fr. *Kyklōps*) + E *-an* — more at CYCLOPS] **1 a** *often cap* : relating to the Cyclopes : like or like that of a Cyclops **b** : fit for a Cyclops : vast and rough : MASSIVE, HUGE **2** : of or relating to a style of stone construction marked typically by the use of large irregular blocks without mortar **3 a** : having or relating to a single median eye or a medially united pair of eyes **b** : of or relating to cyclopia **syn** see HUGE

cyclopean concrete *n* : concrete with embedded large stones

cy·clo·pe·dia *also* **cy·clo·pae·dia** \,sīklә'pēdēә\ *n* -s [short for *encyclopedia, encyclopaedia*] **1** *obs* : the full compass of human learning **2** : a work containing information in all departments of knowledge or on all subjects in a particular department : ENCYCLOPEDIA ⟨a general ~⟩ ⟨a ~ of mechanics⟩

cy·clo·pe·dic *also* **cy·clo·pae·dic** \,sīklә'pēdik, -dēk\ *adj* [*cyclopedia, cyclopaedia* + *-ic*] **1** : being a cyclopedia **2** : of great range or extent : INCLUSIVE ⟨a man of ~ knowledge⟩ — **cy·clo·pe·di·cal·ly** \-dәk(ә)lē, -dēk-, -li\ *adv*

cy·clo·pe·dist *also* **cy·clo·pae·dist** \,sīklә'pēdәst\ *n* -s [*cyclopedia, cyclopaedia* + *-ist*] : a maker of or writer for a cyclopedia

cy·clo·pentadiene \¦== *at* CYCLO- +\ *n* -s [ISV *cycl-* + *pentadiene* (fr. *pent-* + *di-* + *-ene*)] : a colorless liquid unsaturated cyclic hydrocarbon C_5H_6 that is obtained by distillation of coal tar, that polymerizes to its stable dimer on standing, and is used in making plastics and insecticides

cy·clo·pentane \"+\ *n* [ISV *cycl-* + *pentane*] : a liquid saturated cyclic hydrocarbon C_5H_{10} found in petroleum — called also *pentamethylene;* see NAPHTHENE

cy·clo·pen·ta·none \,==+'pentә,nōn\ *n* -s [ISV *cyclopentane* + *-one*] : a liquid ketone C_5H_8O with an odor like that of peppermint

cy·clo·pentene \¦==+\ *n* [ISV *cycl-* + *pentene*] : a liquid unsaturated cyclic hydrocarbon C_5H_8

¹cyclopes *pl of* CYCLOPS

²cy·clo·pes \sī'klō(,)pēz\ *n, cap* [NL, fr. L, pl. of L *Cyclops*] : a genus of edentate mammals including only the So. American silky anteater

cy·clo·pho·rase \,== *at* CYCLO- + 'fō,rās, -āz\ *or* **cyclophorase system** *n* -s [*cycl-* + *phor-* + *-ase*] : a complex of enzymes associated with mitochondria (as of the liver and kidney) that catalyzes oxidations (as of acids participating in the Krebs cycle), oxidative phosphorylation, and various syntheses (as of hippuric acid)

cy·clo·pho·ria \,==+'fōrēә\ *n* -s [NL, fr. *cycl-* + *-phoria*] : a form of heterophoria in which the vertical axis of the eye rotates to the right or left due to weakness of the oblique muscles — **cy·clo·phor·ic** \¦==¦fōrik\ *adj*

cy·cloph·o·rus \sī'kläfәrәs\ *n, cap* [NL, fr. Gk *kyklophoros*, adj., circular, fr. *kykl-* cycl- + *-phoros* -phorous] : a genus of tropical Old World ferns (family Polypodiaceae) having closely crowded circular sori and no indusia

cy·clo·phre·nia \,== *at* CYCLO- + 'frēnēә\ *n* -s [NL, fr. *cycl-* + *-phrenia*] : MANIC-DEPRESSIVE PSYCHOSIS

cy·clo·phyl·lid·ea \,==fә'lidēә\ *n pl, cap* [NL, fr. *cycl-* + *phyll-* + *-idea*] : an order of Cestoda that consists of tapeworms with four suckers on the scolex and the vitelline glands condensed into a mass adjacent to the ovary and that includes most of the medically and economically important tapeworms of the higher vertebrates — **cy·clo·phyl·lid·e·an** \¦===¦==dēәn\ *adj or n*

cy·clo·pia \sī'klōpēә\ *also* **cy·clo·py** \'sīklәpē\ *n, pl* **cy·clopias** *also* **cyclopies** [NL *cyclopia*, fr. L *Cyclop-, Cyclops* + NL *-ia*] : a developmental anomaly characterized by the presence of a single median eye

cyclopian *var of* CYCLOPEAN

cy·clop·ic \(')sī¦kläpik\ *adj* [L *Cyclop-, Cyclops* + E *-ic*] : CYCLOPEAN 3

cy·clo·ple·gia \,== *at* CYCLO- + 'plēj(ē)ә\ *n* -s [NL, fr. *cycl-* + *-plegia*] : paralysis of the ciliary muscle of the eye

¹cy·clo·ple·gic \¦==¦plējik\ *adj* [NL *cycloplegia* + E *-ic*] : producing cycloplegia ⟨a ~ agent⟩ : involving cycloplegia ⟨~ refraction⟩ : being cycloplegic ⟨~ effects⟩

²cycloplegic \"\ *n* -s : a cycloplegic agent

¹cy·clo·poid \'sīklә,pȯid, sī'klō,-\ *adj* [NL *Cyclop-, Cyclops* genus of copepods + E *-oid*] : resembling a water flea — compare CYCLOPS 3

²cyclopoid \"\ *n* -s : a free-swimming larva of many parasitic copepods that resembles a water flea

cy·clo·propane \¦== *at* CYCLO- +\ *n* [ISV *cycl-* + *propane*] : a colorless flammable gaseous saturated cyclic hydrocarbon C_3H_6 made usu. from symmetrical dichloro-propane and zinc and used as a general anesthetic by inhalation — called also *trimethylene*

cy·clops \'sī,kläps\ *n* [L, fr. Gk *Kyklōps*, fr. *kykl-* cycl- + *ōps* eye, face — more at EYE] **1** *pl* **cyclo·pes** \sī'klō(,)pēz\ *usu cap* : one of a race of giants in Greek mythology with a single eye in the middle of the forehead **2** [NL, fr. L] *pl* **cyclopes** : an individual or fetus abnormal in having a single eye or the usual two orbits fused **3** *cap* [NL, fr. L] : a genus of minute free-swimming copepods that have a large median eye, a pear-shaped body tapering posteriorly, and long antennules used in swimming, that are widely distributed and abundant in fresh waters, that are important elements in certain aquatic food chains, and that directly affect man as intermediate hosts of certain parasitic worms — see GUINEA WORM **4** *pl* **cyclops** [NL, fr. L] : a copepod of the genus *Cyclops* : WATER FLEA

cy·clop·ter·i·dae \,sī,kläp'terә,dē\ *n pl, cap* [NL, fr. *Cyclopterus*, type genus (fr. *cycl-* + *-pterus*) + *-idae*] : a family of scorpaenid fishes having the pelvic fins absent or united and modified into a sucking disk — compare LUMPFISH — **cy·clop·te·roid** \(')sī¦kläptә,rȯid\ *adj or n* — **cy·clop·ter·ous** \-tәrәs\ *adj*

cyclopy *var of* CYCLOPIA

cy·clo·ra·ma \,sīklә'ramә, -ämә, -āmә\ *n* -s [*cycl-* + *-orama* (as in *panorama*)] **1** : a large pictorial representation encircling the spectator and often having real objects as a foreground **2** : a curved cloth or wall forming the back of many modern stage settings and used to eliminate shadows and to suggest unlimited space (as of the sky) **3** : something felt to resemble a cyclorama ⟨his last novel a ~ of bawdiness and confusion⟩ ⟨with the ~ of the mountains rising into view as they paddled slowly up the lake⟩ — **cy·clo·ram·ic** \¦==¦ramik\ *adj*

cy·clor·ha·pha \sī'klȯrәfә\ *syn of* CYCLORRHAPHA

cy·clor·rha·pha \"\ *n pl, cap* [NL, fr. *cycl-* + Gk *rhaphē* seam (akin to *rhaptein* to sew) — more at RHAPSODY] : a suborder or other major division of Diptera that comprises flies lacking mandibles and first maxillae and having acephalous larvae and coarctate pupae and that includes the botflies and the common houseflies — **cy·clor·rha·phous** \(')sī¦klȯrәfәs\ *adj*

cy·clo·rubber \¦== *at* CYCLO- +\ *n* [*cycl-* + *rubber*] : CYCLIZED RUBBER

cy·clo·serine \"+\ *n* [*cycl-* + *serine*] : an antibiotic C_3H_4-NO_2NH_2 derived from isoxazole that is esp. active against the tubercle bacillus and is produced by an actinomycete (*Streptomyces orchidaceus*)

cy·clo·silicate \"+\ *n* [*cycl-* + *silicate*] **1** : a class of polymeric silicates sometimes considered a subclass of sorosilicates in which the silicon-oxygen tetrahedral groups are linked by sharing oxygen atoms so as to form rings containing 3, 4, or 6 silicon atoms and 9, 12, or 18 oxygen atoms respectively (as in benitoite or beryl) — called also *ring-silicate;* compare INOSILICATE, NESOSILICATE, PHYLLOSILICATE, SOROSILICATE, TECTOSILICATE **2** : any mineral belonging to the class of cyclosilicates

cy·clo·sis \sī'klōsәs\ *n, pl* **cyclo·ses** \-ō,sēz\ [NL, fr. Gk *kyklōsis* act of surrounding, enveloping, fr. *kykloun* to encircle (fr. *kyklos* ring, circle) + *-ōsis* -osis — more at WHEEL] : the circulatory movement or streaming of protoplasm within a cell

cy·clo·spon·dy·li \,== *at* CYCLO- + 'spändә,lī\ *n pl, cap* [NL, fr. *cycl-* + *-spondyli*] *in some classifications* : the sharks having cyclospondylic vertebrae regarded as a natural group

cy·clo·spon·dyl·ic \¦==¦spän¦dilik\ *also* **cy·clo·spon·dy·lous** \¦==¦spändәlәs\ *adj* [NL *Cyclospondyli* + E *-ic* or *-ous*] : having a single calcified cylinder surrounding the notochord in each vertebral centrum — used esp. of certain sharks

cy·clo·spo·ra·les \,==spә'ra(,)lēz\ [NL, fr. *cycl-* + *spor-* + *-ales*] *syn of* FUCALES

cy·clo·spo·re·ae \,=='spōrē,ē\ *n pl, cap* [NL, fr. *cycl-* + *spor-* + *-eae* — more at SPORE] : a class of brown algae coextensive with the order Fucales and made up of forms having only a sporophytic generation — **cy·clos·po·rous** \(')sī¦kläspәrәs; ¦== *at* CYCLO- + ¦spōrәs\ *adj*

cy·clo·spo·ri·nae \⸗⸗ *at* CYCLO- + spəˈrī(ˌ)nē\ [NL, fr. *cycl-* + *spor-* + *-inae*] *syn of* CYCLOSPOREAE

cy·clo·stage \ˈ⸗⸗+ˌ-\ *n* [*cycl-* + *stage*] : a stage in a bacterial life cycle

¹**cy·clos·to·ma** \sīˈklästəmə\ *n, cap* [NL, fr. *cycl-* + *-stoma*] : a large genus of operculate pulmonate land snails widely distributed chiefly in tropical areas

²**cyclostoma** \"\ [NL, fr. *cycl-* + *-stoma*] *syn of* ²CYCLOSTOMATA

³**cyclostoma** \"\ [NL, fr. *cycl-* + *-stoma*] *syn of* CYCLOSTOMI

¹**cy·clo·sto·ma·ta** \ˌ⸗⸗ *at* CYCLO- +ˈstōməd·ə, -tăm-\ [NL, fr. *cycl-* + *-stomata*] *syn of* CYCLOSTOMI

²**cyclostomata** \"\ *n pl, cap* [NL, fr. *cycl-* + *-stomata*] : an order of bryozoans (class Gymnolaemata) comprising colonial forms with tubular calcareous zooecia having circular apertures without opercula and lacking both avicularia and vibracula

cy·clos·to·mate \(ˈ)sīˈklästəmət\ *also* **cy·clo·stom·a·tous** \ˌ⸗⸗ *at* CYCLO- +ˈstämәd·əs, -tōm-\ *adj* [in sense 1, fr. *cycl-* + *-stomate* or *-stomatous*; in sense 2, *cyclostomate* fr. NL *Cyclostomata; cyclostomatous* fr. NL *Cyclostomata* + E *-ous*] **1** : having a circular mouth **2** : of or relating to the Cyclostomata or Cyclostomi

¹**cy·clo·stome** \ˈ⸗⸗ *at* CYCLO- +ˌstōm\ *adj* [NL *Cyclostomi* or *Cyclostomata*] **1** : of or relating to the Cyclostomi or Cyclostomata **2** : being a cyclostome

²**cyclostome** \"\ *n* -s : one of the Cyclostomi

cy·clos·to·mes \sīˈklästəˌmēz\ [NL, fr. *cycl-* + *-stomes* (fr. Gk *stoma* mouth) — more at STOMACH] *syn of* CYCLOSTOMI

cy·clos·to·mi \-ˌmī\ *n pl, cap* [NL, fr. *cycl-* + *-stomi*] : a class of lowly vertebrates formerly an order or subclass of Pisces but now segregated with certain extinct related forms in a superclass Agnatha that are elongated creatures resembling eels with a large jawless sucking mouth, no limbs or paired fins, a wholly cartilaginous skeleton with persistent notochord, and 6 to 14 pairs of gill pouches supported by a system of cartilaginous rods rudimentary in the hagfishes and that include the lampreys and the hagfishes

cy·clos·to·mous \(ˈ)sīˈklästəməs\ *adj* [*cycl-* + *-stomous*] : CYCLOSTOMATE

cy·clo·stroph·ic \ˌ⸗⸗ *at* CYCLO- +ˈsträfik\ *adj* [*cycl-* + LGk *strophikos* fit to be turned, turned, fr. Gk *stroph-* (stem of *strephein* to turn) + *-ikos* -ic — more at STROPHE] : of cyclic compulsion — used of the component of the deflective force of a wind that is due to the curvature of its path

¹**cy·clo·style** \ˈ⸗⸗+ˌstīl\ *n* -s [fr. *Cyclostyle*, a trademark] : a manifolding machine that utilizes a stencil cut by a graver whose tip is a small rowel

²**cyclostyle** \"\ *vt* -ED/-ING/-S : to manifold by cyclostyle

³**cyclostyle** \"\ *n* -s [*cycl-* + *-style* (as in *peristyle*)] : a structure composed of a circular row of columns about an open court — compare PERISTYLE

cy·clo·system \ˈ⸗⸗+ˌ-\ *n* [*cycl-* + *system*] : a gastropore of a hydrocoral surrounded by a circle of dactylopores

cy·clo·tel·la \ˌ⸗⸗ˈtelə\ *n, cap* [NL, irreg. fr. *cycl-* + L *-ella* (dim. suffix)] : a genus of disk-shaped solitary free-floating diatoms (family Coscinodiscaceae) often causing aromatic odors in water

cy·clo·them \ˈ⸗⸗ˌthem\ *n* -s [*cycl-* + Gk *thema* something laid down — more at THEME] : a stratigraphic unit consisting of a series of beds deposited during a single sedimentary cycle

cy·clo·thu·rus \ˌ⸗⸗ˈth(y)ürəs\ [NL, irreg. fr. Gk *kyklōtos* rounded + NL *-urus*] *syn of* CYCLOPES

cy·clo·thyme \ˈ⸗⸗ˌthīm\ *also* **cy·clo·thym** \-ˌthim\ *n* -s [back-formation fr. NL *cyclothymia*] : a cyclothymic individual

cy·clo·thy·mia \ˌ⸗⸗ˈthīmēə\ *n* -s [NL, fr. G *zyklothymie*, fr. *zyklo-* cycl- + *-thymie* -thymia] : a temperament characterized by alternation of lively and depressed moods believed to predispose the individual toward manic-depressive insanity — opposed to *schizothymia*; compare EXTROVERSION

¹**cy·clo·thy·mic** \ˌ⸗⸗ˈthīmik\ *adj* [NL *cyclothymia* + E *-ic*] : of, relating to, or marked by cyclothymia — compare SYNTONIC

²**cyclothymic** \"\ *n* -s : CYCLOTHYME

cy·clot·ic \(ˈ)sīˈklädik\ *adj* [fr. NL *cyclosis*, after such pairs as NL *neurosis*: E *neurotic*] : exhibiting or being cyclosis ⟨~ movement⟩

cy·clo·tom·ic \ˌ⸗⸗ *at* CYCLO- +ˈtämik\ *adj* : of or relating to cyclotomy

cy·clot·o·my \sīˈklädəmē\ *n* -ES [*cycl-* + *-tomy*] **1** : the mathematical theory of the division of the circle into equal parts or of the construction of regular polygons or analytically of the extraction of the *n*th roots of 1 **2** : incision or division of the ciliary body

cy·clo·to·sau·rus \sīˌklōd·əˈsȯrəs\ *n, cap* [NL, fr. Gk *kyklōtos* rounded (fr. *kyklos* circle, ring) + NL *-saurus* — more at WHEEL] : a genus of labyrinthodonts from the Trias of Germany

cy·clo·tron \ˈsīkləˌträn\ *n* -s [*cycl-* + *-tron*; fr. the circular movement of the particles] : an accelerator in which particles (as protons, deuterons, or ions) are propelled by means of an alternating electric field between electrodes in a constant magnetic field

cy·clus \ˈsīkləs\ *n, pl* **cy·cli** \-ˌklī\ [LL — more at CYCLE] : CYCLE

cy·der \ˈsīdə(r)\ *chiefly Brit var of* CIDER

cy·dip·pe \sīˈdipē\ [NL, fr. L, a mythological girl tricked into marriage by a suitor, fr. Gk *Kydippē*] *syn of* PLEUROBRACHIA

cy·dip·pea \-pēə\ [NL, fr. *Cydippe*] *syn of* CYDIPPIDA

cy·dip·pid \-pəd\ *n* -s [NL *Cydippida*] : a larval ctenophore resembling an adult of the Cydippida

cy·dip·pi·da \-pədə\ *n pl, cap* [NL, fr. *Cydippe* + *-ida*] : an order of Ctenophora comprising forms having two long slender tentacles and unbranched meridional and stomodaeal vessels

cy·dip·pid·ea \-ˌsīdəˈpidēə\ [NL, fr. *Cydippe* + *-idea*] *syn of* CYDIPPIDA

cyd·nid \ˈsidnəd\ *adj* [NL *Cydnidae*] : of or relating to the family Cydnidae ⟨~ bugs⟩

cyd·ni·dae \-nəˌdē\ *n pl, cap* [NL, fr. *Cydnus*, type genus (fr. Gk *kydnos* glorious, renowned, fr. *kydos* glory, renown) + *-idae*; fr. their bright colors — more at KUDOS] : a widely distributed family of chiefly tropical bugs that are related to the stinkbugs and include a number of burrowing bugs with the first two pairs of legs modified for digging in soil

cy·do·nia \sīˈdōnēə\ *n, cap* [NL, fr. L, quince — more at QUINCE] : a monotypic genus of small Asiatic trees (family Rosaceae) having crooked branches, blackish bark, large solitary white or pink flowers, and a fragrant yellow fuzzy fruit somewhat resembling a small apple — see QUINCE; compare CHAENOMELES

¹**cy·do·nian** \(ˈ)sīˈdōnēən, -ōnyən\ *adj, usu cap* [*Cydonia*, city of ancient Crete + E *-an*] **1** : of, relating to, or characteristic of ancient Cydonia **2** : of, relating to, or characteristic of Cydonians

²**cydonian** \"\ *n* -s *cap* : a native or inhabitant of ancient Cydonia

cy·do·ni·um \sīˈdōnēəm\ *n* -s [NL, fr. L *cydoneum (malum)*, quince — more at QUINCE] *pharmacy* : quince seed

cy·e·sis \sīˈēsəs\ *n, pl* **cye·ses** \-ēˌsēz\ [NL, fr. Gk *kyēsis*, fr. *kyein* to be pregnant + *-ēsis* -esis; akin to Gk *koilos* hollow — more at CAVE] : PREGNANCY ⟨two cases of full-term abdominal ~ are described —*Jour. Amer. Med. Assoc.*⟩

cyg·ne·ous \ˈsignēəs\ *adj* [L *cygneus, cycneus*, fr. *cygnus, cycnus* swan] : curved like the neck of a swan

cyg·net \-nət\ *n* -s [ME *sygnett*, fr. MF *cygne* swan (fr. L *cygnus, cycnus*, fr. Gk *kyknos*) + ME *-et*; perh. akin to Skt *śuci* white, shining, Av *saochint-* burning] : a young swan

cyg·nus \-nəs\ *n, cap* [NL, fr. L, swan] : a genus of birds comprising the typical swans

cyke \ˈsīk\ *n* -s [by shortening & alter.] *slang* : CYCLORAMA 2

cyl *abbr* cylinder

cy·las \ˈsīləs\ *n, cap* [NL] : a genus of chiefly tropical weevils including the sweet-potato weevil

cylices *pl of* CYLIX

cyl·i·co·stome \ˈsilə(ˌ)kōˌstōm\ *n* -s [NL *Cylicostomum* genus of worms, fr. Gk *kylik-, kylix* cup + NL *-stomum*; akin to Gk *kalyx* calix, bud — more at CHALICE] : any of several small nematode worms (family Strongylidae) infesting the digestive tract of horses and other equines — called also *small strongyle*; compare STRONGYLE

cyl·in·der \ˈsiləndə(r)\ *n* -s *often attrib* [MF or L; MF *cylindre*, fr. L *cylindrus*, fr. Gk *kylindros*, fr. *kylindein* to roll; akin to OE *sceol* wry, squinting, OHG *scelah*, ON *skjalgr* wry, squinting, L *scelus* crime, wickedness, Gk *skolios* curved, crooked, *skelos* leg, Alb *tshalë* lane; basic meaning: turning, bending] **1** *math* **a** : the surface traced by any straight line moving parallel to a fixed straight line and intersecting a fixed curve **b** : the space bounded by any such surface and two parallel planes cutting all the elements — see VOLUME table **2** : a cylindrical body: as **a** (1) : the turning chambered breech of a revolver (2) : one type of choke boring — see ²CHOKE 3 **b** (1) : a cylindrical chamber in an engine in which a piston is impelled by the pressure or expansive force of the working fluid (2) : the analogous though not cylindrical part in certain abnormal types of engines **c** : a chamber in a pump from which the piston expels the fluid **d** : the rapidly rotating spiked drum of a threshing machine **e** (1) : PLATE CYLINDER (2) : IMPRESSION CYLINDER (3) : BLANKET CYLINDER **f** : CYLINDER SEAL **g** : a cylindrical clay object inscribed with cuneiform inscriptions **h** : a typewriter platen **i** : a cylindrical record of a phonograph or dictating machine **j** : the portion of a cylinder lock that contains the tumblers and keyhole **3** : a pivoted hollow steel shell upon which the balance of a watch is mounted and which is cut away to permit the passage of the rim of the escape wheel **4** : the square prism carrying the cards to the needles in a jacquard loom

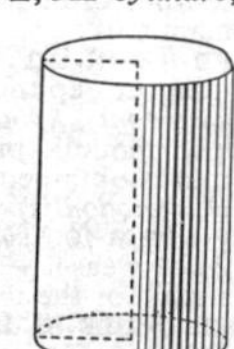
cylinder

cylinder block *n* : ¹BLOCK 1j

cyl·in·dered \-də(r)d\ *adj* : having a cylinder or cylinders ⟨a 6-*cylindered* engine⟩

cylinder front *n* : a desk front having a one-piece lid or cover resembling a longitudinal section of a cylinder

cylinder glass *n* : glass blown in the shape of a cylinder then split and flattened into a sheet

cylinder head *n* : the closed end of an engine or pump cylinder

cylinder lock *n* : a lock with both keyhole and tumbler mechanism in a cylinder separate from the case

cylinder machine *n* : a paper machine in which the sheet is formed on a wire-covered cylinder revolving in a vat of the stock; *esp* : such a machine having several vats and used for making boards each of which is built up by combining as many layers as there are vats

cylinder man *n* **1** : a worker who cures bricks and cinder blocks in steam pressure cylinders to hasten hardening **2** : an optical glass worker who grinds cylinder-shaped lens blanks

cylinder number *n* : the serial number of the cylindrical printing plate on a sheet of rotary-printed British stamps

cylinder oil *n* : a heavy grade of mineral lubricating oil; *esp* : such an oil used for steam-engine cylinders and valves

cylinder planer *n* : a wood surfacer having 1 or 2 rotating cutter cylinders and usu. from 2 to 8 feed rolls for guiding the wood

cylinder press *n* : a printing press in which a rotating cylinder rolls the paper against a printing surface lying on a flat usu. horizontal reciprocating bed — compare ROTARY PRESS

cylinder saw *n* : CROWN SAW

cylinder scale *n* : an automatic indicating scale in which the graduations are on a rotatable cylindrical chart — called also *barrel scale, drum scale*

cylinder seal *n* : a cylinder of stone or other hard material engraved in intaglio upon the curved surface and used esp. in ancient Mesopotamia to roll an identifying impression on wet clay (as in sealing a jar or writing tablet)

cylinder snake *n* : any of several Asiatic burrowing snakes constituting a genus (*Cylindrophis*) of the family Aniliidae

cylindr- *or* **cylindro-** *comb form* [NL, fr. Gk *kylindr-, kylindro-*, fr. *kylindros* — more at CYLINDER] : cylindrical : cylindrical and ⟨*cylindr*arthrosis⟩ ⟨*cylindro*cephalic⟩

cyl·in·dra·ceous \ˌsilənˈdrāshəs\ *adj* [*cylindr-* + *-aceous*] : somewhat like a cylinder

cyl·in·drar·thro·sis \ˌsilənˌdrärˈthrōsəs, səˌlin-\ *n, pl* **cyl·indrar·thro·ses** \-ōˌsēz\ [NL, fr. *cylindr-* + *arthrosis*] : a joint in which the articular surfaces are approximately round

cy·lin·dri·cal \səˈlindrəkəl, -rēk-\ *or* **cy·lin·dric** \-drik, -rēk\ *adj* [*cylindrical* fr. F or Gk; F *cylindrique* (fr. Gk *kylindrikos*, fr. *kylindros* cylinder + *-ikos* -ic) + E *-al*; *cylindric* fr. F *cylindrique* or Gk *kylindrikos* — more at CYLINDER] : relating to or having the form or properties of a cylinder — **cy·lin·dri·cal·i·ty** \səˌlindrəˈkaləd·ē\ *n* -ES — **cy·lin·dri·cal·ly** \səˈlindrək(ə)lē, -rēk-, -li\ *adv* — **cy·lin·dri·cal·ness** \-kəlnəs\ *n* -ES

cylindrical coordinate *n, math* : any of the coordinates in space obtained by constructing in a plane a polar coordinate system and on a line perpendicular to the plane at the pole a linear coordinate system

cylindrical epithelium *n* : COLUMNAR EPITHELIUM

cylindrical harmonic *n* : BESSEL FUNCTION

cylindrical projection *n* : a projection (as of a sphere or a spheroid) on the surface of a cylinder; *specif* : any of numerous map projections of the terrestrial sphere on the surface of a cylinder that is then unrolled as a plane, the parallels and meridians appearing as straight lines perpendicular to each other if the cylinder is tangent over the sphere at the equator and all parallels as well as the points of the poles if shown appearing as the same length as the equator

cylindrical vault *n* : BARREL VAULT

cyl·in·dric·i·ty \ˌsilənˈdrisəd·ē\ *n* -ES [prob. fr. F *cylindricité*, fr. *cylindrique* cylindric + *-ité* -ity] : the quality or state of being cylindrical

cyl·in·drite \ˈsilənˌdrīt, səˈlin-\ *n* -s [ISV *cylindr-* + *-ite*; orig. formed as G *kylindrit*] : a mineral $Pb_3Sn_4Sb_2S_{14}$ consisting of sulfur, lead, antimony, and tin and being dark gray with metallic luster

cy·lin·dro·cap·sa \səˌlindrōˈkapsə\ *n, cap* [NL, fr. *cylindr-* + L *capsa* box — more at CASE] : a genus (the type of the family Cylindrocapsaceae) of freshwater green algae with filaments in which the cells have stratified walls

cy·lin·dro·cap·sa·ce·ae \-ōˌkapˈsāsēˌē\ *n pl, cap* [NL, fr. *Cylindrocapsa*, type genus + *-aceae*] : a family of algae (order Ulotrichales) having unbranched filaments and oogamous sexual reproduction

cy·lin·dro·cellular \səˈlindrō +\ *adj* [*cylindr-* + *cellular*] : made up of cylindrical cells

cy·lin·dro·conical \"+\ *adj* [*cylindr-* + *conical*] : cylindrical with one end tapering to a point

¹**cyl·in·droid** \ˈsilənˌdrȯid, səˈlin-\ *n* -s [*cylindr-* + *-oid*] : a cylinder with elliptic right sections

²**cylindroid** \"\ *also* **cyl·in·droi·dal** \ˌsilənˈdrȯidᵊl\ *adj* : CYLINDRACEOUS

cy·lin·dro·iu·lus \səˌlindrō(ˌ)īˈyüləs\ *n, cap* [NL, fr. *cylindr-* + L *iulus* catkin, fr. Gk *ioulos* (also, downy hair, sheaf of grain); akin to Gk *oulos* curly, *eilyein* to enwrap, enfold — more at VOLUBLE] : a genus of millipedes of the family Julidae including a species (*C. londinensis*) sometimes reported to damage potato crops in Europe

cy·lin·dro·spo·ri·um \səˌlindrōˈspōrēəm\ *n, cap* [NL, fr. *cylindr-* + *-sporium*] : a genus of imperfect fungi (family Melanconiaceae) producing hyaline filiform conidia in acervuli and including many forms that cause leaf and fruit spot diseases and some that are now known to be stages in the life cycles of other fungi — compare COCCOMYCES

cyl·in·dru·ria \ˌsilənˈdrürēə\ *n* -s [NL, fr. ISV *cylindroid* + NL *-uria*] : the presence of casts in the urine

cylix *var of* KYLIX

cym- *or* **cymo-** *also* **kym-** *or* **kymo-** *comb form* [F *cym-, cymo-*, fr. Gk *kym-, kymo-*, fr. *kyma*] **1** : wave ⟨*cymoscope*⟩ **2** : cyme : cluster ⟨*cymoid*⟩

cy·ma *also* **ci·ma** *or* **si·ma** \ˈsīmə\ *n* -s [Gk *kyma* wave, waved molding — more at CYME] **1** : a projecting molding whose profile is a double curve: **a** *or* **cyma rec·ta** \-⸗ˈrektə\ [NL, lit., straight cyma] : such a molding with the upper part concave **b** *or* **cyma re·ver·sa** \-rəˈvərsə\ [NL, lit., reversed cyma] : such a molding with the upper part convex **2** : a double curve formed by the union of a concave line and a convex line

cymagraph *var of* CYMOGRAPH

cymar *var of* SIMAR

cy·ma·rin \ˈsīmərən, ˈsim- *also* səˈma(a)r-\ *n* -s [fr. *Cymarin*, a trademark] : a cardiac glycoside $C_{30}H_{44}O_9$ occurring esp. in plants of the genus *Apocynum*

cy·ma·rose \-(ˌ)rōs *also* -rōz\ *n* -s [ISV *cymarin* + *-ose*] : a sugar $C_7H_{14}O_4$ occurring as a constituent of certain cardiac glycosides (as cymarin); the 3-methyl ether of digitoxose

cy·ma·ti·idae \ˌsīməˈtīəˌdē, ˌsim-\ *n pl, cap* [NL, fr. *Cymatium*, type genus (fr. Gk *kymation*) + *-idae*] : a family of large chiefly tropical gastropod mollusks (suborder Taenioglossa) that includes the typical tritons

cy·ma·ti·um \sīˈmash(ē)əm, səˈ-\ *n, pl* **cyma·tia** \-sh(ē)ə\ [L, fr. Gk *kymation*, dim. of *kyma*] : a crowning molding in classic architecture; *esp* : CYMA

cym·ba \ˈsimbə\ *n, pl* **cym·bae** \-(ˌ)bē, -ˌbī\ [NL, fr. L, boat, fr. Gk *kymbē* boat, bowl, cup] **1** : the upper part of the concha of the ear **2** : a woody durable boat-shaped spathe or other cover around the flower and fruit cluster of certain palms

cym·bal \ˈsimbəl\ *n* -s [ME, fr. OE *cymbal* and MF *cymbale*, both fr. L *cymbalum*, fr. Gk *kymbalon*, fr. *kymbē* boat, bowl, cup — more at HUMP] **1 a** : a large concave brass plate producing a brilliant clashing tone of indefinite pitch and used esp. to accompany the bass drum either in pairs rubbed or struck glancingly together or suspended or mounted singly and struck by drumsticks **b** : a high-pitched mixture stop of an organ **2 a** : CROTALUM **b** : a small tunable cup-shaped instrument used in pairs — called also *ancient cymbals* **3** : TRIANGLE 3c; *specif* : such an instrument with attached rings **4** *archaic* : DOUGHNUT

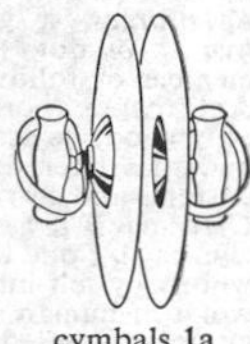
cymbals 1a

cym·bal·ist \-b(ə)ləst\ *n* -s : a performer on cymbals

cymbalom *or* **cymbalon** *var of* CIMBALOM

cym·bid \ˈsimbəd\ *n* -s [NL *Cymbidium*] : CYMBIDIUM 2

cym·bid·i·um \simˈbidēəm\ *n* [NL, fr. L *cymba* boat (fr. Gk *kymbē* boat, bowl, cup) + NL *-idium* — more at HUMP] **1** *cap* : a genus of tropical Old World orchids that are frequently cultivated for their boat-shaped flowers and have narrow leaves and a drooping inflorescence **2** *pl* **cymbidiums** \-mz\ *or* **cymbid·ia** \-dēə\ : a plant or flower of the genus *Cymbidium*

cym·bi·form \ˈsimbəˌfȯrm\ *adj* [NL *cymbiformis*, fr. L *cymba* boat + *-iformis* -iform] : BOAT-SHAPED : convex and keeled ⟨a ~ leaf⟩

cym·bi·um \-bēəm\ *n, cap* [NL, fr. L *cymbium* small cup, fr. Gk *kymbion*, dim. of *kymbē* boat, bowl, cup — more at HUMP] : a genus of marine snails (family Volutidae) comprising the melon shells

cymbling *also* **cymblin** *var of* CYMLING

cym·bo·cephalic *or* **cym·bo·cephalous** \ˈsimbō +\ *adj* [*cymbo-* (fr. L *cymba* boat) + *-cephalic, -cephalous*] *of a head or skull* : having a disproportionately prolonged receding forehead and a projecting occiput — **cym·bo·ceph·a·ly** \" + ˈsefəlē\ *n* -ES

cym·bo·pet·al·um \ˌsimbōˈped·ᵊləm\ *n, cap* [NL, fr. *cymbo-* (fr. L *cymba* boat) + *petalum* petal — more at PETAL] : a genus of tropical American shrubs and small trees (family Annonaceae) with fine-textured green or yellowish wood that includes the sacred earflower of Mexico and Central America

cym·bo·po·gon \-bəˈpōˌgän\ *n, cap* [NL, fr. *cymbo-* (fr. L *cymba* boat) + *-pogon*; fr. the shape of the bracts] : a genus of grasses occurring in warm regions of the Old World and having compound flower clusters of paired racemes enclosed by bracts that resemble spathes — see CITRONELLA GRASS, LEMONGRASS

cyme \ˈsīm\ *n* -s [NL *cyma*, fr. L, young sprout of cabbage, fr. Gk *kyma* wave, young sprout, fetus, anything swollen, fr. *kyein* to be pregnant; akin to *koilos* hollow — more at CAVE] **1** : an inflorescence in which the main and secondary axes always terminate in a single flower whether one flower is produced (as in the wood anemone) or the inflorescence is continued by secondary and tertiary axes (as in the buttercup) **2** : any flower cluster of the cyme type containing several or many flowers (as in pink or phlox) with the first-opening central flower terminating the main axis, subsequent flowers developing from lateral buds, and the inflorescence therefore exhibiting determinate growth — compare CORYMB, RACEME

cyme

cyme·let \-lət\ *n* : CYMULE

cy·mene \-ˌmēn\ *n* -s [F *cymène*, fr. Gk *kyminon* cumin + F *-ène* -ene — more at CUMIN] : any of three isomeric liquid aromatic hydrocarbons $(CH_3)_2CHC_6H_4CH_3$; methyl-isopropyl-benzene; *esp* : the para isomer found in many essential oils (as pine oil and spruce turpentine), obtained as a by-product in the production of sulfite pulp, and made synthetically

cym·ling \ˈsimliŋ\ *or* **cymb·ling** \-m(b)l-\ *also* **cym·lin** \-mlən\ *or* **cymb·lin** *or* **cimb·lin** \-m(b)l-\ *n* -s [prob. alter. of *simnel*] : a summer squash having a scalloped edge

cymo- — see CYM-

cy·mod·o·ce·a·ce·ae \sīˌmädəsēˈāsēˌē\ *n pl, cap* [NL, fr. *Cymodocea*, type genus (fr. L *Cymodoce*, a Nereid) + *-aceae*] : a small family of tropical submerged marine plants (order Naiadales) with slender linear leaves and tiny greenish flowers

cy·mo·gene \ˈsīməˌjēn\ *n* -s [ISV *cymene* + *-o-* + *-gene*] : a flammable easily condensable gaseous petroleum product consisting chiefly of normal butane

¹**cy·mo·graph** *or* **cy·ma·graph** \ˈ⸗⸗ˌgraf\ *n* -s [*cym-* or *cyma* + *-graph*] : an instrument for making tracings of contours (as of profiles or moldings) — **cy·mo·graph·ic** \ˌ⸗⸗ˈ⸗fik\ *adj*

²**cymograph** *var of* KYMOGRAPH

¹**cy·moid** \ˈsīˌmȯid\ *adj* [*cyma* + *-oid*] : like a cyma

²**cymoid** \"\ *adj* [*cym-* + *-oid*] : like a cyme

cy·mo·phane \ˈsīməˌfān\ *n* -s [F, fr. *cym-* + *-phane*] : CHRYSOBERYL; *esp* : an opalescent chrysoberyl

cy·mose \ˈsīˌmōs\ *also* **cy·mous** \-məs\ *adj* [*cyme* + *-ose*, *-ous*] **1** : being, having the form of, or derived from a cyme ⟨~ branching⟩ **2** : of, relating to, or bearing a cyme — **cy·mose·ly** *adv*

cy·mot·ri·chous \(ˈ)sīˈmä·trəkəs\ *adj* [*cym-* + *-trichous*] : having the hair wavy ⟨a ~ race⟩ — **cy·mot·ri·chy** \-kē\ *n* -ES

¹**cym·ric** \ˈkəmrik, ˈkim- *sometimes* ˈsim-\ *also* **kym·ric** \ˈkəm-, ˈkim-\ *adj, usu cap* [W *Cymry* + E *-ic*] **1** : of, relating to, or characteristic of the non-Gaelic Celtic people of Britain; *specif* : WELSH 1b **2** : of, relating to, or characteristic of the language of the Cymric people; *specif* : WELSH 2

²**cymric** *also* **kymric** \"\ *n* -s *cap* : BRYTHONIC; *specif* : the Welsh language

cym·rite \ˈkəmˌrīt, ˈkimˌ- *also* ˈsimˌ-\ *n* -s [W *Cymru* Wales + E *-ite*] : a rare mineral $BaAlSi_3O_8OH$ consisting of a basic aluminosilicate of barium and belonging to the zeolite family

cym·ry *also* **kym·ry** \ˈkəmrē, ˈkim-, -rī\ *n pl, cap* [W *Cymry*, pl. of *Cymro* Welshman, prob. fr. (assumed) OW *combrog* fellow countryman, Welshman, prob. fr. OW *com-* com- + (assumed) OW *brog* region (whence W *bro*); akin to L *com-* and to L *margo* border — more at MARK] : the Brythonic Celts; *specif* : WELSH

cy·mule \ˈsīˌmyül\ *n* -s [*cyme* + *-ule*] : a small cyme or one of very few flowers forming part of a compound cyme

cyn- *or* **cyno-** *comb form* [ME *cyno-*, fr. L, fr. Gk *kyn-, kyno-*, fr. *kyn-, kyōn* dog — more at HOUND] : dog ⟨*cyn*anche⟩

cyn *abbr* cyanide

cy·nan·chum \səˈnaŋkəm\ *n* [NL, fr. Gk *kynanchon* dogbane (*Marsdenia erecta*), fr. *kyn-* cyn- + *-anchon* (fr. *anchein* to choke) — more at ANGER] **1** *cap* : a genus of twining vines (family Asclepiadaceae) with opposite hanging leaves, small greenish or purplish flowers, and long smooth pods **2** -s : the roots of several vines of the genus *Cynanchum* formerly used as an emetic

cyn·a·ra \ˈsinərə\ *n, cap* [NL, fr. Gk *kynara, kinara*, a kind of artichoke] : a genus of herbs (family Compositae) having pinnatifid spiny leaves and large flower heads with fleshy receptacles — see ARTICHOKE, CARDOON — **cyn·a·ra·ceous** \ˌ⸗⸗ˈrāshəs\ *adj* — **cy·nar·e·ous** \səˈna(a)rēəs\ *adj* — **cyn·a·roid** \ˈsinəˌrȯid\ *adj*

cyn·e·get·ic \ˌsinəˈjed·ik\ *adj* [Gk *kynēgetikos*] **:** of or relating to hunting

cyn·e·get·ics \-iks\ *n pl but sing in constr* [L *Cynegetica*, title of a poem (fr. LGk *Kynēgetika*, fr. neut. pl. of Gk *kynēgetikos* of hunting, fr. *kynēgetēs* hunter, fr. *kyn-* cyn- + *hēgeisthai* to lead) + E *-s* — more at SEEK] **:** HUNTING **:** ²CHASE 1b

cyng·ha·nedd \kənˈhä(ˌ)neth\ *n, pl* **cyng·a·nedd·ion** \ˌkəŋəˈnethyən\ [W, fr. *cym-* com- (fr. OW *com-*) + *canu* to sing + *-edd* (n. suffix); akin to L *com-* and to L *canere* to sing — more at CHANT] **1 :** a strict intricate system of alliteration and rhyme used in Welsh poetry ⟨the knowledge of ~ is shared by farm laborer and village craftsman as well as the schoolmaster and parson —Wyn Griffith⟩ **2 :** alliteration or alliteration and rhyme in any of the four patterns of cynghanedd ⟨one rule is common to all the "24 measures": there must be ~ in every line —A.S.D.Smith⟩

¹cyn·ic \ˈsinik, -nēk\ *n* -s [MF or L; MF *cynique*, fr. L *cynicus*, fr. Gk *kynikos*, lit., doglike (prob. influenced in meaning by *Kynosarges*, a gymnasium where Antisthenes taught), fr. *kyn-*, *kyōn* dog + *-ikos* -ic — more at HOUND] **1** *usu cap* **:** a member or follower of a school of philosophers founded by Antisthenes (born *ab*444 B.C.) that taught that virtue is the only good, its essence lying in self-control and independence, and that later developed into a coarse opposition to social customs and current philosophical opinions — contrasted with *Cyrenaic* **2 a :** one who holds views resembling those of the Cynics **b :** one who believes that human conduct is motivated wholly by self-interest **:** a person who expects nothing but the worst of human conduct and motives **:** MISANTHROPE

²cynic \"\ *adj* **1** *usu cap* **:** of or relating to the Cynics **:** resembling the doctrines of the Cynics **2 :** CYNICAL **3** [Gk *kynikos*] **:** like or like that of a dog — now used chiefly in the phrase *cynic spasm*

cyn·i·cal \-nəkəl, -nēk-\ *adj* [¹*cynic* + *-al*] **1 :** having the qualities of a cynic **:** given to faultfinding, sneering, and sarcasm ⟨the younger sister grew more ~, not to say acid, in her ways —Rudyard Kipling⟩ **2 :** given to or affecting disbelief in commonly accepted human values and in man's sincerity of motive or rectitude of conduct **:** accepting selfishness as the governing factor in human conduct ⟨provide a smashing answer for those ~ men who say that a democracy cannot be honest and efficient —F.D.Roosevelt⟩ **3 :** exhibiting feelings ranging from distrustful doubt to contemptuous and mocking disbelief ⟨but people nowadays are so ~ — they sneer at everything that makes life worthwhile —L.P.Smith⟩

syn MISANTHROPIC (or MISANTHROPICAL), PESSIMISTIC, MISOGYNIC (or MISOGYNOUS): CYNICAL often implies a disbelief in sincerity, benevolence, rectitude, or competence ⟨the loneliness which breathes in words like these has often begotten in great rulers a *cynical* contempt of men and the judgments of men —J.R.Green⟩ ⟨he was *cynical* that any good could come of democracy —J.T.Farrell⟩ ⟨the *cynical* opinion, which dissents and says that the less we understand one another the better, will not be considered here —I.A.Richards⟩ MISANTHROPIC suggests dislike and distrust of human beings in general and discomfort at or aversion to their society ⟨he had been the laughingstock of the school even before that day for his inability to conform to their standards, but after that day his loathing for every aspect of youthful high spirits hardened into a *misanthropic* mania —J.C.Powys⟩ PESSIMISTIC connotes a gloomy view of life in general, one without joy or hope ⟨the *pessimistic* sects which despair of social progress and look for a catastrophic ending of the present world order —W.L. Sperry⟩ ⟨official Whig leaders went politically to sleep in their country seats, muttering *pessimistic* prophecies of the impossibility of conquering Napoleon —G.M.Trevelyan⟩ MISOGYNIC and its variants indicate a distrust of and aversion to women on man's part ⟨an old-fashioned bachelor whose *misogynic* views and prejudice against matrimony have been conjecturally traced to his brother Perses having a wife as extravagant as himself —James Davies⟩ ⟨in spite of this modest status of woman, the Greeks were profoundly *misogynous* —H.M. Parshley⟩

cyn·i·cal·ly \-nək(ə)lē, -nēk-, -li\ *adv* **:** in a cynical manner **:** with cynicism

cyn·i·cism \-nəˌsizəm\ *n* -s **1** *usu cap* **:** the doctrine of the Cynics **2 a :** cynical quality ⟨developed the salty ~ that stayed with him throughout his newspaper and political career —Frances Perkins⟩ **b :** an expression of or characteristic of such quality ⟨pungent ~s⟩

cynic spasm *n* **:** RISUS SARDONICUS

¹cyn·i·pid \ˈsinəpəd\ *adj* [NL *Cynipidae*] **:** of or relating to the Cynipidae

²cynipid \"\ *n* -s **:** any insect of the family Cynipidae

cy·nip·i·dae \səˈnipəˌdē\ *n pl, cap* [NL, fr. *Cynip-*, *Cynips*, type genus + *-idae*] **:** a large family of small hymenopterous insects (superfamily Cynipoidea) comprising the gall wasps most of which produce galls on plants (as oaks and rosebushes) in which their larvae develop — see CYNIPS

cyn·i·poid \ˈsinəˌpȯid\ *adj* [NL *Cynipoidea*] **:** of, relating to, or resembling the gall wasps or the Cynipoidea — compare CYNIPIDAE

cyn·i·poi·dea \ˌ==ˈpȯidēə\ *n pl, cap* [NL, fr. *Cynip-*, *Cynips* + *-oidea*] **:** a superfamily of hymenopterous insects (suborder Clistogastra) that are distinguished by greatly reduced wing venation and a coiled retractile ovipositor and that include the gall wasps and several families of parasites of other insects — see CYNIPIDAE

cyn·ips \ˈsinəps\ *n, cap* [NL, prob. fr. L *cinyphes*, *cinyphum* gnat, modif. of Gk *knips* insect infesting fig and oak trees; akin to Gk *sknips*, a kind of small worm, ME *nippen* to nip — more at NIP] **:** a genus (the type of the family Cynipidae) of small gall wasps including a number that form galls on oaks

cyn·ism \ˈsiˌnizəm\ *n* -s [F *cynisme*, fr. LL *cynismus*, fr. Gk *kynismos*, fr. *kyn-* + *-ismos* -ism — more at CYNIC] **:** CYNICISM

cyno- — see CYN-

cyn·o·cephalous *also* **cyn·o·cephalic** \ˌsinō, ˈsīnō, -nə +\ *adj* [*cynocephalous* fr. Gk *kynokephalos*; *cynocephalic* fr. Gk *kynokephalos* + E *-ic*] **:** having a head or face like that of a dog

cyn·o·cephalus \ˌ== +\ *n* [L, fr. Gk *kynokephalos*, fr. *kynokephalos*, adj., fr. *kyn-* cyn- + *-kephalos* -cephalous] **1** *pl* **cynocephali :** a dogheaded being: **a :** one of a fabled race of dogheaded men **b :** BABOON **2** *cap* [NL, fr. L] **a :** a genus of mammals containing the flying lemurs **b** *in former classifications* **:** ¹PAPIO

cyn·o·cram·ba·ce·ae \ˌ==ˌkramˈbāsēˌē\ *n pl, cap* [NL, fr. *Cynocrambe*, type genus + *-aceae*] **:** a family of herbs (order Caryophyllales) coextensive with the genus *Cynocrambe* — **cyn·o·cram·ba·ceous** \ˌ==ˌ=ˈbāshəs\ *adj*

cyn·o·cram·be \ˌ==ˈkram(ˌ)bē\ *n, cap* [NL, fr. Gk *kynokrambē* dog's mercury (*Mercurialis perennis*), fr. Gk *kyn-* cyn- + *krambē* cabbage — more at CRAMBE] **:** a small genus of Old World fleshy herbs constituting a family (Cynocrambaceae) and having simple petioled leaves, inconspicuous apetalous flowers, and globose fruit with a crustaceous pericarp

cyn·o·des·mus \ˌ==ˈdezməs\ *n, cap* [NL, fr. *cyn-* + Gk *desmos* bond — more at DIADEM] **:** a genus of extinct Miocene carnivores apparently derived from *Cynodictis* and on the direct ancestral line of the true dogs and wolves

cyn·o·dic·tis \ˌ==ˈdiktəs\ *n, cap* [NL, fr. *cyn-* + *-dictis* (fr. Gk *diktys*, an unknown Libyan animal mentioned by Herodotus)] **:** a genus of extinct carnivores from the Eocene and Oligocene of Europe that were long-bodied short-legged creatures resembling weasels with retractile claws and presumably ancestral to dogs, foxes, and related forms

cyn·o·don \ˈ==ˌdän\ *n, cap* [NL, fr. Gk *kynodōn* canine tooth, fr. *kyn-* cyn- + *odōn* tooth — more at TOOTH] **:** a genus of creeping grasses having short flat leaves and digitate spikes of one-flowered spikelets — see BERMUDA GRASS

¹cyn·o·dont \ˈ==ˌdänt\ *adj* [Gk *kynodont-*, *kynodōn* canine tooth] **1** *of teeth* **:** having small pulp cavities **2 :** having cynodont teeth ⟨man like the higher apes is ~⟩ **3** [NL *Cynodontia*] **:** of or belonging to Cynodontia

²cynodont \"\ *n* -s **1 :** a reptile or fossil of the group Cynodontia **2 :** a canine tooth

cyn·o·don·tia \ˌ==ˈdänsh(ē)ə\ *n pl, cap* [NL, fr. Gk *kynodont-*, *kynodōn* canine tooth + NL *-ia*] **:** a division of Triassic Therapsida comprising a number of small carnivorous reptiles often with cusps on the teeth that resemble those of mammals

cyn·o·don·tin \ˌ==ˈdäntᵊn, -ntən\ *n* -s [NL *cynodontis* (specific epithet of *Helminthosporium cynodontis*, fr. Gk *kynodont-*, *kynodōn* canine tooth) + E *-in*] **:** a brown crystalline phenolic pigment $C_{15}H_{10}O_6$ derived from anthraquinone that is obtained from fungi of the genus *Helminthosporium* (as *H. cynodontis*)

cy·nog·a·le \səˈnägəlē, sīˈ-\ *n, cap* [NL, fr. *cyn-* + Gk *galē*, *galeē* weasel — more at GALEA] **:** a genus of mammals consisting of the mampalon

cyn·o·glos·si·dae \ˌsinōˈgläsəˌdē, ˌsīn-, -nəˈ-, -lȯs-\ *n pl, cap* [NL, fr. *Cynoglossus*, type genus (fr. Gk *kynoglōssos*, a kind of fish, fr. *kyno-* cyn- + *-glōssos*, fr. *glōssa* tongue) + *-idae* — more at GLOSS] **:** a family of flatfishes comprising the tonguefishes and having small eyes on the left side of the head and the long dorsal and anal fins fused with the caudal fin

cyn·o·glos·sum \ˌ==ˈ=səm\ *n; cap* [NL, fr. Gk *kynoglōsson*, fr. *kyn-* cyn- + *-glōsson* (fr. *glōssa* tongue) — more at GLOSS] **:** a large genus of tall rough herbs (family Boraginaceae) found in most temperate and subtropical regions — see HOUND'S-TONGUE

cy·nog·na·thus \səˈnägnəthəs, sīˈ-\ *n, cap* [NL, fr. *cyn-* + *-gnathus* -gnathous] **:** a genus of large carnivorous therapsid reptiles (suborder Theriodontia) that greatly resembled mammals in form, were presumably near the direct ancestral line of the true mammals, and are known chiefly from remains found in the Karroo formation of the Triassic

cy·noid \ˈsīˌnȯid, ˈsi-\ *adj* [Gk *kynoeidēs*, fr. *kyn-* cyn- + *-oeidēs* -oid] **1 :** resembling a dog **2** [NL *Cynoidea*] **:** of, relating to, or belonging to the Cynoidea

cy·noi·dea \səˈnȯidēə, sīˈ-\ *n pl, cap* [NL, fr. *cyn-* + *-oidea*] *in some classifications* **:** a division of Carnivora comprising mammals that resemble dogs as distinguished from those that resemble bears, the two groups being now usu. combined as the Arctoidea

cy·nol·o·gist \səˈnäləjəst, sīˈ-\ *n* -s **:** one that specializes in the care and training of dogs

cy·nol·o·gy \-jē\ *n* -ES [*cyn-* + *-logy*] **:** scientific study of the dog esp. in respect to its natural history

cyn·o·mol·gus \ˌsinəˈmälgəs, ˌsīn-\ *n, pl* **cynomol·gi** \-ˌgī\ [NL, alter. of *cynamolgus*, fr. L, member of an ancient tribe in Libya, fr. Gk *Kynamolgos*, lit., dog-milker, fr. *kyn-* cyn- + *-amolgos* (fr. *amelgein* to milk) — more at MILK] **:** MACAQUE; *esp* **:** CRAB-EATING MACAQUE — used chiefly in technical literature concerned with poliomyelitis

cyn·o·mo·ri·a·ce·ae \ˌsinōˌmōrēˈāsēˌē, ˌsīn-, -nə-, -mȯr-\ *n pl, cap* [NL, fr. *Cynomorium*, type genus + *-aceae*] **:** a family of plants (order Myrtales) coextensive with the genus *Cynomorium*

cyn·o·mo·ri·um \ˌ==ˈ=rēəm\ *n, cap* [NL, fr. L *cynomorion* broomrape, fr. Gk *kynomorion* dodder, fr. *kyn-* cyn- + *morion* part, member, dim. of *moros* fate, lot — more at MERIT] **:** a genus (the type of the family Cynomoriaceae) of bright red leafless parasitic plants that belong to the order Myrtales, have unisexual flowers borne in heads, and produce edible underground stems which have been used as a dysentery remedy

cyn·o·morph \ˈ==ˌmȯrf\ *adj* [NL *Cynomorpha*] **:** of or belonging to Cercopithecidae

cyn·o·mor·pha \ˌ==ˈ=fə\ *n pl, cap* [NL, fr. *cyn-* + *-morpha*] *in some classifications* **:** a group coextensive with Cercopithecidae — **cyn·o·mor·phic** \ˌ==ˈ=fik\ *adj* — **cyn·o·mor·phous** \-fəs\ *adj*

cyn·o·mys \ˈ==ˌmis\ *n, cap* [NL, fr. *cyn-* + *-mys*] **:** a genus of rodents comprising the prairie dogs

cy·noph·i·list \səˈnäfələst, sīˈ-\ *n* -s [*cyn-* + *-phile* + *-ist*] **:** a dog fancier **:** one that is favorably disposed toward dogs

cyn·o·pi·the·ci·dae \ˌsinōpəˈthēsəˌdē, ˌsīn-, -nəp-, -ēkə-\ [NL, fr. *Cynopithecus*, type genus + *-idae*] *syn of* CERCOPITHECIDAE

cyn·o·pi·the·cus \ˌ==pəˈthēkəs, -ˈpithək-\ *n, cap* [NL, fr. *cyn-* + *-pithecus*] **:** a genus of Old World monkeys (family Cercopithecidae) including only the black ape of Celebes

cy·nos·ci·on \səˈnäsēˌän, sīˈ-, -ēən\ *n, cap* [NL, fr. *cyn-* + *-scion* (modif. of Gk *skiaina*, a sea fish)] **:** a genus of marine fishes (family Sciaenidae) containing the weakfishes and related forms

cy·no·sure \ˈsīnəˌshu̇(ə)r, ˈsin-, -u̇ə; *Brit usu* ˈsinəˌzyu̇- *also* ˈsīn- *or* -ˌzh(y)u̇- *or* -ˌsyu̇-\ *n* -s [MF & L; MF, Ursa Minor, guide, fr. L *cynosura* Ursa Minor, fr. Gk *kynosoura* dog's tail, Ursa Minor, fr. *kynos* (gen. of *kyōn* dog) + *oura* tail; akin to Gk *orrhos* backside — more at HOUND, ASS] **1** *archaic* **:** one that serves to direct or guide **2 :** one that attracts **:** a center of attraction or interest ⟨the council too was a ~ of the nation's hopes —*Time*⟩ ⟨for tradition and digging the ~ of the Wichitas is Devil's Canyon —J.F.Dobie⟩

cyn·o·su·rus \ˌsinəˈs(h)u̇rəs, ˌsīn-\ *n, cap* [NL, fr. Gk *kynosoura* dog's tail] **:** a small genus of European grasses with several-flowered spikelets in panicles — see CRESTED DOGSTAIL

cyn·thia \ˈsinthēə\ [NL, fr. *Cynthia*, goddess of the moon, fr. L, fr. Gk *Kynthia*] *syn of* TETHYUM

cynthia moth *n* **:** a large Asiatic silkworm moth (*Samia cynthia* or *S. walkeri*) introduced into No. America in the 19th century and having a larva that feeds chiefly on the ailanthus

cyn·thi·id \ˈsinthēəd\ *adj or n* [NL *Cynthiidae*] **:** TETHYID

cyn·thi·idae \sinˈthīəˌdē\ [NL, fr. *Cynthia*, type genus + *-idae*] *syn of* TETHYIDAE

cy·on \ˈsīˌän, -īən\ [NL, alter. of *Cuon*] *syn of* CUON

¹cyp \ˈsip, ˈsīp, ˈsēp\ *also* **cy·pre** \-pə(r)\ *n* -s [Haitian Creole] **:** PRINCEWOOD 1

²cyp \"\ *n* -s [by shortening] **:** CYPRIPEDIUM 2

cyp·er·a·ce·ae \ˌsipəˈrāsēˌē, ˌsīp-\ *n pl, cap* [NL, fr. *Cyperus*, type genus + *-aceae*] **:** a large family of monocotyledonous plants (order Graminales) distinguished chiefly by having achenes, solid stems, and 3-ranked stem leaves — compare GRAMINEAE; see SEDGE — **cyp·er·a·ceous** \ˌ==ˈrāshəs\ *adj*

cyp·er·a·les \-ˈrā(ˌ)lēz\ *n pl, cap* [NL, fr. *Cyperus* + *-ales*] *in some classifications* **:** an order of monocotyledonous plants coextensive with the family Cyperaceae

cy·pe·rus \sīˈpirəs, səˈ-\ *n, cap* [NL, fr. L *cyperos*, a kind of rush, fr. Gk *kypeiros*, prob. of Sem. origin; akin to Heb *kōper*, a resin] **:** a genus of plants (family Cyperaceae) having the scales of the spikelet 2-ranked, the flowers all perfect, and the spikelets alike — see CHUFA, PAPYRUS, UMBRELLA PLANT

cy·phel·la \səˈfelə, sīˈ-\ *n* [NL, fr. Gk *kyphella*, pl., hollows of the ears; akin to OE *hūfe* head covering, OHG *hūba*, OS *hūva*, ON *hūfa* hood, cap, bonnet, Gk *kyphos* crooked, bent, ORuss *kubŭ* drinking vessel, OE *hēah* high — more at HIGH] **1** *pl* **cyphel·lae** \-(ˌ)lē\ **:** a small cuplike pit on the lower surface of the thallus of certain lichens (as those of the genus *Sticta*) prob. functioning as a pore **2** *cap* **:** a genus of cup-shaped basidiomycetous fungi (family Thelephoraceae) having the hymenial lining on the inner surface

cy·phel·late \səˈfelət, (ˈ)sī;-, -(ˌ)lāt\ *adj* [NL *cyphella* + E *-ate*] **:** having cyphellae

cy·pher \ˈsīfə(r)\ *chiefly Brit var of* CIPHER

cy·pho·man·dra \ˌsīfəˈmandrə, ˌsif-\ *n, cap* [NL, fr. Gk *kyphōma* hump (fr. *kyphos* crooked, bent) + NL *-andra* — more at CYPHELLA] **:** a genus of So. American shrubs or trees (family Solanaceae) having large simple or divided leaves and rotate or bell-shaped flowers — see TREE TOMATO

cy·pho·nau·tes \-ˈnȯd·(ˌ)ēz\ *n, pl* **cyphonau·tae** \-(ˌ)ā\ [NL, fr. Gk *kyphos* crooked, bent + *nautēs* sailor, fr. *naus* ship — more at NAVE] **:** the free-swimming bivalve larva of certain bryozoans

cy·praea \sīˈprēə, səˈ-\ *n, cap* [NL, fr. L *Cypria* or LL *Cypris*, a name for Venus-Aphrodite, goddess of love, fr. Gk *Kypris*, fr. *Kypros* Cyprus, island in the Mediterranean, her reputed birthplace] **:** a genus (the type of the family Cypraeidae) of gastropod mollusks comprising the typical cowries with smoothly polished often brightly colored shells covered in life by the reflected lobes of the mantle

cy·prae·i·dae \-əˌdē\ *n pl, cap* [NL, fr. *Cypraea*, type genus + *-idae*] **:** a family of marine gastropod mollusks (suborder Taenioglossa) comprising the cowries — see CYPRAEA

cy·prae·i·form \-əˌfȯrm\ *adj* [NL *Cypraea* + E *-iform*] **:** shaped like a cowrie

cy pres \(ˈ)sēˈprā\ *adv (or adj)* [*cy pres (doctrine)*] **:** in accordance with cy pres doctrine

cy pres doctrine *n* [AF *cy pres* as near, so near] **:** the doctrine in the law of charities whereby when it becomes impossible, impracticable, or illegal to carry out the particular purpose of the donor a scheme will be framed by a court or under prerogative powers of a sovereign to carry out the general intention by applying the gift to charitable purposes that are closely related or similar to the original purposes

¹cy·press \ˈsīprəs\ *n* -ES *often attrib* [ME *cipres*, *cypress*, fr. OF *ciprès*, *cyprès*, fr. L *cyparissus*, fr. Gk *kyparissos*, fr. the non-IE source of L *cupressus* cypress] **1 :** a tree of the genus *Cupressus* **2 :** branches or sprigs of cypress used as a symbol of mourning ⟨let the king dismiss his woes . . . and take the ~ from his brows —Matthew Prior⟩ **3 :** any of several coniferous trees related to cypress: **a :** PORT ORFORD CEDAR **b :** YELLOW CEDAR **c :** BALD CYPRESS **d :** a Central-American timber tree (*Podocarpus coriacea*) that produces a fine-grained gray wood **e** *North* **:** JACK PINE 1 **4 :** the wood of cypress **5 :** any of various chiefly herbaceous plants that are not conifers but have flat scaly foliage like that of members of the genus *Cupressus* **6** *or* **cypress green :** a moderate olive green that is greener and duller than forest green (sense 2), greener, darker, and slightly less strong than Lincoln green, and greener and duller than holly green (sense 2)

²cypress \"\ *also* **cy·prus** \-rəs\ *n* -ES [ME *cipres*, *cyprus*, fr. *Cyprus*, island in the Mediterranean] **1 :** any of various rich fabrics imported from or through Cyprus in medieval times; *specif* **:** a rich satin **2 a** *also* **cypress lawn :** a silk or cotton gauze orig. made in Cyprus, usu. dyed black, and used esp. for mourning **b :** a piece of this fabric; *esp* **:** a kerchief worn as a badge of mourning

cy·pressed \-rəst\ *adj* [¹*cypress* + *-ed*] **:** having a growth of cypresses

cypress gilia *n* **:** an herb (*Gilia rubra*) with foliage like that of a cypress

cypress grass *n* **:** a common sedge (*Cyperus diandrus*) of the eastern U.S.

cypress knee *n* **:** one of the outgrowths from the roots of bald cypress that are presumed to aerate the submerged root system

cypress koromiko *n* **:** a New Zealand shrub (*Veronica cupressoides*) with very slender much-forked branches, minute leaves, and tiny flowers

cypress moss *n* **1 :** a moss (*Hypnum cupressiforme*) with foliage like that of a cypress **2 :** a club moss (*Lycopodium alpinum*) growing on mountains of Europe and America

cypress oil *n* **:** a yellowish essential oil from the leaves and young branches of Italian cypress used as an inhalant in whooping cough

cypress pine *n* **:** a tree of the genus *Callitris*

cypress spurge *n* **:** a spurge (*Euphorbia cyparissias*) with foliage resembling that of a cypress that is native to the Old World but is now established as a weed in the eastern U.S.

cypress trout *n* **:** BOWFIN

cypress vine *n* **1 :** a tropical American plant (*Quamoclit pennata*) with red or white tubular flowers and finely dissected leaves that is naturalized in the southern U.S. and used elsewhere as an ornamental garden plant **2 :** CLIMBING FUMITORY

¹cyp·ri·an \ˈsiprēən\ *n* -s [L *Cyprius* native of Cyprus, fr. *Cyprius*, adj. (fr. Gk *Kyprios*, fr. *Kypros* Cyprus) + E *-an*] **1** *often cap* [so called fr. *Cyprus*' being the reputed birthplace of Aphrodite, goddess of love] **:** a lewd person; *specif* **:** PROSTITUTE **2** *usu cap* **:** CYPRIOT **3** *or* **cyprian bee** *usu cap C* **:** a bright yellow fierce-tempered honeybee little raised in the U.S.

²cyprian \"\ *adj* [L *Cyprius* of Cyprus + E *-an*] **1** *often cap* **:** LICENTIOUS **2** *usu cap* **:** CYPRIOT

cyprian earth *or* **cyprian green** *n, often cap C* **:** TERRE VERTE 2

cyp·ri·an·ic \ˌ==ˈanik\ *adj, usu cap* [St. *Cyprian* (Thascius C. Cyprianus) †258 martyred bishop of Carthage + E *-ic*] **:** of, belonging to, or based on the thought of St. Cyprian

cyprian turpentine *n, usu cap C* **:** TURPENTINE 1a

cyp·rid \ˈsiprəd\ *n* -s [NL *Cyprid-*, *Cypris* & NL *Cyprididae*, fr. *Cyprid-*, *Cypris*, type genus + *-idae*] **1 :** a member of the genus *Cypris* or family Cyprididae **2 :** CYPRIS 2

cyprides *pl of* CYPRIS

cyp·ri·di·na \ˌsiprəˈdīnə, -dēnə\ *n, cap* [NL, fr. LL *Cyprid-*, *Cypris*, a name for Venus + NL *-ina* — more at CYPRAEA] **:** a genus (the type of the family Cypridinidae) of commonly bioluminescent marine crustaceans (subclass Ostracoda) having three eyes and a deep anterior notch in the shell — **cyprid·i·noid** \səˈpridᵊnˌȯid\ *adj*

cy·prine \ˈsīprən, -ˌprēn, -ˌprīn\ *n* -s [G *zyprin*, fr. L *cyprum* copper + G *-in* -ine — more at COPPER] **:** a variety of idocrase that is colored blue by copper

¹cyp·ri·nid \ˈsiprəˌnid; səˈprīnəd, -rīn-\ *adj* [NL *Cyprinidae*] **:** of or belonging to Cyprinidae

²cyprinid \"\ *n* -s **:** a cyprinid fish

¹cy·prin·i·dae \səˈprinəˌdē, -rīn-\ *n pl, cap* [NL, fr. *Cyprinus* type genus + *-idae*] **:** a large family (order Ostariophysi) of freshwater fishes (as the carps, barbels, tenches, breams, goldfishes, chubs, dace, shiners, and most of the freshwater minnows) that have a single dorsal fin, a somewhat protractile mouth destitute of teeth except for a few on the pharyngeal bones, the body nearly always covered with cycloid scales, and the air bladder large and divided into two parts

²cyprinidae \"\ *n pl, cap* [NL, fr. *Cyprina*, type genus + *-idae*] *in some classifications* **:** a family of thick-shelled marine bivalve mollusks (suborder Submytilacea) comprising the black quahog and certain related mollusks

cy·prin·o·don \-əˌdän\ *n, cap* [NL, fr. L *cyprinus*, a kind of carp + NL *-odon* — more at CYPRINUS] **:** the type genus of Cyprinodontidae comprising killifishes of tropical fresh and brackish waters that may be an important factor in mosquito control in certain areas

¹cy·prin·o·dont \-əˌdänt\ *adj* [NL *Cyprinodont-*, *Cyprinodon* & *Cyprinodontia* & *Cyprinodontes*] **:** of or belonging to *Cyprinodon*, the Cyprinodontidae, or the Microcyprini

²cyprinodont \"\ *n* -s **:** a cyprinodont fish **:** a killifish, topminnow, or related small soft-finned fish

cy·prin·o·don·tes \ˌ=ˌ==ˈdän(ˌ)tēz\ [NL, fr. *Cyprinodont-*, *Cyprinodon*] *syn of* MICROCYPRINI

cy·prin·o·don·ti·dae \-ˈdäntəˌdē\ *n pl, cap* [NL, fr. *Cyprinodont-* *Cyprinodon*, type genus + *-idae*] **:** a large family (order Microcyprini) of small scaly-headed soft-finned fishes that feed on water plants and insects and include the typical killifishes of the northern hemisphere

¹cyp·ri·noid \ˈsiprəˌnȯid; səˈpri,-, -rī,-\ *adj* [NL *Cyprinoidea*] **:** like or relating to a carp or the Cyprinoidea

²cyprinoid \"\ *n* -s **:** a cyprinoid fish

cyp·ri·noi·dea \ˌsiprəˈnȯidēə\ *n pl, cap* [NL, fr. *Cyprinus* + *-oidea*] **:** a suborder or other division of Ostariophysi comprising the carps and certain related fishes (as suckers and loaches) — **cyp·ri·noi·de·an** \ˌ==ˈ=dēən\ *adj or n*

cy·pri·nus \səˈprīnəs, -rēn-\ *n, cap* [NL, fr. L, carp, fr. Gk *kyprinos*; perh. akin to Skt *śaphara* carp, Lith *šapalas*] **:** the type genus of the family Cyprinidae now usu. restricted to the typical carp

¹cyp·ri·ot \ˈsiprēət, -ēˌät *sometimes* ˈsīp-\ *or* **cyp·ri·ote** \"\, -ēˌōt\ *n* -s *cap* [F *cypriote*, adj. & n., fr. *Cyprus* + F *-i-* + *-ote*] **1 :** a native or inhabitant of Cyprus, an island in the eastern part of the Mediterranean sea **2 :** the ancient or modern Greek dialect of Cyprus

²cypriot *or* **cypriote** \"\ *adj, usu cap* [F *cypriote*] **1 a :** of, relating to, or characteristic of Cyprus **b :** of, relating to, or characteristic of Cypriots **2 :** of, relating to, or characteristic of the Cypriot language

cypriot syllabary *n, usu cap C* **:** a syllabary prob. of Aegean origin in which ancient Cypriot is preserved

cyp·ri·pe·di·um \ˌsiprəˈpēdēəm\ *n* [NL, fr. LL *Cypris*, a name for Venus + NL *-pedium* (modif. of Gk *pedilon* sandal); fr. the shape of the flower; akin to Gk *pod-*, *pous* foot — more at CYPRAEA, FOOT] **1** *cap* **:** a genus of leafy-stemmed terrestrial orchids having large drooping usu. showily colored or marked flowers with a lip that forms an inflated pouch **2** *pl* **cypripe·dia** \-dēə\ **:** a plant or flower of the genus *Cypripedium* or of the genus *Cordula* — see LADY'S SLIPPER **3 :** the dried rhizome and roots of an orchid (*C. parviflorum*) formerly used as a nervine and antispasmodic

cy·pris \'sīprəs\ *n* [NL, fr. LL *Cypris*, a name for Venus — more at CYPRAEA] **1** *cap* **:** a genus (the type of the family Cyprididae) of small ostracod crustaceans that live in stagnant fresh water **2** *pl* **cyp·ri·des** \'siprə,dēz\ **:** a developmental form of a barnacle in which the shell is bivalved as in members of the genus *Cypris*

cypro- *comb form, usu cap* [Gk *Kypro-*, fr. *Kypros* Cyprus] **:** Cyprian (and) ⟨*Cypro*-Phoenician⟩

cy·pro·lith·ic \,sīprō¦lithik, ¦si-, -prə¦-\ *adj, usu cap* [*cypro-* + *-lithic*] **:** AENEOLITHIC

¹cy·prus \'sīprəs\ *adj, usu cap* [fr. *Cyprus*, island in the Mediterranean sea] **:** of or from Cyprus **:** of the kind or style prevalent in Cyprus **:** CYPRIOT

²cyprus *var of* CYPRESS

cyprus cedar *n* [fr. *Cyprus*, island in the Mediterranean] **:** a cedar (*Cedrus libani brevifolia*) of the eastern Mediterranean region that differs from the cedar of Lebanon chiefly in its dwarf habit of growth, shorter leaves, and smaller cones

cyprus earth *or* **cyprus umber** *n, often cap C* **:** RAW UMBER 2

cyprus green *n, often cap C* **:** a strong yellowish green that is yellower and lighter than shamrock and yellower, lighter, and stronger than emerald (sense 2b)

cyps *pl of* CYP

cyp·se·la \'sipsələ\ *n, pl* **cypse·lae** \-,lē\ [NL, fr. Gk *kypselē* hollow vessel, chest, box; akin to Gk *kyphos* bent, crooked — more at CYPHELLA] **:** an achene developed from an inferior bicarpellary ovary fused with the calyx tube (as in the sunflower) — see FRUIT illustration

cyp·sel·i·dae \sip'selə,dē\ [NL, fr. *Cypselus*, type genus + *-idae*] *syn of* APODIDAE

cyp·se·li·form \(')sip¦selə,fȯrm, 'sipsəl-\ *adj* [NL *Cypseliformes*, group of birds including the swift, fr. *Cypselus* + *-iformes*] **:** resembling a swift

cyp·se·line \'sipsə,līn\ *adj* [Gk *kypselos* swift + E *-ine*] **:** of or relating to the swifts

cyp·se·loid \-,lȯid\ *adj* [Gk *kypselos* swift + E *-oid*] **:** resembling a swift

cyp·se·lus \-,ləs\ [NL, fr. L, a kind of swallow, fr. Gk *kypselos* sand martin, swift] *syn of* APUS

¹cyr·e·na·ic \¦sīrə¦nāik, ¦sīr-\ *adj, usu cap* [L *Cyrenaicus*, fr. Gk *Kyrēnaikos*, adj. & n., fr. *Kyrēnaika*, ancient region in Libya (fr. *Kyrēnē*) & *Kyrēnē* Cyrene, ancient Greek city in Libya] **1 a :** of, relating to, or characteristic of Cyrenaica, a region in Libya, Africa **b :** of, relating to, or characteristic of the people of Cyrenaica **2 a :** of, relating to, or characteristic of Cyrene, a city and in ancient times the capital city of Cyrenaica **b :** of, relating to, or characteristic of the people of Cyrene **3 :** of, relating to, or characteristic of the school of philosophers founded by Aristippus of Cyrene

²cyrenaic \"\ *n* -S **1** *cap* **:** a native or resident of Cyrenaica **2** *cap* **:** a native or resident of Cyrene **3** *usu cap* **a :** a member or a follower of a school of philosophers founded by Aristippus of Cyrene who taught that pleasure is the chief end of life — contrasted with *cynic* **b :** one who holds views resembling those of a Cyrenaic

cyr·e·na·i·cism \,==¦nāə,sizəm\ *n* -S *often cap* **:** the doctrine of the Cyrenaics **:** Cyrenaic hedonism

cy·re·ni·an *or* **cy·re·nae·an** \(')sī¦rēnēən\ *adj or n, usu cap* [*Cyrene* + E *-ian, -aean*] **:** CYRENAIC

cy·ril·la \sə'rilə\ *n* [NL, after Domenico Cirillo or *Cyrillo* †1799 It. physician] **1** *cap* **:** a small genus of shrubs and trees (family Cyrillaceae) that have flowers with acute twisted petals and wingless fruit **2** -S **:** a shrub or tree of the genus *Cyrilla*

cyr·il·la·ce·ae \,sirə'lāsē,ē\ *n pl, cap* [NL, fr. *Cyrilla*, type genus + *-aceae*] **:** a family of shrubs and small trees (order Sapindales) with entire coriaceous leaves, small white flowers in racemes, and capsular fruit — **cyr·il·la·ceous** \¦==¦lāshəs\ *adj*

¹cy·ril·li·an \sə'rilēən\ *also* **cy·ril·lic** \-lik\ *adj, usu cap* [*Cyrillus* (Cyril) †444 archbishop of Alexandria + E *-ian* or *-ic*] **:** of, relating to, or based on the thought of Cyril of Alexandria or his followers in his controversy with Nestorius

²cyrillian \"\ *n* -S *cap* **:** a follower of Cyril of Alexandria

cy·ril·li·an·ism \-lēə,nizəm\ *n* -S *often cap* **:** the doctrine of Cyril of Alexandria and his followers that Christ had a thoroughly unified divine-human nature

cy·ril·lic \sə'rilik\ *adj, often cap C* [*Cyrillus* (Cyril) †869 apostle of the Slavs, reputed inventor of the Cyrillic alphabet + E *-ic*] **:** constituting or written in the Cyrillic alphabet

cyrillic alphabet *n, usu cap C* **:** the alphabet based principally on the Greek uncials that was orig. used for writing Old Church Slavonic and that in its modern form with minor variations among the different languages is the alphabet used for Russian and many other Slavic languages and for some non-Slavic languages of the Soviet Union — compare GLAGOLITIC

cyr·o·mys \'sirə,mis\ [NL, fr. Gk *kyros* power, might + NL *-mys* — more at CURIOLOGIC] *syn of* UROMYS

cyrt- *or* **cyrto-** *comb form* [NL, fr. Gk *kyrt-, kyrto-*, fr. *kyrtos* bulging, convex; akin to L *curvus* curved — more at CROWN] **:** bent **:** curved ⟨*cyrtopia*⟩ ⟨*cyrtostyle*⟩ **:** something curved ⟨*cyrtometer*⟩

cyr·ti·dae \'sərdə,dē\ *n pl, cap* [NL, fr. *Cyrtus*, type genus (fr. Gk *kyrtos* bulging, convex) + *-idae*] **:** a family of two-winged flies with small head and greatly enlarged convex thorax whose larvae are parasitic on spiders

cyr·toc·er·a·cone \sər'täsərə,kōn\ *n* -S [NL *Cyrtoceras* + E *cone*] **:** a nautiloid cephalopod shell curved like those of *Cyrtoceras* — **cyr·toc·er·a·con·ic** \¦==¦rə¦känik\ *adj*

cyr·toc·er·as \=='==rəs\ *n, cap* [NL, fr. *cyrt-* + *-ceras*] **:** a genus of Paleozoic nautiloid cephalopods having a conical slightly curved shell with a large body chamber

cyr·to·cer·a·tite \,sərdə'serə,tīt\ *n* -S [NL *Cyrtocerat-*, *Cyrtoceras* + E *-ite*] **:** a fossil cephalopod of the genus *Cyrtoceras* — **cyr·to·cer·a·tit·ic** \¦==¦rə¦tid·ik\ *adj*

cyr·toi·dae \sər'tōi(,)dē\ *n pl, cap* [NL, fr. *cyrt-* + *-idae*] **:** a family of radiolarians widely distributed and often employed as a paleontological index group — compare INDEX FOSSIL

cyr·to·lite \'sərdᵊl,īt\ *n* -S [*cyrt-* + *-lite*] **:** a mineral related to zircon but containing uranium, yttrium, and other rare earths

cyr·tom·e·ter \sər'tämədər\ *n* -S [ISV *cyrt-* + *-meter*; orig. formed as F *cyrtomètre*] **:** an instrument used for delineating or measuring the dimensions of curved surfaces esp. of the chest and head

cyr·to·mi·um \-'tōmēəm\ *n, cap* [NL, fr. Gk *kyrtōma* bulge, convexity (fr. *kyrtos* bulging, crooked, convex) + NL *-ium* — more at CYRT-] **:** a small genus of tropical Asiatic greenhouse ferns (family Polypodiaceae) with anastomosing veins

cyr·to·pia \-'tōpēə\ *n* -S [NL, fr. *Cyrtopia*, genus of crustaceans, fr. *cyrt-* + *-opia*; fr. the resemblance of these larvae to crustaceans of this genus] **:** a larva of certain crustaceans (subclass Ostracoda) characterized by a lengthening of the first pair of antennae and loss of swimming function in the second pair

cyr·to·sis \-'tōsəs\ *n, pl* **cyrto·ses** \-,sēz\ [NL, fr. Gk *kyrtōsis* bulging, fr. *kyrt-* cyrt- + *-ōsis* -osis] **:** a virus disease of cotton characterized by dwarfing, distortion, discolorations, and abnormal branching

cyr·to·style \'sərdə,stīl\ *n* -S [*cyrt-* + *-style*] **:** a circular projecting columned portico

cy·rus \'sīrəs\ *n* -ES [by alter.] **:** SARUS

¹cyst \'sist\ *n* -S [NL *cystis*, fr. Gk *kystis* bladder, pouch; akin to Gk *kysthos* vulva — more at HOARD] **1 :** a sac lacking an opening but having a distinct membrane and developing abnormally in a natural cavity of the body, in the substance of an organ, or in an abnormal structure (as a tumor) **2 a :** a resting spore formed in many algae (as blue-green algae and desmids) by the breaking up of portions of the filaments or by the enclosing of a cell or cell group and their investment by a sheath or envelope — compare STATOSPORE **b :** an air vesicle in certain algae (as the common rockweed) **c :** a structure comparable to a spore formed by certain slime molds **d** (1) **:** a capsule or round sheath formed about certain cells (as some bacteria) when going into a resting stage or becoming transformed into spores (2) **:** the whole structure including the contents of the capsule **3 :** a sac or capsule produced by an animal: as **a :** one that many protozoans and other minute animals secrete about themselves as a prelude to a resting or a specialized reproductive phase **b :** a resistant covering about a parasite produced by the parasite, the host, or by interaction of both

²cyst \"\ *n* -S [alter. (prob. influenced by ¹*cyst*) of ¹*cist*] **:** CIST

cyst- *or* **cysti-** *or* **cysto-** *comb form* [F, fr. Gk *kyst-, kysto-*, fr. *kystis* bladder, pouch] **1 a :** gall bladder ⟨*cysto*colostomy⟩ **b :** urinary bladder ⟨*cyst*itis⟩ ⟨*cysto*tomy⟩ **2 :** sac **:** pouch **:** cyst ⟨*cyst*enchyma⟩ ⟨*cysti*form⟩ ⟨*cysto*phore⟩

-cyst \,sist\ *n comb form* -S [NL *-cyste, -cystis*, fr. Gk *kystis*] **:** bladder ⟨chole*cyst*⟩

cyst·adenoma \¦sist +\ *n, pl* **cystadenomas** *or* **cystadenomata** [NL, fr. *cyst-* + *adenoma*] **:** an adenoma marked by a cystic structure — **cyst·adenomatous** \¦sist +\ *adj*

cyst·a·thionine \,sistə +\ *n* -S [*cyst*eine + *-a-* + *methionine*] **:** a diamino dicarboxylic acid $C_7H_{14}N_2O_4S$ held to be formed as an intermediate in the conversion of methionine to cysteine in the animal organism

cys·tec·to·my \si'stektəmē\ *n* -ES [ISV *cyst* + *-ectomy*] **:** the surgical excision of a cyst; *specif* **:** the removal of all or a portion of the urinary bladder

cys·te·ic acid \'sistēik-\ *n* [ISV *cyst*eine + *-ic*] **:** a crystalline amino acid $HO_3SCH_2CH(NH_2)COOH$ formed by oxidation of cysteine or cystine (as in the outer layers of sheep's wool) and yielding taurine on decarboxylation; β-sulfo-alanine

cys·teine \'si,stēn, -,stēˌēn, 'sistən *also* si'stēən\ *n* -S [ISV, blend of *cystine* and *-eine*; orig. formed as G *zystein*] **:** a crystalline amino acid $HSCH_2CH(NH_2)COOH$ occurring as a constituent of many proteins and of glutathione and readily oxidizable to cystine; β-mercapto-alanine

cys·tic \'sistik, -tēk\ *adj* [F *cystique*, fr. NL *cysticus*, fr. *cystis* cyst + L *-icus* -ic — more at CYST] **1 a :** of or relating to a cyst **b :** of or relating to the urinary bladder or gallbladder **2 :** being a cyst **:** made up of cysts ⟨~ tissue⟩ **3 :** containing a cyst or cysts ⟨a ~ tumor⟩ **:** involving the formation of cysts ⟨~ degeneration⟩ **4 :** enclosed in a cyst **:** ENCYSTED ⟨a ~ worm larva⟩

cys·ti·ca \'sistəkə\ *n pl, cap* [NL, fr. *cyst-* + *-ica* (neut. pl. of *-icus* -ic)] *in former classifications* **:** the larval tapeworms regarded as constituting a natural order

cystic duct *also* **cystic canal** *n* **:** the duct from the gallbladder that unites with the hepatic to form the common bile duct — see DIGESTION illustration

cys·ti·cercal \¦sistə +\ *adj* [NL *cysticercus* + E *-al*] **:** of, relating to, or caused by a cysticercus or cysticerci

cys·ti·cer·ci·a·sis \,sistəsər'sīəsis\ *n, pl* **cysticercia·ses** \-,sēz\ [NL, fr. *cysticercus* + *-iasis*] **:** CYSTICERCOSIS

cys·ti·cer·coid \-ə'sər,kȯid\ *n* -S [ISV *cysticerc-* (fr. NL *cysticercus*) + *-oid*] **:** a larval tapeworm having an invaginated scolex and solid tailpiece — compare COENURUS, CYSTICERCUS, ECHINOCOCCUS

cys·ti·cer·co·sis \-əsər'kōsəs\ *n, pl* **cysticerco·ses** \-ō,sēz\ [NL, fr. *cysticercus* + *-osis*] **:** infestation with or disease caused by cysticerci

cys·ti·cercus \¦sistə +\ *n* [NL, fr. *cyst-* + *-cercus* (fr. Gk *kerkos* tail)] **1** *cap, in former classifications* **:** a genus of parasitic animals comprising the cysticerci when these were not understood to be tapeworm larvae — now often used as though a generic name when referring specif. to the larva ⟨*Cysticercus cellulosae* is the larva of *Taenia solium*⟩ **2** *pl* **cysticerci :** a tapeworm larva consisting of a scolex invaginated into a fluid-filled sac lying in the tissues of an intermediate host and capable of developing into an adult tapeworm when consumed by a suitable definitive host — called also *bladder worm, measle*; compare COENURUS, CYSTICERCOID, ECHINOCOCCUS, PLEROCERCOID

cystic fibrosis *n* **:** MUCOVISCIDOSIS

cys·ti·cid·al \¦==¦sīdᵊl\ *adj* [*cyst-* + *-cide* + *-al*] **:** killing or tending to kill an encysted stage of an organism ⟨a ~ agent such as chlorine⟩

cys·tid \'sistəd\ *n* -S [NL *Cystidea*] **:** any fossil or echinoderm of the class Cystoidea

cys·tid·ea \si'stidēə\ [NL, fr. *cyst-* + *-idea*] *syn of* CYSTOIDEA

cys·tid·e·an \(')si¦stidēən\ *adj or n* [NL *Cystidea* + E *-an*] **:** CYSTOIDEAN

cys·tid·i·um \si'stidēəm\ *n, pl* **cystid·ia** \-dēə\ *or* **cystidiums** [NL, fr. *cyst-* + *-idium*] **:** one of the large inflated and thick-walled cells of the hymenial layer projecting beyond the basidia and paraphyses in certain basidiomycetous fungi

cys·tig·er·ous \(')si¦stijərəs\ *adj* [*cyst-* + *-gerous*] **:** containing or producing cysts ⟨~ tissue⟩

cys·tine \'si,stēn, -,stən\ *n* -S [*cyst-* + *-ine*; fr its discovery in urinary calculi] **:** a colorless crystalline amino acid $[-SCH_2CH(NH_2)COOH]_2$ occurring as a constituent of most proteins (as the keratins in hair, wool, and horn) from which it can be obtained by hydrolysis and yielding cysteine on reduction; β,β′-dithio-di-alanine

cys·ti·nu·ria \,sistə'n(y)u̇rēə\ *n* -S [NL, fr. E *cystine* + NL *-uria*] **:** a familial metabolic defect characterized by the excretion of excessive amounts of cystine in the urine and sometimes resulting in the formation of stones in the urinary tract — **cys·ti·nu·ric** \¦==¦rik\ *adj or n*

-cys·tis \¦sistəs\ *n comb form, pl* **-cystides** [NL, fr. Gk *kystis*] **:** one having (such) a bladder or pouch — esp. in generic names ⟨Macro*cystis*⟩

cys·tit·ic \(')si¦stid·ik\ *adj* [NL *cystitis* + E *-ic*] **:** characteristic of or affected with cystitis

cys·ti·tis \si'stīd·əs\ *n, pl* **cystit·i·des** \-tid·ə,dēz\ [NL, fr. *cyst-* + *-itis*] **:** inflammation of the urinary bladder

cysto- — see CYST-

cys·to·carp \'sistə,kärp, -stō,-\ *n* -S [ISV *cyst-* + *-carp*] **:** the fruiting structure produced in the red algae after fertilization; *esp* **:** such a structure having a special protective envelope (as in *Polysiphonia*) — **cys·to·car·pic** \¦==¦=pik\ *adj*

cys·to·cele \-,sēl\ *n* -S [*cyst-* + *-cele*] **:** hernia of a bladder, esp. the urinary bladder **:** vesical hernia

cys·to·cer·cous \¦==¦sərkəs\ *adj* [*cyst-* + *-cercous* (fr. Gk *kerkos* tail)] *of a cercaria* **:** having a space in the tail into which the body can be retracted

cys·to·flagellata \¦== +\ *n pl, cap* [NL, fr. *cyst-* + *flagellata*] **:** a small suborder of Dinoflagellata comprising a few naked flagellates without furrows and lacking a transverse flagellum that are remarkably medusoid in form — **cys·to·flagellate** \" +\ *adj or n*

cys·tog·e·nous \(')si¦stäjənəs\ *adj* [*cyst-* + *-genous*] **:** cyst-producing ⟨~ glands of a cercaria⟩

cys·to·gram \'sistə,gram, -stō,-\ *n* -S [*cyst-* + *-gram*] **:** a roentgenogram made by cystography

cys·tog·ra·phy \si'stägrəfē\ *n* -ES [F *cystographie*, short for *cystoradiographie*, fr. *cyst-* + *radiographie* radiography] **:** roentgenography of the urinary bladder after injection of a contrast medium

¹cys·toid \'si,stȯid\ *adj* [ISV *cyst-* + *-oid*; prob. orig. formed as F *cystoïde*] **1 :** like a bladder **2** [NL *Cystoidea*] **:** CYSTOIDEAN

²cystoid \"\ *n* -S **1 :** a cystoid structure; *specif* **:** a mass resembling a cyst but lacking a membrane **2 :** CYSTOIDEAN

cys·toid·ea \si'stȯidēə\ *n pl, cap* [NL, fr. *cyst-* + *-oidea*] **:** a class of Paleozoic short-stemmed or stemless pelmatozoan echinoderms formerly considered an order of Crinoidea having the body commonly somewhat globular or egg-shaped and enclosed in calcareous plates that are usu. pierced by a system of pores possibly respiratory in function

¹cys·toi·de·an \(')=¦=dēən\ *adj* [NL *Cystoidea* + E *-an*] **:** of or relating to the Cystoidea

²cystoidean \"\ *n* -S **:** a fossil or echinoderm of the class Cystoidea

cys·to·lith \'sistə,lith, -stō,-\ *n* -S [G *zystolith*, fr. *zyst-* cyst- + *-lith*] **1 :** a calcium carbonate concretion commonly stalked and arising from the cellulose wall of certain cells of higher plants esp. from modified epidermal cells of some flowering plants — compare LITHOCYST **2 :** a urinary calculus — **cys·to·lith·ic** \¦==¦thik\ *adj*

cys·to·lithiasis \¦== +\ *n* [NL, fr. ISV *cystolith* + NL *-iasis*] **:** the presence of calculi in the urinary bladder

cys·to·ma \si'stōmə\ *n, pl* **cystomas** \-məz\ *or* **cystoma·ta** \-məd·ə\ [NL, fr. *cyst-* + *-oma*] **:** a tumor containing cysts — **cys·tom·a·tous** \(')si¦stäməd·əs, -tōm-\ *adj*

cys·tom·e·ter \si'stäməd·ə(r)\ *n* -S [*cyst-* + *-meter*] **:** an instrument designed to measure pressure within the urinary bladder in relation to its capacity — **cys·to·met·ric** \¦sistə¦me·trik\ *adj* — **cys·tom·e·try** \si'stämə·trē\ *n* -ES

cys·to·met·ro·gram \,sistə'me·trə,gram, -stō-, -trō,-\ *n* -S [ISV *cystometro-* (fr. *cystometer*) + *-gram*] **:** a graphic recording of a cystometric measurement — compare CYSTOMETER

cys·to·nec·tae \¦==¦nek(,)tē\ *n pl, cap* [NL, fr. *cyst-* + *-nectae*] *in some classifications* **:** a suborder of siphonophores including only the Portuguese man-of-war — **cys·to·nec·tous** \-ktəs\ *adj*

cys·toph·o·ra \si'stäfərə\ *n, cap* [NL, fr. *cyst-* + *-phora*; fr. the hoodlike sac on the head] **:** a genus of carnivorous mammals including solely the hooded seal

cys·to·phore \'sistə,fō(ə)r\ *n* -S [*cyst-* + *-phore*] **:** the branched stalk that bears the cysts of myxobacteria

cys·top·ter·is \si'stäptərəs\ *n, cap* [NL, fr. *cyst-* + *-pteris*] **:** a genus of ferns (family Polypodiaceae) of the north temperate zone having a hooded or arched indusium partly under the roundish sori — see BLADDER FERN, FRAGILE FERN

cys·to·pus \'sistəpəs\ [NL, fr. *cyst-* + *-pus*] *syn of* ALBUGO

cys·to·pyelitis \¦sistə, -stō +\ *n* [NL, fr. *cyst-* + *pyelitis*] **:** inflammation of the urinary bladder and of the pelvis of one or both kidneys

cys·to·pyelography \" +\ *n* -ES [*cyst-* + *pyelography*] **:** roentgenography of the urinary bladder, the ureter, and the pelvis of the kidney after injection of these organs with a contrast medium

cys·to·pyelonephritis \" +\ *n* [NL, fr. *cyst-* + *pyelonephritis*] **:** inflammation of the urinary bladder and of the cortex and pelvis of one or both kidneys

¹cys·to·scope \'sistə,skōp\ *n* -S [ISV *cyst-* + *-scope*; orig. formed as G *zystoskop*] **:** an instrument that permits visual examination of the bladder and the use of operative devices under visual control — **cys·to·scop·ic** \¦==¦skäpik\ *adj* — **cys·tos·co·pist** \si'stäskəpəst\ *n* -S — **cys·tos·co·py** \-pē\ *n* -ES

²cystoscope \"\ *vt* -ED/-ING/-S **:** to perform cystoscopy on (a patient)

cys·to·spore \'sistə,spō(ə)r\ *n* -S [ISV *cyst-* + *-spore*] **:** an encysted zoospore (as in certain chytridiales)

cys·to·tome \-,tōm\ *n* -S [ISV *cyst-* + *-tome*] **1 :** an instrument used in incising the urinary bladder **2 :** an instrument used in opening the capsule of the lens in cataract operations — **cys·tot·o·my** \si'städ·əmē\ *n* -ES

cys·to·ureteritis \¦sistə, -stō +\ *n* [NL, fr. *cyst-* + *ureter-* + *-itis*] **:** combined inflammation of the urinary bladder and ureters

cys·to·urethrogram \" +\ *n* [*cyst-* + *urethrogram*] **:** a roentgenogram of the urinary bladder and urethra made after injection of these organs with a contrast medium

cyst·ous \'sistəs\ *adj* [¹*cyst* + *-ous*] **:** CYSTIC

cysts *pl of* CYST

-cysts *pl of* -CYST

cyt- *or* **cyto-** *comb form* [G *zyt-, zyto-*, fr. Gk *kyto-*, fr. *kytos* hollow vessel — more at HIDE] **1 :** cell ⟨*cyt*ase⟩ ⟨*cyto*plasm⟩ **2 :** cytoplasm ⟨*cyt*ode⟩ ⟨*cyto*some⟩

cy·tase \'sī,tās, -āz\ *n* -S [ISV *cyt-* + *-ase*; orig. formed as G *zytase*] **:** any of several enzymes found in the seeds of various plants (as cereals) that have the power of making soluble the material of cell walls by hydrolyzing mannan, galactan, xylan, and araban

cy·tas·ter \(')sī¦tastə(r)\ *n* [ISV *cyt-* + *aster* (achromatic substance); orig. formed as G *zytaster*] **1 :** ASTER 3 **2 :** an accessory aster not associated with the chromosomes

cyte \'sīt\ *n* -S [*-cyte*] **:** CELL 5; *specif* **:** a maturing germ cell — compare OOCYTE, SPERMATOCYTE

-cyte \,=\ *n comb form* -S [NL *-cyta*, fr. Gk *kytos* hollow vessel] **:** cell ⟨leuko*cyte*⟩ ⟨peri*cyte*⟩

cyth·er·ea \,sithə'rēə\ [NL, fr. L, epithet of Venus-Aphrodite, fr. Gk *Kythereia*, fr. *Kythēra* Cythera, Greek island associated with Aphrodite] *syn of* CALYPSO

¹cyth·er·e·an \,==¦==ən\ *n* -S *usu cap* [L *Cytherea*, epithet of Venus + E *-an*] **:** a votary of Aphrodite

²cytherean \¦==¦==\ *adj, usu cap* [L *Cytherea* + E *-an*] **:** of or relating to the goddess Venus or to the planet Venus

cyth·er·el·la \,sithə'relə\ *n, cap* [NL, dim. of L *Cytherea*, epithet of Venus] **:** a genus of crustaceans (subclass Ostracoda) with biramous second antennae used for swimming

cyt·i·dine \'sid·ə,dēn, -,dən\ *n* -S [ISV *cyt-* + *-idine*] **:** a crystalline nucleoside $C_9H_{13}N_3O_5$ obtained by hydrolysis of ribonucleic acid and cytidylic acid; 1-D-ribosyl-cytosine

cyt·i·dyl·ic acid \¦sid·ə¦dilik-\ *n* [ISV *cytidine* + *-yl* + *-ic*] **:** a crystalline nucleotide $C_9H_{14}N_3O_8P$ known in various isomeric forms and obtained by hydrolysis of ribonucleic acid; cytidine monophosphate

cyt·i·nus \'sit'nəs\ *n, cap* [NL, fr. Gk *kytinos* flower of the pomegranate, fr. *kytos* hollow vessel, skin + *-inos* -ine — more at HIDE] **:** a genus of reddish or yellow fleshy root parasitic herbs (family Rafflesiaceae) comprising one African and three European species that grow on the roots of plants of the genus *Cistus*

cyt·i·sine \'sid·ə,sēn, -,zēn, -,sən\ *n* -S [NL *Cytisus* + E *-ine*] **:** a bitter crystalline very poisonous alkaloid $C_{11}H_{14}N_2O$ found in many plants of the pea family and formerly used as a cathartic and diuretic — compare ULEXINE

cyt·i·sus \-,səs, -zəs\ *n* [NL, fr. L, a shrub (*Medicago arborea*), fr. Gk *kytisos*] **1** *cap* **:** a large genus of stiff or spiny shrubs (family Leguminosae) native to Europe, northern Africa, and western Asia and having showy racemose flowers with a 2-lipped calyx — see BROOM 1 **2** *pl* **cytisi :** a plant of the genus *Cytisus*

cy·to- *in pronunciations below*, ¦== = ¦sīd·ō *or* ¦sīd·ə *or* ¦sītō *or* ¦sītə\ — see CYT-

cy·to·architectonic \¦== +\ *adj* [*cyt-* + *architectonic*] **:** CYTOARCHITECTURAL

cy·to·architectonics \¦== +\ *n pl but sing or pl in constr* **:** CYTOARCHITECTURE

cy·to·architectural \¦== +\ *adj* **:** of or relating to cytoarchitecture — **cy·to·architecturally** \¦== +\ *adv*

cy·to·architecture \¦== +\ *n* [*cyt-* + *architecture*] **:** the cellular makeup of a bodily tissue or structure

cy·to·blast \'==,blast\ *n* -S [G *zytoblast*, fr. *zyt-* cyt- + *-blast*] **1 :** NUCLEUS 2a **2 :** ALTMANN'S GRANULES **3 :** PROTOPLAST

cy·to·blastema \¦== +\ *n* [NL, fr. *cyt-* + *blastema*] **:** the formative material from which cells formerly were thought to arise — **cy·to·blastemal** \¦== +\ *adj*

cy·to·centrum \¦== +\ *n* [NL, fr. *cyt-* + L *centrum* center — more at CENTER] **:** CENTRAL APPARATUS

cy·to·chemical \¦== +\ *adj* [*cyt-* + *chemical*] **:** of, relating to, or used in cytochemistry ⟨~ methods⟩

cy·to·chemistry \¦== +\ *n* [*cyt-* + *chemistry*] **1 :** microscopical biochemistry **2 :** the chemistry of cells

cy·to·chon·dria \,=='kändrēə\ *n pl* [NL, fr. *cyt-* + *chondr-* + *-ia*] **:** formed bodies in the cytoplasm of a cell — compare MITOCHONDRION

cy·to·chrome \'== +,-\ *n* -S [*cyt-* + *-chrome*] **:** any of several respiratory pigments that occur in animal and plant cells, play a major role in intracellular oxidations (as by oxidizing flavoproteins and being in turn oxidized by means of cytochrome oxidase), and are related chemically to hemoglobin in that they are complexes of iron, a porphyrin, and a protein; *esp* **:** CYTOCHROME C

cytochrome c *n, often cap 2d C* **:** the most abundant and stable of the cytochromes obtained from various sources (as beef heart or yeast)

cytochrome oxidase *n* **:** an iron-porphyrin enzyme important in cell respiration because of its ability to catalyze the oxidation of reduced cytochrome c in the presence of oxygen — called also *respiratory enzyme*

cy·to·chy·le·ma \¦== +\ *n* -S [NL, fr. *cyt-* + *-chylema* (as in *enchylema*)] **:** HYALOPLASM

cy·toc·i·dal \(')sī¦täsədᵊl\ *adj* **:** killing or tending to kill individual cells

cy·tode \'sī,tōd\ *n* -S [ISV *cyt-* + *-ode* (fr. Gk *-ōdēs* like); orig. formed as G *zytode* — more at -ODES] **1 :** an anucleate mass of protoplasm **2 :** an organism normally assuming the form of a cytode (as a bacterium)

cy·to·dendrite \¦== *at* CYTO- +\ *n* [*cyt-* + *dendrite*] **:** a dendrite given off from the body of a nerve cell — distinguished from *axodendrite*

cy·to·diagnosis \¦==+\ *n* [NL, fr. *cyt-* + *diagnosis*] **:** diagnosis based upon the examination of cells found in the tissues or fluids of the body — **cy·to·diagnostic** \¦==+\ *adj*

cy·to·dieresis \¦==+\ *n, pl* **cytodiereses** [NL, fr. *cyt-* + *dieresis* dividing, fr. Gk *diairesis* — more at DIAERESIS] **:** CYTOKINESIS — **cy·to·dieretic** \¦==+\ *adj*

cy·tog·a·my \sī'tägəmē\ *n* -ES [*cyt-* + *-gamy*] **:** cell fusion **:** CONJUGATION 4

cy·to·gene \'== *at* CYTO- +,-\ *n* [*cyt-* + *gene*] **:** a self-duplicating cytoplasmic gene or determinant (as those of certain plant plastids) — compare PLASMAGENE — **cy·to·genic** \¦==+\ *adj*

cy·to·genetic *also* **cy·to·genetical** \¦==+\ *adj* [ISV *cyt-* + *-genetic, -genetical*] **:** of, relating to, concerning, or by the methods of cytogenetics — **cy·to·genetically** \¦==+\ *adv*

cy·to·geneticist \¦==+\ *n* **:** one specializing in cytogenetics

cy·to·genetics \¦==+\ *n pl but sing or pl in constr* [ISV *cyt-* + *genetics*] **:** a branch of biology that deals with the study of heredity and variation by the methods of both cytology and genetics

cy·tog·e·nous \(')sī¦täjənəs\ *adj* [*cyt-* + *-genous*] **:** producing cells — used specif. of lymphatic tissue

cy·to·geography \¦== *at* CYTO- +\ *n* [*cyt-* + *geography*] **:** a branch of biogeography dealing with the distribution of gene complexes among related populations

cy·to·globin \¦==+\ *n* [ISV *cyt-* + *globin;* orig. formed as G *zytoglobin*] **:** a nucleoprotein obtainable from many cells and glandular organs

cy·to·histological *also* **cy·to·histologic** \¦==+\ *adj* **:** of, relating to, or by the methods of cytohistology ⟨~ zonation⟩ ⟨~ diagnosis⟩

cy·to·histology \¦==+\ *n* [*cyt-* + *histology*] **:** the integrated study of cells and tissues

cy·to·kinesis \¦==+\ *n* [NL, fr. *cyt-* + *kinesis*] **1 :** the cytoplasmic changes accompanying karyokinesis **2 :** cleavage of the cytoplasm into daughter cells following nuclear division — **cy·to·kinetic** \¦==+\ *adj*

cy·to·lei·chus \,=='līkəs\ *n, cap* [NL, fr. *cyt-* + *-leichus* (prob. fr. Gk *leichein* to lick, lick up) — more at LICK] **:** a genus (the type of the family Cytoleichidae) of parasitic mites including only the air-sac mite (*C. nudus*)

cy·to·logical *or* **cy·to·logic** \¦==+\ *adj* **:** of, relating to, or by the methods of cytology — **cy·to·logically** \¦==+\ *adv*

cytologic diagnosis *n* **:** cytodiagnosis esp. for the detection of cancer

cy·tol·o·gist \sī'täləjəst\ *n* -S **1 :** one specializing in the study of cells **2 :** a pathologist using cytological techniques in the differential diagnosis of neoplasms

cy·tol·o·gy \-jē, -ji\ *n* -ES [ISV *cyt-* + *-logy*] **1 :** the branch of biology concerned with the study of cells as vital units with reference to their structure, function, multiplication, pathology, and life history ⟨as a procedure for differentiating benign from malignant lesions ~ offers a more precise method of diagnosis than roentgenologic and endoscopic study —*Jour. Amer. Med. Assoc.*⟩ — distinguished from *histology* **2 :** the cytological aspects of a phenomenon, process, or structure considered collectively ⟨the ~ of cancer⟩ ⟨the ~ of mitosis⟩

cy·to·lymph \'== *at* CYTO- +,-\ *n* [ISV *cyt-* + *lymph;* orig. formed as G *zytolymphe*] **:** HYALOPLASM

cy·tol·y·sin \,sītəl'īsᵊn\ *n* -S [ISV *cytolys-* (fr. NL *cytolysis*) + *-in*] **:** a substance (as a hemolysin or one of certain constituents of snake venom) producing cytolysis

cy·tol·y·sis \sī'täləsəs\ *n* [NL, fr. *cyt-* + *-lysis*] **:** the dissolution or disintegration of cells esp. as a pathological process — **cy·to·lytic** \¦sīdᵊl¦id·ik\ *adj*

cy·tol·y·zate \sī'tälə,zāt, -zət\ *n* -S [*cytolyze* + *-ate*] **:** the products resulting from cytolysis

cy·to·lyze \'sīdᵊl,īz\ *vt* -ED/-ING/-S [fr. NL *cytolysis*, after such pairs as ML *analysis*: E *analyze*] **:** to cause to undergo cytolysis

cy·tome \'sī,tōm\ *n* -S [ISV *cyt-* + *-ome;* orig. formed in F] **1 :** the formed inclusions of the cytoplasm **:** chondriome together with ergastic substances **2 :** CHONDRIOME

cy·to·mere \'sīd·ə,mi(ə)r\ *n* -S [ISV *cyt-* + *-mere;* orig. formed as G *zytomer*] **1 :** one of the cells resulting from the division of the schizont in certain coccidia **2 :** the cytoplasmic component of a spermatozoon

cy·tom·e·ter \sī'täməd·ə(r)\ *n* -S [ISV *cyt-* + *-meter*] **:** an apparatus for counting and measuring cells

cy·to·microsome \'== *at* CYTO- +\ *n* [ISV *cyt-* + *microsome;* orig. formed as G *zytomikrosom*] **:** a cytoplasmic microsome **:** MITOCHONDRION

cy·to·morphosis \¦==+\ *n, pl* **cytomorphoses** [NL, fr. *cyt-* + *-morphosis*] **:** the series of developmental changes undergone by a cell during its life

cy·ton \'sī,tän\ *also* **cy·tone** \-,tōn\ *n* -S [*cyt-* + *-on, -one*] **:** CELL; *esp* **:** NERVE CELL

cy·to·path·ic \¦== *at* CYTO- +¦pathik\ *adj* [*cyt-* + *-pathic*] **:** of, relating to, characterized by, or producing pathological changes in cells

cy·to·pathogenic \¦==+\ *adj* [*cyt-* + *pathogenic*] **:** pathologic for or destructive to cells ⟨~ virus⟩ ⟨~ effects⟩

cy·to·pathologic *also* **cy·to·pathological** \¦==+\ *adj* **:** of, relating to, or involving the methods of cytopathology — **cy·to·pathologically** \¦==+\ *adv*

cy·to·pathology \¦==+\ *n* [ISV *cyt-* + *pathology*] **:** a branch of pathology that deals with manifestations of disease on the cellular level

cy·to·pe·nia \,=='pēnēə\ *n* -S [NL, fr. *cyt-* + *-penia*] **:** a deficiency of cellular elements of the blood; *usu* **:** deficiency of a specific element (as granulocytes in granulocytopenia) — **cy·to·pe·nic** \¦==¦nik\ *adj*

cy·toph·a·ga \sī'täfəgə\ *n* [NL, fr. *cyt-* + *-phaga*] **1** *cap* **:** a genus of long flexuous pointed bacteria (order Myxobacterales) showing creeping motility, forming neither fruiting bodies nor microcysts, and being saprophytes of soil and water that vigorously hydrolyze cellulose and aid in the breakdown of plant remains **2** -S **:** any bacterium of the genus *Cytophaga*

cy·to·phag·ic \¦sīd·ə¦fajik\ *also* **cy·toph·a·gous** \(')sī¦täfəgəs\ *adj* [*cyt-* + *-phagic* (fr. *-phagy* + *-ic*) or *-phagous*] **:** of, relating to, or involving phagocytosis ⟨a ~ test⟩ — **cy·toph·a·gy** \sī'täfəjē\ *n* -ES

cy·to·pharynx \¦== *at* CYTO- +\ *n* [ISV *cyt-* + *pharynx*] **:** a channel leading from the surface into the protoplasm of certain unicellular organisms and functioning in ciliates as a gullet

cy·to·phil \'==,fil\ *adj* [ISV *cyt-* + *-phil;* prob. orig. formed as G *zytophil*] **:** having affinity for cells

cy·to·phore \'==,fō(ə)r\ *n* -S [F, fr. *cyt-* + *-phore*] **:** the residual mass of cytoplasm associated with each cluster of spermatozoa in certain invertebrates

cy·to·plasm \'== +,-\ *n* -S [ISV *cyt-* + *-plasm;* orig. formed as G *zytoplasma*] **1 a** *archaic* **:** the fluid ground substance of protoplasm **:** HYALOPLASM **b :** PROTOPLASM — used rarely in modern cytology **2 :** the part of the protoplasm of a protoplast that lies external to the nuclear membrane — distinguished from *karyoplasm, nucleoplasm;* see HYALOPLASM; CELL illustration — **cy·to·plasmatic** \¦==+\ *adj* — **cy·to·plasmic** \¦==+\ *adj* — **cy·to·plasmically** \¦==+\ *adv*

cytoplasmic heredity *or* **cytoplasmic inheritance** *n* **:** the transmission of characters from parent to offspring through the cytoplasm of the germ cell; *also* **:** the characters so transmitted — compare PLASMAGENE, PLASTOGENE

cy·to·plast \'==,plast\ *n* -S [*cyt-* + *-plast*] **:** the cytoplasmic content of a cell — compare PROTOPLAST — **cy·to·plas·tic** \¦==¦=stik\ *adj*

cy·to·poi·e·sis \,==,pȯi'ēsəs\ *n, pl* **cytopoie·ses** \-,sēz\ [NL, fr. *cyt-* + *-poiesis*] **:** production of cells

cy·to·proct \'==,präkt\ *n* -S [*cyt-* + Gk *prōktos* buttocks — more at PROCT-] **:** CYTOPYGE

cy·to·pyge \'==,pīj\ *n* -S [ISV *cyt-* + Gk *pygē* rump; orig. formed as G *zytopyge* — more at PYG-] **:** the point esp. if permanently identifiable at which waste is discharged from the protozoan body

cy·to·reticulum \¦==+\ *n* [NL, fr. *cyt-* + *reticulum*] **1 :** a relatively solid mesh or framework in which the hyaloplasm is suspended according to some theories of protoplasmic structure **2 :** a meshwork of cells and cell processes (as in connective tissues)

cy·to·ryc·tes *also* **cy·tor·rhyc·tes** \,=='rik,tēz\ *n, pl* **cytoryctes** *or* **cytorrhyctes** [NL, fr. *cyt-* + Gk *oryktēs* digger, fr. *orychein, oryssein* to dig — more at ROUGH] **:** any of certain inclusion bodies (as the Guarnieri bodies) orig. considered to constitute a distinct protozoan genus

cy·to·sine \'==,sēn, -,zēn, -,sən\ *n* -S [ISV *cyt-* + *-ose* + *-ine;* orig. formed as G *zytosin*] **:** a crystalline pyrimidine base $C_4H_5N_3O$ obtained esp. by hydrolysis of nucleic acids and also made synthetically; 4-amino-2(1*H*)-pyrimidin-one

cy·to·skeleton \¦==+\ *n* [*cyt-* + *skeleton*] **:** the oriented submicroscopic framework of complex protein fibrils that is believed to be responsible for the mechanical properties of protoplasm

cy·to·some \'==,sōm\ *n* -S [ISV *cyt-* + *-some;* orig. formed as G *zytosom*] **:** the cytoplasmic portion of the cell — distinguished from *nucleus*

cy·tos·po·ra \sī'täspərə\ *n, cap* [NL, fr. *cyt-* + *-spora*] **:** a form genus of parasitic imperfect fungi (family Phyllostictaceae) that produce their spores in pycnidial cavities within a stroma that is either subepidermal or subcortical in the host

cy·tos·po·ri·na \,=,=='rīnə, -'rēnə\ *n, cap* [NL, fr. *Cytospora* + *-ina*] **:** a form genus of imperfect fungi resembling and sometimes included in *Cytospora* but having longer spores

cy·tos·to·mal \(')sī¦tästəməl\ *adj* **:** of or relating to a cytostome

cy·to·stome \'== *at* CYTO- +,stōm\ *n* -S [ISV *cyt-* + *-stome;* orig. formed as G *zytostom*] **:** the mouth of a unicellular organism

cy·to·taxonomic *also* **cy·to·taxonomical** \¦==+\ *adj* **:** of, relating to, or employing the methods of cytotaxonomy — **cy·to·taxonomically** \¦==+\ *adv*

cy·to·taxonomist \¦==+\ *n* **:** one specializing in cytotaxonomy

cy·to·taxonomy \¦==+\ *n* [*cyt-* + *taxonomy*] **1 :** the study of the natural relationships and classification of organisms by methods combining classical systematic techniques with comparative studies of chromosomes **2 :** the karyologic makeup of a kind of organism ⟨the ~ of *Oenothera*⟩

cy·to·toxic \¦==+\ *adj* [in sense 1, fr. *cytotoxin* + *-ic;* in sense 2, fr. *cyt-* + *toxic*] **1 :** of or relating to a cytotoxin **2 :** toxic to cells — **cy·to·toxicity** \¦==+\ *n* -ES

cy·to·toxin \¦==+\ *n* [ISV *cyt-* + *-toxin;* prob. orig. formed as G *zytotoxin*] **:** a substance having a toxic effect upon cells

cy·to·trophoblast \¦==+\ *n* [*cyt-* + *trophoblast*] **:** the inner cellular layer of the trophoblast of an embryonic placental mammal that gives rise to the plasmodial syntrophoblast covering the placental villi — called also *Langhans' layer* — **cy·to·trophoblastic** \¦==+\ *adj*

cy·to·trophoderm \¦==+\ *n* [*cyt-* + *trophoderm*] **:** CYTOTROPHOBLAST

cy·to·tropic \¦==+\ *adj* [*cyt-* + *-tropic*] **1 :** exhibiting cytotropism **2 :** attracted to cells ⟨a ~ virus⟩

cy·tot·ro·pism \sī'tä·trə,pizəm\ *n* -S [ISV *cyt-* + *-tropism;* orig. formed as G *zytotropismus*] **:** the tendency of isolated cells and cell masses to move toward or away from one another

cy·to·zoic \¦== *at* CYTO- +\ *adj* [*cyt-* + *-zoic*] **:** parasitic within a cell — used esp. of protozoans

cy·to·zoon \¦==+\ *n, pl* **cytozoa** [*cyt-* + *-zoon*] **:** a cytozoic animal

cy·to·zyme \'==,zīm\ *also* **cy·to·zym** \-,zim\ *n* -S [F *cytozyme*, fr. *cyt-* + *-zyme* (fr. Gk *zymē* leaven) — more at ZYME] **:** THROMBOPLASTIN

cyt·tar·ia \sə'ta(a)rēə\ *n, cap* [NL, fr. Gk *kyttaros* cell of a honeycomb + NL *-ia;* fr. the pitted appearance of the fungi] **:** a genus of ascomycetous fungi typifying the family Cyttariaceae and comprising the beech fungi that are parasitic on certain evergreen beeches of the southern hemisphere and that have apothecia sunken in the surface of stalked often brightly colored subspherical stromata which are gelatinous at maturity and used as food by the natives of southern So. America

cyt·tar·i·a·ce·ae \=,=rē'āsē,ē\ *n pl, cap* [NL, fr. *Cyttaria*, type genus + *-aceae*] **:** a family of ascomycetous fungi (order Helotiales) that form a pear-shaped stroma with numerous apothecial cavities — see CYTTARIA

cyw·ydd \'kə,wiṯẖ\ *n, pl* **cywydd·au** \kə'wə,ṯẖī\ [W] **1 :** a Welsh verse form in couplets or occas. triplets with rhyme and cynghanedd; *esp* **:** verse consisting of couplets of 7-syllable lines with varying cynghanedd and terminal rhyme that falls alternately on accented and on unaccented syllables **2 :** a poem written in cywydd ⟨found among his loose papers . . . the autograph of a Welsh poem, a ~ by Hopkins himself —W.H.Gardner⟩

cza·pek–dox medium \¦chä(,)pek¦däks-\ *or* **czapek medium** *n, usu cap C&D* [after Friedrich *Czapek* †1921 Czech botanist & Arthur W. *Dox* †1954 Am. chemist] **:** a culture medium for various fungi consisting essentially of a balanced and buffered mixture of inorganic salts, a sugar, and water and being used (1) as a solution or (2) with added agar as a solid — called also respectively (1) *Czapek solution, Czapek-Dox solution,* (2) *Czapek agar*

czar \'z¦är, 'z¦å(r *sometimes* 'ts¦\ *n* -S [NL *czar*, fr. Russ *tsar'*, fr. ORuss *tsĭsarĭ, tsĕsarĭ* emperor, fr. Goth *kaisar*, fr. Gk or L; Gk, fr. L *Caesar* — more at CAESAR] **1** *or* **tsar** *also* **tzar** \'z¦ *also* 'ts\ [*tsar, tzar* fr. Russ *tsar'*] **:** an emperor or king having absolute authority; *specif* **:** the ruler of Russia before the 1917 revolution **2** *also* **tsar** [*tsar* fr. Russ *tsar'*] **:** one having great power or absolute authority **:** BOSS, DICTATOR ⟨gambling ~*s* established a mass of dummy charities to comply with the law —V.W.Peterson⟩; *esp* **:** a person to whom great authority is delegated ⟨his salary as movie ~ ran into six figures —G.W. Johnson⟩

czar·das *or* **csar·das** \'chär,däs(h) *also* zä- *or* -,das *or* -,dəs\ *n, pl* **czardas** *or* **csardas** [Hung *csárdás*] **1 :** a Hungarian couple dance to music in duple time that starts very slowly and ends in a rapid whirl **2 :** music for or suited to the czardas

czar·dom *also* **tsar·dom** *pronunc at* CZAR + dəm\ *n* -S **1 :** the territory ruled by a czar ⟨the ~ of Moscow . . . became aware of itself as the heir of Constantinople —R.M. French⟩ **2 :** the office or authority of a czar ⟨the memorable revolt . . . against the ~ of Speaker Cannon —Allan Nevins⟩

czar·e·vitch *also* **tsar·e·vitch** \'z¦ärə,vich, 'ts¦, ¦är-\ *n* -ES [Russ *tsarevich*, fr. *tsar'* + *-evich* (patronymic suffix)] **:** an heir apparent to the Russian czardom

cza·rev·na *also* **tsa·rev·na** \='revnə\ *n* -S [Russ *tsarevna*, fr. *tsar'* + *-evna* (fem. patronymic suffix)] **1 :** a daughter of a Russian czar **2 :** the wife of a czarevitch

cza·ri·na *also* **tsa·ri·na** \-'rēnə\ *n* -S [prob. modif. of G *zarin*, fr. *zar* tsar (fr. Russ *tsar'*) + *-in* (fem. suffix)] **:** the wife of a Russian czar

czar·ish *also* **tsar·ish** *pronunc at* CZAR + ish *or* ēsh\ *adj* **:** CZARIST

czar·ism *also* **tsar·ism** \" + ,izəm\ *n* -S **1 :** the government of Russia under the czars **2 :** autocratic rule **:** ABSOLUTISM

¹czar·ist *also* **tsar·ist** \'z¦ärəst, 'z¦år- *sometimes* 'ts¦\ *or* **czar·is·tic** *or* **tsar·is·tic** \(')=¦ristik\ *adj* **:** of, relating to, or characteristic of a czar or czarism ⟨the ~ autocracy —Walter Lippmann⟩ ⟨comparisons . . . between the immediate security objectives of the Soviet Union and those of the ~ regime —C.E.Black⟩ **:** DICTATORIAL ⟨gives Bevin ~ powers to shift men and women as he will —*Fortune*⟩

²czarist *also* **tsarist** \"\ *n* -S **:** a supporter of a czar or of czarism

cza·rit·za *also* **tsa·rit·za** \z¦ä'ritsə, ts¦, ¦ä'-, -'rēt-\ *n* -S [Russ *tsaritsa*, fem. of *tsar'*] **:** CZARINA

¹czech *also* **čech** \'chek\ *adj, usu cap* [*Czech* alter. (prob. influenced by Pol *czech*) of earlier *Tshekh, Tschech*, fr. Czech *čech; Čech*, fr. Czech] **1 :** ¹CZECHOSLOVAK 1 **2 :** of, relating to, or characteristic of the Czechs **3 :** of, relating to, or characteristic of the language of the Czechs (sense 1a)

²czech \"\ *n* -S *cap* **1 a :** a native or inhabitant of western Czechoslovakia including Bohemia and Moravia **b :** ²CZECHOSLOVAK **2 :** the Slavic language of the Czechs (sense 1a)

czech·ish \-kish, -kēsh\ *adj, usu cap* **:** CZECH

czech·ize \-,kīz\ *vt* -ED/-ING/-S *often cap* **:** to make Czech **:** cause to acquire Czech traits or characteristics

¹czech·o·slo·vak \¦chekə¦slō,väk, -kō¦-, -,vak,-,våk\ *or* **czech·o·slo·va·ki·an** \¦==(,)=¦=kēən\ *adj, usu cap* [*Czechoslovak* fr. *Czech* + *Slovak; Czechoslovakian* fr. *Czechoslovakia* + E *-an*] **1 :** of, relating to, or characteristic of Czechoslovakia **2 :** of, relating to, or characteristic of the people of Czechoslovakia

²czechoslovak *or* **czechoslovakian** \"\ *n* -S *cap* **:** a native or inhabitant of Czechoslovakia

czech·o·slo·va·kia \¦==(,)=¦=kēə\ *adj, usu cap* [fr. *Czechoslovakia*, country in central Europe] **:** of or from Czechoslovakia **:** of the kind or style prevalent in Czechoslovakia **:** CZECHOSLOVAK

cze·sto·cho·wa \¦chen(t)stə¦kōvə\ *adj, usu cap* [fr. *Częstochowa*, Poland] **:** of or from the city of Czestochowa, Poland **:** of the kind or style prevalent in Czestochowa

¹d \ˈdē\ *n, pl* **d's** *or* **ds** \ˈdēz\ *often cap, often attrib* **1 a :** the fourth letter of the English alphabet **b :** an instance of this letter printed, written, or otherwise represented **c :** a speech counterpart of orthographic *d* (as *d* in *did, raider, Edgar,* or French *duc*) **2 :** 500 — see NUMBER table **3 a :** the keynote of D major or D minor **b :** the tone D **4 :** a printer's type, a stamp, or some other instrument for reproducing the letter *d* **5 :** someone or something arbitrarily or conveniently designated *d* esp. as the fourth in order or class **6 a :** a grade assigned by a teacher or examiner rating a student's work as poor in quality ⟨barely passed geometry with a *D*⟩ **b :** one graded or rated with a D ⟨a *D* student⟩ ⟨a *D* movie⟩ ⟨the theme was a *D*⟩ **7 :** something having the shape of the capital letter D; *specif* **:** a semicircle on a pool table that is about 22 inches in diameter and is used esp. in snooker games

²d *abbr, often cap* **1** dam **2** dame **3** damn **4** date **5** daughter **6** day **7** deacon **8** dead **9** dean **10** deceased **11** deciduous **12** defeated **14** degree **15** dele; delete **16** democratic **17** demy **18** [L *denarius; denarii*] penny; pence **19** density **20** depart; departure **21** department **22** deputy **23** deserted; deserter **24** diameter **25** died **26** differential **27** dime **28** dimensional **29** dinar **30** diopter **31** director **32** discharged **33** distance **34** dividend **35** division **36** doctor **37** dog **38** dollar **39** dominus **40** dorsal **41** dose **42** double **43** dowager **44** drachma **45** driving **46** drizzling **47** duchess; duchy; duke **48** dyne

³d *symbol* **1** *cap* Deuteronomy — used in biblical criticism to designate esp. redactions of biblical material made under the editorship of Deuteronomic writers **2** *cap* deuterium **3** deuteron **4** *cap* D day ⟨wounded in the stomach on the morning of *D* plus three —Laurence Critchell⟩ **5** *cap* duodecimo

d- \(ˌ)dē\ *prefix* [ISV, fr. *dextr-*] **1 :** dextrorotatory — usu. printed in italic ⟨*d*-tartaric acid⟩; compare DEXTR- 2 **2 :** having a similar configuration at a selected asymmetric carbon atom in an optically active molecule to the configuration of dextrorotatory glyceraldehyde — usu. printed as a small capital ⟨D-fructose⟩

¹-d *abbr* ¹-ED — used esp. in standard abbreviations of the past and past participle forms of certain verbs (as *recd* for *received, chgd* for *charged, ltd* for *limited*)

²-d *symbol* — used after the figure 2 or the figure 3 to indicate the ordinal number *second* or *third* or any ordinal number ending with *second* or *third* ⟨May 2*d*⟩ ⟨33*d* St.⟩; compare -ND, -RD

d' \"*d'y*" *is* d(ə)y *or* y *or* j *in sense 1,* j *in sense 2*\ *vb* [by contr.] **1 :** ¹DO ⟨*d*'you know what he wants?⟩ **2 :** DID ⟨*d*'you see what I saw?⟩

-'d \d\ *vb suffix or adj suffix* [by contr.] **:** ¹-ED — now esp. in forms derived from words ending in a vowel ⟨the flicker of one mascara'*d* eyelash —Leslie Charteris⟩

'd \(ə)d\ *vb* [contr. of *had, would, did*] **1 :** HAD ⟨they'*d* gone⟩ **2 a :** ¹WOULD ⟨he'*d* go⟩ **b :** SHOULD **3 :** DID ⟨what'*d* you say?⟩ ⟨where'*d* he go?⟩ ⟨'*d* you see what I saw?⟩

¹da \ˈdä\ *n* -S [Bambara] **:** KENAF

²da \"\ *n* -S *sometimes cap* [short for *dada*] *dial Brit* **:** FATHER ⟨trying to make himself look like my ~ —Frank O'Connor⟩

da *abbr* daughter

DA *abbr* **1** days after acceptance **2** deposit account **3** direct action **4** discharge afloat **5** district attorney **6** documentary bill for acceptance **7** documents against acceptance; documents for acceptance **8** documents attached

¹dab \ˈdab, ˈdaa(ə)b\ *n* -S [ME *dabbe*, prob. of imit. origin] **1 a :** a sudden blow, thrust, or slap **:** POKE, PROD; *also* **:** PECK **b :** a gentle touch or stroke **:** PAT **2 :** an instrument (as a center punch) for dabbing or marking something

²dab \"\ *vb* **dabbed; dabbed; dabbing; dabs** [ME *dabben*, fr. *dabbe*, n.] *vt* **1** *archaic* **a :** to strike with a sudden motion **b :** STAB, PIERCE **c :** PECK **2 a :** to strike or touch lightly **:** PAT ⟨she *dabbed* her eyes with her pocket handkerchief —Rudyard Kipling⟩ **b :** to cause to strike ⟨~ a paintbrush against the surface⟩ **:** apply lightly to (as with a dabber) **3 a** *dial* **:** THROW, THRUST **b** *West* **:** to throw (as a rope) so as to fasten ⟨cowpunchers could ~ their lines on anything that moved —Ross Santee⟩ **4** *also* **daub :** to dress the face of (stone) by picking or fretting **5 :** to apply ink to (a printing surface) with an ink-ball ~ *vi* **1 :** to make a dab ⟨she *dabbed* at her eyes with a . . . handkerchief —*Time*⟩ **2 :** to use a dabber (as in etching) **3 :** DABBLE *vi* 2

³dab \"\ *vt* **dabbed; dabbed; dabbing; dabs** [by alter.] **:** DAUB 1

⁴dab \"\ *n* -S [alter. of *daub*] **1 :** ²DAUB **2 :** a small amount or portion ⟨a little ~ of peas on a plate⟩ **3** *archaic* **:** a wet or dirty cloth

⁵dab \"\ *n* -S [AF *dabbe*] **:** FLATFISH; *esp* **:** any of several flounders of the genus *Limanda* — often used in combination ⟨sand ~⟩

⁶dab \"\ *n* -S [perh. alter. (influenced by ¹ & ²*dab*) of *adept* (a *dab* resulting from incorrect division of *adept*)] *chiefly Brit* **:** a skillful hand **:** EXPERT ⟨a ~ at rationalizing —C.H. Glover⟩

⁷dab *also* **dabb** \"\ *n* -S [Ar *ḍabb* lizard] **:** a large spinytailed agamoid lizard (*Uromastix spinipes* or related species) of Arabia, Egypt, and No. Africa

dab·ber \-bə(r)\ *n* -S **1 :** one that dabs **2 :** a utensil for dabbing: as **a :** a pad used by etchers or engravers to apply ink, ground, or color evenly to a surface **b :** a brush used by stereotypers to force the damped matrix material into the interstices of the matter being molded **c :** a similar brush used in gilding or photography **d :** INK-BALL

dab·ble \ˈdabəl\ *vb* **dabbled; dabbled; dabbling** \-b(ə)liŋ\ **dabbles** [perh. freq. of ³*dab*] *vt* **:** to wet by splashing or by little dips or strokes **:** SPATTER, SPLASH, SPRINKLE ⟨boots *dabbled* with mud⟩ ⟨the moon hung over the harbor *dabbling* the waves with gold —Katherine Mansfield⟩ ~ *vi* **1 a :** to paddle, splash, or play in or as if in water ⟨~ with his fingers in the sand —W.F.Davis⟩ **b** *of a duck* **:** to tilt the body forward and downward in shallow water to obtain food from the bottom **2 :** to work or concern oneself in a superficial way or intermittently according to whim — usu. used with *in* ⟨~ *in* politics⟩ ⟨eternally *dabbling* in diets —Lois Long⟩ **3** *archaic* **:** TAMPER, MEDDLE

dab·bler \-b(ə)lə(r)\ *n* -S **1 :** one that concerns himself only superficially with something **:** one that merely dips into something **:** DILETTANTE **2 :** a duck that frequents shallow water and feeds by dabbling — compare DIVING DUCK

dab·bling·ly *adv* **:** in a dabbling manner

dab·by \-bē\ *adj, usu* -ER/-EST [³*dab* + -*y*] *archaic* **:** wet and adhesive ⟨~ clothes⟩ **:** MOIST, DAMP

dabchick \ˈdab+ˌ-\ *n* [earlier *dapchick*, prob. fr. alter. of *dop* (to dive) + *chick*] **1 :** any of several small grebes: as **a :** LITTLE GREBE **b :** PIED-BILLED GREBE **c :** a small Australian grebe (*Podiceps novae-hollandiae*) **2** *dial Eng* **:** the common gallinule of Europe

dab·er locks \ˈdabə(r),-\ *n pl but sing or pl in constr* [by alter.] **:** BADDERLOCKS

dab-hand *n* [⁶*dab*] *chiefly Brit* **:** EXPERT

da·boia \dəˈbȯiə\ *n* [Hindi *dabоyā*, lit., lurker, fr. *dabnā* to be pressed down, lurk] **1** *also* **da·boya** \"\ -S **:** RUSSELL'S VIPER **2** *cap* [NL, fr. Hindi *daboyā*] *in some esp former classifications* **:** a genus of vipers containing solely the Russell's viper

dabs *pl of* DAB, *pres 3d sing of* DAB

dab·ster \ˈdabstə(r)\ *n* -S [prob. fr. ⁶*dab* + -*ster*] **1** *chiefly dial* **:** one that is esp. skilled **:** EXPERT **2** [prob. influenced in meaning by *dabble*] **:** a dabbler at anything **:** an unskilled hand

¹da ca·po \(ˈ)däˈkä(ˌ)pō, dəˈk-\ *adv (or adj)* [It] **:** from the beginning — used as a direction in music to repeat; abbr. *D.C.*

²da capo \"\ *n, pl* **da capos :** a part repeated or to be repeated da capo in a piece of music

da capo aria *n* **:** ARIA DA CAPO

dac·ca \ˈdakə, ˈdäkə\ *adj, usu cap* [fr. *Dacca*, Pakistan] **:** of or from the city of Dacca, Pakistan **:** of the kind or style prevalent in Dacca

dace \ˈdās\ *n, pl* **dace** *or* **daces** [ME *dace, darce*, fr. MF *dars*, fr. ML *darsus*] **1 :** a small European cyprinoid fish (*Leuciscus leuciscus*) inhabiting chiefly clear quiet streams **2 :** any of many small No. American freshwater fishes of various genera of the family Cyprinidae (as the fallfish or golden shiner) — see HORNED DACE

da·ce·lo \dəˈsē(ˌ)lō\ *n, cap* [NL, anagram of *Alcedo*] **:** a genus of Australasian kingfishers including the kookaburra

da·cent \ˈdāsᵊnt\ *dial Brit var of* DECENT

¹da·cha *or* **dat·cha** \ˈdächə\ *n* -S [Russ *dacha*, lit., act of giving, paying; akin to Ukrainian *dača* gift, Serbo-Croatian *daća* funeral meal, Russ *dat'* to give, Skt *dadāti* he gives — more at DATE] **:** a country house, a summer house, or a villa in Russia

²dacha *var of* DAGGA

da·chi·ar·dite \ˌdäkēˈärˌdīt\ *n* -S [It, fr. Antonio *d'Achiardi* †1902 Ital. mineralogist + It *-ite*] **:** a mineral $(Ca,K_2,Na_2)_3Al_4Si_{18}O_{45}.14H_2O$ belonging prob. to the zeolite group

dachs \ˈdäks, ˈdaks *also* ˈdaks\ *n, pl* **dachs** *or* **dachses** [by shortening] **:** DACHSHUND

dachs·hund \ˈdäksˌhu̇nt, ˈdäk-, -kˌsu̇-, -u̇nd, -ksənt,-ksənd *also* ˈdak- *or* -ks,hənd *or* -kˌsənd; ÷ˈdashənd, ÷ˈdaash-, ÷ˈdaish-, ÷-shˌhau̇nd\ *n, pl* **dachshunds** \-nts,-n(d)z\ *or* **dachshun·de** \-u̇ndə\ [G, fr. *dachs* badger (fr. OHG *dahs*) + *hund* dog, fr. OHG *hunt* — more at TECHNICAL, HOUND] **:** a small dog of a breed of German origin having long drooping ears, commonly a short sleek coat, and the legs short in comparison with the body length and being courageous and tenacious, well adapted for following game (as badgers and foxes) into burrows, and also satisfactory as a house dog

dachs·ie \-ksē\ *n* -S **:** DACHSHUND

¹da·cian \ˈdāshən\ *adj, usu cap* [*Dacia*, ancient Roman province of central Europe (fr. L) + E *-an*] **:** of or relating to Dacia or to the inhabitants of Dacia

²dacian \"\ *n* -S *cap* **:** a native or inhabitant of Dacia

da·cite \ˈdāˌsīt\ *n* -S [G *dazit*, fr. *Dazien* Dacia + G *-it* -ite] **:** an extrusive rock that is sometimes partly glassy and is composed of plagioclase and quartz with biotite, hornblende, or pyroxene — **da·cit·ic** \(ˈ)dāˌsid·ik\ *adj*

da·co- \ˈdākō, -kə\ *comb form, usu cap* [ISV, fr. *Dacia*] **:** Dacian ⟨*Daco*-Romanian⟩

da·coit \dəˈkȯit\ *n* -S [Hindi *ḍakait*, perh. fr. Skt *dakṣa* clever, akin to Skt *dakṣiṇa* right — more at DEXTER] **:** one of a class of criminals in India and Burma who rob and murder in roving gangs

da·coity \-ȯid-ē, -ȯitē, -i\ *n* -ES [Hindi *ḍakaitī*, fr. *ḍakait* dacoit] **:** robbery by dacoits — now used in the Indian penal code of robbery by an armed gang of not less than five men

dacota *or* **dacotah** *usu cap, var of* DAKOTA

dac·que's principle \daˈkāz-\ *n, usu cap D* [after Edgar *Dacqué* †1945 Ger. paleontologist] **:** the theory that different biological groups tend to evolve in the same direction at the same time

Da·cron \ˈdāˌkrän, ˈdaˌ- *sometimes* -ˌkrən\ *trademark* **1** — used for a polyester fiber made in filament and staple form, characterized by its great resilience, and often blended with other fibers in fabrics **2 :** a yarn or fabric made of Dacron fiber

dacry- *or* **dacryo-** *comb form* [NL, fr. Gk *dakry-, dakryo-*, fr. *dakry, dakryon* tear — more at TEAR] **:** of a tear or tears **:** lacrimal ⟨*dacry*oma⟩ ⟨*dacryo*cystitis⟩

da·cryd·i·um \dəˈkridēəm\ *n, cap* [NL, fr. Gk *dakrydion* scammony, lit., little tear, dim. of *dakry* drop, tear; fr. the resinous drops exuded] **:** a genus of Australasian shrubs and trees (family Taxaceae) that resemble those of the genus *Podocarpus* but have orthotropous seeds — see HUON PINE, MOUNTAIN PINE, RIMU

dac·ry·my·ces \ˌdakrəˈmīˌsēz\ *n, cap* [NL, fr. *dacry-* + *-myces*] **:** the type genus of Dacrymycetaceae comprising basidiomycetous fungi with a bifurcate basidium that lacks septa

dac·ry·my·ce·ta·ce·ae \ˌdakrəˌmīsəˈtāsēˌē\ *n pl, cap* [NL, fr. *Dacrymycet-, Dacrymyces*, type genus + *-aceae*] **:** a family of basidiomycetous fungi (order Tremellales) all of which have basidia similar to those of the type genus *Dacrymyces* — see DACRYMYCETALES

dac·ry·my·ce·ta·les \-ˈtā(ˌ)lēz\ *n pl, cap* [NL, fr. *Dacrymycet-, Dacrymyces* + *-ales*] *in some classifications* **:** an order of basidiomycetous fungi coextensive with the family Dacrymycetaceae

dac·ry·o·cyst \ˈdakrēˌō, -rēə+,-\ *n* [ISV *dacry-* + *cyst*] **:** LACRIMAL SAC

dac·ry·o·cystitis \ˌ==(ˌ)=+\ *n* [NL, fr. ISV *dacryocyst* + NL *-itis*] **:** inflammation of the lacrimal sac

dac·ry·on \ˈdakrēˌän\ *n, pl* **dacrya** \-rēə\ [NL, fr. Gk *dakryon* tear — more at TEAR] **:** the point of junction of the anterior border of the lacrimal bone with the frontal bone — see CRANIOMETRY illustration

dac·ry·o·stenosis \ˌdakrēˌō, -rēə+\ *n* [NL, fr. *dacry-* + *stenosis*] **:** a narrowing of the lacrimal duct

dac·tyl \ˈdaktᵊl\ *n* -S [ME *dactile*, fr. L *dactylus*, fr. Gk *daktylos*, lit., finger; fr. the fact that the syllables of the metrical foot are three in number like the joints of the finger] **1 :** a metrical foot of three syllables, the first being stressed and the last two being unstressed (as in "take her up tenderly") **:** a trisyllabic falling cadence — symbol – ᴗ ᴗ for long, short, short in classical prosody or stressed, unstressed, unstressed in English prosody; also óoo; compare ANAPEST **2** [NL *dactylus*, fr. Gk *daktylos* finger, toe] **a :** a finger or toe **b :** DACTYLUS

dactyl- *or* **dactylo-** *comb form* [Gk *daktyl-, daktylo-*, fr. *daktylos*] **:** finger **:** toe **:** digit ⟨*dactyl*itis⟩ ⟨*dactylo*logy⟩

dac·ty·lar \ˈdaktələ(r)\ *adj* [*dactyl-* + *-ar*] **:** of or relating to a dactylus

dactyli *pl of* DACTYLUS

-dac·tyl·ia \dakˈtilēə, -lyə\ *n comb form* -S [NL, fr. Gk *daktylos* + NL *-ia* -y] **:** condition of having (such or so many) digits ⟨hexa*dactylia*⟩ ⟨sclero*dactylia*⟩

¹dac·tyl·ic \(ˈ)dakˈtilik, -lēk\ *adj* [L *dactylicus*, fr. Gk *daktylikos*, fr. *daktylos* dactyl + *-ikos* -ic] **:** having the form of a dactyl ⟨a ~ foot⟩ **:** of or consisting of dactyls ⟨~ verse⟩ — **dac·tyl·i·cal·ly** \-lək(ə)lē, -li\ *adv*

²dactylic \"\ *n* -S **:** a dactylic verse or measure

dactylic pentameter *n* **:** ELEGIAC PENTAMETER

-dactylies *pl of* -DACTYLY

dactylio- *comb form* [prob. fr. F, fr. Gk *daktylio-*, fr. *daktylios*, fr. *daktylos* finger] **1 :** finger ring ⟨*dactylio*logy⟩ **2 :** gem ⟨*dactylio*glyphy⟩

dac·tyl·i·o·man·cy \dakˈtilēəˌman(t)sē\ *n* -ES [prob. fr. F *dactyliomancie*, fr. Gk *daktylio-* dactylio- + F *-mancie* -mancy] **:** divination by means of finger rings

dac·tyl·i·on \-ˈtilēˌän\ *n* -S [NL, fr. Gk *daktylos* finger + *-ion* (dim. suffix)] **:** the tip of the middle finger

dac·tyl·i·o·the·ca \dakˌtilēōˈthēkə\ *n, pl* **dactyliothecas** \-kəz\ *or* **dactyliothe·cae** \-(ˌ)sē\ [L, fr. Gk *daktyliothēkē*, fr. *daktylio-* dactylio- + *thēkē* case, cover — more at TICK] **1 :** a case for a collection (as of rings, gems, or seals) **2 :** a book reproducing illustrations of or cataloging a collection of gems and rings

dac·ty·lis \ˈdaktələs\ *n, cap* [NL, fr. Gk *daktylos* finger; fr. its fingerlike spikelets] **:** a genus of two or three perennial chiefly Eurasian grasses having the 2- to 6-flowered spikelets arranged in a one-sided panicle — see ORCHARD GRASS

-dac·tyl·ism \ˌdaktəˌlizəm\ *n comb form* -S [ISV, fr. Gk *daktylos* finger, toe + ISV *-ism*] **:** -DACTYLIA

dac·ty·lo·gnathite \ˌdaktə(ˌ)lō, -tələ +\ *n* [*dactyl-* + *gnathite*] **:** the distal segment of a maxilliped

dac·tyl·o·gram \dakˈtiləˌgram; ˈ=tə(ˌ)lō-, -tələ,-\ *n* -S [ISV *dactyl-* + *-gram*] **:** an impression taken from a finger **:** FINGERPRINT

dac·tyl·o·graph \-ˌgraf\ *n* -S [*dactyl-* + *-graph*] **:** DACTYLOGRAM

dac·ty·log·ra·pher \ˌdaktəˈlägrəfə(r)\ *n* -S **:** a specialist in dactylography

dac·tyl·o·graph·ic \(ˈ)dakˌtiləˈgrafik; ˈ=tə(ˌ)lō-, -tələ-\ *adj* **:** of or relating to a dactylogram or to dactylography

dac·ty·log·ra·phy \ˌ==ˈlägrəfē\ *n* -ES [*dactyl-* + *-graphy*] **:** the scientific study of fingerprints as a means of identification — compare SIGNALMENT

dac·ty·loid \ˈdaktəˌlȯid\ *adj* [Gk *daktyloeidēs*, fr. *daktyl-* dactyl- + *-eidēs* -oid] **:** resembling a finger in shape

dac·ty·lol·o·gy \ˌ==ˈläləjē\ *n* -ES [Gk *daktyl-* dactyl- + E *-logy*] **:** the art of communicating ideas by signs made with the fingers (as in the manual alphabets of the deaf

dac·ty·lom e·tra \-ˈlämətrə\ *n, cap* [NL, fr. *dactyl-* + *-metra* (fr. Gk *metron* measure) — more at MEASURE] **:** a genus of tropical scyphozoan jellyfishes having a sting that is very painful and that may be dangerous to man — compare FIRE MEDUSA

dac·ty·lo·pi·us \-ˈlōpēəs\ *n, cap* [NL, fr. *dactyl-* + *-pius* (prob. fr. Gk *piōn* fat); fr. the form of the body] **:** a genus of scales containing the cochineal insect and formerly those mealybugs that are now placed in *Pseudococcus*

dac·ty·lop·o·dite \-ˈläpəˌdīt\ *n* [ISV *dactyl-* + *-podite*] **:** the distal segment of certain limbs of arthropods (as the ambulatory limbs of a decapod)

dactylology: one-hand alphabet

dac·tyl·o·pore \dakˈtiləˌpō(ə)r, ˈdaktəl-\ *n* [ISV *dactyl-* + *pore*] **:** one of the pores in hydrozoan corals through which in life the dactylozooids protrude

dac·ty·lop·si·la \ˌ==ˈläpsələ\ *n, cap* [NL, fr. *dactyl-* + *-psila* (fr. Gk *psilos* bare); fr. the bare toes — more at PSIL-] **:** a genus of mammals consisting of the striped opossums

dac·ty·lo·pter·i·dae \ˌdaktə(ˌ)lōˈterəˌdē, -təlapˈ-\ *n pl, cap* [NL, fr. *Dactylopterus*, type genus (fr. *dactyl-* + *-pterus*) + *-idae*] **:** a family (type genus *Dactylopterus*) of the order Scleroparei comprising marine fishes with greatly elongated pectoral fins — see FLYING GURNARD

dac·tyl·o·scop·ic \(ˈ)dakˌtiləˈskäpik; ˈ=tə(ˌ)lō-, -tələ-\ *adj* **:** of or relating to dactyloscopy

dac·ty·los·co·pist \ˌ==ˈläskəpəst\ *n* -S **:** one who practices dactyloscopy

dac·ty·los·co·py \-ˈläskəpē\ *n* -ES [ISV *dactyl-* + *-scopy*] **:** identification by comparison of fingerprints; *also* **:** classification of fingerprints — compare SIGNALMENT

dac·ty·lo·sternal \ˌdaktə(ˌ)lō +\ *adj* [*dactyl-* + *sternal*] *of turtles* **:** having marginal processes suggesting fingers and joining the plastron to the carapace

dac·tyl·o·style \dakˈtiləˌstīl, ˈ=tə(ˌ)lō-,\ *n* -S [*dactyl-* + *-style*] **:** one of a series of minute spicules on the wall of a dactylopore

dac·ty·lo·symphysis \ˌdaktə(ˌ)lō+\ *n* [NL, fr. *dactyl-* + *symphysis*] **:** SYNDACTYLISM

dac·tyl·o·tome \dakˈtiləˌtōm, ˈ=tələ,-\ *n* -S [*dactyl-* + *-tome*] **:** one of a series of shallow slits by which dactylopores open into their associated gastropore

dac·ty·lous \ˈdaktələs\ *adj* [NL *dactylus*] **:** of or relating to a dactylus

-dac·ty·lous \ˈ===\ *adj comb form* [Gk *-daktylos*, fr. *daktylos* finger, toe] **:** having (such or so many) fingers or toes ⟨iso*dactylous*⟩ ⟨mono*dactylous*⟩

dac·ty·lo·zooid \ˌdaktə(ˌ)lō, -tələ+\ *n* [ISV *dactyl-* + *zooid*] **:** a tentacular mouthless zooid in certain hydrozoans that performs tactile and protective functions for the colony

dac·ty·lus \ˈdaktələs\ *n, pl* **dacty·li** \-ˌlī\ [NL, fr. Gk *daktylos* finger, toe] **1 :** DACTYLOPODITE **2 :** the part consisting of one or more joints of the tarsus of certain insects following the enlarged and modified first joint

-dac·ty·ly \ˌdaktəlē, -li\ *n comb form* -ES [NL *-dactylia* — more at -DACTYLIA] **:** -DACTYLIA

da·cus \ˈdākəs\ *n, cap* [NL, fr. Gk *dakos* noxious animal, fr. *daknein* to bite — more at TONGS] **:** a genus of trypetid fruit flies of warm regions including several important pests of cultivated plants (as the melon fly, the oriental fruit fly, and the olive fly)

¹dad \ˈdad, ˈdaa(ə)d\ *n* -S [prob. baby talk, like OHG *todo* father, L *tata*, W *tad*, Gk *tata, tetta*, Skt *tata*] **:** FATHER

²dad \"\ *interj, often cap* [euphemism for *God*] — used as a mild oath

³dad \"\ *vb* **dadded; dadded; dadding; dads** [prob. of imit. origin] *chiefly Scot* **:** BEAT, POUND

⁴dad \"\ *n* -S **1** *chiefly Scot* **:** a heavy blow **:** THUMP **2** *chiefly Scot* **:** LUMP, CHUNK

DAD *abbr* deputy assistant director

¹dada \ˈdaˌda, ˈdä(ˌ)dä *sometimes* ˈdadə\ *n* -S [baby talk — more at DAD] **:** FATHER

²da·da \ˈdä(ˌ)dä\ *or* **da·da·ism** \ˈdä(ˌ)däˌizəm, ˈdäˌdiz-\ *n* -S *usu cap* [*dada* fr. F, fr. (baby talk) *dada* hobby horse, hobby (arbitrarily chosen symbol of the movement), redupl. of *da, dia* giddap; *dadaism* fr. F *dadaïsme*, fr. *dada* + *-isme* -ism] **1 :** the principles or practice in the arts and esp. painting that flourished chiefly in France, Switzerland, and Germany from 1916 to about 1920 and that were based on deliberate irrationality, anarchy, cynicism, and negation of laws of beauty and social organization **2 :** the cult of Dada

da·da·ist \ˈdä(ˌ)däˌist, ˈdäˌdäəst, ˈdädəst\ *n* -S *often cap* **:** a follower of Dada — **da·da·is·tic** \ˌdä(ˌ)däˈistik\ *adj*

dad·ap \ˈdadəp\ *n* -S [Malay *dědap*] **:** any of several Indian trees of the genus *Erythrina* planted for the nitrogen-fixing bacteria on their roots

¹dad–burned \ˈdadˌbərnd\ *adj* [euphemism] **:** ¹DAMNED 2a,2b

²dad–burned \"\ *adv* [euphemism] **:** ²DAMNED

¹dad·dle \ˈdadᵊl, ˈdäd-\ *dial Brit var of* DAWDLE

²dad·dle \ˈdadᵊl\ *n* -S [perh. irreg. fr. ³*dad*] *dial Brit* **:** HAND, FIST

dad·dock \ˈdadək\ *n* -S [origin unknown] *dial* **:** rotten wood — **dad·docky** \-kē\ *adj, dial*

dad·dy \ˈdadē, ˈdaad-, -di\ *n* -ES [¹*dad* + -*y*] **1 :** FATHER ⟨there comes a time to do what our *daddies* did —Hodding Carter⟩ **2** *slang* **:** SUGAR DADDY

daddy longlegs \ˌ==ˈ=ˌ=\ *n pl but sing or pl in constr* **:** any of various animals with long slender legs: as **a :** CRANE FLY **b :** HARVESTMAN

dad·dy·nut \ˈdadēˌnət\ *also* **daddynut tree** *n* **:** AMERICAN BASSWOOD

dade \ˈdād\ *vt* -ED/-ING/-S [origin unknown] *now dial Brit* **:** to lead and support

¹da·do \ˈdā(ˌ)dō *sometimes* ˈdä(-\ *n* -ES [It, die, cube, plinth, perh. fr. Ar *dad* game] **1 a :** the part of a pedestal of a column included between the base and the surbase — called also *die* **b :** the part of the basement of a wall included between the surbase and the base course **c :** the lower part of an interior wall when adorned with moldings or otherwise specially decorated or faced; *also* **:** the molding, facing, or other decoration adorning this part of a wall **2** [²*dado*] **:** a groove made by dadoing **3 :** a rectangular groove in (as a plank)

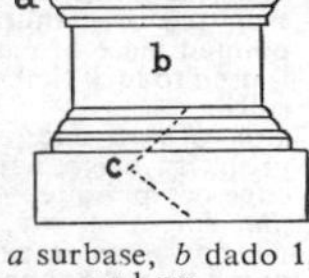

a surbase, *b* dado 1, *c* base

²dado \"\ *vt* **dadoed; dadoed; dadoing; dadoes** *or* **dados** **1 :** to furnish with a dado ⟨a ~*ed* living room⟩ **2 :** to secure by fitting into a groove **:** set into a groove ⟨~ the shelves of the bookcases to make them solider⟩ **3 :** to cut a rectangular groove in (as a plank)

dado cap *n* **:** a molding that caps an interior dado; *often* **:** CHAIR RAIL

dado head *n* **:** a power-saw tool made up of two circular saws of equal diameter and one or more chippers and used for cutting flat-bottomed grooves

dado plane *n* **:** a narrow rabbet plane that has two spurs and often an adjustable fence and that is used for making flat-bottomed grooves in woodwork

dado rail *n* **:** CHAIR RAIL

da·doxy·lon \dəˈdäksə,län, -lən\ *n, cap* [NL, fr. Gk *daid-, dais* firebrand, pine wood (fr. *daiein* to kindle, burn up) + NL *-xylon* — more at TEEN] **:** a form genus of chiefly Paleozoic fossils based on a heterogeneous group of woods which are now known to belong to various families and which are all characterized by alternate pitting on tracheid walls

dads *pl of* DAD, *pres 3d sing of* DAD

dae \ˈdā\ *Scot var of* DO

dae·dal \ˈdēdᵊl\ *adj* [L *daedalus*, fr. Gk *daidalos* — more at CONDOLE] **1 a :** ingeniously formed or working **:** like a maze **:** INTRICATE ⟨this immense, ~ system of artificial segments, of facades, and paths, and bridges —Florence Gould⟩ **b :** SKILLFUL, ARTISTIC, INGENIOUS ⟨words made accessible in a novel and ~ way —*Publishers' Weekly*⟩ **2 :** adorned with many things **:** RICH ⟨through that ~, pristine world sailor and poet spread their fame —John Lehman⟩

dae·da·lea \dēˈdālēə\ *n, cap* [NL, fr. L, fem. of *Daedaleus* of Daedalus, fr. *Daedalus*] **:** a genus of tough pore fungi (family Polyporaceae) of Europe and America usu. growing on dead wood and distinguished from members of the genus *Polyporus* by the labyrinthine lamellae formed by the pores

dae·da·li·an \(ˈ)dēˈdālēən, -lyən\ *or* **dae·da·le·an** \-lēən\ *adj, usu cap* [*Daedalus*, mythical craftsman and inventor of ancient Greece noted esp. for the construction of a labyrinth to contain the Minotaur and for the invention of wings with which he escaped imprisonment (fr. L, fr. Gk *Daidalos*) + E *-ian, -ean*] **1 :** of, relating to, or suggesting the mythological Daedalus ⟨*Daedalian* wings of escape —Curtis Bradford⟩ **2 :** DAEDAL

dae·dal·ic \dēˈdalik\ *adj, usu cap* [*Daedalus* + E *-ic*] **:** DAEDALIAN 1

daemon *var of* DEMON

dae·mon·e·lix \dēˈmänə,liks\ *n, cap* [NL, fr. LL *daemon* + Gk *helix* spiral — more at HELIX] *in some classifications* **:** a genus of large spiral fossils of uncertain systematic position and nature comprising the devil's corkscrews

dae·mo·ni·an \(ˈ)dēˈmōnēən\ *var of* DEMONIAN

daemonic *var of* DEMONIC

daemonology *var of* DEMONOLOGY

dae·na \ˈdänə\ *n* -s [Av *daēnā*] **1** *Zoroastrianism* **:** the moral element in personality **:** CONSCIENCE, SELF **2** *Zoroastrianism* **:** the moral life of man **:** RELIGION

dae·va *or* **de·va** \ˈdāvə\ *or* **dev** \ˈdāv\ *n* -s [*daeva, deva* fr. Av *daēvō*; *dev* fr. Per *dēv*, fr. Av *daēvō*; akin to Skt *deva* god — more at DEITY] *Zoroastrianism* **:** a maleficent supernatural being **:** an evil spirit **:** DEMON

daf·a·dar *or* **duf·fa·dar** \,dəfəˈdär\ *n* -s [Hindi *dafadār* officer, fr. Per *daf'adār*, fr. Ar *daf'ah* time, turn + Per *-dār* holder — more at BHUMIDAR] **:** a noncommissioned officer in the former Indian army or police

¹daff \ˈdaf\ *vi* -ED/-ING/-S [obs. E *daff* fool, coward, fr. ME *daffe*; akin to ME *dafte* gentle, stupid — more at DAFT] *chiefly Scot* **:** to talk or act sportively **:** DALLY, PLAY

²daff \"\ *vt* -ED/-ING/-S [alter. of ¹*doff*] **1** *archaic* **:** to put, turn, or thrust aside — used esp. in the phrase *to daff the world aside* **2** *obs* **:** ¹DOFF 2

daf·fa·dil·ly \ˈdafə,dilē, -li\ *or* **daf·fa·down·dil·ly** \ˌ==,daun̦ˈdil-\ *or* **daf·fo·dil·ly** \ˌ==ˈdil-\ *or* **daf·fo·down·dil·ly** \ˌ==,daun̦ˈdil-\ *n* -ES [*daffadilly, daffodilly* alter. (influenced by *lily*) of *daffodil*; *daffadowndilly, daffodowndilly* alter. of *daffadilly, daffodilly*] *chiefly dial* **:** DAFFODIL

daff·ing \ˈdafin, -fən\ *also* **daff·ery** \-fəri\ *n* [*daffing* fr. gerund of ¹*daff*; *daffery* fr. ¹*daff* + *-ery*] *chiefly Scot* **:** FUN, GAIETY, MERRIMENT

daf·fo·dil \ˈdafə,dil\ *n* -s [prob. fr. D *de affodil* the asphodel, fr. *de*, masc. def. article (fr. MD) + *affodil* asphodel, fr. MF *afrodille*, fr. L *asphodelus*; akin to OHG *thaz*, neut. def. article — more at THAT, ASPHODEL] **1 :** a plant of the genus *Narcissus*; *esp* **:** any of numerous such plants of which the flowers have a large corona elongated into a trumpet (as plants derived from the species *N. pseudo-narcissus*) — called also *trumpet narcissus*; see JONQUIL **1 2** *or* **daf·fo·dile** \-,dīl\ **:** a variable color averaging a brilliant yellow that is greener, lighter, and stronger than lemon yellow (sense 1b) and greener, stronger, and slightly darker than butter yellow — called also *jonquil*

daffodil garlic *n* **:** a European onion (*Allium neapolitanum*) with white flowers

daffodil lily *n* **:** ATAMASCO LILY

daffodil yellow *n* **1 :** DAFFODIL 2 **2 :** CADMIUM YELLOW 2

¹daf·fy \ˈdafē, -fi\ *n* -ES [short for *Daffy's elixir*, an infants' medicine containing gin, after Thomas *Daffy* †1680 Eng. clergyman who first compounded it] **:** a drop of gin **:** GIN

²daffy \"\ *n* -ES [by shortening] **:** DAFFODIL

³daffy \", ˈdaf-\ *adj* -ER/-EST [obs. E *daff* fool + *-y* — more at DAFF] **:** CRAZY, IMBECILE, DAFT ⟨the story is slight, but it has a ~ kind of logic —*N. Y. Times Bk. Rev.*⟩

daf·la \ˈdäflə\ *n, pl* **dafla** *or* **daflas** *usu cap* **1 a :** a primitive people in the Himalaya mountain region of Assam noted for their long houses that hold from 50 to 80 people **b :** a member of such people **2 :** the language of the Dafla people

daft \ˈdaft, ˈdaa(ə)ft, ˈdaift, ˈdäft\ *adj, often* -ER/-EST [ME *dafte* gentle, stupid; akin to OE *gedæfte* mild, gentle, *gedæftan* to put in order, *gedafen* fit, suitable, *gedēfe* suitable, gentle, ME *defte* deft, ON *dafna* to thrive, Goth *gadaban* to happen, *gadofs* fitting, proper, L *faber* smith, OSlav *dobrŭ* good, Arm *darbin* smith] **1 a :** SILLY, FOOLISH ⟨communicating with his friends in his own way . . . making ~ little beckonings and esoteric signals —Osbert Sitwell⟩; *esp* **:** foolishly fond ⟨a man ~ about women⟩ **b :** out of one's mind **:** MAD, INSANE ⟨they had given me so many instructions that I was nearly ~ —Mary Lavin⟩ ⟨in this ~ confusion of inverted values, it soon becomes impossible to determine when virtue is sin and sin, moral perfection —R.K.Merton⟩ **2** *Scot* **:** gay and frivolous **:** FROLICSOME — **daft·ly** \-ftlē, -li\ *adv* — **daft·ness** \-f(t)nəs\ *n* -ES

daf·tar \ˈdəftə(r)\ *n* -s [Hindi, record, office, fr. Per, fr. Ar *daftar, diftar*, fr. Gk *diphthera* prepared hide, parchment, leather — more at DIPHTHERIA] **1** *India* **:** a bundle of official papers **2** *India* **:** a business office

daf·tar·dar *or* **duf·ter·dar** \ˌdəftərˈdär\ *n* -s [Hindi *daftardār*, fr. Per, finance officer, fr. *daftar* + *-dār* holder — more at BHUMIDAR] **:** a revenue officer in India

daft·berry \ˈdaft- — *see* BERRY\ *n* [so called fr. its poisonous and narcotic properties] **:** BELLADONNA 1

daft days \ˈdaft-\ *n pl, Scot* **:** a time of gaiety and merrymaking; *specif* **:** the Christmas season

daft lamb *or* **daft lamb disease** \ˈdaft-\ *n* **:** an abnormality of lambs marked by congenital lesions of the cerebellar cortex by some regarded as genetic anomalies but by others as the result of deficiencies in the maternal diet

¹dag \ˈdag, ˈdaa(ə)g, ˈdaig\ *n* -s [ME *dagge*] **1** *also* **dagge** \"\ **a :** a hanging end or shred **b :** a division in the serrated or foliated edge of a medieval garment **:** an ornamental appliqué attached loosely to a medieval garment **2** *Brit* **:** matted or manure-coated wool — usu. used in pl. **3 a :** a pointed piece of metal that resembles a dagger point and that is used to lock timbers together or for a tooth on coal-breaking rolls

²dag \"\ *vb* **dagged; dagged; dagging; dags** [ME *daggen*, prob. fr. *dagge*, n.] *vt* **1 :** to finish with a jagged or slashed edge or appliqué — used chiefly of medieval garments **2** *now dial Eng* **:** BEMIRE, SOIL **3** *Brit* **:** to cut off the dags from (sheep) ~ *vi* **1 :** DAGGLE **2** *Brit* **:** to remove dags

³dag \"\ *vt* **dagged; dagged; dagging; dags** [ME *daggen*, prob. back-formation fr. *dagger*] *obs* **:** DAGGER, STAB

⁴dag \"\ *n* -s [origin unknown] **:** an obsolete form of large pistol

⁵dag \"\ *n* -s [F *dague*, fr. MF, lit., dagger — more at DAGGER] **:** PRICKET 2b

dag *abbr* decagram

dagaba *var of* DAGOBA

da·ga·me *or* **de·ga·me** \dəˈgä(,)mā\ *n* -s [AmerSp *dagame*] **:** a tropical American timber tree (*Calycophyllum candidissimum*) whose wood is used esp. for building and tools and constitutes one of the lemonwoods of commerce

dag·ba·ne *also* **dag·ba·ni** \dägˈbänē, -nə\ *n* -s *usu cap* **:** DAGOMBA

dag·en·ham \ˈdag(ə)nəm\ *adj, usu cap* [fr. *Dagenham*, England] **:** of or from the municipal borough of Dagenham, England **:** of the kind or style prevalent in Dagenham

dagesh *var of* DAGHESH

¹dag·ga \ˈdagə, ˈdägə\ *also* **da·cha** \ˈdakə, ˈdäkə\ *n* -s [Afrik *dagga*, fr. Hottentot *daga-b*] **1** *Africa* **:** HEMP **1 2 :** either of two relatively nontoxic So. African herbs (*Leonotis leonurus* and *L. orata*) smoked like tobacco — called also *Cape dagga, red dagga, wilde dagga*

²dag·ga \"\ *n* -s [Afrik *dagha* mud, mortar, fr. Bantu *daka*] **:** a mortar used in So. Africa that consists chiefly of clay wetted and packed hard

¹dag·ger \ˈdagə(r), ˈdaag-, ˈdaig-\ *n* -s [ME, prob. modif. of MF *dague*, fr. OProv or OIt *daga*] **1 a :** a short knife used for stabbing — see ANLACE, DIRK, MISERICORD, PONIARD, STILETTO; compare BOWIE KNIFE **b :** something resembling or suggesting a dagger esp. in shape: as (1) **:** the character † used typically to mark the name of a person who is dead and as the second in series of the reference marks — called also *obelisk* (2) **:** the projecting part of a loom rod acting as a stopping device — compare FROG 3i **2 daggers** *pl* **:** HOSTILITY ⟨there's ~*s* in men's smiles —Shak.⟩ **3 :** DOGSHORE **4 :** DAGGER PLANK — **at daggers drawn** *also* **at daggers drawing** *or* **at daggers :** at the point of fighting **:** openly hostile — **look daggers :** to look angrily or as if ready to do violence ⟨they *looked daggers* at each other across the table⟩

daggers 1a

²dagger \"\ *vt* -ED/-ING/-S **1 :** to pierce with a dagger **:** STAB **2 :** to mark with the dagger used in printing

dagger board *also* **dagger plate** *n* **:** a narrow centerboard in some small boats that slides up and down in the trunk instead of pivoting and that can be completely removed when not in use

daggerbush \ˈ==,=\ *n* **:** a plant of the genus *Furcraea*

dagger cocklebur *n* **:** SPINY CLOTBUR

dag·gered \ˈdagə(r)d\ *adj* [ME, fr. ¹*dagger* + *-ed*] *archaic* **:** armed with a dagger

dagger fern *n* **:** CHRISTMAS FERN

dagger moth *n* **:** any of several noctuid moths of *Acronicta* and related genera some of which have a mark suggesting a dagger near the anal angle of the fore wings

dagger plank *n* **:** a diagonal member holding together and bracing launching poppets — called also *dagger*

dagger plant *n* **:** SPANISH BAYONET

dagger rudder *n* **:** a narrow usu. deep rudder

dagging *n* -s [fr. gerund of ²*dag*] **1 :** the act of removing dags **2 :** DAG **2** — usu. used in pl.

dag·gle \ˈdagəl\ *vb* -ED/-ING/-S [freq. of ²*dag*] *vt* **1** *archaic* **:** to wet and soil (as a garment) by dragging in mire **2** *archaic* **:** to make wet by sprinkling or splashing **:** DRAGGLE ⟨clothes *daggled* by the splash of passing vehicles⟩ ~ *vi, archaic* **:** to trail or drag about (as through mud or slush)

dag·gy \ˈgē\ *adj* -ER/-EST [¹*dag* + *-y*] *of sheep* **:** having dags

¹da·ghesh *also* **da·gesh** \ˈdä(,)gesh, -,gāsh *also* -(,)gāsh\ *n* -ES [Heb *dāghēsh*] **:** a point placed in a consonant in pointed writing in the Hebrew alphabet to denote that (1) it is pronounced as a stop rather than as a spirant or that (2) it is pronounced doubled — called also respectively (1) *daghesh lene*, (2) *daghesh forte*

²daghesh *also* **dagesh** \"\ *vt* -ED/-ING/-ES **:** to mark with a daghesh

da·ghe·stan \ˌdagəˈstan, ˌdägəˈstän\ *n* -s *usu cap* [fr. *Daghestan, Dagestan*, autonomous Soviet republic in the Caucasus] **:** a Caucasian rug distinguished by medium pile, fine weave, geometric designs, and mellow colors

da·ghur \däˈgu̇(ə)r\ *n, pl* **daghur** *or* **daghurs** *usu cap* **1 :** a Mongol people inhabiting northwest Manchuria **2 :** a member of the Daghur people

daglock \ˈ=,=\ *n* [¹*dag* + *lock*] **:** a dirty or matted lock of fur, hair, or wool **:** TAGLOCK — see ¹DAG

da·go \ˈdā(,)gō\ *n, pl* **dagos** *or* **dagoes** *sometimes cap* [alter. of earlier *Diego*, fr. *Diego*, a common Spanish given name] **:** a person of Italian or Spanish birth or descent — usu. taken to be offensive

da·go·ba *also* **da·ga·ba** \ˈdägəbə\ *n* -s [Singhalese *dāgoba, dāgaba*, fr. Pali *dhātugabbha*, fr. Skt *dhātugarbha*, lit., having relics inside, fr. *dhātu* element, elemental bodily substance, relics (fr. *dadhāti* he places) + *garbha* womb, interior — more at DO, CALF] **:** a shrine for sacred relics in the Far East

da·gom·ba \dəˈgämbə\ *n* -s *usu cap* **1 :** a Negroid people in the Northern Territories, Ghana, identified primarily by possession of a common language **2 :** a Gur language of the Dagomba people — called also *Dagbane*

dago red *n* [so called fr. its being typically made and drunk by Italians] *slang* **:** an inexpensive red wine

¹dags *pl of* DAG, *pres 3d sing of* DAG

²dags \ˈdagz\ *n pl* [prob. alter. of *dares*, pl. of *dare*] *slang Brit* **:** feats of skill **:** TRICKS — usu. used in the phrase *to do one's dags*

dag-tailed \ˈ=ˌ=\ *adj* [¹*dag*] **:** having dags about the tail

da·guer·re·an \dəˈgerēən\ *adj* [Louis J.M.*Daguerre* †1851 French painter and inventor + E *-an*] **1** *usu cap* **:** of or relating to Daguerre **2 :** of or relating to the daguerreotype

¹da·guerre·o·type \dəˈgerə,tīp, -rō,-, -rēə,-, -rēō,-\ *n* -s [F *daguerréotype*, fr. L.J.M.*Daguerre* + F *-o-* + *-type*] **1 a :** a photograph produced on a silver plate or a silver-covered copper plate which is made sensitive by the action of iodine or iodine and bromine and from which after exposure in the camera a latent image is developed by the vapor of mercury **2 :** the process of producing daguerreotype pictures — **da·guerre·o·typ·ic** \=ˌ=rəˈtipik, -rēō-\ *adj*

²daguerreotype \"\ *vt* -ED/-ING/-S **1 :** to produce or represent by the daguerreotype process **2 :** to impress with great distinctness ⟨the . . . universe around us, all ready to be *daguerreotyped* upon our souls —Benjamin Fine⟩

da·guerre·o·typ·er \-,tīpə(r)\ *or* **da·guerre·o·typ·ist** \-,tīpəst\ *n* **:** one that makes daguerreotypes

da·guerre·o·typy \-,tīpē\ *n* -ES **:** the art or process of producing daguerreotypes

¹dah \ˈdä\ *or* **dao** \ˈdau̇\ *n* -s [Burmese *dā*] **:** a large heavy knife used by the Burmese

²dah \"\ *n* -s [imit.] **:** a dash in radio or telegraphic code — used by operators as an oral representation of the transmitted sound ⟨many a shortwave radio enthusiast soon may fling his dits and ~*s* to remote points of the world —*Science News Letter*⟩

da·ha·be·ah \ˌdä(h)əˈbēə\ *also* **da·ha·bee·yah** \-ēyə\ *or* **da·ha·bi·ah** \-ēə\ *or* **da·ha·bi·eh** \", -ēe\ *n* -s [Ar *dhahabīyah*, lit., golden one] **:** a long light-draft houseboat used on the Nile that is lateen-rigged and is often propelled wholly or partly by engines

da·hi \dəˈhē\ *n* -s [Hindi *dahī*, fr. Skt *dadhi* sour milk; akin to OPruss *dadan* milk, Alb *djathë* cheese, all by redupl. fr. the root of Skt *dhayati* he sucks — more at FEMININE] **:** the curd of soured curdled milk

¹dahl·ia \ˈdalyə *also* ˈdäl- *or* ˈdāl- *sometimes* -lēə; *Brit usu & US sometimes* ˈdāl-\ *n* [NL, fr. Anders *Dahl* †1789 Swedish botanist + NL *-ia*] **1** *cap* **:** a genus of Mexican and Central American tuberous-rooted herbs (family Compositae) having opposite pinnate leaves and rayed flower heads with a pappus of scales, teeth, or awns that are not retrorsely barked **2** -s **:** any plant of the genus *Dahlia*, most of the horticultural varieties being derived from the Central American species (*D. pinnata*) **3** *also* **dahlia violet** -s **a :** one of the methyl violets; *also* **:** a mixture of a methyl violet and fuchsine **b :** one of Hofmann's violets **4** -s **:** a moderate purple that is redder and duller than heliotrope (sense 4a), redder and paler than average amethyst or manganese violet, and bluer and paler than cobalt violet — compare DAHLIA PURPLE

²dahlia \"\ *also* **dahlia wartlet** *n* -s **:** a common large sea anemone (*Tealia crassicornis*) of the Atlantic coasts of Europe

dahlia carmine *n* **:** a dark purplish red that is bluer and less strong than pansy purple, bluer, stronger, and slightly lighter than raisin, and bluer, lighter, and stronger than Bokhara

dahlia purple *n* **1 :** a dark purplish red that is bluer and duller than pansy purple or Bokhara and redder and darker than raisin **2** *of textiles* **:** a deep purple that is redder and deeper than hyacinth violet, deeper than petunia violet, and bluer and stronger than imperial purple (sense 2)

dahlia sunflower *n* **:** a double-flowered horticultural form of a wild sunflower (*Helianthus decapetalus*) of eastern No. America

dahll·ite \ˈdä,līt\ *n* -s [prob. fr. G *dahllit*, fr. Tellef and Johann *Dahll*, 19th cent. Norw. geologists and mineralogists + G *-it* -ite] **:** CARBONATE-APATITE

¹da·ho·me·an \dəˈhōmēən\ *also* **da·ho·man** \-mən\ *or* **da·ho·mey·an** \-mēən, -māən\ *adj, usu cap* [*Dahomey*, former name of Benin, republic in west Africa + E *-an*] **:** of or relating to Dahomey or its inhabitants

²dahomean *also* **dahoman** *or* **dahomeyan** \"\ *n* -s *usu cap* **1 :** a native or inhabitant of Dahomey **2 :** a member of the chiefly Ewe-speaking Dahomean people

da·ho·mey \dəˈhōmē\ *adj, usu cap* [*Dahomey*, former name of Benin, republic in west Africa] **:** of or relating to Dahomey **:** of the kind or style prevalent in Dahomey **:** DAHOMEAN

da·hoon \dəˈhün\ *also* **dahoon holly** *n* -s [origin unknown] **:** an evergreen shrub (*Ilex cassine*) of the southern U.S. — called also *yaupon*

da·hu·ri·an larch \dəˈh(y)u̇rēən-\ *n* [*Dahuria*, region of southern Siberia + E *-an*] **:** a Siberian tree of very irregular growth habit that is sometimes cultivated for its bright green foliage

¹dai·dle \ˈdādᵊl\ *chiefly Scot var of* DAWDLE

²daidle \"\ *also* **dai·dlie** \-d(ᵊ)li\ *n* -s [*daidle*, origin unknown; *daidlie* fr. *daidle* + *-ie*] *Scot* **:** APRON; *esp* **:** PINAFORE

daigh \ˈdāk̲\ *n* -s [ME (northern dial.) *dagh*, fr. OE *dāg, dāh* — more at DOUGH] *Scot* **:** DOUGH

daik·er \ˈdākər\ *vt* -ED/-ING/-S [prob. fr. F *décorer* to decorate, fr. L *decorare* — more at DECORATE] *Scot* **:** to put in order **:** DECORATE ⟨the chaise . . . was elegantly ~*ed* out with evergreens —W.D.Latto⟩

dai·kon \ˈdīkən\ *n* -s [Jap, fr. *dai* big + *kon* root] **:** a radish (*Raphanus sativus longipinnatus*) of Japan with long hard durable roots that are eaten cooked or raw

dail \ˈdāl\ *Scot var of* DEAL

dai·li·ness \ˈdālēnəs, -lin-\ *n* -ES **:** the quality of daily occurrence **:** the quality of being regular, routine, or humdrum

¹dai·ly \ˈdālē, -li\ *adj* [ME *dayly*, fr. OE *dæglic*, fr. *dæg* day + *-lic* -ly — more at DAY] **1 :** occurring or being made, done, or acted upon every day ⟨his ~ work⟩ **:** issued every day or every weekday ⟨a ~ newspaper⟩ **:** of or for every day ⟨a ~ schedule⟩ **2 a :** reckoned by the day ⟨average ~ wage⟩ **b :** covering the period of a day **:** based on a day ⟨~ statistics⟩

²daily \"\ *adv* [ME *dayly*, fr. *dayly*, adj.] **1 :** every day **2 :** day by day **3 :** every weekday ⟨go to work ~⟩

³daily \"\ *n* -ES [¹*daily*] **1 :** a newspaper published every weekday **2** *Brit* **:** a female domestic employee not a resident of the house in which she works **3 dailies** *pl* **:** RUSH 7

daily bread *n* **:** food or provisions necessary for day-to-day survival

daily double *n* **:** a system of betting on horse or dog races in which the bettor must pick the winners of two stipulated races in order to win, such bets forming a pool separate from the ordinary bets

daily dozen *n* [so called fr. its being orig. a set of 12 exercises] **1 :** a series of setting-up exercises to be performed daily **:** WORKOUT **2 :** a set of routine duties or tasks

daim \ˈdam, ˈdām\ *n* -s [F, fr. OF *dain*, fr. (assumed) VL *damus*, alter. of L *dama, damma*] **:** FALLOW DEER

dai·men \ˈdemin, ˈdām-\ *adj* [origin unknown] *chiefly Scot* **:** OCCASIONAL ⟨a ~ one here and there⟩

dai·mi·ate \ˈdīmē,āt, -ēət\ *also* **dai·mi·ote** \-ē,ōt\ *n* -s [*daimio* + *-ate*] **:** the office, power, or territory of a daimyo

dai·mon \ˈdī,mōn\ *n, pl* **daimo·nes** \-,mə,nēz\ *also* **daimons** \-,mōnz\ *sometimes cap* [Gk *daimōn* — more at DEMON] **:** DEMON 1,4 — **dai·mon·ic** \(ˈ)=ˈmänik, -ˈmōn-\ *adj*

dai·mo·ni·on \dīˈmōnē,än\ *n* -s [Gk, fr. neut. of *daimonios* of a demon, fr. *daimon*, *daimōn* demon] **:** an inward mentor conceived as partaking of the nature of a demon or inspired by one

dai·myo *or* **dai·mio** \ˈdīmē,ō, -m(,)yō\ *n, pl* **dai·myos** *or* **daimyo** *or* **dai·mios** *or* **daimio** [Jap *daimyō*, fr. Chin (Pek) *ta⁴* great + *ming²* name] **:** one of the former feudal barons of Japan who were vassals of the shogun but had extensive powers in their own baronies

dain·cha *or* **dhain·cha** \ˈdīnchə\ *n* -s [Beng *dhanicā*] **:** a valuable forage or green-manure plant (*Sesbania aculeata*) planted in tropical regions for soil improvement

daint *adj or n* [by shortening] *obs* **:** DAINTY

dain·ti·fy \ˈdāntə,fī\ *vt* -ED/-ING/-ES [²*dainty* + *-fy*] **:** to make dainty

dain·ti·ly \-tᵊlē, -təlē, -li\ *adv* [ME, fr. ²*dainty* + *-ly*] **:** in a dainty manner: as **a :** with nice attention to taste in food or to personal comfort ⟨sold into a rich house so that she can eat ~ —Pearl Buck⟩ **b :** with nice attention to detail ⟨invitation cards, ~ got up in white and silver —Agnes M. Miall⟩

dain·ti·ness \-tēnəs, -tin-\ *n* -ES **:** the quality or state of being dainty

dain·tith \ˈdāntith\ *n* -s [ME, fr. OF *deintiet, deintié*] *Scot* **:** DELICACY, DAINTY

¹dain·ty \ˈdāntē, -ti\ *n* -ES [ME *deinte* worthiness, pleasure, delicacy, fr. OF *deintié*, fr. L *dignitat-, dignitas* worthiness — more at DIGNITY] **1 :** something delicious to the taste **:** DELICACY ⟨a London ~ — a pyramid of jelly —Virginia Woolf⟩ ⟨the various *dainties* served at supper —E.H.Collis⟩ **2 :** something that arouses favor or excites pleasure **:** something choice or pleasing ⟨sloe-eyed *dainties* in satin skirts and magenta saris —P.C.Jain⟩ **3** *obs* **:** FASTIDIOUSNESS, FUSSINESS

²dainty \"\ *adj* -ER/-EST [ME *deinte*, fr. *deinte*, n.] **1 a** *now dial Brit* **:** pleasant and agreeable **:** FINE ⟨a ~ lass⟩ ⟨~ weather⟩ **b** *obs* **:** UNCOMMON, SCARCE **2 a :** good-tasting **:** SAVORY, PALATABLE ⟨~ bits make rich the ribs —Shak.⟩ **b :** attractively prepared and prettily served to or as if to stimulate a jaded, finicky, or very slight appetite ⟨the ~ crumpets at the tearoom⟩ **3 :** marked by fragile tender beauty, nice or diminutive form, or quaint charm ⟨a ~ Spanish sword —S.P.B.Mais⟩ ⟨~ teacups⟩ **4** *obs* **:** CHARY, SPARING, LOATH, RELUCTANT — used with *of* ⟨let us not be ~ of leave-taking —Shak.⟩ **5 a :** marked by or given to fastidious discrimination and choice or by finical taste **:** shunning anything crude or excessive **:** gently careful and particular ⟨the hungry cannot be ~ —Mary W. Shelley⟩ ⟨the spirit of romance, gross and tawdry in vulgar minds, ~ and refined in the more cultivated —V.L.Parrington⟩ **b :** showing unmanly avoidance of anything rough **:** OVERNICE, SQUEAMISH, PRISSY ⟨steps ~ as those of a French dancing master —George Meredith⟩ ⟨gentry too ~ to risk blisters on their hands —G.W.Johnson⟩ **syn** see CHOICE, NICE

dai·qui·ri \ˈdīkərē, ˈdak- *sometimes* -krē\ *n* -s *often cap* [fr. *Daiquirí*, district in El Caney municipality, Cuba] **:** a cocktail made of rum, lime or sometimes lemon juice, and sugar

dai·ren \(ˈ)dīˈren\ *adj, usu cap* [fr. *Dairen*, Manchuria] **:** of or from the city of Dairen, now forming part of Port Arthur-Dairen, Manchuria **:** of the kind or style prevalent in Dairen

dairy \ˈderē, ˈda(a)r-, ˈdār-, -ri\ *n* -ES *often attrib* [ME *dayerie, deyerie*, fr. *deye* female servant, dairymaid (fr. OE *dæge* kneader of bread) + *-erie* -ery; akin to ON *deigja* dairymaid; derivative fr. the root of OE *dāg* dough — more at DOUGH] **1 :** a room, building, or establishment where milk is kept and butter or cheese is made ⟨the village cheese ~ —*Nat'l Geographic*⟩ **2 :** the department of farming or of a farm that is concerned with the production of milk, butter, and cheese ⟨~ products⟩ ⟨~ farming⟩ **3 :** a dairy farm; *collectively* **:** the cows of a farm **4 :** an establishment for the sale or distribution of milk or milk products

dairy breed *n* **:** a cattle breed developed primarily for the production of milk rather than meat (as the Holstein-Friesian, Jersey, Guernsey, or Ayrshire) and characterized by the ability to convert a large proportion of their food into milk, by angular bodies that do not take on flesh readily, and by comparatively long legs and neck — compare BEEF BREED, DUAL-PURPOSE

dairy cattle *n pl* **:** cattle suitable for milk production; *esp* **:** cattle of one of the dairy breeds

dairy·ing \-rēiŋ, -riŋ\ *n* -s **:** the business of conducting a dairy

dairy lunch *or* **dairy bar** *n* **:** a restaurant specializing in simple dishes made from dairy products

dairymaid \ˈ==,=\ *n* **:** a woman employed on a dairy farm or in a dairy — called also *milkmaid*

dairy·man \-mən, -,man, -,maa(ə)n\ *n, pl* **dairymen :** one who operates a dairy farm or one who works in the dairy industry

dairy shorthorn *n, usu cap D&S* : MILKING SHORTHORN

dairy·wom·an \-ˌwu̇mən\ *n, pl* **dairywom·en** \-ˌwimən\ : a woman who attends to a dairy or sells dairy products

dais \ˈdāəs *also* ˈdīəs *or sometimes* ˈdās *or* ˈdīs\ *n* -ES [ME *deis, dees*, fr. OF *deis*, fr. L *discus* quoit, dish — more at DISH] **1** : a platform raised usu. above the floor of a hall or large room to give distinction or prominence to those occupying it ⟨the principal speakers were seated on the ~⟩ **2** : a raised terrace out of doors ⟨an elevated observation point with a concrete ~ —*Amer. Guide Series: Texas*⟩ **3** : DEAS **4** *archaic* : a canopy over a throne or other seat of state

daise \ˈdāz\ *chiefly Scot var of* DAZE

daisee *or* **daisee jute** *var of* DESI

dai·sied \ˈdāzēd\ *adj* : full of daisies : adorned with daisies ⟨~ lawns⟩

dais·ing \ˈdāziŋ, -zən\ *n* -S [prob. fr. gerund of *daise*] *Scot* : ¹PINE 3

dai·sy \ˈdāzē, -zi\ *n* -ES [ME *daisie, dayeseye*, fr. OE *dægesēge, dægesēage*, fr. *dæg* day + *ēage* eye — more at DAY, EYE] **1** : any of numerous composite plants having flower heads with well-developed ray flowers usu. arranged in a single whorl or a few whorls: as **a** : a low scapose European herb (*Bellis perennis*) having flower heads with small white or pink ray flowers and yellow disk flowers — called also *English daisy* **b** : a rather tall leafy-stemmed perennial herb (*Chrysanthemum leucanthemum*) having larger flower heads than the English daisy and long white ray flowers and being often a troublesome weed esp. in parts of the U.S. — called also *oxeye daisy, white daisy* **c** *Austral* (1) : SWAN RIVER DAISY (2) : any plant of the genus *Vittadinia* **d** *New Zealand* : a plant of the genus *Lagenophora* **e** : any of several wild plants of the genera *Aster* and *Erigeron* **f** : any of various other composite plants — usu. used wth a qualifying term; see AFRICAN DAISY, MICHAELMAS DAISY, SHASTA DAISY **2** : the flower head of any daisy **3** *slang* : a person or thing that is first-rate of its kind ⟨he's a real ~⟩ **4** : a tall drink of a spirituous liquor, lime juice or lemon juice, grenadine or raspberry syrup or curaçao, and carbonated water chilled with cracked or shaved ice and garnished with fruit or mint ⟨rum ~⟩ ⟨gin ~⟩ **5 a** *usu* **daisy ham** : a boned and smoked piece of pork from the shoulder **b** : a cheddar cheese of a certain style and weight

daisybush \ˈ==,=\ *n* : any of certain frost-tender shrubs of the Australasian composite genus *Olearia* with leathery evergreen leaves and flower heads resembling daisies; *esp* : a bushy half-hardy New Zealand shrub (*O. haastii*) sometimes cultivated for its fragrant white flower heads

daisy chain *n* **1** : a string of daisies with stems linked to form a chain; *specif* : such a chain carried by chosen students at a class day or other celebration in some women's colleges **2** : an interlinked series (as of events, items, or steps) ⟨a *daisy chain* of middlemen —*Christian Science Monitor*⟩

daisy cutter *n* **1** *slang* : a horse that carries its feet low in trotting **2** *slang* : a ball (as in cricket or baseball) so batted or bowled that it skims along the ground **3** *slang* : a fragmentation bomb or an antipersonnel bomb

daisy–cutting \ˈ==,==\ *adj* : having the characteristics of a daisy cutter

daisy family *n* : COMPOSITAE

daisy fleabane *n* : any of several white-rayed American plants of the genus *Erigeron* (esp. *E. annuus* and *E. strigosus*)

daisy tree *n* : DAISYBUSH

¹**dak** \ˈdȯk *also* ˈdäk\ *n* -S [Hindi *ḍāk*] **1** : transport or post by relays of men and horses **2** : a post station or traveler's rest house located orig. on post roads ⟨a ~ bungalow⟩

²**dak** *var of* DHAK

da·kar \(ˈ)däˈkär, (ˈ)dä'-, də'-\ *adj, usu cap* [fr. *Dakar*, French West Africa] : of or from Dakar in Senegal : of the kind or style prevalent in Dakar

da·ker \ˈdākə(r)\ *n* -S [MF *dacre*, fr. OF, fr. MD *daker*; akin to MLG *dēker* quantity of ten (hides) — more at DICKER] : ¹DICKER 1

da·ker–hen \" + ,-\ *n* [origin unknown] : CORNCRAKE

dakh·ma \ˈdäkmə\ *n* -S [Per, fr. MPer *dakhmak*, fr. Av *daxma-* funeral place] : TOWER OF SILENCE

da·kin's solution \ˈdākənz-\ *n, usu cap D* [after Henry D. *Dakin* †1952 Eng. chemist] : an antiseptic solution developed during World War I for the treatment of wounds and consisting essentially of an aqueous solution containing from 0.5 percent to 0.6 percent of sodium hypochlorite with 0.4 percent of boric acid added to reduce the alkalinity

¹**da·ko·ta** *also* **da·co·ta** *or* **da·co·tah** \dəˈkōd·ə, -ōtə\ *n, pl* **dakota** *or* **dakotas** *usu cap* [Dakota (Santee dial.) *Dakota*, lit., allies] **1 a** : a Siouan people of the northern Mississippi valley commonly called Sioux and divided into an eastern or forest group comprising the Mdewakanton, Wahpeton, Wahpekute, and Sisseton and a western or prairie group comprising the Yankton, Yanktonai, and Teton **b** : a member of such people **2** : the language of the Dakota people

²**dakota** \" *or* **da·ko·tan** \-tᵊn, -d·ən, -tən\ *adj, usu cap* [in sense 1, fr. ¹*Dakota*; in sense 2, fr. *Dakota* territory, former region of the U.S. including No. & So. Dakota, fr. the *Dakota* Indians] **1** *also* **dacota** *or* **dacotah** *pron at* DAKOTA\ *or* **da·co·tan** *pron at* DAKOTAN\ : of or relating to the Dakota people or their language **2 a** : of or relating to the Dakota territory **b** : of or from the state of No. Dakota or the state of So. Dakota : of the kind or style prevalent in No. Dakota or So. Dakota **c** : of, relating to, or constituting a division of the Cretaceous — see GEOLOGIC TIME table

dakota millet *n, usu cap D* **1** : FOXTAIL MILLET **2** : MILLET 1a

dakotan \"\ *n* -S *cap* [*Dakota (territory)* + E *-an*] : a native or resident of the Dakota territory or No. Dakota or So. Dakota

dak runner *n* [¹*dak*] *India & Burma* : MAIL CARRIER

da–kua \ˈdäk(ə)wə, ˈdak-\ *n* -S [Fijian] **1** : a kauri pine (*Agathis vitiensis*) of the Fiji islands **2** *also* **dakua wood** : the usu. white wood of the dakua used for masts, spars, booms, and flooring

dal \ˈdäl\ *var of* DHAL

dal *abbr* decaliter

da·lag \dəˈläg, ˈdä,l-\ *n* -S [Tag] *Philippines* : MURRAL

da·lai la·ma \ˈdä,līˈlämə, ˈda,-, ˈdä,-, -ˈlämə *also* -(,)lī'l- *or* -(,)lē'l- *or* -,lə'l-; də'lī'l-\ *n, pl* **dalai lamas** *usu cap D&L* [Mongolian *dalai* ocean] : the spiritual head of Tibetan Buddhism

dal·ber·gia \dalˈbərj(ē)ə, -rgēə\ *n, cap* [NL, fr. Nils *Dalberg* †1819 Swedish physician + NL *-ia*] : a large genus of tropical trees (family Leguminosae) with pinnate leaves and paniculate flowers — see BLACKWOOD b

¹**dale** \ˈdāl, *esp before pause or consonant* -āəl\ *n* -S [ME, fr. OE *dæl*; akin to OHG *tal* valley, ON *dalr*, Goth *dal* valley, Gk *tholos* rotunda, OSlav *dolŭ* pit; basic meaning: curving] **1** *chiefly Brit* : a river valley running between hills or through highland **2** : VALE, VALLEY

²**dale** \"\ *n* -S [ME, fr. OE *dāl* — more at DEAL] *Brit* : a portion of land; *specif* : a portion of an undivided common field set off by markers

³**dale** \"\ *n* -S [F *dalle* gutter, stone slab, fr. MF, fr. ON *dæla*; akin to ON *dalr* valley] : a tube, trough, or pipe esp. from a ship's pump

da·lea \ˈdālēə\ *n* [NL, after Samuel *Dale* †1739 Eng. physician and botanist] **1** *cap* : a genus of American herbs or shrubs (family Leguminosae) with pinnate leaves and spikes or heads of mostly purple flowers **2** -S : any plant of the genus *Dalea*

dale–backed \ˈ=ˈ=\ *adj* [¹*dale*] : SWAYBACKED

dal·e·car·li·an \ˌdaləˈkärlēən\ *adj, usu cap* [*Dalecarlia* (Dalarna), region in central Sweden + E *-an*] : of or relating to Dalecarlia in Sweden

d'a·lem·bert's principle \ˌdaləmˈbe(ə)rz-\ *n, usu cap A* [after Jean LeRond *d'Alembert* †1783 Fr. mathematician, its formulator] : a principle in mechanics: the reaction due to the inertia of an accelerated body (as a baseball) is equal and opposite to the force causing the acceleration (as the blow of a bat upon the baseball) and results in a condition of kinetic equilibrium — compare LAW OF MOTION 3

da·ler \ˈdälə(r)\ *n* -S [Dan & Sw, fr. LG, fr. G *taler* — more at DOLLAR] : a Danish or Swedish dollar : RIGSDALER, RIKSDALER

dales \ˈdā(ə)lz\ *n* [so called fr. its having developed in the eastern valleys of the Pennine range, England] **1** *usu cap* : a breed of sturdy surefooted ponies native to northeast England used for farm work and as pack horses **2** *pl* **dales** *often cap* : any animal of the Dales breed

dales·man \ˈdālzmən, -,man\ *n, pl* **dalesmen** *Brit* : one living or born in a dale; *specif* : one of the inhabitants of the river valleys in the north of England

da·leth \ˈdä,leth, -lət\ *also* **da·let** \-,let, -lət\ *n* -S [Heb *dāleth*, prob. pausal form of *deleth* door] **1** : the fourth letter of the Hebrew alphabet — symbol ד; see ALPHABET table **2** : the letter of the Phoenician or of any of various other Semitic alphabets corresponding to Hebrew daleth

da·li·esque \ˌdäleˈesk, ˌdal-,ˌdäl-\ *adj, usu cap* [Salvador *Dali* b1904 Span. painter + E *-esque*] : resembling or suggesting the painting of the surrealist artist Dali : befitting the exotic contents of such painting ⟨a pair of feathers stuck at a *Daliesque* angle in holes pierced in each nostril —*Time*⟩ ⟨a *Daliesque* landscape of stunted pines, twisted cripples of the tree world, and strangely shaped gray-black rocks —Maud Oakes⟩

dal·las \ˈdaləs, *esp S* -lis\ *adj, usu cap* [fr. *Dallas*, Texas] : of or from the city of Dallas, Texas ⟨*Dallas* stores⟩ : of the kind or style prevalent in Dallas

dallas grass *n, usu cap D* : DALLIS GRASS

dal·las·ite \-,sīt\ *n* -S *cap* [*Dallas*, Texas + E *-ite*] : a native or resident of Dallas, Texas

dalles \-lz\ *n pl* [F, pl. of *dalle* gutter — more at DALE] : the rapids in a river confined between walls of a canyon or gorge

dal·li \ˈdä(,)lē, ˈda(-\ *n* -S [prob. of Arawakan origin; akin to Wapisiana *dali* dalli] : any of certain tropical trees of the genus *Virola* of the family Myristicaceae (esp. *V. surinamensis*) that has wood which is used for staves and hard seeds which resemble nutmegs and yield a wax or solid oil

dal·li·ance \ˈdalēən(t)s, -lyə-\ *n* -S [ME *dalyaunce*, fr. *dalyen* to dally + *-aunce* -ance] **1** : PLAY, SPORTIVENESS; *esp* : amorous play (as flirting or caressing) ⟨amatory ~ —R.H.Lowie⟩ **2** : frivolous action : TRIFLING ⟨this short ~ with revolutionary ideas —John Mason Brown⟩

dal·lis grass \ˈdaləs-\ *n, usu cap D* [perh. alter. of *Dallas*, Tex.] : a tall tufted perennial grass (*Paspalum dilatatum*) introduced from the tropics and now common as a pasture and forage grass in the southern U.S.

dallop *var of* DOLLOP

dall porpoise \ˈdȯl-\ *or* **dall's porpoise** *n, usu cap D* [after William H. *Dall* †1927 Am. naturalist] : a common porpoise (*Phocoenoides dalli*) of the coastal waters of western No. America that reaches a length of six feet and is black above with much white on the sides and ventral surface

dall sheep *or* **dall's sheep** *n, usu cap D* [after W.H.*Dall*] : a large white wild sheep (*Ovis montana dalli* or *O. dalli*) of northwestern No. America

¹**dal·ly** \ˈdalē, -li\ *vb* -ED/-ING/-ES [ME *dalyen*, fr. AF *dalier*, perh. of Gmc origin; akin to 16th cent. G *dallen, tallen* to talk foolishly, act frivolously] *vi* **1 a** : to act playfully : PLAY, SPORT, TOY ⟨~*ing* with a glass of wine —Victoria Sackville-West⟩ ⟨the winter that merely *dallies* and trifles —Alfred Buchanan⟩; *esp* : to play amorously ⟨*dallied* with a young Mexican girl —Green Peyton⟩ **b** : to play mockingly ⟨~*ing* with a serious proposition⟩ **2 a** : to waste time (as in frivolity, idleness, or trifling) **b** : LINGER, DELAY, TARRY ⟨while the men *dallied*, the dogs set off —J.T.McNish⟩ ~ *vt* **1** *obs* : to evade or delay by trifling **2** *archaic* : to consume or spend (as time) in dalliance or by dallying — used with *away* ⟨~*ing* away precious time —Sir Walter Scott⟩ **syn** see DELAY

²**dally** \", ˈdäl-\ *vb* -ED/-ING/-ES [Sp *¡dale (vuelta)!* give it a turn!] *vi* : to twist a rope around the saddle horn in roping an animal ⟨his saddle stayed on better when he was ~*ing* if the cinch was attached at the center —S.E.Fletcher⟩ ~ *vt* : to twist (a rope) in a dally ⟨*dallied* the pack-horse rope around his saddle horn —A.B.Guthrie⟩

³**dally** \"\ *n* -ES : a temporary twisting of the rope around the saddle horn in roping an animal

dal·ly·ing·ly *adv* : in a dallying manner

dal·ly·man \ˈ==,man, -,mən\ *n, pl* **dallymen** : a cowboy who uses the dally method of roping

dal·ly wel·ta \ˈ==ˈweltə\ *n, pl* **dally weltas** [by folk etymology fr. Sp. *¡dale vuelta!*] : ³DALLY

dally wel·ter \-tə(r)\ *n* [*dally welta* + *-er*] : DALLYMAN

dal·ma·ni·tes \ˌdalməˈnīd·(,)ēz\ *n, cap* [NL, fr. Johan W. *Dalman* †1826 Swedish naturalist + L *-ites* -ite] : a large genus of trilobites found from the Ordovician to the Devonian in Europe, America, and India

¹**dal·ma·tian** \(ˈ)dalˈmāshən\ *adj, usu cap* [*Dalmatia*, region on the Adriatic sea now included in Yugoslavia + E *-an*] : of or relating to Dalmatia

²**dalmatian** \"\ *n* -S **1** *cap* : a native or inhabitant of Dalmatia **2** *also* **dalmatian dog** *often cap Dalmatian* : a large dog of a breed supposed to have originated in Dalmatia having a white short-haired coat with black or brown spots varying from dime to half-dollar size, standing from 19 to 23 inches high, and weighing from 35 to 50 pounds — called also *coach dog* **3** *cap* : a Romance language developed from colloquial Latin and extinct by the late 19th century that was spoken on the Dalmatian coast and Adriatic islands from Veglia to Ragusa

dalmatian cherry *n, usu cap D* : MARASCA

dalmatian insect powder *n, usu cap D* : pyrethrum (sense 2a) derived from a Dalmatian pyrethrum

¹**dal·mat·ic** \(ˈ)dalˈmad·ik, -atik\ *adj, usu cap* [L *Dalmaticus*, fr. *Dalmatia* + L *-icus* -ic] : ¹DALMATIAN ⟨a ~ robe⟩

²**dalmatic** \=ˈ==\ *also* **dal·mat·i·ca** \-ˈmad·əkə, -atə-\ *n* -S [LL *dalmatica*, fr. fem. of L *Dalmaticus*] **1** : an ecclesiastical outer vestment worn in religious ceremonies orig. by a deacon but now also by some prelates (as bishops) **2 a** : a loose unbelted medieval garment with full sleeves and often with slits up the sides **b** : a similar robe of rich materials worn on state occasions by an English king; *esp* : such a robe worn by a king at his coronation

dalmatic 1

da·lo \ˈdä(,)lō\ *n* -S [Fijian] : TARO 1

dal·ra·di·an \(ˈ)dalˈrādēən\ *adj, usu cap* [*Dalrad-* (alter. of *Dalriada*, ancient region of Scotland) + E *-ian*] : of, relating to, or constituting a division of the Precambrian — see GEOLOGIC TIME table

dal se·gno \ˈdälˈsān(,)yō, dalˈ-,dälˈ-\ *adv* [It] : from the sign — used as a direction in music for the performer to return to the sign that marks the beginning of a repeat

dal·to·ni·an \(ˈ)dȯlˈtōnēən, (ˈ)dälˈ-\ *adj, usu cap* [John *Dalton* †1844 Eng. chemist and physicist + E *-ian*] : of or relating to the English chemist Dalton, his theory of atoms, or his law of multiple proportions

dal·ton·ide \ˈdȯltᵊn,īd, ˈdäl-\ *n* -S [John *Dalton* + E *-ide*] : a chemical compound (as sodium chloride) that conforms to the law of definite proportions : a stoichiometric compound — distinguished from *berthollide*

dal·ton·ism \-ᵊn,izəm\ *n* -S *usu cap* [F *daltonisme*, fr. John *Dalton* †1844 + F *-isme* -ism] **1** : red-green blindness occurring in man as a recessive sex-linked genetic anomaly **2** : COLOR BLINDNESS

dalton's law *n, usu cap D* [after John *Dalton*, its formulator] : LAW OF PARTIAL PRESSURES

dal·yell·ia \dalˈyelēə\ *n, cap* [NL, fr. John G. *Dalyell* †1851 Scot. naturalist + NL *-ia*] : a common genus (the type of the nearly cosmopolitan family Dalyelliidae) of widely distributed rhabdocoel turbellarians with anterior mouth and large dilated pharynx

¹**dam** \ˈdam, ˈdaa(ə)m\ *n* -S [ME, lady, dam, var. of *dame* — more at DAME] : a female parent — used esp. of domestic animals and poultry but sometimes archaically and usu. disparagingly of women

²**dam** \"\ *n* -S [ME; akin to OE for*demman* to dam up, MHG *tam* dam, OHG *temmen* to dam, Goth faur*dammjan* to put a stop to, and perh. to Gk *themeilia* foundations, *tithenai* to place, set — more at DO] **1** : a barrier preventing the flow of water ⟨a lava ~⟩ ⟨beaver ~*s*⟩ ⟨a ~ of drift or other deposits across a valley fed with meltwater —R.F.Flint⟩; *esp* : a barrier (as a bank of earth or a wall of masonry or wood) built across a watercourse to confine and keep back flowing water **2** : a body of water confined or held by a dam (as a millpond or reservoir) ⟨wild geese . . . would rise from the waters of the ~ at my approach —H.V.Morton⟩ ⟨swimming in this ~ is prohibited⟩ **3** : a barrier or obstruction intended to check the flow of liquid, gas, or air: as **a** : a thin sheet of rubber that is stretched around a tooth to keep it dry during dental work **b** : a partition for excluding water, fire, or gas from a section of a mine **c** : a firebrick wall or a stone forming the front of the hearth of a blast furnace **4** *chiefly Brit* : a portable water tank filled from a hose and used in fire fighting

³**dam** \"\ *vt* **dammed; dammed; damming; dams 1** : to provide with a dam : obstruct or restrain the flow of (water) by means of a dam ⟨~ a stream⟩ — often used with *up* **2** : to stop up : block up ⟨the strait pass was *dammed* with dead men —Shak.⟩ : OBSTRUCT, IMPEDE ⟨the futility of trying to ~ the flow of history⟩ — often used with *up* or *back* ⟨~ up an emotion⟩ ⟨~ back his tears⟩ ⟨the tensions *dammed* up by the depression —Oscar Handlin⟩ **syn** see HINDER

⁴**dam** \"\ *n* -S [back-formation fr. *dams*] *Scot* : a piece in checkers; *esp* : KING

dam *abbr* decameter

da·ma \ˈdāmə\ *n* [NL, fr. L *dama, damma* fallow deer, antelope, chamois, perh. of Celt origin; akin to OIr *dam* ox, *dam allaid* stag, W *dafad* sheep, OCorn *dauat*; akin to Gk *damalēs* young bull, Skt *damya* young bull, *dāmyati* he tames — more at TAME] **1** *cap* : a genus of deers consisting of the fallow deer **2** -S [NL (specific epithet of *Gazella dama*), fr.L, fallow deer] : ADDRA

da·ma de no·che \ˌdämə,däˈnō,chā\ *n, pl* **damas de noche** \-məs,-, -məz,-\ [AmerSp, lit., lady of the night] : a West Indian shrub (*Cestrum nocturnum*) with sweet scented yellowish red flowers

¹**dam·age** \ˈdamij, -mēj\ *n* -S [ME, fr. OF, fr. *dam* damage (fr. L *damnum* damage, fine) + *-age* — more at DAMN] **1** : loss due to injury : injury or harm to person, property, or reputation : HURT, HARM ⟨flood ~⟩ ⟨~ resulting from upheavals of nature⟩ ⟨items that may be canceled without ~ to the essential plan⟩ ⟨my poor parents were afraid of social ~ to their child —Rose Macaulay⟩ **2** *obs* : a thing to be regretted : MISFORTUNE, DISADVANTAGE **3 damages** *pl* : the estimated reparation in money for detriment or injury sustained : compensation or satisfaction imposed by law for a wrong or injury caused by a violation of a legal right ⟨bring a suit for ~*s*⟩ ⟨was awarded compensatory ~*s* of $4000⟩ — compare DAMNUM ABSQUE INJURIA; see COMPENSATORY DAMAGES, GENERAL DAMAGES, NOMINAL DAMAGES, PUNITIVE DAMAGES, SPECIAL DAMAGES **4** : EXPENSE, COST, CHARGE **syn** see INJURY

²**damage** \"\ *vb* -ED/-ING/-S [ME *damagen*, fr. MF *damagier*, fr. OF, fr. *damage*, n.] *vt* : to do or cause damage to : HURT, INJURE, IMPAIR ⟨rehabilitation centers for men *damaged* by war⟩ ⟨*damaged* his case by overstating it⟩ ⟨frost severe enough to ~ fruit trees⟩ ~ *vi* : to become damaged ⟨a sturdy cloth that does not ~ easily⟩ **syn** see INJURE

dam·age·able \-jəbəl\ *adj* [MF, fr. OF, fr. *damagier* + *-able*] **1** *obs* : causing damage : HURTFUL **2** : capable of being injured : liable to damage

damage control *n* : procedures and skills employed to maintain or restore watertight integrity, stability, or offensive power in a warship or airplane ⟨the *damage-control* officer⟩

damaging *adj* : causing or able to cause damage : INJURIOUS, DETRIMENTAL ⟨has taken up habits that are very ~ to his health⟩ ⟨~ though wholly circumstantial evidence⟩ ⟨it discredits the authority of science but it is equally ~ to religion —W.R.Inge⟩

dam·ag·ing·ly *adv* : in a damaging manner

dam·an \ˈdamən\ *n* -S [Ar *damān (Isrā'īl)*, lit., sheep of Israel] : the Syrian hyrax

dama pademelon *n* [*dama* + *pademelon*, native name in Australia] : a dark stocky thick-coated and now rare wallaby (*Thylogale eugenii*) of southern and western Australia

damar *var of* DAMMAR

da·ma·ra \ˈdamərə, dəˈmärə\ *n, pl* **damara** *or* **damaras** *usu cap* **1** : a people of South-West Africa including the Herero **2** : a member of the Damara people

¹**dam·a·scene** \ˈdamə,sēn *also* ,==ˈ=\ *n* -S [ME, fr. L *Damascenus*, adj. & n., fr. Gk *Damaskēnos*, fr. *Damaskos* Damascus, Syria] **1** *cap* : a native or inhabitant of Damascus **2** : DAMASK 2b **3** [ME — more at DAMSON] : DAMSON PLUM

²**damascene** \"\ *adj* **1** : of or relating to damask or the art of damascening **2** *usu cap* [L *Damascenus*, adj. & n.] **a** : of, relating to, or characteristic of Damascus **b** : of, relating to, or characteristic of the Damascenes

³**damascene** \"\ *vt* -ED/-ING/-S [alter. (influenced by ¹*damascene*) of earlier *damaskine* — more at DAMASKEEN] **1** : to ornament with wavy patterns (as by welding together bars of iron and steel in the manufacture of Damascus blades) **2** : to ornament (as iron or steel) with inlaid work of precious metals ⟨a Kurdish flintlock *damascened* . . . with gold arabesques —*N.Y. Herald Tribune*⟩

damascened \-nd\ *adj* **1 a** : decorated with wavy patterns ⟨~ swords⟩ **b** : decorated with inlaid work of precious metals ⟨paintings with ~ gold backgrounds⟩ **2** : having an interwoven texture that resembles the markings of a damascened gun barrel — used esp. of certain volcanic glasses

dam·a·scen·er \-nə(r)\ *n* -S : one that damascenes

da·mas·cus \dəˈmaskəs, -maas-, -mäs-\ *adj, usu cap* [fr. *Damascus*, Syria] : of or from Damascus, the capital of Syria : of the kind or style prevalent in Damascus

damascus barrel *n, usu cap D* : a shotgun barrel for use esp. with black-powder cartridges usu. made of strips or rods of iron or steel coiled in a spiral to form a tube and with a speckled or mottled pattern that often runs at right angles to the bore — compare WIRE-WOUND GUN

damascus blade *or* **damascus sword** *n, usu cap D* : a sword made of Damascus steel

damascus iron *or* **damascus twist** *n, usu cap D* : iron made by gunmakers by piling and welding together several bars or wires of iron and steel

damascus steel *or* **damask steel** *n, usu cap Damascus* : steel ornamented with wavy patterns, noted for its hardness and elasticity, and formerly used esp. for making sword blades

damascus ware *n, usu cap D* : a Turkish pottery made with a clear glaze over a white engobe and decorated under the glaze in rich colors

¹**dam·ask** \ˈdaməsk *sometimes* dəˈmask\ *n* -S [ME *damaske*, fr. ML *damascus*, fr. *Damascus*, Syria, where such fabrics were first produced] **1** : a firm lustrous fabric produced with warp-faced and filling-faced satins for figure and ground respectively on one side and with reversed effect on the other, made on jacquard looms usu. of linen, cotton, silk, rayon, or combinations of these fibers, and used for household linen, interior decoration, and clothing **2 a** : DAMASCUS STEEL **b** : the peculiar markings of such steel — compare WATER 7c **3** [*damask (rose)*] : a grayish red that is bluer than bois de rose, bluer, lighter, and stronger than blush rose, and bluer and deeper than Pompeian red or appleblossom

²**damask** \"\ *adj* **1** : made of or resembling damask ⟨~ table linen⟩ **2** : made of or resembling Damascus steel **3** [*damask (rose)*] : of the color damask

³**damask** \"\ *vt* -ED/-ING/-S **1** : DAMASCENE **2** : to weave or adorn with ornamentation characteristic of damask : decorate with variegated pattern or color ⟨on the soft downy bank ~*ed* with flowers —John Milton⟩ ⟨the ~*ed* barge —Elinor Wylie⟩ **3** : to furnish with damask or damask hangings ⟨the columned, ~*ed*, oppressively genteel mansion —Catherine M. Brown⟩ **4** : to make of the color damask **5 a** : to deface (as a book) by marking with lines or figures **b** : to make (a seal) invalid by defacing with a hammer blow

dam·a·skeen \ˈdamə,skēn *also* ,==ˈ=\ *vt* -ED/-ING/-S [fr. earlier *damaskine*, fr. MF *damasquiner*, fr. *damasquin* of Damascus, fr. OIt *damaschino*, fr. *Damasco* Damascus (fr. L *Damascus*) + *-ino* (fr. L *-inus* -ine)] : DAMASCENE

damask rose *n* [fr. obs. *Damask* of Damascus, fr. obs. *Damask* Damascus, fr. ME *Damaske*, fr. L *Damascus*, fr. Gk *Damaskos*] : a large hardy very fragrant pink rose (*Rosa damascena*) of unknown origin that is largely cultivated in Asia Minor as a source of attar of roses and is a parent of many hybrid perpetual roses

damask violet *n* [fr. obs. *Damask* of Damascus] : DAME'S VIOLET

¹**da·mas·sé** \ˌdaməˈsā, ˈ==,=\ *n* -S [F, adj. & n., fr. past part. of *damasser* to damask (weave) fr. MF, fr. *damas* damask, fr. OF, fr. *Damas* Damascus, fr. L *Damascus*] : a damassé fabric esp. of linen

2**damassé** \ˌ==ˈ=\ *adj* [F] **:** woven like damask

dam·bo \ˈdäm(ˌ)bō, ˈdam-\ *n* -s [native name in Africa] **:** a small grassy floodplain in central Africa

dam·brod \ˈdam,(b)räd\ *n* -s [Sc 4*dam* + *brod* board, fr. ME (Scot. dial.) *brodd*, alter. of *bord* — more at BOARD] *Scot* **:** CHECKERBOARD

dame \ˈdām\ *n* -s [ME, fr. OF, fr. L *domina* mistress, lady, fem. of *dominus* master, lord; akin to L *domus* house — more at TIMBER] **1 :** a woman of rank, station, or authority: **a :** the female ruler or head of a body or institution (as a nunnery); *also* **:** a member of certain religious orders of women — used also as a title **b** *archaic* **:** the mistress of a household **:** HOUSEWIFE, WIFE — used also as a title **c :** the wife or daughter of a lord — used formerly also as a form of address but now only as a title prefixed to personified abstractions ⟨*Dame* Care⟩ ⟨*Dame* Fortune⟩ **d** *archaic* **:** the wife or widow of a knight or baronet — used prefixed to prename and surname as a legal title ⟨the will of *Dame* Margaret Murray, widow of Sir John Murray, Bart. —C.R.Hudleston⟩, not as a title of courtesy or a form of address; compare LADY **e :** the mistress of a school — used chiefly in the phrase *dame school* **f :** a matron in charge of a boarding house at Eton College — used also of men **g :** a female member of certain orders of knighthood or of chivalry — used also as a title ⟨*Dame* Myra Hess⟩; compare KNIGHT **2 a :** an elderly woman **:** MATRON ⟨the ancient ~ whose friendship I had so curiously made —William Baucke⟩ ⟨more and more old gaffers and ~*s* hanging loose on society —J.W.Krutch⟩ **b** *Scot* **:** a young unmarried woman **:** GIRL **c** *slang* **:** WOMAN, FEMALE ⟨whiskey, dice, and ~*s* speed the undertaker —Shields McIlwaine⟩ **3 :** a female parent **:** DAM — now used only of animals **4** [MF] *chess, obs* **:** QUEEN **5** *usu cap* **:** a female character in English pantomime played by a male comedian

dame de com·pa·gnie \dämdəkōⁿpányē\ *n, pl* **dames de compagnie** \"\ [F, lit., lady of companionship] **:** a woman who acts as a paid companion

dame school \ˈdām-\ *n* **:** a school in which the rudiments of reading and writing were taught to small children by a woman in her own home ⟨the other girls in the *dame school* which she attended —S.H.Adams⟩

dame's violet \-mz-\ *also* **dame's gilliflower** *or* **dame's rocket** *n* **:** a Eurasian perennial plant (*Hesperis matronalis*) that is widely cultivated for its spikes of showy, single or double, and white or purple flowers which are fragrant in the evening

dame·wort \ˈdām + ˌ-\ *n* -s **:** DAME'S VIOLET

1**dam·fool** \ˌdam, ˌdaa(ə)m+\ *n* [alter. of *damned fool*] **:** one who is extremely foolish — not often in formal use ⟨stand around and let these two ~*s* kill each other —James Jones⟩

2**damfool** *or* **dam·foolish** \"+\ *adj* **:** extremely foolish or stupid ⟨asking ~ questions with ardor —Claud Cockburn⟩ — not often in formal use

dam·i·ana \ˌdamēˈanə, -ˈänə *also* -ˈānə\ *n* -s [AmerSp] **:** the dried leaf of a plant (*Turnera diffusa*) of tropical America, California, and Texas formerly used as a tonic and aphrodisiac

da·mine \ˈdā,mīn, -mən\ *adj* [NL *Dama* + E *-ine*] **:** belonging to or like the fallow deer; *usu* **:** having or being antlers palmate near the tip like those of the fallow deer

dam·kjern·ite \ˈdamkyə(r),nīt\ *n* -s [G *damkjernit*, fr. *Damkjern*, Telemark, Norway, where it was discovered + G *-it* -ite] **:** a melanocratic dike rock with phenocrysts of biotite, pyroxene and barkevikitic hornblende in a groundmass of pyroxene, green hornblende, olivine, magnetite, and considerable calcite

dam·mar *or* **dam·ar** *also* **dam·mer** \ˈdamə(r)\ *n* -s [Malay *damar*] **1 :** any of various hard resins derived esp. from evergreen trees of the genus *Agathis* — compare COPAL, KAURI **2 :** any of various semifossil or recent chiefly East Indian resins; *esp* **:** a soft clear to yellow recent resin obtained chiefly in Malaya from trees of the family Dipterocarpaceae (esp. genera *Shorea*, *Balanocarpus*, and *Hopea*) and used largely in varnishes and printing inks — called also *gum dammar;* see BATU, EAST INDIA RESIN

dammar pine *n* **:** a tree of the genus *Agathis*

dam·me \ˈdamē\ *interj* [alter. of *damn me*] — used as a mild imprecation

dammed *past of* DAM

damming *pres part of* DAM

dam·mit \ˈdamət\ *interj* [alter. of *damn it*] — used as a mild imprecation

1**damn** \ˈdam, ˈdaa(ə)m\ *vb* -ED/-ING/-S [ME *dampnen*, fr. OF *dampner*, fr. L *damnare* to condemn, fr. *damnum* damage, fine, harm, loss; perh. akin to ON *tafn* sacrifice, L *daps* sacrificial feast, Gk *dapanē* expenditure, *daptein* to devour, Skt *dayate* he apportions — more at TIDE] *vt* **1 a** *obs* **:** to adjudge (a person) guilty or culpable **:** sentence judicially **b :** to condemn to a punishment or fate **:** DOOM ⟨if we fail, then we have ~*ed* every man to be the slave of fear —B.M. Baruch⟩ **2 a :** to doom to everlasting punishment in the future world **:** consign to perdition **:** CURSE **b :** to bring about the damnation of **3 :** to condemn as invalid, illegal, immoral, bad, or harmful **:** pronounce adverse judgment upon ⟨~*ing* movies for corrupting the minds of young innocents⟩ ⟨spent three months there and returned with a most ~*ing* report —A.G.N.Flew⟩; *specif* **:** to condemn (a work of art) as a failure **4 :** to bring condemnation or ruin upon **:** RUIN ⟨the story of a . . . minister ~*ed* by his recognition of the mean emotionalism of his church —J.D.Hart⟩ ⟨a democracy is ~*ed* when its leaders are slaves; it is safe when its leaders are not afraid to be free —*New Republic*⟩ **5 :** to invoke damnation upon **:** swear at by using *damn* **:** CURSE — often used to express annoyance, disgust, or surprise ⟨~ him, he ought to have been careful⟩ ⟨well, I'll be ~*ed*⟩ ~ *vi* **:** CURSE, SWEAR — often used interjectionally esp. to express annoyance, disgust, or surprise **syn** see EXECRATE

2**damn** \"\ *n* -s **1 :** the utterance of the word *damn* as a curse **2 :** something of little value — used in various slang or profane phrases ⟨didn't give a ~⟩ ⟨not worth a ~⟩

3**damn** \"\ *adj* [by shortening] **:** 1DAMNED 2a, 2b

4**damn** \"\ *adv* [by shortening] **:** 2DAMNED ⟨Americans . . . will write letters to editors about ~ near anything —*New Yorker*⟩

damna *pl of* DAMNUM

dam·na·bil·i·ty \ˌdamnəˈbiləd·ē, ˌdaam-, -ətē, -i\ *n* -ES **:** the quality or state of being damnable **:** liability to damnation

dam·na·ble \ˈ=nəbəl\ *adj* [ME *dampnable*, fr. MF *damnable*, fr. LL *damnabilis*, fr. L *damnare* + *-abilis* -able] **1 :** liable to damnation **2 :** deserving condemnation **3 :** deserving imprecation **:** DETESTABLE, EXECRABLE ⟨a ~ lie⟩ — often used as a generalized expression of disapproval ⟨a ~ shame⟩ ⟨~ weather⟩ — **dam·na·ble·ness** *n* -ES — **dam·na·bly** \-blē, -bli\ *adv*

damn all *n, slang Brit* **:** NOTHING ⟨hadn't . . . the courage to tell Yeats that he knew *damn all* about the Russian writer —Sean O'Casey⟩

dam·na·tion \damˈnāshən, daamˈ-\ *n* -s [ME *dampnacioun*, fr. OF *dampnation, damnation*, fr. L *damnation-, damnatio*, fr. *damnatus* (past part. of *damnare* to condemn) + *-ion-, -io* -ion — more at DAMN] **1 :** the act of damning or the state of being damned — often used interjectionally esp. to express annoyance or disgust **2 a :** condemnation to everlasting punishment in the future state **b :** the punishment resulting from such condemnation ⟨how can ye escape the ~ of hell —Mt 23:33 (AV)⟩ **3 :** a cause or occasion of damnation **:** a sin leading to or deserving of everlasting punishment ⟨stressing that crime is sin and sin ~ —A.C.Ward⟩ **4** *Roman law* **:** condemnation, sentence, or judgment esp. to pay damages — used esp. in the phrase *legacy by damnation* with reference to the obligation of the heir to do something for or give something to another person

dam·na·tory \ˈ=nə,tōrē, -tȯrē, -ri\ *adj* [L *damnatorius*, fr. *damnatus* + *-orius* -ory] **1 a :** expressing or imposing condemnation **:** CONDEMNATORY ⟨the ~ vehemence we were used to in him —Thomas Carlyle⟩ ⟨the comprehensive, ~ term *parliamentarism* —H.R.Spencer⟩ **b :** occasioning condemnation **:** DAMNING, RUINOUS **2 :** containing, imposing, or consigning to damnation ⟨the ~ clauses of the Athanasian Creed⟩

1**damned** \ˈdamd, ˈdaa(ə)md *also in sense 2* -m; *archaic also* -mnəd\ *adj, sometimes* **damned·er** \-mdə(r)\ *usu* **damned·est** *or* **damnd·est** \-mdəst\ [ME *dampned*, fr. past part. of *dampnen* to damn — more at DAMN] **1 :** doomed or condemned esp. to eternal punishment ⟨~ souls⟩ **2 a :** deserving condemnation **:** calling for execration **:** DAMNABLE, EXECRABLE — often used as a generalized expression of disapproval ⟨a ~ fool⟩ **b :** UNMITIGATED, COMPLETE, UTTER ⟨acted like a ~ idiot⟩ ⟨~ nonsense⟩ — often used as an intensive **c :** EXTRAORDINARY, INCREDIBLE, OUTRAGEOUS — used in the superlative ⟨the *damndest* ruckus you ever heard —Roark Bradford⟩; not often in formal use

2**damned** \-m(d)\ *adv* **:** EXTREMELY, VERY, QUITE ⟨a ~ cold day⟩ ⟨~ glad to see you⟩ ⟨a job ~ well done⟩ ⟨too ~ particular⟩

damned·est *or* **damnd·est** \-mdəst\ *n* -s [fr. superl. of *damned*] **:** UTMOST, BEST — used chiefly in the phrase *do one's damnedest* ⟨dared them to do their ~⟩ ⟨doing his ~ to win⟩

dam·ni·fi·ca·tion \ˌdamnəfəˈkāshən, ˌdaamn-\ *n* -s [F, fr. MF, damage, harm, fr. ML *damnification-, damnificatio*, fr. LL *damnificatus* (past part. of *damnificare*) + L *-ion-, -io* -ion] **:** the action of damnifying **:** an infliction of injury or loss

dam·ni·fy \ˈ==,fī\ *vt* -ED/-ING/-ES [MF *damnifier, damnefier*, fr. OF, fr. LL *damnificare*, fr. L *damnificus* injurious, fr. *damnum* damage, fine + *-i-* + *-ficus* -fic — more at DAMN] **:** to cause loss or damage to **:** DAMAGE, INJURE, WRONG — now chiefly used except in law

damn·ing \ˈdamiŋ, -mēŋ *sometimes* -mn-\ *adj* [fr. pres. part. of 1*damn*] **1 :** bringing damnation ⟨a ~ sin⟩ **2 :** causing or leading to condemnation or ruin ⟨~ evidence of guilt⟩ — **damn·ing·ly** *adv*

dam·no·sa he·re·di·tas *or* **damnosa hae·re·di·tas** \damˈnōsəhəˈredə,tas\ *n* [L, lit., damaging inheritance] **1** *Roman law* **:** an inheritance from a person who dies insolvent and whose debts the heir is bound to discharge **2 :** a harmful or burdensome inheritance ⟨a *damnosa hereditas* from an imperfectly socialized . . . condition —*Times Lit. Supp.*⟩

dam·nous \ˈdamnəs\ *adj* [L *damnosus* hurtful, fr. *damnum* + *-osus* -ous] **:** of, relating to, or involving a damnum — **dam·nous·ly** *adv*

damns *pres 3d sing of* DAMN, *pl of* DAMN

dam·num \ˈdamnəm\ *n, pl* **dam·na** \-nə\ [L — more at DAMN] **:** detriment either to character or property whether involving legal wrong or not **:** harm or loss

damnum abs·que in·ju·ria \-ˌabzkwē(ˌ)inˈyu̇rēə\ *n* [L, lit., damage without wrongdoing] **:** damage without violation of a legal right for which no legal action will lie — compare INJURIA, INJURIA ABSQUE DAMNO

damnum fa·ta·le \-fəˈtā(ˌ)lē\ *n* [L, lit., damage through fate] **:** loss arising from inevitable accident — compare ACT OF GOD

damnum in·fec·tum \-(ˌ)inˈfektəm\ *n* [L, lit., damage not done] **:** loss or damage threatened or anticipated but not yet sustained

damn well *adv* [4*damn*] **:** beyond doubt or question **:** CERTAINLY ⟨had never done it and *damn well* wasn't going to start⟩ ⟨we had better *damn well* be sure⟩ ⟨accustomed to doing as he *damn well* pleased⟩

damnyankee *var of* DAMYANKEE

dam·o·cle·an \ˌdaməˈklēən\ *adj, usu cap* [*Damocles*, 4th cent. B.C. courtier in the retinue of Dionysius the Elder of Syracuse + E *-an* — more at SWORD OF DAMOCLES] **1 :** of or relating to Damocles **2 :** involving imminent danger ⟨the *Damoclean* threat of surpluses and swiftly descending prices —*N.Y.Times*⟩

dam·oi·seau \ˌdaməˈzō, ˈ==,=\ *n, pl* **damoi·seaux** \"\ [MF, fr. OF *damoisel*, fr. (assumed) VL *domnicellus* young aristocrat, dim. of L *dominus* master, lord — more at DAME] *archaic* **:** a young noble not yet made a knight

dam·oi·selle \ˌdaməˈzel, ˈ==,=\ *archaic var of* DAMSEL

damosel *or* **damozel** *var of* DAMSEL

da·mour·ite \dəˈmu̇,rīt\ *n* -s [F *damourite*, fr. A. A. *Damour* †1902 F. chemist + F *-ite*] **:** a variety of muscovite

1**damp** \ˈdamp, ˈdaa(ə)mp, ˈdaimp\ *n* -s [MD or MLG, vapor; akin to OHG *damph* vapor, *demphen* to cause to steam, MHG *dampf, tampf* vapor, *dimpfen* to steam, smoke, OE *dim* — more at DIM] **1 :** a noxious or stifling gas or vapor; *esp* **:** such a gas occurring in coal mines — usu. used in pl; compare BLACKDAMP, FIREDAMP **2** *obs* **:** a dazed or stupefied state **:** STUPOR, INSENSIBILITY **3** MOISTURE: **a :** DAMPNESS, HUMIDITY ⟨*damp*-resisting flour⟩ ⟨that old hostel, rotting down with ~ and time —John Galsworthy⟩ **b** *archaic* **:** FOG, MIST **4 a :** DISCOURAGEMENT, CHECK, DAMPER ⟨no sentiment of shame gave a ~ to her triumph —Jane Austen⟩ ⟨uncertainties that cast a ~ upon trade⟩ **b** *archaic* **:** a depression or dejection of mind or spirit ⟨a secret ~ of grief comes o'er my soul —Joseph Addison⟩ **5 :** a period of humid weather favorable for the moistening and softening of cured tobacco so that it can be handled

2**damp** \"\ *vb* -ED/-ING/-S *vt* **1 a :** to affect with or as if with a noxious gas or vapor **:** CHOKE, STIFLE, EXTINGUISH **b :** to check combustion in (a furnace) while keeping the fire alive: (1) **:** to cover (a fire in a furnace) with damp coal, ashes, or cinders to diminish the generation of heat or steam (2) **:** to stop (a blast) by closing up all the openings in a blast furnace — usu. used with *down* **c** (1) **:** to diminish progressively the vibration or oscillation of (as a string or voltage) (2) **:** to provide (as piano strings) with dampers **2 :** CHECK, RESTRAIN ⟨nothing could ~ his enthusiasm —George Meredith⟩ **:** RETARD ⟨the demand may be ~*ed* by increases in costs —M.D.Ketchum⟩ **:** DEPRESS ⟨nothing could ~ him — even years of failure —Robert Westerby⟩ **3** *obs* **:** to make (mental powers) stupid or dull **:** DAZE **4 :** to make damp **:** MOISTEN ⟨felt the sweat . . . ~*ing* the palms of his hands —Marcia Davenport⟩; *specif* **:** to sprinkle (laundry work) with water and fold for the ironers — usu. used with *down* ~ *vi* **1 :** to become damp **2 :** to diminish progressively in extent of vibration or oscillation ⟨the wave ~*ed* out⟩

3**damp** \"\ *adj* -ER/-EST **1** *obs* **:** belonging to or having the characteristics of a noxious gas or vapor **2 a** *archaic* **:** DAZED, STUPEFIED **b :** having or showing lack of vitality or dejection of spirits **:** DEPRESSED, DULL ⟨the thoughtful expression of a serious able musician, but I thought it a bit ~ —*New Yorker*⟩ ⟨their meandering witless conversations and their ~ love affairs —*Time*⟩ **3 :** slightly or moderately wet **:** MOIST, HUMID ⟨~ weather⟩ ⟨a ~ day⟩ ⟨wipe with a ~ sponge⟩ **syn** see WET

damp course *n* **:** a damp-resisting layer in a masonry wall

damp·en \-pən, -pᵊm\ *vb* **dampened** \-pənd, -pᵊmd\ **dampened** \"\ **dampening** \-p(ə)niŋ\ **dampens** \-pənz, -pᵊmz\ [3*damp* + *-en*] *vt* **1 :** to check or diminish the activity or vigor of **:** DEPRESS, DEADEN, DULL ⟨~*ed* our enthusiasm⟩ ⟨any downturn . . . of the nation's business could ~ the railroad boom —*N.Y.Times*⟩ ⟨nothing here to ~ courage or blunt the zest for life —M.R.Cohen⟩ **2 :** to make slightly wet **:** MOISTEN **:** make damp ⟨a ~ a sponge⟩ ⟨ground barely ~*ed* by showers⟩ **3 :** DAMP *vt* 1c ~ *vi* **1 :** to become damp **:** gather moisture ⟨during the night the ground ~*ed*⟩ **2 :** to become deadened or dulled ⟨soon found their ardor ~*ing*⟩

damp·en·er \-p(ə)nə(r)\ *n* -s **:** one that dampens: as **a :** a device for dampening cloth (as in a laundry) **b :** a worker that dampens articles in preparation for further processing: (1) **:** one that tempers shoe outsoles to facilitate cutting, shaping, and stitching — called also *muller* (2) **:** one that dampens textiles (as hosiery or cloth) for boarding or ironing (3) **:** one that softens hides in warm water **c :** a device for retarding the oscillations of a spring when a load is suddenly applied or removed **d :** any of the rollers on an offset printing press that convey water to nonprinting areas of the printing surface

damp·er \-pə(r)\ *n* -s **1 :** one that checks, lessens, or depresses **:** a dulling or deadening influence, agent, or device ⟨news that put a ~ on the stock market⟩ ⟨served as an effective ~ on further development⟩: as **a :** a valve or movable plate in the flue or other part of a stove, furnace, or fireplace for regulating the draft or in a duct for regulating the flow of air or other gas **b :** one of a set of felted blocks resting on a piano string to keep it silent except when the key is pressed or when the entire set is lifted by a pedal **c :** a device designed to bring a mechanism or a part thereof to rest with minimum oscillation **d** *Brit* **:** SHOCK ABSORBER **2 :** one that moistens (as a device for damping or wetting or a worker that dampens articles) **3** *slang* **:** CASH REGISTER **4** *Austral* **:** a baking-powder bread formed into flat cakes and usu. baked over a campfire

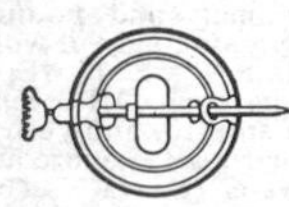

damper 1a

damper pedal *n* **:** the pedal that controls the set of dampers on a piano — called also *loud pedal, sustaining pedal*

damper winding *n* **:** a short-circuited squirrel-cage winding placed in the pole faces and around the pole shoes of synchronous machines, the currents induced in the winding by the periodic variations in synchronous speed having the effect of a damper — called also *amortisseur*

damping *pres part of* DAMP

damping capacity *n* **:** the ability of a material to absorb vibrations ⟨lead has high *damping capacity*⟩ ⟨a tuning fork has low *damping capacity*⟩

damping-off \ˈ==ˌ=\ *n* -s **:** a diseased condition of seedlings or cuttings caused by certain parasitic fungi that invade the plant tissues near the ground and produce wilting usu. associated with rotting of the stem esp. near the ground level

damp·ish \-pish, -pēsh\ *adj* **:** somewhat damp **:** tending to dampness — **damp·ish·ly** *adv*

damp·ly *adv* **:** in a damp manner

damp·ness \-pnəs\ *n* -ES **:** the quality or state of being damp

damp off *vi* **:** to undergo damping-off

1**damp·proof** \ˈ=ˌ=\ *adj* [1*damp* + *proof*] **:** impervious to water vapor or to liquid water when under only slight pressure

2**dampproof** \ˈ=,=\ *vt* -ED/-ING/-S **:** to make dampproof

damp·proof·er \-fə(r)\ *n* **:** one that dampproofs: **a :** a worker that dampproofs masonry walls — called also *waterproofer* **b :** a dampproofing material

damps *pl of* DAMP, *pres 3d sing of* DAMP

damp sheet *n* **:** a curtain in a mine gallery for directing air currents and preventing accumulation of gas

damp–treat \ˈ=,=\ *vt* **:** to treat with a dampproofing material

damp–wood termite *n* **:** any of numerous termites that live in damp decaying wood or moist living wood and do not require a connection with the soil

dampy \-mpē, -pi\ *adj* [1*damp* + *-y*] **:** affected with damp **:** DAMPISH

1**dams** *pl of* DAM, *pres 3d sing of* DAM

2**dams** \ˈdamz\ *n pl but sing in constr* [alter. of earlier *dames*, fr. MF (*jeu de*) *dames*, lit., game of ladies] *Scot* **:** CHECKERS

1**dam·sel** \ˈdamzəl, ˈdaam-\ *n* -s [ME *damesel*, fr. OF *dameisele, damoisele*, fr. (assumed) VL *domnicella* young noblewoman, dim. of L *domina* mistress, lady — more at DAME] **1** *also* **dam·o·sel** *or* **dam·o·zel** \ˈ=mə,zel, ˌ==ˈ=\ **:** a young woman: **a** *archaic* **:** a young unmarried woman of noble or gentle birth **b** *obs* **:** a maid in waiting **:** female attendant **c :** GIRL, MAIDEN, LASS **2 :** an attachment to a millstone spindle for shaking the hopper

2**damsel** \"\ *n* -s [by folk etymology] *dial* **:** DAMSON 1,2

damsel–errant \ˌ==ˈ==\ *n, pl* **damsels–errant :** a female knight-errant

damselfish \ˈ==,=\ *n* **:** any of numerous often brilliantly colored marine fishes of the family Pomacentridae that live almost entirely along coral reefs — called also *demoiselle*

damselfly \ˈ==,=\ *n* **:** any of numerous slender-bodied insects that constitute the suborder Zygoptera of the order Odonata and that are characterized by laterally projecting eyes and by petiolate wings which are folded above the body when at rest

damsite \ˈ=,=\ *n* [2*dam* + *site*] **:** a site for a dam

dam·son \ˈdamzᵊn, ˈdaam-\ *n* -s [ME *damascene, damesene, damson*, fr. L (*prunum*) *Damascenum*, lit., plum of Damascus, fr. neut. of *Damascenus* of Damascus — more at DAMASCENE] **1 :** a rather small compact plum (*Prunus insititia* or *P. domestica insititia*) that has small usu. somewhat acid and dark purple fruits, is native to Asia Minor but now nearly cosmopolitan in cultivation, and is grown in several horticultural forms **2 :** the fruit of the damson **3 :** a moderate violet that is bluer and less strong than Roman purple, redder and darker than Parma violet (sense 2a), and redder and less strong than prelate

damson cheese *n* **:** a preserve made of damson plums peeled, stoned, and cooked with sugar to a consistency of soft cheese

damson plum *n* **:** DAMSON 2; *esp* **:** any comparatively sweet damson that suggests the typical plums in flavor

dam·yankee *also* **damn·yankee** \(ˈ)dam, (ˈ)daam + ˈ==\ *n* -s [contr. of *damned yankee*] **:** a native or inhabitant of the northern states of the U.S. as distinguished from a Southerner — not often in formal use ⟨blaming our troubles, if we were southern, more on the ~ —Lillian Smith⟩ ⟨the South is considered with what seems to this ~ extraordinary fairness —Clifton Fadiman⟩

1**dan** \ˈdan, ˈdaa(ə)n\ *n* -s *usu cap* [ME *dan, daun, daunz*, an honorable title for members of religious orders, fr. MF *dan, danz*, fr. OF, fr. ML *domnus*, fr. L *dominus* lord, master — more at DAME] — used archaically as a title for deities and poets ⟨*Dan* Cupid⟩ ⟨*Dan* Chaucer⟩

2**dan** \", ˈdän\ *n, pl* **dan** *or* **dans** *usu cap* **:** a people of the border region between the Ivory coast and Liberia

dan·a·id \ˈdanē,id, -nā,-\ *n* -s [NL *Danaidae*] **:** one of the Danaidae; *esp* **:** MONARCH BUTTERFLY

da·na·i·dae \dəˈnāə,dē\ *n pl, cap* [NL, fr. *Danaus*, type genus + *-idae*] **:** a small family of large chiefly tropical butterflies having the first pair of legs degenerate in the adult and usu. a disagreeable taste that serves to protect them from predators

da·na·ite \ˈdānə,īt\ *n* -s [J. Freeman *Dana* †1827 Am. chemist + E *-ite*] **:** a mineral consisting of cobaltiferous arsenopyrite

da·na·kil \ˈdanə,kil, ˌ=ˈkēl, dəˈnä,kēl\ *also* **dan·ka·li** \dänˈkä(ˌ)lē\ *n, pl* **danakil** *or* **danakils** *also* **dankali** *or* **dankalis** *usu cap* **1 a :** a Hamitic people of northeast Ethiopia **b :** a member of such people **2 :** 2AFAR 2

da·na·lite \ˈdānə,līt\ *n* -s [James D. *Dana* †1895 Am. geologist + E *-lite*] **:** a mineral $(Fe,Zn,Mn)_8Be_6Si_6O_{24}S_2$ that consists of a reddish or gray silicate and sulfide of iron and beryllium usu. containing also zinc and manganese and that is isomorphous with helvite and genthelvite

dan·a·us \ˈdanēəs, -nāəs\ *n, cap* [NL, after *Danaus*, mythical king of Argos who ordered his daughters to murder their husbands, fr. L, fr. Gk *Danaos*] **:** the type genus of Danaidae comprising the monarch and several other predominantly black-and-orange butterflies chiefly of subtropical regions

dan buoy \ˈdan +,-\ *n, sometimes cap D* [origin unknown] **:** a floating temporary marker buoy (as one used on fishing grounds or in minesweeping and antisubmarine-warfare operations)

dan·bur·ite \ˈdanbə,rīt\ *n* -s [*Danbury*, Conn., its locality + E *-ite*] **:** a mineral $CaB_2(SiO_4)_2$ consisting of a calcium borosilicate that is transparent to translucent and in crystal habit resembles topaz

1**dance** \ˈdan(t)s, ˈdaa(ə)n-, ˈdain-, ˈdȧn-\ *vb* -ED/-ING/-S [ME *dauncen*, fr. OF *dancier*, perh. fr. (assumed) VL *deantiare*, fr. LL *deante* in front of, fr. L *de* from + *ante* in front of — more at DE-, ANTE-] *vi* **1 :** to perform either alone or with others a rhythmic and patterned succession of steps usu. to music **2 :** to move or seem to move nimbly and quickly up and down or about (as from excitement or emotion) **:** LEAP, SPRING, SKIP ⟨a blow that made him ~ with pain⟩ ⟨*danced* for joy at the news⟩ ⟨heart *dancing* with happiness⟩ **3 :** to bob up and down (as in the air or on the surface of water) ⟨motes *dancing* in a beam of light⟩ ~ *vt* **1 :** to perform, execute, or take part in as a dancer ⟨~ a polka⟩ ⟨*danced* the title role in the ballet⟩ **2 a :** to cause to dance **:** lead in a dance **b :** to cause to move up and down with a bouncing jerky motion **:** DANDLE ⟨~ a baby on his knee⟩ **3 :** to bring or accompany into a specified condition or position by dancing ⟨*danced* himself into the favor of the queen⟩ ⟨*danced* the new year in⟩ ⟨*danced* his youth away⟩ — **dance attendance :** to attend assiduously and obsequiously **:** be in waiting or at beck and call **:** court favor — **dance on nothing :** to be hanged — **dance to another tune :** to follow a changed course of action esp. involuntarily

2**dance** \"\ *n* -s *often attrib* [ME *daunce*, fr. OF *dance*, fr. *dancier* to dance] **1 :** rhythmic movement having as its aim the creation of visual designs by a series of poses and tracing of patterns through space in the course of measured units of time, the two components, static and kinetic, receiving varying emphasis (as in ballet, natya, and modern dance) and being executed by different parts of the body in accordance with temperament, artistic precepts, and purpose **:** the art of dancing **2 a :** a round or turn of dancing **b :** a social gathering for the purpose of dancing **3 :** the figure or pattern of a particular form of dancing **:** a coherent series of movement patterns **4 a :** a piece of music by which dancing may be guided (as a jig, minuet, or waltz) **b :** any musical composition in a dance rhythm **5 :** a ceremony among American Indians in which dancing and singing play a conspicuous part — see CORN DANCE, SNAKE DANCE, SUN DANCE, WAR DANCE **6 :** a sequence of more or less rhythmic stereotyped movements habitually made by an animal in response to a particular stimulus ⟨the courting ~ of a prairie chicken⟩; *specif* **:** a series of special steps and turns whereby worker honeybees communicate the whereabouts of food to their fellow workers **7 :** a rhythmic or lively movement suggestive of dancing **8 :** a zigzag fess

dance·abil·i·ty \ˌ⸗⸗əˈbiləd‧ē\ *n* -ES **:** the quality or state of being danceable

dance·able \ˈ⸗⸗əbəl\ *adj* **:** suitable for dancing ⟨tuneful and eminently ~ scores —Winthrop Sargeant⟩

danced *past of* DANCE

dance drama *n* **:** drama conveyed by dance movements sometimes accompanied by dialogue

dance fly *n* **:** a fly of the family Empididae

dance hall *n* **:** a large room set aside or suitable for dances; *esp* **:** a public hall offering facilities for dancing

dance of death : DANSE MACABRE

dance palace *n* **:** a showy dance hall

danc·er \-sə(r)\ *n* -S [ME *dauncer*, fr. *dauncen* to dance + *-er*] **1 :** one that dances; *specif* **:** a professional performer of dances **2 dancers** *pl, slang* **:** STAIRS **3 dancers** *pl, chiefly Scot* **:** AURORA BOREALIS

danc·ery \-s(ə)rē\ *n* -ES **:** a place of entertainment (as a nightclub or dance hall) providing facilities for dancing

dances *pres 3d sing of* DANCE, *pl of* DANCE

dance society *n* **:** a society often found within the communal life of primitive peoples whose function is to perform a ceremonial or ritual dance

¹dan·cet·té *or* **dan·cet·tée** \(ˈ)danˌsed‧(ˌ)ā, ˌdan(t)səˈtā\ *or* **dan·cet·ty** \(ˈ)danˈsed‧ē\ *adj* [prob. modif. of F *denché*, fr. MF, fr. *dent* tooth, fr. L *dent-, dens* — more at TOOTH] *heraldry* **:** having large indentations usu. three in number ⟨a fess ~⟩

²dan·cette \danˈset, ˈ⸗ˌ⸗\ *n* -S [alter. of ¹*dancetté*] **:** an architectural molding or group of moldings with a zigzag pattern in the design **:** CHEVRON MOLDING

dance-walk \ˈ⸗ˌ⸗\ *n* **:** a ballroom step consisting of a simple rhythmic walk

dancing *pres part of* DANCE

dancing disease *n* **:** TARANTISM

dancing girl *n* **:** a girl that dances professionally **:** DANSEUSE; *esp* **:** a female professional dancer of any of several Asiatic countries

dancing-girls \ˈ⸗⸗ˌ⸗\ *n pl but sing or pl in constr* [so called fr. the fancied resemblance of the flowers to ballet dancers] **:** an East Indian herb (*Mantisia saltatoria*) sometimes cultivated in greenhouses for its purple-and-yellow flowers

danc·ing·ly *adv* **:** in a dancing manner

dancy *pron at* DANCE + ē, i\ *adj* -ER/-EST **:** given to or suggestive of dancing esp. when lively ⟨whether the music is dainty . . . or ~ and vigorously expository —Virgil Thomson⟩

dand \ˈdand\ *n* -S [by shortening] *dial Brit* **:** ²DANDY

d&c color \ˌdēənˈsē-\ *n, cap D & 1st C* [abbr. of drug and cosmetic] **:** any of the synthetic dyes that in certified batches are permitted for use in drugs and cosmetics — see DYE table II

dan·de·li·on \ˈdandᵊlˌīən, ˈdaan-, -dəˌlī-,-dēˌlī-, ÷ -ˌlīn\ *n* -S [fr. earlier *dent de lion*, fr. MF, lit., lion's tooth; trans. of ML *dens leonis*; fr. its sharply indented leaves] **1 :** a plant of the genus *Taraxacum* (esp. *T. officinale*) abundant as a weed in meadows, lawns, and cultivated ground throughout Europe, Asia, and No. America **2 :** any of several plants related to and resembling the dandelion — see FALL DANDELION, KRIGIA **3 a :** a brilliant yellow resembling sunflower yellow **b :** a vivid yellow resembling goldenrod (sense 2a)

dandelion coffee *n* **:** a beverage made from the dried roots of the dandelion

¹dan·der \ˈdan(d)ə(r)\ *vi* -ED/-ING/-S [origin unknown] **1** *dial Brit* **:** to walk at a leisurely pace **:** SAUNTER, IDLE **2** *dial Brit* **:** to wander mentally

²dander \-ər\ *n* -S *chiefly Scot* **:** a leisurely walk **:** STROLL

³dan·der \ˈdandə(r), ˈdaan-\ *n* -S [alter. of earlier *dandruff, dandro*] **1 :** DANDRUFF; *specif* **:** minute scales from hair, feathers, or skin that may act as allergens **2 :** ANGER, TEMPER ⟨finally, she got her ~ up and wrote direct to the president —S.V.Benét⟩

⁴dan·der \ˈdan(d)ə(r)\ *n* -S [origin unknown] *dial Brit* **:** a piece of slag **:** a calcined cinder — usu. used in pl. ⟨~*s* from the fire⟩

D and H *abbr* dressed and headed

dan·di·a·cal \(ˈ)danˈdīəkəl\ *adj* [fr. ²*dandy*, after such pairs as E *prosody: prosodiacal*] **:** of, relating to, or suggestive of a dandy **:** DANDIFIED ⟨~ elegance⟩ ⟨a ~ pose⟩ **:** characterized by dandyism — **dan·di·a·cal·ly** \-k(ə)lē\ *adv*

dan·die din·mont terrier \ˌdandēˈdinˌmänt-, -ˌmənt-\ *n, usu cap both Ds* [after *Dandie Dinmont*, character owning 2 such dogs in the novel *Guy Mannering* by Sir Walter Scott †1832 Scottish writer] **:** a terrier of a breed originating on the border between Scotland and England having short legs, long body, pendulous ears, and rough coat, ranging in height from 8 to 11 inches and in weight from 14 to 24 lbs., and being silvery gray or cream to yellowish tan in color and distinctive for its very full topknot of silky light-colored hair

dan·di·fi·ca·tion \ˌdandəfəˈkāshən, ˌdaan-, -ndēf-\ *n* -S **1 :** the action of dandifying or the state of being dandified **2 :** something that dandifies

dan·di·fied \ˈ⸗⸗ˌfīd\ *adj* **1 :** having the dress or manners of a dandy ⟨~ in youth, he became theatrical in later life⟩ **2 :** made or done in the style of a dandy **:** suggestive of dandies ⟨a ~ costume⟩ ⟨walked with a ~ gait⟩

dan·di·fy \-fī\ *vt* -ED/-ING/-ES [²*dandy* + *-fy*] **:** to cause to resemble a dandy **:** make characteristic or suggestive of a dandy

dan·di·ly \-ndəlē, -li\ *adv* **:** in the style or manner of a dandy

dan·di·prat \ˈdandēˌprat\ *n* -S [origin unknown] **1 :** an English silver coin of the 16th century prob. worth twopence **2 a :** a little, insignificant, or contemptible person **:** DWARF, PYGMY **b :** a small boy **:** URCHIN

dan·di·zette *or* **dan·di·sette** \ˌdandēˈzet\ *n* -S [*dandy* + *-zette, -sette* (as in *grisette*)] **:** a female dandy

¹dan·dle \ˈdandᵊl, ˈdaan-, ÷ -nᵊl\ *vb* **dandled; dandled; dandling** \-nd(ᵊ)liŋ\ **dandles** [origin unknown] *vt* **1 :** to move (as a baby) up and down in one's arms or on one's knee **:** toss up and down in or as if in affectionate play **2 :** to treat fondly (as a child) **:** make much of **:** PAMPER, PET ⟨editors, scholars, merchants, even the noble lords and ladies feted and *dandled* him —Max Eastman⟩ **3** *obs* **:** to play or trifle with ~ *vi* **1 :** DANGLE ⟨one leg, even if the hose wrinkle a little, must ~ over the other —Christopher Morley⟩ **2 :** TRIFLE, TOY, PLAY ⟨*dandled* with one art after another⟩

²dandle \"\ *n* -S *NewEng* **:** SEESAW 2

dan·dling·ly *adv* **:** in a dandling manner

D and M *abbr* dressed and matched

D and P *abbr* developing and printing

dan·druff \ˈdandrəf, ˈdaan-\ *n* -S [prob. fr. *dand-* (origin unknown) + *-ruff*, of Scand origin; akin to ON *hrūfa* crust on a wound, scab, Norw *ruva*, ON *hrjūfr* scabby, scurvy; akin to OE *hrēof* rough, scabby, leprous, OHG *riob* leprous, *hriūpi* scabies, *hruf* pock, scurf, Latvian *krāupa* scurf, wart, Lith *kraupùs* rough] **:** a scurf of white or grayish usu. greasy scales forming on and shed from skin surfaces esp. of the scalp — **dan·druffy** \-əfē, -fi\ *adj*

dands *pl of* DAND

¹dan·dy *or* **dan·di** \ˈdandē, ˈdan-\ *n, pl* **dandies** *or* **dandis** [Hindi *ḍā̃ḍī*, fr. *ḍā̃ḍ* oar, pole, staff, fr. Skt *daṇḍa* stick] **1 :** a boatman on the Ganges river **2 :** a palanquin used in India and made with a pole projecting at each end

²dan·dy \ˈdandē, ˈdaan-, -di\ *n* -ES [prob. short for *jack-a-dandy*] **1 :** a man who gives fastidious and exaggerated attention to dress or personal appearance (as by always dressing in the height of fashion or by adopting carefully affected styles of dress) ⟨he became a ~ given to lavender-colored suits with long jackets and brief double-breasted waistcoats —Walter Marsden⟩ **2 :** something esp. excellent in its class ⟨a ~ — good-natured, willing and awfully good at his job —D.B. Putnam⟩ ⟨a little ~ of a tent —*New Yorker*⟩ ⟨this novel is a ~⟩ — not often in formal use **3** [by shortening] **:** DANDY ROLL **4 :** a small 2-masted sailboat with a modified ketch rig **5 :** a device resembling a small capstan used to hoist the trawl in fishing **6 :** a large pail or can usu. mounted on wheels and used for pouring tar or asphalt in road building

³dandy \"\ *adj, usu* -ER/-EST **1 :** of, relating to, or suggestive of a dandy **:** FOPPISH ⟨gave himself ~ airs⟩ ⟨a ~ sort of fellow⟩ **2 :** very good **:** FIRST-RATE, FINE ⟨a ~ new bicycle⟩ ⟨a ~ place for a picnic⟩ ⟨~ weather⟩ — not often in formal use

dandy brush *n* [prob. fr. ²*dandy*] **:** a stiff brush used in cleaning and grooming animals

dan·dy·dom \-dəm\ *n* -S [²*dandy* + *-dom*] **1 :** the state of being a dandy **2 :** the world of dandies

dandy fever \ˈdandē-\ *n* [prob. fr. a West Indian Creole word of African origin; akin to Swahili *kidinga* (*popo*) dengue — more at DENGUE] **:** DENGUE

dandy funk \"-\ *n* [origin unknown] **:** hardtack soaked in water and baked with grease and molasses

dandy horse *n* [²*dandy*] **:** an early 2-wheeled velocipede propelled by pushing with the feet against the ground — called also *hobbyhorse*

dandy horse

dan·dy·ish \ˈdandēish, ˈdaan-, -ndi-\ *adj* [²*dandy* + *-ish*] **:** suggestive of a dandy in manner or appearance **:** FOPPISH — **dan·dy·ish·ly** *adv*

dan·dy·ism \-ndēˌizəm, -diˌiz-\ *n* -S [²*dandy* + *-ism*] **1 :** the style or conduct of a dandy **2 :** the literary or artistic style often associated with the English and French decadents of the last of the 19th century and marked esp. by preciosity of language and refined emotionalism of subject matter

dan·dy·ize \-ndēˌīz, -diˌīz\ *vb* -ED/-ING/-S [²*dandy* + *-ize*] *vt* **:** DANDIFY ~ *vi* **:** to act like a dandy

dandy line *n* [²*dandy* (fishing device)] **:** a fishing line to which are attached crosspieces of whalebone carrying a hook at each end

dan·dy·ling \-ndēliŋ, -dil-\ *n* -S [²*dandy* + *-ling*] **:** an insignificant fop **:** petty dandy

dan·dy·prat *obs var of* DANDIPRAT

dandy roll *also* **dandy roller** *n* [³*dandy*] **:** a light wire-covered roll that rides on the wet web of paper on a fourdrinier machine to compact the sheet and sometimes impress a watermark

dane \ˈdān\ *n* -S [ME *Dan*, fr. ON *Danr*] **1** *cap* **:** a Norseman of Viking times **:** VIKING **2** *cap* **a :** a native or inhabitant of Denmark **b :** a person of Danish descent **3** *usu cap* **:** GREAT DANE 2

danebrog *usu cap, var of* DANNEBROG

dane·geld \ˈdānˌgeld\ *also* **dane·gelt** \-lt\ *n* -S *often cap* [ME *Danegeld*, fr. *Dane* (gen. pl. of *Dan* Dane) + *geld* tribute, payment, fr. OE *gield*; akin to OE *gieldan* to pay, pay for, reward — more at DANE, YIELD] **:** an annual tax believed to have been imposed orig. to buy off the ravages of Danish invaders in England or to maintain forces to oppose them but continued as a land tax usu. of two shillings upon each hide of land

dane gun *n, often cap D* [so called fr. its introduction into Africa by Danish traders] *West Africa* **:** a firearm of obsolete design orig. of European and now of native-village manufacture

dane·law \ˈdānˌlȯ\ *also* **dane·la·ga** \-ˌlägə\ *or* **dane·lagh** \-ˌlȯ\ *n* -S *usu cap* [ME *Dene lawe*, fr. OE *Dena lagu*, lit., Danes' law, fr. *Dena* (gen. of *Dene*, pl., Danes, of Scand. origin; akin to ON *Danr* Dane) + *lagu* law — more at LAW] **1 :** the Danish law formerly in force in the northeastern part of England held by the Danes **2 :** the part of England formerly under the Danelaw

dane's-blood \ˈ⸗ˌ⸗\ *n, pl* **dane's-bloods** *usu cap D* [prob. so called fr. the belief that they grew where Danish blood was spilled] **1** *dial Eng* **:** DANEWORT **2** *dial Eng* **:** PASQUEFLOWER

daneweed \ˈ⸗ˌ⸗\ *n, often cap* **:** DANEWORT

danewort \ˈ⸗ˌ⸗\ *n, usu cap* **:** a dwarf herbaceous elder (*Sambucus ebulus*) of Europe having pink flowers and a nauseous odor

¹dang \ˈdaŋ, -aī-\ *vt* -ED/-ING/-S [euphemism] **:** DAMN vt 5

²dang \-ŋ\ *or* **danged** \-ŋ(d)\ *adj* (*or adv*) [euphemism] **:** DAMNED

³dang \-ŋ\ *n* -S [euphemism] **:** DAMN

⁴dang [ME] *dial past of* DING

⁵dang \daŋ\ *vb* -ED/-ING/-S [by alter.] *dial Brit* **:** ¹DING

danga·rik \ˈdaŋ(g)əˌrik\ *n, pl* **dangarik** *or* **dangariks** *usu cap* **1 :** a Pathan people living in the southern Chitral sector of the northwest frontiers of Pakistan **2 :** a member of the Dangarik people

¹dan·ger \ˈdānjə(r)\ *n* -S [ME *daunger* power, jurisdiction, liability, reluctance, fr. OF *dangier* power, jurisdiction, alter. (influenced by OF *dam* damage, fr. L *damnum*) of *dongier*, fr. (assumed) VL *domniarium, dominiarium* authority, fr. L *dominium* ownership (fr. *dominus* master) + *-arium* -ary — more at DAME, DAMN] **1 a** *archaic* **:** power or authority of a master **:** JURISDICTION ⟨you stand within his ~, do you not? —Shak.⟩ **b** *obs* **:** reach or range esp. of a weapon or missile ⟨out of the shot and ~ of desire —Shak.⟩ **2** *obs* **:** HARM, INJURY, DAMAGE ⟨a sting in him that at his will he may do ~ with —Shak.⟩ **3 :** the state of being exposed to harm **:** liability to injury, pain, or loss **:** PERIL, RISK ⟨pronounced out of ~ the second day after the operation⟩ ⟨a place where children could play without ~⟩ ⟨in ~ of losing his life's savings⟩ **4 :** a case or cause of danger ⟨the ~*s* of the sea⟩

syn DANGER, PERIL, JEOPARDY, HAZARD, and RISK can mean, in common, either the state of being threatened with serious loss or injury or the cause or source of such a threat. DANGER, the general term, implies the contingent evil ⟨troubled by the *danger* that the manuscript might be lost —Carl Van Doren⟩ ⟨realizing that the buffalo in the United States were in *danger* of becoming extinct —*Amer. Guide Series: N.H.*⟩ ⟨the *dangers* of travel by air⟩ ⟨the *danger* of lowering one's standards⟩ PERIL implies more strongly the imminence and fearfulness of the danger ⟨the ship was in deadly *peril* of seizure by mutineers —C.C.Cutler⟩ ⟨the trickle of a clear spring water which is beyond all *peril* of drought —Louis Bromfield⟩ ⟨one fears to say anything when the *peril* of misunderstanding puts a warning finger to the lips —B.N.Cardozo⟩ ⟨the *perils* of modern warfare⟩ JEOPARDY implies exposure to or the position of special susceptibility to extreme danger, as of a man in court accused of a serious offense ⟨to place one's life in *jeopardy* by driving too fast⟩ ⟨one's moral and emotional balance is always in *jeopardy* during wartime⟩ HAZARD, not as strong as *jeopardy*, implies danger from something fortuitous or beyond one's control ⟨needless to say, there are *hazards* connected with brain surgery —H.R.Litchfield & L.H.Dembo⟩ ⟨the protection by insurance or otherwise, against the *hazards* of unemployment, sickness, and old age —*Amer. Guide Series: N.Y.*⟩ ⟨the steeple, with heavy iron cross, is so tall that some consider it a dangerous *hazard* —*Amer. Guide Series: La.*⟩ RISK implies a voluntary placing of oneself in circumstances of doubtful and possibly adverse outcome ⟨to fool around with dynamite to the *risk* of life and limb⟩ ⟨life is a *risk* and all individual plans precarious, all human achievements transient —Irwin Edman⟩ ⟨countries here who want to see the *risk* of another world war extinguished here and now —Benjamin Welles⟩ ⟨for many Americans the *risks* of city life outweighed the attractions —Oscar Handlin⟩

²danger \"\ *vt* -ED/-ING/-S [ME *daungeren*, fr. *daunger*, n.] **1** *obs* **:** to make liable **2** *archaic* **:** ENDANGER

danger angle *n* **:** the angle between two known points as observed from a point marking the limit of safe approach of a ship to a reef, shoal, or other obstruction which can then be passed safely by keeping the known points at an angle, as observed from the ship in her course, greater or less than the danger angle

danger bearing *n* **:** a limiting bearing of any object the passing of which bearing will cause a ship to run into danger

dangerful *adj, obs* **:** DANGEROUS

dan·ger·less \ˈ⸗⸗ləs\ *adj* **:** free from danger **:** lacking danger

danger line *n* **:** a real or imaginary boundary beyond which danger will be encountered

dan·ger·ous \ˈdānj(ə)rəs\ *adj* [ME *daungerous* haughty, trouble-making, hard to please, fr. OF *dangereus* trouble-making, hard to please, fr. *dangier* + *-eus* -ous] **1 :** exposing to danger **:** involving risk **:** demanding caution or care as extremely unsafe **:** HAZARDOUS, PERILOUS ⟨a little learning is a ~ thing —Alexander Pope⟩ ⟨a ~ climb⟩ ⟨~ occupations⟩ ⟨a ~ crossing⟩ **2 :** able or likely to inflict injury **:** causing or threatening harm ⟨a ~ lunatic⟩ ⟨an animal ~ when wounded⟩ **3** *now dial* **:** gravely ill **:** in critical condition ⟨he's in bed but he's not ~⟩

syn HAZARDOUS, PRECARIOUS, PERILOUS, RISKY: DANGEROUS applies to persons or things to be avoided or treated carefully as generally unsafe and likely to cause or be attended by danger ⟨a wide circuit must be made, to avoid a fierce and *dangerous* tribe called Snake Indians —Francis Parkman⟩ ⟨the most *dangerous* waters in the world, the fog-shrouded, berg-haunted Grand Banks, with their swift currents and steep, short seas —*Amer. Guide Series: Mass.*⟩ HAZARDOUS may imply greater operation of chance than DANGEROUS; it is used in reference to situations involving great or continuous risk ⟨life consists largely of *hazardous* leaps in the dark —M.R. Cohen⟩ ⟨the *hazardous* game of secret service in enemy country —Alexander Forbes⟩ Established with the meaning of *insecure* or *uncertain*, PRECARIOUS often adds the implication of attendant dangers ⟨the unorganised mass of London dock laborers who struggled with each other for *precarious* jobs at the dockyard gates —G.M.Trevelyan⟩ ⟨the British army, its communications thus rendered *precarious*, was forced to retreat —Allan Nevins & H.S.Commager⟩ PERILOUS suggests imminent danger ⟨thousands of ships and planes guarding the long, *perilous* sea lanes —F.D.Roosevelt⟩ ⟨burglars who have done a good . . . business are, as a rule, only too glad to enjoy the proceeds in peace and quiet without embarking on another *perilous* undertaking —A. Conan Doyle⟩ RISKY often joins to this suggestion the notion that the danger or risk has been realized in advance and willingly accepted ⟨the control of our universities by propertied interests makes a free and radical inquiry into social affairs a *risky* business for any professor —M.R.Cohen⟩ ⟨so *risky* was travel that the Indiana legislature specifically permitted travelers to carry concealed weapons of any kind —Carl Sandburg⟩

dan·ger·ous·ly *adv* **:** in a manner or to a degree involving danger or risk ⟨was charged with driving ~⟩ ⟨~ wounded⟩

dan·ger·ous·ness \-snəs\ *n* -ES **:** the quality or state of being dangerous

dangerous semicircle *n* **:** the half of the nearly circular area of a cyclonic storm in which the velocity of rotation is added to the velocity of translation and in which a vessel tends to be drawn into the path of the storm center

dangers *pl of* DANGER, *pres 3d sing of* DANGER

dan·ger·some \-jə(r)səm\ *adj, now dial* **:** DANGEROUS

danging *pres part of* DANG

¹dan·gle \ˈdaŋgəl\ *vb* **dangled; dangled; dangling** \-g(ə)liŋ\ **dangles** [prob. of Scand origin; akin to Dan *dangle* to dangle, Sw *dangla*, prob. of imit. origin] *vi* **1 :** to hang loosely esp. with a swinging or jerking motion ⟨hands relaxed and *dangling* over their knee bones —Marjory S. Douglas⟩ ⟨caught hold of the eaves and swung *dangling* there —V.G. Heiser⟩ **2 :** to be a hanger-on **:** hang about as or as if a dependent ⟨a flirt, who liked to keep several beaus *dangling*⟩ —often used with *after* ⟨spent his youth in *dangling* after the ladies⟩ **3 :** to become hanged **4 :** to occur in a sentence esp. at or near the beginning without standing in some normally expected syntactic relation to the rest of the sentence and esp. without modifying the subject (as *lying* in "lying awake, memories crowded into his mind" or *tired* and *happy* in "tired but happy, the bus whisked us home") ⟨*dangling* participle⟩ ⟨*dangling* modifier⟩ ~ *vt* **1 :** to cause to dangle **:** SWING ⟨*dangling* his feet in the water⟩ **2 :** to keep (as hopes) hanging uncertainly **:** hold suspended ⟨*dangling* to them the lures of levity and life —Max Beerbohm⟩

²dangle \"\ *n* -S **1 :** the action of dangling **2 :** something that dangles

dangleberry \ˈ⸗⸗— *see* BERRY\ *n* **:** a huckleberry (*Gaylussacia frondosa*) of the eastern U.S. with pink flowers and sweet blue fruit

dan·gle·ment \ˈ⸗⸗mənt\ *n* -S **:** DANGLE

dan·gler \-g(ə)lə(r)\ *n* -S **:** one that dangles ⟨ear clips, some with diamond ~*s* —*New Yorker*⟩; *esp* **:** a person who dangles about or after a woman

dangle stick *n* **:** a forked green stick used as a pothook in cooking over a campfire — called also *dingle stick*

dan·glin \ˈdäŋˈglēn\ *n* -S [Tag *danglin*] **:** a Philippine tree (*Grewia multiflora*) yielding a coarse bast fiber used for cordage

dan·gling·ly *adv* **:** in a dangling manner

dangs *pl of* DANG, *pres 3d sing of* DANG

da·ni·an \ˈdānēən\ *adj, usu cap* [ML *Dania* Denmark, where typical formations are found (fr. LL *Dani* Danes — of Gmc origin; akin to ON *Danr* Dane — + L *-ia* -y) + E *-an*] **:** of or relating to a subdivision of the European Cretaceous — see GEOLOGIC TIME table

da·nic \ˈdānik *also* ˈdan-\ *adj, usu cap* [ML *Danicus*, fr. LL *Dani* Danes + L *-icus* -ic] **:** DANISH

da·ni·cism \ˈdānəˌsizəm\ *n* -S *often cap* [*Danish* + *-icism* (as in *Gallicism*)] **:** a characteristic feature of Danish occurring in another language

dan·iel \ˈdanyəl, *archaic & dial* -nᵊl\ *n* -S *cap* [after *Daniel*, Hebrew prophet captive in Babylon, famous for his interpretation of Nebuchadnezzar's dreams (Dan 2 & 4) and of the handwriting on the wall before Belshazzar (Dan 5), fr. Heb *Dānīʼēl, Dāniyēl*] **:** an exemplary judge ⟨a *Daniel* come to judgment —Shak.⟩

dan·iell cell \ˈdanyəl-\ *n, usu cap D* [after John F. *Daniell* †1845 Eng. chemist and physicist, its inventor] **:** a primary cell with a constant electromotive force of about 1.1 volts having as its electrodes copper in a copper sulfate solution and zinc in dilute sulfuric acid or zinc sulfate, the two solutions being separated by a porous partition

da·nio \ˈdānēˌō\ *n* -S [NL *Danio*, in older classifications, a genus of cyprinid fishes] **:** any of several small brightly colored cyprinid fishes of southeastern Asia often kept in the tropical aquarium

¹dan·ish \ˈdānish, -nēsh *sometimes* ˈdan-\ *adj, usu cap* [ME *Danyssche*, alter. (influenced by *Dan Dane*) of *Denshe*, fr. OE *Denisc*, fr. *Dene* Danes + *-isc* -ish — more at DANE, DANELAW] **1 a :** of, relating to, or characteristic of Denmark **b :** of, relating to, or characteristic of the Danes **2 :** of, relating to, or characteristic of the Danish language

²danish \"\ *n* -ES *cap* **:** the Germanic language of the Danes — see INDO-EUROPEAN LANGUAGES table

³danish \"\ *or* **danish pastry** *n, usu cap D* **:** a rich pastry made of dough raised with yeast with the shortening rolled in

danish seine *n, usu cap D* **:** a seine arranged to be drawn through the water by a boat somewhat in the manner of a trawl

dan·ism \-ˌnizəm\ *n* -S *often cap* [*Danish* + *-ism*] **:** DANICISM

dan·ite \ˈdaˌnīt\ *n* -S *usu cap* [*Dan*, 5th son of Jacob (Gen 30:6), the eponymous ancestor of the Danites (Judg 13:2) + E *-ite*] **1 :** a member of the Hebrew tribe of Dan **2 :** a member of a secret association of Mormons held to have been pledged to use violent means to destroy their enemies

¹dank \ˈdaŋk\ *adj* -ER/-EST [ME *danke*, adj. & n., prob. of Scand origin; akin to ON *dǫkk* pit, pool, Sw (dial.) *dunken* moist; akin to OHG *tunkal* dark, obscure, ON *dǫkkr* dark, Latvian *danga* mudhole, Hitt *dankuiš* dark, OE *dim* — more at DIM] **1 :** wet or moist esp. in a disagreeable way **:** DAMP, HUMID ⟨~ caves⟩ ⟨the air came up cold and ~ from the surface of the water —Dorothy Sayers⟩ ⟨the ~ hot lowlands of Amazonia⟩ **2 :** RANK ⟨a ~ smell of rotting vegetation⟩ ⟨~ horror, foul and leering —Claudia Cassidy⟩ **syn** see WET

²dank \"\ *n* -S [ME *danke*] **1 :** MOISTURE, WETNESS ⟨the raw ~ of the November afternoon —Marguerite Steen⟩ **2 :** a wet place **:** MARSH ⟨a ~ crisscrossed by the numerous streams of the Pearl river delta —*Amer. Guide Series: La.*⟩

dankali *usu cap, var of* DANAKIL

dank·ish \-kish, -kēsh\ adj : somewhat dank
dank·ly adv : in a dank manner ⟨the cloth stuck ~ to their bodies —Norman Mailer⟩
dank·ness \-knəs\ n -ES : the quality or state of being dank
dan·li \'dän'lē\ n -S [Tag danglin] : DANGLIN
dan·ne·brog or dan·e·brog \'danə,bräg\ n -S usu cap [D Dannebrog, fr. Danne Danes (fr. ON Dana, gen. pl. of Danr Dane) + brog cloth, fr. ON brōk — more at BREECH] 1 : a red swallow-tailed ensign bearing a white cross and being the national flag of Denmark 2 : the red rectangular Danish merchant flag
dan·ne·mo·rite \,danə'mōr,īt\ n -S [Sw dannemorit, fr. Dannemora, Sweden, + Sw -it -ite] : a mineral $(Fe,Mn,Mg)_7Si_8O_{22}(OH)_2$ consisting of a columnar or fibrous amphibole containing iron, magnesium, and manganese
dan·ner process \'danə(r)-\ n, usu cap D [after Edward Danner †1952 Am. inventor] : a process for producing glass cane or tubing by continuous drawing from a rotating refractory cylinder, the diameter of the tubing being determined by the pressure of air passed through the center of the cylinder, the temperature of the glass, and the drawing speed
dan·nock \'danək\ n -S [origin unknown] dial Eng : a hedger's glove of thick untanned leather
dano- comb form, cap [ISV Dan- (fr. LL Dani Danes) + -o-] : Danish and ⟨Dano-Eskimo⟩
dans pl of DAN
dan·sant \dän'sän\ n, pl dansants \-z\ [F, fr. pres. part. of danser to dance, fr. OF dancier — more at DANCE] 1 : an informal or small dance 2 [short for thé dansant] : TEA DANCE
danse d'é·cole \dänsdākōl\ n, pl danses d'école \"\ [F, lit., school dance] : ballet that adheres to traditional rules : classical ballet
danse du ven·tre \dänsdüväntr(ə), -t(rə)\ n, pl danses du ventre \"\ [F, lit., belly dance] : BELLY DANCE
danse ma·ca·bre \dänsmäkäbr(ə), -b(rə)\ n, pl danses macabres \"\ [F, lit., macabre dance] 1 : a medieval dance or procession in which a skeleton representing death leads other skeletons or living persons to the grave — called also dance of death 2 : something that evokes horror as would a danse macabre
dan·seur \(')dän'sər(-), -sə(r, F dänsœr\ n, pl danseurs \-ərz,-ōz,-œr\ [F, lit., dancer, fr. OF, fr. danser, dancier to dance + -eur -or — more at DANCE] : a male ballet dancer
dan·seur no·ble \dänsœrnōbl(ə), -b(lə)\ n, pl danseurs nobles \"\ [F, lit., noble dancer] : the male dancing partner of a ballerina
dan·seuse \(')dän'sə(r)z, -sōz, 'dän'süz, F dänsœz\ n, pl dan·seuses \-ə(r)z(əz),-ōz(əz),-üzəz,-œz\ [F, fem. of danseur] : a female ballet dancer
dan·sker \'danzkə(r), -n(t)sk-\ n -S cap [Dan, fr. dansk, adj., Danish, fr. ON danskr, fr. Danr Dane + -skr -ish] obs : DANE ⟨enquire me first what Danskers are in Paris —Shak.⟩
dan·ta \'dantə, 'dän-\ n -S [Pg & Sp; Pg, tapir, elk, buckskin, fr. Sp de anta of buckskin (in such phrases as adarga de anta shield of buckskin), fr. de of (fr. L, from, down, away) + anta tapir, elk, buckskin — more at DE-, ANTA] : TAPIR
1dan·te·an \'dantēən, 'dän-, =¦==\ adj, usu cap [Dante Alighieri †1321 It. poet + E -an] : DANTESQUE
2dantean \"\ n -S usu cap : a student or admirer of Dante
dan·te chair \'dantē-, 'dän-\ n, usu cap D [after Dante Alighieri] : a folding X-shaped chair of Italian Renaissance style having heavy curved legs and arms and cloth or leather seat and back
dan·tesque \(')dan¦tesk, (')dän¦-\ adj, usu cap [It dantesco, fr. Dante Alighieri + It -esco -esque] : of, relating to, or resembling Dante or his writings ⟨arouse in the reader's mind the memory of some Dantesque scene —T.S.Eliot⟩
dan·tho·nia \dan'thōnēə\ n [NL, irreg. fr. Étienne Danthoine, 19th cent. Fr. botanist & NL -ia] 1 cap : a large genus of tufted erect perennial grasses chiefly of the southern hemisphere and No. America with narrow leaves and small terminal panicles or racemes of densely crowded florets 2 -S : any plant of the genus Danthonia
dan·tist \'dantəst, 'dän-\ n -S usu cap [It dantista, fr. Dante Alighieri + It -ista -ist] : a Dante scholar
dan·ton·esque \,dantə¦nesk\ adj, usu cap [Georges J. Danton †1794 Fr. revolutionist + E -esque] : resembling or in the style of Danton ⟨Dantonesque audacity⟩
dan tuck·er \(')dan'təkə(r)\ n, usu cap D&T [prob. fr. (Old) Dan Tucker, song by Daniel D. Emmett †1904 Amer. composer, to the accompaniment of which it was danced] : an American rustic dance in which extra men singing a song choose partners from a circle formed at a signal by those dancing
dan·ube green \'da(,)nyüb-\ n, often cap D [fr. the Danube river, central Europe] : a dark grayish green to dark yellowish green that is greener than Empire green
da·nu·bi·an \(')da¦n(y)übēən, də'n-\ adj, usu cap [LL Danubius Danube (fr. L Danuvius) + E -an] 1 : of, relating to, characteristic of, or bordering on the Danube river 2 : of, relating to, or characteristic of the nations or peoples near the Danube river 3 : of, relating to, or characteristic of a prehistoric Neolithic culture in the Danube basin
danubian goose n, usu cap D : SEBASTOPOL GOOSE
danubian reed n, usu cap D : GIANT REED
da·nysz phenomenon \'dänish-\ also danysz effect n, usu cap D [after Jan Danysz †1928 Pol.-Fr. physician] : the exhibition of residual toxicity by a mixture of toxin and antitoxin in which the toxin has been added in several increments to an amount of antitoxin sufficient to completely neutralize it if it had been added as a single increment
dan·za \'dän(t)sə, -nzə\ n -S [Sp, fr. OSp dança, fr. OF dance — more at DANCE] : DANCE; specif : a formal or courtly dance
dan·zig \'dan(t)sig, 'dän-, -nzi-, -ik\ or gdansk \gə'dänzk, -dan-, -n(t)sk\ adj, usu cap [fr. Danzig (Gdańsk), city of Poland] : of or from the city of Danzig, Poland : of the kind or style prevalent in Danzig
danzig brandy n, usu cap D : DANZIGER GOLDWASSER
dan·zig·er \-igə(r)\ n -S cap [G, fr. Danzig + -er] : a native or resident of Danzig
dan·zig·er gold·was·ser \G 'däntsigər'gȯlt,väsər\ n, usu cap D&G [G, lit., Danzig goldwater] : a colorless aromatic liqueur mixed with tiny flecks of gold leaf and flavored with citrus peel and various herbs — called also Goldwasser, goldwater
danzig fir n, usu cap D : SCOTCH PINE
dan·zón \dän'sōn\ n, pl danzo·nes \-sō,nās\ [AmerSp, aug. of Sp danza dance — more at DANZA] : a peasant dance; specif : a native Cuban dance of African origin now popularized in Vera Cruz, Mexico
1dao var of DAH
2dao \'dä(,)ō, 'daù\ n -S [Tag & Bisayan] 1 : a very large Philippine tree (Dracontomelon dao) of the family Anacardiaceae with edible fruit and a fibrous bark used for cordage 2 : the rather heavy hard strong wood of the dao characterized by dark brown markings on a lighter ground and much used for veneers and cabinetwork
1dap \'dap\ vb dapped; dapped; dapping; daps [perh. alter. of 2dab] vi 1 : to drop bait or fish by dropping bait gently on the water : DIB ⟨had considerable success dapping with the natural fly —John Buchan⟩ 2 : to dip gently or quickly into water ⟨out in the bay innumerable craft dapped and sailed —Sean O'Dwyer⟩ 3 : REBOUND, BOUNCE, SKIP ~ vt 1 : to cause to jump or skip on or along the surface of water ⟨dapping stones⟩ ⟨dapping her homemade flies in an English chalk stream —E.L.Peterson⟩ 2 : to produce (cup-shaped forms in sheet metal) by the use of special dies and punches 3 : to cut and form a recess in (timbers) for making a joint
2dap \"\ n -S 1 : a bounce esp. of a ball : a skip esp. of a stone over water 2 : the bait used in dapping 3 : a notch cut in one timber to receive another
dap-dap \'dap,däp\ n -S [Tag dapdáp] Philippines : a coral tree (Erythrina indica)
da·pe·di·us \də'pēdēəs\ n, cap [NL, fr. Gk dapedon level surface, ground, fr. da- (akin to Gk domos house) + pedon ground, earth — more at TIMBER, PEDION] : a genus of Mesozoic ganoid fishes of the order Cycloganoidei having a deep laterally compressed body
daph·ne \'daf(,)nē\ n [NL, fr. L, laurel, fr. Gk daphnē; akin to the non-IE source of L laurus laurel] 1 cap : a genus of Eurasian shrubs (family Thymelaeaceae) having tetramerous often fragrant apetalous flowers with a colored calyx resembling a corolla — see MEZEREON, SPURGE LAUREL 2 -S : any plant of the genus Daphne
daph·ne·an \'dafnēən, (')=¦==\ adj, usu cap [Daphne, bashful nymph who was pursued by Apollo and upon her prayer for help was changed into a laurel (fr. L, fr. Gk Daphnē, fr. daphnē laurel) + E -an] : of, relating to, or suggestive of the nymph Daphne : SHY, BASHFUL
daphne lilac n : a small shrub (Syringa microphylla) with small leaves that are pubescent beneath and lilac pink blossoms in small loose pubescent panicles
daphne pink n : a grayish purplish red that is redder, lighter, and stronger than average rose plum, bluer, lighter, and stronger than Aztec maroon, and redder and deeper than tourmaline pink
daphne red n : a grayish to moderate purplish red that is bluer and lighter than heather (sense 2b)
daph·ne·tin \'dafnətən\ n -S [ISV, blend of daphnin and -et-] : a yellow crystalline compound $C_9H_6O_4$ obtained by hydrolysis of daphnin; 7,8-dihydroxy-coumarin
daph·nia \'dafnēə\ n, cap [NL, perh. fr. Daphne, the nymph + NL -ia] : a genus of minute freshwater branchiopod crustaceans (order Cladocera) having imperfect segmentation, very large biramous antennae that are the chief locomotor organs, and a transparent carapace enclosing the body — daph·ni·oid \-nē,ȯid\ adj — daph·noid \-,nȯid\ adj
daph·nid \'dafnəd\ n -S [NL Daphnidae, family of water fleas, fr. Daphnia, type genus + -idae] : any of numerous small active water fleas; esp : any member of Daphnia or a related genus, many of which are used as feed for aquarium fishes
daph·nin \-nən\ n -S [NL Daphne + E -in] : a bitter crystalline glucoside $C_{15}H_{16}O_9$ occurring esp. in plants of the genus Daphne (as D. mezereum)
daph·nite \-,nīt\ n -S [ISV daphn- (fr. Gk daphnē laurel) + -ite; fr. its appearance; orig. formed as G daphnit — more at DAPHNE] : a mineral $(Mg,Fe)_3(Fe,Al)_3(Si,Al)_4O_{10}(OH)_8$ consisting of a basic aluminosilicate of magnesium, iron, and aluminum belonging to the chlorite group
dap joint n : a joint made by dapping two timbers
dapped past of DAP
dap·pen dish \'dapən-\ also dappen glass n [origin unknown] : a small heavy 10-sided piece of glass each end of which is ground into a small cup for mixing dental medicaments or fillings
1dap·per \'dapə(r)\ adj, often -ER/-EST [ME dapyr, fr. MD dapper quick, agile, energetic, strong; akin to OHG tapfar heavy, weighty, ON dapr sad, OSlav debelŭ thick] 1 a : neat and trim in appearance : SPRUCE, SMART ⟨~ in a brown suit and green bow tie —M.W.Straight⟩ b : excessively spruce and stylish ⟨this old giant, intellectually and spiritually shaggy and unkempt . . . makes his splendid sons seem almost ~ —Dorothy C. Fisher⟩ 2 : alert and lively in movement and manners : BRISK, JAUNTY ⟨a ~ wave of the hand⟩ — usu. used of persons small or slight of build — dap·per·ly adv — dap·per·ness n -ES
2dapper \"\ n -S [1dap + -er] : one that daps: as a : one that fishes by dapping b : BUFFLEHEAD c : a circular saw that daps timbers
dap·per·ling \'==,liŋ\ n -S [1dapper + -ling] : a little dapper fellow
dapping pres part of DAP
1dap·ple \'dapəl\ adj [ME dappel (in dappel-gray) — more at DAPPLE-GRAY] : DAPPLED ⟨a ~ horse⟩
2dapple \"\ n -S 1 : one of numerous usu. cloudy and rounded spots or patches of a color or shade different from their background ⟨the distinctive markings of each horse . . . flecks, ~s, stockings —Harry Disston⟩ ⟨clouds and sun throwing gigantic ~s over the varicolored green of the treetops —Tom Marvel⟩ 2 : the quality or state of being dappled : mottled appearance ⟨the ~ of the leaf-filtered light —Anthony West⟩ 3 : a dappled animal (as a horse)
3dapple \"\ vb dappled; dappled; dappling \-p(ə)liŋ\ dapples vt : to mark or variegate with spots or patches of different shade or color ⟨beach plums ~ our dunes and fields with snowy drifts —Christian Science Monitor⟩ ⟨rings of sunlight . . . dappled the dark grass —Truman Capote⟩ ~ vi : to become dappled ⟨sunlight dappling through the great cedar and hemlock tops —Hugh Fosburgh⟩
dappled adj [ME, fr. dappel (in dappel-gray) + -ed] : marked with small spots, patches, or dots contrasting in color or shade with the background ⟨warm and a fine ~ sky —Thomas Gray⟩ ⟨a ~ fawn⟩ syn see VARIEGATED
dap·ple-gray also dappled-gray \'==¦=\ adj [ME dappel-gray, perh. alter. (influenced by ON depill spot) of (assumed) ME appel-gray, lit., apple-gray, prob. trans. of ON apalgrār] : gray variegated with spots or patches of a different shade — used esp. of horses
1daps \'daps\ n pl [origin unknown] now dial Eng : distinctive characteristics : HABITS, LOOKS, MANNERISMS ⟨the very ~ of my old aunt⟩
2daps pres 3d sing of DAP, pl of DAP
1dar \'där\ dial var of DARE
2dar \"\ n -S [Nepali dār, prob. fr. Skt dāru wood — more at TREE] : an Indian timber tree (Boehmeria rugulosa) with soft red wood that is used in Bengal by wood carvers
da·ra·buk·ka \də'räbəkə, ,darə'bükə\ n -S [Ar darābukkah, dirbakkah, darbūkkah] : a kettledrum of northern Africa
da·rak \də'räk\ n -S [Tag darák] Philippines : RICE BRAN
da·rap·skite \də'rap,skīt\ n -S [G darapskit, fr. L. Darapsky, 19th cent. Chilean scientist + G -it -ite] : a mineral $Na_3(NO_3)(SO_4).H_2O$ consisting of a hydrous nitrate and sulfate of sodium
darb \'därb\ n -S [perh. alter. of 6dab] slang : something superlative ⟨a ~ of a black eye⟩ ⟨a regular little ~⟩
dar·bha \'därbə\ n -S [Skt darbha tuft of grass — more at TURF] : KUSA
dar·bies \'därbēz\ n pl [prob. short for obs. (father) Derbies (or Darbies) bonds rigidly bonded indebtedness] Brit : HANDCUFFS
1darby \'därbē\ n -ES [prob. fr. the name Derby or Darby]

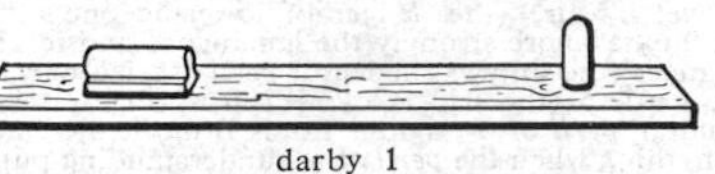

darby 1

1 : a plasterer's float consisting of a long narrow strip of wood with two handles 2 : a trowel with a handle elevated above the blade for use as a darby
2darby \"\ vt -ED/-ING/-ES : to smooth with a darby
dar·by and joan \,därbēən'jō(ə)n, -,jō'an\ n, usu cap D&J [prob. fr. Darby and Joan, stereotypical old married couple in a popular 18th cent. Brit. song] : a happily married couple esp. of advanced years
dar·by·ism \'därbē,izəm\ n -S usu cap [J. N. Darby + E -ism] : the doctrine and practices of the Plymouth Brethren
dar·by·ite \-,īt\ n -S usu cap [John N. Darby †1882 Eng. theologist + E -ite] : one of the Plymouth Brethren following closely the teachings of J. N. Darby
dar·cy \'därsē\ n -S [after Henri P.G. Darcy †1858 Fr. hydraulic engineer] : a unit of porous permeability in physics equal to the permeability of a medium through which the rate of flow of a fluid having one centipoise viscosity under a pressure gradient of one atmosphere per centimeter would be one cubic centimeter per second per square centimeter cross section — compare DARCY'S LAW
dar·cy's law \'därsēz-\ n, usu cap D [after H.P.G. Darcy, its formulator] : a statement in fluid dynamics: the velocity of flow of a liquid through a porous medium due to difference in pressure is proportional to the pressure gradient in the direction of flow
dard \'därd\ n, pl dard \-d\ or dards \-dz\ also dardi \-(,)dē\ usu cap 1 : a member of the stocky broad-shouldered moderately fair frequently brown-haired Indo-Aryan people in the upper valley of the Indus 2 or dar·dic \-rdik\ -S : the complex of languages spoken by the Dards and including Shina, Khowar, Kafiri, Kashmiri, and Kohistani — see INDO-EUROPEAN LANGUAGES table
dar·dan \'därdən\ adj or n, usu cap [L Dardanus, adj., fr. Gk Dardanos, adj.] archaic : TROJAN
dar·da·ni \'därdən,ī, -,ē\ n pl, usu cap [L, fr. Gk Dardanoi] : an ancient Illyrian people esp. noted for their successful raids on Macedonia and the Roman provinces during the 1st century B.C.
dar·da·nian \(')där¦dānēən, -ānyən\ adj, usu cap [L Dardanius Trojan, fr. Gk Dardanios (fr. Dardanos Dardanus, legendary eponymous ancestor of the Trojans) + E -an] : TROJAN
1dare \'da(a)(ə)r, 'de|, |ə\ vb dared or archaic & dial durst \'dərst, 'dəst, 'dəist\ dared; daring; dares or dare; substand pres sing & plural dast \'dast, 'daa(ə)st, 'daist\ archaic pres 2d sing darst \'därst, 'dȧst\ [ME dar (1st & 3d pers. sing. pres. indic. of durren, daren, past dorste, durste), fr. OE dear (infin. — assumed — durran, past dorste); akin to OHG gitar (1st & 3d pers. sing. pres. indic.) dare, Goth gadars (infin. gadaursan), L infestus hostile, Gk tharsein, tharrein to be bold, Skt dharṣati he is bold] vi : to have sufficient courage : be bold enough : be unafraid : VENTURE ⟨try it if you ~⟩ ~ vt 1 : to have the bravery, boldness, or fortitude to contend against, venture, or try ⟨the actress dared the title role⟩ 2 a : to confront boldly : invite the opposition of fearlessly : DEFY ⟨daring the wrath of the family⟩ b : to challenge to perform an action : provoke or goad (a person) into demonstrating courage, power, or skill ⟨to what further frenzies would the gods ~ their victim —Virginia Woolf⟩ ⟨the other boys dared him to dive from the bridge⟩ ~ verbal auxiliary : to be sufficiently bold, brave, or courageous to : be daring enough to ⟨he ~s not pronounce that repentance is followed by full forgiveness in this life —Rev. of Religion⟩ ⟨a few twisted thorn trees . . . which no man ~ cut down —O.S.J.Gogarty⟩ ⟨he durst not stay for fear of some treachery —Ballad Book⟩ syn see FACE
2dare \"\ n -S 1 : an invitation to contend : a challenge to do something dangerous, foolhardy, or unusual ⟨a ~ which it was hard for their rough, pioneer neighbors to resist —M.R. Werner⟩ — often used with take ⟨so foolish he'd always take a ~⟩ 2 : DARING : imaginative or vivacious boldness; esp : VERVE ⟨with a little more ~, the second collection should be better —Time⟩ ⟨each heavenward leap, each architectural ~ —Forum⟩
3dare \"\ n -S [ME dar, alter. (darce being taken as pl.) of darce — more at DACE] archaic : DACE 1
1daredevil \'=,==\ n [1dare + devil] : a person who without apparent fear faces, accepts, or carries out anything unusually dangerous or foolhardy
2daredevil adj : being or befitting a daredevil ⟨a ~ driver⟩ ⟨a ~ escapade⟩ ⟨a ~ attitude toward life⟩ syn see ADVENTUROUS
dare·dev·il·ish \'=,=v(ə)lish, -lēsh\ adj : resembling, befitting, or suggesting a daredevil ⟨a ~ type of person⟩ ⟨a hazardous and ~ action⟩
dare·dev·il·try \'=,=vəl-trē, -ri\ also dare·dev·il·ry \-vəlr-\ n : reckless wildness ⟨the apparent ~ of the circus⟩
dareful adj, obs : DARING
daren't \'da(a)(ə)r(ə)nt, |de|,|ənt\ : dare not
daresay \'=¦=\ vb [ME (I) dar sayen I venture to say] vt : venture to say : think probable : BELIEVE — used in the pres. 1st sing. ⟨I ~ I would have forgotten about the whole thing⟩ ~ vi : SUPPOSE, PRESUME, AGREE — used in the pres. 1st sing. ⟨yes, I ~⟩
dares·n't \'da(a)r|sᵊn(t), 'der|,'där|,'dȧ|,'da|,'daa|,'dai| also |zᵊn-\ [partly contr. of (thou) darst not (fr. ME), partly contr. of (he) dares not] dial : dare not
darg \'därg\ n -S [ME dawerk, daywork, fr. OE dægweorc, fr. dæg day + weorc work — more at DAY, WORK] chiefly Scot 1 : a day's work 2 : a fixed amount of work : TASK
dar·ghin \'därgən\ n, pl darghin or darghins usu cap 1 : a member of a subdivision of the Lezghians of Eastern Dagestan in Ciscaucasia 2 or dar·ghin·i·an \där'ginēən\ -S : a North Caucasic language
da·ri \'därē\ n -S [Ar dhurah] : DURRA
dar·ic \'darik\ n -S [Gk Dareikos, prob. fr. Dareios Darius I †486 B.C. king of Persia + Gk -ikos -ic] : a small gold coin of ancient Persia
1daring adj [fr. pres. part. of 1dare] 1 a : ready, able, or prone to assume or face anything dangerous, risky, or arduous ⟨~ pioneers⟩ ⟨~ acrobats⟩ b : suggestive of, arising from, or prompted by boldness, fearlessness, or audacity ⟨a ~ promise⟩ ⟨a ~ attempt⟩ 2 a : deviating from or contrasting with the conventional or traditional : NOVEL, STRIKING ⟨a ~ yacht designer⟩ ⟨a ~ intellect⟩ b : attracting attention by being brazenly different or loudly unconventional ⟨a ~ neckline⟩ ⟨a ~ exposé⟩ syn see ADVENTUROUS
2daring n -S [fr. gerund of 1dare] : the quality or state of being bold, courageous, or fearless ⟨small in body, he possessed tremendous energy and ~ —E.K.Alden⟩
dar·ing·ly adv : in a daring manner
dar·ing·ness n -ES : the quality or state of being daring
dar·i·ole \'da(a)rē,ōl\ n -S [F, fr. MF, a pastry filled with cream, perh. fr. an assumed dial. word akin to MF dorer to gild + -ole — more at DORY] : a shell of pastry or mold of aspic filled with sweet or savory food
dar·jee·ling \där'jēliŋ\ also darjeeling tea \(')=¦==-\ n -S usu cap Darjeeling [fr. Darjeeling, district in West Bengal, India] : a tea regarded as of high quality grown esp. in the mountainous districts of northern India
1dark \'därk, 'dȧk\ adj -ER/-EST [ME derk, fr. OE deorc; akin to OHG tarchannen to hide, MIr derg red, L fraces dregs of oil, Gk thrassein, thrattein to trouble, disturb, and prob. to Lith darga rainy weather] 1 a : destitute or partially destitute of light : not receiving, reflecting, transmitting, or radiating light ⟨~ as night⟩; also : having no lights burning ⟨the theater was totally ~⟩ b : transmitting only a portion of light, brilliance, or glare ⟨a ~ lampshade⟩ ⟨~ glasses⟩ 2 a : wholly or partially black : somberly hued : of a deep shade ⟨~ earth⟩ ⟨a dark-haired girl⟩ ⟨the ~ robes of the clergy⟩; specif, of color : of low or very low lightness b : made of whole wheat flour ⟨a loaf of ~ bread⟩ or of white flour darkened with spices or other ingredients ⟨~ fruitcake⟩ 3 a : arising from, exhibiting, or motivated by evil traits or desires : WICKED, INIQUITOUS ⟨the ~ side of his character⟩ ⟨the ~ powers that lead to war⟩ b : destitute of sunniness or cheer : GLOOMY, DISMAL, SAD ⟨he's always looking at the ~ side of things⟩ ⟨the ~ days of the war⟩ c : destitute of knowledge or culture : spiritually or intellectually retarded, backward, or primitive : UNREFINED, IGNORANT ⟨the ~ age of poetry among us is almost over —H.A.Overstreet⟩ 4 : not readily perceptible: as a of a celestial body, archaic : barely visible : DIM b : not clear to the understanding : OBSCURE ⟨that makes much which was ~ quite clear to me —John Galsworthy⟩ 5 now dial : unable to see : BLIND ⟨what way would I see . . . and I a ~ woman since the seventh year of my age —J.M.Synge⟩ 6 a of the human complexion : not fair : DUSKY, SWARTHY ⟨brick-red face grew ~er —Kenneth Roberts⟩ ⟨nor had she lost her ~ good looks —Irish Digest⟩ b : having or characterized by a skin rich in melanoid pigments ⟨the ~ races⟩ 7 a : SECRET : not known to the public — used chiefly with keep ⟨he kept his plans ~⟩; see DARK HORSE b : MYSTERIOUS ⟨an imagination that was ~ and rich⟩ c : SECRETIVE, RETICENT ⟨he was always quite ~ about the matter⟩ 8 a of sound : possessing depth and somberness ⟨a woman with a beautifully ~ contralto⟩ ⟨everywhere the ~ laughter of the Negro is to be heard —Amer. Guide Series: Va.⟩ b of an l sound : formed with the tip of the tongue on the teethridge and the rest of the tongue in a position similar to that of a back vowel — compare 1CLEAR 2b c of a vowel : articulated with the back of the tongue higher than its rest position ⟨\ȯ\ and \ü\ are ~⟩ 9 of tobacco : fire-cured or dark air-cured
syn DIM, DUSKY, DUSK, DARKLING, OBSCURE, MURKY, OPAQUE GLOOMY: DARK, the most general and common term of this group, implies a lack or deficiency of light or illumination of whatever kind ⟨it looked dark as pitch, so I gave him to understand that he must strike a light —Herman Melville⟩ ⟨telling me that they were waiting till it was dark to speak to him; that they did not dare to speak to him during the light —Anthony Trollope⟩ DIM suggests darkness enough to render outlines indistinct and shadowy ⟨"Shall I light a taper?" "There is no need. I love this dim light of evening —C.B.Nordhoff & J.N.Hall⟩ ⟨the dim grassy bank amid the tossing trees purple with twilight —G.K.Chesterton⟩ DUSKY and the uncommon

DUSK signify a twilight condition and suggest approaching darkness ⟨but comes at last the dull and *dusky* eve —William Cowper⟩ ⟨during the short period of a total eclipse bright stars may appear in a *dusky* sky —R.M.Sutton⟩ ⟨the *dusk* heavens —John Keats⟩ DARKLING may connote the mysterious, ominous, or uncanny ⟨the *darkling* night, lit only as it was by the slender moon —H.G.Wells⟩ ⟨as on a *darkling* plain swept with confused alarms of struggle and flight, where ignorant armies clash by night —Matthew Arnold⟩ OBSCURE is likely to imply darkness and also concealment, covering, or overshadowing ⟨it does not matter to real culture whether a book be lucid as transparent air, or sullenly *obscure* as pitch-black midnight —J.C.Powys⟩ ⟨a small room, *obscure* because it was heavily curtained —Arnold Bennett⟩ Orig. connoting intense darkness, MURKY now often suggests a blanketing thickness or heaviness ⟨London seemed last winter like an underground city; as if its low sky were the roof of a cave, and its *murky* day a light such as one reads of in countries beneath the earth —L.P. Smith⟩ ⟨a coarse, cheap, and offensive-smelling tobacco. The air was thick and *murky* with the smoke of it —Jack London⟩ OPAQUE, comparatively poor in suggestion, means impervious to light, opposed to *transparent* and *translucent* ⟨*opaque* from rain drawn in slant streaks by wind and speed across the pane, the window of the railway carriage lets nothing be seen but stray flashes of red lights —Richard Jefferies⟩ GLOOMY implies interference with free radiation of light and usu. connotes a pervading cheerlessness ⟨their *gloomy* pathway tended upward, so that, through a crevice, a little daylight glimmered down upon them, or even a streak of sunshine peeped into a burial niche —Nathaniel Hawthorne⟩ **syn** see in addition OBSCURE

²**dark** \"\ *n* -s [ME *derk*, fr. *derk*, adj.] **1 :** absence of light **:** DARKNESS ⟨stumbling about in the ~⟩ **:** a place where or the time when there is little or no light ⟨the fugitives moved into the ~ and waited⟩ **:** NIGHT, NIGHTFALL ⟨we'd better wait till ~ —Zane Grey⟩ **2 a :** something devoid of or not predominantly light, bright, or brilliant **:** something somber or subdued ⟨though still early fall light clothes had given way to winter ~*s*⟩ **b :** a dark or somber hue **:** deep color ⟨in water color the darkest tones can be darker than in fresco, but attempts to rival the ~*s* of oil always looks forced —C.W.H. Johnson⟩ **3 darks** *pl but sing or pl in constr* **:** broadleaf or Havana seed tobacco used for cigar binders — **in the dark 1 :** in secrecy ⟨mostly such transactions were made *in the dark*⟩ **2 :** in ignorance ⟨*in the dark* about a person's intentions⟩

³**dark** \"\ *vb* -ED/-ING/-S [ME *derken*, fr. OE *deorcian* to become dark, grow dim, fr. *deorc* dark] *vi* **1** *obs* **:** to grow dark **:** DARKEN; *specif* **:** to undergo eclipse **2** *dial Eng* **:** EAVESDROP ~ *vt* **:** to make dark **:** DIM, CLOUD ⟨the folk whose shadows ~*ed* the blinds —John Masefield⟩

⁴**dark** \"\ *adv* [¹*dark*] *archaic* **:** DARKLY

dark adaptation *n* **:** the phenomena including dilatation of the pupil, increase in retinal sensitivity, shift of the region of maximum luminosity toward the blue, and regeneration of visual purple by which the eye adapts to conditions of reduced illumination; *sometimes* **:** the time required for the occurrence of these phenomena — compare LIGHT ADAPTATION

dark-adapted \ˈ=,=ˈ=\ *adj* **:** adjusted for vision in dim light **:** having undergone dark adaptation

dark beaver *n* **:** a grayish to moderate brown that is redder and lighter than autumn brown — called also *nutmeg, praline, Santos*

dark box *n* **:** a box from which light is wholly excluded and which is used for storing light-sensitive photographic equipment (as films, plates, paper)

dark cardinal *n* **:** a dark red that is yellower, less strong, and slightly darker than cranberry, lighter, stronger, and slightly yellower than average garnet, and bluer, stronger, and slightly lighter than average wine

dark current *n* **:** the current through a photoelectric or photoconductive cell when an electromotive force is applied in the absence of light

dark·en \ˈdärkən, ˈdȧk-\ *vb* **darkened; darkened; darkening** \-k(ə)niŋ\ **darkens** [ME *derknen, darknen*, fr. *derk*, adj., dark + *-nen* -en] *vi* **1 a :** to grow dark by diminution of light ⟨the theater ~*ed* and the play began⟩ ⟨a cold winter evening ~*ing* down⟩ ⟨suddenly it ~*ed* up and started to rain⟩ **b :** to become obscured ⟨the memory of it ~*s*⟩ **2 :** to undergo or exhibit an emotional, spiritual, or facial change usu. of a disturbed or lowering nature ⟨his expression ~*ed* with anger⟩ ⟨his voice ~*ed* with the words⟩ ⟨his face ~*ing* with suspicion —Dorothy Sayers⟩ **3 :** to grow dark or darker in shading or color ⟨paper ~*ing* at the margins⟩ ~ *vt* **1 a :** to make dark or darker by depriving of light ⟨a cloud of locusts ~*ed* the sky⟩ ⟨~ a room by turning off the light⟩ **b :** to lessen (the illumination) by concealing or standing in the way ⟨a figure ~*ed* the lamplight on the porch —Ellen Glasgow⟩ **2 :** TAINT, TARNISH, BEFOUL ⟨covetousness ~*ed* his mind⟩ ⟨~*ing* a reputation with lies⟩ ⟨an evil genius to ~ the conscience of men and women —V.L.Parrington⟩ **3 :** to make less clear **:** OBSCURE ⟨uncertainty ~*s* the future of radio and television —E.D.Canham⟩; *specif* **:** to hinder or retard the receptivity or vision of ⟨superstitions ~*ing* their minds⟩ **4 :** to deprive (the eyes) in whole or in part of sight ⟨age ~*ing* his eyes⟩ **5 :** to cast a gloom over ⟨~ mirth⟩ ⟨~ his hopes⟩ **:** make unhappy or miserable ⟨a life ~*ed* by afflictions⟩; *specif, obs* **:** to put (a person) in a position bereft of glory or recognition **6 :** to give a dark shade to **:** turn into a dark color ⟨fumes from nearby chimneys had ~*ed* the statehouse dome⟩ ⟨a sun-*darkened* plainsman —R.A.Billington⟩ **syn** see OBSCURE — **darken one's door** *or* **darken the door :** to make an appearance ⟨the first salesman to *darken our door*⟩ — used sometimes with object in pl. ⟨he never *darkened the doors* of the office again⟩

dark·en·er \-k(ə)nə(r\ *n* -s **:** one that darkens

darkening *n* -s **:** an act or instance of becoming or making dark; *specif, chiefly Scot* **:** TWILIGHT, GLOAMING, DUSK

darker *comparative of* DARK

darkest *superlative of* DARK

dark field *n* **:** the dark area that serves as the background for objects viewed in an ultramicroscope

dark-field \ˈ=ˈ=\ *adj* [*dark field*] **:** producing, involving the use of, or relating to a dark field ⟨*dark-field* illumination⟩ ⟨*dark-field* examination⟩ — see ULTRAMICROSCOPE

dark-field microscope *n* **:** ULTRAMICROSCOPE

dark-fired \ˈ=ˈ=\ *adj* **:** FIRE-CURED

dark-ground \ˈ=ˈ=\ *adj* **:** DARK-FIELD

dark horse *n* **1 :** a racehorse whose ability and chances of success in a race are not generally known **2 :** a contestant (as a political candidate) that wins unexpectedly or that although little known is thought to be able to win or make a very good showing

darkie *or* **darkey** *var of* DARKY

darking *pres part of* DARK

dark·ish \ˈdärkish, ˈdȧk-, -kēsh\ *adj* [ME *derkysshe*, fr. *derk*, adj., dark + *-ysshe* -ish] **:** somewhat dark **:** DUSKY

dark lantern *n* **:** a lantern with a single opening which may be closed to conceal the light — called also *bull's-eye*

dar·kle \-kəl\ *vi* **darkled; darkled; darkling** \-k(ə)liŋ\ **darkles** [back-formation fr. ²*darkling*] **1 :** to lurk in the dark **:** lie concealed in or as if in the dark ⟨children playing tag *darkled* in the corners⟩ **2 a :** to grow dark **:** fade into darkness ⟨she watched the last bright-colored daylight ~ slowly against the hills—Agnes S. Turnbull⟩ **b :** to become clouded or gloomy ⟨his face *darkling* with anger⟩

dark lightning *n* **:** a lightning that gives black photographic streaks where white ones ordinarily occur — compare CLAYDEN EFFECT

dark-line spectrum *n* **:** a line spectrum produced by the passage of white light through an ionized gas or vapor

¹**dark·ling** \-kliŋ *also* -kəl-\ *also* **dark·lings** \-ŋz\ *adv* [ME *derkelyng*, fr. *derke, derk* dark + *-lyng* -ling — more at DARK] **:** in the dark ⟨much helpless man . . . roll ~ down the torrent of his fate —Samuel Johnson⟩

²**dark·ling** \"\ *adj* **1 :** done or taking place in the dark ⟨a ~ journey⟩ **2 :** deeply shadowed or shaded **:** DARK, DUSKY ⟨friendly ~ hills —Thomas Wood †1950⟩; *esp* **:** mysteriously, threateningly, or uncannily dark or obscure ⟨a ~ glance⟩ ⟨secret operatives and ~ conspiracies —Archibald MacLeish⟩ **syn** see DARK

darkling beetle *or* **darkling ground beetle** *n* **:** any of numerous mostly hard-bodied black sluggish terrestrial plant-eating beetles (family Tenebrionidae) that are often incapable of flight

dark·lins \-k(ə)lənz\ *adv* [alter. of *darklings*] *dial Brit* **:** DARKLING

dark·ly \-klē, -li\ *adv, sometimes* -ER/-EST [ME *derkly*, fr. OE *deorclīce* (attested only in the meaning "horridly, foully"), fr. *deorc* dark + *-līce* -ly] **:** in a dark manner: as **a :** OBSCURELY, VAGUELY, MYSTERIOUSLY ⟨~ sensing the presence of someone⟩ **b :** with dimmed or obscured vision **:** DIMLY ⟨seeing a ship but ~ against the horizon⟩ **c :** with a dark or blackish color ⟨the storm clouds gathered ~⟩ **d :** with a dark, gloomy, or menacing look or manner ⟨glancing ~ at his opponent⟩ **e :** in the dark **:** SECRETLY ⟨thoughts held ~ in his mind⟩

dark meat *n* **:** dark-colored meat esp. in poultry or game (as the thigh of chicken)

dark·ness *n* -ES [ME *derknesse*, fr. OE *deorcnysse*, fr. *deorc* dark + *-nysse* -ness — more at DARK] **:** the quality or state of being dark: as **a :** the absence in part or in whole of light **:** BLACKNESS, GLOOM ⟨the ~ of night⟩ ⟨the ~ of a cave⟩ **b** (1) **:** absence of moral, religious, or cultural values **:** spiritual backwardness **:** IGNORANCE ⟨peoples living in ~ and superstition⟩ (2) **:** WICKEDNESS, INIQUITY ⟨the powers of ~⟩ **c :** deprivation of sight **:** BLINDNESS **d :** dark quality in shade or color ⟨the somber ~ of pines —*Amer. Guide Series: Vt.*⟩ **e :** PRIVACY, SECRECY ⟨questions of policy kept in ~⟩ **f** (1) **:** lack of clarity **:** OBSCURITY ⟨the ~ of certain passages in a text⟩ (2) **:** imperfect vision or understanding ⟨fanatical ~ of a mind that glimpsed light but could not win it —Carlos Baker⟩ **g** (1) **:** distress caused by misfortune or affliction **:** TROUBLE ⟨my personal life had taken a turn towards ~ —Karl Polanyi⟩ (2) **:** GLOOM ⟨Brahms songs, with their decided ~ of mood —Irving Kolodin⟩

dark of the moon 1 *astron* **:** the period of about a week at the time of a new moon when the moon's light is absent from the nighttime sky **2 :** a period when the moon is not shining or when it is obscured

dark pine *n* **:** a large cypress pine (*Callitris robusta*) of Western Australia that has dark brown furrowed bark and is an important timber tree

dark plaster *n* **:** a plaster made by calcining gypsite without previous grinding

dark reaction *n* **:** a chemical reaction in the absence of light as contrasted with a photochemical reaction

dark red silver ore *n* **:** PYRARGYRITE

darkroom \ˈ=,=\ *n* **:** a room freed from light or lighted by a safelight for handling and processing light-sensitive materials (as plates, films, and paper)

darks *pl of* DARK, *pres 3d sing of* DARK

darkskin \ˈ=,=\ *n* **:** one that has skin of dark brown, red, or black color — **dark-skinned** \ˈ=ˈ=\ *adj*

dark slide *n* **1 :** the removable slide that covers a photographic plate or film in a holder **2 :** a photographic plateholder or sheet-film holder

dark·some \ˈdärksəm, ˈdȧk-\ *adj* [²*dark* + *-some*] **1 :** gloomily somber ⟨a ~ path⟩ ⟨~ prophecies⟩ **:** mysteriously or forbiddingly dark or obscured ⟨a ~ castle⟩ **2** *archaic* **:** not readily understood **:** OBSCURE

dark space *n* **:** any of several regions or layers in the visible-glow discharge of a gas-filled cold-cathode electron tube that remain nonluminous or exhibit low light intensity until the ions in such spaces acquire sufficient energy to excite fluorescence in the tube gas — see ASTON DARK SPACE, CROOKES DARK SPACE, FARADAY DARK SPACE

dark star *n* **:** an invisible but luminous member of a double or multiple system of stars; *esp* **:** the star that causes the primary eclipse in an eclipsing variable

darktown \ˈ=,=\ *n* **:** a usu. urban area inhabited by Negroes — often taken to be offensive

dark wedgwood *n, often cap W* **:** a grayish to moderate purplish blue — distinguished from *light Wedgwood;* called also *flame blue*

dark whites *n pl* **:** swarthy or brunet white people

darky *also* **dark·ie** *or* **dark·ey** \ˈdärkē, ˈdȧk-, -ki\ *n, pl* **darkies** *also* **darkeys** [¹*dark* + *-y, -ie, -ey*] **:** NEGRO — often taken to be offensive

¹**dar·ling** \ˈdärliŋ, ˈdȧl-, -lēŋ\ *n* -s [ME *derling*, fr. OE *dēorling*, fr. *dēore* dear + *-ling* — more at DEAR] **1 a :** one dearly beloved **:** the object of one's love ⟨she was the ~ of his life⟩ — often used as a term of endearment **b :** a favorite esp. of one in power or of a particular power, faction, or group ⟨the cultural ~ of the Communist party⟩ ⟨the king's ~⟩ ⟨Cromwell, more than ever the ~ of his soldiers —T.B. Macaulay⟩ **2 :** something looked upon with especial favor ⟨energy and matter were the scientific ~*s* of the nineteenth century —Norbert Wiener⟩ ⟨cotton shirts will be the ~ of most sportswear departments —*Women's Wear Daily*⟩

²**darling** \"\ *adj, sometimes* -ER/-EST **1 :** dearly beloved **:** FAVORITE ⟨the organization of public balls . . . was another ~ topic of his heart —Sacheverell Sitwell⟩ **2 :** delightfully pleasing **:** SWEET, CUTE, CHARMING ⟨a ~ living room⟩ ⟨a ~ little short story⟩ — **dar·ling·ly** *adv* — **dar·ling·ness** *n* -ES

darling lily \"-\ *n, usu cap D* [fr. *Darling* river, southeastern Australia] **:** an Australian herb (*Crinum flaccidum*) with white flowers and bulbs that yield a substance like arrowroot

darling pea *n, usu cap D* [fr. *Darling* river] **:** either of two Australian plants of the genus *Swainsona* (*S. galegifolia* and *S. greyana*) that have racemose flowers and are poisonous to sheep — called also *poison bush*

darling plum *n, usu cap D* [prob. fr. ²*darling*] **1 :** RED IRONWOOD 1 **2 :** the small black egg-shaped fruit of the red ironwood

dar·ling·to·nia \ˌdärliŋˈtōnēə, -nyə\ *n, cap* [NL, fr. William *Darlington* †1863 Amer. botanist + NL *-ia*] **:** a genus of Californian insectivorous plants (family Sarraceniaceae) characterized by arched and hooded leaves and solitary flowered scapes — see PITCHER PLANT

darm·stadt \ˈdärm,shtät, -,stat\ *adj, usu cap* [fr. *Darmstadt*, Germany] **:** of or from the city of Darmstadt, Germany **:** of the kind or style prevalent in Darmstadt

¹**darn** \ˈdärn, ˈdȧn\ *var of* DERN

²**darn** \"\ *vb* -ED/-ING/-S [prob. fr. F dial. (Channel Islands) *derner, darner* to darn, mend, patch, perh. fr. F dial. (Norman) *darne* piece, fr. Bret *darn;* akin to W *darn* piece, Skt *dīrṇa* torn, OE *teran* to tear — more at TEAR] *vt* **1 :** to mend (a hole or tear in cloth) with interlacing stitches usu. in plain weave ⟨~ woolen socks with matching yarn⟩ **2 :** to embroider by filling in a design or background with geometric patterns or parallel lines of long running or interlacing stitches ⟨the lace was formed by ~*ing* a leaf pattern on a net ground⟩ ~ *vi* **:** to do darning

³**darn** \"\ *n* -s **:** a place darned ⟨a sweater full of ~*s*⟩

⁴**darn** \"\ *or* **durn** \ˈdərn, ˈdən, ˈdəin\ *vb* -ED/-ING/-S [euphemism] *vt* **:** DAMN *vt* 5 ⟨~ him, he won't even try to help⟩ ⟨~ it all⟩ ⟨I'll be ~*ed* if I know⟩ ~ *vi* **:** DAMN

⁵**darn** \"\ *or* **durn** \"\ *adj* [euphemism for ³*damn*] **:** ¹DAMNED 2a, 2b ⟨no ~ thing after another⟩

⁶**darn** \"\ *or* **durn** \"\ *adv* [euphemism for ⁴*damn*] **:** ²DAMNED ⟨he came ~ near killing him⟩

⁷**darn** \"\ *or* **durn** \"\ *n* -s [euphemism] **:** ²DAMN 2

¹**dar·na·tion** \därˈnāshən, dȧˈ-\ *n* -s [euphemism] **:** DAMNATION — often used as a mild imprecation

²**darnation** \(ˈ)=ˈ=\ *adj* **:** ¹DAMNED 2a, 2b ⟨that ~ pump never worked⟩

³**darnation** \"\ *adv* **:** ²DAMNED ⟨a ~ fine time we had⟩

darnd·est *or* **darned·est** \ˈdärndəst, ˈdȧn-\ *or* **durn·dest** *or* **durned·est** \ˈdərn-, ˈdən-, ˈdəin-\ *n* -s [euphemism] **:** DAMNEDEST

¹**darned** \ˈdärnd, ˈdȧnd\ *or* **durned** \ˈdərnd, ˈdənd, ˈdəind\ *adj, sometimes* **darneder** *or* **durneder** *usu* **darndest** *or* **darnedest** *or* **durndest** *or* **durnedest** [euphemism] **:** ¹DAMNED 2

²**darned** \"\ *or* **durned** \"\ *adv* [euphemism] **:** ²DAMNED

dar·nel \ˈdärnᵊl, ˈdȧn-\ *n* -s [ME, prob. fr. an (assumed) MF word akin to F dial. *darnelle, darnèle, daurnale* darnel, cockle, prob. of Gmc origin; akin to MHG *tōre* fool, OE *dysig* foolish — more at DIZZY] **:** any of several grasses of the genus *Lolium;* *esp* **:** BEARDED DARNEL

darn·er \-nə(r)\ *n* -s **1 :** one that darns (as a darning machine) **2 :** DARNING NEEDLE **3 :** a darning egg or similar device

darnick *var of* DORNICK

darning *n* -s **:** articles or parts of articles that have been darned or are to be darned

darning egg *n* **:** an egg-shaped or round object that often has a wood or plastic handle and is used as a support for a curved area during darning

darning needle *n* **1 :** a long needle with a large eye for use in darning **2 :** DRAGONFLY, DAMSELFLY

da·ro·gha *also* **da·ro·ga** \dəˈrōgə\ *n* -s [Hindi *daroga*, fr. Per *dārogha*] *India* **:** a chief officer; *esp* **:** the head of a police, customs, or excise station

dar·rein \dəˈrān, (ˈ)daˈr-\ *adj* [AF *dreyn, derreyn*, fr. OF *darrain, derrein*, fr. (assumed) VL *deretranus*, fr. LL *deretro* back, behind (fr. L *de-* + *retro* back, backward) + *-anus* -an — more at RETRO-] *law* **:** LAST, FINAL

dars *pl of* DAR

dar·sham fern \ˈdärshəm-\ *n, usu cap D* [fr. *Darsham*, Suffolk, England] **:** CREST FERN

¹**dar·shan** \ˈdärshən\ *n, pl* **darsha·nim** \därˈshänəm, -shōn-\ [Heb *darshān* interpreter, fr. *dārash* to inquire, expound] **:** a preacher who expounds Jewish law or scriptures

²**dar·shan** \ˈdärshən, ˈdər-\ *n* -s [Hindi *darśan*, fr. Skt *darśana* act of seeing, view, fr. *dṛś* to see; akin to Gk *derkesthai* to look — more at DRAGON] **:** a blessing held by various Hindus to consist in the viewing of an eminent person (as a religious leader)

dar·so \ˈdär(,)sō\ *n* -s [*d*warf *r*ed *so*rghum] **:** a hybrid grain sorghum of doubtful origin but resulting supposedly from a natural crossing of a sorgo and a kafir and resembling kafir

d'ar·son·val current \ˈdärsᵊn,vȯl-, -val-\ *n, usu D'Arsonval* [after Jacques A. *d'Arsonval* †1940 Fr. physicist] **:** a high-frequency oscillating current of low voltage and high amperage used in diathermy

d'arsonval galvanometer *n, usu D'Arsonval* **:** a moving-coil galvanometer whose coil is provided with a filament suspension or with pivots and hairspring and rotates about a stationary soft-iron core between the poles of a strong permanent magnet

darst *archaic pres 2d sing of* DARE

¹**dart** \ˈdär|t, ˈdȧ|, *usu* |d·+V\ *n* -s [ME, fr. MF, of Gmc origin; akin to OE *daroth* dart, OHG *tart*, ON *darrathr;* perh. akin to Gk *thoos* sharp, Skt *dhārā* blade] **1 a** *archaic* **:** a light spear **:** JAVELIN **b** *archaic* **:** ARROW **c :** a small missile usu. with a shaft pointed and weighted at one end and feathered on the other (as one used in a blowgun or one thrown by hand at a target in the game of darts) **2 a :** something projected with sudden speed; *esp* **:** a sharp glance ⟨the ~ that shot from his eyes was of aggressive honesty —Winston Churchill⟩ **b :** something that sharply or suddenly wounds or pains ⟨~*s* of sarcasm⟩ **3 :** something with a slender pointed shaft or outline: as **a :** a small sharp-pointed shaft of carbonate of lime secreted in the dart sac of a land snail **b :** the guard pin in a watch **c :** a stitched tapering fold used esp. in fitting garments to the curves of the body **d :** an Australian pompano (*Trachinotus botla*) **e :** a pointed element in a wave traced in an electroencephalogram esp. in epilepsy **4 :** a quick movement **:** a sudden jump ⟨she fluttered round, making helpless little ~*s* —Dorothy Sayers⟩ **5** *slang Austral* **a :** PLAN, SCHEME **b :** something particularly to one's taste **6 darts** *pl but sing in constr* **:** a game in which darts are thrown at a target and scored according to their nearness to the bull's-eye

dart 1c

²**dart** \"\ *vb* -ED/-ING/-S [ME *darten*, fr. *dart*, n.] *vt* **1** *obs* **:** to pierce with or as if with a dart **2 :** to throw (an object) with a sudden movement ⟨~ a javelin at the foe⟩ **3 :** to thrust or move with sudden speed ⟨the snake ~*ing* its head this way and that⟩ ⟨who made man, with powers which ~ him from earth to heaven in a moment —Laurence Sterne⟩ ⟨she ~*ed* out her hand like a flash —W.H.Hudson †1922⟩; *specif* **:** to cast (as one's eyes) with suddenness or haste ⟨he shivered and ~*ed* a look over his shoulder —Ellery Queen⟩ **4 :** to furnish with a dart (as the waist of a garment in tapering) ~ *vi* **:** to move, spring, or jump with suddenness or impetuosity ⟨his tongue ~*s* about like a dragonfly —Walter de la Mare⟩ ⟨green eyes ~*ing* over the impassive faces of the judges —Earle Birney⟩ ⟨streets that ~ out at odd angles —*Amer. Guide Series: Ark.*⟩

dart board *n* **:** a large circular board (as of cork) used as a target in the game of darts

dart·er \|d·ə(r),|tə(r)\ *n* -s **1 a :** SNAKEBIRD 1 **b :** BLUE DARTER **2 :** any of numerous small American freshwater fishes closely related to the perches and constituting a subfamily of the family Percidae

dart·ford warbler \ˈdärtfərd-\ *n, usu cap D* [fr. *Dartford*, Kent, England] **:** a dark-colored long-tailed warbler (*Sylvia undata*) of western and southern Europe including the south coast of England

dart·ian \ˈdärd·ēən\ *n* -s *usu cap* [Raymond A. *Dart* b1893 Australian-born anatomist in Union of So. Africa + E *-ian*] **:** AUSTRALOPITHECINE

dart·ing *adj* **1 :** THROWING, CASTING ⟨anger-*darting* eyes⟩ **2 :** making short quick movements ⟨~ fish⟩ **3 :** QUICK, VOLATILE ⟨a ~ intelligence⟩ ⟨a glib, ~ manner of speech —Christopher Rand⟩ — **dart·ing·ly** *adv* — **dart·ing·ness** *n* -ES

dar·tle \ˈdär|d·ᵊl, ˈdȧ|, |tᵊl\ *vb* **dartled; dartled; dartling** \|d·ᵊliŋ,|t(ᵊ)liŋ\ **dartles** [freq. of ²*dart*] *vt* **:** to thrust or dart repeatedly ⟨flames *dartled* the horizon⟩ ~ *vi* **:** to move back and forth repeatedly ⟨an adder's *dartling* tongue⟩

dart·man \ˈdärtmən\ *n, pl* **dartmen :** a soldier armed with darts

dart·moor \ˈdärt,mu̇(ə)r, -mō(-\ *n* -s *usu cap* [fr. *Dartmoor*, region in southwestern England] **:** one of a breed of English hornless long-wooled sheep having a long whitish face similar to that of the Leicester

dartmoor pony *n, usu cap D* [fr. *Dartmoor*, region in England] **:** one of an old breed of hardy English ponies developed in Devonshire

dar·tos \ˈdär,täs, -rd·əs\ *n* -ES [NL, fr. Gk *dartos* flayed, verbal of *derein* to flay — more at TEAR] **:** a thin layer of vascular contractile tissue that contains unstriped muscle fibers but no fat and is situated beneath the skin of the scrotum or beneath that of the labia majora

dar·trose \ˈdär·,trōs *also* -ōz\ *n* -s [F, fr. *dartre* herpes, tetter (fr. MF *dertre*, fr. L *derbita*, of Celt origin; akin to MBret *dervoeden* herpes, W *darwden, tarwden* ringworm) + *-ose;* akin to OE *teter* tetter, OHG *zittaroh* herpes, tetter, Skt *dadru*, a kind of leprosy, skin eruption, OE *teran* to tear — more at TEAR] **:** a disease of the potato and tomato caused by a fungus (*Colletotrichum atramentarium*) and characterized by destruction of the stems esp. towards the base, by yellowing and drying of the foliage, and by development of numerous small black sclerotia in the diseased stem tissue — called also *black dot, black speck*

darts *pl of* DART, *pres 3d sing of* DART

dart sac *n* **:** an eversible appendage of the female reproductive organs in certain land snails

dart thrower *n* **:** THROWING-STICK

dar·vesh \ˈdärvish\ *or* **dar·wish** *also* **dar·wesh** \-rwish\ *n* -ES [Per *darvish*] **:** DERVISH

dar·win barberry \ˈdärwən-, ˈdȧw-\ *n, usu cap D* [after Charles R. *Darwin* †1882 Eng. naturalist] **:** a half-evergreen or evergreen shrub (*Berberis darwinii*) native to So. America but much grown in England that has entire spiny-toothed leaves and orange-yellow flowers in long racemes succeeded by dark purple berries

darwin glass *n, usu cap D* [fr. Jukes-*Darwin*, mining field in western Tasmania] **:** a group of glass objects found in Tasmania and believed to be glassy meteorites

¹**dar·win·i·an** \(ˈ)därˈwinēən, (ˈ)dȧˈw-\ *adj, usu cap* [C. R. *Darwin* + E *-ian*] **:** of or relating to the naturalist Darwin, his theories, or his followers

²**darwinian** \"\ *n* -s *usu cap* **:** one who accepts or advocates Darwinism

darwinian theory *n, usu cap D* **:** DARWINISM

dar·win·ism \ˈdärwə,nizəm, ˈdȧw-\ *n* -s *usu cap* [C. R. *Darwin*, its promulgator + E *-ism*] **:** the theory of the origin and perpetuation of new species of animals and plants holding that organisms tend to produce offspring varying slightly from their parents, that the process of natural selection tends to favor the survival of individuals whose peculiarities render them best adapted to their environment, and that chiefly by the continued operation of these factors new species not only have been and may still be produced but organisms of widely differing groups may have arisen from common ancestors; *broadly* **:** biological evolutionism — compare EVOLUTION 5b, NEO-DARWINISM; LAMARCKISM, MUTATION

[1]**dar·win·ist** \-ˌnəst\ *n* -s *usu cap* [C. R. *Darwin* + E *-ist*] **:** [2]DARWINIAN

[2]**darwinist** \"\ *or* **dar·win·is·tic** \ˌ==ˈnistik, -tēk\ *adj, often cap* **:** [1]DARWINIAN — **dar·win·is·ti·cal·ly** \-tək(ə)lē, -tēk-, -li\ *adv, often cap*

dar·win·ize \ˈ==ˌnīz\ *vb* -ED/-ING/-S *often cap* [C. R. *Darwin* + E *-ize*] *vi* **:** to think in Darwinian terms or ways ⟨a philosopher with a tendency to *Darwinize*⟩ ~ *vt* **:** to convert to or imbue with a Darwinian point of view ⟨Ibsen was *Darwinized* to the extent of exploiting heredity on the stage —G.B.Shaw⟩

darwin's frog *n, usu cap D* [after C. R. *Darwin*] **:** a small Chilean frog (*Rhinoderma darwini*) of the family Brevicipitidae characterized by the male's carrying of the fertilized eggs in his vocal sac

darwin's sheep *n, usu cap D* **:** a central Asiatic wild sheep that is a variety (*Ovis ammon darvini*) of the argali

darwin's tubercle *n, usu cap D* **:** the slight projection occas. present on the edge of the external human ear and assumed by some scientists to represent the pointed part of the ear of quadrupeds

darwin tulip *n, usu cap D* **:** a late-flowering tulip that is single-flowered and tall-growing and has self-colored flowers with a more or less rectangular base

dar·zi \dərˈzē, ˈdär‚zē\ *or* **dur·zee** \dərˈzē\ *n* -s *usu cap* [Hindi *darzī*, fr. Per] **:** a tailor or an urban caste of tailors in Hindu society in India

[1]**das** \ˈdas, ˈdäs\ *n, pl* **dases** *or* **dasses** [Afrik — more at DASSIE] **:** DASSIE 1

[2]**das** \ˈdäs\ *n* -ES [Skt *dāsa* demon, enemy, infidel, slave; prob. akin to Per *dāh* servant, Av *dahyu-*, *daiṅhu-*, *danghu-* land, OPer *dahyu-* land, province, Skt *dasyu* demon, barbarian] **:** a Hindu slave or servant

[3]**das** *pl of* DA

DAS *abbr* delivered alongside ship

da·se·hra *or* **da·sa·ra** *or* **dus·se·rah** \ˈdəsərə\ *or* **da·sa·ha·ra** \ˌdəs(h)əˈhərə\ *or* **da·sa·hra** \ˈdəsərə\ *n* -s *usu cap* [Skt *daśaharā*, lit., one taking away ten (sins), fr. *daśa* ten + *harā*, fem. of *hara* carrier, fr. *harati* he carries, takes; akin to Gk *chortos* pasturage, grass, enclosure — more at TEN, YARD] **:** a 10-day Hindu festival orig. in honor of the Ganges but later of Durga and held in the month Asin

da·sein \ˈdäˌzīn, *G* ˈdäˌ-\ *n* -s *usu cap* [G, lit., existence, being, fr. *dasein* to be present, fr. *da* there, here (fr. OHG *dār*) + *sein* to be, fr. MHG *sīn*, fr. OHG *sīn* to be — more at THERE, IS] *existentialism* **:** factual reality or existence within the spatiotemporal realm

[1]**dash** \ˈdash, -aa(ə)-,-ai-\ *vb* -ED/-ING/-ES [ME *dasshen*, prob. of imit. origin] *vt* **1 :** to knock, hurl, or thrust impetuously, violently, or destructively ⟨~ away your tears⟩ ⟨they ~*ed* water into his face to revive him⟩ ⟨the storm ~*ed* the boat against a reef⟩ ⟨he ~*ed* the door open . . . and fled down the hall —Herbert Gold⟩ ⟨the fury of Pontiac's army ~*ed* itself in vain against the palisades of Detroit —*Amer. Guide Series: Ind.*⟩ **2 :** to break, crush, or smash by striking or knocking ⟨flowers ~*ed* by rain⟩ ⟨the statue was ~*ed* to pieces when it fell⟩ **3 a :** SPLASH, SPATTER ⟨clothes ~*ed* with mud⟩ **b :** BESMIRCH, SULLY ⟨a reputation ~*ed* with rumor⟩ **c :** to spread over carelessly **:** BLOTCH, BESPECKLE ⟨a painting ~*ed* with bright colors⟩ **4 a :** to bring to naught **:** RUIN, FRUSTRATE ⟨the weather ~*ed* his hopes of making the trip⟩ **b :** to put to shame **:** CONFOUND, CONFUSE ⟨~*ed* by her scorn⟩ **c :** to cast down **:** put out of sorts **:** DEPRESS ⟨never one to be ~*ed* when a partridge gets away —Earle Birney⟩ **5 :** MIX, TEMPER ⟨happiness ~*ed* with bitterness⟩; *esp* **:** to enliven, season, or adulterate by adding something of a different quality ⟨a glass of milk was put to his lips, and a new voice said, "I've ~*ed* it with brandy" —Ellen Glasgow⟩ **6** *archaic* **:** CANCEL, ERASE — used with *out* **7 :** to complete, execute, or finish off with haste or rapidity — used with *down* or *off* ⟨~ down a few notes⟩ ⟨~ off a short story⟩ ⟨~ off a drink⟩ **8** [euphemism] **:** [1]DAMN *vt* 5 ~ *vi* **1 a :** to advance suddenly and quickly **:** hurl forward esp. in repeated thrusts ⟨storm clouds ~*ing* low across the sky⟩ ⟨waves ~*ed* against the breakwater⟩ **b :** to move with sudden speed ⟨cars ~*ing* down the highway⟩ ⟨~ upstairs⟩ ⟨the Japanese boat made another attempt to ~ downstream —Nora Waln⟩ **2 :** to make a show of dressing stylishly and acting in a spirited or romantic manner **:** cut a fancy figure **:** appear dashing ⟨a fellow whose only concern is to dress and ~⟩ **syn** see RUSH

[2]**dash** \"\ *n* -ES [ME *dasshe*, fr. *dasshen*, v.] **1 a** *archaic* **:** a violent impact **:** BLOW, STROKE — often used in the phrases *at first dash*, *at a dash*, *at one dash* **b :** a sudden impetuous burst or splash or the sound it produces ⟨a ~ of water⟩ ⟨a ~ of rain⟩ **2** *obs* **:** a sudden demoralizing, crushing, or depressing blow **3 a :** a stroke of a pen esp. when made as a flourish in writing or when drawn through a word to cancel it **b :** the punctuation mark — used to indicate an abrupt shift in the structure of a sentence (as in *the man whom I — but first let me say this*), termination of a sentence when it is syntactically incomplete (as in "*You know very well he —*"), or faltering utterance (as in "*It shows — that he is — clumsy*"), to mark the end of an introductory series and the beginning or resumption of the main structure of the sentence (as in *his colleagues, his friends, his family — all tried to dissuade him*), to set off a repetitive or reinforcing phrase or clause (as in *it was a success — a brilliant success — but it gave him little satisfaction*), a preliminary word group (as in *legend and history — where are we to draw the line between them?*), or a supplementary word group, esp. an afterthought (as in *the object of this organization is to carry on scientific research — on a nonprofit basis*), to set off and emphasize a final word or word group (as in *he never offends anyone — unintentionally*), an appositive (as in *a single blunder — the use of unreliable production figures — invalidates all his conclusions*), or a parenthetical word or word group (as in *the book — though written in haste — reads well*), to separate question and answer (as in *why did he do this? — because he found it necessary*), to indicate change of speaker in dialogue, to join the name of a writer to a quotation or the name of a source to an extract, to introduce explanatory matter, a quotation, or a list, to separate the items in a list, or to set off a heading from the rest of its paragraph or the salutation from the body of a letter **c :** the sign — used to indicate ellipsis or omission (as in *my friend H—, d—d nonsense*, or *1911– —*), to serve as a ditto mark indicating the same author or continuation of the same entry in lists such as bibliographies or catalogs, to join proper names (as in *the Brooklyn—Pittsburgh game*), or to join letters or numbers that indicate the beginning and end points of an inclusive series (as in *A—C, 22—30, 1897—1905*, usu. read as "A to C", "22 to 30", "1897 to 1905") **d :** a mark ' in a musical score denoting that the note over or under which it is placed is to be played very staccato **e :** a graphic character in printing consisting typically of a single horizontal line longer than a hyphen and by printers commonly named according to its width (en ~) ⟨em ~⟩ ⟨2-em ~⟩ **4 :** a small quantity of something added to or giving a particular character or individuality to another **:** TOUCH ⟨his ancestry was chiefly English, with some Scotch and a ~ of both French and Dutch —V.L.Kellogg⟩; *specif* **:** a very small quantity of liquid or dry ingredients variously interpreted as ranging from 3 drops to ¼ teaspoonful added to food or drink **5 :** ostentatious display **:** flashy showiness — usu. used in the phrase *cut a dash* ⟨such a car would cut a ~ anywhere⟩ ⟨the couple cut quite a ~ on the promenade⟩ **6 :** energy in style and action **:** ANIMATION, SPIRIT ⟨the verve and ~ of an old-time cavalry regiment⟩ ⟨the two sisters were not beautiful . . . but they had the ~ . . . that a later generation came to call sex appeal —Robert Shaplen⟩ **7 a :** a sudden onset, rush, or attempt ⟨the dog made a ~ at the passing car⟩ ⟨make a ~ for cover⟩ ⟨established three depots of supplies . . . for a ~ to the Pole —C.O.Paullin⟩ **b** (1) **:** a race short enough to allow the contestants to cover the entire distance at top speed **:** a short swift race or trial of speed ⟨a 100-yard ~⟩ (2) **:** a harness race decided in a single heat **8 a :** a somewhat prolonged click about the duration of three dots on a telegraph sounder forming a letter or part of a letter (as in the Morse code); *also* **:** a correspondingly long buzz by a radiotelegraph transmitter or long blast of a whistle — compare DOT 5b **b :** a wave of a flag through an arc of 90 degrees to the left from vertical as a unit of code in signaling — compare WIGWAG **c :** a flash of a beam from a signal light for about the duration of three dots and representing a letter or part of a letter in a communication system (as the Morse code) — compare DOT 5c **9** [by shortening] **:** DASHBOARD 2 **10 :** a horizontal rule varying in length and used to separate decks of a newspaper headline or to indicate divisions between or within stories **11 :** a mixture (as of mortar) prepared to be dashed against a moist surface to make a finishing coat **syn** see VIGOR

[3]**dash** \", ˈdäsh\ *n* -ES [perh. fr. Pg *das*, 2d pers. sing. of *dar* to give, fr. L *dare* — more at DATE] *Africa* **:** GIFT ⟨~*es* given regularly to his native servant⟩

[4]**dash** \"\ *vt* -ED/-ING/-ES *Africa* **:** to give a gift to (as a native employee)

dashboard \ˈ=ˌ=\ *n* [[1], [2]*dash* + *board*] **1 :** a screen of wood or leather placed on the forepart of a horse-drawn carriage, sleigh, or other vehicle to intercept water, mud, or snow thrown up by the heels of the horses **2 :** a panel extending across an automobile or airplane below the windshield and usu. containing dials, controls, and accessories — called also *instrument board*

dashboard 1

[1]**dashed** \ˈdasht, -aa(ə)-,-ai-\ *adj* [[2]*dash* (mark) + *-ed*] **1** [euphemism] **:** [1]DAMNED 2a, 2b **2 :** made up of a series of dashes ⟨a ~ line⟩ ⟨a ~ pattern⟩

[2]**dashed** \-sht\ *also* **dash·ed·ly** \-shədlē\ *adv* [euphemism] **:** [2]DAMNED

da·sheen \daˈshēn, dəˈ-\ *n* -s [origin unknown] **:** TARO

dash·er \ˈdashə(r), ˈdaash-,ˈdaish-\ *n* -s **:** one that dashes: as **a :** a man or woman who acts in a stylishly clever, forward, or showy manner **b :** a device that usu. consists of a shaft to which paddles are attached and that is used to agitate liquids or semisolids ⟨the ~ of a churn⟩ ⟨the ~ of an ice-cream freezer⟩ — see CHURN illustration **c :** DASHBOARD 1 **d :** an iron plate inside a boiler to prevent the entering cold water from impinging upon the tubes

dasher block *n* **:** a small block situated at the end of the spanker gaff and used for hoisting a ship's colors or signals

dashes *pres 3d sing of* DASH, *pl of* DASH

dashing *adj* [fr. pres. part. of [1]*dash*] **1 :** beating violently **:** SPLASHING ⟨~ waves⟩ **2 :** vigorously active **:** smartly energetic **:** SPIRITED ⟨a ~ young officer⟩ ⟨the most sheerly ~ of all jazz —Wilder Hobson⟩ **3 :** stylishly or elegantly showy ⟨the then gay, ~, and reckless capital of Ireland —Wilmot Harrison⟩ **:** having a smartly impressive appearance ⟨~, newfangled bicycles —*Irish Digest*⟩ **:** brilliantly carried off ⟨a ~ piece of teaching that illuminates his own cast of thought —Charlotte Devree⟩ — **dash·ing·ly** *adv*

dash·ke·san·ite \ˌdashkəˈsaˌnīt\ *n* -s [Russ *dashkesanit*, fr. *Dashkesan*, Azerbaijan, U.S.S.R., its locality + Russ *-it* -ite] **:** a mineral consisting of a chloroaluminosilicate of sodium, potassium, iron, and magnesium $(Na,K)Ca_2(Fe,Mg)_5(Si,Al)_8O_{22}Cl_2$ and belonging near hastingsite in the amphibole group

dash light *n* [[2]*dash* (dashboard)] **:** a light on the dashboard of an automobile

dashpot \ˈ=ˌ=\ *n* **1 :** a device used for cushioning or damping a movement to avoid shock and consisting essentially of a cylinder containing air or a liquid and a piston moving in it **2 :** a device for damping or checking the vibrations of an automatic-indicating scale

dashy \ˈda|shē, ˈdaa|,ˈdai|\ *adj* -ER/-EST [[1]*dash* + *-y*] **:** DASHING 3

da·si \ˈdä(ˌ)sē\ *n* -s [Skt *dāsī*, fem of *dāsa* demon, enemy, infidel, slave — more at DAS] **:** a female Hindu slave or servant **:** a Hindu woman of low caste

dask \ˈdask\ *Scot var of* DESK

das·n't *or* **das·n't** *also* **das·sent** \ˈda|sᵊn(t), ˈdaa|,ˈdai|,ˈdȧ *also* |zᵊn-\ [partly contr. of (*thou*) *darst not* (fr. ME), partly contr. of (*he*) *dares not*] *dial* **:** dare not

dass \ˈdas\ *var of* DESS

dasses *pl of* DAS

das·sie \ˈdasē, ˈdäsē\ *n* -s [Afrik *dassie*, dim. of *das* hyrax, badger, fr. MD, badger; akin to OHG *dahs* badger, Gk *tektōn* carpenter — more at TECHNICAL] **1 :** a hyrax (genus *Procavia*) of southern Africa — called also *das* **2 :** a small sparid fish (*Diplodus sargus*) of African coasts and estuaries that is highly regarded as a sport and table fish and is silvery when young but becomes darker with age and possesses a black spot at the base of the tail — called also *blacktail*

dassie rat *n* **:** a sand-colored diurnal hystricomorph rodent (genus *Petromus* or *Petromys*) of southern African uplands having long silky fur, a bushy tail, and a head suggesting that of a squirrel

dast \ˈdast, -aa(ə)-,-ai-,-ȧ-\ *substand pres sing & pl of* DARE

das·tard \ˈdastə(r)d\ *n* -s [ME, perh. fr. ON *dæstr* exhausted (past part. of *dæsa* to groan, lose one's breath) + ME *-ard*; akin to ON *dasask* to become exhausted — more at DAZE] **1** *obs* **:** DULLARD **2 :** one who shrinks from danger **:** COWARD; *esp* **:** one who carries out malicious or sneaky acts without exposing himself to danger ⟨like a ~ and a treacherous coward —Shak.⟩

das·tard·ize \-tə(r)ˌdīz\ *vt* -ED/-ING/-S *archaic* **:** to make cowardly **:** INTIMIDATE, COW

das·tard·li·ness \-tə(r)dlēnəs, -lin-\ *n* -ES **:** COWARDICE, TREACHERY

das·tard·ly \-lē,-li\ *adj* **:** treacherously cowardly ⟨the ~ brute had trampled on him when he could not turn against him —Anthony Trollope⟩ **:** insidiously or despicably mean ⟨the flood waters have done many ~ things to our residents —K.K.Coleman⟩ **:** BASE ⟨choosing the safe side . . . appeared to me to be playing a rather ~ part —George Borrow⟩ **syn** see COWARDLY

das·tardy \-tə(r)dē\ *n* -ES *archaic* **:** DASTARDLINESS

[1]**da·stur** \dəˈstu̇(ə)r\ *n* -s [Hindi *dastūr* custom, fr. Per] *India* **:** CUSTOM; *also* **:** customary fee

[2]**dastur** \"\ *n* -s [Per *dastūr*] **:** a Parsi high priest

da·stu·ri \-ˈūrē\ *n* -s [Hindi *dastūrī*, fr. Per, fr. *dastūr*] *India* **:** FEE, GRATUITY

dasy- *comb form* [NL, fr. Gk, fr. *dasys* — more at DENSE] **1 :** thick with hair or leaves **:** shaggy **:** woolly ⟨*dasy*phyllous⟩ **2 :** density ⟨*dasy*meter⟩

Das·ya \ˈdasēə\ *n, cap* [NL, fr. Gk *dasys*] **:** a widely distributed genus (the type of the family Dasyaceae) of marine red algae having a filiform sympodially branched thallus — see CHENILLE WEED

dasy·at·i·dae \ˌdasēˈadəˌdē\ *n pl, cap* [NL, fr. *Dasyatis*, type genus (irreg. fr. *dasy-* + Gk *batis* ray, skate) + *-idae*] **:** a family of elasmobranchs (type genus *Dasyatis*) comprising most of the common stingrays

das·y·cla·da·ce·ae \ˌdasəklәˈdāsēˌē\ *n pl, cap* [NL, fr. *Dasycladus*, type genus (fr. *dasy-* + Gk *klados* sprout, branch) + *-aceae* — more at GLADIATOR] **:** a family of coenocytic green algae that are included in Siphonocladales or now more often isolated in a separate order and that have the filaments arranged in whorls about a central axis which is often encrusted with lime — **das·y·cla·da·cean** \ˌ===ˈ=shən\ *adj* — **das·y·cla·da·ceous** \-shəs\ *adj*

das·y·lir·i·on \ˌdasəˈlirēən\ *n* [NL, fr. *dasy-* + Gk *leirion* lily — more at LILY] **1** *cap* **:** a genus of plants (family Liliaceae) related to *Yucca* and *Dracaena* that are native to Mexico and the southwestern U.S. and have a woody stem, stiff sword-shaped leaves, and small white flowers **2** -s **:** any plant of the genus *Dasylirion*

da·sym·e·ter \daˈsimәd·ә(r), dəˈ-\ *n* -s [ISV *dasy-* + *-meter*; prob. orig. formed in G] **:** a thin glass globe weighed in gases to measure their density

das·y·neu·ra \ˌdasəˈn(y)u̇rə\ *n, cap* [NL, fr. *dasy-* + *-neura*] **:** a large widely distributed genus of midges that are typically gall midges having larvae which feed chiefly on plant buds, in leaf curls, or in galls and sometimes cause the destruction of reproductive structures of various plants — see CLOVER SEED MIDGE

das·y·pel·ti·dae \ˌdasəˈpeltəˌdē\ *n pl, cap* [NL, fr. *Dasypeltis*, type genus (fr. *dasy-* + Gk *peltē* small shield) + *-idae* — more at PELTA] **:** an African family of egg-eating snakes containing a single species (*Dasypeltis scaber*) having the hypapophyses of the cervical vertebra extending into the esophagus where they form a rasp used in breaking eggshells — see ELACHISTODONTIDAE

das·y·phyl·lous \ˌdasәˈfiləs\ *adj* [ISV *dasy-* + *-phyllous*] **1 :** having leaves thick or thickly set **2 :** having woolly leaves

[1]**da·syp·o·did** \daˈsipədәd, dəˈ-\ *or* **da·syp·o·doid** \-pə-ˌdȯid\ *adj* [*dasypodid* fr. NL *Dasypodidae*; *dasypodoid* fr. NL *Dasypod-*, *Dasypus* + E *-oid*] **:** of or relating to the Dasypodidae

[2]**dasypodid** \"\ *n* -s **:** one of the Dasypodidae

das·y·pod·i·dae \ˌdasəˈpädəˌdē\ *n pl, cap* [NL, fr. *Dasypod-*, *Dasypus*, type genus + *-idae*] **:** a family of mammals (order Edentata) that comprises the armadillos

das·y·proc·ta \ˌdasəˈpräktə\ *n, cap* [NL, fr. *dasy-* + [2]*-procta*] **:** a genus (the type of the family Dasyproctidae) of hystricomorph rodents comprising the agoutis and having relatively long legs and but three toes on the hind feet — compare PACA — **das·y·proc·tid** \ˌ==ˈ=təd\ *adj or n* — **das·y·proc·tine** \-ˌtīn\ *adj*

das·y·pus \ˈdasəpəs\ *n, cap* [NL, fr. *dasy-* + *-pus*] **:** a genus (the type of the family Dasypodidae) of armadillos that includes the peba and other common armadillos

das·yu \ˈdəs(ˌ)yü\ *n* -s *often cap* [Skt, lit., demon, barbarian — more at DAS] **:** one of the dark-skinned Dravidian aborigines of India that opposed the invasion of the Aryans

dasy·ure \ˈdasēˌyu̇(ə)r\ *n* -s [NL *Dasyurus*] **:** an arboreal carnivorous marsupial of the genus *Dasyurus* — compare NATIVE CAT

dasy·u·rid \ˌdasēˈyu̇rәd\ *n* -s [NL *Dasyuridae*] **:** one of the Dasyuridae

dasy·u·ri·dae \ˌdasēˈyu̇rəˌdē\ *n pl, cap* [NL, fr. *Dasyurus*, type genus + *-idae*] **:** a family of polyprotodont marsupials (type genus *Dasyurus*) that includes the native cats, pouched mice, banded anteater, Tasmanian devil, and related forms

dasy·u·roi·des \ˌdasēyəˈrȯi(ˌ)dēz\ *n, cap* [NL, fr. *Dasyurus* + L *-oides* -oid] **:** a small genus of Australian pouched mice

dasy·u·rus \ˌdasēˈyu̇rəs\ *n, cap* [NL, fr. *dasy-* + *-urus*] **:** a genus of carnivorous more or less arboreal marsupials of Australia and Tasmania that includes several moderate-sized active animals that have white-spotted dark coats and somewhat resemble weasels or martens — see NATIVE CAT

dat *abbr* dative

data *pl of* DATUM

dat·able *or* **date·able** \ˈdādəbəl, -ātə-\ *adj* **:** that may be assigned a date ⟨a datable ~ happening —C.W.Shumaker⟩

[1]**dat·al** \ˈdādᵊl, -ātᵊl\ *adj* [[2]*date* + *-al*] **:** containing a date ⟨the ~ clause of a charter⟩

[2]**da·tal** \ˈdātᵊl\ *n* -s [by alter.] **:** DAYTALE

da·tana \dəˈtanə, -ānə *also* -ānə\ *n* [NL] **1** *cap* **:** an American genus of moths (family Notodontidae) that have the proboscis short and that include several with social larvae that feed on economically important plants — see WALNUT CATERPILLAR, YELLOW-NECKED CATERPILLAR **2** -s **:** any insect of the genus *Datana*

[1]**da·ta·ry** \ˈdād·ərē\ *n* -ES [fr. (assumed) ML *datarius* datary, official of the Roman Curia who added dates to papal letters (whence NL), fr. LL *data* date of a letter + L *-arius* -ary (person) — more at DATE] **:** the cardinal who is head of the datary

[2]**datary** *n* -ES [fr. (assumed) ML *dataria* datary, office of the Roman Curia where dates were added to papal letters (whence NL), fr. LL *data* date of a letter + L *-aria* -ary (thing)] **:** an office of the Roman Curia charged esp. with investigating the fitness of candidates for papal benefices

datch \ˈdach\ *dial Eng var of* THATCH

datcha *var of* DACHA

[1]**date** \ˈdāt, *usu* -ād.+V\ *n* -s [ME, fr. OF, modif. of OIt *dattero* or OProv *datil*, fr. L *dactylus*, fr. Gk *daktylos*, lit., finger] **1 :** the oblong fruit of a palm (*Phoenix dactylifera*) that constitutes a staple food for the people of northern Africa and western Asia and is largely imported into other countries **2** *or* **date palm :** a tall tree with pinnate leaves and large clusters of dioecious flowers that yields the date and is cultivated esp. in many parts of the tropics **3 :** WASHINGTON PALM

[2]**date** \"\ *n* -s [ME, fr. MF, fr. LL *data*, fr. *data* (as in *data Romae* given at Rome), fem. of L *datus*, past part. of *dare* to give; akin to Gk *didonai* to give, Skt *dadāti* he gives] **1 :** a statement or formula affixed (as to a piece of writing, inscription, or coin) that specifies the time (as day, month, and year) and often the place of execution or making ⟨a letter bearing the ~ 3 January 1856⟩ **2 :** the point of time at which a transaction or event takes place or is appointed to take place **:** a given point of time ⟨preparations were sometimes in progress far ahead of the eventful ~ —Della Lutes⟩ ⟨Easter occurs on any ~ between March 22 and April 25⟩ **3 a :** the extent of time that something lasts **:** DURATION ⟨the short ~ of all things sweet —Rebecca P. Parkin⟩ **b** *archaic* **:** TERMINATION, END **4 :** the period of time to which something belongs esp. historically ⟨sculptures of an early ~⟩ ⟨a style belonging to a later ~⟩ **5 a :** an appointment or engagement usu. for a specified time ⟨has a ~ with his lawyer to discuss the sale of a house⟩; *esp* **:** an appointment between two persons of the opposite sex for the mutual enjoyment of some form of social activity ⟨make a ~ with his girl⟩ **b :** an occasion (as an evening) of social activity arranged in advance between two persons of opposite sex **c :** a person of the opposite sex with whom one enjoys such an occasion of social activity ⟨his ~ at the school dance⟩ **syn** see ENGAGEMENT — **to date :** up to the present moment ⟨no election returns have come in *to date*⟩ — **up to date** *also* **down to date 1 :** so as to account for or include present facts or knowledge ⟨the second edition brings the first *up to date*⟩ **2 :** up to the modern or present standard or style ⟨the house was brought *up to date* by the addition of new fixtures⟩ — compare OUT-OF-DATE, UP-TO-DATE

[3]**date** \"\ *vb* -ED/-ING/-S [ME *daten*, fr. MF *dater*, fr. ML *datare*, fr. LL *data*, n.] *vt* **1 a :** to determine or fix the date of origination, fabrication, composition, or occurrence of ⟨~ an early American antique⟩ **:** assign to a particular time or period of time ⟨the start of the Counter Reformation is to be *dated* from this time —R.A.Hall b.1911⟩ **b :** to assign a chronology to ⟨method for *dating* geological periods⟩ **2 :** to note down, record, or mark with the date ⟨bills are *dated* on the day they are made out⟩ ⟨~ the arrival of each new bird⟩ ⟨engine blocks *dated* as they pass off the assembly line⟩; *specif* **:** to write and date ⟨the news dispatch was *dated* from New York⟩ **3** *obs* **:** to put an end to **4 :** to make a date with ⟨she was *dated* several times by her boss⟩ ⟨he didn't go to the dance because all the girls he knew were *dated* up⟩ **:** go on a date with ⟨she *dated* several boys of his acquaintance⟩ **5 a :** to mark strongly or essentially with the qualities typical of a particular period ⟨the manner in which the brushwork is handled ~*s* the work of the great artists⟩ **b :** to make (as a style, an art work, or an artist) only briefly fashionable or artistically appealing **:** limit artistically to a short period of time esp. time in the past **:** quickly deprive of artistic originality or freshness ⟨sentimentality ~*s* most 19th century novelists⟩ ⟨a flashy architectural style ~*s* a house⟩ **6 :** to show up plainly the age of ⟨his button shoes surely ~ him⟩ ~ *vi* **1 :** to reckon chronologically **:** estimate or record the date or chronology ⟨the historian ~*s* by years, the geologist by millions of years⟩ ⟨a machine that ~*s*, weighs, and wraps automatically⟩ **2 :** to become dated and written — usu. used with *from* ⟨a report *dating* from headquarters⟩ **3 a :** ORIGINATE ⟨furniture *dating* as far back as the Revolution⟩ ⟨the manuscript ~*s* not later than the latter half of the 14th century⟩ **b :** to continue in existence **:** EXTEND ⟨a friendship *dating* from college days⟩ ⟨pioneer stock *dating* back to 1640⟩ **4 :** to become dated ⟨a fashion that never seems to ~⟩ ⟨the novel, now a half century old, shows no signs of *dating*⟩

dateable *var of* DATABLE

datebook \ˈ=ˌ=\ *n* **:** a newspaper editor's record of news events to be covered in the future

dated *adj* **1** *obs* **:** having a limit or termination **2 :** provided with a date ⟨~ and stamped documents⟩ **3 a :** spoiled or made invalid or useless by subsequent events or phenomena **:** OBSOLETE ⟨houses burn down, roads are changed, new bridges are built, and a map soon becomes ~ —*Infantry Jour.*⟩ **b :** marked by often hackneyed features, materials, or techniques associated with the immediate and usu. discounted past ⟨a ~ novelist⟩ ⟨~ jazz music⟩ ⟨I find her conclusions ~. She smacks too much of feminism and the selfish twenties —Rhona R. Wilber⟩

date·less \'dātləs\ *adj* **1 a :** having no fixed term **:** ENDLESS ⟨the ~ rise and fall of the tides⟩ **b :** bearing no date ⟨a ~ letter⟩ **c :** of an age or duration so great as to preclude the possiblity of being assigned a date **:** IMMEMORIAL ⟨~ customs⟩ ⟨a spiritual rule of ~ antiquity derived from Rome —G.M. Trevelyan⟩ **d :** of continuously living interest **:** not subject to the adverse effects of the passage of time **:** TIMELESS ⟨few characters are more ~ than Hamlet⟩ **e :** being without a social partner ⟨some of the boys had come to the party ~⟩ **2** *dial Eng* **:** having mental faculties impaired by old age **:** FOOLISH ⟨a poor ~ old man⟩

date letter *n* **:** the alphabetical punch mark placed on pieces of English silver to show the year in which they are assayed

¹dateline \'ˌ\ *n* [²*date* + *line*] **1 :** a line in a written document or a printed publication presenting the date of composition or issue: as **a :** the line at the beginning of a nonlocal news story giving its date and place of origin **b :** a line or space in a publication giving the date of issue, the volume number, and the issue number **2** *usu* **date line :** a hypothetical line on the earth's surface coinciding with the 180th meridian except where it is deflected between north latitudes 48° and 75° and between south latitudes 15° and 51° to avoid dividing places in close intercourse and designated arbitrarily as the place where each calendar day first begins **3 :** DEADLINE 3

date line, indicated in chart by heavy line

²dateline \"\ *vt* **:** to provide with a dateline ⟨a dispatch *datelined* Chicago⟩

datemark \'ˌ\ *n* **:** a marking that indicates the date of a thing; *specif* **:** a mark on gold and silver plate indicating date of manufacture

date mussel *also* **date shell** *n* [¹*date*; fr. its shape and color] **:** a rock-boring bivalve mollusk of the genus *Lithophaga*

date of record *finance* **:** the last date for registered holders of corporate stocks to be entitled to receive a dividend, right, or other benefit

date palm *n* **:** ¹DATE 2

date plum *n* **:** PERSIMMON; *esp* **:** an Asiatic persimmon (*Diospyros lotus*) sometimes cultivated for its small yellow or purplish edible fruits

dat·er \'dād·ə(r), -ātə-\ *n* -s **:** one that dates; *specif* **:** an instrument for stamping dates

dates *pl of* DATE, *pres 3d sing of* DATE

date slip *n* **:** a slip of paper pasted to an endpaper of a circulating library book on which is stamped the date the book is loaned or the date it is due back

date stamp *n* **1 :** an implement or device for stamping a date and often (as on postal matter) related information (as place of origin or receipt) **2 :** the date and related information stamped by a date stamp

date-stamp \'ˌ\ *vt* [*date stamp*] **:** to stamp with a date ⟨the post office *date-stamps* outgoing mail⟩ ⟨he *date-stamped* each letter when he opened it⟩

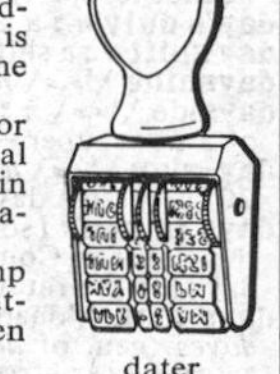

dater

da·til \'dä,tēl\ *n, pl* **dati·les** \-äd·ᵊl,ās, -äd·ē,lās\ [AmerSp *dátil*, fr. Sp, date (fruit), fr. Catal *dàtil*, fr. L *dactylus* — more at DATE] **:** any of several plants and their leaf fibers used for baskets or hats: as **a :** a So. American palm (*Cocos datil*) **b :** a Mexican yucca (*Yucca australis*)

dating *n* -s [fr. gerund of ³*date*] **:** an extension of credit by postdating of a bill or by not dating it until an agreed time

dating nail *n* **:** a broad-headed nail driven into the upper face of a railroad tie or utility pole bearing an indication of the date when the tie was laid

da·tion \'dāshən\ *n* -s [F or L; F, fr. L *dation-, dtio* act of giving, fr. *datus* (past part. of *dare* to give) + *-ion-, -io* -ion — more at DATE] **:** the legal act of giving or conferring

da·tion in pay·ment \ˌdāshənən'pāmənt\ *or* **da·tion en paie·ment** \däsyōⁿnäⁿpeymäⁿ\ [F *dation en paiement*] *civil law* **:** a mode of discharging a debt or claim by the debtor's giving to the creditor with the latter's consent something in full satisfaction of the obligation but of a character different from that orig. called for by the obligation

da·tis·ca \də'tiskə\ *n, cap* [NL] **:** a genus (the type of the family Datiscaceae) of tall herbs resembling hemps and having flowers in clusters in the axils of the leafy branches

dat·is·ca·ce·ae \ˌdad·ə'skāsē,ē\ *n pl, cap* [NL, fr. *Dastica* type genus + *-aceae*] **:** a small family of herbs or trees (order Parietales) having regular often dioecious and apetalous flowers in racemes or spikes and a one-seeded capsule — **dat·is·ca·ceous** \ˌ'skāshəs\ *adj*

da·ti·val \dā'tīvəl, də'- *sometimes* 'dād·|əvəl *or* 'dat| *or* |ēv-\ *adj* [²*dative* + *-al*] **:** connected with the dative case or any of the relations frequently expressed by it **:** of or relating to the dative case

¹da·tive \'dād·|iv, -āt|, |ēv *also* |əv\ *adj* [ME *datif*, fr. L *dativus*, fr. *datus* (past part. of *dare* to give) + *-ivus* -ive — more at DATE] **1** [L *dativus*, trans. of Gk *dotikos*] **a** *of a grammatical case* **:** marking typically the indirect object of a verb (as Latin *mihi* in *da mihi panem* "give me bread" or German *ihm* in *sie gaben ihm wein* "they gave him wine"), the only object of any one of a limited group of verbs (as German *mir* in *er hilft mir* "he helps me"), the object of any of certain prepositions (as German *mir* in *mit mir* "with me" or *ihr* in *zu ihr* "to her"), or a possessor (as German *ihr* in *er küsst ihr die hand* "he kisses her hand") **b** *of a word or word group* **:** standing in any grammatical or semantic relation (as indirect object) that in certain inflected languages is characteristically marked by a dative case form even when this relation is not marked by any inflectional element (as *his son* in "he gave his son a dog") — not now used technically **c :** of or relating to the dative case ⟨a ~ ending⟩ **2 a :** capable of being disposed of as one wishes ⟨a ~ office⟩ **b** [ML *dativus*, fr. L] *of an officer* **:** REMOVABLE — distinguished from *perpetual* **c :** given or appointed and not cast by law upon a person or group; *specif* **:** given or appointed by a magistrate or court or having to do with such an appointment **3** *of chemical bonds* **:** formed by contribution of a pair of electrons by one atom — **da·tive·ly** \|əvlē, -li\ *adv*

²dative \"\ *n* -s [L *dativus*, fr. *dativus*, adj.; trans. of Gk *dotikē* (*ptōsis*)] **:** the dative case of a language or a dative form

dative bond *n* **:** COORDINATE BOND

da·to *or* **dat·to** \'dä(ˌ)tō\ *or* **da·tu** \-)tü\ *n* -s [*dato, datto* fr. Sp *dato*, fr. Tag *dató; datu* fr. Malay] **:** a local headman in many parts of central Malaysia and the southern Philippines

dat·o·lite \'dad·ᵊl,īt\ *n* -s [G *datolith*, fr. Gk *dateisthai* to divide + G *-lith*; fr. its granular structure — more at TED] **:** a mineral $Ca_2B_2Si_2O_8(OH)_2$ consisting of a basic calcium borosilicate commonly occurring in glassy greenish crystals

dat·o·lit·ic \ˌdad·ᵊl|id·ik\ *adj* **:** of or relating to datolite

dat·tock \'dad·ək\ *n* -s [Wolof *detah, ditah*] **1 :** a tropical African tree (*Detarium senegalense*) of the family Leguminosae having rounded to oval pods with a sweet edible pulp and a single oily edible seed **2 :** the hard dark reddish brown intricately figured wood of the dattock

da·tum \'dā|d·əm, 'da|,'dä|,'dá|, |təm\ *n, pl* **da·ta** *see sense 2* \|d·ə,|tə\ [L, something given, fr. neut. of *datus*, past part. of *dare* to give — more at DATE] **1 a :** something that is given either from being experientially encountered or from being admitted or assumed for specific purposes **:** a fact or principle granted or presented **:** something upon which an inference or an argument is based or from which an intellectual system of any sort is constructed ⟨a ~ of experience⟩ ⟨given this ~ it follows that⟩; *specif* **:** SENSE-DATUM **b** (1) *data pl but often sing in constr* **:** material serving as a basis for discussion, inference, or determination of policy ⟨no general appraisal can be hazarded . . . until more *data* is available —*Publishers' Weekly*⟩ (2) **:** detailed information of any kind **2 a** *pl usu* **datums :** a point, line, or surface with reference to which positions (as elevations) are measured or indicated (as a permanent bench mark in leveling or mean sea level in a topographical survey); *specif* **:** the mean low-water mark of all tides assumed as a basis of reckoning but not admitting rigorous scientific determination **b** *pl often* **datums :** a magnitude, figure, or relation supposed to be given, drawn, or known in a mathematical investigation from which other magnitudes, figures, or relations are to be deduced **3 :** DATE **4 :** the sensory basis of a perception or judgment — see SENSE-DATUM

da·tu·ra \də'tùrə, də'tyù-\ *n* [NL, fr. Hindi *dhatūrā* jimsonweed, fr. Skt *dhattūra*] **1** *cap* **:** a genus of widely distributed strong-scented herbs, shrubs, or trees (family Solanaceae) with large funnel-shaped flowers succeeded by spiny capsules — see JIMSONWEED, THORN APPLE; CAPSULE illustration **2** -s **:** any plant or flower of the genus *Datura*

da·tu·ric \-rik\ *adj* [NL *Datura* + E *-ic*] **:** of or relating to the genus *Datura*

dau *abbr* daughter

¹daub \'dób, 'däb\ *vb* -ED/-ING/-s [ME *dauben*, fr. OF *dauber* to whitewash, plaster, prob. fr. (assumed) VL *dalbare*, alter. of L *dealbare*, fr. *de-* + *-albare* (fr. *albus* white) — more at ELF] *vt* **1 :** to cover or coat (as lath, a wall, a building) with soft adhesive matter (as plaster, pitch, mud) **:** PLASTER, CLOSE, SMEAR ⟨~ the crack with plaster⟩ ⟨~ a surface with glue⟩ **2 :** to coat with something that smirches or stains ⟨~*ed* his fingers with ink⟩ **:** SOIL ⟨generally ~*s* himself with soup and grease —Earl of Chesterfield⟩ **3** *obs* **:** to cover with a specious or deceitful exterior ⟨he ~*ed* his vice with show of virtue —Shak.⟩ **4** *dial Eng* **:** to array tastelessly esp. in a gaudy manner **5 :** to apply paint or other coloring material crudely, hastily, or unskillfully to ⟨their faces ~*ed* a savage black —T.B.Costain⟩ ⟨~*ed* her lips with lipstick⟩ **:** apply (colors) in such a way ⟨like an artist ~*ing* unimportant touches of paint on a finished picture —Winifred Bambrick⟩ ~ *vi* **1** *now dial* **:** to put on a false exterior in order to make an impression **2 :** to paint or apply colors in a crude, amateur, or unskillful manner ⟨Awful Arts Club . . . which has been ~*ing* for ten years —Joseph Alger⟩

²daub \"\ *n* -s [ME *dawbe*, fr. *dauben*, v.] **1 :** material (as plaster, mortar, clay, mud) used with straw or hay or roughcast to daub walls ⟨old house . . . built of wattle and ~ —G.E. Fussell⟩ — compare WATTLE **2 :** the act or an instance of daubing ⟨a few hasty ~*s* and the picture was ready⟩ **3 a :** something daubed on; *esp* **:** a viscous sticky application or a daubed spot, smear, or patch of paint **b :** something resembling or suggestive of a hastily or crudely applied touch, smear, or splash of paint ⟨great ~*s* of brilliant-colored fabrics were stretched out on tables —Winifred Bambrick⟩ **4 :** a picture coarsely and unskillfully executed

³daub \"\ *var of* DAB

daube \'dōb\ *n* -s [F] **:** a braised meat stew

dau·ben·to·nia \ˌdōbən'tōnēə\ *n, cap* [NL, fr. Louis J. M. *Daubenton* †1800 Fr. naturalist + NL *-ia*] **:** a genus (coextensive with the family Daubentoniidae) of lemuriform primates comprising solely the aye-aye of Madagascar

dau·ben·ton's plane \'dōbən-,tōⁿz-, dōbäⁿtōⁿz-\ *n, usu cap D* [after L. J. M. *Daubenton*] *anthrop* **:** a plane that passes through the opisthion and the orbital points on a skull

daub·er \'dóbə(r), 'däb-\ *n* -s [ME, fr. AF *daubour*, fr. OF *dauber* to plaster + *-our* -or — more at DAUB] **1 :** one that daubs: as **a :** PLASTERER **b :** a worker who seals with clay the doors of kilns in which brick and tile are burned **c :** LUTER **d :** a crude unskillful painter **e** *slang* **:** SPIRITS, COURAGE ⟨just keep your ~ up an' your mouth shut —Harold Sinclair⟩ ⟨the boys were depressed . . . their ~ was down —Ring Lardner⟩ **f :** MUD WASP **2 :** something (as a brush or pad) used for daubing

daub·ery \-b(ə)rē\ *also* **daub·ry** \-brē\ *n* -ES [¹*daub* + *-ery*, *-ry*] **1 :** the act of daubing **2 a** *archaic* **:** a dauber's work **b** *obs* **:** a misuse of or misrepresentation by words **:** mystifying action

daubing *n* -s [ME, fr. gerund of *dauben* to daub] **1 a :** the material (as clay or mortar) with which something is daubed **b :** ¹DUBBIN **2 :** the action of daubing **3 a :** the action of painting unskillfully or crudely **b :** a painting crudely or unskillfully done **4** *obs* **:** insincere praise **:** FLATTERY

daub·ing·ly *adv* **:** in a daubing manner

dau·bree·ite *or* **dau·bre·ite** \'dóbrē,īt, dō'brā,-\ *n* -s [F *daubréite*, fr. Gabriel A. *Daubrée* †1896 Fr. geologist and mineralogist + F *-ite*] **:** a mineral BiO(OH,Cl) consisting of a yellowish earthy bismuth oxychloride

dau·bree·lite \-ē,līt, -ā,l-\ *n* -s [G. A. *Daubrée* + E *-lite*] **:** a mineral $FeCr_2S_4$ consisting of a black chromium iron sulfide occurring in some meteoric irons (sp. gr. 5.01)

daub·ster \'dóbztə(r), 'däb-, -bst-\ *n* -s [¹*daub* + *-ster*] **:** a bungler in painting **:** DAUBER

dauby \'dóbē, 'däb-\ *adj, usu* -ER/-EST **1 :** of the nature of or like daub or a daub **2 :** crudely executed ⟨a ~ painting⟩ **:** SMEARY, ADHESIVE ⟨a ~ wax⟩

dau·cus \'dókəs\ *n, cap* [NL, fr. L *daucus, daucum*, a kind of parsnip or wild carrot, fr. Gk *daukos, daukon*; perh. akin to Gk *daiein* to ignite, burn; fr. the sharp taste or fr. the combustible sap some species exude — more at TEEN] **:** a genus of chiefly Old World herbs (family Umbelliferae) having compound umbels of mostly white flowers and having prickly fruit — see CARROT, WILD CARROT

daud \'dód, 'dȯd\ *var of* ³·⁴DAD

dau·er·lauf \'daù(ə)r,laùf\ *n, pl* **dauerlaufs** \-fs\ *or* **dauer·läu·fe** \-lóifə\ [G, fr. *dauer-* long-lasting (fr. *dauern* to last, fr. MHG *dūren, tūren*, fr. MLG *dūren*, fr. L *durare*) + *lauf* race, run, running, fr. OHG *louf* — more at DURE, LEAP] **:** a long-distance cross-country ski race of approximately 35 miles — compare LANGLAUF

dauer·modification \ˌdaù(ə)r + \ *or* **dauer·modi·fi·ka·tion** \+ mōdēfēkätsē'ōn\ *n, pl* **dauermodifications** \-shənz\ *or* **dauermodifikati·o·nen** \-ē'ōnən\ [G *dauermodifikation*, fr. *dauer-*, long-lasting, permanent + *modifikation* modification, fr. F *modification* — more at MODIFICATION] **:** an acquired character transmitted through the cytoplasm to several succeeding generations but not incorporated into the permanent heredity of the strain

¹daugh·ter \'dó|d·ə(r), 'dä|, |tə-, *archaic* 'da| *or* 'dä|\ *n* -s [ME *doughter*, fr. OE *dohtor*; akin to OHG *tohter* daughter, ON *dōttir*, Goth *dauhtar*, Gk *thygatēr*, Skt *duhitṛ*] **1 :** a human female having the relation of child to a parent **2 :** a human female descended from remote ancestors **:** female descendant **:** girl or woman of a given lineage **3 :** a female subject to the authority or love of a parent — used esp. as a term of address indicating affectionate interest by an elder **4 :** a female offspring of an animal — used chiefly of pedigreed stock or bloodstock **5 :** something derived from its source or origin as if feminine ⟨the United States is a ~ of Great Britain⟩ **6** *archaic* **:** a young woman **:** MAIDEN ⟨as the lily among thorns, so is my love among the ~*s* —*Song of Sol* 2:2 (AV)⟩ **7 a :** a female native of a specified place or land ⟨~*s* of Egypt⟩ **b :** a female in a spiritual kinship analogous to the physical ⟨~*s* of the church⟩ **8 :** the atomic species that is the immediate product of the radioactive decay of a given element ⟨radon, the ~ of radium⟩

²daughter \"\ *adj* **1 :** having the characteristics of a daughter or relationship of or as if of a daughter **2 :** having the relation of offspring of the first generation **:** resulting from a primary division — used without reference to sex ⟨~ cell⟩ **3 a** *of a manuscript, text, or reading* **:** immediately derived from a previous manuscript, text, or reading **b** *of a language* **:** related to another language in a way that implies a common beginning

daughter-in-law \-ə(r)ən,lò, -ərn-\ *n, pl* **daughters-in-law** \-ə(r)zən-\ [ME *doughter in lawe*] **:** the wife of one's son

daugh·ter·li·ness *pronunc at* DAUGHTERLY + nəs\ *n* -ES **:** the quality or state of being daughterly

daugh·ter·ly \-ərlē, -li, -*R* -əl- *or* -ᵊl-\ *adj* **:** befitting a daughter **:** FILIAL

daughter of mary *usu cap D&M* [after the Virgin *Mary*] **:** GUASTALLINE

daunch \'dónch, -ä-,-á-\ *adj* [ME *daunche*] *now dial* **:** SQUEAMISH

dauncy \'dón(t)sē, 'dän-\ *var of* DONSIE

daun·der *or* **dau·ner** \'dän(d)ər, 'dón-\ *Scot var of* ¹·²DANDER

¹daunt \'dónt, -ä-,-á-\ *vt* -ED/-ING/-S [ME *daunten* (also, to tame), fr. OF *danter*, alter. (prob. influenced by OF *dangier* power, jurisdiction) of *donter*, fr. L *domitare* to tame, fr. *domitus*, past part. of *domare* to tame, conquer — more at DANGER, TAME] **1** *now dial* **:** to get the better of **:** CONQUER, SUBDUE **2 :** to sap the courage of and subdue through fear **:** DISCOURAGE, INTIMIDATE ⟨obstacles that would have ~*ed* a man of less intrepid mind —Adeline Adams⟩ **syn** see DISMAY

²daunt \", -a-\ *n* -s [ME, fr. *daunten*, v.] *now dial Eng* **:** DISCOURAGEMENT

daunt·ing·ly *adv* **:** in a manner or to a degree that daunts ⟨~ difficult —Philip Toynbee⟩

daunt·less \'dóntləs, -'ä-,-'á-\ *adj* **:** marked by courageous resolution **:** incapable of being daunted, intimidated, or subdued ⟨a ~ captain⟩ ⟨a ~ spirit⟩ **syn** see BRAVE

daunt·less·ly *adv* **:** in a dauntless manner

daunt·less·ness *n* -ES **:** the quality of being dauntless **:** COURAGE, BRAVERY

dau·ton \'dóntᵊn, -'ä-,-'a-\ *vt* -ED/-ING/-S [by alter.] *archaic Scot* **:** ¹DAUNT

dau·phin \'dófən, 'dó,faⁿ, 'dō,faⁿ\ *n* -s *often cap* [alter. (influenced by F *dauphin*, fr. OF *dolfin*) of earlier *daulphin*, *dolphin*, fr. ME *dolphyn*, fr. MF *dalfin, dalphin*, fr. *Dalfin, Dolphin*, the surname of certain lords in medieval southeastern France] **1 :** a feudal lord of a French territory or province **2** [MF *dalfin, dalphin*; fr. the fact that the assumption of this title by the eldest sons of the kings of France was a condition of the cession of the Dauphiné to the house of Valois in the 14th cent.] **:** the eldest son of the king of France — used as a title for the eldest sons from the 14th century to 1830

¹dau·phine \dó'fēn, dō'-, 'ˌ\ *n* -s *often cap* [F, fr. MF *daufine, dalfine*, fem. of *dalfin*] **:** DAUPHINESS

²dau·phi·né \ˌdófə¦nā, ¦dōf-\ *adj* [F (*à la*) *Dauphiné*, lit., in the manner of Dauphiné, region in southeastern France] *of potatoes* **:** mashed, shaped into balls, and fried usu. in deep fat

dau·phin·ess \'dófənəs\ *n, pl* **dauphinesses** *often cap* [fr. earlier *daulphinesse, dolphinesse*, fr. *daulphin, dolphyn* dauphin + *-esse* -ess] **:** the wife of the dauphin

¹daur \'dár\ *Scot var of* DARE

²daur \'daù(ə)r\ *n, pl* **daur** \"\ *or* **dau·ri** \-)rē\ *usu cap* **:** a member of certain Manchu-Tungus peoples of the Amur basin related to the Manchus

dau·ri·an \'daùrēən\ *n* -s *usu cap* [²*Daur* + E *-ian*] **:** DAUR

daur·na \'därnə\ [¹*daur* + *na*] *chiefly Scot* **:** dare not

daut *or* **dawt** \'dát, -ó-\ *vt* [origin unknown] *chiefly Scot* **:** to make much of **:** FONDLE, CARESS

daut·ie *or* **dawt·ie** \-ti\ *n* -s [*daut, dawt* + *-ie*] *chiefly Scot* **:** DARLING, DEAR

daut·it \-tət\ *past of* DAUT

dauw \'daù\ *n* -s [obs. Afrik (now *dou*), fr. a native word in southern Africa] **:** BURCHELL'S ZEBRA

dav·ach *or* **dav·och** \'davək\ *n* -s [ME (Sc dial.), fr. ScGael *dabhach* (also, tub); akin to OIr *dabach* tub, land measure] *archaic* **:** any of various ancient Scottish units of land area said to have averaged 416 acres

da·vai·nea \də'vānēə\ *n* [NL, after Casimir J. *Davaine* †1882 Fr. physician] **1** *cap* **:** a genus of very small taenioid tapeworms infesting the intestine of gallinaceous birds and occas. of man **2** -s **:** any tapeworm of the genus *Davainea* — **da·vai·ne·id** \-ēəd\ *adj or n*

dav·ai·ne·i·dae \ˌdavə'nēə,dē\ *n pl, cap* [NL, fr. *Davainea*, type genus + *-idae*] **:** a family of small primitive cyclophyllidean tapeworms (type genus *Davainea*) that are chiefly parasites of birds and that have an armed cushion-shaped rostellum, the suckers also often with hooks, and the larva a cysticercoid — see RAILLIETINA

da·val·lia \də'valēə\ *n* [NL, fr. Edmund *Davall* †1798 Eng. botanist in Switzerland + NL *-ia*] **1** *cap* **:** a genus of Old World tropical ferns (family Polypodiaceae) having scaly creeping rhizomes and ample pinnate or pinnately decompound fronds with marginal sori and cuplike indusia which open toward the leaf apex **2** -s **:** any plant of the genus *Davallia*

da·vao \'dä,vaù, də'v-\ *adj, usu cap* [fr. *Davao*, Philippines] **:** of or from the city of Davao, Philippines **:** of the kind or style prevalent in Davao

da·ven \'dävən, 'dóv-\ *vi* -ED/-ING/-S [Yiddish *davnen* to pray, worship] **:** to recite the prescribed prayers in the daily and festival Jewish liturgies

dav·en·port \'davən,pō|rt, 'davᵊm,p-, 'dabᵊm,p-, -ór|,-ōə|, -ó(ə)|, *usu* |d· + V\ *n* -s [origin unknown] **1 :** a small writing desk **2 :** a large upholstered sofa often convertible into a bed

davenport open for use as a bed

¹da·ver \'dāvər\ *vb* [perh. freq. of *deave*] *vi* **1** *chiefly Scot* **:** to move about as if in a stupor **:** STAGGER **2** *Scot* **:** to wander in mind ~ *vt* **1** *Scot* **:** STUN, DAZE **2** *Scot* **:** CHILL, BENUMB

²da·ver \'dāvə(r), 'dəv-\ *vi* [origin unknown] *dial Eng* **:** FADE, WITHER

¹da·vid·ian \də'vidēən, dā'-\ *n* -s *usu cap* [*David* (Jan) Joris (Joriszoon) †1556 Flemish Anabaptist + E *-ian*] **:** DAVIDIST 2

²da·vid·ian \də'vidēən, da'-,dā'-, -vēd-\ *adj, usu cap* [Jacques Louis *David* †1825 Fr. painter + E *-ian*] **:** of, relating to, or like Jacques Louis David or his paintings

da·vid·ic \(')dā¦vidik, də'v-\ *adj, usu cap* [*David* †ab 973B.C. king of Judah and Israel + E *-ic*] **:** of or relating to King David or his family

da·vid·ist \'dāvədəst\ *n* -s *usu cap* [in sense 1, fr. *David* of Dinant *fl* 1200 Belgian scholastic philosopher + E *-ist*; in sense 2, fr. *David* Joris + E *-ist*; in sense 3, fr. Francis *David* †1579 Transylvanian theologist + E *-ist*] **1 :** a follower of the philosopher David of Dinant **2 :** a follower of the theologist David Joris — called also *Davidian, Jorist* **3 :** a follower of the anti-Trinitarian theologist Francis David

david's-harp \'ˌˌ\ *n, pl* **david's-harps** *usu cap D* [after King *David*, who once charmed King Saul with his harp (1 Sam 16:23—AV); fr. the similarity of its flowering stalk to David's harp in old Biblical illustrations] **:** a Solomon's seal (*Polygonatum multiflorum*)

da·vid·son·ite \'dāvədsə,nīt, ÷ -vəs-\ *n* -s [Thomas *Davidson* †1885 Brit. paleontologist who discovered it near Aberdeen, Scotland + E *-ite*] **:** a greenish variety of beryl

da·vid·son's plum \-sənz-\ *n* [fr. the name *Davidson*] **1 :** the fruit of an Australian tree (*Davidsonia pruriens*) of the family Cunoniaceae having a sharply acid reddish blue juice **2 :** the tree that bears the Davidson's plum

da·vid's squirrel \dä'vēdz-, 'dāvədz-\ *n, usu cap D* [after Abbé Armand *David* †1900 Fr. missionary and naturalist] **:** a grayish cliff-dwelling ground squirrel (*Sciurotamias davidianus*) occurring in several races in mountainous southern China

da·vie·ly \'dāvili\ *adv* [perh. alter. of Sc *davert* (past part. of ¹*daver*) + *-ly*] *Scot* **:** LISTLESSLY

da·vie·sia \dā'vēzh(ē)ə, dō'-\ *n, cap* [NL, fr. Hugh *Davies* †1821 Brit. botanist + NL *-ia*] **:** a large genus of Australasian shrubs (family Leguminosae) having small yellow or purple flowers succeeded by short triangular pods

da·vies·ite \'dāvē,zīt, -və,sīt\ *n* -s [Thomas *Davies* †1891 Eng. mineralogist + E *-ite*] **:** a mineral consisting of a lead oxychloride occurring in minute colorless orthorhombic crystals

da·vi·son·ite \'dāvəsə,nīt\ *n* -s *usu cap* [John M. *Davison* †1915 Amer. chemist and mineralogist + E *-ite*] **:** a mineral $Ca_3Al(PO_4)_2(OH)_3.H_2O(?)$ consisting of a hydrous basic phosphate of calcium and aluminum

da·vit \ˈdāvət *also* ˈdav-; *by most speakers* -vəd· *when a vowel immediately follows, and by seamen sometimes* -āvəd *in all positions*\ *n* -s [alter. of earlier *david,* prob. fr. the name *David*] **:** a fixed or movable crane that projects over the side of a ship or over a hatchway and is used esp. for hoisting ship's boats, anchors, or cargo

1, 1, davits

davoch *var of* DAVACH

da·vy \ˈdāvē\ *n* -ES [by shortening & alter.] *slang* **:** AFFIDAVIT

da·vy jones's locker \ˌdāvēˈjōnz(əz)-\ *n, usu cap D&J* [after *Davy Jones,* legendary spirit of the sea] **:** the bottom of the ocean **:** a grave in the sea ⟨gone down to *Davy Jones's locker*⟩

da·vy lamp \ˈdāvē-\ *n, usu cap D* [after Sir Humphry *Davy* †1829 Eng. chemist, its inventor] **:** an early safety lamp

davy's gray *n, often cap D* [prob. after Sir Humphry *Davy*] **:** STEEL GRAY

¹daw \ˈdȯ, ˈdä\ *vi* **dawed** \-ȧd,-ȯd\ *or sometimes* **dew** \ˈd(y)ü\ **daw·en** \ˈdȧən, ˈdȯən\ *or sometimes* **dawed; dawing; daws** [ME *dawen, dagen,* fr. OE *dagian;* akin to OHG *tagēn* to dawn, ON *daga,* denominatives fr. the root of E *day*] *chiefly Scot* **:** DAWN

²daw \ˈdȯ, *Scot* ˈdȧ *or* ˈdō\ *n* -S [ME *dawe;* akin to OHG *taha* jackdaw] **1 :** JACKDAW **2** *obs* **:** NITWIT, SIMPLETON, FOOL **3** *Scot* **a :** a lazy person **:** SLUGGARD **b :** a slovenly woman **:** SLATTERN

³daw *vt* -ED/-ING/-S [short for *adaw*] *obs* **:** DAUNT

⁴daw \ˈdō\ *n* -S [IrGael & ScGael *dath* color, dye, stain, fr. OIr *dath* color; akin to OIr *date* agreeable] **:** the pinkish yellow color of the eyes of some game fowls

¹daw·dle \ˈdȯdᵊl\ *vb* **dawdled; dawdled; dawdling** \-ȯd-(ᵊ)liŋ\ **dawdles** [origin unknown] *vi* **:** to waste time in idle lingering **:** spend more time than is necessary or usual in doing something ⟨~ over your work⟩ **:** LOITER ⟨*dawdled* about in the vestibule —Jane Austen⟩ ~ *vt* **:** to spend fruitlessly **:** WASTE ⟨*dawdled* my time with . . . symbolic logic —M.R.Cohen⟩ **:** spend lackadaisically ⟨~ away their vacation —Angus Wilson⟩ ⟨~ away four years in college⟩ **syn** see DELAY

²dawdle \"\ *n* -S **1 :** DAWDLER **2 :** the act or an instance of dawdling ⟨a . . . ~ over some of the book catalogs —O.W. Holmes †1935⟩

daw·dler \-ȯd(ᵊ)lə(r)\ *n* -S **:** one that dawdles **:** IDLER

daw·dling·ly *adv* **:** in a dawdling manner

daw·dling·ness *n* -ES **:** the quality or state of being dawdling

dawes' limit \ˈdȯz(əz)-\ *n, usu cap D* [after William R. *Dawes* †1868 Eng. astronomer] **:** an approximate value of the resolving power of a telescope based on the theoretical size of the spurious disk being equal in seconds of arc to 4.56 divided by the aperture of the telescope expressed in inches

¹dawn \ˈdȯn, ˈdän\ *vi* -ED/-ING/-S [ME *dawnen,* prob. back-formation fr. *dawning*] **1 :** to begin to grow light in the morning **:** grow light with or as if with the light of the rising sun ⟨the day ~*s*⟩ **2 :** to make an initial appearance **:** begin to develop ⟨the day of mammals had ~*ed* —W.E.Swinton⟩ ⟨a watery smile ~*ed* on Joe's face —Marguerite Steen⟩ **3 :** to become apparent **:** begin to be perceived or understood — usu. used with *on* ⟨it ~*ed* on me that he was an utter fool⟩ ⟨the truth ~*ed* on him at last —T.B.Costain⟩

²dawn \"\ *n* -S **1 :** the first appearance of light in the morning **:** show of approaching sunrise **:** morning twilight **:** DAYBREAK ⟨by the ~'*s* early light —F.S.Key⟩ **2 :** first appearance **:** OPENING, BEGINNING ⟨~ of the Renaissance⟩ ⟨~ of human consciousness —W.J.Reilly⟩ **3 :** a moderate pink that is yellower and less strong than arbutus pink and bluer and stronger than hydrangea pink

dawn blue *n* **:** a pale blue that is redder and paler than average powder blue or Sistine and greener and paler than average cadet gray

dawn gray *n* **:** a medium gray that is very slightly darker than platinum

dawn-horse \ˈ≈,≈\ *n* [trans. of NL *Eohippus*] **:** a member of the genus *Eohippus*

dawn·ing \ˈdȯniŋ, ˈdän-, -nēn\ *n* -S [ME *dawning, dawening,* alter. (influenced by ME *evening*) of *dawing,* fr. OE *dagung,* fr. *dagian* to dawn + *-ung* -ing — more at DAW] **1 :** DAYBREAK, DAWN ⟨in the gray of cold ~*s* —Ethel Wilson⟩ **2 :** BEGINNING ⟨the ~ of the Gilded Age —J.D.Hart⟩

dawn man *n, often cap D&M* [trans. of NL *Eoanthropus*] **1 :** a primitive extinct man **2 :** PILTDOWN MAN

dawn patrol *n* **1 :** a reconnaissance flight made in the early morning usu. to observe enemy positions or movements **2 :** station personnel who prepare and put on very early morning radio or television programs

dawn pink *n* **:** a grayish purplish pink that is redder, less strong, and slightly darker than average orchid mist and redder and less strong than cameo pink

dawn redwood *n* **:** a Chinese redwood (*Metasequoia glyptostroboides*) resembling the American Coast redwood but having ascending branches and deciduous foliage

dawn stone *n* **:** EOLITH

daw·ny \ˈdȯni, ˈdäni\ *adj* [IrGael *donaidhe;* akin to MIr *dona* wretched] **1** *Irish* **:** in poor health **:** SICKLY **2** *Irish* **:** SMALL, PUNY

daws *pres 3d sing of* DAW, *pl of* DAW

daw·so·nia \dȯˈsōnēə, -nyə\ *n, cap* [NL, fr. *Dawson* Turner †1858 Eng. botanist + NL *-ia*] **:** a genus (the type of the family Dawsoniaceae) of large tufted erect mosses occurring in Australasia and the East Indies and having a dorsiventral capsule and a peristome subtended by numerous filamentous hairs — see DAWSONIALES, GIANT MOSS

daw·so·ni·a·les \(ˌ)dȯˌsōnēˈā(ˌ)lēz\ *n pl, cap* [NL, fr. *Dawsonia* + *-ales*] **:** an order of musci that is closely related to and sometimes included in the order Polytrichales from which it differs chiefly in the form of the capsule and in the size of the gametophore and that is coextensive with the genus *Dawsonia*

daw·son·ite \ˈdȯsᵊnˌīt\ *n* -S [Sir John W. *Dawson* †1899 Canad. geologist + E *-ite*] **:** a mineral $NaAl(CO_3)(OH)_2$ consisting of a basic aluminum sodium carbonate occurring in white bladed crystals (sp. gr. 2.40)

dawt *var of* DAUT

dawtie *var of* DAUTIE

dawt·it \ˈdȧtət, ˈdȯt-\ *past of* DAWT

¹day \ˈdā\ *n* -S [ME, fr. OE *dæg;* akin to OHG *tag* day, ON *dagr,* Goth *dags,* OE *dōgor* day, ON *dægr, dœgn* twelve-hour period, day, night; all prob. fr. a prehistoric Gmc blend of a form or forms akin to Skt *ahn-, ahar* twelve-hour period, day, night and a form or forms akin to L *fovēre* to warm, Gk *tephra* ashes, Skt *dahati* he burns] **1 :** the time of light or interval between one night and the next **:** the time between sunrise and sunset or from dawn to darkness **2 :** the period of the earth's rotation on its axis ordinarily divided into 24 hours, measured by the interval between two successive transits of a celestial body over the same meridian, and taking a specific name from that of the body — see SOLAR DAY, MEAN SOLAR DAY, SIDEREAL DAY **3 a :** CIVIL DAY **b** *among most modern nations* **:** the mean solar day of 24 hours beginning at mean midnight **4 a :** a day set aside for a particular purpose ⟨rent ~⟩ ⟨Monday is wash ~⟩ **b** *sometimes cap* (1) **:** a date on which some notable event occurred or on which the occurrence of a notable event is celebrated ⟨your wedding ~⟩ ⟨New Year's *Day*⟩ (2) **:** a particular day that is identified by reference to or that is commonly associated with some unique historical event ⟨Pearl Harbor *Day*⟩ **c :** the conflict or contention of the day ⟨he was confident he could carry the ~⟩ **d** *archaic* **:** one's set day of the week or month for receiving callers **e** *Scot* **:** TODAY — used with *the* **f** *sometimes cap* **:** a date on which some major event is expected to occur — used with *the* ⟨socialists of the eighties and nineties who . . . yearned for The *Day* —E.R. Bentley⟩ **5 :** DAYLIGHT ⟨at the break of ~⟩ **6 a :** the period of the existence or prominence of a person or thing **:** AGE — usu. used in pl. ⟨in the ~*s* of sailing ships⟩ **b :** the term of one's career, activity, or life **:** LIFETIME ⟨grandfather's stories about sports in his ~⟩ **:** the time during which one's life continues — used in pl. ⟨the general's last ~*s*⟩ **7 a :** a unit of distance traversed in an ordinary day's travel ⟨a ship two ~*s* out of port⟩ **b :** a unit consisting of the labor or output of one individual in one day **8** *obs* **a :** a period of grace esp. for debtors **b :** a space of time **9 a :** the hours or the daily recurring period established by usage or law for work ⟨an 8-hour ~⟩ **b :** a trading session on an exchange ⟨a 3,000,000-share ~⟩ **c :** a conventional unit for calculating pay of railroad employees based on hours worked and distance run **10 :** a division of a window **:** LIGHT **11 :** the time required by a celestial body in turning once on its axis ⟨the moon's ~ is 27 solar days⟩ **12 :** the surface of the ground over a mine — **day after day :** continuously over a period of time measured in days ⟨watching the horizon for a sail *day after day*⟩ **:** for an indefinite or seemingly endless number of days — **day in, day out :** for an indefinite number of successive days without interruption, change, or rest ⟨he does nothing but work *day in, day out*⟩ — **from day to day 1 :** in such a way as to be noticeable or measurable each successive day ⟨he improves *from day to day*⟩ **2 :** without looking further than one day ahead **:** from one day to the next — **this day week :** the same day a week after or before — **without day :** sine die

²day \"\ *vt* -ED/-ING/-S *archaic* **:** to measure by the day

day·ak *also* **dy·ak** \ˈdīˌak, -ˌīək\ *n, pl* **dayak** *or* **dayaks** *usu cap* [Malay *dayak* up-country] **1 a :** any of several Indonesian peoples in the interior regions of Borneo — compare IBAN, KENYA, LAND DAYAK, NGADJU **b :** a member of any of such peoples **2 :** the language of the Dayak peoples

da·yan \dä'yän, dī-, -yōn\ *n, pl* **daya·nim** \-nəm\ *also* **dayans** \-nz\ [Heb *dayyān*] **:** a judge in a rabbinical court **:** an expert in Jewish law to whom rabbis in orthodox Jewish communities refer questions about matters of religious observance

day beacon *n* **:** any of various unlighted structures (as a masonry tower) serving as a daytime aid to navigation

daybed \ˈ≈,≈\ *n* **1 :** a chaise longue of the type made 1680–1780 **2 :** a couch with low head and foot pieces often like chair backs

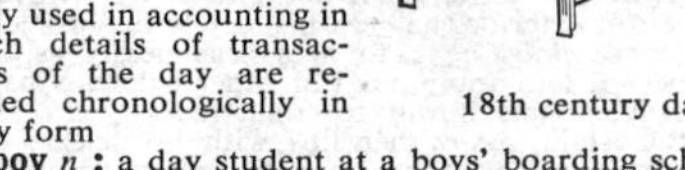

18th century daybed

day·ber·ry \ˈdā- —*see* BERRY\ *n* [fr. earlier *dabberry, deberry*] *dial Eng* **:** a wild gooseberry

day blindness *n* **:** HEMERALOPIA

daybook \ˈ≈,≈\ *n* **1 :** DIARY, JOURNAL **2 :** a book formerly used in accounting in which details of transactions of the day are recorded chronologically in diary form

day boy *n* **:** a day student at a boys' boarding school esp. in Great Britain

daybreak \ˈ≈,≈\ *n* **:** the first appearance of light in the morning or the time of such appearance **:** DAWN

day-by-day \ˌdā(ˌ)bīˈdā, -ˌbəˈ-\ *adj* [ME *day by day* daily, adv.] **:** occurring on each successive day **:** DAILY ⟨*day-by-day* labors of thousands of men and women —H.S.Truman⟩

day camp *n* **:** a camp providing activities and care for children during the daytime only

day coach *n* **:** COACH 1c

daydawn \ˈ≈,≈\ *n, archaic* **:** DAYBREAK

day degree *n* **:** one degree above or below a temperature adopted as a standard (as 42° F for the temperature at which vegetation commences) for a period of 24 hours or its equivalent (as 2° for 12 hours or 4° for 6 hours)

¹daydream \ˈ≈,≈\ *n* [*day* + *dream*] **:** a dream experienced while awake; *esp* **:** a gratifying reverie usu. of wish fulfillment **syn** see FANCY

²daydream \"\ *vi* **:** to engage in daydreams ⟨the chance to ~ about a world which has never existed —Maurice Edelman⟩ ~ *vt* **:** to transport (oneself) by or as if by daydreams ⟨the handyman and the little dancer ~ themselves into the leading parts . . . of the ballet —George Amberg⟩ **:** imagine in or as if in a daydream

day·dream·er \-mə(r)\ *n* **:** one that daydreams

day·dreamy \-mē, -mi\ *adj* **1 :** having the quality of a daydream **2 :** given to daydreams

day drift *n, mining* **:** a drift with one end at the surface so that daylight is admitted

day fighter *n* **:** a short-range fighter-interceptor designed for high-speed interception of enemy aircraft in conditions of good visibility and daylight

dayflower \ˈ≈,≈\ *n* **:** any of several flowers that soon perish: as **a :** a plant of the genus *Commelina; esp* **:** a troublesome weed (*C. communis*) **b :** SPIDERWORT **c :** a rockrose (*Cistus ladaniferus*) of southern Europe with large white yellow-spotted flowers

day gate *n* **:** an inner grating used while a safety vault is open

day in court 1 : a day or opportunity for appearance in a lawsuit **2 :** an opportunity to present one's point of view or argument ⟨Republicans had apparently not bothered to prepare for their biggest *day in court* —*Time*⟩

day jessamine *n* **:** a West Indian aromatic shrub (*Cestrum diurnum*) whose white flowers are sweet-scented by day

day labor *n* [ME *dai labour*] **1 :** labor performed as a daily task **:** labor done or paid for by the day **2 :** laborers hired by the day — usu. used of persons without special training

day laborer *n* **:** one that works by the day or for daily wages esp. as an unskilled laborer

day·less \ˈdāləs\ *adj* **:** lacking daylight

day letter *n* **:** a telegram sent during the day that has a lower priority than a regular telegram

¹daylight \ˈ≈,≈\ *n* [ME, fr. *day* + *light*] **1 :** the light of day as opposed to the darkness of night **:** the light of the sun plus the sky as opposed to that of the moon or to artificial light; *often* **:** the diffused and reflected light of the sun and the sky as distinguished from sunlight and from artificial light **2 :** DAYTIME **3 :** the time of daylight **:** DAYBREAK ⟨arise before ~⟩ **4 a :** knowledge or understanding of something that has been obscure or of something that could not be foretold ⟨the professor's lecture threw some ~ on the problem⟩ **b :** OPENNESS, PUBLICITY ⟨the new diplomacy . . . has to operate in ~ —Dag Hammarskjöld⟩ **5 daylights** *pl* **a** *archaic* **:** EYES **b :** INNARDS ⟨walloped the ~*s* out of him —Dan Polier⟩ ⟨brutishly whacking the ~*s* out of the ball —Frank Gibney⟩; *also* **:** WITS ⟨scare the ~*s* out of you —E.A.McCourt⟩ **6 :** a clear or open space ⟨you could see ~ between the cracks⟩; *esp* **:** the maximum distance between the chase bed and the platen of a platen press

²daylight \"\ *vb* **daylighted; daylighted** *also* **daylit; daylighting; daylights** *vt* **:** to provide or light up (as a classroom) with daylight ~ *vi* **:** to supply daylight

daylight blue *n* **1 :** a pigment prepared by mixing Prussian blue with barium sulfate **2 :** the color of average daylight considered a blue if skylight under average noon sunlight is taken as gray or neutral but closely approximating gray if according to the practice of recent years overcast skylight or sunlight outside the earth's atmosphere is taken as the neutral gray

daylight factor *n* **:** the ratio of the illumination from windows at any point indoors to that out in the open, the test surface being horizontal in each case — called also *window-efficiency ratio*

daylight glass *n* **:** a bluish glass often colored with cobalt that is used with incandescent lamps to absorb the excess radiations in the red part of the spectrum and thus give the effect of daylight

daylight lamp *n* **:** an incandescent or fluorescent lamp that gives an artificial light whose energy distribution approximates that of daylight

daylight saving time *also* **daylight saving** *or* **daylight time** *n* **:** time that is ahead of standard time usu. by one hour but sometimes by two hours and that is used in some places esp. in spring, summer, and fall for the purpose of utilizing all the daylight hours for daytime activities — abbr. *DST*

daylight train *n* **:** DAY TRAIN

daylight vision *n* **:** vision adapted to daylight **:** photopic vision

day lily *n* [so called fr. the fact that each blooms for only one day] **1 a :** a plant of the genus *Hemerocallis* being native to Europe and Asia but cosmopolitan in cultivation and as escapes, having complex tuberous roots and long narrow basal leaves, and bearing short-lived flowers that resemble lilies and are yellow or tawny orange in the wild but under cultivation have developed pinkish and mahogany to purplish forms **b :** the flower of a day lily **2 :** PLANTAIN LILY

day loan *n* **:** a bank loan maturing within a day usu. on an unsecured promissory note — called also *clearance loan, morning loan*

¹daylong \ˈ≈,≈\ *adj* **:** lasting all day ⟨a ~ parade⟩

²daylong \ˈ≈,≈\ *adv* **:** during the entire day ⟨light of the sun pours ~ into the saw grass —Marjory S. Douglas⟩

day·man \ˈdāmən, -ˌman\ *n, pl* **daymen 1 :** a worker paid by time rather than piecework **:** DAY LABORER **2 :** one (as a stagehand or sailor) who works during the daytime

daymare \ˈ≈,≈\ *n* -S [¹*day* + *-mare* (as in *nightmare*)] **:** distress while awake like that experienced in nightmare

daymark \ˈ≈,≈\ *n* **:** a marker visible to pilots as a navigation guide in daylight

daynet *n, obs* **:** CLAPNET

day nettle *n* [*day* prob. by folk etymology fr. a word of Scand origin; akin to ON *akrdāi* hemp nettle, Faroese *dāi,* Norw *dåe, dæe,* Sw *då;* akin to ON *dā* senselessness, *deyja* to die — more at DIE] **:** HEMP NETTLE

day neutral *adj* **:** developing and maturing regardless of relative length of alternating exposures to light and dark periods — compare PHOTOPERIODISM

day nursery *n* **:** a public center for the care and training of young children; *often* **:** NURSERY SCHOOL

day of atonement *usu cap D&A* [trans. of Heb *yōm kippūr*] **:** YOM KIPPUR

day of fire : a unit of ammunition based on the average expenditure of a weapon in a day of combat

day of judgment *usu cap D&J* [trans. of Heb *yōm haddīn* (the) day (of) the judgment] **1 :** JUDGMENT DAY **2 :** ROSH HASHANAH

day of memorial *usu cap D&M* [trans. of Heb *yōm hazzikkārōn* (the) day (of) the memorial] **:** ROSH HASHANAH

day of reckoning : a time when the consequences of a course of mistakes or misdeeds are felt ⟨the flow of wealth . . . hurried overstocking and brought the *day of reckoning* nearer —R.A. Billington⟩

day of supply : a quantity (as of food, clothing or ammunition) taken as the average daily requirement of a body of troops in a given situation

day of the covenant *usu cap D&C* **:** December 16 observed in So. Africa as a legal holiday celebrating the anniversary of the defeat of the Zulu chieftain Dingaan by Dutch immigrants in 1838

day of the lord *usu cap L* [ME] **:** a day inaugurating the eternal universal rule of God: **a** *in the Old Testament* **:** an eschatological day of ultimate judgment bringing final deliverance or doom — called also *day of Yahweh* **b** *in the New Testament* **:** the triumphant day of Christ's return to earth in glory

day order *n* **:** a customer's order to a broker that expires automatically at the close of the day on which it is made if it is not executed or canceled — compare OPEN ORDER

day owl *n* **:** an owl that is partially or wholly diurnal; *esp* **:** SHORT-EARED OWL

day-peep \ˈ≈,≈\ *n, archaic* **:** DAYBREAK

day rate *n* **:** the prescribed amount of pay for a given job of work paid for by the day or hour

dayroom \ˈ≈,≈\ *n* **:** a room (as in a military barracks) fitted up for reading, writing, and recreation

day rule *n* **:** a former order of court in English law allowing a prisoner on civil process to go beyond the prison limits for a single day

days \ˈdāz\ *adv* [ME *dayes,* fr. OE *dæges,* gen. of *dæg* day — more at DAY] **:** in the daytime repeatedly ⟨works ~ and goes to school nights⟩ **:** on any day

day school *n* **:** an elementary or secondary school held on weekdays; *specif* **:** a private school without boarding facilities

day's duty *n* **:** a 24-hour tour of duty on ship

day shift *n* **:** a shift of workers who work during daylight hours

dayshine \ˈ≈,≈\ *n* **:** DAYLIGHT

dayside \ˈ≈,≈\ *n* **:** the staff that works on an afternoon edition of a newspaper — contrasted with *nightside*

day-sign \ˈ≈,≈\ *n* **:** a Maya calendar sign designating one of the 20 successive days making up a uinal

days in bank [so called fr. its originally being the practice of the Court of Common Bank in England] *English law* **:** certain days for the return of writs and the appearance of parties

days·man \ˈdāzmən\ *n, pl* **daysmen 1** [ME *dayesman,* fr. *dayes* (gen. of *day* day set for arbitration) + *-man*] *archaic* **:** UMPIRE, ARBITER ⟨neither is there any ~ betwixt us —Job 9: 33 (AV)⟩ **2** *archaic* **:** DAY LABORER

days of awe *usu cap D&A* [trans. of Heb *yāmīm nōrā'īm,* lit., fearful days] **:** the 10-day period of the Jewish high holidays including Rosh Hashanah and Yom Kippur

days of grace [trans. of L *dies gratiae*] **1 :** the days that immediately follow the day on which a bill or note becomes due on its face and that are allowed to the debtor in which to make payment **2 :** GRACE PERIOD

dayspring \ˈ≈,≈\ *n* [ME, fr. *day* + *spring*] **1** *archaic* **:** the beginning of day **:** DAWN **2 :** the beginning of a new era or order of things ⟨the ~ of their youth —W.B.Yeats⟩

daystar \ˈ≈,≈\ *n* [ME *daysterre,* fr. OE *dægsteorra,* fr. *dæg* day + *steorra* star — more at DAY, STAR] **1 :** MORNING STAR **2 :** SUN 1a

day student *also* **day scholar** *n* **:** a student at a residential school or college who attends classes and other academic exercises but does not live in the institution

day's work *n* **1 :** the amount of work during one day prescribed or required on a given job **:** the legal amount of work in terms of hours as governed by statute or by agreement **2 :** the reckoning and observations made for 24 hours from noon to noon to determine a ship's position

day·tale \ˈdātᵊl\ *n* [*day* + *tale* (count)] *dial Eng* **:** the reckoning esp. of work or wages by the day ⟨a ~ laborer⟩

day tank *n* **:** a tank furnace in which 5 to 10 tons of glass are melted and refined in one day to be hand-shaped the next day

day ticket *n, Brit* **:** a railway ticket good for only one day

daytime \ˈ≈,≈\ *n* **:** the time during which there is daylight

daytimes \-mz\ *adv* [*daytime* + *-s* (adv. suffix)] **:** during the hours of daylight

day-to-day \ˈdādəˌdā, ˈdātə-\ *adj* **1 :** a day at a time in unbroken succession **:** DAILY ⟨newspapers report *day-to-day* events⟩ **2 :** a day at a time without provision for continuance thereafter ⟨life . . . lived on an aimless, *day-to-day* basis —Siegfried Giedion⟩

day-to-day loan *or* **day-to-day money** *n, Brit* **:** CALL LOAN

day·ton \ˈdātᵊn\ *adj, usu cap* [fr. *Dayton,* Ohio] **:** of or from the city of Dayton, Ohio **:** of the kind or style prevalent in Dayton

day·to·ni·an \(ˈ)dāˈtōnēən\ *n* -s *cap* [*Dayton,* Ohio + E *-ian*] **:** a native or resident of Dayton, Ohio

day train *n* **:** a train scheduled to complete its journey during daylight hours — called also *daylight train*

daywoman *var of* DEYWOMAN

daywork \ˈ≈,≈\ *n* **1 :** work paid for at a rate per unit of time worked as distinguished from work done under a wage incentive plan **2 :** work on a day shift

dayworker \ˈ≈,≈≈\ *n* **:** one engaged in daywork

daywrit \ˈ≈,≈\ *n* **:** DAY RULE

¹daze \ˈdāz\ *vt* -ED/-ING/-S [ME *dasen,* fr. ON *dasa* (as in *dasask* to become exhausted); akin to D *dazen* to hesitate, MHG *dæsic* quiet, stupid, ON *dāsi* lazy person, and prob. to OE *demm* injury loss, L *fames* hunger] **1 :** to stupefy esp. by a blow **:** make numb **:** STUN ⟨he swung at him, *dazed* him, and drove him along the bar —Morley Callaghan⟩ **2 :** to confuse or dazzle with light ⟨the whiteness of the walls ~*s* me⟩

syn DAZE, STUN, BEMUSE, STUPEFY, TORPIFY, BENUMB, PARALYZE, and PETRIFY can apply, in common, to a forcefully disturbing experience or influence and mean, in common, to dull or deaden the powers of the mind. DAZE usu. implies a bewilderment or confusion from a blow, a shock, a sudden excess of light, and so on ⟨too stunned and *dazed* by the suddenness with which events had happened during the last twenty-four hours to be able to realize his position —Samuel Butler †1902⟩ ⟨a grief-*dazed* mother⟩ ⟨*dazed* by the lantern glare —Rudyard Kipling⟩ STUN usu. suggests the deprivation of powers of thought, or a usu. momentary loss of consciousness, from a heavy blow or something conceived of as resembling a heavy blow ⟨I was knocked headlong across the floor against the oven handle and *stunned.* I was insensible for a long time

—H.G.Wells⟩ ⟨the swing doors burst open with a crash. There was an instant's *stunned* silence —Nevil Shute⟩ ⟨a world *stunned* and only just beginning to awaken from the stupefying effect of war —Aneurin Bevan⟩ ⟨*stunned* by a sudden declaration of love⟩ BEMUSE implies an addling or muddling of the mind, typically through intoxication ⟨an alcohol-*bemused* tramp⟩ ⟨the noise of London *bemused* her more than the noise of the sea —Ngaio Marsh⟩ ⟨so *bemused* by theories of meaning that we have lost sight of what men do in fact mean —Iredell Jenkins⟩ STUPEFY heightens the implication of stupor or stupidity, implying not so much a blow or shock as some cause like an injury, intoxication, or long-continued grief or anxiety ⟨the ship . . . reeled, trembled, and stopped her way, as if [the heavy sea] had *stupefied* her —Frederick Marryat⟩ ⟨half *stupefied* with sleep and fatigue —Elizabeth Goudge⟩ ⟨a dull misery *stupefied* her thoughts —Ellen Glasgow⟩ TORPIFY is close to STUPEFY but stresses torpor of body resulting in torpor of mind and usu. implying a physical cause ⟨a drug that *torpifies* the rational faculties⟩ BENUMB applies usu. to the effect of cold in deadening the sensations or immobilizing muscle action; in extension, it strongly suggests this effect ⟨it is so cold, so dark, my senses are so *benumbed* —Charles Dickens⟩ ⟨her senses remained *benumbed* by toil —Ellen Glasgow⟩ ⟨Charlotte's cold resolution *benumbed* her courage, and she could find no immediate reply —Edith Wharton⟩ PARALYZE is often used to imply an inability to act or function that results from some dire event ⟨why does danger *paralyze* the will and intelligence of some men —Bernard De Voto⟩ ⟨the grim panic which *paralyzed* business and agriculture in the West —R.A.Billington⟩ PETRIFY emphasizes an immediate strong, figuratively paralyzing effect, usu. of fear, suggesting complete inability to move, think, or speak, and lending itself easily to conversational hyperbole ⟨the *petrifying* effect of fear —E.A.Armstrong⟩ ⟨a tiger, serenely gazing at me barely twenty yards away. I was *petrified* at first —Suresh Vaidya⟩ ⟨I was *petrified* to think my wallet had been lost⟩

²daze \"\ *n* -s **1 :** the state of being dazed ⟨went about in a ~⟩ **2 :** mica or any glittering stone

dazed \'dāzd\ *adj* [fr. past part. of E dial. *daze* to become rotten or spoiled, fr. ME *dasen* to stun] *dial Eng* **:** SPOILED, ROTTEN ⟨~ eggs⟩

daz·ed·ly \'dāzədlē\ *adv* **:** in a dazed manner

daz·ed·ness \-zədnəs\ *n* -ES [ME *dasednes*, fr. *dased* + *-nes* -ness] **:** the quality or state of being dazed **:** DAZE

¹daz·zle \'dazəl\ *vb* **dazzled; dazzled; dazzling** \-z(ə)liŋ\ **dazzles** [freq. of ¹*daze*] *vi* **1 :** to lose clear vision **:** become dim esp. from looking at light that is too bright ⟨the stranger's eyes *dazzled* with the . . . light —Ralph Gustafson⟩ **2 a :** to excite admiration by brilliancy **:** be impressive because of splendor ⟨he ~*s* rather than charms —F.J.Mather⟩ **b :** SHINE ⟨the woods *dazzled* whitely —Truman Capote⟩ **:** REFLECT ⟨the heat ~*s* up from the white slab —R.P.Warren⟩ ~ *vt* **1 :** to overpower (the vision) with light ⟨I *dazzled* his eyes with the brightness of my blade —Padraic Colum⟩ **2 :** to impress deeply, overpower, or confound with showy performance or brilliance ⟨*dazzled* millions with oratory —J.D.Hart⟩ **3** *archaic* **:** eclipse with greater brilliance **:** OUTSHINE — usu. used with *down* or *out*

²dazzle \"\ *n* -s **1 :** the action of dazzling **2 :** something that dazzles ⟨the ~ of the river —Elizabeth Goudge⟩

daz·zle·ment \-zəlmənt\ *n* -s **1 :** the action of dazzling **2 :** the state or condition of being dazzled ⟨drew her hand across her eyes to wipe the ~ away —Kay Boyle⟩

daz·zler \-z(ə)lə(r)\ *n* -s **:** one that dazzles ⟨that dress is a ~⟩

dazzle system *n* **:** a system of painting by which a ship's lines are given a distorted appearance and the course she is steering is made difficult to ascertain (as from a submarine)

daz·zling·ly \-z(ə)liŋlē\ *adv* **:** in a dazzling manner **:** to a dazzling degree

db *abbr* **1** debenture **2** decibel

DB *abbr* daybook

DBA *abbr* doing business as

DBH *abbr, often not cap* diameter at breast height

dbk *abbr* drawback

dbl *abbr* double

DBN *abbr, often not cap* de bonis non

DC *abbr* **1** [It *da capo*] from the beginning **2** decimal classification **3** deputy chief **4** deputy consul **5** deviation clause **6** direct current **7** district court **8** double column **9** *often not cap* double crochet

DCL *abbr or n* -s **:** a doctor of civil law

DD *abbr or n* -s **:** a doctor of divinity

dd *abbr* **1** dated **2** delivered

DD *abbr* **1** days after date **2** days after delivery **3** day's date **4** [L *dedicavit*] he dedicated **5** delayed delivery **6** delivered at docks **7** demand draft **8** [L *Deo dedit*] he gave to God **9** deputy director **10** dishonorable discharge **11** [L *dono dedit*] he gave as a gift

d day *n, usu cap 1st D* [²*d* (abbr. for *day*)] **:** the day set for launching a specific tactical operation

d-day force *n, usu cap 1st D* **:** the force that is trained, equipped, and ready to fight on the day war begins **:** force in being — used esp. of air forces

DDD \ˌdēˌdēˈdē\ *n* -s [*d*ichloro-*d*iphenyl-*d*ichloro-ethane] **:** an insecticide $(ClC_6H_4)_2CHCHCl_2$ closely related chemically to DDT and similar in properties — called also *TDE*

DDD *abbr* **1** [L *dat, dicat, dedicat*] he gives, devotes, and dedicates **2** direct distance dialing **3** [L *dono dedit dedicavit*] he gave and dedicated as a gift

DDS *abbr or n* -s **:** a doctor of dental science **:** a doctor of dental surgery

DDSc *abbr or n* -s **:** a doctor of dental science

DDT \ˌdē(ˌ)dēˈtē\ *n* -s [*d*ichloro-*d*iphenyl-*t*richloro-ethane] **:** a colorless odorless water-insoluble crystalline insecticide $(ClC_6H_4)_2CHCCl_3$ usu. made from chloral and chlorobenzene and used esp. against body lice, houseflies, mosquitoes, and agricultural pests — called also *chlorophenothane, dicophane*

d duct *n, usu cap 1st D* **:** a duct placed in a double-skinned leading edge of an airfoil in order to supply hot air for thermal anti-icing

de *var of* DEE

de- *prefix* [ME, fr. OF *de-, des-*, partly fr. L *de-* from, down, away (fr. *de*) and partly fr. L *dis-*; L *de* akin to OIr *di* from, Gk *dē* now, then, OE *tō* to — more at TO, DIS-] **1 a :** do the opposite of **:** reverse (a specified action) ⟨*de*centralize⟩ ⟨*de*code⟩ **b :** reverse of ⟨*de*calescence⟩ **2 :** remove (a specified thing) from ⟨*de*horn⟩ ⟨*de*louse⟩ **:** remove from (a specified thing) ⟨*de*throne⟩ **3 :** reduce **:** make lower ⟨*de*rate⟩ **4** [L] **:** something derived or compounded from (a specified thing) ⟨*de*compound, n.⟩ **:** derived or compounded from something (of a specified nature) ⟨*de*compound, adj.⟩ — often in grammatical terms (nouns or adjectives) ending in *-al* or *-ative* ⟨*de*adjectival⟩ ⟨*de*verbative⟩ **5 :** get off of (a specified thing) ⟨*de*bus⟩ ⟨*de*train⟩ **6 :** having a molecule characterized by the removal of one or more atoms of (a specified element) — in combining forms occurring in names of chemical compounds ⟨*de*hydro-⟩ ⟨*de*oxy-⟩ **7 :** cause to cease to (perform a specified action) ⟨*de*-emanate⟩

DE *abbr* **1** deckle edged **2** destroyer escort **3** double entry

dea *abbr* deacon

de·acetylate \ˌdē+\ *vt* [*de-* + *acetylate*] **:** to remove acetyl from (a compound) usu. by hydrolysis — **de·acetylation** \"+\ *n*

de·acidification \ˌdē+\ *n* **:** the process of deacidifying

de·acidify \"+\ *vt* [*de-* + *acidify*] **:** to remove acid from **:** reduce the acidity of (as by neutralization)

¹dea·con \'dēkən *sometimes* -kəŋ\ *n* -s [ME *dekne, dekene*, fr. OE *diacon, dēacon*, fr. LL *diaconus*, fr. Gk *diakonos diēkonos*, lit., servant, fr. *dia-, diē-* (alter. of *dia-*) + *-konos* (akin to Gk *enkonein* to be active in service); akin to L *conari* to attempt — more at DIA-] **1 :** a subordinate officer in a Christian church **:** as **a** *Roman Catholicism* (1) **:** a cleric in major orders ranking above a subdeacon and below a priest and having as a principal function close assistance of the celebrant at solemn High Mass and other solemn services (2) **:** one serving as a deacon at solemn High Mass or other solemn services **b :** *Anglicanism* **:** one in orders next below that of priest and now usu. a candidate for ordination to the priesthood **c** *Congregationalism* **:** a layman having some duties similar to those of a ruling elder in Presbyterian churches **d** *Lutheranism* (1) **:** a layman in an office subordinate to that of pastor and elder (2) **:** an assistant minister of a church in which there are several ministers **e** *Mormonism* **:** one ordained to the lowest grade of the Aaronic priesthood who serves as assistant to the teacher **2** *Scot* **a :** the president of an incorporated trade or craft **b :** a proficient workman **:** MASTER **3 :** one of two officers in a Masonic lodge ⟨senior ~⟩ ⟨junior ~⟩ **4 :** a young calf esp. when too young for veal; *also* **:** the hide from such a calf

²deacon \"\ *vt* **deaconed; deaconed; deaconing** \-k(ə)niŋ\ **deacons 1** [so called fr. the former custom in New England Congregational churches of a deacon's reading aloud each line of a hymn before it was sung by the congregation] **:** to read aloud each line of before singing (a psalm or hymn) **2 :** to practice sly deception with usu. short of illegality **3 a :** to pack (fruit or vegetables) with the finest specimens on top **b :** to alter the boundaries of (land) **c :** to adulterate or doctor (an article to be sold) **4 :** to kill (a calf) at or very soon after birth

dea·con·al \-kənᵊl\ *adj* **:** DIACONAL

dea·con·ate \-kənət\ *n* -s **:** DIACONATE

dea·con·ess \-kənəs\ *n* -ES [fr. earlier *deaconisse*, modif. of LL *diaconissa* fr. LGk *diakonissa*, fr. Gk *diakonos* deacon + *-issa* -ess] **1 :** one of an order of women in the early church whose duties resembled those of deacons **2 :** a woman assigned to church work by a bishop of the Church of England or the Protestant Episcopal Church **3 :** a woman serving as a chosen helper in church work (as among the Methodists) **4 :** a member of a sisterhood devoted to works of religion and charity founded at Kaiserswerth in 1836 by Pastor Theodor Fliedner of the German Protestant Church **5 :** a woman in one of various Protestant denominations who has entered an order or sisterhood of deaconesses, who is commissioned or consecrated to a life of service to the church, and who is typically assigned to work as a nurse in a hospital, a benevolent institution, or on a mission field

dea·con process \'dēkən-\ *n, usu cap D* [after Henry *Deacon*, 19th cent. Eng. chemist] **:** a method of obtaining chlorine gas by passing air and hydrogen chloride over a heated catalyst (as copper chloride)

dea·con·ry \-kənrē\ *n* -ES [ME *dekenry*, fr. *dekne, dekene* deacon + *-ry*] **1 :** DIACONATE **2** *Roman Catholicism* **:** a chapel in the city of Rome under the care of a cardinal deacon; *also* **:** the charitable institution to which it was formerly attached

deacons' court *n* **:** a court in some Presbyterian churches consisting of the minister or ministers, elders, and deacons of a congregation

deacon seat *n* **:** a bench usu. of split logs extending along the front of the bunks in a lumberjack's bunkhouse

de·activate \(ˈ)dē+\ *vt* [*de-* + *activate*] **1 :** to make inactive or ineffective **2 a :** to break up (as a military unit) by discharging or reassigning personnel **:** INACTIVATE **b :** to put (as a bomb or mine) in a condition that makes detonation impossible **c :** to deprive of chemical activity ⟨~ a compound by introducing substituents⟩ ⟨~ a catalyst or enzyme⟩ — **de·activation** \(ˌ)dē+\ *n* -s — **de·activator** \(ˈ)dē+\ *n* -s

¹dead \'ded\ *adj, sometimes* -ER/-EST [ME *deed*, fr. OE *dēad*; akin to OHG *tōt* dead, ON *dauthr*, Goth *dauths*; derivative fr. the root of ON *deyja* to die — more at DIE] **1 :** deprived of life **:** having ended existence as a living or growing thing — used of organisms or any of their parts or organs ⟨a ~ wasp⟩ ⟨a ~ rabbit⟩ ⟨~ leaves⟩ ⟨~ of scarlet fever⟩ ⟨~ by his own hand⟩ **2 a** (1) **:** having the appearance of death or of being dead **:** DEATHLY ⟨in a ~ faint⟩ **:** INSENSIBLE ⟨~ to the world⟩ (2) **:** without power to move, feel, or respond **:** NUMB ⟨my arm feels ~⟩ **b :** completely exhausted **:** very tired ⟨after two hours of hiking they were just ~⟩ **c** (1) **:** incapable of feeling or of being stirred emotionally or intellectually **:** impervious esp. to pleas or arguments **:** UNRESPONSIVE ⟨a girl with a heart ~ to pity⟩ ⟨completely ~ and deaf to his father's advice⟩ **:** lacking sensitivity or delicacy of feeling ⟨~ to all sense of honor⟩ (2) *of a sentiment* **:** grown cold **:** EXTINGUISHED ⟨a ~ passion⟩ ⟨a ~ love⟩ **3 a :** not naturally endowed with life **:** INANIMATE, INERT ⟨~ matter⟩ **b :** not producing or sustaining life **:** BARREN, INFERTILE ⟨~ soil⟩ ⟨a ~ rocky waste⟩ **c :** no longer producing or functioning **:** EXHAUSTED, WORKED-OUT ⟨a ~ oil well⟩ ⟨a ~ mine⟩ ⟨a ~ battery⟩ **4 a :** lacking power or effect ⟨a ~ law⟩ **:** no longer of concern **:** no longer having interest, relevance, or significance ⟨a ~ issue⟩ **b** (1) **:** lacking currency **:** DEFUNCT, OBSOLETE ⟨a ~ custom⟩ (2) *of a language* **:** no longer in ordinary spoken use **c :** no longer active **:** EXTINCT ⟨a ~ volcano⟩ **d :** lacking in fervor or warmth ⟨a ~ description⟩ **:** lacking in gaiety, animation, or amusing quality ⟨a very ~ party⟩ **e** (1) **:** lacking in commercial activity **:** QUIET ⟨a ~ produce market⟩ (2) **:** commercially idle or unproductive ⟨~ capital⟩ **:** lacking in salability **:** being unsold ⟨~ stock⟩ **f :** lacking responsiveness or elasticity ⟨a ~ tennis ball⟩ ⟨a ~ string on a viol⟩ **g :** out of action or out of use ⟨a ~ electric circuit⟩ ⟨a ~ telephone line⟩ ⟨~ storage⟩ **h** (1) *of a ball* **:** out of play ⟨in football the ball is ~ after an incompleted forward pass⟩ (2) *of a player* **:** temporarily forbidden to play or make a certain play ⟨a croquet player may be ~ on another player's ball⟩ **i** *printing* (1) **:** being something that has been used or is not to be used ⟨~ copy⟩ ⟨~ type⟩ ⟨~ artwork⟩ (2) **:** being something that is routed or to be routed off as not meant to print ⟨*dead*-metal areas in engravings and electrotypes⟩ **j :** out of play **:** not usable ⟨a hand that is not eligible to win is ~⟩ **k :** having a density greater than water — used of oils distilled from tar **l :** having lost the qualities required for workability ⟨~ plaster will not set hard when mixed with water⟩ ⟨~ stone, yielding a dull thud when struck with the sculptor's hammer⟩ **5 a :** not running or circulating **:** STAGNANT ⟨~ water⟩ ⟨~ air⟩ **b :** not turning ⟨the ~ center of a lathe⟩ ⟨cut between a ~ knife blade and a turning one⟩ **c** *of mail* **:** undeliverable and unreturnable — see DEAD LETTER **6 a :** having no fire, warmth, or glow ⟨a ~ cigar⟩ ⟨a ~ fire⟩ **b :** lacking brilliance or luster **:** DULL ⟨a ~ glossy finish⟩ **c :** lacking tang or taste ⟨a ~ wine⟩ **d :** MUFFLED, DEADENED ⟨a ~ sound⟩ **7 :** having a quality of completeness or finality **8 a** (1) **:** unrelieved by any breaks or deviations **:** absolutely uniform — often used in the phrase *dead level* ⟨the ~ level of a prairie⟩ ⟨reducing all to a ~ level of mediocrity⟩ (2) **:** characterized by the utmost exertion of effort, physical or mental ⟨a ~ pull⟩ **b** (1) **:** completely certain as to outcome **:** INESCAPABLE, UNERRING ⟨a ~ shot with a rifle⟩ **:** EXACT ⟨hit the ~ center of the target⟩ (2) **:** as good as dead **:** DOOMED ⟨a ~ pigeon⟩ (3) **:** IRREVOCABLE, UNRECOVERABLE ⟨a ~ loss⟩ **c :** marked by complete and sudden cessation (as of motion or action) **:** ABRUPT ⟨brought to a ~ stop⟩ ⟨stopped him ~ in his tracks⟩ **d :** COMPLETE, TOTAL, ABSOLUTE ⟨a ~ silence fell⟩ ⟨spoke with ~ certainty of his return⟩ **9 :** being abandoned by its former human occupants **:** DESERTED ⟨a ~ mining town⟩ ⟨~ villages⟩ **10 :** characterized by high absorption of sound **:** ANECHOIC ⟨a ~ wall⟩ **11 :** free from any connection to a source of voltage and free from electric charges **:** having the same potential as that of the ground — used of current-carrying apparatus or circuits that may at other times be alive **12 a :** lacking motion ⟨the ~ spindle of a lathe⟩ **b :** not imparting motion or power although otherwise functioning ⟨the ~ rear axle of a floating transmission⟩ **c :** having the principal function in abeyance ⟨the ~ time between power strokes⟩ **d :** marked by a delay in operation or by inactivity between operations or actions — used in referring to a mechanical or electronic device ⟨~ time of a counter⟩

²dead \"\ *n, pl* **dead** [ME *deed*] **1 :** one that is dead — now usu. used collectively ⟨the ~ and the living⟩ **2 :** the time of greatest quiet **:** the period of profoundest inertness or gloom ⟨the ~ of winter⟩ ⟨when the drum beat at ~ of night —Thomas Campbell⟩ **3 :** something dead **:** as **a** *dead pl* **:** refuse from a mine **b** *slang* **:** an article of dead mail

³dead \"\ *vb* -ED/-ING/-S [ME *deden*, fr. OE *dēadian* to die, fr. *dēad*, adj.] *vi, obs* **:** DIE ~ *vt, chiefly dial* **:** DEADEN

⁴dead \"\ *adv* [¹*dead*] **1 a :** to a degree or in a manner resembling or characteristic of death **:** to the last degree **:** ABSOLUTELY, UTTERLY, ENTIRELY, EXACTLY ⟨~ ripe⟩ ⟨*dead*-tired⟩ ⟨~ certain⟩ **b** *dial Brit* **:** EXTREMELY, VERY ⟨it seems to me ~ strange —C.J.Dennis⟩ **2 :** with suddenness and completeness ⟨he stopped ~⟩ **3 :** DIRECTLY ⟨the police were ~ against the plan⟩ ⟨a *dead*-square opening⟩

⁵dead \'ded, -ē-,-ā-\ *n* -s [ME *dede, deed*, prob. alter. (influenced by *deed*, adj.) of *deeth* — more at DEATH] *dial Brit* **:** DEATH

dead ahead *adj (or adv)* **1 :** directly ahead **2 :** on a forward extension of the fore-and-aft line of a ship

dead air *n* **1** *mining* **:** air deficient in oxygen or containing sufficient carbon dioxide to be unfit for breathing **2 :** silence occurring during a radio or television broadcast

dead-air space *n* **:** a sealed or unventilated air space (as in a hollow wall or ceiling)

dead-alive \ˌdedᵊlˈīv, -edəˈlīv\ *also* **dead-and-alive** \ˌded-ᵊnəˈlīv\ *adj* **:** alive but as if dead **:** DULL, SPIRITLESS

dead angle *n* **:** an angle outside of a fortification that cannot be reached by the direct fire of the defenders

dead-arm \'ˌ=,=\ *n* **:** a fungous disease of the grape caused by an ascomycete (*Cryptosporella viticola*) conspicuous from the death of the main lateral branches — called also *necrosis*

dead asset *n* **:** property carried on accounting books that has neither present nor prospective value — usu. used in pl.

dead axle *n* **:** an axle that carries a road wheel but has no provision for driving it

dead-ball line *n* **:** either of two lines drawn parallel to and not more than 25 yards behind the goal lines to mark the extreme limits of a rugby playing field — see RUGBY illustration

¹deadbeat \'=,=\ *adj* [¹*dead* + *beat* (oscillation)] **1** *of an escapement* **:** without recoil **2 :** APERIODIC — used esp. of highly damped indicators on electrical measuring instruments

²deadbeat \'=,=\ *n* [prob. fr. ⁴*dead* + *beat* (v.)] **1** *chiefly Austral* **:** a man without financial resources **2 :** one that habitually fails to pay his debts or to pay his way **:** SPONGE

dead beat \'=¦=\ *adj* [⁴*dead* + *beat* (past part. of *beat*)] **:** completely beat **:** tired out or hopelessly defeated

dead bird *n* **1 :** a bird or other target (as in trapshooting) regarded as killed **2 :** a mark regarded as already hit **:** SURE THING **3 :** one whose death or failure is or seems inescapable

dead block *n* **:** a buffer on the ends of passenger-train cars and locomotives to absorb shock impacts

dead bolt *n* **:** a lock bolt that is moved positively by turning the knob or key without action of a spring

deadborn \'=¦=\ *adj* [ME *deedborn*, fr. *deed* dead + *born*] *archaic* **:** STILLBORN

dead-bright \'=¦=\ *adj, metalworking* **:** polished so that all tool marks are obliterated **:** BURNISHED

dead-burn \'=¦=\ *vt* **:** to calcine (as a carbonate rock) at a higher temperature and for a longer time than usual with the production of a dense refractory material (as by driving off all carbon dioxide) ⟨*dead-burned* dolomite⟩

dead cat *n* **:** a piece of violent or jeering criticism **:** an insulting or abusive expression of disapproval ⟨the government received a barrage of *dead cats*⟩

dead center *n* **1 :** the position of a crank when the turning moment exerted on it is zero; *esp* **:** either of the two positions at the ends of a stroke in a crank and connecting rod when the crank and rod are in the same straight line **2 :** a center that does not revolve in a machine tool

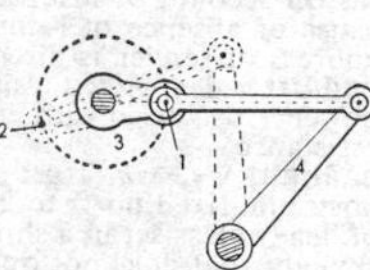

1, 2, dead centers, *3* crank, *4* lever

dead clothes *n pl* [²,⁵*dead*] *Scot* **:** the shroud of a corpse

dead deal *n* [²*dead*] *Scot* **:** the board on which a corpse is laid

dead dog *n* **:** something no longer important ⟨waste time beating a *dead dog*⟩

dead-doing *adj, obs* **:** KILLING, MURDEROUS

dead-drunk \'=¦=\ *adj* **:** so drunk as to be unconscious or unable to move — **dead-drunkenness** \'=¦===\ *n* -ES

dead duck *n* **1 :** a person or thing that has so deteriorated or depreciated as to be practically worthless **2 :** one that is as good as done for ⟨without big advertisers that magazine is a *dead duck*⟩

deaded *past of* DEAD

dead·en \'dedᵊn\ *vb* **deadened; deadened; deadening** \-ed(ᵊ)niŋ\ **deadens** [¹*dead* + *-en*] *vt* **1 :** to make as if dead **:** impair in vigor, force, activity, or sensation **:** BLUNT ⟨~*ed* his feelings⟩ ⟨~ a sound⟩ **2 a :** to lessen the velocity or momentum of **:** RETARD ⟨~ a ship's headway⟩ **b :** to deprive of gloss or brilliancy **:** OBSCURE ⟨~ gilding by a coat of size⟩ **c :** to make vapid or spiritless ⟨~ wine⟩ **d :** to render (as a wall) impervious to sound **:** DEAFEN 3 **e :** to convert (metallic mercury) into a gray powder consisting of minute globules (as by shaking with chalk or a fatty oil) — compare FLOUR 3 **3 a :** to deprive of life **:** KILL **b :** to kill (trees) by girdling **:** clear (land) by thus killing the trees ~ *vi* **:** to become dead **:** to lose life, force, or vigor

dead end \'=¦=\ *n* **1 :** an end (as of a street, pipe, or power line) that has no exit or continuation **2 :** a course of action or policy that leads to nothing further **:** BLIND ALLEY, CUL-DE-SAC

¹dead-end \'=¦=\ *adj* [*dead end*] **1 :** leading nowhere **:** lacking possibilities for advance, progress, or further action ⟨a *dead-end* job⟩ ⟨a *dead-end* policy⟩ **2 :** living in or characteristic of city slums or back streets **:** TOUGH ⟨*dead-end* kids⟩ ⟨a *dead-end* background⟩ **3 :** having a dead end ⟨a *dead-end* street⟩

²dead-end \'=¦=\ *vb* [*dead end*] *vt* **:** TERMINATE ⟨*dead-end* electric transmission lines⟩ ~ *vi* **:** to come to a dead end **:** TERMINATE

dead·en·er \'ded(ᵊ)nə(r)\ *n* -s **:** a log with spikes in the butt end so arranged over a skidway as to retard logs that pass under it

deadening *n* -s **1 :** action that deadens **2 :** something that deadens: as **a :** material used to render a surface (as a wall, floor, or ceiling) impervious to sound **:** PUGGING **b :** a coating (as of glue) to deprive a surface of gloss or brilliancy **3 :** an area on which the trees have been killed esp. by girdling

deadening felt *n* **:** a heavy coarse paper used in building construction to reduce noises

¹dead·er \'dedə(r)\ *comparative of* DEAD

²deader \"\ *n* -s [¹*dead* + *-er*] *slang* **:** CORPSE

deadest *superlative of* DEAD

deadeye \'=,=\ *n* -s **1 :** a rounded wood block that is encircled by a rope or an iron band and pierced with holes to receive the lanyard and is used to set up shrouds and stays and for other purposes **2 :** a dead shot ⟨he's a ~ with that rifle⟩

deadfall \'=,=\ *n* **1 :** a trap constructed so that a gate, log, or other weight falls upon the animal and kills or disables it; *broadly* **:** TRAP, PITFALL **2 :** a gambling den or saloon esp. when crooked **3 :** a forest tree that has fallen from age or decay; *collectively* **:** such fallen trees or branches ⟨making his way through the ~⟩ — compare WINDFALL

dead finish *n, Austral* **:** any of several trees or shrubs (as of the genera *Albizzia* and *Acacia*) that form impenetrable thickets

dead fire *n* [⁵*dead*] **:** SAINT ELMO'S FIRE

dead flat *n* **:** the portion of a ship's transverse form that has the same form as the midship or largest section — called also *straight-of-breadth*

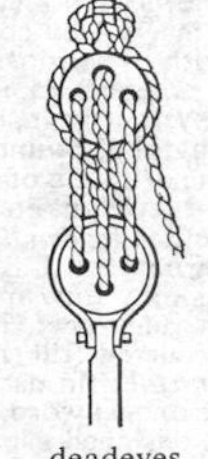

deadeyes

dead fold *n* **:** a fold (as in soft foil) that does not unfold spontaneously

dead freight *n* **1 :** the amount paid by or recoverable from a charterer of a ship for such part of the ship's capacity as he has contracted for but fails to occupy; *also* **:** the unoccupied space in such a ship **2 :** bulky nonperishable freight

dead-front switchboard *n* **:** a switchboard with no live or energized parts on the operating side

dead furrow *n* **:** a double furrow left in the middle of a field or between two lands in plowing

deadgrass \'=¦=\ *n* **:** a deep yellow with a brownish cast — used of a Chesapeake Bay retriever

dead ground *n* **1 :** a low-resistance connection between an electric circuit and the earth **2 :** DEAD SPACE 1

dead hand *n* **1 :** MORTMAIN **2 :** the influence esp. when felt to be oppressive of the dead on the living or of the past on the present

dead handle *n* **:** DEADMAN'S HANDLE

¹deadhead \'=,=\ *n* [¹*dead* + *head*] **1 a :** one that has not paid for a ticket (as for admission to a show or passage on a train); *sometimes* **:** the ticket so received **b** (1) **:** an employee (as of a railroad) riding as a passenger to an assigned point (2) **:** a vehicle (as a freight car or a truck) riding empty **c :** one that does not contribute to the activity of a business or organization ⟨we have several ~*s* on the board of directors⟩ **d :** one who is unfitted or unwilling to advance to a higher rank **2 :** a wholly or partly sunken log **3 :** TAILSTOCK **4 a :** a block of wood used as a buoy **b :** a heavy post on a wharf to which to fasten a hawser **:** BOLLARD

²**deadhead** \"\ *adj* **:** composed of deadheads **:** acting as a deadhead ⟨~ train runs are necessary in the early morning hours⟩

³**deadhead** \"\ *vb* -ED/-ING/-S *vi* **1 :** to act or behave as a deadhead **2 a :** to make a return trip without a load — used esp. of a truck **b :** to drive or ride on a truck making such a trip ~ *vt* **:** to drive or haul (a truck, car, locomotive) as a deadhead

deadheart \ˈ=,=\ *n* **:** a deformed stunted plant of certain crop grasses (as maize and sugarcane) caused by borer attack on the region immediately behind the growing bud and characterized by bushy blanched distorted growth beyond the damaged area

dead heat *n* **:** a race with no single winner

dead-heat \ˈ=ˈ=\ *vi* [*dead heat*] **:** to run a dead heat

dead hole *n* **:** a hole (as in a casting) that does not pass entirely through

dead horse *n* **1 :** advance wages for work ⟨working off a *dead horse*⟩ **:** an old debt ⟨paying for a *dead horse*⟩ **2 :** an exhausted or profitless topic or issue ⟨arguing this question would be beating a *dead horse*⟩ — compare DEAD DOG

deadhouse \ˈ=,=\ *n* [²*dead* + *house*] *archaic* **:** MORGUE, MORTUARY

deading *pres part of* DEAD

dead·ish \ˈdedish\ *adj* [ME *dedisshe*, fr. *deed* dead + *-isshe* -ish] **:** somewhat dead **:** DULL ⟨a ~ sound⟩

de-adjectival \(ˌ)dē+\ *adj* [*de-* + *adjective* + *-al*] **:** derived from an adjective (as *weaken* from *weak*) ⟨a *de-adjectival* verb⟩

dead key *n* **:** a typewriter key (as for an accent or a diacritical mark) that prints when struck but does not move the carriage

deadlatch \ˈ=,=\ *n* **:** a spring-bolt latch in which the bolt is deadlocked against end pressure but may be retracted by either the knob or the key

dead latitude *n* **:** latitude found by dead reckoning

dead leaf *n* **:** FEUILLE MORTE

dead-leaf butterfly *n* **:** any of several tropical Asiatic butterflies (genus *Kallima*) with underside of wings suggesting dead leaves when at rest — compare LEAF BUTTERFLY

dead letter *n* **1 :** something that has lost its force or authority or has fallen into disuse without being formally abolished or declared useless ⟨that law has become a *dead letter*⟩ **2 :** a letter that is received by a post office but that is undeliverable (as on account of insufficient address) and unreturnable because of absence of return address or returnable only when address of sender is discovered upon opening

dead lift *n* **1** *archaic* **:** a situation taxing one's utmost effort or power — usu. used with *at* **2 :** a direct lift without mechanical assistance

deadlight \ˈ=,=\ *n* **1 a :** a metal cover or shutter fitted to air ports and fixed ports to keep out light and water **b :** a piece of heavy glass set in a ship's deck or hull to admit light **2 :** a skylight that does not open **3** *Scot* **:** a luminosity seen over graves **:** CORPSE CANDLE **4 deadlights** *pl, slang* **:** EYES

¹**deadline** \ˈ=,=\ *n* [²*dead* + *line*] **1 :** a line drawn within or around a prison that a prisoner passes only at the risk of being instantly shot **2 :** a line or mark made on the bed of a cylinder press to indicate the limit to which the printing surface may extend **3 :** a fixed time limit **:** a date or time before which something must be done and after which the opportunity passes or a penalty follows ⟨the ~ for filing income tax returns⟩ **:** *specif* **:** the time limit after which copy is not accepted for use in a particular issue of a publication ⟨3 a.m. was the ~ for the newspaper's morning edition⟩ **4 :** a group of military vehicles put aside for repair or periodic maintenance

²**deadline** \ˈ=,=\ *vt* **:** to put aside (as a motor vehicle) for repair or maintenance

dead·li·ness \ˈdedlēnəs, -lin-\ *n* -ES [ME *deedlinesse*, fr. *deedly* deadly + *-nesse* -ness] **:** the state or quality of being deadly

dead load *n* **1 :** a constant load that in structures (as a bridge, car, building, or machine) is due to the weight of the members, the supported structure, and permanent attachments or accessories — compare IMPOSED LOAD, LIVE LOAD **2 :** factory orders prepared by a central control office but not released to the factory for production **:** BACKLOG

¹**deadlock** \ˈ=,=\ *n* [¹*dead* + *lock*] **1 :** a counteraction of things producing entire stoppage **:** a state of inaction or of neutralization caused by the opposition of persons or of factions (as in a government or in a voting body) **:** STANDSTILL **2 :** a device for locking or holding securely together the point and stock rails in a railroad point switch **3 :** a lock having a dead bolt — distinguished from *spring lock* **4 :** a tie score of a game or contest

²**deadlock** \"\ *vt* **:** to bring to a deadlock ~*vi* **:** to reach a deadlock

¹**dead·ly** \ˈdedlē, -li\ *adj* -ER/-EST [ME *deedlich, deedly*, fr. OE *dēadlic*, fr. *dēad* dead + *-lic* -ly — more at DEAD] **1** *obs* **a :** subject to death **b :** being in danger of dying **:** likely to die **c :** INANIMATE **2 :** tending to produce death **:** productive of death ⟨among the Indians, measles, scarlatina, and whooping cough were as ~ as typhus or cholera —Willa Cather⟩ **3 a :** aiming to kill or destroy or involving such an aim ⟨two brave vessels matched in ~ fight —William Wordsworth⟩ **:** lacking possibility of an amicable solution **:** IMPLACABLE ⟨a ~ quarrel⟩ **b :** tending to enervate, vitiate, or smother all force, vitality, influence, or activity ⟨the neglect of form . . . was even *deadlier* to poetry —Peter Viereck⟩ **:** extremely pernicious ⟨the ~ effects of malicious gossip⟩ **:** PENETRATING, DEVASTATING ⟨containing some ~ exposure of human folly or frailty —Daniel George⟩ **4 :** characteristic or suggestive of death or the dead ⟨a ~ paleness spread over her features⟩ **5 :** marked by great precision **:** UNERRING ⟨stories hurled with ~ aim —Green Peyton⟩ **6 :** marked by extreme seriousness and single-minded determination ⟨goes in for careermanship in an impassive, ~ sort of way —James Kelly⟩ **:** notably effective **:** UNFAILING ⟨the ~ efficiency of the famed police force⟩ **:** marked by complete lack of trifling or flippancy ⟨he spoke with ~ seriousness⟩ **7 :** very great **:** COMPLETE, EXTREME ⟨a ~ silence⟩ ⟨a ~ bore⟩ ⟨~ fear⟩

syn MORTAL, LETHAL, FATAL, DEATHLY: DEADLY applies to anything bound or likely to cause death ⟨so poisonous that the drinking of it is *deadly* to all but serpents and hippopotami —Llewelyn Powys⟩ ⟨Hands and his companion locked together in *deadly* wrestle, each with a hand upon the other's throat —R.L.Stevenson⟩ In this sense MORTAL differs from DEADLY only in that it may occur somewhat more frequently in retrospect, in reference to situations in which death has occurred ⟨till that young life being smitten in midheaven with *mortal* cold passed from her —Alfred Tennyson⟩ LETHAL, the strongest word, indicates that which by its quality or quantity is designed esp. to make death certain ⟨the morphia he gave was a full *lethal* dose, and presently the body on the deck found peace —Nevil Shute⟩ FATAL comes between DEADLY and LETHAL in inevitability and may refer to other calamities than death ⟨regarding strychnine, toxicology gives us a very wide range as to *lethal* dosage, depending on the condition and age of the patient. The average *fatal* dose for an adult is, I should say, two grains, though death has resulted from administrations of one grain —W.H.Wright⟩ ⟨the *fatal* policy by which the Empire invited its doom while striving to avert it, the policy of matching barbarian against barbarian —J.R. Green⟩ DEATHLY, once a synonym for DEADLY, is now commonly an intensive meaning "as of death" or "resembling death" ⟨she had a *deathly* fear of Quintal and with reason —C.B.Nordhoff & J.N.Hall⟩

²**deadly** \"\ *adv* [ME *deedliche, deedly*, fr. OE *dēadlice*, fr. *dēadlic*, adj.] **1** *archaic* **:** in a manner to occasion death **:** MORTALLY **:** to death ⟨the groanings of a ~ wounded man —Ezek 30:24 (AV)⟩ **2 :** in an implacable manner **:** to the death **3 :** in a manner or degree produced by or as if produced by death ⟨turned ~ pale⟩ **4 :** in a dead manner **:** as if dead **:** LIFELESSLY **5 :** EXTREMELY, EXCESSIVELY ⟨~ dull⟩

deadly agaric *n* **:** a very poisonous mushroom (as the fly agaric or death cup)

deadly amanita *n* **:** DEATH CUP 2

deadly carrot *n* **:** a large European herb (*Thapsia garganica*) the root of which is emetic and cathartic

deadly nightshade *n* **1 :** BELLADONNA 1 **2 :** BLACK NIGHTSHADE

deadly parallel *n* **:** a comparison of two things part by part (as in parallel columns) that reveals an underlying relationship (as in a case of plagiarism) or a damaging discrepancy

deadly sin *n* **:** one of seven sins of pride, covetousness, lust, anger, gluttony, envy, and sloth regarded by some as the source of other sins and as fatal to spiritual progress

dead mail *n* **:** mail that is undeliverable because of faulty or illegible address and is unreturnable to the sender or that is unclaimed after a certain period of time and that must be sent to the dead-letter branch in the case of first-class mail or to the dead parcel-post branch for disposal

dead·man \-,man, -aa(ə)n\ *n, pl* **deadmen** [ME *deedman*, fr. *deed dead* + *man*] **1 :** CORPSE — now used as one word in place names only ⟨*Deadman's* Bay⟩ **2 :** a buried log serving as an anchor (as for a guy rope) **:** ANCHOR LOG; *also* **:** a stout timber or log used as an anchorage (as for a boom) **3 :** a support that resembles a crutch and is used to hold a pole temporarily while it is being erected or lowered and so permit the workmen to take a fresh grip on the pole **4 :** a fallen tree on the shore **5** *deadmen pl, obs* **:** reef or gasket ends carelessly left dangling under the yard when the sail is furled **6** *or* **deadman control :** a device (as a brake) for controlling a vehicle or machine in case the operator becomes incapacitated

dead man *n* **1 :** the inedible gill filaments of a crab that are discarded in cleaning boiled crabs **2 :** a bottle emptied of beer, wine, or liquor; *also* **:** an empty beer can

deadman brake *n* **:** an automatic emergency brake that goes into action when the driver of a vehicle removes his foot from a pedal

dead man's eye *n, obs* **:** DEADEYE 1

dead-man's-fingers \ˌ=,=ˈ=,==\ *or* **dead-men's-fingers** *n pl but sing or pl in constr* **1 :** any of several European orchids (genus *Orchis*) having pale digitate roots (esp. *O. mascula, O. maculata, O. latifolia*, and *O. morio*) **2 :** any of several other plants: as **a :** BIRD'S-FOOT TREFOIL 1a **b :** CUCKOOPINT **c :** MEADOW FOXTAIL GRASS **3 :** the fruiting bodies of fungi of the genus *Xylaria* (esp. *X. polymorpha*) **4 a :** a fleshy alcyonarian (*Alcyonium digitatum*) usu. lobed or digitate in form **b :** a white or grayish digitately branching sponge (*Chalina arbuscula*) of the Atlantic coast **5 :** DEAD MAN 1

dead man's float *n* **:** a prone floating position with arms extended forward — called also *prone float*

deadman's hand *n* **1 a** *or* **deadman's thumb :** MALE ORCHIS **b :** MALE FERN **c** *also* **deadman's toe :** a palmately branching seaweed (*Laminaria digitata*) **2 :** a poker hand with two pairs either aces and eights or jacks and eights

deadman's handle *n* **:** a handle on a machine having a small button on it which must be kept pressed down by the hand to continue contact so that if the operator is incapacitated contact is broken and the machine stops — called also *dead handle*

dead march \ˈ=ˈ=\ *n* [²*dead*] **:** a piece of solemn funereal music intended to accompany or to suggest a funeral procession

dead marine *n* **:** DEAD MAN 2

¹**deadmelt** \ˈ=ˈ=\ *vt, steel manuf* **:** to keep molten until bubbling ceases and the liquid becomes quiet

²**deadmelt** \"\ *n* **:** the state of deadmelted metal

deadmen's bells *or* **deadman's bells** *n pl, Scot* **:** FOXGLOVE 1

deadmen's bones *n pl but sometimes sing in constr* **:** a toadflax (*Linaria vulgaris*)

deadmen's lines *n pl but sing in constr* **:** SEA LACE

de ad·men·su·ra·ti·o·ne \ˌdāˌäd,men(t)sə,räd·ēˈō,nā, -ˌnē\ *adj* [ML, of admeasurement] **:** commanding admeasurement of dower — used of a writ

dead metaphor *n* **:** a word or phrase that was once metaphoric but that has lost its metaphoric force in common use (as *the head of the house, room and board, time is running out*)

dead mouth *n, of a horse* **:** a mouth no longer sensitive to the bit

dead·ness *n* -ES **:** the quality or state of being dead

dead nettle *n* **1 :** a plant of the genus *Lamium* having leaves resembling those of the nettle but destitute of stinging hairs **2 :** HEMP NETTLE **3 :** HEDGE NETTLE **4 :** RICHWEED 1

dead oil *n* **:** any of various heavy oils (as creosote oil)

de·a·dose \dēˈädə,dōs\ *n, pl* **deadose** *or* **deodoses** *usu cap* **1 :** a Tunican people of south central Texas **2 :** a member of the Deadose people

dead pan \ˈ=ˈ= *in sense 1*, ˈ=,= *in sense 2*\ *n* **1 :** a completely expressionless immobile face ⟨wears a *dead pan* on and off the ice —*Newsweek*⟩ **2 :** a deadpan manner of behavior or of presentation (as of comedy) ⟨a master of *dead pan*⟩

¹**deadpan** \ˈ=,=\ *adj* [*dead pan*] **1 :** having or communicated with an assumed air of earnestness or gravity ⟨~ humor⟩ ⟨an infinitely irritating ~ mockery⟩ ⟨a ~ elegy on a turtle⟩ **2 a :** marked by complete absence of expression or mobility **:** WOODEN, STOLID ⟨a ~ face⟩ ⟨gave his accusers a ~ stare⟩ **b :** giving no sign of emotional or personal commitment or involvement ⟨a ~ presentation of concentration-camp horrors⟩ ⟨a ~ narrative style⟩

²**deadpan** \ˈ=,=\ *adv* **:** in a deadpan manner **:** with deadpan absence of expression ⟨played his role completely ~⟩

³**deadpan** \ˈ=,=\ *vi* **:** to maintain a deadpan manner **:** act in a deadpan manner ⟨*deadpanned* throughout the whole play⟩ ~ *vt* **:** to speak or write in a deadpan manner

dead parking *n* **:** the keeping of a vehicle standing without a driver or operator in attendance

dead pigeon *n* **:** DEAD BIRD

dead plate *n* **:** a stationary steel plate placed at the end of an automatic-stoker grate next to the fire door to collect clinkers

dead pledge *n* **:** MORTGAGE

dead point *n* **:** DEAD CENTER

dead rail *n* **:** one of two rails that are laid across a railroad track-scale platform but not connected with the weighing beam and that permit a locomotive or other load exceeding the capacity of the scale to move across the scale

dead reckoning *n* **1 :** the determination without the aid of celestial observations of the position of a ship or aircraft deduced from the record of the courses sailed or flown, the distance made, and the known or estimated drift **2 :** a procedure attempting to locate something in space or in time (as a goal, a target, an historical event) by deduction unaided by direct observation or direct evidence; *broadly* **:** GUESSWORK

dead rent *n* **:** a fixed rent; *esp* **:** one imposed upon a concessionaire without regard to the yield of his concession

dead rise *n* **:** the rise of the bottom of a midship frame from the keel to the bilge usu. given in inches per foot

dead-rise model *n* **:** a small usu. high-speed power yacht having a flat floor with extreme dead rise and straight sides

dead rising *also* **dead rise line** *n* **:** a curved fore-and-aft line in the sheer plan of a ship passing through the floorheads and showing the dead rise of each head

dead-roast \ˈ=ˈ=\ *vt* **:** to roast (ore) until free from sulfur, arsenic, or other volatile components

dead rope *n* **:** a rope that does not pass over a sheave or reeve through a block

deads *pl of* DEAD, *pres 3d sing of* DEAD

dead sea *n* [fr. the *Dead sea*, salt lake in Palestine, its prototype; trans. of LL *Mare Mortuum*, trans. of Gk *Nekra Thalassa*] **:** a body of water from which beds of rock salt, gypsum, or other evaporites have been precipitated

dead sea apple *n, usu cap D&S* [fr. the *Dead sea*] **1** *or* **dead sea fruit :** APPLE OF SODOM 1a **2 :** a gallnut coming from Asiatic Turkey caused by a gallfly (*Cynips insana*) — called also *mad apple*

dead set *n* **1 :** the position of a hunting dog in pointing his prey **2 :** a determined effort esp. to win or gain a clearly identified objective — usu. used with *at* ⟨made a *dead set* at him and married him⟩ **3 :** an attitude of fixed hostility

dead sheave *n* **:** a hole in the heel of a topmast to receive a top pendant

dead shore *n* **:** an upright shore left in a wall after completion of repairs or alterations

dead short circuit *n* **:** an electrical short circuit of great magnitude arising from large firm contact

dead slow *adv (or adj), naut* **:** so slow as to have only steerageway

dead-smooth \ˈ=ˈ=\ *adj* **1 :** extremely smooth **2 :** smoother than most other implements of the same class ⟨a *dead-smooth* file⟩

dead-soft \ˈ=ˈ=\ *adj* **1** *of steel* **:** very soft; *specif* **:** very low in carbon **2** *of steel* **:** annealed until as soft as possible

dead soldier *n* **:** DEAD MAN 2

dead space *n* **1 :** space that cannot be reached by fire from a given weapon or a given point — called also *dead ground* **2 :** the portion of the respiratory system which is external to the bronchioles and through which air must pass to reach the bronchioles and alveoli — called also *physiologic dead space* **3 :** a space left in the body as the result of a surgical procedure (as that in the chest following excision of a lung or that in an improperly closed surgical wound) **4 :** space (as in a truck or steamer) that is not utilized or occupied

dead's part *n* [²*dead*] *Scots law* **:** the part of a married man's personal property that he may dispose of by will, the rest going to the widow and children — compare JUS RELICTAE, LEGITIM

dead spot *n* **1 :** a locality where activity lags **2 :** a region of poor or no radio reception **:** BLIND SPOT

dead stick *n*, **:** an airplane propeller that has ceased to revolve because the engine has stopped

dead stock *n* **:** farm tools and equipment — opposed to *livestock*

dead-stroke \ˈ=,=\ *adj, of a mechanical device* **:** making a stroke without recoil

dead-stroke hammer *n* **:** a power hammer having a spring interposed between the driving mechanism and the hammerhead or helve to lessen the recoil and reduce the shock

dead thraw *or* **dead throw** *n* [⁵*dead*] *Scot* **:** death throe

dead time *n* **1 :** the short interval which is required for a counting tube to recover its sensitivity after any one discharge and during which it is incapable of further response **2 :** the time lag between a stimulus given to an instrument and the resulting response **3 :** DOWNTIME 2a

deadtongue \ˈ=,=\ *n* [so called fr. its paralyzing effect on the speech organs] *dial Eng* **:** a European water dropwort (*Oenanthe crocata*)

dead to rights *adv* **:** without possibility of escape, excuse, or palliation (as from a charge of guilt) **:** RED-HANDED ⟨we had him *dead to rights*⟩ ⟨caught *dead to rights* on a bribery charge⟩

dead track *n* **1 :** a car or railway track that is no longer used but that has not been removed **2 :** a short section of track usu. at a crossing that is isolated by insulated joints from the track signal circuits

dead wagon *n* [²*dead*] **:** a wagon used to carry the dead

dead wall *n* **:** a wall without openings

dead watch *n* [⁵*dead*] **:** DEATHWATCH

dead water *n* **1 :** standing or still water **2 :** SLACK WATER, NEAP TIDE **3 :** the mass of eddying water formed along a ship's sides in her progress through the water

deadweight \ˈ=ˈ=\ *n* **1** *often* **dead weight :** the unrelieved weight of any inert mass **:** a heavy or oppressive burden **2 :** DEAD LOAD 1 **3 :** a ship's lading including the total weight of cargo, fuel, stores, crew, and passengers

deadweight capacity *or* **deadweight tonnage** *n* **:** the carrying capacity of a ship in tons of 2240 pounds **:** the difference between a ship's displacement light and her displacement loaded

deadweight safety valve *n* **:** a safety valve in which the pressure is caused by a weight acting directly on the valve

deadwood \ˈ=,=; *in sense 1* " *or* ˈ=ˈ=\ *n* **1 :** wood dead on the tree **:** dead branches **2 :** useless personnel or material (as inefficient members of an organization, unsalable stock, or outworn methods) ⟨a definite campaign against human ~ still clogging the system —Ezra Pound⟩ **3 :** solid timbers usu. horizontal and built in at the extreme bow and stern of a ship where the breadth is not such as to permit framing **4 :** bowling pins that have been knocked down but remain on the alley **5 a :** unmatched cards in gin or knock rummy **b :** useless cards (as those that have been discarded) **6 :** type or spacing matter temporarily keyboarded or inserted in typeset matter to make room for something (as a vertical rule in a table) to be inserted later **7** *chiefly West* **:** unquestioned advantage — used esp. in the expression *have the deadwood on* ⟨we've got the ~ on you on a forgery charge —Erle Stanley Gardner⟩

deadwood fence *n, Austral* **:** a heavy fence made of felled trees, heaped logs, or branches

dead wool *n* **1 :** FALLEN WOOL **2 :** wool from dead sheep

dead work *n* **1 :** work which must be done to prepare for future operations but from which there is no direct return (as stripping the surface to expose rock which is to be quarried) **2 dead works** *pl, archaic* **:** UPPERWORKS 1

de ae·qui·ta·te \ˌdē,ekwəˈtād·ē, ˌdā,īkwəˈtäd·ē\ *adv (or adj)* [L, from equity] *law* **:** according to the principles of equity — distinguished from *de jure*

de·aerate \(ˈ)dē + \ *vt* [*de-* + *aerate*] **:** to remove air or gas (as oxygen) from — **de·aeration** \(ˌ)dē + \ *n* -S — **de·aerator** \(ˈ)dē + \ *n* -S

¹**deaf** \ˈdef, *archaic & dial* -ē-\ *adj* -ER/-EST [ME *deef*, fr. OE *dēaf*; akin to OHG *toub* deaf, stupid, ON *daufr* deaf, Goth *daufs* unreceptive to impressions, Gk *typhlos* blind, *typhein* to smoke, L *fumus* smoke — more at FUME] **1 :** lacking or deprived of the sense of hearing either wholly or in part **:** unable to perceive sounds **:** having a sense of hearing that is inadequate for the purposes of daily living **2 :** unwilling to hear or listen **:** determinedly inattentive ⟨none so ~ as those that will not hear⟩ **:** not to be persuaded as to facts, argument, or exhortation — used with *to* ⟨~ to reason⟩ **3** *obs, of a sound* **:** MUFFLED, STIFLED, DEADENED ⟨mocks the dull ear of Time with ~ abortive sound —William Wordsworth⟩ **4** *dial Brit* **:** incapable of bearing **:** having no fruit or kernel **:** STERILE, INFERTILE, BARREN ⟨~ eggs⟩ ⟨~ nutmegs⟩

²**deaf** \"\ *vt* -ED/-ING/-S [ME *deffen*, fr. *deef, deff*, adj.] *archaic* **:** DEAFEN

deaf adder *n* **1 :** any of various harmless snakes; *esp* **:** HOGNOSE SNAKE **2 :** the venomous copperhead **3** *Brit* **:** BLINDWORM 1

deaf-aid \ˈ=,=\ *n* **:** HEARING AID

deaf and dumb *adj* **:** DEAF-MUTE

deaf-and-dumb alphabet *n* **:** MANUAL ALPHABET

deaf ear *n* **:** whitened and empty heads of cereals (as those caused by wheat scab) — usu. used in pl.

deaf-ear crab *n* [so called fr. the belief that juices pressed from this crab will cure deafness] **:** a West Indian fiddler crab (*Uca pugnax vapax*)

deaf·en \ˈdefən\ *vt* **deafened; deafened; deafening** \-f(ə)niŋ\ **deafens 1 :** to make deaf **:** deprive esp. temporarily of the power of hearing **:** daze with noise ⟨~*ed* by the roar of escaping steam⟩ **2** *obs* **:** to make inaudible **:** drown out (a sound) **3 :** to make (a wall, floor, ceiling) impervious to sound (as by filling or lining with sound-absorbent material)

deafened *adj* **:** having become deaf after hearing normally and esp. after learning to speak

¹**deafening** *n* -S **1 :** the action or process of making a floor or wall impervious to sound **2 :** the material with which spaces are filled in the process of soundproofing — called also *pugging*

²**deafening** *adj* **1 :** that deafens **2 :** very loud **:** EARSPLITTING ⟨fell with a ~ crash⟩

deaf·en·ing·ly *adv* **:** in a deafening manner

de·af·fer·en·ta·tion \ˌdē,afə,renˈtāshən\ *n* -S [*de-* + *afferent* + *-ation*] **:** the freeing of a motor nerve from sensory components by severing the dorsal root central to the dorsal ganglion

deaf·ish \ˈdefish\ *adj* **:** slightly deaf **:** HARD-OF-HEARING

deaf·ly *adv* [ME *defly*, fr. *deef, def* deaf + *-ly*] **:** in a deaf manner **:** without hearing **:** without listening

¹**deaf-mute** \ˈ=ˈ=\ *adj* [trans. of F *sourd-muet* or G *taubstumm*] **:** lacking the sense of hearing and the ability to speak — **deaf-mute·ness** *n*

²**deaf-mute** \"\ *n* **:** a person who is deaf-mute

deaf-mut·ism \-ˈmyüd·ˌizəm\ *n* **:** the condition of being a deaf-mute

deaf·ness *n* -ES [ME *deefnesse*, fr. *deef* deaf + *-nesse* -ness — more at DEAF] **:** congenital or acquired lack, loss, or impairment of the sense of hearing whether due to defects in (1) the sound-transmitting mechanism, (2) the organ of Corti or auditory nerve, or (3) the interpretative centers of the brain —

called also respectively (1) *transmission deafness, conduction deafness,* or *conductive deafness,* (2) *perceptive deafness* or *nerve deafness,* and (3) *central deafness, cortical deafness,* or *psychic deafness*

deaf nettle *n* **:** a dead nettle (*Lamium purpureum*)

deaf nut *n* **1 :** a nut with no kernel **2 :** a thing without profit

de-air \(')═¦═\ *vt* [*de-* + *air* (n.)] **:** to remove air from (wet clay) by pugging under vacuum thereby increasing wet strength and density

¹**deal** \'dēl, *esp before pause or consonant* -ēəl\ *n* -s [ME *deel, del,* fr. OE *dǣl;* akin to OE *dāl* division, portion, OHG *teil* part, ON *deild* share, Goth *dails* part] **1** *obs* **:** PART, PORTION, SHARE **2 :** an indefinite quantity, degree, or extent ⟨it makes a good ~ of difference⟩ ⟨it means a great ~ to him⟩ ⟨he hasn't got a great ~ of money⟩ **3 a :** the act, process, or method of distributing cards to players in a card game **b :** the privilege or duty of acting as dealer ⟨it's my ~⟩ **c :** a period in the play of a card game embracing all phases from the shuffle through the determination or scoring of the result — compare HAND 10a(4) **4 :** a large quantity **:** LOT ⟨a ~ of years —Raymond Moley⟩

²**deal** \"\ *vb* **dealt** \'delt\ **dealt** \"\ **dealing** \'dēliŋ\ **deals** \'dē(ə)lz\ [ME *delen,* fr. OE *dǣlan;* akin to OHG *teilen* to divide, ON *deila,* Goth *dailjan;* denominative fr. the root of E ¹*deal*] *vt* **1** *obs* **:** DIVIDE, SEPARATE, SEVER **2 a :** to give as one's share or portion **:** DISTRIBUTE, APPORTION, METE ⟨*dealt* justice to all men⟩ — usu. used with *out* ⟨*dealt* out three sandwiches apiece⟩ **b** (1) **:** to distribute (one or more playing cards) to a player or the players in a card game (2) **:** to distribute the cards for (a specified card game) ⟨~ poker⟩ (3) **:** to act as dealer in (a specified game) ⟨~ craps⟩ **3 :** ADMINISTER, DELIVER, BESTOW ⟨~ the boy a scolding⟩ ~ *vi* **1** *obs* **:** to be a sharer **:** SHARE **2 a :** to distribute the cards in a card game **b :** to have the function or duty of distributing cards to the players in a card game **c :** to act as a dealer in a gambling game **3 a :** to have to do **:** concern oneself **:** TREAT — used with *with* ⟨the book ~*s* with all aspects of the subject⟩ **b :** to become occupied or busy — used with *in* ⟨~*ing* in matters of no concern to him⟩ ⟨fond of ~*ing* in large generalities⟩ **4 :** to act toward a person or regarding a thing **:** DO — used with *by* or *with* ⟨return . . . and I will ~ well with thee —Gen 32:9 (AV)⟩ **5** *archaic* **:** to have dealings — used with *with* ⟨~*ing* with witches —Shak.⟩ **6** *archaic* **:** to act as intermediary **:** make arrangements **:** NEGOTIATE — used with *with* or *between* **7 :** to do a retailing or distributing business **:** TRADE, TRAFFIC — used with *in* before a thing ⟨he ~*s* in flour⟩ and with *with* before a person ⟨he ~*s* fairly with all his customers⟩ **8** *obs* **:** CONTEND, STRUGGLE, QUARREL — used with *with* **9 :** to take action (as in regard to some object, problem, or source of difficulty) **:** come to grips — used with *with* ⟨he may ~ as he pleases with his own property⟩ ⟨had to ~ with a catastrophic inflation⟩ ⟨*dealt* with his problems as they arose⟩ ⟨*dealt* harshly with the rebels⟩ **syn** see DISTRIBUTE, TREAT

³**deal** \"\ *n* -s **1** *obs* **:** DEALINGS, INTERCOURSE **2 a :** an act of buying and selling **:** an offering of a combination of products at a special price ⟨a package ~⟩ **:** a reciprocal arrangement or agreement **:** BARGAIN **b :** treatment received in a transaction from another ⟨a raw ~⟩ or from impersonal forces or circumstances ⟨a rough ~⟩ **c** *usu cap* **:** a particular policy of national administration esp. of economic or politico-economic affairs ⟨Theodore Roosevelt's Square *Deal*⟩ ⟨the New *Deal*⟩ ⟨the Fair *Deal*⟩ **3 :** an often clandestine arrangement to gain mutual advantage for those interested **:** a negotiated settlement of an issue (as a lawsuit) ⟨law . . . has a way of beginning with ideals and ending with ~*s* —H.A.Overstreet⟩

⁴**deal** \"\ *n* -s [MD or MLG *dele* plank; akin to OHG *dili, dilla* plank, plank floor — more at THILL] **1 a** *Brit* **:** a board of fir or pine cut to any of several specified sizes — see DEAL END, SLIT DEAL, STANDARD DEAL, WHOLE DEAL **b** *in the U.S. export trade* **:** sawed yellow-pine lumber nine inches and wider and three, four, or five inches thick **2 :** pine or fir wood **:** deals in the aggregate ⟨a floor of ~⟩

⁵**deal** \"\ *adj* **:** made of deal; *broadly* **:** made of plain unfinished wood ⟨a ~ table⟩

deal apple *n* [⁴*deal*] **:** the cone of the white pine or of the fir

de·alate \dē'ā,lāt, -,lət\ *n* -s [*de-* + *alate*] **:** a dealated insect **:** a mature sexual individual of a kind of insect that undergoes dealation

de·alat·ed \-,lād·əd\ *adj* [*de-* + *alated*] **:** divested of the wings — used of postnuptial adults of certain insects (as ants and termites) that drop their wings after a nuptial flight — **de·ala·tion** \(,)dē,ā'lāshən\ *n* -s

de·al·bate \dē'al,bāt, -'ōl-\ *adj* [L *dealbatus,* past part. of *dealbare* to whitewash — more at DAUB] *bot* **:** covered with an opaque white powder

deal board *n* [⁴*deal*] **:** a fir or pine board **:** DEAL

deal end *n* [⁴*deal*] **:** a deal board less than six feet long — usu. used in pl.

deal·er \'dēlə(r)\ *n* -s [ME *delere,* fr. OE *dǣlere,* fr. *dǣlen* to divide + *-ere* -er — more at DEAL] **1 :** one that divides, distributes, or delivers **2** *obs* **:** NEGOTIATOR, AGENT, GO-BETWEEN **3 :** one that acts or conducts himself in some specified way toward others ⟨noted as a plain ~⟩ **4 :** one that does business **:** TRADER, TRAFFICKER, MIDDLEMAN **:** a person who makes a business of buying and selling goods esp. without altering their condition ⟨a ~ in dry goods⟩ ⟨~ in stocks⟩ ⟨an automobile ~⟩ — compare MANUFACTURER **5 :** one that buys and sells (as securities, commercial paper, or foreign exchange) on his own account — compare BROKER 1b **6 a** *Brit* **:** STOCKJOBBER a — distinguished from *broker* **b :** a member of a stock exchange who buys and sells as principal rather than as agent for a customer **7 a** (1) **:** a person who deals cards (2) **:** a machine or device for dealing cards **b** (1) **:** a gambler or employee of a gambling house who officiates at a game or gaming table (as a stickman, tourneur, croupier, or cashier) (2) **:** the chief among such persons **:** the person in charge of the table (as the stickman in craps or the tourneur at roulette)

dealer acceptance *n* **:** purchase by a retail merchant because of a known demand

dealer help *n* **:** promotional aid (as samples, counter or window displays, briefings for clerks) that is furnished retailers by manufacturers and wholesalers to stimulate sales of advertised products or to gain retailers' goodwill and continued patronage

dealer's choice *n* **:** a card game (as poker) in which the dealer may designate the variant to be played and set the stakes

deal·er·ship \-,ship\ *n* -s **:** an authorized sales agency **:** the business of a distributor ⟨an automobile ~⟩ ⟨a ~ for planes⟩

dealfish \'═,═\ *n* [⁴*deal* + *fish*] **:** any of several long thin fishes of the genus *Trachypterus* inhabiting the deep sea — called also *ribbonfish*

deal frame *n* [⁴*deal*] **:** LOG FRAME

deal in *vt* **:** to include (a specified player) among those to whom cards are dealt ⟨*deal* me *in*⟩

dealing *n* -s [ME *deling,* fr. gerund of *delen* to deal] **1 :** INTERCOURSE, TRAFFIC — usu. used in pl. ⟨~*s* with the devil⟩ **2 :** method of business or manner of conduct ⟨underhand ~⟩

dealing box *n* **:** ²BOX 13

de·alkalization \(,)dē+\ *n* -s **:** the process of dealkalizing

de·alkalize \(')dē+\ *vt* [*de-* + *alkalize*] **:** to remove alkali from **:** reduce the alkalinity of (as by neutralization)

de·alkylate \(')dē+\ *vt* [*de-* + *alkylate*] **:** to remove alkyl groups from (a compound) — **de·alkylation** \(,)dē+\ *n* -s

deal lugger \'dē(ə)l-\ *n, usu cap D* [fr. *Deal,* municipal borough on the Strait of Dover, Kent, England] **:** a lugger formerly common on the southeast coast of England esp. in the ship-tender service

deal off *vi* **:** to deal the last hand of a poker game or the last hand in which one intends to participate

deal out *vt* **:** to omit (a specified player) from those to whom cards are dealt

deal pine *n* [⁴*deal*] **:** WHITE PINE 1a

deals *pl of* DEAL, *pres 3d sing of* DEAL

dealt *past of* DEAL

de·am·bu·la·tion \(,)dē,ambyə'lāshən\ *n* [L *deambulation-, deambulatio,* fr. *deambulatus* (past part. of *deambulare* to walk abroad or about, fr. *de-* + *ambulare* to walk) + *-ion-, -io* -ion — more at AMBLE] **:** the act of walking abroad or about **:** PROMENADE

de·ambulatory \dē+\ *n* [LL *deambulatorium,* fr. L *deambulatus* + *-orium* -ory] **:** AMBULATORY

de·amidate \(')dē+\ *or* **des·amidate** \(')des+\ *vt* [*de-* or *des-* + *amidate*] **:** to remove the amido group from (a compound) — **de·amidation** \(,)dē+\ *or* **des·amidation** \(,)des+\ *n* -s

de·amidization \(,)dē+\ *or* **des·amidization** \(,)des+\ *n* -s **:** the process of deamidizing **:** DEAMIDATION

de·amidize \(')dē+\ *or* **des·amidize** \(')des+\ *vt* [*de-* or *des-* + *amide* + *-ize*] **:** DEAMIDATE

de·am·i·nase \(')dē'amə,nās, -āz\ *also* **des·am·i·nase** \(')de'sam-\ *n* -s [*de-* or *des-* + *amin-* + *-ase*] **:** an enzyme that hydrolyzes amino compounds (as amino acids) with the removal of the amino group

de·aminate \(')dē+\ *vt* [*de-* + *aminate*] **:** to remove the amino group from (a compound)

de·amination \(,)dē+\ *or* **des·amination** \(,)des+\ *n* **:** the process of deaminating ⟨the enzymatic oxidative ~ of glycine to glyoxylic acid and ammonia⟩ — compare AMINOLYSIS 2

de·aminization \(,)dē+\ *n* -s **:** the process of deaminizing **:** DEAMINATION

de·aminize \(')dē+\ *vt* [*de-* + *aminize*] **:** DEAMINATE

¹**dean** *var of* ¹DENE

²**dean** \'dēn\ *n* -s [ME *deen,* fr. MF *deien,* fr. LL *decanus,* lit., chief of ten, fr. L *decem* ten + *-anus* -an — more at TEN] **1** *obs* **:** a chief of 10 men **:** TITHINGMAN 1 **2 a :** a head over 10 monks in a monastery **b :** the head of the chapter or body of canons or prebendaries in a collegiate or cathedral church **c :** a priest of the Roman Catholic Church appointed by a bishop to supervise the affairs of a group of parishes within the diocese — called also *vicar forane* **3 a :** a resident fellow at an English university charged with the discipline rather than the instruction of undergraduates **b :** the head of one of the divisions, faculties, colleges, or schools of a university ⟨the ~*s* of several leading medical colleges⟩ ⟨the ~ of the faculty of arts⟩ ⟨the student must obtain the approval of the appropriate ~*s* and the chairmen of the departments concerned⟩ **c :** an administrative officer at a college or secondary school who counsels students on academic matters (as choice of program, maintenance of academic standing, honors, or failure) and who in addition has some disciplinary authority pertaining to such matters as breach of dormitory rules, unexcused absences, cheating and plagiarism, suspension, or dismissal ⟨~ of men⟩ ⟨~ of women⟩ ⟨~ of freshmen⟩ ⟨~ of the senior class⟩ **4 :** a high officer of the orders of the Thistle and of the Bath who is always a clergyman — compare CHAPLAIN **5 :** the senior of a group of men **:** DOYEN 1a

³**dean** \"\ *vi* -ED/-ING/-S **:** to act as dean ⟨was asked to ~⟩

dea·ner *var of* DEENER

dean·ery \'dēn(ə)rē, -ri\ *n* -ES [ME *denerie,* fr. *deen, den* dean + *-erie* -ery] **1 a :** the office or position of a dean **b :** the residence of a dean **2 :** the jurisdiction of a dean

deanery of christianity *usu cap C* **:** any of various British deaneries comprising certain city or town parishes (as Exeter or Lincoln)

dean·ess \-nəs\ *n* -ES **:** a nun who serves as dean in a convent

dean of a peculiar : a titular dean of the Church of England either without peculiar jurisdiction (as the dean of the Chapels Royal) or with jurisdiction but without a chapter

dean of christianity *usu cap C* **:** a holder of one of certain rural deaneries in England

dean of convocation : the president of a convocation in churches of the Anglican Communion

dean of guild 1 : the head of a guild (as in medieval and some existing European guilds) having the power to summon the members to meetings **2 :** a magistrate of a Scottish burgh or town formerly having jurisdiction of mercantile causes within a burgh and still entrusted with the inspection of and control over the construction, alteration, or repair of buildings

dean of the arches *usu cap D&A* [fr. the Court of *Arches,* the court of appeal for the province of Canterbury] **:** a lay judge in an ecclesiastical court (as the chancery court of the province of York) **:** the official principal of the archbishop of Canterbury

deans *pl of* DEAN, *pres 3d sing of* DEAN

dean schedule \'dēn-\ *n, usu cap D&S* [after Albert F. *Dean* †1933 Am. actuary] **:** a system for measuring the relative fire hazard and determining fire insurance rates for a property by an analysis of location, structural features, occupancy, and exposure

dean's list *n* **:** a list of students receiving special recognition from the dean of a college because of superior scholarship

¹**dear** \'di(ə)r, -iə\ *adj* -ER/-EST [ME *dere* brave, bold, hard, severe, fr. OE *dēor;* prob. akin to OE *dēor* beast — more at DEER] **:** SEVERE, SORE ⟨our *dearest* need⟩ ⟨his *dearest* enemies⟩

²**dear** \"\ *adj* -ER/-EST [ME *dere,* fr. OE *dēore;* akin to OHG *tiuri* costly, ON *dýrr*] **1** *obs* **:** GLORIOUS, WORTHY, HONORABLE **2 :** regarded very affectionately or fondly **:** highly valued or esteemed **:** BELOVED ⟨ran for ~ life⟩ ⟨his son was very ~ to him⟩ ⟨the cause of democracy . . . is so ~ to us —M.R. Cohen⟩ — often used formally or affectionately in address ⟨*Dear* Sir⟩ ⟨my ~ James⟩ ⟨Mother ~⟩ **3 :** LOVING, AFFECTIONATE, FOND ⟨for the ~ love I bear him⟩ **4 a** *obs* **:** SCARCE **b :** high-priced or expensive either absolutely ⟨butter is cheap when it is plentiful and ~ when it is scarce —G.B.Shaw⟩ or relatively ⟨that wretched suit would be ~ at any price⟩ **5** *obs* **:** VALUABLE, IMPORTANT **6 a :** close to the heart **:** present in mind **:** engaging the attention ⟨my ~*est* wish is for your happiness⟩ **b :** HEARTFELT, EARNEST ⟨one whose ~*est* prayer has been granted—G.B.Shaw⟩ **syn** see COSTLY

³**dear** \"\ *adv* [ME *dere,* fr. OE *dēore,* fr. *dēore,* adj.] **1 :** DEARLY ⟨the effort cost him ~⟩ **2 :** FONDLY, AFFECTIONATELY

⁴**dear** \"\ *n* -s [ME *dere,* fr. *dere,* adj.] **1 :** a dear one **:** DARLING, SWEETHEART ⟨that kiss I carried from thee ~ —Shak.⟩ **2 :** a lovable person ⟨pretty little ~*s*⟩ **:** an endearing person or being ⟨carry this in for me, like a ~⟩

⁵**dear** \"\ *vt* -ED/-ING/-S [ME *deren,* fr. *dere,* adj.] **1** *obs* **:** to make dear **:** make high-priced **2 a :** to address as *dear* **b** *obs* **:** ENDEAR

⁶**dear** \"\ *interj* [⁴*dear*] — used typically to express annoyance or dismay

dear·born \'di(ə)r,bōrn, -bərn\ *n* -s *sometimes cap* [after Henry A. S. *Dearborn* †1851 Am. politician and writer who maintained such a carriage] **:** a light 4-wheeled carriage with curtained sides

dearling *obs var of* DARLING

dear·ly *adv* [ME *derely,* fr. OE *dēorlice,* fr. *dēore* dear + *-līce* -ly — more at DEAR] **1 :** in a dear manner: as **a** *obs* **:** PRECIOUSLY, WORTHILY, RICHLY **b :** with affection **:** FONDLY, AFFECTIONATELY ⟨to love one ~⟩ **c :** HEARTILY, EARNESTLY, DEEPLY, KEENLY ⟨the peace we so ~ seek —D.D.Eisenhower⟩ **d :** at a high rate or price ⟨the victory was ~ won⟩

dear·ness *n* -ES [ME *derenesse,* fr. *dere* dear + *-nesse* -ness] **:** the quality or state of being dear: as **a :** LOVABLENESS **:** endearing quality **b :** reciprocal affection **:** FONDNESS **c :** COSTLINESS

dearness allowance *n, India* **:** a bonus or pay increase to meet a rise in the cost of living

¹**dearth** \'dərth, 'dəth, 'dəith\ *n* -s [ME *derthe,* fr. *dere* costly, dear + *-the* -th — more at DEAR] **1** *obs* **:** dearness **:** highness of price **2 :** scarcity that makes dear **:** WANT; *specif* **:** FAMINE ⟨there came a ~ over all the land of Egypt —Acts 7:11 (AV)⟩ **3 :** lack of a present necessity **:** deficiency or inadequate supply of something (as news) or of some quality (as courage)

²**dearth** *vt* -ED/-ING/-S [ME *derthen,* fr. *derthe,* n.] *obs* **:** to make scarce, dear, or high-priced

deary *or* **dear·ie** \'dirē, -ri\ *n, pl* **dear·ies** [⁴*dear* + *-y, -ie*] **:** little dear **:** DARLING — often used as a term of address

deas \'dēs, -ā-,-e-\ *n* -ES [ME *deis, dees* raised table, raised platform — more at DAIS] *Scot* **:** BENCH, SETTLE; *esp* **:** one that can also be used as a table

de·ash \(')dē+\ *vt* [*de-* + *ash* (residue of combustion)] **:** to remove ash from

¹**dea·sil** *also* **dei·seal** *or* **des·sil** \'dēzəl, 'des(h)əl\ *adv* [ScGael *deiseil;* akin to IrGael *deiseal* act of turning to the right, OIr *dess* right hand, south, ScGael *deas,* W *deheu, deau, de* right, south, Bret *dehou* right, south, L *dexter* right — more at DEXTER] **:** RIGHT-HANDWISE, SUNWISE, CLOCKWISE — used esp. of the Masonic rite of circumambulation and also of Masonic floor work that is clockwise; compare WIDDERSHINS

²**deasil** \"\ *n* -s **:** a charm performed by going three times about an object in the direction of the sun and sometimes carrying fire in the right hand

de·aspirate \(')dē+\ *vt* [*de-* + *aspirate*] **:** to pronounce without aspiration

de·assimilation \,dē+\ *n* [*de-* + *assimilation*] **:** CATABOLISM

death \'deth\ *n, pl* **deaths** \-ths *sometimes* -thz\ [ME *deeth, deth,* fr. OE *dēath;* akin to OHG *tōd* death, ON *dauthi,* Goth *dauthus;* derivative fr. the root of ON *deyja* to die — more at DIE] **1 :** the ending of all vital functions without possibility of recovery either in animals or plants or any parts of them **:** the end of life **:** the act, process, or fact of dying **2 a :** the cause or occasion of loss of life ⟨drinking was the ~ of him⟩ **:** a deadly weapon or agency ⟨a cobra with ~ in its fangs⟩ **b** *archaic* **:** PLAGUE — see BLACK DEATH **3** *usu cap* **:** the bringer of death personified and conventionally represented as a skeleton with a scythe **:** the destroyer of life **:** GRIM REAPER **4 a :** the state of being no longer alive ⟨in ~ as in life⟩ **b :** a joyless dull tasteless existence **:** the state of being without full possession or enjoyment of the intellectual or physical faculties ⟨the ~ in life of long years spent in a hospital bed⟩ **c :** cessation or absence of spiritual life variously conceived as alienation from God, deadness to the appeals of spiritual ideals, annihilation of the spirit as a result of sin, or irredeemable damnation — called also *spiritual death* ⟨to be carnally minded is ~ —Rom 8:6 (AV)⟩ **5 :** the passing or destruction of something inanimate ⟨the ~ of the rackety old Third Avenue El —*Newsweek*⟩ or intangible ⟨the ~ of all his hopes⟩ ⟨the ~ of vaudeville⟩ **:** the process of such passing ⟨the ~ of the empire⟩ **:** EXTINCTION ⟨the ~ of a species⟩ **6 :** CIVIL DEATH **7 :** lethal or murderous violence **:** HOMICIDE ⟨merchants of ~⟩ ⟨a man of ~ —Francis Bacon⟩ **8** *Christian Science* **:** the lie of life in matter **:** that which is unreal and untrue **:** ILLUSION — **at death's door :** close to death **:** critically ill **:** in real or apparent danger of dying — **be death on 1 :** to have marked talent for accomplishing or dealing with ⟨his approach shots are erratic but he *is death on* putts⟩ **2 :** to dislike or oppose vigorously ⟨the boss *is death on* latecomers⟩ — **in at the death :** present at the conclusion of an event — **to death** *adv* **:** to the last extremity ⟨tired *to death*⟩ **:** beyond endurance **:** EXCESSIVELY ⟨that kind of plot has been done *to death*⟩ — **to the death 1 :** to death **2 :** as long as life lasts **:** to the end **:** without wavering or compromise ⟨war *to the death*⟩ ⟨follow our leader *to the death*⟩ ⟨hunting a criminal *to the death*⟩

death adder *n* **:** a highly venomous elapid snake (*Acanthophis antarcticus*) of the Australian region having a stout body and a spine on the end of the tail; *also* **:** any of several other related venomous snakes of Australia and Tasmania

death alder *n* [so called fr. its poisonous effect on cattle] **:** a spindle tree (*Euonymus europaeus*)

¹**death angel** *n* **:** AZRAEL

²**death angel** *n* **:** DEATH CUP 1

death apple *n* **:** MANCHINEEL

deathbed \'═,═\ *n* [ME *deeth bed,* fr. *deeth* death + *bed*] **:** the bed in which a person dies **:** the last hours of life ⟨~ baptism⟩

deathbed deed *n, early Scots law* **:** a deed made after contracting a sickness that ended in death within 60 days after the date of granting and without such convalescence as is indicated by the grantor going unsupported to kirk or market

death bell *n* **:** PASSING BELL

death benefit *n* **:** money payable to the beneficiary or estate of a deceased under a policy of life or accident insurance or a pension plan

death bill *n* **:** an ecclesiastical list of dead to be prayed for

deathblow \'═,═\ *n* **:** a mortal blow ⟨he received his ~ in his first battle⟩ **:** a stroke or event that kills, destroys, or puts an end to

death board *n* **:** a plank on which a corpse is laid for sea burial

death camas *n* **:** any of several plants of the genus *Zigadenus* (as *Z. venenosus* and *Z. glaucus*) that cause poisoning of grazing animals in the western U.S.

death candle *n* **:** CORPSE CANDLE

death cell *n* **:** a prison cell for one awaiting execution

death certificate *n* **:** a certificate in which various information (as age, race, occupation) relating to a dead person is given and in which a physician certifies the cause of death

death chamber *n* **:** a room in which a person is dying or lies dead; *specif* **:** a place of execution within a prison

death-come-quickly \,═(,)═'══\ *n, dial Eng* **:** HERB ROBERT

death cord *n* **:** a rope used for hanging a person — called also *death rope*

death cup *n* **1** *also* **death angel :** a very poisonous mushroom (*Amanita phalloides*) of wide distribution ranging in color from pure white (as usu. in the U.S.) to olive or yellow and having a prominent volva at the base **2 :** the prominent cuplike enlargement at the base of the stipe in some fungi of the genus *Amanita* that is characteristic of poisonous forms though present also in some that are harmless

deathday \'═,═\ *n* [ME *deethday,* fr. OE *dēathdæg,* fr. *dēath* death + *dæg* day — more at DAY] **:** the day of a person's death or its anniversary

death duty *n, chiefly Brit* **:** DEATH TAX

death fire *or* **death light** *n* **:** DEADLIGHT 3, CORPSE CANDLE

death·ful \'dethfəl\ *adj* [ME *deethful,* fr. *deeth* death + *-ful*] **1** *archaic* **:** full of or threatening death **:** DEADLY, MURDEROUS, DESTRUCTIVE, BLOODY **2** *archaic* **:** liable to undergo death **:** MORTAL **3 :** like death **:** having the appearance of death **:** DEATHLY ⟨on his ~ face . . . a look of pain and baffled anger —Richard Hofstadter⟩ — **death·ful·ly** \-əlē\ *adv*

death herb *n* **:** BELLADONNA 1

death house *n* **:** the section of a prison for persons awaiting execution

death·in \'dethən\ *n* -s [prob. fr. *death* + *in*] **1 :** a water hemlock (*Cicuta virosa*) of Europe **2 :** a poisonous plant (*Oenanthe phellandrium*) closely related to the water hemlock

death instinct *n* **:** unconscious or biological tendencies toward self-destruction

death knell *n* **1 :** PASSING BELL **2 :** an action or event presaging death or destruction ⟨the coming of the power press was the *death knell* of the hand press⟩

death·less \'dethləs\ *adj* **:** not subject to death, destruction, or extinction **:** IMMORTAL, UNDYING, IMPERISHABLE ⟨~ fame⟩ ⟨~ poems⟩ — **death·less·ly** *adv* — **death·less·ness** *n* -ES

death·like \'═,═\ *adj* **:** DEATHLY

death·li·ness \'dethlēnəs, -lin-\ *n* -ES **:** the quality or state of being deathly

death·ling \-liŋ\ *n* -s **:** one liable to death **:** MORTAL

¹**death·ly** \'dethlē, -li\ *adj* [ME *dethlich* deadly, mortal, fr. OE *dēathlīc* mortal, fr. *dēath* death + *-līc* -ly] **1 :** DEADLY, FATAL, MORTAL, DESTRUCTIVE **2 :** like or having the characteristics of death ⟨a ~ stillness⟩ **3 :** of, relating to, or suggestive of death ⟨I marked each ~ change in him —Robert Browning⟩ **syn** see DEADLY

²**deathly** \"\ *adv* **:** in a way or to a degree resembling or approximating death ⟨~ sick⟩

death march *n* **:** a march (as of prisoners of war) in which those unable to go on are left to die as they fall

death mask *n* **:** a cast taken from the face of a dead person

death penny *n* **1 :** a coin placed with a buried corpse as if to pay passage to the otherworld **2 :** DEATH WEIGHT

death point *n* **:** a limit (as of degree of heat or cold) beyond which an organism or living protoplasm cannot survive

death rate *n* **:** the ratio between number of deaths and number of individuals in a specified population and period of time usu. expressed as number of deaths per hundred or per thousand population

death rattle *n* **:** a rattling or gurgling sound produced by air passing through mucus in the lungs and air passages of one dying

death rope *n* **:** DEATH CORD

death row *n* **:** a row of death cells

deaths *pl of* DEATH

death's-head \'deths,hed\ *n* **1 :** a human skull as the emblem of death **:** the head of Death **2 :** a finger ring bearing the figure of a skull

death's-head moth *n* **:** a very large dark European hawkmoth (*Acherontia atropos*) with markings resembling a human skull on the back of the thorax

death's-herb *n, obs* **:** BELLADONNA 1

deaths·man \'dethsmən\ *n, pl* **deathsmen** *archaic* **:** a man who puts persons to death **:** EXECUTIONER

death–struck \'ˌ=,=\ *also* **death–stricken** \'=,==\ *adj* **:** mortally injured or sick

death tax *n* **:** a tax arising on the transmission of property (as an estate, inheritance, legacy, succession) after the owner's death

deathtrap \'=,=\ *n* **:** a structure or situation that is potentially very dangerous (as by fire) to life ⟨the boat was just seaworthy enough to be a ~ —Padraic Fallon⟩

death·ward \'dethwə(r)d\ *or* **death·wards** \-dz\ *adv* (*or adj*) [ME deethward, fr. *deeth* death + *-ward, -wards*] **:** toward death **:** approaching death

death warrant *n* **1 :** a warrant for the execution of a death sentence **2 :** something that puts an end to the existence or continuance of anything ⟨declared the new law the *death warrant* of unfettered competition⟩

¹deathwatch \'=,=\ *n* [*death* + *watch* (timepiece); fr. the superstition that its ticking presages death] **:** any of several small insects that make a ticking sound: as **: a** *or* **death·watch beetle :** any of various small beetles of the family Anobiidae that are common in old houses where they bore in the woodwork and furniture making a clicking noise probably by knocking the head against the wood **b :** BOOK LOUSE

²deathwatch \'=¦=\ *n* [*death* + *watch* (vigil)] **1 :** a vigil kept with the dead or dying **2 a :** the guard set over a criminal before his execution **b :** a group of press reporters waiting for an expected announcement or break in a big story

deathweed \'=,=\ *n* **:** POVERTYWEED c

death weight *n* **:** a small weight (as a coin) laid on the eyelids of a corpse to keep them closed

death wish *n* **:** the conscious or unconscious desire for the death of another or of oneself

deathworm \'=,=\ *n* **:** a worm that feeds on a buried dead body

deathy \'dethē\ *adj* **:** DEATHLY, DEADLY

de·aurate \dē'ò,rāt\ *vt* -ED/-ING/-S [LL *deauratus*, past part. of *deaurare*, fr. L *de-* + *aurare* to cover with gold, gild, fr. *aurum* gold — more at ORIOLE] *archaic* **:** GILD — **de·aura·tion** \,dē,ò'rāshən\ *n* -S *archaic*

deau·ville sand \'dō,vil-, (')dō¦vēl-\ *n, often cap D* [fr. *Deauville*, Calvados dept., France] **:** a light grayish brown that is redder and paler than average fawn — called also *stucco*

deave \'dēv\ *vt* -ED/-ING/-S [ME *deven*, fr. OE *-dēafian* (as in *ādēafian* to become deaf), fr. *dēaf* deaf — more at DEAF] **1** *dial Brit* **:** to stun or stupefy with noise **:** DEAFEN **2** *dial Brit* **:** BOTHER, CONFUSE

deave·ly \-lī\ *adj, often* -ER/-EST [prob. fr. ¹*deaf* + *-ly*] *dial Eng* **:** LONELY

deb \'deb\ *n* -S [by shortening] **:** DEBUTANTE

deb *abbr* debenture

de·babelization \(¦)dē+\ *n* -S [*de-* + *babelization*] **:** the removal of obstacles to verbal communication ⟨the question still remains whether ~ will be accomplished by the voluntary adoption of a national tongue —K.D.Burke⟩

de·ba·cle \dә'bäkəl, dā'-,dē'-, -ak-,-äk- *sometimes* dā'bäk(lᵊ) *or* dā'bák(lᵊ)\ *n* -S [F *débâcle*, fr. *débâcler* to unbar, unbolt, fr. MF *desbacler*, fr. *des-* de- + *bacler* to bar, bolt, fr. OProv *baclar*, fr. (assumed) VL *bacculare*, fr. (assumed) VL *bacculum* stick, staff, alter. of L *baculum* — more at BACTERIUM] **1 a** (1) **:** a breaking up of ice in a river (2) **:** the rush (as of water and ice) that follows such a breaking up **b :** a violent destructive flood **2 :** a sudden breaking up or breaking loose **:** a violent dispersion or disruption (as of an army or mob) **:** STAMPEDE, ROUT ⟨Custer's ~ on the Little Big Horn —Seth Agnew⟩ **3 :** a sudden breakdown **:** COLLAPSE ⟨the Wall Street ~ of 1929 —Isabel Leighton⟩

de·bag \(')dē+\ *vt* [*de-* + *bag* (trousers)] *Brit* **:** to remove the trousers from as a punishment or in hazing ⟨the new boy was *debagged* and thrown in the fountain⟩

de·bar \dē, dә+\ *vt* [ME *debarren*, fr. MF *desbarrer* to remove the bars from a door, fr. OF, fr. *des-* de- + *barrer* to fasten with a bar — more at BAR] **1 :** to prevent from an action ⟨government contractors *debarred* from sitting in Parliament —J.H.Plumb⟩ **:** shut out **:** EXCLUDE ⟨custom ~s certain persons from marriage⟩ **:** bar from the possession, use, or enjoyment of something ⟨cities like New York ... are *debarred* from a share of modern tax revenues —A.A.Berle⟩ **2 :** to set a barrier or prohibition against ⟨a gate ~s all passage⟩ **:** DEPRIVE ⟨they *debarred* him from the sacrament⟩ **3 :** to exclude from membership in a group or class ⟨the qualifications ~ most of the best applicants⟩ **syn** see EXCLUDE — **debar the tables :** to fence the tables

de·barbarize \(')dē+\ *vt* [*de-* + *barbarize*] **:** to free from barbarousness **:** make no longer barbarous

¹de·bark \dә'bärk,dē'-, -bák\ *vb* -ED/-ING/-S [MF *debarquer*, fr. *de-* + *barque* bark (sailing vessel) — more at BARK] **:** DISEMBARK

²de·bark \(')dē+\ *vt* -ED/-ING/-S [*de-* + *bark* (of a tree)] **:** to remove bark from

³debark \"\ *vt* -ED/-ING/-S [*de* + *bark* (sound made by a dog)] **:** to remove the vocal cords from (a dog) to check barking

de·bar·ka·tion \,dē,bär'kāshən, -bá'- *sometimes* dә,- *or* dē,-\ *n* -S [¹*debark* + *-ation*] **:** DISEMBARKATION

debarkation net *n* **:** a net that may be hung over the side of a ship to enable troops to climb down into small boats

de·bar·ment \dē'bärmənt, dә'-, -bám-\ *n* -S **1 :** the act of debarring **2 :** the state of being debarred

de·bar·rance \-rən(t)s\ *also* **de·bar·ra·tion** \,dē,bä'rāshən, -bá-\ *n* -S **:** the act of fencing the tables in Scottish Presbyterian churches

de·bar·rass \dә'barəs, dē'-\ *vt* -ED/-ING/-ES [F *débarrasser*, fr. MF *desbarrasser*, fr. *de-* + *embarrasser* to embarrass — more at EMBARRASS] **:** to disembarrass esp. by removing what impedes or encumbers ⟨~ed her of her coat and hat⟩

de·base \dә'bās, dē'-\ *vt* -ED/-ING/-S [*de-* + *base* (low, vile); after *abase*] **1** *obs* **:** to lower in esteem by verbal attack **:** DISPARAGE, VILIFY **2 :** to lower in status or esteem ⟨~ himself by physical labor⟩ **:** put to a low or inferior use ⟨a style *debased* by many imitators⟩ **3 :** to lower the quality or character of **:** cause to deteriorate ⟨struggle with Hannibal had ... *debased* the Roman temper —John Buchan⟩ **4 a :** to reduce the intrinsic value of (a coin) by increasing the base-metal content **b :** to reduce the exchange value of (a monetary unit) **:** DEPRECIATE

syn VITIATE, DEPRAVE, CORRUPT, DEBAUCH, PERVERT: DEBASE indicates a drastic and regrettable lowering in worth, value, and dignity and a loss of fine or good qualities ⟨the human values cruelly and systematically *debased* by the Nazis—Vera M. Dean⟩ ⟨Strachey's attitude toward a respected historical figure and his new techniques were soon *debased* by a school of so-called debunking biographers —J.D.Hart⟩ VITIATE is applicable to the introduction or effect of something deleterious and the ensuing destruction of purity, impairment of validity, or enervation of effectiveness ⟨party jealousies *vitiated* the whole military organization —*Times Lit. Supp.*⟩ ⟨his endless muttering *vitiated* every effort I made to think out a line of action —H.G.Wells⟩ DEPRAVE indicates moral deterioration into the obscene and vicious ⟨the servants, wicked and *depraved*, corrupt and deprave the children; the children are bad, full of evil, to a sinister degree —Henry James †1916⟩ CORRUPT indicates bringing about a loss of soundness, purity, and integrity ⟨at sixteen the girl was further *corrupted* by a "perverse and wicked" young man —Edmund Wilson⟩ ⟨the ballot box, *corrupted*, no longer recorded the voice of the people —Oscar Handlin⟩ ⟨to *corrupt* their taste first and try to purify it afterwards —Bertrand Russell⟩ DEBAUCH usu. suggests corrupting and vulgarizing through sensual pleasure or other indulgence with loss of sense of morality, loyalty, duty, integrity, and resolution ⟨she takes them to an enchanted isle, where she *debauches* them with enervating delights and renders them oblivious to their duty —R.A.Hall b. 1911⟩ ⟨readers *debauched* by sentimental and romantic liberalism and naturalism —Douglas Bush⟩ PERVERT suggests a debasing twisting or contorting into an untrue or abnormal condition ⟨those who *pervert* good words to careless misuse may be thought more often ludicrous than harmful —J.M.Barzun⟩ ⟨those who *pervert* honest criticism into falsification of fact —F.D.Roosevelt⟩ ⟨sexually *perverted* during his term in prison⟩

de·based·ness \-sədnəs, -s(t)n-\ *n* -ES **:** the quality or state of being debased

de·base·ment \-smənt\ *n* -S **1 :** the act or process of debasing ⟨the ~ of the coinage⟩ **2 :** the state of being debased **3 :** something that debases

de·bas·er \-sə(r)\ *n* -S **:** one that debases

de·bas·ing·ly *adv* **:** in a debasing manner

dé·bat \dā'bä, *F* dābá\ *n* -S [F, lit., debate, strife, altercation, fr. OF *debat*] **1 :** a type of literary composition popular esp. in medieval times in which two or more usu. allegorical characters discuss or debate some subject — compare TENSON **2 :** an extended discussion, debate, or philosophical argument between two characters in a work of literature

de·bat·able *also* **de·bate·able** \dә'bād·əbəl, dē'-, -ātə-\ *adj* [ML *debatabilis*, fr. ME *debaten* to debate + L *-abilis* -able] **1 :** claimed by more than one country — used of land ⟨the governor ... dispatched troops ... into the ~ territory —H.E.Scudder⟩ **2 a :** open to question or dispute **:** DISPUTABLE, QUESTIONABLE, DOUBTFUL ⟨whether this report is accurate is a ~ question⟩ ⟨the ~ wisdom of your advice⟩ **b :** open to debate ⟨decisions are ~ in closed sessions but binding on members when a parliamentary vote is taken⟩ **:** capable of producing debate ⟨a list of ~ topics for classroom use⟩

¹de·bate \-āt, *usu* -ād·+V\ *n* -S [ME *debat*, fr. OF, fr. *debatre*] **1 a** *obs* **:** a fight or fighting **:** CONTEST **b** *archaic* **:** QUARREL, DISSENSION, STRIFE **2 a :** a contention by means of words or arguments ⟨an evening's ~ among friends⟩ **:** strife in argument **:** CONTROVERSY; *specif* **:** the formal discussion, argumentation, and resolution of a motion before a legislative assembly or other public deliberative body according to the rules of parliamentary procedure **b :** consideration of or reflection upon a problem ⟨paused hesitantly, but after a moment of ~ she went forward⟩ **3 a :** an instance of debating ⟨we have just now engaged in a great ~ —F.D.Roosevelt⟩ **b** (1) **:** a regulated discussion of a proposition between two matched sides as a test of forensic ability (2) **:** a course of study of the methods and techniques of such discussion often taught in schools and colleges

²debate \"\ *vb* -ED/-ING/-S [ME *debaten*, fr. MF *debatre*, fr. OF, fr. *de-* + *batre* to beat, fr. L *battere*, alter. of *battuere* — more at BAT (stick)] *vi* **1** *obs* **:** to engage in combat or strife **:** FIGHT, CONTEND, QUARREL **2 a :** to contend in words **:** DISPUTE **b :** to discuss or examine a question by considering or stating different arguments ⟨Socrates *debated* on the subject of life and death⟩ **3 :** to participate in a debate or other public disputation or discussion **4 :** to reflect upon a question or problem ⟨~ with oneself before deciding to go⟩ **~** *vt* **1 a :** to argue about **:** DISCUSS ⟨the subject was hotly *debated*⟩; *esp* **:** to discuss (a matter of public concern) in a legislative assembly **b :** to engage in debate with (an opponent) ⟨Lincoln *debated* Douglas on this issue⟩ **2 :** to turn over (a matter) in one's mind **:** reflect upon ⟨I held her hand for a moment, *debating* a reply —L.C.Douglas⟩ **3** *archaic* **:** to engage in combat for **:** strive or fight for or over **:** CONTEST **syn** see DISCUSS

debatement *n* -S [MF, fr. *debatre* + *-ment*] *obs* **:** DEBATE, CONTROVERSY, CONFLICT

de·bat·er \dә'bād·ə(r), dē-, -atə-\ *n* -S [ME, fr. *debaten* + *-er*] **:** one that debates

de·bat·ing·ly *adv* **:** in a debating manner

¹de·bauch \dә'bȯch, dē'-, -bäch\ *vb* -ED/-ING/-ES [MF *debaucher*, fr. OF *desbauchier* to scatter, separate, lit., to roughhew (timber for a beam), fr. *des-* de- + *-bauchier* (fr. *bauch, bauc* beam, of Gmc origin; akin to OHG *balko* beam) — more at BALK] *vt* **1** *archaic* **a :** to lead away or seduce from one to whom duty or allegiance is owed **:** lead or seduce esp. to an evil party or action **b :** to seduce from duty or allegiance **:** make disloyal **:** DISAFFECT **2** *obs* **:** to disparage by unfavorable comment **3 a :** to lead astray from what is good or right ⟨a performance *~ed* by an excess of vulgarity⟩ **:** win away from integrity ⟨corrupt the press and ~ the legislatures⟩ **:** corrupt in character or principle ⟨factory methods . . . *~ed* Victorian design —*Country Life*⟩ **b :** to corrupt esp. by intemperance or sensuality **:** to seduce from chastity **4** *obs* **:** to spend lavishly **:** SQUANDER **~** *vi* **:** to indulge excessively in sensual pleasure ⟨a man who never gambled or *~ed*⟩ **syn** see DEBASE

²debauch \"\ *n* -ES [F *débauche*, fr. MF *debauche*, fr. *debaucher*] **1 a :** an act or occasion of debauchery ⟨a night's ~⟩ **b :** an act or occasion of indulging to excess esp. in a violent, emotional, or pleasurable activity ⟨I have had a vast ~ of reading —H.J.Laski⟩ ⟨a ~ of speculation on the stock exchange⟩ **2 :** excess in sensual pleasures **:** DEBAUCHERY ⟨tales of battle and ~ —Max Peacock⟩ **3** *obs* **:** DEBAUCHEE

de·bauched \-cht\ *adj* **:** DISSOLUTE, DEPRAVED ⟨old woman ... with a ~ face —Liam O'Flaherty⟩ — **de·bauched·ly** \-chəd-lē, -chtlē\ *adv* — **de·bauched·ness** \-chədnəs, -ch(t)n-\ *n* -ES

de·bauch·ee \dә'bȯ(,)chē, dē'-, -bä-, -,chi; dә,bȯ'chē, (,)dē,-, -bä-; ¦debə¦shē, -bȯ-, -e(,)bȯ-, -¦shā\ *n* -S [F *débauché*, fr. past part. of *débaucher* to debauch] **:** one given to sensual excesses (as intemperance) ⟨weird orgies . . . of jaded ~s —I.S.Cobb⟩

de·bauch·er \dә'bȯchə(r), dē'-, -bäch-\ *n* -S **:** one that debauches; *esp* **:** one that seduces another from chastity

de·bauch·ery \-ch(ə)rē, -ri\ *n* -ES **1 a :** extreme indulgence in sensuality **:** INTEMPERANCE ⟨nights of riotous ~⟩; *esp* **:** excessive indulgence of sexual desire **b debaucheries** *pl* **:** ORGIES, CAROUSALS **2** *archaic* **:** corruption of fidelity **:** seduction from virtue, duty, or allegiance

debauchment *n* -S [F *débauchement*, fr. MF *debauchement*, fr. *debaucher* to debauch + *-ment*] **1** *obs* **:** the action of debauching **2** *obs* **:** the state of being debauched

de·beak \(')dē+\ *vt* [back-formation fr. *Debeaker*, a trademark] **:** to remove the tip of the upper mandible of (a bird) to prevent cannibalism and fighting

de·bel *or* **de·bell** \dә'bel\ *vt* **debelled; debelled; debelling; debels** *or* **debells** [MF or L; MF *debeller*, fr. L *debellare*] **:** CONQUER, SUBDUE

debellate *vt* -ED/-ING/-S [L *debellatus*, past part. of *debellare*, fr. *de-* + *bellare* to wage war, fr. *bellum* war — more at DUEL] *obs* **:** DEBEL

de·bel·la·tio \,dābə'lād·ē,ō\ *n* -S [LL, fr. L *debellatus* + *-io* -ion] **:** complete subjugation of a belligerent nation usu. involving loss of sovereignty

deb·el·la·tion \,debə'lāshən\ *n* -S [LL *debellation-, debellatio*] **:** the action of debelling

de be·ne es·se \,dā,benē'esē\ *adv* [ML, lit., of well-being] **:** of sufficiency for the present **:** CONDITIONALLY, PROVISIONALLY — used of various things done subject to future exception or avoidance (as the taking of testimony before trial where it may be unavailable at the time of trial)

de·ben·ture \dә'benchə(r), dē'-\ *n* -S [ME *debentur*, fr. L, they are due, 3d pers. pl. pres. pass. of *debēre* to owe — more at DEBT] **1 :** a writing or certificate signed by a public officer as evidence of a debt or of a right to demand or receive a sum of money: as **a :** a voucher from a government official certifying a sum of money to be due to a person (as for stores supplied to the ordnance department) **b :** a customhouse certificate entitling an exporter of imported goods to a drawback of duties paid on their importation **c :** an instrument issued as evidence of debt by a government on the security of the public assets or credit **2 a** *Brit* **:** a security issued by a company other than its shares **:** BOND **b** *or* **debenture bond :** a bond usu. secured by an indenture containing protective provisions but without a specific lien on any asset — now the usual U.S. use; distinguished from *mortgage bond*; compare ³BOND 5b

debenture stock *n* **:** a corporate security issue common in Great Britain that usu. has no fixed maturity date for the principal but that has a fixed claim to interest payments which takes precedence over preferred and common stocks

de·benzylation \(¦)dē+\ *n* -S [*de-* + *benzyl* + *-ation*] **:** the removal of benzyl groups from a compound often by hydrogenation

deb·ile \'debəl, -,bīl, -(,)bil; 'dē,bīl\ *adj* [MF *debile*, fr. L *debilis* weak, feeble — more at DEBILITY] *archaic* **:** marked by debility **:** FEEBLE

de·bil·i·tate \dә'bilə,tāt, dē'-, *usu* -ād·+V\ *vt* -ED/-ING/-S [L *debilitatus*, past part. of *debilitare* to weaken, fr. *debilis* weak] **:** to impair the strength of **:** WEAKEN, ENFEEBLE ⟨a body *debilitated* by disease⟩ ⟨war . . . left a *debilitated* economic plant —C.R.Decker⟩ **syn** see WEAKEN

de·bil·i·ta·tion \dә,bilə'tāshən, (,)dē,-\ *n* -S [MF, fr. L *debilitation-, debilitatio*, fr. *debilitatus* + *-ion-, -io* -ion] **1 :** the act or process of debilitating **2 :** the state of being debilitated **:** WEAKNESS ⟨the greater the ~, the greater the need for protein replenishment —P.R.Cannon⟩

de·bil·i·ta·tive \dә'bilə,tād·iv, dē'-, -,təd-\ *adj, archaic* **:** debilitating in its tendency **:** causing debility

de·bil·i·ty \-ləd·ē, -etē, -i\ *n* -ES [MF *débilité*, fr. L *debilitat-, debilitas*, fr. *debilis* weak (fr. *de* from, away + *-bilis* strength) + *-itat-, -itas* -ity; akin to Gk *beltеros* better, OSlav *bolijī* larger, Skt *bala* strength — more at DE-] **:** the quality or state of being weak, feeble, or infirm; *esp* **:** physical weakness

¹deb·it \'debət, *usu* -əd·+V\ *n* -S *often attrib* [L *debitum* debt — more at DEBT] **1 a :** an entry on the left-hand side of an account constituting an addition to an expense or asset account or a deduction from a revenue, net worth, or liability account **b :** any one of the items on the left-hand side of an account; *also* **:** the sum of these items — opposed to *credit*; abbr. *dr* **c :** a charge against a bank deposit account **2 :** something regarded as disadvantageous or unfavorable ⟨against these successes by the administration there are on the ~ side a number of serious failures⟩ **3 :** an area to which an insurance agent is assigned for the purpose of collecting premiums from the policyholders **syn** see DEBT

²debit \"\ *vt* -ED/-ING/-S **:** to enter upon the left-hand side of an account **:** charge to the debit of ⟨~ a creditor's account⟩ — opposed to *credit*

deb·it·able \'debəd·əbəl\ *adj* **:** that can or should be debited

de·bi·ta la·ico·rum \¦debəd·ə,lāə'kōrəm\ *n pl* [ML] **:** debts of the laity

deb·i·teuse \¦debə¦tüz\ *n* -S [F *débiteuse*, fr. F *débiter* to discharge, yield, sell retail, cut up, (fr. MF *debiter* to cut wood, sell retail, fr. *de-* + *-biter*, of Scand origin; akin to ON *biti* beam, thwart) + *-euse* (fem. of *-eur* -or) — more at BOAT] **:** a rectangular clay block floating upon molten glass in a tank furnace and containing a long slot that shapes glass into a sheet as it is drawn through it

debit note *n* **:** a memorandum of goods returned and debited to a consignor by a consignee

debitor *n* -S [MF & L; MF *debiteur*, fr. L *debitor* — more at DEBTOR] *obs* **:** DEBTOR

de·bitter \(')dē+\ *vt* [*de-* + *bitter* (adj.)] **:** to remove the bitterness from (an edible substance)

de·bit·ter·ize \(')dē'bid·ə,rīz\ *vt* -ED/-ING/-S [*de-* + *bitter* (adj.) + *-ize*] **:** DEBITTER

debit ticket *n* **1 :** an order drawn by an employee of a bank at a depositor's request to pay out money against the depositor's account **2** *or* **debit memo :** a memorandum of a charge (as for service) made by a bank against a depositor's account **3 :** a slip indicating a transaction to be debited to an account or in the general ledger

deb·i·tum \'debəd·əm\ *n, pl* **debi·ta** \-d·ə\ [L — more at DEBT] **:** DEBT

debitum fun·di \-'fən,dī, -'fün,dē\ *n, pl* **debita fundi** [L, lit., debt of an estate] *Scots law* **:** a debt that is a lien on land

de·block \(')dē+\ *vt* [*de-* + *block*] **:** to relax or remove monetary restrictions on (as the transfer of bank funds or currency out of a country)

deboist *adj* [by alter.] *obs* **:** DEBAUCHED

deb·o·nair *also* **deb·o·naire** \¦debə¦na(a)(ə)r, -ne|, |ə\ *adj* [ME *debonere*, fr. OF *debonaire*, fr. *de bon aire, de bonne aire* of good family, lineage, or nature] **1** *archaic* **:** kindly or gentle in disposition or manner **:** COURTEOUS, GRACIOUS ⟨~ and pleasing toward our lieges —Sir Walter Scott⟩ **2 a :** having grace, charm, or urbanity of manner and appearance **b :** LIGHTHEARTED, CAREFREE ⟨life that is gay, brisk, and ~ —H.M. Reynolds⟩ **:** NONCHALANT ⟨his ~ dismissal of serious difficulties —E.M.Earle⟩ — **deb·o·nair·ly** *adv*

deb·o·nair·ness *n* -ES [ME *debonerenesse*, fr. *debonere* + *-nesse* -ness] **:** the quality of being debonair **:** good humor **:** JAUNTINESS, LIGHTHEARTEDNESS

de·bone \(')dē+\ *vt* [*de-* + *bone* (n.)] **:** to remove (bone) from meat

de bo·nis as·por·ta·tis \,dā'bōnə,saspə(r)'täd·əs\ *n* [L, of goods carried away] **:** an action of trespass to recover money damages from one who has taken away or damaged property without right

de bonis non \(,)dā¦bōnə¦snän\ *or* **de bonis non ad·min·i·stra·tis** \dā'bōnə,snänad,minə'sträd·əs\ [L, of the goods not (administered)] **:** concerning the goods of a deceased person not yet administered — used of an administrator or of letters of administration

de bonis pro·pri·is \(,)dā¦bō-nə'sprōprēəs\ [L, out of one's own goods] **:** out of his own pocket — used of a judgment against an administrator or executor to be satisfied out of his own funds

de·bord \dә'bȯ(ə)rd, dē'-\ *vi* -ED/-ING/-S [F *déborder*, fr. MF *desborder*, fr. *des-* de- + *-border* (fr. *bord* shore, bank, edge, board of a ship, fr. OF *bort* edge, end, board of a ship) — more at BORDER] **1** *archaic* **:** to flow beyond its banks — used of a body of water **2** *obs* **:** to go beyond bounds **:** go to excess

de·boshed \-bäsht\ *adj* [by alter.] **:** DEBAUCHED

de·boss \(')dē+\ *vt* [*de-* + *boss* (protruding ornament)] **:** to depress (as a design on a book cover) below the surrounding surface esp. for decoration or lettering — opposed to *emboss*

de·bot effect \də'bō-\ *n, usu cap D* [after R. *Debot*, 20th cent. Belgian scientist] **:** a manifestation of the Herschel effect in which the internal latent image is converted into a surface latent image by the action of red or infrared radiation

de·bouch \dә'büsh, dē-, -bau̇ch\ *vb* -ED/-ING/-ES [F *déboucher*, fr. *dé-* de- (fr. OF *de-, des-*) + *bouche* mouth, opening, fr. OF *boche, bouche*, fr. L *bucca* puffed out cheek, mouth — more at POCK] *vi* **1 :** to march out (as from a wood or defile) into open ground ⟨the three regiments *~ing* from three separate gorges —Rudyard Kipling⟩ **2 :** to emerge into a more open place **:** issue forth **:** pass out into ⟨the tributary *~es* into the main stream⟩ **~** *vt* **:** to lead out into the open **:** cause to emerge **:** DISCHARGE ⟨motor coaches *~ed* a crowd —William Sansom⟩

dé·bou·ché \,dā,bü'shā\ *n* -S [F, fr. past part. of *déboucher*] **:** an opening or passage that can serve as an outlet (as for the debouching of troops)

de·bouch·ment \dә'büshmənt, dē'-, -bau̇ch-\ *n* -S [F *débouchement*, fr. *déboucher* + *-ment*] **1 :** the act or process of debouching **2 :** a mouth or outlet esp. of a river

de·bou·chure \-¦bü¦shu̇(ə)r\ *n* -S [F, fr. *déboucher* + *-ure*] **:** DEBOUCHMENT 2

de·bre·cen \'debrət,sen\ *adj, usu cap* [fr. *Debrecen*, Hungary] **:** of or from the city of Debrecen, Hungary **:** of the kind or style prevalent in Debrecen

de·bride \dә'brēd, dā'-\ *vt* -ED/-ING/-S [F *débrider*, lit., to unbridle, fr. MF *desbrider*, fr. *des-* de- + *bride* bridle, fr. OF, fr. MHG *brīdel* — more at BRIDLE] **:** to cleanse by debridement

de·bride·ment \-d,mäⁿ, -dmənt\ *n* -S [F *débridement*, fr. *débrider* + *-ment*] **:** the surgical removal of lacerated, devitalized, or contaminated tissue

de·brief \dә, dē+\ *vt* [*de-* + *brief*] **:** to interrogate (as a pilot returning from a mission or a government official returning from abroad) in order to obtain useful information or intelligence ⟨where photographs are examined and pilots are *~ed* —Christopher Rand⟩

de·bris \də'brē *also* dā'b- *or* 'dā,b- *sometimes* de'b- *or* 'de,b-\ *n, pl* **debris** \-ēz\ [F *débris*, fr. MF *debris*, fr. *debriser* to break to pieces, fr. OF *debrisier*, fr. *de-* + *brisier* to break — more at BRISANCE] **:** the remains of something broken down or destroyed ⟨swaying buildings and crashing ~ —H.E. Rieseberg⟩ **:** RUINS ⟨the ~ of Alexander's empire —John Buchan⟩: as **a :** an accumulation of loose detached fragments of rock — compare DETRITUS **b :** waste sand and gravel produced by hydraulic mining operations **c :** organic waste from dead or damaged tissue **syn** see REFUSE

debris–avalanche \"+¦-\ *n* **:** a mass of rock fragments and soil that has moved rapidly down a steep mountain slope or hillside and because of its high water content has behaved like an avalanche of snow — compare DEBRIS-SLIDE

debris cone *n* **:** a mound of ice on a glacier protected by an isolated patch of fine rock debris from the more rapid melting that has lowered the surrounding surface

debris glacier *n* **:** a glacier composed of ice that has fallen in fragments from a larger and higher glacier

debris-slide \-,slīd\ *n* **:** a mass of predominantly unconsolidated and incoherent soil and rock fragments that has slid or rolled rapidly down a steep slope when comparatively dry to form an irregular hummocky deposit — compare DEBRIS-AVALANCHE

de bro·glie equation \də¦brō¦glē-, də'brȯyə-\ *n, usu cap B* [after Peter Louis V. *de Broglie*] **:** an equation in physics: the de Broglie wavelength of a moving particle is equal to the Planck constant divided by the momentum of the particle

de broglie wave *n, usu cap B* [after Prince Louis V. *de Broglie* *b*1892 Fr. physicist] **:** the hypothetical wave train that in wave-mechanical theory corresponds to a moving elementary particle (as an electron or proton), moves with it, and gives the particle certain wave properties (as interference and diffraction)

de·bruise \də'brüz, dē'-\ *vt* [ME *debrusen* to break to pieces, fr. OF *debruisier*, fr. *de-* + *bruisier* to break — more at BRUISE] **1** *of a heraldic ordinary* **:** to cross or partly cover (a coat of arms or charge) as if laid over **2** *of a person* **:** to assume or use a heraldic ordinary that crosses or partly covers (a coat of arms or a charge)

debs *pl of* DEB

¹debt \'det, *usu* -ed.+V\ *n* -s [ME *debte*, alter. (influenced in spelling by MF *debte*, fr. OF, alter. — influenced in spelling by L *debitum* — of *dette, dete*) of *dette*, fr. OF *dette, dete*, fr. (assumed) VL *debita*, fr. L, pl. of *debitum* debt, fr. neut. of *debitus*, past part. of *debēre* to owe, fr. *de* from + *habēre* to have — more at DE-, HABIT] **1 :** a neglect or violation of duty **:** FAULT, SIN, TRESPASS ⟨forgive us our ~*s* —Mt 6:12 (RSV)⟩ **2 :** a state of owing ⟨hopelessly in ~⟩ **3 :** something (as money, goods, or services) owed by one person to another ⟨a mortgage ~⟩ **:** something that one person is bound to pay to another or perform for his benefit **:** something owed **:** OBLIGATION ⟨~ of gratitude⟩ **4 :** the common-law action for the recovery of a certain specified sum of money held to be due or of a sum that can be simply and certainly ascertained — called also *action of debt;* compare FORM OF ACTION

syn INDEBTEDNESS, OBLIGATION, LIABILITY, DEBIT, ARREAR, ARREARAGE: DEBT often applies to a single definite amount of money owed; in reference to things other than money it may indicate a definite service or favor equivalent to one rendered ⟨a *debt* of $200 to the store⟩ ⟨the immense *debt* the legal profession and the reading public owe to the publishers for their public spirit in producing these records —Norman Birkett⟩ INDEBTEDNESS in this sense refers to a total due ⟨in practically all states there is either a constitutional or a statutory limitation upon the amount of *indebtedness* that cities may incur —F.A.Ogg & P.O.Ray⟩ ⟨the Canadian government continued to make great progress in the reduction of its huge wartime *indebtedness*—*Collier's Yr. Bk.*⟩ OBLIGATION may suggest a formal expression of INDEBTEDNESS or a formal agreement to pay ⟨a contract is said to be 'performed' or 'discharged' when all the *obligations* have been fulfilled on both sides —Ronald Rubinstein⟩ ⟨to establish conditions under which justice and respect for the *obligations* arising from treaties and other sources of international law can be maintained —*U.N.Charter*⟩ LIABILITY is the term opposite in meaning to *asset* in the terminology of accountants; it applies to any item of indebtedness, as an account payable, tax due, interest payment pledged ⟨*liabilities* may be broadly classified as external and internal, external liabilities being accountabilities due to persons having no basic equity in the business, and internal being amounts due to the owners of the business and pertaining to their equities —*Jour. of Accountancy*⟩ DEBIT in accounting is the opposite of *credit* and designates a sum allotted for any outgo. ARREAR — more often ARREARS — and ARREARAGE refer to an unpaid balance on a debt or account ⟨*arrears* of rent are again becoming a serious problem to local authorities —*New Statesman & Nation*⟩ ⟨*arrearages* piled up rapidly and Congress was forced to pass law after law for the relief of the settlers —D.E.Clark⟩

²debt \"\ *adj* [alter. of ME *dette*, fr. *dette*, n.] *obs* **:** DUE, OWED ⟨to pay ourselves what to ourselves is ~ —Shak.⟩

debt book *n, archaic* **:** an account book in which a record of debts is entered

debted *adj* [alter. of ME *detted*, fr. *dette*, n. + *-ed*] *obs* **:** INDEBTED, OBLIGED

debt·less \'detləs\ *adj* [alter. of ME *detteles*, fr. *dette* + *-les* -less] **:** free from debt

debt monetization *n* **:** expansion of bank deposits through purchases of government securities by commercial banks

debt of honor *n* **:** a debt (as one incurred by betting or gambling) which is not recoverable by law but which the debtor is conventionally considered in honor bound to pay

debt of record **:** JUDGMENT 2b(1)

debt·or \'ded·ə(r), -etə(r) *sometimes* -ed·,ȯ(ə)r *or* -e,tȯ- *or* -ȯ(ə) *esp in the Lord's Prayer*\ *n* -s [alter. of ME *dettour*, *detter*, fr. OF *detur, dettour*, fr. L *debitor*, fr. *debitum* debt + *-or* — more at DEBT] **1 :** one guilty of neglect or violation of duty **:** SINNER ⟨forgive us our debts as we also have forgiven our ~*s* —Mt 6:12 (RSV)⟩ **2 :** one indebted to another: **a :** one under obligation to another ⟨~*s* for our lives to you —Alfred Tennyson⟩ **b :** one owing money to another ⟨founded a colony for the relief of ~*s* —*Univ. of Ga. Press Books*⟩ — opposed to *creditor*

debtor nation *n* **:** a nation whose debts to other countries exceed its foreign investments — compare CREDITOR NATION

debt service *n* **:** the amount of interest and sinking fund payments due annually on long-term debt

de·bub·bliz·er \(')dē'bəbə,līzə(r)\ *n* -s [*de-* + *bubble* + *-ize* + *-er*] **:** one that softens rods and tubes made of plastics and removes bubbles by heating the articles under pressure in an airtight tank of hot water and treating them with a coolant

de·bug \(')dē+\ *vt* [*de-* + *bug* (insect)] **1 :** to remove insects from ⟨~ squash vines⟩ **2 :** to detect and eliminate errors in or malfunctions of ⟨~ a new airplane before it is flown⟩

de·bunk \(')dē+\ *vt* [*de-* + *bunk* (bunkum)] **:** to take the bunk out of ⟨modern writers have ~*ed* the old myths —Bruce Marshall⟩: **a :** to expose the sham pretensions or exaggerated claims of ⟨the authorities were anxious that the natives gain enough literacy to ~ the witch doctors —Jerome Ellison⟩ **b :** to remove the false sentiments from ⟨our modern tendency to ~ traditional standards of honesty, patriotism, and morality —W.C.Nau⟩

de·bunk·er \-kə(r)\ *n* -s **:** one that debunks **:** CRITIC, ICONOCLAST

de·burr \(')dē+\ *vt* [*de-* + *burr* (rough edge)] **:** to remove the burrs from (a piece of machined work)

deburse *vt* -ED/-ING/-S [MF *desbourser* — more at DISBURSE] *obs* **:** DISBURSE

de·bus \də'bəs, (')dē'-\ *vi* [*de-* + *bus* (vehicle)] **:** to get off a bus ⟨when they *debussed*, each company had its piper at the head —Alaric Jacob⟩

¹de·but \'dā(,)byü, dā'b-, də'b-, 'de(,)b-, de'b-; dābü\ *n* -s [F *début*, fr. *débuter* to make one's first appearance, play first, begin, fr. MF *desbuter* to play first, fr. *des-* de- + *-buter* (fr. *but* goal) — more at BUTT (end)] **1 :** a first public appearance (as of an actor or singer) ⟨the Hollywood ~ of an old Broadway favorite⟩ **2 :** a formal entrance into society ⟨had a daughter making her ~ —Hamilton Basso⟩

²debut \"\ *vb* -ED/-ING/-S [F *débuter*] *vi* **:** to make one's debut ⟨the choir ~*ed* the same evening —*Down Beat*⟩ ~ *vt* **:** to present to the public for the first time **:** INTRODUCE ⟨the band ~*s* a new song each week⟩

de·bu·tan·i·za·tion \(¦)dē,byüt³nə'zāshən\ *n* -s **:** the process of debutanizing

de·bu·tan·ize \(')dē'byüt³n,īz\ *vt* -ED/-ING/-S [*de-* + *butane* + *-ize*] **:** to remove by distillation butanes, butenes, and sometimes lighter fractions from (as cracked gasoline)

de·bu·tan·iz·er \-zə(r)\ *n* -s **:** one that debutanizes

de·bu·tant \'debyü,tänt, -yə,-, -tänt *also* 'dāb- *or* -tant *or* -taa(ə)nt *or* -taint; ==¦=\ *n* -s [F *débutant*, fr. pres. part. of *débuter*] **:** one making a debut; *specif* **:** one making his first public appearance or beginning his professional career ⟨one of last year's better ~*s* . . . produces another wholly unconventional and delightful detective story —Anthony Boucher⟩

deb·u·tante \"\ *n* -s [F *débutante*, fem. of *débutant*] **:** one making a debut; *specif* **:** a young woman making her formal entrance into society ⟨walked past flushed groups of ~*s* and their escorts —Raymond Chandler⟩

debutante pink *n* **:** LA FRANCE PINK

de·button \(')dē+\ *vt* [*de-* + *button* (n.)] **:** to remove the calyx and the end of the stem of (an orange) esp. to check disease in storage or shipment

de·bye-hück·el theory \də'bī'hikəl-, -hœk-\ *n, usu cap D&H* [after Peter J. W. *Debye* *b*1884 Dutch physicist and E. *Hückel* *b*1896 Swiss physicist] **:** a theory in physical chemistry: the deviation of solutions of electrolytes from the laws of ideal solutions is due to electrical forces between ions

de·bye-scher·rer method \də'bī'sherə(r)-\ *n, usu cap D&S* [after P. J. W. *Debye* and Paul *Scherrer* *b*1890 Swiss physicist] **:** a method of forming a diffraction pattern by directing a beam of X rays onto an aggregate of small crystals (as in the powdered form of a substance) and by photographing the pattern so formed to provide a means of identifying crystalline substances

debye temperature *n, usu cap D* [after P. J. W. *Debye*] **:** the temperature at which the atomic heat of a pure cubic crystal equals 5.67 calories per gram atom per degree — called also *characteristic temperature*

debye theory *n, usu cap D* [after P. J. W. *Debye*] **:** a theory in wave mechanics: the energy of thermal agitation in a crystal is distributed among the possible systems of standing waves that correspond to the normal modes of elastic vibration

debye unit *also* **debye** *n, usu cap D* [after P. J. W. *Debye*] **:** a unit of electric moment equal to 10^{-18} statcoulomb-centimeter

dec *abbr* **1** decade **2** decani **3** deceased **4** decimal **5** decimeter **6** declaration **7** declared **8** declension **9** declination **10** decorative **11** decrease **12** decrescendo

deca- *or* **dec-** *or* **deka-** *or* **dek-** *comb form* [ME, fr. L, fr. Gk *deka-, dek-*, fr. *deka* ten — more at TEN] **1 :** ten ⟨*decagon*⟩ **2** [F *déca-, déc-*, fr. L *deca-, dec-*] **:** ten times (a specified unit of measure) ⟨*decaliter*⟩ ⟨*decare*⟩ — used in terms belonging to the metric system

dec·a·canth \'dekə,kan(t)th\ *n* -s [*deca-* + *-acanth* (fr. Gk *akantha* thorn) — more at ACANTH-] **:** a 10-hooked cestodarian larva — called also *lycophore;* compare HEXACANTH

dec·a·dal \'dekəd³l\ *adj* [*decade* + *-al*] **:** of or belonging to a decade

dec·ade \'de,kād *also* de'kād *or* də'kād *or* 'dekəd; *the last is most frequent in the sense "division of a rosary" and many who first learned the word in this sense use this pronunciation for all senses; since d and t are identically pronounced in certain intervocalic environments by most U S speakers, some who first learn the word aurally in a context such as "decade of the rosary" originally apprehend the last consonant letter as t and pronounce the word in all its occurrences as if the last consonant letter were t, making the plural for instance* 'dekəts\ *n* -s [ME, fr. MF *décade*, fr. LL *decad-, decas*, fr. Gk *dekad-, dekas*, fr. *deka*] **1 a :** a group or set of 10 ⟨his prisoners were divided into ~*s* —William Godwin⟩ ⟨a ~ of days⟩ ⟨a ~ of proposals⟩ ⟨the fourth ~ in a history⟩ **b :** a period of any 10 years ⟨to last for a ~⟩; *esp* **:** a 10-year period beginning with a year ending in 0 (as 1900–1909) ⟨the ~ of the twenties runs from Jan. 1, 1920 to Dec. 31, 1929⟩ **c :** one of the periods of a century divided in 10 calendric parts each beginning with a year ending in 1 (as 1901–10) ⟨the third ~ of the century runs from Jan. 1, 1921 to Dec. 31, 1930⟩ **d :** a division of the rosary usu. consisting of one Our Father and 10 Hail Marys followed by the minor doxology; *also* **:** one of the sets of rosary beads used to count these prayers and usu. consisting of one large bead and 10 small beads **2 a :** a ratio of 10 to 1 (as in the geometric progression 1, 10, 100, 1000 . . .) **b :** any one of the steps between sets of coils in a resistance box each coil of which has a resistance 10 times that of the corresponding coil in the preceding set

decade box *n* **:** an adjustable assembly of resistor or capacitor units in decimal steps facilitating selection by plug or switch of any multiple of the least unit up to the aggregate of all units

dec·a·dence \'dekədən(t)s, -kəd³n- *also* də'kād³n- *or* dē'kā-\ *n* -s [MF, fr. ML *decadentia*, fr. LL *decadent-, decadens* (pres. part. of *decadere* to fall, sink) + L *-ia* -y — more at DECAY] **1 :** the process of becoming decadent **:** the quality or state of being decadent **:** DETERIORATION ⟨escape the ~ that attends upon old age —G.L.Dickinson⟩ **2 :** the literary movement of the decadents or its animating spirit

dec·a·den·cy \-ənsē, -³n-, -si\ *n* -ES [alter. (influenced by *-cy*) of *decadence*] **:** DECADENCE

¹dec·a·dent \-ənt, -³nt\ *adj* [back-formation fr. *decadence*] **:** marked by decay or decline (as from an earlier condition of excellence or vitality): as **a :** characterized by self-indulgence ⟨a rich and ~ aristocracy⟩ **b :** tending to regress **:** becoming less prominent ⟨shell ornamentation ~⟩ — used chiefly in taxonomic diagnoses **2 a :** of, relating to, or having the qualities characteristic of the decadents **b :** of, relating to, or having the qualities characteristic of a period of decadence — **dec·a·dent·ly** *adv*

²decadent \"\ *n* -s **1 :** one that is decadent; *esp* **:** one characterized by or exhibiting the qualities of those who are degenerating to a lower type or of an age that is on the decline **2 :** one of a group of late 19th century French and English writers whose subjects often tended toward the artificial and abnormal and whose style was marked esp. by refinement and subtlety

dec·a·dent·ism \-,tizəm\ *n* -s [F *décadentisme*, fr. *décadent* decadent (back-formation fr. *décadence*) + *-isme* -ism] **:** DECADENCE 2

de·cad·ic \(')de¦kadik, də'k-\ *adj* [LGk *dekadikos* of the number ten, fr. Gk *dekad-, dekas* group of ten + *-ikos* -ic] **:** of or relating to the decimal system of counting

dec·a·drachm \'dekə,dram\ *n* -s [*deca-* + *drachm*] **:** an ancient Greek silver coin worth 10 drachmas

de·caf·fein·ate \(')dē'ka(,)fē,nāt, -af(ē)ə,n-\ *vt* -ED/-ING/-S [*de-* + *caffeine* + *-ate*] **:** to remove caffeine from ⟨*decaffeinated* coffee⟩

de·caf·fein·ize \-,nīz\ *vt* -ED/-ING/-S [ISV *de-* + *caffeine* + *-ize*] **:** DECAFFEINATE

dec·a·gon \'dekə,gän\ *n* -s [NL *decagonum*, fr. Gk *dekagōnon*, fr. *deka-* deca- + *-gōnon* -gon] **:** a plane polygon of 10 angles and 10 sides — **de·cag·o·nal** \(')de¦kagən³l, -kaig-\ *adj*

a regular decagon

deca·gram \'dekə,gram, -aa(ə)m\ *n* -s [F *décagramme*, fr. *déca-* deca- + *gramme* gram] **:** a metric unit of mass and weight equal to 10 grams — see METRIC SYSTEM table

dec·a·he·dral \¦dekə¦hēdrəl\ *adj* [*decahedron* + *-al*] **:** of or relating to a decahedron

dec·a·he·dron \-rən\ *n, pl* **decahedrons** \-rənz\ *or* **decahe·dra** \-rə\ [ISV *deca-* + *-hedron*] **:** a polyhedron of 10 faces

deca·hy·drate \¦dekə¦hī,drət, -,drāt\ *n* [ISV *deca-* + *hydrate*] **:** a compound with 10 molecules of water — **dec·a·hy·drat·ed** \-ād·əd\ *adj*

dec·a·hy·dro·naphthalene \¦dekə¦hīdrō+\ *n* [ISV *deca-* + *hydr-* + *naphthalene*] **:** a colorless liquid hydrocarbon $C_{10}H_{18}$ obtained by hydrogenation of naphthalene and used as a solvent (as for paints, lacquers, and silicones)

de·caisn·ea \də'kānēə\ *n, cap* [NL, fr. Joseph *Decaisne* †1882 Fr. botanist] **:** a genus of Asiatic shrubs (family Lardizabalaceae) having compound leaves and greenish polygamous flowers in clusters

de·cal \'dē,kal; də'kal, dē'k-; 'dekəl; *sometimes* 'de,kȯl\ *n* -s [by shortening] **:** DECALCOMANIA

dec·a·lage \¦dekə¦läzh, ¦dāk-\ *n* -s [F *décalage* action of putting out of alignment, displacement, removal of a wedge, fr. *décaler* to put out of alignment, shift, remove a wedge from (fr. *dé-* de- — fr. OF *des-* — + *caler* to wedge, chock, fr. *cale* wedge, fr. G *keil*, fr. OHG *kīl*) + *-age* — more at CHINE] **:** the difference between the angles of incidence of the two wings of a biplane that is positive if the incidence of the upper wing is greater than that of the lower

de·calcification \(¦)dē+\ *n* [ISV *de-* + *calcification*] **:** the removal or loss of calcium or calcium compounds (as from bones or soil) ⟨~ of dental tissues by citrate ion is suggested —*Science*⟩

de·calcify \(')dē+\ *vt* [ISV *de-* + *calcify*] **:** to remove calcium or calcium compounds from

de·cal·co·ma·nia \(,)dē,kalkə'mānēə\ *n* -s [F *décalcomanie*, fr. *décalco-* (fr. *décalquer* to copy by tracing, fr. *dé-* off — fr. OF *des-* off, do the opposite of — + *calquer* to trace) + *manie* mania, craze, fr. LL *mania* — more at DE-, CALQUE, MANIA] **1 :** the art or process of transferring pictures and designs typically from specially prepared paper to china, glass, or marble and permanently fixing them thereto **2 a :** a picture or design prepared for transfer by decalcomania **b :** a paper on which designs are printed for transfer printing

de·ca·les·cence \,dēkə'les³n(t)s, ,dek-\ *n* -s [ISV *de-* + *-calescence* (as in *recalescence*)] **:** the decrease in temperature when the rate of heat absorption during transformation exceeds the rate of heat input while heating metal through a transformation range — compare RECALESCENCE

Dec·a·lin \'dekələn\ *trademark* — used for decahydronaphthalene

deca·li·ter \'dekə+ ,-\ *n* -s [F *décalitre*, fr. *déca-* deca- + *litre* liter] **:** a metric unit of capacity equal to 10 liters — see METRIC SYSTEM table

deca·lobate \¦dekə+\ *adj* [prob. fr. (assumed) NL *decalobatus*, fr. NL *deca-* + *lobatus* lobate] **:** having 10 lobes

dec·a·logue *also* **dec·a·log** \'dekə,lȯg *also* -,läg\ *n* -s [ME *decaloge*, fr. LL *decalogus*, fr. Gk *dekalogos*, fr. *deka* ten + *logos* speech, word — more at TEN, LEGEND] **:** a basic set of rules carrying binding authority (as the Ten Commandments found in Exod. 20: 2–17 and Deut. 5: 6–21 which in the biblical account were given by God to Moses on Mount Sinai)

de·cam·er·ous \də'kamərəs, (')de¦k-\ *adj* [*deca-* + *-merous*] **:** having 10 parts or divisions; *specif* **:** having the parts in tens — usu. used of a flower

¹de·cam·e·ter \də'kamǝd·ə(r), -de'-\ *n* [Gk *dekametron*, fr. *deka* ten + *metron* meter, measure — more at TEN, MEASURE] **:** a poetic line of 10 feet

²deca·me·ter \'dekə,mēd·ə(r)\ *n* [F *décamètre*, fr. *déca-* deca- + *mètre* meter] **:** a metric unit of length equal to 10 meters — see METRIC SYSTEM table

dec·a·me·tho·ni·um \,dekəmə'thōnēəm\ *n* -s [*deca-* + *methonium*] **:** the bivalent substituted ammonium ion $[(CH_3)_3N(CH_2)_{10}NCCH_3)_3]^{++}$ derived by methylation of deca-methylene-diamine; *also* **:** any salt containing this ion (as the iodide or bromide used as a muscle relaxant)

de·camp \dē, də +\ *vi* [F *décamper*, fr. MF *descamper*, fr. *des-* de- + *camper* to camp — more at CAMP] **1 :** to break up a camp **:** move away from a camping ground **2 :** to depart suddenly **:** run away ⟨he ~*ed* with the stolen goods⟩ **syn** see ESCAPE

de·camp·ment \-pmənt\ *n* -s [F *décampement*, fr. *décamper* to decamp + *-ment*] **:** the act or process of decamping **:** departure from a camp

dec·an \'dekən\ *n* -s [LL *decanus*, lit., chief of ten — more at DEAN] **:** any of the three divisions of 10 degrees in each sign of the zodiac; *also* **:** the ruler of such a division

¹de·ca·nal \də'kān³l, 'dekən-\ *adj* [ML *decanus* dean (fr. LL, chief of ten) + E *-al*] **1 :** of or relating to a dean or deanery ⟨~ duties⟩ **2 :** of or being the ecclesiastical south side of the choir of a cathedral or church — distinguished from *cantorial*

²dec·a·nal \'dekə,nal\ *n* -s [ISV *decane* + *-al*] **:** a high-boiling liquid aldehyde $CH_3(CH_2)_8CHO$ found in essential oils (as oils of orrisroot and lemongrass) — called also *capraldehyde, capric aldehyde, decylaldehyde*

dec·ane \'de,kān\ *n* -s [ISV *deca-* + *-ane*] **:** any of several isomeric liquid paraffin hydrocarbons $C_{10}H_{22}$; *esp* **:** the normal hydrocarbon $CH_3(CH_2)_8CH_3$

de·ca·ni \də'kā,nī\ *adj* [ML, of the dean, gen. of *decanus* dean] **:** DECANAL 2

dec·a·no·ic acid \¦dekə¦nōik-\ *n* [ISV *decane* + *-oic*] **:** CAPRIC ACID — used in the system of nomenclature adopted by the International Union of Pure and Applied Chemistry

dec·a·nol \'dekə,nȯl, -ōl\ *n* -s [*decane* + *-ol*] **:** any of the decyl alcohols derived from normal decane; *esp* **:** normal decyl alcohol

dec·a·no·yl \¦dekə¦nōəl; de'kanə,wil, -,wēl\ *n* -s [ISV *decan-* (fr. *decanoic acid*) + *-oyl*] **:** CAPRYL 1

de·cant \də'kant, dē'-, -kaa(ə)nt\ *vt* -ED/-ING/-S [NL *decantare*, fr. L *de* from, away + NL *-cantare* (fr. ML *cantus* side, fr. L, iron ring round a carriage wheel) — more at DE-, CANT] **1 a :** to pour (as wine) from the original bottle into another container **b :** to pour (as wine) from one vessel into another **c :** to draw off (a liquid) without disturbing the underlying sediment or precipitate or the lower liquid layers **2 :** to pour out, transfer, or unload as if by pouring ⟨I was ~*ed* from the car —Ursula G. Bower⟩

de·cant·ate \-n,tāt\ *n* -s [*decant* + *-ate*] **:** the liquid decanted

de·can·ta·tion \,dē,kan'tāshən\ *n* -s [NL *decantation-, decantatio*, fr. *decantatus* (past part. of *decantare*) + L *-ion-, -io* -ion] **:** the act or process of decanting ⟨the quality of the sand may be tested . . . for silt by ~ —C.M.Gay⟩

de·cant·er \də'kantə(r), dē'-, -aan-\ *n* -s **:** a vessel used to decant or to receive decanted liquids; *specif* **:** an ornamental glass bottle used esp. for serving wine

de·cap \(')dē¦kap\ *vt* **:** to remove the cap from; *esp* **:** to remove a priming cap from (a cartridge)

de·cap·i·tate \də'kapə,tāt, dē'-, *usu* -ād·+V\ *vt* -ED/-ING/-S [LL *decapitatus*, past part. of *decapitare*, fr. L *de* from, away + LL *-capitare* (fr. *capit-, caput* head) — more at DE-, HEAD] **1 :** to cut off the head of **:** kill by beheading **:** BEHEAD **2 :** to remove summarily from office for political reasons ⟨the incoming administration *decapitated* many officeholders⟩ **3 :** to make ineffective **:** DESTROY ⟨a surprise attack on New York . . . could ~ a wide segment of American business —D.F.Cavers⟩

decanter

de·cap·i·ta·tion \də,kapə'tāshən, (,)dē,-\ *n* -s [ML *decapitation-, decapitatio*, fr. LL *decapitatus* + L *-ion-, -io* -ion] **:** the act or process of decapitating

de·cap·i·ta·tor \də'kapə,tād·ə(r), dē'-, -ātə-\ *n* -s **:** one that decapitates

¹dec·a·pod \'dekə,päd\ *n* -s [NL *Decapoda*] **:** one of the Decapoda **:** a decapod mollusk or crustacean

²decapod \"\ *adj* **:** of or relating to the Decapoda

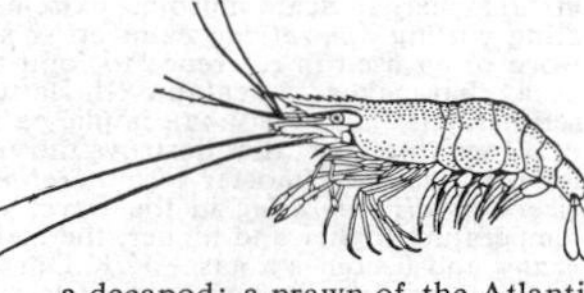

a decapod: a prawn of the Atlantic coast of America

de·cap·o·da \də'kapədə\ *n pl, cap* [NL, fr. *deca-* + *-poda*] **:** an order of Crustaceans (division Eucarida) including the most highly organized crustaceans (as shrimps, lobsters, crabs) having five pairs of thoracic appendages one or more of which are modified into pincers, a pair of movable stalked eyes, mouthparts consisting of a pair of mandibles, two pairs of maxillae, and three pairs of maxillipeds, and the head and thorax fused into a cephalothorax and covered by a carapace that encloses a gill chamber on each side — compare NATANTIA, REPTANTIA **2 :** an order of cephalopod mollusks (subclass Dibranchia) including the cuttlefishes, squids, and members of the genus *Spirula* that are distinguished from the Octopoda by the possession of 10 arms one pair of which is longer than the others and is enlarged at the end and of retractile, stalked suckers with horny rims that are sometimes armed with or replaced by hooks, and an internal horny or calcareous shell — **de·cap·o·dal** \-d³l\ *adj* — **de·cap·o·dan** \-dən\ *adj or n* — **de·cap·o·dous** \-dəs\ *adj*

dec·a·pod·i·form \¦dekə¦pädə,fȯrm\ *adj* [NL *Decapoda* + ISV *-iform*] **:** shaped like a decapod — used of the larvae of insects

de·cap·per \(')dē¦kapə(r)\ *n* **:** an instrument for removing a cap from a cartridge case

de·capsulate \(')dē+\ *vt* -ED/-ING/-S [*de-* + *capsule* + *-ate*] **:** to remove the capsule from ⟨~ a kidney⟩ ⟨~ a poppy head⟩ — **de·capsulation** \(¦)dē+\ *n*

de·carbonate \(')dē+\ *vt* [*de-* + *carbonate*] **:** to remove carbon dioxide or carbonic acid from — **de·carbonation** \(ˌ)dē + \ *n*

de·carbonization \(ˌ)dē + \ *n* **:** the process of decarbonizing

de·carbonize \(ˈ)dē + \ *vt* [ISV *de-* + *carbonize*] **:** to remove carbon from (as an internal-combustion engine)

de·carboxylase \ˌdē + \ *n* [ISV *decarboxyl-* (fr. *decarboxylation*) + *-ase*] **:** any of a group of enzymes that accelerate decarboxylation esp. of alpha-amino acids — distinguished from *carboxylase;* see CODECARBOXYLASE

de·carboxylate \ˌdē + \ *vb* [*de-* + *carboxylate*] *vt* **:** to remove carboxyl from ~ *vi* **:** to lose carboxyl — **de·carboxylation** \ˌdē + \ *n*

de·carburation \(ˌ)dē + \ *n* [ISV *decarbur-* (fr. F *décarburer* to decarburize, fr. *dé-* de- — fr. OF *des-* — + *-carburer* — fr. *carbure* carbide) + *-ation* — more at CARBURANT] **:** DECARBURIZATION

de·carburization \(ˌ)dē + \ *n* **:** the process of decarburizing

de·carburize \(ˈ)dē + \ *vt* [*de-* + *carburize*] **:** to remove carbon from (as the surface of iron alloys)

dec·ar·chy *also* **dek·ar·chy** \ˈdeˌkärkē\ *n* -ES [Gk *dekarchia*, fr. *deka-* deca- + *-archia* -archy] **:** a governing body of 10

dec·are \ˈdeˌk+ˌ-\ *n* -S [F *décare*, fr. *déca-* deca- + *are*] **:** a metric unit of area equal to 10 ares, 1000 square meters, or 0.2471 acre

de·cartelization \(ˌ)dē + \ *n* **:** the act or process of decartelizing

de·cartelize \(ˌ)dē + \ *vt* [*de-* + *cartelize*] **:** to break up or dissolve (as a large industrial trust or monopoly)

deca·stere \ˈdekə +ˌ-\ *n* -S [F *décastère*, fr. *déca-* deca- + *stère* stere] **:** a metric unit of volume equal to 10 cubic meters — see METRIC SYSTEM table

dec·a·stich \ˈdekəˌstik\ *n* -S [*deca-* + *-stich*] **:** a poem or stanza of 10 lines

[1]**dec·a·style** \-ˌstīl\ *adj* [L *decastylos*, fr. Gk *dekastylos*, fr. *deka-* deca- + *-stylos* -style] **:** marked by columniation with 10 columns across the front — compare DISTYLE

[2]**decastyle** \"\ *n* -S **:** a temple or portico having 10 columns in front

de·ca·su·al·i·za·tion \(ˌ)dēˌkazh(əw)ələˈzāshən\ *n* -S **:** the act or process of decasualizing

de·ca·sual·ize \(ˈ)dēˈkazh(əw)əˌlīz\ *vt* -ED/-ING/-S [*de-* + *casual* + *-ize*] **:** to do away with the casual employment of (labor) ⟨the commission *decasualized* 3452 men during the year —Walter Hamshar⟩ **:** eliminate the casuals from ⟨industry will be . . . *decasualized* by making the employment relation more permanent —M.R.Cohen⟩

[1]**deca·syllabic** \ˌdekə +\ *adj* [prob. fr. F *décasyllabique*, fr. Gk *dekasyllabos* decasyllabic (fr. *deka-* deca- + *syllabē* syllable) + F *-ique* -ic — more at SYLLABLE] **:** having or composed of verses that have 10 syllables

[2]**decasyllabic** \"\ *n* -S **:** a line of 10 syllables

[1]**deca·syllable** \ˌdekə + \ *adj* [*deca-* + *syllable*] **:** [1]DECASYLLABIC

[2]**decasyllable** \"\ *n* -S **:** a word or verse having 10 syllables

de·cath·lon \dəˈkathlən, dēˈ-, -ˌlän\ *n* -S [F *décathlon*, fr. *déca-* deca- + Gk *athlon* contest — more at ATHLETE] **:** a 10-event athletic contest; *specif* **:** a composite contest that consists of the 100-meter, 400-meter, and 1500-meter runs, the 110-meter high hurdles, the javelin and discus throws, shot put, pole vault, high jump, and broad jump

dec·at·ing \ˈdekədˌiŋ\ *or* **dec·a·tiz·ing** \-kəˌtīziŋ\ *n* -S [*decating* fr. F *décatir* to steam, remove a stiff finish from (fr. *dé-* de- — fr. OF *des-* — + *catir* to press, fr. assumed VL *coactire* to press together, fr. L *coactus*, past part. of *cogere* to drive together, compel) + E *-ing; decatizing* fr. F *décatir* + E *-ize* + *-ing* — more at COGENT] **:** a textile process for adding luster to cloth (as woolen and worsted) and for setting the nap and size by winding it on perforated rollers and circulating hot water or steam through it

de·cau·date \(ˈ)dēˈkȯˌdāt\ *vt* -ED/-ING/-S [*de-* + L *cauda* tail + E *-ate* — more at COWARD] **:** to deprive of the tail — **de·cau·da·tion** \ˌdēˌkȯˈdāshən\ *n*

de·cau·ville \dəˈkōˌvil, -vēl, -kȯˌvil\ *adj, usu cap* [after Paul *Decauville* †1922 French industrialist who invented equipment for such a railroad] **:** of, relating to, or being a narrow-gauge railroad whose track is mounted in sections upon transverse metal beams and is easily demountable and transportable

[1]**de·cay** \dəˈkā, dēˈ-\ *vb* -ED/-ING/-S [ME *decayen*, fr. ONF *decair*, fr. LL *decadere* to fall, sink, fr. L *de* down, away + *cadere* to fall — more at DE-, CHANCE] *vi* **1 a** *archaic* **:** to decline from a prosperous condition ⟨families . . . ~*ed* into the humble vale of life —Sir Walter Scott⟩ **b :** to pass gradually from a comparatively sound or perfect state to one of unsoundness, imperfection, or dissolution ⟨where wealth accumulates and men ~ —Oliver Goldsmith⟩ **2 :** to decrease in quantity, volume, activity, or force **:** dwindle away ⟨the voices . . . ~*ed* and died out upon her ear —Thomas Hardy⟩ **3 :** to fall into physical ruin ⟨the old house ~*ed* from lack of repairs⟩ **4 :** to decline in health, strength, vigor, or freshness ⟨a mind beginning to ~⟩ **5 :** to undergo decomposition **:** ROT ⟨fruit ~*s* in the sun⟩ ~ *vt* **1** *obs* **:** to cause to decay **:** IMPAIR ⟨infirmity that ~*s* the wise —Shak.⟩ **2 :** to destroy by decomposition **:** ROT ⟨rain and sun ~*ed* the building⟩

syn DECOMPOSE, ROT, PUTREFY, SPOIL, DISINTEGRATE, CRUMBLE: DECAY indicates deteriorating change, often gradual, from a sound condition or perfect state ⟨bruised apples *decaying* quickly⟩ ⟨*decaying* teeth⟩ ⟨with huge machines left to rust and *decay* —*Amer. Guide Series: Texas*⟩ ⟨the Aztec regime and culture collapsed and the native crafts and arts *decayed* —R.W.Murray⟩ DECOMPOSE implies breaking down into components or dissolution through corruption ⟨the strong odor of *decomposing* meat⟩ ⟨action of bacteria in *decomposing* the organic products —A.C.Morrison⟩ ⟨after slaying his colleague, he chemically *decomposed* the body —Leo Guild⟩ ROT, applied to animal or vegetable matter, indicates decaying with corruption, often with offensive foulness; otherwise it may indicate enervation or stagnation ⟨fruit *rotting* in the baskets⟩ ⟨the *rotting* corpses of the Americans and British whom the French allowed to be massacred at Fort William Henry —Cleveland Amory⟩ ⟨it was this garrison life. Half civilian, half military, with all the drawbacks of both. It *rotted* the soul, robbed a man of ambition, faith —Irwin Shaw⟩ PUTREFY may indicate noisome, extremely offensive, or nauseating rotting ⟨*putrefying* cadavers⟩ SPOIL is a less extreme word often used in reference to food to indicate a degree of decay that makes it uneatable ⟨the lettuce will *spoil* if it is not refrigerated⟩ DISINTEGRATE implies a separating of particles or a breaking apart that destroys the entity or integrity of the item in question ⟨mortar *disintegrating* in the old chimney⟩ ⟨icebergs *disintegrating* in the warm water⟩ ⟨if we raise the temperature higher and higher, the metal itself finally *disintegrates* and becomes a gas —K.K.Darrow⟩ ⟨[the] Whig party *disintegrated* into its component elements —H.S.Commager⟩ CRUMBLE implies a slow disintegration with a breaking and falling off of small particles ⟨winter rains had washed and washed against its narrow, faded old bricks until the plaster between them had *crumbled* —Margaret Deland⟩ ⟨still visible, although the stockade itself has long since *crumbled*, are the outlines of the ancient earthworks —*Amer. Guide Series: Mich.*⟩ ⟨Hood's army, *crumbled* in morale and depleted by wholesale desertion —*Amer. Guide Series: Tenn.*⟩

[2]**decay** \"\ *n* -S [ME, fr. *decayen*] **1 a :** the condition of a person or thing that has undergone a decline in strength, soundness, or prosperity or has been diminished in degree of excellence or perfection ⟨arts and letters had fallen into ~⟩ **b :** a progressive failure of strength, soundness, or prosperity **:** a diminishing in degree of excellence or perfection ⟨saw a rapid ~ of moral principles⟩ **2 a :** the material process of dilapidation **:** wasting or wearing away **:** the state of being wasted or worn away **:** RUIN ⟨ancient temples fallen into complete ~⟩ **b** *obs* **:** ruined remains **:** DEBRIS — usu. used in pl. **3** *obs* **:** DESTRUCTION, DEATH, RUIN ⟨sullen presage of your own ~ —Shak.⟩ **4** *obs* **:** a cause of decay ⟨my love was my ~ —Shak.⟩ **5 a :** ROT; *specif* **:** the aerobic decomposition of proteins chiefly by bacteria in which the products of putrefaction are completely oxidized to stable compounds having no foul odors **b :** the product of decay ⟨remove ~ from a tooth⟩ **6 a** *archaic* **:** a decline in health or vigor **b** *obs* **:** the manifestations of age or of decline in health — usu. used in pl. **c** *archaic* **:** a wasting disease; *esp* **:** CONSUMPTION **7 :** decrease in quantity, volume, activity, or force: as **a :** spontaneous decrease in the number of radioactive atoms in radioactive material (as uranium ore) **b :** spontaneous disintegration of an atom, an atomic nucleus, a neutron, or a meson

de·cay·able \-āəbəl\ *adj* **:** capable of or liable to decay

decay constant *n* **:** the constant ratio of the number of radioactive atoms disintegrating in any specified short unit interval of time to the total number of atoms of the same kind still intact at the beginning of that interval

de·cayed·ness \-ā(ə)dnəs\ *n* -ES **:** the quality or state of being decayed

de·cay·less \-āləs\ *adj* **:** being without decay

dec·can \ˈdekən, -ˌkan\ *n* [*Deccan*, the whole peninsula of India south of the Narbada river] **1** *usu cap* **:** a breed of coarse-wooled sheep of southern India **2** -S *often cap* **:** a sheep of the Deccan breed

deccan hemp *n, often cap D* **:** KENAF

decd *abbr* **1** deceased **2** declared **3** decreased

[1]**de·cease** \dəˈsēs, dēˈ-\ *n* -S [ME *deces*, fr. MF, fr. L *decessus* departure, death, fr. *decessus*, past part. of *decedere* to depart, die, fr. *de* from, away + *cedere* to go — more at DE-, CEDE] **:** departure from life **:** DEATH

[2]**decease** \"\ *vi* -ED/-ING/-S [ME *decessen*, fr. *deces*] **:** to depart from life **:** DIE

[1]**deceased** *adj* [fr. past part. of [2]*decease*] **:** DEAD ⟨his ~ wife's sister⟩; *esp* **:** recently dead

[2]**deceased** *n, pl* **deceased :** a dead person ⟨the will of the ~⟩

de·ce·dent \dəˈsēdᵊnt, dēˈ-\ *n* -S [L *decedent-, decedens*, pres. part. of *decedere*] **:** a deceased person

de·ceit \dəˈsēt, dēˈ-, *usu* -ēd· + V\ *n* -S [ME *deceite*, fr. OF, fr. L *decepta*, fem. of *deceptus*, past part. of *decipere* to deceive] **1 :** the act or practice of deceiving (as by falsification, concealment, or cheating) **:** DECEPTION ⟨politics, being the art of ~, suits only little minds —*Encore*⟩ **2 a :** an attempt to deceive **:** a declaration, artifice, or practice designed to mislead another **:** wily device **:** TRICK, FRAUD **b :** any trick, collusion, contrivance, false representation, or underhand practice used to defraud another — see FRAUD **3 :** a disposition to deceive **:** DECEITFULNESS, STRATAGEM, WILE ⟨far from ~ or guile —John Milton⟩

syn DECEIT, DUPLICITY, DISSIMULATION, CUNNING, GUILE can mean, in common, the quality, act, or practice of imposing on credulity by dishonesty, fraud, or trickery. DECEIT implies the intent to mislead and can cover misrepresentation, falsification, fraud, or trickery of any kind ⟨believes that *deceit* and mistrust are the essence of human relationships —Bergen Evans⟩ ⟨they held that the basest trickery or *deceit* was not dishonorable if directed against a foe —*Amer. Guide Series: R.I.*⟩ ⟨there is an element of sham and deceit in every imitation —John Dewey⟩ DUPLICITY usually implies double-dealing, bad faith, or false pretense ⟨preaches honesty but practices *duplicity* —Leo Pfeffer⟩ ⟨so habitual was her *duplicity* that she would gaze softly at you, saying nothing when she was deceiving you —Ethel Wilson⟩ ⟨the cunning and *duplicity* they practiced —W.H.Hudson †1922⟩ DISSIMULATION implies deceit by concealing what one actually is or feels ⟨some in the household were convinced that her ravings and absurd actions were cunning *dissimulation* —E.J.Simmons⟩ ⟨she had revealed of late a chronic habit of *dissimulation*, and it was impossible to decide whether she was lying for diversion or speaking the truth from necessity —Ellen Glasgow⟩ CUNNING implies, in one use, deceit by trickery or stratagem or, in another similar use, an extreme, often vicious shrewdness ⟨with such masterly *cunning* did they lay their measures for the avoidance of every possible chance of detection —George Meredith⟩ ⟨a third-rate, ungenerous person with a low mean *cunning* that is contemptible —H.J.Laski⟩ ⟨a people whose ruthlessness, tenacity, power, and *cunning* are . . . great —D.L.Cohn⟩ ⟨the bear is a favorite animal of the big-game hunter because of its *cunning* and agility —R.E.Trippensee⟩ GUILE stresses, more than *cunning*, a subtle concealment or lack of obviousness of the arts practiced or tricks used ⟨he had not the *guile*, patience, or ruthlessness to make a good Secret Service chief —Karl Robson⟩ ⟨*guile* and trickery —Willa Cather⟩ and occurring most commonly in certain stock phrases, usu. negative, the word has come to have a much weaker sense than *cunning*, implying only artfulness or the use of wiles ⟨his profound innocence, that thorough absence of *guile* —Harvey Breit⟩ ⟨her deceit and illusion were harmless, wholly without *guile* —William Beebe⟩ ⟨she cannot be honest in the legal sense when this minor honesty inhibits her purpose, but this is *guile* rather than dishonesty —Sidney Monas⟩ **syn** see in addition IMPOSTURE

de·ceit·ful \-tfəl\ *adj* [ME *desaitful*, fr. *desait, deceite* deceit + *-ful*] **1 :** having a tendency or disposition to deceive **:** given to deception **:** DISHONEST ⟨she was a ~ scheming little thing —Israel Zangwill⟩ **2 :** tending to deceive **:** DECEPTIVE, MISLEADING ⟨smooth, shining, and ~ as thin ice —S.T.Coleridge⟩ **syn** see DISHONEST

de·ceit·ful·ly \-fəlē, -li\ *adv* [ME *desaitfully*, fr. *desaitful* + *-ly*] **:** in a deceitful manner

de·ceit·ful·ness *n* -ES **:** the quality of being deceitful

de·ceiv·able \-sēvəbəl\ *adj* [ME, modif. (prob. influenced by *deceiven* to deceive) of MF *decevable*, fr. OF, fr. *deceivre, decevoir* + *-able*] **1** *archaic* **:** marked by deceit **:** DECEITFUL, DECEPTIVE **2** *archaic* **:** capable of being deceived **:** liable to be misled — **de·cei·va·bly** \-blē\ *adv, archaic*

de·ceive \dəˈsēv, dēˈ-\ *vb* -ED/-ING/-S [ME *deceiven*, fr. OF *deceivre, decevoir*, fr. L *decipere* to ensnare, deceive, cheat, fr. *de* down, away + *-cipere* (fr. *capere* to take) — more at DE-, HEAVE] *vt* **1** *archaic* **:** to take unawares esp. by craft or trickery **:** ENSNARE, MISLEAD ⟨he it was whose guile . . . *deceived* the mother of mankind —John Milton⟩ **2 a** *obs* **:** to be false to **:** BETRAY ⟨you have *deceived* our trust —Shak.⟩ **b** *archaic* **:** to disappoint (as an expectation) ⟨nor are my hopes *deceived* —John Dryden⟩ **3** *obs* **:** to deprive esp. by fraud or stealth **:** CHEAT, DEFRAUD ⟨*deceived* me of a good sum of money —William Oldys⟩ **4 :** to cause to believe the false **:** DELUDE ⟨when we're young we can be very easily *deceived* —George Meredith⟩ **5** *archaic* **:** to while away (as time, care, or sorrow) **:** BEGUILE ⟨these occupations oftentimes *deceived* the listless hour —William Wordsworth⟩ ~ *vi* **:** to practice deceit **:** be deceitful ⟨his stunning technique that baffles and ~*s* —Eva M. Neumeyer⟩

syn MISLEAD, DELUDE, BEGUILE, BETRAY, DOUBLE-CROSS: DECEIVE indicates an inculcating of one so that he takes the false as true, the unreal as existent, the spurious as genuine ⟨it is a pity to make him the dupe of his more intelligent partner. If he is *deceived*, he has a way of getting his revenge —S.M.Crothers⟩ ⟨disguised Communists trying to *deceive* the ignorant natives —*Americas*⟩ MISLEAD indicates a causing to fall into error of some sort, intentionally or not ⟨I think it was Thrasyllus who tricked her into believing that she was meant. Thrasyllus never told lies but he loved *misleading* people —Robert Graves⟩ ⟨to *mislead* spies, Love and his squad pretended they were on their way to Los Angeles, but at night doubled back to the arroyo, where they surprised Murrieta and his gang —*Amer. Guide Series: Calif.*⟩ DELUDE implies a complete misleading or deceiving so that one remains a fool, dupe, or victim ⟨did he, did all the people who said they didn't mind things, know that they really did? Or were they indeed *deluded*? —Rose Macaulay⟩ ⟨scientists do little to discourage this view, and, indeed, many of them are quite as *deluded* as most laymen are about the subject —M.F.A.Montagu⟩ BEGUILE indicates deceiving or deluding one by subtle allure and wiling one into abandoning doubts or defenses ⟨marshlights to *beguile* mankind from tangible goods and immediate fruitions —Lewis Mumford⟩ ⟨the unique power by which Shakespeare compels 'faith in the emotions expressed' and *beguiles* Bradley and company into their absurdities —F.R.Leavis⟩ BETRAY indicates treacherously or deceitfully leading into enemy hands or into danger or difficulty ⟨the fact that he had *betrayed* his daughter into an ugly position gnawed at his consciousness —Sherwood Anderson⟩ DOUBLE-CROSS applies to deceiving or betraying a friend, partner, or accomplice ⟨De Valera charged that his own trusted negotiators had *double-crossed* him by signing an agreement to take the detested oath of loyalty to the British king without consulting him —Paul Blanshard⟩ ⟨they *double-crossed* the Pasha of Marrakesh, and ordered him to call off the revolt they had inspired —*New Statesman & Nation*⟩

de·ceiv·er \-və(r)\ *n* -S [ME, alter. (influenced by *-er, -ere* -er) of *deceivour*, modif. (influenced by *deceiven*) of MF *deceveur*, fr. OF *decevéor*, fr. OF *deceivre, decevoir* + *-eor* -or] **:** one that deceives

de·ceiv·ing·ly *adv* [ME, fr. *deceiving* (pres. part. of *deceiven*) + *-ly*] **:** in a deceiving manner

de·cel·er·ate \(ˈ)dēˈseləˌrāt, *usu* -ād· + V\ *vb* -ED/-ING/-S [*de-* + *accelerate*] *vt* **1 :** to cause to go progressively slower **:** lessen the speed of **:** slow down **:** RETARD ⟨~ a motor⟩ ⟨~ an automobile⟩ **2 :** to decrease the rate of progress of (as a process or development) ⟨~ erosion of the soil⟩ ⟨~ an educational program⟩ ~ *vi* **1 :** to move at a progressively slower speed **:** slow down ⟨the car *decelerated*⟩ **2 :** to cause something (as a vehicle) to move at a progressively slower speed ⟨the driver *decelerated* quickly⟩

de·cel·er·a·tion \(ˌ)dēˌseləˈrāshən\ *n* -S **1 :** the act or process of decelerating ⟨~ of a truck by braking⟩ ⟨~ of an aging process⟩ **2 :** the rate of decrease in velocity ⟨aeromedical research has shown man's ability to withstand high ~*s*⟩

deceleration lane *n* **:** a speed-change area or lane consisting of added pavement at the edge of through-traffic lanes to permit drivers to diverge from the through-traffic flow without reducing speed until after the diverging maneuver is completed — compare ACCELERATION LANE

de·cel·er·a·tor \(ˈ)dēˈseləˌrād·ə(r)\ *n* -S **:** one that decelerates

de·cel·er·om·e·ter \(ˌ)dēˌseləˈrämədˌə(r)\ *n* -S [*deceleration* + *-o-* + *-meter*] **:** an instrument for measuring the rate of change of speed of a moving vehicle during deceleration

de·cel·er·on \dēˈseləˌrän\ *n* -S [*decelerate* + *-on* (as in *aileron*)] **:** a split lateral control surface combining the functions of aileron and air brakes on an airplane

decem- *comb form* [MF or L; MF, fr. L, fr. *decem* ten] **:** ten ⟨*decem*costate⟩

de·cem·ber \dəˈsembə(r), (ˈ)dēˌs-\ *n* -S *usu cap* [ME *decembre*, fr. OF, fr. L *december* (tenth month), fr. *decem* ten — more at TEN] **:** the 12th month of the Gregorian calendar — abbr. *Dec.*; see MONTH table

de·cem·brist \-ˈ=brəst\ *n* -S *usu cap* [*decembr-* (fr. *december*) + *-ist*; trans. of Russ *dekabrist*; fr. the fact that the uprising occurred in December 1825] **:** one of those who took part in the unsuccessful liberal uprising against the Russian emperor Nicholas I

de·cem·vir \dəˈsemvə(r)\ *n, pl* **decemvirs** \-və(r)z\ *also* **decem·vi·ri** \-vəˌrī\ [L, back-formation fr. *decemviri*, pl., fr. *decem viri* ten men, fr. *decem* ten + *viri*, pl. of *vir* man — more at VIRILE] **:** one of a commission, council, or ruling body of 10; *specif* **:** a member of either of two commissions made up of 10 men each who framed the Roman laws of the Twelve Tables and who had absolute power during their term of office

de·cem·vi·ral \-vərəl\ *adj* [L *decemviralis*, fr. *decemviri* + *-alis* -al] **:** of or relating to decemvirs or a decemvirate

de·cem·vi·rate \-vərət, -əˌrāt\ *n* -S [L *decemviratus*, fr. *decemviri* + *-atus* -ate] **1 :** the office or government of decemvirs **2 :** a body of decemvirs

decence *n* -S [F *décence*, fr. L *decentia*] *obs* **:** appropriateness (as of action or deportment) **:** FITNESS

de·cen·cy \ˈdēsᵊnsē, -nsi\ *n* -ES [L *decentia*, fr. *decent-, decens* (pres. part. of *decēre* to be fitting) + *-ia* -y] **1** *archaic* **a :** suitability or fitness to circumstances ⟨his discourse on the scaffold was full of ~ and courage —David Hume †1776⟩ **b :** orderly condition of society **:** conformity to law ⟨no hundred-headed Riot here we meet, with *Decency* and Law beneath his feet —Robert Burns⟩ **2 :** the quality or state of being decent ⟨only doctors and nurses have the ~ to wear masks —Justina Hill⟩ **:** decent quality, behavior, dress, or deportment **:** DECORUM, PROPRIETY, MODESTY ⟨aid to the victims was simply a matter of common ~⟩ **:** conformity to standards of taste, propriety, or quality ⟨the first story of any real ~ that I ever wrote —Arnold Bennett⟩ **3 :** whatever is proper or becoming **:** standards of propriety ⟨the act was a gross violation of ~⟩ — usu. used in pl. ⟨the *decencies* of normal controversy . . . have been disregarded and men have been publicly criticized —Vannevar Bush⟩ **4 a :** conformity to the standard of living that becomes a person ⟨enabled a gentleman to afford the ~ of burning wood on his own hearth —Oscar Wilde⟩ **b decencies** *pl* **:** the external conditions of decent living ⟨did not provide her . . . children with the *decencies* justified by their inheritance —J.D.Wade⟩ **5 a :** literary decorum or its observance **b decencies** *pl* **:** the established conventions of literary decorum often with special reference to syntactical or grammatical propriety

[1]**de·cen·na·ry** \dəˈsenərē, dēˈ-\ *n* -ES [ML *decennarius* tithingman, fr. *decena, decenna* tithing (fr. L *decem* ten) + L *-arius* -ary] **:** [1]TITHING

[2]**decennary** \"\ *n* -ES [L *decennis* of 10 years + E *-ary*] **:** a period of 10 years

de·cen·ni·ad \-nēˌad\ *n* -S [L *decennium* + E *-ad*] **:** DECENNIUM

[1]**de·cen·ni·al** \-nēəl\ *adj* [L *decennium* + E *-al*] **1 :** consisting of or lasting for 10 years ⟨a ~ interval⟩ **2 :** occurring, appearing, or being made, done, or acted upon every 10 years ⟨~ games⟩ ⟨~ census⟩

[2]**decennial** \"\ *n* -S **:** a decennial anniversary or its celebration

de·cen·ni·al·ly \-əlē, -li\ *adv* **:** every 10 years

de·cen·ni·um \-nēəm\ *n, pl* **decenniums** \-ēəmz\ *or* **decennia** \-ēə\ [L, fr. *decennis* of ten years, fr. *dec-* (fr. *decem* ten) + *-ennis* (fr. *annus* year) — more at ANNUAL] **:** a period of 10 years

de·cent \ˈdēsᵊnt\ *adj, sometimes* -ER/-EST [MF or L; MF, fr. L *decent-, decens*, pres. part. of *decēre* to be fitting, be proper; akin to L *decus* honor, ornament, *dignus* worthy, Gk *dokein* to seem good, seem, think, Skt *daśasyati* he worships, favors] **1** *archaic* **a :** appropriate to circumstances or to social status ⟨the funeral . . . was a ~ solemnity —John Evelyn⟩ **b :** having tasteful appearance or proportions **:** well-formed **:** SHAPELY ⟨her ~ hand —Alexander Pope⟩ **2 :** marked by acceptance as socially unobjectionable, proper, or suitable **:** not questionable or censurable **:** conforming to standards of propriety, etiquette, good taste, or morality ⟨forsake a ~ craft that he may pursue the gentilities of a profession —George Eliot⟩ ⟨his ~ reticence is branded as hypocrisy —W.S.Maugham⟩ **3 a :** free of anything improper or of suggestions of the immodest, lustful, or obscene **:** indicative or suggestive of virtue or propriety ⟨speech in this circle, if not always ~, never became lewd —George Santayana⟩ **b :** not nude **:** clothed with adequate modesty ⟨one of her shoulder straps slipped down, leaving her perfectly ~ by American standards —Santha Rama Rau⟩ **4 :** fairly good but not excellent **:** up to reasonable expectations **:** ADEQUATE, SUFFICIENT, SATISFACTORY ⟨in search of a ~ meal —Robert Shaplen⟩ ⟨vile insanitary barracks to serve as substitutes for ~ human shelter —Lewis Mumford⟩ **:** not poor, scant, questionable, or marginal ⟨only a single fortress put up a ~ resistance —Robert Graves⟩ **5 :** marked by a combination of goodwill, sincerity, tolerance, uprightness, generosity, or fairness **:** not cruel, repressive, or vindictive ⟨the ~ people, the people on the side of the angels, the kind, reasonable, fair-minded people —Gladys B. Stern⟩ **syn** see CHASTE, DECOROUS

de·cent·ly *adv* **:** in a decent manner

de·cent·ness *n* -ES **:** the quality or state of being decent

de·centralism \(ˈ)dē+\ *n* -S [fr. *decentralize*, after E *centralize: centralism*] **:** DECENTRALIZATION

de·centralist \(ˈ)dē+\ *n* -S [prob. fr. F *décentraliste*, fr. *décentraliser* to decentralize + *-iste* -ist] **:** one favoring decentralization, esp. urban decentralization

de·centralization \(ˌ)dē+\ *n* -S [prob. fr. F *décentralisation*, fr. *décentraliser* + *-ation*] **1 :** the dispersion or distribution of functions and powers from a central authority to regional and local governing bodies **2 :** the redistribution of population and industry from urban centers to suburban areas or outlying districts

de·centralize \(ˈ)dē+\ *vt* [prob. fr. F *décentraliser*, fr. *dé-* de- (fr. OF *des-*) + *centraliser* to centralize] **:** to deprive of centralization: as **a :** to disperse or distribute the functions or powers of (as a government) ⟨~ the administration of flood relief⟩ **b :** to cause to withdraw from the center or place of concentration ⟨~ downtown business areas —J.C.Ingraham⟩

de·cephalization \(ˌ)dē+\ *n* -S [*de-* + *cephalization*] **:** decrease or degeneration of organs and parts relating to the head or cephalic regions — opposed to *cephalization*

de·cep·tion \də'sepshən, dē'-\ *n* -s [ME *decepcioun*, fr. MF *deception*, fr. LL *deception-, deceptio*, fr. L *deceptus* (past part. of *decipere* to deceive) + *-ion-, -io* -ion — more at DECEIVE] **1 a :** the act of deceiving, cheating, hoodwinking, misleading, or deluding ⟨resort to falsehood and ~ in avoiding the tax⟩ **b :** the fact or condition of being deceived, fooled, or deluded ⟨the magician's ~ of the audience by clever tricks⟩ **2 a :** a characteristic, arrangement, or situation that deceives or deludes with or without calculated intent **:** FRAUD, ARTIFICE, TRICK ⟨skilled in evasions, ~*s*, and ruses⟩

syn FRAUD, DOUBLE-DEALING, TRICKERY, CHICANE, CHICANERY, SUBTERFUGE: DECEPTION is a general term for any sort of deceiving, by whatever methods or for whatever motive ⟨the *deception* practiced by this corrupt and treacherous group⟩ ⟨the *deception* in this boxer's feints⟩ FRAUD, unless humorously or lightly used, indicates dishonest or even criminal deception, esp. misrepresentation or perversion of the truth in order to defraud ⟨he would sometimes "write in" for articles necessary for his education . . . in order to eke out his pocket money . . . these *frauds* were sometimes . . . in imminent danger of being discovered —Samuel Butler †1902⟩ DOUBLE-DEALING suggests performance of actions incompatible with or contradictory to an ostensible role; sometimes it indicates treachery by secretly aiding a party while professedly a member or ally of its enemy ⟨his *double-dealing* in collaborating secretly with the enemy occupation forces while belonging to the patriot resistance group⟩ TRICKERY indicates use or practice of tricks to deceive, of artful stratagems or crafty ingenuities, and usu. suggests sharp practice or actual dishonesty ⟨they held that the basest *trickery* or deceit was not dishonorable if directed against a foe —*Amer. Guide Series: R.I.*⟩ CHICANE and CHICANERY, the latter being now the more common form, suggest legalistic trickery, esp. trickery by misrepresenting, misleading, confusing, or other shyster devices ⟨the labyrinthine procedure that so delayed justice and helped *chicane* —*Times Lit. Supp.*⟩ ⟨a disintegrating society, rotten and fluid within . . . made . . . *chicane* indispensable to winning riches —Marvin Lowenthal⟩ SUBTERFUGE refers to any shady trick or artifice to conceal, escape, avoid, or evade ⟨whether notes issued by such a bank constituted a *subterfuge* by which the state in effect was emitting bills of credit in the sense forbidden by the Constitution —Harvey Pinney⟩ **syn** see in addition IMPOSTURE

de·cep·tious \-shəs\ *adj* [prob. fr. *deception*, after such pairs as E *faction: factious*] **:** tending to deceive — **de·cep·tious·ly** *adv*

de·cep·tive \-ptiv, -tēv *also* -təv\ *adj* [obs. F or LL; obs. F *déceptif*, fr. LL *deceptivus*, fr. L *deceptus* + *-ivus* -ive] **:** tending to deceive **:** having power to mislead ⟨a ~ appearance⟩ — **de·cep·tive·ly** \-təvlē, -li\ *adv* — **de·cep·tive·ness** \-tivnəs, -tēv- *also* -təv-\ *n* -ES

deceptive cadence *n* **:** a cadence in which the full or final close is evaded by the use of an unexpected or foreign chord as the chord of resolution — called also *false cadence, interrupted cadence, suspended cadence;* see CADENCE illustration

de·cer·e·bel·late \ˌdēˌserə'belət\ *also* **de·cer·e·bel·lat·ed** \-ˌlād·əd\ *adj* [*decerebellate* fr. *de-* + *cerebell-* + *-ate*, adj. suffix; *decerebellated* fr. *de-* + *cerebell-* + *-ate*, vb. suffix + *-ed*] **:** deprived of the cerebellum — **de·cer·e·bel·la·tion** \(ˌ)dēˌserə(ˌ)be'lāshən\ *n* -s

¹de·cerebrate \(ˈ)dē+\ *vt* -ED/-ING/-S [*de-* + *cerebr-* + *-ate*] **:** to remove the cerebrum from; *also* **:** to make incapable of cerebral activity — **de·cerebration** \(ˌ)dē+\ *n* -s

²de·ce·re·brate \ˌdēsə'rēbrət, (ˈ)dē'serəb-\ *adj* **1 :** DECEREBRATED **2 :** characteristic of decerebration ⟨~ rigidity⟩

de·cern \dē'sərn\ *vb* -ED/-ING/-S [ME *decernen*, fr. MF *decerner*, fr. L *decernere* to decree, decide — more at DECREE] *Scots law* **:** to decree by judicial sentence

decerp *vt* -ED/-ING/-S [L *decerpere*, fr. *de* from, away + *-cerpere* (fr. *carpere* to pluck) — more at DE-, HARVEST] *obs* **:** PLUCK, GATHER

de·certification \(ˌ)dē+\ *n* [*de-* + *certification*] **:** the act or process of decertifying

de·certify \(ˈ)dē+\ *vt* [*de-* + *certify*] **:** to withdraw or revoke certification of (as a labor union acting as bargaining agent for a bargaining unit)

de·ces·sion \də'seshən\ *n* [L *decession-, decessio*, fr. *decessus* (past part. of *decedere* to depart, fr. *de* from, away + *cedere* to go) + *-ion-, -io* -ion — more at CEDE] *archaic* **:** WITHDRAWAL, DEPARTURE, DECREASE

dech·en·ite \'dekə,nīt\ *n* -s [G *dechenit*, fr. Heinrich von Dechen †1889 Ger. geologist + G *-it* -ite] **:** DESCLOIZITE

de·chlorinate \(ˈ)dē+ˌ-\ *vt* [*de-* + *chlorinate*] **:** to remove chlorine from ⟨*dechlorinated* water⟩ — **de·chlorination** \(ˌ)dē+\ *n*

de·christianization \(ˌ)dē+\ *n* [prob. fr. F *déchristianisation*, fr. *déchristianiser* + *-ation*] **:** the process of dechristianizing ⟨the last step in the gradual ~ of Europe —Nicolas Zernov⟩

de·christianize \(ˈ)dē+\ *vt* [prob. fr. F *déchristianiser*, fr. *dé-* de- (fr. OF *des-*) + *christianiser* to Christianize, fr. MF, fr. L *christianus* Christian + MF *-iser* -ize] **:** to cause to turn from Christianity **:** deprive of the Christian characteristics

deci- *comb form* [F *déci-*, fr. L *decimus* tenth, fr. *decem* ten — more at TEN] **:** tenth part (of a specified unit of measure) ⟨*decigram*⟩ — chiefly in terms belonging to the metric system

de·cian \'dēsh(ē)ən\ *adj, usu cap* [Gaius Messius Quintus Trajanus *Decius* †A.D.251 Roman emperor + E *-an*] **:** of or relating to the Roman emperor Decius who persecuted the Christians ⟨the *Decian* persecution⟩

deci·are \'desē+ˌ-\ *n* -s [F *déciare*, fr. *déci-* deci- + *are*] **:** a metric unit of area equal to 10 square meters or 11.96 square yards

dec·i·bel \'desə,bel, -ˌbəl\ *n* -s [ISV *deci-* + *bel*] **1** *in electronic communications* **a :** a unit for expressing the ratio of two amounts of electric or acoustic power equal to 10 times the common logarithm of the power ratio — abbr. *db* **b :** a unit for expressing the ratio of the magnitudes of two electric voltages or currents or analogous acoustic quantities (as sound pressure or particle velocity) equal to 20 times the common logarithm of the voltage or current ratio provided that the two voltages or currents are measured on equal resistances **2 :** a unit for measuring the relative loudness of sounds equal approximately to the smallest degree of difference of loudness ordinarily detectable by the human ear the range of which includes about 130 decibels on a scale beginning with 1 for the faintest audible sound

de·cid·able \də'sīdəbəl, dē'-\ *adj* **:** capable of being decided; *specif* **:** capable of being decided as following or not following from the axioms of a logical system — compare DECISION, PROBLEM

de·cide \də'sīd, dē'-\ *vb* -ED/-ING/-S [ME *deciden*, fr. MF *decider*, fr. L *decidere*, lit., to cut off, fr. *de* down, away + *-cidere* (fr. *caedere* to cut) — more at DE-, CONCISE] *vt* **:** to dispel doubt on: **a :** to arrive at a choice or solution concerning which ends uncertainty or contention ⟨~ what to order for breakfast⟩ **b :** to bring definitively and conclusively to an end esp. in matters relating to war ⟨the victory at San Jacinto *decided* the war⟩ **c :** to infer or conclude from available indications and evidence ⟨Washington *decided* . . . that the President could no longer avoid calling the Senator to account —*Economist*⟩ **d :** to choose or select as a future course of action ⟨she *decided* to buy a new hat⟩ ⟨*decided* to read a book instead⟩ **e :** to induce or force (as a person) to arrive at a choice, judgment, or decision ⟨this exordium . . . *decided* Mr. Cruncher —Charles Dickens⟩ ~ *vi* **:** to make a choice or decision esp. a binding or definitive one presumably after consideration **:** come to a conclusion ⟨some learned men, proud of their knowledge, only speak to ~ —Earl of Chesterfield⟩

syn RESOLVE, DETERMINE, RULE, SETTLE: DECIDE is less colorful and has less connotational range than others in this group; in this sense it simply means to come to a decision, presumably after some consideration, or to induce another to come to a decision ⟨the time for deliberation is then passed, he has *decided* —John Marshall⟩ ⟨had finally *decided* Amy to drop the mask of deference —Arnold Bennett⟩ RESOLVE in reference to a person's decisions about his own future actions may imply an earnest and strong-willed attitude ⟨suddenly he *resolved* to say something. He *resolved* to say it so firmly that he determined to say it even if Mr. Britling went on talking all the time —H.G.Wells⟩ but in reference to questions, problems, difficulties, and so on, it appears to stress clear analysis and consideration, with the implication of a final judgment ⟨the task is to *resolve* initial oppositions of interest into some moderate harmony by a process of mutual concessions —J.A.Hobson⟩ ⟨Mr. Fitzpatrick, who did not catch the point at issue very quickly, seemed unable to *resolve* the difficulty —James Joyce⟩ DETERMINE in reference to decisions on personal action implies about the same things as RESOLVE, although it may occas. be somewhat weaker and it may involve more consideration of limitation and choice ⟨she was *determined* that in her house Sophia should have all the freedoms and conveniences that she could have had in her own —Arnold Bennett⟩ ⟨he *resolved* to overcome the one-pawn disadvantage and *determined* on a scheme involving the quick and audacious use of his major pieces⟩ but in reference to less personal and more general matters the word may suggest bounds, limits, classes, or terms and may imply that considerations and judgments involved are decisive in a course, outcome, or judgment ⟨but every atom . . . is a miniature solar system, with electrons in numbers which *determine* the nature of the element —W.R. Inge⟩ ⟨but theories, intellectual systems, notions . . . may themselves create demands or *determine* their directions —Felix Frankfurter⟩ RULE stresses the act of deciding it; may imply a judicial, administrative, or otherwise authoritative positive attitude or procedure and a necessarily binding procedure or precedent set ⟨the procedure was *ruled* out as unparliamentary⟩ ⟨the president *ruled* that such matters should be taken care of in Mr. Smith's office⟩ SETTLE contains less implication than others in this series about procedure for arriving at a decision, more about the finality of the action ⟨the problem of the Pythagorean legend may be said to be *settled*. But the problem of the Socratic legend is still under consideration —Havelock Ellis⟩ ⟨the principle of law is too well *settled* to be disputed, that a court can give no judgment . . . where it has no jurisdiction —R.B.Taney⟩

de·cid·ed \-īdəd\ *adj* [fr. past part. of *decide*] **1 :** free from ambiguity **:** UNQUESTIONABLE, CLEAR-CUT ⟨a ~ advantage⟩ **2 :** free from doubt or wavering **:** DETERMINED, SETTLED ⟨a ~ way of talking and moving —S.H.Adams⟩ — **de·cid·ed·ly** *adv* — **de·cid·ed·ness** *n* -ES

de·cid·er \-də(r)\ *n* -s **:** one that decides

de·cid·ua \də'sijəwə, dē'-\ *n, pl* **decid·uae** \-ˌwē\ [NL, fr. L, fem. of *deciduus* deciduous] **1 :** the part of the mucous membrane lining the uterus that in higher placental mammals undergoes special modifications in preparation for and during pregnancy and is cast off at parturition, being made up in the human of (1) a part lining the uterus, (2) a part enveloping the embryo, and (3) a part participating with the chorion in the formation of the placenta — called also respectively (1) *decidua ve·ra* \-'virə\, (2) *decidua cap·su·lar·is* \-ˌkapsə'la(ə)rəs\ or *decidua re·flexa* \-rə'fleksə\, and (3) *decidua ser·o·ti·na* \-ˌserə'tīnə, -tē-\ **2 :** the part of the mucous membrane of the uterus cast off in the ordinary process of menstruation — called also *decidua men·stru·al·is* \-ˌmenztrə'walə̇s\

de·cid·u·al \-ˌwəl\ *adj* [NL *decidua* + E *-al*] **:** of or involving a decidua **:** having a decidua

decidual cell *n* **:** one of the large irregular cells formed in the decidua of pregnancy

de·cid·u·ary \-ˌwerē\ *adj* [*deciduous* + *-ary*] **:** DECIDUOUS

de·cid·u·a·ta \ˌ=ˌ='wäd·ə, -ād·ə\ *n pl, cap* [NL, fr. *decidua* + *-ata*] **:** the mammals having deciduate placentas

de·cid·u·ate \ˌ='==ˌwət\ *adj* [NL *deciduatus*, fr. *decidua* + L *-atus* -ate] **1** *of a placenta* **:** having the fetal and maternal tissues firmly interlocked so that a layer of maternal tissue is torn away at parturition and forms a part of the afterbirth **2 :** DECIDUOUS

de·cid·u·ous \də'sijəwəs, dē'-\ *adj* [L *deciduus*, fr. *decidere* to fall off, fr. *de* down, away + *-cidere* (fr. *cadere* to fall) — more at DE-, CHANCE] **1 :** falling off or shed at the end of the growing period ⟨~ leaves⟩ ⟨~ fruit⟩, after anthesis ⟨~ flower petals⟩, at certain seasons ⟨the ~ hair of animals⟩ ⟨~ antlers of deer⟩, or at certain stages of development ⟨~ gills⟩ ⟨~ teeth⟩ — opposed to *persistent;* compare CADUCOUS, FUGACIOUS **2 :** having or made up of deciduous parts ⟨a ~ tree⟩ ⟨~ dentition⟩ — compare EVERGREEN **3 :** of passing interest or importance **:** EPHEMERAL, TRANSITORY ⟨there is much that is ~ in books —J.R.Lowell⟩ — **de·cid·u·ous·ly** *adv* — **de·cid·u·ous·ness** *n* -ES

deciduous cypress *n* **:** a bald cypress (*Taxodium distichum*)

deciduous holly *n* **:** BEARBERRY 3

deciduous tooth *n* **:** MILK TOOTH

deci·gram \'desə+ˌ-\ *n* -s [F *décigramme*, fr. *déci-* deci- + *gramme* gram] **:** a metric unit of mass and weight equal to 1/10 gram — see METRIC SYSTEM table

¹dec·ile \'deˌsīl, -ˌsəl\ *n* -s [L *decem* ten + E *-ile* — more at TEN] **:** any one of nine numbers in a series dividing the distribution of the individuals in the series into 10 groups of equal frequency; *also* **:** any one of these 10 groups

²decile \"\ *adj* **:** relating to a decile or division into deciles

deci·liter \'desə+ˌ-\ *n* -s [F *décilitre*, fr. *déci-* deci- + *litre* liter] **:** a metric unit of capacity equal to 1/10 liter — see METRIC SYSTEM table

de·cil·lion \də'silyən\ *n* -s *often attrib* [L *decem* + E *-illion* (as in *million*)] — see NUMBER table

¹dec·i·mal \'desəməl\ *adj* [fr. (assumed) NL *decimalis*, fr. ML, relating to tithes, fr. L *decima* tithe + *-alis* -al — more at DIME] **1 a :** numbered or proceeding by tens **:** based on the number 10 **b :** subdivided into 10th or 100th units ⟨~ coinage⟩ ⟨~ hour⟩ **c :** expressed in a decimal fraction ⟨a ~ equivalent⟩ **2** [ML *decimalis*] **:** of or relating to tithes

²decimal \"\ *n* -s **1 :** a number expressed in the scale of tens **2 :** DECIMAL FRACTION

decimal arithmetic *n* **1 :** the common arithmetic in which numeration proceeds by tens **2 :** calculation with decimals

decimal classification *n* **:** a system of classifying library books and other material whereby the main classes and subclasses are designated by a number composed of three digits and further subdivision is shown by numbers after a decimal point — called also *Dewey classification;* compare EXPANSIVE CLASSIFICATION, LIBRARY OF CONGRESS CLASSIFICATION

decimal fraction *n* **:** a proper fraction in which the denominator is some power of 10 usu. not expressed but signified by a point placed at the left of the numerator (as .2=2/10, .25=25/100, .025=25/1000)

dec·i·mal·ize \-ˌlīz\ *vt* -ED/-ING/-S **:** to reduce to a decimal system ⟨~ the currency⟩

dec·i·mal·ly \-məlē, -li\ *adv* **:** by tens **:** by means of decimals

decimal measure *n* **:** a measure used in a decimal system

decimal notation *n* **:** the expression of numbers through powers of 10; *specif* **:** the common method employing nine digits and zero

decimal place *n* **:** a position of a digit as counted to the right or sometimes to the left of the decimal point in a decimal ⟨carried out to the fourth *decimal place*⟩

decimal point *n* **:** the dot at the left of a decimal fraction

dec·i·mate \'desəˌmāt, *usu* -ād.+V\ *vt* -ED/-ING/-S [L *decimatus*, past part. of *decimare*, fr. *decimus* tenth, fr. *decem* ten — more at TEN] **1 :** to select by lot and kill every tenth man of ⟨~ a regiment⟩ **2 a :** to take a tenth from **:** tax to the amount of one-tenth **b** (1) **:** to take a tenth part of (ore) by means of a sampling device (2) **:** to take every tenth one of ⟨~ carloads⟩ **3 :** to destroy a considerable part of **:** reduce to the point of almost complete extermination ⟨war, which . . . nearly *decimated* the Seminoles —R.F.Warner⟩ **:** decrease greatly ⟨inflation has *decimated* . . . buying power —*New Republic*⟩ **4 :** to rearrange (an alphabet or text) into another sequence by taking every *n*th item until all are taken (as, if *n* is 3 ABCDEFG becomes ADGCFBE if the counting applies to the complete original sequence but ADGECFB if the letters previously taken out are skipped in counting)

decimating factor *n* **:** any direct cause (as starvation or hunting) of reduction in population numbers

dec·i·ma·tion \ˌ=='māshən\ *n* -s [LL *decimation-, decimatio*, fr. L *decimatus* (past part. of *decimare* to pay as a tithe, select by lot and kill every tenth man of) + *-ion-, -io* -ion] **1 a :** the taking of tithes or of a tax of one tenth **b :** the tithe or tax taken **2 :** a selection of every tenth person; *esp* **:** selection by lot for punishment with death **3 :** the destruction of a considerable part **:** reduction to the point of almost complete extermination ⟨~ of the forest Indians, brought about by disease —Farley Mowat⟩ **4 a :** the act of decimating cryptographically **b :** the new sequence resulting from decimating

dec·i·me·ter \'desəˌmēd·ə(r)\ *n* -s [F *décimètre*, fr. *déci-* deci- + *mètre* meter] **:** a metric unit of length equal to 1/10 meter — see METRIC SYSTEM table

dec·i·mo·lar \-ˌmōlə(r)\ *adj* [*deci-* + *molar*] *chem* **:** tenth molar

dec·i·mole \-ˌmōl\ *n* -s [ISV *decim-* (fr. L *decimus* tenth) + *-ole*] **:** DECUPLET 2

dec·i·mo·sex·to \ˌdesə(ˌ)mō'sek(ˌ)stō\ *n* -s [L *decimo sexto, sexto decimo*, abl. of *decimus sextus, sextus decimus* sixteenth, fr. *decimus* tenth + *sextus* sixth — more at SEXT] **:** SIXTEENMO

dec·i·normal \ˌdesə+\ *adj* [*deci-* + *normal*] *of a chemical solution* **:** having one tenth of the normal strength

¹de·cipher \də'sīfə(r), dē's-\ *vt* **deciphered; deciphered; deciphering** \-f(ə)riŋ\ **deciphers** [*de-* + ¹*cipher*; trans. of MF *deschiffrer*] **1 a** *obs* **:** to find out **:** DETECT, DISCOVER ⟨you are both ~*ed* . . . for villains —Shak.⟩ **b** *archaic* **:** to make known **:** INDICATE, REVEAL ⟨his favorite gesture . . . might ~ his whole character —Thomas Holcroft⟩ **2 :** to convert (a cryptic writing) into intelligible form: as **a :** to undo (an encipherment) by reversal of the enciphering procedure **b :** SOLVE ⟨~ a cipher⟩ **c** *obs* **:** to represent by oral description or pictorial art **:** DELINEATE, PORTRAY ⟨with her majesty's name ~*ed* in gold letters —Jonathan Swift⟩ **3 a :** to make out, read, or interpret despite obscuration or partial obliteration ⟨~*ing* the smudged postmark —Arnold Bennett⟩ **b :** to examine and find out or discover the meaning or explanation of (something difficult to understand) ⟨some philosophical message . . . that we fail to ~ —Henri Peyre⟩ **syn** see SOLVE

²decipher \"\ *n* -s **:** a secret message in deciphered form

de·ci·pher·able \də'sīf(ə)rəbəl, (ˈ)dē¦s-\ *adj* **:** capable of being deciphered — **de·ci·pher·ably** \-blē\ *adv*

de·ci·pher·er \də'sīfərə(r), dē's-\ *n* -s **:** one that deciphers

deciphering alphabet *n* [*deciphering* fr. gerund of ¹*decipher*] **:** a substitution alphabet with its cipher component in normal alphabetic order — see ALPHABET 1j, CONJUGATE ALPHABET

de·ci·pher·ment \-fə(r)mənt\ *n* -s **1 :** the act or process of deciphering **2 :** the result of deciphering **:** PLAINTEXT

¹de·ci·sion \də'sizhən, dē'-\ *n* -s [MF, fr. L *decision-, decisio*, fr. *decisus* (past part. of *decidere* to decide) + *-ion, -io* -ion — more at DECIDE] **1 a :** the act of deciding; *specif* **:** the act of settling or terminating (as a contest or controversy) by giving judgment **b :** a determination arrived at after consideration **:** SETTLEMENT, CONCLUSION — see JUDGMENT, PRECEDENT, STARE DECISIS **2 a :** an account or report of a conclusion, esp. of a legal adjudication or judicial determination of a question or cause ⟨a ~ of the Supreme Court⟩ **b :** an announcement (as of a judge) declaring the winner in a contest **3 :** the quality of being decided **:** prompt and fixed determination **:** FIRMNESS ⟨a man of unusual ~⟩ **4 a :** the act of forming an opinion or of deciding upon a course of action ⟨an exhausting ~⟩ **b :** an opinion formed or a course of action decided upon ⟨a favorable ~⟩ **5 :** WIN; *specif* **:** a victory in a boxing match decided on points instead of by a knockout

²decision \"\ *vt* **decisioned; decisioned; decisioning** \-zh(ə)niŋ\ **decisions :** to win a decision over (an opponent) ⟨the champion easily ~*ed* the challenger⟩

de·ci·sion·al \-zhənᵊl, -zhnəl\ *adj* **:** of, relating to, or involving a decision ⟨permeated with ~ . . . elements —Walter Cerf⟩

decisional law *n* **:** the law as determined by reference to the reported decisions of the courts — compare COMMON LAW

de·ci·sion·ism \-zhəˌnizəm\ *n* -s **:** a system of legal philosophy based on the belief that right is what the legislature has determined it to be

decision problem *n* **:** the problem of finding an effective method for deciding whether a given formula is true within the framework of the calculus to which it belongs

de·ci·sive \də'sīsiv, dē's-, -ēv *also* -'sīz- *or* -əv\ *adj* [F *décisif*, fr. MF *decisif*, fr. L *decisus* + MF *-if* -ive] **1 :** having the power or quality of deciding **:** putting an end to ⟨a ~ controversy⟩ **:** CONCLUSIVE ⟨we shall win a complete and ~ victory over the forces of evil —Sir Winston Churchill⟩ **2 :** marked by or displaying decision **:** RESOLUTE, DETERMINED ⟨the clarity that comes from the ~ mind of the man of direct action —J.P.Wood⟩ **3 :** that is beyond doubt **:** UNMISTAKABLE, UNQUESTIONABLE ⟨a ~ superiority⟩ **syn** see CONCLUSIVE

de·ci·sive·ly \-əvlē, -li\ *adv* **:** in a decisive manner

de·ci·sive·ness \-əvnəs\ *n* -ES **:** the quality or state of being decisive **:** RESOLUTENESS

dec·i·stere \'desəˌsti(ə)r\ *n* -s [F *décistère*, fr. *déci-* deci- + *stère* stere] **:** a metric unit of capacity equal to 1/10 cubic meter — see METRIC SYSTEM table

¹deck \'dek\ *n* -s [prob. modif. of (assumed) LG *verdeck* (whence G *verdeck*), fr. (assumed) MLG *vordeck* (trans. of OIt *coperta* or MF *couverte*, lit., cover), fr. MLG *vordecken* to cover, fr. MLG *vor-* (akin to OHG *fir-, fur-* for-) + *decken* to cover (akin to OHG *decken* to cover) — more at THATCH] **1 :** a platform in a ship extending within the hull from side to side and from stem to stern (as the main deck) or extending within or above the hull part of the width or the length (as the bridge deck) and serving as an important element in a ship's structural strength and forming the floor for its compartments **2 :** something resembling the deck of a ship: as **a :** a surface regarded as a floor to stand or move upon — used esp. in the U.S. Navy ⟨the third ~ of the barracks⟩ ⟨flying about 50 feet above the ~⟩ **b :** a story of a building **c :** a floor of a many-tiered stack in a library **d :** the roadway of a bridge **e :** the floor of a boxing ring **f :** a flat floored roofless area adjoining a house or built as a structural part of it and usu. being open on one or more sides **g :** the top of a mansard roof or curb roof when made nearly flat **h** (1) **:** the roof of a railroad passenger car (2) **:** a compartment for livestock in a freight car **i** (1) **:** the lid of the compartment at the rear of the body of an automobile (2) **:** the compartment covered by such a deck **j :** any one of the platforms of a large printing press **3 :** something that is a group or packet usu. containing a specified number or amount: as **a :** PACK 3c **b :** a group or file of tabulation cards usu. punched **c :** a package of cigarettes **d :** a packet containing drugs **e :** a load of market lambs that fills a single-decked railroad shipping car **4 :** duty assignment of officer of the deck ⟨the lieutenant had the ~ that evening⟩ **5 a :** a platform for logs **b :** a pile of logs **6 :** a horizontal division of a newspaper or periodical headline **7 :** FEEDBOARD **8 :** the length of the short triangular deck piece in the bow of a racing shell ⟨led by a ~ to a half-length until there were three quarters of a mile to go —*N.Y. Times*⟩ — **below decks** *adv* **:** in or to a place under the main deck of a ship; *esp* **:** in or to the hold — **between decks** *adv* **:** in the space between the decks of a ship — **on deck** *adv (or adj)* **1 :** on the upper deck **2 a :** ready for duty **:** on hand ⟨every employee had to be *on deck* at nine o'clock⟩ **b :** next in line **:** next in turn ⟨in the fifth inning Jones was at bat and Smith *on deck*⟩

1 2 3 4 5 6 7 8

deck 1: decks of a typical merchant ship, amidships: *1* bridge; 2 boat; *3* promenade; *4* shelter, weather, or superstructure; *5* upper, or freeboard; *6* main, or second; *7* lower, or third; *8* orlop, or fourth

²deck \"\ *vt* -ED/-ING/-S [in senses 3, 4, and 5, fr. ¹*deck;* in senses 1 and 2, fr. D *dekken* to cover; akin to OHG *decken* to cover — more at THATCH] **1** *obs* **:** COVER, ARRAY ⟨~ with clouds the uncolored sky —John Milton⟩ **2 a :** DRESS, APPAREL ⟨the Chinese have ~*ed* themselves for festivity in red —James Cameron⟩ **b :** to clothe with more than ordinary elegance **:** ADORN, EMBELLISH — often used with *out* ⟨~*ed* out with festooned ribbons —Donn Byrne⟩ ⟨an airplane ~*ed* out with an ice-blue interior —*Saturday Rev.*⟩ **3 :** to furnish (as a ship) with or as if with a deck — often used with *in* or *over* **4 :** to load or pile up on a deck ⟨~ up logs⟩ **5 :** FLOOR, FLATTEN ⟨~*ed* every opponent he has fought —Lewis Eskin⟩ **syn** see ADORN

deck beam *n* **:** an athwartship beam supporting a deck

deck boy *n* **:** one who cleans decks and deck fittings of boats

deck bridge *n* **:** a bridge whose supporting elements (as trusses, girders, arches) are below the track or roadway — compare THROUGH BRIDGE

deck chair *n* **:** a folding chair often having an adjustable leg rest

deck curb *n* **:** a curb surrounding or edging a roof deck

deck department *n* **:** the department composed of those members of a ship's personnel whose duties involve the practical handling of the ship, of the lines, and of small boats and the use and maintenance of ground tackle and cargo-handling gear

decke \ˈdekə\ *n, pl* **deck·en** \-ən\ [G, lit., cover, fr. OHG *decki*; akin to OHG *decken* to cover] **:** NAPPE

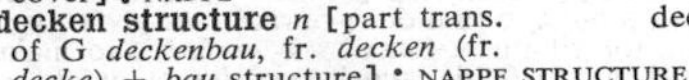
deck chair

decken structure *n* [part trans. of G *deckenbau*, fr. *decken* (fr. *decke*) + *bau* structure] **:** NAPPE STRUCTURE

¹deck·er \ˈdekə(r)\ *n* -s [¹*deck* + *-er*] **1 :** a ship having a specified number of decks or amount of deck space ⟨a single-*decker*⟩ ⟨a half-*decker*⟩ **2 :** something constructed with a specified number of levels, floors, or layers ⟨a double-*decker* sandwich⟩ ⟨the single-*decker* country buses —Evelyn Waugh⟩ **3 :** TENEMENT, APARTMENT ⟨people who live in ~*s*⟩ **4** [²*deck* (to load) + *-er*] **:** one that decks logs **5** [prob. fr. the name *Decker*] **:** WET MACHINE **6 :** an opaque diaphragm having one or more openings and being used to limit the field of a microscope or the slit length of a spectroscope

²decker \ˮ\ *vt* -ED/-ING/-S *papermaking* **:** to pass (pulp) over a wet machine

decker man *n, pl* **decker men :** a paper-mill worker who operates a wet machine — called also *filterman*

deck floor *n* **:** a floor that serves also as a roof

deckhand \ˈ=,=\ *n* **:** a sailor in the deck department who performs manual duties in connection with ship handling

deckhead \ˈ=,=\ *n* **:** the deck overhead **:** the ceiling of a compartment of a ship

deckhouse \ˈ=,=\ *n* **:** a superstructure (as a cabin) built on the upper deck of a ship but not extending to the sides

deck·ie \ˈdekē, -ki\ *n* -s [¹*deck* + *-ie*] *Brit* **:** DECKHAND

decking *n* -s [¹*deck* + *-ing*] **:** the surfacing material of a deck

deck key *n* **:** a key for the lock in the deck of an automobile

¹deck·le \ˈdekəl\ *n* -s [G *deckel*, lit., cover, fr. *decken* to cover, fr. OHG] **1 :** the detachable wooden frame around the outside edges of a papermaker's hand mold **2 a** *also* **deckle strap :** either of the endless rubber bands that run longitudinally upon the edges of the wire of a paper machine and thereby determine the width of the web **b :** the width of the web between deckles **3 :** DECKLE EDGE

²deckle \ˮ\ *vt* **deckled; deckled; deckling** \-k(ə)liŋ\ **deckles 1 a :** to limit the width of (paper) by deckles **b :** to give a deckle edge to **2 :** to equip (as a papermaking machine or hand mold) with deckles

deckle edge *n* **:** the rough untrimmed edge of paper left by the deckle or produced artificially (as by sawing the edges of trimmed sheets)

deck light *n* **:** a glass-covered opening in a deck

deck log *n* **:** a written chronological record of the important data and events of a voyage usu. kept by the quartermaster and signed by the officer of the watch

deck·man \ˈdekmən, -,man\ *n, pl* **deckmen** [¹*deck*] **1 :** a worker who mixes ingredients for paper coatings **2 a :** DECKER 4 **b :** a sawmill worker who operates a bull wheel that pulls cars of logs from pond to mill **c :** a sawmill worker who rolls logs from deck to carriage and positions them for sawing — called also *tripper*

deck molding *n* **:** the molded finish of the edge of a deck (as of a mansard roof) making the junction with the lower elements

decko \ˈde(,)kō\ *var of* DEKKO

deck passage *n* **:** passage (as on a riverboat) without cabin accommodations

deck passenger *n* **:** one that has deck passage

deck pipe *n* **1 :** CHAIN PIPE **2** *or* **deck turret :** MONITOR 6

deck roof *n* **:** a nearly flat roof with no parapet walls

decks *pl of* DECK, *pres 3d sing of* DECK

deck sheet *n* **:** a sheet leading from the clew of a topmast studding sail to the deck forward of the yard

deck stopper *n* **:** a stopper fastened to the deck and used to hold the cable when the anchor is down

deck stringer *n* **:** a strake of plating secured to the deck beams along the outer edge of a ship's deck in order to connect the beams to the side of the ship and to each other

deck tennis *n* [so called fr. its being played on the deck of a ship] **:** a game consisting of tossing a ring or quoit back and forth over a net stretched across a small court that resembles a tennis court

deck watch *n* **:** the officer of the deck's watch

decl *abbr* **1** declaration **2** declension

de·claim \dəˈklām, dēˈ-\ *vb* -ED/-ING/-S [alter. (influenced by *claim*) of earlier *declame*, fr. ME *declamen*, fr. L *declamare*, fr. *de* down, away + *clamare* to cry out; akin to L *calare* to call — more at DE-, LOW (to moo)] *vi* **1 :** to speak or make a speech in a rhetorical manner **:** deliver an oration ⟨some of the province's most illustrious men visited the courthouse and ~*ed* within its four walls —Hazel Y. Grinnell⟩; *specif* **:** to recite a speech or poem as an exercise in elocution ⟨he took to writing verse and was chosen to ~ on occasions both public and private —Raymond Weaver⟩ **2 :** to speak for rhetorical effect or display **:** speak pompously, noisily, or theatrically **:** HARANGUE ⟨in presence of this historical fact it is foolish to ~ about natural rights —V.L.Parrington⟩ **:** INVEIGH ⟨~*ing* against the horrors of the place —C.D.Lewis⟩ ~ *vt* **:** to deliver (as an oration) in a rhetorical manner **:** utter rhetorically ⟨have forgotten the exact moment when he ~*ed* his quotation —Thomas Wood †1950⟩; *specif* **:** to recite as an exercise in elocution ⟨all these people ~*ing* selections from Shakespeare —Ellen Glasgow⟩ — **de·claim·er** \-mə(r)\ *n* -s

de·cla·man·do \ˌdekləˈmän(,)dō, ˌdekləˈman-\ *adv (or adj)* [It, declaiming, fr. L *declamandum*, gerund of *declamare*] **:** in declamatory style — used as a direction in music

dec·la·ma·tion \ˌdekləˈmāshən\ *n* -s [MF or L; MF, fr. L *declamation-, declamatio*, fr. *declamatus* (past part. of *declamare*) + *-ion-, -io* -ion] **1 :** the act or art of declaiming ⟨only in ~ was he unable to match his fellows —A.C.Cole⟩: **a :** the rhetorical delivery of an oration **b :** the recitation of a speech or poem as an exercise in elocution **2 a :** a rhetorical speech **:** HARANGUE ⟨they indulge in vague ~*s* against the existing social order —W.R.Inge⟩ **b :** a speech or poem suitable for recitation as an exercise in elocution **3 :** impassioned delivery or rhetorical style characteristic esp. of a declamation ⟨the impossible cannot be made reasonable even by ~ —W.L. Sullivan⟩ **4 a :** the rhetorical rendering of words in singing **b :** MELODRAMA **c :** ACCENTUATION

declamator *n* -s [ME, fr. L, fr. *declamatus* + *-or*] *obs* **:** one that declaims

de·clam·a·to·ry \dəˈklamə,tōrē, dēˈ-, -,tȯr-, -ri\ *adj* [L *declamatorius*, fr. *declamatus* + *-orius* -ory] **1 :** of, relating to, or having the characteristics of declamation ⟨~ American speech in the 1870's . . . was at bottom noble and pure —George Santayana⟩ ⟨~ exercises⟩ **2 :** marked by rhetorical effect or display **:** STILTED ⟨filled with long ~ speeches as artificial as the improbable plot —O.S.Coad⟩

de·clar·able \dəˈkla(a)rəbəl, dēˈ-, -ler-\ *adj* **:** capable of being declared **:** that must be declared

de·clar·ant \-rənt\ *n* -s [*declare* + *-ant*] **1 :** one that makes a declaration; *specif* **:** an alien who has declared his intention of becoming a citizen of the U.S. by signing the first papers required in the process of naturalization **2 :** DECLARER

dec·la·ra·tion \ˌdekləˈrāshən\ *n* -s [ME *declaracioun*, fr. MF *declaration*, fr. L *declaration-, declaratio*, fr. *declaratus* (past part. of *declarare* to declare, explain) + *-ion-, -io* -ion — more at DECLARE] **1 :** the act of declaring, proclaiming, or publicly announcing **:** explicit assertion **:** formal proclamation ⟨decided that it would be wiser if he left the place till after the ~ of the poll —John Buchan⟩ ⟨the ~ of an extra dividend⟩ **2 a :** the first pleading in a common-law action consisting of the plaintiff's statement in order and at large of his cause of complaint and demand for relief **:** the narration of the plaintiff's case containing a count or counts — compare ALLEGATION, BILL, COMPLAINT 1d, LIBEL **b :** a statement made or testimony given by a witness or by a party to a legal transaction usu. not under oath **c** *Scots law* **:** the voluntary statement made by the accused at his preliminary examination in criminal proceedings, taken in writing, and signed by the accused, the judge, and witnesses **3 a :** something that is declared, proclaimed, or publicly announced **:** formal statement **:** AVOWAL ⟨a ~ of love spiced with a few harsh words —*Atlantic*⟩ **b :** the document containing such a declaration: as (1) **:** a statement or document proclaiming the principles, aims, or policy of a public body ⟨the *Declaration* of Independence⟩ (2) **:** a statement listing property or goods liable to a tax or duty (3) **:** a statement forming part of an insurance policy and containing information regarding the insurance risk **4 a** *in card games* **:** the act of declaring — compare CALL, MELD **b** (1) **:** the make in bridge-whist (2) **:** the final bid in auction bridge (3) **:** the contract in contract bridge **c :** an announcement as to whether he will compete for high, low, or in some cases both high and low that each player in certain forms of high-low poker makes after the final call but before the showdown **5 :** a formal withdrawal of a horse from a race

declaration of rights : a formal declaration enumerating the rights of the citizen — compare BILL OF RIGHTS

declaration of trust *or* **declaration of use :** a usu. written acknowledgment by one holding or taking title to property that he holds the property in trust for or to the use of another

declaration of war : a formal announcement by a sovereign or state of the beginning of hostilities against another

de·clar·a·tive \dəˈkla(a)rəd·iv, dēˈ-, -ler-, -ətiv\ *adj* [MF or L; MF *declaratif*, fr. L *declarativus*, fr. *declaratus* (past part. of *declarare* to declare, explain) + *-ivus* -ive] **1 obs a :** making clear or evident **:** ELUCIDATING **b :** declaring one's opinion **:** COMMUNICATIVE **2 :** having the characteristics of or making a declaration **:** ASSERTIVE ⟨a ~ law⟩ ⟨a letter ~ of his intentions⟩; *specif* **:** constituting a statement that can be either true or false ⟨*he has brown hair, I do not know him*, and Latin *adest* "he is here" are ~ statements⟩ ⟨~ clause⟩ ⟨~ sentence⟩ — **de·clar·a·tive·ly** \-əvlē, -li\ *adv*

de·clar·a·tor \-əd·ə(r)\ *n* -s [modif. of MF or ML; MF *declaratoire* declaratory, fr. ML *declaratorius*] **:** a legal declaration; *specif* **:** a legal action by which a judicial declaration of a fact is obtained

de·clar·a·to·ry \-ə,tōrē, -tȯrē, -ri\ *adj* [prob. fr. ML *declaratorius*, fr. L *declaratus* + *-orius* -ory] **1 :** serving to declare, set forth, or explain **:** being a manifestation of ⟨a philosophy of natural law which regards human law as ~ of divinely established fact —F.S.Cohen⟩ **2 a :** declaring what is the existing law — distinguished from *remedial* **b :** of, relating to, or being an action of declarator **c :** declaring a legal right or establishing a legal interpretation of an instrument ⟨a ~ judgment⟩

de·clare \dəˈkla(a)(ə)r, dēˈ-, -lel, |ə\ *vb* -ED/-ING/-S [ME *declaren*, fr. MF *declarer*, fr. L *declarare*, fr. *de* from, away + *clarare* to make clear, fr. *clarus* clear, bright — more at DE-, CLEAR] *vt* **1** *obs* **:** to make clear **:** EXPLAIN, INTERPRET ⟨I told this unto the magicians but there was none that could ~ it to me —Gen 41:24 (AV)⟩ **2 :** to make known publicly, formally, or explicitly esp. by language ⟨reaffirm on this wider basis the truths which other writers . . . have already *declared* —Herbert Read⟩ **:** announce, proclaim, or publish esp. by a formal statement or official pronouncement ⟨we *declared* rubber a strategic and critical material —W.R.Langdon⟩ ⟨an armistice is called, peace is *declared* —Harrison Forman⟩ **:** communicate to others ⟨here the results of research are presented, here the progress of knowledge is *declared* —Bernard De Voto⟩ **3 :** to make evident or give evidence of **:** serve as a means of revealing **:** MANIFEST, SHOW ⟨a glimpse of his head in outline . . . *declared* his present state of mind —Osbert Sitwell⟩ **4 :** to make a formal acknowledgment of ⟨~ a trust⟩ **5 :** to state emphatically ⟨others ~ that the rains on the mountain sides . . . caused the disaster —C.L.Jones⟩ **:** AFFIRM, ASSERT ⟨happy the country that has no history, ~*s* the proverb —E.H.Collis⟩ **6 a :** to make a full statement of or about (property subject to tax or duty) **b :** to name (a taxable or dutiable item) as being in one's possession or ownership **7 :** SCRATCH 6d **8** *in card games* **a :** to make a bid or announcement naming (a trump suit or no-trump) **b :** to announce or show (scoring cards) **:** MELD **9** *of a cricket team* **:** to announce (its current unfinished innings) closed forthwith **10 :** to make payable esp. by vote of the directors of a corporation ⟨*declared* an extra dividend for the fourth quarter⟩ ~ *vi* **1 :** to make a declaration ⟨poetry . . . evokes rather than merely ~*s* —C.S.Kilby⟩: as **a** *in card games* (1) **:** CALL, BID (2) **:** MELD **b** *of a cricket team* **:** to declare its current unfinished innings closed forthwith **2 :** to make an open and explicit avowal (as of one's opinion or support) **:** announce or proclaim oneself — often used with *for* or *against* ⟨one of the first papers in New England to ~ for Jackson —H.K.Beale⟩ ⟨*declared* against the ancient languages as the staple of American education —Howard M. Jones⟩

syn ANNOUNCE, PUBLISH, ADVERTISE, PROCLAIM, PROMULGATE, BROADCAST: these seven verbs agree in signifying to make known openly or publicly. DECLARE, though often used as an equivalent of *say*, usu. suggests forthrightness or plainness, and often a certain formality, of manner or statement ⟨the visitor *declared* that it was his intention to leave early⟩ ⟨the court *declared* that the interim measures of protection . . . had ceased to operate —*Americana Annual*⟩ To ANNOUNCE is to declare for the first time, esp. something presumably of interest ⟨to *announce* one's arrival⟩ ⟨to *announce* an engagement⟩ ⟨to *announce* a new government economic policy⟩ To PUBLISH is to make public, now generally by means of printing ⟨they may only want to find the Monarchists in a thoroughly compromising position and *publish* it to the world —John Buchan⟩ ⟨if the national government resolves upon some drastic action at ten o'clock it *publishes* the decree at eleven —L.C.Douglas⟩ To ADVERTISE in its most general sense is to call public attention to by widely circulated statements, sometimes with unpleasant publicity or extravagance of statement ⟨deliberately *advertising* his willingness to make concessions —*Time*⟩ ⟨permanent residents also aided materially in *advertising* the territory —R.A.Billington⟩ ⟨to *advertise* one's products in newspapers, on the radio, and on television⟩ To PROCLAIM is to announce usu. orally and loudly and with conclusiveness in a public place or to people at large ⟨to *proclaim* the day a national holiday⟩ ⟨to *proclaim* the independence of the nation⟩ ⟨to *proclaim* one's innocence in the face of public disbelief⟩ To PROMULGATE is to make known to all concerned something that has binding force (as a dogma of the church) or something for which adherents are sought (as a theory or a doctrine) ⟨regulations *promulgated* by executive order —*Americana Annual*⟩ ⟨*promulgates* a brand of heaven-on-earth religion —John Kobler⟩ To BROADCAST is to make known in all directions over a large area, now commonly by radio or television ⟨the book he has written to *broadcast* this conviction —Gordon Harrison⟩ ⟨to *broadcast* the news every hour on the hour⟩ **syn** see in addition ASSERT

— **declare oneself 1 :** to make known one's opinion **:** announce one's position **2 :** to make known one's existence, identity, or true character **3 :** to make a declaration of love **4 :** to register as a member of a political party

de·clared \|(ə)rd, |(ə)d\ *adj* [fr. past part. of *declare*] **:** openly avowed or made known ⟨their ~ and their covert objectives⟩ — **de·clar·ed·ly** \|rədlē, -li\ *adv*

declared trump *n* **:** a trump suit announced in advance of the play in whist

declared value *n* **1 :** the value placed upon imported goods by the importer for clearance through the customhouse **2 :** the value per unit of a shipment as stated by the shipper upon delivery to a carrier usu. to obtain a released or lower rate

declare off *vi* **:** to withdraw esp. from a promise, engagement, or contest **:** back out ⟨no, I *declare off*; I'll fight no more —Oliver Goldsmith⟩

de·clar·er \|rə(r)\ *n* -s **:** one that declares; *specif* **:** the bridge player who plays both his own hand and that of the dummy

de·class \(ˈ)dē+\ *vt* [*de-* + *class* (n.); trans. of F *déclasser*] **:** to remove from a class **:** lower in one's class esp. socially ⟨the psychological effects of being ~*ed* —Francis Downing⟩

¹dé·clas·sé *or* **dé·clas·sée** \ˌdākləˈsā, -laˈ-, -lāˈ-\ *n* -s [F, fr. *déclassé, déclassée*, adj.] **:** one that is déclassé ⟨the younger generation of ~*s* —Willi Frischauer⟩ ⟨treated as a ~, Austria found her credit seriously impaired —*Current History*⟩

²déclassé *or* **déclassée** \ˌ==ˈ=\ *adj* [F *déclassé* (masc.), *déclassée* (fem.), fr. *déclassé*, past part. of *déclasser* to declass, fr. *dé-* de- (fr. OF *des-*) + *classe* class — more at DE-, CLASS] **1 :** fallen or lowered in class, rank, or social position ⟨he was ~ enough to want to work with his hands —*Times Lit. Supp.*⟩ **2 :** of inferior status ⟨it's been a long time since dyed furs were considered ~ —Lois Long⟩

de·classicize \(ˈ)dē+\ *vt* [*de-* + *classicize*] **:** to make less classical ⟨went far toward *declassicizing* Latin prose —H.O. Taylor⟩

de·classification \(ˈ)dē +\ *n* -s **:** the act or process of declassifying

de·classify \(ˈ)dē+\ *vt* [*de-* + *classify*] **:** to remove or reduce the security classification of (as a document or weapon) ⟨admits that any policy-making official may . . . ~ any secret document —Bruce Bliven b.1889⟩

de clau·so frac·to \ˌdā,klō(,)zōˈfrak(,)tō\ [NL, lit., of broken close] **:** of breach of close — used of the old legal action against a trespasser upon real property

de·clen·sion \dəˈklenchən, dēˈ-\ *n* -s [prob. alter. (influenced by *-ion*) of earlier *declenson*, modif. of MF *declinaison* grammatical declension, grammatical inflection, decline, fr. LL *declination-, declinatio* grammatical declension (fr. L, grammatical inflection) & L *declination-, declinatio* grammatical inflection, avoidance, turning aside, fr. L *declinatus* (past part. of *declinare* to inflect grammatically, turn aside) + *-ion-, -io* -ion — more at DECLINE] **1 a :** noun, adjective, or pronoun inflection **b :** a presentation in some prescribed order of the inflectional forms of a noun, adjective, or pronoun **c :** a class of nouns or adjectives having the same type of inflectional forms ⟨Latin nouns of the second ~ have their nominative singular in *-us* or *-um* and their genitive singular in *-ī*⟩ ⟨Latin adjectives of the third ~ such as *facilis*⟩ **2 :** a falling off or away esp. from a standard or a high point of development **:** DECLINE ⟨seems to mark a ~ in his career as an illustrator —F.J.Mather⟩ **:** DETERIORATION ⟨makes me wish to reflect, . . . to see if it is all loss, all ~ —A.C.Benson⟩ **3 :** a bending or sloping downward **:** DESCENT ⟨the ~ of the land from that place to the sea —Thomas Burnet⟩ **4 :** a courteous refusal **:** DECLINATION ⟨his ~ of the nomination⟩

de·clen·sion·al \-chənᵊl, -chnəl\ *adj* **:** of or belonging to grammatical declension — **de·clen·sion·al·ly** \-ᵊl|ē -əl|, |i\ *adv*

de·clin·able \dəˈklīnəbəl, dēˈ-\ *adj* [MF, fr. *decliner* to decline + *-able*] **:** capable of being grammatically declined

dec·li·nate \ˈdeklə,nāt, -,nət\ *adj* [L *declinatus*, past part. of *declinare* to turn aside] **:** bent or curved downward or aside

dec·li·na·tion \ˌ==ˈnāshən\ *n* -s [ME *declinacioun*, fr. MF *declination*, fr. L *declination-, declinatio*, lit., turning aside] **1 :** latitude in the equator system of coordinates corresponding to terrestrial latitude; *specif* **:** angular distance from the celestial equator measured positively northward or negatively southward along a great circle passing through the celestial poles **2 :** a turning aside or swerving **:** DEVIATION ⟨makes his best virtue from the even line with fatal ~ swerve aside —Robert Southey⟩ **3 :** a decline (as from prosperity or vigor) **:** DETERIORATION ⟨something radically deficient in his makeup . . . brought on this moral ~ —Josephine T. Baker⟩ **4 :** a leaning or bending downward **:** INCLINATION ⟨a ~ of the antiquary's stiff backbone acknowledged the preference —Sir Walter Scott⟩ **5 :** a formal refusal **:** NONACCEPTANCE ⟨~*s* of appointments and resignations had been frequent —G.W. Goble⟩ **6 :** the angle formed between a magnetic needle and the geographical meridian when the needle points east or west of true north ⟨east ~⟩ ⟨west ~⟩ — called also *variation*

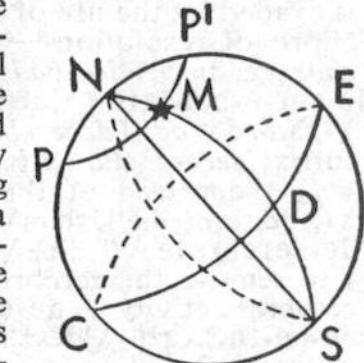

declination: celestial equator, *C E:* celestial poles, *N & S:* star, *M;* declination of star, *DM;* parallel of declination, *P M P'*

dec·li·na·tion·al \ˌ==ˈ=shənᵊl, -shnəl\ *adj* **:** of or relating to declination

declination axis *n* **:** the axis of rotation that is at right angles to the polar axis of an equatorial mounting and that permits pointing the telescope to celestial objects of different declinations

declination circle *n* **:** one of the setting circles of an equatorial mounting fastened to the declination axis to indicate the declination to which the telescope is pointing

declination compass *n* **:** DECLINOMETER

declination parallel *n* **:** PARALLEL OF DECLINATION

de·clin·a·to·ry \dəˈklīnə,tōrē, dēˈ-, -,tȯr-, -ri\ *adj* [ML *declinatorius* denying jurisdiction, fr. L *declinatus* + *-orius* -ory] **:** containing or involving a declination ⟨a ~ motion⟩

declinatory plea *n* [trans. of ML *declinatoria exceptio*] **:** a plea denying the court's jurisdiction; *esp* **:** the plea of benefit of clergy or of sanctuary

de·clin·a·ture \-nəchə(r)\ *n* -s [alter. (influenced by *-ure*) of earlier *declinatour*, fr. *declinatour*, adj., denying jurisdiction, fr. ME (Sc), modif. of ML *declinatorius*] **1** *Scots law* **:** a plea denying jurisdiction **2 :** DECLINATION 5

¹de·cline \dəˈklīn, dēˈ-\ *vb* -ED/-ING/-S [ME *declinen*, fr. MF *decliner* to inflect grammatically, turn aside, sink, fr. L *declinare* to inflect grammatically, turn aside, fr. *de* from, away + *-clinare* to incline — more at DE-, LEAN] *vi* **1 :** to turn aside **:** deviate from or as if from a straight course **:** STRAY ⟨walked in the ways of David his father and *declined* neither to the right hand nor to the left —2 Chron 34:2 (AV)⟩ **2 :** to take a downward direction: as **a :** to slope downward **:** DESCEND ⟨pipes used for the conveyance of gasoline shall ~ to tanks —*Fire Manual (Mass.)*⟩ ⟨the path ~*s* to the track⟩ **b :** to bend down **:** DROOP ⟨eyes . . . *declining* toward the ground —Henry Fielding⟩ **c :** to stoop or descend to what is unworthy ⟨the direful shameful state Adam *declined* into —Edward Taylor⟩ **3 a** *of a celestial body* **:** to sink toward setting ⟨the sun had begun to ~⟩ **b :** to draw toward a close ⟨as the day *declined* the place became insupportable —Ellen Glasgow⟩ **4 :** to tend toward an inferior state or weaker condition **:** become diminished or impaired **:** FAIL ⟨the powers of the mind and body begin with added years to ~ —C.W.Eliot⟩ **5** *obs* **:** INCLINE, TEND ⟨your weeping sister is no wife of mine . . . far more, far more to you do I ~ —Shak.⟩ **6 :** to withhold consent **:** REFUSE ⟨when I invited him he *declined*⟩ ~ *vt* **1 a :** to give in some prescribed order the various grammatical forms of **:** INFLECT — used formerly of any inflected word, now only of a noun, pronoun, or adjective ⟨~ the Latin adjective *bonus*⟩ **b** *obs* **:** to recite formally or in some prescribed order ⟨that you no harsh nor shallow rimes ~ —Michael Drayton⟩ **2** *obs* **a :** to cause to turn aside **:** AVERT ⟨evasions are sought to ~ the pressure of resistless arguments —Samuel Johnson⟩ **b :** to turn aside from **:** AVOID ⟨sinners . . . despairing to ~ their fate —Thomas Ken⟩ **3 :** to cause to bend, bow, or fall **:** bring or move down **:** bend downward ⟨the clover . . . ~*s* its blooms —W.C.Bryant⟩ **4 a :** to refuse to undertake, engage in, or comply with **:** REJECT ⟨sought out the English fleet but it *declined* battle —L.W.Dean⟩ **b :** to refuse courteously or politely **:** not to accept ⟨*declining* the unwanted manuscript —August Frugé⟩ **5 :** to refuse to accept (gambit) or pursue (a line of play) when an opponent in chess offers the opportunity

syn DECLINE, REFUSE, REJECT, REPUDIATE, and SPURN can all mean to turn away something or someone by not consenting to accept, receive, or consider it or him. DECLINE, the most courteous of the terms, is used chiefly in connection with invitations, offers of help, or services ⟨to *decline* an offer of a chairmanship⟩ ⟨to *decline* a formal invitation⟩ ⟨to *decline* to answer personal questions⟩ REFUSE is more positive, implying decisiveness, even ungraciousness ⟨to *refuse* an invitation and insult a friend thereby⟩ ⟨to *refuse* to answer personal questions⟩ ⟨to *refuse* all offers of marriage⟩ REJECT implies a refusal to have anything to do with a person or thing ⟨to *reject* an appeal for help⟩ ⟨*rejecting* with scorn all that can be called mysticism —W.R.Inge⟩ ⟨*rejected* by their mothers, shunted from one boarding home to another, these youngsters have lost faith in the kindliness of adults —Alice Lake⟩

REPUDIATE implies a disowning or rejecting with scorn as untrue, unauthorized, unworthy of acceptance, making false claim, and so on ⟨it is not so easy to *repudiate* one's heritage —A.J.Toynbee⟩ ⟨in permitting the husband to *repudiate* his wife at his own whim —Reuben Levy⟩ ⟨Bradburn had *repudiated* his promise —*Amer. Guide Series: Texas*⟩ SPURN implies even stronger disdain or contempt in rejection than REPUDIATE ⟨a devoted beau whom she had *spurned* for her lover —Joseph Schiffman⟩ ⟨neglected God for years and *spurned* His commandments —Bruce Marshall⟩ ⟨to *spurn* an offer of help⟩

²decline \" *sometimes* 'dē,-\ *n* -S [ME *declyn*, fr. MF *declin*, fr. *decliner* to sink] **1 :** the process of declining **:** a falling off ⟨the reading of books is suffering a ~ —J.D.Adams⟩: **a :** a change to a weaker condition **:** a gradual sinking and wasting away of the physical or mental faculties **b :** a change to an inferior or less favorable state ⟨the ~ of the aristocracy⟩ ⟨the ~ of the small nations⟩ **c** (1) **:** a downward movement or gradual fall (as in price or value) ⟨a late buying movement in these grains eliminated most early ~*s* —*Wall Street Jour.*⟩ **:** DIMINUTION ⟨a ~ in population⟩ (2) **:** a downward course (as of the blood pressure or of a fever) **:** DEFERVESCENCE **2 :** the period during which something is approaching its end or setting ⟨in the ~ of life⟩ **3 :** a downward slope **:** DECLIVITY ⟨constructed on a slight ~ away from the kennels to allow the water to drain away —*Smallholder Encyclopaedia*⟩ **4 a :** any wasting disease ⟨young men who work themselves into a ~ and are driven off in a hearse —R.L. Stevenson⟩; *esp* **:** pulmonary tuberculosis **b** *also* **decline disease :** any progressively deleterious disease or condition of plants — compare QUICK DECLINE

de·clin·er \=ˈ=nə(r)\ *n* -S **:** one that declines

dec·li·nom·e·ter \,deklə'nämәd·ə(r)\ *n* [ISV *declino-* (fr. *declination*) + *-meter*] **:** an instrument for measuring magnetic declination

de·cli·vate \də'klī,vāt, dē'-, 'dekla̤,-, -,vәt\ *adj* [L *declivis* + E *-ate*] **:** inclining downward **:** SLOPING

declive *adj* [F or L; F *déclive*, fr. L *declivis*] *obs* **:** sloping down

de·cli·vent \də'klīvənt, dē'-, 'deklәv-\ *adj* [L *declivis* + E *-ent*] **:** DECLIVOUS

de·cliv·i·tous \də'klivəd·əs, dē'-\ *adj* [*declivity* + *-ous*] **:** having a considerable downward slope **:** moderately steep — **de·cliv·i·tous·ly** *adv*

de·cliv·i·ty \-'klivəd·ē, -ətē, -i\ *n* -ES [L *declivitat-, declivitas*, fr. *declivis* sloping down (fr. *de* down, away + *-clivis*, fr. *clivus* slope, hill) + *-tat-, -tas* -ty; akin to L *clinare* to incline — more at DE-, LEAN] **1 :** downward deviation from the horizontal **:** slope or gradient of a surface **:** INCLINATION ⟨streams of water in the larger valleys of gentler ~ —C.A.Cotton⟩ — opposed to *acclivity* **2 :** a descending slope (as of a hill) **:** a steep or overhanging slope (as of a cliff) ⟨a large village situated just on the ~ of the farther side of the hill —George Borrow⟩

de·cli·vous \-'klīvəs\ *adj* [L *declivis* + E *-ous*] **:** sloping downward — opposed to *acclivous*

de·clutch \(')dē+\ *vi* **:** to disengage a clutch ~ *vt* **:** to put out of action by releasing a clutch

de·coct \də'käkt, dē'-\ *vt* -ED/-ING/-S [L *decoctus*, past part. of *decoquere*, fr. *de* down, away + *coquere* to cook — more at COOK] **1 a :** to prepare by boiling **:** extract the flavor or active principle of by boiling **b :** to steep in hot water **2 a :** to boil down **:** concentrate by or as if by boiling ⟨here we have the thrice . . . ~*ed* essence of the critical study of generations —George Saintsbury⟩ **b** *obs* **:** DIMINISH **3** *obs* **:** KINDLE, EXCITE

de·coc·tion \-'käkshən\ *n* -S [ME *decoccioun*, fr. MF or LL; MF *decoction*, fr. LL *decoction-, decoctio*, fr. L *decoctus* (past part. of *decoquere*) + *-ion-, -io* -ion] **1 :** the act or process of boiling usu. in water so as to extract the flavor or active principle ⟨a substance obtained by ~⟩ — compare INFUSION **2 a :** an extract obtained by decocting **b :** a liquid preparation made by boiling a medicinal plant with water usu. in the proportion of 5 parts of the drug to 100 parts of water ⟨had slept the winter afternoon away, soothed by some ~ of medicinal herbs —Elinor Wylie⟩

decoction process *n* **:** a mashing process in which parts of the mash are removed, boiled, and returned to the main part thereby raising the whole to about 75°C — compare INFUSION PROCESS

de·coc·tive \-'käktiv\ *adj* [*decoct* + *-ive*] **:** relating to or suitable for decoction

de·coc·tum \-'käktəm\ *n, pl* **decoc·ta** \-ktə\ [L, fr. neut. of *decoctus*] **:** DECOCTION 2b

¹de·code \(')dē+\ *vb* [*de-* + ¹*code*] *vt* **1 :** to convert (a message in code) from code into ordinary language **2 :** DECRYPT **3 :** to identify the constituent significant elements of (a message in ordinary language) — compare ¹CODE 3 ~ *vi* **:** to convert a message in code from code into ordinary language

²decode \'dē+,-\ *n* -S **:** a secret message in decoded form

de·coder \(')dē+\ *n* -S **:** one that decodes; *specif* **:** CRYPTOGRAPHER

de·co·ic acid \də'kōik, (')dē¦-\ *n* [*decane* + *-oic*] **:** any of the monocarboxylic acids $C_9H_{19}COOH$ (as capric acid) derived from the decanes

de·coke \(')dē+\ *vt* [*de-* + ¹*coke*] *Brit* **:** DECARBONIZE

¹de·col·late \də'kä,lāt, dē'-, 'dekə,-, -,lət\ *adj* [ME, fr. L *decollatus*, past part. of *decollare* to behead] *archaic* **:** BEHEADED

²de·col·late \-,lāt\ *vt* -ED/-ING/-S [L *decollatus*, past part. of *decollare*, fr. *de* from, away + *-collare* (fr. *collum* neck) — more at DE-, COLLAR] **:** to sever from the neck **:** BEHEAD, DECAPITATE

de·col·lat·ed \də'kä,lād·əd, (')dē¦-, 'dekə,-\ *adj* [fr. past part. of ²*decollate*] **1 :** BEHEADED **2 :** having the apex broken or worn off **:** TRUNCATED — used esp of a spiral shell

de·col·la·tion \,dē,kä'lāshən\ *n* -S [ME *decollacioun*, fr. LL *decollation-, decollatio*, fr. L *decollatus* + *-ion-, -io* -ion] **:** DECAPITATION ⟨the feast of the ~ of St. John the Baptist is Aug. 29⟩

dé·col·le·tage *also* **de·col·le·tage** \(,)dā¦kälə¦täzh, (,)de¦-, -kȯl-, -kōl-, -täzh, ¦=,==¦=; deklə¦t-\ *n* -S [F, action of cutting a low-necked dress, fr. *décolleter* + *-age*] **1 :** the low-cut neckline of a woman's dress ⟨the square ~ . . . finished with a tiny border of oak leaves and acorns in gold —*N.Y. Times*⟩ **2 :** a décolleté dress (a spectacular succession of off-the-shoulder ~*s* —*Newsweek*⟩

décolletage

¹dé·col·le·té *also* **de·col·le·te** \(,)dā¦kälə¦tā, (,)de¦-, -kȯl-, -kōl-, ¦=,==¦=; ¦deklə¦tā\ *adj* [F *décolleté* (masc.), *décolletée* (fem.), past part. of *décolleter* to give a low neckline to, fr. *dé-* de- (fr. OF *des-*) + *collet* collar, fr. OF *colet*, fr. *col* collar, neck (fr. L *collum* neck) + *-et*] **1** *also* **dé·col·le·tée** \"\ **:** wearing a strapless or low-necked dress ⟨she came to the party ~⟩ **2 :** having a low-cut neckline or leaving the neck and shoulders uncovered ⟨a ~ dress⟩

²décolleté *also* **decollete** \"\ *n* -S [F *décolleté*, fr. past part. of *décolleter*] **:** DÉCOLLETAGE

de·color \(')dē+\ *vt* [*de-* + *color*] **:** DECOLORIZE

¹de·colorant \(')dē+\ *n* [*decolor* + *-ant*, n. suffix] **:** a substance that removes color

²decolorant \"\ *adj* [*decolor* + *-ant*, adj. suffix] **:** capable of removing color **:** BLEACHING

de·coloration \(,)dē+\ *n* [F *décoloration*, fr. L *decoloration-, decoloratio*, fr. *decoloratus* (past part. of *decolorare* to discolor, deprive of color, fr. *de* from, away + *colorare* to color, fr. *color*) + *-ion-, -io* -ion — more at DE-, COLOR] **:** DECOLORIZATION

de·col·or·i·za·tion \(,)dē,kələrə'zāshən\ *n* **:** the process of decolorizing

de·col·or·ize \(')dē¦kələ,rīz\ *vt* -ED/-ING/-S [*de-* + *color* + *-ize*] **:** to remove color from (as liquids by adsorption on activated carbon) — compare BLEACH

de·col·or·izer \-zə(r)\ *n* **:** one that decolorizes

de·commission \,dē+\ *vt* [*de-* + *commission*] **:** to remove (as a ship) from service

de·compensate \(')dē+\ *vi* [prob. back-formation fr. *decompensation*] **:** to undergo decompensation

de·compensation \(,)dē+\ *n* [ISV *de-* + *compensation*] **:** loss of compensation; *esp* **:** loss of adequate functional power of a diseased heart after a period of compensation

de·com·pos·abil·i·ty \,dēkəm,pōzə'biləd·ē\ *n* -ES **:** the quality or state of being decomposable

de·com·pos·able \¦==¦pōzəbəl\ *adj* **:** that can be decomposed

de·com·pose \,==ˈpōz\ *vb* [F *décomposer*, fr. *dé-* de- (fr. OF *des-*) + *composer* to compose — more at COMPOSE] *vt* **1 a :** to separate or resolve into constituent parts or elements or into simpler compounds ⟨found that the water was *decomposed* into . . . hydrogen and oxygen —S.F.Mason⟩ **b :** to distinguish by analysis ⟨were I compelled to ~ the motives of my worthy friend —Sir Walter Scott⟩ **2 :** to cause chemical disintegration of (organic matter) **:** ROT ~ *vi* **:** to break up into constituent elements **:** undergo chemical change **:** DECAY, ROT, DISINTEGRATE **syn** see DECAY

decomposed *adj* [fr. past part. of *decompose*] **1 :** in a state of decomposition **2 :** not cohering **:** SEPARATED — used of the crest of birds when the feathers are divergent or of a feather when the barbs do not cohere

de·com·pos·er \-zə(r)\ *n* **:** one that decomposes

¹decomposite \(¦)dē+\ *n* [LL *decompositus* derived from a compound word (trans. of Gk *parasynthetos*), fr. L *de* from, away + *compositus* composite, compound — more at DE-, COMPOSITE] **:** ¹DECOMPOUND

²decomposite \"\ *adj* [LL *decompositus*] **:** ³DECOMPOUND

¹decomposition *n* [prob. fr. ¹*decomposite*, after E *composite*: *composition*] *obs* **:** the combination of composites **:** repeated composition

²de·com·po·si·tion \(¦)dē,kämpə¦zishən\ *n* [prob. fr. F *décomposition*, fr. *décomposer*, after F *composer* to compose: *composition*] **:** the act or process of decomposing **:** the state of being decomposed: **a :** the separation or resolution (as of a substance) into constituent parts or elements or into simpler compounds ⟨~ of mercuric oxide into mercury and oxygen⟩ — compare DISSOCIATION 1a **b :** DISINTEGRATION ⟨~ by fission⟩ **c :** organic decay ⟨the ~ of a dead body⟩ **:** DISSOLUTION ⟨the complete ~ of the opposition⟩

decomposition potential *or* **decomposition voltage** *n* **:** the minimum electromotive force required to cause a steady electrolysis in any solution

¹de·compound \(')dē+\ *n* [*de-* + *compound*, n.; approximate trans. of LL *decompositus* derived from a compound word] **:** any compound that has a compound as one of its parts; *specif* **:** a word that has a compound as one of its immediate constituents (as *newspaperman, railroader*)

²de·compound \(¦)dē+\ *vt* [in sense 1, fr. ¹*decompound*; in sense 2, fr. *de-* + *compound*, v.] **1** *obs* **:** to compound further **:** compound or mix with a compound **2 :** to reduce to constituent parts **:** DECOMPOSE

³decompound \"\ *adj* [¹*decompound*] **1 :** compounded of what is already compound **:** compounded again **2** *of a leaf* **:** having divisions that are themselves compound

de·compress \¦dē+\ *vb* [trans. of F *décomprimer*] *vt* **:** to subject to decompression ~ *vi* **:** to undergo decompression

de·compression \¦dē+\ *n* [prob. fr. F *décompression*, fr. *dé-* de- (fr. OF *des-*) + *compression*] **:** the act or process of releasing from pressure or compression: as **a :** reduction of pressure: (1) **:** the decrease of atmospheric pressure experienced by a workman in an air lock when he is returning to the outside air from a caisson under compression or by an aviator when he ascends to a great height (2) **:** the decrease of water pressure experienced by a diver when he ascends rapidly **b :** an operation or technique employed to relieve pressure upon an organ (as in fractures of skull or spine) or within a hollow organ (as in intestinal obstruction)

decompression chamber *n* **1 :** a chamber in which excessive pressure can be reduced gradually to atmospheric pressure **2 :** a chamber in which an individual can be gradually subjected to decreased atmospheric pressure (as in simulating conditions at high altitudes)

decompression sickness *n* **:** CAISSON DISEASE, AEROEMBOLISM

de·compressive \¦dē+\ *adj* **:** tending toward or for the purpose of decompression

de·concentrate \(¦)dē+\ *vt* **:** to reduce or abolish the concentration of **:** DECENTRALIZE

de·concentration \(¦)dē+\ *n* **:** the act or process of deconcentrating **:** DECENTRALIZATION; *specif* **:** the devolution of power by a central government to local authorities

de·concentrator \(¦)dē+\ *n* **:** a device for removing suspended or dissolved material from feedwater (as for a still or boiler)

de·condition \¦dē+\ *vt* **1 :** to cause to lose fitness ⟨prolonged inactivity ~*s* a person physically⟩ **2 :** to remove the effects of specialized training or unusual habits from **3 :** to cause extinction of (a conditioned response)

de·congest \¦dē+\ *vt* **:** to relieve the congestion of

de·con·ges·tant \,dēkən'jestənt\ *n* -S **:** an agent that relieves congestion (as of mucous membranes)

de·congestion \¦dē+\ *n* [*de-* + *congestion*] **:** the process of relieving congestion

de·congestive \¦dē+\ *adj* [*de-* + *congest* + *-ive*] **:** that relieves congestion ⟨a ~ agent⟩

de·consecrate \(')dē+\ *vt* [prob. trans. of F *déconsacrer*] **:** to remove the sacred character of ⟨the church building was *deconsecrated* and sold⟩ — **de·consecration** \(')dē+\ *n*

de·contaminate \¦dē+\ *vt* **:** to rid of contamination; *specif* **:** to make (as a building or area) harmless to unprotected personnel by the removal, destruction, or neutralization of chemical or biological warfare agents or radioactive material — **de·contamination** \¦dē+\ *n*

¹de·control \¦dē+\ *vt* [*de-* + *control*, n.] **:** to end the control of esp. by governmental agencies ⟨~ the coal industry⟩ **:** remove the controls on ⟨~ meat and dairy products⟩

²decontrol \"\ *n* **:** the abolition of controls, esp. of emergency government controls ⟨the gradual ~ of rents⟩

de·cor *or* **dé·cor** \dā'kō(ə)r, -kō(ə)r, -kȯ(ə)r, -kōə, '=,= *sometimes* də'-\ *n* -S [F *décor*, fr. *décorer* to decorate, fr. L *decorare*] **1 :** ORNAMENTATION, DECORATION ⟨tweed made flashing by the adding of sequins and other incongruous ~ —Lois Long⟩ ⟨clothes with great ~ the stilted platitudes of present-day social thought —Max Lerner⟩ **2 :** stage scenery and furnishings **:** SETS ⟨has written plays in which the audience's chief interest is in the symbolic nature of the ~ —E.R.Bentley⟩ **3 :** pattern of decoration ⟨acquired enough old objects to enable you to establish an integrated ~ for your room —E.F. Robacker⟩ **:** ornamental disposition of accessories in interior decoration ⟨the ~ and the atmosphere of its three dining rooms are like those of a first-class restaurant —Joseph Wechsberg⟩ **4 :** the combination of features or elements that make up the background or milieu characteristic esp. of a place or a period in time ⟨jukeboxes, sports arenas, the couches of psychoanalysts, carnivals — these are the ~ —W.B.C.Watkins⟩ **:** ATMOSPHERE ⟨took . . . the appealing ~ of the Romantic school and fused with it his own kind of gentle and penetrating realism —T.G.Bergin⟩

dec·o·ra·ment \'dek(ə)rəmənt\ *n* -S [LL *decoramentum*, fr. L *decorare* + *-mentum* -ment] **:** ORNAMENT, DECORATION

¹dec·o·rate \'dek(ə)rət, -kə,rāt\ *adj* [ME, fr. L *decoratus*, past part. of *decorare*] *archaic* **:** DECORATED ⟨a fair hall and richly ~ —Sir Richard Burton⟩

²dec·o·rate \'dekə,rāt, *usu* -ād- + V\ *vt* -ED/-ING/-S [L *decoratus*, past part. of *decorare*, fr. *decor-, decus* ornament — more at DECENT] **1 :** to grace with what adorns or honors ⟨they dignified and *decorated* commerce with the splendid virtues of honor and loyalty —Geoffrey Household⟩ ⟨admiration and respect for the liberals who now ~ . . . the U.S. Senate —R.L.Neuberger⟩ **2 :** to furnish or adorn with something becoming, ornamental, or striking **:** EMBELLISH, DECK ⟨some of the farmhouses . . . are *decorated* with climbing roses —Tom Marvel⟩ ⟨the hospital train ghostly white and *decorated* with the red cross —Fred Majdalany⟩ ⟨the knife-edge remarks with which he ~*s* his conversation —Ian Bevan⟩ **3 :** to award a mark of honor (as a medal) to **:** honor with a decoration ⟨*decorated* for valor⟩ **syn** see ADORN

decorated *adj* [fr. past part. of *decorate*] **1 :** ORNAMENTED, ORNATE ⟨when a more ~ style was fashionable in many quarters, bombast and extravagance were common in the press —F.L.Mott⟩ **2** *often cap* **:** of, relating to, or resembling English Gothic architecture in its second phase; *specif* **:** characterized by geometrical bar tracery and floral decoration

dec·o·ra·tion \,dekə'rāshən\ *n* -S [MF or LL; MF, fr. LL *decoration-, decoratio*, fr. L *decoratus* + *-ion-, -io* -ion] **1 :** the act of adorning, embellishing, or honoring **:** ORNAMENTATION ⟨promote the intelligent care of public beauty spots and further ~ of the city with trees and plants —*Amer. Guide Series: Nev.*⟩ **2 :** something that adorns, enriches, or beautifies **:** EMBELLISHMENT, ORNAMENT ⟨a building of steel and stone with aluminum ~*s*⟩ **3 :** a badge of honor (as a medal or a cross); *specif* **:** a U.S. military award usu. of distinctive shape conferred for personal heroism or gallantry — compare SERVICE MEDAL **4 :** GARNITURE 2 **5 :** an arrangement in a work of art of purely sensory elements (as line, color, shape, texture) that stimulates pleasure without regard to meaning

decoration day *n, usu cap both Ds* **:** MEMORIAL DAY

dec·o·ra·tive \'dek(ə)rəd·iv, -rətiv; 'dekə,rād·iv, -ātiv, -ēv *also* -əv\ *adj* [*decorate* + *-ive*] **1 :** of or relating to decoration **:** serving to decorate: as **a :** having a purely ornamental function ⟨its buildings were utilitarian rather than ~ —Green Peyton⟩ **b** *of a work of art* **:** producing immediate sensory satisfaction without regard to meaning ⟨to demand that all art be ~ is . . . a limitation of the material of art —John Dewey⟩ **c :** suitable for decorating or embellishing **:** enhancing in attractiveness ⟨his delight in the use of ~ high-sounding words —Alvin Redman⟩ **2 a** *of a dahlia* **:** having flower heads much doubled with quilled rays **b** *of a chrysanthemum* **:** having loose open flower heads of quilled, flat, or fluted rays — **dec·o·ra·tive·ly** \-əvlē, -li\ *adv* — **dec·o·ra·tive·ness** \-ivnəs, -ēv- *also* -əv-\ *n* -ES

¹dec·o·ra·tor \'dekə,rād·ə(r), -ātə-\ *n* -S [*decorate* + *-or*] **:** one that decorates: as **a** (1) **:** one who plans, designs, and executes interiors and their furnishings (2) **:** one who paints and papers interior walls and paints woodwork and fixtures **b :** one who hand paints, stencils, or transfers decorations on glass, tile, wood, pottery, or such objects as jewelry, furniture, or stemware **c :** one who lays out, traces, or carves lettering or designs on building and monumental stone **d :** one who molds fancy ice cream or who frosts cakes or other confections **e :** one who arranges merchandise displays in retail stores

²decorator \"\ *adj* **:** contributing to a color scheme and style suitable for interior decoration ⟨a selection of ~ fabrics⟩ ⟨~ chair⟩ ⟨a plastic cover in a ~ color —Sylvia Wright⟩

decorator crab *n* **:** any of several spider crabs of the family Majidae that fasten bits of kelp or grasses to their shells; *esp* **:** a widely distributed crab (*Oregonia gracilis*) of the western coast of the U.S.

de·core \də'kō(ə)r, dē'-\ *vt* -ED/-ING/-S [MF *decorer*, fr. L *decorare*] *archaic* **:** DECORATE, BEAUTIFY

de·core·ment \-ōrmənt\ *n* -S [MF, prob. fr. LL *decoramentum*] *archaic* **:** DECORATION

dec·o·rist \'dek(ə)rəst, də'kōr-\ *n* -S [*decorum* + *-ist*] **:** one devoted to artistic decorum ⟨a man of taste and a ~ where *picturesque* effects were concerned —Norman Douglas⟩

dec·o·rous \'dekərəs *also* -krəs; də'kōr-, dē'k-, -'kȯr-\ *adj* [L *decorus*, fr. *decor* beauty, grace; akin to L *decēre* to be fitting — more at DECENT] **:** marked by propriety and good taste esp. in conduct, manners, or appearance **:** characterized by conformity to accepted social standards and by unruffled staidness, correctness, or dignity ⟨when off the air are as ~ and restrained as they are volcanic while performing —G.S. Perry⟩ ⟨the ~ symbols of Victorian art —Ellen Glasgow⟩ ⟨a courtier's laugh, ~, brief, and not too hearty —J.H.Wheelwright⟩

syn DECENT, SEEMLY, PROPER, NICE, COMME IL FAUT, DEMURE: DECOROUS denotes an observance of all proprieties and sometimes connotes dignified or prim formality ⟨we, of course, maintained a most *decorous* exterior; and hence, by all the elderly people of the village, were doubtless regarded as pattern young men —Herman Melville⟩ ⟨the tête-à-tête had proved *decorous* in the extreme, and he had returned the willful maiden to her doorstep without so much as brushing her lips with his —Herman Wouk⟩ DECENT, as here considered detached from matters of sexual morality, suggests the fitting, appropriate, or accustomed, according to good taste or form ⟨the dead face on the pillow, which Dolly had smoothed with *decent* care —George Eliot⟩ ⟨nobody cares a straw for the internal administration of native states so long as oppression and crime are kept within *decent* limits —Rudyard Kipling⟩ SEEMLY stresses lack of discord with propriety and taste and may also suggest a pleasing appearance or manner ⟨for generations the Twyfords had drunk tea here at a *seemly* hour —Sinclair Lewis⟩ ⟨it was reckoned to him a major sin that he forgot his manners, for must not the Lord's work be carried on in *seemly* fashion, and the money changers be scourged from the temple politely? —V.L.Parrington⟩ PROPER stresses unquestioned conformity with social conventions, sometimes a stiff or prissy conformity ⟨Henchard's creed was that *proper* young girls wrote ladies' hand —Thomas Hardy⟩ ⟨but it is only *proper* that you first tell your husband distinctly that you are without any [money], and see what he will do —Thomas Hardy⟩ NICE in this sense suggests a complete and choice correctness in matters social ⟨the small provincial gentry of the West, as drawn by Miss Austen . . . are *nice* in their gentility almost to a fault —G.M.Trevelyan⟩ ⟨we've always been religious, Mother, and *nice* people in Queenborough go to church no matter what they believe —Ellen Glasgow⟩ COMME IL FAUT, more common in the 19th century than the 20th, implies complete correctness in polite society ⟨this remark, if the young lady had made it, would have been perfectly *comme il faut*; but, being made by the young gentleman, it was a most heinous and irremissible offense —T.L.Peacock⟩ DEMURE stresses a modest demeanor more than a staid propriety ⟨but lowering her glance unexpectedly till her dark eyelashes seemed to rest against her white cheeks she presented a perfectly *demure* aspect —Joseph Conrad⟩ ⟨Leora appeared as his assistant, very pretty and *demure* in a nurse's costume —Sinclair Lewis⟩

dec·o·rous·ly *adv* **:** in a decorous manner ⟨pretended to be pleased and applauded ~ —G.B.Shaw⟩

dec·o·rous·ness \-snəs\ *n* -ES **:** the quality or state of being decorous **:** DECORUM

decors *pl of* DECOR

¹de·cor·ti·cate \(')dē¦kō(r)d·ə,kāt, də'k-, -)tə,k-, *usu* -d·+V\ *vt* -ED/-ING/-S [L *decorticatus*, past part. of *decorticare* to remove the bark from, fr. *de* from, away + *-corticare* (fr. *cortic-, cortex* bark) — more at DE-, CORTEX] **1 :** to remove the bark, husk, or other outer covering from **:** HULL, PEEL, SKIN, STRIP ⟨*decorticated* rice⟩ ⟨~ a coconut⟩: as **a :** to remove all or part of the cortex from (as the brain) **b :** to remove the periostracum of (a mollusk) **c :** to separate (fiber) from the woody part of a fiber plant **2 :** FLAY 2 **syn** see SKIN

²de·cor·ti·cate \-ə,kāt, -əkət\ *adj* [L *decorticatus*] **:** without a cortical layer **:** DECORTICATED

de·cor·ti·ca·tion \(')=¦==ˈkāshən\ *n* -S [L *decortication-, decorticatio* removal of bark, fr. *decorticatus* + *-ion-, -io* -ion] **1 :** the act or process of decorticating ⟨the mechanical ~ of the dried black peppercorns —J.W.Parry⟩ **2 :** the medical operation of removing the cortex of an organ, an enveloping membrane, or a constrictive fibrinous covering ⟨the ~ of a lung⟩

de·cor·ti·ca·tor \-,kād·ə(r)\ *n* -S **:** one that decorticates; *specif* **:** a machine for decorticating fiber

de·cor·ti·co·sis \də,kō(r)d·ə'kōsəs\ *n* -ES [NL, fr. L *decorticare* + NL *-osis*] **:** SHELL BARK

de·co·rum \də'kōrəm, dē'k-, -kȯr-\ *n* -S [L, fr. neut. of *decorus*] **1 :** literary and dramatic propriety esp. as formulated and practiced by the neoclassicists: **a :** a literary standard of appropriateness drawn from classical models and justified by nature, which was equated with social custom, and by reason, which was identified with good sense ⟨wishes to subject art and literature to an elaborate set of restrictions in the name of ~ —Irving Babbitt⟩ **b :** a dramatic standard requiring that a character be presented in a way congruous with his presumed type or social condition ⟨according to strict neoclassic ~ only the aristocracy had the right to appear in tragedy —Irving Babbitt⟩ **2 :** propriety and good taste esp. in conduct, manners, or appearance **:** CORRECTNESS ⟨most correct in her conduct, strict in her notions of ~, and with manners that were held a standard of good breeding —Jane Austen⟩ ⟨the whole performance was conducted with perfect ~ —Augustus John› **3 :** the quality or state of being decorous **:** ORDERLINESS ‹the organization's ~ has rarely been shaken —W.F.Longgood› **4 a** *obs* **:** a fitting and appropriate act **b :** an observance or requirement of polite behavior **:** CONVENTION — usu. used in pl. ‹their restoration to the established sobrieties and ~*s* of English life —H.G.Wells› **5** *obs* **:** beauty deriving from fitness or congruousness **:** COMELINESS

de·cou·page *or* **dé·cou·page** \,dākü'päzh, -pázh, '==,=\ *n* -s [F *découpage* action of cutting up, action of cutting out, fr. MF *decoupage,* fr. *decouper* to cut up, cut out, fr. OF *decoper,* fr. *de-* (fr. L *de* from, away) + *coper, couper* to cut — more at DE-, COPE (to contend)] **1 :** the art of decorating surfaces by applying cutouts (as of paper) and then coating with usu. several layers of finish (as lacquer or varnish) **2 :** work produced by decoupage

¹de·coy \də'kȯi, dē'-, 'dē,-\ *n* -s *often attrib* [prob. fr. D *de kooi,* lit., the cage, fr. *de,* masc. def. article (fr. MD, akin to OE *thæt,* neut. def. article) + *kooi* cage, fr. MD *cōie,* fr. L *cavea* — more at THAT, CAGE] **1 :** a pond or pool having net-covered channels into which wild fowl (as ducks) are lured for capture ‹a vast game ~ used to provide sport for the local gentry —O.S.Nock› **2 :** something intended to allure or entice esp. into a trap **:** LURE ‹the commander of that sub . . . took us to be a ~ —H.A.Chippendale›; *specif* **:** an artificial bird used by hunters to attract live birds (as water fowl) within shot **3 :** a person used as a lure: **a :** one employed esp. by the police to induce a suspected person to commit an offense under circumstances that will lead to his detection **b :** one employed to lead another into a position where he may be swindled, robbed, or otherwise injured

decoy 2

²de·coy \'=\ *sometimes* 'dē,-\ *vb* -ED/-ING/-S *vt* **:** to lure by or as if by a decoy **:** ALLURE, ENTICE, ENTRAP ‹the female bird . . . practiced the same arts upon us to ~ us away —John Burroughs› ‹he had ~*ed* her . . . into holding him dearer than her own ambition —Victoria Sackville-West› **~** *vi* **:** to become lured by or as if by a decoy **:** fall into a trap ‹the wind was in the left front, so the old drake ~*ed* from the right rear —*Handbook on Shotgun Shooting*› **syn** see LURE

de·cras·si·fy \(')dē¦krasə,fī\ *vt* -ED/-ING/-ES [*de-* + *crass* + *-i-* + *-fy*] **:** to free from what is crass

de·crat·er \(')dē¦krātə(r)\ *n* -s [*de-* + *crate* + *-er*] *Brit* **:** a machine for unloading bottles or cans from shipping cases — compare RECRATER

¹de·crease \(')dē¦krēs *also* də'-\ *vb* -ED/-ING/-S [ME *decreessen* fr. (assumed) AF *decreistre* (3d pers. pl. pres. indic. *decreissent*), fr. L *decrescere,* fr. *de* from, down, away + *crescere* to grow, increase — more at DE-, CRESCENT] *vi* **:** to grow less esp. gradually **:** become diminished (as in size, amount, or strength) **:** LESSEN, DWINDLE ‹his stock *decreased* as the war went on› ‹his influence slowly *decreased*› **~** *vt* **1 :** to cause to grow less esp. gradually **:** DIMINISH ‹this medicine will ~ his pain› ‹it is necessary to ~ the amount of coal used› **2 :** to remove (a stitch) by knitting two stitches together or by passing a slipped stitch over a knitted stitch

syn LESSEN, DIMINISH, REDUCE, ABATE, DWINDLE: DECREASE, frequently interchangeable with others in this set, may apply to any process of growing less ‹the population of the area is *decreasing*› ‹a steadily *decreasing* income› ‹a rather even crest line, which *decreases* in elevation eastward —C.B.Hitchcock› ‹a *decreasing* chance for victory› ‹*decreasing* intensity› ‹belief in the evolution of man's body has *decreased* among paleontologists —R.W.Murray› LESSEN, meaning simply to become less, is a close synonym for DECREASE except that it is usu. not used with stated numbers ‹the valley widens, hills *lessen* in height —*Amer. Guide Series: Texas*› ‹*lessen* the pain of separation by a very frequent and most unreserved correspondence —Jane Austen› ‹I hoped to obtain your forgiveness, to *lessen* your ill-opinion —Jane Austen› ‹they find that in these quarters the Church is suspected of being an ally of 'capitalism,' and that their influence is *lessened* in consequence —W.R.Inge› ‹the fever is *lessened*› but ‹the fever *decreased* from 101° to 99°› DIMINISH may add to the meaning of DECREASE the notion of loss, of subtraction, sometimes unfortunate ‹with the retreat of the forest, the amount of variety of wild game inevitably *diminished* —*Amer. Guide Series: Minn.*› ‹with the advent of the railroad, trade *diminished* and the town gradually declined —*Amer. Guide Series: La.*› ‹he has shown that he is reluctant to use his prestige to such ends, and his continued refusal to use it *diminishes* his power to do so —R.H.Rovere› REDUCE may heighten suggestion of the role of an agent or agency effecting a change; it may also implicate a lowering of status or significance ‹devices adopted by the government to *reduce* unemployment —*Collier's Yr. Bk.*› ‹medical science has *reduced* the incidence of many communicable diseases virtually to zero —Gertrude Samuels› ‹the yeoman, it has been said, was being steadily *reduced* to a peasant —G.E. Fussell› ABATE may be used to indicate the decrease in intensity, amount, force, or significance of something immoderate or excessive ‹misfortune had *abated* the grandiosity of the Roman temper, and there was a widespread reaction towards simplicity —John Buchan› ‹the long tradition of mutual injury and revenge . . . had left animosities that took long to *abate* —G.M.Trevelyan› ‹physically weakened by a stomach disorder that will not *abate* —Hollis Alpert› DWINDLE may apply to progressive lessening or weakening towards insignificance ‹the last rays of daylight *dwindled* and disappeared —R.L. Stevenson› ‹the Zarafshan had already *dwindled* to an insignificant creek —Douglas Carruthers› ‹the great buffalo herds, once estimated at 60,000,000 head in Texas, have *dwindled* to a few animals —*Amer. Guide Series: Texas*› ‹the place *dwindled* in importance and at present is a small trading village —*Amer. Guide Series: Oregon*›

²de·crease \'dē,krēs *also* dē'- *or* də'-\ *n* -s [ME *decrees,* fr. (assumed) AF *decreis,* fr. (assumed) AF *decreistre,* v.] **1 :** the process of becoming less or the condition resulting from such a process **:** gradual diminution ‹we shall be conscious of a certain ~ in scientific dogmatism —Irving Babbitt› **2 :** the amount by which something decreases **:** DECLINE ‹the ~ in exports for the year was 15 percent› **3** *knitting* **a :** the act of decreasing **b :** the place where decreasing is done

decreasing *adj* [fr. pres. part. of *decrease*] **:** becoming less and less **:** DIMINISHING — **de·creas·ing·ly** *adv*

decreasing cost *n* **:** a decline in the cost per unit or on the average following a rise in the scale of production ‹an industry showing *decreasing costs*›

decreasing function *n* **:** a function whose value decreases as the independent variable increases over a given range

¹de·cree \də'krē, dē'-\ *n* -s [ME, fr. MF *decré, decret,* fr. L *decretum,* fr. neut. of *decretus,* past part. of *decernere* to decide, fr. *de* from, away + *cernere* to sift, discern, decide — more at DE-, CERTAIN] **1 :** an order set forth by one having authority **:** authoritative decision **:** EDICT, LAW ‹he needs to act by executive ~*s* . . . during the next two months —Frank Gorrell› ‹voluntarily entered into a ~ which cut the price of potash —T.W.Arnold› **2 a** (1) **:** an ordinance enacted by council or titular head concerning religious doctrine or discipline ‹a papal ~› (2) **decrees** *pl* **:** a collection of such religious rules **b :** the will of the Deity ‹God's ~› **c :** something allotted by fate **3 :** a judicial decision: **a** *Roman law* (1) **:** a judicial decision of the emperor (2) **:** a command of the praetor enjoining some act or forbearance (3) **:** the judgment in a proceeding of praetorian cognizance **b** (1) **:** a decision or sentence given in a cause by a court of equity, admiralty, probate, or divorce (2) **:** JUDGMENT 2a(1) **c** *Scots law* **:** a final judgment of a civil court

²decree \"\ *vb* **decreed; decreed; decreeing; decrees** [ME *decreen,* fr. *decree,* n.] *vt* **1 :** to command or enjoin authoritatively **:** order or appoint by decree ‹*decreed* that pecan shellers should be paid a minimum of twenty-five cents an hour —Green Peyton› ‹fashion used to be *decreed* by Paris —F.L. Allen› **2 a :** to settle or decide (a legal cause) by a judgment **b :** to determine or order judicially by authority or by decree **:** ADJUDGE **3** *archaic* **:** to determine or decide mentally **:** RESOLVE **~** *vi* **:** to issue a decree **:** ORDAIN ‹as my eternal purpose hath *decreed* —John Milton› **syn** see DICTATE

decree arbitral *n* [alter. (influenced by E ¹*decree*) of earlier *decreet arbitral,* fr. ME (Sc) *decreite arbitrale,* fr. ME *decreite, decret* decreet + *arbitrale, arbitral* arbitral] *Scots law* **:** a sentence proceeding on a submission to arbitration

decree dative *n* [alter. (influenced by E ¹*decree*) of earlier *decreet dative,* fr. *decreet* + *dative*] *Scots law* **:** a decree appointing an executor

decree-law \'=',=\ *n* [trans. of F *décret-loi,* It *decreto legge,* Sp *decreto ley,* & Pg *decreto lei;* It *decreto legge,* Sp *decreto ley,* & Pg *decreto lei* all prob. trans. of F *décret-loi*] **:** a decree of a ruler or ministry having the force of a law enacted by the legislature

decreement *n* -s *obs* **:** DECREE

decree ni·si \-'nī,sī, -'nē(,)sē\ *n* **:** the decree first made upon a petition for a divorce which is made absolute at such time thereafter as may be directed unless cause to the contrary is shown

decree of nullity : a declaration that a marriage has been void from its beginning

de·cre·er \də'krēə(r), dē'-\ *n* -s **:** one that decrees

de·creet \də'krēt\ *n* -s [ME *decret* fr. MF or L; MF *decré, decret,* fr. L *decretum*] **:** DECREE 3c

dec·re·ment \'dekrəmənt\ *n* -s [L *decrementum,* fr. *decrescere* to decrease + *-mentum* -ment — more at DECREASE] **1 a :** the act or process of becoming gradually less **:** DECREASE, DIMINUTION ‹a deer herd suffers no ~ if the legal hunting take is not permitted to exceed 20 percent of the total population —R.E. Trippensee› **b :** the successive diminution of the layers of molecules applied to the faces of the primitive form of crystals by which the secondary forms were held to be produced **2 a :** the quantity lost by diminution or waste **b** *math* **:** a negative increment **c** *physics* **:** the ratio of the maximum amplitude of one oscillation to that of the next in an oscillating system subjected to damping

de·crem·e·ter \'dekrə,mēd·ə(r), də'kremәd·ə-\ *n* [*decrement* + *-meter*] **:** an instrument for measuring the logarithmic decrement of electromagnetic waves

de·crep·it \də'krepət, dē'-, *usu* -əd·+V\ *also* **de·crep·id** \-pəd\ *adj* [ME *decrepit,* fr. MF, fr. L *decrepitus,* prob. from *de* from, down, away + *crepitus,* past part. of *crepare* to crack, creak, break — more at DE-, RAVEN] **1 a :** wasted and weakened by or as if by the infirmities of old age **:** old and feeble ‹the ~ manager who was too ancient and incompetent for more serious employment —Ellen Glasgow› **b :** made useless or impaired by excessive wear or long use **:** WORN-OUT ‹the bus is ~ and the seats and several of the windows are held together with friction tape —John Cheever› **c :** in a state of ruin, dilapidation, or disrepair ‹two or three ~ houses and a forlorn hotel —*Amer. Guide Series: Calif.*› **2 :** lacking power (as for carrying sediment) — used of a stream in the last stage of an erosion cycle **syn** see WEAK

de·crep·i·tate \də'krepə,tāt, dē'-\ *vb* [prob. fr. (assumed) NL *decrepitatus,* past part. of *decrepitare,* fr. L *de* from, away + *crepitare* to crackle — more at DE-, CREPITATE] *vt* **:** to roast or calcine (as salt) so as to cause crackling or until crackling stops **~** *vi* **:** to undergo decrepitation

de·crep·i·ta·tion \=,==='tāshən\ *n* -s [prob. fr. (assumed) NL *decrepitation-, decrepitatio,* fr. (assumed) NL *decrepitatus* + L *-ion-, -io* -ion] **:** the breaking up or crackling of certain crystals upon heating

de·crep·it·ly *adv* **:** in a decrepit manner

de·crep·it·ness *n* -ES **:** the quality or state of being decrepit

de·crep·i·tude \də'krepə,t(y)üd, dē'-\ *n* -s [MF, irreg. fr. *decrepit* + *-tude*] **:** the quality or state of being decrepit: **a :** physical weakness **:** FEEBLENESS, INFIRMITY ‹he had the physically strong man's impatience of ~ —S.H.Adams› ‹the humiliations of ~ and old age —L.P.Smith› **b :** DECAY, DILAPIDATION ‹carvings which turned out to be . . . atrocities in an advanced state of ~ —Mary Austin›

decrepity *n* -ES [MF & ML; MF *decrepité,* fr. ML *decrepitat-, decrepitas,* irreg. fr. L *decrepitus* + *-tat-, -tas* -ty] *obs* **:** DECREPITUDE

de·cres·cence \də'kresən(t)s, dē'-\ *n* -s [L *decrescentia,* fr. *decrescent-, decrescens* (pres. part. of *decrescere* to decrease) + *-ia* -y] **:** the act or process of decreasing; *specif* **:** DECREMENT 1b

¹de·crescendo \¦dā +; *US also & Brit usu* ¦dē+\ *adj (or adv)* [It, lit., decreasing, fr. L *decrescendum,* gerund of *decrescere*] **:** diminishing in volume — used as a direction in music and often indicated by the abbr. *decresc.* or the sign >; compare CRESCENDO

²decrescendo \"\ *n* -s [It, fr. *decrescendo,* adj.] **1 :** a lessening in volume of sound **2 :** a decrescendo musical passage

¹de·crescent \(')dē, də +\ *adj* [alter. (influenced by E ²*crescent*) of earlier *decressant,* prob. fr. AF, pres. part. of *decresser* to decrease, prob. modif. of (assumed) AF *decreistre* (3d pers. pl. pres. indic. *decreissent*), fr. L *decrescere*] **1 :** becoming less by gradual diminution **:** DECREASING **2** *of the moon* **a :** WANING **b** *heraldry* **:** having the horns pointing to the sinister

²decrescent \"\ *n* -s [alter. (influenced by E ¹*crescent*) of earlier *decressant,* prob. fr. (assumed) AF *decressant* decrescent moon, fr. AF *decressant,* pres. part. of *decresser* to decrease] **:** a decrescent moon

heraldic decrescent

¹de·cre·tal \də'krēd·ᵊl, dē'-, -ētᵊl\ *n* -s [ME *decretale,* fr. MF, fr. LL *decretalis,* fr. *decretalis,* adj.] **1 :** an authoritative order **:** DECREE; *esp* **:** a papal epistle replying to some question concerning general ecclesiastical law **2 decretals** *pl* **:** the collection of papal decrees forming the second part of the body of canon law

²decretal \"\ *adj* [LL *decretalis,* fr. L *decretum* decree + *-alis* -al] **1 :** relating to or containing a decree ‹a ~ epistle› **2** *obs* **:** having the binding effect of a decree **3** *obs* **:** DECISIVE, FINAL

de·cre·tal·ist \-ᵊləst\ *n* -s [¹*decretal* + *-ist*] **:** DECRETIST

de·cre·tist \-ēd·əst, -ētə-\ *n* -s [ME *decretiste,* fr. MF or ML; MF, fr. ML *decretista,* fr. L *decretum* decree + *-ista* -ist] **:** one specializing in the study of decretals **:** CANONIST

de·cre·tive \-əv\ *adj* [L *decretum* + E *-ive*] **:** having the force of a decree **:** DECRETORY ‹the ~ will of God›

dec·re·to·ri·al \¦dekrə¦tōrēəl, -kəs, -¦tȯr-\ *adj* [*decretory* + *-al*] **:** DECRETORY

dec·re·to·ry \'dekrə,tōrē, -,tȯr-, -ri; də'krēd·ər-, dē'-, -ētə-\ *adj* [L *decretorius,* fr. *decretus* (past part. of *decernere* to decide) + *-orius* -ory — more at DECREE] **1** *archaic* **:** serving to determine **:** DECISIVE, CRITICAL ‹when the ~ hour of death overtakes you —Cotton Mather› **2** [L *decretum* + E *-ory*] **:** relating to or fixed by a decree, decision, or judgment ‹the ~ rigors of a condemning sentence —Robert South› **3** *obs* **:** POSITIVE, PEREMPTORY

de·cre·tum \də'krēd·əm, -ētəm, dē'-\ *n, pl* **decre·ta** \-ə\ [L — more at DECREE] **:** DECREE, ORDINANCE

de·cri·al \də'krī(ə)l, dē'-\ *n* -s [*decry* + *-al*] **:** DEPRECIATION

de·cri·er \-ī(ə)r\ *n* -s **:** one that decries

de·crown \(')dē+\ *vt* **:** DISCROWN

de·crus·ta·tion \¦dēkrə¦stāshən\ *n* -s [LL *decrustatus* (past part. of *decrustare* to remove the crust of, fr. L *de* from, away + *crustare* to cover with a shell, cover with a crust, fr. *crusta* crust) + E *-ion* — more at DE-, CRUST] **:** the removal of a crust

de·cry \də'krī, dē'-\ *vt* [F *décrier,* fr. OF *descrier,* fr. *des-* de- + *crier* to cry — more at CRY] **1 :** to depreciate officially or publicly **:** reduce the value of esp. by public condemnation ‹the king may at any time ~ . . . any coin of the kingdom —William Blackstone› **2 :** to express strong disapproval of **:** criticize severely **:** DENOUNCE, DISPARAGE ‹citizens of the more advanced democracies . . . ~ dictators and all their works —C.L. Jones› ‹in making his case for pure research . . . he was not ~*ing* applied research —Ritchie Calder›

syn DECRY, DEPRECIATE, DISPARAGE, DEROGATE, DEROGATE (*from*), DETRACT (*from*), BELITTLE, and MINIMIZE can mean, in common, to indicate one's low opinion of something. DECRY implies open condemnation with intent to discredit ‹restraint of emotion was now *decried* in favor of strong expression of feeling —Gilbert Highet› ‹it would be a complete mistake to *decry* love of power altogether as a motive —Bertrand Russell› ‹county editors vying with each other to defend their champions and *decry* their foes —*Amer. Guide Series: Md.*› DEPRECIATE implies a representing of something as of smaller value than it is usu. credited with ‹the Renaissance . . . *depreciated* sculpture and gave the highest place to painting —Herbert Read› ‹the fashion in some quarters during the last few years to *depreciate* the entire scientific outlook —P.W. Bridgman› DISPARAGE implies depreciation usu. by more subtle methods, as slighting or invidious comparison ‹to *disparage* a train by comparing it with a stagecoach —G.B. Shaw› ‹he would sigh, shake his head, *disparage* his importance to anybody, even to himself —Marguerite Young› ‹the notion that Montaigne *disparaged* and sneered at the human race seems . . . absurd to us —L.P.Smith› DEROGATE, often DEROGATE (*from*), and DETRACT (*from*) stress the idea of taking something away from the full or generally recognized quality of a person or thing, esp. quality of merit or reputation ‹readers will inevitably . . . *derogate* what they cannot master —Edith R. Mirrielees› ‹I am not "blaming" the extraterritorial, specifically eastern, archaeologists nor attempting to *derogate* their contributions to southwestern archaeology —W.W. Taylor› ‹the right of the judiciary to review legislative and executive actions and nullify those measures which *derogate from* eternal principles of truth and justice as incarnated in the Constitution —J.P.Roche› ‹his underhanded actions *detract from* his reputation for honesty› ‹to say this in no way *detracts from* the distinguished qualities of the council itself —*Report: (Canadian) Royal Commission on Nat'l Development*› ‹a number of apologetic reservations which *detract from* the force of those forthright statements —Gleb Struve› ‹none of these moral imperfections appeared to *detract* an iota *from* the advantage of a face like an infant Aphrodite —Ellen Glasgow› BELITTLE and MINIMIZE both imply depreciation. BELITTLE suggesting an effort to make contemptibly small in worth, MINIMIZE to make as small as possible ‹Jack Dempsey was not one to underestimate. It was not his habit of mind to *belittle* an antagonist —Gene Tunney› ‹always delighted at a pretext for *belittling* a distinguished contemporary —Edmund Wilson› ‹I did not find anybody *minimizing* the tasks or inclined to exaggerate what had been done —E.P.Snow› ‹an evident tendency on the part of the writers to enlarge on the blessings of nature and to *minimize* her deficiencies —R.H.Brown›

de·crypt \(')dē¦kript *also* də'-\ *vt* -ED/-ING/-S [ISV *de-* + *-crypt* (fr. *cryptogram, cryptograph*); prob. orig. formed as It *decriptare*] **:** to decipher or decode esp. by cryptanalysis — **de·crypt·ment** \-tmənt\ *n* -s

de·cryp·tion \-pshən\ *n* -s [*decrypt* + *-ion*] **1 :** the act or process of decrypting **2 :** the result of decrypting

de·cryptograph \(')dē + *also* də +\ *vt* [*de-* + *cryptograph*] **:** to convert (a cryptogram) into plain language

-dec·tes \¦dek(,)tēz\ *n comb form* [NL, fr. Gk *dēktēs,* fr. *daknein* to bite — more at TONGS] **:** biter — in generic names of animals ‹Mixo*dectes*›

de·cu·bi·tal \də'kyübəd·ᵊl, dē'-, -ətᵊl\ *adj* [*decubitus* + *-al*] **1 :** relating to or resulting from lying down ‹a ~ sore› **2 :** relating to or resembling a decubitus

de·cu·bi·tus \-əd·əs, -ətəs\ *n, pl* **decubi·ti** \-əd·,ī, -ə,tī, -ē\ [NL, fr. L *decubitus,* past part. of *decumbere* to lie down, fr. *de* down, away + *-cumbere* to lie down (akin to *cubare* to lie down) — more at DE-, HIP] **1 :** a position assumed in lying down ‹the dorsal ~› **2 a :** ULCER **b** *or* **decubitus ulcer :** BEDSORE **3 :** prolonged lying down (as in bed)

de·cul·tur·ate \(')dē¦kəlchə,rāt *also* də'k-\ *vt* -ED/-ING/-S [*de-* + ¹*culture* + *-ate*] **:** to deprive of culture or cultural attainments ‹some tribes are extinct, some *deculturated,* and some relatively undisturbed —*Man*›

de·cul·tur·a·tion \(')dē¦kəlchə¦rāshən *also* də¦k-\ *n* -s **:** the process of divesting a tribe or people of their indigenous traits ‹for many native peoples brought involuntarily and reluctantly into contact with western civilization, acculturation is all too often ~ —David Bidney›

de·culture \(')dē+\ *vt* [*de-* + *culture*] **:** DECULTURATE

dec·u·man \'dekyəmən\ *adj* [L *decumanus, decimanus* of the tenth, large, fr. *decumus, decimus* tenth (fr. *decem* ten) + *-anus* -an — more at TEN] **1** *of a wave* **:** extremely large **:** HUGE ‹that ~ wave that took us fore and aft —P.A.Motteux› **2 :** of or relating to the tenth cohort — used esp. of the chief gate of a Roman camp

dec·u·mar·ia \,=='ma(a)rēə\ *n, cap* [NL, fr. L *decumus, decimus* tenth + NL *-aria;* fr. the decamerous flowers] **:** a small genus of woody vines (family Saxifragaceae)

dec·u·mary \'==,merē\ *n* -ES [NL *Decumaria*] **:** a woody vine (*Decumaria barbata*) of the southeastern U.S. with white flowers in compound terminal clusters

de·cum·ben·cy \də'kəmbənsē, dē'-\ *also* **de·cum·bence** \-n(t)s\ *n, pl* **decumbencies** *also* **decumbences** [L *decumbere* + E *-ency, -ence*] **:** the act or position of lying down

de·cum·bent \-nt\ *adj* [L *decumbent-, decumbens,* pres. part. of *decumbere* to lie down, fr. *de-* + *-cumbere* to lie down — more at SUCCUMB] **1 :** lying down **:** RECUMBENT **2** *of a plant stem or shoot* **:** reclining on the ground but with ascending apex or extremity

de·cum·bi·ture \-bə,chü(ə)r, -bəchər\ *n* -s [L *decumbere* to lie down, lie ill + *-it-* (in *decubitus,* past part. of *decumbere*) + E *-ure*] **1** *obs* **:** confinement to a sickbed **2 a :** the time of taking to one's bed from sickness **b :** a horoscope of such a decumbiture

¹dec·u·ple \'dek(y)əpəl\ *n* -s [ME, prob. fr. MF, fr. *decuple,* adj.] **:** a sum 10 times as great as another **:** a tenfold amount **:** the tenth multiple

²decuple \"\ *adj* [F *décuple,* fr. MF *decuple,* fr. LL *decuplus,* fr. L *decem* ten + *-uplus* (as in *quadruplus* quadruple)] **1 :** consisting of 10 **:** being 10 times as great or as many **:** TENFOLD **2 :** taken by tens or in groups of 10

³decuple \"\ *vb* **decupled; decupled; decupling** \-p(ə)liŋ\ **decuples :** to make or become 10 times as much or as many

dec·u·plet \-plət\ *n* -s [²*decuple* + *-et*] **1 :** a combination of 10 of a kind **2 :** a group of 10 notes performed in the time of 8 or 4 of the same musical value — called also *decimole*

de·cu·ri·on \də'kyúrēən, dē'-\ *n* -s [ME *decurioun,* fr. L *decurion-, decurio,* fr. *decuria* decury] **1 :** a Roman cavalry officer in command of 10 men **2 a :** a member of a municipal or colonial senate in ancient Rome **b :** a member of the great council in an Italian city or town

de·cu·ri·on·ate \-nət, -,nāt\ *n* -s [L *decurionatus,* fr. *decurion-, decurio* + *-atus* -ate] **:** the office of a decurion

de·cur·rence \də'kərən(t)s, dē'-\ *also* **de·cur·ren·cy** \-nsē\ *n, pl* **decurrences** *also* **decurrencies** [prob. fr. ML *decurrentia,* fr. L *decurrent-, decurrens* + *-ia* -y] **:** the act or state of running downward **:** downward flow or course

de·cur·rent \-nt\ *adj* [L *decurrent-, decurrens,* pres. part. of *decurrere* to run down, fr. *de* down, away + *currere* to run — more at DE-, CURRENT] **:** running or extending downward — used esp. of a leaf whose base extends downward from its point of insertion and often forms a wing or ridge along the stem — **de·cur·rent·ly** *adv*

decursion *n* -s [LL *decursion-, decursio,* fr. L, military maneuver, fr. *decursus* (past part. of *decurrere*) + *-ion-, -io* -ion] **1** *obs* **:** DECURRENCE **2** [L *decursion-, decursio*] *obs* **:** a military maneuver of classical antiquity; *specif* **:** a procession of armed troops around a funeral pile

de·cur·sive \də'kərsiv, dē'-\ *adj* [NL *decursivus,* fr. L *decursus* + *-ivus* -ive] **:** DECURRENT — **de·cur·sive·ly** \-səvlē\ *adv*

decurt *vt* -ED/-ING/-S [L *decurtare,* fr. *de* from, away + *curtare* to shorten, fr. *curtus* short — more at DE-, CURT] *obs* **:** CURTAIL

¹decurtate *vt* -ED/-ING/-S [L *decurtatus,* past part. of *decurtare* to curtail] *obs* **:** SHORTEN

²de·cur·tate \də'kər,tāt, dē'-, -,tət\ *adj* [L *decurtatus*] **:** CURTAILED, SHORTENED ‹a ~ syllogism has one premise suppressed›

de·curved \də, (')dē+\ *adj* [part trans. of LL *decurvatus,* fr. L *de* down, away + *curvatus,* past part. of *curvare* to bend, curve — more at DE-] **:** curved downward **:** bent down ‹the ~ bill of a curlew›

dec·u·ry \'dekyərē\ *n* -ES [L *decuria,* fr. *decem* ten] **:** a Roman division, company, or body of ten (as cavalrymen, senators, or judges)

¹dec·us·sate \'dekə,sāt, də'k-, dē'k-, *usu* -d·+V\ *vb* -ED/-ING/-S [L *decussatus,* past part. of *decussare,* fr. *decussis* number ten, numeral X, intersection of two lines, irreg. fr. *decem* ten + *ass-, as* copper coin — more at ACE] *vt* **:** to cross, cut, or divide in the form of an X : INTERSECT ~ *vi* : to cross each other in the form of an X : INTERSECT

[2]**dec·us·sate** \", -sət\ *adj* [L *decussatus*, past part. of *decussare*] **1** : shaped like an X ⟨a ~ cross⟩ **2** *bot* : arranged in pairs each at right angles to the next pair above or below ⟨~ leaves⟩ — compare BRACHIATE — **dec·us·sate·ly** *adv*

decussated *adj* [fr. past part. of [1]*decussate*] : DECUSSATE

dec·us·sa·tion \ˌdekəˈsāshən, ˌdēk-\ *n* -s [L *decussation-, decussatio*, fr. *decussatus* + *-ion-, -io* -ion] **1** : an intersection esp. in the form of an X ⟨the ~ of lines⟩ **2** *bot* : the quality or state of being decussate **3 a** : a band of nerve fibers that connects unlike centers of opposite sides of the central nervous system **b** : a crossed tract of nerve fibers passing between centers on opposite sides of the central nervous system : COMMISSURE

dec·yl \ˈdesəl *sometimes* ˈdēs-\ *n* -s [ISV *dec-* (fr. *decane*) + *-yl*] : any of numerous univalent radicals $C_{10}H_{21}$ derived from the decanes by removal of one hydrogen atom; *esp* : the normal radical $CH_3(CH_2)_8CH_2$–

decyl alcohol *n* [ISV *decyl* + *alcohol*] : a monohydroxy alcohol $C_{10}H_{21}OH$ derived from the decanes; *esp* : the colorless to light yellow liquid primary alcohol $CH_3(CH_2)_8CH_2OH$ derived from normal decane that is usu. made by reduction of coconut oil or the fatty acids from this oil and is used chiefly as an intermediate for surface-active agents and perfumes — called also *1-decanol, normal decyl alcohol*

decylaldehyde \ˌ≈≈+\ *n* [ISV *decyl* + *aldehyde*] : DECANAL

dec·yl·ene \ˈ≈≈ˌlēn\ *n* -s [ISV *decyl* + *-ene*] : any of numerous isomeric hydrocarbons $C_{10}H_{20}$ of the ethylene series

de·cyl·ic acid \dəˈsilik-, (ˈ)dē¦-\ *n* [ISV *decyl* + *-ic*] : DECOIC ACID

ded *abbr* dedicated; dedication

dedal *archaic var of* DAEDAL

dedalian *usu cap, archaic var of* DAEDALIAN

de·dans \dəˈdäⁿ\ *n, pl* **dedans** \"\ [F, lit., interior, fr. MF, fr. *dedans*, adv. & prep., within, in, fr. OF *dedenz*, fr. *de* of, from (fr. L, from, away) + *denz* within, in, fr. LL *deintus*, fr. L *de* from, away + *intus* within, in; akin to Gk *entos* within, in, Skt *antastya* intestines; derivative fr. a prehistoric IE word represented by L *in* — more at DE-, IN] **1** : an open gallery that is one of the winning openings placed at the service end of the court in court tennis **2** : the spectators at a court-tennis match

de·den·dum \dəˈdendəm, dēˈ-\ *n* -s [L, neut. of *dedendus*, gerundive of *dedere* to give up, deliver, fr. *de* from, away + *-dere* (fr. *dare* to give); fr. the contrast with the addendum of a gear tooth — more at DE-, DATE] : the root of a gear tooth; *also* : the distance between the dedendum circle and pitch circle of a gear wheel or rack — compare ADDENDUM

dedendum circle *n* : the circle touching the bottom of the spaces between the teeth of a gear wheel

ded·i·cant \ˈdedəkənt\ *n* -s [*dedicate* + *-ant*] : one that dedicates

[1]**ded·i·cate** \-ˌkāt, -ˌkət\ *adj* [ME, fr. L *dedicatus*, past part. of *dedicare* to affirm, dedicate fr. *de* from, away + *dicare* to proclaim, dedicate — more at DE-, DICTION] : DEDICATED — used chiefly of religious dedication ⟨~ mien of a clergyman⟩

[2]**ded·i·cate** \-dəˌkāt, -dē,-, *usu* -ād·+V\ *vt* -ED/-ING/-S [L *dedicatus*, past part. of *dedicare*] **1** : to devote exclusively to the service or worship of a divine being or to sacred uses : set apart with solemn rites **2 a** : to set apart or devote formally or seriously to a definite use, end, or service ⟨the playground was *dedicated* today⟩ ⟨a new nation . . . *dedicated* to the proposition that all men are created equal —Abraham Lincoln⟩ **b** : to commit to something as a constant goal or way of life ⟨we Americans are *dedicated* to improvement —Louis Kronenberger⟩ ⟨she has *dedicated* her life to her husband's comfort⟩ **3** : to inscribe, address, or name by way of compliment, honor, or commemoration ⟨~ a book to a patron⟩; *specif* : to commit (as a person, church, or society) to the protection and intercession of a patron saint **4** : to give, present, or surrender to public use ⟨obliged to ~ a road crossing his land⟩

dedicated *adj* [fr. past part. of [2]DEDICATE] : devoted to a cause, ideal, or purpose : ZEALOUS ⟨a ~ ballet dancer⟩ ⟨a life of ~ patience⟩

ded·i·ca·tee \ˌdedəkəˈtē\ *n* -s [[2]*dedicate* + *-ee*] : one to whom a thing is dedicated

ded·i·ca·tion \ˌdedəˈkāshən, -dēˈ-\ *n* -s [ME *dedicacioun*, fr. L *dedication-, dedicatio*, fr. *dedicatus* + *-ion-, -io* -ion] **1 a** : act or rite of dedicating to a divine being or to a sacred use : solemn appropriation — often distinguished from *consecration* ⟨the ~ of Solomon's temple⟩ **b** : an annual commemoration of a dedication **2** : a devoting or setting aside for any particular purpose; *specif, law* : an appropriation or giving up of property to public use that precludes the owner or others claiming under him from asserting any right of ownership inconsistent with the use for which the property is dedicated **3** : a name and often a message prefixed to a literary, musical, or artistic production, formerly testifying respect to a patron and often recommending the work to his favor, now usu. expressing admiration or affection for a person or for a cause **4** : self-sacrificing devotion to or as if to an ideal or a cause : ZEAL, FAITHFULNESS, ENTHUSIASM ⟨a musical performance marked by technical skill and ~⟩ ⟨requirements for those in the public service should be ability, integrity, and ~⟩

ded·i·ca·tion·al \¦≈≈¦≈shənᵊl, -shnəl\ *adj* : of or relating to dedication

dedication copy *n* : the copy of a book presented by its author to the person to whom it is dedicated

ded·i·ca·tive \ˈ≈≈ˌkād·|iv, -ät|, |ēv *also* |əv; -ˌkəd·iv, -ətiv\ *adj* [[2]*dedicate* + *-ive*] : DEDICATING, DEDICATORY

ded·i·ca·tor \-ˌkād·ə(r), -ātə-\ *n* -s [[2]*dedicate* + *-or*] : one that dedicates

ded·i·ca·to·ri·al \¦≈≈kə¦tōrēəl, -tȯr-\ *adj* [*dedicatory* + *-al*] : DEDICATORY

ded·i·ca·tory \ˈ≈≈≈ˌrē, -ri, *esp Brit* ˈdedi,kāt(ə)ri\ *adj* [[2]*dedicate* + *-ory*] : constituting or serving as a dedication — often used following the noun ⟨the epistle ~⟩

de die in di·em \(ˌ)dāˈdēˌā(ˌ)inˈdē(ˌ)em\ [L] : from day to day

de·differentiate \(ˈ)dē+\ *vi* [back-formation fr. *dedifferentiation*] : to undergo dedifferentiation : lose specialization of form or function

de·differentiation \(ˈ)dē+\ *n* [*de-* + *differentiation*] **1** *biol* **a** : reversion of specialized structures (as cells) to a more generalized or primitive condition often as a preliminary to major physiological or structural change **b** : return of plant cells to a meristematic state (as in the production of phellogen) **2** *biol* : disintegration of specialized habits and adaptations

de·di·mus \ˈdedēməs, ˈdād-\ *or* **dedimus po·tes·ta·tem** \-ˌpōd·əˈstād·əm, -päd·əˈstād-·\ *n* [*dedimus* fr. ME, fr. L, we have given, 1st pers. pl. perf. indic. of *dare* to give; *dedimus potestatem* fr. L, we have given the power; fr. the use of these words in the writ — more at DATE] : a writ to commission a private person to perform some act in place of a judge (as to examine a witness)

de·dit \dāˈdē\ *n* -s [F, fr. OF *desdit*, lit., contradiction, fr. *desdire* to deny, retract, contradict, fr. *des-* de- + *dire* to say, fr. L *dicere* — more at DICTION] *Canadian law* : a sum forfeited by one who has failed in an engagement

ded·i·ti·cian \ˌdedəˈtishən\ *n* -s [L *dediticius* dedititian (fr. *deditus*, past part. of *dedere* to surrender, give up, deliver) + E *-an* — more at DEDENDUM] *Roman law* : a freedman not allowed full citizenship rights because of bad character or grave misconduct during slavery or because as a foreigner he had fought against Rome — **ded·i·ti·cian·cy** \-nsē\ *n* -ES

de·di·tion \dəˈdishən, dēˈ-\ *n* -s [L *dedition-, deditio*, fr. *deditus* (past part. of *dedere* to surrender) + *-ion-, -io* -ion] : act of yielding : SURRENDER

ded·o·lent \ˈdedᵊlənt\ *adj* [L *dedolent-, dedolens*, pres. part. of *dedolēre* to cease to grieve, fr. *de* from, away + *dolēre* to feel pain — more at CONDOLE] *archaic* : feeling no grief or compunction : CALLOUS

de do·lo \(ˈ)dāˈdō(ˌ)lō\ *adj* [L] *law* : of deceit or fraud ⟨an action *de dolo*⟩

de·duce \dəˈd(y)üs, dēˈ-\ *vt* -ED/-ING/-S [L *deducere*, lit., to lead away, fr. *de* from, away + *ducere* to lead — more at DE-, TOW (pull)] **1** : to trace the course or descent of ⟨~ the history of the wool trade⟩ ⟨~ their lineage⟩ **2** : to derive by logical process : INFER: as **a** : to draw (a conclusion) necessarily from given premises : CONSTRUCT ⟨~ a logical result⟩ **b** : to infer (something) about a particular case from a general principle that holds of all such cases **3** *archaic* **a** : BRING, CONDUCT, CONVEY ⟨~ blood to the tissues⟩ **b** : to lead or send out (a colony) **4** : to prove (title to property) by preparing and exhibiting the abstract of title **syn** see INFER

de·duce·ment \-smənt\ *n* -s *obs* : INFERENCE, DEDUCTION

de·duc·i·bil·i·ty \≈,≈səˈbiləd·ē\ *n* -ES : the state or quality of being deducible

de·duc·i·ble \≈ˈ≈səbəl\ *adj* [*deduce* + *-able*] : capable of being deduced : derivable by reasoning as a result or logical consequence

[1]**de·duct** \dəˈdəkt, dēˈ-\ *vb* -ED/-ING/-S [L *deductus*, past part. of *deducere*, lit., to lead away] *vt* **1** : to take (an amount) away from a total : take off : REMOVE ⟨the tax is ~*ed* from the paycheck⟩ — compare SUBTRACT **2** : DEDUCE, INFER ~ *vi* : ABATE, DIMINISH, DETRACT — used with *from* ⟨the noisy street ~*s* from the value of the property⟩

[2]**de·duct** \(ˈ)dē¦-\ *n* -s : an amount deducted : DEDUCTION ⟨resentment of wage earners against the ~*s* —*Jour. Amer. Med. Assoc.*⟩ — not often in formal use

de·duct·ibil·i·ty \dəˌdəktəˈbiləd·ē, (ˌ)dē-, -ətē, -i\ *n* -ES : the state or quality of being deductible

[1]**de·duct·ible** \dəˈdəktəbəl, dēˈ-\ *adj* [*deduct* + *-able*] **1** : capable of being deducted : allowable as a deduction ⟨certain gifts are ~ from the taxable income⟩ **2** : DEDUCIBLE

[2]**deductible** \"\ *n* -s **1** : a clause in an insurance policy relieving the insurer of responsibility for an initial specified small loss of the kind insured against **2** : something that is the subject of a deductible (as a brief initial period of illness or damage to a car costing less than a specified amount to repair)

de·duc·tion \-kshən\ *n* -s [ME *deduccion*, fr. MF or L; MF *deduction*, fr. L *deduction-, deductio*, fr. *deductus* (past part. of *deducere*) + *-ion-, -io* -ion] **1** : an act or process of deducting or deducing: as **a** : an act of taking away : DIMINUTION, SUBTRACTION ⟨~ of all legitimate business expenses⟩ **b** : the deriving of a conclusion by reasoning : inference from evidence; *specif, logic* : inference in which the conclusion follows necessarily from the premises — contrasted with *induction*; compare TRANSFORMATION RULE **c** *archaic* : the leading or sending forth of a colony : establishment of a colony **2** : a product or result of deducting or deducing: as **a** : a conclusion reached by mental deduction : INFERENCE ⟨his behavior confirmed my ~*s* about his upbringing⟩ **b** : something that is or may be subtracted ⟨business expenses are proper ~*s* from one's taxable income⟩ : ABATEMENT **c** *archaic* : an orderly or chronological account

deduction new for old *n* : a subtraction made by a marine underwriter from the total cost of repairs in paying a claim under a hull-insurance policy to allow for the gain in excess of loss to the shipowner resulting from the new material installed during repairing

de·duc·tive \-ktiv, -tēv *also* -təv\ *adj* [[1]*deduct* + *-ive*] **1** : of or relating to deduction : employing deduction in reasoning **2** : capable of being deduced from premises : INFERENTIAL ⟨~ laws⟩ — **de·duc·tive·ly** \-tə̇vlē, -li\ *adv*

deductive method *n* : a method of reasoning by which (1) concrete applications or consequences are deduced from general principles or (2) theorems are deduced from definitions and postulates — compare DEDUCTION 1b; INDUCTION 2

deductory *adj* [[1]*deduct* + *-ory*] *obs* : DEDUCTIVE

de·dust \(ˈ)dē+\ *vt* [*de-* + *dust*, n.] : to remove excessively fine particles of the same material or other material from ⟨~*ing* ground ore⟩

[1]**dee** \ˈdē\ *dial Brit var of* [1]DIE

[2]**dee** *also* **de** \"\ *n* -s **1** : the letter *d* **2** : something having the shape of the letter D: as **a** : a metal ring for holding a saddle strap or belt **b** : either of two hollow semicylindrical metal electrodes in a cyclotron — called also *duant*

[3]**dee** \"\ *or* **deed** \ˈdēd\ *adj* [euphemistic pronunciation of *d—, d—d*] : DAMNED

deece *var of* DIX

[1]**deed** \ˈdēd\ *n* -s [ME *dede*, fr. OE *dǣd*; akin to OHG *tāt* deed, ON *dāth*, Goth *gadeths*; derivative fr. the root of E *do*] **1** : something that is done or effected by a responsible agent : ACT, ACTION ⟨what ~ is this that ye have done? —Gen 44:15 (AV)⟩ ⟨would serve his kind in ~ and word —Alfred Tennyson⟩ **2** : illustrious act : ACHIEVEMENT, EXPLOIT, FEAT ⟨whose ~*s* some nobler poem shall adorn —John Dryden⟩ **3** : PERFORMANCE, DOING ⟨take the will for the ~⟩ — often contrasted with *word* **4** *dial Eng* : DOINGS, ADO ⟨such ~ as never was⟩ **5** *law* : a signed and usu. sealed instrument in writing, duly executed and delivered, containing some transfer, bargain, or contract; *also* : such an instrument before it has been given effect by delivery — often used specifically of an instrument conveying a fee in land as distinguished from a lease, mortgage, or other instruments under seal; compare WILL 6

[2]**deed** \"\ *vt* -ED/-ING/-S : to convey or transfer by deed ⟨he ~*ed* all his estate to his son⟩

[3]**deed** \"\ *adv* [by shortening] : INDEED

deedbox \ˈ≈,≈\ *n* : a strongbox for documents

deed·ful \ˈdēdfəl\ *adj, archaic* : full of deeds or exploits : ACTIVE, STIRRING

deed·i·ly \-dəlē, -li\ *adv* [*deedy* + *-ly*] *dial chiefly Eng* : ACTIVELY, INDUSTRIOUSLY, EARNESTLY

deed·less \-dləs\ *adj, archaic* : not performing or not having performed deeds or exploits : INACTIVE

deed of arrangement *English law* : ARRANGEMENT 6b(2)

deed of assumption *Scots law* : a deed by which a trustee assumes or appoints a new cotrustee

deed of trust *law* : a deed that serves as an evidence of and security for an indebtedness : MORTGAGE

deed poll *n, pl* **deeds poll** [*deed* + *poll* (polled); fr. its having the edge of the paper polled] : a deed made and executed by only one party

deedy \-di\ *adj* -ER/-EST *dial chiefly Eng* : INDUSTRIOUS, ACTIVE, EARNEST

deef \ˈdēf\ *dial var of* DEAF

dee·jay \ˈdē¦jā\ *n* -s [[2]*dee* + *jay* (letter); fr. the initials *D. J.*] : DISC JOCKEY

[1]**deem** \ˈdēm\ *vb* -ED/-ING/-S [ME *demen*, fr. OE *dēman*; akin to OHG *tuomen* to judge, ON *dœma*, Goth *domjan*; denominative fr. the root of E *doom*] *vt* **1 a** *obs* : to sit in judgment upon : DECIDE ⟨at the one side six judges were disposed to view and ~ the deeds of arms that day —Edmund Spenser⟩ **b** *archaic* : ADMINISTER ⟨the deemster was a hard judge and ~*ed* the laws in rigor —Hall Caine⟩ **2** : to come to view, judge, or classify after some reflection : HOLD, THINK ⟨essentially he ~*ed* himself a liberal —Robert Grant †1940⟩ ⟨this criticism I ~ to be without foundation —H.W.Dodds⟩ ⟨it is ~*ed* advisable to refrain from making definite statements until clinical . . . proof is available —H.G.Armstrong⟩ **3** *archaic* : EXPECT, HOPE ⟨a creature . . . whom she ~*ed* to render happy —Lord Byron⟩ ~ *vi* **1** : to form or have an opinion : BELIEVE, SUPPOSE — used with *of* ⟨I cannot ~ otherwise of them —J.P. Kennedy †1870⟩ **2** : to become aware : be cognizant — used with *of* ⟨something unearthly which they ~ not of —Lord Byron⟩ **syn** see CONSIDER

[2]**deem** \"\ *n* -s *obs* : JUDGMENT, SURMISE

[3]**deem** \"\ *n* -s [ME (Sc) *deme* lady, dame, mother, alter. of ME *dame*] *Scot* : GIRL; *specif* : a servant girl

de-emanate \(ˈ)dē +\ *vt* : to deprive of the property of giving off a radioactive emanation ⟨*de-emanate* thorium by heating⟩ — **de-emanation** \(ˈ)dē +\ *n* -s

de-emphasis \(ˈ)dē +\ *n* **1** : lessening of importance : removal from a position of prominence, favor, or special attention : a playing down ⟨a movement for the *de-emphasis* of football in college⟩ **2** : complete or partial suppression of unduly large amplitude components from the output of an oscillating system (as of harsh overtones from a loudspeaker)

de-emphasize \(ˈ)dē +\ *vt* : to reduce in importance esp. in relation to something else : play down : DEFLATE ⟨defense program, accenting science and air power, and *de-emphasizing* army and navy —*Time*⟩

deem·ster \ˈdēmztə(r), -m(p)st-\ *n* -s [ME *demestre* judge — more at DEMPSTER] : one of the two justices of the common-law courts of the Isle of Man — **deem·ster·ship** \ˈ≈≈(r),ship\ *n* -s

de-emulsify *var of* DEMULSIFY

deen \ˈdēn\ *Scot var of* DONE

dee·ner \ˈdēnə(r)\ *n* -s [origin unknown] *slang Austral* : SHILLING

de-energize \(ˈ)dē +\ *vt* : to check the flow of current through (an electrical device)

[1]**deep** \ˈdēp\ *adj* -ER/-EST [ME *deep, dep*, fr. OE *dēop*; akin to OHG *tiof* deep, ON *djūpr*, Goth *diups* deep, OE *dyppan* to dip — more at DIP] **1** : extending far or comparatively far from some level, edge, surface, or area: as **a** : extending downward to a considerable degree ⟨a ~ well⟩ ⟨~ valleys between the ranges⟩ **b** : extending well inward from a surface accepted as outer ⟨a ~ gash in the side of the mountain⟩; *often* : not located superficially within the body ⟨~ pressure receptors in muscles and tendons⟩ **c** : extending well back from a surface accepted as front ⟨a ~ recess behind the organ⟩ ⟨fine ~ closets in every room⟩ **d** : extending far laterally from something expressed or implied that is regarded as central : wide and peripheral ⟨a ~ shrubbery about the house⟩ ⟨~ borders of ecru lace⟩ **e** *sports* : occurring relatively far from the center of activity : located near the outer limits of the playing area ⟨a hit to ~ right field⟩ ⟨the safety man took a ~ position⟩ **2** : having a specified extension in an implied direction usu. downward or toward the back — used postpositively ⟨a canyon a mile ~⟩ ⟨a shelf 20 inches ~⟩ or in combination ⟨cars parked three-*deep*⟩ ⟨knee-*deep* snow⟩ **3** : marked by complexity, intensity, or a high degree of development of pertinent qualities: as **a** : difficult to penetrate or comprehend : RECONDITE ⟨a ~ problem⟩ ⟨the ~*er* questions of the day⟩; *often* : MYSTERIOUS, OBSCURE, DEVIOUS ⟨a ~ dark secret⟩ ⟨~ and deadly plots against civilization⟩ **b** : grave in nature or effect : GRIEVOUS, SERIOUS ⟨a ~ wrong⟩ ⟨in ~*est* disgrace⟩ **c** : of penetrating intellect : WISE, SAGACIOUS ⟨a ~ thinker⟩ ⟨~ clerks she dumbs —Shak.⟩; *often* : CUNNING, SLY, CRAFTY ⟨ah, but he's a ~ one⟩ ⟨they're too ~ for me⟩ **d** : preoccupied with : ENGROSSED, ABSORBED, INVOLVED, ENTANGLED —used postpositively and followed by an explanatory *in* phrase ⟨a man ~ in debt⟩ ⟨~ in her book⟩ **e** : completely developed ⟨~ winter⟩ : UNMIXED, UNALLOYED, EXTREME ⟨~ grief⟩ ⟨~ darkness⟩ : HEAVY ⟨~ sleep⟩ **f** : characterized by close absorption or complete engagement ⟨~ study⟩ ⟨~ thought⟩ **g** : involving heavy liability or great self-indulgence : carried to excess — archaic except of drinking ⟨unable to resist the ~ drinking of his comrades⟩ **h** *of color* : high in saturation and low in lightness : vivid and dark ⟨fuchsia is a much ~*er* color than pink⟩ **i** *of tone* : not high or sharp : rich, full, and heavy ⟨the bass of heaven's ~ organ —John Milton⟩; *specif* : having a low musical pitch or pitch range — used esp. of the human voice ⟨a voice ~ and strong⟩ **4 a** : situated well within the boundaries of ⟨a lodge ~ in the forest⟩; *often* : remote in time or space : hidden away : SECLUDED — used postpositively and followed by *in* ⟨~ in the heart⟩ ⟨found ~ in rural England⟩ **b** : lying or being covered or protected by or as if by a deep layer of something — used postpositively ⟨lanes ~ in snow⟩ ⟨a country ~ in peace⟩ **c** (1) *archaic, of roads* : covered with uncompacted soil : MUDDY, SANDY, BOGGY (2) *of soils* : having a thick covering layer of topsoil ⟨~ sandy loams⟩ **d** : covered, enclosed, or filled to a specified degree — used postpositively, usu. in combination, and with an orienting phrase ⟨cows knee-*deep* in clover⟩ ⟨a box rim-*deep* with junk⟩ **5 a** : moving over or passing through a considerable distance downward ⟨a ~ dive⟩ ⟨a ~ drop from a cliff⟩ **b** (1) : coming from, reaching to, or acting on something (as a part or place) that is far down, back, or within : DEEP-SEATED ⟨a ~ breath⟩ ⟨a ~ strong taproot⟩ ⟨~ therapy⟩ (2) : originating or taking place below the surface of the body ⟨~ pain⟩ ⟨~ reflexes⟩; *often* : involving or operating on mental levels below the conscious ⟨~ neuroses⟩ **6** *now dial Eng* : advanced in time : LATE

syn PROFOUND, ABYSMAL: applied to physical things and situations DEEP is a simple antonym of *shallow* without especial connotation; applied to persons and to mental states, it may imply study, deliberation, penetration, subtlety, or craft ⟨a *deep* thinker⟩ ⟨*deep* scholarship⟩ ⟨a careful editing after a *deep* study of the inner meaning of the work must be undertaken —Warwick Braithwaite⟩ PROFOUND in its occasional use in reference to physical things is likely to indicate great depth, perhaps awe-inspiring ⟨canyons more *profound* than our deepest mountain gorges —Willa Cather⟩ and in its more common use in reference to persons and mental processes to imply thorough penetration into and resolution of weighty and complicated matters and evolving well thought out, just, and correct solutions ⟨a *profound* philosophy⟩ ⟨a *profound* search for truth⟩ ⟨a *profound* lawyer, peculiarly fitted for that high judicial office —Marie B. Owen⟩ ⟨the executive puts on a *profound* air, purses up his lips, looks at the ceiling with penetrating gaze, then trains his ponderous face on the subordinate —H.A.Overstreet⟩ ABYSMAL may describe things of infinite depth or mental conditions or processes showing infinite want, lack, demerit, or fault ⟨*abysmal* ignorance⟩ ⟨Schmaltz is arrogant and assertive; his *abysmal* ignorance is matched only by his conviction of his own influence —M.D.Geismar⟩ ⟨not much happens to starlight in its long passage through the *abysmal* depths of interstellar space —P.W.Merrill⟩ **syn** see in addition BROAD

— **in deep water** : in difficulty : in distress : in a situation with obscure and menacing possibilities

[2]**deep** \"\ *adv* -ER/-EST [ME *depe*, fr. OE *dēope*; akin to OHG *tiufo* deeply; derivative fr. the root of E [1]*deep*] **1** : to a great depth : with depth : far down : PROFOUNDLY, DEEPLY ⟨drink ~⟩ ⟨~-set⟩ ⟨*deep*-versed in books, and shallow in himself —John Milton⟩ **2** : far on (in time) : LATE ⟨~ in the night⟩

[3]**deep** \"\ *n* -s [ME *deep, depe*, fr. OE *dēop* deep water (fr. *dēop*, adj., deep) & OE *dȳpe* depth, sea; akin to OHG *tiufī* depth, Goth *diupei*; derivative fr. the root of E [1]*deep*] **1 a** *now dial Eng* : measurable depth **b** : any of the fathom points on a sounding line that is not a mark : an unmarked estimated fathom measure — see SOUNDING LINE illustration **2** : something that is deep: **a** : a vast or immeasurable extent : ABYSS ⟨the ~ of space⟩ **b** : the extent of surrounding space or time : FIRMAMENT ⟨the azure ~⟩ : OCEAN ⟨the briny ~⟩ **c** : the world of the dead **3** : the middle part : the most intense or characteristic part ⟨~ of winter⟩ ⟨the forest ~*s*⟩ **4** : a profound or not easily fathomed recess (as of thought or feeling) ⟨thy judgments are a great ~ —Ps 36:6 (AV)⟩ **5 a** : one of the deep portions of any body of water; *specif* : a generally long and narrow area in the ocean where the depth exceeds 3000 fathoms ⟨the Aldrich *Deep* in the south Pacific⟩ **b** : a deep channel in a strait or estuary

deep brunswick green *n, often cap B* : a green that is yellower and darker than bottle green, bluer and duller than forest green (sense 1), and yellower, darker, and slightly stronger than evergreen — distinguished from *light Brunswick green* and *middle Brunswick green*

deep buff *n* : a layer of leather found immediately below the top grain layer, produced by splitting off the grain layer, and used chiefly as upholstery leather

deep chrome green *n* : a green that is yellower and duller than holly green (sense 1) or golf green, yellower and less strong than average hunter green — distinguished from *light chrome green* and *medium chrome green*; called also *cinnabar green, Milori green, silk green, zinc green*

deep chrome orange *n* : CHROME SCARLET

deep chrome yellow *n* : a moderate orange yellow that is redder and lighter than yellow ocher — called also *cavalry, yellow orange, medium chrome yellow, middle chrome yellow*

deep culture *n* : a culture produced by a deep inoculation into a solid medium (as gelatin or agar) that is used esp. for the growth of anaerobic bacteria

deep–dish pie *n* : a pie baked in a deep dish and usu. having a fruit filling and no bottom crust

deep–draw \ˈ≈¦≈\ *vt* : to form (sheet metal) into cup-shaped, box-shaped, or cone-shaped articles or shells by forcing into a die (as with a punch press or drop hammer)

deep–dyed \ˈ≈¦≈\ *adj* : THOROUGH, UNRELIEVED, INGRAINED ⟨a *deep-dyed* villain⟩ ⟨a *deep-dyed* Tory⟩

deep·en \ˈdēpən, -pᵊm\ *vb* **deepened** \-pənd, -pᵊmd\ **deepened** \"\ **deepening** \-p(ə)niŋ\ **deepens** \-pənz, -pᵊmz\

vt **:** to make deep or deeper: as **a :** to increase the depth of ⟨~ a well⟩ ⟨~ a channel⟩ **b :** to make more intense ⟨the incident *~ed* the gloom⟩ or more profound ⟨*~ed* the meaning of his life⟩ **c :** to increase in degree ⟨~ sorrow⟩ **d :** to make lower in tone or range of pitch ⟨~ a pipe organ⟩ **~** *vi* **:** to become deeper ⟨the water *~ed* at every step⟩ **:** grow more profound or obscure ⟨with every day the mystery *~s*⟩

deepening *n* -s [fr. gerund of *deepen*] **:** decrease in the central pressure of a cyclone during an interval of time

deep·en·ing·ly *adv* **:** in a deepening manner

deeper *comparative of* DEEP

deepest *superlative of* DEEP

deep etch *n* **:** the etching of an offset printing plate to such a degree that the printing area becomes slightly recessed and thereby productive of sharper definition and longer runs

¹deep-etch \ˈ=ˌ=\ *adj* [*deep etch*] **:** involving the use of plates made by deep etch ⟨printing by *deep-etch* offset⟩

²deep-etch \"\ *vt* [*deep etch*] **:** to produce (a plate) by deep etch

deep fascia *n* **:** a firm fascia that ensheathes and binds together muscles and other internal structures — compare SUPERFICIAL FASCIA

deep fat *n* **:** hot fat deep enough in a cooking utensil to cover the food to be fried ⟨onion rings fried in *deep fat*⟩

deep field *n* **:** LONG FIELD

deep-focus \ˈ=ˌ==\ *adj, of an earthquake* **:** originating at a depth greater than 250 kilometers below the earth's surface

deep freeze *n* **:** a condition of being held in abeyance **:** COLD STORAGE 2 ⟨bill presently in *deep freeze* awaiting a new congress —*Newsweek*⟩

deep-freeze \ˈ=ˌ=\ *vt* **1 :** QUICK-FREEZE **2 :** CHILL, REFRIGERATE

Deepfreeze \"\ *trademark* — used for a freezer for the quick-freezing and storage of food

deep freezer *n* **:** FREEZER 1d(2)

deep fry *vt* **:** to cook by immersing in hot fat — distinguished from *sauté*

deep fryer *n* **:** a utensil suitable for deep frying usu. deep and often with a mesh or perforated compartment in which the food is exposed to the fat

deepgoing \ˈ=ˌ=\ *adj* **:** reaching or penetrating to the heart **:** SERIOUS ⟨~ differences of opinion⟩ **:** FUNDAMENTAL ⟨a ~ theory⟩

deep-grown \ˈ=ˌ=\ *adj, of wool* **:** having a long strong staple

deep·ing \ˈdēpiŋ\ *n* -s [fr. gerund of obs. *deep*, v., to deepen, immerse deeply, fr. ME *depen* to make deep, immerse deeply, fr. OE *dȳpan* to make deep; akin to Goth *gadiupjan* to make deep; causative-denominative fr. the root of E ¹*deep*] *Brit* **:** one of the usu. 6 foot wide sections of which a hand-netted drift net is made ⟨several *~s* are laced side to side to give the required depth to the net⟩

deep·ish \-pish, -pēsh\ *adj* **:** somewhat deep ⟨the theater was a complete little affair with a ~ stage —Ngaio Marsh⟩

deep kiss *n* **:** a kiss involving extensive or intensive contact of the inner lips, tongue, and teeth esp. with prolonged or rhythmic tongue-to-tongue contact

deep·ly *adv* [ME *deepliche*, fr. OE *dēoplīce*, fr. *dēoplīc* deep, fr. *dēop* deep + *-līc* -ly] **1 :** at or to a great depth **:** far below the surface **:** far down **:** far in ⟨sink ~ into mud⟩ **2 :** PROFOUNDLY, THOROUGHLY ⟨~ versed in nuclear theory⟩ **:** not superficially **:** in a high degree ⟨~ hurt by his remark⟩ **3 :** with a tendency to richness and intensity of color ⟨~ tanned face⟩ **4 :** with low or deep tone **:** SONOROUSLY ⟨hounds baying ~⟩ **5 :** with profound skill **:** with cunning ⟨~ laid plot⟩ **6 :** GRAVELY, SERIOUSLY ⟨~ compromised⟩ ⟨~ involved in a scandal⟩

deep·most \-p,mōst, *esp Brit also* -pməst\ *adj, archaic* **:** DEEPEST ⟨from her ~ glen —Sir Walter Scott⟩

deep mourning *n* **:** mourning clothes in which the garments are not only all black but also made of lusterless materials

deepmouthed \ˈ=ˌ=\ *adj* **:** having a deep sonorous voice ⟨~ dogs⟩

deep·ness \-pnəs\ *n* -ES [ME *depnesse*, fr. OE *dēopnes*, fr. *dēop* deep + *-nes* -ness] **:** the quality or state of being deep

deep psychology *n* **:** PSYCHOANALYSIS

deep-rooted \ˈ=ˌ==\ *adj* **:** marked by or having deep roots **:** deeply implanted, embedded, or established and difficult or impossible to alter, decrease, or eliminate ⟨these problems are *deep-rooted* and stubborn —H.S.Truman⟩ ⟨a *deep-rooted* loyalty⟩ **syn** see INVETERATE

deep-root·ed·ness \ˈ=ˌ==nəs\ *n* -ES **:** the quality or state of being deep-rooted

deeps *pl of* DEEP

deep-sea \ˈ=ˌ=\ *adj* [¹*deep* + *sea*] **1 :** of, relating to, occurring in, or for use in the deeper parts of the ocean ⟨*deep-sea* currents⟩ ⟨*deep-sea* fishes⟩ ⟨a *deep-sea* line⟩ **2 :** acting (as by sailing or fishing) or for use in parts of the oceans far from land ⟨*deep-sea* fishermen⟩ ⟨a *deep-sea* tug⟩ — sometimes distinguished from *coastal, longshore*

deep sea *n* [¹*deep* + *sea*] **:** those parts of the oceans in which the water is very deep; *specif* **:** areas in which it has a depth of 1000 fathoms or more — compare ³DEEP 5

deep-sea lead *n* **:** a lead used for sounding in deep water; *specif* **:** the heaviest of sounding leads used in water exceeding 100 fathoms in depth

deep-sea red crab *n* **:** a large light-colored crab (*Geryon quinquedens*) from deep water of the eastern coast of No. and So. America

deep-sea tangle *n* **1 :** DRIFTWEED **2 :** DEADMAN'S HAND 1c

deep-seated \ˈ=ˌ==\ *adj* **1 :** situated, originating, or operating far below the surface **:** not susceptible to surface examination, analysis, or treatment ⟨the inflammation was *deep-seated*⟩ **2 a :** marked by establishment through long habitual practice or usage **:** unlikely to be changed, lessened, or eliminated ⟨easier to overturn the form of government than to uproot a *deep-seated* tradition —A.T.Mahan⟩ **b :** deeply ingrained **:** genuine and lasting as a characteristic **:** essential or as though essential to a character ⟨*deep-seated* preferences cannot be argued about —O.W.Holmes †1935⟩ **3** *of a rock, structure, movement, or process* **:** originating or occurring at depths of more than a few thousand feet below the earth's surface ⟨the origin of *deep-seated* quartzo-feldspathic rocks —*Jour. of Geol.*⟩ **syn** see INVETERATE

deep-sea tube *n* **:** a long tube that reaches to the sea bottom and that is so equipped mechanically that a man within it may perform work on objects outside (as for salvaging purposes)

deep six *n* [perh. so called fr. the idea of submersion under six fathoms of water] **1** *slang* **:** burial at sea ⟨it was not in keeping with the traditions of the navy . . . to give this lad a *deep six* in the darkness of midnight —H.M.Forgy⟩ **2** *slang* **:** DISCARD, OBLIVION — used esp. in the phrase *give it the deep six*

deep-six \ˈ=ˌ=\ *vt* -ED/-ING/-ES [*deep six*] *slang* **:** to discard or throw overboard

deep south *n, often cap D, usu cap S* **:** the southeasterly portion of the U.S. usu. including all states bordering on the Gulf of Mexico and some adjacent regions

deep space *n* **:** the effect esp. in painting of an uninterrupted view into great distance — compare STAGE SPACE

deep stone *n* **:** a light olive brown that is redder, stronger, and slightly lighter than drab, average mustard tan, or sponge —called also *tinsel*

deep tank *n* **:** a portion of a ship's hold bulkheaded off to hold water

deep-waisted \ˈ=ˌ==\ *adj, of a ship* **:** having a low waist ⟨*deep-waisted* with poop and forecastle high above the deck⟩

deepwater \ˈ=ˌ==\ *adj* [¹*deep* + *water*] **:** of, relating to, or characterized by water of considerable depth ⟨a ~ channel⟩; *often* **:** DEEP-SEA, OFFSHORE ⟨~ navigation⟩ ⟨~ sailors⟩

deep water *n* [¹*deep* + *water*] **:** difficulty esp. when serious **:** TROUBLE ⟨he'll find himself in *deep water* if he tries to keep up with the neighbors⟩ **:** PERPLEXITY — often used in pl. and usu. with *in* ⟨I was in *deep waters* before his explanation was well begun⟩

deep waterline *n* **:** the line on a ship's hull to which the water reaches when the ship is loaded to maximum safe capacity

deep·wa·ter·man \ˈ=ˌ===mən\ *n, pl* **deepwatermen :** a ship for navigating deep waters **:** a seagoing ship

deep well *n* **:** a well in which the water level is at a depth exceeding 22 feet beyond which the ordinary suction pump does not operate satisfactorily

deer \ˈdi(ə)r, ˈdiə\ *n, pl* **deer** *also* **deers** [ME, deer, animal, fr. OE *dēor* beast; akin to OHG *tior* wild animal, ON *dȳr*, Goth *dius* wild animal, Lith *dvėsti* to breathe, expire, Skt *dhvaṁsati* he falls to dust, perishes — more at DUST] **1** *obs* **:** ANIMAL; *esp* **:** a quadruped mammal ⟨rats and mice and such small ~ —Shak.⟩ **2 a :** any of numerous ruminant mammals that constitute the family Cervidae, that have two large and two small hoofs on each foot and antlers borne by the males of nearly all and by the females of a few forms, that are represented by numerous species and individuals in most regions except most of Africa and Australia, and that constitute an important source of food in many places for man and the larger carnivorous animals — see CARIBOU, ELK, MOOSE, MUSK DEER, REINDEER; VENISON **b :** any of the small or medium-sized members of the family as distinguished from certain esp. large forms (as elk, moose, or caribou) **3 :** DEERSKIN **4 :** a grayish yellowish brown that is lighter and slightly yellower than olive wood and lighter than acorn — called also *bobolink, camel's hair*

white-tailed deer

deerberry \ˈ=- — *see* BERRY\ *n* **1 :** any of several fruits reputedly eaten by deer; *esp* **:** the extremely acid greenish or yellowish fruit of a rather small branching blueberry (*Vaccinium stamineum*) common in marshy areas in the eastern U.S. **2 :** a plant bearing deerberries

deer brush *n* **:** any of several shrubby plants (as members of the genus *Ceanothus*) that are regularly browsed by deer; *esp* **:** a rapid-growing much-branched semi-evergreen shrub (*C. integerrimus*) that grows in dry upland areas of the western and southwestern U.S. and is a staple browse for mule deer and an important honey plant

deer cabbage *n* **:** a blue-flowered prostrate or decumbent evergreen lupine (*Lupinus diffusus*) of the southern U.S. with unifoliolate leaves

deer dance *n* **:** a mimetic dance widespread among American Indian tribes and performed to appease the deer spirit and thereby effect success in the hunt or cure diseases held to be caused by this spirit

deerdrive \ˈ=ˌ=\ *n* **:** a shoot in which deer are driven past the sportsmen

deer fern *n* **:** a fern (*Blechnum spicant*) of Europe and western No. America that is often cultivated for deer browse and has erect fronds of which the sterile are foliaceous and the fertile are contracted

deerfly \ˈ=ˌ=\ *n* **:** any of numerous small horseflies of *Chrysops* or related genera that usu. have wing markings and include serious bloodsucking pests of deer, man, and livestock some of which are vectors of tularemia

deer-fly fever *n* **:** TULAREMIA

deerfood \ˈ=ˌ=\ *n* **:** WATER SHIELD 1

deer-foot \ˈ=ˌ=\ *n, pl* **deer-foots** [prob. so called fr. the shape of the leaf] **:** VANILLA LEAF 2

deer forest *n* **:** an open or forested but extensive and unenclosed tract set aside for the keeping and hunting of deer

deer grass *n* **1 :** a bunch grass (*Epicampes rigens*) used for forage in the southwestern U.S. **2 :** a plant of the genus *Rhexia* **3 :** DEERHAIR

deerhair *also* **deer's-hair** \ˈ=ˌ=\ *or* **deerhair-bulrush** \ˈ=ˌ=-\ *n* [so called fr. the appearance of its stem] **:** a small club rush (*Scirpus caespitosus*) of Europe, Asia, and No. America with filiform stems

deerherd \ˈ=ˌ=\ *n* [*deer* + *herd* (herdsman)] **:** a keeper of deer

deerhorn \ˈ=ˌ=\ *n* **1 :** the horny material making up the antlers of deer **2 :** a large rough elongated freshwater mussel (*Tritigonia verrucosa*) found in the Mississippi drainage and used for making buttons

deerhorn cactus *n* **:** a night-blooming cereus (*Cereus greggii*) with spiny edible scarlet fruits

deerhound \ˈ=ˌ=\ *n* **:** a large tall dog of a breed developed in Scotland that was formerly much used in hunting deer and has the general conformation of a greyhound but is larger and taller with a rough usu. blue-gray coat

deerkill \ˈ=ˌ=\ *n* [by alter.] **:** KILLDEER

deer laurel *n* **:** BIG LAUREL

deer·let \ˈlət\ *n* -S **1 :** a small deer **2 :** CHEVROTAIN

deer mouse *n* [so called fr. its agility] **:** WHITE-FOOTED MOUSE

deer oak *n* **:** a small shrubby oak (*Quercus sadleriana*) of dry uplands of western U.S. that produces abundant acorns relished by deer, bear, and cattle

deers *pl of* DEER

deer's-ear \ˈ=ˌ=\ *n, pl* **deer's-ear** *or* **deer's-ears :** any of several tall-growing biennial or short-lived perennial herbs (as American columbo) that constitute a genus *Frasera* of the family Gentianaceae and are widely distributed in No. America esp. in warm dry upland areas of the Pacific states — compare DEER'S-TONGUE

deerskin \ˈ=ˌ=\ *n* [ME *deriskyn*, fr. *deri, der, deer* deer + *skyn, skin* skin] **:** leather made from the skin of a deer; *also* **:** a garment of such leather

deerstalker \ˈ=ˌ==\ *n* [so called fr. its suitability to be worn by a person stalking deer] **:** a close-fitting cap with a visor at the front and the back and with earflaps that may be tied up or down

deer's-tongue \ˈ=ˌ=\ *n, pl* **deer's-tongues 1 :** WILD VANILLA — used chiefly commercially **2 :** a tall-growing perennial herb (*Frasera speciosa*) of the Pacific coast of the U.S. with long panicles of greenish white purple-spotted flowers — compare DEER'S-EAR

deer tiger *n* **:** COUGAR

deertongue \ˈ=ˌ=\ *n* **1 :** WILD VANILLA — used chiefly commercially **2 :** a narrow shovel blade for a cultivator

deervetch \ˈ=ˌ=\ *n* **:** a plant of the genus *Lotus*

deer vine *n* **:** TWINFLOWER b

deerweed \ˈ=ˌ=\ *n* **:** any of several bushy herbs of the genus *Lotus* (as *L. scoparius* and *L. purshianus*) occurring in southern California, having trifoliolate leaves and yellow flowers, and being a useful forage plant for arid regions

deerwood \ˈ=ˌ=\ *n* **:** HOP HORNBEAM

deerwort boneset \ˈ=ˌ=-\ *n* **:** WHITE SNAKEROOT

deeryard \ˈ=ˌ=\ *n* **:** a place where deer herd in winter

dees *pl of* DEE

de·e·sis \dēˈēsəs\ *n, pl* **dee·ses** \-(ˌ)sēz\ *usu cap* [Gk *deēsis* entreaty, prayer, fr. *dein* to lack, miss, *deisthai* to beg — more at DEUTER-] **:** a tripartite icon of the Eastern Orthodox Church showing Christ usu. enthroned between the Virgin Mary and St. John the Baptist

de-esterification \(ˈ)dē+\ *n* [*de-* + *esterification*] **:** the process of de-esterifying

de-esterify \(ˈ)dē+\ *vt* [*de-* + *esterify*] **:** to remove ester groups from (as pectin)

de-eth·a·nize \(ˈ)dēˈethəˌnīz\ *vt* -ED/-ING/-S [*de-* + *ethane* + *-ize*] **:** to remove ethane and sometimes lighter fractions from (as cracked gasoline) by distillation — **de-eth·a·niz·er** \-zə(r)\ *n* -S

de-ethicize \(ˈ)dē+\ *vt* [*de-* + *ethicize*] **:** to divest of ethical standards **:** dissociate (as religion) from ethics

deeve \ˈdēv\ *var of* DEAVE

dee·vil \ˈdēvəl\ *Scot var of* DEVIL

dee·vil·ick \-vlək\ *n* -S [Sc *deevil* + *-ick* (dim. suffix)] *Scot* **:** a little devil

de ex·com·mu·ni·ca·to ca·pi·en·do \(ˌ)dā,ekskə,mün-əˈkäd-(ˌ)ō,käpēˈen(ˌ)dō\ *n* [NL, lit., of seizing an excommunicated person] **:** an ancient writ ordering the imprisonment of an excommunicated person until he submitted to the church

def *abbr* **1** defendant; defense **2** deferred **3** deficit **4** defined; definite; definition

de·face \dəˈfās, dēˈ-\ *vt* -ED/-ING/-S [ME *defacen* to disfigure, efface, fr. MF *desfacier, deffacier*, fr. OF, fr. *des-* de- + *-facier* (fr. *face*) — more at FACE] **1 :** to destroy or mar the face or external appearance of **:** DISFIGURE **:** injure, spoil, or mar by effacing important features or portions of ⟨~ an inscription⟩ ⟨~ a bond⟩ **2 :** to impair in value, influence, or effect **3** *obs* **:** DESTROY, EFFACE, ERASE **4** *obs* **a :** DEFAME, DISCREDIT **b :** to face down **:** OUTSHINE ⟨this holy tide of Christmas all others doth ~ —*God Rest You Merry, Gentlemen*⟩

de·face·ment \-smənt\ *n* -S **:** the act of defacing or state of being defaced **:** injury to surface or outward appearance

de·fac·er \-sə(r)\ *n* -S **:** one that defaces

de fac·to \(ˈ)dēˈfak,tō, (ˈ)dāˈ-; (ˈ)dāˈfäk,-\ *adv (or adj)* [L] **1 :** ACTUALLY **:** in fact **:** in reality **2 a :** exercising the powers and demanding the privileges of a regularly and legally constituted authority often with a color of right ⟨a *de facto* court⟩ **b :** existing as the controlling power — used of a government actually functioning as a result of a revolution or rebellion but not yet permanently established or recognized **c :** existing in fact and in opposition to an assumed or fictitious state of affairs ⟨a *de facto* state of war⟩ — distinguished from *de jure*

def·ae·cate *Brit var of* DEFECATE

defailance *or* **defaillance** *n* -S [F *défaillance*, fr. OF *defaillance*, fr. *defaillir* to fail, be lacking + *-ance* — more at DEFAULT] *obs* **:** LACK, OMISSION **:** FAILURE

de·fal·cate \dəˈfal,kāt, dēˈ-, -fȯl-, ˈdē,=,=; ˈdefəl,-; *usu* -ād+V\ *vb* -ED/-ING/-S [ML *defalcatus*, past part. of *defalcare*, fr. L *de-* + *falc-, falx* sickle] *vt* **1** *archaic* **:** to cut off **:** lop off **2** *archaic* **:** to reduce by taking away a part **:** CURTAIL **~** *vi* **:** to take money committed to one's charge

de·fal·ca·tion \(ˌ)dē,falˈkāshən, də,-, -fȯl-, ,defəl-\ *n* -S [ML *defalcation-, defalcatio*, fr. *defalcatus* + L *-ion-, -io* -ion] **1** *archaic* **:** a lopping off **:** CURTAILMENT ⟨sadly puzzled at the ~ of more than one-third of my income —Charles Lamb⟩ **2** *obs* **:** something lopped off **:** DEDUCTION **3 a :** misappropriation of money in one's keeping **b :** a sum of money so misappropriated **4 :** a falling away **:** DEFECTION **:** a failure to meet a promise or an expectation

de·fal·ca·tor *pronunc at* DEFALCATE + ə(r)\ *n* -S **:** one guilty of breach of trust esp. in money matters **:** DEFAULTER

de·falk \dəˈfȯlk, dēˈ-\ *vt* -ED/-ING/-S [ME *defalken*, fr. MF *defalquer*, fr. ML *defalcare* — more at DEFALCATE] *archaic* **:** DEFALCATE

def·a·ma·tion \,defəˈmāshən, -fᵊmˈā- *sometimes* ,dēf-\ *n* -S [alter. (influenced by ¹*defame*) of earlier *diffamation*, fr. ME *diffamacioun*, fr. MF or ML; MF *diffamation*, fr. ML *diffamation-, diffamatio*, fr. L *diffamatus* (past part. of *diffamare*) + *-ion-, -io* -ion] **1** *obs* **:** a bringing into disrepute **:** DISHONOR, DISGRACE **2 :** the act of defaming another or injuring another's reputation by any slanderous communication **:** DETRACTION, CALUMNY, ASPERSION — compare LIBEL, SLANDER

de·fam·a·to·ry \dəˈfamə,tōrē, dēˈ-, -ȯr-, -ri\ *adj* [alter. (influenced by ¹*defame*) of earlier *diffamatory*, fr. ML *diffamatorius*, fr. L *diffamatus* + *-orius* -ory] **:** containing defamation **:** injurious to reputation **:** CALUMNIOUS

¹de·fame \dəˈfām, dēˈ-\ *vt* -ED/-ING/-S [ME *diffamen, defamen*, fr. MF & L; ME *diffamen* fr. MF *diffamer*, fr. OF, fr. L *diffamare*, fr. *dif-* (fr. *dis-*) + *fama* reputation, fame; ME *defamen* fr. MF *defamer*, fr. OF, fr. ML *defamare*, alter. (influenced by *de-*) of L *diffamare* — more at FAME] **1** *archaic* **:** to harm or destroy the good fame of **:** make infamous **:** bring into disgrace ⟨my guilt thy growing virtues did ~ —John Dryden⟩ **2 :** to harm the reputation or good name of by uttering injurious charges **:** LIBEL, SLANDER **3** *archaic* **:** ACCUSE, CHARGE ⟨Rebecca . . . is . . . *defamed* of sorcery —Sir Walter Scott⟩ **syn** see MALIGN

²defame *n* -S [ME, fr. MF *defame, diffame*, fr. OF *diffame*, fr. *diffamer*, v.] **1** *obs* **:** DISHONOR, INFAMY **2** *obs* **:** DEFAMATION, SLANDER

defamed *adj* **1** *obs* **:** DISHONORED **:** of bad repute **2 :** SLANDERED, LIBELED

de·fam·er \-mə(r)\ *n* -S **:** one that defames

de·fam·ing·ly *adv* **:** so as to defame

de·fang \(ˈ)dē+\ *vt* [*de-* + *fang* (n.)] **:** to remove the fangs from (as a poisonous snake)

de·fas·sa \dəˈfasə\ *n, pl* **defassa** [NL (specific epithet of *Kobus defassa*), fr. L, *defassa, defessa*, fem. of *defassus, defessus*, past part. of *defatisci, defetisci* to become tired, weak, fr. *de-* + *fatisci* to become weak, tired; akin to L *fatigare* to weary, fatigue — more at FATIGUE] **:** a large gray African antelope (*Kobus defassa*) having a shaggy coat and spreading ringed horns — called also *waterbuck*

de·fat \(ˈ)dē+\ *vt* [*de-* + *fat* (n.)] **:** to remove fat from — used chiefly as a participle ⟨*defatted* milk powder⟩

¹de·fault \dəˈfȯlt, dēˈ- *sometimes* ˈdē,=\ *n* -S [ME *defaulte*, alter. (influenced by AF *defaulte*, alter. — prob. influenced by OF *defaillir* to be lacking, fail, fr. assumed VL *defallire* — of OF *defaute*) of *defaute*, fr. OF, fr. (assumed) VL *defallita*, fr. fem. of *defallitus*, past part. of (assumed) VL *defallire* to be lacking, fail, fr. L *de-* + (assumed) VL *fallire* to deceive, fail — more at FAIL] **1 :** the absence of something needed **:** LACK, WANT **2 :** failure to do something required by duty or law **:** NEGLIGENCE, NEGLECT ⟨a position of advantage lost by mere ~⟩ **3** *archaic* **:** FAULT: as **a :** WRONGDOING, OFFENSE, MISDEED ⟨pardon our *~s*⟩ **b :** ERROR, IMPERFECTION, FLAW, BLEMISH **4 :** a failure to pay financial debts ⟨salesmen sometimes oversell their prospects thereby laying the ground for later *~s* —H.E.Hoagland⟩ ⟨~ of his loan terms⟩ **5 :** the failure of a defendant or plaintiff to appear at the required time to defend or prosecute an action or proceeding as a result of which a plaintiff may be nonsuited or a defendant may have judgment rendered against him — often used with *in* ⟨the defendant has made no appearance in the case, and is in ~⟩ — see JUDGMENT BY DEFAULT **6 :** failure to compete in or to finish an appointed contest ⟨lose a race by ~⟩ **syn** see FAILURE — **in default of** *prep* **:** in case of failure or lack of **:** in the absence of ⟨*in default of* evidence there was no trial⟩

²default \"\ *vb* -ED/-ING/-S [alter. (influenced by ¹*default*) of ME *defauten*, fr. *defaute*, n.] *vi* **:** to fail to fulfill a contract or agreement, to accept a responsibility, or to perform a duty: as **a :** to fail to meet a financial obligation **b :** to fail to appear in court **:** let a case go by default **c :** to fail to compete in or to finish an appointed contest, esp. an athletic contest; *also* **:** to forfeit a contest by such failure **~** *vt* **1 :** to fail to perform, pay, or make good ⟨~ a loan⟩ **:** OMIT ⟨~ a dividend⟩ **2 :** to call (a defendant or other person whose duty it is to be present in court) and make entry of default for failure to appear **:** enter a default against **3 a :** to fail to compete in or to finish (an appointed contest) **b :** to forfeit (a contest) by such failure **c :** to exclude (a player or team) from a contest by default

de·fault·er \-tə(r)\ *n* -S **:** one that makes or commits a default **:** DELINQUENT: as **a :** one who fails to appear in court when summoned **b :** one who fails to account for money or property entrusted to his care **:** DEFALCATOR, EMBEZZLER **c :** one who fails to pay a debt **d** *Brit* **:** a soldier guilty of a military offense **e** *Brit* **:** a member of the stock exchange who has been publicly declared unable to meet his contracts

de·fau·nate \(ˈ)dēˈfȯ,nāt\ *vt* -ED/-ING/-S [*de-* + NL *fauna* + E *-ate*] **:** to remove a fauna from **:** remove the intestinal protozoans of (termites) — **de·fau·na·tion** \,dē,fȯˈnāshən\ *n* -S

de·fea·sance \dəˈfēzᵊn(t)s, dēˈ-\ *n* -S [ME *defesance*, fr. AF, fr. OF *desfesant, deffesant*, pres. part. of *desfaire, deffaire* to destroy, undo — more at DEFEAT] **1 a :** a rendering null or void **b** (1) **:** the ending of a property interest in accordance with conditions stipulated in the terms of a deed; *also* **:** a collateral deed or instrument stating such a condition of termination (2) **:** the ending of a property interest through a power of termination or an executory limitation **2 :** DEFEAT, OVERTHROW, UNDOING

de·fea·si·ble \-zəbəl\ *adj* [AF, fr. OF *desfais-, deffais-* (stem of *desfaire, deffaire*) + *-ible*] **:** capable of being or liable to being voided, annulled, or undone **:** subject to defeasance esp. by being cut off through the exercise of a power or the happening of an event ⟨a claim to an estate may be ~ so long as the claimant is under 21 and unmarried⟩

[1]**de·feat** \də'fēt, dē'-, *usu* -ēd·+V\ *vt* -ED/-ING/-S [ME *deffeten*, fr. MF *desfait, deffait*, past part. of *desfaire, deffaire* to destroy, fr. OF, fr. ML *disfacere*, fr. L *dis-* + *facere* to do — more at DO] **1** *archaic* **:** UNDO, DESTROY ⟨his unkindness may ~ my life —Shak.⟩ **2** *obs* **:** to mar the looks of **:** DISFIGURE **3 :** to render null and void (as a title to property, a legal claim) **:** NULLIFY, FRUSTRATE ⟨~*ed* hopes⟩ **4 :** to win victory over, check the progress of, or destroy the power of **:** OVERCOME, OVERTHROW ⟨~ an army in battle⟩ ⟨~*ed* the opposing candidate by a large margin⟩ ⟨~*ed* in all his purposes⟩ ⟨the bill was ~*ed* in the senate⟩ **5 :** to decrease the ability of (as a stream) to erode or to maintain a course ⟨a stream ~*ed* by crustal movement⟩ **syn** see CONQUER

[2]**defeat** \"\ *n* -S **1** *archaic* **:** UNDOING **:** DESTRUCTION — often used with *on* ⟨upon whose property and most dear life a damned ~ was made —Shak.⟩ **2 :** frustration by rendering null and void or by prevention of success ⟨the ~ of a plan⟩ **3 :** an overthrow esp. of an army in battle **:** loss of a contest **:** REPULSE, DISCOMFITURE — opposed to *victory*

de·feat·ism \-ēd·,izəm, -ē,tiz-\ *n* -S [F *défaitisme*, fr. *défaite* defeat (fr. MF *deffaite, desfaite*, fr. fem. of *deffait, desfait*, past part.) + *-isme* -ism] **1 :** disbelief in the desirability of victory for one's own side under certain circumstances **2 :** the attitude, policy, or practice of accepting or of being resigned to defeat without any attempt to prevent or forestall it ⟨a mood of ~ overwhelmed them⟩ ⟨~ weakened the nation's ability to resist the enemy⟩

[1]**de·feat·ist** \-ēd·əst, -ētə-\ *n* -S [F *défaitiste*, fr. *défaite* defeat + *-iste* -ist] **:** one who believes in, advocates, or is affected with defeatism **:** one who concedes defeat too readily

[2]**defeatist** \"\ *adj* **:** characterized by defeatism ⟨there was a ~ attitude about the proposal⟩ ⟨such talk is plainly ~⟩

defeatment *n* -S *obs* **:** DEFEAT

[1]**de·fea·ture** \də, dē+\ *n* -S [in sense 1, prob. fr. *de-* + *feature*; in sense 2, fr. [1]*defeat* + *-ure*] **1** *archaic* **:** DISFIGUREMENT ⟨careful hours . . . have written strange ~*s* on my face —Shak.⟩ **2** *obs* **:** DEFEAT

[2]**defeature** \"\ *vt* -ED/-ING/-S **:** DISFIGURE, DEFACE

[1]**defecate** *adj* [ME *deficate*, fr. L *defaecatus*, past part. of *defaecare*, fr. *de-* + *faec-, faex* dregs, lees] *obs* **:** freed from dregs or impurities **:** REFINED, PURIFIED

[2]**def·e·cate** \'defə,kāt, -fē,-, *esp Brit* 'dēf-; *usu* ād·+V\ *vb* -ED/-ING/-S [L *defaecatus*] *vt* **1 :** to free from impurities **:** CLARIFY, PURIFY, REFINE; *esp* **:** to clarify (juice for sugar production) by treating with a reagent (as lime), heating, and separating from scum and sediment **2 :** to free from that which is foreign, nonessential, or corrupting **:** PURGE ⟨~ religion of superstition⟩ **3 :** to discharge through the anus ⟨the seeds were *defecated* undigested⟩ **~** *vi* **:** to discharge feces from the bowels

def·e·ca·tion \,==ˈkāshən\ *n* -S [LL *defaecation-, defaecatio*, fr. L *defaecatus* + *-ion-, -io* -ion] **:** the act or process of defecating: as **a :** separation from impurities (as lees or dregs) **:** purification esp. of sugar **b :** discharge of feces

def·e·ca·tor \'==,kād·ə(r), -ātə-\ *n* -S **:** a tank in which cane juice is defecated **:** CLARIFIER

[1]**de·fect** \'dē,fekt *also* də'f- *or* dē'f-\ *n* -S [ME *defaicte* shortcoming, fr. MF *defect*, fr. L *defectus* lack, fr. *defectus* past part. of *deficere* to desert, fail, be wanting, fr. *de-* + *-ficere* (fr. *facere* to make, do) — more at DO] **1 :** an irregularity in a surface or a structure that spoils the appearance or causes weakness or failure **:** FAULT, FLAW ⟨carefully examine a piece of timber for ~*s*⟩ **:** SHORTCOMING ⟨a moral ~ in his nature⟩ ⟨several ~*s* can be found in this argument⟩ **2** [L *defectus*] **:** want or absence of something necessary for completeness, perfection, or adequacy in form or function **:** DEFICIENCY, WEAKNESS — opposed to *excess* ⟨laziness may be caused by a ~ of health⟩ ⟨a ~ in his hearing⟩ **syn** see ABSENCE, BLEMISH

[2]**de·fect** \də'fekt, dē'- *sometimes* 'dē,f-\ *vi* -ED/-ING/-S [L *defectus*, past part.] **1** *obs* **:** to become deficient **:** FAIL **2 :** to forsake or fall away from a cause or party esp. in order to embrace another **:** DESERT ⟨he ~*ed* to the West⟩

de·fec·ti·bil·i·ty \də,fektə'bilәd·ē, (,)dē,-\ *n* -ES **:** inherent defectiveness **:** tendency to fall short of perfection

defectible *adj*, *obs* **:** liable to defect, failure, or error

de·fec·tion \də'fekshən, dē'-\ *n* -S [L *defection-, defectio*, fr. *defectus* (past part. of *deficere* to desert, fail, be wanting) + *-ion-, -io* -ion — more at DEFECT] **1 :** FAILING, FAILURE, LOSS ⟨fell into a ~ of spirit⟩ **2** *obs* **:** IMPERFECTION, DEFECT **3 :** the act of abandoning a person, cause, or doctrine to whom or to which one is bound by some tie (as of allegiance or duty) **:** DESERTION, APOSTASY

[1]**de·fec·tive** \-ktiv, -tēv *also* 'dē,f- *or* -təv\ *adj* [ME, fr. MF *defectif*, fr. OF, fr. LL *defectivus*, fr. L *defectus* + *-ivus* -ive] **1** *obs* **:** in error **:** at fault **2 :** wanting in something essential **:** falling below an accepted standard in regularity and soundness of form or structure ⟨a ~ imprint⟩ ⟨a ~ pane of glass⟩ or in adequacy of function ⟨a ~ mechanism⟩ ⟨~ eyesight⟩ **:** FAULTY, DEFICIENT, INSUFFICIENT ⟨~ method⟩ **3 a :** lacking one or more of the usual forms of grammatical inflection ⟨the ~ verb *quoth*⟩ **b** *of writing in a Semitic alphabet* **:** lacking a vowel letter to indicate a vowel sound — compare SCRIPTIO DEFECTIVA — **de·fec·tive·ly** \-təvlē, -li\ *adv*

[2]**defective** \"\ *n* -S **1 :** a word that lacks one or more of the usual forms of grammatical inflection ⟨the verb *ought* is a ~⟩ **2 :** a person who is subnormal physically or mentally; *specif* **:** one with marked stigmata or physical defects

defective delinquent *n* **:** an individual of abnormal intelligence who has manifested criminal or esp. psychopathic tendencies

de·fec·tive·ness \-tivnəs, -tēv- *also* -təv-\ *n* -ES **:** the quality or state of being defective

defective number *n* **:** DEFICIENT NUMBER

defective year *n* **:** a common year of 353 days or a leap year of 383 days in the Jewish calendar — see YEAR table

de·fect·less \'dē,fektləs *also* də'f- *or* dē'f-\ *adj* **:** being without a defect

defect of sex : disqualification for service (as jury duty) by reason of being a woman

de·fec·tor \də'fektə(r), dē'-, 'dē,f-\ *n* -S [L, fr. *defectus* (past part. of *deficere* to desert) + *-or* — more at DEFECT] **:** one that defects (as from a party or a doctrine)

de·fec·to·scope \də'fektə,skōp, dē'-\ *n* -S [[1]*defect* + *-o-* + *-scope*] **:** an instrument for detecting structural defects (as in a railroad rail)

defectuous *adj* [ML *defectuosus*, fr. L *defectus* defect + *-osus* -ous — more at DEFECT] *obs* **:** DEFECTIVE

def·e·da·tion \,defə'dāshən\ *n* -S [MF, fr. LL *defoedatus* (past part. of *defoedare* to pollute, fr. L *de-* + *foedare* to make ugly or filthy, fr. *foedus* ugly, filthy) + MF *-ion* — more at BEBUNG] *archaic* **:** POLLUTION, DEFILING

de·feminization \(')dē+\ *n* -S **:** loss of feminine qualities

de·feminize \(')dē+\ *vt* -ED/-ING/-S [*de-* + *feminine* + *-ize*] **:** to divest of feminine qualities or physical characteristics **:** MASCULINIZE

defence *chiefly Brit var of* DEFENSE

de·fend \də'fend, dē'-\ *vb* -ED/-ING/-S [ME *defenden*, fr. OF *defendre*, fr. L *defendere*, fr. *de-* + *-fendere* to strike; akin to OE *gūth* battle, war, OHG *gund-*, ON *gunnr* battle, war, Gk *theinein* to strike, Skt *hanti* he strikes, kills] *vt* **1** *archaic* **:** to ward or fend off **:** drive back or away **:** REPEL **2** *archaic* **:** PREVENT, FORBID, PROHIBIT ⟨which God ~ that I should wring from him —Shak.⟩ **3 :** to drive danger or attack away from **:** secure against attack **:** maintain against force **:** PROTECT, GUARD ⟨men ~*ing* their homes⟩ ⟨~ our shores⟩ — often used with *from* ⟨a floor . . . to ~ the old woman's bones from the dampness —Ellen Glasgow⟩ **4 :** to maintain against argument or hostile criticism **:** UPHOLD, JUSTIFY ⟨~ a theory⟩ ⟨~*ed* his friend's behavior⟩; *specif* **:** to prove valid (as a doctoral thesis) by answering extempore questions asked by experts in an oral examination **5 :** to act as attorney for (an accused person) in criminal proceedings **6 :** to deny or oppose the right of a plaintiff in regard to (a suit or a wrong charged) **:** CONTROVERT **:** OPPOSE, RESIST ⟨~ a claim at law⟩ **:** CONTEST ⟨~ a suit⟩ **~** *vi* **1 :** to take action against attack or challenge ⟨the ~*ing* champion⟩ ⟨he preferred ~*ing* to attacking⟩; *specif* **:** to enter or make a defense in a legal action or suit **2** *in card games* **a :** to play against the high bidder **b :** to bid for the purpose of preventing an opponent from reaching an esp. advantageous bid

syn PROTECT, SHIELD, GUARD, SAFEGUARD: DEFEND may imply warding off what actually threatens or repelling what actually attacks or securing against attack ⟨to *defend* the settlers from the Indians⟩ ⟨the antitrust laws must constantly *defend* the ideal of industrial democracy against all sorts of pressures —T.W.Arnold⟩ PROTECT is somewhat wider and may imply shielding or guarding, sometimes as with a cover, from anything that might injure or destroy ⟨cherished and nurtured to strength by his mother, he may then *protect* and cherish another woman in his turn —Weston La Barre⟩ ⟨a refuge for deer, bear, and wildcats. It is *protected* by a private game warden —*Amer. Guide Series: N.C.*⟩ ⟨the ledge-lined harbor rimmed with well-kept estates affords a *protected* anchorage for a large yachting fleet —*Amer. Guide Series: Conn.*⟩ SHIELD suggests interposition of or as of a shield, screen, or other protective intervention against attack somewhat more imminent and specific than that suggested by PROTECT ⟨who *shielded* himself from importunate callers by an impassable barrage of clerks and secretaries —W.F.Hambly⟩ ⟨innocent, confessing to the crime to *shield* the real murderer, a close friend or relative who had a wife and many children —*Amer. Guide Series: Ariz.*⟩ GUARD implies protecting with vigilance, force, and strength ⟨to *guard* the pass against attack⟩ ⟨secret service men *guarding* the president⟩ ⟨the accumulation of private wealth in Boston, thriftily *guarded* by the canny Whigs —Van Wyck Brooks⟩ SAFEGUARD applies to any strong and careful protective measures against potential dangers and threats ⟨the proletariat, scared by the famine and the floods of the Tiber, looked to him to *safeguard* their precarious livelihood and their scanty pleasures —John Buchan⟩ ⟨tax reforms which will bring the most revenue to the government while *safeguarding* the best interests of our economy and the nation's investors —G.K.Funston⟩ ⟨Marge *safeguards* the reputation of the arresting policeman by riding with him when he takes the girl to the county clink —G.S. Perry⟩ **syn** see in addition MAINTAIN

de·fend·able \-dəbəl\ *adj* **:** DEFENSIBLE

[1]**de·fend·ant** \də'fendənt, dē'-\ *n* -S [ME *defendaunt*, fr. MF *defendant*, pres. part. of *defendre*, fr. OF] **1** *obs* **:** DEFENDER **2 :** a person required to make answer in an action or suit in law or equity or in a criminal action — opposed to *plaintiff;* see DEFEND 6

[2]**defendant** \", 'dē,f-\ *adj* [MF] **1 :** DEFENDING **:** being on the defensive **2** *obs* **:** DEFENSIVE

de·fend·er \də'fendə(r), dē'-\ *n* -S [ME *defendour, defender*, fr. OF *defendeor*, fr. *defendre* + *-eor* -or] **1 :** one that defends **:** PROTECTOR, ADVOCATE, CHAMPION, VINDICATOR, UPHOLDER **2** *Scots law* **a :** a party defendant in a legal proceeding — opposed to *pursuer* **b :** the lawyer acting for a party defendant in a legal proceeding

defender office *n* **:** a staff of lawyers whose duty is to defend poor persons charged with crime; *often* **:** such a staff holding public office

defender of the bond *or* **defender of the marriage tie** [translation of NL *defensor vinculi matrimonii*] *Roman Catholicism* **:** a diocesan official charged with defending the validity of the marriage bond in suits for annulment

defendress *n* -ES [*defender* + *-ess*] *obs* **:** a female defender

de·fen·es·tra·tion \(,)dē,fenə'strāshən\ *n* -S [*de-* + L *fenestra* window + E *-tion* — more at FENESTRA] **:** a throwing of a person or thing out of a window ⟨the Thirty Years' War followed the ~ of deputies at Prague⟩

[1]**de·fense** \də'fen(t)s, dē'-, 'dē,f-\ *n* -S [ME *defens, defense*, fr. OF *defens*, fr. ML *defensum*, fr. L, neut. of *defensus*, past part. of *defendere* to defend; OF *defense* fr. (assumed) VL *defensa*, fr. L, fem. of *defensus* — more at DEFEND] **1 a :** the act of defending ⟨the ~ of Moscow⟩ ⟨to die in ~ of liberty⟩ — opposed to *attack* **b :** a defendant's denial, answer, or plea **:** an opposing or denial of the truth or validity of the plaintiff's or prosecutor's case — compare ANSWER 2c **2 :** capability of resisting attack ⟨a football team weak in ~⟩ **:** practice or manner of self-protection ⟨the body's ~*s* against disease are weakened by hunger⟩ — usu. used in pl. **3 a :** means or method of defending ⟨weapons of ~⟩ **:** defensive plan, policy, or structure ⟨the inadequate ~*s* of the capital were easily penetrated by the enemy troops⟩ — usu. used in pl. **b :** the method and collected facts adopted by a defendant to protect himself against a plaintiff's action **c :** a sequence of moves available in chess to the second player in the opening; *also* **:** any opening having certain characteristic moves for the second player **d :** an argument prepared or advanced to defend an action, policy, or thesis **:** JUSTIFICATION **4 a :** defenders or the positions taken up by them ⟨ran through the ~ for a touchdown⟩ ⟨falsecarding to mislead the ~⟩ **b :** a cricket team's batting power or batsmen — contrasted with *attack* **5 :** a prohibitory ordinance **:** prohibition esp. of fishing or hunting ⟨the ~ months when fish are spawning⟩ — used chiefly in *in defense* ⟨trout streams were put *in defense*⟩

[2]**defense** \"\ *vt* -ED/-ING/-S [ME *defensen*, fr. MF *defenser*, fr. L *defensare*, fr. *defensus*, past part. of *defendere* to defend — more at DEFEND] **1** *obs* **:** to furnish with defenses **:** FORTIFY **2 a :** to impede the progress of (the football player or team in possession of the ball) ⟨he was thoroughly *defensed*⟩ **b :** to break up or defend against (a particular play) ⟨~ the single wing running pass⟩

defense in depth 1 : a tactical system of mutually supporting positions that are each capable of all-round defense and that have sufficient depth to prevent the enemy from achieving freedom of maneuver before his attack is broken up and absorbed **2 :** a strategic succession of defended areas which will permit continuation of a war after forward areas have been lost

de·fense·less \-ləs\ *adj* **:** being without defense **:** helpless against attack — **de·fense·less·ly** *adv* — **de·fense·less·ness** *n* -ES

defenseless mennonite *n*, *usu cap D&M* **:** a member of a conservative middlewestern religious group of Mennonites

de·fense·man \də'fen(t)smən, dē'-, -,man\ *n*, *pl* **defensemen :** a player in an athletic sport (as hockey) assigned to a defensive zone or position

defense mechanism *also* **defense reaction** *n* **1 :** a reaction whereby an organism defends itself (as against disease germs) **2 :** MECHANISM OF DEFENSE

de·fen·si·bil·i·ty \də,fen(t)sə'biləd·ē, (,)dē,-, -ətē, -i\ *n* -ES **:** the quality or state of being defensible

de·fen·si·ble \də'fen(t)səbəl, dē'-\ *adj* [ME, alter. (influenced by LL *defensibilis*, fr. L *defensus* — past part. of *defendere* to defend — + *-ibilis* -ible) of *defensable*, fr. OF, fr. LL *defensabilis*, fr. L *defensare* to defend + *-abilis* -able — more at DEFEND, DEFENSE] **1 :** capable of being defended ⟨a ~ city⟩ **:** EXCUSABLE ⟨his action was ~ under those circumstances⟩ **2** *obs* **:** capable of offering defense — **de·fen·si·bly** \-blē, -li\ *adv*

[1]**de·fen·sive** \də'fen(t)siv, dē'-, 'dē,f-, -sēv *also* -səv\ *adj* [ME, fr. MF *defensif*, fr. ML *defensivus*, fr. L *defensus* (past part. of *defendere* to defend) + *-ivus* -ive] **1 :** serving to defend or protect **:** proper for defense **:** PROTECTIVE, SHIELDING ⟨a moat ~ to a house —Shak.⟩ **2 a :** devoted to resisting or preventing aggression or attack ⟨a ~ alliance⟩ ⟨~ strategy⟩ ⟨~ behavior⟩ — opposed to *offensive* **b** *cricket* **:** concerned with defense of the wicket rather than the scoring of runs — used of a batsman or his play **3** *obs* **:** DEFENSIBLE **4** *bridge* **a :** valuable in defensive play — used of a card that can be expected to win a trick against opponent's contract **b** *of a bid* **:** designed to keep opponent from being the highest bidder — **de·fen·sive·ly** \-sәvlē, -li\ *adv* — **de·fen·sive·ness** \-sivnəs, -sēv- *also* -səv-\ *n* -ES

[2]**defensive** \"\ *n* -S [ME, fr. MF *defensif*, fr. *defensif*, adj.] **1** *obs* **:** something that defends **2 :** a defensive position — **on the defensive :** in a state or posture of defense or resistance **:** in opposition to an actual or expected aggression or attack

defensive allegation *n* **:** a pleading in English ecclesiastical law in which defendant does not deny plaintiff's allegations but avers special circumstances and facts constituting a defense thereby requiring plaintiff to answer upon oath the matter set up in defense

defensive gland *n* **:** REPUGNATORIAL GLAND

de·fen·sor \də'fen(t)sə(r), dē'-, -n,sō(ə)r\ *n* -S [ME *defensour*, fr. L *defensor*, fr. *defensus* (past part. of *defendere* to defend) + *-or* — more at DEFEND] **1** *obs* **:** DEFENDER **2 a** *Roman law* **:** one who voluntarily undertook the defense of a case and gave security to satisfy the judgment **b :** an advocate conducting the defense of a case in court **3** [LL, fr. L] **:** an advocate in the later Roman Empire: **a :** a municipal officer appointed to protect the people from oppression **b :** a layman or member of the clergy appointed to defend the rights and property of the church **4** [LL, fr. L] **:** the patron of a church **:** an officer having charge of the temporal affairs of a church

de·fen·sor·ship \-n(t)sər,ship\ *n* -S **:** the office of defensor

de·fen·so·ry \-n(t)s(ə)rē, -ri\ *adj* [LL *defensorius*, fr. L *defensus* + *-orius* -ory] **:** DEFENSIVE

[1]**de·fer** \də'fər, dē'-, +V -'fər-; -'fə̄, +V -'fər- *or* -'fə̄(r\ *vb* **deferred; deferred; deferring; defers** [ME *deferren, differren*, fr. MF *differer*, fr. L *differre* to postpone, be different — more at DIFFER] *vt* **1 :** DELAY ⟨God . . . will not long ~ to vindicate . . . His name —John Milton⟩: as **a :** to put off (a matter or person to be dealt with) deliberately to a future time ⟨*deferred* payment of a debt⟩ ⟨*deferred* talking with the boy⟩ **b :** to postpone induction of (a person) into military service **2** *obs* **:** to waste (time) by delay **:** PROLONG **~** *vi* **:** to delay to act **:** WAIT, PROCRASTINATE ⟨able to ~ and temporize at leisure —J.A.Symonds⟩

syn POSTPONE, INTERMIT, SUSPEND, STAY: DEFER indicates a delaying or putting off till a later time, often in recognition of developments that prevent proceeding ⟨reluctantly, he made up his mind to *defer* the more exacting examinations until another time —A.J.Cronin⟩ ⟨not more than three or four men could be found to continue the work, and its completion was long *deferred* —*Amer. Guide Series: Mich.*⟩ POSTPONE indicates a deferring, often until some set future time, although to *postpone* indefinitely means to cancel ⟨I think that we had better *postpone* our look round the church until after lunch —Compton Mackenzie⟩ ⟨let us *postpone* a final evaluation of Valla's treatise until after we have considered the handling of the selfsame problem by the English scholastic, Reginald Pecock —G.C.Sellery⟩ INTERMIT suggests halting or delaying for a relatively short interval, usu. with the implication of a quick resumption ⟨seven centuries of hardly *intermitted* war created the Spanish people and they, the most medieval people in western Europe, created the Kingdom of Spain —Bernard DeVoto⟩ SUSPEND indicates a stopping or rendering inoperative for a time, usu. for a reason explicit or implicit in the context ⟨newspaper publication *suspended* during a strike⟩ ⟨shall I *suspend* final decision until I have further evidence? —M.R.Cohen⟩ ⟨had his driving license *suspended* for a month. Too many tickets —Raymond Chandler⟩ STAY suggests stopping activity or progress by or as if by interposing some obstacle ⟨an order *staying* the execution⟩ ⟨in September the injunction was *stayed* and on October 5 set aside by the Supreme Court —*Current Biog.*⟩ ⟨believing that by remaining neutral she could *stay* the forces of war —E.M.Coulter⟩

[2]**defer** \"\ *vb* **deferred; deferred; deferring; defers** [ME *deferen, differren*, fr. MF *defferer, deferer*, fr. LL *deferre*, fr. L, to bring down, bring, fr. *de-* + *ferre* to carry — more at BEAR (to carry)] *vt* **1 :** to refer or submit for determination or decision ⟨he could ~ his job to no one . . . if he did judge wrong, carnage on the carrier deck could be fearful —J.A. Michener⟩ ⟨the court ~*s* its own opinion to that of congress —C.P.Curtis⟩ **2 :** PROFFER, OFFER, TENDER **~** *vi* **:** to submit or yield through authority, respect, force, awe, propriety — used with *to* ⟨he assumed authority . . . everybody *deferred* to him —Ellen Glasgow⟩ **syn** see YIELD

def·er·ence \'def(ə)rən(t)s *also* -fərn-\ *n* -S [F *déférence*, fr. MF *deference*, fr. *deferer* to defer + *-ence*] **:** the act or attitude of deferring **:** a yielding of judgment or preference out of respect for the position, wish, or known opinion of another **:** courteous, complacent, or ingratiating regard for another's wishes ⟨the conquered population should be treated with extreme ~ —N.J.G.Pounds⟩ **syn** see HONOR — **in deference to** *prep* **:** in consideration of **:** in view of ⟨a shorter campaign . . . *in deference to* the belief . . . that television is *the* political weapon —Walter Goodman⟩

[1]**def·er·ent** \-f(ə)rənt\ *n* -S [ME *different*, fr. ML *deferent-, deferens*, fr. L, pres. part. of *deferre* to bring down, bring — more at DEFER] **:** an imaginary circle surrounding the earth in whose periphery, according to Ptolemy, either the celestial body or the center of its epicycle is supposed to move

[2]**deferent** \"\ *adj* [L *deferent-, deferens*, pres. part. of *deferre*] **1 :** serving to carry down or out ⟨a ~ conduit⟩ **2 :** of, relating to, or supplying the vas deferens ⟨~ arteries⟩ **3** [back-formation fr. *deference*] **:** [1]DEFERENTIAL

[1]**def·er·en·tial** \,defə'renchəl\ *adj* [fr. *deference*, after such pairs as E *prudence: prudential*] **1 :** showing or expressing deference ⟨listened with ~ attention⟩ ⟨a ~ bow⟩ **2 :** given to deference ⟨the ~ nature of society —J.G.Pearson⟩ — **def·er·en·tial·ly** \-ch(ə)lē, -li\ *adv*

[2]**deferential** \"\ *adj* [[2]*deferent* + *-ial*] **:** [2]DEFERENT 2

def·er·en·ti·al·i·ty \,defə,renchē'aləd·ē\ *n* -ES **:** the quality or state of being deferential

de·fer·ment \də'fərmənt, dē'-, -'fə̄m-\ *n* -S [[1]*defer* + *-ment*] **:** the act of delaying **:** POSTPONEMENT; *specif* **:** official postponement of induction into military service

de·fer·ra·ble *also* **de·fer·able** \-'fərəbəl *also* -'fə̄rə-\ *adj* [[1]*defer* + *-able*] **:** capable of or suitable for being deferred ⟨much ~ construction⟩ **:** eligible for deferment or such as renders one eligible for deferment esp. from compulsory military service

[2]**deferrable** \"\ *n* -S **:** one that is eligible for deferment

de·fer·ral \-'fərəl *also* -'fə̄rəl\ *n* -S [[1]*defer* + *-al*] **:** DEFERMENT

deferred *adj* [fr. past part. of [1]*defer*] **1 :** put off **:** ALLAYED, POSTPONED ⟨a ~ legal right⟩ **:** withheld for or until a stated time ⟨a ~ payment⟩ **2 :** charged in cases of delayed handling ⟨a ~ rate⟩; *also* **:** handled at a deferred rate ⟨~ telegram⟩

deferred annuity *n* **:** an annuity providing for the first payment to be made to the annuitant at some date later than the end of the first year following purchase

deferred bond *n* **1 :** a bond on which the payment of interest is postponed until some condition has been satisfied **2** *Brit* **:** a bond bearing interest at an increasing rate until a maximum is attained

deferred charge *or* **deferred asset** *n* **:** an expense (as a prepaid insurance premium or an inventory of supplies) that is incurred prior to the fiscal period to which it applies, temporarily carried on the books as an asset, and subsequently charged to expense at the appropriate time — called also *prepaid expense*

deferred credit *or* **deferred income** *or* **deferred liability** *n* **:** income received but not yet earned

deferred delivery *n* **:** delivery specified as deferred for some specified time — used of stocks and bonds ⟨sold, *deferred delivery* ten days⟩

deferred dividend *n* **:** an insurance dividend payable from the surplus accumulated during a given period to those policyholders only who are alive at its expiry and whose policies are then in force

deferred maintenance *n* **:** an amount needed but not yet expended for repairs, restoration, or rehabilitation of an asset

deferred shoot *n* **:** a shoot (as a water sprout) arising from a bud dormant for some time

deferred stock *n*, *chiefly Brit* **:** stock on which no dividend is payable until the happening of some contingent event (as the paying of a dividend on preferred stock)

de·fer·rer *R* də'fər·ər, dē'-, *-R* -'fər·ə(r *also* -'fə̄rə(r\ *n* -S **:** one that defers

deferring *pres part of* DEFER

de·fer·ri·za·tion \(,)dē,ferə'zāshən\ *n* -S [*de-* + L *ferrum* iron + E *-ization* — more at FARRIER] **:** removal of iron (as from water for industry)

defers *pres 3d sing of* DEFER

de·fer·vesce \,dē(,)fər'ves, ¦defər-\ *vi* -ED/-ING/-S [back-formation fr. *defervescence*] **:** to undergo defervescence

de·fer·ves·cence \,=(,)=ˈves³n(t)s\ *n* -S [G *deferveszenz*, fr. L *defervescent-, defervescens*, pres. part. of *defervescere* to stop boiling, cool down, fr. *de-* + *fervescere* to begin to boil, seethe — more at EFFERVESCE] **:** the subsidence of a fever

de·fer·ves·cent \¦=(,)=¦=³nt\ *adj* [back-formation fr. *defervescence*] **:** relating to, characterized by, or causing defervescence

de·fi \(ˈ)dā¦fē\ *n* -s [F *défi*, fr. MF *defi, desfi* — more at DEFY] **:** CHALLENGE, DEFIANCE

de·fi·al \dəˈfī(ə)l, dēˈ-\ *n* -s [¹*defy* + *-al*] *archaic* **:** DEFIANCE

de·fi·ance \dəˈfīən(t)s, dēˈ-\ *n* -s [ME *defyaunce*, fr. OF *desfiance, defiance*, fr. *desfier, defier* to defy + *-ance* — more at DEFY] **1** *obs* **:** a renunciation of allegiance or friendship **2 :** act of defying, putting in opposition, or provoking to combat **:** CHALLENGE **:** a declaration of hostilities **3 :** a state of opposition **:** willingness to fight **:** disposition to resist **:** contempt of opposition ⟨he breathed ~ to my ears —Shak.⟩ — **in defiance of** *prep* **:** in spite of **:** contrary to ⟨*in defiance of* the laws of physics⟩

de·fi·ant \-nt\ *adj* [F *défiant*, fr. OF *desfiant, defiant*, pres. part. of *desfier, defier* to defy] **:** full of defiance **:** BOLD, INSOLENT, UNAFRAID — **de·fi·ant·ly** *adv*

de·fiber \(ˈ)dē+\ *or* **de·fi·ber·ize** \(ˈ)dēˈfībə‚rīz\ *vt* -ED/-ING/-S [*defiber* fr. *de-* + *fiber* (n.); *defiberize* fr. *de-* + *fiber* + *-ize*] **:** DEFIBRATE

de·fi·brate \(ˈ)dēˈfī‚brāt\ *vt* -ED/-ING/-S [*de-* + L *fibra* fiber + E *-ate* — more at FIBER] **:** to separate (as a pulp sheet, waste paper, partly cooked wood) into its fibrous constituents — **de·fi·bra·tion** \‚dē‚fīˈbrāshən\ *n* -s

de·fi·bra·tor \(ˈ)dēˈfī‚brād·ə(r)\ *n* -s **:** a machine that defibrates

de·fi·bri·nate \(ˈ)dē+\ *vt* -ED/-ING/-S [*de-* + *fibrin* + *-ate*] **:** to remove fibrin from (blood) — **de·fi·bri·na·tion** \¦dē+\ *n* -s

deficience *n* -s [LL *deficientia*] *obs* **:** DEFICIENCY

de·fi·cien·cy \dəˈfishənsē, dēˈ-, -si\ *n* -ES [LL *deficientia*, fr. L *deficient-, deficiens* (pres. part. of *deficere* to be lacking) + *-ia* -y] **1 :** the quality or state of being deficient **:** DEFECT, INADEQUACY ⟨so miserably ignorant that his *deficiencies* made him the ridicule of his contemporaries —H.T.Buckle⟩ **2 :** inadequate amount **:** SHORTAGE: as **a :** a shortage of substances (as vitamins) necessary to health **b :** absence of one or more genes from a chromosome

deficiency account *n* **:** an account supplementing the balance sheet of a financially weak enterprise showing estimated realization values of assets and their insufficiency to meet creditors' claims and occas. indicating the causes of the difficulty

deficiency bill *n* **1** *Brit* **:** an advance made to the government by the Bank of England to meet a deficiency **2 :** a legislative bill appropriating supplementary funds to meet a deficiency

deficiency disease *n* **:** a disease caused by a lack of one or more basic nutrients (as amino acids, minerals, or vitamins)

deficiency judgment *n* **:** a judgment for the balance of a debt after the security has been realized and the proceeds applied to payment; *esp* **:** such a judgment following foreclosure of a mortgage

¹**de·fi·cient** \dəˈfishənt, dēˈ-\ *adj* [L *deficient-, deficiens*, pres. part. of *deficere* to be lacking, fr. *de-* + *-ficere* (fr. *facere* to make, do) — more at DO] **1 :** lacking in some quality, faculty, or characteristic necessary for completeness ⟨~ in judgment⟩ **:** not up to a normal standard **:** DEFECTIVE ⟨~ strength⟩ **:** needed to make up completeness ⟨~ by about one quarter of the whole amount⟩ **2 :** having, relating to, or characterized by a gene deficiency — **de·fi·cient·ly** *adv*

²**deficient** \"\ *n* -s **:** one that is deficient ⟨percent of mental ~s institutionalized⟩

deficient number *n* **:** an imperfect number (as 8) that is greater than the sum of its divisors

def·i·cit \ˈdefəsət, *rapid* -fsət, *usu* -əd·+V\ *n* -s [F *déficit*, fr. L *deficit* it is lacking, 3d pers. sing. pres. indic. of *deficere* to be lacking — more at DEFICIENT] **1 :** deficiency in amount or quality ⟨a ~ in yearly rainfall⟩ **:** impairment of capital **:** a falling short esp. of income ⟨a ~ in revenue⟩ — opposed to *surplus* **2 a :** an excess of debit over credit items ⟨a ~ in a nation's balance of international payments⟩ **b :** a loss in business operations ⟨the year's operating ~⟩

deficit financing *n* **:** the financing of government expenditures by borrowing rather than by taxation

deficit spending *n* **:** the spending of public funds raised by borrowing rather than by taxation

de fi·de \(ˈ)dāˈfē‚dā\ *adj* [NL, fr. L, from faith] **:** held as an obligatory article of faith ⟨this doctrine of the Jesuits is not *de fide* —John Dryden⟩

defied *past of* DEFY

de·fi·er \dəˈfī(ə)r, -īə\ *n* -s [*defy* + *-er*] **:** one that defies

defies *pl of* DEFY, *pres 3d sing of* DEFY

defiguration *n* -s [MF *defigurer, desfigurer* to disfigure + E *-ation* — more at DISFIGURE] *obs* **:** DISFIGURATION

¹**def·i·lade** \ˈdefə‚lād, -ād, -ȧd, ‚==ˈ=\ *vt* -ED/-ING/-S [prob. *de-* + *-filade* (as in *enfilade* (v.))] **1 :** to arrange (fortifications) so as to protect the lines from frontal or enfilading fire and the interior of the works from plunging or reverse fire **2 :** to protect by a natural or artificial mask against fire or observation from a given point

²**defilade** \"\ *n* -s [*de-* + *-filade* (as in *enfilade*, n.)] **1 :** the act or process of defilading **2 :** protection from observation or fire from the ground (as by a ridge, embankment, ravine)

¹**de·file** \dəˈfīl, dēˈ-, *esp before pause or consonant* -īəl\ *vt* -ED/-ING/-S [ME *defilen*, alter. (influenced by ME *filen* to defile) of *defoulen* to trample on, violate sexually, defile, fr. OF *defoler, defouler* to trample on, mistreat, fr. *de-* + *foler, fouler* to trample on, lit., to full (as cloth) — more at FULL (to thicken), FILE (to defile)] **1 :** to make filthy **:** DIRTY, BEFOUL ⟨they that touch pitch will be *defiled* —Shak.⟩ **2 :** to corrupt the purity or perfection of **:** DEBASE ⟨not even a tent *defiling* the primeval splendor —R.L.Neuberger⟩ **3 :** to rob of chastity **:** RAVISH, VIOLATE **4 :** to make ceremonially unclean **:** POLLUTE ⟨~ the temple⟩ **5 :** TARNISH, DISHONOR ⟨*defiled* his memory with slander⟩ **syn** see CONTAMINATE

²**defile** \", ˈdē‚f-\ *vi* -ED/-ING/-S [F *défiler*, fr. *dé-* de- (fr. OF *de-, des-*) + *filer* to move in a column or columns (as of troops), fr. OF, to spin, fr. LL *filare*, fr. L *filum* thread — more at FILE (row)] **:** to march off or pass along in a line **:** file off

³**defile** *like* ²DEFILE\ *n* -s [F *défilé*, fr. past part. of *défiler*] **1 :** a narrow passage in which troops can march only in a file or with a narrow front **2 :** a long narrow pass (as between hills, rocks, or cliffs)

de·file·ment \dəˈfīlmənt, dēˈ-\ *n* -s [¹*defile* + *-ment*] **:** the act of defiling or state of being defiled **:** POLLUTION; *also* **:** something that defiles

de·fil·er \dəˈfīlə(r), dēˈ-\ *n* -s **:** one that defiles

de·fil·ing·ly *adv* **:** in a defiling manner

de·fin·abil·i·ty \də‚fīnəˈbiləd·ē, dē‚-\ *n* -ES **:** the quality or state of being definable

de·fin·able \dəˈfīnəbəl, dēˈ-\ *adj* [*define* + *-able*] **:** capable of being defined, limited, or explained **:** DETERMINABLE ⟨~ limits⟩ ⟨~ terms⟩ ⟨~ rules⟩ — **de·fin·ably** \-blē, -li\ *adv*

de·fine \dəˈfīn, dēˈ-\ *vb* -ED/-ING/-S [ME *definen, diffinen*, fr. MF & L; MF *definer, diffiner* to determine, bring to an end, fr. L *definire* to determine, bring to an end, explain, fr. *de-* + *finire* to limit, finish, end, fr. *finis* boundary, end — more at FINAL] *vt* **1** *obs* **:** to bring to an end **:** CONCLUDE; *often* **:** SETTLE ⟨*defined* the controversy⟩ **:** DECIDE, DETERMINE **2 :** to fix, decide, or prescribe clearly and with authority ⟨~ the power of a court by statutory enactment⟩ **3 :** to mark the limits of **:** determine with precision or exhibit clearly the boundaries of ⟨~ the extent of a kingdom⟩ **4 :** to make distinct in outline or features **:** bring into relief ⟨a tree *defined* against the sky⟩ ⟨a well-*defined* impression of an event⟩ ⟨the *defining* power of a lens⟩ **5 a :** to discover and set forth the meaning of (as a word or term); *specif* **:** to formulate a definition of **b :** to determine the essential qualities of (as a concept or thing) **c :** to determine the precise signification of **d :** DESCRIBE, EXPOUND, INTERPRET, EXPLAIN **6 a** *math* **:** to specify the construction or interpretation of (a concept) ⟨~ a conic section by a Cartesian equation⟩ **b :** to set apart in a class by identifying marks **:** CHARACTERIZE, DISTINGUISH ⟨good manners ~ the gentleman⟩ **c :** to establish in the mind so as to orient one's social reactions toward **:** IDENTIFY ⟨~ a situation as hostile⟩ ⟨~ a person as one of the four hundred⟩ ~ *vi* **1** *obs* **a :** to act as a judge in deciding or determining **b :** to deliver a precise opinion **2 :** to formulate one or more precise statements of meaning **:** make a definition **syn** see PRESCRIBE

defined *adj* **:** clearly outlined, characterized, or delimited; *specif, of a culture medium* **:** consisting wholly of chemically identified substances in precisely determined proportions

de·fine·ment \-nmənt\ *n* -s [*define* + *-ment*] **:** the act of defining **:** DEFINITION

de·fin·er \-nə(r)\ *n* -s **:** one that defines

de·fin·i·en·dum \də‚finēˈendəm, ‚dē‚-\ *n, pl* **definien·da** \-də\ [L, neut. of *definiendus*, gerundive of *definire* to determine, bring to an end, explain — more at DEFINE] **:** whatever is being defined **:** the expression that precedes in a nominal definition the symbol of definitional equality — contrasted with *definiens*

de·fin·i·ens \dəˈfinē‚enz, dēˈ-\ *n, pl* **definien·tia** \də‚finēˈench(ē)ə, (‚)dē‚-\ [L, pres. part. of *definire*] **:** whatever serves to define **:** the expression that follows in a nominal definition the symbol of definitional equality — contrasted with *definiendum*

¹**def·i·nite** \ˈdef(ə)nət, *usu* -əd·+V\ *adj* [L *definitus*, past part. of *definire* to limit, determine, bring to an end — more at DEFINE] **1 :** having distinct or certain limits **:** determinate in extent or character **:** LIMITED, FIXED ⟨~ dimensions⟩ ⟨a ~ period⟩ **2 :** marked by absence of the ambiguous, obscure, doubtful, or tentative and by certain clear statement or expression by means of flat positive assertion, careful statement of limitation, or accepted, finished form ⟨whatever qualification of counter doctrine there was in his grouped arguments, there was none in the conclusion; and the ~ conclusion was what men wanted —H.O.Taylor⟩ **3 a** *of a grammatical modifier* **:** typically designating an identified or immediately identifiable person or thing ⟨*this* in "this card", *that* in "that house", *my* in "my father", *Paul's* in "Paul's absence" are ~ modifiers⟩ ⟨the ~ article *the*⟩ **b** *of an adjective form or set of adjective forms* **:** WEAK 8b **c** [F *défini*, fr. L *definitus*] (1) *of a verb form or set of verb forms in French* **:** typically denoting simple occurrence of an action without reference to its completeness or incompleteness, duration, or repetition — usu. used in the phrase *past definite* ⟨*je vis* "I saw" contains a past ~ verb⟩ (2) *of a verb form or set of verb forms in English* **:** PROGRESSIVE 7 **4 a** *of floral organs* **:** constant in number usu. less than 20 and in multiples of the petal number ⟨stamens ~⟩ **b :** CYMOSE **5 :** REAL, ACTUAL ⟨ambition, which had been formless and remote, became ~ —Ellen Glasgow⟩ **:** POSITIVE, COGENT ⟨it is a ~ instrument for maldistribution of the world's income —J.A.Hobson⟩ **syn** see EXPLICIT

²**definite** \"\ *n* -s **:** a definite verb form or set of verb forms in a language

definite failure of issue : the failure of issue determined at a specific time that is or can become certain under the terms of an instrument creating estates in property (as upon the death of a designated person)

definite host *n* **:** DEFINITIVE HOST

definite integral *n* **:** the number obtained by finding an antiderivative of a function, substituting for the variable the first of two given numbers, then the second, and subtracting the second result from the first

definite integration *n* **:** the process of finding the definite integral of a function

def·i·nite·ly *adv* **:** in a definite way or manner **:** DISTINCTLY, UNMISTAKABLY, POSITIVELY

def·i·nite·ness *n* -ES **:** the quality or state of being definite

definite quadratic form *n* **:** a quadratic form that is always positive or always negative for every set of values of the variables involved in it except when all the variables are zero in which case the form has the value zero

definite-time \¦==(=)=¦=\ *adj* **:** having a purposely delayed action, the periods of delay being substantially alike regardless of the magnitude of the operating forces — used esp. of relays

def·i·ni·tion \‚defəˈnishən\ *n* -s [ME *diffinicioun*, fr. MF *diffinition, definition*, fr. L *definition-, definitio*, fr. *definitus* (past part. of *definire* to determine, bring to an end, explain) + *-ion-, -io* -ion — more at DEFINE] **1 :** an act of determining or settling: as **a** *Roman Catholicism* **:** an official ecclesiastical statement concerning a matter of faith or of morals as pertaining to faith **b :** a prescribed or official standard for a commercial product ⟨the ~ for oatmeal prescribes that the amount of nitrogen contained shall not be less than 2.24 percent —*Scientific Monthly*⟩ **c :** the fixing or determination of social character ⟨personal status is a matter of social ~⟩ ⟨society has changed its ~ of women's political rights⟩ **2 :** a word or phrase expressing the essential nature of a person or thing or class of persons or of things **:** an answer to the question "what is x?" or "what is an x?" **3 a :** a statement of the meaning of a word or word group ⟨the ~s in a dictionary⟩ **b :** the action or process of stating the meaning of a word or word group **4 a** *in Aristotelianism* **:** a determination of the real nature of a species by indicating both the genus that includes it and the specific differences or distinguishing marks **b** *in symbolic logic* (1) **:** an equation between a single symbol and a combination of symbols for which it is an abbreviation (as 1 = $_{Df}0'$ reading "1 is the successor of zero" where the special sign of equality indicates that the symbol on the left is always replaceable by the expression on the right) — see RECURSIVE DEFINITION (2) **:** a statement of the meaning to be attached to some symbol of a calculus when that calculus is given some particular interpretation (as $Sxy = x$ is the immediate successor of y) — called also *correlative definition, semantic definition*; see NOMINAL DEFINITION, PERSUASIVE DEFINITION, REAL DEFINITION **5 a :** the action or the power of making definite and clear or of bringing into sharp relief ⟨an emotion beyond ~⟩ ⟨the ~ of a telescope⟩ **b :** distinctness of outline or detail (as in a photograph) **:** clarity esp. of musical sound in reproduction **c :** sharp demarcation of outlines or limits ⟨a problem of clear ~⟩

def·i·ni·tion·al \¦==¦=shən°l, -shnəl\ *adj* **:** relating to definition **:** constituting a definition **:** employed in defining — **def·i·ni·tion·al·ly** \-°lē, -əlē\ *adv*

¹**de·fin·i·tive** \dəˈfinəd·|iv, dēˈ-, -ət|\ *adj* [ME *diffinityf*, fr. MF *diffinitif, definitif*, fr. L *definitivus*, fr. *definitus* + *-ivus* -ive] **1 :** serving to supply a final answer, solution, or evaluation and to end an unsettled unresolved condition ⟨a ~ victory⟩ ⟨~ surgical treatment⟩ **2** *archaic* **:** fixed and unalterable in opinion or judgment **3 :** most authoritative, reliable, and complete usu. with the implication of final and perfected completeness or precision — used of research, scholarship, or criticism esp. of a biographical or historical study or of a text or edition of a literary work or author ⟨~ studies⟩ ⟨it is the ~ book on the ghost or near-ghost towns of the Old West —Vardis Fisher⟩ ⟨~ complete works⟩ ⟨the ~ review of this book has already been written —T.P.Thornton⟩ **4 :** serving to define or specify precisely ⟨~ laws⟩ **:** DISTINGUISHING ⟨the term *communist*, orig. merely ~, has become loosely condemnatory⟩ ⟨species names are often ~ of the species⟩ **5 :** exact, express, and clearly defined; *broadly* **:** real, actual, and positive **:** DEFINITE ⟨the fears and ~ disappointments of the period —Edmund Wilson⟩ ⟨a settled and ~ world order —Aldous Huxley⟩ **6** *biol* **:** COMPLETE **:** fully developed **:** FINAL ⟨a ~ organ⟩ — opposed to *immature, primitive* **7** *of a postage stamp* **:** issued as a regular stamp for the country or territory in which it is to be used — contrasted with *provisional* **syn** see CONCLUSIVE

²**definitive** \"\ *n* -s **1** *archaic* **:** a final judgment or sentence **2 :** a definitive postage stamp

definitive callus *n, bot* **:** callus found in a sieve tube when it becomes or has become functionless

definitive host *n* **:** that host in which the sexual reproduction of a parasite takes place — compare INTERMEDIATE HOST

de·fin·i·tive·ly \|əvlē, -li\ *adv* **:** in a definitive way **:** FINALLY, DECISIVELY, UNALTERABLY

de·fin·i·tive·ness \|ivnəs, |ēv- *also* |əv-\ *n* -ES **:** the quality or state of being definitive

def·i·ni·tize \ˈdefənə‚tīz; dəˈfin-, dēˈ-\ *vt* -ED/-ING/-S **:** to make definite

def·i·ni·tor \ˈdefə‚nīd·ə(r), ‚==ˈ==\ *n* -s [ML, fr. LL, teacher, fr. L *definitus* (past part. of *definire* to determine, bring to an end, explain) + *-or* — more at DEFINE] **1 :** an official charged under canon law with the supervision of ecclesiastical property in one of the districts into which a deanery is divided and with aiding the dean **2 a :** a member of the general chapter in some religious orders **b :** a member of the governing council of some religious orders chosen to aid the superior in the government of the order

de·fin·i·tude \dəˈfinə‚tüd, dēˈ- -ə‚tyüd\ *n* -s [¹*definite* + *-ude*] **:** PRECISION, DEFINITENESS

defis *pl of* DEFI

defix *vt* [ME *defixen*, fr. L *defixus*, past part. of *defigere*, fr. *de-* + *figere* to fasten, thrust in — more at DIKE] *obs* **:** FIX, FASTEN, ESTABLISH

def·la·grate \ˈdeflə‚grāt\ *vb* -ED/-ING/-S [L *deflagratus*, past part. of *deflagrare* to burn down, burn up, fr. *de-* + *flagrare* to burn — more at BLACK] *vt* **:** to cause or initiate deflagration in or of ~ *vi* **:** to burn rapidly **:** undergo deflagration — distinguished from *detonate*

deflagrating spoon *or* **deflagration spoon** *n* **:** a spoon with a long vertical handle used in deflagration experiments

def·la·gra·tion \‚defləˈgrāshən\ *n* -s [L *deflagration-, deflagratio*, fr. *deflagratus* + *-ion-, -io* -ion] **:** the process of deflagrating; *specif* **:** a chemical reaction producing vigorous evolution of heat and sparks or flame and moving through the material (as black powder or smokeless powder) at a speed less than that of sound — distinguished from *detonation*

defla-grat-ing spoon

de·flate \dəˈflāt, (ˈ)dē¦f-, *usu* -ād·+V\ *vb* -ED/-ING/-S [*de-* + *-flate* (as in *inflate*)] *vt* **1 :** to release air or gas from (as a balloon or a tire) — opposed to *inflate* **2 :** to reduce in size or importance **:** PUNCTURE ⟨~ a reputation⟩ ⟨*deflated* hopes⟩ ⟨~ pomposity⟩ **3 :** to reduce (a price level) or contract (a volume of credit) esp. from an abnormally high level ~ *vi* **:** to lose firmness through the escape of air or gas (as of a balloon) **:** COLLAPSE, SAG **syn** see CONTRACT

de·fla·tion \-āshən\ *n* -s [*de-* + *-flation* (as in *inflation*)] **1 :** an act or instance of deflating **:** the state of being deflated **2 :** a contraction in the volume of available money or credit resulting in a decline in the general price level — contrasted with *inflation* **3** [L *deflatus* (past part. of *deflare* to blow off, fr. *de-* + *flare* to blow) + E *-ion* — more at BLOW] **:** WIND EROSION

de·fla·tion·ary \dəˈflāshə‚nerē, dēˈ-, -ri\ *adj* **:** relating to or productive of deflation ⟨~ signs⟩ ⟨~ measures⟩

deflationary gap *n* **:** a deficit in total disposable income relative to the current value of goods produced that is sufficient to cause a decline in prices and a lowering of production — compare INFLATIONARY GAP

¹**de·fla·tion·ist** \-sh(ə)nəst\ *n* -s **:** an advocate of deflation

²**deflationist** \"\ *adj* **:** tending to deflate **:** favoring deflation **:** DEFLATIONARY

de·fla·tive \dəˈflād·iv, (ˈ)dē¦f-\ *adj* **:** DEFLATIONARY

de·fla·tor \-d·ə(r)\ *n* -s **:** one that deflates; *specif* **:** a ratio or percentage by which monetary quantities are reduced to eliminate the effect of higher prices

de·flea \(ˈ)dē¦flē\ *vt* **deflead** \-ēd\ **deflead; defleaing; defleas** [*de-* + *flea* (n.)] **:** to rid of fleas

de·flect \dəˈflekt, (ˈ)dē¦f\ *vb* -ED/-ING/-S [L *deflectere* to bend downward, turn aside, fr. *de-* + *flectere* to bend, turn] *vt* **:** to turn from a straight course or fixed direction: **a :** BEND ⟨~ rays passing through a lens⟩ **b :** to change away from an accustomed, preferred, or likely course, pattern, or way to a goal ⟨~*ed* the course of the stream⟩ ~ *vi* **:** to turn aside **:** deviate from a straight line or from a position, course, or direction ⟨~ from the line of truth and reason —William Warburton⟩ **syn** see TURN

deflected *adj* **:** curved or turned downward ⟨a ~ septum⟩ — see DEFLEXED

de·flec·tion \-kshən\ *n* -s [L *deflexion-, deflexio*, fr. *deflexus* (past part. of *deflectere*) + *-ion-, -io* -ion] **1 a :** a turning aside **:** the state of being turned aside **:** a turning from a straight line or given course **:** a bending esp. downward **:** deviation esp. of a shot from its true course **b :** a result of bending or turning away **:** CURVE, BEND, TURN, DEVIATION **2 :** the bending of one curve away from another or from a straight line **3 a :** the deviation of the neutral axis (as of a beam or girder) under stress from its normal position **b :** the vertical distance between the points of suspension in a suspension bridge and the axis of the lowest part of the chain **4 a :** the horizontal angle between the line of sighting and the axis of the bore of a gun **b :** a setting on the scale of a gunsight such that when the line of sighting is on the aiming point the piece is correctly laid for direction **5 a :** the turning aside or bending of radiation from a straight course ⟨~ of light due to diffraction⟩ ⟨~ of an electron beam in a magnetic field⟩ — called also *deviation* **b :** the angular departure of an indicator or pointer from the zero reading on a scale ⟨~ of an ammeter⟩ **6** [*de-* + *inflection*] **:** the loss of grammatical inflections

deflection bracket *n* **:** BRACKET 5a(2)

deflection offset *n* **:** the distance by which a bomb deviates to right or left of the vertical projection of the airplane path above the ground

deflection shooting *n* **:** the aiming of one's fire in aerial gunnery beyond a moving airplane to compensate for its movement

de·flec·tive \dəˈflektiv, (ˈ)dē¦f-\ *adj* **:** tending to deflect

de·flec·tom·e·ter \də‚flekˈtäməd·ə(r), (‚)dē‚-\ *n* [*deflect* + *-o-* + *-meter*] **:** an instrument for measuring minute deformations in bodies under transverse stress — compare EXTENSOMETER 2

de·flec·tor \dəˈflektə(r), (ˈ)dē¦f-\ *n* -s **:** one that deflects; *esp* **:** a baffle (as in a furnace or ventilating system or on a conveyor) to turn to one side part or all of the forward-moving stream (as of heated air)

de·flexed \-kst\ *adj* [L *deflexus* (past part. of *deflectere* to bend downward, turn aside) + E *-ed* — more at DEFLECT] **1 :** DEFLECTED **2** *biol* **:** turned abruptly downward

de·flex·ion *chiefly Brit var of* DEFLECTION

de·floc·cu·lant *or* **de·floc·cu·lent** \(ˈ)dēˈfläkyələnt\ *n* -s [*deflocculate* + *-ant* or *-ent*] **:** an agent that causes deflocculation; *specif* **:** a chemical (as sodium carbonate) added to a clay slip to minimize settling out

de·floc·cu·late \-‚lāt\ *vt* [*de-* + *flocculate*] **:** to reduce or break up from a flocculent state **:** convert into very fine particles **:** disperse or maintain in a dispersed state — **de·floc·cu·la·tion** \(‚)dē‚fläkyəˈlāshən\ *n* -s

def·lo·rate \ˈdeflə‚rāt, dəˈflōr‚ā-, dēˈ-, -lȯ‚rā-\ *vt* -ED/-ING/-S [ME *defloraten*, fr. LL *defloratus*, past part. of *deflorare* — more at DEFLOWER] **:** DEFLOWER

def·lo·ra·tion \‚defləˈrāshən; də‚flōrˈā-, (‚)dē‚-, -lȯˈrā-\ *n* -s [ME *defloracioun*, fr. LL *defloration-, defloratio*, fr. *defloratus* (past part. of *deflorare* to deprive of virginity, to cull excerpts from) + *-ion, -io* -ion — more at DEFLOWER] **1** *archaic* **:** a gathering or culling of choice literary passages; *also* **:** the resulting collection **:** EPITOME **2** [ME *defloracioun*, fr. MF or LL; MF *defloration*, fr. LL *defloration-, defloratio*] **:** rupture of the hymen (as by sexual intercourse)

de·flo·res·cence \‚defləˈres°n(t)s, ‚dē‚flōrˈe-, ‚dē‚flȯˈre-\ *n* -s [L *deflorescere* to fade, wither (fr. *de-* + *florescere* to blossom) + E *-ence* — more at FLORESCENCE] **:** the fading or disappearance of the eruption in an exanthematous disease

de·flower \(ˈ)dē *also* də+ˈ-\ *vt* [ME *deflouren, defloren*, fr. MF or LL; MF *deflorer* fr. LL *deflorare*, fr. L *de-* + *flor-, flos* flower — more at FLOWER] **1 :** to deprive of virginity **:** VIOLATE, RAVISH **2 :** to take away the prime beauty and grace of **:** rob of the choicest ornament **:** RAVAGE, DESPOIL ⟨notion that any artist who accepts employment is ~*ed* of . . . integrity —*Advertising Age*⟩ **3** [prob. fr. *de-* + *flower*] **:** to deprive or strip of flowers ⟨an earthquake . . . ~*ing* the gardens —Walter Montagu⟩

¹**def·lu·ent** \ˈde‚flüənt, ˈdefləwənt\ *adj* [L *defluent-, defluens*, pres. part. of *defluere* to flow down, fr. *de-* + *fluere* to flow — more at FLUENT] **:** flowing down **:** DECURRENT

²**defluent** \"\ *n* -s **:** something that flows down (as from a lake or icecap)

de·fluorinate \(ˈ)dē+\ *vt* [*de-* + *fluorinate*] **:** to remove fluorine from ⟨*defluorinated* phosphate rock⟩ — **de·fluorina·tion** \(¦)dē+\ *n* -s

de·flu·vi·um \dēˈflüvēəm\ *n* -s [NL, fr. L, alopecia, lit., action of flowing down, fr. *defluere* to flow down] **:** the pathological loss of a part — used of hair, nails, or tree bark

deflux *n* -ES [L *defluxus*, past part. of *defluere*] *obs* **:** DEFLUXION

de·flux·ion \dēˈflәkshən, dēˈ-\ *n* -s [LL *defluxion-, defluxio*, fr. L *defluxus* + *-ion-, -io* -ion] **1 :** DOWNFLOW **2** *obs* **a :** a flowing down of fluid matter (as a copious discharge from the nose in catarrh) **b :** INFLAMMATION **c :** sudden loss of hair

de·foam·er \(ˈ)dēˈfōmə(r)\ *n* -s [*defoam* "to remove the foam from" (fr. *de-* + *foam*, n.) + *-er*] **:** a defoaming agent

de·foam·ing \-miŋ\ *adj* [fr. pres. part. of *defoam*] **:** destroying or preventing the formation of foam ⟨a ~ agent⟩

defoedation *var of* DEFEDATION

de·fo·li·ant \(ˈ)dēˈfōlēənt\ *n* -s [*defoliate* + *-ant*] **:** a chemical spray or dust applied to crop plants (as cotton that is to be harvested with a stripper) to cause the leaves to drop off prematurely

¹de·fo·li·ate \(ˈ)dēˈfōlēˌāt\ *vt* [LL *defoliatus*, past part. of *defoliare*, fr. L *de-* + *folium* leaf — more at BLADE] **:** to strip of leaves **:** cause the leaves of to fall esp. prematurely — **de·fo·li·a·tion** \(ˌ)dēˌfōlēˈāshən\ *n* -s

²de·fo·li·ate \(ˈ)dēˈfōlēət, -ēˌāt\ *or* **de·fo·li·at·ed** \-ēˌād·əd\ *adj* [LL *defoliatus*] **:** deprived of leaves (as by their natural fall)

de·fo·li·a·tor \-ēˌād·ə(r)\ *n* -s **:** one that defoliates: as **a :** an insect that strips plants of their leaves **b :** DEFOLIANT

de·force \(ˈ)dē +\ *vt* [ME *deforcen*, fr. AF *deforcer*, fr. OF *deforcier*, fr. *de-* + *forcier* to force — more at FORCE] **1 :** to keep by force from the rightful owner **:** withhold wrongfully (as the possession of lands or tenements) **2 :** to eject (a person) from possession by force **:** forcibly withhold possession from **:** deprive wrongfully **3** *Scots law* **:** to oppose or resist (an officer) forcibly so as to prevent execution of the law — **de·force·ment** \-smənt\ *n* -s

de·force·or \-sə(r)\ *n* -s [AF *deforceor*, fr. *deforcer* + *-eor* -or] **:** one that deforces

de·for·ciant \dēˈfōrshənt, -fȯr-\ *n* -s [AF, fr. pres. part. of *deforcer*] *English law* **:** one who deforces the rightful owner of an estate

de·forest \(ˈ)dē +\ *vt* [*de-* + *forest* (n.)] **:** to clear of forests **:** remove trees from — **de·forestation** \(ˌ)dē +\ *n* -s — **de·forester** \(ˈ)dē + \ *n* -s

¹de·form \dəˈfȯ(ə)rm, dē-, -ȯ(ə)m\ *adj* [ME *defourme*, fr. L *deformis*, fr. *de-* + *-formis* (fr. *forma* shape, form) — more at FORM] *archaic* **:** DEFORMED, MISSHAPEN, SHAPELESS, HIDEOUS

²deform \"\ *vb* -ED/-ING/-S [ME *deformen*, fr. MF or L; MF *deformer*, fr. L *deformare*, fr. *de-* + *formare* to shape, form — more at FORM] *vt* **1 :** to spoil the form or shape of **:** MISSHAPE, DISTORT ⟨~ the groove walls of a phonograph record⟩ **2 :** to spoil the looks of **:** DISFIGURE, DEFACE ⟨a face ~*ed* by hatred and bitterness⟩ **:** mar the excellence or perfection of ⟨the minor characters are . . . ~*ed* by conditions beyond their power to change —Malcolm Cowley⟩ **:** make offensive ⟨~*ed* by marriage, irritable, acerb —George Meredith⟩ **3 :** to alter the form or shape of: **a** *obs* **:** to unsettle the order of (as ranks of battle) **b :** to change the shape of (a body) by the action of forces **c :** to fold, fracture, compress, or otherwise change the shape or attitude of (rocks) by stresses developed within the earth ~ *vi* **:** to become deformed **:** change in shape ⟨certain metals will ~ permanently without breaking⟩

syn DISTORT, CONTORT, WARP, GNARL: DEFORM, the least specific of this group, applies to any marring or spoiling esp. resulting in disfigurement or loss of some particular good or normal quality or attribute ⟨basaltic and granitic rocks are seen *deformed* side by side in deeply eroded parts of the earth's surface —W.H.Bucher⟩ ⟨he was really hideous, positively *deformed* with malice —Christopher Isherwood⟩ ⟨a dread that it should cramp and *deform* the free operations of his own mind —T.S.Eliot⟩ DISTORT strongly implies a twisting or wrenching away from or out of the natural, regular, or true or, in application to intangibles, an imbalance or lack of reasonable proportion ⟨under such a light the features of the subject are sometimes *distorted*, as in a passport photograph —Hallett Smith⟩ ⟨news was *distorted* in his favor —S.H.Adams⟩ ⟨*distorting* facts to suit theories —R.A.Hall b.1911⟩ CONTORT implies a more involved or intense twisting together or upon itself, suggesting a grotesque or painful result ⟨the boy whose face was *contorted* with fury and frustration —Jean Stafford⟩ ⟨*contorted* thickets of lodgepole pine —*Amer. Guide Series: Oregon*⟩ ⟨their shadows *contorted* themselves grotesquely —Israel Zangwill⟩ WARP is literally a twisting or bending out of a flat plane and figuratively a twisting or wrenching that gives bias, false significance, or abnormal direction ⟨boards *warped* by exposure to the sun and rain⟩ ⟨their lives and minds have been *warped*, twisted and soured —John Lardner⟩ ⟨it degrades the individual and *warps* the nation's moral fabric⟩ GNARL implies, in literal use, the twistings and contortions, knots and protuberances of the roots or branches of an old tree; in extended use it suggests a condition similar to this as in the hands or limbs of the very old, the arthritic, or those who have long done heavy physical work, especially exposed to all weathers ⟨in the old orchard the trees are *gnarled* and broken —Corey Ford⟩ ⟨he was slight, dark, *gnarled*, with a face on him like a knotty piece of old mahogany —Alan Villiers⟩ ⟨the battlefields, *gnarled* by trenches, barbed-wire entanglements, shell holes —H.S.Commager⟩

de·for·ma·tion \ˌdēˌfȯ(r)ˈmāshən, ˌdefə(r)-\ *n* -s [ME *deformacioun*, fr. MF or L; MF *deformation*, fr. L *deformation-, deformatio*, fr. *deformatus* (past part. of *deformare* to deform) + *-ion-, -io* -ion — more at DEFORM] **1 :** the action of deforming or state of being deformed **2 :** change for the worse — opposed in theological use to reformation **3 a :** the process whereby rocks are folded, faulted, sheared, or compressed by earth stresses (as in the growth of mountain ranges) — see DIASTROPHISM **b :** the result of the process **4 :** change in either shape or size of a material body or of a geometrical figure — compare STRAIN 1d

de·for·ma·tion·al \ˌ;=(ˌ)=ˈmāshənᵊl, -shnəl\ *adj* **:** relating to or causing deformation

deformation band *n* **:** a band within an individual cold-worked metal crystal that differs variably from the matrix in orientation

de·for·ma·tive \dəˈfȯ(r)məd·iv, dē-\ *adj* [*deformation* + *-ive*] **:** tending to deform

deformed *adj* [ME, fr. past part. of *deformen* to deform] **1** *obs* **a :** DISFIGURED **b :** FORMLESS, AMORPHOUS **2 a :** distorted or unshapely in form **:** misshapen esp. in body or limbs **:** MONSTROUS, LOATHSOME ⟨a ~ imagination⟩ **b :** subjected to deformation — **de·formed·ly** \-m(ə)dlē\ *adv* — **de·formed·ness** \-mədnəs, -m(d)n-\ *n* -ES

deformed bar *n* **:** a steel bar with surface projections that increase its bond strength when used in reinforced concrete

de·for·me·ter \-ˈfȯ(r)ˌmēd·ə(r)\ *n* [blend of *deformation* and *-meter*] **:** an instrument for measuring small deformations (as of structural materials)

de·for·mi·ty \dəˈfȯ(r)məd·ē, dē-, -ətē, -i\ *n* -ES [ME *deformite*, fr. MF *deformité*, fr. L *deformitat-, deformitas*, fr. *deformis* deformed + *-tat-, -tas* -ty — more at DEFORM] **1 :** the state of being deformed **2 :** a conspicuous departure from regularity in shape or appearance **:** DISFIGUREMENT ⟨acne . . . so pronounced as to amount to positive ~ —H.G.Armstrong⟩ **:** a physical blemish or distortion **:** MALFORMATION ⟨the dwarf's humpbacked ~⟩ **3 a :** the state or result of having deviated from what is accepted as right, proper, or beautiful esp. in art or in moral behavior **:** UGLINESS, DEPRAVITY ⟨all the perversities and *deformities* of humanity —Dudley Fitts⟩ **b :** FLAW, IMPROPRIETY, CORRUPTION ⟨if he attempted decoration, seldom produced anything by ~ —T.B.Macaulay⟩ **4 :** a deformed person or thing ⟨hardly men, mere walking *deformities*⟩

¹de·fraud \dəˈfrȯd, dē-\ *vb* -ED/-ING/-S [ME *defrauden*, fr. MF *defrauder*, fr. L *defraudare*, fr. *de* + *fraudare* to cheat, fr. *fraud-, fraus* fraud, deceit — more at FRAUD] *vt* **:** to take or withhold from (one) some possession, right, or interest by calculated misstatement or perversion of truth, trickery, or other deception ⟨~ the heirs of the bequests⟩ ⟨citizens ~*ed* of their voting rights⟩ ~ *vi* **:** to engage in fraud **syn** see CHEAT

²defraud \"\ *n* -s [ME, fr. *defrauden*, v.] *archaic* **:** DEFRAUDATION

de·frau·da·tion \(ˌ)dēˌfrȯˈdāshən, dəˌ-\ *n* -s [MF, fr. LL *defraudation-, defraudatio*, fr. L *defraudatus* (past part. of *defraudare* to defraud) + *-ion-, -io* -ion] **:** the act of defrauding **:** a taking by fraud or deceit

de·fraud·ment \dəˈfrȯdmənt, dē-\ *n* -s **:** DEFRAUDATION

de·fray \dəˈfrā, dē-\ *vt* -ED/-ING/-S [MF *deffrayer, desfrayer*, fr. *des-* de- + *frayer* to expend, fr. OF, fr. (assumed) OF *frai* expenditure (whence OF *fres*, pl., expenditures), lit., damage caused by breaking something, fr. L *fractum*, neut. of *fractus*, past part. of *frangere* to break — more at BREAK] **1** *obs* **a :** to expend (money) **:** DISBURSE **b :** to avert or appease (as anger, vengeance) by paying off **:** REQUITE, SATISFY **2 :** to pay or to provide for the payment of in money or its equivalent ⟨~ the expenses of a trip⟩ **3** *archaic* **a :** to meet the charges for or expense of **b :** to bear the expenses of (a person) **:** entertain without charge **:** REIMBURSE

de·fray·al \-ā(ə)l\ *n* -s **:** the act of defraying **:** PAYMENT

de·fray·ment \-āmənt\ *n* -s [MF *deffrayement*, fr. *deffrayer* + *-ment*] **:** DEFRAYAL

de·frock \(ˈ)dēˈfräk\ *vt* [*de-* + *frock* (n.)] **:** UNFROCK

de·frost \(ˈ)dē + ;-, də + ˈ-\ *vb* -ED/-ING/-S [*de-* + *frost* (n.)] *vt* **1 :** to thaw out or release from a frozen state ⟨~*ed* the meat for supper⟩ ⟨~*ed* some projects they had been holding in reserve⟩ **2 :** to free or keep free (as a refrigerating unit, a windshield) from ice ~ *vi* **:** to thaw out esp. from a deep-frozen state ⟨heavily sugared foods are the first to ~⟩

de·frost·er \-tə(r)\ *n* -s **:** one that defrosts; *esp* **:** a device for freeing a windshield from frost or ice

deft \ˈdeft\ *adj* -ER/-EST [ME *defte* — more at DAFT] **1 :** characterized by light neat facility and sure quick skill in handling or execution ⟨a ~ waiter⟩ ⟨the ~ handling of suspense —T.S. Eliot⟩ **2** *dial Eng* **:** NEAT, SPRUCE, TRIM **syn** see DEXTEROUS

deft *abbr* defendant

def·ter·dar \ˌdeftərˈdär\ *n* -s [Turk, fr. Per *daftardār* finance officer — more at DAFTARDAR] **:** a Turkish government officer of finance; *specif* **:** the accountant general of a province

deft·ly \ˈdeftlē, -li\ *adv* [ME *defly*, fr. *defte* deft + *-ly*] **:** in a deft manner **:** SKILLFULLY, DEXTEROUSLY, NEATLY

deft·ness \-f(t)nəs\ *n* -ES **:** the quality of being deft **:** DEXTERITY, NEATNESS, QUICKNESS

¹de·funct \dəˈfəŋ(k)t, dēˈ-\ *vi* -s [L *defunctus*, past part. of *defungi* to acquit oneself, die, fr. *de-* + *fungi* to perform, discharge — more at FUNCTION] **:** a dead person — usu. used with *the*

²defunct \dəˈfəŋ(k)t, (ˈ)dē¦f-\ *adj* [L *defunctus*] **:** having finished the course of life or existence **:** DEAD, DECEASED, EXTINCT ⟨a ~ aunt's will⟩ ⟨a ~ journal⟩ ⟨~ economic theory⟩

de·func·tion \dəˈfəŋ(k)shən, dē-\ *n* -s [LL *defunction-, defunctio*, fr. L *defunctus*] **:** DEATH, DECEASE

de·functionalize \(ˈ)dē +\ *vt* [*de-* + *functional* + *-ize*] **:** to deprive of function

de·func·tive \dəˈfəŋ(k)tiv, dē-\ *adj* [L *defunctus* + E *-ive*] **:** FUNEREAL

¹defuse *obs var of* DIFFUSE

²de·fuse *also* **de·fuze** \(ˈ)dē +\ *vt* [*dē* + *fuse, fuze* (n.)] **:** to remove the fuse from (as a mine or bomb)

de·fusion \"+\ *n* [*de-* + *fusion*] **:** a reversal of the fusion between instincts that accompanies maturity

¹de·fy \dəˈfī, dē-\ *vt* -ED/-ING/-ES [ME *defyen*, fr. OF *desfier, defier*, fr. *des-, de-* de- + *fier* to entrust, confide, fr. (assumed) VL *fidare*, alter. of L *fidere* to trust — more at BIDE] **1** *archaic* **a :** to renounce all bonds of faith or obligation with **:** REJECT, REPUDIATE **b :** to declare war against **:** challenge to combat **c :** DESPISE, DISDAIN **2 :** to seek to provoke or goad (a person, agency, or power) into trying to perform, do, or achieve something typically with mocking certainty that the attempt will fail ⟨I ~ him to find the Gate, however well he may think he knows the City —Rudyard Kipling⟩ **3 :** to confront (a person, agency, force) with or as if with a superior resisting force felt as certain to prevail, vanquish, or baffle **:** withstand or contravene (as treatment or influence) with assured power of resistance ⟨the tall erect figure, ~*ing* age, and the perfectly bald scalp ~*ing* the weather —Upton Sinclair⟩ ⟨every great novel has broken many conventions. The greatest of all novels *defies* every formula —Ellen Glasgow⟩ **syn** see FACE

²defy \", ˈdē,fī\ *n* -ES [MF *defi, desfi*, fr. *defier, desfier* to defy, fr. OF] **:** CHALLENGE, DEFIANCE ⟨observers took this to be a form of ~ —Jack Alexander⟩

de·fy·ing·ly *adv* **:** in a defying manner **:** with defiance **:** DEFIANTLY

deg \ˈdeg\ *vt* **degged; degged; degging; degs** [perh. of Scand origin; akin to ON *döggva* to bedew, *dagg-, dögg* dew — more at DEW] *dial Eng* **:** to sprinkle **:** DAMPEN

deg *abbr* degree

dé·ga·gé \ˌdāˌgäˈzhā, -gȧ-\ *adj* [F, fr. past part. of *dégager* to redeem a pledge, disengage, free from, fr. OF *desgagier*, fr. *des-* de- + *gage* pledge, security — more at GAGE] **1 :** free of mental engagement and constraint of manner **:** carefree and indifferent to decorum **:** EASYGOING ⟨I adopted a ~ pose on the arm of a Morris chair —S.J.Perelman⟩ ⟨rather ~ after the nervousness he had shown at dinner —Edmund Wilson⟩ **2 :** marked by a free and easy show of unconcern for strict conventions ⟨the famous slouch hat with the nonchalant ~ air —A.J.Liebling⟩ ⟨a model of crushed pink velvet dipped low over one eye and soaring in a ~ movement on the opposite side —*Hats*⟩ **3** *of the leg* **:** extended with toe pointed in preparation for a ballet step

degame *var of* DAGAME

de·gas \(ˈ)dē +\ *vt* [*de-* + *gas* (n.)] **:** to free from gas **:** remove gas from ⟨~ an electronic tube⟩

de·gasification \(ˈ)dē + \ *n* -s **:** the process of degasifying

de·gasify \(ˈ)dē + ˈ-\ *vt* [*de-* + *gasify*] **:** DEGAS

de gaull·ism \dəˈgōˌlizəm, dē-, -gō,-\ *n, usu cap G* [F *de Gaullisme*, fr. Charles *de Gaulle* b1890 Fr. general & president + F *-isme* -ism] **:** GAULLISM

de gaull·ist \-ˌləst\ *n, usu cap G* [F *de Gaulliste*, fr. C. *de Gaulle* + F *-iste* -ist] **:** GAULLIST

de·gauss \(ˈ)dē +\ *vt* -ED/-ING/-ES [*de-* + *gauss*] **:** to make (a steel ship) effectively nonmagnetic by means of electrical coils carrying currents that neutralize the magnetism of the ship itself and thereby prevent the detonating of magnetic mines — compare DEPERM

de·gen·er·a·cy \dəˈjen(ə)rəsē, dē-, -si\ *n* -ES [*degenerate* + *-cy*] **1 a :** the state of being degenerate **:** DEGRADATION, DEBASEMENT ⟨centuries of ~ and transition —H.O.Taylor⟩ ⟨would it have committed suicide in an isolated act of intellectual and moral ~ —H.J.Morgenthau⟩ **b :** a state or instance of deteriorated or disintegrated energy or control ⟨simplifications and even *degeneracies* —J.A.Thomson⟩ **2 :** the process of becoming degenerate **:** a decline to inferior standards of behavior, morality, culture, or art ⟨our progress in ~ appears to me to be pretty rapid —Abraham Lincoln⟩ ⟨moral ~ followed intellectual degeneration⟩ ⟨how can we prevent the ~ of man in modern civilization —Alexis Carrel⟩ **3 :** sexual perversion

¹de·gen·er·ate \-n(ə)rət, *usu* -əd· + V\ *adj* [ME *degenerat*, fr. L *degeneratus*, past part. of *degenerare* to degenerate, fr. *de-* + *gener-, genus* race, kind — more at KIN] **1 :** having sunk to a lower class or standard or to a state below that normal to a type or to a thing: **a** (1) **:** having declined markedly (as in vigor and stability or in racial or cultural character) from one's ancestors, predecessors, or one's former self ⟨just as the last ~ member of a noble family may be unattractive and uninspiring —W.E.Swinton⟩ (2) **:** losing distinctive racial culture **:** RETROGRADE ⟨the Mayas were ~ but they were stubborn —*Time*⟩ **b :** having deteriorated from a former level **:** DEVITALIZED, CORRUPTED ⟨Savonarola's ecclesiastical superior officer . . . was a monster of perfidy and immorality; and a despairing and ~ world had sunk into servitude beneath him —W.L.Sullivan⟩ ⟨the modern and ~ society, which had rejected the governance of religion —J.C.Ransom⟩ **c :** degraded or debased by loss of moral stability, aesthetic concord, or political integrity ⟨the studies of notorious ~ families prove nothing very significant about the inheritance of degeneracy —R.M.Lindner⟩ ⟨preferred to prop up an effete and ~ dynasty rather than face a vigorous reformed China —G.F.Hudson⟩ ⟨the profession of painting . . . has esthetically, morally, and in certain quarters even politically become a thoroughly ~ one —Huntington Hartford⟩ **d :** having deteriorated progressively (as in the process of evolution) esp. through loss of structure or function — compare DEGENERATION 3b **2 :** characterized by lowered standards ⟨the great wrought nails binding the clapboards are unknown in these ~ days —Herman Melville⟩ **3 :** breaking up into a product of factors of lower degree — used of an algebraic curve or surface **4** *of a gas* **:** characterized by having atoms stripped of most if not all of their electrons as the result of extremely high pressure and temperature in the interior of a very dense star (as a white dwarf) and by being compressed to a density as high as a million times that of water so that the ordinary laws of a perfect gas do not apply **syn** see VICIOUS

²de·gen·er·ate \-nəˌrāt, *usu* -ād· + V\ *vb* -ED/-ING/-S [L *degeneratus*] *vi* **1** *obs* **a :** to show a decline from ancestral or earlier character and quality **b :** to show variation from normal type **2 :** to pass from a higher to a lower type or condition: **a :** to descend to a markedly worse condition in kind or degree **:** worsen conspicuously ⟨the road . . . *degenerated* to little more than a goat track —Michael Swan⟩ ⟨its fine houses one by one *degenerating* into rooming houses —Marcia Davenport⟩ ⟨her fixed mysterious smile *degenerated* into a fatuous stare —J.C.Powys⟩ **b :** to become unstable and sink to some discreditable, despicable, or disastrous state ⟨unfortunately, in practice, rotation in office *degenerated* into the spoils system —E.M.Eriksson⟩ ⟨debate was *degenerating* into partisan squabbling⟩ ⟨lest this international crisis ~ into world war⟩ **c :** to decline to an unworthy secondary status through impairment of essential quality or integrity ⟨the phrase which they have reiterated ad nauseam has *degenerated* into a ponderous platitude —W.F.Hambly⟩ ⟨has not lost its dignity or *degenerated* into mere prettiness —O. Elfrida Saunders⟩ ⟨religion is tending to ~ into a decent formula wherewith to embellish a comfortable life —A.N.Whitehead⟩ **3 :** to decline intellectually or morally or from one's peculiar character or former standards usu. to a shameful or despicable level ⟨mentally and physically the Indians *degenerated* with the taking on of the white men's vices —*Amer. Guide Series: Mass.*⟩ ⟨of heroic stature but ultimately *degenerating* into a typical medieval dictator —R.A.Hall b.1911⟩ **4 :** to decline from a former thriving state or from standards proper to a species or race **:** RETROGRADE ⟨dinosaurs *degenerated* and disappeared⟩ ⟨mallards are prone anyway to ~ into the barnyard type —W.L.McAtee⟩ ⟨all through the evolution of life many forms have *degenerated*, losing their relative autonomy and becoming dependent parasites upon other creatures —Curt Stern⟩ **5 :** to decline in literary, aesthetic, or artistic quality and become altered to a debased substitute or poor imitation ⟨denunciation of the rampant charlatanism into which the surrealist movement has apparently *degenerated* —Bernard Smith⟩ ⟨their metaphor ~*s* into a series of isolated and barren conceits —C.D.Lewis⟩ **6** *biol* **:** to undergo progressive deterioration **:** become of a lower type — see DEGENERATION 3 ~ *vt* **:** to cause to degenerate ⟨the Etruscans were receptive to new ideas and applied them with energy, usually only to ~ them in the end —A.L.Kroeber⟩

³de·gen·er·ate *like* ¹DEGENERATE\ *n* -s [¹*degenerate*] **:** a person declining conspicuously from the normal character or the standard set by his kind in the normal course of development: as **a :** one who is degraded from the normal moral standard ⟨they had rotted in the last two centuries into mere drunkards and dandy ~*s* —G.K.Chesterton⟩ ⟨~*s* are usually about the same type as psychopathics, namely, individuals who intellectually and especially affectively react differently from the average —A.A.Brill⟩ **b :** one who is debased by a psychopathic tendency ⟨he has an urge to kill and destroy women . . . he may be considered a sexual psychopath and ~ —Fred Galvin⟩ **c :** a sexual pervert — not used technically **d :** one showing signs of reversion to an earlier culture stage ⟨it is possible that some of these are cultural ~*s*; most ethnologists, however, prefer to regard the majority as culturally retarded —R.W.Murray⟩

de·gen·er·ate·ly \-ətlē, -li\ *adv* **:** in a degenerate manner

de·gen·er·ate·ness \-ətnəs\ *n* -ES **:** DEGENERACY

de·gen·er·a·tion \dəˌjenəˈrāshən, (ˌ)dē-\ *n* [F or LL; F *dégénération*, fr. LL *degeneration-, degeneratio*, fr. L *degeneratus* + *-ion-, -io* -ion] **1 :** the process of passing from a higher to a lower type: **a :** a lowering of effective power, vitality, or essential quality to an enfeebled and worsened kind or state ⟨that ~ and enhancement were processes that went on side by side in the stream of oral transmission —Douglas Kennedy⟩ ⟨of all the dangers that confront a nation at war this ~ of national purpose . . . is the greatest —*New Republic*⟩ **b :** a sinking to a despicable issue or disintegration ⟨aimed to prevent ~ of interservice rivalries into open hostility⟩ **c :** modification to a lower or inferior cultural stage ⟨the dance as a spectacle is generally regarded as a product of ~, a secularized form of what is really a religious art —Susanne K. Langer⟩ ⟨thus by a process of ~ the original religious insight of primitive man was overpowered and contaminated by demonistic and polytheistic beliefs—David Bidney⟩ **2 a :** intellectual or moral decline tending toward dissolution of character or integrity **:** a progressive worsening of personal adjustment ⟨that Zola's best novels are studies in ~ and failure —C.C.Walcutt⟩ **b :** degenerate condition **:** DEGENERACY ⟨theories explaining artistic genius as rooted in ~⟩ **3 a :** progressive deterioration of physical characters from a level representing the norm of earlier generations or forms ⟨suggests that the small features of the modern Bushman may have resulted from a long process of physical ~ —R.W. Murray⟩ **:** secondary simplification of a part or organism in the course of generations often to the extent of loss of function or complete disappearance of constituent structures ⟨vestigial organs may be interpreted as the product of ~ following alteration of habits⟩ **:** regression of the morphology of a group or kind of organism toward a simpler less highly organized state ⟨the scouring rushes have undergone ~ from treelike Mesozoic ancestors⟩ ⟨parasitisms leads to ~⟩ **b :** deterioration of a tissue or an organ in which its vitality is diminished or its structure impaired; *esp* **:** deterioration in which specialized cells are replaced by less specialized cells (as in fibrosis or in malignancies) or in which cells are functionally impaired (as by deposition of abnormal matter in the tissue) — compare INFILTRATION **4 :** marked decline in excellence of workmanship, originality, technical skill, or decorative quality ⟨~ of human figures used in Polynesian decorative art —*Jour. of the Polynesian Soc.*⟩ **5 :** the process by which part of the power in the output circuit in an amplifying device is caused to act upon the input circuit so as to restrict the amplification, improve linearity, and reduce distortion **:** NEGATIVE FEEDBACK — compare REGENERATION

degeneration disease *n* **:** a virus disease of plants causing a progressive deterioration

de·gen·er·a·tive \dəˈjenəˌrād·iv, dē-, -n(ə)rəl, ¦tiv, -ēv\ *adj* **1 :** undergoing degeneration **:** tending to degenerate ⟨~ conditions of the nervous system —Morris Fishbein⟩ **2 :** having the character of or involving degeneration ⟨the ~ changes which occur in the blood vessels, such as a hardening of the arteries —Lionel Whitby⟩ **3 :** causing or tending to cause degeneration ⟨the continual brutality around me was ~ in its effect —Jack London⟩

degenerative arthritis *n* **:** arthritis of middle age characterized by degenerative and sometimes hypertrophic changes in the bone and cartilage of one or more joints and a progressive wearing down of apposing joint surfaces with consequent distortion of joint position usu. without bony stiffening — compare RHEUMATOID ARTHRITIS

degenerative disease *n* **:** a disease characterized by progressive degenerative changes in tissue (as arteriosclerosis, diabetes mellitus, or hypertrophic arthritis)

de·gen·er·es·cence \dəˌjenəˈresᵊn(t)s, (ˌ)dē,-\ *n* -s [F *dégénérescence*, fr. *dégénérer* to degenerate (fr. L *degenerare*) + *-escence* — more at DEGENERATE] **:** the process of becoming degenerate

degenerous *adj* [L *degener* degenerate (prob. back-formation fr. *degenerare* to degenerate) + E *-ous*] *obs* **:** DEGENERATE

de·germ \(ˈ)dē +\ *vt* -ED/-ING/-S [*de-* + *germ* (n.)] **1 :** to remove germs from (as the skin) **2 :** to remove the germ from (a seed) ⟨~*ed* wheat products⟩

de·ger·ma·tion \ˌdēˌjərˈmāshən\ *n* -s **:** the action or result of degerming the skin

de·germinate \(ˈ)dē + ˈ-\ *vt* [*de-* + *germinate*] **:** DEGERM 2

de·ger·mi·na·tor \(ˈ)dēˈjərməˌnād·ər\ *n* **:** a machine for breaking the kernels of grain or cacao beans and removing the germ

degged *past of* DEG

degging *pres part of* DEG

de·glaciation \(ˌ)dē +\ *n* **:** the inclusive process whereby a glacier or ice sheet shrinks to disappearance; *also* **:** the result of this process

de·glamorization \(¦)dē+\ *n* -s **:** the action of deglamorizing
de·glamorize \(')dē+\ *vt* [*de-* + *glamorize*] **:** to remove the glamor from; *esp* **:** to treat in a way to counteract an accustomed glorification or charm
de·glaze \(')dē+\ *vt* [*de-* + *glaze* (n.)] **:** to remove the glaze from (as pottery or porcelain) so as to give a dull finish — compare DEPOLISH
de·glorify \(')dē + '-\ *vt* [*de-* + *glorify*] **:** to deprive of accustomed glorification
de·glutinate \(')dē + '-\ *vt* [L *deglutinatus*, past part. of *deglutinare*, fr. *de-* + *glutinare* to glue, fr. *glutin-*, *gluten* glue; akin to L *glut-*, *glus* glue — more at CLAY] **1 :** UNGLUE **2** [influenced in meaning by NL *gluten* (substance in flour)] **:** to extract or remove gluten from (as wheat flour) — **de·glutination** \(¦)dē +\ *n*
de·glu·ti·tion \ˌdē,glü'tishən, ˌde,g-\ *n* -s [F *déglutition*, fr. MF *deglutition*, fr. L *deglutitus*, *degluttitus* (past part. of *deglutire*, *degluttire* to swallow down, fr. *de-* + *glutire*, *gluttire* to swallow) + MF *-ion* — more at GLUTTON] **:** the act or process of swallowing (as food) **:** the power of swallowing — **de·glu·ti·tious** \¦==¦=shəs\ *adj*
de·glu·ti·to·ry \də'glüd·əˌtōrē\ *adj* [*deglutition* + *-ory*] **:** serving for or aiding in deglutition
deg·ra·da·tion \ˌdegrə'dāshən\ *n* -s [MF or LL; MF, fr. LL *degradation-*, *degradatio*, fr. *degradatus* (past part. of *degradare* to degrade) + L *-ion-*, *-io* -ion — more at DEGRADE] **1 a :** a canonical punishment in the Roman Catholic Church by which a clergyman is perpetually deprived of all office, titles, benefices, and ecclesiastical rights and privileges **b :** a censure of a Church of England clergyman involving deprivation of office and usu. the exercise of holy orders **c :** reduction to a lower rank, position, or level ⟨stripped of his insignia of rank in an act of public ~ —*United Press*⟩ **d :** demotion or deposition from office ⟨venality eventually brought about the official's ~⟩ **e** *obs* **:** demotion by one or more steps on a college list of precedence imposed as a punishment **f :** lowering or descent in standing, worth, or serviceability ⟨the ~ of reasonable sympathy into sentimentalism —W.R.Inge⟩ ⟨indicative of the early twentieth century's mischievous ~ of the elevated and elevation of the degraded —H.F.Mooney⟩ ⟨two great and not easily reversible evils follow: a conformity-minded speech community . . . and a ~ of the language —I.A.Richards⟩ **2 a :** decline to an inferior state of shamed or shameful distortion, neglect, repudiation, or dissolution **:** abandonment to defeat or corruption ⟨even translation to the screen is not always, as such, a ~ —E.R.Bentley⟩ ⟨the primal emotions of victory and defeat, exaltation and ~ —Allan Nevins⟩ **b :** a despised state of coarsening destitution, inhumane suppression, or demoralized dejection ⟨two centuries of ~ hardly left the freedmen in a position to take up the responsibilities of citizenship —Oscar Handlin⟩ ⟨shocked by the hopeless ~ of the "poor whites" —Edith Wharton⟩ ⟨the last household where I could have found the reckless Ireland of a hundred years ago in final ~ —W.B.Yeats⟩ **3 :** moral or intellectual decadence **:** reduction to ignominy or defilement ⟨three attempts to escape and subsequent punishment educated him in the bestiality and ~ that war brings —Drew Middleton⟩ ⟨the historical principle of cultural development and cultural progress from savagery to civilization as against any theory of cultural retrogression or ~ —David Bidney⟩ ⟨the ~ of art and religion to menial and mountebank offices —Clive Bell⟩ **4** [F *dégradation*, fr. It *digradazione*, fr. LL *degradation-*, *degradatio*] **:** the lessening in size or diminishing in light or color of objects in a drawing or painting to give perspective **5 :** impairment in respect to some physical property: **a :** damage by weakening or loss of some property, quality, or capability ⟨present synthetic rubber tires when used for this purpose are susceptible to a heat buildup that leads to excessive ~ —Roger Adams⟩ **b :** degeneration or arrest of development of any organ or of the body as a whole **c :** transformation into simpler substances or waste **d :** reduction to small lumps or particles ⟨because the ore is loaded only once, ~ is minimized —*Newsweek*⟩ **e :** the weakening of a fabric that brings about a tendency to disintegrate ⟨sodium hydroxide of 10 percent concentration at 85°C for 16 hours caused no apparent ~ of nylon —W.E.Shinn⟩ **f :** change of a soil to a type that is more highly leached or that has sodium replaced by hydrogen **6 :** change of a chemical compound to a less complex compound **7 :** a wearing down by erosion ⟨modifications of the course of the river caused by gradual accretion on the one bank or ~ on the other bank —E.D.Dickinson⟩ — compare AGGRADATION
deg·ra·da·tion·al \¦==¦dāshənᵊl, -shnəl\ *adj* **:** produced by, showing, or relating to degradation from a more to a less complex form or stage ⟨the weathering processes commonly are followed but not always immediately by ~ processes —V.C. Finch & G.T.Trewartha⟩
degradation of energy *physics* **:** the process by which energy becomes less available for doing work — compare CONSERVATION OF ENERGY, DISSIPATION OF ENERGY
deg·ra·da·tive \'degrəˌdād·iv\ *adj* [*degradation* + *-ive*] **:** tending to degradation; *also* **:** DEGRADATIONAL
¹de·grade \də'grād, dē'-; *in senses definable "to make or become lower in grade"*, " *or* 'dē¦g-\ *vb* [ME *degraden*, fr. MF *degrader*, *desgrader*, fr. LL *degradare*, fr. L *de-* + *gradus* step, pace — more at GRADE] *vt* **1 :** to lower in rank, grade, or status: **a :** to reduce from a higher to a lower rank or from a position of dignity or privilege **:** DEMOTE, DEPOSE ⟨the world is weary of statesmen whom democracy has *degraded* into politicians —Benjamin Disraeli⟩ **b :** to strip of rank or honors; *specif* **:** to deprive (a priest) of office, privileges and in the Roman Catholic Church of all that outwardly betokens priesthood **c :** to lower from a superior to an inferior level **:** deprive of standing, efficacy, true function, or exalted status **:** PERVERT ⟨the writer who ~*s* the press to a mere means of material livelihood —J.T.Farrell⟩ ⟨they will claim that the biosystematists are attempting to ~ and wreck the classical concept of the genus —W.H.Camp⟩ ⟨like the grandees of the Classical Renaissance they *degraded* art, which is a religion, to upholstery, a menial trade —Clive Bell⟩ **d :** to lower in grade **:** scale or step down or reduce (as a commercial product) in desirability or salability ⟨because of the exposed area and the formation of callus tissue on its edges it seriously ~*s* logs —*Ecology*⟩ ⟨good honey can easily be *degraded* in quality by unskilled handling and careless presentation —*Brit. Book News*⟩ ⟨turkeys not in prime condition are *degraded*⟩ **2 :** to bring to low esteem or disrepute **:** expose to shame, humiliation, or contempt ⟨he had *degraded* his office by shameless extortion —John Buchan⟩ ⟨a compelled confession demoralizes the confessor and ~*s* the confessed —*Saturday Rev.*⟩ ⟨eagerness of millions of voters to respond to an appeal that does not ~ them or pander to their worst instincts —Elmer Rice⟩ **3 :** to bring low or drag down in moral or intellectual character **:** reduce to dishonor, ignominy, depravity, or moral degeneracy **:** DEBASE, CORRUPT ⟨the Indians who consume peyote buttons do not seem to be physically or morally *degraded* by the habit —Aldous Huxley⟩ ⟨by the end of the 19th century love of country was being unusually *degraded* into contempt for foreigners —Herbert Agar⟩ ⟨an age of compromise, or moral skepticism, and of practiced art in *degrading* the highest of all values into the service of the lowest of all compliances —W.L.Sullivan⟩ **4 :** to lower or impair in respect to some physical property: **a :** to damage by weakening or removing some requisite property ⟨it is recognized that rubber is *degraded* to some extent by contact with copper —D.W. Gay⟩ **b :** to diminish (some pertinent quality or capability) with deteriorating effect ⟨they will, if they obey the physical law, hold that society does work by *degrading* its energies —Henry Adams⟩ **c :** to reduce the definition of (a photographic or projected picture) ⟨in an air photographic system haze and air turbulence ~ the image⟩ **d :** to break up (as coal or ore) into small lumps or into dust **e :** to reduce the strength of (a fabric or textile fiber) giving a tendency to deteriorate or disintegrate ⟨exposure to sunlight ~*s* nylon yarn⟩ **5 :** to wear or scour by erosion ⟨a stream in flood *degrading* its channel⟩ ⟨the surrounding country . . . which has been *degraded* by the processes of denudation —Walter Fitzgerald⟩ **6 :** to reduce the complexity of (a chemical compound) by splitting off one or more groups or larger component parts **:** DECOMPOSE, DEPOLYMERIZE ⟨~ hexose sugars to pentoses⟩ ⟨cellulose is *degraded* by the action of some bacteria⟩ ~ *vi* **1 :** to pass from a higher grade or class to a lower ⟨areas of the forest have *degraded* into scrub⟩ **2 :** to postpone entering the examination for a degree in honors at Cambridge University beyond the usual or required time **3** *biol* **:** DEGENERATE **4** *of a chemical compound* **:** to undergo degradation
²de·grade \'dē,grād\ *n* **:** lumber or a log found to be below grade in quality; *also* **:** a reduction in grade
¹de·grad·ed *pronunc at* ¹DEGRADE + əd\ *adj* [ME, fr. past part. of *degraden*] **1 :** reduced far below ordinary standards of civilized life and conduct: **a :** marked by poverty, helplessness, and apathy ⟨dirty, wild, and ~ as only the worst slaves of antiquity had been —Lewis Mumford⟩ **b :** marked by indulgence in vice or debauchery **:** DEBASED ⟨he so deplorably dissipated and ~, and they so bloomy and idyllic —E.V.Lucas⟩ **c :** fallen far below genuine quality **:** CONTAMINATED, DISTORTED, VULGARIZED ⟨the writer . . . who suffers from what he is bound to consider the ~ and irresponsible taste of his time —*New Yorker*⟩ **2 :** characterized by degeneration of structure or function **3** *of a color* **:** not saturated to the practical maximum — **de·grad·ed·ly** *adv* — **de·grad·ed·ness** *n* -ES
²degraded \"\ *adj* [*de-* + L *gradus* + E *-ed*] *heraldry* **:** standing on steps — used of a cross; compare DEGREE 1b
de·grade·ment \-ādmənt\ *n* -s [obs. F *dégradement*, fr. *dégrader* to degrade + *-ment*] *archaic* **:** DEGRADATION
de·grad·er \-ādə(r)\ *n* -s **:** one that degrades
degrading *adj* **:** that degrades; *esp* **:** that causes human character to become degraded or debased ⟨moralists have often exposed the selfish pursuit of personal gain as a ~ motive in the business life —J.A.Hobson⟩ ⟨war for the most part is ~ and hateful⟩ ⟨the tendency of existentialists to deal with the ~ aspects of human nature⟩ — **de·grad·ing·ly** *adv* — **de·grad·ing·ness** *n* -ES
¹de·grain \(')dē +\ *vt* [*de-* + *grain* (n.)] **:** to remove the grain from
²de·grain \'dē+,-\ *n* **:** a degrained leather
de·gras \dā'grä\ *n, pl* **degras** \-äz\ [F *dégras*, back-formation (influenced by *gras* fat, fr. L *crassus* thick, fat) fr. *dégraisser* to remove the fat from, fr. MF *desgresser*, fr. *des-*, *de-* de- + *gresse*, *graisse* fat, grease — more at CRASS, GREASE] **1 a :** a fatty substance obtained by pressing certain skins following the action of oxidized fish oil on them and used in dressing leather — called also *moellon*; see SOD OIL **b :** a mixture of this substance with other fats or fatty oils (as fish oils) or sometimes wool grease **2 :** WOOL GREASE
de gra·tia \dā'grād·ē,ä, dē'grāsh(ē)ə\ *adv* (*or adj*) [L] *law* **:** by favor
de·grease \(')dē¦grēs, -ēz\ *vt* [*de-* + *grease* (n.)] **:** to treat with an extractant for grease, oil, or fatty matter ⟨a taxidermist *degreasing* specimens for the museum⟩: as **a :** to remove grease and dirt from (wool) with chemicals **b :** to remove grease, oil, or fatty matter from (a metal) with fumes from a hot solvent **c :** to remove excess grease from (hides or skins) by tumbling in solvents in tanning
de·greas·er \"+ə(r)\ *n* **1 :** one employed at degreasing materials in an industrial process **2 :** a solvent or a machine using solvents for degreasing materials, parts, specimens
¹de·gree \də'grē, dē'-\ *n* -s *often attrib* [ME, fr. OF *degré*, fr. (assumed) VL *degradus*, fr. L *de-* + *gradus* step, pace — more at GRADE] **1 a** *obs* **:** one member of a flight of steps or stairs **b** *heraldry* **:** a step (as of a Calvary cross) in a series — called also *grece* **c** *archaic* **:** a steplike member of a series (as of parts of a structure) **:** TIER, BANK **2 a :** a step in a process, course, or classificatory order ⟨shall the shadow go forward ten ~*s* or go back ten ~*s* — 2 Kings 20:9 (AV)⟩ **b :** a stage or point of an advance or retrogression ⟨rising by successive ~*s* to become general manager of the firm⟩ **c :** a measure of damage to tissue caused by disease or other force — compare CLASS 3b, GRADE 1c(3) **3 a :** a grade or point observed in a measuring or estimating of an action, relation, state of being, or mental attitude ⟨at a microphone they are men who know the pecuniary value of words inflated to the right ~ —O.D.Duncan⟩ ⟨the ~ to which the total effect resembles nature —Michael Kitson⟩ **b :** the extent, measure, or scope of an action, condition, or relation ⟨all of our presidents in varying ~*s* have experienced an intoxicating exhilaration in manipulating the levers of power —V.L.Albjerg⟩ ⟨I considered my giddiness and inconstancy when in London as in a great ~ the cause of her unhappiness —Benjamin Franklin⟩ **c :** level in the range and stress or accentuation of an attribute **:** relative efficacy **:** measure or dimension of an essential or distinctive quality ⟨the mental powers of ants differ from those of men not so much in kind as in ~ —John Lubbock⟩ ⟨it is a question of ~ whether I have been negligent —B.N.Cardozo⟩ ⟨most of the distinctions of law are distinctions of ~ —O.W. Holmes †1935⟩ **d :** a grade or point marking the attainment or existence of more or less of a quality, acquirement, or aspect **:** relative intensity ⟨combined literary distinction with a high ~ of historical objectivity —R.W.Van Alstyne⟩ ⟨requiring a high ~ of mastery in the chosen field of study⟩ ⟨the precise ~ of probability⟩ **e :** a positive and unquestionable though undefined quantitative measure and qualitative elevation ⟨the duties owed by the trustee have a ~ of definition and are enforceable before a court of equity —G.B. Hurff⟩ ⟨the religious zeal of the Quakers was always tempered by a ~ of tolerance —*Amer. Guide Series: Pa.*⟩ **f :** one of the forms or sets of forms used in the comparison of an adjective or adverb to denote a particular intensity or level of the quality, quantity, or relation expressed by the adjective or adverb — see COMPARATIVE 1, POSITIVE 2a, SUPERLATIVE 1 **g :** a legal measure of the culpability of one who commits any of certain crimes that depends on attendant circumstances defined by law ⟨an offense in the first ~ is usually the most serious; among the offenses classified in this manner are often found murder or robbery⟩ **h :** one of the legal classes of negligence (as gross, ordinary, or slight) graded according to the determined culpability of the tort-feasor **4 :** a rank or grade of official, ecclesiastical, or social position or advancement ⟨people of low ~ were banished from the capital —E.R. Embree⟩ ⟨clerical hats colored and tasselled according to their ~ —Iain Moncreiffe⟩ ⟨a certain well-to-do air about the man suggested that he was not poor for his ~ —Thomas Hardy⟩ **5 a** *archaic* **:** a particular level, standing, or relative condition esp. as to dignity, reputation, worth ⟨for they that have used the office of a deacon well purchase to themselves a good ~ —1 Tim 3:13 (AV)⟩ **b :** the civil condition or status of a person **6 :** a step in a direct line of descent or in the line of ascent to a common ancestor and thence in line of descent to relatives by consanguinity **7 a :** a grade or class of membership attained in a ritualistic order or society denoting a stage of proficiency often after a set ordeal or examination **b :** the formal ceremonies observed in the conferral of such a distinction **c :** a title conferred upon students by a college, university, or professional school upon completion of a unified program of study carrying a specified minimum of credits, passing of certain examinations, and often completion of a thesis or other independent research project — compare ³ASSOCIATE 4b **d :** an academic title conferred honorarily in recognition of outstanding individual achievement outside the conferring institution ⟨his writings brought him an award of the ~ of Doctor of Humane Letters⟩ **8** *archaic* **:** a position or space on the earth or in the heavens as measured by degrees of latitude **9 :** one of the divisions or intervals marked on a scale of a measuring instrument or a gauge ⟨the length of a ~ depends on the expansion of the thermometric substance used —A.H.Thiessen⟩ **10 :** a 360th measure for arcs and angles **11 a :** the sum of the exponents of the variable factors of a monomial ⟨a^2b^3c is of the sixth ~⟩ **b :** the sum of the exponents of the variables or unknowns of the term of highest degree in a polynomial or polynomial equation **c :** the greatest power of the derivative of highest order in a differential equation after the equation has been cleared of fractions with respect to the derivative ⟨$\frac{d^2y}{dx^2} - 2\left(\frac{dy}{dx}\right)^2 - 4 = 0$ is of the first ~⟩ **12** *music* **a :** a line or space of the staff — compare LEDGER LINE **b :** a step, note, or tone of a scale ⟨the mediant is the third ~ of the scale⟩ **13** *logic* **:** the rank of a predicate according to the number of terms related by it ⟨"before" is a predicate of the second, "between" of the third ~⟩ — **by degrees** *adv* **:** step by step **:** by relatively small stages **:** GRADUALLY ⟨measures raising the minimum of teachers' pay *by degrees*⟩ — **to a degree** *adv* **1 :** to a rather large or remarkable extent **:** in liberal measure **:** HIGHLY, DECIDEDLY, EXCEEDINGLY ⟨but in some things she must have been stupid *to a degree* —I.V.Morris⟩ ⟨a fine classical scholar, of gentlest temper and manners, but easygoing *to a degree* —A.T.Quiller-Couch⟩ **2 :** in a measure **:** in a small way **:** SOMEWHAT ⟨this necessarily involved a departure from strict realism — *to a degree* a denial of reality —G.C.Sellery⟩

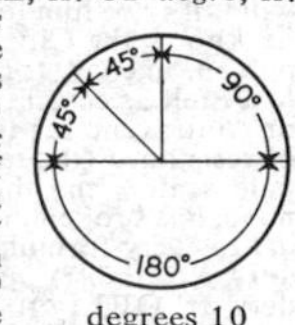

degrees 10

²degree \"\ *vt* **degreed; degreed; degreeing; degrees 1** *obs* **:** to advance by steps or degrees **2 :** to confer a degree upon
degree course *n* **:** a course of studies leading toward a degree **:** an academic subject accepted in partial fulfillment of the requirements for a degree
degree cut *n* **:** STEP CUT
de·greed \-ēd\ *adj* **:** ²DEGRADED
degree-day \=¦=,=\ *n* **:** a unit that represents one degree of declination from a given point (as 65°) in the mean outdoor temperature of one day and is often used in measuring fuel requirements of buildings
de·gree·less \-ēləs\ *adj* **1 :** not divisible into or measurable in degrees **2 :** having no academic degree
de·green \(')dē+\ *vt* [*de-* + *green* (adj.)] **:** to remove green color from (as citrus fruit) by subjection to a specific concentration of ethylene at a specific temperature and relative humidity
degree of curve : a measure of the sharpness of curvature, for U.S. railroads usu. being the angle subtended at the center of curvature by a chord 100 ft. long and for highways by an arc 100 ft. long
degree of freedom 1 : one of a limited number of ways in which a point or a body may move or in which a dynamic system may change, each way being expressed by an independent variable and all requiring to be specified if the physical state of the body or system is to be completely defined **2 :** a capability of variation possessed by a system by reason of the variability of one of its factors (as temperature, pressure, or concentration) ⟨the system water-water vapor has one *degree of freedom* because when either temperature or pressure is arbitrarily fixed the other is no longer variable⟩ — see PHASE RULE **3 :** the number of intervals in which the frequency may be arbitrarily assumed in a statistical distribution with equal intervals of the statistical variable
degree of frost *chiefly Brit* **:** the degree of temperature below the freezing point of water ⟨when the thermometer stands at 20° F there are twelve *degrees of frost*⟩
degree student *n* **:** a college or university student intending to take a degree
degree team *n* **:** a group of members of a ritualistic order who conduct the ceremonies and ritual connected with the working of an initiatory or other particular degree
degreewise \=¦=,=\ *adv* **:** by degrees esp. of the musical diatonic scale
de·gres·sion \dē'greshən\ *n* -s [ME *degressioun*, fr. ML *degression-*, *degressio*, fr. L *degressus* (past part. of *degredi* to go down, fr. *de-* + *-gredi*) to go, step + *-ion-*, *-io* -ion — more at CONGRESS] **1 :** a stepping or movement downward **:** DESCENT — used chiefly as a correlative of progression **2 :** the decrease in rate in degressive taxation
de·gres·sive \-esiv\ *adj* [*degression* + *-ive*] **:** tending to descend or decrease: **a :** based on a plan of taxation in which the rate decreases as the base increases, the rate structure containing some degree of progression in the lower brackets and then tapering off until all income over a certain figure is taxed at the same rate **b :** relating to or characterized by burning (as of solid grains of smokeless powder) in which the surface decreases as the burning advances — opposed to *progressive* — **de·gres·sive·ly** \-səvlē\ *adv*
dé·grin·go·lade \dāgraⁿgōlȧd\ *n* -s [F, lit., tumbling fall, fr. *dégringoler* to tumble (fr. *dé-* de- + *gringoler* to tumble, fr. MF) + *-ade*] **:** rapid decline or deterioration (as in strength, position, or condition) **:** DOWNFALL ⟨what a ~ from the period of that brilliant coterie —*Saturday Rev.*⟩ ⟨the ~ of a theater that once . . . occupied an important position —*Amer. Mercury*⟩
de·growth \'dē+,-\ *n* [*de-* + *growth*] *biol* **:** decrease in mass of an organism esp. at the end of a prolonged period of growth
degs *pres 3d sing of* DEG
de·gu \'dā(,)gü\ *n* -s [AmerSp] **:** any of several small hystricomorphic rodents (genus *Octodon*) of western So. America
de·gue·lia \də'gelēə\ *n* [NL, fr. Galibi *assa-ha-pagara un-deguélé* derris plant + NL *-ia*] *syn of* DERRIS
de·guel·in \-lən\ *n* -s [NL *Deguelia* + E *-in*] **:** a crystalline ketone $C_{23}H_{22}O_6$ that is an active constituent of derris and roots of cube and is closely related to rotenone
de·gum \(')dē+\ *vt* [*de-* + *gum* (n.)] **:** to free from gum or gummy substance; *specif* **:** to free (silk fabric or yarn) from sericin by boiling in a soap solution
de·gust \dē'gəst\ *also* **de·gus·tate** \-'gə,stāt\ *vt* -ED/-ING/-S [*degust* fr. L *degustare*, fr. *de-* + *gustare* to taste; *degustate* fr. L *degustatus*, past part. of *degustare* — more at CHOOSE] **:** TASTE; *esp* **:** to savor or relish as a connoisseur or tester ⟨observes and ~*s* the great world of London —E.K.Brown⟩ — **de·gus·ta·tion** \(,)dē,gə'stāshən\ *n*
de·gus·ta·tor \dē'gə,stād·ə(r)\ *n* -s **:** one that tastes ⟨varieties of oranges rated by ~*s*⟩
de gus·ti·bus \dē'gəstəbəs, dā'güstē,bu̇s\ [L *de gustibus* (*non est disputandum*) there is no disputing concerning tastes] **:** concerning taste ⟨I still detest the sound of him, but *de gustibus* —Jean Stafford⟩ — used elliptically for its full Latin original or its translation
de·hair \(')dē+\ *vt* [*de-* + *hair* (n.)] **:** to deprive of hair **:** UNHAIR; *specif* **:** to remove the hair or wool from (hides or skins)
de haut en bas \dəōtäⁿbä\ *adv* (*or adj*) [F, lit., from top to bottom] **:** with a superior or condescending air ⟨the landlady looked at him *de haut en bas* —D.H.Lawrence⟩
de·hep·a·tize \(')dē'hepə,tīz\ *vt* [*de-* + *hepat-* + *-ize*] **:** to remove the liver from
de·hisce \də'his, dē'-\ *vb* -ED/-ING/-S [L *dehiscere* to split open, gape, fr. *de-* + *hiscere* to gape; akin to *hiare* to yawn, gape — more at YAWN] *vi* **:** to discharge by dehiscence **:** GAPE ~ *vt* **:** to cause to gape
de·his·cence \-sᵊn(t)s\ *n* -s [NL *dehiscentia*, fr. L *dehiscent-*, *dehiscens* (pres. part. of *dehiscere*) + *-ia*] **:** a bursting open: as **a** (1) **:** the bursting open of a capsule, pod, or silique at maturity either between the carpels, through the middle of the carpels, or in some other manner — compare CIRCUMSCISSILE, LOCULICIDAL, SEPTICIDAL, SEPTIFRAGAL (2) **:** the opening of an anther for the discharge of pollen (as by longitudinal slits or pores) **b** *biol* **:** the opening of an organ along a suture or some other definite line for the purpose of discharging its contents **c :** the parting of the sutured lips of a surgical wound
de·his·cent \-sᵊnt, 'dē,h-\ *adj* [L *dehiscent-*, *dehiscens*] **:** characterized by dehiscence **:** opening wide **:** GAPING — used esp. of ripe fruit or fungous fruiting bodies — see FRUIT illustration
deh·kan \'dā,kän\ *n, usu cap* **:** DEHWAR
dehn·stu·fe \'dān,shtüfə\ *n, pl* **dehnstu·fen** \-fən\ [G, fr. *dehnen* to stretch (fr. OHG *dennen*) + *stufe* step, fr. OHG *stuofa* — more at THIN, STEP] *in Indo-European ablaut* **:** a lengthened grade
de·horn \(')dē+\ *vt* [*de-* + *horn* (n.)] **1 :** to deprive of horns **:** prevent the growth of the horns of (cattle) esp. by destroying the undeveloped horn buds with heat or chemicals **2 :** to prune severely (as a fruit tree)
de·horn·er \"+ə(r)\ *n* -s **1 :** one that dehorns cattle **2 a :** a device for removing horns from cattle **b :** a device or chemical for checking the growth of horns in young cattle of horned breeds
de·hors \də'(h)ȯ(ə)r\ *prep* [F, outside, fr. OF, fr. LL *deforis* from the outside, outside, fr. L *de* from + *foris* outside; akin to L *foris*, *fores* door — more at DE-, DOOR] *law* **:** out of (as an agreement, record, or will) **:** foreign to
de·hort \(')dē'hȯ(ə)rt\ *vt* -ED/-ING/-S [L *dehortari*, fr. *de-*

+ *hortari* to urge, exhort — more at YEARN] *archaic* **:** to advise against (an action or policy) **:** DISSUADE — often used with *from*

de·hor·ta·tion \ˌdēˌhȯrˈtāshən\ *n* -s [LL *dehortation-, dehortatio*, fr. L *dehortatus* (past part. of *dehortari*) + *-ion-, -io* -ion] *archaic* **:** DISSUASION

deh·ra dun \ˌderəˈdün\ *adj, usu cap both Ds* [fr. *Dehra Dun*, India] **:** of or from the city of Dehra Dun, India **:** of the kind or style prevalent in Dehra Dun

dehrn·ite \ˈderˌnīt\ *n* -s [*Dehrn*, village near Limburg, Germany, where it was discovered + E *-ite*] **:** a basic phosphate of calcium, sodium, and potassium $(Ca,Na,K)_5(PO_4)_3(OH)$

de·hull \(ˈ)dē+\ *vt* [*de-* + *hull* (n.)] **:** to remove the hulls from (seed)

de·humanization \(ˌ)dē+\ *n* -s **:** the act or process or an instance of dehumanizing

de·humanize \(ˈ)dē+\ *vt* [*de-* + *humanize*] **:** to divest of human qualities or personality **:** make machinelike ⟨*dehumanizing* the masses into unthinking conformity⟩ **:** make impersonal or unconcerned with human values ⟨an abstract, *dehumanized* art⟩

de·humidification \ˌdē+\ *n* -s **:** the process of dehumidifying

de·humidifier \(ˈ)dē+\ *n* -s **:** a substance or apparatus for dehumidifying

de·humidify \(ˈ)dē+\ *vt* [*de-* + *humidify*] **:** to remove moisture from (as the air) **:** DRY

de·husk \(ˈ)dē+\ *vt* [*de-* + *husk* (n.)] **:** HUSK

deh·war \ˈdāˌwär\ *n, pl* **dehwar** *or* **dehwars** *usu cap* [Per *dihwār*, fr. *dih* village (fr. MPer *dēh* land, fr. OPer *dahyu-* land, province) + *-wār* having, possessing (fr. Av *-baro* carrying, bringing); akin to Skt *bharati* he carries — more at DAS, BEAR] **1 :** a Persian racial type recognizable in the population of Baluchistan **2 :** a member of the Dehwar racial type usu. having the status of a laborer or slave

dehydr- *or* **dehydro-** *comb form* [ISV, fr. *de-* + *hydr-*] **1 :** dehydrated ⟨*dehydro*mucic acid $C_4H_2O(COOH)_2$⟩ **2 :** dehydrogenated ⟨*dehydro*abietic acid $C_{19}H_{27}COOH$⟩

de·hy·drant \dēˈhīdrənt\ *n* -s [*dehydrate* + *-ant*] **:** a dehydrating substance

de·hy·drate \dēˈhīˌdrāt, *usu* -ād.+V\ *vb* [*de-* + *hydrate*] *vt* **1 a :** to remove hydrogen and oxygen from (as a compound) in the proportion in which they form water ⟨*dehydrated* castor oil⟩ **b :** to remove chemically combined water or water of hydration from ⟨*dehydrated* alums⟩ **2 :** to remove water or moisture from (as foods or air) **:** render free from water **:** dry completely **:** DESICCATE — compare DEHUMIDIFY **3 :** to deprive of strength, meaning, or vitality ⟨creeps in like the desert wind and ~s the soul —James Jones⟩ **:** make flat, insipid, or uninspiring ⟨touches nothing that he does not ~ —*Economist*⟩ ~ *vi* **:** to lose water or the elements of water **:** become dehydrated **syn** see DRY

de·hy·dra·tion \(ˌ)dēˌhīˈdrāshən\ *n* [*de-* + *hydration*] **1 :** the process of dehydrating; *esp* **:** an abnormal depletion of body fluids resulting from deprivation or loss (as in starvation, hemorrhage, or vomiting) **2 :** the state of being dehydrated **3 :** a procedure designed to reduce the fluid content of body tissues

de·hy·dra·tor *also* **de·hy·drat·er** \dēˈhīˌdrād·ə(r), -ātə-\ *n* -s **:** one that dehydrates or operates dehydrating apparatus: as **a :** an operator of a still for removing water from lubricating oils **b :** an agent (as silica gel) for dehydrating **c :** a device or apparatus for dehydrating **:** DRYER

de·hy·dro \dēˈhī(ˌ)drō\ *adj* [*dehydr-*] **1 :** chemically dehydrated **2 :** DEHYDROGENATED

de·hy·dro·acetic acid \dēˈhīdrō+ . . . -\ *also* **de·hy·dra·cetic acid** \-dr+ . . . -\ *n* [ISV *dehydr-* + *acetic*] **:** a crystalline acid $C_8H_8O_4$ related to pyrone, obtained esp. by heating ethyl acetoacetate, and used as a fungicide, bactericide, and plasticizer

dehydroascorbic acid \"+ . . . -\ *n* [*dehydr-* + *ascorbic*] **:** a crystalline oxidation product $C_6H_6O_6$ of ascorbic acid occurring at times in some foodstuffs (as fruits, vegetables, and milk) that can be reduced to ascorbic acid and thus has potential vitamin C activity

de·hy·dro·cho·late \(ˌ)dēˌhīdrəˈkōˌlāt\ *n* -s [ISV *dehydrocholic* + *-ate*] **:** a salt of dehydrocholic acid

de·hy·dro·cholesterol \dēˈhīdrō+\ *n* [*dehydr-* + *cholesterol*] **:** a crystalline steroid alcohol $C_{27}H_{43}OH$ that occurs chiefly in higher animals and man (as in the skin), that is made synthetically from cholesterol, and that yields vitamin D_3 on irradiation with ultraviolet light — called also *7-dehydrocholesterol*

de·hy·dro·cholic acid \(ˌ)dēˈhīdrə+\ *n* [ISV *dehydr-* + *cholic*] **:** a colorless crystalline acid $C_{23}H_{33}O_3COOH$ made by the oxidation of cholic acid and used often in the form of its sodium salt as a choleretic and diuretic; 3,7,12-triketocholanic acid

de·hy·dro·corticosterone \(ˌ)dēˌhīdrō+\ *n* [ISV *dehydr-* + *corticosterone*] **:** a crystalline triketone $C_{21}H_{28}O_4$ extracted from the adrenal cortex and also made synthetically — called also *11-dehydrocorticosterone;* see CORTISONE

de·hy·dro·cyclization \dēˈhīdrō+\ *n* [*dehydr-* + *cyclization*] **:** cyclization involving dehydrogenation ⟨~ of heptane gives toluene⟩ — called also *cyclodehydrogenation*

de·hy·dro·freezing \"+\ *n* [*dehydr-* + *freezing*] **:** the process of preserving foods by partially dehydrating and then quick-freezing them

de·hy·dro·frozen \"+\ *adj* [*dehydr-* + *frozen*] **:** preserved by dehydrofreezing

de·hydrogenase \(ˌ)dē+\ *n* [ISV *de-* + *hydrogenase*] **:** any of various enzymes that accelerate the removal of hydrogen from metabolites and its transfer to other substances (as diphosphopyridine nucleotide) and thus play an important role in biological oxidation-reduction processes ⟨succinic ~⟩

de·hydrogenate \(ˌ)dē+\ *vt* [*de-* + *hydrogenate*] **:** to remove hydrogen from (a compound) ⟨~ butenes to butadiene⟩ — compare OXIDIZE 1b

de·hydrogenation \(ˌ)dē+\ *n* **:** the process of dehydrogenating

de·hydrogenize \(ˌ)dē+\ *vt* [*de-* + *hydrogenize*] **:** DEHYDROGENATE

de·hypnotize \(ˈ)dē+\ *vt* [*de-* + *hypnotize*] **:** to remove from a state of hypnosis

de·ice \(ˈ)dē+\ *vt* [*de-* + *ice* (n.)] **:** to keep free or rid of ice; *specif* **:** to keep (an airplane) free of ice by applying an antifreeze, by the use of electrical or exhaust-gas heating, or by alternately inflating and deflating air-filled bags overlying wing and tail surfaces — **de·ic·er** \"+ə(r)\ *n* -s

[1]**de·i·cide** \ˈdēəˌsīd\ *n* -s [prob. fr. F *déicide*, fr. MF *deicide*, fr. *dei-* (fr. L, fr. *deus* god) + *-cide* (killing)] **:** the act of killing a divine being or the symbolic substitute of such a being

[2]**deicide** \"\ *n* -s [LL *deicida*, fr. L *dei-* (fr. *deus* god) + *-cida* -cide (killer) — more at DEITY] **:** the killer or destroyer of a god **:** the officiator in certain religious ceremonies in which men or animals considered to be imbued with supernatural qualities are sacrificed

deic·tic \ˈdīktik\ *adj* [Gk *deiktikos*, fr. *deiktos* capable of proof (verbal of *deiknynai* to show) + *-ikos* -ic — more at DICTION] **1 :** showing or pointing out directly ⟨pronouns differ from nouns in that they are essentially ~ —L.H.Gray⟩ **2** *logic* **:** proving directly **:** DIRECT — opposed to *elenctic*

deid \ˈdēd, ˈdād\ *Scot var of* DEAD

de·if·ic \(ˈ)dēˈifik\ *adj* [MF *deifique*, fr. LL *deificus* making divine, divine, holy, fr. L *dei-* (fr. *deus* god) + *-ficus* -fic — more at DEITY] **:** DIVINE, GODLIKE

de·i·fi·ca·tion \ˌdēəfəˈkāshən\ *n* -s [ME *deificacioun*, fr. LL *deification-, deificatio*, fr. *deificatus* (past part. of *deificare* to deify, fr. *deificus*) + L *-ion-, -io* -ion] **1 :** the act or an instance of deifying ⟨~ of material values⟩ **:** the state of being deified ⟨the emperor's ~ was proclaimed⟩ **2 :** the process of becoming one with a deity **:** absorption (as of the soul) into Deity — **de·if·i·ca·to·ry** \dēˈifəkəˌtōrē\ *adj*

de·i·fi·er \ˈdēəˌfī(ə)r\ *n* -s **:** one that deifies

de·i·form \-ˌfȯrm\ *adj* [ML *deiformis*, fr. L *deus* god + *-iformis* -iform — more at DEITY] **:** conforming to the nature of God **:** having the form of a god ⟨the universe shows no evidence of being ~ —R.W.Sellars⟩

de·i·fy \ˈdēəˌfī\ *vb* -ED/-ING/-ES [ME *deifyen*, fr. MF *deifier*, fr. LL *deificare* — more at DEIFICATION] *vt* **1 :** to make a god of **:** enroll among the national or tribal deities ⟨~*ing* their emperor became their link with the divine⟩ **2 :** to make godlike in appearance or character **:** TRANSFIGURE **3 :** to glorify or exalt as of supreme worth or excellence ⟨*deified* . . . the railroad builder, the gold-hungry miner —Leo Cherne⟩ ⟨*deifies* the political state⟩ ~ *vi* **:** to become divine **:** assume the status of a deity ⟨failed to completely ~ —Thornton Wilder⟩

deign \ˈdān\ *vb* -ED/-ING/-S [ME *deynen, deignen*, fr. OF *deignier* to consider worthy, deign, fr. L *dignare, dignari*, fr. *dignus* worthy — more at DECENT] *vi* **:** to think it appropriate to one's dignity **:** CONDESCEND ⟨did not even ~ to contradict —Louis Auchincloss⟩ ⟨~*ed* to cast an eye upon humble me —George Meredith⟩ ~ *vt* **1** *obs* **:** to condescend to receive or accept ⟨I fear my Julia will not ~ my lines —Shak.⟩ **2 :** to condescend to give or offer ⟨never so much as ~*ing* a glance —George Meredith⟩

dei ju·di·ci·um \ˌdāˌēyüˈdikēəm\ *n, cap D* [ML, judgment of God] *law* **:** trial by ordeal

deil \ˈdē(ə)l\ *n* -s [ME *del*, alter. of *devel* — more at DEVIL] *Scot* **:** DEVIL

deil's buckie *n, Scot* **:** a mischievous person **:** imp of Satan

dein- *or* **deino-** — see DIN-

dei·no·ce·pha·lia \ˌdīnōsəˈfālyə\ *n pl, cap* [NL, fr. *din-* + *cephal-* + *-ia*] **:** a suborder of Therapsida comprising reptiles known from Permian fossils of southern Africa and Russia that had massive skulls and heavy legs and included the largest of the reptiles foreshadowing mammals, some exceeding the modern rhinoceros in size — **dei·no·ce·pha·lian** \ˌ≈≈≈ˈfālyən\ *adj or n*

dei·no·don \ˈdīnəˌdän\ *n, cap* [NL, fr. *din-* + *-odon*] **:** a genus of immense carnivorous saurischian dinosaurs of the upper Cretaceous of Alberta that with *Tyrannosaurus* and related genera constitutes a distinct family chiefly of No. America — **dei·no·dont** \-ˌdänt\ *adj or n*

de in·of·fi·ci·o·so tes·ta·men·to \ˌdāˌinəˌfikēˈō(ˌ)sō,testəˈmen,tō\ *adj* [L] *civil law* **:** concerning an inofficious or undutiful will — used of a form of action for setting aside such a will

dei·no·the·ri·an \ˌdīnōˈthirēən\ *adj* [NL *Deinotherium* + E *-an*] **:** of or relating to the genus *Deinotherium*

dei·no·the·ri·um \ˌ≈≈ˈēəm\ *n, cap* [NL, fr. *din-* + *-therium*] **:** a genus (usu. coextensive with the family Deinotheriidae and suborder Deinotherioidea of the order Proboscidea) comprising Miocene and Pliocene mammals of Europe and Asia related to but often larger than the elephants and distinguished by a pair of tusks directed downward from the decurved apex of the lower jaw

De–ion \(ˈ)dēˈīən, (ˈ)dēˈīˌän\ *trademark* — used for a circuit breaker that extinguishes the arc following the opening of a circuit by removing ions from the gap by means of an oil vapor produced by the arc

de·ionization \(ˌ)dē+\ *n* **:** the process of deionizing

de·ionize \(ˈ)dē+\ *vt* [*de-* + *ionize*] **:** to remove ions from (as water by ion exchange) **:** DEMINERALIZE, DESALT — **de·ion·iz·er** \-zə(r)\ *n* -s

deip·nos·o·phist \dīpˈnäsəfəst\ *n* -s [fr. *the Deipnosophists*, a work depicting a banquet where long discussions take place, written by Athenaeus *fl* A.D. 200 Graeco-Egyptian writer, fr. Gk *Deipnosophistai*, lit., culinary experts, pl. of *deipnosophistēs*, fr. *deipnon* meal (prob. of non-IE origin) + *sophistēs* wise man, sophist — more at SOPHIST] **:** a person skilled in table talk

dei·rid \ˈdīrəd\ *n* -s [Gk *deire*, *derē* neck, throat + E *-id* — more at DER-] **:** either of a pair of sensory papillae in the lateral cervical region of certain nematodes usu. considered tactile organs

deiseal *var of* DEASIL

de·ism \ˈdēˌizəm\ *n* -s *sometimes cap* [F *déisme*, fr. L *deus* god + F *-isme* -ism — more at DEITY] **:** a rationalistic movement of the 17th and 18th centuries whose adherents generally subscribed to a natural religion based on human reason and morality, on the belief in one God who after creating the world and the laws governing it refrained from interfering with the operation of those laws, and on the rejection of every kind of supernatural intervention in human affairs

de·ist \ˈdēəst\ *n* -s *often cap* [F *déiste*, fr. L *deus* god + F *-iste* -ist] **:** an adherent of deism

de·is·tic \(ˈ)dēˈistik, -tēk\ *also* **de·is·ti·cal** \-təkəl, -tēk-\ *adj, sometimes cap* **:** relating to or characteristic of deists or deism **:** professing deism ⟨~ belief⟩ — **de·is·ti·cal·ly** \-tək(ə)lē, -tēk-, -li\ *adv*

dei·ters' cell \ˈdīd·ə(r)z-, -(r)s(ǝz)-\ *n, usu cap D* [after Otto F. K. *Deiters* †1863 Ger. physician] **1 :** one of the modified supporting cells prolonged into a process ending in a terminal plate that are placed among and alternate with the outer hair cells of the organ of Corti **2 :** a spider cell of the neuroglia

deiters' nucleus *n, usu cap D* [after O. F. K. *Deiters*] **:** a nucleus in the medulla oblongata on the inner side of the restiform body receiving fibers from the semicircular canals by way of the vestibular nerve and concerned in maintaining equilibrium and muscular tone and in conjugate movement of the eyes

deith \ˈdēth\ *Scot var of* DEATH

de·i·ty \ˈdēəd·ē, -ətē, -i *sometimes* ˈdāə-\ *n* -ES [ME *deitee*, fr. MF *deité*, fr. LL *deitat-, deitas* (prob. trans. of Gk *theotēs*), fr. L *deus* god + *-itat-, -itas* -ity; akin to OE *Tīw*, god of war, OHG *Zio*, ON *Týr*, god of war, Goth *sinteins* daily, L *divus* divine, god, *dies* day, *Juppiter*, god of the sky, Gk *dios* heavenly, *Zeus*, god of the sky, Skt *deva* god, *dyaus* sky, day; basic meaning: sky] **1 a** *often cap* **:** divine nature or rank **:** the essential nature of a god or of a supreme being **:** DIVINITY, GODHEAD, GODHOOD ⟨doctrines of the ~ of Christ⟩ **b** *cap* **:** SUPREME BEING, [2]GOD ⟨entering into communion with the *Deity*⟩ **2 :** a god or goddess ⟨the tutelary ~ of the village —J.G.Frazer⟩ **3 a :** a person or thing that is exalted or revered as supremely good or great ⟨such established American *deities* as Daniel Boone, Kit Carson —J.D.Hart⟩ ⟨a world in which power is the ~⟩ **b :** one that holds or wields supreme power or influence in some field ⟨the *deities* of the banking world⟩

déjà vu *or* **déjà vue** \ˌdāzhäˈvǖ\ *n* [F, adj., already seen] **:** PARAMNESIA b

[1]**de·ject** \dəˈjekt, dēˈ-\ *vt* -ED/-ING/-S [ME *dejecten*, fr. L *dejectus*, past part. of *dejicere* to throw down, fr. *de-* + *-jicere* (fr. *jacere* to throw) — more at JET] **1** *archaic* **:** to cast down **:** bend down **:** OVERTHROW **2 a** (1) *obs* **:** to lower esp. in rank or condition **:** ABASE, HUMBLE (2) *archaic* **:** to reduce esp. in force, degree, or quality **:** WEAKEN, LESSEN **b :** to make gloomy **:** DISPIRIT, DISHEARTEN ⟨nor think, to die ~*s* my lofty mind —Alexander Pope⟩ **syn** see DISCOURAGE

[2]**deject** \"\ *adj* [ME, fr. L *dejectus*] *archaic* **:** DEJECTED ⟨make livers pale and lustihood ~ —Shak.⟩

de·jec·ta \-ktə\ *n pl* [NL, fr. L, neut pl. of *dejectus*] **:** EXCREMENTS ⟨the ~ of the sick may be a source of infection⟩

dejected *adj* **1 :** cast down in spirits **:** DEPRESSED, MOURNFUL ⟨grew timorous and ~ —William Bartram⟩ **2 a** *obs, of the eyes* **:** DOWNCAST ⟨her eyes ~ and her hair unbound —Alexander Pope⟩ **b** *archaic* **:** thrown down **:** PROSTRATE ⟨looking at her ~ pillar —Henry James †1916⟩ **3** *obs* **:** lowered in rank, estate, or condition **:** HUMBLED, ABASED ⟨the ~ state wherein he is —Shak.⟩ **syn** see DOWNCAST

de·ject·ed·ly *adv* **:** in a dejected manner **:** SADLY

de·ject·ed·ness *n* -ES **:** the quality or state of being dejected **:** DEJECTION

de·jec·tion \dəˈjekshən, dēˈ-\ *n* -s [ME *dejeccioun*, fr. LL & L; LL *dejection-, dejectio* act of lowering or pulling down, abject condition, humiliation, fr. L, purging, ejection, degradation, fr. *dejectus* + *-ion-, -io* -ion] **1** *obs* **:** the act of lowering or the condition of being lowered in rank, estate, or circumstances **:** ABASEMENT, HUMILIATION **b :** a lowering of strength **:** diminution esp. of appetite **2 :** lowness of spirits **:** DEPRESSION, MELANCHOLY ⟨slumped down on the wall, the picture of ~ —O.E.Rölvaag⟩ **3** [prob. fr. F, fr. MF, fr. L] **a :** DEFECATION **b :** FECES, EXCREMENT **syn** see SADNESS

dé·jeu·ner \ˌdāzhəˈnā, F dāzhœnā\ *n* -s [F, fr. MF *desjeuner*, fr. *desjeuner* to breakfast, fr. OF, fr. (assumed) VL *disjejunare* to break one's fast — more at DINE] **1 :** breakfast or lunch **2 :** a service for serving individual breakfasts on a tray

de ju·re \(ˈ)dēˈjurē, (ˈ)dāˈjü,rā; (ˈ)dāˈyü,rā\ *adv (or adj)* [L] **:** by right **:** of right **:** by a lawful title ⟨recognition extended *de jure* to the new government⟩ — distinguished from *de gratia* and *de facto* **2 :** by law — distinguished from *de aequitate*

deka- *or* **dek-** — see DECA-

de·ka·brist \dəˈkäbrəst, ˈdekəb-\ *n* -s *usu cap* [Russ, fr. *dekabr'* December (fr. ORuss *dekębrĭ*, fr. MGk *dekembris, dekembrios*, fr. L *december*) + *-ist* (fr. F *-iste* & G *-ist*) — more at DECEMBER] **:** DECEMBRIST

dek·a·drachm \ˈdekəˌdram\ *n* -s [Gk *deka-* deca- + E *drachm*] **:** DECADRACHM

dek·an \ˈdekən\ *n* -s [Gk *dekanos*, fr. *deka* ten; fr. the ten days of each subdivision — more at TEN] **:** one of 36 equal subdivisions of the equatorial belt of the celestial sphere including the ecliptic and the stars contained in it — used in ancient Egyptian astronomy — **dek·an·al** \ˈdekənᵊl\ *adj*

dek·ar \dəˈkär\ *n* -s [G, fr. F *décare* — more at DECARE] **:** DECARE

dekarchy *var of* DECARCHY

de·kay's snake \dəˈkāz-\ *n, usu cap D & 1st K* [after James E. *DeKay* †1851 Am. naturalist and writer] **:** a small brown harmless colubrid snake (*Storeria dekayi*) of No. America

de kho·tin·sky cement \ˌdēkəˈtinzkē-\ *n, sometimes cap D & usu cap K* [after Achilles *de Khotinsky* †1933 Am. industrial designer] **:** a thermoplastic cement resistant to water and most chemicals that is made by heating shellac and pine tar and used esp. in cementing glass, porcelain, metal, wood, and plastics

[1]**dek·ko** \ˈde(ˌ)kō\ *n* -s [Hindi *dekho* look!, imper. pl. of *dekhnā* to see, fr. Skt *dṛś* to see; akin to Skt *dṛṣṭi* seeing, sight, eye — more at DRAGON] *slang Brit* **:** LOOK, PEEP ⟨got out to have a ~ —J.B.Smyth⟩

[2]**dekko** \"\ *vt* -ED/-ING/-ES *slang Brit* **:** to look at ⟨~*ed* the front page —Richard Llewellyn⟩

del \ˈdel\ *n* -s [short for *delta*; fr. its being symbolized by an inverted Greek delta] **:** an operator upon a function of three variables (as *x, y,* and *z*) interpreted as coordinates in a right-handed rectangular system for obtaining the partial derivatives of the function, for multiplying these derivatives by the unit vectors (as I, J, K) along the axes, and for adding the results ⟨the vector differential operator (read ~) is defined by

$$\nabla = I\frac{\delta}{\delta x} + J\frac{\delta}{\delta y} + K\frac{\delta}{\delta z}$$

—Leigh Page⟩ — symbol ∇

del *abbr* **1** delegate **2** delete **3** [L *delineavit*] he drew **4** deliver

de·labialization \(ˌ)dē+\ *n* [*de-* + *labialization*] **:** the pronouncing of a sound without lip rounding

de·la·foss·ite \ˌdeləˈfōˌsīt\ *n* -s [F, fr. Gabriel *Delafosse* †1878 Fr. mineralogist + F *-ite*] **:** a mineral $CuFeO_2$ consisting of an oxide of copper and iron formerly found in quantity at Bisbee, Arizona, and in small amounts elsewhere

de·laine \dəˈlān, dēˈ-\ *n* -s [F (*mousseline*) *de laine* muslin of wool] **1 :** a lightweight dress fabric of wool or wool and cotton made in prints or solid colors **2** *usu cap* [by shortening] **:** DELAINE MERINO

delaine merino *n, pl* **delaine merinos** *usu cap D&M* **:** a sheep of an American strain of the Merino breed noted for its smooth body and long fine fleece

de·laminate \(ˈ)dē+\ *vb* [*de-* + *laminate*] *vi* **1:** to split into constituent layers **2** *of an embryo* **:** to undergo delamination ~ *vt* **:** to split (as a laminated plastic) along a plane of lamination

de·lamination \(ˌ)dē+\ *n* [*de-* + *lamination*] **1 :** separation (as of plywood) into constituent layers **2 :** gastrula formation which is typical of meroblastic eggs with discoidal cleavage and in which the endoderm is split off as a layer from the inner surface of the blastoderm and the archenteron is represented by the space between this endoderm and the underlying yolk mass

de·lapse \dəˈlaps, dēˈ-\ *vi* [L *delapsus*, past part. of *delabi* to descend, slip down, fr. *de-* + *labi* to slide — more at SLEEP] *archaic* **:** to slip down **:** DESCEND, LAPSE

de·late \-ˈlāt\ *vt* -ED/-ING/-S [L *delatus* (suppletive past part. of *deferre* to bring down, bring, report, indict, accuse), fr. *de-* + *latus*, suppletive past part. of *ferre* to bear — more at DEFER, TOLERATE] **1 a** *chiefly Scot* **:** to inform against **:** ACCUSE, DENOUNCE ⟨*delating* villagers suspected of witchcraft from the pulpit⟩ **b** *archaic* **:** to carry or spread abroad **:** make public **:** REPORT, RELATE **2 a** *medieval Roman law* **:** to offer or tender (as an inheritance) for acceptance **b** *archaic* **:** DELEGATE, REFER, TRANSFER

de·lateralization \(ˌ)dē+\ *n* [*de-* + *lateralization*] *phonetics* **:** replacement of a lateral by a nonlateral sound

de·la·tion \dəˈlāshən, dēˈ-\ *n* -s [L *delation-, delatio*, fr. *delatus* + *-ion-, -io* -ion] **:** an act or instance of delating; *usu* **:** ACCUSATION, DENOUNCEMENT

de·la·tive \-ād·iv\ *adj* [L *delatus* + E *-ive*] *of a grammatical case* **:** denoting motion down from

de·la·tor \-ād·ər *also* -āˌtō(ə)r\ *n* -s [L *delator*, fr. *delatus* + *-or*] **:** ACCUSER; *esp* **:** a professional informer — **del·a·to·ri·an** \ˌdeləˈtōrēən, -tȯr-\ *adj*

de·la·tyn·ite \dəˈlatᵊnˌīt\ *n* -s [G *delatynit*, fr. *Delatyn*, Ukraine + G *-it* -ite] **:** an amber high in carbon but lacking sulfur that is found at Delatyn in the Carpathian mountains of Galicia

[1]**del·a·ware** \ˈdeləˌwa(ə)(ə)r, -ˌwe|, |ə; -ˌwə(r)\ *n, pl* **delaware** *or* **delawares** *usu cap* [fr. the *Delaware* river] **1 a :** an Indian people of New Jersey, New York, and parts of eastern Pennsylvania and northern Delaware **b :** a member of such people **2 :** the Algonquian language of the Delaware people

[2]**delaware** \"\ *adj, usu cap* [fr. *Delaware*, middle Atlantic state of the U.S., fr. the *Delaware* river, after Thomas West, Lord *Delaware* (Baron *De La Warr*) †1618 colonial administrator in America] **:** of or from the state of Delaware **:** of the kind or style prevalent in Delaware

[3]**delaware** \"\ *n* -s *usu cap* [fr. *Delaware* state] **:** one of a breed of white dual-purpose fowls used esp. for broiler production that have faint black barring on hackles and tail and developed in Delaware from off-color sports produced in a cross between barred Plymouth Rock and New Hampshire fowls

[1]**del·a·war·e·an** *or* **del·a·war·i·an** \ˌ≈≈ˈwa(a)rēən, -wer-\ *adj, usu cap* [*Delaware* state + E *-an* or *-ian*] **:** of, relating to, or characteristic of Delaware or Delawareans

[2]**delawarean** *or* **delawarian** \"\ *n* -s *cap* **:** a native or resident of the state of Delaware

[1]**de·lay** \dəˈlā, dēˈ-\ *n* -s [ME *delaye*, fr. OF *delaie*, fr. *delaier*] **1 :** the act or practice of delaying **:** PROCRASTINATION, LINGERING ⟨~ in aircraft production⟩ ⟨~ and uncertainty could cripple our industries⟩ **2 a :** the state or an instance of being delayed ⟨the ~*s* incident to diplomacy⟩ **b :** the time during which something is delayed ⟨a ~ of 30 minutes⟩

[2]**delay** \"\ *vb* -ED/-ING/-S [ME *delayen*, fr. OF *delaier*, fr. *de-* + *laier* to leave, alter. of *laissier*, fr. L *laxare* to slacken, loosen, untie, fr. *laxus* slack, loose — more at SLACK] *vt* **1 :** to put off **:** prolong the time of or before **:** POSTPONE, DEFER ⟨we decided to ~ our departure until the weather improved⟩ **2 a :** to stop, detain, or hinder for a time **:** check the motion of, lessen the progress of, or slow the time of arrival of ⟨the mails were ~*ed* by heavy snows⟩ ⟨the upper house is ~*ing* the passage of important bills⟩ **b :** to cause to be slower or to occur more slowly than normal **:** RETARD — usu. used as a past participle ⟨~*ed* resolution in pneumonia⟩ ⟨a heavy child, ~*ed* in walking⟩ **3** *archaic* **:** to put (a person) off **:** make (a person) wait (as for a payment due) ~ *vi* **:** to move or act slowly, intermittently, or incessantly

syn DELAY, RETARD, SLOW, SLACKEN, and DETAIN agree in meaning to make someone or something behind in schedule or usual rate of movement or progress. DELAY implies a holding back, as by interference, esp. from completion or arrival ⟨a storm *delayed* the ship for an hour⟩ ⟨the opening of the school year had been *delayed* by an epidemic —*Amer. Guide Series: Minn.*⟩ ⟨the symptoms of poisoning may be *delayed* for several days —H.G.Armstrong⟩ ⟨a criminal court jury on which I served *delayed* a verdict all afternoon —C.G.Jameson⟩ RETARD implies a reduction of speed or rate of motion often by interference ⟨snow *retarded* the car considerably⟩ ⟨shortages of labor continue to *retard* production —*Americana Annual*⟩ ⟨other factors *retarded* progress toward a stable economy —*Collier's Yr. Bk.*⟩ ⟨secrecy in research is bound to *retard* the growth of science as a whole —Hartley Shawcross⟩ SLOW, often with *down* or *up*, and SLACKEN also imply a reduction in speed or rate, SLOW often implying intention, SLACKEN stressing an easing up, letting up, or relaxation of effort ⟨as we turned into Compton Street together he *slowed* his step —G. W.Brace⟩ ⟨lack of coordination in the past has *slowed* extensive conservation of water resources —*Amer. Guide Series: Texas*⟩ ⟨perhaps existence was *slowing down* a trifle —Sylvia Berkman⟩ ⟨a bounty of $150 on every live Indian brought in somewhat *slowed up* the general shooting —Marjory S. Douglas⟩ ⟨their rate of growth *slackens* as they age —L.P.Schultz⟩ ⟨the river broadens, *slackening* its pace as it spreads out and turns —Ted Sumner⟩ ⟨economic expansion had *slackened* —Oscar Handlin⟩ DETAIN implies a holding back or being held back beyond an appointed or reasonable time, whether deliberate or not ⟨I slipped my arm around her slender body to *detain* her —W.H.Hudson †1922⟩ ⟨on the voyage thither they were *detained* in Honolulu —R.S.Kuykendall⟩ ⟨after being *detained* in England by the war then raging with Spain, White returned to Roanoke Island —*Amer. Guide Series: N.C.*⟩

syn DELAY, PROCRASTINATE, LAG, LOITER, DAWDLE, DALLY, and DILLYDALLY mean, in common, to move or act slowly so that expected progress is not made or prospective work is left undone or unfinished. DELAY suggests putting off ⟨do not *delay* in sending for your copies. Fill out the attached form today —*Current History*⟩ ⟨genuine success seemed as usual to *delay* and postpone itself —Arnold Bennett⟩ ⟨to *delay* foolishly until all opportunity is past⟩ PROCRASTINATE suggests blameworthy delay as from laziness, indifference, or habitual inertia ⟨to fumble, to vacillate, to *procrastinate* and so let war come creeping upon us almost unawares —W.A.White⟩ ⟨to *procrastinate* in letter writing and lose friends⟩ LAG implies a failure to maintain a required or desirable speed ⟨for half the race the one who finally won had *lagged* behind the others, conserving his strength⟩ ⟨work on the fort had *lagged* —*Amer. Guide Series: Ark.*⟩ ⟨confidence in the administration *lagged* until enemies of the regime were emboldened recently to attempt a revolution —P.P.Kennedy⟩ LOITER implies a delay while in progress, esp. walking, often suggesting a lingering about or an aimless sauntering ⟨a child *loitering* on the way to school⟩ ⟨after breakfasting he walked down the hill and *loitered* about the little streets —Willa Cather⟩ DAWDLE implies a slighter delay in progress than LOITER but connotes more strongly an aimlessness or a taking of more time than is necessary ⟨I did not hurry the rest of the way home; but neither did I *dawdle* —V.G.Heiser⟩ ⟨the sun *dawdles* intolerably on the threshold like a tedious guest —Jan Struther⟩ DALLY and, more strongly, DILLYDALLY suggest wasting time in trifling, pottering, or vacillation ⟨while the men *dallied*, the dogs set off briskly of their own accord —J.T.McNish⟩ ⟨they *dallied* to make mud pies or just to get themselves as muddy as time permitted —*English Digest*⟩ ⟨because the government had *dillydallied* with new export rules, trading in hides and skins had all but stopped —*Time*⟩ ⟨the protagonist is a maundering fellow who *dillydallies* too much in getting his murdering done —Margery Bailey⟩

[3]**delay** *vt* -ED/-ING/-S [MF *delayer*, fr. (assumed) VL *delicare*, for L *deliquare* to clarify, strain, decant, fr. *de-* + *liquare* to melt, strain — more at LIQUATE] *obs* **:** ALLAY: as **a :** MITIGATE, ASSUAGE **b :** WEAKEN, TEMPER, DILUTE

delayed-action *also* **delay-action** \=ˈ=ˌ==\ *adj* **1 :** tending to act or become effective only after some usu. predetermined period of time **2** *of an explosive projectile* **:** detonating some time after it strikes the target

delayed action *n* [*delayed-action*] **:** a device for automatically releasing the shutter of a camera after a certain period of time to enable the photographer to appear in the picture

delayed dormant spray *n* **:** a pesticidal spray applied esp. to fruit trees after the green bud tips begin to show but before they are exposed ¼ to ½ inch

delayed subject *n* **:** a subject following its verb when an expletive or an anticipatory subject precedes (as *five people* in "there are five people here" or *to believe that* in "it is easy to believe that")

de·lay·er \dəˈlāə(r), dēˈ-\ *n* -S **:** one that delays

delaying *adj* **:** causing or involving delay — **de·lay·ing·ly** *adv*

delaying action *n* **:** a defensive military action in which advance of an enemy is delayed by fighting as long as possible without the defensive force becoming involved in decisive battle that would imperil its withdrawal

delay line *n, electronics* **:** a device put in series with a transmission line to introduce a time lag in signals traversing it

del cre·de·re \(ˈ)delˈkrādərē\ *adj* [It, of belief, of trust] *of a commission merchant or agent or an agency agreement* **:** relating to or guaranteeing performance or payment by third persons to the principal in connection with sales or transactions entered into by such merchant or agent for the principal usu. in return for higher commissions

deld *abbr* delivered

[1]**de·le** \ˈdē(ˌ)lē, -ēlī\ *vt* **deled; deled; deleing; deles** [L, imper. sing. of *delēre* to wipe out, destroy — more at DELETE] **1 :** to remove (as a word or character) from typeset matter **:** ERASE **2 :** to mark (as matter for deletion) with a dele

[2]**dele** \"\ *n* -S **:** a mark that is usu. made in a margin and that indicates something is to be deled

de·lead \(ˈ)dē+\ *vt* [*de-* + *lead* (n.)] **:** to remove lead from ⟨~ a chemical⟩

de·lec·ta·bil·i·ty \də,lektəˈbilədē, dē,-, -ətē, -i\ *n* -ES **:** delectable quality or condition

de·lec·ta·ble \=ˈ=təbəl\ *adj* [ME, fr. MF, fr. L *delectabilis*, fr. *delectare* to delight + *-abilis* -able — more at DELIGHT] **1 :** highly pleasing **:** DELIGHTFUL **2 :** deliciously flavored **:** SAVORY **syn** see DELIGHTFUL

de·lec·ta·ble·ness \-bəlnəs\ *n* -ES **:** the quality of being delectable

de·lec·ta·bly \-blē, -bli\ *adv* [ME, fr. *delectable* + *-ly*] **:** in a delectable manner

de·lec·tate \dəˈlek,tāt, dēˈ-\ *vb* -ED/-ING/-S [L *delectatus*, past part. of *delectare* — more at DELIGHT] *vt* **:** DELIGHT, PLEASE, ENTERTAIN ~ *vi* **:** to obtain pleasure from or take pleasure in something

de·lec·ta·tion \,delәkˈtāshən; ,dē(,)lek-, di(-\ *n* -S [ME *delectacioun*, fr. MF or L; MF *delectation*, fr. L *delectation-*, *delectatio*, fr. *delectatus* + *-ion-*, *-io* -ion] **1 :** DELIGHT **2 :** PLEASURE, DIVERSION, ENJOYMENT **syn** see PLEASURE

de·lec·tus \dəˈlektəs\ *n* -ES [L, selection, fr. *delectus*, past part. of *deligere* to choose out, select, fr. *de-* + *-ligere* (fr. *legere* to gather) — more at LEGEND] **:** a book of selected passages esp. for learners of Latin or Greek

delectus per·so·nae \-pə(r)ˈsō(,)nē, -,nī\ *n* [L, choice of person] **:** the selection of a person satisfactory to oneself for a position involving trust and confidence in the other's character, capacities, or responsibility — used in the phrase *right of delectus personae*

de·lee·rit \dəˈlērət\ *adj* [fr. past part. of Sc *deleer*, *delier*, prob. fr. F *délirer* to be delirious, fr. MF *delirer*, fr. L *delirare* to be crazy, be delirious, dote, rave — more at DELIRIUM] *Scot* **:** out of one's senses; *specif* **:** INTOXICATED

del·e·ga·ble \ˈdeləgəbəl, -lēg-\ *adj* [[2]*delegate* + *-able*] **:** that can be delegated ⟨~ responsibilities⟩

del·e·ga·cy \-gəsē, -si\ *n* -ES [[1]*delegate* + *-cy*] **1 a :** the act of delegating or state of being delegated **:** appointment as delegate **b :** deputed power **2 :** a body of delegates **:** DELEGATION; *specif* **:** a special permanent committee at Oxford University

de·legalize \(ˈ)dē+\ *vt* [*de-* + *legalize*] **:** to remove the status of statutory authorization from

del·e·gant \ˈdeləgənt, -lēg-\ *n* -S [L *delegant-*, *delegans*, pres. part. of *delegare* to delegate] **:** one that delegates

[1]**del·e·gate** \ˈdeləgət, -lēg-, -,gāt, *usu* -d·+V\ *n* -S [ME *delegat*, fr. ML *delegatus*, fr. L, past part. of *delegare* to delegate, fr. *de-* + *legare* to send — more at LEGATE] **:** a person sent and empowered to act for another **:** DEPUTY, REPRESENTATIVE, COMMISSIONER: as **a :** a representative to a convention or conference (as of a political party) **b :** a member of a committee for some branch of university business at Oxford University **c :** a representative of a U.S. territory in the House of Representatives who has the right to debate but not to vote **d :** a member of the lower house of the legislature of Maryland, Virginia, or West Virginia

[2]**del·e·gate** \-,gāt, *usu* -ād·+V\ *vt* -ED/-ING/-S [L *delegatus*, past part. of *delegare*] **1 :** to entrust to another **:** TRANSFER, ASSIGN, COMMIT ⟨power *delegated* by the people to the legislature⟩ ⟨one may ~ one's authority to a competent assistant⟩ **2 :** to send (someone) as one's representative or as a delegate **:** COMMISSION, DEPUTE ⟨*delegated* her to watch over the sleeping children⟩ ⟨the union will ~ three representatives to the convention⟩ **3** *Roman & civil law* **:** to assign (a debtor of oneself) to a creditor as a debtor in place of oneself

[3]**del·e·gate** \-,gət, -,gāt\ *adj* [L *delegatus*] *archaic* **:** DELEGATED

del·e·ga·tee \,deləgəˈtē\ *n* -S **:** one to whom a debtor is delegated

del·e·ga·tion \,deləˈgāshən, -lēˈ-\ *n* -S [L *delegation-*, *delegatio*, fr. *delegatus* + *-ion-*, *-io* -ion] **1 :** the act of investing with authority to act for another **:** appointment of a delegate or delegates **2 :** one or more persons appointed or chosen to represent others (as in a convention or congress) **:** a body of delegates **:** DEPUTATION **3 :** LETTER OF DELEGATION; *also* **:** the transfer of a debt or credit by such a letter **4** *Roman & civil law* **:** a novation wherein a debtor extinguishes his debt by substituting a debt owed him for the one he owes his creditor

del·e·ga·tor \ˈ==,gād·ə(r)\ *n* -S **:** DELEGANT

del·e·ga·to·ry \ˈ==gə,tōrē, -tôr-, -ri\ *adj* [LL *delegatorius*, fr. L *delegatus* + *-orius* -ory] **:** of, relating to, or involving delegation of authority **:** conveying power or authority to one that has no independent right to it ⟨various ~ acts required to establish modern public-health services⟩

de le·ge fe·ren·da \(,)dāˈlā,jāfəˈrendə\ *adj* (*or adv*) [L, by means of a law to be made] **:** being on the basis of new law

deles *pres 3d sing of* DELE, *pl of* DELE

del·es·se·ria \,deləˈsirēə\ *n, cap* [NL, fr. Benjamin *Delessert* †1847 Fr. banker and botanist + NL *-ia*] **:** a genus (the type of the family Delesseriaceae of the order Ceramiales) of red algae with flat thalli that often simulate the leaves of higher plants — **del·es·se·ri·a·ceous** \ˈ==;=rēˈāshəs\ *adj*

de·lete \dəˈlēt, dēˈ-, *usu* -ēd·+V\ *vt* -ED/-ING/-S [L *deletus*, past part. of *delēre* to wipe out, destroy, fr. *de-* + *-lēre* (fr. the root of *linere* to smear) — more at LIME] **:** to reduce to nullity: as **a** *archaic* **:** DESTROY, ANNIHILATE **b :** to reject by physically obscuring (as by blotting out, scratching out, or cutting out) or by excluding or marking for exclusion during further processing (as retyping or printing) ⟨~ the third paragraph⟩ ⟨his name was *deleted* from the list⟩ **:** ERASE, EXPUNGE, DELE **c :** to eliminate as a factor or a matter for consideration ⟨new processes will probably ultimately ~ this crop from the economy⟩ ⟨it is impossible to ~ religious considerations and retain a clear view of colonial history⟩ **syn** see ERASE

del·e·te·ri·ous \,deləˈtirēəs, -tēr- *sometimes* -ter-, *esp Brit* ˈdēl-\ *adj* [Gk *dēlētērios*, fr. *dēleisthai* to hurt; akin to L *dolare* to hew — more at CONDOLE] **:** HURTFUL, DESTRUCTIVE, NOXIOUS, PERNICIOUS ⟨~ plants⟩ ⟨~ effects of excessive drinking⟩ **syn** see PERNICIOUS

del·e·te·ri·ous·ly *adv* **:** in a deleterious manner

del·e·te·ri·ous·ness *n* -ES **:** the quality of being deleterious **:** HARMFULNESS ⟨arguments about the ~ of smoking⟩

[1]**deletery** *adj* [Gk *dēlētērios*] *obs* **:** DELETERIOUS, POISONOUS

[2]**deletery** *n* -ES [ML or Gk; ML *deleterium*, fr. Gk *dēlētērion*, fr. neut. of *dēlētērios*] **1** *obs* **:** something deleterious or poisonous **2** *obs* **:** ANTIDOTE

de·le·thal·ize \(ˈ)dēˈlēthə,līz\ *vt* -ED/-ING/-S [*de-* + *lethal* + *-ize*] **:** to make nonlethal

de·le·tion \dəˈlēshən, dēˈ-\ *n* -S [L *deletion-*, *deletio*, fr. *deletus* (past part. of *delēre* to wipe out, destroy) + *-ion-*, *-io* -ion — more at DELETE] **1 :** an act of deleting, blotting out, or erasing **:** DESTRUCTION, EXTINCTION **2 a :** something deleted esp. from written matter **:** a deleted passage **:** ERASURE ⟨~*s* by the censor⟩ **b :** DEFICIENCY 2b; *esp* **:** a large deficiency not including either end of a chromosome

de·leveling \(ˈ)dē+\ *n* [*de-* + *leveling*] **:** alteration of the elevation of a part of the earth's surface

delf \ˈdelf\ *also* **delft** \-lft\ *or* **delph** \-lf\ *n* -S [ME *delf*, fr. OE *gedelf*, fr. *delfan* to dig — more at DELVE] **1 a** *now dial Eng* **:** EXCAVATION; *usu* **:** MINE, QUARRY **b :** POND; *also* **:** DRAIN, DITCH **2 :** a square heraldic bearing used as an abatement and supposed to represent a square sod

delft \ˈdelft\ *also* **delf** \-lf\ *or* **delph** \"\ *n* -S [short for *delftware, delphware*] **1 a :** DELFTWARE 1 **b :** glazed pottery esp. when blue and white **2** *or* **delft blue** *also* **delf blue :** a variable color averaging a grayish purplish blue that is bluer, lighter, and stronger than regimental, redder, lighter, and stronger than average navy blue, and very slightly redder and darker than Wedgwood blue (sense 2) — called also *Dutchware blue*

delftware *also* **delphware** \ˈ=,=\ *n* [*Delft*, Netherlands, where it originated + E *ware*] **1 :** a soft but strong tin-glazed Dutch faience decorated on the unfired glaze in blue or sometimes polychrome orig. in imitation of oriental porcelain but later with genre scenes; *also* **:** a similar but harder English ware **2** *Brit* **:** glazed and decorated earthenware

del·hi \ˈdelē, -li *sometimes* -l,hī *or* -l,hē\ *adj, usu cap* [fr. *Delhi*, India] **:** of or from the city of Delhi, India **:** of the kind or style prevalent in Delhi

delhi belly *n, usu cap D* [so called fr. its high incidence among Am. troops in the Delhi area during World War II] **:** DYSENTERY

delhi boil *n, usu cap D* [so called fr. its former high incidence among British troops in the Delhi area] **:** leishmaniasis of the skin

de·lia \ˈdēlēə, -lyə\ *n pl, usu cap* [Gk *Dēlia*, fr. neut. pl. of *Dēlios* of Delos] **:** a festival with games that was celebrated by the ancient Greeks every fourth year at Delos in honor of Apollo and was noted for musical contests

de·li·an \-ən\ *adj, usu cap* [L *Delius* of Delos (fr. Gk *Dēlios*, fr. *Dēlos*, island in the Aegean) + E *-an*] **:** of or relating to the island of Delos, held in antiquity to be the birthplace of Apollo and Artemis

delian problem *n, usu cap D* [so called fr. the problem posed by the judgment of the Delian oracle in ancient Greece that a plague in Athens could be brought to an end by doubling the size of a cubical altar to Apollo] **:** the problem of finding the edge of a cube the double in volume of a given cube

delibate *vt* -ED/-ING/-S [L *delibatus*, past part. of *delibare* to take away, decrease, taste, enjoy, fr. *de-* + *libare* to pour out, take out, taste — more at LIBATION] *obs* **:** to take a little of **:** dabble in **:** SIP — **delibation** *n* -S *obs*

de·lib·er·ant \dəˈlib(ə)rənt, dēˈ-\ *n* -S [[2]*deliberate* + *-ant*] **:** one who deliberates

[1]**de·lib·er·ate** \dəˈlib(ə)rə|t, dē-, *chiefly in substand speech* -bər|t; *usu* |d· + V\ *adj* [L *deliberatus*, past part. of *deliberare* to deliberate, alter. (influenced by *liberare* to free) of (assumed) *delibrare*, fr. *de-* + *libra* scale, pound — more at LIBERATE] **1 :** characterized by or resulting from slow careful thorough calculation and consideration of effects and consequences **:** not hasty, rash, or thoughtless ⟨a ~ judgement⟩ ⟨there is no ~ study of it; haphazard thoughts occupy the place of rational conclusions —Herbert Spencer⟩ **2 :** characterized by presumed or real awareness of the implications or consequences of one's actions or sayings or by fully conscious often willful intent ⟨~ mischief⟩ ⟨a ~ lie⟩ ⟨it was no accidental meeting of fugitive glances . . . a ~ communication —Joseph Conrad⟩ **3 :** slow, unhurried, and steady as though allowing time for decision on each individual action involved ⟨a ~ man, slow to anger but ruthless when aroused⟩ ⟨he had not heard her heavy ~ tread on the now uncarpeted stair —Willa Cather⟩ ⟨~ in speech⟩

syn CONSIDERED, ADVISED, PREMEDITATED, DESIGNED, STUDIED: DELIBERATE always indicates full awareness of what one is doing and, used precisely, implies careful and unhurried consideration of procedures or consequences ⟨before the U.S. could obtain an admission from Palmerston that the attack on the *Caroline* had been *deliberate* and official —S.E.Morison & H.S.Commager⟩ ⟨cautious, *deliberate*, methodical, he was in no danger, she felt, of plunging precipitately into marriage — Ellen Glasgow⟩ ⟨her methodicalness made her suicide more *deliberate*. Her self-possession was frightening —W.S. Maugham⟩ CONSIDERED, not usu. applied to questionable acts, suggests careful study and soundness and maturity of judgment ⟨in my *considered* opinion⟩ ⟨a fitting object to be called, by those who suspect all men of *considered* opinions and of wide systematized views, a dogmatist —*Contemporary Rev.*⟩ ADVISED, now used mostly with deprecatory modifying adverbs, means so well thought out that possible criticisms and objections can be readily answered and doubts resolved ⟨the very proper young man felt well *advised* to sound out the parents before proposing to the girl⟩ PREMEDITATED emphasizes previous planning and intent but does not necessarily indicate consideration of consequences ⟨both first and second degree murder (laying aside the exceptions which I thought it unnecessary to state) require an intent to kill, but in the one instance it is deliberate and *premeditated* intent and in the other it is not —B.N.Cardozo⟩ DESIGNED indicates intent and plan, perhaps despite appearances of spontaneity and naturalness ⟨perhaps the humor of this ruling was more unwitting than *designed* —B.N.Cardozo⟩ STUDIED connotes absence of spontaneity and presence of cool deliberateness, painstaking effort, or careful attention ⟨the student began to feel that the teacher's oppression of him was a *studied* effort⟩ ⟨the themes of these chaste exercises are often of a *studied* thinness. You may find that the author is disclaiming, almost anxiously, the idea of tarnishing the minute mirror of his sensibilities with any breath of thought —C.E.Montague⟩ **syn** see in addition SLOW, VOLUNTARY

[2]**de·lib·er·ate** \-ˈlibə,rāt, *usu* -ād·+V\ *vb* -ED/-ING/-S [L *deliberatus*] *vt* **:** to ponder or think about with measured careful consideration and often with formal discussion before reaching a decision or conclusion ⟨he is *deliberating* what to do⟩ ⟨the committee *deliberated* the matter⟩ ~ *vi* **:** to ponder issues and decisions carefully often with the aid of counsel and formal consultation ⟨the jury *deliberated* throughout the night⟩ ⟨a club *deliberating* on what to do with the extra money in its treasury⟩ **syn** see THINK

de·lib·er·ate·ly \-ˈlibər(ə)tlē, -brət-, -li\ *adv* **:** in a deliberate manner **:** with deliberation

de·lib·er·ate·ness \-bər(ə)tnəs, -brət-\ *n* -ES **:** calm well-poised slowness (as of thought, speech, or bodily movement) ⟨shrewd Dutch ~⟩

de·lib·er·a·tion \də,libəˈrāshən, dē,-\ *n* -S [ME *deliberacioun*, fr. MF or L; MF *deliberation*, fr. L *deliberation-*, *deliberatio*, fr. *deliberatus* + *-ion-*, *-io* -ion] **1 :** the act of weighing and examining the reasons for and against a choice or measure **:** careful consideration **:** mature reflection ⟨after careful ~ he decided to study medicine rather than law⟩ **2 :** a discussion and consideration by a number of persons of the reasons for and against a measure — often used in pl. ⟨the House concluded its ~*s* and its members hurried home to mend political fences⟩ **3 :** the quality or state of being deliberate **:** DELIBERATENESS **4** *obs* **:** RESOLUTION, DECISION, DETERMINATION

[1]**de·lib·er·a·tive** \=ˈ==,rād·|iv, -āt|, |ēv *also* |əv; -b(ə)rəd·|, -rət|\ *adj* [L *deliberativus*, fr. *deliberatus* + *-ivus* -ive] **:** of, relating to, or marked by deliberation **:** proceeding or acting by discussion and examination **:** engaged in or devoted to deliberation ⟨a ~ body⟩ — see DELIBERATIVE ASSEMBLY — **de·lib·er·a·tive·ly** \|əvlē, -li\ *adv* — **de·lib·er·a·tive·ness** \|əvnəs\ *n* -ES

[2]**deliberative** *n* -S *obs* **:** a deliberative discourse or topic

deliberative assembly *n* **:** a nonlegislative organization that conducts meetings according to parliamentary law

de·lib·er·a·tor \-bə,rād·ə(r)\ *n* -S **:** one that deliberates

de·libidinize \ˌdē+\ *vt* [*de-* + *libidinize*] **:** to free of erotic significance

del·i·ble \ˈdeləbəl\ *adj* [alter. (influenced by *-ible*) of earlier *deleble*, fr. L *delebilis*, fr. *delēre* to wipe out, destroy + *-bilis* capable or worthy of (being acted upon) — more at DELETE] **:** capable of being deleted

del·i·ca·cy \ˈdeləkəsē, -lēk-, -si\ *n* -ES [ME *delicacie*, fr. *delicat* delicate + *-cie* -cy] **1** *obs* **a :** the quality or state of being pleasurable or agreeable **b :** addiction to sensuous pleasure or luxury **:** INDULGENCE; *also* **:** luxurious treatment or care **c :** PLEASURE, GRATIFICATION **2 :** something that is dainty or delicate and gives uncommon pleasure; *esp* **:** something pleasing to eat that is accounted rare or luxurious ⟨fresh fruit in winter was once a ~ available only to the very rich⟩ **3 a :** fineness or daintiness of form, texture, or constitution ⟨the cobwebby ~ of fine lace⟩ ⟨the ~ of the long filament that the silkworm spins⟩ ⟨a slender figure of great ~⟩ **b :** want of vigor or robustness **:** susceptibility to ill-health or injury **:** FRAILTY, WEAKNESS, TENDERNESS ⟨an appearance of over-refinement and ~⟩ ⟨the ~ of the tea rose renders it useless for northern gardens⟩ **4 :** nicety, fineness, or subtle expressiveness of manipulation or touch ⟨the ~ of a pianist's touch⟩ **5 a :** precise and refined perception and discrimination ⟨the ~ of his taste in art⟩ **b :** extreme sensitivity **:** capacity for reacting to minute changes or with great precision — used chiefly of devices and mechanisms ⟨a balance of such ~ that moisture from the breath would activate it⟩ ⟨the ~ of a fine watch movement⟩ **6 a :** nice sensibility esp. as to the decorous, honorable, modest, or kindly; *specif* **:** gentle consideration of the feelings of others **b :** excessive fastidiousness **:** SQUEAMISHNESS ⟨hunger knows no ~⟩ **7 :** the quality or state of requiring careful, precise, or tactful procedure ⟨the ~ of the present international situation⟩

[1]**del·i·cate** \-kət, *usu* -əd·+V\ *adj, sometimes* -ER/-EST [ME *delicat*, fr. L *delicatus* pleasing to the senses, voluptuous, pampered, dainty; akin to L *delicere* to allure — more at DELIGHT] **1 :** gratifying to the senses **:** sensuously pleasing: as **a :** generally agreeable or pleasant **:** DELIGHTFUL ⟨the most ~ air — Grecian air, pellucid —Richard Jefferies⟩ ⟨a ~ garden⟩ **b :** pleasing to the sense of taste or smell esp. without being heady, obtrusive, or intense ⟨a tea with a peculiarly ~ aroma⟩ ⟨a ~ blend of spices⟩ **:** subtly savory ⟨~ cookery⟩ ⟨~ dishes to tempt an invalid⟩ **c :** delightful to see esp. because of fine dainty charming color, lines, or proportions ⟨her face . . . was as ~ as porcelain —Ellen Glasgow⟩ **2** *obs* **:** characterized by or addicted to self-indulgence or ease **:** luxury-loving **:** VOLUPTUOUS; *also* **:** SLOTHFUL **3 a :** marked by or given to keen sensitivity of impression and analysis, fine discrimination, subtle distinction, nice appreciation; *also* **:** calling for observation and judgment with these qualities ⟨this ~ moralist, so sensitive to historical pathos —Cecil Sprigge⟩ ⟨a task so ~ exacts the scholar and philosopher —B.N. Cardozo⟩ **b :** marked by or given to fastidiousness esp. by exacting or squeamish tastes or prim interests and pursuits **:** likely to be repelled by the crude or gross; *also* **:** calling for fastidious treatment ⟨not a book for the ~ reader, but . . . not pornographic —Charles Lee⟩ **c :** strongly marked by or given to scruples, strict ethics, propriety, honor, punctilio, or finer feelings **4 a :** capable of or marked by precise or minute perception, detection, measure, discernment, or judgment **b** *of an instrument or device* **:** exhibiting great delicacy or extreme sensitivity **:** capable of reacting to or registering (as by deflection of a balance) a minute effect, force, or quantity ⟨an impulse so small as to be almost undetectable with even the . . . most ~ instruments —A.C.Morrison⟩ **c :** calling for or involving meticulously careful measurement, treatment, or calculation ⟨a ~ process⟩ ⟨~ tests for contamination⟩ **:** liable to being easily unsettled or mishandled; *sometimes* **:** precariously or very unevenly balanced ⟨the ~ interdependence of our credit-built finance and industry —Norman Angell⟩ **5 a :** marked by precise skillful meticulous technique or operation or by execution with adroit finesse in meeting uncommon difficulties or dangers; *also* **:** requiring such technique, operation, or execution ⟨a marvelously precise chart . . . the calculations were ~, minute, exquisitely clear —Sinclair Lewis⟩ **b :** marked by very fine structure, texture, finish, organization, or integration produced by or as if by immaculate or meticulous craftsmanship ⟨~ feminine handwriting —George Meredith⟩ ⟨a ~ celestial chain of sapphires —Elinor Wylie⟩ ⟨~ lace⟩ **c :** frail, fragile, or easily torn, bruised, damaged, or hurt ⟨a ~ butterfly wing⟩; *often* **:** lacking in physical strength and stamina **:** tending to suffer fatigue or illness from slight causes **:** WEAK, SICKLY **d :** marked by fine subtlety **:** having qualities perceived and appreciated only by the cultivated **:** not crude or obvious ⟨an irony so quiet, so ~, that many readers never notice it —J.B.Priestley⟩ **e :** marked by or given to elaborate tact, cautious judgment, and prudent discreetness to avoid offense, conflict, or difficulty ⟨~ semidiplomatic relationships with belligerent and neutral powers —W.B.Hesseltine⟩ ⟨he went off, ~ as always, so we could talk about it —Ernest Hemingway⟩; *also* **:** requiring such characteristics **:** SENSITIVE, UNCERTAIN, PRECARIOUS ⟨a ~ position, one requiring great tact —J.T.Farrell⟩

⟨one's spiritual concerns are rather ~ for a stranger to meddle with —Herman Melville⟩ **syn** see CHOICE

[2]**delicate** \"\ *n* -s [ME *delicat*, fr. L *delicatus* voluptuary, fr. *delicatus*, adj.] **:** one that is delicate: as **a** *obs* **:** a luxurious or fastidious person **b** *obs* **:** a delight esp. of the senses **:** LUXURY **c** *archaic* **:** a table delicacy

del·i·cate·ly *adv* [ME *delicatly*, fr. *delicat* + *-ly*] **:** in a delicate manner **:** with delicacy: as **a :** with fastidiousness ⟨picking ~ at the morsels on her plate⟩ **b :** with nice consideration ⟨words ~ chosen to avoid further offense⟩ **c :** gently and precisely ⟨stepping ~ from hummock to hummock⟩

del·i·cate·ness *n* -ES **:** the quality or state of being delicate **:** PRECARIOUSNESS, FRAGILITY, REFINEMENT, DELICACY

del·i·ca·tesse \ˌ==kəˈtes\ *n* -s [F *délicatesse*, fr. MF *delicatesse*, prob. fr. OIt *delicatezza*, fr. *delicato* delicate, dainty, tasty (fr. L *delicatus* pleasing to the senses, voluptuous) + *-ezza* -ess — more at DELICATE] **:** DELICACY, TACT

del·i·ca·tes·sen \-sᵊn\ *n pl* [G *delikatessen* (formerly spelled *delicatessen*), pl. of *delikatesse* delicacy, fr. F *délicatesse*] **1 :** ready-to-eat food products (as cooked or processed meats, cheeses, prepared salads, canned foods, preserves, relishes) **2** *sing, pl* **delicatessens** [*delicatessen* (*store*)] **:** a store where delicatessen are sold either to be taken out or to be eaten on the premises (as in sandwiches)

de·lice \dəˈlēs\ *n* -s [ME, fr. OF, fr. L *delicium*, fr. *delicere* to allure — more at DELIGHT] *archaic* **:** something giving pleasure; *esp* **:** DELICACY

del·i·chon \ˈdelə̇ˌkän\ *n, cap* [NL, anagram of *Chelidon*] **:** a genus of swallows with feathered feet that includes the European martin (*D. urbica*)

[1]**de·li·cious** \də̇ˈlishəs, dēˈ-\ *adj* [ME, fr. OF, fr. LL *deliciosus*, fr. L *deliciae* delight (fr. *delicere* to allure) + *-osus* -ose — more at DELIGHT] **1 a :** affording great pleasure **:** DELIGHTFUL, ENCHANTING ⟨a stroll through the ~ spring landscape⟩ ⟨a ~ breeze cooled our heated foreheads⟩ **b :** appealing to one of the bodily senses **:** affording an enjoyable sensory reaction esp. involving the sense of taste or smell ⟨a ~ dessert⟩ ⟨a ~ mouth-watering smell drifted from the kitchen⟩ **c :** delightfully amusing ⟨her ~ impudence and enchanting grace held them spellbound⟩ **2** *obs* **:** characterized by or addicted to self-indulgent or sensuous pleasure **:** seeking voluptuous enjoyment **:** LUXURIOUS **syn** see DELIGHTFUL

[2]**delicious** \"\ *also* **delicious apple** *n, pl* **deliciouses** *or* **delicious** *often cap* **:** a largely red apple of American origin and superior form, aroma, and flavor that is much grown in warmer apple-producing sections; *broadly* **:** any of several apples having qualities in common with the delicious and possibily derived from it — usu. used in combination ⟨golden ~⟩ ⟨double-red ~⟩

de·li·cious·ly *adv* [ME, fr. *delicious* + *-ly*] **:** in a delicious manner ⟨~ flavored sauce⟩ **:** so as to produce delight ⟨a ~ exciting situation⟩

de·li·cious·ness *n* -ES [ME *deliciousnesse*, fr. *delicious* + *-nesse* -ness] **:** the quality or state of being delicious **:** DELIGHT

de·lict \də̇ˈlikt, dēˈ- *also* ˈdēˌ-\ *n* -s [L *delictum* fault, fr. neut. of *delictus*, past part. of *delinquere* to fail, offend — more at DELINQUENT] **:** a wrong or improper act **:** OFFENSE: **a :** an offense or transgression against law — chiefly used in the civil and Scots law to designate civil wrongs corresponding closely to the torts of English law **b :** an act of a sovereign state that is considered under the law of nations to be an offense or injury against another state — **de·lic·tu·al** \=ˈlikchəwəl, (ˈ)dēˌ-\ *adj*

de·lic·tum \=ˈliktəm\ *n, pl* **delic·ta** \-tə\ [L] **:** DELICT

de·lie·ret \dəˈlērə̇t\ *var of* DELEERIT

[1]**de·light** \də̇ˈlīt, dēˈ-, *usu* -īd·+V\ *n* -s [ME *delit*, fr. OF *delit*, *deleit*, fr. *delitier*, *deleitier*] **1 :** a high degree of gratification of mind or sense **:** a high-wrought state of pleasurable feeling **:** lively pleasure **:** JOY ⟨filled with ~ at the thought of pleasant days ahead⟩; *also* **:** extreme satisfaction ⟨he took ~ in his new accomplishment⟩ **2 :** something that gives great pleasure or gratification ⟨Heaven's last, best gift, my ever new ~ —John Milton⟩ ⟨the new car is a perfect ~⟩ **3** *archaic* **:** the power of affording pleasurable emotion or felicity ⟨of more ~ than hawks or horses be —Shak.⟩ **syn** see PLEASURE

[2]**delight** \"\ *vb* -ED/-ING/-S [ME *deliten*, fr. OF *delitier*, *deleitier*, fr. L *delectare*, fr. *delectus* past part. of *delicere* to allure, fr. *de-* + *-licere* (fr. *lacere* to allure); akin to OE *lǣl* switch, L *laqueus* snare] *vi* **1 :** to have or take great satisfaction or pleasure **:** become greatly pleased or rejoiced—used with *in* or an infinitive ⟨love *delights* in praises —Shak.⟩ ⟨I *delight* to do thy will, O my God —Ps 40:8⟩ **2 :** to give keen enjoyment or pleasure **~** *vt* **1 :** to give joy or satisfaction to **:** affect very pleasurably **:** please highly **:** GRATIFY ⟨a beautiful scene ~*s* the eye⟩ ⟨their gifts ~*ed* the children⟩ **2** *obs* **:** to take delight in **:** ENJOY **syn** see PLEASE

delighted *adj* **1** *obs* **:** DELIGHTFUL **2 :** highly pleased **:** GRATIFIED **:** JOYOUS — **de·light·ed·ly** *adv* — **de·light·ed·ness** *n* -ES

de·light·er \-īd·ə(r), -ītə-\ *n* -s **:** one that gives or takes delight

de·light·ful \-ītfəl\ *adj* **1 :** highly pleasing **:** affording great pleasure and satisfaction ⟨a ~ day in the country⟩ **2** *obs* **:** experiencing delight

syn DELICIOUS, DELECTABLE, LUSCIOUS: DELIGHTFUL, very wide in its applications, may describe anything that gives keen lively pleasure to mind, heart, or senses ⟨this is the most charming and *delightful* book I have read in many a day —H.S.Canby⟩ ⟨he was a high-spirited ornamental youth with soft melting eyes, as good as he was beautiful, and so *delightful* to women that it was said they all longed to bite him —J.A. Froude⟩ ⟨for rest and recreation a warm, equable climate is doubtless most *delightful* —Ellsworth Huntington⟩ ⟨sex must be treated from the first as natural, *delightful* and decent —Bertrand Russell⟩ DELICIOUS commonly refers to that which is tasted, smelled, or otherwise savored with maximum pleasure and keenest appreciation ⟨the fish was *delicious;* the manner of cooking them in the ground preserving all the juices and rendering them exceeding sweet and tender —Herman Melville⟩ ⟨among the irises and roses and nodding tufts of lilac . . . snuffing in . . . the *delicious* scent —Virginia Woolf⟩ ⟨her gestures *delicious* in their modest and sensitive grace —Arnold Bennett⟩ DELECTABLE, a rather literary word, is close to DELICIOUS but may apply to what enraptures a refined or discriminating taste ⟨it was spicy sherry, and we drank out of the halves of fresh citron melons. *Delectable* goblets —Herman Melville⟩ ⟨the sweet cloister, with its walls of silver, surrounded by silvery herbage, all *delectable* beyond conception —H.O. Taylor⟩ ⟨its scoring is *delectable*, with the subtlest of balances, mixed colors and shifting sonorities —*Musical America*⟩ LUSCIOUS suggests a lush richness of taste, flavor, fragrance, or coloring ⟨the *luscious* figs, the grapes, oozy with southern juice —Nathaniel Hawthorne⟩ ⟨Renoir, whose appetizing La Source — an amply bosomed nude sitting beside a running fountain — showed the *luscious* tints and easy symbolism —*Time*⟩ ⟨the quatrains of wine and flowers translated for us in *luscious*, seductive rhyme —Donn Byrne⟩ LUSCIOUS may suggest overtones of excess or extravagance, as of coloring, fleshy ripeness, full-blown luxuriance, or voluptuousness ⟨others amuse themselves with *luscious* sonnets to Bessies and Jessies —*Publ's Mod. Lang. Assoc. of America*⟩ ⟨she was a blonde, who must once have been quite *luscious* and who was by no means even now undesirable — smooth and round, with a pink complexion that sometimes looked like strawberries and cream, sometimes a little blowsy —Edmund Wilson⟩ DELECTABLE and LUSCIOUS are more common in humorous and ironic uses than DELIGHTFUL and DELICIOUS ⟨one of the most *delectable* bees that ever buzzed in a bonnet —C.E.Montague⟩ ⟨a droll and *luscious* nasality —Thomas Wolfe⟩

de·light·ful·ly \-ītf(ə)lē, -li\ *adv* **:** in a delightful manner **:** in such a way or to such a degree as to be esp. pleasant ⟨~ gentle breezes⟩ ⟨a ~ restful season⟩

de·light·ful·ness \-fəlnə̇s\ *n* -ES **:** the quality of being delightful

de·light·ing *adj* **:** giving delight — **de·light·ing·ly** *adv*

de·light·less \-tlə̇s\ *adj* **:** being without delight **:** JOYLESS

de·light·some \-ītsəm\ *adj* **:** very pleasing **:** DELIGHTFUL ⟨Elizabeth Barrett Browning found melancholy capable of being ~ —I.J.C.Brown⟩ — **de·light·some·ly** *adv*

de·lignification \(ˈ)dē+\ *n* [*de-* + *lignin* + *-fication*] **:** removal of lignin from woody tissue (as by natural enzymatic or industrial chemical processes) — **de·lignify** \(ˈ)dē+\ *vt*

de·lime \(ˈ)dē+\ *vt* [*de-* + *lime* (n.)] **:** to free from lime; *esp* **:** to remove lime previously used as a dehairing agent from hides or skins preparatory to tanning

de·limer \" +\ *n* -s **:** a tannery worker who removes from hides the lime that was used for dehairing

de·limit \(ˈ)dē, də̇+\ *vt* [F *délimiter*, fr. L *delimitare*, fr. *de-* + *limitare* to limit — more at LIMIT] **1 :** to fix or determine the limits of ⟨the commission ~*ed* the frontier through the disputed region⟩ **2 :** to serve as a boundary to or between ⟨a river ~*ing* the plain⟩ ⟨social custom ~*s* propriety and impropriety⟩

de·lim·i·tate \(ˈ)dēˈlimәˌtāt, də̇ˈ-\ *vt* [L *delimitatus*, past part. of *delimitare* to delimit] **:** DELIMIT — **de·lim·i·ta·tion** \(ˌ)dēˌliməˈtāshən\ *n* -s — **de·lim·i·ta·tive** \(ˈ)dēˈliməˌtād·iv\ *adj*

de·limiter \(ˈ)dē, də̇+\ *n* -s **:** one that delimits

delineament *n* -s [L *delineamentum*, fr. *delineare* + *-mentum* -ment] *obs* **:** DELINEATION

[1]**de·lin·e·ate** \də̇ˈlinēˌāt, dēˈ-, *usu* -ād·+V\ *vt* [L *delineatus*, past part. of *delineare*, fr. *de-* + *lineare* to draw a line, make straight, fr. *linea* line — more at LINE] **1 a :** to indicate by lines drawn in the form or figure of **:** represent by sketch, design, or diagram **:** sketch out **:** PORTRAY, PICTURE; *specif* **:** to represent in drawing and engraving by lines (as with pen, pencil, or graver) **b :** to represent with accuracy and minute attention to detail **2 :** to describe in detail esp. with sharpness or vividness ⟨I do not intend to . . . ~ their wars, or describe their political backgrounds —W.H.Camp⟩ ⟨a good many nouns and adjectives have also been expended in *delineating* Abbott as a theater personality —Gilbert Millstein⟩ **syn** see REPRESENT

[2]**de·lin·e·ate** \-ēə̇t\ *adj* [L *delineatus*] *archaic* **:** DELINEATED

de·lin·e·a·tion \=ˈ=nēˈāshən\ *n* -s [LL *delineation-*, *delineatio*, fr. L *delineatus* + *-ion-*, *-io* -ion] **1 a :** the act of representing, portraying, or describing (as by lines, diagrams, sketches) **:** a drawing in outline ⟨the ~ of a scene⟩; *esp* **:** representation in drawing and engraving by means of lines as distinguished from representation by means of tints and shades **b :** accurate and precise graphic representation as distinguished from that which is careless or sketchy as to details **2 :** the act of delineating verbally ⟨the ~ of final metaphysical truth is no part of this lecture —A.N.Whitehead⟩ **3 :** something (as a diagram, picture, description) made by delineating ⟨a photographic ~ of low life —T.S.Eliot⟩

de·lin·e·a·tive \=ˈ=nēˌād·iv, -ēəd·-\ *adj* **:** serving or tending to delineate

de·lin·e·a·tor \-ˌād·ə(r), -ātə-\ *n* -s **1 :** one that delineates **2 a :** a surveying odometer that records distances and delineates a profile (as of a road) **b :** a person who makes perspective drawings from an architect's plans **c :** a row of light reflectors mounted on posts esp. on curves along the edge of a highway to guide traffic at night

de·lin·quence \də̇ˈliŋkwən(t)s, dēˈ-, -link-\ *archaic var of* DELINQUENCY

de·lin·quen·cy \-nsē, -nsi\ *n* -ES [LL *delinquentia*, fr. L *delinquent-*, *delinquens* (pres. part. of *delinquere*) + *-ia* -y] **:** the quality or state of being delinquent: as **a :** failure, omission, or violation of duty **:** transgression of law **b :** MISDEED, FAULT, OFFENSE **:** MISFEASANCE, MALFEASANCE, MISDEMEANOR; *often* **:** a tendency to commit such offenses — usu. distinguished from *crime* on the basis of an implied psychological rather than a judicial attitude toward the offender **c :** a debt on which payment of interest or principal is in arrears — used esp. of taxes and mortgage loans

[1]**de·lin·quent** \-nt\ *n* -s [MF, fr. pres. part. of *delinquer* to do wrong, fail, fr. L *delinquere*] **:** a delinquent individual **:** a transgressor against duty or law esp. in a degree not constituting crime; *specif* **:** JUVENILE DELINQUENT **syn** see CRIMINAL

[2]**delinquent** \"\ *adj* [L *delinquent-*, *delinquens*, pres. part. of *delinquere* to fail, offend, fr. *de-* + *linquere* to *leave* — more at LOAN] **1 a :** failing in duty **:** offending by neglect or violation of duty or of law **b** (1) **:** in arrears in payment of debt or interest thereon ⟨~ debtor⟩ (2) **:** past due and unpaid ⟨~ taxes⟩ **2 :** of or relating to a delinquent or delinquency — **de·lin·quent·ly** *adv*

de·lint \(ˈ)dē+\ *vt* -ED/-ING/-S [*de-* + *lint* (n.)] **:** to free (as cottonseed) from lint or linters — **de·linter** \(ˈ)dē+\ *n* -s

del·i·quesce \ˈdeləˈkwes\ *vi* [L *deliquescere*, fr. *de-* + *liquescere* to become fluid, melt, fr. *liquēre* to be fluid — more at LIQUID] **1 :** to melt away **:** disappear as though by melting: **a :** dissolve gradually and become liquid by attracting and absorbing moisture from the air **b :** to become soft or liquid with age — used of certain plant structures (as some mushrooms) **2 :** to divide repeatedly ending in fine divisions — used esp. of the veins of a leaf

del·i·ques·cence \-sən(t)s\ *n* -s **:** the act or process of deliquescing; *also* **:** the resultant state or liquid product

del·i·ques·cent \ˈ==ˈ=sənt\ *adj* [L *deliquescent-*, *deliquescens*, pres. part. of *deliquescere* to become liquid, melt] **:** of, relating to, or exhibiting deliquescence **:** tending or liable to deliquesce

de·liq·ui·ate \də̇ˈlikwēˌāt, dēˈ-\ *vi* -ED/-ING/-S [alter. of earlier *deliquate*, fr. L *deliquatus*, past part. of *deliquare* to clarify, strain, fr. *de-* + *liquare* to melt, liquefy, strain; akin to L *liquēre* to be fluid — more at LIQUID] *archaic* **:** DELIQUESCE

[1]**de·liq·ui·um** \-wēəm\ *n* -s [L, fr. *delinquere* to fail, offend — more at DELINQUENT] *archaic* **:** a failure of vitality **:** a fainting or sinking away

[2]**deliquium** \"\ *n* [LL, act of melting, fr. L *de-* + *-liquium* (fr. *liquēre* to be fluid) — more at LIQUID] *archaic* **:** DELIQUESCENCE

de·lir·a·ment \də̇ˈlirəmənt, dēˈ-\ *n* -s [ME, fr. L *deliramentum*, fr. *delirare* to be crazy + *-mentum* -ment — more at DELIRIUM] *archaic* **:** an insane fancy **:** CRAZE, DELUSION

del·i·ra·tion \ˌdeləˈrāshən\ *n* -s [L *deliration-*, *deliratio*, fr. *deliratus* (past part. of *delirare* to be crazy) + *-ion-*, *-io* -ion] *archaic* **:** abnormal state of mind **:** DELIRIUM; *often* **:** irrational action or speech

[1]**de·lir·i·ant** \də̇ˈlirēənt, dēˈ-\ *adj* [*delirium* + *-ant*] **:** producing or tending to produce delirium

[2]**deliriant** \"\ *n* -s **:** a deliriant agent

de·lir·i·ous \də̇ˈlirēəs, dēˈ-\ *adj* [*delirium* + *-ous*] **1 :** of, relating to, or characteristic of delirium ⟨~ mutterings⟩ **2 :** affected with delirium ⟨the ~ children⟩ **:** wandering in mind esp. temporarily and as a result of physical disease ⟨he is ~ from fever⟩ **3 :** tending to induce delirium esp. in the form of wild excitement or enthusiasm ⟨the ~ quality of her voice⟩ — **de·lir·i·ous·ly** *adv* — **de·lir·i·ous·ness** *n* -ES

de·lir·i·um \-rēəm\ *n, pl* **deliriums** \-mz\ *also* **delir·ia** \-rēə\ [L, fr. *delirare* to be crazy, fr. *de-* + *lira* furrow, track — more at LEARN] **1 :** a transient mental disturbance that is characterized by confusion, disorientation, disordered speech, restlessness, excitement, and often delusions and hallucinations and sometimes occurs in the course of a mental illness but is usu. associated with high fever, toxemia, or injury **2 :** frenzied excitement or wild enthusiasm ⟨the year was 1924, the great Florida land boom was just gathering ~ in the region of Sarasota —R.L.Taylor⟩; *also* **:** an instance or expression of it ⟨a veritable ~ of symbol hunting —Joseph Frank⟩ **syn** see MANIA

delirium tre·mens \=ˈ===ˈtrēmənz *also* -ˌmenz *sometimes* -ˈtremənz\ *n* [NL, lit., trembling delirium] **:** a violent delirium induced by excessive and prolonged use of alcoholic liquors and characterized by terrifying hallucinations, mental confusion, restlessness, sweating, and tremor

de·list \(ˈ)dē+\ *vt* [*de-* + *list* (n.)] **:** to remove from a list (as from one indicative of approval); *often* **:** to remove (a security) from the list of securities that may be dealt in on a particular exchange

del·i·tes·cence \ˌdeləˈtesən(t)s\ *also* **del·i·tes·cen·cy** \-nsē\ *n, pl* **delitescenc·es** *also* **delitescen·cies :** delitescent state **:** OBFUSCATION, CONCEALMENT, OBSCURATION

del·i·tes·cent \ˈ==ˈ=sənt\ *adj* [L *delitescent-*, *delitescens*, pres. part. of *delitescere* to hide, be hidden, fr. *de-* + *litescere* (fr. *latescere* to hide, incho. of *latēre* to hide) — more at LATENT] **:** lying hidden **:** OBFUSCATED, LATENT

[1]**de·liv·er** \də̇ˈlivə(r), dēˈ-\ *vb* **delivered; delivered; delivering** \-v(ə)riŋ\ **delivers** [ME *deliveren*, fr. OF *delivrer*, fr. LL *deliberare*, fr. L *de-* + *liberare* to free — more at LIBERATE] *vt* **1 :** to set free from restraint **:** set at liberty **:** release or liberate esp. from control **:** rescue from actual or feared evil **:** FREE, SAVE ⟨he that taketh warning shall ~ his soul —Ezek 33:5 (AV)⟩ — often used with *from* or *out of* ⟨~*ed* him from captivity⟩ **2 :** GIVE, TRANSFER **:** yield possession or control of **:** make or hand over **:** make delivery of **:** COMMIT, SURRENDER, RESIGN — often used with *up* or *over*, *to* or *into* ⟨thou shalt ~ Pharaoh's cup into his hand —Gen 40:13 (AV)⟩ ⟨the constables have ~*ed* her over —Shak.⟩ **3 a :** to assist (a parturient female) in giving birth ⟨she was ~*ed* of a fine boy⟩ ⟨the doctor has ~*ed* several thousand women in his long career⟩; *also* **:** to aid in the birth of ⟨sometimes it is necessary to ~ a child with forceps⟩ **b :** to give birth to ⟨she ~*ed* a pair of healthy twins after a short labor⟩ **4 a :** to disburden (as oneself) in words **:** give forth in words **:** UTTER, SPEAK, ENUNCIATE ⟨he ~*ed* his speech effectively⟩ **b :** to make known to another **:** COMMUNICATE ⟨they ~*ed* their ultimatum to the enemy⟩ **5 :** to send (something aimed or guided) to an intended destination ⟨~*ing* a short uppercut to the jaw⟩ ⟨the frigate ~*ed* a smashing broadside⟩ ⟨the pitcher ~*ed* a curve to the batter⟩ **6** *archaic* **:** to unload (as a ship) of cargo **:** EMPTY **7 :** to bring (as votes) to the support of a particular candidate or cause ⟨couldn't ~ the votes of his ward⟩ **~** *vi* **1 :** to set one free **:** DISBURDEN ⟨a deliverance which does not ~ —R.W.Emerson⟩ **2 :** UTTER, DISCOURSE ⟨he ~*ed* beautifully but his speech had little real content⟩; *sometimes* **:** to express an opinion or judgment **3 :** to give birth to offspring ⟨patients that repeatedly ~ prematurely present special problems⟩ **syn** see FREE, RESCUE — **deliver a jail :** to clear a jail by bringing all the prisoners to trial — **deliver the goods :** to give results that are promised, expected, or desired

[2]**deliver** \"\ *adj* [ME (also, free), fr. MF *delivre*, fr. *delivrer* to free] *archaic* **:** NIMBLE, SPRIGHTLY, ACTIVE

de·liv·er·abil·i·ty \=ˌ=v(ə)rəˈbiləd·|ē, -ət|, |i\ *n* -ES **:** ability to be delivered (as on demand)

de·liv·er·able \=ˈ=v(ə)rəbəl\ *adj* **:** suitable for, ready for, or in condition for delivery usu. immediately

de·liv·er·ance \-v(ə)rən(t)s, -vərn-\ *n* -s [ME *deliveraunce*, fr. OF *delivrance*, fr. *delivrer* to free, deliver + *-ance* — more at DELIVER] **1 :** the act of delivering or state of being delivered: as **a :** the act of freeing or state of being freed (as from restraint, captivity, peril) **:** RESCUE, LIBERATION, RELEASE ⟨He hath sent me to heal the brokenhearted, to preach ~ to the captives —Lk 4:18 (AV)⟩ ⟨their ~ from the flood seemed a miracle⟩ **b :** the delivery of offspring **c** *archaic* **:** the act of speaking **:** UTTERANCE, DELIVERY **d :** the act of disburdening (as by uttering one's thoughts) **2 :** something delivered or communicated: as **a :** an opinion or decision expressed publicly **b** (1) **:** a legal opinion, verdict, or decision expressed publicly (2) *Scots law* **:** an interlocutory order or decree

delivered *adj* **:** including the cost of delivery ⟨~ prices will vary somewhat⟩

delivered price *n* **:** a price for which a seller agrees to deliver merchandise to a purchaser at a designated place and which usu. includes the f.o.b. price at the shipping point plus lawful transportation charges actually incurred in delivery

de·liv·er·er \-v(ə)rə(r)\ *n* -s [ME *deliverere*, fr. MF, fr. *delivrer* + *-ere* -er] **:** one that delivers: as **a :** one that liberates or rescues **:** PRESERVER **b :** one that gives up or transfers (as letters or goods) **c :** one that utters or recites **d :** one that delivers something (as parcels or mail)

de·liv·er·ly \-və(r)lē\ *adv* [ME, fr. [2]*deliver* + *-ly*] *archaic* **:** ACTIVELY, NIMBLY, DEFTLY

de·liv·ery \-v(ə)rē, -ri\ *n* -ES [ME *deliverie*, fr. *deliveren* to deliver + *-ie* -y] **1 :** a delivering from restraint **:** RESCUE, RELEASE, LIBERATION ⟨~ of a captive from a dungeon⟩ **2 a :** the act of delivering up or over **:** transfer of the body or substance of a thing **:** SURRENDER ⟨an agreement to make ~ of the bonds⟩ **b :** the physical and legal transfer of a shipment from consignor to carrier, between carriers, and from transport agency to consignee **c :** the act of putting property into the legal possession of another ⟨the ~ of a fort⟩ ⟨~ of hostages⟩ whether involving the actual transfer of the physical control of the object from one to the other or being constructively effected in various other ways (as by the handing over of something symbolical of the thing sought to be delivered) **d :** an act or instance of delivery ⟨we are prepared to make daily *deliveries*⟩ **:** something delivered at one time or in one unit ⟨each ~ will include five gross of assorted novelties⟩ **e :** a truck or other vehicle used for delivering merchandise esp. to retail customers **f :** an organization that engages to deliver goods (as retail parcels) within a local area **3 a :** the act of giving birth **:** the expulsion or extraction of a fetus and its membranes **:** PARTURITION **b :** the procedure of delivering the fetus and placenta by manual, instrumental, or surgical means **4 :** utterance esp. of words **:** a delivering esp. of a speech; *often* **:** manner or style of uttering in speech or song **:** ENUNCIATION **5 a :** the act or manner of sending forth, discharging, or throwing (as a baseball) **b :** a pitched or bowled ball **6** *archaic* **:** the act of exerting one's strength or limbs **:** bodily poise **:** BEARING **7** *obs* **:** the act of communicating **:** STATEMENT, NARRATION, ACCOUNT **8 :** the manner or form of output of a textile machine ⟨~ of the untwisted sliver⟩ **9 :** a part of certain printing presses that receives and stacks the printed sheets

delivery boy *n* **:** a person employed by a retail store to deliver small orders to customers on call

delivery cylinder *n* **:** a cylinder (as in a rotary offset printing press) that conveys the printed paper to the delivery

delivery desk *n* **:** a desk in a library from which books are handed or sent to readers and borrowers upon request

de·liv·ery·man \-ˌman, -ˌmaa(ə)n, -mən\ *n, pl* **deliverymen :** a person who delivers wholesale or retail goods to customers usu. over a regular local route

delivery room *n* **1 :** a hospital room esp. equipped for the delivery of pregnant women **2 :** the room or section of a library in which books are issued to and returned by borrowers

[1]**dell** \ˈdel\ *n* -s [ME *dele*, *delle;* akin to Fris, MD & MLG *delle* valley, MHG *telle* ravine, Goth ib*dalja* mountain slope, OE *dæl* valley — more at DALE] **1 :** a small secluded natural hollow or valley usu. covered with trees or turf **2** *obs* **:** a deep pit in the ground

[2]**dell** \"\ *n* -s [D *del*, fr. MD *delle*, *dille* gossip, frivolous girl, fr. *dillen* to gossip, prattle] *archaic slang* **:** a young woman; *usu* **:** TRULL, DRAB, WENCH

[1]**del·la–crus·can** \ˈdeləˈkrəskən\ *adj, usu cap D&C* [Accademia *della Crusca*, Florentine academy founded 1582 for the cultivation of the Italian language and literature (fr. It, lit., academy of chaff) + E *-an*] **1 a :** of, relating to, or resembling the Accademia della Crusca or the literary style it championed **b :** of, relating to, or resembling the style of a school of chiefly expatriate English writers of affected rhetorically ornate poetry in the late 18th century **2 :** affectedly pedantic — used of writings or literary style

[2]**della–cruscan** \"\ *n* -s *usu cap D&C* **:** a member of the Accademia della Crusca or the Della-Cruscan school

del·la rob·bia blue \ˈdeləˈräbēə-, -rōb-\ *n, often cap R* [after *Della Robbia*, family of Ital. painters and sculptors of the 15th and 16th cents.] **:** a variable color averaging a light blue that is redder and deeper than average forget-me-not (sense 2a)

della robbia ware \"-\ *also* **della robbia** *n, usu cap D&R* [after Luca *della Robbia* †1482 Florentine sculptor who developed the process] **:** sculptured glazed and colored terra-cotta work produced in Florence by the workshop of Luca della Robbia and his nephews and followers

dells \ˈdelz\ *n pl* [by folk etymology] **:** DALLES

del mar pine \ˈdelˌmär-\ *n, usu cap D&M* [fr. *Del Mar*, village near San Diego, Calif.] **:** TORREY PINE

del·mon·i·co potatoes \delˈmänə̇(ˌ)kō-\ *n pl, usu cap D* [fr. the *Delmonico* restaurants, New York City, after Lorenzo *Delmonico* †1881 Am. restaurateur] **:** hashed or sliced potatoes baked in cream sauce with butter and chives and with or without grated cheese

delmonico steak *also* **delmonico** *n* -s *usu cap D* [fr. the *Delmonico* restaurants] **:** CLUB STEAK

de·localization \(ˈ)dē+\ *n* -s **:** the state of being delocalized **:** the act of delocalizing

de·localize \(ˈ)dē+\ *vt* [*de-* + *localize*] **1 :** to remove from its place **2 :** to free from the limitations of locality or from connection with a particular place **:** free from provincialism or localism

de·lo·mor·phous \ˌdēlōˈmȯrfəs\ *or* **de·lo·mor·phic** \-fik\ *adj* [Gk *dēlo-* (fr. *dēlos* clear, visible, evident) + E *-morphous, -morphic* — more at ADEL-] **:** having a definite or fixed form ⟨the parietal cells of the cardiac glands are ~⟩

de·lo·nix \dəˈlōniks\ [NL] *syn of* POINCIANA

de·lo·ren·zite \ˌdeləˈrenˌzīt, ˌdel-\ *n* -s [It, fr. G. *De Lorenzo* *b*1871 It. geologist + It *-ite*] **:** a mineral approximately (Y,U,Fe)(Ti,Sn)$_3$O$_8$ consisting of an oxide chiefly of titanium, tin, yttrium, uranium, and iron

de·loul \dəˈlül\ *n* -s [F, fr. Ar *dhahūl* well-tamed] **:** a swift Arabian riding camel **:** DROMEDARY

de·louse \(ˈ)dē+\ *vt* -ED/-ING/-S [*de-* + *louse* (n.)] **1 :** to remove lice from **2 :** to free from something suggestive of lice in unpleasant or harmful character ⟨*delousing* a mine field⟩ ⟨comic book publishers will find it pays to ~ their own output⟩

¹delph *var of* DELF

²delph *var of* DELFT

¹del·phi·an \ˈdelfēən\ *or* **del·phic** \-fik, -fēk\ *adj, usu cap* [*Delphian* fr. *Delphi*, town in ancient Greece (fr. L, fr. Gk *Delphoi*) + E *-an*; *Delphic* fr. L *Delphicus*, fr. Gk *Delphikos*, fr. *Delphoi* + *-ikos* -ic] **1 :** of or relating to Delphi in ancient Greece or to the oracle located there **2 :** PROPHETIC, ORACULAR **3 :** characterized by obscurity or ambiguity ⟨*Delphian* pronouncements of certain government agencies⟩

²delphian \"\ *n* -s *usu cap* **:** a native or inhabitant of Delphi

del·phin \ˈdelfən\ *adj, cap* [fr. the *Delphin* classics; *Delphin* fr. ML *delphinus* dauphin, fr. MF *dalphin*; fr. the words *in usum Serenissimi Delphini* "for the use of the most serene Dauphin" inscribed on the title page — more at DAUPHIN] **:** of or relating to the Delphin classics, an edition of the Latin classics prepared in the reign of Louis XIV of France

del·phi·nap·ter·us \ˌ==ˈnaptərəs\ *n, cap* [NL, fr. L *delphinus* dolphin + Gk *apteros* wingless — more at APTEROUS] **:** the genus of cetaceans that consists solely of the beluga

del·phine \ˈdelˌfīn, -ˌfən\ *adj* [L *delphinus* dolphin — more at DOLPHIN] **:** of or relating to the dolphins

delphine blue B *n, usu cap D&B* **:** a mordant dye — see DYE table 1 (under *Mordant Blue 56*)

del·phin·i·dae \delˈfinəˌdē\ *n pl, cap* [NL, fr. *Delphinus*, type genus + *-idae*] **:** a family of moderate to small-sized toothed whales including the dolphins, grampuses, and usu. the porpoises — see PHOCAENIDAE — **del·phi·noid** \ˈ=fəˌnȯid\ *adj or n*

del·phin·i·din \delˈfinədən\ *n* -s [ISV, blend of *delphinin* and *-id*] **:** an anthocyanidin that occurs widely in plants in the form of glycosides (as delphinin) and is usu. obtained as the dark violet or brownish red crystalline chloride $C_{15}H_{11}ClO_7$ (as by hydrolysis of the glycosides or by synthesis from pyrogallol derivatives)

del·phi·nin \ˈ=fənən\ *n* -s [ISV *delphin-* (fr. NL *Delphinium*) + *-in*] **:** a violet crystalline anthocyanin pigment $C_{41}H_{38}O_{21}$ that is a glycoside of delphinidin found in larkspur

del·phi·nine \-ˌnēn, -ˌnən\ *n* -s [NL *Delphinium* (genus name of *Delphinium staphisagria*) + E *-ine*] **:** a poisonous crystalline alkaloid $C_{33}H_{45}NO_9$ obtained esp. from seeds of the stavesacre

del·phin·i·um \delˈfinēəm\ *n* [NL, fr. Gk *delphinion* larkspur, dim. of *delphin-, delphis* dolphin; fr. the shape of the nectary — more at DOLPHIN] **1** *cap* **:** a large genus of chiefly perennial erect branching herbs (family Ranunculaceae) that are widely distributed in temperate parts of the northern hemisphere, have palmately divided leaves and irregular flowers in showy spikes, and include several containing extremely poisonous substances **2** *pl* **delphiniums** \-mz\ *also* **delphin·ia** \-nēə\ **:** any plant of the genus *Delphinium; esp* **:** a cultivated perennial plant of this genus — compare LARKSPUR

delphinium blue *n* **:** a variable color averaging a brilliant blue

del·phi·nus \ˈ=fīnəs\ *n, cap* [NL, fr. L, dolphin — more at DOLPHIN] **:** a genus of marine mammals that includes the common dolphin and is the type of the family Delphinidae

-del·phis \ˈdelfəs\ *n comb form* [NL, fr. Gk *delphis* — more at DOLPHIN] **:** dolphin — in generic names ⟨Cyrto*delphis*⟩

delphware *var of* DELFTWARE

dels *pl of* DEL

del·sar·ti·an \(ˈ)delˈsärdēən\ *adj, usu cap* [François A.N.C. *Delsarte* †1871 Fr. teacher of dramatic and musical expression who invented the system + E *-ian*] **:** of, relating to, or having the characteristics of a system or method of using body movements to express emotional concepts

delt \ˈdelt\ *vt* [origin unknown] *Scot* **:** PAMPER

delt *abbr* [L *delineavit*] he drew

¹del·ta \ˈdeltə\ *n* -s [ME *deltha*, fr. Gk *delta*, of Sem origin; akin to Heb *dāleth* 4th letter of the Hebrew alphabet — more at DALETH] **1 :** the fourth letter of the Greek alphabet — symbol Δ or δ; see ALPHABET table **2 :** any of various things felt to resemble a capital Δ: as **a :** the alluvial deposit at the mouth of a river commonly forming a nearly flat fan-shaped plain of considerable area traversed by many separate branches in which the river distributes itself downstream and resulting from the accumulation of stream-borne sediment supplied more rapidly than it can be carried away by offshore and alongshore currents **b :** the closed figure produced by connecting three electrical coils or circuits successively end for end esp. in a three-phase system **c :** the triangular terminus of a pattern in a fingerprint formed either by bifurcation of a ridge or by divergence of two ridges that are parallel beyond it **3 :** an increment of a variable — symbol Δ

²delta \"\ *usu cap* — a communications code word for the letter *d*

³delta *or* **δ-** \"\ *adj* **1 :** of or relating to one of four or more closely related chemical substances ⟨δ-yohimbine⟩ — used somewhat arbitrarily to specify ordinal relationship or to specify a particular physical form, esp. an allotropic modification (as in δ-iron), or an isomeric or stereoisomeric form (as in δ-benzene hexachloride) **2 :** fourth in position in the structure of an organic molecule from a particular group or atom or having a structure characterized by such a position ⟨δ-hydroxy acids⟩ ⟨δ-lactones⟩ **3 :** fourth in order of brightness — used of a star in a constellation

delta connection *n* **:** a mesh connection for connecting electrical apparatus to a three-phase circuit, the three corners of the delta as represented being connected to the three wires of the supply circuit — compare OPEN-DELTA CONNECTION, STAR CONNECTION, T CONNECTION

delta fan *n* **:** FAN DELTA

del·ta·fi·ca·tion \ˌ==fəˈkāshən\ *n* -s [¹*delta* + *-fication*] *geol* **:** the formation of a delta

del·ta·ic \(ˈ)delˈtāik\ *or* **del·tic** \ˈ=tik\ *adj* [¹*delta* + *-ic*] **1 :** of, like, relating to, or typical of a delta ⟨~ deposits⟩ ⟨~ accumulation of silt⟩; *also* **:** constituting a delta ⟨a ~ area⟩ **2** *often cap* **:** arising or originating in the Nile delta ⟨early ~ civilization⟩ ⟨the *Deltaic* dynasties of ancient Egypt⟩

delta iron *n* **:** an iron that is stable between 1400°C and the melting point and is characterized by a body-centered cubic crystal structure — compare GAMMA IRON

del·ta·ite \ˈdeltəˌīt\ *n* -s *often cap* [¹*delta* (Gk letter) + *-ite*; fr. the triangular appearance of the crystals in cross section] **:** a mineral $Ca_2Al_2(PO_4)_2(OH)_4.H_2O$ consisting of a basic hydrous phosphate of calcium and aluminum

delta lake *n* **:** a lake surrounded by deltaic deposits

delta plain *n* **:** the level or nearly level surface of a delta

delta plateau *n* **:** a raised delta plain

delta process *n, math* **:** the process of differentiation that employs deltas

delta ray *n* **:** an electron ejected by an ionizing particle (as an alpha particle) in its passage through matter

del·tar·i·um \delˈta(a)rēəm\ *n, pl* **deltar·ia** \-rēə\ [NL, fr. Gk *delta* + NL *-arium*] **:** DELTIDIUM 2

delta shoreline *n* **:** a shoreline produced by the building forward of a delta into a lake or sea

del·ta·tion \delˈtāshən\ *n* -s [¹*delta* + *-ation*] **:** DELTAFICATION

delta wing *n* **:** a triangular swept-back airplane wing with straight trailing edge — **delta-winged** \ˈ==ˈ=\ *adj*

del·thy·ri·al \(ˈ)delˈthīrēəl\ *adj* [NL *delthyrium* + E *-al*] **:** of, relating to, or constituting a delthyrium

del·thy·ri·um \ˈ=ˈrēəm\ *n, pl* **delthy·ria** \-rēə\ [NL, prob. irreg. fr. Gk *dēlos* clear, visible, evident + *thyrion* little door, dim. of *thyra* door — more at ADEL-, DOOR] **:** the opening between the beak and the hinge through which the pedicle of certain brachiopods extends

del·tid·i·al \(ˈ)delˈtidēəl\ *adj* [NL *deltidium* + E *-al*] **:** of, relating to, constituting, or functioning as a deltidium

del·tid·i·um \ˈ=ˈdēəm\ *n, pl* **deltid·ia** \-dēə\ [NL, fr. Gk *delta* + NL *-idium*] **1 :** a plate partly or wholly closing the delthyrium of certain brachiopods — called also *pseudodeltidium* **2 :** a pair of plates not homologous with the pseudodeltidium that perform the same function in other brachiopods — called also *deltidial plates*

del·ti·ol·o·gist \ˌdeltēˈäləjəst\ *n* -s **:** a person whose hobby is deltiology

del·ti·ol·o·gy \-əjē\ *n* -ES [Gk *deltion* small writing tablet (dim. of *deltos* writing tablet) + E *-logy*; akin to L *dolare* to hew — more at CONDOLE] **:** the hobby of collecting postcards

del·to·ceph·a·lus \ˌdeltəˈsefələs\ *n, cap* [NL, fr. *delto-* (fr. Gk *delta*) + *-cephalus*] **:** a large genus of leafhoppers containing one member (*D. dorsalis*) that is an important vector of rice dwarf

del·to·he·dron \-ˈhēdrən\ *n, pl* **deltohe·dra** \-drə\ [NL, fr. *delto-* + *-hedron*] **:** a solid (as a crystal) that is bounded by 12 quadrilateral faces and is a hemihedral form of the isometric system related to the tetrahedron — called also *deltoid dodecahedron, tetragonal tristetrahedron*

deltohedron

¹del·toid \ˈdelˌtȯid\ *or* **del·toi·de·us** \ˈ=ˈdēəs\ *n, pl* **deltoids** \-dz\ *or* **deltoi·dei** \-dēˌī\ [*deltoid* fr. NL *deltoides*, fr. Gk *deltoeidēs* delta-shaped, fr. *delta* + *-oeidēs* -oid; *deltoideus*, NL, alter. of *deltoides*] **:** a large triangular muscle that covers the shoulder joint, serves to raise the arm laterally, arises from the upper anterior part of the outer third of the clavicle and from the acromion and spine of the scapula, and is inserted into the outer side of the middle of the shaft of the humerus

²deltoid \"\ *adj* [NL *deltoides*, fr. Gk *deltoeidēs*] **1 :** shaped like a capital delta **:** TRIANGULAR ⟨a ~ leaf⟩ ⟨the ~ muscle of the shoulder⟩ — see LEAF illustration **2 :** constituting or formed like a river delta

del·toi·dal \(ˈ)delˈtȯidᵊl\ *adj* **1 :** DELTOID **2 :** relating to or resembling a river delta

deltoid dodecahedron *n* **:** DELTOHEDRON

deltoid ligament *n* **:** a strong radiating ligament of the inner aspect of the ankle binding the base of the tibia to the bones of the foot

de·lude \dəˈlüd, dēˈ-\ *vt* -ED/-ING/-S [ME *deluden*, fr. L *deludere*, fr. *de-* + *ludere* to play — more at LUDICROUS] **1 :** to lead from truth or into error **:** mislead the mind or judgment of **:** impose on **:** DECEIVE, TRICK **:** make a fool of ⟨they *deluded* themselves with belief in their own superiority⟩ **2** *obs* **a :** to trifle with (one) as if acting seriously **:** MOCK **b :** to frustrate or disappoint **c :** EVADE, ELUDE **syn** see DECEIVE

de·lud·er \-də(r)\ *n* -s **:** one that deludes

de·lud·ing·ly *adv* **:** in a manner calculated to delude

¹del·uge \ˈdel(ˌ)yüj *also* ˈde(ˌ)lüj *or* ˈdelyəj *sometimes* ˈdāl(ˌ)yüj *or* ˈdā(ˌ)lüj *or* |zh\ *n* -s [ME, fr. MF, fr. L *diluvium*, fr. *diluere* to wash away, fr. *di-* (fr. *dis-* apart) + *-luere* (fr. *lavere* to wash) — more at DIS-, LYE] **1 a :** an overflowing of the land by water **:** INUNDATION, FLOOD **b :** a drenching rain **:** DOWNPOUR **2 :** an irresistible rush of something (as in overwhelming numbers, quantity, or volume) ⟨a ~ of mail⟩ ⟨a ~ of offers⟩ **3 :** a forceful jet of water (as from a fire hose)

²del·uge \" *sometimes* dəˈlüj\ *vt* -ED/-ING/-S **1 :** to overflow with water **:** INUNDATE, FLOOD ⟨torrential rains *deluged* the region⟩; *sometimes* **:** DRENCH ⟨they were *deluged* before they could reach shelter⟩ **2 :** to overwhelm as if with a deluge **:** OVERRUN, SWAMP ⟨the empire was *deluged* with mercenaries⟩ ⟨he was *deluged* with letters⟩ ⟨I shall ~ the reader with examples, hundreds of them —Anna G. Hatcher⟩ **syn** see OVERPOWER

deluge set *n* **:** a large monitor nozzle used in fire fighting to produce a deluge

del·u·gi·nous \(ˈ)delˈyüjənəs, -eˈlü-\ *adj* **:** like a deluge

de lu·na·ti·co in·qui·ren·do \ˌdāˌlüˈnädˌē(ˌ)kō(ˌ)inkwēˈren(ˌ)dō\ *n* [LL, for inquiring concerning the lunatic] **:** a writ directing an inquiry as to whether a person named in the writ is insane

del·un·dung \ˈdelənˌdəŋ, dəˈl-\ *n* -s [Malay *dĕlundong*] **:** LINSANG

de·lu·sion \dəˈlüzhən, dēˈ-\ *n* -s [ME *delusioun*, fr. L *delusion-, delusio*, fr. *delusus* (past part. of *deludere* to delude) + *-ion-, -io* -ion — more at DELUDE] **1 :** act of deluding or state of being deluded; *often* **:** a misleading of the mind ⟨such pleasures end in ~⟩ **:** an abnormal mental state characterized by occurrence of delusions **2 :** something that is falsely or delusively believed or propagated **:** false belief or a persistent error of perception occasioned by false belief or mental derangement **:** customary or fixed misconception ⟨cling to a ~⟩: as **a :** a false conception and persistent belief unconquerable by reason in something that has no existence in fact **b :** a false belief regarding the self or persons or objects outside the self that persists despite the facts and is common in paranoia, schizophrenia, and psychotic depressed states ⟨~*s* of grandeur⟩

de·lu·sion·al \-zhənᵊl, -zhnəl\ *adj* **:** relating to, based on, or marked by delusions

de·lu·sion·ary \-zhəˌnerē\ *adj* **:** resulting in or marked by delusions ⟨~ hopes⟩ ⟨~ insanity⟩

de·lu·sion·ist \-zhənəst\ *n* -s **:** one given to deluding or to having delusions

de·lu·sive \dəˈlüs|iv, dēˈ-, |ēv *also* -üz| *or* |əv\ *adj* [*delusion* + *-ive*] **1 :** apt or fitted to delude **:** DECEPTIVE, BEGUILING **2 :** constituting a delusion **:** DELUSIONAL — **de·lu·sive·ly** \|əvlē, -li\ *adv* — **de·lu·sive·ness** \|əvnəs\ *n* -ES

de·lu·so·ry \-üs(ə)rē, -üz(-, -ri\ *adj* [*delusion* + *-ory*] **:** DECEPTIVE, DELUSIVE

de·luster \(ˈ)dē+\ *vt* [*de-* + *luster* (n.)] **:** to reduce the brightness of (as yarns or fabrics); *esp* **:** to add pigment to the spinning solution of (rayons)

de·lus·ter·ant \(ˈ)dēˈləst(ə)rənt, dəˈ-\ *also* **de·lus·trant** \-tr-\ *n* -s **:** a chemical agent for reducing the brightness of yarns and fabrics

de·lu·vi·al \dəˈlüvēəl, dēˈ-\ *adj* [by alter.] **:** DILUVIAL

de·lu·vi·um \-vēəm\ *n, pl* **deluviums** \-mz\ *also* **delu·via** \-vēə\ [NL, by alter.] **:** DILUVIUM

¹de·luxe \dəˈlu̇ks, dēˈ-, -ləks, -lüks\ *adj* [F, lit., of luxury] **:** notably luxurious or elegant **:** sumptuous or elaborate (as in materials, style, or workmanship) ⟨a ~ edition of a book⟩ ⟨accommodations ~⟩ ⟨a ~ train⟩

²deluxe \"\ *adv* [F *de luxe*] **:** in a deluxe manner **:** LUXURIOUSLY, SUMPTUOUSLY ⟨traveling ~⟩

del·vaux·ite \delˈvōˌksīt, -vōk,-sīt\ *n* -s [G *delvauxit*, modif. (influenced by G *-it* -ite) of F *delvauxine*, fr. J.S.P.J. *Delvaux de Feuffe* *b ab* 1782 Belgian chemist who first described it + F *-ine*] **:** a mineral approximately $Fe_4(PO_4)_2(OH)_6nH_2O$ consisting of an ill-defined hydrous phosphate of iron

¹delve \ˈdelv\ *vb* -ED/-ING/-S [ME *delven*, fr. OE *delfan* to dig, bury; akin to OS *bidelban* to bury, OHG *telban* to dig, Lith *delba* crowbar, Russ *dolbit'* to chisel] *vt* **1** *archaic* **:** to make (as a ditch or hole) by digging **:** EXCAVATE **2 a** *now chiefly dial Brit* **:** SPADE ⟨~ a garden⟩ **b :** to dig into **:** explore by or as if by digging ⟨*delving* the garnered lore of centuries⟩ ~ *vi* **1 a :** to dig or labor with or as if with a spade; *often* **:** to labor as a drudge **b :** to seek laboriously (as in books or records) for information **2** *of a slope or sloping way* **:** to make a sudden descent **:** DIP **syn** see DIG

²delve \"\ *n* -s [partly fr. *delf*, partly fr. ¹*delve*] **1 a** *archaic* **:** a place dug **:** PIT, DEN **b :** a surface depression **:** HOLLOW **2 :** an act of digging

delv·er \-və(r)\ *n* -s [ME, fr. OE *delfere*, fr. *delfan* to dig + *-ere* -er] **:** one that delves (as a device for clearing ditches)

delving *n* -s **:** careful and detailed investigation

dely *abbr* delivery

dem \ˈdem\ *chiefly Brit var of* DAMN

dem- *or* **demo-** *comb form* [*dem-* fr. L, fr. Gk *dēm-, dēmo-*, fr. *dēmos* deme, populace; *demo-* fr. MF, fr. LL, fr. Gk *dēm-, dēmo-*; akin to OIr *dām* retinue, company, Skt *dayate* he apportions — more at TIDE] **:** people **:** populace **:** population ⟨*demo*graphy⟩ ⟨*dem*oid⟩

dem *abbr* **1** demand **2** *often cap* democratic **3** demurrage **4** demy

-de·ma \ˌdəmə\ *n comb form* [NL, fr. Gk *demas* body, bodily build; akin to Gk *demein* to build — more at TIMBER] **:** one having (such) a body — in generic names of insects ⟨Dasy*dema*⟩

de·magnetization \(ˌ)dē+\ *n* **:** the process of demagnetizing or state of being demagnetized

de·magnetize \(ˈ)dē+\ *vt* [*de-* + *magnetize*] **:** to deprive of magnetic properties — **demagnetizer** *n*

dem·a·gog·ic \ˌdeməˈgäj|ik, -ˈgäg|ik, |ēk *also* -mē|- *or* -mi|- *or* |ək *sometimes* -gōg|\ *also* **dem·a·gog·i·cal** \|əkəl, |ēk-\ *adj* [Gk *dēmagōgikos*, fr. *dēmagōgos* + *-ikos* -ic, ical] **:** characteristic of or like a demagogue ⟨a ~ concept of Americanism⟩ ⟨took ~ advantage of a press interview⟩ ⟨the use of ~ terminology⟩ **:** tending or aiming to gain personal or partisan advantage by arousing or appealing to popular passions or prejudices esp. by making specious or extravagant claims, promises, or charges **:** RABBLE-ROUSING ⟨a ~ attack on the "plutocracy"⟩ ⟨a ~ manner of speech⟩ ⟨~ laws that he never meant to implement⟩ — **dem·a·gog·i·cal·ly** \|ək(ə)lē, -li\ *adv*

dem·a·gog·ism *also* **dem·a·gogu·ism** \ˈ==ˌgäˌgizəm *also* ˈ==ˈ=,-gō,-\ *n* -s **:** DEMAGOGUERY

¹dem·a·gogue *or* **dem·a·gog** \ˈ==ˌgäg *sometimes* -ˌgȯg\ *n* -s [Gk *dēmagōgos*, fr. *dēm-* dem- + *agōgos* leading, fr. *agein* to lead — more at AGENT] **1 :** a leader or orator in ancient times who championed the cause of the common people **:** a leader of the popular or plebeian party or faction in the state **2 :** one who employs demagogic methods; *esp* **:** a political leader who seeks to gain personal or partisan advantage by specious or extravagant claims, promises, or charges **:** RABBLE-ROUSER ⟨play statesman one moment and ~ the next —*Economist*⟩

²demagogue *or* **demagog** \"\ *vi* -ED/-ING/-S **:** to act the part of a demagogue **:** behave like a demagogue

dem·a·gogu·ery \ˈ==ˌgäg(ə)rē, -ri *also* ˈ==ˈ=(=)= *sometimes* -ˌgōg-\ *n* -ES **:** the principles or practices of demagogues **:** demagogic character ⟨oversimplification and single-minded pursuit of an inflammatory issue are characteristics of modern ~ —*New Republic*⟩

dem·a·gogy \ˈ==ˌgäj|ē, -gōj|, -gäg|, |i *sometimes* -gōg|\ *n* -ES [Gk *dēmagōgia*, fr. *dēmagōgos* + *-ia* -y] **:** demagogic action or character **:** DEMAGOGUERY ⟨principles warped by ~⟩

demain *or* **demaine** *obs var of* DEMESNE

¹de·mand \dəˈmand, dēˈ-, -maa(ə)nd, -mȧnd\ *n* -s [ME *demaunde*, fr. MF *demande*, fr. *demander*] **1 a :** the act of demanding or asking esp. with authority **:** a peremptory request ⟨wishes turned into ~*s* for obedience⟩ **b** (1) **:** the asking or seeking for what is due or claimed as due (2) **:** the right or title in virtue of which something may be claimed ⟨hold a ~ against a person⟩ (3) **:** a thing or amount claimed to be due **2** *archaic* **:** earnest inquiry **:** QUESTION, QUERY **3 a :** a manifested desire for ownership or use (as of a commodity) **:** a need or request for a commodity **b :** willingness and ability to purchase a commodity or service **c :** the quantities of goods or of a service that would be purchased at each of various possible prices at a given time **d :** the sum spent on or the quantity purchased of a commodity or service **4 a :** a seeking or state of being sought after esp. with authority or insistence ⟨his eloquence brought him into frequent ~ as an occasional speaker —Ella Lonn⟩ ⟨nickel is in great ~⟩ **b :** urgent need **:** REQUIREMENT ⟨increased ~*s* for manpower⟩ **5 :** something that is demanded esp. by right or as due **:** the substance of or matter presented in a claim ⟨~*s* that are justifiable and reasonable⟩ **6 :** the requirement of work or of the expenditure of some resource ⟨~*s* that overtax a piece of machinery⟩ ⟨equal to any ~*s* his old ship was likely to make on his competence —Joseph Conrad⟩ **7 :** a crude peremptory order to relinquish esp. without regard to legal right ⟨a kidnapper's ~*s* for money⟩ **8 :** the electricity load (as of an individual consumer or power plant) usu. indicated in kilowatts and averaged over a period of time **9 :** DEMAND BID — **on demand** *adv* **:** upon presentation and request for payment

²demand \"\ *vb* -ED/-ING/-S [ME *demaunden*, fr. MF *demander*, fr. LL *demandare* to demand, fr. L, to entrust, commit, fr. *de-* + *mandare* to commit to one's charge, order — more at MANDATE] *vi* **:** to make a demand **:** ASK, INQUIRE — used with *of* ~ *vt* **1** *obs* **:** to ask (a person) authoritatively or formally for information **2 :** to call for urgently and importunately or peremptorily and imperiously ⟨he no longer ~*ed* such recognition. Instead he prayed for it —Sherwood Anderson⟩ **3 a :** to ask or call for legally **:** make legal claim to as a rightful owner **b :** to claim as due, just, or fit ⟨the harpooner was ~*ing* the beam that he had paid for —H.A.Chippendale⟩ **c :** to ask or call for with force or authority and with expectation of compliance ⟨~ obedience to the rules⟩ **4 a :** to ask with authority or earnestness to be informed of ⟨~ the cause of her sorrow —Shak.⟩ **b :** to ask to see **:** bid (a person) to appear authoritatively or insistently ⟨the crowd ~*ed* the star⟩ **5 :** to call for as useful, necessary, or requisite **:** make imperative **:** NECESSITATE, REQUIRE ⟨the fire that the cool evenings of early spring ~*ed* —Mary Austin⟩ ⟨questions that ~ discussion of cultural conditions —John Dewey⟩ **6 :** to summon into court

syn REQUIRE, CLAIM, EXACT: DEMAND may suggest peremptory imperative communication or strongly necessitous indication ⟨Antonius tomorrow will *demand* your tribute —Alfred Tennyson⟩ ⟨the sun . . . *demanded* attention in a manner that would take no denial —C.S.Forester⟩ ⟨instincts which the conventions of good manners and the imperatives of morality *demand* that they should repress —Aldous Huxley⟩ REQUIRE is more likely to stress the fact of necessity or compulsiveness than the manner of communication or indication, and may seem less strident but more coolly insistent and exigent ⟨the duty of self-preservation *requires* us to be mentally as well equipped as the French, Germans, and Americans —W.R.Inge⟩ ⟨the government of the U.S. which in the administrations of Washington, Adams, and Jefferson *required* the services of slightly more than one thousand civilian employees —Alan Barth⟩ CLAIM may indicate a demand or request for due delivery or appropriate concession or recognition based on right, warrant, or sanction and calculated to overcome resistance or reluctance ⟨in Naples the beggars *claim* an alms noisily and as though by right —Aldous Huxley⟩ ⟨authoritarian methods now . . . come to us *claiming* to serve the ultimate ends of freedom and equity —John Dewey⟩ EXACT suggests not asking, claiming, or demanding but instead obtaining or forcing delivery, execution, or concession of what is sought ⟨the mistake of *exacting* reparation in money and then lending Germany money with which to pay —H.S. Truman⟩ ⟨kept a keen eye on her court and *exacted* prompt and willing obedience from king and archbishops —Henry Adams⟩

de·mand·able \-dəbəl\ *adj* **:** subject to being demanded

de·mand·ant \-dənt\ *n* -s [ME *demaundaunt*, fr. MF *demandant*, fr. pres. part. of *demander*] **1 :** the plaintiff in a real action at law; *also* **:** any plaintiff **2 :** one who makes a demand or claim **3 :** one who interrogates or asks questions ⟨refer his ~*s* to a history of the case⟩

demand bid *n* **:** a bridge bid obligating one's partner to certain responses (as an opening bid of two in a suit)

demand bill *or* **demand draft** *n* **:** SIGHT DRAFT

demand charge *n* **:** the part of a bill for electric power based on the amount of power that the customer requires to be kept available to him

demand curve *n* **:** a graphical presentation of the quantities of a good or service that will be purchased at each of various possible prices at a given time

demand deposit *n* **1 :** a bank deposit that is subject to payment by check and that may be withdrawn without notice **2 :** a bank deposit payable within 30 days

demand factor *n* **:** the ratio of the maximum demand during an assigned period upon an electric-power system to the load actually connected during that time expressed usu. in per cent

demanding *adj* **:** unremittingly severe or difficult in making demands **:** EXACTING, TAXING — **de·mand·ing·ly** *adv*

demand limiter *n* **:** CURRENT LIMITER

demand-load factor *n* **:** load factor at time of maximum electric-power demand

demand loan *n* **:** CALL LOAN

demand meter *n* **:** a meter used for measuring electric-power demand

demand note *n* **1 :** a note payable on demand **2 :** one of the notes composing the issues of paper money authorized by Congress in 1861–62

demand rate *n* : a rate (as of electric power) based on the maximum amount that a customer requires to be kept available to him

demands *pl of* DEMAND, *pres 3d sing of* DEMAND

demand schedule *n* : [1]DEMAND 3c

demand system *n* : an oxygen-dispensing system which automatically adjusts the rate of flow to the demand of a flyer's body as the altitude changes

de·manganize \(ˈ)dē+\ *vt* [*de-* + *manganize*] : to remove manganese or manganese compounds from

de·man·i·an system \dəˈmănēən-, -man-\ *also* **demanian vessel** *n* [after Johannes G. *de Man* †1930 Du. zoologist + E *-ian*] : a group of tubes near the anus of certain female nematodes that secrete a sticky substance which protects the eggs or functions during copulation

de·man·sia \dəˈman(t)sēə, dēˈ-\ *n, cap* [NL, irreg. fr. Anton van *Diemen* †1645 governor-general of Dutch East Indies + NL *-ia*] : a genus of snakes (family Elapidae) comprising the venomous Australian brown snake and related forms

de·man·toid \-ˈman,tȯid\ *n* -s [G, fr. obs. G *demant* diamond (fr. MHG *diemant*, fr. OF *diamant*) + *-oid* — more at DIAMOND] : a green variety of andradite that has a brilliant luster and is used as a gem

de·mar·cate \dəˈmär,kāt, dēˈ-, ˈdē(,)=,=, -mȧ,k-, *usu* -ād·+V\ *vt* -ED/-ING/-S [back-formation fr. *demarcation*] **1** : to mark by bounds : determine the boundary of : DELIMIT ⟨the frontier with Yugoslavia had not yet been *demarcated* exactly — *Collier's Yr. Bk.*⟩ **2** : to set apart clearly or distinctly as if by definite limits or boundaries : DISCRIMINATE ⟨the distinction between influence and imitation ~*s* equally the imaginatively creative from the merely cerebrally inventive writer —Elizabeth Bowen⟩ **syn** see DISTINGUISH

de·mar·ca·tion *also* **de·mar·ka·tion** \,dē(,)märˈkāshən, -mȧˈk-\ *n* -s [Sp *demarcación* & Pg *demarcação*, fr. *demarcar* to delimit (fr. *de-* — fr. L — + *marcar* to mark, fr. It *marcare*, of Gmc origin; akin to Goth *marka* boundary) + Sp *-ción*, Pg *-ção* -tion — more at MARK] **1** : the act or process of demarcating : the act of ascertaining and setting a boundary or limit : DELIMITATION ⟨a distinct ~ between the clear and glacial waters⟩ **2** : SEPARATION, DISTINCTION — often used in the phrase *line of demarcation* ⟨sharp lines of ~ between successive rock strata⟩

demarcative *adj* : serving to point out or draw attention to a significant dividing place ⟨language with ~ stress⟩

de·mar·ca·tor \dəˈmär,kād·ər, dēˈ-, (ˈ)dē(,)=,==, -mȧ,kād·ə(r), -ātə-\ *n* -s : one that demarcates

de·march \ˈdē,märk\ *n* -s [Gk *demarchos*, fr. *dēmos* deme, populace + *-archos* -arch — more at DEM-] : a ruler of a deme

de·marche \dāˈmärsh, -mȧsh, ˈ=,=\ *n, pl* **demarches** \-shəz\ [F *démarche*, lit., walk, gait, fr. MF *demarche*, fr. *demarcher* to trample, march, fr. OF *demarchier*, fr. *de-* + *marchier* to trample, march — more at MARCH] **1** : PROCEEDING, STEP : MOVE, COUNTERMOVE : course of action : MANEUVER ⟨she caught on to that ~ and . . . we always landed where we didn't want to go —Frederick Packard⟩ **2** : a diplomatic move, countermove, or maneuver ⟨to visit an ambassador may be considered a ~, to visit his wife is merely an act of courtesy —G.H.Stuart⟩ ⟨began the necessary diplomatic ~*s* at Rome to secure their exclusive title —S.E.Morison⟩; *esp* : an oral or written diplomatic representation ⟨the two governments joined to present a vigorous ~ in their neighbor's capital⟩ ⟨made a solemn ~ insisting on withdrawal of all troops⟩ **3 a** : any formal or informal representation or statement of views to a public official ⟨opposition leaders made a ~ to the prime minister about police terror⟩ **b** : a verbal sally

dem·a·ree \ˈdemə(,)rē\ *vt* **demareed**; **demareed**; **demareeing**; **demarees** [after George W. *Demaree* †1915 Am. beekeeper who developed the method] : to remove the queen from the brood of (a strong colony of bees) to prevent swarming

de·mar·ga·rin·ate \(ˈ)dē¦märj(ə)rə,nāt *sometimes* -rg(-\ *vt* -ED/-ING/-S [*de-* + *margarin* + *-ate*] : DESTEARINATE

de·mark \dəˈmärk, dēˈ-, -mȧk, ˈdē,=\ *vt* [*de-* + *mark*] : DEMARCATE

de·mast \(ˈ)dē+\ *vt* [*de-* + *mast* (n.)] : to remove or strip masts from (a ship)

de·materialize \¦dē+\ *vb* [*de-* + *materialize*] *vt* : to make immaterial ~ *vi* : to become immaterial : VANISH

de·mat·i·a·ce·ae \də,mad·ēˈāsē,ē, (,)dē,-\ *n pl, cap* [NL, fr. *Dematium*, type genus (fr. Gk *demation* small cord, rope, dim. of *dema* band) + *-aceae*] : a family of imperfect fungi (order Moniliales) having hyphae, conidia, or both that are dark colored, brownish, or black — **de·mat·i·a·ceous** \=¦==¦āshəs\ *adj*

demd \ˈdemd\ *chiefly Brit var of* DAMNED

deme \ˈdēm\ *n* -s [Gk *dēmos* deme, populace — more at DEM-] **1 a** : a unit of local government in ancient Attica — compare PHRATRY, PHYLE **b** : a commune in modern Greece **2** : a local population of closely related organisms — usu. used in combination ⟨gamo*deme*⟩ ⟨topo*deme*⟩

[1]**de·mean** \dəˈmēn, dēˈ-\ *vt* [ME *demenen*, fr. OF *demener* to conduct, guide, treat, fr. *de-* + *mener* to lead, drive, fr. L *minare* to drive (animals), fr. *minari* to threaten — more at MOUNT] **1** *obs* : MANAGE : carry on : deal with **2** : to conduct or behave (oneself) ⟨he might have been observed to ~ himself as a person with nothing to do —Henry James †1916⟩ **3** *now dial* : MALTREAT **syn** see BEHAVE

[2]**demean** \"\ *n* -s [ME *demene*, fr. *demenen*, v.] : BEHAVIOR, MIEN

[3]**demean** *or* **demeane** *obs var of* DEMESNE

[4]**de·mean** \dəˈmēn, dēˈ-\ *vt* [*de-* + *mean* (adj.)] : to lower in status, condition, reputation, or character : DEGRADE, DEBASE ⟨her son would ~ himself by a marriage with an artist's daughter —W.M.Thackeray⟩ ⟨~*ed* his position by bullying and browbeating officers of the army —*N.Y.Times*⟩

de·mean·or \-nə(r)\ *n* -s *see -or in Explan Notes* [earlier *demeanure*, fr. [1]*demean* + *-ure*] **1** : behavior toward others : outward manner : CONDUCT ⟨obsequious in speech and in ~ toward his superiors —D.C.Buchanan⟩ **2** : BEARING, MIEN : facial appearance ⟨an ancient . . . ~ —R.L.Stevenson⟩

de me·di·e·ta·te lin·guae \dā,medēəˈtäd·āˈliŋ,gwī\ *adj* [L, (composed) of half of (one's own) tongue] *of a jury* : constituted half of aliens and half of citizens or subjects — referring to an arrangement that before 1870 might be claimed in an English civil or criminal case by one alien born or by a foreign merchant

de·me·gor·ic \¦dēmə¦gȯrik\ *adj* [Gk *dēmēgorikos*, fr. *dēmēgoros* popular orator (fr. *dēm-* dem- + *-ēgoros*, fr. *-agorein* to speak publicly) + *-ikos* -ic — more at CATEGORY] : of or relating to public speaking

de·mem·bra·tion \¦dē(,)memˈbrāshən\ *n* -s [ML *demembration-*, *demembratio*, fr. LL *demembratus* (past part. of *demembrare* to dismember, fr. *de-* of + *membrum* limb) + *-ion-*, *-io* -ion — more at MEMBER] *Scots law* : the crime of maliciously severing a limb from the body of a person

[1]**de·ment** \dəˈment, dēˈ-\ *vt* -ED/-ING/-S [LL *dementare*, fr. L *dement-*, *demens* out of one's mind, mad, fr. *de-* + *ment-*, *mens* mind — more at MIND] *archaic* : to deprive of reason

[2]**dement** \"\ *n* -s [MF, fr. L *dement-*, *demens*] : one who is demented

de·men·tate \-ˈ=,tāt\ *vt* -ED/-ING/-S [LL *dementatus*, past part. of *dementare*] *archaic* : DEMENT

de·men·ta·tion \,dē(,)menˈtāshən\ *n* -s [LL *dementation-*, *dementatio*, fr. *dementatus* + L *-ion-*, *-io* -ion] *archaic* : the process of dementing or state of being demented

de·ment·ed \dəˈmentəd, dēˈ-\ *adj* **1** : having dementia : of unsound mind : DERANGED **2** : marked by or arising from dementia ⟨~ screams⟩ ⟨~ conduct⟩ — **de·ment·ed·ly** *adv* — **de·ment·ed·ness** *n* -ES

dé·men·ti \,dāmäⁿˈtē, =ˈ=(,)=\ *n* -s [F, contradiction, denial, fr. MF *demanti*, fr. *dementir* to contradict, fr. OF *desmentir*, fr. *des-* dis- + *mentir* to tell a lie, fr. LL *mentire*, fr. L *mentior*, fr. *ment-*, *mens* mind — more at MIND] : an official or formal denial of the truth of a report — used esp. in diplomacy

de·men·tia \dəˈmench|ə, *also* |ēə\ *n* -s [L, fr. *dement-*, *demens* mad + *-ia* — more at DEMENT] **1** : a condition of deteriorated mentality that is characterized by marked decline from the individual's former intellectual level and often by emotional apathy — contrasted with *amentia* **2** : MADNESS ⟨the ~ of national hatreds —*Times Lit. Supp.*⟩ **syn** see INSANITY

de·men·tial \|(ē)əl\ *adj* : relating to or involving dementia

dementia par·a·lyt·i·ca \-,parəˈlid·əkə\ *n, pl* **dementi·ae paralyti·cae** \|ē,ē...,sē\ [NL, lit., paralytic dementia] : GENERAL PARESIS

dementia prae·cox *also* **dementia pre·cox** \-ˈprē,käks\ *n, pl* **dementiae prae·co·ces** \-ˈprēkə,sēz\ [NL, lit., premature dementia] : SCHIZOPHRENIA

dem·e·rara greenheart \¦demə¦ra(a)rə-, -rär-\ *n, cap D* [fr. *Demerara* county, British Guiana] : BEBEERU

demerara sugar *n, usu cap D* : a coarse light-brown raw sugar

[1]**demerit** *n* -s [ME *demerite*, fr. L *demeritum*, fr. neut. of *demeritus*, past part. of *demerēre* to deserve, fr. *de-* + *merēre* to deserve — more at MERIT] *obs* : MERIT, DESERT; *also* : a deserving or praiseworthy act

[2]**demerit** *vt* -ED/-ING/-S **1** *obs* : to be worthy of : DESERVE, MERIT **2** *obs* : to obtain by merit : EARN

[3]**de·merit** \(ˈ)dē +\ *n* -s [ME, fr. MF *demerite*, fr. *de-* dis- + *merite* merit — more at MERIT] **1** *obs* : an act that incurs blame or censure : OFFENSE — usu. used in pl. **2 a** : a quality or characteristic that deserves blame : CULPABILITY ⟨they see no merit or ~ in any man or any action —Edmund Burke⟩ **b** : lack of merit ⟨it was not wholly from ~, it was in part because of different merit, that he refused our exile —W.B.Yeats⟩ **3** : FAULT, DEFECT, IMPERFECTION ⟨it has the merit of quickness, but the ~*s* of inaccuracy, ambiguity, and slackness — F.C.Avis⟩ ⟨if the work seems to have a conspicuous ~ at first hearing, it is the overindulgence of a passion for display work —Irving Kolodin⟩ **4** : a mark usu. entailing a loss of privilege given to an offender by one in authority (as a teacher or an officer) ⟨~*s* for traffic violations⟩ ⟨a ~ system designed to ensure discipline⟩ **5** *Hinduism, Buddhism, & Jainism* : the accrual of evil consequences that determine the number and forms of an individual's future earthly reincarnations : bad karma

[4]**demerit** \"\ *vb* -ED/-ING/-S *vt* **1** *obs* : to divest of merit : DISPARAGE **2** *archaic* : to deserve not to have or to lose : fail to merit **3** : to lower (a person) in rank or status ⟨an employee reprimanded or ~*ed* for continued tardiness⟩ ~ *vi*, *obs* : to deserve or incur guilt or blame

de·meritorious \(ˈ)dē +\ *adj* [*de-* + *meritorious*] : BLAMEWORTHY ⟨~ conduct⟩ — **de·meritoriously** \(ˈ)dē +\ *adv*

Dem·er·ol \ˈdemə,rȯl, -rōl\ *trademark* — used for meperidine

de·mer·sal \dəˈmərsəl, (ˈ)dē¦-\ *adj* [L *demersus* (past part. of *demergere* to sink, fr. *de-* + *mergere* to dip, sink, plunge) + E *-al* — more at MERGE] : bottom-dwelling — used of marine organisms (as fishes)

demes *pl of* DEME

de·mesmerize \(ˈ)dē +\ *vt* [*de-* + *mesmerize*] : to bring out of a hypnotic state

[1]**de·mesne** \dəˈmān, dēˈ-, -mēn\ *n* -s [ME, alter. (influenced by AF *demesne*, alter. of OF *demaine*) of *demeyne*, fr. OF *demaine* — more at DOMAIN] **1 a** : legal possession of land as one's own — used chiefly in the phrase *to hold in demesne* **b** *obs* : POSSESSION : POWER, SOVEREIGNTY **2** *Old English law* : an estate or land of which the owner was in possession including all an owner's land except that which was held by freehold tenants or sometimes only that actually occupied by the owner **3 a** : the land attached to a mansion or country house ⟨a celebrated ~ of 400 acres and a Georgian mansion⟩; *also* : the house and land together **b** : landed property : ESTATE ⟨the cattlemen's noble, unfenced ~ —John McCarten⟩ **c** : region in general : TERRITORY ⟨the vast ~ that lies to the west⟩ **4** : realm, province, or range esp. of interests or activity ⟨through the exact ~*s* of grammar —W.S.Maugham⟩

[2]**demesne** \"\ *adj* : of or belonging to a demesne : DEMESNIAL ⟨a high ~ wall⟩

de·mesn·i·al \-nēəl\ *adj* : of or belonging to a demesne

de·methylate \(ˈ)dē +\ *vt* [*de-* + *methylate*] : to remove methyl from (a compound) — **de·methylation** \(¦)dē +\ *n*

demi- *in pronunciations below*, ¦== = ¦demē *or* (*usu not before vowels*) ¦demə *sometimes* ¦de,mī\ *prefix* [ME, fr. *demi*, fr. MF, fr. LL *demedius*, alter. (influenced by L *medius*) of L *dimidius*, prob. back-formation fr. *dimidiare* to halve — more at DIMIDIATE] : half: as **a** : of less than full size ⟨*demi*cannon⟩ ⟨*demi*pike⟩ : shortened ⟨*demi*robe⟩ — compare SEMI- **b** *heraldry* : having only one half depicted, usu. the upper or foremost half but sometimes the dexter or the sinister half ⟨*demi*angel⟩ ⟨*demi*lion⟩ **c** : half in quantity or value ⟨*demi*barrel⟩ ⟨*demi*groat⟩ **d** : inferior in quality ⟨*demi*luster⟩ **e** : one that partly belongs to (a specified type or class) ⟨*demi*beast⟩ ⟨*demi*deity⟩ ⟨*demi*lawyer⟩ **f** : partial : incomplete ⟨*demi*nudity⟩ ⟨*demi*toilet⟩

demi·bastion \¦== +\ *n* [*demi-* + *bastion*] : a half bastion consisting of one face and one flank

demi·brassard *or* **demi·brassart** \¦== +\ *n* [*demi-* + *brassard*, *brassart*] : armor for the upper arm from shoulder to elbow — see BRASSARD

demi·cannon \¦== +\ *n* [MF *demi canon*, fr. *demi* half + *canon* cannon — more at DEMI-, CANNON] : an obsolete cannon having a bore of about 6½ inches and carrying a ball weighing from 30 to 36 pounds

demi·canton \¦== +\ *n* [F *demi-canton*, fr. *demi-* (fr. *demi* half) + *canton*] : one of the two divisions into which each of the three Swiss cantons Appenzell, Basel, and Unterwalden are separated

de·mi·ca·rac·tère \dəmēkȧrȧkteer, ¦demē,karək¦te(ə)r\ *adj* [F, lit., half-character] : of, involving, or resembling a character dance that uses classical technique as a basis for interpretation

demi·circle \ˈ== *at* DEMI- + ,-\ *n* [F *demi-cercle*, fr. MF *demi cercle*, fr. *demi* half + *cercle* circle — more at CIRCLE] *archaic* : SEMICIRCLE

demi·culverin \¦== +\ *n* [MF *demie coulevrine*, fr. *demie* (fem. of *demi* half) + *coulevrine* culverin — more at CULVERIN] : a culverin of about 4½ inches bore for ball of 9 to 13 pounds

demies *pl of* DEMY

demi·glace \ˈ== + ,-\ *n* [F, lit., half glaze, fr. *demi-* (fr. *demi* half) + *glace* glaze, ice — more at GLACE] : espagnole sauce simmered down, degreased, strained, and usu. seasoned with dry wine

demi·god \ˈ== + ,-\ *n* [*demi-* + *god*; trans. of L *semideus*] **1** : a mythological divine or semidivine being (as the offspring of a deity and a mortal) thought to possess less power than a god — compare HERO **2** : one so preeminent in intellect, power, ability, beneficence, or appearance as to seem to approach the divine ⟨modern propaganda machines can quickly build even an inconspicuous character into a ~ —*Reporter*⟩

demi·goddess \ˈ== + ,-\ *n* [*demi-* + *goddess*] : a female demigod

demi·john \ˈ== + ,jän\ *n* [by folk etymology fr. F *dame-jeanne*, lit., Lady Jane] : a narrow-necked bottle of glass or stoneware holding from one to 10 gallons that is enclosed in wickerwork and has one or two wicker handles — compare CARBOY

demijohn

demi·lance \ˈ== + ,-\ *n* [MF *demie lance*, fr. *demie* (fem. of *demi* half) + *lance*] **1** : a short light lance used chiefly in the 15th and 16th centuries **2** : a light cavalryman carrying a demilance

demi·lancer \¦== +\ *n* : DEMILANCE 2

de·militarization \(¦)dē, də +\ *n* : the act, process, or result of demilitarizing

de·militarize \də, (ˈ)dē +\ *vt*, *see -ize in Explan Notes* [*de-* + *militarize*] **1** : to do away with the military organization and potential of ⟨*demilitarized* the vanquished country and its satellites⟩ : prohibit (as a zone or frontier area) from being used for any military purpose ⟨the treaty ~*s* a fifty-mile strip on either side of the border⟩ **2** : to deprive of military characteristics or purposes ⟨~ atomic energy⟩

[1]**demi·lune** \ˈ== *at* DEMI- + ,lün\ *or* **demilune of hei·den·hain** \-ˈhīdᵊn,hīn\ *or* **demilune of gia·nuz·zi** \-jəˈnüt(,)sē\ *n, cap H&G* [*demilune* fr. F *demi-lune*, fr. *demi-* (fr. *demi* half) + *lune* moon, fr. L *luna*; *Heidenhain* after R.P.H. *Haidenhain* †1897 Ger. physiologist; *Gianuzzi* after Giuseppe *Gianuzzi* †1876 It. physiologist — more at DEMI-, LUNA] : one of the small crescentic groups of granular deeply staining zymogen-secreting cells lying between the clearer mucus-producing cells and the basement membrane in the alveoli of mixed salivary glands

[2]**demilune** \"\ *adj* [F *demi-lune*] : SEMILUNAR, CRESCENT

demi·metope \¦== +\ *n* [*demi-* + *metope*] : an incomplete usu. one-half metope (as at the corner of a frieze)

de·mi·mon·dain \¦demē(,)män¦dān, -(,)mōn¦-; dəmēmōⁿdaⁿ\ *adj* [F *demi-mondain*, fr. *demi-monde*] : of or belonging to the demimonde

demi·mon·daine \"; dəmēmōⁿden\ *n* -s [F *demi-mondaine*, fr. fem. of *demi-mondain*] : a woman of the demimonde : a kept woman

demi·monde \¦demē¦mänd, -mōnd; dəmēmōⁿd\ *n* -s [F *demi-monde*, fr. *demi-* (fr. *demi* half) + *monde* world, fr. L *mundus* — more at DEMI-, MUNDANE] **1 a** : a class of women on the fringes of respectable society characterized by liaisons with and economic dependence upon wealthy lovers but not engaged in open prostitution and usu. striving to present an appearance of respectability **b** : the class of prostitutes : COURTESANS ⟨the city's ~ grew during the war⟩ **2** : a member of the demimonde : DEMIMONDAINE ⟨the richer ~*s* . . . joined London society in its glittering and fashionable parade —Hollis Alpert⟩ **3 a** : a group (as within a profession) characterized by dealings of doubtful legality or propriety or by cheap commercialism or hack work and often by conspicuous lack of financial success ⟨the ~ of letters⟩ ⟨the artistic ~⟩; *also* : the area in which such a group resides or is concentrated **b** : any group engaged in activity of doubtful or twilight legality or propriety ⟨the political ~ of international fascism —Edmond Taylor⟩

de·mineralization \(ˈ)dē +\ *n* **1** : the process of demineralizing **2** : removal or loss of minerals (as salts of calcium) from the body esp. by disease

de·mineralize \(ˈ)dē +\ *vt* [*de-* + *mineralize*] : to remove the mineral matter from (as water) : DEIONIZE, DESALT

de·mineralizer \(ˈ)dē +\ *n* : an apparatus for demineralizing water

[1]**demi·pique** \ˈ== *at* DEMI- + ,pēk\ *adj* [alter. (influenced by F *pique* pike) of *demipeak*, fr. *demi-* + *peak*] : having a peak of about half the height of that of an older style of saddle — used of an 18th century war saddle

[2]**demipique** \"\ *n* -s : a demipique saddle

de·mi-plié \dəmēpleā; ¦demē¦pleā, ¦===¦=\ *adj* [F, lit., half bent, fr. *demi-* + *plié*, past part. of *plier* to bend — more at PLY] : comprising a slight bending of the knee in ballet

de·mi-pointe \dəmēpwaⁿt, ¦demē¦pwant\ *n* [F, fr. *demi-* + *pointe* point, toe — more at POINT] : HALF-TOE

demi·rep \ˈdemē,rep\ *n* [*demi-* + *rep*] : DEMIMONDAINE

demi·rhumb \ˈ== *at* DEMI- + ,-\ *n* [*demi-* + *rhumb*] : a halfway point between rhumbs on the compass card

demi·sang *also* **demi·sangue** \ˈ== + ,saŋ\ *n* -s [AF *demy sangue*, fr. *demy* half (fr. MF *demi*) + *sangue* blood, fr. OF, fr. L *sanguen*, var. of *sanguin-*, *sanguis*] **1** : HALF BLOOD **2** : the offspring of full-blood parents of different races : HALF-BREED **3** : a cross between a Thoroughbred stallion and a native English or French mare, esp. one of the heavier French mares : GRADE 5

[1]**de·mise** \dəˈmīz, dēˈ-\ *vb* -ED/-ING/-S [ME *demisen*, fr. MF *demis*, past part.] *vt* **1** : to convey (as an estate) by will or by lease ⟨premises *demised* for a period of 10 years⟩ **2** *obs* : RELEASE : let go **3** *obs* : CONVEY, GIVE **4** : to transmit (as a title or the sovereignty) by succession or inheritance ⟨declare the crown voluntarily *demised*⟩ ~ *vi* **1** : to demise the sovereignty **2** : DIE, DECEASE **3** : to pass by descent or bequest ⟨the property *demised* to the king⟩

[2]**demise** \" *sometimes* dəˈmēz\ *n* -s [MF, fem. of *demis*, past part. of *demettre* to put away, dismiss, fr. L *demittere* to send down, lower, fr. *de-* from, down, away + *mittere* to send — more at DE-, SMITE] **1** : the conveyance of an estate (as by lease for a number of years) **2** : transference of the sovereignty to a successor (as by death or abdication) — used usu. in the phrase *demise of the crown* ⟨the appointment of a regent at the unexpected ~ of the crown⟩ **3 a** : DEATH ⟨the lady's ~ had been ascribed to apoplexy —Alan Hynd⟩ **b** : end of existence or being ⟨when the Roman Empire perished, neither contemporaries nor posterity acknowledged its ~ —A.J.Toynbee⟩ : discontinuance or cessation of activity or operation ⟨a paper . . . published daily until its recent unlamented journalistic ~ —Victor Riesel⟩

demise and re·de·mise \-ˈrēdə,mīz\ *n* : a conveyance by mutual leases made from one to another of the same land or of some profit or burden arising from the land

demi-sec \¦== *at* DEMI- + ¦sek\ *adj* [F, fr. *demi-* (fr. *demi* half) + *sec* — more at DEMI-] *of champagne* : containing five to seven percent sugar by volume : drier than doux and sweeter than sec

demise charter *n* : a bareboat charter

demi·semiquaver \¦== +\ *n* [*demi-* + *semiquaver*] : THIRTY-SECOND NOTE

demi·semitone \¦== +\ *n* [*demi-* + *semitone*] : QUARTER TONE

demi·sphere \ˈdemə + ,-\ *n* [*demi-* + *sphere*] : HEMISPHERE

demiss *adj* [L *demissus*, past part. of *demittere* to send down, lower, drop — more at DEMISE] **1** *obs* : HUMBLE, SUBMISSIVE **2** *obs* : BASE, DEGRADED **3** *obs* : cast down : DEJECTED

[1]**de·miss·ion** \dəˈmishən, dēˈ-\ *n* [MF, fr. L *demission-*, *demissio*, act of sending down, lowering] **1** : the act of resigning or giving up (as an office or dignity) : RELINQUISHMENT **2** : a sending away : DISMISSAL, DISCHARGE ⟨a sudden and unexpected ~⟩

[2]**demission** \"\ *n* [L *demission-*, *demissio*, act of sending down, lowering, fr. *demissus* + *-ion-*, *-io* -ion] **1** *archaic* : ABASEMENT, DEGRADATION **2** *obs* : a lowering of the spirits : DEJECTION

[1]**de·mit** \dəˈmit, dēˈ-, *usu* -id·+V\ *vb* **demitted**; **demitted**; **demitting**; **demits** [MF *demettre* to put away, dismiss — more at DEMISE] *vt* **1** *archaic* : to let go : DISMISS **2** : to give up (as an office) : RESIGN ~ *vi* : to relinquish office or membership usu. voluntarily : RESIGN, WITHDRAW

[2]**de·mit** \", ˈdē,-\ *or* **di·mit** \dəˈ-, ˈdi,-\ *n* -s : a letter or other document certifying that a person has honorably demitted (as from a Masonic lodge)

[3]**de·mit** \dəˈmit, dēˈ-, *usu* -id·+V\ *or* **di·mit** \dəˈ-\ *vt* **demitted** *or* **dimitted**; **demitted** *or* **dimitted**; **demitting** *or* **dimitting**; **demits** *or* **dimits** [L *demittere* to send down, lower — more at DEMISE] **1** : to put or let down : send down : LOWER **2** *obs* : HUMBLE, ABASE

demi·tasse \ˈdemē,tas, -mə,-, -,täs,-,tȧs\ *n* -s [F *demi-tasse*, fr. *demi-* (fr. *demi* half) + *tasse* cup — more at DEMI-, TASS] : a small cup of coffee usu. taken black; *also* : the cup in which it is served

demi·tint \ˈ== *at* DEMI- + ,-\ *n* [*demi-* + *tint*] : a tone intermediate between high light and deep shade : a medium tone; *also* : the part of a painting or engraving that exhibits such a tone — called also *half tint*

demi·toilet \¦==+\ *n* [*demi-* + *toilet*] : dress that is somewhat elaborate but less so than full dress

demi·tone \ˈ==+,-\ *n* [*demi-* + *tone*] : SEMITONE

demi·urge \ˈdemē,ərj, *esp Brit* ˈdē-\ *n* -s [LL *demiurgus*, fr. Gk *dēmiourgos*, lit., one who works for the people, fr. *dēmios* of the people (fr. *dēmos* people) + *-ourgos* worker (akin to *ergon* work) — more at DEM-, WORK] **1** *usu cap* **a** *in Platonism* : the subordinate god who fashions the sensible world in the light of eternal ideas **b** *in some Gnostic systems* : an inferior not absolutely intelligent deity who is the creator of the material world and is frequently identified with the creator God of the Old Testament **2** : something (as an institution, idea, or individual) conceived as an autonomous creative force or decisive power ⟨that too was a gain in spiritual balance, provided the machine was not conceived as a ~ that ruled all other human needs —Lewis Mumford⟩

demi·ur·geous \¦==¦ərjəs\ *adj* : DEMIURGIC

demi·ur·gic \-jik\ *or* **demi·ur·gi·cal** \-jəkəl\ *adj* [Gk *dēmiourgikos*, fr. *dēmiourgos* + *-ikos* -ic, -ical] : relating to or having the characteristics of a demiurge : FORMATIVE, CREATIVE ⟨a demon of a man, a full-blooded exuberant Philistine, with a ~ brain and a bull's body —Van Wyck Brooks⟩ — **demi·ur·gi·cal·ly** \-jək(ə)lē\ *adv*

demi·ur·gism \ˈ==(,)ər,jizəm, ,==ˈ=,-\ *n* -s : belief in or the philosophy of a demiurge

de·mi-vierge \,demēvēˈeərzh, dəmēvyerzh\ *n* -s [F, lit., half virgin, fr. *demi-* (fr. *demi* half) + *vierge* virgin, fr. L *virgin-*, *virgo* — more at DEMI-, VIRGIN] : a girl or woman who engages in lewd or suggestive speech and usu. promiscuous petting but retains her virginity

demi·vol \'⸗⸗ *at* DEMI- + ,väl\ *n* [F *demi-vol,* fr. *demi-* + *vol*] *heraldry* **:** a single wing used as a bearing

demi·wolf \'⸗⸗+,-\ *n* [*demi-* + *wolf*] **:** a mongrel dog; *specif* **:** the offspring of a dog and a wolf

demj *abbr* demijohn

dem·me \'demē, -mi\ *chiefly Brit var of* DAMME

dem·ni·tion \dem'nishən\ *n* -S [euphemism] **:** DAMNATION

demo \'de(,)mō\ *n* -S *usu cap* [by shortening] **:** DEMOCRAT

demo- — see DEM-

¹de·mob \(')dē'mäb, dǝ'-\ *vt* [by shortening] *chiefly Brit* **:** DEMOBILIZE ⟨when he was *demobbed* he decided to start at the beginning again —*Irish Digest*⟩

²demob \"\ *n* [by shortening] *chiefly Brit* **:** DEMOBILIZATION ⟨~ pay⟩

de·mobilization \(')dē, dǝ +\ *n* **:** the act or process of demobilizing: as **a :** the reduction (as of forces, equipment, or resources) from a war basis to a peace basis ⟨the rapid ~ of factories⟩ **b :** the disarming of troops previously mobilized ⟨demonstrations against the slowness of ~ —*Current Biog.*⟩ **c :** release from the armed services ⟨upon ~ he entered local politics⟩

de·mobilize \(')dē, dǝ +\ *vt* — *see -ize in Explan Notes* [*de-* + *mobilize*] **1 a :** to put on a peacetime footing or in a condition not prepared for war ⟨ships returning to port to be *demobilized*⟩ **b :** to disband or break up the organization of (as troops) ⟨the reserves were *demobilized* at once⟩ ⟨one of his best bands, *demobilized* a few years ago, was a powerhouse . . . outfit —Wilder Hobson⟩ **c :** to discharge from service with the armed forces ⟨he was *demobilized* in 1919 with the grade of captain —*Current Biog.*⟩ **2 :** to remove restrictions from **:** relax the governing rules and regulations of ⟨it allows us to mobilize and ~ our industrial combinations according to the actual necessities of the day —T.W.Arnold⟩ ⟨we shall never ~ the more highly integrated control that now exists over banking, credit, and the securities markets —*New Republic*⟩

de·moc·ra·cy \dǝ'mäkrǝsē, dē'-, -si\ *n* -ES [MF *democratie,* fr. LL *democratia,* fr. Gk *dēmokratia,* fr. *dēm-* dem- + *-kratia* -cracy] **1 a :** government by the people **:** rule of the majority **b** (1) **:** a form of government in which the supreme power is vested in the people and exercised by them directly (as in the ancient Greek city-states or the New England town meeting) — called also *direct democracy* (2) **:** a form of government in which the supreme power is vested in the people and exercised by them indirectly through a system of representation and delegated authority in which the people choose their officials and representatives at periodically held free elections — called also *representative democracy* **2 :** a community or state in which the government is controlled by the people; *specif* **:** a state in which the supreme power is held and exercised directly by the people rather than by their elected agents ⟨in a ~ the people meet and exercise their government in person; in a republic, they assemble and administer it by their representatives and agents —James Madison⟩ — compare REPUBLIC **3** *usu cap* **a :** the principles and policies of the Democratic party in the U.S. **b :** the Democratic party or its members **4 :** the common people esp. when regarded as the source of government **5 :** political, social, or economic equality **:** the absence or disavowal of hereditary or arbitrary class distinctions or privileges ⟨~ stands at a midway point, with personal freedom limited only by another concept — that of equality —Louis Wasserman⟩ **6 :** a state of society characterized by tolerance toward minorities, freedom of expression, and respect for the essential dignity and worth of the human individual with equal opportunity for each to develop freely to his fullest capacity in a cooperative community **7 :** control through representation by the rank and file esp. in industry — see INDUSTRIAL DEMOCRACY

dem·o·crat \'demǝ,krat, *usu* -ad·+V\ *n* -S [F *démocrate,* fr. *démocratie,* after such pairs as F *aristocratie* aristocracy: *aristocrate* aristocrat] **1 :** an adherent or advocate of democracy; *esp* **:** one who believes in or practices social equality **2** *usu cap* **a :** a member of a political party advocating democracy; *esp* **:** a member of the Democratic party of the U.S. **3 :** DEMOCRAT WAGON

dem·o·crat·ic \¦⸗⸗¦krad·|ik, -at|, |ēk *also* |ǝk\ *also* **dem·o·crat·i·cal** \|ǝkǝl, |ēk-\ *adj* [*democratic* fr. MF *democratique,* fr. ML *democraticus,* fr. Gk *dēmokratikos,* fr. *dēm-* dem- + *-kratikos* -cratic; *democratical* fr. MF *democratique* + E *-al*] **1 a :** favoring, characterized by, or based upon the principles of democracy ⟨no church constitution has proved in practice so ~ as that of Scotland —J.R.Green⟩ **b :** of, relating to, or favoring a political system in which the supreme power is held and exercised by the people ⟨a ~ country⟩ — opposed to *authoritarian* **2** *often cap* **:** of or relating to one of the two major political parties in the U.S. evolving in the early 19th century from the anti-Federalists and the Democratic-Republican party and associated in modern times with policies of broad social reform and internationalism in foreign affairs — compare REPUBLICAN 2b **3 :** relating or appealing to or having the characteristics of the broad masses of the people ⟨a ~ art⟩ **4 :** favoring or disposed to favor social equality **:** disregarding or overcoming class distinctions **:** not snobbish or socially exclusive ⟨~ tastes⟩ ⟨bombs are completely ~. They are no respecters of persons, and do not distinguish between a hovel and a mansion —John Mason Brown⟩ **5 :** favoring the assessment of individuals upon their own merits and capacities **:** emphasizing the individual's potentiality for development ⟨promotion in industry along ~ lines⟩ — **dem·o·crat·i·cal·ly** \|ǝk(ǝ)lē, |ēk-, -li\ *adv*

democratic centralism *n* **:** a communist system or principle of hierarchic organization that seeks to combine democratic participation of the rank and file in the discussion of policy and the election of officers and of delegates to the next higher unit with strict obedience by the members and lower bodies to the decisions of the higher units and with absolute authority residing in fact at the apex of the hierarchic structure and strict discipline being enforced

democratic-republican \¦⸗⸗¦⸗⸗¦⸗⸗⸗\ *adj, usu cap D & R* **:** of or relating to a major American political party of the early 19th century favoring a strict interpretation of the constitution to restrict the powers of the federal government and emphasizing states' rights

de·moc·ra·tism \dǝ'mäkrǝ,tizǝm, dē'-\ *n* -S [*democrat* + *-ism*] **:** the theory, system, or principles of democracy

de·moc·ra·ti·za·tion \⸗,⸗⸗tǝ'zāshǝn, -,tī'-\ *n* -S **:** the act or process of making or becoming democratic ⟨this great ~ of music has been made possible, thanks to the radio and the phonograph —*Christian Science Monitor*⟩

de·moc·ra·tize \⸗'⸗⸗,tīz\ *vt* -ED/-ING/-S *see -ize in Explan Notes* [F *démocratiser,* fr. *démocrate* + *-iser* -ize] **:** to make democratic (as in character or principle) **:** give popularity to **:** make available to the masses ⟨efforts to ~ occupied territories since the war —E.O.Melby⟩ ⟨to recommend plans to ~ scientific research in that country —*Current Biog.*⟩ ⟨books and art and music are all to be *democratized* —E.C.Lindeman⟩

democrat wagon *n, sometimes cap D* **:** a light farm wagon or ranch wagon that has two or more seats and is usu. drawn by two horses

de·moc·ri·te·an \⸗¦⸗⸗¦tēǝn\ *adj, usu cap* [*Democritus* †*ab*362 B.C. Gk. philosopher + E *-ean*] **:** of, relating to, or in the manner of Democritus or his materialist philosophy — compare ATOMISM

dé·mo·dé \¦dā(,)mō¦dā\ *adj* [F, fr. *dé-* (fr. OF *de-, des-* de-) + *mode* fashion + *-é* (past part. ending) — more at MODE] **:** no longer fashionable **:** OUT-OF-DATE, OUTMODED ⟨a short jacket of astrakhan, slightly ~ owing to its leg-of-mutton sleeves —Louis Bromfield⟩ ⟨classical formulas of exploitation are ~ —C.L.Sulzberger⟩

dem·o·dec·tic \¦demǝ¦dektik\ *adj* [irreg. fr. NL *Demodic-, Demodex* + E *-ic*] **1 :** of or relating to the genus *Demodex* **2 :** caused by mites of the genus *Demodex*

demodectic mange *n* **:** mange caused by mites of the genus *Demodex* that burrow in the hair follicles (as esp. of dogs) causing pustule formation and spreading bald patches — called also *red mange*

de·mod·ed \(')dē¦mōdǝd, dǝ'-\ *adj* [trans. of F *démodé*] **:** DÉMODÉ

dem·o·dex \'demǝ,deks, 'dēm-\ *n* [NL, fr. Gk *dēmos* fat + *dēx,* a wood worm] **1** *cap* **:** a genus (coextensive with a family Demodicidae) of minute elongated cylindrical mites with the legs greatly reduced that live in the hair follicles esp. about the face of man and various furred mammals and in the latter often cause follicular mange **2** -ES **:** any mite of the genus *Demodex* **:** FOLLICLE MITE

dem·o·di·co·sis \,⸗⸗dǝ'kōsǝs\ *n, pl* **demodico·ses** \-,sēz\ [NL, irreg. fr. NL *Demodic-, Demodex* + *-osis*] **:** DEMODECTIC MANGE

de·modulate \(')dē, dǝ +\ *vt* [*de-* + *modulate*] **1 :** to extract the intelligence from (a modulated radio signal) **2 :** DETECT 3c

de·modulation \(')dē, dǝ +\ *n* **1 :** extraction of the intelligence from a modulated radio signal **2 :** DETECTION 2d

de·modulator \(')dē, dǝ +\ *n* **1 :** a device for converting a modulated radio signal into the original modulating signal — called also *detector* **2 :** DETECTOR e(2), e(3)

de·mog·ra·pher \dǝ'mägrǝfǝ(r), dē'-\ *n* -S **:** one who specializes in demography

de·mo·graph·ic \¦dēmǝ¦grafik, ¦dem-\ *adj* [F *démographique,* fr. *démographie* + *-ique* -ic] **:** of or relating to demography **:** relating to the dynamic balance of a population esp. with regard to density and capacity for expansion or decline ⟨~ pressures determining trends⟩ — **de·mo·graph·i·cal·ly** \-fǝk(ǝ)lē\ *adv*

de·mog·ra·phy \dǝ'mägrǝfē, dē'-\ *n* -ES [F *démographie,* fr. *démo-* dem- + *-graphie* -graphy] **:** the statistical study of the characteristics of human populations esp. with reference to size and density, growth, distribution, migration, and vital statistics and the effect of all these on social and economic conditions

de·moid \'dē,mȯid\ *adj* [*dem-* + *-oid*] **:** common or abundant esp. in a given geological formation — used of fossils

dem·oi·selle \,dem(w)ǝ'zel, '⸗⸗,⸗\ *n* -S [F, fr. OF *dameisele, damoisele* — more at DAMSEL] **1 :** a young lady **:** DAMSEL **2 a :** a crane (*Anthropoides virgo*) of rather small size with long flowing secondaries and breast feathers and white plumes behind the eyes that is widely distributed in Asia, No. Africa, and southeast Europe **b :** LOUISIANA HERON **3 :** DAMSELFLY; *esp* **:** one of the genus *Agrion* **4 :** DAMSELFISH **5 :** EARTH PILLAR

de moi·vre's theorem \dǝ'mȯivǝ(r)z-\ *n, cap D&M* [after Abraham *De Moivre* †1754 Fr. mathematician] **:** a theorem of complex numbers: the *n*th power of a complex number has for its absolute value and its argument respectively the *n*th power of the absolute value and *n* times the argument of the given complex number

de·mo·lay \,dēmǝ'lā\ *n* -S *usu cap D&M* [after Jacques B. *de Molay* †1314 Fr. grand master of the Knights Templar] **:** a member of the Order of DeMolay for Boys sponsored by Masonic orders as a secret society for boys aged 14 to 21

de·mol·ish \dǝ'mälish, dē'-, -lēsh\ *vt* -ED/-ING/-ES [MF *demoliss-,* stem of *demolir* to demolish, fr. L *demoliri,* fr. *de-* + *moliri* to construct, set in motion, toil, fr. *moles* mass, massive structure — more at MOLE] **1 a :** to pull or tear down (as a building) **:** RAZE ⟨built in 1706 and ~*ed* in 1859 to make way for the present building —*Amer. Guide Series: N.J.*⟩ **b :** to break to pieces or apart usu. with force or violence **:** ruin completely **:** SHATTER, SMASH ⟨~*ing* the fortifications and the harbor⟩ **2 a :** to do away with **:** put an end to **:** DESTROY ⟨his research has been painstaking and he ~*es* a good many legends —Fletcher Pratt⟩ ⟨a filibuster which would effectively ~ the issue —*Current Biog.*⟩ **b :** to divest of any claim or pretense to merit, truth, credence, or acceptability ⟨I heard him on another occasion ~ a city financier of more wealth than probity —David Williamson⟩ **c :** to eat up ⟨they ~*ed* the roast⟩ **syn** see DESTROY

dem·o·li·tion \,demǝ'lishǝn, ,dē-\ *n* -S [MF & L; MF, fr. L *demolition-, demolitio,* fr. *demolitus* (past part. of *demoliri* to demolish) + *-ion-, -io* -ion] **1 :** the act or process of demolishing or the state of being demolished **2 demolitions** *pl, obs* **:** RUINS, REMAINS **3 a :** destruction of structures, areas, or targets esp. in warfare by means of explosives ⟨~ of vital communication units⟩ ⟨~ experts⟩ **b demolitions** *pl* **:** the explosives used for such destruction

demolition bomb *n* **:** a bomb used against installations and materiel — used esp. of heavy bombs and bombs for which a lapse of time between impact and detonation is desirable

¹de·mon *also* **dae·mon** \'dēmǝn\ *n* -S [ME *demon,* fr. LL & L; LL *daemon, demon* evil spirit, fr. L *daemon* spirit, fr. Gk *daimōn* spirit, deity; prob. akin to Gk *daiesthai* to distribute — more at TIDE] **1 :** an attendant, ministering, or indwelling power or spirit **:** DAIMONION, GENIUS ⟨the only one of our five authors who writes because he has a ~ —*New Republic*⟩ **2 a :** an evil spirit **:** DEVIL ⟨a magical observance whose aim is to banish the ~*s* of pain, psychosis and bad luck —Paul Bowles⟩ **b :** an undesirable or evil emotion, trait, or state personified ⟨melancholy is a kind of ~ that haunts our island —Joseph Addison⟩ **3** *in late biblical Judaism and early Christianity* **a :** a pagan spirit **b :** an unclean spirit or evil superhuman being below a god but believed to be capable of inhabiting and actuating the bodies of men **4** *usu* **daemon :** a supernatural being in ancient Greek mythology whose nature is intermediate between that of a god and that of a man **:** an inferior divinity **5 :** one that possesses extraordinary drive, enthusiasm, or effectiveness in respect to some activity or function ⟨he is a positive ~ for work —William Ridsdale⟩

²demon \"\ *adj* **1 :** of, relating to, or involving demons ⟨~ worship⟩ ⟨the ~ herd⟩ **2 a :** being a demon **:** possessed of a demon ⟨a ~ lover⟩ **b :** having the characteristics of a demon ⟨the ~ driver of the village —Sinclair Lewis⟩

demon *abbr* **1** demonstration **2** demonstrative

de·monetization \(¦)dē+\ *n* [F *démonétisation,* fr. *démonétiser* to demonetize + *-ation*] **:** the process of demonetizing or the state of being demonetized ⟨the ~ of silver⟩

de·monetize \(')dē+\ *vt, see -ize in Explan Notes* [F *démonétiser,* fr. *dé-* de- (fr. OF *de-, des-*) + L *moneta* coin + F *-iser* -ize — more at MINT] **1 :** to abandon use of (a metal) as a monetary standard **2 :** to deprive (as a coin or stamp) of value for official payment

¹de·mo·ni·ac \dǝ'mōnē,ak, dē'- *also* -'män- *sometimes* ¦dēmǝ¦nī,ak *or* -īǝk\ *also* **de·mo·ni·a·cal** \¦dēmǝ¦nīǝkǝl\ *adj* [*demoniac* fr. ME *demoniak,* fr. LL *daemoniacus,* fr. Gk *daimoniakos,* fr. *daimonios* of a daimon, fr. *daimōn-, daimōn* demon; *demoniacal* fr. LL *daemoniacus* + E *-al* — more at DEMON] **1 :** influenced or produced by a demon **:** possessed by an evil spirit ⟨through the ~ ambivalence of the passions, which make actions a pursuit of chimeras —Fritz Kaufmann⟩ ⟨a lunatic who is thinking of some ~ buffoonery in his muddled brain —Liam O'Flaherty⟩ **2 :** of, belonging to, or having the characteristics of a demon **:** FIENDISH, DEVILISH ⟨possessed with ~ energy⟩ — **de·mo·ni·a·cal·ly** \-k(ǝ)lē, -li\ *adv*

²demoniac \"\ *n* -S [ME *demoniak,* fr. LL *daemoniacus,* fr. *daemoniacus,* adj.] **:** one regarded as possessed by an evil spirit

de·mo·ni·an *or* **dae·mo·ni·an** \dǝ'mōnēǝn, dē'-, -nyǝn\ *adj* [*demon* + *-ian*] **:** DEMONIAC 2

de·mon·ic *also* **dae·mon·ic** \-'mänik, -nēk *also* -nǝk *or* -mōn-\ *or* **de·mon·i·cal** \-nǝkǝl, -nēk-\ *adj* [*demonic, daemonic* fr. LL *daemonicus,* fr. Gk *daimonikos,* fr. *daimon-, daimōn* daimon + *-ikos* -ic; *demonical* fr. LL *daemonicus* + E *-al*] **1 :** DEMONIAC 2 ⟨~ energy⟩ ⟨a *daemonic* gift for blackmail and sabotage —*Economist*⟩ **2** *usu* **daemonic :** activating or compelling like an indwelling or ministering force **:** having extraordinary genius ⟨some physical rebellion . . . sets loose the pent-up *daemonic* powers —P.E.More⟩

de·mon·i·cal·ly \-nǝk(ǝ)lē, -nēk-, -li\ *adv* **:** in a demonic manner **:** DIABOLICALLY

de·mon·iza·tion \,dēmǝnǝ'zāshǝn\ *n* -S [ML *daemonizatus* (past part. of *daemonizare*) + E *-ion*] **:** the act of changing into or giving the characteristics of a demon ⟨their superstition is evident in the ~ of religion, faith, cult —Paul Tabori⟩

de·mon·ize \'⸗⸗,nīz\ *vt* -ED/-ING/-S [ML *daemonizare,* fr. LL *daemon* + L *-izare* -ize — more at DEMON] **1 :** to convert into a demon **:** instill the principles, power, or fury of a demon into ⟨man *demonized* by war⟩ **2 :** to control or possess by a demon

de·mon·olog·ic \¦dēmǝnǝ¦läjik\ *or* **de·mon·olog·i·cal** \-jǝkǝl\ *adj* **:** of or relating to demonology — **de·mon·olog·i·cal·ly** \-jǝk(ǝ)lē\ *adv*

de·mon·ol·o·gist \,⸗⸗'nälǝjǝst\ *n* -S **:** one who specializes in demonology

de·mon·ol·o·gy *also* **dae·mon·ol·o·gy** \-jē\ *n* -ES [*demon, daemon* + *-o-* + *-logy*] **1 :** a branch of learning that deals with demons or with popular beliefs in or superstitions about demons or evil spirits; *also* **:** a treatise on demons or on beliefs in demons **2 :** belief in demons; *specif* **:** a systematized religious doctrine of evil spirits

de·mon·o·ma·nia \,dēmǝnǝ'mānēǝ\ *n* [*demon* + *-o-* + *mania*] **:** a delusion of being possessed by evil spirits

demon stinger *n* **:** a variably colored scorpaenid fish (*Inimicus japonicus*) of coral reefs of the tropical Pacific having long venomous dorsal spines

de·mon·stra·bil·i·ty \dǝ,mänstrǝ'bilǝd·|ē, dē,-, -lǝt|, |i; ,demǝn-\ *n* -ES **:** the quality of being demonstrable

de·mon·stra·ble \dǝ'mänstrǝbǝl, dē'-; 'demǝn-\ *adj* [ME, fr. L *demonstrabilis,* fr. *demonstrare* to demonstrate + *-abilis* -able] **1 :** capable of being demonstrated ⟨~ and systematically classifiable truths —Havelock Ellis⟩ **2 :** APPARENT, EVIDENT, PALPABLE ⟨uttering ~ nonsense —Aldous Huxley⟩ — **de·mon·stra·ble·ness** *n* -ES — **de·mon·stra·bly** *adv*

demonstrance *n* -S [ME *demonstraunce,* fr. MF *demonstrance, demostrance,* fr. *demonstrer, demostrer* to demonstrate (fr. L *demonstrare*) + *-ance*] *obs* **:** DEMONSTRATION

de·mon·strant \-strǝnt\ *n* -S [*demonstrate* + *-ant*] **:** one making or participating in a public demonstration

dem·on·strat·able \¦demǝn¦strād·ǝbǝl\ *adj* **:** DEMONSTRABLE ⟨easily ~ aural and visual proof —R.D.Darrell⟩

dem·on·strate \'demǝn,strāt *sometimes* dǝ'män,- *or* dē'män,-, *usu* -ād·+V\ *vb* -ED/-ING/-S [L *demonstratus,* past part. of *demonstrare,* fr. *de-* + *monstrare* to show — more at MUSTER] *vt* **1 a** *obs* **:** INDICATE **:** point out **b :** to manifest clearly, certainly, or unmistakably **:** show clearly the existence of ⟨even if both sides ~ a will to agree —*New Republic*⟩ **2 a :** to make evident or reveal as true by reasoning processes, concrete facts and evidence, experimentation, operation, or repeated examples ⟨*demonstrated* that the geologic agencies are not explosive and cataclysmal but steady and patient —C.W. Eliot⟩ **b :** to illustrate or explain in an orderly and detailed way esp. with many examples, specimens, and particulars ⟨~ the essentials of the theistic position —W.R.Inge⟩ **3 :** to show or prove to a prospective customer (as by actual operation) the special value or merits of (an article or product) ~ *vi* **1 :** to make a demonstration; *specif* **:** to make a public display of sentiment for or against a person or cause ⟨students *demonstrating* for the ouster of the dictator⟩ **2 :** to teach or explain by demonstration **syn** see PROVE, SHOW

dem·on·stra·tion \,demǝn'strāshǝn\ *n* -S [ME *demonstracioun,* fr. MF or L; MF *demonstration,* fr. L *demonstration-, demonstratio,* fr. *demonstratus* + *-ion-, -io* -ion] **1 :** the act of making known or evident by visible or tangible means: as **a** *obs* **:** INDICATION, SIGN **b :** an expression or display (as of feelings) **:** SHOW, MANIFESTATION ⟨no one was called upon to make any great ~ of gratitude on receiving a gift —Havelock Ellis⟩ **2 :** the act, process, or means of demonstrating to the intelligence: as **a :** conclusive evidence ⟨seek for a ~ of his guilt⟩ **b :** a proof by experiment ⟨a lecture ~ of the neutralization of an acid by a base⟩ **c :** exhibition of methods of manufacture by means of specimens, examples, or specific instances ⟨~*s* in shingle making and other frontier crafts —*Amer. Guide Series: Texas*⟩ **d :** illustration of the practical application of theories or methods ⟨an early ~ of satisfactory housing within the limitations of the average city block —*Amer. Guide Series: N.Y. City*⟩ ⟨a ~ school for student teachers to observe approved teaching practices⟩ **3 :** an exhibition of armed force or a movement indicating an attack to show readiness for combat or to divert attention from the real point of attack ⟨tying down the main enemy forces with ~*s,* feints, or limited attacks —*Military Engineer*⟩ **4 :** a public display of group feeling (as of approval, sympathy, or antagonism) esp. towards a person, cause, or action of public interest ⟨while the delegates are howling and conducting their ~*s,* the leaders may be quietly engaged in the highest statesmanship —D.D.McKean⟩ **5 :** a logical proof; *specif* **:** one in which the conclusion is the immediate sequence of reasoning from axiomatic or established premises **6** *Roman law* **:** the first of the four principal parts of the formula or order of reference to a magistrate in which the general background and subject matter of a case in litigation was set forth — compare INTENTION 1c(1) **7 :** a showing to a prospective buyer or buyers (as by actual operation) of the merits of an article or product

dem·on·stra·tion·al \¦⸗⸗¦⸗shǝn°l, -shnǝl\ *adj* **:** relating to or based on demonstration ⟨~ methods in farming⟩

¹de·mon·stra·tive \dǝ'mänstrǝd·|iv, dē'-, |t| *sometimes* 'demǝn,strā\ *adj* [ME, fr. MF or L; MF *demonstratif,* fr. L *demonstrativus,* fr. *demonstratus* + *-ivus* -ive] **1 a :** demonstrating or manifesting as real and true **:** making evident **:** exhibiting conclusively ⟨the oath of office . . . is completely ~ of the legislative opinion on this subject —John Marshall⟩ **b :** characterized by, established by, or employing demonstration ⟨scientific honesty, however, makes us admit that where ~ knowledge ends only guessing begins —M.R.Cohen⟩ **2** *of a word or morpheme* **:** pointing out the person or thing that is directly or indirectly referred to and distinguishing it from others of the same class (as *this* in "who's this?", *that* in "that dog", *here* meaning "in this place") ⟨~ pronoun⟩ ⟨~ adjective⟩ ⟨~ adverb⟩ **3 :** EPIDEICTIC **4 a :** given to or characterized by a display of sentiment or feeling **:** expressed openly ⟨the reception of the young aviator in the capital of France was cordial and ~ —Kenneth Colegrove⟩ **b :** EFFUSIVE, EXUBERANT — **de·mon·stra·tive·ly** \|ǝvlē, -li\ *adv* — **de·mon·stra·tive·ness** \|ǝvnǝs\ *n* -ES

²demonstrative \"\ *n* -S **:** a demonstrative word or morpheme

demonstrative legacy *n* **:** a legacy made payable out of a designated fund or asset

dem·on·stra·tor *pronunc at* DEMONSTRATE + ǝ(r)\ *n* -S [F or L; F *démonstrateur,* fr. L *demonstrator,* fr. *demonstratus* + *-or*] **:** one that demonstrates or makes a demonstration: as **a :** a teacher or teacher's assistant in a professional school or a science department who demonstrates the principles and theories studied (as by means of experiments, dissections, physical and chemical preparations) **b :** one that demonstrates an article or product to a prospective buyer; *also* **:** an article or product (as an automobile or vacuum cleaner) used in a demonstration **c :** one engaged in a public demonstration ⟨~*s* protesting the pact⟩

de·moralization \dǝ, (¦)dē +\ *n* **:** the act or process of demoralizing **:** a demoralized state ⟨the ~ of peace was more difficult to combat than the madness of war —Ellen Glasgow⟩

de·moralize \dǝ, (')dē +\ *vt* [*de-* + *moral* + *-ize*] **1 :** to corrupt or undermine in morals or moral principle **:** PERVERT, DEPRAVE **2 a :** to destroy the morals or morale of **:** deprive of self-reliance **:** weaken in courage, fortitude, or spirit **:** render untrustworthy in efficiency and discipline ⟨the prisoners carried on an endless war of nerves against their captors, taunting them, *demoralizing* them in dozens of different ways —Peter Blake⟩ ⟨the objective of a given campaign is to ~ enemy troops so that they will surrender or desert —L.W. Doob⟩ **b :** to upset or destroy the working order, proper functioning, or normal activity of ⟨powerful earth currents are induced that sometimes ~ the telegraph service —Waldemar Kaempffert⟩ ⟨foreclosures were further *demoralizing* an already desperate real-estate market —F.D.Roosevelt⟩ **3 :** to cast into disorder or confusion **:** BEWILDER, PERPLEX ⟨do many art critics deliberately set out to deceive and confuse and ~ the public? —Huntington Hartford⟩ ⟨the declarer was so *demoralized* that he discarded spades from both hands —*London Times*⟩

de mor·gan's theorem \dǝ'mȯrgǝnz-, dē'-\ *n, usu cap D&M* [after Augustus *De Morgan* †1871 Eng. mathematician] **:** one of a pair of theorems in logic: the denial of a conjunction is equivalent to the alternation of the denials and the denial of an alternation is equivalent to the conjunction of the denials

¹de·mos \'dē,mäs\ *n* -ES [Gk *dēmos* deme, populace — more at DEM-] **1 a :** the people of an ancient Greek usu. democratic state **b** *sometimes cap* **:** the common people **:** POPULACE ⟨~ ruled in the age of the common man⟩ **2 :** the people of a nation considered as a political unit as distinguished from a tribe or kinship group — compare ETHNOS

²demos *pl of* DEMO

de·mo·spon·gea *or* **de·mo·spon·gia** \,dēmǝ'spǝnjēǝ\ *syn of* DEMOSPONGIAE

de·mo·spon·gi·ae \-jē,ē\ *n pl, cap* [NL, alter. of *Desmospongiae*] **:** a large class of Porifera comprising the majority of living sponges and being characterized by complex structure with a skeleton of tetraxial or simple siliceous spicules or of fibers of spongin or of both

de·mos·the·ne·an \də¦mästhə¦nēən, (ˈ)dē¦-\ *or* **de·mos·the·ni·an** \¦dēməs¦thēn-, ¦dem-\ *adj, usu cap* [*Demosthenes* †322 B.C. Greek orator + E *-ean, -ian*] : DEMOSTHENIC ⟨a species of *Demosthenean* eloquence⟩

de·mos·then·ic \¦dēməs¦thenik, ¦dem-\ *adj, usu cap* [L *Demosthenicus*, fr. Gk *Dēmosthenikos* of Demosthenes, fr. *Dēmosthenes* + Gk *-ikos* -ic] : of or relating to the Athenian orator Demosthenes : resembling or suggesting his oratorical style or effectiveness; *esp* : oratorically impassioned and moving ⟨*Demosthenic* passages occur in Pitt's speeches —Gilbert Highet⟩

de·mote \də, dē+ˈmōt, *usu* -ōd·+V\ *vt* -ED/-ING/-S [*de-* + *-mote* (as in *promote*)] : to reduce to a lower grade or rank ⟨~ a pupil⟩ ⟨a soldier *demoted* from sergeant to corporal⟩ : relegate to a subordinate or less important position — opposed to *promote* — **de·mo·tion** \-ōshən\ *n* -S

1de·mot·ic \dəˈmäd·|ik, dēˈ-, -ät|\ *adj* [Gk *dēmotikos*, fr. *dēmotēs* commoner (fr. *dēmos* deme, populace) + *-ikos* -ic — more at DEM-] **1** : of or relating to the people : POPULAR, COMMON — used esp. of language ⟨the attempt to create beauty out of city life and style out of the ~ English which is spoken therein —Cyril Connolly⟩ **2 a** : written in, constituting, or belonging to a simplified form of the ancient Egyptian hieratic writing used at first chiefly for business and social purposes but later also for religious and literary works : ENCHORIAL, EPISTOLOGRAPHIC **b** : written in, constituting, or belonging to a relatively simple rapidly written cursive form of any of various systems of writing **3** : of, belonging to, or connected with the form of Modern Greek that is based on colloquial use and is characterized by free acceptance of loanwords and simplification of inflections — compare KATHAREVUSA

2demotic \"\ *n* -S : the demotic form of Modern Greek

demotic egyptian *n, cap E* : the stage of the Egyptian language that immediately preceded Coptic and that is known from writings in demotic characters dating approximately from the 8th century B.C. to the 3d century A.D.

de·mot·ist \ˈəst\ *n* -S [*demotic* (*Egyptian*) + *-ist*] : a student of demotic writings

de·mount \(ˈ)dē¦maunt\ *vt* [*de-* + *mount* (to assemble)] **1** : to remove from a mounted position ⟨~*ed* the tire from the wheel⟩ **2** : to take apart or to pieces esp. carefully or systematically with the purpose of reassembly : DISASSEMBLE ⟨~ an airplane motor⟩ ⟨~ a watch⟩

1de·mount·able \-təbəl\ *adj* [*demount* + *-able*] **1** : capable of being demounted ⟨~ wheel⟩ ⟨a planetarium with a ~ sky⟩ **2** : designed to allow disassembly with minimum damage to component parts ⟨a ~ house⟩

2demountable \"\ *n* : a demountable building

demp·ster \ˈdemztər, -m(p)st-\ *n* -S [ME *dempster*, *demestre* judge, fr. *demen* to judge + *-ster* — more at DEEM] *old Scots law* : an officer whose duty it was to pronounce the doom of the court

1de·mul·cent \dəˈməlsənt, dēˈ-\ *adj* [L *demulcent-*, *demulcens*, pres. part. of *demulcēre* to caress, soothe, fr. *de-* + *mulcēre* to caress, soothe] : SOOTHING, SOFTENING ⟨~ expectorants which give a protective coating to the throat —*Therapeutic Notes*⟩

2demulcent \"\ *n* -S : a substance (as tragacanth, acacia, or flaxseed) usu. of a mucilaginous or oily character capable of soothing an inflamed or abraded mucous membrane or protecting it from irritation

de·mul·si·bil·i·ty \də,məlsəˈbiləd·ē, dē,-\ *n* -ES [*demulsify* + *-ibility*] : the ability to be demulsified being sometimes expressed as the rate at which a liquid (as an oil) separates from an emulsion

de·mul·si·fi·ca·tion \-səfəˈkāshən\ *n* -S : the process of demulsifying

de·mul·si·fy \dəˈməlsə,fī, dēˈ-\ *also* **de-emulsify** \¦dē+\ *vt* -ED/-ING/-ES [*de-* + *emulsify*] : to convert into a form that resists emulsification : BREAK *vt* 9e

1de·mur *R* dəˈmər, dēˈ-, +V-mər·; *-R* -mə̄, + *suffixal vowel* -mər· *also* -mər, +V *in a following word* -mər· *or* -mə̄ *also* -mər\ *vb* **demurred**; **demurred**; **demurring**; **demurs** [ME *demeoren*, *demeren* to linger, wait, fr. OF *demorer* (3d pers. pl. pres. indic. *demeurent*), fr. L *demorari* to linger, retard, fr. *de-* + *morari* to linger, retard, fr. *mora* delay — more at MEMORY] *vi* **1** *law* : to interpose a demurrer **2** : to object or have scruples : take exception — often used with *to* or *at* ⟨it would seem hazardous to ~ to a proposition which is so widely accepted —Samuel Alexander⟩ **3** *archaic* : to suspend proceedings or judgment in view of a doubt or difficulty : put off the determination or conclusion of an affair : DELAY, HESITATE ~ *vt* **1** *obs* : to cause delay to : put off **2** *obs* : to doubt or hesitate about **3** *archaic* : to object to

syn SCRUPLE, BALK, JIB or GIB, SHY, BOGGLE, STICK, STICKLE, STRAIN: DEMUR indicates delaying through personal doubt, uncertainty, objection, or exception ⟨we are bound to challenge many of our colleagues in the university who *demur* on academic grounds to the inclusion of theology —Walter Moberly⟩ ⟨they had been seated about the middle room with *demurring* and unwillingness to take seats, for politeness —Pearl Buck⟩ SCRUPLE implies reluctance to assent or proceed because of doubts about rightness, morality, propriety, or wisdom ⟨he does not *scruple* to ask the most abominable things of you —George Meredith⟩ ⟨Greece and in particular Athens was overrun by philosophers, who . . . did not *scruple* to question the foundations of social and moral obligation —G.L.Dickinson⟩ BALK indicates an obstinate stopping short, as though some sort of limit had been reached or check encountered ⟨one of the Marauder mules *balked* at the bottom of every rugged Burma hill —Dave Richardson⟩ ⟨minds can be pushed just so far and so fast, then they *balk* —Russell Lord⟩ JIB (GIB) may suggest balking and drawing back or away ⟨his soldiers, many of whom had served with Antony, *jibbed* at the attack on their old leader —John Buchan⟩ SHY implies starting or recoiling away in fright, like a frightened horse, or in wary suspicion or squeamish distaste ⟨she *shied* away from him like a startled Thoroughbred⟩ ⟨even the hardiest pioneer is likely to *shy* at the Valley of Death and put off going there to the very end —W.P.Webb⟩ BOGGLE may indicate shying away from in sudden alarm or with fussy scruple ⟨Lord Cardigan *boggled* at the incredible order, then squared his shoulders and took the Brigade to destruction —Anthony West⟩ ⟨when a native begins perjury he perjures himself thoroughly. He does not *boggle* over details —Rudyard Kipling⟩ ⟨but I do *boggle* at putting my tongue in my cheek and teaching what I know to be nonsense —Paul Roberts⟩ STICK indicates demurring because of conscientious scruples ⟨to *stick* at nothing in accomplishing his ends⟩ STICKLE involves refusing to accept because of something felt to be offensive or contrary to principles ⟨presumably that is his method — so the reader, eager to get good things where he can, will not *stickle* at it —K.D.Burke⟩ STRAIN in this sense indicates demurring at the unacceptable; it is often used in situations involving standards and tastes sharply varied by whimsical caprice ⟨to *strain* at a gnat and swallow a camel⟩

2demur \"\ *n* -S [ME *demure*, *demere* delay, abode, fr. OF *demore*, fr. *demorer*] **1** : difficulty in making up one's mind : IRRESOLUTION, INDECISION, UNCERTAINTY ⟨after some delay and ~, the door grudgingly turned on its hinges —Charles Dickens⟩ **2** : the act of objecting or taking exception : PROTEST ⟨to accept without ~⟩ ⟨rather than be brought into court he will pay without ~ —G.B.Shaw⟩ **syn** see SCRUPLE

1de·mure \dəˈmyu̇(ə)r, dēˈ-, -u̇ə\ *adj* -ER/-EST [ME, perh. fr. MF *demorer*, *demourer* to linger, wait] **1** : marked by quiet modesty, sedate reserve, restraint, or sobriety : not demanding attention : RETIRING, SHY ⟨by hustling male assistants very energetic and rapid, instead of by ~ anemic virgins —Arnold Bennett⟩ ⟨the recurring flash of mischief in its ~ and marvelously dainty humor —*Times Lit. Supp.*⟩ **2** : affectedly modest, reserved, or serious : PRIM, COY ⟨had a knack of adopting a ~ ingenue air —W.M.Thackeray⟩ ⟨linen, nonchalant and swank and cut with ~ and deceitful simplicity —Lois Long⟩ **syn** see DECOROUS

2demure *vi, obs* : to look demurely

de·mure·ly *adv* [ME, fr. *demure* + *-ly*] : in a demure manner : with affected or coy gravity or meekness : MODESTLY, PRIMLY ⟨pale fair hair that she ~ parted in the middle —Edmund Wilson⟩

de·mure·ness *n* -ES : the quality of being demure

de·mur·i·ty \dəˈmyu̇rəd·ē, dēˈ-\ *n* -ES [1*demure* + *-ity*] : DEMURENESS

de·mur·ra·ble \dəˈmər·əbəl, dēˈ- *also* -mərə-\ *adj* [1*demur* + *-able*] : susceptible of being demurred to (as in a legal action)

de·mur·rage \-ˈmər·|ij, -mə·r|, |ēj *also* -mər|\ *n* -S [1*demur* (to delay) + *-age*] **1 a** : the detention of a ship by the freighter beyond the time allowed in her charter party for loading, unloading, or sailing — compare LAY DAY **b** : a charge assessed for detaining a freight car, truck, or other vehicle beyond the free time stipulated for loading or unloading **2** : a storage charge on goods in transit not called for within a reasonable or set time; *also* : the delay in collecting such goods

de·mur·ral \-ˈmər·əl *also* -mərəl\ *n* -S [1*demur* + *-al*] : the act or an instance of demurring : OBJECTION, PROTEST, DISSENT

de·mur·rant \-ˈmər·ənt *also* -mərə-\ *n* -S [1*demur* + *-ant*] : one that interposes a demurrer

demurred *past of* DEMUR

1de·mur·rer \-ˈmər·ə(r), -mə·rə(r) *also* -mərə(r\ *n* -S [MF *demorer* to delay, linger, wait — more at DEMUR] **1** : a pleading by a party to a legal action that assumes the truth of the matter alleged by the opposite party and sets up that it is insufficient in law to sustain his claim or that there is some other defect on the face of the pleadings constituting a legal reason why the opposing party should not be allowed to proceed further **2** : an objection or exception : DEMUR 2 ⟨the only ~ one might register . . . would be in relation to the dangerous generalizations of the author's last chapter —J.J.Sweeney⟩

2de·mur·rer \-ˈmər·ə(r) *also* -mərə(r\ *n* -S [1*demur* + *-er*] : one that demurs

demurring *pres part of* DEMUR

demurs *pres 3d sing of* DEMUR, *pl of* DEMUR

demy \dəˈmī\ *n* -ES [ME, fr. *demi* half — more at DEMI-] **1 a** : a 15th century gold coin of Scotland weighing from 50 to 53 grains **b** : a unit of value equivalent to one demy coin ⟨a gold half-*demy* was issued⟩ **2** : a scholar on the foundation at Magdalen college, Oxford, orig. receiving half the allowance of a fellow **3** : a size of paper commonly 16 × 21, 15½ × 20, or 17½ × 22½ inches

de·my·e·li·nate \(ˈ)dē¦mīələ,nāt, dəˈ-\ *vt* [*de-* + *myelin* + *-ate*] : to remove myelin from or destroy the myelin of ⟨a disease that ~*s* the cranial nerves⟩

de·my·e·li·na·tion \(¦)dē,mīələˈnāshən, də,-\ *n* : the state of being demyelinated

de·my·e·lin·i·za·tion \(¦)dē,mīələnəˈzāshən, də,-\ *n* -S : DEMYELINATION

de·my·ship \dəˈmī,ship\ *n* [*demy* + *-ship*] : a scholarship at Magdalen college, Oxford

de·mythologize \(¦)dē+\ *vb* [*de-* + *mythologize*] *vt* : to divest (a writing) of mythological forms in order to uncover the meaning underlying such forms ~ *vi* : to separate the meaning of a writing from the mythological forms in which it is expressed — **de·mythologization** \(¦)dē+\ *n* -S

1den \ˈden\ *n* -S [ME, fr. OE *denn;* akin to OE *denu* valley, OHG *tenni* threshing floor, Gk *thenar* palm of the hand, Skt *dhanu* sandy shore] **1** : the lair of a wild animal, esp. of a beast of prey ⟨a fox ~⟩ **2** : a cavern or hollow used esp. as a place of concealment or refuge ⟨a robber's ~ in the side of a mountain⟩ **3** *dial Brit* : a narrow glen or ravine : DINGLE **4** : a comfortable usu. secluded room provided in a dwelling for study, reading, or leisure ⟨every home that could afford one had a ~, with leather armchair, pennants on the wall —*Time*⟩ **5** : a place that is usu. small and dimly lit and that serves as or resembles a hideout or a center of secret activity ⟨the ~*s* where the gangs lived —S.H.Adams⟩ ⟨the amusement ~*s* of New York and Hollywood —R.L.Taylor⟩ ⟨gambling ~*s*⟩ ⟨a ~ of iniquity⟩ ⟨an opium ~⟩ **6** : the home, base, or goal in certain games **7** : a subdivision of a cub-scout pack of the Boy Scouts of America made up of two or more cub scouts and corresponding to a boy-scout patrol — see DEN MOTHER

2den \"\ *vb* **denned**; **denned**; **denning**; **dens** [ME *dennen*, fr. *den* lair] *vi* **1** : to live in or as if in a den ⟨there were hill folk who *denned* in log cabins with dirt floors and no windows —Vance Randolph & G.P.Wilson⟩ **2** : to retire to a den (as for hibernating) — often used with *up* ⟨the young bears ~ up together during the second winter —R.E.Trippensee⟩ ~ *vt* : to drive or pursue (an animal) into a den ⟨cold weather had *denned* up the coons for good —Hugh Fosburgh⟩ ⟨his dogs drove hard and long and never quit until the fox was killed or *denned* —*Red Ranger*⟩

den *abbr* denotation; denotative

denar *var of* DINAR

de·nar·i·us \dəˈna(a)rēəs, dē-, -ˈnär-\ *n, pl* **denar·ii** \-rē,ī, -rē(,)ē\ [ME, fr. L — more at DENIER] **1** : a small silver coin of ancient Rome orig., under the Republic, equivalent to 10 bronze asses but later debased until by the late Empire its silver content became only a wash on copper **2** : a gold coin of the Roman Empire equivalent to 25 denarii **3** : 3DENIER 1

denarius of Julius Caesar, 44 B.C.

denarius dei \-ˈdē,ī, ˈdā(,)ē\ *n, pl* **denarii dei** *sometimes cap 2d D* [NL] : GOD'S PENNY

1denary *n* -ES [L *denarius*, fr. *denarius* adj.] *obs* : the number ten : a group of ten

2de·na·ry \ˈdēnərē, ˈden-\ *adj* [L *denarius* — more at DENIER] : containing ten : based on or proceeding by tens : TENFOLD

de·nasalization \(¦)dē, də+\ *n* : the act or an instance of denasalizing

de·nasalize \(ˈ)dē, də+\ *vt* [*de-* + *nasalize*] : to eliminate nasality from ⟨in a choked *denasalized* voice —Natacha Stewart⟩

de·nationalization \(¦)dē, də+\ *n* : the act of denationalizing or the state of being denationalized

de·nationalize \(ˈ)dē, də+\ *vt, see -ize in Explan Notes* [*de-* + *nationalize*] **1** : to divest or deprive (as a people) of national character or rights **2** : to free from ownership or domination by the national government ⟨the coal industry was *denationalized*⟩ : free from obligation to serve the interests of any particular nation in preference to the universal good

de·naturalization \(¦)dē, də+\ *n* : the act of denaturalizing or the state of being denaturalized

de·naturalize \(ˈ)dē, də+\ *vt* [*de-* + *naturalize*] **1** : to make unnatural : take away or alter the true or proper nature of : alienate from nature ⟨it was landscape *denaturalized* . . . and with all that was left adapted to a decorative purpose —*N.Y. Herald Tribune*⟩ **2** [F *dénaturaliser*, fr. *dé-* de- (fr. OF *de-*, *des-*) + *naturaliser* to naturalize] : to deprive of the rights and duties of a subject or citizen — opposed to *naturalize*

de·na·tur·ant \dəˈnāchərənt, dēˈ-\ *n* -S [*denature* + *-ant*] : a denaturing agent

de·na·tur·a·tion \də,nāchəˈrāshən, (,)dē,-\ *n* -S : the process of denaturing — used esp. of proteins ⟨~ of egg white by heat leads to coagulation⟩

de·nature \(ˈ)dē, də+\ *vb* -ED/-ING/-S [*de-* + *nature* (n.)] *vt* **1** : to deprive of natural qualities or characteristics : change the nature of ⟨a simplified but not *denatured* form of one of the world's existing major languages —I.A.Richards⟩ **2** : to so modify (a native protein) esp. by heat, acid, alkali, or ultraviolet radiation that some of the original properties (as solubility and specific activity) no longer are present or present in the same degree owing to a change in molecular structure **3** : to add nonfissionable material to (fissionable material) so as to render unsuitable for use in an atomic bomb without processing but not to affect value as a source of atomic power ~ *vi* : to become denatured — used esp. of proteins

denatured alcohol *n* : ethyl alcohol made unfit for drinking but still suitable for industrial or domestic purposes and freed from internal revenue tax in many countries (as the U. S.): as **a** : alcohol to which have been added sufficient malodorous and obnoxious substances (as products from the destructive distillation of wood or from petroleum) to prevent completely its use or recovery for beverage purposes but not for many industrial uses (as for an antifreeze) — called also *completely denatured alcohol* **b** : alcohol to which have been added small amounts of substances (as methanol, benzene, or acetaldehyde) that do not prevent its use in industry and the arts for specialized purposes (as for solvents) — called also *specially denatured alcohol;* compare METHYLATED SPIRIT

de·na·tur·ize \(ˈ)dē¦nāchə,rīz, dəˈn-\ *vt* -ED/-ING/-S *see -ize in Explan Notes* [ISV *de-* + *nature* + *-ize*] : DENATURE

de·na·zi·fi·ca·tion \(¦)dē,nätsəfə¦kāshən, -nat- *sometimes* -näzə- *or* -nazə-\ *n* -S : the process of denazifying or the state of being denazified

de·na·zi·fy \(ˈ)dēˈnätsə,fī, -nat- *sometimes* -näzə,- *or* -nazə,-\ *vt* -ED/-ING/-ES [*de-* + *nazify*] : to rid of nazism and its influence : free or pronounce free of the charge of nazism

den·bigh·shire \ˈdenbə,shi(ə)r, -iə, -,shə(r)\ *or* **den·bigh** \-bē, -bi\ *adj, usu cap* [fr. *Denbighshire* or *Denbigh*, county of Wales] : of or from the county of Denbigh, Wales : of the kind or style prevalent in Denbigh

den chief *n* : a boy scout who cooperates with a den mother in supervising a cub-scout den of the Boy Scouts of America

den dad *n* : a male adult leader of a cub-scout den of the Boy Scouts of America

dendr- *or* **dendro-** *comb form* [NL *dendr-*, fr. Gk *dendr-*, *dendro-* tree, fr. *dendron;* akin to Gk *drys* tree — more at TREE] : tree ⟨*dendro*philous⟩ : resembling a tree ⟨*dendr*axon⟩

den·drag·a·pus \denˈdragəpəs\ *n, cap* [NL] : a genus of grouses (family Tetraonidae) comprising the blue grouses

den·dras·pis \-ˈdraspəs\ *n, cap* [NL, fr. *dendr-* + L *aspis* asp — more at ASP] : a genus of African elapid snakes comprising the mambas

den·dri·form \ˈdendrə,fȯrm\ *adj* [*dendr-* + *-iform*] : resembling a tree in structure ⟨~ sponge⟩

den·drite \ˈden,drīt\ *n* -S [*dendr-* + *-ite*] **1** : a branching figure resembling a tree produced on or in a mineral or stone (as in the moss agate) by an oxide of manganese or other foreign mineral; *also* : the mineral or stone so marked **2** : a crystallized arborescent form (as of gold or silver) **3** : any of the protoplasmic processes of a nerve cell that conduct impulses toward the cell body and that are usu. branched and comparatively short : an afferent fiber of a neuron — compare AXON

den·drit·ic \(ˈ)den¦drid·ik\ *also* **den·drit·i·cal** \-d·əkəl\ *adj* : resembling a dendrite : branching like a tree : ARBORESCENT ⟨~ snow crystals⟩ ⟨~ pigment-bearing cells in the skin⟩ ⟨a ~ drainage system⟩ — **den·drit·i·cal·ly** \-d·ək(ə)lē\ *adv*

den·drob·a·tes \denˈdräbəd·,ēz\ *n, cap* [NL, fr. *dendr-* + *-bates;* prob. influenced by Gk *dendrobatein* to climb trees] : a genus of toothless mostly small brightly colored tropical American frogs of the family Ranidae having a poisonous skin secretion that has been used by certain Central American Indians as an arrow poison

den·drobe \ˈden,drōb\ *n* -S [NL *Dendrobium*] : an orchid of the genus *Dendrobium*

den·dro·bi·um \denˈdrōbēəm\ *n* [NL, fr. *dendr-* + *-bium*] **1** *cap* : a genus of epiphytic orchids that are chiefly native to tropical and subtropical Asia and have stems resembling canes and racemose flowers in which the labellum is connate with or articulate to the base of the column **2** -S : any plant of the genus *Dendrobium*

den·dro·calamus \,den(,)drō+\ *n, cap* [NL, fr. *dendr-* + L *calamus* reed — more at CALAMUS] : a small genus of large Asiatic bamboos with long panicles of globular clusters of flowers succeeded by small fruits with thick hard walls

den·dro·chi·ro·ta \,dendrō,kīˈrōd·ə\ *n pl, cap* [NL, fr. *dendr-* + *-chirota* (fr. LGk *chirōtos* furnished with hands, fr. Gk *cheir* hand) — more at CHIR-] : an order of holothurians having tube feet and tentacles which branch like a small tree and occurring in shallow water thoughout the world but esp. in temperate and cold regions — **den·dro·chi·rote** \-ˈkī,rōt\ *adj or n*

dend·ro·chronological \¦den(,)drō+\ *adj* : relating to or concerned with dendrochronology — **den·dro·chronologically** \¦=(,)=+\ *adv*

den·dro·chronologist \¦=(,)=+\ *n* : a specialist in dendrochronology

den·dro·chronology \¦=(,)=+\ *n* [*dendr-* + *chronology*] : the science of dating events, intervals of time, and variations in environment in former periods by study of the sequence of and differences between rings of growth in trees and aged wood

den·dro·coe·lum \,dendrōˈsēləm\ *n, cap* [NL, fr. *dendr-* + *-coelum*] : a common genus of Old World triclad turbellarians to which the common white planarian (*Procotyla fluviatilis*) was formerly assigned

den·dro·co·lap·tid \,=(,)=kəˈlaptəd\ *n* -S [NL *Dendrocolaptidae*] : a bird of the family Dendrocolaptidae

den·dro·co·lap·ti·dae \,=(,)=kəˈlaptə,dē\ *n pl, cap* [NL, fr. *Dendrocolaptes*, type genus (fr. *dendr-* + *-colaptes* (fr. Gk *kolaptein* to peck) + NL *-idae*] : a large family of tropical American birds (suborder Tyranni) that are closely related to the ovenbirds, are of climbing habit, and creep over trees from which they dig out insects — see WOODHEWER — **den·dro·co·lap·tine** \¦=(,)=kə¦lap,tīn, -,tən\ *adj*

den·droc·o·pos \denˈdräkəpəs\ *n, cap* [NL, fr. Gk *dendrokopos* woodcutter, fr. *dendr-* + *-kopos* (fr. the stem of *koptein* to smite, cut off) — more at CAPON] : a large genus of woodpeckers that are widely distributed in temperate parts of the northern hemisphere, and are all black or blackish brown with white markings and more or less red about the head

den·droc·to·nus \-ˈdräktənəs\ *n, cap* [NL, fr. *dendr-* + Gk *ktonos* murder; fr. their destructiveness] : a genus of small bark beetles that are esp. destructive to mature coniferous trees and that have a large prothorax, short clubbed elbowed antennae, serrated tibiae, and spiny elytra

den·dro·cyg·na \,dendrōˈsignə\ *n, cap* [NL, fr. *dendr-* + *-cygna* (fr. L *cygnus, cycnus* swan) — more at CYGNET] : a genus of long-legged ducks comprising the tree ducks and having long strong claws used in perching and a peculiar whistling call

den·dro·date \ˈdendrə+,-\ *n* [*dendr-* + *date*] : a date (as of an archaeological site) obtained by dendrochronology

den·dro·gae·an *or* **den·dro·ge·an** \¦dendrō¦jēən\ *adj, usu cap* [NL *Dendrogaea*, *Dendrogea*, a biogeographic realm (fr. *dendr-* + *-gaea*, *-gea*) + E *-an*] : of, relating to, or being a biogeographic realm or region that includes all of the Neotropical region except temperate So. America

den·dro·gram \ˈdendrə,gram\ *n* -S [*dendr-* + *-gram*] : a branching diagrammatic representation of the interrelations of a group of items sharing some common factors (as of natural groups connected by a common ancestral form)

den·dro·graph \ˈ==,graf\ *n* -S [*dendr-* + *-graph*] : an instrument for the automatic recording of changes in tree diameter

den·dro·graph·ic \¦==¦grafik\ *adj* : of or relating to dendrography

den·drog·ra·phy \denˈdrägrəfē\ *n* -ES [*dendr-* + *-graphy*] : the recording of tree growth by a dendrograph

den·dro·hyrax \,dendrō+\ [NL, fr. *dendr-* + Gk *hyrax* mouse, shrew mouse — more at SOREX] *syn of* PROCAVIA

den·droi·ca \denˈdrȯikə\ *n, cap* [NL, fr. *dendr-* + *-oica* (fr. Gk *oikos* house, dwelling place) — more at VICINITY] : a genus of brightly colored No. American warblers (family Parulidae) including the Blackburnian, yellow, and magnolia warblers

den·droid \ˈden,drȯid\ *also* **den·droid·al** \(ˈ)=¦=dᵊl\ *adj* [*dendroeidēs*, fr. *dendr-* tree + *-oeidēs* -oid, -oidal] **1** : resembling a tree in form : ARBORESCENT **2** *of graptolites* : forming many-branched colonies

den·drol·a·gus \denˈdräləgəs\ *n, cap* [NL, fr. *dendr-* + Gk *lagōs* hare] : the genus consisting of the tree wallabies

den·dro·log·ic \¦dendrə¦läjik\ *or* **den·dro·log·i·cal** \-jəkəl\ *adj* : relating to dendrology

den·drol·o·gist \denˈdräləjəst\ *n* -S : a specialist in dendrology

den·drol·o·gy \-jē\ *n* -ES [*dendr-* + *-logy*] **1** : the study of trees **2** : a treatise on trees

den·drom·e·ter \denˈdrämәd·ə(r)\ *n* -S [*dendr-* + *-meter*] : any of several devices for measuring trees *esp* : one for measuring diameters and heights indirectly utilizing principles based on the relation of the sides of similar triangles — compare DENDROGRAPH

den·dron \ˈdendrən, -,drän\ *n, pl* **dendrons** \-nz\ *also* **den·dra** \-,drə\ [NL, fr. Gk, tree — more at DENDR-] : DENDRITE

-den·dron \¦dendrən, -,drän\ *n comb form, pl* **-dendrons**

\-nz\ *also* **-den·dra** \-drə\ [L, fr. Gk, fr. *dendron* — more at DENDR-] **1 :** tree — esp. in generic names of plants ⟨Lirio*dendron*⟩ ⟨Trocho*dendron*⟩ **2 :** treelike formation ⟨neuro*dendron*⟩ **3 :** stem : part of a stem ⟨Schizo*dendron*⟩

den·droph·a·gous \(ˈ)den¦dräfəgəs\ *adj* [*dendr-* + *-phagous*] **:** feeding on trees — used of insects

den·droph·i·lous \-fələs\ *adj* [*dendr-* + *-philous*] **:** tree-loving : living in or on trees ⟨~ plants⟩

den·droph·y·sis \den'dräfəsəs\ *n, pl* **dendrophy·ses** \-ˌsēz\ [NL, fr. *dendr-* + *-physis* (as in *paraphysis*)] **:** an arboreally branched hyphal thread in certain fungi that resembles a paraphysis

[1]**dene** \ˈdēn\ *n* -s [ME *dene*, fr. OE *denu* valley; akin to OE *denn* den — more at DEN] **1** *Brit* **:** VALLEY — often used in place names **2** *Brit* **:** a deep wooded valley; *esp* **:** one with a stream flowing through it

[2]**dene** \"\ *n* -s [ME *den, denne;* prob. akin to OE *dūn* down (hill) — more at DOWN] *Brit* **:** a sandy tract or low sand hill by the sea

[3]**dé·né** \dāˈnā\ *n, pl* **déné** *or* **dénés** *usu cap* [F, fr. Déné] **1 a :** an Athapaskan people occupying most of the interior of Alaska and northwestern Canada **b :** a member of such people — compare PACIFIC ATHAPASKAN **2 :** the language of the Déné people — called also *Northern Athapaskan*

den·e·ga·tion \ˌdenəˈgāshən\ *n* -s [ME *denegacioun*, fr. MF or L; MF *denegation*, fr. L *denegation-, denegatio*, fr. *denegatus* (past part. of *denegare* to deny) + *-ion-, -io* -ion — more at DENY] **:** DENIAL, REFUSAL

denehole \ˈ≈,≈\ *n* [prob. fr. [1]*dene* + *hole*] **:** an ancient excavation found chiefly in Essex and Kent in England and in the valley of the Somme in France consisting of a shaft sunk to the Chalk formation and enlarged into a room or rooms

de·ner·vate \ˈdēˈnərˌvāt, dəˈ-\ *vt* -ED/-ING/-S [*de-* + *nerve* + *-ate*] **:** to deprive of nerve supply (as by cutting a nerve)

de·ner·va·tion \ˌdēnərˈvāshən\ *n* **:** the act of denervating or the state of being denervated

den·gue \ˈdeŋ(ˌ)gē, -(ˌ)gā, -ŋgi *also* -ŋē *or* -ŋi; *S often* -ŋ-(ˌ)gyü\ *also* **dengue fever** *n* -s [Sp *dengue*, prob. of African origin; akin to Swahili *kidinga* (*popo*) dengue, Giryama *kidhinghidhyo* fever, Rabai *dengeleka* go around, be dizzy] **:** an acute infectious disease characterized by sudden onset, headache, racking joint pain, and a rash and caused by a virus transmitted by mosquitoes of the genus *Aedes* chiefly in tropical and semitropical regions — called also *breakbone fever*

de·ni·able \dəˈnīəbəl, dēˈ-\ *adj* [*deny* + *-able*] **:** capable of being denied

de·ni·al \-ˈnī(ə)l\ *n* -s [*deny* + *-al*] **1 :** refusal to grant, assent to, or sanction **:** rejection of something requested, claimed, or felt to be due ⟨~ of his visiting privileges⟩ ⟨~ of passports to undesirables⟩ **2 a :** refusal to admit the truth of a statement, charge, or imputation **:** assertion that something alleged is untrue ⟨his ~ that he took the money⟩ ⟨her ~ that her son was involved⟩ **b :** refusal to accept or acknowledge the reality or validity of a thing or idea ⟨his ~ of the divine right of kings⟩ **3 :** refusal to acknowledge a person or thing as standing in a certain relationship or as having a certain character **:** DISAVOWAL, REPUDIATION ⟨a renegade's ~ of his leader⟩ ⟨the baron's ~ of his weakling son⟩ **4 :** the opposing by the defendant of an allegation of the opposite party in a law suit **5** *dial Eng* **:** HINDRANCE, HANDICAP, DISADVANTAGE ⟨his lame hand was a great ~ to him⟩ **6 :** a restriction or limitation upon one's own activity or desires **:** SELF-DENIAL ⟨the three thousand which he had hoarded at the price of sacrifice and ~ —William Faulkner⟩ **7 :** a bridge bid indicating inability to raise or support a partner's bid **8** *logic* **:** NEGATION

denial of the antecedent : the logical fallacy of inferring the negation of the consequent of an implication from the negation of the antecedent (as in "if it rains then the game is canceled but it has not rained therefore the game is not canceled") — compare AFFIRMATION OF THE CONSEQUENT

de·nicotinize *also* **de·nicotine** \(ˈ)dē, də +\ *vt* -ED/-ING/-S [*denicotinize* fr. *de-* + *nicotine* + *-ize; denicotine* fr. *de-* + *nicotine* (n.)] **:** to remove part of the nicotine from (tobacco)

denied *past of* DENY

[1]**de·ni·er** \dəˈnī(ə)r, -īə\ *n* -s [ME, fr. *denyen* to deny + *-er*] **:** one that denies

[2]**denier** *n* -s [MF *denier* to deny — more at DENY] *obs* **:** DENIAL 4

[3]**de·nier** \dəˈni(ə)r, -niə; dənˈyā *also* ˈdenyə(r) *or* -enēə(r); *in sense 2 usu* ˈdenyə(r) *or* -enēə(r) *also* -enˌyā *or* -enēˌā\ *n* -s [ME *denere*, fr. MF *denier*, fr. L *denarius*, Roman silver coin originally equivalent to ten asses, fr. *denarius* containing ten, fr. *deni* ten by ten (fr. the base of *decem* ten) + *-arius* -ary — more at TEN] **1 :** a small coin of France and western Europe from the time of Pepin the Short to the French Revolution, orig. of silver, later of billon, and finally of copper; *also* **:** a unit of value equal to one denier **2 a :** a unit of fineness for silk, rayon, or nylon yarn equal to the fineness of a yarn weighing 0.05 gram for each 450 meters of length or one gram for each 9000 meters ⟨9000 meters of a 15-*denier* yarn weigh 15 grams⟩ ⟨15-*denier* yarn is finer than 30-*denier* yarn⟩ **b :** the fineness of a silk, rayon, or nylon yarn or fabric

de·nier à dieu \dənyāadyœ̄\ *n, pl* **deniers à dieu** \"\ *sometimes cap 2d D* [F] **:** GOD'S PENNY

denies *pres 3d sing of* DENY

den·i·grate \ˈdenəˌgrāt, -nēˌ- *sometimes* ˈdēn-; *also* dəˈnīˌg- *or* dēˈ- *sometimes* -ˈniˌg-; *usu* -ād- + V\ *vt* -ED/-ING/-S [L *denigratus*, past part. of *denigrare* to blacken, fr. *de-* + *nigrare* to blacken, fr. *nigr-, niger* black] **1 :** to cast aspersion on the character or reputation of **:** belittle maliciously **:** DEFAME, SULLY ⟨*denigrating* his efforts and subjecting him to scorn —Manfred Nathan⟩ ⟨~ the values of living —Stephen Spender⟩ **2 :** to make black **:** DARKEN ⟨fog *denigrated* with factory smoke⟩

den·i·gra·tion \ˌdenəˈgrāshən, -nēˈ- *sometimes* ˌdēn-; *also* ˌdēˌnīˈ-\ *n* -s **1** *obs* **:** the act of denigrating **2 :** a sullying of reputation or character **:** DEFAMATION, DEGRADATION ⟨the ~ of man to his former animal level —G.L.Steibel⟩

den·i·gra·tor *pronunciation at* DENIGRATE + ə(r)\ *n* -s **:** one that denigrates

den·i·gra·to·ry \ˈdenəgrəˌtōrē, -ˌtȯr-, -ri; dəˈnīg-, -ˈnig-\ *adj* **:** DEFAMATORY

den·im \ˈdenəm\ *n* -s [F (*serge*) *de Nîmes* serge of Nîmes, France] **1 :** a firm durable twilled usu. cotton fabric woven with colored warp and white filling threads; *also* **:** such a fabric woven in colored stripes **2 denims** *pl* **:** overalls or trousers usu. of dark blue denim for work or rough use

den·i·so·nia \ˌdenəˈsōnēə\ *n, cap* [NL, fr. Sir William T. *Denison* †1871 Australian statesman and governor of New South Wales + NL *-ia*] **:** a genus of venomous Australian snakes (family Elapidae) including the copperhead

de·nitrate \(ˈ)dē +\ *vt* [*de-* + *nitrate* (n.)] **:** to remove nitric acid, nitrates, the nitro group, or nitrogen oxides from — **de·nitration** \¦dē +\ *n*

de·nitrator \(ˈ)dē +\ *n* **:** one that denitrates: as **a :** an apparatus in which denitration is conducted **b :** one who operates denitrator towers for the recovery of nitric acid in the manufacture of trinitrotoluene

de·nitrification \(¦)dē +\ *n* **:** the act or process of denitrifying; *specif* **:** a process by which nitrates or nitrites are reduced with the formation of nitrites, nitrogen oxides, ammonia, or free nitrogen and which is commonly brought about (as in the soil or in sewage) by denitrifying bacteria usu. resulting in the escape of nitrogen into the air

de·nitrifier \(ˈ)dē +\ *n* **:** a denitrifying agent (as a denitrifying bacterium)

de·nitrify \(ˈ)dē +\ *vt* [*de-* + *nitrify*] **:** to deprive of or free from nitrogen or its compounds; *also* **:** to convert (nitrates or nitrites) into compounds of lower oxidation states **:** subject to denitrification

denitrifying bacteria *n pl* **:** various bacteria that bring about denitrification — used esp. of forms that reduce nitrates to nitrites or nitrites to nitrogen gas (as many common putrefactive organisms of manure and soil); see ACHROMOBACTER

de·nitrogenate \(¦)dē +\ *vt* [*de-* + *nitrogenate*] **:** to reduce the stored nitrogen in the body of by forced breathing of pure oxygen for a period of time esp. as a measure designed to prevent development of aeroembolism — **de·nitrogenation** \(¦)dē +\ *n*

de·nitrogenize \(¦)dē +\ *vt* [*de-* + *nitrogenize*] **:** DENITROGENATE

den·i·za·tion \ˌdenəˈzāshən\ *n* -s **:** the act of making one a denizen **:** the process of being made a denizen

denize *vt* -ED/-ING/-S [prob. by alter. (influence of *-ize*)] *obs* **:** DENIZEN

[1]**den·izen** \ˈdenəzən *also* -əsən\ *n* -s [ME *deynseen, denysen*, fr. MF *denzein*, fr. OF, inner, fr. *denz* in, within (fr. LL *deintus* within, from within, fr. L *de* from, away + *intus* within, fr. *in*) + *-ein* -an (fr. L *-anus*) — more at DE-, IN] **1 : a :** a dweller in a certain place or region **:** INHABITANT, RESIDENT ⟨~*s* of the village⟩ ⟨the ~*s* of the bayous love a holiday —R.M.Hodesh⟩ **2 :** one admitted to residence in a foreign country; *esp* **:** an alien admitted by favor to all or a part of the rights of citizenship **3 :** one that has been naturalized — used esp. of a word, animal, or plant **4 a :** one that remains in a place temporarily or for a period of time **b :** one that occupies or goes to a place frequently **:** HABITUÉ ⟨~*s* of out-of-town theaters⟩

[2]**denizen** \"\ *vt* -ED/-ING/-S **:** to make (one) a denizen **:** admit to residence with certain rights and privileges

den·mark \ˈdenˌmärk, -ˌmäk\ *adj, usu cap* [fr. *Denmark*, kingdom in northwestern Europe] **:** of or from Denmark **:** of the kind or style prevalent in Denmark

den mother *n* **:** a female adult leader of a cub-scout den of the Boy Scouts of America

denned *past of* DEN

[1]**den·ner** \ˈdenər\ *Scot var of* DINNER

[2]**den·ner** \ˈdenə(r)\ *n* -s [[1]*den* + *-er*] **:** a boy who serves as leader of a cub-scout den of the Boy Scouts of America

den·net \ˈdenət\ *n* -s [prob. fr. the name *Dennet*] **:** a light open 2-wheeled carriage with the body suspended on leather braces that is drawn by one horse — compare WHISKEY

denning *pres part of* DEN

denn·staedt·ia \denˈsted·ēə, -tād-\ *n, cap* [NL, fr. August W. *Dennstaedt*, 19th cent. Ger. botanist + NL *-ia*] **:** a genus of chiefly tropical ferns (family Polypodiaceae) having tripinnate fronds and globular sori with sporangia in elevated receptacles and with cup-shaped indusia — **denn·staedt·i·oid** \(ˈ)≈¦≈ēˌȯid\ *adj*

de·nom·i·nal \dəˈnämənᵊl, dēˈ-\ *adj* [*de-* + *nominal*] **:** DENOMINATIVE 3

[1]**de·nom·i·nate** \-ˈnäməˌnāt, *usu* -ād- + V\ *vt* [L *denominatus*, past part. of *denominare*, fr. *de-* + *nominare* to name — more at NOMINATE] **1 :** to give a name to **:** call by a name **:** DESIGNATE, CALL ⟨a fact is a fact and all evidence so *denominated* has the prestige of science —R.M.Weaver⟩ ⟨anger ~*s* a state of mind —W.F.Hambly⟩ **2** *archaic* **:** to serve to distinguish **:** INDICATE, DENOTE **3 :** to express or designate in some denomination ⟨exchange certificates *denominated* in dollars or pounds —R.F.Mikesell⟩

[2]**de·nom·i·nate** \-ˌnət, -ˌnāt\ *adj* [L *denominatus*] **1** *archaic* **:** DENOMINATED, CALLED **2 :** having a specific name or denomination **:** specified in the concrete as opposed to the abstract ⟨*7 feet* is a ~ quantity, while 7 is an abstract quantity or number⟩

de·nom·i·na·tion \dəˌnäməˈnāshən, dēˌ-\ *n* -s [ME *denominacioun*, fr. MF or LL; MF *denomination*, fr. LL *denomination-, denominatio*, fr. L, metonymy, fr. *denominatus* + *-ion-, -io* -ion] **1 :** the act of denominating or naming **2 :** that by which something is denominated or styled **:** APPELLATION, NAME, DESIGNATION, TITLE; *esp* **:** a general name for a class of like individuals **:** CATEGORY ⟨a sort of tribute under the ~ of presents —Tobias Smollett⟩ **3 :** a class or society of individuals called by the same name; *esp* **:** a religious group or a community of believers called by the same name ⟨Presbyterians form one ~ of Christians⟩ **4 :** a value or size naming one of a particular series of values or sizes (as of monetary issues, stamps, units of weight or measure) ⟨bills in $5 and $10 ~*s*⟩ ⟨liter is a metric ~⟩ **5 :** the suit or no-trump named in a bridge bid **syn** see CLASS, RELIGION

de·nom·i·na·tion·al \≈¦≈≈¦shənᵊl, -shnəl\ *adj* **1 :** of or relating to a denomination **:** supported in part and either actually or nominally controlled by a particular religious denomination ⟨a ~ school⟩ **2 :** of or relating to denominationalism **3 :** PARTISAN, SECTARIAN — **de·nom·i·na·tion·al·ly** *adv*

de·nom·i·na·tion·al·ism \-nᵊlˌizəm, -nəˌliz-\ *n* -s **1 :** denominational spirit or policy **:** devotion to denominational principles or interests **2 :** the emphasizing of denominational differences to the point of being narrowly exclusive **:** SECTARIANISM

de·nom·i·na·tion·al·ize \-nᵊlˌīz, -nəˌlīz\ *vt* -ED/-ING/-S **:** to make denominational

[1]**de·nom·i·na·tive** \dəˈnäməˌnād·iv, dēˈ-, -ˌnə¦, ¦t¦, ¦ēv *also* ¦əv\ *adj* [*denominate* + *-ive*] **1 :** conferring a denomination or name **2** *of a word or term* **:** characterized by or referring to certain marks or qualities which determine the naming of the subject possessing them ⟨connotative names have hence been also called ~ because the subject which they denote is denominated by, or receives a name from, the attribute which they connote —J.S.Mill⟩ **3** [*de-* + L *nomin-, nomen* name, noun + E *-ative*] **:** derived from a noun or an adjective ⟨the ~ verbs *lengthen* and *sweeten* come from *length* and *sweet*⟩ — **de·nom·i·na·tive·ly** \¦əvlē, -li\ *adv*

[2]**denominative** \"\ *n* [*de-* + L *nomin-, nomen* name, noun + E *-ative*] **:** a word derived from a noun or an adjective

de·nom·i·na·tor \-ˈnäməˌnād·ə(r), -ātə-\ *n* -s **1 :** the part of a fraction that is below the horizontal or slanting line signifying division and that in fractions with numerator 1 indicates into how many parts the unit is supposed to be divided **:** DIVISOR **2** *archaic* **:** one that denominates **3 :** a common trait ⟨only a single ~ do they share —Osbert Sitwell⟩ **:** the average level (as of taste or opinion) **:** STANDARD ⟨manufacturers catering to a safely low ~ of public taste —*Time*⟩ — see COMMON DENOMINATOR

de·not·able \dəˈnōd·əbəl, dēˈ-, -ōtə-\ *adj* [*denote* + *-able*] **:** capable of being denoted

denotate *vt* [L *denotatus*, past part. of *denotare* — more at DENOTE] *obs* **:** DENOTE

de·no·ta·tion \ˌdēnōˈtāshən\ *n* -s [L *denotation-, denotatio*, fr. *denotatus* + *-ion-, -io* -ion] **1 a :** the act or process of signifying ⟨the ~ of plural forms by adding *-s*⟩ **b :** demarcation and explanation ⟨the ~ of the methods used⟩ **2 :** MEANING ⟨the ~ of an expression⟩; *esp* **:** direct specific meaning as distinct from additional suggestion — compare CONNOTATION 1 **3 a :** a term specifying or denoting a thing **:** NAME ⟨*mind* is the ~ for a faculty, *brain* for an organ⟩ **b :** SIGN, INDICATION ⟨visible ~*s* of divine wrath⟩ **4 :** the totality of things to which a term in logic is applicable — called also *extension;* contrasted with *connotation*

de·no·ta·tive \ˈdēnōˌtā¦d·¦iv, ¦t¦, ¦ēv *also* ¦əv; dəˈnōd·ə¦, dēˈ-, -ōtə¦\ *adj* **1 :** having the power of denoting **:** marking off **:** DESIGNATING **2** *logic* **:** bearing a denotation — **de·no·ta·tive·ly** \¦əvlē, -li\ *adv* — **de·no·ta·tive·ness** \¦əvnəs\ *n* -ES

denotative definition *n* **:** OSTENSIVE DEFINITION

de·no·ta·tum \ˌdēnōˈtād·əm\ *n, pl* **denota·ta** \-ād·ə\ [NL, fr. L, neut. of *denotatus*] **:** an actually existing object referred to by a word, sign, or linguistic expression — contrasted with *designatum*

de·note \dəˈnōt, dēˈ-, *usu* -ōd- + V\ *vt* -ED/-ING/-S [MF *denoter*, fr. L *denotare*, fr. *de-* + *notare* to mark, note — more at NOTE] **1 :** to serve as indication of **:** show by signs the presence or existence of **:** BETOKEN ⟨symptoms that ~ tuberculosis⟩ ⟨thickets of aspen, willow, and cottonwood ~ underlying water —*Amer. Guide Series: Wash.*⟩ **2 :** to serve as an arbitrary mark for **:** designate as a sign **:** MARK ⟨red flares *denoting* danger⟩ ⟨the slanting strokes at the bottom ~ the number —Edward Clodd⟩ ⟨a flag flown upside down to ~ distress⟩ **3** *obs* **:** write down **:** DESCRIBE **4 :** to make known **:** ANNOUNCE ⟨*denoting* his feelings clearly⟩ **5 a :** serve as linguistic expression of the notion of **:** MEAN ⟨*mono-* may ~ "one" or "single"⟩ **b :** to designate by an indicated symbol ⟨let me ~ by T the lapse of time —K.K.Darrow⟩ **c** *logic* **:** to stand for **:** signify by way of denotation **:** NAME ⟨the name . . . is said to signify the subjects *directly*, the attributes *indirectly;* it ~*s* the subjects and . . . *connotes* the attributes —J.S.Mill⟩ **syn** see MEAN

de·note·ment \-tmənt\ *n* -s **:** the act or means of denoting

de·no·tive \dəˈnōd·iv, dēˈ-\ *adj* **:** serving to denote **:** DENOTATIVE

de·noue·ment \ˌdāˌnüˈmäⁿ, ≈ˈ≈ˌ≈ *also* ˈ≈≈ˌ≈ *sometimes* dəˈnümənt *or* -ˌmänt; dānüˈmäⁿ\ *n* -s [F *dénouement*, lit., action of untying, fr. MF *desnouement*, fr. *desnouer* to untie (fr. OF *desnoer*, fr. *des-* de- + *noer* to tie, knot, fr. L *nodare*, fr. *nodus* knot) + *-ment* — more at NET] **1 :** the final outcome, result, or unraveling of the main dramatic complication in a play or other work of literature ⟨many of the better stories are written round, rather than towards, their ~*s* —*Times Lit. Supp.*⟩ ⟨in the ~ the girl commits suicide⟩ **2 :** the outcome or result of any complex situation or sequence of events ⟨the whole devious development of Soviet-German relations until the final dramatic ~ of the treaty —*Economist*⟩

de·nounce \dəˈnaun(t)s, dēˈ-\ *vt* -ED/-ING/-S [ME *denouncen, denounsen*, fr. OF *denoncier* to proclaim, pronounce, announce, fr. L *denuntiare*, fr. *de-* + *nuntiare* to report, announce, fr. *nuntius* messenger] **1 :** to pronounce (as a person, idea, course of conduct, political philosophy) to be blameworthy or evil **:** stigmatize or charge esp. publicly, unequivocally, and indignantly **:** inveigh against publicly ⟨*denounced* this perversion of his teaching with justifiable indignation —W.R.Inge⟩ ⟨~ the menaced proprietors as enemies of mankind —G.B.Shaw⟩ **2** *archaic* **:** to announce publicly and formally or solemnly; *sometimes* **:** to declare or publish (something calamitous) **3 :** to inform against **:** declare or make known (as a culprit) to authorities ⟨*denounced* the conspirators to the authorities⟩ **4 a** *obs* **:** to indicate by or as if by omen **:** PORTEND, AUGUR **b** *archaic* **:** to announce (as punishment, judgment, or other impending evil) in a warning or threatening manner **5 :** to proclaim formally and publicly the termination of (as a treaty, truce, pact) ⟨*denounced* the arrangement with their former ally⟩ **6** [Sp *denunciar*, lit., to proclaim, announce, fr. L *denuntiare*] *Mexican law* **:** to offer for record legal notice of a claim for a mining concession covering (a described area of land the mining rights for which are held by the government) **syn** see CRITICIZE

de·nounce·ment \-smənt\ *n* -s [MF *denoncement*, fr. *denoncier* + *-ment*] **1 :** the act of denouncing: **a** *obs* **:** DECLARATION, ANNOUNCEMENT **b :** DENUNCIATION **c :** public accusation **2** *Mexican law* **a :** the act of denouncing a mining claim; *also* **:** the record or documentary proof of such action **b :** the claim so denounced

de·nounc·er \-sə(r)\ *n* -s **:** one that denounces

de no·vo \dēˈnō(ˌ)vō, (ˈ)dēˈ-, (ˈ)dāˈ-\ *adv* [L] **:** ANEW, AFRESH **:** over again ⟨a case tried *de novo*⟩

[1]**dens** *pl of* DEN, *pres 3d sing of* DEN

[2]**dens** \ˈdenz\ *n, pl* **den·tes** \-nˌtēz\ [L — more at [1]TOOTH] **:** a tooth or anatomical part resembling a tooth; *specif* **:** ODONTOID PROCESS

densate *vt* -ED/-ING/-S [L *densatus*, past part. of *densare* to thicken, fr. *densus*] *obs* **:** CONDENSE — **densation** *n, obs*

dense \ˈden(t)s\ *adj* -ER/-EST [L *densus;* akin to Gk *dasys* thick with hair or leaves, Hitt *dassuš* strong] **1 a :** marked by an arrangement of parts or units so crowded or massed together as to defy penetration **:** notably lacking empty spaces or unfilled intervals ⟨the backs of the pinafores were ~ with buttons —Natacha Stewart⟩ ⟨if I went into ~ jungle, by the time I was out of sight I was also lost —Agnes N. Keith⟩ **b :** crowded very close together **:** massed together with little or no intervening space and consequently obstructing easy penetration through **:** concentrated in large numbers in a limited space ⟨every balcony, every housetop was crammed with a ~ mass of spectators —J.G.Frazer⟩ ⟨~ hardwood hammocks alternate with vast swamps —*Amer. Guide Series: Fla.*⟩ ⟨the ~ print of the directory —Jean Stafford⟩ **2** *biol* **:** COMPACT ⟨a ~ flower spike⟩ **3 a :** insensible or dull ⟨human error's ~ and purblind faith —P.B.Shelley⟩ **b :** mentally dull **:** SLOW-WITTED, THICK-HEADED **c :** EXTREME, INTENSE ⟨~ stupidity⟩ **4 a :** marked by solidly interwoven texture, by texture permitting thick matting, by deep dark color, by opaqueness or other obstruction to passage of light, or by massive concentration ⟨a ~ fabric⟩ ⟨lost in a ~ fog⟩ ⟨the heart is a ~ organ for X-ray purposes⟩ ⟨her pallor made her dark hair seem *denser* —Edith Wharton⟩ **b :** marked by presentation without lighter or less significant passages and demanding concentration to follow or comprehend ⟨her prose . . . so ~ . . . that it is all but impenetrable —*New Yorker*⟩ **5** *math* **:** having between any two elements at least one element and hence an infinity of elements ⟨a set of proper fractions arranged in order of size is ~⟩ **6 :** possessing relatively great retarding power upon light waves and consequently relatively great refractive power — used esp. of optical glass **7 :** having high or relatively high density — used of a photographic negative or a positive transparency **syn** see CLOSE, STUPID

dense·ly *adv* **:** in a dense manner

dens·en \-sən\ *vb* **densened; densened; densening** \-s(ə)niŋ\ **densens** *vt* **:** to make dense **~** *vi* **:** to become dense

dense·ness \-snəs\ *n* -ES **:** the quality or state of being dense **:** DENSITY

den·si·fi·ca·tion \ˌden(t)səfəˈkāshən\ *n* -s **:** the act or process of making dense

den·si·fi·er \ˈ≈≈ˌfī(ə)r\ *n* -s **:** a densifying agent ⟨concrete ~⟩

den·si·fy \-ˌfī\ *vt* -ED/-ING/-ES **:** to make dense or denser; *specif* **:** to increase the natural density of (wood) by application of pressure and usu. impregnation with a resin or other material

den·sim·e·ter \denˈsimәd·ə(r)\ *n* -s [ISV *densi-* (fr. L *densus* dense) + *-meter*] **:** an instrument for determining density or specific gravity — **den·si·met·ric** \¦den(t)sə¦me·trik\ *adj* — **den·si·met·ri·cal·ly** \-k(ə)lē\ *adv*

den·si·tom·e·ter \ˌden(t)səˈtämәd·ə(r)\ *n* -s [*density* + *-o-* + *-meter*] **1 :** DENSIMETER **2 :** an instrument for measuring optical density; *specif* **:** an instrument usu. photoelectric or visual for measuring photographic density by means of the light transmitted or the light reflected — **den·si·to·met·ric** \¦≈sәd·ə¦me·trik\ *adj* — **den·si·tom·e·try** \ˌ≈səˈtämə·trē\ *n* -ES

den·si·ty \ˈden(t)səd·ē, -sәtē, -)stē, -i\ *n* -ES [F or L; F *densité*, fr. L *densitat-, densitas*, fr. *densus* + *-itat-, -itas* -ity] **1 :** the quality or state of being dense **:** closeness of texture or consistency **:** a crowded condition ⟨a fog of great ~⟩ ⟨the great ~ of growth in the jungle⟩ ⟨made difficult by the ~ of his style⟩ **2 a :** the mass of a substance per unit volume **b :** the distribution of a quantity (as mass, electricity, or energy) per unit usu. of space (as area, length, or volume) — see ENERGY DENSITY, FLUX DENSITY, SURFACE DENSITY **c :** the average number of individuals or units per space unit ⟨a ~ of population of about 100 per square mile⟩ **3 :** extreme stupidity **4** *of an inflorescence* **:** COMPACTNESS **5 a :** the degree of opacity of any translucent medium **:** the common logarithm of the opacity **b :** the degree of darkening of a photographic film or positive transparency approximately proportional to the mass of metallic silver or dye per unit area

density altitude *n* **:** the altitude that corresponds to a given air density in a standard atmosphere

density of freight traffic *or* **density of passenger traffic :** the amount of traffic carried over a certain transport route in a given unit of time usu. computed by dividing total ton-miles or passenger-miles by the length of route

density rule *n* **:** a set of specifications for grading lumber based on the width of annual rings

[1]**dent** \ˈdent\ *n* -s [ME, stroke, blow, alter. of *dint* — more at DINT] **1** *now dial Eng* **:** STROKE, BLOW **2 :** a depression or hollow such as is made by a blow or by pressure **:** INDENTATION ⟨a ~ in a fender⟩ ⟨the touch of his finger made a ~ in the swollen flesh⟩ **3 :** DENT CORN **4 :** an impression or effect often having a minimizing or weakening influence ⟨a sizable ~ in the literary consciousness of the American reading public —John Barkham⟩ ⟨a ~ in the weekly budget⟩ ⟨the Texas drought made no appreciable ~ on total production —*Reporter*⟩ ⟨nor has any really effective ~ been made into the problem of shortages —F.M.Hechinger⟩

[2]**dent** \"\ *vb* -ED/-ING/-S [ME *denten*, alter. of *dinten* — more at DINT] *vt* **1 :** to make a dent in or on **:** INDENT ⟨the car hood was ~*ed* in⟩ ⟨~*ed* his fender in the collision⟩ **2 :** to make an impression or have an effect upon esp. with a weakening result ⟨such actions ~*ed* his political influence⟩ **~** *vi* **:** to form a dent by sinking inward **:** show dents **:** become dented ⟨tin ~*s* easily⟩

[3]**dent** \"\ *n* -s [MF, tooth, fr. L *dent-, dens* — more at TOOTH] **1 :** an indentation or notch **2 a** *in machinery* **:** a tooth esp. of a card or gear wheel or in a lock **b :** one of the fine flat wires which compose a reed in a loom and between which the warp threads pass; *also* **:** the space between two such wires by which

the number of practicable warp ends is determined **3** [F, fr. MF] **:** a mountain peak that resembles a tooth in shape

dent- *or* **denti-** *or* **dento-** *comb form* [ME *denti-*, fr. L *dent-, denti-*, fr. *dent-, dens*] **1 :** tooth **:** teeth ⟨*dent*algia⟩ ⟨*denti*form⟩ **2 :** dental and ⟨*denti*lingual⟩ ⟨*dento*surgical⟩

dent *abbr* dental; dentist; dentistry

¹den·tal \ˈdentᵊl\ *adj* [L *dentalis*, fr. *dent-, dens* tooth + *-alis* -al] **1 :** of or relating to the teeth or dentistry ⟨~ formula⟩ ⟨~ student⟩ **:** used for the care of the teeth or in dentistry ⟨~ paste⟩ ⟨~ file⟩ **2** *of a speech sound* **a :** articulated with the tip or blade of the tongue against or near the upper front teeth ⟨English \th\ and \th\ and French \t\ and \d\ are ~ sounds⟩ **b :** articulated either thus or alveolarly ⟨English \t\ and \d\ and\s\ and\z\ are ~ sounds⟩ — compare INTERDENTAL, LABIODENTAL

²dental \ˈ"\ *n* -s **1 :** DENTIL **2 :** a dental consonant **3 :** TOOTH — not often in formal use **4 :** a part (as a nerve or artery) supplying the teeth or the adjoining parts of the head

dental arch *n* **:** the curve of the row of teeth in each jaw

dental artery *n* **:** any of the several small arteries derived from the internal maxillary artery that supply the teeth and adjacent parts

den·ta·le \denˈta(ˌ)lē, -tā-,-tä-\ *n, pl* **denta·lia** \-lēə\ [NL, fr. neut. of L *dentalis* dental] **:** DENTARY

dental engine *n* **:** a dentist's drilling machine for rotating drills, burs, or other instruments at high speed

dental floss *n* **:** a flat waxed thread used to clean between the teeth

dental formula *n* **:** an abridged expression of number and kind of teeth of mammals, the kind of teeth being represented by *i* (incisor), *c* (canine), *pm* (premolar) or *b* (bicuspid), and *m* (molar) and the number in each jaw written like a fraction, the figures above the horizontal line showing the number in the upper jaw, and those below the number in the lower jaw, a dash separating the figures representing the teeth of each side of the jaw ⟨the *dental formula* of adult man is $i\,\frac{2-2}{2-2}$, $c\,\frac{1-1}{1-1}$, *b* or $pm\,\frac{2-2}{2-2}$, $m\,\frac{3-3}{3-3} = 32$⟩

dental hygienist *n* **:** one who assists a dentist in his professional duties; *esp* **:** one who cleanses teeth and performs other routine care on the patient

den·ta·li·i·dae \ˌdentᵊlˈīəˌdē\ *n pl, cap* [NL, fr. *Dentalium*, type genus + *-idae*] **:** a family of tooth shells that have the foot trilobate — see DENTALIUM

dental index *n, anthrop* **:** a measure of the relative size of teeth obtained as a ratio of the dental length to the distance from the nasion to the basion multiplied by 100

den·tal·i·ty \denˈtalәd.ē\ *n* -ES *phonetics* **:** dental quality

den·ta·li·um \-ˈtālēәm\ *n* [NL, fr. L *dentalis* dental + *-ium*] **1** *cap* **:** the type genus of Dentaliidae comprising a number of widely distributed tooth shells **2** *pl* **dentaliums** \-mz\ *or* **denta·lia** \-lēә\ **:** any mollusk or shell of the genus *Dentalium*; *broadly* **:** TOOTH SHELL, SCAPHOPOD

den·tal·i·za·tion \ˌdentᵊləˈzāshən\ *n* -s **:** the act of dentalizing

den·tal·ize \ˈdentᵊlˌīz\ *vt* -ED/-ING/-s **:** to make (a speech sound) dental **:** change (a speech sound) into a dental

dental length *n* **:** the distance from the anterior surface of the first premolar tooth to the posterior surface of the last molar

dental·ly \-ᵊlē\ *adv* **:** in a dental manner

dental nerve *n* **:** any of the nerves arising from the superior and inferior maxillary nerves that supply the teeth and adjacent parts

dental pad *n* **:** a firm ridge replacing the incisors in the upper jaw of cud-chewing herbivores

dental papilla *n* **:** the mass of mesenchyme that occupies the cavity of each enamel organ and gives rise to the dentin and the pulp of the tooth

dental plate *n* **1 :** any of various flattened often sharp-edged plates replacing teeth (as in certain worms) or representing fused teeth (as in parrot fishes and related forms) **2 :** DENTURE

dental preterit *n* **:** a past tense formed by the addition of a suffix containing a dental or alveolar consonant — used esp. of Germanic weak verbs

dental pulp *n* **:** the highly vascular sensitive tissue occupying the central cavity of a tooth

dental ridge *or* **dental lamina** *n* **:** a linear zone of epithelial cells of the covering of each embryonic jaw that grows down into the developing gums and gives rise to the enamel organs of the teeth

dental sac *n* **:** the mesenchymal investment of the developing tooth and enamel organ that differentiates into cementoblasts about the dentin and forms a connective tissue sheath about the enamel organ

dental star *n* **:** a marking on the incisor teeth of horses used in judging their age that appears in the lower central incisors at about eight years

dental surgeon *n* **:** DENTIST; *esp* **:** one engaging in oral surgery

dental technician *n* **:** one that engages in the construction of dental replacements or appliances (as bridges, inlays, dentures) from impressions taken by the dentist

den·tar·ia \denˈta(a)rēə\ *n* [NL, fr. L *dent-, dens* tooth + NL *-aria* — more at TOOTH] **1** *cap* **:** a small genus of herbs (family Cruciferae) with pungent scaly or toothed roots **2** -s **:** any plant of the genus *Dentaria* — compare CORALWORT CRINKLEROOT

den·ta·ry \ˈdentərē\ *n* -ES [*dent-* + *-ary*] **:** either of a pair of membrane bones of the lower jaw of most vertebrates, in lower forms being restricted to the distal area but in recent higher mammals forming the body of the mandible

den·tate \ˈdenˌtāt\ *or* **den·tat·ed** \-ˌtād.əd\ *adj* [L *dentatus*, fr. *dent-, dens* tooth + *-atus* -ate, -ated] **:** having teeth or pointed conical projections ⟨a ~ leaf margin⟩ — **den·tate·ly** \-ātlē\ *adv*

-den·tate \ˌdenˌtā|t, -tə|, *usu* |d· + V\ *adj comb form* [NL *-dentatus*, fr. L *dentatus*] **:** having (such or so many) toothlike projections **:** -toothed ⟨multi*dentate*⟩ ⟨quadri*dentate*⟩

dentate fissure *or* **dentate sulcus** *n* **:** a fissure of the mesial surface of each cerebral hemisphere extending from behind the posterior end of the corpus callosum forward and downward to the recurved part of the hippocampal convolution — called also *hippocampal fissure*

dentate nucleus *n* **:** a large laminar nucleus of gray matter forming an incomplete capsule within the white matter of each cerebellar hemisphere

den·ta·tion \denˈtāshən\ *n* -s **1 :** the quality or state of being dentate **2 :** an angular projection like a tooth

dent corn *n* [¹*dent*] **1 :** an Indian corn forming a distinct variety (*Zea mays indentata*) and having kernels that contain both hard and soft starch and become indented at maturity — compare FLINT CORN **2 :** the kernels of dent corn

dented *past of* DENT

den·tel \ˈdentᵊl\ *n* -s [F *dentelle*, lit., small tooth, fr. OF — more at DENTELLE] **:** DENTIL

den·te·lat·ed *or* **den·tel·lat·ed** \ˈdentᵊlˌād.əd\ *adj* [modif. (influenced by E *-ate* & *-ed*) of F *dentelé*, fr. *dentelle*] **:** having fine serrations or serrated markings **:** DENTICULATE

den·telle \denˈtel, dänˈ-\ *n* -s [F, fr. MF, lit., small tooth, fr. OF, dim. of *dent* tooth, fr. L *dent-, dens* — more at TOOTH] **1 a :** LACE **b :** LACEWORK **2 :** a lacy style of book-cover decoration featuring angular or toothed outlines around fine detail

dentes *pl of* DENS

den·tex \ˈdenˌteks\ *n* -ES [NL, fr. L *dentex, dentix*, a kind of marine fish] **:** a European marine sparid fish (*Dentex dentex*) or a related fish

denti- — see DENT-

den·ti·cle \ˈdentəkəl\ *n* -s [ME, fr. L *denticulus*, dim. of *dent-, dens* tooth — more at TOOTH] **1 :** a small tooth or other conical pointed projection ⟨the ~s of sharkskin⟩ **2 :** DENTIL

den·tic·u·lar \(ˈ)denˈtikyələ(r)\ *adj* [L *denticulus* + E *-ar*] **:** like a denticle **:** DENTICULATE

den·tic·u·late \-ˌlāt, -lət\ *or* **den·tic·u·lat·ed** \-ˌlād.əd\ *adj* [L *denticulatus*, fr. *denticulus* + *-atus* -ate] **1 :** having small teeth **:** covered with small pointed projections ⟨a ~ shell⟩; *sometimes* **:** repeatedly notched **:** SERRATE ⟨margin of propodium ~⟩ **2 :** cut into dentils ⟨*denticulated* Doric cornice⟩ **3 :** finely dentate ⟨a ~ leaf⟩ — **den·tic·u·late·ly** *adv*

den·tic·u·la·tion \(ˌ)denˌtikyəˈlāshən\ *n* -s **1 :** the state of being denticulate **2 :** a diminutive tooth or denticle

den·ti·cule \ˈdentəˌkyül\ *n* -s [MF, fr. L *denticulus* small tooth] **:** the member in which dentils are cut

den·ti·fi·ca·tion \ˌ==fəˈkāshən\ *n* -s [ISV *dent-* + *-fication*] **:** formation of or conversion into dental structure

den·ti·form \ˈdentəˌfórm\ *adj* [*dent-* + *-form*] **:** having the form of a tooth or of teeth

den·ti·frice \ˈdentəfrəs\ *n* -s [MF, fr. L *dentifricium*, fr. *dent-* + *-fricium* (fr. *fricare* to rub) — more at BRINE] **:** a powder, paste, or liquid used in cleaning the teeth

den·tig·er·ous \(ˈ)denˈtijərəs\ *adj* [*dent-* + *-gerous*] **:** bearing teeth or structures resembling teeth

dentigerous cyst *n* **:** an epithelial cyst containing fluid and one or more imperfect teeth usu. thought to result from defects in the enamel-forming structures

den·til \ˈdentᵊl, -nˌtil\ *n* -s [obs. F *dentille*, fr. MF, dim. of *dent* tooth — more at DENT] **:** a small rectangular block in a series projecting like teeth (as under the corona of a cornice esp. in the Ionic, Corinthian, and composite orders)

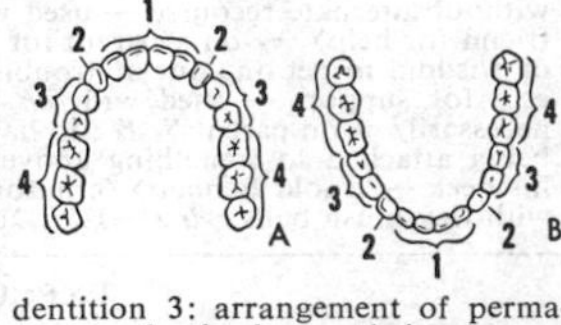

dentils

den·ti·labial \ˌdentə+\ *adj or n* [*dent-* + *labial*] **:** LABIODENTAL

dentil band *n* **:** a molding in the bed molding of a cornice resembling a row of dentils with the interdentils filled up solid; *also* **:** one of diminished projection as if the dentils had been stripped away

¹den·ti·lingual \ˌdentə +\ *adj* [*dent-* + *lingual*] *of a speech sound* **:** articulated with tongue and teeth; *specif* **:** INTERDENTAL

²dentilingual \ˈ"\ *n* **:** a dentilingual consonant

den·tin \ˈdentᵊn, -tən\ *or* **den·tine** \ˈdenˌtēn, ==ˈ=\ *n* -s [*dent-* + *-in, -ine*] **:** a calcareous material similar to bone but harder and denser that composes the principal mass of a tooth, is formed by the odontoblasts of the surface of the dental papilla, and consists of a matrix containing minute parallel tubules which open into the pulp cavity and during life contain processes of the cells of the pulp — compare CEMENTUM, ENAMEL; see TOOTH illustration

den·ti·nal \(ˈ)denˈtēnᵊl, ˈdentᵊnəl\ *adj* **:** of or relating to dentin

dentinal fiber *n* **:** one of the minute processes of the dental pulp that project into the dentinal tubules

dentinal papilla *n* **:** DENTAL PAPILLA

dentinal sac *n* **:** DENTAL SAC

dentinal tubule *n* **:** one of the minute parallel tubules of the dentin of a tooth that communicate with the dental pulp — see DENTINAL FIBER

¹den·ti·nasal \ˌdentə +\ *adj* [*dent-* + *nasal*] **:** both dental and nasal — used of the sound \n\

²dentinasal \ˈ"\ *n* **:** the sound \n\

denting *pres part of* DENT

den·tin·o·blast \denˈtēnəˌblast, -nō,-\ *n* [*dentin* + *-o-* + *-blast*] **:** a mesenchymal cell that forms dentin

den·tin·o·genesis \ˌ=ˈ== +,-\ *n* [NL, fr. *dentino-* (fr. ISV *dentin*) + *-genesis*] **:** the formation of dentin

den·tin·o·gen·ic \(ˈ)=ˌ=ˈjenik\ *adj* [*dentin* + *-o-* + *-genic*] **:** forming dentin

den·ti·noid \denˈtēˌnóid\ *n* -s [*dentin* + *-oid*] **:** the immature still uncalcified matrix of dentin

den·ti·no·ma \ˌdentəˈnōmə\ *n, pl* **dentinomas** \-məz\ *also* **dentinoma·ta** \-məd.ə\ [NL, fr. ISV *dentin* + NL *-oma*] **:** an odontoma containing dentin

den·ti·ros·tral \ˌdentəˈrästrəl\ *or* **den·ti·ros·trate** \-ˌstrāt, -ˌstrət\ *adj* [*dent-* + *-rostral, rostrate*] **1 :** having a toothed or notched bill **2** [NL *Dentirostres* + E *-al* or *-ate*] **:** of or relating to the Dentirostres

den·ti·ros·tres \ˌ==ˈräˌstrēz\ *n pl, cap* [NL, fr. *dent-* + *-rostres* (fr. L *rostrum* beak) — more at ROSTRUM] *in former classifications* **:** a group of passerine birds to which various limits have been assigned

den·tist \ˈdentəst\ *n* -s [F *dentiste*, fr. *dent* tooth + *-iste* -ist — more at DENT] **:** one whose profession it is to treat diseases of the teeth and associated tissues and to make and insert replacements for lost or damaged parts — called also *dental surgeon;* compare EXODONTIST, ORTHODONTIST

den·tis·try \-təstrē, -ri\ *n* -ES **1 :** the art or profession of a dentist **:** dental science and practice **2 :** something that is made by or under the supervision of a dentist (as inlays or dentures) **:** work done by a dentist

den·ti·tion \denˈtishən\ *n* -s [L *dentition-, dentitio*, fr. *dentitus* (past part. of *dentire* to cut teeth, fr. *dent-, dens* tooth) + *-ion-, -io* -ion — more at TOOTH] **1 :** the development and cutting of teeth **:** TEETHING **2 :** the character of the teeth as determined by their form and arrangement ⟨carnivorous ~⟩ **3 :** the number, kind, and arrangement of teeth of an individual; *collectively* **:** TEETH

dentition 3: arrangement of permanent teeth of a human being: upper, *A;* lower, *B; 1* incisors, *2* canines, *3* bicuspids, *4* molars

dento- — see DENT-

den·to·facial \ˌdentə +\ *adj* [*dent-* + *facial*] **:** of or relating to the dentition and face

den·toid \ˈdenˌtóid\ *adj* [*dent-* + *-oid*] **:** like or resembling a tooth

dents *pl of* DENT, *pres 3d sing of* DENT

den·tu·lous \ˈdenchələs\ *adj* [back-formation fr. *edentulous*] **:** having teeth — opposed to *edentulous*

den·ture \ˈdenchə(r)\ *n* -s [F, fr. MF, fr. *dent* tooth + *-ure*] **1 :** a set of teeth **2 :** an artificial replacement of one, several, or all of the natural teeth; *esp* **:** one not permanently anchored in the mouth — compare BRIDGE 4e

den·ty \ˈdentī\ *chiefly Scot var of* DAINTY

¹de·nu·dant \dəˈn(y)üdᵊnt, dēˈ-\ *adj* [*denude* + *-ant*] **:** DENUDING

²denudant \ˈ"\ *n* -s **:** an agency that denudes

¹de·nu·date \ˈdē(ˌ)n(y)üˌdāt, ˈdenyə,-, dəˈn(y)ü,-, dēˈ-, *usu* -d.+V\ *vt* -ED/-ING/-s [L *denudatus*, past part. of *denudare* — more at DENUDE] **:** to lay bare **:** DENUDE

²de·nu·date \ˈ", -dət\ *adj* [L *denudatus*] **:** DENUDED, BARE

de·nu·da·tion \ˌdē(ˌ)n(y)üˈdāshən, ˌdenyəˈ-\ *n* -s [LL *denudation-, denudatio*, fr. L *denudatus* + *-ion-, -io* -ion] **1 :** the act of denuding or the state of being denuded **:** EXPOSURE, DIVESTITURE **2 :** the laying bare of rocks or a formation through the removal of overlying material by erosion; *also* **:** the entire process of erosion whereby the land is worn down **3 :** complete destruction of trees and humus in a forest **:** BURNOUT

de·nu·da·tion·al \ˌ=ˈ=shənᵊl, -shnəl\ *adj* **:** of or relating to denudation

de·nu·da·tive \ˈdē(ˌ)n(y)üˌdā|d.|iv, ˈdenyə,-; dəˈn(y)üdə|t|, dēˈ-\ *adj* **:** causing denudation

de·nude \dəˈn(y)üd, dēˈ-\ *vt* -ED/-ING/-s [L *denudare*, fr. *de-* + *nudus* bare — more at NAKED] **1 a :** to divest of all covering **:** make bare or naked **:** STRIP, DEPRIVE ⟨~ him of clothing⟩ ⟨a room *denuded* of pictures⟩ **b :** to lay bare by erosion; *also* **:** ERODE ⟨rolling hills are soon marred by *denuded* banks —*Amer. Guides Series: Minn.*⟩ **c :** to divest or strip (land) of forests (as by lumbering or by fire) **2 :** to divest entirely or partially (as of an attribute, right, purpose, possession) **:** make useless **:** WEAKEN ⟨the world *denuded* by ceaseless activity —Harold Rosenberg⟩ **syn** see STRIP

de·nud·er \-də(r)\ *n* -s **:** one that denudes

de·numerable \də, dē +\ *adj* [*de-* + *numerable*] **:** countable even though infinite — used of any class whose elements may be numbered successively (as the system of cardinal numbers) — **de·nu·mer·a·bly** \-blē\ *adv*

de·nun·ci·ate \dəˈnənsēˌāt, dēˈ- *sometimes* -nchē,-, *usu* -ād.+V\ *vb* -ED/-ING/-s [L *denuntiatus*, past part. of *denuntiare* — more at DENOUNCE] **:** DENOUNCE

de·nun·ci·a·tion \=ˌ=ˈāshən\ *n* -s [L *denuntiation-, denuntiatio*, fr. *denuntiatus* + *-ion-, -io* -ion] **1 :** the act of denouncing **:** the utterance with which something is denounced **2 a** *archaic* **:** official announcement **:** PROCLAMATION **b** *archaic* **:** solemnly pronounced warnings of punishments or imminent evils **c** *Scots law* **:** the act of denouncing publicly as a rebel (as by blowing blasts on a horn) preliminary to enforcing the judgment of a court **d :** the act of formally giving information to a public prosecutor that another has committed a crime **e :** the act of inveighing against something or someone as evil ⟨praise of a glorious past that is dead, and ~s of a decadent present —G.L.Dickinson⟩ **f :** the action of giving formal notice of the termination of a treaty **g :** the furnishing of information in an ecclesiastical court by one other than the accuser

de·nun·ci·a·tive \dəˈnənsēˌā|d.iv, dēˈ-, -ēə|, |tiv *sometimes* -nchē-\ *adj* [LL *denuntiativus*, fr. L *denuntiatus*, + *-ivus* -ive] **:** DENUNCIATORY — **de·nun·ci·a·tive·ly** \|əvlē, -li\ *adv*

de·nun·ci·a·tor \-ēˌād.ə(r), -ˌātə-\ *n* -s [MF *denonciateur*, fr. L *denuntiator* police officer, fr. *denuntiatus* + *-or*] **:** one that denounces, publishes, or proclaims: **a :** one that proclaims intended or coming evil **b :** one that threatens or accuses

de·nun·ci·a·to·ry \-ēəˌtōrē, -ˌtór-, -ri\ *adj* **:** marked by or given to denunciation ⟨all his plays are contemptuous of people and ~ of human existence —*Times Lit. Supp.*⟩ **:** ACCUSING, THREATENING ⟨~ language⟩

¹den·ver \ˈdenvə(r)\ *adj, usu cap* [fr. *Denver*, Colorado] **:** of or from Denver, the capital of Colorado **:** of the kind or style prevalent in Denver

²denver \ˈ"\ *n* -s *often cap* **:** BATTLESHIP GRAY

den·ver·ite \ˈdenvəˌrīt\ *n* -s *cap* [*Denver*, Colorado + E *-ite*] **:** a native or resident of Denver, Colorado

denver sandwich *n, usu cap D* **:** WESTERN SANDWICH

de·ny \dəˈnī, dēˈ-\ *vt* -ED/-ING/-ES [ME *denyen*, fr. OF *denier, denoier*, fr. L *denegare*, fr. *de-* + *negare* to say no, deny — more at NEGATION] **1 a :** to declare untrue **:** assert to be untenable **:** CONTRADICT ⟨the suspect *denied* the charge⟩ ⟨~*ing* that the explanation was true⟩ **b** *logic* **:** to assert the negative or contradictory of **2 :** to refuse to recognize or acknowledge **:** withhold acknowledgment from **:** disclaim connection with, allegiance to, or responsibility to or for **:** DISAVOW, RENOUNCE ⟨an apostate ~*ing* his faith⟩ **3 a :** to turn down or give a negative answer to (a person) ⟨hard to ~ an eager child⟩ ⟨~*ing* the petitioners⟩ **b :** to refuse to grant **:** WITHHOLD ⟨the king *denied* his vassal's plea⟩ ⟨the leave was *denied* to him⟩ ⟨*denied* the child the candy⟩ **c :** to restrain (oneself) from gratification of wishes or desires **:** restrain (oneself) from self-indulgence ⟨~*ing* herself any fun in life⟩ **4** *archaic* **a :** DECLINE — used with an infinitive **b :** to refuse or withhold permission to **:** preclude occasion for or occurrence of **5 a** *obs* **:** to withhold acceptance of **b** *obs* **:** to withhold admittance to, greeting to, or acknowledgment of **c :** to withhold acknowledging presence of to a caller ⟨the doctor did not wish to see the woman and told the nurse to ~ him⟩ **6 :** to refuse to accept the existence, truth, or validity of ⟨~*ing* the appearances of gods⟩ ⟨~*ing* witchcraft as an effective force⟩ **7 :** to make a bridge bid in no-trump or a suit different from (that bid by one's partner) in order to show inability to raise or support the partner's bid ⟨~*ing* his partner's spades⟩

syn GAINSAY, CONTRADICT, NEGATIVE, TRAVERSE, IMPUGN, CONTRAVENE: DENY implies a refusal, usu. outspoken, to accept as true, to grant or concede, or to acknowledge the existence or the claims of ⟨*deny* an accusation⟩ ⟨*deny* the possibility of peaceful coexistence⟩ ⟨history cannot be *denied* —James King⟩ GAINSAY, not now common in speech, implies opposition by a disputing of what someone else has said ⟨it cannot be *gainsaid* that cormorants are fish-eaters —C.L. Barrett⟩ ⟨no one would *gainsay* the right of anyone, the royal American right, to protest —W.A.White⟩ CONTRADICT, implying a flatter denial of the truth of an assertion, or a fact that lends itself to assertion, than does GAINSAY, commonly suggests that the contrary of an assertion is true or that the assertion is totally untrue ⟨nobody would have *contradicted* an assertion that it really was so —Thomas Hardy⟩ ⟨sales of that sort *contradicted* the spirit of the Homestead Act —R.A. Billington⟩ NEGATIVE is variable in its force but is often a mild term implying a refusal to assent ⟨it was not due to the banks that their request for loans was *negatived* —L.W.Mints⟩ ⟨he emphatically *negatived* the movement to nominate him as vice-president —Jonas Viles⟩ TRAVERSE, chiefly a legal term in this sense, implies a formal denial, as of the truth of an allegation or the justice of an indictment ⟨to *traverse* the decision of the House in rejecting a reasoned amendment on the second reading of the bill —T.E.May⟩ ⟨it *traverses* the theory of the Court in the Belmont and Pink cases —E.S.Corwin⟩ IMPUGN implies very strongly a direct, commonly insulting, disputing, questioning, or contradicting ⟨did not hesitate to challenge when he considered his honor *impugned* —J.A. Robertson⟩ ⟨his accuracy had often been *impugned*, his authority challenged —Osbert Sitwell⟩ ⟨to *impugn* the reality of the world as known to science —W.R.Inge⟩ CONTRAVENE implies strongly a coming into conflict but implies less strongly than the other terms an intentional opposition, suggesting rather some inherent incompatibility ⟨he could not strike out in any direction without wounding his wife or his friends, without *contravening* some loyalty that had become sacred to him —Van Wyck Brooks⟩ ⟨the power to abrogate actions of the constituent republics which *contravene* laws or decrees of the central government —F.A.Ogg & Harold Zink⟩

de·ny·ing·ly *adv* **:** in a denying manner

de·o·dand \ˈdēəˌdand\ *n* -s [AF *deodande*, fr. ML *deodandum*, fr. L *Deo dandum* that must be given to God] **:** a thing that by English law before 1846 was forfeited to the crown and thence to pious uses because it had been the immediate cause of the death of a person

de·o·dar \ˈdēəˌdär\ *or* **deodar cedar** *or* **de·o·da·ra** \ˌdēəˈdärə\ *n* -s [Hindi *deodār*, fr. Skt *devadāru*, lit., timber of the gods, fr. *deva* god + *dāru* wood — more at DEVA, TREE] **:** an East Indian cedar (*Cedrus deodara*) highly valued for its size and appearance as well as for its timber

¹de·odor·ant \dēˈōdərənt\ *adj* [*de-* + *odor* + *-ant*] **:** destroying or masking offensive odors

²deodorant \ˈ"\ *n* -s **:** any of various preparations or solutions (as a soap or disinfectant) that destroy or mask unpleasant odors; *esp* **:** a cosmetic that neutralizes perspiration odors

de·odor·i·za·tion \(ˌ)dēˌōdərəˈzāshən, -ˌrīˈz-\ *n* -s **:** the act or process of deodorizing or the state of being deodorized

de·odor·ize \dēˈōdəˌrīz\ *vt* [*de-* + *odor* + *-ize*] **1 :** to eliminate or neutralize the offensive odor of ⟨he extracts the solvents from the dry-cleaned garments and . . . dries and *deodorizes* the extracted garments —*Opportunity & a Future*⟩; *specif* **:** to apply to or treat with a deodorant **2 :** to make (a reprehensible act or fact) more acceptable or palatable by placing in a pleasant light esp. by misrepresenting, glossing over, or evading ⟨their buccaneering was *deodorized* by the fact that their victims were Madagascar pirates —*N.Y. Herald Tribune Bk. Rev.*⟩ ⟨~ the unpleasant fact that in laboratories all over the world devices to rip out the heart and soul of man are being systematically . . . developed —Norman Cousins⟩

de·odor·iz·er \-zə(r)\ *n* -s **:** DEODORANT

de·on·tic \(ˈ)dēˈäntik\ *adj* [Gk *dent-, deon* that which is obligatory, fr. neut. of pres. part. of *dein* to lack, be needful — more at DEUTER-] **:** of or relating to obligation ⟨~ propositions⟩ — **de·on·ti·cal·ly** \-tᵊk(ə)lē\ *adv*

de·on·to·log·i·cal \(ˌ)dēˌäntəˈläjəkəl, -tᵊlˈä-\ *adj* **1 :** of, relating to, or based on deontology **:** DEONTIC **2 :** that considers moral obligations to be knowable by intuition and without reference to conceptions of the good ⟨a ~ ethical theory⟩ — contrasted with *axiological*

de·on·tol·o·gist \(ˌ)dēˌänˈtäləjəst\ *n* **1 :** a specialist in deontology **2 :** a philosopher advocating a deontological theory of ethics — contrasted with *axiologist*

de·on·tol·o·gy \-jē\ *n* [Gk *deont-, deon* + E *-logy*] **:** the theory or study of duty or moral obligation **:** the ethics of duty

¹de·operculate \ˌdē +\ *adj* [*de-* + *operculate*] **1 :** lacking an operculum — used of the capsule of a moss or hepatic after the lid has fallen **2 :** having an operculum that does not separate from the capsule — used of mosses

²de·oper·cu·late \ˌdēōˈpərkyəˌlāt\ *vi* -ED/-ING/-s [*de-* + NL *operculum* + E *-ate*] **:** to shed or cast off the operculum — used of mosses and liverworts

de·ordination \(ˈ)dē +\ *n* [LL *deordination-, deordinatio*, fr. L *de-* + *ordination-, ordinatio* order — more at ORDINATION] **:** departure from a natural or normal order **:** DISORDER

deo vo·len·te \ˌdā(ˌ)ōvōˈlenˌtā, ˌdē(ˌ)ōvəˈlentē\ *usu cap D* [L] **:** God being willing **:** with God's sanction — abbr. *DV*

de·oxidant \(ˈ)dē +\ *n* -s [*deoxid*ate + *-ant*] **:** DEOXIDIZER

de·oxidate \(ˈ)dē +\ *vt* [*de-* + *oxidate*] *archaic* : DEOXIDIZE
de·oxidation *also* **de·oxidization** \(ˌ)dē +\ *n* : the process of deoxidizing or state of being deoxidized
de·oxidize \(ˈ)dē +\ *vt* [*de-* + *oxidize*] : to remove oxygen from (as molten metals) : reduce from the state of an oxide — **de·ox·i·diz·er** \-zə(r)\ *n*
de·oxy \(ˈ)dēˈäksē\ *or* **des·oxy** \(ˈ)deˈzäksē,-eˈsä-\ *adj* [*deoxy-*] : containing less oxygen in the molecule than the compound to which it is closely related ⟨~ sugars⟩
deoxy- *or* **desoxy-** *comb form* [ISV, fr. *de-* or *des-* + *oxy-*] : containing less oxygen in the molecule than the compound to which it is closely related; *esp* : derivable from another compound by the removal of one oxygen atom ⟨*deoxy*nucleotide⟩ ⟨*desoxy*benzoin $C_{14}H_{12}O$⟩
de·oxy·cholate \dēˌäksē +\ *n* [*deoxy-* + *cholate*] : a salt or ester of deoxycholic acid
de·oxy·cholic acid \(ˌ)dēˌäksē +. . .-\ *n* [*deoxy-* + *cholic*] : a crystalline acid $C_{23}H_{37}(OH)_2COOH$ found esp. in bile and used as a choleretic and digestant and in the synthesis of adrenocortical hormones (as cortisone); 3,12-dihydroxy-cholanic acid
de·oxy·corticosterone \(ˌ)dēˌäksē +\ *n* [ISV *deoxy-* + *corticosterone*; orig. formed as G *desoxykortikosteron*] : a colorless crystalline steroid hormone $C_{21}H_{30}O_3$ occurring in the adrenal cortex that can be prepared synthetically and is used in the form of its acetate in the treatment of adrenal cortical insufficiency — called also *cortexone, deoxycortone*
de·oxy·cor·tone \(ˌ)dēˌäksēˈkȯrˌtōn\ *n* -S [by shortening] : DEOXYCORTICOSTERONE
de·oxy·ephedrine \(ˌ)dēˌäksē +\ *n* [*deoxy-* + *ephedrine*] : METHAMPHETAMINE
de·oxygenate \(ˌ)dē +\ *vt* [*de-* + *oxygenate*] : to remove oxygen (as free or loosely combined oxygen) from (as water, sewage, or blood) — **de·oxygenation** \"+\ *n* -S
deoxygenated *adj, of blood* : having the hemoglobin in the reduced state : VENOUS
de·oxy·pentose \(ˌ)dēˌäksē +\ *n* [*deoxy-* + *pentose*] : an aldose $C_4H_9O_3CHO$ having one less alcohol-type oxygen atom in the molecule than a pentose
deoxypentose nucleic acid *n* : any of various nucleic acids yielding a deoxypentose on hydrolysis; *esp* : DEOXYRIBONUCLEIC ACID
de·oxy·ribonuclease \(ˌ)dēˌäksē +\ *n* [*deoxy-* + *ribonuclease*] : a crystalline enzyme found esp. in the pancreas that hydrolyzes deoxyribonucleic acid to nucleotides
de·oxy·ribonucleic acid \"+ . . . -\ *n* [*deoxyribose* + *nucleic acid*] : any of various nucleic acids that yield deoxyribose as one product of hydrolysis, are found in cell nuclei and esp. genes, and are associated with the transmission of genetic information — abbr. *DNA*; called also *thymonucleic acid*; compare RIBONUCLEIC ACID
de·oxy·ri·bo·nu·cleo·protein \(ˌ)dēˌäksēˌrī(ˌ)bōˌn(y)üklē(ˌ)ō +\ *n* [*deoxyribonucleic* + *-o-* + *protein*] : a nucleoprotein that yields a deoxyribonucleic acid on hydrolysis
de·oxy·ribose \(ˌ)dēˌäksē +\ *n* [ISV *deoxy-* + *ribose*] : any of several sugars $C_5H_{10}O_4$ having one of the alcoholic hydroxyl groups of ribose replaced by hydrogen; *esp* : a sugar $HOCH_2(CHOH)_2CH_2CHO$ that is a constituent of nucleic acids
de·ozonize \(ˈ)dē +\ *vt* [*de-* + *ozonize*] : to remove ozone from — **de·ozon·iz·er** \-zə(r)\ *n*
dep *abbr* **1** depart; departure **2** department **3** deponent **4** deposed **5** deposit **6** depot **7** deputy
de pa·ce et pla·gis \(ˌ)dāˈpäˌkā(ˌ)etˈpläˌgēs\ *n* [ML, of peace and wounds] : an ancient appeal available in cases of breach of the peace and of assault
de·paint \dəˈpānt\ *vt* [ME *depeinten, depainten*, fr. OF *depeint*, past part. of *depeindre* to paint, fr. L *depingere* to paint, depict] **1** *archaic* : to delineate in colors or words **2** *obs* : to adorn with color or painted figures
de·palatalization \(ˌ)dē +\ *n* [*de-* + *palatalization*] *phonetics* : the loss of palatalization : the failure to palatalize
de·pancreatize \(ˈ)dē +\ *vt* [*de-* + *pancreat-* + *-ize*] : to deprive of the pancreas and thereby induce inability to utilize glucose and impair the digestion of fats — compare INSULIN
de·paraffinize \(ˈ)dē +\ *also* **de·paraffin** \(ˈ)dē +\ *vt* [*de-* + *paraffinize* or *paraffin* (n.)] : to remove paraffin from (a section of tissue prior to microscopic examination)
¹de·part \dəˈpär\t, dē'-, -pȧl, *usu* \d·+V\ *vb* -ED/-ING/-S [ME *departen* to divide, go away, fr. OF *departir*, fr. *de-* + *partir* to divide, go away, fr. L *partire, partiri* to divide, fr. *part-, pars* part — more at PART] *vi* **1 a** : to go forth or away : set forth : LEAVE ⟨the train ~*ed* from the station⟩ **b** *obs* : to leave and go — used with *into* **c** : to pass away : DIE, PERISH **2 a** : to turn aside : DEVIATE ⟨the river ~*ed* from its original course a few miles downstream⟩ ⟨his second account markedly ~*ed* from the first⟩ ⟨a homogeneous population that ~*s* reluctantly from long-accepted institutions —*Amer. Guide Series: Pa.*⟩ **b** *obs* : DESIST **3** *law* : to make a departure in pleading ~ *vt* **1** *obs* **a** : DIVIDE, SEPARATE, SUNDER **b** : deal out : DISTRIBUTE **c** : SHARE **2** : to go away from or out of : LEAVE ⟨~ the city for a summer cottage⟩ ⟨ships . . . ~ the land-locked harbor at the rate of one an hour —Franc Shor⟩ **syn** see GO, SWERVE — **depart with** *archaic* : to give up : SURRENDER ⟨willingly *departed with* a part —Shak.⟩
²depart \"\ *n* [ME, fr. MF, fr. *departir*] **1** *archaic* **a** : DEPARTURE **b** : DEATH **2** *old chem* : the separation of one metal (as gold) in an alloy from another
departed *n, pl* **departed** [fr. past part. of ¹*depart*] : one who has died ⟨the likeness of the ~ preserved on stone —*Amer. Guide Series: Fla.*⟩ ⟨the graves of the ~⟩
dé·par·te·ment \dāpärtəmäⁿ\ *n, pl* **départements** \-äⁿ(z)\ [F] : DEPARTMENT 2a(1)
de·part·ment \dəˈpärtmənt, dē'-, -pȧt-\ *n* -S [F *département*, fr. MF *departement*, fr. *departir* to divide + *-ment* — more at DEPART] **1** : appointed sphere or province (as of activity or thought) ⟨Pope's own peculiar ~ of literature —T.B.Macaulay⟩ **2 a** : a discrete territorial or functional division or section of a larger organized or systematized whole ⟨good taste . . . goes into every ~ of life —Elspeth Betjeman⟩: as (1) : the largest administrative subdivision in France and some of the French colonies presided over by a prefect (2) [AmerSp *departamento*, fr. F *département*] : a similar territorial division in some Central and So. American countries **b** : an administrative division or branch of a national or municipal government ⟨the welfare ~⟩ **c** : a discrete branch of instruction or study in a school or college ⟨the English ~⟩ ⟨the ~ of modern languages⟩ **d** (1) : a division of a business concern handling a major function ⟨the accounting ~⟩ (2) : a division of a store handling a distinct class of merchandise ⟨the furniture ~⟩ ⟨dry goods ~⟩ **e** (1) : a territorial subdivision for the administration, training, and tactical control of military units stationed within its limits (2) *usu cap* : such a former subdivision of the possessions of the United States outside the continental limits **3** : a regular column or feature devoted to a particular subject in a publication or radio program
de·part·men·tal \dəˌpärtˈmentᵊl, -pȧt-, ˌdēˌ-, ˌdēˌp-\ *adj* : of or relating to a department — **de·part·men·tal·ly** \-ntᵊlē, -li\ *adv*
de·part·men·tal·ism \dəˌ≈ˈ≈ˌizəm, (ˌ)dēˌ-\ *n* -S : strong emphasis upon or partiality for division into departments esp. at the expense of the whole (as in an educational institution) ⟨exaggerated ~ which splits the university into sections —*Report: (Canadian) Royal Commission on Nat'l Development*⟩
de·part·men·tal·i·za·tion \dəˌ≈ˌ≈≈əˈzāshən, (ˌ)dēˌ-, -ˌīˈz-\ *n* -S : the process of departmentalizing or of being departmentalized ⟨the importance of ~ of your store cannot be overemphasized —*Jewelers' Circular-Keystone*⟩ ⟨breaks away from the ~ of knowledge —*School & Society*⟩
de·part·men·tal·ize \dəˌ≈ˈ≈≈ˌīz, (ˌ)dēˌ-\ *vt* -ED/-ING/-S : to divide or form into departments ⟨a highly *departmentalized* school organization⟩ : handle according to departmental divisions ⟨*departmentalizing* the costs⟩
departmental store *n, Brit* : DEPARTMENT STORE
de·part·men·ta·tion \dəˌpärtmənˈtāshən, (ˌ)dēˌ-, -pȧt-\ *n* -S : the process of departmentalizing an enterprise for gaining efficiency and coordination : the grouping of tasks into departments and subdepartments and delegating of authority for accomplishment of the tasks
de·part·ment·ize \-ˈ≈mənˌtīz\ *vt* -ED/-ING/-S : DEPARTMENTALIZE ⟨department stores have taught all other types of retailers the value of *departmentizing* the business —J.B.Swinney⟩
department stamp *or* **departmental stamp** *n* : an official postage stamp issued for use in a particular government department, as one of a series issued in the U.S. 1873–79
department store *n* : a store that carries several lines of merchandise and that is organized into separate departments for the purpose of promotion, service, accounting, and control
departs *pres 3d sing of* DEPART, *pl of* DEPART
de·par·ture \dəˈpärchər, dē'-, -pȧchə(r\ *n* -S [¹*depart* + *-ure*] **1** *obs* : DIVISION, SEPARATION **2 a** : removal from a place : the act of going away ⟨postpone ~ of its troops from Italy —*Collier's Yr. Bk.*⟩ **b** (1) : a setting out (as on a journey or a course of action or thought) ⟨anticipate his ~ for England⟩ ⟨we need a fairly definite point of ~ for intelligent discourse —Robert Humphrey⟩ (2) : a beginning of a new course of thought or action ⟨the purchase by the state of property for purely esthetic purposes was a new ~ —*Amer. Guide Series: N.Y.*⟩ **c** : a ship's position in latitude and longitude at the beginning of a voyage as a point from which to begin dead reckoning usu. ascertained by taking cross bearings of landmarks **3** *archaic* : removal from life : DEATH ⟨the time of my ~ has come —2 Tim 4:6 (RSV)⟩ **4** : the distance due east or west made by a ship in its course reckoned in plane sailing as the product of the distance sailed and the sine of the angle made by the course with the meridian — compare DEAD RECKONING **5 a** : deviation or divergence esp. from a rule, course of action, plan, or purpose ⟨a ~ from official procedure⟩; *also* : something that has deviated or diverged ⟨in nature most ~*s* from normal cannot survive long —W.F.Hollander⟩ **b** *law* : the desertion by a party to any pleading of the ground taken by him in his last antecedent pleading and the adoption of another **6** *surveying* : the projection on the east-west axis of a course in a plane survey, being equal to the length of the course multiplied by the sine of its bearing
departure track *or* **departure yard** *n* : a track or group of tracks where outgoing freight cars are made ready for movement in trains
de·pasturage \də, dē+\ *n* : pasturing or right of pasture of grazing animals
de·pasture \"+\ *vb* [*de-* + *pasture*] *vi, now chiefly Austral* : to feed on pasture : GRAZE ~ *vt* **1** *archaic* : to denude of pasture by too constant grazing **2** *now chiefly Austral* : put to graze : PASTURE **3** *archaic* : to use for pasture
¹de·pau·per·ate \dəˈpȯp(ə)rət, dēˈ-\ *adj* [ME *depauperat*, fr. ML *depauperatus*, past part. of *depauperare*, fr. L *de-* + *pauperare* to impoverish, fr. *pauper* poor — more at POOR] **1** : IMPOVERISHED **2** *biol* : falling short of natural development or size: **a** : inferior in growth or differentiation as compared with the norm of a strain or group ⟨~ maize⟩ **b** : including few kinds of organisms — used of local floras and faunas ⟨a ~ island avifauna⟩
²de·pau·per·ate \-ōpəˌrāt\ *vt* [ML *depauperatus*] : to make poor — **de·pau·per·a·tion** \dəˌpȯpəˈrāshən, (ˌ)dēˌpȯ-\ *n* -S
de·pauperization \də, dē+\ *n* : the process of becoming depauperate or the quality or state of being depauperate
de·pauperize \"+\ *vt* [*de-* + *pauperize*] : to make depauperate
dé·pay·sé \ˌdāˌpā(ˌ)päˈzā\ *adj* [F, fr. past part. of *dépayser* to remove (a person) from his element, fr. OF *despaisier* to exile, fr. *des-* de- + *pais* region, country, fr. ML *pagensis* of a region, fr. L *pagus* region, district, village + *-ensis* -ese — more at PAGAN] : situated in unfamiliar surroundings : being out of one's element : DISPLACED : ASTRAY ⟨lived in hope of being instructed to drive me to Biarritz, where among the other hired-car chauffeurs . . . he would feel less ~ —A.J.Liebling⟩
de·pend \dəˈpend, dēˈ-\ *vi* -ED/-ING/-S [ME *dependen*, fr. MF *dependre* to hang down, be contingent or conditioned, modif. of L *dependēre*, fr. *de-* + *pendēre* to hang — more at PENDANT] **1** : to be contingent: **a** : to require something as a necessary condition — used with *on* or *upon* ⟨we ~ on food to keep us alive⟩ ⟨his life ~*s* on his undergoing an operation⟩ ⟨the merit of his piece ~*ed* on the brilliant things which arose under his pen as he went along —Matthew Arnold⟩ **b** : to become conditioned or based (as by subjection or relatedness) — used with *on* or *upon* ⟨sciences ~ on one another⟩ ⟨prices ~ upon supply and demand⟩ **2 a** : to hang in suspense : be pending or undecided ⟨matters of greatest moment were ~*ing* —John Milton⟩ **b** *obs* : to wait in suspense **c** *obs* : to be imminent : IMPEND **3** : to have a connection or relationship as a subordinate part or appurtenance — used with *on* or *upon* **4 a** : to trust, rely, or place belief or hope often without alternate recourse — used with *on* or *upon* ⟨~ on a friend for help⟩ ⟨~ on a parent for funds⟩ ⟨~ on your skill or wisdom to get one out of trouble⟩ **b** : to be dependent esp. for support — used with *on* or *upon* ⟨small children necessarily ~ on parents⟩ **5** : to hang down : be held up by being attached to something above ⟨a star was ~*ing* from his neck —Arnold Bennett⟩ ⟨crimson plush curtains intricate with tiny plush balls ~*ing* —T.W.Duncan⟩

syn HANG, HINGE, TURN: DEPEND is the general term to indicate a contingent relationship involving existence, nature, or characteristics ⟨the future of the American university *depends* primarily on keeping a proper balance between these four traditional elements of strength —J.B.Conant⟩ ⟨the conviction that winning the best satisfactions of later life will *depend* on possessing this power to think —C.W.Eliot⟩ HANG may refresh the now faded metaphor explicit in the etymology of DEPEND ⟨a good deal . . . *hangs* on the meaning, if any, of this short word *full* —T.S.Eliot⟩ ⟨the Crewe of today — a borough whose life no longer *hangs* on railway prosperity —*Times Lit. Supp.*⟩ HINGE may suggest resting on a cardinal or pivotal point, with a decisive swing in one direction or another as imminent ⟨on the outcome of the motion to dismiss the indictment . . . *hinge* issues of fundamental importance —*Nation*⟩ TURN may be less vivid in suggesting a cardinal point ⟨our continued backing of Chiang Kai-shek, and therefore his future, *turn* on the reactions of the conference committee —*New Republic*⟩ These words are completely interchangeable except in the few sentences in which unusual attention is paid to the implications of the metaphors involved.
syn see in addition RELY
de·pend·abil·i·ty \dəˌpendəˈbiləd-ē, (ˌ)dēˌ-, -ətē, -i\ *n* -ES : the quality or state of being dependable
de·pend·able \dəˈpendəbəl, dēˈ-\ *adj* : worthy or capable of being depended upon : TRUSTWORTHY **syn** see RELIABLE
de·pend·able·ness *n* -ES : DEPENDABILITY
de·pend·ably \-blē, -li\ *adv* : in a dependable manner
de·pen·dence *or* **de·pen·dance** \-endən(t)s\ *n* -S [MF *dependance*, fr. *dependre* + *-ance*] **1** *archaic* : the quality or state of being undecided or undetermined **2 a** : the quality or state of depending upon or being dependent upon something else **b** : the quality or state of being influenced, conditional upon, or necessitated by something else ⟨scarcely a single incident which has any necessary ~ upon any one other —E.A.Poe⟩ ⟨the relation of a logical consequent to its antecedent or of an effect to its cause is one of ~⟩ **c** : the quality or state of being subject or subservient to or needful of the use, activity, assistance, direction, or approval of another or others — used with *on* or *upon* ⟨the nation's ~ upon its self-sacrificing men⟩ ⟨the modern age's ~ upon luxury goods⟩; *specif* : inability to provide for oneself ⟨a child's ~ upon its parents⟩ **3** : RELIANCE, TRUST ⟨place ~ upon old and trusted friends⟩ ⟨for a knowledge of Celtic law . . . ~ must be placed mainly on the written records —John MacNeill⟩ **4** : something on which one relies : the object of one's trust ⟨he was her sole ~⟩ ⟨cotton was the earliest crop . . . but ultimately rice became the chief ~ —R.H.Brown⟩ **syn** see TRUST
de·pen·den·cy \-dənsē, -si\ *n* -ES [MF *dependance* + E *-y*] **1 a** : DEPENDENCE 2 ⟨their ~ on the crown of England —Francis Bacon⟩ ⟨~ in the infant increases in evolutionary sequence —Weston La Barre⟩ **b** : the condition of receiving assistance from the community for the necessities of life : the condition of being on relief **2** : something that is dependent or in dependence upon something else: as **a** : something necessarily consequent upon something else **b** : a geographically separate territorial unit under the jurisdiction of but not formally annexed by a nation — compare COLONY 1b, MANDATE 4b **3** : a building (as a stable or a kennel) appurtenant to a main dwelling ⟨a double driveway leads to the palace and its *dependencies* —*Amer. Guide Series: Va.*⟩ **4** : the state of having dependents ⟨deferred from army service because of his ~⟩
¹de·pen·dent \dəˈpendənt, (ˈ)dēˌp-\ *adj* [ME *dependant*, fr. MF, pres. part. of *dependre* to depend] **1** : hanging down ⟨a ~ bough⟩ ⟨lamps ~ from the ceiling⟩ **2 a** : determined or conditioned by something else : CONTINGENT ⟨a conclusion that is ~ on a premise⟩ **b** : unable to exist, sustain oneself, or act suitably or normally without the assistance or direction of another or others ⟨smelting operations were ~ on charcoal —Desmond Sprague⟩ ⟨a girl who remained excessively ~ on her parents even after marriage —Ruth & Edward Brecher⟩ ⟨the maple sugar and syrup crop, so ~ on weather conditions —*Amer. Guide Series: N.H.*⟩ ⟨traffic . . . has been ~ on ferries to cross five rivers —*Americana Annual*⟩ ⟨a child is pretty ~ on companionship⟩ **c** : connected in a subordinate relationship : subject to the jurisdiction of another ⟨~ territories⟩ **d** : lacking the necessary means of support and receiving aid from others (as from persons outside the immediate family or from a private or public welfare agency) ⟨a program of assistance for ~ children⟩ **e** *of a clause* : SUBORDINATE 2b **f** *of a compound* : belonging to the tatpurusha class **3** *obs* : IMPENDING **4** *phonetics* : COMBINATIVE — used of sound change — **de·pen·dent·ly** *adv*
²de·pen·dent *also* **de·pen·dant** \dəˈpendənt, dēˈ-\ *n* -S [MF *dependant*, fr. *dependant*, pres. part.] **1** *archaic, usu dependant* : something attached to something else : APPURTENANCE, DEPENDENCY **2** : one that depends or is dependent; *esp* : one relying on another for support ⟨a man taxed according to

EXECUTIVE DEPARTMENTS OF THE UNITED STATES

DEPARTMENT	TITLE OF CHIEF	DATE OF CREATION	FUNCTIONS
Department of State	Secretary of State	July 27, 1789, as Dept. of Foreign Affairs; Sept. 15, 1789, under present name	conduct of foreign relations
Department of the Treasury	Secretary of the Treasury	Sept. 2, 1789	administration of national fiscal policies
*Department of Defense	Secretary of Defense	July 26, 1947, as National Military Establishment; Aug. 10, 1949, under present name	responsibility for national defense and security
Department of Justice	Attorney General (office created Sept. 24, 1789)	June 22, 1870	enforcement of federal laws; provision of legal counsel in federal cases; interpretation of laws for other departments
Department of the Interior	Secretary of the Interior	March 3, 1849	conservation and development of natural resources of U.S. and territories; guardianship of American Indians
Department of Agriculture	Secretary of Agriculture	May 15, 1862; made executive department Feb. 9, 1889	acquisition and diffusion of useful information on agricultural subjects; supervision of national forests; administration of price support programs
Department of Commerce	Secretary of Commerce	Feb. 14, 1903, as the Dept. of Commerce and Labor; reorganized Mar. 4, 1913, under present name	promotion and development of foreign and domestic commerce
Department of Labor	Secretary of Labor	Mar. 4, 1913	administration and enforcement of statutes designed to promote welfare of wage earners
Department of Housing and Urban Development	Secretary of Housing and Urban Development	Sept. 9, 1965	supervision and coordination of federal programs relating to housing and urban renewal
Department of Transportation	Secretary of Transportation	Oct. 15, 1966	administration and coordination of federal agencies and programs dealing with transportation
Department of Energy	Secretary of Energy	August 4, 1977	administration of agencies promoting energy conservation and development
Department of Education	Secretary of Education	October 17, 1979; upon abolition of Dept. of Health, Education, and Welfare (created April 11, 1953), assumed education functions	administration of agencies promoting educational programs and policies
Department of Health and Human Services	Secretary of Health and Human Services	October 17, 1979; upon abolition of Dept. of Health, Education, and Welfare (created April 11, 1953), assumed health and welfare functions	administration of welfare, social security, and health agencies

*The Department of the Army, created Aug. 7, 1789, as the Department of War and the Department of the Navy, created April 30, 1789, lost executive status July 26, 1947, on merger under their present names in the newly created National Military Establishment. The Department of the Air Force was created Sept. 18, 1947, as a third subordinate department of the National Military Establishment.

the number of ~s he has⟩ ⟨~s were defined as those persons unable to care for themselves —J.F.Cuber⟩

dependent covenant *or* **dependent contract** *n* **:** a contract not enforceable until a connecting stipulation is performed

dependent differentiation *n* **:** differentiation of a tissue or structure in response to factors outside itself (as differentiation of ectoderm into a lens in the presence of an optic cup)

dependent variable *n* **:** the variable for which an equation that contains more than one variable is solved

de·pend·ing·ly *adv* **:** in a depending manner

de·per·di·tion \ˌdē(ˌ)pər'dishən\ *n* [F *déperdition*, fr. LL *deperdition-, deperditio* loss, fr. L *deperditus* (past part. of *deperdere* to destroy, lose, fr. *de-* + *perdere* to lose) + *-ion-, -io* -ion — more at PERDITION] *archaic* **:** LOSS, DESTRUCTION

de·pé·ret's law \də'pāˌrāz-\ *n, usu cap D* [after Charles J.J.Depéret †1929 Fr. geologist] **:** a principle in zoology: body size tends to increase within a natural group with increasing evolutionary development

dep·er·i·tion \ˌdepə'rishən\ *n* -s [ML *deperitus* (past part. of *deperire* to perish, fr. L *de-* + *perire* to perish) + E *-ion* — more at PERISH] *archaic* **:** destructive process **:** waste and wear

de·perm \(ˈ)dē¦pərm\ *vt* -ED/-ING/-S [*de-* + *permanent* magnetism] **:** to demagnetize partly (a ship's steel hull) as a precaution against magnetic mines by surrounding in dry dock with a large coil through which is sent an alternating current very strong at first but gradually diminishing in intensity — compare DEGAUSS

de·personalization \(ˌ)dē+\ *n* **1 :** the act or process of depersonalizing or the quality or state of being depersonalized **2 :** loss of the sense of personal identity or of recognition of self

de·personalize \(ˈ)dē+\ *vt, see -ize in Explan Notes* [*de-* + *personalize*] **1 :** to deprive of personality ⟨our complex society necessarily ~s people —H.W.Dodds⟩ ⟨a *depersonalized* production system⟩ **2 :** to make impersonal ⟨an attempt to ~ his feeling in order to write about it more clearly⟩

depeter *var of* DEPRETER

de·phleg·mate \(ˈ)dē'flegˌmāt\ *vt* -ED/-ING/-S [*de-* + *phlegm* + *-ate*] **1** *archaic* **:** to deprive (a spirit or an acid) of phlegm (sense 3) **:** free from an excess of water esp. by distillation **2 :** to rectify (a liquid) by distillation — **de·phleg·ma·tion** \ˌdēˌfleg'māshən\ *n* -s

de·phleg·ma·tor \(ˈ)dē'flegˌmād·ə(r)\ *n* -s **:** an apparatus used in fractional distillation as a partial condenser to cool the mixed vapors and thus condense the higher-boiling portions

de·phlogisticate \¦dē+\ *vt* [*de-* + *phlogisticate*] **:** to remove phlogiston from

de·phosphorization \(ˌ)dē+\ *n* -s **:** the process of dephosphorizing or the state of being dephosphorized

de·phosphorize \(ˈ)dē+\ *vt* [*de-* + *phosphorize*] **:** to remove phosphorus from (as steel)

de·phos·pho·ryl·ate \(ˈ)dē'fäsfərəˌlāt\ *vt* -ED/-ING/-S [*de-* + *phosphoryl* + *-ate*] **:** to remove the phosphate portion of (an organic compound of phosphoric acid) by hydrolysis (as with the aid of a phosphatase)

de·phosphorylation \(ˌ)dē+\ *n* **:** the process of dephosphorylating or the state of being dephosphorylated

de·pict \də'pikt, dē'-\ *vt* -ED/-ING/-S [L *depictus*, past part. of *depingere* to paint, depict, fr. *de-* + *pingere* to paint — more at PAINT] **1 a :** to form a likeness of by drawing or painting **b :** to represent, portray, or delineate in other ways than in drawing or painting ⟨elaborate carvings ~*ing* the history of the pioneer period —*Amer. Guide Series: Oregon*⟩ ⟨five 16th century tapestries ~*ing* the story of Vulcan and the loves of Venus and Mars —*Amer. Guide Series: N.C.*⟩ ⟨the quiet, unspectacular work of the United Nations . . . is ~*ed* in dozens of on the spot films —*Dun's Rev.*⟩ ⟨the countryside . . . has always been ~*ed* to us through art and photography as blazing with clear color —Virgil Thomson⟩ ⟨an annual pageant . . . ~*s* the Mormon migration to Utah —*Amer. Guide Series: Texas*⟩ ⟨bronze grillwork over the entrance ~*s* the evolution of mail transportation —*Amer. Guide Series: La.*⟩; *specif* **:** to portray in words **:** DESCRIBE ⟨a magazine article ~*ed* his beloved father, then deceased, as a mean, hard-fisted miser —Beverly Smith⟩ ⟨the neuroses which they have ~*ed* with relentless misanthropy —Harrison Smith⟩ **2 :** to represent by mapping **syn** see REPRESENT

de·pic·tion \-kshən\ *n* -s [LL *depiction-, depictio*, fr. L *depictus* + *-ion-, -io* -ion] **:** REPRESENTATION, DELINEATION, PORTRAYAL, DESCRIPTION

de·pig·ment \(ˈ)dē¦pigmənt, -'pigˌment\ *vt* [*de-* + *pigment* (n.)] **:** to cause to undergo depigmentation **:** deprive of pigment

de·pigmentation \(ˌ)dē+\ *n* [*de-* + *pigmentation*] **:** loss of normal pigmentation (as from skin or feathers)

dep·i·late \'depəˌlāt\ *vt* -ED/-ING/-S [L *depilatus*, past part. of *depilare*, fr. *de-* + *pilus* hair — more at PILE] **:** to remove hair from

dep·i·la·tion \ˌdepə'lāshən\ *n* -s [MF or ML; MF, fr. ML *depilation-, depilatio*, fr. L *depilatus* + *-ion-, -io* -ion] **:** the act or process of depilating or the state of being depilated; *specif* **:** the removal of the hair, wool, or bristles from an animal skin by chemical or mechanical methods in the processing of leather

¹de·pil·a·to·ry \də'piləˌtōrē, dē'-, -ȯr-, -ri\ *adj* [prob. fr. F *dépilatoire*, fr. MF *depilatoire*, fr. L *depilatus* + MF *-oire* -ory] **:** having the power to remove hair

²depilatory \"\ *n* -ES **1 :** a cosmetic for the temporary removal of undesired hair **2 :** a chemical preparation usu. of sulfide used to remove hair, wool, or bristles from hides

de·pil·i·tant \-lətənt\ *n* -s [irreg. (influence of such words as *excitant, irritant*) fr. *depilate* + *-ant*] **:** an agent used in leather making to loosen hair before depilating

dep·i·lous \'depələs\ *adj* [L *depilis* (fr. *de-* + *-pilis*, fr. *pilus* hair) + E *-ous* — more at PILE] **:** HAIRLESS

de·plane \(ˈ)dē+\ *vb* [*de-* + *plane* (airplane)] *vi* **:** to descend from a plane after a flight ~ *vt* **:** to remove from or cause to descend from a plane after a flight

de plano \dā'plä(ˌ)nō\ *adv* [L] **:** beyond argument **:** MANIFESTLY; *also* **:** in a summary way **:** as a matter of course — usu. used in legal documents

de·plasmolysis \¦dē+\ *n* [NL, fr. *de-* + *plasmolysis*] **:** swelling of the cytoplasm of a previously plasmolyzed cell **:** reversal of plasmolysis

de·plenish \də+'-, (ˈ)dē+'-\ *vt* [*de-* + *plenish*] **:** to deprive of furniture, stock, or other contents ⟨a ~*ed* house⟩ ⟨a ~*ed* purse⟩

de·plet·able \də'plēd·əbəl, dē'-, -lētə-\ *adj* **:** capable of becoming depleted or exhausted ⟨~ assets⟩ ⟨~ resources⟩

de·plete \də'plēt, dē'-, *usu* -lēd·+V\ *vt* -ED/-ING/-S [L *depletus*, past part. of *deplēre*, fr. *de-* + *plēre* to fill — more at FULL] **1 :** to empty (as the blood vessels) of a principal substance ⟨a body *depleted* by excessive blood loss⟩ ⟨tissues *depleted* of vitamins⟩ **2 :** to lessen in number, quantity, significant content, or force or in vital power or value as a result of such lessening **:** exhaust (as a mine) of its valuable content or (a country) of its strength or resources ⟨army, crumbled in morale and *depleted* by wholesale desertion —*Amer. Guide Series: Tenn.*⟩ ⟨the house whose air was lifeless and *depleted* —Ethel Wilson⟩ ⟨sick and *depleted* children —Robert Payne⟩ ⟨leaves *depleted* of starch —*Experiment Station Record*⟩

syn DEPLETE, DRAIN, EXHAUST, IMPOVERISH, and BANKRUPT can mean, in common, to deprive a thing in whole or in part of what is essential to its existence or total functioning or power. DEPLETE can signify merely a lessening in number, quantity, or force, but generally stresses a consequent loss, or potential loss, in effective functioning from such a lessening ⟨cattle herds *depleted* by the heavy slaughter last year —*Time*⟩ ⟨under conditions of sustained or repeated injury the body may be so *depleted* that it no longer can withstand infection and new stresses —W.K.Livingston⟩ ⟨has not the soil been *depleted* of its riches? —G.R.Stewart⟩ DRAIN implies a gradual depletion and ultimate deprivation in force, or vigor, or in elements that provide it ⟨the summer had *drained* the last reserve of her strength —Ellen Glasgow⟩ ⟨a burden of arms *draining* the wealth and the labor of all peoples —D.D.Eisenhower⟩ ⟨excesses *drained* the last element of decency from him⟩ EXHAUST stresses the total loss of force or vigor or of elements that provide it ⟨cultivated ground is *exhausted* after only two or three harvests and a new plot must then be cleared —C.D. Forde⟩ ⟨evidently the old ideas had been *exhausted* and the time was ripe for new ideologies and a new order —R.W.Murray⟩ ⟨a person *exhausted* by constant worry⟩ IMPOVERISH implies a depletion or a draining of what is essential to richness or productiveness ⟨alleging that mechanization helps to *impoverish* the soil and thus to reduce the output of crops or animal products —*Farmer's Weekly (So. Africa)*⟩ ⟨ignorance of the Bible, of mythology, and of ancient literature in general *impoverishes* our understanding of much of the poetry of the past —C.S.Kilby⟩ ⟨an *impoverished* imagination⟩ BANKRUPT implies total impoverishment or total loss of effectiveness ⟨astronomical sums of time are so great that they *bankrupt* the imagination —D.C.Peattie⟩ ⟨*bankrupt* a creative power by constant hack work⟩

de·ple·tion \-ēshən\ *n* -s [LL *depletion-, depletio* bloodletting, fr. L *depletus* + *-ion-, -io* -ion] **:** the act or process of depleting or the state of being depleted: as **a** (1) **:** the reduction or loss of blood, body fluids, chemical constituents, or stored materials from the body (as by hemorrhage or malnutrition) (2) **:** a debilitated state caused by excessive loss of body fluids or other constituents **b** (1) **:** the reduction in capital value that results from the consumption or diminution of an asset (as an oil well or a mine) (2) **:** the measure or amount of exhaustion of such an asset — distinguished from *amortization* and *depreciation* (3) **:** the utilization of a natural resource (as a water reservoir, a stand of timber) at a rate greater than the rate of replenishment

depletion ration *n* **:** a basic experimental ration designed to exhaust the body reserve of a specific nutrient while maintaining other dietary requirements in balance

de·ple·tive \-ēd·iv\ *adj* [L *depletus* + E *-ive*] **:** tending to deplete

de·plor·abil·i·ty \dəˌplōrə'biləd·ē, dē-, -ȯr-, ətē, -i\ *n* -ES **:** the quality or state of being deplorable

de·plor·able \=ˈ==bəl\ *adj* [F *déplorable*, fr. MF *deplorable*, fr. *deplorer* to deplore + *-able*] **:** fit to be deplored **:** LAMENTABLE ⟨a ~ lack of tact⟩ ⟨a ~ intellectual confusion —C.I. Glicksberg⟩ ⟨uniforms of the servants were sleazy and often dirty and the service ~ —Virginia A. Oakes⟩ **:** WRETCHED, UNFORTUNATE ⟨in a truly ~ condition, only less filthy than the prison itself —C.B.Nordhoff & J.N.Hall⟩ **:** ABOMINABLE ⟨the food is ~ for a healthy man —John Buchan⟩ — **de·plor·a·ble·ness** \-lnəs\ *n* -ES — **de·plor·ably** \-blē, -li\ *adv*

dep·lo·ra·tion \ˌdeplə'rāshən; ˌdēˌplōr'ā-, -ō'rā-\ *n* -s [L *deploration-, deploratio*, fr. *deploratus* (past part. of *deplorare*) + *-ion-, -io* -ion] **:** the act of deploring **:** LAMENTATION

de·plore \də'plō(ə)r, -ō(ə)r, -ōə, -ō(ə)\ *vt* -ED/-ING/-S [MF or L; MF *deplorer*, fr. L *deplorare*, fr. *de-* + *plorare* to wail, lament, prob. of imit. origin] **1** *obs* **:** to regard or abandon as hopeless **2 a :** to feel or express deep grief for **:** sorrow over ⟨~ the death of a close friend⟩ **b :** to regret strongly ⟨I ~ that I cannot conform to that practice —Tor Ulving⟩ **c :** to consider as very unfortunate or to be strongly lamented ⟨they ~ the fifteen years of slow whittling away of basic liberties —E.A.Mowrer⟩ ⟨their zeal to ~ the inferior position to which men have shoved women —Paul Engle⟩ **3** *obs* **:** to tell of or recount with sorrow

syn DEPLORE, LAMENT, BEWAIL, and BEMOAN agree in signifying to show grief or sorrow for something. DEPLORE usu. implies keen and profound regret for, but as commonly implies strong grieving objection to, esp. the irreparable, calamitous, or unavoidable ⟨helping the process of moral decay which he *deplores* —*New Republic*⟩ ⟨he *deplores* the fact that there is dissension within the Church —Robert Corkey⟩ ⟨how profoundly a man, holding that view, must *deplore* the whole course of academical literary study —A.T.Quiller-Couch⟩ ⟨purists *deplore* slang —*Quarterly Jour. of Speech*⟩ LAMENT implies a vehement demonstration of sorrow suggesting mourning but without tears or similar manifestation, usu., however, implying passionate utterance ⟨his yelling rose into an indignant *lament* as he waved his arms more wildly —Paul Bowles⟩ ⟨jails where the members were given ample time to *lament* their errors —R.A.Billington⟩ ⟨we need not gloat or *lament* about the limitations of finite minds —A.G.N.Flew⟩ BEWAIL and BEMOAN imply intense sorrow finding an outlet in words or cries, BEWAIL usu. suggesting a loud and BEMOAN a lugubrious expression of grief or, in popular use, grievance or complaint ⟨valet *bewailing* the loss of his wages —Samuel Alexander⟩ ⟨the large number who *bewail* the materialistic tendencies of modern life —*Times Lit. Supp.*⟩ ⟨he *bemoaned* their fate, his mood steadily growing gloomier and gloomier —O.E.Rölvaag⟩ ⟨as ready as any tycoon to *bemoan* the woes of being wealthy —*Time*⟩

de·plor·er \-ōrə(r), -ȯrə-\ *n* -s **:** one that deplores something

de·plor·ing·ly *adv* **:** in a deploring manner

¹de·ploy \də'plȯi, dē'p- *also* 'dēˌp-\ *vb* -ED/-ING/-S [F *déployer*, fr. L *displicare* to scatter — more at DISPLAY] *vt* **1 a :** to extend (a military or naval unit) in width or in both width and depth ⟨he ~*ed* his squad on both sides of the road⟩ **b :** to place or arrange (armed forces) in battle disposition or formation or in locations appropriate for their future employment ⟨~ forces to check aggressions⟩ **2 :** to extend or place as if deploying troops ⟨~*ing* the editors . . . in various phases of political reporting —*Newsweek*⟩ ⟨harried roadmasters ~ equipment and work gangs along the grade in military fashion —R.L.Neuberger⟩ ~ *vi* **:** to move in or as if in deployment ⟨the squad ~*ed* and made a dash for the hill —Hanama Tasaki⟩ ⟨the staff ~*ed* to their phones —*Time*⟩

²deploy \=ˈ= *or* 'dēˌp-\ *n* -s **:** the power to use esp. in deployment ⟨two other weapons in the ~ of the Soviet block . . . propaganda and internal revolution —D.W.Mitchell⟩

de·ploy·ment \=ˈ=mənt\ *n* -s [F *déploiement*, fr. MF *deploiement*, fr. *deployer* + *-ment*] **:** the act or movement of deploying or the state of being deployed

de·plu·mate \(ˈ)dē¦plüˌmāt, -mət\ *or* **de·plu·mat·ed** \-ˌmād·əd\ *adj* [*deplumate* fr. ML *deplumatus*, past part. of *deplumare*; *deplumated* fr. ML *deplumatus* + E *-ed*] **:** destitute of feathers

de·plu·ma·tion \ˌdēˌplü'māshən\ *n* -s [ML *deplumatus* + E *-ion*] **:** the stripping or falling off of feathers

de·plume \(ˈ)dē+\ *vt* [ME *deplumen*, fr. MF *deplumer*, fr. ML *deplumare*, fr. L. fr. *de-* + *pluma* feather — more at FLEECE] **1 :** to pluck off the feathers of **:** deprive of plumage **2 :** to strip of possessions, honors, or attributes

depluming mite *n* **:** an itch mite (*Knemidokoptes gallinae*) that attacks poultry feeding about the bases of the feathers and causing a mangy condition

de·polarization \(ˌ)dē+\ *n* **1 :** the process of depolarizing **2 :** the state of being depolarized

de·polarize \(ˈ)dē+\ *vt* [*de-* + *polarize*] **1 :** to cause (polarized radiation) to become partially or wholly unpolarized (as by scattering) **2 :** to prevent, decrease, or remove polarization of (as a dry cell) esp. by adding a substance that prevents accumulation of reaction products **3 :** DEMAGNETIZE

de·polarizer \(ˈ)dē+\ *n* **:** something that depolarizes; *specif* **:** a substance that reacts with the products accumulating at one of the electrodes of a cell and thus prevents polarization

de·polish \(ˈ)dē+\ *vt* [*de-* + *polish* (n.)] **:** to remove or destroy the smoothness, gloss, or polish of (as by sand blasting, acid, or grinding) **:** ROUGHEN

de·po·lym·er·ase \ˌdēpə'liməˌrās, -āz\ *n* -s [*depolymerize* + *-ase*] **:** any of various enzymes (as nucleases) that bring about depolymerization

de·polymerization \(ˌ)dē+\ *n* **:** the process of depolymerizing

de·polymerize \"+\ *vt* [ISV *de-* + *polymerize*] **:** to decompose (macromolecular compounds) by various means (as by hydrolysis) into relatively simple compounds (as monomers) — opposed to *polymerize* ⟨starch and gelatin are easily *depolymerized*⟩ ⟨*depolymerized* nucleic acids⟩

de·pone \də'pōn, dē'-\ *vb* -ED/-ING/-S [ML *deponere*, fr. L, to put down, fr. *de-* + *ponere* to put — more at POSITION] *vt* **:** to assert under oath **:** TESTIFY **syn** see SWEAR

¹de·po·nent \də'pōnənt, (ˈ)dē¦p-\ *adj* [LL *deponent-, deponens*, fr. pres. part. of L *deponere* to put down; trans. of Gk *apothetikos*] *of a verb* **:** occurring with passive or middle voice forms but with active voice meaning ⟨the ~ verbs in Latin and Greek⟩

²deponent \"\ *n* -s [in sense 1, fr. LL *deponent-, deponens*; trans. of Gk *apotheton*; in sense 2, fr. ML *deponent-, deponens*, pres. part. of *deponere*] **1 :** a deponent verb **2 :** one who depones **:** one who gives evidence esp. in writing

de·po·nen·tial \¦depə¦nenchəl\ *adj* **:** of, relating to, or characteristic of a deponent verb ⟨a ~ ending⟩ **:** DEPONENT

de·popularize \(ˈ)dē+\ *vt* [*de-* + *popularize*] **:** to cause to be no longer popular

¹de·populate \(ˈ)dē+\ *vb* [L *depopulatus*, past part. of *depopulari, depopulare*, fr. *de-* + *populari, populare* to ravage, perh. fr. *populus* people — more at PEOPLE] *vt* **1** *obs* **:** to lay waste **:** DEVASTATE, RAVAGE **2 :** to deprive wholly or partly of inhabitants (as by war or pestilence) **:** reduce the population of ⟨the Black Death . . . *depopulated* parts of Europe in the 15th century —V.M.Ehlers & E.W.Steel⟩ ⟨the cities almost *depopulated* of Spaniards gone to seek the greater riches of Mexico —Marjory S. Douglas⟩ ~ *vi* **:** to become less populous

²de·pop·u·late \(ˈ)dē¦päpyələt\ *adj* [L *depopulatus*] *archaic* **:** DEPOPULATED

de·population \(ˌ)dē+\ *n* [ME *depopulacioun* devastation, fr. L *depopulation-, depopulatio*, fr. *depopulatus* + *-ion-, -io* -ion] **:** the act of depopulating or the state of being depopulated: **a** *archaic* **:** DEVASTATION ⟨the Danes . . . infested those parts with wide ~ —John Milton⟩ **b :** reduction of population ⟨the causes of ~ are physical, political, and economic —G.B. Longstaff⟩

de·populator \(ˈ)dē+\ *n* [ME, devastator, fr. L *depopulator*, fr. *depopulatus* + *-or*] **:** one that depopulates

¹de·port \də'pō(ə)r|t, dē'-, -ō(ə)r|,-ōə|,-ō(ə)|, *usu* |d·+V\ *vt* -ED/-ING/-S [MF *deporter* to behave, support, spare, fr. L *deportare* to carry away, exile, fr. *de-* + *portare* to carry — more at PORT (to carry)] **1 :** CARRY, DEMEAN, CONDUCT ⟨teaching the child how to ~ himself in public⟩ **2** [L *deportare*] **a :** to carry away or off **:** TRANSPORT ⟨200 miners . . . were forcibly ~*ed* from their homes —Zechariah Chafee⟩ **b :** to send out of the country **:** sentence to legal deportation ⟨~*ing* criminals⟩ ⟨in Moscow whither he had been ~*ed* —Louis Bromfield⟩ **syn** see BANISH, BEHAVE

²deport *n* -s [MF, fr. *deporter*] *obs* **:** BEARING, DEPORTMENT

de·port·abil·i·ty \dəˌpōrd·ə'biləd·ē, (ˌ)dē,- -pō(r)|,-pōə|, |tə-, -ətē, -i\ *n* -ES **:** the state of being liable to deportation

de·port·able \də'pōrd·əbəl, (ˈ)dē¦p-, -ō(r)|,-ōə|, |tə-\ *adj* **1 :** subject to deportation ⟨any alien who fails to give the required notices . . . is also ~ —*Harvard Law Rev.*⟩ **2 :** carrying the punishment of deportation ⟨cases of illegal entry, criminality . . . and other ~ offenses —F.A.Ogg & P.O.Ray⟩

de·por·ta·tion \ˌdēˌpōr'tāshən, -ō(r)'-,-ōə'- *also* -ˌpə(r)'-\ *n* -s [MF & L; MF, fr. L *deportation-, deportatio*, fr. *deportatus* + *-ion-, -io* -ion] **:** the act or an instance of deporting or the state of being deported: as **a** *Roman law* **:** permanent banishment of a condemned criminal esp. to an island with resultant loss of citizenship and forfeiture of property — compare EXILE, RELEGATION **b :** the removal from a country of an alien whose presence in the country is unlawful or is held to be prejudicial to the public welfare — compare EXTRADITION, TRANSPORTATION

de·port·ee \dəˌpōr¦tē, dē-, ¦dēˌpōr¦tē, -ȯr|,-ōə|,-ō(ə)|, |d·¦ē; ¦dēpə(r)¦tē\ *n* -s **:** one who has been deported, is about to be deported, or is under sentence of deportation

de·port·ment \də'pōrtmənt, -ȯrt-,-ōət-,-ō(ə)t-\ *n* -s [F *déportement*, fr. MF *deportement*, fr. *deporter* to behave + *-ment* — more at DEPORT] **:** the manner in which one deports himself **:** CARRIAGE, BEHAVIOR, CONDUCT ⟨a stranger clad in black, and of a clerical ~ —Owen Wister⟩ ⟨all the thousand and one artificialities which go to make up feminine ~ —Max Peacock⟩ ⟨he placed his feet, one before the other, with the care of a young woman practicing ~ —Fred Majdalany⟩ ⟨their teacher had trained them in ~ and manners —Gladys Skelley⟩

de·pos·able \də'pōzəbəl, dē'-\ *adj* [*depose* + *-able*] **:** capable of being deposed ⟨a czar of high finance as ~ as any other dictator⟩

de·pos·al \-ōzəl\ *n* -s [ME, prob. fr. *deposen* + *-al*] **:** the act of deposing or the process of being deposed esp. from a throne ⟨the ~ of James II and the ascension of William of Orange —Frank Thilly⟩

de·pose \də'pōz, dē'-\ *vb* -ED/-ING/-S [ME *deposen*, fr. OF *deposer*, modif. (influenced by *poser* to put, place) of LL & L *deponere* (perfect stem *depos-*); LL *deponere* to remove from office or authority, fr. L, to lay aside, put down — more at DEPONE] *vt* **1 :** to remove from a throne or other high position **:** divest or deprive of office or rank **:** DETHRONE ⟨striving to ~ the king in favor of his brother⟩ ⟨*deposed* from his post as prime minister —*Time*⟩ ⟨they *deposed* Philip Carteret as governor —*Amer. Guide Series: N.J.*⟩ ⟨*deposed* as unfit to hold office⟩ **2** *obs* **a :** to take away **:** REMOVE **b :** DIVEST, DISPOSSESS **c :** to lay aside **:** divest oneself of **3 :** to let fall **:** put down **:** DEPOSIT ⟨she carelessly *deposed* costly trinkets on the table —Arnold Bennett⟩ ⟨the practice . . . of *deposing* the sacrament in a carved recess —Francis Berry⟩ **4 a** [ME *deposen*, fr. ML *depos-*, perfect stem of *deponere* to assert under oath, fr. L, to put down] **:** to say under oath **:** TESTIFY; *esp* **:** to give witness of by an affidavit or other sworn statement in writing ⟨~ before the court that he had seen the man in the act of murder⟩ **b :** AFFIRM, ASSERT ⟨a fat grocer was *deposing* that he thought it was I who had stolen five feet of pork sausages from him —Carolyn Hannay⟩ **c** *obs* **:** to put under oath **:** call upon as witness ~ *vi* [ME *deposen*, fr. ML *depos-*, perfect stem of *deponere* to assert under oath] **:** to bear witness **:** make a deposition **:** TESTIFY ⟨he was a bit shaky when it came his turn to ~⟩ **syn** see SWEAR

de·pos·er \-zə(r)\ *n* -s **:** one who deposes; *esp* **:** one that testifies

¹de·pos·it \də'päzət, dē'-, *usu* -əd·+V\ *vb* **deposited** \-zəd·əd, -z(ə)təd\ **depositing** \-zəd·iŋ, -z(ə)tiŋ\ **deposits** \-zəts\ [L *depositus*, past part. of *deponere* to put down, lay aside — more at DEPONE] *vt* **1 a :** to place, cache, or entrust esp. seriously and carefully (as for safekeeping, pledging or guaranteeing performance, or recording) ⟨until the last voter ~*ed* his ballot —R.M.Lovett⟩ **b :** to place in deposit in a bank or similar institution **c :** to set down or place esp. carefully or safely or in care or custody ⟨the maid had . . . ~*ed* a huge decanter on the table —A.N.Whitehead⟩ ⟨the adventurous gentlemen . . . were safely ~*ed* at their inn in London —T.B.Macaulay⟩ ⟨~*ed* in a clean hospital bed —Allen Churchill⟩ ⟨a giant wave lifted the tiny craft completely over the beached ship and ~*ed* it still intact, on the other side —*All Hands*⟩ **2** *archaic* **:** to lay aside or give up **:** rid oneself of **3 :** to lay down or let fall or drop by a natural process **:** foster the accretion or accumulation of as a natural deposit ⟨the intervening seasons had ~*ed* a thick layer of refuse over the vacant lot⟩ ⟨the wind ~*ed* a film of dust over the furniture⟩ ⟨in . . . hogs fed on copra . . . the cocoanut oil globules had been ~*ed* by nature in the tissues —V.G. Heiser⟩ ~ *vi* **1 :** to become precipitated **:** SETTLE **2 :** to make a deposit; *also* **:** to become deposited ⟨the zirconium metal . . . ~*s* on the filament —Samuel Glasstone⟩ **syn** see SET

²deposit \"\ *n* -s [L *depositum*, fr. neut. of *depositus*, past part.] **1 a :** the state of being deposited in trust or safekeeping **b :** the state of being deposited to one's credit in a bank **2 :** something placed (as in a bank or in someone's hands) for safekeeping: as **a :** money that is deposited in a bank or with a banker, that is subject to order, and that creates the relationship of creditor and debtor **b :** something given as a pledge or security (as a forfeit) ⟨post a ~ of money as evidence of his good faith —*Canadian Citizenship Series*⟩ ⟨~*s* which some librarians require from borrowers . . . returnable when the depositor ceases to use the library —W.C.B.Sayers⟩ ⟨a five-cent ~ on a soda bottle⟩ **c** *Roman & civil law* **:** a bailment of goods to be kept gratuitously for the bailor and without any benefit to the bailee or depositary — see IRREGULAR DEPOSIT, NECESSARY DEPOSIT, QUASI DEPOSIT, SEQUESTRATION, VOLUNTARY DEPOSIT **d :** a partial and first payment on account of the purchase price of property **3** [ML *depositum*] **:** a place of deposit **:** DEPOSITORY **4 :** the act of depositing ⟨is to come into force upon the ~ of ratifications with the government —Vera M.Dean⟩ ⟨ritual is . . . a slow ~, as it were, of people's imaginative insight into life —Susanne K.Langer⟩ **5 a :** something laid, placed, or thrown down; *esp* **:** matter deposited by some natural process ⟨the muddy and sandy ~*s* at the river's mouth⟩ ⟨the walls of the house are . . . less discolored by the ~ of carbon than usual in most towns —Richard Jefferies⟩ **b :** a natural accumulation (as of iron ore, coal, or gas) ⟨~*s* of phosphates suitable for agricultural fertilizer were discovered near Oruro —*Americana Annual*⟩

deposit account *n* **1** *Brit* **:** a bank account requiring advance notice of withdrawals and earning interest **:** SAVINGS ACCOUNT **2 :** the bank account of any depositor

deposit administration *n* **:** a plan for retaining retirement contributions made by employers in a special fund held by the ensurer to be applied toward the purchase of annuities as employees reach retirement

1de·pos·i·tary \-zə,terē, -ri\ *n* -ES [LL *depositarius*, fr. L *depositus* + *-arius* -ary] **1 :** one that receives a deposit : one with whom a depositor makes his deposit; *specif* **:** a bailee in a deposit **2 :** DEPOSITORY

2depositary \"\ *adj* **:** being or acting as a depositary ⟨a ~ bank⟩ ⟨a ~ agent⟩

de·pos·i·ta·tion \də,päzə'tāshən, (')dē,-\ *n* -S ['*deposit* + *-ation*] **1 :** the act of depositing : DEPOSIT **2** *Scots law* **:** an agreement by which an owner of personal property gives possession of it to another for safekeeping to be restored upon demand

deposit banking *n* **:** banking in which bank credit is in the form of deposits instead of the issue of notes

deposit copy *n* **:** a copy of a publication deposited by legal requirement in any of certain specified libraries

deposit currency *n* **:** checks and other credit instruments drawn on deposits in banks and used as a medium of exchange

deposited *past of* DEPOSIT

depositing *pres part of* DEPOSIT

dep·o·si·tion \,depə'zishən *also* ,dēp-\ *n* -S [ME & LL; ME *deposicioun* dismissal, testimony, fr. LL *deposition-, depositio* act of putting down, laying away, dismissal, testimony, burial, fr. LL & L *depositus* (past part. of LL *deponere* to remove from office or authority & L, to lay aside, put down) + L *-ion-, -io* -ion — more at DEPONE] **1 :** the act of deposing or the process of being deposed (as a sovereign from a throne) **:** deprivation of authority ⟨the forceful ~ of the vice-regent⟩; *specif* **:** the depriving of a clergyman of an ecclesiastical office or the suspension of a clergyman from the ministry **2 a :** an alleging or a giving of testimony **:** a testifying esp. before a court **b :** an opinion asserted **:** a statement made **:** something alleged **:** DECLARATION, TESTIMONY, ALLEGATION; *specif* **:** testimony taken down in writing under oath or affirmation in reply to interrogatories before a competent officer to replace the viva voce testimony of the witness or to supply necessary information for pretrial procedure — compare AFFIDAVIT **3** [L *depositus* + E *-ion*] **:** DEPOSITION FROM THE CROSS **4 :** the act or process of depositing or the state of being deposited: as **a** *obs* **:** a putting down or laying aside (as of a burden) **b :** a giving over or committing for safekeeping ⟨~ of the valuables into the hands of police⟩ **c :** a placing or a laying or throwing down often by a natural process ⟨glaciers caused denudation . . . more widely than ~ —Samuel Van Valkenberg & Ellsworth Huntington⟩ ⟨pneumoconiosis involves the ~ of foreign particles in the substance of the lungs⟩ **d :** PRECIPITATION ⟨the . . . ~ of metals on cotton from salt solutions —R.S.Horsfall & L.G.Lawrie⟩ ⟨sedimentary rocks . . . formed by the ~ of solids from the waters —S.F. Mason⟩ **5 :** BURIAL **:** interment (as of a saint's body) in a new place; *also* **:** a festival commemorating a burial **6** ['*deposit* + *-ion*] **:** something deposited **:** DEPOSIT, SEDIMENT ⟨excavation revealed more than one type of ~ in the dry river bed⟩

dep·o·si·tion·al \¦==¦zishənᵊl, -shnəl\ *adj* **:** of, relating to, or made by, deposition ⟨the present erosional and ~ topography of semiarid regions —P.G.Worcester⟩

deposition from the cross : a work of art representing Christ's descent from the cross

deposit money *n* **:** bank demand deposits which can be used as money through drawing checks

deposit of faith [trans. of ML *depositum fidei*] **:** the body of revealed truth in the Scriptures and tradition proposed by the Roman Catholic Church for the belief of the faithful

de·pos·i·tor \də'päzəd·ə(r), -z(ə)tə-\ *n* -S [LL, fr. L *depositus* + *-or*] **:** one that deposits; *esp* **:** one that makes a bank deposit or has money in deposit at a bank

1de·pos·i·to·ry \-zə,tōrē, -ȯr-, -ri\ *n* -ES ['*deposit* + *-ory*] **1 :** a person or group with which something and esp. something nonmaterial is deposited for preservation or safekeeping ⟨a ~ of ancient tradition⟩ **2** [LL *depositorium*, fr. L *depositus* + *-orium* -ory] **a :** a place where something is deposited or stored (as for safekeeping or convenience) ⟨an official ~ for U.S. government publications —*Bull. of Bates Coll.*⟩ ⟨the original furniture is stored away in hidden *depositories* of the château —Arnold Bennett⟩ ⟨Congress officially became the ~ of Burma's gift to America —Cecil Hobbs⟩; *specif* **:** a bank chosen for the depositing of government funds — compare DEPOSITORY LIBRARY **b :** a device consisting of a bank vault and a mechanism on the outside wall of the bank building through which deposits may be inserted into the vault during the hours the bank is closed

2depository \"\ *adj* **:** of or relating to a depository

depository bond *n* **:** a bond that is often required from a bank for deposits of state and municipal governments and that guarantees the amount of the deposit in the event of the bank's insolvency

depository library *n* **1 :** a library legally designated to receive at no cost except postage all or a selected list of U.S. government publications **2 :** a library designated by the United Nations to receive all or a selected list of its publications

deposit premium company *or* **deposit premium mutual** *n* **:** a mutual insurance company issuing policies at a stated premium often with provision for assessment

deposits *pres 3d sing of* DEPOSIT, *pl of* DEPOSIT

deposit slip *n* **:** a slip accompanying a bank deposit and containing a list of checks or cash deposited, the date, and depositor's signature

deposit station *n* **:** a place (as a school, firehouse, or store) at which a public library maintains a small collection of books; *also* **:** the collection of books maintained there

de·pos·i·tum \-zəd·əm\ *n* -S [in sense 1, fr. L; in sense 2, fr. ML, fr. L — more at DEPOSIT] **1 :** DEPOSIT 2, 3 **2 :** the faith and doctrine committed to the Christian church — archaic except in law and theology

de·po·si·tum mi·se·ra·bi·le \",mizə'rabə(,)lē\ *or* **depositum ne·ces·sa·ri·um** \-,nesə'sa(a)rēəm\ *n, pl* **deposi·ta misera·bi·lia** \-zəd·ə,mizərə'bilēə\ *or* **deposita necessa·ria** \-rēə\ [L] **:** NECESSARY DEPOSIT

1de·pot *in senses 1 & 2* 'de(,)pō *also* 'dē-; *in sense 3* 'dē- *sometimes* 'de-; *in all senses: archaic* 'dā(,)pō,\ *n* -S [F *dépôt*, fr. L *depositum* deposit] **1 :** a place organized for the reception, classification, storage, issue, or maintenance of military or naval supplies or equipment or for the reception, classification, detention, or forwarding of military or naval replacements **2 a :** a place at which things may be stored, collected, deposited, or cached or from which they may be conveniently distributed ⟨archiving is . . . the accumulation of material in a convenient ~ —M.B.Emeneau⟩ ⟨turning their house into a mere ~ for dilapidated objects —F.M.Ford⟩ ⟨a gasoline ~⟩ ⟨an auto-parts distribution ~ —*Newsweek*⟩ **b :** STORE, COLLECTION, DEPOSIT, CACHE ⟨we had the ship's stores and there was a food ~ on the north side of the island —H.A.Chippendale⟩ **3 a :** RAILROAD STATION **b :** a bus station **c :** an air terminal

2depot \"\ *vt* -ED/-ING/-S **:** to place (supplies) in a depot **:** CACHE ⟨that spring the first need was to ~ additional supplies for the dog-sledging parties —G.deQ.Robin⟩

3depot \"\ *adj, physiol* **:** STORED, REPOSITORY; *also* **:** adapted for prolonged action ⟨~ fat⟩ ⟨~ penicillin⟩ ⟨~ insulin⟩

depot ship *n* **:** a supply and repair ship in a flotilla of small naval vessels (as destroyers or submarines)

depr *abbr* depreciation

dep·ra·va·tion \,deprə'vāshən\ *n* -S [MF, fr. L *depravation-, depravatio* perversion, fr. *depravatus* + *-ion-, -io* -ion] **1** *obs* **:** DEFAMATION, CALUMNY **2 :** the act or process of depraving or the state of being depraved **:** CORRUPTION, PERVERSION, DEGENERACY, DEPRAVITY; *also* **:** an instance of this

de·prave \də'prāv, dē'-\ *vt* -ED/-ING/-S [ME *depraven*, fr. MF *depraver* to calumniate, pervert, fr. L *depravare* to pervert, distort, fr. *de-* + *-pravare* (fr. *pravus* crooked, wrong, bad) — more at PRAIRIE] **1 :** to speak ill of **:** DEPRECIATE, MALIGN **2 :** to make bad **:** ⟨things that would ~ the judgment rather than make it more discriminating⟩: as **a** *obs* **:** to pervert the meaning of by misconstruing **b** *archaic* **:** to make (a word or a text) corrupt **c :** to bring about the moral debasement of **d** *obs* **:** to reduce (coinage) in value **3** [by alter.] *obs* **:** DEPRIVE **syn** see DEBASE

de·praved \-vd\ *adj* **:** marked by debasement, corruption, perversion, or deterioration ⟨asserted that the present evils of society are the consequence of vicious institutions rather than of ~ human nature —V.L.Parrington⟩ ⟨scavenger birds with ~ habits⟩ — **de·praved·ly** \-v(ə)dlē\ *adv* — **de·praved·ness** \-v(ə)dnəs\ *n* -ES

depraved appetite *n* **:** PICA 2

de·prave·ment \-vmənt\ *n* -S **:** DEPRAVATION

de·prav·er \-və(r)\ *n* -S **:** one that depraves

de·prav·i·ty \-ravəd·ē, -ətē, -i\ *n* -ES **1 :** the quality or state of being depraved; *specif* **:** the state of sinfulness natural to unregenerate man according to certain religions **2 :** a corrupt act or practice

dep·re·cate \'deprə,kāt, -rē,-, *usu* -ād·+V\ *vt* -ED/-ING/-S [L *deprecatus*, past part. of *deprecari* to avert by prayer, intercede for fr. *de-* + *precari* to pray — more at PRAY] **1** *obs* **:** SUPPLICATE, BESEECH **2 a** *archaic* **:** to pray against (as an evil) **b :** to seek to avert (as by supplication) ⟨smilingly placed himself opposite him, with the look of one who ~*s* an expected reproof —J.C.Powys⟩ ⟨it would bring about the war we all dread and ~ —A.L.Guérard⟩ **3 :** to disapprove of often with mildness ⟨a man who advocates aesthetic effort and ~*s* social effort —Thomas Hardy⟩ ⟨shook her head, *deprecating* such wit —Arnold Bennett⟩ **4** [influenced in meaning by *depreciate*] **:** DEPRECIATE ⟨a shy self-*deprecating* manner⟩ ⟨insisted that he was merely a private citizen and *deprecated* any public honors paid to him —Robert Graves⟩ **syn** see DISAPPROVE

deprecating *adj* **:** depreciating or tending to depreciate; *esp* **:** APOLOGETIC ⟨he managed a ~ smile at the compliment⟩ — **dep·re·cat·ing·ly** *adv*

dep·re·ca·tion \,==ˈkāshən\ *n* -S [MF & L; MF, prayer, fr. L *deprecation-, deprecatio* prayer, act of averting by prayer, fr. *deprecatus* + *-ion-, -io* -ion] **1 :** a prayer that an evil may be removed or prevented **2 :** an act of deprecating: **a :** an often mild expression of disapproval **b :** depreciation esp. of oneself

dep·re·ca·tive \'==,kā|d·|iv, -,kə|, |t|, |ēv *also* |əv\ *adj* [LL *deprecativus*, fr. *deprecatus* + *-ivus* -ive] **:** DEPRECATORY — **dep·re·ca·tive·ly** \|əvlē, -li\ *adv*

dep·re·ca·to·ry \-,kə,tōrē, -ȯr-, -ri\ *adj* [LL *deprecatorius*, fr. L *deprecatus* + *-orius* -ory] **:** DEPRECATING

de·pre·cia·ble \də'prēsh(ē)əbəl, (')dē¦p-\ *adj* **:** that can or may depreciate in valuation

de·pre·ci·ate \də'prēshē,āt, dē'-, *usu* -ād·+V\ *vb* -ED/-ING/-S [LL *depretiare* (often spelled *depreciare* in later MSS), fr. *de-* + *pretium* price — more at PRICE] *vt* **1 :** to lessen in price or estimated value **:** lower the worth of ⟨the owner's right to ~ such property —*Jour. of Accountancy*⟩ — opposed to *appreciate* **2 :** to represent as of little value or claim to esteem **:** UNDERVALUE, DISPARAGE, BELITTLE ⟨objected to scholars *depreciating* the craftsmen —S.F.Mason⟩ ~ *vi* **:** to become depreciated **:** fall in value or esteem ⟨perishable goods ~ rapidly⟩ ⟨a *depreciating* currency⟩ **syn** see DECRY

de·pre·ci·at·ing·ly *adv* **:** in a way that depreciates

de·pre·ci·a·tion \də,prēshē'āshən, (,)dē,-\ *n* -S [*depreciate* + *-ion*] **:** the act or process of depreciating or the state of being depreciated **:** loss of value ⟨the rapid ~ of currency⟩ ⟨made some bitter remarks in ~ of his enemies⟩ ⟨estimated the degree of ~ in a car after a year's use⟩

depreciation accounting *n* **:** a branch of accounting that deals with systematically distributing or allocating the cost or other basic value of a fixed asset over its estimated useful life by periodic charges to expense or against revenue

depreciation charge *n* **:** an amount in accounting that is commonly a fixed percentage of the original cost of a property and that is periodically charged off to expense or against revenue in order to compensate for the depreciation of the property

depreciation insurance *n* **:** insurance that is added to a fire insurance policy by endorsement and that covers the difference between the actual cash value and the replacement cost of the insured property

de·pre·cia·tive \də'prēshē,ād·iv, dē'-, -sh(ē)əd·-\ *adj* **:** DEPRECIATING, DISPARAGING — **de·pre·cia·tive·ly** \-d·əvlē\ *adv*

de·pre·ci·a·tor \-shē,ād·ə(r)\ *n* -S [LL *depretiator* (often spelled *depreciator* in later MSS), fr. *depretiatus* + L *-or*] **:** one that depreciates

de·pre·ci·a·to·ry \-sh(ē)ə,tōrē\ *adj* **:** DEPRECIATING, DISPARAGING

dep·re·date \'deprə,dāt\ *vb* -ED/-ING/-S [LL *depraedatus*, past part. of *depraedari*, fr. L *de-* + *praedari* to plunder — more at PREY] *vt* **:** to lay waste **:** prey upon **:** PLUNDER, PILLAGE, DESPOIL ⟨*depredating* the surrounding countryside⟩ ~ *vi* **:** to make depredations **:** PLUNDER ⟨if you ~ in that country, we'll have to clash —J.E.Haley⟩

dep·re·da·tion \,deprə'dāshən\ *n* -S [ME *depredacioun*, fr. MF or LL; MF *depredation*, fr. LL *depraedation-, depraedatio*, fr. *depraedatus* + L *-ion-, -io* -ion] **1 a :** the act of depredating or the state of being depredated **:** an act of plundering, despoiling, or making inroads **b depredations** *pl* **:** RAVAGES ⟨trying to ease the ~*s* of the disease⟩ **2** *Scots law* **:** the forcible driving away of cattle in large numbers

dep·re·da·tor \'deprə,dād·ə(r)\ *n* -S [LL *depraedator*, fr. *depraedatus* + L *-or*] **:** one that plunders or despoils **:** PILLAGER

dep·re·da·to·ry \'deprədə,tōrē; də'predə-, dē'-; 'deprə,dād·ərē\ *adj* **:** tending to depredate **:** characterized by depredation **:** PLUNDERING

deprehend *vt* [L *deprehendere*, fr. *de-* + *prehendere* to lay hold of, seize — more at PREHENSILE] **1** *obs* **:** SEIZE, CAPTURE **2** *obs* **:** to take by surprise **3** *obs* **:** PERCEIVE, DETECT — **deprehension** *n* -S *obs*

de·press \də'pres, dē'-\ *vt* -ED/-ING/-ES [ME *depressen*, fr. MF *depresser*, fr. L *depressus*, past part. of *deprimere* to press down, fr. *de-* + *-primere* (fr. *premere* to press) — more at PRESS] **1 :** to put down or overcome forcibly **:** CRUSH, SUBJUGATE **2 :** to press down ⟨~ a typewriter key⟩ **:** LOWER: as **a :** to cause to sink, fall, or assume a lower level, position, point, situation, or attitude ⟨~*ed* the mounted gun⟩ ⟨~*ed* areas below sea level⟩ ⟨where the highway goes through cities you will find, perhaps, a ~*ed* express street . . . a bridge overhead —William Carter⟩ ⟨raise or ~ the roadbed at the crossing of a highway —B.N.Cardozo⟩ **b :** to lessen, diminish, impoverish, or depreciate the activity, strength, level, yield, or significance of ⟨confederates in Canada supplied cash for buying gold, shipping it to England and selling it in order to ~ Federal currency values —C.H.Coleman⟩ ⟨it has tended to ~ the culture of the minority below the point at which a full understanding of poetry becomes possible —C.D.Lewis⟩ ⟨able to ~ irritability of the heart muscle by the use of such a drug as procaine⟩ ⟨any number of factors can ~ germination in plants⟩ ⟨an injection to ~ the excretion⟩ **c :** to lower in spirit or mood **:** press down into dejection **:** make sad or downcast **:** DISCOURAGE, DISPIRIT ⟨the mere volume of work was enough to crush the most diligent of rulers and ~ the most vital —John Buchan⟩ **d :** to lessen or lower in value, esp. market value; *also* **:** to lower in marketability **e** *math* **:** to lower (as an equation) in degree **3 :** to cause (certain ore or gangue minerals) to sink while other minerals float — compare FLOTATION 3

syn OPPRESS, WEIGH (*down*), WEIGH (*on*), or WEIGH (*upon*): DEPRESS may stress the fact of lowering but does not stress the cause or agency involved. In reference to persons and their feelings it stresses dejection and discouragement ⟨she had been *depressed* by the failing trade of the shop —Arnold Bennett⟩ ⟨war had blighted his past, *depressed* his present and clouded his future with grave doubts —E.T.Weir⟩ OPPRESS stresses the fact of a weight or burden calculated to lower but does not stress the effect ⟨the butler, *oppressed* by the heat of the weather —G.B.Shaw⟩ ⟨the dismaying sense of it [the compulsion of a war period] . . . *oppressed* the mind —J.G. Cozzens⟩ WEIGH (*down*), WEIGH (*on*), and WEIGH (*upon*) are used to cover in-between situations; they suggest continuing concern with an urgent oppressive matter calculated to depress ⟨I know too well my own inefficiency; it has *weighed on* me from youth —Havelock Ellis⟩ ⟨Walter's mind had cleared itself of the depression which had *weighed on* him so heavily —T.B.Costain⟩

1de·pres·sant \-sᵊnt\ *adj* **:** causing depression **:** tending to depress: as **a :** making unhappy **:** DISPIRITING ⟨a fatal accident always has a ~ effect on a crowd —Ken Purdy⟩ **b :** creating economic depression ⟨other government policies were ~ —R.C.Leffingwell⟩ **c :** lowering or tending to lower functional or vital activity ⟨a drug with a ~ effect on heart rate⟩

2depressant \"\ *n* -S **:** something that depresses: as **a :** a reagent (as cyanide) that depresses in ore flotation **b :** an agent that causes the lessening or depressing of some specified property ⟨pour-point ~⟩ ⟨foam ~⟩ ⟨perspiration ~⟩ **c :** an agent that reduces exaggerated functional activity (as irritability or spasm) of tissues ⟨a ~ of intestinal spasm⟩

depressed *adj* **1 a :** DEJECTED, DISPIRITED **b :** DEPRESSIVE **2 a :** vertically flattened ⟨a ~ cactus⟩ **b :** having the central portion lower than the margin ⟨a ~ pustule⟩ **c :** lying flat or prostrate ⟨~ herb⟩ **d :** dorsoventrally flattened **3 a :** being in, suffering from, or caused by a state or period of economic depression ⟨a ~ industry⟩ ⟨~ areas⟩ ⟨~ conditions⟩ **b :** economically or socially below standard, oppressed, or underprivileged ⟨peasants are deserting the villages and streaming into the towns to form the kind of ~ proletariat that existed in England during the industrial revolution —George Woodcock⟩ ⟨the ~ peoples of the ghetto⟩; *esp* **:** constituting or belonging to the lowest social and economic class usu. characterized by unsatisfactory living and working conditions ⟨the most notable of the ~ classes in India is the class of untouchables⟩ **syn** see DOWNCAST

depressed arch *n* **:** DROP ARCH

depressed center car *or* **depressed well car :** a railroad flatcar constructed with a low center section and used to handle oversized loads which otherwise would not clear tunnels or other way structures

depressed fracture *n* **:** a fracture esp. of the skull in which the fragment is depressed below the normal surface

de·press·ibil·i·ty \də,presə'biləd·ē, (,)dē,-, -ətē, -i\ *n* -ES **:** the quality or state of being depressed **:** susceptibility to being depressed

de·press·ible \də'presəbəl, dē'-\ *adj* **:** capable of being depressed

depressing *adj* **:** that depresses **:** causing esp. emotional depression ⟨hot weather is enervating and severe cold although temporarily stimulating is permanently ~ —C.C.Furnas⟩ ⟨a ~ sense of all the stupidity —Floyd Dell⟩ ⟨that is a ~ book⟩ — **de·press·ing·ly** *adv* — **de·press·ing·ness** *n* -ES

de·pres·sion \-eshən\ *n* -S [in sense 1, fr. ME *depressioun*, fr. ML *depression-, depressio*, fr. LL, act of pressing down, fr. L *depressus* (past part. of *deprimere* to press down) + *-ion-, -io* -ion; in other senses, partly fr. MF & LL; MF *depression* act of pressing down, lowering, fr. LL *depression-, depressio*; partly fr. *depress* + *-ion* — more at DEPRESS] **1 a :** the angular distance of a celestial object below the horizon **b** (1) **:** the angular distance of an object beneath the horizontal plane that passes through the observer (2) *med* **:** a displacement downward or inward **2 :** the act of depressing or the quality or state of being depressed: as **a** *archaic* **:** ABASEMENT, HUMBLING, DEGRADATION ⟨the ~ of a haughty nobleman⟩ **b :** a pressing down **:** LOWERING, SINKING ⟨a quick ~ of the typewriter key⟩ ⟨recommend a ~ of the roadway where it goes under the bridge⟩ ⟨a rapid ~ of the mercury in the thermometer⟩ **c :** the state of feeling depressed **:** DISPIRITEDNESS, DEJECTION ⟨a chronic ~ of mind⟩ ⟨a physical reaction marked by ~ and languor⟩ **d** (1) **:** reduction, diminution, impoverishment, or depreciation in activity, strength, amount, quality, force, yield, value, or significance ⟨a ~ in trade⟩ ⟨a series of confiscations which completed the ~ of the English interest in the south —F.M.Stenton⟩ ⟨~ in Indian arts which may result in their disappearance —*Report: (Canadian) Royal Commission on Nat'l Development*⟩ ⟨as a surface mulch sawdust causes a ~ of nitrates⟩ (2) **:** a lowering of vitality or functional activity **:** the state of being below normal in physical or mental vitality **3 :** an instance of depression: as **a :** a region of low barometric pressure surrounded by higher pressures **:** LOW **b** (1) **:** a place or part that is depressed ⟨a slight ~ at the base of my left forefinger —Sidney Lovett⟩ (2) **:** ³HOLLOW 1 ⟨an open-air auditorium located in a natural ~ encircled by magnolias, oaks and sweet gum —*Amer. Guide Series: La.*⟩ **c :** a period of low general economic activity marked by mass unemployment, deflation, a decreasing use of resources, and a low level of investment **4 :** a mental disorder of psychoneurotic or psychotic proportions characterized by sadness, retardation of motor and certain vegetative processes, feelings of inadequacy and self-depreciation, and often by suicidal attempts — compare MANIC-DEPRESSIVE PSYCHOSIS **syn** see SADNESS

de·pres·sion·al \-shənᵊl, -shnəl\ *adj* **:** of or relating to depression or a depression

de·pres·sion·ary \-shə,nerē\ *adj* **:** DEPRESSIONAL ⟨such unemployment . . . will tend to cause a ~ movement in the whole economy —Gabriel Kolko⟩

depression of the dew point : the number of degrees that the dew point is lower than the temperature

depression slide *n* **:** a glass slide that has a concavity in one surface over which a cover glass can be placed and that is used in biology for hanging-drop cultures and for the microscopic study of small specimens

depression spring *n* **:** a spring where the earth's surface is coincident with the water table

1de·pres·sive \də'presiv, dē'-, -sēv *also* -səv\ *adj* [*depress* + *-ive*] **:** tending to depress **:** involving, marked by, or affected with depression **:** DEPRESSING — **de·pres·sive·ly** \-səvlē, -li\ *adv*

2depressive \"\ *n* -S **:** one who is depressed; *specif* **:** one afflicted with manic-depressive psychosis in its depressive phase

de·pres·sor \-sə(r)\ *n* -S [LL, fr. L *depressus* + *-or*] **:** something that depresses: as **a :** a muscle that depresses or draws down a part — compare LEVATOR **b :** a device or appliance that depresses a part ⟨a tongue ~⟩ **c :** a nerve or nerve fiber that decreases the activity or the tone of an organ **d :** DEPRESSANT **e :** a substance (as a drug) that lowers blood pressure **f :** a substance that retards or prevents a chemical reaction or process

depressor nerve *n* **:** a nerve whose stimulation tends to decrease the activity or tone of the part or organ that it innervates

depressure *n* [*depress* + *-ure*] *obs* **:** DEPRESSION

dep·re·ter \'deprəd·ə(r)\ *or* **dep·e·ter** \-pəd·-\ *n* -S [origin unknown] **:** a finish for a plastered wall made by pressing small stones in the soft plaster

de·priv·able \də'prīvəbəl, dē'-\ *adj* **:** subject to or capable of being deprived

de·priv·al \-vəl\ *n* -S **:** the act of depriving or the state of being deprived **:** DEPRIVATION ⟨assigns to them no punishment but the ~ of the Beatific Vision —G.G.Coulton⟩

dep·ri·va·tion \,deprə'vāshən *also* ,dē,prī'- *sometimes* ,dēprə'-\ *n* -S [NL *deprivation-, deprivatio*, fr. ML *deprivatus* (past part. of *deprivare* to deprive) + L *-ion-, -io* -ion] **1 a :** the act of depriving or the state of being deprived ⟨evidence that had been produced regarding the ~ of civil liberties in the area —*Collier's Yr. Bk.*⟩; *specif* **:** removal from an office, dignity, or benefice ⟨several months had been allowed him before he incurred suspension, several months more before he incurred ~ —T.B.Macaulay⟩ **b :** an act of depriving or an instance of being deprived ⟨the treatment of these slave laborers was stated in general terms not difficult to translate into concrete ~*s* —R.H.Jackson⟩ **2 :** the process of losing or the condition of having lost essentials vital to the body ⟨oxygen ~⟩ ⟨vitamin ~⟩

de·prive \də'prīv, dē'-\ *vt* -ED/-ING/-S [ME *depriven*, fr. ML *deprivare*, fr. L *de-* + *privare* to deprive — more at PRIVATE] **1** *obs* **:** to take away **:** REMOVE, DESTROY ⟨'tis honor to ~ dishonored life —Shak.⟩ **2 a :** to take something away from **:** DIVEST, BEREAVE ⟨last year's farm law that ~*s* farmers of soil conservation payments —*Wall Street Jour.*⟩ ⟨the proposed boundary settlement would permanently ~ that country of Silesia and East Prussia —Marshall Knappen⟩ **b :** to take an office, dignity, or benefice from **:** remove from office ⟨the Archbishop, accused of incontinence, would be *deprived* and sent to the Tower —Edith Sitwell⟩ **3 :** to keep from the possession, enjoyment, or use of something ⟨threatened to ~ American citizens of rights guaranteed them under the federal constitution —F.L.Mott⟩

syn DEPRIVE, DISPOSSESS, DISINHERIT, and BEREAVE can mean, in common, to prevent one from possessing. DEPRIVE, the most comprehensive of these words, usu. implies a taking away of what one has, owns, or has a right to ⟨to *deprive* a person of a week's wages⟩ ⟨I had *deprived* myself of rest and health —Mary W.Shelley⟩ ⟨the feeling that the system under which we live *deprives* the majority of the chance of a decent life —C.D. Lewis⟩ DISPOSSESS usu. applies to a removing or dislodging of a person in usu. illegitimate possession, less often implies a depriving of possessions, sometimes implies a deprivation of rights, qualities, or properties ⟨the family was *dispossessed* of their apartment and their furniture piled in the street⟩ ⟨he would at least try to *dispossess* her of the pistol —E.M. Lustgarten⟩ ⟨an attempt to *dispossess* nonproperty owners of voting rights⟩ DISINHERIT suggests an heir being deprived of the right to inherit an estate; in extension it often implies a robbing or divesting of a right, prerogative, or privilege, esp. acquired by birth ⟨*disinherited* by an angry father on his deathbed⟩ ⟨*disinherited* of all rights to citizenship or a decent livelihood⟩ BEREAVE means to deprive of something as by robbery, stripping, or seizing, usu. implying suddenness or surprise and now tending to occur in the form *bereaved* when loss by death is implied, in the form *bereft* when such things as hope, peace, friends, or intelligence are implied ⟨*bereaved* of both her parents and without a home of her own —Gabrielle Long⟩ ⟨the comedians full of jokes and *bereft* of humor —Bernard Kalb⟩ ⟨*bereft* of all hope of recovery⟩ ⟨to feel extremely *bereaved* after the death of a loved one⟩

deprived *adj* **:** marked by deprivations esp. of the necessities of life or of healthful environmental influences ⟨a childhood that was unhappy and ~, the family living a good deal off charity⟩ ⟨boys from a ~ environment, wherein the family life reveals a pattern of neglect, personality distortion, moral degradation and disregard for law —J.P.Murphy⟩

de·prive·ment \-vmənt\ *n* -S **:** DEPRIVATION

de·priv·er \-və(r)\ *n* -S [ME *deprivere*, fr. *depriven* + *-ere* -er] **:** one that deprives

de pro·fun·dis \ˌdāprōˈfu̇ndəs, -prəˈ-, -ˈfən-; ˌdē...ˈfən-; *sometimes* -ùn,dēs\ *n* -ES [fr. *de profundis* 130th Psalm, fr. ME, fr. LL, out of the depths, the first 2 words of the psalm (Ps 129 in the Vulgate)] **:** a profound and esp. agonized expression of despair or misery ⟨if this ill-fated woman . . . could be enabled to write her confession, this *de profundis* would be different and would perhaps disclose agonies of soul never known before —*N.Y. Times*⟩

de·pro·pa·ni·za·tion \(ˌ)dē,prōpənəˈzāshən\ *n* -S **:** the process of depropanizing

de·pro·pa·nize \(ˈ)dē¦prōpə,nīz\ *vt* -ED/-ING/-S [*de-* + *propane* + *-ize*] **:** to remove propane and sometimes lighter fractions from (as cracked gasoline) by distillation — **de·pro·pa·niz·er** \-zə(r)\ *n* -S

de·pro·tein·i·za·tion \(ˌ)dē,prō,tēnəˈzāshən, -ōd·ēənəˈ-\ *n* -S **:** the process of deproteinizing

de·pro·tein·ize \(ˈ)dēˈprō,tē,nīz, -ōd·ēə,n-\ *vt* -ED/-ING/-S [*de-* + *protein* + *-ize*] **:** to remove protein from ⟨*deproteinized* blood⟩ ⟨*deproteinized* rubber⟩

dep·side \ˈdep,sīd, -,səd\ *n* -S [ISV *deps-* (fr. Gk *depsein* to knead) + *-ide* — more at DIPHTHERIA] **:** any of a class of esters formed by the condensation of two or more molecules of phenolic carboxylic acids

dep·si·done \-psə,dōn\ *n* -S [ISV *depside* + *-one*] **:** any of a class of chemical compounds that are esters like depsides and are also cyclic ethers

dept *abbr* **1** department **2** deponent **3** deputy

dept·ford \ˈdetfə(r)d\ *adj, usu cap* [origin unknown] **:** of or relating to a No. American Indian culture of coastal Georgia and northwestern Florida of about A.D. 700–900 characterized by slender cooking pots that have conical bases and are decorated by check stamping

deptford pink *n, usu cap D* [fr. *Deptford*, England] **:** a European wild pink (*Dianthus armeria*) that is naturalized in America and that has small bright pink flowers

depth \ˈdepth\ *n, pl* **depths** \-ps *also* -pt(h)s\ [ME, prob. fr. *dep* deep + *-th* — more at DEEP] **1 a :** something that is deep **:** a deep place **:** a deep part of something; *esp* **:** the deepest part — often used in pl. ⟨treasures in the ~s of the ocean⟩ **b :** a profound or intense or often the most profound or intense state (as of thought or feeling) — often used in pl. ⟨in the ~s of misery⟩ ⟨the ~s of reflection⟩; *also* **:** a reprehensibly low social, moral, or intellectual condition — often used in pl. ⟨criticism . . . having fallen to such ~s, it is hardly surprising that our standards of literature and the arts have fallen with it —Huntington Hartford⟩ **c :** the inner esp. midmost or more or less remote or unfathomable part — often used in pl. ⟨the ~s of the forest⟩ ⟨disappeared in the ~ of the crowd⟩ **d :** the part marked by the greatest, the most intense, or the severest degree (as of cold) — often used in pl. ⟨in the ~s of winter⟩ ⟨the ~s of the night⟩ ⟨in the lowest ~s of servility and superstition —T.L.Peacock⟩; *also* **:** the worst part — often used in pl. ⟨the ~s of the slums⟩ ⟨the ~ of the depression⟩ **2 a :** the perpendicular measurement downward from a surface ⟨the ~ of the river⟩ **:** the extent or measurement from the top downward ⟨the ~ of a mine shaft⟩ **b** (1) *of a square sail* **:** the extent from the headrope to the footrope (2) *of a staysail or boom sail* **:** the length of the after leech — compare ¹DROP 2b(2) ²HOIST 3b **c :** the distance between upper and lower or between dorsal and ventral points of a body **d :** the direct linear measurement from the point of viewing, from the usual position of an observer, or toward the back from a position usu. considered the front ⟨wishing he could measure the ~ of the sky⟩ ⟨the house lot was 200 ft. in ~⟩ ⟨the ~ of the crowd was considerable⟩; *specif* **:** the space from front to rear occupied by a military formation or position including front and rear elements **e :** a great distance into something immeasurable conceived of as extending from the observer — often used in pl. ⟨the ~s of space⟩ **3 a :** the quality of being deep or of having considerable extension downward or inward **b :** the quality of being profound (as in insight) or full (as of knowledge) **:** ACUTENESS, PENETRATION ⟨a certain ripeness of wisdom, a certain pertinency and ~ of meaning —P.E.More⟩ ⟨says much for the ~ of the impression he had received —Richard Garnett †1906⟩ ⟨Shakespeare gives the greatest width of human passion; Dante the greatest altitude and greatest ~ —T.S.Eliot⟩ **c :** the quality of being abstruse ⟨the great ~ of such thought left the ordinary brain tired and confused⟩ **d :** the quality of being intense or complete (as in moral quality or state of feeling) ⟨the ~ of a man's unrighteousness⟩ ⟨impossible to share another's ~ of grief⟩ ⟨no one knew the ~ of his guilt⟩ **e :** the quality of being low in pitch usu. with fullness of tone ⟨the vitality and ~ of the sound that reached the ear —Jack Gould⟩ **f :** physical intensity ⟨a great ~ of stillness in the woods⟩; *specif* **:** the degree of departure from colorlessness that is characteristic of the concentration or efficiency of a bulky color produced by increasing from zero the thickness of its layers or from white of a surface color **4** *archaic* **:** the number of attributes that an abstract conception or notion includes **:** CONNOTATION **5 :** the degree of engagement between a wheel and a pinion in a clock or watch — **beyond one's depth** *or* **out of one's depth 1 :** in water that is deeper than one's height **2 :** beyond the limit of one's mental capability — **in depth 1 :** extending over or for a considerable distance into an area **2** *of military defense* **:** extended for some distance forward from a primary combat zone and usu. supported by successive lines of defenders and materiel ⟨organize defense *in depth* —J.H.Plumb⟩ **3 :** in marked thoroughness **:** covering a great number and often a maximum of elements, considerations, or relevant matters ⟨here *in depth* is a portrait of Spain as it was and is —*NY Times Book Rev.*⟩ ⟨making a study *in depth* of the effects of the broadcast —Gilbert Seldes⟩

depth charge *or* **depth bomb** *n* **:** a projectile to be exploded underwater against submarines or other underwater targets

depth–charge *or* **depth–bomb** \ˈ≈,≈\ *vt* [*depth charge* or *depth bomb*] **:** to attack, damage, or destroy with a depth charge

depth gauge *n* **:** a gauge for measuring the depth of holes, grooves, or concavities

depth·ing tool \ˈdepthiŋ,-\ *n* **:** a tool for arranging a wheel and pinion of a watch at their proper working depth

depth interview *n* **:** an interview designed to probe attitudes, feelings, or motives not usu. tapped by the asking of standard or prepared questions

depth·less \-pt(h)ləs\ *adj* **1 :** immeasurable in depth **:** deep or profound beyond description ⟨new insight into the ~ nature of her loneliness —Ethel Waters⟩ ⟨the ~ misery and heroism of the people they served —*Time*⟩ **2 :** lacking significant depth **:** SHALLOW, SUPERFICIAL ⟨it promises to make life impersonal, mechanized and ~ —*Time*⟩

depth of compensation : the depth below the earth's surface at which the topographic inequalities are compensated by variations in rock density so that all columns of rock or of rock and water above that depth have approximately equal weights

depth of definition : DEPTH OF FOCUS 1

depth of engagement : the depth of thread contact measured radially of the mating parts of an external and an internal thread

depth of field : the range of distances of the object in front of a camera lens or other image-forming device measured along the axis of the device throughout which the image has acceptable sharpness

depth of focus 1 : the range of distances of the image behind a camera lens or other image-forming device measured along the axis of the device throughout which the image has acceptable sharpness **2 :** DEPTH OF FIELD — not used technically

depth of hold : the distance from the underside of the tonnage deck plank amidships to the ceiling of the hold of a ship

depth of thread : the distance between the crest and the base of a screw thread measured radially

depth·om·e·ter \depˈthäməd·ə(r)\ *n* [*depth* + *-o-* + *-meter*] **:** an instrument for measuring the depth of water

depth perception *n* **:** the ability to judge more or less accurately the distance of objects away from the observer and the spatial relationship of objects at different distances and angles away from the observer

depth psychology *n* **:** PSYCHOANALYSIS

depths *pl of* DEPTH

depth–sounder \ˈ≈,≈≈\ *n* **:** an instrument (as a bathymeter or fathometer) for measuring mechanically the depth of water beneath a ship

depth table *n* **:** a table used in the appraisal of real estate that shows in percentages the variations of land value attributable to differences in the depth of lots

dep·u·rant \ˈdepyərənt, dəˈpyu̇r-\ *n* -S [ML *depurant-, depurans*, pres. part. of *depurare*] **:** an agent or means used to effect purification

dep·u·rate \ˈdepyə,rāt\ *vt* -ED/-ING/-S [ML *depuratus*, past part. of *depurare*, fr. L *de-* + *purare* to purify, fr. *purus* clean, pure — more at PURE] **:** to free from impurities or heterogeneous matter **:** PURIFY, CLEANSE — **dep·u·ra·tion** \ˌdepyəˈrāshən\ *n* -S

dep·u·ra·tor \ˈdepyə,rād·ə(r)\ *n* -S **:** one that purifies

de·purge \(ˈ)dē+\ *vt* [*de-* + *purge*] **:** to restore previous social and political status (as eligibility for public office) to (a formerly purged person)

depurse *vt* [*de-* + *purse* (n.)] *obs* **:** DISBURSE — **depursement** *n* -S

dep·u·ta·tion \ˌdepyəˈtāshən\ *n* -S [ME, fr. LL *deputation-, deputatio* delegation of powers, fr. *deputatus* (past part. of *deputare*) + L *-ion-, -io* -ion] **1 a** *obs* **:** appointment or ordination esp. to an office **b** *obs* **:** COMMISSION 1a, WARRANT 2c **c :** an appointment as gamekeeper on an English estate often made as a way of giving hunting privileges **2 a :** the act of deputing **:** the act of appointing a deputy or representative **b :** the office of deputy or delegate **3 a :** a person or group deputed to act on one's behalf ⟨the larger nations sent ~s to the peace conference⟩ **b :** a group acting as a unit ⟨waved to a halt by ~s of rugged, villainous-looking men —Mollie Panter-Downes⟩ ⟨a ~ of season-ticket holders protested to the management —O.S.Nock⟩ — **dep·u·ta·tion·al** \ˌdepyəˈtāshənᵊl, -shnəl\ *adj*

dep·u·ta·tive \ˈ≈≈,tād·iv\ *adj* [*deputation* + *-ive*] **:** of, relating to, or having the character or authority of a deputy

¹**dep·ute** \ˈdəˌpyüt\ *n* -S [ME, fr. MF, past part. of *deputer*] *now Scot* **:** DEPUTY

²**de·pute** \dəˈpyüt, dēˈ-, *usu* -üd·+V\ *vt* -ED/-ING/-S [ME *deputen*, fr. MF *deputer* to appoint, fr. LL *deputare* to allot, destine, fr. L, to esteem, consider, lit., to cut off, fr. *de-* + *putare* to prune, esteem, consider, think — more at PAVE] **1** *obs* **:** APPOINT, DEVOTE **2 :** DELEGATE ⟨the duty of keeping in touch with the constituencies . . . was *deputed* to the party agents —H.J.Hanham⟩ ⟨he had been *deputed* to meet us and had forgotten —John Masters⟩ ⟨a body of men *deputed* to report the invasion of Europe —Richard Dimbleby⟩

dep·u·tize \ˈdepyə,tīz *also* ÷ -pə-\ *vb* -ED/-ING/-S *see -ize in Explan Notes* [*deputy* + *-ize*] *vt* **1 :** to appoint as deputy **:** make into a deputy esp. by an official swearing in **2 :** to entrust to a deputy ⟨friends would like to see him ~ part of his mountainous work to lieutenants —Li Shu-Fan⟩ ~ *vi* **1 :** to act as deputy ⟨a dearth of princes who could ~ for the sovereign —*Times Lit. Supp.*⟩ **2 :** to act or function as a substitute in another's place ⟨if photography was ever allowed to ~ for art . . . in the end it would either supplant or completely corrupt art —Douglas Cooper⟩

dep·u·ty \ˈdepyəd·ē, -ətē, -i *also* ÷ -pə-\ *n* -ES *often attrib* [ME, fr. MF *deputé*, *depute*, past part. of *deputer* to appoint — more at DEPUTE] **1 :** a person appointed, nominated, or elected as the substitute of another and empowered to act for him, in his name, or in his behalf **:** DELEGATE, REPRESENTATIVE ⟨the hostess left for awhile but picked a ~ hostess to take care of things in her absence⟩ ⟨each alderman has a ~ in the common council of London⟩; *specif* **:** a member of the lower house of certain legislative assemblies — compare GENERAL DEPUTY, LORD LIEUTENANT, SPECIAL DEPUTY, VICEROY **2 a :** a second in command or an assistant who usu. takes charge when his superior is absent ⟨a ~ supervisor⟩ ⟨a ~ editor⟩ ⟨a ~ marshal⟩ **b :** DEPUTY CHIEF **c :** DEPUTY SHERIFF **3 :** one who supervises such matters as shoring and bratticing in an English coal mine

deputy chief *n* **1 :** an official in a police or fire department usu. second in command **2 :** the rank of a deputy chief

deputy sheriff *n* **:** an assistant appointed to receive and serve writs and sometimes to act in place of the sheriff

deputy surveyor *n* **:** MINERAL SURVEYOR

de·queen \(ˈ)dē+\ *vt* [*de-* + *queen* (n.)] **:** to remove the queen from (a hive of bees) — compare SUPERSEDURE

der- *or* **dero-** *comb form* [NL, fr. Gk *der-*, fr. *derē, deirē;* akin to OSlav *griva* mane, Skt *grīvā* neck, L *vorare* to devour — more at VORACIOUS] **:** neck **:** throat ⟨*deradenitis*⟩ ⟨*Derotremata*⟩

der *abbr* derivation; derivative; derived

de·racialization \(ˌ)dē, də +\ *n* **:** the act or process of deracializing

de·racialize \(ˈ)dē, də +\ *vt* [*de-* + *racial* + *-ize*] **1 :** to attenuate or eliminate distinctive racial qualities of ⟨may ultimately ~ themselves through education and interbreeding⟩ **2 :** to free from appeal to race ⟨until local authorities ~ their outlook, the segregation problem won't be solved⟩

de·rac·i·nate \dəˈrasᵊn,āt, dēˈ-\ *vt* -ED/-ING/-S [F *déraciner* (fr. MF *desraciner*, fr. *des-* + *racine* root, fr. LL *radicina*, fr. *radic-, radix* root + *-ina*, fem. of *-inus* -ine) + E *-ate* — more at WORT] **1 :** to pull out by the roots **:** EXTIRPATE **2 :** to separate from one's environment **syn** see EXTERMINATE

deracinated *adj* **:** physically, mentally, or emotionally separated from one's racial, social, or intellectual group **:** free from racial characteristics or influence ⟨as ~ as migrants from another country⟩

de·rac·i·na·tion \də,rasᵊnˈāshən, (ˌ)dē,-\ *n* -S **1 :** the act or process of deracinating **2 :** detachment from one's background (as from homeland, customs, traditions)

¹**de·raign** \dəˈrān, dē-\ *vt* -ED/-ING/-S [ME *dereynen, deraynen*, fr. OF *deraisnier* to defend, champion, fr. *de-* + *raisnier* to speak, plead, fr. (assumed) VL *rationare*, fr. L *ration-, ratio* reckoning, calculation, reason — more at REASON] *archaic* **:** to defend or prove (a claim) or settle (a dispute) esp. in personal combat

²**deraign** /"/ *vt* -ED/-ING/-S [MF *desrengier* to get out of place, disarrange — more at DERANGE] *archaic* **:** to discharge from a religious order — **deraignment** *n* -S *obs*

¹**de·rail** \dəˈrāl, (ˈ)dēˈ-, *esp before pause or consonant* -āəl\ *vb* -ED/-ING/-S [F *dérailler*, fr. *dé* (fr. OF *des-, de-* de-) + *rail*, fr. E — more at RAIL] *vt* **1 :** to cause (a railroad engine or car) to run off the rails of the track **2 :** to throw off course (as a plan or project) **:** INTERRUPT, DIVERT ⟨new trade barriers could ~ British planning —*Atlantic*⟩ ⟨addiction to alcohol, which ~*ed* his career —Val Adams⟩ ~ *vi* **:** to leave the rails

²**de·rail** \ˈdē,r-,dəˈr-,dēˈr-\ *also* **de·rail·er** \dəˈrālə(r), dēˈ-\ *n* **:** a device for guiding railway cars or locomotives off the rails at selected points when in danger of collision or other accident

de·rail·ment \dəˈrā(ə)lmənt, dēˈ-\ *n* -S [F *déraillement*, fr. *dérailler* + *-ment*] **:** an act or instance of derailing or of being derailed **:** derailed state

de·range \dəˈrānj, dēˈ-\ *vt* -ED/-ING/-S [F *déranger*, fr. OF *desrengier* to get out of place, disarrange, fr. *des-* de- + *reng, renc* line, place, row — more at RANK] **1 a :** to put out of place or order **:** DISARRANGE ⟨war *deranged* the lines of communication and transportation⟩ ⟨hatless, with tie *deranged* —G.W.Stonier⟩ ⟨excessive erosion tends to ~ the continental water system —Russell Lord⟩ **b :** to throw into disorder or confusion **:** UPSET ⟨the arrival of guests *deranged* all his plans⟩ ⟨the music brought back memories and *deranged* her poise⟩ **2 :** to disturb the operation or functioning of ⟨even slight damage to the hearing mechanism may ~ it⟩ **3 :** to break in upon **:** INTERRUPT, DISTURB **syn** see DISORDER

de·range·able \-jəbəl\ *adj* **:** capable of being deranged

deranged *adj* **:** DISARRANGED, DISORDERED, UNBALANCED; *esp* **:** CRAZY, INSANE

de·range·ment \-jmənt\ *n* -S [F *dérangement*, fr. *déranger* + *-ment*] **:** the state of being deranged **:** DISARRANGEMENT, CONFUSION, DISORDER; *esp* **:** INSANITY

de·rat \(ˈ)dē +\ *vt* [*de-* + *rat* (n.)] **:** to rid of rats

de·rate \(ˈ)dē +\ *vt* [*de-* + *rate*] **1 :** to reduce or eliminate rates on ⟨the Local Government Act of 1929 *derated* British agricultural holdings⟩ **2 :** to lower the rated capability of (electrical apparatus) because of deterioration, inadequacy, age, or obsolescence

de·ration \(ˈ)dē +\ *vt* [*de-* + *ration*] **:** to cease to ration (as a commodity)

derationing *n* **:** a stopping or cancellation of rationing

de·rat·i·za·tion \(ˌ)dē,rad·əˈzāshən\ *n* -S **:** the ridding of rats

de·ray \diˈrā\ *n* -S [ME, fr. OF *desrei*, fr. *desreer*, to disturb, put in disorder, prob. alter. of *desaree* — more at DISARRAY] *now dial Brit* **:** DISORDER, DISTURBANCE, CONFUSION; *specif* **:** disorderly merriment

der·bied *pronunc at* ¹DERBY +d\ *adj* **:** wearing a derby

derbies *see* ¹DERBY\ *var of* DARBIES

¹**der·by** \ˈdərbē, -ōb-,-əib-, -bi, *in Brit speech usu* ˈdȧb-; *in the US* ˈdärb- & ˈdȧb- *are seriously used by many for Brit places, persons, or things having "derby" or "Derby" as or in their name*\ *n* -ES [fr. the *Derby*, famous horse race run at Epsom Downs, England; after Edward Stanley †1834, 12th earl of *Derby*, who founded it in 1780] **1 a** *usu cap* **:** any of certain traditionally prominent horse races held annually and usu. restricted to three-year-olds **b :** a race or contest open to all comers or all who fall within some specified category (as boys under a certain age or size) and offering prizes to winners ⟨a salmon ~⟩ ⟨bicycle *derbies*⟩ **c :** a field contest or trial for hounds or bird dogs classified as two-year-olds; *often* **:** a dog eligible to compete in such a derby **2 a** *or* **derby hat** *sometimes cap D* **:** a stiff felt hat with a dome-shaped crown and a rather narrow somewhat rolled brim — called also *bowler* **b :** a woman's hat (as of stiff straw or fabric) more or less resembling the felt derby **c :** a mute for trumpet or trombone in the shape of a derby used by jazz players **3** [*derby (vamp)*] **a** *often cap* **:** a low-heeled short-vamped usu. buckled sport shoe for men **b** *Brit* **:** BLUCHER ⟨a *derby*-front shoe⟩

derby 2a

²**derby** *see* ¹DERBY\ *adj, usu cap* [in sense 1, fr. *Derby*, county borough in England; in sense 2, fr. *Derby* county, England] **1 :** of or from the county borough of Derby, England **:** of the kind or style prevalent in Derby **2 :** DERBYSHIRE

³**derby** *see* ¹DERBY\ *or* **derby cheese** *n* -ES *often cap D* **:** a hard-pressed mild-flavored English cheese that is prepared from whole sweet cow's milk and resembles but is moister and flakier than cheddar

derby blue *n, often cap D* [so called fr. the characteristic color of Derby China] **:** a dark violet that is bluer, lighter, and stronger than plum purple (sense 2) and bluer and stronger than average blue plum — called also *elderberry*

Derby China *trademark* — used for a highly ornamented china

derby flycatcher *n, usu cap D* [after Edward S. Stanley, 13th earl of *Derby* †1851 Eng. zoologist] **:** a large conspicuously marked tyrant flycatcher (*Pitangus sulphuratus*) found in tropical America and northward to southern Texas

der·by·lite \ˈdərbē,līt\ *n* -S [Orville A. *Derby* †1915 Am. geologist + E *-lite*] **:** a mineral probably $Fe_6Ti_6Sb_2O_{23}$ consisting of an iron antimonate and titanate in black prismatic orthorhombic crystals (sp. gr. 4.53)

derby red *n, often cap D* [prob. fr. *Derby (China)*] **1 :** vermilion or a color resembling it **2 :** CHROME RED 1

¹**der·by·shire** \ˈ≈≈,shi(ə)r, -iə, -,shə(r) — *see* ¹DERBY\ *adj, usu cap* [fr. *Derbyshire*, England] **:** of or from the county of Derby **:** of the kind or style prevalent in the county of Derby

²**derbyshire** \"\ *or* **derbyshire cheese** *n, usu cap D* **:** ³DERBY

derbyshire chair *n, usu cap D* **:** an English country chair of Jacobean style with arched top rail and open back

de·realization \(ˌ)dē, də+\ *n* [*de-* + *realization*] **:** loss of a sense of the reality of one's environment

de·re·cha·zo \ˌderəˈchä(ˌ)sō\ *n* -S [Sp, fr. *derecho* right hand (fr. *derecho*, adj., right, fr. L *directus* straight, direct) + *-azo*, suffix used to denote a blow of a (specified) nature — more at DIRECT] **:** a close pase in bullfighting done with the muleta in the right hand — compare NATURAL

de·re·ism \ˈdēˈrē,izəm, ˈdāˈrā,-\ *n* -S [L *de re* away from reality + E *-ism*] **:** thinking directed away from reality and not following ordinary rules of logic — compare AUTISM

de·re·is·tic \¦≈≈¦istik\ *adj* **:** characterized by or involving dereism — **de·re·is·ti·cal·ly** \-tək(ə)lē\ *adv*

¹**der·e·lict** \ˈderə,likt\ *adj* [L *derelictus*, past part. of *derelinquere* to forsake wholly, abandon, fr. *de-* + *relinquere* to leave — more at RELINQUISH] **1 :** abandoned esp. by the owner or occupant **:** FORGOTTEN, UNUSED, RUN-DOWN ⟨a ~ hill farm⟩ ⟨books that lie ~ on the top shelf⟩ ⟨a house now ~ beyond redemption —*Country Life*⟩ **2 :** lacking in a sense of duty **:** REMISS, NEGLECTFUL ⟨school boards that were ~ in opening and maintaining public schools —C.S.Stine⟩ ⟨voters who feel that they would somehow be ~ in their civic duty . . . if they did not vote selectively —R.H.Rovere⟩ ⟨~ behavior toward racial minorities —H.L.Ickes⟩

²**derelict** \"\ *n* -S **1 a :** a thing voluntarily abandoned or willfully cast away by its owner with the intention of not retaking it and rightly claimed by the first person who takes possession of it; *specif* **:** a boat abandoned on the high seas **b :** a tract of land left dry by the sea or other body of water receding from its former bed **2 :** a person abandoned or forgotten **:** one that is not a responsible or acceptable member of society ⟨chronic ne'er-do-wells, useless ~s of society, seldom hired and then not for long —F.L.Allen⟩

der·e·lic·tion \ˌderəˈlikshən\ *n* -S [L *dereliction-, derelictio*, fr. *derelictus* + *-ion-, -io* -ion] **1 a :** an intentional abandonment ⟨~ of sins —Jeremy Taylor⟩ — now used chiefly in law **b :** the state of being abandoned **2** *obs* **:** failure esp. of physical or mental powers **3 :** a recession of water (as of the sea) so that land above high-water mark is left dry **4 a :** intentional or conscious neglect (as of principles) ⟨~ of duty⟩ **:** deviation esp. from conventional conduct **:** DELINQUENCY **b :** FAULT, SHORTCOMING **syn** see FAILURE

de·requisition \də, dē +\ *vt* [*de-* + *requisition*] **:** to release from requisition; *specif* **:** to release from government control

de·res·i·nate \(ˈ)dēˈrezᵊn,āt\ *vt* [*de-* + *resinate*] **:** to remove resin from — **de·res·i·na·tion** \(ˌ)dē,rezᵊnˈāshən\ *n* -S

de·restrict \(ˌ)dē +\ *vt* [*de-* + *restrict*] **:** to remove restrictions from ⟨trading in Canadian dollar securities was ~*ed*⟩; *specif* **:** to remove a speed limit from (a road)

derf \ˈdərf\ *adj* [ME, of Scand origin; akin to ON *djarfr* bold; akin to OE *deorfan* to labor, perish, OS *derbi* strong, OFris *derve* bold, Arm *derbuk* rough, stiff, Lith *dirbti* to work; basic meaning: to work] *Scot* **:** BOLD, DARING

derham *var of* DIRHEM

de·ride \dəˈrīd, dēˈ-\ *vt* -ED/-ING/-S [L *deridēre*, fr. *de-* + *ridēre* to laugh — more at RIDICULOUS] **:** to laugh at with contempt **:** turn to ridicule or make sport of **:** MOCK ⟨sardonic wisecracks in which supposedly lofty ideals are mercilessly *derided* —*Times Lit. Supp.*⟩ **syn** see RIDICULE

de·rid·ing·ly *adv* **:** in a deriding manner

de ri·gueur \də(,)rēˈgər, -ˌriˈ-, +V -ər-; -gə̄, +V -ər-, -ə̄(r\ *adj* [F] **:** prescribed or required by fashion, etiquette, or custom esp. among sophisticated or informed persons **:** PROPER ⟨instructions as to when and where a silk hat is *de rigueur* —André Maurois⟩ ⟨the *de rigueur* luggage of a salesman —Bernard Kalb⟩ ⟨a type of architecture that became *de rigueur* for suburban homes⟩ ⟨at which it is *de rigueur* to drink as much champagne as possible —Robert Shaplen⟩

deringer *var of* DERRINGER

de·rip·ia \dəˈripēə\ [NL] *syn of* JUGULARES

de·ris·i·ble \dəˈrizəbəl, dēˈ-\ *adj* [*derision* + *-ible*] **:** worthy of derision or scorn

de·ri·sion \-izhən\ *n* -S [ME *derisioun*, fr. MF *derision*, fr. LL *derision-, derisio*, fr. L *derisus* (past part. of *deridēre* to deride) + *-ion-, -io* -ion — more at DERIDE] **1 a :** a laughing at what seems ridiculous or contemptible **:** the use of ridicule, mockery, or scorn to belittle or to show contempt **b :** a state of being derided ⟨a social life which . . . wins its way from ~ to acceptance —Samuel Alexander⟩ **2 :** an object of derision or scorn **:** LAUGHINGSTOCK ⟨I was a ~ to all my people —Lam 3:14 (AV)⟩

de·ri·sive \dəˈrīsiv, dēˈ-, ǀēv *also* ǀəv *sometimes* -rizǀ *or* -rīzǀ *or* -risǀ\ *adj* [*derision* + *-ive*] **1 :** expressing or characterized by derision **:** JEERING ⟨~ taunts —Alexander Pope⟩ **2 :** causing derision **:** RIDICULOUS — **de·ri·sive·ness** *n* -ES

de·ri·sive·ly \ǀəvlē, -li\ *adv* **:** in a derisive manner **:** with derision

de·ri·so·ry \-rīs(ə)rē, -rīz(-,-riz(-, -ri\ *adj* [LL *derisorius*, fr. L *derisus* + *-orius* -ory] **1 :** expressive of derision **:** DERISIVE ⟨scornful ~ smiles —Katherine A. Porter⟩ **2 :** worthy of derision **:** RIDICULOUS ⟨~ sales of contemporary verse —Cyril Connolly⟩ ⟨a ~ excuse for an automobile —A.J.Liebling⟩

de·riv·abil·i·ty \dəˌrīvəˈbilədˌē, dē,-\ *n* **:** the quality or state of being derivable

de·riv·able \-ˈ=vəbəl\ *adj* **1** *obs* **:** TRANSMISSIBLE **2 :** that can be derived **:** OBTAINABLE ⟨pleasure ~ from home life⟩; *specif* **:** capable of being known by inference (as from premises or data) **:** DEDUCIBLE **3 :** capable of being traced (as from a source) — **de·riv·ably** \-blē\ *adv*

¹der·i·vate \ˈderəvə̇t, -ˌvāt\ *adj* [L *derivatus*, past part. of *derivare* to draw off, derive — more at DERIVE] **:** DERIVED, DERIVATIVE — **der·i·vate·ly** *adv*

²derivate \"\ *n* -S **:** something derived (as a thing, word, idea) **:** DERIVATIVE ⟨faith in the possibility of science . . . is an unconscious ~ from medieval theology —A.N.Whitehead⟩

der·i·va·tion \ˌderəˈvāshən\ *n* -S [MF & L; MF, fr. L *derivation-, derivatio*, fr. *derivatus* + *-ion-, -io* -ion] **1 a** *historical linguistics* (1) **:** the formation of a word from an earlier word or base usu. by the addition of an affix usu. noninflectional (as in *rebuild* from *build* or *boyish* from *boy*), functional change (as in *picnic*, vb., from *picnic*, n.), or back-formation (as in *peddle* from *peddler*) (2) **:** an act of ascertaining or stating the derivation of a word (3) **:** ETYMOLOGY 1a **b** *descriptive linguistics* (1) **:** the relation of a word to its base as expressed usu. in terms of presence of an affix (as in *peddler*, base *peddle*, or *teaches*, base *teach*), vowel alternation (as in *rode*, base *ride*, or *song*, base *sing*), consonant alternation (as in *spent*, base *spend*, or German *halb* \hälp\ "half", base *halb-* \hälb\), difference of accent (as in *convict* \kənˈvikt\, base *convict* \ˈkän,vikt\), absence of one or more sounds (as in French *gris* \grē\, masc., "gray", base *grise* \grēz\, fem.), suppletion (as in *better*, base *good*), or zero difference (as in *sheep*, pl., base *sheep*, sing.) (2) **:** the relation of a word to its base when the two do not belong to the same inflectional paradigm (as in *peddler*, base *peddle*, *song*, base *sing*, *convict* \kənˈvikt\, base *convict* \ˈkän,vikt\) **2** *obs* **:** a handing on or transmission from a source **3 a :** the source from which a thing is derived **:** ORIGIN ⟨a style of writing which has long forgotten its ~ —Maurice Edelman⟩ ⟨hats of French ~⟩ **b :** ORIGINATION, DESCENT ⟨distinguished by ~ from royal ancestors⟩ **4** *obs* **a :** a drawing off of water from its main channel (as for irrigation) **b :** the drawing of inflammation or fluid out of or away from a diseased part of the body **5 :** something that is derived **:** DERIVATIVE, DEDUCTION ⟨the painting seems more like a copy than a ~⟩ ⟨a belief that proved to be an entirely false ~⟩ **6 a :** the act or process of deriving from or as if from an original source ⟨the rational ~ of human law from the law of nature —G.H.Sabine⟩ **b :** an instance or result of being derived ⟨Martha's Vineyard . . . was granted by ~ from the crown of England to Thomas Mayhew —L.C.M.Hare⟩ **7 :** a sequence of statements (as in logic or mathematics) showing that a certain result (as a formula) is a necessary consequence of previously accepted statements

der·i·va·tion·al \ˌderəˈvāshənᵊl, -shnəl\ *adj* **1 :** relating to derivation **2** *linguistics* **:** of, relating to, used in, or characterized by derivation — distinguished from *inflectional*

der·i·va·tion·ist \ˌderəˈvāsh(ə)nə̇st\ *also* **de·riv·a·tist** \dəˈrivəd·ə̇st, dēˈ-\ *n* -S *archaic* **:** EVOLUTIONIST

¹de·riv·a·tive \dəˈrivəd·ǀiv, dēˈ-, -vətǀ\ *adj* [LL *derivativus*, fr. L *derivatus* + *-ivus* -ive] **1** *linguistics* **:** formed by derivation **2 :** made up of or marked by elements or qualities derived from something else (as from an ultimate source) **:** arising from, obtained by, used in, or consisting of derivation **:** lacking originality ⟨~ ecclesiastical structures with which the landscape . . . was dotted in a time when people did not know how to build —G.N.Shuster⟩ ⟨~ presentation of already available data rather than an original contribution —*English Language Teaching*⟩ ⟨artists who spend most of their time with other artists . . . their work thins out, becomes ~, lacks the individual contour —Sidney Alexander⟩ **3 :** SECONDARY, DERIVATIONAL ⟨not only in their direct success but in the ~ benefits that would flow from them —Elmer Davis⟩

²derivative \"\ *n* -S **1 :** a word formed by derivation **2 :** something that derives from, grows out of, or results from an earlier or fundamental state or condition ⟨the sonata form (itself a ~ of opera) —Kingsley Martin⟩ ⟨nostalgia is a fine ~ from any book —Lewis Nichols⟩ **3 :** DERIVATIVE OF A FUNCTION **4 a :** a chemical substance that is so related structurally to another substance as to be theoretically derivable from it even when not so obtainable in practice ⟨the methoxy ~ of naphthalene⟩ **b :** a substance that can be made from another substance in one or more steps ⟨nitration of benzene to the *meta*-dinitro ~⟩ **5 :** one that holds derivative citizenship

derivative action *or* **derivative suit** *n* **:** a suit by a shareholder to enforce a corporate cause of action based upon a right of the corporation

derivative citizenship *n* **:** citizenship derived from that of another (as from a person who holds citizenship by virtue of naturalization)

derivative deposit *n* **:** a bank deposit consisting of the proceeds of a loan credited to the depositor's account — compare PRIMARY DEPOSIT

derivative hybrid *n, bot* **:** the progeny of a cross between a hybrid and either one of its parent species

de·riv·a·tive·ly \ǀəvlē, -li\ *adv* **:** by derivation

de·riv·a·tive·ness \ǀivnə̇s\ *n* -ES **:** the quality or state of being derivative

derivative of a function : the limit if it exists of the quotient of an increment of a dependent variable to the corresponding increment of an associated independent variable as the latter increment tends to zero without being zero

de·riv·a·ti·za·tion \-ˌrivəd·əˈzāshən\ *n* -S **:** the process of derivatizing

de·riv·a·tize \-ˈrivə,tīz\ *vt* -ED/-ING/-S [*derivative* + *-ize*] **:** to convert (a chemical compound) into a derivative usu. for the purpose of identification

de·rive \dəˈrīv, dēˈ-\ *vb* -ED/-ING/-S [ME *deriven* to come (as from a source), receive (as from a source), divert (as water) into a different channel, fr. MF *deriver*, fr. L *derivare* to divert (as water) into a different channel, derive (one word from another), fr. *de-* + *-rivare* (fr. *rivus* stream, brook) — more at RISE] *vt* **1 a :** to take or receive esp. from a source ⟨an English loanword *derived* from German⟩ ⟨the river ~s its name from an Indian chief⟩ ⟨the mills ~ their power from the falls⟩ ⟨he ~s much of his income from investments⟩ **b :** to obtain or gain through heredity or by transmission from environment or circumstance ⟨he *derived* his enthusiasm for the theater from his father⟩ ⟨*deriving* certain dignity from battles fought and won —Richard Llewellyn⟩ ⟨the word *girl* is *derived* from Middle English *girle*⟩ **c :** to acquire, get, or draw (as something pleasant or beneficial) ⟨the satisfaction *derived* from a sense of sharing in creative activities —John Dewey⟩ ⟨the mutual benefits that nations can ~ from trading which flows in both directions —*Lamp*⟩ **d :** ADAPT ⟨a movie *derived* from a novel⟩ **e :** to obtain (a substance) actually or theoretically from a parent substance (as by substitution or hydrolysis) — compare ²DERIVATIVE 4 **2** *archaic* **:** to divert (as water) from its source or normal course **3 :** to gather or arrive at (as a conclusion) by reasoning and observation: **a :** to obtain inductively ⟨ideas *derived* from nature⟩ **:** INFER **b :** DEDUCE ⟨propositions *derived* from axioms⟩ **4** *archaic* **:** to pass along **:** TRANSMIT **5** *archaic* **:** to cause to come ⟨inconvenience that will be *derived* to them from stopping all imports —Thomas Jefferson⟩ **6 :** to trace the origin, descent, or derivation of ⟨we can ~ English *chauffeur* from French⟩ ⟨~ *toaster* from *toast*⟩ ⟨an early theory *derived* speech from involuntary cries⟩ **7 :** to be descended or formed from ⟨all were probably *derived* from the same ancestral stock —M.F.A. Montagu⟩ **:** be a derivative of ⟨the plural is normally *derived* from the singular⟩ ~ *vi* **1** *archaic* **:** DESCEND 3 **2 :** to have or take origin **:** ORIGINATE **:** STEM, EMANATE **:** come as a derivative — usu. used with *from* ⟨all knowledge ~s from sensations —J.H.Randall⟩ ⟨half of his income ~s from wheat⟩ ⟨the social stratum from which he *derived* —Carl Van Doren⟩ ⟨stories *deriving* from his experiences in Africa⟩ **syn** see SPRING

derived *adj* **1 :** formed or developed out of something else **:** DERIVATIVE **:** reflected or secondary in character **:** not original or primary ⟨the belief that individuals are alone real, that classes and organizations are secondary and *derived* —John Dewey⟩ **2 :** brought from elsewhere **:** not native ⟨*derived* fossils⟩

derived curve *n* **:** the graph of the derivative of a function of one variable whose graph is the given curve — called also *first derived curve*

derived function *n, math* **:** the derivative of a given function — called also *first derived function*

derk \ˈderk\ *chiefly Scot var of* DARK

derm \ˈdərm, -ə̄m,-əim\ *n* -S [NL *derma* & *dermis*] **1 :** DERMIS **2 :** SKIN 2a **3 :** CUTICLE 1a

derm- *or* **derma-** *or* **dermo-** *comb form* [NL, fr. Gk *derm-, dermo-*, fr. *derma*, fr. *derein* to skin — more at TEAR] **1 :** skin ⟨*derm*algia⟩ ⟨*derma*hemia⟩ ⟨*dermo*skeleton⟩ **2 :** dermal and ⟨*dermo*humeral⟩

-derm \ˌdərm, -ə̄m,-əim\ *n comb form* -S [prob. fr. F *-derme*, fr. Gk *derma*] **:** skin **:** covering **:** integument ⟨blasto*derm*⟩

¹der·ma \ˈdərmə, -ə̄mə,-əimə\ *n* -S [NL, fr. Gk *derma* skin — more at DERM-] **1 :** DERMIS 1 **2 :** the inner part of the skin of which leather is made, the fat cells and tissues determining the character of leather that can be produced

²der·ma \"\ *n pl but often sing in constr* [Yiddish *derme*, pl. of *darm* intestine, gut, fr. MHG, fr. OHG *darm, daram;* akin to OE *thearm* gut, OFris *therm*, ON *tharmr* gut, Gk *tormos* hole — more at TERM] **:** beef casing — see KISHKE

-der·ma \ˈdərmə, -ə̄mə,-əimə\ *n comb form, pl* **-dermas** \-məz\ *or* **-derma·ta** \-məd·ə,-mətə\ [NL, fr. Gk *dermat-, derma*] **1 :** skin **:** covering **:** integument ⟨sarco*derma*⟩ **2 :** skin or skin ailment of a (specified) type ⟨sclero*derma*⟩ **3 :** one having a (specified) type of skin — in generic names ⟨Helo*derma*⟩

der·ma·cen·tor \ˈdərmə,sentər, ˌ==ˈ==\ *n, cap* [NL, fr. *derm-* + Gk *kentōr* goader, fr. *kentein* to sting, prick, goad] **:** a large widely distributed genus of ornate eyed ticks (family Ixodidae) including a number that attack man and other mammals and several that are vectors of important diseases (as anaplasmosis of cattle, piroplasmosis of dogs, and Rocky Mountain spotted fever of man)

der·mal \ˈdərməl\ *adj* [*derm-* + *-al*] **1 :** of or relating to skin, esp. to the dermis **:** CUTANEOUS **2 :** EPIDERMAL

dermal ossicle *n* **:** a small bone or concretion lying within the skin (as in various reptiles or the extinct ground sloths)

dermal pore *n* **:** one of the minute openings in the surface of a sponge that give access to the incurrent canals **:** OSTIUM

der·ma·nys·sid \ˌdərməˈnisə̇d\ *adj* [NL *Dermanyssidae*] **:** of or relating to the Dermanyssidae

der·ma·nys·si·dae \ˌ==ˈnisə,dē\ *n pl, cap* [NL, fr. *Dermanyssus*, type genus + *-idae*] **:** a family of parasitic mites having the chelicerae adapted for piercing and including several economically important forms (as the chicken mite and the tropical rat mite)

der·ma·nys·sus \-ˈnisəs\ *n, cap* [NL, fr. *derm-* + *-nyssus* (fr. Gk *nyssein* to prick)] **:** the type genus of Dermanyssidae comprising a number of blood-sucking mites that are parasitic on birds — see CHICKEN MITE

der·map·tera \(ˌ)dərˈmaptərə\ *n pl, cap* [NL, fr. *derm-* + *-ptera*] **:** an order of insects consisting of the earwigs and usu. a few related forms parasitic on bats or rats — **der·map·ter·an** \(ˈ)=ˈ=tərən\ *adj or n* — **der·map·ter·ous** \-tərəs\ *adj*

dermasurgery \ˈ==ˌ=(=)=\ *n* [*derm-* + *surgery*] **:** a branch of embalming that deals with the restoration of mutilated or destroyed features or members

dermat- *or* **dermato-** *comb form* [Gk, fr. *dermat-, derma*] **:** skin **:** hide ⟨*dermat*odynia⟩ ⟨*dermato*logy⟩

-der·ma·ta \ˈdərməd·ə, -ə̄m-,-əim-, -ətə\ *n pl comb form* [NL, fr. Gk *dermat-, derma*] **:** ones having a (specified) type of skin — in names of taxonomic categories of animals larger than a genus ⟨Sclero*dermata*⟩

der·ma·tit·ic \ˌdərməˈtid·ik, ˌdə̄m-,ˌdəim-, -ˈtitik\ *adj* [NL *dermatitis* + E *-ic*] **:** relating to dermatitis

der·ma·ti·tis \ˌ==ˈtīd·ə̇s, -ītə̇s\ *n, pl* **dermatiti·ses** \-sə̇z\ *or* **dermatit·i·des** \-ˈtid·ə,dēz\ [NL, fr. *dermat-* + *-itis*] **:** inflammation of the skin typically marked by reddening, swelling, oozing, crusting, or scaling

der·ma·to·bia \-ˈtōbēə\ *n, cap* [NL, fr. *dermat-* + *-bia*] **:** a genus of botflies whose larvae live under the skin of domestic mammals and sometimes of man in tropical America

der·mat·o·cranium \(ˌ)dərˌmad·ə, ˌdərməd·ə +\ *n* [NL, fr. *dermat-* + *cranium*] **:** the part of the skull that develops in the form of membrane bone — compare CHONDROCRANIUM

der·mat·o·gen \(ˌ)dərˈmad·əjən, -ˌjen, ˈdərməd·ə-\ *n* -S [ISV *dermat-* + *-gen*] **1 :** the outer primary meristem of a plant or plant part that according to the histogen theory gives rise to epidermis **2 :** the outer apical meristem of a root tip — called also PROTODERM

der·mato·glyph·ic \(ˌ)dərˌmad·əˈglifik, ˌdərməd·ə-\ *adj* [back-formation fr. *dermatoglyphics*] **:** of or relating to dermatoglyphics

der·mato·glyph·ics \-ks\ *n pl but sing or pl in constr* [*dermat-* + Gk *glyphein* to carve + E *-ics* — more at CLEAVE] **1 :** skin patterns; *specif* **:** patterns of the specialized skin of the inferior surfaces of the hands and feet **2 :** the science of the study of skin patterns

der·mat·o·graph \(ˌ)dərˈmad·ə,graf, ˈdərməd·ə-\ *n* [*dermat-* + *-graph*] **:** an instrument for producing markings on the skin: as **a :** a crayon used by surgeons to outline internal organs on the body surface ⟨sketch the outline of the liver with a ~ on the abdominal skin⟩ **b :** a crayon used to test for allergies

der·mat·o·graph·ia \(ˌ)dərˌmad·əˈgrafēə, ˌdərməd·əˈ-\ *or* **der·ma·tog·ra·phism** \ˌdərməˈtägrə,fizəm\ *n* -S [*dermatographia*, NL, fr. *dermat-* + *-graphia* -graphy; *dermatographism* fr. *dermat-* + *-graph* + *-ism*] **:** DERMOGRAPHIA

der·ma·tog·ra·phy \ˌdərməˈtägrəfē\ *n* -ES [ISV *dermat-* + *-graphy*] **:** anatomical description of the skin

der·mat·o·histology \(ˌ)dərˌmad·ə, ˌdərməd·ō +\ *n* [*dermat-* + *histology*] **:** histology of the skin

der·ma·toid \ˈdərmə,tȯid\ *adj* [ISV *dermat-* + *-oid*] **:** resembling skin

der·mat·o·log·ic \(ˌ)dərˌməd·əˈläjik, ˌdərməd·əˈ-\ *or* **der·mat·o·log·i·cal** \-jəkəl\ *adj* **:** of or relating to dermatology

der·ma·tol·o·gist \ˌdərməˈtäləjə̇st\ *n* -S **:** a specialist in dermatology; *usu* **:** a physician practicing in the field of dermatology

der·ma·tol·o·gy \-jē\ *n* -ES [*dermat-* + *-logy*] **:** a branch of science that is concerned with the skin, its structure, functions, and diseases

der·ma·tome \ˈdərmə,tōm\ *n* -S [ISV *derm-* + *-tome*] **1 :** an instrument for cutting skin for use in grafting **2 a :** the lateral wall of a somite from which the dermis is produced **b :** a segmental skin area delimited by nerve supply

der·mat·o·mere \(ˌ)dərˈmad·ə,mi(ə)r, ˈdərməd·ə,-\ *n* -S [ISV *dermat-* + *-mere*] **:** DERMATOME 2

der·ma·tom·ic \ˌdərməˈtämik\ *also* **der·ma·to·mal** \-ˈtōməl\ *or* **der·mat·o·mat·ic** \(ˌ)dərˌmad·əˈmad·ik, ˌdərməd·əˈ-\ *adj* **:** of or relating to a dermatome

der·mat·o·my·ces \(ˌ)dərˌmad·əˈmī,sēz, ˌdərməd·əˈ-\ *n, pl* **dermatomyce·tes** \-ˌmīˈsēd·ēz\ [NL, fr. *dermat-* + *-myces*] **:** DERMATOPHYTE

der·mat·o·my·co·sis \-ˌmīˈkōsə̇s\ *n, pl* **dermatomyco·ses** \-ˌsēz\ [NL, fr. *dermat-* + *mycosis*] **:** a disease of the skin caused by infection with a fungus

der·mat·o·my·o·si·tis \-ˌmīəˈsīd·ə̇s\ *n* [NL, fr. *dermat-* + *myositis*] **:** a chronic inflammation of the skin, subcutaneous tissue, and skeletal muscles of unknown cause

der·mat·o·path·ia \-ˈpathēə\ *also* **der·ma·top·a·thy** \ˌdərməˈtäpəthē\ *n, pl* **dermatopathias** *also* **dermatopathies** [NL *dermatopathia*, fr. *dermat-* + *-pathia* -pathy] **:** disease of the skin — **der·mat·o·path·ic** \(ˌ)dərˌmad·əˈpathik, ˌdərməd·əˈ-\ *adj*

der·mat·o·phyte \(ˌ)dərˈmad·ə,fīt, ˈdərməd·ə,-\ *n* -S [ISV *dermat-* + *-phyte*] **:** a fungus parasitic upon the skin or skin derivatives (as hair or nails) of man or lower animals — compare DERMATOMYCOSIS — **der·mat·o·phyt·ic** \(ˌ)dər,mad·əˈfid·ik, ˌdərməd·əˈ-\ *adj* — **der·mat·o·phy·to·sis** \-ˌfīˈtōsə̇s\ *n*

der·mat·o·phy·tid \ˌdərˌmad·əˈfīd·əd, ˌdərməd·əˈ-\ *n* -S **:** a skin eruption associated with a fungus infection; *esp* **:** one considered to be due to allergic reaction

der·ma·top·sy \ˈdərmə,täpsē\ *n* -ES [ISV *dermat-* + *-opsy*] **:** sensitiveness of the skin to light (as in some worms) — **der·ma·top·tic** \ˌ==ˈtäptik\ *adj*

der·ma·to·sclerosis *n, pl* **dermatoscleroses** \(ˌ)dər,mad·ə, ˌdərməd·ə+\ [NL, fr. *dermat-* + *sclerosis*] **:** SCLERODERMA

der·ma·to·sis \ˌdərməˈtōsə̇s\ *n, pl* **dermato·ses** \-ˌsēz\ [NL, fr. *dermat-* + *-osis*] **:** a disease of the skin

der·mat·o·some \(ˌ)dərˈmad·ə,sōm, ˈdərməd·ə,-\ *n* -S [ISV *dermat-* + *-some;* orig. formed as G *dermatosom*] **:** one of the ranked particulate elements joined by cytoplasm that in one theory of cell-wall structure are held to make up the plant cell wall; *broadly* **:** a structural unit of cellulose in a plant cell wall

der·mat·o·tome \-ˌtōm\ *n* -S [*dermat-* + *-tome*] **:** DERMATOME 2

dermatotropic *var of* DERMOTROPIC

-der·ma·tous \ˌdərməd·əs, -ə̄m-,-əim-, -mətəs\ *adj comb form* [NL *-dermata* + E *-ous*] **:** having a (specified) type of skin ⟨sclero*dermatous*⟩

der·mes·tes \dərˈme,stēz\ *n, cap* [NL, fr. Gk *dermēstēs* worm that eats skin or leather, fr. *derm-* + *-ēstēs* (fr. *esthiein* to eat); akin to Gk *edmenai* to eat — more at EAT] **:** the type genus of Dermestidae — see LARDER BEETLE, MUSEUM BEETLE

¹der·mes·tid \dərˈmestə̇d\ *adj* [NL *Dermestidae*, fr. *Dermestes*, type genus + *-idae*] **:** of or relating to the Dermestidae

²dermestid \"\ *n* -S **:** a beetle of the family Dermestidae

der·mes·ti·dae \-tə,dē\ *n pl, cap* [NL, fr. *Dermestes*, type genus + *-idae*] **:** a family of small beetles that have clubbed antennae and are very destructive both as larvae and adults to organic material of animal origin (as dried meats, fur, wool, or insect collections)

-der·mia \ˈdərmēə, -ə̄m-,-əim-\ *n comb form* -S [NL, fr. Gk *derma* skin + NL *-ia* — more at DERM-] **:** skin or skin ailment of a (specified) type ⟨pachy*dermia*⟩

der·mic \ˈdərmik\ *adj* [*derm-* + *-ic*] **:** DERMAL

der·mis \ˈdərmə̇s, -ə̄m-,-əim-\ *n* -ES [*-dermis*] **1 :** the sensitive vascular inner mesodermic layer of the skin made up chiefly of white fibrous connective tissue with some smooth muscle and elastic tissue and numerous nerves and sensory receptors — called also *corium, cutis* **2 :** the uppermost layer of the thallus of many lichens that consists of one or more layers of irregular flattened hyphal cells with somewhat gelatinous walls

-der·mis \ˌ==\ *n comb form* -ES [LL, fr. Gk, fr. *derma* skin] **:** layer of skin or tissue ⟨endo*dermis*⟩

dermo- — see DERM-

der·mo·blast \ˈdərmə,blast\ *n* -S [ISV *derm-* + *-blast*] **:** dermatomes (sense 2a) as a group

der·mo·branchia *or* **der·mo·branchiata** \ˌdərmə+\ [NL, fr. *derm-* + *branchia, -branchiata*] *syn of* NUDIBRANCHIA

der·mo·branchiate \ˌ==+\ *adj* [NL *Dermobranchia* + E *-ate*] **:** NUDIBRANCHIATE

der·moch·e·lys \dərˈmäkələs\ *n, cap* [NL, fr. *derm-* + Gk *chelys* tortoise — more at CHELYS] **:** a genus (the type of the family Dermochelidae) of large marine turtles including only the leatherback

der·mo·dermaptera \ˌdərmə+\ [NL, fr. *derm-* + *Dermaptera*] *syn of* DIPLOGLOSSATA

der·mog·e·nys \(ˌ)dərˈmäjənə̇s\ *n, cap* [NL, fr. *derm-* + Gk *genys* jaw, cheek — more at CHIN] **:** a genus of Siamese halfbeaks including one (*D. pusillus*) sometimes kept in a tropical aquarium

der·mo·graph·ia \ˌdərməˈgrafēə\ *or* **der·mog·ra·phism** \(ˌ)dərˈmägrə,fizəm\ *n* -S [*dermographia*, NL, fr. *derm-* + *-graphia* -graphy; *dermographism* fr. *derm-* + *-graph* + *-ism*] **:** a condition in which pressure or friction on the skin gives rise to a transient raised usu. reddish mark so that a word traced on the skin becomes visible — **der·mo·graph·ic** \ˌdərməˈgrafik\ *adj*

der·moid \ˈdər,mȯid\ *also* **der·moi·dal** \(ˈ)=ˌ=dᵊl\ *adj* [*derm-* + *-oid, -oidal*] **:** made up of cutaneous elements esp. of ectodermal derivatives ⟨a ~ tumor⟩ **:** resembling skin

dermoid cyst *also* **dermoid** *n* -S **:** a frequently ovarian cystic tumor containing skin and skin derivatives (as hair or teeth)

der·mo·muscular \ˌdərmə+\ *adj* [*derm-* + *muscular*] **1 :** of or relating to both skin and musculature **2 :** combining the function of skin and muscle ⟨certain cells in the body wall of lower invertebrate animals are ~⟩

der·mop·tera \dərˈmäpt(ə)rə\ *n pl, cap* [NL, fr. *derm-* + *-ptera*] **:** a small order of eutherian mammals comprising the flying lemurs — **der·mop·ter·an** \(ˈ)=ˈ=t(ə)rən\ *adj or n* — **der·mop·ter·ous** \-t(ə)rəs\ *adj*

der·mo·skeleton \ˌdərmə+\ *n* [*derm-* + *skeleton*] **1 :** EXOSKELETON **2 :** the portion of the vertebrate skeleton that develops as membrane bone

der·mo·tactile \ˌ==+\ *adj* [*derm-* + *tactile*] **:** of or relating to the tactile sensitivity of the skin

der·mo·trop·ic \ˌdərməˈträpik\ *also* **der·mat·o·trop·ic** \(ˌ)dərˌmad·əˈträpik, ˌdərməd·əˈ-\ *adj* [*derm-* or *dermato-* + *-tropic*] **:** attracted to, localizing in, or entering by way of the skin ⟨~ viruses⟩ — compare NEUROTROPIC

derms *pl of* DERM

-derms *pl of* -DERM

¹dern \ˈdern, ˈdərn\ *adj* [ME *derne*, fr. OE *dyrne, dierne;* akin to OS *derni* secret, OHG *tarni*, L *firmus* firm — more at FIRM] **1** *now chiefly dial* **a :** HIDDEN, SECRET **b :** CRAFTY, UNDERHANDED **2** *now chiefly dial* **:** DREAR, DARK, SOMBER, DIRE **3** *dial Eng* **:** EARNEST, DETERMINED

²dern \"\ *vb* -ED/-ING/-S [ME *dernen*, fr. OE *dyrnan;* akin to OHG *ternen, tarnen* to hide, conceal, OS *dernian;* denominatives fr. the root of OE *dyrne* secret, hidden] *now chiefly Scot* **:** HIDE, CONCEAL

³dern \ˈdərn, -ə̄n,-əin\ *dial var of* DARN

¹der·nier \ˈdərnēər, (ˈ)dernˌyā\ *adj* [F, fr. OF *derrenier*, fr. *darrain, derrein* — more at DARREIN] *archaic* **:** LAST, FINAL

²der·nier \(ˈ)dernˌyā\ *n* -S [F, fr. *dernier* last] **:** the third of the three columns on a roulette layout on which one may bet and which embraces the numbers 25 to 36 inclusive

der·nier cri \ˌdern,yāˈkrē\ *n* [F, lit., last cry] **:** the latest or most authoritative thing **:** the last word; *specif* **:** the newest fashion ⟨strapless gowns were the *dernier cri*⟩ **syn** see FASHION

dernier res·sort *or* **dernier re·sort** \-ərəˈzō(ə)r, -rəˈsō-\ *n* [F *dernier ressort*] **:** a last resort or expedient

dero \ˈde(ˌ)rō\ *n, cap* [NL] **:** a genus of small aquatic oligochaete worms (family Naididae) having an expanded anal hood from which project two pairs of cylindrical ciliated gills

dero- — see DER-

¹der·o·gate \ˈderə,gāt, *usu* -ād·+V\ *vb* -ED/-ING/-S [L *derogatus,* past part. of *derogare,* fr. *de-* + *rogare* to ask, ask the people about a law — more at RIGHT] *vt* **1** *obs* **:** to annul or repeal in part (as a law or sentence) **:** restrict the force of (a law) **2 :** to make to seem inferior **:** lower in esteem **:** DISPARAGE, DECRY ⟨it is the aim of this paper to ~ a somewhat condescending attitude toward Oriental philosophy that is prevalent among a number of western thinkers —Jack Kaminsky⟩ **3** *archaic* **:** to take away (a part or quality of something) so as to do injury to the whole — used with *from* ~ *vi* **1 :** to place something at a disadvantage or in disesteem esp. by taking part of it away **:** DETRACT — used with *from* ⟨increase the authority of each dominion and not ~ from it —R.G.Menzies⟩ ⟨some are trying to ~ from his reputation as a leader⟩ **2 :** to deviate or go astray (as from a principle or standard) — used with *from* **syn** see DECRY

²der·o·gate \-,gət,-,gāt\ *adj* [L *derogatus*] *archaic* **:** INFERIOR, DEBASED

derogately *adv, obs* **:** DEROGATORILY

der·o·ga·tion \,derə'gāshən\ *n* -S [ME *derogacioun,* fr. MF or L; MF *derogation,* fr. L *derogation-, derogatio,* fr. *derogatus* + *-ion-, -io* -ion] **1 :** partial repeal (as of a law, contract, treaty) — used with *of* or *to* **2 a :** a taking away, lessening, or detraction esp. of power, reputation, value — used with *of* or *from* ⟨a serious ~ of his influence and prestige⟩ ⟨it is no necessary ~ from his book that the humor is about the humor of alumni magazines and college reunions —Howard M. Jones⟩ **b :** DISPARAGEMENT, DETRIMENT ⟨without ~ to his high rank⟩

de·rog·a·tive \də'rägəd·iv *also* 'derə,gād·-\ *adj* [ME, fr. MF or LL; MF *derogatif,* fr. LL *derogativus,* fr. L *derogatus* + *-ivus* -ive] **:** tending to derogate — used with *to* or *of*

derogator *n* -S [LL, fr. L *derogatus* + *-or*] *obs* **:** DETRACTOR

de·rog·a·to·ri·ly \də¦rägə¦tōrəlē, dē¦-, -ōr-, -li\ *adv* **:** in a derogatory manner

de·rog·a·to·ri·ness *pronunc at* DEROGATORY + nəs\ *n* -ES **:** the quality of being derogatory

de·rog·a·to·ry \də'rägə,tōrē, dē'-, -ōr-, -ri\ *adj* [LL *derogatorius,* fr. L *derogatus* + *-orius* -ory] **1 :** characterized by or tending toward derogation **:** DISPARAGING, DETRACTING, DEGRADING, DEPRECIATORY — used with *to, from,* or *of* ⟨the crude fact of money-making was still regarded as ~ —Edith Wharton⟩ ⟨express his feelings on the tender or emotional side without feeling it ~ to his manhood —Bram Stoker⟩ **2 :** expressive of low estimation or reproach **:** DISDAINFUL ⟨trying to discredit the speaker by making ~ remarks about his appearance⟩ ⟨a child hostile and ~ toward everyone⟩ ⟨few of the Normans who received large estates in England deserve to be called adventurers, in the ~ sense of the word —F.M.Stenton⟩

derogatory clause *n* **:** a clause in a legal document (as a will) making any future altering or canceling document invalid except upon the recital of the clause word for word and its formal revocation

der·o·trem·a·ta \,derə·'tremədə, -rēm-\ *n pl, cap* [NL, fr. *der-* + *-tremata*] *in some esp former classifications* **:** a division of tailed amphibians typically retaining gill slits but not external gills when adult and comprising the Cryptobranchidae and Amphiumidae — **der·o·trem·ate** \¦==¦=mət, -,māt\ *or* **der·o·trem·a·tous** \-mədəs\ *adj* — **der·o·treme** \'derə-,trēm\ *n* -S

¹de·rout \(ʹ)dē, də+\ *vt* [obs. F *dérouter,* fr. OF *desroter, desrouter,* fr. *des-* de- + *rote, route* troop, band, defeat — more at ROUT (troop)] **:** to rout completely

²derout \"\ *n* [F *déroute,* fr. OF *desrote, desroute,* fr. *desroter, desrouter*] **:** utter defeat **:** ROUT

der·ren·ga·de·ra \(,)de,reŋgə'derə\ *n* -S [AmerSp, fr. Sp *derrengar* to injure the back or kidneys, fr. (assumed) VL *derenicare,* fr. L *de-* + *ren* kidney] **:** MAL DE CADERAS

¹der·rick \'derik, -rēk\ *n* -S [after *Derick* (first name unknown) *fl ab*1600 hangman at Tyburn, England] **1** *obs* **a :** HANGMAN **b :** GALLOWS **2 :** any of various hoisting apparatus employing a tackle rigged at the end of a beam: as **a** *obs* **:** a tackle rigged at the outer quarter of a mizzen yard **b :** a spar standing on end and carrying at the upper end a hoisting tackle, the upper end being also secured by guys sometimes in such a manner as to permit adjustments of the angle of the spar to the horizontal **c :** a crane consisting of a pivoting mast having fastened to its lower end a boom carrying at its outer end a hoisting tackle, the outer end also being secured by a tackle to the head of the mast so as to permit raising and lowering of the end of the boom **d :** a fixed arm or bracket projecting from a wall with a hoisting tackle at its end (as over a warehouse door) **3 a :** the framework or tower over a deep drill hole (as that of an oil well) for supporting the tackle for boring or for hoisting and lowering **b :** a tall three-legged staging erected to support a hoisting tackle (as in building construction)

derrick 3a

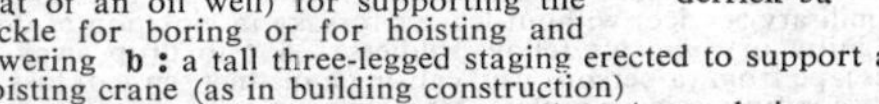

²derrick \", *esp in pres part* -rək\ *vt* -ED/-ING/-S **:** to hoist, convey, or load by means of a derrick

derricking *adj* **:** operating like a derrick in the raising and lowering of the jib ⟨a ~ crane⟩

der·rick·man \-mən, -,man\ *n, pl* **derrickmen 1 :** a worker who operates a derrick **2 :** a member of a crew that rigs oil-well derricks and assists with the drilling of wells

derrick post *n* **:** KING POST 2

der·ri·en·gue \,derē'eŋ,gā\ *n* -S [MexSp] **:** a highly fatal paralytic disease of cattle and sometimes other livestock that occurs in the Pacific coast states of Mexico and is caused by a virus related to or identical with that of rabies and prob. transmitted by the bite of vampire bats

¹der·rière \,derē¦e(ə)r, (ʹ)der¦ye-, -eə\ *adj* [F, fr. OF *deriere,* fr. L *de retro* from the back] **:** BACK, BEHIND — used in ballet of a movement, the execution of a step, or motion of arms or legs

²der·riere *or* **der·rière** \"\ *n* -S [F, fr. *derrière,* adj.] **:** BUTTOCKS, RUMP ⟨a wide tuck starts three inches below the pocket flaps and dips well below the ~ —Lois Long⟩ ⟨you should pull up with your chest, in with your diaphragm, and down with your ~ —Maribel Y. Vinson⟩

der·ring–do \¦deriŋ¦dü, -rēŋ-\ *n, pl* **derrings–do** [alter. of ME *dorring don, durring don* daring to do (taken as a n.), fr. pres. part. of *dorren, durren* to dare + *don* to do — more at DARE, DO] **1 :** daring action **:** DARING, COURAGE, BRAVERY ⟨the first airmail flight — a deed of *derring-do* by an army pilot —*Time*⟩ **2 :** BRAVADO ⟨the days of *derring-do* when swords flashed in rescue of beautiful highborn maidens —J.D. Hart⟩

der·rin·ger \'derənjə(r)\ *n* -S [after Henry *Deringer,* 19th cent. Am. inventor] **:** a short-barreled pocket pistol

der·ris \'derəs\ *n* [NL, fr. Gk, leather covering, skin, fr. *derein* to skin — more at TEAR] **1** *cap* **:** a large genus of tropical Old World shrubs and woody vines (family Leguminosae) including several that are used as sources of native fish poisons and arrow poisons and commercially as sources of rotenone and related insecticidal substances **2** -ES **:** any plant of the genus *Derris* (esp. *D. elliptica*) **3** -ES **:** a preparation of derris roots and stems that contains rotenone and rotenoids and is esp. important as an insecticide

¹der·ry \'derē, -ri\ *adj, usu cap* [by shortening] **:** LONDONDERRY

²derry \"\ *n* -ES [origin unknown] *Austral* **:** DISLIKE, AVERSION — usu. used with *on* ⟨her father had an unaccountable ~ on the family⟩

de·ru·ta \dā'rüd·ə\ *n, usu cap* [fr. *Deruta,* village in Perugia province, Italy, where it is produced] **:** an Italian majolica ware

der·vish \'dərvish, -əv-,-əiv-, -vēsh *sometimes* 'derv- *or* 'deəv-\ *n* -ES [Turk *derviş,* lit., beggar, fr. Per *darvēsh*] **1 :** a member of any Muslim religious fraternity of monks or mendicants noted for its forms of devotional exercises (as group repetition of religious formulas or concerted bodily movements often leading to a kind of trance or ecstasy) — often used with a qualifier such as *howling, whirling, dancing;* compare FAKIR **2 :** something that whirls or dances with or as if with the abandon of a dervish ⟨the most blinding of the snow ~*es* that whirled across him —W.V.T.Clark⟩ ⟨a very ~ dance of fury —Brendan Behan⟩

der·vish·hood \-sh,hu̇d\ *n* -S **:** the status of or the condition of being a dervish

der·vish·ism \-sh,izəm\ *n* -S **:** the principles or practices of the dervishes

des *pl of* DE

des- *prefix* [F *dés-,* fr. OF *des-* — more at DE-] **1 :** DE- 1 — esp. before vowels ⟨*desamidate*⟩ **2 :** DE- 6 — esp. before vowels ⟨*desiodo-*⟩ ⟨*desoxy-*⟩

des *abbr* **1** deserted; deserter; desertion **2** design; designed **3** desired

desa *also* **des·sa** \'desə\ *n* -S [Jav *désa,* fr. Skt *deśa* place, country] **:** a village community in Java, Bali, or Madura formerly relatively independent

de·sa·cral·i·za·tion \(,)dē,sākrələ'zāshən\ *n* -S **:** the act of desacralizing or state of being desacralized

de·sa·cral·ize \(ʹ)dē'sākrə,līz\ *vt* -ED/-ING/-S [*de-* + *sacral* + *-ize*] **:** to divest ceremonially of supernatural qualities or a taboo and render nonsacred

de·salinization *also* **de·salination** \(ʹ)dē+\ *n* -S [*de-* + *salinization* or *salination*] **:** removal of salt (as from water) **:** reduction of the salt content (as of soil by leaching)

de·salt \(ʹ)dē+\ *vt* [*de-* + *salt* (n.)] **:** to remove salt from (as sea water) **:** DEIONIZE, DEMINERALIZE — **de·salter** \"+\ *n* -S

desamidate *var of* DEAMIDATE

desamination *var of* DEAMINATION

de·sanctify \(ʹ)dē+\ *vt* [*de-* + *sanctify*] **:** to divest of sanctification

de·sand \(ʹ)dē+\ *vt* [*de-* + *sand* (n.)] **:** to remove sand from

de·sargues's theorem \dā'zärgz-\ *n, usu cap D* [after Gérard *Desargues* †1662 Fr. mathematician] **:** a theorem in geometry: if the junction lines of corresponding vertices of two triangles are concurrent the junction points of the corresponding sides lie on the same straight line, the converse also being true

de·saturate \(ʹ)dē+\ *vb* [*de-* + *saturate*] *vt* **:** to cause to become unsaturated ⟨the polarizer helps remove scattered light that ~*s* color in the picture —*Eastman Kodak Monthly Abstract Bull.*⟩ ~ *vi* **:** to become unsaturated — **de·saturation** \"+\ *n*

desc *abbr* descendant

de·scale \(ʹ)dē+\ *vt* [*de-* + *scale* (n.)] **:** to free from scale

des·ca·mi·sa·do \,de,skamə'sä(,)dō\ *n* -S [Sp, fr. *descamisado* poor, fr. *des-* dis- (fr. L *dis-*) + *camisa* shirt + *-ado* -ate (fr. L *-atus*) — more at CAMISA] **1 a :** an extreme liberal of the Spanish revolution of 1820–23 **b :** a violent revolutionist **2** [AmerSp, fr. Sp] **:** an Argentine worker esp. when poor and underprivileged

¹des·cant \'de,skant, -kaa(ə)nt\ *or* **dis·cant** \'di,-\ *n* -S [ME *dyscant,* fr. ONF & ML; ONF *descant,* fr. ML *discantus,* fr. L ¹*dis-* + *cantus* song — more at CHANT] **1 a :** a melody or counterpoint sung above the plainsong of the tenor **b :** the art of composing or improvising contrapuntal part music; *also* **:** the music so composed or improvised **c :** the upper voice (as soprano, treble) in part music **d :** a superimposed counterpoint to a hymn tune or other simple melody sung typically by some or all of the sopranos **2 :** a song or strain of melody ⟨the birds in vain their amorous ~ join —Thomas Gray⟩ **3 a :** a musical prelude in which a theme is varied **b :** discourse or comment on a theme felt to resemble variations on a musical air **:** OBSERVATION, REMARK ⟨provides a noble ~ on the theme of our human mystery —*Times Lit. Supp.*⟩ **4** *obs* **a :** variation from what is customary or an instance of it **b :** carping criticism **5 :** an extended and often warmly enthusiastic expression of one's convictions or interests

²des·cant \'de,skant, də's-,de's-, -kaa(ə)nt\ *vi* -ED/-ING/-S **1 a :** to sing or play a descant **b :** SING, WARBLE **2 :** to discuss discerningly and at considerable length on a subject evoking one's keen interest ⟨on that favorite poet of mine, Sir Thomas Wyat, I ~*ed* in a former lecture —A.T.Quiller-Couch⟩ ⟨~*ing* on her love of flowers, a passion that was among her prettiest originalities —Edith Sitwell⟩ ⟨the temptation to ~ in detail on tidbits —R.T.House⟩ **:** DILATE — used with *on* or *upon* **syn** see DISCOURSE

des·cant·er *pronunc at* ²DESCANT +ə(r)\ *n* -S **:** one that descants

des·cant·ist *pronunc at* ¹DESCANT +əst\ *n* -S **:** one proficient in descant

descant recorder *n, chiefly Brit* **:** SOPRANO RECORDER

descant viol *n* **1 :** TREBLE VIOL **2 :** PARDESSUS DE VIOLE

des·cartes's rule of signs \(ʹ)dā¦kärts-, -kāts-\ *usu cap D* [after René *Descartes* †1650 Fr. philosopher and mathematician] **:** a rule of algebra: in an algebraic equation with real coefficients, $F(x) = 0$, arranged according to powers of x, the number of positive roots cannot exceed the number of variations in the signs of the coefficients of the various powers and the difference between the number of positive roots and the number of variations in the signs of the coefficients is even

des·cart·ian \(ʹ)dā¦kärd·ēən\ *adj, usu cap* [R. *Descartes* + E *-ian*] **:** CARTESIAN

des·ce·met's membrane \(ʹ)de¦sm¦āz, ¦desə¦m¦\ *n, usu cap D* [after Jean *Descemet* †1810 Fr. anatomist] **:** a transparent highly elastic apparently structureless membrane lined with endothelium and covering the inner surface of the cornea

de·scend \də'send, dē'-\ *vb* -ED/-ING/-S [ME *descenden,* fr. OF *descendre,* fr. L *descendere,* fr. *de-* + *-scendere* (fr. *scandere* to climb) — more at SCAN] *vi* **1 :** to go or come down: **a :** to pass from a higher place or spatial level to a lower one **:** move downward ⟨these fish winter up the river . . . and ~ to the sea . . in the spring —*Biol. Abstracts*⟩ ⟨the river ~*s* 18 feet in one mile⟩ ⟨the paper ~*s* from one roller onto another⟩ **b :** to appear or enter from above or from a spiritual realm ⟨to her it seemed that a god had ~*ed* from the blue sky personally to aid her —Charles Beadle⟩ ⟨he felt a great being ~*ing* into him and strengthening him —W.B.Yeats⟩; *specif* **:** to settle down like a blanket or curtain ⟨the sound that irresistibly you make when death is about to ~ —F.M.Ford⟩ **c** *archaic* **:** to withdraw or retreat from social intercourse and seclude oneself in personal or mental absorption **d** *of the testes of a mammal* **:** to pass from the abdominal cavity into the scrotum **2 :** to pass in discussion from what in logical order precedes or from what is the more comprehensive or universal ⟨descend to causes, ~ to consequences⟩ ⟨the writer ~*s* from the general to the particular —*Times Lit. Supp.*⟩ **3 a :** to come down or spring from a stock or source **:** ORIGINATE, DERIVE ⟨the family ~*ed* from Scotch-Irish immigrants who came to America in the 18th century⟩ ⟨historians report that he ~*ed* from an ancient family of noble lineage⟩ **b :** to pass by inheritance ⟨that kingship was divinely ordained to ~ according to strict hereditary principles —J.H.Plumb⟩ ⟨heirlooms which have ~*ed* in families since the original Pennsylvania Dutch immigrants arrived —V.R.Tortora⟩ **c :** to pass by transmission **:** take origin or pattern or acquire character from a precursor ⟨songs ~*ed* from early ballads⟩ ⟨if, as some scholars believe, Greek liturgical music ~*s* from the hymns to the Olympian gods —*N.Y.Times*⟩ **4 :** to incline, lead, or extend downward **:** form or follow a downgrade ⟨the coastal mountains ~*ed* precipitously to the very edge of the Pacific —R.A.Billington⟩ ⟨the road ~*s* to the flatland⟩ **5 a :** to swoop or pounce down or make a sudden attack — usu. used with *on* or *upon* ⟨the plague ~*ed* upon them⟩ ⟨if the enemy ~*ed* on his country⟩ **b :** to converge or materialize as if from above with disconcerting abruptness or in formidable array — used with *on* or *upon* ⟨one evening the police ~*ed* quietly, without warning, on a dozen or so drive-in taverns —Green Peyton⟩ ⟨over a hundred newspaper reporters from all over America ~*ed* upon that amazed little southern town to cover the trial —R.W.Murray⟩; *also* **:** to make a startling or exciting visitation ⟨the most famous visitors, licit or otherwise, to ~ on the island —Horace Sutton⟩ **c :** to pour down or in with beneficent effect — used with *on* or *upon* ⟨then fame and royalties ~*ed* upon him —E.A. Weeks⟩ **6 :** to proceed in a sequence or gradation from higher to lower or from more remote to nearer or more recent ⟨this list is arranged in ~*ing* order of the reliability of the information —R.N.Denney⟩ ⟨we shall expect to find the curves of art and spiritual fervor ascending and ~*ing* together —Clive Bell⟩ **7 a :** to sink in status or dignity **:** demean or degrade oneself by indulgence in pettiness or unworthy behavior **:** STOOP ⟨ashamed of myself for having ~*ed* to a kind of wheedling —Kenneth Roberts⟩ ⟨his successor, after failing to dominate, ~*ed* to reckless abuse —Raymond Moley⟩ **b :** to worsen and sink in condition or estimation **:** become degraded **:** DEGENERATE ⟨the family ~*ed* from comparative prosperity to poverty⟩ ⟨her autobiography ~*s* to a dragging pedestrianism⟩ ⟨his attacks ~ to a level almost indistinguishable from personal character assassination —Martin Gardner⟩ **c :** to pass from higher to lower musical notes or tones ~ *vt* **1** *obs* **:** to cause to descend **:** bring down ⟨power to raise some and ~ others⟩ **2 a :** to pass, move, or climb down or down along ⟨~*ed* the steps with senile deliberation —Arnold Bennett⟩ **b :** to journey downstream along (a stream) or toward the foot of (a lake) **3 :** to extend down along ⟨a raw scar ~*s* the side of the mountain showing the course of a slide⟩ ⟨vertical tucks ~*ing* the bodice —Lois Long⟩

syn DISMOUNT, ALIGHT: these have in common a sense of getting or coming down from a height. One DESCENDS when one goes or climbs down a slope or incline, as of a mountain, hill, ladder, stair, tree, and so on. One DISMOUNTS by getting off (the back of a horse or other ridable animal, a bicycle, motorcycle, or similar vehicle). One ALIGHTS when one dismounts with a certain springing lightness or grace or when one gets down from a carriage, gets out of a car or off a plane.

de·scend·ance *also* **de·scend·ence** \-ndən(t)s\ *n* -S [MF *descendance,* fr. OF, fr. *descendre* + *-ance*] **1 :** descent from a particular ancestor **2 :** derivation from predecessors

de·scend·an·cy *or* **de·scend·en·cy** \-dənsē, -si\ *n* -ES [F *descendance* (fr. OF) + E *-y*] *archaic* **:** lineal descent

¹de·scend·ant *also* **de·scend·ent** \-dənt\ *adj* [MF & L; MF *descendant,* fr. L *descendent-, descendens,* pres. part. of *descendere*] **1 :** DESCENDING 1 **2 :** proceeding from an ancestor or source ⟨eighth in the ~ line from the original immigrant⟩

²descendant *also* **descendent** \"\ *n* -S [F & L; *descendant,* fr. L *descendent-, descendens,* fr. *descendent-, descendens,* pres. part.] **1 a :** one that is descended from another or from a common stock ⟨the ~*s* of King David⟩ ⟨the several cultivated ~*s* of the native persimmon⟩ — distinguished from *ancestor, ascendant* **b :** a lineal or collateral blood relative usu. of a later generation — compare ISSUE **2 :** something that derives its character directly from a precursor or prototype ⟨the vertebral column is the altered ~ of the notochord⟩; *esp* **:** an offshoot from an antecedent practice or idea ⟨the modern signet ring is a ~ of the scarab ring —Elizabeth W. King⟩ ⟨the maypole dance is said to be a ~ of an ancient fertility dance⟩ **3 :** a follower or disciple who shows close adherence to the principles and methods of an earlier master in some literary, learned, or artistic specialty ⟨though not all the ~*s* of Kant agree —J.G.Gray⟩ — **in the descendant** *also* **on the descendant :** DECLINING, WANING

de·scen·den·tal \¦dē,sen¦dentᵊl\ *adj* [¹*descendent* + *-al* (as in *transcendental*)] **:** EMPIRICAL, POSITIVISTIC — opposed to *transcendental* — **de·scen·den·tal·ism** \,=,=ᵊ=,izəm\ *n* -S — **de·scen·den·tal·ist** \-əst\ *n* -S — **de·scen·den·tal·is·tic** \,=,=ᵊ='istik\ *adj*

¹descender *n* -S [ME, fr. MF *descendre* to descend — more at DESCEND] *law, obs* **:** DESCENT **:** title of descent

²de·scend·er \də'sendə(r), dē'-\ *n* -S [*descend* + *-er*] **1 :** one that descends ⟨the solitary ~ from the train —James Schuyler⟩ **2 a :** the part of a lowercase letter (as q, p, y, *j*) that is lower than the lowest part of an x-height letter (as o, a, e); *also* **:** a corresponding short tail to a letter whose lower limit does not exceed or markedly exceed the lower limit of an x-height letter **b :** a descending letter or character (as g and ;); *also* **:** the descending part of a descending character

de·scend·ibil·i·ty \=,=də'biləd·ē\ *n* -ES **:** the property or condition of being descendible

de·scend·ible \=ʹ=dəbəl\ *adj* [ME *descendable,* fr. MF, fr. *descendre* to descend + *-able*] **1 :** descending or being capable of descending from an ancestor to an heir **:** DEVISABLE **2 :** admitting descent ⟨a downgrade safely ~ only with tire chains⟩

de·scend·ing \'də,sendiŋ, də's-\ *adj* **1 :** that descends **:** moving or directed downward ⟨following are the amounts contributed by classes in ~ order⟩ ⟨does not distinguish ascending and ~ lineal relatives —G.M.Foster⟩ ⟨~ infection from the kidney —*Therapeutic Notes*⟩ ⟨the ~ interval of the minor third occurs with special prominence and frequency —*Amer. Guide Series: Minn.*⟩ **2 :** having a descender ⟨a ~ letter⟩ **3** *heraldry* **:** in a head-downward position ⟨a dolphin ~⟩

descending aorta *n* **:** the part of the aorta from the arch to its bifurcation that passes downward in the thoracic and abdominal cavities

descending diphthong *n* **:** FALLING DIPHTHONG

descending line *n* **:** the portion of a line of direct descent that represents descendants of a given individual — compare CONSANGUINITY 1

de·scend·ing·ly *adv* **:** in a downward direction; *specif* **:** southward in the sky

descending node *n* **:** the node passed as an astronomical body goes south

descending raceme *n* **:** a scorpioid cyme

descending rhythm *n* **:** FALLING RHYTHM

descends *pres 3d sing of* DESCEND

de·scen·sion \də'senchən, dē'-\ *n* -S [ME *descensioun,* fr. MF *descension,* fr. L *descension-, descensio,* fr. *descensus* (past part. of *descendere* to descend) + *-ion-, -io* -ion — more at DESCEND] **1** *archaic* **:** downward motion or direction **2 :** the part of the zodiac in which in astrology a planet's influence is thought to be least — opposed to *exaltation* **3** *obs* **:** descent from an ancestor **4 :** descent from rank, station, or prosperity **:** ABASEMENT, CONDESCENSION

de·scen·sion·al \-chənᵊl,-chnəl\ *adj* **1 :** relating to descension **:** moving or directed downward **2 :** involving or produced by processes of disintegration of rock and aggregation of particles in beds ⟨sand produced by the disintegration of granite is a ~ deposit⟩

de·scen·sion·ist \-ch(ə)nəst\ *n* -S **:** one who holds the descension theory

descension theory *n* **:** the theory that ore deposits have been formed of material carried down in solution from above

de·scen·sive \-n(t)siv\ *adj* [*descension* + *-ive*] **:** tending to descend

de·scen·sus \-n(t)səs\ *n* -ES [NL, fr. L, *descent,* fr. *descensus,* past part. of *descendere*] *med* **:** DESCENT, PROLAPSE

¹de·scent \də'sent, dē'-\ *n* -S [ME, fr. MF *descente,* fr. *descendre* to descend — more at DESCEND] **1 :** the act or process of descending from a higher to a lower level, rank, or state ⟨a parachute ~⟩ ⟨during their ~ of the ski run⟩ ⟨some thirty-two separate rapids and cataracts in its final furious ~ —Tom Marvel⟩ ⟨~ by chromatic intervals⟩ ⟨ascent and ~ between the physical and spiritual worlds —*Times Lit. Supp.*⟩ **2 a :** a decline or comedown in station, respectability, or living conditions ⟨the ~ to being junior partners of the newcomer to world power —D.W.Brogan⟩ ⟨~ of the family to actual shabbiness⟩ **b :** a stepping down or stooping to an inferior level (as of intellectual elevation, dignity, self-respect) ⟨look around among my books for a further ~ from philosophy to literature —O.W.Holmes †1935⟩ ⟨~ from self-justification to self-deception⟩ ⟨a sudden ~ . . . from the sublimity of his highfalutin critical terminology —*Times Lit. Supp.*⟩ **c** *logic* **:** passage from the more general to the more particular **3 a :** derivation from an ancestor **:** BIRTH ⟨only three alternatives are known, namely, patrilineal, matrilineal, or bilateral ~, and every culture incorporates one of these rules or some combination thereof —G.P.Murdock⟩; *usu* **:** the established connection between an individual and his progenitors or the stock from which he is descended **:** EXTRACTION, LINEAGE ⟨of Pilgrim stock, eighth in ~ through his mother from a governor of the colony⟩ ⟨people of Polish ~⟩ **b** *obs* **:** DESCENDANT ⟨our ~ . . . born to certain woe, devoured by death —John Milton⟩ **c :** transmission or devolution of an estate by inheritance usu. but not necessarily in the descending line **d :** the fact or process of originating by generation from an ancestral stock (as a species or genus) **e :** the shaping or development in nature and character by transmission from a source **:** DERIVATION, ORIGINATION ⟨the home of an active legal science which could trace a faint but sure ~ from Roman law —R.W.Southern⟩ ⟨there was a line of ~ from these ideas to the Fascist movement —Cecil Sprigge⟩ ⟨native American voices tracing their ~ from the Know-Nothings of yesterday —T.H.White b.1915⟩ **4 a :** an inclination downward **:** an inclined or sloping surface : DECLIVITY ⟨it appears that the water is broken nowhere by striking against the rocks, and that therefore the ~ is perpendicular —Anthony Trollope⟩ **b** : a descending way (as a downgrade or stairway) **c** *obs* : the lowest part ⟨from the extremest upward of thy head to the ~ and dust below thy foot —Shak.⟩ **5 a** : a sudden disconcerting appearance (as for a visit) ⟨unprepared for the ~ of his in-laws⟩ **b** : a hostile raid or predatory assault ⟨the ~ of the Assyrians upon Israel⟩ ⟨~ of the locusts⟩ **6** : a step downward in a scale of gradation; *specif* : one generation in an ancestral line or genealogical scale ⟨his pedigree shows 11 ~*s*⟩ **7** : a former method of distillation in which the material was heated in a vessel having its outlet underneath so that the vapors produced were forced to descend

²de·scent \(ˈ)dēˈsent\ *vt* [*de-* + *scent* (n.)] : to rid of scent

descent cast *n, English law* : the descent of an estate to an heir by the death of one who held it adversely to the real owner which prior to 1833 barred the latter's right of entry so that he could recover only by suing — compare ADVERSE POSSESSION

des·champ·sia \dəˈshampsēə\ *n, cap* [NL, fr. Jean L. A. Loiseleur-*Deslongchamps* †1849 Fr. botanist + NL *-ia*] : a genus of perennial grasses of cold and temperate regions having loose or compact panicles with 2-flowered spikelets

des·cha·pelles coup \ˌdāshəˈpel(z)-\ *n* [after Guillaume *Deschapelles* †1847 Fr. authority on whist] : the lead of a high card (as a king) in whist or bridge in the hope that an opponent will win it and make the next-higher card good for an entry in one's partner's hand

des·cloi·zite \dāˈklȯiˌzīt, dəˈ-\ *n* -s [F *descloizite*, fr. A.L.O.L. *Des Cloizeaux* †1897 Fr. mineralogist + F *-ite*] : a mineral (ZnCu)Pb(VO$_4$)(OH) consisting of a basic vanadate chiefly of lead and zinc and varying in color from cherry red to brown and black (hardness 3.5, sp. gr. 5.9–6.2)

des·cort \deˈskȯ(ə)r\ *n* -s [F, fr. OF, lit., discord — more at DISCORD] **1** : a medieval French lyric in which the stanzas are unlike **2** : a poem in old Provençal literature with stanzas in different languages

des·cri·able \dəˈskrīəbəl, dēˈ-\ *adj* [*descry* + *-able*] : capable of being descried

des·cri·al \-ī(ə)l\ *n* -s [*descry* + *-al*] : the act or process of descrying; *esp* : discovery or disclosure of something recondite or to be held secret

de·scrib·abil·i·ty \dəˌskrībəˈbiləd·ē, dē,-, -ətē, -i\ *n* -ES : capability of being described

de·scrib·able \=ˈ=bəbəl\ *adj* : capable of being described — **de·scrib·ably** \-bəblē, -li\ *adv*

de·scribe \dəˈskrīb, dēˈ-\ *vt* -ED/-ING/-S [L *describere*, fr. *de-* + *scribere* to write — more at SCRIBE] **1** : to represent by words written or spoken for the knowledge or understanding of others: **a** : to communicate verbally from the results of personal observation an account of salient identifying features of (something existing in space) ⟨unable to find words to ~ the mountain scene⟩ ⟨in 1886 a Boston surgeon . . . *described* the condition now called appendicitis —Morris Fishbein⟩; *specif* : to observe and narrate simultaneously with the action (as for radio or television) ⟨*describing* a football game to an unseeing audience⟩ **b** : to transmit a mental image, an impression, or an understanding of the nature and characteristics of (something immaterial) : present distinctly by means of properties and qualities ⟨the unique character of the artistic quality of a work . . . cannot be defined or even *described* —T.M. Greene⟩ ⟨there were so many things he wanted to ~ —James Joyce⟩ ⟨like Mark Twain he exhibits rather than ~*s* his characters: their speech is a portrait —Marvin Lowenthal⟩ **c** : to make clear by expounding esp. in a minute way ⟨had traveled in the principal countries of the world and *described* what it was like to live in a police state —Victor Boesen⟩ ⟨~ the life of the past from the various scraps of the fossil forms —W.E.Swinton⟩ **d** : to distinguish by a definitive label or other designation or by an individualizing phrase or similitude — used with *as* and a complement ⟨few doctors would ~ themselves as scientists⟩ ⟨the State is often rightly *described* as a machine: its total effect is inhuman —Herbert Read⟩ **e** : to convey an image or notion of : EXPRESS, SIGNIFY, DENOTE ⟨we have indicated that jealousy ~*s* a state of tension among various interests of the personality —Abram Kardiner⟩ ⟨while the natural sciences grow more modest in admitting that their laws ~ only probabilities —Reinhold Niebuhr⟩ **2** *obs* : to write down : INSCRIBE, TRANSCRIBE **3** : to represent by a drawing, figure, model, or picture : PORTRAY, DELINEATE ⟨and when the curves thus brilliantly drawn ~ vividly some object in life toward which we have pleasing associations we get a complex pleasure —Roger Fry⟩ **4** : to mark out : trace or traverse the outline of ⟨each planet ~*s* an ellipse with the sun in one focus —S.F.Mason⟩ ⟨while he *described* a big smooth arc with the muleta —Barnaby Conrad⟩ ⟨butted amidships he *described* a somersault backward⟩ **5** *obs* : to portion out : DISTRIBUTE ⟨ye shall therefore ~ the land into seven parts —Josh 18:6 (AV)⟩ **6** *archaic* : to discover by observation : ESPY, PERCEIVE **syn** see RELATE

de·scrib·er \-bə(r)\ *n* -s **1** : one that describes **2** *Brit* : an instrument giving details about trains moving or scheduled to move between given points

descried *past of* DESCRY

des·cri·er \dəˈskrī(ə)r, dēˈ-, -īə\ *n* -s : one that descries

descries *pres 3d sing of* DESCRY

de·script \dəˈskript, (ˈ)dēˈs-\ *adj* [L *descriptus*, past part. of *describere*] **1** *archaic* : DESCRIBED **2** *archaic* : INSCRIBED

descripta *pl of* DESCRIPTUM

de·scrip·tion \dəˈskripshən, dēˈ-\ *n* -s [ME *descripcioun*, fr. MF or L; MF *description*, fr. L *description-, descriptio*, fr. *descriptus* + *-ion-, -io* -ion] **1** : the act or an instance of describing: as **a** : a describing or a representation produced by a describing of something material or immaterial ⟨~ of things is a mode of classification which in turn furnishes material for a more general classification —V.F.Lenzen⟩ ⟨the meticulous ~*s* of the rocks of each of the Paleozoic systems —*Amer. Jour. of Science*⟩ ⟨reading a ~ of a murderer and looking at his picture both enable one to say "so that's what he's like" —J.M.Shorter⟩; *specif* : composition intended primarily to present to the mind or imagination graphically and in detail a unit of objective or subjective experience (as a scene, person, sensation, emotion) — used in textbooks in distinguishing a separate literary genre; compare EXPOSITION ⟨it is the purpose of such ~*s* that explains why their typical merits and demerits are what they are — namely: exactness, minuteness, accuracy, detail, fullness, sketchiness, misleadingness —S.E.Toulmin & K. Baier⟩ **b** : a statement of the properties of a thing or its relations to other things serving to identify it : a univocal designation of an object by means of a phrase beginning with *the* or *a* (as "the present king of the Belgians" or "a house next to my office") **c** : a descriptive statement or account — often contrasted with *analysis* and *valuation* **d** : an individualizing or identifying designation (as a name, label, epithet) ⟨the ~ "wax" is a misnomer since the substance is a fat —J.N.Goldsmith⟩ **2** *obs* **a** : INSCRIPTION **b** : ENROLLMENT **3** : kind or character esp. as determined by salient features ⟨each state may still confer them upon an alien, or . . . upon any class or ~ of persons —R.B.Taney⟩ ⟨opposed to any tax of so radical a ~⟩ **4** *obs* : pictorial representation **5 a** : a tracing out of a geometrical figure **b** : a traversing of a course ⟨the rocket's ~ of a high arching curve⟩ **6** : a specification of the boundaries of a piece of land with sufficient accuracy for legal purposes (as in preparing a deed of transfer) **syn** see TYPE

de·scrip·tion·ist \-sh(ə)nəst\ *n* -s **1** : one proficient in description **2** : DESCRIPTIVIST

de·scrip·tion·less \-shənləs\ *adj* : being without description

de·scrip·tio per·so·nae \dəˈskripshēˌōpə(r)ˈsō(ˌ)nē\ *n* [L, description of the person] : matter merely descriptive of the persons of the parties and not essential to the validity of a legal document — compare DESIGNATIO PERSONAE

¹de·scrip·tive \dəˈskriptiv, dēˈ-, -tēv *also* -təv\ *adj* [LL *descriptivus*, fr. L *descriptus* + *-ivus* -ive] **1** : serving to describe : characterized by description : representational through presentation of observed facts ⟨a minute anatomical and generally ~ account of the large fulvous orangutan —E.A.Poe⟩ ⟨outjutting formations have been given ~ names: the Devil's Chair is 80 feet high —*Amer. Guide Series: Minn.*⟩ ⟨purely ~ poetry —Yvor Winters⟩ — distinguished from *critical, evaluative*, and *theoretical* **2 a** : referring to, constituting, or concerned with empirical things or events or with their parts, characteristics, or functions ⟨~ expressions⟩ ⟨~ disciplines⟩ **b** : factually grounded or informative rather than normative, prescriptive, emotive, aprioristic, or analytical ⟨~ judgments⟩ ⟨~ theories⟩ ⟨that this meaning shall be called "~" when the responses evoked are cognitions and shall be called "emotive" when the responses evoked are attitudes —Asher Moore⟩ **3 a** *of a modifying word* : expressing the quality, kind, or condition of what is denoted by the modified term ⟨*hot* in "hot water" and *sick* in "a sick man" are ~ adjectives⟩ — distinguished from *limiting* **b** *of a modifier, esp a clause* : NONRESTRICTIVE **c** *of a compound* : belonging to the karmadharaya class **4** : characterized by or connected with description of the structure of a language at a particular time usu. with rigorous exclusion of historical and comparative judgments ⟨~ linguistics⟩ ⟨~ grammar⟩ ⟨a ~ study⟩ — compare COMPARATIVE 4a **5** : characterized by kinship name classes that apply in part only to lineal relatives (as grandfather, father, son, grandchild) and in part only to collateral relatives (as uncle, cousin, nephew) regardless of the sex of the connecting relatives ⟨regarded most European systems as ~ and those of primitive peoples as classificatory —R.H.Lowie⟩ — compare CLASSIFICATORY — **de·scrip·tive·ly** \-təvlē, -li\ *adv* — **de·scrip·tive·ness** \-təvnəs\ *n* -ES

²descriptive \"\ *n* -s : a distinctive word, phrase, or sentence applied to a particular product in advertising

descriptive anatomy *n* : anatomy dealing with the character, form, size, and position of organs and parts

descriptive bibliography *n* : a bibliographical record in complete detail of the physical characteristics and publishing history of the books of a related series properly including an account of internal printing variants requisite for textual criticism

descriptive botany *n* : a branch of botany dealing with the systematic description or diagnostic characters of plants

descriptive cataloging *n* : a library procedure by which a book or other item is identified and described by recording such items as author, title, imprint, and collation — contrasted with *subject cataloging*

descriptive geometry *n* : the theory of geometry treated by means of projections; *specif* : the theory of projecting an exactly defined body so as to deduce both projective and metrical properties from its projections, the projections usu. being made on two planes at right angles to each other

de·scrip·tiv·ism \-təˌvizəm\ *n* -s **1** : a theory of ethics according to which only descriptive or empirical statements are meaningful **2** : advocacy or use of the methods of descriptive linguistics

de·scrip·tiv·ist \-vəst\ *n* -s **1** : an advocate of descriptivism **2** : a specialist in descriptive linguistics

de·scrip·tiv·is·tic \=ˌ==ˈvistik\ *adj* : of, relating to, or based on descriptivism — **de·scrip·tiv·is·ti·cal·ly** \-tək(ə)lē\ *adv*

de·scrip·tor \dəˈskriptə(r) *also* -ˌtȯ(ə)r *or* -ȯ(ə)\ *n* -s [LL, describer, fr. L *descriptus* + *-or*] : an identifying sign or symbol

de·scrip·to·ry \-t(ə)rē\ *n* -ES [L *descriptus* + E *-ory*] : DESCRIPTIVE

de·scrip·tum \dəˈskriptəm, dēˈ-\ *n, pl* **descrip·ta** \-tə\ [L, fr. neut. of *descriptus*, past part. of *describere* to describe — more at DESCRIBE] *philos* : something that is described

de·scrive \dəˈskrīv, -rēv\ *vt* -ED/-ING/-S [ME *descriven*, fr. OF *descrivre*, fr. L *describere*] *Scot* : DESCRIBE ⟨let me fair Nature's face ~ —Robert Burns⟩

¹des·cry \dəˈskrī, dēˈ-\ *vt* -ED/-ING/-S [ME *descrien*, fr. OF *descrier* to proclaim, decry — more at DECRY] **1 a** : to spy out or come to see esp. with watchful attention and careful observation of the distant, uncertain, or obscure ⟨the grass was high in the meadow, and there was no ~*ing* her —George Eliot⟩ **b** : to attain to the realization or understanding of : DISCOVER ⟨examine the legend in a more critical spirit and ~ the reasons for Toscanini's preeminence —*Times Lit. Supp.*⟩ **2** *obs* **a** : to make known (as one's name) : DECLARE **b** : BETRAY **3** *obs* : CHALLENGE **4** *obs* : DECRY **syn** see SEE

²descry *n* -ES *obs* : discovery or view from afar

de·scum \(ˈ)dē+\ *vt* [*de-* + *scum* (n.)] : to rid of scum

des·cu·rain·ia \ˌdeskyəˈrānēə, ˌdāsk-\ *n, cap* [NL, fr. François *Déscourain* †1740 Fr. botanist + NL *-ia*] : a genus of annual or biennial herbs (family Cruciferae) of America and Europe differing from members of the genus *Sisymbrium* in having a pubescence of stellate or forked hairs and comprising the tansy mustards — see TANSY MUSTARD

de·seam \(ˈ)dē+\ *vt* [*de-* + *seam* (n.)] : to chip out or flame-cut seams or other similar surface defects from (semifinished metal)

de·sea·son·al·ize \(ˈ)dēˈsēz(ᵊ)nəˌlīz, dēˈ-\ *vt* [*de-* + *seasonal* + *-ize*] : to adjust (as an industry) to continuous rather than seasonal operation

¹des·e·crate \ˈdesəˌkrāt, -sē,-, *usu* -ād·+V\ *vt* -ED/-ING/-S [*de-* + *-secrate* (as in *consecrate*, v.)] **1 a** : to violate the sanctity of by diverting from sacred purpose, by contaminating, or by defiling ⟨they *desecrated* the shrine outright — bargaining with the Moslem merchants —*Time*⟩ ⟨it would ~ the Lincoln Memorial to have an obviously false voice speak from the statue there —*N.Y. Times Mag.*⟩ ⟨the quivering host whose house has been profaned and whose religion *desecrated* —W.L.Sullivan⟩ **b** : to divest of sacred character or treat as unhallowed ⟨many cemeteries were *desecrated*⟩ **2** *archaic* : to dedicate (someone or something) to false gods : condemn to an evil fate **3** : to treat (an object of veneration, reverent devotion, or admiration) irreverently or contemptuously often in a way to provoke outrage on the part of others ⟨[his] great memory . . . has been *desecrated*. . . . —Margery Allingham⟩ ⟨Americans love the scenic outdoors, and they do not want to see it *desecrated* —R.L.Neuberger⟩ **4** : to make desolate ⟨churned up lawns and drives, and *desecrated* houses with their broken windows —S.P.B.Mais⟩

²des·e·crate \-ˌkrət, -krāt\ *adj* [*de-* + *-secrate* (as in *consecrate*, adj.)] : DESECRATED

des·e·crat·er *or* **des·e·cra·tor** \-ˌkrād·ə(r)\ *n* -s : one that desecrates

des·e·cra·tion \ˌ==ˈkrāshən\ *n* -s **1** : the act or an instance of desecrating ⟨I have heard this chorus sung in a uniform fortissimo right from the beginning. What a ~ —Warwick Braithwaite⟩ ⟨the United Nations Flag of Authority may be subject to ~*s* —*World Flag Encyc.*⟩ **2** : the condition of being desecrated **syn** see PROFANATION

de·seed \(ˈ)dē+\ *vt* [*de-* + *seed* (n.)] : to remove the seed from

de·segmentation \(ˌ)dē+\ *n* [*de-* + *segmentation*] *zool* : coalescence of distinct segments : loss of segmentation

de·segregate \(ˈ)dē+\ *vb* [*de-* + *segregate*] *vt* : to rid of segregation : to end the practice of segregation in ⟨two more counties . . . *desegregated* their schools —*New Republic*⟩ ⟨impetus to ~ this swimming pool came from a court order —*Jour. of Social Issues*⟩ **~** *vi* : to effect or implement desegregation ⟨few Southern universities . . . *desegregated* without being required to do so —K.B.Clark⟩

de·segregation \(ˌ)dē+\ *n* : the act of desegregating : the process of effecting an end to the practice of segregation ⟨urbanization . . . may make ~ easier —J.B.Martin⟩ ⟨the process of ~ has been going forward steadily . . . in school districts throughout the country —J.W.Waring⟩ — compare INTEGRATION

de·se·mer \ˈdāzəmə(r)\ *n* -s [G, fr. LG, alter. of MLG *bisemer, besemer*, of Baltic origin; akin to Lith *bezmėnas*, of Slav origin; akin to ORuss *bezmĕnŭ* desemer, small weight, Pol *bezmian, przezmian* balance without pans, perh. of Turkic origin; akin to Turk *batman* small weight] : an ancient balance : STEELYARD

de·sensitization \(ˌ)dē, də+\ *n* : the process of desensitizing ⟨~ consists in the gradual specific neutralizing of the sensitizing antibody —A.F.Coca⟩

de·sensitize \(ˈ)dē, də+\ *vb* [*de-* + *sensitize*] *vt* **1** : to render (a sensitized or hypersensitive individual) insensitive or nonreactive to a sensitizing agent ⟨*desensitized* to an allergenic pollen by repeated injections of an extract of that pollen⟩ **2** : to render (a photographic material) less sensitive or completely insensitive to radiation **3** : to make portions of (an offset plate) repellent to ink **4** : to render insensible to some sensation or emotion or insensitive or callous to inhumanity, injustice, degradation ⟨they have been so successfully *desensitized* that they are unable to recognize the most obvious facts —Alfred Kantorowicz⟩ **5** : to free (as by psychotherapy) of the emotional charge investing a complex

de·sensitizer \"+\ *n* : a desensitizing agent: as **a** : a drug that reduces sensitivity to pain ⟨a ~ which makes it possible to drill and fill teeth painlessly —*Industrial & Engineering Chemistry*⟩ **b** : a chemical (as a dye) that reduces the sensitivity of a photographic material to radiation

des·er·et \ˌdezəˈret, *usu* -ed·+V\ *adj, usu cap* [fr. *Deseret*, nickname for the state of Utah and from 1849–1850 official Mormon name for the Utah territory, fr. *deseret* honeybee, coined in the *Book of Mormon* (Ether 2:3)] : of or from Utah territory or the state of Utah

¹des·ert \ˈdezə(r)t, *usu* \|d·+V\ *n* -s [ME, fr. OF, fr. LL *desertum*, fr. L, neut. of *desertus*, past part. of *deserere* to desert, fr. *de-* + *serere* to join together — more at SERIES] **1 a** *archaic* : a wild uninhabited and uncultivated tract : a desolate unoccupied plain or coast or pathless woodland : WILDERNESS, WASTE **b** : any of the formerly unsettled regions of the U.S. between the Mississippi river and the Rocky mountains thought to be arid and uninhabitable **2 a** : a region in which the vegetation is so scanty as to be incapable of supporting any considerable population (as a region perpetually cold or covered with snow or ice or a region located in the interior of a continent and characterized by scanty rainfall esp. of less than 10 inches annually) **b** : a more or less barren tract incapable of supporting any considerable population without an artificial water supply **c** : an area of an ocean believed to be devoid of marine life **3** : a secluded place for secret worship by the Huguenots during the years 1715–1802 when Protestantism was under proscription in France **4** : a desolating or forbidding prospect (as from pathless emptiness, bleak unrelieved changelessness or monotony, futility of effort, or destitution of mental or spiritual animation or stimulation) ⟨tiny figures lost in an immense ~ of darkness —Beverley Nichols⟩ ⟨lost in a ~ of doubt⟩ ⟨eagles still soar between the summit of Parnassus and the Corinthian gulf, but they look down upon a ~ of human history —Mark Van Doren⟩

²des·ert \", *in sense 1 usu like* ³DESERT\ *adj* [ME, fr. OF, fr. L *desertus*] **1** *archaic* : DESERTED ⟨the boat deck was utterly ~ —Waldo Frank⟩ **2 a** : desolate and sparsely occupied or unoccupied : INHOSPITABLE ⟨so ~ a country as the Highlands of Scotland —Adam Smith⟩ **b** : uncultivated and uninhabited : barren like a desert ⟨one could scarcely find a more ~ tract for a settler⟩ **3** : having its habitat in a desert ⟨~ flora and fauna⟩ **4** : peculiar to or adapted to life in a desert ⟨sturdy ~ boots⟩

³de·sert \dəˈzər\|t, dēˈ-, -zə̄\|, -zəi\|, *usu* \|d·+V\ *n* -s [ME *deserte*, fr. OF, fr. fem. of *desert* (past part. of *deservir* to deserve), fr. L *deservitus*, past part. of *deservire* to serve zealously — more at DESERVE] **1 a** : the quality or fact of being worthy of or deserving of rewards or recompense or of requital or punishment ⟨the concept of ~ is essentially indefinable except in terms of existing practices and ideas —G.H.Sabine⟩ **b** : a complex of actions calling for such returns ⟨in the midst is seated Justice to award to each according to his ~ —Carleton Brown⟩ **2 a** : reward or punishment deserved or earned by one's qualities or acts ⟨not weighing our ~*s* but pardoning our offenses —*Missale Romanum*⟩ ⟨by dint of much caballing and much dwelling upon his own ~*s* he triumphed over his enemies —Virginia Woolf⟩ **b deserts** *pl* : awards due for superior or inferior qualities of art or workmanship ⟨book reviewers . . . frequently praise the first venture of a writer beyond its just ~*s* —Harrison Smith⟩ **3** : worthiness or excellence of character as adduced by a good course of conduct ⟨he won the appointment on grounds of ~ rather than through family prestige⟩ **syn** see DUE

⁴desert \"\ *vb* -ED/-ING/-S [F *déserter*, fr. LL *desertare*, fr. L *desertus*, past part. of *deserere* to desert — more at ¹DESERT] *vt* **1** : to withdraw from or leave permanently or less often temporarily (as a place) : QUIT ⟨farmers continue to ~ the land to take up factory work⟩ ⟨the smile ~*ing* his broad face —T.B.Costain⟩ ⟨phrases which never ~ the memory —T.S. Eliot⟩ **2 a** : to turn away from (what has previously engaged one) esp. by withdrawing support or disrupting bonds of attachment or duty : reject in order to take up something else : ABANDON ⟨who, 30 years before, upon being ~*ed* by her lover had taken to her bed —Margaret Deland⟩ ⟨coming at last to ~ the Prohibition party⟩ ⟨he ~*ed* prose for the compensating rhythms of poetry —Tyrus Hillway⟩ **b** : to leave behind or give up (as a person) — used with *to* ⟨forced to ~ the rest of the miners to their fate⟩ **c** : to renounce marital relations by quitting the company of (one's spouse) **3 a** : to break away from or break off association with (some matter involving legal or moral obligation or some object of loyalty) : BETRAY ⟨not propose to ~ the 100-year-old Monroe Doctrine —A.H.Vandenberg †1951⟩ ⟨would be a calamity if these sciences ~*ed* the ideal of accurate and verifiable systematic knowledge for its own sake —M.R.Cohen⟩ **b** : to abandon (military service) without leave : forsake in violation of duty ⟨guilty of ~*ing* his fellow soldiers⟩ **4** : to drop away or escape from (a person) usu. causing a distinct sense of loss or discomfiture : leave in the lurch : FORSAKE ⟨all sense of courtly etiquette ~*ing* him —T.B.Costain⟩ **~** *vi* **1** : to quit one's post, leader, or service without leave ⟨the native guides quietly ~*ed* during the night⟩ ⟨the more liberal members of the party began ~*ing*⟩ **2** : to change one's allegiance ⟨he gave fear of a return of Nazism as the reason for his ~*ing* to the Communists⟩ **3 a** : to quit military service without right ⟨determined to ~⟩ : absent oneself without leave from proper post, station, or duty with the intent to remain away permanently **b** : to leave one's proper place to avoid hazardous duty or to shirk important service : accept appointment or enlist in the same or another armed service without first being regularly separated : enter a foreign armed service without authorization by the U.S. **c** *of an officer* : to quit one's post without leave and with intent to remain away permanently after tendering one's resignation but before due notice of acceptance of it has been received

desert armor *n* : a concentration of pebbles and boulders on the surface of the ground in a desert resulting from removal of sand and dust particles by the wind and protecting the underlying material from further wind erosion

desert bat *n* : PALLID BAT

desert candle *n* : a plant of the genus *Eremurus*

desert cat *n* : any of several small wildcats of arid regions: as **a** : a widely distributed Asiatic wildcat (*Felis bieti*) **b** : KAFFIR CAT **c** : a pale sandy-colored bay lynx of desert parts of western No. America

desert date *n* : BITO

deserted *adj* : left without the accustomed occupants, company, or support : ABANDONED, FORSAKEN ⟨found shelter in a ~ shack⟩ ⟨stood there, motionless, without desire, like a ship at sea, ~ of all winds —L.P.Smith⟩ — **de·sert·ed·ly** *adv* — **de·sert·ed·ness** *n* -ES

de·sert·er *pronunc at* ³DESERT + ə(r)\ *n* -s [F & L; F *déserteur*, fr. L *desertor*, fr. *desertus* + *-or*] : one who forsakes a duty, a cause, or anyone to whom he owes service; *esp* : a member of a military force who deserts

desert fever *or* **desert rheumatism** *n* : a mild form of coccidioidomycosis resembling influenza

desert fox *n* **1** : a fox (*Vulpes leucopus*) of the western deserts of Asia **2** : the kit fox (*Vulpes macrotis*) of the southwestern U.S.

desert gum *n* : any of several trees of the genus *Eucalyptus* (esp. *E. rudis*)

desert holly *n* : a low saltbush (*Atriplex hymenelytra*) of arid regions of the southwestern U.S. and Mexico with smooth bluish green or silvery prickly-edged foliage that is often used for Christmas decoration

de·ser·tic \dəˈzərd·ik, deˈ-\ *adj* : belonging or peculiar to or having the distinctive character of a desert ⟨the red ~ hills dotted with juniper —D.C.Peattie⟩ : found in a desert ⟨a ~ soil may be rich in nutrients⟩ ⟨a ~ climate⟩

des·er·tic·o·lous \ˌdezə(r)ˈtikələs\ *adj* [¹*desert* + *-i-* + *-colous*] : dwelling in a desert

de·ser·tion \dəˈzer\|shən, dēˈ-, -zə̄\|, -zəi\|\ *n* -s [MF or LL; MF, fr. LL *desertion-, desertio*, fr. L *desertus* + *-ion-, -io* -ion] **1** : the act or an instance of deserting: **a** : abandonment of a person to whom one is obligated or bound by agreement ⟨we resolved to make the dash for the summit in spite of their ~⟩ **:** abandonment of that to which a degree of loyalty is considered due (as a post of duty, employment engaged for, a cause, a political party) **:** DEFECTION **b :** a deserting from the military or naval service **c :** the intentional and substantial abandonment permanently or for a period of time stated by law without legal excuse and without consent of one's duties arising out of a status (as that of husband and wife or parent and child) **2 :** a state of being deserted or forsaken **:** DESOLATION **3 :** one who deserts ⟨all the ~s gave themselves up⟩

desert ironwood *n* **1 :** a small leguminous tree (*Olneya tesota*) of the southwestern U.S. and Mexico with odd-pinnate leaves and purplish white flowers in short racemes — called also *Sonora ironwood* **2 :** the hard wood of the desert ironwood

desert lark *n* **:** any of several larks (as of the genus *Ammomanes*) inhabiting the deserts of Asia and Africa

desert lemon *n* **:** an Australian tree (*Eremocitrus glauca*) of the family Rutaceae bearing a small acid fruit

de·sert·less \dəˈzərtləs\ *adj* [³*desert* + *-less*] **1 :** UNDESERVING **2** *obs* **:** UNDESERVED — **de·sert·less·ly** *adv*

desert lily *n* **:** a bulbous herb (*Hesperocallis undulata*) of the family Liliaceae of the southwestern U.S. with narrow sword-shaped leaves and showy racemose flowers

desert locust *n* **:** a destructive migratory locust (*Schistocerca gregaria*) of southwestern Asia and parts of northern Africa

desert lynx *n* **:** CARACAL

desert mahogany *n* **:** a widely distributed mountain mahogany (*Cercocarpus ledifolius*) that grows as a large shrub or small tree on dry gravelly uplands of the western U.S. and is an important browse for deer

desert milkweed *n* **:** any of several plants of the genus *Asclepias* that grow in the dry regions of southwestern U.S. (esp. *A. subulata* and *A. erosa*)

desert mouse *n* **:** a small brown mouse (*Pseudomys hermannsburgensis*) of the central desert of Australia

des·ert·ness \ˈdezə(r)tnəs\ *n* -ES [ME *desertnes*, fr. ²*desert* + *-nes* -ness] **:** the condition of being like a desert ⟨that air of spellbound ~ which so significantly invests the isles —Herman Melville⟩

desert palm *n* **:** WASHINGTON PALM

desert pavement *n* **:** a natural mosaic of closely-packed pebbles, cobblestones, and boulders commonly found in a desert where the wind has swept away all smaller particles

desert pea *n* **:** STURT'S DESERT PEA

desert peach *n* **:** a thorny thicket-forming large shrub or small tree (*Prunus andersonii*) of dry uplands of the Pacific and Intermountain states that is locally important as browse for sheep and goats

desert plant *n* **:** a plant suited to the environment of arid regions of little rainfall that often stores water in its tissues or hollow center and reduces transpiration by total or seasonal leaflessness or by a densely hairy, waxy, varnished, or otherwise modified leaf **:** a xerophilous plant

desert plume *n* **:** a perennial herb (*Stanleya pinnata*) of the family Cruciferae of the southwestern U.S. with pinnatifid leaves, spirally coiled anthers, and long stalked seedpods — called also *prince's-plume*

desert rat *n* **1 :** any of several pale-coated active rodents found in deserts (as the American kangaroo rat or certain southern African rodents) **2** *West* **:** one who has lived much on the desert esp. as a prospector

desert rod *n* **:** any of several herbs of the genus *Eremostachys* (family Labiatae) found in arid regions of western and central Asia

deserts *pl of* DESERT, *pres 3d sing of* DESERT

desertscape \ˈ==,=\ *n* [¹*desert* + *-scape*] **1 :** a scenic view of a desert **2 :** a pictorial representation of a scenic view of a desert

desert soil *n* **:** any of a group of zonal soils that develop under sparse shrub vegetation in warm to cool arid climates and have a light-colored surface soil usu. underlain by calcareous material and a hardpan layer

desert sore *n* **:** an ulcer of unknown cause affecting chiefly the extremities and occurring in desert regions of the tropics

desert sparrow *n* **:** a black-throated sparrow (*Amphispiza bilineata*) of arid parts of southwestern No. America

desert sweet *n* **:** FERN-BUSH

desert-thorn \ˈ==,=\ *n* [¹*desert* + *thorn*] **:** MATRIMONY VINE

desert tortoise *n* **:** a large burrowing turtle (*Gopherus agassizii*) of arid regions of the western U.S. — compare TESTUDINIDAE

desert trumpet *n* **:** a tall perennial plant (*Eriogonum inflatum*) of arid uplands of the western U.S. with silvery leaves and the upper part of the nodes inflated

desert trumpet flower *n* **:** a perennial herb (*Datura meteloides*) of the southwestern U.S. with erect showy tubular rose-white flowers and spiny fruit

desert varnish *or* **desert polish** *n* **:** a dark coating or polish found on rocks and pebbles after long exposure in desert regions

¹**des·ert·ward** \ˈdezə(r)t·wə(r)d\ *adv* [¹*desert* + *-ward*] **:** toward a desert

²**desertward** \"\ *adj* **:** sloping toward a desert **:** lying near to a desert

desert willow *n* **:** a shrub or low tree (*Chilopsis linearis*) of the family Bignoniaceae resembling a willow, having showy purplish flowers and long seed pods, and occurring in dry regions of southwestern No. America — called also *flowering willow*

desertworthy \ˈ==,==\ *adj* **:** capable of functioning competently in a desert

de·serve \dəˈzərv, dēˈ-, -zəv, -zəiv\ *vb* -ED/-ING/-S [ME *deserven*, fr. OF *deservir*, fr. L *deservire* to serve zealously, fr. *de-* + *servire* to serve — more at SERVE] *vt* **1 a :** to come to be rightfully worthy of, to be fairly entitled to, or to be able to claim rightfully by virtue of actions done or qualities displayed ⟨we have the poetry we ~, just as we have the painting we ~ —Herbert Read⟩ ⟨rebels ~ no consideration —Kenneth Roberts⟩ ⟨a people indifferent to their civil liberties do not ~ to keep them —W.O.Douglas⟩; *also* **:** to be so circumstanced as to undergo as one's just due **:** have due as requital ⟨a drunken driver ~s to have his driving license suspended⟩ ⟨he ~s to lose because of his unsportsmanlike tactics⟩ **b :** to be rightfully qualified (as by excellence, utility, wrongness, or other special character) to have or receive **:** qualify for on the basis of right or justice ⟨a laboratory that hardly *deserved* the name⟩ ⟨the question ~s dispassionate consideration —Vera M. Dean⟩ ⟨what crimes ~ the death penalty?⟩ ⟨that his country's new society *deserved* all his energies —Jay Leyda⟩ ⟨acute and liberating observations which ~ to be widely disseminated —M.R.Cohen⟩ **2** *obs* **:** to be or prove of service to **:** BENEFIT **3 :** to win by reason of worthy performance or earn by reason of untoward performance ⟨they cannot command prosperity or continuing employment, but they are certainly doing their best to ~ them —Sam Pollock⟩ ⟨I do not know how he had *deserved* our disrespect —Mary Austin⟩ **4** *obs* **:** to give in return ~ *vi* **1 :** to be worthy, fit, suitable for some reward or requital **:** have acted in a worthy way ⟨that the Tudor translators have become recognized as they ~ —T.S.Eliot⟩ ⟨as one who had *deserved* well of his country —G.L.Dickinson⟩ **2** *obs* **:** to be of service

syn EARN, MERIT, RATE: DESERVE may suggest one's being rightfully entitled to reward for actions done or qualities exhibited in particular situations calling for special notice or evaluation ⟨if he [Dr. Johnson] inserts the poems of some who can hardly be said to *deserve* such an honor —William Cowper⟩ ⟨liberty is easier to win than to *deserve*, and if it is treated as either a license or a vacuum, the police will come or the walls will fall in —Curtis Bok⟩ ⟨a second point *deserves* renewed emphasis —Zechariah Chafee⟩ EARN may suggest a due reward or recompense according to a systematic or regulated plan of evaluation ⟨since he has not missed any hours of work I suppose that he has *earned* his salary, but from the caliber of his work I do not think that he deserves it⟩ ⟨advanced work . . . by men already graduates of theological schools *earns* the degree of Master or Doctor of Theology —*Official Register of Harvard Univ.*⟩ More certainly than the others in this set EARN suggests previous sustained expenditure of energy, effort, and time ⟨we had *earned* that right . . . no group of men can grant other men rights of any kind; they are achieved —H.D. Skidmore⟩ MERIT may be used in reference to lasting traits, rather than sustained action, more readily than EARN ⟨the idle politicos of the country do not *merit* our trust, but her zealous partisans have earned it⟩ MERIT highly stresses the fact of worthiness fit for reward or consideration but implies less about the fact of being rewarded than the others of this group ⟨a boost which in a sense it does *merit* —T.S.Eliot⟩ ⟨if hope's familiar whispers *merit* faith —William Wordsworth⟩ RATE in this sense may stress the idea of being fit or suited for some special reward or consideration in addition to what is officially earned and paid or conferred through rank, status, or connection ⟨important statesmen in the United States have usually *rated* eulogistic titles —E.C.Smith⟩ ⟨not that I *rated* the governor's suite on my own —Bennett Cerf⟩

de·served \-vd\ *adj* **:** such as one deserves ⟨a ~ reputation⟩ ⟨a ~ rebuke⟩ — **de·serv·ed·ly** \-vədlē, -li\ *adv* — **de·serv·ed·ness** \-vədnəs\ *n* -ES

de·serv·er \-və(r)\ *n* -S **:** one who deserves

¹**deserving** *n* -S [ME, fr. gerund of *deserven*] **:** DESERT, MERIT

²**deserving** *adj* [fr. pres. part. of *deserve*] **:** MERITORIOUS, WORTHY ⟨rewarding ~ workers⟩ ⟨the causes most ~ of help⟩ ⟨a charlatan ~ of the severest penalty⟩; *specif* **:** meriting financial assistance ⟨scholarship aid for needy and ~ students⟩ — **de·serv·ing·ly** *adv* — **de·serv·ing·ness** *n* -ES

-deses *pl of* -DESIS

de·sex \(ˈ)dē, də+\ *vt* [*de-* + *sex* (n.)] **1 :** to castrate or spay **2 :** to de-emphasize or minimize appeals to sexual interest in

de·sexualization \(ˈ)dē, də+\ *n* **:** the act or an instance of desexualizing ⟨the view that this ~ necessarily results in the choice of a higher, more socially acceptable channel of expression —G.S.Blum⟩

de·sexualize \(ˈ)dē, də+\ *vt* [*de-* + *sexualize*] **1 :** to deprive of sexual characters or power **:** UNSEX, CASTRATE **2** *psychoanalysis* **a :** to divest of sexual quality by diverting the libido to other goals (as in sublimation) **b :** to withdraw (sexual libido) from the genital to other areas of the body (as in perversions)

deshabille *var of* DISHABILLE

¹**de·si** \ˈdāsē, ˈdesē\ *adj* [Bengali *desī*, fr. Skt *deśīya*, fr. *deśa* point, country, district, fr. *diśati* he points out — more at DICTION] *India* **:** INDIGENOUS ⟨~ fowl⟩ ⟨~ goat⟩

²**desi** \"\ *also* **dai·see** \ˈdāsē\ *or* **daisee jute** *n* -S [Bengali *desī* indigenous] **:** an Indian jute obtained from Jew's mallow

desiatin *var of* DESSIATINE

¹**des·ic·cant** \ˈdesəkənt, -sēk-\ *adj* [L *desiccant-*, *desiccans*, pres. part. of *desiccare* to dry up] **:** DRYING, DESICCATIVE

²**desiccant** \"\ *n* -S **:** a drying agent (as sulfuric acid, silica gel)

¹**des·ic·cate** \-kə̇t, -ˌkāt, *usu* |d·+V\ *adj* [ME, fr. L *desiccatus*] **:** DESICCATED ⟨a ~ romance —Allen Tate⟩

²**des·ic·cate** \ˈdesə̇ˌkāt, -sē-, *usu* -ād·+V\ *vb* -ED/-ING/-S [L *desiccatus*, past part. of *desiccare* to dry up, fr. *de-* + *siccare* to dry, fr. *siccus* dry — more at SACK] *vt* **1 :** to dry up or cause to dry up **:** deprive or exhaust of moisture; *esp* **:** dry thoroughly ⟨artificial *desiccating* of timber in an oven with a current of hot air⟩ ⟨the surgeon removed a suspect mole by electrodesiccation and thoroughly *desiccated* the immediately adjoining tissue with a needle electrode⟩ ⟨requiring a *desiccated* hermetically sealed container⟩ **2 :** to preserve (a food) by drying **:** DEHYDRATE ⟨one cup of *desiccated* coconut⟩ **3 a :** to drain of vitality; *esp* **:** to divest of vigor, spirit, passion, or a capability of evoking mental or emotional excitement ⟨a charming little romance . . . not *desiccated* and compressed within the pages of a book —Elinor Wylie⟩ ⟨Mr. Copland's musical style — a deft fusion of ingredients assembled from Debussy and Satie and of *desiccated* elements of American folk music —Winthrop Sargeant⟩ **b :** to divest of spontaneity, animating or interesting properties, or stimulating capacity ⟨a secret-police system first unsettles, then ~s, then calcifies a free society —E.B. White⟩ ⟨the lopsidedly historical approach to literature which dominated and *desiccated* American academic studies for many years —G.H.Genzmer⟩ ⟨the thoughts and behavior of Londoners whose lives were *desiccated* by war —James Stern⟩ **c :** to divest of or divorce from aesthetic sensitivity and human sensibilities and abandon to intellectual aridity ⟨the typical scholar filled with such learning has been caricatured as an absent-minded and *desiccated* personality —C.F.Richards⟩ ~ *vi* **:** to become dried up **:** undergo a desiccating or divesting process ⟨some very small poikilotherms ~ and encapsulate for protection —Samuel Brody⟩ ⟨English philosophy, lost in the aridities of logical positivism and semantics, has tended to become pedantically *desiccated* —*Times Lit. Supp.*⟩ **syn** see DRY

³**desiccate** *like* ¹DESICCATE\ *n* -S **:** a product of or residue from desiccation

desiccated *adj* **1 :** dried up **:** ANHYDROUS ⟨each gram of *desiccated* liver contains the equivalent of not less than 0.05 mg of riboflavin⟩ ⟨half-filled boxes of ~ Spanish cigars —Janet Flanner⟩ **2 :** lacking vitality, spirit, spontaneity, or emotional vigor ⟨a prissy and emotionless creature . . . settles into a mold of ~ snobbery —C.J.Rolo⟩

des·ic·ca·tion \ˌ==ˈkāshən\ *n* -S [LL *desiccation-*, *desiccatio*, fr. L *desiccatus* + *-ion-*, *-io* -ion] **1 :** the act or process of desiccating or the state of being or becoming desiccated: **a :** a complete or nearly complete deprivation of moisture or of water not chemically combined (as by vaporization or evaporation) **:** DEHYDRATION ⟨attributed to some preconsolidation in the soils, particularly the clays, due to compaction by ~ —Mason Lockwood⟩ ⟨partial ~ of landlocked seas at many stages of geological history has given rise to extensive deposits of gypsum and rock salt —W.G.Fearnsides⟩ ⟨for industrial purposes enzymes are rarely purified beyond the stage of simple extraction and ~ of the extract —A.K.Balls⟩ ⟨from the long-wave diathermy machine two distinct currents are obtained which produce ~ and electrocoagulation respectively —W.H.Schmidt⟩ **b :** destitution of vitality from having been or having become desiccated; *esp* **:** deterioration through deprivation or loss of animating, stimulating, or inspiring qualities ⟨the prevalent ~ of the study of philosophy in universities —T.S.Eliot⟩ ⟨research, which alone preserves science from ~ and death —A.L.Guérard⟩ **2 :** a bit of desiccated matter ⟨ringed glasses, clotted tub drains, ~s of paste on toothbrushes —Philip Wylie⟩

desiccation crack *n* **:** MUD CRACK

desiccation polygon *n* **:** a structure bounded by mud cracks found in sedimentary rocks and mud flats

¹**des·ic·ca·tive** \ˈ==ˌkā|d·|iv, -kə|, dəˈsikə|, dēˈs-, |t|, |ēv *also* |əv\ *adj* [LL *desiccativus*, fr. L *desiccatus* + *-ivus* -ive] **:** drying up or tending to dry up ⟨intense ~ characteristics⟩

²**desiccative** \"\ *n* -S *archaic* **:** a desiccative agent

des·ic·ca·tor \ˈdesəˌkād·ə(r), -ˌātə-\ *n* -S **1 :** a container (as a glass jar) fitted with an airtight cover and containing at the bottom some desiccating agent (as calcium chloride) ⟨when a substance to be dried would be decomposed by high temperature it is dried in a ~⟩ **2 :** a machine or apparatus for desiccating fruit, milk, or other food usu. by the aid of heat and sometimes in a vacuum

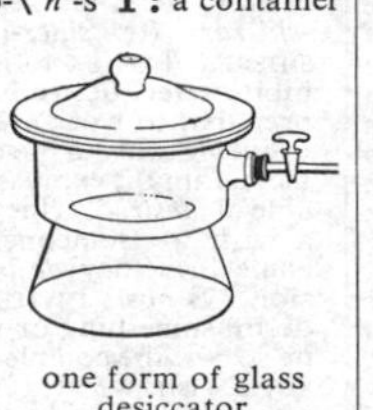

one form of glass desiccator

des·ic·ca·to·ry \ˈ==ˌkəˌtōrē, dəˈsi-,dē-ˈsi-, -ōr-, -ri\ *adj* **:** DESICCATIVE

desiderable *adj* [ME, fr. L *desiderabilis*, fr. *desiderare* to long for, miss, desire + *-abilis* -able — more at DESIRE] *obs* **:** PLEASING, DESIRABLE

de·sid·er·ant \dəˈsidərənt, dēˈ-, -ˈzi-\ *adj* [L *desiderant-*, *desiderans*, pres. part. of *desiderare*] *archaic* **:** DESIROUS

¹**desiderate** *n* -S [L *desideratum*, neut. of *desideratus*, past part. of *desiderare*] *obs* **:** a thing desired

²**de·sid·er·ate** \dəˈsidəˌrāt, dēˈ- *also* -ˈzi-; *usu* -ād·+V\ *vt* -ED/-ING/-S [L *desideratus*, past part. of *desiderare*] **1 :** to seek or advocate earnestly or call for as essential ⟨the author's practice may not achieve the scope he ~s for the complete "historiography of ideas" —J.L.Adams⟩ ⟨just what and how, for instance, the monastic teaching orders he ~s would teach —F.R.Leavis⟩ **2 :** to entertain or express a longing for or a wish to have or attain ⟨to think these two might negotiate peaceably is to ~ an impossibility⟩

de·sid·er·a·tion \=,=dəˈrāshən\ *n* -S [L *desideration-*, *desideratio*, fr. *desideratus* + *-ion-*, *-io* -ion] **1 :** the act or an instance of desiderating **2 :** DESIDERATUM

¹**de·sid·er·a·tive** \=ˈ=də,rā|d·iv, -d(ə)rə|\ *adj* [LL *desiderativus*, fr. L *desideratus* + *-ivus* -ive] **1 :** relating to or denoting desire, esp. a wish to do ⟨the intellect does not include the emotional and immediately ~ elements of human nature —H.O.Taylor⟩ **2 a** *of a verb or verb form* **:** derived from or belonging to the inflectional paradigm of a verb and expressing a desire to perform the action denoted by that verb ⟨the ~ Latin verb *esurire* "to be hungry" is from *edere* "to eat"⟩ **b :** of or relating to a desiderative verb or verb form ⟨a ~ suffix⟩

²**desiderative** \"\ *n* -S **:** a desiderative verb or verb form

de·sid·er·a·tum \=,=dəˈrä|d·əm, -rā|, -rá|, |təm\ *n, pl* **desiderata** \|d·ə,|tə\ [L, neut. of *desideratus*, past part. of *desiderare* to desire — more at DESIRE] **:** something desired as essential or needed **:** something that is sought for or aimed at ⟨the correct reverberation is not, of course, the whole ~ behind concert-hall acoustics —E.G.Richardson⟩ ⟨detached individuality does not seem to be a ~ of the Vedantic mind —Robert Bierstedt⟩ ⟨the concept that peace of mind is the great ~ —Warren Weaver⟩

des·i·de·ri·um \ˌdesəˈdirēəm, -ezə-\ *n, pl* **desideria** \-ēə\ [L, fr. *desiderare* to desire] **:** an ardent desire or longing; *esp* **:** a feeling of loss or grief for something lost

de·sight \ˈdē+ ,-\ *n* [*de-* + *sight*] **:** an unsightly object **:** EYESORE

¹**de·sign** \dəˈzīn, dēˈ-\ *vb* -ED/-ING/-S [MF *designer*, fr. L *designare*, lit., to mark out, fr. *de-* + *signare* to mark — more at SIGN] *vt* **1 a :** to conceive and plan out in the mind ⟨a savage on seeing a watch would at once conclude that it was ~*ed* —Samuel Butler †1902⟩ **b :** DEVOTE, CONSIGN, DESTINE ⟨a city ~*ed* to destruction⟩ ⟨grants ~*ed* in his will for making amends⟩ **c :** to make up one's mind to set apart **:** settle in mind to reserve ⟨mementos of his travels that he had ~*ed* for friends⟩ **d :** to plan or have in mind as a purpose **:** INTEND, PURPOSE, CONTEMPLATE ⟨he was sociable by disposition, and I believe he ~*ed* particularly to shine in the world of talk and manners —Osbert Sitwell⟩ ⟨when some other foreign power ~*ed* division or seizure —Roger Burlingame⟩ **e** *archaic* **:** to have in mind or include as a matter of consideration **f :** to devise or propose for a specific function ⟨a book ~*ed* primarily as a college textbook⟩ ⟨a program obviously ~*ed* as a first approach to this problem⟩ **g :** to create, plan, or calculate for serving a predetermined end **:** prepare or lay out deliberately ⟨the challenging problem of ~*ing* a college curriculum for young women⟩ ⟨a little group of members which is ~*ed* for study, propaganda, and energetic canvassing —R.M.Dawson⟩ ⟨~*ed* to form a frame for what was to come after —E.M.Lustgarten⟩ **2 a** *obs* **:** to indicate with a distinctive mark or sign **b** *archaic* **:** to indicate by name or distinctive phrase **c :** to designate for office or function ⟨~*ing* a friend to act as substitute⟩ ⟨the other parties named and ~*ed* in the summons⟩ **d** *archaic* **:** ASSIGN, GRANT **3** [MF *desseigner*, fr. It *disegnare*, fr. L *designare*] **a** *archaic* **:** to make a drawing or sketch of (an object or scene) **b :** to outline or sketch in proportion for creating a work of art or to serve as a pattern in the practical arts ⟨she has ~*ed* the dances for several Broadway hits⟩ ⟨a curious woman whose dresses always looked as if they had been ~*ed* in a rage —Oscar Wilde⟩ **c :** to plan and plot out the shape and disposition of the parts of and the structural constituents of **:** draw the plans for ⟨he ~*ed* many buildings and bridges⟩ **d :** to create, fashion, execute, or construct according to plan ⟨he was also a clever artist and ~*ed* scenes with a flair for color —Winifred Bambrick⟩ ⟨buildings of the institution are so ~*ed* that each patient's room opens upon a porch —*Amer. Guide Series: Mich.*⟩ **e :** to originate, draft, and work out, set up, or set forth **:** DEVISE, CONTRIVE ⟨a landscaping authority to ~ the city's park system⟩ ⟨can start to ~ and execute a foreign policy without fear —H.W.Barber⟩ ⟨like most Communist propaganda it was very cleverly ~*ed* —Patrick McMahon⟩ ⟨knows how to ~ a part so that it develops and acquires momentum in performance —Brooks Atkinson⟩ **f :** to plan or produce with special intentional adaptation to a specific end — used in passive or participial form ⟨statutes are ~*ed* to meet the fugitive exigencies of the hour —B.N.Cardozo⟩ ⟨slogans are normally ~*ed* to get action without reflection —A.E.Stevenson b.1900⟩ ⟨marriage was a social institution ~*ed* to fit instinct into a legal framework —Bertrand Russell⟩ ⟨would do it for $5000, a price . . . ~*ed* to discourage offers —Elsa Maxwell⟩ ~ *vi* **1 :** to conceive a plan for making something **2 :** to draw, lay out, or otherwise prepare a design or designs ⟨those who ~ for the home⟩ ⟨in ~*ing* for motion pictures there is also the problem of geography —Cedric Gibbons⟩: **a :** to draw a preliminary figure, outline, or sketch (as for a machine, structure, or work of art) **b :** to fashion a work of art **c :** to fashion a decorative figure or pattern **3 :** to plan or intend to start out on a trip or course ⟨this ship ~s for Guam⟩ ⟨the young man ~s for law⟩ **syn** see INTEND, ¹PLAN

²**design** \"\ *n* -S [MF *dessein*, fr. It *disegno*, fr. *disegnare* to mark out] **1 :** a mental project or scheme in which means to an end are laid down **:** PLAN ⟨morality also, like religion, is a product of human ~ —Benjamin Farrington⟩ ⟨had no rivals among the secular rulers of Europe for largeness of ~s —R.W.Southern⟩ **2 a :** a particular purpose held in view by an individual or group **:** a planned intention ⟨my ~ in writing this preface is to forestall certain critics⟩ ⟨he has ambitious ~s for his son⟩ **b :** deliberate purposive planning ⟨what superficially may appear to be a masterpiece of ~ was likely to have been just an empirical policy of muddling through —*Times Lit. Supp.*⟩ ⟨his clumsiness is due to inattention rather than ~⟩ ⟨battle was joined apparently more by accident than ~ —John Buchan⟩; *also* **:** direction toward an ultimate end ⟨the teleological, which shows the marks of ~ in nature, and from them argues to a great designer —*Encyc. Americana*⟩ — opposed to *accident* **3 a :** a deliberate undercover project or scheme entertained with discreditable or hostile and often dishonest, treacherous, sinister, or seductive intent ⟨each camp accusing the other of imperialist ~s⟩ ⟨eager to ferret out any subversive ~s⟩ ⟨a declaration of a ~ upon his life —John Locke⟩ **b designs** *pl* **:** such a scheme contemplating some rapacious or disruptive aggression or some illicit encroachment — used with *on* or *against* ⟨the United States has no . . . ~s against any of its neighbors anywhere —A.H.Vandenberg †1951⟩ ⟨has ~s on the money⟩ **4 :** a preliminary sketch or outline (as a drawing on paper or a modeling in clay) showing the main features of something to be executed **:** DELINEATION ⟨a textile ~ and its specifications constitute the complete working plan for the manufacture of a fabric —Alfred Higgins & R. L. La Vault⟩ **5 a :** a painter or sculptor's preliminary drawing or model ⟨he made two or three charming and blasphemous ~s —W.B.Yeats⟩ **b :** a scheme for the construction, finish, and ornamentation of a building as embodied in the plans, elevations, and other architectural drawings pertaining to it **c :** a conceptual outline or sketch according to which the elements of a literary or dramatic composition or series are developed ⟨his sense of structure, both in the general ~ of *Paradise Lost* and *Samson*, and in his syntax —T.S.Eliot⟩ ⟨it is now widely agreed that such compositions as *Moby Dick* and *Billy Budd* are complete ~s —Nathalia Wright⟩ ⟨the main ~s of the poem, an imaginative control of dispersed material —*Times Lit. Supp.*⟩ **d :** a settled coherent program followed or imposed; *usu* **:** an underlying scheme that governs functioning, developing, or unfolding **:** PATTERN, MOTIF ⟨his ad-libbing . . . is not unfortified by ~ because he is far too fine a professional ever to trust entirely to chance —John Mason Brown⟩ ⟨whether or not there be a ~, . . . in nature, a man's biography frequently discloses haunting glimpses of a pattern —Perry Miller⟩ **6 a :** the arrangement of elements that make up a work of art, a machine, or other man-made object ⟨systematic art instruction begins with the study of ~, which includes little except the perception and creation of formal relations —Hunter Mead⟩ ⟨made her decide to introduce choreographic ~ into her free skating —*Current Biog.*⟩ **b :** the process of selecting the means and contriving the elements, steps, and procedures for producing what will adequately satisfy some need ⟨industrial ~⟩ ⟨included in ~ are the arrangement of the basic text page, choice of typeface, title page, and special pages —Joseph Blumenthal⟩; *specif* **:** the drawing up of specifications as to structure, forms, positions, materials, texture, accessories, decorations in the form of a layout for setting up, building, or

fabrication ⟨the ~ of the ship's bridge⟩ ⟨his experiments were noted for their simple ~⟩ ⟨the problems of stability were corrected by better ~ in duplicating equipment —R.O.Jordan⟩ **c** : structural constitution or fundamental framework of a musical composition ⟨unacceptable to our sense of melodic ~ —P.H.Lang⟩ ⟨inflated music with ambitious and mystical programmatic ~*s* —Nicolas Slonimsky⟩ **7 a** : a visual arrangement or disposition of lines, parts, figures, details usu. unified by an implicit key or clue of signification or an artistic motif (as in engravings, medals, textiles, metalwork) ⟨linoleum in a great number of ~*s*⟩ ⟨the ~*s* on the reverse of our coins⟩ ⟨an iron balustrade with a ~ of bows and arrows that rises from the eaves of the house —*Amer. Guide Series: Maine*⟩ **b** : a pattern or figuration applied to a surface (as of a vase) : DECORATION ⟨porcelain with carved or engraved floral ~*s*⟩ ⟨a gold-tooled ~ impressed on bookbindings⟩ **syn** see INTENTION, PLAN

³design \"\ *adj* : used as a basis for anticipating practical problems and solving them at the engineering stage — used chiefly in highway designing ⟨the ~ speed of a highway⟩

des·ig·na·ble \ˈdezignəbəl, |ēg *sometimes* -es|\ *adj* [L *designare* to mark out + E *-able*] : DISTINGUISHABLE, IDENTIFIABLE ⟨the probability that two parts of the subject might be designated or ~ by the same term —J.T.Krumpelmann⟩

de·sig·na·do \ˌdesig'nä(ˌ)dō, -ezi-\ *n* -s [Sp. fr. *designado*, past part. of *designar* to designate, fr. L *designare*] : one legally appointed or elected in some Spanish-American countries to succeed the president

designata *pl of* DESIGNATUM

des·ig·nat·able \ˈdez|ig,nād·əbəl, -ēg-, -ātə- *sometimes* -es|\ *adj* : capable of being designated

¹des·ig·nate \-ˌnā|t, -ˌnə|, *usu* |d·+V\ *adj* [L *designatus*, past part. of *designare*] : chosen for an office but not yet installed — used after the noun ⟨called president-elect or president-*designate*⟩ ⟨the pledges of the governor ~⟩

²des·ig·nate \-ˌnāt, *usu* -ād·+V\ *vt* -ED/-ING/-S [L *designatus*, past part. of *designare*, lit., to mark out — more at DESIGN] **1 a** : to point out the location of ⟨a marker *designating* the crest of the flood waters⟩ **b** : to make known directly as if by sign : SIGNIFY, INDICATE ⟨any reasonable task *designated* by the employer⟩ **c** : to distinguish as to class : DENOMINATE, IDENTIFY, LABEL ⟨the area we ~ as that of spiritual values —J.B.Conant⟩ **d** : SPECIFY, STIPULATE ⟨sending food packages to *designated* recipients in Europe⟩ ⟨a gift *designated* by the donor to be used for faculty compensation⟩ **2 a** : to call by a distinctive title, term, or expression ⟨a particle having approximately the mass of a proton but having no charge and so *designated* as a neutron —W.V.Houston⟩ ⟨the four parts were *designated A, B, C,* and *D* in the diagram⟩ **b** : to declare to be : CHARACTERIZE ⟨areas *designated* as strategic⟩ **3** : to name esp. to a post or function **4 a** : to decide upon : NOMINATE, DELEGATE, APPOINT; *esp* : to assign officially by executive or military authority ⟨the operating agency last *designated* by the president⟩ ⟨the tanks had been *designated* to exploit a breakthrough of the enemy's defenses —R.D.Gardner⟩ **b** : to induct in a rank or position ⟨the supreme council is *designated* as the highest organ of state power⟩ ⟨the duke had been *designated* as king of a puppet state⟩ **c** : to choose and set apart (as by public will or in the process of government administration) ⟨a successful *designating* petition places the name of the candidate on the primary ballot —*Bk. of Civic Definitions*⟩ ⟨control dams *designated* for construction⟩ ⟨finally Queen Victoria was asked to ~ a site—B.K.Sandwell⟩ **5** : to serve as a name of : stand for : DENOTE ⟨associate . . . the names with the persons they ~ —Weldon Kees⟩ ⟨names are now given bacteria as a sort of shorthand to ~ a whole series of complicated reactions —Justina Hill⟩ **6** *logic* : to refer to (an abstract or a concrete entity) — used of a sign, word, or linguistic expression

syn NAME, NOMINATE, ELECT, APPOINT: DESIGNATE may apply to choosing or detailing a person or group for a certain post by a person or group having power or right to choose ⟨the following deputies were *designated* by the three ministers to carry on the council's work —*Americana Annual*⟩ ⟨the vice-chairman is elected from among the commissioners, and the president *designates* the chairman —*Current Biog.*⟩ NAME differs little from DESIGNATE except that it may more strongly imply public announcement and less strongly suggest official action ⟨the president-elect has not yet *named* his secretary of state⟩ ⟨*named* to the position of general manager⟩ ⟨a council of the realm to advise him and to *name* his successor in the event of his death —*Current Biog.*⟩ NOMINATE today often indicates presentation of a candidate for the approval of or rejection by those who make final decisions ⟨the parties *nominate* their presidential candidates during the summer⟩ ⟨President Truman *nominated* him for promotion to full admiral, an advancement confirmed by the Senate —*Current Biog.*⟩ ELECT may apply to definitive selection by a qualified group from among persons nominated or offering themselves as candidates ⟨*elected* by a large majority of the voters⟩ ⟨*elected* to membership in a general meeting of the club⟩ APPOINT indicates selection without election by a qualified person or group, with or without confirmation by another instrumentality ⟨the president *appoints* postal officials⟩ ⟨by constitutional provision the chief executive *appoints*, not independently (except in a few instances as indicated above), but "by and with the advice and consent of the senate"; to speak with complete accuracy, he nominates, the Senate confirms (by a majority vote of the members present), and he thereupon *appoints* —F.A.Ogg & P.O.Ray⟩

des·ig·na·tion \ˌ==ˈnāshən\ *n* -s [ME *desygnacion*, fr. L *designation-, designatio*, fr. *designatus* + *-ion-, -io*, -ion] **1** : the act of indicating or identifying by a mark, letter, or sign or by classification or specification ⟨contriving new characters for the ~ of sounds alien to the language⟩ ⟨anciently the law was that the mere repetition of a slander was not actionable if the repetition was accompanied by a ~ of the author —B.N.Cardozo⟩ **2 a** : a distinguishing name : a title earned or awarded ⟨for years the county seat had no proper ~⟩ ⟨as a writer of light verse; but this ~ isn't good enough —Charles Jackson⟩ **b** : NAMING ⟨perhaps the honor that touched him most deeply was the ~ during his last years of the new laboratory —C.H.Herty⟩ ⟨the ~ of degrees for women graduates puzzled the more liberal educators —*Amer. Guide Series: Texas*⟩ **3 a** : appointment or assignment to a post ⟨his next ~ was a second secretaryship at Panama City⟩; *also* : nomination for a political office ⟨seeking to win the Republican primary ~⟩ **b** : delegation, engagement, or allocation for a service ⟨his ~ by Chile and Argentina as umpire of a commission⟩ ⟨the revision of the rest of Matthew and of Genesis and all of Exodus by the ~ of different sections to various members of the committee —I.M.Price⟩ **c** *archaic* : a natural leaning that contributes to one's fitness **4** *obs* : end in view **5** : an allotment of bottom for planting oysters; *also* : the space so allotted **6** *logic* : the relation between a sign, word, or linguistic expression and the object referred to; *also* : MEANING, CONNOTATION

des·ig·na·tio per·so·nae \ˌdezig'nāshē,ōpə(r)ˈsō(ˌ)nē\ *n* [L, designation of the person] : matter designating the persons who are parties to and essential to the validity of a document — compare DESCRIPTIO PERSONAE

¹des·ig·na·tive \ˈdez|ig,nā|d·|iv, |ēg-, -ˌnə|, |t|, |ēv *also* |əv *sometimes* ˈdes|\ *adj* [LL *designativus*, fr. L *designatus* + *-ivus* -ive] : serving to designate or indicate

²designative \"\ *n* -s : something designative

des·ig·na·tor \-ˌnād·ə(r), -ātə-\ *n* -s [LL, fr. L *designatus* + *-or*] : one that designates; *esp* : a designative sign in semantics

des·ig·na·to·ry \-ˌnə,tōrē, -ōr-, -ri\ *adj* : DESIGNATIVE

des·ig·na·tum \ˌdezig'nād·əm\ *n, pl* **designa·ta** \-d·ə\ [L, neut. of *designatus*, past part. of *designare* to designate, design, lit., to mark out — more at DESIGN] : something that is referred to by a word, sign, or linguistic expression whether actually existing or not : the class of objects referred to by a sign, including the null class — contrasted with *denotatum*

design bedding *n* : an arrangement of herbaceous plants in a definite pattern of contrasting foliage or blossom ⟨the atrocities of *design bedding* still persist in some public gardens as geometric figures or stylized objects stiffly painted in varied colors of leaf and flowers⟩ — distinguished from *carpet bedding*

de·signed \dəˈzīnd, dēˈ-\ *adj* : done, performed, or made with purpose and intent often despite an appearance of being accidental, spontaneous, or natural ⟨style . . . is more than the deliberate and ~ creation —Havelock Ellis⟩ **syn** see DELIBERATE

de·sign·ed·ly \-nədlē, -li\ *adv* : with definite purpose : PURPOSIVELY, DELIBERATELY

des·ig·nee \ˌdezig'nē *sometimes* -esi-\ *n* -s [*designate* + *-ee*] : one who is designated or delegated ⟨the favorite-son ~ of the New York delegation⟩ ⟨one of the plant supervisors is a union ~⟩

de·sign·er \dəˈzīnə(r), dēˈ-\ *n* -s **1** : one who conceives plans (as large-scale plans or those for public or social projects) ⟨the ~*s* of the Fourth Republic provided what France wanted —*Time*⟩ ⟨it is strange that resistance to this proposition seems strongest among some of the most audacious social ~*s* —Curt Stern⟩ ⟨the planners and ~*s*, the inciters and leaders without whose evil architecture the world would not have been so long scourged —R.H.Jackson⟩ **2** : one whose work is creating or laying out designs or reproducing designs made by others for products of mechanical, industrial, or practical arts or for architectural structures ⟨a famous industrial ~⟩ ⟨better planners, urban ~*s*, and landscape artists in our schools —J.L.Sert⟩ **3 a** : one who plans, produces, or creates utilitarian or aesthetic objects ⟨ceramic ~*s*⟩ ⟨an outstanding book ~ planned the format⟩ ⟨dress ~⟩ **b** : one who plans and directs the fashioning of theatrical stage settings, costumes, and ballet settings

de·sign·er·ship \-ˌship\ *n* -s : the office or function of a designer : accomplishment as designer

de·sign·ful \-nfəl\ *adj* : full of design : INTENTIONAL — **de·sign·ful·ly** \-f(ə)lē\ *adv*

¹designing *n* [fr. gerund of ¹*design*] : the art of making designs or sketches ⟨studied ~ under experts⟩

²designing *adj* [fr. pres. part. of ¹*design*] **1** : practicing forethought **2** : concealing under a complaisant manner crafty or evil designs esp. for advancing one's own interests : SCHEMING ⟨~ woman⟩ ⟨a selfish and ~ nation, obsessed with the dark schemes of European intrigue —Sir Winston Churchill⟩ ⟨a ~ Providence⟩ — **de·sign·ing·ly** *adv*

de·sign·less \-nləs\ *adj* : being without a design — **de·sign·less·ness** *n* -ES

design patent *n* : a patent granted to one who has invented any new, original, and ornamental design for an article of manufacture ⟨under a *design patent* the appearance of the article rather than its mechanical function receives protection —*Harvard Law Rev.*⟩

designs *pres 3d sing of* DESIGN, *pl of* DESIGN

de·silicate \(ˈ)dē+\ *vt* [*de-* + *silicate*] : to remove silica or silicate from; *esp* : to cause to undergo desilication

de·silication \(ˌ)dē+\ *n* -s : removal of silica from a magma esp. by interaction with limestone and its transfer to the enveloping wall rock where it is fixed in the form of various silicates

de·silt \(ˈ)dē+\ *vt* [*de-* + *silt* (n.)] : to remove suspended silt from (the water of a stream) ⟨a basin for ~*ing* water⟩

de·silverization \(ˌ)dē+\ *n* -s : the act or a process of desilverizing

de·silverize *also* **de·silver** \"+\ *vt* [*desilverize* fr. *de-* + *silver* + *-ize*; *desilver* fr. *de-* + *silver*] : to remove the silver from : free from silver ⟨*desilverizing* lead ores⟩ — **de·silverizer** \"+\ *n* -s

des·i·nence \ˈdezənən(t)s, -esə-\ *n* -s [MF, fr. ML *desinentia*, fr. L *desinent-, desinens* + *-ia*] : TERMINATION ⟨the ~ of a verse⟩; *often* : ENDING c (1) ⟨any Russian inflectional form comprehends a stem and a ~ —Roman Jakobson⟩

des·i·nent \-nənt\ *adj* [L *desinent-, desinens*, pres. part. of *desinere* to leave off, cease, fr. *de-* + *sinere* to leave — more at SITE] : TERMINAL

des·i·nen·tial \ˌ==ˈnenchəl\ *adj* **1** : TERMINAL **2** : of, relating to, or being an inflectional ending

de·sip·i·ence \dəˈsipēən(t)s, dēˈ-\ *also* **de·sip·i·en·cy** \-nsē\ *n, pl* **desipiences** *also* **desipiencies** [L *desipientia*, fr. *desipient-, desipiens* + *-ia*] : relaxed dallying in enjoyment of foolish trifles

de·sip·i·ent \-pēənt\ *adj* [L *desipient-, desipiens*, pres. past. of *desipere* to be foolish, fr. *de-* + *-sipere* (fr. *sapere* to have taste, be wise) — more at SAGE] : indulging in desipience ⟨and smiled to see ~ Horace play —Timothy Dwight⟩

de·sir·abil·i·ty \də,zīrəˈbiləd·ē, dē,-, -ətē, -i\ *n* -ES **1** : the quality, fact, or degree of being desirable or of having worth ⟨they considered the chances and ~ of revolution⟩ **2 desirabilities** *pl* : a desirable condition ⟨we had understood and studied certain *desirabilities* in a truly integrated staff —D.D. Eisenhower⟩

¹de·sir·able \-ˈzīrəbəl\ *adj* [ME, fr. MF, fr. *desirer* + *-able*] **1** : capable of arousing desire: **a** : having the power to attract or bring into demand : of such properties or qualities as to be wished for or sought ⟨one of the city's most ~ neighborhoods⟩ ⟨a plant species that may prove to be commercially ~⟩; *often* : so valuable or excellent as to assure being desired or selected **b** : such as to awake urgent or passionate longing or craving ⟨there are circumstances in which a scoop of dirty water can be supremely ~⟩; *esp* : exciting erotic longing ⟨she was never more ~ than at this moment⟩ **2 a** : worth seeking or doing as advantageous, beneficial, or wise : ADVISABLE, EXPEDIENT ⟨having the footnotes at the back of the book is not nearly so ~⟩ ⟨even if the highest education were ~ for all, which I doubt —Bertrand Russell⟩ ⟨~ freedom and individual responsibility of the elective system —*Official Register of Harvard Univ.*⟩ **b** : suited to the purposes and objectives of normal society ⟨however ~ a common language for all the world may be —I.A.Richards⟩ ⟨the personal opinion of the judge as to what is ~ or undesirable legislation —M.R.Cohen⟩

²desirable \"\ *n* -s : one that is desirable ⟨a balanced diet and adequate rest are basic ~*s* for any convalescent⟩ : a person or thing that merits or attracts desire or favorable attention and consideration ⟨fostering the ~*s* and weeding out the undesirables⟩; *often* : a person regarded as of high social standing and eligibility ⟨moving always in a small circle of ~*s* he scarcely knew the lower world of clubs and theaters and balls existed⟩

de·sir·able·ness \-bəlnəs\ *n* -ES : the fact or quality of being desirable : DESIRABILITY ⟨I am quite ready to accept the ~ of government liability —O.W.Holmes †1935⟩

de·sir·ably \-blē, -bli\ *adv* : in a desirable place or manner : to a desirable extent or degree : in accordance with what is considered desirable ⟨land ~ situated in a sheltered river valley⟩

¹de·sire \dəˈzī(ə)r, dēˈ-\ *vb* -ED/-ING/-S [ME *desiren*, fr. OF *desirer*, fr. L *desiderare* to long for, miss, desire, fr. *de-* + *-siderare* (fr. *sider-, sidus* star, constellation) — more at SIDEREAL] *vt* **1** : to long or hope for : wish for earnestly : exhibit or feel desire for : COVET ⟨men who ~ success must be prepared to work⟩ ⟨he *desired* her approval above all things⟩ ⟨*desiring* only a peaceful haven⟩ **2 a** : to ask or call for (something) : express a wish for : REQUEST ⟨maid services available if *desired*⟩ ⟨they ~ an immediate answer⟩ **b** : to express a wish to (someone) : ASK, REQUEST, ENTREAT ⟨~ him to come in⟩ ⟨they *desired* the conference to reconsider its decision⟩ **3** *obs* : INVITE **4** *archaic* : to feel the loss of ~ *vi* : to desire something or the fulfillment of some aim ⟨he can be, if he so ~*s*, the complete master of his own cabinet —H.J.Laski⟩

syn WISH, WANT, CRAVE, COVET: DESIRE, WISH, and WANT are often used with identical intent though in such situations, usu. everyday ones where the degree of intensity of longing or need is not at issue, DESIRE and WISH occur more frequently than WANT as seeming to confer more dignity on the subject or implying more respectfulness ⟨we can definitely order anything you *wish*⟩ ⟨a position *desired* by young lady —*advt*⟩ DESIRE in more general use, however, emphasizes the strength or ardor of feeling and often implies strong intention or aim ⟨more than any other thing on earth he *desired* to fight for his country —W.A.White⟩ ⟨unions which *desired* to avail themselves of the benefits of the law —*Collier's Yr. Bk.*⟩ ⟨the waitress should not ask if wine is *desired*⟩ WISH is less strong, often suggesting a not usu. intense longing for an object unattained, unattainable, or questionably attainable ⟨Newton's law of gravitation could not be *wished* into existence —H.A.Overstreet⟩ ⟨not to have property, if one *wished* it, was almost a certain sign of shiftlessness —Van Wyck Brooks⟩ WANT is a less formal term than WISH and so is often interchangeable with it in situations where dignity of the subject or respectfulness is not at issue, though generally WANT implies a need or lack ⟨those who *wanted* to live long —Morris Fishbein⟩ ⟨the French *wanted* European unity —*N.Y. Times*⟩ CRAVE implies strongly the force of physical or mental appetite or need (as of hunger, thirst, love, or ambition) ⟨to *crave* peace and security after war⟩ ⟨that eternal *craving* for amusement —Donn Byrne⟩ ⟨what he *craved* was books of poetry and chivalry —E.A.Weeks⟩ COVET implies a strong, eager desire, often inordinate and envious and often for what belongs to another ⟨where water is the most *coveted* and essential resource because its supply is limited —*Amer. Guide Series: Texas*⟩ ⟨we hate no people, and *covet* no people's land —Wendell Willkie⟩

²desire \"\ *n* -s [ME, fr. MF *desir*, fr. *desirer*] **1** : conscious impulse toward an object or experience that promises enjoyment or satisfaction in its attainment ⟨with Freud all human behavior seems to be the outcome of ~ — that is, of the search for pleasure —H.M.Parshley⟩ ⟨in all Indian thought since Buddhism, the original sin has been ~, which ensnares the spirit in material incarnation —Weston La Barre⟩ **2 a** : an enduring and passionate longing or intense yearning : an urgently impelling motive toward attainment : CRAVING, APPETENCY ⟨a ~ of serfs to get rid of the feudalism that has held them in a vise from time out of mind —W.O.Douglas⟩ ⟨the ~ for adventure⟩ ⟨if a plebiscite confirms the people's ~ for independence —Vera M. Dean⟩ ⟨humility is the most difficult of all virtues to achieve; nothing dies harder than the ~ to think well of oneself —T.S.Eliot⟩ **b** (1) : a strong physical inclination (2) : erotic urge : sexual attraction or appetite ⟨the full lips thrust out and taut like the flesh of animals distended by fear or ~ —Willa Cather⟩ ⟨~ is the natural consequence of the sexual instinct —W.S.Maugham⟩ **c** : a striving after in intent : a deliberate choice or preference ⟨the conductor's ~ to follow the composer's instructions to the letter⟩ ⟨he expressed a ~ to avoid compulsory measures⟩ **3** : an asking or formal request for some action : PETITION ⟨the yeas and nays of the members of either house on any question shall, at the ~ of one fifth of those present, be entered on the journal —*U.S. Constitution*⟩ **4** : something that is desired : an object of longing ⟨then the leaders got hold of it, took it to pieces and remodeled it closer to the heart's ~ —S.H.Adams⟩

syn APPETITE, APPETENCY *or* APPETENCE, CONCUPISCENCE, LUST, PASSION, URGE: DESIRE is a general term applicable to any wish or longing of any sort ⟨the *desire* for change, for novelty, for a relief from the monotony of every day —Aldous Huxley⟩ ⟨a *desire* for admiration in general —Herbert Spencer⟩ ⟨the geisha is only what she has been made in answer to foolish human *desire* for the illusion of love mixed with youth and grace, but without regrets or responsibilities —Lafcadio Hearn⟩ APPETITE applies to a desire strongly calling for satisfaction; it may be wide in its application ⟨it gave men a familiarity with the method and outline of Aristotle's logic, and whetted their *appetite* for more —R.W.Southern⟩ ⟨young Nathaniel Bowditch, the future navigator, first fed his *appetite* for mathematical science —S.E.Morison & H.S.Commager⟩ It is likely to be used in reference to sensual desires and needs ⟨the collected guns and women, and his sexual *appetite* was awesome —E.D.Radin⟩ ⟨*appetites* for expensive clothes and jewelry, good food, strong liquor and weak women —Alan Hynd⟩ APPETENCY and APPETENCE may suggest appetite marked by strong craving ⟨the liquid shine of the workmen's eyes, like the eyes of drinking men when they smell liquor, bright with *appetence* —Mary Austin⟩ ⟨that gnawing dissatisfaction which his purely physical *appetencies* create in him again and again —R.W.Stallman⟩ CONCUPISCENCE may apply to any strong craving but commonly applies to strong or inordinate sexual desire ⟨the principle of sin was designated by the Schoolmen as "*concupiscence*", which included inordinate desires in general, the sexual passion being the prominent element —G.P.Fisher⟩ LUST may apply to any exigent desire but commonly is used in reference to crass craving for something unsanctioned, esp. illicit or inordinate sex ⟨no greed for the land or wealth of any other people, no vulgar ambition, no morbid *lust* for material gain at the expense of others —Sir Winston Churchill⟩ ⟨he had the *lust* for money as Martinez had for women —Willa Cather⟩ ⟨in his morning litany he could pray to be kept from lasciviousness, but when night came *lust* might come with it —Carl Van Doren⟩ PASSION indicates compelling, intense emotion or desire or its ardent fulfillment, often in matters sexual ⟨this consuming *passion* for law made him govern himself, keep in restraint the fierce wrath which leaped up within him —H.E.Scudder⟩ ⟨the *passion* of Giovanni and Annabella is not shown as an affinity of temperament due to identity of blood; it hardly rises above the purely carnal infatuation —T.S.Eliot⟩ ⟨and she loved him with a full, happy *passion* that responded frankly and generously to his —Rose Macaulay⟩ URGE is used of a persistent desire or inclination seeking satisfaction ⟨the *urge* of "backward" peoples to move rapidly from feudalism to industrialism, to acquire modern and expensive technology in a hurry and thus drastically raise their living standards —W.G.Carleton⟩ ⟨the *urges* of dishonest hired girls, prostitutes who didn't want to be reformed, or shiftless husbands —Barbara Klaw⟩

desired *adj* [ME, fr. past part. of *desiren*] **1** : that is longed or hoped for **2** : predetermined to be suitable or satisfactory : prescribed as requisite : RIGHT ⟨once the ~ level is obtained, the helicopter is in a standstill or hovering attitude —S.A. Constantino⟩ ⟨sawed to the ~ width⟩ — **de·sired·ness** \-ī(ə)rdnəs, -īəd-, -īrəd-\ *n* -ES

de·sire·ful \-ī(ə)rfəl, -īəf-\ *adj* [ME, fr. *desire* + *-ful*] **1** *archaic* : DESIRABLE **2** *archaic* : filled with desire : EAGER

de·sire·less \-ī(ə)rləs, -īəl-\ *adj* : being without desire

de·sir·er \-īrə(r)\ *n* -s [ME, fr. *desiren* + *-er*] : one that desires

desires *pres 3d sing of* DESIRE, *pl of* DESIRE

desiring *pres part of* DESIRE

de·sir·ing·ly *adv* : LONGINGLY, YEARNINGLY

de·sir·ous \-ī(ə)rəs\ *adj* [ME, fr. OF *desireus, desirous*, fr. *desir* + *-eus*, *-ous* -ous] **1 a** : impelled or governed by desire : eagerly wishing : SOLICITOUS ⟨the committee is ~ you should select a suitable speaker⟩ ⟨~ to ask his help⟩ **b** : eager to obtain : COVETOUS **2** *obs* : expressive of desire **3** *obs* : eager and spirited esp. in combat **4** *archaic* : DESIRABLE, DELECTABLE — **de·sir·ous·ly** *adv* — **de·sir·ous·ness** *n* -ES

desis *pl of* DESI

-de·sis \ˌdəsəs\ *n comb form, pl* **-de·ses** \ˌdə,sēz\ [NL, fr. Gk *desis*, fr. *dein* to bind + *-sis* — more at DIADEM] : binding ⟨arthro*desis*⟩

de·sist \dəˈzist, dēˈ-, -ˈsi-\ *vb* -ED/-ING/-S [MF *desister*, fr. L *desistere*, fr. *de-* + *sistere* to stand, stop, fr. *stare* to stand — more at STAND] *vi* : to give over or leave off : refrain from or forbear continuing an action, activity, or endeavor under way — often used with *from* or *in* ⟨he had made two attempts to shave but his hand had been so unsteady that he had been obliged to ~ —James Joyce⟩ ⟨~*ed* in his effort to press love upon her —Sherwood Anderson⟩ ⟨the city has been ordered to ~ from further levies⟩ — compare CEASE AND DESIST ORDER ~ *vt, obs* : to cease from : DISCONTINUE **syn** see STOP

de·sis·tance *also* **de·sis·tence** \-tən(t)s\ *n* -s : the act of desisting : cessation of action ⟨pending ~ from violence⟩

de·si·tion \-ˈzishən, -ˈsi-\ *n* -s [ML *desition-, desitio*, fr. L *desitus* (past part. of *desinere* to leave off, cease) + *-ion-, -io* -ion — more at DESINENT] *archaic* : a cessation of being

des·i·tive \ˈdezəd·iv, -esə-\ *adj* [L *desitus* + E *-ive*] : concluding or expressing a conclusion ⟨a ~ proposition⟩

de·size \(ˈ)dē, də+\ *vt* [*de-* + *size* (n.)] : to remove size or sizing from (cloth)

¹desk \ˈdesk\ *n* -s [ME *deske*, fr. ML *desca*, modif. of It *desco* board, table, fr. L *discus* dish, disk, quoit — more at DISH] **1 a** : a table, frame, or case that has a sloping or horizontal surface esp. for writing and reading and is often provided with drawers, compartments, and pigeonholes **b** *obs* : BOOKCASE, BOOKSHELF **c** : a reading table or lectern to support the book from which the liturgical service is read that differs from the pulpit from which the sermon is preached **d** : a table, counter, stand, or booth at which a person (as an editor, a police sergeant, a clerk) performs his duties ⟨speeding — at least for first offenders — can be settled for a set fine at the violations ~ —J. C. Ingraham⟩ ⟨leave your key at the ~ when you are out of the hotel⟩ **e :** a music stand **2 a** *Scot* **:** a pew or seat in a church **b :** a seating position according to rank in an orchestra ⟨a first-*desk* violinist⟩ **3 a :** a division of a complex organization that specializes in and is responsible for a particular phase of that organization's activity ⟨the city ~ of a metropolitan newspaper⟩ ⟨the head of the State Department's Northeast Asian ~⟩ **b :** a person officiating at or heading such a desk

²desk \"\ *adj* **1 :** engaged at or suitable for use at a desk ⟨no mere ~ executive⟩ ⟨a ~ dictionary⟩ ⟨a ~ chair⟩ ⟨he was a ~ colonel⟩ **2 :** given to theorizing without technical knowledge or experience of field conditions ⟨~ strategists⟩

deskbound \'=,=\ *adj* **:** tied down to work at a desk ⟨an officer ~ in Washington by a heart condition⟩

de·skill \(')dē+\ *vt* [*de-* + *skill* (n.)] **:** to mechanize or break down (as an operation) so that performance may require little or no skill

desk jobber *n* **:** DROP SHIPPER

desk·man \'desk,man, -,mən\ *n, pl* **deskmen 1 :** a supervisor or director of operations performing his duties at a desk: **a :** an official in charge of a desk in a government department **b :** a police sergeant on duty at the desk in a police station **c :** a hotel room clerk **2 :** a newsman who works primarily at a desk processing news and preparing copy

desk pad *n* **:** a pad for use on the writing surface of a desk

desk room *n* **:** rented desk space in a business office

desk shoe *n* **:** a cushioning rubber cap to be slipped on each foot of a metal desk

desk work *n* **:** work usu. performed at a desk

de·slime \(')dē+\ *vt* -ED/-ING/-S [*de-* + *slime* (n.)] **:** to remove slime from ⟨*desliming* of fine coal⟩

desm- *or* **desmo-** *comb form* [NL, fr. Gk, band, bond, fr. *desmos*, fr. *dein* to bind] **:** bond **:** ligament ⟨*desm*algia⟩ ⟨*desmo*graphy⟩

des·ma \'dezmə\ *n, pl* **desma·ta** \-mədə, -mətə\ [NL, fr. Gk, bond, fr. *dein* to bind — more at DIADEM] **:** an irregularly branched sponge spicule

des·ma·chyme \'dezmə,kīm\ *n* -S [NL *desma* + Gk *chymos* juice — more at CHYME] **:** connective tissue of sponges

des·ma·cyte \-,sīt\ *n* -S [NL *desma* + E *-cyte*] **:** one of the long fusiform cells forming a fibrous network in sponge cortex

des·man \'dezmən\ *n* -S [short for Sw *desmansråtta*, fr. *desman* musk (fr. MLG *desem, dessmer*) + *råtta* rat; akin to OE *disma* musk, OS *desemo*, MHG *tiseme, tesem*, all fr. a prehistoric WGmc word borrowed fr. ML *bisamum* musk, of Sem origin; akin to Heb *beśem* pleasant aroma] **1 a :** an aquatic insectivorous mammal (*Desmana moschata*) of Russia that resembles a mole **b :** a related animal (*Galemys pyrenaicus*) of the Pyrenees **2 :** the fur or pelt of a desman

des·man·thus \dez'man(t)thəs\ *n, cap* [NL, fr. Gk *desmē* bundle (fr. *dein* to bind) + NL *-anthus* — more at DIADEM] **:** a genus of American herbs or shrubs (family Leguminosae) with sensitive bipinnate leaves and small whitish flowers

des·ma·res·tia \,dezmə'restēə, ,dām-, -sch(ē)ə\ *n, cap* [NL, fr. A. G. *Desmarest* †1838 Fr. naturalist + NL *-ia*] **:** a genus of small feathery and usu. lithophytic brown algae (order Desmarestiales) that occur commonly in colder seas of both hemispheres esp. on rocky shores — **des·ma·res·ti·a·ceous** \;==;=tē;āshəs, -chē;-\ *adj*

des·ma·res·ti·a·les \,demə,restē'ā(,)lēz, ,dām-, -schē'ā-\ *n pl, cap* [NL, fr. *Desmarestia* + *-ales*] **:** an order of much-branched brown algae (class Heterogeneratae) with a single growing apex to each filament and complex pseudo-parenchymatous specialization of the basal part of the thallus — see DESMARESTIA

des·mid \'dezməd\ *n* -S [NL *Desmidium, Desmidiaceae* & *Desmidiales*] **:** any of numerous unicellular or colonial green algae that belong to the order Zygnematales esp. to the family Desmidiaceae or to this together with the Mesotaeniaceae, and that lack asexual means of spore formation, have platelike green chromatophores, and differ from diatoms mainly in lacking a siliceous skeleton

desmids

des·mid·i·a·ce·ae \(,)dez,midē'āsē,ē\ *n pl, cap* [NL, fr. *Desmidium*, type genus (fr. *desm-* + *-idium*) + *-aceae*] **:** a family of unicellular or colonial algae (order Zygnematales) comprising the placoderm desmids — compare MESOTAENIACEAE — **des·mid·i·a·ceous** \(;)=;==;āshəs\ *adj*

des·mid·i·a·les \-'ā(,)lēz\ *n pl, cap* [NL, fr. *Desmidium* + *-ales*] *in some classifications* **:** an order comprising the desmids and including the Desmidiaceae and sometimes also the Mesotaeniaceae

des·mid·i·ol·o·gy \-dē'äləjē\ *n* -ES [NL *Desmidium* + E *-o-* + *-logy*] **:** a branch of botany that deals with desmids

des·mine \'dez,mēn, -,mən\ *n* -S [Gk *desmē* bundle + E *-ine*] **:** STILBITE

desmo- — see DESM-

des·mo·cranium \,dezmə+\ *n* [NL, fr. *desm-* + *cranium*] **:** the earliest mesenchymal precursor of the chondrocranium

des·mo·cyte \'==,sīt\ *n* -S [*desm-* + *-cyte*] **:** any of certain elongated interstitial cells (as a fibroblast)

des·mo·di·um \dez'mōdēəm\ *n* [NL, prob. irreg. fr. Gk *desmos* band, bond + NL *-ium* — more at DESM-] **1** *cap* **:** a large genus of coarse chiefly tropical and perennial leguminous herbs comprising the tick trefoils and having stipulate pinnate leaves, racemose flowers, and indehiscent fruits that separate into one-seeded segments and often stick to anything touching them — see BEGGARWEED, TELEGRAPH PLANT **2** -S **:** a plant of the genus *Desmodium*

¹des·mo·dont \'dezmə,dänt\ *adj* [NL *Desmodontidae*] **:** of or belonging to the family Desmodontidae

²desmodont \"\ *n* -S **:** a bat of the family Desmodontidae **:** VAMPIRE BAT

des·mo·don·ta \,=='däntə\ *n pl, cap* [NL, fr. *desm-* + *-odonta*] *in some classifications* **:** an order of Lamellibranchia comprising bivalve mollusks having no lateral teeth on the shell and the cardinal teeth often reduced or absent

des·mo·don·ti·dae \-tə,dē\ *n pl, cap* [NL, fr. *Desmodont-, Desmodus*, type genus + *-idae*] **:** a small family of bats (suborder Microchiroptera) comprising the true vampire bats

des·mo·dus \'dezmədəs\ *n, cap* [NL, fr. *desm-* + *-odus*] **:** the type genus of Desmodontidae comprising a number of common So. Amer. bloodsucking bats — see VAMPIRE

des·mo·gen \'dezməjən, -,jen\ *n* -S [*desm-* + *-gen*] **:** vascular meristematic tissue

des·mog·na·thae \dez'mägnə,thē\ *n pl, cap* [NL, fr. *desm-* + *-gnathae*] *in former classifications* **:** a primary division of birds having the maxillopalatines united directly or by ossifications in the nasal septum and including the ducks, geese, herons, storks, totipalmate birds, birds of prey, parrots, and most picarian birds — **desmognathism** \-,thizəm\ *n* -S — **des·mog·na·thous** \(')=;==thəs\ *adj*

des·mog·na·thus \-nəthəs\ *n, cap* [NL, fr. *desm-* + *-gnathus*] **:** a genus of small dark salamanders (family Plethodontidae) common and widely distributed in the eastern U.S. — see DUSKY SALAMANDER

des moines \dē'mȯin, də'-, *chiefly by outsiders* -nz\ *adj, usu cap D & M* [fr. *Des Moines*, Iowa] **:** of or from Des Moines, Iowa **:** of the kind or style prevalent in Des Moines

des·moines·ian \-n(z)ēən\ *adj, usu cap* [*Des Moines*, Iowa + E *-ian*] **:** of, relating to, or constituting a subdivision of the Pennsylvanian — see GEOLOGIC TIME table

des moines squash *n, usu cap D & M* **:** ACORN SQUASH

des·mo·kon·tae \,dezmō'kän(,)tē\ *n pl, cap* [NL, fr. *desm-* + *-kontae* (fr. Gk *kontos* pole)] **:** a class of chiefly solitary and motile algae (division Pyrrophyta) that have the cell wall divided vertically into two valves which are not in turn divided into plates like those of members of the class Dinophyceae

des·mo·lase \'dezmə,lās, -āz\ *n* -S [NL *desmolysis* + E *-ase*] **:** an enzyme (as aldolase) capable of breaking or forming a carbon-to-carbon bond in a molecule and playing a role in respiration and fermentation — often distinguished from *hydrolase*

des·mol·y·sis \dez'mäləsəs\ *n, pl* **desmoly·ses** \-,sēz\ [NL, fr. *desm-* + *-lysis*] **:** a chemical reaction in which a carbon-to-carbon double bond is broken (as by the action of a desmolase) — **des·mo·lyt·ic** \;dezmə;lidik\ *adj*

des·mon·cus \dez'mäŋkəs\ *n, cap* [NL, fr. *desm-* + Gk *onkos* barbed hook — more at ANGLE] **:** a genus of pinnate-leaved prickly climbing palms found from Mexico to Brazil — see JACITARA PALM

des·mo·neme \'dezmə,nēm\ *n* -S [*desm-* + *-neme*] **:** a nematocyst having a long coiled tube that wraps about projecting parts of the prey when extruded

des·mo·sco·lex \,dezmə'skō,leks\ *n, cap* [NL, fr. *desm-* + *-scolex*] **:** a genus (the type of the family Desmoscolecidae) that comprises minute marine worms having a globular head with four movable setae and a ringed pseudosegmented body and being usu. considered highly specialized nematodes

des·mose \'dez,mōs *also* -,mōz\ *n* -S [ISV *desm-* + *-ose*] **:** any fibril connecting the division centers in mitosis esp. in protozoans — see CENTRODESMOSE, PARADESMOSE

des·mo·spon·gia \,dezmə'spənjēə, -pän-\ *or* **des·mo·spon·gi·ae** \-jē,ē\ [NL, fr. *desm-* + *-spongia, -spongiae*] *syn of* DEMOSPONGIAE

des·mo·trope \'dezmə,trōp\ *n* -S [*desm-* + *-trope*] **:** a form of a chemical element related to another by desmotropism

des·mo·trop·ic \;==;träpik\ *adj* [*desm-* + *-tropic*] **:** of, relating to, or exhibiting desmotropism

des·mot·ro·pism \dez'mä·trə,pizəm\ *or* **des·mot·ro·py** \-trəpē\ *n, pl* **desmotropisms** *or* **desmotropies** [*desm-* + *-tropism, -tropy*] **:** tautomerism in which both tautomeric forms have been isolated

de·socialization \(;)dē, də+\ *n* -S **:** deprivation of the capacity for social intercourse

de·socialize \(')dē, də+\ *vt* [*de-* + *socialize*] **:** to deprive of sociality ⟨industrialization tends to ~ man⟩

de·soil \(')dē+\ *vt* [*de-* + *soil* (n.)] **:** to free from dirt

¹des·o·late \'desələt *also* -ez| *sometimes* |lət; *usu* -əd·+V\ *adj* [ME *desolat*, fr. L *desolatus*, past part. of *desolare* to abandon, desert, fr. *de* from, away + *-solare* (fr. *solus* alone) — more at DE-, SOLE] **1 :** devoid of inhabitants and visitors **:** DESERTED, ABANDONED ⟨a ~ ghost town⟩ **2** *obs* **a :** DESTITUTE **b :** lacking goodness **:** DISSOLUTE **3 a :** bereaved, forsaken, or abandoned esp. of or by one very dear and consequently inconsolable and crushed by grief ⟨this lady leaning at her window ~, pouring out her abandoned heart —George Meredith⟩ **b :** joyless, disconsolate, and sorrowful through or as if through some separation, destitution, or grief ⟨depressed and ~ of soul . . . and filled with anxious fear —William Wordsworth⟩ **c :** expressing or arising from such grief or sorrow ⟨a low ~ wail which made the terrible scream seem only the quick expression of an endless grief —Bram Stoker⟩ **4 a :** showing the effects of abandonment and neglect **:** RUINED, DILAPIDATED ⟨a ~ old house with sagging floors and broken shutters⟩ **b :** devoid of anything suggesting or furthering life **:** LIFELESS, BARREN, STARK ⟨passing through a ~ once-wooded area that had been ravaged by fire⟩ ⟨~ with crags and alkali —*Amer. Guide Series: Calif.*⟩ ⟨the empty, ~, endless waste —O.E.Rölvaag⟩ **c :** devoid of anything cheering, comforting, or suggesting warmth, comfort, pleasant human relations, or hope **:** DISHEARTENING, CHEERLESS ⟨the stormy howling of the wind in that avenue of great trees at night was wild and ~ —Thomas Wolfe⟩ ⟨a ~ memory of the sterile idle life I had lived —Edmund Wilson⟩ ⟨this wild, ~ lake . . . a very picture of unbroken solitude —John Burroughs⟩ **syn** see ALONE, DISMAL

²des·o·late \|ə,lāt, *usu* -ād·+V\ *vt* -ED/-ING/-S [ME *desolaten*, fr. L *desolatus* deserted, past part. of *desolare* to abandon, desert] **:** to make desolate: **a :** to deprive partially or wholly of inhabitants **:** DEPOPULATE ⟨the mines never again operated, and three townships in the vicinity were *desolated* —*Amer. Guide Series: Vt.*⟩ **b :** to lay waste **:** RAVAGE ⟨Hitler *desolated* British cities with bombs —F.L.Allen⟩; *also* **:** to leave in a ruined or barren state ⟨boulders left by mining operations ~ the valley⟩ **c :** to forsake or leave alone — used in the past participial form ⟨the bulletin board listing casualties was haunted by *desolated* wives⟩ **d :** to rob of joy and contentment; *esp* **:** to leave grief-stricken and wretched ⟨so obsessed with gambling that they ruin their own lives, ~ their families, and alienate their friends —C.B.Davis⟩

des·o·late·ly \|ələtlē, -tli\ *adv* **:** in desolate state, manner, or mood **:** in grief-stricken loneliness **:** without comforting circumstance or prospect **:** CHEERLESSLY, DISCONSOLATELY

des·o·late·ness \|ələtnəs\ *n* -ES **:** the quality or state of being desolate **:** LONELINESS, BLEAKNESS

des·o·lat·er *or* **des·o·la·tor** \|ə,lād·ə(r), -ātə-\ *n* -S **:** one that brings desolation

desolating *adj* **:** that desolates: **a :** SADDENING ⟨a ~ letter⟩ **b :** DEJECTING, DISPIRITING, DEPRESSING ⟨the most ~ spectacle of human indiscipline it is possible to conceive —H.G.Wells⟩ ⟨people like myself who frequent the movies testify to their ~ romantic morality —G.B.Shaw⟩ — **des·o·lat·ing·ly** *adv*

des·o·la·tion \,desə'lāshən *also* -ezə-\ *n* -S [LL *desolation-, desolatio*, fr. *desolatus* + L *-ion-, -io* -ion] **1 :** the action of desolating ⟨Europe was living in a state of anarchy . . . until it erupted into the pitiful ~ and slaughter of World War I —D.F.Fleming⟩ **2 a :** the condition of being desolated **:** a state of ruin, dilapidation, devastation ⟨the Indians fled into the Great Smoky mountains, leaving ruin and ~ behind —*Amer. Guide Series: N.C.*⟩ **b :** a condition of shocking abandonment to confusion and disintegration or of forbidding natural barrenness and bleakness ⟨an appearance of ~ . . . dead cypress masts rise above thick gray underbrush; in others the boggy surface is littered with charred logs and stumps —*Amer. Guide Series: N.C.*⟩ ⟨little to distract the eye from the awful surrounding dreariness and ~ except the bleaching skeletons of horses —*Amer. Guide Series: Ariz.*⟩ **3 a :** gloomy lifeless barren wasteland ⟨bleak, gray, God-forsaken, the empty ~ stretched on every hand —O.E.Rölvaag⟩ **b :** a stark area repellent by reason of wild empty barrenness ⟨nothing was visible but an opaque mist veiling an immense, sun-brown ~ —James Hilton⟩ **c :** an area seeming empty and often repellent because of lacking the presence of man or evidence of his handiwork ⟨the unconquerable ~ of the Yorkshire moors —Ellen Glasgow⟩ **4 a :** disconsolate sorrow from bereavement, abandonment, or loss ⟨he put his trembling hands to his head and gave a ringing scream, the cry of ~ —George Eliot⟩ **b :** dejection **:** dreary sadness ⟨thoughts that climb from ~ toward the genial prime —William Wordsworth⟩

de·sonation \;dē+\ *n* -S [*de-* + *sonant* + *-ation*] **:** DEVOICING

de son tort \dəsōⁿtȯr\ *adj* [F] **:** as a result of his own wrong act — used of persons assuming a responsibility (as of trusteeship) without rightful authority ⟨executor *de son tort*⟩

de·sophisticate \;dē+\ *vt* [*de-* + *sophisticate*] **:** to divest of sophistication ⟨Joyce . . . is said to have *desophisticated* language —F.R.Leavis⟩ — **de·sophistication** \"+\ *n* -S

de·sorb \(')dē+\ *vt* [*de-* + *sorb*] **:** to free from a sorbed state **:** remove (a sorbed substance) by the reverse of adsorption or absorption — **de·sorb·able** \-əbəl\ *adj*

de·sorption \(')dē+\ *n* -S [fr. *desorb*, after E *absorb: absorption*] **:** the process of desorbing

de·sor's larva \də'zȯrz|-\ *or* **de·sor larva** \-r|-\ *n, usu cap D* [after Édouard *Desor* †1882 Fr. geologist and archeologist] **:** LARVA OF DESOR

desoxy *var of* DEOXY

desoxy- — see DEOXY-

desp *abbr* despatch

¹de·spair \də'spa(a)|(ə)r, dē'-, -pe|, |ə\ *vb* -ED/-ING/-S [ME *despeiren*, fr. MF *desperer* (assumed AF 3d pers. pl. pres. indic. *despeirent*), fr. L *desperare*, fr. *de-* + *sperare* to hope; akin to L *spes* hope and prob. to OE *spēd* success — more at SPEED] *vi* **1 :** to lose hope utterly ⟨sailors are too sanguine to ~, even at the last moment —Frederick Marryat⟩ ⟨to resign or ~ you must first of all have an aim that you cannot attain —Stefan Schimanski⟩; *also* **:** to give up all expectation — used with *of* ⟨I should ~, however, of any successful analysis of problems at once so large and so difficult within the limits of this paper —B.N.Cardozo⟩ ⟨we ~*ed* of mastering the idiomatic niceties of the language⟩ **2 :** to give up hope for or belief in the success, progress, or achievement — used with *of* ⟨~*ed* of man —Karl Meyer⟩ ⟨~ of people who do not like poetry⟩ ~ *vt, obs* **:** to lose hope for

²despair \"\ *n* -S [ME *despeir*, fr. (assumed) AF *despeir*, fr. (assumed) OF *despeir* (whence OF *despoir*), fr. *desperer*, v. (3d pers. pl. pres. indic. *despeirent*)] **1 :** utter loss of hope **:** complete domination by feelings of hopelessness, futility, or defeat, wildly and bitterly expressed or quietly and pervasively dominant **:** complete loss of expectation of something wished for ⟨his ~, which may find expression in . . . suicide —Rudyard Kipling⟩ ⟨subject to alternating moods of elation and ~⟩ ⟨with the apathy of entire ~ he simply assented to whatever measures they suggested —Sheridan Le Fanu⟩; *often* **:** a fit of despair — usu. used in pl. ⟨the hopes, the ~*s* that accompanied our labors⟩ **2 a :** something that constitutes a cause for despair ⟨an incorrigible child is the ~ of his parents⟩ **b :** something that causes bafflement and loss of hope that it can be successfully emulated, comprehended, or otherwise acted upon in the desired way ⟨his nondescript features are the ~ of caricaturists⟩ ⟨play on words is the translator's ~ —J.C.Swaim⟩ ⟨the theory of induction is the ~ of philosophy —A.N.Whitehead⟩

despaired *adj* [ME *despeired*, fr. past part. of *despeiren*] **:** no longer hoped for **:** UNHOPED — often used with *of*

de·spair·ful \|rfəl, |əf-\ *adj* **:** full of despair **:** HOPELESS — **de·spair·ful·ly** \-əlē, -li\ *adv*

despairing *adj* **:** given to, arising from, or marked by despair, vanished hope, vain wild hopes ⟨tauntingly repelling the last ~ claim of a condemned culprit —H.T.Cockburn⟩ **syn** see DESPONDENT

de·spair·ing·ly *adv* **:** in a despairing manner

de·spair·ing·ness *n* -ES **:** the quality or state of being despairing

despatch *var of* DISPATCH

de·specialization \(;)dē+\ *n* **:** the act of despecializing

de·specialize \(')dē+\ *vb* [*de-* + *specialize*] *vi* **:** to reverse or reduce specialization ~ *vt* **:** to divest of specialization

de·spe·ci·ate \(')dē;spēs(h)ē,āt\ *vt* -ED/-ING/-S [*de-* + *species* + *-ate*] **:** to remove the characteristic antigenicity of (a foreign protein) by chemical or other treatment — **de·spe·ci·a·tion** \(;)dē,spēs(h)ē;āshən\ *n* -S

de·specificate \(;)dē+\ *vt* [*de-* + *specificate*] **:** to divest of specific signification — **de·specification** \"+\ *n*

de·spect \də'spekt\ *n* -S [L *despectus*, fr. *despectus* past part. of *despicere* to look down upon, despise — more at DESPISE] *archaic* **:** CONTEMPT

desperacy *n* -ES [*desperate* + *-cy*] *obs* **:** DESPERATION

des·per·a·do \,despə'rä|(,)dō, -rā|, -rā|\ *n, pl* **desperadoes** *also* **desperados** [prob. alter. (influenced by Sp *-ado*, as in *renegado*) of ²*desperate*] **1** *obs* **:** one in despair or in desperate straits **2 :** a bold or violent criminal; *typically* **:** a bandit of the western frontier ⟨bands of *desperadoes* lay in wait every few miles along the highway —Green Peyton⟩

des·per·a·do·ism \-ō,izəm\ *n* -S **:** a wave or period of unusual activity by desperadoes

¹des·per·ate \'desp(ə)rə|t, -pər|t, *usu* |d·+V\ *adj* [L *desperatus*, past part. of *desperare* to despair — more at DESPAIR] **1 :** having lost hope **:** yielding to despair ⟨he seemed, somehow, helpless and ~, as if he had come to the end of his tether —Rose Macaulay⟩ **:** giving no ground for hope ⟨the prospect was not only grim, it was ~. Britain stood alone; Dunkirk, for all its heroism, had been a disaster —H.S.Commager⟩ **2 a :** moved by despair ⟨there is reason to believe that they jumped overboard of their own will, made ~ at the sight of the sacrifice of a brother —B.N.Cardozo⟩ **:** likely to seize at wild vain hopes ⟨act with the folly and extravagance of ~ men —Adam Smith⟩ **:** involving the adoption of grim, rash, or otherwise extreme measures to escape defeat or frustration ⟨they have gradually lost faith in their own traditional ways and are ready for any ~ attempt to catch up with modern civilization —M.H.Trytten⟩ **b :** arising from or indicative of extreme need or pressure of circumstance ⟨those artists whom the presage of an early death stimulates to a ~ activity —Roger Fry⟩ ⟨had conceived the ~ idea of seeking the family fortune in the United States —Helen B. Woodward⟩ **c :** facing the worst with resolution and disregard of the cost ⟨it found her despairing **:** it left her ~ —two different states —Charlotte Brontë⟩; *esp* **:** exerting one's last ounce of energy in a do-or-die effort ⟨the ~ gallantry of our naval task forces marked the turning point in the Pacific —G.C.Marshall⟩ ⟨there is such a thing as a ~ pursuit of Truth; a pursuit fierce, relentless, absorbing —J.C.Powys⟩ **d :** suffering extreme need or anxiety ⟨the old lady was ~ for money —Mary R. Rinehart⟩ ⟨~ for something to do —F.L.Keefe⟩ ⟨in sudden terror at his tone, ~ to please him —B.A.Williams⟩ **3 a** (1) **:** devoid of any reasonable hope of betterment, solution, success, or salvation ⟨that *A* is in affluent circumstances while *B* is in ~ straits, with heavy responsibilities —W.M. Sibley⟩ ⟨for many institutions, the financial stringency which had been ~ during the war —T.L.Hungate⟩ (2) **:** practically irretrievable **:** UNCOLLECTIBLE ⟨a ~ debt⟩ **b :** fraught with extreme danger or impending disaster **:** CRUCIAL ⟨on all the fighting fronts the Allies were in a ~ situation due to lack of adequate materiel —G.C.Marshall⟩ ⟨the question of defense has been ~ for Israel from the day it became a state in 1948 —Claire Sterling⟩ **c :** suited to or incited by an all but hopeless situation ⟨the bitter, ~ striving unto death of the oppressed race —Rose Macaulay⟩ ⟨iron plates which Renwick had a ~ time getting because of the war —James Dugan⟩ **4 :** of extreme intensity **:** OVERPOWERING, OVERMASTERING, VEHEMENT ⟨I take ~ likes and dislikes —John Buchan⟩ ⟨a ~ languor descended heavily upon her, and she slept —Elinor Wylie⟩ ⟨two archrivals may be seen avoiding each other with ~ zeal —R.D.Altick⟩ **5 :** SHOCKING, OUTRAGEOUS ⟨everywhere there was a ~ grime and greasiness —William McFee⟩ ⟨sentimentality is a ~ word to hurl at an artist of any kind —Herbert Read⟩ **syn** see DESPONDENT

²desperate \"\ *n* -S **1** *archaic* **:** a person in desperate condition or circumstances **2** *obs* **:** a desperate character **:** DESPERADO 2

³desperate \"\ *adv, dial* **:** DESPERATELY

⁴des·per·ate \-pə,rāt\ *vt* -ED/-ING/-S **:** to render desperate

des·per·ate·ly \-pərtlē, -p(ə)rət-, -li\ *adv* **1 :** in a desperate manner: **a :** so as to leave little hope (as of recovery or escape) **:** DANGEROUSLY ⟨became ~ ill with pneumonia⟩ ⟨the old fixation, the result of 14 years together, still ~ influences her mind and body —Leslie Rees⟩ **b :** with an intensified or all-out last-ditch effort in refusal to give up a struggle or purpose ⟨~ fighting asthma⟩ ⟨figures struggling ~ among the countless corpses that floated in the heavy seas —H.E. Rieseberg⟩ ⟨grasping ~ at any straw to stave off starvation⟩ **c :** in utter indifference to consequences or danger **:** with reckless abandon ⟨the tough cruel but ~ brave Arab slavers —Rodney Gilbert⟩ **d :** with a degree of obligation or pressure of necessity not to be denied or delayed **:** URGENTLY, INDISPENSABLY, COMPELLINGLY ⟨I emphasize the religious element in our national inheritance because I believe it is the one which ~ needs to be reexamined and recovered —Ruth Suckow⟩ ⟨~ needed potash in the soil⟩; *also* **:** with unyielding insistence ⟨~ ambitious to make up for lost time —Gerald Priestland⟩ ⟨I wanted ~ to be popular⟩ **2 a :** to such a degree or such a degree of intensity as to bring dismay or distress close to despair **:** APPALLINGLY, FRIGHTFULLY, SHOCKINGLY ⟨~ poor, they lived mostly on fat pork and cornbread⟩ ⟨all houses and cellars were ~ overcrowded —J.H.Plumb⟩ **b :** to a superlative degree **:** EXTREMELY, INTENSELY ⟨one must get ~ tired of a climate which knows no winter or summer —Vernon Bartlett⟩ ⟨never was the need for the proper discharge of this task so ~ urgent —*Publ's Mod. Lang. Assoc. of Amer.*⟩ ⟨consistently entertaining, and at times it is, in fact, ~ funny —C.J.Rolo⟩ ⟨I'm ~ sorry, sir⟩ **c :** with undue complication of detail or protraction **:** TORTUOUSLY ⟨it darkens toward the end and winds up in a ~ contrived coincidence —*Time*⟩

des·per·ate·ness \-p(ə)rətnəs, -pərt-\ *n* -ES **:** DESPERATION

des·per·a·tion \,despə'rāshən\ *n* -S [ME *desperacioun*, fr. MF or L; MF *desperation*, fr. L *desperation-, desperatio*, fr. *desperatus* + *-ion-, -io* -ion] **1 :** the quality or state of being desperate ⟨disillusionment and disgust may become ~ —*Times Lit. Supp.*⟩ **:** a loss or abandonment of hope and surrender to misery or dread ⟨he shivered with fear and with cold, and a ~ began to possess him —Farley Mowat⟩; *also* **:** a strong urgency ⟨the very ~ of this dire need for some glimpse into that darkness which is the future —F.L.Mott⟩ **2 :** adoption of a last resource : a seizing on any action or means that offer any hope of success regardless of consequences : extreme recklessness ⟨with all the ~ of a fox caught by wire netting in a fowl run —J.C.Powys⟩ ⟨she had had the courage of ~, and that had saved her from failure —Ellen Glasgow⟩

de·spic·a·bil·i·ty \də,spikə'bilәd·ē, -ətē, -i *also* ,despək- *or* ,de,spik-\ *n* -ES : DESPICABLENESS

de·spic·a·ble \də'spikəbəl *also* 'despək- *or* 'de,spik-\ *adj* [LL *despicabilis*, fr. L *despicari* to look down upon, despise + *-abilis* -able; akin to L *despicere* to despise — more at DESPISE] **1** : deserving to be despised : meriting hatred, scorn, or loathing ⟨the immorality of James's court was hardly more ~ than the imbecility of his government —J.R.Green⟩ **2** *obs* : CONTEMPTUOUS **syn** see CONTEMPTIBLE

de·spic·a·ble·ness *n* -ES : the quality or state of being despicable

de·spic·a·bly \-blē, -li\ *adv* : in a despicable manner : with contempt

despiciency *n* -ES [L *despicientia*, fr. *despicient-*, *despiciens* (pres. part. of *despicere* to look down upon, despise) + *-ia* — more at DESPISE] *obs* : a looking down upon : CONTEMPT

de·spiralization \(')dē, də+\ *n* [*de-* + *spiralization*] *biol* : the uncoiling of the helical chromonema that is esp. evident toward the end of the meiotic prophase — **de·spiralize** \(')dē, də+\ *vi*

despiritualization \(')dē+\ *n* : the process of despiritualizing

de·spiritualize \(')dē+\ *vt* [*de-* + *spiritualize*] : to deprive of spiritual character or influence ⟨~ education and you devitalize life —W.L.Sullivan⟩

de·spis·able \də'spīzəbəl, dē'-\ *adj* [ME, fr. MF, fr. *despis-* (stem of *despire*) + *-able*] : DESPICABLE

de·spis·al \-zəl\ *n* -S : intense dislike : CONTEMPT, DESPISING ⟨this modern ~ of the pun —Clemence Dane⟩

de·spise \də'spīz, dē'-\ *vt* -ED/-ING/-S [ME *despisen*, fr. OF *despis-*, stem of *despire*, fr. L *despicere*, fr. *de-* + *spicere*, *specere* to look — more at SPY] **1 a** : to look down on : think of (a person) as objectionable, reprehensible, discreditable, disgraceful : hold oneself above : regard as an inferior ⟨that the young are in full revolt against them, and that the child born now may grow up to ~ them —*Times Lit. Supp.*⟩ **b** : to feel disrespect or aversion toward or disgust of : DISDAIN, DETEST ⟨despised the poor whites as creatures distinctly inferior to Negroes —H.L.Mencken⟩ **2 a** : to regard (something) as negligible, worthless, distasteful, a nuisance, a disgrace ⟨health comes first and good looks are not to be *despised* —J.M.Barzun⟩ ⟨submariners have always *despised* the need to evade in order to survive —S.D.Cutter⟩ ⟨they ~ all forms of organized religion, yet luxuriate in theology historically considered —*N.Y.Herald Tribune Bk. Rev.*⟩ : think of or look on with shame, repugnance, disgust : LOATHE ⟨that the spirit of Charity which neither ~*s* nor fears the nations of another creed and color —J.L.Cranmer-Byng⟩ **b** : to ignore or scorn as not worth taking steps to avoid or counter : SPURN ⟨he was in a state to ~ consequences —Arnold Bennett⟩ **3** *now dial* : DISLIKE, SCORN ⟨~ to vote for a party controlled from the outside —R.B.Vance⟩

syn CONTEMN, SCORN, DISDAIN, SCOUT: DESPISE, implying any emotional reaction from strong disfavor to loathing, stresses the judging of a thing as mean, petty, worthless, or repulsive, and a consequent, often derisive, looking down upon it ⟨when the inferior creature appreciates us, we cease to *despise* her —George Meredith⟩ ⟨an enemy . . . he loathed and hated, never *despised* —Laura Krey⟩ ⟨to *despise* certain foods⟩ CONTEMN suggests a somewhat harsher though more intellectual judgment and condemnation than DESPISE ⟨his own early drawings of moss roses and picturesque castles — things that he now mercilessly *contemned* —Arnold Bennett⟩ ⟨the human need of entertainment as a counterbalance in modern life is *contemned* by the serious novelists as "escapism" —A.C. Ward⟩ SCORN implies quick, indignant or profound contempt, esp. vocal or visible ⟨they *scorn* decorative chrome on the body, and remove it ruthlessly to reduce the car to its cleanest lines —*Lamp*⟩ ⟨the Welshmen so *scorned* the Saxons that they refused to extend to them the blessings of Christianity in the third century—O.S.J.Gogarty⟩ DISDAIN suggests a supercilious and visible contempt for or aversion to something regarded as unworthy ⟨the psychiatric patient is *disdained* and ridiculed by his fellow inmates —R.S.Banay⟩ ⟨despised by those superior persons who *disdain* her as old-fashioned —M.R.Cohen⟩ SCOUT stresses the rejection or dismissal with ridicule of anything (as a person or idea) one considers unworthy of consideration ⟨his Majesty will be most provoked if his ideas are *scouted* —C.S.Forester⟩ ⟨we scorned presentiments and *scouted* occult influences —F.W.Crofts⟩

de·spised·ness \-zədnəs, -z(d)n-\ *n* -ES : the quality or state of being despised

de·spise·ment \-zmənt\ *n* -S : DESPISAL

de·spis·er \-zə(r)\ *n* -S [ME, fr. *despisen* + *-er*] : one that despises

de·spis·ing·ly *adv* : in a despising manner : SCORNFULLY

¹de·spite \də'spīt, dē'-, *usu* -īd+V\ *n* -S [ME, fr. OF *despit*, fr. L *despectus* — more at DESPECT] **1** : the feeling or attitude of despising : CONTEMPT ⟨the ~ in which cunners are held is a convention —*Yale Rev.*⟩ **2** : ill will, aversion, or indignation toward another esp. accompanied with a desire to vex or harm : MALICE, GRUDGE, SPITE ⟨the whites mingle freely with these redskins, bearing them no such ~ —Horace Kephart⟩ **3** : an act showing contempt or defiance ⟨to say that these habitually coincide is surely doing ~ to our judgment —T.S.Omond⟩ : HARM ⟨I know of no government which stands to its obligations, even in its own ~, more solidly —Sir Winston Churchill⟩ ⟨when, in ~ of American opinion and interests, things go awry —D.W.Brogan⟩ **syn** see MALICE

²despite \"\ *vb* -ED/-ING/-S [ME *despiten*, fr. MF *despitier*, fr. L *despectare*, fr. *despectus*] *vt* **1** *archaic* : to treat with contempt **2** *obs* : to vex or injure spitefully ~ *vi*, *obs* : to show despite or contempt

³despite \"\ *prep* [(*in*) *despite* (*of*)] : without deterrence or prevention by : NOTWITHSTANDING : without being blocked, balked, or thwarted by : in spite of ⟨he managed to hold his position until retirement ~ failing health⟩ ⟨privateers were fitted out in American ports ~ official opposition —D.G. Munro⟩ ⟨generous ~ their own economic troubles —Arthur Rucker⟩

de·spite·ful \-ītfəl\ *adj* [ME *dispitful*, fr. *despit* + *-ful*] **1** *obs* : CONTEMPTUOUS : INSOLENT ⟨backbiters, haters of God, ~, proud, boasters —Rom 1:30 (AV)⟩ **2** : expressing malice or contemptuous hate : MALEVOLENT ⟨a ~ fiend⟩

de·spite·ful·ly \-əlē, -li\ *adv* [ME *despitfully*, fr. *despitful* + *-ly*] **1** *obs* : CONTEMPTUOUSLY **2** : MALICIOUSLY, MALEVOLENTLY, ABUSIVELY ⟨bless them that curse you, pray for them that ~ use you —Lk 6:28 (AV)⟩

de·spite·ful·ness *n* -ES : MALICE, CRUELTY

de·spit·e·ous \də'spid·ēəs, (')de¦s-\ *adj* [ME, alter. of *despitous*, fr. MF *despiteus*, fr. *despit* + *-eus* -ous] *archaic* : full of or moved by ill will : CONTEMPTUOUS, DESPITEFUL; *broadly* : MALICIOUS, CRUEL, PITILESS

de·spit·e·ous·ly *adv* [ME, fr. *despiteous* + *-ly*] *archaic* : DESPITEFULLY

¹de·spoil \də'spȯil, dē'-, *esp before pause or consonant* -ȯiəl\ *vt* -ED/-ING/-S [ME *despoylen*, fr. OF *despoillier*, fr. L *despoliare*, fr. *de-* + *spoliare* to strip, rob, plunder — more at SPOIL] **1** : to strip of belongings or possessions : PLUNDER, PILLAGE ⟨the English buccaneers . . . fell upon their cities and ~*ed* them —F.J.Haskin⟩ ⟨the great northern war involving Sweden, Denmark, and Russia completely ~*ed* Poland —J.S.Davenport⟩ **2** *obs* : to strip of garments or armor : DISROBE **3** : to deprive or divest coercively or wantonly — used with *of* ⟨monasteries were occasionally ~*ed* of their land and revenues —Owen & Eleanor Lattimore⟩ ⟨that Colombia had been ~*ed* of the Isthmus of Panama⟩ ⟨only the Etruscans ~*ed* the Sirens of all birdlike attributes—Norman Douglas⟩ **4** : to strip of what is of value : DENUDE ⟨the ~*ing* of the land by their primitive methods of subsistence farming —Jean Fortt⟩; *also* : to strip away ⟨magnificent stands of pine ~*ed* by loggers⟩ **5** : to wrest away, blast, or wreck as if by predatory raid ⟨her maternal instincts, stimulated and then ~*ed*, were increased, and when she loved it was always with an anxious and protective love —Susan Ertz⟩ ⟨you have disagreed and argued without calling each other liars and thieves, without ~*ing* our best traditions—A.E.Stevenson b. 1900⟩ **syn** see RAVAGE

²despoil \"\ *n* -S [MF *despoille*, fr. *despoillier*] **1** *archaic* : DESPOILING **2** *obs* : BOOTY

de·spoil·er \-ȯilə(r)\ *n* -S [ME *despoyler*, fr. *despoylen* + *-er*] : one that despoils ⟨no criminal was thought to be worse than a ~ of tombs⟩ ⟨warning against Communism as the No. 1 ~ of the democratic ideal —*Time*⟩

de·spoil·ment \-ȯi(ə)lmənt\ *n* -S : DESPOLIATION ⟨the ~ of colored women by white men is likewise held in the spotlight—H.M.Gloster⟩ ⟨the ~ and division of Poland⟩

de·spoliation \də, dē +\ *n* -S [LL *despoliation-*, *despoliatio*, fr. L *despoliatus* (past part. of *despoliare*) + *-ion-*, *-io* -ion] : a stripping or plundering : condition of being despoiled : SPOLIATION ⟨residents fear ~ of their charming community⟩

¹de·spond \də'spänd, dē'-\ *vi* -ED/-ING/-S [L *despondēre*, to promise, betroth, despair, fr. *de-* + *spondēre* to promise solemnly — more at SPOUSE] : to feel utter discouragement : undergo deep depression of spirits at vanishing hope, courage, or confidence

²despond \" *sometimes* 'de,spänd\ *n* -S : DESPONDENCY

de·spon·dence \-dən(t)s\ *n* -S **1** : DESPONDING ⟨his sudden ~ surprised us⟩ **2** : DESPONDENCY ⟨often the prey of doubt and fear, of bleak ~, stark anxiety —Walter de la Mare⟩

de·spon·den·cy \-dənsē, -si\ *n* -ES **1** : condition of being despondent : discouragement and dejection inducing apathetic inertia ⟨I found him in a state, if not of ~, of dejection —O.S.J.Gogarty⟩ **2** : an instance or cause of a despondent condition ⟨those nearest him noticed a ~ and indecision in his bearing —S.H.Adams⟩

¹de·spon·dent \-dənt\ *adj* [L *despondent-*, *despondens*, pres. part. of *despondēre*] : feeling extreme discouragement, dejection, or depression : experiencing or expressing an all but complete loss of hope or sense of defeat ⟨~ about his health, he killed himself⟩

syn FORLORN, HOPELESS, DESPAIRING, DESPERATE: DESPONDENT indicates utter discouragement and suggests either mournful or sullen dejection ⟨something dark and cold had settled over her thoughts. She could not shake it off though she told herself that it was unreasonable for her to feel so *despondent* —Ellen Glasgow⟩ ⟨Twain was filled with a *despondent* desire, a momentary purpose even, to stop writing altogether —Van Wyck Brooks⟩ FORLORN connotes pitiful, hopeless dejection, often resulting from a betrayal, calamity, or bereavement ⟨poor Columbine, *forlorn* and betrayed and dying, out in the cold at midnight — sinking down to hell, perhaps — was making her last frantic appeal —George du Maurier⟩ ⟨suggested by the portrait of Beatrice Cenci; and, in fact, there was a look somewhat similar to poor Beatrice's *forlorn* gaze out of the dreary isolation and remoteness, in which a terrible doom had involved a tender soul —Nathaniel Hawthorne⟩ Applied to actions or situations, it suggests a pathetic inadequacy certain of frustration or defeat ⟨spoke . . . with a *forlorn* effort at dignity —Sinclair Lewis⟩ HOPELESS suggests ending of hope and struggle and may imply dejection or resignation ⟨the little *hopeless* community of beaten men and yellow defeated women —Sherwood Anderson⟩ ⟨realizing now that pleading was useless, the men quieted down, and we resigned ourselves to the situation in that mood of *hopeless* apathy that comes over men powerless to help themselves —C.B.Nordhoff & J.N.Hall⟩ Of actions, it indicates impossibility of success and makes no implication about the spirit of the actors ⟨no body of men would stand against them, so *hopeless* was the enterprise —H.G.Wells⟩ DESPAIRING may suggest a situation in which a last, wild, vain hope is harbored ⟨tauntingly repelling the last *despairing* claim of a condemned culprit —H.T.Cockburn⟩ ⟨the author of 'Friendship's Garland' ended with a *despairing* appeal to the democracy, when his jeremiads evoked no response from the upper class, whom he called barbarians, or from the middle class, whom he regarded as incurably vulgar —W.R.Inge⟩ Applied to people, DESPERATE describes conditions in which reasonable hope is gone, or reckless action is considered ⟨now inhabited by a band of brigands, outlawed by government, strong in discipline, furious from penury, reckless by habit, *desperate* in circumstance — a crew which feared not God nor man nor devil —J.L.Motley⟩ ⟨driven from their cabins and little holdings, their crops and cattle taken from them, they were everywhere around *desperate* with poverty, and discontented equally with their own landlords and the restraints put upon them by the government —Anthony Trollope⟩ ⟨he felt *desperate*. He was ready to pay any price —Arnold Bennett⟩ Used with situations, it indicates wild crucial importunateness and exigency ⟨he is in a more *desperate* way financially than ever. He can borrow no more, and his debtors are clamoring —Gertrude Atherton⟩ ⟨when a country is in *desperate* straits, and everything hangs on the issue of a single battle —W.H.Mallock⟩ Of actions, it indicates motivation by despair ⟨the king's *desperate* efforts could hardly save his army from utter rout —J.R.Green⟩ ⟨such cries of terror and consternation on the part of the bird, tacking to the right and left, and making the most *desperate* efforts to escape —John Burroughs⟩

²despondent \"\ *n* -S : one who desponds

de·spond·ent·ly *adv* : in a despondent mood, manner, or tone

desponding *adj* **1** : DESPONDENT ⟨I feel quite ~ about the election tonight —Emily Eden⟩ **2** : causing despondency —

de·spond·ing·ly *adv*

desponsories *n pl* [modif. (influenced by L *desponsare*) of Sp *desposorios*, fr. *desposar* to marry, betroth, fr. L *desponsare* to betroth, fr. *de-* + *sponsa* spouse — more at SPOUSE] **1** *obs* : BETROTHAL **2** *obs* : a writing formally announcing a betrothal

des·pot \'despət, -,spät, *usu* ¦d· + V\ *n* -S [MF *despot*, *despote*, fr. Gk *despotēs* master, lord, despot; akin to Skt *dampati* lord of the house; both from a prehistoric compound whose first and second constituents are akin respectively to L *domus* house and to L *potis* able — more at TIMBER, POTENT] **1 a** : a Byzantine emperor or a prince of his imperial house : a vassal prince — used as a title of honor or address **b** : a bishop or patriarch of the Eastern Orthodox Church **c** : a petty Christian ruler tributary to the Turks after the Turkish conquest of Constantinople ⟨the ~ of Morea⟩ **d** : an Italian hereditary prince or military leader during the Renaissance **2 a** : a ruler with absolute or virtually absolute power and authority : AUTOCRAT ⟨Lord Curzon, the most enigmatic and greatest of those benevolent ~*s* —W.B.Willcox⟩ **b** : a ruler exercising absolute power abusively, oppressively, or tyrannously : TYRANT ⟨as a ~ he ruled by the force of arms⟩ **3 a** : a person having recognized and complete governance or authority and usu. domineering or oppressive ⟨affection by itself can turn an old nurse into a cranky ~ —Joyce Cary⟩ **b** : an animal or thing that seems to hold dominance and strict control ⟨it is not necessarily the strongest bird which becomes ~ —E.A.Armstrong⟩ ⟨the tireless machine is the ~ of our age —Waldemar Kaempffert⟩

des·po·tate \-,pə,tāt\ *also* **des·po·tat** \-tat\ *n* -S [F *despotat*, fr. *despote* + *-at* -ate] : a state or principality ruled by a despot

des·pot·ic \de'spädik, (')de¦s-, -ätl, |ēk\ *also* **des·pot·i·cal** \|əkəl\ *adj* [F *despotique*, fr. Gk *despotikos*, fr. *despotēs* + *-ikos* -ic, -ical] **1** : belonging to or having the character of an absolute ruler ⟨God's universal law gave to the man ~ power over his female —John Milton⟩ ⟨the introduction of European civilization was forced from above by ~ rulers chiefly for military and political reasons —M.R.Cohen⟩ **2** : ruling as or ruled by a despot ⟨the government of China was based upon natural law and was that of a ~ emperor —A.E.Nuquist⟩ ⟨moved from a feudal to a ~ order —K.A.Wittfogel⟩; *esp* : exhibiting imperious and usu. oppressive exercise of absolute power ⟨his administration remained arrogant and ~⟩ **3** : generally domineering and arbitrary ⟨as ~ as an old-time schoolmaster⟩ **syn** see ABSOLUTE

des·pot·i·cal·ly \|ək(ə)lē, |ēk-, -li\ *adv* : in a despotic manner : as a despot ⟨the company town implies a hierarchy ~, if benevolently, guiding the lives of those beneath —W.H. Whyte⟩ ⟨ruling his kingdom ~⟩

des·po·tism \'despə,tizəm *also* -pəd·,iz-\ *n* -S [F *despotisme*, fr. *despote* despot + *-isme* -ism] **1 a** : rule by a despot : TYRANNY ⟨~ is a perversion of sovereignty in which the interests of a governing class usurp the place belonging to the general interest —G.H.Sabine⟩ ⟨an excess of law is ~, from which free men revolt —S.B.Pettengill⟩ **b** : arbitrary or despotic exercise of power : any harsh or oppressive arbitrary domination ⟨under the parental ~ of the Confucian code of ethics —*Times Lit. Supp.*⟩ ⟨warnings against educational ~⟩ ⟨that ~ is one of the major biological principles; that whenever two birds are together invariably one is despot —W.C.Allee⟩ ⟨game fads sweep film circles, achieve a social ~ which lasts for weeks —Leo Rosten⟩ **2 a** : a system of government in which the ruler has unlimited power : ABSOLUTISM, AUTOCRACY ⟨the conception of government by naked, overwhelming power alone — power itself ungoverned by anything beyond the whims of its possessors . . . is of course the conception of tyranny or ~ —J.T.Dunlop⟩ ⟨the old ~ of the czars⟩ **b** : a despotic state ⟨that Communism is the surest way yet found to continue the old Asian ~*s* in modern times —*New Yorker*⟩ ⟨under the ~ of Cromwell —Hilaire Belloc⟩

des·pot·ist \-pəd·əst, -pətə-\ *n* -S : an advocate or supporter of despotism

des·po·tize \-pə,tīz, -pəd·,īz\ *vi* -ED/-ING/-S [F *despotiser*, fr. *despote* + *-iser* -ize] : to act the despot

des·pu·mate \'despyü,māt, də's-\ *vb* -ED/-ING/-S [L *despumatus*, past part. of *despumare* to skim off, fr. *de-* + *spuma* froth — more at SPUME] *vt*, *archaic* : to clarify (as wine or honey) by removing a surface scum : SKIM ~ *vi*, *archaic* : to cast off a scum : work off impurities in foam or scum

des·pu·ma·tion \,despyü'māshən\ *n* -S [LL *despumation-*, *despumatio*, fr. L *despumatus* + *-ion-*, *-io* -ion] *archaic* : the act of discharging impurities from the body fluids; *sometimes* : matter so discharged

des·qua·mate \'deskwə,māt\ *vi* -ED/-ING/-S [L *desquamatus*, past part. of *desquamare*, fr. *de-* + *squama* scale — more at SQUAMA] : to peel off in the form of scales : scale off ⟨he came down with scarlet fever and did not finish *desquamating* until . . . Christmas —Frank Sullivan⟩ ⟨thus a particular skin patch may redden and ~ each time a barbiturate is taken —R.W.Gerard⟩ — **des·qua·ma·tion** \,deskwə'māshən\ *n* -S

des·qua·ma·tive \'deskwə,mād·iv, də'skwamәd·-\ *adj* : attended by or causing desquamation

des·qua·ma·to·ry \'deskwəmə,tōrē, də'skwamə,-\ *adj* : characterized by or used for desquamation

¹dess \'des\ *n* -ES [prob. of Celt origin; akin to OIr *dais* heap] **1** *dial Brit* : LEDGE, SHELF **2** *dial Brit* : PILE, STACK ⟨a ~ of hay⟩

²dess \"\ *vt* -ED/-ING/-ES *dial Brit* : to arrange or pile up in layers

des·sa \'desə\ *var of* DESA

des·sert \də'zər|t, -zə|, -zəi|, *usu* |d· + V\ *n* -S *often attrib* [MF, fr. *desservir* to clear the table, fr. *des-* de- + *servir* to serve, fr. L *servire* — more at SERVE] **1** : a course of fruit, pastry, pudding, ice cream, or cheese served at the close of a meal — compare SAVORY, SWEET **2** *Brit* : a fresh fruit served after a sweet

dessert fork *n* : a fork slightly smaller than a dinner fork

dessert knife *n* : a knife slightly smaller than a dinner knife

dessert raisin *n* : a selected usu. light-colored raisin that is dried in the cluster esp. for eating out of hand

dessertspoon \=',=,=\ *n* **1** : a spoon intermediate in size between a teaspoon and a tablespoon used in eating dessert and sometimes soup or cereals **2** : DESSERTSPOONFUL ⟨add a ~ of sugar⟩

des·sert·spoon·ful \=',=,=,=,=\ *n* **1** : as much as a dessertspoon will hold **2** : a unit of measure equal to about 2½ fluidrams

dessert wine *n* : a still usu. sweet straw-colored to red wine containing over 14 percent and frequently 20 to 21 percent alcohol by volume (as port, tokay, and muscatel) often served with dessert or between meals — compare APPETIZER WINE, SPARKLING WINE, TABLE WINE

des·sia·tine \¦des(h)yə¦tēn\ *or* **des·sa·tine** \-sə¦-\ *or* **de·sia·tin** *also* **de·sya·tin** \-s(h)yə¦tin\ *n* -S [Russ *desyatina* tithe, unit of land area, fr. *desyat'* ten; akin to L *decem* ten — more at TEN] : a Russian unit of land area equal to 2.7 acres

dessil *var of* DEASIL

¹des·sous \də'sü\ *n*, *pl* **dessous** \-ü(z)\ [F, fr. *dessous*, adv. & prep., underneath, below, fr. OF *desoz*, fr. *de-* + *soz* below, underneath, fr. L *subtus*, fr. *sub* under — more at SUB-] : UNDERWEAR

²dessous \"\ *adj* [F, adv., underneath] *ballet* : UNDER — used of the movement in which the working leg passes behind the supporting leg

des·sus \də'sü\ *adj* [F, adv., above, fr. OF *desus*, fr. *de-* + *sus* under, fr. L *susum*, *sursum* — more at SURSUM-] *ballet* : OVER — used of the movement in which the working leg passes in front of the supporting leg

de·stabilize \(')dē + \ *vt* [*de-* + *stabilize*] : to make unstable : cause or allow to fluctuate ⟨booms and depressions, both of which ~ the position of labor today —Eduard Heimann⟩; *specif* : to tend to increase economic fluctuations in ⟨that the use of replacement cost depreciation for tax purposes would be a *destabilizing* influence —J.F.Due⟩

¹destain *var of* DISTAIN

²de·stain \(')dē + \ *vt* [*de-* + *stain* (n.)] : to selectively remove stain from (a specimen for microscopic study)

de·sta·lin·ize \(')dē'stälə,nīz, -tal- *also* -tȯl- *or* -tȧl- *sometimes* -lyə,- *or* -l(,)(y)ē,- *or* ¦dē(,)stä'lē,- *or* ¦dē(,)sta'lē,- *or* ¦dē(,)stä'lē,-\ *vb* -ED/-ING/-S [*de-* + Joseph *Stalin* (Dzhugashvili) †1953 Russ. political leader + E *-ize*] *vi* : to deflate the influence of Stalin as a Soviet leader of heroic stature by revelations of disastrous state policies and ruthless self-aggrandizement ~ *vt* : to offset and reverse the influence of Stalin on (as sports)

de·ste·a·rin·ate \(')dē¦stēərə,nāt, -stir-\ *vt* -ED/-ING/-S [*de-* + *stearin* + *-ate*] : to remove the lower melting-point components from (a fatty oil)

de·sterilize \(')dē + \ *vt* [*de-* + *sterilize*] : to release (gold) from an insulated condition in the treasury to useful service (as in forming the base for further credit expansion through deposit in a central bank)

des·thio·biotin \,dez,thīə +\ *n* [*des-* + *thi-* + *biotin*] : a crystalline acid $C_{10}H_{18}N_2O_3$ obtained from biotin by removal of sulfur and held to be a precursor of biotin in some organisms (as many yeasts and bacteria)

de·stigmatize \(')dē + \ *vt* [*de-* + *stigmatize*] : to clear of a stigma

de stijl \də'stī(ə)l, -tā(ə)l\ *n*, *usu cap S* [D *De Stijl*, lit., the style, a magazine published by members of the school] : a school of art founded in Holland in 1917 producing work that typically used rectangular forms, the primary colors plus black and white, and asymmetric balance and that had wide application in architecture and practical design

¹des·ti·nate \'destənət, -,nāt\ *adj* [ME, fr. L *destinatus*, past part. of *destinare*] **1** *archaic* : ordained by fate **2** : set apart for : INTENDED

²des·ti·nate \-,nāt\ *vt* -ED/-ING/-S [L *destinatus*, past part.] **1** *archaic* **a** : DESIGNATE **b** : DOOM **2** *archaic* : to predetermine as an act of fate or by divine decree **3** *archaic* : to design or intend

des·ti·na·tion \,destə'nāshən\ *n* -S [LL & L; LL *destination-*, *destinatio* goal, from L, act of establishing, determination, purpose, fr. *destinatus* + *-ion-*, *-io* -ion] **1 a** : the act of appointing, setting aside to a purpose, or predetermining ⟨the clubs discuss the probable ~ of offices with that air of secret knowledge —H.J.Laski⟩ **b** *archaic* : the fact of being designated **2** : purpose for which something is destined : predetermined end, object, or use ⟨to find the mainstream of one's period and its source of flow, dominant direction, and presumable ~ —Louis Kronenberger⟩ **3** : a place which is set for the end of a journey or to which something is sent : place or point aimed at ⟨when buying your plane tickets always buy through to your farthest ~ —Richard Joseph⟩ **4** *Scots law* **a** : the nomination of successors to movable or heritable property in a certain order made by the will of a decedent **b** : the series of heirs so succeeding **5** : the purpose to which property or money is intended to be applied **6** : one that receives in a form recognizably like its original form a message transmitted through any medium and by any set of signals

des·tine \'destən\ *vt* -ED/-ING/-S [ME *destinen*, fr. OF *destiner*, fr. L *destinare* to make fast, determine, destine, fr. *de-* + *-stinare* (akin to *stare* to stand) — more at STAND] **1 a** : to fix or decree beforehand : PREORDAIN — used orig. of a divine foreordaining or a decreeing by fate ⟨he was not *destined* to attain the throne⟩ **b** : to direct and impel inescapably on a fixed course : PREDETERMINE — used of an inevitable ordering in human eventualities, usu. followed by *to* and an infinitive, sometimes by *for* ⟨whose star in the Navy was bright and *destined* to grow brighter still —Burke Wilkinson⟩ ⟨*destined* to occupy a niche of some importance in the history of American music —Virgil Thomson⟩ ⟨he foretold the telescope and the microscope — inventions which were *destined* not to occur until centuries after his death —R.D.Altick⟩ ⟨the now somnolent villages which in the past seemed *destined* for an active commercial development —*Amer. Guide Series: Maine*⟩ **2 :** to determine the future condition, use, or action of: **a :** to designate, assign, or dedicate in advance ⟨where forces *destined* to invade Normandy would eventually be gathered —J.P.Baxter⟩ ⟨the librarianship, with its meagre income, to which I had been originally *destined* —L.P.Smith⟩ ⟨funds *destined* for scholarship endowments⟩ ⟨*destined* by his parents for the ministry⟩; *broadly* **:** INTEND ⟨a scheme of decoration however appropriate to its *destined* setting —C.W.H.Johnson⟩ **b :** to direct, devise, or set aside for a specific purpose or end ⟨boats were ordered made ready at Fort Pitt for an expedition *destined* for the Illinois posts —P.M.Angle⟩ ⟨freight *destined* for Israeli ports⟩

des·ti·nez·ite \ˌdestəˈnāˌzīt\ *n* -s [F *destinezite*, fr. Pierre *Destinez*, 19th cent. Belgian mineralogist + F *-ite*] **:** DIADOCHITE

des·ti·ny \ˈdestənē, -ni\ *n* -ES [ME *destinee*, fr. MF, fr. OF, fr. fem. of *destiné* (past part. of *destiner*), fr. L *destinatus*] **1 :** that to which any person or thing is destined: as **a :** predetermined state **:** condition foreordained by divine will or by human will **:** unavoidable lot **:** FATE, DOOM ⟨reconciled to one's ~⟩ **b :** culminating condition or end indicated as probable, inevitable, or having been reached **:** FORTUNE, GOAL ⟨manifest ~⟩ ⟨unhappy ~⟩ **2 a :** the predetermined course of events often conceived as a resistless power or agency **:** the foreordained future whether in general or of an individual ⟨pursued by ~⟩ ⟨turn aside ~⟩ **b :** continuing activity and functional behavior that tend to determine eventual status esp. as to progress or decadence — usu. used in pl. ⟨we could not tolerate control by a European power over the ~ of the former Spanish possessions⟩ ⟨that a man should manage the *destinies* of a corporation while owning only a minute fraction of its stock —F.L.Allen⟩ **3 :** a real or imaginary power or agency conceived as predetermining the course of events and choice of alternatives ⟨our helplessness, at least with respect to those events over which *Destiny* presides —Lucius Garvin⟩ ⟨the leader is simply the man whom ~ . . . has placed in such a position that he alone can assume the supreme leadership —Barbara & Robert North⟩ ⟨a flash of Free Will, pure and simple, which instantly gives place . . . to the dominion of what we call *Destiny* —Joseph Furphy⟩ **syn** see FATE

¹des·ti·tute \ˈdestəˌtüt, -stəˌtyüt, *usu* \|d· + V\ *adj* [ME *destitut*, fr. L *destitutus*, past part. of *destituere* to set away, leave alone, forsake, fr. *de-* + *-stituere* (fr. *statuere* to set) — more at STATUTE] **1** *obs* **:** ABANDONED **2 :** bereft or divested ⟨a city street ~ of trees⟩ ⟨no danger of our becoming ~ of facts —S.C.Pepper⟩ **:** bare or empty ⟨a lake ~ of fish⟩ **:** lacking any provision or showing a want ⟨a new religion of authority singularly ~ of safeguards against self-deception —W.R. Inge⟩ **:** subject to a lack or deficiency ⟨of all men alive he is possibly the most completely ~ of the mystical sense —W.L. Sullivan⟩ ⟨~ of all sense of personal dignity⟩ **:** possessing or showing no vestige ⟨as ~ of conscience as a snake —W.L. Sullivan⟩ — used with *of* **3 :** lacking possessions and resources; *esp* **:** lacking the necessaries of life **:** suffering extreme want ⟨the death of a ~ widow from starvation —Julian Maclaren-Ross⟩ ⟨homes for the ~⟩ ⟨the result was impoverished villages in India, hideous and ~ towns in England —Lewis Mumford⟩ ⟨in a ~ condition for clothes⟩ **syn** see POOR

²destitute \"\ *vt* -ED/-ING/-S [L *destitutus*] **1** *obs* **:** FORSAKE **2 a :** to deprive or divest — used with *of* ⟨the accident will ~ us of all our liquid assets⟩ **b** *archaic* **:** to deprive of office **:** DEPOSE **3** *archaic* **:** to lay waste **:** DEVASTATE **4** *obs* **:** to make void **:** FRUSTRATE

des·ti·tute·ly *adv* **:** in a destitute condition

des·ti·tute·ness *n* -ES **:** the state of being destitute

des·ti·tu·tion \ˌdestəˈtüshən, -stəˈtyü-\ *n* -s [ME *destitucioun*, fr. MF or L; MF *destitution*, fr. L *destitution-*, *destitutio*, fr. *destitutus* + *-ion-*, *-io* -ion] **1 :** state of being deprived of or lacking something **:** destitute condition ⟨many historic dwellings remain, sinking stage by stage from indigence to squalor, from squalor to grimy ~ —Lewis Mumford⟩ ⟨and what ~ of the spirit did he owe to his harsh memories of his father —Charles Lee⟩; *usu* **:** deprivation of the necessaries of life **:** poverty esp. when extreme ⟨forgotten men and women living at or below the ~ level —R.H.S.Crossman⟩ **2** *archaic* **:** dismissal from office

destn *abbr* destination

de·stock \(ˈ)dē + \ *vb* [*de-* + *stock*] *vt* **1** *Africa* **:** to remove livestock from ⟨~ an overgrazed range⟩ **2** *Africa* **:** to reduce the number of (livestock) on a range ~ *vi*, *Africa* **:** to remove stock from a range or pasture

de·ston·er \(ˈ)dē + \ *n* -s [*de-* + *stone* + *-er*] **:** a worker who operates machines that remove hard particles from vegetables prior to freezing

de·stool \(ˈ)dē + \ *vt* [*de-* + *stool* (n.)] **:** to depose from office (a West African chief) — contrasted with *enstool* — **de·stool·ment** \" + . . . mənt\ *n* -s

des·trier \ˈdestrēər, (ˈ)deˈstri(ə)r\ *n* -s [ME, fr. OF, fr. *destre* right hand, fr. L *dextera*, *dextra*, fr. *dexter* right; fr. the fact that the knight's horse was led by the squire with his right hand — more at DEXTER] **:** a large powerful horse used as a war horse by a medieval knight

de·stroy \dəˈstrȯi, dēˈ-\ *vb* -ED/-ING/-S [ME *destroyen*, *destruyen*, fr. OF *destruire*, fr. (assumed) VL *destrugere*, alter. (influenced by L *destructus*, past part. of *destruere*) of L *destruere* to tear down, destroy, fr. *de-* + *struere* to pile up, build; akin to L *sternere* to spread out, scatter — more at STREW] *vt* **1 :** to ruin the structure, organic existence, or condition of: as **a :** to pull or tear down **:** RAZE, DEMOLISH ⟨~*ed* the altars of the gods⟩ **b** *obs* **:** to lay waste **:** DESOLATE **c :** to ruin completely or injure or mutilate beyond possibility of use (as by tearing, breaking, burning, or erosion) ⟨priceless art ~*ed* by fire⟩ ⟨water may undermine and ~ the riverbank⟩ **d :** to ruin as if by ripping to shreds ⟨~*ed* a goodly number of existing reputations —H.J.Laski⟩ **e :** to deprive of position, prestige, and reputation and of the power to oppose or offer resistance **:** reduce to political, financial, or professional impotence or ruin **:** defeat and discredit fully ⟨an author can weather the most damning criticisms but he is ~*ed* when he is ignored completely —Bennett Cerf⟩ **2 :** to bring to naught by putting out of existence: **a :** to take the life of **:** put to death **:** KILL ⟨the plague ~*ed* men by the thousands⟩ **b :** to cause to vanish **:** ABOLISH ⟨~ one's love⟩ **c :** COUNTERACT, NULLIFY, NEUTRALIZE ⟨the moon ~*s* the light of the stars⟩ **d :** to subject to a crushing defeat **:** wipe out **:** ANNIHILATE ⟨building a war machine capable of ~*ing* the enemy⟩ **3** *Irish* **:** DISTRESS, DEPRESS, PLAGUE ⟨and you ~*ed* with the grief has come on you —Mary Deasy⟩ ~ *vi* **1 :** to have the effect of destroying something or someone ⟨it is proverbially easier to ~ than to construct —T.S.Eliot⟩ **2 :** to become destroyed ⟨wear nothing that ~*s* easily⟩

syn DEMOLISH, RAZE, RUIN, UNDO, WRECK, WRACK, DILAPIDATE: DESTROY implies any force that smashes, tears down or apart, kills, or annihilates ⟨*destroy* a house⟩ ⟨*destroy* a document by burning it⟩ ⟨*destroy* a friendship by deceit⟩ ⟨*destroy* a bridge by blowing it up⟩ ⟨*destroy* a mood⟩ DEMOLISH implies more a pulling or smashing to pieces; in its frequent application to the smashing or tearing down of buildings or other structures it implies complete wreckage to the point of a heap of ruins ⟨a building *demolished* by a bomb⟩ ⟨a car *demolished* by a train at a railroad crossing⟩ RAZE implies a leveling whether by sudden destruction or an orderly process ⟨the governor formulated a plan to *raze* the old State prison and transfer the inmates to other institutions —*Current Biog.*⟩ ⟨in 1865 a Gulf hurricane *razed* the town —*Amer. Guide Series: Texas*⟩ ⟨the hotel was *razed*, and its colonial pillars were sent to Grand Rapids —*Amer. Guide Series: Mich.*⟩ RUIN usu. suggests a usu. total bringing to an end of the wholeness, value, beauty, well-being, or opportunities of someone or something as by fire, collision, or misuse, or by the loss of something essential to happiness or success ⟨*ruin* a car by neglect⟩ ⟨beauty *ruined* by dissipation⟩ ⟨big planters *ruined* by the failure of the Bank of Tallahassee —Marjory S. Douglas⟩ ⟨it is he who decides how loud or soft the music will be at any given moment, and therefore it is he who can make or *ruin* everything by the merest touch of the dials —Aaron Copland⟩ ⟨because of the destruction of the plantation system the Civil War *ruined* the town —*Amer. Guide Series: Texas*⟩ UNDO, in this comparison, is a more neutral synonym for RUIN ⟨an inordinate impulsion to *undo* his rivals —H.O.Taylor⟩ ⟨the cost of reequipping his many theaters proved one of the causes of his financial *undoing* —*Americana Annual*⟩ ⟨the battle left him untouched; it was the peace that *undid* him —Virginia Woolf⟩ ⟨to *undo* a lifetime of effort⟩ WRECK suggests a ruining as by a crash or by being shattered; in figurative use, it implies an injuring past all hope of repair or reconstruction ⟨the collision *wrecked* the car beyond repair⟩ ⟨she . . . *wrecked* several saloons with stones and iron bars —C.M.Thomas⟩ ⟨warned that if private educational institutions were *wrecked* it would be a disaster to the country —A.J.Schaefer⟩ ⟨attempting to degrade and *wreck* the classical concept of the genus —W.H.Camp⟩ ⟨*wreck* plans for a new school⟩ WRACK, now infrequent in this connection and even then archaic or largely in poetic use, suggests an overwhelming catastrophe or widespread ruin ⟨the seas . . . *wracking* whole fleets in pride like river toys —F.T.Palgrave⟩ ⟨a civilization *wracked* by its own evil ways⟩ DILAPIDATE, in earlier use implying ruin by wastefulness as well as neglect, now generally implies ruin, esp. of a building, mainly through neglect, suggesting a run-down, tumbledown condition ⟨they tax the country according to their pleasure, and *dilapidate* the estates of the King's friends —Sir Walter Scott⟩ ⟨a *dilapidated* old shack of a house⟩ ⟨its cities were *dilapidated*, its public buildings run down and dirty —Carleton Beals⟩ ⟨an old and *dilapidated*-looking car —Francis Stuart⟩

de·stroy·able \-ȯiəbəl\ *adj* **:** capable of being destroyed

de·stroy·er \-ȯi(ə)r, -ȯiə\ *n* -s [ME *destroyer*, *destruyer*, fr. *destroyen*, *destruyen* to destroy + *-er*] **1 :** a destroying agent or agency **2 :** a small fast warship armed with usu. 5-inch guns, depth charges, torpedoes, mines, and sometimes guided missiles — called also *can*, *tin can*

destroyer escort *n* **:** an antisubmarine warship similar to a destroyer but smaller and not as fast

destroyer leader *n* **:** a large destroyer — compare FRIGATE

destroying angel *n*, *often cap D&A* **1 :** a variably colored extremely poisonous mushroom (*Amanita phalloides*) that grows esp. in open woodlands and along field margins and in its white form is sometimes mistaken for the common edible agarics; *also* **:** a related poisonous mushroom (*A. verna*) **2 :** DANITE 2

de·stroy·ing·ly *adv* **1 :** in the role of destroyer **2 :** with destructive effect

de·struct \dəˈstrəkt, dēˈ-\ *vb* -ED/-ING/-S [back-formation fr. *destruction*] **:** DESTROY

de·struc·ti·bil·i·ty \-ˌstrəktəˈbilədē, -ətē, -i\ *n* -ES **:** the quality of being destructible

de·struc·ti·ble \-ˈstrəktəbəl\ *adj* [*destruction* + *-ible*] **:** capable of being destroyed **:** liable to destruction

de·struc·tion \-kshən\ *n* -s [ME *destruccioun*, fr. MF *destruction*, fr. L *destruction-*, *destructio*, fr. *destructus* (past part. of *destruere* to tear down) + *-ion-*, *-io* -ion — more at DESTROY] **1 :** the action or process of destroying a material or immaterial object: **a :** demolition or complete ruin ⟨~ of dead files by a government department⟩ ⟨bombers accomplished ~ of the city⟩ **b :** killing or annihilation ⟨~ of sheep by dogs and wild animals⟩ ⟨inflicted ~ on enemy units⟩ **c :** a bringing to an end **:** ELIMINATION, ERADICATION ⟨measures toward ~ of the dictatorship⟩ ⟨was his real purpose in creating this painting the ~ of religion rather than the furtherance of it —Huntington Hartford⟩ **d :** IMPAIRMENT, DISRUPTION, DISINTEGRATION ⟨~ of the universities by the Nazi regime⟩ ⟨the ~ of European civilization through internal strife⟩ **e :** INVALIDATION ⟨any act aimed at the ~ of any of the rights and freedoms set forth herein —*U.N. Declaration of Human Rights*⟩ **2 a :** the fact or experience of or subjection to being destroyed ⟨Albania . . . suffered whole or partial ~ of 1600 of its villages —*Current Biog.*⟩ ⟨Macbeth seemed eager for his own ~⟩ ⟨a study of communistic ideology and prospects of its gradual ~⟩ ⟨voluntary muscular movements become sluggish and finally tissue ~ and death may occur at temperatures of −25°F to −50°F —H.G.Armstrong⟩ **b :** loss of prestige and reputation **:** descent into a state of ignominy and degradation ⟨resolved on the teacher's personal ~ because of his stand on civil rights⟩ **c :** a condition of having been destroyed ⟨coffee planting on steep slopes has resulted in serious land ~ —P.E.James⟩ ⟨with economic and social ~ as the penalty for dissent —Archibald MacLeish⟩ ⟨the ~ resulting from the hurricane⟩ **3 :** a destroying agency **:** a cause of ruin ⟨alcohol is likely to be his ~⟩

de·struc·tion·al \-shənᵊl, -shnəl\ *adj* **:** resulting from destructive agencies ⟨~ erosion⟩

de·struc·tion·ism \-shəˌnizəm\ *n* -s **:** advocacy or a policy of destroying an institution or regime

de·struc·tion·ist \-sh(ə)nəst\ *n* -s **1 :** one who delights in destroying **2 :** an advocate of destroying existing institutions

¹de·struc·tive \dəˈstrəktiv, dēˈ-, -tēv *also* -təv\ *adj* [MF *destructif*, fr. LL *destructivus*, fr. L *destructus* + *-ivus* -ive] **1 :** having the capability, property, or effect of destroying **:** causing destruction: **a :** tending to bring about demolition or devastation ⟨~ storms are rare in Maine⟩ ⟨insects ~ of many trees⟩ ⟨abuse of mankind's scientific genius for ~ ends —Vera M. Dean⟩ **b :** tending to take life or promote death **:** dangerously injurious to a living being **:** DEADLY, ANNIHILATIVE ⟨a cavalry that checked to fire exposed itself to a ~ volley —Tom Wintringham⟩ ⟨an exceedingly ~ type of joint lesion known as a Charcot joint —G.A.Bennett⟩ ⟨otters are very ~ of salmon and trout —F.D.Smith & Barbara Wilcox⟩; *specif* **:** prompting one to destroy another or oneself ⟨passionate feeling is desirable, provided it is not ~ —Bertrand Russell⟩ ⟨harbors aggressive and ~ instincts to kill⟩ ⟨self-*destructive* human behavior⟩ **c :** tending to impair, damage, or wreck **:** productive of evil results **:** DELETERIOUS ⟨sharp or persistent inflations, deep and dragging depressions, are not corrective but ~ —*Defense Against Recession*⟩ **2 :** designed or tending to destroy, clear away, eliminate, or invalidate ⟨~ of firmly established ideas⟩ ⟨a ~ standard⟩ — opposed to *constructive* **3** *logic* **:** retroactively negating (as when the denial of a consequent invalidates the antecedent: if A is B, then C is D; but C is not D; hence A is not B) — **de·struc·tive·ly** \-kt**ə**vlē, -li\ *adv*

²destructive \"\ *n* -s **1 :** a destructive agent or force **2 :** one destructive of an accepted norm

destructive distillation *n* **:** distillation involving decomposition of a substance (as wood, coal, or a hydrocarbon oil) by heat in a closed container (as a retort) and collection of the volatile products produced **:** CARBONIZATION — compare CRACKING, PYROLYSIS

de·struc·tive·ness \-ktəvnəs\ *n* -ES **:** the quality of being destructive **:** capacity for destruction ⟨the awesome ~ of the atom bomb⟩

destructive sorites *n* **:** a process of reasoning that involves the denial of the first of a series of dependent propositions as a consequence of the denial of the last

de·struc·tiv·i·ty \ˌdēˌstrəkˈtivədē, dəˌ-, -ətē, -i\ *n* -ES **:** capacity for destruction

de·struc·tor \dəˈstrəktə(r), dēˈ-\ *n* -s [LL *destructor* destroyer, fr. L *destructus* + *-or*] **1 :** a furnace or oven for the burning of refuse **:** INCINERATOR **2 a :** a device for destroying a missile or a part thereof at a desired time in its flight **b :** an explosive device for enabling quick destruction of matériel to prevent its falling into the hands of the enemy

de·stru·do \-ˈstrü(ˌ)dō\ *n* -s [NL, fr. L *destruere* to destroy — more at DESTROY] **:** DEATH WISH

de·sublimate \(ˈ)dē+\ *vt* [*de-* + *sublimate*] **:** to undo a sublimation of — **de·sublimation** \(ˌ)dē+\ *n*

de·substantival \(ˌ)dē+\ *adj* [*de-* + *substantival*] **:** derived from a substantive ⟨*bookish* from *book* is a ~ adjective⟩ ⟨*methodize* is a ~ verb⟩

des·ue·tude \ˈdeswēˌtüd, -swəl, \|·ˌtyüd *also* deˈsüəl *sometimes* ˈdezw- *or* ˈdeˌsü- *or* ˈdesˌyü-\ *n* -s [F or L; F *désuétude*, fr. L *desuetudo*, fr. *desuetus*, past part. of *desuescere* to become unaccustomed, fr. *de-* + *suescere* to become accustomed; akin to L *suus* one's own — more at SUICIDE] **1 :** discontinuance from use, practice, exercise, or functioning ⟨as to the Scottish statute it is presumably abrogated by ~ —Frederick Pollock⟩ ⟨vexing myself today over the gradual ~ of our correspondence —A.T.Quiller-Couch⟩ ⟨figureheads . . . are being used again after long years of ~ —John Woodyatt⟩ ⟨there are those who foresee total ~ for our society with the profit motive thus wantonly eliminated —Irwin Edman⟩ **2 :** a state of protracted suspension or of apparent abandonment ⟨an ancient custom that has fallen into ~⟩ ⟨we all have this profound unconscious, but it falls into atrophy and ~ because most of us do not utilize it —L.K.Anspacher⟩ **:** a state of disuse or neglect attended by deterioration ⟨what energy and vision may do for an old school fast falling into ~ —J.P.Marquand⟩ **:** outmoded or discarded status ⟨the purely speculative and seemingly impractical things should have fallen into disfavor and disrepute, if not positive ~ —F.X.Meehan⟩

de·sugar *also* **de·sugarize** \(ˈ)dē+\ *vt* [*desugar* fr. *de-* + *sugar*, n.; *desugarize* fr. *de-* + *sugar*, n. + *-ize*] **:** to remove sugar from

de·sulfonate \(ˈ)dē+\ *vt* [*de-* + *sulfonate*] **:** to remove sulfonic groups from (a sulfonated substance) — **de·sulfonation** \(ˌ)dē+\ *n*

de·sul·fo·vibrio \(ˌ)dēˌsəlfə+\ *n*, *cap* [NL, fr. *de-* + *sulfo-* + *vibrio*] **:** a genus of curved motile anaerobic bacterial rods (family Spirillaceae) that reduce sulfates to hydrogen sulfide and include at least one form (*D. halohydrocarbonoclasticus*) capable of increasing the flow of oil wells by raising the gas pressure and enlarging the flow channels in the rock

de·sulfurization *also* **de·sulfuration** \(ˌ)dē, də+\ *n* **:** the process of desulfurizing

de·sulfurize *also* **de·sulfur** \(ˈ)dē, də+\ *vt* [*de-* + *sulfurize* or *sulfur* (n.)] **:** to remove sulfur or sulfur compounds from (as molten metals or petroleum oils) by suitable agents — compare SWEETEN — **de·sulfurizer** \"+\ *n*

de·sul·tor \dəˈsəltə(r), dēˈ-\ *n*, *pl* **desultors** \-(r)z\ *or* **desulto·res** \ˌdesəlˈtōrˌēz\ [L, fr. *desultus* + *-or*] **:** a rider trained to leap from one horse to another (as in the circensian games)

des·ul·to·ri·ly \ˌdesəlˈtōrəlē, -tȯr-, -li *also* -ezə-\ *adv* **:** in a desultory manner ⟨for another six years he ~ attended lectures in arts as well as canon law —G.C.Sellery⟩ ⟨a trollop of soldiery oozed ~ across the square, out of step —Bruce Marshall⟩

des·ul·to·ri·ness *n* -ES **:** the quality of being desultory

des·ul·to·ri·ous \-rēəs\ *adj* [L *desultorius*] *archaic* **:** DESULTORY

des·ul·to·ry \ˈdesəlˌtōrē, -tȯr-, -ri *also* -ezə-\ *adj* [L *desultorius*, fr. *desultor*, fr. *desultus* (past part. of *desilire* to leap down, fr. *de-* + *-silire*, fr. *salire* to leap) + *-orius* -ory — more at SALLY] **1 :** lacking steadiness, fixity, regularity, or continuity **:** ERRATIC, WAVERING, SHIFTING ⟨~ whistling of trains —Edmund Wilson⟩ ⟨their one small cannon boomed a ~ fire to distract the attention of the Mexicans —Green Peyton⟩ ⟨lived for some time in regular contact with each other and in ~ contact with the surrounding larger American community —Ethel Albert⟩ **2 :** marked by lack of definite plan or method, sustained purpose, or regular persistent logical procedure or continuity **:** showing unsteadiness, inconsistency, or incoherence ⟨make reading have a purpose instead of being ~ —Bertrand Russell⟩ ⟨already they appeared to be strangers to each other and their last conversations grew more and more ~ —Ngaio Marsh⟩ **3 :** not connected with the main subject **:** not cogently relevant **:** DIGRESSIVE ⟨certain comments of a more or less ~ character seem to need making here —Samuel Alexander⟩ **syn** see RANDOM

de·superheat \(ˈ)dē, də+\ *vb* [*de-* + *superheat*] *vt* **:** to lower the temperature of (superheated steam or other vapor) ~ *vi* **:** to desuperheat steam

de·superheater \(ˌ)dē, də+\ *n* **:** a coil, wire-mesh baffle, spray nozzle, or other device to cool superheated steam

de·surface \(ˈ)dē, də+\ *vt* [*de-* + *surface* (n.)] **:** to remove a surface layer from; *esp* **:** to strip of topsoil

de·swell \(ˈ)dē+\ *vb* [*de-* + *swell*] *vt* **:** to reduce swelling of (as the fiber of a textile) usu. by abstraction of water ~ *vi* **:** to become contracted — used esp. of colloids

desyatin *var of* DESSIATINE

des·yl \ˈdezəl, -esəl\ *n* -s [*des*oxybenzoin + *-yl*] **:** a univalent radical $C_6H_5COCH(C_6H_5)$— derived from desoxybenzoin by removal of one hydrogen atom from the methylene group; alpha-phenyl-phenacyl

de·synapsis \ˌdē+\ *n* [NL, fr. *de-* + *synapsis*] **:** failure of synapsis due to separation of homologous chromosomes after initial pairing in meiosis — compare ASYNAPSIS — **de·synaptic** \"+\ *adj*

de·synonymize \"+\ *vt* [*de-* + *synonymize*] **:** to deprive of synonymous character **:** differentiate meanings of (words often used as close synonyms or as interchangeable, as *semantics* and *semasiology*)

det *abbr* **1** detached; detachment **2** detail **3** detective **4** determine; determiner

de·tach \dəˈtach, dēˈ-\ *vt* -ED/-ING/-ES [F *détacher*, fr. OF *destachier*, fr. *des-* de- + *-tachier* (as in *atachier* to attach) — more at ATTACH] **1 :** to separate esp. from a larger mass and usu. without violence or damage ⟨~ a stamp from a sheet⟩ — opposed to *attach* **2 :** DISENGAGE, WITHDRAW ⟨~*ed* himself from the embrace⟩ **3 :** to separate from a parent organization for a special object or use ⟨~ a ship from a fleet⟩

syn DISENGAGE, ABSTRACT, PRESCIND: DETACH stresses the fact of separation, parting, removal, or isolation; it is unlikely to suggest forcible action ⟨I rose, and *detaching* the silver ornament from my cloak presented it to him —W.H.Hudson †1922⟩ ⟨I brought my face close and aroused no sign of life. Then I reached up and slowly *detached* the butterfly from its resting place —William Beebe⟩ DISENGAGE suggests an extricating or freeing of something involved, enmeshed, or entangled, literally or figuratively ⟨gently *disengaging* himself from her enfolding arms —Charles Dickens⟩ ⟨the taxi *disengaged* itself from the traffic —Dan Wickenden⟩ ⟨psychology, also, was beginning to *disengage* itself from its dependence on general philosophy —A.N.Whitehead⟩ ABSTRACT indicates a withdrawing, gathering, or separating out from a mass or body; it is used more often of intangibles than tangibles ⟨I suspect that some of these early chapters will be *abstracted* from the autobiography and be reprinted again and again —*Book-of-the-Month Club News*⟩ ⟨the Church of England, which might be supposed able to *abstract* the question from its worldly confusions, is of two minds also —Virginia Woolf⟩ PRESCIND indicates a separating or detaching mentally for purposes of consideration or philosophic analysis ⟨can anyone forget the great and gentle Buddha who, *prescinding* from any belief in soul or self, gave to thousands of millions of people a code of conduct? —*Times Lit. Supp.*⟩

de·tach·abil·i·ty \=ˌ=əˈbilədē, -ətē, -i\ *n* -ES **:** the quality or state of being detachable

de·tach·able \=ˈ=əbəl\ *adj* **:** capable of being or designed to be detached **:** capable of being separated or withdrawn without loss or damage — **de·tach·ably** \-blē, -li\ *adv*

dé·ta·ché \ˌdāˌtaˈshā, dāˈtaˌshā\ *adv (or adj)* [F, lit., detached, fr. past part. of *détacher*] **:** NONLEGATO — used as a direction to players of bowed instruments

detached \dəˈtacht, dēˈ-\ *adj* [fr. past part. of *detach*] **1 :** standing by itself **:** SEPARATE, UNCONNECTED, ISOLATED; *specif* **:** not sharing any wall with another building ⟨a ~ house⟩ **2 :** UNBIASED, ALOOF ⟨a ~ view of the affair⟩ ⟨a ~ mood⟩ **3 :** DÉTACHÉ **syn** see INDIFFERENT

detached core *n* **:** the part of a compressed anticlinal or synclinal fold of rock that may be separated or pinched off from the main body of the strata

de·tached·ly \-chədlē, -chtlē, -li\ *adv* **:** in a detached manner

detached meristem *n*, *bot* **:** a meristematic region that originates directly from an apical meristem but because of the differentiation of intervening tissue becomes discontinuous with it

de·tach·ed·ness \-chədnəs, -ch(t)n-\ *n* -ES **:** the quality or state of being detached

detached service *n* **:** military service away from one's assigned organization ⟨during the course of their study the men are on *detached service* from their units —*Technical Education News*⟩ — compare TEMPORARY DUTY

de·tach·ment \-chmənt\ *n* -s [F *détachement*, fr. *détacher* + *-ment*] **1 :** the act or fact of detaching **:** SEPARATION ⟨~ of a leaf from a twig⟩ **2 a :** the dispatch of a body of troops or part of a fleet from the main body for a special mission or service **b :** the portion so dispatched **c :** a permanently organized separate unit usu. smaller than a platoon and different in composition from normal units ⟨a medical ~⟩ **3 :** indifference to worldly concerns or partisan opinion **:** absence of emotional bias **:** neutrality of feeling **:** UNWORLDLINESS ⟨saintly ~⟩ ⟨the ~ necessary to an historian⟩

¹de·tail \dəˈtāl, dēˈ-, ˈdē,-, *esp before pause or consonant* -āəl\ *n* -s [F *détail*, fr. OF *detail* piece cut off, small quantity, fr. *detaillier* to cut in pieces, fr. *de-* (fr. L *dis-* apart, to pieces) + *taillier* to cut — more at DIS-, TAILOR] **1 a :** extended treatment of or attention to particular items ⟨careful attention to ~⟩ ⟨give the argument without going into ~⟩ **b** *archaic* **:** a narrative that relates minute points **:** a particularized account **2 :** a part of a whole: as **a :** a small and subordinate part **:** PARTICULAR, ITEM, CIRCUMSTANCE ⟨this is only a ~⟩ ⟨ask for the ~s of a scheme⟩ **b :** a portion considered independently of the parts considered together ⟨reproduce a ~ of a painting⟩ ⟨elaborate in ~⟩ **c :** a minor part (as the cornice, caps of the buttresses, capitals of the columns of a building) **3 :** DETAIL DRAWING **4 a :** a written list of military duties for the day either for the entire command or for any portion; *also* **:** the distribution of the daily orders to the officers **b :** selection for a particular task of a person or a body of persons; *also* **:** the person or body selected or the task to be performed **5 :** the small elements of a photographic image corresponding to the small elements of the original subject ⟨strong lighting to achieve clarity of ~⟩ **syn** see ITEM, PART

²detail \"\ *vb* -ED/-ING/-S [F *détailler*, lit., to cut in pieces, fr. OF *detaillier*] *vt* **1 :** to relate in particulars **:** report minutely and distinctly ⟨~ a new drug⟩ **2 :** ENUMERATE, SPECIFY ⟨~ all the facts in a case⟩ **3 :** to assign (a person, a military unit) to a particular task ⟨the first sergeant will ~ the platoons for fatigue duty⟩ ⟨an infantry officer ~*ed* to an air-force unit during maneuvers⟩ **4 :** to furnish with detailing ⟨beautifully ~*ed* hats⟩ ⟨trimmings that ~ slips and petticoats⟩ ~ *vi* **:** to make detail drawings

detail drawing *n* **:** a separate large-scale drawing of a small part of a machine or structure; *esp* **:** WORKING DRAWING

detailed *adj* [ˈ*detail* + *-ed*] **:** marked by abundant detail or by thoroughness in treating small items or parts ⟨the ~ study of history should be supplemented by brilliant outlines —Bertrand Russell⟩ **syn** see CIRCUMSTANTIAL

de·tailed·ly \-l(ə)dlē, -li\ *adv* **:** in a detailed manner **:** item by item **:** THOROUGHLY

de·tailed·ness \-l(ə)dnəs\ *n* -ES **:** the quality or state of being detailed **:** PARTICULARITY

de·tail·er \-lə(r)\ *n* -s [²*detail* + *-er*] **1 :** one that makes detail drawings **:** one that elaborates general outlines (as of a building design) into specifics **2 :** one that details (as prescription drugs)

detail fracture *n* **:** a rail fracture from external cause that begins at or near the top surface of the rail and progresses crosswise

detailing *n* -s [fr. gerund of ²*detail*] **:** the smaller elements of design and finish (as on garments or building interiors)

detail man *n* **:** a representative of a drug manufacturer who introduces new drugs to professional users (as physicians or pharmacists)

de·tain \dəˈtān, dēˈ-\ *vt* -ED/-ING/-S [ME *deteynen*, fr. MF *detenir*, fr. OF, fr. L *detinēre*, fr. *de* from, away + *-tinēre* (fr. *tenēre* to hold) — more at DE-, THIN] **1 :** to hold or keep in or as if in custody ⟨~*ed* by the police for questioning⟩ **2** *archaic* **:** to keep back (as something that is due) **:** WITHHOLD **3 :** to restrain esp. from proceeding **:** hold back **:** STOP, DELAY ⟨~*ed* by an accident⟩ **4 :** to hold the attention of ⟨the introduction . . . will ~ the reader as effectively as many of the selected passages that follow —*Brit. Book News*⟩ **syn** see DELAY, KEEP

de·tain·ee \dəˌtāˈnē, dēˌ-; ˌdēˌt-\ *n* -s **:** a person (as an enemy alien) held in custody for political reasons

de·tain·er \dəˈtānə(r), dēˈ-\ *n* -s [modif. (influenced by E *detain*) of AF *detener* (infin. used as n.), fr. *detener*, *detenir* to detain, fr. L *detinēre*] **1 :** a keeping in one's possession; *specif* **:** the withholding from the owner of something which is rightfully his but which through lawful circumstances has come into the possession of the holder **2 :** detention in custody **3 :** a writ authorizing the keeper of a prison to continue to keep a person in custody

de·tain·ing·ly *adv* [*detaining* (pres. part. of *detain*) + *-ly*] **:** in a detaining manner

de·tain·ment \-nmənt\ *n* -s **:** DETENTION

de·tassel \(ˈ)dē+\ *vt* **:** to remove the tassels that bear the staminate flowers of (corn) thereby preventing self-pollination

de·tect \dəˈtekt, dēˈ-\ *vt* -ED/-ING/-S [ME *detecten*, fr. L *detectus*, past part. of *detegere* to uncover, detect, fr. *de* from, away + *tegere* to cover — more at THATCH] **1 :** to discover the true esp. hidden or disguised character of (a person) ⟨~ a hypocrite⟩ ⟨potential crack-ups who should have been ~*ed* at the induction center —S.L.A.Marshall⟩ **2 :** to discover or determine the existence, presence, or fact of ⟨~ the presence of alcohol in blood⟩ ⟨radar devices to ~ enemy planes⟩ ⟨his keen eyes ~*ed* a slight movement in the bushes⟩ **3** *radio* **a :** to determine the presence of (a signal) **b :** RECTIFY **c :** to convert (a modulated wave or current) into the original modulating wave or current **:** DEMODULATE **syn** see DISCOVER

de·tect·able \-əbəl\ *adj* **:** capable of being detected

de·tec·ta·phone \-ktəˌfōn\ *n* -s [*detect* + connective *-a-* + *-phone*] **:** a telephonic apparatus with an attached microphone transmitter used esp. for listening secretly

de·tect·er \-ktə(r) *also* ˈdē,t-\ *n* -s [by alter. (influenced by E *-er*)] **:** DETECTOR

de·tec·tion \dəˈtekshən, dēˈ-\ *n* -s [ME *deteccyon*, fr. LL *detection-*, *detectio* act of revealing, fr. L *detectus* (past part. of *detegere* + *-ion-*, *-io* -ion] **1 :** the act of detecting **:** the laying open of what was concealed or hidden or of what tends to elude observation **:** DISCOVERY ⟨~ of a thief⟩ ⟨the ~ of fraud⟩ ⟨techniques of crime ~⟩ **2** *radio* **a :** determination of the presence of a signal **b :** RECTIFICATION **c :** extraction of the intelligence from a signal **d :** conversion of a modulated wave or current into the original modulating wave or current — called also *demodulation*

¹de·tec·tive \dəˈtektiv, dēˈ-, -ktēv, *also* -ktəv\ *adj* [*detect* + *-ive*] **:** fitted for, employed for, or concerned with detection ⟨~ ability⟩ ⟨~ fiction⟩

²detective \"\ *n* -s **:** one employed or engaged in detecting lawbreakers or getting information that is not readily or publicly accessible **:** an investigator of private esp. illicit or criminal affairs **:** a plainclothes police officer

de·tec·tor \-ktə(r)\ *n* -s [LL, revealer, fr. L *detectus* + *-or*] **:** one that detects: as **a :** an arrangement in a lock designed to prevent forcing and to indicate any tampering **b :** an indicator showing the depth of the water in a boiler **c :** a device for indicating improper functioning or condition of a facility (as a railroad switch or signal) or to assure proper functioning **d :** a device for detecting the presence of electric waves or of radioactivity **e** *radio* (1) **:** a device for determining the presence of a signal (2) **:** a rectifier of high-frequency current (as a cat whisker and crystal or a vacuum tube) (3) **:** a device for extracting the intelligence from a signal (4) **:** DEMODULATOR 1

detector bar *n* **:** a device used to keep a railroad switch locked in position while a train is passing over it

detector car *n* **:** a self-propelled car equipped with a special mechanism for detecting flaws in rails and marking the rail for replacement

de·temporize *or* **de·temporalize** \(ˈ)dē+ˈ-\ *vt* [*detemporize* fr. *de-* + L *tempor-*, *tempus* time + E *-ize*; *detemporalize* fr. *de-* + *temporalize* — more at TEMPORAL] **:** to dissociate from a particular historical time **:** make timeless ⟨war fiction that tries to disengage itself from its own historical background, to ~ and depersonalize its time-bound characters —Robert Pick⟩

de·tent \dəˈtent, (ˈ)dēˌt-\ *n* -s [F *détente*, fr. MF *destente*, fr. *destendre* to slacken, release, fr. OF, fr. *des-* de- + *tendre* to stretch, fr. L *tendere* — more at THIN] **:** a part of a mechanism (as a catch, pawl, dog, or click) that locks or unlocks a movement: as **a :** the part of a watch or clock that detains a wheel or a lever when moved in one direction but releases it on its return excursion **b :** the set lever in a stem-set watch **c :** the hook that locks and unlocks the striking mechanism in a clock

dé·tente \(ˈ)dāˈtä(ⁿ)nt, dāˈtäⁿt\ *n* -s [F, détente, detent] **1 :** a slackening or relaxing; *esp* **:** an easing or relaxation of strained relations and political tensions between nations **2** *phonetics* **:** OFF-GLIDE, RELEASE

de·ten·tion \dəˈtenchən, dēˈ-\ *n* -s [MF or LL; MF, fr. LL *detention-*, *detentio* retention, fr. L *detentus* (past part. of *detinēre* to detain) + *-ion-*, *-io* -ion — more at DETAIN] **1 :** the act or fact of detaining: **a :** a holding in custody ⟨~ of a tardy pupil after school hours⟩ **b :** a holding back ⟨the ~ of a motorist by a traffic officer⟩ **2 :** the state of being detained ⟨~ in jail⟩ **:** enforced delay ⟨accidental ~ on a journey⟩; *esp* **:** a period of temporary custody prior to disposition by a court ⟨the ~ of juvenile delinquents⟩ **3** *civil law* **:** a bare physical control without the mental element of intention required for possession

detention home *n* **:** a house of detention for juvenile delinquents usu. under supervision of the local juvenile court

de·ten·tive \-entiv\ *adj* [fr. *detention*, after E *retention*: *retentive*] **:** having the function of detaining

dé·te·nu *or* **dé·te·nue** \ˌdātᵊnˈ(y)ü, *F* dātnü\ *n* -s [F *détenu* (masc.), *détenue* (fem.), fr. *détenu*, past part. of *détenir* to detain, fr. OF *detenir* — more at DETAIN] **:** a detained person; *esp* **:** a political prisoner in India

de·ter \dəˈtər, dēˈ-, +V -ər-; -ˈtə̄, +V -ər- *or* -ə̄(r\ *vt* **deterred; deterred; deterring; deters** [L *deterrēre*, fr. *de* from, away + *terrēre* to frighten — more at DE-, TERROR] **1 :** to turn aside, discourage, or prevent from acting by fear or consideration of dangerous, difficult, or unpleasant attendant circumstances or consequences **2 :** INHIBIT ⟨painting to ~ rust⟩ **syn** see DISSUADE

de·terge \dəˈtərj, dēˈ-, -əj,-əij\ *vt* -ED/-ING/-S [F or L; F *déterger* to cleanse, fr. L *detergēre* to wipe off, cleanse, fr. *de* from, away + *tergēre* to rub off, wipe off — more at TERSE] **:** to wash off **:** CLEANSE

de·ter·gency \-jənsē, -si\ *n* -ES [*detergent*, adj. + *-cy*] **:** cleansing quality or power

¹de·ter·gent \-jənt\ *adj* [F or L; F *détergent*, fr. L *detergent-*, *detergens*, pres. part. of *detergēre*] **:** CLEANSING

²detergent \"\ *n* -s **:** a cleansing agent: as **a :** SOAP **b :** an inorganic alkali, an alkaline salt (as a sodium phosphate or a sodium silicate), or a mixture of such compounds for use esp. in cleaning metals (as in dairy equipment) — called also *alkaline detergent* **c :** any of a large number of synthetic water-soluble or liquid organic surface-active agents for use in washing that resemble soaps in the ability to emulsify oils and hold dirt in suspension but differ in other respects (as in nonprecipitation of calcium and magnesium salts from hard water and in chemical composition) — called also *synthetic detergent*; see ANIONIC DETERGENT, CATIONIC DETERGENT, NONIONIC DETERGENT; compare WETTING AGENT **d :** an oil-soluble substance that holds insoluble foreign matter in suspension and is used in lubricating oils and dry-cleaning solvents

de·te·ri·o·ra·ble \dəˈtirēərəbəl, dēˈ-\ *adj* [*deteriorate* + *-able*] **:** liable to deteriorate

de·te·ri·o·rate \dəˈtirēəˌrāt, dēˈ-, *chiefly in substand speech* -irēˌāt *sometimes* -irəˌrāt; *usu* -ād+V\ *vb* -ED/-ING/-S [LL *deterioratus*, past part. of *deteriorare*, fr. L *deterior* worse, fr. *de* down, away + *-ter* (suffix as in L *uter* which of two) + *-ior* (comparative suffix) — more at DE-, WHETHER, -ER] *vt* **:** to make inferior in quality or value **:** IMPAIR ⟨laxity ~s discipline⟩ ~ *vi* **:** to grow worse ⟨the weather had *deteriorated* during the night —Nevil Shute⟩ **:** become impaired in quality, state, or condition **:** DEGENERATE ⟨idle houses ~⟩

de·te·ri·o·ra·tion \dəˌtirēəˈrāshən, dēˌ-, *chiefly in substand speech* -irēˈā- *sometimes* -irəˈrā-\ *n* -s [LL *deterioration-*, *deterioratio*, fr. *deterioratus* + L *-ion-*, *-io* -ion] **:** the action or process of deteriorating or state of having deteriorated **:** gradual impairment

de·te·ri·o·ra·tion·ist \-sh(ə)nəst\ *n* -s **:** one who holds that the world and mankind are deteriorating

de·te·ri·o·ra·tive \-ˈtirēəˌrā|d·|iv, -ˌrəl, |t|, |ēv *also* |əv\ *adj* **:** tending to deteriorate **:** DETERIORATING

de·te·ri·o·ra·tor \-ˌrād·ə(r), -ātə-\ *n* -s **:** one that deteriorates

de·te·ri·o·rism \-ˌrizəm\ *n* -s [L *deterior* worse + E *-ism*] **:** the belief in universal deterioration — compare MELIORISM

de·ter·ma \dəˈtərmə\ *n* -s [native name in Guiana] **:** a Central American tree (*Ocotea rubra*) valued for its light strong wood

de·ter·ment \dəˈtərmənt, dēˈ-, -tə̄m-\ *n* -s [*deter* + *-ment*] **1 :** the action of deterring **2 :** DETERRENT

de·ter·min·abil·i·ty \dəˌtərmənəˈbiləd·ē, (ˌ)dēˌt-, -tə̄m-, -təim-, -ətē, -i *also* -mn-\ *n* -ES **:** the quality or state of being determinable or determinate

¹de·ter·min·able \dəˈtərmənəbəl, dēˈ-, -tə̄m-,-təim- *also* -mn-\ *adj* [ME, fr. *determinen* to determine + *-able*] **1 :** capable of being determined, definitely ascertained, or decided upon **:** JUDICABLE **2 :** liable to be terminated **:** TERMINABLE — **de·ter·min·able·ness** *n* -ES — **de·ter·min·ably** \-blē, -li\ *adv*

²determinable \"\ *n* -s **:** a logical attribute or the name of a logical attribute (as color) of which certain more specific characters or their names are determinates (as red)

determinable fee *n* **:** a fee so qualified that it terminates upon the happening of a contingency or failure of a qualification

de·ter·mi·na·cy \-mənəsē, -si\ *n* -ES [*determinate* + *-cy*] **1 :** the quality or state of being determinate **2 a :** the condition of being definitely and unequivocally characterized **:** EXACTNESS ⟨the ~ of a logical statement⟩ **b :** the condition of being determined or necessitated ⟨the conflict between freedom of the will and universal ~⟩

¹de·ter·mi·nant \-nənt\ *adj* [L *determinant-*, *determinans*, pres. part. of *determinare* to limit, determine] **:** serving to determine **:** DETERMINATIVE

²determinant \"\ *n* -s **1 :** a fact, circumstance, or situation which identifies or aids diagnosis or determines the nature of something or which fixes, determines, or conditions an outcome or issue **:** FACTOR ⟨there is no eternal ~ of obscenity, lasciviousness, indecency . . . the meanings of these terms change with the times —J.T.Farrell⟩ ⟨a semiconsciousness that education is the most important function of the state and the chief ~ of its way of life —Stephen Duggan⟩ **2 :** a determining bachelor of arts **3 :** a square array of numbers with which is associated a value that is the algebraic sum of all of the different products that can be formed by taking as factors an element from each column in succession, each one from a different row, the signs of the products being positive or negative depending upon whether the number of interchanges in the row indices necessary to restore them to natural order is even or odd **4** *logic* **:** a qualifying adjective or phrase **:** a mark or attribute distinguishing some class which falls under a more general concept **:** DIFFERENTIA **5 a :** a hypothetical aggregate of biophores conceived as comparable to the gene of more recent biological theory **b :** GENE; *broadly* **:** a comparable but subordinate agent (as a plasmagene or plastogene) **6 :** RADICAL 2c **7 :** ²DETERMINATIVE 3 **8** *archeol* **:** a trait or complex that is diagnostic of a cultural unit (as a component, aspect, phase) **9 :** one of the chemical groupings that together determine the specific reactivity of an antigen or antibody **syn** see CAUSE

de·ter·mi·nan·tal \ə̇ˌ=ˌ=ˈnantᵊl\ *adj* **:** relating to, consisting of, or expressed in determinants

¹de·ter·mi·nate \dəˈtərmənət, dēˈ-, -|tə̄m-,-təim-, *usu* -nəd·+V\ *adj* [ME *determinat*, fr. L *determinatus*, past part. of *determinare* to limit, determine] **1 :** having defined limits **:** not uncertain **:** fixed by a rule or by some specific and constant cause **:** ESTABLISHED, DEFINITE ⟨~ variations in animals⟩ **2 :** definitely settled **:** fixed by authority or consent **:** INVARIABLE, ARBITRARY ⟨a ~ order of precedence⟩ **3 :** determined by resolving, deciding, or coming to a conclusion about **:** DEFINITIVE ⟨a ~ answer to the problem⟩ **4** *of a number* **:** having a fixed value — opposed to *indeterminate* **5 :** CYMOSE **6** *embryol* **:** undergoing determinate cleavage — **de·ter·mi·nate·ly** *adv* — **de·ter·mi·nate·ness** *n* -ES

²de·ter·mi·nate \-ˌnāt, *usu* -ād+V\ *vt* -ED/-ING/-S [L *determinatus*, past part. of *determinare*] **1** *obs* **a :** to fix the boundaries or limits of **b :** to bring to an end **2** *obs* **:** to decide or settle (an issue) **3** *obs* **:** to guide or determine the course or end of **4 :** to find out for certain **:** ASCERTAIN **5 :** to fix the identity of **:** IDENTIFY

³determinate *like* ¹DETERMINATE\ *n* -s [¹*determinate*] **:** a logical character that is a further determination of some more general attribute — see ²DETERMINABLE

determinate cleavage *n* **:** cleavage (sense 4a) in which each cell division irreversibly separates portions of the zygote with specific and distinct potencies for further development — compare INDETERMINATE CLEAVAGE, MOSAICISM

determinate evolution *or* **determinate variation** *n* **:** ORTHOGENESIS 1

determinate growth *n* **1 :** growth in which the axis being limited by the development of the terminal flower bud or other reproductive structure does not continue to elongate indefinitely (as in a cymose inflorescence and in certain mosses) — compare INDETERMINATE GROWTH **2 :** growth that proceeds only during part of the vegetative season and then ceases

de·ter·mi·na·tion \dəˌtərməˈnāshən, dēˌ-, -tə̄m-,-təim-\ *n* -s [ME *determinacioun*, fr. ML *determination-*, *determinatio*, fr. L, boundary, end, fr. *determinatus* + *-ion-*, *-io* -ion] **1 :** the settling and ending of a controversy esp. by judicial decision **:** CONCLUSION, DECISION ⟨the contending parties came to a ~⟩ **2 :** the resolving of a question by argument or reasoning; *specif* **:** a disputation in English universities formerly held by those just made bachelors of arts as a condition of proceeding toward the master's degree **3** *archaic* **:** a bringing or coming to an end **:** TERMINATION **4 a :** the act of deciding definitely and firmly esp. regarding a course of action; *also* **:** the result of such an act of decision **:** fixed resolution **:** PURPOSE **b :** the power or habit of deciding definitely and firmly **:** ability to persist against opposition or attempts to dissuade or discourage **:** RESOLUTENESS ⟨men of great courage and ~⟩ **5 :** a fixing of the position, magnitude, or character of something: as **a :** the act, process, or result of an accurate measurement (as of weight, volume, intensity) ⟨a ~ of the salt in sea water⟩ ⟨a ~ of the orbit of a planet⟩ **b :** an identification of the taxonomic position of a plant or animal **6** *logic* **a :** the act of defining a concept or notion by giving its essential constituents **b :** the addition of a differentia to a concept or notion, thus limiting its extent **c :** a differentia added **7 :** an unvarying and often conclusive tendency toward an end ⟨a ~ of capital toward investment in transport industries⟩ **8 :** the fixation of the destiny of undifferentiated embryonic tissue **:** field formation

¹de·ter·mi·na·tive \ə̇ˈ==ˌnā|d·|iv, -ˌnəl, |t|, |ēv *also* |əv\ *adj* [prob. fr. ML *determinativus* definite, fr. LL, relating to the crisis of a disease, fr. L *determinatus* + *-ivus* -ive] **1 :** having power or tendency to determine **:** LIMITING, SHAPING, DIRECTING, CONCLUSIVE **2 :** fixing or tending to determine the specific character **3** *of a compound word* **:** belonging either to the karmadharaya class or to the tatpurusha class **syn** see CONCLUSIVE

²determinative \"\ *n* -s **1 :** one that serves to determine **2 :** a sign attached to a word in any of various forms of writing (as hieroglyphic and cuneiform) to indicate its class, number, or other feature, thereby often serving to distinguish the word from its homographs — compare RADICAL 2c **3 :** a usu. suffixal sound or sequence of sounds added to a root and producing a longer root or base sometimes with perceptibly modified meaning to which derivational affixes or inflectional endings may be added (as *d* in reconstructed Indo-European *gheud-* "to pour", represented by Latin *fudi* "I have poured" and Gothic *giutan* "to pour", contrasted with reconstructed Indo-European *gheu-* "to pour", represented by Sanskrit *homa* "sacrifice", Greek *cheein* "to pour", *chylos* "juice") **4 :** a word belonging to any of several classes differently constituted by different grammarians but typically either consisting of certain uses of the definite article and of demonstrative adjectives and pronouns or including the definite article, demonstrative adjectives, demonstrative pronouns, and some limiting adjectives other than demonstratives **5 :** a determinative compound **6 :** CLASSIFIER 2

determinative judgment *n* [trans. of G *bestimmende urteilskraft*] *in Kantianism* **:** a judgment that proceeds from a general concept or universal principle and designates the particulars which are to be subsumed under the general — contrasted with *reflective judgment*

de·ter·mi·na·tive·ly \|əvlē, -li\ *adv* **:** in a determinative manner

de·ter·mi·na·tor \-ˌnād·ə(r), -ātə-\ *n* -s [MF & LL; MF *determinateur*, fr. LL *determinator*, fr. L *determinatus* + *-or*] **:** DETERMINER

de·ter·mine \dəˈtərmən, dēˈ-, -tə̄m-,-təim-\ *vb* **determined; determined; determining** \-m(ə)niŋ\ **determines** [ME *determinen*, fr. MF *determiner*, fr. L *determinare* to limit, determine, fr. *de* from, away + *terminare* to limit, fr. *terminus* limit, boundary — more at DE-, TERM] *vt* **1 a :** to fix conclusively or authoritatively ⟨a council was set up to ~ national policy⟩ **b :** to settle a question or controversy about **:** decide by judicial sentence ⟨the court heard and *determined* the plea⟩ **c :** to come to a decision concerning as the result of investigation or reasoning ⟨an attempt to ~ the date of his death⟩ **d :** to settle or decide by choice of alternatives or possibilities ⟨~ the list of guests to be invited⟩ **e :** to set up as a goal or purpose **:** resolve upon ⟨when did Thoreau ~ to become a man of letters —H.S.Canby⟩ **2 a :** to fix the form or character of beforehand **:** ORDAIN, FOREORDAIN **b :** to establish causally **:** bring about as a result **:** REGULATE ⟨demand ~s the price⟩ **3 :** to set bounds or limits to: as **a :** to fix the boundaries of **b :** to limit in extent or scope **c :** to put or set an end to **:** bring to a close **:** TERMINATE ⟨~ an estate⟩ **d** *logic* **:** to define or limit by adding a differentia **4 :** to direct or control the end or course of: as **a :** to turn to a definite resolution or intention **:** cause to come to a decision ⟨opposition only *determined* her further⟩ **b :** to give a definite direction, impetus, or bias to ⟨what we notice ~s what we do —William James⟩ **5 a :** to obtain definite and firsthand knowledge of as to character, location, magnitude, or quantity ⟨~ the salt in sea water⟩ **b :** to discover the taxonomic position of (a plant or animal) **:** ascertain the generic and specific names of **6** *embryol* **:** to cause or elicit determination of ~ *vi* **1 :** to come to a decision **:** RESOLVE ⟨the boy *determined* on becoming a painter⟩ **2 :** to come to an end **:** expire or become void **:** END, TERMINATE ⟨membership in the order ~s with the death of the sovereign⟩ **3 :** to dispute a question or maintain a thesis as formerly required at some European universities of those completing the assumption of a bachelor's degree **4** *obs* **:** to have a course (as toward an end) **:** TEND **syn** see DECIDE, DISCOVER

de·ter·mined \-mənd\ *adj* [fr. past part. of *determine*] **:** DECIDED, RESOLUTE ⟨even the most ~ realist has more than a streak in him of romanticist —John Galsworthy⟩ **:** BENT ⟨~ to get a rich husband⟩ — **de·ter·mined·ly** \-n(d)dlē, -li\ *adv* — **de·ter·mined·ness** \-n(d)nəs\ *n* -ES

de·ter·min·er \-mənə(r)\ *n* -s **:** one that determines: as **a :** an inheritance factor **:** GENE, DETERMINANT **b :** a word belonging to a group of limiting noun modifiers that in English consists of *a, an, any, each, either, every, neither, no, one, some, the, that, those, this, these, what, whatever, which, whichever*, possessive adjectives (as *my*), and possessive-case forms (as *Joe's*) and is characterized by occurrence before descriptive adjectives modifying the same noun (as *that* in "that big yellow house" or *his* in "his new car")

de·ter·mi·nism \-məˌnizəm\ *n* -s [ISV *determine* + *-ism*] **1 a :** the doctrine that all acts of the will result from causes which determine them either in such a manner that man has no alternative modes of action or that the will is still free in the sense of being uncompelled — called also *ethical determinism*; compare INDETERMINISM **b :** the theory that all occurrences in nature are determined by antecedent causes or take place in accordance with natural laws — called also *cosmological determinism* **c :** a belief in predestination — called also *theological determinism*; compare FATALISM **2 :** a theory that regards a certain order of phenomena (as economic, geographical, or social factors) as the primary or determining causes for cultural change, social evolution, or the appearance of certain culture traits — compare ECONOMIC INTERPRETATION OF HISTORY **3 :** the quality or state of being determined: **a :** a natural process wherein all events are determined **b :** the determination of mental processes

de·ter·mi·nist \-ˌnəst\ *n* -s [ISV *determine* + *-ist*] **:** an adherent of determinism

de·ter·mi·nis·tic \ˌ≈ˌ≈¦nistik\ *adj* : relating to or implying determinism — **de·ter·mi·nis·ti·cal·ly** \-tək(ə)lē\ *adv*
deterred *past of* DETER
de·ter·rence \də'tər·ən(t)s, dē'-, -tə·rə- *also* -terə- *or* -tərə-; *esp in emphatic positions* -tərn- *or* -tern-\ *n* -s [*deter* + *-ence*] : the act or process of deterring; *esp* : the restraint and discouragement of crime by fear (as by the exemplary punishment of convicted offenders)
¹**de·ter·rent** \-nt\ *adj* [L *deterrent-, deterrens,* pres. part. of *deterrēre* to deter] **1** : serving to deter ⟨the ~ effect of high prices on buying⟩ **2** : relating to deterrence ⟨a ~ view of punishment⟩ — **de·ter·rent·ly** *adv*
²**deterrent** \"\ *n* -s : something that deters ⟨many . . . people feel that corporal punishment . . . does act as a ~ to potential offenders —W.T.McGrath⟩ ⟨U.S. superiority in atomic weapons seemed a ~ to all-out war —*New Statesman & Nation*⟩
deterring *pres part of* DETER
deters *pres 3d sing of* DETER
¹**de·ter·sive** \də'tərsiv *also* -rziv\ *adj* [MF *detersif,* fr. L *detersus* (past part. of *detergēre* to wipe off, cleanse) + MF *-if* -ive — more at DETERGE] : CLEANSING, DETERGENT
²**detersive** \"\ *n* -s : a cleansing agent : DETERGENT
de·test \də'test, dē'-\ *vt* -ED/-ING/-S [ME *detesten,* fr. L *detestari,* lit., to curse while calling a deity to witness, fr. *de* from, down, away + *testari* to be a witness, testify, invoke as a witness, fr. *testis* witness — more at DE-, TESTIS] **1** : to dislike intensely : ABHOR, LOATHE, HATE ⟨she delights in wrangles, noises, drafts, and almost everything that older people ~ —E.K. Brown⟩ **2** *obs* : CURSE, DENOUNCE, CONDEMN **syn** see HATE
de·test·able \-stəbəl, *archaically with stress on first syllable*\ *adj* [ME, fr. MF, fr. L *detestabilis,* fr. *detestari* + *-abilis* -able] : worthy of being detested : very odious : deserving abhorrence : ABOMINABLE ⟨~ vices⟩ — **de·test·able·ness** *n* -ES — **de·test·ably** \-blē, -li\ *adv*
de·tes·ta·tion \ˌdē,te'stāshən *sometimes* də,- *or* ˌde,-\ *n* -s [ME *detestacion,* fr. MF & L; MF *detestation,* fr. L *detestation-, detestatio,* fr. *detestatus* (past part. of *detestari*) + *-ion-, -io* -ion] **1** *obs* : public or formal denunciation **2** : the act or feeling of detesting : extreme hatred or dislike : ABHORRENCE, LOATHING ⟨~ of civil war⟩ **3** : an object of hatred or contempt ⟨the ~ of all honest men⟩
de·throne \də'thrōn, dē'-\ *vt* : to remove or drive from a throne : divest of royal or supreme authority and dignity : DEPOSE — **de·throne·ment** \-mənt\ *n* -s
de·tin \(')dē+\ *vt* : to remove or recover tin from
det·i·net \'detᵊn,et\ *n* -s [L, he detains, 3d pers. sing. pres. indic. act. of *detinēre* to detain — more at DETAIN] : a common-law action alleging merely that the defendant is withholding the money or chattels demanded — compare DETINUIT
det·i·nue \-tᵊn,(y)ü\ *n* -s [ME *detenewe,* fr. MF *detenue* detention, fr. fem. of *detenu,* past part. of *detenir* to detain — more at DETAIN] **1** : detention of something due; *esp* : the un lawful detention of a personal chattel from another **2** : a common-law action for the recovery of a personal chattel or its value wrongfully detained; *also* : the writ used for this action — compare TROVER
de·tin·u·it \də'tinyəwət\ *n* -s [L, he has detained, 3d pers. sing. perf. indic. act. of *detinēre*] : an action for replevin where the plaintiff already has the goods sued for — compare DETINET
detn *abbr* **1** detention **2** determination
det·o·na·bil·i·ty \ˌdetᵊnə'bilәd·ē, -ed·ən-,-etən- *sometimes* ˌdē-\ : the quality or state of being detonable
det·o·na·ble \'detᵊnəbəl, -ed·ən-,-etən- *sometimes* 'dē-\ *adj* [*detonate* + *-able*] : capable of being detonated
det·o·nat·abil·i·ty \ˌ≈ˌād·ə'bilәd·ē, ˌ≈≈ˌnā-\ *n* -ES : DETONABILITY
det·o·nat·able \'≈≈ˌ≈bəl, ˌ≈≈¦≈≈\ *adj* : DETONABLE
det·o·nate \'≈≈ˌāt, '≈≈ˌnāt, *usu* -ād·+V\ *vb* -ED/-ING/-S [L *detonatus,* past part. of *detonare* to thunder down, fr. *de* down, away + *tonare* to thunder — more at DE-, THUNDER] *vi* : to explode almost instantaneously : undergo detonation — distinguished from *deflagrate* ~ *vt* : to cause to detonate ⟨~ TNT⟩ ⟨~ an atom bomb⟩
det·o·na·tion \ˌ≈≈'āshən, ˌ≈≈'nā-\ *n* -s [F *détonation,* fr. ML *detonation-, detonatio,* fr. L *detonatus* + *-ion-, -io* -ion] **1 a** : the action or process of detonating; *specif* : a chemical reaction producing vigorous evolution of heat and sparks or flame and moving through the material detonated (as a high explosive such as dynamite or TNT) at a speed greater than that of sound — distinguished from *deflagration* **b** : a violent explosion **2** : abnormally rapid combustion in an internal-combustion engine that replaces or occurs simultaneously with normal combustion and is manifested by loss of power, overheating, rough operation, and a characteristic knock
det·o·na·tive \'≈≈ˌād·iv, '≈≈ˌnā|, '≈≈ə|, '≈≈nə|, |t|, |ēv *also* |əv\ *adj* : having the property of detonating or characterized by detonation : EXPLOSIVE
det·o·na·tor \'≈≈ˌād·ə(r), '≈≈ˌnād·ə(r), -ātə-\ *n* -s : one that detonates: as **a** : a device (as a blasting cap) used for detonating a high-explosive charge **b** *Brit* : TORPEDO 4d **c** : an explosive (as mercury fulminate) that is more sensitive to heat or shock than the common high explosives and is used in small quantity to detonate another explosive
de·torsion \(')dē+\ *n* [*de-* + *torsion*] : the removal of torsion; *specif* : correction of abnormal twist (as of the intestine)
de·tort \də'tȯ(ə)rt\ *vt* -ED/-ING/-S [L *detortus,* past part. of *detorquēre,* fr. *de* from, away + *torquēre* to twist — more at DE-, TORTURE] *archaic* : TWIST, DISTORT, PERVERT — **de·tor·tion** \-ȯrshən\ *n* -s *archaic*
¹**de·tour** \'dē,tù(ə)r, dē't-, də't-, -üə\ *n* -s [F *détour,* fr. OF *destor,* fr. *destorner, destourner* to divert, turn aside, fr. *des-* de- + *torner, tourner* to turn — more at TURN] : a turning aside : a circuitous route : a deviation from a direct course or the usual procedure ⟨the ~s of the Mississippi⟩; *specif* : a roundabout way temporarily replacing part of a route
²**detour** \"\ *vb* -ED/-ING/-S *vi* : to proceed by a detour ⟨pits intervened and obliged the party to ~ around them⟩ ~ *vt* **1** : to send by a circuitous route : deflect from a straight course ⟨heavy trucks were ~*ed* to avoid the bridge⟩ **2** : to avoid by going around : BYPASS ⟨either flying above or ~*ing* storms⟩
de·toxicant \(')dē + '-\ *n* -s [*detoxicate* + *-ant*] : a detoxicating agent
de·tox·i·cate \(')dē'täksə,kāt\ *vt* -ED/-ING/-S [*de-* + L *toxicum* poison + E *-ate* — more at TOXIC] : DETOXIFY — **de·tox·i·ca·tion** \(,)dē,täksə'kāshən\ *n* -s — **de·tox·i·ca·tor** \(')dē'täksə,kād·ə(r)\ *n* -s
de·tox·i·fi·ca·tion \(,)dē,täksəfə'kāshən\ *n* -s [alter. (influenced by E *-fication*) of *detoxication*] : the act of detoxifying or the state of being detoxified
de·tox·i·fi·er \(')dē'täksə,fī(ə)r\ *n* -s [*detoxify* + *-er*] : DETOXICANT
de·tox·i·fy \-,fī\ *vt* -ED/-ING/-ES [fr. *detoxification,* after such pairs as E *magnification: magnify*] : to remove the poison or effect of poison from
de·tract \də'trakt, dē'-\ *vb* -ED/-ING/-S [ME *detracten,* fr. L *detractus,* past part. of *detrahere* to take away, withdraw, disparage, fr. *de* from, away + *trahere* to pull — more at DE-, DRAW] *vt* **1** *archaic* : to speak ill of : DISPARAGE, BELITTLE **2** *archaic* : to take away (a part) from something so as to lessen its value or importance **3** : DIVERT, DRAW ⟨these exaggerated reports tend to ~ attention from the real issue —John Scott⟩ ~ *vi* : to diminish the importance, value, or praiseworthiness of something : DEROGATE ⟨far above our poor power to add or to ~ —Abraham Lincoln⟩ — often used with *from* ⟨any attempt to give a rational proof of the mysteries of religion really ~s from faith —Frank Thilly⟩ **syn** see DECRY
de·tract·er \-ktə(r)\ *n* -s [by alter.] : DETRACTOR
de·tract·ing·ly *adv* : in a detracting manner
de·trac·tion \də'trakshən, dē'-\ *n* -s [ME *detraccioun,* fr. MF *detraction,* fr. LL *detraction-, detractio,* fr. L, withdrawal, fr. *detractus* (past part. of *detrahere*) + *-ion-, -io* -ion] **1** : the uttering of material (as false or slanderous charges) that is likely to damage the reputation of another : DEFAMATION, DISPARAGEMENT **2** : a taking away : SUBTRACTION ⟨a ~ from the dignity of the legislature⟩
syn SLANDER, BACKBITING, CALUMNY, SCANDAL: DETRACTION, the least colorful of this group, is likely to stress the fact of damage to reputation, esteem, or credit and to leave unstressed motives for or kinds of malicious utterance ⟨I have no thought to paint the failings of our law in lurid colors of *detraction.* I have little doubt that its body is for the most part sound and pure —B.N.Cardozo⟩ ⟨no momentary happiness to have one enclosure where the voice that speaks in envy or *detraction* is not heard; which malice may not enter —William Wordsworth⟩ SLANDER, often legal or legalistic in suggestion, likewise connotes actual definite harm to the victim and suggests oral utterance of damaging statements, either quite maliciously and with full realization of their effect or quite carelessly and without consideration ⟨a *slander,* with which envy prompts the malignity of persons in their senses to asperse wittier than themselves —William Cowper⟩ ⟨this charge cannot be excused as a reckless *slander.* It was a deliberate falsehood, a lie —*New Republic*⟩ Sometimes SLANDER may involve statements true in fact but usu. not uttered and hence having the nature of the defamatory when uttered ⟨it is not hypocrisy to conceal the desires or imaginings which one would never act upon. To tell these is not true disclosure of oneself, but *slander* —H.O. Taylor⟩ BACKBITING suggests continued mean criticism, belittling, and unfair attacks on an absent friend, colleague, or associate by one from whom loyalty and fairness could be expected ⟨jealousy and intrigue and *backbiting,* producing a poisonous atmosphere of underground competition —Bertrand Russell⟩ CALUMNY may stress the purposive malice of the agent and the fact of his deliberate use of falsehood or misrepresentation ⟨these *calumnies,* indeed, could find credit only with the undiscerning multitude; but with these *calumnies* were mingled accusations much better founded —T.B.Macaulay⟩ ⟨a fellow . . . telling people that I was a consummate hypocrite. He could know nothing of it . . . I had given him no ground for that particular *calumny* —Joseph Conrad⟩ SCANDAL suggests gossipy repetition of and emphasis on discreditable details, esp. lurid ones, that defame ⟨I saw him coming out of the brush with that oldest girl of Trinidad's, only Sunday night. The reappearance of the priest upon the scene cut short further *scandal* —Willa Cather⟩ ⟨she was reconciled to the facts, but when she knew or suspected that they might be a subject of *scandal* among people who would be "sorry for her", she felt the situation intolerable —Havelock Ellis⟩
de·trac·tive \-ktiv, -tēv *also* -təv\ *adj* [MF *detractif,* fr. L *detractus* + MF *-if* -ive] **1** : tending to detract : given to detraction ⟨~ influences on the volume of foreign investment⟩ **2** : DEFAMATORY, CALUMNIOUS — **de·trac·tive·ly** \-tәvlē\ *adv*
de·trac·tor \-ktə(r)\ *n* -s [ME *detractour,* fr. MF & L; MF *detracteur,* fr. L *detractor,* fr. *detractus* + *-or*] : one that detracts esp. habitually : DEROGATOR, DEFAMER, CALUMNIATOR
de·trac·to·ry \-kt(ə)rē, -ri\ *adj* [LL *detractorius,* fr. L *detractus* + *-orius* -ory] : DETRACTIVE
¹**de·train** \(')dē'trān\ *vb* -ED/-ING/-S [*de-* + *train,* n.] *vi* : to get off a railroad train ⟨the tourists ~*ed* wearily⟩ ~ *vt* : to remove from a railroad train ⟨~*ed* the troops and supplies as near the front as possible⟩ — **de·train·ment** \-mənt\ *n* -s
²**detrain** \"\ *n* [*de-* + *train* (v.)] : DECONDITION 2
dé·tra·qué \ˌdā,trä'kā\ *adj* [F, past part. of *détraquer* to cause to stop functioning properly, fr. MF *detraquer* to divert from one's course, fr. *de-* (fr. OF *des-*) + *-traquer* (fr. *trac* track) — more at TRACK] : DERANGED, PSYCHOPATHIC
de·trash \(')dē+\ *vt* -ED/-ING/-ES [*de-* + *trash,* n.] : to remove the leaves and tops from (sugarcane stalks) before crushing
detrect *vt* [L *detrectare, detractare,* fr. *de* from, away + *tractare* to pull violently — more at DE-, TREAT] *obs* : to draw back from : REFUSE
de·trib·al·i·za·tion \(¦)dē,trībələ'zāshən\ *n* -s : the breaking down of a tribal organization esp. through culture contact
de·trib·al·ize \(')dē'trībə,līz\ *vt* -ED/-ING/-S [*de-* + *tribal* + *-ize*] : to cause to relinquish tribal customs : estrange or alienate from a tribe : ACCULTURATE ⟨*detribalized* natives working in mines⟩
det·ri·ment \'de·trəmənt\ *n* -s [ME, fr. MF or L; MF, fr. L *detrimentum,* fr. *detri-* (fr. *deterere* to wear out, impair, fr. *de* from, away + *terere* to rub) + *-mentum* -ment — more at DE-, THROW] : injury or damage or something that causes it : MISCHIEF, HURT ⟨study without ~ to one's health⟩
¹**det·ri·men·tal** \ˌde·trə¦mentᵊl\ *adj* : causing detriment : HARMFUL, DAMAGING ⟨~ effects of a drug⟩ ⟨reports ~ to a reputation⟩ **syn** see PERNICIOUS
²**detrimental** \"\ *n* -s **1** : a detrimental person or thing **2** *slang* : an ineligible suitor
det·ri·men·tal·ly \-ᵊlē, -ᵊli\ *adv* : in a detrimental manner
det·ri·men·tal·ness *n* -ES : detrimental quality
de·tri·tal \də'trīd·|ᵊl, dē'-, -īt|\ *adj* [*detritus* + *-al*] : of, relating to, or resulting from detritus
detrital rock *n* : rock composed mostly of constituents of clastic origin
de·trit·ed \|əd\ *adj* [L *detritus* worn down (past part. of *deterere* to wear down, wear out) + E *-ed*] **1** : worn down ⟨a ~ coin⟩ **2** : resulting from disintegration : DETRITAL
de·tri·tion \-rishən\ *n* -s [ML *detrition-, detritio,* fr. L *detritus* (past part. of *deterere*) + *-ion-, -io* -ion] : a wearing off or away by or as if by rubbing or by disintegration ⟨~ of sea cliffs⟩
de·tri·tus \-rīd·əs, -ītəs\ *n, pl* **detritus** [F *détritus,* fr. L *detritus,* past part. of *deterere*] **1** : loose material that results directly from rock disintegration or abrasion esp. when composed of rock fragments **2** : a product of disintegration or wearing away : fragment or fragmentary material ⟨the ~ of a conflagration⟩ ⟨ballads formed from the ~ of an old epic poem⟩ ⟨a ~ of broken-down bodily tissue⟩
detritus tank *n* : a chamber for removing the large heavy suspended matter from sewage
de·triv·o·rous \-rivərəs\ *adj* [*detritus* + *-vorous*] : feeding on animal wastes ⟨certain protozoans living on the skin of fishes and feeding on the mucous secretion are ~⟩
de·troit \də'trȯit, dә'-, *usu* -ȯid·+V\ *adj, usu cap* [fr. *Detroit,* city in Michigan] : of or from the city of Detroit, Michigan : of the kind or style prevalent in Detroit
de·troit·er \-ȯid·ə(r),-ȯitə(r)\ *n* -s *cap* : a native or resident of Detroit, Michigan
de trop \də'trō\ *adj* [F] : too much or too many : in the way : SUPERFLUOUS, UNWANTED ⟨a topcoat was *de trop* with the thermometer standing at 72 degrees —Irving Kolodin⟩
de·truck \(')dē+\ *vb* [*de-* + *truck,* n.] *vi* : to get down from a truck ~ *vt* : to unload (as troops) from a truck
de·trude \də'trüd, dē'-\ *vt* -ED/-ING/-S [L *detrudere,* fr. *de* from, down, away + *trudere* to thrust, push — more at DE-, THREAT] : to thrust or force down, out, or away
de·truncate \də-, dē- +\ *vt* [L *detruncatus,* past part. of *detruncare,* fr. *de* from, away + *truncare* to cut off, mutilate — more at DE-, TRUNCATE] : TRUNCATE — **de·trun·ca·tion** \ˌdē +\ *n*
de·tru·sion \-üzhən\ *n* -s [LL *detrusion-, detrusio,* fr. L *detrusus* (past part. of *detrudere*) + *-ion-, -io* -ion] : the action of thrusting outward or downward
de·tru·sive \-üsiv *also* -üziv\ *adj* [fr. *detrusion,* after such pairs as E *intrusion: intrusive*] : tending to thrust out or down
de·tru·sor \-üzə(r), -üsə-\ *or* **detrusor muscle** *n* -s [NL, fr. L *detrusus* + *-or*] : the outer largely longitudinally arranged musculature of the bladder wall
de·tu·ba·tion \ˌdē,t(y)ü'bāshən\ *n* -s [*de-* + *tube* + *-ation*] : EXTUBATION
de·tumescence \¦dē+\ *n* -s [L *detumescere* to cease swelling (fr. *de* down, away + *tumescere* to swell up) + E *-ence* — more at DE-, TUMESCENT] : diminution of swelling : subsidence of tumescence
de·tune \(')dē+\ *vt* : to put (a radio receiver) out of tune or resonance (as by varying capacity or inductance)
de·tur \'dē,tər, -tù(ə)r\ *n* -s [L, let there be given, 3d pers. sing. pres. subj. pass. of *dare* to give — more at DATE] : a specially bound book awarded to a student for meritorious work
deturb *vt* -ED/-ING/-S [L *deturbare* to throw down, beat down, fr. *de* down, away + *turbare* to disturb — more at DE-, TURBID] *obs* : to throw down or out
de·turgescence \¦dēt+\ *n* [*de-* + *turgescence*] : DETUMESCENCE
deturn *vt* [ME *deturnen,* fr. MF *detourner, destourner,* fr. OF *destorner, destourner* — more at DETOUR] *obs* : to turn aside : DIVERT
deturpate *vb* -ED/-ING/-S [L *deturpatus,* past part. of *deturpare* to disfigure, fr. *de* from, away + *turpare* to disfigure, defile, fr. *turpis* ugly, foul, shameful — more at DE-, TURPITUDE] *vt, obs* : DEBASE, DEFILE ~ *vi, obs* : to become vile or debased
¹**deuce** \'d(y)üs\ *n* -s [MF *deus* two, fr. OF, fr. L *duos,* accus. masc. of *duo* two — more at TWO] **1 a** (1) : the face of a die that bears two spots (2) : a playing card bearing an index number 2 or having two pips : TWOSPOT **b** (1) : a cast of dice yielding a point of two (2) **deuces** *pl* : a pair of deuces in a poker hand **2** [so called fr. the two successive points or games that must be won] : a tie in tennis in points toward a game or in games toward a set immediately below the minimum score needed for one side to win (as at 40 points or 5 games in lawn tennis) requiring scoring of two consecutive points by one side to win the game or set; *also* : a subsequent tie in a game in which deuce has occurred — compare ADVANTAGE **3** [prob. fr. *deuce* two at dice (as the lowest throw)] **a** *obs* : bad luck : PLAGUE — used chiefly as a mild oath **b** : DEVIL, DICKENS, HELL — used chiefly as a mild oath ⟨the ~ you say⟩ ⟨what the ~ is he up to now⟩ and as an intensive with *in* ⟨where in the ~ is he⟩ **c** : something notable of its kind — used quasi adverbially ⟨a ~ of a lovely day⟩ ⟨we had one ~ of a time getting there on schedule⟩ **4** : any of various things of which the number two forms an important identification (as a two-dollar bill, a 2000-watt spotlight, or a score of two strokes on a hole at golf)

deuces 1a (2)

²**deuce** \"\ *vt* -ED/-ING/-S : to bring the score of (a tennis game or set) to deuce
deuce-ace \'≈¦≈\ *n* -s [MF *deus as,* fr. OF, fr. *deus* two, deuce + *as* ace] **1** : a throw of dice of two and one **2** *archaic* : bad luck : low condition
¹**deuced** \'d(y)üsәd, -st\ *adj* [*deuce* (devil) + *-ed*] : DARNED, CONFOUNDED, DEVILISH ⟨you're in a ~ fix now⟩
²**deuced** \"\ *or* **deuc·ed·ly** \-sədlē, -li\ *adv* : DAMNABLY, DEVILISHLY; *often* : VERY, REMARKABLY, EXTREMELY ⟨a ~ clever girl⟩ ⟨he was *deucedly* well-fixed⟩
deuces wild *n* : a variety of poker and certain other card games in which each deuce may be made to represent any other card designated by the holder of the deuce
deuk \'dyük\ *n* -s [ME (Sc) *duke,* fr. OE *dūce* — more at DUCK] *Scot* : ¹DUCK 1
de·us ex ma·chi·na \¦dāə,sek'smakәnә, ¦dēə-; ¦dā,ù,sek'smäkәnə; ÷ -,smә'shēnә\ *n* [NL, a god from a machine, trans. of Gk *theos ek mēchanēs*] : a person or thing that appears or is introduced (as into a story) suddenly and unexpectedly and provides an artificial or contrived solution to an apparently insoluble difficulty
deut- *or* **deuto-** *comb form* [ISV, short for *deuter-*] **1** : second in a regular series of chemical compounds ⟨*deut*oxide⟩ **2** : second ⟨*deuto*mala⟩ : secondary ⟨*deuto*plasm⟩ — esp. in biological terms
¹**deuter-** *or* **deutero-** *comb form* [alter. (influenced by LL *deutero-*) of earlier *deutro-,* fr. ME, modif. of LL *deutero-,* fr. Gk *deuter-, deutero-,* fr. *deuteros* second; prob. akin to L *dudum* formerly, Gk *dein* to lack, miss, Gk (Homeric) *deuesthai* to be in need of, Skt *dūra* far] **1** : second : secondary ⟨*deuter*agonist⟩ ⟨*deutero*plasm⟩ **2** : belonging to any of various classes of chemical substances regarded as secondary products of decomposition ⟨*deutero*porphyrin⟩ ⟨*deutero*proteose⟩
²**deuter-** *or* **deutero-** *comb form* [ISV fr. *deuterium*] : DEUTERIUM ⟨*deuter*ide⟩ ⟨*deutero*chloroform⟩
deu·ter·ag·o·nist \ˌd(y)üd·ə'ragənəst, -raig-\ *n* -s [Gk *deuteragōnistēs,* fr. *deuter-* ¹deuter- + *agōnistēs* combatant, actor — more at AGONIST] **1** : the actor taking the part of second importance in a classical Greek drama **2** : a person who serves as a foil to another
deu·ter·anomalous \¦d(y)üd·ər +\ *adj* [NL *deuteranomalia* + E *-ous*] : exhibiting deuteranomaly
deu·ter·anomaly \"+\ *n* -ES [NL *deuteranomalia,* fr. ¹*deuter-* + L *anomalia* anomaly] : trichromatism in which an abnormally large proportion of green is required to match the spectrum — compare PROTANOMALY, TRICHROMAT
deu·ter·an·ope \'d(y)üd·ərə,nōp\ *n* -s [ISV, back-formation fr. *deuteranopia*] : an individual affected with deuteranopia
deu·ter·an·o·pia \ˌ≈≈≈'nōpēə\ *n* -s [NL, fr. ¹*deuter-* + ²*a-* + *-opia*] : red-green blindness believed due to a defect in the optic nerve that interferes with normal transmission of red and green sensations and marked by confusion of purplish red and green — compare PROTANOPIA
deu·ter·an·op·ic \¦≈≈≈¦näpik, -nōp-\ *adj* [*deuteranopia* + *-ic*] : characterized by or affected by deuteranopia ⟨~ vision⟩ ⟨a ~ person⟩
deu·ter·at·ed \'d(y)üd·ə,rād·əd\ *also* **deu·ter·ized** \-,rīzd\ *adj* [*deuterated* fr. ²*deuter-* + *-ate* + *-ed; deuterized* fr. ²*deuter-* + *-ize* + *-ed*] : containing deuterium esp. as a constituent of a chemical compound
deu·ter·a·tion \ˌd(y)üd·ə'rāshən\ *or* **deu·ter·i·za·tion** \ˌd(y)üd·ərə'zāshən\ *n* -s [*deuteration* fr. ²*deuter-* + *-ation; deuterization* fr. ²*deuter-* + *-ize* + *-ation*] : the introduction of deuterium esp. into a chemical compound
deuteri- *or* **deuterio-** *comb form* [ISV, fr. *deuterium*] : deuterium : containing deuterium — in names of chemical compounds ⟨*deuterio*ammonia⟩
deu·ter·ic \(')d(y)ü¦terik\ *adj* [¹*deuter-* + *-ic*] : PAULOPOST — **deu·ter·i·cal·ly** \-rək(ə)lē\ *adv*
deu·ter·ide \'d(y)üd·ə,rīd\ *n* -s [²*deuter-* + *-ide*] : a binary compound of deuterium with a more electropositive element or radical analogous to a hydride
deu·te·ri·um \d(y)ü'tirēəm\ *n* -s [¹*deuter-* + *-ium*] : the isotope of hydrogen that has atoms of twice the mass of ordinary light hydrogen atoms, that occurs naturally in very small amounts in water, and that is used in nuclear reactions and as a tracer in chemical and biological investigations — called also *heavy hydrogen;* symbol *D,* H^2, or ^2H
deuterium oxide *n* : heavy water D_2O composed only of deuterium and oxygen
deu·tero-canonical \¦d(y)üd·ə(,)rō+\ *adj* [NL *deuterocanonicus* deuterocanonical (fr. ¹*deuter-* + LL *canonicus* belonging to the canon of Scripture) + E *-al* — more at CANONIC] : of, belonging to, or constituting a second or later canon — used esp. by Roman Catholics (1) of those scriptural books in the canon fixed by the Council of Trent that are found only in the Septuagint and not in the Hebrew and constitute the Apocrypha of most Protestants and (2) of the following portions of the New Testament: Mark 16:9–20, Luke 22:43, 44, John 7:53–8:11, Hebrews, James, 2 Peter, 2 and 3 John, Jude, and Revelation
deu·ter·o·cone \'d(y)üd·ərə,kōn\ *n* [¹*deuter-* + *cone*] : the cusp of a mammalian premolar corresponding in position to the protocone of a true molar
deu·ter·o·co·nid \¦≈≈≈¦kōnəd\ *n* -s [*deuterocone* + *-id*] : the cusp of a mammalian premolar corresponding in position to the protoconid
deu·ter·og·a·my \ˌd(y)üd·ə'rägəmē\ *n* -ES [LGk *deuterogamia,* fr. Gk *deuter-* ¹deuter- + *-gamia* -gamy] **1** : DIGAMY **2** : secondary pairing of sexual cells or nuclei that replaces direct copulation in many fungi, algae, and higher plants
deu·tero·genesis \¦d(y)üd·ə(,)rō+\ *n* [¹*deuter-* + *genesis*] : the appearance of a new adaptive character late in life — compare CENOGENESIS
deu·tero-malay \"+\ *n* -s *cap M* [¹*deuter-* + *Malay*] : a Malaysian whose physical appearance distinguishes him from the proto-Malay and from Veddoid or negritoid types but who is often described as having southern Mongoloid characteristics — called also *Malayan, Malaysian* — **deu·tero-malayan** *or* **deu·tero-malaysian** \"+\ *adj, usu cap M*
deu·ter·o·my·ce·tes \ˌd(y)üd·ə(,)rō,mī'sēd·ēz\ [NL, fr. ¹*deuter-* + *-mycetes*] *syn of* FUNGI IMPERFECTI
deu·ter·on \'d(y)üd·ə,rän\ *also* **deu·ton** \'d(y)ü,tän\ *n* -s [*deuteron* fr. *deuterium* + *-on; deuton* fr. *deuterium* + *-on*] : the nucleus of the deuterium atom that consists of one proton and one neutron and is used as a projectile in nuclear bombardments (as with a cyclotron) — symbol *d*
deu·ter·o·nom·ic \¦d(y)üd·ərə¦nämik\ *adj, usu cap* [*Deuteronomy,* the fifth book of the Old Testament (alter. — influenced by LL *Deuteronomium* — of earlier *Deutronome,* fr. ME *Deutronomie,* modif. of LL *Deuteronomium,* fr. Gk *Deuteronomion,* fr. *deuter-* ¹deuter- + *-nomion* — fr. *nomos* law) + E *-ic* — more at NIMBLE] : of, relating to, or in the style of the biblical book of Deuteronomy

deu·ter·on·o·mist \d(y)üd·ə'ränəmə̇st\ *n* -s *usu cap* [*Deuteronomy* + E *-ist*] : a writer or editor of the book of Deuteronomy, one of its versions, or Deuteronomic portions of the Old Testament of the Bible

deu·ter·os·co·py \-'räskəpē\ *n* -ES [¹*deuter-* + *-scopy*] **1** *obs* : something seen or perceived only at a second view **2** *archaic* : CLAIRVOYANCE

deu·ter·o·sto·ma·ta \,d(y)üd·ərə'stōməd·ə\ [NL, fr. ¹*deuter-* + *-stomata*] *syn of* DEUTEROSTOMIA

¹**deu·ter·o·stome** \'====,stōm\ *adj* [NL *Deuterostomia*] : of or relating to Deuterostomia

²**deuterostome** \"\ *n* -s : an animal belonging to the group Deuterostomia

deu·ter·o·sto·mia \,===='stōmēə\ *n pl, cap* [NL, fr. ¹*deuter-* + *-stomia*] *in many classifications* : a major division of the animal kingdom comprising all bilateral animals (as the chordates) that lack ectomesoderm and have indeterminate cleavage and a mouth that does not arise from the blastopore

deu·ter·ot·o·kous \¦d(y)üd·ə¦rädˑəkəs\ *adj* [¹*deuter-* + *-tokous*] : exhibiting deuterotoky : producing both male and female offspring parthenogenetically

deu·ter·ot·o·ky \,==='==kē\ *n* -ES [¹*deuter-* + *-toky*] : the parthenogenetic production of both males and females — compare ARRHENOTOKY, THELYTOKY

deu·ter·o·tonic \¦d(y)üd·ərə+\ *adj* [¹*deuter-* + *tonic*] : characterized by accent on the second syllable — contrasted with *prototonic*

deu·ter·o·zooid \"+\ *n* [¹*deuter-* + *zooid*] : a zooid produced by budding or fission from a primary zooid

deuto- — see DEUT-

deu·to·cerebral \¦d(y)üd·(,)ō+\ *adj* [*deutocerebrum* + *-al*] : of or relating to the deutocerebrum

deu·to·cerebrum \"+\ *n* [NL, fr. *deut-* + *cerebrum*] : the midsection of the brain of most arthropods formed by the paired ganglia of the second true segment and consisting of paired antennary and olfactory lobes; *esp* : the median lobes of the insect brain that innervate the antennal segment

deu·to·ma·la \"+¦mālə\ *n, pl* **deutoma·lae** \-,lē\ [NL, fr. *deut-* + *mala*] : either member of the second pair of mouthparts of a diplopod — **deu·to·ma·lal** \-āləl\ *or* **deu·to·ma·lar** \-ālə(r)\ *adj*

deu·tom·er·ite \d(y)ü'tämə,rīt\ *n* -s [ISV *deut-* + *mer-* (fr. Gk *meros* part) + *-ite* — more at MERIT] : the posterior segment of the trophozoite of certain gregarines

deuton *var of* DEUTERON

deu·to·nymph \'d(y)üd·ō+\ *n* [*deut-* + *nymph*] : a second larval form occurring in the development of most mites — compare PROTONYMPH, TRITONYMPH — **deu·to·nymphal** \¦==+\ *adj*

deu·to·plasm \'===+\ *n* -s [ISV *deut-* + *-plasm*; orig. formed as F *deutoplasme*] : the nutritive inclusions of protoplasm; *esp* : the yolk reserves of an egg — **deu·to·plas·mic** \¦==¦plazmik\ *adj*

deu·to·plasmolysis \¦d(y)üd·(,)ō+\ *n* [*deutoplasm* + *-o-* + *-lysis*] : elimination of part of the yolk content of an egg following fertilization or during cleavage

deut·ovum \d(y)üd·'ōvəm, -ü'tō-\ *n* [NL, fr. *deut-* + *ovum*] : the inactive incompletely developed larva of a mite after the rupture of the outer eggshell

deut·sche mark \¦dȯichə¦märk\ *also* **deutsch·mark** \'dȯich-,m-\ *n* -s [G *deutsche mark*, lit., German mark] **1** : the German mark as established in 1948 by the German Federal Republic — see MONEY table **2** : a coin representing one deutsche mark

deut·zia \'d(y)ütsēə, 'dȯit-\ *n* [NL, fr. Jean *Deutz* †1784? Dutch patron of botanical researches + NL *-ia*] **1** *cap* : a genus of ornamental shrubs (family Saxifragaceae) that are native to Asia and Central America but widespread in cultivation and that have short-stalked toothed opposite leaves, usu. shreddy bark, and white or sometimes pink flowers mostly in panicles or cymes **2** -s : any shrub of the genus *Deutzia*

¹**dev** *var of* ¹DEVA

²**dev** *var of* DAEVA

dev *abbr* **1** developed; developer **2** deviation

¹**de·va** \'dāvə\ *or* **dev** \'dev\ *n* -s [Skt *deva* — more at DEITY] : a divine being or god in Hinduism and Buddhism

²**deva** *var of* DAEVA

de·va·chan \dā'vächən\ *n* -s [perh. irreg. fr. Skt *devāc* directed toward the gods, fr. *deva*] *theosophy* : a state intermediate between two earth lives into which the ego enters after leaving kamarupa — **de·va·cha·nic** \¦dävə¦chänik\ *adj*

de·va·da·si \,dävə'däsē\ *n* -s [Skt *devadāsī* female servant of a god, fr. *deva* + *dāsī* dasi] : a dancing girl and courtesan of a Hindu temple

¹**de·val** \də'väl, -vȯl\ *vi* -ED/-ING/-S [ME *devalen* to descend, sink, fr. MF *devaler*, fr. (assumed) VL *devallare*, fr. L *de* down, away + (assumed) VL *-vallare* (fr. L *valles, vallis* valley) — more at DE-, VALE] *chiefly Scot* : to leave off : CEASE ⟨it rained the whole day and never ~*ed*⟩

²**deval** \"\ *n* -s *Scot* : CESSATION, PAUSE

de·va·lo·ka \,dävə'lōkə\ *n* -s [Skt, fr. *deva* + *loka* world — more at LEA] *Hinduism & Buddhism* : a world of gods : HEAVEN

de·valorize \(')dē+\ *vt* -ED/-ING/-S [F *dévaloriser*, fr. *dé-* de- (fr. OF *des-*) + *valor-* (alter. — influenced by ML *valor* — of *valeur* value, fr. ML *valor*) + *-iser* -ize — more at VALOR] : to diminish the value of : DEVALUE

de·valuate \(')dē+\ *vb* [*de-* + *value*, n. + *-ate*] : DEVALUE

de·valuation \(¦)dē+\ *n* -s [*devaluate* + *-ion*] **1** : an official reduction in the exchange value of a currency by a lowering of its gold equivalency **2** : a lessening esp. of status or stature : a reduction or minimizing esp. of importance : DECLINE

de·value \(')dē+\ *vb* [*de-* + *value*, n.] *vt* **1** : to institute the devaluation of (money) **2** : to cause or be responsible for a devaluation of (as a person or a literary work); *sometimes* : to divest of value or esteem ~ *vi* : to institute devaluation

de·va·na·ga·ri \,dävə'nägərē\ *n, usu cap* [Skt *devanāgarī*, fr. *deva* + *nāgarī* Nagari] : the alphabet having as a characteristic feature long horizontal strokes on the tops of most of the characters that is usu. employed for Sanskrit and is also used as a literary hand for various modern languages of central, western, and northern India — see ALPHABET table; NAGARI

de·vance \də'van(t)s\ *vt* -ED/-ING/-S [MF *devancer*, fr. OF *devancier, davancier*, fr. *devant, davant* in front, forward, after OF *avant* before: *avancier* to advance] *archaic* : FORESTALL, ANTICIPATE, OUTSTRIP

de·vant \də'vä͞n\ *adv* [F, fr. OF *devant, davant*, fr. *de* from (fr. L *de*) + *avant* before, fr. L *abante* — more at DE-, ADVANCE] : in front : FORWARD — used in ballet of the execution of a step or of the movement of an arm or leg in front of the body

de·vast \də'vast\ *vt* -ED/-ING/-S [MF or L; MF *devaster*, fr. L *devastare* to devastate] : DEVASTATE

dev·as·tate \'devə,stāt, *usu* -ād.+V\ *vt* -ED/-ING/-S [L *devastatus*, past part. of *devastare*, fr. *de* from, away + *vastare* to lay waste, fr. *vastus* empty, waste — more at WASTE] **1** : to lay waste : RAVAGE ⟨whole countries *devastated* by storm and cold⟩ ⟨man has stripped the hills, *devastated* the valleys⟩ **2** : OVERPOWER, OVERCOME, OVERWHELM ⟨he was *devastated* by grief⟩ ⟨her constant mischief *devastated* the classroom⟩ **syn** see RAVAGE

devastating *adj* [fr. pres. part. of *devastate*] : serving, tending, or having the power to devastate; *broadly* : highly effective ⟨a ~ portrait of human folly⟩ — **dev·as·tat·ing·ly** *adv*

dev·as·ta·tion \,devə'stāshən\ *n* -s [LL *devastation-, devastatio*, fr. L *devastatus* + *-ion-, -io* -ion] **1** : the action of devastating or state of being devastated : a laying waste : DESOLATION ⟨the ~*s* of war⟩ **2** : DEVASTAVIT 1

dev·as·ta·tive \'devə,stād·iv\ *adj* : tending to cause devastation : DESTRUCTIVE

dev·as·ta·tor \-d·ə(r)\ *n* -s [It & LL; It *devastatore*, fr. LL *devastator*, fr. L *devastatus* + *-or*] : one that devastates

dev·as·ta·vit \,devə'stāvə̇t, -äv-\ *n* -s [L, he has laid waste, 3d pers. sing. perf. indic. act. of *devastare*] **1** : mismanagement or waste of the goods of a deceased person by his executor who may thereby be liable **2** : a writ whereby a remedy for devastavit is sought

deve *var of* DEAVE

de·vein \(')dē+\ *vt* [*de-* + *vein*, n.] : to remove the dark dorsal vein from (shrimp)

¹**de·vel** \'dävəl\ *n* -s [origin unknown] *Scot* : a severe blow

²**devel** \"\ *vt, Scot* : to strike forcibly

develin *var of* DEVILING

de·vel·op *also* **de·vel·ope** \də'veləp, dē'-\ *vb* -ED/-ING/-S [F *développer*, fr. OF *desveloper, desvoleper, desvoloper*, fr. *des-* de- + *veloper, voleper, voloper* to wrap up] *vt* **1 a** : UNFOLD, UNFURL — used only as a past participle and now only of flags **b** : to change the form of (a surface) by applying point by point to a specified surface; *specif* : to unroll (a developable surface) on a plane in this way without stretching any element **c** : to lay out (as a representation) in or evolve (as an idea) into a clear, full, and explicit presentation (as in a drawing or specification); *specif* : to determine (as by calculating or drafting) the precise size and shape of (a sheet metal blank from which an article is to be formed) **2** : to make clear by or as if by unfolding some enclosing, enveloping, or obscuring cover **3 a** : EXPOUND, EXPLAIN ⟨~*ing* the thesis with great skill⟩ **b** : to make visible or manifest **c** : to treat (as a dye intermediate applied to a fiber) with an agent to cause the appearance of color : subject (as a fiber impregnated with dye intermediate) to the action of an agent to produce color; *also* : to produce (color or color-producing dye) by such a method **d** : to cause (writing in secret ink) to become visible (as by the action of heat or chemicals) **e** : to subject (exposed photograph material) to a usu. chemical treatment designed to produce a visible deposit in matter previously modified by radiation; *also* : to render (a photographic image) visible by such a method **f** *obs* : DISCLOSE, REVEAL; *also* : DETECT, DISCOVER **g** : to express (as a mathematical equation or a formula) in expanded form **h** : to elaborate (a piece of music) by means of development **4** : to open up : cause to become more completely unfolded so as to reveal hidden or unexpected qualities or potentialities **5 a** : to make (something latent) active : cause to increase or improve : promote the growth of ⟨he ~*ed* his muscles by exercise, his mind by reading and study⟩ **b** : to make actually available or usable (something previously only potentially available or usable) ⟨~*ing* the natural resources of the region⟩ ⟨an engine that ~*s* 100 horsepower⟩: as (1) : to convert (as raw land) into an area suitable for residential or business purposes ⟨they ~*ed* several large tracts on the edge of town⟩; *also* : to alter raw land into (an area suitable for building) ⟨the subdivisions that they ~*ed* were soon built up⟩ (2) : to prepare (a mineral-bearing deposit) for the extraction of ore (as by driving mine workings and passageways and providing power, ventilation, and other equipment) **c** : to move (a chess piece) from the original position to one providing more opportunity for effective use ⟨~*ed* the rook as soon as possible⟩ **6 a** : to cause to unfold gradually : conduct through a succession of states or changes each of which is preparatory for the next ⟨he ~*ed* his argument point by point⟩ **b** : to expand by a process of growth ⟨a precocious child that ~*ed* mature breasts when 8 years old⟩ ⟨they ~*ed* a strong militant organization⟩ **c** : to cause to grow and differentiate along lines natural to its kind ⟨warm rains and summer suns ~ the grain⟩ ⟨the zygote is gradually ~*ed* into the adult plant or animal⟩ **7** : to acquire usu. gradually ⟨~*ing* a taste for dry wines⟩ ⟨he ~*ed* a strong dislike for his mother-in-law⟩; *often* : to have (something) unfold or differentiate within one — used esp. of diseases and abnormalities ⟨too many children ~*ed* tuberculosis⟩ ~ *vi* **1 a** : to go through a process of natural growth, differentiation, or evolution by successive changes from a less perfect to a more perfect or more highly organized state : advance from a simpler form or state of existence to one more complex either in structure or function ⟨a blossom ~*s* from a bud⟩ ⟨the fever ~*s* normally⟩ ⟨the embryo ~*s* into a well-formed animal⟩ **b** : to acquire secondary sex characters ⟨she is ~*ing* rapidly for a girl of 12⟩ **c** : EVOLVE, DIFFERENTIATE; *broadly* : GROW **2 a** : to become gradually visible or manifest ⟨as the photographic negative ~*s*⟩ ⟨his interest ~*ed* as he watched her⟩ **b** : to become apparent : come to light ⟨it ~*s* that neither one paid the bill⟩ ⟨they waited to see what would ~ next⟩ **3** : to develop one's pieces in chess **syn** see MATURE, UNFOLD

de·vel·op·abil·i·ty \=,=ləpə'biləd·ē\ *n* : capacity or suitability for development

de·vel·op·able \='=ləpəbəl\ *adj* : capable of being developed

developable surface *n* [trans. of F *surface développable*] : a surface that may be imagined flattened out upon a plane without stretching any element

developed black BH *n, often cap D& 1st B* [*developed* fr. past part. of *develop*] : DIAMINE BLACK BH

developed dye *n* : any of a group of direct azo dyes that after application to the fiber can be further diazotized and coupled on the fiber to form shades faster to washing — called also *diazo dye*; compare AZOIC DYE

de·vel·oped·ness \-p(t)nə̇s, -pədn-\ *n* -ES : the quality or state of being developed

de·vel·op·er \-pə(r)\ *n* -s **1** : a person who develops something esp. habitually or as an occupation: as **a** : a worker who develops photographic materials (as films and prints) **b** : a person who develops real estate; *often* : one that improves and subdivides land and builds and sells residential structures thereon **2** : something that develops or is used in developing: as **a** : a chemical agent used to produce a dye by reaction with a dye or dye intermediate on the fiber — see DYE table I **b** : a chemical bath or reagent used in developing exposed photographic materials

developing dye *n* [*developing* fr. pres. part. of *develop*] : a dye produced on the fiber; *esp* : DEVELOPED DYE

developing-out paper \=,===¦=,==\ *n* : a photographic paper coated with silver halide gelatin emulsion on which the image is invisible until developed

de·vel·op·ment *also* **de·vel·ope·ment** \də'veləpmənt, dē'-\ *n* -s **1** : the act, process, or result of developing : the state of being developed : a gradual unfolding by which something (as a plan or method, an image upon a photographic plate, a living body) is developed ⟨a new ~ in poetry⟩ : gradual advance or growth through progressive changes : EVOLUTION ⟨a stage of ~⟩ : a making usable or available ⟨well worth ~⟩ **2 a** : the whole process of growth and differentiation by which the potentialities of a zygote, spore, or embryo are realized; *broadly* : ONTOGENY **b** : the gradual differentiation of an ecological community or a natural group; *sometimes* : PHYLOGENY **3** : the process of or position attained in developing chess pieces **4** *logic* : an expansion by means of which all the elements contained in a given expression are made explicit **5** : work done in developing a mine **6 a** : the elaboration of a musical theme, subject, or idea by rhythmic, melodic, tonal, or harmonic modifications **b** *or* **development section** : the section of a musical movement where this elaboration occurs (as in the sonata form) **7** : a method of reducing grade in railroading by increasing the length of a line between two predetermined points that differ much in elevation **8** : a developed tract of land; *esp* : a subdivision having necessary utilities (as water, gas, electricity, roads)

de·vel·op·men·tal \də¦veləp¦ment°l, dē¦-\ *adj* **1** : of, relating to, or constituting development ⟨~ processes⟩ ⟨~ stages⟩ ⟨~ questions⟩ : serving to develop ⟨~ concessions for the region⟩ ⟨a long-range ~ program⟩ ⟨~ aid for backward areas⟩; *broadly* : EXPERIMENTAL ⟨a ~ series of tests⟩ ⟨the ~ stages of military aviation⟩ **2** : designed to further growth (as of a child) or to bring about improvement (as of a skill) by gradual training adapted to the learner's physical and mental development ⟨~ reading⟩ — **de·vel·op·men·tal·ly** \-°lē,°li\ *adv*

developmental anatomy *n* : the anatomy of the embryo or fetus

de·vel·op·men·tal·ist \=,=='==ə̇st\ *also* **de·vel·op·ment·ist** \='== məntə̇st\ *n* -s : EVOLUTIONIST; *usu* : an exponent of or specialist in any school of philosophic evolution

developmental pueblo *adj, usu cap D&P* : of, relating to, or constituting the early Pueblo stages of the 8th to 11th centuries A.D. during which the architecture was developing toward the complexity of the Great Pueblo period

developmental quotient *n* : a number expressing the development of a child determined by dividing his maturity age by his chronological age and multiplying by 100 — abbr. *DQ*

development area *n, Brit* : any of certain areas in which the government encourages the establishment of new industries particularly in order to increase industrial diversification and stability

de·vel·op·pé \də̇¦velə¦pā, ¦dāv(ə)(,)lō¦pā\ *n* -s [F, fr. past part. of *développer* to develop] *ballet* : an unfolding of the free leg into the air

develops *pres 3d sing of* DEVELOP

devels *pl of* DEVEL, *pres 3d sing of* DEVEL

de·verb·al \(')dē+\ *adj* [*de-* + *verb* + *-al*] : DEVERBATIVE

¹**de·verb·a·tive** \(')dē¦vərbəd·iv\ *adj* [*de-* + *verb* + *-ative*] : derived from a verb ⟨the ~ noun *developer* is derived from *develop*⟩ : used in derivation from a verb ⟨the ~ suffix *-er* in *developer*⟩

²**deverbative** \"\ *n* -s : a deverbative word

de·vertebrated \(')dē+\ *adj* [*de-* + *vertebrated*, past part. of *vertebrate*] : lacking stamina — **de·vertebration** \(¦)dē+\ *n* -s

de·vest \də'vest, (')dē'-\ *vb* [MF *desvestir, devestir*, fr. ML *disvestire*, fr. L *dis-* + *vestire* to dress, fr. *vestis* garment — more at WEAR] *vt* **1 a** *obs* : UNCLOTHE **b** *law* : to take away (as property, an authority, or title) : ALIENATE, DIVEST **c** : to deprive or dispossess (as a person) of a vested right — now used only in law **2** *obs* : to cast off : DISCARD, ABANDON ~ *vi, of a title or estate* : to become devested

de·vi \'dā(,)vē\ *n* -s [Skt *devī*, fem. of *deva* — more at DEVA] *Hinduism* : GODDESS — used in India as a title following the personal name of a married woman

de·vi·a·ble \'dēvēəbəl\ *adj* [*deviate* + *-able*] : capable of deviating or of being deflected

de·vi·ance \'dēvēən(t)s\ *n* -s [*deviate* + *-ance*] : deviant quality or state : DEVIANCY, DEVIATION

de·vi·an·cy \-ənsē\ *n* -ES [*deviant* + *-cy*] : the character or behavior of a deviant

¹**de·vi·ant** \-ənt\ *adj* [LL *deviant-, devians*, pres. part. of *deviare* to deviate] : deviating esp. from some accepted norm ⟨seriously ~ conduct⟩ : characterized by deviation (as from a standard of conduct) ⟨~ children⟩

²**deviant** \"\ *n* -s : something that deviates from a norm; *esp* : a person who differs markedly (as in intelligence, social adjustment, or sexual behavior) from what is considered normal or acceptable in the group of which he is a member

¹**de·vi·ate** \'dēvē,āt, *usu* -ād.+V\ *vb* -ED/-ING/-S [LL *deviatus*, past part. of *deviare*, fr. L *de* from, away + LL *-viare* (fr. L *via* way, road) — more at DE-, VIA] *vi* : to diverge or turn aside : veer esp. from an established way or toward a new direction ⟨he *deviated* from the path⟩ ⟨*deviating* to the south⟩ : stray esp. from a standard, principle, or topic ⟨she never *deviated* from her first account⟩ ⟨*deviating* sharply from the traditional approach⟩ : turn aside from a previous, usual, normal, or acceptable course (as of conduct) ⟨party principles permit no one to ~⟩ ⟨whenever I *deviated* I felt guilty⟩ ~ *vt* : to turn (something) out of a previous course : cause to deviate ⟨he would ~ rivers, turn the scorched plains of Lombardy into fertile pastures —F.M.Godfrey⟩ ⟨a deep iron keel will tend to ~ the compass during heeling over⟩ **syn** see SWERVE

²**de·vi·ate** \-vē¦ət, -ē,āt, *usu* ¦d·+V\ *n* -s [LL *deviatus*, past part. of *deviare*] : something that differs noticeably from the average or normal range of its kind: as **a** : a person that is a deviant; *esp* : SEXUAL PERVERT **b** : any item of a statistical distribution that differs significantly from the norm

³**deviate** \"\ *also* **de·vi·at·ed** \-ē,ād·əd, -ātəd\ *adj* [*deviate* fr. LL *deviatus*; *deviated* fr. LL *deviatus* + E *-ed*] : characterized by or given to significant departure from the behavioral norms of a particular society

de·vi·a·tion \,dēvē'āshən\ *n* -s [LL *deviation-, deviatio*, fr. *deviatus* + L *-ion-, -io* -ion] : an act or instance of deviating : DEFLECTION, VEERING, DIVERGENCE: as **a** : deflection of the needle of a compass caused by magnetic influences within the ship or airplane in which it is mounted **b** *in the old Ptolemaic system* : a motion of the deferent toward and from the ecliptic **c** (1) : the divergence laterally unless otherwise stated of a projectile from the plane of departure caused by extraneous factors (as drift, wind) (2) : the divergence of a projectile from the mean direction of a number of shots fired at the same target — called also *deviation from the center of impact* (3) : the angular measurement between a burst and a target as measured from an observation post **d** : voluntary and unnecessary departure of a ship from the regular and usual course of a specific voyage, such departure releasing underwriters of insurance on the ship from further responsibility **e** : DEFLECTION 5a **f** : the algebraic difference found by subtracting some fixed number (as the arithmetic mean of a series of statistical data) from any item of the series **g** : evolutionary differentiation involving interpolation of new stages in the ancestral pattern of morphogenesis — compare ANABOLY, ARCHALLAXIS **h** : departure from an established body of principles, a system of beliefs, an ideology, or a party line; *specif* : departure from strict Marxist doctrine ⟨he was expelled from the Communist party for ~⟩ **i** : noticeable or marked departure from accepted societal norms of behavior

de·vi·a·tion·al \¦==¦=shən°l, -shnəl\ *adj* : involving or tending toward deviation esp. from political party principles — **de·vi·a·tion·al·ism** \,==='=shən°l,izəm, -shnə,li-\ *n* -s

de·vi·a·tion·ism \-shə,nizəm\ *n* -s : defection or divergence from a party line esp. of the Communist party

¹**de·vi·a·tion·ist** \-sh(ə)nə̇st\ *n* -s : one who departs from the principles of an organization (as a political party) with which he is affiliated ⟨~*s* in Communist countries⟩

²**deviationist** *adj* : of or relating to deviationism or deviationists

deviation warranty *n* : an implied warranty underlying all contracts of ocean marine insurance that a ship will not depart from the customary route between the ports for which insurance is granted

de·vi·a·tive \'dēvē,ād·iv, -vēəd·iv\ *adj* : tending to deviate

de·vi·a·tor \-,ād·ə(r)\ *n* -s [*deviate* + *-or*] : something that deviates or causes to deviate; *sometimes* : DEVIATIONIST

de·vice \də'vīs, dē'-\ *n* -s [ME *devis, devise*, fr. OF *devis* will, intention & OF *devise* dividing line, difference, wish, fr. *deviser* to divide, regulate, tell — more at DEVISE] **1** : something that is formed or formulated by design and usu. with consideration of possible alternatives, experiment, and testing : something devised or contrived : CONTRIVANCE, INVENTION, PROJECT, SCHEME: as **a** : a scheme to deceive or overreach : ARTIFICE, STRATAGEM **b** : something fanciful, elaborate, or intricate in design (as a trinket or a musical motive) **c** : something in a literary work designed to achieve a particular artistic effect (as a figure of speech, a special method of narration, or use of words or word sounds) **d** *archaic* : MASQUE, SPECTACLE **e** : a piece of equipment or a mechanism designed to serve a special purpose or perform a special function ⟨a ~ for measuring heat release⟩ ⟨an improved steering ~⟩ **2** : WILL, DESIRE, INCLINATION, PURPOSE — now used only in pl. ⟨left to his own ~*s*⟩ **3 a** : an emblematic design typically of one or more figures with a motto that is used esp. as a heraldic bearing denoting the historical situation, the ambition, or the desire of the person adopting it; *sometimes* : MOTTO **b** : an emblematic figure that is used to identify usu. an organization (as a publisher or navigation line) **4** *archaic* : INVENTION, DEVISING **5** *obs* : CONVERSATION, CHAT

de·vice·ful \-sfəl\ *adj* : full of devices; INGENIOUS — **de·vice·ful·ly** \-fəlē\ *adv*

¹**dev·il** \'devəl *sometimes* -(,)vil, *dial or as a mild imprecation* 'divəl\ *n* -s *often attrib* [ME *devel, devil*, fr. OE *dēofol*, fr. LL *diabolus*, fr. Gk *diabolos*, lit., slanderer, fr. *diaballein* to throw across, discredit, slander, fr. *dia* through, across + *ballein* to throw; akin to OE *cwellan*, to kill, OHG *quellan* to well, gush, Skt *galati* it drips — more at DIA-] **1** *sometimes cap* : the personal supreme spirit of evil and unrighteousness in Jewish and Christian theology : the tempter and spiritual enemy of mankind who is the adversary of God although subordinate to him and able to act only by his sufferance and is represented frequently as the leader or prince of all apostate angels and as ruler of hell — called also *Apollyon, Beelzebub, Lucifer, Satan*; usu. used with *the* and often used as a mild imprecation or expression of surprise, vexation, or emphasis ⟨the ~ you say⟩ ⟨the ~ take it⟩ **2** : one of the superhuman followers of the devil : a lesser evil or malignant spiritual being: as **a** : a heathen god or idol — used chiefly in scriptural and Christian clerical writings **b** *in the Bible* : a malignant spirit possessing and responsible for the state of a demoniac **3 a** : an extremely and malignantly wicked person : a human fiend; *often* : a person cantankerously self-centered and without regard for

the rights of others **b** *archaic* **:** a great evil ⟨the ~ drunkenness —Shak.⟩ **4 a :** a person of notable energy, recklessness, and dashing spirit ⟨all those young ~*s* that followed Prince Charlie⟩ **b :** a person thought of as misconducting himself more from youthful folly and exuberance of spirits than from real wickedness ⟨both my cousins were perfect ~*s* as boys⟩ **c :** a person exhibiting marked intensity in some line of conduct **:** one excessively addicted or attracted to ⟨a ~ for gambling⟩ ⟨a ~ with the ladies⟩; *often* **:** one regarded as atypical ⟨a gentleman but a queer ~ all the same⟩ **5 a :** FELLOW, MAN — usu. used with *poor* ⟨poor ~*s* sleeping on park benches and in subways⟩ ⟨my uncle, poor ~, lost his wife in a wreck only weeks after their marriage⟩ ⟨poor ~*s* who make life sweeter for the rest by sweeping the streets, collecting the garbage, cleaning the sewers⟩ **b :** PRINTER'S DEVIL **c :** a junior legal counsel working usu. without pay **6 a :** an ill-tempered, vicious, or ugly creature ⟨a big bay stallion that was a perfect ~⟩ — often used in vernacular names of animals; see TASMANIAN DEVIL **b :** a firecracker or similar firework **c :** something very provoking, difficult, or trying ⟨most game birds are ~*s* to bring down without a good dog⟩ **:** a perturbed, disordered, or distressing state ⟨they found themselves in a ~ of a mess⟩ ⟨there was a ~ of a high sea running that day⟩ **7 :** a mood, passion, or quality that possesses, incites, or disturbs ⟨the victim of a moody ~ within his own heart⟩ — compare BLUE DEVIL 1 **8 :** a highly seasoned dish esp. of broiled or fried meat (as chops or meaty bones) **:** a grill with cayenne pepper **9 :** any of various machines, appliances, or devices: as **a :** a machine for tearing or shredding something or for grinding material into bits (as stock for papermaking, woolen for shoddy, or fur for felt) **b :** an iron fire basket or grate for open-air use **c :** a machine for making wooden screws **d :** a drag for clearing plowed ground **10 :** a seam in a ship's hull on or below the waterline **11** *India & Africa* **:** DUST DEVIL **12 :** POWER, EFFICACY, STING — used esp. of cricket bowling or a bowled ball ⟨you will never take wickets unless you put more ~ in your bowling⟩ **13** *Christian Science* **:** the opposite of Truth **:** a belief in sin, sickness, and death **:** EVIL, ERROR — **between the devil and the deep sea** *or* **between the devil and the deep blue sea :** between two equally objectionable or hazardous alternatives **:** between two comparable evils — **devil and all :** everything right or wrong; *esp* **:** everything bad — **devil of it :** a vexatious or mischief-making feature **:** something to be regretted or deplored — used with *the* ⟨the *devil of it* was that we could easily have come early⟩ ⟨they only did it for the *devil of it*⟩ — **devil's own time :** a very bad experience **:** a painful drawn-out struggle — used with *the* ⟨had the *devil's own time* with yellow fever⟩ — **devil to pay :** serious trouble **:** grave mischance or mischief — used with *the* ⟨there'll be the *devil to pay* when her father finds out⟩ — **in the devil :** EVER — used as an intensive ⟨where *in the devil* did he go⟩

2**devil** \"\ *vb* **deviled** *or* **devilled; deviled** *or* **devilled; deviling** *or* **devilling** \-v(ə)liŋ, -vil-\ **devils** *vt* **1 :** TEASE, ANNOY, TORMENT, HAZE; *esp* **:** to pester with importunities ⟨~*ing* her mother for a new dress⟩ **2 :** to chop (food) fine and mix with hot seasoning or sauce usu. after cooking — now usu. used as a past participle ⟨a tasty ~*ed* crab⟩ ⟨~*ed* eggs⟩ **3 :** to tear to pieces in a devil ⟨~ rags⟩ ~ *vi* **:** to serve or function as a devil (as in a printshop or to a lawyer)

devil among the tailors : a firework that emits sparks, stars, and finally whirling imps

devil and the tailors *n* **:** FOX AND GEESE 1b

devil bolt *n* **:** a sham or faulty bolt sometimes used in contract shipbuilding

devil chaser *n* **:** a ranting moral reformer

devil–club *var of* DEVIL'S CLUB

devil dance *n* **1 :** a grotesque and often obscene impersonation of an evil spirit usu. with the aid of a mask that is important in Asiatic curative rites and stage dramas and popular in European carnivals as a remnant of medieval miracle plays **2 :** APACHE DEVIL DANCE

devil–dancer \ˈ=,=\ *n* **:** a performer of devil dances; *esp* **:** a professional performer of such dances

devil–devil \ˈ==,==\ *n* **:** CHARM, SPELL **:** magical incantation — used chiefly in pidgin English

devil–diver \ˈ==,==\ *n* **:** a dabchick or other small grebe

devil–dodger \ˈ==,==\ *n, slang* **:** PREACHER; *esp* **:** a military chaplain

devil dog *n* **:** MARINE

dev·il·dom \ˈdevəldəm\ *n* -s **:** the realm, rule, or power of the devil **:** diabolic influence or condition

devil drum *n* **:** a drum used in ceremonies (as of propitiation) of various primitive societies

devil duster *n* **:** DUST DEVIL

dev·il·er *also* **dev·il·ler** \ˈdev(ə)lə(r)\ *n* -s **:** one that devils or operates a devil

devil–fire \ˈ==,=\ *n* **1 :** WILL-O'-THE WISP **2 :** SAINT ELMO'S FIRE

devilfish \ˈ==,=\ *n* **1 :** any of several extremely large rays of the genera *Manta* and *Mobula* (family Mobulidae) that are widely distributed in warm seas; *esp* **:** a ray (*Manta birostris*) that is common in the Gulf of Mexico and along the southern coasts of the U.S. though probably cosmopolitan in warm seas, that may be 15 to 20 feet wide and several feet thick with a weight considerably in excess of one ton, that has a pair of movable cephalic lobes used in guiding small fishes into the nearly toothless mouth, and that reproduces viviparously usu. producing a single young at a birth **2 :** OCTOPUS; *broadly* **:** any large cephalopod

devilfish

devil–god \ˈ==,=\ *n* **1 :** a devil worshiped as a god **2 :** a heathen deity — used chiefly in Christian clerical writings

devil grass *n* **:** BERMUDA GRASS

devil horse *var of* DEVIL'S HORSE

devil–in–a–bush *or* **devil–in–the–bush** \ˈ====ˈ=\ *n* **1 :** LOVE-IN-A-MIST 1 **2 :** HERB PARIS

devil–in–a–mist \ˈ====ˈ=\ *n* **:** LOVE-IN-A-MIST 1

1**dev·il·ing** \ˈdevəliŋ\ *n* -s [ˈ*devil* + *-ling*] **1 :** a young devil **:** IMP **2** *also* **dev·e·lin** *or* **dev·i·lin** \-v(ə)lən\ [*develin, devilin,* alter. of *deviling*] *dial Eng* **:** the common European swift (*Apus apus*)

2**dev·il·ing** \ˈdev(ə)liŋ\ *adj* [fr. *deviling, devilling,* pres. part. of 2*devil*] **:** TEASING, PESKY, IMPORTUNATE

1**dev·il·ish** \ˈdev(ə)lish, -lēsh\ *adj* **1 :** resembling, typical of, or relating to the devil **:** DIABOLICAL ⟨~ tricks and stratagems⟩ **2 :** like or like that of a devil esp. in daring and rakishness or in arrogant disregard for the rights of others ⟨sheer ~ courage⟩ ⟨a ~ gang of young roughs⟩; *often* **:** EVIL, VICIOUS ⟨their ~ program⟩ ⟨their ~ practices⟩ **3 :** EXTREME, EXCESSIVE ⟨he was in a ~ hurry⟩ — **dev·il·ish·ly** *adv* — **dev·il·ish·ness** *n* -ES

2**devilish** \"\ *adv* **:** EXCESSIVELY, DEVILISHLY ⟨he's tough, sir, — tough, and ~ sly —Charles Dickens⟩

dev·il·ism \-və,lizəm\ *n* -s **:** devilish practice, doctrine, or quality

devil ivy *n* **:** IVY-ARUM

dev·il·ize \ˈdevə,līz\ *vt* -ED/-ING/-S **:** to make a devil of **:** cause to become devilish

dev·il·kin \-vəlkən\ *n* -s **:** a little devil **:** IMP

deviller *var of* DEVILER

de·vil·lite \dəˈvē,līt, -vi,-\ *n* -s [F *devilline* devillite (fr. Henri Étienne Sainte-Claire *Deville* †1881 Fr. chemist + F *-ine*) + E *-ite*] **:** a mineral $Cu_4Ca(SO_4)_2(OH)_6{\cdot}3H_2O$ consisting of a hydrous basic sulfate of copper and calcium found in Cornwall and elsewhere in dark green 6-sided platy crystals

devil lore *n* **:** DEMONOLOGY; *often* **:** a body of folk belief and custom concerning evil spirits or devils

devil·man \ˈ==,man, -,mən\ *n, pl* **devilmen :** DEVILER

devil–may–care \ˈ=,=ˈ=\ *adj* **1 :** RECKLESS, ROISTERING, ROLLICKING **:** careless of authority ⟨a crew of *devil-may-care* swashbucklers⟩ ⟨an arrogant *devil-may-care* attitude⟩ **2 :** RAKISH, INFORMAL, CASUAL ⟨hat worn at a *devil-may-care* angle⟩

dev·il·ment \ˈdevəlmənt *sometimes* -,ment\ *n* -s **:** devilish conduct; *often* **:** reckless mischief **:** TEASING ⟨his ~ at school remained undiscovered for several years⟩

devil ray *n* **:** DEVILFISH 1

dev·il·ry \ˈdevəlrē, -ri\ *or* **dev·il·try** \-l·tr-\ *n* -ES [ME *devilrie, develrie,* fr. *devil, devel* devil + *-rie* -ry] **1 a :** WITCHCRAFT **:** action performed with the help of the devil **:** diabolic art **b :** works of the devil **:** behavior typical of the devil ⟨fighting on the side of God against all the ~ of hell⟩ **c :** behavior felt to be suitable to a devil **:** extreme wickedness **:** gross or malignant cruelty ⟨the determined ~ of fanatics⟩ **d :** reckless unrestrained raffish conduct **:** irregular behavior that is mischievous, teasing, and unconsidered rather than vicious or dictated by evil intent **2 :** an act of devilry; *usu* **:** an act of studied malignancy or cruelty

devils *pl of* DEVIL, *pres 3d sing of* DEVIL

devil's advocate *n* [trans. of NL *advocatus diaboli*] **1** *Roman Catholicism* **:** an official of the Congregation of Rites whose duty is to point out defects in the evidence upon which a demand for beatification or canonization rests or in the character of the person for whom the honor is sought — called also *promoter of the faith;* compare POSTULATOR **2 :** a critic who picks flaws to evoke controversy or to bring out the whole truth **3 :** a champion of the worse cause for the sake of argument

devil's–apple \ˈ=ˈ=,==\ *n, pl* **devil's–apples 1 :** JIMSONWEED **2 :** MANDRAKE 1 **3 :** MAYAPPLE

devil's–apron \ˈ=ˈ=,==\ *n, pl* **devil's–aprons :** a kelp of the genus *Laminaria* (esp. *L. saccharina* of the Atlantic ocean) having a large flat leathery thallus shaped somewhat like an apron

devil's bit *n* [ME *develesbite* (trans. of ML *morsus diaboli*), fr. *develes* (gen. of *devel* devil) + *bite, bitt* bit, bite — more at BIT] **:** any of various plants with premorse rootstocks: **a** *also* **devil's bit scabious :** SCABIOUS 1; *esp* **:** a common purple or white flowered scabious (*Scabiosa succisa* or *Succisa pratensis*) that is native to Europe but naturalized in eastern No. America and that yields a blue dye from the leaves — compare WOAD **b :** any of several New World blazing stars (as *Chamaelirium luteum, Liatris spicata,* or *Aletris farinosa*) — compare BUTTON SNAKEROOT, COLICROOT

devil's–bite \ˈ=ˈ=,=\ *n, pl* **devil's–bites :** AMERICAN HELLEBORE 1

devil's–bones \ˈ=ˈ=,=\ *n pl* **1** *slang* **:** DICE **2** *sing or pl in constr* **:** a wild yam (*Dioscorea paniculata*)

devil's book *n* **:** DEVIL'S PICTURE BOOK

devil's buckie *n* **:** DEIL'S BUCKIE

devil's–claw \ˈ=ˈ=,=\ *n, pl* **devil's–claws 1 a :** UNICORN PLANT **b :** a cat's-claw (*Acacia greggii*) **2 :** a strong split hook used on a ship to grasp a link of a chain cable and act as a stopper; *also* **:** any of several hooked devices (as a grapnel or ice anchor)

devil's club *or* **devil–club** *n* **:** a spiny shrub (*Oplopanax horridus*) of the family Araliaceae with large simple petiolate lobed leaves and crowded terminal umbels of flowers

devil's coachhorse *n, chiefly Brit* **:** any of several rove beetles

devil's corkscrew *n* **:** any of certain large spiral fossils from Nebraska previously reported as fossil plants or animals but now usu. regarded as sediment-filled burrows of extinct rodents, possibly beavers

devil's–cotton \ˈ=ˈ=,==\ *n, pl* **devil's–cottons :** a shrub or small tree (*Abroma augusta*) of the East Indies that yields fiber used for cordage

devil's darning needle *n* **1 a :** DRAGONFLY **b :** DAMSELFLY **2 :** VIRGIN'S BOWER b **3 devil's darning needles** *pl* **:** any of certain grasses of the genus *Stipa; esp* **:** ESPARTO

devil's dozen *n, dial* **:** THIRTEEN

devil's dung *n* [trans. of G *teufelsdreck*] **:** ASAFETIDA

devil's dyke *n, usu cap both Ds* **:** any of several prehistoric British earthworks

devil's–fig \ˈ=ˈ=,=\ *n, pl* **devil's–figs 1 :** PRICKLY POPPY **2 :** PRICKLY PEAR

devil's–finger \ˈ=ˈ=,==\ *n, pl* **devil's–fingers :** BELEMNITE

devil's–flax \ˈ=ˈ=,=\ *n, pl* **devil's–flaxes :** a toadflax (*Linaria vulgaris*)

devil's food cake *also* **devil's food** *n* [so called fr. the contrast in color with angel food cake] **:** a rich dark chocolate cake

devil's–grandmother \ˈ=ˈ=,=,==\ *n, pl* **devil's–grandmothers :** a woolly herb (*Elephantopus tomentosus*) with bluish flowers — called also *elephant's-foot, tobaccoweed*

devil's–grass \ˈ=ˈ=,=\ *n, pl* **devil's–grasses 1 :** COUCH GRASS 1a **2 :** JOINT GRASS 1 **3 :** BERMUDA GRASS

devil's–grip \ˈ=ˈ=,=\ *n, pl* **devil's–grips 1 :** CARPETWEED **2 :** a malformation of sheep that consists of an indentation near the withers and down behind the shoulder as if a string had been put round that part of the sheep and tightened **3 :** EPIDEMIC PLEURODYNIA

devil's–gut *n, pl* **devil's–guts** \ˈ=ˈ=,=\ **:** DODDER; *broadly* **:** any of several weedy or destructive creeping plants (as dodder laurel or a bindweed) — usu. used in pl. but often sing. in constr.

devil's–hair \ˈ=ˈ=,=\ *n, pl* **devil's–hairs :** the common American virgin's bower (*Clematis virginiana*)

devil's–hand \ˈ=ˈ=,=\ *n, pl* **devil's–hands :** an ornamental Mexican tree (*Chiranthodendron pentadactylon*) of the family Sterculiaceae having bright red flowers with five stamens arranged like the fingers of a hand

devil's–head–in–a–bush \ˈ==,===ˈ=\ *n* **:** FLOWER-OF-AN-HOUR

devil's–horn \ˈ=ˈ=,=\ *n, pl* **devil's–horns 1** *dial Eng* **:** STINKHORN **2 :** UNICORN PLANT

devil's horse *n, South & Midland* **:** PRAYING MANTIS

devil's ironweed *n* **:** any of several American plants of the genus *Lactuca*

devil's ivy *n* **:** any of several climbing tender perennial plants of the family Araceae (as some members of the genus *Philodendron*) that are grown as ornamental foliage plants

devil's–knitting–needles \ˈ=ˈ=ˈ==,==\ *n, pl* **devil's–knitting–needles :** ESPARTO 1

devil's mark *n* **:** a spot on the body of a person held guilty of witchcraft that was supposed to be insensible because the devil had touched it in sealing his bargain with the witch

devil's mass *n* **:** indiscriminate cursing

devil's milk *n* [trans. of G *teufelsmilch* or D *duivelsmelk*] **1 :** any of several plants having acrid milky juice (as the spurges *Euphorbia peplus* and *E. helioscopia* or the celandine) **2 :** the juice of a devil's milk plant usu. having reputed curative power (as on warts) or other remarkable attributes in folklore

devils on horseback [so called fr. the similarity to angels on horseback] **:** a dish consisting of oysters or pieces of chicken liver seasoned, wrapped in bacon, and broiled or fried **:** PIGS IN BLANKETS

devil's paintbrush *n* **:** ORANGE HAWKWEED; *broadly* **:** any of certain hawkweeds that are naturalized as weeds in the eastern U.S.

devil's paternoster *n* **1 :** the Lord's Prayer recited backward (as in late medieval witchcraft) **2 :** a muttering or grumbling of curses

devil's picture book *n* **:** playing cards — called also *devil's book;* formerly usu. used in pl.

devil's–pitchforks \ˈ=ˈ=,=\ *n pl but sing or pl in constr* [so called fr. the shape of the fruit] **:** BEGGAR-TICKS

devil's–plague \ˈ=ˈ=,=\ *n, pl* **devil's–plagues :** WILD CARROT

devil's–rattlebox \ˈ=ˈ=,==\ *n, pl* **devil's–rattleboxes** [so called fr. the rattling of the ripe seeds in the pod] **:** a bladder campion (*Silene latifolia*)

devil's–root \ˈ=ˈ=,=\ *n, pl* **devil's–roots :** CLOVER BROOMRAPE

devil's shoestring *n* **1 :** CATGUT 3a **2 devil's shoestrings** *pl* **:** the dried leaves and stems of the catgut formerly used as an anthelmintic — called also *turkey pea*

devil's slide *n* **:** the path of an avalanche down a steep slope **:** a long narrow mass of scree or talus descending a precipitous mountainside

devil's–snuffbox \ˈ=ˈ=,=\ *n, pl* **devil's–snuffboxes** *dial* **:** a fungus (as a puffball or corn smut) that releases clouds of minute spores when jarred or broken

devil's tattoo *n* **:** a drumming with or as if with fingers or feet

devil's toenail *n* **1 :** BELEMNITE **2 :** STYLOLITE

devil's–tongue \ˈ=ˈ=,=\ *n, pl* **devil's–tongues 1 :** a prickly pear (*Opuntia compressa*) **2 :** a foul-smelling somewhat fleshy tropical bulbous herb (*Hydrosme rivieri* or *Amorphophallus rivieri*) of the family Araceae that is sometimes grown in the greenhouse for its large leaves and showy dark red spathe surrounding a long spadix — called also *snake palm*

devil's trumpet *n* **:** JIMSONWEED

devil's–walking–stick \ˈ=ˈ=ˈ==,=\ *n, pl* **devil's–walking–sticks :** HERCULES'-CLUB 3

devil's–weed \ˈ=ˈ=,=\ *n, pl* **devil's–weeds :** KING DEVIL

devil theory *n* **:** a theory in history and political economy: wars and other crises result not from objective causes but from the vicious conduct of individuals in power

deviltry *var of* DEVILRY

dev·il·ward \ˈdevəlwə(r)d\ *adv (or adj)* **:** toward the devil

devilwood \ˈ==,=\ *n* [prob. so called fr. the fact that it is very hard to cut or split] **:** a small tree (*Osmanthus americanus*) of the southern U.S. that is related to the olive and has whitish bark and panicles of dull white flowers which are succeeded by dark purple fruits — called also *American olive*

de·vi·ous \ˈdēvēəs *also* -vyəs\ *adj* [L *devius,* fr. *de* from, away + *-vius* (fr. *via* way, road) — more at DE-, VIA] **1 :** located off the highroad **:** OUT-OF-THE-WAY, REMOTE, RETIRED ⟨shipwrecks upon ~ coasts⟩ **2 a :** deviating from a straight line **:** WINDING, ROUNDABOUT, CIRCUITOUS ⟨a ~ path along the ridge⟩ **b :** moving without a fixed course **:** ERRANT, ROVING ⟨~ breezes⟩ **3 a :** deviating from a right, accepted, or common course **:** ASTRAY, ERRING ⟨~ arguments⟩ ⟨a ~ conscience⟩; *often* **:** seeking or advancing toward a right, accepted, or common end by roundabout means ⟨the ways of the Lord are ~⟩ **b :** hard to pin down or bring to agreement ⟨a ~ man⟩; *often* **:** SHIFTY, TRICKY, UNSCRUPULOUS, UNFAIR ⟨his ~ treatment of the allies⟩ ⟨a ~ attack on his character⟩ — **de·vi·ous·ly** *adv* — **de·vi·ous·ness** *n* -ES

de·vir·gin·ate \(ˈ)dēˈvərjə,nāt\ *also* **de·vir·gin·ize** \-,nīz\ *vt* -ED/-ING/-S [L *devirginatus,* past part. of *devirginare* to deflower, fr. *de* from, away + *-virginare* (fr. *virgin-, virgo* girl, virgin) — more at VIRGIN] **:** to deprive of virginity or of virginal quality — **de·vir·gi·na·tion** \(ˌ)dē,vərjəˈnāshən\ *n* -s — **de·vir·gi·na·tor** \(ˈ)dēˈvərjə,nād·ə(r)\ *n* -s

devis *pl of* DEVI

de·vis·abil·i·ty \də,vīzəˈbilәd·ē, dē,-\ *n* -ES **:** the quality or state of being devisable

de·vis·able \=ˈ=zəbəl\ *adj* [AF, fr. OF *deviser* to distribute, divide, regulate + *-able*] **1 :** capable of being devised or bequeathed ⟨lands, tenements and hereditaments, be not ~ by testament —*Act 27 Henry VIII*⟩ **2 :** capable of being devised, contrived, or invented

de·vis·al \=ˈ=zəl\ *n* -s **:** DEVISING

de·vi·sat vel non \ˈdevə,sat,velˈnän\ *n* [NL, he bequeaths or not] **:** a written document that sets forth the questions of fact pertinent to the validity of an alleged will and is sent from a court of probate or chancery having jurisdiction to allow or disallow a will to a court of common law having a jury so that the answers of the jury after trial will be recorded thereon and returned to the original court for the proper judgment as to the validity of the will

1**de·vise** \dəˈvīz, dēˈ-\ *vb* -ED/-ING/-S [ME *devisen,* fr. OF *deviser* to divide, regulate, tell, modif. of (assumed) VL *divisare,* fr. L *divisus,* past part. of *dividere* to divide — more at DIVIDE] *vt* **1 a :** to form in the mind by new combinations of ideas, new applications of principles, or new arrangement of parts **:** formulate by thought **:** CONTRIVE, INVENT, PLAN, SCHEME ⟨~ an engine⟩ ⟨*devising* a new style in hats⟩ **b** *archaic* **:** SUPPOSE, IMAGINE, GUESS **c :** to plan to obtain or bring about **:** scheme for **:** PLOT — used esp. of objectives felt to be evil or unworthy ⟨the traitors *devised* the death of the king⟩ ⟨*devising* a plot to overthrow the government⟩ **2** *obs* **:** to describe fully **:** relate in detail **:** RECOUNT **3 :** to give by will — now used esp. of real estate; compare BEQUEATH 1a **4** *obs* **:** DRAW, DESIGN, DELINEATE ⟨that dear cross upon your shield *devised* —Edmund Spenser⟩ ~ *vi* **1 :** to form a scheme **:** develop a plan or intent **:** DESIGN, CONTRIVE, DETERMINE — now used chiefly as a present participle ⟨the *devising* spirit, the scheming brain⟩ **2** *obs* **:** to talk together **:** CONVERSE **syn** see CONTRIVE, WILL

2**devise** \"\ *n* -s [MF, fr. OF, division, deliberation, wish, will, testament, fr. *deviser* to divide, regulate] **1 :** the act of giving or disposing of property by will — now used technically only of real property but formerly used as well of the bequest of personal estate **2 :** a will or clause of a will disposing of real property **3 :** property given by will

3**de·vise** \dəˈvēzə\ *n, pl* **devi·sen** \-zən\ *sometimes cap* [G, fr. F, motto, fr. MF, heraldic device, fr. OF, dividing line — more at DEVICE] **:** foreign exchange in readily available form

de·vi·see \,devəˈzē; dəˈvīˈzē, dēˈ-\ *n* -s [ˈ*devise* + *-ee*] **:** one to whom a devise of property is made — compare DEVISOR

de·vis·er \dəˈvīzə(r), dēˈ-\ *n* -s [ME *diviser,* alter. (influenced by ME *-er, -ere -er*) of *devysour,* fr. MF *deviseur,* fr. OF *deviseor,* fr. *deviser* to divide, regulate + *-eor* -or] **:** one that devises (as by planning, inventing, designing, or preparing) — compare DEVISOR

de·vi·sor \,devəˈzȯ(ə)r; dəˈvīzər, dēˈ-, -ˈvīˈzȯ(ə)r\ *n* -s [AF, fr. OF *deviser* to distribute, divide + *-or, -our* -or] **:** a person who devises property in a will — compare DEVISEE

de·vitalization \(ˌ)dē+\ *n* **:** an act of devitalizing **:** the condition of being devitalized ⟨~ of two affected teeth was necessary⟩ ⟨insect attack may cause ~ and leaf drop⟩ ⟨the ~ of Western influence on Eastern nations⟩

de·vitalize \(ˈ)dē+\ *vt* [*de-* + *vitalize*] **:** to deprive of life or vitality: as **a :** to deprive of force or effectiveness ⟨catchy tunes are often *devitalized* by constant repetition⟩ ⟨his clumsy presentation ~*s* his argument⟩ **b :** to refine (as foodstuffs) to the point that essential or desirable constituents are lost ⟨the processor that ~*s* our food and then restores a part of what he has thrown away⟩ **c :** to destroy the pulp of and usu. remove the pulp from (as a tooth)

de·vitaminize \(ˈ)dē+\ *vt* [*de-* + *vitamin* + *-ize*] **:** to deprive (as food) of vitamins esp. by cooking or hulling

de·vitrification \(ˌ)dē+\ *n* [F *dévitrification,* fr. *dévitrifier*] **:** the action or process of devitrifying or state of being devitrified; *specif* **:** the conversion of glassy matter into crystalline (as by slow cooling or by pressure, action of water, or chemical changes)

de·vitrify \(ˈ)dē+\ *vb* [F *dévitrifier,* fr. *dé-* de- (fr. OF *des-*) + *vitrifier* to vitrify] *vt* **:** to deprive of glassy luster and transparency; *esp* **:** to change (as a glass, glassy rock, or enamel) from a vitreous to a crystalline condition ~ *vi* **:** to change from a vitreous to a crystalline condition usu. with loss of transparency and luster

devize *obs var of* DEVISE

de·vocalize \(ˈ)dē+\ *vt* [*de-* + *vocalize*] **:** DEVOICE

de·voice \(ˈ)dē+\ *vt* [*de-* + *voice,* v.] **:** to pronounce without vibration of the vocal cords (a sound that is voiced in certain other positions or was formerly voiced)

devoid \dəˈvȯid, dēˈ-\ *adj* [ME, prob. short for *devoided,* past part. of *devoiden* to get rid of, depart from, fr. MF *desvuidier* to empty, fr. OF, fr. *des-* dis- + *vuidier* to empty — more at VOID] **1** *obs* **:** VOID, EMPTY, VACANT ⟨when I awoke, and found her place ~ —Edmund Spenser⟩ **2 a :** not having or using **:** LACKING — used with *of* ⟨desert sand . . . ~ of humus —W.B.Fisher⟩ ⟨her somewhat sallow face ~ of makeup —Erle Stanley Gardner⟩ ⟨absolutely ~ of any ambition —L.P.Smith⟩ ⟨echoing phrases ~ of substance —W.L. Sullivan⟩ ⟨~ of teeth —R.W.Murray⟩ **b :** free from **:** unimpaired by — used with *of* ⟨love is never quite ~ of sentimentality —W.S.Maugham⟩ ⟨a conscience ~ of offense — Acts 24:16 (AV)⟩ ⟨a dignity of manner ~ of all stiffness —Anthony Trollope⟩

de·voir \dəvˈwär, -wȯ(ə)r, ˈdev,w-; dəˈvȯ(i)(ə)r\ *n* -s [ME, alter. (influenced by MF *devoir,* fr. OF *devoir, deveir*) of *dever,* fr. OF *devoir, deveir,* fr. *devoir, deveir,* v., to owe, be obliged, be supposed, fr. L *debēre* — more at DEBT] **1 a :** an act or conduct that may be required or expected of one **:** assigned task **:** DUTY ⟨I'm a part-time detective. My ~ is to study . . . people —Christopher Morley⟩ **b** *obs* **:** utmost effort **:** best endeavor **c :** an act of civility or respect ⟨a birthday ~ to the founder⟩; *often* **:** a formal act of greeting or leave-taking **:** RESPECTS — now usu. used in pl. ⟨he paid his ~*s* to his hostess and hurried down the steps⟩ **2 devoirs** *pl, obs* **:** money due for payment of duties or customs

dev·o·lute \'devə,lüt *also* -vəl,yüt\ *vt* -ED/-ING/-S [L *devolutus,* past part. of *devolvere*] : DEVOLVE

dev·o·lu·tion \,devə'lüshən *also* -vəl'yü-\ *n* -S [ML *devolution-, devolutio,* fr. LL, corruption, fr. L *devolutus* (past part. of *devolvere*) + *-ion-, -io* -ion] **1** : transference from one individual to another: as **a** : a passing or devolving (as of property, qualities, power, or rights) upon a successor ⟨the ~ of the crown⟩ **b** : delegation or conferral (as of authority, responsibility, or tasks) esp. to a subordinate ⟨~ of functions in industry⟩ **c** *in ecclesiastical law* : transfer of power and privilege in a particular case because of nonfeasance or misfeasance (as when the filling of a vacant benefice passes to the church because the patron failed to nominate or presented an unworthy candidate) **d** : the delegation or surrender of powers formerly held by a central government to regional or local authorities — compare DECENTRALIZATION **e** *Scots law* (1) : the reference of a matter to an umpire by arbiters who disagree (2) : the devolving of a purchase at auction upon the next highest bidder when the highest bidder fails to make good his bid **2 a** : descent or passage through a series (as of stages in development) **b** : retrograde evolution : DEGENERATION — **dev·o·lu·tion·ary** \-shə,nerē\ *adj*

dev·o·lu·tion·ist \-sh(ə)nəst\ *n* -S : an advocate or practicer of devolution esp. in government : a person favoring a high degree of autonomy in local government

de·volve \də'välv, dē'-, -vȯlv *also* -vä(u)v *or* -vȯv\ *vb* -ED/-ING/-S [ME *devolven* to roll down, fr. L *devolvere,* fr. *de* down, away + *volvere* to roll — more at DE-, VOLUBLE] *vt* **1** *archaic* : to roll onward or downward **2** *obs* : to cause to pass down, descend, be transferred, or changed (as by the course of events or operation of law) **3** : to transfer from one person to another : hand down — usu. used with *upon,* sometimes with *to* or *into* ⟨The God-Father . . . having *devolved* his potency upon men —Weston La Barre⟩ ⟨the risk of . . . *devolving* a measure of authority to people who are poor and politically immature —A.C.Jones⟩ ~ *vi* **1** : to pass by transmission or succession ⟨his estate *devolved* on a distant cousin⟩ : fall or be passed usu. as an obligation or responsibility ⟨after the general fell, command *devolved* upon the colonel⟩ ⟨the chairmanship shall ~ in strict order of seniority⟩ **2 a** : to flow or roll from a situation viewed as higher to one that is lower ⟨streams *devolving* from the mountains⟩ **b** *archaic* : to proceed from one point or condition into another as if by flowing or unrolling

[1]**dev·on** \'devən\ *usu cap, var of* DEVONSHIRE

[2]**devon** \"\ *n* [*Devon,* county in England where it originated] **1** *usu cap* : a breed of vigorous red dual-purpose cattle that is commonly divided into (1) a predominantly beef type variety which produces meat of fine quality and (2) a strictly dual-purpose variety which has satisfactory meat conformation and produces moderate quantities of rich milk — called also (1) *North Devon,* (2) *South Devon* **2** -S *often cap* : any animal of the Devon breed

[1]**de·vo·ni·an** \də'vōnēən, dē'-, -nyən\ *adj, usu cap* [*Devon,* county in England + E *-ian*] **1** : of or relating to Devonshire or Devon in England **2** : of or relating to the period of the Paleozoic that follows the Silurian and is next below the Mississippian or the system of rocks formed during this period which are commonly separable into marine and nonmarine facies and are characterized by abundant preservation of fossils including ferns, lycopods, horsetails, and a few gymnosperms as plants and abundant lower fishes and some air-breathing invertebrates — see GEOLOGIC TIME table

[2]**devonian** \"\ *n* -S *usu cap* **1** : a native or inhabitant of Devonshire **2** : the Devonian period or system of rocks

dev·on·shire \'devən,shi(ə)r, -iə, -,shə(r)\ *or* **dev·on** \'devən\ *adj, usu cap* [fr. *Devonshire, Devon,* county in England] : of or from the county of Devon, England : of the kind or style prevalent in Devon

devonshire cream *n, usu cap D* : cream allowed to rise on milk, set by heating and then cooling, and skimmed from the underlying skim milk

devon wrestling *also* **devonshire wrestling** *n, usu cap D* : a system of wrestling in which catching hold the opponent's strong loose linen jacket or any part of his body above the waist is permitted, in which two shoulders and one hip or two hips and one shoulder must touch ground simultaneously to constitute a fall, and in which contestants get up on their feet and the bout recommences if a man is thrown other than on his back

dé·vot \dā'vō, -vȯ\ *n* -S [F, fr. *dévot* devout, fr. OF *devot* — more at DEVOUT] : a man who is a devotee

[1]**de·vote** \də'vōt, dē'-, *usu* -ōd·+V\ *adj* [partly fr. ME *devot* devout; partly fr. L *devotus* devoted, past part. of *devovēre* — more at DEVOUT] *archaic* : DEVOTED, DEVOUT

[2]**devote** \"\ *vt* -ED/-ING/-S [L *devotus,* past part. of *devovēre,* fr. *de* from, away + *vovēre* to vow — more at DE-, VOW] **1 a** : to set apart by a solemn act of appropriation : dedicate or consecrate esp. formally ⟨she vowed to ~ her child to God's service⟩ **b** : to provide (something) for use ⟨a chapel was *devoted* to the worship of each sect⟩ **2 a** : to give up (as time, money, thought, effort) to the cause, for the benefit, or to the advancement of something regarded as deserving support, improvement, or aid ⟨she *devoted* large sums to the care of the poor⟩ ⟨*devoting* all their thoughts to planning an escape⟩ **b** : to attach the attention or center the activities of (oneself) wholly or chiefly on a specified object, field, or objective : attach (oneself) to : set (oneself) on ⟨she *devoted* herself to her invalid sister⟩ **3 a** : to consign to the powers of evil : give over to destruction : DAMN, DOOM **b** *obs* : EXECRATE, CURSE **syn** see DIRECT

[3]**devote** *n* -S [prob. fr. [1]*devote*] *obs* : DEVOTEE

[4]**dé·vote** \dā'vȯt\ *n* -S [F, fr. fem. of *dévot* devout] : a woman who is a devotee

devoted *adj* [fr. past part. of [2]*devote*] : consecrated to a purpose; *broadly* : ARDENT, ZEALOUS, DEVOUT — **de·vot·ed·ly** *adv* — **de·vot·ed·ness** *n* -ES

de·vo·tee \,devə'tē, -vō',- *also* -'tā *sometimes* də,vō'tē *or* dē-'vō'tē *or* ,dē,vō'tē\ *n* -S [[2]*devote* + *-ee*] **1** : a person preoccupied with religious duties and ceremonies; *often* : one vowed, consecrated, or given over to esp. zealous and vigorous practice of his religion **2** : an ardent or zealous follower, supporter, or enthusiast (as of a cause, an art, a sport) : VOTARY

de·vote·ment \də'vōtmənt, dē'-\ *n* -S : the act of devoting or state of being set apart by or as if by a vow : DEDICATION

de·vo·tion \-ōshən\ *n* -S [ME *devocioun,* fr. OF *devotion,* fr. LL *devotion-, devotio,* fr. L, devotement, fr. *devotus* (past part. of *devovēre*) + *-ion-, -io* -ion] **1 a** : earnestness and zeal in the performance of religious duties and observations : religious fervor : REVERENCE, PIETY **b** : an act evincing religious devotion; *usu* : an act of prayer or supplication — now usu. used in pl. ⟨spent half the night at her ~*s*⟩ **c devotions** *pl* : prayers or service of worship usu. intended for private nonliturgical services ⟨a book of daily ~*s*⟩ **d** *obs* : an offering (as of money) devoted in worship : OBLATION; *often* : alms given from religious motives **2** : the act of devoting or quality of being devoted ⟨~ of such talents to the public service⟩ ⟨his ~ to the cause of justice is well known⟩ : ardent love or affection ⟨their ~ was beautiful to behold⟩ : strong attachment : ZEAL, ARDOR, ENTHUSIASM **3** *archaic* **a** : devoted service **b** : disposal or power of disposal : beck and call ⟨the . . . rabble were wholly at the ~ of those incendiaries —Edmund Burke⟩ **4** *obs* : something (as a cause) to which a person or thing is devoted : PURPOSE, MISSION **syn** see FIDELITY

[1]**de·vo·tion·al** \-shən°l, -shnəl\ *adj* : relating to, suited to, used in, or characterized by devotion (as religious devotion) ⟨dedicated to the ~ life⟩ ⟨a ~ exercise⟩ ⟨the priest considered it more ~ to hear than to say mass⟩ — **de·vo·tion·al·ly** \-°lē, -əlē, -li\ *adv*

[2]**devotional** \"\ *n* -S : a short worship service esp. when preceding or incorporated into a meeting (as of a club or discussion group) that is not predominantly religious

de·vo·tion·al·ism \-°l,izəm, -ə,li-\ *n* -S : the quality or state of one markedly characterized by religious devotion

de·vo·tion·al·ist \-°ləst, -ələst\ *n* -S : one that is characterized by marked religious devotion

de·vo·tion·ary \-shə,nerē\ *archaic var of* DEVOTIONAL

devoto *n* -ES [It, fr. *devoto* devout, fr. LL *devotus*] *obs* : DEVOTEE

de·vour \də'vau̇(ə)r, dē'-, -auə, *chiefly S* -au̇wə(r\ *vt* -ED/-ING/-S [ME *devouren,* fr. MF *devourer,* fr. L *devorare,* fr. *de* down, away + *vorare* to eat greedily, swallow up — more at DE-, VORACIOUS] **1** : to eat up with greediness : consume ravenously : feast upon like a wild beast or a glutton ⟨~*ed* everything on his plate⟩ **2** : to seize upon and destroy or appropriate greedily, selfishly, or wantonly : swallow up : use up : CONSUME, ENGULF, WASTE, ANNIHILATE ⟨~*ed* by fire⟩ ⟨the raging water ~*ed* the riverbank⟩ **3** : to prey upon : ABSORB — usu. used passively ⟨a man ~*ed* by remorse⟩ **4** : to enjoy with avidity; *often* : to take in eagerly by the senses or mind ⟨~*ing* the book⟩ ⟨~*ed* that graceful figure as though engraving it permanently on his mind⟩ **syn** see EAT

de·vour·er \-au̇rə(r)\ *n* -S [ME, fr. *devouren* + *-er*] : one that devours: as **a** : a gluttonous eater **b** : a destructive agent : DESTROYER **c** : an avid reader

devouring *adj* [ME, fr. pres. part. of *devouren*] : GREEDY, AVID, CONSUMING ⟨fierce ~ affection⟩ — **de·vour·ing·ly** *adv* — **de·vour·ing·ness** *n* -ES

de·vour·ment \-au̇(ə)rmənt, -auəm-\ *n* -S : an act of devouring

de·vout \də'vau̇t,dē'-, *usu* -au̇d·+V\ *adj* [ME *devout, devot,* fr. OF *devot,* fr. LL *devotus,* fr. L, devoted, past part. of *devovēre* to devote — more at DEVOTE] **1** : devoted to religion or to religious feelings, duties, or exercises : given to devotion : PIOUS, REVERENT, RELIGIOUS ⟨a ~ man, and one that feared God —Acts 10: 2 (AV)⟩ **2** : expressing devotion or piety ⟨a ~ posture⟩ **3** : warmly devoted : HEARTY, SINCERE ⟨~ wishes for continued prosperity⟩

syn PIOUS, RELIGIOUS, PIETISTIC, SANCTIMONIOUS: DEVOUT stresses a genuine feeling, a mental or emotional attitude about religion leading to solemn reverence and fitting observance of rites and practices ⟨I was often *devout,* my eyes filling with tears at the thought of God and for my sins —W.B.Yeats⟩ ⟨a *devout* man, with a childlike trust in God —C.B. Nordhoff & J.N.Hall⟩ PIOUS may suggest faithful and fervent performance of the duties of one's religion rather than inner, genuine feelings or attitudes; it may also be used in connection with hypocrisy ⟨happy, as a *pious* man is happy when, after a long illness, he goes once more to church —Robert Hichens⟩ ⟨were *pious* Christians, taking their faith devoutly. But such religious emotion as was theirs, was reflected rather than spontaneous —H.O.Taylor⟩ ⟨a hypocrite — a thing all *pious* words and uncharitable deeds —Charles Reade⟩ RELIGIOUS may suggest genuine faith and adherence to a way of life consonant with religion ⟨he was a *religious* soul rather than a speculative intellect, and he measured all things by the principles of primitive Christianity —V.L.Parrington⟩ ⟨but Henry was a simple man, and a *religious.* On his knees before his confessor, he had learned that God was his friend —Francis Hackett⟩ ⟨they are not *religious:* they are only pew renters —G.B.Shaw⟩ Commonly derogatory, PIETISTIC stresses the emotional or ritualistic rather than the intellectual attitudes on religion and similar matters ⟨an emotional person with *pietistic* inclinations that nearly carried him over at different times to the Plymouth Brethren, to the Wesleyan Methodists, and to the Countess of Huntingdon's connection —H.G.Wells⟩ ⟨his kneeling on a stage, in front of a crowded house, as was recorded in the press, to receive the blessing of a visiting cardinal, was, to Sean, a humiliating thing for the head of a republican state to do. The *pietistic* Spaniard in him, Sean thought —Sean O'Casey⟩ SANCTIMONIOUS now always implies pretension to or appearance of exaltedness, or some other hypocrisy ⟨better in appearance anyway than that *sanctimonious* fellow, the missionary, who had passed straight from world service to one of the more exclusive tribes in the Congo —Ellen Glasgow⟩ ⟨if it only takes some of the *sanctimonious* conceit out of one of those pious scalawags —Robert Frost⟩

de·vout·ly *adv* [ME, fr. *devout* + *-ly*] : in a devout manner : REVERENTLY, SINCERELY, EARNESTLY, DEEPLY

de·vout·ness *n* -ES [ME *devoutnes,* fr. *devout* + *-nes* -ness] : a devout quality or state; *esp* : religious devotion

de·vove \də'vōv\ *vt* -ED/-ING/-S [L *devovēre*] *archaic* : DEVOTE, DEDICATE

devow *vt* -ED/-ING/-S [MF *devouer,* fr. *de-* (as in *devot* devout) + *vouer* to vow — more at VOW, v.] **1** \də'vau̇\ *obs* : to dedicate esp. by a vow : DEVOTE **2** \(')dē¦v-\ [*de-* + *vow,* v.] **a** *obs* : RENOUNCE, DISAVOW **b** : to release from a vow

de·vulcanize \(')dē+\ *vt* [*de-* + *vulcanize*] : to treat (vulcanized scrap rubber) for recovery of original plastic properties even though vulcanizing agents are not removed — compare RECLAIMED RUBBER

de·vulcanizer \"+\ *n* : one that devulcanizes

[1]**dew** \'d(y)ü\ *n* -S [ME, fr. OE *dēaw;* akin to OHG *tou* dew, ON *dögg* dew, Gk *thein* to run, Skt *dhavate* it flows] **1** : moisture condensed upon the surfaces of cool bodies esp. at night ⟨~ glistening in the early morning light⟩ ⟨the ~*s* of night⟩; *broadly* : small deposits of water that are produced by condensation of water vapor in the free atmosphere, by condensation of vapor directly from the ground, or less often by exudation of water through the leaf pores of a plant particularly at night upon the surfaces of cool bodies and in calm weather under an unclouded sky and more rapidly upon surfaces freely radiating heat and that remain as fluid water or frost according to the temperature **2** : something felt to resemble dew as in purity, freshness, or power to refresh ⟨the golden ~ of sleep —Shak.⟩ ⟨a lad in the ~ of his youth⟩ ⟨the ~ of God's grace lay over them⟩ **3** : moisture esp. when appearing in minute droplets: as **a** : TEARS **b** : SWEAT, PERSPIRATION **c** : a distilled liquor; *broadly* : an alcoholic beverage — usu. used with a qualifying term **d** : droplets of water produced by a plant in transpiration

[2]**dew** \"\ *vb* -ED/-ING/-S [ME *dewen,* fr. *dew,* n.] *vt* : to wet with or as if with dew : BEDEW ⟨every sense in slumber ~*ing* —Sir Walter Scott⟩; *esp* : to apply a fine spray of water to (woolen or worsted cloth) ~ *vi, archaic* : to fall or form as dew

[3]**dew** *past of* DAW

de·wa·li *or* **di·wa·li** *or* **di·va·li** \də'wälē, -'vä-\ *n* -S *usu cap* [Hindi *divālī,* fr. Skt *dīpālī, dīpāvalī,* lit., row of lights, fr. *dīpa* light, lamp + *ālī, āvalī* row; akin to Skt *dīdeti* he shines — more at ADEL-] : a Hindu festival of lights held late in October

de·wan \də'wän\ *n* -S [Hindi *dīwān,* fr. Per, account book — more at DIVAN] *India* : a chief officer: as **a** : a minister of finance under the former Muslim rule **b** : the prime minister of an Indian state

de·wa·nee *or* **de·wan·ny** *or* **di·wa·ni** \-nē\ *n, pl* **dewanees** *or* **dewannies** *or* **diwanis** [Hindi *dīwānī,* fr. *dīwān*] : the office or jurisdiction of a dewan; *specif* : the right to collect the revenues of Bengal, Bihar, and Orissa that was acquired by the East India Company in 1765

dew·ar \'d(y)üə(r), -ůə-\ *or* **dewar flask** *or* **dewar vessel** *n* -S *usu cap D* [after Sir James *Dewar* †1923 Scot. chemist and physicist who invented it] : a usu. glass or metal container with at least two walls that has the space between the walls evacuated so as to prevent the transfer of heat, often has a coating (as silvering) on the inside to reduce radiation, and is used esp. for storing liquefied gases (as liquid air) or for investigations at low temperatures — compare VACUUM BOTTLE

Dewar flasks

de·water \(')dē+\ *vt* [*de-* + *water,* n.] : to remove water from (as by draining, pressing, pumping)

de·wax \(')dē¦waks\ *vt* [*de-* + *wax,* n.] : to remove wax from; *specif* : to remove paraffin wax from (oil) usu. by chilling, pressing, or treating with a solvent — **de·wax·able** \-səbəl\ *adj*

dewbeam \'=,=\ *n* : a ray of light reflected from dew

dew-beater \'=,==\ *n, dial Eng* : a large thick-soled shoe

dew·ber·ry \'d(y)ü- — *see* BERRY\ *n* **1** : any of several sweet edible berries related to and resembling blackberries and including several distinct horticultural forms developed in cultivation **2** : a trailing or decumbent bramble of the genus *Rubus* (as the European *R. caesius* or the American *R. hispidus, R. flagellaris,* and *R. trivialis*) that bears dewberries

dew bit *n, dial Eng* : a snack before breakfast

dew bow \-bō\ *n* : a rainbow seen in dewdrops

dew·cap \'=,=\ *n* : a tube extending beyond the objective of a telescope to retard the deposition of dew on the object glass and to prevent entrance of light from the side

dewclaw \'=,=\ *n* : a vestigial digit not reaching to the ground on the foot of a mammal or a claw or hoof terminating such a digit (as on the inner aspect of a dog's foot or the false hoof of a deer, pig, or other hoofed mammal) — **dew·clawed** \-ōd\ *adj*

1 dewclaw

dewcup \'=,=\ *n* : LADY'S-MANTLE

dew-drink *also* **dew-cup** \'=,=\ *n, dial Brit* : an early morning allowance of beer to harvesters taken before they begin work

dewdrop \'=,=\ *n* **1** : a drop of dew **2** : a low unarmed perennial herb (*Dalibarda repens*) of the family Rosaceae having entire leaves, 5-petalled white flowers like those of the strawberry, and fruits of several dry achenes enclosed in the enlarged calyx **3** : a small decorative bit of material suggesting a dewdrop (as a glass bead or button or a drop-shaped rhinestone) **4** : a drinking vessel for small animals that releases water by drops

dewdrop grass *n* : a small creeping perennial herb (*Dichondra repens*) that is related to the morning-glory, is cosmopolitan in warm regions esp. in low moist areas, and has been used in lawns as a substitute for grass

dewed *past of* DEW

dew·er \'d(y)üə(r), -ůə-\ *n* -S : an operator of a textile machine that brushes or sprays water on woolen or worsted cloth during the finishing process

dew·ey·an \'d(y)üēən\ *adj, usu cap* [John *Dewey* †1952 Am. philosopher and educator + E *-an*] : of or relating to John Dewey, his followers, or his philosophy, esp. his pragmatism and instrumentalism

dew·ey classification \'d(y)üē-, -üi-\ *or* **dewey decimal classification** *n, usu cap 1st D* [after Melvil *Dewey* †1931 Am. librarian] : DECIMAL CLASSIFICATION

dew·ey·lite \-,līt\ *n* -S [Chester *Dewey* †1867 Am. clergyman and scientist + E *-lite*] : a mineral $Mg_3Si_2O_5(OH)_4$ occurring as a hydrous amorphous resinous magnesium silicate (hardness 2–3.5, sp. gr. 2.0–2.2)

dewfall \'=,=\ *n* [so called fr. the erroneous belief that dew comes down like rain] **1** : formation of dew; *also* : the time when dew begins to deposit **2** : the amount of moisture deposited during one period of dewfall ⟨a very heavy ~⟩

dewflower \'=,==\ *n* : any of several dayflowers; *esp* : COMMELINA 2

dew·i·ly \'d(y)üəlē, -li\ *adv* [*dewy* + *-ly*] : in a dewy manner ⟨gazed ~ into his eyes⟩

de·windt·ite \də'wint·,īt\ *n* -S [F, fr. Jean *Dewindt,* 20th cent. Belg. geologist + F *-ite*] : a mineral $Pb_3(UO_2)_5(PO_4)_4(OH)_4 \cdot 10H_2O$ consisting of a hydrous basic phosphate of lead and uranium

dew·i·ness \'d(y)üēnəs, -üin-\ *n* -ES [*dewy* + *-ness*] : the quality or state of being dewy

dewing *pres part of* DEW

de·witt \də'wit\ *vt* -ED/-ING/-S *usu cap D & often cap W* [after Jan and Cornelis *De Witt* †1672 Dutch statesmen murdered by a mob] *archaic* : LYNCH

[1]**dew·lap** \'d(y)ü,lap\ *n* -S [ME *dewlappe,* fr. [1]*dew* + *lappe* lap — more at LAP (loose part)] **1 a** : a pendulous fold of skin under the neck of bovine animals **b** : a corresponding fold on various other animals — see DOG illustration, GOOSE illustration **c** : a strip of hide cut to hang free from the neck or brisket of cattle as an identification mark **2** : a flaccid fold of fat or flesh on the human throat **3** : one of the two triangular or squarish areas just above the ligule that form the hinge of the blade joint in the sugarcane leaf

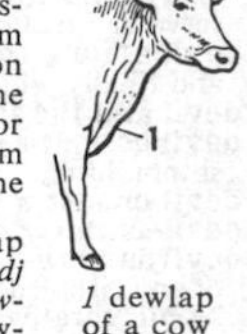

1 dewlap of a cow

[2]**dewlap** \"\ *vt* : to mark (cattle) with a dewlap

dew·lapped \-pt\ *also* **dew·lap·py** \-pē\ *adj* [*dewlapped* fr. ME, fr. *dewlappe* + *-ed; dewlappy* fr. [1]*dewlap* + *-y*] : furnished with a dewlap

dew·less \'d(y)üləs\ *adj* : being without dew

de·wool \(')dē+\ *vt* **dewooled** *or* **dewoolled; dewooled** *or* **dewoolled; dewooling; dewools** [*de-* + *wool,* n.] : to remove the wool from

de·worm \"+\ *vt* [*de-* + *worm,* n.] : to free from worms

dew plant *n* **1** : [1]ICE PLANT **2** : a sundew (*Drosera rotundifolia*) that has rounded leaves and white or rarely pink flowers and is widely distributed in the northern hemisphere

dew point *n* : the temperature at which a vapor begins to condense — used esp. of water vapor in the atmosphere

dew-point hygrometer *n* : a hygrometer for determining the dew point usu. by measuring the temperature of a liquid being cooled in a highly polished silver vessel at the moment when drops of moisture condense on the outer wall of the vessel

dew poison *n, Midland* : a cutaneous rash (as ringworm, athlete's foot, or a rash caused by penetration of hookworms) attributed to the toxic action of dew on the bare skin

dew pond *n* : a shallow artificial pond on the English downs filled and kept up chiefly by the condensation of dew and mist and used to provide water for cattle

dewret *also* **dewrot** \'=,=\ *vt* **dewretted; dewretted; dewretting; dewrets** [*dewret* fr. [1]*dew* + *ret* (to soak); *dewrot* by folk etymology (influence of *rot,* v.) fr. *dewret*] : to ret (flax or hemp) by exposure to rain, dew, and sun

dews *pl of* DEW, *pres 3d sing of* DEW

dew snail *n, dial Eng* : SLUG

dewtry *n* -ES [Marathi *dhutrā,* fr. Skt *dhattūra*] **1** *obs* : JIMSONWEED **2** *obs* : stramonium or an extract of stramonium apparently formerly used as an aphrodisiac

dew web *n, dial* : SPIDER WEB; *usu* : one found outdoors and covered with dew

dew worm *n* : an earthworm suitable for use as bait : NIGHT CRAWLER

dewy \'d(y)üē, -üi\ *adj* -ER/-EST [[1]*dew* + *-y*] **1** : moist with dew : BEDEWED ⟨a ~ lawn⟩ **2** : accompanied or modified by dew ⟨a ~ light⟩ ⟨~ coolness of evening⟩ **3** : resembling or suggestive of dew (as in moistness, freshness, or purity) ⟨~ tears⟩ ⟨~ sleep⟩ ⟨a ~ maiden⟩

dewy-eyed \'==,=\ *adj* : naïvely credulous : exhibiting childlike innocence and trust; *sometimes* : artfully presenting an effect of innocence, trust, and credulity

dex·i·id \'deksēəd\ *adj* [NL *Dexiidae*] : of or relating to the family Dexiidae

dex·i·idae \dek'sīə,dē\ *n pl, cap* [NL, fr. *Dexia,* type genus (perh. fr. Gk *dexia* right hand, fr. fem. of *dexios*) + *-idae*] : a family of muscoid flies that are closely related to the tachina fly and have larvae which are parasitic in insects and other small arthropods

dex·io·trop·ic \¦deksēō¦träpik\ *or* **dex·i·ot·ro·pous** \¦deksē¦ä·trəpəs\ *also* **dex·tro·trop·ic** \¦dekstrō¦träpik\ *or* **dex·trot·ro·pous** \dek'strä·trəpəs\ *adj* [*dexiotropic* fr. *dexio-* (fr. Gk *dexios*) + *-tropic; dexiotropous* fr. *dexio-* + *-tropous; dextrotropic* fr. *dextr-* + *-tropic; dextrotropous* fr. *dextr-* + *-tropous*] : turning to the right : DEXTRAL — used esp. of certain shells, of spiral cleavage patterns, or of the movement of volvox colonies

[1]**dex·ter** \'dekstə(r)\ *adj* [L; akin to OHG *zeso* relating to or situated on the right, Goth *taihswa,* Gk *dexiteros, dexios,* Skt *dakṣiṇa* relating to or situated on the right, L *decēre* to be fitting — more at DECENT] **1** : relating to or situated on the right ⟨the ~ wing of a fowl⟩ **2** : being or relating to the side of a heraldic shield or escutcheon at the right of the person wearing it **3** : appearing or facing toward the right or considered of good omen : AUSPICIOUS, FORTUNATE ⟨on sounding wings a ~ eagle flew —Alexander Pope⟩

[2]**dexter** \"\ *adv* : on the right side

[3]**dexter** \"\ *n* [prob. after Mr. *Dexter,* 19th cent. Irish stockbreeder who originated it] **1** *usu cap* : a breed of small short-legged hardy cattle originating from the Kerry breed of Ireland, being usu. chiefly black or sometimes red, and carrying in heterozygous condition the gene that when homozygous causes the bulldog calf — compare ACHONDROPLASIA **2** -S *often cap* : any animal of the Dexter breed

dexter base point *n* : the lower dexter part of the field of an escutcheon — see POINT illustration

dexter chief point *n* : the upper dexter part of the field of an escutcheon — see POINT illustration

dex·ter·i·ty \dek'sterəd·ē, -ətē, -i\ *n* -ES [MF or L; MF *dexterité,* fr. L *dexteritat-, dexteritas,* fr. *dexter* skillful, relating to or situated on the right + *-itat-, -itas* -ity] **1 :** readiness and grace in physical activity **:** skill and ease in using the hands **:** expertness in manual acts ⟨~ with the chisel⟩ ⟨it seemed impossible that the clarinetists could be doing more than improvisations, playing as they did with such reckless ~ —J.S.Bowman⟩ **2 :** readiness in the use or control of the mental powers **:** quickness and skill in managing any complicated or difficult affair **:** ADROITNESS ⟨~ in argument⟩ **3 :** RIGHT-HANDEDNESS

dex·ter·ous \'dekst(ə)rəs\ *or* **dex·trous** \-trəs\ *adj* [L *dexter* skillful, relating to or situated on the right + E *-ous*] **1 :** DEXTRAL **2 a :** skillful and active with the hands **:** deft and skillful in manipulation ⟨a ~ hand⟩; *broadly* **:** adroit and competent in the use of the limbs and body esp. in the performance of a task ⟨a ~ worker⟩ **b** *of a tool or machine* **:** designed for easy efficient operation; *often* **:** operated with sure expertness **3 a :** mentally adroit and skillful **:** quick at inventing expedients **:** EXPERT, CLEVER ⟨a ~ manager⟩ **b** *obs* **:** FOXY, CRAFTY, UNSCRUPULOUS **4 :** done with dexterity **:** SKILLFUL, ARTFUL ⟨~ management⟩ ⟨~ intrigue⟩ ⟨a ~ résumé of the play⟩

syn ADROIT, DEFT, FEAT, HANDY: these adjectives signify in common having or showing readiness or skill in the use of one's hands, limbs, or body. DEXTEROUS (or DEXTROUS) may imply expertness, cunning, and knowledge, with accompanying facility or agility ⟨one of the most *dexterous* novelists now writing, with an enviable command of styles —Saul Bellow⟩ ⟨by force or by *dexterous* diplomacy —Walter Moberly⟩ ⟨seized one corner of the blanket, and with a *dexterous* twist and throw unrolled it —C.G.D.Roberts⟩ ADROIT stresses artfulness, often a deceptive artfulness, in one's dexterity, and may indicate ability to cope well with likely situations ⟨an exceptionally *adroit* pianist —Douglas Watt⟩ ⟨a visionary and an idealist, he was at the same time the most thoroughly realistic and *adroit* political leader since Lincoln —Allan Nevins & H.S.Commager⟩ DEFT stresses lightness, neatness, and sureness of touch ⟨Angus seemed appallingly at home, and he waltzed off with the prettiest girl, sliding, swinging, *deft* —Sinclair Lewis⟩ ⟨there was a shifting of gears, and with . . . *deft* manipulations he reversed the car in the narrow road —W.H.Wright⟩ ⟨the lore of all men he knew, and was *deft* in every cunning, save the dealings of the sword —William Morris⟩ FEAT, archaic except in dialect, suggests deftness and grace in movement or execution of a task ⟨the *featest* fellow at the dance⟩ HANDY suggests a degree of skill, even though a lack of training, in performance of a wide variety of tasks, generally involving such activities as carpentry, plumbing, or general repairing ⟨to be *handy* around the house when the plumbing goes bad or the roof leaks⟩ ⟨as men become more *handy* at manipulating labels and symbols —Clive Bell⟩ ⟨*handy* at playing bridge, writing a sonnet, or cleaning the cellar⟩

dex·ter·ous·ly *adv* **:** in a dexterous manner **:** with dexterity

dex·ter·ous·ness *n* -ES **:** the quality or state of being dexterous

dextr- *or* **dextro-** *comb form* [LL, fr. L *dextr-, dexter*] **1 a :** right ⟨*dextr*ad⟩ **:** on or toward the right ⟨*dextro*rotatory⟩ **b :** dextral and ⟨*dextro*sinistral⟩ **2** *usu* **dextro-**, *usu ital* **:** dextrorotatory — in names of chemical compounds ⟨*dextrose*⟩ ⟨*dextro*-tartaric acid⟩; symbol (+)- ⟨(+)-tartaric acid⟩; compare D-

dex·trad \'dek,strad\ *adv* [*dextr-* + *-ad*] **:** toward the right side **:** DEXTRALLY

[1]**dex·tral** \'dekstrəl\ *adj* [ML *dextralis* southern, on the right, fr. L *dextr-, dexter* + *-alis* -al] **:** of or relating to the right **:** inclined to the right: as **a :** RIGHT-HANDED **b** *of certain flatfishes* **:** having the right side turned uppermost **c** *of a gastropod shell* **:** having the whorls turning from the left toward the right as viewed with the apex toward the observer or having the aperture open toward the observer to the right of the axis when held with the spire uppermost

[2]**dextral** \"\ *n* -S **:** a person exhibiting dominance of the right hand and eye **:** a typical right-handed individual

dex·tral·i·ty \dek'stralәd·ē\ *n* -ES **1 :** the quality or state of having the right side or certain of its parts (as the hand or eye) different from and usu. more efficient than the left or its corresponding parts; *also* **:** RIGHT-HANDEDNESS **2 :** the condition of being dextral ⟨in some snails ~ appears to be a simple Mendelian dominant⟩

dex·tral·ly \'dekstrəlē, -li\ *adv* **:** toward the right ⟨a ~ coiled shell⟩ ⟨the hands of a watch viewed from in front rotate ~⟩ — compare CLOCKWISE

dextral shell *n* **:** a spiral gastropod shell the whorls of which turn from left to right

dex·tran \'dek,stran, -strən\ *n* -S [ISV *dextr-* + *-an*] **:** any of numerous polysaccharides $(C_6H_{10}O_5)_n$ that yield only glucose on hydrolysis but differ otherwise from starch and glycogen (as in molecular structure): as **a :** any such polysaccharide of very high molecular weight usu. obtained by fermentation of sugar with bacteria of the genus *Leuconostoc* (as *L. mesenteroides*) — called also *native dextran* **b :** any such polysaccharide of reduced molecular weight obtained by controlled acid hydrolysis of native dextran as a white amorphous powder and used esp. in physiological saline as a plasma substitute — called also *clinical dextran*

dex·trin \'dekstrən\ *also* **dex·trine** \-,strēn, -strən\ *n* -S [F *dextrine*, fr. *dextr-* + *-ine* -in, -ine] **:** any of various water-soluble dextrorotatory gummy polysaccharides obtained from starch by the action of heat, acids, or enzymes as a yellow or white powder or granules, capable of yielding maltose or glucose by further hydrolysis, and used as adhesives, as sizes for paper and textiles, as gum substitutes, and in making syrups and beer — called also *British gum*

dex·trin·ate \'dekstrə,nāt\ *vt* -ED/-ING/-S **:** to convert into or impregnate with dextrin ⟨a *dextrinated* mash⟩

dex·trin·i·za·tion \,dekstrənə'zāshən\ *n* -S **:** an act or process of dextrinizing

dex·trin·ize \'dekstrə,nīz\ *vt* -ED/-ING/-S **:** to convert (starch) into dextrins

dex·trino·gen·ic \¦dekstrənō¦jenik\ *adj* [*dextrin* + *-o-* + *-genic*] **:** producing dextrins ⟨~ activity of α-amylase⟩

dextrinogenic enzyme *n* **:** AMYLASE 2a

dex·tro \'dek(,)strō\ *adj* [*dextr-*] **:** DEXTROROTATORY

dex·tro·amphetamine \¦dek(,)strō +\ *n* [*dextr-* + *amphetamine*] **:** the dextrorotatory isomer of amphetamine used in the form of the sulfate or hydrochloride as a central nervous system stimulant

dex·tro·car·dia \,dekstrō'kärdēə\ *n* -S [NL, fr. *dextr-* + *-cardia*] **:** an abnormal condition in which the heart is situated on the right side and the great blood vessels of the right and left sides are reversed — **dex·tro·car·di·al** \¦==¦=dēəl\ *adj*

dex·troc·u·lar \(')dek¦sträkyələ(r)\ *adj* [*dextr-* + *ocular*] **:** using the right eye habitually or more effectively than the left — **dex·troc·u·lar·i·ty** \(,)=,==¦larəd·ē\ *n* -ES

dex·tro·glucose \¦dekstrō +\ *n* [*dextr-* + *glucose*] **:** DEXTROSE

dex·tro·gyrate \" +\ *or* **dex·tro·gyre** \'dekstrō,jī(ə)r\ *also* **dex·tro·gyratory** \¦dekstrō +\ *or* **dex·tro·gy·rous** \¦dekstrō¦jīrəs\ *adj* [*dextrogyrate* fr. *dextr-* + *gyrate*, adj.; *dextrogyre* ISV *dextr-* + *-gyre* (fr. L *gyrus* gyre); *dextrogyratory* fr. *dextr-* + *gyratory*; *dextrogyrous* fr. *dextr-* + *-gyrous* (fr. *gyre* + *-ous*)] **:** DEXTROROTATORY

dex·tro·pimaric acid \¦dekstrō + ...-\ *n* [ISV *dextr-* + *pimaric*] **:** a crystalline resin acid $C_{19}H_{29}COOH$ found esp. in oleoresins from pine trees

dex·tro·position \" +\ *n* -S [NL *dextroposition-, dextropositio*, fr. *dextr-* + L *position-, positio* position] **:** displacement to the right — used chiefly of the aorta

dex·tro·rotation \" +\ *n* [*dextr-* + *rotation*] **:** right-handed or clockwise rotation — used chiefly of the plane of polarization of light; opposed to *levorotation*; compare OPTICAL ROTATION

dex·tro·rotatory *also* **dex·tro·rotary** \" +\ *adj* [*dextr-* + *rotatory* or *rotary*] **:** turning toward the right hand or clockwise; *esp* **:** rotating the plane of polarization of light toward the right hand ⟨~ crystals⟩ ⟨~ sugar solutions⟩ — abbr. *dextro-*, *d-*; opposed to *levorotatory*; compare OPTICALLY ACTIVE

dex·trorse \'dek,strȯrs\ *also* **dex·tror·sal** \(')dek¦strȯrsəl\ *adj* [*dextrorse* fr. NL *dextrorsus*, fr. L *dextrorsum, dextrorsus* toward the right side, fr. *dexter* relating to or situated on the right + *versus*, past part. of *vertere* to turn; *dextrorsal* fr. NL *dextrorsus* + E *-al* — more at DEXTER, WORTH] **1 :** *of a plant or its parts* **:** twining spirally upward around an axis from left to right: **a :** twining clockwise (as in the hop) when the observer's point of view is felt to be within or above the spiral **b :** twining counterclockwise (as in the morning glory) when the observer's point of view is felt to be outside the spiral — compare SINISTRORSE **2 :** DEXTRAL **c** — **dex·trorse·ly** *adv*

dex·trose \'dek,strōs *also* -ōz\ *n* -S [ISV *dextr-* + *-ose*] **:** dextrorotatory glucose obtained usu. by acid hydrolysis of starch as sweet crystals of the anhydrous compound or of the monohydrate $C_6H_{12}O_6.H_2O$ and used chiefly in foods and beverages, in making caramel, and in intravenous feeding — called also *corn sugar, grape sugar*

dex·tro·sinistral \¦dek(,)strō +\ *adj* [*dextr-* + *sinistral*] **1 :** extending from the right toward the left ⟨a ~ line⟩ **2 :** naturally left-handed but trained to use the right hand in writing — **dextrosinistrally** *adv*

dextrotropic *or* **dextrotropous** *var of* DEXIOTROPIC

dextrous *var of* DEXTEROUS

dex·tro·version \¦dekstrō +\ *n* -S [*dextr-* + ML *version-, versio* action of turning — more at VERSION] **:** movement or turning to the right (as of the eyes)

[1]**dey** *or* **deye** \'dī\ *n, pl* **deyes** [ME *deye*, fr. OE *dǣge* kneader of bread — more at DAIRY] *now chiefly Scot* **:** DAIRYMAID

[2]**dey** \'dā\ *n* -S [F, fr. Turk *dayı*, lit., maternal uncle] **:** a ruling official of the Ottoman empire in northern Africa; *esp* **:** a governor of Algiers before the French conquest in 1830

deywoman \'=,==\ *n, pl* **deywomen** [[1]*dey* + *woman*] *now chiefly dial* **:** DAIRYMAID

de·zinc \(')dē +\ *vt* [*de-* + *zinc*, n.] **:** DEZINCIFY

de·zincification \(¦)dē +\ *n* [*de-* + *zinc*, n. + *-i-* + *-fication*] **:** the action or process of dezincifying

de·zincify *also* **de·zinkify** \(')dē +\ *vt* [back-formation fr. *dezincification*] **:** to remove zinc from **:** free from zinc

DF *abbr* **1** damage free **2** dead freight **3** [ML *Defensor Fidei*] Defender of the Faith **4** direction finder; direction finding

DFDT \,dē,ef,dē'tē\ *n* -S [*di*fluoro-*d*iphenyl-*t*richloro-ethane] **:** a white solid compound $(FC_6H_4)_2CHCCl_3$ that is a partial fluorine analogue of DDT and is held to be less toxic to animals and fish than DDT and more toxic to flying insects

d flat \'=¦=\ *n, usu cap D* **1 :** the keynote of D-flat major **2 :** the tone a half step below D

d-flat major \'=,=¦==\ *n, usu cap D* **:** the major musical key having a signature of five flats

DFP \¦dē,ef¦pē\ *abbr or n* -S diisopropyl fluorophosphate

dft *abbr* **1** defendant **2** draft

dftg *abbr* drafting

dg *abbr* decigram

DG *abbr* **1** degaussing **2** [LL *Dei gratia*] by the grace of God **3** [LL *Deo gratias*] thanks to God **4** directional gyro **5** director general

dghai·sa \'dīsə\ *n* -S [Maltese *dgħajsa*] **:** a small boat resembling a gondola that is common in Malta

dgt *abbr* daughter

dhai \'dä,ē, 'dī\ *n* -S [Hindi *dhāī*, fr. (assumed) Skt *dhātṛkā*, fr. *dhayati* he sucks — more at FEMININE] *India* **:** WET NURSE; *also* **:** MIDWIFE

dhaincha *var of* DAINCHA

dhak *also* **dak** \'däk, 'dōk\ *n* -S [Hindi *ḍhāk*] **:** an East Indian tree (*Butea frondosa*) whose flowers yield a yellow dye

dhal \'däl\ *n* -S [Hindi *dāl*] *India & East Indies* **:** PIGEON PEA

dha·man \'dämən\ *n* -S [Hindi *dhāman*, fr. Skt *dharmaṇa*] **:** an Indian tree (*Grewia tiliaefolia*) with reddish brown strong flexible wood used for wheel axles and spokes and for athletic equipment

dhan \'dən\ *n* -S [Hindi, fr. Skt *dhana*, fr. *dadhāti* he puts, places — more at DO] *India* **:** property or wealth; *specif* **:** the village cattle

dha·ra·na \'därənə\ *n* -S [Skt *dhāraṇa*, lit., act of holding, fr. *dhārayati*] *Hinduism, Buddhism, Jainism* **:** fixed attention; *esp* **:** a state of mental concentration on an object without wavering

dha·ra·ni \'därə(,)nē\ *n, pl* **dharanis** *or* **dharani** [Skt *dhāraṇī*, lit., act of holding, remembering, fr. *dhārayati* he holds — more at FIRM] *Hinduism & Mahayana Buddhism* **:** MANTRA

dhar·ma \'dərmə\ *n* -S [Skt, lit., that which is established, fr. *dhārayati* he holds — more at FIRM] **1** *Hinduism* **a** (1) **:** social custom regarded as one's duty ⟨some ~ such as not eating beef and respecting Brahmans is common to all Hindus —Talcott Parsons⟩ (2) **:** caste custom; *esp* **:** the religious custom of the castes having a sacrament of spiritual regeneration **b :** civil and criminal law **c :** the body of cosmic principles by which all things exist **:** NATURE: (1) **:** essential function ⟨it is the ~ . . . of a stone to be hard, of fire to burn, of a tiger to be fierce, just as it is the ~ of a king to punish and to protect, of a Brahman to study and pray —Seymour Vesey-Fitzgerald⟩ (2) **:** NATURAL LAW (3) **:** MORAL LAW, JUSTICE ⟨the ruler so inaugurated was regarded not as a temporal autocrat but as the instrument of ~ —D.M.Brown⟩ **d :** conduct appropriate to one's essential nature, establishing the morally sound life that is one of man's four ends **:** RIGHTEOUSNESS, RELIGION — opposed to *adharma* **2** *Buddhism* **a :** ideal truth esp. as taught by Buddha **b** *Hinayana* **:** an element of existence **:** one of the minute brief appearances of which any experienced object is made up **3** *Jainism* **:** the uncreated and eternal substance that is the necessary condition of movement for souls and matter **:** the ontological principle of movement ⟨~ is compared to water, through which and by which fish are able to move —Heinrich Zimmer⟩ — compare ADHARMA

dhar·ma·ka·ya \,dərmə'kāyə\ *n* -S [Skt *dharmakāya*, fr. *dharma* + *kāya* body; akin to Skt *cinoti* he gathers, heaps up — more at POET] **:** the ideal body or the essence of the Absolute in the Buddhist doctrine of trikaya

dhar·ma·shas·tra \-'shästrə\ *or* **dhar·ma·sas·tra** \-'sästrə\ *n* -S [Skt *dharmaśāstra*, fr. *dharma* + *śāstra* shastra — more at SHASTRA] **:** a Brahmanical collection of rules of life often in the form of a metrical law book

dhar·ma·su·tra \-'sü·trə\ *n* -S [Skt *dharmasūtra*, fr. *dharma* + *sūtra* sutra — more at SUTRA] **:** any of the early lawbooks of Brahmanism

dharm·sa·la \(,)dərm'sä(,)lä\ *or* **dharm·sha·la** \-'shä-\ *n* -S [Hindi *dharmsālā*, fr. Skt *dharmaśālā*, fr. *dharma* + *śālā* hall, house — more at HALL] *India* **:** a building devoted to a religious or charitable purpose; *esp* **:** a shelter for travelers

dhar·na *also* **dhur·na** \'dərnə\ *n* -S [Hindi *dharnā*] *India* **:** a method of appealing for justice by fasting even to the point of death while seated at the door of the offender

dhau·ra \'dȯrə\ *n* -S [Marathi *dhāvḍā* dhauri] **:** DHAWA

dhau·ri \'dȯrē\ *n* -S [Hindi *dhāṛī*] **1 :** DHAWA **2 :** an East Indian red-flowered shrub (*Woodfordia floribunda*) of the family Lythraceae that yields a gum resembling tragacanth

dha·wa *or* **dha·va** \'dävə\ *n* -S [Hindi *dhāvā*, fr. Skt *dhava*] **:** an East Indian tree (*Anogeissus latifolia*) of the family Combretaceae that is used for timber and tanning and is a source of a gum

dhe·gi·ha \'dāgē,hä\ *n, pl* **dhegiha** *or* **dhegihas** *usu cap* **1 :** a Siouan language of the Omaha, Ponca, Osage, Kansa, and Quapaw peoples **2 a :** the peoples speaking Dhegiha **b :** a member of any of such peoples

dhikr \'dikər\ *n, pl* **dhikrs** *or* **dhikr** [Ar, mention, recitation, remembrance] **1 :** the ritual formula of a Sufi brotherhood recited devotionally in praise of Allah and as a means of attaining ecstatic experience **2 :** the recitation of the dhikr; *also* **:** the period of such recitation

dhim·mi \'dimē\ *n, pl* **dhimmis** *or* **dhimmi** [Ar *dhimmīy*] **:** a person living in a region overrun by Muslim conquest who was accorded a protected status and allowed to retain his original faith

dho·bi *also* **dho·bie** \'dōbē\ *n* -S [Hindi *dhobī*; akin to Skt *dhāvaka* chobi, *dhāvati* he washes, *dhavala* white, Gk *thoos* bright, shining] **:** a member of a low caste of India employed as washermen **:** WASHERMAN

dhobie itch *n* [so called fr. the belief that the disease is transmitted by newly washed clothes] **:** ringworm attacking moist parts of the body (as the groin)

dhole \'dōl\ *n, pl* **dholes** *also* **dhole** [perh. fr. Kanarese *tōḷa* wolf] **:** a fierce wild dog (*Cuon dukhunensis*) of India that hunts in packs and may attack even large and fierce animals (as the tiger)

dholl \'däl\ *var of* DHAL

dho·luo \'dō'lü(,)ō\ *n, usu cap* **:** LUO 2

dho·ni *also* **do·ni** \'dōnē\ *n* -S [Hindi *ḍonī*, Marathi *ḍoṇī*, Kanarese *dōṇi*, *ḍōṇi*, & Telugu *dōne*, fr. Skt *droṇī* trough, tub, fr. *dru* wood, tree — more at TREE] **:** a fishing or coastwise trading boat of India

dhoo·ly \'dülē\ *var of* DOOLY

dhoon \'dün\ *n* -S [Hindi *dūn*] *India* **:** VALLEY; *esp* **:** a valley in the Siwalik hills

d-horizon \'dē=¦==\ *n, usu cap D* **:** a soil layer that sometimes occurs beneath the B-horizon or the C-horizon if present, that has not been subjected to weathering, and that may consist of the unmodified mineral matter from which the more superficial layers developed or of a different complex of mineral matter

dho·ti \'dōtē\ *or* **dhoo·tie** *or* **dhu·ti** \'dütē\ *n* -S [Hindi *dhotī*] **1 :** a long loincloth worn by Hindu men **2 :** a fabric used for dhotis

dhow *also* **dow** \'daů\ *n* -S [Ar *dāwa, dau*, prob. of Indic origin; akin to Marathi *dāw* dhow] **:** an Arab lateen-rigged boat of the Indian ocean usu. having a long overhang forward, a high poop, and an open waist

dhu'l-hij·ja \dül'hi(,)jä\ *n, usu cap D&H* [Ar *dhū-l-ḥijjah*, lit., the one of the pilgrimage] **:** the 12th month of the Muhammadan year — see MONTH table

dhu'l-qa'·dah \-'kä-(,)dä\ *n, usu cap 1st D&Q* [Ar *dhū-l-qa'dah*, lit., the one of the sitting] **:** the 11th month of the Muhammadan year — see MONTH table

dhow

dhurra *var of* DURRA

dhur·rie \'dərē\ *n* -S [Hindi *darī*] **:** a thick cotton cloth or carpet made in India

dhur·rin *also* **dur·rin** \'dürən\ *n* -S [*dhurra* + *-in*] **:** a crystalline cyanogenetic glucoside $C_{14}H_{17}NO_7$ found in durra at a certain stage in its growth

dhya·na \dē'änə, 'dyä-\ *n* -S [Skt *dhyāna*, fr. *dhyāti* he thinks — more at SEMANTICS] *1 Hinduism, Buddhism, Jainism* **:** MEDITATION; ESP **:** an uninterrupted state of mental concentration upon a single object **:** higher contemplation **2** *usu cap* **:** a Mahayana school of Buddhism relying on meditation as a method of enlightenment — compare CH'AN

di- *comb form* [ME, fr. MF, fr. L, fr. Gk; akin to OE *twi-* — more at TWI-] **1 :** twice **:** twofold **:** double ⟨*di*chromatic⟩ **2 :** containing two atoms, radicals, or groups (of a specified kind) ⟨*di*chloride⟩ **3 :** being a Greek coin or unit of value worth two specified units ⟨*di*stater⟩ ⟨*di*drachma⟩

DI *abbr* drill instructor

Di *symbol* didymium

dia- *also* **di-** *prefix* [ME, fr. OF, fr. L, fr. Gk, *dia*; akin to L *dis-* — more at DIS-] **1 :** through **:** during ⟨*dia*chronic⟩ **:** across ⟨*dia*ctinic⟩ **2 :** made of **:** consisting of — in names of compounded medicines ⟨*dia*codion⟩

dia *abbr* diameter

di·a·ban·tite \,dīə'ban,tīt\ *n* -S [modif. (influenced by *-ite*) of G *diabantachronnyn*, irreg. fr. G *diabase* + Gk *chrōnnyein* to stain] **:** a mineral approximately $(Mg,Fe,Al)_3(SiAl)_2O_5(OH)_4$ consisting of a basic silicate of magnesium, iron, and aluminum

di·a·base \'dīə,bās\ *n* [F, fr. Gk *diabasis* act of crossing over, fr. *diabainein* to cross over, fr. *dia-* + *bainein* to go — more at COME] **1** *archaic* **:** DIORITE **2** *chiefly Brit* **:** an altered basalt **3 :** a hypabyssal rock of the composition of gabbro but with an ophitic texture consisting of labradorite laths involved in a matrix of augite with magnetite a common accessory

di·a·bas·ic \¦dīə¦bāsik\ *adj* **:** consisting of or resembling diabase **:** OPHITIC

di·a·bat·ic \¦dīə¦bad·ik\ *adj* [Gk *diabatos* passable (fr. *diabainein* to cross over) + E *-ic*] *physics* **:** involving the transfer of heat ⟨~ flow of air⟩ — opposed to *adiabatic*

di·a·be·tes \,dīə'bēd·|ēz, -ēt|, |,əs, |,is *sometimes* -bēd·,ēz *or* -bē,tēz\ *n, pl* **diabetes** [L, fr. Gk *diabētēs* compass, siphon, diabetes, fr. *diabainein* to walk or stand with legs wide apart, to cross over] **:** any of certain abnormal conditions characterized by the secretion and excretion of excessive amounts of urine ⟨bronze ~⟩; *esp* **:** DIABETES MELLITUS — see DIABETES INSIPIDUS

diabetes in·sip·i·dus \-in'sipədəs\ *n* [NL, lit., insipid diabetes] **:** a disorder of the pituitary gland characterized by intense thirst and the excretion of great amounts of dilute urine

diabetes mel·li·tus \-'melәd·әs, -'melətəs\ *n* [NL, lit., honey-sweet diabetes] **:** a familial constitutional disorder of carbohydrate metabolism involving inadequate secretion or utilization of insulin, characterized by hyperglycemia, glycosuria, polyuria, and marked by thirst, hunger, itching, weakness, loss of weight, and when severe acidosis and coma

[1]**di·a·bet·ic** \¦dīə¦bed·|ik, |t|, |ēk *sometimes* -bē|\ *adj* [prob. fr. F *diabétique*, fr. *diabète* diabetes (fr. L *diabetes*) + *-ique* -ic] **:** of, relating to, or concerning diabetes or diabetics: as **a :** afflicted with diabetes **b :** indicating, occurring in, caused by, or resulting from diabetes ⟨~ gangrene⟩ ⟨~ sugar⟩ ⟨~ coma⟩ **c :** suitable for diabetics ⟨~ food⟩

[2]**diabetic** \"\ *n* -S **:** a person having diabetes

di·a·be·to·gen·ic \,dīə¦bēd·ə¦jenik, -ētə-\ *adj* [*diabetes* + *-o* + *-genic*] **:** producing diabetes

dia·ble·rie \dē'äblə(,)rē, -'ab-, =¦==', ='==_ri\ *n* -S [F, fr. OF *diablerie, deablerie*, fr. *diable, deable* devil (fr. LL *diabolus*) + *-erie* -ery — more at DEVIL] **1 a :** actions or behavior of devils ⟨~ of a satyr⟩ **:** dealings with the devil or devils **:** black magic **:** WITCHCRAFT, SORCERY, DEVILRY ⟨practicing witchcraft and ~⟩ **b :** a quality or air of black magic or of dealings with the devil ⟨~ of gothic romance⟩ **2 a :** an infernal scene esp. as represented in words or painting **:** representation of devils ⟨a collection of ~*s*⟩ **b :** demon lore ⟨stories of ~⟩ **3 a :** mischievous conduct or manner **:** lighthearted and ingenious mischievousness **:** ⟨full of wit and ~⟩ **b :** WICKEDNESS ⟨house-burnings, assassinations, and other pieces of ~⟩

dia·blo \'dyäblō, 'thy-\ *n* -S [Sp, fr. LL *diabolus*] **:** DEVIL

dia·blo·tin \dē¦äblō¦taⁿ\ *n* -S [F, lit., imp, dim. of *diable*] **1** *West Indies* **:** BLACK-CAPPED PETREL **2 :** any of various dainties (as croutons, frozen custards, chocolate bonbons in paper) — usu. used in pl.

diabol- *or* **diabolo-** *comb form* [ME *deabol-*, fr. MF *diabol-*, fr. LL, fr. Gk, fr. *diabolos* — more at DEVIL] **:** devil ⟨*diabol*ism⟩ ⟨*diabolo*cracy⟩

dia·boleite \¦dīə+\ *n* [*dia-* + *boleite*] **:** a mineral $Pb_2CuCl_2(OH)_4$ consisting of a basic chloride of lead and copper

di·a·bol·ic \¦dīə¦bälik, -lēk\ *or* **di·a·bol·i·cal** \-lәkəl, -lēk-\ *adj* [*diabolic* fr. ME *deabolik*, fr. MF *diabolique*, fr. LL *diabolicus*, fr. *diabolus* devil + L *-icus* -ic; *diabolical* fr. MF *diabolique* + E *-al* — more at DEVIL] **1 :** of or relating to the devil or devils ⟨Lucifer is . . . forced to reassume his ~ shape —*Modern Language Rev.*⟩ ⟨~ lore⟩ **:** derived from the devil ⟨~ arts⟩ ⟨difference between the angelic and the ~ temperament —G.B.Shaw⟩ **:** being under the influence of devils ⟨*diabolical* sorcerers —Herman Melville⟩ **:** resembling a devil ⟨a ~ figure⟩ **:** being a devil ⟨a ~ visitor⟩ **:** suggestive of devils or hell ⟨fires lit up a truly ~ scene⟩ **2 :** resembling that of devils **:** befitting or characteristic of a devil typically in having or showing cunning, ingenuity, cruelty, or wickedness **:** DEVILISH, FIENDISH ⟨the cold calculation and the ~ art of these statesmen⟩ ⟨his expression changing to something *diabolical* —Rudyard Kipling⟩ — **di·a·bol·i·cal·ly** \-lәk(ə)lē, -lēk-, -li\ *adv* — **di·a·bol·i·cal·ness** *n* -ES

di·ab·o·lism \dī'abə,lizəm\ *n* -S [*diabol-* + *-ism*] **1 a :** dealings with the devil **:** demonic possession **:** SORCERY ⟨conducting experiments in ~⟩ **b :** action or practice instigated or aided by the devil ⟨~ was rampant in the universe —Carl Van Doren⟩ **c :** evil conduct or intent **:** EVIL ⟨deeds of black misunderstanding rather than ~ —*Newsweek*⟩ **2 :** belief in or doctrine concerning devils; *esp* **:** a religious doctrine or a perversion of religious doctrine involving the worship of devils

di·ab·o·list \-ləst\ *n* -s [*diabol-* + *-ist*] **:** one who teaches or practices diabolism **:** one who worships the devil
di·ab·o·lize \-,līz\ *vt* -ED/-ING/-s [*diabol-* + *-ize*] **1 :** to make diabolical **:** subject to diabolical influence ⟨his associations degrade and ~ him⟩ **2 :** to represent as diabolical ⟨newspapers *diabolized* the enemy soldiers⟩
di·ab·o·lo \dī'abə,lō, dē'-\ *n* -s [fr. *Diabolo*, a trademark] **:** a game in which an hourglass-shaped top is balanced and spun on a string stretched between the tips of two sticks; *also* **:** the top used in this game
di·a·bol·o·gy \,dīə'bäləjē\ *or* **di·a·bo·lol·o·gy** \,dīəbə'läl-, (,)dī,abə'läl-\ *n* -ES [*diabology* blend of *diabol-* and *-logy*; *diabolology* fr. *diabol-* + *-logy*] **1 :** the study of the devil or of belief in devils **2 :** the theory or doctrine of devils **:** devil lore
¹di·a·bo·lo·nian \,dīəbə'lōnyən, (,)dī,abə-\ *n* -s [*diabol-* + *-onian* (as in *Babylonian*)] **:** a follower of the devil
²di·a·bo·lo·nian \¦dīəbə¦l-, (¦)dī¦abə-\ *adj* **:** DEVILISH, DIABOLIC
di·a·brot·i·ca \,dīə'bräd·əkə\ *n, cap* [NL, fr. Gk *diabrōtikē*, fem. of *diabrōtikos* corrosive, fr. (assumed) *diabrōtos* (verbal of *diabibrōskein* to consume, corrode, fr. *dia-* + *bibrōskein* to devour) + *-ikos* -ic — more at VORACIOUS] **:** a genus of small destructive leaf-eating beetles (family Galerucidae) that are usu. greenish yellow with spots or stripes — compare CUCUMBER BEETLE
¹dia·caus·tic \¦dīə¦kȯstik\ *adj* [prob. fr. F *diacaustique*, fr. *dia-* + *caustique* caustic, fr. L *causticus* — more at CAUSTIC] **:** relating to a caustic curve or caustic surface formed by refraction — compare CATACAUSTIC
²diacaustic \"\ *n* -s **:** a diacaustic curve or surface
di·acetate \(')dī+\ *n* [*di-* + *acetate*] **1 :** a salt, ester, or acylal containing two acetate groups ⟨ethylene ~⟩ **2 :** ACETOACETATE
di·acetic acid \¦dī+-\ *n* [*di-* + *acetic*] **:** ACETOACETIC ACID
di·acetin \(')dī+\ *n* [ISV *di-* + *acetin*] **:** ACETIN b
diacetone alcohol *also* **di·acetone** \"+\ *n* [*di-* + *acetone*] **:** a liquid keto alcohol $CH_3COCH_2C(OH)(CH_3)_2$ made usu. by alkaline condensation of acetone and used chiefly as a solvent (as in lacquer formulations) and in hydraulic brake fluids
¹di·acetyl \(¦)dī+\ *adj* [ISV *di-* + *acetyl*] **:** containing two acetyl groups
²di·acetyl \"+\ *n* -s **:** BIACETYL
diacetylmorphine *pronunc for* DIACETYL +\ *n* [ISV *diacetyl* + *morphine*] **:** HEROIN
dia·chronic \¦dīə¦kränik\ *or* **dia·chro·nis·tic** \¦dīəkrə¦nistik, -(,)krä¦n-; (¦)dī¦akrə¦n-\ *or* **di·ach·ro·nous** \(')dī'akrənəs\ *adj* [*diachronic*, ISV *dia-* + *chronic*; orig. formed as F *diachronique*; *diachronistic* fr. *dia-* + *-chronistic* (as in *synchronistic*); *diachronous* fr. *dia-* + *-chronous*] **:** considering or embracing phenomena (as the sounds of a language) as they occur, change, or develop over a period of time — contrasted with *synchronic* ⟨~ descriptions of a language are properly built up by a comparison of synchronic descriptions of the same language at different historical periods —D.W. Reed⟩ — **dia·chron·i·cal·ly** \¦dīə¦kränək(ə)lē\ *adv* — **di·ach·ro·nous·ly** \(')dī¦akrənəslē\ *adv*
di·ach·ro·ny \dī'akrənē\ *n* -ES [ISV *dia-* + *-chrony* (as in *synchrony*); prob. orig. formed as F *diachronie*] **1 :** diachronic analysis or point of view **:** diachronic arrangement or treatment — contrasted with *synchrony* **2 :** change extending through time
di·ach·y·lon \dī'akə,län, -ələn\ *also* **di·ach·y·lum** \-ələm\ *n, pl* **diachylons** *also* **diachy·la** \-ələ\ [*diachylon* fr. ME *diaquilon*, fr. ML, fr. LL *diachylon*, a kind of medicine, fr. Gk, neut. of *diachylos* juicy, fr. *dia-* + *chylos* juice; *diachylum*, NL, alter. of ML *diaquilon* — more at CHYLE] **:** a plaster that is made of litharge and either olive oil or olive oil and lard and hence consists essentially of lead oleate and small amounts of glycerin and oleic acid and that is used for excoriated surfaces and wounds and as an adhesive
¹di·acid \(')dī+\ *or* **di·acid·ic** \¦dīə¦sidik\ *adj* [¹*di-* + *acid* (adj.)] **1 :** able to react with two molecules of a monobasic acid or one of a dibasic acid to form a salt or ester — used esp. of bases **2 :** containing two hydrogen atoms replaceable by basic atoms or radicals — used esp. of acid salts
²di·acid \(')dī+\ *n* [ISV *di-* + *acid* (n.)] **:** an acid (as sulfuric acid or oxalic acid) having two acid hydrogen atoms
di·a·clase \'dīə,klās, -āz\ *n* -s [ISV *dia-* + *-clase* (fr. Gk *klasis* breaking); orig. formed in F — more at -CLASIA] *geol* **:** JOINT, FRACTURE — **di·a·clas·tic** \¦dīə¦klastik\ *adj*
di·a·cle \'dī(ə)kəl\ *n* -s [ME (Sc dial.), prob. alter. (influenced by *-cle*, as in *receptacle*) of *dyal* dial — more at DIAL] *chiefly Scot* **:** a pocket compass
dia·cli·nal \¦dīə¦klīn°l\ *adj* [*dia-* + *-clinal*] *geol* **:** crossing a fold ⟨a ~ river⟩
di·a·co·di·um \,dīə'kōdēəm\ *n* -s [NL, fr. L *diacodion*, fr. Gk *dia kōdeiōn* out of poppyheads, fr. *dia* through, out of + *kōdeiōn*, gen. pl. of *kōdeia* poppyhead — more at DIA-, CODEINE] **:** a syrup of poppies formerly used as a narcotic
di·a·coele \'dīə,sēl\ *n* -s [*dia-* + *-coele*] **:** the third ventricle of the brain
di·ac·o·nal \(')dī¦akən°l\ *also* dē'a-\ *adj* [LL *diaconalis*, fr. *diaconus* deacon + L *-alis* -al — more at DEACON] **:** of or relating to a deacon ⟨an astute showman lurks behind that ~ exterior —G.P.Meyer⟩
di·ac·o·nate \dī'akənət, dē'-, -,nāt\ *n* -s [LL *diaconatus*, fr. *diaconus* deacon + L *-atus* -ate] **:** the office or period of office of a deacon **:** DEACONSHIP; *also* **:** a body or board of deacons
di·a·con·i·con \,dīə'känə,kän, -əkən\ *also* **di·a·con·i·cum** \-əkəm\ *n, pl* **diaconi·ca** \-əkə\ [LL & LGk; LL *diaconicum*, fr. LGk *diakonikon*, fr. neut. of *diakonikos* of a deacon, fr. Gk, serviceable, fr. *diakonos* deacon, servant + *-ikos* -ic — more at DEACON] *Eastern Church* **:** the sacristy at the right or north side of the bema opposite to the prothesis
di·a·cran·te·ri·an \,dīə,kran¦tirēən\ *also* **di·a·cran·ter·ic** \-¦terik\ *adj* [*dia-* + Gk *krantēres* wisdom teeth + E *-ian* or *-ic*] **:** having the back teeth separated by an interval from the front ones ⟨the hognose snake is ~⟩ — opposed to *syncranterian*
¹di·a·crit·ic \¦dīə¦krid·|ik, -it|, |ēk\ *or* **di·a·crit·i·cal** \|əkəl, |ēk-\ *adj* [*diacritic* fr. Gk *diakritikos* separative, able to distinguish, fr. *diakritos* separated (verbal of *diakrinein* to separate, distinguish, fr. *dia-* + *krinein* to separate) + *-ikos* -ic; *diacritical* fr. Gk *diakritikos* + E *-al* — more at CERTAIN] **1 :** serving as a diacritic **2 a :** serving to separate or distinguish **:** DISTINCTIVE ⟨the ~ elements in culture —S.F.Nadel⟩ **b :** capable of distinguishing or discerning ⟨students of superior ~ powers⟩
²diacritic \"\ *n* -s **:** a modifying mark or sign over, under, after, or through an orthographic or phonetic character or combination of characters indicating a phonetic or semantic value different from that given the unmarked or otherwise marked character — compare ACCENT 5a
di·acromyodi \(¦)dī+\ *n pl, cap* [NL, fr. *di-* + *Acromyodi*] *in some classifications* **:** a group of passerine birds having the intrinsic syringeal muscles attached to both ends of the bronchial half rings — **di·acromyodian** \"+\ *adj* — **di·acromyodous** \"+\ *adj*
di·ac·ti·nal \(')dī¦aktənəl, ¦dī,ak¦tīn°l\ *also* **di·ac·tine** \(')dī¦ak,tīn, -,tən\ *adj* [*di-* + *-actinal*, *-actine*] *zool* **:** having two rays **:** pointed at both ends
di·ac·tine \(')dī'ak,tīn, -,tən\ *or* **di·act** \'dī,akt\ *also* **di·ac·tin** \(')dī'aktən\ *n* -s [*di-* + Gk *aktin-, aktis* ray — more at ACTIN-] **:** a sponge spicule having two pointed arms
di·ac·tin·ic \,dī,ak¦tinik, -ī¦k-\ *adj* [*dia-* + Gk *aktin-, aktis* + E *-ic*] **:** capable of transmitting actinic rays
di·ac·tin·ism \(')dī'aktə,nizəm\ *n* -s **:** the property of transmitting actinic rays
¹di·ad \'dī,ad, -īəd\ *var of* DYAD
²diad *also* **dy·ad** \"\ *adj* [¹*diad*] *crystallog* **:** having symmetry that results in repetition after every 180° rotation ⟨a ~ axis⟩
di·a·dac·tic \¦dīə¦daktik\ *adj* [¹*diad* + *-actic* (as in *syntactic*)] *geol* **:** having reference to a bedding sequence in sediments or sedimentary rocks that is characterized by the repetition of a pair of unlike laminae ⟨the ~ structure of varved clay⟩
di·a·del·phous \¦dīə¦delfəs\ *adj* [*di-* + *-adelphous*] *of stamens* **:** united by the filaments into two fascicles (as in Dutchman's-breeches and most legumes) — compare MONADELPHOUS, POLYADELPHOUS

¹di·a·dem \'dīə,dem, -ədəm\ *n* -s [ME *diademe*, fr. OF, fr. L *diadema*, fr. Gk *diadēma*, fr. *diadein* to bind on both sides, bind around, fr. *dia* through, across + *dein* to bind; akin to Alb *dua* sheaf, Skt *dāman* rope — more at DIA-] **1 :** CROWN; *specif* **:** an ornamental headband worn (as by Eastern monarchs) as a badge of royalty ⟨the regal ~ —John Milton⟩ **2 :** an emblem of regal power or dignity **:** SOVEREIGNTY, EMPIRE
²diadem \"\ *vt* -ED/-ING/-s **:** to adorn with a diadem **:** CROWN

diadem 1

di·a·de·ma \,dīə'dēmə\ [NL, fr. L, diadem] *syn of* CENTRECHINUS
di·a·de·ma·toi·da \,dīə,dēmə'tȯidə\ [NL, *Diademat-, Diadema* + *-oida*] *syn of* CENTRECHINOIDA
diadem monkey *n* **:** PLUTO MONKEY
diadem spider *n* [so called fr. its crown-shaped markings] **:** a European garden spider (*Aranea diadema*)
dia·derm \'dīə,dərm\ *n* -s [*dia-* + *-derm*] **:** a blastoderm in the stage in which only ectoderm and endoderm are present
dia·dermal \¦dīə+\ *or* **dia·dermatic** \"+\ *or* **dia·dermic** \"+\ *adj* [*dia-* + *dermal* or *dermatic* or *dermic*] **:** acting through the skin ⟨~ allergy⟩ ⟨a ~ ointment⟩
diadic *var of* DYADIC
di·ad·o·chite \dī'adə,kīt\ *n* -s [G *diadochit*, fr. Gk *diadochos* succeeding, relieving (fr. *diadechesthai* to succeed, relieve, fr. *dia-* + *dechesthai* to take, receive) + G *-it* -ite; akin to L *decēre* to be fitting, proper — more at DECENT] **:** a mineral $Fe_2(PO_4)(SO_4)(OH).5H_2O$ consisting of a basic hydrous ferric phosphate and sulfate that is brown or yellowish in color
di·ad·o·cho·kinesia \dī¦adə,kō, ¦dīə¦dōkō+\ *or* **di·ad·o·ko·kinesia** \"+\ *n* -s [*diadochokinesia* fr. NL, fr. Gk *diadochos* + NL *-kinesia*; *diadokokinesia* fr. NL, alter. of *diadochokinesia*] **:** the normal power of alternating diametrically opposite muscular actions (as flexion and extension of a limb) — **di·ad·o·cho·kinetic** \"+\ *adj*
di·ad·o·cho·kinesis \"+\ *n* [NL, fr. Gk *diadochos* + NL *-kinesis*] **:** DIADOCHOKINESIA
di·ad·ro·mous \(')dī¦adrəməs\ *adj* [*dia-* + *-dromous*] **1 :** migratory between salt and fresh waters — used of a fish; compare ANADROMOUS, CATADROMOUS **2 :** having venation that radiates like the spokes of a fan ⟨the ~ leaf of a gingko⟩
di·aene \'dī,ēn\ *n* -s [*di-* + *triaene*] **:** a triaene with one ray reduced or absent
di·aer·e·sis \dī'erəsəs, *esp Brit* -'i(ə)r-\ *also* **di·er·e·sis** \-'er-\ *n, pl* **diaere·ses** *also* **diere·ses** \-ə,sēz\ [LL *diaeresis*, fr. Gk *diairesis*, fr. *diairein* to divide (fr. *dia-* + *hairein* to take) + *-sis* — more at HERESY] **1 :** the resolution of one syllable into two esp. by separating the vowel elements of a diphthong or by resolving a *w* or *y* sound into a vowel — opposed to *syneresis* **2 :** the mark ¨ placed over a vowel (as over the second of two adjacent vowels) to indicate that the vowel is pronounced in a separate syllable (as in *naïve*, *Boëthius*, *Brontë*) — compare UMLAUT **3** *prosody* **:** the break caused by the coincidence of the end of a foot with the end of a word — distinguished from *caesura* **4 :** DIVISION 15
di·ae·ret·ic *also* **di·eret·ic** \¦dīə¦red·ik\ *adj* [Gk *diairetikos*, fr. *diairetos* divided (verbal of *diairein* to divide) + *-ikos* -ic] **:** of or relating to diaeresis or division
diag *abbr* **1** diagonal **2** diagram
di·a·gen·e·sis \,dīə'jenəsəs\ *n, pl* **diagene·ses** \-ə,sēz\ [NL, fr. *dia-* + L *genesis*] **1** *mineralogy* **:** recombination or rearrangement resulting in a new product (as in the formation of larger crystalline grains from smaller ones) **2 :** the reconstructive process by which changes are produced in sedimentary rocks during or immediately after their deposition and which is caused by such forces as the weight of overlying strata or hot waters
di·a·ge·net·ic \¦dīəjə¦ned·ik\ *adj* [*dia-* + *-genetic*] **:** caused by or relating to diagenesis ⟨~ changes that are taking place in these sediments —V.T.Allen⟩
dia·geotropic \¦dīə+\ *adj* [*dia-* + *geotropic*] **:** characterized by diageotropism
dia·geotropism *or* **dia·geotropy** \"+\ *n, pl* **diageotropisms** *or* **diageotropies** [*dia-* + *geotropism* or *geotropy*] **:** the tropistic tendency of growing organs (as branches, rhizomes, or roots) to assume a position with its axis at right angles with the line of gravity
di·a·glyph \'dīə,glif\ *n* -s [Gk *diaglyphos* hollowed out, fr. *diaglyphein* to scoop out, fr. *dia-* + *glyphein* to carve — more at CLEAVE] **:** INTAGLIO
di·a·glyph·ic \¦dīə¦glifik\ *also* **di·a·glyp·tic** \-¦gliptik\ *adj* [Gk *diaglyphos* & *diaglyptos* hollowed out + E *-ic*] **:** of or relating to sculpture or engraving formed by depressions in the general surface — opposed to *anaglyphic*
di·ag·nos·able *or* **di·ag·nose·able** \'dīəg,nōsəbəl, -ïēg- *also* -ōzə- *or* ,==¦===\ *adj* **:** capable of being diagnosed
di·ag·nose \'dīəg,nōs, -ïēg- *also* -ōz *or* ,==¦=\ *vb* -ED/-ING/-s [back-formation fr. *diagnosis*] *vt* **1 :** to identify (as a disease or condition) by symptoms or distinguishing characteristics **2 :** to determine the causes of or the nature of by diagnosis ⟨the teacher *diagnosed* and corrected the boy's reading difficulties⟩ ⟨roots of the change may not easily be *diagnosed* —Max De Schauensee⟩ ⟨an attempt to explain or ~ . . . the concrete historical situation of literary criticism at the present time —F.A. Pottle⟩ ~ *vi* **:** to make a diagnosis
di·ag·no·sis \,==¦nōsəs\ *n, pl* **diagno·ses** \-ō,sēz\ [NL, fr. Gk *diagnōsis*, fr. *diagignōskein* to distinguish, fr. *dia-* + *gignōskein* to know — more at KNOW] **1 :** the art or act of identifying a disease from its signs and symptoms; *also* **:** the decision reached ⟨a ~ of pneumonia⟩ — see DIFFERENTIAL DIAGNOSIS **2 :** a concise technical description of a taxonomic entity giving its distinguishing characters **3 :** investigation or analysis of the cause or nature of a condition, situation, or problem ⟨heat-flow measurements in the earth can aid in our ~ of the earth's condition —A.E.Benfield⟩ **:** a statement or conclusion about the nature or cause of a phenomenon ⟨Arnold's ~ of the national characteristics —Herbert Read⟩
¹di·ag·nos·tic \¦==¦nästik, -tēk\ *adj* [Gk *diagnōstikos*, fr. *diagnōstos* to be distinguished (fr. *diagignōskein* to distinguish) + *-ikos* -ic] **1 :** adapted to or used for the furthering of diagnosis **:** employing or marked by the methods of diagnosis **:** concerned with diagnosis ⟨~ reading tests⟩ ⟨a ~ clinic⟩ ⟨~ social work⟩ ⟨~ information⟩ **2 :** serving to distinguish, identify, or determine **:** DISTINCTIVE: as **a :** characteristic of or indicating the presence of a particular disease ⟨a ~ sign of yellow fever —*Amer. Guide Series: La.*⟩ **b :** distinctive of the species or other group to which an animal or plant belongs ⟨a ~ character⟩ **c :** serving to identify a mineral or fossil ⟨colored by impurities so that the property is not ~ —W.J. Miller⟩ **:** indicative of the conditions of origin or the geologic age of a formation ⟨some minerals are ~ of certain source rocks —F.J.Pettijohn⟩
²diagnostic \"\ *n* -s **1 a :** the art or practice of diagnosis — often used in pl. ⟨his rare skill in ~s —T.B.Macaulay⟩ **b :** a diagnostic conclusion, opinion, or explanation ⟨a false ~⟩ **2 :** a distinguishing mark ⟨the true ~ of modern gentility is parasitism —G.B.Shaw⟩
di·ag·nos·ti·cal·ly \-tək(ə)lē, -tēk-, -li\ *adv* **:** by means of diagnosis **:** in a diagnostic manner
di·ag·nos·ti·cate \,==¦stə,kāt\ *vb* -ED/-ING/-s **:** DIAGNOSE
di·ag·nos·ti·cian \-,nä'stishən *sometimes* -,nō'-\ *n* -s **:** one that makes diagnoses; *esp* **:** a specialist in medical diagnostics
¹di·ag·o·nal \(')dī¦agən°l, -aig-, -g(°)n°l, -gnəl\ *adj* [L *diagonalis*, fr. Gk *diagōnios* from angle to angle (fr. *dia-* + *-gōnios*, fr. *gōnia* angle) + L *-alis* -al; akin to Gk *gony* knee — more at KNEE] **1 a :** joining two nonadjacent vertices of a rectilinear or polyhedral figure **:** running across from corner to corner **b :** passing through two nonadjacent edges of a polyhedron ⟨a ~ plane⟩ **2 a :** inclined obliquely from a reference line (as the vertical or an axis) ⟨wood with a ~ grain⟩ ⟨a map with a number of ~ lines⟩ ⟨a ~ white cross on a blue ground⟩ **b :** having diagonal markings or parts ⟨a ~ weave⟩ **3** *crystallog* **a :** having reference to certain axes of the isometric system which are the intersections between the principal and the secondary planes of symmetry **b :** having reference to the directions bisecting the angles between lateral axes in the tetragonal and hexagonal systems — **di·ag·o·nal·ly** \-gən°lē, -gnəl, |i\ *adv*

²diagonal \"\ *n* -s **1 :** a straight line joining any two nonadjacent vertices of a polygon or any two vertices of a polyhedron not in the same face **2 a :** a diagonal direction **:** a diagonal row, arrangement, or pattern ⟨water bugs skated hither and thither in apparently purposeless ~s —S.E.White⟩ ⟨neckties with colorful ~s⟩ **b :** a twill weave **:** a twilled fabric esp. of wool **c :** a line of squares running obliquely across a chessboard or checkerboard ⟨one bishop moves along white ~s⟩ **d :** something lying in a diagonal positon (as in an inclined plane) ⟨its gable wall rises from the falling ~ of the ground —*Amer. Guide Series: Md.*⟩ **3 :** the secondary mirror in a Newtonian reflecting telescope that is used to bring the focus to the side of the tube and is usu. a flat mirror but sometimes a totally reflecting 45 degrees prism **4 :** the symbol / used esp. to denote "or" (as in *and/or*), "and or" (as in *straggler/deserter form*), "per" (as in *feet/second*), "in" or "of" (as in *U. S. Embassy/Paris*), "shilling" (as in *6/8d*), or "for" (as in 2/39) to indicate division (as in *birth/death ratio*) or the end of a line of verse or of a display line when quoted in running text, to separate terms of quantity (as in 5 *tons/7 cwts/57 lbs*) or the figures of a date (as in 1/9/56), or to enclose phonemic rather than phonetic symbols — called also *oblique, scratch comma, separatrix, slant, slash, slash mark, solidus, virgule* **5 :** an inclined member of a truss or bracing system excepting the end post of a truss and the top chord of a roof truss whose top chords are inclined

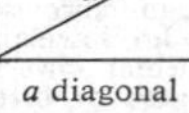

a diagonal

diagonal biped *n* **:** a foreleg and the opposite hind leg of a quadruped — called also *diagonals*
diagonal bond *n* **:** a masonry bond in which the headers are laid diagonally
diagonal bracing *n* **:** a member of a wooden case or crate placed at an angle to adjacent members to add strength
diagonal bridging *n* **:** CROSS BRIDGING
diagonal eyepiece *n* **:** ZENITH EYEPIECE
diagonal fraction *n* **:** a fraction in which numerator and denominator are separated by a diagonal (as 1/7)
diagonal pitch *n* **:** the distance between the center of a rivet in one row and that of the nearest rivet in the next row in riveted joints having two or more rows of staggered rivets
diagonal rib *n* **:** one of the ribs in a groined arch springing from the corners in a diagonal direction
diagonal stratification *n* **:** CROSS-BEDDING
diagonial *adj or n* [Gk *diagōnios* + E *-al*] *obs* **:** DIAGONAL, OPPOSITE
¹di·a·gram \'dīə,gram, -raa(ə)m\ *n* -s [Gk *diagramma*, fr. *diagraphein* to mark out by lines, fr. *dia-* + *graphein* to write — more at CARVE] **1 :** a line drawing made for mathematical or scientific purposes **:** a mechanical drawing or geometrical figure **2 :** a graphic design that explains rather than represents **:** a drawing that shows arrangement and relations (as of parts to a whole, relative values, origins and development, chronological fluctuations, distribution) **:** CHART, GRAPH ⟨a ~ of the nervous system⟩ — see BLOCK DIAGRAM
²diagram \"\ *vt* **diagramed** *or* **diagrammed**; **diagramed** *or* **diagrammed**; **diagraming** *or* **diagramming**; **diagrams :** to represent by or put into the form of a diagram ⟨he *diagrammed* his route on the tablecloth —Willa Cather⟩
diagram factor *n, engin* **:** a numerical coefficient by which the area of an ideal indicator diagram or its mean effective pressure must be multiplied to approximate that of the probable actual indicator diagram or the probable actual mean effective pressure
di·a·gram·mat·ic \¦dīəgrə¦mad·|ik, -mat|, |ēk\ *also* **di·a·gram·mat·i·cal** \|əkəl, |ēk-\ *adj* [*diagram* + *-atic*, *-atical* (as in *epigrammatic*, *epigrammatical*)] **:** being or relating to a diagram **:** showing by diagram **:** GRAPHIC — **di·a·gram·mat·i·cal·ly** \|ək(ə)lē, |ēk-, -li\ *adv*
di·a·gram·ma·tize \,dīə'gramə,tīz\ *vt* -ED/-ING/-s **:** to make a diagram of **:** DIAGRAM
di·a·gram·me·ter \'dīə,gram,mēd·ə(r)\ *n* -s [*diagram* + *-meter*] **:** an instrument for measuring diagrams; *esp* **:** one for measuring the ordinates of indicator diagrams
di·a·graph \'dīə,graf\ *n* -s [F *diagraphe*, fr. Gk *diagraphein* to mark out by lines — more at DIAGRAM] **:** a drawing instrument combining a protractor and scale — **di·a·graph·ic** \¦==¦grafik\ *adj*
di·a·gui·ta \,dēə'gēd·ə\ *n, pl* **diaguita** *or* **diaguitas** *usu cap* [Sp, of AmerInd origin] **:** CALCHAQUI
di·a·gui·te \-d·ē\ *adj, usu cap* [*Diaguita*] **:** of or relating to the Calchaqui people
dia·heliotropism \¦dīə+\ *n* [*dia-* + *heliotropism*] **:** diaphototropism in response to sunlight
dia·ki·ne·sis \,dīəkə'nēsəs, -,kī'-\ *n, pl* **diakine·ses** \-ē,sēz\ [NL, fr. *dia-* + *-kinesis*] **:** the final stage of the meiotic prophase immediately preceding formation of the metaphase plate and distinguished by marked contraction of the bivalents — **dia·ki·net·ic** \¦==(,)=¦ned·ik\ *adj*
¹di·al \'dī(ə)l\ *n* -s [ME *dyal*, fr. L *dies* day + ME *-al* — more at DEITY] **1 :** the face of a sundial whether horizontal, vertical, or inclined **2 a** *obs* **:** any of various timepieces (as a clock or watch) **b** *obs* **:** a mariner's compass **3 a :** the graduated face of a timepiece on which the time in hours and minutes and sometimes seconds is shown usu. by pointers or hands **b** *slang Brit* **:** the human face **4 a :** a face (as of a measuring instrument) upon which some measurement (as of force, pressure, speed) or other number is registered usu. by means of graduations and a pointer ⟨the hand of the ~ points to 50 pounds pressure⟩ **b :** a disk usu. with a knob or slot that may be turned to make electrical connections or to regulate the operation of a machine and typically with a series of markings around its border to serve as a guide for the operation ⟨increase the volume by turning the left-hand ~⟩ — see DIAL TELEPHONE **5 :** a lapidary's instrument for cutting a range of facets on a gem having a rod which holds the gem and turns on a ball-and-socket joint and a graduated dial and index at the other end for gauging the inclination between facets

dial 3a

²dial \"\ *vb* **dialed** *or* **dialled**; **dialed** *or* **dialled**; **dialing** *or* **dialling**; **dials** *vt* **1 :** to measure with or as if with a dial *specif* **:** to survey with a dial or circumferentor **2 a :** to manipulate a telephone dial so as to place a call to (a telephone number or subscriber) ⟨for a weather forecast one may ~ ST 1-0100⟩ ⟨~ the newspaper office⟩ **b :** to manipulate a dial so as to operate, regulate, or select ⟨~ a radio⟩ ⟨~ your favorite program⟩ ~ *vi* **1 a :** to manipulate a dial (as of a telephone or a television set) **b :** to make a call on a dial telephone **2 :** to tune, control, or regulate a radio or other apparatus by means of a dial ⟨many a radio owner, having ~*ed* into this discourse . . . ~*ed* out again —*Time*⟩
Dial \", 'dī,al\ *trademark* — used for diallylbarbituric acid
-di·al \-'dī,al\ *n suffix* -s [ISV, fr. *di-* + *-al*] **:** containing two aldehyde groups replacing two methyl groups at the ends of an aliphatic hydrocarbon chain ⟨heptanedi*al* $OCH(CH_2)_5CHO$⟩
dial *abbr* **1** dialect; dialectal **2** dialectic; dialectical; dialectics
di·al·able \'dī(ə)ləbəl\ *adj* **:** capable of being dialed
di·al bird \'dī(ə)l-\ *n* [by folk etymology fr. Hindi *dahiyāl*] **:** any of several songbirds of India (as the magpie robin) related to the European robin
di·al·de·hyde \(')dī+\ *n* [*di-* + *aldehyde*] **:** a chemical compound containing two aldehyde groups
¹dialect *n* -s [Gk *dialektos* debate, conversation, variety of language distinguished from other varieties of common origin] *obs* **:** ¹DIALECTIC 1
²di·a·lect \'dīə,lekt\ *n* -s *often attrib* [MF *dialecte*, fr. L *dialectus*, fr. Gk *dialektos*, fr. *dialegesthai* to converse — more at DIALOGUE] **1 :** a variety of language that is used by one group of persons and has features of vocabulary, grammar, or pronunciation distinguishing it from other varieties used by other groups: as **a :** a local or regional variety of language

distinguished by features of vocabulary, grammar, and pronunciation from other local or regional varieties and constituting together with them a single language of which no one variety is standard ⟨the Attic, Ionic, Aeolic, and Doric ~*s* of ancient Greek⟩ ⟨the Bavarian, Alemannic, and Franconian ~*s* of Old High German⟩ **b :** one of two or more cognate languages ⟨French and Italian are Romance ~*s*⟩ ⟨Russian and Bulgarian are Slavic ~*s*⟩ ⟨English and Sanskrit are Indo-European ~*s*⟩ **c :** a local or regional variety of a language chiefly oral and orally transmitted and differing distinctively in vocabulary, grammar, and pronunciation from other local or regional varieties and from the standard language ⟨the Lancashire ~ of English⟩ ⟨the Neapolitan ~ of Italian⟩ ⟨he knows the ~ of the southern mountains well⟩ — see MIDLAND DIALECT, NORTHERN, SOUTHERN; compare IDIOLECT

☞ In this dictionary the label *dial* is *dialect* sense 1c and is affixed to words and senses to indicate, when in combination with a specific regional label, a specific regional pattern of use and, when unqualified, a regional pattern too complex for summary, usu. including several regional varieties of American or of American and British English

d : a variety of a language that is used by the members of an occupational group in speech or writing directly concerned with their occupation and that differs from other varieties of the same language chiefly or solely in containing technical terminology ⟨the ~ of the atomic physicist⟩ **e :** a variety of a language ordinarily and habitually used by a group of persons whose identity is fixed by some factor other than geography (as social class ⟨peasant ~⟩, educational level ⟨he speaks and writes the standard ~ of his language⟩, or first language ⟨Italian-American ~⟩) **2 :** manner or means of expressing oneself esp. in language or in one of the fine arts **:** PHRASEOLOGY, STYLE ⟨this book is writ in such a ~ as may the minds of listless men affect —John Bunyan⟩ ⟨no composer of the first rank has been able to say all he wanted to without remolding the current musical language into at least a distinct ~ of his own to say it in —Gerald Abraham⟩ **3 :** the features of vocabulary, grammar, and pronunciation that distinguish a dialect (sense 1c or 1e) from the standard language ⟨some playwrights use more ~ than others⟩

syn PATOIS, CREOLE, JARGON, LINGO, SLANG, ARGOT, CANT, VERNACULAR, PATTER, along with DIALECT, are used in different meanings with varying degrees of exactness and with dissimilar value judgments involved. DIALECT is often used to designate the regional forms of a language ⟨Yorkshire *dialect*⟩ ⟨the *dialects* of Texas⟩ ⟨the following outline of Anglo-Saxon grammar is restricted to the West Saxon *dialect* —J.W.Bright⟩ This word may or may not connote marked difference from a received standard language or marked preference for that received standard language. PATOIS is likely to suggest a regional dialect, esp. one used by the unlettered ⟨the *patois* of the peasantry around Carcassonne⟩ The word is of French origin and its use is likely to be more common in Romance language areas than elsewhere. CREOLE is used mainly in reference to languages that come into existence when a politically or economically subordinate group adopts the language of a dominant group, usu. with very considerable modification ⟨the *creole* of Haiti⟩ JARGON may apply to a quickly evolved mixed linguistic form for simple communication between speakers of different languages, like Bêche-de-Mer or Pidgin English. JARGON may also signify a phase of language containing an undue number of words unfamiliar to the average speaker ⟨the technical *jargons* of sport —C.E. Montague⟩ ⟨the proper meaning of *jargon* is writing that employs technical words not commonly intelligible —Ernest Gowers⟩ LINGO, a word more common in preceding centuries than now, is often derogatory and stresses the incomprehensibility of a strange language or unfamiliar phase of one's own language ⟨a *lingo* that few people understand or care about —C.C.Furnas⟩ SLANG is likely to indicate a complex of words and constructions preferred within a limited group, esp. an informal one, to the standard language, and often more or less forceful or novel in their suggestion. ARGOT sometimes refers specif. to the forms of speech used in criminal groups ⟨the professional criminal speaks one or more *argots* in addition to colloquial English —D.W.Maurer⟩ CANT, which usu. has derogatory implications, may be applied to the language of thieves and their companions, or to the special languages of artisans or even of learned or professional groups, esp. if one wishes to ridicule, although JARGON is perhaps more common in designating the language of the latter. ⟨the pseudoscientific *cant* which is talked about the "Baconian philosophy" —T.H. Huxley⟩ VERNACULAR, with less suggestion of the derogatory than the others in this group, denotes the simple, colloquial, everyday speech of the commoner in contrast to more bookish and erudite speech ⟨his gumption, to use the *vernacular* word —William James⟩ PATTER may suggest fast, glib, voluble speech, ostensibly spontaneous, to lull or deceive ⟨the dispute resembles a conjuror's *patter* — its primary purpose is to divert attention from what is going on elsewhere —*Economist*⟩ ⟨the *patter* of a professional guide —H.S.Canby⟩ **syn** see in addition LANGUAGE

di·a·lec·tal \ˌdīəˈlektᵊl\ *adj* **:** of, belonging to, or characteristic of a dialect ⟨the ~ structure of the Eastern States —Hans Kurath⟩ — **di·a·lec·tal·ly** \-tᵊlē, -li\ *adv*

di·a·lec·tal·ism \ˌ==ˈ=ᵊlˌizəm\ *n* -s **:** a characteristic feature of a dialect ⟨beginning to impose Castilian ~*s* on eastern León —W.J.Entwistle⟩

dialect atlas *n* **:** LINGUISTIC ATLAS

dialect geographer *n* **:** LINGUISTIC GEOGRAPHER

dialect geography *n* **:** LINGUISTIC GEOGRAPHY

di·a·lec·tic \ˌdīəˈlektik, -tēk\ *n* -s [alter. (influenced by L *dialectica*) of ME *dialetik*, fr. MF *dialetique*, fr. L *dialectica*, fr. Gk *dialektikē*, fr. fem. of *dialektikos*, adj.] **1 :** the theory and practice of weighing and reconciling juxtaposed or contradictory arguments for the purpose of arriving at truth esp. through discussion and debate: **a** *pre-Socratic philos* (1) **:** argument by critical examination of logical consequences (as the contradictory consequences of antinomies) (2) **:** sophistic reasoning **:** ERISTIC **b** *Socratic philos* **:** discussion and reasoning by dialogue as a method of intellectual investigation **c** *Platonism* (1) **:** logical analysis or division of things into genera and species (2) **:** the discipline that investigates the eternal ideas esp. in their relation to those of the good, the true, and the beautiful **d** *Aristotelianism* **:** a method of arguing with probability on any given problem as an art intermediate between rhetoric and strict demonstration **e** *Stoicism* **:** formal logic as contrasted with rhetoric and grammar **2 a** *Kantianism* **:** the logic of appearances and of illusions dealing with paralogisms, antinomies, and transcendental ideas as these arise through logical fallacies, perceptual errors, or the endeavor to use the principles of the understanding applicable only within experience for determination of such transcendental objects as the soul, the world, and God **b** *Hegelianism* **:** a logical development progressing from less to more comprehensive levels that on its subjective side is the passage of thought from a thesis through an antithesis to a synthesis that in turn becomes a thesis for further progressions ultimately culminating in the absolute idea and on its objective side is an analogous development in the process of history and the cosmos **3** *Marxism* **a :** the process of self-development or unfolding (as of an action, event, idea, ideology, movement, or institution) through the stages of thesis, antithesis, and synthesis in accordance with the laws of dialectical materialism — usu. used in pl. but sing. or pl. in constr. **b :** a method that regards change in nature and history as taking place in this way — usu. used in pl. but sing. or pl. in constr. **4 :** any systematic reasoning, exposition, or argument esp. in literature that juxtaposes opposed or contradictory ideas and usu. seeks to resolve their conflict ⟨the brilliant *dialectics* and irony of this comedy⟩ **:** play of ideas **:** cunning or hairsplitting disputation ⟨subtlety was foreign and *dialectics* distasteful to his character —S.H.Adams⟩ **:** argumentative skill ⟨his speech was a remarkable display of *dialectics*⟩ — usu. used in pl. but often sing. in constr. **5 :** the dialectical tension or opposition between two interacting forces or elements ⟨the ~ between Nature and Spirit —Joseph Frank⟩

di·a·lec·ti·cal \ˌdīəˈlektəkəl, -tēk-\ *also* **di·a·lec·tic** \-tik, -tēk\ *adj* [MF & L; MF *dialectique, dialetique*, fr. L *dialecticus*, fr. Gk *dialektikos*, fr. *dialektos* debate, conversation + -*ikos* -ic, -ical — more at DIALECT] **1 a :** of or relating to dialectic ⟨the ~ method⟩ ⟨the ~ process in history⟩ **:** marked by a dynamic inner tension, conflict, and interconnectedness of its parts or elements ⟨all educational situations are ~ at the core —G.E.Mueller⟩ **:** MUTUAL, RECIPROCAL ⟨a . . . fruitful ~ interplay between literary history and literary criticism —C.I.Glicksberg⟩ **b :** practicing, devoted to, or employing dialectic ⟨a ~ philosopher⟩ **:** regarding or interpreting from the point of view of dialectic ⟨a ~ approach to the problems of cultural change⟩ ⟨his thought . . . became to some extent ~; he began to conceive of life . . . as a whole which depends upon the conflict of the parts —*New Republic*⟩ **c :** of or relating to logical or systematic disputation or debate ⟨displayed great forensic and ~ skill⟩ ⟨an argument used as a ~ weapon in campaign oratory⟩ **2 :** DIALECTAL

di·a·lec·ti·cal·ly \-tək(ə)lē, -tēk-, -li\ *adv* **1 :** in a dialectical manner **:** in accordance with or on the basis of dialectic ⟨views the problem ~, in all its many-sided complexity⟩ ⟨Marxists believe that culture and economics are ~ interactive and interdependent —Melvin Rader⟩ **2 :** as regards argumentative or reasoning skill **:** LOGICALLY ⟨very agile ~, as shown by his persuasive speeches⟩

dialectical materialism *n* **1 :** the theory of reality advanced by Karl Marx and Friedrich Engels and adopted as the official Soviet philosophy combining elements of traditional materialism with the method of Hegel's dialectic and maintaining the independent objective reality of matter and its priority both in time and logical importance over mind **2 :** HISTORICAL MATERIALISM

dialectical theology *n* **:** neoorthodoxy esp. as holding against rationalism that man's attempts to know God by his own reasoning reach contradictory conclusions and must give way to a faith that awaits God's word

di·a·lec·ti·cian \ˌdīəˌlekˈtishən *sometimes* -ˌlək-\ *n* -s [MF *dialecticien*, fr. L *dialectica* + MF -*ien* -ian] **1 :** one who is skilled in or practices dialectic **:** LOGICIAN, REASONER **2 :** DIALECTOLOGIST

di·a·lec·to·log·i·cal \ˌdīəˌlektəˈläjəkəl\ *adj* **:** of or belonging to dialectology — **di·a·lec·to·log·i·cal·ly** \-jək(ə)lē\ *adv*

di·a·lec·tol·o·gist \ˌdīəˌlekˈtäləjəst *sometimes* -ˌlək-\ *n* -s **:** a specialist in dialectology

di·a·lec·tol·o·gy \-jē\ *n* -ES [ISV *dialect* + -*o* + -*logy*] **1 :** the systematic study of dialect **2 :** the body of data available for use in the systematic study of a dialect or group of related dialects

dialects *pl of* DIALECT

dialed \ˈdī(ə)ld\ *adj* [[1]*dial* + -*ed*] **:** provided with a dial ⟨a radium-*dialed* watch⟩

dial feed *n* **:** a circular conveyor that carries successive workpieces into position for action of a punch press or some other machine tool

dial gauge *or* **dial indicator** *n* **:** a gauge consisting of a circular graduated dial and a pointer actuated by a member that contacts with the part being calibrated

dialing *also* **dialling** *n* -s [fr. gerund of [2]*dial*] **1 :** the art of constructing sundials **2 :** the measurement of time by sundials

di·a·lis·ter \ˌdīəˈlistə(r)\ *n, cap* [NL, fr. Gk *dia* through + *hylistēr* filter, fr. *hylazein* to filter, fr. *hylē* mud, dregs; akin to Gk *hyein* to rain — more at DIA-, SUCK] **:** a genus of minute gram-negative parasitic strictly anaerobic bacteria (family Bacteroidaceae) growing only in fresh sterile tissue or ascitic fluid, the cells occurring singly, in pairs, or in short chains

[1]**di·alkyl** \(ˈ)dī+\ *n* [*di-* + *alkyl*] **:** a compound of two alkyl radicals with a metal ⟨zinc ~*s*⟩

[2]**dialkyl** \"\ *adj* [*di-* + *alkyl*] **:** containing two alkyl groups in the molecule

di·alkylamine \(ˌ)dī+\ *n* [*di-* + *alkylamine*] **:** an amine (as dimethylamine) containing two alkyl groups attached to amino nitrogen

di·al·lage \ˈdīəlij\ *n* -s [F, fr. Gk *diallagē* change, fr. *diallag-*, aorist stem of *diallassein* to interchange, exchange, change, fr. *dia-* + *allassein* to change, fr. *allos* other — more at ELSE] **:** a dark green or bronze-colored laminated pyroxene common in certain igneous rocks (hardness 4, sp. gr. 3.2–3.35) — **di·al·lag·ic** \ˌdīəˈlajik\ *adj*

dialled *past of* DIAL

di·al·lel \ˈdīəˌlel\ *adj* [Gk *diallēlos* reciprocating, confused, in a circle, fr. *di' allēlōn* through one another, fr. *dia* through + *allēlōn* of one another — more at PARALLEL] **:** mating according to a system in which each female is bred to each of two or more males in order to determine the relative importance of sire and dam in the transmission of certain qualities to the offspring

di·al·le·lon \ˌdīəˈlēˌlän\ *n, pl* **dialle·la** \-lə\ [Gk *diallēlon*, neut. of *diallēlos*] *logic* **:** definition in a circle

di·al·le·lus \-ləs\ *n, pl* **dialle·li** \-ˌlī\ [NL, fr. Gk *diallēlos*] **:** a reasoning in a circle

dial lock *n* **:** COMBINATION LOCK

di·al·lyl \(ˈ)dīˈaləl\ *adj* [ISV *di-* + *allyl*] **:** containing two allyl groups

di·al·lyl·barbituric acid \"+ . . . -\ *n* [*diallyl* + *barbituric*] **:** a white crystalline compound $C_{10}H_{12}N_2O_3$ used as a sedative and hypnotic

dialog *var of* DIALOGUE

di·a·log·ic \ˌdīəˈläjik, ¦ēk *sometimes* -lōg¦ *or* -lăg¦\ *or* **di·a·log·i·cal** \¦əkəl, ¦ēk-\ *adj* [LL *dialogicus*, fr. Gk *dialogikos* of discourse, fr. *dialogos* debate, discourse + -*ikos* -ic, -ical — more at DIALOGUE] **1 :** having reference to or characterized by dialogue **:** consisting of dialogue or a dialogue ⟨~ writing⟩ ⟨the ~ form preferred by philosophers⟩ **2 :** taking part in dialogue — **di·a·log·i·cal·ly** \¦ək(ə)lē, ¦ēk-, -li\ *adv*

di·al·o·gism \dīˈaləˌjizəm *sometimes* ˈdīəˌlōˌgi- *or* -ˌläˌg-, *in sense 1*\ *n* -s [LL *dialogismos*, fr. Gk, fr. *dialogos* + -*ismos* -ism] **1** *archaic* **a :** the expression of an author's ideas by means of a dialogue between two or more characters **b :** DIALOGUE 2 **2 :** a disjunctive conclusion inferred from a single premise (as in "gravitation may act without contact; therefore, either some force may act without contact or gravitation is not a force")

di·al·o·gist \dīˈaləjəst *also* ˈdīəˌlōgə- *or* ˈdīəˌläg-\ *n* -s [LL *dialogista*, fr. L *dialogus*] **1 :** one who participates in a dialogue **2 :** a writer of dialogues

di·a·lo·gis·tic \ˌdīəlōˈjistik *also* -(ˌ)lōˈgis-\ *or* **di·a·lo·gis·ti·cal** \-təkəl\ *adj* [Gk *dialogistikos*, fr. (assumed) *dialogistos* (verbal of *dialogizesthai* to debate, argue, fr. *dialogos* + -*izesthai* -ize) + -*ikos* -ic] **:** DIALOGIC

di·al·o·gite \dīˈaləˌjīt\ *n* -s [G *dialogit*, fr. Gk *dialogē* enumeration, estimate (fr. *dialegein* to pick out, fr. *dia-* + *legein* to speak) + G -*it* -ite] **:** RHODOCHROSITE

di·al·o·gize \dīˈaləˌjīz *also* -dīəˌlōˌgīz *or* ˈdīəˌläˌg-\ *vi* -ED/-ING/-S [Gk *dialogizesthai*] **:** DIALOGUE

[1]**di·a·logue** \ˈdīəˌlōg *also* -läg\ *also* **di·a·log** \"\ *n* -s [ME *dialoge, dialogue*, fr. OF, fr. L *dialogus*, fr. Gk *dialogos*, fr. *dialegesthai* to converse, fr. *dia-* + *legesthai*, pres. middle infin. of *legein* to speak — more at LEGEND] **1 :** a written composition in which two or more characters are represented as conversing or reasoning on some topic ⟨the essay . . . is in the form of a ~ between two philosophers —*Times Lit. Supp.*⟩ **2 a** (1) **:** an instance of conversational exchange **:** TALK 1b ⟨he had just come from an angry ~ with his quarrelsome neighbor⟩ (2) **:** oral communication **:** CONVERSATION 3a(1) ⟨pleasant ~ improves any dinner⟩ **b :** an exchange of ideas and opinions; *esp* **:** a serious colloquy conducted or presented to entertain or instruct ⟨should be useful . . . in providing a genuine ~ between the English and the American intelligentsia —Stephen Spender⟩ — see DUOLOGUE; compare MONOLOGUE **3 :** the conversational element of literary or dramatic composition ⟨~ in which each phrase fits and reveals a character perfectly —Stanislaus Joyce⟩ **4 a** *obs* **:** a musical composition for two or more alternating voices typically in question and answer form **b :** any musical arrangement suggestive of a conversation ⟨the first movement, with its lovely initial ~ between wind and strings —Cecil Gray⟩

[2]**dialogue** \"\ *vb* -ED/-ING/-S *vi* **:** to take part in a dialogue ~ *vt* **:** to express in dialogue ⟨and *dialogued* for him what he would say —Shak.⟩

dialogue mass *n, often cap D & M, Roman Catholicism* **:** a low mass in which the congregation recites aloud the responses that are usu. given by the server

dial press *n* **:** a punch press with a dial-feed motion

dials *pl of* DIAL, *pres 3d sing of* DIAL

-dials *pl of* -DIAL

dial telegraph *n* **:** a telegraph in which letters and numbers or other symbols are placed upon the border of a circular dial plate at each station, the apparatus being so arranged that the needle or index of the dial at the receiving station copies the movements of that at the transmitting station

dial telephone *n* **:** a telephone from which connections may be automatically completed without the aid of an exchange operator by revolving a dial marked with numbers and letters into positions corresponding to the units of the desired telephone number

dial tone *n* **:** a characteristic tone emitted by a dial telephone as a signal that the system is ready for dialing

di·a·lu·ric acid \ˌdīəˈlůrik-\ *n* [ISV *di-* + *alloxan* + *uric*] **:** crystalline heterocyclic acid $C_4H_4N_2O_4$ formed by the reduction of alloxan or the oxidation of uric acid; 5-hydroxybarbituric acid

dialy- *comb form* [NL, fr. Gk *dialyein* to separate] **:** separated ⟨*dialy*carpic⟩ ⟨*dialy*petalous⟩

di·a·ly·pet·a·lae \ˌdīəlēˈped·ᵊlˌē\ [NL, fr. *dialy-* + -*petalae*] *syn of* CHORIPETALAE

di·a·ly·pet·a·lous \¦===¦ped·ᵊləs\ *adj* [*dialy-* + -*petalous*] **:** CHORIPETALOUS

di·a·lyse \ˈdīəˌlīz\ *chiefly Brit var of* DIALYZE

di·al·y·sis \dīˈaləsəs\ *n, pl* **dialy·ses** \-əˌsēz\ [NL, fr. Gk, separation, dissolution, fr. *dialyein* to break apart, dissolve (fr. *dia-* + *lyein* to loosen) + -*sis* — more at LOSE] **1 :** the separation of substances in solution by means of semipermeable membranes (as of parchment, cellophane, or living cells) through which the smaller molecules and ions diffuse readily whereas the larger molecules and colloidal particles diffuse very slowly or not at all, such separations being important in nature (as in living organisms and in soils) and having many applications (as in blood fractionation or in the recovery of sodium hydroxide in the manufacture of viscose) — used esp. of the separation of noncolloids from colloids (as proteins); see ELECTRODIALYSIS; compare OSMOSIS, ULTRAFILTRATION **2** *bot* **:** the separation of parts which are normally united esp. in the same floral whorl

di·a·lyt·ic \ˌdīəˈlid·ik\ *adj* [Gk *dialytikos* able to sever, destructive, fr. *dialytos* capable of dissolution (fr. *dialyein* to dissolve) + -*ikos* -ic] **:** being or manifesting dialysis

di·a·lyz·able \ˈdīəˌlīzəbəl\ *adj* **:** capable of being dialyzed or of dialyzing; *esp* **:** capable of diffusing through a dialyzing membrane

di·al·y·zate \dīˈaləˌzāt\ *or* **di·al·y·sate** \-ˌsāt\ *n* -s [ISV *dialyze, dialyse* + -*ate*] **:** a product of dialysis — used either of the material that has failed to diffuse through the membrane or of the diffusate

di·a·lyze \ˈdīəˌlīz\ *vb* -ED/-ING/-S [fr. NL *dialysis*, after such pairs as NL *analysis* **:** E *analyze*] *vt* **:** to subject to dialysis **:** separate or obtain by dialysis ~ *vi* **:** to undergo dialysis **:** diffuse through a suitable membrane

di·a·lyz·er \-zə(r)\ *n* -s **:** an apparatus in which dialysis is carried out consisting essentially of one or more containers for liquids separated into compartments by membranes in any of various forms (as a sheet, bag, or tube)

a laboratory dialyzer

diam *abbr* diameter

dia·magnet \ˈdīə+\ *n* -s [back-formation fr. [1]*diamagnetic*] **:** a substance that exhibits diamagnetism

[1]**dia·magnetic** \"+\ *adj* [*dia-* + *magnetic*] **:** having a magnetic permeability less than that of a vacuum **:** having negative magnetic susceptibility ⟨~ bodies are feebly repelled by a strong magnet⟩ — compare PARAMAGNETIC — **dia·magnetically** \"+\ *adv*

[2]**dia·magnetic** \"+\ *n* -s **:** DIAMAGNET

dia·magnetism \"+\ *n* [*dia-* + *magnetism*] **:** the property of being diamagnetic **:** the characteristic phenomena exhibited by diamagnetic bodies

[1]**di·a·man·té** \ˌdēəˌmänˈtā\ *adj* [F, fr. past part. of *diamanter* to set with diamonds or paste brilliants, fr. *diamant* diamond — more at DIAMOND] **:** decorated with diamanté

[2]**diamanté** \"\ *n* -s **:** sparkling decoration consisting usu. of paste brilliants or glass used esp. on evening gowns; *also* **:** a fabric so decorated

di·a·man·tif·er·ous \ˌdī(ə)mənˈtif(ə)rəs, ˌdēəm-\ *adj* [F *diamantifère*, fr. *diamant* diamond + -*i-* + -*fère* -ferous] **:** DIAMONDIFEROUS

di·a·man·tine \ˌdīəˈmanˌtīn, -tēn, -antᵊn\ *adj* [F *diamantin*, fr. *diamant* diamond + -*in* -ine] **:** consisting of or resembling diamond

di·a·mat \ˈdīəˌmat\ *n* -s [*dialectical materialism*] **:** DIALECTICAL MATERIALISM

di·amb \ˈdīˌam *also* -mb\ *or* **di·iamb** \(ˈ)dīˈīˌa-\ *n, pl* **diambs** *or* **diiambs** \-mz\ *n* -s [LL *diiambus*, fr. Gk *diiambos*, fr. *di-* + *iambos* iamb] **:** a metrical foot consisting of two iambs **:** an iambic dipody reckoned as a single compound foot **:** a double iamb — **di·am·bic** \(ˈ)dīˈambik\ *or* **di·iam·bic** \ˌdīˌīˈa-\ *adj*

di·am·e·ter \dīˈaməd·ə(r), -mətə-\ *n* -s [ME *diametre*, fr. MF, fr. L *diametros*, fr. Gk *diametros*, fr. *dia-* + -*metros* (fr. *metron* measure) — more at MEASURE] **1 a :** a chord passing through the center of a figure or body (as a circle, conic section, sphere, cube) **b :** a line that bisects each of a system of parallel chords of a curve **c :** a unit of magnification of microscopic and telescopic observations equal to the number of times the linear dimensions of the object are increased ⟨a magnification of eight ~*s* means the dimensions are increased in the ratio of 8:1⟩ **2 a :** the length of a straight line through the center of an object **:** THICKNESS ⟨a tree two feet in ~ at the base of the trunk⟩ ⟨a rope one inch in ~ measured at its greatest dimension⟩ **b :** the distance through a column at its base used in architecture as a standard measure for all parts of an order — see MODULE **c :** one of the maximal breadths of a part of the body

diameter tape *n* **:** a measuring tape so scaled that when it encircles a tree trunk the diameter is read directly

di·am·e·tral \(ˈ)dīˈamə·trəl\ *adj* [MF, fr. *diametre* + -*al*] **1 :** of or relating to a diameter **:** located at the diameter **:** constituting a diameter ⟨the ~ plane⟩ **2** *obs* **:** DIAMETRIC 2

diametral curve *or* **diametral surface** *n* **:** any line or surface that bisects a system of parallel chords of a curve or surface

diametral pitch *n* **:** a ratio equal to the pitch diameter of a gear in inches divided by the number of teeth in the gear

diametral plane *n* **1 :** a plane bisecting a system of parallel chords of a quadric surface; *specif* **:** any plane through the center of a sphere **2** *of a linear complex* **:** a plane conjugate to a point at infinity

di·a·met·ric \ˌdīəˈme·trik, -rēk\ *or* **di·a·met·ri·cal** \-rəkəl, -rēk-\ *adj* [Gk *diametrikos*, fr. *diametros* + -*ikos* -ic, -ical] **1 :** DIAMETRAL 1 **2 :** completely opposed or opposite as if at the opposite end of a diameter ⟨in ~ contradiction to his claims⟩

di·a·met·ri·cal·ly \-rək(ə)lē, -rēk-, -li\ *adv* **1 :** as if at opposite ends of a diameter ⟨differing ~ from the earlier conception⟩ **:** COMPLETELY, UTTERLY ⟨ideas ~ opposite to his own⟩ **2 :** at or along the diameter **:** in the direction of the diameter

di·amide \(ˈ)dī+\ *n* [ISV *di-* + *amide*] **1 :** any compound containing two amido groups **2 :** HYDRAZINE

di·amidine \"+\ *n* [*di-* + *amidine*] **:** any compound containing two amidino groups (as stilbamidine)

diamido- *comb form* [ISV, fr. *di-* + *amid-*] **:** containing two amido groups — esp. in names of inorganic acids ⟨*diamido*phosphoric acid $HPO_2(NH_2)_2$⟩

di·amine \(ˌ)dī+\ *n* [ISV *di-* + *amine*] **:** any compound containing two amino groups

diamine black BH *n, often cap D&B* **:** a direct blue disazo dye that can be converted into a navy blue or black developed dye on the fiber — called also *developed black BH;* see DYE table I (under *Direct Blue 2*)

diamine dye *n, often cap 1st D* : any of numerous direct dyes — see DYE table I

diamine oxidase *n* : HISTAMINASE

diamino- *comb form* [ISV *di-* + *amin-*] : containing two amino groups — used in names of organic compounds ⟨2,6-*diamino*purine⟩

di·ami·no \¦dī¦mē(,)nō, (ˈ)dī¦amə,nō\ *adj* [*diamino-*] : relating to or containing two amino or substituted amino groups

di·ami·no·diphenyl sulfone \"+ . . . -\ *n* [ISV *diamino-* + *diphenyl*] : a crystalline compound $(NH_2C_6H_4)_2SO_2$ that like certain of its derivatives is used in the treatment of leprosy; 4, 4′-sulfonyl-di-aniline

Di·a·mi·no·gen \¦dīə¦mēnəjən, -jen\ *trademark* — used for a direct dye; see DYE table I (under *Direct Blue 126*)

di·ammonium \¦dī+\ *adj* [*di-* + *ammonium*] : containing two ammonium radicals

diammonium phosphate *n* : AMMONIUM PHOSPHATE

1**di·a·mond** \ˈdī(ə)mənd\ *n* -s [ME *diamaunt, diamaunde,* fr. MF *diamant, diamande,* fr. LL *diamant-, diamas,* alter. of (assumed) VL *adimant-, adimas* hardest iron or steel, diamond, fr. Gk *adamant-, adamas*] **1 a** : native carbon crystallized in the isometric system often in the form of octahedrons with rounded edges and usu. nearly colorless that when transparent and more or less free from flaws is highly valued as a precious stone because having high refractive and dispersive powers it shows when faceted a remarkable brilliance and play of prismatic colors and that when off-color or flawed is invaluable for industrial purposes (as for use in wire dies, abrasive powder, rock drills, and turning tools) because it is the hardest substance known (hardness 10, sp. gr. 3.52) — see WATER 7a; BRILLIANT 1, ROSE, TABLE DIAMOND; BORT **b** : a piece of this material **c** : a crystalline mineral that is like diamond in brilliance — used with a qualifying name; see ALENÇON DIAMOND **d** : crystallized carbon similar to the native but produced by artificial means **2** *obs* : a very hard substance : ADAMANT **3 a** : something that resembles a diamond (as in value, rarity, or brilliance) **b** : a person possessing very high character or other fine qualities **4** : a square or rhombus-shaped configuration usu. having a distinctive orientation (as by having a diagonal perpendicular to the horizontal) **5** : something shaped like a diamond; *specif* : any of the small diamond-shaped marks at regular intervals on the cushions of an American billiard table to aid the player in calculating the angles of his shots **6 a** : a red lozenge impressed on a playing card; *also* : a card marked with such lozenges **b diamonds** *pl but sing or pl in constr* : the suit comprising cards so marked **c** *bridge* : an odd trick won or contracted for with diamonds trumps ⟨four ~s bid and made⟩ **7** : a tool holding a diamond; *specif* : any of several instruments varying in shape, size, and surfaces featuring diamond bonded on a metallic base and used typically in dental work and for cutting glass **8** : an old size of printing type (approximately 4½ point) between brilliant and pearl — compare POINT SYSTEM **9 a** : the area of a baseball or softball field enclosed in a square with a base at each corner — called also *infield* **b** : the entire playing field in baseball or softball **10** : something ornamented or set with a diamond; *specif* : an engagement ring set with a diamond solitaire **11** : RERAILER **12 diamonds** *pl but sing in constr* : DIAMOND-SKIN DISEASE — **diamond in the rough** : a person of sterling character or other exceptional qualities but lacking in social graces or refinement of manner

diamond 4

2**diamond** \"\ *adj* **1** : consisting or made of diamond **2** : BRIGHT, SPARKLING ⟨the ~ dawn of a golden winter day —L.C. Stevens⟩ **3** : ornamented or set with a diamond ⟨~ tiara⟩ **4** : shaped like a diamond : having diamond-shaped figures or parts ⟨~ weave⟩ **5** : of, relating to, or marking a 60th or a 75th anniversary

3**diamond** \"\ *vt* -ED/-ING/-S : to adorn with or as if with diamonds ⟨the grass is ~*ed* with cobwebs of dew —Stuart Kinzie⟩

di·a·mond albumin test \ˈdī(ə)mənd-\ *n, usu cap D* [after Louis S. *Diamond* b1920 Am. parasitologist] : a test for blocking antibodies (as in the Rh system) by use of red blood cells suspended in concentrated serum albumin — compare RH FACTOR

diamond anniversary *n* : a 60th or 75th anniversary

1**diamondback** \ˈ=(=)=,=\ *n* **1** : DIAMONDBACK RATTLESNAKE **2** : DIAMONDBACK TERRAPIN **3** : DIAMONDBACK MOTH

2**diamondback** \ˈ=(=)=,=\ *also* **diamond-backed** \ˈ=(=)=¦=\ *adj* : having marks like diamonds or lozenges on the back

diamondback moth *n* : a nearly cosmopolitan moth (*Plutella xylostella*) of European origin whose larva is a pest on cruciferous crops — called also *cabbage moth*

diamondback rattlesnake *n* : the largest and most deadly snake (*Crotalus adamanteus*) of No. America inhabiting the southern U.S. and sometimes attaining a length of eight feet

diamondback terrapin *n* : any of several terrapins constituting a genus *Malaclemys* and formerly widely distributed in salt marshes along the Atlantic and Gulf coasts from Buzzards Bay southward but now exterminated from much of the northern part of their range — see TERRAPIN illustration

diamondback water snake *n* : a harmless water snake (*Natrix rhombifera*) of southern No. America having a series of dark diamond-shaped marks along the back

diamond ball *n* : SOFTBALL

diamond bird *n* **1** : any of several Australian flower-peckers (genus *Pardalotus*) sometimes kept as cage birds — called also *diamond sparrow, pardalote* **2** : DIAMOND SPARROW 1

diamond bracket *n* : BRACKET 4b

diamond canker *n* : a virus disease of stone-fruit trees characterized esp. by corky roughening and thickening of the bark and by progressive weakening of the tree

diamond cement *n* : a cement used for setting diamonds (as a solution of mastic and isinglass in alcohol)

diamond chip *n* : CHIP 1e(2)

diamond crossing *n* : a railroad crossing in which the rails cross obliquely forming a diamond-shaped center

diamond dash *n* : a graphic character —◆— sometimes used to mark page or column divisions in printed matter — called also *swell dash*

diamond die *n* : a wiredrawing die made of diamond for drawing fine wire of hard metals (as tungsten)

diamond dove *n* : a small Australian dove (*Geopelia cuneata*) often kept as a cage or aviary bird that is largely gray and brown with the wings dotted with white

diamond dresser *n* : a tool carrying industrial diamond for dressing or truing the surface of a grinding wheel

diamond drill *n* : a usu. annular drill faced with bort diamonds and used for rock boring

diamond dust *n* : powdered or crushed diamond used as an abrasive — called also *diamond powder*

diamond dye *n, often cap 1st D* : any of several mordant or acid dyes — see DYE table I

di·a·mond·ed \ˈdī(ə)məndəd\ *adj* **1** : 2DIAMOND 4 ⟨the windows had ~ panes —Edith Sitwell⟩ **2** : adorned with or as if with diamonds ⟨he went ever gold-laced, highly powdered, scented, and ~ —Charles Reade⟩ : DIAMONDIZED

diamond-fish \ˈ=(=)=,=\ *n, Austral* : DEVILFISH 1

diamond flounder *n* : a large mottled brown flatfish (*Hypsopsetta guttulata*) of the coast of California — called also *diamond turbot*

diamond flower *n* : a low-growing tufted Portuguese annual herb (*Ionopsidium acaule*) of the family Cruciferae with rounded leaves and light violet flowers

diamond hitch *n* : a knot used in tying a pack on an animal so that the interlacing ropes form a diamond on the top of the pack

di·a·mon·dif·er·ous \¦dī(ə)mən¦dif(ə)rəs\ *adj* [*diamond* + *-i-* + *-ferous*] : yielding diamonds ⟨~ earth⟩

diamond indentor *or* **diamond indenter** *n* : an instrument for measuring hardness by the depth of the indentation made by a pyramidal diamond point under a given load

diamonding *n* -s [1*diamond* + *-ing*] : a distortion in wood usu. occurring during drying and resulting in a change in cross section from rectangular to diamond shape

di·a·mond·ize \ˈdī(ə)mən,dīz\ *vt* -ED/-ING/-S **1** : to set with diamonds : ADORN, ENRICH **2** : to change into diamond

diamond jubilee *n* : a diamond anniversary or its celebration

diamond knot *n* : a diamond-shaped knot tied in the strands of a rope used esp. to provide a foothold on a footrope

diamond-leaf laurel *n* : an Australian tree (*Pittosporum rhombifolium*) resembling a laurel of pyramidal habit

diamond mortar *n* : a small steel mortar used for pulverizing hard substances

diamond paste *n* : diamond dust in a jelly or oil used as an abrasive

diamond pencil *n* : a tool tipped with diamond (as for ruling gratings on metal)

diamond plate *n* **1** : a steel plate spread with diamond dust and oil for rubbing down gems **2** : a diamond-shaped plate or strap in a ship forming a connection and brace for the flanges of two frames or beams where they cross

diamond knot

diamond point *n* **1** : an instrument (as a stylus or cutting tool) with a diamond tip **2 a** : a diamond-shaped figure formed by intersecting rails at a railroad diamond crossing **b** : one of the acute angles formed at this crossing

diamond-point \ˈ=(=)=,=\ *or* **diamond-pointed** \¦=(=)=¦==\ *adj* : having a point that is diamond-shaped or rhombus-shaped ⟨~ tool⟩

diamond-point chisel *n* : a cold chisel having a diamond-shaped cutting face for cutting V grooves or sharp internal corners

diamond powder *n* : DIAMOND DUST

diamond rattlesnake *n* : DIAMONDBACK RATTLESNAKE

diamonds *pl of* DIAMOND, *pres 3d sing of* DIAMOND

diamond saw *n* : a circular disk in the edge of which diamond dust or carbon diamonds are set to form a saw suitable for cutting hard material (as stone)

Di·a·mond·scope \ˈ=(=)=,skōp\ *trademark* — used for a low-power microscope fitted with a special illuminator for use in examining diamonds

diamond-skin disease *also* **diamond skin** *n* : a mild urticarial form of swine erysipelas characterized by 4-angled red patches on the skin

diamond snake *n* **1** : a snake of a variety of the carpet snake restricted to parts of the east coast of Australia and distinguished by smaller size, darker color, and reduction of the pattern to diamond-shaped clusters of spots **2** *in Tasmania* : COPPERHEAD 1b

diamond sparrow *n* **1** : an Australian weaverbird (*Zonaeginthus guttatus*) having white-spotted sides and a bright red tail base — called also *firetail* **2** : DIAMOND BIRD 1

diamond stack *n* : a smokestack with a diamond-shaped top used on early steam locomotives

diamond tooth *n* : a compound tooth for crosscut saws

diamond truer *n* : a grinding wheel truer consisting usu. of a short steel rod inserted in a wooden handle and having in its free end a carbon diamond : DIAMOND DRESSER

diamond turbot *n* : DIAMOND FLOUNDER

diamond wedding *n* : a diamond anniversary of a wedding

diamond wheel *n* : a grinding wheel for very hard materials (as gems or tungsten carbide) using diamond dust as abrasive

diamondwork \ˈ=(=)=,=\ *n* : masonry in which pieces are set so as to form diamond-shaped patterns on the surface

di·a·morphine \¦dīə+\ *n* [*diacetyl* + *morphine*] : HEROIN

di·ana \dīˈanə\ *n* -s *often cap* [fr. the name *Diana*] : SQUILL BLUE

di·ana butterfly \(ˈ)dī¦anə-\ *n, usu cap D* [NL *diana* (specific epithet of *Speyeria diana*), fr. L *Diana,* Roman goddess of the moon, moon; fr. the silvery crescents on the wings] : a large butterfly (*Speyeria diana*) mainly of the southern Appalachian region, the male being brown above with a fulvous border and the female bluish black with blue spots

diana monkey *n, usu cap D* [NL *diana* (specific epithet of *Cercopithecus diana*), fr. L *Diana;* fr. the white crescent on the forehead] : a white-bearded monkey (*Cercopithecus diana*) of western Africa

di·an·drous \(ˈ)dī¦andrəs\ *adj* [*di-* + *-androus*] **1** : having two stamens **2** *of a moss* : having two antheridia associated with each bract

di·ane pigment \(ˈ)dī¦an-\ *n, usu cap D* [prob. fr. the name *Diane*] : either of two organic pigments — see DYE table I (under *Pigment Blue 25* and *Pigment Orange 16*)

di·anisidine \¦dī+\ *n* [ISV *di-* + *anisidine*] : BIANISIDINE — used chiefly commercially ⟨~ blue⟩

di·a·nite \ˈdīə,nīt\ *n* -s [G *dianit,* fr. NL *dianium* new metal held to be contained in dianite (fr. L *Diana* + *-ium*) + G *-it* -ite] : a variety of columbite

di·a·no·et·ic \¦dīənō¦ed·ik\ *adj* [Gk *dianoētikos,* fr. *dianoētos* (verbal of *dianoeisthai* to think) + *-ikos* -ic] : of or relating to dianoia : INTELLECTUAL

dianoetic virtue *n, Aristotelianism* : INTELLECTUAL VIRTUE

di·a·noia \¦dīəˈnȯiə *also* -ōiyə\ *n* -s [Gk, fr. *dianoeisthai* to have in mind, think, fr. *dia-* + *nous* mind] **1** : the capacity for, process of, or result of discursive thinking **2** : OPINION 6 — contrasted with *noesis*

di·an·the·ra \dīˈan(t)thərə\ [NL, fr. *di-* + *-anthera*] *syn of* JUSTICIA

di·an·thus \dīˈan(t)thəs\ *n* [Gk *dios* heavenly + NL *-anthus* — more at DEITY] **1** *cap* : a very large and horticulturally important Old World genus of herbs (family Caryophyllaceae) including the pinks and carnations and distinguished by the cylindrical many-veined calyx with bracts at its base **2** -ES : any plant or flower of the genus *Dianthus* **3** -ES : a grayish to moderate red that is yellower and darker than Cambridge red

di·a·pasm \ˈdīə,pazəm\ *n* -s [L *diapasma,* fr. Gk *diapasma,* fr. *diapassein* to sprinkle, fr. *dia-* + *passein* to sprinkle — more at QUASH] *archaic* : a perfume of powdered aromatic herbs sometimes made into little balls and strung together

di·a·pa·son \,dīəˈpāzᵊn, -āsᵊn, *attrib* ¦==¦==\ *n* -s [ME *dyapason,* fr. L *diapason,* fr. Gk (*hē*) *dia pasōn* (*chordōn symphōnia*) the concord through all the notes, fr. *dia* through + *pasōn,* gen. pl. fem. of *pas* all — more at DIA-, PAN-] **1 a** (1) : the interval or consonance of the octave in Greek music (2) : a part in music sounding such a consonance (3) *obs* : complete accord, harmony, or agreement **b** (1) : a burst of harmonious sound : MELODY, STRAIN ⟨the sweet ~ of their girlish voices⟩ (2) : any full deep outburst of sound ⟨ugly, deep-throated sounds wove themselves together in a ~ of protest —Hodding Carter⟩ ⟨the foghorn sent deep ~s of sound rolling through the fog⟩ **c** : one of the two principal foundation stops in the organ extending through the complete scale of the instrument **d** (1) : the entire compass of musical tones (2) : the entire compass, scope, or range (as of an activity or other phenomenon) ⟨the vast ~ of his poetic talent⟩ ⟨the unchanging ~ of life in a small country town⟩ **2 a** : TUNING FORK **b** : a measure for determining the construction (as of flutes, oboes, organ pipes) so that the correct pitches may be produced **c** : a standard of pitch — see DIAPASON NORMAL

di·a·pa·son·al \¦dīə¦pāzᵊnᵊl, -äs|, |nəl\ *adj* : relating to or like a diapason

diapason normal *n* [F, lit., normal diapason] : the standard pitch adopted by the French government in 1859 establishing A above middle C as 435 vibrations per second — called also *French pitch, international pitch, low pitch*

1**di·a·pause** \ˈdīə,pȯz\ *n* [Gk *diapausis* pause, fr. *diapauein* to conclude, pause (fr. *dia-* + *pauein* to stop) + *-sis* — more at PAUSE] : a period of spontaneous dormancy independent of environmental conditions interrupting developmental activity in an embryo, larva, or pupa or arresting reproductive activity in an adult insect and usu. occurring during hibernation or aestivation; *sometimes* : a comparable period of dormancy intervening between two periods of activity in other forms (as in certain mammalian embryos) ⟨after the ~ of winter —P.H.Holloway⟩

2**diapause** \"\ *vi* : to undergo diapause — used chiefly as the present participle ⟨*diapausing* larvae⟩

di·a·pe·de·sis \,dīəpəˈdēsəs\ *n, pl* **diapede·ses** \-ē,sēz\ [NL, fr. Gk *diapēdēsis* act of leaping through, oozing through, fr. *diapēdan* to leap through, ooze through (fr. *dia-* + *pēdan* to leap) + *-sis* — more at PEDESIS] **1** : the passage of blood cells through capillary walls into the tissues; *esp* : active amoeboid passage of leukocytes between the enclosing endothelial cells **2** : loss of blood (as through a mucous membrane) without detectable gross lesions — **di·a·pe·det·ic** \¦==¦ded·ik\ *adj*

di·a·pen·sia \,dīəˈpensēə\ *n* [NL, perh. irreg. fr. Gk *dia pente* by fives + NL *-ia;* fr. the five-leaved calyx] **1** *cap* : a genus (the type of the family Diapensiaceae) of boreal dwarf evergreen plants with small crowded coriaceous leaves and flowers on short peduncles **2** -s : any plant of the genus *Diapensia*

di·a·pen·si·a·ce·ae \,dīə,pensēˈāsē,ē\ *n pl, cap* [NL, fr. *Diapensia,* type genus + *-aceae*] : a family (coextensive with the order Diapensiales or included in Ericales) of chiefly north temperate low evergreen plants having pentamerous flowers and epipetalous stamens and the ovary trilocular — compare GALAX, PYXIDANTHERA — **di·a·pen·si·aceous** \,==¦==¦āshəs\ *adj*

di·a·pen·si·a·les \,dīə,pensēˈā(,)lēz\ *n pl, cap* [NL, fr. *Diapensia* + *-ales*] *in some classifications* : an order of low evergreen plants distinguished from those of the order Ericales by a tricarpellate ovary and stamens in two whorls of which one is reduced to staminodia — see DIAPENSIACEAE

di·a·pen·te \,dīəˈpentē, -en·,tē\ *n* -s [ME, fr. L, fr. Gk (*hē*) *dia pente* (*chordōn symphōnia*) the concord through five notes, fr. *dia* through + *pente* five — more at DIA-, FIVE] : the interval or consonance of the fifth in ancient music

1**di·a·per** \ˈdī(ə)pə(r)\ *n* -s [ME *diapre,* fr. MF *diapre, diaspre,* fr. ML *diasprum,* prob. fr. neut. of *diasprus* made of diaper, fr. MGk *diaspros* pure white, fr. Gk *dia* through, throughout + MGk *aspros* white — more at DIA-, ASPER] **1** : a fabric with a distinctive pattern: **a** : a rich silk fabric **b** *also* **diaper cloth** : a soft usu. white linen or cotton fabric used for tablecloths, towels, and now chiefly for infants' wear **2 a** *archaic* : a towel or napkin **b** : a basic garment for infants consisting usu. of a piece of folded cloth or other absorbent material drawn up between the legs and fastened about the waist **3** : an allover pattern consisting of one or more small repeated units of design (as geometric figures) connecting with one another or growing out of one another with continuously flowing or straight lines

2**diaper** \"\ *vb* **diapered; diapered; diapering** \-p(ə)riŋ\ **diapers** [ME *diapren,* fr. MF *diaprer, diasprer,* fr. *diapre, diaspre*] *vt* **1** : to ornament with diaper designs : weave (cloth) in diaper patterns : make (a figure) in diaper pattern **2** : to put on or change the diaper of (an infant) ~ *vi* : to draw diaper patterns (as on cloth)

examples of diaper pattern

diapered *adj* [ME *diapred,* fr. past part. of *diapren*] : having a design of or resembling a diaper pattern

diapering *n* -s : the act of ornamenting with diaper; *also* : the work or ornamentation

diaper rash *n* : an inflammation of the buttocks of infants; *esp* : the condition caused by exposure to excessive urinary ammonia

diaper service *n* **1** : a business concern that supplies and launders diapers **2** : the supplying and laundering of diapers carried out by a diaper service

diaphan- *or* **diaphano-** *comb form* [ME *diaphan-,* fr. MF, fr. *diaphane*] : transparent ⟨*diaphanoscopy*⟩ : transparency ⟨*diaphanometer*⟩

1**di·a·phane** \ˈdīə,fān\ *adj* [MF, fr. ML *diaphanus*] *archaic* : DIAPHANOUS

2**diaphane** \"\ *n* -s **1** : a diaphanous substance **2** : a complex resinous medium for microscopic mounts having a rather low refractive index and comparatively slight tendency to react with stains

di·aph·a·ne·i·ty \(,)dī,afəˈnēəd·ē, ,dīəfə-\ *n* -ES [F *diaphanéité,* fr. *diaphane* diaphanous + *-ité* -ity] : the quality or state of being diaphanous; *specif* : the ability of a mineral to transmit light

di·aph·a·nie \dīˈafənē\ *n* -s [F, fr. *diaphane* + *-ie* -y] : the art of imitating stained glass with translucent paper

di·aph·a·nom·e·ter \dī,afəˈnäməd·ə(r)\ *n* -s [*diaphan-* + *-meter*] : an instrument for measuring transparency (as of air or liquids) — **di·aph·a·no·met·ric** \=,==nō¦me·trik\ *adj*

di·aph·a·no·scope \dīˈafənō,skōp\ *n* -s [ISV *diaphan-* + *-scope*] : a device for examining the accessory nasal sinuses of domestic animals — **di·aph·a·nos·co·py** \=,==ˈnäskəpē\ *n* -ES

di·aph·a·nous \(ˈ)dīˈafənəs\ *adj* [ML *diaphanus,* fr. Gk *diaphanēs,* fr. *diaphainein* to show through, fr. *dia-* + *phainein* to show — more at FANCY] **1** : characterized by such fineness and delicacy of texture as to permit seeing through usu. with a high degree of clarity ⟨~ gowns of chiffon, lace, or net⟩ ⟨~ water through which fish may be clearly seen⟩ **2** : composed or arranged to permit ready perception or comprehension of an inner or veiled essence or substance ⟨I like ~ illusions, with the shapes of things as they are showing not too faintly through them —L.P.Smith⟩ **3** : characterized by extreme delicacy of form : ETHEREAL ⟨poetic and ~ landscapes —Wolfgang Born⟩ ⟨the fantastic, the ~, airy scherzo, nimble-footed and delicate, like a fairy's dance —Hugo Leichtentritt⟩ **4** : INSUBSTANTIAL, VAGUE ⟨the ~ possibility, becoming each day more amorphous —Donn Byrne⟩ **syn** see CLEAR

di·aph·a·nous·ly *adv* : in a diaphanous manner

di·aph·a·nous·ness *n* -ES : the quality or state of being diaphanous

di·a·phone \ˈdīə,fōn\ *n* -s [*dia-* + *-phone*] **1** : all the variants of a phoneme that occur in all utterances of all speakers of a language (in French the tongue-trilled *r* used by some speakers and the uvula-trilled *r* used by other speakers belong to the same ~) **2** : a fog signal similar to a siren **3** : a powerful pipe-organ stop of peculiar construction of 8-foot, 16-foot, or 32-foot pitch

di·a·pho·neme \,dīəˈfō,nēm, ˈdīə(,)fō,n-\ *n* [*dia-* + *phoneme*] : a category or a member of a category consisting of the entire range of dialectal variants of an allophone — **di·a·pho·ne·mic** \¦dīəfō¦nēmik\ *adj*

1**di·a·phon·ic** \¦dīə¦fänik\ *adj* [*diaphony* + *-ic*] : of or relating to diaphony

2**diaphonic** \"\ *adj* [*diaphone* + *-ic*] **1** : of or relating to a diaphone **2** : using a single symbol for an entire diaphone ⟨a ~ transcription⟩

di·aph·o·ny \dīˈafənē\ *also* **di·a·pho·nia** \,dīəˈfōnēə\ *n, pl* **diaphonies** *also* **diaphonias** [ML *diaphonia,* fr. Gk *diaphōnia,* fr. *diaphōnos* dissonant, (fr. *dia-* + *-phōnos,* fr. *phōnē* sound) + *-ia* — more at BAN] **1** *Greek music* : DISSONANCE — opposed to *symphony* **2** *medieval music* : ORGANUM 2b

di·aph·o·rase \dīˈafə,rās, -āz\ *n* -s [G *diaphoros* different + E *-ase*] : a flavoprotein enzyme capable of oxidizing the reduced form of diphosphopyridine nucleotide or of triphosphopyridine nucleotide at the expense of some nonphysiological electron acceptor (as the dye methylene blue)

di·a·pho·re·sis \,dīəfəˈrēsəs\ *n, pl* **diaphore·ses** \-ē,sēz\ [LL, fr. Gk *diaphorēsis,* fr. *diaphorein* to dissipate by perspiration (fr. *dia-* + *phorein* to carry, fr. *pherein* to carry) + *-sis* — more at BEAR] : PERSPIRATION; *esp* : profuse perspiration artificially induced

1**di·a·pho·ret·ic** \¦==¦red·ik\ *adj* [LL *diaphoreticus,* fr. Gk *diaphorētikos,* fr. *diaphorētos* (verbal of *diaphorein*) + *-ikos* -ic] : having the power to increase perspiration

2**diaphoretic** \"\ *n* -s : an agent inducing sweating

di·aph·o·rite \dīˈafə,rīt\ *n* -s [G *diaphorit,* fr. Gk *diaphoros* different + G *-it* -ite] : a mineral $Pb_2Ag_3Sb_3S_8$ consisting of sulfide of lead, silver, and antimony in orthorhombic crystals

dia·phototropism \¦dīə+\ *n* [*dia-* + *phototropism*] : the tropistic tendency of leaves to turn their upper surfaces to face a source of illumination

1**di·a·phragm** \ˈdīə,fram, -raa(ə)m\ *n* -s [ME *diafragma,* fr. LL *diaphragma,* fr. Gk, partition, diaphragm, fr. *diaphrassein, diaphrattein* to barricade, fr. *dia-* + *phrassein, phrattein* to enclose, fence in — more at FARCE] **1** : a body partition of muscle and connective tissue; *specif* : the partition separating the chest and abdominal cavities in mammals that by its contraction and relaxation varies the relative size and the internal pressure of these cavities and thereby plays an important role in such activities as breathing, defecation, and parturition and that in man has the form of an obliquely placed domed sheet, higher in front than behind, attached to the xiphoid cartilage, the six or seven lower ribs and their cartilages, and the lumbar vertebrae — see HICCUP **2** : a dividing membrane or thin partition esp. in a tube **3** : any of various more or less rigid partitions in the bodies or shells of invertebrate animals: as **a** : the membrane separating the heart from the rest of the body of an insect **b** : a calcareous partition extending into the cavity of the shell of a slipper limpet **c** : a chitinous shelf extending from the hydrotheca about the base of a hydranth **d** : a partition dividing the zooecia of some bryozoans into two chambers **4 a** : the constriction in the neck of the nucule in the stoneworts **b** : a transverse septum in a stem (as at the nodes of a scouring rush or in the pith of some woody stems) **5** : a device (as a perforated plate) that limits the aperture of a lens or optical system : STOP — see IRIS DIAPHRAGM **6** : a thin flexible often metallic disk that vibrates when struck by sound waves (as in a microphone) or that vibrates to produce sound waves (as in a telephone receiver or loudspeaker) **7** : a thin plate or partition between parallel parts of a structural steel member (as of a bridge) used to give rigidity to the member **8** : a molded cap usu. of thin rubber fitted over the uterine cervix to act as a mechanical contraceptive barrier **9** : a moving grid of lead strips used for producing sharper X-ray images by eliminating the oblique rays that pass through them before reaching the film

²diaphragm \"\ *vt* -ED/-ING/-S **1** : to equip with a diaphragm : fit a diaphragm to **2** : to cut down the aperture of (a lens or mirror) by means of a diaphragm

di·a·phrag·mat·ic \¦dīəfrag¦mad·ik, -fraig-, -at\|, \|ēk *also* -frə¦m- *sometimes* -frag¦m-\ *adj* [F *diaphragmatique*, fr. MF, fr. Gk *diaphragmat-, diaphragma* + MF *-ique* -ic] : of, involving, or resembling a diaphragm — **diaphragmatically** \|ək(ə)lē, \|ēk-, -li\ *adv*

diaphragmatic respiration *n* : inspiration and expiration produced chiefly by movements of the diaphragm — distinguished from *costal respiration*

diaphragm horn *n* : a foghorn that produces a loud signal by the vibration of a disk diaphragm

diaphragm pump *n* : a pump having a flexible diaphragm in place of a piston

diaphragm shutter *n* : a camera shutter that opens from and closes to the center

diaphragm valve *n* : a valve opened or closed by pressure of or against a diaphragm

di·aph·y·se·al \dī,afə'sēəl, -¦zē- *also* ¦dīə¦fizēəl\ *or* **di·a·phys·i·al** \¦dīə¦fizēəl\ *adj* [*diaphyseal* alter. of *diaphysial; diaphysial* fr. NL *diaphysis* + E *-al*] : of, relating to, or involving a diaphysis

di·aph·y·sis \dī'afəsə̇s\ *n, pl* **diaphy·ses** \-ə,sēz\ [NL, fr. Gk, ridge on the shaft of the tibia, fr. *diaphyesthai* to grow between, be connected with (fr. *dia-* + *phyesthai*, mid. of *phyein* to bring forth) + *-sis* — more at BE] : the shaft of a long bone — distinguished from *epiphysis*

di·a·pir \'dīə,pi(ə)r\ *n* -S [irreg. fr. Gk *diapeirein* to drive through, pierce, fr. *dia-* + *peirein* to pierce; akin to Gk *poreuein* to convey — more at FARE] : an anticlinal fold in which a mobile core has broken through the more brittle overlying rocks — **di·a·pir·ic** \¦dīə¦pirik\ *adj*

di·apophysis \¦dī+\ *n, pl* **diapophyses** [NL, fr. *dia-* + *apophysis*] : a transverse process of a vertebra in higher vertebrates that is an outgrowth of the neural arch and often articulates with the tubercle of a rib; *esp* : one of the dorsal pair of transverse processes when two or more pairs of transverse processes are present

di·a·por·tha·ce·ae \,dīə,pȯr'thāsē,ē\ [NL, fr. *Diaporthe*, type genus + *-aceae*] *syn of* VALSACEAE

di·a·por·the \,dīə'pȯrthē\ *n, cap* [NL, fr. Gk *diaporthein* to destroy completely, fr. *dia-* + *porthein* to destroy] : a genus of ascomycetous fungi (family Valsaceae) having fusoid or ellipsoid hyaline 2-celled ascospores borne in perithecia that are embedded in diffuse or isolated stromata

dia·positive \¦dīə+\ *n* [*dia-* + *positive*] : a photographic positive made on a transparent support (as a lantern slide or a small transparency of an aerial photograph used in the preparation of contour maps)

¹di·ap·sid \(')dī¦apsə̇d\ *adj* [NL *Diapsida*] : of or relating to the Diapsida

²diapsid \"\ *n* -S : any reptile of the subclass Diapsida

di·ap·si·da \dī'apsədə\ *n pl, cap* [NL, fr. *di-* + *-apsida* (fr. Gk *hapsid-, hapsis* arch, loop) — more at APSIS] *in some classifications* : a subclass of reptiles having two pairs of temporal openings in the skull and including the extinct dinosaurs and pterosaurs, the crocodiles and rhynchocephalians, and usu. the lizards and snakes — compare PARAPSIDA — **di·ap·si·dan** \(')dī¦apsədᵊn\ *adj or n*

di·ap·to·mid \dī'aptəmə̇d\ *n* -S [NL *Diaptomidae*, family of copepods, fr. *Diaptomus*, type genus + -idae] : a copepod of the genus *Diaptomus* or the family Diaptomidae

di·ap·to·mus \-məs\ *n, cap* [NL, perh. fr. *di-* + Gk *haptein* to grasp, fasten + *ōmos* shoulder — more at APSIS, HUMERUS] : a genus (the type of the family Diaptomidae) of widely distributed freshwater copepods

di·ap·to·sauria \dī,aptə'sȯrēə\ [NL, fr. *di-* + *-apto-* (fr. Gk *haptein* to fasten) + *-sauria*] *syn of* ARCHOSAURIA

di·arch \'dī,ärk\ *adj* [*di-* + Gk *archē* beginning, origin — more at ARCHI-] : having two xylem groups

diarchy *var of* DYARCHY

di·ar·i·al \(')dī¦a(a)rēəl\ *adj* [*diary* + *-al*] : of or resembling a diary

di·a·rist \'dīərə̇st\ *n* -S : one who keeps a diary

di·a·ris·tic \¦dīə¦ristik\ *adj* : in the style of a diary ⟨~ account⟩ : like that of a diarist ⟨~ talent⟩

di·a·rize \'dīə,rīz\ *vb* -ED/-ING/-S *see -ize in Explan Notes* [*diary* + *-ize*] *vi* : to keep or write in a diary ⟨~ for an hour each evening⟩ ~ *vt* : to record in a diary ⟨~ the affairs of the hour⟩

di·ar·rhea *or* **di·ar·rhoea** \,dīə'rēə\ *n* -S [ME *diaria*, fr. LL *diarrhoea*, fr. Gk *diarrhoia*, lit., act of flowing through, fr. *diarrhein* to flow through, fr. *dia-* + *rhein* to flow — more at STREAM] : an abnormal frequency of discharge of more or less fluid intestinal evacuations due to infectious, fermentative, or toxic causes or physiologic disturbances — **di·ar·rhe·al** *or* **di·ar·rhoe·al** \¦dīə¦rēəl\ *or* **di·ar·rhe·ic** *or* **di·ar·rhoe·ic** \-ēik\ *also* **di·ar·rhet·ic** *or* **di·ar·rhoet·ic** \-red·ik\ *adj*

di·ar·rhee \¦dīə¦rē, (')dī¦rē\ *n* -S [by shortening] *dial* : DIARRHEA

di·arsenide \(')dī+\ *n* [*di-* + *arsenide*] : an arsenide containing two atoms of arsenic

di·ar·thro·di·al \¦dī,är¦thrōdēəl\ *adj* [*di-* + *arthrodial*] : of, relating to, or exhibiting diarthrosis

di·arthrosis \¦dī+\ *n, pl* **diarthroses** [NL, fr. Gk *diarthrōsis*, fr. *diarthroun* to joint, articulate (fr. *dia-* + *arthroun* to fasten by a joint, fr. *arthron* joint) + *-sis* — more at ARTHR-] : a form of articulation that permits considerable change in position and spatial relationship between the articulated parts : a freely movable joint (as the arthrodia, the ginglymus, the pivot joint, the condyloid joint, the enarthrosis)

di·articular \¦dī+\ *adj* [*di-* + *articular*] : of or involving two joints

¹di·a·ry \'dī(ə)rē, -ri\ *n* -ES [L *diarium*, fr. *dies* day + *-arium* -ary — more at DEITY] **1** : a register or record of events, transactions, or observations kept daily or at frequent intervals : JOURNAL; *esp* : a daily record of personal activities, reflections, or feelings **2** : a book intended or used for a diary

²diary \"\ *adj* [L *dies* day + E *-ary*] : lasting one day ⟨~ fever⟩

di·aryl \(')dī+\ *adj* [*di-* + *aryl*] : containing two aryl groups esp. in place of hydrogen

di·arylamine \¦dī+\ *n* -S [*di-* + *aryl* + *amine*] : an amine (as diphenylamine) containing two aryl groups attached to amino nitrogen

di·as·chi·sis \dī'askəsə̇s\ *n, pl* **diaschi·ses** \-ə,sēz\ [NL, fr. Gk, division, fr. *diaschizein* to sever (fr. *dia-* + *schizein* to split) + *-sis* — more at SHED] : the breaking up of a pattern of brain activity by a localized injury that temporarily throws the whole activity out of function though destroying only part of a structure

di·a·schis·ma \,dīə'skizmə\ *n* -S [NL, fr. Gk *diaschisma*, fr. *diaschizein* to sever] **1** : one of several minute intervals in ancient Greek music **2** : a small musical interval (as that between C and D double flat in pure intonation) that together with the schisma comprises the syntonic comma

dia·schistic \¦dīə+\ *adj* [*dia-* + *schistic*] **1** *of chromosomes* : apparently separating longitudinally in one division but transversely in another during atypical meiosis — compare ANASCHISTIC **2** *of rock* : DIFFERENTIATED — opposed to *aschistic*

di·as·cia \dī'ash(ē)ə\ *n, cap* [NL, fr. *di-* + Gk *askos* wineskin, bladder, belly + NL *-ia*; fr. the two sacs that grow on the corolla — more at ASCUS] : a genus of chiefly annual southern African herbs (family Scrophulariaceae) having 2-lipped flowers with the lower lip 2-spurred

di·a·scope \'dīə,skōp\ *n* -S [ISV *dia-* + *-scope*] : a plate of glass pressed against the skin so as to expel the blood from a part and show anatomical changes — **di·a·scop·ic** \¦dīə¦skäpik\ *adj* — **di·as·co·py** \dī'askəpē\ *n* -ES

di·a·scor·di·um \,dīə'skȯrdēəm\ *n, pl* **diascor·dia** \-ēə\ [NL, fr. Gk *dia* through, by means of + Gk *skordion* garlic germander, fr. *skordon* garlic; akin to Alb *hurdhë, hudhrë* garlic, OE *scort* short — more at DIA-, SHORT] : a stomachic and astringent electuary made from the dried leaves of the water germander or other herbs

di·a·skeu·ast *also* **di·a·sceu·ast** \,dīə'skyü,ast, -,əst\ *n* -S [Gk *diaskeuastēs*, fr. *diaskeuazein* to make ready, revise, edit, fr. *dia-* + *skeuazein* to make ready, fr. *skeuos* vessel, implement — more at SKEUOMORPH] : one who makes a revision : EDITOR

Di·a·sone \'dīə,sōn\ *trademark* — used for sulfoxone sodium

di·as·pid \dī'aspə̇d\ *adj* [NL *Diaspididae*] : of or relating to the Diaspididae

di·as·pi·di·dae \dī,aspə'dī(,)dē\ *n pl, cap* [NL, fr. *Diaspid-, Diaspis*, type genus (fr. *dia-* + *-aspid-, -aspis*) + *-idae*] : a family of scales that have a one-jointed beak and a female which secretes a firm scaly covering over herself and her eggs and that comprise the armored scales

di·as·pine \dī'a,spīn, -,spə̇n\ *adj* [NL *Diaspinae* subfamily of scales, fr. *Diaspis*, type genus + *-inae*] : DIASPID

di·as·po·ra \dī'asp(ə)rə, -'aas-\ *n* -S [Gk, dispersion, scattering, fr. *diaspeirein* to scatter, spread about, fr. *dia-* + *speirein* to sow, scatter — more at SPORE] **1** *usu cap* **a** : the settling of scattered colonies of Jews outside Palestine after the Babylonian exile **b** : the area outside Palestine settled by Jews ⟨in Israel or in the *Diaspora*⟩ **c** : the Jews living outside Palestine or modern Israel **d** : the state of the Jews living scattered in the Gentile world **2** : a dispersion (as of people of a common national origin or of common beliefs) : spread (as of a national culture) : EXILE, SCATTERING, MIGRATION **3** : the people of one country dispersed into other countries ⟨certain sections of the Armenian ~ scattered over the world could be attracted —Walter Kolarz⟩ **4** : the dispersion of Christians isolated from their own communion

di·a·spore \'dīə,spō(ə)r\ *n* -S [Gk *diaspora* dispersion, scattering] **1** : a mineral consisting of aluminum hydrogen oxide $HAlO_2$ and occurring in white lamellar masses with pearly luster or in prismatic orthorhombic crystals **2** : DISSEMINULE; *esp* : one specialized for dispersal

diaspore clay *n* : a rock consisting of diaspore bonded by fireclay

di·a·stase \'dīə,stās\ *n* -S [F, fr. Gk *diastasis* separation, fr. *diistanai* to separate, fr. *dia-* through, apart + *histanai* to set, cause to stand — more at DIA-, STAND] **1** : AMYLASE; *esp* : a mixture of amylases obtained usu. as a yellowish white amorphous powder from malt and used chiefly in desizing textiles and converting starch to maltose **2** : ENZYME

di·a·sta·sic \¦dīə¦stāsik\ *adj* [ISV *diastase* + *-ic*] : DIASTATIC

di·as·ta·sis \dī'astəsə̇s, -'aas-\ *n, pl* **diasta·ses** \-ə,sēz\ [NL, fr. Gk, separation] **1** *med* : an abnormal separation of parts normally joined together **2** *physiol* : the rest phase of cardiac diastole occurring between filling of the ventricle and the start of auricular contraction

-diastasis \"\ *n comb form, pl* **-diastases** [NL, fr. Gk *diastasis* separation] **1** : disintegration ⟨myelo*diastasis*⟩ **2** : displacement ⟨adeno*diastasis*⟩

di·a·stat·ic \¦dīə¦stad·ik\ *adj* [irreg. (influence of Gk *diastatikos* disintegrating) fr. *diastase* + *-ic*] : relating to or having the properties of diastase : AMYLOLYTIC ⟨~ activity of flour⟩ — **di·a·stat·i·cal·ly** \-ək(ə)lē\ *adv*

di·a·stem \'dīə,stem\ *n* -S [LL *diastema*, fr. Gk *diastēma* interval, fr. *diistanai* to separate — more at DIASTASE] **1** : an interval in ancient Greek music **2** : DIASTEMA 1 **3** : a minor interruption in sedimentation with little or no erosion before deposition is resumed — compare DISCONFORMITY, UNCONFORMITY — **di·a·stem·ic** \¦dīə¦stemik\ *adj*

di·a·ste·ma \,dīə'stēmə\ *n, pl* **di·a·ste·ma·ta** \-tēməd·ə, -tem-\ [NL, fr. LL, interval] **1** : the modified cytoplasm in the equatorial plane during mitosis that indicates the division plane of the cell **2** : a space between teeth in a jaw — **di·a·ste·mat·ic** \¦dīəstə¦mad·ik\ *adj*

di·aster \(')dī+\ *n* -S [ISV *di-* + *-aster*] : a stage in mitotic cell division when the chromosomes, having split and separated, group themselves near the poles of the spindle preparatory to forming the new nuclei — **di·astral** \"+\ *adj*

dia·stereoisomer \¦dīə+\ *or* **dia·ster·e·o·mer** \¦dīə¦sterēəmə(r), -tir-\ *n* -S [*dia-* + *stereoisomer*] : an isomer exhibiting diastereoisomerism — distinguished from *enantiomorph*

dia·stereoisomeric \¦dīə+\ *or* **di·a·ster·e·o·mer·ic** \¦dīə¦sterēō¦merik, -tir-\ *adj* : of, relating to, or exhibiting diastereoisomerism

dia·stereoisomerism \¦dīə+\ *n* -S : optical isomerism of compounds whose molecules contain more than one asymmetric atom and do not exhibit mirror-image relationship (as glucose and galactose or *meso*-tartaric acid and *dextro*-tartaric acid) — distinguished from *enantiomorphism*; compare ASYMMETRIC CARBON ATOM

di·a·stim·e·ter \,dīə'stiməd·ə(r)\ *n* -S [ISV *diasti-* (fr. Gk *diastasis* interval, separation) + *-meter* — more at DIASTASE] : an instrument for measuring distances

di·as·to·le \dī'astə(,)lē, -'aas-, -,lī\ *n* -S [Gk *diastolē* dilatation, fr. *diastellein* to expand, be dilated, fr. *dia-* + *stellein* to make ready, start out, send — more at STALL] **1 a** : the passive rhythmical expansion or dilatation of the cavities of the heart during which they fill with blood — compare SYSTOLE **b** : the rhythmical expansion of a pulsating vacuole **2** *prosody* : a lengthening of a short quantity or syllable **3** : EXPANSION

di·a·stol·ic \¦dīə¦stälik, -lēk\ *adj* : of, relating to, or occurring during diastole

diastolic pressure *n* : the lowest arterial blood pressure of a cardiac cycle occurring during diastole of the heart — compare SYSTOLIC PRESSURE

dia·stomatic \¦dīəstō¦mad·ik\ *adj* [*dia-* + *stomatic*] : STOMATAL

di·as·tro·phe \dī'astrəfē\ *n* -S [Gk *diastrophē* twisting, distortion, fr. *diastrephein* to twist about, distort, fr. *dia-* + *strephein* to turn, twist — more at STROPHE] : a deformation of the earth's crust

di·a·stroph·ic \¦dīə¦sträfik\ *adj* : of, having reference to, or caused by diastrophism

di·as·tro·phism \dī'astrə,fizəm\ *n* -S : the process of deformation that produces in the earth's crust its continents and ocean basins, plateaus and mountains, folds of strata, and faults — compare EPEIROGENY, OROGENY

di·a·style \'dīə,stīl\ *n* -S [L *diastylos* having a space of three diameters between columns, fr. Gk, fr. *dia-* through, apart + *stylos* column — more at DIA-, STYLE] : intercolumniation of three diameters — see INTERCOLUMNIATION illustration

di·a·tes·sa·ron \,dīə'tesərən, -,rän\ *n* -S [ME *dyatessaron*, fr. L *diatessaron*, fr. Gk (*hē*) *dia tessarōn* (*chordōn symphōnia*) the concord through four notes, fr. *dia* through + *tessarōn*, gen. of *tessares, tettares* four — more at FOUR] **1** : the interval of a fourth in ancient Greek music **2** *obs* : an electuary compounded of four medicines **3** : a harmony of the four Gospels edited and arranged into a single connected narrative

di·a·ther·mal \¦dīə¦thərməl\ *adj* [*dia-* + *thermal*] : DIATHERMIC

di·a·ther·man·cy \,dīə'thərmənsē\ *or* **di·a·ther·ma·cy** \-məsē\ *n* -ES [*diathermancy* fr. F *diathermansie*, fr. Gk *dia-* + *thermansis* heating, fr. *thermainein* to heat, fr. *thermos* hot; *diathermacy* fr. F *diathermasie*, fr. Gk *diathermasia* heating effect, fr. *diathermainein* to heat through, fr. *dia-* + *thermainein* — more at WARM] : the ability to transmit infrared radiation — compare ATHERMANCY

di·a·ther·ma·nous \¦dīə¦thərmənəs\ *adj* [F *diathermane*, irreg. (influence of *diaphane* diaphanous) fr. Gk *diathermainein*] : transmitting infrared radiation — compare ATHERMANOUS

di·a·ther·mic \¦dīə¦thərmik, -ēm-,-əim-, -mēk\ *adj* [F *diathermique*, fr. *dia-* + *thermique* thermic] **1** : DIATHERMANOUS **2** : of or relating to diathermy ⟨~ treatment⟩

di·a·ther·my \'==,=mē, -mi\ *n* -ES [ISV *dia-* + *-thermy*] : the generation of heat in tissue for medical or surgical purposes by the application of high-frequency electric currents of various wavelengths by means of electrodes and other instruments — see ELECTROCOAGULATION, SHORTWAVE THERAPY

di·ath·e·sis \dī'athəsə̇s\ *n, pl* **diathe·ses** \-ə,sēz\ [NL, fr. Gk, lit., arrangement, disposition, fr. *diatithenai* to arrange, dispose, fr. *dia-* + *tithenai* to set, put, place — more at DO] **1** : a bodily tendency or constitutional predisposition toward some abnormality or disease ⟨hemorrhagic ~⟩ ⟨tubercular ~⟩ **2** : an innate disposition toward or aptitude for some particular mental development **3** *of a verb* : VOICE 7

di·a·thet·ic \¦dīə¦thed·ik\ *adj* [fr. NL *diathesis*, after such pairs as LL *antithesis*: E *antithetic*] : of or relating to a diathesis; *specif* : of or belonging to the voice of a verb

di·a·tom \'dīə,täm *sometimes* -əd·əm *or* -ətəm\ *n* -S [NL *Diatoma*] : any of the unicellular or colonial algae constituting a class (Bacillariophyceae), having a silicified cell wall that persists as a skeleton after death and forms diatomite, and forming a large part of the plankton of both fresh and salt water — see FRUSTULE, GIRDLE e(1), VALVE

di·at·o·ma \dī'ad·əmə\ *n, cap* [NL, fr. Gk *diatomē*, fem. of *diatomos* cut in half, fr. *diatemnein* to cut through, fr. *dia-* + *temnein* to cut — more at TOME] : a genus of freshwater diatoms (family Diatomaceae) that sometimes cause aromatic or disagreeable odors in water

¹di·a·to·ma·ce·ae \,dīəd·ə'māsē,ē, (,)dī,ad·ə-\ [NL, fr. *Diatoma*, type genus + *-aceae*] *syn of* BACILLARIACEAE

²diatomaceae \"\ *n pl, cap* [NL, fr. *Diatoma*, type genus + *-aceae*] : a family of rectangular diatoms

di·a·to·ma·ceous \¦dīəd·ə¦māshəs, (¦)dī,ad·ə-\ *adj* [NL ¹*Diatomaceae* + E *-ous*] **1** : BACILLARIACEOUS **2** : consisting of or abounding in diatoms or their siliceous remains ⟨~ silica⟩

diatomaceous earth *n* : DIATOMITE

di·a·to·ma·les \,dīəd·ə'mā(,)lēz, (,)dī,ad·ə-\ *n pl, cap* [NL, fr. *Diatoma* + *-ales*] *in some classifications* : an order coextensive with the class Bacillariophyceae

di·a·to·me·ae \,dīə'tōmē,ē\ [NL, fr. *Diatoma* + *-eae*] *syn of* BACILLARIOPHYCEAE

di·atomic \¦dī+\ *adj* [ISV *di-* + *atomic*] **1** : consisting of two atoms : having two atoms in the molecule **2** : having two replaceable atoms or radicals

di·at·o·min \dī'ad·əmə̇n\ *n* -S [*diatom* + *-in*] : a yellow or yellowish brown pigment found in certain algae and diatoms — called also *phycoxanthin*

di·a·tom·ist \'dīə,täməst, dī'ad·əm- *sometimes* 'dīəd·əm-\ *n* -S [*diatom* + *-ist*] : one who studies diatoms

di·at·o·mite \dī'ad·ə,mīt\ *n* -S [ISV *diatom* + *-ite*] : a light friable siliceous material resembling chalk that is derived chiefly from the remains of diatoms and is used as a filter aid, adsorbent, filler (as for paints and plastics), and abrasive, and for thermal insulation — called also *diatomaceous earth*; compare KIESELGUHR, TRIPOLI

diatom ooze *n* : deep-sea deposits rich in diatoms

di·a·ton·ic \¦dīə¦tänik, -nēk\ *adj* [LL *diatonicus*, fr. Gk *diatonikos*, fr. *diatonos* stretching, extending (fr. *diateinein* to stretch out, extend, fr. *dia-* + *teinein* to stretch) + *-ikos* -ic — more at THIN] **1** *of a Greek tetrachord* : comprising two steps and a half step — distinguished from *chromatic* and *enharmonic* **2** : relating to a standard major or minor scale of eight tones to the octave without chromatic deviation — **di·a·ton·i·cal·ly** \-nək(ə)lē, -nēk-, -li\ *adv*

di·a·ton·i·cism \,dīə'tänə,sizəm\ *also* **di·a·ton·ism** \'dīə,tä,nizəm, dī'ad·ə,n-\ *n* -S **1** : the quality or state of being diatonic **2** : the use of diatonic harmony — contrasted with *chromaticism*

di·a·tor·ic \¦dīə¦tȯrik\ *adj* [G *diatoros* pierced (fr. *diateirein* to pierce, fr. *dia-* + *teirein* to bore, turn) + E *-ic* — more at THROW] : having a recess in its base for attachment to the dental plate — used of an artificial tooth

di·a·traea \,dīə'trēə\ *n, cap* [NL, irreg. fr. Gk *diateirein*] : a genus of moderate-sized dull-colored moths (family Pyralididae) producing boring larvae that are serious pests in a number of crop plants esp. in warm regions — see SOUTHERN CORNSTALK BORER

di·a·treme \'dīə,trēm\ *n* -S [*dia-* + Gk *trēma* hole — more at THROW] : a small generally circular volcanic vent produced by gaseous explosion usu. preceded by deep-seated rock fusion by hot gases

di·a·tribe \'dīə,trīb\ *n* -S [L *diatriba*, fr. Gk *diatribē* pastime, study, discourse, fr. *diatribein* to spend (time), wear away, fr. *dia-* + *tribein* to rub — more at THROW] **1** *archaic* : a prolonged discourse or discussion **2** [F, fr. MF, prolonged discourse, fr. L *diatriba*] **a** : a bitter, abusive, and usu. lengthy speech or piece of writing ⟨the melancholy ~s of the old prophets —Richard Chase⟩ ⟨a ~ against Nero —Berthe M. Marti⟩ **b** : bitter and abusive speech or writing ⟨to be irritated or offended by such ~ —*Time*⟩ **3** : ironical or satirical criticism

di·a·trop·ic \¦dīə¦träpik\ *adj* : characterized by diatropism

di·at·ro·pism \dī'a·trə,pizəm\ *n* -S [ISV *dia-* + *-tropism*] : the tropistic tendency of certain plant organs to place themselves transversely to the line of action of a stimulus — compare DIAGEOTROPISM, DIAPHOTOTROPISM

di·a·try·ma \,dīə'trīmə\ *n, cap* [NL, fr. *dia-* + Gk *tryma, trymē* hole] : a genus of large flightless Eocene birds from Wyoming and New Mexico having much reduced wings, large head and powerful beak, and long massive legs and constituting with extinct related forms (as *Gastornis*) an order of birds probably most nearly related to the surviving cariamas and bustards

di·au·los \dī'aù,läs, dē'ō,l-\ *n, pl* **diau·li** \-aù,lē, -ō,lī\ [Gk, fr. *di-* + *aulos* pipe, reed instrument like an oboe, racecourse — more at ALVEOLUS] : the double course for footraces in ancient Greece in which the contestants ran down one side of the stadium, turned round a goal, and returned to the starting point

di·axon \(')dī+\ *also* **di·axone** \"+\ *n* -S [*di-* + *axon, axone*] : a nerve cell with two axons — **di·ax·on·ic** \¦dī,ak¦sänik\ *adj*

diaz- *or* **diazo-** *comb form* [ISV, fr. *di-* + *az-*] **1** *usu diazo-* : containing the group N_2 united to carbon in one organic radical ⟨*diazo*acetic ester $N_2CHCOOC_2H_5$⟩ **2** *diazo-* : containing diazonium ⟨*diazo*benzenesulfonic acid $^{+}N_2C_6H_4SO_3^{-}$⟩

di·a·zine \'dīə,zēn, dī'az-, -zə̇n\ *n* -S [ISV *di-* + *az-* + *-ine*] **1** : any of three parent compounds $C_4H_4N_2$ containing a ring composed of four carbon atoms and two nitrogen atoms and distinguished by indication of the positions of the nitrogen atoms or by trivial names: **a** : PYRIDAZINE **b** : PYRIMIDINE **c** : PYRAZINE **2** : any of a large class of derivatives of the three parent diazines

¹di·azo \(')dī¦a(,)zō, -¦ā-\ *adj* [*diaz-*] **1** : relating to or containing the group N_2 united to carbon in one organic radical — distinguished from *disazo*; compare AZO **2** : relating to or containing diazonium **3** : of or relating to a diazotype ⟨~ paper⟩

²diazo \"\ *n* -S : any diazo compound — usu. used commercially

di·azo·amino \"+\ *adj* [*diazoamino-*] : containing the group $-N{=}N{-}NH{-}$

diazoamino- *comb form* [ISV *diaz-* + *amin-*] : containing the group $-N{=}N{-}NH{-}$ united to organic radicals ⟨*diazoamino*benzene $C_6H_5N{=}NNHC_6H_5$⟩

di·az·o·ate \dī'azō,āt, -'āz-, -ōə̇t\ *or* **di·az·o·tate** \-,tāt\

n -s [*diazoate* fr. *diaz-* + *-ate; diazotate* fr. *di-* + *azote* + *-ate*] **:** a salt of a diazoic acid

di·azo·dinitrophenol \(ˈ)dīˌa(ˌ)zō, -ā(ˌ)zō+\ *n* -s [*diaz-* + *dinitrophenol*] **:** a yellow solid diazo oxide $(NO_2)_2C_6H_2N_2O$ made by diazotization of picramic acid and used as an initiating explosive in mixtures

diazo dye *or* **diazo color** *also* **diazo** *n* **:** DEVELOPED DYE — see DYE table I (under *Direct*)

diazo fast yellow GG *n, usu cap D&F&Y* **:** a fluorescent brightener — see DYE table I (under *Fluorescent Brightener 5*)

di·a·zo·ic acid \ˌdīəˈzōik-\ *n* [ISV *diaz-* + *-ic*] **:** any of a class of acids containing a diazo group united with hydroxyl; *esp* **:** an aromatic acid of the general formula ArN=NOH (as benzene-diazoic acid C_6H_5N=NOH) obtained in the form of salts by treating a diazonium chloride with alkali

di·azo·imide \(ˈ)dīˌa(ˌ)zō, -ā(ˌ)zō+\ *n* -s [ISV *diaz-* + *imide*] **:** AZIDE; *esp* **:** an aromatic azide

di·a·zole \ˈdīəˌzōl, dīˈaz-\ *n* -s [ISV *diaz-* + *-ole*] **1 :** either of two parent compounds $C_3H_4N_2$ containing a ring composed of three carbon atoms and two nitrogen atoms: **a :** PYRAZOLE **b :** IMIDAZOLE **2 :** a derivative of either parent diazole

di·a·zo·ma \ˌdīəˈzōmə\ *n, pl* **di·a·zo·ma·ta** \-mədˌə\ [L, fr. Gk *diazōma*, lit., girdle, fr. *dia-* + *zōma* girdle — more at ZONE] **:** a passage in the auditorium of an ancient Greek theater dividing the lower from the upper rows of seats for convenience of access — see THEATER illustration

di·azo·methane \(ˈ)dīˌa(ˌ)zō, -ā(ˌ)zō+\ *n* [ISV *diaz-* + *methane*] **:** a yellow odorless poisonous explosive gaseous compound CH_2N_2 used chiefly as a methylating agent (as for converting organic acids into their methyl esters) and in converting organic acids into the next higher homologues

di·a·zo·ni·um \ˌdīəˈzōnēəm\ *n* -s [ISV *diaz-* + *-onium*] **:** the univalent cation $-N_2^+$ composed of two nitrogen atoms united to carbon in one organic radical; *esp* **:** a cation ArN_2^+ (as benzenediazonium) obtained in the form of salts by diazotizing an arylamine and used chiefly in the manufacture of azo dyes — compare DIAZ-

diazo oxide *n* **:** any of a class of compounds (as diazodinitrophenol) that contain a diazo group and an oxygen atom attached to ortho positions of an aromatic nucleus and are formed by the action of nitrous acid on *ortho*-aminophenols with loss of water, a few of these compounds finding use as initiating explosives and in diazotypes — called also *diazophenol*

di·azo·phenol \(ˈ)dīˌa(ˌ)zō, -ā(ˌ)zō+\ *n* -s [ISV *diaz-* + *phenol*] **:** DIAZO OXIDE

diazo process *n* **:** the process of making diazotypes

diazo reaction *n* **:** a reaction in which a diazo compound is made or used; *specif* **:** a reaction in various diseases (as typhoid fever) consisting of a red discoloration of the urine on addition of diazobenzenesulfonic acid

di·azo·sulfonate \(ˈ)dīˌa(ˌ)zō, -ā(ˌ)zō+\ *n* -s [*diaz-* + *sulfonate*] **:** a salt of a diazosulfonic acid

di·azo·sulfonic acid \"+ . . . -\ *n* [*diaz-* + *sulfonic*] **:** any of a class of aromatic acids that contain a diazo group united with a sulfonic acid group, have the general formula ArN=NSO₃H, and are obtained in the form of salts by treating a diazonium salt with a sulfite

di·az·o·tiz·able \dīˈazəˌtīzəbəl\ *adj* **:** capable of being diazotized

di·az·o·ti·za·tion \dīˌazətəˈzāshən\ *n* -s **:** the process of diazotizing

di·az·o·tize \dīˈazəˌtīz\ *vt* -ED/-ING/-S [*di-* + *azote* + *-ize*] **:** to convert (a chemical compound) into a diazo compound; *esp* **:** to convert (an arylamine) into a diazonium salt by the action of nitrous acid in acid solution

di·az·o·type \-ˌtīp\ *n* [*diaz-* + *-type*] **:** a photograph or photocopy produced on a surface (as paper) by coating with a solution containing a diazo compound that is decomposed on exposure to light, the compound in the unexposed parts being then converted to a colored image formed by an azo dye by developing esp. with an alkaline solution or gaseous ammonia

¹dib \ˈdib\ *vi* **dibbed; dibbed; dibbing; dibs** [perh. fr. obs. *dib* to dab, pat, prob. alter. of *dab*] **:** to fish by letting the bait bob and dip lightly

²dib \"\ *n* -s [short for *dibstone*] **1** *Brit* **a dibs** *pl but sing in constr* **:** the game of jacks **b :** a knucklebone or jack used in playing jacks — usu. used in pl. **2 dibs** *pl, slang* **:** money esp. in small amounts **3 dibs** *pl* **:** CLAIM, RESERVATION, RIGHTS — used with *on* ⟨I have ~s on that piece of cake⟩

³dib \"\ *var of* ³DUB

di·basic \(ˈ)dī+\ *adj* [*di-* + *basic*] **1 :** having two hydrogen atoms capable of replacement by basic atoms or radicals — used of acids (as oxalic or sulfuric acid) **2 :** containing two atoms of a univalent metal or their equivalent ⟨~ sodium phosphate Na_2HPO_4⟩ **3 :** having two basic hydroxyl groups **:** able to react with two molecules of a monobasic acid — used of bases and basic salts — **di·basicity** \(ˌ)dī+\ *n* -ES

dib·a·tag \ˈdibəˌtag\ *n* -s [Somali *dabatag, dibtag*] **:** a small gazelle (*Ammodorcas clarkei*) of northeastern Africa having a long neck and tail and in the male short ringed recurved horns — called also *Clarke's gazelle*

dib·ber \ˈdibə(r)\ *n* -s [by alter.] **:** DIBBLE

¹dib·ble \ˈdibəl\ *n* -s [ME *debylle*] **:** a small hand implement used to make holes in the ground for plants, seeds, or bulbs

²dib·ble \"\ *vb* **dibbled; dibbled; dibbling** \-b(ə)liŋ\ **dibbles** *vt* **:** to plant with a dibble **:** make holes in (soil) with or as if with a dibble (as for planting) **~** *vi* **:** to work with a dibble (as in planting)

³dibble \"\ *vi* -ED/-ING/-S [freq. of obs. *dib* to dab — more at DIB] **1 :** DABBLE 1b **2 :** ¹DIB

dib·bler \ˈdib(ə)lə(r)\ *n* -s **:** one that dibbles; *esp* **:** a machine having two wheels with long rounded projections on their rims that make spaced holes in a row for transplants

dibble

dibbuk *var of* DYBBUK

dibenz- *or* **dibenzo-** *comb form* [ISV, fr. *di-* + *benz-*] **:** containing two benzene rings — in names of organic compounds ⟨*dibenz*acridine⟩ ⟨*dibenzo*furan⟩

di·benz·anthracene \ˌdī(ˌ)benz+\ *n* [*dibenz-* + *anthracene*] **:** an orange-brown crystalline actively carcinogenic cyclic hydrocarbon $C_{22}H_{14}$ found in trace amounts in coal tar — called also *1,2:5,6-dibenzanthracene, dibenz[a,h]anthracene*

dibhole \ˈ≈,≈\ *n* [³*dib* + *hole*] *Brit* **:** a drainage hole at the bottom of a mine shaft

di·borane \(ˈ)dī+\ *n* [*di-* + *borane*] **:** a gaseous compound B_2H_6 of boron and hydrogen that has a repulsive odor, is formed by reaction between a metal hydride and a boron halide usu. in ether solution, and decomposes rapidly in water to boric acid and hydrogen — called also *diborane(6)*

di·bothriocephalus \(ˌ)dī+\ [NL, fr. *di-* + *bothri-* + *-cephalus*] *syn of* DIPHYLLOBOTHRIUM

di·bot·ry·on \dīˈbä·trēˌän, -ˌən\ *n, cap* [NL, fr. *di-* + Gk *botryon* cluster of berries] **:** a genus of parasitic fungi (family Dothideaceae) having hyaline 2-celled spores borne in perithecia formed in dark stromata — see BLACK KNOT

di·brach \ˈdīˌbrak\ *n* -s [LL *dibrachys*, adj., fr. Gk, fr. *di-* + *brachys* short — more at BRIEF] **:** PYRRHIC

di·branch \ˈdīˌbraŋk\ *n* -s [NL *Dibranchia*] **:** one of the Dibranchia

di·bran·chia \dīˈbraŋkēə\ *n pl, cap* [NL, fr. *di-* + Gk *branchia* gills — more at BRANCHIA] **:** a subclass or order of Cephalopoda including the squids and octopuses, being characterized by 2 gills, 2 auricles, 2 nephridia, an apparatus for emitting an inky fluid, and either 8 or 10 cephalic arms bearing suckers or hooks, and comprising all living cephalopods except those of the genus *Nautilus* — **di·bran·chi·ate** \(ˈ)≈ˈ≈kēət, -ēˌāt\ *adj or n*

di·bran·chi·a·ta \(ˌ)≈,≈kēˈäd·ə, -ād·ə\ [NL, fr. *di-* + *branchi-* + *-ata*] *syn of* DIBRANCHIA

dibrom- *or* **dibromo-** *comb form* [ISV, fr. *di-* + *brom-*] **:** containing two atoms of bromine — in names of chemical compounds ⟨*dibromo*acetic acid⟩; compare BROM-

di·bromide \(ˈ)dī+\ *n* [*di* + *bromide*] **:** a binary compound containing two atoms of bromine combined with an element or radical

¹dibs *pres 3d sing of* DIB, *pl of* DIB

²dibs \ˈdibz\ *n pl but sing in constr* [Ar] **:** a sweet syrup made from grape juice or from dates and used in the East

dibstone \ˈ≈,≈\ *n* [¹*dib* + *stone*] **1 :** DIB 1b **2 dibstones** *pl but sing in constr, archaic* **:** the game of jacks

di·bu·caine \(ˈ)dīˈbyüˌkān\ *n* -s [*di-* + *butoxy-* + *-caine*] **:** a local anesthetic $C_{20}H_{29}N_3O_2$ that is administered parenterally as the bitter crystalline hydrochloride

di·butyl \(ˈ)dī+\ *adj* [*di-* + *butyl*] **:** containing two butyl groups in the molecule

dibutyl phthalate *n* **:** a colorless oily ester $C_6H_4(COOC_4H_9)_2$ used chiefly as a solvent and plasticizer

di·cac·i·ty \dīˈkasəd·ē\ *n* -ES [L *dicacitas*, fr. *dicac-, dicax* satirical, sarcastic, witty (fr. *dicere* to say) + *-itas* -ity — more at DICTION] *archaic* **:** RAILLERY **:** biting wit

di·cae·i·dae \dīˈsēəˌdē\ *n pl, cap* [NL *Dicaeum*, type genus + *-idae*] **:** a family of passerine birds containing the flower-peckers

di·calcium \(ˈ)dī+\ *adj* [*di-* + *calcium*] **:** containing two atoms or equivalents of calcium in the molecule

dicalcium phosphate *n* **:** CALCIUM PHOSPHATE 1a(2)

di·camp·to·don \dīˈkamptəˌdän\ *n, cap* [NL, fr. *di-* + *campto-* + *-odon*] **:** a genus of large salamanders (family Ambystomidae) of the Pacific coast of No. America

di·carbocyanine \"+\ *or* **dicarbocyanine dye** *n* [*di-* + *carb-* + *cyanine*] **:** any of certain cyanine dyes in whose structure the two heterocyclic rings are joined by a five-carbon chain (as =CH—CH=CH—CH=CH—); *specif* **:** such a dye containing two quinoline rings — called also *pentamethine*

di·carboxylic \(ˌ)dī+\ *adj* [*di-* + *carboxylic*] **:** containing two carboxyl groups in the molecule

dicaryon *var of* DIKARYON

dicaryophase *var of* DIKARYOPHASE

dicaryophyte *var of* DIKARYOPHYTE

dicaryotic *var of* DIKARYOTIC

di·cast *or* **di·kast** \ˈdīˌkast, ˈdi,-\ *n* -s [Gk *dikastēs* judge, juror, fr. *dikazein* to judge, fr. *dikē* right, judgment — more at DICTION] **:** a member of the highest court of law of ancient Athens who performed the functions of both judge and jury — **di·cas·tic** *or* **di·kas·tic** \(ˈ)dīˌkastik, diˈk-\ *adj*

di·cas·tery *or* **di·kas·tery** \dīˈkast(ə)rē, ˈdīˌk-, diˈk-\ *n* -ES [Gk *dikastērion* court of law, fr. *dikastēs*] **:** the court composed of the dicasts; *also* **:** the place where the court sat

¹di·catalectic \(ˌ)dī+\ *adj* [*di-* + *catalectic*] *prosody* **:** composed of two catalectic members

²dicatalectic \"\ *n* **:** a dicatalectic verse

di·catalexis \(ˌ)dī+\ *n* [*di-* + *catalexis*] *prosody* **:** catalexis occurring twice within a line

¹dice \ˈdīs\ *n, pl* **dice** *usu pl in constr, often attrib* [fr. pl. of ²*die*] **:** ²DIE — **no dice :** of no avail **:** no use **:** FUTILE ⟨falls in love with her . . . but it is *no dice* —Philip Hamburger⟩

²dice \"\ *vb* -ED/-ING/-S [ME *dycen*, fr. *dyce, dees*, pl. of *dee* die — more at DIE] *vt* **1 a :** to cut into dice ⟨~ bread⟩ ⟨*diced* potatoes⟩ **b :** to ornament with square markings or make in a pattern of small squares **:** CHECKER ⟨*diced* leather⟩ ⟨*diced* stockings⟩ **2 a :** to bring into some usu. unfavorable condition by playing dice games ⟨~ himself into debt⟩ **b :** to lose by dicing **:** throw away **c** *Austral* **:** to cast aside **:** REJECT ⟨*diced* by her sweetheart⟩ **3** *mil* **a :** to map (an area) by taking aerial photographs **b :** to fly as low as possible over to obtain detailed photographs of (a territory or objective) ⟨~ a target⟩ **~** *vi* **1 a :** to play games with dice **:** GAMBLE ⟨you may not even ~ for drinks in the bar —Malcolm Lowry⟩ **b :** to take a chance ⟨the temptation to ~ with death —*Newsweek*⟩ **2** *of glass* **:** to break into small pieces **:** SHATTER

dice board *n* **:** a board on which dice are thrown

dicebox \ˈ≈,≈\ *n* **:** a box from which dice are thrown

dice cup *n* **:** a small cup or box in which dice are shaken by hand and from which they are then thrown

dice girl *n* **:** a girl who acts as dealer at various dice games

di·cen·tra \dīˈsen·trə\ *n* [NL, fr. *di-* + *-centra* (fr. Gk *kentron* sharp point) — more at CENTER] **1** *cap* **:** a genus of No. American and Asiatic herbs (family Fumariaceae) with dissected leaves and irregular flowers — see BLEEDING HEART, DUTCHMAN'S-BREECHES **2** -s **:** any plant of the genus *Dicentra* (esp. *D. spectabilis*)

di·centric \(ˈ)dī+\ *adj* [*di-* + *-centric*] *biol* **:** having two centromeres

di·ceph·a·lus \(ˈ)dīˈsefələs\ *n, pl* **dicepha·li** \-ˌlī\ [NL, fr. *di-* + *-cephalus*] **:** a fetal anomaly having two distinct heads

dic·er \ˈdīsə(r)\ *n* -s [ME *dycer*, fr. *dycen* to dice + *-er*] **1 :** one who gambles at dice games **2** *slang* **:** a man's hat; *esp* **:** DERBY **3 a :** a machine that dices food (as fruits and vegetables) **b :** one that operates such a machine **4 :** GRAINER 1d

di·cer·as \ˈdīsərəs, dīˈserəs\ *n, cap* [NL, fr. *di-* + *-ceras*] **:** a genus (the type of the family Diceratidae) of Jurassic lamellibranchs with the umbones of both valves produced and spirally curved and the hinges thick and bearing prominent teeth

dicerion *var of* DIKERION

di·cer·ous \ˈdisərəs, (ˈ)dīˈserəs\ *adj* [Gk *dikerōs* having two horns, fr. *di-* + *-kerōs* (fr. *keras* horn) — more at HORN] **:** having two tentacles or antennae

dich- *or* **dicho-** *comb form* [LL *dicho-*, fr. Gk *dich-, dicho-*, fr. *dicha*; akin to Gk *di-* — more at DI-] **:** in two **:** apart **:** asunder ⟨*dicho*gamy⟩

di·cha·pet·a·lum \ˌdīkəˈped·ᵊləm\ *n, cap* [NL, fr. Gk *dicha* in two + Gk *petalon* leaf — more at PETAL] **:** a genus (the type of the family Dichapetalaceae) of African and Malagasy shrubs that have coriacious leaves and small regular flowers borne in compound cymes or in umbels

di·cha·si·al \(ˈ)dīˈkāzh(ē)əl\ *adj* [NL *dichasium* + E *-al*] **:** of, relating to, or of the nature of a dichasium

di·cha·si·um \dīˈkāzh(ē)əm\ *n, pl* **dicha·sia** \-(ē)ə\ [NL, irreg. fr. Gk *dichasis* division, halving, fr. *dichazein* to divide in half (fr. *dicha* in two) + *-sis*] **:** a cymose inflorescence that produces two main axes (as in a dichotomous cyme) — compare MONOCHASIUM, POLYCHASIUM

di·chel·y·ma \dīˈkeləmə\ *n, cap* [NL] **:** a genus of aquatic mosses (family Fontinalaceae) resembling those of the genus *Fontinalis* but distinguished by a midrib in the leaves and including one (*D. capillaceum*) that is common on stems of shrubs in swamps

di·chlamydeous \ˌdī+\ *adj* [*di-* + *chlamyd-* + *-eous*] **:** having both calyx and corolla (as a rose)

di·chlone \ˈdīˌklōn\ *n* -s [*dichloro-* naphthoquinone] **:** a yellow crystalline compound $C_{10}H_4Cl_2O_2$ used as a fungicide and algicide; 2,3-dichloro-1,4-naphthoquinone

dichlor- *or* **dichloro-** *comb form* [ISV *di-* + *chlor-*] **:** containing two atoms of chlorine — in names of chemical compounds ⟨*dichloro*ethylene⟩; compare CHLOR-

di·chloramine \(ˈ)dī+\ *n* [ISV *di-* + *chloramine*] **1 :** an unstable compound $NHCl_2$ formed from ammonia by chlorination but not known in the pure state — called also *chlorimide* **2 :** any chloramine (sense 1) or chloramide (sense 1) having two chlorine atoms attached to the nitrogen atom; *esp* **:** DICHLORAMINE-T

dichloramine-T *n* **:** a yellow crystalline compound $CH_3C_6H_4SO_2NCl_2$ used esp. formerly as an antiseptic; *para*-toluenesulfon-dichlor-amide — called also *dichloramine;* compare CHLORAMINE-T

di·chloride \(ˈ)dī+\ *n* [*di-* + *chloride*] **:** a binary compound containing two atoms of chlorine combined with an element or radical

di·chlo·ro·acetic acid \(ˌ)dīˌklōrō+ . . . -\ *n* [ISV *dichlor-* + *acetic*] **:** a strong high-boiling liquid acid $CHCl_2COOH$ obtained esp. by chlorination of acetic acid

di·chlo·ro·benzene \"+\ *n* [ISV *dichlor-* + *benzene*] **:** any of three isomeric compounds $C_6H_4Cl_2$ made by chlorinating benzene: as **a :** ORTHODICHLOROBENZENE **b :** PARADICHLOROBENZENE

di·chlo·ro·butane \"+\ *n* [*dichlor-* + *butane*] **:** a liquid compound $Cl(CH_2)_4Cl$ made usu. from tetrahydrofuran and used chiefly in making adiponitrile for the manufacture of nylon — called also *1,4-dichlorobutane*

di·chlo·ro·diethyl ether \"+ . . . -\ *n* [*dichlor-* + *diethyl*] **:** DICHLOROETHYL ETHER

di·chlo·ro·di·flu·o·ro·methane \(ˌ)dīˌklōrōˌdīˌflü(ə)rō+\ *n* [*dichlor-* + *difluor-* + *methane*] **:** a nontoxic nonflammable easily liquefiable gas CCl_2F_2 made from carbon tetrachloride by reaction with antimony trifluoride and used as a refrigerant in refrigerators and air-conditioning units and as a propellant in aerosols

di·chlo·ro·ethyl ether \(ˌ)dīˌklōrō+ . . . -\ *also* **di·chlor·ethyl ether** \ˌdīklōr+ . . . -\ *n* [*dichlor-* + *ethyl*] **:** a liquid ether $(ClCH_2CH_2)_2O$ that has an odor like chloroform, is made usu. by dehydration of ethylene chlorohydrin, and is used chiefly as a solvent and as a fumigant for insects; bis(2-chloroethyl) ether — called also *beta, beta'-dichlorodiethyl ether*

dichloroethyl sulfide \"+ . . . -\ *also* **di·chlor·ethyl sulfide** \ˌdīklōr+ . . . -\ *n* **:** MUSTARD GAS

di·chlo·ro·hydrin \(ˌ)dīˌklōrō+\ *or* **di·chlor·hydrin** \ˌdīklōr+\ *n* [ISV *dichlor-* + *-hydrin*] **:** either of two liquid compounds $C_3H_6Cl_2O$ made by the action of hydrochloric acid on glycerol or of hypochlorous acid on allyl chloride, distinguished as alpha- or alpha-gamma-dichlorohydrin $CH_2ClCHOHCH_2Cl$ and beta- or alpha-beta dichlorohydrin $CH_2ClCH_2ClCH_2OH$, and used chiefly in organic synthesis and as solvents

di·chlo·ro·phenarsine \(ˌ)dīˌklōrō+\ *n* [*dichlor-* + *phen-* + *arsine*] **:** an arsenical used in the form of its white powdery hydrochloride $HOC_6H_3(AsCl_2)NH_2.HCl$ in the treatment of syphilis esp. as an adjuvant to penicillin

di·chlo·ro·phenoxyacetic acid \"+ . . . -\ *n* [*dichlor-* + *phenoxyacetic*] **:** a white crystalline compound $Cl_2C_6H_3OCH_2COOH$ made from 2,4-dichloro-phenol and chloroacetic acid that is a growth regulator for plants and is used esp. in the form of salts and esters as a weed killer — usu. used with initial numbers ⟨2,4-*dichlorophenoxyacetic acid*⟩; called also *2,4-D*

dicho- — see DICH-

di·chog·a·mous \(ˈ)dīˈkägəməs\ *or* **di·cho·gam·ic** \ˌdīkōˈgamik\ *adj* [*dich-* + *-gamous, -gamic*] **:** characterized by or relating to dichogamy

di·chog·a·my \dīˈkägəmē\ *n* -ES [G *dichogamie*, fr. *dich-* + *-gamie* -gamy] **:** production of male and female reproductive elements of hermaphroditic plants or animals at different times ensuring cross-fertilization

di·chon·dra \dīˈkändrə\ *n* [NL, fr. *di-* + *-chondra* (fr. Gk *chondros* grain)] **1** *cap* **:** a genus of chiefly tropical perennial herbs (family Convolvulaceae) having slender creeping stems, cordate-orbicular to reniform entire leaves, and very small obscure greenish yellow to white flowers borne in the leaf axils and including some (esp. *D. repens* or its varieties) that are naturalized or used as a ground cover and substitute for lawn grasses in parts of the southern U.S. **2** -s **:** any plant of the genus *Dichondra*

di·choph·y·sis \dīˈkäfəsəs\ *n* -ES [NL, fr. *dich-* + Gk *physis* nature — more at PHYSIC] **:** a regularly and dichotomously branching sterile hyphal end in the hymenium of certain fungi

dich·optic \(ˈ)dīˈkäptik, (ˈ)di;-\ *adj* [*dich-* + *optic*] *zoo* **:** having the borders of the compound eyes separate — compare HOLOPTIC

di·cho·ree \(ˈ)dīˌkōrˌē, ˌdīkəˈrē\ *n* -s [F *dichorée*, fr. L *dichoreus*, fr. *di-* + *choreus* trochee — more at CHOREUS] **:** DITROCHEE

di·chorial \(ˈ)dī+\ *adj* [*di-* + *chorial*] **:** having two chorions and two placentas — used esp. of human fraternal twins

di·cho·ri·san·dra \(ˌ)dīˌkōrəˈsandrə\ *n, cap* [NL, fr. *di-* + Gk *chōris* of a different kind + NL *-andra*] **:** a genus of tropical American herbs (family Commelinaceae) with sheathing leaves and blue or purple racemose or paniculate flowers

di·chot·o·mal \(ˈ)dīˈkäd·əməl, -ätə- *sometimes* dəˈk-\ *adj* **:** of, relating to, or situated in a dichotomy — used esp. of the central flower in a dichasium

di·cho·tom·ic \ˌdīkəˈtämik *sometimes* ˌdik-\ *adj* **:** of, relating to, or involving dichotomy — **di·cho·tom·i·cal·ly** \-mək(ə)lē\ *adv*

di·chot·o·mist \dīˈkäd·əməst, -ätə- *sometimes* dəˈk-\ *n* -s [Gk *dichotomia* dichotomy + E *-ist*] **:** one that dichotomizes **:** DUALIST

di·chot·o·mi·za·tion \(ˌ)dīˌkäd·əməˈzāshən, -ätə-, -ˌmīˈz- *sometimes* dəˌ≈-\ *n* -s **:** the act or action of dichotomizing **:** the condition of being dichotomized

di·chot·o·mize \≈ˈ≈≈ˌmīz\ *vb* -ED/-ING/-S [LL *dichotomos* + E *-ize*] *vt* **1 :** to divide into two parts, classes, or groups ⟨~ all answers into those right and those wrong⟩ ⟨~ the animal world into vertebrate and invertebrate⟩ **2 :** to separate into several parts **~** *vi* **1 :** to become readily dichotomized **:** split readily into two groups or classes **2 :** to form or grow into a dichotomy

di·chot·o·mo·siphon \(ˌ)≈,≈≈(ˌ)mō+\ *n, cap* [NL, fr. Gk *dichotomos* + *siphōn* tube, pipe, siphon — more at SIPHON] **:** a monotypic genus of erect tough fibrous coenocytic aquatic green algae (family Vaucheriaceae) that cause clogging of screens at water-pumping stations in some areas

di·chot·o·mous \(ˈ)dīˈkäd·əməs, -ätə- *sometimes* dəˈk-\ *adj* [LL *dichotomos*, fr. Gk, fr. *dich-* + *-tomos* (fr. *temnein* to cut) — more at TOME] **1 :** dividing into two parts or groups **:** readily susceptible to dichotomy **:** readily dividing into pairs successively **:** showing a dual arrangement **2 :** relating to, involving, or proceeding from dichotomy ⟨a ~ division⟩ — **di·chot·o·mous·ly** *adv*

dichotomous key *n, biol* **:** a key to classification based on a choice between two alternative characters

di·chot·o·my \≈ˈ≈≈mē, -mi\ *n* -ES [Gk *dichotomia*, fr. *dichotomein* to cut in half (fr. *dichotomos*) + *-ia* -y] **1 a :** division into two parts, classes, or groups esp. into two groups mutually exclusive or opposed by contradiction ⟨a ~ into the good and the evil⟩ **b :** division into two **:** a splitting into two parts or groups **:** differentiation into two contrasted or sharply opposed groups ⟨~ between practice and theory⟩ ⟨a ~ between written and spoken evidence⟩ **2 :** the phase of the moon or an inferior planet in which just half its disk appears illuminated **3 a :** FORKING, BIFURCATION; *esp* **:** repeated bifurcation (as of the stem of a plant or a vein of the body) **b :** a system of branching in which the main axis forks repeatedly into two branches (as in the thallus of the seaweed *Dictyota dichotoma* and in many liverworts) forming a helicoid axis when the corresponding member of each pair is suppressed or a scorpioid axis when alternate members of adjacent pairs are suppressed — see FALSE DICHOTOMY, SYMPODIUM **c :** branching of an ancestral line into two more or less equal diverging branches **4 :** fee splitting by doctors

di·cho·triaene \ˌdīkō+\ *n* -s [*dich-* + *triaene*] **:** a sponge spicule with dichotomously branched rays

di·chro·ic \(ˈ)dīˈkrōik\ *also* **di·chro·it·ic** \ˌ≈≈ˈid·ik\ *adj* [Gk *dichroos* two-colored (fr. *di-* + *-chroos* -chroous) + E *-ic, -itic*] **1 :** having the property of dichroism ⟨a ~ crystal⟩ ⟨a ~ mirror⟩ **2 :** DICHROMATIC

dichroic fog *n, photog* **:** a clouded effect or stain that is greenish by reflected light and reddish by transmitted light and is due to the deposition of very finely divided silver usu. on the surface of a film or plate during processing

di·chro·ism \ˈdīkrōˌizəm\ *n* -s [Gk *dichroos* + E *-ism*] **1 :** pleochroism in which the colors are unlike when a crystal is viewed in the direction of two different axes **2 a :** the property of some bodies of differing in color with the thickness of the transmitting layer or of some liquids of differing in color with the degree of concentration of the solution **b :** the property of some surfaces of reflecting light of one color and transmitting light of other colors **3 :** DICHROMATISM

di·chro·ite \-ōˌīt\ *n* -s [F, fr. Gk *dichroos* + F *-ite*] **:** CORDIERITE

di·chro·mat \ˈdīkrōˌmat\ *n* -s [back-formation fr. *dichromatic*] **:** one that requires only two primary colors to be mixed in order to match the spectrum as he sees it **:** one affected with dichromatism — compare MONOCHROMAT, TRICHROMAT

di·chromate \(ˈ)dī+\ *n* [ISV *di-* + *chromate*] **:** a salt of dichromic acid — called also *bichromate*

di·chro·mat·ic \ˌdī+\ *adj* [*di-* + *chromatic*] **1 :** having or exhibiting two colors **2 :** having two color varieties or color phases independently of age or sex ⟨a ~ bird⟩ ⟨a ~ insect⟩ **3 a :** relating to or exhibiting dichromatism **b :** characteristic of a dichromat

di·chro·ma·tism \dīˈkrōməˌtizəm\ *n* -s [*dichromatic* + *-ism*] **1 :** the state or condition of being dichromatic **2 :** partial color blindness in which only two of the fundamental colors or two colors and their combinations are perceptible

di·chro·ma·top·sia \(ˌ)dīˌkrōməˈtäpsēə\ *n* -s [NL, fr. *di-* + *chromat-* + *-opsia*] : DICHROMATISM 2

di·chromic \(ˈ)dī+\ *adj* [*di-* + *chromic*] : containing two atoms of chromium or their equivalents in the molecule

dichromic acid *n* : an acid $H_2Cr_2O_7$ known only in solution and esp. in the form of its salts (as potassium dichromate) most of which are orange or red

di·chro·nous \ˈdīkrənəs\ *adj* [LL *dichronus, dichronos*, fr. Gk *dichronos*, fr. *di-* + *-chronos* -chronous] *prosody* **1** : consisting of or lasting through two morae : DISEMIC **2** : COMMON 9c

di·chro·scope \ˈdīkrəˌskōp\ *also* **di·chro·i·scope** *or* **di·chro·o·scope** \dīˈkrōə,-\ *n* -s [*dichro-, dichroi-, dichroo-* (fr. *dichroism*) + *-scope*] : an instrument for examining crystals (as gems) for pleochroism — **di·chro·scop·ic** \ˌ⸗⸗ˈskäpik\ *adj*

dicht \ˈdikt\ *Scot var of* ²DIGHT

dicing *n* -s [ME *dycing*, fr. gerund of *dycen* to dice — more at DICE] **1** : the throwing of dice esp. in a gambling game **2** : ornamentation or an ornamenting in squares or cubes

dicing board *n* : DICE BOARD

¹**dick** \ˈdik\ *n* -s [fr. the nickname *Dick*, by shortening & alter. fr. *Richard*] **1** *chiefly Brit* : FELLOW, MAN, CHAP ⟨he's a queer ~, for sure⟩ **2** *dial Eng* : a leather apron and bib **3** : PENIS — usu. considered vulgar **4** [by shortening & alter.] : DETECTIVE ⟨a house ~ in one of the busiest hotels⟩

²**dick** \"\ *n* -s [ME *dick, dike* — more at DIKE] **1** *dial Brit* : DIKE **2** *dial Brit* : DITCH

³**dick** \"\ *n* -s [by shortening & alter.] *slang Brit* : DECLARATION ⟨I'll take my ~ he's wrong⟩ : a declared standard (as of value) ⟨a shipment not up to ~⟩

dick·cis·sel \dikˈsisəl, ˈ⸗,⸗⸗\ *n* -s [imit.] : a common migratory finch (*Spiza americana*) that breeds throughout the central U.S., is brownish streaked with black and gray above with black throat, white chin, and yellowish breast, and feeds chiefly on weed seeds and grasshoppers

dick·ens \ˈdikənz\ *n* -ES [prob. fr. the name *Dickens*, euphemism for *devil*] **1 a** : DEVIL, DEUCE — used as a more or less meaningless intensive; often used interjectionally; usu. used with *the* ⟨I cannot tell what the ~ his name is —Shak.⟩ ⟨very mad and swearing like the ~⟩ **b** : worst disadvantage or difficulty : most serious part ⟨the ~ of it was that we had no money⟩ **2** : CHILD; *esp* : an exceptionally active and mischievous child

¹**dick·en·si·an** \diˈken(t)sēən, -kenzē-\ *adj, usu cap* [Charles J. H. *Dickens* †1870 Eng. novelist + E *-ian*] : characteristic of or having the qualities of the writings of Charles Dickens with respect to humor and pathos in the portrayal of odd often extravagant and picturesque character types usu. from the lower economic strata of 19th century English society ⟨the novel verges on the *Dickensian*: there is pathos, there is humor, and, above all, there is excellent characterization, with a tendency to noble caricature —John Cournos⟩ ⟨the *Dickensian* squalor of London's slums —*Time*⟩

²**dickensian** \"\ *n* -s *usu cap* : an ardent admirer or student of the works of Charles Dickens

¹**dick·er** \ˈdikə(r)\ *n* -s [ME *dyker*; akin to MLG *dēker* quantity of ten (hides), MHG *techer, decher*; all fr. a prehistoric WGmc word borrowed fr. L *decuria* quantity of ten, fr. *decem* ten — more at TEN] **1** : the number or quantity of 10 esp. of hides or skins **2** *obs* : a large quantity : LOT

²**dicker** \"\ *vi* **dickered**; **dickered**; **dickering** \-k(ə)riŋ\ **dickers** [origin unknown] : to seek to arrive at a workable arrangement by bargaining : discuss negotiations and arrangements : HAGGLE, BARGAIN ⟨a trapper ~*ing* for a higher price for his furs⟩ ⟨~*ing* with members of the opposition for their support⟩ ⟨~*ing* in connection with the merger between the companies⟩

³**dicker** \"\ *n* -s **1** : BARTER; *often* : goods bartered **2** : a swap made after haggling and bargaining : an act or session of haggling or bargaining : a political deal : negotiation with concessions offered and discussed ⟨a ~ for his saddle⟩ ⟨~s being argued in the lobbies outside the assembly room⟩

¹**dick·ey** *also* **dicky** \ˈdikē, -ki\ *n, pl* **dickeys** *also* **dickies** [fr. the nickname *Dicky*, dim. of *Dick*] **1** : any of various articles of clothing: as **a** *dial Eng* : PETTICOAT **b** : a man's separate or detachable shirtfront usu. worn under a jacket in place of a shirt and sometimes in addition to a shirt esp. with clerical garments **c** *chiefly New Eng* : a detachable shirt collar **d** : a small fabric insert that is worn to fill in the neckline of a dress, jacket, or other garment and give the appearance of a blouse **2** : one of various animals: **a** *dial Brit* : a male donkey : JACK **b** (1) *also* **dickeybird** *or* **dickybird** \ˈ⸗⸗,⸗\ : a small bird (as a sparrow or a canary) (2) *dial Eng* : HEDGE SPARROW **3** *chiefly Brit* **a** *also* **dickey box** : the seat for the driver at the front of a carriage **b** : a seat at the back of a carriage or automobile : RUMBLE SEAT **4** : a supplementary device used in textile manufacturing; *esp* : an additional roll used to keep the working rolls clear in textile manufacturing

dickey 1d

²**dickey** *or* **dicky** \"\ *adj* [origin unknown] : of poor quality : being in bad condition : SHAKY, WEAK ⟨a ~ leg⟩ ⟨communications that are in a ~ state⟩

dick·in·son·ite \ˈdikənsəˌnīt\ *n* -s [William *Dickinson*, 19th cent. Am. clergyman and mineralogist + E *-ite*] : a green mineral $H_2Na_6(Mn,Fe,Ca,Mg)_{14}(PO_4)_{12}.H_2O$ consisting of foliated hydrous acid phosphate chiefly of manganese, iron, and sodium (sp. gr. 3.34)

dick·ite \ˈdiˌkīt\ *n* -s [Allan B. *Dick* †1926 Eng. mineralogist + E *-ite*] : a mineral $Al_2Si_2O_5(OH)_4$ consisting of a basic silicate of aluminum found relatively well crystallized in clays : a polymorph of kaolinite

dicks *pl of* DICK

dick·so·nia \dikˈsōnēə\ *n, cap* [NL, fr. James *Dickson* †1822 Eng. botanist + NL *-ia*] : a large genus of tropical tree ferns (family Cyatheaceae) having bipinnatifid or tripinnatifid fronds and marginal or submarginal sori with a surrounding membranous cup-shaped indusium and including one species (*D. antarctica*) that is often cultivated — **dick·so·ni·oid** \-nēˌȯid\ *adj*

dick test \ˈdik-\ *n, usu cap D* [after George F. *Dick* †1967 and Gladys H. *Dick* †1963 Am. physicians] : a test to determine susceptibility or immunity to scarlet fever made by injecting scarlet fever toxin into the skin

dick toxin *n, usu cap D* [after George F. and Gladys H. *Dick*] : the erythrogenic toxin of the scarlatinal streptococcus

dickty *var of* DICTY

dicky rice weevil \ˈdikē-\ *n* [prob. fr. the nickname *Dicky*] : a weevil (*Malenterpes spinipes*) common in Australia and New Zealand whose adults feed on foliage and whose larvae feed on the roots of citrus and other fruit trees

di·cli·nism \(ˈ)dīˈklīˌnizəm\ *or* **di·cli·ny** \ˈdīˌklīnē\ *n, pl* **diclinisms** *or* **diclinies** [*di-* + *-clinism, -cliny*] : the condition of being diclinous

di·cli·nous \(ˈ)dīˈklīnəs\ *adj* [*di-* + *-clinous*] : having the stamens and pistils in separate flowers — compare MONOCLINOUS, DIOECIOUS, MONOECIOUS

di·coc·cous \(ˈ)dīˈkäkəs\ *adj* [*di-* + *-coccous* (fr. Gk *kokkos* grain, seed)] : composed of two coherent one-seeded carpels ⟨a ~ capsule⟩

di·co·lic \(ˈ)dīˈkōlik\ *adj* [Gk *dikōlos* (fr. *di-* + *-kōlos*, fr. *kōlon* limb, colon) + E *-ic* — more at COLON] : of, relating to, or having two cola ⟨~ verse⟩

di·colon \(ˈ)dī+\ *n, pl* **dicola** [*di-* + ²*colon*] : a verse or rhythmic period having two cola

di·con·dyl·i·an \ˌdī(ˌ)känˈdilēən\ *adj* [*di-* + *condyle* + *-ian*] : having two occipital condyles

di·con·dyl·ic \-lik\ *adj* [*di-* + *condyle* + *-ic*] : having two articulatory condyles — used chiefly of joints between segments of the limbs of insects

di·co·phane \ˈdīkəˌfān\ *n* -s [*dichloro-diphenyl-ethane*] : DDT

di·cot \ˈdīˌkät\ *or* **di·cot·yl** \ˈdīˌkädᵊl, dīˈk-, -ätᵊl\ *n* -s [by shortening] : DICOTYLEDON

di·cotyledon \(ˌ)dī+\ *n* [NL *dicotyledones*] : a plant having two cotyledons : a member of the subclass Dicotyledoneae — compare MONOCOTYLEDON

di·cot·y·le·do·ne·ae \(ˌ)dīˌkädᵊlˈēdōnēˌē\ *n pl, cap* [NL, alter. of *Dicotyledones*, fr. *di-* + *cotyledones*, pl. of *cotyledon*] : a subclass of Angiospermae comprising seed plants (as cactuses and oaks) that produce an embryo with two cotyledons and have net-veined leaves, stems with secondary thickening resulting in annual ring formation in woody perennials, and floral organs usu. arranged in cycles of four or five, including most of the deciduous woody plants of temperate climates and the majority of herbaceous flowering plants, and commonly being divided into Archichlamydeae and Metachlamydeae — compare MONOCOTYLEDONEAE

di·cot·y·le·do·nes \(ˌ)dīˌkäd·ᵊlˈēdᵊnˌēz\ *n pl, cap* [NL] *in some classifications* : DICOTYLEDONEAE

di·cotyledonous *also* **di·cotyledonary** \(ˈ)dī+\ *adj* [*dicotyledon* + *-ous* or *-ary*] : of, relating to, or characteristic of the subclass Dicotyledoneae; *often* : having paired cotyledons — contrasted with *monocotyledonous*; compare POLYCOTYLEDONOUS

di·cot·y·les \dīˈkädᵊlˌēz\ [NL, fr. *di-* + *-cotyles* (fr. Gk *kotylos* cup, anything hollow)] *syn of* TAYASSU

di·co·tyl·i·dae \ˌdīkəˈtiləˌdē\ [NL, fr. *Dicotyles*, type genus + *-idae*] *syn of* TAYASSUIDAE

di·cot·y·lous \(ˈ)dīˈkädᵊləs\ *adj* [by contr.] : DICOTYLEDONOUS

di·cou·ma·rol \dīˈk(y)üməˌrōl, -ōl\ *or* **di·cou·ma·rin** \-ˌrən\ *n* -s [*dicoumarol* fr. *Dicumarol*, a trademark; *dicoumarin* fr. *di-* + *coumarin*] : a white crystalline compound $C_{19}H_{12}O_6$ that is obtained from spoiled sweet clover hay or made synthetically, is the actual pathogenic agent in sweet clover disease, and is used as an anticoagulant (as in the treatment of embolism); 3,3′-methylene-bis(4-hydroxy-coumarin) — called also *bishydroxycoumarin*

di·cra·na·les \ˌdīkrəˈnā(ˌ)lēz\ *n pl, cap* [NL, fr. *Dicranum* + *-ales*] : a widely distributed order of Musci comprising mosses with erect gametophores, a usu. acrocarpous sporophyte, and a capsule with 16 peristome teeth — see DICRANUM

di·cra·num \dīˈkrānəm\ *n, cap* [NL, fr. Gk *dikranon*, neut. of *dikranos* two-headed, fr. *di-* + *-kranos* (fr. *kranion* skull, head) — more at CRANIUM] : a large genus (the type of the family Dicranaceae) comprising mosses of the order Dicranales that have costate leaves, a cleft or bifid peristome, and long-stalked capsules

¹**di·cro·coe·lid** \ˌdīkrəˈsēləd\ *adj* [NL *Dicrocoeliidae*] : of or relating to the Dicrocoeliidae

²**dicrocoelid** \"\ *n* -s : a worm of the family Dicrocoeliidae

di·cro·coe·li·i·dae \ˌdīkrəsəˈlīəˌdē\ *n pl, cap* [NL *Dicrocoelium*, type genus + *-idae*] : a family of small to medium-sized, flattened or more or less cylindrical digenetic trematode worms that as adults parasitize the biliary ducts or occas. other viscera of vertebrates

di·cro·coe·li·um \ˌ⸗⸗ˈsēlēəm\ *n, cap* [NL, fr. Gk *dikroos, dikrous, dikros* forked, cloven + NL *-coelium* (fr. Gk *koilia* cavity, fr. *koilos* hollow) — more at CAVE] : a widely distributed genus comprising small lanceolate digenetic trematodes of the livers of ruminants or occas. other mammals including man and being the type of the family Dicrocoeliidae

di·cros·to·nyx \dīˈkrästəˌ(ˌ)niks\ *n, cap* [NL, irreg. fr. Gk *dikroos, dikrous, dikros* + NL *-onyx*] : a genus consisting of the pied lemmings

di·crot·ic \(ˈ)dīˈkräd·ik\ *also* **di·cro·tal** \-rōdᵊl, -räd-\ *or* **di·cro·tous** \ˈdīkrəd·əs\ *adj* [Gk *dikrotos* (fr. *di-* + *-krotos*, fr. *krotein* to beat, knock, rattle) + E *-ic* or *-al* or *-ous* — more at CROTAL] **1** *of the pulse* : having a double beat (as in certain febrile states in which the heart is overactive and the arterial walls lacking in tone) — compare MONOCROTIC **2** : being or relating to the second expansion of the artery that occurs during the diastole of the heart — **di·cro·tism** \ˈdīkrəˌtizəm\ *n* -s

di·cru·ri·dae \dīˈkrürəˌdē\ *n pl, cap* [NL, fr. *Dicrurus*, type genus (fr. Gk *dikroos, dikrous, dikros* + NL *-urus*) + *-idae*] : a family of Old World passerine birds that are usu. black with rather large hooked bills, short metatarsi and small toes, long wings, and a tail with 10 rectrices and usu. a deep fork — see DRONGO

dict *abbr* **1** dictaphone **2** dictation **3** dictator **4** dictionary

dicta *pl of* DICTUM

dic·ta·men \dikˈtāmən\ *n, pl* **dic·tam·i·na** \-taməna\ [LL, fr. L *dictare* to pronounce, assert, dictate — more at DICTATE] : RULE, PRONOUNCEMENT ⟨the ~ of reason⟩ ⟨the *dictamina* of a master⟩

Dic·ta·phone \ˈdiktəˌfōn\ *trademark* — used for a phonographic instrument combining a recorder and reproducer for use in dictating

dic·ta·phon·ic \ˌ⸗⸗ˈfänik, -ˈfōn-\ *adj, of speech* : reproduced with extreme accuracy ⟨the dialogue in the play is a little less ~ than it was in the book —John Mason Brown⟩

¹**dic·tate** \ˈdikˌtāt *also* ⸗ˈ⸗; *usu* -ād·+V\ *vb* -ED/-ING/-S [L *dictatus*, past part. of *dictare* to pronounce, assert, dictate, freq. of *dicere* to say — more at DICTION] *vi* **1** : to speak, recite, or read off for a person to write down or transcribe or for a machine to record for later transcription ⟨*dictating* too fast for the secretary to transcribe⟩ ⟨*dictating* into the machine⟩ **2** : to speak or act commandingly or domineeringly, imposing orders, injunctions, and terms authoritatively or autocratically ⟨a stern father and husband always *dictating* to his family⟩ : PRESCRIBE, COMMAND ⟨to act spontaneously as the heart ~s —Bertrand Russell⟩ ⟨as the situation ~s⟩ ~ *vt* **1** : to speak, recite, or read off (something) for a person to write down or transcribe or for a machine to record ⟨*dictating* a letter to the secretary⟩ ⟨*dictating* test questions to a class⟩ ⟨*dictating* a statement to the reporters⟩; *sometimes* : to compose while speaking **2 a** : to issue as an order usu. peremptorily ⟨the duke *dictating* what part each should take⟩ **b** : to command or impose authoritatively : PRESCRIBE, ENJOIN : direct forcefully or irresistibly ⟨*dictating* peace terms to the vanquished⟩ **c** : to require or determine necessarily ⟨the weight of the floor ~s use of heavy supports⟩ ⟨an arrangement *dictated* by the situation⟩ **d** : to bring into being, form, determine, or influence commandingly ⟨patroness who has set herself up to ~ public taste —Lillian de la Torre⟩ **e** : to designate authoritatively, overriding possible opposition ⟨a president strong enough to ~ his successor⟩

syn PRESCRIBE, ORDAIN, DECREE, IMPOSE: DICTATE implies an authoritative direction, usually peremptory, or intended as not to be questioned ⟨groups trying to *dictate* who shall and who shall not be retained on the faculties of the colleges and universities of the nation —W.T.Gossett⟩ ⟨he continued . . . to *dictate* the lives of the parishioners —Willa Cather⟩ ⟨the avarice which *dictated* every detail of their lives —Marcia Davenport⟩ PRESCRIBE implies a formulated rule, law, or order and an authoritative pronouncement ⟨my teachers should have *prescribed* to me, 1st, sincerity; 2d, sincerity; 3d, sincerity —H.D.Thoreau⟩ ⟨the terms *prescribed* by law —John Marshall⟩ ⟨driven to describe paths round the sun by exactly the same forces as *prescribed* the orderly motions of the planets —James Jeans⟩ ORDAIN implies enactment or institution by a supreme and unquestioned authority or power, usually suggesting the authoritatively definitive settlement of a question ⟨in this same period Parliament . . . *ordained* that everyone who died should be buried in English cloth —G.M. Trevelyan⟩ ⟨nature inexorably *ordains* that the human race shall perish of famine if it stops working —G.B.Shaw⟩ ⟨a code of rigid and inflexible rules, arbitrarily *ordained*, and to be blindly obeyed —Havelock Ellis⟩ DECREE implies a pronouncement by a governmental authority, a divine power, or an authoritative force ⟨complainant must so state his case that . . . court can *decree* upon it —*Detroit Law Jour.*⟩ ⟨Apollo *decreed* that nobody should believe her, although she spoke the truth —Maxwell Nurnberg & Morris Rosenblum⟩ ⟨blue eyes which his parents' chromosomes *decreed* for him —Ralph de Toledano⟩ IMPOSE implies a subjecting to what must be borne, endured, or submitted to, or a compelling prescription of something upon someone or a dictatorial forcing of something ⟨to *impose* impossible taxes on a poverty-stricken people⟩ ⟨to *impose* limitations on hours of work —*Amer. Guide Series; N.H.*⟩ ⟨we are willing therefore to believe that destiny is *imposed* upon us —Archibald MacLeish⟩

²**dic·tate** \ˈ⸗,⸗ *sometimes* ⸗ˈ⸗\ *n* -s [L *dictatum*, fr. neut. of *dictatus*] **1 a** : an authoritative rule : a prescription or injunction authoritatively pronounced (as in scripture or law) : a directive given cogency by conscience, reason, virtue, or other ruling principle ⟨the ~s of good taste⟩ ⟨~s of common sense⟩ **b** : a command by one in authority ⟨the ruler's ~s⟩ **2** *archaic* : material uttered for another's transcription **3** *obs* : DICTUM, MAXIM, PRECEPT **4** : DIKTAT

dic·tat·ing·ly *adv* [*dictating* (pres. part. of *dictate*) + *-ly*] : in a dictating manner

dictating machine *n* : a usu. electronic machine used esp. for the recording (as on a wax cylinder, a disc, or a tape) of dictated matter to be transcribed later in typed form

dic·ta·tion \dikˈtāshən\ *n* -s [LL *dictation-, dictatio*, fr. L *dictatus* + *-ion-, -io* -ion] **1** : the act of uttering authoritatively : PRESCRIPTION : arbitrary command : necessitous injunction or requirement : forceful formation or shaping ⟨they would tolerate no outside ~ in matters concerning their own parishes —V.L.Parrington⟩ ⟨duty's stern ~ —W.S.Gilbert⟩ **2 a** : the act of uttering words to be written by another; *also* : manner of dictating **b** : the playing or singing of music so that it may be reproduced either orally or in written notation usu. by a student for the purpose of training the hearing to accurate appreciation of musical tones **3** : matter (as words or music) that has been presented by dictation ⟨the secretary took ~ all morning long⟩

dic·ta·tive \ˈdikˌtād·iv, ⸗ˈ⸗⸗\ *adj* : DICTATORIAL

dic·ta·tor \ˈdikˌtād·ə(r), -ātə- *also* ⸗ˈ⸗⸗\ *n* -s [L, fr. *dictatus* + *-or*] **1 a** : a chief magistrate appointed in emergencies and given absolute authority by the senate of ancient Rome **b** : a person granted absolute emergency power in a later republic ⟨making the general ~ of the state during the invasion⟩ ⟨when ~s resist the temptation to become despots —F.L.Schuman⟩ **c** : one enjoying complete autocratic control or leadership ⟨the secretary was actually the ~ of the party⟩ ⟨making him ~⟩; *often* : a supreme sometimes autocratic arbiter ⟨a ~ in the world of British art —DeLancey Ferguson⟩ **d** : one ruling absolutely, typically with brutality, oppression, and ruthless suppression of opposition ⟨political ~s who attempt to accomplish by calculated brutality and aggression what they lack the intelligence and magnanimity to consummate —Lewis Mumford⟩ **2** : one that dictates (as to a secretary or recording machine)

dic·ta·to·ri·al \ˌdiktəˈtōrēəl, -tȯr-\ *adj* [L *dictatorius* (fr. *dictatus* + *-orius* -ory) + E *-al*] **1** : befitting or belonging to a dictator ⟨given ~ power but using it sparingly⟩ : ruled by a dictator ⟨a ~ government⟩ **2** : characteristic of an autocratic dictator : oppressive to or contemptuous of others ⟨imperious and ~, he knew how to command but not to obey —V.L.Parrington⟩ ⟨began a ~ rule that lasted for the duration of the war —*Amer. Guide Series: La.*⟩ — **dic·ta·to·ri·al·ly** \-ēəlē, -li\ *adv* — **dic·ta·to·ri·al·ness** *n* -ES

dictatorian *adj* [L *dictatorius* + E *-an*] : DICTATORIAL 1

dic·ta·tor·ship \dikˈtād·ə(r),ship, -ātə- *also* ˈ⸗⸗⸗,⸗\ *n* -s **1** : the office or term of office of a dictator **2** : absolute authority or power ⟨there should not be a ~, that is, social choice conforming only to the will of one man —H.M.Somers⟩ ⟨the exploitation of labor by industrial ~ —Roger Burlingame⟩ **3** : a form of government in which a dictator or small clique has absolute power without effective constitutional limitations ⟨after the revolution the country became a ~ under a former army officer⟩ : a despotic state ⟨a war between a democracy and a ~⟩

dictatorship of the proletariat : the assumption of political power by the proletariat with concomitant repression of previously controlling or governing classes that in Marxist philosophy is considered an essential preliminary to establishment of the classless state

dic·ta·to·ry \ˈdiktəˌtōrē, -tȯr-, -ri\ *adj* [L *dictatorius*] : DICTATORIAL

dic·ta·tress \ˈdikˌtā·trəs, ⸗ˈ⸗⸗\ *n* -ES [*dictator* + *-ess*] : a female dictator

dic·ta·trix \dikˈtā·triks\ *n, pl* **dictatri·ces** \-ā·trəˌsēz, ˌdiktəˈtrī(ˌ)sēz\ [L, fem. of *dictator*] : DICTATRESS

dic·ta·ture \dikˈtāchər, ˈdiktəˌchü(ə)r\ *n* -s [L *dictatura*, fr. *dictatus* + *-ura* -ure] : office of a dictator : DICTATORSHIP; *also* : a body of dictators

dictier *comparative of* DICTY

dictiest *superlative of* DICTY

dic·tion \ˈdikshən\ *n* -s [LL & L; LL *diction-, dictio* word, fr. L, delivery in public speaking, fr. *dictus* (past part. of *dicere* to say) + *-ion-, -io* -ion; akin to OE *tēon* to accuse, OHG *zīhan* to accuse, ON *tjā* to show, Goth *gateihan* to tell, L *dicare* to dedicate, Gk *deiknynai* to show, *dikē* right, judgment, Skt *diśati* he shows] **1** *obs* **a** : WORD, PHRASE **b** : verbal expression or description **2** : choice of words esp. with regard to correctness, clearness, or effectiveness : wording used ⟨very careless ~ in the essay⟩ ⟨a new ~ for poetry⟩ ⟨trite ~ is so common in these pages —H.N.Fairchild⟩ **3 a** : vocal expression : ENUNCIATION; *esp* : clear, accurate, and pleasing delivery in public speaking **b** : pronunciation and enunciation of words in singing

dic·tio·nary \ˈdikshəˌnerē, -ri\ *n* -ES *often attrib* [ML *dictionarium*, fr. LL *diction-, dictio* word + L *-arium* -ary] **1** : a reference book containing words usu. alphabetically arranged along with information about their forms, pronunciations, functions, etymologies, meanings, and syntactical and idiomatic uses ⟨a general ~ of the English language⟩ ⟨a monolingual ~⟩ — compare VOCABULARY ENTRY **2 a** : a reference book listing terms or names important to a particular subject or activity along with discussion of their meanings and applications ⟨a law ~⟩ ⟨a ~ of sports⟩; *broadly* : an encyclopedic listing ⟨a ~ of dates⟩ **b** : a reference book giving for words of one language equivalents in another ⟨an English-French ~⟩ ⟨a bilingual ~⟩ **c** : a reference book listing terms as commonly spelled together with their equivalents in some specialized system (as of orthography or symbols) ⟨a ~ of shorthand⟩ ⟨a pronouncing ~⟩ **3 a** : a general comprehensive list, collection, or repository ⟨a ~ of biography⟩ ⟨a usage ~⟩ **b** : vocabulary in use (as in a special field) : TERMINOLOGY ⟨the ~ of literary criticism⟩ **c** : a vocabulary of accepted terms ⟨in the ~ of the French Academy⟩ **d** : a vocabulary of the written words used by one author ⟨systematic *dictionaries* of individual authors —Hillis Miller⟩ **e** : LEXICON 4

dictionary catalog *n* : a catalog having its entries (as author, title, or subject) arranged in a single alphabet

dictionary definition *n* : a definition reporting established meanings or uses of words or symbols — compare STIPULATIVE DEFINITION

Dic·to·graph \ˈdiktəˌgraf\ *trademark* — used for a telephonic instrument for picking up sounds in one room and transmitting them to another or recording them

dic·tum \ˈdiktəm\ *n, pl* **dic·ta** \-tə\ *also* **dictums** \-təmz\ [L, fr. neut. of *dictus*, past part. of *dicere* to say — more at DICTION] **1** : SAYING, STATEMENT: **a** : an authoritative pronouncement often formal and definitive ⟨awaiting the king's ~ on the case⟩ : a statement in summation uttered with the intent or hope of acceptance as definitive ⟨a critic's *dicta* about art⟩ **b** : a formal statement of a principle or proposition ⟨a philosopher's ~ on the nature of good⟩ **c** : an opinionative statement uttered as though authoritatively and objectively ⟨the subjectivity and authoritarianism of many of his *dicta* —Thomas Pyles⟩ : MAXIM ⟨a would-be professor must heed the ~ "Publish or perish" —M.M.Hunt⟩ **2** : an opinion expressed by a judge on a point not necessarily arising or involved in a case in question or necessary for determining the rights of parties involved — see OBITER DICTUM; compare PRECEDENT, STARE DECISIS

dic·tum de om·ni et nul·lo \ˌdiktəmdāˈämnēˌetˈnü(ˌ)lō\ [L, maxim of all and none] : an axiom in logic: whatever may be affirmed or denied of a class may be affirmed or denied of every member of it

dic·ty *or* **dick·ty** \ˈdiktē\ *adj* -ER/-EST [origin unknown] *slang* : HIGH-TONED, SNOBBISH; *often* : very good : very pleasing

dicty- *or* **dictyo-** *comb form* [NL, fr. Gk *dikty-, diktyo-*, fr. *diktyon*, fr. *dikein* to throw] : net ⟨*dictyo*some⟩

dic·tyn·i·dae \dikˈtinəˌdē\ *n pl, cap* [NL, fr. *Dictyna*, type genus (irreg. fr. Gk *diktyon* net) + *-idae*] : a family of spiders that spin irregular webs composed partly of threads curled by means of the calamistrum

dic·ty·o·cau·lus \ˌdiktēōˈkȯləs\ *n, cap* [NL, fr. *dicty-* + Gk *kaulos* stem, penis — more at HOLE] : a genus of small slender lungworms (family Metastrongylidae) infesting mammals (as ruminants) and often causing severe bronchial symptoms or even pneumonia in young animals

dic·ty·o·gen \ˈdiktēəˌjen, -ˌjən\ *n* -s [NL *dicty-* + E *-gen*]

: a monocotyledonous plant having net-veined leaves (as *Smilax rotundifolia*) — **dic·ty·og·e·nous** \ˌ==ˈäjənəs\ *adj*

dic·ty·o·kinesis \ˌdiktē(ˌ)ō+\ *n* [NL, fr. *dicty-* + *kinesis*] : fission of the Golgi apparatus as a normal reproductive process

dic·ty·o·ne·ma \ˌ=tēəˈnēmə\ *n, cap* [NL, fr. *dicty-* + *-nema*] : a genus of graptolites common in Ordovician and Silurian formations

dic·ty·o·ni·na \-əˈnīnə\ *n pl, cap* [NL, fr. Gk *diktyon* net + NL *-ina* — more at DICTY-] *in some classifications* : an order of Hyalospongiae comprising those members of the Hexasterophora with hexactine spicules fused into a rigid network — **dic·ty·o·nine** \ˈ===ˌnīn\ *adj or n*

dic·ty·oph·o·ra \ˌdiktēˈäf(ə)rə\ *n, cap* [NL, fr. *dicty-* + *-phora*] : a genus of stinkhorn fungi closely related to those of the genus *Phallus* but distinguished by an indusium that hangs like a skirt from below the pileus

dic·ty·o·siphon \ˈdiktēə+\ *n, cap* [NL, fr. *dicty-* + Gk *siphōn* tube, pipe, siphon — more at SIPHON] : a genus (the type of the family Dictyosiphonaceae) of brown algae (order Dictyosiphonales) having filiform fronds that taper to acute points — **dic·ty·o·siphonaceous** \"+\ *adj*

dic·ty·o·siphonales \ˌdiktēə+\ *n pl, cap* [NL, fr. *Dictyosiphon* + *-ales*] : an order of brown algae having a profusely branched cylindrical sporophyte which at maturity is differentiated internally into two or three regions

dic·ty·o·some \ˈdiktēəˌsōm\ *n* -S [ISV *dicty-* + *-some*; orig. formed as It *dictiosoma*] : GOLGI BODY

dic·ty·o·sper·mum scale \ˌ===ˈspərməm-\ *n* [*dictyospermum* fr. NL *Dictyospermum* (syn. of *Aneilema*), fr. *dicty-* + *-spermum*] : a widely distributed rounded armored scale (*Chrysomphalus dictyospermi*) that is particularly destructive to citrus

dic·ty·o·spore \ˈdiktēə+ˌ\ *n* [*dicty-* + *spore*] : a multicellular spore of certain fungi that has both longitudinal walls and cross septa — **dic·ty·o·spor·ous** \ˌ==əˈspōrəs, ˌ==ˈäspərəs\ *adj*

dic·ty·o·stele \ˈdiktēəˌstēl *also* ˌ===ˈstēlē\ *n* -S [*dicty-* + *stele*] : a stele in which the vascular cylinder is broken up by leaf gaps into a longitudinal series or network of vascular strands around a central pith (as in many ferns) — **dic·ty·o·ste·lic** \ˌ===ˈstēlik\ *adj* — **dic·ty·o·ste·ly** \ˈ===ˌstēlē\ *n* -ES

dic·ty·o·ta \ˌdiktēˈōd·ə\ *n, cap* [NL, fr. Gk *diktyōtē*, fem. of *diktyōtos* latticed, made like a net, fr. *diktyon* net — more at DICTY-] : the type genus of Dictyotaceae comprising brown algae with the thallus dichotomously branched

dic·ty·o·ta·ce·ae \ˌdiktēəˈtāsēˌē\ *n pl, cap* [NL, fr. *Dictyota*, type genus + *-aceae*] : a family of brown algae (order Dictyotales) that have an erect flattened parenchymatous thallus, oogamous sexual reproduction, and asexual reproduction by nonmotile spores — **dic·ty·o·ta·ceous** \ˌ===ˈtāshəs\ *adj*

dic·ty·o·ta·les \ˌdiktēəˈtā(ˌ)lēz\ *n pl, cap* [NL, fr. *Dictyota* + *-ales*] : an order of dichotomously branched parenchymatous brown algae (class Isogeneratae) that grow from apical cells

dic·ty·ox·y·lon \ˌdiktēˈäksəˌlän, -lən\ *n, cap* [NL, fr. *dicty-* + *-xylon*] : a form genus represented by Paleozoic fossil stems exhibiting radiating wedges of wood

di·cy·an·diamide \ˌdīˌsīˈan+\ *also* **di·cy·an·o·diamide** \(ˌ)dīˌsīə(ˌ)nō+\ *n* -S [ISV *di-* + *cyan-* + *diamide*] : a colorless crystalline water-soluble compound $H_2NC(=NH)NHCN$ formed by polymerization of cyanamide and used chiefly in making melamine and guanidine — called also *cyanoguanidine*

di·cyanide \(ˈ)dī+\ *n* [*di-* + *cyanide*] : a chemical compound containing two cyano groups combined with an element or radical

di·cyanine \"+\ *n* [*di-* + *cyanine*] : any of various blue cyanine dyes derived from quinoline

di·cyanogen \ˌdī+\ *n* [*di-* + *cyanogen*] : CYANOGEN 2

di·cy·cle \ˈdīˌsikəl, -ˌsək-, -ˌsēk- *sometimes* -ˌsīk-\ *n* [*di-* + *cycle*] : a velocipede having the two wheels parallel instead of in the same line

di·cy·clic \(ˈ)dīˈsīklik, -ˈsik-\ *adj* [*di-* + *cyclic*] **1 a** : having two whorls **b** : BIENNIAL 2 **2** : BICYCLIC 2 **3** : having two maxima of population each year — used chiefly of planktonic organisms — **di·cy·cly** \ˈdīˌsīklē\ *n* -ES

di·cyc·li·ca \dīˈsikləkə, -ˈsīk-\ *n pl, cap* [NL, fr. *di-* + L *cyclica*, neut. pl. of *cyclicus* cyclic — more at CYCLIC] *in some classifications* : a division of Crinoidea comprising forms in which the cup of the calyx has a basal and an infrabasal series of ossicles

di·cyclopentadiene \(ˌ)dī+\ *n* [*di-* + *cycl-* + *pentadiene*] : a liquid tricyclic hydrocarbon $C_{10}H_{12}$ formed from cyclopentadiene on standing and yielding cyclopentadiene on boiling

di·cy·e·ma·ta \ˌdīˌsīˈēməd·ə\ [NL, fr. *Dicyema*, genus of Mesozoa + *-ata*] *syn of* DICYEMIDA

¹di·cy·e·mid \ˌdīˌsīˈēməd\ *adj* [NL *Dicyemida*] : of or relating to the Dicyemida

²dicyemid \"\ *n* -S : one of the Dicyemida

di·cy·e·mi·da \ˌ=ˌ=ˈēmədə\ *n pl, cap* [NL, fr. *Dicyema*, genus of Mesozoa (fr. *di-* + Gk *kyēma* embryo; fr. the 2 types of larvae produced at different stages) + *-ida*] : an order or other division of Mesozoa comprising minute ciliated vermiform internal parasites of cephalopod mollusks and occurring in a nematogen phase in the young host and in a rhombogen phase in the sexually mature host — compare ORTHONECTIDA

di·cyn·o·don \(ˈ)dīˈsinəˌdän, -ˈsīn-\ *n, cap* [NL, fr. *di-* + *cyn-* + *-odon*] : a genus of heavily built small to moderately large Permian reptiles (order Therapsida) that were presumably herbivorous and semiaquatic or marsh-dwelling forms and that had the teeth reduced to a pair of large canines in the male only and the jaws covered by a horny beak

¹di·cyn·o·dont \-ˌdänt\ *adj* [NL *Dicynodont-*, *Dicynodon* & *Dicynodontia*] : of or relating to the Dicynodontia

²dicynodont \"\ *n* -S : a reptile of the suborder Dicynodontia

di·cyn·o·don·tia \(ˌ)=ˌ==ˈdänch(ē)ə\ *n pl, cap* [NL, fr. *Dicynodont-*, *Dicynodon* + *-ia*] : a suborder of Therapsida including a widely distributed group of apparently herbivorous Permian and Triassic reptiles with reduced dentition — compare DICYNODON

did [ME *did*, *dide*, fr. OE *dyde*] *past of* DO

di·dact \ˈdīˌdakt\ *n* -S [back-formation fr. ²*didactic*] : a didactic person

¹di·dac·tic \dīˈdaktik, -tēk, *Brit usu & US sometimes* dəˈd-\ *n* -S [Gk *didaktikos* apt at teaching] **1** *archaic* **a** : a didactic treatise **b** : a didactic writer **2 didactics** *pl but sing or pl in constr* : systematic instruction : PEDAGOGY; *sometimes* : TEACHINGS

²di·dac·tic \(ˈ)dīˈd-, *Brit usu & US sometimes* dəˈd-\ *also* **di·dac·ti·cal** \-təkəl, -tēk-\ *adj* [Gk *didaktikos* apt at teaching, fr. *didaktos* taught, able to be taught (fr. *didaskein* to teach) + *-ikos* -ic] **1** : fitted or intended to teach : concerned with or functioning in the conveyance of instruction: as **a** : teaching some moral lesson ⟨the ~ aspect of the Mysteries is often overlooked⟩ **b** *of literature or other art* : intended to convey instruction and information as well as pleasure and entertainment ⟨~ poetry⟩ ⟨a fine piece of ~ writing⟩; *often* : overburdened with instructive or factual matter to the exclusion of graceful and pleasing detail : pompously dull and erudite : DRY ⟨his writing became increasingly arid and ~ as he withdrew from normal social life⟩ ⟨to write a ~ play is to suppose . . . the public in need of your advice —E.R.Bentley⟩ **c** : involving lecture and textbook instruction rather than demonstration and laboratory study ⟨a purely ~ course⟩ ⟨both ~ and laboratory instruction are used⟩ **d** *of grammar* : NORMATIVE **2** : making moral observations : urging the acceptance of moral conclusions : MORALISTIC — **di·dac·ti·cal·ly** \-tək(ə)lē, -tēk-, -li\ *adv*

didactic analysis *n* : the psychoanalysis of one who will himself employ psychoanalysis in treatment or research

di·dac·ti·cism \-ˈ=təˌsizəm\ *n* -S : didactic method or quality; *often* : PEDANTRY

di·dac·tive \(ˈ)dīˈdaktiv, dəˈd-\ *adj* [Gk *didaktos* + E *-ive*] *archaic* : DIDACTIC

di·dac·tyl *or* **di·dac·tyle** \(ˈ)dīˈdaktəl\ *also* **di·dac·ty·lous** \-tələs\ *adj* [*di-* + *-dactyl*, *-dactyle*, *-dactylous* (fr. Gk *daktylos* finger)] : having only two digits on each extremity — **di·dac·ty·lism** \-ˈ=təˌlizəm\ *n* -S

di·dac·ty·la \-tələ\ *n pl, cap* [NL, fr. *di-* + *-dactyla* (fr. Gk *daktylos* finger)] *in some classifications* : a primary division of Marsupialia comprising forms in which the 2d and 3d pedal digits are bound together — compare POLYPROTODONTIA

di·dap·per \ˈdīˌdapə(r)\ *n* -S [ME *dydoppar*, prob. alter. of OE *dūfedoppa* pelican, fr. *dūfan* to dive + *-doppa* diver — more at DIVE, DOP] : a dabchick or other small grebe

di·das·cal·ic \ˌdīˌdaˈskalik, -ˈidəˌ-, ˌdidəˈ-\ *adj* [LL *didascalicus*, fr. Gk *didaskalikos*, fr. *didaskalos* teacher (fr. *didaskein* to teach) + *-ikos* -ic — more at DOCILE] **1** *archaic* : intended to teach (as a moral lesson) : MORALISTIC, DIDACTIC **2** : of, relating to, or contained in a didascaly

di·das·ca·ly \dīˈdaskəlē, dəˈ-\ *n* -ES [Gk *didaskalia*, lit., teaching, instruction, fr. *didaskalos* + *-ia* -y] : any of various catalogs of Greek drama with names of authors and dates in the form of the original inscriptions or as later published by Alexandrian scholars

did·der \ˈdidə(r)\ *vi* -ED/-ING/-S [ME *didderen*] *dial Brit* : QUIVER, SHAKE, TREMBLE

did·dle \ˈdidᵊl\ *vb* **diddled; diddled; diddling** \-id(ᵊ)liŋ\ **diddles** [origin unknown] *vi* **1 a** *chiefly Scot* : to move rapidly back and forth : JIGGLE ⟨the fiddler's elbow *diddled* madly during the jig⟩ **b** *dial Brit* : to dance with a bouncing bobbing movement **2** : COPULATE — usu. considered vulgar **3** : to waste time : LOAF : DAWDLE **~** *vt* **1** *chiefly dial* : to move with short rapid motions **2** *chiefly dial* : DANDLE *vt* 1 **3** : to copulate with — usu. considered vulgar **4 a** : SWINDLE, CHEAT ⟨he will not ~ his employers⟩ **b** : HOAX, DELUDE ⟨when he forgot his part he *diddled* the audience into believing another actor had slipped⟩

diddle away *vt* : to waste (as time) in trifling : potter away ⟨they *diddled away* the afternoon and had nothing to show for it⟩

¹did·dle-dad·dle \ˈdidᵊlˌdadᵊl\ *n* -S [origin unknown] : FUSSING, TRIFLING, FIDDLE-FADDLE

²diddle-daddle \"\ *vi* **diddle-daddled; diddle-daddled; diddle-daddling** \-ad(ᵊ)liŋ\ **diddle-daddles** : DAWDLE, TRIFLE

did·dle·dee \ˈdidᵊlˌdē\ *n* -S [origin unknown] *Falkland islands* : RED CROWBERRY

did·dle·dees \-ēz\ *n pl* [origin unknown] *NewEng* : fallen pine needles

did·dler \ˈdid(ᵊ)lə(r)\ *n* -S : one that diddles; *specif* : CHEAT

did·dy \ˈdidi\ *n* -ES [alter. of *titty*] *dial Eng* : TEAT

diddy box *var of* DITTY BOX

di·del·phia \dīˈdelfēə\ *or* **didel·phes** \-ˌfēz\ [NL, fr. *di-* + Gk *delphys* womb + NL *-ia*, *-es* — more at DOLPHIN] *syn of* MARSUPIALIA

¹di·del·phi·an \(ˈ)=ˈ=fēən\ *adj* [NL *Didelphia* + E *-an*] : MARSUPIAL

²didelphian \"\ *or* **di·delph** \ˈdīˌdelf\ *n* -S : MARSUPIAL

di·del·phic \(ˈ)dīˈdelfik\ *adj* [*di-* + Gk *delphys* womb + E *-ic*] **1 a** : having or relating to a double uterus **b** : having the female genital tract completely doubled (as certain worms) **2** [NL *Didelphia* + *-ic*] : MARSUPIAL

¹di·del·phid \(ˈ)dīˈdelfəd\ *adj* [NL *Didelphidae*] : of or relating to the Didelphidae or to *Didelphis* or to members of this family or genus

²didelphid \"\ *n* -S : a marsupial of the family Didelphidae or genus *Didelphis* : OPOSSUM

di·del·phi·dae \dīˈdelfəˌdē\ *n pl, cap* [NL, fr. *Didelphis*, type genus + *-idae*] : a family of marsupial mammals comprising the New World opossums

di·del·phine \(ˈ)dīˈdelfən\ *adj* [NL *Didelphia* + E *-ine*] : of or relating to the Didelphidae or the Marsupialia

di·del·phis \=ˈ=fəs\ *n, cap* [NL, irreg. fr. *di-* + Gk *delphys* womb] : the type genus of Didelphidae which includes the Virginia opossum and a few related marsupials of tropical America

di·del·phy·i·dae \ˌdīˌdelˈfīəˌdē\ [NL, fr. *Didelphys*, type genus + *-idae*] *syn of* DIDELPHIDAE

di·del·phys \=ˈ=fəs\ [NL, alter. of *Didelphis*] *syn of* DIDELPHIS

did·ger·i·doo *or* **did·jer·i·doo** \ˌdijərēˈdü\ *n* -S [imit.] : a large musical pipe of the Australian aborigines made from bamboo or a hollow sapling

di·di·dae \ˈdidəˌdē\ [NL, fr. *Didus*, type genus + *-idae*] *syn of* RAPHIDAE

didie *var of* DIDY

di·din·i·um \dīˈdinēəm\ *n* [NL, fr. *di-* + Gk *deinos* terrible + NL *-ium* — more at DIN-] **1** *cap* : a genus of carnivorous protozoans (order Holotricha) that feed on paramecia **2** *pl* **didiniums** \-mz\ *or* **didin·ia** \-nēə\ : any protozoan of the genus *Didinium*

di·dip·lis \dīˈdipləs\ [NL] *syn of* PEPLIS

di·diploid \(ˈ)dī+\ *n* [*di-* + *diploid*] *biol* : an amphidiploid or autotetraploid

did·na \ˈdidnə\ [by shortening & alter.] *chiefly Scot* : did not

didn't \ˈdidᵊn(t), *chiefly substand* (ˈ)dint\ [by contr.] : did not

di·do \ˈdī(ˌ)dō\ *n, pl* **didoes** *or* **didos** [origin unknown] **1** : an absurd, foolish, or mischievous act : TRICK, PRANK, CAPER — usu. used in pl. and often in the phrase *cut didoes* ⟨such sums were too vast, and the economic *didoes* too complex, for comprehension —Michael Scully⟩ ⟨the sun had cut no *didoes* sufficiently serious to interrupt continent-to-continent radio broadcasting —*Newsweek*⟩ ⟨his harmless *didoes* that once scared me to death —Bennett Cerf⟩ **2 a** : an article of little worth : TRINKET **b** : a frivolous article of dress : FRILL, FURBELOW

di·dodecahedron \ˌdī+\ *n* [*di-* + *dodecahedron*] : DIPLOID 1

di·dot \(ˈ)dēˈdō\ *adj, usu cap* [after François-Ambroise *Didot* †1804 Fr. printer and publisher who devised it] : of or relating to a typographical point system commonly used in Europe

di·drachm \ˈdī+ˌ-\ *or* **di·drachma** \(ˈ)dī+\ *n* -S [LL & Gk; LL *didrachmon*, *didrachma*, fr. Gk *didrachmon*, fr. *di-* + *-drachmon* (fr. *drachmē* drachm) — more at DRAM] : an ancient Greek silver coin worth two drachmas — **di·drachmal** \(ˈ)dī+\ *adj*

di·dric \ˈdiˌdrik\ *or* **die·dric cuckoo** *or* **die·drik cuckoo** \ˈdē|-\ *n* -S [Afrik *diedrik*, of imit. origin] : a small African cuckoo (*Chrysococcyx caprius*) lustrous emerald green above and largely white below

didst *archaic past 2d sing of* DO

diduce *vt* -ED/-ING/-S [L *diducere*, fr. *di-* (fr. *dis-* ¹dis) + *ducere* to lead, draw — more at TOW] **1** *obs* : to draw apart **2** *obs* : EXPAND, ENLARGE

diduction *n* -S [L *diduction-*, *diductio*, fr. *diductus* (past part. of *diducere*) + *-ion-*, *-io* -ion] **1** *obs* : a drawing apart : SEPARATION **2** *obs* : DILATATION

di·duc·tor \(ˈ)dīˈdəktə(r)\ *n* -S *often attrib* [L *diductus* + E *-or*] : a divaricator muscle in arthropomatous brachiopods

di·dus \ˈdīdəs\ [NL, prob. modif. of E *dodo*] *syn of* RAPHUS

di·dy *or* **di·die** \ˈdīdē, -īdi\ *n, pl* **didies** [baby-talk alter. of *diaper*] : DIAPER 2b

didym- *or* **didymo-** *comb form* [Gk, fr. *didymos*, fr. *dyo* two — more at TWO] **1** : twin ⟨*didymolite*⟩ **2** : testicle ⟨*didymitis*⟩

di·dym·i·um \dīˈdimēəm\ *n* -S [NL, fr. *didym-* + *-ium*] : a mixture of rare-earth elements that is freed from cerium, contains chiefly neodymium and praseodymium usu. associated with lanthanum, was once regarded as an element (symbol *Di*), and is used in coloring glass for optical filters

did·y·mo·lite \ˈdidəməˌlīt\ *n* -S [*didym-* + *-lite*] : a mineral consisting of a calcium aluminum silicate $Ca_2Al_6Si_9O_{29}$ occurring in dark gray monoclinic twinned crystals

did·y·mous \ˈdidəməs\ *also* **did·y·moid** \-ˌmȯid\ *or* **did·y·mate** \-ˌmāt, -māt\ *adj* [*didymous* fr. Gk *didymos*; *didymoid*, *didymate* fr. *didym-* + *-oid* or *-ate*] *biol* : growing in pairs : TWIN, TWOFOLD

di·dy·na·mia \ˌdīdəˈnāmēə\ *n pl, cap* [NL, fr. *di-* + Gk *dynamis* power + NL *-ia* — more at DYNAMIC] *in former classifications* : a class of plants including those having flowers with four stamens disposed in pairs of unequal length — **di·dy·na·mi·an** \ˌ==ˈnāmēən\ *or* **di·dy·nam·ic** \-ˈnamik\ *adj*

di·dy·na·mous \(ˈ)dīˈdinəməs\ *adj* [NL *Didynamia* + E *-ous*] : having four stamens disposed in pairs of unequal length — used esp. of plants of the families Scrophulariaceae and Labiatae — **di·dyn·a·my** \-mē\ *n* -ES

¹die \ˈdī\ *vb* **died; died; dy·ing** \ˈdīiŋ\ **dies** [ME *dien*, *deyen*, fr. or akin to ON *deyja* to die; akin to OS *dōian* to die, OHG *touwen* to die, Goth *diwans* mortal, OIr *duine* human being, Arm *di* corpse] *vi* **1** : to pass from physical life : suffer total and irreversible loss of the bodily attributes and functions that constitute life : EXPIRE, PERISH ⟨*died* in a fire⟩ ⟨may yet ~ at his brother's hand⟩ ⟨*dying* of old age⟩ ⟨likely to ~ from lack of care⟩ **2 a** : to pass out of existence : come to an end : become lost or extinct : become extinguished : CEASE ⟨his secret *died* with him⟩ ⟨their anger *died* at these words⟩ ⟨the bill *died* in committee⟩ **b** : to pass gradually out of existence : become imperceptible or extinct in the course of an appreciable period : recede and grow fainter : disappear or subside gradually — often used with *out*, *down*, or *away* ⟨in the course of millennia the dinosaurs *died* out⟩ ⟨the wind often ~*s* down at sunset⟩ ⟨childish voices *dying* away in the distance⟩ **c** : to disappear gradually in another surface — used esp. of moldings that become incorporated in a sloped or curved face (as of a building) **3** : to suffer spiritual death : become spiritually lost : become damned ⟨whosoever lives and believes in me shall never ~ —Jn 11:26 (RSV)⟩ **4 a** : to suffer or face the pains of death ⟨the martyr in spirit is ready to ~ every day for his faith⟩ **b** : to be brought to or as if to the point of death by intensity of emotion (as desire, envy, shame, embarrassment) **c** : to lose vitality : grow faint ⟨their hearts *died* at that uncanny cry⟩ **d** : to languish esp. from weakness, discouragement, or boredom ⟨simply *dying* from fatigue⟩ **e** : to long keenly or desperately : want exceedingly — usu. used with *for* or an infinitive ⟨*dying* for a smoke⟩ ⟨*dying* to go⟩ **5** : to become indifferent : cease to be subject ⟨~ to worldly things⟩ ⟨let them ~ unto sin⟩ **6** : to pass into an inferior state or situation: as **a** : to become flat : lose characteristic desired qualities (as sparkle or bouquet) — used chiefly of beverages ⟨the more delicate wines tend to ~ early⟩ **b** : to cease from functioning : STOP ⟨the motor *died* on the hill⟩ **c** *of a baseball player* : to be on base at the end of an inning **~** *vt* : to suffer in dying : come to death by — used with a cognate object ⟨*dying* a natural death⟩ ⟨*died* a shameful death⟩ — **die game 1** : to die while courageously struggling **2** : to persist valiantly to the end in behalf of a lost cause — **die hard 1** : to be long in dying as if struggling against death or destruction ⟨such rumors *die hard*⟩ **2** : to fight a hopeless fight : continue resistance against hopeless odds ⟨hard-shell conservatism *dies hard*⟩ — **die in bed** *or* **die in one's bed** : to die of disease or old age — **die in harness** : to die while still actively engaged in one's work or duty — **die in one's boots** *or* **die with one's boots on** *also* **die in one's shoes** *or* **die with one's shoes on** : to die otherwise than from disease or old age; *esp* : to die as a result of the violent act of another — **die laughing** : to laugh without restraint, immoderately, or to the point of physical distress — **die on the vine** : to fail to be productive of a planned or desired result esp. because of lack of concerted effort or enthusiasm ⟨he had sound ideas but they usually *died on the vine*⟩ ⟨the plan to draft the mayor as a candidate for governor *died on the vine*⟩

²die \"\ *n, pl* **dice** \-īs\ *or* **dies** \-īz\ [ME *dee*, fr. MF *dé*, perh. fr. Ar *dad* game] **1 a** *pl dice* : a small cube (as of ivory, bone, or plastic) marked distinctively on each face with one to six spots and used in pairs in various games and in gambling by being shaken and thrown to come to rest at random on a flat surface ⟨made a killing with loaded *dice*⟩ **b** *dice pl* : any of various games played with dice; *esp* : a gambling game so played **2** *pl dice* : a small cubical piece (as of food) — usu. used in pl. ⟨cut the meat into *dice*⟩ **3** *pl usu dice* : something determined by or as if by a cast of dice : CHANCE, FORTUNE, FATE ⟨there is no turning back now; the ~ is cast⟩ ⟨the *dice* appear to be loaded against a victory this year⟩ **4** *pl dies, Scot* : PLAYTHING, TOY **5** *pl dies* : DADO 1a **6** *pl dies* : any of various tools or devices for imparting a desired shape, form, or finish to a material: as **a** (1) : one of a pair of cutting or shaping tools that when moved toward each other produce a certain desired form in or impress a desired device on an object by pressure or by a blow, this tool being the larger of the pair or the part into which the punch enters — called also *matrix* (2) : a device composed of a pair of such tools (3) : a set of dies (as a set of triple-action dies including the matrices, punches, springs) that make up the complete tool **b** : a hollow internally threaded screw-cutting tool made in one piece or composed of several cutting parts, often adjustable as to distance, and used for forming screw threads (as on bolts) — compare DIE HEAD, DIESTOCK, SPRING DIE **c** : a knife or cutter used to cut out blanks (as for soles in shoemaking) **d** : the mold in which a die casting, a powdered-metal casting, or a drop forging is made **e** : a block of hard metal or precious stone with a perforation of definite shape that is used in making wire and rod by drawing or extrusion **f** : a perforated block through which plastic material is forced to make it assume a desired shape: as (1) : such a block through which clay is forced in molding bricks (2) : the metal end of a cookie press or cake decorator that is pierced with various designs through which dough or frosting can be forced out into fancy shapes **g** : a heavy iron ring or block on which ore is crushed (as in an edge mill or a stamp mill) **h** (1) : a metal block with a design in intaglio into which a matching counterpart forces material (as paper or board) to be die-stamped or embossed — compare COUNTER, PLATE (2) : a comparable device used to stamp, emboss, or mold a seal (as on paper or wax) **i** : a rigid assembly of steel cutting and creasing rules with which flat sheets of paperboard are stamped out before being folded into cartons **7** *pl dies* : a block of metal on which the design of a postage stamp is engraved and which is used in making the repeated impressions that form the printing plate

dice

³die \"\ *vt* **died; died; dieing; dies** : to cut or shape with a die — often used with *out* ⟨~*ing* out leather for wallets⟩

die away *vi* : FAINT, SWOON ⟨I could have *died away* with embarrassment⟩

¹die-away \ˈ=ˌ=ˌ=\ *adj* [*die away*] : having a languid air : LANGUISHING ⟨a *die-away* glance⟩ ⟨*die-away* airs and graces⟩

²die-away \"\ *n* -S [*die away*] : a gradual fading out (as of a sound)

dieb \ˈdēb\ *n* -S [Ar *dhi'b*, *dhib* wolf, jackal] : a jackal (*Canis anthus*) of No. Africa

die back *vi, of a plant or plant part* : to die from the top toward the base — used esp. of woody plants and of only part of their aboveground structure

dieback \ˈ=ˌ=\ *n* -S [*die back*] **1** : a diseased condition in woody plants in which peripheral parts are killed either by parasites or by other agencies (as winter injury) **2** : EXANTHEM 2

die break *also* **die crack** *n* : a defect or blemish on a coin or medal caused by a crack in the die

diecase \ˈ=ˌ=\ *n* : MATRIX CASE

¹die-cast \ˈ=ˌ=\ *vt* [²*die* + *cast*] : to make by forcing molten metal (as a zinc, tin, lead, or aluminum alloy) into a die

²die-cast \"\ *adj* : made by die-casting ⟨a *die-cast* seal⟩

die casting *n* : a part made by die-casting

die chaser *n* : a threading die or one of the cutters of a composite die or a die head

dieck·mann reaction *or* **dieckmann condensation** \ˈdēkmən-, -ˌmän-\ *n, usu cap D* [after Walter *Dieckmann* †1925 Ger. chemist] : a base-catalyzed condensation of an open-chain dicarboxylic ester to form a cyclic keto ester (as 2-keto-cyclopentane-carboxylic ester)

di·ec·ta·sis \dīˈektəsəs\ *n* -ES [LGk *diektasis*, fr. Gk *diekteinein* to stretch out, fr. *dia-* + *ekteinein* to stretch — more at ECTASIS] *prosody* : lengthening by an interpolated syllable

die-cut \ˈ=ˌ=\ *vt* : to cut with dies

died *past of* DIE

die down *vi, of a plant* : to undergo death of the aboveground portions — used chiefly of a normal seasonal behavior of herbaceous perennials, less often of winterkilling of semihardy woody plants ⟨the spring bulbs ripen their foliage and *die down* soon after blooming⟩ ⟨buddleias *die down* each winter in the north but bloom from new wood the next season⟩

diedric cuckoo *or* **diedrik cuckoo** *var of* DIDRIC

dief·fen·bach·ia \ˌdēfənˈbakēə, ˈ=ˌ==ˌ=\ *n* [NL, fr. Ernst *Dieffenbach* †1855 Ger. naturalist & NL *-ia*] **1** *cap* : a small genus of tropical American erect plants (family Araceae) with long sheathing or clasping petioles and united stamens **2** -S : any plant of the genus *Dieffenbachia*

die-forge \ˈ=ˌ=\ *vt* : DROP-FORGE

di·e·gue·ño \ˌdēəˈgān(ˌ)yō\ *n, pl* **diegueño** *or* **diegueños** *usu* *cap* [Sp, fr. San Diego, Cal. + Sp *-eño* (suffix denoting an inhabitant)] **1 a :** an Indian people of southern California **b :** a member of such people **2 :** a Yuman language of the Diegueño people

diehard \ˈ⸗,⸗\ *n* -s [¹*die* + *hard*] **:** one that dies hard: as **a :** an irreconcilable opponent of a measure, situation, or condition ordinarily accepted as tolerable, normal, or desirable; *esp* **:** an extreme conservative who resists to the last any alteration in the political system **b :** SCOTTISH TERRIER

die-hard \"\ *adj* [¹*die* + *hard*] **:** offering extreme resistance to change ⟨*die-hard* optimism⟩ **:** completely and determinedly fixed ⟨*die-hard* conservatives⟩ ⟨a few *die-hard* colonists continued to farm⟩ **syn** see CONSERVATIVE

die-hard·ism \" + ,izəm\ *n* -s **:** the principles or attitudes of a political diehard

die head *also* **die holder** *n* **:** a device that holds a threading die when chasing threads on work revolving in a machine or that itself revolves and chases threads on work held stationary in a machine

di·el \ˈdīəl, ˈdēəl\ *adj* [irreg. fr. L *dies* day + E *-al* — more at DEITY] **:** involving a 24-hour period that usu. includes a day and the adjoining night — used chiefly in ecology ⟨fluctuating ~ light cycles⟩ ⟨a mild ~ periodicity⟩

diel·drin \ˈdēldrən\ *n* -s [*Diels*-Alder reaction + *-in*] **:** a white crystalline insecticide consisting chiefly or entirely of the epoxide $C_{12}H_8Cl_6O$ obtained by oxidation of aldrin

¹**di·electric** \ˌdī +\ *n* -s [*dia-* + *electric*] **1 :** a nonconductor of direct electric current **2 :** a substance in which a steady electric field can be set up with a negligible flow of current

²**dielectric** \"\ *adj* [*dia-* + *electric*] **:** relating to or having the properties of a dielectric ⟨~ material⟩ — **di·electrically** \ˌdī +\ *adv*

dielectric absorption *n* **:** ABSORPTION 3

dielectric constant *n* **:** a measure of the ability of a dielectric material to store electrical potential energy under the influence of an electric field, measured by the ratio of the capacitance of a condenser with the material as dielectric to its capacitance with vacuum as dielectric

dielectric heating *n* **:** the rapid and uniform heating throughout a nonconducting material by means of a high frequency electromagnetic field, the heat resulting from the dissipation of energy in the rapid reversal of the polarization of the molecules — compare INDUCTION HEATING

dielectric loss *n* **:** energy loss in a dielectric due to an alternating electric field

dielectric strength *n* **:** the maximum intensity of electric field that a given dielectric can sustain without disruptive discharge, usu. expressed in kilovolts per millimeter

diels–al·der reaction \ˈdēlsˈäldə(r)-\ *n, usu cap D&A* [after Otto *Diels* †1954 & Kurt *Alder* †1958 Ger. chemists] **:** an addition reaction in which a diene unites with the double or triple bond of an unsaturated compound to form a 6-membered ring (as in tetrahydro-phthalic anhydride)

diemaker \ˈ⸗,⸗⸗\ *n* **:** a worker who makes cutting and shaping dies — called also *diesinker*

die·me·nia \dēˈmēnēə\ [NL, fr. Anton Van *Diemen* †1645 Dutch governor of Batavia who sent out the expedition that discovered Tasmania + NL *-ia*] *syn of* DEMANSIA

di·encephalic \(ˌ)dī +\ *adj* [NL *diencephalon* + E *-ic*] **:** of, relating to, or involving the diencephalon

di·encephalon \ˌdī +\ *n* -s [NL, fr. *dia-* + *encephalon*] **:** the posterior subdivision of the forebrain — called also *between-brain, thalamencephalon*

di·ene \ˈdī,ēn, ⸗ˈ⸗\ *n* -s [ISV, fr. *-diene*] **:** a chemical compound containing two double bonds; *esp* **:** DIOLEFIN ⟨conjugated ~s like 1,3-butadiene⟩

-diene \ˌdī,ēn, ⸗ˈ⸗\ *n suffix* -s [ISV, fr. *di-* + *-ene*] **:** chemical compound containing two double bonds ⟨hexa*diene*⟩

die·ner \ˈdēnə(r)\ *n* -s [G, servant, fr. MHG *dienære*, fr. *dienen* to serve (fr. OHG *thionōn*) + *-ære* -er — more at THEOW] **:** a laboratory helper esp. in a medical school

di·en·es·trol *also* **di·en·oes·trol** \ˌdīəˈneˌstrōl, -rōl\ *n* -s [*diphenol* + *estrogen, oestrogen* + *-ol*] **:** a white crystalline estrogenic diphenol $[HOC_6H_4C(=CHCH_3)-]_2$ containing two hydrogen atoms fewer than diethylstilbestrol

diene synthesis *n* **:** DIELS-ALDER REACTION

diene value *n* **:** a numerical measure of the conjugated double bonds in a fatty acid or fat (as a drying oil) that is calculated from the amount of maleic anhydride capable of reacting with a known weight of the acid or fat

di·eno·phile \dīˈēnə,fīl, ⸗ˈ⸗⸗,⸗\ *n* -s [*diene* + *-o-* + *-phile*] **:** the olefinic or acetylenic component (as maleic anhydride) that is seeking a diene in the Diels-Alder reaction

di·entamoeba \(ˌ)dī +\ *n, cap* [NL, fr. *di-* + *Entamoeba*] **:** a genus of commensal amoebas of the human intestine distinguished by the presence of two nuclei in the trophozoite

die off *vi* **:** to be removed severally or in numbers by death ⟨her few remaining kinfolk *died off* one by one⟩

die-off \ˈ⸗,⸗\ *n* -s [*die off*] **:** a sudden sharp decline of a population (as of rabbits or game birds) not directly due to hunting or other human activity

die proof *n* **:** proof of a postage stamp made directly from a die

di·er \ˈdī(ə)r, -īə\ *n* -s **:** one that dies

dieresis *var of* DIAERESIS

die·ri \ˈdirē\ *n, pl* **dieri** *or* **dieris** *usu cap* **1 a :** a primitive people near Lake Eyre, Australia, having marriage customs in which a woman is pledged a husband at birth and in which the custom of pirraura exists **b :** a member of such people **2 :** the language of the Dieri people

dier·vil·la \dirˈvilə\ *n, cap* [NL, after M. *Dierville*, 18th cent. Fr. surgeon] **:** a genus of shrubs (family Caprifoliaceae) comprising the bush honeysuckles and having 2-lipped flowers and long-beaked capsular fruits

dies *pres 3d sing of* DIE, *pl of* DIE

di·es co·mi·ti·a·lis \ˌdē,āskə,mid·ēˈälə̇s\ *n, pl* **dies comitia·les** \-ä,lās\ [L, lit., comitial day] **:** any of the 190 days of each year on which the people under the Roman republic could meet for legislation or election

¹**die·sel** \ˈdēzəl, -ēsəl\ *adj, sometimes cap* [after Rudolf *Diesel* †1913 Ger. mechanical engineer and inventor] **1 :** relating to the diesel cycle or engine **2 :** equipped with or driven by a diesel engine ⟨a ~ truck⟩

²**diesel** \"\ *n, sometimes cap* **1 :** DIESEL ENGINE **2 :** a vehicle (as a truck, locomotive, or ship) driven by a diesel engine

diesel cycle *n, sometimes cap D* **:** an ideal-engine cycle during which the working substance successively undergoes adiabatic compression, constant-pressure heating, adiabatic expansion, and constant-volume cooling — compare DIESEL ENGINE, OTTO CYCLE

diesel–electric \ˌ⸗⸗ˈ⸗⸗\ *adj, sometimes cap D* **:** of, relating to, or employing the combination of a diesel engine driving an electric generator

diesel–electric locomotive *also* **diesel–electric** *or* **diesel locomotive** *n, sometimes cap D* **:** an electric locomotive having electric generators powered by diesel engines for the production of its own electric power

diesel engine *n, sometimes cap D* **:** an internal-combustion engine in which air is compressed to a temperature sufficiently high to ignite fuel injected directly into the cylinder where the combustion and expansion actuate a piston

diesel–engined \ˌ⸗⸗ˈ⸗⸗\ *adj, sometimes cap D* **:** driven by a diesel engine

die·sel·i·za·tion \ˌdēzələˈzāshən, -ēsə-, -lī'z-\ *n* -s *sometimes cap* **:** the act of dieselizing

die·sel·ize \ˈ⸗⸗,līz\ *vt* -ED/-ING/-S *sometimes cap* **:** to equip with a diesel engine or with diesel-electric locomotives

diesel oil *also* **diesel fuel** *n, sometimes cap D* **:** a heavy mineral oil used as fuel in diesel engines

die set *n* **1 :** a set of cutting, shaping, or combination dies **2 :** a punch-press accessory for maintaining proper alignment between punch and die block

di·es fas·tus \ˌdē,ā|sˈfästəs\ *n, pl* **dies fas·ti** \-,stē\ [L, lit., court day] **1 :** a day on which Roman religious law permitted secular activities or an auspicious day for such activities **2 :** any of the 40 days of each year on which the praetors under the Roman republic could exercise their general powers in holding court; *broadly* **:** DIES COMITIALIS

die shoe *n* **:** a metal block inserted between the lower half of a cutting or shaping die and the bed of a press to spread the blow and avoid wear

die·sinker \ˈ⸗,⸗⸗\ *n* **1 :** DIEMAKER **2 :** a vertical milling machine used in diesinking

die·sinking \ˈ⸗,⸗⸗\ *n* **:** the art or process of forming cutting and shaping dies

di·e·sis \ˈdīəsə̇s\ *n, pl* **die·ses** \-ə,sēz\ [L, fr. Gk, fr. *dïienai*, to drive through, let go through (fr. *dia-* + *hienai* to let go, send, throw) + *-sis* — more at JET] **1 a** *in ancient Greek music* **:** LIMMA **b :** ENHARMONIC DIESIS **c :** ⁴SHARP c(1), c(2) **2 :** DOUBLE DAGGER — compare REFERENCE MARK

di·es ju·ri·di·cus \ˌdē,āsyüˈridə̇kəs\ *n, pl* **dies juridi·ci** \-ə̇,kē\ [L] **:** COURT DAY — compare DIES NON

dies ne·fas·tus \-āsneˈfästəs\ *n, pl* **dies nefas·ti** \-,stē\ [L, lit., nor-court day] **:** a day on which secular activities were forbidden in ancient Rome; *specif* **:** a day on which the courts were closed and it was illegal (as for the praetors) to transact public judicial affairs

di·es non \ˌdē,āˈsnōn, ˈdī,ēzˈnän\ *also* **di·es non ju·ri·di·cus** \ˌdē,āˈsnōnyüˈridə̇kəs\ *n, pl* **dies nons** \-nz\ *also* **dies non juridi·ci** \-də,kē\ [L *dies non juridicus* nonjuridical day] **1 :** a day on which the courts do not ordinarily sit or carry on business **2 :** a day on which general business may not lawfully be transacted

die–stamp \ˈ⸗,⸗\ *vt* **:** to form or cut out esp. from sheet stock or to emboss by means of a die

die stamper *n* **:** a worker who performs die-stamping (as of metal or stationery)

di·ester \ˈdī+,-\ *n* [ISV *di-* + *ester*] **:** a compound containing two ester groupings

die·stock \ˈ⸗,⸗\ *n* **:** a stock to hold dies used for cutting threads (as on screws or pipe)

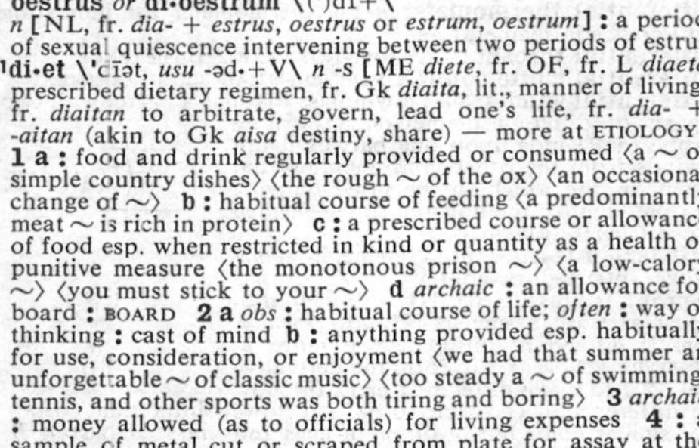

diestock: *1* diestock; *2* die

di·estrous *or* **di·estrual** *also* **di·oestrous** *or* **di·oestrual** \(ˈ)dī+\ *adj* [NL *diestrus, dioestrus* + E *-ous* or *-al*] **:** of, relating to, or exhibiting diestrus

di·estrus *or* **di·estrum** *also* **di·oestrus** *or* **di·oestrum** \(ˈ)dī+\ *n* [NL, fr. *dia-* + *estrus, oestrus* or *estrum, oestrum*] **:** a period of sexual quiescence intervening between two periods of estrus

¹**di·et** \ˈdīət, *usu* -əd·+V\ *n* -s [ME *diete*, fr. OF, fr. L *diaeta* prescribed dietary regimen, fr. Gk *diaita*, lit., manner of living, fr. *diaitan* to arbitrate, govern, lead one's life, fr. *dia-* + *-aitan* (akin to Gk *aisa* destiny, share) — more at ETIOLOGY] **1 a :** food and drink regularly provided or consumed ⟨a ~ of simple country dishes⟩ ⟨the rough ~ of the ox⟩ ⟨an occasional change of ~⟩ **b :** habitual course of feeding ⟨a predominantly meat ~ is rich in protein⟩ **c :** a prescribed course or allowance of food esp. when restricted in kind or quantity as a health or punitive measure ⟨the monotonous prison ~⟩ ⟨a low-calory ~⟩ ⟨you must stick to your ~⟩ **d** *archaic* **:** an allowance for board **:** BOARD **2 a** *obs* **:** habitual course of life; *often* **:** way of thinking **:** cast of mind **b :** anything provided esp. habitually for use, consideration, or enjoyment ⟨we had that summer an unforgettable ~ of classic music⟩ ⟨too steady a ~ of swimming, tennis, and other sports was both tiring and boring⟩ **3** *archaic* **:** money allowed (as to officials) for living expenses **4 :** a sample of metal cut or scraped from plate for assay at the British mint

²**diet** \"\ *vb* -ED/-ING/-S [ME *dieten*, fr. MF *dieter*, fr. *diete*] *vt* **1 :** to cause to take food **:** FEED **:** provide for consumption **2 :** to cause to eat and drink according to prescribed rules **:** regulate the food of; *often* **:** to cause to eat sparingly **3** *archaic* **:** to provide with meals **:** BOARD **~** *vi* **:** to eat according to prescribed rules; *often* **:** to eat sparingly ⟨she said she ~*ed* but she didn't lose a pound⟩ ⟨the Lenten fast is often an occasion for many to ~ seriously⟩

³**diet** \"\ *n* -s [ME *dyet*, fr. ML *dieta*, fr. L *dies* day — more at DEITY] **1** *archaic, chiefly Scot* **a :** a day's journey **b :** the itinerary of a journey **:** JOURNEY **2** *Scot* **a :** a day set for an event (as a meeting); *specif* **:** the day on which a person is cited to appear in court **b :** a session or sitting of a court or assembly **3 a** *archaic* **:** a formal conference of notables meeting to attend to affairs of the realm **b** (1) **:** a formal public assembly esp. of the estates or governing body of a realm or of a confederation; *specif* **:** one of the great formal assemblies of councillors of the Holy Roman Empire ⟨the *Diet* of Worms condemned Luther as a heretic⟩ ⟨the *Diet* of Augsburg of 1530⟩ (2) **:** the estates or members participating in such a diet **c :** a legislative assembly **:** the national parliament or provincial legislature of a state (as Denmark, Germany, Japan, Paraguay)

¹**di·e·tary** \ˈdīə,terē, -ri\ *n* -ES [ME *dietarie*, fr. *diete* + *-arie* -ary (n. suffix)] **1** *obs* **:** a rule of diet; *also* **:** a treatise or discourse on such rules **2 :** an allowance or quantity of food provided or eaten by an individual, group, or population in accord with medical or other orders, availability, or social and economic controls ⟨the American ~⟩ ⟨the ~ changes according to need and age⟩

²**dietary** \"\ *adj* [¹*diet* + *-ary* (adj. suffix)] **:** of or related to a diet or to the rules of diet ⟨~ foods⟩ ⟨~ habits⟩ ⟨a ~ disease⟩ ⟨~ cuisine⟩

dietary law *n* **:** any of the laws relating to the fitness for consumption of various foods and to the prohibition of various combinations and contacts (as that of milk with meat) that are observed by orthodox Jews

dietary standard *n* **:** the food in the diet usu. expressed in terms of digestible nutrients supposed to be best adapted for man under different conditions

di·et·er \ˈdīəd·ə(r), -ītə-\ *n* -s **1** *obs* **:** a person who supervises and prescribes a diet or dietary **2 :** one that diets; *esp* **:** a person that consumes a reduced allowance of food in order to lose weight ⟨one of the food preparations most demanded by ~s —Vance Packard⟩

di·e·tet·ic \ˌdīəˈted·|ik, -et|, |ēk\ *also* **di·e·tet·i·cal** \|ə̇kəl, |ēk-\ *adj* [LL *diaeteticus*, fr. Gk *diaitētikos*, fr. *diaita* diet + *-ētikos* -etic, -etical — more at DIET] **1 :** of or relating to diet or the kind and quantity of food to be eaten ⟨~ rules⟩ **:** belonging to dietetics ⟨~ studies⟩ **2 :** adapted (as by elimination of sugar or salt) for use in special diets ⟨~ sweets⟩ ⟨a ~ canned tuna⟩

di·e·tet·i·cal·ly \|ə̇k(ə)lē, |ēk-, -li\ *adv, archaic* **1 :** in the diet **2 :** in respect to or from the point of view of dietetics ⟨~ adequate meals⟩

di·e·tet·ics \ˌ⸗⸗ˈted·|iks, -et|, |ēks\ *n pl but sing or pl in constr* [Gk *diaitētikē*, fr. fem. of *diaitētikos*] **:** the science or art of applying the principles of nutrition to the feeding of individuals or groups under different economic conditions or for hygienic or therapeutic purposes

di·ethanolamine \(ˌ)dī+\ *n* [*di-* + *ethanolamine*] **:** a colorless deliquescent crystalline or liquid amino alcohol $(HOCH_2CH_2)_2NH$ used similarly to ethanolamine (sense 1); bis-(2-hydroxyethyl)-amine

di·ether \(ˈ)dī+\ *n* [*di-* + *ether*] **:** a chemical compound containing two atoms of oxygen with ether linkages

di·ethyl \(ˈ)dī+\ *adj* [ISV *di-* + *ethyl*] **:** containing two ethyl groups in the molecule

di·ethylamine \(ˈ)dī+\ *n* [ISV *diethyl* + *amine*] **:** a colorless flammable volatile liquid base $(C_2H_5)_2NH$ having a fishy odor and used (chiefly in synthesis (as of accelerators for vulcanization)

di·eth·yl·car·bam·a·zine \ˌdī,ethəl,kärˈbamə,zēn, -,zən\ *n* **:** an anthelmintic derived from piperazine and administered in the form of its crystalline citrate $C_{10}H_{21}N_3O.C_6H_8O_7$

di·ethylene glycol \(ˈ)dī+ . . . -\ *n* [*di-* + *ethylene*] **:** a sweet toxic hygroscopic syrupy compound $O(CH_2CH_2OH)_2$ made from ethylene oxide (as by reaction with ethylene glycol) and used chiefly as solvent, humectant, and plasticizer and in the production of polyester resins — called also *diglycol*

diethyl ether *n* **1 :** ETHER 3a **2 :** an ether containing two ethoxy groups ⟨the *diethyl ether* $C_6H_4(OC_2H_5)_2$ of pyrocatechol⟩

diethyl ketone *n* **:** PENTANONE b

diethyl phthalate *n* **:** a colorless liquid ester $C_6H_4(COOC_2H_5)_2$ used chiefly as a solvent and plasticizer

diethyl·stilbestrol *also* **diethyl·stilboestrol** \(ˌ)⸗ˌ⸗⸗+\ *n* [ISV *diethyl-* + *stilbestrol, stilboestrol*] **:** a colorless crystalline diphenol $[HOC_6H_4C(C_2H_5)=]_2$ derived from stilbene and used as a potent estrogen in medicine and in livestock and poultry feed — called also *stilbestrol*

diethyl sulfate *n* **:** the ethyl sulfate $(C_2H_5)_2SO_4$

di·et·ic \(ˈ)dīˌed·ik\ *adj, archaic* **:** of or relating to diet

di·e·tine \ˌdīəˌtēn, ˌdēə-\ *n* -s [F *diétine*, fr. *diète* diet (fr. ML *dieta*) + *-ine* — more at DIET] **:** a subordinate or local assembly or diet; *specif* **:** a onetime local assembly of Polish nobles that elected deputies to the national diet

dieting *pres part of* DIET

di·e·ti·tian *also* **di·e·ti·cian** \ˌdīəˈtishən\ *n* -s [*dietitian* irreg. fr. ¹*diet* + *-ician*; *dietician* alter. (influenced by *-ician*) of *dietitian*] **:** a person qualified in or practicing dietetics usu. after technical training ⟨a hospital ~⟩

diet kitchen *n* **:** a kitchen in which special diets are prepared (as in a hospital) or where outpatients are instructed concerning diets and their preparation

diet list *n* **:** a list of foods and beverages permitted to a person on a diet usu. giving the absolute or relative quantities of different items that may be taken

diet loaf *n, Scot* **:** SPONGE CAKE

die·tl's crisis \ˈdēd·ᵊlz-\ *n, usu cap D* [after Joseph *Dietl* †1874 Pol. physician] **:** an attack of violent pain in the kidney region accompanied by chills, nausea, vomiting, and collapse that is caused by kinking of the ureter and is usu. associated with floating kidney

di·e·to·therapy \ˌdīəd·ō+\ *n* [¹*diet-* + *-o-* + *therapy*] **:** a branch of dietetics concerned with therapeutic uses of food and diet

die·trich·ite \ˈdē·tri,kīt\ *n* -s *usu cap* [G *dietrichit*, fr. Dr. *Dietrich* 19th cent. Austrian scientist who analyzed it + G *-it* -ite] **:** a mineral $(Zn,Fe,Mn)Al_2(SO_4)_4.22H_2O$ consisting of a hydrous sulfate of aluminum and one or more of the metals zinc, iron, and manganese

diets *pl of* DIET, *pres 3d sing of* DIET

diet·ze·ite \ˈdētsə,īt\ *n* -s [G *dietzeit*, fr. August *Dietze* †*ab*1893 Ger. chemist + G *-it* -ite] **:** a yellow mineral $Ca_2(IO_3)_2(CrO_4)$ commonly in fibrous or columnar form (hardness 3–4, sp. gr. 3.70)

die–up \ˈ⸗,⸗\ *n* -s [fr. *die up*, v.] *West* **:** a widespread destruction of range livestock caused usu. by some untoward natural phenomenon (as drought or blizzard); *sometimes* **:** an animal dead in a die-up ⟨salvaging the hides of *die-ups*⟩

diewise \ˈ⸗,⸗\ *adv* **:** in the shape of a die **:** with perfectly square corners **:** CUBICALLY

diff *abbr* **1** difference **2** different **3** differential

dif·fa \ˈdifə\ *n* -s [Ar *ḍiyāfah* hospitality] **:** an Arabic reception or banquet

dif·far·re·a·tion \(ˌ)di,farēˈāshən\ *n* -s [L *diffarreation-*, *diffarreatio*, fr. *dif-* (fr. *dis-*) + *-farreation-*, *-farreatio* (as in *confarreation-*, *confarreatio* confarreation) — more at CONFARREATION] **:** the Roman ceremony of divorce performed by a pontiff who dissolves a marriage that had been celebrated by confarreation

¹**dif·fer** \ˈdifə(r)\ *vb* **differed; differed; differing** \-f(ə)riŋ\ **differs** [ME *differen*, fr. MF or L; MF *differer* to postpone, be different, fr. L *differre*, fr. *dif-* (fr. *dis-*) + *ferre* to carry — more at BEAR] *vi* **1 a :** to be unlike or distinct in one or more respects or characteristics ⟨the engines ~ greatly in power and endurance⟩ **:** be unlike in nature or form ⟨details of the two statements ~⟩ — often used with *from* ⟨the law of one state ~*s* from that of another⟩ **b :** to display variety or exist in variety **:** change from time to time or from one instance or occasion to another **:** VARY ⟨though ingredients ~, the basic process of manufacture remains the same⟩ **2 :** to be of unlike or opposite opinion **:** disagree in sentiment ⟨persecution of men who ~ on religious matters⟩ — used with *with* ⟨~*s* with the army on the use of air power⟩ or sometimes with *from* ⟨I ~ from him concerning an essential part . . . of religion —W.E.Gladstone⟩ **3** *archaic* **:** DISPUTE, QUARREL **~** *vt* **:** to make different or unlike **:** DIFFERENTIATE ⟨something it is that ~*s* thee and me —Abraham Cowley⟩

syn VARY, DISAGREE, DISSENT: DIFFER stresses the fact of unlikeness in kind or nature or in opinion, but conveys no implication of degree of difference ⟨the houses *differ* only in minor details⟩ ⟨day *differs* from day in respect of the importance of the public events they bring forth —C.E.Montague⟩ ⟨all business men and economists admit that there are grave defects in the present working of our economic system. But they *differ* widely in their diagnosis —J.A.Hobson⟩ VARY, often interchangeable with DIFFER, may call attention to readily apparent differences and may suggest some range among them ⟨tasks may be *varied* slightly, as when a worker in a cigarette factory is shifted from the job of packing and weighing —Aldous Huxley⟩ ⟨the form of political control *varied* widely from country to country, and depended both on the traditions of the different states and on their position with respect to the new balance of power —C.E.Black & E.C. Helmreich⟩ ⟨the strength and direction of sea currents *vary* considerably at different times of the year —W.H.Dowdeswell⟩ DISAGREE stresses lack of agreement and may call up notions of incompatibility, unfitness, or disharmony ⟨one can *disagree* with his views, but one can't refute them —Henry Miller⟩ ⟨the authorities *disagree* about the procedure to be followed in initiating inquiry —F.S.C.Northrop⟩ DISSENT applies to difference of opinion between persons ranging from withholding of assent to strong or formal expression ⟨we may all agree that a world auxiliary language would help. The cynical opinion, which *dissents* and says that the less we understand one another the better, will not be considered here —I.A. Richards⟩ ⟨he *dissented* vigorously from and refused to sign the award —*Americana Annual*⟩

²**differ** \"\ *n* -s [by shortening] *dial* **:** DIFFERENCE

¹**dif·fer·ence** \ˈdifərn(t)s, -f(ə)rən-, *-R sometimes* -fən-\ *n* -s [ME, fr. MF, fr. L *differentia*, fr. *different-, differens* + *-ia*] **1 a :** the quality or state of being different ⟨great ~ between the two ideas⟩ **b :** an instance of differing in nature, form, or quality ⟨~*s* in the manufacturing process result in a wide variety of flavors⟩ **:** a property or characteristic in which things or persons differ ⟨~*s* in color and texture between the two fabrics⟩ **c** *archaic* **:** a characteristic that distinguishes one person or thing from another or from the general ⟨an absolute gentleman full of the most excellent ~*s* —Shak.⟩ **d :** DIFFERENTIA 1 **e :** the element or factor that separates or distinguishes two contrasting situations or events ⟨water is the ~ between profit and loss to these farmers⟩ **2 :** distinction or discrimination in preference or choice ⟨the law should make no ~ between the rich and the poor⟩ **3 :** disagreement in opinion **:** DISSENSION, CONTROVERSY ⟨there has never been any ~ between the two men⟩ **:** an instance of disagreement or a point upon which there is disagreement ⟨nationalists have always used force to settle their ~*s* —H.S.Fowler⟩ **4 a :** the degree or amount by which things differ in quantity or measure ⟨10 cents ~ in price⟩; *specif* **:** the result obtained by subtracting one magnitude, number, or function from another of the same kind **b :** the amount payable to or by a seller on the occasion of the sale of securities or commodities orig. purchased by him as a speculation without intention to take physical possession and representing the change in price **c :** the amount paid or allowed for the delivery of a quality of produce better or poorer than that on which the contract price is based **5 :** an addition to or change in a coat of arms to distinguish the bearings of two persons which would otherwise be the same — compare AUGMENTATION 6, CADENCY MARK **6 :** a significant change in a situation **:** a significant effect on a situation ⟨what's the ~ whether I go or not⟩ ⟨streamlining did not make much ~⟩ **syn** see DISSIMILARITY

²**difference** \"\ *vt* -ED/-ING/-S [ME *differencen*, fr. *difference*, n.] **1 a :** to make different **:** differentiate or distinguish in nature or character ⟨every individual has something that ~*s* it from another —John Locke⟩ **b :** to make a distinction between (as in the mind) **:** DISCRIMINATE, DIFFERENTIATE ⟨~ gods from men —George Chapman⟩ **2 :** to make a heraldic difference in (a coat of arms)

difference limen *or* **difference threshold** *n* **:** JUST-NOTICEABLE DIFFERENCE

difference table *n* **:** an auxiliary table to facilitate interpolation between the numbers of the principal table giving approximate differences in values of the tabulated function corresponding to certain submultiples (as tenths) of the constant smallest increment of the independent variable in the table

difference tone *n* **:** a combination tone whose frequency is equal to the difference between the frequencies of the two tones generating it

dif·fer·en·cy \-nsē\ *n* -ES [L *differentia*] *archaic* : DIFFERENCE

1**dif·fer·ent** \ˈdifərnt, -f(ə)rənt, *-R sometimes* -fənt\ *adj* [MF, fr. L *different-, differens,* pres. part. of *differre* to carry apart, be different, fr. *dif-* (fr. *dis-*) + *ferre* to carry — more at BEAR] **1 :** partly or totally unlike in nature, form, or quality ⟨two men could hardly be more ~⟩ : having at least one property not possessed by another (of a specified pair or larger group) ⟨no thing is ~ from itself⟩ — used with *from* ⟨small, neat hand, very ~ from the captain's tottery characters —R.L.Stevenson⟩ or with *than* ⟨~ than any other piece we've done lately —*Harper's*⟩ ⟨vastly ~ in size than it was twenty-five years ago —N.M. Pusey⟩ or chiefly Brit. with *to* ⟨a very ~ situation to the . . . one under which we live —Sir Winston Churchill⟩ **2 :** not the same : distinct or separate (from another or from others in a group) ⟨studying the behavior of males in ~ age groups⟩ : VARIOUS, SEVERAL ⟨~ members of your group could then tell . . . stories about these heroes —L.J.Davidson⟩ : ANOTHER ⟨not liking the first book, he tried a ~ one⟩ **3 :** being out of the ordinary : UNUSUAL, SPECIAL ⟨advertising that strives continually to be ~⟩

syn DIFFERENT, DIVERSE, DIVERGENT, DISPARATE, and VARIOUS agree when they modify plural nouns and mean unlike in kind or character. DIFFERENT sometimes implies little more than separateness and sometimes implies contrast ⟨many *different* kinds of food⟩ ⟨*different* points of view⟩ DIVERSE implies marked difference and decided contrast ⟨*diverse* tendencies among the arts have given rise to opposed theories —John Dewey⟩ ⟨the important problems which arise when two different groups having *diverse* languages and cultures meet —T.A.Sebeok⟩ ⟨a curious fusion of *diverse* elements —Carl Van Vechten⟩ DIVERGENT, often used in the sense of markedly different, implies a movement away from sameness or similarity, usu. implying impossibility of again coming together as for close association, agreement, or reconciliation ⟨he recognized that labor and capital have *divergent* interests —M.R. Cohen⟩ ⟨a great part of the quarrel between science and religion arises from *divergent* opinions not about the world as it is, but about what it will be —W.R.Inge⟩ ⟨either the concepts of the great Powers coincide and they are in agreement, or their concepts are *divergent* and they therefore cannot agree among themselves as to . . . action —M.S.Fairchild⟩ DISPARATE usu. implies an unequivocal difference, usu. as between in congruous or incompatible things ⟨a nation believing in free speech can't federate with a nation believing in kept speech, and nobody should even consider raising a federal roof over two such *disparate* ideas —*New Yorker*⟩ ⟨the *disparate* elements of the medieval personality were as yet unblended —H.O.Taylor⟩ VARIOUS commonly lays stress on the number of kinds or the variety within one whole ⟨*various* people dropped in for tea⟩ ⟨a personality that is *various* and interesting⟩

2**different** \"\ *adv* : DIFFERENTLY ⟨they do things ~ here⟩

dif·fer·en·tia \ˌdifəˈrench(ē)ə\ *n, pl* **differenti·ae** \-chē,ē\ [L, difference — more at DIFFERENCE] **1 :** the characteristic or quality that distinguishes one species from others of the same genus; *broadly* **:** a distinguishing characteristic ⟨the chief *differentiae* between man and the brute creation —A.T. Quiller-Couch⟩ **2 :** a trope in medieval music

dif·fer·en·tia·bil·i·ty \ˌdifəˌrench(ē)əˈbiləd·ē\ *n* -ES **:** the property or quality of being differentiable ⟨the results of assuming ~ —E.G.Phillips⟩

dif·fer·en·tia·ble \ˌdifəˈrench(ē)əbəl\ *adj* [*differentiate* + *-able*] **1 :** capable of being differentiated **2 :** possessing a differential coefficient or derivative

1**dif·fer·en·tial** \ˌdifəˈrenchəl\ *adj* [prob. fr. F *différentiel*, fr. MF *differentiel*, fr. *different* + *-iel* -ial] **1 a :** of, relating to, or constituting a difference or distinction : DISTINGUISHING **:** making a difference or distinction between individuals or classes ⟨~ legislation such as income tax laws⟩ **b :** based upon or resulting from a differential ⟨~ freight charges⟩ **c :** functioning or proceeding differently or at a different rate (as among members of a group or parts of a whole) ⟨~ melting results in an occasional sunken pool in the surface of the glacier⟩; *specif* **:** resulting from crustal movements whereby one part of the earth's crust is displaced in relation to other parts **2 :** relating to or involving a differential or differentiation **3 :** relating to quantitative differences (as of motion, area, pressure, or leverage) : producing effects by reason of such differences

2**differential** \"\ *n* -S **1 a :** an arbitrary increment of an independent variable **b :** the product of the derivative of a function of one variable by the increment of the independent variable **c :** the sum of the products of each partial derivative of several variables by the arbitrary increment of the corresponding variable **2 a :** a difference between transportation rates over two routes to the same point or over routes to different points competing for the same traffic often allowed to one or more of a number of carriers in order to insure equality in the distribution of traffic among competing lines — compare DIFFERENTIAL ROUTE **b :** an amount added to or deducted from a basic transportation rate, fare, or charge — compare PORT DIFFERENTIAL **3 a :** a difference in wage rate for similar work of comparable quality and granted or imposed as a reflection of varying circumstances (as in location or time of work) or of varying status (as of race or sex) ⟨a shift ~ consisting of additional pay for night work⟩ **b :** a difference in wage reflecting difference in job duties, complexity of tasks, volume or quality of production, level of skill required **4 :** the price difference between the basic grade and a superior or inferior grade of a commodity deliverable on a contract **5 a :** DIFFERENTIAL GEAR **b :** PLANET DIFFERENTIAL **6 :** the amount or degree by which comparable individuals or classes of individuals differ in some particular respect ⟨wide ~s in living standards between the two countries⟩ : a difference between comparable things ⟨price ~ between regular and high-test gasoline⟩ **7 :** DIFFERENTIAL BLOOD COUNT

differential analyzer *n* **:** a computer and esp. an analog computer for the mechanical solution of complicated nonlinear differential equations

differential association *n* **:** abnormal distribution of personal associations; *specif* **:** a theory in sociology: continuous contact with criminals is chiefly responsible for the development of criminal behavior in an individual

differential blood count *or* **differential count** *n* **:** an enumeration of the number of each kind of white blood cell in 100 cells counted — called also *differential white count*

differential brake *n* **:** a band brake acting on the difference of two motions or tensions and tending to be self-tightening when the rotating part turns in the normal direction

differential calculus *n* **:** a branch of mathematics dealing fundamentally with the rate of change of functions with respect to the variables on which they depend

differential chain block *or* **differential block** *n* **:** a chain-operated differential pulley

differential diagnosis *n* **:** the distinguishing of a disease or condition from others presenting similar symptoms

differential duties *n pl* **:** duties imposed unequally on the same products according to the sources of or methods of getting these products

differential equation *n* **:** an equation containing differentials or derivatives of functions

differential fertility *n* **:** variation in fertility of different groups or classes in the population ⟨relation of economic status to *differential fertility*⟩

differential gear *or* **differential gearing** *n* **1 :** an arrangement of gears forming an epicyclic train for connecting two shafts or axles in the same line, dividing the driving force equally between them, and permitting one shaft to revolve faster than the other when required (as by the driving wheels of an automobile that is moving in a curve), the speed of the main driving member being always equal to the algebraic mean of the speeds of the two shafts **2 :** PLANET DIFFERENTIAL

differential geometry *n* **:** geometry that involves the calculus in its development

differential grasshopper *also* **differential locust** *n* **:** a destructive grasshopper (*Melanoplus differentialis*) common in the western U.S.

differential indexing *n* **:** a method used on a dividing engine for dividing a circle into subdivisions otherwise unobtainable by utilizing the difference between simultaneous movements of index plate and index crank

dif·fer·en·tial·ly \ˌdifəˈrenchəlē, -li\ *adv* **:** in a differential manner **:** so as to constitute or create a differential **:** so as to make distinction between different individuals or types

differential motion *n* **:** a mechanism (as a differential screw or a differential chain block) having two driving elements so arranged that the net motion of the follower is the difference between the two motions that it would have if either driver acted alone

differential operator *n, math* **:** a prescribed combination or sequence of operations involving differentiation

differential piece-rate system *n* **:** a method of wage payment whereby after tests have set a standard time for a task the worker receives a high piece rate for doing the job in task time and a lower piece rate if he takes longer than task time

differential psychology *n* **:** the study of differences between human beings either as individuals or in groups esp. through the use of tests

differential pulley *n* **:** a tackle consisting of a fixed upper double block with pulleys of different diameters fixed together on the same axis, a movable single lower pulley that carries the load, and an endless cable or chain that passes around all the pulleys and hangs in a loop for operating the mechanism which is used to achieve a very high mechanical advantage

differential rate *n* **:** a transportation rate obtained by deducting a differential from or adding it to a standard rate

differential refraction *n, astron* **:** the change of the apparent place of one object relative to a second object near it due to atmospheric refraction; *also* **:** the correction necessary to fix the two places accurately

differential route *n* **:** a carrier (as a railroad or steamship line) allowed to give a lower rate than some of its competitors in order to equalize a competitive disadvantage

differential screw *n* **:** a screw having two parts of slightly different pitch cut on the same barrel each working in a nut so that when the screw is turned the nuts have a very slow relative motion

differential thermometer *n* **:** a thermometer for indicating difference in temperature

differential threshold *n* **:** JUST-NOTICEABLE DIFFERENCE

differential white count *n* **:** DIFFERENTIAL BLOOD COUNT

differential windlass *n* **:** a windlass that has a barrel with two parts of different diameters, a hoisting rope that winds upon one part as it unwinds from the other, and a pulley that sustains the weight to be lifted hanging in the bight of the hoisting rope — called also *Chinese windlass*

differential windlass: *A* barrel; *B* pulley

1**dif·fer·en·ti·ate** \ˌdifəˈrenchēˌāt *sometimes* -n(t)sē-; *usu* -ād.+V\ *vb* -ED/-ING/-S [prob. fr. (assumed) NL *differentiatus*, past part. of (assumed) NL *differentiare*, fr. L *differentia* difference — more at DIFFERENCE] *vt* **1 :** to form the derivative of **2 :** to make different : mark or show a difference in ⟨possible to ~ lava flows of similar color but of different ages and to ~ certain lake sediments from lava flows —R.G.Ray & W.A.Fischer⟩ **3 :** to effect a difference in as regards classification : develop differential characteristics in ⟨what *differentiated* a laborer from another man? —Sherwood Anderson⟩ **4 :** to cause differentiation of in the course of development ⟨in the olive the flower parts are *differentiated* . . . in the spring —H.T.Hartmann⟩ **5 :** to express the specific difference of : DISCRIMINATE ⟨~ prose and poetry⟩ **6 :** to cause differentiation of staining in (a specimen for microscopic examination) ~ *vi* **1 :** to recognize a difference ⟨unable to ~ even between the narrowest ellipse and the circle —R.S.Woodworth⟩ **2 :** to become distinct or different in character : develop differences **3 :** to undergo differentiation **syn** see DISTINGUISH

2**dif·fer·en·ti·ate** \-ēət\ *n* -S **:** a differentiation rock

dif·fer·en·ti·a·tion \ˌ==ˌ==ˈāshən\ *n* -S [prob. fr. (assumed) NL *differentiation-, differentiatio*, fr. (assumed) NL *differentiatus* + L *-ion-, -io* -ion] **1 :** the act or process or result of differentiating: as **a :** the process or result of forming the derivative of a function **b :** the act of distinguishing or describing a thing by giving its differentia or specific difference **c :** the enhancement of microscopically visible differences between tissue or cell parts by partial selective decolorization or removal of excess stain (as in regressive staining) **d :** the development of a discriminating conditioned response with a positive response to one stimulus and absence of the response on the application of similar but discriminably different stimuli **2 :** development from the one to the many, the simple to the complex, or from the homogeneous to the heterogeneous ⟨~ of Latin into vernaculars⟩ **3 a :** modification of different parts of the body for performance of particular functions; *also* **:** specialization of parts or organs in the course of evolution **b :** RACIATION **c :** the sum of the processes whereby apparently indifferent cells, tissues, and structures attain their adult form and function — compare DETERMINATION **4 :** the total of processes by which various rock types are produced from a common magma; *also* **:** a result of such processes **5 :** the process whereby a social organization or culture or any of its parts becomes more complex through the growth of distinct societal functions, the development of privileged roles appropriate to individual capacity, the separation of social groups into class strata, and the establishment of political and religious structures; *also* **:** the result of such process

dif·fer·en·ti·a·tor \ˌ==ˈ==ˌād·ə(r), -ātə-\ *n* -S **:** one that differentiates

dif·fer·ent·ly *pronunc at* DIFFERENT +lē *or* li\ *adv* [ME, fr. *different* + *-ly*] **1 :** in a different way or manner — often used with *from* or chiefly Brit. with *to* followed by a substantive ⟨~ from us⟩ ⟨~ to us⟩ or with *than* followed by a substantive or a clause ⟨~ than we do⟩ **2 :** OTHERWISE ⟨very soon you will know ~⟩

dif·fer·ent·ness *n* -ES **:** the quality or state of being different

differing *pres part of* DIFFER

dif·fer·ing·ly *adv* **:** in a differing manner

differs *pres 3d sing of* DIFFER, *pl of* DIFFER

dif·fi·cile \ˌdēfēˈsē(ə)l, ˈdif-, *archaic* dəˈfisəl\ *adj* [MF, fr. L *difficilis* difficult, fr. *dif-* (fr. *dis-*) + *-ficilis* (fr. *facilis* easy) — more at FACILE] **1 a** *obs* **:** hard to do or manage : DIFFICULT **b :** hard to understand **2 :** hard to deal with : PERVERSE, STUBBORN, UNREASONABLE

1**dif·fi·cult** \ˈdifə|(ˌ)kəlt *sometimes* -fē| *or* -fi|\ *adj* [back-formation fr. *difficulty*] **1 :** hard to do, make, or carry out : attended with or requiring effort, trouble, or painstaking ; not easy : ARDUOUS ⟨a ~ climb⟩ ⟨a ~ task⟩ ⟨such a situation is ~ to imagine⟩ ⟨nesting places very ~ of access⟩ **2 :** hard to deal with, manage or overcome : involving difficulties ⟨~ days lie ahead⟩: **a :** hard to understand : PUZZLING, OBSCURE ⟨~ reading⟩ ⟨a ~ text⟩ **b :** hard to approach : PERVERSE, STUBBORN ⟨a ~ child⟩ ⟨a ~ disposition⟩ ⟨~ music⟩ **c :** hard to obtain or produce ⟨getting a ~ living on worn-out lands⟩ **d :** HAMPERING, AWKWARD ⟨a fine performance under ~ circumstances⟩ **e :** causing pain or embarrassment ⟨the family had a ~ time after the father's death⟩ **syn** see HARD

2**difficult** \"\ *vt* -ED/-ING/-S **1** *obs* **:** to render difficult : IMPEDE **2** *chiefly Scot* **:** to place in difficulties : PERPLEX

dif·fi·cult·ly *adv* **:** with difficulty — usu. used before adjectives in *-able* and *-ible* ⟨a ~ soluble salt⟩

dif·fi·cult·ness *n* -ES **:** the quality or state of being difficult

dif·fi·cul·ty \-ˌkəltē, -ti *also* -ˌkə-\ *n* -ES [ME *difficulte*, fr. L *difficultas*, irreg. (influence of L *facultas* skill, ability) fr. *difficilis* difficult — more at DIFFICILE, FACULTY] **1 a :** the quality or state of being difficult or hard to do or to overcome : ARDUOUSNESS ⟨the ~ of a task⟩ **b :** unusual or laborious effort ⟨the ~ of climbing those steep stairs⟩ **2 :** a thing hard to do or to overcome : something that causes labor or perplexity and requires skill and perseverance in mastering, solving, or achieving : a hard enterprise : OBSTACLE, IMPEDIMENT ⟨the *difficulties* of a science⟩ **3 :** a show of reluctance : OBJECTION, CAVIL, DEMUR ⟨he made no ~ in granting the request⟩ **4 :** embarrassment of affairs ⟨in days of ~ and pressure —Alfred Tennyson⟩: as **a** *usu pl* **:** embarrassment in financial affairs ⟨spent wildly and suddenly found himself in *difficulties*⟩ **b :** a falling out : DISAGREEMENT, CONTROVERSY ⟨labor *difficulties* grew out of bad working conditions⟩

syn DIFFICULTY, HARDSHIP, RIGOR, and VICISSITUDE can mean in common something obstructing one's goal and demanding effort or endurance to overcome. DIFFICULTY, the most widely applicable of the terms, applies to any condition, situation, experience, or task which presents a problem hard to solve ⟨we ventured, however, over all these *difficulties*, and I took her to wife September 1st, 1730 —Benjamin Franklin⟩ ⟨*difficulties* occur and have to be surmounted —T.D.Weldon⟩ ⟨Galileo's *difficulties* with the church had nothing to do with his experiments —M.R.Cohen⟩ ⟨there are always *difficulties* between a man's dream and its achievement⟩ HARDSHIP stresses suffering, toil, or privation that is unusual or hard to bear, esp. in the pursuit of a goal ⟨the first decade in the history of Minnesota's newspapers brought them great *hardships* —*Amer. Guide Series: Minn.*⟩ ⟨they face the *hardships* of their comfortless lives with stolid indifference —P.E.James⟩ ⟨she insisted on sharing the *hardships* on equal terms with soldiers —*Current Biog.*⟩ RIGOR usu. applies to a hardship imposed upon one, as by ambition, a religion, a tyrannical government, or a trying climate ⟨anything which might soften the *rigor* of his prison —J.H.Wheelwright⟩ ⟨the *rigor* of parental authority —Abram Kardiner⟩ ⟨the *rigors* of the weather —Alexis Carrel⟩ ⟨a European custom which nowhere survived the *rigors* of the frontier —W.P.Webb⟩ VICISSITUDE, in this connection, applies to a difficulty or hardship incident to life or a career or course of action ⟨the dwarfing *vicissitudes* of poverty —Francis Hackett⟩ ⟨the *vicissitudes* of living, such as faulty diets, infections, intoxications, traumata, emotional stresses, overwork, laziness —A.J.Carlson & E.J.Stieglitz⟩ ⟨the *vicissitudes* of political persecution and exile —*Times Lit. Supp.*⟩

dif·fi·da·tion \ˌdifəˈdāshən\ *n* -S [ML *diffidation-, diffidatio*, fr. *diffidatus* (past part. of *diffidare* to renounce one's vassalage, renounce friendship, fr. L *dif-* — fr. *dis-* — + *fides* faith) + L *-ion-, -io* -ion — more at FAITH] *archaic* **:** a renunciation of faith or allegiance : formal severing of peaceful relations

diffide *vb* -ED/-ING/-S [L *diffidere* — more at DIFFIDENT] *vi, obs* **:** to lack faith : DISTRUST ~ *vt, obs* **:** to have no faith in : DOUBT, DISTRUST

dif·fi·dence \ˈdifədən(t)s *also* -dᵊn- *or* -ˌden-\ *n* -S [L *diffidentia*, fr. *diffident-, diffidens* + *-ia*] **:** the quality or state of being diffident: **a** *archaic* **:** DISTRUST **:** want of confidence : doubt of the power or disposition of others ⟨that affliction . . . weighed me down even to a ~ of God's mercy —John Donne⟩ **b :** distrust of oneself or one's own powers : lack of self-reliance : MODESTY : modest reserve : BASHFULNESS ⟨it is good to speak on such questions with ~ —T.B.Macaulay⟩

diffidency *n* -ES [L *diffidentia*] *obs* **:** DIFFIDENCE

dif·fi·dent \ˈdifədənt *also* -dᵊnt *or* -ˌdent\ *adj* [L *diffident-, diffidens*, pres. part. of *diffidere* to mistrust, fr. *dif-* (fr. *dis-*) + *fidere* to trust — more at BIDE] **1** *archaic* **:** lacking trust : DOUBTFUL, DISTRUSTFUL **2 :** lacking confidence in oneself : distrustful of one's own powers : TIMID **3 :** characterized by modest reserve ⟨one should feel ~ . . . when offering to comment on any Hindu myth —Heinrich Zimmer⟩ **syn** see SHY

dif·fi·dent·ly *adv* **:** in a diffident manner

dif·fi·dent·ness *n* -ES **:** the quality or state of being diffident

dif·flu·ence *also* **dif·lu·ence** \ˈdiˌflüən(t)s, -ˌfləwən-\ *n* -S **1 :** a flowing off or away ⟨~ of glaciers into new channels⟩ **2 :** DISSOLUTION

dif·flu·ent \-nt\ *adj* [L *diffluent-, diffluens*, pres. part. of *diffluere* to flow away or apart, dissolve, fr. *dif-* (fr. *dis-*) + *fluere* to flow — more at FLUENT] **1 :** flowing away or off ⟨~ rivers⟩ — opposed to *confluent* **2 :** readily dissolving : DELIQUESCENT

dif·flu·gia \dəˈflüjēə\ *n* [NL, irreg. fr. L *diffluere* + NL *-ia*] **1** *cap* **:** a genus of protozoans related to *Amoeba* but having an ovoid shell of cemented sand grains **2** -S **:** any protozoan of the genus *Difflugia*

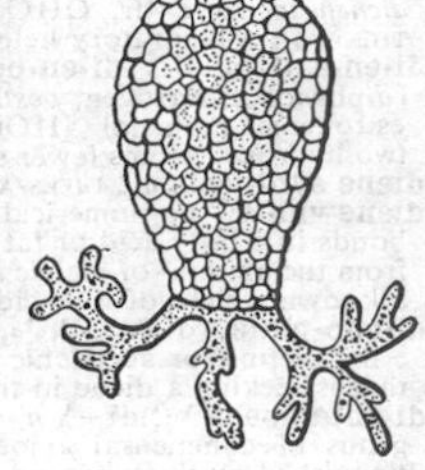

difflugia 2

difform *adj* [ML *difformis*, fr. L *dif-* (fr. *dis-*) + *-formis* -form] **1** *obs* **:** UNLIKE, DISSIMILAR **2 :** irregular in form : ANOMALOUS

dif·for·mi·ty \(ˈ)diˈfȯrməd·ē\ *n* -ES [MF or ML; MF *difformité*, fr. ML *difformitat-, difformitas*, fr. *difformis* + L *-itat-, -itas* -ity] **:** irregularity or diversity of form : lack of conformity

dif·fract \dəˈfrakt\ *vb* -ED/-ING/-S [back-formation fr. *diffraction*] *vt* **:** to break or separate into parts; *specif* **:** to cause to undergo diffraction ~ *vi* **:** to undergo diffraction

dif·frac·tion \-kshən\ *n* -S [NL *diffraction-, diffractio*, fr. L *diffractus* (past part. of *diffringere* to break to pieces, fr. *dif-* — fr. *dis-* apart — + *-fringere*, fr. *frangere* to break) + *-ion-, -io* -ion — more at DIS-, BREAK] **:** a modification which light undergoes in passing by the edges of opaque bodies or through narrow slits or in being reflected from ruled surfaces and in which the rays appear to be deflected and produce fringes of parallel light and dark or colored bands; *also* **:** a similar modification of other waves (as sound waves and electromagnetic waves) that occurs whenever the full wave front is not brought to a focus or utilized and that results in the curvature of waves around objects in their path — see ELECTRON DIFFRACTION

diffraction disk *n* **:** SPURIOUS DISK

diffraction grating *n* **:** GRATING 3

diffraction pattern *n* **:** an often photographic pattern produced by diffraction (as of light, X rays, or electrons) — compare LAUE PATTERN

dif·frac·tom·e·ter \ˌdiˌfrakˈtäməd·ə(r)\ *n* [*diffraction* + *-o-* + *-meter*] **:** an instrument for measuring the diameters of small particles in a microscope field by means of the diffraction rings which appear to surround them — **dif·frac·to·met·ric** \diˌfraktəˈme·trik\ *adj* — **dif·frac·to·met·ri·cal·ly** \-trək(ə)lē\ *adv*

dif·fu·sate \dəˈfyüˌzāt\ *n* -S [ISV *diffuse* + *-ate*] **:** a product of diffusion: as **a :** the material that passes through the membrane in dialysis; *also* **:** the liquid into which such material diffuses — sometimes called also *dialyzate* **b :** the material that passes through a suitable barrier in gaseous diffusion (as for the separation of isotopes of volatile uranium compounds)

1**dif·fuse** \dəˈfyüs\ *adj* [ME, fr. MF or L; MF *difus* scattered, spread out, fr. L *diffusus*, past part. of *diffundere* to spread out, pour out, scatter, fr. *dif-* (fr. *dis-*) + *fundere* to pour — more at FOUND] **1** *obs* **a :** CONFUSED **b :** hard to understand : DIFFICULT **2 :** poured or spread out : WIDESPREAD : not concentrated or restrained : COPIOUS, FULL **3 :** VERBOSE, PROLIX ⟨a ~ writer⟩ **4 :** spreading widely or loosely ⟨~ branches⟩ **5 :** not localized : SCATTERED ⟨~ sclerosis⟩ **6 :** moving in many directions ⟨~ radiation⟩ **7 :** having the whole chorionic surface studded with villi ⟨whales and horses have ~ placentas⟩ **syn** see WORDY

2**dif·fuse** \dəˈfyüz *sometimes* dī-\ *vb* -ED/-ING/-S [MF or L; MF *diffuser*, fr. L *diffusus*, past part.] *vt* **1 a :** to pour out and permit or cause to spread freely (as a fluid out of a container) ⟨a drop of dye *diffused* through water⟩ ⟨gas being *diffused* through the air⟩ : spread out : permit to spread over a wide area or through a large space ⟨the all-pervasive spirit of sweetness and light *diffused* through the universe —V.L. Parrington⟩ **b :** to make widely perceptible, known, or familiar : send out : EXTEND, SCATTER, BROADCAST ⟨in place of the present chaos universities must again ~ a definite culture —Walter Moberly⟩ **c :** to spread out into many areas, spheres, agencies, and activities often with consequent reduced concentration or effectiveness ⟨a state in which power is concentrated will . . . be more bellicose than one in which power is *diffused* —Bertrand Russell⟩ ⟨it is like dynamite exploded in the open. Its force is *diffused* by going in all directions —*Saturday Rev.*⟩ **2 :** to subject (as a light beam) to diffusion : treat by diffusion **3 :** to break up and distribute (incident light) by reflection (as from a rough surface) ~ *vi* **1 :** to spread out : pass or become transmitted often with slow tingeing or permeation ⟨culture traits are able to

~ apart from the migration of peoples —Brewton Berry〉 **2 :** to undergo diffusion 〈a gas in solution ~*s* from a region of greater to one of less concentration〉 **syn** see SPREAD

dif·fused \-zd\ *adj* **:** spread out or abroad **:** DISPERSED, DIFFUSE 〈a widely ~ opinion〉 — **dif·fus·ed·ly** \-zədlē, -li\ *adv* — **dif·fus·ed·ness** \-zədnəs\ *n* -ES

dif·fuse·ly \də'fyüslē, -li\ *adv* [ME, fr. *diffuse* + *-ly*] **:** in a diffuse manner

diffuse nebula *n* **:** any of the numerous luminous or dark formations or irregularly distributed dust and gas seen within the Milky Way galaxy and in other spiral galaxies but not including the planetary nebulae

dif·fuse·ness \-üsnəs\ *n* -ES **:** the quality or state of being diffuse

diffuse placenta *also* **diffused placenta** *n* **:** a placenta made up of villi diffusely scattered over almost the whole surface of the chorion (as in whales, swine, and horses)

diffuse–porous \¦=¦=¦==\ *adj* **:** having vessels distributed more or less uniformly thoughout an annual ring and not varying greatly in size — used of certain woody stems and roots (as those of maples and birches); compare RING-POROUS

dif·fus·er \də'fyüzə(r) *sometimes* dī'-\ *n* -S **:** one that diffuses: as **a :** a chamber surrounding a turbine wheel commonly provided with stationary vanes into which the fluid is discharged **b :** a device (as a reflector placed above an electric lamp or a vaned shield placed below) to distribute the light from a concentrated source uniformly **c :** a device through which air or other gas is admitted in minute bubbles into sewage or water undergoing treatment **d :** a device for diffusing spray or vapor (as in a carburetor) **e :** a device for reducing the velocity and increasing the static pressure of a fluid passing through a system, usu. made in the form of a chamber having an effective cross section which increases in the direction of flow **f :** a screen (as of cloth or frosted glass) used to soften lighting (as in a motion-picture or television studio) **g :** a device (as a louver with slats at different angles) for deflecting air in various directions from an outlet to effect mixture with room air (as for heating or cooling a room)

dif·fus·ibil·i·ty \də,fyüzə'biləd·ē *sometimes* (,)dī,-\ *n* -ES **:** the capability of being diffused

dif·fus·ible \də'fyüzəbəl *sometimes* dī'-\ *adj* **:** capable of diffusing or of being diffused — **dif·fus·ibly** \-blē, -li\ *adv*

dif·fu·sion \də'fyüzhən *sometimes* dī'-\ *n* -S [LL *diffusion-, diffusio*, fr. L *diffusus* + *-ion-, -io* -ion] **1 :** the action of diffusing or the state of being diffused **:** SPREADING, DISPERSION 〈the ~ of knowledge〉 **2 :** DIFFUSENESS, PROLIXITY **3 a :** the process whereby particles (as molecules and ions) of liquids, gases, or solids intermingle as the result of their spontaneous movement caused by thermal agitation and in dissolved substances move from a region of higher concentration to one of lower concentration — see GASEOUS DIFFUSION **b :** reflection of light by a rough reflecting surface **:** transmission of light through a translucent material **:** SCATTERING **4 :** the spread of linguistic or cultural elements from one area, tribe, or people to others through contact 〈the ~ of tobacco from the New World to the Old World〉 **5 a :** the process of slightly scattering a portion of the image-forming light to give a pleasing artistic softness to a photograph **b :** IRRADIATION 1c(3) **6 :** a radio broadcast — **dif·fu·sion·al** \-zhənᵊl, -zhnəl\ *adj*

diffusion coefficient *or* **diffusion constant** *n* **:** the quantity of a substance that in diffusing from one region to another passes through each unit of cross section per unit of time when the volume-concentration gradient is unity — called also *diffusivity*

diffusion disk *also* **diffusing disk** *n* **:** a piece of transparent material having special markings or embossings used with a photographic lens to give a soft focus or diffused effect to the image

dif·fu·sion·ism \-zhə,nizəm\ *n* **:** a theory in anthropology: widely separated cultural similarities are evidence of historical contact

dif·fu·sion·ist \-zhənəst\ *n* **:** one who emphasizes the role of diffusion in the history of culture: **a :** an advocate of diffusionism — contrasted with *evolutionist* **b :** a student of diffusion within a circumscribed geographical area esp. in America

diffusion pressure deficit *n* **:** the algebraic sum of all the forces tending to cause water to move into a plant cell

diffusion pump *n* **:** a vacuum pump for producing extremely high vacuums by diffusing gas into a jet of vapor of mercury or some heavy oil by which the gas is carried off and which is separated from the gas by condensation

diffusion–transfer process *n* **:** any of several document-copying photographic processes in which a facsimile of the original document is produced by development of a photographic image, by transfer by diffusion of the silver salts in the undeveloped areas to a receiving paper, and by development of the transferred image

dif·fu·sive \-üs|iv, -üz|, |ēv *also* |əv\ *adj* **1 :** having the quality of diffusing **:** tending to diffuse **:** characterized by diffusion **2** *obs, of a people or group* **:** acting as a mass of individuals having authority diffused throughout the entire membership — **dif·fu·sive·ly** \|əvlē, -li\ *adv* — **dif·fu·sive·ness** \|ivnəs, |ēv-\ *n* -ES

dif·fu·siv·i·ty \də,fyü'sivəd·ē, -'zi- *sometimes* (,)dē,-\ *n* -ES **1 :** DIFFUSION COEFFICIENT **2 :** the quantity of heat passing normally through a unit area per unit time divided by the product of specific heat, density, and temperature gradient

dif·fu·sor \də'fyüzə(r) *sometimes* dī'-\ *n* -S **:** DIFFUSER

diffluence *var of* DIFFLUENCE

difluor- *or* **difluoro-** *comb form* [ISV *di-* + *fluor-*] **:** containing two atoms of fluorine — in names of chemical compounds 〈1,1-*difluoro*ethane〉; compare FLUOR-

di·fluoride \(')dī+\ *n* [*di-* + *fluoride*] **:** a compound containing two atoms of fluorine combined with an element or radical

[1]**dig** \'dig\ *vb* **dug** \'dəg\ *or archaic* **digged** \'digd\ **dug** *or archaic* **digged; digging; digs** [ME *diggen*, perh. of imit. origin] *vi* **1 :** to turn up, loosen, or remove earth **:** DELVE 〈~ for buried treasure〉 〈*digging* in the garden〉 **2 :** to work hard or laboriously **:** DRUDGE 〈*digging* away at his geometry lessons〉 **3 a :** to penetrate below the surface in search of something hidden or buried **:** pierce deeply — used with *into* 〈~ into the facts of a case〉 〈*digging* into the history of mankind〉 **b :** to advance or progress by or as if by removing or pushing aside material **:** BURROW 〈if we ~ down through the strata of English historical writing —B.R.Redman〉 **4** *slang* **:** LODGE, DWELL 〈this is the inn where I ~ —John Galsworthy〉 **5** *of a tool* **:** to cut deeply into material being worked on because of some fault (as being ill-set or held at a wrong angle) **6 :** to run hard 〈the runner on first base ~*s* for second with the first pitch〉 ~ *vt* **1 :** to break up (earth) with a hard implement (as a spade, hoe, mattock) **:** pierce, loosen, or turn over (the soil) 〈~ a field for planting〉 **2 a :** to bring to the surface or get by digging **:** UNEARTH 〈~ potatoes〉 **b :** to bring to light or out of hiding — often used with *out* or *up* 〈~ up facts〉 **3 :** to hollow out (as a well) **:** form (as a ditch) by removing earth **:** EXCAVATE 〈~ a trench〉 〈~ a foundation〉 **4 :** to drive down so as to penetrate **:** THRUST 〈*dug* his fingers into the soft earth〉 **5 :** POKE, PROD 〈he *dug* me in the ribs with his sharp little elbow〉 **6** *slang* **a :** to listen to or look at **:** pay attention to 〈~ that fancy hat〉 **b :** UNDERSTAND, APPRECIATE 〈what I don't ~ over there is the British money —Jimmy Durante〉 **c :** LIKE, ADMIRE 〈a very corny gag, but people seem to ~ it —*Down Beat*〉 — **dig into** *vt* **:** to take a substantial part from (a supply) **:** eat into **:** DEPLETE 〈forced to *dig into* savings to pay current debts〉

syn DIG, DELVE, SPADE, GRUB, EXCAVATE, EXHUME, and DISINTER mean, in common, to use a spade or similar implement in breaking up the ground to a point below the surface and turning or removing the earth or bringing to the surface anything below it. DIG, the commonest of the terms, implies a loosening of earth around or under something so as to bring it to the surface or any disturbing of earth to penetrate it in some way 〈*dig* worms〉 〈*dig* for gold〉 〈*dig* a bone up〉 〈*dig* into a cliff〉 DELVE implies more commonly the use of a spade or efforts comparable to the use of one and suggests strongly a laborious digging around in or in among something 〈lab scientists *delve* into the secrets of nature —*Investor's Reader*〉 〈to *delve* into the mysteries of prehistoric man —E.J. Sawyer〉 〈*delve* beneath these superficialities —William Petersen〉 〈*delve* among the old records in the city archives —F.L. Pattee〉 SPADE may apply to the manual preparation of soil for planting, to turning over and loosening the ground 〈*spade* the garden early〉 〈*spade* in the fertilizer〉 GRUB usu. does not imply deep digging but rather suggests laborious dirty digging around in surface soil or dirt, or any dirty, groveling work resembling it 〈scorning to *grub* the soil, they live off the produce of their herds —Jean & Franc Shor〉 〈a group of ragpickers haphazardly *grubbing* about among a pile of human refuse —*Times Lit. Supp.*〉 〈*grubbing* around Etruscan cemeteries —Robert Graves〉 〈he *grubs* for the answers in the memory heap of five decades —*Time*〉 EXCAVATE implies making a hollow in, into, or through something, usu. by spade, shovel or machine 〈the powerful stream . . . *excavated* a new channel —*Amer. Guide Series: Wash.*〉 〈an expedition of the Witte Memorial Museum of San Antonio *excavated* caves, the contents of which revealed the culture of a sedentary people —*Amer. Guide Series: Texas*〉 〈*excavate* a cliff〉 EXHUME implies the removal of something buried 〈the ungrateful task of *exhuming* antiquities —*Americas*〉 〈trees buried by the gray unweathered outwash gravels and *exhumed* through erosion of the valley train by the Rio Ameghino —R.L.Nichols & M.M.Miller〉 DISINTER implies the exhuming of something buried by human hands 〈the urns *disinterred* at Walsingham —A.T.Quiller-Couch〉 〈bodies were *disinterred* from battlefields —*Amer. Guide Series: N.C.*〉

[2]**dig** \"\ *n* -S **1 a :** THRUST, POKE 〈gave the horse a good ~ in the side〉 **b :** a verbal thrust **:** a cutting remark esp. containing a veiled allusion 〈why all the small ungracious ~*s* and hedging of good report with evil suspicion —Philip Burnham〉 **2 :** a plodding and laborious student **:** GRIND **3** *dial Eng* **:** a tool for digging **4** [by shortening] **:** DIGGER 4 **5 digs** *pl, Brit* **:** DIGGINGS 3b **6 :** a site at which an archaeological excavation is made; *also* **:** the excavation itself and the conduct of the project as a whole 〈on their return from some fruitful ~ in the Nile valley —David Garnett〉 **7 :** a push of the ball of the foot against the floor in dancing

[3]**dig** \"\ *n* -S [ME *digge*] *now dial Eng* **:** DUCK

dig *abbr* digest

di·gallic acid \(')dī+ . . .-\ *n* [ISV *di-* + *gallic*] **1 :** a crystalline phenolic ester acid $C_{14}H_{10}O_9$ obtained as a decomposition product of tannins or made synthetically and yielding two molecules of gallic acid on hydrolysis — called also *meta-digallic acid* **2 :** GALLOTANNIN — used chiefly in pharmacy

di·gam·ba·ra \di'gəmbərə\ *n* -S *cap* [Skt, lit., sky-clad, naked] **:** a member of a major Jain sect formed in the 3d century B.C. and distinguished by its original abandonment of all worldly possessions including clothes and by its denial that women can attain salvation

di·gametic \¦dī+\ *adj* [*di-* + *gametic*] **:** forming two kinds of germ cells (as one with and one without the X chromosome) **:** heterozygous for sex

di·gam·ma \dī'gamə, 'dī,g-\ *n* [L, fr. Gk, fr. *di-* + *gamma*; fr. its resemblance to two capital gammas placed on top of each other] **1 :** a letter of the original Greek alphabet representing a sound approximately that of English *w* which early fell into disuse except in writing the western dialects and in numerical notation where it represented the number 6 — called also *vau*; symbol F, ϝ **2 :** the sound represented by the letter ϝ

di·gam·mat·ed \dī'ga,mād·əd\ *adj* **1 :** having the Greek letter digamma **2 :** inferred to have had a *w*-sound of which actual orthographic evidence does not survive — used of a Greek word or root or of the vowel following the inferred sound 〈the number of ~ roots in Homer —R.C.Jebb〉 **3 :** printed with digamma inserted where its sound is believed orig. to have been employed 〈a ~ edition of Homer〉

dig·a·my \'digəmē\ *n* -ES [LL *digamia*, fr. LGk, fr. *digamos* married twice (fr. Gk, adulterous, fr. *di-* + *-gamos* -gamous) + Gk *-ia* -y] **:** a legal second marriage after the termination of a first marriage (as by death or divorce of the spouse) — called also *deuterogamy*; distinguished from *bigamy*

[1]**di·gastric** \(')dī+\ *n* -S [NL *digastricus*, fr. *di-* + *gastricus* gastric — more at GASTRIC] **:** either of a pair of digastric muscles that extend from the anterior inferior margin of the mandible to the temporal bone and serve to open the jaw

[2]**digastric** \"\ *adj* [NL *digastricus*, fr. *digastricus*, adj.] **1** *of a muscle* **:** having two bellies separated by a median tendon **2 :** of or relating to a digastric

dig–dig *var of* DIK-DIK

dig down *vi* **:** to pay money out of one's own pocket 〈the customers will not *dig down* for such entertainment〉

di·ge·nea \dī'jēnēə\ *n pl, cap* [NL, fr. *di-* + Gk *genea* race, descent — more at KIN] **:** a subclass of Trematoda commonly divided into the orders Gasterostomata and Prosostomata, comprising forms with a complex life cycle involving alternation of sexual reproduction as an internal parasite of a vertebrate with asexual reproduction in a mollusk, and often including developmental stages in still other hosts — compare ASPIDOGASTREA 1, MONOGENEA — **di·ge·ne·ous** \(')dī¦jēnēəs\ *adj*

di·genesis \(')dī+\ *n* [NL, fr. *di-* + *genesis*] **:** successive reproduction by sexual and asexual methods

di·genetic \¦dī+\ *adj* [in sense 1, fr. *di-* + *genetic*; in sense 2, fr. NL *Digenetica*] **1 :** of or relating to digenesis **2 :** of or relating to the Digenea

di·ge·net·i·ca \,dījə'ned·əkə\ *syn of* DIGENEA

di·genic \(')dī+\ *adj* [*di-* + *-genic*] *biol* **:** induced by two genes — used of phenotypic effects manifested only when two nonallelic controlling genes interact

dig·e·nite \'dijə,nīt\ *n* -S [G *digenit*, fr. *di-* + L *genus* kind + G *-it* -ite — more at KIN] **:** a mineral $Cu_{2-x}S$ consisting of an isometric copper sulfide having a variable deficiency in copper

[1]**di·gest** \'dī,jest *sometimes* -,jəst\ *n* -S [ME *Digest* compilation of Roman laws ordered by Justinian, fr. LL *Digesta*, pl., fr. L, collection of writings arranged under various headings, fr. neut. pl. of *digestus*, past part. of *digerere* to divide, distribute, arrange, digest, fr. *di-* (fr. *dis-* apart) + *gerere* to bear, carry — more at DIS-, CAST] **1 :** a short summation of or the compressed kernel of a body of information: as **a :** a compilation of legal rules, statutes, or decisions systematically arranged **b :** a literary condensation or abridgment **c :** a periodical usu. of small format that characteristically prints condensed versions of articles previously published elsewhere 〈on the shelves were ~*s* and pulp magazines〉 **2 :** a product of digestion; *specif* **:** a mixture of breakdown products of a complex organic substance (as meat) resulting from the controlled action of one or more enzymes — see DIGEST MEDIUM **syn** see COMPENDIUM

[2]**di·gest** \(')dī¦jest *also* də'j-\ *vb* -ED/-ING/-S [ME *digesten*, fr. L *digestus*, past part.] *vt* **1** *obs* **:** SEPARATE, DISTRIBUTE **:** dispose separately or in parts or groups **2 :** to distribute or arrange systematically **:** work over and classify **:** reduce to portions for ready use or application; *specif* **:** CODIFY 〈~ the laws〉 **3 :** to think over and arrange systematically in the mind **:** receive in the mind and consider **:** COMPREHEND **4 a :** to subject to or transform by digestion **:** convert (food) into absorbable form **b :** to cause or aid the digestion of (food) 〈pancreatic enzymes ~ most of the protein〉 **c :** to break down in vitro in a manner similar to digestion in vivo 〈sugars are ~*ed* by yeasts〉 **5 :** to appropriate or assimilate mentally 〈read, mark, learn, and inwardly ~ them —*Bk. of Com. Prayer*〉 **6 :** to bear patiently **:** be reconciled to **:** BROOK 〈~ many insults〉 **7** *obs* **:** to cause to generate pus **8 :** to change the nature of (a substance) by various means: as **a :** to soften or decompose by heat and moisture or chemicals often under pressure **:** COOK **b :** to extract soluble ingredients from (as plant or animal materials) by warming with a liquid — compare MACERATE 3a **c :** to decompose by chemicals (as acids) without heating **9 :** to compress (a piece of literature or a body of information) into a short summary form containing the essential core of the matter ~ *vi* **1 a :** to digest food 〈don't bother me; I'm resting and ~*ing*〉 **b :** to become digested **:** undergo digestion 〈soft-boiled eggs ~ easily〉 **2** *obs* **:** to generate pus **:** SUPPURATE

di·ges·ta \də'jestə, dī'-\ *n pl* [NL, fr. neut. pl. of L *digestus*] **:** something undergoing digestion (as food in the stomach)

di·ges·tant \də'jestənt, dī'-\ *n* -S **:** DIGESTIVE 1

di·gest·er \-tə(r)\ *n* -S **1 :** one that digests or makes a digest **2 :** a medicine or an article of food that aids digestion **3 a** *also* **di·ges·tor** \"\ **:** a vessel or apparatus for digesting **:** COOKER, AUTOCLAVE **b :** a vessel in which cellulosic pulp is produced usu. from wood chips by cooking with chemicals under pressure **c :** a covered tank in which digestion of sewage sludge is carried out **4 :** RECOVERER

digester tankage *or* **digester meal tankage** *n* **:** tankage for feeding livestock

di·gest·ibil·i·ty \də,jestə'biləd·ē, (,)dī,-, -ətē, -i\ *n* -ES **:** the fitness of a foodstuff or nutrient for digestion; *often* **:** the percentage of a foodstuff taken into the digestive tract that is absorbed into the body

di·gest·ible \də'jestəbəl, (')dī¦j-\ *adj* [ME, fr. MF or LL; MF, fr. LL *digestibilis*, fr. L *digestus* + *-ibilis* -ible] **:** capable of being digested — **di·gest·ible·ness** *n* -ES — **di·gest·ibly** \-blē,-bli\ *adv*

digestible nutrient *n* **:** any of the three basic classes of foodstuffs carbohydrate, fat, or protein; *esp* **:** the part of a protein that has actually undergone digestion and assimilation as distinguished from the part rejected in feces

di·ges·tion \də'jes(h)chən, dī'-\ *n* -S [ME *digestioun*, fr. MF *digestion*, fr. L *digestion-, digestio*, fr. *digestus* + *-ion-, -io* -ion] **1 :** the action or process of digesting; *also* **:** the power of digesting **2** *obs* **:** the generation of pus **:** SUPPURATION **3 :** the process of making food absorbable by dissolving it and breaking it down into simpler chemical compounds that occurs in the living body chiefly through the action of secretions containing enzymes (as the saliva and the gastric, pancreatic, and intestinal juices in the alimentary canal of higher animals) **4 :** the process in sewage treatment by which organic matter in sludge is decomposed by anaerobic bacteria with the release of a burnable mixture of gases (as methane with carbon dioxide) **5 :** partial or complete solution of rock in magma — **di·ges·tion·al** \də'jes(h)chənᵊl, (')dī¦j-\ *adj* — **digestionally** *adv*

diagrammatic figure of digestive organs of man, as seen from the front: *a* esophagus; *b* cardiac end of stomach; *c* pyloric end of stomach; *d* duodenum; *e, f* convolutions of small intestine; *g* cecum; *g′* vermiform appendix; *h* ascending colon; *i* transverse colon; *k* descending colon; *l* sigmoid flexure; *m* rectum; *n* anus; *o, o* lobes of liver, raised and turned back; *p* hepatic duct; *q* cystic duct; *r* gallbladder; *s* common bile duct; *t* pancreas; *u* pancreatic duct, entering the duodenum with the common bile duct

digestion coefficient *also* **digestibility coefficient** *n* **:** the proportion of a nutrient taken into the digestive tract that is actually digested — compare BIOLOGICAL VALUE

[1]**di·ges·tive** \də'jestiv, -tēv *also* dī'- *or* -təv\ *n* -S [ME, fr. MF *digestif*, fr. *digestif*, adj.] **1 a :** something (as a food or drug) that aids digestion **:** DIGESTER **b** *Brit* **:** a thin slightly sweet biscuit or wafer **2** *obs* **:** a substance that promotes suppuration

[2]**di·ges·tive** \də'j- *also* (')dī¦j-\ *adj* [MF or L; MF *digestif*, fr. L *digestivus*, fr. *digestus* (past part. of *digerere* to divide, distribute, arrange, digest) + *-ivus* -ive — more at DIGEST] **:** relating to digestion **:** having the power to cause or promote digestion 〈~ ferments〉 — **di·ges·tive·ly** \-təvlē, -li\ *adv* — **di·ges·tive·ness** \-tivnəs, -tēv- *also* -təv-\ *n* -ES

digestive gland *n* **:** a gland in an animal or plant that secretes digestive enzymes

digest medium *n* **:** a biological culture medium prepared from or containing a digest

digestor *var of* DIGESTER

digests *pl of* DIGEST, *pres 3d sing of* DIGEST

digesture *n* -S [[2]*digest* + *-ure*] *obs* **:** DIGESTION

digged *archaic past of* DIG

dig·ger \'digə(r)\ *n* -S [ME, fr. *diggen* to dig + *-er*] **1 :** one that digs in the ground: as **a :** MINER **b :** a tool for digging **c :** a machine for digging 〈trench ~〉 〈posthole ~〉 **d :** a plow used in England with a short high abruptly curved moldboard for turning and breaking up the furrow slice of soil **2** *usu cap* **:** a member of a short-lived equalitarian group that began in 1649 to cultivate certain English common lands as a protest against private property **3** *or* **digger indian** *usu cap D & I* **a :** BANNOCK **b :** PAIUTE 1 **4** [fr. earlier *digger* gold miner (i.e. a typical Australian)] **a :** AUSTRALIAN; *esp* **:** an Australian or New Zealand soldier of World War I **b** *Austral* **:** PAL, BUDDY **5** *slang* **:** one that buys theater tickets for speculative brokers

digger pine *n, usu cap D* **:** a California pine (*Pinus sabiniana*) with sparse foliage and nuts formerly used as food by the Digger Indians — called also *bull pine, gray pine*

digger wasp *n* **:** a burrowing wasp; *specif* **:** any of numerous usu. solitary wasps chiefly of the superfamily Sphecoidea that dig nest burrows in the soil and provision them with living insects or spiders which they paralyze by stinging

dig·ging \'digiŋ, -gēŋ\ *n* -S [fr. gerund of *dig*] **1 diggings** *pl* **:** material taken out of an excavation **2** *usu* **diggings** *pl but sing or pl in constr* **:** a place of excavating **:** a place where ore, metals, or precious stones are got by digging (as by placer mining) **3 diggings** *pl* **a :** PLACE, PREMISES 〈he hasn't been seen around these ~*s* lately〉 **b** *chiefly Brit* **:** quarters or lodgings esp. for a student or other single person

digging stick *n* **:** a primitive agricultural implement consisting of a pointed stick sometimes weighted with a perforated stone or equipped with a crossbar upon which the digger steps

[1]**dight** \'dīt, *Scot* 'dikt *or* 'dī(k)t\ *vt* **dighted** *or* **dight; dighted** *or* **dight; dighting; dights** [ME *dighten*, fr. OE *dihtan* to arrange, dictate, compose (verse or prose); akin to OFris *dichta* to arrange; both fr. a prehistoric Anglo-Frisian word borrowed fr. L *dictare* to dictate, compose (verse or prose) — more at DICTATE] **1** *obs* **:** APPOINT, ORDER, ASSIGN **2** *archaic* **:** DRESS, ADORN **3** *chiefly Scot* **a :** to put in order **:** REPAIR **b :** to wipe clean **c :** SWEEP **d :** WINNOW

[2]**dight** \"\ *n* -S *chiefly Scot* **:** WIPE, RUB

[3]**dight** *var of* DITE

dig·i·lan·ide \,dijə'la,nīd, -,nəd\ *or* **dig·i·lan·id** \-,nəd\ *n* -S [fr. *Digilanid*, a trademark] **:** LANATOSIDE; *also* **:** a mixture of the lanatosides

dig in *vt* **:** to cover by digging **:** BURY 〈*dig in* fertilizer〉 ~ *vi* **1 :** to prepare a defensive position by digging trenches 〈the troops had no time to *dig in* before the attack came〉 **2 :** to hold stubbornly to a position **3 a :** to go resolutely to work **b :** to begin eating **:** fall to **4 :** to run hard

dig·it \'dijət, *usu* -əd·+V\ *n* -S [ME, fr. L *digitus* finger, toe — more at TOE] **1 a :** any one of the whole numbers from one through nine **b :** one of the 10 arabic numerals by which all numbers may be expressed; *often* **:** any of the arabic numerals with the exception of the cipher **2 :** a unit of length based on the breadth of a finger and equal in English measure to ¾ inch **3 :** one of the divisions in which the limbs of amphibians and all higher vertebrates terminate numbering typically five on each limb but often reduced (as in the horse where the whole foot consists of an enormously developed middle digit) and having typically a series of bony phalanges which in most mammals do not exceed three in number and usu. bearing a horny nail at the tip which may be modified into a claw or hoof : a finger or toe **syn** see NUMBER

1**dig·i·tal** \'dijəd·əl, -ət·əl\ *adj* [L *digitalis*, fr. *digitus* + *-alis* -al] **1** : of or relating to the fingers ⟨~ technique of a pianist⟩ ⟨~ grasp⟩ or toes : DIGITATE **2** : performed with a finger ⟨~ examination⟩ **3 a** : of or relating to calculation by numerical methods or by discrete units **b** : of or relating to the representation of data by numerical digits or discrete units — **dig·i·tal·ly** \-əlē, -əli\ *adv*

2**digital** \"\ *n* -s **1** : FINGER **2** : a key (as of an organ) to be played by the finger **3** : the terminal joint of the pedipalpus of a spider

digital computer *n* : a computer that operates with numbers expressed directly as digits in a decimal, binary, or other system

dig·i·tal·in \,dijə'talən *sometimes* -tāl- *or* -täl- *or* -tȧl-\ *n* -s [NL *digitalis* + E *-in*] **1** : a white crystalline steroid glycoside $C_{36}H_{56}O_{14}$ obtained from seeds of the purple foxglove **2** : a mixture of the glycosides of digitalis varying in composition according to the method of preparation from the leaves or seeds

dig·i·tal·is \-ləs\ *n* [NL, fr. L, adj.] **1** *cap* : a genus of Eurasian herbs of the family Scrophulariaceae that have alternate leaves and racemes of showy bell-shaped flowers **2** -ES : the dried leaf of the purple foxglove containing the active principles digitoxin and gitoxin and constituting a powerful cardiac stimulant and a diuretic used principally in diseases of the heart to correct lost compensation

dig·i·tal·i·za·tion \,dijə,taləˈzāshən\ *n* -s : the administration (as in heart disease) of digitalis until the desired physiologic adjustment is attained; *also* : the bodily state so produced

dig·i·ta·lize \'dijəd·əl,īz, ,dijə'ta,līz\ *vt* -ED/-ING/-S [NL *digitalis* + E *-ize*] : to subject (a person) to digitalization

dig·i·tal·ose \,dijə'ta,lōs *also* -ōz\ *n* -s [ISV *digitalin* + *-ose*] : a sugar $C_7H_{14}O_5$ obtained esp. from digitalin by hydrolysis; the 3-methyl derivative of D-fucose

dig·i·tar·ia \,dijə'ta(a)rēə\ *n, cap* [NL, fr. L *digitus* finger + NL *-aria* — more at TOE] : a genus of grasses found in warm regions and having one-flowered spikelets in one-sided digitately arranged racemes — see CRABGRASS

dig·i·tate \'dijə,tāt\ *also* **dig·i·tat·ed** \-ād·əd\ *adj* [*digit* + *-ate, -ated*] **1** : having digits **2** : resembling a finger; *specif* : having divisions arranged like fingers of a hand — used esp. of compound leaves (as those of lupine or horse chestnut) having lobes that extend to the point of insertion of the petiole — **dig·i·tate·ly** *adv*

dig·i·ta·tion \,dijə'tāshən\ *n* -s **1** : the state of being digitate : a division into fingers or digitiform processes **2** : a process that resembles a finger

digiti *pl of* DIGITUS

digiti- *comb form* [F, fr. L *digitus* finger, toe — more at TOE] **1** : digit : finger or toe ⟨*digiti*grade⟩ **2** : finger ⟨*digiti*form⟩ **3** : digitately ⟨*digiti*pinnate⟩

dig·i·ti·gra·da \,dijəd·ə'grādə\ *n pl, cap* [NL, fr. *digiti-* + *-grada* (neut. pl. of *-gradus* -grade)] *in former classifications* : a group consisting of the digitigrade Carnivora

1**dig·i·ti·grade** \'dijəd·ə,grād\ *adj* [F, fr. *digiti-* (fr. L *digitus* finger, toe) + *-grade* — more at TOE] *of an animal* : walking upon the digits with the posterior part of the foot more or less raised — opposed to *plantigrade*

2**digitigrade** \"\ *n* : a digitigrade animal

dig·i·ti·nervate *also* **dig·i·ti·nerved** \,dijəd·ə+\ *adj* [*digiti-* + *nervate* or *nerved*] : having veins that emerge from the petiole and spread out like fingers : straight-veined ⟨a ~ leaf⟩

dig·i·ti·pinnate \"+\ *adj* [*digiti-* + *pinnate*] : having digitate leaves of which the leaflets are pinnate : digitately pinnate

dig·i·tize \'dijə,tīz\ *vt* -ED/-ING/-S : to put (data) into digital notation (as for use in a digital computer) : convert to digital form — **dig·i·tiz·er** \-zə(r)\ *n* -s

dig·i·to·gen·in \,dijəd·ə'jenən, ,==ˈtäjən-\ *n* -s [blend of *digitonin* and *-gen*] : a crystalline steroid sapogenin $C_{27}H_{44}O_5$ obtained by hydrolysis of digitonin

dig·i·to·nide \,dijə'tō,nīd\ *n* -s [*digitonin* + *-ide*] : a sparingly soluble complex of digitonin and some other compound ⟨cholesterol ~⟩

dig·i·to·nin \-'tōnən\ *n* -s [ISV *digit-* (fr. NL *Digitalis*) + *-onin* (as in *saponin*)] : a crystalline steroid saponin $C_{56}H_{92}O_{29}$ occurring in the leaves and seeds of purple foxglove

dig·i·to·plantar \,dijəd·ə+\ *adj* [*digito-* (fr. L *digitus* finger, toe) + *plantar*] : of or relating to the toes and the plantar surface of the foot

dig·i·tox·i·gen·in \,dijə,täksə'jenən, ,==,=ˈsijən-\ *n* -s [ISV, blend of *digitoxin* and *-gen*] : a crystalline steroid lactone $C_{23}H_{34}O_4$ obtained esp. by hydrolysis of digitoxin

dig·i·tox·in \,==ˈtäksən\ *n* [ISV *digi-* (fr. NL *Digitalis*) + *toxin*] : a poisonous crystalline steroid glycoside $C_{41}H_{64}O_{13}$ occurring as the most active principle of digitalis and used similarly to digitalis; *also* : a mixture of cardiotonic glycosides obtained from digitalis and consisting chiefly of digitoxin — see LANATOSIDE a

dig·i·tox·ose \-'täk,sōs *also* -ōz\ *n* -s [ISV *digitoxin* + *-ose*] : a sugar $CH_3(CHOH)_3CH_2CHO$ obtained by the hydrolysis of several glycosides of digitalis (as digitoxin or gitoxin); 2,6-di-deoxy-D-allose

digits *pl of* DIGIT

dig·i·tus \'dijəd·əs\ *n, pl* **digi·ti** \-jə,tī\ [NL, fr. L, finger, toe — more at TOE] : any of various small processes on insects; *esp* : the claw-bearing terminal segment of the tarsus

di·glos·sia \dī'gläsēə\ *n* [NL, fr. *di-* + *-glossia*] : the condition of having the tongue bifid

1**di·glot** \'dī,glät\ *adj* [Gk *diglōttos*, fr. *di-* + *-glōttos* -glot] : BILINGUAL 1

2**diglot** \"\ *n* -s : a bilingual publication

di·glucoside \(')dī+\ *n* [*di-* + *glucoside*] : a compound with two molecules of glucose

di·glyceride \"+\ *n* [ISV *di-* + *glyceride*] : a diester of glycerol

di·glycerol *or* **di·glycerin** \"+\ *n* [*di-* + *glycerol* or *glycerin*] : a viscous hygroscopic liquid polyhydroxy ether $O(CH_2CHOHCH_2OH)_2$ made by dehydration of glycerol and used esp. in making rosin esters for varnishes

di·glycol \"+\ *n* [ISV *di-* + *glycol*] : DIETHYLENE GLYCOL

di·glycolic acid *or* **di·glycollic acid** \(,)dī+ . . . -\ *n* [ISV *di-* + *glycolic, glycollic*] : a crystalline dicarboxylic acid $O(CH_2COOH)_2$ regarded as the ether of glycolic acid, formed from a salt of chloroacetic acid by reaction with calcium hydroxide, and used in making plasticizers and resins

di·glyph \'dī,glif\ *n* -s [Gk *diglyphos* doubly indented, fr. *di-* + *-glyphos* (fr. *glyphein* to carve or hollow out) — more at CLEAVE (split)] : a projecting ornamental face like the triglyph but having only two grooves

di·glyphic \(')dī+\ *adj* [*di-* + *glyphic*] : having two siphonoglyphs ⟨~ polyps⟩

dignation *n* -s [ME *dignacion*, fr. MF or L; MF *dignation*, fr. L *dignation-, dignatio*, fr. *dignatus* (past part. of *dignare, dignari* to consider worthy, deign) + *-ion-, -io* -ion — more at DEIGN] *obs* : the act of showing esteem esp. to an inferior : CONDESCENSION

dig·ni·fi·cation \,dignəfə'kāshən\ *n* -s [MF, fr. LL *dignificatus* (past part. of *dignificare*) + MF *-ion*] : a dignifying or being dignified

dig·ni·fied \'dignə,fīd\ *adj* : showing or expressive of dignity in appearance, manner, or language ⟨his appearance was anything but ~; he was short and very fat, and had little or no appearance of neck —Anthony Trollope⟩ — **dig·ni·fied·ly** \-ī(ə)dlē, -li\ *adv* — **dig·ni·fied·ness** \-ī(ə)dnəs\ *n* -ES

dig·ni·fy \-,fī\ *vt* -ED/-ING/-ES [MF *dignefier, dignifier*, fr. LL *dignificare*, fr. L *dignus* worthy + *-ficare* -fy — more at DECENT] **1** : to invest with dignity or honor : make illustrious : give distinction to : EXALT, ENNOBLE ⟨your worth will ~ our feast —Ben Jonson⟩ **2** : to confer dignity upon by changing name, appearance, or character ⟨~ a style with imagery⟩ ⟨~ thievery by calling it kleptomania⟩

dig·ni·tar·i·al \,dignə'terēəl\ *adj* : of or belonging to a dignitary

1**dig·ni·tary** \'dignə,terē, -ri\ *n* -ES [*dignity* + *-ary*] : one who possesses exalted rank or holds a position of dignity or honor ⟨a diplomatic ~⟩

2**dignitary** \"\ *adj* : of, belonging to, or having a dignity ⟨a ~ title⟩

dig·ni·ty \'dignəd·ē, -ətē, -i\ *n* -ES [ME *dignete, dignite*, fr. OF *digneté, dignité*, fr. L *dignitat-, dignitas*, fr. *dignus* worthy + *-itat-, -itas* -ity — more at DECENT] **1** : the quality or state of being worthy : intrinsic worth : EXCELLENCE ⟨the ~ of this act was worth the audience of kings —Shak.⟩ ⟨all human beings are born free and equal in ~ and rights —*U.N. Declaration of Human Rights*⟩ **2** : the quality or state of being honored or esteemed : degree of esteem : HONOR ⟨rose to the ~ of a judgeship⟩ **3 a** : high rank, office, or position ⟨aspir'd to ~ —Edmund Spenser⟩ **b** *archaic* : RANK, DEGREE ⟨clay and clay differs in ~, whose dust is both alike —Shak.⟩ **c** : a particular office, rank, or title of honor ⟨Napoleon persuaded the Archduke Maximilian . . . to accept the Mexican imperial ~ —*Times Lit. Supp.*⟩ **d** *Eng law* : a title of honor that is an incorporeal hereditament or real property **4** *archaic* **a** : one holding high rank : DIGNITARY ⟨in spite of pope or *dignities* of church —Shak.⟩ **b** : persons of high rank as a body **5** : formal reserve of manner, appearance, behavior, or language : behavior that accords with self-respect or with regard for the seriousness of occasion or purpose : GRAVITY, POISE ⟨watched him kindly but with ~, as well-treated animals who have an assured position always do —Mary Webb⟩

di·go·nal \(')dī'gōn·əl\ *adj* [*di-* + Gk *gōnia* angle + E *-al*] *of an axis of symmetry of a crystal* : TWOFOLD, DIAD

di·go·neu·tic \,dīgə'n(y)üd·ik\ *adj* [*di-* + (assumed) Gk *goneutos* (verbal of *goneuein* to produce, generate) + E *-ic*; akin to Gk *gignesthai* to be born — more at KIN] : having two broods in one year : BIVOLTINE — **di·go·neu·tism** \,dīgə'n(y)üd·,izəm\ *n* -s

di·gonial \(')dī+\ *adj* [*di-* + *gonial*] : BIGONIAL

di·go·nop·o·rous \,dīgə'näpərəs, -,gä'-\ *adj* [*di-* + *gon-* + *-porous* (fr. Gk *poros* passage) — more at FARE] : having separate orifices for the male and female reproductive organs ⟨~ hermaphroditic gastropods⟩

dig out *vt* **1** : to make hollow by digging ⟨*dig out* a mud-filled spring⟩ **2** : to get by searching or rummaging : bring out of storage ⟨*dig* a book *out* of the attic⟩ ~ *vi* : to set out or go at full speed ⟨the rabbit *dug out* for the woods⟩ : depart hastily ⟨he didn't say where he was going, just *dug out*⟩

di·gox·i·gen·in \(,)dī,gäksə'jenən, -'sijən-\ *n* -s [ISV, blend of *digoxin* and *-gen*] : a crystalline steroid lactone $C_{23}H_{34}O_5$ obtained by hydrolysis of digoxin

di·gox·in \dī'gäksən\ *n* -s [ISV *dig-* (fr. NL *Digitalis*) + *toxin*] : a poisonous bitter crystalline cardiotonic steroid glycoside $C_{41}H_{64}O_{14}$ obtained from the leaves of a foxglove (*Digitalis lanata*) and used similarly to digitalis — see LANATOSIDE c

di·gram \'dī,gram, -aa(ə)m\ *n* [*di-* + *-gram*] : a group of two successive letters or other symbols

di·graph \'dī,graf, -aa(ə)f,-aif,-af\ *n* [*di-* + *-graph*] **1** : a group of two successive letters whose phonetic value is a single sound (as *ea* in *bread*, *ng* in *thing*) or whose value is not the sum of a value borne by each in other occurrences (as *ch* in *chin*, where the value is \t\+\sh\) **2** : any group of two successive letters

di·graphic \(')dī+\ *adj* **1** : of or belonging to a digraph **2** *cryptology* : taking two letters at a time — see PLAYFAIR CIPHER — **di·graphically** \"+\ *adv*

di·gress \(')dī'gres *also* də'g-\ *vi* -ED/-ING/-ES [L *digressus*, past part. of *digredi*, lit., to go apart, fr. *di-* (fr. *dis-* apart) + *-gredi* to step, go (fr. *gradi*) — more at DIS-, GRADE] **1** *archaic* : to step or turn aside : DEVIATE, DIVERGE, SWERVE **2** : to turn aside from the main subject of attention or course of argument in writing or speaking ⟨I shall not pursue these points further for fear of ~*ing* too far from my main theme —R.J.Spilsbury⟩ **3** *obs* : TRANSGRESS **syn** see SWERVE

di·gres·sion \dī'greshən *also* də'-\ *n* -s [ME *digressioun*, fr. MF *digression, disgression*, fr. L *digression-, digressio*, fr. *digressus* + *-ion-, -io* -ion] **1** *archaic* : an act or instance of digressing : a going aside **2 a** : the act of digressing in a discourse or other usu. organized literary work ⟨other flights and ~*s* I find yet more doubtful than the humorous —B.N. Cardozo⟩ **b** : the portion of the discourse in which such a digression is made ⟨a lengthy ~ on the subject of free trade interrupted the main point of the speech⟩ **3** *obs* : TRANSGRESSION — **di·gres·sion·al** \-shən·əl\ *adj*

di·gres·sive \(')dī,gresiv, də'g-, -sēv *also* -səv-\ *adj* [L *digressivus*, fr. *digressus* + *-ivus* -ive] **1** : of the nature of a digression ⟨a ~ chapter on a subject entirely different from that of the bulk of the book⟩ **2** : characterized by digressions ⟨the book is amusingly ~: there are satirical thrusts at women's fashions and some neatly turned couplets —E.H.Dewey⟩ — **di·gres·sive·ly** \-səvlē, -li\ *adv* — **di·gres·sive·ness** \=ˈ=sivnəs, -sēv- *also* -səv-\ *n* -ES

digs *pres 3d sing of* DIG, *pl of* DIG

digue \'dēg\ *n* -s [MF *digue, dike*, fr. MD *dijc*; akin to OE *dīc* dike, ditch — more at DIKE] : EMBANKMENT, DIKE

dig up *vt* : to find or obtain or bring to light esp. with difficulty ⟨I'll *dig up* the money somehow⟩ ⟨*dig up* evidence in support of a case⟩ ~ *vi* : to make a money contribution ⟨taxpayers had to *dig up* to keep [the unemployed] on . . . relief —T.W. Arnold⟩

di·gyn·ia \dī'jinēə, -'gi-\ *n pl, cap* [NL, fr. *di-* + *-gynia*] : *in former classifications* : an order of plants including those having flowers with two pistils — **di·gyn·ian** \(')=ˈ==ən\ *adj* — **di·gy·nous** \(')=ˈjīnəs, -ˈgī-\ *adj*

dihal- *or* **dihalo-** *comb form* [ISV *di-* + *hal-*] : containing two atoms of a halogen — in names of chemical compounds ⟨*dihalo*hydrin⟩

di·halide \(')dī+\ *n* [*di-* + *halide*] : a compound containing two atoms of halogen combined with an element or radical

1**di·he·dral** \(')dī'hēdrəl\ *adj* [*di-* + *-hedral*] **1** : having or formed by two plane faces ⟨a ~ angle⟩ **2 a** *of a kite or an airplane* : having wings that make with one another a dihedral angle esp. when the angle between the upper sides is less than 180° **b** *of airplane wing pairs* : inclined at a dihedral angle to each other

2**dihedral** \"\ *n* -s **1** : a mathematical figure formed by two intersecting planes **2** : the angle between an aircraft supporting surface and a horizontal transverse line; *esp* : the angle between (1) an upwardly inclined wing or (2) a downwardly inclined wing and such a line — called also respectively (1) *positive dihedral* or (2) *negative dihedral*

dihedral angle *n* **1** : the angle between two intersecting planes **2** : 2DIHEDRAL 2

di·hexagonal \,dī+\ *adj* [ISV *di-* + *hexagonal*] *crystallog* : being or relating to a symmetrical 12-sided figure the alternate angles of which are equal — used esp. in naming forms of the hexagonal system

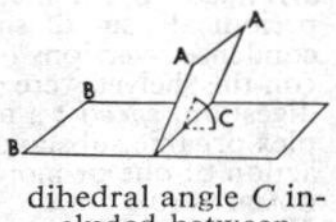

dihedral angle *C* included between planes *A A* and *B B*

dihexagonal–dipyramidal *adj* : of or characterized by the symmetry of the class of crystals in the hexagonal system having a vertical hexad axis, six horizontal diad axes, six vertical planes, and a horizontal plane of symmetry

dihexagonal prism *n* : a prism any horizontal section of which is dihexagonal

dihexagonal pyramid *n* : a pyramid any horizontal section of which is dihexagonal

di·hexa·he·dral \(')dī,heksə'hēdrəl\ *adj* [*di-* + *hexahedral*] : of or relating to a dihexahedron

di·hexa·he·dron \-drən\ *n* -s [ISV *di-* + *hexahedron*] : a form of crystal having 12 faces (as a double 6-sided pyramid)

1**di·hybrid** \(')dī+\ *n* [ISV *di-* + *hybrid*] : an individual or strain that is heterozygous for two factors (as recessive genes)

2**dihybrid** \"+\ *adj* : of, relating to, or being a dihybrid

dihydr- *or* **dihydro-** *comb form* [ISV *di-* + *hydr-*] : combined with two atoms of hydrogen — in names of chemical compounds ⟨*dihydro*naphthalene⟩

di·hydrate \(')dī+\ *n* [ISV *di-* + *hydrate*] : a chemical compound with two molecules of water ⟨calcium sulfate ~ $CaSO_4.2H_2O$⟩

di·hydrated \(')dī+\ *adj* [*di-* + *hydrated*] : combined with two molecules of water

di·hydrazone \(')dī+\ *n* [*di-* + *hydrazone*] : a compound containing two hydrazone groupings =NNHR — compare OSAZONE

di·hydric \(')dī+\ *adj* [ISV *di-* + *-hydric*] **1** *archaic* : containing two atoms of acid hydrogen **2** : DIHYDROXY — used esp. of alcohols and phenols

di·hy·drite \dī'hī,drīt\ *n* -s [G *dihydrit*, fr. *di-* + *hydr-* + *-it* -ite] : PSEUDOMALACHITE

di·hy·dro \(')dī'hī(,)drō\ *adj* [*dihydr-*] : combined with two atoms of hydrogen

di·hydrochloride \(,)dī+\ *n* [*di-* + *hydrochloride*] : a chemical compound with two molecules of hydrochloric acid ⟨quinine ~ $C_{20}H_{24}N_2O_2.2HCl$⟩

di·hy·dro·co·de·inone \(,)dī,hīdrōkō'dēə,nōn\ *n* -s [*dihydr-* + *codeine* + *-one*] : a crystalline habit-forming compound $C_{18}H_{21}NO_3$ derived from codeine and used as an analgesic and cough sedative

di·hy·dro·er·go·cor·nine \dī'hīdrō,ərgō'kȯr,nēn, -,nən\ *n* [ISV *dihydr-* + *ergocornine* alkaloid from ergot (*ergo-* + *corn-* — fr. G *korn* grain, fr. OHG — + *-ine*) — more at CORN] : a hydrogenated derivative $C_{31}H_{41}N_5O_5$ of an alkaloid from ergot that is used in the treatment of peripheral vascular diseases and hypertension

di·hy·dro·ergotamine \,dī,h|īdrō, dī,h|+\ *n* [ISV *dihydr-* + *ergotamine*] : a crystalline compound $C_{33}H_{37}N_5O_5$ made by hydrogenating ergotamine and used in the treatment of migraine headaches

di·hydrogen \(')dī+\ *adj* [*di-* + *hydrogen*] : containing two atoms of hydrogen in the molecule

di·hy·dro·mor·phi·none \(,)dī,hīdrō'mȯrfə,nōn\ *n* -s [*dihydr-* + *morphine* + *-one*] : a crystalline ketone $C_{17}H_{19}NO_3$ derived from morphine that is about five times as active biologically as morphine

di·hy·dro·streptomycin \,dī,h|īdrō, dī,h|+\ *n* [ISV *dihydr-* + *streptomycin*] : an antibiotic $C_{21}H_{41}N_7O_{12}$ made by hydrogenating streptomycin and considered by some authorities to be less toxic than streptomycin with which it is often administered chiefly in the treatment of tuberculosis, tularemia, and infections caused by gram-negative organisms

di·hy·dro·tachysterol \"+\ *n* [*dihydr-* + *tachysterol*] : a crystalline alcohol $C_{28}H_{45}OH$ used in the treatment of hypocalcemia (as in hypoparathyroidism)

di·hy·droxy \,dī,hī'dräksē\ *adj* [*dihydroxy-*] : containing two hydroxyl groups in the molecule

dihydroxy- *comb form* [ISV *di-* + *hydroxy-*] : containing two hydroxyl groups — in names of chemical compounds ⟨*dihydroxy*succinic acid⟩

diiamb [LL *diiambus*, fr. Gk *diiambos*, fr. *di-* + *iambos* iamb] *var of* DIAMB

di·iam·bus \,dī,ī'ambəs\ *n, pl* **diiam·bi** \-,bī\ [LL] : DIAMB

diiod- *or* **diiodo-** *comb form* [ISV *di-* + *iod-*] : containing two atoms of iodine — in names of chemical compounds ⟨*diiodo*fluorescein⟩; compare IOD-

di·iodide \(')dī+\ *n* [*di-* + *iodide*] : a compound containing two atoms of iodine combined with an element or radical

di·io·do·hy·droxy·quinoline \dī'īə,dō,hī,dräksē+\ *or* **di·io·do·hy·droxy·quin** \-,hī'dräksēkwən\ *n* [*diiodohydroxyquinoline* fr. *diiod-* + *hydroxyquinoline*; *diiodohydroxyquin* short for *diiodohydroxyquinoline*] : a colorless to tan crystalline compound $C_9H_5I_2NO$ used esp. in the treatment of amebic dysentery

di·io·do·methane \(,)dī,īə,dō+\ *n* [ISV *diiod-* + *methane*] : METHYLENE IODIDE

di·io·do·tyrosine \"+\ *n* [ISV *diiod-* + *tyrosine*] : a crystalline amino acid $HOC_6H_2I_2CH_2CH(NH_2)COOH$ obtained by hydrolysis of thyroglobulin and of proteins from corals and sponges and held to be a precursor of triiodothyronine and thyroxine in the thyroid gland — called also *3,5-diiodotyrosine, iodogorgoic acid*

di·isobutylene \(')dī+\ *n* [*di-* + *isobutylene*] : a liquid mixture containing the two octylenes 2,4,4-trimethyl-1-pentene and 2,4,4-trimethyl-2-pentene obtained from isobutylene by reaction with acid catalysts and used as an intermediate (as for plastics)

di·isocyanate \"+\ *n* [ISV *di-* + *isocyanate*] : a compound containing two isocyanate groups in the molecule and sometimes used in making resins and plastics ⟨tolylene ~ $CH_3C_6H_4(NCO)_2$⟩

di·isopropyl \"+\ *adj* [ISV *di-* + *isopropyl*] : containing two isopropyl groups in the molecule

diisopropyl fluorophosphate *n* [ISV *diisopropyl* + *fluorophosphate*] : a volatile irritating liquid ester $[(CH_3)_2CH]_2PO_3F$ that acts as a nerve gas by inhibiting cholinesterases and as a myotic and that is used chiefly in treating glaucoma — called also *DFP, isoflurophate*

di·jon \(')dē'zhō^n\ *adj, usu cap* [fr. *Dijon*, city in France] : of or from the city of Dijon, France : of the kind or style prevalent in Dijon

di·judicate \(')dī+\ *vb* -ED/-ING/-S [L *dijudicatus*, past part. of *dijudicare* to decide, fr. *di-* (fr. *dis-* apart) + *judicare* to judge — more at DIS-, JUDGE] *vi* : to make a judicial decision : DECIDE, DETERMINE ~ *vt* : to judge between : decide on

di·judication \(,)dī+\ *n* -s [L *dijudication-, dijudicatio*, fr. *dijudicatus* + *-ion-, -io* -ion] : the act or action of dijudicating

di·ka \'dēkə\ *n* -s [Mpongwe *odika*, a condiment, prob. dika bread] **1** : WILD MANGO **2 a** *also* **dika nut** : the fruit or seed of the African wild mango **b** : DIKA BREAD

dika bread *n* : a somewhat acid and astringent paste that is prepared by grinding and heating the seeds of the African wild mango usu. together with pepper and other spices and that is a staple food of some African peoples

dik·age *also* **dyk·age** \'dīkij\ *n* -s [*dike*, v. + *-age*] : the digging of dikes

di·karyon *also* **di·caryon** \(')dī+\ *n* [ISV *di-* + *karyon*] **1** : a pair of associated but unfused haploid nuclei brought together in a cell by the union of plus and minus hyphae (as in the rust fungi) and capable of carrying on conjugate division prior to their ultimate fusion **2** : a cell having or a mycelium made up of cells each having a dikaryon — compare HOMOKARYON

di·kary·ophase *also* **di·cary·ophase** \dī'karēə,fāz\ *n* [*di-* + *kary-* + *phase*] : the phase of the life cycle of a fungus (as the rusts) characterized by the dikaryotic condition — **di·kary·opha·sic** \(,)dī,karēə'fāzik\ *adj*

di·kary·ophyte *also* **di·cary·ophyte** \dī'karēə,fīt\ *n* -s [*di-* + *kary-* + *-phyte*] : the dikaryotic mycelium as a whole in fungi (as the rusts) — used esp. to distinguish such a mycelium from that having a single diploid nucleus in each cell — **di·cary·ophyt·ic** \(,)dī,karēə'fid·ik\ *adj*

di·kary·ot·ic *also* **di·cary·ot·ic** \dī,karē'äd·ik\ *adj* [*di-* + *kary-* + *-otic*] : of or relating to the dikaryon

dikast *var of* DICAST

dik–dik \'dik,dik\ *or* **dig–dig** \'dig,dig\ *n* -s [native name in East Africa] : any of several small East African antelopes (genera *Madoqua, Rhynchotragus*) of the size of a large rabbit

1**dike** *or* **dyke** \'dīk\ *n* -s [ME, fr. OE *dīc* ditch, dike; akin to MHG *tīch* pond, dike, ON *dīki* swamp, ditch, L *figere* to fasten, pierce, Lith *diegti* to prick] **1 a** : an artificial watercourse (as for drainage) **b** *now dial Brit* : any natural or artificial watercourse ⟨Thames, the king of ~*s* —Alexander Pope⟩ **c** : POOL, POND **2 a** *dial Brit* : a wall or fence of turf or stone **b** : a bank usu. of earth constructed to control or confine water : LEVEE ⟨the ~*s* of Holland prevent the sea from flooding the land⟩ **c** : a barrier preventing passage esp. protecting against or excluding something undesirable ⟨the legions were a ~ against the barbarian hordes⟩ **3 a** *dial Brit* : a bank of earth thrown up from a ditch **b** : a raised causeway **c** [so called fr. its standing up like a wall in places where the material that once surrounded it has been eroded away] : a tabular body of igneous rock that has been injected while molten into a fissure — see COMPOSITE DIKE

2**dike** *or* **dyke** \"\ *vb* -ED/-ING/-S [ME *diken*, fr. *dike*, n.] *vt* : to surround or protect with a dike; *also* : to drain by a dike or ditch ~ *vi* : to work as a ditcher : DIG : work at making a dike

3**dike** \"\ *vt* -ED/-ING/-S [perh. alter. of 2*deck*] *chiefly Midland* : to dress in fine clothes — usu. used with *out* or *up* ⟨all *diked* out for the party⟩

dike·grave \'dīk,grāv\ *n* -s [modif. of D *dijkgraaf*, fr. MD *dijcgrāve*, fr. *dijc* dike + *grāve* overseer; akin to OE *dīc* ditch, dike — more at BURGRAVE] : an officer in Holland in charge of dikes

dike·let \'dīklət\ *n* -s *geol* : a small dike approximately an inch in width

dike-loup·er \'dī,klaủpə(r), -lōp-,-lüp-\ *n* -s [¹*dike* + E dial. *louper* leaper, fr. E dial. *loup* to leap + E *-er* — more at LOUP] *dial Brit* : one that jumps fences

dik·er *also* **dyk·er** \'dīkə(r)\ *n* -s [ME *dikere*, fr. *diken* to dike + *-ere* -er] : one that makes or works upon dikes

dike·reeve *also* **dyke·reeve** \'dī,krēv\ *n* -s [perh. alter. (influenced by E *reeve*) of *dikegrave* — more at REEVE (official)] : an English official in charge of the drains, sluices, and sea walls in a district of fen or marshy land

dike ridge *n* **1** *geol* : a hogback in which the formation resistant to erosion is a dike **2** *geol* : a small wall-like ridge on a glacier resulting from differences in the rate of melting **3** *geol* : any small wall-like ridge (as one along a shore) resulting from differences in the rate of erosion

di·ke·ri·on \thē'kēryȯn\ *or* **di·ce·ri·on** \dī'sirē,än\ *n, pl* **dike·ria** \-yä\ *or* **dice·ria** \-ēə\ [NGk *dikērion*, fr. Gk *di-* + LGk *kērion* wax candle, fr. Gk, honeycomb, fr. *kēros* wax — more at CEREUS] *Eastern Orthodox Church* : a two-branched candlestick symbolizing the divine and human natures in Christ used by the bishop for blessing during the service — compare TRIKERION

di·ketene \(')dī+\ *n* [*di-* + *ketene*] : an unsaturated pungent liquid lactone $C_4H_4O_2$ made by spontaneous dimerization of ketene in solution and used chiefly in making derivatives of acetoacetic acid

diketo- *comb form* [ISV *di-* + *ket-*] : containing two ketone groups — in names of chemical compounds ⟨*diketo*adipic acid⟩; compare KET-

di·ketone \(')dī+\ *n* [ISV *di-* + *ketone*] : a chemical compound containing two ketonic carbonyl groups

di·ke·to·piperazine \'dī,k|ēd·(,)ō, dī,k|+\ *n* [ISV *diketo-* + *piperazine*] **1** : a crystalline compound $C_4H_6N_2O_2$ that is obtainable from two molecules of glycine by dehydration and may be regarded as a cyclic dipeptide; 2,5-piperazine-dione **2** : any of various cyclic compounds formed similarly to diketopiperazine from alpha-amino acids other than glycine or obtained by partial hydrolysis of proteins

dik·kop \'di,käp\ *n* -s [Afrik, fr. *dik* thick (fr. D, fr. MD *dicke*) + *kop* head, fr. D, fr. MD *cop, coppe* drinking vessel, skull; akin to OHG *dicki* thick — more at THICK, CUP] *Africa* : STONE CURLEW

dik·tat \dik'tät\ *n* -s *sometimes cap* [G, lit., something dictated, fr. NL *dictatum*, fr. L, neut. of *dictatus*, past part. of *dictare* to dictate — more at DICTATE] : a harsh decision or settlement unilaterally imposed esp. on a defeated or subject people or nation ⟨the treaty was regarded by the vanquished as a ~⟩

dil *abbr* dilute; dilution

di·lacerate \(')dī, də+\ *vt* [L *dilaceratus*, past part. of *dilacerare*, fr. *di-* (fr. *dis-* apart) + *lacerare* to tear — more at DIS-, LACERATE] : to tear apart or in pieces

di·laceration \(')dī, də+\ *n* [NL *dilaceration-, dilaceratio*, fr. L *dilaceratus* + *-ion-, -io* -ion] **1** : the action of dilacerating or the state of being dilacerated **2** : injury (as partial fracture) of a developing tooth resulting in a curve in the long axis as development continues

di·lactone \(')dī +\ *n* [*di-* + *lactone*] : a chemical compound containing two lactone groupings

di·lamb·do·dont \(')dī,lamdə,dänt\ *adj* [NL *Dilambdodonta*, category of insectivorous mammals recognized in some classifications, fr. *di-* + Gk *lambda* (Λ) + NL *-odonta*] : having two Λ-shaped transverse ridges on the molar teeth

Di·lan·tin \dī'lant°n, də'-, -tən\ *trademark* — used for diphenylhydantoin

di·lap·i·date \də'lapə,dāt, *usu* -ād+V\ *vb* -ED/-ING/-S [L *dilapidatus*, past part. of *dilapidare* to throw away, squander, destroy, fr. *di-* (fr. *dis-* apart) + *lapidare* to throw stones, fr. *lapid-, lapis* stone — more at DIS-, LAPIDARY] *vt* **1** : to bring (as a building) into a condition of decay or partial ruin ⟨a ruined house *dilapidated* by marauders⟩ ⟨furniture is *dilapidated* by use —Janet Flanner⟩ — now usu. used in the past participle **2** *archaic* : to impair or ruin (as a fortune or estate) by waste or abuse : SQUANDER ~ *vi* : to become dilapidated ⟨the house was neglectfully allowed to ~⟩ **syn** SEE DESTROY

dilapidated *adj* [fr. past part. of *dilapidate*] : decayed, deteriorated, injured, or fallen into partial ruin esp. because of neglect or misuse ⟨the old house still had an air of ~ grandeur⟩ ⟨a ghost town of ~ buildings —*Amer. Guide Series: Calif.*⟩ ⟨a ~ notice that the place was for sale —Bram Stoker⟩

di·lap·i·da·tion \-,lapə'dāshən\ *n* -s [ME *dilapidacion*, fr. LL *dilapidation-, dilapidatio* action of squandering, fr. L *dilapidatus* + *-ion-, -io* -ion] **1** : the act of dilapidating or the state of being dilapidated ⟨the wreck of a ship in the last stages of ~ —R.L.Stevenson⟩ **2** *Eng law* **a** : ecclesiastical waste whether permissive or voluntary : waste of a building (as a parsonage) committed to the charge of ecclesiastical persons **b** : the charge for repairing such waste **3** : the natural disintegration and breaking away of rock from a cliff or mountainside; *also* : the resulting debris

di·lap·i·da·tor \-ˌ=ˌ=ˌād·ə(r), -ātə-\ *n* -s [*dilapidate* + *-or*] : one that causes or permits dilapidation

di·lat·abil·i·ty \(,)dī,lād·ə'biləd·ē, də,-\ *n* -ES : the property of being dilatable

di·lat·able \(')dī|lād·əbəl, də'l-\ *adj* : capable of being dilated; *esp* : EXPANDABLE

di·la·tan·cy \də'lāt°nsē, dī'-, -si\ *n* -ES [*dilatant* + *-cy*] : the property of being dilatant

di·la·tant \-āt°nt\ *adj* [L *dilatant-, dilatans* dilating, pres. part. of *dilatare* to dilate] **1** : having the property of increasing in volume when changed in shape because of an increase of the space between the particles **2** : increasing in viscosity and setting to a solid as a result of deformation by expansion, pressure, or agitation — opposed to *thixotropic* ⟨~ quicksands⟩

dil·a·ta·tion \,dilə'tāshən, ,dīl-\ *n* -s [ME *dilatacioun*, fr. MF *dilatation* enlargement, fr. LL *dilatation-, dilatatio*, fr. L *dilatatus* (past part. of *dilatare* to dilate) + *-ion-, -io* -ion] **1** : amplification in writing or speech esp. by the addition of discussion, illustration, or detail **2 a** : the condition of being stretched beyond normal dimensions esp. as a result of overwork or disease ⟨~ of the heart⟩ or of abnormal relaxation ⟨~ of the stomach⟩ **b** : DILATION 2 **3** : the act of expanding or the state of being expanded : enlarging or spreading **4** : a dilated part or formation **5 a** : a change in volume of a rock body under confining pressure ⟨an increase in volume is positive ~ and a decrease is negative ~⟩ **b** : the strain produced by such pressure change — **dil·a·ta·tion·al** \ˌ=ˌ='shən°l, -shnəl\ *adj*

di·la·ta·tive \(')dī|lād·əd·iv, də'l-; 'dilə,tā-, 'dīlə-\ *adj* [L *dilatatus* + E *-ive*] : DILATIVE

dil·a·ta·tor \'dilə,tād·ə(r), 'dīl-\ *n* -s [prob. fr. F *dilatateur*, fr. *dilatater* to dilate + *-ateur* -ator (fr. OF *-atour*)] : ²DILATOR b

¹di·late \(')dī|lāt, də'l-, ÷ ¦dīə¦l-; *usu* -ād·+V\ *vb* -ED/-ING/-S [ME *dilaten*, fr. MF *dilater* to enlarge, comment at length, fr. L *dilatare* to enlarge, spread out, fr. *di-* (fr. *dis-* apart) + *-latare* (fr. *latus* wide) — more at DIS-, LATITUDE] *vt* **1** *archaic* : to describe or set forth lengthily or in detail ⟨~ at full what hath befallen of them and thee till now —Shak.⟩ **2** *obs* : to extend or diffuse through a wide space **3 a** : to enlarge or expand in bulk or extent ⟨matter is *dilated* by heat⟩ : WIDEN, EXTEND ⟨enrich and ~ our cultural heritage⟩ **b** : to widen or cause to be stretched (a contracted duct or part) ~ *vi* **1** : to comment at length : expand discussion : DISCOURSE — usu. used with *on* or *upon* ⟨he ~s on themes of love and death⟩ **2** : to expand or become wide : SWELL ⟨the pupil of the eye is able to ~ and contract⟩ **syn** SEE DISCOURSE, EXPAND

²dilate \"\ *adj* [ME *dilat*, fr. *dilaten*, v., after such pairs as ME *desolaten* to desolate: *desolat* desolate] : DILATED : EXPANDED

dilated *adj* [fr. past part. of ¹*dilate*] : expanded laterally : FLATTENED; *specif, of parts of insects* : having a broad expanded border — **di·lat·ed·ly** *adv* — **di·lat·ed·ness** *n* -ES

di·la·tion \dī'lāshən, də'-, ÷,dīə'l-\ *n* -s [¹*dilate* + *-ion*] **1** : the act of dilating or the state of being dilated : EXPANSION, DILATATION **2** : the action of stretching or enlarging an organ or part of the body ⟨~ of the cervix⟩ ⟨~ of the pupil by atropine⟩

di·la·tive \(')dī|lād·iv, də'l-, ÷¦dīə¦l-\ *adj* : causing dilation : tending to dilate ⟨the ~ factor is a disadvantage in acute glaucoma —*Americana Annual*⟩

dil·a·tom·e·ter \,dilə'tämәd·ər, ,dīl-\ *n* [ISV *dilate* + *-o-* + *-meter*] : an instrument for measuring thermal dilatation or expansion esp. in determining coefficients of expansion of liquids or solids — **dil·a·to·met·ric** \ˌdilәtə¦me·trik\ *adj* — **dil·a·to·met·ri·cal·ly** \-trə-k(ə)lē\ *adv* — **dil·a·tom·e·try** \,dilə'tämə·trē\ *n* -ES

dilatometer

¹dil·a·tor \'diləd·ə(r)\ *n* -s [ME *dilatour*, modif. of MF *dilatoire* delay, fr. OF, fr. *dilatoire*, adj., causing delay, fr. LL *dilatorius*] **1** *archaic* : a legal delay **2** *archaic* : DILATORY DEFENSE

²di·la·tor *also* **di·lat·er** \(')dī¦lād·ə(r), də'l-, -ātə-\ *n* -s [¹*dilate* + *-or* or *-er*] : one that dilates: as **a** : an instrument for expanding a tube, duct, or cavity ⟨a urethral ~⟩ **b** : a muscle that dilates a part **c** : a drug (as a vasodilator) causing dilation

dil·a·to·ri·ly \¦dilə¦tōrəlē, -tȯr-, -li\ *adv* : in a dilatory manner

dil·a·to·ri·ness \'dilə,tōrēnəs, -tȯr-, -rin-\ *n* -ES : the quality or state of being dilatory

dil·a·to·ry \'dilə,tōrē, -tȯr-, -ri, *chiefly dial* -,ter-\ *adj* [LL *dilatorius* causing delay, fr. L *dilatus* (suppletive past part. of *differre* to postpone, delay) (fr. *di-* — fr. *dis-* apart — + *latus* carried, suppletive past part. of *ferre* to carry) + *-orius* -ory — more at DIS-, TOLERATE] **1** : tending or having the intent to cause delay ⟨obstructive and ~ tactics⟩ **2** : characterized by procrastination or delay : TARDY : SLOW ⟨he is ~ in answering letters⟩ ⟨~ payment of bills⟩ **syn** SEE SLOW

dilatory defense *or* **dilatory plea** *n* : a defense or plea which is intended to defeat the pending action or proceeding without involving any decision on the merits of the case

dilatory motion *n* : a motion made for the purpose of evading or superseding a question before a legislative body

Di·lau·did \dī'lȯdəd, də'l-\ *trademark* — used for dihydromorphinone

dil·do \'dil(,)dō\ *n* -s [origin unknown] **1 a** : PHALLUS **b** *usu* **dil·doe** \"\ : an object serving as a penis substitute for vaginal insertion **2** *obs* — used as refrain syllables in a song **3** *obs* : a weak or effeminate man **4** : a cylindrical curl usu. of a wig or peruke **5** [prob. so called fr. its shape] : a West Indian spiny cactus (*Lemaireocereus hystrix*) with columnar joints and pink flowers

¹di·lem·ma \də'lemə *sometimes* dī'-\ *n* -s [LL, fr. LGk *dilēmmat-, dilēmma*, prob. back-formation fr. Gk *dilēmmatos* involving two assumptions, fr. *di-* + *-lēmmatos* (fr. *lēmmat-, lēmma* assumption) — more at LEMMA] **1** : an argument that offers an opponent a choice between two or more alternatives but that is equally conclusive against him no matter which alternative he chooses **2 a** : a choice or a situation involving choice between equally unsatisfactory alternatives ⟨the ~ was whether to lower prices or to accept fewer sales⟩ **b** : a difficult problem : a problem seemingly incapable of a satisfactory solution ⟨the modern ~; what to do to spend all this time —Peggy Bennett⟩ **3** : an argument that contains a premise consisting of the conjunctive affirmation of two hypothetical propositions and a disjunctive premise **syn** SEE PREDICAMENT

²dilemma \"\ *vt* -ED/-ING/-S *archaic* : to place in a dilemma

dil·em·mat·ic \¦dilə¦mad·ik *sometimes* ¦dīl-\ *also* **dil·em·mat·i·cal** \-d·əkəl\ *or* **dil·lem·mic** \də'lemik *sometimes* (')dī¦l-\ *adj* [*dilemmatic* fr. LGk *dilēmmat-, dilēmma* + E *-ic*; *dilemmatical* fr. LGk *dilēmmat-, dilēmma* + E *-ical*; *dilemmic* fr. *dilemma* + *-ic*] : of or containing a dilemma

dil·e·pid·i·dae \,dilə'pidə,dē\ *n pl, cap* [NL, fr. *Dilepid-, Dilepis*, type genus (fr. *di-* + *-lepis*) + *-idae*] : a family of cyclophyllidean tapeworms having a hooked rostellum and unarmed suckers and including a number of common parasites of birds and mammals

¹dil·et·tante \,dilə'täntē, -'tan-,-'taan-,-'tán-, -nti *sometimes* -lē'- *or* -n·,tä; ¦ˌ=ˌ=¦tänt, -¦tant, -¦taa(ə)nt, -¦tánt\ *also* **dil·et·tant** *three syllables*\ *or* **dil·le·tante** *like* DILETTANTE\ *n, pl* **dilet·tantes** \-ntēz, -ntiz, -n(t)s *sometimes* -n·,täz\ *or* **dilet·tan·ti** \-n(·,)tē,-nti\ *also* **dilet·tants** \-n(t)s\ *or* **dille·tantes** *like* DILETTANTES\ *or* **dille·tan·ti** \-n(·,)tē,-nti\ [It *dilettante*, fr. pres. part. of *dilettare* to delight, fr. L *delectare* — more at DELIGHT] **1 a** : an admirer or lover of the arts **b** : a person who has discrimination or taste esp. in aesthetic matters : CONNOISSEUR **2 a** : a person who cultivates an art or branch of knowledge as a pastime without pursuing it professionally **b** : a person who pursues an art or branch of knowledge sporadically, superficially, or frivolously

²dilettante \¦=ˌ=¦=(,)=, ¦=ˌ=¦=\ *adj* : of or characteristic of a dilettante : AMATEURISH

dil·et·tant·ish \¦=ˌ=¦t . . . ntish, -ntēsh\ *also* **dil·et·tan·te·ish** \¦=ˌ=¦t . . . ntēish, -nti·ish\ *adj* : of, characteristic of, or like a dilettante

dil·et·tant·ism \,=ˌ='t . . . n,tizəm\ *also* **dil·et·tan·te·ism** \-ntē,izəm, -nti,iz-\ *n* -s : the quality or procedure characteristic of dilettantes

dil·et·tant·ist \¦=ˌ=¦t . . . ntəst\ *adj* : DILETTANTISH

¹dil·i·gence \'diləjən(t)s\ *n* -s [MF, care, persevering application, haste, fr. L *diligentia* care, persevering application, fr. *diligent-, diligens* + *-ia* -y] **1 a** *obs* : caution or care **b** : persevering application : devoted and painstaking application to accomplish an undertaking : ASSIDUITY ⟨the proverbial ~ of the bee⟩ **c** *obs* : an act of labor or exertion **d** *obs* : speed or haste ⟨go hence with ~! —Shak.⟩ **e** *obs* : persistent effort to please **2 a** *Scot law* (1) : a process or warrant of the court to attach the person or property of a defendant to secure a judgment (2) : a process or warrant to enforce the appearance in court of a party or witness or to compel the production of a document (3) : the process of execution to enforce a judgment already entered **b** : the attention and care required of a person (as of a party to a contract) ⟨~ that may be required of a bailee⟩ — opposed to *negligence*

²dil·i·gence \¦dilə¦zhäⁿs, ¦dēl-, 'diləjən(t)s\ *n, pl* **dili·gences** \-äⁿs(əz),-ən(t)səz\ [F, lit., haste] : a large closed public horse-drawn carriage formerly used esp. for long journeys

dil·i·gen·cia \,dilə'jen(t)sēə, -nchə, *or as Sp*\ *n* -s [Sp, trans. of F *diligence*] : ²DILIGENCE

dil·i·gen·cy \'diləjənsē, -si\ *n* -ES [L *diligentia*] : ¹DILIGENCE

dil·i·gent \-nt\ *adj* [ME, fr. MF, fr. L *diligent-, diligens*, pres. part. of *diligere* to esteem highly, love, fr. *di-* (fr. *dis-* apart) + *-ligere* (fr. *legere* to choose, gather) — more at DIS-, LEGEND] **1** : characterized by steady, earnest, attentive, and energetic application and effort in a pursuit, vocation, or study : not lackadaisical ⟨a ~ investigator⟩ ⟨a ~ search⟩ **2** *archaic* : CAREFUL, OBSERVANT, HEEDFUL ⟨be you watchful, and let us be ~ —J.A.Froude⟩ **syn** SEE BUSY

dil·i·gent·ly *adv* [ME, fr. *diligent* + *-ly*] : in a diligent manner : CAREFULLY, ASSIDUOUSLY, INDUSTRIOUSLY

dil·i·gent·ness *n* -ES : DILIGENCE

¹dill \'dil\ *n* -s [ME *dile*, fr. OE; akin to OS *dilli* dill, OHG *tilli*, Dan *dild*] **1** : any of several plants of the family Umbelliferae; *esp* : a European herb (*Anethum graveolens*) with aromatic foliage and seeds both of which are used in flavoring pickles and other foods **2** : DILL PICKLE

²dill \"\ *vt* -ED/-ING/-S [ME *dillen*, prob. fr. *dul* dull, adj.] *dial Brit* : CALM, SOOTHE

dill apiole *n* : APIOLE 1b

dil·le·nia \də'lēnēə\ *n, cap* [NL, fr. Johann J. Dillen †1747 Ger. botanist in England + NL *-ia*] : a genus of East Indian trees and shrubs (family Dilleniaceae) having panicles of large showy white or yellow flowers with numerous stamens

dil·le·ni·a·ce·ae \də,lēnē'āsē,ē\ *n pl, cap* [NL, fr. *Dillenia*, type genus + *-aceae*] : a family of chiefly tropical shrubs, trees, and climbers (order Parietales) with leathery leaves sometimes replaced by phylloclades and cymose inflorescences — **dil·le·ni·a·ceous** \¦=ˌ=¦āshəs\ *adj*

dil·le·ni·ad \də'lēnē,ad\ *n* -s [NL *Dillenia* + E *-ad*] : a dilleniaceous plant

dilletante *var of* DILETTANTE

dil·ling \'dilən\ *n* -s [origin unknown] **1** *now dial Eng* : the youngest child of a family — often used as a term of endearment **2** *dial Eng* : the smallest and weakest pig of a litter

dil·lisk *or* **dil·lesk** \'diləsk\ *n* -s [IrGael *duileasg*] *Irish* : DULSE

dill oil *n* : either of two essential oils derived from the common dill: **a** *or* **dillseed oil** : a colorless or pale yellow oil having a sweetish acrid taste that is obtained from the dried ripe fruits of the dill and is used as an aromatic carminative and as a flavoring agent **b** *or* **dillweed oil** : a similar oil obtained from the whole dill plant and used as a flavoring agent

dill pickle *n* : a large pickle seasoned with fresh dill or dill juice

dillseed \'=ˌ=\ *n* : the seed of the dill plant used for flavoring pickles

dil·lue \də'lü\ *vt* -ED/-ING/-S [Corn *dyllo* to discharge, set free] *dial Eng* : to separate (tin ore) by washing in a hand sieve

dill water *n* : a distilled aqueous solution of the volatile constituents of dill — called also *gripe water*

dillweed \'=ˌ=\ *n* [¹*dill*] **1** : MAYWEED **1 2** : DILL

¹dil·ly \'dilē, -li\ *n* -ES [by shortening & alter.] **1** *obs* : ²DILIGENCE **2** *now dial Eng* : any of various horse-drawn vehicles (as a light wagon or cart) **3** : a haulage system on a short incline in a mine

²dilly \"\ *n* -ES [origin unknown] *dial Eng* : DUCK

³dilly \"\ *n* -ES [short for *daffadilly*] : DAFFODIL

⁴dilly \"\ *n* -ES [by shortening & alter.] **1** : SAPODILLA 1 **2** : a small tree (*Mimusops emarginata*) of Florida and the West Indies having hard dark brown wood susceptible of a fine polish and small edible fruits — called also *wild dilly, wild sapodilla*

⁵dilly \"\ *adj* [perh. blend of *dippy* and *silly*] *slang chiefly Austral* : SILLY, FOOLISH

⁶dilly \"\ *n* -ES [obs. slang *dilly*, adj., delightful, irreg. fr. E *del-* (fr. *delightful*) + *-y*] : one that is remarkably good or successful or strikingly different : something spectacular or extraordinary ⟨a ~ of a trial novel —Donald Gordon⟩ ⟨a ~ of a doll who, off screen, looks younger, is even prettier, and is just as witty —Helen Colton⟩ ⟨I have a long-standing and legitimate interest in middle names having been christened with a ~ myself —Alfred Gilliland Miller⟩ ⟨another joker was the Veterans of Future Wars — some guys in Princeton cooked that ~ up —Martin Dibner⟩ — not often in formal use

⁷dilly \"\ *vi* -ED/-ING/-ES [by shortening] : DILLYDALLY

dilly bag *n* [Australian *dhilla* hair] *Austral* : a mesh bag of native fibers used for carrying various articles and usu. having a drawstring

dil·ly·dal·li·er *pronunc at* DILLYDALLY +ə(r)\ *n* -s : one that dillydallies

dil·ly·dal·ly \¦dilē¦dalē, -ili¦dali\ *vi* -ED/-ING/-ES [redupl. of *dally*] : to act with unusual or improper slowness : waste time by loitering or delay ⟨for a month the governor had *dillydallied* over the choice of a successor⟩ **syn** SEE DELAY

dil·ly·man \'dilēmən, -lim-\ *also* **dilly boy** *n, pl* **dil·ly·men** [¹*dilly*] : a mineworker who starts and brakes the movement of cars on a dilly — called also *incline man*

di·lo \'dē(,)lō\ *n* -s [Fijian] : POON

dilse \'dils\ *Scot var of* DULSE

dilucidate *vt* -ED/-ING/-S [LL *dilucidatus*, past part. of *dilucidare*, fr. L *di-* (fr. *dis-* apart) + LL *lucidare* to make clear, fr. L *lucidus* clear, shining — more at DIS-, LUCID] *obs* : to make clear : ELUCIDATE — **dilucidation** *n* -s

di·lu·en·do \,dil(y)ə'wen(,)dō\ *adj* (*or adv*) [It, lit., diluting, fr. L *diluendum*, gerund of *diluere* to dilute] : dying away — used as a direction in music

¹dil·u·ent \'dilyəwənt\ *n* -s [L *diluent-, diluens*, pres. part. of *diluere* to wash away, dilute] : a diluting agent: as **a** : a volatile liquid (as toluene) used along with solvents in coating materials (as cellulose lacquers) esp. for reducing the cost — compare THINNER b **b** : an inert substance (as powdered talc) added to a mixture esp. for reducing the concentration of active ingredients (as in an insecticidal dust) — compare EXTENDER 1, FILLER 1a(1)

²diluent \"\ *adj* [L *diluent-, diluens*, pres. part. of *diluere*] : making thinner or less concentrated by admixture : DILUTING

di·lu·tant \dī¦lüt°nt, də¦ *also* ¦l¦yü-\ *n* -s : DILUENT

¹di·lute \(')dī¦lüt, də¦'l- *also* |l¦yü- *or* |l'yü-; *usu* -üd·+V\ *vb* -ED/-ING/-S [L *dilutus*, past part. of *diluere* to wash away, dilute, dissolve, partly fr. *di-* (fr. *dis-* apart) + *-luere* (fr. *lavere* to wash) and partly fr. *di-* (fr. *dis-* apart) + *luere* to atone for (akin to Gk *lyein* to unbind, release) — more at DIS-, LYE, LOSE] *vt* **1** : to make inferior or reduce (as in power or effect) ⟨the quality of the novel is *diluted* by the bad writing⟩ : make inferior (as in quantity or quality) : DEBASE ⟨~ the purity of a theory —H.W.Spiegel⟩ **2 a** (1) : to make thinner or more liquid by admixture (as with water) (2) : to make less concentrated : diminish the strength, activity, or flavor of (as by thinning or introducing an inert substance) ⟨~ wine⟩ ⟨~ combustible gases with carbon dioxide⟩ **b** : to change (something immaterial) by mixture with extraneous or foreign elements esp. with a resulting debasement ⟨Christianity . . . generously *diluted* with pagan beliefs —C.L.Jones⟩ ~ *vi* : to become diluted ⟨the iced coffee *diluted* rapidly⟩ **syn** SEE THIN

²dilute \"\ *adj* [L *dilutus*, past part. of *diluere*] **1** : deprived of its natural or proper force or quality : WEAK, ENFEEBLED ⟨a ~ form of democracy⟩ **2** : DILUTED, THIN : of relatively low strength or concentration — usu. contrasted with *concentrated* ⟨a ~ solution⟩ **3** : characterized genetically by reduced pigmentation — **di·lute·ly** *adv* — **di·lute·ness** *n* -ES

³di·lute \", 'dil,yü-\ *n* -s : an individual exhibiting reduced pigmentation

di·lut·ed \(')dī¦lüd·əd, də¦'l-, -ütəd *also* |l¦yü- *or* |l'yü-\ *adj* [fr. past part. of ¹*dilute*] : reduced in strength, concentration, quality, or purity ⟨~ alcohol⟩ : THIN, WEAK, ATTENUATED ⟨a ~, doubtful, questioning faith⟩ — **di·lut·ed·ly** *adv* — **di·lut·ed·ness** *n* -ES

dil·u·tee \¦dilyə¦tē; dī¦lü¦tē, ¦dī¦(,)lü-, də¦lü- *also* |l¦yü- *or* |l(,)yü-\ *n* -s : an unskilled worker performing a task previously a part or process of a skilled operation — compare DILUTION 2

di·lut·er *or* **di·lu·tor** *like* ¹DILUTE +ə(r)\ *n* -s : one that dilutes

di·lu·tion \dī¦lüshən, də¦ *also* |l'yü-\ *n* -s [¹*dilute* + *-ion*] **1 a** : the act of diluting or the state of being diluted ⟨the ~ of paint with thinner⟩ ⟨the sermon was a weak ~ of familiar ideas⟩ **b** : something that is diluted : a diluted substance ⟨lower ~s of serum showing no agglutination⟩ **2** : the breakdown of skilled jobs or operations into separate processes requiring little or no skill to perform **3** : the process of disposing of sewage by allowing it to mix with a large volume of water **4** : a reduction in value of a corporation's shares occurring when new shares are issued without the receipt of full consideration

di·lu·vial \də¦lüvēəl, (')dī¦lü-, -vyəl *also* |l'yü- *or* |l¦yü-\ *adj* [LL *diluvialis*, fr. L *diluvium* flood + *-alis* -al] **1 a** : of, concerning, or relating to a flood or deluge, esp. the deluge described in the Bible **b** : resembling a flood : FLOODING **2** : effected or produced by a flood or deluge of water : of or characterized by diluvium **3** *usu cap* : of or belonging to the epoch during which man has existed

di·lu·vial·ist \-ləst\ *n* -s : a believer in diluvianism

di·lu·vian \-ēən,-yən\ *adj* [L *diluvium* + E *-an*] : DILUVIAL

di·lu·vian·ism \-,nizəm\ *n* -s : a theory in geology: many geological phenomena can be explained by a former universal deluge

di·lu·vion \-vēən,-vyən\ *n* -s [LL *diluvion-, diluvio* flood, fr. L *diluere* to wash away + *-ion-, -io* -ion — more at DELUGE] : DILUVIUM

di·lu·vi·um \-vēəm\ *n, pl* **diluviums** \-vēəmz\ *also* **dilu·via** \-ēə\ [L, flood — more at DELUGE] **1** : DRIFT 2g **2** *archaic* : any geological deposit produced by a flood of more than ordinary power

¹dim \'dim\ *adj* **dimmer**; **dimmest** [ME, fr. OE; akin to OHG *timber* dark, ON *dimmr* dark, gloomy, MIr *dem* black, dark, Gk *themerōpis* grave-looking, Skt *dhamati* he blows] **1 a** : not bright : emitting a limited or insufficient amount of light ⟨the moon is ~ on a cloudy night⟩ **b** : of a dull or subdued shade or tint : lacking brightness or clarity ⟨the iris was of a peculiar soft or ~ and tender red —W.H.Hudson †1922⟩ **c** : lacking pronounced, clear-cut, or vigorous quality or character ⟨~ affairs with women in which he flirts in a scared way —Anthony West⟩ **d** *slang* : BORING, DULL ⟨a pretty ~ celebration⟩ **2 a** : seen indistinctly : without clear outlines or details : scarcely visible ⟨the ~ distances of his own Mississippi river country —Sherwood Anderson⟩ **b** : indistinctly or faintly perceived by the senses : of low volume or strength ⟨the ~ strumming of a guitar⟩ ⟨strawberry leaves sent up their sweet ~ smell —Edith Sitwell⟩ **c** : perceived by the mind indistinctly or with difficulty ⟨a ~ awareness of his environment⟩ : indistinctly known or remembered ⟨the ~ centuries of the later empire —Roger Fry⟩ : sensed or perceived weakly in an emotional or intuitional manner ⟨led . . . early man to a ~ feeling for symbolism —Edward Sapir⟩ : of a hazy or indefinite nature ⟨claimed some ~ relationship with Houdini —R.G.G. Price⟩ **d** : having little prospect of favorable result or outcome ⟨a ~ future⟩ : unlikely to be fulfilled or realized ⟨the ~ expectancy that he might return —Ann Ryan⟩ **e** : characterized by an unfavorable, skeptical, pessimistic, disapproving, or unenthusiastic attitude — usu. used in the phrase *take a dim view of* ⟨he takes a ~ view of human nature⟩ ⟨the villagers take a ~ view of people who try to impress them⟩ **3 a** : not perceiving clearly and distinctly with one of the senses (as sight) ⟨eyes grown ~ with age⟩ **b** : dull and weak in understanding or comprehension ⟨big and overdeveloped and ~ in her wits —Louis Bromfield⟩ **syn** see DARK

²dim \"\ *vb* **dimmed; dimmed; dimming; dims** [ME *dimmen*, fr. *dim*, adj.] *vt* **1** : to make dim ⟨~ the theater lights⟩ ⟨the years could not ~ his early love⟩ ⟨the incident *dimmed* the prospects for peace⟩ **2** : to reduce the light from (headlights) by switching to the low beam **~** *vi* : to become dim ⟨her fame and beauty *dimmed* rapidly⟩ ⟨the way the lights ~ in a farmhouse during a storm —John Cheever⟩ **syn** see OBSCURE

³dim \"\ *n* -s **1** *archaic* : DIMNESS, DUSK **2 a** : PARKING LIGHT ⟨put his lights on the ~ and pulled into the curb —Erle Stanley Gardner⟩ **b** : LOW BEAM

dim *abbr* **1** dimension **2** [L *dimidium*] half **3** diminished **4** diminuendo **5** diminutive

dim·ble \'dim(b)əl\ *n* -s [perh. alter. of *dingle*] *dial Eng* : a ravine with a watercourse : DINGLE

dime \'dīm\ *n* -s [ME, fr. MF *dime, disme*, fr. L *decima*, fr. fem. of *decimus* tenth (adj.), fr. *decem* ten — more at TEN] **1** *archaic* : a tenth or tithe **2 a** : a coin of the U.S. first issued in 1796 and worth $\frac{1}{10}$ dollar **b** : the sum of ten cents ⟨the price of admission was only a ~⟩ **c dimes** *pl, archaic* : money or financial gain ⟨no matter about her temper — has she got the ~*s* —Mary J. Holmes⟩ **d** : a petty sum of money ⟨they made hardly a ~⟩ ⟨they hadn't lost a ~ on the deal —Nelson Algren⟩ **3** : a Canadian ten-cent piece — **a dime a dozen** : plentiful or commonplace to the point of having little value ⟨heroes were *a dime a dozen* that day —*Infantry Jour.*⟩ — **on a dime** *adv* : in a very small area ⟨this car can turn *on a dime*⟩ : INSTANTLY ⟨stopped *on a dime*⟩

di·me·don \'dīmə,dän\ *or* **di·me·done** \-,dōn\ *n* -s [ISV *dime-* (fr. *dimethyl*) + *d-* (fr. *dihydr-*) + *-one*] : a crystalline diketone $C_8H_{12}O_2$ made by reaction of mesityl oxide and ethyl malonate and used in the analysis of aldehydes with which it forms insoluble derivatives; 5,5-dimethyl-1,3-cyclohexanedione

dime museum *n* : a collection of often lurid and sensational curiosities, monstrosities, and freaks exhibited for a low price of admission

di·men·hy·dri·nate \,dī,men'hīdrə,nāt\ *n* -s [*dime-* (fr. *dimethyl*) + *-n-* (fr. *amine*) + *-hydrin-* (fr. *diphenhydramine*) + *-ate*] : a crystalline compound $C_{17}H_{22}NO.C_7H_6ClN_4O_2$ made by reaction of diphenhydramine with 8-chloro-theophylline and used in the prevention or treatment of motion sickness and postoperative nausea

dime novel *n* **1** : an inexpensive paper-bound melodramatic novel of adventure popular in the U.S. from about 1860 to World War I — compare ³DREADFUL **2** : a cheap sensational and often lurid novel

¹di·men·sion \də'menchən *sometimes* dī'-\ *n* -s *often attrib* [ME *dimensioun*, fr. MF *dimension*, fr. L *dimension-, dimensio*, fr. *dimensus* (past part. of *dimetiri* to measure out, fr. *di-* — fr. *dis-* apart) + *metiri* to measure) + *-ion-, -io* -ion — more at DIS-, MEASURE] **1 a** : measure in a single line (as length, breadth, height, thickness, or circumference) : one of the three coordinates of position; *specif* : the physical characteristic of length, breadth, or thickness ⟨a line has one ~ (length), a plane has two ~*s* (length and breadth), and a cube has three ~*s* (length, breadth, and thickness)⟩ — usu. used in pl. **b** : the quality of spatial extension ⟨~ is a common trait of all matter⟩ : MAGNITUDE, SIZE ⟨the town's modest ~*s* and leisurely ways —Jane Shellhase⟩ **c (1)** : the range over which or the degree to which something extends : EXTENT, SCOPE, PROPORTIONS ⟨the vast ~*s* of the disaster⟩ ⟨music grown to the ~*s* of a great art⟩ — usu. used in pl. **(2)** : the quality, character, or moral or intellectual stature proper to or belonging to a person ⟨reduced to his own natural ~*s* —J.G.Lockhart⟩ — usu. used in pl. **(3)** *chiefly in literature and art* : lifelike or realistic quality ⟨a portrayal from which the character of Hamlet emerges bloodless, without ~⟩ : largeness of vision or thought ⟨reasoned convictions give his work a ~ lacking in the plays of lesser men⟩ **d (1)** : the particular set of circumstances or environmental factors within which someone or something exists or with reference to which something is viewed ⟨for a social novelist . . . time is the ~ in which his materials exist —Granville Hicks⟩ **(2)** : one of the elements or factors making up a complete personality or entity ⟨no other character in the book has more than one ~⟩ : one of the planes of organization or one of the aspects of a cultural phenomenon ⟨every human situation has environmental, organic, and social ~*s*⟩ ⟨preoccupation with geography at the expense of other ~*s* of dialectal diversity —Glenna R. Pickford⟩ : an independent variable or a combination of variables ⟨a psychological test measuring ~*s* of personality⟩ : QUALITY, ASPECT, TRAIT **2** *archaic* : the act or an instance of measuring : MEASUREMENT **3** *obs* : bodily form or proportions ⟨hath not a Jew hands, organs, ~*s*? —Shak.⟩ **4** : one of a set of coordinates containing the number of coordinates necessary and sufficient to distinguish any one of the elements of a magnitude or aggregate from all others : one of the three coordinates of momentum **5** : one of the fundamental units or powers thereof that enter into the makeup of a derived unit ⟨the gram, the square of the centimeter, and the −2 power of the second are the ~*s* of the erg⟩ **6** : wood or stone cut to pieces of specified size: as **a** : yard lumber usu. over two inches and under five inches thick and of any width **b** : hardwood in small squares of varying length and thickness for the use esp. of manufacturers of furniture **c** : blocks or slabs of natural stone used chiefly for the construction of masonry walls and memorials **syn** see SIZE

²dimension \"\ *vt* **dimensioned; dimensioned; dimensioning** \-ch(ə)niŋ\ **dimensions 1** : to make or form (as by cutting or planing) to the required dimensions ⟨the shaft is ~*ed* to fit any wheel⟩ **2** : to figure with dimensions and sometimes also with tolerances (as an architectural plan or a working drawing) : indicate the dimensions on (a drawing)

di·men·sion·al \-chən°l, -chnəl\ *adj* **1** : of or relating to dimension ⟨the ~ stability of properly set nylon fabrics precludes trouble due to shrinkage —H.R.Mauersberger⟩ **2 a** : having dimension ⟨never matures as a ~ character; he is pasty, bland, faceless —Norman Cousins⟩ **b** : having a specified number of dimensions

dimensional analysis *n* : a method of analysis in which physical quantities are expressed in terms of their fundamental dimensions that is often used when there is not enough information to set up precise equations

di·men·sion·al·i·ty \=,=chə'naləd-ē\ *n* -ES : the quality or state of having dimension : SIZE, MAGNITUDE ⟨~ is the common attribute of all matter⟩

di·men·sion·al·ly \='menchən°lē, -chnəlē, -li\ *adv* : with respect to dimension ⟨glass is a ~ stable material⟩

di·men·sioned \-chənd\ *adj* [¹*dimension* + *-ed*] : having dimension : having a specified number of dimensions ⟨three-*dimensioned*⟩

di·men·sion·less \-nləs\ *adj* : having no dimensions

di·men·sive \-n(t)siv\ *adj* [L *dimensus* (past part. of *dimetiri* to measure out) + E *-ive* — more at ¹DIMENSION] *archaic* : DIMENSIONAL

di·mer \'dīmə(r)\ *n* -s [ISV *di-* + *-mer*] : a compound formed by the union of two molecules of a simpler compound : a polymer formed from two molecules of a monomer ⟨diisobutylene is the ~ of isobutylene⟩

di·mer·cap·rol \,dī(,)mər'ka,prōl, -rōl\ *n* -s [irreg. fr. *di-mercapto-propanol*] : a colorless viscous oily compound $CH_2(SH)CH(SH)CH_2OH$ with an offensive odor developed as an antidote to lewisite but now used in treating poisoning by compounds of arsenic and heavy metals (as mercury and gold); 2,3-di-mercapto-1-propanol — called also *BAL, British anti-lewisite*

di·mer·ic \(')dī'merik\ *adj* [*dimerous* + *-ic*] **1** *biol* **a** : consisting of two parts : DIMEROUS ⟨a ~ chromosome⟩ **b** : involving or mediated by two factors ⟨~ inheritance⟩ ⟨a ~ character⟩ **2** [*dimer* + *-ic*] : of or relating to a dimer

di·me·ride \'dīmə,rīd, -rəd\ *n* -s [*dimer* + *-ide*] : DIMER

dim·er·ism \'dimə,rizəm\ *n* -s [ISV *dimerous* + *-ism*] : the quality or state of being dimerous

di·mer·i·za·tion \,dīmərə'zāshən\ *n* -s [ISV *dimer* + *-ization*] : the process of dimerizing or the state of being dimerized

di·mer·ize \'dīmə,rīz\ *vb* -ED/-ING/-S [back-formation fr. *dimerization*] : to polymerize to a dimer

dim·er·ous \'dimərəs\ *adj* [NL *dimerus*, fr. L *di-* + NL *-merus* -merous] : consisting of two parts: as **a** *of certain insects* : having the tarsi two-jointed **b** *of flowers* : having two members in each whorl

dimes *pl of* DIME

dime store *n* : FIVE-AND-TEN

dim·e·ter \'dimad-ə(r)\ *n* [LL *dimeter, dimetrus*, n., dimeter, *dimeter, dimetrus*, adj., being a dimeter, fr. Gk *dimetros* being a dimeter, fr. *di-* + *-metros* (fr. *metron* meter, measure) — more at MEASURE] : a line consisting of two metrical feet or of two dipodies

di·me·thoxy- \,dīmə'thäksē, -me¦-\ *comb form* [ISV *di-* + *methoxy-*] : containing two methoxy groups ⟨*dimethoxy*benzene $C_6H_4(OCH_3)_2$⟩

di·methyl \(')dī+\ *adj* [ISV *di-* + *methyl*] : containing two methyl groups in the molecule

dimethyl·acetylene \(,)dī,methəl+\ *n* [ISV *dimethyl* + *acetylene*] : BUTYNE b

di·meth·yl·amine \(,)dī,methələ'mēn, -thə'laman\ *n* [ISV *dimethyl* + *amine*] : an easily condensable gaseous compound $(CH_3)_2NH$ having a strong ammoniacal odor made by catalytic reaction of methanol with ammonia or methylamine and used chiefly in organic syntheses (as of vulcanization accelerators for rubber)

dimethylamino- *comb form* [ISV *dimethyl* + *amin-*] : containing the univalent group $(CH_3)_2N-$ derived from dimethylamine ⟨*p-dimethylamino*benzaldehyde⟩

di·meth·yl·aniline \(,)dī,methəl+\ *n* [ISV *dimethyl* + *aniline*] : a yellowish to brownish oily liquid compound $C_6H_5N(CH_3)_2$ made by methylating aniline and used chiefly as an intermediate (as in dye manufacture)

di·meth·yl·benzene \"+\ *n* [ISV *dimethyl* + *benzene*] : XYLENE 1

dimethyl ether *n* [ISV *dimethyl* + *ether*] **1** : METHYL ETHER 1 **2** : an ether containing two methoxy groups

di·meth·yl·formamide \(,)dī,methəl+\ *n* [*dimethyl* + *formamide*] : a liquid compound $HCON(CH_3)_2$ used esp. at elevated temperatures as solvent for certain polymeric materials in producing synthetic fibers

di·meth·yl·glyoxime \"+\ *n* [ISV *dimethyl* + *glyoxime*] : a crystalline compound $CH_3C(NOH)C(NOH)CH_3$ used as an analytical reagent esp. for precipitating nickel and palladium

dimethyl ketone *n* [ISV *dimethyl* + *ketone*] : ACETONE

di·meth·yl·ol·urea \dī¦methə,lōlyü'rēə, -lōl-\ *n* [*dimethyl* + *-ol* + *urea*] : a crystalline compound $CO(NHCH_2OH)_2$ formed as the first stage in making urea-formaldehyde resins and used chiefly in making adhesives and in treating textiles and wood

dimethyl phthalate *n* : a colorless liquid ester $C_6H_4(COOCH_3)_2$ used chiefly as a plasticizer and insect repellent

dimethyl sulfate *n* [ISV *dimethyl* + *sulfate*] : the methyl sulfate $(CH_3)_2SO_4$

di·meth·yl·tubocurarine \(,)dī,methəl+\ *n* : the dimethyl ether of tubocurarine used in the form of a salt (as the chloride $C_{40}H_{48}Cl_2N_2O_6$) as a skeletal muscle relaxant

dimetient *adj* [L *dimetient-, dimetiens*, pres. part. of *dimetiri* to measure out — more at DIMENSION] *obs* : DIAMETRAL

di·metric \(')dī+\ *adj* [*di-* + Gk *metron* measure + E *-ic*] : tetragonal or hexagonal — compare CRYSTAL SYSTEM

dimetric projection *n* : an axonometric projection in which only two faces are equally inclined to the plane of projection

di·met·ro·don \dī'me·trə,dän\ *n, cap* [NL, fr. *di-* + *metr-* (fr. Gk *metron* measure) + *-odon*] : a genus of No. American Lower Permian synapsid reptiles comprising terrestrial carnivores of moderate size distinguished by a curious crest or dorsal sail supported by greatly elongated neural spines of the vertebrae

dim·i·ca·tion \,dimə'kāshən\ *n* -s [L *dimication-, dimicatio*, fr. *dimicatus* (past part. of *dimicare* to fight, fr. *di-* — fr. *dis-* apart — + *micare* to flash) + *-ion-, -io* -ion; akin to W *dirmygu* to despise, Per *miža, muža* eyelash, Gk *omichlē* mist — more at DIS-, MIST] *archaic* : CONTEST, STRIFE

¹di·mid·i·ate \də'midē,āt\ *vt* -ED/-ING/-S [L *dimidiatus*, past part. of *dimidiare*, fr. *di-* (fr. *dis-* apart) + *-midiare* (fr. *medius* mid) — more at DIS-, MID] **1** *archaic* : to halve or reduce to the half **2** *heraldry* : to represent the half of : cut in two : HALVE

²di·mid·i·ate \-ēət\ *adj* [L *dimidiatus*, past part. of *dimidiare*] : divided into two equal parts : HALVED **2** *biol* : consisting of only one half of the normal : seeming to lack one half or to have one part smaller than the other ⟨~ elytra that cover only half the abdomen are common among certain families of beetles⟩

di·mid·i·a·tion \-,midē'āshən\ *n* -s [LL *dimidiation-, dimidiatio* action of halving, fr. L *dimidiatus* + *-ion-, -io* -ion] : a formation of marshaling by joining the dexter half of one heraldic shield with the sinister half of another divided per pale or sometimes per bend

di·min·ish \də'minish, -nēsh, *esp in pres part* -nəsh\ *vb* -ED/-ING/-ES [ME *deminishen*, alter. (influenced by ME *menusen, minishen* to lessen) of *diminuen*, fr. MF *diminuer*, fr. L *diminuere*, fr. *di-* (fr. *dis-* apart) + *minuere* to lessen — more at DIS-, MINISH, MINOR] *vt* **1** : to make less or cause to appear less : reduce in size, number, or degree ⟨losses and desertions sharply ~*ed* the forces at Washington's disposal⟩ ⟨a tiny figure, rather stooped and ~*ed* by constant ill health —May Sarton⟩ ⟨the passing years did not ~ their friendship⟩ **2** *obs* : to take away or subtract **3** : to lessen the authority, dignity, importance, or reputation of ⟨his society destroyed, his country defeated, his emperor ~*ed* —W.M.Hitzig⟩ : detract from : DISPARAGE, BELITTLE ⟨began to ~ the skill of the local skaters —S.H.Adams⟩ **4** *archit* : to cause to taper ⟨a ~*ed* column⟩ **~** *vi* **1** : to become less : DWINDLE ⟨his form . . . ~*ed* to a speck on the road —Thomas Hardy⟩ ⟨his interest in the subject had steadily ~*ed*⟩ **2** *archit* : TAPER ⟨a curious tower ~*ing* in five stages to an octagonal cupola⟩ **syn** see DECREASE

di·min·ish·able \-shəbəl\ *adj* : capable of being diminished

diminished *adj* [fr. past part. of *diminish*] **1** : made less or decreased **2** *of a musical interval* : made one half step less than perfect or minor ⟨a ~ fifth⟩

diminished arch *n* : an arch having less height than half its width (as a segmental or three-centered arch) — compare DROP ARCH

diminished seventh *n* **1** : a chord comprised of three superimposed minor thirds — see SEVENTH CHORD illustration **2** : an interval less by one half step than the minor seventh

diminished shaft *n* : the shaft of a tapering column

diminished triad *or* **diminished chord** *n* : a triad consisting of a minor third and diminished fifth — see TRIAD illustration

di·min·ish·ing·ly *adv* [*diminishing* (pres. part. of *diminish*) + *-ly*] : in a diminishing manner : DECREASINGLY ⟨the rain continued, but ~, all that night⟩

diminishing returns *n pl* : a rate of yield that at a certain point fails to increase in proportion to additional investments of labor or capital — see LAW OF DIMINISHING RETURNS

diminishing rule *n* : a template for contouring a shaft

diminishing stile *n* : a stile that is narrower in one part than in another (as in many glazed doors)

di·min·ish·ment \-shmənt\ *n* -s : DIMINUTION

¹di·min·u·en·do \də,min(y)ə'wen(,)dō\ *adv (or adj)* [It, lit., diminishing, fr. L *diminuendum*, gerund of *diminuere*] : with gradually diminishing volume or intensity : DECRESCENDO — used as a direction in music; abbr. *dim.* or *dimin.*

²diminuendo \"\ *n, pl* **diminuendos** *or* **diminuendoes** [It, fr. *diminuendo*, adj.] **1** : a gradual decrease in volume or intensity esp. of sound **2** : a musical passage, phrase, or note played with diminishing volume or force

diminute *adj* [ME *diminut*, fr. L *diminutus*, past part. of *diminuere*] *obs* : DIMINISHED, DIMINUTIVE — **diminutely** *adv, obs*

dim·i·nu·tion \,dimə'n(y)üshən, ÷ -myə'nish-\ *n* -s [ME *diminucioun*, fr. MF *diminution*, fr. L *diminution-, diminutio*, alter. (influenced by L *diminuere* to diminish) of *deminution-, deminutio*, fr. *deminutus* (past part. of *deminuere* to diminish, fr. *de* from, away + *minuere* to lessen) + *-ion-, -io* -ion — more at DE-, MINOR] **1** : the act, process, or an instance of diminishing : DECREASE ⟨experienced no ~ of his physical powers⟩ **2** *archaic* : a lowering in estimation : DEGRADATION, DEPRECIATION **3** : the reduction to smaller note values of the repetition of, imitation of, or answer to a musical subject or phrase — opposed to *augmentation* **4 a** : the defacing of part of a heraldic shield **b** : DIFFERENCE 5 **5** : omission or incompleteness in a record sent up by a lower court in proceedings for review **6** : the tapering or diminishing of a column or some other part of a building; *also* : the amount of such diminishing

di·min·u·ti·val \də¦minyə¦tīvəl\ *adj* [*diminutive*, n. + *-al*] : ²DIMINUTIVE 1

¹di·min·u·tive \də'minyəd-|iv, -yət|\ *n* -s [ME *diminutif*, fr. LL *diminutivum*, alter. (influenced by L *diminuere*) of *deminutivum*, fr. *deminutivus*, adj., fr. L *deminutus* + *-ivus* -ive] **1** : a diminutive word or affix ⟨*Jeanie* is a ~ of *Jean*⟩ **2** *heraldry* : any of several ordinaries corresponding in characteristic shape and position in the shield with other ordinaries which are greater in width ⟨the bendlet is a ~ of the bend, being one half its width⟩ **3** : a diminutive object or individual : a small variety or replica ⟨such water flies, ~*s* of nature —Shak.⟩

²diminutive \"\ *adj* [MF *diminutif*, fr. LL *diminutivus*, alter. (influenced by L *diminuere*) of *deminutivus*] **1** : indicating small size and sometimes the quality or condition of being loved, lovable, pitiable, or contemptible — used of affixes (as *-ette, -ie, -kin, -let, -ling, -y*) and of words formed with them (as *kitchenette, Jeanie, lambkin, streamlet, witling, sonny*); contrasted with *augmentative* **2** : small esp. in size : TINY ⟨all was on a ~ scale, like a doll's house⟩ ⟨~ in stature⟩ **3** *archaic* : diminishing or tending to diminish; *also* : DISPARAGING **syn** see SMALL

di·min·u·tive·ly \|əvlē, -li\ *adv* **1** : in a diminutive manner : in a way expressing diminution **2** : to a very small degree : by a very little

di·min·u·tive·ness \|ivnəs\ *n* -ES : extreme smallness or littleness

di·mis·sion \də'mishən, dī'-\ *n* -s [ME, conveyance by lease, fr. ML *dimission-, dimissio*, fr. L, dismissal, discharge, fr. *dimissus* (past part. of *dimittere* to dismiss) + *-ion-, -io* -ion] : dismissal or discharge ⟨a letter of ~⟩

dim·is·so·ri·al \¦dimə¦sōrēəl, -sȯr-\ *n* -s [NL *dimissorialis* dimissory and commendatory, fr. ML *dimissorius* dimissory and commendatory + L *-alis* -al] : a letter from a pope, bishop, abbot, or other high ecclesiastical official authorizing the ordination of the bearer — called also *dimissory letter*

dim·is·so·ry \'dimə,sōrē, -sȯr-, -ri *sometimes* də'misər- *or* dī'm-\ *adj* [ML *dimissorius* dimissory and commendatory, fr. LL, submitting a matter to a higher court, fr. L *dimissus* (past part. of *dimittere* to dismiss) + *-orius* -ory] : dismissing or granting leave to depart

dimissory letter *n* [trans. of ML *dimissoriae litterae*] **1** : a letter given by a bishop dismissing a clergyman to another diocese and recommending him for reception there **2** : DIMISSORIAL

¹di·mit \də'mit\ *vt* **dimitted; dimitted; dimitting; dimits** [ME *dimitten* to convey by lease, fr. ML *dimittere*, fr. L, to dismiss, renounce — more at DISMISS] : ¹DEMIT

²dimit *var of* DEMIT

dim·i·ty \'dimad-ē, -ətē, -i\ *n* -ES [alter. of ME *demyt*, prob. fr. MGk *dimitos* of double thread, fr. LGk, fr. Gk *di-* + *mitos* thread of the warp; perh. akin to Gk *mitra* headband — more at MITER] : a sheer cotton fabric of plain weave that is usu. checked or striped by corded effects which are made by weaving two or more threads as one and that is used for clothing and curtains and in a heavier weight for bedspreads

dim·ly *adv* [ME, fr. ¹*dim* + *-ly*] : in a dim manner : FAINTLY, INDISTINCTLY, UNCLEARLY ⟨foghorns sounding ~ in the distance⟩ ⟨crooked little side streets, ~ lit by gas lamps —John Durant⟩ : VAGUELY, HAZILY, OBSCURELY ⟨only ~ aware of the meaning of these large events⟩

dimmed *past of* DIM

dimmed·ness \'dimdnəs, -m(d)n-\ *n* -ES [*dimmed* (past part. of *dim*) + *-ness*] : the quality or state of being dimmed

¹dimmer *comparative of* DIM

²dim·mer \'dimə(r)\ *n* -s **1** : a device for causing an electric light to burn less brightly (as during a stage play); *esp* : a choke coil, rheostat, or transformer connected to the light **2 dimmers** *pl* **a** : PARKING LIGHTS **b** : headlights on low beam

dimmest *superlative of* DIM

dim·met *or* **dim·mit** \'dimət\ *n* -s [irreg. fr. ¹*dim*] *dial Eng* : TWILIGHT, DUSK

dimming *pres part of* DIM

dim·mish \'dimish\ *adj* : somewhat dim

dim·ness *n* -ES [ME *dimnesse* darkness, obscurity, fr. OE *dimnes*, fr. *dim* dim, dark + *-nes* -ness] **1** : the quality or state of being dim **2** : something that is dim

di·molecular \¦dī+\ *adj* : BIMOLECULAR

di mol·to \də'mōl(,)tō, dē'-\ *adv* [It] : very much — used as a direction in music

di·mo·ric \(')dī¦mōrik, -mȯr-, -mär-\ *adj* [*di-* + *mora* + *-ic*] : DISEMIC

di·morph \'dī,mȯrf\ *n* -s [prob. back-formation fr. *dimorphism, dimorphous*] : either of the two crystalline forms of a dimorphous substance ⟨calcite and aragonite are ~*s*⟩

¹di·mor·phic \(')dī¦mȯrfik\ *adj* [*dimorphous* + *-ic*] **1 a** : DIMORPHOUS 1 **b** : occurring in two distinct forms ⟨~ leaves of emergent plants⟩ ⟨a sexually ~ butterfly⟩ **2** : combining qualities of two kinds of individuals in one — used chiefly by breeders of fancy-colored canaries

²dimorphic \"\ *n* -s : a dimorphic individual

di·mor·phism \(')dī'mȯr,fizəm\ *n* -s [ISV *dimorph-* (fr. Gk *dimorphos*) + *-ism*] : the condition or property of being dimorphic or dimorphous: as **a** : difference (as of form, color, size) between two individuals or kinds of individuals that might be expected to be similar or identical ⟨the floating and submerged leaves of aquatic plants may exhibit considerable ~⟩ ⟨in certain marine invertebrates sexual ~ is so extreme that the male is reduced to a minute parasite in the kidney of the female⟩ — compare POLYMORPHISM **b** : crystallization in two different forms

di·mor·phite \-,fīt\ *n* -s [obs. E *dimorphine* dimorphite (fr. It *dimorfina*, fr. *dimorf-* — fr. Gk *dimorphos* — + *-ina* -ine) + E *-ite*] : a mineral As_4S_3 consisting of arsenic sulfide originally thought to be one of two dimorphous substances

di·mor·pho·the·ca \(,)dī,mȯrfə'thēkə\ *n* [NL, fr. *dimorpho-* (fr. Gk *dimorphos*) + *-theca*] **1** *cap* : a genus of southern African herbs or subshrubs (family Compositae) with terminal solitary white, purple, orange, or yellow flower heads similar to those of plants of the genus *Calendula* and with conspicuously toothed leaves **2** -s : any plant of the genus *Dimorphotheca* — called also *African daisy, cape marigold, star of the veldt*

di·mor·phous \(')dī¦mȯrfəs\ *adj* [Gk *dimorphos* having two forms, fr. *di-* + *-morphos* -morphous] **1** : crystallizing in two different forms **2** : DIMORPHIC 1b — **di·mor·phous·ly** *adv*

dim out *vt* : to darken (as a city) by imposition of a dimout

dimout \'=,=\ *n* -s [*dim out*] : a restriction limiting the use of lighting or the showing of lights at night esp. during the threat of an air raid; *also* : a condition of partial darkness produced by such restriction ⟨the continuing crisis gradually imposes a ~ on the sources and channels of public information —H.D. Lasswell⟩ — compare BLACKOUT

¹dim·ple \'dimpəl\ *n* -s [ME *dympull*; akin to OHG *tumphilo* whirlpool, OE *dyppan* to dip — more at DIP] **1** : a slight natural indentation or hollow in the surface of some part of the human body (as on a cheek or the chin) **2** : a depression or indentation on any surface ⟨the pool's dark surface breaks into ~s —William Wordsworth⟩; *specif* **:** such a depression in a building material (as for the recessing of nailheads) **3 :** a slight mound in a building material (as for the holding of metal lath away from the flat surface to which it is applied in plastering)

²**dimple** \"\ *vb* **dimpled; dimpled; dimpling** \-p(ə)liŋ\ **dimples** *vt* **1 :** to produce dimples in **:** mark with dimples ⟨large, heavy drops that *dimpled* the smooth stream —Marguerite Steen⟩ **2 :** to form a conical depression around (a rivet hole in sheet metal) in order to countersink the rivet head ~ *vi* **:** to exhibit or form dimples esp. in the cheeks in the act of smiling ⟨she *dimpled* up at them, shyly —Mary McCarthy⟩ **:** ripple or break into ripples ⟨a little stream that ran *dimpling* all the way⟩

dim·ply \-p(ə)lē, -li\ *adj, often* -ER/-EST [¹*dimple* + *-y*] **:** having dimples **:** DIMPLED ⟨her face grew ~ with joy⟩

dimps \'dim(p)s\ *n* -ES [irreg. fr. ¹*dim*] *dial Brit* **:** DUSK, TWILIGHT

¹**dimpsy** \-sē\ *n* -ES [*dimps* + *-y*, n. suffix] *dial Eng* **:** DUSK

²**dimpsy** \"\ *adj* [*dimps* + *-y*, adj. suffix] *dial Eng* **:** DIM, DARK

dims *pres 3d sing of* DIM, *pl of* DIM

dim–sighted \'=¦==\ *adj* **:** having dim sight **:** lacking perception — **dim–sight·ed·ness** *n* -ES

dimwit \'=,=\ *n* -S **:** a stupid or very undiscerning person **:** FOOL, BLOCKHEAD

dim–witted \'=¦==\ *adj* **:** having little or no discernment **:** not mentally bright **:** STUPID ⟨a *dim-witted* remark⟩ ⟨the poor *dim-witted* girl —Louis Bromfield⟩ — **dim–wit·ted·ly** *adv* — **dim–wit·ted·ness** *n* -ES

di·mya \dī'mīə\ [NL, fr. *di-* + *-mya*] *syn of* DIMYARIA

di·my·ar·ia \,dī,mī'a(a)rēə\ *n pl, cap* [NL, fr. *di-* + *-myaria*] *in some classifications* **:** a division of Lamellibranchia comprising the bivalve mollusks with both anterior and posterior adductor muscles, sometimes used synonymously with Isomyaria but commonly including also Heteromyaria — compare MONOMYARIA — **di·my·ar·i·an** \,dī,mī¦a(a)rēən\ *adj or n* — **di·my·ar·ic** \-ī¦arik\ *adj*

¹**din** \'din\ *n* -S [ME, fr. OE *dyne*; akin to OHG *tuni* din, ON *dynr*, Skt *dhvanati* it roars] **:** a loud noise; *esp* **:** a welter of confused or discordant sounds **:** CLAMOR, UPROAR ⟨a ~ of whistles, catcalls . . . and trumpets —Whitney Balliett⟩

syn DIN, UPROAR, PANDEMONIUM, HULLABALOO, BABEL, HUBBUB, and RACKET mean, in common, a disturbingly loud or confusing sound or mélange of sounds. DIN stresses an extreme, usu. painful and prolonged, extremely distracting loudness, sometimes, however, applying to a noise or mélange of noises which, though not necessarily painful, totally or almost totally occupies the consciousness ⟨it made a *din* like all the boiler factories in the world and all the backfiring motors in creation trying to drown each other's noise out —W.F.Jenkins⟩ ⟨the general had forbidden the tolling of funeral bells so that the incessant mournful *din* might not pound perpetually at our ears —Kenneth Roberts⟩ ⟨the air was full of the usual tropic *din:* mosquitoes humming, cicadas trilling, bullfrogs twanging like guitars—R.A.W.Hughes⟩ UPROAR and PANDEMONIUM both imply tumult or the wildest disorder, usu. among persons but often among animals or the elements. UPROAR usu. implies disordered shouting or the clamor of an arguing, fighting, or protesting crowd ⟨it is the tenants of this upper gallery who, for their shilling, make all the noise and *uproar* for which the English playhouses are so famous —Eugene Burr⟩ ⟨two thousand choristers from 70 choral societies . . . beefed, brayed, and bellowed . . . the only listeners to the enormous *uproar* were sundry critics —*Sydney (Australia) Bulletin*⟩ ⟨often throw the parliamentary debates into an *uproar* —Paul Blanshard⟩ PANDEMONIUM is stronger than UPROAR, stressing a complete disorder and implying the noisy boisterousness of a crowd breaking bounds and running riot ⟨by this time the mob had its blood up, and *pandemonium* broke loose —Bertrand Russell⟩ ⟨their temple for the next hundred years was a *pandemonium* of contending priests —*Times Lit. Supp.*⟩ ⟨the result of his inflammatory speech was *pandemonium* in the hall⟩ HULLABALOO, often interchangeable with DIN or UPROAR, seldom suggests earsplitting noise or turmoil, but suggests rather noise attendant upon great excitement, esp. that disturbing peace and quiet, often applying to a quick storm of protest, a torrent of sudden sensational gossip, or an outburst of noisy passion ⟨the current political *hullabaloo* —*New Republic*⟩ ⟨the building was planned for nine stories, but the residents of the St.-Germain quarter raised such a *hullabaloo* against its towering bulk that one story was left off —Janet Flanner⟩ ⟨the music stopped and the familiar *hullabaloo* was reestablished in the room —Jean Stafford⟩ BABEL signifies a confusion esp. of mixed languages or vocal qualities, usu. strongly stressing the total meaninglessness or purposelessness of the noise ⟨young and old, fat and thin, all laughed and shouted in a *babel* of tongues —Winifred Bambrick⟩ ⟨among the *babel* of contradictory claims —Ruth Benedict⟩ ⟨must we fall into the jabber and *babel* of discord while victory is still unattained? —Sir Winston Churchill⟩ HUBBUB suggests the noisy and incessant movement of a busy bustling market place, seldom implying painful or disturbing noise or turmoil ⟨the *hubbub* about national politics —Leon Halden⟩ ⟨listening far into the night to the *hubbub* of voices —Howard Troyer⟩ ⟨further *hubbub* in the Beverly Hills sector was occasioned when headlines featured a well-known literary figure's suicide gesture —Bennett Cerf⟩ RACKET stresses the psychological effects of a noise more than its character, implying annoyance or disturbance and applying to any noise that strikes one as excessive or inordinate ⟨he could hear the *racket* in the street — loud now, the cries, the honkings, the vendors, the rattle of carriage wheels over cobbles, the harsh clang of the extra streetcars —Barnaby Conrad⟩ ⟨the children had police whistles and cap pistols and made a terrible *racket* in the street⟩

²**din** \"\ *vb* **dinned; dinned; dinning; dins** *vt* **1 :** to assail or deafen with loud noise or outcry ⟨*dinned* his ears with shrill reproaches and complaints⟩ **2 :** to utter or sound with great insistence **:** impress by or as if by insistent repetition — often used with *into* ⟨*dinned* the official doctrines into their minds⟩ ~ *vi* **:** to make a loud noise **:** make a din **:** RESOUND ⟨a hundred horns *dinned* in protest as traffic ground to a stop⟩ ⟨the jukebox was *dinning* —Ralph Ellison⟩

din– *or* **dino–** *also* **dein–** *or* **deino–** *comb form* [NL, fr. Gk *dein-, deino-*, fr. *deinos* — more at DIRE] **:** terrible **:** mighty ⟨*Dein*odon⟩ ⟨*Deino*therium⟩ ⟨*Din*ornis⟩ ⟨*dino*saur⟩

din *abbr* dinar

di·nan·de·rie \də'nandərē, ,dē,nan'drē\ *n* -S [F, fr. MF, fr. *dinandier* coppersmith (fr. OF, fr. *Dinand* — now *Dinant* — town in Belgium + OF *-ier* -er) + *-ie* -y] **:** decorative objects of brass, copper, or bronze chiefly for ecclesiastical or domestic use such as were made in the 13th to 15th centuries

di·nan·tian \də'nanchən\ *adj, usu cap* [ISV *dinant-* (fr. *Dinant*, town in Belgium) + *-ian*] **:** of or relating to a division of the Carboniferous of Europe — see GEOLOGIC TIME table

dinaphth– *or* **dinaphtho–** *also* **dinaphtha–** *comb form* [ISV *di-* + *naphth-* or *naphtho-* or *naphtha-* (fr. *naphthalene*)] **:** containing two naphthalene nuclei ⟨*dinaphtha*zine⟩ ⟨*dinaphtho*thiophene⟩ — compare NAPHTH- 2

di·naphthyl \(')dī+\ *adj* [ISV *di-* + *naphthyl*] **:** containing two naphthyl groups in the molecule

di·nar *also* **de·nar** \də'när, dē'-, -nò(ə)r, 'dē,n-\ *n* -S [Ar *dīnār*, fr. Gk *dēnarion* denarius, modif. of L *denarius*] **1 :** a gold coin first struck in the late 7th century A.D. which was for several centuries the basic monetary unit in territories under Muslim control **2 a :** any one of several monetary units: as (1) **:** a subsidiary unit in Iran (2) **:** the basic unit in Algeria, Bahrain, Iraq, Jordan, Kuwait, Libya, Southern Yemen, Tunisia, and Yugoslavia — see MONEY table **b :** a coin or a note representing one dinar

di·nar·ic \də'narik\ *adj, usu cap* [L *dinaricus*] **:** of or belonging to the mountainous region in Yugoslavia lying east of the Adriatic

di·nas brick \'dēnəs-\ *n, usu cap D* [after *Craig-y-Dinas*, Wales] **:** a refractory silica brick made from an impure sandstone containing lime and clay and formerly used in furnace crowns

dinas clay *n, usu cap D* [after *Craig-y-Dinas*, crag near Neath river, South Wales, where it is found] **:** a disintegrated sandstone formerly used for making refractory brick

din·der \'dində(r)\ *n* -S [alter. of ³*denier*] **:** a small ancient coin found on the site of a Roman settlement in England — usu. used in pl.

¹**din·dle** \'din(d)ᵊl\ *vi* -ED/-ING/-S [ME *dindlen*, of imit. origin] *dial Brit* **:** VIBRATE

²**dindle** \"\ *n* -S *Scot* **:** VIBRATION, TREMOR

³**dindle** \"\ *n* -S [perh. alter. of *dandelion*] **1** *dial Eng* **:** SOW THISTLE **2** *dial Eng* **:** HAWKWEED **3** *dial Eng* **:** DANDELION 1

¹**dine** \'dīn\ *vb* -ED/-ING/-S [ME *dinen*, fr. OF *disner, diner* to dine, breakfast, fr. (assumed) VL *disjejunare* to break one's fast, fr. L *dis-* + LL *jejunare* to fast, fr. L *jejunus* fasting, hungry] *vi* **:** to eat a meal, esp. the principal meal of the day **:** take dinner — often used with *on* or *upon* ⟨*dined* elegantly on truffled goose livers⟩ or *off* ⟨*dining* off a hamburger . . . washed down with two cups of coffee —Hamilton Basso⟩ ~ *vt* **:** to give a dinner to **:** FEED ⟨often *dined* a dozen guests at his table⟩ **:** provide a feast for ⟨he was wined and *dined* at every stage of his triumphal tour⟩

²**dine** \"\ *n* -S [ME, fr. *dinen*, v.] **:** DINNER

³**di·né** \də'nā\ *n, pl* **diné** *or* **dinés** *usu cap* [Navaho, lit., people] **:** NAVAHO

dine out *vi* **:** to eat a meal away from home esp. in a restaurant

din·er \'dīnə(r)\ *n* -S **1 :** one that dines **2 a :** a railroad dining car **b :** a roadside short-order restaurant that has a long counter and usu. booths and that often resembles a dining car

din·er·gate \dī'nərgət\ *n* -S [*din-* + *-ergate*] **:** the soldier form of ants with polymorphic castes that is distinguished by a greatly enlarged head

di·ner·ic \(')dī¦nerik, də'n-\ *adj* [*di-* + LGk *nēron, nēros* water + E *-ic*; akin to Gk *naein* to flow — more at NOURISH] **:** of or relating to the interface between two mutually immiscible liquids (as oil and water) contained in the same vessel

di·nero \də'ne(,)rō\ *n* -S [Sp, fr. L *denarius* Roman silver coin originally equivalent to ten asses — more at ³DENIER] *slang* **:** MONEY ⟨Man! You should have that old gal's ~ —Martin Dibner⟩

di·nette \(')dī¦net, *usu* -ed·+V\ *n* -S [¹*dine* + *-ette*] **:** a small space usu. off a kitchen or pantry and often containing a built-in table and seats that is used for informal dining; *also* **:** a set of furniture consisting of a small-sized table and chairs suitable for use in such a space

di·neutron \(')dī+\ *n* [*di-* + *neutron*] **:** a neutral particle of twice the neutron's mass that is produced by collision of tritons and that is very unstable and quickly disintegrates into two neutrons

¹**ding** \'diŋ\ *vb* **dinged** \-ŋd\ *or dial* **dang** \'daŋ\ **dinged** *or dial* **dang**; **dinging; dings** [ME *dingen*, fr. (assumed) OE *dingan* (whence OE *dencgan* to beat); akin to OHG *tangal* hammer, OSw *diunga* to beat, OE *dynt* blow — more at DINT] *vt* **1** *dial* **:** BEAT, STRIKE, KNOCK **2** *dial* **:** to throw violently **:** DASH, FLING, DRIVE ⟨I have been trying to ~ you out of my head —Charles Gibbon⟩ **3** *dial* **:** to get the better of **:** SURPASS, OVERCOME ⟨we'll ~ the Campbells yet in their own town —R.L.Stevenson⟩ **4 :** DAMN 5 ⟨~ my buttons if she ain't more Southern than any of our own gals —A.W.Tourgee⟩ ~ *vi* **1** *obs* **:** to throw or fling oneself violently about **:** BOUNCE **2** *Scot, of rain* **:** to fall heavily — usu. used with *on*

²**ding** \"\ *n* -S *dial* **:** BLOW, STROKE ⟨he give me a ~ across the ear —H.E.Bates⟩

³**ding** \"\ *vb* -ED/-ING/-S [prob. imit.] *vt* **:** to talk, urge, or impress with tiresome repetition — often used in the phrase *to ding into the ears;* compare DIN 2 ~ *vi* **:** to make a ringing sound **:** CLANG ⟨the bell ~*ing* and the engine giving off quiet chuffs like a giant breathing —Helen Eustis⟩

⁴**ding** \"\ *n* -S **:** the sound of dinging — often used as part of a song refrain and often reduplicated ⟨when birds do sing, hey *ding a ding, ding* —Shak.⟩

din·gaan's day \'diŋ,gänz-\ *n, cap both Ds* [after *Dingaan fl*1838 Zulu chieftain defeated by the Afrikaners on Dec. 16, 1838] **:** DAY OF THE COVENANT

ding–a–ling *n* -S [imit.] **:** TING-A-LING

ding an sich \,diŋ(,)än'zik\ *n, pl* **dinge an sich** \,diŋə(-\ [G] **:** THING-IN-ITSELF

ding·bat \'diŋ,bat, *usu* -ad·+V\ *n* [origin unknown] **:** a typographical ornament (as a bullet or star) used typically to call attention to an opening sentence or to make a break between two paragraphs

¹**ding·dong** \'diŋ,dȯŋ, -,däŋ\ *n* [imit.] **1 :** the ringing sound produced by or as if by repeated strokes on a bell or some other metallic object — often used in oral imitation of such a sound ⟨hark! now I hear them, ~ bell —Shak.⟩ ⟨the bell goes ~⟩ **2 :** a bell or other metallic object (as a steel triangle) that makes a ringing sound ⟨every Monday mawnin', when the ~ sounds —*Midnight Special*⟩ **3 :** a verse or poem having a singsong monotonous character **:** JINGLE ⟨who would hold the order of the almanac so fast but for the ~, "thirty days hath September, etc." —R.W.Emerson⟩

²**dingdong** \'=¦=\ *adv* **:** with zeal **:** earnestly or heartily ⟨fell to work ~⟩

³**dingdong** \'=,=\ *vi* **1 :** to make a dingdong sound ⟨heard the whistle wail mournfully, heard the bell ~*ing* —A.W. Somerville⟩ **2 a :** to repeat an action with monotonous or mechanical regularity ⟨a good engineer . . . , but not adjusted to ~*ing* up and down the river at all —Richard Bissell⟩ **b :** to talk, urge, or scold tediously or insistently **:** DIN ⟨kept on ~*ing* in my ears —W.H.Hudson †1922⟩

⁴**dingdong** \'=,=\ *adj* **1 :** of, belonging to, or resembling the ringing sound made by a bell or other metallic object ⟨the ~ chime of cathedral bells⟩ **2 :** marked by a rapid exchange or alternation (as of blows) ⟨six weeks of ~ fighting with heavy tank and infantry losses —Arthur Davies⟩ — often used of a close contest or competition ⟨a ~ struggle in which both players were reaching great heights —*Sydney (Australia) Morning Herald*⟩

dingdong theory *n* **:** a theory that language originated out of a natural correspondence between objects of sense perception and the vocal noises which were a part of early men's reaction to them — compare BOWWOW THEORY, POOH-POOH THEORY

¹**dinge** \'dinj\ *n* -S [origin unknown] **:** a dent made by a blow **:** a surface depression **:** DINT ⟨the vertical frown had left an ineradicable ~ between her eyebrows —Gladys Schmitt⟩

²**dinge** \"\ *vt* **dinged; dinged; dingeing; dinges** *dial Brit* **:** to make a dinge or depression in **:** BATTER ⟨one of the gentlemen . . . held a *dinged* silk hat in his hand —James Joyce⟩

³**dinge** \"\ *vt* **dinged; dinged; dingeing; dinges** [back-formation fr. *dingy*, adj.] **:** to make dingy

⁴**dinge** \"\ *n* -S [back-formation fr. *dingy*, adj.] **:** DINGINESS ⟨the ~ and dust of these crumbling halls⟩ **:** DEPRESSION ⟨his mood threw a ~ even over the children —John Galsworthy⟩

⁵**dinge** \"\ *n* -S [back-formation fr. *dingy*, adj.] *slang* **:** NEGRO — usu. used disparagingly

¹**ding·er** \'diŋə(r)\ *n* -S [prob. fr. ¹*ding* + *-er*] *slang* **:** HUMDINGER

²**ding·er** \"\ *n* -S [prob. fr. ³*ding* + *-er*] *railroad slang* **:** a yardmaster or one who performs the duties of a yardmaster

ding·ey *like* DINGHY\ *archaic var of* DINGHY

dinghy \'diŋ|ē, 'diŋk|, 'diŋg|, |i\ *n* -ES [Bengali *ḍiṅgi* & Hindi *ḍiṅgī*, dim. of *ḍiṅgā* boat; perh. akin to Skt *droṇī* trough, tub — more at DHONI] **1 :** a rowboat or sailboat used to carry passengers or cargo on the coasts of India esp. in sheltered waters around the peninsula **2 :** any of various small boats propelled by oars, sails, or motors: as **a :** a man-of-war's or merchant ship's small boat **b :** a rowboat used as a tender and lifeboat in a yacht **c :** a sailboat or yacht used in racing **d :** an inflatable rubber life raft used by fliers forced to parachute into the sea

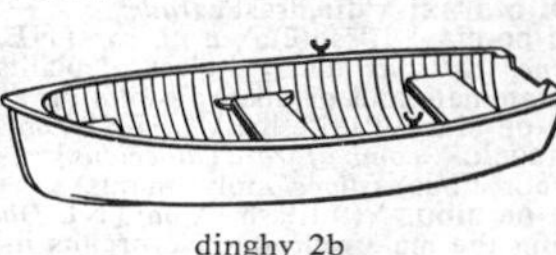
dinghy 2b

dingier *comparative of* DINGY

dingiest *superlative of* DINGY

din·gi·ly \'dinjəlē, -li\ *adv* **:** in a dingy manner

din·gi·ness \-jēnəs, -jin-\ *n* -ES **:** the condition of being dingy ⟨he was appalled by the ~ of the house⟩

dinging *pres part of* DING

dinging hammer *n* [*dinging* prob. fr. gerund of ¹*ding*] **:** BUMPING HAMMER

¹**din·gle** \'diŋgəl\ *n* -S [ME, abyss] **1 :** a narrow dale or dell **2 :** a small secluded well-wooded ravine or valley

²**dingle** \"\ *n* -S [origin unknown] **1** *North* **:** a storm door or protecting weather shed at the entrance of a camp or house **2** *North* **:** a roofed-over passageway between the cooking and sleeping areas of a logging camp often used as a storeroom

din·gle·ber·ry \'diŋgəl-— *see* BERRY\ *n* [*dingle-* (of unknown origin) + *berry*] **1 :** a shrub (*Vaccinium erythrocarpus*) of the southeastern U.S. **2 :** the globose dark red edible berry of the dingleberry

din·gle·bird \'diŋgəl,=\ *n* [*dingle-* (of imit. origin) + *bird*] *Austral* **:** BELLBIRD

dingle stick *n* [by alter.] **:** DANGLE STICK

ding·man \'diŋmən\ *n, pl* **dingmen** [prob. fr. ¹*ding* + *man*] **:** ⁴BUMPER 1d(1)

din·go \'diŋ(,)gō\ *n* -ES [native name in Australia] **:** a wild dog (*Canis dingo*) of Australia with a wolfish face, bushy tail, and usu. a reddish brown color supposed to have been introduced by man at a very early period

ding–on \'diŋ,än\ *n* [Sc *ding on*, v., to continue raining heavily, fr. ¹*ding* + *on*] *Scot* **:** a heavy rainstorm

dings *pres 3d sing of* DING, *pl of* DING

ding–toed \'diŋ¦tōd\ *adj* [*ding-* (of unknown origin) + *toed*] *NewEng* **:** PIGEON-TOED

din·gus \'diŋ(g)əs\ *n* -ES [D or G; D *dinges*, prob. fr. G *dings*, fr. gen. of *ding* thing, fr. OHG — more at THING] **1 :** something (as a gadget) whose common name is unknown or forgotten ⟨various slides and clips that replaced the tiepin of yesteryear are in turn being replaced . . . by a new sort of ~ adapted from army insignia —*New Yorker*⟩ ⟨the bell-shaped ~ on the end of an old electric-light cord —G.C.Furnas⟩ **2 :** PENIS — often considered vulgar

¹**dingy** *like* DINGHY\ *archaic var of* DINGHY

²**din·gy** \'dinjē, -ji\ *adj, usu* -ER/-EST [origin unknown] **:** DIRTY, SOILED, DISCOLORED ⟨~ white doors fastened with long iron bars —Rudyard Kipling⟩ ⟨shabby in attire, ~ of linen —W.M. Thackeray⟩ **:** dark, dull, or drab in color or appearance ⟨a nasty, ~ night⟩ **:** SHABBY, MEAN, SQUALID ⟨flashed from ~ obscurity into splendor —H.G.Wells⟩ ⟨the ~ loneliness of his life —*Punch*⟩ ⟨had no record of ~ conspiracy —T.E.M. McKitterick⟩ ⟨to make mean treaties and . . . accept the *dingiest* peace —Francis Hackett⟩

¹**din·ich·thy·id** \(')dī¦nikthēəd\ *adj* [NL *Dinichthys* + E *-id*] **:** of or relating to the genus *Dinichthys*

²**dinichthyid** \"\ *n* -S **:** a fish or fossil of the genus *Dinichthys*

din·ich·thys \dī'nikthəs\ *n, cap* [NL, fr. *din-* + *-ichthys*] **:** a genus of large Devonian fishes (subclass Arthrodira) known from both Europe and America and esp. abundant in parts of Ohio attaining a length of 30 feet and having the anterior bony armor reduced

dining *pres part of* DINE

dining alcove *n* [*dining* fr. gerund of ¹*dine*] **:** a recess usu. off a living room used as a dining area — compare DINETTE

dining car *n* **:** a railroad car which contains tables or counters and seats and usu. a kitchen and in which meals are served

dining hall *n* **1 :** a large dining room (as in a college) **2 :** a building containing a dining hall

dining room *n* **:** a room used for the taking of meals

dining table *n* **:** a table at which meals are taken

di·nitrate \(')dī+\ *n* **:** a chemical compound containing two nitrate groups

di·nitrile \(')dī+\ *n* [ISV *di-* + *nitrile*] **:** an organic chemical compound (as adiponitrile) containing two cyano groups

dinitro– *comb form* [ISV *di-* + *nitr-*] **:** containing two nitro groups

di·ni·tro·benzene \(,)dī,nī·trō+\ *n* [ISV *dinitro-* + *benzene*] **:** any of three isomeric toxic crystalline compounds $C_6H_4(NO_2)_2$ formed by nitration of benzene or nitrobenzene; *esp* **:** the yellow meta isomer used chiefly as a dye intermediate

di·ni·tro–or·tho–cresol \(,)dī,nī·trō,ȯrthō+\ *n* [ISV *dinitro-* + *orth-* + *cresol*] **:** a yellow crystalline compound $(NO_2)_2C_6H_2(CH_3)OH$ used esp. as an insecticide and herbicide; 4,6-dinitro-*o*-cresol — called also *DNOC*

di·ni·tro·phenol \(,)dī¦nī·trō+\ *n* [ISV *dinitro-* + *phenol*] **:** any of six isomeric crystalline compounds $(NO_2)_2C_6H_3OH$ formed by nitration of phenol or nitrophenols: as **a :** the yellowish isomer formed as an intermediate step in making picric acid and used chiefly as an intermediate (as for sulfur dyes and photographic developers) — called also *2,4-dinitrophenol* **b :** a yellow commercial mixture usu. of three of the isomers

di·ni·tro·toluene \"+\ *n* [ISV *dinitro-* + *toluene*] **:** any of six isomeric toxic crystalline compounds $CH_3C_6H_3(NO_2)_2$ formed by nitration of nitrotoluenes: as **a :** the yellow isomer obtained as the sole first product from *para*-nitrotoluene and used chiefly in making dyes and explosives — called also *2,4-dinitrotoluene* **b :** a commercial mixture of two or more of the isomers

¹**dink** \'diŋk\ *adj* [origin unknown] *Scot* **:** TRIM, NEAT — used esp. of dress

²**dink** \"\ *vt* -ED/-ING/-S *Scot* **:** to dress elegantly **:** ADORN

³**dink** \"\ *n* -S [by shortening & alter. fr. *dinghy*] **:** a small boat; *esp* **:** one used in duck shooting

⁴**dink** \"\ *vt* -ED/-ING/-S [origin unknown] **:** to cut out with a die — see DINKING DIE

⁵**dink** \"\ *n* -S [prob. back-formation fr. *dinky*] *slang* **:** a small round close-fitting skullcap with a button on top often traditionally worn by freshmen during their first term at school or college **:** BEANIE

⁶**dink** \"\ *vt* -ED/-ING/-S [prob. imit.] **:** to hit (a tennis ball) into an opponent's court close to the net with so little force that he cannot reach it before it bounces twice

⁷**dink** \"\ *n* -S **:** a drop shot in tennis which falls close to the net

⁸**dink** \"\ *n* -S [prob. alter. of *dick*] **:** PENIS — usu. considered vulgar

din·ka \'diŋkə\ *n, pl* **dinka** *or* **dinkas** *usu cap* [modif. of Dinka *jieng* people] **1 a :** a numerous and powerful Negro people of the Nile valley inhabiting the country to the south of Khartoum and noted for their herds of humped cattle, goats, and sheep **b :** a member of such people **2 :** the language of the Dinka people

dink·er \'diŋkə(r)\ *n* -S [⁴*dink* + *-er*] **:** one that cuts various shapes from cloth, leather, or other material by means of a dinking die

dink·ey *or* **dinky** \'diŋkē, -ki\ *n, pl* **dink·eys** *or* **dink·ies** [prob. fr. *dinky*] **:** a small locomotive used esp. for hauling freight, logging, and shunting

dinking die *n* [*dinking* fr. gerund of ⁴*dink*] **:** a cutting punch either hand or machine operated used without a matrix to cut out various shapes (as from leather, cloth, paper)

¹**din·kum** \'diŋkəm\ *adj* [prob. fr. E dial. *dinkum*, n., work] **1** *Austral* **:** AUTHENTIC, GENUINE **2** *Austral* **:** fair and square

²**dinkum** \"\ *adv, Austral* **:** TRULY, HONESTLY

dinkum oil *n, slang Austral* **:** the truth

dinky \'diŋkē, -ki\ *adj, usu* -ER/-EST [¹*dink* + *-y*] **1** *chiefly Brit* **:** NEAT, SMART, SPRUCE **:** CUTE, PRETTY ⟨exemplified ~ femininity, with stylish cut and gay colors —Sam Pollock⟩ **2 :** SMALL, INSIGNIFICANT ⟨the ~ little engine switched loaded cars —John Faulkner⟩

din·ky–di \¦diŋkē¦dī\ *adj* [alter. of *dinkum*] **1** *Austral* **:** LOYAL, TRUE **2** *Austral* **:** DINKUM

din·le *Scot var of* DINDLE

din·mont \'din,mänt\ *n* -S [ME *dynmont*] *Scot* **:** a wether between one and two years old or between the first and second shearing

din·na \'dinə\ [Sc *din-* (fr. *dae*) + *na*] *Scot* **:** do not

dinned *past of* DIN

din·ner \'dinə(r)\ *n* -S *often attrib* [ME *diner*, fr. OF *disner, diner*, fr. *disner, diner* to dine — more at ¹DINE] **1 :** the principal meal of the day eaten about midday or in the evening; *also* **:** a formal feast or banquet in honor of some person or event **2 :** TABLE D'HÔTE 2

dinner cloth *n* **:** a tablecloth esp. of fine fabric or lace for an elaborate or formal dinner

dinner clothes *n pl* **:** conventional attire for formal or semiformal dinners or social occasions — compare EVENING DRESS

dinner fork *n* **:** a large fork with 3 or 4 tines

dinner jacket *or* **dinner coat** *n* **1 :** TUXEDO 1a **2 :** a usu. light-colored shawl-collared jacket esp. for formal or semiformal summer or tropical wear worn with dark trousers and black tie

dinner jacket 2

dinner knife *n* **:** a large table knife usu. with a steel or silver blade and a handle of any of a number of materials
dinner pail *or* **dinner bucket** *n* **:** a pail in which a worker carries his lunch or dinner
dinner plate *n* **:** a large plate usu. 10 inches in diameter used for the main course of a meal
dinner ring *n* **:** a usu. large and elaborate woman's ring with one large stone or a cluster of stones worn for afternoon and evening occasions
dinner table *n* **:** DINING TABLE
dinnertime \ˈ==,=\ *n* **:** the time at which it is customary to eat dinner
dinner wagon *n* **:** a small wheeled table with shelves that is used for the service of a dining room — see TEA CART
dinnerware \ˈ==,=\ *n* **:** china, glassware, or tableware (as flatware and hollow ware) used in table service
dinning *pres part of* DIN
¹dino- — see DIN-
²dino- *comb form* [NL, fr. Gk *dinos* rotation, whirling, whirlpool; perh. akin to OIr *dían* rapid, Skt *dīyati* he soars] **1 :** whirling ⟨*Dino*bryon⟩ **2 :** whirlpool **:** eddy ⟨*Dino*capsales⟩ ⟨*Dino*philus⟩
di·nob·ry·on \dīˈnäbrēən, -ē,än\ *n, cap* [NL, fr. ²*dino-* + L *bryon* moss, fr. Gk — more at BRY-] **:** a genus of plantlike flagellates (order Chrysomonadina) having delicate cuplike tests and sometimes living water supplies
di·no·cap·sa·les \,dīnō,kapˈsā(,)lēz\ *n pl, cap* [NL, fr. ²*dino-* + L *capsa* box, case + NL *-ales* — more at CASE] **:** an order of yellow-green or greenish brown algae (class Dinophyceae) having a temporary naked motile stage but otherwise forming irregular colonies within a common envelope
di·no·cap·sin·e·ae \-pˈsinē,ē\ *n pl, cap* [NL, fr. ²*dino-* + L *capsa* + NL *-ineae*] *in some classifications* **:** a subclass of yellow-green algae equivalent to the order Dinocapsales
di·no·ce·pha·lia \-ōsəˈfālyə\ *syn of* DEINOCEPHALIA
di·noc·er·as \dīˈnäsərəs\ *n, cap* [NL, fr. *din-* + *-ceras*] *syn of* UINTATHERIUM
di·no·cer·a·ta \,dīnōˈserəd·ə\ *n pl, cap* [NL, fr. *Dinocerat-, Dinoceras*] **:** a small order of primitive ungulate mammals of the Paleocene and Eocene — compare UINTATHERIUM — **di·noc·er·ate** \(ˈ)dīˈnäsərət, dəˈn-\ *adj or n*
di·no·coc·ca·les \,dīnō(,)käˈkā(,)lēz\ *n pl, cap* [NL, fr. ²*dino-* + L *coccum* berry + NL *-ales* — more at COCC-] **:** an order of unicellular yellow-green algae (class Dinophyceae) lacking vegetative cell divisions and forming new cells by the production of motile or nonmotile spores similar to the parent cells
di·nod·er·us \dīˈnädərəs\ *n, cap* [NL, prob. fr. *din-* + Gk *deros* skin; akin to Gk *derma* skin — more at DERM-] **:** a genus of chiefly tropical small cylindrical beetles (family Bostrychidae) that have the dorsal surface covered with short dense erect hairs and that live as borers in woody plants (as bamboos)
di·no·flagellata \ˌdīnō+\ *n pl, cap* [NL, fr. *dino-* + *flagellum* + *-ata*] **:** an order of chiefly marine usu. solitary plantlike flagellates that are typically enclosed in a cellulose envelope which may be simple and smooth or variously sculptured and divided into plates, that have one transverse flagellum running in a groove about the body, one posterior flagellum extending out from a similar median groove, usu. a single nucleus, and yellow, brown, or occas. green chromoplasts, and that constitute a significant element in marine plankton, including certain brilliantly luminescent forms (as noctilucas), important elements of marine food chains (as many peridinians), and most of the flagellates that cause red tide (as members of the genus *Gymnodinium*) — see DINOPHYCEAE — **di·no·flagellate** \"+\ *adj or n*
di·no·flagellatae \"\ [NL, fr. *dino-* + *flagellum* + *-atae* (fr. L, fem. pl. of *-atus* -ate)] *syn of* DINOFLAGELLATA
di·no·fla·gel·li·da \,dīnōfləˈjeləda\ [NL, fr. *dino-* + *flagellum* + *-ida*] *syn of* DINOFLAGELLATA
di·no·hy·us _ōˈhīəs\ *n, cap* [NL, fr. *din-* + *-hyus* (fr. Gk *hys* hog, swine) — more at SOW (female hog)] **:** a genus of extinct giant pigs (family Entelodontidae) of the Lower Miocene of Nebraska some of which exceed the modern bison in size
¹di·no·my·id \ˌdīnōˌmīəd\ *adj* [NL *Dinomys* + E *-id*] **:** of or relating to the genus *Dinomys* or family Dinomyidae
²dinomyid \"\ *n* -S **:** a dinomyid rodent
di·no·mys \ˈdīnō,mis\ *n, cap* [NL, fr. *din-* + *-mys*] **:** a genus of Peruvian hystericomorph rodents (the type of the family Dinomyidae) resembling the pacas
di·no·phil·ea \,dīnōˈfilēə\ *n pl, cap* [NL, fr. *Dinophilus*, genus coextensive with the group Dinophilea, prob. fr. *dino-* + *-philus*] **:** a small group of minute vermiform invertebrate animals inhabiting salt water or brackish water, constituting a single genus, and being considered of uncertain systematic position or included as a class in Trochelminthes
di·no·phy·ce·ae \-ˈfisē,ē, -fis-\ *n pl, cap* [NL, fr. *dino-* + *-phyceae*] **:** a class of the division Pyrrophyta coextensive with the order Dinoflagellata
di·no·phys·i·da·les \-,fizəˈdā(,)lēz\ *n pl, cap* [NL, prob. irreg. fr. *Dinophysis*, genus belonging to the order Dinophysidales (fr. *dino-* + Gk *physis* nature) + *-ales* — more at PHYSIC] **:** an order of algae (class Dinophyceae) having the cell wall made up of a definite number of plates arranged in a fixed pattern and vertically divided into two similar halves or valves — compare DESMOKONTAE
di·no·pi·the·cus \-,pəˈthēkəs, -ˈpithəkəs\ *n, cap* [NL, fr. *din-* + *-pithecus*] **:** a genus of extinct Pleistocene African baboons that were nearly the size of gorillas
di·nor·nis \dīˈnȯrnəs\ *n, cap* [NL, fr. *din-* + *-ornis*] **:** the type genus of Dinornithidae comprising the largest of the moas
di·nor·ni·thid \(ˈ)dīˈnȯrnəthəd\ *or* **di·nor·nith·ic** \ˌ==ˈnithik\ *adj* [*dinornithid* fr. NL *Dinornithidae*; *dinornithic* fr. NL *Dinornith-, Dinornis* + E *-ic*] **:** of or relating to the Dinornithidae
di·nor·nith·i·dae \,dī,nȯrˈnithə,dē\ *n pl, cap* [NL, fr. *Dinornith-, Dinornis*, type genus + *-idae*] **:** a family of extinct ratite birds that are related to the emus and cassowaries though usu. placed in a distinct order — see DINORNIS, MOA
di·no·saur \ˈdīnə,sō(ə)r, -ō(ə)\ *n* -S [NL *Dinosauria*] **1 :** one

restored skeleton of a dinosaur

of the Dinosauria **2 :** any of various large extinct reptiles
di·no·sau·ria \,dīnəˈsȯrēə\ *n pl, cap* [NL, fr. *din-* + *-sauria*] **:** a group of extinct reptiles widely distributed from the Triassic to the Mesozoic initially differing little from the generalized long-tailed quadrupedal common ancestors of modern birds and crocodilians but later becoming specialized for chiefly terrestrial carnivorous or herbivorous modes of life into distinct bipedal and quadrupedal types, the latter including the largest known land animals — compare BRONTOSAURUS, DIPLODOCUS, ORNITHISCHIA, SAURISCHIA, THECODONTIA
¹di·no·sau·ri·an \-ēən\ *n* -S [NL *Dinosauria* + E *-an*] **:** DINOSAUR
²dinosaurian \ˌ==ˈ===\ *adj* [NL *Dinosauria* + E *-an*] **:** of, relating to, or like the Dinosauria
di·no·sau·ric \,dīnəˈsȯrik\ *adj* [*dinosaur* + *-ic*] **:** of the size or nature of a dinosaur **:** HUGE, ENORMOUS
di·no·there \ˈdīnə,thi(ə)r\ *n* -S [NL *Dinotherium*] **:** one of the Deinotherioidea — compare DEINOTHERIUM
di·no·the·ri·um \,dīnəˈthirēəm\ *syn of* DEINOTHERIUM
di·no·tri·cha·les \,dīnōtrəˈkā(,)lēz\ *n pl, cap* [NL, fr. *Dinotrich-, Dinothrix*, genus belonging to the order Dinotrichales (fr. *dino-* + *-thrix*) + *-ales*] **:** an order of yellow-green algae (class Dinophyceae) that are immobile and form a branching system of nearly cylindrical cells
dins *pl of* DIN, *pres 3d sing of* DIN

din·some \ˈdin(t)səm\ *adj* [ˈ*din* + *-some*] *chiefly Scot* **:** NOISY
DIN system \ˌdē,īˈen-\ *n* [*DIN* fr. G, abbr. of *Deutsche Industrie-Normen* (lit., German industry standards), standards for industrial products established by the Deutscher Normenausschuss, a German organization for the establishment and registration of standards in all branches of industry] **:** a system for determining the speed of photographic materials in terms of the logarithm of the reciprocal of the exposure required to obtain a density of 0.1 above fog density
¹dint \ˈdint\ *n* -S [ME, fr. OE *dynt*; akin to ON *dyttr* blow, *detta* to fall, Alb *gdhent* I chop wood] **1** *archaic* **:** BLOW, STROKE ⟨sharp-smitten with the ~ of armed heels —Alfred Tennyson⟩ **:** a clap of thunder **2 :** FORCE, POWER ⟨the ~ of pity —Shak.⟩ — now used chiefly in the phrase *by dint of* ⟨by ~ of patience and hard work . . . he gained the top of the mountain —S.E.White⟩ **3 :** a mark left by a blow or pressure **:** DENT, NOTCH ⟨produced a deep ~ in the car fender⟩ **:** a small hollow or indentation **:** IMPRESSION, IMPRINT ⟨does not make any deep ~ in their minds —Walter Moberly⟩ **4** *dial Brit* **:** a jarring blow **:** ATTACK **5** *Scot* **:** a momentary chance
²dint \"\ *vt* -ED/-ING/-S [ME *dinten*, fr. ¹*dint*] **1** *obs* **:** STRIKE, BEAT **2 :** to make a mark or cavity on or in by a blow or by pressure ⟨a financial nut not even a sledge hammer would ~ —J.H.Gray⟩ **3 :** to impress or drive in with force ⟨~*ed* the pointed nails into his own finger tips —Clemence Dane⟩ **:** IMPRINT
di·nucleotide \(ˈ)dī+\ *n* [ISV *di-* + *nucleotide*] **:** a nucleotide consisting of two mononucleotides in combination
di nuo·vo \dēn ˈwō(,)vō, ,dēnəˈw-\ *adv* [It] **:** ANEW — used as a direction in music
¹di·oc·e·san \(ˈ)dīˈäsəsən *also* -əzən *sometimes* dəˈä- *or* dēˈä-\ *adj* [ME, fr. ML *diocesanus*, alter. of LL *dioecesanus*, fr. *dioecesis* + L *-anus* -an] **1 a :** belonging to a diocese and subject to the bishop of the diocese ⟨priests are divided into two categories, ~ and religious —P.H.Furfey⟩ **b :** restricted or devoted to a diocese ⟨he has never been able to be contentedly ~ or even insular —*Times Lit. Supp.*⟩ ⟨a book authorized for ~ use⟩ **c :** formed of dioceses ⟨advocating a ~ system⟩ **d :** being the seat of the bishop of a diocese ⟨a ~ city⟩ **2 a :** governing a diocese ⟨powers possessed by virtue of his position as ~ bishop⟩ **b :** entrusted with ecclesiastical enactments or discipline, administrative business, or missions of a diocese ⟨canons enacted at a ~ convention⟩ ⟨the bishop convokes a ~ synod⟩ **3 :** maintained by or serving a diocese ⟨attended ~ schools⟩ ⟨~ visitor to religious communities⟩
²diocesan \"\ *n* -S [ME, fr. ML *diocesanus*, fr. *diocesanus*, adj.] **1 :** a bishop having jurisdiction over a diocese **2** *archaic* **:** one of the clergy or the people of a diocese ⟨humble ~*s* of the old bishop⟩
diocesan conference *n* **:** a body in the Anglican communion that consists of all the clergy of a diocese and of elected representatives of the laity and that under the presidency of the bishop transacts certain diocesan business — called also *diocesan convention*
diocesan court *n* **:** CONSISTORY 6
diocesan curate *n* **1 :** a clergyman of the Church of Ireland at the disposal of the bishop to give help in emergencies to parish clergy **2 :** an assistant priest to a pastor appointed by the bishop of a diocese
di·o·cese \ˈdīəsəs *also* -ī,sēz *or* -ī,sēs *sometimes* -ī,sis\ *n, pl* **dio·ces·es** \-ī,səsəz, -ī,sēzəz, -ī,sēsəz, ÷ -ī,sēsəz *sometimes* -ī,sisəz *or* ÷ dīˈäsəsəz\ [ME *diocise*, fr. MF *diocese*, *diocise*, fr. LL *diocesis*, alter. of *dioecesis*, fr. L, administrative division of a country, fr. Gk *dioikēsis* administrative division of a country, administration, fr. *dioikein* to keep house, administer, govern (fr. *dia* through + *oikein* to have one's dwelling place, keep house, fr. *oikos* house) + *-sis* — more at DIA-, VICINITY] **1 a :** the circuit or extent of a bishop's jurisdiction **:** the district in which a bishop has ecclesiastical authority — compare EPARCHY **b :** sphere of authority **2 :** an administrative division of a country; *esp* **:** a division of a prefecture of the Roman Empire
diocesian *obs var of* DIOCESAN
diocess *obs var of* DIOCESE
di·o·coel \ˈdīə,sēl\ *n* -S [prob. alter. of *diacoele*] **:** the cavity of the developing diencephalon that later gives rise to the third ventricle of the brain
di·octahedral \(ˈ)dī+\ *adj* [*di-* + *octahedral*] **1 :** having 16 faces; *esp* **:** octahedral with tetrahedral summits **2 :** having two of the three available octahedrally coordinated positions occupied ⟨a ~ mica⟩
di·oc·to·phy·ma \(,)dī,äktəˈfīmə\ [NL, fr. *diocto-* (irreg. fr. Gk *dionkoun* to distend) + *-phyma* (fr. Gk *phyma* tumor)] *syn of* DIOCTOPHYME
di·oc·to·phy·ma·ti·na \-,fīməˈtīnə\ *n pl, cap* [NL, fr. *Dioctophymat-, Dioctophyma* + *-ina*] **:** a suborder of Enoplida (being sometimes considered a separate order and including solely the kidney parasite (*Dioctophyme renale*) distinguished from related nematodes by the absence of both setae and buccal stylet — compare DORYLAIMINA, ENOPLINA
di·oc·to·phy·me \-ˈfī(,)mē\ *n, cap* [NL, fr. *diocto-* (irreg. fr. Gk *dionkoun* to distend, fr. *dia-* + *onkoun* to raise, distend, fr. *onkos* bulk, mass) + *-phyme* (fr. Gk *phyma* tumor, fr. Gk *phyein* to bring forth, grow); akin to Gk *enenkein* to carry — more at ENOUGH, BE] **:** a genus (coextensive with a family Dioctophymidae) of nematode worms including a single form (*D. renale*) which is a destructive parasite of the kidney of dogs, other mammals, and occas. man — see DIOCTOPHYMATINA
di·octyl \(ˈ)dī+\ *adj* [ISV *di-* + *octyl*] **:** containing two octyl groups in the molecule
dioctyl phthalate *n* **:** an oily liquid ester $C_6H_4(COOC_8H_{17})_2$ used chiefly as a plasticizer; bis-(2-ethyl-hexyl) phthalate
di·ode \ˈdī,ōd\ *n* -S [ISV *di-* + *-ode*] **1 :** an electron tube having two electrodes, a cathode and an anode **2 :** an electrical rectifier that consists of a semiconducting crystal (as of germanium or silicon) with two terminals and that is analogous in use to an electron tube diode — called also *crystal diode*
di·o·dia \dīˈōdēə\ *n, cap* [NL, fr. Gk *diodos* thoroughfare (fr. *dia-* + *hodos* way) + NL *-ia*; fr. the frequent growth of these plants by the wayside — more at CEDE] **:** a genus of mostly American weedy herbs of the family Rubiaceae with opposite leaves and small tubular solitary axillary flowers — see BUTTONWEED 1
di·odon \ˈdīə,dän\ *n, cap* [NL, fr. *di-* + *-odon*] **:** the type genus of Diodontidae comprising the typical porcupine fishes — **di·odont** \-,dänt\ *adj or n*
di·o·done \-,dōn\ *n* -S [irreg. fr. *diiod-* + *pyridone*] **:** IODOPYRACET
di·odon·ti·dae \,==ˈdäntə,dē\ *n pl, cap* [NL, fr. *Diodont-, Diodon*, type genus + *-idae*] **:** a family of blocky to nearly spherical plectognath fishes that live in warm shallow seas and have the body covered with spines and the teeth fused into a cutting plate in each jaw —see PORCUPINE FISH
Di·o·do·quin \dīˈōdəkwən\ *trademark* — used for diiodohydroxyquinoline
di·o·do·re·an \ˌdīəˌdōrēən, -dȯr-\ *adj, usu cap* [*Diodorus* Cronus, 4th cent. B.C. Greek philosopher (Megarian school) + E *-ean*] **:** of or relating to the Megarian philosopher Diodorus Cronus or his contributions to modal logic
Di·o·drast \ˈdīə,drast\ *trademark* — used for iodopyracet
di·oe·cia \dīˈēsh(ē)ə\ *n pl, cap* [NL, fr. *di-* + *-oecia*] *in former classifications* **:** a class of plants including those having staminate and pistillate flowers on different individuals
di·oe·cian \(ˈ)dīˈēshən\ *adj* [NL *Dioecia* + E *-an*] **:** DIOECIOUS
dioecio- *comb form* [*dioecious*] **:** dioeciously ⟨*dioecio*dimorphous⟩ ⟨*dioecio*polygamous⟩
di·oe·cious \(ˈ)dīˈēshəs\ *adj* [NL *Dioecia* + E *-ous*] **1 :** having the male reproductive organs in one individual and the female in another — compare DICLINOUS **2** *of a seed plant* **:** having staminate and pistillate flowers borne on different individuals — **di·oe·cious·ly** *adv*
di·oe·cism \dīˈē,sizəm\ *n* -S [ISV *dioec-* (fr. NL *Dioecia*) + *-ism*] **:** the condition of being dioecious
di·oe·cy \ˈdī,ēsē\ *n* -ES [ISV *dioec-* (fr. NL *Dioecia*) + *-y*] **:** DIOECISM
dioestrous *or* **dioestrual** *var of* DIESTROUS
dioestrus *or* **dioestrum** *var of* DIESTRUS
di·og·e·ne·an \(ˌ)dīˌäjəˈnēən\ *or* **di·o·gen·ic** \ˌdīəˈjenik\ *adj, usu cap* [*Diogenes* †323 B.C. Greek philosopher + E *-ean* or *-ic*] **:** characteristic of, attributed to, or associated with the philosopher Diogenes
di·og·e·nes crab \dīˈäjə(,)nēz-\ *n, usu cap D* [so called fr. its habit of living in an empty shell as Diogenes is reputed to have lived in a tub] **:** a terrestrial hermit crab (*Cenobita diogenes*) abundant in the West Indies and destructive to crops
di·og·e·nite \-,nīt\ *n* -S [G *diogenit*, fr. Gk *diogenēs* born of or descended from Zeus (fr. *Di-, Zeus* Zeus, god of the sky + *-genēs* born) + G *-it* -ite — more at DEITY, -GEN] **:** an achondritic meteorite composed essentially of orthopyroxene
-di·o·ic \ˌdīˈōik, -ōek\ *adj suffix* [ISV *di-* + *-oic*] **:** containing two carboxyl groups in place of two methyl groups ⟨hexane*dioic* acid $HOOC(CH_2)_4COOH$⟩
di·oi·cous \(ˈ)dīˈȯikəs\ *adj* [NL *dioicus*, fr. *di-* + *-oicus* (fr. Gk *oikos* house) — more at VICINITY] **:** having archegonia and antheridia on separate plants — compare DIOECIOUS, HETEROICOUS, MONOICOUS, PAROICOUS, SYNOICOUS
di·ol \ˈdī,ōl, -ōl\ *n* -S [ISV *-diol*] **:** a chemical compound (as a glycol) containing two hydroxyl groups
-di·ol \"\ *n suffix* -S [ISV *di-* + *-ol* (alcohol)] **:** chemical compound containing two hydroxyl groups ⟨1,5-pentane*diol*⟩
di·olefin *also* **di·olefine** \(ˈ)dī+\ *n* -S [ISV *di-* + *olefin*] **:** any of a series of aliphatic hydrocarbons C_nH_{2n-2} (as allene, butadiene, isoprene) containing two double bonds — called also *alkadiene, diene* — **di·olefinic** \(ˌ)dī+\ *adj*
di·o·ma·te \,dēəˈmäd·ē\ *n* -S [AmerSp] **:** GATEADO
di·o·me·dea \,dīəˈmēdēə\ *n, cap* [NL, prob. fr. L, fem. of *diomedeus* of Diomedes, fr. *Diomedes* (fr. Gk *Diomēdēs*), mythical or legendary Greek warrior; prob. fr. the story that Diomedes' companions were turned into birds in Italy after his return from the Trojan War] **:** a genus of albatrosses
di·o·me·de·idae \,dīəməˈdīə,dē, -ˈmēdē-\ *n pl, cap* [NL, fr. *Diomedea*, type genus + *-idae*] **:** a family of large sea birds (order Procellariiformes) comprising the albatrosses
-di·one \ˈdī,ōn\ *n suffix* -S [ISV *di-* + *-one*] **:** chemical compound containing two carbonyl groups — in names of diketones or di-oxo compounds that are not true diketones ⟨butane*dione*⟩ ⟨2,6-piperidine-*dione*⟩
di·o·nin \ˈdīənən\ *or* **di·o·nine** \-,nēn, -,nən\ *n* -S [G *dionin*, a former trademark] **:** ethylmorphine or its hydrochloride
dionise *n* -S [ME *diones*, fr. MF *dionise*, fr. L *dionysias*, fr. Gk, of Dionysus, fr. *Dionysos* Dionysus] *obs* **:** a precious stone dark with red streaks reputed when dissolved in water to prevent drunkenness
di·o·ny·sia \,dīəˈnizh(ē)ə, -nish(ē)ə, -nisēə\ *n pl, usu cap* [L, fr. Gk, fr. neut. pl. of *dionysios* of Dionysus, fr. *Dionysos* Dionysus, god of an orgiastic religion and of wine] **:** any of the Greek religious festivals held in honor of Dionysus esp. in Attica: as **a :** the lesser festival which was held in the autumn and from which the Greek drama is said to have originated **b :** the great festival which was held in the spring and at which plays were regularly given from the time of Pisistratus — compare BACCHANALIA 1
di·o·nys·i·ac \ˌdīəˌniˌsē,ak *also* -nī| *or* |zē-\ *also* **di·o·ny·si·a·cal** \-,nəˈsīəkəl, -,nī;-; ,dīəˈniˌsē,akəl, -nī|, |zē-\ *or* **di·o·ny·sic** \ˌdīəˈnisik, -nis-\ *adj* [*dionysiac* fr. LL *dionysiacus*, fr. Gk *dionysiakos*, fr. *Dionysia*; *dionysiacal* fr. LL *dionysiacus* + E *-al*; *dionysic* fr. L *Dionysus* (fr. Gk *Dionysos*) + E *-ic*] **1** *usu cap* **:** relating to the Greek mythical god Dionysus or the Dionysia ⟨in the cruder of Dionysiac mysteries the devotees drank of the fruit of the vine —K.S.Latourette⟩ **2** *often cap* **:** DIONYSIAN 2b ⟨the ~ rapture, . . . gives place to Apolline serenity —Hunter Mead⟩ ⟨the ~ character of hot jazz —R.L. Shayon⟩ — **di·o·ny·si·a·cal·ly** \ˌdīəˌniˈsīək(ə)lē, -,nī;-; ,dīəˈniˌsē,akəlē, -nī|, |zē-\ *adv, often cap*
di·o·nys·i·an *in sense 1* ˌdīəˈnisēən, *in sense 2* -nizhən *or* -nishən *or* -nīsēən\ *adj* [in sense 1, fr. *Dionysius* (personal name) + E *-an*; in sense 2, fr. L *Dionysia* + E *-an*] **1** *usu cap* **a** [*Dionysius* the Elder †367 B.C. Greek tyrant and his son *Dionysius* the Younger *fl* 345 B.C. Greek tyrant] **:** of or relating to the elder or the younger Dionysius ⟨*Dionysian* cruelty⟩ **b** [*Dionysius* Exiguus, 6th cent. Roman monk and scholar born in Scythia who introduced the method of reckoning the Christian era from the supposed date of the birth of Christ] **:** of or relating to Dionysius Exiguus ⟨the ~ period of 532 years after which the moon's changes recur on the same days of the week and month⟩ **c** [*Dionysius* the Areopagite *fl* A.D. 500 Greek author of *The Celestial Hierarchy* and other Neoplatonic Christian works that greatly influenced medieval thought] **:** of or relating to Dionysius the Areopagite **2 a** *usu cap* **:** devoted to the worship of the god Dionysus or connected with the Dionysia **:** DIONYSIAC 1 ⟨the Eleusinian, the *Dionysian*, and the Orphic rites were the most important mystery religions of Greece —G.E.Mylonas⟩ ⟨the most radical departure from the rationalistic interpretation of life and history is to be found in the *Dionysian* religious tradition —Reinhold Niebuhr⟩ **b** *usu cap* [trans. of G *dionysisch*] **:** of a character symbolized by the god Dionysus or the cult of his myth and worship: (1) **:** of a sensuous, frenzied, orgiastic, or Bacchic character **:** unbounded, lawless, or irrational in nature — contrasted with *Apollonian* ⟨Nietzsche had used the terms *Dionysian* and Apollonian to separate the creative-passionate from the critical-rational —J.M.Barzun⟩ ⟨the *Dionysian* experience, our ecstatic participation in the divine life —Sheldon Cheney⟩ (2) **:** pregnant with strength **:** creatively striving **:** PASSIONATE **:** FAUSTIAN ⟨the unleashed fury of *Dionysian* dynamics, —C.H.Cardinal⟩
di·o·ön \dīˈō,än\ *n, cap* [NL, fr. *di-* + *-oön* (fr. Gk *ōion* egg) — more at EGG] **:** a genus of plants (family Cycadaceae) having a somewhat conical trunk crowned by a large tuft of pinnate leaves with spine-tipped pinnae
di·o·phan·tine \ˌdīəˌfantˈn, -an,tīn\ *adj, usu cap* [*Diophantus*, 3d cent. A.D. Greek mathematician of Alexandria + E *-ine*] **:** of or relating to Diophantus
diophantine equation *n, usu cap D* **:** a polynomial equation for which the unknowns are to be rational numbers
di·op·side \dīˈäp,sīd, -,səd\ *n* -S [F, irreg. fr. *di-* + Gk *opsis* appearance, sight — more at OPTIC] **:** a pyroxene $CaMgSi_2O_6$ that contains calcium and magnesium but little or no aluminum, that varies in color from white to green, and that when transparent is sometimes used in jewelry — **di·op·sid·ic** \ˌdī,äpˈsidik\ *adj*
di·op·sis \dīˈäpsəs\ *n, cap* [NL, fr. *di-* + *-opsis*] **:** a genus of two-winged flies (group Acalyptrata) of the Old World tropics having the head produced into long lateral club-shaped projections bearing the antennae and eyes
di·op·tase \dīˈäp,tās, -āz\ *n* -S [F, prob. fr. LGk *dioptos* transparent (fr. Gk *dia-* + *optos* visible, fr. *opsesthai* to be going to see) + F *-ase* (as in *euclase*) — more at OPTIC] **:** a mineral $CuSiO_2(OH)_2$ consisting of hydrous copper silicate and occurring in emerald-green crystals and massive (hardness 5, sp. gr. 3.47)
di·op·ter \dīˈäptər, ˈdī,ä-\ *n* -S [MF & L; MF *dioptre*, fr. L *dioptra*, fr. Gk, fr. *dia-* + *-optra* (akin to *opsesthai* to be going to see)] **1** *obs* **:** an optical instrument invented by Hipparchus for taking altitudes and leveling **2** *archaic* **:** a stand or disk revolving about a vertical axis and carrying a lens or prism, leveling sights, or the index arm of a circle according to the kind of instrument to which it was applied **:** ALIDADE **3** *also* **di·op·tre** \"\ **:** a unit of measurement of the refractive power of a lens equal to the reciprocal of the focal length in meters **4 :** an instrument used in craniometry for making projections of the skull
di·op·tom·e·ter \,dī,äpˈtämәd·ә(r)\ *n* -S [*dia-* + *opto-* + *-meter*] **:** an instrument used in measuring the accommodation and refraction of the eye — **di·op·tom·e·try** \-mə·trē\ *n* -ES
di·op·tral \(ˈ)dīˈäptrəl\ *adj* [L *dioptra* + E *-al*] **:** relating to a diopter or to the focal power in diopters
di·op·trate \dīˈäp,trāt, -,trət\ *adj* [*dia-* + *optr-* (irreg. fr. Gk *opsesthai* to be going to see) + *-ate*] **:** divided by a transverse line or septum — used of the compound eyes of certain insects (as water beetles) and of ocelli on the wings of certain moths and butterflies
dioptre *var of* DIOPTER
¹di·op·tric \(ˈ)dīˈäptrik\ *also* **di·op·tri·cal** \-rәkәl\ *adj* [*dioptric* fr. Gk *dioptrikos* of an optical instrument used for taking altitudes, fr. *dioptra* + *-ikos* -ic; *dioptrical* fr. Gk *dioptrikos* + E *-al*] **1 a :** that effects or serves in refraction of a beam of light **:** REFRACTIVE; *specif* **:** that assists vision by refracting

and focalizing light ⟨a ~ apparatus formed of ~ prisms⟩ ⟨the ~ mechanism of an insect's eye⟩ ⟨the ~ power of a lens⟩ **b :** produced by means of refraction ⟨the ~ images of objects in space that are formed on the retinas of the two eyes —Otto Glasser⟩ **2** *archaic* **:** TRANSPARENT ⟨discrepancy between the ~ certainty of the understanding and the immediate insight of the conscience —James Martineau⟩ — **di·op·tri·cal·ly** \-rək(ə)lē\ *adv*

²dioptric \"\ *n* -s **:** DIOPTER 1, 3

di·op·trics \dī'äptriks\ *n pl but sing in constr* [trans. of Gk *dioptrika*, neut. pl. of *dioptrikos*] *archaic* **:** a branch of optics dealing with the refraction of light esp. by lenses

di·op·try \'dī,äptrē\ *n* -ES [ISV *dioptr-* (fr. *diopter*) + *-y*] **:** focal power expressed in diopters

di·o·rama \,dīə'ramə, -rämə, -râmə\ *n* -s [F, fr. *dia-* + *-orama* (as in *panorama*, fr. E)] **1 a :** a scenic representation in which a partly translucent painting is seen from a distance through an opening, the light shining through the painting being varied to achieve varying effects (as of changes in weather) **b :** a building used for an exhibition of such representations **2 a :** a scenic representation (as of a theatrical stage) in which sculptured figures and lifelike details are displayed usu. in miniature so as to blend indistinguishably with a realistic painted background **b** *chiefly Brit* **:** an imagined succession of brilliant scenes or episodes imperceptibly merging one into another like a pageant in miniature ⟨the style of Macaulay . . . is a ~ of political pictures —Walter Bagehot⟩ **3 a :** a scale model usu. under glass exhibiting with precise detail some phenomenon of nature or the layout of some engineering project ⟨a ~ indicating how a dam and powerhouse will look on completion⟩ **b :** a life-size exhibit of a wildlife specimen or scene mounted in the midst of realistically reproduced natural surroundings merging into a painted background ⟨recessed ~s of Colorado wildlife —Catherine L. Barker⟩ **c :** a miniature set used in television to represent a location that cannot be constructed in its actual size in the studio

di·o·ram·ic \,dīə'ramik\ *adj* **:** peculiar to or suggesting a diorama

di·ordinal \(')dī+\ *adj* [*di-* + *ordinal*] **:** of or relating to two orders

dioristic *adj* [Gk *dioristikos* capable of distinguishing, fr. *diorizein* to distinguish, delimit, fr. *dia-* + *horizein* to separate, bound, define — more at HORIZON] *obs* **:** serving to distinguish

di·o·rite \'dīə,rīt\ *n* -s [F, irreg. fr. Gk *diorizein* to distinguish + F *-ite*] **:** a granular crystalline igneous rock commonly of acid plagioclase and hornblende, pyroxene, or biotite — **di·o·rit·ic** \,dīə'ridik\ *adj*

di·or·tho·sis \,dī,ȯr'thōsəs\ *n, pl* **diortho·ses** \-ō,sēz\ [NL, fr. Gk *diorthōsis* correction, making straight, fr. *diorthoun* to correct, make straight, fr. *dia-* + *orthoun* to set straight, set upright, fr. *orthos* straight — more at ORTH-] *archaic* **:** a correcting or revision esp. of a text

di·or·thot·ic \,dī ȯr'thäd·ik\ *adj* [Gk *diorthōtikos*, fr. *diorthoun*] *archaic* **:** CORRECTIVE

di·os·co·rea \,dīə'skōrēə\ *n* [NL, irreg. fr. Pedanius *Dioscorides*, 1st cent. A.D. Greek physician] **1** *cap* **:** a genus of mostly tropical twining herbs (family Dioscoreaceae) including the yams and having net-veined leaves and small dioecious flowers **2** -s **:** the dried rhizome of a wild yam (*Dioscorea paniculata*) formerly used in hepatic disorders and rheumatism

di·os·co·re·a·ce·ae \,dīə,skōrē'āsē,ē\ *n pl, cap* [NL, fr. *Dioscorea*, type genus + *-aceae*] **:** a family of twining herbs and shrubs (order Liliales) comprising the yams and related plants — see TAMUS

di·os·cu·ric \,dīə'skyùrik\ *adj* [Gk *Dioskouroi* sons of Zeus, namely the twin heroes or demigods of Greek mythology known in Latin as Castor and Pollux and in Greek as Castor and Polydeuces, sons of Zeus and Leda (fr. *Dios*, gen. of *Zeus* Zeus, god of the sky + *kouroi*, pl. of *kouros*, *koros* boy, son) + E *-ic;* akin to L *crescere* to grow — more at DEITY, CRESCENT] **:** like Castor and Pollux of classical mythology **:** TWIN

di·ose \'dī,ōs *also* -ōz\ *n* -s [*di-* + *-ose*] **:** any of a class of monosaccharides containing two carbon atoms, glycolaldehyde being the only member — called also *biose*

di·os·gen·in \,dī,äz'jenən, dī'äzjən-\ *n* -s [*dios-* (fr. NL *Dioscorea*) + *-genin*] **:** a crystalline steroid sapogenin $C_{27}H_{42}O_3$ obtained chiefly in Mexico from locally available yams and used as a starting material for the synthesis of steroid hormones (as cortisone)

di·os·ma \dī'äzmə\ *n* [NL, irreg. fr. Gk *dios* heavenly + NL *-osma* — more at DEITY] **1** *cap* **:** a small genus of southern African heathlike shrubs of the family Rutaceae with fragrant foliage and small white or pinkish flowers **2** -s **:** any plant of the genus *Diosma* **3** -s **:** BUCHU

di·os·phenol \,dī,äs+\ *n* -s [ISV *dios-* (fr. *diosma*) + *phenol;* prob. orig. formed in G] **:** a crystalline hydroxy terpenoid ketone $C_{10}H_{16}O_2$ obtained from the essential oil of buchu — called also *buchu camphor*

di·os·py·ros \,dīə'spīrəs\ *n, cap* [NL, fr. L, a plant, prob. gromwell, fr. Gk, fr. *Dios* (gen. of *Zeus*) + *pyros* wheat — more at FURZE] **:** a genus of trees and shrubs (family Ebenaceae) found throughout the warmer parts of the world that have beautiful and valuable wood, leaves alternate and leathery, and fruit a 1- to 10-seeded berry — see EBONY, PERSIMMON

di·otic \(')dī+\ *adj* [*di-* + *-otic*] **:** affecting or relating to the two ears **:** BINAURAL

di·oto·car·dia \(,)dī,ōd·ə'kärdēə\ [NL, fr. *di-* + *oto-* (fr. Gk *ōt-*, *ous* ear, auricle of the heart) + *-cardia* — more at EAR] *syn of* ASPIDOBRANCHIA

di·ovular \(')dī+\ *adj* [*di-* + *ovular*] **:** BIOVULAR

di·ox·ane \dī'äk,sān *also* **di·ox·an** \-,san, -sən\ *n* -s [ISV *di-* + *ox-* + *-ane*] **:** a flammable irritating water-soluble liquid cyclic diether $C_4H_8O_2$ obtainable from ethylene glycol and used as a solvent and dispersing agent — called also *para-dioxane, 1,4-dioxane*

di·ox·ide \dī'äk,sīd, -,səd\ *n* [ISV *di-* + *oxide*] **:** an oxide containing two atoms of oxygen in the molecule — usu. distinguished from *peroxide* ⟨carbon ~⟩ ⟨manganese ~⟩

di·ox·o·lane \dī'äksə,lān\ *n* -s [*dioxol* chemical compound having the formula $C_3H_4O_2$ (ISV *di-* + *ox-* + *-ol*) + *-ane*] **1 :** a water-soluble liquid cyclic acetal $C_3H_6O_2$ made usu. from formaldehyde and ethylene glycol that is capable of polymerizing to poly-acetal resins having essentially the open-chain structure $(-OCH_2OCH_2CH_2-)_x$ — called also *1,3-dioxolane* **2 :** a derivative of dioxolane made usu. by reaction of an aldehyde or ketone with formaldehyde, many such derivatives being capable of polymerizing to useful products (as supports for photographic emulsions)

dioxy- *comb form* [ISV *di-* + *oxy-*] **:** containing two oxy groups

¹dip \'dip\ *vb* **dipped** *also archaic* **dipt; dipped** *also archaic* **dipt; dipping; dips** [ME *dippen*, fr. OE *dyppan;* akin to LG *düppen* to wash, OHG *tupfen* to wash, OIr *domain* deep, Lith *dubus* deep, hollow] *vt* **1 a :** to thrust, plunge, or slip momentarily or partially under the surface of a liquid or an adhesive substance so as to moisten, drench, cool, color, or coat **:** IMMERSE, SOUSE, DUCK ⟨ate clams *dipping* each in melted butter⟩ ⟨*dipped* my arms and face in the water trough⟩ ⟨the small parts are *dipped* in a primer paint —John Kobler⟩ **b :** to alter or move in a way to suggest immersion or the effect of immersion in a liquid ⟨you have constantly to ~ your hand in your pocket⟩ **2 a** *archaic* **:** to immerse in baptizing **b** *obs* **:** to wet as if by immersing ⟨a cold shuddering dew ~s me all over —John Milton⟩ **3 a :** to color by dipping (as in a dye) **b :** to make (a candle) by repeated immersion of a wick in melted fat or wax **c :** to immerse (as a sheep or hog) in an antiseptic or parasiticidal solution (as for the cure of the itch) **d :** to rub (snuff) on the teeth and gums with a brush or stick **e :** to immerse (candies) for the purpose of coating **4 :** to lift a portion of by reaching below the surface with an open utensil or something shaped to hold liquid **:** LADLE ⟨the cook *dipped* our soup from the kettle⟩ ⟨men who ~ ore out of freighters with an electric shovel⟩ **5** *Brit* **a** *archaic* **:** INVOLVE, IMPLICATE ⟨*dipt* in the rebellion —John Dryden⟩ **b :** MORTGAGE **c :** to involve in financial difficulty ⟨she was *dipped* as badly as her father —John Galsworthy⟩ **6 a :** to lower and then raise again ⟨put the helm alee and ~ the sail⟩ **b :** to haul (an ensign) part way down and then raise again in salute ⟨merchant ships salute each other by *dipping* the flag⟩ **c :** to swing (a signal flag) from vertical to somewhat below horizontal and then back to vertical **d :** to lower or cause to drop down somewhat and usu. temporarily ⟨he had to ~ his head to enter the cave⟩ ⟨*dipping* his chin into his muffler⟩ **e** *chiefly Brit* **:** to dim or lower the beam of (automobile headlights) **~** *vi* **1 a :** to immerse oneself **:** plunge into a liquid and quickly emerge ⟨the ship's bow *dipped* gently into the wave⟩ ⟨the sound of oars *dipping* rhythmically⟩ ⟨after the rain the ruts *dipped* in and out of the puddles —Helen B. Woodward⟩ ⟨the whale *dipped* playfully under the waves⟩ **b :** to immerse something into a processing liquid or finishing material ⟨waterproofing the surface of bisque ware is done in the *dipping* house⟩ **2 a :** to descend rather sharply **:** drop a slight distance ⟨the sun *dipped* at that moment below the horizon⟩ ⟨in Michigan three small tornadoes *dipped* to the ground, leveling barns —Seth King⟩ ⟨I saw purple martins pairing, *dipping*, and swooping —E.A. Weeks⟩ ⟨that the familiar prose ~s into the ordinary —E.T. Williams⟩ **b :** to make an abrupt slight downward movement ⟨we would one day enter to look round, ~ over the hill, and push the gate to the locked garden —G.W.Stonier⟩ ⟨fine brows *dipping* down with annoyance —Harriet La Barre⟩; *also* **:** to bring about a lowering of something ⟨salutes of the ensign are made by *dipping* —H.A.Calahan⟩ **c** (1) *of an ensign* **:** to become dipped ⟨regimental colors do ~ in salute —Elbridge Colby⟩ (2) *of a ship* **:** to dip its ensign **d :** to extend downward or below the surface ⟨branches that ~ in the water⟩ **e** *of a plane* **:** to drop suddenly before climbing **f :** to veer sharply ⟨the road follows the irregular shoreline and ~s back occasionally into the wooded hill country —*Amer. Guide Series: Minn.*⟩ **g :** to perform a dip in dancing **h :** to perform the gymnastic exercise constituting a dip **i :** to decline moderately and usu. temporarily ⟨prices *dipped* to a lower level before recovering⟩ ⟨commodity markets *dipped* but losses were not extensive —*Wall Street Jour.*⟩ **3 a :** to reach down inside or below a surface esp. for the purpose of withdrawing a part of the contents ⟨he *dipped* into the pocket and drew out a mixed collection —Dorothy Sayers⟩ ⟨one crane *dipped* five decks deep into No. 2 hold where the cars were carried —Vernon Pizer⟩ **b :** to appropriate a portion of something intangible ⟨that she had *dipped* in the wells of blissful oblivion —George Meredith⟩ ⟨not aware that in unjust suspicion a man ~s into himself for the colors he is painting —Francis Hackett⟩ **c :** to make an inroad for funds — used with *into* ⟨temptation of *dipping* into the public treasury to please constituents —Herbert Koshetz⟩ **d :** to dip snuff **4 a :** to make a slight or cursory subjective excursion **:** delve casually, aimlessly, or tentatively here and there — usu. used with *into* ⟨having *dipped* into the past we turn to the present⟩ ⟨the novel digressing here ~s into a bit of maudlin sentimentality⟩ ⟨I *dipped* into philosophy⟩ **b :** to read by sampling random disconnected passages or in the manner of browsing ⟨an ideal volume for *dipping* —B.R.Redman⟩ — usu. used with *into;* distinguished from *skim* ⟨it is a better book to ~ into than to read from cover to cover —Jane G. Mahler⟩ **c :** to explore or sample briefly or tentatively ⟨warily *dipping* into the possibilities of clairvoyance and telepathy⟩ **5 :** to incline downward **:** have a downward slant ⟨his landing lights *dipped* into the blackness and then *dipped* more steeply —Ira Wolfert⟩: **a :** to tilt or slope downward from the horizontal ⟨at this point in the trail land began to ~ the other way⟩ ⟨a forested cliff ~s steeply to the shore⟩ **b** *geol* **:** to incline downward from the plane of the horizon ⟨underlying the area are sedimentary rocks *dipping* gently eastward —M.A.Clement⟩ ⟨frequently, however, coal seams ~ steeply —H.R.Cox⟩ **c :** to tip downward ⟨the magnetic needle ~s in the direction of the earth's magnetism⟩ **d :** to take a course downgrade **:** have a downward pitch ⟨the narrow highway ~s and ascends like a crazy roller coaster —*Amer. Guide Series: Conn.*⟩ **6 :** to engage in reaching down and lifting out something from a liquid ⟨the whey that separates from the curd before *dipping*⟩ ⟨*dipping* on the turpentine plantation begins about April first⟩ **7** *archaic* **:** DIB

syn DIP, IMMERSE, SUBMERGE, DUCK, SOUSE, and DUNK may mean to plunge a thing into water or other liquid or may apply to any figurative action suggesting this. DIP implies a momentary or partial plunging or a cursory or short-lived looking or entering into (as into a subject) ⟨*dip* a finger in water⟩ ⟨*dip* a collar in starch⟩ ⟨*dip* into archaeology⟩ ⟨to *dip* into a doorway for a moment⟩ IMMERSE implies a total covering with liquid or a total engrossing or engaging (as in a study) ⟨*immerse* the clothes in a solution of dye⟩ ⟨become *immersed* in the study of history⟩ SUBMERGE implies total and often prolonged immersion or a sinking to a low level, grade, or status ⟨a barren, low-lying plain often partially *submerged* by the Mississippi —*Amer. Guide Series: Minn.*⟩ ⟨a boat *submerged* in four feet of water⟩ ⟨personality has been *submerged* by organization on all sides —W.P.Webb⟩ ⟨the older agrarian simplicity of New England was being *submerged* by the industrial revolution —V.L.Parrington⟩ ⟨the *submerged* lower classes⟩ DUCK implies a sudden plunging and withdrawal ⟨*duck* your head under water⟩ ⟨while he *ducks* into the doctor's office and back out again —*Advertising Age*⟩ ⟨*duck* under a low doorway⟩ SOUSE stresses a thorough soaking or can apply, figuratively, to any kind of saturating and, popularly, to intoxication ⟨she *soused* her hands in disinfectant before she touched him —*New Yorker*⟩ ⟨after being *soused* in the Atlantic ocean —T.B.Aldrich⟩ ⟨they ought to have *soused* the conscience in repentance or good resolutions —*Times Lit. Supp.*⟩ ⟨he hurries to *souse* himself in cheap red wine —*Time*⟩ DUNK applies to the dipping and soaking of something (as a doughnut) in a beverage; in extension, it is similar to DIP, DUCK, or IMMERSE ⟨*dunk* toast in her tea⟩ ⟨men dangling from lines, being *dunked* in the cold sea as the ship rolled —P.B.Cronk⟩

— **dip one's fingers into :** to obtrude oneself into participation in

²dip \"\ *n* -s **1 :** an act of dipping: as **a :** a brief immersion ⟨gaining a little with every ~ of the oars⟩ ⟨an earthenware cup ready for a ~ in the glaze tub⟩; *specif* **:** a plunge into the water for sport or exercise ⟨guests lingered on the beach, gossiping . . . and taking ~s —Alec Waugh⟩ ⟨either take ~s in little side eddies or hug the banks and wade in timidly—John Mason Brown⟩ **b :** a casual or experimental delving into a book or subject ⟨~s into heraldry⟩; *also* **:** a transient experimental or tentative excursion ⟨his early ~ into politics⟩ ⟨it is a Victorian-type novel, loosely constructed, with ~s into sentimentality —Ruth Suckow⟩ **c** *archaic* **:** CURTSY **d :** a reaching down into for withdrawing a portion ⟨a ~ in the punch bowl⟩ ⟨a ~ into the president's emergency fund⟩ **e :** a lowering in position ⟨a flag salute is one ~ of the ensign —C.D.Lane⟩ ⟨a ~ of a wigwag signal flag to the right indicates a dot⟩ **f :** a moderate decrease ⟨a 3 percent ~ in the claims for unemployment compensation⟩ ⟨how to account for ~s in his popularity⟩ ⟨tonight's forecast is for a ~ to 33°⟩; *specif* **:** a moderate and usu. temporary decline (as in prices or revenue) ⟨predictions of a business ~⟩ ⟨a sharper-than-seasonal production ~⟩ **g :** a gymnastics exercise on the end of the parallel bars in which the performer, resting on his hands, lets his arms bend until his chin is level with the bars and then raises himself by straightening his arms **h** (1) **:** a ballroom step in which the dancer bends one knee slightly and extends the other leg forward or backward (2) **:** a square-dance step in which the dancer bends forward and passes under an arch **2 :** inclination downward: **a :** downward slope, turn, or sag **:** divergence downward from the horizontal **:** PITCH ⟨the ~ of the lines from ship to pier⟩; *also* **:** decline from a level (as of performance) ⟨her graph of accomplishment was destined for a downward ~ —*Saturday Rev.*⟩ **b :** a sharp downward course or tilting ⟨a sudden ~ and rise out of a dingle —*Amer. Guide Series: Conn.*⟩ ⟨plotting the ~ of the indicator of a pressure gauge⟩ **c :** the angle that a stratum, sheet, vein, fissure, fault, or similar geological feature makes with a horizontal plane as measured in a plane normal to the strike **d :** position of an ensign hoisted part way to the yardarm or other point of hoist ⟨on the order "fox at the dip" the code flag for the letter *f* was hoisted two thirds of the way⟩ **e :** an abrupt but curved lowering of the belly of an archery bow on each side of the handle **3 a :** the vertical angle contained between the sensible horizon and a line to the visible horizon at sea, the latter because of the convexity of the earth's surface and the elevation of the observer being below the former **b :** the angle formed with the horizon by a magnetic needle free to rotate in the vertical plane of the magnetic meridian that is 0° at the magnetic equator and 90° at the magnetic poles — called also *inclination* **4 :** depth of submergence (as of a ship, oar, paddle wheel) **5 a :** a low spot with rather steeply sloping sides; *esp* **:** a hollow among hills or a gap in a ridge **b :** a pronounced depression in a surface or path ⟨the ~ that was destined to be the bed of Lake Superior —*Amer. Guide Series: Minn.*⟩; *specif* **:** a sharp depression in a highway at the point of crossing of a dry stream bed found chiefly in the western states **6 :** something obtained by or used in dipping: **a :** a candle made by repeated dippings of a wick in a fat or wax **b :** a stick or frayed twig dampened and used for dipping tobacco snuff ⟨with a snuff ~ in her mouth⟩ **c :** a portion dipped at one time ⟨writing steadily, one ~ of ink after another⟩ ⟨a double ~ of ice cream⟩; *specif* **:** as much snuff as clings to a dip at one dipping **d :** the viscid exudation constituting crude turpentine dipped from incisions in certain pine trees — compare SCRAPE 5 **7 :** a liquid or semiliquid flavoring or savory sauce into which solid food is dipped or which is served esp. on a dessert or on pie ⟨whip up chive cream cheese into a ~ for potato chips⟩ ⟨a ~ of sweetened cream on cobbler⟩ **8 a :** a liquid preparation into which objects may be dipped or immersed (as for cleansing, coloring, staining, or coating) ⟨a varnish ~ serves to bind the whole unit together —*Purchasing News*⟩; *specif* **:** an insecticide or parasiticide for use in a dipping tank **b :** a vat or tank in which such a dip is used ⟨a U-shaped sheep ~ with a 30-foot swim⟩ **c :** a moistening and flavoring solution through which some tobaccos are drawn **9** *slang* **:** PICKPOCKET **10 :** DIPHEAD **11** *slang* **:** a man's hat **12 :** a receptacle from which the contents may be dipped ⟨individual salt ~s⟩ **13** *Brit* **:** a small opening covered by a hinged flap in the floorboards of a theatrical stage for plugging leads into electric cables underneath

di·par·tite \(')dī'pär,tīt, -pȧ| *also* |d·,īt; *usu* -īd· +V\ *adj* [*di-* + L *partitus*, past part. of *partire, partiri* to divide — more at PART] **:** separated into parts **:** DIVIDED — **di·partition** \,dī +\ *n* -s

dip circle *n* **1 :** an inclinometer (sense 1) whose indications depend on a magnetized needle **2 :** DIP NEEDLE 2

¹dipcoat \'=,=\ *n* [²*dip* + *coat*, n.] **:** a vaporproof and waterproof coating applied over a wrapped container or item by dipping in molten wax

²dipcoat \"\ *vt* [²*dip* + *coat*, v.] **:** to coat by complete immersion in a proofing or finishing material

dip-dye \'=,=\ *vt* **1 :** to dye (knit goods) after knitting **2 :** to dye (furs) by completely immersing in the dye bath — compare TIP

di·pentene \(')dī+\ *n* [ISV *di-* + *pentene*] **:** a liquid terpene hydrocarbon $C_{10}H_{16}$ found in many essential oils (as Levant wormseed oil), usu. obtained along with other terpenoids from certain turpentines, and used chiefly as a solvent and dispersing agent (as for resins and varnishes); *dl*-limonene — called also *cajeputene*

di·pep·ti·dase \dī'peptə,dās, -āz\ *n* -s [ISV *dipeptide* + *-ase*] **:** any of various enzymes (as in yeast, kidney, and malt) that hydrolyze dipeptides but not polypeptides

di·peptide \(')dī+\ *n* [ISV *di-* + *peptide;* prob. orig. formed as G *dipeptid*] **:** a peptide that yields two molecules of amino acid on hydrolysis

di·pet·a·lo·ne·ma \(,)dī,ped·ᵊlō'nēmə\ *n, cap* [NL, fr. *di-* + *petal-* + *-nema*] **:** a genus of tropical filarial worms whose adults occur in connective tissue and skin of man and apes and monkeys and whose microfilariae occur in their blood — see DIPETALONEMATIDAE

di·pet·a·lo·ne·mat·i·dae \-ᵊl(,)ōnə'madə,dē\ *n pl, cap* [NL, fr. *Dipetalonemat-, Dipetalonema*, type genus + *-idae*] **:** a family of filarial worms distinguished from Filariidae by possession of slender larvae with no anterior spines and including most filarial worms parasitic in man and domestic animals

di·pet·al·ous \(')dī¦ped·ᵊləs\ *adj* [NL *dipetalus*, fr. *di-* + *-petalus* -petalous] **:** having two petals

di pet·to \dē'ped·(,)ō\ *adv (or adj)* [It] **:** from the chest — used of the natural singing voice; compare FALSETTO

dip fault *n* **:** a geologic fault whose trend is at right angles to the strike

dip-grained \'=¦=\ *adj, of wood* **:** having undulations in the fibers such as occur around knots

di·phase \'dī +,-\ *adj* **1 :** having two phases **2 :** TWO-PHASE

di·phasic \(')dī+\ *adj* [ISV *di-* + *phase* + *-ic*] **:** DIPHASE

diphead \'=,=\ *also* **dipheading** \'=,==\ *n* **:** a drift inclined along the dip of a coal seam

di·phen·an \dī'fenən\ *n* -s [*di-* + *phen-* + *-an*] **:** a crystalline ester $C_6H_5CH_2C_6H_4OOCNH_2$ administered in the treatment of pinworms; *para*-benzyl-phenyl carbamate

di·phen·hydramine \,dī,fen+\ *n* [*di-* + *phen-* + *hydr-* + *amine*] **:** a white crystalline amine $(C_6H_5)_2CHOCH_2CH_2N(CH_3)_2$ used in the form of its hydrochloride to treat allergy symptoms

di·phenol \(')dī+\ *n* [ISV *di-* + *phenol*] **:** a chemical compound containing two phenolic hydroxyl groups (as pyrocatechol and resorcinol)

¹di·phenyl \(')dī+\ *adj* [ISV *di-* + *phenyl*] **:** containing two phenyl groups in the molecule

²diphenyl \"\ *n* **:** BIPHENYL — used chiefly commercially

diphenylamine \(¦)=¦== + *pronunc at* AMINE\ *n* [ISV *diphenyl*, adj. + *amine*] **:** a crystalline pleasant-smelling compound $(C_6H_5)_2NH$ made usu. by heating aniline with aniline hydrochloride and used chiefly in the manufacture of dyes and in stabilizing explosives

di·phen·yl·amine·chlor·ar·sine \"+,klōr'är,sēn, -,sən\ *n* [*diphenylamine* + *chlor-* + *arsine*] **:** ADAMSITE

diphenyl black base *n, often cap D & both Bs* **:** a crystalline diamine $C_6H_5NHC_6H_4NH_2$ — see DYE table I (under *Oxidation Base 2*)

di·phen·yl·chlo·ro·ar·sine \(¦)=¦==+,klōrō'är,sēn, -,sən\ *also* **di·phen·yl·chlor·ar·sine** \+,klōr'är-\ *n* [*diphenyl* + *chlor-* + *arsine*] **:** a colorless crystalline arsenical $(C_6H_5)_2AsCl$ used during World War I esp. by the Germans for producing a toxic smoke causing sneezing and vomiting

diphenyl dye *n, often cap 1st D* **:** any of numerous direct dyes — see DYE table I

di·phen·yl·en·im·ine \(,)dī,fenᵊl,ē'nimən\ *n* **:** CARBAZOLE

diphenyl ether *n* **1 :** PHENYL ETHER **2 :** an ether containing two phenoxy groups

di·phen·yl·guanidine \(,)=,==+\ *n* [*diphenyl* + *guanidine*] **:** a crystalline compound $(C_6H_5NH)_2C{=}NH$ made by reaction of aniline and cyanogen chloride and used as an accelerator of vulcanization — called also *1,3-diphenylguanidine*

di·phen·yl·hydantoin \"+\ *n* [*diphenyl* + *hydantoin*] **:** a crystalline compound $C_{15}H_{12}N_2O_2$ used in the form of its sodium salt in the treatment of grand mal epilepsy

diphenyl ketone *n* [ISV *diphenyl* + *ketone*] **:** BENZOPHENONE

di·phen·yl·methane \(,)=,==+\ *n* [ISV *diphenyl* + *methane*] **:** a crystalline hydrocarbon $(C_6H_5)_2CH_2$ that has an odor suggesting geranium, that is made usu. from benzene (as by reaction with benzyl chloride), that is used chiefly as a perfume in soaps, and that is the parent of some synthetic dyes

diphenyl oxide *n* **:** PHENYL ETHER — used chiefly commercially

di·phen·yl·thio·carbazone \(,)=,==+,thītō+\ *n* [ISV *diphenyl* + *thi-* + *carb-* + *az-* + *-one*] **:** DITHIZONE

di·phen·yl·thiourea \(,)=,==+\ *n* [*diphenyl* + *thiourea*] **:** THIOCARBANILIDE

di·phosgene \(')dī+\ *n* [ISV *di-* + *phosgene*] **:** a liquid compound $ClCOOCCl_3$ made by chlorinating methyl formate and used in World War I as a poison gas; trichloro-methyl chloroformate

di·phosphate \(')dī+\ *n* [ISV *di-* + *phosphate*] **1 :** PYROPHOSPHATE **2 :** a salt containing two phosphate radicals

di·phos·pho·pyr·i·dine nucleotide \(,)dī,fäsfō'pirə,dēn-\ *n* [*diphosphopyridine* fr. *di-* + *phosph-* + *pyridine*] **:** a coenzyme $C_{21}H_{27}N_7O_{14}P_2$ of numerous dehydrogenases that occurs in most cells and plays an important role in all phases of intermediary metabolism as an oxidizing agent or when in the reduced form as a reducing agent for various metabolites — called also *codehydrogenase I, coenzyme I, cozymase, DPN;* compare PYRIDINE NUCLEOTIDE

di·phos·phor·ic acid \,dī+. . .-\ *n* [*di-* + *phosphoric*] **:** PYROPHOSPHORIC ACID

di·phos·pho·thiamine *also* **di·phos·pho·thiamin** \(,)dī-,fäsfō +\ *n* [*di-* + *phosph-* + *thiamine*] **:** COCARBOXYLASE

diph·the·ria \dif'thirēə, ÷dip'-, -thēr-\ *n* -s [NL, fr. F *diphthérie*, fr. Gk *diphthera* piece of leather (prob. fr. *depsein* to knead) + F -*ie* -ia (fr. L -*ia*); fr. the toughness of the false membrane; akin to Gk dial. (Argos) *dephidastai* (pl.) fullers, Arm *top'el* to beat] **1 :** an acute highly contagious disease chiefly of young children that is marked by the formation of a false membrane upon any mucous surface esp. of the throat where it causes swelling and obstruction and possibly suffocation and that is caused by a bacterium (*Corynebacterium diphtheriae*) which produces a toxin causing inflammation of internal organs, esp. the heart and nervous system **2 :** any of several diseases of animals characterized by the formation of false membranes (as fowl pox and calf diphtheria) — **diph·the·ri·al** \(ˈ)ˌ=ˈ=rēəl\ *or* **diph·the·ri·an** \-ēən\ *adj*

¹diph·ther·ic \(ˈ)=ˈtherik, -thir-\ *adj* [*diphtheria* + *-ic*] **:** DIPHTHERITIC

²diphtheric \"\ *n* -s **:** one suffering from diphtheria

diph·the·rit·ic \ˌ=thəˈrid·ik -rit|, |ēk\ *adj* [obs. E *diphtheritis* diphtheria (fr. NL, fr. F *diphthérite*, fr. Gk *diphthera* + F *-ite* -itis) + E *-ic*] **:** typical of, attendant on, or produced by infection with diphtheria ⟨a ~ membrane⟩ **:** resembling diphtheria esp. in the formation of a false membrane ⟨~ dysentery⟩ **:** affected with diphtheria ⟨a ~ child⟩

¹diph·the·roid \ˈ=thəˌrȯid\ *adj* [*diphtheria* + *-oid*] **:** resembling diphtheria

²diphtheroid \"\ *n* -s **:** a bacterium that resembles the bacterium of diphtheria but does not produce diphtheria toxin

¹diph·thong \ˈdifˌthȯŋ, ÷ˈdip-, *also* -thäŋ\ *n* -s [alter. (influenced by Gk *diphthongos*) of ME *diptonge*, fr. MF *diptongue*, fr. LL *dipthongus*, fr. Gk *diphthongos*, fr. *di-* + *phthongos* voice, sound] **1 :** a gliding monosyllabic speech item that starts at or near the articulatory position for one vowel and moves to or toward the position for another (as the vowel combination that forms the last part of *toy*) and that is usu. indicated in phonetic transcription by two symbols representing often only approximately the beginning and ending limits of the glide (as kau̇ or kau̇ or kaw or kaw for *cow*, tȯi or tȯy for *toy*, yät for *yacht*, wīz for *wise*) **2 :** DIGRAPH **3** [so called fr. their pronunciation as diphthongs in classical Latin] **:** a form of the ligature æ or œ — a printer's term

²diphthong \"\ *vb* -ED/-ING/-S **:** DIPHTHONGIZE

diph·thong·al \(ˈ)=ˈ=(g)əl\ *adj* **:** of or relating to a diphthong **:** having the character of a diphthong — **diph·thong·al·ly** \-(g)əlē, -li\ *adv*

diph·thong·ic \-(g)ik\ *adj* **:** DIPHTHONGAL

diph·thong·iza·tion \ˌ=ˌ=(g)əˈzāshən, -ˌ(g)īˈz-\ *n* -s **:** the act of diphthongizing or the state of being diphthongized

diph·thong·ize \ˈ=ˌ=(g)īz\ *vb* -ED/-ING/-S *vi, of a simple vowel* **:** to change into a diphthong ~ *vt* **:** to pronounce as a diphthong

diphy- *or* **diphyo-** *comb form* [NL, fr. Gk *diphy-*, fr. *diphyēs*, fr. *di-* + *-phyēs* (fr. *phyein* to bring forth, produce) — more at BE] **:** twofold **:** double **:** bipartite ⟨*diphy*odont⟩ ⟨*diphyo*zooid⟩

diphy·cercal \ˌdifē, -fə+\ *adj* [*diphy-* + *-cercal*] **1** *of a tail fin* **:** having the upper and lower portions alike or nearly so and the vertebral column extending to the tip without any upturning ⟨in lungfish and crossopterygians this symmetry is attained by the evolution of a ~ tail —A.S.Romer⟩ **2 :** having a diphycercal tail fin

diphy·cer·cy \ˈ=ˌsərsē, -rkē\ *n* -ES [*diphy-* + *-cercy*] **:** the state of being diphycercal

diph·y·es \ˈdifēˌēz\ *n, cap* [NL, fr. Gk *diphyēs* double] **:** a genus of oceanic hydrozoans of the order Siphonophora having two large swimming bells at the upper end of a stock that bears the polyps

diphy·genic \ˌdifēˈjenik, -fə-\ *adj* [*diphy-* + *-genic*] **:** following either of two alternate courses of embryonic development

di·phyletic \ˌdī+\ *adj* [*di-* + *phyletic*] **:** derived from two lines of descent **:** marked by or based on duality as to source ⟨calling for reconsideration of the ~ origin of the dinosaurs⟩

di·phyl·la \dīˈfilə\ *n, cap* [NL, fr. *di-* + *-phylla* (fr. Gk *phyllon* leaf); fr. the bifoliate nose leaf — more at BLOW (to blossom)] **:** a genus of bloodsucking bats of the family Desmodontidae — see VAMPIRE 3

di·phyl·leia \ˌdīfəˈlīə, -lē(y)ə\ *n, cap* [NL, fr. *di-* + *-phylleia* (fr. Gk *phyllon* leaf)] **:** a small genus of perennial herbs (family Berberidaceae) with a single basal peltate leaf and two cauline leaves all deeply 2-cleft, 6-petaled white flowers, and globose or oblong berries

di·phyl·lid·ea \ˌdīfəˈlidēə\ *n pl, cap* [NL, fr. *di-* + *phyll-* + *-idea*] **:** an order of Cestoda comprising tapeworms with two bothria on the scolex and dorsal and ventral rostellar hooks and including only a few parasites of elasmobranch fishes

di·phyl·lo·both·ri·a·sis \(ˌ)dīˌfilō(ˌ)bäˈthrīəsəs\ *n* -ES [NL, fr. *Diphyllobothrium* + *-iasis*] **:** infestation with or disease caused by the fish tapeworm (*Diphyllobothrium latum*)

di·phyl·lo·both·ri·i·dae \-īəˌdē\ *n pl, cap* [NL, fr. *Diphyllobothrium*, type genus + *-idae*] **:** a family of pseudophyllidean tapeworms (type genus *Diphyllobothrium*) having a complex life history with more than one intermediate host and the scolex of the adult usu. grooved and lacking suckers or hooks

di·phyl·lo·both·ri·um \-ˈbäthrēəm\ *n, cap* [NL, fr. *di-* + *phyll-* + *bothrium*] **:** a large genus of pseudophyllidean tapeworms comprising a number of parasites of fish-eating birds and mammals and including the common fish tapeworm (*D. latum*) of man

di·phyllous \(ˈ)dīˈfiləs\ *adj* [NL *diphyllus*, fr. *di-* + *-phyllus* -phyllous] **:** having two leaves

¹di·phy·odont \(ˈ)dīˈfīəˌdänt\ *adj* [ISV *diphy-* + *-odont*] **:** having deciduous and permanent sets of teeth successively ⟨a ~ mammal⟩; *also* **:** marked by the development of two such sets ⟨~ dentition⟩ — opposed to *monophyodont*

²diphyodont \"\ *n* -s **:** a diphyodont animal ⟨most mammals are ~*s*⟩

diphyo·zooid \ˌdifēō+\ *n* -s [*diphy-* + *zooid*] **:** one of the free-swimming sexual zooids of siphonophores

di·pic·ryl·amine \dīˌpikrəlˈəmēn\ *n* [ISV *di-* + *picryl* + *amine*] **:** HEXANITRODIPHENYLAMINE

dip–iron \ˈ=ˌ=(=)\ *n* **:** an implement used in removing resin from cups attached to trees tapped for resin production

dip joint *n* **:** a joint running in the same direction as the dip of the strata

dipl- *or* **diplo-** *comb form* [Gk, fr. *diploos* — more at DOUBLE] **1 :** double **:** twofold ⟨*diplo*coccus⟩ ⟨*dipl*opia⟩ **2 :** diploid ⟨*diplo*some⟩

dipl *abbr* **1** diploma **2** diplomatic

dip·la·can·thi·dae \ˌdipləˈkan(t)thəˌdē\ *n pl, cap* [NL, fr. *Diplacanthus*, type genus + *-idae*] **:** a family of primitive placoderm fishes (subclass Acanthodii) having two dorsal fins — see DIPLACANTHUS

dip·la·can·thus \-thəs\ *n, cap* [NL, fr. *dipl-* + *-acanthus*] **:** the type genus of Diplacanthidae comprising small Devonian fishes with two strong spines between the pectoral fins

dip·la·cu·sis \ˌdipləˈkyüsəs\ *n, pl* **diplacu·ses** \-üˌsēz\ [NL, fr. *dipl-* + Gk *akousis* hearing, fr. *akouein* to hear + *-sis* — more at HEAR] **:** the hearing of a single tone as if it were two tones of different pitch

dip·la·de·nia \ˌdipləˈdēnēə\ *n, cap* [NL, fr. *dipl-* + Gk *aden-*, *adēn* gland + NL *-ia*; fr. the pair of nectar glands — more at ADEN-] **:** a genus of tropical So. American woody vines (family Apocynaceae) having large varicolored racemose flowers

di·pla·net·ic \ˌdīpləˈned·ik\ *adj* [*di-* + Gk *planētikos* migratory, fr. *planēt-*, *planēs* wanderer (fr. *planan* to cause to wander, *planasthai* to wander) + *-ikos* -ic — more at FLOOR] *of a fungus* **:** having two swarming periods each with a different form of zoospore and separated by an encysted stage (as in the Saprolegniales) — compare MONOPLANETIC — **di·plan·e·tism** \dīˈplanəˌtizəm\ *n* -s

dip·lar·throus \(ˈ)diˈplärthrəs\ *adj* [*dipl-* + *arthr-* + *-ous*] **:** having each or most of the tarsal or carpal bones of one row articulating with more than one bone of the other row — used esp. of certain ungulate mammals; opposed to *taxeopodous*

di·pla·sic \(ˈ)dīˈplā|zik, -la|, |sik\ *adj* [Gk *diplasios* twofold (fr. *di-* + *-plasios* -fold) + E *-ic* — more at FOLD] *in classical prosody* **:** two to one in proportion **:** having a thesis twice the length of the arsis

di·pla·sio·coe·la \(ˌ)dīˌplāzēōˈsēlə\ *n pl, cap* [NL, fr. *diplasio-* (fr. Gk *diplasios*) + *-coela* (fr. Gk *koilos* hollow) — more at CAVE] **:** a suborder of Salientia including the families Ranidae, Polypedatidae, and Brevicipitidae and having the anterior surface of the first seven vertebrae concave and the eighth vertebra biconcave, a firm median fusion of the shoulder girdle, and no ribs — **di·pla·sio·coe·lid** \ˌ=ˌ===ˈ=ləd\ *adj or n* — **di·pla·sio·coe·lous** \-ləs\ *adj*

di·plec·trum \dīˈplektrəm\ *n, cap* [NL, fr. *di-* + *plectrum*] **:** a genus of small marine and brackish-water fishes (family Serranidae) widely distributed along the warmer parts of both coasts of the Americas — compare SANDFISH

di·ple·gia \dīˈplēj(ē)ə\ *n* -s [NL, fr. *di-* + *-plegia*] **:** paralysis of corresponding parts (as the legs) on both sides of the body

di·pleu·ru·la \dīˈplu̇r(y)ələ\ *n, pl* **dipleurulas** \-ləz\ *or* **di·pleuru·lae** \-ˌlē\ [NL, fr. *dipleura* bilaterally symmetrical organisms (fr. *di-* + *-pleura*) + *-ula*] **1 :** a hypothetical bilaterally symmetrical echinoderm larva sometimes regarded as a common ancestor of echinoderms and chordates **2 :** a larval echinoderm (as a bipinnaria or an echinopluteus) — not used technically

¹di·plex \ˈdīˌpleks\ *adj* [alter. (influenced by *di-*) of *duplex*] **:** allowing telecommunication of two independent signals simultaneously by a single station or antenna or on a single carrier frequency without mutual interference ⟨~ radio and television transmission⟩ ⟨~ reception⟩ — distinguished from *duplex*

²diplex \"\ *vt* -ED/-ING/-ES **:** to effect diplex transmission or reception of

di·plex·er \-sə(r)\ *n* -s **:** a combining network (as an impedance bridge or a filter circuit) allowing operation of diplex transmission (as of a radar and a communication transmitter) ⟨a simple ~ may be used to feed the picture signal and the sound signal into the same antenna—*Radio Corp. of Amer. Rev.*⟩

dip·lo·bacillus \ˌdiplō+\ *n, pl* **diplobacilli** [NL, fr. *dipl-* + *bacillus*] **:** any of certain small aerobic gram-negative rod-shaped bacilli that are related to the genus *Hemophilus* and are parasitic on mucous membranes

dip·lo·bi·ont \ˌdiplōˈbīˌänt, dəˈplōbēˌänt\ *n* -s [*dipl-* + *-biont*] **:** an organism in which a haploid generation alternates with a usu. morphologically dissimilar diploid generation — compare DIPLOHAPLONT — **dip·lo·bi·on·tic** \ˌdiplōˌbīˈäntik, dəˌplōbēˈäntik\ *adj*

dip·lo·blas·tic \ˌdiplōˈblastik\ *adj* [*dipl-* + *-blastic*] **:** having two germ layers — used of embryos and of lower invertebrates (sponges and coelenterates) that lack a true mesoderm

dip·lo·car·dia \ˌdiplōˈkärdēə\ *n, cap* [NL, fr. *dipl-* + *-cardia*] **:** a common American genus of earthworms (family Megascolecidae) often abundant in moist forest soil

dip·lo·car·di·ac \ˌdiplōˈkärdēˌak\ *adj* [*dipl-* + *-cardiac* (fr. Gk *kardia*) — more at HEART] **:** having the heart completely divided so that one side is systemic and the other is pulmonary

dip·lo·car·pon \ˌdiplōˈkärˌpän\ *n, cap* [NL, fr. *dipl-* + *-carpon* (fr. Gk *-karpon*, neut. of *-karpos* -carpous)] **:** a genus of fungi (family Microthyriaceae) with shield-shaped perithecia and unequally two-celled hyaline ascospores — see BLACK SPOT

dip·lo·caulescent \ˌdiplō+\ *adj* [*dipl-* + *caulescent*] **:** having axes of the second order — used of a plant that cannot reproduce until after the production of secondary axes; compare HAPLOCAULESCENT, TRIPLOCAULESCENT

dip·lo·chlamydeous \ˌdiplō+\ *adj* [*dipl-* + *chlamydeous*] **:** DICHLAMYDEOUS

dip·lo·chromosome \"+\ *n* [*dipl-* + *chromosome*] **:** a chromosome with four chromatids

dip·lo·coc·cal \ˌdiplōˈkäkəl\ *or* **dip·lo·coc·cic** \-äksik\ *adj* [*diplococcus* + *-al* or *-ic*] **:** of, or relating to diplococci or the genus *Diplococcus* **:** caused by diplococci

dip·lo·coc·coid \-ˈkäˌkȯid\ *adj* [*diplococcus* + *-oid*] **:** resembling a diplococcus

dip·lo·coc·cus \ˌdiplōˈkäkəs\ *n* [NL, fr. *dipl-* + *-coccus*] **1** *pl* **diplococ·ci** \-äˌkī, -ākē, -äkˌsī, -äksē\ **:** a pair of adherent cocci (sense 2) **2** *cap* **:** a genus of gram-positive somewhat elongated encapsulated bacteria (family Lactobacillaceae) that occur usu. in pairs and sometimes in chains, are parasitic growing best in the animal body but poorly in artificial media, and include serious pathogens, as the pneumococcus (*D. pneumoniae*) **3** *pl* **diplococci :** any bacterium of the genus *Diplococcus*

di·plo·dia \dəˈplōdēə\ *n, cap* [NL, irreg. fr. *diploos* double; fr. the 2-celled spores] **:** a large form genus of imperfect fungi (of the family Sphaeropsidaceae, order Sphaeropsidales) having carbonous pycnidia and brown 2-celled spores — see DRY ROT 2b

di·plod·o·cus \dəˈplädəkəs\ *n* [NL, fr. *dipl-* + *-docus* (fr. Gk *dokos* beam, bar, fr. *dekesthai*, *dechesthai* to take, receive); akin to L *decēre* to be fitting, be proper — more at DECENT] **1** *cap* **:** a genus of very large herbivorous saurischian dinosaurs (suborder Sauropoda) from the Upper Jurassic of Colorado and Wyoming **2** -ES **:** any animal of the genus *Diplodocus*

dip·lo·dus \ˈdiplədəs\ *n, cap* [NL, fr. *dipl-* + *-odus*] **:** a genus of deep-bodied fishes (family Sparidae) including a number of typical sargos

dip·loe \ˈdipləˌwē\ *n* -s [NL, fr. Gk *diploē*, fr. *diploos* double] **:** the cancellous bony tissue between the tables of the skull

dip·lo·et·ic \ˌdipləˈwed·ik\ *adj* [*diploe* + connective *-t-* + *-ic*] **:** DIPLOIC

dip·lo·gangliate \ˌdiplō+\ *adj* [*dipl-* + *gangliate*] **:** having the ganglia arranged in pairs

dip·lo·genesis \ˌdiplō+\ *n* [NL, fr. *dipl-* + *genesis*] **:** a hypothetical production of changes in the germ plasm corresponding to acquired modification of somatic structure — compare LAMARCKISM — **dip·lo·genetic** \"+\ *adj*

dip·lo·gen·ic \ˌdiplōˈjenik\ *adj* [*dipl-* + Gk *genos* race, kin + E *-ic* — more at KIN] **:** partaking of the nature of two bodies

dip·lo·glos·sa·ta \ˌdiplō(ˌ)gläˈsäd·ə, -ˈsād-ə\ *n pl, cap* [NL, fr. *dipl-* + Gk *glōssa* tongue + NL *-ata* — more at GLOSS (interpretation)] **:** a suborder of Dermaptera including the single genus *Hemimerus* of ectoparasites on African rats

dip·lo·glossate \ˌdiplō+\ *adj* [*dipl-* + Gk *glōssa* tongue + E *-ate*] *of certain lizards* **:** having the end of the tongue retractile into the basal portion

dip·lo·haplont \ˌdiplō+\ *n* [ISV *dipl-* + *haplont*] **:** an organism in which a haploid generation alternates with a usu. morphologically similar diploid generation — compare DIPLOBIONT — **dip·lo·hap·lon·tic** \ˌdiplōˌhaˈpläntik\ *adj*

dip·lo·he·dral \ˌdiplōˈhēdrəl\ *adj* [*diplohedron* + *-al*] **:** of or relating to a diplohedron

dip·lo·he·dron \-ən\ *n* -s [ISV *dipl-* + *-hedron*] **:** DIPLOID 1

di·plo·ic \dəˈplōik, (ˈ)diˈp-\ *adj* [ISV *diploe* + *-ic*] **:** of or relating to the diploe

¹dip·loid \ˈdiˌplȯid\ *n* -s [*dipl-* + *-oid*] **1 :** an isometric crystalline form that has 24 similar quadrilateral faces arranged in pairs and that is a hemihedral form of the hexoctahedron — called also *diplohedron* **2** [²*diploid*] **a :** a diploid cell **b :** an individual or generation characterized by the diploid chromosome number

diploid 1

²diploid \"\ *adj* [ISV *dipl-* + *-oid*; prob. orig. formed in G] **:** double or twofold in appearance or arrangement **:** having the basic chromosome number doubled ⟨typical ~ somatic cells⟩ **:** comprising twice the number of chromosomes present in typical gametes ⟨the chromosome complement is ~ before reduction⟩ — compare HAPLOID, POLYPLOID

dip·loi·dal \dəˈplȯidᵊl, (ˈ)diˈp-\ *adj* [¹*diploid* + *-al*] **:** belonging to or characterized by the symmetry of the class of isometric crystals having diad axes parallel to the crystallographic axes, triad axes in the directions of the cube body diagonal, and axial mirror-image planes of symmetry

dip·lo·id·i·on \ˌdiplōˈidēˌän, -ēən\ *n* -s [Gk *diploïdion*, dim. of *diploïd-*, *diploïs* double cloak, fr. *diploos* double] **:** an ancient Greek chiton for women having the part above the waist double and the outer fold hanging loose

dip·loid·i·za·tion \ˌdiˌplȯidəˈzāshən\ *n* -s **:** the act or process of diploidizing or the state of being diploidized

dip·loid·ize \ˈdiˌplȯiˌdīz\ *vb* -ED/-ING/-S *vt* **:** to make diploid (as by hyphal fusions in certain fungi) ~ *vi* **:** to become diploid

dip·loi·dy \ˈdiˌplȯidē\ *n* -ES [ISV *diploid* + *-y*] **:** the condition of being diploid

dip·lo·karyon \ˌdiplō+\ *n* [ISV *dipl-* + *karyon*; orig. formed in G] **:** a nucleus possessing twice the diploid number of chromosomes **:** a tetraploid nucleus — **dip·lo·kar·y·ot·ic** \ˌdiplōˌkarēˈäd·ik\ *adj*

¹di·plo·ma \dəˈplōmə\ *n, pl* **diplo·mas** \-məz\ [L, passport, document conferring an honor or privilege, fr. Gk *diplōma* passport, folded paper, something doubled, fr. *diploun* to double, fr. *diploos* double] **1** *pl also* **diploma·ta** \-məd·ə, -mətə\ **:** an historical or state document **:** CHARTER ⟨in a ~ of Hlothhere, king of Kent — the first English charter of which a contemporary text has survived —F.M.Stenton⟩ **2 :** a letter or writing usu. under seal conferring some honor or privilege ⟨the council's peace prize was handed to him and along with it a ~⟩ **3 :** a document bearing record of graduation from or of a degree conferred by an educational institution

²diploma \"\ *vt* -ED/-ING/-S **:** to furnish with a diploma ⟨too many ~*ed* illiterates⟩

di·plo·ma·cy \dəˈplōməsē, -si\ *n* -ES [F *diplomatie*, fr. *diplomatique* diplomatic, after F *aristocratique* aristocratic: *aristocratie* aristocracy] **1 a :** the art and practice of conducting negotiations between nations for the attainment of mutually satisfactory terms ⟨the technique of direct ~, whereby responsible members of governments deal with each other face to face instead of through ambassadors or other intermediaries —N.F.Busch⟩ ⟨secondly, there is the other kind of ~ . . . : the search for agreement between friends on policies and tactics and timing —Lester Pearson⟩ — compare DIPLOMATIC AGENT **b :** the procedures, methods, and forms employed in conducting such negotiations ⟨colleges having specific courses in ~⟩ ⟨forget that ~ is itself a skilled profession — Llewellyn Woodward⟩ ⟨resolved to make a career of ~⟩ **c :** the skillful or successful settlement of differences between peoples ⟨~ is the peaceful resolution of disputes between autonomous groups —M.J.Herskovits⟩ **d :** a statesman's or nation's policies and strategies in conducting foreign relations ⟨when the ~ of certain aggressive statesmen was employed to isolate a particular enemy so as to facilitate his defeat —C.J. Friedrich⟩ **2 :** adroitness or artfulness in securing advantages without arousing hostility **:** address or tact in conduct of affairs ⟨he is a kind man, but simpleminded in the extreme; he has no gift for ~ —Elinor Wylie⟩ **3 :** the diplomatic corps ⟨members of UN ~⟩

diploma mill *n* **:** an institution of higher education operating without supervision of a state or professional agency and granting diplomas which are either fraudulent or because of the lack of proper standards worthless

diploma piece *n* **1 :** a finished piece of work by a new member of an academy or society of art and presented by him to the organization upon election to membership **2 :** an academic project (as a thesis or dissertation) undertaken for the purpose of obtaining a diploma rather than from interest in the subject

dip·lo·mat \ˈdipləˌmat, *usu* -ad·+V\ *n* -s [F *diplomate*, back-formation fr. *diplomatique* diplomatic] **1 :** one employed or skilled in diplomacy ⟨the modern ~ will look upon himself as a liaison officer who will promote cooperation and understanding on all sides —C.J.Friedrich⟩ **2 :** DIPLOMATIST 2

¹diplomate *vt* -ED/-ING/-S [¹*diploma* + *-ate*, v. suffix] *obs* **:** to give a title, a degree, or a privilege to by means of a diploma

²dip·lo·mate \ˈdipləˌmāt\ *n* -s [¹*diploma* + *-ate*, n. suffix (one acted upon)] **:** one who holds a diploma; *esp* **:** a physician certified as qualified generally or as a specialist by an agency recognized as professionally competent to grant such certification (as the American Board of Anesthesiology)

¹dip·lo·mat·ic \ˌdipləˈmad·ik, -at|, |ēk\ *adj* [in sense 1, fr. NL *diplomaticus*, fr. L *diplomat-*, *diploma* document conferring an honor or privilege + *-icus* -ic; in other senses, fr. F *diplomatique* connected with the documents that regulate international relations, fr. NL *diplomaticus*] **1 :** relating to the deciphering, age, authenticity, signatures, or textual emendations of writings of former times **:** PALEOGRAPHIC; *esp* **:** exactly reproducing the original — used of a copy or edition of a text or document ⟨their own translation is based on the critical, ~ text of Henri Lestienne (Paris, 1907), which provides all of Leibnitz's own alterations—Nicholas Rescher⟩ **2 a :** concerned or connected with international relations ⟨a ~ assignment in So. America⟩ ⟨~ techniques for preventing war⟩ **:** engaged or skilled in international relations ⟨a ~ expert⟩ ⟨sent over a ~ group to Europe⟩ **b :** belonging to or proper to the personnel responsible for the conduct of international relations ⟨~ secretaries and consuls⟩ ⟨~ privileges and immunities⟩ ⟨a breach of ~ etiquette⟩ ⟨the right of ~ sanctuary⟩ **:** composed of such personnel ⟨a ~ group⟩ **3 :** employing tact and conciliation ⟨tried a ~ approach before using strong-arm methods⟩ ⟨a ~ way of dealing with a touchy personal relationship⟩ **syn** see SUAVE

²diplomatic \"\ *n* -s **1** *archaic* **:** a diplomatic agent **:** DIPLOMATIST **2** *also* **dip·lo·mat·ics** \-ks\ *pl but sing in constr*, *archaic* **:** the art of international diplomacy **3 diplomatics** *pl but sing in constr* **:** critical study of official documents of history (as ancient registers, decrees, charters, treaties, judicial records) esp. of medieval times

diplomatic agent *n* **:** an agent employed by a state in its diplomatic service or in its intercourse or negotiation with other states

dip·lo·mat·i·cal·ly \-ək(ə)lē, |ēk, -li\ *adv* **1 :** according to the rules of diplomacy **2 :** in a diplomatic manner ⟨and ~ allowed a prince to beat him at chess —Elinor Wylie⟩ **:** TACTFULLY

diplomatic corps *n* [trans. of F *corps diplomatique*] **:** the whole body of diplomatic agents attached to a foreign legation at the seat of government including ambassadors, envoys, ministers, and their attachés and secretaries

diplomatic immunity *n* **:** freedom from arrest, taxation, payment of customs charges, and submission to police regulations usu. accorded by international law to diplomatic agents, their families, and servants

diplomatic pouch *n* **:** a mail pouch that is sealed shut in transit and is used for carrying communications between a legation and its home office

diplomatic service *n* **:** a branch of the foreign service that employs diplomatic agents and is concerned with foreign legations

di·plo·ma·tist \dəˈplōməd·əst, -mətəst\ *n* -s [fr. ¹*diplomatic*, after such pairs as E *dramatic*: *dramatist*] **1 :** DIPLOMAT ⟨churchmen were the natural intermediaries in this business, and a good clerical ~ might reasonably expect a bishopric —F.M.Stenton⟩ ⟨the greatest of the German professional ~*s* of the interwar period —H.J.Morgenthau⟩ **2 :** one who is dexterous, tactful, or artful in meeting situations (as in managing men) without arousing antagonism

di·plo·ma·tize \-məˌtīz\ *vb* -ED/-ING/-S [in sense 1 (transitive), fr. L *diplomat-*, *diploma* + E *-ize*; in other senses, fr. ¹*diplomatic*, after such pairs as E *dramatic*: *dramatize*] *vt* **1** *archaic* **:** to confer a diploma upon **2 :** to treat or manage with diplomacy **:** aid in the manner of a diplomatist ~ *vi* **:** to act like a diplomat or with adroitness and tact **:** practice diplomacy

dip·lo·nephridia \ˌdiplō+\ *n pl* [NL, fr. *dipl-* + *nephridia* (pl. of *nephridium*)] **:** nephridia in whose formation both the ectoderm and mesoderm take part

dip·lo·neural \"+\ *adj* [*dipl-* + *neural*] **:** supplied by two different nerves

dip·lont \ˈdiˌplänt\ *n* -s [ISV *dipl-* + *-ont*] **:** an organism with somatic cells having the diploid chromosome number, only the gametes being haploid — compare HAPLONT, SPOROPHYTE — **di·plon·tic** \(ˈ)diˈpläntik\ *adj*

dip·lo·parthenogenesis \ˌdiplō+\ *n* [NL, fr. *dipl-* + *parthenogenesis*] **:** parthenogenesis characterized by the production of diploid offspring from unreduced primordial cells

dip·lo·phase \ˈdiplōˌfāz\ *n* [*dipl-* + *phase*] **:** the diploid phase (as the sporophyte) in the life cycle of certain organisms

di·plo·pia \dəˈplōpēə\ *n* -s [NL, fr. *dipl-* + *-opia*] **:** a disorder of vision in which two images of a single object are seen owing to unequal action of the eye muscles

di·plop·ic \dəˈpläpik, (ˈ)diˈp-, -lōp-\ *adj* [*diplopia* + *-ic*] **:** relating to or affected with diplopia

¹dip·lo·pod \ˈdipləˌpäd\ *n* -s [NL *Diplopoda*] **:** one of the Diplopoda **:** MILLIPEDE

²diplopod \"\ *adj* **:** of or relating to the Diplopoda

di·plop·o·da \dəˈpläpədə\ *n pl, cap* [NL, fr. *dipl-* + *-poda*] **:** a class of arthropods comprising the millipedes — **dip·lo·pod·ic** \ˌdipləˈpädik\ *adj* — **di·plop·o·dous** \dəˈpläpədəs, (ˈ)diˈp-\ *adj*

di·plo·sis \dəˈplōsəs\ *n, pl* **diplo·ses** \-ōˌsēz\ [NL, fr. Gk *diplōsis* action of doubling, fr. *diploun* to double (fr. *diploos* double) + *-sis* — more at DOUBLE] **1 :** the alchemical process of increasing the amount of a precious metal by transmutation **2 :** restoration of the somatic chromosome number by fusion of two gametes in fertilization — compare HAPLOSIS

dip·lo·some \ˈdiplə,sōm\ *n* -S [*dipl-* + *-some*] **:** a double centriole

dip·lo·somite \ˈdiplō+\ *n* [*dipl-* + *somite*] **:** one of the typical structural units of a diplopod, each bearing two pairs of appendages and representing two fused true segments

dip·lo·sphene \ˈdiplō,sfēn\ *n* -S [*dipl-* + Gk *sphēn* wedge — more at SPHEN-] **:** HYPOSPHENE

dip·lo·spon·dy·li \,diplōˈspändə,lī\ [NL, fr. *dipl-* + *-spondyli*] *syn of* NOTIDANI

dip·lo·spondylic \,diplō+\ *also* **dip·lo·spondylous** \"+\ *adj* [*dipl-* + *spondylic, spondylous*] **:** EMBOLOMEROUS

dip·lo·spor·ous \ˈdiplə;spōrəs, dəˈplīspərəs\ *adj* [*dipl-* + *-sporous*] **:** being or belonging to diplospory

dip·lo·spory \ˈdiplə,spōrē, dəˈplīspərē\ *n* -ES [*dipl-* + *-spory*] **:** reproduction by means of unreduced spores

dip·lo·ste·mo·nous \ˈdiplō;stēmənəs, -tem-\ *adj* [prob. fr. (assumed) NL *diplostemonus*, fr. NL *dipl-* + (assumed) NL *-stemonus* -stemonous] **:** having the stamens in two whorls each of which has the same number as the petals and usu. an inner stamen opposite each petal and an outer one opposite each sepal — compare OBDIPLOSTEMONOUS

dip·lo·stom·u·lum \,diplōˈstämyələm\ *n, pl* **diplostomu·la** \-lə\ [NL, fr. *dipl-* + Gk *stoma* mouth + NL *-ulum* — more at STOMACH] **:** a modified metacercaria occurring unencysted esp. in the lens of the eye of fishes

dip·lo·tax·is \,=ˈtaksəs\ *n, cap* [NL, fr. *dipl-* + *-taxis*] **:** a genus of Old World weedy herbs (family Cruciferae) with alternate pinnatifid leaves and yellow racemose flowers — see WALL ROCKET

dip·lo·te·gia \,diplōˈtējēə\ *n* -S [NL, fr. *dipl-* + *-tegia* (fr. Gk *tegos* roof) — more at THATCH] **:** a capsule developed in seed plants from an inferior ovary (as in iris)

dip·lo·tene \ˈdiplō,tēn\ *n* -S [ISV *dipl-* + *-tene;* orig. formed as F *diplotène*] **:** the stage of the meiotic prophase immediately following pachytene during which the homologous chromosomes tend to repel one another

dip·lo·zo·ic \ˈdiplə;zōik\ *adj* [*dipl-* + *-zoic*] *of an animal* **:** combining a double set of vital structures in one unit

dip·lo·zo·on \,dipləˈzō,än\ *n, cap* [NL, fr. *dipl-* + *-zoon*] **:** a genus of monogenetic trematode worms parasitic upon the gills of fishes (as minnows) and unique among animals in that two larvae fuse together permanently at the middle of their bodies forming an individual shaped like an X and only double individuals thus formed are capable of becoming sexually mature

di·plu·ra \dəˈplu̇rə\ *n pl, cap* [NL, fr. *dipl-* + *-ura*] **:** ENTOTROPHI — **di·plu·ran** \-rən\ *n* -S

dipmeter \ˈ=,==\ *n* **:** an instrument designed for determining the direction and angle of dip of geological formations

dip mold *n* **:** an open-top one-piece mold used in pattern molding in glassmaking

dip needle *n* **1** *or* **dipping needle :** a magnetic needle pivoted to rotate in the vertical plane of the magnetic meridian with its rotation axis through its center of gravity so that it points in the direction of the earth's magnetic intensity **2 :** an instrument similar to a dip needle but with a counterweight so adjusted as to give the needle maximum sensitivity to changes in the magnetic dip

dip needle 1

dip net *n* **:** a small bag net usu. with a rigid support about the mouth and a long handle used to scoop small fishes and other aquatic life from the water

dipnetter *n* **:** one who fishes with a dip net

dipnetting *n* **:** fishing by means of a dip net

[1]**di·pneu·mo·na** \dīˈn(y)ümənə, dipˈn-\ *n pl, cap* [NL, fr. neut. pl. of *dipneumonus* dipneumonous] **1** *in some classifications* **:** a group of lungfishes including the genera *Protopterus* and *Lepidosiren* in which the lung is double and the lateral rays of the archipterygium are vestigial or absent **2** *in some classifications* **:** a division of holothurians having two branching respiratory organs

[2]**dipneumona** \"\ [NL, fr. neut. pl. of *dipneumonus*] *syn of* DIPNEUMONES

di·pneu·mone \(ˈ)dī,n(y)ü,mōn, (ˈ)dipˈn-\ *adj* [NL *Dipneumones*] *of a spider* **:** having one pair of book lungs **:** DIPNEUMONOMORPH

di·pneu·mo·nes \dīˈn(y)ümə,nēz, dipˈn-\ *n pl, cap* [NL, fr. *di-* + *-pneumones* (fr. Gk *pneumones*, pl. of *pneumōn*, *pneumōn* lung) — more at PNEUMONIA] *in some classifications* **:** a division of spiders comprising those with a single pair of lungs

di·pneu·mo·no·morph \-mənō,mȯrf\ *adj* [NL *Dipneumonomorphae*] **:** of or relating to the Dipneumonomorphae

di·pneu·mo·no·mor·phae \(,)=,===ˈmȯr,fē\ *n pl, cap* [NL, fr. *di-* + *pneumon-* + *-morphae*] **:** a suborder of Araneida comprising spiders that have a single pair of book lungs

di·pneu·mo·nous \(ˈ)=;=mənəs\ *adj* [NL *dipneumonus*, fr. *di-* + *-pneumonus* (fr. Gk *pneumon-*, *pneumōn* lung)] **1 :** having two respiratory organs **2 :** belonging to or characteristic of the Dipneumona

dip·neust \ˈdip,n(y)üst\ *n* -S [NL *Dipneusti*] **:** a fish of the order Dipneusti

dip·neus·tal \(ˈ)dip;n(y)üstᵊl\ *adj* [NL *Dipneusti* + E *-al*] **:** of or relating to the Dipneusti

dip·neus·ti \dipˈn(y)üsti\ *n pl, cap* [NL, fr. *di-* + *-pneusti* (irreg. fr. Gk *pneustikos* of breathing, fr. *pnein* to breathe) — more at PNEUMATIC] **:** an order of Choanichthyes coextensive with Dipnoi — see LUNGFISH

dip·neus·tid \-təd\ *adj* **:** DIPNEUSTAL

[1]**dip·no·an** \ˈdipnəwən\ *adj* [NL *dipnoi* + E *-an*, adj. suffix] **:** belonging to the Dipnoi

[2]**dipnoan** \"\ *n* -S [NL *Dipnoi* + E *-an*, n. suffix] **:** one of the Dipnoi

dip·noi \ˈdip,nȯi, -pnə,wī\ *n pl, cap* [NL, fr. masc. pl. of *dipnous* having two apertures for breathing] **:** an order or other division of Choanichthyes including a number of fossil fishes known from the Devonian and later formations and three surviving genera, *Neoceratodus*, *Protopterus*, and *Lepidosiren*, comprising aberrant fishes that have overlapping cycloid scales and dermal fin rays, a largely cartilaginous skeleton with a persistent notochord, an autostylic skull, paired fins of the archipterygial type, gills covered by an operculum, and in addition a lung or pair of lungs communicating with the ventral side of the esophagus by a short tube

dip·noid \ˈdip,nȯid\ *adj or n* [NL *Dipnoi* + E *-oid*] **:** DIPNOAN

dip·no·ous \ˈdipnəwəs\ *adj* [NL *dipnous* having two apertures for breathing, fr. Gk *dipnoos*, fr. *di-* + *-pnoos* (fr. *pnoē* breath, fr. *pnein* to breathe)] **1 :** having both lungs and gills **2 :** DIPNOAN

di·pode \ˈdī,pōd\ *adj* [Gk *dipod-*, *dipous*] **:** BIPED

di·pod·ic \(ˈ)dī;pädik\ *adj* [*dipody* + *-ic*] **:** of, relating to, or composed of a dipody or dipodies ⟨a ~ verse⟩ ⟨poem . . . with ~ instead of short feet —Evelyn H. Scholl⟩

[1]**di·po·did** \ˈdipədəd\ *n* -S [NL *Dipodidae*] **:** a rodent of the family Dipodidae

[2]**dipodid** \"\ *adj* **:** of or relating to the Dipodidae

di·pod·i·dae \dīˈpädə,dē\ *n pl, cap* [NL, fr. *Dipod-*, *Dipus*, type genus + *-idae* — more at DIPUS] **:** a family of myomorph rodents comprising the Old World jerboas and sometimes related forms

di·pod·o·mys \-də,mis\ *n, cap* [NL, fr. *dipodo-* (fr. Gk *dipod-*, *dipous* having two feet, fr. *di-* + *pod-*, *pous* foot) + *-mys* — more at FOOT] **:** a genus of sciuromorph rodents consisting of the No. American kangaroo rats

dip·o·dy \ˈdipədē\ *n* -ES [LL *dipodia*, fr. Gk, lit., condition of having two feet, fr. *dipod-*, *dipous* + *-ia* -y] **:** a prosodic unit or measure of two feet; *esp* **:** one in an accentual meter in which the stress or arsis of one of the feet is notably stronger than that of the other

di·po·lar \ˈdī,pōlə(r)\ *adj* [*di-* + *polar*] **:** of, relating to, or having a dipole

dipolar ion *n* **:** an ion charged both positively and negatively (as that of an amino acid in solution) **:** an amphoteric ion ⟨the *dipolar ion* $^{+}H_3NCH_2COO^{-}$ of glycine⟩ — called also *zwitterion;* compare BETAINE 1a, INNER SALT

di·pole \ˈdī,pōl\ *n* [ISV *di-* + *pole*] **1 a :** a pair of equal and opposite electric charges or magnetic poles of opposite sign separated esp. by a small distance **b :** a body or system (as a molecule) having such charges **2 :** a radio or television antenna consisting of two equal horizontal metal rods in line with each other and with their slightly separated adjacent ends connected to the input terminals of the transmitter or receiving set — see FOLDED DIPOLE

dipole moment *n* [ISV *dipole* + *moment*] **:** the electric moment of an electric dipole or the magnetic moment of a magnetic dipole

di·potassium \ˈdī+\ *adj* [*di-* + *potassium*] **:** containing two atoms of potassium in the molecule

dipped *adj* [fr. past part. of [1]*dip*] *of a horse's back* **:** excessively sloped between withers and croup

dip·pel's oil \ˈdipəlz-\ *n, usu cap D* [after Johann K. *Dippel* †1734 Ger. theologian and alchemist who prepared it] **:** BONE OIL 1

dip·per \ˈdipə(r)\ *n* -S [ME *dippere*, a diving bird, fr. *dippen* to dip + *-ere* -er — more at [1]DIP] **1 :** one that dips: **a** *usu cap* **:** a member of a religious sect that practices baptism by immersion **:** BAPTIST, ANABAPTIST, DUNKER **b :** a worker who dips articles into a processing solution (as cleaner, bleach, dye) or into a finishing solution (as color, glaze, paint); *also* **:** a worker who immerses animals in a dip **c :** a worker who builds up articles (as candles, candies, rubber gloves, match tips) by successive dipping into the forming solution **d :** one who only dips into a book ⟨few bona fide readers but many ~s⟩ **e :** one who dips snuff **f :** one who dips from cups the gum exuded from pine trees in the making of turpentine **g** *slang* **:** PICKPOCKET **2 :** any of several birds notable for their skill in diving: as **a :** WATER OUZEL **b** *or* **dipper duck :** BUFFLEHEAD **3 :** something that is used for dipping: **a :** a cup with a long handle for dipping liquids (as drinking water) **b :** the holder for immersing the collodionized glass plate in the silver bath in photoengraving **c :** a receptacle attachable to a palette for holding varnish or other medium **d :** the grab, bucket, or scoop of any of several kinds of excavating machines; *also* **:** the machine itself **4** *Brit* **:** a switch for dimming automobile headlights

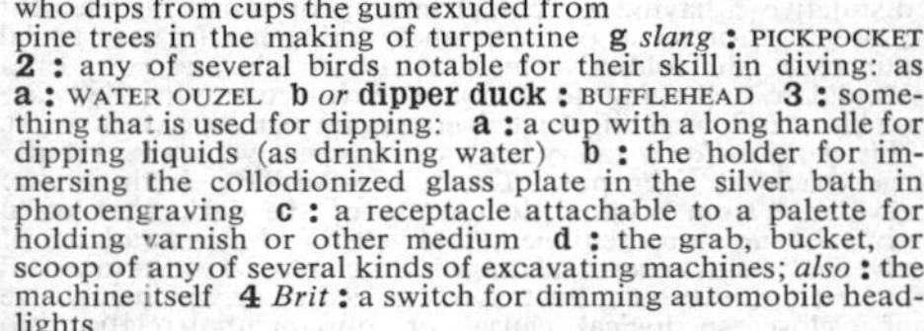

dipper 3a

dipper clam *n* [prob. so called fr. the spoon-shaped receptacle near the umbones] **:** a surf clam (*Spisula solidissima*)

dipper dredge *also* **dipper shovel** *n* **:** a floating dredging machine with a single machine-operated bucket working on an arm

dip·per·ful \-(r),fu̇l\ *n* -S **:** the full quantity a dipper holds

dipper gourd *n* **1 :** a gourd shaped like a dipper; *esp* **:** such a fruit borne by the bottle gourd **2 :** a plant that bears dipper gourds

dipper stick *n* **1 :** a revolving dipper shovel **2 :** the shaft that connects the dipper to the boom in an excavating machine

dip·pi·ness \ˈdipēnəs\ *n* -ES *slang* **:** dippy behavior, appearance, or effect

dipping *n* -S [ME *dippinge*, fr. *dippen* to dip + *-inge* -ing — more at [1]DIP] **:** the liquid preparation in which a thing is dipped

dipping frame *n* **:** a frame used for dipping (as in dipping tallow candles and in dyeing)

dipping lug *n* **:** a lugsail in which the tack is made fast to the deck forward of the mast and the yardarm must be dipped and hoisted again on the other side of the mast in tacking — see LUGSAIL illustration

dip·ping·ly *adv* [*dipping* (pres. part. of [1]*dip*) + *-ly*] **:** with dipping movements

dipping needle *var of* DIP NEEDLE

dipping rod *n* **:** DIVINING ROD

dipping stick *n* **:** DIP 6b

dipping tank *n* **:** a tank or race arranged for complete immersion of an animal in an insecticide

dip pipe *n* **:** a pipe that conveys hot coal gas from retorts in gas manufacturing and discharges through its turned-down upper end into a water seal or into a hydraulic main for removing solubles or condensable impurities

dip·py \ˈdipē\ *adj* -ER/-EST [origin unknown] **1** *slang* **:** mildly insane **:** slightly out of one's mind **:** MAD ⟨a girl feeling ~ about the boy next door⟩ **2** *slang* **:** FOOLISH ⟨a ~ scheme for making money⟩ **:** ODD, QUEER ⟨wearing a very ~ hat on the top of a bun⟩

dip·ri·on·i·dae \,diprēˈänə,dē\ *n pl, cap* [NL, fr. *Diprion*, type genus (fr. *di-* + *-prion*) + *-idae*] **:** a small family of sawflies that have many-jointed antennae serrate in the female and pectinate in the male and that include various serious pests of coniferous trees

di·prismatic \ˈdī+(,)=;==\ *adj* [*di-* + *prismatic*] **:** doubly prismatic

dip rope *n* **:** a seaman's rope tailed with chain for clearing hawse or for mooring

di·propellant \ˈdī+\ *n* [*di-* + *propellant*] **:** BIPROPELLANT

di·propyl \(ˈ)dī+\ *adj* [ISV *di-* + *propyl*] **:** containing two propyl groups in the molecule

dipropyl ketone *n* **:** BUTYRONE

di·pro·so·pus \,dīprəˈsōpəs\ *n* -ES [NL, fr. Gk *diprosōpos* having two faces, fr. *di-* + *-prosōpos* -prosopous] **:** a fetal anomaly with two faces

di·pro·to·don \dīˈprōd·ə,dän\ *n, cap* [NL, fr. *di-* + *prot-* + *-odon*] **1** *cap* **:** a monotypic genus of Australian Pleistocene herbivorous marsupials related to the kangaroos, resembling a rhinoceros in size, and walking on four legs — see DIPROTODONTIA **2** -S **:** any animal or fossil of the genus *Diprotodon*

[1]**di·pro·to·dont** \(ˈ)dī;prōd·ə,dänt\ *adj* [NL *Diprotodont-*, *Diprotodon*] **:** belonging to Diprotodontia

[2]**diprotodont** \"\ *n* -S [NL *Diprotodont-*, *Diprotodon*] **:** a diprotodont mammal

di·pro·to·don·tia \(,)dī,prōd·əˈdänch(ē)ə\ *n pl, cap* [NL, fr. *Diprotodont-*, *Diprotodon* + *-ia*] *in many classifications* **:** a suborder of Marsupialia comprising the kangaroos, phalangers, koala, wombats, the extinct giants of the genus *Diprotodon*, and other marsupials that are all almost exclusively herbivorous, have only one well-developed pair of lower incisors, but usu. have three pairs of upper incisors — compare POLYPROTODONTIA

dips *pl of* DIP, *pres 3d sing of* DIP

dip·sa·ca·ce·ae \,dipsəˈkāsē,ē\ *n pl, cap* [NL, fr. *Dipsacus*, type genus + *-aceae*] **:** a family of chiefly southern European herbs (order Rubiales) having the flowers in heads as in the Compositae but with the stamens separate — **dip·sa·ca·ceous** \;=;=ˈkāshəs\ *adj*

dip·sa·ce·ae \dipˈsāsē,ē\ [NL, prob. alter. of *Dipsacaceae*] *syn of* DIPSACACEAE

dip·sa·ceous \(ˈ)dip;sāshəs\ *adj* [NL *Dipsaceae* + E *-ous*] **:** DIPSACACEOUS

dip·sa·cus \ˈdipsəkəs\ *n, cap* [NL, fr. Gk *dipsakos* teasel, diabetes, fr. *dipsa* thirst] **:** a genus (the type of the family Dipsacaceae) of Old World prickly herbs comprising the teasels

dip·sad·i·dae \dipˈsadə,dē\ [NL, fr. *Dipsad-*, *Dipsas*, genus of snakes (fr. L *dipsad-*, *dipsas* dipsas) + *-idae*] *syn of* AMBLYCEPHALIDAE

dip·sa·do·mor·phi·dae \,dipsə(,)dōˈmȯrfə,dē\ [NL, fr. *Dipsadomorphus*, genus of snakes (fr. *dipsado-* — fr. L *dipsad-*, *dipsas* dipsas — + *-morphus* — fr. Gk *-morphos* -morphous) + *-idae*] *syn of* BOIGIDAE

dip·sas \ˈdipsəs\ *n, pl* **dip·sa·des** \-sə,dēz\ [ME *dipsas*, fr. L *dipsad-*, *dipsas*, fr. Gk, fr. *dipsa* thirst] **:** a serpent with a bite anciently supposed to produce intense thirst

[1]**dip·sey** *or* **dip·sie** *or* **dip·sy** \ˈdipsē, -si\ *adj* [by alter.] **:** DEEP-SEA ⟨a ~ line⟩

[2]**dipsey** *or* **dipsie** *or* **dipsy** \"\ *n, pl* **dipseys** *or* **dipsies** **1 :** DEEP-SEA LEAD **2 :** a sinker attached to a fishing line

dip shift *n* **:** the component of the shift parallel with the dip of a fault

dip slip *n* **:** the part of a fault displacement that is recorded by the separation of originally continuous beds or veins measured straight down the dip and in the plane of the fault

dip-slip fault *n* **:** a geologic fault the displacement of which is predominantly a dip slip

dip slope *n* **:** a land surface inclined in the same direction and at the same angle as the dip of the underlying rocks

dip·so \ˈdip(,)sō\ *n* -S [by shortening] **:** DIPSOMANIAC

dip·so·ma·nia \,dipsəˈmānēə, -sō'-, -nyə\ *n* -S [NL, fr. *dipso-* (fr. Gk *dipsa* thirst) + *mania*] **:** an uncontrollable often periodic craving for alcoholic liquors; *also* **:** ALCOHOLISM — compare CHRONIC ALCOHOLISM

dip·so·ma·ni·ac \-nē,ak\ *n* -S [fr. NL *dipsomania*, after E *mania: maniac*] **:** one affected with dipsomania — **dip·so·ma·ni·a·cal** \;==mə;nīəkəl\ *adj*

dip·so·sau·rus \,dipsōˈsȯrəs\ *n, cap* [NL, fr. *dipso-* (fr. Gk *dipsa* thirst) + *-saurus*] **:** a genus of small iguanid lizards including one form (*D. dorsalis*) that inhabits the desert regions of the southwestern U. S. and feeds on buds and flowers

dipstick \ˈ=,=\ *n* -S **1 :** DIP 6b **2 :** a graduated wooden stick or metal rod for indicating depth (as of oil in a crankcase or gasoline in a tank)

dip stream *n* **:** a stream flowing in the direction of the geologic dip of the rocks it traverses

dip switch *n, Brit* **:** a switch for dimming or lowering automobile headlight beams

dip·sy doo·dle \;dipsē;düdᵊl\ *also* **dipsy doo** \-dü\ *n* -S *often attrib* [origin unknown] **1** *slang* **:** a bewildering plunge and lag by turns ⟨the *dipsy doodle* price of rice shows how unsound the country's economy is⟩ **2** *slang* **:** artfully deceptive or shady manipulation ⟨not theorists, not the advocates of any alien philosophies or political *dipsy doo* —Joseph W. Martin⟩ **3 :** a very slow curve on a pitched ball in baseball

dipt *archaic past of* DIP

dip tank *n* **1 :** DIPPING TANK **2 :** a tank (as of paint) into which objects are dipped for finishing

dip·ter \ˈdiptə(r)\ *n* -S [NL *Diptera*] **:** DIPTERON

dipter- *or* **diptero-** *comb form* [NL, fr. Gk *dipteros*] **1 :** two-winged **:** dipterous ⟨*dipteral*⟩ **2 :** Diptera ⟨*dipterology*⟩

dip·tera \ˈdipt(ə)rə\ *n pl, cap* [NL, fr. Gk, neut. pl. of *dipteros* having two wings, fr. *di-* + *-pteros* -pterous] **:** a large order of winged or rarely wingless insects including the true flies (as the housefly), mosquitoes, midges, gnats, and related forms and a few specialized parasitic forms with the anterior wings usu. functional and the posterior pair reduced to small club-shaped structures, mouthparts adapted for sucking, lapping, or piercing or vestigial, and cylindrical or spindle-shaped segmented often headless, eyeless, and legless larvae that pass through a complex metamorphosis — see BRACHYCERA, HALTER, NEMATOCERA — **dip·ter·an** \-rən\ *n or adj*

dip·ter·al \-t(ə)rəl\ *adj* [L *dipteros* dipteral (fr. Gk *dipteros* having two wings) + E *-al*] **:** marked by columniation consisting of a completely surrounding double row of free columns ⟨a ~ Greek temple⟩ — see PSEUDODIPTERAL; COLUMNIATION illustration

dip·ter·ist \-t(ə)rəst\ *n* -S [NL *Diptera* + E *-ist*] **:** a specialist in the study of Diptera

dip·ter·o·carp \ˈdiptərō,kärp\ *n* -S [NL *Dipterocarpus*] **:** a plant of the genus *Dipterocarpus* or of the family Dipterocarpaceae

dip·ter·o·car·pa·ce·ae \,==(,)=,kärˈpāsē,ē\ *n pl, cap* [NL, fr. *Dipterocarpus*, type genus + *-aceae*] **:** a family of trees (order Parietales) chiefly of tropical Asia yielding valuable wood and aromatic oils and resins and distinguished by having 2-winged fruit — **dip·ter·o·car·pa·ceous** \;==(,)=,=;pāshəs\ *adj*

dip·ter·o·car·pous \;===;kärpəs\ *adj* [*dipterocarp* + *-ous*] **:** of or relating to the genus *Dipterocarpus* or to the family Dipterocarpaceae

dip·ter·o·car·pus \,===ˈ==\ *n, cap* [NL, fr. *dipter-* + *-carpus*] **:** a large genus (the type of the family Dipterocarpaceae) of tall trees ranging from India to the Philippines where they are important as timber — see GURJUN BALSAM

dip·tero·cecidium \;diptə(,)rō+\ *n* [NL, fr. *dipter-* + *cecidium*] **:** a gall caused by an insect of the order Diptera

dip·ter·ol·o·gy \,diptəˈräləjē\ *n* -ES [ISV *dipter-* + *-logy*] **:** a branch of entomology which relates to Diptera

dip·ter·on \ˈdiptə,rän\ *n, pl* **dip·tera** \-t(ə)rə\ [Gk, neut. of *dipteros* having two wings] **:** one of the Diptera

dip·ter·os \-tə,räs\ *n, pl* **dip·ter·oi** \-,rȯi\ [L, dipteral, fr. Gk, having two wings] **:** a dipteral building

dip·ter·ous \ˈdipt(ə)rəs\ *adj* [NL *dipterus*, fr. Gk *dipteros* having two wings] **1 :** having two wings or winglike appendages **2 :** of or relating to the Diptera

dip·ter·us \"\ *n, cap* [NL, fr. Gk *dipteros* having two wings] **:** a genus of Devonian dipnoan fishes of Scotland and America having ganoid scales, two short dorsal fins, and a heterocercal tail

dip·ter·yx \ˈdiptə(,)riks\ *n, cap* [NL, fr. *di-* + *-pteryx;* fr. the wing-shaped lobes of the calyx] **:** a small genus of tropical American trees (family Leguminosae) having opposite pinnate leaves and the calyx with the two upper petaloid lobes like wings — see TONKA BEAN

dip toast *n* **:** toast drenched with milk, cream, or melted butter

dip·tote \ˈdip,tōt\ *n, pl* **dip·totes** \-ōts\ *or* **dip·to·ta** \dipˈtōd·ə\ [LL *diptoton* noun with only two cases, fr. Gk *diptōton*, neut. of *diptōtos* having only one form for two cases, fr. *di-* + *-ptōtos* (fr. *piptein* to fall, influenced in meaning by Gk *ptōsis* case) — more at SYMPTOM] **:** a noun or adjective with only two cases

dip tube *n* **:** a glass or plastic device used for removing debris from the bottom of an aquarium

dip·tych \ˈdip(,)tik, -,tēk\ *n* -S [LL *diptycha*, pl., fr. Gk, fr. neut. pl. of *diptychos* folded, doubled, fr. *di-* + *-ptychos* (akin to Gk *ptychē* fold, layer)] **1 :** a 2-leaved hinged tablet folding together to protect writing on its waxed surfaces used by the ancient Romans for everyday writing **2** *usu pl* [ML *diptychum* list of the dead for whom prayers were said at mass, fr. LL *diptycha*, pl., 2-leaved tablet] **a :** a 2-leaved tablet containing in one part the names of living and in the other those of dead persons commemorated in eucharistic services **b :** the catalog or list of such persons **c :** the intercession in the course of which the commemoration was made **3 :** a picture or series of pictures (as an altarpiece) painted on two tablets connected by hinges — compare TRIPTYCH **4 a :** a literary work consisting of two contrasting parts (as a narrative telling the same story from two opposing points of view) ⟨a ~, a pastoral in which the author narrates the birth of Christ . . . first as it has impressed the rich countryman Asveer, then as it has been seen by the skeptic Nicodemus —François Closset⟩ **b :** any work made up of two matching parts treating complementary or contrasting pictorial phases of one general topic ⟨the first volume of a ~ *Vegetation and Flora of the Sonoran Desert* —F.E.Egler⟩

dip tube

di·pus \ˈdīpəs\ *n, cap* [NL, fr. Gk *dipous* jerboa, fr. *dipous* having two feet, fr. *di-* + *pous* foot — more at FOOT] **:** the type genus of Dipodidae comprising the typical jerboas with but three toes on each hind foot

dipware \ˈ=,=\ *n* **:** pottery decorated by being dipped in slip

di·py·lid·i·um \,dī,pīˈlidēəm, ,dīpəˈl-\ *n, cap* [NL, fr. *di-* + Gk *pylid-*, *pylis* little gate (dim. of *pylē* gate) + NL *-ium*] **:** a genus of taenioid tapeworms including the common double-pored tapeworm (*D. caninum*) that is a cosmopolitan parasite of dogs, cats, and other carnivores and occas. infests man

dip·y·lon \ˈdipə,län\ *adj, often cap* [*Dipylon*, gateway on the west side of ancient Athens, near which pottery in this style has been found] **:** distinctive of an elaborate stage of ancient Greek pottery making and decorating in the geometric style marked by pictures of funerals

di·pyramid \(ˈ)dī+\ *n* [*di-* + *pyramid*] **:** a crystal consisting of two pyramids base to base, the one geometrically a mirror image of the other with respect to the horizontal plane of symmetry ⟨~s occur in the tetragonal, hexagonal, and orthorhombic systems and may have corresponding orthorhombic, tetragonal, ditetragonal, hexagonal, or dihexagonal symmetry⟩

di·pyramidal \(;)dī+\ *adj* [*dipyramid* + *-al*] **1 :** having the shape of a dipyramid **2 :** having symmetry such that the general form is a dipyramid — used of certain of the 32 classes of symmetry

di·pyre \ˈdī,pī(ə)r\ *n* -S [F, fr. *di-* + Gk *pyr* fire; fr. the double effect of fire in fusing it and making it phosphorescent — more at FIRE] : MIZZONITE; *specif* : a variety of scapolite with the components marialite and meionite in a ratio of about 3:2

dir *abbr* **1** direction; directional **2** director

di·radical \(ˈ)dī+\ *n* -s [*di-* + *radical*] : BIRADICAL

dir·ca \ˈdərkə\ *n* [NL, fr. L *Dirce*, a fountain near Thebes in Boeotia, fr. Gk *Dirkē*] **1** *cap* : a genus of shrubs (family Thymelaeaceae) having tough fibrous bark and clusters of yellow flowers — see LEATHERWOOD 1a **2** -s : any plant of the genus *Dirca*

[1]**dird** \ˈdird\ *n* -s [prob. short for *dirdum*] *Scot* : a powerful blow or stroke

[2]**dird** \"\ *vb*, *Scot* : BUMP, BOUNCE, JOLT

dir·dum \ˈdirdəm\ *n* -s [ME (northern dial.) *durdan*, fr. ScGael, grumbling, hum, dim. of *durd* hum, word, sound; akin to IrGael *dordan* hum, buzz, *dord* humming, buzzing] **1** *Scot* : UPROAR, FUSS **2** *Scot* **a** : REBUKE, SCOLDING **b** : BLAME, PUNISHMENT **3** *Scot* : a piece of bad luck : MISFORTUNE

dire \ˈdī(ə)r, -īə\ *adj* -ER/-EST [L *dirus*; akin to Gk *dedienai* to fear, *deos* fear, *deinos* terrible, Av *dvaēthā* threat, Skt *dveṣṭi* he hates] **1 a** : exciting horror or terror esp. because of the great suffering or loss or devastating ruin actually caused or only threatened ⟨the ~ days of bombing raids⟩ ⟨if South America were to seek her imports elsewhere, it would be a ~ blow to us —Gustave Weigel⟩ ⟨the ~ fate which the Lord had seen fit to visit upon her sinful employers —W.H.Wright⟩ **b** : inducing mental suffering or depression by reason of concern with a dreaded eventuality or a grievous circumstance : AFFLICTIVE, PAINFUL ⟨palsied by the ~ news of the president's death⟩ **c** : oppressive to the feelings or spirit : DISMAL, CHEERLESS ⟨the heavy drag of winter is then at its most ~ —F.M.Ford⟩ ⟨despite its ~ point of view, the book jests and jostles with life —*Time*⟩ **2** : warning of disaster to come : OMINOUS, SINISTER ⟨in the fight against foot-and-mouth disease proposals to substitute vaccination for eradication evoked ~ forecasts⟩ **3 a** : demanding immediate action to fend off disastrous con sequences : EXIGENT, URGENT ⟨spokesmen talked about the ~ need for school buildings, which had been at least equally ~ during the previous two years —W.L.Miller⟩ ⟨this was due to ~ necessities elsewhere and not to direct intent or indifference —Herbert Feis⟩ **b** : close to the utmost limit of sufferance : most acute : EXTREME, DESPERATE ⟨scope is left for instantaneous action, but only in the *direst* emergency —A.P.Ryan⟩ ⟨while their means were always modest there was no trace of ~ poverty —J.T.Ellis⟩ ⟨left his family in ~ financial straits⟩ **syn** see FEARFUL

[1]**di·rect** \dəˈrekt *also* dīˈr- *sometimes* ˈdī,r- — *compare* [2]DIRECT\ *vb* -ED/-ING/-S [ME *directen*, fr. L *directus*, past part. of *dirigere* to set straight, direct, guide — more at DRESS] *vt* **1 a** *obs* : to dedicate to a person **b** *obs* : to write to a person **c** : to mark or label the outer surface of (a message or package to be delivered) with the name and residence or place of business of the intended recipient : SUPERSCRIBE **d** : to supply with a heading, statement, or other indication of a specific addressee or desired recipient ⟨the auditors' certificate ~*ed* to the stockholders⟩ **e** : to impart orally ⟨the speaker ~*ed* a side remark to the gallery⟩ **f** : to adapt and arrange in expression so as to have particular applicability or appeal : ANGLE — used with *to* or *at* ⟨a lawyer who ~*s* his appeals to intelligence and character⟩ **2** : to cause to turn, move, or point undeviatingly or to follow a straight course with a particular destination or object in view: **a** : to dispatch, aim, or guide usu. along a fixed path ⟨X rays are ~*ed* through a portion of the body⟩ ⟨wavelengths ~*ed* to southeast Asia⟩ ⟨sensitivity to humor ~*ed* toward himself⟩ ⟨to Peru was ~*ed* one of the main currents of Spanish colonial conquest —P.E.James⟩ ⟨that Locke's influence upon his successors was primarily to ~ them to empiricism —J.W.Yolton⟩; *also* : ASSIGN, ALLOT ⟨many industries ~ part of their earnings to academic scholarship funds⟩ **b** : to devote with concentration — used usu. with *to* or *toward* ⟨has he found that he must have someone else toward whom he can ~ his mind and in whom he can expand himself —H.A.Overstreet⟩ ⟨~*ing* their whole attention toward the international conflict⟩ **c** : to aim fixedly : concern or involve oneself primarily or totally with — used with *to* or *toward* ⟨ecclesiastical policy was ~*ed* primarily toward the liberation of the church from the fetters of secular interest and state expediency —H.D.Hazeltine⟩ ⟨applied research may be defined as research ~*ed* to the end of reducing the degree of empiricism in a practical art —J.B.Conant⟩ **d** : to point, extend, or project esp. upward or downward ⟨in these mammoths the tusks are vertically ~*ed* at their bases —A.S.Romer⟩ **e** : to engage in or launch hostilely : FOCUS — used with *against* or *at* ⟨our policy is not ~*ed* against any country or doctrine but against hunger, poverty, desperation, and chaos —G.C. Marshall⟩ ⟨if atomic or biological warfare should be ~*ed* against us⟩; *also* : to institute for possible launching or application ⟨binding agreements of a much more specific character ~*ed* at a potential aggressor —Vera M. Dean⟩ **3** : to show or point out the way for ⟨a guide ~*s* tourists to the marine museum⟩ ⟨the map ~*s* us to the left⟩ **4** : to regulate the activities or course of: **a** : to guide and supervise ⟨~*ed* the floor strategy in the House of Representatives⟩ ⟨the archaeologist ~*ing* the excavations⟩; *specif* : to carry out the organizing, energizing, and supervising of esp. in an authoritative capacity ⟨~*ed* the building and arming of an underground network⟩ ⟨not only public propaganda, but also cultural infiltration, is ~*ed* from the same source —A.T.Bouscaren⟩ **b** : ADMINISTER, CONDUCT ⟨ably ~*ed* music and language departments⟩ ⟨while in office he ~*ed* vigorous prosecutions of racketeers⟩ **c** : to dominate and determine the course of ⟨will not find it preposterous that the past should be altered by the present as much as the present is ~*ed* by the past —T.S.Eliot⟩ **d** : to assist by giving advice, instruction, and supervision ⟨the major professor ~*s* graduate students' thesis research⟩; *specif* : to lend a refining, cultivating, or inspiring influence to ⟨~ American taste and mold the genius of the young republic —Van Wyck Brooks⟩ **e** : to train and lead performances of (a musical or dramatic aggregation); *also* : to lead a group in presenting (a ballet, opera, concert, play, or motion picture) **5 a** : to request or enjoin esp. with authority ⟨the judge ~*ed* the clerk to pass him the paper⟩ ⟨the resolution ~*ed* the commission to prepare proposals⟩ ⟨I ~ my executors to present my library intact to my alma mater⟩; *also* : to issue an order to ⟨Lee ~*ed* Jackson to make a wide march to the southwest —T.R.Hay⟩ **b** : to prescribe esp. by formal or mandatory instruction or legal enactment ⟨a court order ~*ing* that the person be brought to a court hearing⟩ ⟨postal inspectors ~*ed* destruction of the obscene matter⟩ ~ *vi* **1** : to point out, prescribe, or determine a course or procedure ⟨however chance shall ~⟩ ⟨the ~*ing* agencies of society — the family, the city, the church, the school, the workshop, and above all the state —J.M.Cameron⟩ ⟨the old theological notion that there is in the universe besides ourselves some ~*ing* power that means well by us —J.W.Beach⟩ **2** : to direct an orchestra or chorus or a dramatic group or performance ⟨equally clever at composing and ~*ing*⟩

syn ADDRESS, DEVOTE, APPLY: these four verbs have in common a reflexive use signifying to turn or bend one's attention, energies, or efforts to something. DIRECT and ADDRESS are not significantly different; one can *direct* or *address* oneself to a task, to one's work, or to the study of something; one can *direct* or *address* one's attention, one's remarks, one's writings to something or someone. DIRECT may possibly stress more an aim or intent, ADDRESS more an appeal to or claim upon attention or interest ⟨asked myself to what purpose I should *direct* my energies —M.R.Cohen⟩ ⟨to *direct* my endeavors . . . toward the object of my search —Mary W. Shelley⟩ ⟨speakers *addressed* themselves to a common question —H.W.Sams⟩ ⟨a story *addressed* not only to one's sense of excitement and the exotic but also to his sense of honor and humanity —Charles Lee⟩ DEVOTE often adds the implication of persistence or of personal dedication ⟨at Cornell he *devoted* himself primarily to his studies and to athletics —*Current Biog.*⟩ ⟨*devoted* himself chiefly to the affairs of this school for the next eight or ten years of his life —S.P.Chase & R.E.Ham⟩ APPLY stresses often an intentional turning of the attention or energies, often a concentration or concentrated application; one APPLIES oneself to a task when, after consideration, he determines upon doing the task, or when he directs his whole attention to it, esp. for some time ⟨he cannot *apply* himself to study —Charles Clairmont⟩ ⟨after having received a careful education . . . he *applied* his attention to practical military subjects —*Encyc. Americana*⟩ **syn** see in addition COMMAND, CONDUCT

[2]**di·rect** \dəˈrekt *also* (ˈ)dī¦r-, *rapid* ˈdre-; *after a monosyllabic prefix* -dī- *occurs less often than in other environments, pronunciations like* dī¦rektəˈnində,rekt (*"direct and indirect"*) *being frequent*\ *adj sometimes* -ER/-EST [ME, fr. L *directus* straight, direct, fr. past part. of *dirigere*] **1 a** : proceeding from one point to another in time or space without deviation or interruption : not crooked, oblique, reflected, refracted, or circuitous ⟨~ blows of the gavel⟩ ⟨disintegrated by the ~ heat⟩ ⟨exposed to the ~ force of the hurricane⟩ **b** : leading by the short or shortest way to a point or end ⟨a ~ route⟩ ⟨~ means⟩ ⟨~ rays⟩ ⟨~ and speedy passenger service to the coast⟩ **c** *obs* : moving or extending at a right angle to a surface ⟨a ship needs a ~ wind to enter⟩ **d** : transmitted back and forth without an intermediary ⟨engaged in a ~ exchange of recriminations⟩ ⟨no ~ communication with the flooded area⟩ **e** : assigned in the postal service for separate delivery to a particular addressee rather than routed according to street address ⟨a letter deposited in a ~ pouch⟩ **f** : capable of being allocated to a particular portion or process of an undertaking and so treated in cost accounts; *specif* : chargeable to a particular job — compare DIRECT COST, DIRECT LABOR **2 a** : operating or guided without digression or obstruction ⟨while he gives his more ~ attention to something nearer at hand —Nathaniel Hawthorne⟩ ⟨her letters . . . are a ~ reflection of her personality —R.A.Hall b. 1911⟩ ⟨~ expansion of consumption is of utmost urgency —*New Republic*⟩ **b** : stemming immediately from a source ⟨having no ~ authority over factory employment policies⟩ **c** : being or passing in a straight line of descent from parent to offspring : LINEAL ⟨only a collateral relative, not his ~ ancestor⟩ ⟨the examiner should not overvalue the influence of ~ heredity —H.G.Armstrong⟩ **d** : clear-cut and distinctive : having no compromising or impairing element : GENUINE, OUT-AND-OUT ⟨an undertaking having a ~ social purpose⟩ ⟨the soldier's pleasures are simple and ~ —Fred Majdalany⟩ ⟨hoping to avoid ~ involvement in the war⟩ **e** : blunt and unqualified : delivered point-blank : CATEGORICAL ⟨his petition for a salary increase was met with a ~ rebuff⟩ ⟨get back to your post. That's a ~ order —Irwin Shaw⟩ ⟨evidence from original documents of the dark ages often give the lie ~ to sentimental novelists⟩ **f** *cryptanalysis, of alphabetic sequences* : arranged or employed in traditional order : not reversed **3 a** : characterized by or giving evidence of a close esp. logical, causal, or consequential relationship ⟨there is a ~ personal tie which assures the beginning of real understanding between individuals —D.J.Shank⟩ ⟨most scientific discoveries now have a ~ bearing on security⟩ ⟨for 20 years in ~ association with the library⟩ ⟨a hundred different complications in which we shall have a ~ interest —F.D. Roosevelt⟩ **b** : INEVITABLE, UNEQUIVOCAL ⟨one ~ result of improving the living conditions was a rise in the birthrate⟩ **c** : serving to get to the point : EFFECTIVE ⟨raising funds would be a ~*er* way of helping the cause⟩ **d** : communicating explicitly often with brusqueness : going straight to the point ⟨before any inquiry so ~ as to demand a positive answer was addressed to her —Jane Austen⟩ ⟨keeps the play ~, uncluttered, and so brisk that the long and familiar story does not make martyrs of its audience —Henry Hewes⟩ ⟨her choreography is ~, nowhere obscured by extraneous devices⟩ **e** : frank, natural, and positive : STRAIGHTFORWARD ⟨a charming, lively person who had a ~ mind, said what he thought and believed others did the same —*Times Lit. Supp.*⟩ ⟨that one's relations with others should be ~ and not diplomatic —A.C.Benson⟩ ⟨it often told you a great deal that was both too ~ and too elusive for words —Willa Cather⟩ **f** *of the object of a verb* : being the one that is the primary goal of an action (*him* in "I saw him" and *me* in "he hit me" are ~ objects) or that results from an action (*a house* in "we built a house" is the ~ object) **4** : marked by absence of an intervening agency, instrumentality, or influence : IMMEDIATE: **a** : made, carried on, or effected without any intruding factor or intervening step ⟨~ loans⟩ ⟨relying less and less on ~ observation of nature —Eric Newton⟩ ⟨some ~ borrowing of Anglo-Norman into English⟩ ⟨until the breaking off of ~ negotiations⟩ **b** : effected by the votes of the people or the electorate and not by representatives ⟨elected for 7 years by ~ suffrage —*Statesman's Yr. Bk.*⟩ ⟨institutions of ~ democracy — popular initiative, the referendum, and the recall —C.A.M.Ewing⟩ ⟨the ~ election of senators —E.P.Herring⟩ **c** : unhampered by divergent, intervening, or separative forces ⟨he had more ~ access to the governor than the legislators⟩ ⟨prefer the more ~ American approach to human problems —David Daiches⟩ **d** : effected by one object or substance in contact with another with no insulating or obstructing element between ⟨~ contact with another metal must be avoided⟩ ⟨there is no ~ connection between the apartments⟩ **e** : consisting of or reproducing the exact words of a real or supposed original speaker ⟨the words in quotation marks in the sentence *He said, "I can come"* are ~ quotation⟩ ⟨~ discourse⟩ **f** (1) : being without intermediate logical steps ⟨~ proofs⟩ (2) : independent of intermediate representations, percepts, images, or sense data ⟨~ knowledge of things⟩ **g** : not requiring an intermediate host for completion : MONOXENOUS — used of the life cycle or development of a parasitic organism **h** : capable of dyeing without the aid of a mordant : SUBSTANTIVE — see DIRECT DYE **5 a** : experienced personally without associative effort of anyone else ⟨his account of the battle contains much ~ evidence⟩ ⟨whereas to conceal ~ pain was a virtue, to conceal vicarious pain was a sin —Jan Struther⟩; *specif* : FIRSTHAND ⟨from ~ experience with youngsters at camp⟩ **b** : active, personal, and responsible ⟨taking ~ charge of the distribution of relief funds⟩ ⟨the ordinary worker has a ~ part in the production process⟩; *specif* : not deputed or to be deputed ⟨few were willing to assume ~ responsibility⟩ **6 a** *of a celestial body* : moving in the general planetary direction from west to east : not retrograde **b** *of a binary star* : following the direction of increasing position angle : COUNTERCLOCKWISE **7** *of a sundial* : having a vertical face and facing squarely toward one of the cardinal points of the compass

[3]**di·rect** \dəˈrekt *also* dīˈ-, *rapid* ˈdre-\ *adv* [ME, fr. *direct*, adj.] : in a direct way: **a** : from point to point without deviation : by the short or shortest way ⟨by helicopter it is now possible to go ~ from port to airport in forty minutes —Ivor Jones⟩ ⟨despatching individual books ~ to individual teachers —James Britton⟩ **b** : from the source or the original without interruption or diversion ⟨broadcast ~ from ringside⟩ ⟨the writer must take his material ~ from life —Douglas Stewart⟩ **c** : mechanically joined or in mesh : mechanically or electrically in contact ⟨*direct*-controlled by the helmsman⟩ **d** (1) : without any intervening agency or step : without any intruding or diverting factor ⟨some enter a career ~ from college⟩ ⟨refusal to negotiate ~ with the puppet regime⟩; *specif* : without use of a broker or other middleman ⟨butter that is sold ~ without going through the exchanges —Geoffrey Shepherd⟩ (2) : EXPLICITLY, UNEQUIVOCALLY ⟨the right information ~ from his office⟩ ⟨in reporting news the television camera brings the event and the personalities ~ to the public —*Collier's Yr. Bk.*⟩ (3) : VERBATIM ⟨translated ~ from the Russian text⟩

[4]**direct** \"\ *n* -s [[2]*direct*] **1** : a character sometimes put at the end of a musical staff or page of music on a line or space corresponding to the position of the first note of the next staff as a warning to the performer — called also *custos* **2** : a direct package of postal matter

di·rect·able \dəˈrektəbəl *also* dīˈ-, *rapid* ˈdre-\ *adj* : capable of being directed

direct–acting \¦≡¦≡, ¦≡,≡¦≡\ *adj* : involving direct action without the intervention of other working parts ⟨*direct-acting* engine⟩ ⟨*direct-acting* pump⟩

direct action *n* : action that seeks to achieve an end directly and by the most immediately effective means as opposed to the use of diplomatic exchange or negotiation; *specif* : action by organized labor to obtain ends by means of boycott, sabotage, or striking — contrasted with *political action*

direct bearing *n* : direct vertical support for any structural element in a construction

direct black *n* : any of various direct dyes that dye cotton black — see DYE table I

direct cell division *n* : AMITOSIS

direct cerebellar tract *n* : a tract of fibers in the posterior lateral part of the spinal cord that is external to the crossed pyramidal tract, that arises from the cells of the nucleus dorsalis, and that passes through the restiform body of the medulla to the cerebellum

direct–connected \¦≡¦≡≡, ¦≡,≡¦≡≡\ *adj*, *of machines* : being on a common shaft : DIRECT-COUPLED

direct contempt *n* : a contempt occurring in the presence of a court in session or so near as to interfere with the administration of justice or in the presence of a judge acting in a judicial capacity; *also* : a contempt directly obstructing a legislative body in the actual exercise of its lawful legislative powers — compare CONSTRUCTIVE CONTEMPT

direct control *n* : a control that is directly imposed upon the manufacturing, pricing, and distribution of specific goods in contrast with an indirect or general control (as a credit and fiscal policy) that affects the economy in its entirety and specific goods only indirectly

direct cost *also* **direct charge** *n* : a cost that may be computed and identified directly with a product, function, or activity and that usu. involves expenditures for raw materials and direct labor and sometimes specific and identifiable items of overhead — contrasted with *indirect cost*

direct–coupled \¦≡¦≡≡, ¦≡,≡¦≡\ *adj* **1** *of belting or gearing* : coupled without intermediate connections **2** *of an electric circuit* : having conductive rather than inductive or capacitive coupling

direct current *n* : an electric current flowing in one direction only and substantially constant in value — abbr. *D.C.*; compare ALTERNATING CURRENT

direct deep black EW *n*, *usu cap both Ds&B* : a trisazo dye derived from benzidine and used esp. for dyeing cotton and leather and as a biological stain — called also *chlorazol black E*, *direct black EW*; see DYE table I (*under Direct Black 38*)

direct democracy *n* : DEMOCRACY 1b(1)

direct development *n* : development without a metamorphosis

direct distance dialing *n* : the dialing of a telephone number outside the local calling area by using initial code numbers to make a direct connection — abbr. *DDD*

direct drive *n* : a drive whose driving and driven parts are direct-connected

direct–driven \¦≡¦≡≡, ¦≡,≡¦≡\ *adj* : driven by another machine to which it is direct-connected

direct dye *n* : a water-soluble dye usu. of the azo class that is used in alkaline or neutral solution esp. for dyeing cellulosic material (as cotton or paper) directly — see DYE table I

directed *adj* [fr. past part. of [1]*direct*] **1** : having a positive or negative sense — used of a line segment or vector **2** : subject to regulation by a guiding and supervising agency ⟨a ~ economy that would permit an increased volume of capital investments on the part of the state —C.A.L.Rich⟩ ⟨a ~ study program for gifted children⟩

di·rect·ed·ly *adv* : under guidance and supervision

di·rect·ed·ness *n* -ES : subjection to a guiding or motivating influence ⟨the interplay within the individual of these two ~*es* —Adam Curle⟩

directed number *n* : a number preceded by a plus or minus sign

directed verdict *n* : a verdict that the jury is instructed by the court to find when the facts proved do not admit in the court's opinion of any reasonable doubt

di·rect·ee \də¦rek¦tē, dī¦r-, ¦dī,rek¦-\ *n* -s [[1]*direct* + *-ee*] : one who receives direction

directer *comparative of* DIRECT

directest *superlative of* DIRECT

direct evidence *n* : evidence that if true immediately establishes the fact to be proved by it

direct examination *n* : the first examination of a witness in the orderly course by the party calling him and upon the merits

direct exchange *n* : FIXED EXCHANGE

direct finder *n* : DIRECT VIEWFINDER

direct fire *n* [[3]*direct* + *fire*, v.] : gunfire by direct aiming on a visible target

direct–fire \¦≡¦≡, ¦≡,≡¦≡\ *vt* : to fire without provision for preheating the air or gas ⟨some furnaces are *direct-fired*⟩

direct–geared \"\ *adj* : connected for power transmission by a gear on the power shaft of one machine meshing with a gear on the driving or following shaft of another machine

direct grant school *n*, *in England & Wales* : a private secondary school that receives a direct grant from the ministry of education and in return binds itself to obey certain conditions with reference to admission of pupils

directing *pres part of* DIRECT

directing piece *n* : BASE PIECE

direct initiative *n* : the legislative initiative where a proposed measure is submitted directly to the voters — distinguished from *indirect initiative*; compare INITIATIVE 3b

direct investment *n* : investment of capital in physical assets or in ownership of a whole enterprise — contrasted with *portfolio investment*

[1]**di·rec·tion** \dəˈrekshən *also* dīˈ-, *rapid* ˈdre-\ *n* -s [MF & L; MF, fr. L *direction-*, *directio*, fr. *directus* (past part. of *dirigere* to direct, guide) + *-ion-*, *-io* -ion — more at DRESS] **1 a** : guidance or supervision of action, conduct, or operation ⟨the whole system of life had its culmination in the church; and parson and squire presided over its ~ —C.E.Raven⟩ ⟨under whose ~ this paper was written⟩ ⟨the doctrine that government should move forward toward ~ of the economy⟩; *specif* : chief executive function ⟨he was put in charge and given overall ~ of the program⟩ **b** : the art and technique of directing a stage play, a motion picture, or a television program consisting of the selection of the effects to be produced, the means to produce these effects, and the management and training of the cast **c** : the art and technique of directing the performance of an orchestra, opera, or concert or of a chorus or other musical group ⟨the musicianly ~ . . . helped illumine the score —Miles Kastendieck⟩ **d** : a word or phrase usu. in Italian or a sign indicating the appropriate tempo, mood, or intensity of a passage or movement in a musical score **2** *archaic* : the address placed on the outside of a letter or package to be delivered : SUPERSCRIPTION ⟨pray send me Grandmamma's ~. I must write to her —W.M.Thackeray⟩ **3 a** : something that is imposed as authoritative instruction or bidding ⟨the senate had been voting according to ~ for so long that they seemed to have lost the power of independent decision —Robert Graves⟩ ⟨he gave orders all round and men quickly obeyed—relieved at ~ —Harris Downey⟩ **b** : an explicit instruction : ORDER, COMMAND ⟨a report prepared at the ~ of the president⟩ — often used in pl. ⟨the author's stage ~*s* to actors and cameramen⟩ ⟨~*s* appear on the package⟩ **c** : the charge or instruction given on a point of law by a judge to a jury **4** *obs* : administrative capacity **5 a** : the property of space by which given two positions others may be generated or determined in the same dimension and relation, the aspect of progression being usu. implicit **b** : the line or course on which something is moving or is aimed to move or along which something is pointing or facing ⟨the ~ of a current is that toward which the water moves, which is the reverse of the way winds are named —G.W.Mixter⟩ ⟨follow the ~ of the arrow⟩ **c** : a line or course extending away from a given point through space and often designated by the point of the compass toward which it extends ⟨from the tower sweeping views in all ~*s*⟩ ⟨below the falls the river meanders in a southeasterly ~⟩ **d** : the shortest path toward the vicinity or source — used in the expression *in the direction of* ⟨throwing grenades in the ~ of the voices⟩ **e** : a position on a line extending through space toward a point of the compass ⟨from what ~ will the attack come⟩ ⟨protests poured in from all ~*s*⟩; *also* : a point of view or an angle from which something may be considered ⟨the three authors attack the same subject from three different ~*s*⟩ **f** : the angle between a true north-south line passing through the position of the observer and a great circle passing through both this position and a given point on the surface of the earth : BEARING **g** : the path of either the longest straight line that can be drawn along a sheet or band of paper or a straight line crossing this at right angles from edge to edge **6 a** : a channel or direct course of thought or action ⟨the outbreak of war gave another ~ to his activities⟩ ⟨the ~*s* in which voters can express their will are limited⟩ ⟨with business expanding in all ~*s*⟩ **b** : a course of progress, development, or evolution showing a distinct tendency or trend ⟨his latest

title indicates the ~ his historical studies have taken⟩ ⟨the existence of the censorship deters men . . . from essaying new ~*s* in drama —A.B.Walkley⟩ ⟨it is because culture molds the specific ~ and activities of the personality —Abram Kardiner⟩; *also* : tenor of a saying or writing ⟨I had felt and written to him in the same general ~ —O.W.Holmes †1935⟩ **c** : a path or course esp. of thought or effort marked by a specific aim or design ⟨the introduction of printing in Italy in 1462 gave a new ~ to scholarship —R.A.Hall b. 1911⟩ ⟨ideals are not meant to be reached; they merely indicate the ~ of movement —Edward Sapir⟩ ⟨even those who do not accept the letter of his dogma are in accord with the ~ taken by his thought —W.L.Sperry⟩; *also* : a pointing of thought or effort on a predetermined path or course ⟨his ~ toward a life of asceticism and contemplation was already clear —W.P.Clancy⟩ ⟨there the boy began to give ~ to the instinct for arranging nature that later was translated into a delightful profession —José Gómez-Sicre⟩ ⟨a deep uncertainty about goals and obligations pervades all classes and all levels of culture. Our society has lost ~ —Walter Moberly⟩ **d** : an onward path determined through inclination or guidance pointing toward some attainment ⟨the conspiracy gained momentum and ~ —R.C.Doty⟩ ⟨slow to make up his mind what his ~ as a writer ought to be⟩ ⟨stood about idly on the street corners without purpose or ~ in their lives —Oscar Handlin⟩ **e** : determinative guiding or governing design ⟨cultivate the historical sense and a sense of ~, and read some good books on the history of law; at least, the law has ~ —Caroline Slade⟩ **7** : the way of advancement, furtherance, or cultivation : AIM, PURPOSE, OBJECTIVE — used in the expression *in the direction of* ⟨gains made in the ~ of integration⟩ ⟨a significant step in the ~ of cooperation between the executive and congress in treaty making —Vera M. Dean⟩ ⟨advocate of reforms particularly in the ~ of equalizing the legal status of men and women —H.W.H.Knott⟩ **8** : an indicated sphere or role in which something may be regarded : a particular respect ⟨a few pencil portraits do exist which show that he had great talent in this ~ —Herbert Read⟩ ⟨much of the literature (geographical, historical, and economic) on Czechoslovakia is biased in one ~ or another —*Geog. Jour.*⟩ **9** *archaic* : DIRECTORATE 1 **10** : a calculation by reference to a horoscope of the times when events will happen **11** *in equity practice* : the part of a bill containing the address to the court **12** : the lateral pointing of an artillery piece — compare ELEVATION **13** : one of the cardinal points which among some peoples include the zenith, nadir, and center and intermediate points of the compass

²di·rec·tion \"\ *vt* **directioned**; **directioned**; **directioning** \-sh(ə)niŋ\ **directions** : to give a direction to : direct along a line ⟨strangely ~*ed* water —D.L.Morgan⟩

di·rec·tion·al \-shənᵊl, -shnəl\ *adj* **1** : relating to direction in space: **a** : moving, aiming, or leading in some particular direction ⟨a strictly ~ flight on a great circle⟩ ⟨~ lines showing winds and ocean currents⟩ **b** : suitable or used for detecting the direction in which or from which signals are received ⟨plot position by ~ radio⟩ ⟨flying on the beam of a ~ radio range⟩ **c** : so designed that performance depends on direction or is restricted in direction : more effective in some directions than others ⟨a polarized ~ electromagnet controls the position and shape of the tail flame —J.K.Elderkin⟩ ⟨the use of ~ broadcasting techniques had made it possible to increase the number of radio stations —F.L.Mott⟩; *specif* : narrowly selective as to direction in the emission or reception of signals ⟨a highly ~ microphone picks up sounds coming from a single direction⟩ ⟨that a Geiger-Müller tube cannot be made ~ enough and still retain any measure of workable sensitivity —*Surgical Forum*⟩ **d** *of sound* : controlled for giving depth and realism in motion pictures by the use of several sound tracks recorded at different parts of the set or location **e** : indicating the direction in which something lies or the direction to take or about to be taken ⟨a ~ airway marker⟩ ⟨~ arrows for facilitating movement of traffic⟩ ⟨flashing ~ signals for motorcars and trucks⟩ **2** : relating to direction (as of thought, effort, or culture): **a** : aimed or moving in the direction of one or another object, objective, or condition ⟨the picture presented is frankly chaotic; it is hard to recognize in it any unifying pattern, any ~ trends —V.G.Childe⟩ ⟨the ~ quality of cultural change⟩ **b** : constitutive of purpose or motivation **3 a** : consisting of or imposing direction or guidance ⟨the ~ role that profits play under capitalism⟩ **b** : suitable or contributory to the direction of dramatic performance ⟨good plays and even good ~ ideas frequently take on a distressingly ragged aspect in performance —H.E.Clurman⟩ **c** *of an oil-well drilling* : made at an angle with the vertical

directional filter *n* : an electric filter designed to divide the band of frequencies available for carrier currents about midway using one portion of the band for east-to-west transmission and the other portion for west-to-east transmission

directional gyro *n* : an air-driven free gyroscope with rotor spinning on a horizontal axis that when manually set to some one direction maintains that fixed direction despite maneuvers of its conveyor and thereby indicates any deviation from the course

di·rec·tion·al·i·ty \də̇,rekshə'naləd·ē, (,)dī,-\ *n* -ES **1** : the property of directional selectivity or precision ⟨a scintillation counter was devised in such a fashion as to give a ~ of fifteen degrees and adequate sensitivity —*Surgical Forum*⟩ **2** : maintenance of direction ⟨among these properties is that of ~ —C.K.Kluckhohn⟩

di·rec·tion·al·ize \də̇'reksh(ə)nə,līz, dī'-\ *vt* -ED/-ING/-S : to guide or govern as to direction

di·rec·tion·al·ly \-nəlē, -li\ *adv* : as to or with reference to direction

direction angle *n* : an angle made by a given line with an axis of reference; *specif* : one of the three angles made by a straight line with the three axes of a rectangular coordinate system

direction cosine *n* : one of the cosines of the three angles between a directed line in space and the positive directions of the axes of a rectangular Cartesian coordinate system — usu. used in pl.

direction finder *n* : a radio receiving device permitting determination of the direction from which received radio waves come to it, typically consisting of a coil antenna mounted on a vertical axis so that it can be rotated freely

direction finding *n* : the finding of the azimuth of a distant transmitter by the use of a direction finder

direction indicator *n* : a compass that assists an airplane pilot in flying a predetermined course by direct reading and comparison of two indicators one of which is set for the desired heading while the other shows the actual heading so that when the two indicators point alike the airplane is flying the desired course

di·rec·tion·ize \-shə,nīz\ *vt* -ED/-ING/-S : to impel in a particular direction

di·rec·tion·less \-ənlə̇s\ *adj* **1** : having no discernible direction **2** : having no guiding purpose

direction post *n, Brit* : GUIDEPOST

directions *pl of* DIRECTION, *pres 3d sing of* DIRECTION

direction test *n* : a psychological test measuring an individual's success in following simple or complex directions

direction word *n* : CATCHWORD 1a

direction indicator: *1* index setting knob, *2* pointer, *3* reference index

¹di·rec·tive \də̇'rektiv, -tēv *also* dī'- *or* -təv\ *adj* [MF & ML; MF *directif*, fr. ML *directivus*, fr. L *directus* (past part. of *dirigere* to direct, guide) + *-ivus* -ive — more at DRESS] **1** : serving or qualified to lead, guide, or govern thought or action usu. by prompting and impelling rather than by dominating ⟨the ~ power of conscience⟩ ⟨experimenting to find which is superior, the permissive or the ~ method of teaching⟩ ⟨every manager who has at least one subordinate engages in the ~ function —Harold Koontz & Cyril O'Donnell⟩ **2** : serving to point direction ⟨the ~ power of a magnetized needle⟩ ⟨the ~ function of a compass⟩; *specif* : DIRECTIONAL 1c ⟨a more ~ aerial⟩ **3** : pointing the way : concentrating or focusing on an objective : selective as to tendency or trend ⟨like the realities of the external environment they exercise a ~ influence on the development of behavior patterns —Ralph Linton⟩ **4** : of or relating to psychotherapy or counseling in which the counselor introduces information, content, or attitudes not previously expressed by the client

²directive \"\ *n* -S **1** : something that serves to direct, guide, and usu. impel toward an action, attainment, or goal: **a** : a pronouncement urging or banning some action or conduct : BIDDING ⟨leaders became too fond of passing down ~*s* to the members instead of calling for a vote⟩; *also* : a sharp or peremptory word of command ⟨"keep your head down!" . . . and a heavy hand on top of his head added persuasion to the ~ —Helen Nielsen⟩ **b** : an assignment, instruction, or injunction by a superior ⟨the verdict of the people in the recent election constituted a ~ —B.C.Reece⟩ **c** : an advisory instruction or set of directions ⟨progress has been hampered by inadequate coordination, lack of clear ~*s* —*Economist*⟩ ⟨dependent on the ~*s* of the guidebook and the hotel porter⟩ **d** : an ideological, traditional, cultural, or moral influence or principle : EXEMPLAR ⟨folk wisdom preserves many ~*s* —L.J.Davidson⟩ ⟨they were not trained in a school of science which accepts Marxism-Leninism as the supreme ~ —C.P.Fitzgerald⟩ **e** : a communication that initiates or governs action, conduct, or procedure **f** : an authoritative instrument that promulgates a program or regulation or directs or prohibits certain acts and that is issued by a high-level official body or competent official as a broad policy statement to be developed by technicians or as an explicit instruction with details; *usu* : such an instrument of a national regime or international body esp. of a head of a government or an administrative bureau whose decrees have the force of an executive order ⟨a relatively new administrative device called the "~" . . . was frequently used by the president and other high officials to explain, modify, or amplify an order —C.O.Johnson⟩ ⟨he issued a stream of ~*s* that in their entirety imposed a far-reaching social revolution upon Japan —Allan Taylor⟩ ⟨~*s* which actually have the force of law —H.W. Sumners⟩ **2** : DIRECTIVE MESENTERY

directive antenna *n* : an antenna that radiates or receives better in some directions than in others

di·rec·tive·ly \-tə̇vlē, -li\ *adv* : so as to guide : with directive methods ⟨taught a psychology class ~⟩

directive mesentery *n* : either member of one or more pairs of mesenteries in actinians that differ from other mesenteries in the arrangement of the muscles and serve to determine the longitudinal plane of the body

di·rec·tive·ness \-tivnə̇s, -tēv- *also* -təv-\ *n* -ES : the quality of being directive; *specif* : the character of being determined in direction of development (as toward definitely organized structure) ⟨impressed by the apparent ~ of evolution —*Brit. Book News*⟩

di·rec·tiv·i·ty \də̇,rek'tivəd·ē, (,)dī,-\ *n* -ES **1** : DIRECTIVENESS **2** : the property of being directional or a measure of that property (as the front-to-back ratio of microphone response) : ORIENTATION; *specif* : a measure of the property in an antenna, loudspeaker, microphone, or other transducer used for sound transmission or reception by which its performance in one direction is better than that in another

direct labor *n* **1** : labor (as machine operators) applied directly to a product in the manufacturing process so that the cost is computable, identifiable, and chargeable directly to the specific product — called also *productive labor*; compare INDIRECT LABOR **2** : the wages paid to workers classed as direct labor

direct laying *n* : the laying of an artillery piece with the line of sighting directly upon the target

direct lighting *n* : lighting in which the greater part of the luminous flux goes directly from the fixture toward the area to be illuminated

direct loss by fire : loss traceable to fire as the proximate cause : loss that is caused by smoke or by water used in extinguishing a fire

¹di·rect·ly \də̇'rek(t)lē *or* -li *or* (*rapid in senses other than 6*) 'dre- *or* (*esp in senses other than 6*) (')dī¦re-; *in sense 6 often* 'drekl- *in both the US & England and chiefly substand South* tə̇'rekl-\ *adv* [ME, fr. ²*direct* + *-ly*] **1 a** : without any intervening space or time : next in order : SQUARELY, EXACTLY ⟨~ opposite the city hall⟩ ⟨~ in the center of the room⟩ ⟨during the decade ~ before his birth⟩ ⟨he holds a position ~ below that of the president⟩ **b** : in a straight line : without deviation of course ⟨the turnpike here runs ~ east and west⟩ ⟨a dredged channel allows boats to get in and out ~⟩ : by the shortest way ⟨we headed ~ into the mountain country⟩ **2 a** : straight on along a definite course of action without deflection or slackening ⟨proceeds to go ~ to a children's hospital⟩ ⟨the problem being ~ attacked⟩ ⟨~ or by the most circuitous routes the fountain of happiness is what all living entities fumble and grope toward —J.C.Powys⟩ **b** : purposefully or decidedly and straight to the mark ⟨~ engaged in replacing muscle power with machine power⟩ : in a straightforward manner without hesitation, circumlocution, or equivocation : plainly and not by implication ⟨he ~ criticizes contemporary society⟩ : in unmistakable terms : UNQUALIFIEDLY ⟨deals ~ with the stated purpose of the book —Stanley Newman⟩ **c** : without divergence from the source or the original ⟨that the only valid method of painting was to paint ~ from nature and to imitate nature as closely as possible —Michael Kitson⟩ **d** : simultaneously and exactly or equally ⟨that certain types of costs are neither ~ variable with output nor entirely fixed —Harold Koontz & Cyril O'Donnell⟩ **3** : in close relational proximity ⟨increased interest in art may be ~ traceable to present easy and lucrative employment⟩ ⟨new evidence bearing ~ on the question of guilt⟩ ⟨~ concerned in the founding of the university⟩ **4 a** : without any intervening agency or instrumentality or determining influence : without any intermediate step ⟨writes ~ in Spanish⟩ ⟨paints ~ on canvas⟩ ⟨take part in the government either ~ or through freely chosen representatives⟩ **b** : in the exact words of the original : VERBATIM ⟨permitted to take notes but enjoined not to quote anything ~⟩ **5 a** : in independent action without any sharing of authority or responsibility ⟨the initial steps in the process of demilitarization and democratization were handled ~ by the American occupying forces —C.E.Black & E.C.Helmreich⟩ **b** : FACE-TO-FACE : in person ⟨dealing ~ with the strikers⟩ **6 a** : without a moment's delay : at once : IMMEDIATELY ⟨get a doctor ~⟩ **b** : after a little : in a little while : SHORTLY, PRESENTLY ⟨we'll discuss that ~; first we must act on this motion⟩

²directly *like sense 6 of* ¹DIRECTLY\ *conj, chiefly Brit* : immediately after : as soon as ⟨apparently written ~ their agreement was made —K.J.Fielding⟩ ⟨~ we enter it we breast some new wave of emotion —Virginia Woolf⟩

direct mail *n* : printed matter prepared to solicit trade or contributions and sent directly through the mails to individuals (as letters, cards, circulars, catalogs, house periodicals)

direct material *n* : material used in manufacturing processes which becomes an integral part of the product and the cost of which is identifiable and chargeable directly to it — compare INDIRECT MATERIAL

direct method *n* : a teaching method that seeks to dispense with theoretical discussion and historical considerations in favor of concrete observation and practical experience; *specif* : a method of teaching a language through conversation, discussion, and reading in the language itself without translation and without the study of formal grammar

di·rect·ness *n* -ES **1 a** : the character of being true in course toward a target or goal ⟨rivaling a hawk in ~ of aim⟩ ⟨stared at her youngest niece with concentrated ~ —J.C.Snaith⟩ **b** : strict pertinence or distinct forthrightness : straightforwardness often with a degree of abruptness or brusqueness ⟨his sledgehammer ~ had often served him better than nice legal knowledge —Thomas Hardy⟩ **2** : closeness to actual experience and consequent vividness or incisiveness ⟨described Ireland's troubles with a searing ~ that has rarely been equalled —*Time*⟩ **3** : open frankness and naturalness : freedom from barriers of pretense and pretension and from adornment and prettiness ⟨created an atmosphere of ~ between herself and all men and women —Eden Phillpotts⟩ ⟨what people take for rudeness is really ~ —Ian Bevan⟩

di·rec·toire \də̇,rek¦twär, dē¦r-, ¦dē,r-\ *adj, usu cap* [F, fr. *Directoire*, the body of five men that held executive power in France from 1795–1799, fr. *directoire* directory (book — influenced in meaning by *directeur* director), fr. MF, fr. ML *directorium* — more at DIRECTORY] : of, relating to, or imitative of the kind or style prevalent in France during the French Revolution: as **a** *of women's clothes* : imitative of classic dress and marked by a picturesque hat with a flaring brim and a décolleté gown usu. with short sleeves and a skirt hanging straight down like a tube from a waistline just under the bust **b** *of furniture* : transitional between the Louis Seize style and the Empire style and not sharply distinguishable from the latter

di·rec·tor \də̇'rektə(r) *also* (')dī¦r-, *rapid* 'dre-\ *n* -S [LL, fr. L *directus* (past part. of *dirigere* to direct) + *-or* — more at DRESS] **1** : one that directs: as **a** : the head or chief of an organized occupational group (as a bureau, foundation, institute, school) ⟨the ~ of the budget⟩ ⟨orientation of new school ~*s* is the responsibility of the county superintendent⟩ ⟨thousands of ~*s* of religious education now at work —J.O. Nelson⟩ ⟨a department of public relations headed by a ~ —R.F.Harlow & M.M.Black⟩ **b** : one of a group of persons entrusted by the shareholders of a corporation with the final overall control and direction of the corporate enterprise ⟨final authority in a corporation of this sort lies with a board of ~*s* —P.M.Sweezy⟩ **c** : one that supervises the production of a show (as for stage, screen, or radio transmission) with responsibility for action, lighting, music, rehearsals and generally for giving substance to the conception of the author — compare PRODUCER 4a **d** : CONDUCTOR 6 **e** : a college teacher that directs students individually in the choice of a program and in special projects (as research for a thesis or practice teaching) — compare ADVISER **f** : the head judge in a fencing match **2** [trans. of F *directeur*, fr. MF *directeur* director, fr. LL *director*] : a member of the French Directory of 1795–99 **3** : an instrument grooved to guide and limit the motion of a surgical knife **4** : a computing machine for controlling gunfire that automatically and continuously predicts the future position of the target and computes the ballistically correct firing data **5** *Brit* : a device to hold in position an unattended fire hose emitting a jet of water

di·rec·tor·al \-t(ə)rəl\ *adj* : DIRECTORIAL

di·rec·tor·ate \də̇'rekt(ə)rə̇t *also* dī'-, *rapid* 'dre-, *usu* -ə̇d·+V\ *n* -S [F *directorat*, fr. LL *director* + F *-at* -ate] **1** : the office or occupancy of the office of director (as of an agency) ⟨served during the ~ of his predecessor⟩ **2** : ²DIRECTORY 2a ⟨a perpetuating ~ which subordinates the making of laws and the processes of the courts to the orders of the executive —F.D. Roosevelt⟩ **3 a** : a board of directors of a corporation ⟨two subsidiary funds, each with its own ~ and administrative staff —Craig Thompson⟩ **b** : membership on a board of directors ⟨was required to resign his ~*s* before accepting the appointment⟩ **4** : an executive staff in charge of a program, bureau, department, or major subdivision ⟨astronautics ~⟩ ⟨four main ~*s* deal with the various aspects of local government —Brian Chapman⟩ ⟨a 4-man aircraft ~ created to speed up production⟩

director general *n, pl* **directors general** *also* **director generals** : a chief executive or administrator placed in overall charge of a bureau, department, or agency esp. in a national government or organization with international orientation

di·rec·to·ri·al \də̇¦rek¦tōrēəl, ¦dī,r-, -tȯr-\ *adj* [LL *directorius* + E *-al* — more at DIRECTORY] **1** : serving to direct : DIRECTIVE, DIRECTORY ⟨reading ~ books in preparation for citizenship⟩ ⟨how far the council shall go in exercising these ~ powers —J.E.Pate⟩ **2 a** : belonging to or having the function or qualities of a director ⟨his earlier ~ assignments⟩ ⟨employed in a ~ position at a large automobile plant —Paul Moor⟩ **b** : adapted to or connected with the direction or directorship of dramatic or theatrical production ⟨a new ~ genius⟩ ⟨richly fulfilling his high ~ promise⟩ : characteristic of a skilled director ⟨an ambitious melodrama bristling with fine ~ touches —*Time*⟩ **3** [F, fr. LL *directorius* (influenced in meaning by F *Directoire*, 18th cent. executive body) + F *-al* — more at DIRECTOIRE] : belonging to a directory or body of directors : done, constituted, or administered by a directory ⟨during the period France was under ~ government⟩

di·rec·to·ri·al·ly \-ēəlē, -li\ *adv* : in a directorial function or manner

di·rec·to·ri·um \də,rek'tōrēəm, (,)dī,-, -tȯr-\ *n, pl* **directo·ria** \-ēə\ [ML, directory, guidebook] : ORDO

di·rec·tor·ship *pronunc at* DIRECTOR + ,ship\ *n* **1** : the office of director **2** : a position as a director esp. on a board of directors

¹di·rec·to·ry \də̇'rekt(ə)rē, -ri *also* dī'-, *rapid* 'dre-\ *adj* [ME, fr. LL *directorius*, fr. L *directus* (past part. of *dirigere* to direct) + *-orius* -ory — more at DRESS] **1** : serving to direct : DIRECTIVE; *specif* : providing guidance that is advisory and authoritative but not compulsory **2** *of a law* **a** : directing what is to be done **b** : directing how a thing shall be done rather than what shall be done — opposed to *mandatory* **3** *usu cap* [trans. of F *Directoire*] : DIRECTOIRE

²directory \"\ *n* -ES **1** [ML *directorium* guidebook, fr. neut. of LL *directorius*] : a compilation, index, or treatise serving to direct or guide: **a** : a collection of directions, rules, or ordinances **b** : a book of directions for the conduct of worship; *specif, usu cap* : a Presbyterian book of rules for public worship used in the Church of Scotland and certain Presbyterian and Congregational churches elsewhere **c** : ORDO **d** : an alphabetical or classified list containing the names and addresses of the inhabitants or organizations of a locality or the names, location, and identifying data of persons or organizations connected with a particular profession or occupation or that are subscribers of a particular service ⟨a city ~ is usually an annual or biennial publication⟩ ⟨a ~ of manufacturers —*Eastman Kodak Monthly Abstract Bull.*⟩ ⟨an annual ~ of "who is who" among the publishers, reviewers, publications, and organizations interested in literary material —Anne J. Richter⟩ **e** : a tablet or sectional strips on the wall of the entry of a building bearing the names of occupants with indication of the floor level and room numbers of each **2** [fr. *Directory*, French executive body, trans. of F *Directoire* — more at DIRECTOIRE] **a** : a small governing body with executive power often unconstitutional and of a military character ⟨the French ~ of the First Republic⟩ ⟨to make sure that the cabinet did what it was supposed to do, they set up a ~, or shadow cabinet, behind it —Leigh White⟩ **b** : a body of directors : DIRECTORATE

direct package *n* : a package of sorted mail containing matter to be distributed from a single post office

direct positive *n* : a positive in photography that is made directly by exposure to light and by development without the use of a negative

direct primary *n* : a preliminary election at which direct nominations of candidates for office are made usu. by a plurality vote by the qualified voters under the same procedures as used in final elections

direct printing *n* : the process of printing textiles by passing them between a succession of rollers having different colors and different parts of the pattern

direct process *n* : a process that yields metal by a single working from the ore — compare INDIRECT PROCESS

direct product *n* : SCALAR PRODUCT

direct proportion *n* : a proportion of two variable quantities when the ratio of the two quantities is constant

direct pyramidal tract *n* : a tract of descending fibers in the upper half of the spinal cord that is traceable from the cerebral cortex of the same side and that is situated next to the anterior median fissure

direct reduction *n* : a reduction of a syllogistic argument to the first figure by converting or obverting one or more of its propositions or by converting or obverting and interchanging the premises — contrasted with *indirect reduction*

direct rein *n* : the use of a rein in such a way as to place tension on the bit and move a horse's head toward the direction in which it is intended to move — compare INDIRECT REIN

di·rec·tress \də̇'rektrə̇s, dī'-\ *n* -ES [*director* + *-ess*] : a female director ⟨the social ~ said hopefully, "You're a bridge player" —Walter Hackett⟩

di·rec·trice \də̇¦rek¦trēs\ *n* -S [F, fr. ML *directric-, directrix*] : DIRECTRESS ⟨had been the ~ of wardrobe of a ballet company⟩ ⟨could let its managing ~ draw a lavish stipend —Leslie Charteris⟩

di·rec·trix \də'rektriks, dī'-\ *n, pl* **directrixes** \-ksəz\ *also* **directri·ces** \də'rektrə,sēz, dī-; də,rek'trī(,)sēz, (,)dī,-\ [ML, fem. of LL *director* — more at DIRECTOR] **1** *archaic* **:** DIRECTRESS **2 :** a fixed curve with which a generatrix maintains a given relationship in generating a geometric figure; *specif* **:** a straight line the distance to which from any point of a conic section is in fixed ratio to the distance from the same point to a focus **3 :** the center line of the field of fire of an artillery piece

directs *pres 3d sing of* DIRECT, *pl of* DIRECT

direct salesman *n* **:** a house-to-house peddler or canvasser

direct selling *n* **:** the selling by a manufacturer or other producer or his agent to any other than a jobber or middleman **:** selling directly to a consumer

direct service *n, of social workers* **:** active service on cases and work with patients as distinguished from staff functions

direct syllogism *n* **:** a syllogism proceeding from a rule and the subsumption of a case under that rule to the result of the rule in that case

direct take *n* **:** an instant replacement of one picture with another in television transmission with no interval

direct tax *n* **:** a tax exacted directly from the person on whom the ultimate burden of the tax is expected to fall ⟨property, income, gift, inheritance, and poll taxes are generally included under *direct taxes*⟩

direct tide *n* **:** high tide at any given place on one side of the earth accompanied by high tide on the opposite side

direct viewfinder *n* **:** a finder in which the subject is viewed directly through a lens or sight

direct-vision spectroscope *n* **:** a spectroscope utilizing an Amici prism so that the observer looks in the direction of the light source

direct white 2GT *n, usu cap D&W* **:** a fluorescent brightener — see DYE table I (under *Fluorescent Brightener 34*)

direct-writing company *n* **1 :** an insurance company with which a policyholder directly insures his property — called also *originating company;* distinguished from *reinsurance company* **2 :** an insurance company that solicits and services business directly with the public through its own employees rather than through local agents

dire·ful \'dī(ə)rfəl, -īəf-\ *adj* **1 a :** exciting horror or terror **:** DREADFUL, FRIGHTFUL, DIRE ⟨entered upon a career of vengeance so ~ that London was shocked —G.W.Johnson⟩ **b :** oppressive to feelings or spirit **:** DISMAL ⟨the ~ sound of air-raid sirens⟩ **2 :** warning of disaster to come **:** OMINOUS ⟨seeing himself trapped, he filled the air with ~ cries⟩ — **dire·ful·ly** \-f(ə)lē, -li\ *adv* — **dire·ful·ness** \-fəlnəs\ *n* -ES

dire·ly \'dī(ə)rlē, -īəl-, -li\ *adv* **:** in a dire manner: **a :** DREADFULLY, FRIGHTFULLY **b :** DISMALLY **c :** OMINOUSLY

di·remp·tion \də'rem(p)shən\ *n* -S [L *diremption-, diremptio,* fr. *diremptus* (past part. of *dirimere* to take apart, separate, fr. *dir-* — fr. *dis-* apart — + *-imere,* fr. *emere* to take, buy) + *-ion-, -io* -ion — more at DIS-, REDEEM] **:** SEPARATION, DISJUNCTION **:** division into two ⟨because it does make that vast ~ of our world into a One and a Many —H.B.Alexander⟩

dire·ness \'dī(ə)rnəs, -īən-\ *n* -ES **:** the quality of being dire or of being dreadful to look upon or contemplate or of presaging coming disaster

di·rep·tion \də'repshən\ *n* -S [MF or L; MF, fr. L *direption-, direptio,* fr. *direptus* (past part. of *diripere* to tear apart, plunder, fr. *di-* — fr. *dis-* apart — + *-ripere,* fr. *rapere* to seize and carry off) + *-ion-, -io* -ion — more at DIS-, RAPID] **1** *obs* **:** a tearing apart or away **2** *archaic* **:** DESPOLIATION

direr *comparative of* DIRE

direst *superlative of* DIRE

dire wolf *n* **:** a large lupine mammal (*Canis dirus* or *Aenocyon dirus*) found in Pleistocene deposits of No. America

¹dirge \'dərj, -ōj, -əij\ *n* -S [ME *dirige, derge,* fr. L *dirige* (sing. pres. imper. act. of *dirigere* to direct, make straight), the first word of an antiphon adapted from Ps 5:9 (Vulgate) that opens the first nocturn in the Office of the Dead — more at DRESS] **1** *archaic* **:** the Office of the Dead in the Roman Catholic Church **2 a :** a psalm sung for a departed soul in the Roman Catholic Church; *also* **:** a requiem mass **b :** a song or hymn expressing grief or a solemn sense of loss esp. to accompany funeral or memorial rites **c :** any slow solemn and mournful piece of music **3 a :** a piece of writing resembling a dirge in being expressive of deep and solemn grief or sense of loss; *esp* **:** a poem of this kind **b :** any sorrowful or lugubrious literary expression

²dirge \"\ *vb* -ED/-ING/-S *vt* **1** *archaic* **:** to sing a dirge for **2** *archaic* **:** to sing as if a dirge ~ *vi* **:** to give forth a dirge or a sound like or having the effect of a dirge

dirge·ful \-jfəl\ *adj* **:** full of lamentation **:** FUNEREAL, MOURNFUL

dir·gie \'dirjē\ *n* -S [ME *derge, dirige* — more at DIRGE] **1** *Scot* **:** DIRGE 2 **2** *Scot* **:** a funeral feast

dir·hem \dər'(h)em\ *also* **dir·ham** *or* **der·ham** \-am\ *n* -S [Ar *dirham,* fr. L *drachma* drachma — more at DRAM] **1 a :** a Muslim unit of weight orig. established in Arabia as equal to two thirds of the Attic drachma or nearly 45 grains, later used with varying values in Persia, Turkey, and No. Africa, but by the 1930s found as a chief unit only in Egypt, there being equal to about 41 grains **2 a :** a silver coin of Muslim countries the first issues of which in the 8th century weighed one dirhem **b :** a unit of value equivalent to the value of a dirhem coin orig. $^1/_{10}$ of a dinar **c :** the silver 50-fils piece of Iraq

di·rhin·ic \(')dī¦rinik, -rīn-\ *adj* [*di-* + *rhin-* + *-ic*] **:** affecting both nostrils alike

di·riá \,dirē'ä\ *n, pl* **diriá** *or* **diriás** *usu cap* [Sp *diriá, dirián, diriano,* of AmerInd origin] **1 :** an Indian people of southwestern Nicaragua **2** *also* **dir·i·an** \-'ēən\ **:** a member of the Diriá people

dir·i·ge \'dirə,jē\ *n* -S [ME — more at DIRGE] *archaic* **:** DIRGE 1

dir·i·gi·bil·i·ty \,dirəjə'bilədē, də,rij-\ *n* -ES **1 :** the property of being dirigible **2 :** susceptibility to control ⟨usurpation is a crime to which men are tempted by human ~ —H.G.Wells⟩

¹dir·i·gi·ble \'dirəjəbəl, də'rij-\ *adj* [L *dirigere* to direct, make straight + E *-ible* — more at DRESS] **:** that can be directed **:** STEERABLE ⟨a ~ balloon⟩ ⟨a ~ torpedo⟩

²dirigible \"\ *n* -S [*dirigible (balloon)*] **:** AIRSHIP

di·ri·gisme \dērēzhēs|m(ᵊ), -ēz-, |mə\ *n* -S [F, fr. *diriger* to direct (fr. L *dirigere*) + *-isme* -ism — more at DRESS] **:** economic planning and control by the state ⟨a middle course between ~ and laissez-faire⟩

di·ri·ment impediment \'dirəmənt-\ *n* [L *diriment-, dirimens,* pres. part. of *dirimere* to take apart, interrupt, destroy — more at DIREMPTION] **:** a disability that makes void a marriage contracted without the required legal solemnities

¹dirk \'dərk, -ōk,-əik\ *n* -S [alter. of Sc *durk*] **1 :** a long straight-bladed dagger formerly carried esp. by the Scottish Highlanders **2 :** a short sword formerly worn by British junior naval officers

²dirk \"\ *vt* -ED/-ING/-S **:** to stab with a dirk

dirk dance *n* **:** a leaping dance over and around a dirk or dagger done esp. by Manxmen

dirk knife *n* **:** a clasp knife having a large blade like that of a dirk

¹dirl \'dirl\ *vb* -ED/-ING/-S [prob. alter. of *thirl*] *vt, Scot* **:** to pierce with pain or emotion ~ *vi* **1** *Scot* **:** to emit a rattling or ringing sound esp. when struck **2** *Scot* **:** to tremble or quiver esp. with pain or emotion

²dirl \"\ *n* -S **1** *Scot* **:** a powerful blow **:** JOLT **2** *Scot* **:** a vibration of sound or motion ⟨put your ear to the ground and you'll hear the ~ of their feet —J.M.Barrie⟩

dirndl \'dərndᵊl *also* 'dir-\ *n* -S [short for G *dirndlkleid,* fr. G dial. (Bavarian) *dirndl* girl (dim. of *dirne,* fr. OHG *thiorna* maid, virgin) + *kleid* dress; akin to OS *thiorna* maid, MD *dierne* maid, maidservant, ON *therna* maidservant, OE *thegn* servant, thane — more at THANE] **1 :** a dress style marked by a tight bodice, short sleeves, low neck, and gathered skirt and copied from Alpine peasant costume **2** *also* **dirndl skirt :** a full skirt gathered or pleated on a tight waistband

di·ro·filaria \¦dī(,)rō+\ *n, cap* [NL, fr. *diro-* (fr. L *dirus* ominous, dreadful) + *Filaria* — more at DIRE] **:** a genus of filarial worms (family Dipetalonematidae) — see HEARTWORM

¹dirt \'dər|t, 'dō|, 'dəi|, *usu* |d·+V\ *n* -S *often attrib* [alter. of ME *drit,* fr. ON, excrement; akin to OE *drītan* to defecate, OHG *trizan,* ON *drīta* to defecate, L *foria* diarrhea, Serb *driskati* to have diarrhea, Lith *derkti* to defecate] **1 a :** EXCREMENT ⟨warm steamy knobbles of sheep ~ getting crushed between my toes —Janet Frame⟩ **b :** mud or waste matter mixed with water ⟨in summer there is dust, and in winter there is ~ —Jane Austen⟩ **c :** a foul or filthy substance that by adhering to a thing makes it unclean or foul ⟨the crew gutted the catch and hosed the ~ through the scuppers⟩; *esp* **:** an accumulation of dust, grit, refuse, waste, or litter ⟨how to remove . . . ~ consisting of dust, pollen, and sooty particles —*Pliotron*⟩ ⟨under its accumulated rust and ~ of five centuries —G.G.Coulton⟩ **d :** grime, spot, or stain resulting from travel, work, a fall, or other ordinary experience or from use ⟨a chance to wash the ~ off his face⟩ ⟨guaranteed to remove ~ from upholstery⟩ **e** *archaic* **:** something worthless ⟨is yellow ~ the passion of thy life? —Alexander Pope⟩ **f :** a person to be treated with contempt ⟨he's got beautiful manners. Doesn't chuck the stuff at you as if you were ~ like young Willis —Dorothy Sayers⟩ **g :** visible foreign matter that disfigures finished paper **2 a** (1) **:** EARTH, GROUND **:** loose or packed soil or sand ⟨tons of rock and ~ slid into the canal⟩ ⟨replacing ~ roads with macadam⟩ (2) **:** the surface of the ground ⟨alarmed at the first sound we hit the ~⟩ **b :** land as property ⟨a rare good little farm; a sound bit of ~ that is, sir —Adrian Bell⟩ **c :** a substance that is dug or comes from the earth ⟨mining gold by means of ~ washing⟩ **d** (1) **:** alluvial earth, gravel, and similar material in placer mining (2) **:** broken ore and in coal mines slate and other foreign matter **e** *dial Eng* **:** foul or flammable mine air **3 a :** an abject or filthy state **:** SQUALOR ⟨ignorance and ~ are not necessary concomitants of poverty⟩ **b :** moral obliquity **:** CORRUPTION, CHICANERY ⟨the ~ of jealousy⟩ ⟨there's more ~ to be uncovered at the capital⟩ **c :** moral uncleanness; *esp* **:** licentiousness of language or theme ⟨this leaves a rather amorphous concept of what obscenity may be . . . . Its one essential quality is ~ for ~'s sake —Curtis Bok⟩ ⟨a quite mistaken belief that to make his reader smell ~ is realism —H.J.Laski⟩ **d :** common scandalous gossip about discreditable personal behavior; *esp* **:** malicious or slanderous gossip ⟨a writer as much interested in writing ~ as in reporting the news⟩ **e :** suppressed information whose disclosure would be highly damaging ⟨the thought . . . investigations should be started only after the most careful consideration and when there was real prospect of turning up ~ —Vance Johnson⟩ **f :** an underhanded or despicable trick — used as the object of *do* ⟨wanting to do him ~, she sent his wife a poison-pen letter⟩ **4 :** dirty weather

²dirt \"\ *vt* -ED/-ING/-S **1** *archaic* **:** to make foul **:** DIRTY ⟨don't dog's-ear nor ~ them —R.H.Barham⟩ **2 :** to cover with dirt; *esp* **:** to draw soil up around the base of

dirt band *n* **:** a dark-colored layer or zone in a glacier representing a former surface where dust or other debris accumulated

dirt bed *n* **:** a buried soil often containing leaves and stems in a state of partial decay and sometimes occurring between sheets of glacial drift (as in some parts of the Mississippi basin)

dirtbird \'=,=\ *n* [¹*dirt* (weather); fr. its habit of chirping before rain] **:** GREEN WOODPECKER

dirtboard \'=,=\ *n* **:** a guard placed on a carriage so as to keep dirt from the axle arm

¹dirt cheap *adj* **:** exceedingly cheap

²dirt cheap *adv* **:** at an exceedingly low price

dirt dauber *or* **dirtdobber** \'=,=\ *n, chiefly South & Midland* **:** MUD DAUBER

dirt·en \'dərtᵊn\ *adj* [in sense 1, alter. of ME *driten,* fr. OE, past part. of *drītan* to defecate — more at DIRT; in sense 2, fr. ¹*dirt* + *-en* (as in *earthen*)] **1** *dial Eng* **:** DIRTY, FILTHY **2** *dial Eng* **:** made of dirt

dirt farmer *n* **:** a farmer who works on the soil

dirt·i·ly \'dər|d·ᵊlē, 'dō|, 'dəi|, |t|, |əlē,|ᵊli,|əli\ *adv* **1 a :** in a foul or filthy manner ⟨a ~ robed camel driver⟩ **b :** with a dirty color or a sprinkling of dirt ⟨ill-modeled from some ~ glossy substance of a livid color —Ngaio Marsh⟩ **2 :** in a disgraceful, dishonest, or base manner **:** SORDIDLY, DESPICABLY ⟨as ~ drunk as usual —John Steinbeck⟩

dirt·i·ness \|d·ēnəs, |t|, |in-\ *n* -ES **:** the quality or state of being dirty **:** FOULNESS: as **a :** obscenity or licentiousness of language **b :** moral obliquity **:** SORDIDNESS

dirt line *n* **:** a layer appearing as a line in the front of a glacier and made up of earth that settled and was covered by a snowfall

dirtplate \'=,=\ *n* **:** DIRTBOARD

dirt poor *adj* **:** lacking practically all the essentials of life or the resources for supporting life **:** DESTITUTE ⟨Rembrandt's last, *dirt poor* years —*Time*⟩ ⟨Greece had been *dirt poor* for centuries —Claire Sterling⟩

dirts *pl of* DIRT, *pres 3d sing of* DIRT

¹dirty \'dər|d·ē, 'dō|,'dəi|, |t|, |i\ *adj* -ER/-EST [¹*dirt* + *-y*] **1 :** characterized by the presence of dirt or impurities: **a :** not clean or pure **:** soiled, defiled, or begrimed with dirt **:** overlaid or intermixed with dirt, impurities, or foreign matter ⟨the stage roustabouts' dungarees were convincingly ~⟩ **b :** likely to befoul, defile, or begrime with dirt ⟨put them on the *dirtiest* job in the camp⟩; *specif* **:** that befouls the hold of a transport ship ⟨a tanker carrying such ~ cargo as crude oil, diesel oil, or asphalt is not subjected to this high rate of corrosion⟩ **c** *of work* **:** consisting of drudgery that is tedious, disagreeable, and unrecognized or thankless and usu. makes the course easy for someone else ⟨she did, as always, quietly, complacently, the ~ work while her sisters fussed over their wardrobes⟩ **d :** requiring onerous or repulsive action that is most sordid, least rewarded, and most risky of the assignments made by the principal in an undertaking ⟨a male accomplice was sitting out there playing it safe, sending the girl in to do the ~ work —Erle Stanley Gardner⟩ ⟨determined that the bourgeois liberals should not use them for the ~ work at the barricades and then shove them . . . aside —Stringfellow Barr⟩ **e :** contaminated with infecting organisms ⟨~ wounds⟩ **2 :** characterized by unfairness, baseness, or evil **:** LOW, CONTEMPTIBLE, HATEFUL: **a :** repugnant to a sense of decency ⟨a mob . . . may lynch a Negro . . . and apparently enjoy the ~ business —C.C.Furnas⟩ **b** (1) **:** marked or characterized by dishonorable, unscrupulous, or treacherous dealing ⟨her father was a kind of ~ dog . . . he married a rich woman and left this kid to get along as best she could —Susan Ertz⟩ (2) **:** obtained through dishonest, corrupt, or inhumane dealing ⟨refused to legally name the higher-ups who got the millions in ~ money —Mike Stern⟩ **c :** marked by moral corruption or by criminality ⟨those who regard politics as a ~ business would do well to remember that war is a *dirtier* business —John Lodge⟩ ⟨called wire tapping a ~ business —*Newsweek*⟩ **d :** given to or characterized by covert attempts to harass or disable opposing players in violation of the rules of the sport or game **:** UNSPORTSMANLIKE ⟨a ~ hockey player⟩ ⟨overemphasis on winning is liable to produce ~ football⟩ **e :** violating ordinary standards of fair play in deadly combat ⟨a teacher of jujitsu and ~ fighting to recruits⟩ **f :** highly regrettable, distressing, or grievous ⟨it's a ~ shame you weren't given a fair chance⟩ **3 a :** characterized by expressed or suggested obscenity or indecency **:** BAWDY, SMUTTY ⟨anecdotes of a type that can be called earthy but not ~ —Sidney Lovett⟩ ⟨Shakespeare was the *dirtiest* of English authors if you knew the vocabulary —D.W.Brogan⟩ ⟨sniggering at ~ postcards —John Masters⟩ **b :** offensive and to be shunned or applied only with repugnance by reason of an implicit offensive idea ⟨but discipline? Ah, that's a ~ word and used only to describe the old Prussian army —*Time*⟩ ⟨for years in the entertainment business "documentary" has been a ~ word —Marya Mannes⟩ **4 :** rough and murky on sea or land or in the air; *esp* **:** stormy with squally winds and low visibility ⟨it developed into a ~ night. Fog shut down, reducing visibility to zero, and an unusually heavy tide was running —C.C.Hanks⟩ **5 a** *of color or light* **:** CLOUDED, SULLIED **:** DULLISH, DINGY **:** not clear and bright ⟨he was not ~ white, as I had often found whales of the smaller size to be, but pure white —H.A.Chippendale⟩ **b :** characterized typically by a husky, rasping, or raw tonal quality — usu. used of jazz or of the singing or playing of musical tones that are slightly off-key **6 a :** conveying ill-natured resentment ⟨the two girls give me a ~ look like it was my fault or something —Ring Lardner⟩ ⟨this is not meant as a ~ crack at the American railroads —Richard Joseph⟩ **b :** expressive of contempt **:** intended to affront, humiliate, or insult **:** SCURRILOUS, ABUSIVE ⟨quick to strike back at being called a ~ name⟩ ⟨some of the ~ epithets applied to immigrants from foreign countries⟩ **7** *printing* **a** *of copy* **:** difficult to follow because heavily emended or marked or poorly written **b** *of typesetting or a proof* **:** full of errors or heavily marked with corrections of errors — opposed to *clean;* compare FOUL 8 **c** *of a type case* **:** FOUL 13 **8** *of an atom bomb or hydrogen bomb* **:** having considerable fallout

syn FILTHY, FOUL, NASTY, SQUALID: DIRTY is a general term applicable to anything sullied or defiled ⟨the window so *dirty* you could hardly see the new houses opposite —George du Maurier⟩ ⟨he was *dirty* and bloodstained and his clothes were bedaubed with mud and weeds as though he had been in the river —Dorothy Sayers⟩ FILTHY intensifies the offensive suggestions of DIRTY ⟨tenements — rickety wooden structures five or six stories high, dark, ill-ventilated, and *filthy,* breeders of disease and nurseries of vice —Allan Nevins & H.S.Commager⟩ ⟨he was constantly drunk, *filthy* beyond all powers of decent expression . . . as disreputable an old wretch as was at that time to be found in New York —Leslie Stephen⟩ FOUL, the strongest term in this group, suggests revolting loathsomeness ⟨the stagnant water looked uninviting. Over its face lay a thick mantle of green slime, from which swelled curious bladder islands of floating fatty pink. The Arabs explained that the Turks had thrown dead camels into the pool to make the water *foul* —T.E.Lawrence⟩ ⟨Van Gogh knew the paleotechnic city in its most complete gloom, the *foul* bedraggled gaslighted London of the seventies —Lewis Mumford⟩ NASTY may imply highly repugnant qualities, esp. those repugnant to a fastidious person ⟨the *nasty* stench of the place turned me sick; if ever a man smelled fever and dysentery, it was in that abominable anchorage —R.L.Stevenson⟩ ⟨I wonder why he really did hide himself like that. Something *nasty,* I suppose; was he a leper? —G.K. Chesterton⟩ ⟨would they, pray, explain why instead of sharing their beds with decent women of their own class . . . they squandered all their virile energy on greasy slave girls and *nasty* Asiatic-Greek prostitutes? —Robert Graves⟩ SQUALID adds to DIRTY the suggestions of slovenliness or neglect ⟨magnified hovels, piled story upon story, and *squalid* with the grime that successive ages have left behind them —Nathaniel Hawthorne⟩ All these terms may describe things reprehensible morally ⟨public office in this country has become a *dirty* and *nasty* thing. Its attainment in most cases implies chicanery and deceit —M.L.Ernst⟩ ⟨I oughtn't to sell Max out like that. It would be utterly *filthy* —Dashiell Hammett⟩ ⟨secret murder was their object — black, *foul,* midnight murder —Anthony Trollope⟩ ⟨he has treated such malice with the stony contempt the utterances of *squalid* politicians and journalists deserve —*New Republic*⟩ All these terms but SQUALID apply often to unpleasant weather.

²dirty \"\ *adv* -ER/-EST **:** DIRTILY, BASELY

³dirty \"\ *vb* -ED/-ING/-ES *vt* **1 :** to make filthy **:** SOIL ⟨he *dirtied* his new clothes in the coal cellar⟩ **2 a :** to stain with dishonor **:** SULLY, TARNISH ⟨but with Jackson the common man poured into the White House and *dirtied* more than the carpets . . . theft on a great scale appeared for the first time —*Times Lit. Supp.*⟩ **b :** to debase or degrade by distorting the real nature of ⟨their religion took most of the rural whites' pleasures away from them, ~*ing* sex and the human body until it was a nasty thing —Lillian Smith⟩ ~ *vi* **:** to become soiled ⟨soft cloths ~ easily⟩ — **dirty one's hands :** to sully one's moral uprightness or good reputation ⟨a man who had never *dirtied his hands* with political intrigue —Bruce Marshall⟩

dirty al·lan \-'alən\ *n, sometimes cap D & A* [origin of *allan* unknown; called dirty fr. its habit of eating the excrement of smaller gulls] **:** PARASITIC JAEGER

dirty linen *n* **:** private or domestic matters whose exposure in public would bring shame or embarrassment — compare WASH ONE'S DIRTY LINEN IN PUBLIC

dis *var of* DIX

¹dis- *prefix* [ME *dis-, des-,* fr. OF & L; OF *des-, dis-,* fr. L *dis-,* lit., apart, to pieces; akin to OE *te-* apart, to pieces, OHG *zi-, ze-,* Goth *dis-* apart, Gk *dia* through, Alb *tsh-* apart, L *duo* two — more at TWO] **1 a :** do the opposite of **:** reverse (a specified action) ⟨*dis*join⟩ ⟨*dis*establish⟩ ⟨*dis*own⟩ ⟨*dis*qualify⟩ **b :** deprive of (a specified character, quality, or rank) ⟨*dis*able⟩ ⟨*dis*prince⟩ **:** deprive of (a specified object) ⟨*dis*frock⟩ **c :** exclude or expel from ⟨*dis*bar⟩ ⟨*dis*castle⟩ **2 :** opposite of **:** contrary of **:** absence of ⟨*dis*union⟩ ⟨*dis*affection⟩ **3 :** not ⟨*dis*honest⟩ ⟨*dis*loyal⟩ **4 :** completely ⟨*dis*annul⟩ **5** [by folk etymology] **:** DYS- ⟨*dis*function⟩ ⟨*dis*trophy⟩

²dis- *prefix* [MF, fr. ML, alter. (influenced by Gk *dis-* twice, double, fr. *dis* twice) of L *di-,* fr. Gk — more at BIS, TWI-] **1 :** DI- 1 **2 :** DI- 2 ⟨*disazo*⟩

dis *abbr* **1** discharge; discharged **2** disciple **3** discipline **4** disconnect **5** discontinued **6** discount **7** distance **8** distribute

di·sa \'dīsə\ *n* [NL] **1** *cap* **:** a genus of showy tropical African terrestrial orchids with tuberous rootstocks and dark green leaves **2** -S **:** any plant of the genus *Disa*

dis·ability \¦dis *sometimes* -iz+\ *n* [¹*dis-* + *ability*] **1 a** *archaic* **:** inability to do something **b** (1) **:** the condition of being disabled **:** deprivation or lack esp. of physical, intellectual, or emotional capacity or fitness; *also* **:** an instance of such a condition **:** a particular weakness or inadequacy ⟨he appeared sullen, melancholy, tongue-tied — a ~ stemming in part from a speech defect —H.M.Ledig-Rowohlt⟩ ⟨concluded that his *disabilities* were his best defense —M.W.Straight⟩ (2) **:** the inability to pursue an occupation or perform services for wages because of physical or mental impairment ⟨suffering from total ~⟩ ⟨receives a ~ pension⟩ (3) **:** the period of duration of such a condition ⟨receives monthly payments during his ~⟩ (4) **:** a physical or mental illness, injury, or condition that incapacitates in any way ⟨as a result of a personal accident . . . he lost his right arm, but he overcame this ~ —O.S.Nock⟩ (5) **:** a material object or condition that hinders, impedes, or incapacitates **:** HANDICAP ⟨the placement of the elevators is not so serious a ~ on the upper floors —Lewis Mumford⟩ **2 a :** lack of legal qualification to do a thing **:** legal incapacity, incompetence, or disqualification ⟨~ of infancy⟩ ⟨a law placing severe *disabilities* upon Catholics and Jews⟩; *also* **:** an instance or cause of such incapacity **b** (1) **:** a nonlegal disqualification, restriction, or discrimination ⟨nominally free, but actually subject to numerous social and economic *disabilities*⟩ ⟨a person with even the most tenuous Communist affiliation from years ago may suffer *disabilities* that could ruin his entire future career —A.H.Sulzberger⟩ (2) **:** DISADVANTAGE ⟨discussed the benefits and *disabilities* of price controls⟩ ⟨the special *disabilities* under which the industry operates⟩

disability clause *n* **:** a clause in a life-insurance contract providing that the policy continue in full force without payment of premiums if the policyholder becomes totally and permanently disabled and sometimes providing also for fixed monthly payments to the policyholder during the period of disability

disability insurance *n* **:** insurance against loss of income due to partial or total disability — compare ACCIDENT INSURANCE, HEALTH INSURANCE

dis·able \də'sābəl *also* -'zā-\ *vt* **disabled; disabled; disabling** \-b(ə)liŋ\ **disables** [ME *disablen,* fr. ¹*dis-* + *able* (adj.)] **1 :** to deprive of legal right or qualification **:** make legally incapable or incompetent **:** DISQUALIFY **2 :** to make incapable or ineffective **:** INCAPACITATE ⟨heavy financial losses *disabling* him from the execution of his plans⟩ ⟨~ a bomb⟩; *esp* **:** to deprive of physical, moral, or intellectual strength ⟨an English winter . . . *disabled* my mother like a mortal sickness —Sylvia T. Warner⟩ ⟨~*s* the rich as completely as the poor —G.B.Shaw⟩ **3** *obs* **a :** to deprive of what gives value **:** impair in worth ⟨I have *disabled* mine estate —Shak.⟩ **b :** to declare incompetent or invalid **:** DISPARAGE ⟨he *disabled* my judgment —Shak.⟩ **syn** see WEAKEN

disabled *adj* [fr. past part. of *disable*] **:** incapacitated by or as if by illness, injury, or wounds **:** CRIPPLED ⟨~ war veterans⟩; *also* **:** broken down ⟨~ cars⟩

dis·able·ment \-bəlmənt\ *n* -S [ME, fr. *disablen* + *-ment*] **1 :** deprivation of legal right or qualification **:** INCAPACITY **2 :** the act of disabling or becoming disabled or the state of being disabled ⟨the temporary ~ of most of her reasoning faculties —Elinor Wylie⟩

dis·abler \-b(ə)lə(r)\ *n* -s : one that disables ⟨heart disease is a major ~⟩

dis·abuse \ˌdisəˈbyüz\ *vt* [F *désabuser,* fr. *dés-* ¹dis- + *abuser* to abuse — more at ABUSE] : to set free from mistakes (as in reasoning or judgment) : UNDECEIVE : set right ⟨*disabused* us of the old belief that the universe revolved about the home of man —P.E.More⟩ ⟨he couldn't however ~ his mind of the idea —F.M.Ford⟩ **syn** see RID

di·saccharide *also* **di·saccharose** \(ˈ)dī+\ *n* [*di-* + *saccharide, saccharose*] : any of a class of sugars (as sucrose, lactose, or maltose) that yield on hydrolysis two monosaccharide molecules

disaccommodate *vt* [¹*dis-* + *accommodate*] *archaic* : DISCOMMODE

¹**dis·accord** \ˌdis+\ *vi* [ME *disacorden,* fr. MF *desacorder,* fr. *desacort* disagreement, lack of harmony, fr. *des-* ¹dis- + *acort* agreement — more at ACCORD] : to fail to be in accord or harmony : DISAGREE

²**disaccord** \"\ *n* : DISAGREEMENT : lack of harmony ⟨the economic and political systems of the country are in complete ~⟩

dis·accredit \ˌdis+\ *vt* [¹*dis-* + *accredit*] : to deprive of accreditation — **dis·accreditation** \"+\ *n*

dis·accustom \ˌdis +\ *vt* [MF *desaccoustumer,* fr. OF *desacostumer,* fr. *des-* ¹dis- + *acostumer* to accustom — more at ACCUSTOM] **1** *archaic* : to abandon as a custom **2** : to free from a habit

disaccustomed *adj* : UNACCUSTOMED

dis·acidify \ˌdis +\ *vt* [¹*dis-* + *acidify*] : to free from acid

dis·acknowledge \ˌdis+\ *vt* [¹*dis-* + *acknowledge*] : to refuse to acknowledge : DENY, DISOWN **syn** see DISCLAIM

dis·acknowledgment \"+\ *n* : the refusal to acknowledge : DISCLAIMING, DISOWNING, DENIAL

dis·acquaintance \ˌdis+\ *n* [fr. obs. *disacquaint* to make unfamiliar, estrange (fr. ¹*dis-* + *acquaint*) + *-ance*] : loss of acquaintance or association ⟨long ~ with army life⟩

disadvance *vt* [alter. (influenced by *ad-*) of ME *disavauncen,* fr. MF *desavancer,* fr. OF *desavancier,* fr. *des-* ¹dis- + *avancier* to move forward, advance — more at ADVANCE] *obs* : to cause to draw back : STOP, CHECK

¹**dis·advantage** \ˌdis+\ *n* [alter. (influenced by *ad-*) of ME *disavauntage,* fr. MF *desavantage* unfavorable condition, fr. OF, fr. *des-* ¹dis- + *avantage* advantage — more at ADVANTAGE] **1** : loss or damage esp. to reputation, credit, or finances : PREJUDICE, DETRIMENT ⟨his attempts to reach his enemy's face were greatly to the ~ of his own —G.B.Shaw⟩ ⟨spread reports to the ~ of the candidate⟩ **2 a** : the state or fact of being without advantage : an unfavorable, inferior, or prejudicial condition ⟨found himself at a ~ among his polished, cultivated friends⟩ **b** : an unfavorable or prejudicial quality or circumstance : HANDICAP ⟨the machine has two serious ~*s*⟩ ⟨the work has the ~ of being written in a tedious style⟩

²**disadvantage** \"\ *vt* : to place at a disadvantage : affect unfavorably : HARM ⟨their commercial interests were *disadvantaged* by the colonial relationship⟩ ⟨seriously *disadvantaged* by the general fall of raw material prices⟩

disadvantaged *adj* : lacking in the basic resources or conditions (as standard housing, medical and educational facilities, civil rights) believed to be necessary for an equal position in society ⟨a ~ class or section of the populace⟩ — compare UNDERPRIVILEGED

dis·advantageous \(ˌ)dis+, *also* ˌdisəd,v-\ *adj* [¹*dis-* + *advantageous*] **1** : constituting a disadvantage : UNFAVORABLE, PREJUDICIAL ⟨a ~ trait⟩ ⟨found the terms of sale ~⟩ **2** : tending to diminish esteem : DISPARAGING, DEROGATORY ⟨his action was viewed in a ~ light by many⟩ — **disadvantageously** *adv* — **disadvantageousness** *n* -ES

disadventure *n* [alter. (influenced by *ad-*) of ME *disaventure,* fr. MF *desaventure,* fr. OF, fr. *des-* ¹dis- + *aventure* chance, adventure — more at ADVENTURE] *obs* : MISHAP

disadventurous *adj* [¹*dis-* + *adventurous*] *obs* : DISASTROUS, UNFORTUNATE

dis·advise \ˌdis+\ *vt* [¹*dis-* + *advise*] **1** : to advise against ⟨~ a long journey⟩ **2** : to dissuade (a person)

¹**dis·affect** \ˌdis +\ *vt* [¹*dis-* + *affect* (have affection for)] **1** *archaic* : to lack affection for : be alienated from : DISLIKE **2** : to alienate or diminish the affection or loyalty of : fill with discontent and unrest ⟨all hands were ~*ed* by the example of the ringleaders —R.L.Stevenson⟩ **syn** see ESTRANGE

²**disaffect** *vt* [¹*dis-* + *affect* (act upon)] *obs* : DERANGE, DISORDER

disaffected *adj* [fr. past part. of ¹*disaffect*] : filled with discontent and a sense of grievance esp. against those in authority : MUTINOUS, REBELLIOUS, DISLOYAL ⟨I . . . did my best to rally the ~ villains to a sense of their duty —C.B.Nordhoff & J.N.Hall⟩ ⟨in an age of ballistic warfare a ~ territory is . . . a liability —*Newsweek*⟩ — **dis·af·fect·ed·ly** *adv* — **dis·af·fect·ed·ness** *n* -ES

dis·affection \ˌdis+\ *n* [¹*dis-* + *affection* (feeling)] **1** : the state of being disaffected : alienation of loyalty or affection : ESTRANGEMENT ⟨the problem that is created by the ~ of the intellectual . . . from the popular culture —J.L.Blaw⟩; *esp* : the state of being disaffected toward those in authority ⟨the order caused much ~ among the troops⟩ **2** : lack of affection : DISLIKE, HOSTILITY, DISCONTENT ⟨except for a few expressions of ~, the British people were pleased with the engagement —*Current Biog.*⟩

dis·affiliate \ˌdis+\ *vb* [¹*dis-* + *affiliate*] *vt* : DISASSOCIATE, DETACH ⟨*disaffiliated* himself from the gangster-ridden organization⟩ ~ *vi* : to terminate an affiliation ⟨six rebel locals *disaffiliated* from the international union⟩

dis·affiliation \"+\ *n* : the act or an instance of disaffiliating

dis·affinity \ˌdis+\ *n* [¹*dis-* + *affinity*] : absence of affinity : OPPOSITION ⟨the ~ between the teachings of Plato and Aristotle⟩

dis·affirm \ˌdis+\ *vt* [¹*dis-* + *affirm*] **1** : to assert the contrary of : CONTRADICT, DENY — used of something asserted **2** *law* : to refuse to confirm : REPUDIATE, ANNUL, REVERSE ⟨~ a judicial decision⟩ — opposed to *affirm*

dis·affirmance \"+\ *n* : the act of disaffirming : DENIAL, NEGATION, REPUDIATION, ANNULMENT, REVERSAL

dis·affirmation \(ˌ)dis+\ *n* : DISAFFIRMANCE

dis·afforest \ˌdis+\ *vt* [ML *disafforestare,* fr. L *dis-* ¹dis- + ML *afforestare* to afforest — more at AFFOREST] *Eng law* : to reduce from the privileges of a forest to the state of ordinary land : exempt from forest laws

dis·aggregate \(ˈ)dis +\ *vt* [¹*dis-* + *aggregate*] : to destroy the aggregation of : separate into component parts ⟨an easily *disaggregated* sandstone⟩

dis·aggregation \(ˌ)dis +\ *n* **1** : the separation of an aggregate into its component parts **2** : DISSOCIATION 1b(1)

dis·agio \(ˈ)dis+\ *n* [¹*dis-* + *agio*] : AGIO; *esp* : the agio charged for exchange of depreciated or foreign currency

dis·agree \ˌdis+\ *vi* [ME *disagreen,* fr. MF *desagreer,* fr. *des-* ¹dis- + *agreer* to agree — more at AGREE] **1** : to fail to agree : lack harmony : be unlike or at variance ⟨the two accounts ~ with each other⟩ **2 a** : to differ in opinion : hold discordant views ⟨~*ing* on virtually every topic⟩ **b** : to refuse to agree : DISSENT ⟨by an overwhelming vote the Senate *disagreed* with the House motion⟩ **3** : to be unsuitable : be harmful because of incompatibility ⟨fried foods ~ with me⟩ ⟨the damp climate seriously *disagreed* with her⟩ **syn** see DIFFER

dis·agreeability \"+\ *n* : the quality or state of being disagreeable : UNPLEASANTNESS

dis·agreeable \"+\ *adj* [ME *disagreable,* fr. ¹*dis-* + *agreable* agreeable] **1** *obs* : DISAGREEING : not conformable : INCONGRUOUS **2** : causing discomfort, displeasure, or repugnance : UNPLEASANT, OFFENSIVE ⟨had a most ~ journey home⟩ ⟨a ~ odor⟩ ⟨a ~ predicament⟩ **3** : marked by ill temper or irritability : PEEVISH ⟨a most ~ old man⟩ — **disagreeableness** *n* -ES

disagreeables \-bəlz\ *n pl* : disagreeable things ⟨in spite of my anxiety about Laurence's illness and the ~ resulting from it —Richard Aldington⟩ ⟨ready to put up with a host of ~ for the sake of having at her house the original Dr. Johnson —Virginia Woolf⟩

dis·agreeably \ˌdis+\ *adv* : in a disagreeable manner : UNPLEASANTLY, OFFENSIVELY ⟨~ surprised by the visit of the police⟩

dis·agreement \"+\ *n* [ME, fr. *disagreen* + *-ment*] **1** : the act or an instance of disagreeing ⟨his verbal ~ provoked a duel of words⟩ ⟨rumors of these ~*s* soon reached the public⟩ **2 a** : the state of being at variance : DISPARITY, INCONGRUITY ⟨the clear ~ between the testimony of the two sides⟩ **b** : difference of opinion ⟨~ in matters of religion⟩

dis·allow \ˌdis+\ *vb* [ME *disallowen,* partly fr. MF *desallouer* to refuse praise, reprimand (fr. *des-* ¹dis- + *allouer* to approve) partly fr. ME ¹*dis-* + *allowen* to allow — more at ALLOW] *vt* **1** *archaic* : to refuse to commend or approve : disapprove of **2** : to deny the force, truth, or validity of ⟨~*ing* the philosophical concept of free will⟩ ⟨tax officials ~*ed* the company's claim⟩ **3** : to refuse to allow : REJECT ⟨~*ed* his timid request to take the afternoon off⟩ **4** [AF *desallower,* fr. MF *des-* ¹dis- + *allouer* to approve] : VETO ⟨~*ing* the charter⟩ — used chiefly of British parliamentary practice ⟨the king in council ~*ed* colonial statutes harmful to the British interest⟩ ⟨the Canadian federal government has not ~*ed* the Quebec statute⟩ ~ *vi, obs* : to refuse approval or sanction — used with *of* **syn** see DISCLAIM

dis·allowance \"+\ *n* : the act of disallowing : refusal to admit or permit : REJECTION ⟨the taxpayer was notified of the ~ of his claim for refund⟩

dis·ally \(ˌ)dis+\ *vt* [¹*dis-* + *ally*] *archaic* : to free from an alliance : SEVER

dis·amenity \ˌdis+\ *n* [¹*dis-* + *amenity*] : DISADVANTAGE, UNPLEASANTNESS ⟨a reasonable division of *disamenities* seems eminently fair —Christopher Hollis⟩

dis·anchor \(ˈ)dis+\ *vb* [ME *disancren,* fr. MF *desancrer,* fr. OF, fr. *des-* ¹dis- + *ancrer* to anchor, fr. *ancre* anchor, fr. L *ancora* — more at ANCHOR] *vt, archaic* : to loosen from anchorage ~ *vi, archaic* : to weigh anchor

dis·animate \(ˈ)dis+\ *vt* [¹*dis-* + *animate*] **1** *archaic* : to deprive of life **2** *archaic* : to deprive of spirit : DISHEARTEN

dis·annex \(ˌ)dis+\ *vt* [ME *disannexen,* fr. ¹*dis-* + *annexen* to annex — more at ANNEX] : to undo the annexation of

dis·annul \ˌdis+\ *vt* [¹*dis-* + *annul*] **1** : to annul completely : make void or of no effect : CANCEL, DESTROY ⟨*disannulled* the reforms conceded by earlier rulers⟩ **2** *obs* : to deprive esp. by an annulment of title

dis·anoint \ˌdis+\ *vt* [¹*dis-* + *anoint*] : to invalidate the consecration of ⟨~ a king⟩

dis·ap·pear \ˌdisəˈpi(ə)r, -iə\ *vi* [¹*dis-* + *appear*] **1** : to cease to appear or to be perceived : pass from view either suddenly or gradually ⟨the fantastic vision appeared and as swiftly ~*ed*⟩ ⟨the moon ~*ed* behind a cloud⟩ **2** : to cease to be ⟨ancient evils have ~*ed*⟩ : become lost ⟨the book I left on this table has ~*ed*⟩ : cease to be known ⟨he ~*ed* without a trace two years ago⟩ **syn** *see* VANISH

dis·ap·pear·ance \ˌ==ˈpirən(t)s\ *n* **1** : the act or an instance of disappearing : removal from sight : VANISHING ⟨the ~ of his name from the list of players⟩ ⟨the ~ of stately old mansions⟩ ⟨made a sudden ~ from the party⟩ **2** : the depletion or diminution of world or national stocks or supplies (as of cotton, wheat) ⟨with the present rate of ~ the national marketing quota for the new crop of cotton would be 10 million bales⟩; *also* : the amount of such depletion ⟨the total annual ~ of wheat averaged 721 million bushels⟩

disappearing bed *n* : a bed that can be concealed (as in a recess or closet) when not in use

disappearing carriage *n* : a carriage for heavy coast guns on which the gun is raised above the parapet for firing and upon discharge is lowered automatically behind the parapet for protection

disappearing stair *n* : a stair built to swing upward and be concealed in a space in the ceiling

dis·ap·point \ˌdisəˈpȯint\ *vb* [MF *desapointier,* fr. *des-* ¹dis- + *apointier* to arrange, settle — more at APPOINT] *vt* **1** *archaic* : to remove from office **2** : to thwart or defeat the expectation or hope of ⟨expected a profitable year, but was badly ~*ed*⟩ ⟨I was much ~*ed* in him⟩ : FRUSTRATE, BALK ⟨~*ed* their best hopes⟩ **3** *obs* : UNDO, NULLIFY, DESTROY ~ *vi* : to cause disappointment ⟨somewhere, life had ~*ed* —Mollie Panter-Downes⟩

disappointed *adj* **1** : defeated in expectation or hope : BALKED, THWARTED ⟨a ~ hope⟩ **2** *obs* : not adequately appointed or prepared : UNEQUIPPED — **dis·ap·point·ed·ly** *adv*

disappointing *adj* : failing to come up to expectations — **dis·ap·point·ing·ly** *adv*

dis·ap·point·ment \ˌdisəˈpȯintmənt\ *n* **1** : the act or an instance of disappointing : the state or condition of being disappointed : failure of expectation or hope : FRUSTRATION **2** : one that disappoints ⟨he is a ~ to his parents⟩ ⟨the party was a great ~⟩

dis·approbation \(ˌ)dis+\ *n* [¹*dis-* + *approbation*] : the act or state of disapproving or the state of being disapproved : CONDEMNATION, DISAPPROVAL

dis·approbative \(ˌ)dis+\ *adj* [¹*dis-* + *approbative*] : DISAPPROBATORY

dis·approbatory \"+\ *adj* [¹*dis-* + *approbatory*] : containing or expressing disapprobation : DISAPPROVING ⟨cast a ~ glance at the boy⟩

dis·approval \ˌdis+\ *n* : DISAPPROBATION, CENSURE

dis·approve \"+\ *vb* [¹*dis-* + ¹*approve*] *vt* **1** *obs* : DISPROVE **2** : to pass unfavorable judgment upon : regard as wrong : CONDEMN ⟨I ~ his conduct⟩ **3** : to refuse approval to : decline to sanction : REJECT ⟨the treaty was *disapproved* by the senate⟩ ~ *vi* : to feel or express disapproval — often used with *of* ⟨*disapproved* of his attitude⟩

syn DISAPPROVE and DEPRECATE mean in common to feel or express an objection to or condemnation of (something or someone). DISAPPROVE implies an attitude of dislike or distaste and an unwillingness to accept though not necessarily connoting an expression of condemnation ⟨*disapprove* of a friend's actions⟩ ⟨*disapprove* of a fashion in dresses⟩ ⟨Lawrence *disapproved* of too much knowledge, on the score that it diminished men's sense of wonder —Aldous Huxley⟩ DEPRECATE, as here compared, usu. strongly implies regret, profound, diffident, or apologetic, often carrying also the idea of belittling ⟨it is customary to *deprecate* the literary achievement of the past decade —James Laughlin⟩ ⟨he *deprecates* the kind of criticism which is out to destroy long-established reputations —Daniel George⟩ ⟨I not only *deprecate,* I deplore, monkeyshines in Congress —H.L.Ickes⟩ ⟨the man who knows he too has been successful but can't help *deprecating* his position as an artist —Taliaferro Boatwright⟩

dis·ap·prov·ing·ly *adv* : in a disapproving way : CENSORIOUSLY ⟨eyed him ~⟩ ⟨spoke ~ of his methods⟩

dis·arm \dəs, (ˈ)dis+, *also* dəz *or* (ˈ)diz +\ *vb* [ME *desarmen,* fr. MF *desarmer,* fr. OF, fr. *des-* ¹dis- + *armer* to arm — more at ARM] *vt* **1 a** : to divest of arms ⟨methodically ~*ing* the captured troops⟩ **b** : to deprive of a means of attack or defense ⟨~ a city by razing its walls⟩ ⟨~ a ship⟩ **c** : to deprive of the capacity or means of inflicting material injury **d** : to make harmless (as a mine or bomb) by removing a fuse or other actuating device **2 a** : to make powerless : deprive of means or disposition to harm, criticize, or be hostile ⟨~*ed* the administration's foes by a series of reform laws⟩ ⟨~*ed* criticism by frank avowal of his errors⟩ **b** : to win over by persuasive words or acts ⟨~ her angry father with winning smiles and caresses⟩ ~ *vi* **1** : to lay aside arms **2** : to reduce materially or to a peace footing the military establishment of a country (as at the close of a war)

dis·armament \"+\ *n* [modif. (influenced by *armament*) of F *désarmement,* fr. *désarmer* + *-ment*] : the laying aside or depriving of arms; *esp* : the reduction of a military establishment to some minimum set by some specified authority ⟨the ~ of the defeated aggressor nation must be complete⟩

disarming *adj* : tending to allay or remove a critical or hostile attitude : INGRATIATING ⟨a ~ smile⟩ ⟨~ frankness⟩ ⟨dressed with the ~ simplicity that made her so noticeable —Morley Callaghan⟩ — **dis·arm·ing·ly** *adv*

dis·arrange \ˌdis+\ *vt* [¹*dis-* + *arrange*] : to unsettle or disturb the order or due arrangement of : to throw out of order ⟨sufficient to disturb and ~ her whole inner life —Ellen Glasgow⟩ ⟨her clothing was ripped and violently *disarranged* —J.P.Brown⟩ **syn** see DISORDER

dis·arrangement \"+\ *n* [¹*dis-* + *arrangement*] : the act of disarranging or the state of being disarranged : CONFUSION, DISORDER

¹**dis·array** \ˌdis+\ *n* -S [ME *disaray,* fr. MF *desarroi,* fr. OF *desareer*] **1** : a lack of order or sequence ⟨those dark and noisome hulks anchored in forlorn ~ —Kenneth Roberts⟩ **2** : a confused state in which orderly disposition has been broken or lost : DISARRANGEMENT ⟨the ~ into which society had been thrown by this deplorable affair —Edith Wharton⟩ **3** : incomplete or disorderly dress **syn** see CONFUSION

²**disarray** \"\ *vt* [ME *disarayen,* fr. MF *desarroyer,* fr. OF *desareer,* fr. *des-* ¹dis- + *areer* to prepare, provide, put in order — more at ARRAY] **1** : to throw into disorder : put out of array ⟨the child had ~*ed* the bedcovers⟩ **2** : to take off the dress of : UNROBE ⟨called to ~ the queen⟩ **3** *archaic* : DESPOIL, STRIP — used with *of*

dis·articulate \ˌdis +, *also* ˌdisə(r)ˈt-\ *vb* [¹*dis-* + *articulate*] *vi* : to become disjointed or severed : become separated joint from joint ~ *vt* : DISJOINT, SEVER, SUNDER

dis·articulation \ˌdis +, *also* ˌdisə(r),t-\ *n* [¹*dis-* + *articulation*] **1** : the act of disarticulating; *specif* : amputation or separation of a body part at a joint **2** : a condition of lack of unity or integration : DISJOINTEDNESS ⟨the ~ of society⟩

dis·assemble \ˌdis+\ *vb* [¹*dis-* + *assemble*] *vt* : to take apart : separate into constituent parts ⟨~ a watch⟩ ~ *vi* : to come apart ⟨automobile sections ~⟩

dis·assembly \"+\ *n* [¹*dis-* + *assembly*] **1** : the state or condition of being disassembled **2** : the act or process of disassembling or taking apart ⟨the careful ~ of a lens⟩

disassembly line *n* : a grouping of slaughtering equipment and workers so that carcasses for dismemberment are passed from worker to worker until completely dismembered

dis·assimilate \ˌdis +\ *vt* [¹*dis-* + *assimilate*] : to subject to catabolism — **dis·assimilation** \"+\ *n* — **dis·assimilative** \"+\ *adj*

dis·associate \ˌdis + \ *vb* [¹*dis-* + *associate*] *vt* : to detach from association : DISSOCIATE ⟨*disassociated* himself from the business⟩ ~ *vi* : to terminate an association ⟨deliberately *disassociated* from the circle of his old friends⟩

dis·association \"+\ *n* : the act, process, or an instance of disassociating : the state of being disassociated : DISSOCIATION ⟨the false ~ of the individual and the social —R.M.MacIver⟩

¹**di·sas·ter** \dəˈzastə(r), ˌaas-,ˌais-,ˌas *also* dəˈs|; -ˈs- *is less frequent in "disastrous" than in "disaster", probably because three identical sounds (here, S-sounds) within as many syllables cause a stronger tendency to dissimilation than do two*\ *n* -S *often attrib* [MF & OIt; MF *desastre,* fr. OIt *disastro,* fr. *dis-* ¹dis- (fr. L) + *astro* star, fr. L *astrum,* fr. Gk *astron* — more at STAR] **1** *obs* **a** : an unpropitious or baleful aspect of a planet or star **b** : PORTENT : malevolent influence of a heavenly body **2 a** : a sudden calamitous event producing great material damage, loss, and distress ⟨a flood ~⟩ ⟨a mine ~⟩ ⟨such a war would be the final and supreme ~ to the world —Archibald MacLeish⟩ **b** : a sudden or great misfortune : CALAMITY ⟨the loss of his wife was the culminating ~ of the trip⟩ **c** : a complete failure : FIASCO ⟨only his skillful direction saved the play from being an unqualified ~⟩

syn CALAMITY, CATASTROPHE, CATACLYSM: these words refer to events of great misfortune, duress, and loss, and they are often interchangeable. DISASTER may connote the sudden and unexpected, with attendant notions of lack of foresight ⟨accidents to various ships thwarted this attempt, and brought about a battle *disastrous* to him —A.T.Mahan⟩ The misfortunes of a disaster may be measurable ⟨taking the atom bomb out of the realms of unimaginable horror and showing it as a measurable *disaster* —*Economist*⟩ CALAMITY may heighten suggestions of lasting emotion, affliction, grief at loss ⟨a disaster, for me a *calamity* —John Galsworthy⟩ ⟨revolving this last chapter of *calamity* suddenly opened where happiness had promised —George Meredith⟩ CATASTROPHE is often stronger than DISASTER or CALAMITY ⟨which spell discomfort when one cycle, distress when two, *catastrophe* when all cycles are in the depression phase —E.R.Dewey & E.F.Dakin⟩ It may suggest finality ⟨has Europe been engulfed at last by irrevocable tragedy? Has the fair continent . . . been overtaken at last by irremediable *catastrophe* —T.R.Ybarra⟩ CATACLYSM suggests an upheaval that overwhelms, shatters, and submerges an established order; it usu. applies to the general or universal rather than to the limited or personal ⟨it is not clear whether the Norman Conquest and the Russian Revolution are *cataclysms* or forms of political activity —J.C.Rees⟩ ⟨the impact of war and defeat on the South was immediate and *cataclysmic* —Allan Nevins & H.S.Commager⟩ All of these words and their derivatives are used less precisely in milder situations ⟨a considerable incident. Almost a *disaster* —Joseph Conrad⟩ ⟨live down its small *calamities* —Frederic Morton⟩ ⟨to save the city from the *catastrophic* mismanagement of its own officials —T.E.Dewey⟩ ⟨the *cataclysmic* race, with two real chariots, each drawn by four Arabian horses —*Time*⟩

²**disaster** *vt* -ED/-ING/-S *obs* : to bring harm upon : INJURE, RUIN

disaster area *n* : an area officially declared to be the scene of an emergency created by a disaster and therefore qualified to receive certain types of governmental aid (as emergency loans and relief supplies)

di·sas·trous \-trəs *sometimes* -tərəs\ *adj* [MF & OIt; MF *desastreux,* fr. OIt *disastroso,* fr. *disastro* disaster + *-oso* (fr. L *-osus* -ous)] **1** *archaic* : subject to or affected by disaster : UNLUCKY, ILL-FATED **2** *archaic* : full of unfavorable stellar influences : UNPROPITIOUS, ILL-BODING **3** : attended by or productive of suffering or disaster : very unfortunate : CALAMITOUS ⟨a ~ day⟩ ⟨a ~ termination⟩ **syn** see UNLUCKY

di·sas·trous·ly *adv* : in a disastrous manner : CALAMITOUSLY, UNLUCKILY ⟨the battle ended ~ for the enemy⟩

di·sas·trous·ness *n* -ES : the quality or state of being disastrous

dis·au·xiny \dīˈsȯksənē\ *n* -ES [¹*dis-* + *auxin* + *-y*] : a disturbance in auxin relations of plants sometimes associated with disease

dis·avouch \ˌdis+\ *vt* [¹*dis-* + *avouch*] *archaic* : DISAVOW

dis·avow \ˌdis+\ *vt* [ME *desavowen,* fr. MF *desavouer,* fr. OF, fr. *des-* ¹dis- + *avouer* to avow — more at AVOW] **1** : to refuse to own or acknowledge : deny responsibility for, approbation of, or validity of : DISCLAIM, REPUDIATE, DISOWN ⟨~*ed* the actions of his subordinates⟩ ⟨~*ed* any desire for independence⟩ **2** *obs* : REFUSE, DECLINE **syn** see DISCLAIM

dis·avowal \"+\ *n* : the act or an instance of disavowing : REPUDIATION ⟨the official ~ of the minister's actions⟩ ⟨his ~ of responsibility for the incident⟩

dis·azo \(ˈ)dīˈsa(ˌ)zō\ *adj* [*disazo-,* fr. ²*dis-* + *azo-*] : containing two azo groups in the molecule — distinguished from *diazo* ⟨~ dyes⟩

dis·balance \dəˈsbalən(t)s, (ˈ)di|sˈba-, |ˈspa-,|ˈspa-\ *n* [¹*dis-* + *balance*] : lack of balance : IMBALANCE ⟨the ~ of power between the great and small states⟩ ⟨traumatic experiences which threw his personality into ~ —Wenzell Brown⟩

dis·band \dəˈsˈband, (ˈ)di|sˈb|, |ˈsp|,|ˈsp|, |aand\ *vb* [MF *desbander,* fr. *des-* ¹dis- + *bande* troop — more at BAND] *vt* **1** : to break up the organization of : DISSOLVE ⟨the dance group was ~*ed* after a farewell concert⟩; *esp* : to dismiss as a body from military service ⟨~ an army⟩ **2** *obs* : to release from a band or army : DISCHARGE **3** *obs* : to send away : DISMISS, DIVORCE ~ *vi* : to break up an organization ⟨the company gave its last performances in 1943 and has since ~*ed* —Anatole Chujoy⟩ : break ranks : DISPERSE, SCATTER ⟨the troops ~*ed* in the greatest disorder⟩

dis·band·ment \-n(d)mənt\ *n* -S : the act of disbanding or the state of being disbanded ⟨the symphony orchestra faced the prospect of ~⟩

¹**dis·bar** \dəˈsˈbär, (ˈ)di|sˈb|, |ˈsp|,|ˈsp|, |ä(r\ *vt* [¹*dis-* + *bar* (v.)] : to exclude from a place or condition : DISQUALIFY, DEBAR ⟨his age and poor health *disbarred* him from further service in the senate⟩ ⟨automatically ~*s* it from strict classification as a sonata —A.E.Wier⟩ **syn** see EXCLUDE

²**disbar** \"\ *vt* [¹*dis-* + *bar* (court)] : to expel from the bar or the legal profession : deprive (an attorney) of legal status and privileges

disbark *vb* -ED/-ING/-S [prob. fr. MF *desbarquer, debarquer* — more at DEBARK] *obs* : DISEMBARK

dis·bar·ment \-ärmənt, -äm-\ *n* -S [²*disbar* + *-ment*] : the act or an instance of disbarring : the state of being disbarred

dis·be·lief \ˌdisbəˈlēf, -spə-\ *n* [¹*dis-* + *belief*] : the act of disbelieving : mental refusal to accept (as a statement or proposition) as true ⟨listened to him with shocked ~⟩

dis·be·lieve \-ēv\ *vb* [¹*dis-* + *believe*] *vt* : to hold not to be true or real : reject or withhold belief in ⟨~ his professions of sincerity⟩ ⟨~ the existence of ghosts⟩ ~ *vi* : to withhold or reject belief — used with *in* ⟨~*s* in the sanctity of the status quo —W.C.Brownell⟩

dis·be·liev·er \-və(r)\ *n* **:** one that disbelieves **:** an unbeliever esp. in the doctrines of a religion

disbelieving *adj* **:** refusing to believe **:** withholding belief **:** UNBELIEVING — **dis·be·liev·ing·ly** *adv*

dis·bod·ied \dəs'bädēd, (')dis'b-, \|spä-, \|spä-\ *adj* [fr. past part. of obs. *disbody* to disembody, fr. ¹*dis-* + *body* (n.)] **:** DISEMBODIED ⟨while we rode we were ~, unconscious of flesh or feeling —T.E.Lawrence⟩

dis·bow·el \dəs'bau̇(ə)l, (')dis'bau̇-, \|'spau̇-, \|spau̇-\ *vt* **disbowelled; disbowelled; disbowelling; disbowels** [ME *disbowelen*, fr. ¹*dis-* + *bowel* (n.)] *archaic* **:** DISEMBOWEL

dis·branch \dəs'brlanch, (')dis'br\|, \|'spr\|, \|spr\|, \|aa(ə)n-, \|ain-,\|ān-\ *vt* [MF *desbrancher*, fr. *des-* ¹dis- + *branche* branch — more at BRANCH] **:** to divest of a branch **:** tear off (as a branch)

dis·bud \dəs'bəd, (')dis'bəd, \|'spəd,\|spəd\ *vt* **disbudded; disbudded; disbudding; disbuds** [¹*dis-* + *bud* (n.)] **1 :** to deprive of buds or shoots for the purpose of training **:** thin out flower buds to improve the quality of bloom of **2 :** to dehorn (cattle) by destroying the undeveloped horn bud

dis·bur·den \dəs'bərdᵊn, (')dis'b\|, \|'sp\|,\|sp\|, \|ǝd-,\|ǝid-\ *vb* [¹*dis-* + *burden* (n.)] *vt* **1 a :** to rid of a burden or load **:** DISENCUMBER ⟨~ a pack animal⟩ **b :** to relieve of something burdensome or oppressive to the mind ⟨enabled to ~ himself of some of his anxieties —R.J.B.Sellar⟩ ⟨~ your conscience by confession⟩ **2 :** to get rid of (a burden) **:** UNLOAD ⟨~*ed* their merchandise in the city square⟩ ~ *vi* **:** to get rid of a burden or load **:** DISCHARGE, UNLOAD ⟨vessels ~*ing* at a dock⟩

dis·burs·al \dəs'bərsəl, dəs'sp\|, \|ǝs-,\|ǝis-\ *n* -s **:** the act or an instance of disbursing **:** DISBURSEMENT ⟨made large ~*s* of money daily⟩

¹**dis·burse** \-s\ *vt* -ED/-ING/-s [MF *desbourser*, fr. OF *desborser*, fr. *des-* ¹dis- + *borser* to get money, fr. *borse* purse, fr. LL *bursa* oxhide — more at PURSE] **1 a :** to expend esp. from a public fund **:** pay out ⟨*disbursed* over $5,000,000 for roads and other improvements⟩ ⟨party bosses *disbursed* money freely in strategic election districts⟩ **b :** to pay in settlement of **:** DEFRAY ⟨his father's readiness to ~ such a thumping bill —George Meredith⟩ **2 :** DISTRIBUTE ⟨his will *disbursed* property to the value of approximately $35,000,000 —R.S. Boardman⟩ ⟨the hundred kilograms of uranium . . . was to be *disbursed* under strictly bilateral agreement —John Lear⟩ **syn** see SPEND

²**disburse** \"\ *n* -s *archaic* **:** DISBURSEMENT

dis·burse·ment \-smənt\ *n* -s [MF *desboursement*, fr. *desbourser* + *-ment*] **:** the act of disbursing ⟨~ of the loan has been completed⟩; *also* **:** something that is disbursed **:** funds paid out ⟨made large ~*s* for research and development⟩

dis·burs·er \-sə(r)\ *n* -s **:** one that disburses ⟨foundations and other ~*s* of research money should deal directly with universities —S.E.Harris⟩

disc *var of* DISK

disc- *or* **disci-** *or* **disco-** *comb form* [L *disc-*, *disco-* & ML *disci-*, fr. Gk *disk-*, *disko-*, fr. *diskos* quoit — more at DISH] **1 :** disk ⟨*Discina*⟩ ⟨*disci*gerous⟩ ⟨*disco*mycete⟩ **2 :** phonograph record **:** recording ⟨*disco*graphy⟩ ⟨*disco*phile⟩

disc *abbr* **1** discharged **2** disconnect **3** discount **4** discovered

dis·cal \'diskəl\ *adj* **:** like or relating to a disk

dis·cal·ce·ate \(')di'skalsēət\ *adj* [L *discalceatus*, fr. *dis-* ¹dis- + *calceatus*, past part. of *calceare* to furnish with shoes, shoe, fr. *calceus* shoe, half boot, fr. *calc-*, *calx* heel — more at CALK] **:** DISCALCED

dis·calced \(')di'skalst\ *adj* [part trans. of L *discalceatus*] **:** UNSHOD, BAREFOOTED ⟨~ friars⟩ — compare CALCED

discal cell *n* **1 :** a large cell near the base of the wing of a butterfly or moth **2 :** a cell between the branches of the media in the two-winged fly

discamp *vb* [MF *descamper* — more at DECAMP] *vt*, *obs* **:** to drive from a camp ~ *vi*, *obs* **:** DECAMP

discandy *vi* [¹*dis-* + *candy*] *obs* **:** MELT, DISSOLVE

discant *var of* DESCANT

dis·can·tus \də'skantəs\ *n*, *pl* **discantus** [ML — more at DESCANT] **:** DESCANT

¹**dis·card** \də'skärd, 'di,s-, -kȧd\ *vb* -ED/-ING/-s [¹*dis-* + *card* (n.)] *vt* **1 a :** to remove (a playing card) from one's hand to prepare for drawing or to reduce the hand to the number specified **b :** to play (any card except a trump) from a suit different from the one led **2 :** to drop, dismiss, let go, or get rid of as no longer useful, valuable, or pleasurable ⟨a butterfly who has ~*ed* his chrysalis —A.T.Quiller-Couch⟩ ⟨on reaching Vancouver he had . . . ~*ed* his lightweight suits —V.G.Heiser⟩ ⟨the painful process of ~*ing* cherished illusions —Laurence Binyon⟩ ~ *vi* **:** to discard a playing card

syn SHED, SLOUGH, CAST, MOLT, SCRAP, JUNK: DISCARD indicates dispensing with, letting go of, getting rid of, as not immediately useful; it is not a forceful word and may connote only the mild action of getting rid of a playing card from one's hand ⟨he sorted and re-sorted his cargo, always finding a more necessary article for which a less necessary had to be *discarded* —Willa Cather⟩ ⟨the song appeared in a draft of the play's first act, and was later *discarded* from the revised versions —H.V.Gregory⟩ ⟨modern research, which *discards* obsolete hypotheses —W.R.Inge⟩ SHED, SLOUGH, CAST, and MOLT may all suggest an animal's discarding an old skin or integument. SHED suggests divesting oneself or letting go of something outworn, rough or callow, or burdensome ⟨some words *shedding* old meanings and acquiring new ones —*Times Lit. Supp.*⟩ ⟨as he mellowed, he *shed* such vulgarity —*Times Lit. Supp.*⟩ ⟨though statesmen may try to *shed* their responsibility —J.A.Hobson⟩ SLOUGH suggests the throwing off of the deleterious, objectionable, or disadvantageous ⟨in the face of death Sonya seemed transformed, *sloughing* off all earthly dross —E.J.Simmons⟩ ⟨as though her gaunt and worldly air had been only a mockery she began to *slough* it off —Louis Bromfield⟩ CAST may be more forceful in its suggestion and imply rejection and repudiation ⟨an Englishman like the Ethiopian cannot change his skin any more than a leopard can *cast* off his spots —Stuart Cloete⟩ ⟨the Mexican Revolution of 1820 *cast* off the shackles of Spanish mercantilism —R.A.Billington⟩ MOLT may imply casting off of feathers, skin, or other covering, esp. during a period of difficulty or transition ⟨the belief that social change can be effected without revolution or unpleasantness, that society can *molt* its outer covering and become new in shape and spirit —J.D.Hart⟩ SCRAP and JUNK suggest discarding as worthless in existent form or operation, as an automobile or a ship is scrapped or junked. SCRAP is milder and less summary and final in its suggestion ⟨most modern literary theory would be inclined to *scrap* the prose-poetry distinction —René Wellek & Austin Warren⟩ ⟨the idea of *scrapping* our two military academies or drastically altering them —C.T.Lanham⟩ JUNK is a more forthright term, more drastic in indicating a demonstrated lack of serviceability, validity, or worth ⟨the South has never been able to understand how the North, in its astonishing quest for perfection, can *junk* an entire system of ideas almost overnight —Donald Davidson⟩

²**dis·card** \"*,* *sometimes* "*,*\ *n* **1** *card games* **:** the act of discarding; *also* **:** the card or cards discarded **2 :** a person or thing cast off: as **a :** a person that is cast off or rejected by society **:** one that is economically or socially degraded or abased ⟨the West had been the land of new hope . . . for the ~*s* of industrialism —F.L.Allen⟩ ⟨finds his characteristic hero and characteristic story among the ~*s* of society —R.P.Warren⟩ **b :** the rejected top portion of an ingot **c :** a book or other publication officially withdrawn from a library collection as unfit for further use or as no longer needed — **into the discard** *adv* **:** into disuse or oblivion **:** out of consideration or existence ⟨sword and spear and battle-ax have gone *into the discard* of time —Tom Wintringham⟩

dis·car·nate \də'skärnət, -,nāt\ *adj* [¹*dis-* + *-carnate* (as in *incarnate*)] **:** having no physical body **:** INCORPOREAL ⟨~ intelligence thinking in self-sufficient silence on first and last things —Irwin Edman⟩ ⟨believe in the existence of ~ spirits⟩

dis·case \dəs, (')dis+\ *vb* [¹*dis-* + *case* (n.)] **:** UNDRESS

disc cultivator *n* **:** a cultivator consisting of discs that are grouped in sets and paired so that the discs of each pair incline in opposite directions

disced *past of* DISC

dis·cept \də'sept\ *vi* -ED/-ING/-s [L *disceptare* to separate, decide between, debate, fr. *dis-* apart + *-ceptare* (fr. *captare* to chase, strive to seize) — more at DIS-, CATCH] **:** DEBATE, DISCUSS, DISAGREE ⟨as he ~*s* and distinguishes, classifies his kinds of tragedy, his orders of comedy —*Times Lit. Supp.*⟩

dis·cep·ta·tion \,di,sep'tāshən\ *n* -s [ME *deceptacioun*, fr. L *disceptation-*, *disceptatio*, fr. *disceptatus* (past part. of *disceptare*) + *-ion-*, *-io* -ion] *archaic* **:** CONTROVERSY, DISPUTATION, DISCUSSION

dis·cern \də'sərn, \|ǝn,\|ǝin *also* -'z\ *vb* -ED/-ING/-s [ME *discernen*, fr. MF *discerner*, fr. L *discernere* to separate, distinguish between, fr. *dis-* apart + *cernere* to sift — more at DIS-, CERTAIN] *vt* **1 a :** to make out with the eyes (as something obscure or distant) **:** DETECT, DESCRY ⟨could ~ a narrow path winding up the mountainside⟩ ⟨a convoy of 30 vessels was ~*ed* this morning by our forces —Sir Winston Churchill⟩ **b :** to detect or discover with other senses than vision ⟨~*ed* a strange unfamiliar odor in the room⟩ ⟨~*ed* the muffled sobbing of a child⟩ **2 :** to sense or come to know or recognize mentally esp. something that is hidden or obscure ⟨the inductive apprehension of a truth imperfectly ~*ed* —B.N.Cardozo⟩ ⟨the ability to ~ and analyze the essentials of complicated questions —K.C.Wheare⟩ **3 :** DISTINGUISH: as **a** *obs* **:** to mark as separate and distinct **:** put a distinguishing mark upon **b :** to recognize or identify as separate and distinct **:** DIFFERENTIATE, DISCRIMINATE ⟨~ right from wrong⟩ ⟨~ the false from the genuine⟩ ~ *vi* **:** to see or understand the difference **:** make distinction ⟨~ between good and evil⟩ **syn** see SEE

dis·cern·er \-nə(r)\ *n* -s **:** one that discerns

dis·cern·ible *or* **dis·cern·able** \-nəbəl\ *adj* [*discernible* alter. (influenced by LL *discernibilis*, fr. L *discernere* + *-ibilis* -ible) of *discernable*; *discernable* fr. MF, fr. *discerner* + *-able*] **:** capable of being discerned by the senses or the understanding **:** DISTINGUISHABLE ⟨a ~ trend⟩ ⟨there was ~ the outline of an old trunk —Floyd Dell⟩ — **dis·cern·ible·ness** \-bəlnəs\ *or* **dis·cern·able·ness** *n* -ES

dis·cern·ibly *or* **dis·cern·ably** \-blē, -li\ *adv* **:** in a discernible manner

discerning *adj* **:** revealing insight and understanding **:** DISCRIMINATING ⟨a ~ critic⟩ ⟨~ criticism⟩ — **dis·cern·ing·ly** *adv*

dis·cern·ment \-nmənt\ *n* -s [MF *discernement*, fr. *discerner* + *-ment*] **1 :** the act of discerning ⟨his quick ~ of his opponent's weaknesses⟩ **2 :** the quality of skill in discerning esp. that which is hidden or obscure **:** readiness and accuracy in discriminating **:** keenness of insight ⟨a novel of depth and ~⟩ ⟨displayed ~ and courage⟩

dis·cerp \də'sərp, -'zerp\ *vt* -ED/-ING/-s [ME *discerpen*, fr. L *discerpere*, fr. *dis-* apart + *-cerpere* (fr. *carpere* to pick, pluck) — more at DIS-, HARVEST] **1 :** to tear apart **:** DISMEMBER **2** *archaic* **:** to tear off **:** sever from a whole

dis·cerp·ible \-pəbəl\ *adj*, *archaic* **:** DISCERPTIBLE

dis·cerp·ti·ble \-ptəbəl\ *adj* [L *discerptus* (past part. of *discerpere*) + E *-ible*] **:** capable of being torn to pieces or pulled apart **:** separable into parts ⟨cannot be told by poetry or by music . . . nor is ~ in logic —Robert Bridges †1930⟩

dis·cerp·tion \-pshən\ *n* -s [LL *discerption-*, *discerptio*, fr. L *discerptus* + *-ion-*, *-io* -ion] **:** the act of discerping **:** a pulling to pieces; *also* **:** something that is severed or separated

disc furrower *n* **:** a land furrower in which the customary shoe is replaced by a pair of concave discs set at an angle to the line of draft

disc go-devil *n* **:** RIDGE BUSTER

¹**dis·charge** \dəs(h)'chärj, 'dis(h),ch-, -chȧj\ *vb* -ED/-ING/-s [ME *dischargen*, fr. MF *descharger*, fr. OF *deschargier*, fr. LL *discarricare*, fr. L *dis-* ¹dis- + LL *carricare* to load — more at CHARGE] *vt* **1 :** to relieve of a charge, load, or burden: **a :** to empty of a cargo **:** UNLOAD ⟨~ a ship⟩ **b** *archaic* **:** to rid or deprive esp. of something that burdens **c :** to free from something that burdens **:** EXEMPT **:** release from an obligation ⟨*discharged* from further payment of taxes⟩ **d** *obs* **:** to clear of an accusation or charge **:** ACQUIT, EXONERATE **e :** to project the missile of **:** FIRE ⟨~ a gun⟩ **f :** to relieve the electrical tension or release the energy of by withdrawal or emission of that which charges ⟨~ a Leyden jar⟩ ⟨~ a storage battery⟩ **2 a :** to let go **:** clear out **:** REMOVE ⟨~ a cargo⟩ ⟨the train ~*s* passengers⟩ **b :** to send forth (as a projectile) **:** SHOOT **:** let fly **:** FIRE ⟨~ an arrow⟩ **c :** to set at liberty **:** release from confinement, custody, or care ⟨~ a prisoner⟩ ⟨*discharged* from parole⟩ ⟨~ a patient from the hospital⟩ **d (1) :** to give outlet to **:** pour forth **:** EMIT ⟨the river ~*s* its waters into the bay⟩ ⟨a motor ~*s* a certain amount of fumes⟩ ⟨a boil *discharging* pus⟩ **(2) :** to release or give vent to (as a pent-up emotion or repressed impulse) ⟨sometimes impossible . . . to ~ our emotions upon their proper objects —T.V.Smith⟩ ⟨into her diary she *discharged* her fury and brooding loneliness⟩ **(3) :** UTTER, PRONOUNCE ⟨he *discharged* a string of oaths⟩ ⟨*discharging* abuse on all his critics⟩ **3 a (1) :** to dismiss from employment **:** terminate the employment of ⟨a rich man can ~ anyone in his employment who displeases him —G.B.Shaw⟩ **(2) :** to end formally the service of **:** release from duty ⟨~ a soldier⟩ ⟨~ a jury⟩ ⟨~ a committee with thanks to its members⟩ **b (1) :** to get rid of (as a debt or duty) by paying or performing ⟨he *discharged* his liabilities⟩ **:** FULFILL, EXECUTE ⟨~ one's duties effectively⟩ **(2)** *obs* **:** to act the part of ⟨not a man in all Athens able to ~ Pyramus but he —Shak.⟩ **c** *obs* **:** to get rid of (as an office or obligation) by doing away with **d (1)** *obs* **:** to make a settlement with (as a creditor) ⟨the present money to ~ the Jew —Shak.⟩ **(2)** *archaic* **:** to pay for **:** PAY **e :** to set aside **:** dismiss legally **:** ANNUL ⟨~ a court order⟩ **f :** to release (a legislative committee) from further consideration of a bill in order to bring it before the house for action ⟨they moved to ~ the committee⟩ **4** *now chiefly Scot* **:** PROHIBIT, FORBID **5 a :** to receive and distribute (as the weight of a wall above an opening) **b :** to relieve (as an opening or the lintel spanning an opening) from the weight of a wall **6 a :** to bleach out or to remove (color or dye) in dyeing and printing textiles usu. by a chemical process ⟨~ the blue color from a dyed fabric⟩ **b :** to remove the color from (a dyed fabric) in this manner **7 :** to cancel the record of the loan of (a library book) upon its return ~ *vi* **1 :** to throw off or deliver a load, charge, or burden **:** UNLOAD **2 a :** to go off (as of a gun) **b :** RUN ⟨some dyes ~⟩ **c :** to emit or give vent to fluid or other contents ⟨the water pipe ~*s* freely⟩ **syn** see DISMISS, FREE, PERFORM

²**discharge** \dis(h),ch-, dəs(h)'ch-\ *n* -s [ME, fr. MF *descharge*, fr. OF, fr. *deschargier*] **1 a :** the act of relieving of something that oppresses (as an obligation, accusation, penalty) **:** ACQUITTANCE, DISMISSAL, RELEASE ⟨ask for the ~ of a debtor⟩ **b :** something that discharges or releases (as from imprisonment, an obligation, or a liability); *esp* **:** a certification of release or payment ⟨produced his ~ as evidence⟩ **2 :** the state or fact of being discharged or relieved (as of a debt, obligation, or accusation) **:** ACQUITTAL, EXONERATION ⟨received a full ~ from responsibility for the incident⟩ **3 :** the act of discharging **:** removal of a load **:** UNLOADING ⟨the ~ of a ship⟩ ⟨the ~ of a cargo⟩ **4 :** legal release from confinement **:** LIBERATION ⟨ordering a conditional ~ of the alien on habeas corpus —*Harvard Law Rev.*⟩ **5 :** a firing off **:** expulsion of a charge **:** EXPLOSION ⟨a ~ of arrows⟩ ⟨an artillery ~⟩ **6 a :** a flowing or issuing out; *also* **:** a rate of flow **:** EMISSION, VENT ⟨a rapid ~ of water from a pipe⟩ ⟨a ~ of spores from a fungus⟩ **b :** something that is emitted or evacuated ⟨a purulent ~ from a wound⟩ ⟨profuse intestinal ~*s*⟩ **7 :** the act of removing or getting rid of an obligation or liability (as by the payment of a debt or the performance of a trust or duty) **:** FULFILLMENT, ACCOMPLISHMENT ⟨active in the ~ of his professional functions⟩ **8 a :** release or dismissal esp. from an office or employment ⟨the ~ of a worker⟩ **b (1) :** the dismissal of a court's mandate **(2) :** the release of a bankrupt as a result of bankruptcy proceedings and after his estate has been settled **c :** complete separation from the military service; *also* **:** the certificate verifying the service performed and the separation **9 a :** a composition used for removing color from a dyed fabric **:** a discharging agent **b :** the removal of color from a dyed fabric ⟨acid ~ of Turkey red⟩ **c :** the effect produced on a dyed fabric by discharging ⟨a white ~ is obtained⟩ **10 a :** the equalization of a difference of electric potential by a transfer of electricity, the character of the equalization being determined by the medium through which it occurs, by the amount of difference of potential, and by the form of the terminal conductors on which the difference exists — see BRUSH DISCHARGE, DISRUPTIVE DISCHARGE, GLOW DISCHARGE, OSCILLATORY DISCHARGE **b :** the converting of the chemical energy of a voltaic cell or battery into electrical energy **11 :** the transfer of an impulse from nerve fiber to effector

³**discharge** \"\ *adj* **:** of, relating to, or produced by the process of discharging in dyeing and printing textiles

dis·charge·able \-jəbəl\ *adj* **:** capable of being discharged

dischargeable weight *n* **:** all weight that can be consumed or discharged and still leave an airship in safe operating condition with a specified reserve of fuel, oil, water ballast, and provisions and with normal crew

discharge coefficient *n* **:** COEFFICIENT OF DISCHARGE

discharged *past of* DISCHARGE

dis·charg·ee \,dis(h),chär'jē, dəs(h)'ch-, -chȧ'-\ *n* -s [¹*discharge* + *-ee*] **:** one who has been discharged

discharge lamp *n* **:** an electric lamp in which discharge of electricity between electrodes causes luminosity of the enclosed metallic vapor (as sodium or mercury) or gas (as neon) or in which the luminosity of the enclosed gas is enhanced by phosphors (as in the fluorescent lamp)

discharge printing *n* **:** a process of printing textiles already dyed a solid color by bleaching out a pattern usu. producing a white or light-colored design on a dark background — compare ¹DISCHARGE 6

dis·charg·er *pronunc at* ¹DISCHARGE +ə(r)\ *n* -s **:** one that discharges: as **a :** an instrument for discharging a Leyden jar or electrical battery by making a connection between the two surfaces **b :** SPARK GAP 2 **c :** a device for discharging the tied bundles of grain from a binder

discharges *pres 3d sing of* DISCHARGE, *pl of* DISCHARGE

discharge tube *n* **:** an electron tube which contains gas or vapor at low pressure and through which conduction takes place when a high voltage is applied

discharging *pres part of* DISCHARGE

discharging arch *n* **:** RELIEVING ARCH

disc harrow *n* **:** a harrow that breaks up plowed or rough land by means of discs arranged at an angle with the line of draft

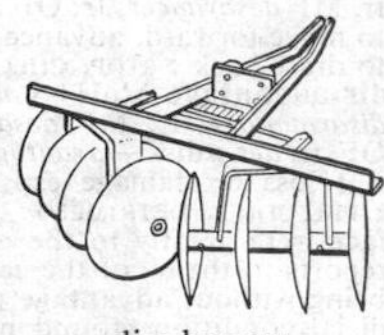
disc harrow

disc hiller *n* **:** a cultivator attachment having two series of discs arranged to throw topsoil around the roots of crops

disci *pl of* DISCUS

disci- — see DISC-

dis·ci·flo·ral \'dis(k)ə'flōrəl, -lȯr-\ *also* **dis·ci·flo·rous** \-rəs\ *adj* [*disc-* + *floral* or *-florous*] **:** having flowers with the receptacle enlarged into a conspicuous disc (as in the Rutaceae and other families of dicotyledons)

dis·ci·form \'dis(k)ə,fȯrm\ *adj* [*disc-* + *-form*] **:** of round or oval shape ⟨a ~ skin lesion⟩ **:** DISCOID

dis·cig·er·ous \(')di'sijərəs\ *adj* [*disc-* + *-gerous*] **:** having a disk ⟨~ woody tissue of conifers⟩

dis·ci·na \də's(k)īnə\ *n*, *cap* [NL, fr. *disc-* + *-ina*] **:** a genus of recent African inarticulate brachiopods having a disk-shaped shell whose ventral valve is perforated by the pedicle — **dis·ci·noid** \'dis(k)ə,nȯid\ *adj*

dis·cinct \də'siŋ(k)t\ *adj* [L *discinctus*, fr. past part. of *discingere* to ungird, fr. *dis-* ¹dis- + *cingere* to gird — more at CINCTURE] **:** loosely dressed; *also* **:** LOOSE, NEGLIGENT

discing *pres part of* DISC

¹**dis·ci·ple** \də'sīpəl\ *n* -s [ME, fr. OE *discipul* & OF *deciple*, *desciple*, fr. LL *discipulus* personal follower of Jesus Christ in his lifetime (fr. L) & L *discipulus* pupil, perh. fr. (assumed) L *discipere* to grasp, comprehend, fr. L *dis-* ¹dis- + *-cipere* (fr. *capere* to seize) — more at HEAVE] **1 :** one who receives instruction from another **:** one who accepts the doctrines of another and assists in spreading or implementing them **:** FOLLOWER: as **a :** a professed follower of Christ in his lifetime; *esp* **:** one of the twelve apostles **b :** a convinced adherent of a school (as in philosophy, art, or politics) ⟨a ~ of Kant⟩ ⟨a ~ of Rubens⟩ ⟨a ~ of Jefferson⟩ **2** *usu cap* **:** a member of the Disciples of Christ who reject human creeds and sectarian names, hold the Bible alone to be the rule of faith and practice, celebrate the Lord's Supper every Sunday, baptize believers by immersion only and regard baptism with faith and repentance as essential to salvation, employ a congregational polity, and have been closely associated with the Churches of Christ

²**disciple** \"\ *vt* -ED/-ING/-s **1** *obs* **:** TEACH, TRAIN **2** *obs* **:** PUNISH, DISCIPLINE **3** *archaic* **:** to make a disciple of **:** CONVERT

dis·ci·plin·able \'disə'plinəbəl, 'disəplən-, 'displən-, də'siplən-\ *adj* [MF, fr. LL *disciplinabilis*, fr. L *disciplina* teaching, instruction + *-abilis* -able — more at DISCIPLINE] **1 :** capable of being disciplined or instructed **:** TEACHABLE **2 :** liable or deserving to be disciplined **:** subject to disciplinary punishment ⟨a ~ offense⟩

dis·ci·plin·al \'disəplənᵊl, -,plin-, 'displən-, də'siplən-\ *adj* **:** of or relating to discipline **:** constituting discipline **:** DISCIPLINARY ⟨~ measures⟩

dis·ci·plin·ant \'disəplənənt, -,plinənt, 'displən-, də'siplən-\ *n* -s [Sp & It; Sp *disciplinante*, fr. It, fr. ML *disciplinant-*, *disciplinans*, pres. part. of *disciplinare* to discipline — more at DISCIPLINE] **:** FLAGELLANT; *esp* **:** a member of a Spanish order noted for its severe discipline

¹**dis·ci·pli·nar·i·an** \,disəplə'nerēən, -na(a)r-, -nār- *also* ,disp-\ *n* -s [¹*discipline* + *-arian*] **1** *usu cap* **:** an early English Puritan with Calvinistic leanings **2 :** one who disciplines **:** one who enforces order ⟨a strict ~ in school⟩

²**disciplinarian** \"\ *adj* **1** *usu cap* **:** of or relating to the Disciplinarians **2 :** of or relating to discipline

dis·ci·pli·nary \'disəplə,nerē, -ri *also* -sp- *sometimes* də'sip-\ *adj* [¹*discipline* + *-ary*] **1** *obs* **:** of or relating to ecclesiastical discipline or legislation **2 :** of or relating to discipline ⟨in a certain classroom ~ problems were frequent —A.A.Hanson⟩ **:** strict in enforcing discipline ⟨if the mother is a cold, unforgiving, stern, and ~ one —Carl Binger⟩ **:** designed to correct or punish breaches of discipline ⟨took ~ action against three inspectors charged with taking bribes⟩ ⟨set up a committee to consider ~ measures against the senator⟩ **3** *archaic* **:** of, relating to, or serving the ends of teaching **4 :** of or relating to a discipline **:** regarded as a particular field of study ⟨political science in a formal ~ sense is of very recent origin in Japan —R.E.Ward⟩ **5 :** marked by discipline **:** DISCIPLINED, ORDERED ⟨Rousseau's view of life is above all emotional, that of Plato's supremely ~ —Irving Babbitt⟩

disciplinary barracks *n pl but usu sing in constr* **:** a military prison organized with a system of suspension of sentences, paroles, and restoration to duty

dis·ci·plin·a·to·ry \'dis(ə)plənə,tōrē, ,disə'plin-, də'siplən-\ *adj* [LL *disciplinatorius*, fr. *disciplinatus* disciplined (past part. of *disciplinare* to discipline) + L *-orius* -ory — more at DISCIPLINE] **:** DISCIPLINARY

¹**dis·ci·pline** \'disəplən, -,plin *sometimes* -splən\ *n* -s [ME, fr. MF & L; MF *discipline*, *descepline*, fr. L *disciplina*, lit., teaching, instruction, alter. of *discipulina*, fr. *discipulus* pupil — more at DISCIPLE] **1** *obs* **:** TEACHING, INSTRUCTION, TUTORING **2 :** a subject that is taught **:** a branch of learning **:** field of study ⟨such traditional ~*s* as history, literature, political science —W.R.Steckel⟩ **3 :** training or experience that corrects, molds, strengthens, or perfects esp. the mental faculties or moral character ⟨will submit willingly to severe ~ in order to acquire some coveted knowledge or skill —Bertrand Russell⟩ ⟨the valuable intellectual ~ of close research into a limited topic⟩ ⟨needs the ~ of hard work and early rising⟩ ⟨to learn to dance is the most austere of ~*s* —Havelock Ellis⟩ **4 :** PUNISHMENT: as **a :** chastisement self-inflicted as mortification or imposed as a penance or as a penalty **b :** an instrument of chastisement; *specif* **:** WHIP, SCOURGE **c :** punishment by one in authority esp. with a view to correction or training ⟨schoolboys kept in line by floggings and other severe ~⟩ **5 a :** control gained by enforcing obedience or order (as in a school or army) **:** strict government to the end of effective action ⟨maintained the strictest ~ in the barracks and the field⟩ **b :** behavior in accordance with the rules (as of an organization) **:** prompt and willing obedience to the orders of superiors **:** systematic, willing, and purposeful attention to the performance of assigned tasks **:** orderly conduct ⟨commended

the ~ of these veteran troops⟩ ⟨lack of ~ was made plain by the students' listless, apathetic recitation⟩; *also* **:** behavior (as of students or soldiers) regarded in terms of its conformity with an ideal or actual code or set of rules ⟨poor ~⟩ ⟨good ~⟩ **c :** conduct in accordance with a self-imposed rule or set of rules **:** SELF-CONTROL, SELF-RESTRAINT ⟨with a remarkable ~ she avoided all reference to this incident in the pages of her diary⟩ ⟨the sixty-six-pound free luggage allowance . . . forces me into a ~ in selecting what to take along —Richard Joseph⟩ **6 :** a rule or system of rules governing conduct or action **:** system of regulation ⟨in these revolutions the ~*s*, such as food rationing, either collapsed or near-collapsed —Herbert Hoover⟩: as **a :** a body of laws relating to conduct and church government **:** practical rules as distinguished from dogmatic formulations ⟨to introduce the Presbyterian polity and ~⟩ **b :** a body of purely ecclesiastical laws or practices that may be altered to meet new conditions ⟨changes in the Roman Catholic ~ relating to fasting⟩ **7 a :** an orderly or regular pattern of behavior ⟨watching the ~ of the tides, with their evident rhythm —Clare Leighton⟩ **b :** METHOD, APPROACH ⟨argued that the ~ of science differs from that of the humanities⟩

²**discipline** \“\ *vt* -ED/-ING/-S [ME *disciplinen*, fr. MF & LL; MF *discipliner*, fr. LL *disciplinare*, fr. *disciplina*] **1 :** to inflict suffering on or to penalize for the sake of discipline, regularity, order, or rule. as **a :** to whip or punish corporally in order to subjugate, mortify, or inflict penance on ⟨saw a dozen wretched creatures *disciplining* themselves with whips⟩ **b :** to punish or penalize in any way often by infliction of extra tasks or by loss of privileges ⟨cadets *disciplined* by confinement to quarters⟩ **c :** to inflict ecclesiastical censures and penalties upon **2 :** to train by instruction or exercise (as for the performance of some task) ⟨attention which modern education does not ~ the majority of our citizens to give —R.M. Weaver⟩ ⟨endless practice . . . had *disciplined* his muscles and nerves into beautiful coordination —P.B.Sears⟩ **:** train (the mental faculties) in habits of order, sobriety, and precision ⟨a *disciplined* mind⟩ ⟨a *disciplined* imagination⟩ **:** make effective by restraint ⟨so ~*s* his writing as to make every word count —Coleman Rosenberger⟩ **3 a :** to bring (a group) under control **:** govern strictly **:** train to habits of order **:** DRILL ⟨poorly armed and *disciplined* troops⟩ **b :** to impose order or measure upon **:** bring into order ⟨the enormous, confused, and unruly material has . . . been *disciplined* into a single coherent narrative —Walter Millis⟩ **syn** see PUNISH, TEACH

dis·ci·plin·er \-nə(r)\ *n* -S **1 :** one that disciplines **2** *cap* **:** DISCIPLINARIAN 1

dis·cip·u·lar \də'sipyələ(r)\ *adj* [L *discipulus* pupil + E *-ar* — more at DISCIPLE] **:** of, relating to, or befitting a disciple ⟨his ~ patience —Henry Morley⟩

dis·cis·sion \də'sishən\ *n* -S [LL *discission-, discissio* act of cutting apart, fr. L *discissus* (past part. of *discindere* to cut apart, fr. *di-* — fr. *dis-* apart — + *scindere* to cut, split) + *-ion-, -io* -ion — more at DIS-, SHED] **:** an incision of the capsule of the lens of the eye (as in treating cataract)

disc jockey *or* **disk jockey** *n* **:** a person who conducts and announces a radio or television program of musical recordings often with interspersed comments not relating to music

¹**dis·claim** \də'sklām\ *n* [ME *disclaime*, fr. AF, fr. *disclaimer, desclamer*] *archaic* **:** DISCLAMATION

²**disclaim** \“\ *vb* [AF *disclaimer, desclamer*, fr. *des-* ¹dis- + *claimer, clamer*, fr. OF *clamer* to cry out, complain, claim — more at CLAIM] *vi* **1 :** to renounce or repudiate a legal claim **:** make a disclaimer **2 a** *obs* **:** to disavow all part or share **:** make public denunciation or dissent **b :** to utter denial ⟨Catherine colored, and ~*ed* again —Jane Austen⟩ **3** *obs* **:** to cry out or declaim ~ *vt* **1 :** to renounce a legal claim to **:** deny or repudiate any interest in or connection with **2 :** to deny or disavow (as a connection with or responsibility for) ⟨~*ed* any knowledge of the contents of the letter⟩ **:** REPUDIATE, DISOWN ⟨~*ed* the libelous pamphlet⟩ ⟨~*ing* any ill will toward him⟩ **3 :** to deny or reject the right, validity, or authority of ⟨~*ed* the charge that he received financial backing from oil interests⟩ **:** DENY, DISPUTE ⟨accords wisdom to his hands . . . but ~*s* the wisdom of the heart —Ernest Ansermet⟩ **:** RENOUNCE, REPUDIATE ⟨~*ed* the authority of the supreme pontiff⟩ **4** *archaic* **:** to deny (as a claim) **:** REFUSE **5 a** *of a herald* **:** to denounce or make infamous (as one bearing arms without right or one usurping the title of esquire or gentleman) by proclamation **b :** to disown any claim to (as a right to bear arms) **:** DISAVOW, RENOUNCE

syn DISCLAIM, DISAVOW, REPUDIATE, DISOWN, DISACKNOWLEDGE, and DISALLOW can mean, in common, to refuse to admit, accept, or approve. DISCLAIM implies a refusal to admit or accept a claim, esp. anything claimed or likely to be claimed in one's favor or against him ⟨*disclaim* any responsibility for a crime⟩ ⟨the ordinary qualifications of the novelist, all pretension to which he entirely *disclaims* —Richard Garnett⟩ ⟨responded with characteristic modesty, *disclaiming* any right to special honor —D.G.Mandelbaum⟩ ⟨*disclaim* any intention of leaving⟩ DISAVOW is close to DISCLAIM but usu. applies to denial of responsibility for something besides refusal to accept or approve ⟨this Court always had *disavowed* the right to intrude its judgment upon questions of policy or morals —O.W.Holmes †1935⟩ ⟨the error of . . . putting forth in a permanent form work that I might subsequently wish to *disavow* —Havelock Ellis⟩ ⟨*disavow* the harsh materialism of mines and factories —*Time*⟩ REPUDIATE is usu. to disclaim responsibility for what one has previously or implicitly acknowledged or accepted ⟨a wise graduate student . . . accepted the degree for what it ostensibly stood for, and straightway *repudiated* everything it actually stood for —Bruce Dearing⟩ ⟨a law which everyone recognizes in fact, though everyone *repudiates* it in theory —G.L.Dickinson⟩ DISOWN implies repudiation of something with which one has previously stood in close relationship, often implying disinheritance or abjuration ⟨Keith and his followers were *disowned* by the orthodox Quakers —*Amer. Guide Series: Pa.*⟩ ⟨*disown* an erring son⟩ ⟨*disown* earlier obligations contracted in his name by friends⟩ DISACKNOWLEDGE is milder than disown, usu. applying to repudiation of something by denying any knowledge of it ⟨*disacknowledge* any responsibility to the community⟩ ⟨*disacknowledge* a signature on a note⟩ DISALLOW implies the withholding or taking away of sanction or approval, sometimes implying rejection or condemnation ⟨its duty of *disallowing* any proceedings which would infringe the rules of financial procedure —T.E.May⟩ ⟨if he is going to drive while intoxicated . . . his right to a driving license must be *disallowed* —Lucius Garvin⟩

dis·claim·ant \-mənt\ *n* **:** one who makes a disclaimer

dis·claim·er \-mə(r)\ *n* [AF *disclaimer* to disclaim] **1 a :** a denial or disavowal of legal claim (as in pleading where a defendant denies any interest in or claim to the subject of the action) **:** renunciation of a title, claim, interest, estate, or trust **:** relinquishment, waiver of, or formal refusal to accept an interest or estate **b** (1) **:** a writing by which a patentee that has by inadvertence, accident, or mistake claimed more than he had a right to claim as new disclaims such parts as he chooses not to claim or hold under the patent (2) **:** a clause in an original or reissue application referring to matter to which the disclaimant does not choose to claim title **:** a writing made to avoid the continuation of an interference **2 a :** a disavowal (as of pretensions, claims, or opinions) **:** DENIAL ⟨his first defense was a ~ of the authorship —S.H.Adams⟩ ⟨frowned in grave ~ of responsibility —Marguerite Steen⟩ **b :** REPUDIATION, DISOWNMENT ⟨his contemptuous ~ of stuff he did not keep —George Meredith⟩ **3** *heraldry* **a :** a proclamation by a herald of the illegitimacy of a person's right to bear arms or to be known by the title of esquire or gentleman **b :** a disavowal of any claim to such a right or title

dis·cla·ma·tion \,disklə'māshən\ *n* -S [ML *disclamatus* (past part. of *disclamare* to disclaim, prob. fr. AF *disclaimer, desclamer*) + E *-ion*] **1** *Scots law* **:** the act of a tenant or vassal who disclaims **2 :** DISAVOWAL, RENUNCIATION, DISCLAIMER

dis·clam·a·to·ry \də'sklamə,tōrē\ *adj* [ML *disclamatus* + E *-ory*] **:** having the character of a disclaimer ⟨his lordship waved a ~ hand —Max Peacock⟩ ⟨a shocked and most ~ tone —Charles Reade⟩

dis·climax \(')dis, dəs+\ *n* [¹*dis-* + *climax*] **:** a relatively stable ecological community that often includes kinds of organisms (as species) foreign to the region and that has displaced the climax because of disturbance esp. by man or domesticated animals — compare SUBCLIMAX

discloak *vt* [¹*dis-* + *cloak* (*n*.)] *obs* **:** UNCLOAK

¹**dis·close** \də'sklōz\ *vb* [ME *disclosen, desclosen*, fr. MF *desclor-*, stem of OF *desclore*, fr. ML *disclaudere* to open, fr. L *dis-* ¹dis- + *claudere* to close — more at CLOSE (adj.)] *vt* **1** *obs* **:** to open up **:** UNCLOSE **2 a :** to expose to view ⟨the curtain rises to ~ once again the lobby —J.T.Winterich⟩ **:** lay open or uncover (something hidden from view) ⟨excavations *disclosed* many artifacts⟩ **b :** to make known **:** open up to general knowledge ⟨her appearance *disclosed* an amazing vocal and acting talent⟩ ⟨a complete review of the literature fails to ~ a single comprehensive treatise on the subject —H.G.Armstrong⟩; *esp* **:** to reveal in words (something that is secret or not generally known) **:** DIVULGE ⟨the adventurer did not ~ his true objective⟩ ⟨*disclosed* that an exchange of views had taken place between the two governments⟩ **syn** see REVEAL

²**disclose** *n, obs* **:** DISCLOSURE

dis·clo·sure \də'sklōzhə(r)\ *n* **1 :** the act or an instance of disclosing **:** the act or an instance of opening up to view, knowledge, or comprehension **:** EXPOSURE ⟨a bill to require fuller ~ of stockholder groups in proxy contests —*Wall Street Jour.*⟩ ⟨his self-respect required a public ~ of his motives and actions⟩ **2 :** something that is disclosed **:** REVELATION, DIVULGATION ⟨these lurid ~*s* produced a scandal and led to the arrest of City Hall officials⟩ **3 :** a statement or description of an invention and its method of operation in a patent application

discloud *vt* [¹*dis-* + *cloud* (n.)] *obs* **:** UNCLOUD

disco- — see DISC-

dis·co·blas·tic \¦diskō¦blastik\ *adj* [*disc-* + *-blastic*] **:** MEROBLASTIC

dis·co·blastula \¦diskō+\ *n* [NL, fr. *disc-* + *blastula*] **:** BLASTODERM

dis·cob·o·lus *also* **dis·cob·o·los** \də'skäbələs\ *n, pl* **discob·o·li** \-,lī, -,lē\ *also* **discob·o·loi** \-,lȯi\ [L & Gk; L *discobolus*, fr. Gk *diskobolos*, fr. *diskos* quoit + *-bolos* (fr. *ballein* to throw) — more at DISH, DEVIL] **:** a discus thrower

dis·co·carp \'diskə,kärp\ *n* -S [NL *discocarpium*, fr. *disc-* + *-carpium*] **:** APOTHECIUM

dis·co·ceph·a·li \,diskō'sefə,lī\ *n pl, cap* [NL, fr. *disc-* + *-cephali*] **:** a small order of spiny-finned fishes comprising the remoras and having the dorsal fin modified into a flat sucking disk on top of the head used for adhering to the bodies of other fishes (as sharks and swordfishes)

dis·co·ceph·a·lous \¦==¦fələs\ *adj* [*disc-* + *-cephalous*] **:** having a sucker on the head — compare DISCOCEPHALI

dis·co·dac·ty·lous \¦==¦daktələs\ *adj* [*disc-* + *-dactylous*] **:** having sucking disks on the toes (as the tree frogs)

dis·co·dri·lid \,diskō'drīləd\ *n or adj* [NL *Discodrilidae* family of annelid worms, fr. *disc-* + Gk *drilos* earthworm + NL *-idae*] **:** BRANCHIOBDELLID

dis·co·gastrula \¦diskō+\ *n* [NL, fr. *disc-* + *gastrula*] **:** a gastrula derived from a blastoderm

¹**dis·co·glos·sid** \¦diskō¦gläsəd\ *adj* [NL *Discoglossidae*] **:** of or relating to the Discoglossidae or to toads of this family

²**discoglossid** \“\ *n* -S **:** one of the Discoglossidae

dis·co·glos·si·dae \,==¦gläsə,dē\ *n pl, cap* [NL, fr. *Discoglossus*, type genus (fr. *disc-* + *-glossus*, fr. Gk *glōssa* tongue) + *-idae* — more at GLOSS] **:** a family of Old World toads characterized by a fixed disklike tongue and having as well-known representatives the obstetrical toad and the fire-bellied toad — **dis·co·glos·soid** \¦==¦glä,sȯid\ *adj*

dis·cog·ra·pher \də'skägrəfə(r)\ *n* -S **:** one that compiles discographies **:** a specialist in discography

dis·co·graph·i·cal \¦diskə¦grafəkəl\ *also* **dis·co·graph·ic** \-fik\ *adj* **:** of or relating to discography

dis·cog·ra·phy \də'skägrəfē\ *n* -ES [F *discographie*, fr. *disc-* + *-graphie* -graphy] **1 :** a descriptive compilation of phonograph records by classes; *also* **:** a list of recordings of one composer or by one performer **2 :** the history or description of recorded music

¹**dis·coid** \'dis,kȯid\ *adj* [LL *discoides* quoit-shaped, fr. Gk *diskoeidēs*, fr. *disk-* disc- + *-oeidēs* -oid] **1 :** like a disk or discus **:** flat and circular ⟨a ~ body⟩ **2 :** relating to or having a disk: as **a** *of a composite floret* **:** situated in the floral disk **:** being a disk floret **b** *of a composite flower head* **:** having only tubular florets

²**discoid** \“\ *n* -S **1 :** something shaped like a discus or disk ⟨the concept of the galactic system as a stellar ~ . . . was soon abandoned —Harlow Shapley⟩ **2 :** DISCOIDAL

¹**dis·coi·dal** \də'skȯidᵊl, 'di,s-\ *adj* [LL *discoides* + E *-al*] **:** of, like, or producing a disk ⟨~ cleavage⟩ ⟨a ~ sponge⟩: as **a** *of a gastropod shell* **:** having the whorls form a flat coil ⟨snails of the genus *Planorbis* are ~⟩ **b :** having the villi restricted to one or more disklike areas ⟨most insectivores, bats, rodents, and primates have ~ placentas⟩ — see METADISCOIDAL

²**discoidal** \“\ *n* -S **:** a disk-shaped stone artifact found in No. America that was probably used by the Indians in games

discoidal cleavage *n* **:** meroblastic cleavage in which a disk of cells is produced at the animal pole of the zygote (as in bird eggs) — compare SUPERFICIAL CLEAVAGE

dis·coi·dea \də'skȯidēə\ [NL, fr. *disc-* + *-oidea*] *syn of* DISCOPLACENTALIA

dis·co·lichen \¦diskō+\ *n* [NL *Discolichenes*] **:** a member of the Discolichenes — compare BASIDIOLICHEN

dis·co·lichenes \“+\ *n pl, cap* [NL, fr. *disc-* + *Lichenes*] **:** a subgroup of ascolichens having an open rather flat and rounded or cup-shaped spore fruit — compare PYRENOLICHENES

dis·co·lith \'diskə,lith\ *n* -S [*disc-* + *-lith*] **:** a discoidal coccolith — compare TREMALITH

¹**dis·color** \dəs, (')dis+\ *vb* [ME *discolouren*, fr. MF *descolourer, descolorer*, fr. LL *discolorari* to change color, fr. L *discolor* of another color, fr. *dis-* ¹dis- + *color* — more at COLOR] *vt* **1 :** to alter the hue or color of **:** TARNISH ⟨a long row of ~*ed* frame houses⟩ **:** change to a different color **:** STAIN, TINGE ⟨~*ed* the water, changing it to a dull red⟩ **2 :** to change the intellectual or moral complexion or appearance of esp. for the worse ⟨~*ing* the luster of a glorious name⟩ **3 :** to deprive of color or coloring **:** DULL, FADE, STREAK ⟨a dress ~*ed* by the sun⟩ ~ *vi* **:** to change color **:** STAIN, FADE ⟨it will not ~ or stain if given reasonable care⟩

²**discolor** \“\ *n* [ME *discolour*, fr. *discolouren*, v.] *archaic* **:** change of color esp. for the worse **:** STAIN

³**discolor** \“\ *adj* [L, of another color, variegated] **:** of two or more colors **:** VARIEGATED

dis·coloration \dəs, ¦dis+\ *n* **1 :** the act of discoloring or state of being discolored **:** change of hue or appearance **2 :** a discolored spot or formation **:** STAIN ⟨a small ~ on the finger⟩ ⟨~*s* caused by microscopic marine organisms⟩

discolored *adj* [ME *discoloured*, fr. past part. of *discolouren* to discolor — more at DISCOLOR] **1 :** changed in color **:** STAINED, FADED ⟨~ teeth⟩ ⟨~ walls⟩ **2** *obs* **:** of different colors **:** VARIEGATED — **dis·col·ored·ness** *n* -ES

dis·col·or·ment \də'skələ(r)mənt, 'di,s-\ *n* -S **:** DISCOLORATION

dis·com·bob·u·late \,diskəm'bäb(y)ə,lāt\ *vt* -ED/-ING/-S [prob. alter. of *discompose* or *discomfit*] **:** UPSET, CONFUSE, DISCONCERT ⟨the offensive had *discombobulated* all the German defensive arrangements —A.J.Liebling⟩

dis·co·medusae \¦diskō+\ *n pl, cap* [NL, pl., fr. *disc-* + *medusae*, pl. of *medusa*] *in some classifications* **:** a large order of Scyphozoa equivalent to the modern orders Rhizostomae and Semaeostomeae, or more broadly, nearly equivalent to Scyphozoa — **dis·co·medusan** \“+\ *adj or n* — **dis·co·medusoid** \“+\ *adj*

¹**dis·com·fit** \də'skəmfə̇|t, *in dial speech in the southern US & the Brit Isles* ¦diskəm¦fi|; *usu* |d·+V\ *vt* -ED/-ING/-S [ME *disconfiten, discomfiten*, fr. OF *desconfit*, past part. of *desconfire* to destroy, defeat, fr. *des-* ¹dis- + *confire* to prepare — more at COMFIT] **1 a** *archaic* **:** to defeat in battle **:** put to rout **:** OVERTHROW ⟨~*ed* the pagans in two great battles⟩ ⟨pictured the ground . . . as strewn with the ~*ed* —Stephen Crane⟩ **b :** to defeat or rout (an opponent) in any way ⟨in the ensuing debate he utterly ~*ed* his less agile adversary⟩ ⟨~*ed* all her rivals in the race for colonies⟩ **:** frustrate the plans of **:** THWART, FOIL ⟨completely ~*ed*, the would-be robbers fled the scene⟩ **2 :** to cause perplexity or embarrassment to **:** DISCONCERT, UPSET ⟨completely ~*ed* by the unexpected question⟩ **:** ABASH ⟨hung his head in shame and looked quite ~*ed*⟩ **syn** see EMBARRASS

²**dis·com·fit** \də'skəmfə̇t\ *n* -S [ME *discomfite*, fr. *discomfiten*, v.] *archaic* **:** ROUT, OVERTHROW, DISCOMFITURE

dis·com·fi·ture \də'skəmfə,chu̇(ə)r, -ùə, -,chə(r)\ *n* -S [ME *discomfiture*, fr. MF *desconfiture*, fr. OF, fr. *desconfit* + *-ure*] **1 a :** defeat in battle **:** ROUT, OVERTHROW ⟨might well have been the scene of the ~ of the pursuing Egyptian chariotry —G.W.Murray⟩ **b :** defeat or rout of any kind ⟨the defeated candidate attributed his ~ to the disloyalty of party lieutenants⟩ ⟨the champion picked himself up from the floor, grinning wryly at his own ~⟩ **:** FRUSTRATION, DISAPPOINTMENT ⟨great hopes destined to end in ~⟩ **2 :** the state of being disconcerted or abashed **:** CONFUSION, EMBARRASSMENT ⟨blushed and lowered her eyes in evident ~⟩ ⟨smiling blandly at my ~⟩ **3 :** DISARRAY, DAMAGE, INJURY, INCONVENIENCE ⟨plunged through countless . . . hedges and ditches, without apparent ~ to her muslin —George Meredith⟩ ⟨the Waterside Workers' Federation has repeatedly demonstrated its strength, often to the ~ of the entire commonwealth —E.P.Hohman⟩

¹**dis·comfort** \dəs+\ *vt* [ME *discomforten*, fr. MF *desconforter*, fr. OF, fr. *des-* ¹dis- + *conforter* to comfort — more at COMFORT] **1** *archaic* **:** DISCOURAGE, DEJECT, GRIEVE, DISMAY ⟨his funerals shall not be in our camp, lest it ~ us —Shak.⟩ **2 :** to cause bodily or mental discomfort to **:** make uncomfortable or uneasy ⟨the tart rejoinder did not ~ him⟩

²**discomfort** \“\ *n* [ME, fr. MF *desconfort*, fr. OF, fr. *desconforter*] **1** *archaic* **a :** DISTRESS **b :** something that causes sorrow or distress **:** GRIEF, TROUBLE, MISFORTUNE ⟨'tis no ~ in the world to fall —Robert Herrick †1674⟩ **2 :** lack of comfort **:** uncomfortable condition **:** mental or physical uneasiness less intense and less localized than pain **:** EMBARRASSMENT, ANNOYANCE ⟨the ~ of a bad cold⟩ ⟨reducing to an acceptable range the ~*s* incident to business cycles —Clark Warburton⟩ ⟨he gave every sign of intense ~⟩

dis·comfortable \dəs+\ *adj* [ME, fr. MF *desconfortable*, fr. *desconforter* + *-able*] **1** *archaic* **:** causing mental discomfort or discouragement **:** affording no comfort **2** *archaic* **:** lacking in physical comfort **:** causing physical discomfort or inconvenience **3** *archaic* **:** feeling discomfort **:** UNCOMFORTABLE ⟨some among us . . . seemed most ~ because of the skimpiness of the rags they wore —Kenneth Roberts⟩

dis·comfortably \“+\ *adv* **:** in a discomfortable manner

discomforting *adj* [ME, fr. pres. part. of *discomforten*] **:** causing discomfort ⟨a thoroughly ~, disturbing book⟩ — **dis·com·fort·ing·ly** *adv*

dis·commend \¦dis+\ *vt* [ME *discommenden*, fr. ¹*dis-* + *commenden* to commend — more at COMMEND] **1 :** to mention with disapproval **:** DISAPPROVE ⟨seldom ~ anything . . . or do it but moderately —Isaac Newton⟩ ⟨I shall . . . commend and ~ this book —*John o'London's Weekly*⟩ **:** DISPRAISE — opposed to *commend* **2 :** to speak of as not meriting consideration, adoption, or favor ⟨the book is ~*ed* to students⟩ **:** cause to be viewed unfavorably ⟨an act that ~*s* him to all honest men⟩ — opposed to *recommend*

dis·commendable \¦dis+\ *adj, archaic* **:** deserving disapproval, blame, or unfavorable comment

dis·commendation \(¦)dis, dəs+\ *n, archaic* **:** BLAME, CENSURE, REPROACH, DISPRAISE

dis·com·mode \,diskə¦mōd\ *vt* -ED/-ING/-S [MF *discommoder*, fr. *dis-* ¹dis- + *commode* convenient — more at COMMODE] **:** to cause inconvenience to **:** INCONVENIENCE, TROUBLE ⟨I don't think the war has *discommoded* him too seriously —L.C. Douglas⟩

dis·commodious \¦dis+\ *adj* [¹*dis-* + *commodious*] **:** INCONVENIENT, TROUBLESOME ⟨a very ~, untimely accident⟩ — **discommodiously** *adv* — **discommodiousness** *n* -ES

dis·commodity \“+\ *n* [¹*dis-* + *commodity*] **1** *archaic* **a :** INCONVENIENCE, DISADVANTAGEOUSNESS ⟨you go about, in rain or fine, at all hours, without ~ —Charles Lamb⟩ **b :** something that is inconvenient **:** DISADVANTAGE, TROUBLE ⟨*discommodities* visited upon a stiff-necked disobedient people⟩ **2 :** a substance or action having no utility — opposed to *commodity*

dis·common \dəs, (')dis+\ *vt* [ME *discomenen*, fr. ¹*dis-* + *comen, commun* common (n.) — more at COMMON] **1** *obs* **:** to exclude or banish from a community of interest; *specif* **:** to deprive of citizenship or of church fellowship **2** *at Oxford and Cambridge Universities* **:** to forbid (a tradesman) to deal with undergraduates **3 a :** to deprive of the right of common (as of pasture) **b :** to deprive of commonable quality (as land by enclosing it)

dis·commons \“+\ *vt* -ED/-ING/-ES [¹*dis-* + *commons*] **:** to deprive of the right to commons in an English college ⟨could not dine in hall, as he was ~*ed* for persistent absence from lectures —Thomas Hughes⟩

discommune *vt* [¹*dis-* + *commune*] *obs* **:** to exclude from community or association of interests

dis·compose \¦dis+\ *vt* [¹*dis-* + *compose*] **1 :** to destroy the composure or serenity of **:** deprive of equanimity or stability **:** AGITATE, DISCONCERT ⟨do not be *discomposed* by the opinions of inept persons —Norman Douglas⟩ ⟨he was still *discomposed* by the girl's bitter and sudden retort —James Joyce⟩ **2 :** to disturb the order of **:** DISARRANGE, DISARRAY ⟨the wind ruffled her hair, *discomposed* her dress⟩ **3** *obs* **:** to discharge from service **:** DISPLACE; *also* **:** to derange the health of

syn DISQUIET, DISTURB, PERTURB, AGITATE, UPSET, FLUSTER, FLURRY: DISCOMPOSE indicates a causing loss of self-control, self-confidence, or poise ⟨her look so *discomposed* him that he stopped, wandered, and began anew —Charles Dickens⟩ ⟨the even temperament of his mind was never *discomposed*, and at each moment he was able always to decide, and to do, what the moment required —J.A.Froude⟩ DISQUIET denotes a making uneasy, a causing loss of security and peace of mind ⟨Roylance drove a motorcar well but audaciously, so that he *disquieted* the nerves of those who accompanied him —John Buchan⟩ ⟨he was indubitably . . . restless and *disquieted*, his disquietude sometimes amounting to agony —Matthew Arnold⟩ DISTURB now applies to the effect of care, strain, conflict, worry, or disappointment in interfering with or confusing accustomed mental and nervous processes ⟨nothing is more *disturbing* than the upsetting of a preconceived idea —Joseph Conrad⟩ ⟨I slept, indeed, but I was *disturbed* by the wildest dreams —Mary W. Shelley⟩ ⟨a very badly *disturbed* child, one whom it would take a long, tough struggle to straighten out —J.N.Bell⟩ PERTURB applies to the worrisome or disturbing results of uncertainty, disappointment, or danger ⟨in this *perturbed* state of mind, with thoughts that could rest on nothing, she walked on —Jane Austen⟩ ⟨and a presence of mind which no emergency can *perturb* —C.W.Eliot⟩ AGITATE suggests show of obvious signs of nervous excitation and loss of self-control and calm ⟨she was too *agitated* to sit down. She lit a cigarette but her lips trembled and she could not smoke it —Audrey Barker⟩ ⟨Clara was so *agitated* that she was incoherent —Margaret Deland⟩ ⟨an infernal spirit which *agitates* them and makes them tremble —J.G.Frazer⟩ UPSET applies to any nervous unsettling, slight or serious ⟨what *upset* me in the . . . trial was not the conviction, but the methods of the defense —H.J. Laski⟩ ⟨Prospero, *upset* by a plot to murder him, philosophizing on the insubstantial quality of life —C.S.Kilby⟩ FLUSTER suggests confused or bewildered agitation in which one cannot act decisively or entirely rationally ⟨the Sognings were a people of even temperament, not easily *flustered*; they bore the affliction with remarkable calmness and fortitude —O.E.Rölvaag⟩ FLURRY suggests natural agitation, excitement, or confusion induced by haste, rush, and concern ⟨thoughts, with their attendant visions, which occupied and *flurried* her too much to leave her any power of observation —Jane Austen⟩ ⟨he recognized her and sat down immediately, *flurried* and confused by his display of excitement —Liam O'Flaherty⟩

discomposed \-zd\ *adj* **:** DISORDERED, DISTURBED, DISQUIETED ⟨looked about with a wandering and ~ countenance⟩ — **dis·com·pos·ed·ly** \-zədlē, -li\ *adv*

dis·composure \¦dis+\ *n* **1 :** DISORDER, DISARRANGEMENT ⟨his royal robe covered his wounds, there was no stain nor ~ —Robinson Jeffers⟩ **2 :** the state of being disturbed or upset in feelings : AGITATION, PERTURBATION ⟨his trembling voice and flushed cheeks revealed his profound ~⟩ **3** *obs* : derangement of health

dis·co·my·cete \ˌdiskōˈmīˌsēt, -ˌmīˈsēt\ *n, pl* **discomyce·tes** \ˌ==ˌmīˈsēd·ēz\ [NL *Discomycetes*] : a fungus of the group Discomycetes

discomycetes *n pl, cap* [NL, fr. *disc-* + *-mycetes*] *in some classifications* : a group of fungi of the class Ascomycetes in which the fruiting body is disklike or cup-shaped (as in Pezizales) — **dis·co·my·ce·tous** \ˌ==ˌmīˈsēd·əs, ˌ== mīˈsēd·əs\ *adj*

dis·co·nan·thae \ˌdiskəˈnanˌthē\ *n pl, cap* [NL, fr. *disc-* + connective *-n-* + *-anthae* (fr. Gk *anthos* flower) — more at ANTHOLOGY] *in some classifications* : a division of Siphonophora comprising jellyfishes with a round flat many-chambered float (as members of the genera *Veletta* and *Porpita*) — **dis·co·nan·thous** \ˌdiskəˈnan(t)thəs\ *adj*

¹dis·con·cert \dəˈskän(t)sə(r)|t, -nˌsər|, -nˌsə̄|, -nˌsəi|; ˈdis,-kän(t)sə(r)|; *usu* |d·+V\ *n* [¹*dis-* + *concert*] : lack of concert : the state of being disconcerted ⟨there was a brief ~ of the whole gay company —E.A.Poe⟩

²dis·con·cert \ˌdiskənˈsər|t, -ˈsə̄|, -ˈsəi|, *usu* |d·+V\ *vt* -ED/-ING/-S [obs. F *disconcerter*, alter. (influenced by L *dis-* ¹dis-) of MF *desconcerter*, fr. *des-* ¹dis- + *concerter* to concert — more at CONCERT] **1** : to break up the concert or arrangement of : throw into confusion : DISARRAY, UPSET, FRUSTRATE, DISTURB ⟨~*ing* enemy plans by a sudden offensive⟩ ⟨confessed that the eerie howls ~*ed* his slumbers —Rex Ingamells⟩ **2** : to disturb the composure or shake the complacency of : RUFFLE, EMBARRASS ⟨~*ed* his academic cronies by confessing that inspiration was most often induced in him by a pint of beer —Herbert Read⟩ ⟨in an interview with Washington, he succeeded chiefly in ~*ing* that most just of men —A.L.Kroeber⟩ **syn** see EMBARRASS

disconcerted *adj* : marked by loss of self-possession or composure : PERTURBED, EMBARRASSED ⟨look at each other dumbly, quite ~ —G.B.Shaw⟩ ⟨was somewhat ~ to learn that her daughter was a suffragist —Margaret A. Barnes⟩ : put out ⟨was a little ~ not to find the missing book⟩ — **disconcertedly** *adv* — **disconcertedness** *n* -ES

disconcerting *adj* : causing loss of composure or self-possession : DISTURBING, EMBARRASSING ⟨this ~ stare often caused people to falter nervously in their speech —Jean Stafford⟩ ⟨a ~ habit of greeting friends ferociously and strangers charmingly —Herb Caen⟩ — **dis·con·cert·ing·ly** *adv* — **disconcertingness** *n* -ES

dis·con·cer·tion \ˌdiskənˈsərshən, -sə̄sh-,-səish-\ *n* -S : the action of disconcerting or state of being disconcerted : DISCOMPOSURE, PERTURBATION

dis·con·cert·ment \-ˈsərtmənt, -sə̄t-,-səit-\ *n* -S : DISCONCERTION

dis·confirm \ˌdis+\ *vt* [¹*dis-* + *confirm*] : to establish as untrue or invalid : DISPROVE ⟨~ a philosophical assertion by appeal to sense experience⟩ — opposed to *confirm*

dis·confirmation \ˌdis, dəs+\ *n* : the act, process, or an instance of disconfirming

dis·con·form \ˌdiskənˈfō(ə)rm\ *adj* [¹*dis-* + *conform*] : not conformable — usu. used with *to*

dis·conformable \ˌdis+\ *adj* [¹*dis-* + *conformable*] **1** *archaic* : not conformable : DISAGREEING — used with *from* or *to* **2** : of or relating to a disconformity ⟨~ contact of Middle Devonian on Middle Silurian limestones —C.O.Dunbar⟩

dis·conformity \ˌdis+\ *n* [¹*dis-* + *conformity*] **1** *archaic* : lack of conformity or correspondence : NONCONFORMITY — used with *to* or *with* **2** : a break in a sequence of sedimentary rocks all of which have approximately the same dip indicating an interruption in sedimentation generally by an interval of erosion — compare DIASTEM 3, UNCONFORMITY

dis·congruity \ˌdis+\ *n* [¹*dis-* + *congruity*] : INCONGRUITY

¹dis·connect \ˌdis+\ *vb* [¹*dis-* + *connect*] *vt* : to sever the connection of or between : DETACH ⟨~ the fuse from a bomb⟩ : SEPARATE, DISUNITE ⟨~ church and state⟩ ~ *vi* : to terminate a connection

²disconnect \"\ *n* -S [by shortening] : DISCONNECTING SWITCH

disconnected *adj* : not connected : DISUNITED ⟨Congress . . . gives the impression of . . . a confusing sum of ~ local forces —Samuel Lubell⟩ : lacking logical or organic connection : DISJOINTED ⟨throwing down her pen after having written a few ~ lines —H.A.Overstreet⟩ — **disconnectedly** *adv* — **disconnectedness** *n*

disconnecting switch *n* : a switch that isolates a circuit or one or more pieces of electrical apparatus after the current has been interrupted by other means

dis·connection \ˌdis+\ *n* [¹*dis-* + *connection*] : the act of disconnecting or state of being disconnected : SEPARATION, DETACHMENT ⟨a curious feeling of loneliness or ~ from the busy crowds about him⟩

dis·con·nec·tor \"+\ *n* : DISCONNECTING SWITCH

dis·consider \ˌdis+\ *vt* [¹*dis-* + *consider*] : to deprive of consideration or esteem ⟨it was the sort of exploit that ~*ed* a young man for good with the more serious classes —R.L. Stevenson⟩ : view without regard or respect ⟨when humanity is ~*ed* the public is not protected, nor is the professional code honored —*Spectator*⟩

¹dis·con·so·late \dəˈskän(t)s(ə)lət, ˈdiˌs-, *usu* -əd·+V\ *adj* [ME *disconsolat*, fr. ML *disconsolatus*, fr. L *dis-* ¹dis- + *consolatus*, past part. of *consolari* to console — more at CONSOLE] **1** : lacking consolation : deeply dejected and dispirited : hopelessly sad : being beyond consolation ⟨a ~ parent⟩ **2** : inspiring dejection : SADDENING, CHEERLESS ⟨set up a wall . . . to shut off the ~ hills and the monotonous sea —M.R.Cohen⟩ : indicating or suggestive of dejection ⟨retired . . . with a ~ step —T.L.Peacock⟩ **syn** see DOWNCAST

²disconsolate *vt* -ED/-ING/-S *obs* : to make disconsolate

dis·con·so·late·ly *adj* : in a disconsolate manner ⟨gazed ~ at the smoking ruins of his house⟩ ⟨rows of cypresses standing ~ beside the brooding river⟩

dis·con·so·late·ness *n* -ES : the quality or state of being disconsolate : DEJECTION, DISPIRITEDNESS

dis·con·so·la·tion \dəˌskän(t)səˈlāshən, ˌdiˌ-\ *n* [¹*dis-* + *consolation*] : the state of being disconsolate

dis·consonant \dəs, (ˈ)dis+\ *adj* [¹*dis-* + *consonant*] : not agreeing : DISCORDANT, DISSIMILAR

¹dis·content \ˌdis+\ *adj* [¹*dis-* + *content* (adj.)] : DISCONTENTED — usu. used with *with* ⟨~ with his prospects and station in life⟩

²discontent \"\ *n* : one who is discontented : one who has a grievance : MALCONTENT ⟨his following had diminished to less than a dozen ~*s*⟩

³discontent \"\ *vt* [¹*dis-* + *content* (v.)] : to inspire feelings of grievance or dissatisfaction in : make discontented : DISPLEASE ⟨inflation . . . corrupted the civil service . . . , ~*ed* and disheartened the soldiers —C.P.Fitzgerald⟩

⁴discontent \"\ *n* [¹*dis-* + *content* (n.)] : lack of contentment : a sense of grievance or thwarted aspirations or desires : DISSATISFACTION ⟨abolitionists encouraged agitators to come south and stir up ~ —Helen B. Woodward⟩ ⟨unless such aid reaches down to the masses . . ., it will not be effective in preventing social ~*s* —Dexter Perkins⟩ : restless yearning or aspiration for improvement or perfection : inquietude of mind ⟨though yet young, he had sunk into a groove extremely deep, and had forgotten nearly all divine ~ —Arnold Bennett⟩

discontented *adj* : DISSATISFIED, UNSATISFIED, MALCONTENT : uneasy in mind ⟨hardly a ~ face to be seen —Thomas Gray⟩ ⟨~ with his position⟩ — **discontentedly** *adv* — **discontentedness** *n* -ES

discontenting *adj* **1** : causing discontent : DISSATISFYING, DISPLEASING ⟨a most ~ kind of activity⟩ **2** *obs* : DISCONTENTED

dis·contentment \ˌdis+\ *n* : DISCONTENT

dis·continuance \ˌdis+\ *n* [ME *discontinuaunce*, fr. ¹*dis-* + *continuaunce* continuance — more at CONTINUANCE] **1** : the act or an instance of discontinuing the use or practice of ⟨there were no automobiles to cause a ~ of walking —Morris Fishbein⟩ ⟨an appeal for the ~ of the electoral college⟩ : the state of being discontinued ⟨~ of dueling had changed the pattern of German university life⟩ : CESSATION, SHUTDOWN, CLOSURE ⟨a ~ of bus service between the two towns⟩ ⟨the site of the state fair until its recent ~⟩ ⟨almost 40 percent of small business ~*s* involve simply a change of ownership —*Nation's Business*⟩ : INTERRUPTION ⟨an intercourse renewed after many years' ~ —Jane Austen⟩ **2** *obs* : temporary absence **3** [ME *discontinuaunce*, fr. AF, fr. MF *dis-*, *des-* ¹dis- + *continuance* — more at CONTINUANCE] **a** : a breaking off or interruption of an estate upon an alienation made esp. by a tenant in tail of a larger estate than he was entitled to **b** : the termination of an action by the failure of the plaintiff to properly continue it or by the entry of a discontinuing order on his motion — compare DISMISS *vt* 4b **c** : the interruption of the proceedings in an action that follows where a party does not answer all the material allegations of the previous pleading and the opposite party fails to take judgment for the part unanswered

dis·continuation \"+\ *n* [MF, fr. ML *discontinuation-*, *discontinuatio*, fr. *discontinuatus* (past part. of *discontinuare*) + L *-ion-*, *-io* -ion] : DISCONTINUANCE

dis·continue \"+\ *vb* [ME *discontinuen*, fr. MF *discontinuer*, fr. ML *discontinuare*, fr. L *dis-* ¹dis- + *continuare* to continue — more at CONTINUE] *vt* **1 a** : to break off : give up : TERMINATE ⟨found it necessary to ~ her course in Spanish⟩ ⟨*discontinued* bus service between the two points⟩ : end the operations or existence of ⟨the school was *discontinued* after a sharp drop in enrollments⟩ ⟨*discontinued* the business after the death of his partner⟩ : cease to use ⟨*discontinued* the pattern after it proved unsatisfactory⟩ **b** *obs* : to cease to attend, frequent, or occupy **c** : to break the continuity of : SEVER ⟨in regard to the mountains it was contended that a gap does not ~ the general line of the range —*Encyc. Americana*⟩ **d** (1) : to cease to publish ⟨~ an unprofitable journal⟩ (2) : to cease to subscribe to ⟨~ the morning newspaper⟩ **2** : to abandon or terminate by a discontinuance or by other legal action ~ *vi* : to cease to continue : come to an end; *specif* : to cease to be published ⟨the magazine will ~ after the next issue⟩ **syn** see STOP

dis·continuity \ˌdəs, ˌdis+\ *n* [ML *discontinuitas*, fr. *discontinuus* + L *-itas* -ity] **1** : lack of continuity or cohesion : disunion of parts ⟨from chapter to chapter . . . there is a sense of ~, of failure on the author's part to "follow through" —Carlos Lynes⟩ **2** : a break in continuity : GAP ⟨microscopic *discontinuities* in the foil —N.A.Cooke⟩ ⟨conceived of the organic species as a hierarchy of creatures with comparatively large *discontinuities* between their ranks —S.F.Mason⟩ **3** *math* : a point or value of the argument at which a function is not continuous **4** : the boundary between two layers within the earth which display different physical properties made known by analysis of earthquake records **5** : a rapid change in meteorological elements in a short distance or a short time

dis·continuous \ˌdis+\ *adj* [ML *discontinuus*, fr. L *dis-* ¹dis- + *continuus* continuous — more at CONTINUOUS] **1** *obs* : causing discontinuity : GAPING ⟨with ~ wound —John Milton⟩ **2 a** : not continuous : marked by breaks or gaps ⟨a ~ mosaic of better watered and settled territory, embedded . . . in wide expanses of arid or semiarid land —*Geog. Jour.*⟩ ⟨the boy received a very jumbled and ~ schooling —Louis Kronenberger⟩ : not continued : DISCRETE, SEPARATE ⟨here and there were conspicuous elevations . . . but they were ~ features, not useful as regional boundaries —R.H.Brown⟩ : lacking logical or organic sequence or coherence ⟨a series of ~ events⟩ ⟨the tone poem is gay and always entertaining, but a trifle ~⟩ **b** *math* : having one or more discontinuities — used of a variable or a function **c** *of a linguistic form* : consisting of parts that are separated by other linguistic units of the same order or by parts of such units (as French *ne . . . pas* "not" in *je ne sais pas* "I do not know") ⟨~ morphemes⟩ ⟨~ phonemes⟩ — **discontinuously** *adv* — **discontinuousness** *n* -ES

discontinuous easement *n* : an easement or servitude that requires an act of man for its exercise or enjoyment (as a right of way or right to draw water) — compare CONTINUOUS EASEMENT

discontinuous phase *n* : DISPERSED PHASE

discontinuous variation *n, biol* : abrupt variation in which there are few or no intermediate forms

¹dis·convenience \ˌdis+\ *n* [ME, fr. LL *disconvenientia* fr. L *disconvenient-*, *disconveniens* (pres. part. of *disconvenire* to disagree, be inconsistent, fr. *dis-* ¹dis- + *convenire* to come together, agree) + *-ia* -y — more at CONVENE] *dial* : INCONVENIENCE

²disconvenience \"\ *vt, dial* : INCONVENIENCE

dis·convenient \ˌdis+\ *adj* [¹*dis-* + *convenient*] *now dial* : INCONVENIENT

dis·co·phile \ˈdiskəˌfīl\ *n* -S [*disc-* + *-phile*] : one who is devoted to the study and collecting of phonograph records

dis·coph·o·ra \dəˈskäf(ə)rə\ *or* **dis·coph·o·rae** \-fəˌrē\ *n pl, cap* [NL, fr. *disc-* + *-phora*, *-phorae*] *in some classifications* : a group of jellyfishes: **a** : a group coextensive with Scyphozoa **b** : a group coextensive with Discomedusae

dis·coph·o·rous \dəˈskäf(ə)rəs, (ˈ)diˌs-\ *adj* [in sense 1, fr. *disc-* + *-phorous*; in sense 2, fr. NL *Discophora* + E *-ous*] **1** *zool* : bearing a disk or disklike structure **2** : of or relating to the Discophora

dis·co·placenta \ˌdiskō+\ *n* [NL, fr. *disc-* + *placenta*] : a discoidal placenta — **dis·co·placental** \"+\ *adj* — **dis·co·placentalian** \"+\ *adj*

dis·co·placentalia \"+\ *n pl, cap* [NL, fr. *disc-* + *Placentalia*] : mammals having discoidal placentas

dis·cop·o·dous \dəˈskäpədəs, (ˈ)diˌs-\ *adj* [*disc-* + *-podous*] *zool* : having the foot disk-shaped

¹dis·cord \ˈdiˌskȯrd, -ō(ə)d\ *n* -S [ME *descord*, *discorde*, partly fr. OF *descort* (fr. *descorder*); partly fr. OF *descorde*, fr. L *discordia*, fr. *discord-*, *discors* discordant + *-ia* -y] **1 a** (1) : lack of harmony or agreement between persons : DISUNITY, DISAGREEMENT, DISSENSION ⟨must we fall into the jabber and babel of ~ while victory is still unattained —Sir Winston Churchill⟩ (2) : CONFLICT, STRIFE ⟨~ among the barons of the border country reached the point of daily raids, ambushes, and kidnappings⟩ **b** : lack of harmony or agreement between things or ideas : CONTRAST, DIFFERENCE, OPPOSITION ⟨the glaring ~ between the architecture of the two buildings⟩ ⟨the ~ between the idealist and materialist philosophies⟩ **2 a** : a combination of musical sounds which strike the ear harshly due either to an unprepared dissonance or to an effect of false intonation or tuning **b** : the interval between two discordant notes; *also* : a discordant note **c** : DISSONANCE **3** : any harsh or unpleasant sound ⟨the braying of automobile horns and other daily ~*s* of city life⟩

syn STRIFE, CONFLICT, CONTENTION, DISSENSION, VARIANCE: DISCORD may indicate sustained inharmonious disagreement marked by quarreling, factiousness, antagonism ⟨the meeting broke up in *discord*⟩ ⟨the *discord* among the brawling barons⟩ ⟨the controversies arising from this situation are bitter, and the *discord* is ominously apparent —H.A.Wagner⟩ DISCORD indicates the fact of existent disharmony, perhaps pointless; STRIFE may designate competition in a hectic struggle for victory or supremacy ⟨all must live together in harmony as good neighbors or in *strife* as bad neighbors —*Saturday Rev.*⟩ ⟨as the war drew to its end he, like Lincoln, sought to heal the wounds caused by internecine *strife* —H.A.Bridgman⟩ CONFLICT indicates existence of opposition or rivalry with desire or impetus to victory or mastery but not necessarily with the surging activity associated with STRIFE ⟨the medieval *conflicts* between England and France⟩ ⟨the age-old *conflict* between city and village —A.R.Williams⟩ ⟨the *conflict* of passion, temper, or appetite with the external duties —T.S.Eliot⟩ ⟨the union and *conflict* of two very different human impulses, the one urging men towards mysticism, the other urging them towards science —Bertrand Russell⟩ CONTENTION may suggest bickering quarrelsome altercation in words; it usu. does not apply to physically active strife ⟨*contention* about the new zoning laws⟩ ⟨*contention* between free trade and tariff groups⟩ ⟨the *contentions* and turmoils preceding Kentucky's admission into the Union —E.M.Coulter⟩ DISSENSION is likely to stress the existence of disharmony and noisy truculent antipathy between groups, with or without strife ⟨the party was split by internal *dissension* on religious, racial, and intellectual questions —*Amer. Guide Series: N. Y.*⟩ ⟨reports of internal *dissension* in Venezuela: a "moderate" group in the Venezuelan army threatened to revolt against the Gallegos government —*Current Biog.*⟩ VARIANCE may indicate a clash of opinion, temperament, or character that make for strife, discord, or cold hostility ⟨sectarian *variances* in the town had delayed the erection of a house of worship —*Amer. Guide Series: Vt.*⟩ ⟨the unwillingness of young men interested in the ministry to accept the required strict orthodoxy at *variance* with twentieth century viewpoints —*Current Biog.*⟩

²dis·cord \", dəˈskȯ(ə)rd, -ˈskō(ə)d\ *vi* -ED/-ING/-S [ME *discorden*, fr. OF *descorder*, *discorder*, fr. L *discordare*, fr. *discord-*, *discors* discordant, at odds, fr. *dis-* ¹dis- + *cord-*, *cor* heart — more at HEART] : to be at variance : DISAGREE, DIFFER ⟨several of his disclosures ~ strongly with my personal knowledge —E.J.Wayland⟩

dis·cor·dance \dəˈskȯrdᵊn(t)s, ˈdiˌs-, -ō(ə)d-\ *n* -S [ME *discordaunce*, fr. MF *descordance*, fr. OF, fr. *descorder* + *-ance*] **1** : the state or an instance of being discordant : lack of harmony : DISAGREEMENT ⟨the still unsolved ~ between Spaniard and Indians —P.E.James⟩ : lack of internal harmony : INCONGRUITY ⟨the violence and ~ of his imagery —C.D. Lewis⟩ **2** : discord of sounds : DISSONANCE **3** *geol* **a** : angular unconformity **b** : a discordant junction (as of valleys)

dis·cor·dan·cy \dəˈskȯ(r)dᵊnsē, -si\ *n* -ES : DISCORDANCE, DISPARITY ⟨the maze of apparent *discordancies* in the text —R.H.Popkin⟩

dis·cor·dant \dəˈskȯrdᵊnt, (ˈ)diˌs-, -ō(ə)d-\ *adj* [ME, fr. MF, fr. OF *discordant*, *descordant*, fr. L *discordant-*, *discordans*, pres. part. of *discordare* to discord — more at DISCORD] **1 a** : being at variance : DISAGREEING ⟨views ~ with present-day ideas⟩ : being at variance with each other : INHARMONIOUS, ANTAGONISTIC ⟨the various dissevered and ~ elements of feudal society —W.J.Shepard⟩ : not conforming with : INCONGRUOUS ⟨the ~ element in the picture was his face, which belied his garb —John Buchan⟩ **b** : marked by lack of inner harmony or agreement of its parts ⟨a poetry that . . . is not only confused and ~ but negative in its emphasis —C.I.Glicksberg⟩ **c** : marked by inner discord ⟨a ~ family⟩ : QUARRELSOME ⟨a ~, savage people⟩ **2** : relating to a discord : DISSONANT ⟨~ tones⟩ : HARSH, JARRING ⟨I heard a horrid ~ cry, something between a bray and a yell —George Borrow⟩ : making inharmonious sounds ⟨a ~ crowd . . . shouting and laughing —Hugh Walpole⟩ **3** : lacking conformity or parallelism of bedding or structure — used of geologic strata **4** *of twins* : dissimilar in respect to one or more particular characters — compare CONCORDANT — **dis·cor·dant·ly** *adv* — **dis·cor·dant·ness** *n* -ES

discording *adj* [ME, fr. pres. part. of *discorden* to discord] : DISCORDANT

¹dis·count \ˈdiˌskau̇nt\ *n* -S [modif. (influenced by ¹*dis-* & ¹*count*) of F *décompte*, fr. OF *descont*, fr. *desconter*] **1** : an abatement or reduction made from the gross amount or value of anything: as **a** (1) : a reduction made from a price made to a specific customer or class of customers — see TRADE DISCOUNT (2) : a proportionate deduction from an account as debt usu. made for cash or prompt payment — see CASH DISCOUNT **b** : a deduction made for interest in advancing money upon or purchasing a bill or note not due : payment in advance of interest upon money **2** : the rate of interest charged in discounting **3** : the act or an instance of discounting ⟨to employ bank funds in the ~ of bills of exchange⟩ **4** : a deduction in billiards of one point from the score of one player for every point made by his opponent **5** : a deduction taken or allowance made (as for the specious element in a story or something that qualifies the truth of an assertion) ⟨we may . . . have to make very heavy ~, or even sometimes to reject our author's conclusions altogether —G.G.Coulton⟩ ⟨after all the ~*s* are taken, timeliness remains a chief quality of good reporting —F.L.Mott⟩; *also* : an objectionable feature : DRAWBACK, HINDRANCE ⟨he does . . . mention smells and some other ~*s* to a pleasant day —*Times Lit. Supp.*⟩ — **at a discount 1** : below par : below the nominal value ⟨the bond sold *at a discount*⟩ **2** : out of favor : poorly or lightly esteemed ⟨utopias and visionaries were *at a discount* in this sober workaday world⟩ : with reservations ⟨his continual complaints . . . must be taken . . . *at a discount* —Hilaire Belloc⟩

²dis·count \"*also* dəˈs-\ *vb* -ED/-ING/-S [modif. of F *décompter*, fr. OF *desconter*, fr. ML *discomputare*, fr. L *dis-* ¹dis- + *computare* to reckon, compute — more at COUNT] *vt* **1 a** : to deduct esp. from an account, debt, or charge : make an abatement of ⟨~ a bill for early payment⟩ **b** : to offer for sale at a discount : sell at a discount ⟨dealers were heavily ~*ing* last year's unsold models⟩ **2** : to lend money upon, deducting the discount or allowance for interest ⟨banks ~ negotiable paper⟩ **3 a** : to leave out of account : DISREGARD, OMIT ⟨the influence of Hawaii on the American house is minute, ~*ing* the spectacle . . . of flapping shirttails printed with gaudy flora —T.H.Robsjohn-Gibbings⟩ **b** : to make a deduction in evaluating the significance or worth of : view as unimportant : MINIMIZE, DISPARAGE, DEPRECIATE, UNDERRATE ⟨~*ing* his offense as a pardonable action under the circumstances⟩ ⟨his mature judgment and long experience were ~*ed* by his juniors⟩ ⟨never ~ the fellow's cunning and ingenuity⟩ : DIMINISH, LESSEN ⟨the value of his criticism was ~*ed* by his ignorance of the subject⟩ **c** (1) : to make a deduction in evaluating the truth or validity of : make allowance (as for bias or exaggeration) in ⟨he ~*ed* seventy-five percent of all stable gossip —Gerald Beaumont⟩ ⟨~ some of the more enthusiastic claims made for the new drug⟩ (2) : to view with doubt or skepticism : DISBELIEVE ⟨I ~ the story that the brave bull gored Miss McCormick . . . because . . . she was an author —C.V.Little⟩ **d** : to anticipate or take into account (as a future event) in present calculations or planning ⟨mail came chiefly from those organized groups whose opposition had already been ~*ed* —*Time*⟩ ⟨businessmen had already ~*ed* the inflationary effects of the price increase⟩ **4** : to give a discount to in billiards ~ *vi* : **1** : to lend or make a practice of lending money, abating the discount ⟨banks ~ for 60 or 90 days⟩ **2** : to make allowance ⟨~*ing* for Richard's modesty —S.E.Hyman⟩

dis·count·able \ˈ=ˌ=əbəl *or* =ˈ===\ *adj* : capable of being discounted ⟨a ~ note⟩ ⟨the evident bias of the book is ~⟩ : set apart for discounting ⟨within the ~ period⟩

discount broker *n* : one who makes a business of discounting commercial paper usu. as an agent

discount company *n* : a company that discounts commercial accounts receivable : COMMERCIAL CREDIT COMPANY

discount day *n* : the weekday when a bank discounts bills

¹dis·countenance \dəs, (ˈ)dis+\ *vt* [¹*dis-* + *countenance* (n.)] **1** : to put out of countenance : put to shame : ABASH, DISCONCERT ⟨the republic soon confirmed the doubters and *discountenanced* its few friends —C.P.Fitzgerald⟩ **2** : to refuse to look with favor upon : use one's influence against : discourage by evidence of disapproval ⟨the intrenched interests *discountenanced* the teaching of reading and writing to the working classes —Helen Sullivan⟩

²discountenance \"\ *n* [¹*dis-* + *countenance*] : the act of discountenancing ⟨American actions gave discouragement and ~ to the Bolshevik and anarchist elements —Ward Moore⟩

dis·count·er \ˈdiˌskau̇ntə(r) *also* dəˈs-\ *n* -S : one that discounts; *specif* : the operator of a discount house

discount house *n* **1** : a firm selling branded goods (as consumer durables) at a discount from list prices **2** *Brit* : BILL BROKER

discount market *n* : an open market in which negotiable instruments (as acceptances, bills, and notes) are discounted — compare BANK DISCOUNT

discount rate *n* : the interest on an annual basis deducted in advance for a bank or other loan; *also* : the charge levied by central banks for advances and rediscounts

discounts *pl of* DISCOUNT, *pres 3d sing of* DISCOUNT

dis·cour·age \dəˈskər·ij, -kə·r|, |ēj, *esp in pres part* |əj\ *vb* -ED/-ING/-S [MF *descorager*, *descourager*, fr. OF *descoragier*, fr. *des-* ¹dis- + *corage* courage — more at COURAGE] *vt* **1** : to deprive of courage or confidence : DISHEARTEN, DEJECT ⟨loss of the bastion greatly *discouraged* the besieged garrison⟩ ⟨a succession of failures *discouraged* the young inventor⟩ **2 a** : to seek to check, hinder, or deter by disfavoring ⟨~ gambling by legislative enactment⟩ : DETER, HINDER ⟨a condition of feudal anarchy *discouraged* the growth of trade⟩ ⟨the aridity of the soil *discouraged* agriculture⟩ **b** : to attempt to dissuade from some action : dampen or lessen the boldness or zeal of for some action ⟨*discouraged* his son from pursuing a literary career⟩ ⟨a table-high platform . . . with a rail around it to ~ souvenir snatchers —Green Peyton⟩ ~ *vi* : to lose courage or heart ⟨I don't ~ easily⟩

syn DISCOURAGE, DISHEARTEN, DISPIRIT, DEJECT: DISCOURAGE implies loss of courage, confidence, and resolution, along with the sapping effect of fear and doubt and inability to muster up further hope and determination ⟨these accidents did great damage, and *discouraged* the French mariners to such a degree, that they became more afraid of their own guns than of those of the English —Tobias Smollett⟩ DISHEARTEN is a close synonym of DISCOURAGE; it may indicate temporary loss of heart or courage ⟨the days came, but not the visitor, though Lucetta repeated her dressing with scrupulous care. She was *disheartened* —Thomas Hardy⟩ ⟨a difficult undertaking that might have *disheartened* one less buoyant —Vera M. Dean⟩ DISPIRIT may indicate enervation, depriving of all cheer, and surrender to gloom ⟨in quelling a local Armenian revolt he was badly wounded. Sick and *dispirited,* he gave up his Arabian plan —John Buchan⟩ ⟨the shabby, *dispiriting* spectacle of Versailles, with its base greeds and timidities —C.E.Montague⟩ DEJECT implies a general casting down of spirits and a driving away of hope and cheer ⟨I pitied poor Miss Read's unfortunate situation. She was generally *dejected,* seldom cheerful, and avoided company —Benjamin Franklin⟩ ⟨the *dejected* appearance that is usually found only in the faces of old men who have been disappointed in life —Liam O'Flaherty⟩ **syn** see in addition DISSUADE

dis·cour·aged·ly *adv* **:** in a discouraged manner **:** with feelings of discouragement **:** DEJECTEDLY

dis·cour·age·ment \-jmənt\ *n* -s [MF *descouragement,* fr. OF *descoragement,* fr. *descoragier* + *-ment*] **1 :** the act of discouraging ⟨the encouragement of free enterprise and ~ of monopolies —*Current Biog.*⟩ **:** the state of being discouraged **:** DEPRESSION ⟨there are moments of ~ in us all —William James⟩ **2 :** something that discourages **:** something that tends to deter **:** DETERRENT ⟨rather an incentive than a ~ to vice —Rose Macaulay⟩

discouraging *adj* **:** lessening courage **:** DISHEARTENING ⟨gave a ~ picture of local economic conditions⟩ **:** DETERRING, HINDERING ⟨repeated accidental applications were found to have a ~ effect on warts —Ben Riker⟩ — **dis·cour·ag·ing·ly** *adv* — **dis·cour·ag·ing·ness** *n* -ES

discouraging card *n* **:** one's lowest card of a suit in bridge when played or discarded as a signal to one's partner not to lead that suit

[1]**dis·course** \ˈdi͵skō(ə)rs, -ō(ə)rs,-ōəs,-ó(ə)s *also* dəˈs-\ *n* -s [ME *discours,* modif. (influenced by *cours* course) of ML & LL *discursus;* ML, argument, course, fr. LL, conversation, fr. L, act of running about, fr. *discursus,* past part. of *discurrere* to run about, fr. *dis-* about, apart + *currere* to run — more at DIS-, CURRENT] **1** *archaic* **a :** the act, power, or faculty of thinking consecutively and logically **:** the process of proceeding from one judgment to another in logical sequence **:** the reasoning faculty **:** RATIONALITY ⟨he that made us with such large ~ —Shak.⟩ **b :** the capacity of proceeding in an orderly and necessary sequence — used chiefly in the phrase *discourse of reason* ⟨a beast that wants ~ of reason —Shak.⟩ **2** *obs* **:** progression or course esp. of events **:** course of arms **:** COMBAT **3 a :** verbal interchange of ideas ⟨we need to have a fairly definite point of departure for intelligent ~ —Robert Humphrey⟩; *often* **:** CONVERSATION ⟨let your ~ with men of business be short and comprehensive —George Washington⟩ **b :** an instance of such interchange ⟨his ~s with his puritan colleagues —Sidney Lovett⟩ **4 a :** the expression of ideas; *esp* **:** formal and orderly expression in speech or writing ⟨what seemed sapient ~ . . . is rather puerile chatter now —G.W.Johnson⟩ ⟨the forms of ~⟩ **b :** a talk or piece of writing in which a subject is treated at some length usu. in an orderly fashion ⟨the lecture . . . is an acute and suggestive ~ upon a subject that has always occupied his attention —Bliss Perry⟩ ⟨the preacher, who would interrupt his ~ to denounce a dormant worshiper —*Amer. Guide Series: Mich.*⟩ **5** *obs* **a :** power of conversing **:** conversational ability **b :** ACCOUNT, NARRATIVE, TALE **c :** social familiarity; *also* **:** familiarity with a subject **6** *linguistics* **:** connected speech or writing consisting of more than one sentence

syn TREATISE, TRACTATE, DISQUISITION, DISSERTATION, THESIS, MONOGRAPH: DISCOURSE is applicable to well formulated or coherently arranged serious and systematic treatment of a subject in writing or speaking ⟨the sermon was a *discourse* on the apostle's thoughts⟩ ⟨a learned *discourse* on the effect of the tariff⟩ TREATISE is likely to refer to a formal methodical written exposition, often more detailed but less pointed and persuasive than a discourse ⟨a scholarly and comprehensive *treatise*⟩ ⟨there are several excellent *treatises* on Thoreau's literary sources —H.S.Canby⟩ TRACTATE, now not much used, means and implies about the same things as TREATISE, but may be somewhat contentious ⟨the fabulists were right, he reflected, when they took beasts to illustrate their *tractates* of human morality —Aldous Huxley⟩ DISQUISITION may apply to a discussion more exploratory and investigative than definitive ⟨many of Burke's reflections on the theme of history are of a purely empirical character, being *disquisitions* about the direction human affairs are likely to follow if certain conditions are (or are not) fulfilled —*Times Lit. Supp.*⟩ DISSERTATION is likely to imply examination, usu. academic, of a subject, and discussion at length; often the word applies to treatises written to attest fitness for higher university degrees ⟨a tradition has developed that a *dissertation* in economics must be a sizable tome —H.R.Bowen⟩ ⟨the reason, perhaps, why scholarly *dissertations* upon literature are so often merely scholastic enumerations of minutiae —John Dewey⟩ THESIS may designate the statement, explanation, and defense of a proposition ⟨Miss L——'s extremely suggestive *thesis* is that the transition from Elizabethan-Jacobean to later Caroline comedy is primarily economic —T.S.Eliot⟩ It is often used in reference to essays written by candidates for the master's degree. MONOGRAPH may refer to a learned treatise on a limited subject ⟨a *monograph* on the earliest Roman coins⟩ ⟨a *monograph* on this subspecies⟩

[2]**discourse** \ˈ=ˌ=, ˈ=ˌ=\ *vb* -ED/-ING/-S *vi* **1 a :** to express oneself in esp. oral discourse **:** talk in a continuous or formal manner ⟨we talk in the bosom of our family in a way different from that in which we ~ on state occasions —J.L.Lowes⟩ **b :** TALK, CONVERSE ⟨let us ~ beneath this knotty carob tree —Norman Douglas⟩ **2** *obs* **:** REASON **~** *vt* **1** *archaic* **:** to expose or set forth in speech or writing **:** treat of **:** NARRATE, TELL, DISCUSS **2 :** PLAY, PERFORM ⟨an orchestra *discoursed* soft, seductive music —A.W.O'Neil⟩ ⟨eloquently *discoursed* and invested with the necessary virtuosity —*Current Biog.*⟩ **3** *obs* **:** to talk to **:** confer with **:** converse with

syn DISCOURSE, EXPATIATE, DILATE, and DESCANT can mean, in common, to talk more or less formally and at length upon a subject. DISCOURSE implies the manner of a lecturer, suggesting also detailed, ordered discussion ⟨to *discourse* knowledgeably about the laws of nature today requires a formidable apparatus of mathematics —*Times Lit. Supp.*⟩ ⟨*discourses* in his usual manner on the technique and value of mystical contemplation —Gerald Bullett⟩ EXPATIATE implies ranging over a subject, often without restraint and sometimes at will, connoting more copiousness in the product than does DISCOURSE ⟨was forever *expatiating* on the close resemblance between the methods of art, as shown especially in painting, and the methods of moral action —Havelock Ellis⟩ ⟨in another lecture I shall *expatiate* on the idea —William James⟩ ⟨he *expatiated* on the theme that organization produces the great thinker —H.J.Laski⟩ DILATE implies an enlarging upon the details of a subject of discourse ⟨as it is not right to damp a native enthusiasm, Redworth let him *dilate* on his theme —George Meredith⟩ ⟨he reverted to his conversation of the night before, and *dilated* upon the same subject with an easy mastery of his theme —Elinor Wylie⟩ DESCANT stresses free comment, often connoting a delight in the expression of one's views ⟨*descanted* again and again on the virtues of silence —Max Herzberg⟩ ⟨loves to *descant* on personalities—princes, statesmen, poets —G.K.Anderson⟩

discourse analysis *n* **:** structural analysis of texts larger than one sentence

dis·cours·er \ˈ=ˈ=ə(r), ˈ==-\ *n* -s **:** one that discourses ⟨Switzerland's brilliant Protestant ~ on religious and ethical problems —*Time*⟩

discourses *pl of* DISCOURSE, *pres 3d sing of* DISCOURSE

dis·cour·sive \ˈ=ˈ=siv, -sēv *also* -səv-\ *adj* **1 a** *obs* **:** characterized by reason or reasoning **:** RATIONAL **b :** ARGUMENTATIVE, EXPOSITORY ⟨material quoted for critical, satirical, ~, . . . and scholarly purposes —Margaret Nicholson⟩ **2** *obs* **:** constituting or containing dialogue or discourse **:** CONVERSATIONAL — **dis·cour·sive·ly** \-sȯvlē, -li\ *adv* — **dis·cour·sive·ness** \-sivnəs, -sēv- *also* -səv-\ *n* -ES

dis·cour·teous \dəs, (ˈ)dis+\ *adj* [[1]*dis-* + *courteous*] **:** lacking courtesy or good manners **:** UNCIVIL, RUDE ⟨distant and at times ~ to his associates⟩ **syn** see RUDE

discourteously *adv* **:** in a discourteous manner

discourteousness *n* -ES **:** the quality or state of being discourteous **:** RUDENESS

dis·courtesy \dəs, (ˈ)dis+\ *n* [[1]*dis-* + *courtesy*] **:** rudeness of behavior or language **:** ill manners **:** INCIVILITY ⟨complained of inattention and ~ on the part of her students⟩; *also* **:** a rude act ⟨committed the grave ~ of not first removing my spurs —R.H.Davis⟩

dis·cous \ˈdiskəs\ *adj* [*disc-* + *-ous*] **:** DISCOID 2

dis·cov·er \dəˈskəvə(r)\ *vb* **discovered; discovered; discovering** \-v(ə)riŋ\ **discovers** [ME *discoveren, discuren,* fr. OF *descovrir,* fr. LL *discooperire,* fr. L *dis-* [1]dis- + *cooperire* to cover — more at COVER] *vt* **1 a :** to make known (something secret, hidden, unknown, or previously unnoticed) **:** EXPOSE, DISCLOSE ⟨~*ed* to his friend the sad state of his fortunes⟩ ⟨the novelist Emily Brontë had to ~ these absurdities to the girl Emily —Mark Schorer⟩ **b :** to reveal the identity of ⟨God, when he ~*ed* himself to the Israelites in Egypt —G.G.Coulton⟩ ⟨~*ing* himself to the lovely culprit as her adoring and magnanimous lover —T.L.Peacock⟩ **c** *archaic* **:** to make manifest (as a characteristic or attribute) **:** EXHIBIT, DISPLAY, MANIFEST ⟨the very attempt towards pleasing everybody ~*s* a temper . . . often false and insincere —Edmund Burke⟩ **d :** to disclose to view (something hidden, covered, or previously unseen); *specif* **:** to reveal on a theater stage when the curtain rises or when flats are parted or raised — used only in the past participial form ⟨at curtain wife and mother-in-law are ~*ed* packing fragile articles into a barrel —Saul Bellow⟩ **e** *archaic* **:** to disclose unwittingly (as by one's actions) **2 :** to remove or lift a covering from **:** UNCOVER **3 a :** to obtain for the first time sight or knowledge of ⟨~*ed* a large bay that now bears his name⟩ ⟨~*ed* the circulation of the blood⟩ ⟨~*ed* a number of writers who afterward gained wide recognition —*Current Biog.*⟩ **b :** to detect the presence of **:** FIND, DISCERN ⟨~*ed* arsenic in the patient's sleeping potion⟩ ⟨~ slights in the most innocent remarks —Joyce Cary⟩ **c :** to find out **:** ASCERTAIN ⟨~*ed* he had lost his purse⟩ **d** *archaic* **:** to get sight of **:** SIGHT, ESPY **e** *archaic* **:** EXPLORE, RECONNOITER **~** *vi* **1 :** to make a discovery ⟨the rumor is false, as far as I can ~⟩ **2** *obs* **a :** EXPLORE, RECONNOITER **b :** LOOK, DISCERN **c :** to make admission **:** CONFESS

syn ASCERTAIN, DETERMINE, DETECT, UNEARTH, LEARN: DISCOVER means to come to know something not previously known, either by purposive search and investigation or by accident ⟨a careful search at last *discovered* a small whirlpool —O.S.Nock⟩ ⟨we shall never know who first *discovered* how to pound up metal-bearing rock and heat it in the fire —Tom Wintringham⟩ ASCERTAIN usu. indicates purposively directed study and investigation to find the truth or discover the facts ⟨scientific experiment has *ascertained* how many trials are needed by a rat to grasp the idea that by taking a particular turn or giving a special push he can penetrate from one chamber of his prison house to a more desirable one —C.H.Grandgent⟩ ⟨it has been *ascertained* by test borings that salt extends for 2200 feet below the surface —*Amer. Guide Series: La.*⟩ DETERMINE may stress intent to decide or establish the truth definitively ⟨the executor must assemble all available records to *determine* the decedent's assets and liabilities —Richard Gehman⟩ ⟨his duties for the next seven years included inspecting ships, including nearly all the largest vessels in the world, to *determine* seaworthiness and compliance with laws —*Current Biog.*⟩ DETECT may apply to discovering something well hidden, masked, or present only in trace quantities ⟨it was he who first *detected* the small variations in hundreds of stars closely packed into the globular clusters —Leon Campbell⟩ ⟨the shadowy passages, often hard to *detect* —J.W. Schaefer⟩ ⟨still feebler is the final sonant, as in *bid, bed, bad.* So weak is it that few hearers would *detect* its complete omission —C.H.Grandgent⟩ UNEARTH indicates bringing to light something lost, hidden, or otherwise very hard to trace, often after intensive investigation ⟨and the Index of Design division of the project has *unearthed* and reproduced many valuable examples of early American design —*Amer. Guide Series: Wash.*⟩ ⟨when a legislative committee began an investigation of the activities of the previous session, the Yazoo land fraud was *unearthed* —Sidney Warren⟩ LEARN in this sense may indicate a being told or otherwise acquiring knowledge with little effort or intention ⟨go at once to your father, and *learn* where you stand —L.C.Douglas⟩ ⟨it is said that the young lieutenant who directed the bombardment was a staunch Episcopalian and that he was horrified when he *learned* that he had shelled his own church —*Amer. Guide Series: La.*⟩ **syn** see in addition REVEAL

—discover check *chess* **:** to produce a check by moving an intervening man

dis·cov·er·able \-v(ə)rəbəl\ *adj* **:** capable of being discovered, found out, or perceived **:** ASCERTAINABLE

discovered check *n* **:** a position in chess in which check has been discovered

dis·cov·er·er \-v(ə)rə(r)\ *n* -s [ME *discoverer, discurer,* fr. OF *descovreur,* fr. *descovrir* + *-eur* -or] **1** *obs* **a :** INFORMER **b :** SCOUT, SPY **2 :** one who first finds out the existence or truth of something hitherto unknown (as by exploration, experiment, research, reasoning) **3 :** one that discovers a vein or lode and makes the first location thereon — compare FREE MINER, LOCATOR

dis·covert \dəs, (ˈ)dis+\ *adj* [[1]*dis-* + *covert*] *law* **:** not covert **:** not under coverture

dis·coverture \dəs+\ *n* -s **:** the state of being discovert

dis·cov·ery \dəˈskəv(ə)rē, -ri\ *n* -ES [*discover* + *-y* (as in *recovery*)] **1 a :** the act, process, or an instance of gaining knowledge of or ascertaining the existence of something previously unknown or unrecognized ⟨the ~ of a new chemical element⟩ ⟨his ~ of a strange tribe of pygmies⟩ **b** (1) *archaic* **:** the act of making known **:** REVELATION, DISCLOSURE (2) *obs* **:** display or manifestation esp. of a quality or attribute **c** *drama* **:** RECOGNITION **d :** the act or an instance of finding or finding out (as something that was lost or hidden) ⟨police announced ~ of the missing money⟩ ⟨for fear of ~ he changed his lodgings every night⟩ **e** *obs* **:** EXPLORATION, RECONNAISSANCE, INVESTIGATION ⟨to make a more perfect ~ of the island —Daniel Defoe⟩ **f :** the act of exposing the opponent's king to check by moving an intervening piece **2 :** something that is discovered (as by being brought to light, disclosed, or ascertained) ⟨brought home valuable *discoveries* including a large plant of exotic coloring and foliage⟩ **3 :** the disclosure in practice or in pretrial procedures by a party to an action or proceeding of facts or documents which will afford material evidence in determining the rights of the party asking it **4 :** the original finding of part of a vein or lode that is a prime requisite in the valid location of a mining claim

discovery bond *n* **:** a fidelity bond covering losses discovered during the term of the bond regardless of when any dishonest act is committed

discovery day *n, usu cap both Ds* **:** COLUMBUS DAY

discovery well *n* **:** the first well to produce oil in a new field

disc plow *n* **:** a plow adapted esp. for work in sticky or hard dry soils by replacement of the moldboard plow bottom with one or more concave steel discs

dis·create \(ˌ)dis, dəs+\ *vt* [[1]*dis-* + *create*] **:** to reduce to chaos **:** ANNIHILATE

[1]**dis·credit** \dəs+\ *vt* [[1]*dis-* + *credit* (v.)] **1 :** to refuse to accept as true **:** DISBELIEVE ⟨contradicts the oath of witnesses whom we have no reason to ~ —Irving Bacheller⟩ **2 :** to deprive of credibility **:** destroy confidence or trust in **:** cause disbelief in the accuracy or authority of ⟨his careful researches ~*ed* the claims of his predecessors⟩ **:** designate as inaccurate or unreliable **3 :** to deprive of good repute **:** bring into discredit **:** make less reputable **:** DISGRACE ⟨the decadent and tyrannical past that they are so energetically trying to ~ —James Cameron⟩ ⟨thoroughly ~*ed* by his role in the recent police scandals⟩

[2]**discredit** \"\ *n* [[1]*dis-* + *credit* (n.)] **1 :** loss of credit or reputation **:** DISESTEEM, REPROACH ⟨I knew stories to the ~ of England —W.B.Yeats⟩ **2 :** lack or loss of belief or confidence **:** DISBELIEF, DOUBT ⟨contradictions cast ~ on his testimony⟩

dis·creditable \dəs+\ *adj* **:** not creditable **:** injurious to reputation **:** DISGRACEFUL, DISREPUTABLE ⟨war is enormously ~ to those who order it to be waged —Aldous Huxley⟩ ⟨his marks . . . were not at all ~ —J.P.Marquand⟩

dis·creditably \"+\ *adv* **:** in a discreditable manner

discredited *adj* **:** having had its credit taken away **:** deprived of credit ⟨a ~ theory⟩ **:** brought into disrepute ⟨a ~ politician⟩; *also* **:** lacking in credit or repute **:** UNRESPECTED ⟨in Honduras a night attack is a ~ maneuver —R.H.Davis⟩

dis·creet \dəˈskrēt, *usu* -ēd.+V\ *adj, sometimes* -ER/-EST [ME *discreet, discret,* fr. MF *discret,* fr. OF, fr. ML *discretus,* fr. L, past part. of *discernere* to separate, distinguish between — more at DISCERN] **1 :** possessed of or displaying discernment or good judgment in conduct and esp. in speech **:** PRUDENT, CIRCUMSPECT, TACTFUL; *esp* **:** capable of preserving prudent silence (as with respect to confidences or delicate matters) ⟨his trusted ~ aide⟩ **2 a :** marked by, reflecting, or suggesting prudence, circumspection, or reticence **:** CAUTIOUS, UNOBTRUSIVE ⟨a ~ silence⟩ ⟨~ inquiries⟩ ⟨followed her at a ~ distance⟩ **b :** not showy **:** UNPRETENTIOUS, MODEST ⟨the warmth and ~ elegance of a civilized home—Joseph Wechsberg⟩ **:** RESTRAINED, MUTED ⟨her playing yesterday was extremely ~ in the sense of sonority and tonal impact —Olin Downes⟩ **:** not offensively vivid or strong ⟨perfumes became more "massive" and less ~ —T.F.Brady⟩ **3** *Scot* **:** observant of decencies **:** CIVIL, POLITE — **dis·creet·ness** *n* -ES

dis·creet·ly *adv* [ME *discretly,* fr. *discret, discreet* + *-ly*] **:** in a discreet manner: as **a :** TACTFULLY, PRUDENTLY ⟨his utterances never gave offense, being ~ academic⟩ **b :** with restraint **:** JUDICIOUSLY, CAREFULLY, UNOBTRUSIVELY ⟨rouge ~ applied to the cheek —Edward Sapir⟩ ⟨do not let a canary's claws grow too long . . . but trim them ~ —Emily Holt⟩

dis·crep·ance \dəˈskrepən(t)s\ *n* -s [ME *discrepaunce,* fr. MF *discrepance,* fr. L *discrepantia,* fr. *discrepant-, discrepans* (pres. part. of *discrepare*) + *-ia* -y] **:** DISCREPANCY

dis·crep·an·cy \-nsē, -si\ *n* -ES [L *discrepantia*] **1 :** the quality or state of being discrepant **:** DIFFERENCE, DISAGREEMENT ⟨its inveterate tendency to seek out areas of ~ rather than of agreement —Harriet de Onís⟩ **2 :** an instance of being discrepant **:** DIFFERENCE, VARIATION, INCONSISTENCY ⟨wide *discrepancies* of income⟩ ⟨discovered certain *discrepancies* in his financial reports⟩

dis·crep·ant \-nt\ *adj* [L *discrepant-, discrepans,* pres. part. of *discrepare* to sound differently or discordantly, disagree, fr. *dis-* [1]dis- + *crepare* to rattle, crack, creak — more at RAVEN] **:** at variance **:** DISCORDANT, DISAGREEING, CONTRARY, DIFFERENT ⟨widely ~ statements⟩ — **dis·crep·ant·ly** *adv*

dis·cre·pate \ˈdiskrə͵pāt\ *vb* -ED/-ING/-S [L *discrepatus,* past part. of *discrepare*] **:** DISCRIMINATE, DISTINGUISH

dis·crete \dəˈskrēt, (ˈ)di͵s-, *usu* -ēd.+V\ *adj* [ME, fr. L *discretus* — more at DISCREET] **1 a :** possessed of definite identity or individuality **:** constituting a separate entity **:** DETACHED, SEPARATE ⟨the conclusion that gases are made of ~ units (molecules) —Lancelot Hogben⟩ **:** having no organic or reciprocal relationship with others of its kind ⟨human traits and abilities are not ~, like sticks in a bundle, but interact with each other in highly complex ways —*Educational Research Bull.*⟩ **:** concerned with distinct or disconnected parts **b :** characterized by discrete lesions ⟨~ smallpox⟩ — compare CONFLUENT 2b **2 :** consisting of distinct, unconnected, or unrelated parts **:** NONCONTINUOUS ⟨regarded society as a ~ mass of individuals guided by blind egotism⟩ **3** *logic* **a :** containing a clause that expresses exception or opposition by means of particles like *but, though, yet* ⟨"I resign my life but not my honor" is a ~ statement⟩ **b :** individually distinct but not generically different **c :** having no content in common **:** not overlapping — used specif. of individuals **4** *math* **:** capable of assuming, containing, or involving only a finite or countably infinite number of values, items, or objects **:** COUNTABLE **syn** see DISTINCT

dis·crete·ly *adv* **:** in a discrete manner **:** SEPARATELY **:** in an unrelated manner ⟨the events occur ~, as they would to someone who, though situated within this society, did not have any ongoing, extended relationship with it —Isaac Rosenfeld⟩

dis·crete·ness *n* -ES **:** the quality of being discrete: as **a :** SEPARATENESS ⟨the simple sentence tends to emphasize the ~ of phenomena within the structural unity —R.M.Weaver⟩ **b :** the quality of consisting of a number of individual parts ⟨in order to cast lots, the dice must have some quality of ~ in the form of two or more "sides" —C.J.Erasmus⟩

dis·cre·tion \dəˈskreshən *sometimes* ÷ -ˈrēsh-\ *n* -s [ME *discrecioun,* fr. MF & LL; MF *discretion,* fr. LL *discretion-, discretio,* fr. L *discretus* (past part. of *discernere* to separate, distinguish between) + *-ion-, -io* -ion — more at DISCERN] **1 :** the quality of being discreet **:** PRUDENCE, CIRCUMSPECTION TACT, WARINESS ⟨use care and ~ in your choice of a cleaner —Richard Joseph⟩ **:** RESTRAINT, MODERATION, DELICACY ⟨plays with ~, even with beauty, but gives no impression of being a complicated person —E.R.Bentley⟩; *esp* **:** cautious reserve esp. in speech ⟨a manservant who exuded ~ from every pore —Basil Thompson⟩ **:** ability to maintain a secret **:** SECRECY ⟨~ is a trait of primary importance in a public official⟩ ⟨promises of complete ~ have been exchanged only a few minutes before —Henri Bonnet⟩ **2** *archaic* **:** the act or faculty of discerning, discriminating, or judging **:** DISCERNMENT ⟨it is not in mortal ~ to fathom her craft —Charlotte Brontë⟩ **3 a :** power of decision **:** individual judgment ⟨it is a matter that I cannot leave to anyone's ~ —Upton Sinclair⟩ **b :** power of free decision or choice within certain legal bounds ⟨for students of constitutional law the royal ~ in Australia has an illuminating history —Alexander Brady⟩ ⟨subject to the president's ~⟩; *specif* **:** the latitude of decision within which a court or judge decides questions arising in a particular case not expressly controlled by fixed rules of law according to the circumstances and according to the judgment of the court or judge (as in suspension of a sentence or the amount of a fine) **:** ability to make decisions which represent a responsible choice and for which an understanding of what is lawful, right, or wise may be presupposed — see AGE OF DISCRETION **4 a** *obs* **:** the act of separating or distinguishing **b** *archaic* **:** the quality or state of being separate and distinct **:** DISCRETENESS **5** *Scot* **:** POLITENESS, CIVILITY **syn** see PRUDENCE — **at discretion** *adv* **1 :** according to one's judgment or pleasure **:** at will ⟨allowing students to come and go *at discretion*⟩ **2 :** at the mercy of an antagonist ⟨forced to surrender *at discretion*⟩

dis·cre·tion·al \-shənᵊl, -shnəl\ *adj* **:** DISCRETIONARY — **dis·cre·tion·al·ly** \-ᵊlē, -əlē, -li\ *adv*

dis·cre·tion·ar·i·ly \ˈ=ˌ=shə͵nerəlē, -li\ *adv* **:** in a discretionary manner **:** according to one's discretion

dis·cre·tion·ary \ˈ=ˈ=shə͵nerē, -ri\ *adj* **1 :** left to discretion or individual judgment **:** exercised at one's own discretion ⟨an ambassador with ~ powers⟩ **2** *archaic* **:** characterized by discretion **:** DISCREET

[1]**dis·cre·tive** \dəˈskrēd.iv, ˈdiskrəd.-\ *adj* [LL *discretivus,* fr. L *discretus* (past part. of *discernere* to separate, distinguish between) + *-ivus* -ive — more at DISCERN] **1 :** DISCRETE 3 **2** *archaic* **:** marking distinction **:** DISCRIMINATIVE, DISTINGUISHING — **dis·cre·tive·ly** *adv*

[2]**discretive** *n* -s *obs* **:** a discretive proposition or conjunction

disc ridge buster *n* **:** RIDGE BUSTER

dis·crim·i·na·bil·i·ty \də͵skrim(ə)nəˈbiləd.ē\ *n* -ES **1 :** the quality of being discriminable ⟨the ~ of the various senses of a word⟩ **2 :** ability to discriminate ⟨pressure receptivity and ~ are very high in the lips and parts of the hands and feet where there are no hairs —F.A.Geldard⟩

dis·crim·i·na·ble \dəˈskrim(ə)nəbəl\ *adj* [[2]*discriminate* + *-able*] **:** capable of being discriminated ⟨treated as ~ aspects of institutional life within cultures —J.L.Blau⟩

dis·crim·i·na·bly \-blē, -li\ *adv* **:** in a discriminable manner

[1]**dis·crim·i·nant** \-m(ə)nənt\ *adj* [L *discriminant-, discriminans,* pres. part. of *discriminare*] **:** DISCRIMINATING

[2]**discriminant** \"\ *n* -s **:** a mathematical expression that provides a criterion for the behavior of another more complicated expression, relation, or set of relations — **dis·crim·i·nan·tal** \də͵skriməˈnantᵊl\ *adj*

[1]**dis·crim·i·nate** \dəˈskrim(ə)nət, *usu* -əd.+V\ *adj* [L *discriminatus*] **1** *archaic* **:** having the difference marked **:** distinguished by certain tokens **:** DISTINCT **2 :** marked by discrimination **:** carefully distinguishing ⟨~ travelers who de-

mand only the finest⟩ — **dis·crim·i·nate·ly** *adv* — **dis·crim·i·nate·ness** *n* -ES

²**dis·crim·i·nate** \-mə,nāt, *usu* -ād.+V\ *vb* -ED/-ING/-S [L *discriminatus*, past part. of *discriminare* to divide, distinguish, fr. *discrimin-, discrimen* division, distinction, decision, fr. *discernere* to separate, distinguish between — more at DISCERN] *vt* **1 a :** to mark or perceive the distinguishing or peculiar features of **:** recognize as being different from others ⟨depth perception may be defined as the ability to appreciate or ~ the third dimension —H.G.Armstrong⟩ **:** distinguish between or among ⟨whenever you have learned to ~ the birds, or the plants, . . . it is as if new and keener eyes were added —John Burroughs⟩ **b :** to serve to distinguish **:** DISTINGUISH, DIFFERENTIATE ⟨these curious markings ~ the bird from all related species⟩ **c :** to make out **:** ANALYZE, DISCERN, DEMARCATE ⟨he can very well ~ what the word means to him —Bernard Pares⟩ ⟨he is able to ~ eight stages in the poet's philosophical development⟩ **2 :** to distinguish (as objects, ideas, or qualities) by discerning or exposing their differences ⟨a warped mind that cannot ~ good from evil ways⟩; *esp* **:** to distinguish (one like object) from another by discerning or exposing the minute differences ⟨a dictionary of *discriminated* synonyms⟩ ~ *vi* **1 a :** to make a distinction **:** distinguish accurately ⟨~ between fact and fancy⟩ ⟨a climber must learn to ~ as to when compass bearings are necessary and when they are not —K.A. Henderson⟩ **b :** to use discernment or good judgment ⟨to expect that children should . . . ~ without experience, and save themselves by their own wits —R.A.W.Hughes⟩ **2 :** to make a difference in treatment or favor on a class or categorical basis in disregard of individual merit ⟨~ in favor of your friends⟩ ⟨habitually ~ against a certain nationality⟩ **syn** see DISTINGUISH

discriminating *adj* **1 a :** constituting a distinctive trait **:** DISTINGUISHING ⟨the ~ mark of this species is its varicolored plumage⟩ **b :** making a distinction **:** separating into constituent parts **:** ANALYTICAL ⟨there is a unifying as well as a ~ phase of judgment —John Dewey⟩ **2 :** capable of making fine discriminations (as in respect to quality) **:** careful or fastidious in selection **:** DISCERNING, JUDICIOUS ⟨a ~ and severe critic of the output of younger poets⟩ ⟨~ buyers⟩ ⟨~ taste⟩ — **dis·crim·i·nat·ing·ly** *adv*

discriminating duties *n pl* **:** DIFFERENTIAL DUTIES

dis·crim·i·na·tion \də̇,skrimə'nāshən\ *n* -S [LL *discrimination-, discriminatio* act of contrasting opposite thoughts, separation, distribution, fr. L *discriminatus* + *-ion-, -io* -ion] **1 a :** the act or an instance of discriminating: as (1) **:** the making or perceiving of a distinction or difference ⟨incapable of ~ between the imaginary and the real⟩ ⟨the same name was applied to both instruments with little ~⟩ (2) **:** recognition, perception, or identification esp. of differences ⟨the eye is capable of much finer ~ of detail —Otto Glasser⟩ **:** critical evaluation or judgment ⟨the public would need to be educated in the ~ of cider —*English Digest*⟩ **b** *psychol* **:** the process by which two stimuli differing in some aspect are responded to differently **:** DIFFERENTIATION **2** *archaic* **:** something that discriminates **:** a distinguishing mark **3 :** the quality of being discriminating **:** the power of finely distinguishing (as in respect to quality) **:** good or refined taste **:** DISCERNMENT ⟨nobody should reproach them for reading indiscriminately . . . only by so doing can they learn ~ —*Times Lit. Supp.*⟩ **4 :** the act, practice, or an instance of discriminating categorically rather than individually ⟨waged a lifelong campaign to end ~ against women⟩ ⟨relieved the working class of economic and political ~*s* found in other countries —T.S. Barclay⟩: as **a :** the according of differential treatment to persons of an alien race or religion (as by formal or informal restrictions imposed in regard to housing, employment, or use of public community facilities) **b :** the act or practice on the part of a common carrier of discriminating (as in the imposition of tariffs) between persons, localities, or commodities in respect to substantially the same service — **dis·crim·i·na·tion·al** \-;==;'nāshənᵊl, -shnəl\ *adj*

discrimination box *n* **:** a laboratory apparatus in which the experimental subject responds discriminatively to cues in order to gain a reward or avoid a punishment

discrimination time *n* **:** REACTION TIME

dis·crim·i·na·tive \də̇'skrimə,nād·|iv, -m(ə)nə|, |t|, |ēv *also* |əv\ *adj* [L *discriminatus* + E *-ive*] **1** *archaic* **:** DISTINGUISHING, DISTINCTIVE **2 :** making or observing distinctions **:** DISCERNING, DISCRIMINATING ⟨the eye . . . is the . . . subtlest, the supplest, the most ~, and the most docile of our organs —I.A. Richards⟩ **3 :** DISCRIMINATORY, DIFFERENTIAL ⟨it permitted tariffs which were grossly ~ —Mabel R. Gillis⟩ — **dis·crim·i·na·tive·ly** \|əvlē, -li\ *adv*

dis·crim·i·na·tor \-mə,nād·ə(r), -ātə-\ *n* -S [LL, fr. L *discriminatus* + *-or*] **:** one that discriminates; *specif* **:** a circuit that can be adjusted to accept or reject signals of different characteristics (as amplitude, frequency) — often used to describe a circuit in an FM receiver in which the FM signal is converted to an AM signal

dis·crim·i·na·to·ri·ly \də̇'skrim(ə)nə¦tōrəlē, -tòr-, -li\ *adv* **:** in a discriminatory manner

dis·crim·i·na·to·ry \də̇'skrim(ə)nə,tōrē, -tòr-, -ri\ *adj* **:** DISCRIMINATIVE; *esp* **:** applying or favoring discrimination in treatment ⟨a ~ tax⟩ ⟨~ attitudes toward minority groups⟩

dis·crown \dəs, (')dis+\ *vt* [¹*dis-* + *crown* (n.)] **:** to deprive of a crown; *specif* **:** DEPOSE

discs *pl of* DISC, *pres 3d sing of* DISC

disct *abbr* discount

dis·cul·pate \'di(,)skəl,pāt, də̇'s-\ *vt* -ED/-ING/-S [ML *disculpatus*, past part. of *disculpare*, fr. L *dis-* ¹dis- + *culpare* to blame, fr. *culpa* fault — more at CULPA] **:** EXCULPATE

dis·cum·ber \dəs, (')dis+\ *vt* [prob. by alter.] **:** DISENCUMBER

dis·cur·sion \də̇'skərzhən *sometimes* -rsh-\ *n* -S [MF (also, act of running about), fr. LL *discursion-, discursio* act of running about, motion, course, fr. L *discursus* (past part. of *discurrere* to run about) + *-ion-, -io* -ion — more at DISCOURSE] **1 :** discursive reasoning **2 :** a turning away from the main subject **:** ROVING, ROAMING, DIGRESSION ⟨each chapter returns there after a ~ into Asia, Africa or America —Gerald Sykes⟩

dis·cur·sive \də̇'skər|siv, -kə̄|, -kəi|, |ēv *also* |z| *or* |əv\ *adj* [ML *discursivus*, fr. L *discursus* + *-ivus* -ive] **1 a :** passing from one topic to another **:** ranging over a wide field **:** RAMBLING, DIGRESSIVE, DESULTORY, CHATTY ⟨a sprawling book, ~ and prolix —Brendan Gill⟩ **b :** proceeding logically or coherently from topic to topic ⟨no flaming into meaning but a steady ~ commentary in the course of which the meaning is eloquently conveyed —David Daiches⟩ **2 :** reasoning from premises to conclusions or proceeding from particulars to generalizations **:** utilizing or based upon analytical reasoning — contrasted with *intuitive* **3 :** passing from one place to another **:** ROAMING, ROVING ⟨entered into a life eternally ~ in search of superior grazing lands —J.B.Cabell & A.J.Hanna⟩ — **dis·cur·sive·ly** \|əvlē, -li\ *adv* — **dis·cur·sive·ness** \|ivnə̇s, |ēv- *also* |əv-\ *n* -ES

discursive reason *n* **:** the faculty of drawing inferences

dis·cur·tain \dəs, (')dis+\ *vt* [¹*dis-* + *curtain* (n.)] *archaic* **:** to divest of a curtain or cover **:** UNVEIL

dis·cus \'diskəs\ *n, pl* **discuses** \-skəsə̇z\ *also* **dis·ci** \'di,s(k)ī\ [L — more at DISH] **1 a :** a disk of metal and wood, thicker in the center than at the perimeter and used for hurling for distance **b :** a field event in which a discus of about 4½ pounds is hurled for distance from a circle about 8 feet in diameter **2 :** DISK 2, 3, 4

discus 1a

-discus \"\ *n comb form* [NL, fr. L *discus*] **:** organism with a (specified) form of disk — in generic names ⟨Cephalo*discus*⟩

discus pro·lig·er·us \-prō'lijərəs\ *n* [NL, lit., offspring-bearing disk] **:** CUMULUS 3

¹**dis·cuss** \də̇'skəs\ *vb* -ED/-ING/-ES [ME *discussen*, fr. LL & L *discussus*; LL, past part. of *discutere* to examine, investigate, fr. L, to dash to pieces, scatter, fr. *dis-* apart + *-cutere* (fr. *quatere* to shake, strike) — more at DIS-, QUASH (crush)] *vt* **1** *obs* **:** to clear away by breaking up or scattering **:** DISPEL, DISSIPATE **2 a** *obs* **:** to examine and pass upon judicially **:** TRY **b** (1) **:** to investigate (as a question) by reasoning or argument **:** argue by presenting the various sides of **:** DEBATE ⟨a committee of pilots and geographers ~*ed* the project but reached no conclusion⟩ ⟨the cabinet met in emergency session to ~ the draft law⟩ (2) **:** to discourse about **:** present in detail **:** EXPOUND ⟨a book that ~*es* the transmission of acquired characteristics⟩ ⟨in his afterword, Eban ~*ed* his views on Zionism and on the cures for anti-Semitism —*Current Biog.*⟩ (3) **:** to converse or talk about **:** exchange views or information about ⟨~*ing* what we'd do after graduation⟩ **3** *obs* **:** to make clear or open **:** EXPLAIN **:** disclose in speech **:** DECLARE ⟨~ the same in French unto him —Shak.⟩ **4 :** to consume (food or drink) with zest ⟨we settled down to ~ a plentiful supper of roast and boiled beef and mutton —W.H.Hudson⟩ **5 :** EXCUSS 3 ~ *vi* **:** to hold discussion **:** ARGUE, CONVERSE ⟨he would be squatting in the grass ~*ing* with someone —Helen Rich⟩

syn ARGUE, DEBATE, DISPUTE, AGITATE: these verbs all mean to discourse about something in order to arrive at the truth or to convince others. DISCUSS implies a reasoned conversational examining, esp. by considering pros and cons, in an attempt to clarify or settle ⟨*discuss* plans for a party⟩ ⟨*discuss* terms of a peace treaty⟩ ⟨they *discussed* the best way of raising money⟩ ARGUE usu. implies conviction and the often heated adducing of evidence or reasons in support of one's cause or opinion ⟨pros and cons of "mercy killing" are no longer very seriously *argued* in medical circles —W.T.Fitts & Barbara Fitts⟩ ⟨deep-seated preferences cannot be *argued* about — you cannot *argue* a man into liking a glass of beer —O.W.Holmes †1935⟩ DEBATE stresses formal or, often, public argument between opposing parties, although it can apply to a deliberation in one's own mind ⟨the . . . question was hotly *debated* in the spring parliamentary election campaign —*Collier's Yr. Bk.*⟩ ⟨the 82d Congress took many actions affecting social welfare and hotly *debated* a number of further measures —*Americana Annual*⟩ ⟨I held her hand for a moment, *debating* a reply —L.C.Douglas⟩ DISPUTE (in its older use signifying to debate) is to argue or to argue about, usu. contentiously ⟨the students *disputed* forensically this day a twofold question —Noah Webster⟩ ⟨Scotchmen and Irishmen anxious for disputation, who in previous centuries would probably have *disputed* about the classics or theology —E.L.Anderson⟩ AGITATE stresses vigorous argument toward a practical objective, an active propaganda in the interests of a change of some kind ⟨what Doc was *agitating* for . . . was recognition of battle exhaustion as an illness —Fred Majdalany⟩ ⟨the nine million refugees and expellees . . . are discontented with their economic plight and *agitate* for the recovery of their old homes —S.B. Fay⟩ ⟨the Senate was *agitating* an investigation of the department —E.M.Coulter⟩

²**discuss** *n* -ES *obs* **:** DISCUSSION, DEBATE

dis·cus·sant \-sᵊnt\ *n* -S **:** one who discusses; *esp* **:** one who takes part in a formal or prearranged discussion (as a symposium) ⟨the implicit expectation that a ~ should look for weaknesses or shortcomings in the paper on which he has been asked to comment —J.J.Honigmann⟩

dis·cuss·er \-sə(r)\ *n* -S **:** one that discusses

dis·cuss·ible \-səbəl\ *adj* **:** capable of being discussed

dis·cus·sion \də̇'skəshən\ *n* -S [ME *discussioun*, fr. MF & LL; MF *discussion*, fr. LL *discussion-, discussio* examination, investigation, fr. L, act of shaking, fr. *discussus* + *-ion-, -io* -ion] **1 a :** consideration of a question in open usu. informal debate **:** argument for the sake of arriving at truth or clearing up difficulties ⟨nothing promotes intellect like intellectual ~ —Walter Bagehot⟩ **b :** a formal or orderly treatment of a topic in speech or writing **:** EXPOSITION, DISCOURSE ⟨a recognized scholar . . . whose ~ . . . embodies the finest fruits of contemporary opinions and research —E.H.Swift⟩ **2** *obs* **:** dissipation or resolution esp. of a tumor **3 :** the exhaustion of legal remedies against a principal debtor or his property before recourse is had to the surety

dis·cus·sion·al \-shənᵊl, -shnəl\ *adj* **:** of or relating to discussion

discussion of heirs *Scots law* **:** the exhaustion of remedies against heirs for debts due by a deceased person in the order of their legal liability

dis·cus·sive \də̇'skəsiv\ *adj, archaic* **:** relating to debate or discussion

disc weeder *n* **1 :** an edged disc attachment to a cultivator that cuts off weeds and pulverizes surface soil **2 :** a cultivator with discs for use on intertilled row crops

¹**dis·dain** \də̇s'd|ān, də̇'st| *sometimes* də̇z'd|\ *n* -S [ME *dedeyn, disdeigne*, fr. OF *desdaing, desdeing*, fr. *desdeignier*] **1 :** a feeling of contempt and aversion for something regarded as unworthy of or beneath one **:** haughty indifference or insolence **:** SCORN, CONTEMPT ⟨~ and scorn ride sparkling in her eyes —Shak.⟩ **2** *obs* **:** keen resentment due to injured pride **:** INDIGNATION **3** *obs* **:** something that provokes contempt

²**disdain** \"\ *vb* -ED/-ING/-S [ME *desdeynen*, fr. MF *desdeignier*, fr. (assumed) VL *disdignare*, fr. L *dis-* ¹dis- + *dignare* to consider worthy — more at DEIGN] *vi* **1 :** to experience disdain ⟨let us in America not ~ —D.M.Friedenberg⟩ **2** *obs* **:** to take offense **:** feel indignation or distaste ~ *vt* **1 a :** to look with scorn on ⟨did not ~ that rich rolling land⟩ ⟨~*ed* him for the coward he was⟩ **b :** to be unwilling because of disdain — used with a following infinitive ⟨he ~*ed* to cheat her⟩ ⟨we might well ~ to have any part in this affair⟩ **c :** to treat with contempt as being of little worth or consequence or as unworthy of oneself ⟨~*ed* shooting the unarmed fleeing men —*Time*⟩ ⟨~*ing* snakes, insects, and other hazards of the trip⟩ **2** *archaic* **:** to incite to scorn or anger **:** OFFEND **syn** see DESPISE

disdained *adj* [¹*disdain* + *-ed*] *obs* **:** DISDAINFUL

dis·dain·er \-nə(r)\ *n* -S **:** one that disdains

dis·dain·ful \-nfəl\ *adj* **:** full of or expressing disdain **:** haughtily indifferent **:** SCORNFUL, CONTEMPTUOUS **syn** see PROUD

dis·dain·ful·ly \-fəlē, -li\ *adv* **:** in a disdainful manner **:** with disdain

dis·dain·ful·ness \-fəlnə̇s\ *n* -ES **:** the quality or state of being disdainful

dis·diapason \dəs, (¦)dis+\ *n* -S [L, fr. Gk *dis dia pasōn* twice through all — more at DIAPASON] **:** FIFTEENTH 4b

¹**dis·ease** \də̇'z|ēz, *in sense 1a* də̇'s| *or* (')di¦s|\ *n* -S *often attrib* [ME *disese*, fr. MF *desaise*, fr. *des-* ¹dis- + *aise* ease — more at EASE] **1 a** *obs* **:** lack of ease **:** DISCOMFORT, UNEASINESS, TROUBLE, DISTRESS **b** (1) **:** an impairment of the normal state of the living animal or plant body or of any of its components that interrupts or modifies the performance of the vital functions, being a response to environmental factors (as malnutrition, industrial hazards, or climate), to specific infective agents (as worms, bacteria, or viruses), to inherent defects of the organism (as various genetic anomalies), or to combinations of these factors **:** SICKNESS, ILLNESS (2) **:** a particular instance or kind of such impairment ⟨baby-pig ~⟩ ⟨hampered by her ~⟩ **:** MALADY, AILMENT — compare HEALTH **c :** disorder or derangement (as of the mind, moral character, public institutions, or the state) **d :** an alteration that impairs the quality of a product usu. caused by the action of microorganisms ⟨the ~*s* of wine⟩ **2 a** *obs* **:** a cause of discomfort or harm **b :** an organism that causes disease — used chiefly in plant pathology

²**disease** \"\ *vt* -ED/-ING/-S [ME *disesen*, fr. MF *desaisier*, fr. *desaise*, n.] **1** *obs* **:** to deprive of ease **:** make uncomfortable **:** DISTRESS **2 :** to affect or infect with disease **:** DERANGE, DISORDER

diseased *adj* [ME *disesed*, fr. past part. of *disesen*] **:** affected with or as if with a disease **:** lacking health or soundness **:** SICKLY, FEVERED, DISORDERED ⟨hopelessly ~ lungs⟩ ⟨your trade requires you to read a mass of abominable stuff that it would be ~ to enjoy —Bernard De Voto⟩ ⟨a world ~ and decadent⟩ ⟨the evil imaginings of ~ minds⟩ **syn** see UNWHOLESOME

dis·eas·ed·ly \-ēz(ə̇)dlē\ *adv* **:** in a diseased manner **:** as though affected by disease

dis·eas·ed·ness \-ēzə̇dnə̇s, -ēz(d)n-\ *n* -ES **:** diseased condition **:** disordered state **:** SICKNESS

dis·ease·ful \-ēzfəl\ *adj* [ME *diseseful*, fr. *disese* + *-ful*] **1** *obs* **:** causing uneasiness, discomfort, or trouble **2 :** DISEASED, UNHEALTHY

disease germ *n* **:** a minute organism (as a bacterium or virus) that causes disease

disease rating *n* **:** a numerical expression of relative severity or incidence of a plant disease usu. based on comparison of conditions observed with certain arbitrary standards (as sizes and frequency of lesions) of severity or incidence

dis·economy \¦dis+\ *n* [¹*dis-* + *economy*] **:** lack of economy **:** increase in costs or any factor responsible for such increase

dis·edge \dəs, (')dis+\ *vt* [¹*dis-* + *edge* (n.)] **:** to deprive of an edge **:** BLUNT, DULL

dis·edification \dəs, (¦)dis+\ *n* **:** an act or instance of disedifying; *also* **:** disedified state

dis·edify \dəs, (')dis+\ *vt* [¹*dis-* + *edify*] **:** to injure the piety or morals of **:** shock the higher sensibilities or religious feelings of — used chiefly as a participle

di·selenide \(')dī+\ *n* [*di-* + *selenide*] **:** a compound containing two atoms of selenium combined with an element or radical

di·sem·a·tism \dī'semə,tizəm\ *n* -S [*di-* + Gk *sēmat-, sēma* sign + E *-ism* — more at SEMANTICS] **:** the use in conjunction of two systems of writing (as the ideographic and the phonetic)

dis·embalm \¦dis+\ *vt* [¹*dis-* + *embalm*] **:** to bring from obscurity to prominence or from disuse into use **:** DISINTER

dis·embark \¦dis+\ *vb* [MF *desembarquer*, fr. *des-* ¹dis- + *embarquer* to embark — more at EMBARK] *vt* **:** to remove (as cargo) to shore from on board a ship **:** LAND, DEBARK ⟨~*ed* the troops during the night⟩ ~ *vi* **:** to go ashore out of a ship or boat **:** leave a ship; *broadly* **:** to get out of any vehicle — **dis·embarkation** \dəs, (¦)dis+\ *or* **dis·embarkment** \¦dis+\ *n*

dis·embarrass \¦dis+\ *vt* [¹*dis-* + *embarrass*] **:** to free from embarrassment, impediment, or superfluity **:** CLEAR, EXTRICATE, RELIEVE ⟨~*ing* ourselves of preconceptions⟩ ⟨working for the balance of eighteenth-century rhythms and he soon learns how to ~ these of . . . pomposity —Edmund Wilson⟩ **syn** see EXTRICATE

dis·embarrassment \"+\ *n* **:** a disembarrassed state **:** a freeing from impeding or superfluous matter

dis·embellish \¦dis+\ *vt* [*dis-* + *embellish*] **:** to deprive of adornment

dis·embodied \¦dis+\ *adj* **:** lacking substance, solidity, or reality that would normally be expected to be present ⟨~ beliefs and ideals⟩ ⟨a life in which people are trained to hide their passions and act generally in a ~ way —David Riesman⟩

dis·embodiment \"+\ *n* **:** an act or instance of disembodying or the state of being disembodied

dis·embody \"+\ *vt* [¹*dis-* + *embody*] **1 :** to divest of the body, corporeal existence, or reality **2** *archaic* **:** to discharge (a body of troops) from military service

dis·em·bogue \¦disə̇m¦bōg, -,sem-\ *vb* **disembogued; disembogued; disemboguing; disembogues** [modif. of Sp *desembocar*, fr. *des-* (fr. L *dis-* ¹dis-) + *embocar* to put into the mouth, fr. *en* (fr. L *in*) + *-bocar* (fr. *boca* mouth, fr. L *bucca* cheek, mouth) — more at IN, POCK] *vi* **1** *obs* **a :** to pass through a narrow channel (as a strait or the mouth of a river) into the open sea **b :** to come forth as if from a channel **:** EMERGE **2 a** *of a body of water* **:** to discharge water through an outlet or mouth; *often* **:** to flow to a specified place — used with *into* ⟨streams *disemboguing* into the sea⟩ **b :** to discharge contents as if they were flowing water ~ *vt* **1** *of a body of water* **:** to pour out (as waters) or discharge (itself) through an outlet or into another body of water ⟨a swift stream *disemboguing* its waters through a rocky outlet⟩ ⟨the river *disembogued* itself into the sea⟩ **2** *archaic* **:** to pour out (as contents) like water from a stream **:** empty (as oneself) by such pouring

dis·embosom \¦dis+\ *vt* [¹*dis-* + *embosom*] **:** UNBOSOM, UNBURDEN

dis·embowel \¦dis+\ *vt* [¹*dis-* + *embowel*] **1 :** to take out the bowels of **:** EVISCERATE; *also* **:** to tear, slash, or rip so that the bowels protrude **2 :** to exhaust of content **:** remove the substance of — **dis·embowelment** \"+\ *n* -S

dis·embroil \¦dis+\ *vt* [¹*dis-* + *embroil*] **:** to bring out of a confused condition or situation **:** UNTANGLE, EXTRICATE

dis·emburden \¦dis+\ *vb* -ED/-ING/-S [¹*dis-* + *emburden*] **:** DISBURDEN

di·seme \'dī,sēm\ *n* -S [back-formation fr. *disemic*] **:** a disemic syllable

di·se·mic \(')dī¦sēmik, -sem-\ *adj* [*di-* + *-semic*] *prosody* **:** equal to or having the length of two morae

dis·employ \¦dis+\ *vt* [¹*dis-* + *employ*] **:** to dismiss from or put out of employment ⟨workers ~*ed* by the shift from a war to a peace economy —Leopold Lippman⟩ — **dis·employment** \"+\ *n*

dis·enable \¦dis+\ *vt* [¹*dis-* + *enable*] **:** DISQUALIFY, INCAPACITATE — **dis·enablement** \"+\ *n* -S

dis·enchant \¦dis+\ *vt* [MF *desenchanter*, fr. *des-* ¹dis- + *enchanter* to enchant — more at ENCHANT] **:** to free from enchantment **:** DISILLUSION

dis·enchanter \"+\ *n* **:** one that disenchants

dis·enchantingly \"+\ *adv* **:** so as to disenchant **:** tending to produce disenchantment

dis·enchantment \"+\ *n* **:** an act of disenchanting; *also* **:** the condition of one disenchanted **:** DISILLUSIONMENT

dis·encourage \¦dis+\ *vt* [¹*dis-* + *encourage*] **:** DISCOURAGE — **dis·encouragement** \"+\ *n*

dis·encumber \¦dis+\ *vt* [MF *desencombrer*, fr. *des-* ¹dis- + *encombrer* to encumber — more at ENCUMBER] **:** to free from encumbrance or from anything that clogs, impedes, or obstructs **:** DISBURDEN ⟨I have ~*ed* myself from rhyme —John Dryden⟩ ⟨~*ing* the mind of prejudices⟩ **syn** see EXTRICATE

dis·encumberment \"+\ *or* **dis·encumbrance** \"+\ *n* -S **:** an act of disencumbering or the state of being disencumbered

dis·endow \¦dis+\ *vt* [¹*dis-* + *endow*] **:** to strip (as an established church) of endowment — **dis·endower** \"+\ *n* — **dis·endowment** \"+\ *n*

dis·enfranchise \¦dis+\ *vt* [¹*dis-* + *enfranchise*] **:** DISFRANCHISE — **dis·enfranchisement** \"+\ *n*

¹**dis·engage** \¦dis+\ *vb* [F *désengager*, fr. MF *desengager*, fr. *des-* ¹dis- + *engager* to engage — more at ENGAGE] *vt* **1 :** to release from anything that engages, engrosses, involves, or entangles **:** FREE, LIBERATE **2 a :** to free from a pledge or obligation — now used only as a past participle **b :** to extricate from something that entangles ⟨*disengaging* the rope from the gear⟩ **c :** to loosen or detach from something clung to ⟨gently *disengaged* the baby fingers wrapped about his thumb⟩ **d :** to remove (troops) from combat ⟨*disengaged* the first battalion⟩ ~ *vi* **1 :** to release or detach oneself **2 :** to shift one's blade from one side of an opponent's blade to the other in fencing **3 :** to withdraw from combat **syn** see DETACH

²**disengage** \"\ *n* -S **:** the act of disengaging in fencing

disengaged *adj* **:** not engaged **:** being at leisure **:** free from occupation or care

dis·engagement \"+\ *n* **1 :** the act of disengaging or state of being disengaged **:** DETACHMENT **2 :** freedom from ties, occupation, or constraint in mode of life or in manner **:** EASE **:** RELAXATION **3 :** the cancellation of an engagement of marriage

dis·enjoy \¦dis+\ *vt* [¹*dis-* + *enjoy*] **:** to take no pleasure in (as an achievement); *sometimes* **:** to be bored with (as oneself) — **dis·enjoyment** \"+\ *n*

dis·enroll \¦dis+\ *vt* [¹*dis-* + *enroll*] **:** to remove (as a name) from a roll; *broadly* **:** to release (an individual) from membership in an organization (as from a military reserve) — **dis·enrollment** \"+\ *n*

¹**dis·entail** \¦dis+\ *vt* [¹*dis-* + *entail*] **:** to free (as property) from entail **:** break the entail of (an estate)

²**disentail** \"\ *or* **dis·entailment** \"+\ *n* **:** the act or process of disentailing

dis·entangle \¦dis+\ *vb* [¹*dis-* + *entangle*] *vt* **:** to free from entanglement **:** straighten out **:** EXTRICATE, UNRAVEL ⟨~ a skein of yarn⟩ ⟨*disentangling* the threads of a plot⟩ ~ *vi* **:** to become disentangled ⟨shake your line free and let it ~ gradually⟩ **syn** see EXTRICATE

dis·entanglement \"+\ *n* **:** an act of disentangling or the state of being disentangled

dis·entangler \"+\ *n* **:** one that disentangles

dis·enthrall *also* **dis·enthral** \¦dis+\ *vt* [¹*dis-* + *enthrall, enthral*] **:** to free from bondage

dis·enthrone \¦dis+\ *vt* [¹*dis-* + *enthrone*] **:** DETHRONE, DEPOSE — **dis·enthronement** \"+\ *n*

dis·entitle \¦dis+\ *vt* [¹*dis-* + *entitle*] **:** to deprive of title, claim, or right

dis·entomb \¦dis+\ *vt* [¹*dis-* + *entomb*] **:** to take out from or as if from a tomb **:** bring to light **:** DISINTER — **dis·entombment** \"+\ *n*

dis·entrance \¦dis+\ *vt* [¹*dis-* + *entrance* (to put into a trance)] **:** DISENCHANT

dis·entwine \¦dis+\ *vb* [¹*dis-* + *entwine*] **:** UNTWINE, DISENTANGLE

dis·envenom \¦dis+\ *vt* [¹*dis-* + *envenom*] **:** to free from venom

dis·equilibrate \(¦)dis, dəs+\ *vt* [¹*dis-* + *equilibrate*] **:** to put out of balance **:** cause disequilibrium in

dis·equilibration \"+\ *n* **:** the quality or state of being disequilibrated

dis·equilibrium \dəs, (¦)dis+\ *n* [¹*dis-* + *equilibrium*] **:** loss or lack of equilibrium **:** imbalanced state **:** INSTABILITY; *esp* **:** a condition of imbalance in economic affairs in which normally self-correcting forces are ineffective or inoperative

dis·establish \¦dis+\ *vt* [¹*dis-* + *establish*] **:** to alter the existent state of (as by ceasing to use or support or by withdrawing recognition from) ⟨daylight saving time was largely ~*ed* after the war⟩; *esp* **:** to deprive (a church) of the status and privileges of an established church

dis·establisher \"+\ *n* **:** an advocate of disestablishment

dis·establishment \"+\ *n* **:** the act or process of disestablishing or the state of being disestablished; *specif* **:** the act of a state in sundering the relationships between it and its established church

dis·establishmentarian \"+\ *n* **:** an advocate of disestablishment

dis·establishmentarianism \"+\ *n* **:** adherence to or advocacy of the principle of disestablishment

¹**dis·esteem** \¦dis+\ *vt* [¹*dis-* + *esteem* (v.)] **:** to consciously lack esteem for **:** regard with disfavor or slight contempt ⟨the healthy mind cannot help but ~ the abnormal⟩ ⟨~*ing* all his favors⟩

²**disesteem** \"\ *n* [¹*dis-* + *esteem* (n.)] **:** the act of disesteeming or the condition of being disesteemed **:** DISLIKE, DISFAVOR, DISREPUTE

dis·estimation \dəs, (¦)dis+\ *n* [¹*dis-* + *estimation*] **:** DISESTEEM

di·seur \R dē'zər, di'-, +V -zər-; -R -zə̄, +V -zər- *or* -zə̄ *also* -zə̄r\ *n, pl* **diseurs** \-ər(z), -ə̄(z)\ [F, fr. OF, fr. *dis-* (stem of *dire* to speak, say, fr. L *dicere*) + *-eur* -or — more at DICTION] **:** a skilled and usu. professional reciter (as of verse spoken to music)

di·seuse \R -'zə̄|z, -'zər|z, -'zə|z, -R -'zə̄|z\ *n, pl* **diseuses** \|z(əz)\ [F, fem. of *diseur*] **:** a skilled and usu. professional woman reciter (as a monologist); *usu* **:** a woman who recites verse or other text to music

dis·faith \dəs, (')dis+\ *n* [¹*dis-* + *faith*] **:** DISTRUST **:** lack of faith

dis·fashion \dəs, (')dis+\ *vt* [¹*dis-* + *fashion*] **:** DISFIGURE

¹**dis·favor** \dəs, (')dis+\ *n* [prob. fr. MF *desfaveur*, fr. *des-* ¹*dis-* + *faveur* favor — more at FAVOR] **1 a :** DISPLEASURE, DISAPPROVAL, DISLIKE ⟨he had nothing but ~ for his associates⟩ **b** *obs* **:** a disobliging act **:** UNKINDNESS **2 :** the state or fact of not being favored or in favor: as **a :** absence of esteem **:** DISREPUTE, DISREGARD ⟨the poor . . . grown familiar with ~ —H.W.Longfellow⟩ **b :** the condition of being deprived of favor or under displeasure ⟨long in ~ at court⟩ **c :** absence or loss of that which favors one's standing or cause **:** DETRIMENT, DISADVANTAGE ⟨he acted to his own ~⟩ **syn** see DISLIKE

²**disfavor** \"\ *vt* [¹*dis-* + *favor* (v.)] **:** to withhold or withdraw favor from **:** regard with disesteem **:** DISCOUNTENANCE ⟨his system was ~*ed* by most people —*Encyc. Americana*⟩

dis·fea·ture \də'sfēchə(r), (')di¦s-\ *vt* [¹*dis-* + *feature* (n.)] **:** to mar the features of **:** DEFACE — **dis·fea·ture·ment** \-mənt\ *n* -s

¹**dis·fellowship** \dəs, (')dis+\ *n* [¹*dis-* + *fellowship*] **:** exclusion from or lack of fellowship

²**disfellowship** \"\ *vt* **:** to exclude from fellowship, esp. from religious communion

dis·figuration \dəs, (¦)dis+\ *n* **:** DISFIGUREMENT

dis·figure \dəs, (')dis+\ *vt* [ME *disfiguren*, fr. MF *desfigurer*, fr. *des-* ¹*dis-* + *figure* — more at FIGURE] **1 :** to make less complete, perfect, or beautiful in appearance or character **:** DEFACE, DEFORM, MAR ⟨~ a landscape with billboards⟩ ⟨his face seamed and *disfigured* by time⟩ **2** *obs* **:** to disguise by changing the figure or appearance of **3** *archaic* **:** to carve (a peacock) at table

dis·fig·ure·ment \-mənt\ *n* -s **1 :** the act of disfiguring or the state of being disfigured **:** DEFACEMENT **2 :** something that disfigures **:** BLOT

dis·fig·ur·er \-ə(r)\ *n* **:** one that disfigures

dis·fig·ur·ing·ly *adv* **:** in a disfiguring manner

dis·forest \dəs, (')dis+\ *vt* [in sense 1, modif. (infl. by ME *forest*) of ML *disafforestare*; in sense 2, fr. ¹*dis-* + *forest* (n.) — more at DISAFFOREST] **1 :** DISAFFOREST **2 :** DEFOREST — **dis·forestation** \dəs, (¦)dis+\ *n*

dis·form \dəs, (')dis+\ *vb* [¹*dis-* + *form*] *vt* **:** *obs* **:** DEFORM ~ *vi* **:** to change or lose form or order

dis·franchise \dəs, (')dis+\ *vt* -ED/-ING/-S [ME *disfraunchisen*, fr. ¹*dis-* + *fraunchisen* to franchise — more at FRANCHISE] **1 a :** to deprive (as a corporation) of a franchise or of some privilege or immunity previously specifically granted ⟨the company will be *disfranchised* if it fails to maintain regular passenger service⟩ **b :** to deprive of a statutory or constitutional right; *esp* **:** to deprive (a person) of the right to vote **2 :** to deprive (as a person) of a privilege, right, or pleasure ⟨any unconscious confusion of mate with mother tends to ~ him of enjoyment —Weston La Barre⟩ **3 :** to remove (a person) from membership in a corporation — **dis·fran·chise·ment** \-mənt, -chəzmənt *sometimes* -chəsm *or* də,sfra(a)n'chī- *or* ,di,sfra(a)n'chī- *or* ,disfrən'chī\ *n* — **dis·franchiser** \dəs, (')dis+\ *n*

dis·frock \dəs, (')dis+\ *vt* [¹*dis-* + *frock* (n.)] **:** UNFROCK

disfunction *var of* DYSFUNCTION

dis·furnish \dəs, (')dis+\ *vt* [MF *desfourniss-*, stem of *desfournir*, fr. *des-* ¹*dis-* + *fournir* to furnish — more at FURNISH] **1 :** to make (as a person) destitute of possessions **:** STRIP, DIVEST **2** *Midland* **:** DISCOMMODE, DEPRIVE, INCONVENIENCE — **dis·furnishment** \"+\ *n*

dis·garnish \dəs, (')dis+, *or* -sk- *instead of* -sg-\ *vt* [ME *disgarnysshen*, fr. MF *desgarniss-*, stem of *desgarnir*, fr. *des-* ¹*dis-* + *garnir* to furnish, garnish — more at GARNISH] *archaic* **:** to deprive of something that garnishes **:** DESPOIL

dis·garrison \dəs, (')dis+, *or* -sk- *instead of* -sg-\ *vt* [¹*dis-* + *garrison* (n.)] **:** to remove a garrison from

dis·gavel \dəs, (')dis+, *or* -sk- *instead of* -sg-\ *vt* [¹*dis-* + *gavel* (to subject to gavelkind)] **:** to deprive of or relieve from the tenure of gavelkind

dis·generic \¦dis+\ *adj* [¹*dis-* + *generic*] **:** belonging to different genera — opposed to *congeneric*

disgenic *var of* DYSGENIC

dis·gorge \dəs, (')dis+, *or* -sk- *instead of* -sg-\ *vb* [MF *desgorger*, fr. *des-* ¹*dis-* + *gorge* gorge, throat — more at GORGE] *vt* **1 a :** to discharge by the throat and mouth **:** VOMIT **b :** to discharge violently, confusedly, or as a result of force ⟨the volcano ~*s* lava⟩ ⟨day after day the tourist buses *disgorged* their multitudes —Mollie Panter-Downes⟩ **2 :** to discharge the contents of (as the stomach) **:** EMPTY **3 :** to remove sediment from (champagne) after secondary fermentation in the bottle is complete and before the addition of dosage ~ *vi* **:** to discharge contents; *esp* **:** to give up illicit or ill-gotten gains

dis·gorge·ment \-mənt\ *n* -s [MF *desgorgement*, fr. *desgorger* + *-ment*] **:** an act or instance of disgorging

dis·gorg·er \-ə(r)\ *n* **:** one that disgorges; *specif* **:** an implement for extracting a hook from a fish

¹**dis·grace** \dəs'g|rās, də'sk|\ *vt* -ED/-ING/-S [MF *disgracier*, fr. OIt *disgraziare*, fr. *disgrazia*] **1 a** *obs* **:** to spoil the appearance of **:** mar in outward seeming **:** DISFIGURE **b** *archaic* **:** to cause to seem inferior by comparison ⟨thy whiteness . . . shall ~ the swan —Robert Browning⟩ **2 :** to bring as an accompaniment reproach or shame to **:** reflect discredit upon ⟨his behavior *disgraced* his family⟩ ⟨such manners are enough to ~ anyone⟩ **3** *obs* **:** to treat discourteously **:** UPBRAID, REVILE **4 :** to put (as a person) to shame or out of favor **:** cast reproach upon **:** bring to dishonor ⟨seeking to ~ his enemies⟩; *specif* **:** to dismiss as discredited esp. from court

²**disgrace** \"\ *n* [MF, fr. OIt *disgrazia*, fr. *dis-* (fr. L *dis-* ¹dis-) + *grazia* grace, fr. L *gratia* — more at GRACE] **1 a :** loss of grace, favor, or honor **:** the condition of one fallen from grace or honor usu. through some indecorous, dishonest, or immoral action ⟨a courtier in ~⟩ ⟨the divorce suit ending in ~ for all⟩ **b :** the often widespread ill repute attendant on some fall from grace ⟨the colonel's ~ spread through the whole post⟩ **2 :** something causing a fall from grace **:** a person, act, thing, or condition causing loss of grace ⟨the child's manners were a ~⟩ ⟨the mayor's conduct in office is a ~⟩ **3 a** *obs* **:** an action of degradation **b** *obs* **:** a specific action or instance indicating rebuke, degradation, downfall **c :** an expression or utterance condemning the indecorous, dishonest, or immoral **d** *obs* **:** disapproval or utterance of disapproval **e :** ill luck **:** MISFORTUNE **f :** the act of marring or disfiguring **g :** the condition of being unsightly **syn** see DISHONOR

dis·grace·ful \-āsfəl\ *adj* **1** *obs* **:** lacking grace or charm **2 :** bringing or involving disgrace **:** causing shame **:** SHAMEFUL, DISHONORABLE, UNBECOMING — **dis·grace·ful·ly** \-fəlē, -li\ *adv* — **dis·grace·ful·ness** \-fəlnəs\ *n*

dis·grac·er \-āsə(r)\ *n* **:** one that disgraces

dis·gra·cious \dəs'grāshəs, (')dis¦g-, də'skr-, (')di¦skr-\ *adj* [MF *disgracieux*, fr. OIt *disgrazioso*, fr. *disgrazia* + *-oso* -ous] **1** *obs* **:** out of favor **:** in disgrace; *sometimes* **:** DISGRACEFUL **2 :** lacking in consideration **:** UNGRACIOUS, INCONSIDERATE, UNKIND

dis·grade \dəs'grād, (')dis¦g-, də'skr-, (')di¦skr-\ *vt* [ME *disgraden*, fr. MF *desgrader*, *degrader* — more at DEGRADE] **:** DEGRADE

disgregate *vb* [LL *disgregatus*, past part. of *disgregare*, fr. L *dis-* ¹dis- + *gregare* to collect, fr. *greg-*, *grex* flock — more at GREGARIOUS] **:** SEPARATE, DISINTEGRATE, SCATTER

dis·grun·tle \dəs'grənt°l, də'skr-\ *vt* -ED/-ING/-S [¹*dis-* + *gruntle* (to grumble)] **:** to put in bad humor **:** arouse peevish dissatisfaction in — **dis·grun·tle·ment** \-mənt\ *n* -s

dis·grun·tled·ly \-°ldlē, -li\ *adv* **:** in a disgruntled manner

dis·guis·able \dəs'gīzəbəl, də'skī- *sometimes* dəz'gī-\ *adj* **:** suitable for disguising **:** capable of being disguised

dis·guis·al \-īzəl\ *n* -s **:** the act of disguising

¹**dis·guise** \-īz\ *vt* -ED/-ING/-S [ME *disgisen*, fr. MF *desguiser*, fr. OF, fr. *des-* ¹dis-) + *-guiser* (fr. *guise* manner) — more at GUISE] **1 :** to change the customary dress or appearance of **:** furnish with a false appearance or an assumed identity ⟨the noblemen *disguised* as hall porters look through you or past you —C.E.Montague⟩ **2** *obs* **:** to transform esp. for the worse **:** DEFORM, DISFIGURE **3 :** to deny or obscure the existence, identity, or true state or character of **:** CONCEAL ⟨a *disguised* tax⟩ ⟨hate is *disguised* beneath all the fine phrases —Bertrand Russell⟩ ⟨I see no reason for *disguising* my settled conviction —G.G.Coulton⟩ **4** *archaic* **:** to affect or change by liquor **:** INTOXICATE

syn DISSEMBLE, CLOAK, MASK: DISGUISE, the most general of these four terms, stresses the fact of concealment of identity by usu. temporary alteration of appearance or by usu. temporarily presenting a false appearance as by assuming another's identity ⟨had not been able to *disguise* their disapproval —Archibald Marshall⟩ ⟨no judgment is so persuasive as when it is *disguised* as a statement of facts —R.P. Blackmur⟩ ⟨our author, *disguised* as Jonathan Oldstyle —Saxe Commins⟩ DISSEMBLE stresses more the intent to deceive, esp. as to one's own thoughts or feelings, usu. carrying a stronger implication of successful deception than does DISGUISE and often suggesting something censurable ⟨I account him faithful in the pulpit who *dissembles* nothing that he believes for fear of giving offense —William Cowper⟩ ⟨smiling in the face of misfortune in order to *dissemble* the truth to the world —Clare Sheridan⟩ ⟨a crafty child given to frequent *dissembling*⟩ CLOAK and MASK are often interchangeable with DISGUISE although both usu. carry the suggestion of only partial though deceptive concealment. CLOAK carries strongly the idea of covering something up usu. with the intent of misleading or in an attempt to make something unacceptable seem acceptable ⟨who *cloaks* the wisdom of her "uplift" talks in warm humanity —Muriel Segal⟩ ⟨intolerance and public irresponsibility cannot be *cloaked* in the shining armor of rectitude and righteousness —A.E.Stevenson †1965⟩ MASK adds to CLOAK the idea of a certain obviousness in the covering and suggests even more strongly the unacceptableness of the thing masked, sometimes suggesting, correlatively, not only a neutral or even acceptable quality in the disguise as opposed to the thing masked but often a quality that positively ornaments or embellishes ⟨his pessimism . . . became an obvious pose, an attempt to *mask* his porky complacence —Granville Hicks⟩ ⟨the usual disorderly bustle which *masks* the deadly efficiency of the French people —Osbert Sitwell⟩ ⟨the windows were *masked* by long cretonne drapes⟩

²**disguise** \"\ *n* -s [ME *disgise*, fr. *disgisen*, v.] **1 :** unfamiliar or uncharacteristic style of dress or apparel assumed to conceal one's identity ⟨a king in ~⟩; *often* **:** something used to conceal one's identity or counterfeit another's (as a masker's costume) ⟨grotesque ~*s* at carnival balls⟩ **2 a :** an outward form that misrepresents the true nature or identity of a person or thing **:** a deceptive appearance ⟨blessings in ~⟩ **b :** pretentious appearance **:** artifice or insincerity esp. in manners or speech **:** PRETENSE ⟨throw off all ~⟩ **c :** a misleading lack of correspondence between appearance and reality **:** DECEPTION, SPECIOUSNESS ⟨without fear of evil or ~ —P.B.Shelley⟩ **3 :** the act of disguising **:** assumption of an appearance to hide the truth ⟨spoke with ~⟩ **4** *obs* **:** a change of manner by drink **:** INTOXICATION **5** *obs* **:** MASQUERADE

dis·guised \-īzd\ *adj* [ME *disgised*, fr. past part. of *disgisen* to disguise — more at DISGUISE] **1 :** altered by or for disguise **:** dressed in disguise **:** OBSCURED, COVERT **2 :** INTOXICATED — **dis·guised·ly** \-īzədlē, -li\ *adv*

dis·guise·less \-īzləs\ *adj* **:** UNDISGUISED, UNOBSCURED, OPEN

dis·guise·ment \-īzmənt\ *n* -s [MF *desguisement*, fr. *desguiser* + *-ment*] **1 :** a disguised state **:** the act of disguising **2 :** something that disguises **:** DISGUISE; *sometimes* **:** added ornamentation or decoration that alters the appearance

dis·guis·er \-īzə(r)\ *n* -s [ME *disgiser*, fr. *disgisen* + *-er*] **:** one that disguises

disguising *n* -s [ME *disgising*, fr. gerund of *disgisen*] *archaic* **:** MASQUE, MASQUERADE

¹**dis·gust** \dəs'gəst, də'skə- *sometimes* dəz'gə-\ *n* -s [MF *desgoust*, fr. *desgouster*] **1 a :** marked aversion or repugnance toward food or toward a particular dish or kind of food **:** NAUSEA, SQUEAMISHNESS ⟨from that day to this he never smelled cooking beans without ~⟩ **b :** physical or emotional reaction comparable to nausea that is excited by exposure to something highly distasteful or loathsome ⟨their cruelty excited our ~⟩ ⟨impossible to see such wounds without ~⟩ **2** *archaic* **a :** a state or outbreak of mutual ill feeling or annoyance **:** QUARREL, DISAGREEMENT **b :** something that offends **:** a source of displeasure or repugnance **:** VEXATION, TRIAL, ANNOYANCE

²**disgust** \"\ *vb* -ED/-ING/-S [MF *desgouster*, fr. *des-* ¹*dis-* + *goust* taste, fr. L *gustus*; akin to L *gustare* to taste — more at CHOOSE] *vt* **1** *obs* **:** to experience intense dislike for **2 a :** to excite queasiness or strong physical distaste in **:** sicken the stomach of **:** NAUSEATE **b :** to provoke (one) to loathing, repugnance, or aversion **:** be offensive to the taste or sensibilities of ⟨your thoughtlessness ~*s* me⟩ ⟨~*ed* with her careless work⟩ ⟨he was ~*ed* at her answer⟩ ⟨everyone is ~*ed* by their behavior⟩ **3 :** to cause or arouse effective aversion in **:** cause (one) to lose an interest or intention through exciting distaste ⟨his failures ~*ed* him against further efforts⟩ ~ *vi* **:** to cause disgust ⟨too rich food soon ~*s*⟩

syn DISGUST, SICKEN, and NAUSEATE agree in meaning to arouse extreme distaste in (a person). DISGUST implies extremely offended sensibilities or a strong repugnance or aversion ⟨*disgusted* at what she thought of as the vulgarity of the men —Sherwood Anderson⟩ ⟨the majority of women that he meets offend him, repel him, *disgust* him —H.L.Mencken⟩ ⟨they were not *disgusted* at the torture of slaves —W.R.Inge⟩ SICKEN suggests a disgust so strong that one is affected physically, as by a turning of the stomach ⟨the national propaganda of all the belligerent nations *sickened* me —Bertrand Russell⟩ ⟨his unctuous morality, which *sickens* later ages —Roy Lewis & Angus Maude⟩ NAUSEATE is stronger still, suggesting a loathsomeness that provokes vomiting ⟨in letter after letter, she rinsed herself in the dirty tub-water of her miseries. It . . . *nauseated* one erstwhile friend —*Time*⟩ ⟨*nauseated* by a manifestly hypocritical saintliness⟩

disgusted *adj* **:** affected by disgust **:** disturbed physically or mentally by something distasteful — **dis·gust·ed·ly** *adv* — **dis·gust·ed·ness** *n* -ES

dis·gust·ful \-tfəl\ *adj* **1 :** provoking disgust **:** DISGUSTING **2 :** resulting from or accompanied by disgust ⟨~ curiosity —R.L.Stevenson⟩ — **dis·gust·ful·ly** \-fəlē\ *adv*

disgusting *adj* **:** causing disgust **:** SICKENING, REVOLTING, NAUSEATING, LOATHSOME — **dis·gust·ing·ly** *adv* — **dis·gust·ing·ness** *n* -ES

¹**dish** \'dish\ *n* -ES *often attrib* [ME, fr. OE *disc* plate; akin to OS *disk* table, OHG *tisc* dish, table; all fr. a prehistoric WGmc word borrowed fr. L *discus* dish, disk, quoit, fr. Gk *diskos*, fr. *dikein* to throw] **1 a :** a large shallow more or less concave vessel (as a platter) in which food is brought to the table for serving; *broadly* **:** any open vessel (as a tureen) similarly used ⟨a deep vegetable ~⟩ **b** *obs* **:** ALMS DISH 1 **c** *archaic* **:** a drinking vessel **d dishes** *pl* **:** table utensils — used esp. of those of pottery or china as distinguished from glass drinking vessels and metal implements but sometimes used inclusively ⟨I'll get out the ~*es* while you lay the silver⟩ ⟨you must wash the ~*es* before you go out⟩ **2 a :** food prepared for the table in a particular fashion ⟨a ~ of boiled potatoes⟩; *often* **:** food prepared according to a specified cuisine ⟨tasty Armenian ~*es*⟩ **b :** something (as a literary work) resembling a dish of food esp. in combining varied ingredients properly blended and seasoned ⟨the yeastiest ~ on TV this season —*Time*⟩ **c :** CUP OF TEA ⟨marriage was scarcely his ~⟩ **d** *slang* **:** an alluring young woman ⟨what a ~ my blind date turned out to be⟩ **3 a :** the contents of a dish; *usu* **:** food or drink served in a dish ⟨a ~ of strawberries⟩ **b :** the capacity of a dish **:** the quantity measured by a dish **:** DISHFUL **c** *dial Brit* **:** a trough about 28 inches long, 4 inches deep, and 6 inches wide in which ore is measured **d** *dial Brit* **:** the portion of a mine's product that is paid to the landowner or proprietor **e** *dial Brit* **:** a gallon of tin ore ready for the smelter **4 a :** any of various shallow concave vessels (as an evaporating dish); *broadly* **:** something that in shallow concavity is felt to resemble a dish (as a hollow in land or one between the eyes of certain mammals) **b :** the state of being concave or the degree of concavity present ⟨the ~ of a wheel⟩ **c** *slang* **:** HOME PLATE **d :** a microwave antenna that is often paraboloid in form and usu. highly directive in wave reflection

²**dish** \"\ *vb* -ED/-ING/-ES *vt* **1 a :** to put (as food for serving) into a dish or dishes — often used with *up* **b :** to present for acceptance — usu. used with *up* ⟨~*ed up* another explanation⟩ **c :** to make widely known **:** DISSEMINATE — usu. used with *up* ⟨~*ing* up the latest scandal⟩ **2 a :** to make concave like a dish ⟨a boiler with both ends ~*ed*⟩ — often used with *in* ⟨several car tops were ~*ed* in by the concussion⟩ **b :** HOLLOW ⟨~ a gutter⟩ — often used with *out* **3** *chiefly Brit* **a :** CIRCUMVENT, OUTWIT, CHEAT **b :** DEFEAT, RUIN **4 :** to get rid of **:** set aside **:** SHELVE ~ *vi* **1 :** to become concave in the middle — used esp. of spoke wheels ⟨the rim hit a rock and the wheel ~*ed*⟩ **2** *of a horse* **:** to swing the forefeet sideways in trotting **3** *slang* **:** to talk casually **:** CHAT, CHATTER

dis·ha·bille \¦disə¦bē(ə)l, -is,(h)a¦-, -is,(h)ä¦-, -is,(h)a¦-, ÷-isha¦-, ÷-ish,a¦-, ÷-ish,ä¦-, ÷-ish,a¦-, -¦bil, -¦bē\ *or* **des·ha·bille** *\with* e *instead of* i *of the first syllable of, or with* -āz(,)- *instead of* -is- *or* -is,(h) *of, the preceding pronunc; or as, or with approximation to, F* (F dāzābēyā)\ *n* -s [F *déshabillé*, fr. past part. of *déshabiller* to undress, fr. *dés-* ¹dis- + *habiller* to dress — more at HABILIMENT] **1 a** *archaic* **:** NEGLIGEE **b :** the state of being dressed in a loose or careless style **2 :** disorder or dishevelment of body or mind

dis·hallow \dəs, (')dis+\ *vt* [¹*dis-* + *hallow*] **:** to violate the sanctity of ⟨~ the Sabbath with their conduct⟩ **:** PROFANE

dis·harmonic *or* **dis·harmonious** *also* **dis·harmonical** \¦dis+\ *adj* [¹*dis-* + *harmonic* or *harmonious* or *harmonical*] **1 :** lacking in harmony **:** not harmonic or harmonious **2 a :** having a combination of bodily characters that results in an unusual form or appearance ⟨the ~ skeletal remains of certain European fossil hominids may result from interbreeding of separate distinct races⟩ **b :** ALLOMETRIC **c :** constituting a folded geologic structure in which the form of the fold in deeper beds differs from that in the overlying beds

dis·har·mo·nism \dəs'härmə,nizəm, (')dis'-\ *n* -s **:** disharmonic state **:** DISHARMONY

dis·harmonize \dəs, (')dis+\ *vt* [¹*dis-* + *harmonize*] **:** to make disharmonic

dis·harmony \"+\ *n* [¹*dis-* + *harmony*] **1 :** lack of harmony **:** DISCORD **2 :** something incongruous **:** an instance of disharmonic condition or behavior

dishaunt *vt* [MF *deshanter*, fr. *des-* ¹*dis-* + *hanter* to frequent, dwell — more at HAUNT] *obs* **:** to absent oneself from

dish board *n* **:** DRAINBOARD

dishcloth \'=,=\ *n* **1 a :** a cloth used for washing dishes **b** *Brit* **:** DISH TOWEL **2 :** PURPLE TRILLIUM

dishcloth gourd *n* **1 :** the fruit of any of several gourds of the genus *Luffa* (esp. *L. cylindrica*) distinguished by a fibrous interior that is dried and used like a sponge or cloth — called also *luffa, sponge gourd* **2 :** a plant that bears dishcloth gourds

dishclout \'=,=\ *n* **1** *Brit* **:** DISHCLOTH 1 **2** *chiefly Brit* **:** a weak or dull person

dish cross *n* **:** a low cross-shaped stand that is used for holding dishes at the table and that consists usu. of adjustable silver bars with a small lamp being placed beneath the center to keep the food hot

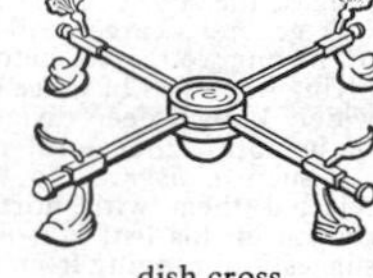
dish cross

dis·hearten \dəs, (')dis+\ *vt* [¹*dis-* + *hearten*] **:** to deprive of courage and hope **:** depress the spirits of **:** DEJECT, DISCOURAGE **syn** see DISCOURAGE

disheartening *adj* **:** inducing disheartenment, discouragement, or dejection — **dis·heart·en·ing·ly** *adv*

dis·heart·en·ment \-t°nmənt\ *n* -s **:** the state of being disheartened **:** DESPONDENCY

dished *adj* [fr. past part. of ²*dish*] **1 a :** depressed at or toward the center **:** CONCAVE ⟨a ~ face⟩ **b** *of a wheel* **:** having the hub inset in respect to the rim so that the joining structure (as spokes) forms a blunt cone with rim as base and hub as apex **2** *of vehicle wheels* **:** nearer together at the bottom than at the top

dished patch *n* **:** a piece of dished metal (as plate) used for patching usu. by welding

dished plate *n* **:** a concave metal plate shaped to allow for contraction (as after welding) and to increase resistance to force applied to the convex surface

¹**dis·helm** \dəs, (')dis+\ *vt* [¹*dis-* + *helm* (helmet)] **:** to deprive of a helm or of a helmet

²**dishelm** \"\ *vt* [¹*dis-* + *helm* (steering apparatus)] **:** to deprive (a ship or boat) of the rudder

dish·er \'dishə(r)\ *n* -s **:** one that dishes; *esp* **:** an ice-cream scoop

¹**dis·her·i·son** \(')dis'herəsən, -əzən\ *n* -s [ME *desertison, disheretison, disherison*, fr. OF *desheriteison, deseriteison*, fr. *desheriter, deseriter*] **:** the act of disinheriting **:** DISINHERITANCE

²**disherison** \"\ *vt* -ED/-ING/-S **:** DISINHERIT

dis·her·it \dəs'herət, (')dis¦h-\ *vt* -ED/-ING/-S [ME *deseriten, disheriten*, fr. OF *deseriter, desheriter*, fr. *des-* ¹*dis-* + *heriter* to inherit, fr. L *hereditare* to inherit — more at INHERIT] *archaic* **:** DISINHERIT

disheritor *n, obs* **:** a person who disinherits another

dishes *pl of* DISH, *pres 3d sing of* DISH

di·shev·el \də'shevəl\ *vt* **disheveled** *or* **dishevelled**; **disheveled** *or* **dishevelled**; **disheveling** *or* **dishevelling** \-v(ə)liŋ\ **dishevels** [back-formation fr. *disheveled*] **1 :** to let (as the hair) hang loosely or in disorder **2 :** to cause disarray in (as a person) ⟨the wind tugged at and ~*ed* her⟩ ⟨like the fair flower ~*ed* in the wind —William Cowper⟩

disheveled *or* **dishevelled** *adj* [ME *discheveled*, part trans. of MF *deschevelé*, fr. OF, past part. of *descheveler* to disarrange the hair, fr. *des-* ¹*dis-* + *-cheveler* (fr. *chevel* hair of the head, fr. L *capillus*)] **:** being in loose disorder or disarray **:** DISARRANGED, RUFFLED ⟨~ hair⟩; *also* **:** marked by disarray or disorder **:** UNTIDY ⟨a ~ movie that charges futilely about —John McCarten⟩ **syn** see SLIPSHOD

di·shev·el·ment \-vəlmənt\ *n* -s **:** a disheveled state **:** DISORDER
dish–face \ˈ=,=\ *n* **:** a dish-faced animal
dish–faced \ˈ=ˈ=\ *adj* **:** having the face somewhat concave — used esp. of certain dogs, cattle, horses, and hogs
dish·ful \ˈdish,fu̇l\ *n, pl* **dishfuls** [ME, fr. *dish* + *-ful*] **:** the content of a dish **:** SERVING ⟨ate several heaping ~s of ice cream⟩
dish garden *n* **:** a miniature garden that is planted in a shallow dish
dish gravy *n* **:** meat juice usu. collected on the platter and served as gravy
dishing *pres part of* DISH
di·shiv·er \də̇+\ *vt* [ˈ*dis-* + *shiver*] *archaic* **:** SHIVER
dishmop \ˈ=,=\ *n* **:** a device for washing dishes consisting usu. of a head of fine soft cotton thread bound to a short wooden handle
dish mustard *n* [so called fr. the round flat pods] **:** PENNYCRESS

dishmop

dis·hoard \dəs, (ˈ)dis+\ *vi* [ˈ*dis-* + *hoard*] **:** to put money or goods previously withheld into circulation — **dis·hoard·er** \-ə(r)\ *n*
dish of tea : CUP OF TEA
dis·home \dəs, (ˈ)dis+\ *vt* [ˈ*dis-* + *home* (n.)] **:** to deprive of a home
ˈ**dishonest** *vt* [ME *dishonesten*, fr. MF *deshonester*, modif. (influenced by *deshoneste*) of L *dehonestare*, fr. *de-* + *honestare* to honor — more at HONEST] *obs* **:** to make dishonest **:** DEFAME, DISHONOR, DEFILE
²**dis·honest** \dəs, (ˈ)dis+\ *adj* [ME, fr. MF *deshoneste*, fr. *des-* ˈ*dis-* + *honeste* honest — more at HONEST] **1** *obs* **a :** DISHONORABLE, SHAMEFUL **b :** INDECENT, UNCHASTE, LEWD **c :** DISFIGURED, REPULSIVE, UNSEEMLY **2 :** characterized by lack of truth, honesty, probity, or trustworthiness or by an inclination to mislead, lie, cheat, or defraud **:** FRAUDULENT ⟨~ politicians⟩ ⟨hoarding his ~ gains⟩ ⟨a ~ report on his earnings⟩
syn DECEITFUL, LYING, MENDACIOUS, UNTRUTHFUL: DISHONEST may apply to any breach of honesty or trust, as lying, deceiving, cheating, stealing, or defrauding ⟨a *dishonest* answer⟩ ⟨while it would be *dishonest* to gloss over this weakness, one must understand it in terms of the circumstances that conspired to produce it —Lewis Mumford⟩ ⟨a *dishonest* clerk fired for stealing⟩ DECEITFUL may imply an intent or inclination to mislead with the specious or spurious and conceal or distort truth or fact ⟨a *deceitful* schemer⟩ ⟨*deceitful* testimony⟩ ⟨educators, above all others, ought to be able to look behind the fine phrase and the fair words, to lift the hooded robe or tear away the *deceitful* mask, and to expose double-talk for what it is —B.G.Gallagher⟩ LYING describes a disposition to falsehood, a habit of telling lies ⟨a *lying* scoundrel⟩ ⟨silly newspapers and magazines for the circulation of *lying* advertisements —G.B.Shaw⟩ MENDACIOUS, a rather literary term, is a close synonym for LYING; it may have benign or bland overtones ⟨nothing would suit him but that they should go aboard the ships that caught his interest where the masters, hearing his quality, set out wine and told him *mendacious* tales of their trade —J.H.Wheelwright⟩ UNTRUTHFUL is milder than LYING and may center attention on the fact of discrepancy from truth or fact without suggestion of motive ⟨an *untruthful* explanation for the accident⟩ ⟨an *untruthful* account of the affair⟩
dis·honestly \"+\ *adv* [ME, fr. *dishonest* + *-ly*] **1** *obs* **:** DISHONORABLY, UNCHASTELY **2 :** in a deceptive or fraudulent manner **:** with dishonesty
dis·honesty \"+\ *n* [ME *deshonestee, dishonestee*, fr. MF *deshonesté*, fr. *des-* ˈ*dis-* + *honesté* honesty — more at HONESTY] **1** *obs* **a :** DISHONOR, SHAME **b :** LEWDNESS, UNCHASTITY **2 :** lack of honesty, probity, or integrity in principle **:** lack of fairness and straightforwardness **:** disposition to defraud, deceive, or betray **:** FAITHLESSNESS **3 :** a dishonest act **:** FRAUD **:** a deviation from probity
ˈ**dis·honor** \"+\ *n* [ME *dishonour*, fr. OF *deshonor, deshoneur*, fr. *des-* ˈ*dis-* + *honor, honeur* honor — more at HONOR] **1 :** lack or loss of honor or a condition characterized by such lack or loss **2 a :** the state of one who has offended against honor **:** SHAME, DISGRACE, IGNOMINY ⟨a traitor to his kind, wrapped in ~ as in a cloak⟩ **b :** loss of prestige or place; *esp* **:** the obscure and disregarded state of one that has fallen from a position of prominence ⟨a courtier in ~⟩ **c :** strong speech in condemnation or other expressions of disapproval or scorn **:** INSULT ⟨exposed to ~ by every hack writer⟩ **3 :** a person, thing, or action bringing dishonor and sacrificing or endangering good repute ⟨the professor's conduct is a ~ to the university⟩ **4 :** the nonpayment or nonacceptance of commercial paper by the party on whom it is drawn
syn DISREPUTE, DISGRACE, SHAME, IGNOMINY, OBLOQUY, OPPROBRIUM, ODIUM, INFAMY: these words all involve loss of esteem and good repute and resulting denigration or hatred. DISREPUTE is the mildest in the group and means no more than loss of praise and popularity with ensuing desuetude or marked but not necessarily extreme dislike ⟨this author is now in *disrepute* and his works are no longer read⟩ ⟨the secretary fell into *disrepute* and was suspended but not discharged⟩ DISHONOR implies lost honor. It may imply general loss of respect and deference formerly accorded ⟨Belisarius, once courted, now exposed to *dishonor*⟩ It may suggest the scorn of the cowardly, corrupt, or untrustworthy ⟨the general's career will always be tarnished by the *dishonor* of having retreated before inferior forces⟩ DISGRACE, implying utter loss of grace or favor, is a strong term and implies widely known deep disfavor incurred by something improper or immoral ⟨the moral reputation of these Grandisons was . . . such a *disgrace* to the noble name they bore, that she rejected them with horror —George Meredith⟩ SHAME is central in this list; it is usable in various situations and with suggestions ranging from those of DISHONOR to those of INFAMY ⟨to soften the *shame* of this defeat in battle⟩ ⟨the lasting *shame* of a quisling or a Judas⟩ In this series SHAME is unusual in implying that inner feelings of guilt are likely to be experienced by the victim, along with scornful or hateful feelings of others ⟨*shame* is a reaction to other people's criticism. A man is shamed either by being openly ridiculed and rejected or by fantasying to himself that he has been made ridiculous —Ruth Benedict⟩ The extreme feelings attached to the following words blur their exact meanings and make comments on them difficult and inexact: IGNOMINY may imply something more intense than *scorn*, deeper than DISGRACE and may add notions of hatred and contempt ⟨he cast the pork solemnly upon the dunghill, with every attendant circumstance of *ignominy* —G.G.Coulton⟩ ⟨the *ignominy* [of being horsewhipped] he had been compelled to submit to —George Meredith⟩ OBLOQUY connotes strong widespread hatred and contempt for an important or well-known figure found guilty of something hateful, base, or shocking ⟨that unmerited *obloquy* had been brought on him by the violence of his minister —T.B.Macaulay⟩ ⟨all the *obloquy* which Weed's corruption had excited —H.S.Commager⟩ OPPROBRIUM may carry with it the suggestion of general condemnation for the fraudulent or the brutal, or a specific instance of them ⟨the name "educator", for many intelligent people, has become a term of *opprobrium* —C.H.Grandgent⟩ ⟨the *opprobrium* conveyed by the term headhunter —V.G.Heiser⟩ ODIUM is quite similar; it may occasionally suggest more lasting and less specific resentment, blame, and hatred ⟨whatever *odium* or loss her maneuvers incurred she [Queen Elizabeth] flung upon her counselors —J.R.Green⟩ INFAMY is perhaps the strongest of this group; it suggests long-lasting and extreme ill fame with attendant hatred, loathing, and contempt ⟨I have come, not from obscurity into the momentary notoriety of crime, but from a sort of fame to a sort of eternity of *infamy* —Oscar Wilde⟩ ⟨December 7, 1941, a date which will live in *infamy* —F.D.Roosevelt⟩ ⟨long remember the *infamy* of this kidnap-murder⟩
²**dishonor** \"\ *vt* [ME *deshonouren*, fr. MF *deshonorer, deshonerer*, fr. *des-* ˈ*dis-* + *honorer, honerer* to honor — more at HONOR] **1 :** to deprive of honor **:** treat with indignity or as unworthy in the sight of others **:** stain the character or reputation of **2 :** to violate the chastity of **:** DEBAUCH, RAPE **3 :** to bring reproach or shame on **:** DISGRACE ⟨his behavior ~*ed* his family⟩ **4 :** to refuse to accept or pay (as a draft, bill, check, or note that is duly presented for acceptance or payment)
dis·honorable \"+\ *adj* [prob. fr. MF, fr. *des-* ˈ*dis-* + *honorable*] **1 :** lacking honor **:** not honorable **:** bringing or deserving dishonor **:** SHAMEFUL, DISGRACEFUL ⟨the ~ conduct of trusted men⟩ ⟨a man ~ in thought and deed⟩ **2** *obs* **:** lacking esteem **:** DISESTEEMED, UNHONORED ⟨to find ourselves ~ graves —Shak.⟩
dishonorable discharge *n* **:** a discharge (as from employment or a position of trust or responsibility) without favorable recommendation; *specif* **:** a formal release without honor from military service given as a result of a sentence by a court-martial
dis·honorableness \dəs, (ˈ)dis+\ *n* -ES **:** the quality or state of being dishonorable
dis·honorably \dəs, (ˈ)dis +\ *adv* **:** in a dishonorable manner ⟨~ used his position for personal gain⟩
dis·honorer \"+\ *n* **:** one that dishonors
dis·horn \dəs, (ˈ)dis+\ *vt* [ˈ*dis-* + *horn* (n.)] **:** to remove the horns from
dis·horse \dəs, (ˈ)dis+\ *vb* [ˈ*dis-* + *horse* (n.)] **:** DISMOUNT
dis·house \dəsˈhau̇z, (ˈ)dis¦h-\ *vt* [ˈ*dis-* + *house* (n.)] **1 :** to deprive of a house **:** put out of a house **2 :** to clear (an area) of houses
dish out *vt* **1 :** to serve (food) from a dish **:** distribute in portions at table ⟨she *dished out* the chowder⟩ **2 a :** GIVE, PROVIDE, RELEASE ⟨*dishing out* important news releases⟩ ⟨those doctors who *dish out* opiates at the slightest provocation⟩ **b** *slang* **:** to present in glib, effusive, or exuberant outpourings ⟨that salesman could really *dish it out*⟩ ⟨you could *dish out* a memorized spiel —W.L.Gresham⟩
dishpan \ˈ=,=\ *n* **:** a large flat-bottomed orig. round or oval pan used for washing dishes; *broadly* **:** something (as a boat or a reflector) felt to resemble a dishpan
dishpan hands *n pl but sing or pl in constr* **:** a condition of dryness, redness, and scaling of the hands resulting typically from the constant exposure to, sensitivity to, or overuse of cleaning materials and other substances that are used in housework
dishrag \ˈ=,=\ *n* **1 :** DISHCLOTH **2** *or* **dishrag gourd :** DISHCLOTH GOURD **3 :** a pivoting of a dance couple under raised joined hands
dish ring *n* **:** a ring-shaped stand formerly used under dishes of hot food — called also *potato ring*
dish top *n* **:** a table top with a raised molded edge
dish towel *n* **:** a cloth for drying dishes
dish turner *n* **:** a worker who turns wooden dishes on a lathe
dish turning *n* **:** the process of turning wooden dishes on a lathe
ˈ**dishwash** \ˈ=,=\ *n* **1** *obs* **:** DISHWATER **2 :** NONSENSE
²**dishwash** \ˈ=,=\ *vi* **:** to cleanse dishes and other table and cookery utensils by washing esp. as a regular task or means of livelihood
dishwasher \ˈ=,==\ *n* **:** one that washes dishes: **a :** a worker employed to wash dishes (as in a restaurant) **b :** a contrivance or machine for washing dishes (as by means of jets of cleaning solution and water)
dishwater \ˈ=,==\ *n* **:** water in which dishes have been or are to be washed; *also* **:** any of various things felt to resemble dishwater (as in dullness, weakness, or uncleanness)
dishwatery \ˈ=,===\ *adj* **:** like dishwater esp. in weak or attenuated character ⟨~ speeches⟩
dis·identify \¦dis+\ *vt* [ˈ*dis-* + *identify*] **:** to rid of identity or characteristic qualities; *also* **:** DISSOCIATE
di·silane *also* **di·silicane** \(ˈ)dī+\ *n* -s [*di-* + *silane* or *silicane*] **:** a liquid compound Si_2H_6 of silicon and hydrogen that is spontaneously flammable in air
di·silicate \(ˈ)dī+\ *n* [*di-* + *silicate*] **:** a silicate containing two atoms of silicon in the molecule ⟨sodium ~⟩
di·silicide \(ˈ)dī+\ *n* [*di-* + *silicide*] **:** a compound containing two atoms of silicon combined with an element or radical
dis·illude \¦dis+\ *vt* -ED/-ING/-S [ˈ*dis-* + *illude*] **:** DISILLUSION
ˈ**dis·illusion** \¦dis+\ *n* [ˈ*dis-* + *illusion*] **1 :** the lack or loss of faith in illusions or in hopes previously held **:** DISENCHANTMENT ⟨facile ~ of our romantic intellectuals —*New Republic*⟩ **2 :** the state of having lost faith or illusions; *also* **:** an instance of this ⟨romantic ~s and tangled, tragic problems —H.E. Salisbury⟩
²**disillusion** \"\ *also* **dis·il·lu·sion·ize** \,==ˈ=zhə,nīz\ *vt* **disillusioned** *also* **disillusionized; disillusioned** *also* **disillusionized; disillusioning** \-zh(ə)niŋ\ *also* **disillusionizing; disillusions** *also* **disillusionizes :** to free from or deprive of illusion **:** DISENCHANT ⟨~*ed* his fans by his sloppy play⟩ — **dis·il·lu·sion·ist** \,==ˈ=zhənə̇st, -zhnə̇st\ *n* — **dis·il·lu·sion·iz·er** \-zhə,nīzə(r)\ *n* -s
dis·illusionary \¦dis+\ *or* **dis·illusive** \"+\ *adj* **:** constituting or tending to induce disillusion ⟨~ practices⟩
dis·il·lu·sion·ment \,disə̇ˈlüzhənmənt *also* -səlˈyü-\ *n* -s **1 :** the state or process of being disillusioned ⟨the ~ of youth at the way the world was run —Agnes Repplier⟩ ⟨another novel about ~ with communism —Granville Hicks⟩ **2 :** an instance of being disillusioned ⟨a study of the ~s of the Australian radio world —Leslie Rees⟩
dis·imagine \¦dis+\ *vt* [ˈ*dis-* + *imagine*] **:** to dispel from existence in the imagination
dis·impassioned \¦dis+\ *adj* [ˈ*dis-* + *impassioned*] **:** divested of warmth of passion or feeling **:** CALM, COOL, DISPASSIONATE
dis·imprison \¦dis+\ *vt* [ˈ*dis-* + *imprison*] **:** to release from confinement — **dis·imprisonment** \"+\ *n*
dis·improve \¦dis+\ *vb* [ˈ*dis-* + *improve*] *vt* **:** to make worse ~ *vi* **:** to become worse — **dis·improvement** \"+\ *n*
dis·incarnate \¦dis+\ *or* **dis·incarnated** \"+\ *adj* [ˈ*dis-* + *incarnate, incarnated*] **:** free of or freed from the demands of the body **:** DISEMBODIED
dis·incarnation \dəs, (¦)dis+\ *n* [ˈ*dis* + *incarnation*] **:** the quality or state of being disincarnate
dis·incentive \¦dis+\ *n* [ˈ*dis-* + *incentive*] **:** something that stands in the way esp. of economic progress or production ⟨excessive taxes form a major ~ to industrial expansion in many states⟩
dis·inclination \dəs, (¦)dis+\ *n* [ˈ*dis-* + *inclination*] **:** a state of unwillingness **:** lack of inclination **:** DISTASTE, DISLIKE — usu. used with *to*, occas. with *for* ⟨a distinct ~ to stir from the hammock⟩ ⟨my ~ to reading arose early in life⟩
dis·incline \¦dis+\ *vt* [ˈ*dis-* + *incline*] **:** to turn away the inclination of **:** make unwilling or averse ⟨his background ~s him from needless disciplining of his subordinates⟩
disinclined *adj* **:** unwilling because of lack of inclination or through mild doubt or disapproval ⟨~ to go out⟩ ⟨~ to accept his story⟩ **:** lacking desire ⟨~ for conversation⟩
syn DISINCLINED, INDISPOSED, HESITANT, RELUCTANT, LOATH (or LOTH), and AVERSE can mean, in common, not having or not seeming to have the full will or desire to do, or have to do with, a thing indicated or implied. DISINCLINED implies a lack of taste or inclination ⟨*disinclined* to go to the movies⟩ ⟨the Italian, so affable as a rule, was rather preoccupied and *disinclined* for talk —Norman Douglas⟩ ⟨the various writers are *disinclined* to come to real grips with the vexed question of public control in industry —M.R.Cohen⟩ INDISPOSED implies an unfavorable, often hostile or unsympathetic attitude ⟨they were *indisposed* to put money into foolish enterprises⟩ HESITANT implies a holding back as through fear, uncertainty, or irresolution ⟨he smiled, in a *hesitant* way, as though not sure how Walter would take such familiarity on his part —T.B.Costain⟩ ⟨*hesitant* about spending the money required to build an experimental plant —Harold Griffin⟩ RELUCTANT implies a holding back through unwillingness ⟨he was *reluctant* to speak out, afraid to let his emotions seize upon his speech —V.L.Parrington⟩ ⟨worked only one shift, because workers were *reluctant* to change their accustomed hours —*Time*⟩ ⟨his passionate appeal to their loyalty wrested a *reluctant* assent to the prosecution of the war —J.R.Green⟩ LOATH connotes a prospective act incompatible with one's feelings, convictions, or makeup ⟨Frederick stood at the door, *loath* to go without some shred of victory to take with him —Irwin Shaw⟩ ⟨*loth* to perjure himself⟩ ⟨publishers have been *loath* to publish translations of anything except our surefire sex-and-mayhem fiction —W.H.Whyte⟩ AVERSE suggests a turning away from something distasteful or repugnant ⟨the adventurers, though not *averse* to courting, being unwilling to entangle themselves in a matrimonial alliance —Herman Melville⟩ ⟨not insensible to the power of female beauty, nor *averse* from excess in wine —T.B.Macaulay⟩ ⟨politicians . . . *averse* from political suicide —W.K.Hancock⟩ ⟨slow of speech, tenacious of opinion, and *averse* . . . to innovation of any sort —C.B.Nordhoff & J.N. Hall⟩
dis·incorporate \¦dis¦==,rāt\ *vt* [ˈ*dis-* + *incorporate*] **:** to deprive of corporate powers, rights, or existence **:** divest of the condition of a corporate body
dis·incorporation \¦dis+\ *n* **:** the quality or state of being disincorporated
dis·infect \¦dis+\ *vt* [MF *desinfecter*, fr. *des-* ˈ*dis-* + *infecter* to infect — more at INFECT] **:** to free from infection esp. by destroying harmful microorganisms; *broadly* **:** to relieve of some undesirable quality ⟨he must ~ his speech of emotional overtone —Irwin Edman⟩ **:** CLEANSE
ˈ**dis·in·fec·tant** \,disə̇nˈfektənt\ *n* -s [F *désinfectant*, fr. pres. part. of *désinfecter* to disinfect] **:** an agent that frees from infection; *esp* **:** a chemical that destroys vegetative forms of harmful microorganisms but not ordinarily bacterial spores — used esp. of substances suitable for application to inanimate objects; compare GERMICIDE
²**disinfectant** \¦==¦==\ *adj* [F *désinfectant*, pres. part.] **:** serving or tending to disinfect **:** suitable for use in disinfecting
disinfecting candle *n* **:** a cylinder or cone of a combustible mixture usu. containing sulfur or formaldehyde that is burned for disinfecting purposes
dis·infection \¦dis+\ *n* **:** the act or process of disinfecting
dis·infective \"+\ *adj* **:** DISINFECTANT
dis·infector \"+\ *n* **:** one that disinfects; *esp* **:** an apparatus for applying disinfectants
dis·infest \¦dis+\ *vt* [ˈ*dis-* + *infest*] **:** to rid (as a house, a plant, or the intestine) of infestation **:** free from infesting insects, rodents, or other small animals — **dis·infestation** \(¦)dis+\ *n*
dis·in·fes·tant \,disə̇nˈfestənt\ *n* -s **:** a disinfesting agent
dis·in·fes·tor \-tə(r)\ *n* -s **:** an agent or apparatus for disinfesting
dis·infeudation \dəs, (¦)dis+\ *n* [ˈ*dis-* + *infeudation*] **:** release from feudal tenure or obligation
dis·inflate \¦dis+\ *vb* [ˈ*dis-* + *inflate*] **:** DEFLATE
dis·inflation \"+\ *n* [*dis-* + *inflation*] **:** a reversal of inflationary pressures manifested by a leveling off or a moderate decline in prices **:** DEFLATION — **dis·inflationary** \"+\ *adj*
dis·ingenuity \dəs, (¦)dis+\ *n* [ˈ*dis-* + *ingenuity*] **:** disingenuous state, behavior, or act
dis·ingenuous \¦dis+\ *adj* [ˈ*dis-* + *ingenuous*] **:** not ingenuous **:** lacking in candor or frankness; *often* **:** unworthily or meanly artful **:** giving a false appearance of simple frankness — **dis·ingenuously** \"+\ *adv* — **dis·ingenuousness** \"+\ *n*
dis·inhabit \¦dis+\ *vt* [ˈ*dis-* + *inhabit*] *archaic* **:** DISPEOPLE
dis·in·her·i·son \,disə̇nˈherəsən, -rəzən\ *n* -s [alter. (influenced by *disinherit*) of *disherison*] **:** DISHERISON
dis·inherit \¦dis+\ *vt* [ME *disinheriten*, fr. ˈ*dis-* + *inheriten* to inherit — more at INHERIT] **1 :** to deprive (an heir apparent) of the right to inherit **:** prevent deliberately (as by making a will) from coming into possession of a property right or title that would otherwise devolve on the heir by law or custom in the course of descent **2 a :** to deprive of natural or human rights ⟨the ~*ed* millions behind the iron curtain⟩ **b :** to deprive of special privileges previously held ⟨as the peoples of Asia and Africa stir and gradually ~ the colonial powers⟩
syn see DEPRIVE
dis·inheritance \"+\ *also* **dis·in·her·i·ta·tion** \¦disə̇n,herəˈtāshən\ *n* -s **:** an act of disinheriting or the state of being disinherited
dis·inhibition \dəs, (¦)dis+\ *n* [ˈ*dis-* + *inhibition*] **:** loss of a conditioned reflex (as by the action of interfering stimuli)
dis·inhibitory \¦dis+\ *adj* [ˈ*dis-* + *inhibitory*] **:** tending to overcome esp. psychological inhibition ⟨~ drugs⟩
dis·inhume \¦dis+\ *vt* [ˈ*dis-* + *inhume*] **:** DISINTER
dis·in·sec·ti·za·tion \,disə̇n,sektə̇ˈzāshən\ *n* -s [ˈ*dis-* + *insect* + *-ization*] **:** removal of insects (as from an aircraft) ⟨a ~ squad⟩
dis·integrable \də̇s+\ *adj* [*disintegrate* + *-able*] **:** capable of being disintegrated
dis·integrate \də̇s+\ *vb* [*dis-* + *integrate*] *vt* **1 :** to break or decompose (something) into constituent elements or into parts ⟨their attacks gradually *disintegrated* the government⟩ **2 a :** to reduce (rock) to particulate matter (as by weathering) **b :** to shatter (as a building) suddenly into bits (as by exploding) **c :** to cause disintegration of (an atomic nucleus) ~ *vi* **1 :** to break or separate into constituent elements or parts ⟨with the rise of nationalism, the colonial empires *disintegrated*⟩ **2 a** *of rock* **:** to become reduced to particulate matter usu. through the action of natural forces ⟨the older strata gradually ~⟩ **b** *of a structure* **:** to shatter suddenly **:** fly to bits ⟨the flaming building suddenly *disintegrated*⟩ ⟨the plane hit the ground and *disintegrated*⟩ **c :** to deteriorate by or as if by breaking into constituent parts ⟨asked if he thought theater was *disintegrating* —Louise Mace⟩ ⟨an actor long since *disintegrated* by the blacklist —Murray Kempton⟩ ⟨the *disintegrating* features of an aging woman —Philip Wylie⟩ **d :** to undergo disintegration — used of an atomic nucleus, a neutron, or a meson **syn** see DECAY
dis·integration \dəs, (,)dis+\ *n* **1 :** the act or process of disintegrating or state of being disintegrated ⟨~ of personality⟩; *specif* **:** a change in the composition of an atomic nucleus whether occurring spontaneously (as in the ejection of particles from the nucleus in radioactivity) or as a result of bombardment by particles (as by neutrons or protons) **2 :** the transformation of an elementary particle into others (as of a neutron into a proton and electron)
disintegration constant *n* **:** DECAY CONSTANT
dis·in·te·gra·tion·ist \-sh(ə)nə̇st\ *n* **:** a person who favors disintegration esp. of a social structure or order
dis·integrative \də̇s+\ *adj* **:** tending to induce disintegration ⟨~ influences⟩
dis·integrator \də̇s+\ *n* **:** one that disintegrates (as a machine for grinding or pulverizing); *specif* **:** a substance used in tablet formulations to cause the tablet to break up on contact with moisture and exert its medicinal action promptly
dis·in·te·grous \də̇ˈsintəgrəs, ¦disə̇nˈtegrəs\ *adj* [*disintegrate* + *-ous*] **:** lacking cohesion
dis·inter \¦dis+\ *vt* [ˈ*dis-* + *inter*] **1 :** to take out of the grave or tomb **:** to dig up **:** EXHUME **2 :** to bring out of concealment **:** bring from obscurity into view **:** UNEARTH ⟨plays . . . remained unknown . . . until *disinterred* by a painstaking bibliophile —Saxe Commins⟩ **syn** see DIG
disinteress *vt* -ED/-ING/-ES [F *désintéresser*, fr. *dés-* ˈ*dis* + *intéresser* to interest — more at INTEREST] *obs* **:** DISINTEREST
ˈ**dis·interest** \dəs, (ˈ)dis+\ *vt* [ˈ*dis-* + *interest* (v.)] **:** to divest of interest or interested motives ⟨criminal case histories, which usually have a way of ~*ing* theater audiences —G.J. Nathan⟩
²**disinterest** \"\ *n* [ˈ*dis-* + *interest* (n.)] **1 :** something contrary to interest **:** DISADVANTAGE ⟨to the ~ of the public⟩ **2 :** DISINTERESTEDNESS **:** lack of self-interest ⟨the highest honor is ~ —James Martineau⟩ **3 :** lack of interest **:** APATHY, UNCONCERN ⟨two soldiers with slovenly ~ on their unlighted faces —Bruce Marshall⟩ ⟨the monumental ~ of the voters —Don Shoemaker⟩
disinterested *adj* **1 :** lacking or revealing lack of interest **:** INDIFFERENT, UNINTERESTED, APATHETIC, UNCONCERNED **2 :** not influenced by regard to personal advantage **:** free from selfish motive **:** not biased or prejudiced ⟨a ~ decision⟩ ⟨~ sacrifices⟩ **syn** see INDIFFERENT
dis·interestedly \dəs, (ˈ)dis+\ *adv* **:** in a disinterested manner; *usu* **:** without bias or selfish motive
dis·interestedness \"+\ *n* **:** disinterested state; *usu* **:** freedom from bias or selfish motives
disinteresting *adj* **:** not interesting
dis·interment \¦dis+\ *n* **1 :** the act of disinterring **:** EXHUMATION **2 :** something brought to light
dis·intoxication \¦dis+\ *n* [*dis-* + *intoxication*] **:** the freeing of an individual from an intoxicating agent (as an addict from a drug) stored in the body
dis·invest \¦dis+\ *vb* [ˈ*dis-* + *invest*] *vt* **:** to subject to disinvestment ~ *vi* **:** to engage in disinvestment (as by selling capital assets)

dis·investment \"+\ *n* **:** consumption of capital (as by uncompensated deterioration of assets or using up of stored inventory) ⟨~ in the economic sense occurs when national consumption exceeds national income —J.O.Kamm⟩; *sometimes* **:** withdrawal of capital from investment or from an investment
disinvite *vt* [*dis-* + *invite*] *obs* **:** to recall an invitation to
dis·in·vol·ture \,disən'välchə(r), -vōl-,-vōl-\ *n* -s [F *désinvolture*, fr. It *disinvoltura*, fr. *disinvolto* unconstrained, unembarrassed (fr. past part. of *disinvolgere* to unwrap, fr. *dis-* [1]dis- — fr. L *dis-* — + *involgere* to wrap) + *-ura* -ure; It *disinvolto*, trans. of Sp *desenvuelto*] **:** an unconstrained free and easy manner
dis·involve \¦dis+\ *vt* [[1]*dis-* + *involve*] **:** to relieve from involvement **:** DISENTANGLE
dis·jas·kit *also* **dis·jas·ked** \dəs'jaskət\ *adj* [perh. alter. of *dejected*] **1** *Scot* **:** DEPRESSED, DEJECTED **2** *Scot* **:** BROKEN-DOWN, DILAPIDATED
dis·ject \dəs'jekt\ *vt* -ED/-ING/-S [L *disjectus*, past part. of *disjicere*, fr. *dis-* apart + *-jicere* (fr. *jacere* to throw) — more at DIS-, JET] **:** to scatter about **:** DISPERSE
dis·jec·ta mem·bra \dəs¦jektə'membrə\ *n pl* [L] **:** scattered parts; *usu* **:** literary fragments or disjointed quotations
dis·jec·tion \dəs'jekshən\ *n* -s **:** the act of scattering or state of being scattered **:** DISPERSION
dis·join \dəs, (')dis+\ *vb* [MF *desjoin-*, stem of *desjoindre*, fr. L *disjungere*, fr. *dis-* [1]dis- + *jungere* to join — more at YOKE] *vt* **:** to bring to an end the joining of **:** SEPARATE, DISUNITE, PART, SUNDER ⟨that marriage, therefore, God himself ~*s* —John Milton⟩ ⟨~*s* the physical cause from the final end —A.N.Whitehead⟩ ~ *vi* **:** to become detached **:** SEPARATE, PART ⟨the bivalents ~ normally —*Genetics*⟩
dis·join·able \-nəbəl\ *adj* **:** fit or suitable for disjoining
disjoined *adj, of a heraldic cross* **:** voided with the voiding extending through the ends of the four arms so as to leave only the sides of the arms outlined
[1]**dis·joint** \dəs, (')dis+\ *adj* [ME *disjoynt*, fr. MF *desjoint*, past part. of *desjoindre* to disjoin — more at DISJOIN] **1** *obs* **:** DISJOINTED **2 :** having no members in common ⟨~ sets⟩
[2]**dis·joint** \dəs, (')dis+\ *vb* [ME *disyointen*, fr. MF *desjoint*, past part.] *vt* **1 :** to separate the parts of **:** break up into divisions **:** disturb or undo the connections, order, or coherence of **:** DISLOCATE ⟨her work suffers from her reluctance to come to absolute grips with her subject, and this reluctance ~*s* her writing —*New Yorker*⟩ **2 :** to undo the joining of **:** DISUNITE ⟨Great Britain, ~*ed* from her colonies —Thomas Jefferson⟩ **3 :** to separate at junctures or joints **:** dissect, carve, or break into pieces at the joints ⟨~ a frying chicken⟩ ~ *vi* **:** to separate at the joints
disjointed *adj* **1 :** separated at or as if at the joint **:** DISLOCATED ⟨a ~ hip⟩ **2 :** DISCONNECTED, DISORDERED ⟨a ~ society⟩; *esp* **:** INCOHERENT ⟨~ words⟩ ⟨~ conversation⟩ — **dis·joint·ed·ly** *adv* — **dis·joint·ed·ness** *n*
dis·joint·ly \dəs'jȯintlē, (')dis¦j-\ *adv* [[1]*disjoint* + *-ly*] **1 :** in a disjointed state **:** SEPARATELY — opposed to *conjointly* **2 :** DISCONNECTEDLY, INCOHERENTLY
dis·join·ture \dəs, (')dis+\ *n* **:** absence of connection **:** SEPARATION
[1]**dis·junct** \dəs'jəŋ(k)t, (')dis¦j-\ *adj* [L *disjunctus*, past part. of *disjungere* to disjoin — more at DISJOIN] **:** marked by separation of or from usu. contiguous parts or individuals ⟨little isolated worlds, as abruptly ~ and unexpected . . . as a palm-shaded well in the Sahara —*Scientific Monthly*⟩: as **a :** DISCONTINUOUS — now used almost entirely of distributions (as of statistical or natural populations) ⟨genera that are ~ between New and Old World xerophytic areas⟩ ⟨the ~ distribution of the king crabs⟩ **b :** relating to melodic progression by intervals larger than a major second — contrasted with *conjunct* **c** *of certain insects* **:** having head, thorax, and abdomen separated by deep constrictions
[2]**dis·junct** \'dis,jəŋ(k)t\ *n* -s **:** any of the alternatives comprising a logical disjunction
dis·junction \dəs, (')dis+\ *n* [ME *disjunccioun*, fr. L *disjunction-, disjunctio*, fr. *disjunctus* + *-ion-, -io* -ion] **1 :** the act of disjoining or state of being disjoined **:** DISUNION, SEPARATION, PARTING ⟨the ~ of soul and body⟩ **2 :** the relation of the terms or clauses of a logical proposition or judgment expressing alternatives; *also* **:** a statement of such a proposition usu. taking the form (1) *p* v *q* meaning *p* or *q* or both or (2) *p* + *q* meaning *p* or *q* but not both — called also respectively (1) *inclusive disjunction*, (2) *exclusive disjunction* **3 :** an area of discontinuity between areas in which populations of a specified organism are present
dis·junctional \"+\ *adj* **:** involving disjunction **:** by means of disjunction
[1]**dis·junctive** \dəs'jəŋ(k)tiv\ *n* -s [LL & L *disjunctivus*, adj.] **1 :** a disjunctive conjunction **2** *in Hebrew orthography* **:** a disjunctive accent **3 :** DISJUNCTION 2; *broadly* **:** a situation involving alternate choices
[2]**dis·junc·tive** \dəs'=,=, (')dis¦==\ *adj* [L *disjunctivus*, fr. *disjunctus* + *-ivus* -ive] **1 a :** tending to disjoin **:** involving disjunction **:** SEPARATIVE **b** *of a vowel* **:** epenthesized in a cluster of consonants to facilitate pronunciation ⟨the parasitic vowel \ə\ in the pronunciation \'athə,lēt\ of *athlete* is ~⟩ **2** [LL *disjunctivus*, fr. L] **a** *of a conjunction* **:** expressing an alternative, contrast, or opposition between the meanings of the words or word groups that it connects ⟨the ~ conjunctions *or* in "peas or beans", *either . . . or* in "either milk or cream", *but* in "small but important", and *though* in "they went on playing ball though it was raining"⟩ — contrasted with *copulative* **b :** pleading or marked by mutually exclusive alternatives joined by "or" ⟨the ~ statement *the defendant knew or ought to have known*⟩ ⟨~ pleading⟩ **3** *of a pronoun form* **:** stressed and not attached to the verb as an enclitic or proclitic (as French *moi, lui, toi, soi*) — contrasted with *conjunctive* **4** *in Hebrew orthography* **:** indicating that the word marked is separated to a greater or less degree rhythmically and grammatically from the word which follows it — used of an accent; opposed to *conjunctive* — **dis·junc·tive·ly** \-təvlē\ *adv*
disjunctive legacy *n, Roman law* **:** a legacy of the same thing given to two or more persons that is expressed in separate clauses with the latter gift or gifts apparently encroaching on the first gift
dis·junc·tiv·i·ty \(,)dis,jəŋ(k)'tivəd·ē, dəs-\ *n* -ES **:** disjunctive state or quality
disjunct motion *n, music* **:** a succession of notes in a part progressing by intervals larger than a major second
dis·junc·tor \dəs'jəŋ(k)tə(r)\ *n* -s **1 :** a device for disconnecting an electrical circuit **2 :** a small cellulose body interposed between the conidia of certain fungi that ultimately breaks down and sets them free
disjunct species *n pl* **:** different logical species falling coordinately under a single genus
disjunct tetrachord *n* **:** either of two successive tetrachords in which the lowest tone of one is one step from the highest tone of the other
dis·juncture \dəs, (')dis+\ *n* [ME, modif. (influenced by L *disjunctus*) of MF *desjointure*, fr. *desjoint* (past part. of *desjoindre* to disjoin) + *-ure* — more at DISJOIN] **:** DISJUNCTION
dis·june \dəs'jün\ *n* -s [ME (Sc dial.) *disione*, fr. MF *desjun*, *desjeun*, fr. *desjuner*, *desjeuner* to breakfast, fr. (assumed) VL *disjejunare* to break one's fast] *Scot* **:** BREAKFAST
[1]**disk** *or* **disc** \'disk\ *n* -s *often attrib* [L *discus* dish, disk, quoit — more at DISH] **1** *archaic* **:** DISCUS 1 **2 :** the seemingly flat figure or image of a celestial body as it appears in the heavens **3 :** any of several more or less rounded and flattened plant structures: as **a :** the central portion of the flower head of a typical composite composed of closely packed tubular flowers — see DISCOID **b** *usu disc* **:** an enlargement of the torus surrounding, beneath, or above the pistil of some flowers **c :** the curved spore-bearing surface of an apothecium; *also* **:** one of the central upper portion of the pileus of a mushroom **d :** one of the adhesive circular enlargements at the ends of the tendrils in the Virginia creeper, Boston ivy, and similar plants by which they climb flat surfaces; *also* **:** any similar adhesive surface (as the base of a pollinium) **4 :** any of various rounded and flattened animal anatomical structures: as **a :** the flattened circumoral part of a coelenterate (as a sea anemone) **b** *usu disc* **:** the body of an echinoderm **c :** the area of modified plumage surrounding the eye of an owl **d :** a mammalian red blood cell **e :** OPTIC DISK **f :** INTERVERTEBRAL DISK **5 :** a thin circular object ⟨a metal ~⟩: as **a :** DISCOIDAL **b :** a round dish used in the Eastern Orthodox Church to hold the host **c :** a small tablet with glycerogelatin base used in eye medication; *also* **:** a small medicated mass of sugar and egg albumen used in homeopathic practice **d :** [3]PUCK 2a **e :** one of the circular wooden pieces used in shuffleboard **f** *usu disc* **:** a phonograph record **6 :** a rotating abrasive device used in dentistry **7 :** a circular symbol used by ancient Egyptians to represent the sun **8** *usu disc* **:** one of the concave circular hardened steel tools with sharpened edge that make up the working part of a disc harrow or plow; *often* **:** an implement employing such tools **:** DISC HARROW, DISC PLOW **9** *usu disc* **:** a small flat woman's hat of oval shape usu. worn forward on the head

head of chamomile, *d* disk, *r* rays

[2]**disk** *or* **disc** \"\ *vt* -ED/-ING/-S **1 :** to cultivate with a disc harrow or disc cultivator **2** *usu disc* **:** to record on a phonograph disc
disk barrow *n* **:** a flat circular tumulus of the Bronze Age
disk bat *n* [so called fr. the appearance of the suckers] **:** any of several tropical American bats (family Thyropteridae) distinguished by the presence on the thumbs and on the soles of the hind feet of suckers by which they can hang from a smooth surface — called also *disk-wing bat*
disk bit *n* **:** a rotary drill bit consisting of sharp-edged disks set vertically
disk brake *n* **:** a friction brake in which the surfaces that rub together are in the form of disks
disk cipher *n, cryptology* **:** a cipher using the cipher disk
disk clutch *n* **:** a friction clutch in which the friction is between two parallel flat plates or sets of such plates
disk crank *n* **:** a balanced crank consisting of a disk revolving about its center and having a crankpin secured eccentrically in it
disk drill *n* **1 :** a primitive drill in which the shaft is weighted by a disk and which is operated by a strap or bow **2** *usu* **disc drill :** a drill for sowing grain or seeds using discs as furrow openers
di·skel·i·on \dī'skelēən, də'-, -ē,än\ *n* -s [NL, fr. *di-* + *-skelion* (as in *triskelion*)] **:** a figure like the triskelion but with only two radiating members
disk engine *n* **:** any of various rotary engines in which the piston or its equivalent is a rotating or wobbling disk
disk·er \'diskə(r)\ *n* -s **:** a worker who readies automobile bodies for painting
disk·ery \-kərē\ *n* -ES [[1]*disk* + *-ery*] *slang* **:** a phonograph-record manufacturer
disk flower *also* **disk floret** *n* **:** one of the tubular flowers in the disk of a composite plant — see COMPOSITE illustration
disk grinder *n* **:** a grinding machine equipped with one or more abrasive-coated disks that usu. revolve at high speed
diskindness *n* [[1]*dis-* + *kindness*] *obs* **:** UNKINDNESS
disk jockey *var of* DISC JOCKEY
disk·less \'diskləs\ *adj* **:** lacking a disk
disklike *or* **disclike** \'=,=\ *adj* **:** circular and nearly flat ⟨a ~ acetabulum⟩
disk meter *n* **:** a meter for measuring fluids that has a disk that controls the alternate filling and emptying of the measuring chambers
disk of confusion : CIRCLE OF CONFUSION
dis·ko·gram \'diskə,gram\ *n* -s [[1]*disk* + *-o-* + *-gram*] **:** a roentgenogram of an intervertebral disk made after injection of a radiopaque substance — **dis·kog·ra·phy** \də'skägrəfē\ *n* -ES
disk pile *n* **:** a steel pile having a disk on its lower end to give increased supporting power
disk sander *n* **:** a machine having one or more flat circular disks faced with abrasive for smoothing wood surfaces (as floors)
disk-shaped \'=,=\ *adj* **:** flat and circular
disk signal *n* **:** an automatic block signal indicating train movements by the positions of colored disks
disk telegraph *n* **:** DIAL TELEGRAPH
disk-urchin \'=,==\ *n* **:** a flattened sea urchin (as a sand dollar or a keyhole urchin)
disk valve *n* **:** a valve opened or closed by a disk; *often* **:** a suction valve operated by a flexible disk (as of rubber or leather)
disk wheel *n* **1 :** a disk having a spiral on its flat face for engaging with a worm wheel **2 :** a wheel presenting a solid convex or concave surface from hub to rim
disk-wing bat *n* **:** DISK BAT
dis·leaf *or* **dis·leave** \dəs, (')dis+\ *vt* **disleafed** *or* **disleaved; disleafed** *or* **disleaved; disleafing** *or* **disleaving; disleafs** *or* **disleaves** [[1]*dis-* + *leaf* (n.)] *archaic* **:** to remove the leaves from **:** strip of leaves ⟨the cankerworm that annually *disleaved* the elms —J.R.Lowell⟩
disleal *adj* [[1]*dis-* + *leal*] *obs* **:** DISLOYAL, PERFIDIOUS
dis·likable *or* **dis·likeable** \dəs, (')dis+\ *adj* **:** such as to provoke dislike **:** UNLIKABLE
dis·likably *or* **dis·likeably** \"+\ *adv* **:** in a dislikable manner
[1]**dis·like** \dəs, (')dis+\ *vt* [[1]*dis-* + *like* (v.)] **1** *archaic* **:** to awaken dislike in **:** DISPLEASE **2 :** to regard with dislike **:** feel aversion for **:** DISAPPROVE ⟨the two . . . *disliked* each other by instinct —Henry Adams⟩ **3** *obs* **:** to show aversion to
[2]**dislike** \"\ *n* **1 :** a feeling of positive aversion (as to something unpleasant, uncongenial, or offensive) **:** DISAPPROBATION, REPUGNANCE, DISPLEASURE, DISFAVOR ⟨our determined ~ of hard work⟩ **2** *obs* **:** DISCORD, DISSENSION
syn DISLIKE, DISTASTE, AVERSION, and DISFAVOR agree in designating a state of mind or feeling marked by an inner shunning or avoiding of something or a finding of it unpleasant or positively repugnant. DISLIKE may, on the one hand, imply the mere finding of something unpleasant or, on the other, a reacting to it with detestation ⟨known . . . for his *dislike* of large social functions —*Current Biog.*⟩ ⟨an aristocratic disdain and *dislike* of the bourgeoisie, whose virtues and shortcomings are alike displeasing to both the upper and the lower classes —W.R.Inge⟩ ⟨concerning phobias, care should be exercised in differentiating between mere aversion and *dislike* and morbid unreasonable fear or dread —H.G.Armstrong⟩ ⟨I don't mean *dislike*, or find distasteful, or have an aversion for; I mean hate —Hamilton Basso⟩ DISTASTE stresses a squeamishness or repugnance ⟨viewing liquor and tobacco with *distaste* —John Lawler⟩ ⟨a disdain amounting at times to a violent physical *distaste* for practically every human component of their lives —Florence Bullock⟩ ⟨the individual's *distaste* for his occupation —H.G.Armstrong⟩ AVERSION is stronger, stressing avoidance or a desire to evade or escape ⟨they stared at each other with instinctive repudiation, *aversion* almost —Margery Sharp⟩ ⟨the natural human *aversion* to cold, noise, vibration, high places, rapid ascents and descents, and the unfriendly and lonesome environment at high altitude —H.G. Armstrong⟩ DISFAVOR is the weakest of these four nouns, usu. suggesting no feeling stronger than disapproval though sometimes it may imply contempt or disdain as motives ⟨to look with *disfavor* upon frivolous conduct in public⟩ ⟨his father's *disfavor* prevented his asking for an allowance until more amicable relations should be established⟩
[3]**dislike** *adj* [[1]*dis-* + *like* (adj.)] *obs* **:** UNLIKE
dis·like·ful \dəs'līkfəl, (')dis¦l-\ *adj* **:** DISAGREEABLE
disliken *vt* [[3]*dislike* + *-en*] *obs* **:** to make unlike **:** DISGUISE
dis·lik·er \-kə(r)\ *n* **:** one that dislikes
disliking *n* [fr. gerund of [1]*dislike*] **:** DISLIKE, DISAPPROVAL
dis·limb \dəs, (')dis+\ *vt* [[1]*dis-* + *limb* (n.)] **:** DISMEMBER
dis·limn \dəs, (')dis+\ *vb* [[1]*dis-* + *limn*] **:** DIM ⟨the nocturnal pageant has ~*ed* and vanished —Thomas De Quincey⟩
dis·link \dəs, (')dis+\ *vt* [[1]*dis-* + *link*] **:** DISUNITE, UNCOUPLE, UNLINK, SEPARATE
dis·load \dəs, (')dis+\ *vb* [[1]*dis-* + *load*] **:** UNLOAD, DISBURDEN
dis·lo·ca·ble \'di(,)slōkəbəl *also* 'disləˌk- *or* də'slō- *or* 'di'slōk-\ *adj* [*dislocate* + *-able*] **:** subject to dislocation
[1]**dis·lo·cate** \'dis(,)lō,kāt *also* 'dislə,k- də'slō- *or* 'di'slō- *sometimes* ,dis¦lō'k- *or* ,dislə'k-; *usu* -ād·+V\ *vt* [ML *dislocatus*, past part. of *dislocare*, fr. L *dis-* [1]dis- + *locare* to place — more at LOCATE] **1 :** to put out of place: as **a :** to put (a body part) out of order by displacing a bone from its normal connections with another bone or other bones ⟨he slipped and *dislocated* his shoulder⟩; *also* **:** to displace (a bone) from normal connections with another bone or other bones ⟨the humerus was completely *dislocated* in the fall⟩ **b :** to displace from a former or proper place **:** move away from contiguous items **:** REMOVE ⟨*dislocating* whole sections in his revision⟩ **c :** to alter the position of in respect to contiguous items without removal to a distance **:** SHIFT ⟨major earth movements may occur without *dislocating* the strata locally⟩ **2 :** to cause confusion in **:** cause to deviate from a normal or predicted course, situation, or relationship **:** DISORDER, DISARRANGE, DISTURB ⟨economies *dislocated* by war⟩ ⟨revolution accomplished gradually by *dislocating* the internal structure of the empire⟩
[2]**dislocate** \"\ *adj, archaic* **:** DISLOCATED
[3]**dislocate** \"\ *n* -s **:** a stunt executed from a kip position on the flying rings in which the head is dropped backward, the body is straightened by arching the back and extending the hips, and the legs are made to describe an arc in the air
dislocated *adj* **1 :** put out of position **:** DISPLACED, DISARRANGED **2 :** put out of order **:** DISRUPTED
dis·lo·cat·ed·ly *adv* **:** in disorder **:** in or as if in the wrong place
dis·lo·cat·ed·ness *n* -ES **:** the quality or state of being dislocated
dis·lo·ca·tion \,di(,)slō'kāshən, ,dislə'k-\ *n* [ME *dislocacioun*, fr. MF *dislocation*, fr. ML *dislocatus* + MF *-ion*] **:** the act of dislocating or state of being dislocated: as **a :** displacement of one or more bones at a joint **:** LUXATION **b :** displacement of rocks by movement along a fracture **:** FAULT **c :** a discontinuity in the otherwise normal lattice structure of a crystal **d :** disruption of an established order (as in social, economic, or political affairs) ⟨postwar industrial ~*s*⟩
dis·lo·ca·tor *pronunc at* [1]DISLOCATE +ə(r)\ *n* **:** one that dislocates
dis·lo·ca·to·ry \'di(,)slōkə,tōrē, də'slōk-, (')di'slōk- *also* 'disləˌk-, *chiefly Brit* 'dislə,kātəri\ *adj* **:** causing or resulting from dislocation
dis·lodge \dəs, (')dis+\ *vb* [ME *disloggen*, fr. MF *desloger*, fr. *des-* [1]dis- + *loger* to lodge — more at LODGE] *vt* **1 a :** to drive out of a dwelling place ⟨the wave of crisis that *dislodged* them from their native land —M.J.Clark⟩; *sometimes* **:** to drive (a wild animal) from a lair or hiding place **b :** to force to leave or give up an advantage or favorable position ⟨they gathered proxies and *dislodged* him at the next stockholders' meeting⟩ ⟨attempting to ~ the leftist faction in the union⟩ ⟨occupied the rugged mountains . . . from which the Japanese never succeeded in *dislodging* them —*Current Biog.*⟩ **c :** to cause to shift from a fixed position esp. by exertion of physical effort on ⟨a sharp blow *dislodged* the lid⟩ ⟨*dislodging* a shower of pebbles as he slid down the hill⟩ **2** *obs* **:** to shift the quarters or station of (a military force) **:** move from one position to another ~ *vi* **:** to move from a place previously occupied **:** leave a lodging place ⟨the bone may ~ from his throat without surgery⟩
dis·lodgment *or* **dis·lodgement** \"+\ *n* **:** the act or process of dislodging or state of being dislodged
dislogistic *var of* DYSLOGISTIC
dis·loyal \dəs, (')dis+\ *adj* [MF *desloial*, fr. OF *deslëal*, fr. *des-* [1]dis- + *lëal* loyal — more at LOYAL] **:** not loyal **:** marked by lack of adherence to a sovereign, leader, country, principle, or cause claiming allegiance or by lack of adherence to vows, obligations, or promises esp. in friendships or marriage ⟨great party people think . . . openmindedness *disloyal* —G.B.Shaw⟩ **syn** see FAITHLESS
dis·loyalist \"+\ *n* **:** a person lacking in loyalty; *usu* **:** one supporting an enemy of the established government
dis·loyally \"+\ *adv* **:** in a disloyal manner **:** UNFAITHFULLY **:** with disregard to the dictates of loyalty
dis·loyalty \"+\ *n* [modif. (influenced by MF *desloial*) of MF *desloiauté*, fr. OF *deslëauté*, fr. *deslëal* + *-té* -ty] **1 :** lack of loyalty or fidelity **:** violation of allegiance **2 :** a disloyal act or thought
dis·luster \dəs, (')dis+\ *vb* [[1]*dis-* + *luster*] *vt* **:** to deprive of luster ~ *vi* **:** to lose luster
dis·mail \dəs, (')dis+\ *vt* [ME *dismailen*, fr. MF *desmaillier*, fr. *des-* [1]dis- + *maille* mail — more at MAIL] *archaic* **:** to divest of armor
[1]**dis·mal** \'dizməl\ *adj, often* -ER/-EST [ME, fr. *dismal*, n., set of 24 days (two in each month) identified as unlucky in medieval calendars, fr. AF, fr. ML *dies mali*, lit., evil days, fr. L *dies* (pl. of *dies* day) + *mali* (pl. of *malus* evil, bad) — more at DEITY, SMALL] **1 a** *obs, of a day* **:** UNLUCKY, ILL-OMENED, SINISTER **b** *obs* **:** bringing disaster or calamity **:** DREADFUL, OMINOUS **2 :** marked by, showing, or causing gloom, dejection, somberness, or depression of spirits **:** utterly wanting in anything cheering, gladdening, encouraging, or inspiring ⟨tones so ~ as to make woe itself more insupportable —William Cowper⟩ ⟨the ~ prison twilight —Charles Dickens⟩ **3 :** marked by weakness, ineptness, sparseness, impoverishment, or dullness **:** lacking interest or merit ⟨the tonal monotony, the ~ vocal ineffectiveness —E.T.Canby⟩
syn DREARY, CHEERLESS, DISPIRITING, BLEAK, DESOLATE: DISMAL and DREARY are often interchangeable. DISMAL may indicate extreme gloominess or somberness utterly depressing and dejecting ⟨*dismal* acres of weed-filled cellars and gaping foundations —Felix Morley⟩ ⟨rain dripped . . . with a *dismal* insistence —T.B. Costain⟩ ⟨the most *dismal* prophets of calamity —J.W.Krutch⟩ DREARY may differ in indicating what discourages or enervates through sustained gloom, dullness, tiresomeness, or futility, and wants any cheering or enlivening characteristic ⟨the most *dreary* solitary desert waste I had ever beheld —William Bartram⟩ ⟨it was a hard *dreary* winter, and the old minister's heart was often heavy —Margaret Deland⟩ ⟨had the strength been there, the equipment was lacking. Harding's *dreary* appreciation of this was part of his tragedy —S.H.Adams⟩ CHEERLESS stresses absence of anything cheering and is less explicit than but as forceful as the others in suggesting a pervasive disheartening joylessness or hopelessness ⟨he would like to have done with life and its vanity altogether . . . so *cheerless* and dreary the prospect seemed to him —W.M.Thackeray⟩ DISPIRITING refers to anything that disheartens or takes away morale or resolution of spirit ⟨it was such *dispiriting* effort. To throw one's whole strength and weight on the oars, and to feel the boat checked in its forward lunge —Jack London⟩ BLEAK is likely to suggest chill, dull, barren characteristics that dishearten and militate against any notions of cheer, shelter, warmth, comfort, brightness, or ease ⟨the *bleak* upland, still famous as a sheepwalk, though a scant herbage scarce veils the whinstone rock —J.R.Green⟩ ⟨the sawmill workers of the *bleak* mountain shack towns —*Amer. Guide Series: Calif.*⟩ ⟨the *bleak* years of the depression —J.D.Hicks⟩ DESOLATE applies to that which disheartens by being utterly barren, lifeless, uninhabitable or abandoned, and remote from anything cheering, comforting, or pleasant ⟨a semibarren, rather *desolate* region, whose long dry seasons stunted its vegetation —Tom Marvel⟩ ⟨some *desolate* polar region of the mind, where woman, even as an ideal, could not hope to survive —Ellen Glasgow⟩
[2]**dismal** \"\ *n* -s **1 dismals** *pl* **:** low spirits **:** extreme dejection **:** BLUES — used with *the* ⟨suffering from an attack of the ~*s*⟩ **2** *South* **:** SWAMP
dis·mal·i·ty \diz'maləd·ē\ *n* -ES **:** the quality or state of being dismal **:** DISMALNESS; *also* **:** a dismal occurrence or feeling
dismal jim·my \-'jimi\ *or* **dismal jem·my** \-'jemi\ *n, usu cap J* [fr. *Jimmy, Jemmy*, nickname for *James*] *slang Brit* **:** a man noted for depressing pessimistic predictions and frame of mind
dis·mal·ly \'dizməlē, -li\ *adv* **:** in a dismal manner ⟨a frightened child crying ~ in a corner⟩ ⟨trying to make out with a ~ inadequate money intake —F.L.Allen⟩ ⟨~ wrong in some of his . . . dogmas —W.H.Chamberlin⟩
dis·mal·ness \-məlnəs\ *n* -ES **:** the quality or state of being dismal **:** GLOOMINESS
dismal science *n* **:** POLITICAL ECONOMY **:** ECONOMICS
dis·mantle \dəs, (')dis+\ *vt* [MF *desmanteler*, lit., to deprive of a cloak, fr. *des-* [1]dis- + *mantel* cloak — more at MANTLE] **1 :** to strip or deprive of dress or covering **:** DIVEST, UNCLOAK **2 :** to strip of furniture and equipment or significant contents ⟨~ a house that is to be razed⟩ ⟨~ a ship before scrapping it⟩;

specif : to strip of guns, walls, and defenses ⟨~ a fort⟩ ⟨~ a town⟩ **3** : to wear down : RAZE, DESTROY; *also* : ANNUL, RESCIND ⟨~ price controls after the war⟩ **4** : to take to pieces : DISMOUNT **syn** see STRIP

dis·man·tle·ment \-ˈ==mənt\ *n* -s : the act of dismantling or the state of being dismantled; *esp* : deprivation of defenses

dis·man·tler \dəˈsmant(ə)lə(r), -maan-\ *n* -s : one that dismantles; *esp* : one who disassembles

dis·mask \dəs, (ˈ)dis+\ *vb* [MF *desmasquer*, fr. *des-* ¹dis- + *masque* mask — more at MASK] *archaic* : UNMASK

dis·mast \dəs, (ˈ)dis+\ *vt* [¹*dis-* + *mast* (n.)] : to remove the mast from : carry away or break off the mast of ⟨a ship ~*ed* in the storm⟩ — **dis·mast·ment** \-mənt\ *n* -s

¹**dis·may** \dəˈs|mā *sometimes* dəzˈ|\ *vb* -ED/-ING/-s [ME *dismayen*, fr. (assumed) OF *desmaiier* (whence Sp *desmayar* to dishearten, depress), fr. OF *des-* ¹dis- + *-maiier* (as in *esmaiier* to dismay, fr. — assumed — VL *exmagare*, fr. L *ex* out of, from + a word stem of Gmc origin; akin to OHG *magan* to be able) — more at EX-, MAY] *vt* **1 a** : to take away the courage or resolution of with alarm or fear : DAUNT ⟨shocked and ~*ed* . . . by the condescension and contempt to be found at every turn —H.J.Morgenthau⟩ **b** : to check suddenly the enthusiasm of : DISILLUSION, DISENCHANT ⟨the boy was ~*ed* to see his idol drunk and in disarray⟩ **c** : UPSET, PERTURB, ALARM ⟨the naive scientific belief that the whole is nothing but its parts which so ~*ed* and irritated Goethe —Philip Toynbee⟩ **2** : to put to rout : SUBDUE ~ *vi, obs* : to become daunted, disheartened, or terrified

syn APPALL, HORRIFY, DAUNT: DISMAY indicates disconcerting, disabling, unnerving, or depriving of morale and initiative through blended fear, dread, perplexity, or discouragement ⟨who in one lifetime sees all causes lost, herself *dismayed* and helpless —Muriel Rukeyser⟩ ⟨an opponent that more than once puzzled Roosevelt, and in the end flatly *dismayed* him —H.L.Mencken⟩ APPALL suggests striking with overwhelming dread or with powerlessness before the monstrous, enormous, or shocking ⟨*appalled* by the magnitude of the tragedy —C.G.Bowers⟩ ⟨the ruffians were so utterly *appalled*, not only by the false powers of magic, but by veritable powers of majesty and eloquence, that they let her do what she would —Charles Kingsley⟩ ⟨the immense modern Cosmos in which we live — the great Creation of granite, planned in such immeasurable proportions, and moved by so pitiless a mechanism, that it sometimes *appalls* even its own creators —L.P.Smith⟩ HORRIFY indicates striking with horror at the ghastly or gruesome or revulsion at the hideously offensive; weakened, it is a synonym for *shock* ⟨to developed sensibilities the facts of war are revolting and *horrifying* —Aldous Huxley⟩ ⟨she *horrified* London society by pouring hot tea on a gentleman who displeased her —*Amer. Guide Series: Va.*⟩ ⟨Massachusetts owners, *horrified* by the loss of profits —*Amer. Guide Series: Mass.*⟩ DAUNT indicates a cowing, subduing, disheartening, or frightening in a venture requiring courage ⟨no adventure *daunted* her and risks stimulated her —Havelock Ellis⟩ ⟨the attempt to draw the future frontiers of Europe is a *daunting* and ticklish enterprise —*Times Lit. Supp.*⟩

²**dismay** \"\ *n* -s **1 a** : sudden loss of courage or resolution by reason of alarm or fear : CONSTERNATION ⟨facing with ~ a force too powerful to resist⟩ **b** : sudden loss of enthusiasm for something : DISILLUSIONMENT, DISENCHANTMENT **c** : PERTURBATION, ALARM ⟨views with ~ the fact that one of his sons may choose to become a composer —Huntington Hartford⟩ **2** *obs* : a condition or a result that dismays : DESTRUCTION, RUIN **syn** see FEAR

dis·mayed·ness \-ā(ə)dnəs\ *n* -ES : the quality or state of being dismayed : DISMAY

dis·may·ful \-āfəl\ *adj* : TERRIFYING, APPALLING, ALARMING — **dis·may·ful·ly** \-f(ə)lē\ *adv*

dis·may·ing·ly *adv* : in a dismaying manner ⟨since then . . . things had changed ~ for the worse —Joseph Wechsberg⟩

disme \ˈdīm\ *n* -s [fr. obs. E, tenth, fr. obs. F, fr. MF — more at DIME] : a U.S. ten-cent coin struck in 1792

dis·member \dəs, (ˈ)dis +\ *vt* -ED/-ING/-s [ME *dismembren*, fr. OF *desmembrer*, fr. *des-* ¹dis- + *membre* member, limb — more at MEMBER] **1 a** : to cut or tear off or disjoin the limbs, members, or parts of ⟨found a ~*ed* corpse in the rubbish heap⟩ ⟨piece by piece Mexico was being ~*ed* —R.A.Billington⟩ **b** : to tear into pieces : take apart roughly or divide (a whole) into sections or separate units ⟨~*ed* an old apple barrel —P.K.Thomajan⟩; *also* : MANGLE, MUTILATE ⟨amounts to ~*ing* the facts in order to make them fit a rather farfetched preconception —J.O.Nelson⟩ **c** : DISMANTLE ⟨~*ed* their wagons, loaded them upon rafts —*Amer. Guide Series: Oregon*⟩ **2** *obs* : LOP, SEVER **3** *archaic* : to deprive of membership **4** : to make (a tributary of a river) into an independent stream by a change of geologic conditions (as the submergence of the lower part of a valley)

dis·mem·ber·ment \dəˈsmembə(r)mənt\ *n* -s : the act of dismembering or the state of being dismembered : division into separate parts or units : SEPARATION : MUTILATION ⟨the ~ of great estates —F.B.Millett⟩ ⟨the ~ of the Roman Empire —*Encyc. Americana*⟩ ⟨investigation revealed the ~ of the body after death⟩

¹**dis·miss** \dəˈsmis\ *vb* -ED/-ING/-ES [modif. (influenced by *dis-*) of L *dimissus*, past part. of *dimittere*, fr. *di-* (fr. *dis-* apart) + *mittere* to send — more at DIS-, SMITE] *vt* **1 a** : to grant or furnish leave to depart : permit or cause to leave ⟨after instructing him, the master ~*ed* the servant⟩ **b** : to send away severally : DISBAND, DISPERSE ⟨~ one's retainers⟩; *specif* : to order (a military unit) to break ranks at the end of a formation **2 a** : to divorce (a wife) by sending away or repudiating **b** : REJECT ⟨forlorn as a ~*ed* suitor⟩ **3** : to send or remove from employment, enrollment, position, or office ⟨editors and journalists who express opinions in print that are opposed to the interests of the rich are ~*ed* —G.B.Shaw⟩ ⟨reserves the right to ~ a student at any time if his conduct is considered unsatisfactory —*Bull. of Meharry Med. Coll.*⟩; *specif* : to discharge (a military officer or cadet) without honor by reason of a sentence to dismissal by a general court-martial **4 a** : to put out of one's mind : cease further consideration of : refuse to consider seriously ⟨scarcely had the thought formed itself in my mind before I ~*ed* it as utterly incredible —W.H.Hudson †1922⟩ ⟨the older view . . . may now be ~*ed* as antiquated —Edward Sapir⟩ ⟨we may ~ these harmonizers as plainly ignorant of the history of religion —M.R.Cohen⟩ **b** : to put (a legal action or a party) out of judicial consideration : refuse to hear or hear further in court **5** : to put out (a batsman) in cricket ~ *vi* : to break ranks : DISPERSE ⟨when the drill was over the company ~*ed*⟩

syn DISCHARGE, CASHIER, DROP, SACK, FIRE, BOUNCE: DISMISS in the sense of letting go from employment, position, or service is more comprehensive in its use than any of its synonyms and less suggestive or rich in connotation ⟨spoke of the sovereign as receiving and holding all revenues, appointing and *dismissing* ministers, making treaties —F.A.Ogg & Harold Zink⟩ ⟨*dismissed* the night watchers from the room, and remained with her alone —George Meredith⟩ DISCHARGE is a more stringent term in reference to cessation of employment; it suggests a more positive and forceful termination, usu. permanent and often for cause ⟨you took workmen under pressure of the most extravagant assurances of competency, and found yourself next day involved in the necessity of *discharging* them for egregious ignorance of what they had been hired to do —Mary Austin⟩ ⟨although there was some evidence supporting the employer's claim that the employee was *discharged* for incompetence, the company has the obligation . . . to act in such a manner that there can be no doubt that they are *discharging* him and not merely laying him off —*Digest of Labor Relations Development*⟩ CASHIER is used in situations involving formal, decisive, summary dismissal with discredit from high position ⟨the few sentimental fanatics who . . . proceeded upon the assumption that academic freedom was yet inviolable, and so got themselves *cashiered*, and began posturing in radical circles as martyrs —H.L.Mencken⟩ ⟨it wasn't every decade that the republic fathered an Oriental proconsul or that a president *cashiered* him —Theodore Morrison⟩ DROP, SACK, FIRE and BOUNCE are all more or less informal. DROP is the mildest and is close to DISMISS in colorlessness ⟨he learned that he had been *dropped* from the army on May 31, 1834, for overstaying his leave of absence —W.J.Ghent⟩ SACK may indicate summary dismissal as contentious, incompetent, or no longer useful ⟨"If you insist on going beyond your authority—" "You can *sack* me" —Dorothy Sayers⟩ FIRE may indicate sudden, peremptory, and very decisive dismissal ⟨he was *fired* that afternoon when his drinking came to the boss's attention⟩ BOUNCE may imply being kicked out, that is, being dismissed abruptly and forcefully ⟨Wallace had to *bounce* him and 20 other AAA employees because too many people complained that the group was trying to change the world too fast —*Time*⟩ **syn** see in addition EJECT

²**dismiss** *n* -ES *obs* : DISMISSAL

dis·mis·sal \dəˈsmisəl\ *n* -s **1** : the act of dismissing or the fact or state of being dismissed ⟨requesting the ~ of a new employee for incompetence⟩ ⟨Ross's robust ~ of Kant's theory of knowledge —*Times Lit. Supp.*⟩ **2** : the church rite of dismissing a congregation after a eucharistic service

dismissal wage *n* : a sum paid in addition to salary or wages to an employee discharged through no fault of his own : SEVERANCE PAY

dis·missed time \dəˈs|mist-, (ˈ)diˈs|\ *n* : time provided in some communities for the religious education of students or for recreation one day a week by the early dismissal of schools

dis·miss·ing·ly \=ˈ===\ *adv* : in a manner that dismisses ⟨they picked things up and shoved them ~ aside —Mary-Carter Roberts⟩

dis·mis·sion \dəˈsmishən\ *n* -s [modif. (influenced by *dis-*) of L *dimission-, dimissio*, fr. *dimissus* + *-ion-, -io* -ion] **1** : the act of dismissing or of being dismissed **2** *archaic* : the document or the form of expression by which an act of dismissing is effected

dis·mis·sive \dəˈsmisiv, (ˈ)diˈs-\ *adj* **1** : giving dismissal or serving to dismiss : REJECTING, REPUDIATING **2** : DISDAINFUL

dis·moded \dəˈsmōdəd, (ˈ)diˈs-\ *adj* [¹*dis-* + *moded*] : OUTMODED

¹**dis·mount** \dəs, (ˈ)dis+\ *vb* [prob. modif. (influenced by *dis-* & *mount*) of MF *desmonter*, fr. *des-* ¹dis- + *monter* to mount — more at MOUNT] *vi* **1** *obs* : to come down : DESCEND **2** : to alight from or as if from a horse ⟨I preferred to ~ to ease the horse's burden —Ana Beker⟩ ⟨I took a taxi to within a third of a mile of the stadium, ~*ing* when my vehicle could no longer advance —A.J.Liebling⟩ ~ *vt* **1 a** : to remove often forcibly from a mount or a mounting or something felt to resemble one of these ⟨enabling the ~*ed* motorist to reach his urban destination by swift public transport —Lewis Mumford⟩; *esp* : UNHORSE ⟨I should like to ~ my men . . . and send the horses to the rear —Oliver La Farge⟩ **b** *obs* : to bring or force down from a height; *also* : to deprive of honor or authority : DEGRADE **2** *archaic* : to alight from (as a horse) **3** : to take down or apart from an assembled condition : DISASSEMBLE ⟨~ a revolver for cleaning⟩ **syn** see DESCEND

²**dismount** \"\ *n* : the act of dismounting; *specif* : movement to the floor from a position on a gymnastics apparatus

dis·mount·able \-əbəl\ *adj* : capable of being dismounted : removable from a carriage or mounting : easily disassembled

dis·mutation \ˌdis+\ *n* [¹*dis-* + *mutation*] : a process of simultaneous oxidation and reduction : DISPROPORTIONATION — used esp. of compounds taking part in biological processes ⟨~ of pyruvate to acetate and lactate⟩

dis·mutative \dəs, (ˈ)dis +\ *adj* : relating to or causing dismutation

dis·na \ˈdiznə\ [by alter.] *chiefly Scot* : does not

dis·nature \dəs, (ˈ)dis +\ *vt* [ME *disnaturen*, fr. MF *desnaturer*, fr. *des-* ¹dis- + *nature* — more at NATURE] : to make unnatural : deprive of a natural quality or appearance

dis·ney·esque \ˌdiznēˈesk\ *adj, usu cap* [Walter E. *Disney* b1901 American cartoonist and producer of animated motion-picture cartoons + E *-esque*] : resembling or having the character of an animated cartoon made by the Walt Disney studios ⟨the animals take part in circus acts of the most . . . *Disneyesque* nature —May L. Becker⟩ ⟨it has nothing in novelty on a *Disneyesque* railroad that runs 38 miles south of Myitkyina —*Newsweek*⟩

dis·obedience \ˌdis+\ *n* [ME, fr. MF *desobedience*, fr. *des-* ¹dis- + *obedience*] : refusal to obey or negligence in obeying a command : violation or disregard of a rule or prohibition ⟨the lads try to excel one another in mischief and ~ —Willa Cather⟩ ⟨that peculiar taint of barbarism which makes men prefer occasional ~ to systematic liberty —H.T.Buckle⟩

dis·obedient \"+\ *adj* [ME, fr. MF *desobedient*, fr. *des-* ¹dis- + *obedient*] **1 a** : refusing or neglecting to obey : disobeying an order or rule **b** : characterized by habitual disobedience : UNRULY ⟨a woman cursed with noisy and ~ boys⟩ **2** *archaic* : not yielding : INTRACTABLE — **dis·obediently** \"+\ *adv*

dis·obey \"+\ *vb* [ME *disobeyen*, fr. MF *desobeir*, fr. *des-* ¹dis- + *obeir* to obey — more at OBEY] *vt* : to refuse to obey : neglect to obey : transgress the commands, prohibitions, or rules of : violate the laws of ⟨a child prone to ~ a parent⟩ ⟨a driver who consistently ~*s* traffic regulations⟩ ⟨~*ing* one's conscience⟩ ~ *vi* : to be disobedient : refuse or fail to obey orders or to abide by rules or laws ⟨often punished for ~*ing*⟩

dis·obligation \dəs, (ˌ)dis+\ *n* [¹*dis-* + *obligation*] **1** *archaic* : an act that purposely inconveniences or offends : AFFRONT **2** *archaic* : the state or sensation of being disobliged : GRUDGE

dis·oblige \ˌdis +\ *vt* [F *désobliger*, fr. MF *desobliger*, fr. *des-* ¹dis- + *obliger* to oblige — more at OBLIGE] **1** : to go purposely counter to the wishes of : be unaccommodating to ⟨had promised to do a friend a favor but was finally forced to ~ him for lack of time⟩ **2 a** : to cause inconvenience to : put out : INCOMMODE ⟨the action was not offensive to him but proved somewhat *disobliging*⟩ **b** : AFFRONT, OFFEND ⟨not wishing to ~ a man who could be of so much help to him⟩ — **dis·oblig·er** \-ə(r)\ *n*

dis·oblig·ing·ly *adv* : in a manner that disobliges : UNACCOMMODATINGLY

dis·occupation \dəs, (ˌ)dis +\ *n* [¹*dis-* + *occupation*] : the state of being idle or unoccupied : INACTIVITY, LEISURE

di·sodium \(ˈ)dī +\ *adj* [*di-* + *sodium*] : containing two atoms of sodium in the molecule

disodium phosphate *or* **disodium hydrogen phosphate** *n* : SODIUM PHOSPHATE 1b

di·somatic \ˌdī +\ *adj* [*di-* + *somatic*] : characterized by disomaty

di·so·ma·ty \dīˈsōməd·ē\ *n* -ES [*disomatic* + *-y*] : duplication in somatic cells of the chromosome number through a division of chromosomes without subsequent nuclear division

di·some \ˈdīˌsōm\ *n* -s [F, fr. *di-* + *-some* (body)] : a chromosome set having members paired (as in a normal somatic cell)

di·so·mic \(ˈ)dīˈsōmik\ *adj* [*di-* + *-somic*] **1** : having one or more chromosomes duplicated but not an entire genome duplicated **2** : of, relating to, or characterized by a disome

di·so·mus \dīˈsōməs\ *n, pl* **diso·mi** \-ˌmī\ *or* **disomuses** [NL, fr. *di-* + *-somus*] : a 2-bodied monster

dis·operation \dəs, (ˌ)dis +\ *n* [¹*dis-* + *-operation* (as in *cooperation*)] : any harmful effect other than direct competition of the aggregation or crowding of two or more organisms or kinds of organism in a limited area that is manifested directly (as through accumulation of toxic wastes) or indirectly (as through alteration of the habitat by growth or feeding habits of one or more members of the population)

dis·operative \"+\ *adj* [¹*dis-* + *-operative* (as in *cooperative*)] : hostile to or hindering cooperation ⟨the balance between the cooperative, altruistic tendencies and those which are ~ and egoistic —M.F.A.Montagu⟩ ⟨working in ~ conditions⟩

disopinion *n* [¹*dis-* + *opinion*] *obs* : DISESTEEM

dis·orb \dəs, (ˈ)dis +\ *vt* -ED/-ING/-s [¹*dis-* + *orb* (orbit)] : to throw (as an asteroid or comet) out of its normal orbit

¹**dis·order** \dəs, (ˈ)dis +, *sometimes* dəz *or* (ˈ)diz +\ *vb* [¹*dis-* + *order* (v.)] *vt* **1 a** : to disturb the order of : DISARRANGE **b** : to disturb the regular or normal functions of (as the body or mind) : cause a disordered condition in ⟨eating enough to ~ his digestive system⟩ ⟨events shocking enough to ~ the mind⟩ **2** *archaic* : DISCONCERT : DISCOMPOSE ~ *vi* : to fall into disorder or confusion : become disordered

syn DISORDER, DISARRANGE, DERANGE, DISORGANIZE, UNSETTLE, and DISTURB can mean to undo the fixed or proper order of something. DISORDER implies the alteration to its marked detriment of a given, desirable, or proper order, applying commonly to what depends upon being properly ordered for its best functioning or effectiveness ⟨to *disorder* the carefully arranged contents of a drawer⟩ ⟨reasoning *disordered* by strong emotion⟩ ⟨a country *disordered* by war⟩ DISARRANGE implies merely the changing of a fixed, desirable, or neat order or arrangement ⟨*disarranged* his carefully brushed hair⟩ ⟨*disarrange* the normal functioning of the household⟩ DERANGE implies a marked throwing out of proper order of parts which exist in their best state or function best in a given order or interrelationship, differing from the previous words in implying a resulting confusion or a destruction of normal or healthy conditions ⟨within the power of man irreparably to *derange* the combinations of inorganic matter and organic life —Russell Lord⟩ ⟨the news of his cousin Anne's engagement . . . *deranged* his best plan of domestic happiness —Jane Austen⟩ ⟨[war] lays its blight on whole peoples, *deranges* their life —C.E. Montague⟩ DISORGANIZE implies the destruction of the order and functioning of an organization of interrelated things, suggesting, therefore, a disordering that runs through an entire system, breaking it up or seriously impeding its full operation or effectiveness ⟨world economy and national currencies in 1948 were highly *disorganized* and unbalanced —*Collier's Yr. Bk.*⟩ ⟨an expenditure which would *disorganize* his whole scheme of finance —John Buchan⟩ ⟨the normal metabolic activity of this organ is *disorganized* by infections —H.R. Litchfield & L.H.Dembo⟩ UNSETTLE suggests a disordering or disarrangement of a fixed or desirable order, or a calm attendant upon such an order, and a resulting instability and often turbulence ⟨learned enough of it to *unsettle* his religious beliefs —R.A.Hall b.1911⟩ ⟨war *unsettles* the institutions and practices of even the firmest culture⟩ ⟨*unsettle* the thoughts⟩ DISTURB implies a force that unsettles or disarranges; often it suggests an interruption that affects a settled order or condition ⟨the headlights also *disturbed* the slumbers of the night —Sherwood Anderson⟩ ⟨those emotions which *disturb* the reason —Virginia Woolf⟩ ⟨the warps and strains of civilized life, with its excessive industrialism and militarism, seem to *disturb* the wholesome balance of even the humblest elements of the possessive and aesthetic instincts —Havelock Ellis⟩ ⟨a noise that *disturbs* one's thoughts⟩

²**disorder** \"\ *n* [¹*dis-* + *order* (n.)] **1** : a condition marked by lack of order, system, regularity, predictability, or dependability : the act or fact of disturbing, neglecting, or breaking away from a due order ⟨the scientific view . . . regards ~ and inexplicable irregularity as a scandal —W.R.Inge⟩ ⟨those rooms are all in ~, there has been hurried packing —Charles Dickens⟩ **2 a** : breach of public order : disturbance of the peace of society **b** : MISCONDUCT, MISDEED, MISDEMEANOR ⟨she had been a sinner from her early youth and . . . continued her ~*s* even until an advanced age —Willa Cather⟩ **c** : an instance of such disorder or misconduct ⟨widespread lawlessness in the 1850's appeared . . . in lynchings of abolitionists and in the ~*s* in Kansas —H.E.Davis⟩ **3** : a derangement of function : an abnormal physical or mental condition : SICKNESS, AILMENT, MALADY ⟨an intestinal ~⟩ ⟨suffering from a nutritional ~ caused by lack of calcium and phosphorus —*Time*⟩ **syn** see CONFUSION

disordered *adj* **1** *obs* : morally reprehensible : UNRULY **2** : marked or characterized by disorder: as **a** : lacking a visible order or organization ⟨the country was ~ for years, but gradually white traders . . . began to establish a foothold in the region of the Lower Congo —Tom Marvel⟩ **b** : existing in turmoil : lacking a central organizing control ⟨a ~ country with a history of successive revolutions⟩ **c** (1) : not functioning in an organically normal orderly healthy way ⟨during hysterical conditions various functions of the human body are ~⟩ (2) : mentally unbalanced ⟨a ~ patient⟩ : not functioning in a sane manner ⟨a ~ mind⟩ — **dis·or·dered·ly** *adv* — **dis·or·dered·ness** *n*

dis·orderliness \"+\ *n* : the quality or state of being disorderly ⟨it gives a certain typical ~ to our behavior which baffles some foreign observers —Dean Acheson⟩

¹**dis·orderly** \"+\ *adv* [¹*dis-* + *orderly* (adv.)] *archaic* : in a disorderly manner : without law or order : IRREGULARLY, CONFUSEDLY, TURBULENTLY

²**disorderly** \"\ *adj* [¹*dis-* + *orderly* (adj.)] **1 a** : not complying with the restraints of law and order : UNRULY, TURBULENT ⟨a weak government and a ~ people⟩ **b** : constituting a public nuisance by reason of behavior that violates public order or is offensive to public decency; *esp, of a person* : guilty of disorderly conduct **2** : not in order : marked by disorder : DISARRANGED : lacking a reasonable or apparent system ⟨a ~ array of books⟩ ⟨romantic artists were rather expected to live ~ lives at odds with God, man, the Devil, and various mistresses —*New Yorker*⟩ ⟨help correct ~ market conditions —*Federal Reserve System*⟩ ⟨the usual ~ bustle that masks the deadly efficiency of the French people —Osbert Sitwell⟩

disorderly conduct *n, law* : one of a wide range of petty offenses chiefly against public order and decency that fall short of indictable misdemeanors, that are usu. provided for by municipal ordinances, and that are tried before a magistrate

disorderly house *n* : BROTHEL

disorders *pl of* DISORDER, *pres 3d sing of* DISORDER

dis·ordinate \dəs, (ˈ)dis+\ *adj* [ME *disordinat*, fr. ¹*dis-* + *ordinat* ordinate — more at ORDINATE] *archaic* : INORDINATE, IMMODERATE

dis·organization \dəs, (ˌ)dis +\ *n* [F *désorganisation*, fr. *désorganiser* + *-ation*] : the act of disorganizing or the quality or state of being disorganized ⟨accomplish the total ~ of the existing government⟩ ⟨suffering from a ~ of mind incident to mild hysteria⟩

dis·organize \dəs, (ˈ)dis +\ *vt* [F *désorganiser*, fr. *dés-* ¹dis- + *organiser* to organize, fr. ML *organizare* — more at ORGANIZE] : to destroy the organic structure or regular or systematic arrangement of : deprive of organization : throw into disorder or confusion : DISARRANGE ⟨an attempt to ~ the government failed⟩ ⟨I became so jumpy and *disorganized* that I am unable to concentrate on anything —John Willig⟩ **syn** see DISORDER

disorganized *adj* : lacking coherence, system, or central guiding principle or agency ⟨analyzing the needs of the country's ~ areas⟩ ⟨two thousand pages of ~, muddy prose —*Saturday Rev.*⟩

dis·organizer \dəs, (ˈ)dis +\ *n* : one that disorganizes or disrupts

dis·orient \dəs, (ˈ)dis +\ *vt* [F *désorienter*, fr. *dés-* ¹dis- + *orienter* to orient — more at ORIENT] **1 a** : to cause to lose bearings ⟨by the time he had made three turns, one to the right and two to the left, he was totally ~*ed* and had to seek directions⟩ **b** : to cause to lose identity **2** : to confuse (as in one's sense of what is right or proper) to the point of causing to act irrationally or of preventing from acting purposively or sensibly ⟨it has ~*ed* and confused the electorate —Daniel James⟩ **3** : to cause to deviate from correct or normal alignment ⟨~ magnetic domains by heat⟩

dis·orientate \dəs, (ˈ)dis +\ *vt* [¹*dis-* + *orient* + *-ate*] **1** : to turn from the east or from an eastward course **2** : DISORIENT

dis·orientation \dəs, (ˌ)dis+\ *n* **1** : the state of being disorientated ⟨takes for granted that we all recognize our homelessness, that we all believe the rootlessness and ~ of his hero to be typical —H.E.Clurman⟩ **2** : an often transient state of mental confusion esp. as to time, place, or identity resulting from a toxic condition caused by disease, drugs, or other agency — compare DELIRIUM

disoriented *adj* **1 a** : markedly displaced from a normal, usual, or accustomed relationship with others or with the world ⟨his fellow employees are all badly ~ . . . and include a homicidal pastrymaker, a sluttish salesgirl, and a former German petty functionary —*New Yorker*⟩ **b** : confused as to aim or purpose ⟨the present ~ condition of the world —*Yale Rev.*⟩ **2** : having no fixed or accustomed relationship with society or its more common ideologies : at sea ⟨a poet and intellectual of the most sophisticated and ~ type⟩ **3** : wandering in the mind : having no rational grasp of time, place, or one's own identity ⟨he was conscious but ~ and close to death —John Kobler⟩

disour *n* -s [ME, fr. OF *diseur* — more at DISEUR] *obs* : STORYTELLER, JESTER

dis·own \dəs, (ˈ)dis +\ *vt* [¹*dis-* + *own*] **1 a** : to refuse to acknowledge as belonging to oneself : REPUDIATE ⟨the man ~*ed* the gun when he found it had been used to kill⟩ ⟨faithlessly ~*ing* a friend if it profited him to do so⟩ **b** : to dismiss or expel from the Society of Friends **2 a** : DENY, DISCLAIM

⟨I cannot ~ that I should like to go⟩ ⟨the prime minister ~*ed* any intention of pursuing a policy of isolation —*Collier's Yr. Bk.*⟩ **b :** to refuse to acknowledge the validity of ⟨the Jacobites ~*ed* any king but James II or a descendant⟩ ⟨every president ~*s* and disparages the doctrine of the indispensable man —R.H.Rovere⟩ **syn** see DISCLAIM

dis·own·ment \-mənt\ *n* -s **:** the act of disowning or the state of being disowned

disp *abbr* **1** dispatch; dispatcher **2** dispensary; dispenser

dis·palatalization \dəs, (ˈ)dis +\ *n* [¹*dis-* + *palatalization*] *phonetics* **:** a depriving of palatal quality

dis·par·age \dəˈsparij, -rēj *also* -per-, *esp in pres part* -rəj\ *vt* -ED/-ING/-S [ME *disparagen*, fr. MF *desparagier*, fr. OF, fr. *des-* ¹dis- + *-paragier* (fr. *parage* extraction, lineage, high birth, fr. *per* peer + *-age*) — more at PEER (equal)] **1 a** *obs* **:** to lower or degrade esp. by marriage to one socially inferior **b :** to lower in esteem or reputation **:** diminish the respect for ⟨the Labor party, in turn, is being carried further to the left . . . in an effort to ~ the Tory party —*New Republic*⟩ **c :** DISCOURAGE, DISHEARTEN **2 a** *obs* **:** to discredit or bring reproach upon by comparing with something inferior **:** lower in rank by actions or words **b :** to speak slightingly of **:** run down **:** DEPRECIATE ⟨I get very hot under the collar when I hear this country *disparaged* —Victor Ross⟩ ⟨I do not wish to ~ the bouillabaisse, which is a dish for heroes —A.T.Quiller-Couch⟩ **syn** see DECRY

dis·par·age·ment \-jmənt\ *n* -s [MF *desparagement*, fr. *desparagier* + *-ment*] **1 a :** diminution of esteem or standing **:** INDIGNITY, DISGRACE **b** *archaic* **:** marriage to one of an inferior social position; *also* **:** dishonor by reason of such a marriage ⟨it was regarded as no ~ for the daughter of a duke . . . to espouse a distinguished commoner —T.B.Macaulay⟩ **2 a :** the expression of a low opinion of something **:** DETRACTION ⟨these comparisons are certainly not to be taken in any way as a ~ : rather as a compliment —Douglas Stewart⟩ **b :** low opinion **:** CONTEMPT ⟨every age seems to develop a certain ~ of its immediate predecessor —P.H.Muir⟩

dis·par·ag·er \-jə(r)\ *n* -s **:** one that disparages ⟨hater of war and ~ of nationalism —W.P.Hall⟩

dis·par·ag·ing·ly *adv* **:** in a manner that disparages ⟨these mythological figures are occasionally described almost ~ as belonging "only to a story" —F.G.Hawley⟩

¹dis·par·ate \dəˈsparət *also* -ˈsper- *or* ˈdisp(ə)r-; *usu* -əd.+V\ *n* -s [L *disparatum*, fr. neut. of *disparatus*] **:** something disparate **:** one of two or more things so unequal or unlike that they cannot be compared with each other — usu. used in pl.

²disparate \"\ *adj* [L *disparatus*, past part. of *disparare* to separate, fr. *dis-* ¹dis- + *parare* to make ready, prepare — more at PARE] **1 a :** distinct in quality or character **:** UNEQUAL, DISSIMILAR ⟨cast as a young lady who has three ~ personalities —John McCarten⟩ ⟨connecting ~ thoughts purely by means of resemblances in the words expressing them —S.T. Coleridge⟩ ⟨a series of ~ biological essays strung loosely within a historical framework —L.C.Eiseley⟩ ⟨such ~ attractions as grand opera and game fishing —M.A.Santin⟩ **b :** comprising markedly dissimilar and unequal elements **:** not homogeneous ⟨a ~ aggregate of creeds, prayers, and songs —Joseph Kerman⟩ ⟨this most ~ genius of the middle ages —H.O.Taylor⟩ ⟨a poet's mind . . . is constantly amalgamating ~ experience —T.S.Eliot⟩; *specif, of polygamy and polyandry* **:** characterized by inequality of the plural partners **2** *of two or more statements* **:** having no definitive relation in common **:** connected only by some notion of great generality or by some interest of extreme catholicity — opposed to *connex* **3 :** indicating or stimulating dissimilar points on the retina of each eye **syn** see DIFFERENT

dis·par·ate·ly *adv* **:** in a disparate manner ⟨taken ~, item by item —R.H.Pearce⟩

dis·par·ate·ness *n* -ES **:** the quality or state of being disparate

dis·pa·ra·tum \ˌdispəˈrāˌd·əm, -rā\ *n*, *pl* **dispara·ta** \|d·ə\ [L — more at DISPARATE] **:** a disparate term or concept in logic

dis·par·i·ty \dəˈsparəd·ē, -ətē, -i *also* -per-\ *n* -ES [MF *desparité*, fr. LL *disparitat-, disparitas*, fr. L *dis-* ¹dis- + LL *paritat-, paritas* parity — more at PARITY] **:** the state of being disparate **:** marked difference (as in age, rank, grade, condition, quantity, quality, or kind) **:** DISSIMILARITY, INEQUALITY ⟨shocking ~ between the rich and the poor —A.E.Stevenson b.1900⟩ ⟨the present ~ between the military resources and her [Poland's] will to fight —O.D.Tolischus⟩ ⟨the tragicomic ~ which exists between man's aspirations and his accomplishments, between his yearning and his attaining —B.R.Redman⟩

dis·park \dəs, (ˈ)dis +\ *vt* [¹*dis-* + *park* (n.)] **:** to throw open (a private park); *esp* **:** to convert (a park) to something else than a private park ⟨Henry VIII decided to ~ the Duchy parks and turn them more profitably into pasture —A.L. Rowse⟩

dis·part \dəs, (ˈ)dis+\ *vb* [It & L; It *dispartire* to divide, separate, fr. L *dispertire, dispartire* to distribute, divide, fr. *dis-* ¹dis- + *partire* to divide, distribute — more at PART] *vt* **1** *archaic* **:** to put or force apart **:** SEPARATE, DIVIDE ⟨what face is this . . . peering through the ~*ed* branches? —R.L.Stevenson⟩ **2** *obs* **:** to divide into parts or portions ~ *vi, archaic* **:** to open up **:** SEPARATE, DIVIDE

dis·passion \dəs, (ˈ)dis+\ *n* [¹*dis-* + *passion*] **:** freedom from or lack of strong feeling **:** CALMNESS, DISPASSIONATENESS ⟨his own experience . . . is a deeply horrifying one, but he presents it with a noble ~ —M.R.Ridley⟩

dis·passionate \"+\ *adj* [¹*dis-* + *passionate*] **:** free from the influence of passion or strong feeling: **a :** equitable of disposition **:** CALM, COOL, COMPOSED ⟨it was his fate in life to have his equanimity mistaken for pluck, whereas it was actually something much more ~ and much less virile —James Hilton⟩ **b :** calm in judgment **:** uninfluenced by prejudice, favoritism, or partisanship **:** JUDICIAL ⟨plumes himself upon this spirit, even when he is sufficiently ~ to perceive the ruin it works —Charles Dickens⟩ **syn** see FAIR

dis·passionately \"+\ *adv* **:** in a dispassionate manner ⟨a scientist . . . does not praise or censure; he ~ studies the forces at work —Irving Kristol⟩

dis·passionateness \"+\ *n* **:** the quality or state of being dispassionate

dis·passioned \"+\ *adj, obs* **:** free from passion **:** DISPASSIONATE

¹dis·patch \dəˈspach *sometimes* ˈdi,s- *or* **des·patch** \dəˈs-\ *vb* -ED/-ING/-ES [Sp *despachar* or It *dispacciare*, fr. Prov *despachar* to get rid of, fr. MF *despeechier* to set free, fr. OF, fr. *des-* ¹dis- + *-peechier* (as in *empeechier* to hinder) — more at IMPEACH] *vt* **1 a :** to send off or away (as to a special destination) with promptness or speed often as a matter of official business ⟨~ a letter to one's superior reporting on progress⟩ ⟨~ troops to the scene of conflict⟩ ⟨~ a messenger to the king requesting military assistance⟩ ⟨organized and ~*ed* a motorcade over the proposed route —*Amer. Guide Series: Fla.*⟩ **b :** to perform the job of dispatcher of ⟨employed to ~ buses at a terminal⟩ ⟨~ seamen in a hiring hall⟩ ⟨the starter is better equipped to ~ elevators to maintain an even flow of traffic —*Dun's Rev.*⟩ ⟨truck ~*ing* and maintenance, which he had learned as a motor transport officer in the army, being the only trade he knew —Oakley Hall⟩ **2 a :** to get rid of (as by sending away) **:** DISMISS, DISCHARGE ⟨with the heavyset girl ~*ed* amid gaiety —Harriet LaBarre⟩ **b :** to put to death **:** KILL ⟨promptly seized the trap and ~*ed* the bear with one blow on the head —*Amer. Guide Series: Vt.*⟩ **c** *obs* **:** to rid or free oneself of **d** *obs* **:** to do away with (life) **3 a :** to dispose of rapidly or efficiently (as a piece of business) **:** execute quickly ⟨anxious to ~ the matter at hand and get on to other business⟩ **b :** to eat with avid concentration **:** clean up by eating ⟨~ a seven-course dinner without effort or pause⟩ ⟨the salad and frozen pudding were ~*ed* as promptly as the roast had been —Willa Cather⟩ ~ *vi, archaic* **:** to make haste **:** HASTEN **syn** see KILL, SEND

²dispatch \"\ *or* **despatch** \"\ *n* -ES [Sp *despacho* or It *dispaccio*, resp. fr. Sp *despachar* & It *dispacciare*] **1 :** the act of dispatching: as **a** *obs* **:** DISMISSAL, DISCHARGE; *esp* **:** official dismissal **b :** the act of putting to death **:** KILLING ⟨her well-planned loathing of Scarpia, and her equally determined ~ of him once her plan of action was clear —*Saturday Rev.*⟩ **c** (1) **:** prompt settlement or disposal (as of an item of business) ⟨concerned more with grievances and their redress than with the ~ of the crown's business —T.E.May⟩ (2) **:** quick riddance **d :** a sending off esp. to a particular destination ⟨requested the ~ of two companies to the front⟩ ⟨the ~ of goods trains from important centers of traffic —O.S.Nock⟩ **:** SHIPMENT ⟨fine white clay being bagged for ~ to the potteries —L.D. Stamp⟩ **2 a :** a message dispatched or sent with speed; *esp* **:** an important official message often in cipher sent by an officer of the diplomatic, military, or naval service of a government ⟨his military record brought him three mentions in ~*es* —*Current Biog.*⟩ ⟨~ to the war department via the state department from . . . the consul at Tsingtao —J.D.Morris⟩ **b :** a news item sent with promptness or speed by a correspondent to a newspaper or news agency **3 :** promptness or exactness and efficiency ⟨the gallery stages its auctions with such ~ and charm that one might be attending a cunningly directed play —*New Yorker*⟩ **4** *Brit* **:** EXPRESS 1c **syn** see HASTE

dispatch boat *n* **:** an official boat for the conveying of dispatches

dispatch box *or* **dispatch case** *n* **1 :** an oblong box or case usu. with a lock for carrying dispatches or other papers **2** *chiefly Brit* **:** a stiff case (as of metal) in the style of a brief-case

dis·patch·er *also* **des·patch·er** \-chə(r)\ *n* -s **:** one that dispatches or expedites usu. as a vocation: as **a :** an employee of a transportation company who directs the departures of trains, planes, buses, trucks, boats, or other vehicles according to traveling conditions and in the best interests of efficient service **b :** one that assigns jobs to waiting seamen in a hiring hall **c :** one that expedites repair service or delivery of materials or goods within a plant or for customers **d :** a telephone local test deskman who directs the locating, testing, and clearing of trouble on subscriber lines **e :** one that upon receiving reports of forest fire from lookouts organizes men and equipment to combat it **f :** one that directs the departure of passenger elevators (as from the main floor of a large building) ⟨worked as ~ at a big hotel⟩ **g :** one that receives information about crimes and transmits it by radio to police patrols **h :** one that directs the movement of oil or gas into and through pipeline systems or the disposition of loads and generating capacity on an electric power system **i :** a telegraph worker who directs the flow of messages during times of wire shortage or emergency or who assigns additional personnel when needed **j :** MOTOR BOSS

dis·patch·ful \-chfəl\ *adj, archaic* **:** fitted to achieve or bent upon achieving an end with dispatch; *also* **:** HASTY

dis·patch·ment \-chmənt\ *n* -s **:** the act of dispatching ⟨the first ~ of workers to the U.S. —*Nassau (Bahamas) Guardian*⟩

dispatch money *n* **:** a money allowance given to a charterer of a ship by the owner of it for any shortening in the lay days stipulated in the contract between them

dispatch note *n* **:** a tag required on a parcel-post package in international mail giving facts (as weight, postage, names of sender and addressee, and sender's directions to the foreign post office if the parcel is undeliverable) that are essential to the handling of the package

dispatch rider *n* **:** a bearer of military dispatches traveling usu. by motorcycle

dis·pauper \dəs, (ˈ)dis+\ *vt* [¹*dis-* + *pauper* (n.)] **:** to deprive of the claim of a pauper to public support **:** deprive of the privilege of suing in forma pauperis

dis·pauperize \"+\ *vt* [¹*dis-* + *pauperize*] **:** to free from pauperism or from paupers

dis·peace \dəs, (ˈ)dis+\ *n* [¹*dis-* + *peace*] **:** DISSENSION, STRIFE, TURMOIL ⟨~ between the two countries⟩ ⟨even marriage offered no lasting balm to his inner ~ —J.B.Noss⟩

dis·pel \dəˈspel\ *vt* **dispelled; dispelled; dispelling; dispels** [L *dispellere*, fr. *dis-* ¹dis- + *pellere* to push, drive, strike — more at PULSE] **:** to drive away by scattering **:** clear away **:** DISSIPATE ⟨~ a mist⟩ ⟨~ one's doubts by ascertaining the facts⟩ ⟨~ illusions⟩ **syn** see SCATTER

dis·pel·ler \-lə(r)\ *n* -s **:** one that dispels

dispend *vt* -ED/-ING/-S [ME *dispenden*, fr. OF *despendre*, fr. L *dispendere* to weigh out — more at DISPENSE] **1** *obs* **:** SPEND, EXPEND **2** *obs* **:** DISTRIBUTE, DISPENSE

dis·pen·di·ous \dəˈspendēəs, (ˈ)di¦s-\ *adj* **:** EXPENSIVE, COSTLY; *also* **:** EXTRAVAGANT — **dis·pen·di·ous·ly** *adv*

dis·pens·abil·i·ty \də,spen(t)səˈbiləd·ē, (,)di,-, -ətē, -i\ *n* -ES **:** the quality or state of being dispensable ⟨his ~ to his corporation and his corporation's indispensability to him are bound to remain the crux of his problem —John McDonald⟩

dis·pens·able \dəˈspen(t)səbəl, (ˈ)di¦s-\ *adj* [ML *dispensabilis*, fr. L *dispensare* + *-abilis* -able] **1** *obs* **a :** REMITTABLE **b :** PARDONABLE, ALLOWABLE **2 :** capable of being dispensed with **:** not essential ⟨the communications machines will render excess and ~ whole assembly lines and whole echelons of supervisory employees —Irwin Edman⟩ — **dis·pen·sa·ble·ness** *n* -ES — **dis·pen·sa·bly** *adv*

dis·pen·sa·ry \dəˈspen(t)s(ə)rē, -ri\ *n* -ES [ML *dispensaria* storeroom, pantry, fr. L *dispensare* to distribute + *-aria* -ary] **1 :** a place where medicines or medical or dental aid are dispensed to ambulant patients ⟨a ~ in an industrial plant⟩ **2 :** a liquor store in some southern states (as So. Carolina) where by the dispensary law intoxicating liquors are sold but not to be drunk on the premises

dis·pen·sa·tion \ˌdispənˈsāshən, ˌdi,spen-\ *n* -s [ME *dispensacioun*, fr. ML, LL, & L; ML *dispensation-, dispensatio* exemption, pardon, fr. LL, arrangement, administration, fr. L, distribution, fr. *dispensatus* (past part. of *dispensare* to distribute) + *-ion-, -io* -ion — more at DISPENSE] **1 a** (1) **:** ORDERING, ADMINISTRATION, MANAGEMENT ⟨under the new ~ private distillers are first to be licensed and then gradually bought out —D.W.McConnell⟩; *specif* **:** a divine ordering and administration of worldly affairs (2) **:** a system of principles, promises, and rules divinely ordained and administered **:** the divine economy ⟨the Mosaic ~⟩ ⟨the Christian ~⟩ (3) **:** a period of history during which a particular divine revelation has predominated in the affairs of mankind (4) **:** any general state or ordering of things ⟨the triumph of the predatory dog-eat-dog ~ —John Gassner⟩ **b :** an arrangement or provision esp. of providence or nature; *also* **:** FAVOR ⟨the 400 merino sheep that he had purchased by special ~ from the Escurial royal flock of Spain —*Amer. Guide Series: Vt.*⟩ **2 :** a dispensing with or doing without something **:** remission of a sin **:** exemption from a rule of civil or ecclesiastical law or from an impediment, vow, or oath **3 a :** the act of dispensing **:** a dealing out **:** DISTRIBUTION ⟨a ship's pharmacist concerns himself with the ~ of medicines⟩ **b :** something dispensed or distributed ⟨one of the most remarkable cultural ~*s* in the country's history, the paperback book —T.E.Cooney⟩ **4 :** formal authorization by a fraternal organization (as for the purpose of forming a chapter) ⟨four other Freemasons met to petition the Grand Lodge of Louisiana for a ~ to organize a lodge at Brazoria —*Amer. Guide Series: Texas*⟩ — **dis·pen·sa·tion·al** \ˌ=(ˌ)=ˈsāshənᵊl, -shnəl\ *adj*

dis·pen·sa·tion·al·ism \ˌ=(ˌ)=ˈ=(=)=ˌizəm\ *n* -s **:** adherence to or advocacy of a system of interpreting history in terms of a series of God's dispensations

dispensative *adj* [ML *dispensativus*, fr. L *dispensatus* + *-ivus* -ive] **1** *obs* **:** ADMINISTRATIVE **2** *obs* **:** granting or serving to grant dispensation

dispensator *n* -s [ME *dispensatour*, fr. ML *dispensator*, fr. L, household manager, treasurer, fr. *dispensatus* + *-or*] **1** *obs* **:** DISPENSER **2** *obs* **:** one that manages or administers

¹dis·pen·sa·to·ry \dəˈspen(t)sə,tōrē, -tȯr-, -ri\ *n* -ES [ML *dispensatorium*, fr. L *dispensatus* + *-orium* -ory] **1 :** a book or medicinal formulary containing a systematic description of most of the drugs and preparations used in medicine — compare PHARMACOPOEIA **2 :** DISPENSARY

²dispensatory *adj* [ML *dispensatorius*, fr. L *dispensatus* + *-orius* -ory] *obs* **:** DISPENSATIVE

¹dispense *n* -s [ME, expense, expenditure, supplies, fr. MF *despense*, fr. ML *dispensa*, fr. fem. of L *dispensus*, past part. of *dispendere* to weigh out] *obs* **:** EXPENSE, EXPENDITURE

²dis·pense \dəˈspen(t)s\ *vb* -ED/-ING/-S [ME *dispensen*, fr. ML, LL, & L; ML *dispensare* to exempt, pardon, grant a dispensation, fr. LL, to administer, fr. L, to distribute, fr. *dispensus*, past part. of *dispendere* to weigh out, fr. *dis-* ¹dis- + *pendere* to weigh — more at SPAN] *vt* **1 a :** to deal out in portions **:** DISTRIBUTE, GIVE, PROVIDE ⟨*dispensing* alms among the poor⟩ ⟨~ goodwill with each kindness⟩ **b :** ADMINISTER ⟨~ the sacraments⟩ ⟨~ justice in his own special way⟩ **c :** to deal with **:** HANDLE ⟨the smaller roles were *dispensed* by equally capable actors⟩ **2 :** to give dispensation (as from a vow) **:** RELEASE, EXEMPT ⟨~ a friend from keeping a promise⟩ ⟨in exceptional circumstances the dean of the faculty may . . . ~ the candidate from the oral examination —*Durham Univ. Calendar*⟩ **3 a :** to put up (a prescription or medicine) **b :** to prepare and distribute (medicines) to the sick ~ *vi* **1 a** *archaic* **:** to grant permission by exempting one from a law or obligation or the penalty for its infringement or neglect **b** *obs* **:** PERMIT, ALLOW **2 a :** to grant or arrange for special exemption from a law or obligation — used with *with* ⟨asked the king to ~ with statutes that prevented immediate action against the enemy⟩ **b :** to set aside or disregard something — used with *with* **c :** to do without something — used with *with* ⟨made an analysis of production to see how many men and jobs could be *dispensed* with⟩ ⟨~ with all formalities and get to the business at hand⟩ **3 :** to be rid **:** do away — used with *with* ⟨trying to ~ with the futile necessity of eating three times a day⟩ ⟨the design reduced framing at least 25 percent and *dispensed* with foundation and wooden sills —*Monsanto Mag.*⟩ **4** *obs* **:** HANDLE, DEAL **syn** see DISTRIBUTE

³dispense *n* -s *obs* **:** DISPENSATION

dis·pens·er \dəˈspen(t)sə(r)\ *n* -s [ME *dispenser, dispensour*, fr. *dispensen* + *-er* & *-our* -or] **:** one that dispenses ⟨a ~ of favors⟩ ⟨a ~ of justice⟩: as **a** *archaic* **:** a steward or manager of a household **b :** PHARMACIST **c :** one in charge of a dispensary (sense 2) in one of certain southern states **d :** a container that extrudes, sprays, or feeds out in convenient units something (as facial tissues, tape, perfume, pills) usu. sold or acquired in multiple units or in bulk **e :** a usu. mechanical device for vending merchandise (as candy, gum, or postage stamps) ⟨a soft-drink ~⟩

dispensible *adj, obs* **:** DISPENSABLE

dispensing power *n* **:** the authority of a judge or an executive (or certain of his agents) to suspend the operation of a specific statute or rule of law where the interests of justice can be better served by such action

dis·people \dəs, (ˈ)dis+\ *vt* [¹*dis-* + *people* (n.)] **:** DEPOPULATE ⟨a plague that nearly ~*s* a country⟩ ⟨~ the woods of all game⟩

di·spermic \(ˈ)dī+\ *adj* [*di-* + *-spermic*] **:** of, relating to, or involving dispermy

di·spermous \"+\ *adj* [*di-* + *-spermous*] **:** having or producing two seeds

di·sper·my \ˈdī,spərmē\ *n* -ES [ISV *di-* + *-spermy*] **:** the entrance of two spermatozoa into one egg — compare MONOSPERMY, POLYSPERMY

dis·per·sal \dəˈspər|səl, -pə̄s|, -pəis| *sometimes* |zəl\ *n* -s **:** the act or result of dispersing **:** DISPERSION, DISTRIBUTION; *esp* **:** the process or result of spreading by active migration or of passive transfer of organisms from one place to another

dispersal area *n* **:** an area adjacent to an airfield runway connected to the runway by taxi strips and used for parking airplanes in widely separated positions to protect them from enemy air attacks

dispersal bay *or* **dispersal point** *n* **:** a dispersed parking place for an airplane in a combat area usu. protected from enemy air attack by earth or concrete revetments

dis·per·sant \|sᵊnt\ *n* -s **:** a dispersing agent; *esp* **:** a substance (as a polyphosphate) for promoting the formation and stabilization of a dispersion of one substance in another — compare EMULSIFIER, SURFACE-ACTIVE AGENT

¹dis·perse \dəˈspərs, -pə̄s, -pəis\ *vb* -ED/-ING/-S [ME *dysparsen*, fr. MF *disperser*, fr. L *dispersus*, past part. of *dispergere* to scatter, fr. *dis-* ¹dis- + *-spergere* (fr. *spargere* to strew, scatter) — more at SPARK] *vt* **1 a :** to cause to break up and go in different ways **:** send or drive into different places **:** SCATTER ⟨his command was *dispersed* by a bayonet charge —T.R.Hay⟩ **b :** to cause to become spread widely **:** DISTRIBUTE ⟨the party left the bus and *dispersed* themselves to various hotels⟩ ⟨*dispersing* barges and crews along the route as convenient —C.S.Forester⟩; *esp* **:** to separate and distribute (as troops or planes) over a large area to avoid offering the enemy a concentrated target **c :** DISSIPATE, DISPEL ⟨the sun *dispersing* the vapors of the night⟩ ⟨this explanation had at least *dispersed* the feeling of weirdness that had gripped the colony —O.E. Rölvaag⟩ **2 :** to spread or distribute from a fixed or constant source: as **a :** to spread abroad from a center of supply or control **:** DISSEMINATE ⟨~ news throughout the state⟩ ⟨80 percent of the discharge of this river at Baghdad is *dispersed* in these marshes —Wilfred Thesiger⟩ **b :** to cause to diverge **c :** to break up (light) into colors of the spectrum by refraction or diffraction **d :** to distribute (as finely divided particles) more or less evenly throughout a liquid, gaseous, or solid medium with the formation of a two-phase system ⟨~ a pigment in an oil by grinding⟩ ~ *vi* **1 a :** to break up and move or scatter to different places or go in different directions ⟨the crowd *dispersed* at the first shot⟩ ⟨his senses . . . seemed to be *dispersing* hopelessly and uncontrollably all about him —Hanama Tasaki⟩ **b :** to become dispersed ⟨the particles *dispersed* throughout the mixture⟩ **2 :** to dispel itself **:** DISSIPATE ⟨the fog *dispersed* toward morning⟩ **syn** see SCATTER

²dis·perse \dəˈs-, (ˈ)di¦s-\ *adj* [L *dispersus*] **:** widely distributed by dispersion **:** DISPERSED ⟨vitamin B is so ~ in rice polishings that ten tons of raw material yields only an ounce of vitamin —A.C.Morrison⟩

dispersed harmony \(ˈ)=¦=-\ *n* **:** OPEN HARMONY

dis·persed·ly \dəˈspər|sədlē, -pə̄|, -pəi|, |stlē, -li\ *adv* **:** in a dispersed manner

dis·persed·ness \|sədnəs, |s(t)n-\ *n* -ES **:** the state of being dispersed

dispersed phase *or* **disperse phase** *n* **:** the phase in a two-phase system that consists of finely divided particles (as colloidal particles), droplets, or bubbles of one substance distributed through another substance — called also *discontinuous phase, internal phase*

disperse dye *or* **dispersed dye** *n* **:** an insoluble dye used in the form of a dispersion (as in water) for dyeing acetate and other synthetic fibers — see DYE table I

dis·pers·er \dəˈspərsər, -pə̄sə(r, -pəisə(r\ *n* -s **:** one that disperses

disperse system *n* **:** a two-phase system consisting of a dispersion medium and a dispersed phase **:** COLLOID 1b **:** DISPERSION 4b

dis·pers·ibil·i·ty \də,spərsəˈbiləd·ē, (,)di,s-, -pə̄s-,-pəis-, -lətē, -i\ *n* -ES **:** the quality or state of being dispersible

dis·pers·ible \-səbəl\ *adj* **:** capable of being dispersed

dis·per·sion \dəˈspər|zhən, -pə̄|, -pəi|, |shən\ *n* -s [ME *dispersioun*, fr. MF *dispersion*, fr. L *dispersion-, dispersio*, fr. *dispersus* + *-ion-, -io* -ion] **1** *usu cap* **:** DIASPORA 1a **2 :** the act or process of dispersing or the state of being dispersed: **a :** the scattering of the values of a frequency distribution from their average **b :** the spreading of troops, weapons, vehicles, or airplanes over a wide area to avoid offering the enemy a concentrated target **c :** the spreading of chemical agents in warfare by means of a bursting charge in a container **d :** the scattering of projectiles or bombs fired or released under apparently identical conditions **3 a :** the selective separation of a nonhomogeneous emission in accordance with some characteristic (as wavelength, particle mass, speed, or energy); *esp* **:** the separation of light into colors by refraction or diffraction with formation of a spectrum **b :** a measure of the degree of dispersion for any region of the spectrum commonly being the derivative of the separation with respect to the chosen characteristic (as wavelength) — compare DISPERSIVE POWER **4 a :** a dispersed substance **:** DISPERSED PHASE **b :** a system (as an emulsion or suspension) consisting of a dispersed substance and the medium in which it is dispersed **:** COLLOID 1b **:** DISPERSE SYSTEM

dispersion medium *n* **:** the liquid, gaseous, or solid phase in a two-phase system in which the particles of the dispersed phase are distributed — called also *continuous phase, external phase*

dis·per·si·ty \|səd·ē\ *n* -ES [²*disperse* + *-ity*] **:** the state or the degree of chemical dispersion

dis·per·sive \|siv, |ziv\ *adj* [¹*disperse* + *-ive*] **:** of or belonging to dispersion **:** tending to disperse ⟨the modern society and the modern economy have such a ~ tendency —E.S.Griffith⟩ — **dis·per·sive·ly** \|səvlē, |zə-\ *adv* — **dis·per·sive·ness** \|sivnəs, |zi-\ *n* -ES

dispersive power *n* **:** the power of a transparent medium to separate different colors of light by refraction as measured by the difference in refractivity for two specified widely differing wavelengths divided by the refractivity at some specified intermediate wavelength

dis·per·soid \ ˌsȯid\ *n* -s [²*disperse* + *-oid*] **1 :** matter in a form produced by dispersion **:** DISPERSE SYSTEM **:** COLLOID 1b **2 :** DISPERSED PHASE

dis·personify \ˌdis+\ *vt* [¹*dis-* + *personify*] **:** to consider or call impersonal

dis·petal \dəs, (ˈ)dis+\ *vt* [¹*dis-* + *petal* (n.)] **:** to remove petals from **:** deprive of petals

dis·pharynx \dəs+\ *n, cap* [NL, fr. ¹*dis-* + *pharynx*] **:** a genus of spiruroid nematodes including destructive parasites of the proventriculus and gizzard of gallinaceous birds and usu. having intermediate stages in sow bugs

di·sphenoid \(ˈ)dī+\ *n* [*di-* + *sphenoid*] **1 :** a wedge-shaped crystal form of the tetragonal or orthorhombic system having four like triangular faces that correspond in position to alternate faces of the tetragonal or orthorhombic dipyramid and being symmetrical about each of three mutually perpendicular diad axes of symmetry in all classes except the tetragonal-disphenoidal in which the form is generated by an inverse tetrad axis of symmetry **2 :** a form of crystal bounded by eight scalene triangles arranged in pairs **:** the tetragonal scalenohedron — **di·sphenoidal** \(ˌ)dī+\ *adj*

dis·phol·i·dus \dəˈsfäləd əs\ *n, cap* [NL, fr. ¹*dis-* + *-pholidus* (fr. Gk *pholid-, pholis* scale of a reptile) — more at PHOLID-] **:** a genus of boigid snakes that includes the boomslang

di·spireme *also* **di·spirem** \(ˈ)dī+\ *n* [*di-* + *spireme*] **:** a supposed late phase in mitotic division characterized by association of each set of daughter chromosomes into a spireme and now usu. considered an observational artifact

di·spirit \də, (ˈ)di+\ *also* **dis·spirit** \də, (ˈ)di(s)+\ *vt* [¹*dis-* + *spirit* (n.)] **1** *obs* **:** to take away the vigor or force from **2 :** to deprive of cheerful or sanguine spirits **:** DEPRESS, DISCOURAGE ⟨~*ed* by their futile efforts —C.H.Grandgent⟩ ⟨a sparsely settled community laid out on ~*ing* flat lands —*Amer. Guide Series: N.Y. City*⟩ **syn** see DISCOURAGE

dispirited *adj* **1 :** marked by gloom of spirit, by a sense of personal defeat, or by a pessimistic outlook **:** DISCOURAGED, DEPRESSED, DOWNCAST ⟨had never seen a more ~ man than he when he lost the election⟩ **2 a :** lacking independent vigor or forcefulness **:** flaccid in moral quality ⟨the weakness doesn't lie in the pessimism of the younger writers so much as it lies in their rather ~ correctness and conformity —Malcolm Cowley⟩ **b :** lacking an essential spirit **:** FLAT **:** LIFELESS ⟨the black gummy ~ air —R.P.Warren⟩ **syn** see DOWNCAST

di·spir·it·ed·ly *adv* **:** in a dispirited manner ⟨working ~ at a job he would never finish⟩

di·spir·it·ed·ness *n* **:** the quality or state of being dispirited **:** DEJECTION, DEPRESSION

dispiriting *adj* **:** acting to dispirit **:** DISCOURAGING, DISHEARTENING, CHEERLESS ⟨one person whose struggle for existence was more hopeless and ~ than his —Erskine Caldwell⟩ ⟨no ~ rows of tenements are to be seen —Ellery Sedgwick⟩ **syn** see DISMAL

di·spir·it·ing·ly *adv* **:** in a dispiriting manner

di·spir·it·ment \-mənt\ *n* -s **:** the state of being dispirited or disheartened **:** DISCOURAGEMENT

dis·pit·e·ous \dəˈspid·ēəs, (ˈ)dis-\ *adj* [alter. of *despiteous*] *archaic* **:** CRUEL, SPITEFUL, PITILESS — **dis·pit·e·ous·ly** *adv*

dis·place \dəs, (ˈ)dis+\ *vt* [prob. fr. MF *desplacer*, fr. *des-* ¹*dis-* + *place* — more at PLACE] **1 a :** to remove from the usual or proper place **:** put out of place; *specif* **:** to expel or force to flee from home or homeland ⟨the war has *displaced* thousands of people⟩ **b :** to remove from an office or position of dignity **:** DISCHARGE, DEPOSE **c** *obs* **:** to drive away **:** BANISH **d :** to shift or redirect from a previous or usual objective or form of outlet ⟨in every society there are hatreds and frustrations which the movement of events ~*s* on chosen victims —Max Lerner⟩ **2 :** to crowd out **:** take the place of esp. by force **:** move from place by occupying the space **:** SUPPLANT ⟨the Bishop's Bible that immediately *displaced* the Great Bible as the ecclesiastical version in use in the churches —I.M.Price⟩ ⟨today, when barns have been *displaced* by garages —*Amer. Guide Series: Minn.*⟩; *specif* **:** to set free from chemical combination by taking the place of ⟨zinc ~*s* the hydrogen of dilute acids⟩ **3 :** to put (an object) in place of another **:** substitute (one thing) for another ⟨an effort . . . to ~ the American shoe with the English boot —*Encyc. Americana*⟩ **4 :** to subject to percolation **syn** see REPLACE

dis·place·able \-əbəl\ *adj* **:** that can be displaced

displaced person *n* **:** a person expelled, deported, or impelled to flee from his country of nationality or habitual residence by the forces or consequences of war or oppression — abbr. *DP*

displaced speech *n* **:** the use of a word to refer to something that is not present

dis·place·ment \-mənt\ *n* **1 a :** the act or process of displacing or the state of being displaced ⟨sideward ~ of the foundation of a house by earth pressure⟩ ⟨the final ~ of an ancient and unjust law⟩ ⟨the uneven ~ of population and consequent disorganization of tribal village life —Tom Marvel⟩ **:** DEPOSITION ⟨the ultimate ~ of the autocratic ruler⟩ **:** DISLOCATION ⟨the ~ of a knee joint⟩ **b :** PERCOLATION 1d **2 :** the quantity in which or the degree to which something is displaced: as **a :** the volume or weight of a fluid (as water) displaced by a floating body (as a ship) of equal weight **b :** the difference between the initial position of a geologic body and its later position along a geologic fault **c :** the distance from a neutral or equilibrium point to any specified point of a path in vibratory motion **d :** PISTON DISPLACEMENT **3 a :** the electric intensity in a dielectric medium under electric influence multiplied by the dielectric constant of the medium **b :** the product of this multiplication divided by 4π **4 :** a vector drawn from an initial position of a material particle to any subsequent position **5 a :** redirection of an emotion or impulse from its original object (as an idea or person) to something that is more acceptable **b :** SUBLIMATION 1b

displacement angle *n* **:** angular phase change in the terminal voltage of an alternator when the orig. open external circuit is closed upon a load

displacement current *n* **:** a limited shifting of electric components that occurs within a dielectric when a voltage is applied to or removed from it (as in charging or discharging a capacitor) and that corresponds to the current in the circuit supplying the voltage

displacement law *n* **:** any of three statements in physics or chemistry: (1) WIEN'S DISPLACEMENT LAW or (2) the emission of an alpha particle by an atom reduces the atomic number by two while the emission of a beta particle increases it by one or (3) ionization of an element causes both its spectrum and its chemical properties to resemble those of the element whose atomic number is less by one, two, or more according as the ionization is single, double, or higher

displacement pump *n* **:** a pump (as an air lift or pulsometer) that raises or transfers a fluid by direct displacement with no transformation of the kinetic energy due to the fluid's motion into potential energy due to pressure

displacement theory *n* **:** WEGENER HYPOTHESIS

dis·pla·cen·cy \dəˈsplās³nsē\ *n* -ES [ML *displacentia*, alter. of L *displicentia*, fr. *displicent-, displicens* (pres. part. of *displicēre* to displease) + *-ia* -y — more at DISPLEASE] *archaic* **:** DISLIKE, DISSATISFACTION, DISPLEASURE

dis·placer \dəˈsplāsə(r), (ˈ)diˌs-\ *n* **:** one that displaces; *specif* **:** PERCOLATOR b

dis·pla·cive \dəˈsplāsiv, (ˈ)diˌs-\ *adj, of a crystal* **:** affected by, resulting from, or causing displacement

displant *vt* [MF *desplanter*, fr. *des-* ¹*dis-* + *planter* to plant, fr. LL *plantare*] **1** *obs* **:** to take (a plant) out of the ground **2** *obs* **a :** to deprive (as a town or settlement) of inhabitants **:** destroy the essential character of (as a town or settlement) **b :** to remove from a place (as of habitation or a colony or a settlement) **:** root out **:** DISPLACE; *also* **:** SUPPLANT

¹dis·play \dəˈsplā *sometimes* ˈdiˌs-\ *vb* -ED/-ING/-S [ME *displayen*, fr. AF *despleier*, fr. L *displicare* to scatter, fr. *dis-* ¹dis- + *plicare* to fold — more at PLY] *vt* **1** *obs* **a :** to spread or stretch out or wide **:** UNFOLD **b :** DEPLOY 1 **2 a :** to spread before the view **:** exhibit to the sight or mind **:** give evidence of **:** SHOW, MANIFEST, DISCLOSE ⟨~*ed* the flag for all to see⟩ ⟨~ a map on the table⟩ ⟨~ one's appreciation⟩ ⟨~ criminal tendencies⟩; *specif* **:** to put on exhibition ⟨these reproductions have been ~*ed* throughout Canada —*Report: (Canadian) Royal Commission on Nat'l Development*⟩ ⟨two model houses were ~*ed* for a week⟩ **b :** to exhibit conspicuously ⟨~ a gift for ham acting⟩ **c :** to set forth (as in representation or narrative) **:** DESCRIBE, DEPICT ⟨the canvases ~*ed* shabby acrobats —*Time*⟩ **d :** to set in display in printing **3** *obs* **:** DISCOVER, DESCRY ~ *vi* **1 :** to make a display **:** act as one making a show or demonstration **2 :** to present or advertise something by means of a display **syn** see SHOW

²display \"\ *n* -s *often attrib* **1** *obs* **:** a presentation by representation or narrative **:** DESCRIPTION **2 a :** an exhibiting or showing of something **:** an unfolding or opening out to view **:** EXHIBITION, MANIFESTATION ⟨want no ~ of emotion —Henry Adams⟩; *specif* **:** the means by which radar echoes or other information is given to an operator in visual form in communications **b :** ostentatious show **:** exhibition for effect ⟨the Church of the Brethren or the Mennonite Church, neither of which countenances worldly ~ —*Amer. Guide Series: Pa.*⟩ ⟨making a disgusting ~ in front of company⟩ **c :** composition designed to catch the eye (as by the use of lines of uneven length or different type sizes or styles) and typically used in title pages, advertising brochures, and magazine covers ⟨~ composition⟩ ⟨~ typefaces⟩; *also* **:** printed matter so composed ⟨the local press gave top ~ to the murder story⟩ **d :** an often artistic conspicuous eye-catching construction or assemblage by which something (as merchandise or collector's items) is exhibited or advertised ⟨his pictures are on ~ at the art gallery⟩; *also* **:** the use of such constructions or assemblages ⟨~ is the key to self-service sales —*Printers' Ink*⟩ **3 :** a stereotypic pattern of behavior exhibited esp. by male birds in the breeding season that serves to initiate specific responses in another individual (as a possible breeding partner or a potential territorial rival) ⟨the males congregate on a low knoll serving as a ~ ground —J.M.Flagler⟩

syn PARADE, ARRAY, POMP: DISPLAY may suggest a spectacular spreading out in or as if in exhibition to impress by extent, detail, beauty, number, or lavishness ⟨the *display* of political partisanship on the part of the Hamilton-Jefferson faction —J.C.Fitzpatrick⟩ ⟨fine editions that make an impressive *display* in an oilman's library —Green Peyton⟩ ⟨a fine *display* of camellias in bloom —*Amer. Guide Series: La.*⟩ ⟨an imitation of the jousts of the middle ages, providing *displays* of horsemanship —*Amer. Guide Series: N.C.*⟩ PARADE may indicate ostentatious flaunting, usu. sustained, to impress, dazzle, or awe another ⟨he does not make the least *parade* of his wealth or his gentility —J.C.Snaith⟩ ⟨in the ritornello, with its *parade* of themes, one immediately recognizes the orchestral opulence and virtuosity of the incomparable Toscanini —Abram Chasins⟩ ARRAY may suggest order and brilliancy in display of or as if of marshaled ranks of soldiers ⟨we look up at this facade and see a magnificent *array* of saints, all ordered in their appropriate niches; we recognize Homer, Dante, Shakespeare and several others —Herbert Read⟩ ⟨today's motorists come in all seasons to revel in such an *array* of splendors as few other roads of the state can offer —Maynard Leahey⟩ POMP, once often used of a ceremonial process or pageant, now suggests spectacular brilliance or splendid ostentation often accomplished with vain or lofty punctiliousness ⟨a *pomp* of flaming colors —F.D.Ommanney⟩ ⟨the *pomp* of nations that pretend to be sovereign —C.W.Ferguson⟩

display advertising *n* **:** advertising not under classified headings in a newspaper or magazine; *esp* **:** advertising that utilizes various kinds of display techniques or devices (as large print, colorful makeup, or a large spread)

display artist *n* **:** one who prepares advertising displays for windows or interiors of business concerns

displayed *adj* [ME, fr. past part. of *displayen*] **:** having wings spread out — used of a heraldic representation of a bird of prey, esp. an eagle

display key *n* [*display* (*room*)] **:** a key generally used in hotel rooms to prevent any unwarranted entrance and that when used to operate a given lock of a master-keyed lock system prevents the lock from being opened by any other key except an emergency key

display line *n* **:** matter set in one line in nontext often ornamental type

dis·play·man \dəˈsplāmən, -ˌman\ *n, pl* **displaymen :** DISPLAY ARTIST

display pipe *n* **:** a pipe forming part of an organ case; *sometimes* **:** a dummy pipe

displays *pres 3d sing of* DISPLAY, *pl of* DISPLAY

display window *n* **:** a large window usu. in the front of a store for the display of merchandise

disple *vt* -ED/-ING/-S [ME *dissplyen*, alter. of *disciplinen*] *obs* **:** DISCIPLINE

displeasant *adj* [ME *displesaunt*, fr. MF *desplaisant*, pres. part. of *desplaire, desplaisir*] **1** *obs* **:** DISPLEASING **2** *obs* **:** DISPLEASED

dis·please \dəˈsplēz, (ˈ)diˌs-\ *vb* [ME *displesen*, fr. MF *desplais-*, stem of *desplaisir, desplaire*, fr. (assumed) VL *displacēre*, alter. of L *displicēre*, fr. *dis-* ¹dis- + *-plicēre* (fr. *placēre* to please) — more at PLEASE] *vt* **1 :** to incur the disapproval of esp. as accompanied by annoyance, aversion, or dislike ⟨a rich man can discharge anyone in his employment who ~*s* him —G.B.Shaw⟩ ⟨the verdict *displeased* the judge⟩ **2 :** to arouse unpleasant feelings in **:** be offensive to ⟨the colors of the picture *displeased* her the most⟩ ~ *vi* **:** to give displeasure or offense ⟨it is best to always ~ if it can be decently avoided⟩

dis·pleased·ly \-z(ə)dlē, -li\ *adv* **:** in a manner that shows one's displeasure

displeasing *adj* [ME *displesing*, fr. pres. part. of *displesen* to displease] **1 :** causing displeasure ⟨~ behavior⟩ **2 :** lacking in pleasing quality or effect ⟨~ voice⟩

dis·pleas·ing·ly *adv* **:** in a displeasing manner ⟨making ~ cutting remarks about one's friends⟩

dis·pleas·ing·ness *n* **:** the quality or state of being displeasing

¹dis·pleasure \dəs, (ˈ)dis+\ *n* [ME *displesure*, alter. (influenced by *plesure, plesire* pleasure) of *displesire*, fr. MF *desplaisir*, fr. *des-* ¹dis- + *plaisir* pleasure — more at PLEASURE] **1 :** the feeling of one that is displeased **:** DISAPPROVAL, DISLIKE, DISFAVOR, INDIGNATION ⟨not anxious to incur further government ~ —H.C.Atyeo⟩ **2 a :** DISCOMFORT, UNEASINESS **b :** PAIN, SORROW, UNHAPPINESS ⟨pleasure and ~ are intensive quantities —Lucius Garvin⟩ **3** *archaic* **:** something that displeases **:** a cause of irritation or annoyance **:** OFFENSE, INJURY

²displeasure \"\ *vt, archaic* **:** DISPLEASE

dis·plenish \dəs, (ˈ)dis+\ *vt* [*dis-* + *plenish*] *Scot* **:** to divest or strip (as a house or farm) of contents and equipment **:** DEPLENISH

displenishing sale *n, Scot* **:** a disposal sale esp. of farm or household goods

displicence *n* -s [L *displicentia*] *obs* **:** DISPLICENCY

dis·plic·en·cy \dəˈsplis³nsē, ˈdisplǝs-\ *n* -ES [L *displicentia* — more at DISPLACENCY] *archaic* **:** DISSATISFACTION, AVERSION, DISCONTENT

dis·plode \dəˈsplōd\ *vb* -ED/-ING/-S [L *displodere*, fr. *dis-* apart + *-plodere* (fr. *plaudere* to clap, beat, applaud) — more at DIS-] *archaic* **:** to discharge explosively **:** EXPLODE — **dis·plo·sion** \-ōzhən\ *n* -s

dis·plume \dəs, (ˈ)dis+\ *vt* [¹*dis-* + *plume* (n.)] **:** DEPLUME

dis·pone \dəˈspōn\ *vt* -ED/-ING/-S [ME *disponen* to set in order, arrange, dispose, fr. L *disponere* — more at DISPOSE] *Scots law* **:** to dispose of, grant, or transfer (real or personal property) legally — **dis·pon·er** \-nər\ *n* -s

dis·pon·ee \ˌdis(ˌ)spōˈnē, dəˌs-\ *n* -s [*dispone* + *-ee*] *Scots law* **:** one to whom property is disponed

dis·pon·ible \dəˈspōnəbəl\ *adj* **:** capable of being placed, arranged, or disposed of as one wishes **:** AVAILABLE

dis·pope \dəs, (ˈ)dis+\ *vt* -ED/-ING/-S [¹*dis-* + *pope* (n.)] **:** to depose from the office of pope

di·sporous \(ˈ)dī+\ *adj* [*di-* + *-sporous*] **:** having two spores

¹dis·port \də+\ *n* -s [ME, fr. MF *desport*, fr. *desporter*] **1 a :** PLAY, SPORT, DIVERSION **b :** a pastime or game **2** *archaic* **:** MIRTH, AMUSEMENT, DELIGHT **syn** see ²PLAY

²disport \"\ *vb* -ED/-ING/-S [ME *disporten*, fr. MF *desporter*, fr. *des-* ¹dis- + *porter* to carry — more at PORT (to carry)] *vt* **1 :** DIVERT, AMUSE, ENTERTAIN ⟨converted one of the stables . . . into a billiard room and here the youths ~*ed* themselves to their hearts' content —Thomas Wall⟩ ⟨sea lions bark and ~ themselves before a gallery of enthusiasts —*Amer. Guide Series: N.Y. City*⟩ **2 :** to make a fine display of ⟨the town ~*ed* three bright shiny new hacks with rumbling wheels —W.A.White⟩ ⟨gave the . . . critics an opportunity to ~ their innocence of Christian knowledge or culture —*Time*⟩ **3 :** to conduct or behave (oneself) **:** DEPORT ⟨~*ed* himself like the high-bred virtuoso he is —*Musical Digest*⟩ ⟨equip a man to ~ himself gracefully in the domain of American speech —*Saturday Rev.*⟩ ~ *vi* **:** to amuse or divert oneself esp. in a light, frolicsome, lively, or wanton way ⟨do you dig in the garden, ride horses, ~ at dude ranches, or amble around the countryside? —*Better Homes & Gardens*⟩ ⟨in this den he would ~ among books, radios, tape recorders —Murray Schumach⟩ **syn** see PLAY

di·sportive \də+\ *adj, archaic* **:** SPORTIVE

di·spo·rum \(ˈ)dīˈspōrəm, ˈdispər-\ *n* [NL, fr. *di-* + *-sporum* (fr. Gk *sporos* seed) — more at SPORE] **1** *cap* **:** a small genus of herbs of the family Liliaceae with leafy branching stems, small terminal greenish, yellow, or purplish flowers, and oval berries **2** *pl* **dispo·ra** \-rə\ *or* **disporums** \-rəmz\ **:** a plant of the genus *Disporum*

dis·pos·abil·i·ty \dəˌspōzəˈbiləd·ē, (ˌ)diˌs-, -ətē, -i\ *n* -ES **:** the quality or state of being disposable ⟨the ~ of paper napkins is their great recommendation⟩

dis·pos·able \dəˈspōzəbəl\ *adj* [*dispose* + *-able*] **1 :** free to be used as occasion requires **:** not assigned to any special use ⟨needs all ~ air-combat units for the Mediterranean front —*New Republic*⟩ **2 :** capable of being disposed of easily; *esp* **:** designed to be thrown away after use with only negligible loss ⟨fabrics from which are made ~ napkins, towels, and diapers —S.B.Hunt⟩ — **dis·pos·able·ness** *n* -ES

disposable income *n* **:** the personal income that is left after the deduction of personal taxes and that is available for consumption and savings

disposable weight *n* **:** all weights on an aircraft other than the fixed weight

¹dispos·al \dəˈspōzəl\ *n* -s [*dispose* + *-al*] **1 :** the act or process of disposing: as **a :** orderly or systematic placement, distribution, or arrangement ⟨the ~ of troops along the ridge⟩ ⟨the pitching of the tent and the ~ of the gear under cover⟩ **b :** the regulation of the fate or condition of something **:** ADMINISTRATION, DISPENSATION **c :** the transference of something into new hands or to a new place **:** BESTOWAL ⟨the ~ of political offices by patronage⟩ ⟨worrying about the ultimate ~ of one's property⟩ **d :** a discarding or throwing away ⟨the ~ of the dirty paper napkins⟩ ⟨the ~ of all the rubbish on the desk⟩ **:** DESTRUCTION ⟨the ~ of all enemy aircraft by concentrated flak⟩; *esp* **:** the discarding or destroying of garbage or sewage or its transformation into something useful (as fertilizer) or innocuous (as by incineration) **2 :** the power or authority to dispose of or use at one's convenience **:** discretionary use, command, or control — used esp. in the phrase *at the disposal of* ⟨a plane was always at the ~ of the president⟩ ⟨Congress had at its ~ the means of alleviating the high cost of living —*Current Biog.*⟩ ⟨the shortness of the period at our ~ —D.C.Buchanan⟩ ⟨the effectiveness of the central organization depended in the last resort on the amount of money it had at its ~ —H.J.Hanham⟩

²disposal \"\ *or* **disposal unit** *n* -s [garbage-*disposal* (*unit*)] **:** DISPOSER c

disposal field *n* **:** an area of ground under whose surface the overflow from a septic tank is distributed in drain tile to be absorbed in the soil

¹dis·pose \dəˈspōz\ *vb* -ED/-ING/-S [ME *disposen*, fr. MF *disposer*, modif. (influenced by *poser* to put, place) of L *disponere* to set in order, arrange (perfect stem *dispos-*), fr. *dis-* ¹dis- + *ponere* to put, place — more at POSITION, POSE] *vt* **1 a :** to give a tendency to ⟨night air was thought to ~ one to sickness⟩ **:** put in a frame of mind or feeling that is favorable (as to an act or a condition) ⟨the remark *disposed* him to like the man immediately⟩ **b :** to put into a condition (as for a particular action) **:** make ready **:** PREPARE ⟨troops *disposed* for immediate withdrawal⟩ **2 a :** to put in place or order **:** distribute and arrange esp. for greatest effectiveness, economy, ease, or conformity to a pattern ⟨she carried an armful of books; these she *disposed* within reach —Elinor Wylie⟩ ⟨branches and leaves were *disposed*, not as combinations of color in mass, but as designs in line —Laurence Binyon⟩ ⟨the general who *disposed* his forces so as to counteract a greater force —W.E.Channing⟩ **b** *obs* **:** REGULATE, DETERMINE, ORDER, MANAGE **c** *archaic* **:** deal out **:** assign to a use **:** bestow for a purpose **:** dispose of **d** *obs* **:** to assign to a particular place or position ~ *vi* **1 :** to arrange or settle a matter finally or definitively **:** make disposition; *esp* **:** to regulate the fate or condition finally or definitively ⟨man proposes but God ~*s*⟩ **2** *obs* **:** BARGAIN **syn** see SET — **dispose of 1 a :** to place, distribute, or arrange esp. in an orderly or systematic way (as according to a pattern) ⟨the men *disposed of* the weapons in convenient quickly accessible places⟩ **b :** to apportion or allot (as to particular purposes) freely or as one sees fit ⟨she has been allowed to *dispose of* her time in the most idle and frivolous manner —Jane Austen⟩ **2 a :** to transfer into new hands or to the control of someone else (as by selling or bargaining away) **:** RELINQUISH, BESTOW ⟨*dispose of* some property to a man all too anxious to buy⟩ ⟨*dispose of* public offices to all his political friends⟩ **b** (1) **:** to get rid of **:** throw away **:** DISCARD ⟨*dispose of* a lot of old clothes by burning them⟩ ⟨*dispose of* the trash in several barrels⟩ (2) **:** to treat or handle (something) with the result of finishing or finishing with ⟨the article *disposed of* the matter in two paragraphs⟩ ⟨the ability of supervisors and employees to *dispose of* differences —*Annual Report Pa. Railroad*⟩ **:** COMPLETE, DISPATCH ⟨they had quickly *disposed of* the meal⟩ **c :** DESTROY ⟨*disposed of* three enemy planes in an afternoon⟩

²dispose *n* -s **1** *obs* **:** the disposal or the power or right of disposal **2** *obs* **:** DISPOSITION; *also* **:** DEMEANOR

dis·posed \-zd\ *adj* [ME, fr. past part. of *disposen*] **1 :** having a particular temperament, disposition, or tendency or being of a particular frame of mind or condition of bodily health ⟨a dog that is ~ to bite⟩ ⟨a man generally ~ to love his fellow men⟩ ⟨a man well ~ in all physical qualities⟩ ⟨a young boy already criminally ~⟩ ⟨those ~ to violate or evade the decrees of the sovereign —M.R.Cohen⟩ **2** *obs* **:** MERRY, JOLLY, MIRTHFUL, HAPPY

dis·pos·ed·ly \-zədlē, -li\ *adv* **:** in a dignified manner ⟨a stout man moving ~ along the promenade⟩

dis·pos·er \-zə(r)\ *n* -s **:** one that disposes: as **a** *archaic* **:** MANAGER, DIRECTOR **b** *archaic* **:** DISPENSER **c :** an electrical device that forms part of a sink drain and disposes of garbage by grinding it up to be flushed through the house drainpipes

dis·pos·ing·ly *adv* **:** in a disposing manner

dis·po·si·tio \ˌdispəˈzishē,ō, -zid·ē,ō\ *n* -s [L] **:** the rhetorical and logical arrangement of the matter or the discrete elements of a discourse esp. in classical and Renaissance rhetorical systems

dis·po·si·tion \ˌdispəˈzishən\ *n* -s [ME *disposicioun*, fr. MF *disposition*, fr. L *disposition-, dispositio*, fr. *dispositus* (past part. of *disponere* to set in order, arrange) + *-ion-, -io* -ion — more at DISPOSE] **1 :** the act or the power of disposing or disposing of or the state of being disposed or disposed of: as **a :** ADMINISTRATION, CONTROL, MANAGEMENT; *often* **:** divine dispensation ⟨received the law by the ~ of angels —Acts 7:53 (AV)⟩ **b :** a placing elsewhere, a giving over to the care or possession of another, or a relinquishing ⟨saw to the ~ of all surplus goods by shipment to needy countries⟩ ⟨the ~ of the garbage was always a problem⟩ **:** the power of so placing, giving, ridding oneself of, relinquishing, or doing with as one wishes **:** discretionary control — used esp. in the phrase *at the disposition of*; *specif* **:** the transfer of property from one to another (as by gift, barter, or sale or by will) or the scheme or arrangement by which such transfer is effected **c :** an ordering or arranging or a state of being ordered or arranged usu. systematically or in an orderly way and esp. of the parts of a whole **:** orderly preparation or placing **:** ARRANGEMENT ⟨the ~ of the parts of his argument made his speech forceful and tidy⟩ ⟨the ~ of the artillery was shown on the map⟩ **2 a :** the prevailing tendency, aspect, mood, or inclination of one's spirits ⟨with large blue eyes that . . . showed her thoughts and ~*s* —Hugh Walpole⟩ ⟨woke up in a nasty ~⟩ **:** the complex of attitudes, proclivities, and responses conditioning conduct **:** PROPENSITY ⟨his ~ was to make the worst of bad fortune⟩ ⟨conservatism with them is not so much a program as a ~ or attitude or temper —Daniel Aaron⟩ **:** temperamental makeup ⟨a man of broad sympathies and a genial ~⟩ **b** (1) *obs* **:** physical condition **:** HEALTH (2) *archaic* **:** CONSTITUTION, NATURE **c :** the inclination, tendency, or power of anything to act in a certain manner under given circumstances ⟨the ~ of sugar to dissolve in water⟩ ⟨the ~ to war or to peace in human societies seems to be a matter of economic, political, social, and psychological structurings of the society itself —Weston LaBarre⟩ **3 :** the number and types of stops in an organ **:** the makeup of an organ **4 dispositions** *pl* **:** strategical or tactical military plans ⟨the general perfected his ~*s* for the campaign⟩ **5 :** the sentence given to or treatment prescribed for a juvenile offender ⟨boys 12 to 16 who were sent to his ward for routine observation pending ~ by the courts —Charles Grutzner⟩

syn COMPLEXION, TEMPERAMENT, PERSONALITY, INDIVIDUALITY, TEMPER, CHARACTER: DISPOSITION refers to one's accustomed attitudes and moods in reacting to life around one ⟨as ages of fierceness have overlaid what is naturally kindly in the *dispositions* of ordinary men and women —Bertrand Russell⟩ ⟨the taint of his father's insanity perhaps appeared in his unbalanced *disposition* —E.S.Bates⟩ COMPLEXION blends together notions involving mood and attitude and ideas about ways of thinking ⟨the rationalist mind, radically taken, is of a doctrinaire and authoritative *complexion:* the phrase 'must be' is ever on its lips —William James⟩ ⟨great thinkers of various *complexion*, who differing in many fundamental points, all alike assert the relativity of truth —Havelock Ellis⟩ TEMPERAMENT may suggest individual proclivities, esp. as colored by feeling and emotion and esp. in matters social or creative ⟨the electric amenities that pass between artistic *temperaments* at different tensions still find free play —J.L.Lowes⟩ ⟨melancholy was the dominant note of his *temperament* . . . a melancholy tempered by recurrences of faith and resignation and simple joy —James Joyce⟩ PERSONALITY stresses those traits the composite of which tends to individualize one in his society, often those which attract, which give popularity, ready appeal, or decisive or compelling interest ⟨the *personality* of the brilliant secretary of the treasury is not clearly defined. The inner man . . . is unfortunately neglected —J.C.Miller⟩ ⟨by sheer *personality* he has so far propped up a somewhat artificial arrangement with the smaller parties —*Economist*⟩ INDIVIDUALITY stresses an individualizing and distinguishing composite of traits ⟨an *individuality*, a style of its own —Willa Cather⟩ ⟨detected for the first time, beneath the dehumanized drudge, the stirrings of a separate and perhaps capricious *individuality* —Arnold Bennett⟩ TEMPER may indicate the frame of mind with which one makes choices and decisions, faces difficulties or problems, or controls and governs himself ⟨a less dogmatic *temper* is becoming apparent among the scientists themselves —Irving Babbitt⟩ ⟨after four years of fighting, the *temper* of the victors was such that they were quite incapable of making a just settlement —Aldous Huxley⟩ CHARACTER may suggest the deep, fundamental, and established complex of moral traits, the genuine and lasting individualizing inner nature of a person ⟨that inexorable law of human souls that we prepare ourselves for sudden deeds by the reiterated choice of good or evil that determines *character* —George Eliot⟩ ⟨*character*, or what is fixed, hard, and resistant in human nature, cannot be expressed lyrically —*Times Lit. Supp.*⟩

dis·po·si·tion·al \ˌdispəˈzishənᵊl, -shnəl\ *adj* **:** of, belonging to, or characterizing the disposition ⟨~ statements, namely statements to the effect that a mentioned thing, beast, or person has a certain capacity, tendency or propensity, or is subject to a certain liability —Gilbert Ryle⟩

dis·po·si·tioned \ˌdispəˈzishənd\ *adj* **:** having a particular disposition ⟨a friendly-*dispositioned* person, anxious to help⟩

dispositions *pl of* DISPOSITION

dispositios *pl of* DISPOSITIO

dis·pos·i·tive \dəˈspäzəd·iv, -pōz-\ *adj* [L *dispositus* (past part. of *disponere* to set in order, arrange) + E *-ive* — more at DISPOSE] **1** *archaic* **:** having the capacity or quality of giving a tendency or inclination to something **2 :** disposing or belonging to the disposition or direction of something **:** of or belonging to disposal or control

dispositively *adv, obs* **:** as a possibility **:** in respect to a tendency or to a future eventuality

dis·pos·i·tor \dəˈspäzəd·ə(r)\ *n* -s [L, arranger, fr. *dispositus* + *-or*] **:** a planet which is in astrology lord of the sign where another planet is

dis·possess \ˌdis +\ *vt* [MF *despossesser*, fr. *des-* ¹dis- + *possesser* to possess — more at POSSESS] **1 a :** to put out of possession esp. of property or land — usu. used with *of* before the thing taken away ⟨~ a man of his goods and chattels⟩ **b :** to strip of possessions ⟨a depression in which many people found themselves ~*ed*⟩ **2 a :** to put out of occupancy **:** EJECT, OUST **b :** to drive out **:** BANISH ⟨~*ing* the French from the southern shores of the Mediterranean —Percy Winner⟩ **3** *archaic* **:** to free from possession by an evil spirit **syn** see DEPRIVE

dispossessed *adj* **:** deprived of physical or spiritual security (as by the loss of property, rank, faith, or patriotic ties) **:** physically or spiritually homeless ⟨made a living out of shepherding ~ people from one country to another —James Stern⟩ ⟨a ~ man in every sense, abandoned by a feckless wife, deprived of spiritual zest by isolation —*Time*⟩

dis·possession \ˌdis +\ *n* **:** the act of dispossessing or the state of being dispossessed ⟨Alexander proposed to himself nothing short of complete ~ of Darius in favor of himself as captain general of Hellas —*Encyc. Americana*⟩ ⟨waves of ~ that have marked American history — Indian driven out by pioneer, pioneer displaced by planter, planter superseded by speculator —Paul Pickrel⟩; *specif* **:** legal ouster

dispossess notice *n* **:** an official notice from an owner (as of a house or store) to one in possession to evacuate the premises within a certain time

dis·pos·ses·sor \"+\ *n* **:** one that dispossesses someone of something

dis·possessory warrant \ˌdis+...-\ *n* [*dispossess* + *-ory*] **:** a warrant giving authority to dispossess (as by eviction)

dis·post \dəˈspōst, (ˈ)diˈs-\ *vt* [¹*dis-* + *post* (position)] **:** to remove from a position

dis·po·sure \dəˈspōzhə(r)\ *n* -s [*dispose* + *-ure*] *archaic* **:** DISPOSAL, DISPOSITION

dis·prais·al \ˌdis'prāzəl, (ˈ)diˈs-\ *n* -s **:** DISPRAISE

¹dis·praise \-āz\ *vt* [ME *dispraisen*, fr. OF *despreisier*, *desprisier*, fr. *des-* ¹dis- + *preisier*, *prisier* to praise — more at PRAISE] **:** to notice or comment on with disapprobation or some degree of censure **:** DISPARAGE, DEPRECIATE ⟨*dispraising* it in a few light easy sentences of condemnation —Arnold Bennett⟩ — **dis·prais·er** \-zə(r)\ *n*

²dispraise \"\ *n* **:** the act of dispraising **:** DISPARAGEMENT, DEPRECIATION ⟨her addiction to withering ~ and her parsimony when dispensing appreciation —C.J.Rolo⟩

dis·prais·ing·ly *adv* **:** in a dispraising manner **:** with dispraise ⟨he usually spoke ~ of anyone who disagreed with him⟩

di·spread *or* **dis·spread** \də +\ *vb* [¹*dis-* + *spread*] **:** to spread abroad or out **:** spread in different directions **:** open out **:** EXPAND ⟨the morning sun ~ his beams⟩ ⟨a peacock with tail ~⟩

dis·privilege \dəs, (ˈ)dis+\ *vt* [¹*dis-* + *privilege*] **:** to deprive of privilege, a privilege, or normal privileges ⟨members of *disprivileged* ethnic minorities —Jerome Himelhoch⟩

dis·prize \dəˈsprīz, (ˈ)diˈs-\ *vt* [MF *despriser*, fr. OF *despreisier*, *desprisier* — more at DISPRAISE] **1** *obs* **:** UNDERVALUE, UNDERESTIMATE **2 :** to hold in contempt **:** DESPISE ⟨the pangs of *disprized* love —Shak.⟩

¹dis·profit \dəs, (ˈ)dis+\ *vt* [¹*dis-* + *profit* (v.)] *archaic* **:** to prove to be a loss or detriment to

²disprofit \"\ *n* [¹*dis-* + *profit* (n.)] *archaic* **:** DAMAGE, DETRIMENT, LOSS

dis·proof \dəs, (ˈ)dis +\ *n* [¹*dis-* + *proof*] **1 :** a proving that something is other than someone says or maintains **:** CONFUTATION, REFUTATION ⟨offering evidence in ~ of a claim⟩ **2 :** evidence that disproves or tends to disprove ⟨he would not believe even with the ~ before his eyes⟩

¹dis·proportion \ˌdis+\ *n* [¹*dis-* + *proportion*] **1 :** absence of proportion **:** lack of symmetry or proper relation ⟨~ between a maternal pelvis and a fetal head⟩ **:** DISPARITY ⟨a ~ between the large head and the average-size body⟩ **:** a relationship in which there is this absence or lack ⟨a supply in ~ with the demand⟩ **2 :** an instance of disproportion ⟨the paintings . . . abound in bad drawing and ~*s* —Aldous Huxley⟩

²disproportion \"\ *vt* **:** to make out of proportion **:** cause to be unsuitable in quantity, form, or fitness **:** MISMATCH

dis·proportionable \ˌdis +\ *adj, archaic* **:** DISPROPORTIONAL, DISPROPORTIONATE

dis·proportional \"+\ *adj* **:** DISPROPORTIONATE — **dis·proportionality** \"+\ *n* — **dis·proportionally** \"+\ *adv* — **dis·proportionalness** \"+\ *n*

¹dis·proportionate \"+\ *adj* [¹*dis-* + *proportionate*] **:** not properly or pleasingly proportioned **:** out of proportion **:** UNSYMMETRICAL ⟨making a case ~ to facts —J.B.May⟩ ⟨an influence quite ~ to their relatively small numbers —William Petersen⟩ — **dis·proportionately** \"+\ *adv* — **dis·proportionateness** \"+\ *n*

²disproportionate \"+\ *vt* **:** to subject to disproportionation ~ *vi* **:** to undergo disproportionation

disproportionated rosin *n* **:** a substance consisting essentially of dehydrogenated resin acids (as dehydro-abietic acid) together with hydrogenated resin acids (as dihydro-abietic acid) obtained by heating rosin or by treating it with acid and used chiefly in the form of a soap as an emulsifier in making GR-S-type rubber

dis·pro·por·tion·a·tion \ˌdisprə,pōrshəˈnāshən, -pȯr-\ *n* **:** the transformation of a substance into two or more dissimilar substances usu. by a process involving simultaneous oxidation and reduction **:** DISMUTATION ⟨~ of hydrogen peroxide to water and molecular oxygen⟩

dis·provable \dəs, (ˈ)dis +\ *adj* **:** capable of being disproved ⟨making outrageous assertions that were manifestly and easily ~⟩

dis·prove \"+\ *vt* [ME *disproven*, fr. MF *desprover*, fr. *des-* ¹dis- + *prover* to prove — more at PROVE] **1 a :** to prove to be other than is claimed or maintained **:** show to be fake **:** REFUTE ⟨the defendant's claims were *disproved* by the evidence⟩ **b** *archaic* **:** to prove wrong a claim or assertion by (a person) **2** *obs* **:** to disapprove of **:** DISALLOW

syn REFUTE, CONFUTE, REBUT, CONTROVERT: DISPROVE is the most general of these terms in implying only the demonstration of the falsity, invalidity, or erroneousness of an argument or claim ⟨charges of this kind have the peculiar advantage that even when *disproved* or shown to be manifestly absurd, they leave a stain behind them —J.A.Froude⟩ ⟨the final values of life, the ultimate meanings of experience, are just those that no man can prove, and that no man can *disprove* either —George Hedley⟩ ⟨he argues . . . that scientific thinking proper can do nothing to *disprove* Christian doctrines —W.P.Alston⟩ ⟨the authenticity of this runic writing . . . is far from *disproved* —*Amer. Guide Series: Minn.*⟩ REFUTE usu. suggests disproof of an argument or claim by careful logical or legal method as by the presenting of evidence, authoritative opinion, testimony of witnesses, or closely reasoned argument, or disproof by a fact or method acceptable to logic or legal process ⟨to *refute* all claims against the man by convincing circumstantial evidence⟩ ⟨the president's power to see that the laws are faithfully executed *refutes* the idea that he is to be a lawmaker —*Current History*⟩ ⟨one can disagree with his views, but one can't *refute* them . . . every particle of him asseverates the truth which is in him —Henry Miller⟩ ⟨with respect to that other, more weighty accusation, of having injured Mr. Wickham, I can only *refute* it by laying before you the whole of his connection with my family —Jane Austen⟩ ⟨the universe *refutes* our closet rationalizations and our kitchen diagrams —W.L.Sullivan⟩ CONFUTE suggests more the attempt to overwhelm or the actual overwhelming of someone else's arguments by any method even though it may be legitimate refutation ⟨the dialectical arguments employed by the Sophists . . . were designed to *confute* their adversaries rather than to establish true knowledge —Frank Thilly⟩ ⟨hypotheses which may be *confuted* by experience —A.J.Ayer⟩ ⟨to *confute* the too-frequent misstatement that poor laws came in with the Reformation —G.G. Coulton⟩ ⟨ignorance of the law excuses no man . . . because it is an excuse every man will plead, and no man can tell how to *confute* him —Robert Just⟩ REBUT throws stress upon the act of opposing an argument or claim as well as suggesting a certain formality of method although not necessarily implying successful refutation ⟨the author carefully examined and *rebutted*, point by point, many of the arguments —M.F.A. Montagu⟩ ⟨this presumption could be *rebutted* only by clear and convincing evidence to the contrary —*U.S. Code*⟩ ⟨he *rebuts* the legend about the Italian not being a good fighter —*Times Lit. Supp.*⟩ CONTROVERT like REBUT stresses the act of opposing but suggests such opposition as in denial or contradiction as much as in refutation, suggesting often a certain valiant effort to refute, although like REBUT not necessarily implying success ⟨a number of character witnesses . . . testified . . . and the prosecution did not try to *controvert* what they said —St. Clair McKelway⟩ ⟨delivering her opinion on every subject in so decisive a manner as proved that she was not used to have her judgment *controverted* —Jane Austen⟩ ⟨the two series of experiments, one which favors their view, the other *controverting* it —*Annual Rev. of Med.*⟩ ⟨reasons of a new kind to *controvert* the dangerous arguments of their opponents —M.F.A.Montagu⟩ ⟨the thesis which is maintained by one school and *controverted* by another —A.J.Ayer⟩ ⟨a few *controvert* and reject it by reasoning —J.A.Hobson⟩

dis·provided \ˌdis +\ *adj* [¹*dis-* + *provided*] *archaic* **:** UNPROVIDED **:** UNSUPPLIED

¹di·spunge \dəˈspənj\ *vt* -ED/-ING/-S [¹*dis-* + *spunge*, obs. var. of *sponge*] *archaic* **:** to pour down upon

²dispunge *vt* -ED/-ING/-S [¹*dis-* + *-punge* (as in *expunge*)] *obs* **:** EXPUNGE

dis·punishable \dəs, (ˈ)dis+\ *adj* [AF, fr. ¹*dis-* (fr. OF *des-* ¹dis-) + *punishable*, fr. MF *punissable* — more at PUNISHABLE] *archaic* **:** not punishable

dis·put·abil·i·ty \də,spyüd·əˈbiləd·ē, |tə-, -ətē, -i; ,dispyə|, ,di,spyü|\ *n* -ES **:** the quality or state of being disputable

dis·put·able \dəˈspyüd·əbəl, |tə-; ˈdispyə|, ˈdi,spyü|\ *adj* [MF, fr. L *disputabilis*, fr. *disputare* to discuss, examine + *-abilis* -able — more at DISPUTE] **1 :** capable of being disputed or contested **:** liable to be called in question ⟨presenting many ~ claims to the committee⟩ ⟨a speech full of ~ statements⟩ **2** *obs* **:** ARGUMENTATIVE, CONTENTIOUS — **dis·put·able·ness** \-bəlnəs\ *n* -ES

dis·put·ably \-blē, -li\ *adv* **:** in a disputable manner

¹dis·pu·tant \dəˈspyütᵊnt; ˈdispyəd·ənt, -yətənt\ *n* -s [L *disputant-*, *disputans*, pres. part. of *disputare*] **:** one that disputes **:** one engaged in a dispute **:** CONTROVERSIALIST ⟨attempting to make peace between the ~*s*⟩ ⟨the ~*s* on both sides were ignorant of the matter they were disputing about —Havelock Ellis⟩

²disputant \"\ *adj* [L *disputant-*, *disputans*, pres. part.] **:** DISPUTING **:** engaged in controversy

dis·pu·ta·tio \ˌdispəˈtād·ē,ō\ *n, pl* **disputati·o·nes** \-,tād·ēˈō,nās\ [L] **:** disputation or a disputation esp. in medieval or Renaissance rhetorical principle or practice

dis·pu·ta·tion \ˌdispyəˈtāshən, -(,)spyüˈ-\ *n* -s [ME *disputacioun*, fr. L *disputation-*, *disputatio*, fr. *disputatus* (past part. of *disputare*) + *-ion-*, *-io* -ion] **1 :** the act of disputing **:** CONTROVERSY, DEBATE ⟨there is a familiar ~ among painters and critics over the relative merits of modern and traditional art —*Atlantic*⟩ ⟨in a heated ~ with another driver who had dented his front fender⟩; *specif* **:** a formal rhetorical exercise in which somebody propounds and defends a thesis or in which two parties reason in opposition to each other **2** *obs* **:** interchange esp. conversational

dis·pu·ta·tious \ˌdispyəˈtāshəs, -(,)spyüˈ-\ *adj* [*disputation* + *-ous*] **1 a :** inclined to dispute **:** apt to wrangle or cavil **:** ARGUMENTATIVE, CONTENTIOUS ⟨the wrangling of many ~ . . . councils of French churchmen —H.O.Taylor⟩ ⟨man by his nature is a ~ and fighting animal —Horace Sutton⟩ **b :** marked by disputation ⟨philosophers loll in their ~ ease —R.P.Warren⟩ ⟨had a ~ time at the meeting⟩ **2 :** CONTROVERSIAL ⟨a paper so concise, so lacking in ~ matter —D.C. Peattie⟩ — **dis·pu·ta·tious·ly** *adv* — **dis·pu·ta·tious·ness** *n* -ES

dis·pu·ta·tive \dəˈspyüd·əd·iv, -ütətiv\ *adj* [LL *disputativus*, fr. L *disputatus* + *-ivus* -ive] **1 :** DISPUTATIOUS ⟨the journalism of all pioneer communities has been abusive and ~ and personal —*Scribner's*⟩ **2 :** of or belonging to disputation — **dis·pu·ta·tive·ly** *adv* — **dis·pu·ta·tive·ness** *n* -ES

¹dis·pute \dəˈspyüt, *usu* -üd·+V\ *vb* -ED/-ING/-S [ME *disputen*, fr. OF *desputer*, fr. L *disputare* to examine, discuss, fr. *dis-* ¹dis- + *putare* to prune, esteem, consider, think — more at PAVE] *vi* **1 :** to contend in argument **:** argue for or against something asserted or maintained **:** engage in a disputation **:** DEBATE ⟨*disputing* with opposing firms over what constituted ethical trade practices⟩; *often* **:** to argue irritably or with irritating persistence **:** WRANGLE ⟨a bitter old man much given to *disputing* over any suggestion made by others⟩ **2** *obs* **:** to struggle against something **:** FIGHT ~ *vt* **1 a :** to make the subject of disputation **:** argue pro and con **:** DEBATE ⟨the charge of treason would be *disputed* before a government committee⟩ **b :** to call into question (as the validity or the existence of something) ⟨its right to issue authoritative orders for the settlement of a conflict is *disputed* —*Economist*⟩ ⟨the bravery of the people has never been *disputed* —H.T.Buckle⟩; *also* **:** to oppose by argument or assertion **:** CONTROVERT ⟨likely to ~ any propositions not to his liking⟩ **c** *obs* **:** to argue or contend in favor of **:** MAINTAIN **d** *obs* **:** to influence, persuade, or argue into or out of a belief or action by a process of disputation **2 a :** to struggle against **:** OPPOSE, RESIST ⟨trying to ~ the man's entry into the house⟩ **b :** to strive or contend about **:** CONTEST ⟨~ a former enemy's possession of land⟩ ⟨~ a victory⟩ ⟨during the Revolutionary War this territory was much *disputed* on both sides of the river —A.C.Flick⟩ ⟨the dogs were *disputing* ownership of a bone —T.B.Costain⟩ **syn** see DISCUSS

²dis·pute \" *also* ˈdi,s-\ *n* -s **1 a :** verbal controversy **:** strife by opposing argument or expression of opposing views or claims **:** controversial discussion **:** DEBATE; *also* **:** an instance of such controversy ⟨was investigating the frontier ~*s* of Greece with the adjacent countries —*Current Biog.*⟩ **b :** a wrangling altercation **:** QUARREL **2** *obs* **:** physical combat **:** STRUGGLE, FIGHT — **in dispute :** in the process of being disputed

dis·put·er \dəˈspyüd·ə(r), -ütə-\ *n* -s [ME *disputar*, fr. *disputen* to dispute + *-ar* -er] **:** one that disputes esp. quarrelsomely

dis·qualification \dəs, (ˌ)dis+\ *n* [¹*dis-* + *qualification*] **1 :** the act of disqualifying or the state of being disqualified ⟨protesting his ~ from office under the new law⟩ **2 :** something that disqualifies or incapacitates ⟨a crime conviction is automatically a ~ for that public office⟩ ⟨his ~ for the team was a bad knee⟩

dis·qualify \dəs, (ˈ)dis+\ *vt* [¹*dis-* + *qualify*] **1 :** to deprive of the qualities, properties, or conditions necessary for a purpose **:** make unfit ⟨a bad back *disqualified* him from competition⟩ ⟨he remains . . . psychologically *disqualified* for appreciating the fears and despairs that today afflict so large a part of the world —H.S.Commager⟩ **2 :** to deprive of a power, right, or privilege **:** DISBAR ⟨a conviction of perjury *disqualified* him from being a witness⟩ ⟨he was *disqualified* for citizenship by certain controversial restrictions⟩ ⟨two infringements of the rules will ~ a player from further participation in the game⟩

dis·quantity \dəs, (ˈ)dis+\ *vt* -ED/-ING/-ES [¹*dis-* + *quantity* (n.)] **1** *obs* **:** to reduce in quantity **:** DIMINISH, LESSEN **2 :** to utter without accurate distinction of metrical quantity — used of syllables of quantitative verse

¹dis·quiet \dəs, (ˈ)dis+\ *vt* [¹*dis-* + *quiet* (v.)] **:** to take away the peace, rest, easy frame of mind, or normal relaxation of by disturbing, stirring up, making restless or uneasy, or alarming ⟨why should we ~ ourselves in vain in the attempt to direct our destiny —S.M.Crothers⟩ ⟨each day brought ~*ing* news of war threats⟩ ⟨felt a ~*ing* shame about the act⟩ ⟨all questions about the future of mankind are ~*ing*⟩ ⟨~*ing* symptoms of illness⟩ **syn** see DISCOMPOSE

²disquiet \"\ *n* [¹*dis-* + *quiet* (n.)] **1 :** the lack of quiet or of tranquillity in body or mind **:** UNEASINESS, RESTLESSNESS, ANXIETY ⟨instead of inspiring you, she filled you with ~ —R.H.Davis⟩ ⟨even in less . . . hostile hands, the capacity for a surprise attack with fusion weapons would be a source of ~ —H.A.Kissinger⟩ ⟨to spread suspicion and ~ —Evelyn G. Cruickshanks⟩ **2** *obs* **:** an instance of disquiet **:** DISTURBANCE

³disquiet \"\ *adj* [¹*dis-* + *quiet* (adj.)] *archaic* **:** DISQUIETED

disquieted *adj* **:** DISTURBED, UNEASY — **dis·qui·et·ed·ly** *adv* — **dis·qui·et·ed·ness** *n* -ES

dis·quieten \"+\ *vt* [¹*dis-* + *quieten*] **:** DISQUIET ⟨~*ing* rumors of war⟩

dis·qui·et·ing·ly *adv* **:** in a manner that disquiets ⟨the ~ close sounds of gunfire⟩

dis·qui·et·ly *adv* **:** in a turbulent manner **:** UNPEACEFULLY, RESTLESSLY ⟨all ruinous disorders follow us ~ to our graves —Shak.⟩

disquietment *n* -s *obs* **:** DISQUIET

dis·qui·et·ness \="==\ *n* **:** UNEASINESS

dis·quietude \dəs, (ˈ)dis+\ *n* [³*disquiet* + *-ude* (as in *quietude*)] **:** lack of peace or tranquillity **:** UNEASINESS, AGITATION, ANXIETY ⟨there was rest now, not ~, in the knowledge —Ellen Glasgow⟩ ⟨the initial mild ~ developed soon into outright fear⟩

dis·qui·si·tion \ˌdiskwəˈzishən\ *n* -s [L *disquisition-*, *disquisitio* inquiry, investigation, fr. *disquisitus* (past part. of *disquirere* to inquire diligently, to investigate, fr. *dis-* ¹dis- + *-quirere*, fr. *quaerere* to seek, inquire) + *-ion-*, *-io* -ion] **:** a formal or systematic inquiry into or discussion of a subject **:** an elaborate analytical or explanatory essay or discussion ⟨with long and profound ~*s* on questions of social economics —Carolyn Hannay⟩ ⟨pedantic ~*s* about the nature of his conservatism —H.A.Kissinger⟩ **syn** see DISCOURSE

dis·qui·si·tion·al \ˌ==ˈzishənᵊl, -shnəl\ *adj* **:** of, belonging to, resembling, or being a disquisition

dis·quis·i·tive \dəˈskwizəd·iv\ *adj* [L *disquisitus* + E *-ive*] **:** INQUIRING, INVESTIGATIVE ⟨a man with a ~ and discerning mind⟩

dis·quis·i·tor \-zəd·ə(r)\ *n* -s [L *disquisitus* + E *-or*] *archaic* **:** a writer of a disquisition **:** RESEARCHER

disrank *vt* [¹*dis-* + *rank* (n.)] *obs* **:** to throw into disorder

dis·rate \dəs, (ˈ)dis+\ *vt* [¹*dis-* + *rate* (n.)] **:** to reduce to a lower rating, rank, or class; *esp* **:** DEMOTE ⟨~ a noncommissioned officer⟩

¹dis·regard \ˌdis+\ *vt* [¹*dis-* + *regard* (v.)] **1 a :** to treat without fitting respect or attention ⟨flouting convention and ~*ing* his own clerical position —Oscar Handlin⟩ **b :** to treat as unworthy of regard or notice ⟨~ the rudeness of an associate⟩ ⟨~*ing* with broad tolerance the aberrations of the youthful mind⟩ **2 :** to give no thought to **:** pay no attention to ⟨the artistic merit . . . was ~*ed* in a storm of protest against the use of nude figures —*Amer. Guide Series: Pa.*⟩ ⟨~*ing* for a moment the practical aspects of the case in order to discover the principle at work⟩ **syn** see NEGLECT

²disregard \"\ *n* [¹*dis-* + *regard* (n.)] **:** the act of disregarding or the state of being disregarded; *esp* **:** intentional slight or neglect ⟨his flip ~ for the consequences of his actions —Arthur Knight⟩ ⟨they acted with complete ~ of danger —*Current Biog.*⟩ ⟨treated his former friend with withering ~⟩

dis·regardant \ˌdis+\ *adj* [¹*disregard* + *-ant* (as in *regardant*)] **:** DISREGARDFUL

dis·regardful \ˌdis+\ *adj* [¹*dis-* + *regardful*] **:** NEGLECTFUL, HEEDLESS ⟨a procedure ~ of the true issue at stake⟩ ⟨~ of one's responsibilities⟩ — **dis·regardfully** \"+\ *adv* — **dis·regardfulness** \"+\ *n*

dis·relate \ˌdis+\ *vt* [¹*dis-* + *relate*] **:** to break the relationship between or among **:** DISUNITE ⟨tends to ~ the components of immediate experience —D.S.Savage⟩

disrelated *adj* **:** UNRELATED ⟨trying to control the operations of corporations largely by means of negative and ~ rules —*World Social Economic Planning*⟩

dis·relation \"+\ *n* [¹*dis-* + *relation*] **:** lack of a fitting or proportionate connection or relationship ⟨the danger lies in the ~ between its newly acquired powers and its characteristic methods and techniques —E.C.Lindeman⟩; *also* **:** DISUNITY, DISSOCIATION ⟨lads, whose every gesture . . . bespoke a lethargic ~ with their surroundings —Adrian Bell⟩

¹dis·relish \dəs, (ˈ)dis+\ *vb* [¹*dis-* + *relish* (v.)] *vt* **1** *obs* **:** to take away the flavor of or give a bad flavor to **:** make distasteful **2 :** to find unpalatable or objectionable **:** DISLIKE

⟨murdered six persons he ~*ed* —John Sack⟩ ⟨however much our riper and sophisticated judgment may ~ the fact, it is the trick . . . in a story which assures it immortality —Marvin Lowenthal⟩ **3** *archaic* : DISGUST **~** *vi, obs* : to be distasteful or objectionable

²disrelish \"\ *n* [¹*dis-* + *relish* (n.)] : lack of relish : DISTASTE ⟨a ~ for some kinds of food⟩ : DISLIKE ⟨~ of him as a human being does not prevent the author from recognizing his intellect —Leonidas Dodson⟩

dis·remember \¦dis+\ *vt* [¹*dis-* + *remember*] : FORGET ⟨I ~ what he was praying for at the time —Helen Eustis⟩ ⟨for a minute I ~*ed* where I was —Shelby Foote⟩

dis·remembrance \"+\ *n* [¹*dis-* + *remembrance*] : DISREGARD, OBLIVION ⟨has fallen into ~ because he made so many enemies during his lifetime —Leon Edel⟩

dis·repair \¦dis+\ *n* [¹*dis-* + *repair*] : the quality or state of being in need of repair ⟨here were several crumbling stone buildings . . . and a mile or two distant a newer homestead also in ~ —George Farwell⟩ ⟨the human personality in states of hopeless, neurotic ~ —*Time*⟩ ⟨the house had fallen into ~⟩

dis·reputability \dəs, (¦)dis+\ *n* : the quality or state of being disreputable

¹dis·reputable \dəs, (¦)dis+\ *adj* [¹*dis-* + *reputable*] **1** : not reputable or decent : UNRESPECTABLE ⟨like a man who deals in something ~ — pornographic books or illegal operations —Graham Greene⟩ ⟨the penniless daughter of a woman too ~ to bring her up —Louis Auchincloss⟩ **2** : in bad condition : markedly worn, dirty, or tattered ⟨wearing an old ~ coat⟩ ⟨a very ~ armchair in the sitting room —*Current Biog.*⟩ — **dis·reputableness** \"+\ *n*

²disreputable \"\ *n* -s : a disreputable person

dis·reputably \"+\ *adv* : in a disreputable manner

dis·reputation \dəs, (¦)dis+\ *n* [¹*dis-* + *reputation*] *archaic* : loss or lack of a good reputation or good name : DISHONOR, DISREPUTE, DISCREDIT

¹disrepute *vt* [¹*dis-* + *repute* (v.)] *obs* : to bring into discredit : DISESTEEM

²dis·repute \¦dis+\ *n* [¹*dis-* + *repute* (n.)] : a condition in which there is an absence or lack of esteem or good reputation : low estimation ⟨the habit of pub-crawling — so much the fashion when I was their age — seems to have happily fallen into ~ —M.P.O'Connor⟩ ⟨the viola has also been held in ~ from the fact that it is often played by inferior violinists —A.E.Wier⟩ ⟨these treaties gradually fell into ~ —Vera M. Dean⟩ **syn** see DISHONOR

¹dis·respect \¦dis+\ *vt* [¹*dis-* + *respect* (v.)] : to have disrespect for : show disrespect to or for ⟨the man's remark gave us every reason for ~*ing* and profoundly disliking him⟩ ⟨~*ing* the law by violating it⟩

²disrespect \"\ *n* [¹*dis-* + *respect* (n.)] **1 a** : lack of respect or reverence ⟨had an enormous ~ for party-line intelligentsia —*Newsweek*⟩ ⟨a ~ for authority⟩ **b** : an instance or act of disrespect : INCIVILITY, DISCOURTESY ⟨she regarded the remark as a ~⟩ **2** : an expression or sentiment of disrespect ⟨in the speech the mayor paid his extended ~*s* to his enemies⟩

dis·respectable \"+\ *adj* [¹*dis-* + *respectable*] : not conforming to conventional standards of conduct : not respectable ⟨~ poems, straight off the street —Randall Jarrell⟩

dis·respectful \"+\ *adj* [¹*dis-* + *respectful*] : lacking proper respect in speech or action : showing disesteem or contempt ⟨remarks that were ~ of the law⟩ ⟨~ of a man's rights⟩ : UNCIVIL, DISCOURTEOUS ⟨~ in the presence of elders⟩ — **dis·respectfully** \"+\ *adv* — **dis·respectfulness** \"+\ *n*

disrespective *adj* [¹*dis-* + *respective*] *obs* : DISRESPECTFUL

disrest *n* [¹*dis-* + *rest*] *obs* : UNREST, DISQUIET

dis·robe \dəs, (¦)dis+\ *vb* [MF *desrober*, fr. OF, fr. *des-* ¹dis- + *robe* robe, garment — more at ROBE] *vt* **1 a** : to divest of a robe **b** : to remove the clothing from : UNDRESS ⟨the medical officer requested that the patient ~ himself before the examination⟩ **2** : to divest or strip of (something that clothes, decorates, or dignifies) ⟨has given us a certain view of kings, queens, and princes, *disrobed* of their formalities —C.G. Bowers⟩ **~** *vi* **1** : to divest oneself of a robe **2** : to undress oneself ⟨on cold nights the children *disrobed* before the fire⟩ — **dis·rob·er** \-ə(r)\ *n*

dis·roof \dəs, (¦)dis+\ *vt* [¹*dis-* + *roof* (n.)] : UNROOF

dis·root \dəs, (¦)dis+\ *vt* [¹*dis-* + *root* (n.)] **1** : to tear up the roots of : tear up by the roots ⟨replanted the ~*ed* shrubbery⟩ **2** : to dislodge esp. from a fixed position

disrump *vb* [L *disrumpere*] *obs* : DISRUPT

¹dis·rupt \dəs'rəpt\ *adj* [L *disruptus*] DISRUPTED

²disrupt \"\ *vt* -ED/-ING/-S [L *disruptus, diruptus*, past part. of *disrumpere, dirumpere*, fr. *dis-* apart + *rumpere* to break — more at DIS-, REAVE] **1 a** : to break apart : RUPTURE ⟨the suction tube was left in to draw off gas lest he become distended and ~ his wound —*Time*⟩ ⟨three periods of faulting ~*ed* the rocks —*Univ. of Ariz. Record*⟩ ⟨many communications routes remained unsafe or ~*ed* —*Americana Annual*⟩ **b** : to throw into disorder or turmoil ⟨the speech totally ~*ed* the meeting⟩ ⟨India was not ~*ed* by the Japanese War —Christopher Rand⟩ ⟨she would hate to have the job, because it will ~ her domestic coziness —David Sylvester⟩ **c** : to destroy the unity or wholeness of ⟨the party was ~*ed* by the defection of a large group of radical members⟩ **2** : to interrupt to the extent of stopping, preventing normal continuance of, or destroying ⟨that experience ~*ed* my interest in the life about me —Jack McLaren⟩ ⟨she had ~*ed* a bridge game by permanently hiding up the ace of spades —Scott Fitzgerald⟩ ⟨traffic on the main railway lines was largely ~*ed* during the war —*Collier's Yr. Bk.*⟩

dis·rupt·er *also* **dis·rup·tor** \-tə(r)\ *n* -s : one that disrupts

dis·rup·tion \dəs'rəpshən\ *n* -s [*disruption-, disruptio*, fr. *disruptus* + *-ion-, -io* -ion] **1** : the act or process of disrupting : the state of being disrupted ⟨bandaged the leg tightly to prevent ~ of the partly healed wound⟩ ⟨he was . . . the center of intrigues framed against the royal power and directed toward the ~ of the state —Hilaire Belloc⟩ ⟨the sixteenth century of our era saw the ~ of western Christianity and the rise of modern science —A.N.Whitehead⟩ ⟨foresee the speedy ~ and eventual collapse of our economic life —Lewis Mumford⟩

dis·rup·tion·ist \-sh(ə)nəst\ *n* -s **1** : one who favors disruption (as among groups constituting a political party) **2** : DISRUPTER

¹dis·rup·tive \-ptiv, -tēv *also* -təv\ *adj* [²*disrupt* + *-ive*] : causing or tending to cause disruption ⟨~ movements trying to go faster than the main body of the party wishes to go —Harry Walston⟩ ⟨pragmatically, religion is necessary to the average individual to overcome the shattering ~ anticipation of death, of disaster, and of destiny —B.K.Malinowski⟩ — **dis·rup·tive·ly** \-təvlē, -li\ *adv* — **dis·rup·tive·ness** \-tivnəs, -tēv- *also* -təv-\ *n* -ES

²disruptive *n* -s : HIGH EXPLOSIVE

disruptive discharge *n* : a discharge through an insulating material subjected to an electrostatic stress with an accompanying breaking down or rupture of the material

dis·rupture \dəs, (¦)dis+\ *n* [²*disrupt* + *-ure* (as in *rupture*)] : DISRUPTION ⟨~ of telephone service⟩

dis·ruptured \"+\ *adj* : broken up : SPLIT, DIVIDED

diss \'dis\ *n* -ES [Ar *dīs*] : a reedy grass (*Ampelodesma tenax*) common in the Mediterranean region that is used in basketry and cordage making

diss- *or* **disso-** *comb form* [NL, fr. Gk, fr. *dissos, dittos*; akin to Gk *dyo* two — more at TWO] : double ⟨*dissoconch*⟩ ⟨*dissophyte*⟩

diss *abbr* dissertation

dis·satisfaction \də(s), (¦)di(s)+\ *n* [¹*dis-* + *satisfaction*] **1** : the quality or state of being dissatisfied, unsatisfied, or discontented : uneasiness, disturbance, or distress resulting from a lack of gratification ⟨~ with the world in which we live and determination to realize one that shall be better —G.L.Dickinson⟩ ⟨had grown discouraged with his son-in-law but did not openly voice his ~ —Sherwood Anderson⟩ **2** : DISPLEASURE ⟨~ with inflation was not confined to organized labor —*Collier's Yr. Bk.*⟩

dis·satisfactory \"+\ *adj* [¹*dis-* + *satisfactory*] : UNSATISFACTORY

dissatisfied *adj* : expressing or showing dissatisfaction ⟨a ~ scowl on his face⟩ ⟨a ~ complaint⟩ — **dis·satisfiedly** \"+\ *adv* — **dis·satisfiedness** \"+\ *n*

dis·satisfy \də(s), (')di(s)+\ *vt* [¹*dis-* + *satisfy*] : to fail to satisfy : fail to provide with something desired, expected, or hoped for or to the extent desired, expected, or hoped for : frustrate wishes or expectations of ⟨a ~*ing* dinner⟩ ⟨we cannot prove that it is better to be a human being *dissatisfied* than a pig satisfied —H.J.Muller⟩ ⟨*dissatisfied* with the dollar a day he earned —*Current Biog.*⟩ ⟨a book that is one part superb and two parts stimulating yet ~*ing* —J.F.McComas⟩

dis·sa·va \də'sävə\ *n* -s [Sinhalese *disāwa*] : one of the district governors of Ceylon

dis·save \də(s), (')di(s)+\ *vi* [¹*dis-* + *save*] : to engage in or practice dissaving — **dis·saver** \"+\ *n*

dissaving *n* : the use of past savings for current consumption : consumption in excess of income ⟨the savings of those still rich are offset by the ~*s* of the poorer ones —*Canadian Jour. of Economics & Political Science*⟩

dis·scepter \də(s), (')di(s)+\ *vt* [¹*dis-* + *scepter* (n.)] *archaic* : to deprive of a scepter

dis·seat \də(s), (')di(s)+\ *vt* [¹*dis-* + *seat*] *archaic* : UNSEAT

dis·sect \də'sekt *also* ÷(')dī¦s-\ *vb* -ED/-ING/-S [L *dissectus*, past part. of *dissecare* to cut apart, fr. *dis-* apart + *secare* to cut — more at DIS-, SAW] *vt* **1** : to divide or separate into parts **2 a** : to cut so as to separate into pieces or to expose the several parts and their locations and connections esp. with precision and deftness for scientific examination; *specif* : to separate or follow along natural lines of cleavage (as through connective tissue) ⟨~ out the regional lymph nodes⟩ ⟨a ~*ing* aneurysm⟩ **b** : to divide and separate into different phases, items, or parts and to examine, interpret, or evaluate minutely ⟨~*ing* the claims of John Quincy Adams to the support of abolitionists —William MacDonald⟩ ⟨those words which it is the business of criticism to ~ and reassemble —T.S.Eliot⟩ **c** : to cut or divide (land) into hills and ridges with valleys between — used esp. of a river **d** : to break up for colors in printing **3** : to separate out for special attention or different treatment or consideration : isolate out — used with *out* ⟨pupils . . . often could not ~ out the subject or object in a Miltonic sentence —H.R.Warfel⟩ **~** *vi* **1** : to make a medical dissection **2** : to analyze and evaluate something in great detail **syn** see ANALYZE

dissected *adj* **1** : cut into parts or sections ⟨a ~ map⟩ **2 a** *of a leaf* : cut deeply into many fine lobes or divisions **b** : divided into hills and ridges by valleys and gorges ⟨a ~ plateau⟩

dissecting room *n* : a room (as in a hospital or medical school) where anatomical dissecting is performed for instruction, research, or analysis

dis·sec·tion \-kshən\ *n* -s [prob. fr. F, fr. MF, fr. L *dissectus* + MF *-ion*] **1** : the act or process of dissecting or the state of being dissected ⟨sharpened the big carving knife, beamed at the turkey, and pretended to be absorbed in its ~ —Anne Green⟩ **2 a** : a detailed critical analysis of something (as of a type represented in a novel) ⟨although there were novels on a great variety of themes, the two characters most favored for ~ were American businessmen or young ladies uncertain of their identity —Harrison Hayford⟩ **b** (1) : the surgical removal along the natural lines of cleavage of tissues which are or might become diseased — compare BLOCK DISSECTION (2) : the digital separation of tissues (as in heart-valve operations) — compare FINGER FRACTURE **c** : the process of erosion whereby a land surface is cut by gullies, ravines, canyons, or other kinds of valleys **3 a** : something (as a part or the whole of an animal or plant) that has been dissected **b** : an anatomical specimen prepared in this way

dis·sec·tion·al \-kshənᵊl, -shnəl\ *adj* : DISSECTIVE ⟨in setting, personalities, and ~ treatment, this part is reminiscent of . . . novels of psychopathic provincial people —Dorothy Chamberlain⟩

dis·sec·tive \-ktiv\ *adj* : of or relating to dissection ⟨it is only ~ analysis and knowledge of history that reveal the compositeness of any culture —A.L.Kroeber⟩

dis·sec·tor \-tə(r)\ *n* -s [L *dissectus* + E *-or*] : one that dissects

Dissector \"\ *trademark* — used for an image dissector

dissed *past of* DIS

dis·seise *or* **dis·seize** \də(s)'sēz, (')di(s)¦s-\ *vt* -ED/-ING/-S [ME *disseisen*, fr. ML *disseisiare* & AF *disseisir*, fr. OF *dessaisir* to dispossess, fr. *des-* ¹dis- + *saisir* to put in possession of — more at SEIZE] : to deprive of seisin; *usu* : to wrongfully dispossess or oust (as one in freehold possession of land) — used with *of*, formerly with *from*

dis·seis·ee *or* **dis·seiz·ee** \də(s)¦sē'zē, ¦di(s),s-\ *n* -s [AF *disseisi*, fr. pres. part. of *disseisir*] : a person disseised — contrasted with *disseisor*

dis·seisin *or* **dis·seizin** \də(s), (')di(s)+\ *n* -s [ME *dysseysyne*, fr. ML *disaissina* & AF *disseisine*, fr. OF *dessaisine* dispossession, fr. *des-* ¹dis- + *saisine* seisin — more at SEISIN] : the act of disseising or the state of being disseised

dis·sei·sor *or* **dis·sei·zor** \də(s)¦sē¦zȯ(ə)r, ¦di(s),s-\ *n* -s [ME *disseiser*, fr. AF *disseisour*, fr. *disseisir* + *our* -or] : one that disseises another — contrasted with *disseisee*

dis·sel·boom \'disəl,büm, -,bōm\ *n* -s [Afrik, fr. D, fr. *dissel* tongue or shaft of a wagon (fr. MD) + *boom* pole, tree, fr. MD; akin to OS *thīsla* tongue or shaft of a wagon, OE *thīxl*, OHG *dīhsala*, ON *thīsl* tongue or shaft of a wagon, OSlav *tęgnąti* to pull, and to OHG *boum* tree — more at BEAM] *Africa* : the pole of a horse-drawn wagon

¹dis·semblance \də'semblən(t)s\ *n* [ME, fr. MF *dessemblance*, fr. *dessembler* to be unlike (fr. *des-* ¹dis- + *-sembler*, as in *resembler* to resemble) + *-ance* — more at RESEMBLE] : lack of resemblance : DISSIMILITUDE

²dissemblance \"\ *n* [*dissemble* + *-ance*] : the act or the art of dissembling : DISSIMULATION

dis·sem·ble \də'sembəl\ *vb* **dissembled**; **dissembled**; **dissembling** \-b(ə)liŋ\ **dissembles** [alter. (influenced by MF *dessembler* to be unlike) of *dissimule*] *vt* **1** : to hide under a false appearance : conceal with intent to deceive : FEIGN ⟨the propagandist . . . is a man so convinced of the truth of a certain proposition that he ~*s* the facts that tell against it —Katharine F. Gerould⟩ **2** *obs* : OVERLOOK, IGNORE **3** *archaic* : to put on the appearance of : make pretense of : SIMULATE ⟨he soon *dissembled* a sleep —*Tatler*⟩ **~** *vi* : to put on a false appearance : conceal facts, motives, intentions, or feelings under some pretense ⟨we are all brought up to have a strict regard for the truth, but in adult life we learn to ~⟩ **syn** see DISGUISE

dis·sem·bler \-b(ə)lə(r)\ *n* -s : one that dissembles ⟨we shall have to become ~*s* — saying one thing while knowing in our own minds that it is a lie —Asher Moore⟩

dis·sem·bling·ly \-b(ə)liŋlē\ *adv* : in a manner that dissembles

dissembly *n* -ES [by alter.] *obs* : ASSEMBLY

dis·sem·i·nate \də'semə,nāt, *usu* -ād+V\ *vb* -ED/-ING/-S [L *disseminatus*, past part. of *disseminare*, fr. *dis-* ¹dis- + *seminare* to sow, fr. *semin-, semen* seed — more at SEMEN] *vt* **1 a** : to spread or send out freely or widely as though sowing or strewing seed : make widespread ⟨as citizens devoted to the use of books and as librarians and publishers responsible for *disseminating* them —*Amer. Library Assoc. Bull.*⟩ ⟨distrusting the great city twenty miles away that *disseminated* its virus through the outlying villages and farms —V.L.Parrington⟩ **b** : to foster general knowledge of : BROADCAST, PUBLICIZE ⟨unlicensed preachers went about the country *disseminating* heresies and notorious errors —G.G.Coulton⟩ ⟨*disseminating* information about the latest scientific discoveries⟩ ⟨~ the latest events, regardless of the inconclusive shape they are in —Harvey Breit⟩ **2 a** : to disperse throughout in small particles : distribute in every part : DIFFUSE, PERMEATE ⟨reported that copper was *disseminated* through the rock⟩ **b** : to spread out : extend widely : strew or scatter over a large area or into many places ⟨silt from the Amazon is *disseminated* for hundreds of miles⟩ ⟨*disseminated* multiple sclerosis⟩ **~** *vi* : to spread widely : become found widely ⟨seeds, wind-borne, ~ over quite a wide area from the parent plant⟩ **syn** see SPREAD

dis·sem·i·na·tion \də,semə'nāshən\ *n* -s [L *dissemination-, disseminatio*, fr. *disseminatus* + *-ion-, -io* -ion] : the action or process of disseminating : the state of being disseminated : DIFFUSION ⟨the ~ of ideas⟩ ⟨devoted himself to the ~ of a modified form of Darwinism —S.F.Mason⟩

dis·sem·i·na·tor \də'semə,nād·ə(r), -ātə-\ *n* -s [LL, fr. L *disseminatus* + *-or*] : one that disseminates ⟨wild birds may also serve as ~*s* of infection —E.H.Barger & L.E.Card⟩ ⟨the newspaper . . . still the most important news ~ —R.E. Wolseley⟩

dis·sem·i·nule \-,nyüℓ\ *n* -s [*disseminate* + *-ule*] : a part or organ of a plant that ensures propagation (as a seed or spore)

dis·sen·sion *also* **dis·sen·tion** \də'senchən\ *n* -s [ME *dissensioun, dissencioun*, fr. MF *dissension*, fr. L *dissension-, dissensio*, fr. *dissensus* (past part. of *dissentire*) + *-ion-, -io* -ion] **1** : disagreement in opinion esp. partisan and contentious : breach of friendship : QUARRELING ⟨continued ~ in the ranks of the party —J.G.Colton⟩ ⟨one of the unions fraught with disharmony and ~ —Honor Tracy⟩ **2** *archaic* : dissent from religious doctrine or practice **syn** see DISCORD

¹dis·sent \də'sent\ *vi* -ED/-ING/-S [ME *dissenten*, fr. L *dissentire*, fr. *dis-* ¹dis- + *sentire* to feel — more at SENSE] **1** : to withhold assent : not to approve : OBJECT ⟨~*ing* to the most outrageous invasion of private right ever set forth as a decision of the court —J.P.Boyd⟩ **2 a** : to differ in opinion : DISAGREE ⟨~ from the prevailing opinion⟩ ⟨all who ~ from its orthodox doctrines are scoundrels —H.L.Mencken⟩ **b** *archaic* : to be in discord : QUARREL **c** : to differ from an established church in the matter of doctrines, rites, or government ⟨~*ing* from the Church of England⟩ **syn** see DIFFER

²dissent \"\ *n* -s **1 a** : difference of opinion : NONAGREEMENT, NONCONCURRENCE, DISAGREEMENT: as (1) : religious dissension or nonconformity (2) : a justice's statement with or without an accompanying opinion of nonconcurrence with a decision of the majority of the justices of a court **b** : an instance of such disagreement or nonconcurrence ⟨his major ~*s* have now become the law —Francis Biddle⟩ **2** *obs* : DISPARITY, DIVERSITY, DIFFERENCE

dis·sen·ta·ne·ous \¦dis°n·¦tānēəs\ *adj* [L *dissentaneus*, fr. *dissentire* + *-aneus* (as in *subterraneus* subterranean) — more at SUBTERRANEAN] *archaic* : being at variance : DISCORDANT

dis·sent·er \də'sentə(r)\ *n* -s **1** : one that dissents ⟨always finds himself drawn to the ~, the rebel, the nonconformist —Sara H. Hay⟩; *esp* : a person who worships in a communion other than that of an established state church **2** *usu cap* : an English nonconformist

dis·sen·tience \də'sench(ē)ə|n(t)s\ *n* : the quality or state of being dissentient : DISAGREEMENT

¹dis·sen·tient \|nt\ *n* -s [L *dissentient-, dissentiens*, pres. part. of *dissentire* to dissent — more at DISSENT] : one that dissents ⟨gained him a vote of confidence with only four ~*s* —E.A. Peers⟩

²dissentient \"\ *adj* [L *dissentient-, dissentiens*, pres. part.] : not concurring : DISSENTING, DISAGREEING ⟨such suppression does not carry with it the destruction of recalcitrant individuals but only of their powers of ~ action —Samuel Alexander⟩

dis·sent·ing·ly *adv* : in a manner that shows or expresses dissent

dis·sen·tious \də'senchəs, (')di¦s-\ *adj* [irreg. fr. *dissension* + *-ous*] : marked by dissensions : FACTIOUS — **dis·sen·tious·ly** *adv*

dis·sen·tive \də'sentiv\ *adj* : marked by dissent : DISAGREEING ⟨an interest in reform and an occasional ~ attitude socially and religiously —Allan Holaday⟩

dis·sep·i·ment \də'sepəmənt\ *n* [L *dissaepimentum* partition, fr. *dissaepire, dissepire* to separate, divide (fr. *dis-* apart + *saepire, sepire* to fence in) + *-mentum* -ment — more at DIS-, SEPIMENT] : a separating tissue : PARTITION: as **a** : SEPTUM **b** : TRAMA **c** : one of the transverse calcareous partitions between the radiating septa of a coral **d** : a crossbar between branches of a lace bryozoan colony **e** : a similar support of a graptolite

dis·sep·i·men·tal \də¦sepə¦mentᵊl\ *adj* : of or relating to a dissepiment

dis·sert \də'sərt\ *vi* -ED/-ING/-S [L *dissertus*, past part. of *disserere*, fr. *dis-* ¹dis- + *serere* to place, arrange, join together — more at SERIES] : to give a dissertation : speak at some length and in detail : DISCOURSE ⟨I am not going to ~ on Hood's humor; I am not a fair judge —John Ruskin⟩

dis·ser·tate \'disə(r),tāt\ *vi* -ED/-ING/-S [L *dissertatus*, past part. of *dissertare*, freq. of *disserere*] : DISSERT

dis·ser·ta·tion \,disə(r)'tāshən\ *n* -s [L *dissertation-, dissertatio*, fr. *dissertatus* + *-ion-, -io* -ion] **1** *obs* : DISCUSSION, DEBATE **2** : an extended usu. systematic oral or written treatment of a subject : TREATISE, DISQUISITION; *specif* : a substantial paper that is submitted to the faculty of a university by a candidate for an advanced degree that is typically based on independent research and that if acceptable usu. gives evidence of the candidate's mastery both of his own subject and of scholarly method — see THESIS **syn** see DISCOURSE

dis·ser·ta·tion·al \¦disə(r)¦tāshənᵊl, -shnəl\ *adj* : of, relating to, or consisting of a dissertation

dis·ser·ta·tive \'disə(r),tād·iv\ *adj* : of, relating to, or consisting of a dissertation

dis·serve \də(s), (')di(s)+\ *vt* [¹*dis-* + *serve*] : to serve ill or falsely or be of inadequate service to ⟨if I am not *disserved* by my memory . . . Mr. Hayes used to intersperse this cycle of spirituals with readings —J.M.Conly⟩ : INJURE, DAMAGE, HARM ⟨*disserving* the very democracy in which he ardently believes —*New Republic*⟩ ⟨has *disserved* his art by a self-conscious preachment —Parker Tyler⟩

dis·service \"+\ *n* [¹*dis-* + *service*] : ill service : INJURY, HARM, MISCHIEF ⟨charts what is called "passenger *disservice*" — all the things which go to delay flights or otherwise incommode the passenger —R.P.Cooke⟩ ⟨there would be no greater ~ to the American people than to underestimate the gravity of the dangers —A.E.Stevenson⟩ ⟨it does a country great ~ to claim for it a perfection to which it cannot aspire —Richard Joseph⟩

dis·serviceable \"+\ *adj* : tending or calculated to do disservice : INJURIOUS, HARMFUL ⟨dismisses . . . all such checks as the referendum as ~ interventions of a crude electorate —*Contemporary Rev.*⟩

dis·serviceably \"+\ *adv* : in a disserviceable manner

disses *pres 3d sing of* DIS, *pl of* DISS

dissettle *vt* [¹*dis-* + *settle*] *obs* : UNSETTLE

dis·sever \də+\ *vb* [ME *deseveren, disseveren*, fr. OF *dessevrer*, fr. LL *disseparare*, fr. L *dis-* ¹dis- + *separare* to separate — more at SEPARATE] *vt* : SEVER, DISUNITE, SEPARATE, PART ⟨he loved knowledge; yet he would not ~ it from its value in the art of living —H.O.Taylor⟩ ⟨great wastes of empty land ~*ed* the single farm from the rest of the world —Oscar Handlin⟩ ⟨Henchard's wife was ~*ed* from him by death —Thomas Hardy⟩; *also* : to divide or cut into parts or separate units ⟨the ~*ed* carcass of the chicken⟩ **~** *vi* : to dissever two or more things ⟨deep beneath the surface of the legal system . . . are these attractions and repulsions, uniting and ~*ing* as in one unending paradox —B.N.Cardozo⟩

dis·severance \"+\ *n* [ME *deseveraunce, disseveraunce*, fr. MF *dessevrance*, fr. *dessevrer* + *-ance*] : the act of dissevering : the state of being dissevered : SEPARATION ⟨complete selfishness and ~ from anything that might cause her discomfort —Amy Loveman⟩

dis·severation \"+\ *n* -s [*dissever* + *-ation*] : DISSEVERANCE

dis·si·dence \'disədən(t)s, -dᵊn-\ *n* -s [L *dissidentia*, fr. *dissident-, dissidens* + *-ia* -y] : DISSENT, DISAGREEMENT, CONTENTION ⟨arresting people for political ~ —Peggy Durdin⟩ ⟨confronted by religious revolts or ~ —G.C.Sellery⟩

¹dis·si·dent \-ənt, -ᵊnt\ *adj* [L *dissident-, dissidens*, pres. part. of *dissidēre* to sit apart, disagree, fr. *dis-* apart + *-sidēre* (fr. *sedēre* to sit) — more at DIS-, SIT] **1 a** : not agreeing : DISSENTING : not concurring ⟨psychological theory, like economic theory, is in the hands of several ~ schools —J.S.Gambs⟩; *esp* : differing often contentiously with an established political or religious system or belief of a country or people ⟨~ elements within the Thai navy attempted to overthrow Pibul's regime —*Current Biog.*⟩ ⟨the aristocrats and ~ politicians demanded that the army demagogue be removed —D.M. Friedenberg⟩ **b** : QUARRELSOME, CONTENTIOUS ⟨what a united, aggressive minority can do to a ~, lethargic majority —*Time*⟩ **2** : clashingly unharmonious ⟨an aesthetic jungle of ~, competing buildings —Lewis Mumford⟩ — **dis·si·dent·ly** \-əntlē, -li\ *adv*

²dissident \"\ *n* -s : one that is dissident ⟨the Labor government . . . had been forced by a number of Labor ~*s* to announce a reduction in the period of national service

—Woodrow Wyatt⟩ ⟨had two ~s burned alive in 1575 —George Willison⟩ ⟨protect the constitutional rights of pacifists and other wartime ~s —Dwight MacDonald⟩

dis·sight \də(s), (ˌ)di(s)+\ *n* [¹*dis-* + *sight*] **:** an unsightly object

dis·sil·ient \də'silyənt, -lēənt\ *adj* [L *dissilient-, dissiliens,* pres. part. of *dissilire,* fr. *dis-* apart + *-silire* (fr. *salire* to leap) — more at DIS-, SALLY] **:** springing apart; *specif* **:** bursting open (as the ripe capsules of the balsam)

dis·similar \də(s), (ˈ)di(s)+\ *adj* [¹*dis-* + *similar*] **:** not similar **:** UNLIKE ⟨Americans who had been reared in the most ~ places and born into the most ~ families —Oscar Handlin⟩ ⟨completely ~ cultures —K.E.Read⟩ ⟨the military requirements are not ~ from those for defense —Fletcher Pratt⟩ ⟨those pumps . . . were not ~ to those once familiar to everyone on a farm —J.B.Conant⟩ — **dis·similarly** \"+\ *adv*

dis·similarity \də(s), (ˈ)di(s)+\ *n* **:** the quality or state of being dissimilar **:** difference in appearance or nature **:** UNLIKENESS, HETEROGENEITY ⟨progress toward full union has remained stalled because of *dissimilarities* between the Belgian and the Netherlands economies —*Americana Annual*⟩

syn DISSIMILARITY, UNLIKENESS, DIFFERENCE, DIVERGENCE, DIVERGENCY, and DISTINCTION all mean lack of agreement or correspondence in appearance, quality, or nature, or an instance of this. DISSIMILARITY and UNLIKENESS, the most general terms in this group, are often interchangeable; DISSIMILARITY, however, often stresses the lack of agreement or correspondence more than UNLIKENESS which often applies more to a lack of resemblance as among things in the same species or in some other more or less uniform category ⟨there are often not mere *unlikenesses* but marked *dissimilarities* of belief between members of the same religious group⟩ ⟨what a *dissimilarity!* In the ground of the two lives, a likeness; in all their circumstance, what *unlikeness!* —Matthew Arnold⟩ ⟨a noticeable *unlikeness* between twins⟩ DIFFERENCE implies a quality or feature which marks one thing as apart from another — want of resemblance in one or more particulars, a want of identity, or a disagreement or cause of disagreement ⟨dwell with satisfaction upon the poet's *difference* from his predecessors —T.S.Eliot⟩ ⟨*differences* in the type of ware manufactured by the various crafts —H.E.Steele⟩ ⟨an obvious *difference* between the statesman and the politician⟩ ⟨settle the *differences* between hostile nations⟩ DIVERGENCE or DIVERGENCY usu. applies to things which have or have had much in common, implying strongly a cleavage or a purposeful separation in path or character ⟨one university system might show considerable *divergence* from another —J.B.Conant⟩ ⟨in the old days I demanded agreement; I am now amused by *divergence* —A.C.Benson⟩ ⟨his *divergence* from his sister in this sphere of religion was never so wide as she feared —Matthew Arnold⟩ ⟨increasing *divergencies* between British and French policies —Sumner Welles⟩ ⟨the *divergencies* between these three passages are obvious —A.P.d'Entrèves⟩ DISTINCTION implies a difference, usu. in a detail, brought out by close observation or analysis ⟨the natural *distinction* between literary and graphic art —John Ruskin⟩ ⟨he had lost all sense of the *distinction* between reality and illusion —Van Wyck Brooks⟩ ⟨these *distinctions* in national character are rooted in some quality of human nature —J.A.Hobson⟩

dis·sim·i·late \də'siməˌlāt, (ˈ)di's-, *usu* -ād·+V\ *vb* -ED/-ING/-S [¹*dis-* + *-similate* (as in *assimilate*)] **:** to make or become dissimilar **:** undergo or cause to undergo dissimilation

dis·sim·i·la·tion \də'simə'lāshən, (ˌ)diˌsimə¦l-\ *n* -S [¹*dis-* + *-similation* (as in *assimilation*)] **:** the act of making or the process of becoming dissimilar: as **a :** CATABOLISM — contrasted with *assimilation* **b :** the development of dissimilarity between two identical or closely related sounds in a word; *also* **:** the loss or dropping of one of two such sounds (as in Vulgar Latin *pelegrinus,* from Latin *peregrinus* or as in the pronunciation \'gəvənər\ instead of \'gəvərnər\ for *governor* by speakers of English who do not ordinarily "drop" their *r's*) — compare ASSIMILATION 4

dis·similative \dəs, (ˈ)dis+\ *adj* **:** belonging to or causing dissimilation

dis·sim·i·la·to·ry \də'simələˌtōrē, (ˈ)di's-, -tȯr-, -ri\ *adj* **:** of, relating to, or caused by dissimilation

dis·similitude \¦di(s)+\ *n* [L *dissimilitudo,* fr. *dissimilis* unlike (fr. *dis-* ¹dis- + *similis* like) + *-tudo* -tude — more at SAME] **:** lack of resemblance **:** DISSIMILARITY; *also* **:** an instance or example of dissimilarity

dis·simulate \də, (ˈ)di+\ *vb* [L *dissimulatus,* past part. of *dissimulare,* fr. *dis-* ¹dis- + *simulare* to simulate — more at SIMULATE] **:** to hide under a false appearance **:** DISSEMBLE ⟨during the first three centuries . . . the cross of Christ is invariably *dissimulated* under the form of an object which recalls its image —Eugene Goblet d'Alviella⟩ ⟨a man trained to conceal or ~ all strong feeling⟩ ⟨as a politician he was not good at *dissimulating*⟩

dis·simulation \də, (ˌ)di+\ *n* [ME *dissimulacioun,* fr. MF *dissimulation,* fr. L *dissimulation-, dissimulatio,* fr. *dissimulatus* + *-ion-, -io* -ion] **:** the act of dissembling or the fact of being dissembled ⟨some of these may recognize themselves in these pages . . . but I believe that I have been careful enough in ~ that they will not be recognized by others —J.A.Pike⟩ **:** false pretense ⟨try to keep my detachment from becoming so complete a lie that I myself am deceived by it . . . but one thing can be gained by ~, and that is an increment in dignity —Isaac Rosenfeld⟩ **syn** see DECEIT

dis·simulative \də, (ˈ)di+\ *adj* **:** belonging to, consisting of, or marked by dissimulation ⟨the ~ arts⟩

dis·simulator \"+\ *n* [L, fr. *dissimulatus* + *-or*] **:** DISSEMBLER

dissimule *vb* -ED/-ING/-S [ME *dissimulen,* fr. MF *dissimuler,* fr. L *dissimulare*] *obs* **:** DISSEMBLE

dissing *pres part of* DIS

dissipable *adj* [L *dissipabilis,* fr. *dissipare* + *-abilis* -able] *obs* **:** capable of being dissipated

¹**dis·si·pate** \'disəˌpāt, *usu* -ād·+V\ *vb* -ED/-ING/-S [L *dissipatus,* past part. of *dissipare,* fr. *dis-* ¹dis- + *-sipare* (fr. *supare* to throw); akin to OE *geswōpe* trash, ON *sōpl* broom, *svāf* spear, Skt *svapū* broom, OSlav *sypati* to shake; basic meaning: throwing, shaking] *vt* **1 a :** to break up and drive off (as a crowd) **:** SCATTER, DISPERSE ⟨~ the enemy forces by unremitting gunfire⟩ **b :** to cause to disappear esp. by dispersion or diffusion **:** cause to spread out or spread thin to the point of vanishing **:** DISPEL, DISSOLVE ⟨the morning sun *dissipated* the night mists⟩ ⟨if this absorbed heat is not *dissipated,* the surfaces of the combustion chambers would become red hot —Ernest Venk⟩ ⟨a bright light *dissipated* the darkness of the night —W.H.G.Kingston⟩ ⟨familiarity . . . *dissipated* the prejudice born of ignorance —Oscar Handlin⟩ ⟨the common bond which drew them together is *dissipated* by the divergent interests of adult life —Carmen Rosa⟩ **2 a :** to expend aimlessly or foolishly ⟨~ our energies in trivial occupations⟩ ⟨the union would be *dissipating* its bargaining power — using it wastefully instead of conserving it —S.H.Slichter⟩ **b :** to spend so as to have no further possession of ⟨had a small patrimony . . . but that he *dissipated* before he left college —George Meredith⟩; *also* **:** to lose by squandering ⟨*dissipated* the family fortune in only a few years of wild living⟩ ~ *vi* **1 a :** to separate into parts and scatter or disappear **:** DISPERSE, VANISH ⟨mist will usually ~ in the sun's rays⟩ ⟨the crowd lost interest and *dissipated*⟩ **b :** to spread out so that an original identity is lost ⟨the skirts flowed down to ~ . . . where they touched the floor —Elizabeth Bowen⟩ ⟨the river *dissipated* in several smaller streams⟩ **2 :** to be extravagant or dissolute in the pursuit of physical pleasure; *esp* **:** to drink alcoholic beverages excessively ⟨paying with a hangover for his extended *dissipating* of the night before⟩ **syn** see SCATTER, WASTE

²**dissipate** *adj* [L *dissipatus*] *obs* **:** thinly dispersed **:** SCATTERED

dissipated *adj* **1 :** given to dissipation and having a resultant deteriorated condition of physical health ⟨the young baronet was weak and ~ —Humphry Bullock⟩ ⟨so deplorably ~ and degraded —E.V.Lucas⟩ **2 :** marked by or fostering intemperance and dissipation ⟨a ~ society⟩ ⟨more than half the seamen remaining were more or less unwell from a long sojourn in a ~ port —Herman Melville⟩ — **dis·si·pat·ed·ly** *adv* — **dis·si·pat·ed·ness** *n* -ES

dis·si·pat·er \'disəˌpād·ə(r), -ātə-\ *n* -S **:** one that dissipates

dis·si·pa·tion \ˌdisə'pāshən\ *n* -S [L *dissipation-, dissipatio,* fr. *dissipatus* + *-ion-, -io* -ion] **1 :** the act of dissipating or the state of being dissipated: **a :** a scattering or spreading out or being scattered or spread out to the point of destroying an original identity **:** DISPERSION, DIFFUSION ⟨the ~ of the enemy's forces in battle⟩ ⟨the ~ of the mist⟩ ⟨the ~ of gloom⟩ ⟨the ~ of ignorance⟩ **b** *archaic* **:** DISINTEGRATION, DISSOLUTION **c :** wasteful expenditure ⟨the ~ of one's energies⟩ ⟨the quick ~ of his fortune in foolish investments⟩ **d :** dissolute or intemperate living ⟨passing one's life in a round of ~⟩; *esp* **:** excessive drinking **2 :** AMUSEMENT, DIVERSION ⟨my only ~ is an occasional Sunday concert —Havelock Ellis⟩ ⟨amidst the innumerable conflicting impulses and attractions and ~s of life —P.E.More⟩

dissipation of energy : a physical process (as the cooling of a body in the open air) by which energy becomes not only unavailable but irrecoverable in any form — compare CONSERVATION OF ENERGY, DEGRADATION OF ENERGY

dis·si·pa·tive \'disəˌpād·iv\ *adj* **:** of or relating to dissipation **:** tending to dissipate ⟨the loss characteristics of the ~ material —*Technical News Bull.*⟩ **:** marked by dissipation esp. of energy ⟨aluminum consumed in various ~ uses —D.D. Blue⟩ ⟨a ~ system⟩ — **dis·si·pa·tiv·i·ty** \ˌdisəpə'tivəd·ē\ *n* -ES

dis·si·pa·tor \'disəˌpād·ə(r), -ātə-\ *n* -S **:** DISSIPATER; *specif* **:** a part of a glacier in which the loss by melting exceeds the gain by the accumulation of snow

dissite *adj* [L *dissitus,* fr. *dis-* apart + *situs* placed — more at DIS-, SITE] *obs* **:** lying apart **:** REMOTE

disso- — see DISS-

dis·sociability \də, (ˌ)di+ — *see* DISSOCIABLE\ *n* **:** the quality of being dissociable or being capable of dissociation

dis·so·cia·ble \ *in sense 1* də'sōshəbəl *or* (ˈ)di¦s-, *in sense 2* " *or* -ōs(h)ēəb-\ *adj* [in sense 1, fr. ¹*dis-* + *sociable;* in sense 2, fr. L *dissociabilis,* fr. *dissociare* + *-abilis* -able] **1 :** UNSOCIABLE **2 :** capable of being dissociated **:** SEPARABLE

dis·social \də(s), (ˈ)di(s)+\ *adj* [¹*dis-* + *social*] **:** unfriendly to society **:** UNSOCIAL, SELFISH ⟨motivated by ~ feelings into ~ and aggressive behavior⟩

¹**dis·so·ci·ant** \də'sōs(h)ēənt\ *adj* [L *dissociant-, dissocians,* pres. part. of *dissociare*] **:** producing or resulting from dissociation; *specif, of bacteria* **:** MUTANT

²**dissociant** \"\ *n* -S **:** a dissociant substance or individual

¹**dis·so·ciate** \də'sōs(h)ēə¦t, (ˈ)di¦sō-, -ōshə¦, -ōs(h)ē,ā¦, *usu* ¦d·+V\ *adj* [L *dissociatus,* past part.] **:** DISSOCIATED ⟨perched on the edge of the old sofa in the living room . . . she would appear oddly ~ from her surroundings —Frances G. Patton⟩

²**dis·so·ci·ate** \-ōs(h)ēˌāt, *usu* -ād·+V\ *vb* -ED/-ING/-S [L *dissociatus,* past part. of *dissociare* to separate from fellowship, disunite, estrange, fr. *dis-* ¹dis- + *sociare* to join, share, fr. *socius* companion — more at SOCIAL] *vt* **1 :** to cut off (as from society) **:** separate esp. from association or union with another **:** disconnect from association with another ⟨~s him from the company of cynics —Marya Mannes⟩ ⟨modern architecture cannot be *dissociated* from town or community planning —*Report: (Canadian) Royal Commission on Nat'l Development*⟩ ⟨*dissociated* themselves from the saloons and the distillers —M.R.Cohen⟩ ⟨never possible to ~ the meaning of words from the words themselves —Samuel Alexander⟩ **2 :** to separate into discrete units or parts **:** DISUNITE ⟨those two elements of feeling which Freud says have become *dissociated* in the life of modern man —Irving Howe⟩ ⟨nor are Joyce's characters merely the sum of the particles into which their experience has been *dissociated* —Edmund Wilson⟩; *specif* **:** to subject to chemical dissociation ~ *vi* **1 :** to undergo dissociation **2** *of bacteria* **:** to mutate esp. reversibly

dissociated *adj* **1 :** having nothing to do with **:** not connected **:** UNRELATED ⟨inflationary rises resulting from causes ~ from money —*Current Biog.*⟩ **2 :** giving evidence of or marked by psychological dissociation ⟨a ~ personality⟩ ⟨a ~ idea⟩

dis·so·ci·a·tion \dəˌsōsē'āshən, (ˌ)diˌsō-, -ōshē-— *compare* ASSOCIATION\ *n* -S [L *dissociation-, dissociatio,* fr. *dissociatus* + *-ion-, -io* -ion] **1 :** the act or process of dissociating or the state of being dissociated **:** SEPARATION, SEPARATENESS, DISUNION: as **a :** the process by which a chemical combination breaks up into simpler constituents usu. capable of recombining under other conditions — used esp. of the action of heat or other forms of energy on gases and of solvents upon dissolved substances ⟨~ of ammonia at high temperatures⟩ ⟨electrolytic ~⟩; compare DECOMPOSITION a, IONIZATION **b** (1) **:** isolation, abstraction, or extraction from the total perceptual field of some element which is to be separately observed or analyzed (2) **:** the separation of an idea or activity from the main stream of consciousness or of behavior esp. as a mechanism of ego defense (3) **:** the decompensation of defense permitting fragmentation of the ego into disunited parts (as under hypnosis or in psychotic states) **2 :** the property inherent in certain biological stocks of differentiating into two or more distinct and relatively permanent strains (as the rough and smooth strains of certain bacteria); *also* **:** such a strain

dissociation constant *n* **:** a constant that depends upon the equilibrium between the dissociated and undissociated forms of a chemical combination; *esp* **:** IONIZATION CONSTANT — symbol *K*

dis·so·cia·tive \də'sōs(h)ēˌād·iv, (ˈ)di¦sō-, -ōshəd·iv, -ōs(h)ēəd·iv\ *adj* **:** of, relating to, or tending to produce dissociation ⟨a ~ chemical reaction⟩ ⟨the ~ phenomena associated with schizophrenia⟩; *specif* **:** tending to produce nonsocial or antisocial behavior ⟨~ emotions in the adolescent⟩

dis·so·conch \'disə+,-\ *n* [*diss-* + *conch*] **:** the larval shell of a bivalve mollusk in the veliger stage

dis·sog·e·ny \də'säjənē\ *also* **dis·sog·o·ny** \-ägə-\ *n* -ES [ISV *diss-* + *-geny* or *-gony;* orig. formed as G *dissogonie*] **:** the occurrence of sexual maturity at two distinct periods in the life of an individual (as in the larva and again in the adult of certain ctenophores)

dis·sol·u·bil·i·ty \dəˌsälyə'bilədˌē, *archaic* ˌdisəly-\ *n* **:** the quality or state of being dissoluble ⟨the ~ of sugar⟩

dis·sol·u·ble \də'sälyəbəl, *archaic* 'disəly-\ *adj* [L *dissolubilis,* fr. *dissolvere* to dissolve + *-bilis* -able] **:** capable of being dissolved: **a :** capable of being disintegrated or decomposed ⟨matter is ~⟩ **b :** soluble in a liquid ⟨sugar is ~ in water⟩ **c :** capable of being disunited or disconnected ⟨a ~ bond between the two⟩ **d :** liable to be dispersed or terminated ⟨a ~ bank of mist⟩ ⟨a ~ contract⟩

dis·so·lute \'disəˌlü¦t, -sələ *also* -səlˌyü¦, *usu* ¦d·+V\ *adj* [L *dissolutus,* past part. of *dissolvere* to loosen, dissolve, relax, destroy — more at DISSOLVE] **1 a** *obs* **:** REMISS, NEGLIGENT, CARELESS **b** *archaic* **:** lacking energy, consistency, or firmness **:** LOOSE **2 :** lacking restraint **:** unrestrained or lawless in conduct ⟨the ~ condition of masterless men —Frank Thilly⟩; *esp* **:** loose in morals or conduct **:** WANTON, PROFLIGATE, LICENTIOUS ⟨the obscenity used in their books and the tendency to deal with the ~ and degrading aspects of human nature —Wallace Fowlie⟩ **3** *obs* **:** DISJOINED, DISCONNECTED, SEPARATE, DISSOLVED — **dis·so·lute·ly** *adv* — **dis·so·lute·ness** *n* -ES

dis·so·lu·tion \ˌdisə'lüshən *also* -səl'yü-\ *n* [ME *dissolucioun,* fr. MF & L; MF *dissolution,* fr. L *dissolution-, dissolutio,* fr. *dissolutus* + *-ion-, -io* -ion] **1 :** the act or the process of dissolving or breaking up: as **a :** separation into component parts ⟨the ~ of the phoneme into simultaneous distinctive features —John Lotz⟩ **b :** DISINTEGRATION, DECAY ⟨the old hostelry, then not many years from its final ~ —A.W.Long⟩; *esp* **:** the extinction of life in the human body **:** DECEASE, DEATH ⟨grew convinced of his friend's approaching ~ —Elinor Wylie⟩ **c :** termination or destruction by breaking down, disrupting, or dispersing ⟨the ~ of the republic⟩ ⟨the ~ of a treaty⟩ ⟨the ~ of American urban life —Richard Hofstadter⟩ ⟨he saw his lifework threatened with ~ through the political and shortsighted muddling —J.C.Fitzpatrick⟩ **d :** final dispersion (as of an organized group) ⟨the power of ~ of a legislature at will possessed by the colonial governor —O.P. Field⟩ **e :** LIQUEFACTION ⟨the ~ of ice⟩ **f :** SOLUTION 2a **g :** the final liquidation of a business **2 :** the process of becoming or the state of being relaxed or loosened or a becoming or being dissolute: as **a** *obs* **:** a becoming lax **:** ENFEEBLEMENT **b :** a loosening or a loss of restraint esp. in moral behavior **:** DISSOLUTENESS, PROFLIGACY **c :** the dissolving of a tie or connection ⟨the ~ of the partnership⟩ **3 :** an instance or product of dissolution or something dissolved or dissolute: as **a :** SOLUTION 2b **b** *obs* **:** a dissolute or profligate act **:** EXTRAVAGANCE, EXCESS **c :** an opening in rock produced by the solution of part of the rock

dis·sol·u·tive \də'sälyəd·iv, 'disəˌlü¦ *also* 'disəlˌyü¦\ *adj* [ME, fr. LL *dissolutivus,* fr. L *dissolutus* + *-ivus* -ive] **:** of or relating to dissolution

dis·solv·abil·i·ty \=¦=+ (*with sounds as in* DISSOLVE) + ə'bilədˌē *or* -ətē *or* -i\ *n* **:** the quality of being dissolvable

dis·solv·able \=¦=+əbəl\ *adj* **:** capable of being dissolved esp. by liquefaction or of being broken up and dispersed ⟨a soap not easily ~ in cold water⟩ ⟨inclined to think marriage a too easily ~ union⟩ ⟨a committee ~ at the will of the president⟩

¹**dis·solve** \də'z¦älv, ¦ȯlv *also* ¦ä(ú)v *or* ¦ȯv *sometimes* də's¦\ *vb* [ME *dissolven,* fr. L *dissolvere,* fr. *dis-* ¹dis- + *solvere* to loosen, release, dissolve — more at SOLVE] *vt* **1 a :** to cause to disperse or disappear **:** get rid of **:** do away with **:** DESTROY ⟨a direct hit had *dissolved* one of the destroyers —R.L.Schwartz⟩ ⟨poetry ~s traditional preconception —Harold Rosenberg⟩ ⟨help to ~ some of the rancor —Edward Shils⟩ **b** *obs* **:** to cause the death of **:** KILL **c :** UNDO, END ⟨*dissolved* their alliance⟩ **:** break the continuity of **:** DISCONNECT, DISUNITE ⟨~ a marriage⟩ ⟨~ a bond⟩ **d :** to separate into component parts **:** DISINTEGRATE, DECOMPOSE ⟨the American Tobacco Company was *dissolved* into smaller units —*Amer. Guide Series: N.C.*⟩ ⟨this would ~ a vocabulary into an infinite number of nonce words —Weston La Barre⟩ **e :** to bring to an end by dispersal or by causing the dissociation of **:** TERMINATE ⟨the king's former power to ~ parliament⟩ ⟨he had *dissolved* army courts —*Farmer's Weekly (So. Africa)*⟩ ⟨~ a partnership⟩ **f :** to destroy the influence or effect of by counteracting **:** ANNUL, ABROGATE ⟨~ an injunction⟩ **2 a :** to cause to pass into solution ⟨the difference in content of *dissolved* gases in cold and warm waters —R.E.Coker⟩ **b :** MELT, LIQUEFY ⟨the heat *dissolved* the candles into opaque pools of wax⟩ **c :** to cause to be emotionally moved **:** melt emotionally ⟨the news *dissolved* her so completely she ran from the room weeping⟩; *also* **:** to unstring emotionally and totally — used esp. in the phrase *dissolved in tears* **d :** to totally occupy **:** IMMERSE ⟨his life was *dissolved* in a round of frivolities⟩ **e :** to fade out (a shot in a motion-picture or television sequence) in a dissolve **3** *archaic* **:** to set free **:** RELEASE, DETACH **4 :** to clear up **:** SOLVE ⟨~ the mystery⟩ ~ *vi* **1 a :** to waste away or become dissipated **:** become broken up or decomposed **:** VANISH, DISAPPEAR ⟨the mist . . . *dissolved* as it touched the valleys —Han Suyin⟩ ⟨she would simply have *dissolved* like a slug with salt poured on it —Jean Stafford⟩ ⟨our goals themselves were in flux and . . . we should only find them *dissolving* in our hands —Brand Blanshard⟩ **b :** to break up **:** DISPERSE ⟨the assembly *dissolved*⟩ ⟨orders . . . direct the soldiers to ~ before a stronger force —W.O.Douglas⟩ ⟨the interim committees *dissolved* as soon as the regular committees returned from vacation⟩ **c :** to fade away **:** fall to nothing **:** lose power ⟨his strength *dissolved* before her irresistible charm⟩ ⟨the solidity of the main characters seems almost to ~ —John Lehmann⟩ **2 a :** to become fluid **:** MELT, LIQUEFY ⟨ice cream *dissolving* in the sun⟩ **b :** to pass into solution ⟨sugar ~s in liquid⟩ **c :** to melt or be overcome emotionally ⟨the father *dissolved* in grief⟩; *also* **:** to become totally unstrung emotionally — used esp. in the phrase *dissolve into tears* **d :** to resolve itself as if by dissolution ⟨on closer inspection the street riot *dissolved* into a mob of students struggling to get into an empty store building to see an exhibition of books —Robert Payne⟩ — **dis·solv·er** \-və(r)\ *n*

²**dissolve** \"\ *n* -S **:** a superimposing of one motion-picture or television shot upon another on a screen in which the overlapped shot is gradually darkened as the emergent shot is brightened usu. to indicate a lapse of time or change of scene — called also *lap dissolve;* compare FADE, WIPE

dissolved bone *n* **:** a phosphatic fertilizer made by treating ground bone or bone meal with sulfuric acid

¹**dis·sol·vent** \-vənt\ *n* [L *dissolvent-, dissolvens,* pres. part. of *dissolvere*] **:** something that is dissolvent ⟨a corrosive ~ upon traditional orthodoxy —F.H.A.Micklewright⟩ ⟨industrial democracy, itself a product of cultural dissolution, is a ~ of decadent cultures —Waldo Frank⟩

²**dissolvent** \"\ *adj* [L *dissolvent-, dissolvens,* pres. part.] **1 :** SOLVENT 2 **2 :** tending to dissipate or to destroy by slow degrees ⟨its respect for the rights of religious dissent has proved a ~ force both for bigotries and hostilities —Max Lerner⟩

dis·solv·ing·ly *adv* **:** in a dissolving manner

dissolving shutter *n* **:** a camera attachment used in motion pictures and television for producing dissolves

dis·so·nance \'disənən(t)s\ *also* **dis·so·nan·cy** \-sənənsē, -si\ *n, pl* **dissonances** *also* **dissonancies** [MF or LL; MF, fr. LL *dissonantia,* fr. L *dissonant-, dissonans* + *-ia* -y] **1 :** a mingling of discordant sounds **:** DISCORD ⟨the ~ of the two bands playing different pieces too close to each other⟩; *specif* **:** a harsh or clashing musical interval or combination of notes ⟨varying the flow of harmonious progressions with occasional jarring ~⟩ — compare CONSONANCE **2 a :** lack of agreement **:** INCONGRUITY, DISCREPANCY **b :** DISSIDENCE, CONTENTION, STRIFE ⟨frustrations of the preceding hours, and . . . the occasional ~s that those could but produce between him and her —Elizabeth Bowen⟩ **c :** an instance or example of such incongruity or such dissidence ⟨the mingling of bitter comedy and stark tragedy produces sharp ~s —F.B. Millett⟩ **3 :** an unresolved musical note or chord; *specif* **:** an interval not included in a major or minor triad or its inversions — compare CONSONANCE 2b

dis·so·nant \-sənənt\ *adj* [MF or L; MF, fr. L *dissonant-, dissonans,* pres. part. of *dissonare* to disagree, be discordant, fr. *dis-* ¹dis- + *sonare* to sound — more at SOUND] **1 :** marked by dissonance **:** DISCORDANT ⟨clamor of voices ~ and loud —H.W.Longfellow⟩ ⟨on white grounds, at least two shades often ~ of blue are used together —*Women's Wear Daily*⟩ ⟨held the ~ factions together and patiently built it into a potent political machine —*Time*⟩ **2 :** INCONGRUOUS, DISSIDENT, DISCREPANT ⟨even his discussion of experimental science has touches of medievalism, which are peculiarly ~ —H.O.Taylor⟩ **3 :** disagreeable or unsatisfying in sound ⟨the ~ noises from the badly tuned piano⟩; *specif* **:** harmonically unresolved — contrasted with *consonant* — **dis·so·nant·ly** *adv*

disspirit *var of* DISPIRIT

disspread *var of* DISPREAD

dis·suad·able \də'swādəbəl\ *adj* **:** capable of being dissuaded

dis·suade \-ād\ *vt* -ED/-ING/-S [MF or L; MF *dissuader,* fr. L *dissuadēre,* fr. *dis* ¹dis- + *suadēre* to advise, urge — more at SUASION] **1 a** *archaic* **:** to advise or exhort against (an action) **b :** to advise (a person) against something — usu. used with *from* ⟨a faithful monitor persuading us to whatever in conduct is gentle, honorable, of good repute, and so silently *dissuading* us from base thoughts, low ends, ignoble gains —A.T.Quiller-Couch⟩ **2 :** to divert by advice or persuasion **:** turn from something by reasoning ⟨~ a friend from making a grave mistake⟩ ⟨could easily ~ immigrant labor from unionism —*Amer. Guide Series: N.J.*⟩ ⟨if humanity can be *dissuaded* from suicide —Sumner Welles⟩

syn DISSUADE, DETER, DISCOURAGE, and DIVERT can mean in common to turn (one) aside from a purpose or project. DISSUADE suggests the method of argument, advice, or exhortation, implying coaxing or wheedling rather than bullying or browbeating ⟨he wrote a book to *dissuade* people from the use of tobacco —H.E.Scudder⟩ ⟨were not easily *dissuaded* and sought to have their way several times —A.N.Dragnich⟩ DETER usu. suggests fear as the cause of the turning aside though it can apply to any influence or consideration that alters the purpose or plan ⟨not *deterred* by threat of retaliation⟩ ⟨lured by desire, and yet *deterred* by conscience or want of decision —Theodore Dreiser⟩ ⟨his pride . . . must *deter* him from such foul misconduct —Jane Austen⟩ DISCOURAGE implies a deterring by undermining spirit or enthusiasm or weakening the intent or sense of purpose in some way ⟨strict laws *discourage* if they do not prevent crime⟩ ⟨nothing in these standards that will prohibit or *discourage* bakers from making improvements in the nutritional or other qualities of their products —*Americana Annual*⟩ ⟨the public was exhorted to avoid and *discourage* panic —H.G.Wells⟩ DIVERT implies the turning aside of the interest toward a new object or the turning of the attention in a new direction ⟨*divert* a person by flattery from causing a scandal⟩ ⟨*divert* a child from mischief by a toy⟩

dis·suad·er \-də(r)\ *n* -s **:** one that dissuades from a course of action

dis·sua·sion \-āzhən\ *n* -s [MF or L; MF, fr. L *dissuasion-, dissuasio*, fr. *dissuasus* (past part. of *dissuadēre*) + *-ion-, -io* -ion] **:** the act of dissuading **:** exhortation against something ⟨the man was bent upon squandering his money and no ~ would prevent it⟩

¹dis·sua·sive \-āsiv, -āz|\ *adj* [*dissuasion* + *-ive*] **:** tending to or intended to dissuade **:** expostulating against some action ⟨~ advice⟩ ⟨she made slight ~ gestures with her . . . hands —Mary Norton⟩ — **dis·sua·sive·ly** \|əvlē\ *adv* — **dis·sua·sive·ness** \|ivnəs\ *n* -ES

²dissuasive \"\ *n* -s **:** a dissuasive argument, treatise, or exhortation

dis·sunder \də+\ *vt* [¹*dis-* + *sunder*] *archaic* **:** SUNDER, SEVER, SEPARATE

dissyllable *var of* DISYLLABLE

dis·symmetrical *also* **dis·symmetric** \ˈdi(s)+\ *adj* **:** characterized by dissymmetry — **dis·symmetrically** \"+\ *adv*

dis·symmetry \də(s), (ˈ)di(s)+\ *n* [¹*dis-* + *symmetry*] **1 :** the absence of or the lack of symmetry **:** ASYMMETRY; *specif* **:** ENANTIOMORPHISM **2 :** biradial symmetry

dist- *or* **disto-** *or* **disti-** *comb form* [*distant*] **:** distal ⟨*disto*clusion⟩ — opposed to *proximo-*

dist *abbr* **1** distance **2** distilled **3** distinguished **4** district

dis·tad \ˈdi,stad\ *adv* [*distant* + *-ad*] **:** DISTALLY

¹dis·taff \ˈdi,sta|f, -taa(ə)|,-tai|,-tȧ|\ *n, pl* **distaffs** \|fs,|vz\ [ME *distaf*, fr. OE *distæf*, fr. *dis-* bunch of flax (akin to MLG *dise* bunch of flax on a distaff) + *stæf* staff — more at DIZEN, STAFF] **1 a :** a staff for holding the bunch of flax, tow, or wool from which thread is drawn in spinning by hand or with the spinning wheel **b :** woman's work, authority, or domain ⟨a man fitter for the ~ than for war⟩ **2 a** *archaic* **:** WOMAN, FEMALE; *esp* **:** a female heir **b :** the mother's side of a family ⟨tracing their descent by ~⟩ — compare SWORD SIDE

distaff 1a

²distaff \"\ *adj* **:** of or relating to a woman **:** FEMALE ⟨cooking, sewing, and such ~ matters⟩ ⟨~ applicants must be high-school graduates— *Springfield (Mass.) Daily News*⟩ ⟨a golf swing that is the ~ counterpart of the male champion's⟩ ⟨the entries in the golf tournament were largely on the ~ side⟩; *esp* **:** consisting of, derived from, or related to the mother or female line ⟨the ~ side of the family⟩ ⟨the ~ branch of a family⟩ — compare SPEAR

dis·taff·er \|fə(r)\ *n* -s *slang* **:** WOMAN

dis·tain \dəˈstān\ *vt* -ED/-ING/-S [ME *disteynen*, fr. MF *desteindre* to take away the color of, fr. OF, fr. *des-* ¹dis- + *teindre* to dye, color, fr. L *tingere* to wet, dye — more at TINGE] **1** *archaic* **:** to tinge with a color different from the natural and proper one **:** STAIN, DISCOLOR **2** *archaic* **:** DEFILE, DISHONOR, SULLY

dis·tal \ˈdistᵊl\ *adj* [*dist-* + *-al*] **1 :** remote from the point of attachment or origin, from a point conceived of as central, or from the point of view: as **a :** located away from the center of the body ⟨the ~ end of a bone⟩ — opposed to *proximal* **b :** located away from the mesial plane of the body — opposed to *mesial* **2 :** physical or social rather than sensory — opposed to *proximal*

distal convoluted tubule *n* **:** the convoluted portion of the vertebrate nephron that lies between the loop of Henle and the collecting tubule in intimate association with the afferent vessel, that resembles the proximal convoluted tubule in structure though lacking the striated border, and that is concerned esp. with concentration of the urine

dis·ta·le \dəˈsta(,)lē, -ā(,)lē, -ä(,)lē\ *n, pl* **distal·ia** \-lēə\ [NL, fr. *dist-* + L *-ale* (neut. of *-alis* -al)] **:** any of the distal row of carpal or tarsal bones

dis·tal·ly \ˈdistəlē\ *adv* **:** toward or near a distal part or end

¹dis·tance \ˈdistən(t)s\ *n* -s [ME *distaunce*, fr. OF *destance, distance*, fr. L *distantia*, fr. *distant-, distans* (pres. part. of *distare* to stand apart, be distant) + *-ia* -y — more at DISTANT] **1** *obs* **:** DISCORD, DISSENSION, QUARREL **2 a** (1) **:** a portion of time between two events or between an event and the present **:** INTERVAL ⟨the ~ between birth and death⟩ ⟨not sure he could endure the ~ to the time of his release from captivity⟩ (2) **:** separation in time ⟨it is impossible to judge, at this ~, whether most of these cases would pass for willful murder at the present day —G.G.Coulton⟩ **b :** the degree or amount of separation between two points, lines, surfaces, or objects in geometrical space measured along the shortest path joining them ⟨the ~ between the two houses was exactly one mile⟩ ⟨the ~ between the eyes varies with individuals⟩: (1) **:** the space between troops in ranks, vehicles, or units measured from front to rear — contrasted with *interval* (2) **:** the space between the foremasts of adjacent ships in column, line, or line of bearing (3) **:** the amount of space between the eye and an object of perception **c :** an extent of space measured linearly along a route **:** the length esp. of a surface or road traveled or to be traveled ⟨the Gambia river, navigable for ocean vessels for a ~ of 150 miles —*Americana Annual*⟩ ⟨he did not know the ~ he had walked⟩ ⟨whoever guided the Stevens Party in 1844 would have kept as close as possible to the point of this hill in order to save ~ —G.R.Stewart⟩ ⟨a considerable ~ of highway⟩ ⟨followed for a ~ by a stray dog⟩ **d :** an extent or degree of figurative advance or movement away or along from a point considered primary or original ⟨they carried Puritan severity quite a ~ —John Gould⟩ ⟨the firm is now quite a ~ from what it was when it was founded⟩ **e :** a portion (as of landscape) extended in breadth and depth esp. viewable all at once **:** EXPANSE ⟨a ~ of field, woods, and diluted November sky did indeed stretch without any other feature —Elizabeth Bowen⟩ ⟨a country of flat plains and great ~s⟩ **f** *in racing* (1) **:** COURSE, ROUTE ⟨was able to run the ~ in record time⟩ (2) **:** an extent or length of the track marked by a post or flag placed in the last part of a racecourse which a horse in a heat race must reach by the time the winner crosses the finish line or be disqualified for later heats **3 a :** the quality or state of being distant or spatially remote ⟨~ lends enchantment⟩ **b :** remoteness in nonspatial relationships **:** the quality or state of being distant or not near or not close in ways other than spatial ⟨the gradual elimination of the ~ between a character and a writer's sympathy for that character —J.B.Ludwig⟩: as (1) **:** personal and esp. emotional or moral separation or lack of involvement **:** absence of intimacy or familiarity ⟨the sensitive young hero, shiveringly conscious of his ~ from the school community around him —Anthony Quinton⟩; *also* **:** COLDNESS, RESERVE ⟨an unusual ~ between the two formerly inseparable friends⟩ (2) **:** the degree of separation from immediate succession or close blood relationship ⟨the ~ between the duke and the throne was not great⟩ ⟨a great ~ between the two cousins⟩ (3) **:** AESTHETIC DISTANCE ⟨trying to preserve the ~ between the play and the audience⟩ **c :** DIFFERENCE, DISPARITY ⟨the spiritual, economic, and social ~s between city dweller and farmer —*Amer. Guide Series: Minn.*⟩ **4 a :** a distant point or region or its representation in drawing or painting **:** a point not near or close ⟨the house was at a ~ from his work⟩ ⟨I can see things from a great ~, and look back across a fairly wide gulf of years —Harold Nicolson⟩ **b :** the representation of distance or spatial separation in drawing or painting **:** PERSPECTIVE; *also* **:** the background of a visual view — often used in pl. ⟨shaded ~s⟩ — **go the distance** *or* **last the distance :** to complete a specified course or a succession of commitments **:** last out a series of events or a course of action — **keep one's distance** *or* **keep at a distance :** to stay aloof **:** maintain an attitude of reserve — **know one's distance :** to avoid undue familiarity

²distance \"\ *vt* -ED/-ING/-S **1 a :** to place or keep at a distance ⟨to one who contrives to ~ himself from contemporary emotional disputation —*Times Lit. Supp.*⟩ ⟨apartness in space is the most common factor in such *distancing* of the potential aesthetic object —Hunter Mead⟩ **b :** to cause to appear remote or as if at a distance **2 a :** to leave far behind **:** OUTSTRIP ⟨they both intended to take the road to Irkutsk, and being well mounted hoped to ~ the Emir's scouts —W.H.G.Kingston⟩; *specif* **:** to beat by a distance in racing **b :** to surpass greatly **3 :** to declare disqualified for later heats in racing because of losing one heat by a distance or more

³distance \"\ *adj* **:** intended for or designed to facilitate the clearer perception of things at a distance ⟨~ glasses⟩

distance flag *n* **:** a flag held at a distance pole in a racecourse

distance language *n* **:** a mode of communication (as by means of drums or horns) for use beyond the range of the articulate voice

dis·tance·less \-ləs\ *adj* **1 :** lacking the effect of distance ⟨in the clear atmosphere the mountains seemed ~⟩ **2 :** not allowing an extended view or visibility ⟨a foggy ~ day⟩

distance meter *n* **:** a photographic range finder

distance pole *n* **:** the pole that indicates the distance on a racecourse

distance rate *n* **:** a transportation rate or scale of rates (as most passenger rates) that increases with or is affected by the distance of transportation

distance receptor *n* **:** a receptor for physiological stimuli (as light or sound) produced by distant objects — compare CONTACT RECEPTOR

distance ring *n* **:** a ring (as one shrunk on a piston) to separate two other rings

distances *pl of* DISTANCE, *pres 3d sing of* DISTANCE

distance signal *n* **:** one of a system of signals in the shape of spheres, cones, or cylinders used for communication at sea (as when conditions of wind prevent use of signal flags)

dis·tant \ˈdistənt\ *adj* [ME, fr. MF, fr. L *distant-, distans*, pres. part. of *distare* to stand apart, be distant, fr. *dis-* apart + *stare* to stand — more at DIS-, STAND] **1 a :** separated away in space **:** situated at some distance ⟨set up a pole a mile ~ from the beginning mark⟩ ⟨the ridge of hills some miles ~ —*Amer. Guide Series: Mich.*⟩ ⟨traveling to a more ~ place⟩; *also* **:** at a great distance **:** FAR-OFF ⟨the ship was headed for ~ countries⟩ ⟨would like to escape to some ~ spot⟩ **b :** separated by intervals of greater or less regularity ⟨when he smiled he showed a row of ~ teeth⟩ ⟨a grove of ~ trees⟩; *also* **:** being far apart **:** separated by a great distance from each other ⟨communication was difficult between such ~ places⟩ **c :** separated in a relationship other than spatial (as that of time, blood, or character) ⟨heartbeats that were ~ and very feeble⟩ ⟨in those ~ years when scholars will be able to write the history of the Far East with access to all the sources —Robert Payne⟩ ⟨a ~ relative⟩ ⟨willful blindness to ~ consequences —A.L.Guérard⟩ **2 :** different in kind ⟨a play far ~ from the one he first wrote⟩ ⟨pieces by far ~ composers⟩ **3 :** reserved or aloof in personal relationship **:** not cordial **:** somewhat haughty **:** COLD ⟨treated all people with a ~ politeness⟩ ⟨a ~ manner⟩ **4 :** coming from or going to a distance ⟨~ voyages⟩; *also* **:** concerned with or directed toward things at a distance ⟨~ thoughts⟩ ⟨a ~ look in the eye⟩ — **dis·tant·ly** *adv* — **dis·tant·ness** *n* -ES

distant signal *or* **distant block signal** *n* **:** a railroad signal placed at a distance that will allow adequate advance warning of the setting of a home signal at which the train must stop — called also *approach signal*

¹dis·taste \dəˈstāst, (ˈ)di|s-\ *vb* [¹*dis-* + *taste* (v.)] *vt* **1 a** *obs* **:** to dislike the taste of **:** DISRELISH **b** *archaic* **:** to feel repugnance for or aversion to **2 a** *obs* **:** to cause a physical distaste in **:** DISGUST, NAUSEATE **b** *archaic* **:** to cause aversion or repugnance in **:** OFFEND, DISPLEASE **3** *obs* **:** to deprive of taste or relish **:** make unsavory ~ *vi, obs* **:** to become distasteful **:** taste offensive

²distaste \"\ *n* [¹*dis-* + *taste* (n.)] **1 a :** dislike of food or drink **:** DISRELISH **b :** DISINCLINATION, DISLIKE, AVERSION, REPUGNANCE ⟨~s are equally legitimate, including a distaste for music itself —Virgil Thomson⟩ ⟨a ~ for work⟩ ⟨a ~ for book and thought —A.C.Benson⟩ **c** *obs* **:** mutual aversion **:** ALIENATION, ESTRANGEMENT **2** *obs* **:** DISCOMFORT, UNEASINESS, DISTRESS **3** *obs* **:** a cause of offense **:** OFFENSE **syn** see DISLIKE

distasted *adj, now dial* **:** DISLIKED, DISAPPROVED

dis·taste·ful \-āstfəl\ *adj* **1 a :** unpleasant or disgusting to the taste **:** NAUSEOUS, LOATHSOME ⟨a ~ plate of cold and underdone food⟩ **b :** OFFENSIVE, DISAGREEABLE ⟨the truth proved ~⟩ ⟨a succession of ~ chores⟩ **2 :** showing distaste or aversion ⟨viewed the cold and greasy potatoes on his plate with a ~ expression on his face⟩ **syn** see HATEFUL

dis·taste·ful·ly \-fəlē, -li\ *adv* **:** in a distasteful manner

dis·taste·ful·ness \-fəlnəs\ *n* **:** the quality or state of being distasteful

dis·tel·fink \ˈdis(h)tᵊl,fiŋk\ *n* -s [PaG *dischdelfink*, lit., goldfinch, fr. G *distelfink*, fr. *distel* thistle (fr. OHG *distila*) + *fink* finch, fr. OHG *finco, fincho* — more at THISTLE, FINCH] **:** a traditional Pennsylvania Dutch design motif in the form of a stylized bird

¹dis·temper \dəs +\ *vt* [ME *distempren, destempren*, fr. LL *distemperare* (to mix badly), fr. L *dis-* ¹dis- + *temperare* to temper, mingle properly — more at TEMPER] **1 :** to throw out of order or proper or smoothly working adjustment **:** afflict with a distemper **:** DISORDER, DERANGE ⟨no sophism is too gross to delude minds ~*ed* by party spirit —T.B.Macaulay⟩ ⟨he has seldom been grievously ~*ed* by repressions, guilt, despondency, or philosophical doubt —C.J.Rolo⟩ **2** *archaic* **a :** to make unhealthy **:** SICKEN **b :** to derange the mind of **:** make insane **3** *archaic* **:** to deprive of even temper or moderation **:** make ill-humored

²dis·temper \" *sometimes* ˈdi+,-\ *n* [partly fr. ¹*distemper*, partly fr. ¹*dis-* + *temper*] **1 :** bad or ill humor **:** bad temper **:** ill feeling **2 :** a disordered or abnormal bodily state usu. of an animal: as **a :** a highly contagious virus disease of dogs, minks, wolves, and foxes that is marked by fever, skin eruptions, acute respiratory inflammation frequently passing into pneumonia and sometimes by symptoms referable to invasion and demyelination of nervous tissue; *also* **:** any of certain allied and ill-distinguished virus infections of dogs — compare HARD PAD **b :** STRANGLES **c :** PANLEUCOPENIA **d :** a severe frequently fatal infectious nasopharyngeal inflammation of rabbits **3** *obs* **:** INTOXICATION **4 a :** disorder or derangement esp. civil or political or a particular disorder, affliction, or derangement ⟨in the middle ages . . . resistance was an ordinary remedy for political ~*s* —T.B.Macaulay⟩ ⟨the ~*s* of monarchy were the great subjects of apprehension and distress —J.R.Newman⟩ **b** *archaic* **:** unpleasant or inclement condition (as of weather or climate)

³dis·temper \dəs +\ *vt* -ED/-ING/-S [ME *distemperen*, fr. MF *destemprer*, fr. ML *distemperare*, fr. L *dis-* ¹dis- + *temperare* to mingle properly] **1 a** *obs* **:** to dilute with or soak, steep, or dissolve in a liquid **b** *archaic* **:** to corrupt or impair by dilution or by a counteragent **2 a :** to mix (colors or ingredients) to produce distemper for painting **b :** to paint in or with distemper

⁴dis·temper \" *sometimes* ˈdi+,-\ *n* -s **1 :** a process of painting in which the pigments are mixed with an emulsion of egg yolk, with size, or with white of egg, or when distinguished from tempera with size only as a vehicle and usu. used for scene painting or the decoration of usu. plaster walls and ceilings **2 a :** the paint or the prepared ground used in the distemper process of painting **b :** a painting done in distemper **c :** a pigment used esp. for distemper paint **3 :** any of a number of paints or coloring materials using water as a vehicle (as whitewash, calcimine, or cement wash)

distemperate *adj* [ME *distemperat*, fr. ML *distemperatus*, past part. of *distemperare*] **1** *obs* **:** being out of order **:** not functioning normally **2** *obs* **:** INTEMPERATE, IMMODERATE

dis·temperature \dəs, (ˈ)dis+\ *n* **1 :** DISTEMPER **2** *archaic* **:** lack of moderation **:** EXCESS, INTEMPERATENESS

distempered *adj* [ME, fr. past part. of *distemperen*] **1 :** DISORDERED, UNHEALTHY ⟨a ~ national economy⟩ **2 :** suggesting disease (as in color or appearance) ⟨moldy ~ walls⟩ — **dis·tem·pered·ly** *adv* — **dis·tem·pered·ness** *n* -ES

distempering *n* -s **:** ⁴DISTEMPER 2a

dis·tem·per·oid \dəˈstempə,rȯid\ *adj* [²*distemper* + *-oid*] **:** resembling distemper; *specif* **:** of, relating to, or being a strain of canine distemper virus attenuated by passage through ferrets and used to develop immunity in dogs and other susceptible hosts to natural distemper infection

dis·tend \dəˈstend\ *vb* [ME *distenden*, fr. L *distendere*, fr. *dis-* apart + *tendere* to stretch — more at DIS-, THIN] *vt* **1** *archaic* **:** to extend in one direction **:** lengthen out **:** spread apart **2 a :** to stretch out or extend in more than one direction ⟨the main outlines of the land yet lay clearly ~*ed* before them —Norman Douglas⟩ **b :** to enlarge from internal pressure **:** SWELL, DILATE, BLOAT ⟨the bat's body was so ~*ed* that it appeared spherical —R.L.Ditmars & A.M.Greenhall⟩ ⟨a ~*ed* bladder⟩ ⟨~*ed* nostrils⟩ **c :** to make larger or increase beyond a due, expected, or reasonable proportion ⟨the ~*ed* profits of the enemy trade —F.L.Paxson⟩ ⟨a much-*distended* land power —W.G.East⟩ ⟨this simple drama as it has been ~*ed* into a spectacle to catch the eye of Broadway —John Mason Brown⟩ **:** unduly increase or magnify the importance of ⟨print headlines that attract the reader, even if the facts of the story have to be ~*ed* —Jean Hills⟩ ~ *vi* **:** to become larger, expanded, or inflated **:** SWELL, ENLARGE ⟨her eyes seemed to ~ with surprise⟩ **syn** see EXPAND

distended *adj* **:** greatly enlarged **:** SWOLLEN, BULGING, DILATED — **dis·tend·ed·ly** *adv* — **dis·tend·ed·ness** *n* -ES

dis·ten·si·bil·i·ty \də,sten(t)səˈbilədē, (,)di,s-\ *n* -ES **:** the quality or state of being distensible **:** the capacity of stretching

dis·ten·si·ble \dəˈsten(t)səbəl\ *adj* [LL *distensus* (past part. of L *distendere*) + E *-ible*] **:** capable of being distended, extended, or dilated **:** able to stretch or expand or to be stretched or expanded ⟨its stomach . . . is extraordinarily ~ —R.E. Coker⟩ ⟨the arterial walls are . . . not rigid but elastic and ~ —F.A.Faught⟩

dis·tensile \dəs+\ *adj* [LL *distensus* + E *-ile* (as in *tensile*)] **1 :** DISTENSIBLE **2 :** causing distension

dis·ten·sion *or* **dis·ten·tion** \dəˈstenchən\ *n* -s [L *distention-, distentio*, fr. *distentus* + *-ion-, -io* -ion] **:** the act of distending or the state of being distended esp. unduly or abnormally ⟨~ of the abdomen, vomiting, and localized pain and swelling —Morris Fishbein⟩

dis·ten·sive \-n(t)siv\ *adj* [*distension* + *-ive*] **:** DISTENSIBLE

¹distent *adj* [L *distentus*, past part. of *distendere* to distend — more at DISTEND] *obs* **:** spread out **:** DISTENDED

²dis·tent \dəˈstent\ *n* -s [L *distentus*, fr. *distentus*, past part.] **:** BREADTH, DISTENSION

¹disterminate *vt* [L *disterminatus*, past part. of *disterminare*, fr. *dis-* ¹dis- + *terminare* to bound, limit, terminate — more at TERMINATE] *obs* **:** to separate by forming a boundary

²disterminate *adj* [L *disterminatus*] *obs* **:** marked off **:** SEPARATED

dis·thene \ˈdis,thēn, ˈdīs-\ *n* -s [F *disthène*, fr. *di-* + Gk *sthenos* force — more at STHENIC] **:** CYANITE

dis·throne \dəs, (ˈ)dis+\ *vt* [¹*dis-* + *throne* (n.)] **:** DETHRONE ⟨a queen *disthroned*⟩

disthronize *vt* -ED/-ING/-S [¹*dis-* + *throne* + *-ize*] *obs* **:** DETHRONE

disti- — see DIST-

dis·tich \ˈdi(,)stik, -,stēk\ *n* -s [L *distichon*, fr. Gk, fr. neut. of *distichos* with two rows, of two verses, fr. *di-* + *stichos* row, line, verse; akin to Gk *steichein* to go — more at STAIR] **:** a strophic unit or unit of verse consisting of two lines and usu. comprising a sense unit

dis·ti·chal \ˈdistəkəl, -tēk-\ *adj* **:** of, relating to, or comprising a distich

dis·tich·lis \dəˈstikləs\ *n, cap* [NL, irreg. fr. Gk *distichos*] **:** a small genus of American grasses found along seashores and in alkaline regions and having creeping rhizomes, distichous leaves, and several-flowered spikes in small panicles — see SALT GRASS

dis·ti·chous \ˈdistəkəs\ *adj* [L *distichus* fr. Gk *distichos* with two rows] **1** *of plant or animal parts* **:** disposed in two vertical rows **:** two-ranked ⟨a grass with ~ leaves⟩ **2 :** divided into two distinct segments **:** BIPARTITE ⟨~ antennae⟩ — **dis·ti·chous·ly** *adv*

dis·till *also* **dis·til** \dəˈstil\ *vb* **distilled; distilled; distilling; distills** *also* **distils** [ME *distillen*, fr. MF *distiller*, fr. LL *distillare*, alter. of L *destillare*, fr. *de-* down + *stillare* to drip, trickle, fr. *stilla* drop; akin to G *stieren* to stare, ON *stira* to stare, L *stiria* icicle, Lith *stýrti* to stiffen, OE *stān* stone — more at DE-, STONE] *vt* **1 a :** to send or pour forth in small quantities **:** INFUSE ⟨snowy . . . blossoms that ~ their fragrance through the countryside —*Amer. Guide Series: Va.*⟩ **b :** to let fall or precipitate in drops or in a wet mist ⟨some caves are dry, others ~ water from invisible rifts or pendent beards —Norman Douglas⟩ **2 a :** to subject to or transform by distillation ⟨~ molasses into rum⟩ **b :** to get, extract, or make by distillation, by a process suggesting distillation, or as if by distillation ⟨a strong drink ~*ed* from grain⟩ ⟨~ gasoline from crude oil⟩ ⟨~ coal tar from coal⟩ ⟨basic truths must be discovered and ~*ed* out of the available mass of mental acrobatics, common sense, horse sense, and nonsense —P.M.Mazur⟩ ⟨they manage to ~ comedy out of the spiritual loneliness of the characters they are playing —Brooks Atkinson⟩ ⟨a 1500-page narrative ~*ed* from 168 bound volumes of his papers —A.S. Henning⟩ **c :** to obtain an extract from (as a plant) by infusion and distillation ⟨making medicines by ~ing herbs she had gathered⟩ **d :** to remove by distillation — usu. used with *out* or *off* ⟨~ impurities from the elixir⟩ ⟨~ off the impurities⟩ ⟨the heavy oil left after gasoline and light oils are ~*ed* off the crude —*Newsweek*⟩ **e :** to make concentrated by abridgment and purification or by the extraction of an essential or typical portion **:** CONCENTRATE, PURIFY ⟨~ the information before presenting it to the committee⟩ ⟨she ~*s* the lore of the ancients and the learning of modern specialists into a literary form palatable to a wide public —W.E.D.Allen⟩ ⟨a lyric poet works in a more ~*ed* medium than narrative prose —Cyril Connolly⟩ **3** *obs* **:** DISSOLVE, MELT ~ *vi* **1 a :** to fall or materialize in drops or in a fine moisture **:** DROP, TRICKLE ⟨water ~*ing* over the rocks from the moist undergrowth⟩ **b :** to fall, appear, or materialize slowly or in small quantities at a time as if by distillation ⟨spiritual values ~ slowly from the interaction of sensation, emotion, or thought —G.R.Harrison⟩ **2 :** to undergo distillation **:** condense or drop from a still after distillation ⟨a liquor that ~*s* easily⟩ **3 :** to perform distillation

dis·till·able \-ləbəl\ *adj* **:** capable of being distilled esp. without chemical change ⟨alcohol is ~⟩

dis·till·age \-lij\ *n* -s [*distill* + *-age*] **:** the product of distillation

dis·til·land \ˈdistə,land\ *n* -s [L *distillandum*, neut. of *distillandus*, gerundive of *distillare*] **:** material to be or being distilled — compare DISTILLATE

dis·til·late \ˈdistə,lāt, -,lət *also* dəˈstilət; *usu* |d·+V\ *n* -s [ISV *distill* + *-ate*] **1 :** the usu. liquid product that is condensed from vapor during distillation (as of petroleum) — compare DISTILLAND **2 :** something resembling a distillate in being a concentration, an abstract, or an essence ⟨the very ~ of idolatry —D.C.Williams⟩ ⟨this book is the clear sparkling ~ of the wide experience gained during a lifetime —A.C.Morrison⟩ ⟨this book is a ~ of facts —*N.Y. Times Book Rev.*⟩ ⟨put into their letters the ~ of their wisdom and nobility —G.W. Johnson⟩

dis·til·la·tion \,distəˈlāshən\ *n* -s [ME *distillacioun*, fr. L *distillation-, distillatio*, fr. *distillatus* (past part. of *distillare* to distill) + *-ion-, -io* -ion] **1 :** the process of driving off gas or vapor from liquids or solids by heating (as in a still or retort) and condensing to liquid products, such processes being used esp. for purification, fractionation, or the formation of new substances by decomposition **:** RECTIFICATION — see AZEOTROPIC DISTILLATION, DESTRUCTIVE DISTILLATION, EXTRACTIVE DISTILLATION, MOLECULAR DISTILLATION; compare EVAPORATION, SUBLIMATION **2 :** DISTILLATE ⟨every paragraph is a ~ of wide reading, sound judgment, and unemotional reasoning —*Times Lit. Supp.*⟩ ⟨these translations . . . can be accepted as genuine ~*s* of the Orient —G.P.Meyer⟩

distilled green *n* **:** VERDIGRIS 4

distilled liquor *n* **:** an alcoholic liquor (as brandy, whiskey, gin, rum, or arrack) obtained by distillation from wine or other fermented fruit juice or plant juice or from a starchy material (as various grains) that has first been brewed — called also *hard liquor*

distilled water *n* **:** water that has been freed of dissolved or suspended solids and from organisms by distillation (as for medical or chemical purposes)

dis·till·er \dəˈstilə(r)\ *n* -s **:** one that distills: as **a :** one that distills alcoholic liquors **b :** a distilling apparatus **:** STILL

distillers' beer *n* **:** WASH 6b (1)

distillers' grains *n pl* **:** the residue from the manufacture of alcohol or alcoholic beverages distilled from grains and used as livestock feed

distillers' solubles *n pl but often sing in constr* **:** the dissolved remains and fine particles left after the solid grains have been strained from the residue from alcoholic distillation; *esp* **:** such remains and particles when dehydrated and used as a source of vitamins and minerals in animal rations

dis·till·ery \də'stil(ə)rē, -ri\ *n* -ES [*distill* + *-ery*] **1** *archaic* **:** DISTILLATION **2 :** the building and works where distilling (as of alcoholic liquors) is carried on

dis·till house \də'stil-\ *n, archaic* **:** a building used for distilling; *also* **:** DISTILLERY

distilling *n* -S [fr. gerund of *distill*] **:** the making of distilled liquors as a business

distilling flask *n* **:** a glass usu. round-bottomed flask for holding a substance to be distilled

dis·till·ment *or* **dis·til·ment** \də'stilmənt\ *n* -S *archaic* **:** DISTILLATION

distills *pres 3d sing of* DISTILL

distils *pres 3d sing of* DISTIL

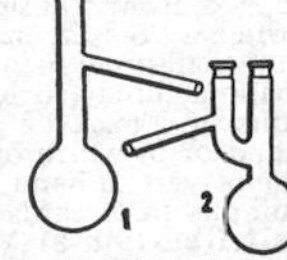

distilling flasks: *1* common type, *2* Claisen flask

dis·tinct \də'stiŋ(k)t\ *adj, often* -ER/-EST [ME, fr. MF, fr. L *distinctus*, past part. of *distinguere* to distinguish — more at DISTINGUISH] **1 a** *obs* **:** discriminated by a visible sign **:** marked out **:** DISTINGUISHED **b :** characterized by qualities individualizing or distinguishing as apart from, unlike, or not identical with another or others ⟨things similar in effect but wholly ~ in motive —Hilaire Belloc⟩ **2 :** capable of being easily perceived: as **a :** capable of being readily seen, felt, or heard through sharp, clear, unmistakable impression **:** not blurred, obscured, or indefinite ⟨the slender and fragile tracery that must be preserved unventilated and ~ —B.N. Cardozo⟩ ⟨her last death shriek ~ among a thousand —William Wordsworth⟩ **b :** capable of being easily grasped or comprehended by the mind because of clear cogent appearance or presentation ⟨a promise that Mr. Nicholls should have a ~ refusal —Virginia Woolf⟩ ⟨left us with a clear and ~ idea of human nature —*Times Lit. Supp.*⟩ **3** *archaic* **:** notably marked or decorated **4 a :** NOTABLE, UNUSUAL ⟨so overrun with camera'ed foreigners that it is a ~ achievement to get an unencumbered photo —William Petersen⟩ **b :** UNEQUIVOCAL, UNQUESTIONABLE ⟨a ~ liberal⟩ ⟨hot, dry summers . . . with drought a ~ possibility —W.B.Johnston & I.Crkvencic⟩

syn SEPARATE, SEVERAL, DISCRETE: these words agree in referring to two or more things not the same or not blended or united. DISTINCT is likely to stress characteristics that distinguish or that indicate that the thing modified is apart from or different from others ⟨probably to Guido de Bres . . . the Dutch Reformed Church owed the beginning of its sturdy life, and that it did not become a mere limb of either the French Calvinistic, or German Reformed body, but grew as a "shield and blessing to both" with a *distinct* and rooted life of its own —J.L.Motley⟩ ⟨Mrs. Yeobright, who, possessing two *distinct* moods in close contiguity, a gentle mood and an angry, flew from one to the other without the least warning —Thomas Hardy⟩ Often interchangeable with DISTINCT, SEPARATE may stress lack of connection or difference in identity between two things ⟨a part of the citizens seceded from the main body, and formed a *separate* community on the neighboring marshes —W.H.Prescott⟩ ⟨this rupture of the supposed continuity of nature and the reestablishment of ethics and aesthetics as *separate* and autonomous realms —J. W.Krutch⟩ ⟨she had a command of hand, a nicety and force of touch, which is an endowment *separate* from pictorial genius, though indispensable to its exercise —Nathaniel Hawthorne⟩ In older, archaic, or formal English SEVERAL may also indicate distinctness, difference, or separation from similar items ⟨her knowledge of three *several* tongues —Elinor Wylie⟩ ⟨a network of concrete highways upon the *several* states —W.H.Hamilton⟩ DISCRETE forcefully stresses individuality and lack of connection despite apparent similarities ⟨*discrete* quantity consists of the separate and unjointed units. Continuous quantity resists and even defies description in terms of disjunct ultimate units —Josiah Royce⟩ ⟨the conclusion that gases are made up of *discrete* units (molecules) —Lancelot Hogben⟩ ⟨by confining his operations to those aspects of reality which had, so to say, market value, and by isolating and dismembering the corpus of experience, the physical scientist created a habit of mind favorable to *discrete* practical inventions —Lewis Mumford⟩ **syn** see in addition EVIDENT

dis·tinc·tio \də'stiŋ(k)t(s)ē,ō, -)shē,ō\ *also* **dis·tinc·tion** \-)shən\ *n, pl* **distincti·o·nes** \-,=tsē'ō,nās, -shē'ō,nēz\ *also* **distinctions** \-shənz\ [ML *distinction-, distinctio* section, division, fr. L] **:** a phrase in a Gregorian melody indicated by markings in the text

dis·tinc·tion \də'stiŋ(k)shən\ *n* -S [ME *distinccioun*, fr. OF *distinction*, fr. L *distinction-, distinctio*, fr. *distinctus* (past part. of *distinguere* to distinguish) + *-ion-, -io* -ion — more at DISTINGUISH] **1 a** *archaic* **:** a part of a divided whole **:** CATEGORY, SECTION **b** *obs* **:** the act of separating into parts **:** PARTITION, DIVISION **c :** CLASS, GRADE, RANK ⟨Mr. Hemingway's . . . prose is of the first ~ —Edmund Wilson⟩ **2 a :** the act of distinguishing a difference **:** DISCRIMINATION, DIFFERENTIATION ⟨not interested in ~s between philosophic entities⟩ ⟨without ~ as to race, sex, language, or religion —Vera M. Dean⟩ **b :** the object or result of distinguishing or discriminating ⟨the ~s of degree had lost much of their rigidity —Douglas Bush⟩ ⟨the line of ~ between the citizen and the subject —R.B.Taney⟩ ⟨crooked crooks and honest crooks, a ~ which does represent a difference —Gerald Carson⟩ **:** CONTRAST ⟨he was pretty reasonable in ~ to the other men⟩ ⟨the classical economists in ~ to the modern price theorists —Paul Mattick⟩; *also* **:** special favor ⟨full commissions are payable to the galleries to the same extent as if sold to other bidders, without ~ or preference shown to such consignors or agents —*Parke-Bernet Galleries Catalog*⟩ **c** *archaic* **:** the faculty of distinguishing **:** DISCERNMENT **3 :** something that distinguishes one thing from another **:** a distinguishing quality or mark **:** DIFFERENTIA ⟨the ~ between good and evil⟩ ⟨a ~ between the two men was their manner of treating inferiors⟩ **4 :** the quality or state of being distinguishable or distinct: as **a :** DIFFERENCE, DISPARITY ⟨the ~ between the twins was great enough to eliminate the usual identification trouble⟩ **b** *obs* **:** CLEARNESS, DISTINCTNESS **5 a :** the quality or state of being distinguished or of having distinguished oneself ⟨the man's ~ was in his entire bearing⟩ **b :** EMINENCE, SIGNIFICANCE ⟨a politician of some ~ in the town⟩ ⟨looking for actions that would reveal his guilt, but found none of ~⟩ **:** special honor or regard ⟨graduated from college with ~⟩ ⟨grant him the ~ he deserves⟩ **c :** the mark or indication of special honor or regard ⟨has the ~ of being both rich and handsome⟩ **d :** worthiness or fitness for special or professional honor or recognition ⟨accomplished the difficult task with rare ~⟩ **6 :** the act of giving special recognition (as by honoring) ⟨Urban received him with great ~ —*Encyc. Americana*⟩ **syn** see DISSIMILARITY

dis·tinc·tion·less \-ləs\ *adj* **:** lacking distinctions

¹dis·tinc·tive \də'stiŋ(k)tiv, -tēv *also* -təv\ *adj* [ML *distinctivus*, fr. L *distinctus* + *-ivus* -ive] **1 a :** serving to distinguish **:** setting apart from others **:** INDIVIDUALIZING ⟨a ~ characteristic of the type is a tendency to procrastinate⟩ **b :** CHARACTERISTIC, PECULIAR ⟨actions ~ of a brutal man⟩ ⟨a call that was almost ~ to the catbird⟩ ⟨the moist, salt air of the Cape is said to turn the shingles on roofs and walls to a ~ gray —Jackson Rivers⟩ **:** SPECIAL ⟨not only was homicide frequent but the tough hombres of the town added a ~ touch in their manner of disposing of the body —*Amer. Guide Series: Texas*⟩ **c :** having or giving style or distinction ⟨a woman with a talent for wearing consistently ~ clothes⟩ ⟨an old ~ residential quarter —*Amer. Guide Series: N.Y. City*⟩ **2** *archaic* **:** having the ability to distinguish **:** DISCRIMINATING **3** *phonetics, of a feature of speech* **:** capable of making a segment of utterance different in meaning as well as in sound from an otherwise identical utterance **:** that makes or helps to make a speech item a phoneme rather than an allophone **4 :** DISJUNCTIVE 4 **syn** see CHARACTERISTIC

²distinctive \"\ *n* -S **:** DISJUNCTIVE 2

distinctive insignia *n* **:** the distinctive metal badges or other devices authorized for wear by members of a regiment or battalion of the U.S. Army

dis·tinc·tive·ly \-təvlē, -li\ *adv* **:** in a distinctive manner ⟨a bird with ~ mottled coloring⟩ ⟨a man ~ attired⟩

dis·tinc·tive·ness \-tivnəs, -tēv- *also* -təv-\ *n* -ES **:** the quality or state of being distinctive

dis·tinct·ly \də'stiŋ(k)tlē, -ŋklē, -li\ *adv* [ME, fr. *distinct* + *-ly*] **:** in a distinct manner: as **a** *obs* **:** SEPARATELY **b :** with distinctness **:** not confusedly **:** without a blending or merging of one thing with another ⟨the efforts of the writers to paint ~ and separately these six heads —Irving Babbitt⟩ ⟨that which is clearly and ~ conceived as the truth —C.W.Hendel⟩ **c :** CLEARLY, OBVIOUSLY, UNEQUIVOCALLY ⟨the end which Charles ~ proposed to himself —T.B.Macaulay⟩ ⟨the younger of the two boys is ~ the brighter⟩ **:** DECIDEDLY ⟨the boy was ~ angry when he lashed out with his fists⟩ **d :** DISTINCTIVELY ⟨his characters are ~ Irish —*Univ. of Arizona Record*⟩ ⟨the swamp forests are a ~ southern plant community —*Amer. Guide Series: N.C.*⟩

dis·tinct·ness \-ŋtnəs, -ŋkn-\ *n* -ES **:** the quality or state of being distinct

dis·tin·gué \¦dē,stan¦gā, ¦di,s-, -taiŋ-, də¦=,=, dē¦=,=\ *adj* [F, fr. past part. of *distinguer*] **1 :** distinguished in manner or bearing **:** marked by an appearance of distinction ⟨a rather ~ foreign diplomat with graying temples and a black homburg⟩ **:** giving distinction ⟨black is always ~ for evening wear⟩ **2 :** special to a group laying claim to distinction **:** superior fashionably or culturally ⟨it was agreed that her manners were fine, and her air ~ —W.M.Thackeray⟩

dis·tin·guish \də'stiŋgwish, -wēsh, *chiefly in pres part* -wəsh; ÷ -ŋw-\ *vb* -ED/-ING/-ES [MF *distinguer*, fr. L *distinguere*, fr. *dis-* ¹dis- + *-stinguere* (akin to L *instigare* to urge on, stimulate) — more at STICK] *vt* **1 a :** to perceive as being separate or different **:** recognize a difference in ⟨able to ~ normally confused sounds⟩ **b** *obs* **:** to draw fine distinctions in respect to **2 a :** to mark as separate or different (as one thing from another) **:** make a difference between **:** DISCRIMINATE ⟨the concept of culture . . . ties some phenomena and interpretations together; it dissimilates and ~es others —A.L.Kroeber⟩ ⟨he was slightly built, shy, deferential almost, with nothing in his dress to ~ him from his workmen —G.S. Gale⟩ ⟨the church was ~ed by the absence of a tower⟩ ⟨a man ~ed by a shock of wild white hair⟩; *also* **:** to make clearly visible ⟨street lamps and lighted windows ~ the hills and valleys that are obscured in the day by tenements and apartment houses —*Amer. Guide Series: N.Y. City*⟩ **b :** to separate into kinds, classes, or categories (as by logical division) ⟨unable to ~ the notes into anything more than high or low⟩ **c :** to set above or apart from others **:** make eminent **:** give prestige to ⟨he has ~ed himself by negotiating a number of international trade agreements —*Amer. Guide Series: Tenn.*⟩ ⟨the New Jersey Constitution is ~ed as one of the briefest in the country —*Amer. Guide Series: N.J.*⟩ ⟨men who had ~ed themselves in action in several significant battles⟩ **d** *obs* **:** to separate or divide into portions or sections **:** mark (parts) as separate **e :** to make identifiable or discernible as a separate entity **:** mark off **:** CHARACTERIZE ⟨once writers were a class apart, ~ed by ink-stained fingers, unkempt hair, and a predilection for drinking cheap wine in cellars —Edward Uhlan⟩ ⟨nothing ~es the taste of an age more clearly than the language which it admires —R.W.Southern⟩ **3 a :** to perceive, discern, or descry (something easily confused or blended with adjacent things) ⟨I glanced seaward . . . and ~ed nothing except a single green light, minute and far away, that might have been the end of a dock —Scott Fitzgerald⟩ ⟨unable to ~ road markings in the fog⟩ **b :** to pick out or single out ⟨the examiner must be careful to ~ the excitable individuals —H.G. Armstrong⟩ **4** *archaic* **:** to pay special attention to **:** note especially **5** *obs* **:** to argue subtly and speciously ~ *vi* **:** to perceive a difference **:** exercise discrimination ⟨a judge ~es between cases apparently similar⟩ — **distinguish of** *obs* **:** DISTINGUISH

syn DISTINGUISH, DIFFERENTIATE, DISCRIMINATE, and DEMARCATE can mean, in common, to point out or mark the differences between things that are or seem to be very much and often confusingly alike. DISTINGUISH implies a reason for confusion as between two things having an extremely close relationship or connection ⟨nothing more profoundly *distinguishes* the Hellenic from the modern view of life than the estimate in which women were held by the Greeks —G.L.Dickinson⟩ ⟨he must be taught to *distinguish* between the truth and his imagination —Mary Austin⟩ ⟨a child under four will hardly *distinguish* between yesterday and a week ago —Bertrand Russell⟩ ⟨Dr. Dunham *distinguished* between the terms *public relations* and *publicity* —T.F.Reidy⟩ DIFFERENTIATE implies the possession of a distinguishing character or characters or the ascertainment of the differences between things easily confused ⟨his immaculate appearance *differentiates* him from his fellow workers⟩ ⟨classes small enough to enable the teacher to *differentiate* the strong and the willing from the sluggards —C.H.Grandgent⟩ ⟨he *differentiates* industrial, political, and moral activities —D.S.Robinson⟩ DISCRIMINATE can imply the possession of obvious distinguishing characteristics ⟨his gift of fine oratory *discriminates* him from other statesmen⟩ but usu. implies the power to discern differences, often slight, between similar things ⟨irritated by the wasp's inability to *discriminate* a house from a tree —E.K.Brown⟩ ⟨no dictionary *discriminates* perfectly among these finely shaded distinctions in trade vocabularies —Ben Riker⟩ DEMARCATE, implying the literal setting of boundaries, can be used to suggest a distinguishing between things as if by marking them off ⟨how shall we *demarcate* reproduction from growth —G.H. Lewes⟩

dis·tin·guish·abil·i·ty \=,==ə'biləd-ē, -ətē, -i\ *n* -ES **:** the quality or state of being distinguishable

dis·tin·guish·able \-shəbəl\ *adj* **1 :** capable of being distinguished **:** SEPARABLE, DIVISIBLE, DISCERNIBLE ⟨have maintained that dialectic and rhetoric are ~ stages of argumentation —R.M.Weaver⟩ ⟨an essay with a meaning that was not always ~⟩ ⟨a project ~ into four separate stages of progress⟩ **2** *obs* **:** DISTINGUISHED, DISTINCTIVE, EMINENT — **dis·tin·guish·able·ness** \-nəs\ *n* -ES

dis·tin·guish·ably \-blē, li\ *adv* **:** in a distinguishable manner

dis·tin·guished \-sht\ *adj* **1 a :** marked by eminence and distinction **:** noted for significant achievement or great dignity ⟨under the general's ~ leadership⟩ ⟨his name was placed on the roster of ~ statesmen⟩ ⟨a ~ figure in American architecture⟩ ⟨a ~ career as a mathematical logician —M.R.Cohen⟩ ⟨~ for his facility in languages⟩ **b :** marked by excellence in quality ⟨many facets of the mind and personality of the greatest scientist of our time presented in a ~ translation —I.B.Cohen⟩ ⟨it is not ~, but has the clarity of action and plot demanded by oral storytelling —*N.Y. Herald Tribune Bk. Rev.*⟩ ⟨a book ~ for its handling of an intricate period in history⟩ **2 :** befitting an eminent person **:** conferring dignity ⟨blue eyes made bluer by dark hair with a ~ streak of gray —Eva Gabor⟩ ⟨wearing a ~ velvet-collared coat⟩ — **dis·tin·guished·ly** \-shtlē, -shədlē, -li\ *adv*

distinguishing *adj* **:** serving to separate or set apart from others in nature, character, or quality **:** marking off as different **:** DISTINCTIVE ⟨the really ~ feature of the directories is their great accuracy —*Report of Amer. Tel. & Tel. Co.*⟩ ⟨it was . . . a ~ characteristic of the Greek religion that it did not concern itself with the conscience at all —G.L. Dickinson⟩ — **dis·tin·guish·ing·ly** *adv*

distinguishing flag *n* **1 :** any of certain flags flown to indicate the presence of an officer of high rank or of the holder of a high governmental office — used in the British navy and the U.S. Army; compare PERSONAL FLAG **2 :** a flag flown to identify the headquarters of a major unit of the U.S. Army that does not have an organizational color or standard **3 :** a flag indicative of the ownership of a vessel (as the house flag of a commercial ship or the private signal of a yacht)

distinguishing pennant *n* **:** any of a number of pennants that various naval officers are entitled to fly as an indication of their rank or command (as the broad pennant of a British commodore or a command pennant in the U.S. Navy)

dis·tin·guo \də'stiŋ(,)gwō\ *n* -S [L, I distinguish, 1st pers. sing. pres. indic. of *distinguere*] **:** a quibbling distinction

dis·ti·style \'distə,stīl\ *n* [*dist-* + *style*] **:** one of the blade-shaped accessory parts of the male genitalia of certain insects

distn *abbr* distillation

disto- — see DIST-

dis·to·clu·sion \¦distə¦klüzhən\ *n* -S [*dist-* + *occlusion*] **:** malposition of a lower tooth or teeth distal to the upper when the jaws are closed

dis·toe·chu·rus \,distə'kyürəs\ *n, cap* [NL, fr. Gk *distoichos* in two rows + NL *-urus*] **:** a genus of marsupial mammals consisting of the pen-tailed phalanger

dis·to·ma \'distəmə\ [NL, fr. *di-* + *-stoma*] *syn of* FASCIOLA

di·sto·ma·ta \dī'stōməd·ə\ *n pl, cap* [NL, fr. *di-* + *-stomata*] *in some classifications* **:** a large suborder of Prosostomata comprising flukes with oral and ventral suckers and with the reproductive organs mostly posterior to the ventral sucker — **di·sto·mate** \-ō,māt, -ōmət\ *adj* — **di·stome** \'dī,stōm\ *adj or n*

dis·to·mat·i·dae \,distə'mad·ə,dē\ [NL, fr. *Distomat-, Distoma*, type genus + *-idae*] *syn of* FASCIOLIDAE

di·sto·ma·to·sis \,dī,stōmə'tōsəs\ *also* **di·sto·mi·a·sis** \,dīstō'mīəsəs\ *n, pl* **distomato·ses** \-ō,sēz\ *also* **distomiases** \-ī,ə,sēz\ [NL, fr. *Distomata* + *-osis* or *-iasis*] **:** infestation with or disease caused by digenetic trematode worms; *specif* **:** LIVER ROT

di·stomatous \(')dī+\ *adj* [*di-* + *-stomatous*] **1 :** having two mouths or suckers **2 :** of or relating to Distomata

dis·tom·i·dae \də'stämə,dē\ [NL, fr. *Distoma*, type genus + *-idae*] *syn of* FASCIOLIDAE

dis·to·mum \'distəməm\ [NL, fr. *di-* + *-stomum*] *syn of* FASCIOLA

dis·tort \də'stȯr|t, -stȯ(ə)|, *usu* |d.+V\ *vt* -ED/-ING/-S [L *distortus*, past part. of *distorquēre*, fr. *dis-* ¹dis- + *torquēre* to twist — more at TORTURE] **1 :** to twist out of the true meaning **:** alter or pervert to give a false or unnatural picture or account ⟨his ~ed account of Mrs. Lincoln had become thoroughly embedded in Lincoln literature —Ruth P. Randall⟩ ⟨~ing the news to make it sensational⟩ ⟨do not ~ their writings in order to conform to the prejudices and values of any group —*New School for Social Research Bull.*⟩ **2 a** *obs* **:** to twist or wrench out of a straight position **b :** to twist out of a natural, normal, or original shape or condition **:** wrench into an unnatural shape or condition ⟨a car whose frame is ~ed by a collision⟩ ⟨in playing, he ~ed the music out of all recognition⟩ ⟨putting ideas on paper seems to ~ our perspectives —E.S.McCartney⟩ ⟨a judgment ~ed by strong feeling⟩ ⟨a face ~ed by pain⟩ **c :** to twist or make misshapen mentally or morally ⟨delusions of various kinds ~ed his outlook on life⟩ ⟨falling into a ~ed pattern of behavior⟩ **syn** see DEFORM

distorted *adj* **:** TWISTED, DEFORMED — **dis·tort·ed·ness** *n* -ES

dis·tort·ed·ly *adv* **:** in a distorted manner ⟨a ~ inadequate conception of self-interest —Edgar Johnson⟩

dis·tor·tion \|shən\ *n* -S [L *distortion-, distortio*, fr. *distortus* + *-ion-, -io* -ion] **1 :** the act of distorting: as **a :** an altering or perverting that essentially falsifies true or accurate facts or true significance ⟨a gross ~ of the news for propaganda purposes⟩ **b :** a twisting or deforming out of a natural, normal, or original shape, form, or condition ⟨a ~ of the car chassis resulting from collision⟩ ⟨~ of the sort that later became so striking a feature of Cubist painting —Edgar Levy⟩ ⟨~ of the economic structure of the country⟩ **c** *psychoanalysis* **:** the censorship of unacceptable unconscious impulses so that they are unrecognizable to the ego in the manifest dream content **2 :** the quality or state of being distorted or the product of distortion ⟨the pain showed in the ~ of the facial muscles⟩ ⟨most of the books about the Orinoco are spiced with enough ~ and fake adventure to nauseate anyone who knows the country —Marston Bates⟩ ⟨the economic ~ and confusion which will be an inevitable aftermath of the war —L.G. Melville⟩: as **a :** a distorted form or image ⟨a painter who paints not observed objects but colorful ~s of them⟩; *also* **:** distorted dream content **b :** a lack of proportionality between corresponding dimensions of an object or its optical image resulting from spherical aberration or other defects in the optical system **c :** the change in wave form of a composite wave train (as a signal over a telephone line or radio) due to unequal speed of transmission or nonproportional attenuation of different frequencies **3 :** a sound or sound-producing current introduced into an electrical system that results in falsified reproduction of the original current or sound — **dis·tor·tion·al** \|shənᵊl, |shnəl\ *adj*

dis·tor·tion·ist \|sh(ə)nəst\ *n* -S **:** one that practices distortion esp. in painting

dis·tor·tion·less \|shənləs\ *adj* **:** free of distortion

dis·tor·tive \|d·iv\ *adj* **:** causing or marked by distortion ⟨what they offer as pure facts are actually descriptions with . . . ~ interpretation —S.C.Pepper⟩

distr *abbr* distribute; distribution; distributive; distributor

¹dis·tract \də'strakt, (')di¦s-\ *adj* [ME, fr. L *distractus*, past part.] **1** *obs* **:** drawn apart or pulled to pieces; *also* **:** DIVERTED **2 a** *obs* **:** experiencing confusion of mind **:** DISTRAUGHT **b** *archaic* **:** INSANE, MAD

²dis·tract \də'strakt\ *vt* -ED/-ING/-S [ME *distracten*, fr. L *distractus*, past part. of *distrahere*, lit., to draw or pull apart, fr. *dis-* apart + *trahere* to draw, pull — more at DIS-, DRAW] **1 a :** to draw or cause to turn away (from an original position, goal, purpose, direction, association, or interest) ⟨the last thing he wanted was to be ~ed from his present high purpose —Archibald Marshall⟩ ⟨Roeder and his associates were not at once ~ed from the sawmill —*Amer. Guide Series: Wash.*⟩ **b** *obs* **:** to draw apart or away **:** DIVIDE, SEPARATE; *also* **:** DISPERSE **c :** to draw (the sight, mind, or attention) to a different object or compellingly and confusingly attract in divergent directions at once ⟨irritated and ~ed during the first part of the concert by the entrance of late concertgoers⟩ ⟨they have ~ed our eyes from the pastoral beauty of another Ireland —Sean O'Faolain⟩ **d :** to provide amusement or diversion for ⟨the excursion to the zoo served to ~ him for at least one afternoon⟩ **2 a :** to stir up or confuse with conflicting emotions or motives or unsettling worries **:** HARASS, CONFOUND ⟨she was ~ed by the uncertainty of her future⟩ **b :** to disrupt or cause dissension in by reason of divergent or conflicting desires, aims, or motives ⟨shifting governments and violent oppositions, whose component groups found advantage in forming connections with interests and groups within the ~ed company —*Times Lit. Supp.*⟩ ⟨the famous "Elizabethtown Controversy" which long ~ed the politics of New Jersey —E.P.Tanner⟩ ⟨the Christian Church . . . ~ed by an internecine conflict —W.R.Inge⟩ **3 :** to unsettle the reason of **:** make insane **:** MADDEN **syn** see PUZZLE

distracted *adj* **1 :** intensely worried **:** harassed or confused by conflicting feelings **2 :** maddened or deranged esp. by grief or anxiety ⟨for six weeks or more before his death he was ~, not childish but really raving —Thomas Gray⟩ — **dis·tract·ed·ness** *n* -ES

dis·tract·ed·ly *adv* **:** in the manner of one that is distracted: as **a :** DISTRAUGHTLY ⟨the mother of the lost child could do nothing but pace ~ up and down the room until the child was found⟩ **b :** to the point of mental disorder ⟨felt it was foolish to love so ~ as the two young people did⟩

dis·tract·er *or* **dis·trac·tor** \-ktə(r)\ *n* -S **:** one that distracts

dis·tract·ibil·i·ty \də,straktə'biləd-ē, -ətē, -i\ *n* -ES **:** susceptibility to distraction

dis·tract·ible \də'straktəbəl\ *adj* **:** capable of being distracted **:** having one's attention readily diverted ⟨described by his teacher as lovable but extremely restless and ~ —Edwin Powers & Helen Witmer⟩

dis·tract·ing·ly *adv* **:** in a distracting manner ⟨she looked ~ provocative and she knew it —Winifred Bambrick⟩

dis·trac·tion \də'strakshən\ *n* -S [ME *distraccioun*, fr. L *distraction-, distractio*, fr. *distractus* (past part. of *distrahere* to distract) + *-ion-, -io* -ion — more at DISTRACT] **1 :** the act of distracting or the state of being distracted: **a :** diversion of the attention ⟨where he felt he could live more cheaply and with fewer ~s from his scholarly labors —Kemp Malone⟩ **b :** DISORDER, DISSENSION ⟨a unified organization bothered by only minor ~s that were easily resolved⟩ **c :** mental derangement **:** MADNESS ⟨drove her adoring audiences to ~ and tears —Roma Lipsky⟩ ⟨goaded to ~⟩ **d :** agitation from violent usu. conflicting emotions **:** PERTURBATION ⟨an inward ~ drove her to pacing the room like a mad woman⟩; *also* **:** PERPLEXITY, CONFUSION ⟨faced the problem with ~ showing in his uncertain words and troubled countenance⟩ **e :** AMUSEMENT, ENTERTAINMENT, RECREATION ⟨the need for relaxation and ~ was not forgotten —*Report: (Canadian) Royal Commission on Nat'l Development*⟩ ⟨obsessed by the pursuit of pleasure, driven by the insatiable craving for ~ —A.J.Cronin⟩ **2 :** something that distracts esp. by diverting or amusing ⟨offering all kinds of ~*s* to the bored vacationer⟩

dis·trac·tive \-ktiv\ *adj* **:** causing distraction

distracts *pres 3d sing of* DISTRACT

dis·train \də'strān\ *vb* -ED/-ING/-S [ME *distreynen*, fr. OF *destreign-, destrein-*, stem of *destreindre* to press, oppress, force, fr. ML *distringere* to compel, distrain, fr. L, to hinder, molest, fr. *dis-* ¹dis- + *stringere* to draw tight, press together — more at STRAIN] *vt* **1 a** (1) **:** to coerce or punish by levying a distress (2) **:** to levy a distress upon in order to obtain payment of a debt by sale of the goods taken **b :** to seize as a pledge or indemnification **:** take possession of as security (as on nonpayment of rent or the reparation of an injury done) **:** take by distress ⟨~ goods for rent or an amercement⟩ **c** *obs* **:** to seize by force **:** CONFISCATE **2** *obs* **a :** CONFINE, CONSTRICT, BIND **b :** DISTRESS, AFFLICT, TORMENT **3** *obs* **:** REND, TEAR ~ *vi* **:** to levy a distress — often used with *upon* or *on*

dis·train·able \-nəbəl\ *adj* [AF *distreignable*, fr. OF *destreign-* + *-abie*] **:** subject to distraint; *also* **:** recoverable by distraint

dis·train·ee \ˌdiˌstrā'nē, dəˌs-\ *n* -S [*distrain* + *-ee*] **:** one who is distrained

dis·train·er \də'strānər\ *or* **dis·trai·nor** \"", ˌdiˌstrā'nȯ(ə)r, dəˌstrā'nȯ(ə)r\ *n* -S [AF *destreinor*, fr. OF *destrein-* + *-or*] **:** one who distrains

dis·traint \də'strānt\ *n* -S [fr. *distrain*, after such pairs as E *constrain: constraint*] **:** the act or proceeding of distraining

dis·trait \də'strā, (ˈ)di¦s-, (ˈ)dē¦s-\ *adj* [F, fr. L *distractus*, past part. of *distrahere* to distract — more at DISTRACT] **1 :** INATTENTIVE, ABSTRACTED ⟨Marcus Aurelius could sit for hours in the amphitheater, bored and ~, it is true, but with unmoved serenity —Agnes Repplier⟩ **2 :** anxiously or apprehensively divided or withdrawn in attention **:** DISTRAUGHT, UPSET ⟨so ~ he was unable to listen to the speaker for worrying what was going to happen if he lost his job⟩ ⟨at the bad news the woman became so ~ she was incapable of answering simple questions coherently⟩

dis·traite \-āt, *usu* -ād·+V\ *adj* [F, fem. of *distrait*] **:** DISTRAIT — used of a female ⟨made her as ~ as a mother bird —Elizabeth Bowen⟩

dis·traught \də'strȯt, *usu* -ȯd·+V\ *adj* [ME, modif. of L *distractus* — more at DISTRACT] **1 a :** beset with doubt or mental conflict **:** deeply troubled **:** DISTRACTED, FRANTIC ⟨he must always be doing something, seeking relief in a factitious gaiety and nervous garrulity . . . a man beset and ~ —S.H. Adams⟩ ⟨in his ~ state he allows himself to be hit by a truck —H.M.Jones⟩ ⟨~ with grief for the dead queen —Edna S. V. Millay⟩; *also* **:** thrown into confusion or disorder (as through indecision, dissension, or lack of clear direction) ⟨the affairs of the U.N. itself are tangled and ~ —*Reporter*⟩ ⟨the post-revolutionary period which was more excited with aspirations, and nearly as ~ with terrors as our present epoch —*Times Lit. Supp.*⟩ **b :** mentally deranged **:** CRAZED ⟨she waited, pacing back and forth, pale and almost ~ —P.I.Wellman⟩ ⟨as if thou wert ~ and mad with terror —Shak.⟩ **2** *obs* **:** torn apart **:** SEPARATED ⟨his greedy throat . . . ~ —Edmund Spenser⟩ — **dis·traught·ly** *adv*

¹dis·tress \də'stres\ *n* -ES [ME *destresse*, fr. OF *destresse, destrece*, fr. (assumed) VL *districtia*, fr. L *districtus* (past part. of *distringere* to hinder, molest) + *-ia* -y — more at DISTRAIN] **1 a :** the act or remedy of distraining **:** the seizure and detention of the goods of another by way of pledge for the reparation of an injury or the performance of a duty or in order to obtain satisfaction of a claim (as for rent, taxes, or an injury) by the sale of the goods seized **b :** the thing taken by distraining **:** something that is seized to procure satisfaction **2** *obs* **:** the act or the condition of straining or forcing **:** STRESS, CONSTRAINT, COMPULSION **3 a :** an oppressed or distressed state **:** PAIN, SUFFERING **:** anguish of body or mind **:** TROUBLE, NEED ⟨each side sees its own security and prosperity in the insecurity, destitution, and ~ of the other —Isaac Deutscher⟩ ⟨in great ~ for money —*Encyc. Americana*⟩ ⟨poetry, that immortal medium fallen into ~, if not disrepute or desuetude —Harvey Breit⟩ ⟨these days when the world is in tension and ~ because of the conflict of two ideologies —R.D. Jacobs⟩ **b :** a painful situation **:** MISFORTUNE, CALAMITY **:** great trouble **:** ADVERSITY, AFFLICTION ⟨suffered most severely in the interwar years from unemployment and economic ~ —L.D.Stamp⟩ **c :** a cause of sorrow ⟨her son's dissolute ways were a ~ to her⟩ ⟨their greatest ~ was poverty⟩ **4 a :** a state of danger or necessity ⟨a ship in ~⟩ ⟨respiratory ~⟩; *also* **:** evidence of such a state **b :** an indication of weakness or incipient failure in a structure subjected to stress

syn SUFFERING, MISERY, AGONY, DOLOR, PASSION: these nouns designate in common the condition of one in great trouble or in mental or physical pain. DISTRESS commonly implies conditions or circumstances that cause physical or mental stress or strain, suggesting strongly the need of assistance; in application to a mental state, it implies the strain of fear, anxiety, shame, or the like ⟨the *distress* of the underprivileged —Oscar Handlin⟩ ⟨the personal *distress* of those who cannot emotionally readjust themselves to new views —M.R.Cohen⟩ ⟨the spring and summer of 1842 brought severe *distress* to many in County Mayo in the form of famine —J.T.Ellis⟩ SUFFERING applies esp. to human beings, implying an awareness of distress and often a conscious endurance ⟨the losses and hardships and *sufferings* entailed by war —Bertrand Russell⟩ ⟨the *suffering* of unhappy adolescence⟩ MISERY stresses the unhappy or wretched conditions attending distress or suffering as well as the distress itself, often suggesting an unalleviated or chronic suffering ⟨the stench and *misery* of poverty —Harrison Smith⟩ ⟨anguish that wept aloud; *misery* that could find no voice; sorrow that was dumb —Oscar Wilde⟩ AGONY suggests intense, usu. unbearable, pain or suffering ⟨fell with a scream of mortal *agony* —F.V.W.Mason⟩ ⟨she suffered *agonies* of mortification —Margaret Deland⟩ ⟨the *agonies* of an impaled beetle —Rudyard Kipling⟩ DOLOR, a literary word, applies chiefly to mental suffering involving sorrow, somber depression, or anxiety, often intense ⟨heaviness is upon them, and *dolor* thickens the air they walk through —Waldo Frank⟩ ⟨accept national and local calamities, such as invasions, droughts, famines . . . with a quiet *dolor* which suggests passivity and stoicism —*New Republic*⟩ ⟨the "happy child" she was though underlaid by *dolor* —Louise Nicholl⟩ PASSION is now rare in this sense except in application to the suffering of Christ before and during the crucifixion ⟨the *passion* of Our Lord⟩

²distress \"\ *vt* **distressed** *also archaic* **distrest**; **distressed** *also archaic* **distrest**; **distressing**; **distresses** [ME *destressen*, fr. MF *destresser, destrecer*, fr. *destresse, destrece*] **1 a :** to subject to great strain or difficulties; *esp* **:** to bring to dire and painful esp. economic straits ⟨~*ed* companies would get technical advice, loans, government contracts and fast tax amortizations to help them diversify their products and find new markets —*Time*⟩ ⟨public housing for ~*ed* families of veterans, servicemen, government employees —*Current Biog.*⟩ ⟨relief shipments to Europe and other ~*ed* war areas —Harry Truman⟩ **b :** to afflict or exhaust esp. with strain or discomfort **c :** to cause pain or suffering to **:** oppress with calamity **:** make miserable **:** PAIN, HARASS ⟨wild speculation and unwholesome overexpansion . . . caused several bank failures and a ~*ing* public debt —*Amer. Guide Series: N.C.*⟩ ⟨the sight of blood, in fact, always ~*ed* him —Charles Lee⟩; *also* **:** to cause to worry or be troubled **:** UPSET, DISTURB ⟨the bitter remarks ~*ed* the sensitive boy considerably⟩ ⟨it ~*es* me somewhat to hiss at trolley-car conductors who . . . were my personal heroes some decades back —Horace Sutton⟩ ⟨stories not involving military security occasionally ~*ed* Captain Lee to the point where he felt it necessary to call in an offending correspondent and explain to him that some stories were better left unprinted —E.L.Jones⟩ **:** TROUBLE, BOTHER ⟨the ~*ing* accumulation of down and dust —Emily Holt⟩ **2 a :** to force or compel by or as if by inflicting pain or suffering ⟨men who can neither be ~*ed* nor won into a sacrifice of duty —Alexander Hamilton⟩ **b** *obs* **:** to rout in battle **:** OVERWHELM **3** *archaic* **:** to levy a distress upon **:** DISTRAIN

³distress \"\ *adj* [¹*distress*] **1** *of merchandise* **:** sold or offered for sale at a sacrifice **:** disposed of cheaply because of financial necessity ⟨the weaker the market becomes, the more ~ merchandise comes on the market —E.B.Weiss⟩ ⟨the resulting so-called ~ cargoes of spot gasoline, offered through brokers, often have a strong depressing effect on prices —Harold Fleming⟩ **2 :** involving distress goods ⟨a ~ sale⟩

distress call *n* **:** SOS

dis·tressed \-est\ *adj* **1 :** afflicted with trouble, pain, or grief **2 :** purposely marred to give the appearance of great age — used of furniture or leather — **dis·tressed·ly** \-esədlē,-estlē, -li\ *adv* — **dis·tressed·ness** \-esədnəs, -es(t)n-\ *n* -ES

distresses *pl of* DISTRESS, *pres 3d sing of* DISTRESS

dis·tress·ful \-esfəl\ *adj* **:** causing distress ⟨for four years lived in heroic if somewhat ~ isolation —*Amer. Guide Series: N.H.*⟩ ⟨wandering into the past as a refuge from the ~ present —Rebecca West⟩ — **dis·tress·ful·ly** \-fəlē, -li\ *adv* — **dis·tress·ful·ness** \-lnəs\ *n* -ES

distressing *pres part of* DISTRESS

dis·tress·ing·ly *adv* **:** in a manner that distresses ⟨a ~ meager income for such a large family⟩ ⟨the transition at times is ~ swift —B.N.Cardozo⟩ ⟨she had grown ~ deaf —Osbert Sitwell⟩

distress signal *n* **:** an emergency signal (as a flare, flag, or SOS) used by one in distress or in need of help

dis·trib·ut·able \də'stribyədəbəl, -yətə-\ *adj* **:** capable of being distributed ⟨income ~ to a beneficiary —Benjamin Harrow⟩

¹dis·trib·u·tary \-yəˌterē\ *adj* [*distribute* + *-ary*] **:** DISTRIBUTIVE; *esp* **:** of or relating to a distributary

²distributary \"\ *n* -ES **1 a :** a river branch flowing away from the main stream and not rejoining it — contrasted with *tributary* **b :** one of the channels of a braided stream **2 :** an irrigation canal or ditch leading away from the main canal; *esp* **:** one of the smaller conduits by which irrigation water is delivered directly to the consumer from the larger branches of the system

dis·trib·ute \də'stribyət, -i(ˌ)byüt, *also* -ˌbət; *usu* -d·+V; *Brit often* 'distriˌbyüt\ *vb* **distributed** \-yəd·əd, -yətəd\ **distributed** \"\ **distributing** \-yəd·iŋ, -yətiŋ\ **distributes** \-yəts, -yüts\ [ME *distributen*, fr. L *distributus*, past part. of *distribuere*, fr. *dis-* ¹dis- + *tribuere* to give, allot — more at TRIBUTE] *vt* **1 a :** to divide among several or many **:** deal out **:** apportion esp. to members of a group or over a period of time **:** ALLOT ⟨the American Relief Administration *distributed* nearly five million tons of foodstuffs —*Current Biog.*⟩ ⟨the problem of how to ~ taxes equitably among the various economic groups —*Collier's Yr. Bk.*⟩ ⟨precipitation is not ample, but is *distributed* throughout the year —G.G.Weigend⟩ **b :** DISPENSE, ADMINISTER ⟨~ justice⟩ ⟨lamented that the great fields of private law, where justice is *distributed* between man and man, should be left without a caretaker —B.N.Cardozo⟩ **2 a :** to spread out or scatter so as to cover a surface or a space ⟨*distributing* the seed over the lawn⟩ ⟨*distributing* the ink evenly over the print⟩; *also* **:** to give out or deliver esp. to the members of a group ⟨*distributing* magazines to subscribers⟩ ⟨the U.N. secretariat, which *distributed* a 125-page questionnaire to member governments —*Current Biog.*⟩ **b :** to place or position usu. so as to be properly apportioned over or throughout an area ⟨the blood vessels *distributed* throughout the arm⟩ ⟨he seems chunkier than the 175 pounds *distributed* over his five feet ten inches would indicate —W.B.Furlong⟩ ⟨the various factories *distributed* throughout the city —*Amer. Guide Series: N.H.*⟩ ⟨a widely *distributed* company —Marquis James⟩ ⟨our Indians are not evenly *distributed* —Juan Comas⟩ **c** *logic* **:** to use (a term) so as to convey information about every member of the class named ⟨the proposition "all men are mortal" ~*s* a universal affirmative subject, here "man", but does not ~ the predicate⟩ **3 a :** to divide or separate esp. into classes, orders, kinds, or species **:** CLASSIFY, ASSORT ⟨spend a good deal of time *distributing* his specimens into their proper classes⟩ **b** (1) **:** to separate the units of (as typeset matter or handset matrices) and return to the proper storage places (2) *of a keyboard slugcasting machine* **:** to return (matrices) automatically to the proper magazine channels **4 :** to market (a commodity) under a franchise in a particular area esp. at wholesale ~ *vi* **:** to make distribution **:** spread out

syn DISTRIBUTE, DISPENSE, DIVIDE, DEAL, and DOLE can agree in meaning to give out, usu. in shares, to each person or thing of a group of persons or things. DISTRIBUTE implies (1) an apportioning of something among many by separating it into parts, units, or amounts and assigning each part, etc., to its appropriate person or place or (2) a spreading or scattering of something more or less evenly over an area ⟨*distribute* their possessions among their children⟩ ⟨*distribute* profits among corporation members⟩ ⟨*distribute* different size nails to their appropriate containers⟩ ⟨*distribute* loam over a lawn⟩ DISPENSE carries no strong implication, as does DISTRIBUTE, of the lessening of a whole by subdivision or scattering but suggests a giving of a carefully weighed and measured portion as a right or due, or in answer to a need ⟨*dispense* drugs to plague victims⟩ ⟨the host is *dispensing* drinks —Agnes M. Miall⟩ ⟨he liberally *dispensed* hospitality to all . . . with whom he came into contact —E.H.Collis⟩ ⟨*dispense* justice⟩ ⟨*dispense* charity⟩ DIVIDE stresses the separation of a whole into parts in order to dispense to or share among each of a group, equality of shares usu. being implied in default of other specification ⟨*divide* a cake among 10 guests⟩ ⟨*divide* profits evenly among themselves⟩ ⟨*divide* the spoils of war⟩ DEAL, usu. with *out*, stresses a giving out piece by piece or in suitable portions ⟨*deal* out the day's ration of water⟩ ⟨*deal* out paper plates to the picnickers⟩ DOLE, frequently with *out*, still often implies a dispensing of alms to the needy but more commonly now suggests merely a dispensing in scanty, usu. niggardly, portions ⟨mother collects the paychecks and *doles* out allowances to all hands —J.H.Fenton⟩ ⟨there cannot be in this republic any class of human beings in practical subjection to another class, with power in the latter to *dole* out to the former just such privileges as they may choose to grant —O.K. Fraenkel⟩ ⟨a prince *doling* out favors to a servile group of petitioners —Theodore Dreiser⟩

dis·trib·ut·ed·ly *adv* **:** in a distributed manner

dis·trib·u·tee \dəˌstribyə'tē\ *n* -S [*distribute* + *-ee*] **:** one to whom something is or is to be distributed; *esp* **:** one sharing in or entitled to share in an estate

distributer *var of* DISTRIBUTOR

dis·tri·bu·tion \ˌdistrə'byüshən\ *n* -S [ME *distribucioun*, fr. L *distribution-, distributio*, fr. *distributus* + *-ion-, -io* -ion] **1 a :** the act or process of distributing or the condition of being distributed **:** APPORTIONMENT, ALLOTMENT ⟨the ~ of money among creditors⟩ ⟨the ~ of the cards to the players⟩ ⟨a twice yearly ~ of the profits among the stockholders⟩ **b :** the process of apportionment by which the value of a product is divided and imputed to the various factors of production as payment for their use **c :** the apportionment in a student's program (as required in some American universities) of a certain number of courses to widely different departments or fields of learning for breadth of training — compare CONCENTRATION 1d **d :** the apportionment by a court of the personal property of an intestate or its proceeds among those entitled to it according to the statutes of distribution **2 a :** a spreading out or scattering over an area or throughout a space ⟨the ~ of the seed over the field⟩ ⟨the ~ of the oil throughout the engine parts⟩ **b :** the position, placement, or arrangement (as of a mass or the members of a group) over an area or throughout a space or unit of time **:** the frequency of occurrence **:** ARRANGEMENT ⟨the ~ of iron ore in So. America⟩ ⟨~ of eclipses over a thousand years⟩ ⟨the ~ of the stars⟩ ⟨the ~ of population⟩ ⟨the ~ of the nation's wealth⟩ **c :** the natural geographic range of a kind of organism (as a species) or category of organisms (as an order); *sometimes* **:** the range of such a kind or category in geologic time **d :** the occurrence of a linguistic item in terms of context or geography ⟨the ~ of the allophones of /t/ in English⟩ **e :** the disposition or arrangement in rational groups or classes **:** CLASSIFICATION ⟨the accurate ~ of several rare zoological specimens⟩ **f :** delivery or conveyance (as of newspapers or goods) to the members of a group ⟨the ~ of telephone directories to customers⟩ ⟨in charge of company sales and ~⟩ **3 a :** something distributed ⟨supported his family only with the help of charitable ~*s*⟩ **b :** an array in statistics of the instances of a variable arranged by classes according to their value ⟨the ~ showed the heights of all the men in the regiment given at one-inch intervals⟩ **c :** PROBABILITY DENSITY FUNCTION **4 :** the status of a term in logic with respect to its being distributed or undistributed **5 :** a device, mechanism, or system by which something is distributed (as from a main source): as **a :** the operations regulating the passage of the working fluid (as steam) through an engine cylinder including admission, cutoff, release, exhaust, and compression **b :** the pattern of branching and termination of a nerve, artery, or other ramifying structure **c :** the part of an electric supply system between bulk power sources (as generating stations or transformation stations tapped from transmission lines) and the consumers' service switches **6 :** the marketing or merchandising of commodities ⟨the mail-order ~ of books⟩ ⟨keeping track of all ~ costs of a manufactured article for a year⟩ **7 :** the manner in which the suits in a pack of playing cards are divided in one player's hand or in which one suit is divided among the hands of all the players ⟨a hand with 4-3-3-3 ~ contains four cards in one suit and three cards in each of the other suits⟩

dis·tri·bu·tion·al \ˌdistrə¦byüshənᵊl, -shnəl\ *adj* **1 :** of or relating to distribution **2 :** of or relating to the trick-winning value of long suits and trumps rather than high cards — **dis·tri·bu·tion·al·ly** \-ᵊl|ē,-əl|ē, |i\ *adv*

distribution board *n* **:** PANELBOARD 3

distribution box *n* **:** a contrivance used to equalize the flow of septic-tank effluent into the various tile lines of the disposal field

distribution coefficient *or* **distribution ratio** *n* **:** the ratio of the amounts of solute dissolved at equilibrium in two immiscible liquids

distribution cost *n* **1 :** cost incurred by a producer incident to activities connected with placing a finished product in the hands of a customer (as the expense of selling, advertising, shipping) **2 :** any cost incurred by a wholesaler, retailer, or distributor

distribution curve *n* **:** a graph of the frequencies of different values of a variable in a statistical distribution

distribution function *n* **:** the expression of a relationship between the values and the corresponding frequencies of a variable in a statistical distribution

dis·trib·u·tism \də'stribyəˌtizəm\ *n* -S **:** the theory or practice of distributing private property (as land) to the maximum degree among individual owners **:** AGRARIANISM

dis·trib·ut·ist \-yəd·əst\ *n* -S **:** an advocate of distributism

¹dis·trib·u·tive \də'stribyəd·|iv, -yət|\ *adj* [ME, fr. MF *distributif*, fr. LL *distributivus*, fr. L *distributus* (past part. of *distribuere* to distribute) + *-ivus* -ive — more at DISTRIBUTE] **1 :** of or relating to distribution: as **a :** serving to divide and assign in portions **:** dealing a proper share to each of a group ⟨serving both a collective and ~ function in the charity organization⟩ **b :** spreading out, covering, diffusing, or scattering more or less evenly over an area or throughout a space ⟨you may interpret the word "salvation" in any way you like, and make it as diffuse and ~, or as climacteric and integral a phenomenon as you please —William James⟩ **c :** engaged in or concerned with distribution esp. of goods ⟨the ~ and service trades⟩ ⟨he had founded the Ceylonese cooperative movement, which was to become the major ~ agency for foodstuffs in the island —*Current Biog.*⟩ **2** *of a word* **:** referring singly and without exception to the members of a group ⟨*each, every, either, neither*, and *none* are ~⟩ **:** referring to a single member of a group ⟨*which* in "which one of the men" is ~⟩ **:** expressing division of a group into smaller groups ⟨the ~ Latin word *bini* "two by two"⟩ or individuals ⟨the ~ Latin word *singuli* "one by one"⟩ **3 :** taken in its full extension — used of a term in logic **4 :** producing the same element when operating on a whole as when operating on each part and collecting the results ⟨multiplication is ~ relative to addition since $a(b+c)=ab+ac$⟩ — **dis·trib·u·tive·ness** \-nəs\ *n* -ES

²distributive \"\ *n* -S **:** a distributive word

distributive fault *n* **:** one of two or more closely associated parallel geologic faults — called also *step fault*

distributive function *n* **:** a function of the sum of two or more variables that is equal to a sum each term of which is the same function of one of the variables **:** any function F such that $F(u+v)=F(u)+F(v)$

distributive justice *n* **:** the justice that is concerned with the apportionment of privileges, duties, and goods in consonance with the merits of the individual and in the best interest of society

dis·trib·u·tive·ly \|əvlē, -li\ *adv* **1 :** in a distributive manner ⟨not predicating something about the class as such but about its membership ~ —Jørgen Jørgensen⟩ ⟨marine vertebrates . . . have their body weight supported ~ by water displacement, instead of having it concentrated on two or four columns of leg bone —Weston La Barre⟩ **2 :** as individuals or separate units **:** INDIVIDUALLY, SEPARATELY ⟨their potential rights, which, taken ~, are imperceptible, amount collectively to a most important interest —John Marshall⟩

distributive operation *n* **:** a mathematical operation obeying a distributive principle

distributive principle *also* **distributive law** *n* **:** a mathematical principle expressed by a distributive formula (as $a(b+c+d)=ab+ac+ad$)

dis·trib·u·tiv·ism \|əˌvizəm\ *n* -S **:** DISTRIBUTISM

dis·trib·u·tiv·i·ty \dəˌstribyə'tivəd·ē\ *n* -ES **:** the quality of being mathematically or logically distributive

dis·trib·u·tor *also* **dis·trib·ut·er** \də'stribyəd·|ə(r), -yət|\ *n* -S **1 :** one that distributes ⟨bill ~*s* may cover the same territory, leaving circulars at the same houses —H.E.Agnew⟩ ⟨if the lawn is large some type of seed ~ may well be used —C.E. Millar & L.M.Turk⟩ **2 a :** one that markets a commodity; *esp* **:** WHOLESALER **b :** an apparatus for directing the secondary current from the induction coil to the various spark plugs of a multicylinder engine in their proper firing order — compare TIMER **c :** a device for spreading sewage over the surface of a filter **d :** CARRIER 2d

dis·trib·u·tor·ship \-ˌship\ *n* -S **:** a franchise granted by a manufacturer or company to market its goods esp. at wholesale in a particular area; *also* **:** an office or business concern having such a franchise

¹district *adj* [L *districtus*, fr. past part. of *distringere* to hinder, molest — more at DISTRAIN] *obs* **:** RIGOROUS, STRICT

²dis·trict \'di(ˌ)strikt, -ˌstrēkt\ *n* -S *often attrib* [F, fr. MF, fr. ML *districtus* coercive action, justice, jurisdiction, area of jurisdiction, district, fr. *districtus*, past part. of *distringere* to compel — more at DISTRAIN] **1** *obs* **:** the territory under a feudal lord's jurisdiction **2 :** a territorial division (as of a nation, state, county, or city) marked off or defined for administrative, electoral, judicial, or other purposes: as **a :** an administrative unit established as a quasi-municipal corporation for the performance of a special governmental function or functions ⟨park ~⟩ ⟨water supply ~⟩ ⟨fire protection ~⟩ ⟨a police ~⟩ ⟨a postal ~⟩ ⟨a ~ school⟩ — see CONGRESSIONAL DISTRICT, DRAINAGE DISTRICT, ELECTION DISTRICT, MAGISTERIAL DISTRICT **b :** the most important administrative unit of a province or presidency in British India **c :** one of the subdivisions of the United States or of the individual states served by a particular federal or state court **d :** an ecclesiastical division of an English parish made under the Church Building Acts and having its own church and pastor **e :** an urban or rural subdivision of a British administrative county constituted by the Local Government Act of 1894 and having an urban or rural district council **f :** an area usu. comprising several subordinate territories that is demarcated by a commercial firm for convenience of sales promotion, assignment to sales representatives, or distribution ⟨a ~ sales manager⟩ ⟨a ~ representative⟩ **3 :** an area, region, or tract or a portion of one of these usu. marked by a distinguishing quality, set of characteristics, devotion to a distinguishing purpose, or habitation by a more or less homogeneous group ⟨a barren ~⟩ ⟨a wooded ~⟩ ⟨a shopping ~⟩ ⟨a residential ~⟩ ⟨the Italian ~⟩ **4 :** a subdivision of an embryonic field determined for the production of a specific definitive structure

³district \"\ *vt* -ED/-ING/-S **:** to divide or organize into districts ⟨attending to a new ~*ing* of the city⟩ ⟨the area was ~*ed* according to population figures only⟩ ⟨interlocking problems of zoning and school ~*ing* —Merrill Folsom⟩

district attorney *n* **:** the prosecuting officer of a district who is appointed by the president in federal districts but generally elective in counties

district check *n* **1 a :** a plaid or a fabric design in checks that is peculiar to or presumed to be special to the dress of a Scottish district **b** an imitation or variation of such a design **2 :** a fabric with a district check

district council *n* **:** the local governing body of a rural or urban district in Great Britain and of certain administrative districts in Australia and parts of British Africa

district court *n* **:** a court of first instance having jurisdiction in certain cases within a judicial district; *esp* **:** the U.S. federal court of first instance

district heating *n* **:** the distribution of heat by steam or otherwise from a central plant to buildings more or less widely distributed — compare ¹CENTRAL 4a

district judge *n* **:** the judge of a district court

district leader *n* **:** the party leader or boss of an American assembly district or ward

district manager *n* **:** one who supervises the sales activity in a district

district superintendent *n* **:** an official of the Methodist Church appointed by a bishop to have the oversight of the churches and the preachers in a district

district visitor *n* **:** a woman worker in a Church of England parish who gives voluntary assistance to the rector (as by visiting and reporting cases of sickness)

di·strin·gas \də'stringəs, -,gas\ *n* -ES [ML, that you distrain 2d pers. sing. pres. subj. of *distringere*] **:** a writ commanding the sheriff to distrain a person by his goods or chattels

¹**dis·trust** \də'strəst, (')dis-\ *vb* [ME *distrusten* to suspect, fr. ¹*dis-* + *trusten* to trust — more at TRUST] *vt* **1 :** to have no trust or confidence in **:** MISTRUST ⟨~ the sword as a cure for all ills —John Buchan⟩ ⟨he ~*ed* mathematics and the art of deductive logic that went with it —S.F.Mason⟩ **2 :** to suspect of evil consequences or designs **:** feel wary or suspicious of ⟨it would deprive him of the enormous personal satisfaction of ~*ing* what he doesn't know and despising what he has never seen —E.B.White⟩ ⟨the Cistercians disliked and ~*ed* Abelard —Henry Adams⟩ ~ *vi, obs* **:** to have no trust or confidence

²**distrust** \"\ *n* [¹*dis-* + *trust*] **:** the lack or absence of trust **:** SUSPICION, WARINESS ⟨the Swiss, with their traditional ~ of personal power —*Current Biog.*⟩ ⟨an atmosphere of ~ and suspicion has been allowed to permeate the government —Vannevar Bush⟩ ⟨his self-criticism, his ~ of his own ideas —Harold Callender⟩ ⟨growing ~ of the efficacy of parliamentary bodies —John Dewey⟩

dis·trust·ful \-fəl\ *adj* **1 :** having or showing distrust **:** SUSPICIOUS, WARY ⟨vigilant and ~ superintendence —Thomas Jefferson⟩ ⟨a man of ~ nature⟩ ⟨my experience as a judge in other fields of law has made me ~ of rules of thumb generally —B.N.Cardozo⟩ **2** *archaic* **:** causing or arousing distrust — **dis·trust·ful·ly** \-fəlē, -li\ *adv* — **dis·trust·ful·ness** \-lnəs\ *n* -ES

dis·trust·ing·ly *adv* **:** in a distrustful manner

dis·trust·less \-ləs\ *adj, archaic* **:** having no distrust or suspicion **:** UNSUSPECTING, INNOCENT

dis·tune \dəs, (')dis+\ *vt* [¹*dis-* + *tune*] **:** to put out of tune

¹**dis·turb** \də'stərb, -təb, -təib\ *vb* -ED/-ING/-S [ME *disturben, destourben,* fr. OF & L; OF *destorber, destourber,* fr. L *disturbare,* fr. *dis-* ¹*dis-* + *turbare* to throw into disorder, disturb, make turbid — more at TURBID] *vt* **1 a** *obs* **:** to turn or distract (a person) by disturbance **b :** to interfere with (as by hindering or causing to turn from a course or to stop) ⟨~ the sequence of events⟩ ⟨~ a man's reflections by shouting⟩ ⟨a synthetic plant hormone which ~*s* plant growth and eventually destroys it —*Collier's Yr. Bk.*⟩ ⟨he failed to ~ the dominant current of thought —A.N.Whitehead⟩ ⟨another factor was beginning to ~ the tenor of life in their curious household —T.B.Costain⟩; *specif* **:** to interfere with in the lawful enjoyment of a right **c** (1) **:** to break into the preoccupations of or command the attention of esp. annoyingly or disquietingly ⟨she had ~*ed* an antique god in his sylvan haunt —G.B.Shaw⟩ ⟨she sat outside his door, and none of us dared ~ her —George Meredith⟩ (2) **:** to alter the position or arrangement of **:** move from place **:** ⟨he found that the papers on his desk had been ~*ed*⟩ **:** cause to move, wave, bend, or otherwise change position ⟨the wind ~*ing* the grass⟩ ⟨the coal seams were later ~*ed* by the crushing of the valley —L.D.Stamp⟩ ⟨no bone was broken and no joint was ~*ed* —Arthur Morrison⟩ ⟨how is my relation to the environment ~*ed* —John Dewey⟩ **2 a :** to destroy the rest, tranquillity, or settled state of **:** stir up **:** AGITATE, TROUBLE ⟨strikes and war talk ~*ing* the country⟩ ⟨that fact poisons me, ~*s* my serenity —John Reed⟩ ⟨the most calculated, among contemporary writings, to ~ the reader, to startle and excite him —Wallace Fowlie⟩ ⟨a few passages of verse . . . have still the power to ~ our hearts —Edward Sapir⟩ ⟨the ~*ed* state of the country —*Americana Annual*⟩ **b :** to upset the mental or emotional composure of **:** deprive of mental or emotional peace **:** DISQUIET ⟨his passion for his cause ~*ed* me —W.A.White⟩ ⟨the times are too upset and ~*ing* —Louis Bromfield⟩ **c :** to throw into confusion or disorder ⟨his incompetence ~*ed* the once smoothly running system⟩ **d :** to rouse esp. from thought or sleep ⟨~ a scholar in his study⟩ **:** ALARM ⟨afraid of ~*ing* the sleeping animal⟩ **e :** to put to inconvenience ⟨do not ~ yourself to get supper for us⟩ ~ *vi* **:** to cause disturbance

syn see DISCOMPOSE, DISORDER

²**disturb** *n* -S *obs* **:** DISTURBANCE

dis·tur·bance \də'stərbən(t)s, -təb-, -təib-\ *n* -S [ME *destourbaunce, disturbaunce,* fr. OF *destorbance, destourbance,* fr. *destorber, destourber* + *-ance*] **1 :** the act or process of disturbing or the state of being disturbed **2 a :** an interruption of a state of peace or quiet **:** an agitating or agitation esp. of the mind or feelings ⟨understandable that the awkward age should be for the girl a period of painful ~ —H.M.Parshley⟩ **b :** the hindering or disquieting of a person in the lawful and peaceable enjoyment of his right ⟨the ~ of an easement⟩ **c :** an interference with a planned, ordered, or regular procedure, state, or habit **:** INTERRUPTION ⟨hated the ~ of his privacy⟩ ⟨the ~ of his routine always made him grouchy⟩ **:** a moving out of place ⟨the ~ of his papers⟩ **:** ALTERATION ⟨an obesity related to endocrine ~*s*⟩ ⟨some basic ~ of the body's chemistry —G.W.Gray b. 1886⟩; *also* **:** COMMOTION ⟨looked out of the window to see what the ~ was all about⟩ **:** DERANGEMENT ⟨a certain appalling ~ in the body politic⟩ ⟨market ~*s* to which the less integrated and smaller business enterprises frequently find it difficult or even impossible to adjust —A.D.H.Kaplan⟩ ⟨the large-scale and national ~*s* which so disrupted affairs —*Collier's Yr. Bk.*⟩ **d :** a movement of the earth's crust (as in crustal crumpling to form a mountain range) **:** DIASTROPHISM; *also* **:** the result of such movement **e :** a local variation from the average or normal wind conditions; *esp* **:** a cyclone or tornado **f :** abnormal variation from a mental or emotional norm ⟨the disturbed personality is not always aware of the ~⟩

dis·tur·bant \-bənt\ *adj* [L *disturbant-, disturbans,* pres. part. of *disturbare* to disturb — more at DISTURB] **:** DISTURBING ⟨pouring forth ~ and gusty heresies —V.L.Parrington⟩

dis·turbed \-bd\ *adj* **1 :** marked by a variable degree of pathological variation from a mental or emotional norm **:** showing symptoms of emotional illness or personality abnormality ⟨the handling of ~ children —George Edwards⟩ ⟨~ and backward children — aggressive, neurotic, recessive —Avima Dushkin⟩ **2 :** designed for or occupied by disturbed patients ⟨a ~ ward⟩

disturbed area *n* **:** the area within which an earthquake shock is appreciable by the unaided senses

dis·turbed·ly \-b(ə)dlē\ *adv* **:** in a disturbed manner

dis·turb·er \-bə(r)\ *n* -S [ME, fr. *disturben* to disturb + *-er*] **:** one that disturbs; *specif* **:** an English bishop who unlawfully refuses to examine and admit the patron's clerk to a benefice

dis·turb·ing·ly *adv* **:** in a disturbing manner **:** in a way that upsets or agitates emotionally or tends to throw into disorder ⟨a ~ long drought⟩ ⟨a ~ large incidence of petty thievery⟩

dis·turnpike \dəs, (')dis+\ *vt* [¹*dis-* + *turnpike* (n.)] **:** to convert into a toll-free road

di·style \'dī,stīl, 'di,-\ *adj* [¹*di-* + *-style*] **:** marked by columniation with two columns across the front — compare DECASTYLE, DODECASTYLE, ENNEASTYLE, HEPTASTYLE, HEXASTYLE, OCTASTYLE, PENTASTYLE, TETRASTYLE

distyle in an·tis \-ə'nantəs, -,i'n-, -'an-,tēs\ *adj* [L *in antis* between antas] **:** having two columns between two antas

di·substituted \(')dī+\ *adj* [*di-* + *substituted*] **:** having two substituent atoms or groups in the molecule ⟨~ barbiturates⟩

di·sulfate \(')dī+\ *n* [*di-* + *sulfate*] **1 :** PYROSULFATE **2 :** BISULFATE **3 :** a compound containing two sulfate groups

di·sulfide \(')dī+\ *n* [*di-* + *sulfide*] **1 :** a compound containing two atoms of sulfur combined with an element or radical ⟨iron ~⟩ **2 :** an organic compound containing the bivalent group –SS– composed of two sulfur atoms united to carbon atoms ⟨diethyl ~⟩

di·sul·fi·ram \dī'səlfə,ram\ *n* -S [*disulfide* + tetraethylthiu*ram*] **:** TETRAETHYLTHIURAM DISULFIDE — used esp. of the drug

disulfo- *comb form* [ISV *di-* + *sulf-*] **1 :** containing two sulfonic acid groups esp. replacing hydrogen **2 :** DITHI-

di·sulfonate \(')dī+\ *n* [*di-* + *sulfonate*] **:** a compound containing two sulfonate groups

di·sulfonic acid \(¦)dī+. . .-\ *n* [*di-* + *sulfonic*] **:** a compound containing two sulfonic acid groups

di·sulfuric acid \(¦)dī+. . .-\ *n* [*di-* + *sulfuric*] **:** PYROSULFURIC ACID

dis·unification \dəsh, ¦dish + ,(y)ü . . . ; dəs, ¦dis + ,yü . . .\ *n* the act or process of disunifying or the state of being disunified **:** the destruction of concord or harmony among a group **:** the breaking up of a unified whole into separate often dissident parts

dis·uniform \dəsh, (')dish+¦yü . . . ; dəs, (')dis+¦yü . . .\ *adj* [¹*dis-* + *uniform*] *archaic* **:** not uniform **:** lacking uniformity

dis·unify \"+\ *vt* [¹*dis-* + *unify*] **:** to destroy the unity of: **a :** to bring about a lack of concord or harmony in or among ⟨humanity, already profoundly perplexed and *disunified* —J.D. Ratcliff⟩ **b :** to break up (a unified whole) into separate often dissident parts ⟨set out deliberately to divide and ~ this nation —S.A.Mitchell⟩

dis·union \"+\ *n* [¹*dis-* + *union*] **1 :** the termination or destruction of union **:** DISJUNCTION, SEPARATION ⟨the ~ of the body and soul at death⟩ ⟨looking forward to the ~ of the two parts of the organization⟩; *esp* **:** the termination of political union ⟨the Southerners favoring ~ prior to the Civil War⟩ **2 a :** the quality or state of being disunified **:** DISUNITY ⟨some of the remaining 10 towns were held by Macedonian garrisons, some by local tyrants, a state of ~ equally gratifying to Macedonia and intolerable to Greek patriots —*Encyc. Americana*⟩ ⟨he thought political unity sufficient in spite of religious ~ to secure the monarchy —Hilaire Belloc⟩ **b :** ALIENATION, DISSENSION ⟨a group torn by ~⟩

dis·unionist \"+\ *n* **:** one who favors disunion; *specif* **:** an American secessionist

dis·unite \¦dish + (y)ü..., ¦dis + yü...\ *vb* [¹*dis-* + *unite*] *vt* **1 :** to destroy the unity of **:** DIVIDE, SEPARATE ⟨might we not ~ our war effort by trying prematurely to unite our peace effort —A.H.Vandenberg †1951⟩ ⟨a league of *disunited* nations —E.B.White⟩ ⟨the family was deeply *disunited,* and each member unhappy for a different reason —George Santayana⟩ **2 :** to alienate in spirit **:** destroy the concord or harmony between or among ⟨attempted to ~ the members of the club by gossip⟩ ~ *vi* **:** to fall apart or separate into individual units **:** become disunified or disjoined

disunited *adj, of a horse or its gait* **:** using the legs in the wrong order when cantering or galloping

dis·unity \dəsh, (')dish + ¦(y)ü...; dəs, (')dis + ¦yü...\ *n* [¹*dis-* + *unity*] **:** the state of being disunified in spirit **:** lack of concord, harmony, or a cooperative spirit **:** ALIENATION, DISSENSION ⟨states . . . are destroyed by their folly, weakness, ~ —John Strachey⟩ ⟨the unpreparedness of the West, its woeful ~, and its pitiful mutual incriminations —Hans Kohn⟩ ⟨the much more difficult kind of ~ made by deep cleavages of race, religion, or culture —Margery Perham⟩

dis·usage \" + \ *n* [ME, fr. ¹*dis-* + *usage*] **:** DISUSE

¹**disuse** \" +\ *vt* [ME *disusen,* fr. ¹*dis-* + *usen* to use — more at USE] **1** *archaic* **:** to make unaccustomed or unused **:** DISACCUSTOM **2 :** to discontinue the use or practice of **:** DISCARD, ABANDON — now used chiefly in the past participial form ⟨a golf course long *disused*⟩ ⟨a *disused* initiation rite⟩ ⟨the baroque scroll pediment had been *disused* on exteriors before the revolution —Fiske Kimball⟩

²**disuse** \"\ *n* [¹*dis-* + *use*] **:** cessation of use, practice, or exercise **:** DESUETUDE ⟨intellectual vigor has been circumscribed by the ~ of the scholar's language —A.A.Hill⟩ ⟨the mine ultimately fell into ~⟩ ⟨combat intelligence had atrophied by ~ —Shipley Thomas⟩ ⟨we should die of idiocy through ~ of our mental faculties if we did not fill our heads with romantic nonsense out of illustrated newspapers and novels and plays and films —G.B.Shaw⟩

dis·utility \¦dish + (y)ü..., ¦dis + yü...\ *n* [¹*dis-* + *utility*] **:** the absence or lack of utility; *specif* **:** the quality of causing inconvenience, discomfort, or pain or of thwarting the satisfaction of desires

dis·valuable \dəs, (')dis+\ *adj* [¹*dis-* + *valuable*] **:** characterized by disvalue

dis·valuation \dəs, (¦)dis+\ *n* [¹*dis-* + *valuation*] **:** the action of losing value **:** DEPRECIATION ⟨they faced the problem of living in a world which was in process of ~ —R.M.Weaver⟩

¹**dis·value** \dəs, (')dis+\ *vt* [¹*dis-* + *value* (v.)] **1** *archaic* **:** UNDERVALUE, DEPRECIATE **2 :** to consider of little value **:** DISESTEEM ⟨in civilized man the variety of the valued and *disvalued* increases greatly —E.L.Thorndike⟩

²**disvalue** \"\ *n* [¹*dis-* + *value* (n.)] **1** *obs* **:** DISESTEEM, DISREGARD **2 :** a negative value; *specif* **:** one that is positively detrimental (as an evil) ⟨has chosen on the contrary to pair every value exactly with its corresponding ~ —P.B.Rice⟩ ⟨the artist, in projecting an individual experience, or his own interpretation of it, is indicating values to be salvaged, ~*s* to be avoided —*Jour. of Aesthetics*⟩

disweapon *vt* [¹*dis-* + *weapon* (n.)] *obs* **:** DISARM

disworship *n* [ME, fr. ¹*dis-* + *worship*] *obs* **:** a withholding or deprivation of honor **:** DISHONOR

di·syllabic *or* **dis·syllabic** \¦dī, ¦di +\ *adj* [F *dissyllabique,* fr. *dissyllabe* (fr. MF *dissilabe*) + *-ique* -ic] **:** consisting of or having two syllables only ⟨a ~ word⟩ ⟨an iambic foot is ~⟩

di·syllabify *or* **dis·syllabify** \"+\ *vt* [*dissyllable,* disyllable + *-i-* + *-fy*] **:** DISYLLABIZE

di·syl·la·bism *or* **dis·syl·la·bism** \dī'silə,bizəm, di'-\ *n* [F *dissyllabisme,* fr. *dissyllabe* + *-isme* -ism] **:** the quality or state of being disyllabic

di·syllabize *or* **dis·syllabize** \(')dī, (')di+\ *vt* [*dissyllable, dissyllable* + *-ize*] **:** to make two syllables of

di·syllable *or* **dis·syllable** \(')dī, (')di+\ *n* [part trans. of MF *dissilabe,* fr. ML *dissyllabus* of two syllables, alter. (influenced by Gk *dis-* twice, double, fr. *dis* twice) of L *disyllabus,* fr. Gk *disyllabos,* fr. *di-* + *-syllabos* (fr. *syllabē* syllable) — more at BIS, TWI-] **:** a linguistic form consisting of two syllables (as *many, repeat*)

¹**dit** *or* **ditt** \'dit\ *vt* **ditted; ditted; ditting; dits** *or* **ditts** [ME *ditten,* fr. OE *dyttan;* akin to Icel *dytta* to repair, stop up (as a crack) — more at DOT] *Scot* **:** to close up **:** obstruct the course of

²**dit** \"\ *n* -S [alter. (influenced by *ditty*) of ME *dite,* fr. MF *dit* word, speech, poem, song, fr. L *dictum* saying, dictum — more at DICTUM] *archaic* **:** DITTY, SONG

³**dit** \'dē\ *n, pl* **dits** \-ē(z)\ [F, fr. OF, word, speech, poem, song] **:** a short usu. didactic sometimes satirical poem in old French literature often dealing with homely subjects

⁴**dit** \'dit, *usu* -id·+V\ *n* -S [imit.] **:** a dot in radio or telegraphic code — used by operators as an oral representation of the transmitted sound; compare DAH

di·ta \dē'tä\ *n* -S [Tag *ditâ*] **1 :** a forest tree (*Alstonia scholaris*) of eastern Asia and the Philippines the bark of which was formerly used as an antiperiodic **2 :** the bark of the dita tree **3 :** UPAS 1a

di·tal \'dēd·ᵊl, 'di|,'dī|\ *n* -S [It *dito* finger (fr. L *digitus*) + E *-al* (as in *pedal*) — more at TOE] **:** a key by which the pitch is raised a half step in a harp guitar

dital harp *n* **:** a harp guitar provided with a dital

di·ta·li \dē'tälē\ *n pl* [*ditali* fr. It, pl. of *ditale,* lit., thimble, fingerstall] **:** elbow-shaped pieces of macaroni

di·ta·li·ni \,dēd·ᵊl'ēnē\ *n pl* [It, pl. of *ditalino,* dim. of *ditale*] **:** elbow-shaped pieces of macaroni that are shorter than ditali

¹**ditch** \'dich\ *n* -ES *often attrib* [ME *dich,* fr. OE *dīc* dike, ditch — more at DIKE] **1 :** a long narrow excavation dug in the earth **2 a :** a trench for guarding or fencing enclosures **b :** a trench for conveying water for drainage or irrigation **c :** the area at either side of a road usu. consisting of a drainage trench ⟨a car headed for the ~⟩ **3** *chiefly Irish* **:** a bank of earth from an excavation **4 :** a natural or artificial usu. narrow watercourse or waterway **5 :** the ground bounding a bowling green sometimes consisting of a shallow trench **6 :** a borrow pit of a road **7 :** a trough for disposing of the drilling fluid in rotary drilling of an oil well

²**ditch** \"\ *vb* -ED/-ING/-ES [ME *dichen,* fr. *dich,* n.] *vt* **1 a :** to enclose with a ditch ⟨a pasture hedged and ~*ed*⟩ **b :** to dig a ditch in (as for drainage or irrigation) **2 :** to cause (a train) to derail **:** drive (a car) into the ditch **3 a :** to discard, dismiss, or abandon as no longer useful or desirable **:** get rid of ⟨~*ed* the old policy when it proved ineffective⟩ ⟨~ his fiancée⟩ **b** *slang* **:** to hide, put away, or put aside with the intent of recovery ⟨~ the stolen goods⟩ **c** *slang* **:** to get away from or avoid by artifice or stratagem ⟨~*ed* me by sneaking out the back door⟩ ⟨let's ~ school today⟩ **4 :** to make a forced landing of (an aircraft) on water ~ *vi* **1 :** to dig a ditch **2** *dial* **:** to clean or repair a ditch **3 :** to make a forced landing of an aircraft on water

ditch bank blade *n* **:** a weed and grass cutter comprising a hooked blade at the end of a long wooden handle

ditch boss *n* **:** an official in the western U.S. having the authority to apportion irrigation water

ditchbur \'ˌ=,=\ *n* **:** COCKLEBUR

ditch check *n* **:** a small usu. wood or concrete dam placed at frequent intervals below the surface of a road ditch to prevent erosion

ditch crowfoot *n* **:** CURSED CROWFOOT

ditchdigger \'=,==\ *n* **1 :** one that digs ditches **2 a :** one employed at menial and usu. hard physical labor **b :** DITCHER 2

ditchdigging \'=,==\ *n* **:** the occupation of a ditchdigger

ditch·er \'dichə(r)\ *n* -S [ME *dicher,* fr. *dichen* to make a ditch + *-er* — more at DITCH] **1 :** a workman who digs or repairs ditches **2 :** a machine that digs ditches and usu. piles the dirt in a bank to the side (as by means of a conveyor belt)

ditch fern *n* [ME *diche fern*] **:** ROYAL FERN

ditch grass *n* **:** a slender branching marine aquatic plant (*Ruppia maritima*) with linear leaves like those of grasses

ditching car *n* **:** a railroad car equipped for excavation

ditch·less \'dichləs\ *adj* **:** lacking a ditch

ditch·man \'dichmən\ *n, pl* **ditchmen :** a ditcher in a mine

ditch millet *n* **:** a grass (*Paspalum scrobilatum*) grown esp. in India, Africa, and Australia and said to poison the milk of cows that eat it

ditch moss *n* **:** WATERWEED a

ditch reed *n* **:** a tall reed of the genus *Phragmites* (*P. communis*) that has creeping rhizomes, broad flat leaves, and a large bushy panicle, is widely distributed in moist areas throughout most of No. America, and has been used for weaving mats, screens, and lattices and for making arrow shafts

ditch rider *n* **:** a person who patrols and inspects irrigation systems and distributes water to farmers

ditch stonecrop *n* **:** a common American perennial weed (*Penthorum sedoides*) with united carpels, flowers in loose spikes, and scattered leaves

ditch sunflower *n* **:** TICKSEED SUNFLOWER

ditchwater \'=,==\ *n* [ME *dich water,* fr. *dich* ditch + *water*] **1 :** foul stagnant water collected in a ditch **2 :** something regarded as typically dull and lifeless ⟨writing as dull as ~⟩

¹**dite** *vt* -ED/-ING/-S [ME *diten,* fr. OF *ditier,* fr. L *dictare* to pronounce, assert, dictate — more at DICTATE] **1** *obs* **:** INDITE, COMPOSE **2** *obs* **:** INDICT

²**dite** \'dīt\ *n* -S [alter. of *doit*] *dial* **:** a small amount **:** MITE, BIT

di·ten·tion \(')dī¦tenchən\ *n* -S [*divided* at*tention*] **:** a mode of attention in which ideational reactions are distorted by the unconscious intrusion of elements of feeling and emotion — compare COTENTION

di·ten·tive \-entiv\ *adj* **:** of, relating to, or marked by ditention

di·terpene \(')dī+\ *n* [*di-* + *terpene*] **:** any of a class of terpenes $C_{20}H_{32}$ containing twice as many atoms in the molecule as monoterpenes; *also* **:** a derivative of such a terpene

¹**di·terpenoid** \"+\ *adj* [*diterpene* + *-oid*] **:** resembling a diterpene in molecular structure

²**diterpenoid** \"\ *n* -S **:** a diterpene or diterpene derivative (as phytol or abietic acid)

di·tetragonal \¦dī+¦=,==\ *adj* [ISV *di-* + *tetragonal*] **1 :** relating to or being a prism in the tetragonal system that has eight similar faces whose alternate interfacial angles only are equal; *also* **:** relating to or being a pyramid corresponding to such a prism **2 :** relating to or being a type of symmetry that requires a ditetragonal pyramid or dipyramid

di·the·ism \'dīthē,izəm, (')dī'th-\ *n* -S [*di-* + *-theism*] **:** belief in or theory of the existence of two gods or of two original principles, one good and one evil (as in Manichaeism) — **di·the·is·tic** \¦dīthē¦istik\ *or* **di·the·is·ti·cal** \-stəkəl\ *adj*

di·the·ist \'dī(,)thēəst, (')dī'th-\ *n* **:** an advocate or adherent of ditheism

di·thematic \¦dī+\ *adj* [*di-* + *thematic*] **:** having or characterized by two themes ⟨a ~ chess problem⟩

¹**dith·er** \'dith|ə(r) *sometimes* -th|\ *vb* **dithered; dithered; dithering** \|(ə)riŋ\ **dithers** [alter. of *didder*] *vi* **1 :** SHIVER, SHAKE, TREMBLE ⟨the ~*ing* of grass —Wallace Stevens⟩ **2 :** to act or move nervously, hesitantly, confusedly, or without clear purpose ⟨the stage manager was ~*ing* in the wings⟩ **:** act indecisively **:** VACILLATE, WAVER ⟨faced with unpleasant choices she merely ~*s*⟩ **3 :** BABBLE ⟨~*ing* on the phone⟩ ~ *vt* **:** to cause confusion, concern, or nervous agitation in ⟨wild rumors of war ~*ed* the population⟩

²**dither** \"\ *n* -S **1** *dial Eng* **:** a trembling, shaking, or quivering esp. with cold **2 :** a state of strong excitement or agitation ⟨the outbreak of war threw all parties into a ~⟩ — **dith·ery** \|(ə)rē\ *adj*

dithered *adj* **:** being in a state of confusion or excitement **:** DAZED

dithi- *or* **dithio-** *comb form* [ISV *di-* + *thi-*] **:** containing two atoms of sulfur usu. in place of two oxygen atoms ⟨*dithi*ane⟩ ⟨*dithio*benzoic acid⟩

di·thio \(')dī¦thī(,)ō\ *adj* [*dithi-*] **:** relating to or containing two atoms of sulfur usu. in place of two oxygen atoms ⟨~ compound⟩

di·thio·carbamate \¦dī,thīō+\ *n* [*dithiocarbamic* + *-ate*] **:** a salt of dithiocarbamic acid or of one of its organic derivatives

di·thio·carbamic acid \"+. . .-\ *n* [ISV *dithi-* + *carbamic*] **:** an unstable acid NH_2CSSH known best in the form of salts and disubstituted organic derivatives (as salts of the dimethyl derivative) that are made from carbon disulfide (as by reaction with ammonia or amines) and that in many cases are used as fungicides or accelerators of vulcanization

-di·thi·o·ic \¦dī,thī¦ōik\ *adj comb form* [ISV *dithi-* + *-ic*] **:** containing two atoms of sulfur replacing two oxygen atoms in the molecule of an acid ⟨phosphoro*dithioic* acid $H_3PO_2S_2$⟩

-di·thi·ol \¦dī'thī,ōl, -ōl\ *n comb form* -S [ISV *dithi-* + *-ol*] **:** containing two mercapto groups replacing hydrogen ⟨1,2-ethane*dithiol* CH_2SHCH_2SH⟩

di·thionate \(')dī+\ *n* -S [ISV *dithionic* + *-ate*] **:** a salt of dithionic acid

di·thionic acid \¦dī+. . .-\ *n* [ISV *di-* + *thionic*] **:** a strong dibasic acid $H_2S_2O_6$ made by oxidizing sulfurous acid but known only in solution and in the form of salts

di·thi·o·nite \dī'thīə,nīt\ *n* -S [*dithion-* + *-ite*] **:** HYDROSULFITE

di·thi·o·nous acid \(')dī¦thīənəs-\ *n* [*di-* + *thion-* + *-ous*] **:** HYDROSULFUROUS ACID — used in the nomenclature adopted by the International Union of Pure and Applied Chemistry

di·thi·zone \dī'thī,zōn\ *n* -S [*diphenylthiocarbazone*] **:** a bluish black crystalline compound $C_6H_5N{=}NCSNHNHC_6H_5$ used for the colorimetric determination of heavy metals (as lead) — called also *diphenylthiocarbazone*

di·thra·nol \'dīthrə,nōl, 'dith-, -nōl\ *n* -S [*dihydroxyanthranol*] **:** ANTHRALIN

dith·y·ramb \'dith|ə,ram, |ē,-, -raa(ə)m *sometimes* -ith|\ *n* -

[Gk *dithyrambos*, prob. of non-IE origin] **1 :** a choric poem, chant, or hymn of ancient Greece sung by revelers at the festival in honor of the god Dionysus **2 :** a poem in an inspired wild irregular strain **3 :** a statement or piece of writing in an exalted impassioned style usu. in praise of something ⟨went into ~s over the beauty of the landscape⟩

¹dith·y·ram·bic \ˌ==ˈrambik, -bēk\ *adj* [Gk *dithyrambikos*, fr. *dithyrambos* + *-ikos* -ic] **1 :** of or relating to dithyrambs **:** composing dithyrambs **2 :** like a dithyramb esp. in being impassioned and elevated ⟨he grew ~ in speaking of the candidate's merits⟩ — **dith·y·ram·bi·cal·ly** \-bək(ə)lē, -bēk-, -li\ *adv*

²dithyrambic \"\ *n* -s **:** DITHYRAMB

di·thy·rid·i·um \ˌdīˌthīˈridēəm, ˌdithəˈr-\ *n* -s [NL, fr. *di-* + Gk *thyridion*, dim. of *thyra* door — more at DOOR] **:** a larva of certain taeníoid tapeworms consisting of a scolex invaginated into an elongated solid body

diting *pres part of* DITE

dition *n* -s [MF, fr. L *dicion-*, *dicio* word of command, command, dominion, fr. *dicere* to say + *-ion-*, *-io* -ion — more at DICTION] *obs* **:** DOMINION, RULE

dit·o·kous \ˈdidəkəs\ *adj* [Gk *ditokos* having borne two at one birth, fr. *di-* + *tokos* childbirth, offspring] **1 :** producing two eggs or young at a time ⟨pigeons are generally ~⟩ **2 :** producing two kinds of young ⟨~ worms⟩

di·tone \ˈdīˌtōn\ *n* [Gk *ditonon*, fr. neut. of *ditonos* having two tones, fr. *di-* + *tonos* tone — more at TONE] **:** the Greek musical interval of a major third comprehending two major steps, corresponding to the ratio 81:64, and being slightly larger than the modern major third — **di·ton·ic** \(ˈ)dīˈtänik\ *adj*

ditonic comma *n* [trans. of NL *comma ditonicum*] **:** the difference in pitch between two musical tones respectively twelve perfect fifths and seven octaves from the same tone and represented by the ratio of 531,441:524,288 — called also *Pythagorean comma*

di·trem·a·ta \dīˈtremədə\ [NL, fr. *di-* + *-tremata*] *syn of* THERIA

di·trem·a·tous \(ˈ)dīˈtremədəs\ *adj* [*di-* + Gk *trēmat-*, *trēma* hole + E *-ous* — more at THROW] **1 :** having the two genital openings separate — used of freshwater pulmonate snails **2 :** having the genital and anal openings separate — used of viviparous fishes

di·triglyph \(ˈ)dī+\ *n* [F *ditriglyphe*, fr. *di-* + *triglyphe* triglyph] **:** a horizontal division in the Doric architectural style assumed to contain two triglyphs: as **a :** a single metope with its limiting triglyphs **b :** two metopes with one whole and two half triglyphs, equaling an intercolumniation **c :** the wide middle intercolumniation found in some porticoes **d :** the space from the vertical axis of one metope to that of the next but one — **di·triglyphic** \ˌdī+ˈ==ik\ *adj*

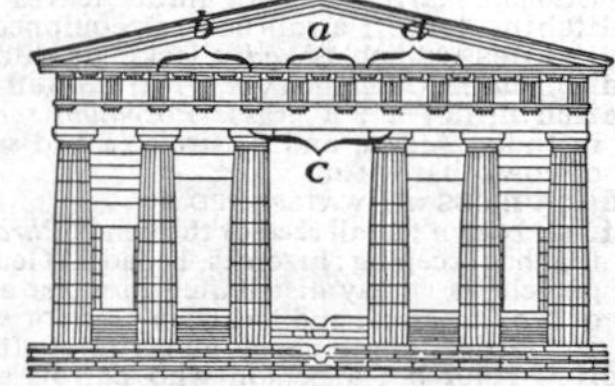

ditriglyph, showing portions included according to senses *a*, *b*, *c*, and *d*

di·trigonal \(ˈ)dī+\ *adj* [ISV *di-* + *trigonal*] *of a six-sided prism or pyramid* **:** having only the alternate interfacial angles equal — see SCALENOHEDRON illustration — **di·trigonally** \"+\ *adv*

di·tro·che·an \(ˈ)dīˈtrōkēən, ˌdī(ˌ)trōˈk-\ *adj* **:** of, containing, or consisting of a ditrochee

di·trochee \(ˈ)dī+\ *n* [LL & Gk; LL *ditrochaeus*, fr. Gk *ditrochaios*, fr. *di-* + *trochaios* trochee — more at TROCHEE] **:** a double trochee **:** a trochaic dipody reckoned as a single measure or compound foot

dits *pres 3d sing of* DIT, *pl of* DIT

ditt *var of* DIT

dit·tan·der \dəˈtandə(r), ˈditᵊn-\ *n* -s [AF *ditaundere*, alter. of OF *ditan*] **1 :** CRETAN DITTANY **2 :** a perennial European pepperwort (*Lepidium latifolium*) with sepals broadly white-margined from the base

dit·ta·ny \ˈditᵊnē\ *n* -ES [ME *diptannus*, *ditoyne*, fr. ML & MF; ML *diptannus* & MF *ditan*, fr. L *dictamnus*, *dictamnum*, fr. Gk *diktamnon*, perh. fr. *Diktē*, mountain in Crete] **1 :** CRETAN DITTANY **2 :** FRAXINELLA **3 :** a small aromatic herb (*Cunila origanoides*) of the family Labiatae **4 :** BASTARD DITTANY

dit·tay \ˈdiˌtā, -ˌti\ *n* -s [ME (Sc dial.), fr. MF *dité*, *ditié*, past part. of *diter*, *ditier* to compose, indict — more at DITE] *Scots law* **:** the matter charged in an indictment; *also* **:** the indictment itself

ditted *past of* DIT

ditting *pres part of* DIT

¹dit·to \ˈdid·(ˌ)ō, -i(ˌ)tō\ *n*, *pl* **dittos** *also* **dittoes** [It *ditto*, *detto* (past part. of *dire* to say), fr. L *dictus*, past part. of *dicere* to say — more at DICTION] **1 a :** a thing mentioned previously or above — used to avoid repeating a word ⟨mamma polar bears clutching infant ~s —Mollie Panter-Downes⟩; abbr. *do;* often symbolized by inverted commas, apostrophes, or other small marks **b :** a ditto mark **2** *dittoes pl, Brit* **:** clothes of one material or color throughout ⟨a dark-colored suit of ~es⟩ **3 :** a duplicate or close copy ⟨he is the ~ of his father⟩

²ditto \"\ *vb* -ED/-ING/-ES *vt* **:** to repeat the action or statement of ⟨the second speaker ~*ed* his argument⟩ **~** *vi* **:** to repeat an act or statement

³ditto \"\ *adv* **:** as before or aforesaid **:** in the same manner ⟨I shall act ~⟩

dit·to·graph \ˈdid·ōˌgraf, -itō-, -ráf\ *n* -s [Gk *dittos*, *dissos* twofold + E *-graph*] **:** a letter or letters or words unintentionally repeated in copying or printing

dit·tog·ra·phy \diˈtägrəfē\ *n* -ES [Gk *dittographia*, *dissographia*, fr. *dittos*, *dissos* + *-graphia* -graphy] **:** the unintentional repetition of letters or words in copying or printing (as in literature for literature)

dit·tol·o·gy \-täləjē\ *n* -ES [Gk *dittologia*, *dissologia* repetition of a word, fr. *dittos*, *dissos* + *-logia* -logy] **:** a double reading or twofold interpretation (as of a biblical text)

¹dit·ty \ˈdid·ē, -itˌ|i\ *n* -ES [ME *dite*, fr. OF *ditié* composition, poem, moral tract, fr. past part. of *ditier* to compose, indict — more at DITE] **1 :** a song or short poem intended to be sung; *esp* **:** one of a simple unaffected character ⟨a plaintive ~ sung by a Highland lass⟩ **2** *obs* **:** the words or subject of a song as distinguished from its tune

²ditty \"\ *vb* -ED/-ING/-ES *vi*, *obs* **:** SING **~** *vt*, *obs* **:** to celebrate in song **:** set to music **:** SING ⟨with his soft pipe, and smooth-*dittied* song —John Milton⟩

ditty bag *n* [origin unknown] **:** a small bag used esp. by sailors to hold thread, needles, tape, or other small articles of gear

ditty box \"-\ *also* **did·dy box** \-idē, |i\ *n* [origin unknown] **:** a box used for the same purpose as a ditty bag

dit·y·len·chus \ˌdidᵊlˈeŋkəs\ *n*, *cap* [NL, fr. Gk *ditylos* having two humps (fr. *di-* + *tylos* callus, lump, penis) + *enchos* spear, lance — more at THOLE] **:** a genus of small slender nematode worms (family Tylenchidae) including serious plant parasites (as the potato rot nematode and the bulb eelworm) as well as a number of harmless soil forms and commensals

di·um·vi·rate \dīˈəmvərət, -rāt\ *n* -s [by alter. (influence of *di-*)] **:** DUUMVIRATE

di·ure·sis \ˌdīyəˈrēsəs\ *n*, *pl* **diure·ses** \-ēˌsēz\ [NL, fr. LL *diureticus*, after Gk *ourēsis* uresis — more at URETIC, URESIS] **:** an increased excretion of urine

¹di·uret·ic \ˌdīyəˈred·|ik, -et|, |ēk\ *adj* [ME, fr. MF or LL; MF *diuretique*, fr. LL *diureticus*, fr. Gk *diourētikos*, fr. (assumed) *diourētos* (verbal of *diourein* to urinate, have diuretic properties, fr. *dia-* + *ourein* to urinate) + *-ikos* -ic — more at URINE] **:** tending to increase the flow of urine — **di·uret·i·cal·ly** \|ək(ə)lē, |ēk, -li\ *adv*

²diuretic \"\ *n* -s [ME, fr. *diuretic*, adj.] **:** an agent that increases the flow of urine

¹di·ur·nal \(ˈ)dīˈərnᵊl, -ˈən-, -ˈəin-\ *adj* [ME *diurnall*, fr. L *diurnalis* — more at JOURNAL] **1 a :** repeated or recurring every day **:** DAILY ⟨the ~ round of tasks and cares⟩ **b :** going through its changes in a day; *specif* **:** having a recurrent daily cycle of change ⟨~ rotation of the heavens —D.J.Price⟩ **2 a :** performed in or belonging to the daytime ⟨black bats, inverted in ~ slumber —P.M.Hubbard⟩ ⟨the city's ~ noises faded with the night⟩ **b :** chiefly active during the daytime ⟨hunting dogs are mainly ~ animals —James Stevenson-Hamilton⟩ — compare NOCTURNAL **3** *of a flower* **a :** opening during the day and closing at night **b :** lasting only a day **:** EPHEMERAL **4** *of a sign of the zodiac* **:** UNEVEN ⟨the 1st, 3d, and 5th are ~ signs⟩ — **di·ur·nal·ly** \-ᵊlē, -ᵊli\ *adv*

²diurnal \"\ *n* -s **1** *obs* **:** a small volume containing the services for the canonical hours which are said in the daytime **2** *archaic* **:** DAYBOOK, DIARY **3** *archaic* **:** a daily newspaper or journal

diurnal arc *n* **:** the portion of the diurnal circle of a celestial body that is above the observer's horizon ⟨the *diurnal arc* of the sun is its apparent path from sunrise to sunset⟩

diurnal circle *n* **:** the apparent circle or parallel of declination described by a celestial body in consequence of the earth's rotation

di·ur·nal·ist \=ˈ=nᵊləst\ *n* -s [²*diurnal* + *-ist*] *archaic* **:** JOURNALIST

diurnal motion *n* **:** the apparent westward motion of the celestial sphere and celestial bodies resulting from the rotation of the earth; *also* **:** the earth's rotation

diurnal parallax *n* **:** GEOCENTRIC PARALLAX

di·ur·na·tion \ˌdī(ˌ)ərˈnāshən\ *n* -s [L *diurnus* of the day, daily + E *-ation* (as in *hibernation*) — more at JOURNAL] **1 :** the habit of sleeping or being quiescent by day ⟨the ~ of bats⟩ **2 :** a daily recurrent fluctuation in an ecological community (as the vertical movement of plankton)

di·u·tur·nal \ˌdīyüˈtərnᵊl\ *adj* [L *diuturnus* (fr. *diu* lasting a long time, a long time ago) + E *-al*] **:** of long continuance **:** LASTING

di·u·tur·ni·ty \ˌ==ˈ=nəd·ē\ *n* -ES [ME *diuturnite*, fr. L *diuturnitat-*, *diuturnitas*, fr. *diuturnus* + *-itat-*, *-itas* -ity] **:** the quality or state of being continuous or lasting

¹div \ˈdiv\ *n* -s [Per *dēv* — more at DAEVA] **:** DAEVA

²div *substand past of* DIVE

div *abbr* **1** divergence **2** diversion **3** divide **4** dividend **5** divine; divinity **6** [It *divisi*] separate **7** division **8** divorce

di·va \ˈdēvə\ *n*, *pl* **divas** \-vəz\ *or* **di·ve** \-ˌvā\ [It, lit., goddess, fr. L, fem. of *divus* god — more at DEITY] **:** PRIMA DONNA 1

diva blue *n* **:** a moderate blue that is redder and duller than average copen and redder and deeper than azurite blue or Dresden blue

di·va·gate \ˈdīvəˌgāt, ˈdiv-\ *vi* -ED/-ING/-S [LL *divagatus*, past part. of *divagari*, fr. L *di-* (fr. *dis-* apart) + *vagari* to wander — more at DIS-, VAGARY] **1 :** to wander about or stray from one place or subject to another ⟨now he *divagated* into the field of literature⟩ **2 :** DIVERGE ⟨natural science *divagated* more and more from metaphysics —George Boas⟩

di·va·ga·tion \ˌ==ˈgāshən\ *n* -s [LL *divagation-*, *divagatio*, fr. *divagatus* + L *-ion-*, *-io* -ion] **:** the act or fact of divagating: as **a :** DIGRESSION ⟨numerous ~s of the plot⟩ **b :** DEVIATION, DIVERGENCE ⟨fashionable ~s from classic literary norms⟩

di·valent \(ˈ)dī+\ *adj* [ISV *di-* + *valent*] **:** BIVALENT

divali *usu cap*, *var of* DEWALI

di·van *in sense 3* ˈdīˌvan *or* -vaa(ə)n *sometimes* dīˈv- *or* dəˈv- *or* ˈdīvən; *in other senses the preceding pronunciations having heavy stress in the last syllable, and* dəˈvän *or* dēˈ- *or* -ˈvän, *are frequent*\ *n* -s [Turk, fr. Per *dīwān* account book] **1** *or* **di·wan** \dēˈwän, dəˈ-, -ˈwän\ **a :** a Muslim council of state; *specif* **:** the Turkish privy council that was presided over by the sultan or grand vizier **b :** COUNCIL ⟨meet the family . . . in full ~ —Sir Walter Scott⟩ **2** *or* **diwan a :** a room or hall where a divan is held **b :** a Muslim court of justice **c :** SMOKING ROOM **3 a :** a large low couch with no back or ends **b :** SOFA, DAVENPORT **c :** a couch usu. without back or arms and often designed for use as a bed **4** *or* **diwan :** a collection of poems esp. in Persian or Arabic; *specif* **:** a series of poems by one author

di·variant \(ˈ)dī+\ *adj* [ISV *di-* + *variant*] **:** BIVARIANT

¹di·var·i·cate \dīˈvarəˌkāt, dəˈ-\ *vb* -ED/-ING/-S [L *divaricatus*, past part. of *divaricare*, fr. *di-* (fr. *dis-* apart) + *varicare* to straddle — more at DIS-, PREVARICATE] *vi* **1 :** to spread apart **:** diverge from each other ⟨at this spot the two roads ~⟩ **2 :** to divide or break up into distinct parts **~** *vt* **1** *obs* **:** to cause to divide into branches **2 :** to stretch or spread apart ⟨*divaricated* two fingers of his hand⟩ **syn** see BRANCH

²di·var·i·cate \(ˈ)dīˈvarəkət, dəˈv-\ *adj* [L *divaricatus*] **:** widely diverging or spreading apart — used esp. of branches and wings — **di·var·i·cate·ly** *adv*

di·var·i·ca·tion \(ˌ)dīˌvarəˈkāshən, dəˌ-\ *n* -s [ML *divarication-*, *divaricatio*, fr. L *divaricatus* (past part. of *divaricare*) + *-ion-*, *-io* -ion] **1 :** the process or fact of separating into parts or branching out ⟨~ of dialects from a common tongue⟩; *also* **:** one of the branches or subdivisions made by such separation **2 a :** a disagreement or divergence of opinion ⟨~ of philosophical systems⟩ **3 :** the action or an instance of stretching or spreading apart (as the legs)

di·var·i·ca·tor \=ˈ==əˌkād·ə(r)\ *n* -s **:** one that divaricates; *esp* **:** a muscle that causes divergence or separation of parts (as one of those which open the shell of brachiopods)

divd *abbr* dividend

¹dive \ˈdīv\ *vb* **dived** \ˈdīvd\ *or* **dove** \ˈdōv\, *substand* \ˈdəv\ *or substand* **div** \ˈdiv\ **dived; diving; dives** [ME *diven*, *duven*, fr. OE *dȳfan* (vt) to dip & *dūfan* (vi) to dive; OE *dȳfan*, causative fr. the root of *dūfan*; akin to MLG *bedūven* to be covered, ON *dȳfa* to dip, OHG *tobal* narrow valley, OSlav *dupina* cave, OE *dyppan* to dip — more at DIP] *vi* **1 a :** to plunge into water headfirst **:** thrust the body under or deeply into water or other fluid; *specif* **:** to execute a dive **b :** SUBMERGE ⟨the submarine *dived*⟩ **2 a :** to descend or fall precipitously ⟨the mercury *dived* to eight below zero⟩ **b :** to plunge one's hand into something ⟨*dived* into her pocketbook⟩ **c** *of a plane* **:** to descend in a dive — compare GLIDE **3 a :** to plunge into or explore some matter or subject ⟨~ into the heart of the matter⟩ **b :** to throw oneself into some activity **:** make a vigorous start ⟨*dived* into his food⟩ ⟨~ boldly into a strange new profession⟩ **c :** to plunge or dash (as for shelter) into some place or across some space ⟨bystanders *dived* for cover⟩ **:** lunge esp. with the intent of seizing something ⟨*dived* for his legs⟩ **~** *vt* **1 a** *archaic* **:** to plunge (a person or thing) into water **b :** to thrust (as the hand or anything held) into something ⟨~ his hand into the earth —Mollie Panter-Downes⟩ **2 :** to cause (as an airplane or submarine) to descend ⟨*dived* his plane through the sonic barrier⟩ **3** *archaic* **:** to penetrate or explore by or as if by diving ⟨he ~*s* the hollow, climbs the steeps —R.W.Emerson⟩ **syn** see PLUNGE

²dive \"\ *n* -s **1 :** the act or an instance of diving: as **a** (1) **:** a plunge into water executed in a prescribed manner and consisting of a takeoff (as from a springboard), an evolution in the air, and entry into the water either headfirst (as in a swan dive or jackknife) or feet first (as in a somersault or gainer) — called also *fancy dive* (2) **:** a submerging esp. of a submarine (3) *of an airplane* **:** a steep descent with or without power in which the airspeed attained is greater than the maximum speed in horizontal flight (4) **:** a headfirst leap in tumbling into the air from the mat or over a piece of apparatus followed immediately by a forward roll **b :** a plunge into or exploration of some matter or subject ⟨undismayed by his first ~ into calculus⟩ **c :** a plunge or dash (as for shelter) into some place or across some space ⟨made a ~ for the ditch⟩ **:** a lunge esp. with the intent of seizing something ⟨made a ~ for the gun⟩ **d :** a sharp decline (as of stocks or intangible values) ⟨morale took a ~ as the news spread⟩ **2 :** a disreputable resort for drinking or entertainment ⟨this is a respectable roadhouse; this is no ~ —Erskine Caldwell⟩ **3** *slang* **:** a pretended knockout resulting from collusion between two prizefighters ⟨took a ~ in the third round⟩

³dive *pl of* DIVA

dive-bomb \ˈ=ˌ=\ *vt* **:** to bomb by making a steep dive toward the target before releasing the bomb **~** *vi* **:** to engage in dive-bombing

dive bomber *n* **:** a bomber designed for dive-bombing

dive brake *n* **:** a retractable usu. hinged flap that may be extended into the airstream to increase the aerodynamic drag and thereby reduce the speed of a diving airplane

divekeeper \ˈ=ˌ==\ *n* **:** a keeper of a dive

di·vel \(ˈ)dīˈvel, dəˈv-\ *vt* **divelled; divelled; divelling; divels** [L *divellere*, fr. *di-* (fr. *dis-* apart) + *vellere* to pluck, pull — more at DIS-, VULNERABLE] *archaic* **:** to tear asunder or draw apart

di·vel·lent \dīˈvelənt, dəˈ-\ *adj* [L *divellent-*, *divellens*, pres. part. of *divellere*] *archaic* **:** drawing or tending to draw apart

di·vel·li·cate \dīˈveləˌkāt, dəˈ-\ *vt* -ED/-ING/-S [L *di-* (fr. *dis-* apart) + *vellicatus*, past part. of *vellicare* to pluck, twitch, fr. *vellere* to pluck, pull] *archaic* **:** to tear apart **:** break off **:** DETACH

div·er \ˈdīvə(r)\ *n* -s **1 :** one that dives **2 a :** a person who stays under water (as in salvage work) for long periods by having air supplied from the surface **b :** a fancy diver — compare DIVE 1a(1) **c :** any of various birds skillful in diving (as the grebe, sea duck, auk or penguin); *specif* **:** LOON **d** *slang chiefly Brit* **:** PICKPOCKET

diverb *n* [prob. fr. L *di-* (fr. *dis-* apart) + E *-verb* (as in *proverb*)] *obs* **:** a proverbial expression **:** PROVERB

di·verge \dəˈvərj, (ˈ)dīˈv-, -vōj, -vəij\ *vb* -ED/-ING/-S [ML *divergere*, fr. L *di-* (fr. *dis-* apart) + *vergere* to bend, incline — more at DIS-, WRENCH] *vi* **1 a :** to move or extend in different directions from a common point **:** draw apart ⟨these two roads ~ like the branches of a Y⟩ — opposed to *converge* **b :** to become different in character or form **:** differ in opinion ⟨dialects of the same language have *diverged* so widely that their relationship is no longer apparent⟩ **2 a :** to turn aside or lead away from a particular route or direction ⟨*diverging* from his direct path —Thomas Hardy⟩ **b :** to turn aside or deviate from a particular policy, course of action, subject, or line of thought **:** DIGRESS ⟨~ to another topic⟩ **:** differ in form, character, or opinion ⟨the traditions recorded there ~ from those that my mother handed down —George Santayana⟩ **~** *vt* **:** to cause to take a different direction **:** DEFLECT ⟨~ a compass needle⟩ **syn** see SWERVE

di·verge·ment \=ˈ=mənt\ *n* -s *archaic* **:** DIVERGENCE

di·ver·gence \dəˈvərjən(t)s, dīˈ-, -vōj-, -vəij-\ *n* -s [ML *divergere* + E *-ence*] **1 a :** a drawing apart (as of lines extending from a common center) ⟨an angle is formed by the ~ of straight lines⟩ **b :** a difference or disagreement in form, character, opinion ⟨growing ~ of opinion between the two countries⟩ — opposed to *convergence* **c :** the acquisition of dissimilar characters by related organisms or strains under the influence of unlike environments **2 a :** a turning aside or departure from a direction, course, policy **:** DEVIATION, DIGRESSION ⟨~ from a theoretical norm⟩ **3 :** dissemination of the effect of activity of a single nerve cell through multiple synaptic connections — compare CONVERGENCE **4 :** the depletion of air in a layer or region of the atmosphere due to outflowing winds **syn** see DISSIMILARITY

di·ver·gen·cy \-nsē, -si\ *n* -ES **:** DIVERGENCE

di·ver·gent \dəˈvərjənt, -vōj-, -vəij- *also* dəˈv- *or* ˈdīˈv-\ *adj* [ML *divergent-*, *divergens*, pres. part. of *divergere*] **1 a :** diverging from each other **:** radiating from a common center ⟨~ lines⟩ ⟨the ~ evolution of two species⟩ **:** SPREADING ⟨~ branches⟩ — opposed to *convergent* **b :** differing from each other or from a standard **:** DEVIATING, DEVIANT ⟨how to reconcile these ~ statements⟩ ⟨frowned on his ~ behavior⟩ **2 :** relating to or being an infinite sequence that does not have a limit or an infinite series whose partial sums do not have a limit **3 :** causing divergence of rays ⟨a ~ lens⟩ **syn** see DIFFERENT

di·ver·gent·ly *adv* **:** in a divergent manner

diverging lens *n* **:** a lens that causes divergence of rays and has a virtual focus for parallel rays — compare CONVERGING LENS

di·verg·ing·ly *adv* **:** in a diverging manner

diverging meniscus *n* **:** a meniscus lens that is thicker at the edge than in the center — see LENS illustration

¹di·vers \ˈdīvə(r)z *sometimes* -və(r)s *or* -ˌvərz *or* -ˌvōz *or* -ˌvəiz\ *adj* [ME *divers*, *diverse* — more at DIVERSE] **1** *obs* **:** different in kind or species **:** DIVERSE **2 :** more than one but indefinite in number **:** SEVERAL, VARIOUS, SUNDRY ⟨~ styles of musical expression —Virgil Thomson⟩

²divers \"\ *pron*, *pl in constr* [ME *divers*, *diverse*, fr. *divers*, *diverse*, adj.] **:** an indefinite number more than one (as of persons or objects) ⟨~ of the enemy were captured⟩

³divers *pl of* DIVER

di·verse \dīˈvərs, dəˈv-, -vōs, -vəis\ *adj* [ME *divers*, *diverse*, fr. OF & L; OF *divers*, fr. L *diversus*, fr. past part. of *divertere* to turn aside, go different ways, differ — more at DIVERT] **1 :** differing from one another **:** UNLIKE, DISTINCT ⟨offered ~ judgments on the matter⟩ ⟨a people of such ~ racial origins⟩ **2** *obs* **:** DIVERS 2 **3 :** having or capable of having various forms or qualities ⟨the exceedingly ~ nature of man⟩ **:** composed of unlike or distinct elements ⟨a most ~ group of politicians⟩ **syn** see DIFFERENT

di·verse·ly *adv* [ME, fr. *diverse* + *-ly*] **:** in a diverse manner **:** in different ways **:** VARIOUSLY ⟨treated the subject most ~⟩

di·verse·ness *n* -ES [ME *diversenes*, fr. *diverse* + *-nes* -ness] **:** DIVERSITY

diversi- *comb form* [ME, fr. MF, fr. L, fr. *diversus*] **:** different **:** diverse **:** diversely ⟨*diversi*form⟩ ⟨*diversi*foliate⟩

di·ver·si·fi·ca·tion \dəˌvərsəfəˈkāshən, -vōs-, -vəis- *also* (ˌ)dīˌ-\ *n* -s [ML *diversification-*, *diversificatio*, fr. *diversificatus* (past part. of *diversificare* to diversify) + L *-ion-*, *-io* -ion — more at DIVERSIFY] **1 :** the act or process of diversifying or becoming diversified **:** the state of being diversified ⟨~ of our population⟩ **2 a :** the practice of spreading investments among a variety of securities or classes of securities **b :** the act or policy of increasing the variety of products or manufactures (as of a manufacturing concern)

diversified *adj* **1 :** having variety of character, of form, or of the elements of composition ⟨~ musical program ranging from classical to modern⟩ ⟨~ scenery⟩ **2 a :** having investments distributed among a variety of securities **b :** producing a variety of crops or manufactures

di·ver·si·form \dəˈvərsəˌfȯrm, dīˈ-\ *adj* [*diversi-* + *-form*] **:** varied or differing in form

di·ver·si·fy \dəˈvərsəˌfī, -vōs-, -vəis- *also* dīˈ-\ *vb* -ED/-ING/-ES [ML *diversificare*, fr. LL *diversificus* varied, fr. L *diversi-* + *-ficus* -fic] *vt* **1 a :** to make diverse (as in character, form, quality) **:** give variety to **:** VARIEGATE ⟨~ the educational program by introducing new subjects⟩ ⟨skyscrapers which now ~ the skyline —P.E.James⟩ **b :** to distribute (as investments) among different kinds of securities **c :** to increase the variety of the products or manufactures of ⟨seeking manufacturing plants to ~ a predominantly agricultural economy —*Wall Street Jour.*⟩ **2** *obs* **:** to differentiate or distinguish (one) from another **~** *vi* **:** to produce variety **:** VARY; *specif* **:** to produce a variety of crops or of manufactures ⟨low wheat prices forced farmers to ~⟩

di·ver·sion \dəˈvərzhən, dīˈ-, -vōj, -vəi|, *Brit often & US sometimes* |shən\ *n* -s [F, fr. MF, fr. LL *diversion-*, *diversio*, fr. L *diversus* (past part. of *divertere* to turn aside, go different ways, differ) + *-ion-*, *-io* -ion — more at DIVERT] **1 a :** the act or an instance of diverting from one course or use to another ⟨charged the board with ~ of public funds⟩ **b :** the act or an instance of diverting (as the mind or attention) from some activity or concern ⟨recommended ~ of his mind from business⟩ **c :** a turning aside of one's attention, course, or concern **:** DEVIATION, DIGRESSION ⟨a ~ from the main highway⟩ ⟨mars the story by a ~ into irrelevant material⟩ **2 a :** something that turns the mind from serious concerns or ordinary matters and relaxes or amuses **:** RELAXATION, AMUSEMENT, PASTIME ⟨hiking is a favorite ~⟩ **b :** the turning of the mind to pleasure **:** the act of receiving pleasure or amusement ⟨life consisted . . . entirely of ~ —V.G.Heiser⟩ ⟨a play performed for our ~⟩ **c :** VARIATION 5 **3 :** the act or an instance of drawing the attention and force of an enemy from the point of the principal operation (as by an attack or feint which diverts attention) **4 a :** the act or process of changing the route or destination of a shipment while in transit — compare RECONSIGNMENT **b** *Brit* **:** DETOUR **c :** a channel constructed to divert water from one course or body of water to another

di·ver·sion·al \-nᵊl\ *adj* **:** used for or tending to produce diversion or recreation ⟨~ activities for tuberculosis patients⟩

di·ver·sion·ary \-ˌnerē, -ri\ *adj* **1 :** tending to draw attention away from the principal or most important concern **2** *of a military operation* **:** intended to draw the enemy's forces away from the point of principal attack

di·ver·sion·ist \-ˌnəst\ *n* -s **:** one that engages in irregular military action, sabotage, or subversive and disruptive activity behind enemy lines or that engages in such activity against his own government

di·ver·si·ty \dəˈvərsəd·ē, dīˈ-, -vəs-,-vəis-, -ətē, -i\ *n* -ES [ME *diversite*, fr. MF *diversité*, fr. L *diversitat-, diversitas*, fr. *diversus* + *-itat-, -itas* -ity] **1 :** the condition of being different or having differences **:** VARIETY ⟨much ~ in their choices⟩ ⟨~ of opinion⟩ **2 :** an instance of being different **:** a point of difference ⟨the climatic *diversities* result in a great variety of plant life⟩ **3** *archaic* **:** a variety, kind, or species esp. of plants or animals **4 :** diversity of state or national citizenship esp. in determining the jurisdiction of a court **syn** see VARIETY

diversity factor *n* **:** the ratio of the sum of the maximum power demands of the subdivisions of any electric power system to the maximum demand of the whole system measured at the point of supply

diversity reception *n* **:** a method of radio reception in which the best signal impulse is automatically selected from among those available (as those produced by several antennas in different locations)

di·vers·ly *pronunc at* ¹DIVERS + lē *or* li\ *adv* [ME, fr. *divers* + *-ly* — more at DIVERSE] **:** in divers ways **:** VARIOUSLY

diversory *n* -ES [L *diversorium*, alter. (influenced by *divertere*) of *deversorium*, fr. *deversus* (past part. of *devertere* to turn aside, go aside, turn in at an inn, lodge, fr. *de-* + *vertere* to turn) + *-orium* -ory — more at WORTH] *obs* **:** a place of shelter by the wayside

diver's palsy *or* **diver's paralysis** *n* **:** CAISSON DISEASE

¹**di·vert** \dəˈvər|t, dīˈ-, -vǝ̄|, -vəi|, *usu* |d.+V\ *vb* -ED/-ING/-S [ME *diverten*, fr. MF & L; MF *divertir*, fr. L *divertere* (also *divortere*) to turn aside, go different ways, differ, fr. *di-* (fr. *dis-* away, apart) + *vertere* to turn — more at WORTH] *vi* **:** to turn aside from a course or purpose **:** DEVIATE ⟨traffic was forced to ~ to side streets⟩ ⟨was trained as a surgeon, but ~*ed* to diplomacy⟩ **:** DIGRESS ⟨~*ed* drearily to the figure he would cut —George Meredith⟩ **~** *vt* **1 a :** to turn from one course, direction, objective, or use to another ⟨~ a stream to a new channel⟩ ⟨~ tax money to his own pocket⟩ **:** turn aside **:** DEFLECT ⟨~ calamity from his own head⟩ **b :** to turn or draw (as the mind or the attention) from one occupation or concern to another **:** DISTRACT ⟨grief did not ~ him from his duty⟩ ⟨Bunker Hill . . . had ~*ed* General Gage's mind —Kenneth Roberts⟩ **2 a :** to give pleasure or amusement to **:** ENTERTAIN ⟨the people ~*ed* themselves with games⟩ **b :** excite mirth in ⟨he was ~*ed*, though his face betrayed no sign of his amusement —C.B.Kelland⟩ **3** *archaic* **:** to while away (the time) **syn** see AMUSE, DISSUADE, TURN

²**di·vert** \diˈvert\ *n* -S *Scot* **:** ENTERTAINMENT, DIVERSION

di·vert·ed·ly *adv* **:** with amusement **:** AMUSEDLY

di·vert·ible \dəˈvər|d·əbəl, dīˈ-, -vǝ̄|,-vəi|, |təb-\ *adj* **:** capable of being diverted

di·ver·ti·cle \|d·əkəl, |təˈ-\ *n* -S [L *diverticulum* — more at DIVERTICULUM] *archaic* **:** BYWAY, BYPATH

di·ver·tic·u·lar \ˌdīvə(r)ˈtikyələ(r)\ *adj* [NL *diverticulum* + E *-ar*] **:** consisting of or resembling a diverticulum

di·ver·tic·u·late \-lət, *usu* -əd.+V\ *also* **di·ver·tic·u·lat·ed** \-ˌlād·əd, -ātəd\ *adj* [NL *diverticulum* + E *-ate, -ated*] **:** having a diverticulum

di·ver·tic·u·lec·to·my \ˌdīvə(r)ˌtikyəˈlektəmē, -mi\ *n* -ES [ISV *diverticul-* (fr. NL *diverticulum*) + *-ectomy*] **:** the surgical removal of a diverticulum

di·ver·tic·u·li·tis \-ˈlīd·əs, -ītəs\ *n* -ES [NL, fr. *diverticulum* + *-itis*] **:** inflammation of a diverticulum

di·ver·tic·u·lo·sis \-ˈlōsəs\ *n* -ES [NL, fr. *diverticulum* + *-osis*] **:** an intestinal disorder characterized by the presence of many diverticula

di·ver·tic·u·lum \ˌdīvə(r)ˈtikyələm\ *n, pl* **diverticu·la** \-lə\ [NL, fr. L, bypath, prob. alter. of *deverticulum*, fr. *devertere* to turn aside, go aside + *-i-* + *-culum* -cle — more at DIVERSORY] **1 :** a pocket or closed branch opening off a main passage **2 a :** an abnormal pouch or sac opening from a hollow organ (as the intestine or bladder) **b :** a blind tube or sac branching off from a cavity or canal of the body **3 :** one of the filaments arising from the fused cells of a fertilized procarp and giving rise to carpospores in certain red algae **4 :** a branch produced laterally on the mycelium of a fungus (as of the genus *Pythium*)

di·ver·ti·men·to \dəˌvərd·əˈmen(ˌ)tō, -ver-, dēˌver-\ *n, pl* **divertimen·ti** \-n(ˌ)tē\ [It, lit., diversion, amusement, fr. *divertire* to divert, amuse (fr. F *divertir*) + *-mento* -ment — more at DIVERT] **1 :** an instrumental musical composition having from 4 to 10 movements that is written as a chamber work in the form of a dance suite or in the form and style of symphonic music **:** SERENADE **2 :** DIVERTISSEMENT 1

diverting *adj* **:** giving pleasure or causing mirth **:** AMUSING, ENTERTAINING ⟨a ~ story⟩ — **di·vert·ing·ly** *adv* — **di·vert·ing·ness** *n* -ES

divertise *vt* -ED/-ING/-S [F *divertiss-*, stem of *divertir* to divert — more at DIVERT] *obs* **:** DIVERT, ENTERTAIN

di·ver·tise·ment \dəˈvərd·ə̇mənt, -əzm-\ *n* -S [F *divertissement*, fr. MF, fr. *divertiss-* + *-ment*] **1 :** DIVERSION, AMUSEMENT, RECREATION ⟨jam sessions and nightclubbing, among other ~*s* —Bernard Kalb⟩ **2 :** DIVERTISSEMENT 1

di·ver·tisse·ment \dəˈvərd·əsmənt, -əzm-, F dēvertēsmäⁿ\ *n* -S [F, lit., diversion, amusement] **1 a :** a suite of ballet numbers used as an interlude in a full-length ballet, opera, or similar program **b :** a light diverting piece of music **c :** an episode in a fugue **d :** a potpourri of airs **2 :** DIVERTIMENTO 1 **3 a :** an activity or performance that gives pleasure and entertainment to participants or audience **:** DIVERSION, ENTERTAINMENT ⟨such ~*s* as horse racing, dog racing, and swimming⟩ **b :** an artistic or intellectual production of a light, informal, and entertaining character ⟨detective story . . . has an honorable history as an intellectual ~ —Anthony Boucher⟩

di·ver·tive \dəˈvərd·iv, dī-\ *adj, archaic* **:** tending to divert **:** AMUSING, INTERESTING

di·ver·tor *or* **di·vert·er** \-d·ə(r)\ *n* -S **:** a resistor used to divert part of an electric current (as one connected in shunt with the series winding or with the commutating-pole winding of a machine

diverts *pres 3d sing of* DIVERT, *pl of* DIVERT

¹**di·ves** \ˈdīˌvēz\ *n, pl* **di·ves·es** \-ēzəz\ *usu cap* [ME, fr. L, rich, rich man (often interpreted as a proper noun in Luke 16), prob. fr. *divus* divine, god (the gods being distributors of largess) — more at DEITY] **:** a rich man **:** a rich worldling

²**dives** *pres 3d sing of* DIVE, *pl of* DIVE

dives costs \"-\ *n pl, usu cap D* [L *dives* rich man] **:** ordinary costs allowed in English law to a successful plaintiff by a chancery court as distinguished from costs on a reduced scale allowed to one suing in forma pauperis

di·vest \dīˈvest, dəˈ-\ *vt* -ED/-ING/-S [alter (influenced by L *di-*, fr. *dis-* ¹dis-) of *devest*] **1 a :** to undress or strip esp. of clothing, ornament, or equipment ⟨~ him of his clothes⟩ ⟨trees ~*ed* of summer finery⟩ **b :** to dispossess or deprive esp. of possessions, qualities, rights ⟨compelled to ~ himself of his holdings⟩ **2 a** *archaic* **:** to lay aside **:** ABANDON **b :** to take away (possessions or vested rights) **:** DEVEST **syn** see STRIP

di·ves·ti·tive \-stəd·iv\ *adj* [*divestiture* + *-ive*] *law* **:** having the function or effect of divesting ⟨a ~ fact puts an end to a right altogether —T.E.Holland⟩

di·ves·ti·ture \-stəˌchu̇(ə)r, -ˌchər\ *n* -S [*divest* + *-iture* (as in *investiture*)] **1 :** the act of divesting or state of being divested **2 :** the compulsory transfer of title or disposal of interests (as stock in a corporation) upon government order

di·vest·ment \-s(t)mənt\ *n* -S **:** DIVESTITURE

di·vid·able \dəˈvīd·əbəl\ *adj* **:** DIVISIBLE

¹**di·vide** \dəˈvīd\ *vb* -ED/-ING/-S [ME *dividen*, fr. L *dividere*, fr. *di-* (fr. *dis-* apart) + *-videre* to separate — more at DIS-, WIDOW] *vt* **1 a :** to separate into two or more parts, areas, groups **:** split up ⟨~ the city into wards⟩ **b** (1) **:** to separate into classes, categories, or divisions **:** CLASSIFY ⟨~ the field of history into epochs⟩ (2) *logic* **:** to separate (classes or class terms) by abstraction or by restriction of denotation **:** DISTINGUISH **c :** to pass through **:** cleave in passage ⟨the swift ship *dividing* the waves⟩ **2 a :** to separate into parts or portions and give out in shares **:** DISTRIBUTE ⟨~ the profits among the several owners of the business⟩ — sometimes used with *up* ⟨they *divided* up the remaining food⟩ **b :** to possess, enjoy, or make use of in common **:** share in ⟨~ the blame with his companion⟩ **c :** to separate into parts or portions and assign to or set apart for various dispositions, concerns, or activities ⟨~ his time between the office and the golf course⟩ **3 a :** to cause to be separate, distinct, or apart from one another ⟨deep gulf which . . . ~*s* the living from the dead —W.R.Inge⟩ **:** keep apart by or as if by a partition ⟨stone walls ~ the fields⟩ **b :** to separate into opposing sides or parties **:** disunite in opinion or interest **:** set at variance **:** cause to disagree ⟨no controversy had ever so *divided* the country⟩ ⟨students were *divided* on the issue⟩ **c** *Brit* **:** to call (a parliamentary body) to a vote on a question or issue **4 a :** to mark divisions on **:** GRADUATE ⟨~ a sextant⟩ **b** (1) **:** to subject to mathematical division (2) **:** to locate one or more points on (a line or its extension) **c** *obs* **:** to play or sing in a florid style **:** perform divisions upon (as a melody) **~** *vi* **1** *archaic* **:** to make distinctions (as in logic) ⟨~ with reason between self-love and society —Francis Bacon⟩ **2 :** to perform mathematical division **3 a** (1) **:** to become separated into parts ⟨each of the four chromosomes ~*s* longitudinally —J.B.Grace⟩ (2) **:** to branch out **:** FORK, DIVERGE ⟨the railway ~*s* here into two lines⟩ (3) **:** to become separate from another part ⟨Collier county . . . *divided* from Lee county in 1923 —*Amer. Guide Series: Fla.*⟩ **b :** to become separated (as in opinion or interest) ⟨on these issues the court *divided*⟩ **:** become disunited ⟨the party *divided* into warring factions⟩ **c :** to vote by separating into two groups with those in favor in one group and those opposed in another ⟨the House again *divided*, and the bill was passed by 11 votes⟩ **4 a** *archaic* **:** to have a share **:** PARTAKE ⟨you shall in all ~ with us —Shak.⟩ **b :** to give out something in portions or shares ⟨having plenty, he ~*s* with others⟩ **syn** see DISTRIBUTE, SEPARATE

²**divide** \"\ *n* -S **1 :** a division or distribution esp. of spoils or assets **2 a :** a dividing ridge or section of high ground between two basins or areas of drainage **:** WATERSHED **b :** a point or line of division (as between differing situations or sets of circumstances) ⟨a period marking the ~ between two eras of American history⟩

divided *adj* **1 a** (1) **:** separated into parts or pieces ⟨finely ~ particles of steel⟩ (2) **:** consisting of distinct parts or divisions ⟨a book ~ into 30 chapters⟩ **b :** separated into distinct divisions, sections, classes, groups **c** *of a leaf* **:** cut into distinct parts by incisions extending to the base or to the midrib — compare CLEFT, PARTED **d :** subjected to logical division **e** *of a road* **:** having the stream of traffic moving in one direction separated (as by a strip of planted land) from that moving in the opposite direction **2 a :** separated into opposing sides or groups **:** at variance with each other **:** DISUNITED ⟨the allies were sharply ~ over this issue⟩ **b :** distributed among two or more specified objects or individuals ⟨the population is about equally ~ between Swedes and Norwegians⟩ **:** directed or moved (as by affection, inclination, duty) toward conflicting interests, states, or objects ⟨~ loyalties kept him aloof from the struggle⟩ **c :** DIVISI **3 :** separated by distance from another **:** kept apart ⟨familiar objects from which she had never dreamed of being ~ —James Joyce⟩ **4** *Hindu law* **:** separated or freed from the bond or obligation of the joint family ⟨a ~ brother⟩ — **di·vid·ed·ness** *n* -ES

divided highway *n* **:** a highway of four or more traffic lanes having two roadways with a median strip between them separating opposing traffic streams — called also *dual highway*

di·vid·ed·ly *adv* **:** in a divided manner **:** SEPARATELY, INDIVIDUALLY ⟨viewed the matter ~ from the standpoints of their several interests⟩

divided pitch *n* **:** the distance between corresponding points in two adjacent threads measured parallel to the axis in a multiple-threaded screw — compare PITCH, SCREW THREAD

divided skirt *n* **:** a woman's garment that gives the appearance of a flared skirt but is divided and seamed in the manner of trousers

divided skirt

divided stop *n* **:** an organ stop so arranged that the treble and bass registers may be drawn independently of one another

div·i·dend \ˈdivəˌdend *sometimes* -ˌdənd *or* -dᵊnd\ *n* -S [ME *divident*, fr. L *dividendum* something to be divided, neut. of *dividendus*, gerundive of *dividere* to divide — more at DIVIDE] **1 a :** an individual share of something distributed among a number of recipients **b :** a share in a pro rata distribution (as of profits) to stockholders **c :** a share of surplus allocated to a policyholder in a participating insurance policy generally representing a return of a portion of the premium not needed to meet losses and expenses and a distribution of earnings from investment **d :** a bonus item given to a customer with each purchase of a set number of items ⟨a book ~ given with every four books purchased⟩ **e :** the return or reward resulting from an activity, effort, or undertaking ⟨better training was paying big ~*s* in increased efficiency⟩ **f :** something received unexpectedly or in addition to that which is usual or that which is expected or sought **:** BONUS ⟨three fine stories in the book, and, as a ~, all happen to be true⟩ **g :** a portion of a mixed iced drink remaining after the regular servings have been poured out ⟨there's a ~ here for someone before I mix another round⟩ **2** [AF *dividende*, fr. L *dividendum*] **a obs :** the act or an instance of dividing (as profits or spoils) among a number of individuals **b :** a pro-rata distribution of money, securities, or other property; *esp* **:** such a distribution to corporate shareholders or to creditors of a bankrupt estate — see STOCK DIVIDEND **3** *math* **:** a number or quantity to be divided **4** *archaic* **:** a body of land in one patent or survey — **dividend off :** EX DIVIDEND — **dividend on :** CUM DIVIDEND

dividend warrant *n* **:** an order (as a check payable to a shareholder) in which a dividend is paid

di·vid·er \dəˈvīdə(r)\ *n* -S **1 :** one that divides **2** *usu* **dividers** *pl* **:** an instrument for measuring or marking (as in dividing lines and transferring dimensions) **:** COMPASS **3 :** one of a series of transverse timbers in a mine shaft which help to resist lateral pressure on the wall plates and divide the shaft into compartments — called also *bunton* **4 :** a prow on the outer end of the cutter bar of a mower or binder that parts off the crop to be cut **5 :** the second incisor tooth of a horse situated between the center and corner incisors on each side — compare NIPPER **6 :** a piece of material (as paperboard) placed between adjacent articles in a shipping case to prevent damage **7 :** a device that divides dough into equal portions (as for rolls); *also* **:** a bakery worker who operates such a device **8 :** a mechanical device used in knitting for equalizing the amount of yarn in each loop of a course **9 :** something serving as a partition between separate spaces within a larger area ⟨a low bookcase ~ between living room and dining area⟩

dividers

divides *pres 3d sing of* DIVIDE, *pl of* DIVIDE

dividing *adj* [fr. pres. part. of ¹*divide*] **:** serving to separate (as regions) ⟨the ~ line between two estates⟩ **:** serving to divide (as into parts) ⟨a ~ machine⟩ — **di·vid·ing·ly** *adv*

dividing engine *or* **dividing machine** *n* **:** a machine for graduating circles (as for surveying instruments) or bars (as for scales) or for spacing off and cutting teeth in wheels

dividing head *n* **:** INDEX HEAD

dividing network *n* **:** CROSSOVER NETWORK

dividing plate *n* **:** INDEX PLATE

divi-divi \ˌdivēˌdivē, ˌdēvēˌdēvē\ *n, pl* **divi-divi** *or* **divi-divis** [Sp *dividivi*, of Cariban origin; akin to Cumanagoto *diwidiwi* divi-divi] **1 :** a small tree (*Caesalpinia coriaria*) of tropical America **2 :** the twisted astringent pods of the divi-divi tree that yield a large proportion of tannin

di·vid·u·al \dəˈvijəwəl\ *adj* [L *dividuus* (fr. *dividere* to divide) + E *-al* — more at DIVIDE] **1** *archaic* **:** SEPARATE, DISTINCT **2** *archaic* **:** DIVISIBLE, DIVIDED **3** *archaic* **:** divided among or shared by a number ⟨the moon . . . her reign with thousand lesser lights ~ holds —John Milton⟩ — **di·vid·u·al·ly** *adv, archaic*

di·vid·u·ous \-wəs\ *adj* [L *dividuus*] *archaic* **:** DIVISIBLE, SEPARABLE, DIVIDED

div·il \ˈdivəl\ *dial var of* DEVIL

div·i·na·tion \ˌdivəˈnāshən\ *n* -S [ME *divinacioun*, fr. L *divination-, divinatio*, fr. *divinatus* (past part. of *divinare* to divine) + *-ion-, -io* -ion — more at DIVINE (v.)] **1 :** the art or practice that seeks to foresee or foretell future events or discover hidden knowledge usu. by means of augury or by making use of a psychical condition of the diviner in which supernatural powers are assumed to cooperate (as in the case of a spiritualistic medium or a crystal gazer); *also* **:** an instance of this practice **2 :** unusual insight or intuitive perception ⟨the brilliant ~*s* of the ancient Greeks in the field of atomic theory⟩

div·i·na·tor \ˈdivəˌnād·ə(r)\ *n* -S [LL, fr. L *divinatus* + *-or*] **:** one that practices divination **:** DIVINER

di·vin·a·to·ry \dəˈvinəˌtōrē, -ˈvīn-; ˈdivən-; *chiefly Brit* ˈdivəˌnātəri\ *adj* [*divination* + *-ory*] **:** of or relating to divination **:** used in divination ⟨~ lots⟩ **:** using or depending upon intuition or perception ⟨mysterious and ~ healing powers —*Jour. Amer. Med. Assoc.*⟩

¹**di·vine** \dəˈvīn *sometimes* dēˈ-\ *adj, sometimes* -ER/-EST [ME *devin, divin*, fr. MF, fr. L *divinus*, fr. *divus* divine, god + *-inus* -ine — more at DEITY] **1 a :** of or relating to God **:** proceeding from God ⟨the ~ will⟩ ⟨~ judgment⟩ **b :** of or relating to a god **:** having the nature of a god ⟨the custom of killing the ~ king upon any serious failure of his . . . powers —J.G. Frazer⟩ **:** proceeding from a god ⟨the ~ strength of Achilles⟩ **:** like a god or like that of a god ⟨~ capacity for love⟩ **2 a :** devoted or addressed to God **:** RELIGIOUS, HOLY, SACRED ⟨summoned the people to ~ worship⟩ **b** *obs* **:** relating to divinity or theology **:** concerned with sacred things **3 a :** supremely good or admirable ⟨admired the writings of the ~ Shakespeare⟩ ⟨her pies were simply ~⟩ **b :** having a sublime or inspired character ⟨in her role as the mother, woman is regarded as ~ —R.N.Dandekar⟩

²**divine** \"\ *n* -S [ME *divine, devine*, fr. ML *divinus*, fr. L, soothsayer, fr. *divinus*, adj.] **1 :** a minister of the gospel **:** PRIEST, CLERGYMAN ⟨a Puritan ~⟩ **2 :** one skilled in divinity **:** THEOLOGIAN ⟨great Protestant ~*s* such as Luther, Calvin, Melanchthon, and Zwingli⟩ **3 :** a priest, theologian, or spiritual guide of a non-Christian religion **4** *often cap* **:** something having the qualities and attributes of an ultimate reality that is regarded as sacred ⟨man's relation to the ~⟩

³**divine** \"\ *vb* -ED/-ING/-S [ME *devinen, divinen*, fr. MF & L; MF *deviner*, fr. L *divinare*, fr. *divinus* soothsayer] *vt* **1 a :** to discover or make known by divination ⟨she *divined* the fall of the city⟩ **b :** to discover or locate (as water) by means of a divining rod **2 a :** to perceive, make out, or discover intuitively or through keenness of insight ⟨*divined* her unhappiness before she had uttered a word⟩ ⟨no other critic has so well *divined* the poet's essential meaning⟩ **b** *archaic* **:** to be or give a sign or indication of (future events or something unknown) **:** PORTEND ⟨all things wait for and ~ him —R.W.Emerson⟩ **~** *vi* **1 a :** to prophesy with supernatural aid ⟨a Cassandra, *divining* of evils to come⟩ **b :** to use or practice divination ⟨*divined* in tent-shaking rites to discover the . . . cause of illness or death —*Amer. Anthropologist*⟩ **2 a :** CONJECTURE, SUPPOSE, INFER ⟨I either know them or ~ by the root —O.W.Holmes †1935⟩ **b :** to perceive, recognize, or acquire understanding concerning some fact or circumstance esp. by insight or intuition ⟨all the time only too well *divining* —John Galsworthy⟩ **syn** see FORESEE

divine decree *n* **:** DECREE 2b

divine healing *n* **:** healing attributed to the direct agency of God usu. in response to faith

divine liturgy *n, often cap D&L* **:** LITURGY 1

di·vine·ly *adv* **1 a :** in a divine or godlike manner **b :** to a supreme degree ⟨~ beautiful⟩ **:** supremely well **:** EXCELLENTLY ⟨she danced ~⟩ **2 :** by the agency or influence of God ⟨we are ~ endowed with certain rights⟩

di·vine·ness \-īnnəs\ *n* -ES **:** the quality or state of being divine **:** superhuman or supreme excellence **:** DIVINITY

divine office *n, often cap D&O* **:** the daily office for the canonical hours of prayer; *esp* **:** BREVIARY 2b

¹**di·vin·er** \dəˈvīnə(r)\ *n* -S [ME *devinour, divinour*, fr. MF *devineor*, fr. LL *divinator*, fr. L *divinatus* (past part. of *divinare* to divine) + *-or* — more at DIVINE (v.)] **:** one that practices divination **:** SOOTHSAYER, ORACLE; *specif* **:** one that seeks to discover the location of water or minerals underground with the aid of a divining rod

²**diviner** *comparative of* DIVINE

divine right *n* **1 :** the right of a king to rule as set forth by the theory of government that his right to govern came directly from God, that he could do no wrong, and that neither he nor his heirs could forfeit their right to the throne and to the obedience of the people **2 :** a right or claim (as to a certain privilege or possession) supposed to proceed from God

divine service *n* **:** the worship of God; *specif* **:** a public service for worship

divinest *superlative of* DIVINE

diving *adj* [fr. pres. part. of ¹*dive*] **:** that dives or is used for diving ⟨swam over to the ~ raft⟩

diving beetle *n* **:** a beetle of the family Dytiscidae habitually living under water and rising to the surface to obtain air

diving bell *n* **:** an early diving apparatus consisting of a steel cylinder or box open only at the bottom and supplied with compressed air by a hose

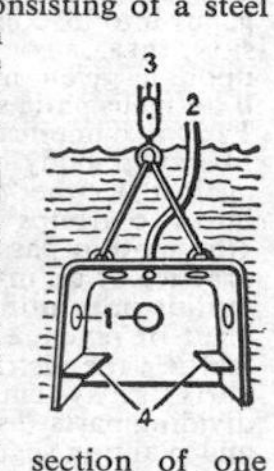

section of one form of diving bell: *1* windows, *2* air tube, *3* hoisting tackle, *4* seats

diving board *n* **:** SPRINGBOARD

diving boat *n* **:** a small boat specially fitted for tending deep-sea divers

diving buck *n* [trans. of Afrik *duikerbok*] **:** DUIKER 1

diving duck *n* **:** any of various ducks that frequent deep waters and obtain their food by diving — compare DABBLER

diving petrel *n* **:** any of several diving birds of the southern hemisphere that somewhat resemble auks in appearance and habits and constitute the family Pelecanoididae

diving plane *also* **diving rudder** *n* **:** a rudder or plane structure hung on a horizontal axis on a submarine for steering it in an upward or downward direction

diving suit *or* **diving dress** *n* **:** a waterproof suit used in diving; *esp* **:** one that has a helmet and that is supplied with air pumped through a tube to enable the diver to breathe under water

di·vin·i·fy \dəˈvinəˌfī\ *vt* -ED/-ING/-ES [L *divinus* divine + E *-ify* — more at DIVINE] **:** to make divine **:** DEIFY

divining *pres part of* DIVINE

divining rod *n* **:** a forked rod believed to divine the presence of water or minerals by dipping sharply downward when held over a vein

di·vin·i·ty \dəˈvinəd·ē, -ətē, -i\ *n* -ES [ME *devinite, divinite*, fr. MF *devinité, divinité*, fr. L *divinitat-, divinitas*, fr. *divinus* divine + *-itat-, -itas* -ity — more at DIVINE] **1 :** the quality or state of being divine **:** nature or essence of God **:** GODHEAD ⟨the ~ of Jesus⟩ **2 :** DEITY, GOD **:** ultimate reality ⟨there's a ~ that shapes our ends —Shak.⟩ **3 :** a celestial being inferior to the supreme God but superior to man ⟨one of the subservient *divinities*⟩ **4 :** the science of divine things **:** the science that deals with God, his laws and moral government, and the way of salvation **:** THEOLOGY **5 a** *also* **divinity fudge :** fudge made from whipped whites of eggs, white or brown sugar, and nuts **b :** a frosting made of whipped whites of eggs, corn syrup, sugar, and flavoring beaten until of the right consistency to spread

divinity calf *n* [so called fr. its use in the binding of theological books] **:** a style of bookbinding featuring calf stained dark brown and blind title and decoration

divinity circuit binding *n* **:** a style of bookbinding that is often used for Bibles and hymnbooks and that is characterized by rounded corners on both book and cover and by a flexible leather cover with projecting flaps bent over to protect the edges of the leaves — called also *circuit binding, yapp binding*

divinity school *n* **:** SEMINARY 2b(4)

di·vin·i·ty·ship \-ˌship\ *n* **:** the quality or state of being divine **:** the status of a divinity

di·vi·ni·za·tion \ˌdivənəˈzāshən, -ˌnīˈ-\ *n* -s **:** the act, process, or an instance of investing with a divine character or of making into an object of worship **:** DEIFICATION, GLORIFICATION ⟨~ of the state is a feature of his political thought⟩

div·i·nize \ˈcivə,nīz\ *vt* -ED/-ING/-S [F *diviniser*, fr. *divin* divine + *-iser* -ize — more at DIVINE] **:** to deify or clothe with a divine character **:** EXALT, GLORIFY ⟨the romantic poets *divinized* nature⟩

¹di·vinyl \(ˈ)dī+\ *n* [ISV *di-* + *vinyl*] **:** BUTADIENE

²divinyl \"\ *adj* **:** containing two vinyl groups in the molecule

di·vi·nyl·acetylene \(ˌ)=,==+\ *n* [¹*divinyl* + *acetylene*] **:** a liquid hydrocarbon $CH_2{=}CHC{\equiv}CCH{=}CH_2$ formed by trimerization of acetylene and used in surface coatings since it polymerizes to a hard resin on contact with air

di·vi·nyl·benzene \"+\ *n* [¹*divinyl* + *benzene*] **:** a liquid hydrocarbon $C_6H_4(CH{-}CH_2)_2$ obtained usu. as a mixture containing the ortho, meta, and para isomers and used in polymerization (as with styrene for making ion-exchange resins)

di·vi·sa \dəˈvēsə, -ēzə\ *n* -s [Sp, lit., emblem, heraldic device, fr. fem. of *diviso* (obs. past part. of *dividir* to divide), fr. L *divisus*] **:** colored ribbons denoting the breeder that are attached by a barb to a bull's withers as it enters the bullfighting arena

di·vi·si \dəˈvēzē\ *adj* [It, pl. of *diviso* (past part. of *dividere* to *divide*), fr. L *divisus* divided — more at DIVISION] **:** SEPARATE — used as a direction in music for orchestral players reading the same musical staff to divide into two or more voice parts; abbr. *div.*

di·vis·i·bil·i·ty \də,vizəˈbiləd-ē, -ətē, -i\ *n* -ES **:** the quality or state of being divisible

di·vis·i·ble \dəˈvizəbəl\ *adj* [LL *divisibilis*, fr. L *divisus* + *-ibilis* -ible] **:** capable of being or liable to be divided or separated — **di·vis·i·ble·ness** \-nəs\ *n* -ES

divisible contract *n* **:** a contract containing agreements one of which can be separated from the other so that one part may be valid or enforceable although another is void or so that a right may accrue on one and not on another

divisible offense *n* **:** an offense the commission of which involves the commission of one of a lesser grade so that on the former there can be an acquittal and on the latter a conviction

divisible surplus *n* **:** the part of the annual surplus fund of an insurance company which is available for payment in the form of dividends to policyholders

di·vi·sion \dəˈvizhən\ *n* -s [ME *devisioun*, fr. MF *division*, fr. L *division-*, *divisio*, fr. *divisus* (past part. of *dividere* to divide) + *-ion-*, *-io* -ion — more at DIVIDE] **1 a :** the act, process, or an instance of dividing into parts or portions **:** PARTITION ⟨made a ~ of his empire⟩ ⟨~ of the day into hours, minutes, seconds⟩ **:** the state of being divided ⟨remarked on the peculiar geographic ~ of the state⟩ **b :** the act, process, or an instance of dividing or distributing among a number **:** DISTRIBUTION, APPORTIONMENT ⟨protested his method of ~ of the profits⟩ **c** *obs* **:** ARRANGEMENT, DISPOSITION ⟨never set a squadron in the field, nor the ~ of a battle knows —Shak.⟩ **2 :** one of the parts, sections, or groupings into which a whole is divided **3 a :** the elementary organic unit of combined arms that is tactically and administratively a self-contained unit capable of independent action **b :** a military unit made up normally of five battle groups **c** (1) **:** one of the groups usu. of four ships into which a fleet or large squadron is divided (2) **:** the basic unit of men for administration aboard ship and ashore **d :** a tactical subdivision of a squadron of ships or aircraft **4** *obs* **:** a portion of land allotted to an individual settler or to a group of settlers **5 :** a definite portion of a nation, state, county, or other political unit marked off for administrative, judicial, or other purposes: as **a :** an election district in Great Britain **b :** a subdivision of a province or presidency in British India **6 :** a segment of a transportation system (as a railroad, truckline, pipeline, or airline) designated by management as a semi-independent or autonomous operating unit **7 :** a group of organisms forming part of some larger group; *specif* **:** a major primary category of the plant kingdom — compare PHYLUM **2 8 a :** a subordinate administrative unit of the executive department of the U.S. government usu. ranking below a bureau **b :** a subordinate unit of state and local government **9 :** a competitive class or category (as in boxing and wrestling) based on age, weight, skill, or other standard of eligibility **10 :** a major administrative unit in an education institution of organization usu. embracing several departments ⟨the ~ of modern languages⟩ **11 :** a major administrative unit of an industrial enterprise comprising at least several departments or constituting a complete integrated unit for a specific purpose ⟨the radio ~ of an aviation corporation⟩ **12 a :** something that divides, separates, or marks off ⟨the ~s of the compass mark off its 32 points⟩ **:** a dividing line **b :** the act, process, or an instance of separating or keeping apart (two objects or individuals) ⟨used a screen to complete the ~ of the dining room from the kitchen⟩ **:** the state of being separated **:** SEPARATION ⟨the lovers mourned their hopeless ~⟩ **13 :** the condition or an instance of being divided in opinion or interest **:** DISAGREEMENT, DISUNITY ⟨attempted to exploit the ~s between the two countries⟩ **14 :** the process of finding how many times one number or quantity is contained in another **15 :** the separation of a genus into its constituent species — compare FALLACY OF DIVISION, TREE OF PORPHYRY **16 a :** a florid instrumental variation upon a given melody of 17th and 18th century England **b :** a melismatic song or phrase of the 17th and 18th centuries **17 :** a numerical determination of those members of a deliberative body that are for a motion and those who are against it either by a rising vote or by a physical separation into two groups ⟨a ~ was being taken⟩ ⟨the results of the ~⟩ ⟨the motion passed without a ~ —T.B.Macaulay⟩ **18 :** the practice or an instance of dividing words or word elements in writing or printing by the use of a hyphen **19 :** the apportionment of revenue among carrier participants sharing interline traffic **:** the distribution of revenue or expense among various parts of a system or organization **20 :** plant propagation by dividing parts (as of a crown or a clump of suckers or tubers) and planting segments capable of producing roots and shoots **syn** see PART

di·vi·sion·al \-zhənᵊl, -zhnəl\ *adj* **1 :** that divides **:** marking or noting a division ⟨the ~ line between two states⟩ **2 :** constituting a division or an aliquot part **:** FRACTIONAL ⟨American ~ coins include the dime and the nickel⟩ **3 :** of or relating to a division ⟨the ~ artillery⟩ — **di·vi·sion·al·ly** \-ᵊlē, -əl|, |i\ *adv*

divisional title *n* **:** a title page immediately preceding a major division of a book — called also *part title*

di·vi·sion·ary \-zhə,nerē\ *adj* **:** DIVISIONAL

division bar *n* **:** a structural or nonstructural element connecting or aligning two panels or pieces of glass

division bell *n* **:** a bell rung to summon members of a deliberative body when a vote is to be taken — compare DIVISION 17

division center *n, biol* **:** the structure at the center of the aster or central body **:** CENTRIOLE

division fence *n* **:** a fence separating adjacent areas of the same farm or ranch — distinguished from *line fence*

di·vi·sion·ism \-zhə,nizəm\ *n* -s *often cap* **1 :** the theory or practice of breaking color in painting — compare NEO-IMPRESSIONISM **2 :** the neo-impressionist use of small strokes or dots of pure color juxtaposed on a canvas — compare POINTILLISM

¹di·vi·sion·ist \-zh(ə)nəst\ *n* -s [*division* + *-ist*] **1 :** one that advocates division or disunion ⟨the ~s objected to the existing boundary line⟩ **2** *often cap* **:** an adherent or practitioner of divisionism **:** NEO-IMPRESSIONIST

²divisionist \"\ *adj, often cap* **:** of or relating to divisionism **:** NEO-IMPRESSIONIST

division of labor **:** the separation of labor into its components or into various distinct processes and their apportionment among different individuals, groups, or machines for the purpose of increasing productive efficiency: as **a :** the distribution of occupations or vocations among the members of society ⟨*division of labor* in this tribe is limited to the separation between hunters and farmers⟩ **b :** the breaking up of technical tasks (as in a modern factory) into their component parts or processes and their distribution to specific individuals, groups, or machines **c :** specialization in the production of a specific commodity or group of commodities by a particular region or country

division of powers 1 : SEPARATION OF POWERS **2 :** the principle that sovereignty should be divided between the federal government and the states esp. as expressed by the Constitution of the U.S.

division point *n* **:** the location of a railroad division headquarters

divisions *pl of* DIVISION

division viol *n, obs* **:** VIOLA DA GAMBA

division wall *n* **:** a wall subdividing a building into major portions — compare FIRE WALL, PARTY WALL

di·vi·sive \dəˈvīs|iv, |ēv *also* -viz| *or* -vis| *or* |əv *sometimes* -vīz|\ *adj* [ML *divisivus*, fr. L *divisus* (past part. of *dividere* to divide) + *-ivus* -ive — more at DIVIDE] **1** *archaic* **:** having the quality of separating or distinguishing **:** DISTRIBUTIVE, ANALYTICAL **2 :** creating or tending to create disunity or dissension ⟨criticized his ~ activities in a time of peril⟩ — **di·vi·sive·ly** \|əvlē, -li\ *adv* — **di·vi·sive·ness** \|ivnəs, |ēv- *also* |əv-\ *n* -ES

di·vi·sor \-ˈvīzə(r)\ *n* -s [ME *diviser*, *divisor*, fr. L *divisor*, fr. *divisus* + *-or*] **1 :** the number by which the dividend is divided **2 :** any of various devices for apportioning the water in an irrigating ditch to the holders of water rights in the ditch

di·vi·so·ry \-īz(ə)rē, -ri\ *adj* [L *divisus* + E *-ory*] **1 :** of or relating to division or distribution ⟨~ actions in law relate to the partition of property⟩ **2 :** DIVISIVE 2 ⟨did not understand the ~ issues of the day —W.A.White⟩

di·vi·su·ral line \dəˈvizhərəl-\ *n* [L *divisura* division, fork of a tree (fr. *divisus* + *-ura* -ure) + E *-al*] *of a moss* **:** the median line along which the peristome teeth split

¹di·vorce \dəˈvō(ə)rs, -ó(ə)rs, -ōəs, -ó(ə)s\ *n* -s *often attrib* [ME *devors*, *divors*, *divorse*, fr. MF *divorse*, *divorce*, fr. L *divortium*, fr. *divortere*, *divertere* to turn aside, go different ways, leave one's husband — more at DIVERT] **1 :** a legal dissolution in whole or in part of a marriage relation usu. by a court or other body having competent authority: **a :** an absolute dissolution of a valid marriage made by decree of court for lawful cause arising after the marriage — called also *divorce a vinculo matrimonii*; distinguished from *annulment* **b** *among some non-Christian peoples* **:** a formal separation of man and wife by the act of one party or by consent according to established custom — see TALAK **c :** DECREE OF NULLITY **d :** a divorce a mensa et thoro — compare JUDICIAL SEPARATION, SEPARATION 4a **2 :** disunion of things closely united ⟨the ~ between ownership and management in the corporate system —David Fellman⟩ **:** a complete or final separation ⟨demanded the ~ of the subsidiary from the parent firm⟩

²divorce \" *sometimes* dīˈ- *in vt sense 1*\ *vb* -ED/-ING/-S [MF *divorcer*, fr. *divorce*] *vt* **1 :** SEPARATE, DISUNITE ⟨proposed to ~ church and state⟩ ⟨*divorced* himself from the position taken by his colleagues⟩ ⟨when the second rocket ~s itself from the first spent rocket —William Stringer⟩ **2 :** to get rid of (one's spouse) by divorce **:** dissolve the marriage contract of either wholly or partly **:** separate by divorce **3** *archaic* **:** to put away **:** REMOVE, BANISH **~** *vi* **:** to obtain a divorce **syn** see SEPARATE

di·vorce·able \-səbəl\ *adj* **:** capable of or subject to being divorced

di·vor·cée *also* **di·vor·cee** \də,vōrˈsā, -vórˈ-, -vōəˈ-, -vó(ə)ˈ-, -sē\ *n* -s [F, fr. fem. of *divorcé*, past part. of *divorcer*] **:** a divorced woman

di·vorce·ment \dəˈvōrsmənt, -vórs-,-vōəs-,-vó(ə)s-; *sometimes* dīˈ- — *see* ²DIVORCE\ *n* -s **1** *archaic* **:** the act or an instance of divorcing **:** dissolution of marriage ties **:** DIVORCE **2 :** the act, process, or an instance of separating things closely joined ⟨claimed the ~ of theory from practice had gone to extreme lengths⟩ **:** the state of being separated ⟨too long have art and the church lived in ~ from each other —J.F. Hayward⟩

divorce mill *n* **:** a jurisdiction in which divorce is allowed upon liberal grounds and in which the legal requirements (as residence within the jurisdiction) are easily met

di·vorc·er \-sə(r)\ *n* -s **:** one that divorces or produces a divorce

div·ot \ˈdivət, *usu* -əd-+V\ *n* -s [origin unknown] **1** *Scot* **a :** a square of turf or sod used in covering cottages **b :** a piece of peat used for fuel **2 :** a piece of turf dug from a golf fairway in making a stroke

di·vo·to \dəˈvō(ˌ)tō, dēˈ-, -vōd-(ˌ)ō\ *adv* (*or adj*) [It, devout, fr. LL *devotus* — more at DEVOUT] **:** with religious emotion — used as a direction in music

divs *pl of* DIV

di·vul·gate \dəˈvəl,gāt, dīˈ-; ˈdivə-,ˈdīvə-\ *vt* -ED/-ING/-S [L *divulgatus*, past part. of *divulgare*] **1** *obs* **:** DIVULGE 1 **2** *archaic* **:** DISCLOSE, REVEAL

di·vul·ga·tion \(ˌ)dī,vəlˈgāshən, də,vəl-, ˌdivəl-\ *n* -s [LL *divulgation-*, *divulgatio*, fr. L *divulgatus* + *-ion-*, *-io* -ion] **:** the act or an instance of divulging or spreading abroad **:** PUBLICATION, DISCLOSURE

di·vulge \dəˈvəlj *also* dīˈ-\ *vt* -ED/-ING/-S [ME *divulgen*, fr. L *divulgare*, fr. *di-* (fr. *dis-* ¹dis-) + *vulgare* to make known, publish — more at VULGATE] **1** *archaic* **:** to make public **:** spread abroad **2 :** to tell or make known (a secret or confidence or what had been previously unknown) ⟨knew of the conspiracy, yet did not ~ it⟩ ⟨*divulged* to me his dearest hopes⟩ **syn** see REVEAL

di·vulge·ment \-jmənt\ *n* -s **:** DIVULGENCE

di·vul·gence \-jən(t)s\ *n* -s **:** the act or an instance of divulging **:** REVELATION, DISCLOSURE ⟨forbids the ~ of classified information⟩

di·vulse \dīˈvəls, dəˈ-\ *vt* -ED/-ING/-S [L *divulsus*, past part. of *divellere* — more at DIVEL] **:** to pull or tear apart **:** REND — now used chiefly in surgery

di·vul·sion \-lshən\ *n* -s [L *divulsion-*, *divulsio*, fr. *divulsus* + *-ion-*, *-io* -ion] **:** the act or an instance of tearing or pulling apart or away from — now used chiefly in surgery

di·vul·sive \-lsiv\ *adj* [L *divulsus* + E *-ive*] **:** tending to divulse

di·vul·sor \-lsə(r)\ *n* -s **:** ²DILATOR a

div·vers \ˈdivə(r)z\ *n pl but sing in constr* [*divinity* + *-er* (Oxford Univ. slang suffix) + *-s* (representing pl. *moderations*)] *slang Brit* **:** an examination in biblical literature and history required of every Oxford undergraduate up to 1932

¹div·vy \ˈdivē, -vi\ *n* -ES [by shortening & alter. fr. *dividend*] *slang* **:** DIVISION, DISTRIBUTION ⟨a four-way ~ of the profits⟩

²divvy \"\ *vb* -ED/-ING/-ES *vt, slang* **:** DIVIDE, SHARE, DISTRIBUTE ⟨absent when the money was *divvied*⟩ — often used with *up* ⟨*divvied* up the loot and fled⟩ **~** *vi, slang* **:** to divide or distribute among a number — often used with *up*

diwali *usu cap, var of* DEWALI

¹diwan *var of* DIVAN

²di·wan \dēˈwän, dəˈ-, -ˈwȧn\ *var of* DEWAN

diwani *var of* DEWANEE

dix \ˈdēs\ *also* **dis** \"\ *or* **deece** \"\ *n, pl* **dixes** *also* **dises** *or* **deeces** \ˈdēsəz\ [F *dix* ten, fr. L *decem* — more at TEN] **:** the lowest trump (as the nine or seven) in some card games (as pinochle, bezique, klaberjass) that in certain circumstances is exchangeable for a higher trump and has a scoring value of ten

dix·e·nite \ˈdiksə,nīt, dīˈze,n-\ *n* -s [*di-* + *xen-* + *-ite*] **:** a manganese arsenite and silicate $(MnOH)_2Mn_5SiO_3(AsO_3)_2$ occuring in black hexagonal scales

¹dix·ie \ˈdiksē, -si\ *adj, usu cap* [fr. *Dixie*, nickname for the southern states of the U.S.] **:** of or related to the southern states of the U.S., ⟨a *Dixie* lullaby⟩

²dix·ie \"\ *or* **dixy** \"\ *n, pl* **dixies** [Hindi *degcī*, dim. of *degcā* kettle, pot] *Brit* **:** a mess tin or oval pot often used in camp for cooking or boiling (as tea); *specif* **:** a 12-gallon camp kettle

Dixie \"\ *trademark* — used for a paper cup used esp. for ice cream or beverages

dix·ie·crat \-,krat\ *n* -s *usu cap, often attrib* [*Dixie* Democrat] **:** a member of a secessionist party of southern Democrats who bolted the Democratic party because of its advocacy of civil-rights legislation in the U.S. presidential campaign of 1948 — compare REPUBLOCRAT — **dix·ie·crat·ic** \ˌ==ˈkrad-ik\ *adj, usu cap*

dix·ie·land \-,land, -,laa(ə)nd\ *also* **dixie** *n* -s *usu cap* [fr. *Dixieland*, *Dixie* the South, its origin (in New Orleans)] **:** jazz music characterized by two beats to the measure with strong afterbeats, a small combination of instruments in the band (as cornet, clarinet, trombone, piano, and drums), and a style of performance consisting of lyrical solo choruses, improvised solo choruses, and polyphonic improvisation by the entire group

di·zain \dēˈzaⁿ, dəˈzān\ *or* **di·zaine** \dəˈzān\ *n* -s [F *dizain*, fr. *dix* ten — more at DIX] **:** a poem or stanza of ten lines

¹di·zen \ˈdīzᵊn, ˈdiz-\ *vt* -ED/-ING/-S [fr. earlier *disen* to dress a distaff with flax, fr. (assumed) ME, fr. MD, fr. or akin to MLG *dise* bunch of flax on a distaff] *archaic* **:** to dress gaudily or with finery **:** BEDIZEN ⟨'tis the vulgar great who come ~*ed* with gold and jewels —R.W.Emerson⟩

²diz·en *or* **diz·zen** \ˈdizᵊn\ *Scot var of* DOZEN

di·zo·ic \(ˈ)dīˈzōik\ *adj* [*di-* + *-zoic*] **:** having two young — used of a sporocyst containing two sporozoites

di·zygotic \ˌdī+\ *adj* [*di-* + *zygotic*] *of twins* **:** FRATERNAL

diz·zard \ˈdizə(r)d\ *n* -s [prob. alter. of *disour*] **1** *obs* **:** JESTER **2** *now dial* **:** BLOCKHEAD, NITWIT

diz·zi·ly \ˈdizəlē, -li\ *adv* [ME *disyly*, fr. *disy* + *-ly*] **:** in a dizzy manner **:** in such a way, manner, or degree as to cause dizziness or vertigo ⟨looked down from a ~ high bridge⟩ **:** with a sensation of giddiness ⟨~ tried to comprehend his terrible message⟩ **:** in an unsteady or uncertain way ⟨tottered ~ across the floor⟩

diz·zi·ness \-zēnəs, -zin-\ *n* -ES [ME *dysinesse* folly, vertigo, fr. OE *dysignes* folly, fr. *dysig* foolish + *-nes* -ness] **:** the condition of being dizzy; *esp* **:** a sensation of unsteadiness accompanied by a feeling of movement within the head **:** GIDDINESS — compare VERTIGO

¹diz·zy \ˈdizē, -zi\ *adj* -ER/-EST [ME *disy*, fr. OE *dysig* foolish, stupid; akin to OHG *tusig* stupid, MLG *dūsich* stunned, dizzy, OE *dwǣs* stupid, foolish MLG *dwas* stupid, foolish, ON *dos* quiet, *dusa* to be quiet, L *furere* to rage, *fumus* smoke — more at FUME] **1 :** FOOLISH, SILLY, INANE, HEEDLESS — not often in formal use **2 a :** having a whirling sensation in the head with a tendency to fall **:** GIDDY ⟨round and round they danced until ~⟩ **b :** mentally confused or dazed **:** being in a whirl ⟨could juggle mathematical formulas in such a way as to make the ordinary man ~ —A.W.Long⟩ **3 a** (1) **:** causing or tending to cause dizziness or giddiness **:** VERTIGINOUS ⟨gazing down from those ~ heights⟩ (2) **:** confusing or tending to confuse mentally **:** making one's head swim ⟨~ and exuberant rhetoric⟩ **b :** caused by or associated with dizziness ⟨his fever rose enveloping him in a ~ mist⟩ **c :** whirling or moving with extreme rapidity ⟨drawn into the ~ vortex of the whirlpool⟩ **d :** exceeding normal or reasonable limits **:** EXTREME, IMMODERATE ⟨prices continued to rise at a ~ rate⟩

²dizzy \"\ *vt* -ED/-ING/-ES **1 :** to make dizzy or giddy **:** cause a swimming sensation in the head of **:** DAZE ⟨we were *dizzied* by the beating wind —T.E.Lawrence⟩ **2 :** to make unsteady in thought or mind **:** CONFUSE, STUPEFY, BEWILDER ⟨prospects so brilliant as to ~ the mind⟩ ⟨the disaster *dizzied* her brain and paralyzed her will⟩

dizzying *adj* **1 :** causing or tending to cause dizziness or giddiness **:** CONFUSING, BEWILDERING ⟨ten years of ~ reverses of policy⟩ **2 :** DAZZLING, BRILLIANT ⟨crowned a ~ career with this triumph⟩

diz·zy·ing·ly *adv* **:** in a dizzying manner ⟨watching the rows of waist-high corn curve ~ away from him as he passed them —Florette Henri⟩

DJ *abbr* **1** disc jockey **2** district judge **3** *often not cap* dust jacket

dja·kar·ta *or* **ja·kar·ta** \jəˈkärd-ə\ *adj, usu cap* [fr. *Djakarta*, Indonesia] **:** of or from Djakarta, the capital of Indonesia **:** of the kind or style prevalent in Djakarta

djal·ma·ite \ˈjalmə,īt\ *n* -s [Pg *djalmaita*, fr. *Djalma* Guimarães, 20th cent. Brazilian mineralogist + Pg *-ita* -ite] **:** an isometric oxide of uranium, tantalum, columbium, and other minerals closely related to betafite

dja·ti \ˈjäd-ē\ *n* -s [Malay *jati*] *in the Malay peninsula* **:** TEAK

djave *var of* NJAVE

dje·bel *or* **je·bel** \ˈjebəl\ *n* -s [Ar *jebel*] **:** a hill in northern Africa

djellaba *var of* JELLABA

djen·kol·ic acid \(ˈ)jen|ˈkälik-, -eŋ|-\ *n* [*djenkol* (*bean*) velvet bean (fr. Java *djenkol*) + *-ic*] **:** a crystalline amino acid $CH_2[SCH_2CH(NH_2)COOH]_2$ obtained esp. from the velvet bean

djerma *usu cap, var of* DYERMA

djibbah *var of* JIBBA

djig·ga \ˈjigə\ *n* -s [of African origin — more at CHIGGER] **:** CHIGOE 1

djinn *or* **djinni** *also* **djin** *var of* JINNI

djok·ja·kar·ta \ˌjäkyəˈkärd-ə\ *or* **jog·ja·kar·ta** \ˈjägy-\ *or* **jok·ya·kar·ta** \ˈjäky-\ *adj, usu cap* [fr. *Djokjakarta*, Indonesia] **:** of or from the city of Djokjakarta, Indonesia **:** of the kind or style prevalent in Djokjakarta

dju·ka \ˈjükə\ *n, pl* **djuka** *or* **djukas** *usu cap* [D, of AmerInd origin] **1 :** a Bush Negro people of Dutch Guiana **2 :** a member of the Djuka people

dk *abbr* **1** dark **2** deca-; deka- **3** deck **4** dock **5** duck

dkg *abbr* decagram

dkl *abbr* decaliter

dkm *abbr* decameter

dks *abbr* decastere

dkt *abbr* docket

dl- \(ˈ)dēˈel\ *prefix* [ISV *d-* + *l-*] **1** *also* **d,l- :** consisting of equal amounts of the dextro and levo forms of a specified compound — usu. printed in italic ⟨*dl*-tartaric acid⟩; compare RACEMIC **2 :** consisting of equal amounts of the D- and L- forms of a specified compound — usu. printed as small capitals ⟨DL-fructose⟩; compare RACEMIC

dl *abbr* deciliter

DL *abbr* **1** day letter **2** demand loan **3** dominical letter

d layer *n, usu cap D* **1 :** a layer that may exist within the D region of the ionosphere; *also* **:** D REGION **2 :** D-HORIZON

dld *abbr* delivered

d line *n, usu cap D* **:** a yellow persistent first line of the principal series of the sodium spectrum constituting in the Fraunhofer lines a doublet whose nearly equal components have wavelengths 5895.93 and 5889.96 angstroms respectively

D Litt *abbr or n* -s [L *doctor litterarum*] **:** a doctor of letters

DLO *abbr* **1** dead letter office **2** dispatch loading only

dlvy *abbr* delivery

dly *abbr* **1** daily **2** delivery

dm *abbr* **1** decimeter **2** drum

DM *abbr* **1** [It *destra mano*] right hand **2** deutsche mark

d major *n, usu cap D* **:** the major musical key having a signature of two sharps

d-mark \ˈdē,märk\ *n, usu cap D* [G] **:** DEUTSCHE MARK

DMD *abbr or n* -s [NL *dentariae medicinae doctor*] **:** a doctor of dental medicine

DME *abbr or n* -s [*distance measuring equipment*] **:** an electronic device that informs the pilot of an airplane of its distance from a particular ground station

d minor *n, usu cap D* **:** the minor musical key having a signature of one flat

dn *abbr* **1** down **2** dun

DN *abbr* debit note

DNA *abbr* deoxyribonucleic acid

dne·pro·dzer·zhinsk \ˌneprōd(ə)r(t)ˈzhinzk, -n(t)sk\ *adj, usu cap* [fr. *Dneprodzerzhinsk*, U.S.S.R.] **:** of or from the city of Dneprodzerzhinsk **:** of the kind or style prevalent in Dneprodzerzhinsk

dne·pro·pe·trovsk \-pəˈtrȯfsk\ *adj, usu cap* [fr. *Dnepropetrovsk*, U.S.S.R.] **:** of or from the city of Dnepropetrovsk **:** of the kind or style prevalent in Dnepropetrovsk

d net *n, cap D* **:** a net with an orifice shaped like the letter D used for collecting bottom plankton

DNOC \ˌdē,en(ˌ)ōˈsē\ *abbr or n* -s dinitro-ortho-cresol

dns *abbr* dominus

¹do \(ˈ)dü, ˌdə *or* +V ˌdəw\ *vb, past 1st & 3d sing* **did** \(ˈ)did, ˌdəd\ *or substand* **done** \ˈdən\ *or archaic* **didst** \(ˈ)di|dzt, ˌdə|, |dst,|tst\ *pl* **did** *or substand* **done** *or archaic* **didst** \(ˈ)di|dzt, ˌdə|, |dst,|tst\ *pl* **did** *or substand* **done**; *past part* **done**; *pres part* **do·ing** \ˈdüiŋ\ *pres 1st sing* **do**; *2d sing* **do** *or archaic* **do·est** \ˈdüəst\ *or archaic* **dost** \(ˈ)dəst\ *3d sing* **does** \(ˈ)dəz\ *or now chiefly substand* **do** *or archaic* **do·eth** \ˈdüəth\ *or archaic* **doth** \(ˈ)dəth\ *pl* **do** [ME don, fr. OE *dōn;* akin to OFris *duā, duān* to do, OS *dūan*, OHG *tuon* to do, L *-dere* to put, *facere* to make, do, Gk *tithenai* to place, set, Skt *dadhāti* he puts, places, sets, OSlav *dĕti* to lay; basic meaning: setting, placing] *vt* **1** *archaic* : CAUSE, MAKE — used with an infinitive following the object ⟨~ me not before my time to die —Edmund Spenser⟩ **2** : to bring to pass : carry out ⟨it is my earnest desire to know the will of Providence . . . and if I can learn what it is I will ~ it —Abraham Lincoln⟩ **3** : PUT ⟨he *did* the diadem on —Philemon Holland⟩ — now usu. used in the phrase *do to death* ⟨had been hounded down and *done* to death as heretics —Stringfellow Barr⟩ **4** : to perform (as an action) by oneself or before another : EXECUTE ⟨you're bound to ~ much more walking . . . than you're accustomed to —Richard Joseph⟩ ⟨watched the natives ~ a sacred dance⟩ **5 a** : to be the cause of : bring about as a result : EFFECT ⟨his vacation *did* him a great deal of good⟩ ⟨the portrait . . . *does* him great injustice —Mary R. Mitford⟩ **b** : to give freely : RENDER, PAY ⟨have not sought the honor you have *done* me —A.E.Stevenson b.1900⟩ ⟨pilgrims having *done* their homage to the tomb —Virginia Woolf⟩ **6** : to bring to an end : COMPLETE, FINISH ⟨when she had *done* washing, it was a soft white silky fleece —Seumas O'Kelly⟩ ⟨work waiting for them back on the . . . prairies when the fun was *done* —F.B.Gipson⟩ **7** : to put forth in achieving an end : EXERT ⟨treason has *done* his worst —Shak.⟩ ⟨he *did* his best to win the race⟩ ⟨a place where there are men *~ing* thinking —Woodrow Wilson⟩ **8** : to wear out esp. by physical exertion : EXHAUST, TIRE ⟨men and horses . . . were pretty well *done* by the time we got in —C.A.Murray⟩ **9** : to bring (as a work of art) into existence esp. through the exercise of thought or imagination ⟨he's going to ~ an article on you —Barnaby Conrad⟩ ⟨the . . . paintings were *done* under the immediate influence of his academic masters —Herbert Read⟩ ⟨the commission to ~ a work for the . . . Music Festival —Ross Parmenter⟩ **10 a** : to play the part of (as a character in a play) ⟨*did* the leading lady in several comedies⟩ **b** : to act in or serve as producer of ⟨told one of the directors . . . that she would have *done* my play —Thomas Wolfe⟩ ⟨they were *~ing* a purely musical program —Jack Gould⟩ **11** : to take advantage of : treat unfairly ⟨a great bookseller who . . . charges very high prices, he has *done* me many a time —H.J. Laski⟩; *esp* : CHEAT ⟨had played the dirty trick on the farmer and *done* him out of his woodland —Dorothy C. Fisher⟩ ⟨they *did* him out of his share of the fortune⟩ **12** : to convert from one language or literary form to another — usu. used with *into* ⟨~ a book from Latin into English⟩ ⟨a prose essay *done* into rhyming couplets⟩ **13** : to treat or deal with in any way typically with the sense of preparation or with that of care or attention: as **a** (1) : to put in order : CLEAN ⟨was *~ing* the parlor when the phone rang⟩ (2) : to make ready for use : WASH ⟨*did* the dishes right after supper⟩ **b** (1) : to make ready for cooking or serving ⟨~ the beets with vinegar⟩ (2) : COOK ⟨likes his steak well *done*⟩ **c** : SET, ARRANGE ⟨her hair is *done* in that ugly pompadour of the period —J.P. Marquand⟩ **d** : to apply cosmetics to ⟨she had *done* her face and fixed her . . . hair —Hamilton Basso⟩ **e** : DECORATE, FURBISH ⟨*did* the front bedroom in blue⟩ ⟨*did* the dining room over⟩ **14 a** : to be occupied with or employed in : work at esp. as a vocation ⟨wanted to go on *~ing* chemistry all his life —J.B.S.Haldane⟩ ⟨hardly knows what he wants to ~ when he finishes college⟩ **b** : to prepare or work out esp. by studying ⟨*did* his lessons faithfully⟩ **15 a** : to pass over (as distance) : COVER, TRAVERSE ⟨*did* 300 miles on the second day of their trip⟩ ⟨the car *did* 18 miles to the gallon of gasoline⟩ **b** : to travel at a speed of ⟨two cars *~ing* 80 on the turnpike⟩ **16** : to visit and explore as or as if a sightseer : TOUR ⟨tried to ~ England in a month⟩ ⟨spent all afternoon *~ing* one wing of the museum⟩ **17** : to satisfy the needs of : SERVE, SUFFICE ⟨our coats would ~ us for the goalposts —Mary Purcell⟩ **18** : to serve (as a term of imprisonment) under restraint : UNDERGO ⟨was *~ing* five years for forgery⟩ **19** : to approve esp. by custom, opinion, or propriety — usu. used in the passive voice and with a negative ⟨you oughtn't to say a thing like that . . . it's not *done* —Dorothy Sayers⟩ **20** : to provide esp. for the physical comfort of — usu. used with *well* ⟨the largish restaurant was full of lunchers all *~ing* themselves exceedingly well —Arnold Bennett⟩ **21** — used as a substitute verb to avoid repetition of a verb ⟨I . . . chose my wife as she *did* her wedding gown —Oliver Goldsmith⟩ often in a conclusion to a condition ⟨if you have anything more to say, ~ it now⟩ ~ *vi* **1** : to conduct oneself : ACT, BEHAVE ⟨never knew him to ~ like this before —J.M.MacDonald⟩ ⟨~ as I say⟩ **2 a** : to get along : FARE ⟨men who wish to ~ well in the world —R.M.Weaver⟩ ⟨how are your crops *~ing?*⟩ ⟨the airlines were *~ing* pretty well —Richard Witkin⟩ **b** : to be as regards health : FEEL ⟨how do you ~⟩ **3** : to take place : go on : HAPPEN ⟨should get to know more about . . . Africa and what's *~ing* there —Emory Ross⟩ **4** : to carry on business or affairs : MANAGE ⟨how shall we ~ for money for these wars —Shak.⟩ **5** : to come to or make an end : FINISH ⟨worked busily for a few minutes and when he had *done*, the stretcher was a rectangle —Norman Mailer⟩ ⟨he had *done* with speech for that evening and gave us no reply —Arnold Bennett⟩ **6** : to exert oneself : be active : WORK ⟨let us then be up and *~ing* —H.W.Longfellow⟩ **7** *obs* : to continue with an action that one is already performing : proceed with an action that one has prepared to perform : go ahead — used in the imperative to express encouragement or incitement **8 a** : to be adequate or sufficient : answer the purpose : SERVE ⟨said this country would ~ for dairy farming —Ellen Glasgow⟩ ⟨an ordinary trout rod of about five ounces . . . will ~ nicely —Pete Barrett⟩ ⟨will not ~ as a translation —R.A.Fowkes⟩ **b** : to be fitting or appropriate : conform to custom or propriety ⟨it would never ~ to neglect official obligations —W. F. de Morgan⟩ **9** — used as a substitute verb to avoid repetition of a verb ⟨when beauty lived and died as flowers ~ now —Shak.⟩ often in a reply to a question ⟨did you go to the movies? I *did*⟩ **10** — used in the imperative after an imperative verb to add emphasis ⟨be quiet, ~⟩ ~ *verbal auxiliary* **1 a** *archaic* — used with the infinitive without *to* to form periphrastic present and past tenses virtually interchangeable with the corresponding simple tenses; now used in biblical or ecclesiastical language ⟨I ~ set my bow in the cloud —Gen 9:13(AV)⟩ or in legal or parliamentary language ⟨the motion for adjournment, in order to supersede a question, must be simply that the House ~ now adjourn —T.E.May⟩ or in poetry ⟨so offers he to give what she *did* crave —Shak.⟩ or in British dialect ⟨ye ~ be always with the hounds —Charles Lever⟩; not used with *be* in American English or in standard British English, nor with *have* in the literal sense of "possess" in standard British English **b** — used with the infinitive without *to* to form periphrastic present and past tenses now more generally current and acceptable than the corresponding simple tenses in declarative sentences with inverted word order ⟨fervently ~ we pray —Abraham Lincoln⟩ or in interrogative sentences ⟨*did* you hear that⟩ or in negative sentences ⟨we ~ not know⟩ ⟨*don't* you see⟩; not used with *be* in American English or in standard British English, nor with *have* in the literal sense of "possess" in standard British English **c** — used with full stress with the infinitive without *to* to form periphrastic present and past tenses expressing greater emphasis than the corresponding simple tenses ⟨just as I expected, you *did* forget my birthday⟩; not used with *be* in American English or in standard British English, nor with *have* in the literal sense of "possess" in standard British English **2 a** — used with full stress with the infinitive without *to* to form a periphrastic imperative expressing greater emphasis than the simple imperative ⟨~ be careful⟩ **b** — used with the infinitive without *to* to form a periphrastic imperative now used to the exclusion of the simple imperative in negative sentences ⟨please ~ not enter⟩ ⟨*don't* be foolish⟩ — **do by** : to deal with : TREAT ⟨publishers always *do* handsomely *by* the nursery set —Katharine T. Kinkead⟩ — **do one's block** *Austral* : to lose one's head : become flustered, excited, or angry — **do proud** : to give cause for pride or gratification ⟨looks magnificent, *does* you *proud* anywhere on earth —*N.Y. Times Mag.*⟩ — **do withal** *obs* : to help or prevent it ⟨they fell sick and died; I could not *do withal* —Shak.⟩ — **to do** : necessary to be done ⟨ten thousand times I've done my best and all's *to do* again —A.E.Housman⟩

2do \'dü\ *n, pl* **dos** *or* **do's** \'düz\ **1** *now chiefly dial* : fuss and commotion : ADO ⟨a great deal of ~ and a great deal of trouble —Sir Walter Scott⟩ **2** *archaic* : DEED, DUTY — used esp. in the phrase *to do one's do* **3** *chiefly Brit* **a** : a festive get-together : AFFAIR, PARTY ⟨it is fashionable to support the public school system with an annual ~ —A.C.Spectorsky⟩ **b** : a military engagement : SHOW ⟨he was at Dieppe for the big ~ —Robert Trout⟩ **4** : a command or entreaty to do something ⟨the basic *~s* and don'ts of mental health —Peg Bradner⟩ **5** *Austral* : GO, SUCCESS ⟨looks a bit of a gamble to me but if you think you can make a ~ of it —Vance Palmer⟩

3do *also* **doh** \'dō\ *n, pl* **dos** *or* **do's** \'dōz\ [It *do*] **1** : the first tone of the diatonic scale in solmization : TONIC **2** : the tone *C* in the fixed-do system of solmization

4do \"\ *n* -s [Jap *dō*] : any of numerous regions or large districts each containing several provinces into which Japan was formerly divided

do *abbr* ditto

DO *abbr* **1** defense order **2** delivery order **3** district officer **4** duty officer

DOA *abbr* dead on arrival

do·ab \'dō,äb\ *n* -s [Per *dōāb*, fr. *dō two* (fr. MPer) + *āb* water, fr. OPer *āpi-;* akin to Av *dvā-* two, Skt *dva*, and to Av *āp-* water — more at TWO] : a tract of land between two rivers : INTERFLUVE

do·able \'düəbəl\ *adj* [ME, fr. *don* to do + *-able* — more at DO] : that can be done : PRACTICABLE ⟨likes to . . . get something done that is not considered ~ —Otis Ferguson⟩

do–all *n* -s *obs* : a general manager : FACTOTUM

doat *var of* DOTE

do away *vt, archaic* : to put an end to : DESTROY ⟨a dislike which not all his fortune and consequence might *do away* —Jane Austen⟩ — **do away with** **1** : to put an end to : ABOLISH, DISCONTINUE ⟨the motor did not *do away with* steam power —Roger Burlingame⟩ ⟨attempted to *do away with* the entire civic art program —Jules Langsner⟩ **2** : to put to death : KILL ⟨thousands of persons have been *done away with* in this manner —*Manchester Guardian Weekly*⟩

1dob \'däb\ *var of* DAB

2dob \"\ *var of* DAUB

1dob·ber \'däbə(r)\ *n* -s [D, fr. MD, float; perh. akin to OE *dūfan* to dive — more at DIVE] *dial* : a float to a fishing line

2dobber \"\ *n* -s [1*dob* + *-er*] : a dabchick or other small grebe

dob·bin \'däbən\ *n* -s [fr. *Dobbin*, alter. of *Robin*, nickname for Robert] : a farm horse : a quiet plodding family horse ⟨he is no agile cow pony but is more like some comfortable ~ —G.R.Stewart⟩

dob·by *also* **dob·bie** \'däbē, -bi\ *n* -ES [prob. fr. *Dobby*, nickname for *Robert*] **1** *dial Brit* : a silly person : DOLT **2** *dial Brit* : a brownie or sprite believed to possess powers of good and evil **3 a** (1) : a loom attachment resembling a jacquard for weaving small figures usu. about 12 to 16 threads and seldom more than 30 threads (2) : a loom having such an attachment **b** : a fabric or figured weave made with a dobby

do·be *or* **do·bie** *or* **do·by** \'dōbē, -bi\ *n, pl* **dobes** *or* **dobies** [by shortening & alter.] : ADOBE

do·bell's solution \(')dō¦belz-\ *n, usu cap D* [after Horace B. *Dobell* †1917 Eng. physician] : an aqueous solution of sodium borate, sodium bicarbonate, glycerin, and phenol used as a spray for the nose and throat

do·ber·man pin·scher \¦dōbə(r)mən'pinchə(r), *rapid –R sometimes* -b(ə)m-\ *also* **doberman** *n* -s *usu cap D* [after Ludwig *Dobermann*, 19th cent. Ger. dog breeder] : a short-haired working dog of a breed of German origin characterized by medium size, long slender head with moderate stop, strong arched neck, deep chest and compact trunk with the back rather short and lower at rump than shoulder, long strong legs terminating in compact feet, and typically by a black coat with rusty brown markings

do·bie man \'dōbē-\ *n* [origin unknown] : one who blasts rock, coal, or ore from a quarry or mine

do·bla \'dōblə\ *n* -s [Sp — more at DOUBLOON] : an old Spanish gold coin

do·blon \də'blōn\ *n, pl* **doblons** \-ōnz\ *or* **doblo·nes** \-ōnēz, -ō,näs\ [Sp *doblón* — more at DOUBLOON] : an old gold coin of Spain and Spanish America worth two gold escudos

do·bos torte \'dō,bōs(h)-\ *also* **dobos** *n* -ES *usu cap D* [after Jozsef C. *Dobós* †1928 Hung. pastry chef] : a torte made of multiple thin layers of sponge cake often containing ground hazelnuts, put together with a mocha-chocolate filling, and topped with caramel glaze

do·bra \'dōbrə, 'dȯb-\ *n* -s [Pg, fr. fem. of obs. *dobro* (now *dobre*) double, fr. L *duplus* — more at DOUBLE] **1** : any of various former Portuguese coins; *specif* : a gold coin of the 18th and early 19th centuries equivalent to 12,800 reis — compare JOHANNES **2** : a unit of value equivalent to one dobra coin ⟨a half-*dobra* coin⟩

dob·son \'däbsən\ *n* -s [prob. fr. the name *Dobson*] : HELLGRAMMITE

dobsonfly \'==,=\ *n* : a winged insect of the family Corydalidae distinguished by the very long slender mandibles of the male and the large carnivorous aquatic larvae — compare HELLGRAMMITE

do·bu·an \'dō,büən, dō'b-\ *n, pl* **dobuan** *or* **dobuans** *usu cap* [*Dobu* island + E *-an*] **1** : a member of a Melanesian people of Dobu island, Territory of Papua **2** *or* **do·bu** \'dō,bü\ -s : the language of the Dobuans

doc \'däk\ *n* -s [by shortening] **1** : DOCTOR — used chiefly as a familiar term of address **2** *slang* : DOCUMENT

doc·cia ware \'dōch(ē)ə-\ *n, usu cap D* [fr. *Doccia*, town near Florence, Italy + E *ware*] : fine porcelain ware produced in or of the kind produced in the Italian town of Doccia

1do·cent \'dōs*nt\ *adj* [L *docent-, docens*, pres. part of *docēre* to teach — more at DOCILE] : serving to instruct : TEACHING, INSTRUCTIVE

2do·cent \,dōs*nt *or, esp with reference to German institutions,* dō(t)'sent *or* də(t)'s-\ *n* -s [G *dozent* (formerly spelled *docent*), fr. L *docent-, docens*, pres. part.] : TEACHER, LECTURER: as **a** : a college or university teacher or lecturer holding a rank inferior to that of a professor **b** : a person who conducts guided groups through a museum or art gallery and discusses and comments on the exhibits — **do·cent·ship** \-,ship\ *n*

do·ce·tae \dō'sē,tē\ *n pl, usu cap* [Gk *Dokētai*, fr. *dokein* to seem good, seem, think — more at DECENT] : an early Christian sect that adhered to the doctrine of Docetism

do·ce·tic \dō's¦ēd·ik, ¦ed·-\ *or* **do·ke·tic** \dō'k¦ \ *also* **do·ce·tist** \dō'sēd·əst\ *adj, often cap* **1** : relating to, held by, or like the Docetists **2** : of, espousing, or relating to Docetism — **do·ce·ti·cal·ly** \-d·ək(ə)lē\ *adv*

do·ce·tism \dō'sēd·,izəm, 'dōsə,ti-\ *n* -s *usu cap* : an early Christian doctrine advanced by the Docetae that Jesus Christ appeared to men in a spiritual body and that since he had no actual human body he only seemed to suffer and die on the cross

do·ce·tist \dō'sēd·əst\ *also* **do·cete** \'dō,sēt\ *n* -s *usu cap* : a person adhering to or believing in some form of Docetism

doch–an–dor·rach *or* **doch–an–dor·ris** \¦d(y)äkən¦dōrəs, -där-\ *n* [ScGael & IrGael *deoch an doruis*, lit., drink of the door] *Scot & Irish* : a parting drink : STIRRUP CUP

1doch·mi·ac \'däkmē,ak\ *adj* [Gk *dochmiakos*, fr. *dochmios*] : of, relating to, or composed of the dochmius

2dochmiac \"\ *n* -s : DOCHMIUS

doch·mi·a·cal \(')däk¦mīəkəl, ¦däkmē¦ak-\ *adj* [Gk *dochmiakos* + E *-al*] : of or relating to dochmiac verse

doch·mi·us \'däkmēəs\ *n, pl* **doch·mii** \-ē,ī\ [L, fr. Gk *dochmios*, fr. *dochmos, dochmios* slanted, oblique; akin to Skt *jihma* slanted, oblique] *prosody* : a foot of five syllables typically having the first and fourth short and the rest long

doch·ter \'dōktər, 'däk-\ *n* -s [ME *doghter, doughter* — more at DAUGHTER] *Scot* : DAUGHTER

doc·i·bil·i·ty \,däsə'biləd·ē, ,dōs-\ *n* -ES [LL *docibilitas*, fr. *docibilis* + L *-itas* -ity] *archaic* : TEACHABLENESS, DOCILITY

doc·i·ble \'==bəl\ *adj* [LL *docibilis*, fr. L *docēre* to teach + *-ibilis* -ible] : easily taught or managed : TEACHABLE

doc·ile \'däsəl *sometimes* 'dä(,)sil *or* 'dä,sīl, *Brit usu & US sometimes* 'dō,sīl\ *adj* [L *docilis*, fr. *docēre* to teach (causative fr. the root of L *decēre* to be fitting) + *-ilis* -ile — more at DECENT] **1** : TEACHABLE ⟨~ pupils looking for instruction —H.O.Taylor⟩ **2** : TRACTABLE, OBEDIENT ⟨a good ~ lass ever ready to help her fellows⟩; *often* : lacking in independence : SUBMISSIVE ⟨the ~ masses of an enslaved nation⟩ **syn** see OBEDIENT

doc·ile·ly \-səl(l)¦ē, -,sill¦, -,sīll¦, ¦i\ *adv* : in a docile manner : with docility

do·cil·i·ty \dä'siləd·ē, dō'-,də'-, -ətē, -i\ *n* -ES [MF or L; MF *docilité*, fr. L *docilitat-, docilitas*, fr. *docilis* + *-itat-, -itas* -ity] : the quality or state of being docile

doc·i·mas·tic \¦däsə¦mastik\ *also* **doc·i·mas·ti·cal** \-təkəl\ *adj* [Gk *dokimastikos* of or for scrutiny, fr. *dokimazein* to assay, test] *archaic* : of or relating to docimasy

doc·i·ma·sy \'däsəməsē\ *or* **doc·i·ma·sia** \,däsə'māzh(ē)ə\ *n, pl* **docimasies** *or* **docimasias** [NL *docimasia*, fr. Gk *dokimasia* examination, scrutiny, test, fr. *dokimazein* to assay, test, approve (fr. *dokimos* approved, tested, fr. *dokein* to seem good, seem, think) + *-ia* -y — more at DECENT] **1** *archaic* : the art or practice of assaying ores **2** : determination as to whether a dead infant was stillborn by placing the body in water in which it sinks unless the infant has expanded the lungs in respiration

do·cious \'dōshəs\ *adj* [by alter.] *dial* : DOCILE

doc·i·ty \'däsəd·ē\ *n* [prob. contr. of *docility*] *dial* : ability to comprehend quickly : mental energy or vigor : TEACHABLENESS

1dock \'däk\ *n* -s [ME *dock, docke*, fr. OE *docce;* akin to MD, MLG, & ODan *docke* dock, ScGael *dogha* burdock] **1** : any of certain coarse weedy plants with long strong taproots that constitute the genus *Rumex*, that are sometimes used as table greens, and that have long been used in folk medicine — often used with a qualifying or descriptive adjective; see BITTER DOCK, SOUR DOCK **2** : any of several usu. broad-leaved weedy plants (as members of the genera *Arctium, Petasites, Tussilago*, or *Malva*)

2dock \"\ *n* -s [ME *dok, docke* fr. OE *-docca* (as in *fingirdocca* finger muscle); akin to Fris *dok* bundle, ball, OHG *tocka* doll, ON *dokka* girl, bundle] **1 a** : the solid part of an animal's tail as distinguished from the hair : the part of a tail left after clipping the hair or cropping the end **b** : the part of the body of certain animals adjacent to the base of the tail: (1) : RUMP (2) : VULVA **2** : a docking esp. of wages; *also* : the amount docked

3dock \"\ *vt* -ED/-ING/-S [ME *docken*, fr. *dok, docke* (end of tail)] **1 a** : to cut off the end of some body part of; *specif* : to remove part of the tail of (a horse or lamb) ⟨*~ed* lambs are cleaner and command a premium on the market⟩ **b** : to cut (as a tail) short ⟨nobody'd ~ his cattle's ears that close —H.L.Davis⟩ ⟨the boxer's tail should be *~ed* and ears cropped soon after birth⟩ **2** : to cut short: as **a** : to take away a part of : ABRIDGE, LESSEN, REDUCE ⟨while it has been necessary . . . to ~ some [of the writings] . . . nothing of crucial import has been omitted —W.B.Scott⟩ ⟨if we grow absorbed in work . . . to the exclusion of . . . human elements, we ~ and maim our lives —A.C.Benson⟩ **b** : to bring (an entail) to an end **c** : to subject (as wages) to a deduction; *often* : to cheapen (market livestock) by assessing a deduction from weight or in price as a penalty for defects **3** : to deprive (as a person) of some benefit ordinarily due esp. as a penalty for a fault ⟨he was *~ed* $10 for repeated tardiness⟩ — often used with *of* ⟨~ him of the small pleasures of childhood —Samuel Butler †1902⟩

4dock \"\ *n* -s [prob. fr. MD *docke* dock, ditch, fr. L *ductio* act of conducting — more at DOUCHE] **1 a** *archaic* : natural or artificial inlet or hollow in which a ship can be received : MOORING, HARBOR **b** : a usu. artificial basin or enclosure in connection with a harbor or river for the reception of ships and equipped with means for controlling the water height — see DRY DOCK, FLOATING DOCK, WET DOCK **c** : the waterway extending between two piers or projecting wharves or cut into the land for the reception of ships **d** : a series of slips and adjoining wharves, offices, and other buildings — often used in pl. **2** : a place for the loading or unloading of materials (as from ships or carts) or for their storage: as **a** : WHARF **b** : a raised platform used for loading or unloading wheeled freight carriers (as trucks or railway cars) **c** : an elevated platform where sawed lumber is stored at the sawmill until shipped; *also* : DOLLYWAY **d** : the space usu. under the floor of the stage in which scenery is stored in a theater **3 a** : scaffolding enclosing and giving access to exterior parts of an aircraft **b** : a place or building equipped for the inspection and repair of aircraft; *broadly* : HANGAR **syn** see WHARF

5dock \"\ *vb* -ED/-ING/-S *vt* **1** : to haul or guide (as a ship) into a dock (as for repairing, cleaning, or loading) **2** : to supply (as a port) with a dock ~ *vi* : to come or go into dock ⟨the ship *~ed* here⟩

6dock \"\ *n* -s [Flem *docke, dok* cage] : the place in court where a prisoner stands or sits — **in the dock** : on trial ⟨it is the civilization that permits such acts that should be *in the dock*⟩ ⟨but you cannot put a dog *in the dock* —*Manchester Guardian Weekly*⟩

7dock \"\ *vt* -ED/-ING/-S [origin unknown] : to perforate (as a cracker) before baking

1dock·age \-ij,-ēj\ *n* -s [4*dock* + *-age*] **1** : a charge for the use of a dock **2** : docking facilities **3** : the docking of ships

2dockage \"\ *n* -s [3*dock* + *-age*] **1** : a deduction (as from wages, a going price, or the recorded weight of a salable commodity) taken or withheld (as by an employer or purchaser) as compensation for some defect **2** : the foreign material in market grain (as wheat) that is readily removable by ordinary cleaning devices

dockage period *n* [1*dockage*] : the period during which water and current conditions allow a ship to enter or leave a dock (as in a particular harbor or port)

dockboard \'=,=\ *n* [4*dock* + *board*] : a movable often metal plate for bridging the gap between a motor truck or freight car and a loading platform

dock boss *or* **docking boss** *n* [3*dock*] : a foreman who checks carloads of newly mined coal to estimate the amount of slate and other foreign matter that has been included in order to establish a rate of dockage — called also *gager*

dock brief *n* [6*dock*] *English law* : a brief from a prisoner in the dock who is unable to provide counsel for himself; *also* : the privilege granted such a prisoner at the discretion of the trial judge of selecting a barrister from among those present to represent him for a nominal fee

dock·en \'däkən\ *n* -s [ME *doken* (pl. of *dock, docke*), fr. OE *doccan*, pl. of *docce* dock — more at DOCK] **1** *chiefly Scot* : 1DOCK **2** *chiefly Scot* : something of small value ⟨I don't care a ~ —John Buchan⟩

1dock·er \'däkə(r)\ *n* -s [3*dock* + *-er*] : one that docks: as **a** : a worker that docks the tails of animals **b** : a device for docking tails esp. of lambs

2docker \"\ *n* -s [4*dock* + *-er*] : one connected with docks or wharves; *usu* : a dock laborer : LONGSHOREMAN

3docker \"\ *n* -s [7*dock* + *-er*] : a stamp for cutting out and perforating dough in making certain unleavened breads (as crackers)

1dock·et \'däkət, *usu* -əd·+V\ *n* -s [ME *doggette*] **1** : a document containing the heads or a summary of a writing: as **a** : an abstract of a proposed letters patent of the throne of England **b** : an abridged entry of a judgement or proceeding in an action at law **c** *Brit* : a form accompanying merchandise and containing data relevant to its disposal (as owner's name or date, time, and place of delivery) : LABEL, TICKET; *also* : a British customhouse warrant certifying payment of duties or facts entitling the holder to a delivery order **d** : a memorandum or identifying statement about a document that is placed on its outer surface or cover **2** : LIST: as **a** (1) : a list of dockets of a court or quasi-judicial body or a session of one of these (2) : a book of original entries kept by the clerk of a court or quasi-judicial body and containing a formal list of the names of parties and minutes of proceedings in each case in that court or body (3) : a record containing a list of causes waiting to be tried in a court or quasi-judicial body **b** : a calendar of matters to be acted on by any formally organized body (as a board of directors or a legislative assembly) : AGENDA **c** : a sequence of things to be presented, dealt with, or done whether formally listed or not ⟨on the Broadway ~ for early this season —J.P.Shanley⟩ ⟨anyone who has a tailor-made cloth coat on his or her Christmas ~ —*New Yorker*⟩ **3** : the documents relating to a particular matter or topic ⟨the

~ of the case — a manila folder as big as the phone book, bulging with forms, applications, vouchers —Bernard Taper〉; *broadly* **:** a mass of documents

²docket \"\ *vt* -ED/-ING/-S **:** to inscribe (as a document or bill) with or in a docket **:** endorse with an abstract; *esp* **:** to make a brief abstract of (a legal matter) and inscribe it in a list

dockhand \'=,=\ *n* [*⁴dock* + *hand*] **:** a freight handler **:** STEVEDORE, LONGSHOREMAN

dockhead \'=,=\ *n* [*⁴dock* + *head*] **:** the foremost part of a dock

docking *pres part of* DOCK

docking block *n* [fr. gerund of *⁵dock*] **:** one of the heavy timbers on which a ship rests when in dry dock

docking bridge *n* **:** a raised platform on a large ship near the stern

docking keel *n* **:** either of two keels placed near and parallel to the bilge keels of some ships and between them and the main keel and used for supporting the ship in dry dock

dock·i·za·tion \,däkə'zāshən\ *n* -S **:** conversion of an area (as of waterfront) into docks

dock·ize \'dä,kīz\ *vt* -ED/-ING/-S [*⁴dock* + *-ize*] **:** to equip (a river) with docks or (a harbor) for docking

dock·land \'dä,kland\ *n* [*⁴dock* + *land*] *Brit* **:** the part of a port occupied by docks; *often* **:** the blighted residential section adjacent to docks — **dock·land·er** \-də(r)\ *n*

dock·mack·ie \'däk,makē\ *n* -S [prob. fr. D, fr. Lenape *dogekumak*] **:** a No. American shrub (*Viburnum acerifolium*) with white flowers succeeded by red berries — called also *arrowwood, mapleleaf viburnum*

dock·man \'däkmən\ *n, pl* **dockmen** [*⁴dock* + *man*] **:** a worker at a dock: as **a :** one that helps to catch and cast off mooring lines **b :** DOCKER **c :** a person in charge of placing or assembling shipments on a dock

dockmaster \'=,==\ *n* [*⁴dock* + *master*] **:** a person in charge of a dock; *esp* **:** one that supervises the actual docking of a ship

dock receipt *n* [*⁴dock*] **:** a receipt issued by a shipping company for cargo delivered at the pier and later exchanged for a bill of lading

docks *pl of* DOCK, *pres 3d sing of* DOCK

dockside \'=,=\ *n, often attrib* [*⁴dock* + *side*] **:** the shore or area adjacent to a dock 〈a destructive ~ fire〉 〈the price was quoted as landed at ~〉 〈planning improvements for the municipal ~〉

dockside switcher *n* [*⁴dock*] **:** a small locomotive designed for switching work in close quarters around waterfront and industrial areas

dock spike *n* [*⁴dock*] **:** a spike usu. from 6 inches to 2 feet in length and from ½ inch to 1 inch square in section with a wedge-shaped point and often barbed like a rag bolt

dock-tailed \'=,=\ *adj* [*²dock* + *tailed*] **:** having a docked tail 〈*dock-tailed* lambs bring better prices〉

dockwalloper \'=,===\ *n* [*⁴dock*] **1 :** a loafer about docks who picks up casual employment **2 :** a freight handler on a dock

dockwalloping \'=,===\ *n* -S **:** the work of a dockwalloper

dockyard \'=,=\ *n* [*⁴dock* + *yard*] **1 :** a storage place for naval stores or timber for shipbuilding with facilities for building or repairing ships **2** *Brit* **:** NAVAL SHIPYARD — **dock·yard·man** \-mən\ *n, pl* **dockyardmen**

doc·o·glos·sa \,däkə'gläsə, -lȯsə\ *n pl, cap* [NL, fr. Gk *dokos* beam + NL *-glossa*] **:** a suborder of Aspidobranchia comprising primitive marine gastropods having a conical shell, paired nephridia and osphradia, a long radula, and no operculum and including the true limpets and certain related mollusks — **doc·o·glos·san** \;==;=sən\ *adj* — **doc·o·glos·sate** \-sət\ *adj*

doc·o·sane \'däkə,sān\ *n* -S [ISV *docos-* (fr. *do-* — as in *dodeca-* — + *-cos-* — fr. *eicosa-*) + *-ane*] **:** a paraffin hydrocarbon of the formula $C_{22}H_{46}$; *esp* **:** the crystalline normal isomer $CH_3(CH_2)_{20}CH_3$

doc·o·sa·no·ic acid \;däkəsə;nōik-\ *n* [*docosane* + *-o-* + *-ic*] **:** BEHENIC ACID

doc·quet *archaic var of* DOCKET

¹doc·tor \'däktə(r)\ *n* -S [ME *doctour*, fr. MF & ML; MF *doctour, docteur*, fr. ML *doctor*, fr. L, teacher, fr. *doctus* (past part. of *docēre* to teach) + *-or* — more at DOCILE] **1 a :** a religious scholar who is eminent in theological learning and personal holiness and usu. an expounder and defender of established doctrine 〈Christ disputed with the ~s〉 〈St. Jerome was one of the great ~s of the church〉 **b** *archaic* **:** a person competent by reason of skill and knowledge to teach or expound authoritatively a subject or field of knowledge; *broadly* **:** a person who teaches or expounds something — used with *of* **c :** a person who has earned one of the highest academic degrees (as a PhD) conferred by a university usu. by spending several years in advanced study of a specialized field, by writing an acceptable dissertation, and by passing numerous rigorous examinations **d :** a person awarded an honorary doctorate (as an LLD or LittD) by a college or university **2 :** one skilled or specializing in healing arts: **a :** a practitioner of medicine, dentistry, or veterinary medicine **b :** a person who has completed a course of study in one of these fields and been duly licensed to practice his profession **c :** PHYSICIAN — distinguished from *surgeon* **d :** a medicine man in a primitive culture; *broadly* **:** any practitioner (as a rainmaker or shaman) of mysterious or magic arts in such a culture **3** *archaic slang* **:** a loaded die **4 :** a recurrent cool breeze; *esp* **:** a tropical sea breeze **5 :** material added to produce a desired effect: **a :** something added to food or drink to improve its apparent quality (as acid to certain candies) **b :** DOCTOR SOLUTION **6 :** a mechanical contrivance or attachment for remedying a difficulty esp. when makeshift and used in an emergency: as **a** *or* **doctor blade :** a blade (as of metal, wood, or plastic) for spreading a coating (as of glue on layers of material being laminated) or for scraping a surface (as for removing ink from the nonprinting part of an intaglio printing surface or lint from a textile printing roll) **b :** a small engine for providing water for a boiler system **:** DONKEY ENGINE **c :** a tool used for electroplating surfaces that cannot conveniently be placed in a bath **d :** a soldering tool **e :** a knife for scraping up and incorporating rubber dough in a mixing machine **7 a** *slang* **:** a ship or camp cook **b :** a person who puts things in or restores things to order: as (1) **:** a repairer of broken or disordered items, esp. of mechanical apparatus or systems — used often with a qualifying attributive 〈a first= rate loom ~〉 (2) **:** PLAY DOCTOR **c :** a person in charge (as of a situation) **:** one responsible for decisions to be made — used chiefly in the phrase *you're the doctor* **8 :** any of several brightly colored artificial flies used by anglers

²doctor \"\ *vb* **doctored; doctored; doctoring** \-t(ə)riŋ\ **doctors** *vt* **1 a :** to confer a doctorate upon **:** make (someone) a doctor **b :** to address or refer to as "Doctor" 〈a false humility that made him ~ all his associates〉 **2 a :** to treat (a patient or ailment) as a physician **:** apply remedies to 〈faithfully ~*ed* her old mother〉 〈~*ed* his boil〉 **b :** to restore to good condition **:** MEND, REPAIR 〈he tinkered with the old clock until he finally ~*ed* its strike〉 **3 a :** to adapt or modify for a desired end by alteration or special treatment 〈~*ed* the play by tightening its whole structure and abridging the last act〉 **b :** to conceal the real state or actual quality of by deceptive alteration (as with chemicals) 〈~*ing* poor wine to get a better price〉 〈hoping to ~ the election returns〉 — often used with *up* 〈you'll have to ~ up your plans if you hope to fool anybody〉 ~ *vi* **1 :** to practice medicine 〈my grandfather ~*ed* in the backwoods country for over 50 years〉 **2** *dial* **:** to take medicine or medical treatment 〈~*ing* for the asthma〉 〈she ~*ed* with my nephew all that winter〉

doc·tor·al \'däkt(ə)rəl\ *also* **doc·to·ri·al** \(')däk;tōrēəl\ *adj* **:** of, relating to, or characteristic of a doctor or doctorate 〈a ~ hood〉 〈~ candidates〉 — **doc·tor·al·ly** \-əlē, -li\ *adv*

doc·to·rand \;däktə;rand\ *also* **doc·to·ran·dus** \,däktə'randəs\ *n, pl* **doctorands** \-n(d)z\ *also* **doctoran·di** \,=='ran,dī\ [ML *doctorandus*, gerundive of *doctorare*] **:** a candidate for a doctorate

doc·tor·ate \'däkt(ə)rə|t, -ktə,rā|, *usu* |d.+V\ *n* -S [ML *doctoratus*, fr. *doctoratus*, past part. of *doctorare* to become a doctor, fr. *doctor*] **:** the degree, title, or rank of a doctor

doctorbird \'==,=\ *n* [prob. so called fr. the resemblance of the bill to a surgical needle] **1 :** GREEN TODY **2 :** a curve-billed hummingbird (*Sericotes holosericeus*) of the West Indies; *broadly* **:** any of various West Indian hummingbirds

doctor book *n* **:** a book intended to supplement the knowledge of the individual in matters of home medication usu. helping to identify common ailments and suggesting simple medication that can be undertaken without the supervision of a physician

doctorfish \'==,=\ *n* [so called fr. the sharp spines on each side of the tail] **:** SURGEONFISH

doctor gum *n* **1 :** POISONWOOD 1 **2 :** a gum obtained from the doctor-gum tree and used locally for medicinal purposes

doc·tor·hood \'däktə(r),hu̇d\ *n* -S **:** doctoral position or rank

doc·tor·ize \-tə,rīz\ *vt* -ED/-ING/-S **:** to confer the degree of doctor on

doc·tor·ly \-tə(r)lē\ *adj* **:** like a doctor **:** befitting a doctor

doctors *pl of* DOCTOR, *pres 3d sing of* DOCTOR

doc·tor·ship \-tə(r),ship\ *n* **1 :** DOCTORATE **2** *archaic* **:** the position, function, or characteristics of a doctor; *sometimes* **:** LEARNING, SCHOLARSHIP

doctor solution *n* **:** a solution made by adding litharge to sodium hydroxide solution and used in sweetening petroleum distillates (as naphtha) by reaction with any malodorous sulfur compounds (as mercaptans) present

doctor test *n* **:** a test with doctor solution for detecting the presence of undesirable sulfur compounds in petroleum distillates (as naphtha)

doc·tress \'däktrəs\ *also* **doc·tor·ess** \-t(ə)rəs\ *n* -ES [*doctor* + *-ess*] **:** a female medicine man or witch doctor

¹doc·tri·naire \;däktrə;na(a)|(ə)r, -ne|, |ə\ *n* -S [F, fr. *doctrine* doctrine, teaching + *-aire* -ary (fr. L *-arius*)] **1 :** a member of a French political party that persisted from about 1815 to 1830, advocated a constitutional monarchy, and was opposed both to the ultraroyalists and to the revolutionists **2 :** one who attempts to put into effect some esp. political doctrine or theory with little or no regard for practical difficulties

²doctrinaire \"\ *adj* **:** relating to or characteristic of a doctrinaire **:** stubbornly devoted to some particular doctrine or theory without regard to practical considerations **:** DOGMATIC 〈an atonal composition in the ~ sense —Winthrop Sargeant〉

doc·tri·nair·ism \,=='na(a)ˌrizəm, -'ne,r-\ *n* -S **:** the principles or practices of a doctrinaire **:** stubborn attachment to a doctrine or theory without regard to its practicality

¹doc·tri·nal \'däktrən°l, *Brit often & US sometimes* däk'trīn°l\ *n* -S [ME, fr. MF, fr. *doctrinal*, adj.] **1** *obs* **:** a manual of instruction **2 doctrinals** *pl, archaic* **:** matters of doctrine or instruction

²doc·tri·nal \'däktrən°l, *Brit often & US sometimes* (')däk;trīn°l\ *adj* [ME, fr. MF or LL; MF, fr. LL *doctrinalis*, fr. L *doctrina* teaching + *-alis* -al] **1 a :** of, relating to, or preoccupied with doctrine 〈quibbling and hairsplitting over ~ minutiae〉 〈Milton was a ~ poet —Douglas Bush〉 **b :** containing or involving something taught and to be believed 〈those who seek ~ support of spending now turn to the statistics of national income —H.L.Lutz〉 **2** *obs* **:** relating to teaching **:** DIDACTIC — **doc·tri·nal·ly** \-°lē, -°li\ *adv*

doc·tri·nal·i·ty \,däktrə'naləd·ē\ *n* -ES **:** doctrinal character

doc·tri·nar·i·an \,däktrə'na(a)rēən, -ner-\ *n* -S [modif. of F *doctrinaire* + E *-ian*] **:** DOCTRINAIRE

doc·tri·nar·i·ly \;däktrə;nerəlē, -na(a)r-\ *adv* **:** with respect to basic principles and outlook 〈~ opposed to the present government〉

doc·tri·nar·i·ty \,däktrə'narəd·ē\ *n* -ES **:** DOCTRINALITY

doc·tri·nary \'däktrə,nerē\ *adj* [F *doctrinaire*] **:** of, relating to, or holding certain basic usu. abstract doctrines or theories

doc·trine \'däktrən\ *n* -S [ME, fr. MF & L; MF, fr. L *doctrina*, fr. *doctor* teacher] **1** *archaic* **:** TEACHING, INSTRUCTION 〈He . . . said unto them in his ~, Hearken —Mark 4:2(AV)〉 **2 a :** something that is taught **:** something that is held, put forth as true, and supported by a teacher, a school, or a sect 〈the ~ and lore of the early fathers〉 **b :** a principle or position or the body of principles in any branch of knowledge **:** a principle of faith **:** TENET, DOGMA 〈the ~ of atoms〉 〈Christian ~〉 **c :** a principle of law established through past decisions and interpretations 〈the ~ of caveat emptor〉 **d :** a formulation of the principles on which a government proposes to base its actions or policy in some matter esp. in the field of international relations 〈the Truman ~〉 〈the Monroe ~〉 **3** *obs* **:** LEARNING, KNOWLEDGE

syn DOGMA, TENET: DOCTRINE may indicate a formulated theory supported or not controverted by evidence, backed or sanctioned by authority, and proposed for acceptance; it may refer to authoritative teaching accepted by a body of believers or adherents 〈the *doctrine* of Einstein, which sweeps away axioms so familiar to us that they seem obvious truths, and substitutes others which seem absurd because they are unfamiliar —Havelock Ellis〉 〈there was also a nascent theory of sound waves; and out of it there grew a tremendous mathematical *doctrine* of waves which nowadays has almost come to dominate the physics of these times —K.K.Darrow〉 DOGMA applies to authoritative teaching or ruling laid down or promulgated as true and unquestionable 〈those who rejected the Marxist *dogma* found it easy to accept the dogma of those racists who represented Hitler as a modern synthesis of Frederick the Great, Bismarck, Nietzsche, and Kaiser Wilhelm II —Quincy Howe〉 〈he sees orthodox science, despite all its achievements, become now the most dangerous enemy of a true philosophy, because its *dogmas* are least often questioned —J.W.Krutch〉 〈the *dogma* of the bodily assumption of the Virgin Mary〉 TENET may apply to any principle or opinion generally believed, whether taught and actively maintained or not 〈the other *tenet* of his materialism is that supernaturalism, though it may have a certain practical justification for the majority of men, has no rational basis —Vivian J. McGill〉 〈sympathy for the afflicted, a Christian *tenet*, has done much to alleviate the sufferings of these unfortunate people —V.G. Heiser〉

doctrine of correspondence : the theory in Swedenborgianism that natural objects correspond to or participate in transcendent archetypes — compare PARTICIPATION

doctrine of descent : a theory in biology: all animals and plants are direct descendants of previous animals or plants — opposed to *special creation*

doctrine of signatures : a theory in old natural philosophy: the outward appearance of a body signalizes its special properties (as of magic or healing virtue) and there is a relationship between the outward qualities of a medicinal object and the diseases against which it is effective

doc·trin·ism \-,nizəm\ *n* -S **:** devotion to or enunciation of doctrine — **doc·trin·ist** \-nəst\ *n* -S

¹doc·u·ment \'däkyəmənt\ *n* -S [ME, fr. MF, fr. LL & L; LL *documentum* official paper, fr. L, lesson, example, fr. *docēre* to teach + *-mentum* -ment — more at DOCILE] **1** *obs* **:** something taught **:** TEACHING, INSTRUCTION **2 a** *archaic* **:** something (as a writing) that serves to demonstrate or prove something **:** PROOF, EVIDENCE **b :** an original or official paper relied upon as the basis, proof, or support of something **c documents** *pl* **:** the bill of lading and policy of insurance and sometimes other papers that evidence or effect the shipment of goods, their insurance, the transfer of title to the consignee, and other procedures and that are annexed to a documentary bill of exchange **d documents** *pl* **:** SHIP'S PAPERS **e :** a formal or official writing or personal identification **:** an identity card (as of a seaman) **f** (1) **:** a writing (as a book, report, or letter) conveying information (2) **:** a material substance (as a coin or stone) having on it a representation of the thoughts of men by means of some conventional mark or symbol **g :** DOCUMENTARY **h :** a publication of federal, state, or local government — chiefly in library usage **3** *archaic* **:** a piece of information **:** LESSON; *often* **:** a warning or admonition

²doc·u·ment \-,ment, -mənt — *see* ²-MENT\ *vt* -ED/-ING/-S **1** *obs* **:** TEACH, SCHOOL, INSTRUCT **2 :** to evidence by documents **:** furnish documentary evidence of 〈carefully ~*ing* his claims〉 **3 :** to furnish with documents **4 a :** to furnish (a ship) with ship's papers as required by law for the manifesting of ownership and cargo **b :** to annex to (a bill of exchange) the shipment documents — see DOCUMENTARY BILL **5 a :** to provide with factual or substantial support for statements made or a hypothesis proposed; *esp* **:** to equip with exact references to authoritative supporting information (as by means of footnotes or other textual annotation) 〈pointed out, and ~*ed* in his book, that great progress has been made in the professional study of world affairs —F.M.Hechinger〉 〈~ a thesis〉 **b :** to construct or produce (as a movie or novel) with a high proportion of details closely reproducing authentic situations or events 〈my desire to compose a highly ~*ed* picture of the modern world —R.P.Warren〉

doc·u·ment·able \;däkyə;mentəbəl\ *adj* **:** capable of demonstration by documentary evidence

doc·u·men·tal \-nt°l\ *adj* **:** DOCUMENTARY

doc·u·men·tal·ist \,=='=əst\ *n* -S **:** a specialist in documentation of recorded knowledge

doc·u·men·tar·i·an \,däkyəmən-'terēən, -,men-\ *n* -S **:** a person who employs or advocates the stressing of documentary presentation (as in photographic art or fiction)

doc·u·men·tar·i·ly \;==(,)=;terəlē\ *adv* **1 :** by means of documents 〈a ~ verifiable incident in American history〉 **2 :** in a documentary manner 〈quiet ~ unhighlighted acting —H.E.Clurman〉

doc·u·men·ta·rist \,däkyə'mentərəst\ *n* -S **:** a specialist in documentary presentation (as of theatrical or literary material)

¹doc·u·men·ta·ry \;däkyə;mentər|ē, |i *also* ;==;men·tr| *or* 'däkyəmən,ter|\ *adj* [*¹document* + *-ary*] **1 :** being or consisting of documents **:** contained or certified in writing 〈~ evidence〉 **2 :** of, relating to, or employing documentation in literature or art 〈~ annotations〉 〈a careful ~ writer〉; *broadly* **:** having or claiming the objective quality, authority, or force of documentation in the representation of a scene, place, or condition of life or of a social or political problem or cause **:** FACTUAL, OBJECTIVE, REPRESENTATIONAL — used of works of literature, the theater, art, photography, radio and TV programs

²documentary \"\ *n* -ES **:** a documentary presentation (as a film or novel)

documentary bill *or* **documentary draft** *also* **document bill** *n* **:** a bill of exchange drawn on a consignee of goods and having appended to it the shipment documents by way of collateral security for its payment

documentary stamp *n* **:** a revenue stamp issued for use on documents

doc·u·men·ta·tion \,däkyəmən-'tāshən, -,men-\ *n* -S **1** *archaic* **:** INSTRUCTION, ADMONITION **2 :** the act or an instance of furnishing or authenticating with documents **3 a :** the provision of ship's papers to a ship **b :** the provision of documents in substantiation; *also* **:** documentary evidence (as in a treatise) **c** (1) **:** the use of historical documents esp. in the writing of history or of works relying on the authenticity of historical information (2) **:** conformity to historical or objective facts (as in writing or painting) (3) **:** the provision of footnotes, appendices, or addenda referring to or containing documentary evidence in verification of facts or in support of theory in a piece of writing (as a biography or history) **4 :** the assembling, coding, and disseminating of recorded knowledge comprehensively treated as an integral procedure utilizing semantics, psychological and mechanical aids, and techniques of reproduction including microcopy for giving documentary information maximum accessibility and usability

document board *n* **:** smooth and flexible paperboard of a kind usable for protective folders for documents and letters

documentize *vt* -ED/-ING/-S *obs* **:** to furnish with evidence **:** TEACH, ADMONISH

document of title : a document affording evidence of title to property; *specif* **:** any document that is used in the ordinary course of business as proof of the possession or control of goods or that imparts authority in the possessor of the document to transfer or receive the goods in question

documents *pl of* DOCUMENT, *pres 3d sing of* DOCUMENT

¹dod *or* **dodd** \'däd\ *vt* **dodded; dodded; dodding; dods** *or* **dodds** [ME *dodden*] **1** *dial Brit* **:** to lop or clip hair or wool from 〈it is time to ~ the sheep〉 **2** *dial Brit* **:** POLL

²dod \"\ *n* -S **1 :** a perforated metal plate through which clay is forced to mold it to a desired shape **2 :** an annular die for making drainpipe

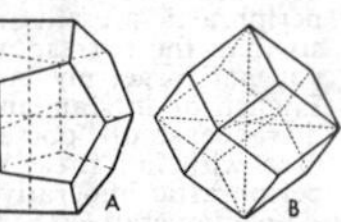
dod for pipe

³dod \"\ *interj* [euphemism for *God*] — used as a mild oath esp. as an intensive with a verb

do·da \'dōdə\ *n* -S [native name in India] **:** FOUR-HORNED ANTELOPE

dodad *var of* DOODAD

¹dod·der \'dädə(r)\ *n* -S [ME *doder*; akin to MLG *doder, dodder* dodder, MHG *toter* dodder, yolk, OHG *totoro* yolk, OS *dodro*, OE *dydring* yolk, Norw *dudra* to tremble, Gk *thyssetai* to tremble, *thysanos* tassel, Skt *dodhat-* shaking, raging, L *fumus* smoke — more at FUME] **:** any of certain plants comprising the genus *Cuscuta* with seeds that germinate and produce elongated seedlings which come in contact with stems of a suitable host plant and which obtain nourishment through haustoria — called also *love vine*

²dodder \"\ *vi* **doddered; doddered; doddering** \-d(ə)riŋ\ **dodders** [alter. of earlier *dadder*, fr. ME *dadiren*] **1 :** to tremble or shake (as from weakness or age) **:** become enfeebled 〈we . . . have no excuse for ignoring a sick and ~*ing* church school —Iva Kilpatrick〉 〈in the pulpit a ~*ing* priest was preaching —Bruce Marshall〉 **2 :** to progress feebly and unsteadily 〈an old man ~*ing* down the walk〉

dod·dered \'dädə(r)d\ *adj* [prob. alter. of *dodded*] **1 :** deprived of branches through age or decay 〈a ~ oak〉 **2 :** SHATTERED, INFIRM **:** enfeebled esp. by age 〈auld, feckless, ~ men —R.L.Stevenson〉

dod·der·er \'dädərə(r)\ *n* -S **:** one that dodders; *esp* **:** a person enfeebled and doddering from weakness or age

doddering *adj* **:** feeble and dull esp. from age

dodder laurel *n* [*¹dodder*] **:** a parasitic plant of the genus *Cassytha* found commonly along tropical coasts — called also *devil's-guts, woevine*

dodder oil *n* **:** CAMELINE OIL

dodder seed *n* **:** the seed of the gold of pleasure that yields cameline oil

dod·dery \'däd(ə)rē\ *adj* [*²dodder* + *-y*] **:** unsteady or trembling esp. by reason of age or weakness **:** DODDERING

dod·die *or* **dod·dy** \'dädē\ *n, pl* **doddies** [*¹dod* + *-ie, -y*] **1** *chiefly Scot* **:** a hornless cow or bull **2 :** ABERDEEN ANGUS

¹dod·dle \'däd°l\ *adj or n* [*¹dod* + *-le*] **:** POLLARD

²doddle \"\ *vb* **doddled; doddled; doddling** \-d(°)liŋ\ **doddles** [prob. alter. of *dodder*] *vi, now dial* **:** DODDER, TODDLE ~ *vt, chiefly Midland* **:** to shake or nod (as the head)

dod·dy mitten \'dädē-\ *n* [prob. so called fr. the resemblance of a mitten to the head of a doddie] *Scot* **:** MITTEN 1

dod·dy·poll \'dädē,pōl\ *n* [alter. (influenced by *¹dod*) of ME *dotypolle, dotepol*, prob. fr. *dote* fool (fr. *doten* to dote) + *polle, pol* poll — more at DOTE, POLL] *now dial Eng* **:** BLOCKHEAD

dodeca- *or* **dodec-** *comb form* [L *dodeca-*, fr. Gk *dōdeka-*, *dōdek-*, fr. *dōdeka, dyōdeka*, fr. *dyō, dyo* two + *deka* ten — more at TWO, TEN] **:** twelve 〈*dodeca*hedron〉 〈*dodec*yl〉

do·dec·a·gon \dō'dekə,gän\ *n* -S [Gk *dōdekagōnon*, fr. *dōdeka-* + *-gonon* -gon] **:** a polygon of 12 sides — **do·de·cag·o·nal** \;dōdə;kagən°l, ;dō,de;-\ *adj*

do·deca·he·dral \(;)dō;dekə;hēdrəl\ *adj* [*dodecahedron* + *-al*] **:** relating to or like a dodecahedron

dodecahedral cleavage *n* **:** cleavage in a mineral parallel to the faces of the rhombic dodecahedron

do·deca·he·dron \(,)dō,dekə'hēdrən\ *n, pl* **dodecahedrons** \-nz\ *or* **dodecahe·dra** \-rə\ [Gk *dōdekaedron*, fr. *dōdeka-* dodeca- + *-edron* -hedron] **:** a solid having 12 plane faces and commonly in either of two forms: (1) with 12 equal regular pentagonal faces or (2) with 12 equal rhombic faces — called also respectively (1) *regular dodecahedron*, (2) *rhombic dodecahedron*

dodecahedrons: pentagonal, *A*; rhombic, *B*

do·deca·hydrate \(;)dō;dekə+\ *n* [*dodeca-* + *hydrate*] **:** a compound with 12 molecules of water

do·de·cam·er·ous \;dōdə;kamərəs\ *adj* [*dodeca-* + *-merous*] **:** having the whorls of floral parts in twelves — often written *12-merous*

do·de·cane \'dōdə,kān\ *n* -S [ISV *dodeca-* + *-ane*] **:** any of the oily paraffin hydrocarbons having the formula $C_{12}H_{26}$; *esp* **:** the normal isomer $CH_3(CH_2)_{10}CH_3$ occurring in some petroleums

¹do·dec·a·ne·sian \(;)dō;dekə;nēzhən, -ēsh-; ;dōdək-\ *or*

do·dec·a·nese \-ēz,-ēs\ *also* **do·dec·a·ne·san** \-ēs°n,-ēz°n\ *adj, usu cap* [fr. *Dodecanese* islands] **:** of, relating to, or produced in the Dodecanese islands in the Aegean

²**dodecanesian** \"\ *or* **dodecanese** \"\ *n* -s *cap* **:** a native or inhabitant of the Dodecanese islands

do·dec·a·no·ic acid \(,)dō¦dek|ə¦nōik-, ¦dōdək|-\ *n* [*dodecane* + *-o-* + *-ic*] **:** LAURIC ACID

do·dec·ant \'dō,dekənt, 'dōdək-, dō'dek-\ *n* -s [*dodeca-* + *-ant*] **:** any of the 12 parts into which the space about the center of a hexagonal crystal is divided by the four axial planes

do·deca·phon·ic \(,)dō¦dekə¦fänik\ *adj* [*dodeca-* + *phon-* + *-ic*] **1 :** *of musical composition* **:** composed by using as a device the mechanical application of a particular numerical arrangement of the successive notes of the chromatic scale **2 :** of, relating to, or involved in the composition of dodecaphonic music ⟨a ~ technique⟩ ⟨the ~ tradition —Howard Taubman⟩

do·deca·pho·nism \dō'dekə,fō,nizəm, -fä-; ,dōdə'kafə,n-\ *n* -s **:** musical composition employing dodecaphonic techniques

do·deca·pho·nist \-,nəst\ *n* -s **:** an exponent of dodecaphonic techniques in musical composition; *esp* **:** a composer who uses these techniques

do·deca·pho·ny \dō'dekə,fōnē, -,fänē; ,dōdə'kafənē\ *n* -ES [*dodeca-* + *-phony*] **:** the practice of dodecaphonic composition

do·de·car·chy \'dōdə,kärkē\ *n* -ES [*dodeca-* + *-archy*] **:** a ruling body of 12

do·deca·se·mic \(,)dō¦dekə¦sēmik\ *adj* [LL *dodecasemus* (fr. Gk *dōdekasēmos*, fr. *dōdeka-* dodeca- + *-sēmos*, fr. *sēma* sign) + E *-ic* — more at SEMANTICS] *prosody* **:** comprising 12 morae ⟨a dactylic tripody is ~⟩

¹**do·deca·style** \dō'dekə,stīl\ *n* -s [Gk *dōdekastylos*, fr. *dōdeka-* dodeca- + *stylos* pillar — more at STOIC] **:** a dodecastyle structure (as a portico)

²**dodecastyle** \"\ *adj* **:** marked by columniation with 12 columns across the front — compare DISTYLE

do·deca·syllabic \(,)dō¦dekə+\ *adj* [*dodeca-* + *syllabic*] **1 :** having or composed of 12 syllables **2 :** of or related to a dodecasyllable

do·deca·syllable \dō'dekə+,-, (,)dō,dekə+'-\ *n* [*dodeca-* + *syllable*] **1 :** a line of 12 syllables **2 :** a word consisting of 12 syllables

do·de·cath·eon \,dōdə'kathēən\ *n* [NL, fr. Gk *dōdekatheon* primrose, fr. neut. of *dōdekatheos* of twelve gods, fr. *dōdeka-* dodeca- + *theos* god — more at THEISM] **1** *cap* **:** a genus of No. American and Asiatic herbs (family Primulaceae) having basal leaves and scapose nodding flowers with reflexed corolla and monadelphous stamens **2** -s **:** any plant of the genus *Dodecatheon*

do·deca·tonal \(,)dō¦dekə+\ *adj* [*dodeca-* + *tonal*] **:** DODECAPHONIC

do·dec·u·ple scale \(')dō'dekyəpəl-\ *n* [*dodeca-* + *-uple* (as in *octuple*)] **:** the twelve-tone chromatic scale

do·dec·u·plet \dō'dekyəplət, -,plet\ *n* -s [*dodeca-* + *-uplet* (as in *octuplet*)] **:** 12 musical notes performed in the time of the same value

do·de·cyl \'dōdə,sil\ *n* -s [ISV *dodeca-* + *-yl*] **1 :** an alkyl radical $C_{12}H_{25}$ derived from a dodecane by removal of one hydrogen atom; *esp* **:** the normal radical $CH_3(CH_2)_{10}CH_2$— **2 :** a mixture of branched-chain alkyl radicals averaging $C_{12}H_{25}$ in composition — used chiefly industrially ⟨benzene substituted by ~⟩

dodecyl alcohol *n* **:** LAURYL ALCOHOL 1

dod·gas·ted \'däd,gastəd\ *adv* (*or adj*) [euphemism for *God blasted*] — used as a mild oath

¹**dodge** \'däj\ *vb* -ED/-ING/-s [origin unknown] *vi* **1 a** *obs* **:** to behave evasively in speech or action **:** haggle over terms **:** PARLEY **b :** to evade responsibility or a duty esp. by trickery or deceit ⟨she *dodged* again, she lied again, and felt no guilt —Ethel Wilson⟩ **c :** to minimize a presentation (as of facts) **:** present something less harshly or forcefully than might be possible ⟨he never ~s, never seeks refuge in platitudinous generalities —*Saturday Rev.*⟩ **d :** to move to and fro or from place to place usu. in an irregular course ⟨had to ~ backward and forward between London, Scotland, and Ireland —*Times Lit. Supp.*⟩ ⟨*dodging* in and out among the crowd⟩ ⟨*dodged* in long zigzag leaps⟩; *often* **:** to make a sudden movement in a new direction (as to evade a blow) ⟨he *dodged* behind the door⟩ **2 :** to step backward in striking order — used of a bell in change ringing ~ *vt* **1 :** to evade (as a responsibility) usu. subtly and without positive repudiation ⟨that's *dodging* the question⟩ ⟨the fact that these deficiencies exist ought not to be *dodged* —Dexter Perkins⟩ ⟨those young men who ~ the draft⟩ **2 :** to evade by a sudden or by repeated shift of place or position ⟨*dodging* a hail of bullets⟩ **:** avoid an encounter with (as by suddenly turning aside) ⟨she *dodged* him in the crowd⟩ **3** *archaic* **:** to follow (as a person) stealthily concealing oneself from view **:** DOG **4 :** to reduce the intensity of (a portion of a photograph) by selectively shading or selectively masking by chemical means during printing — compare BURN IN

syn DODGE, PARRY, SIDESTEP, DUCK, SHIRK, FENCE, and MALINGER agree in meaning to avoid or evade by some maneuver or shift. DODGE implies quickness of movement or a sudden shift of position esp. in an unexpected direction (as in evading a blow or pursuit) ⟨I looked up just in time to *dodge* a window frame falling from a fourth-story apartment —T.P. Whitney⟩ ⟨the trouble has often been diagnosed, but it is always being *dodged* or minimized by the moralist —E.M. Forster⟩ ⟨he hides in a dream world, *dodging* all responsibility —Ruth Blodgett⟩ PARRY implies a warding off (as of a blow) as by turning the object aside, extending commonly to any adroitness in defending oneself ⟨the Modoc bands *parried* thrust after thrust of the Federal troops —*Amer. Guide Series: Oregon*⟩ ⟨a new species of general, to *parry* a kind of enemy that was not described in the textbooks —*Time*⟩ ⟨developing some adroitness in *parrying* awkward questions from the press —Edmond Taylor⟩ SIDESTEP implies a refusal to face by suddenly or ingeniously moving out of the way (as of something that threatens) ⟨a man who *sidesteps* difficulties by quick thinking —Hazel Sullivan⟩ ⟨Thomas *sidestepped* the snare which besets the prose playwright —Kenneth Tynan⟩ ⟨he realized that every single speaker, with two courageous exceptions, had *sidestepped* the issue —H.A.Overstreet⟩ DUCK, close to SIDESTEP, implies avoidance or evasion by or as if by bobbing down the head or suddenly stooping out of the way, suggesting possibly more purposeful evasion than SIDESTEP ⟨the way for a reviewer to *duck* such a question —*Newsweek*⟩ ⟨on the whole the major studios have *ducked* controversy, seldom fighting censorship —*Saturday Night*⟩ ⟨certainly some ministers and teachers have *ducked* the facts of life —McGeorge Bundy⟩ SHIRK implies evasion by means that suggest laziness, cowardice, or sneakiness ⟨that is my duty and I shall not *shirk* it —H.S.Truman⟩ ⟨a war which must be fought out and not *shirked* —Walter Moberly⟩ ⟨the critic cannot forgo the attempt nor *shirk* the responsibility —C.I. Glicksberg⟩ ⟨does not *shirk* the horrors of his scene —W.E. Allen⟩ FENCE, usu. figurative, in this context suggests any dexterous purposeful maneuver to avoid an issue or to ward something off (as embarrassing questions) ⟨spent much time in *fencing* on the witness stand⟩ ⟨it is rather odd that, after successfully *fencing* with police, prosecutors, and other officials for weeks, she should have made a slip and mentioned Halloran's name —E.D.Radin⟩ ⟨the president showed a new capability for *fencing* with the press —*Time*⟩ MALINGER implies a shirking or delaying by pretense of illness, weakness, or incapacity ⟨a *malingering* old colonel . . . pleading dysentery —*Time*⟩ ⟨*malingering* was rare, however, if we adhere to the definition that it is an act or behavior in an otherwise normal individual for the purpose of evading military duty —W.C. Menninger⟩ ⟨tried to escape it for more than ten juvenile years of my life, often successfully by playing truant day after day, or by *malingering* —F.N.Souza⟩

²**dodge** \"\ *n* -s **1 :** an act or means of evading **2 a :** avoidance (as of contact) by sudden evasive bodily movement ⟨he made a sudden ~ aside as the door swung to⟩ **b :** an artful device to evade, deceive, or trick **:** a crafty or subtle evasion ⟨the surprising ~s used to escape taxation⟩ ⟨just another ~ to get out of working⟩ **c :** an expedient or scheme ⟨through the ~s and changes of Latin America's most dangerously significant revolution —Duncan Aikman⟩ ⟨penny-pinching ~s⟩; *often* **:** a method, technique, or way of life that tends to effect an end usu. with notable or increased effectiveness ⟨if you think the jingle ~ is easy —H.D.Quigg⟩ ⟨got into the cowboy ~ because it looked more promising than cotton picking —Martin Levin⟩ ⟨making use of a new market ~ to increase unit sales⟩ **3 :** a backward step or one of a series of zigzags taken by a bell in change ringing **syn** see TRICK — **on the dodge** *slang* **:** living without settled abode to escape arrest

dodge ball *n* **:** a game in which players formed around a circle try to hit opponents within the circle with a large ball and in which the player or team staying unhit longest is the winner

dodge chain *n* [fr. *Dodge Chain*, a trademark] **:** an accurately pitched cable chain in which detachable bearing blocks are inserted between the links

dodge chain

Dodg·'em \'däjəm\ *trademark* — used for an amusement ride consisting of small electric cars which are steered about in an enclosure and may be frequently bumped into each other

dodg·er \'däjə(r)\ *n* -s **1 :** one that dodges **:** HAGGLER; *usu* **:** one who plays fast and loose or uses tricky devices **2 :** a small handbill **:** CIRCULAR, THROWAWAY **3 a** *South* **:** CORN DODGER **b** *slang Austral* **:** BREAD; *broadly* **:** FOOD **4 :** a device or chemical used for photographic dodging **5 :** a canvas or wood screen to protect lookouts on a ship from spray

dodg·ery \'däj(ə)rē\ *n* -ES **:** TRICKERY, ARTIFICE, *also* **:** EXPEDIENT

dodgy \'däjē\ *adj* -ER/-EST **:** full of dodges **:** EVASIVE, TRICKY

dod·kin \'dädkən\ *n* -s [AF *doydekyn*, fr. MD *duitkijn*, dim. of *duit* doit — more at DOIT] *archaic* **:** DOIT

dod·man \'dädmən\ *n* -s [origin unknown] *dial Eng* **:** SNAIL

do·do \'dō(,)dō\ *n, pl* **dodoes** *or* **dodos** [Pg *doudo*, fr. *doudo* silly, stupid] **1 a :** a large heavy flightless extinct bird (*Raphus cucullatus*, syn. *Didus ineptus*) related to the pigeons but larger than a turkey, that had dark ash-colored plumage with the breast and tail whitish, the rudimentary wings being yellowish white with black-tipped coverts, the bill blackish, and the legs yellow; that inhabited forests and laid a single large white egg in a nest of grass; and that was present in great numbers on the island of Mauritius prior to the arrival of European settlers but became extinct by 1681 **b :** a similar and apparently closely related bird of the neighboring island of Réunion that became extinct under similar circumstances at a slightly later date **2 a :** a person who is simplemindedly unaware of changing conditions and new ideas **:** a dull stupid person **b** *slang* **:** a flight cadet who has not yet soloed **3** *also* **dodo ball :** an illegally weighted bowling ball

dodo

do·do·naea \,dōd°n'ēə\ *n, cap* [NL, after Rembert *Dodoens* (*Dodonaeus*) †1585 Dutch botanist] **:** a genus of tropical shrubs or trees (family Sapindaceae) with alternate gummy leaves and reticulated capsules

do·do·nae·an \,dōd°n'ēən\ *or* **do·do·ne·an** \", də'dōnēən\ *also* **do·do·ni·an** \də'dōnēən\ *or* **do·do·nae·ic** \,dōd°n'ēik\ *adj* [L *Dodonaeus* (fr. Gk *Dōdōnaios*, fr. *Dōdōnē* Dodona, town and oracle in northwestern Greece) + E *-an, -ian* or *-ic*] **:** of or relating to the ancient oracle of Zeus at Dodona on Mount Tomarus in Epirus

dodo split *n* **:** a spare formation in bowling in which the headpin and either the 7 or 10 pin are left standing

do down *vt, Brit* **:** to get the better of (as by trickery) **:** OVERCOME ⟨if it's a game of skill you'll *do* me *down* —W.J.Locke⟩ ⟨hope you don't think I'm *doing* you *down* over selling the house —Clemence Dane⟩

do·drans \'dō,dranz\ *n, pl* **dodran·tes** \dō'dran,tēz\ [L, three quarters of an as, three quarters, alter. of (assumed) *dequadrans*, fr. *de* from + *quadrans* quarter of an as, quarter — more at DE, QUADRANT] **:** a unit of six syllables in Greek and Latin prosody of which either the last four or the first four form a choriambus and the other two are of indeterminate quantity — symbol (o o –◡◡– or –◡◡– o o)

dod-rot \(')däd'rät\ *vt* [euphemism for *God rot*] **:** DAMN — used as a mild oath ⟨*dod-rot* their souls —P.E.Green⟩ ⟨that *dod-rotted* old lady —R.D.Saunders⟩

¹**dods** *pres 3d sing of* DOD, *pl of* DOD

²**dods** \'dädz\ *n pl* [ScGael *dod* + E *-s*] *Scot* **:** a grouchy mood **:** SULKS

do·dunk \'dō,dəŋk\ *n* -s [origin unknown] *NewEng* **:** a stupid person **:** DULLARD

doe \'dō\ *n, pl* **does** *or* **doe** [ME *do, doo*, fr. OE *dā*; akin to G dial. (Alemannic) *tē* doe and perh. to Skt *dhayati* he sucks — more at FEMININE] **1 a :** the adult female fallow deer **b :** the female esp. when adult of any of various mammals of which the male is called buck (as most deers, antelope, goat, rabbit, and rat) — compare COW, HIND **2 :** ALMOND 6a

doe·ling \'dōliŋ\ *n* -s [¹*doe* + *-ling*] **:** a young unbred female goat

do·er \'düə(r), 'dü(ə)r, 'düə\ *n* -s [ME, fr. *don* to do + *-er* — more at DO] **1 :** one that does **:** one that performs or executes ⟨a thinker or a ~ —Sinclair Lewis⟩ **2 :** a domestic animal considered in terms of its capacity to respond to proper care and feeding — used with a qualifying adjective ⟨those steers are very poor ~s⟩ ⟨it doesn't pay to hold over any but your best ~s⟩ **3** *Austral* **:** ECCENTRIC

does *pres 3d sing of* DO

doeskin \'=,=\ *n* [ME *doskin*, fr. *do* + *skin*] **1 :** the skin of does or leather made of it; *also* **:** soft glove leather tanned from sheep or lambskins by a formaldehyde and alum process **2 :** a compact coating and sportswear fabric napped and felted for a smooth surface and made in satin weave of wool or worsted or in twill weave of cotton or rayon

doeskin brown *n* **:** MONKEY SKIN

does·n't \'dəz°nt, *rapid* 'dəd\ [by contr.] **:** does not

doest *archaic pres 2d sing of* DO

doeth *archaic pres 3d sing of* DO

DOF *abbr* delivery on field

¹**doff** \'däf, 'dȯf\ *vb* -ED/-ING/-s [ME *doffen*, fr. *don* to do + *offe, off* off] *vt* **1 a :** to divest oneself of (clothing) **:** take off (one's clothes); *esp* **:** to lift (the hat) **b :** to lay aside **:** rid oneself of ⟨retailers have ~*ed* their rose-colored glasses —Gene Boyo⟩ **2** *obs* **:** to put off (as an unwelcome petitioner) **:** turn away **3 :** to remove (material) from a textile-manufacturing machine ⟨~ full bobbins from a spinning frame⟩ ⟨~ cotton from a carding machine⟩ ~ *vi* **1** *obs* **:** to take off clothing **:** UNDRESS **2** *archaic* **:** to take off or raise the hat

²**doff** \"\ *n* -s **:** the act of removing material from a textile-manufacturing machine; *also* **:** material so removed

doff·er \-fə(r)\ *n* -s **1 a :** a small roller usu. covered with wire teeth used to strip material from another roller or cylinder on textile machinery; *esp* **:** a roller on a carding machine **b :** a machine or device for doffing bobbins **c :** a device for stripping cotton from the spindle of a mechanical cotton picker **2 :** a textile worker who removes full bobbins or cones from machines and puts in empty ones

doffing *adj* **:** relating to or used in the process of removing material from a doffer or carder ⟨~ comb⟩ ⟨~ cylinder⟩

do for \'düfə(r), -,fȯ..\ *vt* **1 :** to attend to the wants and needs of **:** take care of; *esp* **:** to act as the domestic servant of ⟨during her illness she was *done for* by a neighbor⟩ **2 :** to bring about the death or ruin of **:** DESTROY, KILL ⟨a gash in the side of the helmet which would have *done for* a man of lesser breed —Richard Joseph⟩

do·fun·ny *or* **doo·fun·ny** \'dü,fənē\ *n* [¹*do* + *funny*] **:** DOODAD, GADGET

¹**dog** \'dȯg *sometimes* 'däg\ *n* -s [ME *dog, dogge*, fr. OE *docga*] **1 a :** a carnivorous mammal (*Canis familiaris*) of the family Canidae that has been kept in a domesticated state by man since prehistoric times, is undoubtedly descended from some unknown wild member of the genus *Canis* possibly the common wolf, varies in its artificially produced breeds far more than any other mammal (as in form, size, color, and length and character of coat), and is kept chiefly for sporting use or as a guard or companion or esp. formerly for light draft and other labor; *broadly* **:** any animal of the family Canidae **b :** a male dog — opposed to *bitch* **2 a :** a mean worthless fellow **:** CUR, WRETCH, RASCAL ⟨~ of an unbeliever —Sir Walter Scott⟩ **b :** a sportive or roguish fellow **:** BIRD, CHAP ⟨a gay old ~⟩ **c :** FELLOW — used with a qualifying adj. ⟨a lazy ~⟩ ⟨a very sad ~⟩ **3 :** any of various usu. simple mechanical devices for holding, gripping, or fastening something: as **a :** any of various devices consisting essentially of a spike, rod, or bar of metal with a ring, hook, claw, or lug at the end used in various ways (as by driving or embedding in an object or hooking to an object) **b :** either of the hooks of a pair of sling dogs **c :** an iron for holding wood in a fireplace **:** FIREDOG, ANDIRON **d :** a clamp in a lathe for gripping the piece of work and for communicating motion to it from the faceplate **e :** STOP, DETENT, CLICK **f :** a drag for the wheel of a vehicle **g :** a short heavy sharp-pointed steel hook with a ring at one end **h :** a steel projection on a log carriage or on an endless chain that conveys logs into a sawmill **i :** the hammer in a gunlock **4 a** (1) **:** DOGFISH (2) **:** DOG SALMON (3) **:** PRAIRIE DOG **b** (1) **:** SUN DOG (2) **:** WATER DOG 4 (3) **:** FOGBOW **c** (1) **:** DOGSHORE (2) **:** DOGWATCH **d :** HOT DOG **5 :** ostentatious display **:** affected stylishness or dignity ⟨there was a lot of ~ about the affair⟩; *often* **:** dress and behavior not characteristic of or suited to one's station — used esp. in the phrase *put on the dog* **6 :** dogskin used as fur **7 dogs** *pl, slang* **:** FEET **8 :** something inferior of its kind ⟨you call your agent but the only scripts available are real ~s —Paul Newman⟩ **9 dogs** *pl* **:** RUINATION, DESTRUCTION — used with *the* ⟨it's enough to drive anyone to the ~s⟩ ⟨everything is going to the ~s around here⟩ **10 :** PROMISSORY NOTE **11 a :** a poor investment; *usu* **:** a stock or bond not worth its price **b :** a domestic animal of inferior quality or performance **c :** a sluggish horse or a racehorse that does not do well in competition **d :** a low-grade beef animal **e :** a slow-moving or undesirable piece of merchandise — compare RUNNER **f :** a poor-quality motor vehicle **:** LEMON; *esp* **:** a badly worn used car **g** *slang* **:** a woman inferior in looks, character, or accomplishments; *sometimes* **:** PROSTITUTE **h** *slang* **:** a theatrical or musical flop **:** a poor, hackneyed, or outmoded presentation **12** *usu cap* **:** any of certain American Indian peoples: as **a :** CHEYENNE **b :** FOX **13 dogs** *pl* **:** dog racing **14 :** one of the wooden sawhorses placed on a racetrack near the rail when the track is soft to keep horses out of the mud during workouts

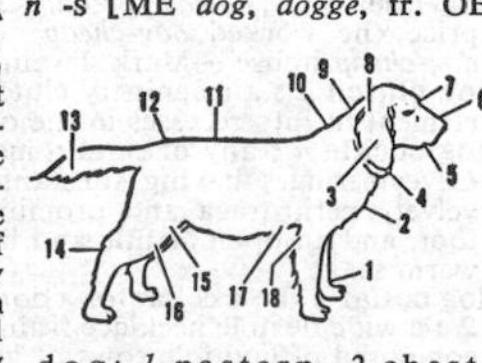

dog: *1* pastern, *2* chest, *3* leather, *4* dewlap, *5* flews, *6* muzzle, *7* stop, *8* occiput, *9* crest, *10* withers, *11* loin, *12* rump, *13* feather, *14* hock, *15* stifle, *16* knee, *17* brisket, *18* elbow

²**dog** \"\ *vb* **dogged** \-gd\ **dogged** \"\ **dogging; dogs** *vt* **1 a :** to hunt or track like a hound **:** follow insidiously or indefatigably ⟨she *dogged* him until he gave in and married her⟩ **b :** to chase with a dog **c :** to worry as if by dogs **:** HOUND ⟨he was *dogged* by financial worries⟩ **2 :** to fasten with a dog — sometimes used with *down* ⟨a sailor *dogged* down the hatch⟩ **3** *South & Midland* **:** DAMN, DARN ⟨well ~ my boot⟩ ⟨~ it all⟩ ~ *vi, archaic* **:** to follow slavishly or pertinaciously — **dog it 1** *slang* **:** to run away **2** *slang* **:** to fail to try one's best **:** loaf on the job **:** GOLDBRICK — **dog the watches :** to change the order of night watches by means of dogwatches

³**dog** \"\ *adv* **:** EXTREMELY, VERY, UTTERLY — often used in combination ⟨dog-poor⟩ ⟨dog-tired⟩ ⟨dog-lame⟩

⁴**dog** \"\ *adj* **1 :** of or for dogs ⟨~ diseases⟩ ⟨~ breeders⟩ ⟨a ~ collar⟩ **:** CANINE **2 :** MALE — used chiefly of carnivorous mammals ⟨a ~ otter⟩ **3 :** MONGREL, SPURIOUS, INFERIOR ⟨~ rhyme⟩; *esp* **:** unlike that used by native speakers or writers ⟨~ Latin⟩ ⟨~ French⟩

⁵**dog** \"\ *usu cap* — a communications code word for the letter *d*

dog alley *n, Midland* **:** DOGTROT

do·ga·na \dō'gänə\ *n* -s [It, fr. Ar *dīwān*, fr. Per, account book] **:** an Italian customhouse

dog ape *n* **:** a baboon or related monkey

do·ga·res·sa \,dōgə'resə\ *n* -s [It, fr. It dial. (Venice), fr. L *ducatrix* female leader, fem. of *duc-, dux* leader — more at DUKE] **:** the wife of a doge

dogbane *also* **dog's-bane** \'=,=\ *n, pl* **dogbanes** *also* **dog's-banes 1 :** a plant of the genus *Apocynum* **2 :** WOLFSBANE 1

dogbane family *n* **:** APOCYNACEAE

dog bent *or* **dog's bent** *n* [so called fr. its being eaten by sick dogs, supposedly as an emetic] **:** a common grass (*Agrostis canina*) with slender culms, narrow leaves, and a long-awned lemma

¹**dog·ber·ry** \'dȯg,berē *sometimes* 'däg-\ *n, pl* **dogberrys** *usu cap* [fr. *Dogberry*, a foolish constable in Shakespeare's *Much Ado about Nothing*] **:** a blundering official; *often* **:** POLICEMAN, CONSTABLE

²**dogberry** \'=—*see* BERRY\ *n* [¹*dog* + *berry*] **1 :** any of certain small fruits usu. considered inferior or unfit for human consumption (as the chokeberry, prickly wild gooseberry, certain rose hips, or the fruit of the mountain ash); *esp* **:** the fruit of the red dogwood **2 :** any plant (as certain dogwoods, mountain ash, or yellow clintonia) that bears dogberries

dogberry tree *n* **:** RED OSIER 2

dog biscuit *n* **:** a hard dry cracker for dogs containing cereal and other vegetable nutrients together with meat and bone meals and flavoring; *sometimes* **:** a hard coarse cracker (as hardtack) for human consumption

dogbit \'=,=\ *adj, South & Midland* **:** bitten by a dog

dogbody \'=,==\ *n* [so called fr. its square stern] **:** a square-sterned boat similar to a chebacco boat

¹**dog·bolt** \'=,bōlt\ *n* [ME *doggebolde*, perh. fr. *dogge* dog + *bolde* bold — more at DOG, BOLD] *archaic* **:** wretched fellow **:** mean contemptible person

²**dogbolt** \"\ *n* [¹*dog* + *bolt*] **1 :** a long slim bolt for uniting two parts at right angles or for securing girders to a supporting post by being driven through one piece then bent and driven into the other **2 :** a bolt used to hold the work in machining

³**dogbolt** \"\ *vt* **:** to secure with a dogbolt

dog brier *n* [trans. of L *sentis canis*] **:** DOG ROSE

dog bur *n* **:** a hound's-tongue (*Cynoglossum officinale*); *also* **:** WILD COMFREY

dog button *n* [so called fr. its having been used to poison dogs] **:** NUX VOMICA

dog cabbage *or* **dog's cabbage** *n* **:** a fleshy southern European herb (*Cynocrambe prostrata*) often eaten as a potherb

dog camomile *n* **:** MAYWEED

dog carrier *n* **:** a ventilated crate with a handle on the top for transporting small or medium-sized dogs

dogcart \'=,=\ *n* **1 :** a cart drawn by a dog or dogs **2 :** a light usu. one-horse carriage that is commonly two-wheeled and high with two transverse seats set back to back

dogcart 2

dogcatcher \'=,==\ *n* **1 :** one that catches dogs; *specif* **:** a person employed or elected to catch and get rid of the stray dogs of a community **2** *slang* **:** a member of a train crew sent to relieve another who is temporarily prohibited by law from further train operation because of having worked 16 hours consecutively

dog-cheap \ˈ=¦=\ *adv (or adj)* **1 :** CHEAPLY **:** for a very low price ⟨he worked *dog-cheap*⟩ ⟨if you come across another *dog-cheap* house —Mark Twain⟩ **2** *archaic* **:** in little repute
dog clutch *n* **:** a machinery clutch in which projections of one element fit into recesses in the other
dog cockle *n* **:** any of certain marine bivalve mollusks (family Glycymeridae) having substantial rounded shells with dark velvety periostraca and prominent hinge teeth, a crescentic foot, and an open mantle and living chiefly on the bottom of warm seas
dog collar *n* **1 :** a collar for a dog **2 :** *slang* **:** CLERICAL COLLAR **2 :** a wide flexible necklace fitting the neck snugly that is often composed of multiple rows of gems or beads
dog daisy *n* **:** any of several composite plants having flower heads with white rays (as certain daisies, the mayweed, or the field chamomile)
dog dance *n* **:** a ceremonial dance among certain western No. American Indians; *esp* **:** one in which eating of dog meat was a feature
dog dandelion *n* **:** FALL DANDELION
dog day *n* [back-formation fr. *dog days,* trans. of LL *dies caniculares,* trans. of Gk *hēmerai kynades;* fr. their being reckoned in ancient times from the heliacal rising of the Dog Star (Sirius)] **1 a dog days** *pl* **:** the period between early July and early September when the hot sultry weather of summer usu. occurs **b :** a day in dog days **:** a hot sultry day **2 dog days** *pl* **:** a period marked by dull lack of progress ⟨the *dog days* following any major upheaval⟩
dog-day cicada *n* **:** any of several large American cicadas (genus *Tibicen*) having a prolonged trilling note that is heard esp. in late summer
dog disease *n* **:** DISTEMPER 2a
dog dollar *n* **:** a silver dollar of the Netherlands that circulated in New Jersey, Pennsylvania, and Maryland about 1700 and had on the obverse a lion rampant
dog·dom \ˈ=dəm\ *n* -s **:** the world of dogs or of dog fanciers
doge \ˈdōj, *It* ˈdòòjā\ *n, pl* **dog·es** \ˈdōjəz\ [It, fr. It dial. (Venice), fr. L *duc-, dux* leader — more at DUKE] **:** the chief magistrate in the former republics of Venice (697–1797) and Genoa (1339–1797 and 1802–5) — **doge·ship** \ˈdōj,ship\ *n*
¹dog-ear *also* **dog's-ear** \ˈ=,=\ *vt* **:** to disfigure or damage with a dog-ear ⟨a book for me is something to be read . . . I want to *dog-ear* it, to underline it, to annotate it —John Mason Brown⟩
²dog-ear *also* **dog's-ear** \ˈ"\ *n, pl* **dog-ears** *also* **dog's-ears 1 :** the corner of a leaf esp. of a book turned down like the ear of a fox terrier **2 :** the small bight made in the leech rope of a sail in reefing
dog-eared *also* **dog's-eared** *adj* **1 :** having dog-ears ⟨a *dog-eared* book⟩ **2 :** WORN, SHABBY, DISFIGURED ⟨a somewhat *dog-eared* . . . duke, a bit run down —Clifton Fadiman⟩
¹dog-eat-dog \¦=¦=ˈ=\ *adj* **:** marked by ruthless self-interest ⟨a *dog-eat-dog* business from start to finish, with each side playing a fast and underhanded game —F.B.Gipson⟩
²dog-eat-dog *n* **:** ruthless self-interest ⟨a raw tough city where *dog-eat-dog* was the law —*New Republic*⟩
dogey *var of* DOGIE
dogface \ˈ=,=\ *n* **:** an army soldier; *esp* **:** INFANTRYMAN
dog-faced ape \ˈ=,fāst-\ *or* **dog-faced baboon** *n* **:** BABOON
¹dogfall \ˈ=,=\ *n* [¹*dog* + *fall*] **1 :** a falling in wrestling of both contestants in which neither is given an advantage **2 :** an inconclusive result to any kind of contest **:** DRAW, TIE **3 :** a throw of a steer resulting in a position with his feet still under him
²dogfall \ˈ"\ *vt* -ED/-ING/-S **:** to put (a steer) down by roping or bulldogging with his feet under him
dog fennel *n* **1 :** MAYWEED 1 **2 :** an annual weed (*Eupatorium capillifolium*) with dissected leaves and a lax elongate inflorescence
¹dogfight \ˈ=,=\ *n* [¹*dog* + *fight*] **1 :** a fight between or as if between dogs **:** MELEE; *broadly* **:** a fiercely disputed contest ⟨political ~s and skulduggery⟩ **2 :** a fight in aerial warfare between two or more fighter planes usu. maneuvering at close quarters
²dogfight \ˈ"\ *vi* **:** to engage in an aerial dogfight ~ *vt* **:** to dogfight with
dogfish \ˈ=,=\ *n* [ME *dokefyche,* fr. *doke, dogge* dog + *fyche, fissh* fish — more at DOG, FISH] **1 :** any of various small sharks (as of the families Squalidae, Carcharhinidae, and Scyliorhinidae) that often appear in schools near shore, that are destructive to fish and fishing gear, and that have livers valued for oil and flesh often made into fertilizer — see SMOOTH DOGFISH, SPINY DOGFISH **2 :** any of various other fishes: as **a :** BOWFIN **b :** the New World burbot **c :** BLACKFISH 1f **3 :** a mud puppy (*Necturus maculosus*)
dog flea *n* **:** a flea (*Ctenocephalides canis*) feeding chiefly on dogs and cats
dog flower *n* **1 :** DAISY 1b **2 :** PURPLE TRILLIUM
dog fly *n* **:** STABLE FLY 1
dogfoot \ˈ=,=\ *n* [so called fr. the appearance of the flower panicles] **:** ORCHARD GRASS
dog·ged \ˈdògəd *sometimes* ˈdäg-\ *adj* [ME, fr. *dog, dogge* dog + *-ed* — more at DOG] **1** *obs* **:** DOGLIKE; *esp* **:** exhibiting unattractive qualities (as belligerence) sometimes attributed to dogs **2 :** obstinately determined **:** UNSHAKABLE, UNREMITTING ⟨~ determination⟩ ⟨resumed his ~ efforts⟩ **syn** see OBSTINATE
dog·ged·ly \-gədlē, -li\ *adv* [ME, fr. *dogged* + *-ly*] **:** in a dogged manner
dog·ged·ness \-gədnəs\ *n* -ES **:** the quality or state of being dogged **:** RESOLUTENESS
¹dog·ger \-gə(r)\ *n* -s [ME *doggere,* perh. fr. MD *dogge* fishing boat] **:** a broad-bowed two-masted fishing boat used esp. by the Dutch in the North sea
²dogger \ˈ"\ *n* -s [¹*dog* (contrivance) + *-er*] **:** a worker who attaches dogs (as to logs), moves articles mechanically by dogs, or fastens articles (as stock to be machined) into dogs that will hold them for further processing
³dogger \ˈ"\ *adj, usu cap* [fr. *dogger,* a kind of ironstone prevalent in strata of this period, of unknown origin] **:** of, relating to, or constituting a subdivision of the European Jurassic — see GEOLOGIC TIME table
¹dog·ger·el *also* **dog·grel** \ˈdòg(ə)rəl, ˈdäg-\ *adj* [ME *dogerel*] **1** *of poetry* **:** quickly contrived, loose, and often irregular esp. if also burlesque or comic **2** *of poetry* **:** trivial or bad ⟨not poetry but mere ~ verse⟩
²doggerel *also* **doggrel** \ˈ"\ *n* -s **1 :** doggerel verse **2 :** a poem in doggerel
dog·gery \ˈdògərē, -ri *sometimes* ˈdäg-\ *n* -ES [¹*dog* + *-ery*] **1 :** doglike behavior; *usu* **:** mean or mischievous actions **2 a :** DOGS **b :** RABBLE, MOB **3** *archaic slang* **:** a low grogshop
dogging *pres part of* DOG
dog·gish \-gish,-gēsh\ *adj* [ME *doggissh,* fr. *dogge* dog + *-issh* -ish — more at DOG] **1 :** like a dog esp. in bad qualities **:** CURRISH, SNAPPISH, SULKY **2 :** stylish in a showy way **:** DASHING — **dog·gish·ly** *adv* — **dog·gish·ness** *n* -ES
dog·gle \ˈdägəl\ *n* -s [origin unknown] *Scot* **:** a child's marble
dog·go \ˈdò(,)gō *sometimes* ˈdä(-\ *adv* [prob. fr. *dog* + *-o*] *slang* **:** quietly out of sight esp. in concealment — used chiefly in the phrase *to lie doggo*
¹dog·gone \ˈdäg¦gän *also* ˈdòg¦gòn — *many who have* ò *in* "*dog*" *and/or* "*gone*" *have* ä *in both syllables of* "*doggone*"\ *vt* -ED/-ING/-S [euphemism for *God damn*] **:** ¹DAMN 5 ⟨~ him⟩ ⟨I'll be *doggoned* if I'll go⟩
²doggone \ˈ"\ *or* **dog·goned** \-n(d)\ *adj* -ER/-EST [euphemism for *God damn, God damned*] **:** DAMNED 2 ⟨go and use up all the towels, every ~ one of them —Sinclair Lewis⟩ ⟨one of the *doggonedest* quirks there is in human nature —W.J.Reilly⟩
³doggone \ˈ"\ *or* **doggoned** \ˈ"\ *adv* [euphemism for *God damn, God damned*] **:** DAMNED ⟨has been pretty ~ self-centered —James Kelly⟩ ⟨is not the country too *doggoned* big? —*New Republic*⟩
⁴doggone \ˈ"\ *n* -s [euphemism for *God damn*] **:** ²DAMN 2 ⟨doesn't give a ~ what happens⟩
dog grass *also* **dog's grass** *n* [so called fr. its being eaten by sick dogs] **1 :** DOG BENT **2 :** COUCH GRASS 1a **3 :** YARD GRASS
dog grate *n* **:** a movable metal frame or basket orig. supported on dogs or andirons that is used for burning logs or coal in a fireplace
doggrel *var of* DOGGEREL
¹dog·gy \ˈdògē, -gi *sometimes* ˈdäg-\ *adj* **doggier; doggiest** [ME, fr. *dogge* dog + *-y* (adj. ending) — more at DOG] **1 :** like or like that of a dog ⟨a ~ odor⟩ **2 a** *of wool* **:** straight, lustrous, and inferior in quality **:** like the hair of a dog **b** *of a bitch* **:** masculine in conformation **3 :** interested or specializing in or fond of dogs ⟨the country club and ~ sets⟩ ⟨a book of interest to all ~ experts⟩ **4 :** DASHING, STYLISH; *often* **:** pretentiously fashionable
²doggy \ˈ"\ *or* **doggie** \ˈ"\ *n, pl* **doggies** [¹*dog* + *-y, -ie* (dim. suffix)] **1 :** a small dog — used also as a pet name or calling name for any dog **2** *usu* **doggie :** DOGFACE
doghead \ˈ=,=\ *n* **:** the hammer of a gunlock
dogheaded \ˈ=¦==\ *adj* **:** having a head shaped like that of a dog ⟨~ bears⟩
dog hip *or* **dog hep** *n, dial Brit* **:** the fruit of the dog rose
dog hobble *n* [so called fr. its tough interlacing branches that obstruct the progress of dogs] **:** DOG LAUREL
doghole \ˈ=,=\ *n* **1 :** a place fit only for dogs **2 :** a mean miserable abode **3 :** a small opening (as in a mine) **4** *West* **:** a small inlet on the coast where ships tie up in order to load lumber
dog hook *n* **:** any of various hooks used in logging
doghouse \ˈ=,=\ *n* **1 :** a shelter for a dog **:** KENNEL **2 :** something felt to resemble a kennel esp. in form or compactness: as **a :** a shed for workmen to store and change clothes (as at a pithead or oil-well drilling); *also* **:** TOOLSHED **b :** the housing of a machine part **c :** a shelter over the cockpit or deck of a boat **d :** an entry chamber through which the batch is fed into a glass furnace **e** *slang* **:** CABOOSE 3 **f** *slang* **:** CIRCUMFLEX 1 ⟨ô is sometimes called ~ o⟩ — **in the doghouse** *adv (or adj)* **:** in a state of disfavor or repudiation ⟨put *in the doghouse* for getting drunk the other night⟩ ⟨has been *in the doghouse* with the administration for months⟩
dog hysteria *n* **:** CANINE HYSTERIA
do·gie *also* **do·gey** *or* **do·gy** \ˈdōgē, -gi\ *n* -s [origin unknown] *chiefly West* **:** a motherless calf in a range herd; *sometimes* **:** a poor or inferior adult animal
dogies *pl of* DOGY
dog in the manger [so called fr. the fable of the dog who would not allow a horse or ox to eat the hay in a manger, even though he did not want it himself] **:** a person who selfishly withholds from others something that he himself cannot use or does not need
dog iron *n* **1** *South & Midland* **:** ANDIRON **2 :** a short bar of iron having its ends bent at right angles for use as a cramp or joggle (as to hold together timbers or stones) **3 :** a short bar of iron with an eye at one end for driving or fitting into a timber or stone to hold it or lift it

dog iron 3

dog killer \ˈ=,==\ *n* **:** a person in charge of killing mad or unwanted dogs
dog laurel *n* **:** an evergreen shrub (*Leucothoe editorum*) of the southern U.S. with racemose white flowers
dog leech *n* **1** *archaic* **:** QUACK 1 **2** *archaic* **:** one that treats dogs' diseases
¹dogleg \ˈ=,=\ *n* **1 :** tobacco of poor quality marketed in twists **2 :** something having an abrupt angle felt to resemble the hind leg of a dog: as **a** *or* **dogleg hole :** a golf hole having an angled fairway that offers the player a choice of following the fairway or risking a shot across the rough **b :** KINK ⟨a ~ in a cable⟩ ⟨a ~ in pipe⟩ **c :** a course (as of an airplane) involving movement first in one direction then in another; *also* **:** an abrupt change in course or direction
²dogleg \ˈ"\ *also* **doglegged** \ *US usu* -¦legəd, *Brit usu* -gd\ *or* **dog's-leg** *adj* **:** crooked or bent like a dog's hind leg; *specif, of stairs* **:** consisting of two or more flights connected by a platform or platforms and running in opposite directions without an intervening well
³dogleg \ˈ"\ *vi* [¹*dogleg* (course)] **:** to proceed along a dogleg course
dogleg fence *n* **:** WORM FENCE
dog letter *var of* DOG'S LETTER
dog lichen *n* **:** a common foliose lichen (*Peltigera canina*) that has the thallus brownish green above and whitish beneath and fruiting bodies resembling the teeth of a dog and that was formerly believed to cure hydrophobia
doglike \ˈ=,=\ *adj* **:** felt to resemble a dog **:** characteristic of a dog esp. in dumb devotion ⟨a ~ affection⟩
dog lily *n* **:** SPATTERDOCK 1
dog louse *n* **:** either of two lice that infest dogs: **a :** a bird louse (*Trichodectes canis*) **b :** a sucking louse (*Linognathus setosus*)
dog·ly \ˈdòglē *sometimes* ˈdäg-\ *adj* **:** CANINE
dog·ma \ˈdògmə *also* ˈdägmə\ *n, pl* **dogmas** \-məz\ *also* **dogma·ta** \-məd·ə,-mətə\ [L, fr. Gk, fr. *dokein* to seem good, seem, think — more at DECENT] **1 a :** something held as an established opinion; *esp* **:** one or more definite and authoritative tenets **b :** a code or systematized formulation of such tenets (as by a theoretician or a school of art or philosophy) ⟨pedagogical ~⟩ ⟨communist ~⟩ **c :** a point of view or alleged authoritative tenet put forth as dogma without adequate grounds **:** an arrogant or vehement expression of opinion **2 :** a doctrine or body of doctrines of theology and religion formally stated and authoritatively proclaimed by a church **syn** see DOCTRINE
dog·man \ˈdògmən *sometimes* ˈdäg-; *in sense "specialist"* -,man\ *n, pl* **dogmen 1 :** KENNELMAN **2 :** a dog fancier or specialist ⟨the best ~ among our local veterinarians⟩
¹dog·mat·ic \dòg¦mad·|ik -at|, |ēk *also* däg-\ *n* -s [Gk *dogmatikos,* fr. *dogmatikos,* adj.] **1** *archaic* **:** DOGMATIST **2** *archaic* **:** DOGMATICS
²dogmatic \(ˈ)=¦=\ *also* **dog·mat·i·cal** \(ˈ)=¦=|əkəl, |ēk-\ *adj* [LL *dogmaticus,* fr. Gk *dogmatikos,* fr. *dogmat-, dogma* + *-ikos* -ic] **1 a :** characterized by or given to the use of dogmatism ⟨a ~ critic⟩ **:** asserting a matter of opinion as if it were fact **:** directly affirmed rather than qualified, debated, or discovered by induction ⟨a ~ statement⟩ **b :** excessively positive in manner or utterance **2 a :** based on or proceeding from a priori truths or assumptions rather than empirical evidence **:** DEDUCTIVE ⟨~ philosophy⟩ **b :** of or relating to a school using a dogmatic approach ⟨a ~ physician⟩ **3 :** of, relating to, or constituting established and authorized doctrine **:** DOCTRINAL ⟨~ writings of the early fathers⟩ — **dog·mat·i·cal·ly** \|ək(ə)lē, |ēk-, -li\ *adv* — **dog·mat·i·cal·ness** \-kəlnəs\ *n* -ES
dog·ma·ti·cian \,dògmə'tishən *also* ,däg-\ *n* -s **:** a specialist in dogmatics or dogmatism
dog·mat·i·cism \dòg'mad·|ə,sizəm, -at| *also* däg-\ *n* -s **:** DOGMATISM 1
dog·mat·ics \|iks,|ēks\ *n pl but sing or pl in constr* **:** a branch of theology dealing with religious doctrines **:** DOGMATIC THEOLOGY
dogmatic theology *n* **:** doctrinal theology that seeks to present the intellectual content of a religious faith and to explicate its meaning from the base of authoritative doctrines generally regarded as derived from revelation **:** DOGMATICS
dog·ma·tism \ˈdògmə,tizəm *also* ˈdäg-\ *n* -s [F *dogmatisme,* fr. MF, fr. L *dogmat-, dogma* + MF *-isme* -ism] **1 a :** positiveness in assertion in matters of opinion **:** statement of a view or belief as if it were an established fact; *often* **:** marked positiveness of statement when unwarranted or arrogant **b :** the use of dogmatic statement as a method of exposition ⟨the ~ of Emerson's writings⟩ **2 a :** a viewpoint or system of ideas based upon insufficiently examined premises **b :** a doctrine that insists upon the existence of certain truths and is opposed to skepticism **c :** philosophy grounded in principles preponderantly established by reason to the neglect of recourse to experience; *specif* **:** an epistemologically uncritical philosophical system
dog·ma·tist \-məd·əst, -mətə-\ *n* -s [MF & ML; MF *dogmatiste,* fr. ML *dogmatista,* fr. Gk *dogmatistēs,* fr. *dogmatizein*] **1 :** a person who believes in or propounds dogmatism **:** a member of a dogmatic school (as of philosophy) **2** *archaic* **:** a propounder of new dogma **3 :** a person who dogmatizes or employs dogmatic methods of exposition; *sometimes* **:** a presumptuously dogmatic person
dog·ma·ti·za·tion \,=məd·ə'zāshən, -mətə-, -mə,tī'z-\ *n* -s **:** an act or instance of dogmatizing
dog·ma·tize \ˈ=mə,tīz\ *vb* -ED/-ING/-S [F *dogmatiser,* fr. LL *dogmatizare* to lay down an opinion, fr. Gk *dogmatizein,* fr. *dogmat-, dogma* + *-izein* -ize] *vi* **:** to speak or write dogmatically **:** make declarations or contend confidently or arrogantly about matters that are open to question ⟨had no wish to ~ concerning the best mode of living —V.L.Parrington⟩ ~ *vt* **:** to state as a dogma or dogmatically — **dog·ma·tiz·er** \-zə(r)\ *n* -s
dogmeat \ˈ=,=\ *n* **1** *also* **dog's meat :** meat for or fit only for dogs; *sometimes* **:** OFFAL, CARRION **2 a :** dog flesh used as food **b :** inferior table meat; *broadly* **:** something disliked
dog mercury *var of* DOG'S MERCURY
dog mint *n* **:** WILD BASIL
dogmouth *var of* DOG'S-MOUTH
dog nail *n* **1 :** a nail with a head that fits flush in a countersink **2 :** a nail with a head projecting considerably on one side
dog nap *n* **:** a brief sleep
dog·nap \ˈdòg,nap *sometimes* ˈdäg-\ *vt* **dognapped; dognapped; dognapping; dognaps** [¹*dog* + *-nap* (as in *kidnap*)] **:** to steal or lure away (a dog) — **dog·nap·per** \-apə(r)\ *n* -s
dog nettle *n* **1 :** HEMP NETTLE **2 :** an annual dead nettle (*Lamium purpureum*) having deep green or purplish leaves, a hairy calyx, and a ring of hairs inside the slender corolla tube
do·gon \ˈdō,gän\ *n, pl* **dogon** *or* **dogons** *usu cap* **1 :** a people located in the central bend of the Niger and noted for their woodcarving esp. of masks **2 :** a member of the Dogon people
do-good \ˈ=,=\ *or* **do-good·ing** \ˈ=¦=iŋ\ *adj* **:** designed sometimes impracticably and overzealously toward bettering the conditions under which others live ⟨*do-good* schemes⟩ ⟨little patience with the *do-gooding* type of foreign aid —*Time*⟩ — **do-good·ism** \-,izəm\ *n* -s
do-good·er \ˈ=¦=ə(r)\ *n* -s **:** an earnest usu. impractical-minded humanitarian bent on promoting welfare work or reform — commonly used with a derogatory implication of naïveté or blundering ineffectualness
dog paddle \ˈ=,==\ *n* **:** an elementary form of swimming often learned by children in which the arms reach forward alternately in the water, the head remains above water, and the legs maintain a kicking motion
dog-paddle \ˈ"\ *vi* [*dog paddle*] **:** to swim clumsily esp. using the dog paddle
dog parsley *or* **dog's parsley** *n* **1 :** FOOL'S PARSLEY **2 :** WILD CHERVIL 1
dogplate \ˈ=,=\ *n* **:** FACEPLATE
dog plum *n* **:** CAPE ASH
dog point *n* **:** the usu. blunted cylindrical thread-free point of a screw designed to clamp or hold
dog poison *n* **:** FOOL'S PARSLEY
do·gra \ˈdōgrə\ *n, pl* **dogra** *or* **dogras** *usu cap* **:** one of a group of hill dwellers in the Dogra district between Punjab and Kashmir
dog·rib \ˈdò,grib *sometimes* ˈdä,-\ *n, pl* **dogrib** *or* **dogribs** *usu cap* [trans. of Déné *Thlingchadinne*] **1 a :** an Athapaskan people of the region between Great Slave Lake and Great Bear Lake, Canada **b :** a member of such people **2 :** a language of the Dogrib people
dog robber *n, slang* **:** an officer's orderly
dog rose *n* **:** a common European wild rose (*Rosa canina*) with stout hooked prickles, five to seven leaflets, and light pink single flowers that is often used as a grafting stock
dog run \ˈ=,=\ *n* **:** DOGTROT 2
¹dogs *pl of* DOG, *pres 3d sing of* DOG
²dogs \ˈdògz *sometimes* ˈdägz\ *n, pl* **dogs** [by folk etymology fr. LaF *dos gris,* lit., gray back] *South* **:** SCAUP DUCK
dog's age *n* **:** a long time
dog salmon *n* **1 :** a salmon (*Oncorhynchus keta*) that occurs abundantly in streams of the American Pacific coast from the Sacramento northward and also on the Asiatic side and that is the common large salmon in Japan — called also *chum salmon* **2 :** any of various other salmons (as the king salmon, the silver salmon, or the humpback salmon)
dogs-and-cats \¦==¦=\ *n pl but sing or pl in constr* **:** RABBIT=FOOT CLOVER
dog's-bane *var of* DOGBANE
dog's bent *var of* DOG BENT
dog's cabbage *var of* DOG CABBAGE
dog's camomile *n* **:** MAYWEED
dog's chance *n* **:** a bare chance in one's favor — usu. used negatively ⟨he didn't have a *dog's chance* of proving his innocence⟩
dog screw *n* **:** a screw with an eccentric head or with one side of its head removed that is used for attaching a watch in a case
dog's death *n* **:** a miserable end; *often* **:** a dishonorable or shameful death
dog's-ear *var of* DOG-EAR
dog's-eared *var of* DOG-EARED
dog's grass *var of* DOG GRASS
dog shark *n* **:** DOGFISH 1
dogshore \ˈ=,=\ *n* **:** a short timber between a block bolted to the ground ways and a similar block on one of the bilge ways to hold a ship while the keelblocks and shores are removed before launching
dogskin \ˈ=,=\ *n* **1 a :** the skin of the dog **b :** leather from it **2 :** leather (as from sheepskins or goatskins) resembling dogskin ⟨a pair of ~ gloves⟩
dogsled \ˈ=,=\ *or* **dog sledge** *n* **:** a sled drawn by dogs
dogsleep \ˈ=,=\ *n* **1** *obs* **:** pretended sleep **2 :** fitful sleep **:** DOZING
dog's-leg *var of* DOGLEG
dog's letter *also* **dog letter** *n* [trans. of L *littera canina;* fr. the fancied resemblance of the trilled *r* to the growl of a dog] **:** the letter *r*
dog's life *n* **:** a miserable drab existence
dog's meat *var of* DOGMEAT 1
dog's mercury *also* **dog mercury** *n* **:** a European perennial weedy plant (*Mercurialis perennis*) with greenish flowers
dog's-mouth *also* **dogmouth** \ˈ=,=\ *n, pl* **dog's-mouths** *also* **dogmouths** \-ths,-thz\ [so called fr. the appearance of the bearded palate that closes the throat of the corolla] **:** SNAPDRAGON 1a
dog snapper *n* **:** a brightly marked silvery or coppery snapper (*Lutjanus jocu*) common in the West Indies and on the Florida coast
dog's nose \ˈ=,=\ *n, pl* **dog's noses :** a mixed drink of malt liquor and spirits; *esp* **:** a hot drink of spiced porter laced with gin or rum
dog soldier *n* [trans. of Cheyenne *Hotámitániu*] **1 :** a member of one of the war societies of the Cheyenne **2 :** a U.S. cavalryman in the period of the Plains Indian wars **3** *slang* **:** SOLDIER, DOGFACE
dog's parsley *var of* DOG PARSLEY
dog spike *n* **:** a dog-nail railroad spike
dogstail *also* **dogtail grass** *n* **1 :** a grass of the genus *Cynosurus; esp* **:** CRESTED DOGSTAIL **2 :** YARD GRASS
dog standard *or* **dog stander** *n, dial Eng* **:** TANSY RAGWORT
dog stinkhorn *n* **:** a basidiomycetous fungus (*Mutinus caninus*) of the order Phallales
dog's-tongue \ˈ=,=\ *n, pl* **dog's-tongues 1 :** HOUND'S=TONGUE **2 :** WILD VANILLA
dog's tooth *n* **:** a string course in masonry with the bricks laid so that one corner projects
dog's-tooth bond *n* **:** a bond in masonry in which no through bonds are introduced and in which headers overlap one another from opposite sides
dog's-tooth grass *n* **1 :** COUCH GRASS 1a **2 :** BERMUDA GRASS
dog's-tooth violet *var of* DOGTOOTH VIOLET
dog-stopper \ˈ=,==\ *n* **:** an extra cable stopper for relieving the strain on a deck stopper of a ship
dog tag *n* **1 :** a metal disk or plate on a dog collar bearing a license registration number **2 :** a military identification tag — usu. used in pl.
dogtail *n* **:** or **dogtail trowel** *n* **:** a molder's small usu. heart-shaped trowel with a curved handle
dog tapeworm *n* **:** a tapeworm (*Dipylidium caninum*) occurring in dogs and cats and occas. in man — called also *double-pored tapeworm*
dog tent *n, slang* **:** SHELTER TENT, PUP TENT
dog tick *n* **:** any of several ticks infesting dogs and commonly other animals: as **a :** AMERICAN DOG TICK **b :** LONE STAR

TICK **c** : a common European tick (*Ixodes ricinus*) that is a vector of canine piroplasmosis **d** : an Australian tick (*Ixodes holocyclus*) that chiefly infests marsupials and that may cause respiratory paralysis in dogs or man by its bite **e** : BROWN DOG TICK

dog–toes \'ˌ=,=\ *n pl but sing or pl in constr* : PUSSYTOES

[1]**dogtooth** \'=,=\ *n, pl* **dogteeth** [ME *dogge toothe,* prob. trans. of L *dens caninus*] **1** *often* **dog tooth** : CANINE TOOTH, EYETOOTH **2** : an architectural ornament common in early English Gothic that consisted usu. of four leaves radiating from a raised point at the center

[2]**dogtooth** \'=,tüth, -th\ *vt* : to decorate with dogteeth

dogtooth spar *n* : a variety of calcite that occurs in acute crystals resembling the tooth of a dog

dogtooth tuna *n* : a medium-sized scaleless tuna (*Gymnosarda nuda*) of the Southwest Pacific ocean that is distinguished by a large mouth with prominent powerful teeth

dogtooth 2

dogtooth violet *also* **dog's-tooth violet** *or* **dogtooth** *n* : a plant of the genus *Erythronium:* as **a** : a European bulbous herb (*Erythronium denscanis*) with two mottled basal leaves and a solitary nodding purple flower appearing in early spring **b** : any of several related American spring-flowering plants: as (1) : a yellow-flowered low-growing woodland plant (*E. americanum*) (2) : a white-flowered or pinkish purple-flowered plant (*E. albidum*) of similar habit

dog town *n* **1** : a community of prairie dogs **2** *slang* : a city commonly used for theatrical tryouts before a play receives metropolitan presentation

dogtown grass *n* : a needle grass (*Aristida longiseta*) of the western U.S.

dog tree *n* : any of several Old World trees and shrubs: as **a** : RED DOGWOOD 1 **b** : a spindle tree (*Euonymus europaeus*) **c** : an elder (*Sambucus nigra*) **d** : GUELDER ROSE **e** : a common alder (*Alnus glutinosa*)

dogtrick \'=,=\ *n, archaic* : a scurvy knavish trick

[1]**dogtrot** \'=,=\ *n* [*dog* + *trot*] **1** : a quick easy gait suggesting that of a dog **2** *South & Midland* : a roofed passage similar to a breezeway; *esp* : one connecting two parts of a cabin ⟨born in a ~ cabin in Kentucky⟩

[2]**dogtrot** \"\ *vi* : to move or progress at a dogtrot

dog tune *n, slang* : a poor song of little musical worth

dog typhus *n* : STUTTGART DISEASE

dogvane \'=,=\ *n* : a small vane carried on the weather rail aboard ship to indicate the direction of the wind

dog violet *n* [trans. of NL *viola canina*] **1** : a leafy-stemmed blue-flowered violet (*Viola canina*) found throughout the northern portions of the Old World **2** : any of several closely related plants of the genus *Viola* (esp. *V. conspersa*)

dog wagon *n* [(*hot*) *dog*] : a small restaurant often specializing in short orders that occupies a converted vehicle (as a streetcar or bus) or that is built to suggest such a vehicle

dog warp *n* : a rope with a strong hook for moving logs

dogwatch \'=,=\ *n* **1** : either of two watches of two hours on shipboard that extend from 4 to 6 and from 6 to 8 p.m. and make an odd number of watches in a day so that crew members who work on a rotating watch system will not stand the same watches every day **2 a** : any of various night shifts; *esp* : the last shift of an organization which is on duty at all times (as a police department) **b** : LOBSTER SHIFT

dog wheel *n* **1** : a wheel turned by dog power **2** : RATCHET WHEEL

dog whelk *also* **dog winkle** *n* : any of certain thick-shelled marine snails: as **a** : BASKET SHELL 2 **b** : any of numerous members of the genus *Thais* that feed chiefly on other mollusks

dog whistle \'=,=\ *n* : a whistle to call or direct a dog; *esp* : one sounding at a frequency inaudible to the human ear

dogwood \'=,=\ *n* **1 a** : a tree or shrub of the genus *Cornus:* as (1) : FLOWERING DOGWOOD (2) : RED DOGWOOD 1 (3) : RED OSIER 2 **b** : the hard tough wood of any dogwood of the genus *Cornus* resembling boxwood in qualities and uses and including some woods that are also classed as boxwoods **2** : any of various trees and shrubs felt to resemble those of the genus *Cornus:* as **a** *Brit* (1) : SPINDLE TREE (2) : GUELDER ROSE **b** : POISON SUMAC **c** : STRIPED MAPLE **d** : any of several Australian shrubs and trees: as (1) : a large leguminous shrub (*Jacksonia scoparia*) having leafless drooping branches and sweet-scented yellow or orange pealike flowers — called also *native broom, stinkwood* (2) : BOOBYALLA 2; *also* : any of several other trees or shrubs of the family Rubiaceae **e** : JAMAICA DOGWOOD **3** : a light brown to moderate yellowish brown that is very slightly redder than Mosul

dogwood borer *n* : a larval clearwing moth (*Thamnosphecia scitula*) that tunnels in the cambium of flowering dogwood

dogwood family *n* : CORNACEAE

dogwood winter *n, South & Midland* : a brief spell of wintry weather in spring

dog wrench *n* : a wrench with a crank handle

[1]**do·gy** \'dōgē\ *n* -ES [by folk etymology fr. LaF *dos gris,* lit., gray back] *Midland* : SCAUP DUCK

[2]**dogy** *var of* DOGIE

doh *var of* DO

doig·té \dwä'tā\ *n* -S [F, fr. *doigt* finger, fr. L *digitus* — more at TOE] : FINGERING

doiled \'dȯi(ə)ld\ *adj* [ME *dold*] *dial Brit* : CONFUSED, DAZED

doi·ly \'dȯilē, -li\ *n* -ES [fr. *Doily* or *Doyley* fl1712 London draper] **1** *obs* : a light woolen fabric **2 a** *archaic* : a small napkin (as one provided at table with a fruit course) **b** : a small often decorative piece (as of linen, lace, or paper) usu. serving as a mat beneath some object (as a vase) either for ornament or to protect an underlying surface **3** *slang* : TOUPEE 2

do in \(')dü'in\ *vt* **1 a** : to bring about the defeat or destruction of : inflict great injury upon : RUIN ⟨an agent sent to *do in* the current government —Herbert Gold⟩ ⟨the stock-market crash *did* him *in* —Thomas Whiteside⟩ **b** : to bring about the death of : KILL ⟨after twice trying to *do* him *in* with gas —Alexander Woollcott⟩ **c** : to bring almost to the point of exhaustion : wear out ⟨would see I was *done in* and tell me to stop working —Frank Sargeson⟩ **2** : to take in : CHEAT ⟨one feels as though one has been somehow swindled and *done in* —Aldous Huxley⟩

doi·na \'dȯinə\ *n, pl* **doinas** \-nəz\ *also* **doi·ne** \-,ne\ [Romanian *doină*] : a Romanian folk song usu. in the form of a lament

doing *n* -S [ME, fr. gerund of *don* to do — more at DO] **1 a** : the act of performing or executing : ACTION ⟨art is primarily not a contemplation but a ~ —Havelock Ellis⟩ ⟨any such grandiose plan will take some ~ —Green Peyton⟩ **b** : the result of such an action ⟨the picture and the story I recognized as my father's ~ —Ben Riker⟩ **2 doings** *pl* **a** : things that are done or that occur : ACTS, DEEDS, EVENTS ⟨the daily ~*s* of the forge and field and market —H.O.Taylor⟩ **b** *dial* : social activities ⟨went to the ~*s* at the schoolhouse Saturday night⟩ **3 doings** *pl, dial* : materials for a dish or meal : food esp. when made up into a dish ⟨a breakfast of corn ~*s* and flapjacks⟩

[1]**doit** \'dȯit\ *n* -S [D *duit,* fr. MD *duit, doyt;* akin to ON *thveiti* small coin, *thveita* to hew — more at WHITTLE] **1** : an old Dutch coin equal to ⅛ stiver or about ½ farthing **2** : a small amount : TRIFLE, BIT, WHIT

[2]**doit** \"\ *vb* -ED/-ING/-S [prob. alter. of [1]*dote*] *vi, dial Brit* : [1]DOTE 1 ~ *vt, Scot* : PERPLEX

doit·ed \-əd, -ət\ *adj* [ME (Sc dial.), prob. alter. of *doted,* past part. of *doten* to dote — more at DOTE] *chiefly Scot* : turned to dotage : CONFUSED

doit·kin \-kən\ *n* -S [AF *doydekyn* — more at DODKIN] : DOIT

doit·ri·fied \'dȯitrə,fēt\ *adj* [blend of *doited* and *petrified*] *Scot* : DAZED

do·jo \'dō(,)jō\ *n* -S [Jap *dojō*] : a speckled brownish loach (*Misgurnus anguillicaudata*) of eastern Asia that is sometimes kept as a scavenger in the tropical aquarium — compare WEATHERFISH

doke \'dōk\ *n* -S [prob. alter. of *dalk,* fr. ME, perh. dim. of ME *dale* — more at DALE] *dial Eng* : a depression or indentation; *esp* : DIMPLE

doketic *often cap, var of* DOCETIC

dol \'dōl\ *n* -S [L *dolor* pain — more at DOLOR] : a unit for the measurement of pain intensity usu. taken as one tenth of the range of increasing sensation from that produced by the least perceptible stimulus to that at which further increase in stimulation causes no further increase in sensation

dol *abbr* **1** [It *dolce*] soft; sweet **2** dollar

do·lab·rate \dō'labrət, 'dalə,brāt\ *adj* [LL *dolabratus,* fr. L *dolabra* mattock, pickax + *-atus* -ate] : DOLABRIFORM

do·lab·ri·form \dō'labrə,fȯrm\ *adj* [L *dolabra* + E *-iform*] : shaped like the head of an ax or hatchet

do·lan·tal \də'lantᵊl\ *n* -S [alter. of *dolantin*] : meperidine hydrochloride

do·lan·tin \-tᵊn\ *n* -S [ISV *dol-* (fr. L *dolor* pain) + *ᵊanti-* + *-in* — more at DOLOR] : meperidine hydrochloride

dol·can \'dälkən\ *n* -S [alter. of *dulciana*] : an 8-foot pipe-organ stop similar to the dulciana

[1]**dol·ce** \'dōl(,)chā, -,chē\ *adj* (*or adv*) [It, lit., sweet, fr. L *dulcis* — more at DULCET] : SOFT, SMOOTH — used as a direction in music — **dol·ce·men·te** \,dōlchä'mentē, -n(,)tā\ *adv*

[2]**dolce** \"\ *n, pl* **dol·ci** \-(,)chē\ [It, fr. *dolce,* adj.] **1** : a sweet dessert **2** : a very soft flute pipe-organ stop of either 8-foot or 4-foot pitch

dolce cornet *n* : a pipe-organ mixture of soft singing quality of tone

dol·ce far nien·te \,dōlchē,färnē'entē, -(,)chā,-, -ärn'ye-, -en(,)tā\ *n* -S [It, lit., sweet doing nothing] : delightful relaxation in carefree indolence

dol·ci·an \'dälsēən, 'dōl-,'dȯl-\ *or* **dul·ci·an** \'dəl-\ *also* **dol·ci·no** \dōl'chē(,)nō\ *n* -S [*dolcian, dulcian* alter. of *dulciana; dolcino* fr. It, modif. of ML *dulciana* — more at DULCIANA] **1** : a small musical instrument sounding like a bassoon and used in the 16th and 17th centuries **2** *also* **dul·zi·an** \'dəlzēən\ : a pipe-organ stop sounding like a bassoon

[1]**dol·cis·si·mo** \dōl'chēsə,mō, -chis-\ *adj* (*or adv*) [It (superl. of *dolce* sweet), fr. L *dulcissimus,* superl. of *dulcis* sweet — more at DULCET] : very sweet or soft — used as a direction in music

[2]**dolcissimo** \"\ *n* -S [It, *dolcissimo,* adj.] : an extremely soft pipe-organ stop of flute quality

dol·drum \'dōldrəm, 'däl- *sometimes* 'dȯl-\ *n* -S [prob. akin to OE *dol* foolish, silly — more at DULL] **1 doldrums** *pl* **a** : a spell of listlessness or despondency : BLUES **b** : a state of bafflement : QUANDARY **2** *archaic* : a sluggish or slow-witted person **3 doldrums** *pl* **a** : a region over the ocean near the equator abounding in calms, squalls, and light baffling winds **b** : the calms met with in that region **4 doldrums** *pl* **a** : condition of inactivity, retardation, or stagnation: **a** : a downswing, slump, or slack period (as in business or industry) ⟨through the economic ~*s* of the late forties —Drew Middleton⟩ ⟨bring the antiques business out of the depression ~*s* —Alice Winchester⟩ : a period of sagging or falling off (as in sales or financial or political activity) **b** : a deterioration to a low ebb of vigor, creative power, or effectiveness ⟨that American fiction is at present in the ~*s* is borne out anew —Amy Loveman⟩

[1]**dole** \'dōl\ *n* -S [ME, fr. OE *dāl* division, separation, share, lot; akin to OE *dǣl* part, share, lot — more at DEAL] **1 a** *archaic* : one's allotted share or portion ⟨hath not our great Queen my ~ of beauty trebled —Alfred Tennyson⟩ **b** *archaic* : one's lot in life : one's destiny or fate ⟨happy man be his ~, say I; every man to his business —Shak.⟩ **c** *dial Eng* : an allotment of land in a common **2 a** (1) : a giving or distribution of food, money, or clothing to the needy ⟨the weekly ~ at a parish charity station⟩ (2) : a direct distribution of government funds made at regular intervals to the unemployed : UNEMPLOYMENT INSURANCE ⟨all his family was on the ~ —Margaret Kennedy⟩ ⟨it was as well to starve or live on the ~ in the Old World as the New —Oscar Handlin⟩ **b** : something distributed at intervals as charity : a ration for the needy ⟨people able and willing to work forced to accept ~*s*⟩ **c** : something portioned out and distributed in driblets or pittances **d** *obs* : a blow or some dire treatment administered ⟨dealing ~ among his foes —John Milton⟩ **e** : a gratuitous bestowal; *specif* : a distribution of sustaining or subsidizing contributions ⟨the country's industrial recovery is an illusion; it is living on an American ~⟩

[2]**dole** \"\ *vt* -ED/-ING/-S [ME *dolen,* fr. *dole,* n.] **1** : to give or distribute as a charity — used often with *out* ⟨he gathered all the blankets, pillows, pieces of clothing, and other supplies . . . and *doled* them out to the distraught, homeless natives of the island —Clay Blair⟩ **2** : to give or deliver in small portions (as in driblets) guardedly or calculatingly : PARCEL — used with *out* ⟨puts all my money in the bank and just ~*s* out a few dollars to me once in a while —Lucy M. Montgomery⟩ **3** : to give or deliver in equal portions or according to a prescribed allotment — used with *out* ⟨stopped his scribbling long enough to ~ out sheets and mattress covers, shelter half and blankets, pack and all the rest of it —James Jones⟩ **syn** see DISTRIBUTE

[3]**dole** \"\ *n* -S [ME *dol, doel, del,* fr. OF, fr. LL *dolus* pain, grief, alter. (influenced by L *dolus* fraud, deceit) of L *dolor* — more at TALE, DOLOR] **1 a** : GRIEF, SORROW ⟨deep questioning, which probes to endless ~ —George Meredith⟩ **b** : bad luck : MISFORTUNE **2** *obs* : mourning clothes **syn** see SORROW

[4]**dole** \"\ *vi* -ED/-ING/-S [ME *dolen,* fr. MF *doloir,* fr. L *dolēre* to feel pain, grieve — more at CONDOLE] : LAMENT, MOURN

[5]**dole** \"\ *n* -S [in sense 1, fr. ME, prob. fr. MD *doel* trench used as a landmark; in sense 2, prob. fr. Fris *dōl* goal, fr. OFris *dōl;* both akin to OHG *tuolla* small valley, ON *dæll* inhabitant of a valley, OE *dæl* valley — more at DALE] **1** *now dial Brit* : a landmark or boundary marker **2** *now dial Brit, in some children's games* : GOAL

[6]**dole** \"\ *n* -S [MF *dol,* fr. L *dolus* fraud, deceit — more at TALE] **1** *obs* : TRICKERY **2** *Scots law* : criminal intent : MALICE

dole chaser *n* [[1]*dole*] *Austral* : a vagrant living on food issued by dole stations

dole cupboard *n* [[1]*dole*] : an ecclesiastical cupboard to contain bread or other supplies for the poor of the parish

dole·ful \'dōlfəl\ *adj* **dolefuller; dolefullest** [ME *dolful, doelful, delful,* fr. *dol, doel, del* dole + *-ful* — more at DOLE (grief)] **1 a** : causing grief or affliction : WOEFUL, LAMENTABLE ⟨a head and heart full of ~ thoughts, anxieties, and fears —Nathaniel Hawthorne⟩ **b** : attended with or indicating grief or a morose or despairing attitude : CHEERLESS ⟨in the *dolefullest* dumps after flunking⟩ ⟨abandoning the argument, she gave a ~ shake of her head⟩ **c** : DISCONSOLATE ⟨the ~ one is obviously the defeated competitor⟩ **2 a** : expressing mourning or lamentation ⟨the body is carried around in front of the mourners, who are singing a very ~ dirge —W.H.Goodenough⟩ **b** : evoking sadness or gloom : inducing depression of spirits : LUGUBRIOUS ⟨he was constitutionally gloomy, a congenital pessimist who always saw the ~ side of any situation —W.A.White⟩ — **dole·ful·ly** \-fəlē, -li\ *adv* — **dole·ful·ness** \-lnəs\ *n* -ES

dole·fuls \-fəlz\ *n pl* : BLUES — used with *the*

do·lent \'dōlənt\ *adj* [ME, fr. MF, fr. L *dolent-, dolens,* pres. part. of *dolēre* to feel pain, grieve — more at CONDOLE] : SORROWFUL — **do·lent·ly** *adv*

do·len·te \dō'lentē, -n(,)tā\ *adj* (*or adv*) [It, fr. L *dolent-, dolens*] : SORROWFUL — used as a direction in music

do·len·tis·si·mo \,dō,len'tisə,mō\ *adj* (*or adv*) [It, superl. of *dolente*] : most mournful — used as a direction in music

dol·er·ite \'dälə,rīt\ *n* -S [F *dolérite,* fr. Gk *doleros* deceitful (fr. *dolos* deceit) + *-ite;* fr. its being easily mistaken for diorite — more at TALE] **1** : a coarse basalt **2** *Brit* : DIABASE 3 **3** : a dark igneous rock whose constituents are not determinable megascopically — **dol·er·it·ic** \,dälə'ridik\ *adj*

dol·er·oph·a·nite \,dälə'räfə,nīt\ *also* **dol·er·o·phane** \'dälərə,fān, dō'ler-\ *n* -S [*dolerophanite* fr. *dolerophane* + *-ite; dolerophane* fr. It *dolerofano,* fr. Gk *doleros* deceitful + It *-fano* (fr. Gk *phainesthai* to appear)] : a basic copper sulfate $Cu_2(SO_4)O$ of volcanic origin occurring in brown monoclinic crystals

doles *pl of* DOLE, *pres 3d sing of* DOLE

doles·man \'dōlzmən\ *n, pl* **dolesmen** : one who receives a dole

dole·some \'dōlsəm\ *adj* [[3]*dole* + *-some*] : DOLEFUL ⟨the ~ realms of darkness and of death —Alexander Pope⟩ — **dole·some·ly** *adv*

do·less \'düləs\ *adj* [[1]*do* + *-less*] *dial* : lacking energy or ambition : SHIFTLESS

dolia *pl of* DOLIUM

do·li ca·pax \,dō,lī'kä,paks\ *adj* [L, capable of deceit] : old enough or of sufficient intelligence and sane enough to be legally responsible for wrongful acts — opposed to *doli incapax*

dolich- *or* **dolicho-** *comb form* [NL, fr. Gk, fr. *dolichos* — more at INDULGE] **1** : long ⟨*dolicho*cephalic⟩ **2** : narrow ⟨*dolicho*hieric⟩

dol·i·cho·blond \,dälə(,)kō,-lē(-+\ *n* [*dolich-* + *blond*] : a longheaded blond person

dol·i·cho·ceph·al \,=ˌ=(,)='sefəl\ *n, pl* **dolichocephals** \-əlz\ *also* **dolichocepha·li** \-ə,lī\ [NL *dolichocephalus,* fr. *dolich-* + *-cephalus*] : a dolichocephalic person

dol·i·cho·ce·phal·ic \'=ˌ=(,)=sə'falik\ *also* **dol·i·cho·ceph·a·lous** \-'sefələs\ *adj* [*dolichocephalic* fr. NL *dolichocephalus* + E *-ic; dolichocephalous* fr. NL *dolichocephalus*] : having a relatively long head with a cephalic index of less than 75 — **dol·i·cho·ceph·a·lism** \,=ˌ=(,)='sefə,lizəm\ *n* -S — **dol·i·cho·ceph·a·ly** \-fəlē\ *n* -ES

dol·i·cho·cra·ni·al \'=ˌ=(,)='krānēəl\ *also* **dol·i·cho·cra·nic** \-nik\ *adj* [ISV *dolich-* + *cranial, cranic;* orig. formed as G *dolichokran*] : having a relatively long head with a cranial index of less than 75 — **dol·i·cho·cra·ny** \'=ˌ=(,)=,krānē\ *n* -ES

dol·i·cho·facial \,=ˌ=(,)=+\ *adj* [*dolich-* + *facial*] : LEPTOPROSOPIC

dol·i·cho·glos·sus \,=ˌ=(,)='gläsəs, -lȯs-\ *n, cap* [NL, fr. *dolich-* + *-glossus* (fr. Gk *glōssa* tongue) — more at GLOSS] : a genus of hemichordate worms differing from those of *Balanoglossus* in lacking liver sacs and in having a long proboscis with a single pore — compare ENTEROPNEUSTA

dol·i·cho·hi·er·ic \'=ˌ=(,)=;hī;erik\ *adj* [*dolich-* + *-hieric*] : having a relatively long narrow sacrum with a sacral index of less than 100 — compare PLATYHIERIC, SUBPLATYHIERIC

dol·i·cho·id \'dälə,kȯid\ *adj* [*dolich-* + *-oid*] *anthrop* : tending to be long and narrow

dol·i·cho·mor·phic \,dälәkō;mȯrfik, -lēk-\ *adj* [*dolich-* + *-morphic*] : ECTOMORPHIC, ASTHENIC — opposed to *brachymorphic* — **dol·i·cho·mor·phy** \'=ˌ=,mȯrfē\ *n* -ES

dol·i·cho·pel·lic \'=ˌ=(,)=;pelik\ *adj* [*dolich-* + *-pellic*] : having a pelvis relatively long dorsoventrally with a pelvic index of 95 or more — **dol·i·cho·pel·ly** \'=ˌ=(,)=,pelē\ *n* -ES

dol·i·chop·o·did \,dälə'käpədəd\ *adj* [NL *Dolichopodidae*] : of or relating to the Dolichopodidae

dol·i·cho·pod·i·dae \,dälәkō'pädə,dē, -lēk-\ *n pl, cap* [NL, fr. *Dolichopod-, Dolichopus,* type genus (fr. *dolich-* + *-pus*) + *-idae*] : a large family of small bristly usu. metallic green long-legged two-winged flies that feed on other insects and mites

dol·i·chop·o·dous \,dälə'käpədəs\ *adj* [*dolich-* + *-podous*] : having a relatively long foot

dol·i·cho·prosopic \'dälə(,)kō, -lē(-+\ *adj* [*dolich-* + *prosop-* + *-IC*] : LEPTOPROSOPIC

dol·i·cho·psyl·li·dae \,=ˌ=kō'silə,dē, -,käp's-\ *n pl, cap* [NL, fr. *Dolichopsylla,* type genus (fr. *dolich-* + Gk *psylla* flea) + *-idae*] : a family of fleas chiefly of temperate zones including many that attack rodents and act as vectors of plague among rodents — see CERATOPHYLLUS

dol·i·chos \'dälə,käs\ *n* [NL, fr. L, a leguminous plant, fr. Gk, lit., racecourse, fr. *dolichos* long — more at INDULGE] **1** *cap* : a genus of chiefly tropical vines (family Leguminosae) having a bearded style and the keel of the corolla coiled **2** -ES : any plant of the genus *Dolichos*

dol·i·cho·saur \'dälәkō,sȯ(ə)r, -lēk-\ *n* -S [NL *Dolichosaurus*] : a lizard of the genus *Dolichosaurus*

dol·i·cho·sau·rus \,=ˌ=='sȯrəs\ *n, cap* [NL, fr. *dolich-* + *-saurus*] : a genus (the type of the family Dolichosauriidae) of small long-necked aquatic fossil lizards from the Upper Cretaceous of England closely related to the recent Varanidae

dol·i·cho·so·ma \-'sōmə\ *n, cap* [NL, fr. *dolich-* + *-soma*] : a genus of slender limbless extinct amphibians (order Aistopoda) from the Carboniferous and Permian of Europe

dol·i·cho·sty·lous \'=ˌ=;stīləs\ *adj* [*dolich-* + *-stylous*] : long-styled (as certain dimorphic or trimorphic flowers)

dol·i·chu·ran·ic \,dälәkyü'ranik\ *adj* [*dolich-* + *uran-* + *-ic*] : having an upper alveolar arch index of less than 110

dol·i·chu·ric \,dälə'kyürik\ *adj* [NL *dolichurus* + E *-ic*] : having a redundant syllable ⟨~ hexameter⟩

dol·i·chu·rus \,dälə'kyürəs\ *n, pl* **dolichu·ri** \-ü,rī\ [NL, fr. Gk *dolichouros,* lit., long-tailed, fr. *dolich-* + *-ouros* *-urous*] : a dactylic hexameter with an actual or apparent redundant syllable in the last foot

do·li·idae \də'līə,dē\ [NL, fr. *Dolium,* type genus + *-idae*] *syn of* TONNIDAE

do·li in·ca·pax \,dō,lī'iŋkə,paks, -iŋk-\ *adj* [L, incapable of deceit] : incapable of guilt — opposed to *doli capax*

do·li·ne *also* **do·li·na** \də'lēnə\ *n* -S [Russ *dolina* plain, valley, bottomland, fr. *dol* valley; akin to OSlav *dolŭ* pit, hole, valley — more at DALE] : SINK 5

doling *pres part of* DOLE

do·li·o·form \'dōlēə,fȯrm\ *adj* [L *dolium* large jar, cask + E *-o-* + *-form* — more at DOLIUM] : shaped like a barrel

do·li·ol·i·dae \,dōlē'älə,dē\ *n pl, cap* [NL, fr. *Doliolum,* type genus + *-idae*] : a small family of oceanic tunicates coextensive with the suborder Cyclomyaria

do·li·o·lum \də'līələm\ *n, cap* [NL, fr. L, small cask, dim. of *dolium*] : a genus of free-swimming oceanic tunicates developing with alternation of generations and having a cask-shaped transparent body surrounded by complete muscular rings

dolittle \'=,=\ *n* -S [[1]*do* + *little*] : IDLER

[1]**do·li·um** \'dōlēəm\ *n, pl* **do·lia** \-ēə\ [L; akin to ORuss *delva, delvi* cask, L *dolare* to hew — more at CONDOLE] : an earthenware cask or jar of Roman antiquity sometimes large enough to hold a man — compare PITHOS

[2]**dolium** \"\ [NL, fr. L, large jar, cask] *syn of* TONNA

[3]**dolium** \"\ *n, pl* **dolium** *or* **doliums** [NL, fr. L, large jar, cask] : a mollusk of the genus *Tonna* : TUN SHELL

doll \'däl, 'dȯl\ *n* -S *often attrib* [prob. fr. *Doll,* nickname for *Dorothy*] **1 a** : a small-scale figure of a human being (as of a baby or child) used esp. as a child's plaything ⟨busy dressing and undressing her ~*s*⟩ ⟨~ clothes⟩ **b** : PUPPET 1a **c** : a small carved or molded figure serving as a cult object or representing a nursery-story or cartoon character ⟨carrying a Mickey Mouse ~ for good luck⟩ **2 a** : a young woman with pretty babyish face and often frilly clothes that is sometimes featherbrained, frivolous, or giddy ⟨the most stuck-up ~ in the world —Willa Cather⟩ **b** *slang* : WOMAN ⟨a realm where men are guys, women are ~*s,* and gambling . . . is a profession —John Mason Brown⟩ **c** *slang* : PARAMOUR **d** *slang* : a male who is an object of female admiration ⟨he is tall, handsome, and muscular. In short, he's a ~ —Ethel Merman⟩ **e** : a sweet kind good-natured woman

dol·lar \'dälə(r)\ *n* -S *often attrib* [alter. of earlier *daler,* fr. D or LG, fr. G *taler,* short for *joachimstaler,* fr. Sankt *Joachimsthal* (Jáchymov), town in northwestern Bohemia, Czechoslovakia, where the first talers were made] **1** : an old German taler coin **2** : any one of a number of coins of various countries patterned after the taler: as **a** : a Spanish or Spanish-American peso or piece of eight **b** : any of several coins issued in the U.S. (as a silver coin issued 1794–1935, after 1837 weighing 412.5 grains or 26.730 grams of silver .900 fine, and a gold coin issued 1849–89, weighing 25.8 grains or 1.6718 grams of gold .900 fine) — see TRADE DOLLAR **c** : a silver coin of Canada issued since 1935 chiefly for commemorative purposes **d** : any of several British coins issued for use in certain territories of the Commonwealth (as a silver coin for Hong Kong issued 1866–68 and a silver coin issued at intervals between 1903 and 1926 for the Straits Settlements) — called also *British dollar* **3 a** : the basic monetary unit of the U.S. serving as a medium, standard, or basis of foreign exchange ⟨provided the ~*s* required as credit to finance reconstruction in war-devastated areas⟩ ⟨a loan to enable a country to pay in ~*s* for additional imports from the U.S.⟩ ⟨the area of American minor satellites and its accompanying ~ bloc would have to be indicated —O.S.Knauth⟩ **b** : any of various basic monetary units — see MONEY table **4 a** : a currency bill representing one dollar **b** : a token representing one dollar **5** : PESO **6** : YUAN **7** *slang Brit* : CROWN 8a (3) **8** : the commercial interests of the U.S. in trade in foreign countries ⟨whether the flag will follow the ~⟩

dollar-and-cent *or* **dollars-and-cents** \¦==¦=\ *adj* **:** expressed or expressible in money **:** measurable in or calculated hardheadedly in terms of money value exclusively or in exact amount of money ⟨from the *dollars-and-cents* approach⟩
dollar area *n* **:** the area of the world where the U.S. dollar is used as a basis for exchange and currencies can be converted freely into dollars
dollar averaging *n* **:** a practice of investing a uniform sum in common stocks periodically regardless of the level of prices
dollar-a-year \¦===¦=\ *adj* **:** compensated by a token salary (as one dollar a year) usu. for government service ⟨a *dollar-a-year* man⟩
dollar bird *n* [so called fr. the light spot, about the size of a Straits dollar, on its open wing] **:** a roller (*Eurystomus orientalis*) found from Manchuria to Ceylon and Australia
dollar day *n* **:** a day on which the merchants of a locality make special offerings of goods and services for one dollar; *broadly* **:** a day on which bargain prices in many lines are offered
dol·lar·dee \ˈdälə(r),dē\ *n* -s [origin unknown] **:** BLUEGILL
dollar diplomacy *n* **1 :** diplomacy used by a country to promote its financial or commercial interests abroad **2 :** diplomacy that seeks to strengthen the power of a country or effect its purposes in foreign relations by the use of its financial resources
dollarfish \ˈ==,=\ *n* [so called fr. its shape and the silver color of the young] **1 :** a small marine butterfish (*Poronotus triacanthus*) of the family Stromateidae with a laterally compressed body common in summer on the Atlantic coast of the northern and middle U.S. — called also *harvest fish* **2 :** LOOKDOWN
dollar gap *also* **dollar shortage** *n* **:** the amount of additional dollar receipts required by a country to equal dollar payments that must be made for imports from dollar nations or to meet other obligations
dollarleaf \ˈ==,=\ *n* **1 :** FALSE WINTERGREEN **2 :** a prostrate round-leafed tick trefoil (*Desmodium rotundifolium*)
dollar mark *or* **dollar sign** *n* **:** a mark $ or $ placed before a number to indicate that it stands for dollars
dollar of account : the U.S. dollar reckoned on the London stock exchange at four shillings (instead of actual exchange value) for facility of calculation
dollar spot *n* **:** a disease of golf-green and lawn grasses caused by a fungus (*Sclerotinia homeocarpa*) and characterized by areas in the turf about two inches in diameter that are first brownish but become bleached straw colored and finally coalesce to form large irregular patches — compare GREASE SPOT
dollarwise \ˈ==,=\ *adv* [*dollar* + *-wise*] **:** in terms of dollars **:** so far as values are translatable into money equivalents
doll baby *n* **1 :** a child's doll **2 :** DOLL 2a **3 :** SWEETHEART — used chiefly as a pet name
doll carriage *also* **doll buggy** *n* **:** a child's small-scale baby carriage for play with a doll
doll cheeses *n pl* **:** CHEESE 4
doll·dom \ˈdäldəm, ˈdȯl-\ *n* -s **:** the realm of dolls
dollface \ˈ=,=\ *n* **:** a person having a face with a smooth prettiness and childish expression suggestive of a doll
dollhouse \ˈ=,=\ *n* **1 :** a child's small-scale toy house **2 :** a dwelling so small as to suggest resemblance to a house for dolls
dolli·er \ˈdäliə(r)\ *n* -s [²*dolly* + *-er*] *Brit* **:** a worker who scours or polishes with a dolly
doll·ish \ˈdälish, ˈdȯl-, -lēsh\ *adj* **:** like a doll; *specif* **:** pretty but rather empty-headed — **doll·ish·ly** \-ləshlē, -lēsh-, -shli\ *adv* — **doll·ish·ness** \-lishnəs, -lēsh-\ *n* -ES
¹**dol·lop** \ˈdäləp\ *also* **dal·lop** \ˈdal-\ *n* -s [origin unknown] **1** *obs* **:** a tuft or clump esp. of grass **2 a :** a lump or blob of a semiliquid, mushy, or plastic substance ⟨drop a ~ of ice cream or of whipped cream on a piece of pie⟩ ⟨a ~ of stew hit me on the back of the neck —Allan Ashbolt⟩ **b :** a dash or splash or a small portion of a liquid; *specif* **:** a small drink ⟨lingering over a few ~*s* of brandy⟩ **c :** a slight admixture or one of several interspersed bits ⟨the author has essayed a charming fantasy with a ~ of satire —Lee Rogow⟩ ⟨experimental novels . . . served up in ~*s* of bogus poetic prose —J.B.Priestley⟩ **3** *dial Brit* **:** SLUT, TROLLOP
²**dollop** \″\ *also* **dallop** \″\ *vb* -ED/-ING/-S *vt* **1** *chiefly Brit* **:** to serve in dollops **2** *chiefly Brit* **:** to admix with a dollop or intersperse with dollops ~ *vi* **:** PLOP ⟨salt water ~*ed* over the boat's side⟩
dol·lo's law \ˈdä(,)lōz-\ *n, usu cap D* [after Louis *Dollo* †1931 Belgian paleontologist] **:** a generalization in biology: characters lost in the course of evolution are never regained in the original form
doll out *vt* **:** to doll up
doll post *n* **:** a railroad signal consisting of a short post mounted on a bracket
dolls *pl of* DOLL
doll's-eyes \ˈ=,=\ *n pl* **:** the fruits of a white baneberry (*Actaea brachypoda*)
doll's head *n* **:** a projection of the top rib that fits into a corresponding hollow in the breech of a gun
doll up *vi* **:** to dress oneself in formal, elegant, or fancy attire and personal adornments ⟨insisted that he must *doll up* for this party⟩ ~ *vt* **1 :** to array in elegance, extravagance, or showy outfit ⟨all *dolled up* in top hat and tails, dancing attendance on a certain show girl —Polly Adler⟩ **2 :** to make more attractive with a freshening up and addition of decorative details ⟨a country schoolhouse all *dolled up* by the pupils for a Christmas party⟩
¹**dolly** *also* **doll·ey** *or* **doll·ie** \ˈdälē, ˈdȯl-, -li\ *n, pl* **dollies** *also* **dolleys** [*doll* + *-y, -ey, -ie*] **1 a** *dial Eng* **:** an untidy woman **b** *slang* **:** an attractive young woman **:** DOLL **c** *cricket* **:** SITTER **2 :** DOLL 1a — a child's term **3 a :** a hand-operated wooden-pronged instrument that washes clothes by turning and pounding them in a tub **b :** a contrivance turning on a vertical axis by a handle or winch used in mining operations to give a circular motion to the ore to be washed **:** STIRRER **c :** a large mortar and pestle for crushing ore **d :** a machine for scouring textiles (as woolens and worsteds) during manufacture **4 a :** a block put between the head of a pile and the ram of a pile driver **b :** a heavy steel bar with a cupped head for holding against the head of a rivet while the other end is being headed **c :** a shaped metal block used as an anvil in sheet-metal work (as in reshaping an automobile fender) **5 a :** an auxiliary car (as one attached to a cable and used to push a standard car up an incline) **b :** a compact narrow-gauge railroad locomotive used for moving construction trains and for switching **6 a :** a small cart or wheeled platform used to move freight in terminals or in loading and unloading **b :** a platform on a roller or on wheels or casters used for transporting heavy objects (as logs, girders, or machines) short distances or for supporting a person working under an automobile **c :** a small wheeled truck used to support the tail of an airplane when moving the latter on the ground **d :** a wheeled platform on which a motion-picture or television camera is mounted for ready movement about a set **e :** a standard that is swung down in position to support the forward part of a semitrailer when it is detached from a truck tractor

dolly 3a

²**dolly** \″\ *vb* -ED/-ING/-ES *vt* **1 :** to treat with a dolly: **a** *dial Eng* **:** to wash (clothes) with a dolly **b :** to crush (rock) with a dolly **2 :** to move (a camera) about on a dolly **3 :** to convey on a dolly ⟨movers *dollied* away the file cabinets⟩ ~ *vi* **:** to move the camera about on a dolly while shooting a scene for motion pictures or television ⟨we *dollied* in for a close-up of the two faces⟩ ⟨~ out for a long shot⟩; *also, of a camera* **:** to be moved on a dolly ⟨the camera can pan or ~ along with the subject⟩
³**dol·ly** \ˈdälē\ *n* -ES [Hindi *ḍālī*, lit., basket, tray] *India* **:** a present or offering (as of fruit, flowers, or confections)
dolly bar *n* **:** DOLLY 4b
dolly block *n* **:** DOLLY 4c
dollyhead \ˈ==,=\ *n* [¹*dolly* + *head*] **:** an artificial model (as of papier-mâché) of a head made by a furrier for filling out the scalp of a skin
dol·ly·man \ˈ==mən\ *n, pl* **dollymen** [¹*dolly* + *man*] **:** one who works with a dolly **:** BUCKER
dolly-mop \ˈ==,=\ *n* [¹*dolly* (woman)] *slang Brit* **:** STRUMPET, DRAB
dolly shot *n* [¹*dolly*] **:** a motion-picture or television shot taken while the dolly on which the camera is mounted is moving
dolly tub *n* [¹*dolly*] *dial Eng* **:** a washtub for washing with a dolly
dolly var·den \¦dälē'värdᵊn, ¦dȯl-\ *n, cap D&V* [after *Dolly Varden*, gaily dressed coquette in *Barnaby Rudge* (1841), novel by Charles Dickens †1870 Eng. novelist] **1 :** a 19th century clothing style for women consisting of a print dress with a white fichu, tight bodice, and skirt with panniers, and a beflowered hat with a wide drooping brim **2 :** a large char (*Salvelinus malma*) that is olivaceous in color with round red or orange spots, attains a length of two or three feet and a weight of 20 pounds, is closely related to or possibly a variety of the eastern brook trout, and has an extensive range in streams west of the Cascade Range from the upper Sacramento northward, in the Columbia basin east to Montana, and in northern Japan as well as in coastal salt waters
dolly varden crab \¦==¦==-\ *n, usu cap D&V* **:** CALICO CRAB
dollyway \ˈ==,=\ *n* [¹*dolly* + *way*] **:** an elevated runway from a sawmill to the drying yard over which lumber is moved
dol·ma \ˈdōlmə, -,mä\ *n* -s [Turk, lit., something stuffed, fr. *dolma* stuffed] **:** a vegetable shell (as of eggplant, green pepper, or zucchini) or a grape or cabbage leaf stuffed with a mixture of meat, rice, herbs, and seasonings and boiled
dol·man \ˈdōlmən, ˈdōl-,ˈdäl-\ *n* -s [alter. of earlier *doliman*, fr. F, fr. Turk *dolama*, lit., act of winding, fr. *dolamak* to wind] **1 :** a long robe with sleeves worn by Turks **2 a :** a woman's wrap like a cape in vogue in the 19th century with wide sleeves cut in one piece with the body **b :** a woman's coat or jacket with similarly wide sleeves **3** [G, fr. Turk *dolama*] **:** a short jacket distinctive of many hussar uniforms usu. worn slung across one shoulder and fastened with a cord or chain
dolman sleeve *n* **:** a sleeve that is very wide at the armhole and tight at the wrist, is either set into a deep armhole or cut in one piece with the bodice, and is used in women's clothing

dolman sleeve

dol·men \ˈdōlmən, ˈdōl-,ˈdäl-\ *n* -s [F, irreg. fr. Bret *tōl, taol* table (fr. L *tabula* board, plank) + *maen, mēn* stone — more at TABLE, MENHIR] **:** a prehistoric monument consisting of two or more upright stones supporting a horizontal stone slab found esp. in Britain and France and thought to be a tomb
dol·o·me·des \,däləˈmē(,)dēz\ *n, cap* [NL, fr. Gk *dolomēdēs* crafty, wily] **:** a genus of large long-legged spiders (family Pisauridae) common in wet places and able to move freely over the surface of water
do·lo·mite \ˈdōlə,mīt, ˈdäl-, *usu* -īd·+V\ *n* -s [F, fr. Déodat de *Dolomieu* †1801 Fr. geologist & F *-ite*] **1 :** a mineral $CaMg(CO_3)_2$ consisting of a calcium magnesium carbonate found in rhombohedral crystals and in extensive beds as a compact limestone that is often crystalline granular and either white or clouded — called also *bitter spar* **2 :** a limestone or marble rich in magnesium carbonate
do·lo·mit·ic \¦==¦mid·ik\ *adj* **1 :** containing dolomite **2 :** containing magnesium ⟨a pressure-hydrated ~ lime⟩
do·lo·mit·i·za·tion \,==,mīd·ə'zāshən, -,məd-·\ *n* -s **:** the process of converting into dolomite
do·lo·mit·ize \ˈ==,mīd·,īz, -,mə,tīz\ *vt* -ED/-ING/-S **:** to convert into dolomite
Dol·o·phine \ˈdälə,fēn, -,fən\ *trademark* — used for methadone
do·lor \ˈdōlə(r), *archaic* ˈdäl-\ *n* -s *see -or in Explan Notes* [ME *dolour*, fr. MF, fr. L *dolor*, fr. *dolēre* to feel pain, grieve — more at CONDOLE] **1** *obs* **:** physical pain — used in old medicine as one of five cardinal symptoms of inflammation **2 :** mental suffering or anguish **:** SORROW ⟨and yet nationally we go into the ~*s* whenever somebody remarks that we are weak in "preparation for citizenship" —W.W.Waymack⟩ **3** *obs* **:** LAMENTATION **syn** see DISTRESS
doloriferous *adj* [ML *doloriferus*, alter. of LL *dolorifer*, fr. L *dolor* + *-i-* + *-fer* -ferous] *obs* **:** producing pain
do·lo·rif·ic \¦dōlə¦rifik *sometimes* ¦däl-\ *adj* [MF *dolorifique*, fr. ML *dolorificus*, fr. L *dolor* + *-i-* + *-ficus* -fic] **:** causing pain or grief
do·lor·i·fuge \dəˈlȯrə,fyüj\ *n* -s [*dolor* + *-i-* + *-fuge*] **:** something that banishes or mitigates grief
do·lo·ri·met·ric \¦dōlərə¦me·trik, ¦dälərə-, də¦lȯrə-\ *adj* **:** using or obtained by dolorimetry — **do·lo·ri·met·ri·cal·ly** \-trək(ə)lē\ *adv*
do·lo·rim·e·try \,dōləˈrimə·trē, ,däl-\ *n* -ES [*dolor* + *-i-* + *-metry*] **:** a method of measuring intensity of pain perception in degrees ranging from unpleasant to unbearable by using heat applied to the skin as a gauge
do·lo·ro·so \,dōləˈrō(,)sō\ *adj (or adv)* [It, fr. LL *dolorosus*] **:** SORROWFUL, PLAINTIVE — used as a direction in music
do·lo·rous \ˈdōlərəs *sometimes* ˈdälər- *or* dəˈlōr- *or* dəˈlȯr-\ *adj* [ME, fr. MF *dolereus*, fr. LL *dolorosus*, fr. L *dolor* pain + *-osus* -ous] **1 :** occasioning pain ⟨washed down with wine of ~ acerbity —Nathaniel Hawthorne⟩ **2 a :** causing mental suffering or distress ⟨women and children howling and weeping — a most ~ sight —Dorothy Thompson⟩ **b :** highly regrettable **:** DEPLORABLE, LAMENTABLE ⟨the causes which have brought the world to its present ~ pass —P.E.More⟩ **3 :** marked by deep misery **:** WOEFUL ⟨during the ~ years of the depression —Amy Loveman⟩ **4 :** expressive of sorrow or affliction **:** DOLEFUL, LUGUBRIOUS ⟨that ~ aspect of human nature which in comedy is best portrayed by Molière —T.S. Eliot⟩ ⟨~ ballads of death and violence⟩ — **do·lo·rous·ly** *adv* — **do·lo·rous·ness** *n* -ES
dol·os \ˈdä,läs\ *n, pl* **do·los·se** \dəˈläsə\ [Afrik] **:** a knucklebone of a sheep or goat used by Kafir witch doctors in divining — usu. used in pl.
do·lose \ˈdō,lōs, dōˈl-\ *also* **do·lous** \ˈdōləs\ *adj* [L *dolosus* cunning, deceitful, fr. *dolus* fraud, deceit + *-osus* -ose, -ous — more at TALE] *Roman, civil, & Scots law* **:** characterized by criminal intent
¹**dol·phin** \ˈdälfən, ˈdȯl-\ *n* -s [ME, fr. MF *dophin, doffin, daufin*, fr. OF *dalfin*, fr. OProv, fr. ML *dalfinus*, alter. of L *delphinus*, fr. Gk *delphin-, delphis, delphin;* akin to Gk *delphys* womb; fr. its shape; akin to Skt *garbha* womb, Av *garəwa-*] **1 a :** any of various small toothed whales of the family Delphinidae that have the snout more or less elongated into a beak and the neck vertebrae partially fused — distinguished from *porpoise* **b :** PORPOISE 1 **2 :** either of two active pelagic spiny-finned fishes constituting the genus *Coryphaena* (family Coryphaenidae) which are widely distributed in tropical and temperate seas and the commoner of which (*C. hippurus*) usu. becomes about six feet long and is esteemed as food and noted for its brilliant colors when it is taken out of the water and is dying **3 :** one of the handles above the trunnions of an ancient cannon for lifting it **4 : a** mass of iron or lead hung from the yardarm on ancient Greek ships of war to be dropped on the deck of an enemy's vessel **5 a** *archaic* **:** a wreath or strap of plaited cordage around a mast to aid in supporting the yard **b :** a mooring spar or buoy furnished with a ring to which boats may fasten their cables **c :** a mooring post on a wharf or beach — called also *bollard* **d :** a cluster of piles driven into the bottom of a harbor and bound firmly together for the mooring of boats **e :** a permanent fender around a heavy boat just below the gunwale **f :** SPLINE WEIGHT **6 :** a cluster of piles to which a boom is secured (as for protecting a bridge pier) **7 a** *or* **dolphin butterfly** *or* **dolphin fishtail :** BUTTERFLY 3g(2) **b :** a synchronized swimming stunt in which the body from a back floating position is arched and goes down headfirst to describe a complete circle back to the starting position
²**dolphin** \″\ *vi* -ED/-ING/-S **:** to swim in a series of plunges like a dolphin
³**dolphin** *obs var of* DAUPHIN
dolphinfish \ˈ==,=\ *n* **:** DOLPHIN 2
dolphin flower *n* [so called fr. the shape of the nectary] **:** either of two larkspurs (*Delphinium consolida* and *D. ajacis*)
dolphin oil *n* **:** an unsaturated fatty oil obtained from the body, head, or jaw of a dolphin and used esp. as a fine lubricant — compare PORPOISE OIL
dolphin striker *n* **:** a vertical spar under the end of the bowsprit of a sailboat to extend and support the martingale — called also *martingale;* see SHIP illustration
dols *pl of* DOL
dolt \ˈdōlt\ *n* -s [prob. akin to OE *dol* foolish, silly — more at DULL] **:** a heavy stupid fellow **:** BLOCKHEAD, NUMSKULL
dolthead \ˈ=,=\ *n* **:** BLOCKHEAD
dolt·ish \ˈdōltish, -tēsh\ *adj* **:** like a dolt **:** BLOCKISH, STUPID — **dolt·ish·ly** *adv* — **dolt·ish·ness** *n* -ES
do·lus \ˈdōləs\ *n* [L — more at TALE] **1** *Roman, civil, & Scots law* **:** the doing of anything that is contrary to good conscience **:** the use of a trick, stratagem, artifice, or device to deceive another **:** DECEIT **2** *Roman, civil, & Scots law* **:** evil or criminal intent similar to malice at the common law in the law of crimes **:** willful and wanton misconduct in the law of delicts **:** FRAUD, DECEPTION
dolus bo·nus \-ˈbōnəs\ *n* [L, good deceit] *Roman, civil, & Scots law* **:** simple cunning or sagacity in bargaining or in other transactions that is not actionable or punishable as fraud or misrepresentation or ground for rescinding the transaction induced by it
dolus ma·lus \-ˈmäləs, -ˈmāl-\ *n* [L, bad deceit] *Roman, civil, & Scots law* **:** fraud and misrepresentation that is actionable and punishable or is ground for rescinding the transaction resulting from it
¹**dom** \ˈdäm\ *n* -s [L *dominus* master — more at DAME] — often used as a title before the names of Benedictine and some other monks and canons regular
²**dom** \ˈdōm\ *n* -s *usu cap* [Hindi *ḍom*, fr. Skt *ḍoma, ḍomba* man of a low caste of musicians — more at ROMANY] **:** a member of a Hindu caste of untouchables that are like gypsies in their habits, engage in blacksmithing, tinsmithing, and basket-making, and cremate the dead
³**dom** \ˈdōm\ *n* -s [F *doum* — more at DOOM PALM] **:** DOOM PALM
-dom \dəm\ *n suffix* -s [ME, fr. OE *-dōm;* akin to OS *-dōm* -dom, OHG *-tuom*, ON *-dōmr;* all fr. a prehistoric Gmc noun represented by OE *dōm* judgment — more at DOOM] **1 a :** dignity **:** office ⟨duke*dom*⟩ **b :** realm **:** jurisdiction ⟨king*dom*⟩ ⟨Christen*dom*⟩ **c :** geographical area ⟨Anglo-Saxon*dom*⟩ **2 :** state, condition, or fact of being ⟨free*dom*⟩ ⟨martyr*dom*⟩ **3 :** those having a (specified) office, occupation, interest, or character ⟨official*dom*⟩ ⟨dog*dom*⟩ ⟨stamp*dom*⟩
dom *abbr* **1** domestic **2** dominion **3** dominus
DOM *abbr* [ML *Deo optimo maximo*] to God, the best and greatest
do·main \dōˈmān *also* dəˈ-\ *n* -s [MF *demaine, domaine*, fr. L *dominium*, fr. *dominus* master, owner — more at DAME] **1** *archaic* **:** landed property which one has in his own right **:** DEMESNE 2 **2 a :** the possessions of a sovereign, feudal lord, nation, or commonwealth ⟨built up the ~*s* of the Papal States—R.A.Hall b. 1911⟩ ⟨the great Forest of Galtres . . . was a royal ~ —Edwin Benson⟩ ⟨the buffaloes and bears marched in single file, as did also the Indians when traveling beyond the ~ of their nation —S.C.Williams⟩ **b :** a territory possessed and governed of right or over which authority is exercised of right ⟨the Roman Church has had a far greater ~ and longevity than the Roman Empire —Weston La Barre⟩ ⟨where great cattle ~*s* stretched over seemingly endless miles —*Amer. Guide Series: Texas*⟩ **c :** field of control or range of governance ⟨our highways and roads have been in the ~ of state and local governments —T.H.White b. 1915⟩ ⟨poetical works belong to the ~ of our permanent passions —Matthew Arnold⟩ — see EMINENT DOMAIN, PUBLIC DOMAIN **d :** a region distinctively marked or wholly overspread or dominated by some physical feature ⟨a ~ of peaks, forests, and roaring rivers —R.L.Neuberger⟩ **3 a :** a distinctly delimited sphere of knowledge or of intellectual, institutional, or cultural activity (as a humanistic or scientific discipline, a form of artistic creation, a department of research) ⟨the ~ of biblical scholarship⟩ ⟨psychiatry seems unwilling merely to resist invasion of its ~ —Bernard DeVoto⟩ ⟨the ~ of ascertainable fact should be clearly distinguished from the ~ of personal opinion —Stuart Hampshire⟩ **b :** a circumscribed realm of human concern ⟨in the ~ of rural economy⟩ ⟨argot is really a dialect whose ~ is social instead of regional —A.L.Guérard⟩ **c :** one's peculiar and exclusive function or field of active cultivation and responsibility ⟨without intruding on the expert's ~ —S.L.A.Marshall⟩ ⟨problems which were formerly regarded as belonging exclusively to the ~ of philosophers —W.V.Houston⟩ ⟨intellectual qualities which liberal education has typically staked out for itself as its own special ~ —H.D.Gideonse⟩ **4 a :** a mathematical aggregate to which a variable is confined ⟨the ~ of real numbers⟩ ⟨the ~ of rational numbers⟩ **b :** an aggregate of elements each of which is a first element of an ordered pair **5 :** a small region of a ferromagnetic substance that contains many atoms all oriented in the same direction so that the group as a whole acts as a completely saturated magnet, the relative orientations of these regions determining the magnetization of the magnet **6** *logic* **a :** the realm of applicability of an idea or notion or the range of values within which a variable may govern **b** *for a relation R* **:** the class of things *x* for which there is at least one thing *y* such that *xRy* holds ⟨the ~ of *father of* is the class of male parents⟩ **7 :** the segment of speech throughout which a linguistic feature such as grammatical agreement or a pitch or stress contour extends **syn** see FIELD
do·main·al \-nᵊl\ *adj* **:** DOMANIAL
¹**do·mal** \ˈdōməl\ *adj* [in sense 1, fr. L *domus* house + E *-al;* in sense 2 & 3, fr. ¹*dome* + *-al*] **1** *archaic* **:** relating to a house **2 :** shaped like a dome ⟨a ~ arrangement of the strata far beneath the ocean floor —R.E.Hardwicke⟩ ⟨a ~ eruption⟩ **3 :** RETROFLEX — **do·mal·ly** \-əlē\ *adv*
²**domal** \″\ *n* -s **:** a domal speech sound
domal mountain *n* **:** DOME MOUNTAIN
do·ma·ni·al \dōˈmānēəl\ *adj* [ML *domanialis*, fr. L *dominium* domain + *-alis* -al — more at DOMAIN] **1 :** constituting or belonging to a domain or to a particular domain (as a manor) **:** held in one's own hands as possessor by free tenure — distinguished from *alodial* and *feudal* **2 :** having or belonging to a domain
do·mat·ic \(ˈ)dō¦mad·ik\ *adj* [ISV ¹*dome* + *-atic* (as in *prismatic*)] **:** belonging to a crystallographic class of symmetry of the monoclinic system that is characterized by a dome **:** CLINODOMATIC
do·ma·tium \dōˈmāsh(ē)əm\ *n, pl* **doma·tia** \-(ē)ə\ [NL, fr. Gk *dōmation* small house, bedroom, dim. of *dōma* house; akin to Gk *domos* house — more at TIMBER] **:** a portion of a plant (as on or in a leaf) modified to form a chamber or other form of shelter for insects, mites, or fungi
dom·beya \dämˈbāə, ˈdämbēə\ *n, cap* [NL, after Joseph *Dombey* †1794 Fr. botanist] **:** a genus of African shrubs or small trees (family Sterculiaceae) having palmately nerved leaves, showy flowers with five petals, and capsular fruit
dom·dan·iel \dämˈdanyəl\ *n* -s *usu cap* [fr. *Domdaniel*, fictitious submarine chamber in Arabic tales translated by Jacques Cazotte †1792 Fr. writer & Dom Denys Chavys, 18th cent. Fr. monk of Arabian origin] *archaic* **:** a den of iniquity
¹**dome** \ˈdōm\ *n* -s [F, It & L; F *dôme* dome, cathedral, fr. It *duomo* cathedral, fr. ML *domus* church, fr. L, house — more at TIMBER] **1 a** *archaic* **:** a stately building **:** MANSION **b :** RESORT, RETREAT — used esp. with *pleasure* ⟨the pleasure ~*s* of Reno or Las Vegas —Jack Goodman⟩ **2 :** a vaulted circular roof or ceiling **3** *obs* **:** a cathedral church **4 a :** a natural formation, a structure, or a projecting part arched and rounded that has some resemblance to a cupola or vaulted ceiling of a building: **a :** the upper part of a reverberatory furnace **b :** the roof of a vaulted cavern **c :** a rounded mountaintop or vast mound of ice **d :** an overhanging hemispherical space or area ⟨the sun seeming to hang in a coppery ~⟩ ⟨projected on the ~ of the planetarium⟩ **e :** the vertical chamber on the top of a steam boiler or of a tank car **f :** the hemispherical or cylindrical roof of an astronomical observatory providing for rotation of the observing slit to any part of the sky **g (1) : a** glass-enclosed compartment built into the roof of a railroad

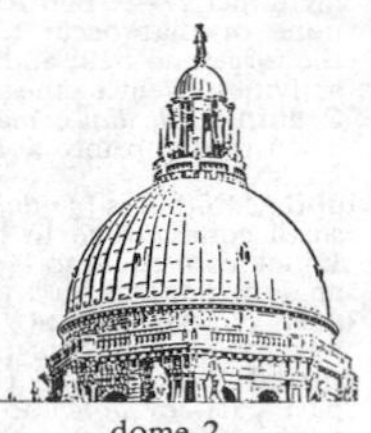
dome 2

car to permit upper-deck passengers an unobstructed view in every direction ⟨adopted the ~ car as standard equipment⟩ (2) : ASTRODOME **h** : the arching periphery of the carcass of a pneumatic tire **i** : a concave approximately quarter-spherical usu. plaster structure backing and overhanging a theatrical stage **5** : the back inside cap or case of a jointed-case watch **6 a** : a form of crystal composed of planes parallel to a lateral axis which meet above in a horizontal edge like a roof — see BRACHYDOME, CLINODOME, MACRODOME, ORTHODOME **b** : a form of crystal composed of only two faces intersecting along and astride of a symmetry plane regardless of the orientation of the line of their intersection **7 a** : a doubly plunging anticline that is broad in comparison with its length and consequently approximately circular or elliptical in plan : a quaquaversal fold ⟨the Ozark ~ is many miles in diameter⟩ ⟨some small and steep-sided salt ~s in Louisiana⟩ ⟨at the top of a ~ oil and gas may have collected⟩ **b** : a rock mass in domical form ⟨the granite ~s of the Yosemite⟩ **c** : a rounded snow peak **d** : a broad gently sloping volcano — called also *shield volcano, volcanic dome* **8** : a rounded isolated elevation on the ocean bottom at depths greater than 100 fathoms **9** *chiefly slang* : a person's head **10** : a ball-shaped or mushroom-shaped clothing accessory: **a** : a raised button **b** : SNAP FASTENER **11** : a rounded-arch element in the wave tracing in an electroencephalogram

²**dome** \"\ *vb* -ED/-ING/-S *vt* **1** : to cover with or as if with a dome **2** : to press, bend, or thrust up into a dome ⟨upward pressure from underlying magma ~s the surface —*Jour. of Geology*⟩ ⟨shaping the cover with a *doming* mallet⟩ ~ *vi* **1** : to swell upward or outward like a dome **2** : to arch overhead in a dome (as of the sky)

dome bed *n* : a bed with a dome-shaped canopy

domed \-md\ *adj* **1** : having an arched and rounded shape like that of an approximately hemispherical dome ⟨his ~ forehead, great white moustache —John Galsworthy⟩ ⟨red and blue ~ precision-prism lenses⟩ **2** : constructed or roofed with a dome ⟨topped by a ~ belfry⟩

dome light *n* : a light in the ceiling (as of an automobile)

dome mountain *n* : a mountain range resulting from dissection of a structural dome (as the Black Hills in So. Dakota) — called also *domal mountain*

do·ment \'dümənt, -,ment\ *n* -S [¹*do* + *-ment*] *dial Eng* : CELEBRATION, ENTERTAINMENT, AFFAIR

dome of silence : a furniture caster consisting of a single large ball in a retainer

dom·er \'dōmə(r)\ *n* -S : an operator or a machine that shapes box tops

¹**domes·day** \'dümz,dā, 'dōm-\ *archaic var of* DOOMSDAY

²**domesday** \"\ *adj* [fr. the 11th cent. *Domesday (Book)*] : of or relating to the 11th cent. Domesday Book or the time of its compilation

domesday book *n, usu cap D&B* [fr. the *Domesday Book*, a Latin census of England property compiled by order of William the Conqueror 1085–86] : a census compiled usu. from a comprehensive survey of a geographical sector ⟨a sort of *Domesday Book*, in which the merits and demerits of each individual were recorded —J.W.Waterhouse⟩

¹**do·mes·tic** \də'mestik, dō'-, -tēk\ *adj* [MF *domestique*, fr. L *domesticus*, fr. *domus* house — more at TIMBER] **1** *obs* : enjoying intimate status (as in a household) : being familiar as if at home **2 a** : relating to the household or the family : concerned with or employed in the management of a household or private place of residence — distinguished from *public* ⟨affects the house at large and the course of ~ affairs —Herbert Spencer⟩ ⟨the servant has risen in the world and become a ~ worker —Gabriel Ullstein⟩ **b** : connected with the supply, service, and activities of households and private residences — distinguished from *industrial* ⟨coke as a fuel for ~ heating plants⟩ ⟨sewing, interior decoration, and other ~ arts⟩ ⟨a scarcity of ~ help⟩ **c** : suited to the physical requirements and livability of a private dwelling ⟨the community, which possesses a ~ architecture of charm and distinction —*Amer. Guide Series: N.C.*⟩; *also* : engaged in designing private dwellings ⟨both an ecclesiastical and a ~ architect⟩ **d** : belonging to or incumbent on the family or members of the family ⟨~ status⟩ ⟨the ~ chastity required is recommended in effect to produce an equilibrium population —G.E.Hutchinson⟩ : participated in by or emanating from members of a family ⟨there seemed no place for myself in this ~ tableau —Christopher Isherwood⟩ ⟨under strict ~ orders not to sit out of doors —John Buchan⟩ **e** : peculiar to or affecting the intimate relations and amenities of a family group living together ⟨Diderot never achieved ~ happiness, either in his marriage or in his many affairs of the heart —J.S.Schapiro⟩ ⟨there are others beside Charles Lamb who are peculiarly sensitive to the charm of the ~ —John Dewey⟩; *also* : associated with family obligations and harmony ⟨her many ~ virtues⟩ ⟨weighed down with ~ worries⟩ **f** : dealing with the intimate life of a family group ⟨we have the ~ epic dealing with the details of modern life which pass daily under our eyes —Matthew Arnold⟩ ⟨~ drama of the sentimental kind⟩ **3** : relating and limited to one's own country or the country under consideration or its internal affairs and interests **4 a** : belonging or occurring within the sphere of authority or control or the fabric or boundaries of the indicated nation or sovereign state : INTERNAL ⟨charts of ~ as well as foreign waters⟩ ⟨once a state has assumed such an obligation the matter ceases to be within its ~ jurisdiction —Quincy Wright⟩; *specif* : involving activities of or within the national government ⟨a ~ power struggle between the president and the congress⟩ **b** : affecting the welfare of or experienced or participated in by the citizenry of the indicated country ⟨a depression that proved one of our worst ~ calamities⟩ ⟨evincing a major interest in ~ politics⟩ ⟨painting the ~ scene in somber colors⟩; *also* : living and occupied within one's own country ⟨the various forms of entertainment available to ~ vacationers⟩ ⟨all the critics, ~ and foreign —S.P.Sherman⟩ **c** : carried on, operating or serving, produced, or distributed within the bounds of the indicated country or region ⟨the ~ shipping industry declined after 1939⟩ ⟨the acknowledged power of a state to regulate its police, its ~ trade —John Marshall⟩ ⟨~ corporations, that is, those chartered by the state in which they do business —M.S.Kendrick⟩ ⟨short trip services by a ~ airline⟩ ⟨formerly scornful of the quality of our ~ wines⟩ ⟨caves used for the ripening of a ~ Roquefort-type cheese⟩ ⟨cats of various breeds, some ~, some imported⟩; *also* : applying only within these bounds ⟨~ airmail rates⟩ ⟨~ prices of oil products⟩ **d** : INDIGENOUS ⟨~ snails representing 12 species of the family Bulimidae⟩ **e** : domiciled in the home state of the regulatory authority concerned — used of an insurance company **5 a** : living near or about the habitations of man ⟨rats, roaches, and other ~ vermin⟩ **b** : DOMESTICATED, TAME **6** : devoted to home duties and pleasures ⟨author of blood-and-thunder novels, yet quite ~ in his tastes⟩

²**domestic** \"\ *n* -S **1** *obs* : HOUSEMATE **2** *obs* : a native citizen **3** : a household servant **4** : an article of domestic manufacture: as **a** : common cotton cloth (as sheeting) **b** : an American-made rug as distinguished from an Oriental rug **c domestics** *pl* : household linens and bedding

do·mes·ti·ca·ble \-tə̇kəbəl, -tēk-\ *adj* [*domesticate* + *-able*] : capable of being domesticated

do·mes·ti·cal \-kəl\ *adj* [ME *domysticall*, fr. MF *domestique* + ME *-al* — more at DOMESTIC] *archaic* : DOMESTIC

do·mes·ti·cal·i·ty \də,mestə'kaləd·ē, dō,-\ *n* -ES : DOMESTICITY

do·mes·ti·cal·ly \-'mestə̇k(ə)lē, -tēk-, -li\ *adv* **1** : in a domestic or familiar way **2** : in domestic territory **3** : with respect to domestic affairs ⟨~ he proposed a conservative program⟩

domestic animal *n* : any of various animals (as the horse, ox, or sheep) which have been domesticated by man so as to live and breed in a tame condition — compare FERAE NATURAE

domestic architecture *n* : the architecture of single or multiple dwellings

¹**do·mes·ti·cate** \də'mestə,kāt, dō'- *usu* -ād.+V\ *vb* -ED/-ING/-S [¹*domestic* + *-ate*] *vt* **1 a** : to bring into domestic use : ADOPT, NATURALIZE ⟨a European custom *domesticated* here⟩ **b** : to bring into a degree of conformity and comfortable accommodation with one's home environment ⟨an alien philosophy difficult to ~ here⟩ **2** : to cause to be domestically engaged, inclined, or adapted ⟨offering home economics to ~ the female prisoners⟩ ⟨whether she could ~ her explorer husband⟩ **3 a** : to adapt (an animal or plant) to life in intimate association with and to the advantage of man or another species usu. by modifying growth and traits through provision of food, protection from enemies, and selective breeding during generations of living in association and often to the extent that the domesticated form loses the ability to survive in nature ⟨the fungi *domesticated* by certain ants produce special bromatia on which the ants feed⟩ ⟨man *domesticated* the dog⟩ **b** : to subject to the control and service of man ⟨settled communities were made possible by *domesticating* watercourses⟩ **4 a** : to bring to the level (as of understanding) of ordinary people : FAMILIARIZE ⟨he *domesticated* the fairy tale and gave it a townsman's home —Robert Lynd⟩ **b** : to force into a mold of accepted conduct or thought : make conform ⟨this deliberate attempt of the universities to ~ our poets, if not to tame them —Conrad Aiken⟩ ~ *vi* **1** *archaic* **a** : to live in the same household **b** : to settle in or become habituated to an ordered household **c** : to make one's home : SETTLE **2** : to obtain a charter of incorporation in a particular state ⟨an unlicensed foreign corporation doing business in the state without *domesticating*⟩

²**domes·ti·cate** \-stə̇kə̇t, -stə,kāt, *usu* \|d.+V\ *n* -S : a domesticated animal or plant

domesticated *adj, Brit* : experienced in the duties of housekeeping and the details of household management

do·mes·ti·ca·tion \-,mestə'kāshən\ *n* -S : the action or process of domesticating or the state of being domesticated ⟨according to Hahn, ~ involves free breeding in captivity —R.H.Lowie⟩ ⟨the ant's ~ of the aphid⟩ ⟨carbon monoxide ... has been a hazard to man since the ~ of fire —Berton Roueché⟩ ⟨what might be expected to result from the ~ in a free environment of the inchoate idealisms of English Puritanism —V.L.Parrington⟩

do·mes·ti·ca·tive \-'mestə,kād·iv, -tə̇kəd-\ *adj* : tending to domesticate

do·mes·ti·ca·tor \-tə,kād·ə(r)\ *n* -S : one that domesticates

domestic bill *n* : INLAND BILL

domestic cat *n* : CAT 1a

domestic economy *n* : the theory and practice of household management

domestic factor *n* : a factor doing business in the same state or country as his principal — compare FOREIGN FACTOR

domestic fowl *n* **1** : POULTRY **2** : a bird of one of the breeds developed from the jungle fowl (*Gallus gallus*) including some specialized for meat production and others for egg laying, for fighting, or purely for ornament or show : CHICKEN — see BANTAM, BRAHMA, GAME FOWL, LEGHORN

do·mes·tic·i·ty \(,)dō,me'stisəd·ē, də,-, -ətē, -i\ *n* -ES [¹*domestic* + *-ity*] **1** : the quality or state of being domestic or domesticated ⟨a royal family living in unpretentious ~⟩ ⟨the untidy ~ of pigeons —Lewis Mumford⟩ **2** : domestic activities or life ⟨making a hobby of ~⟩ **3 domesticities** *pl* : domestic affairs ⟨she bore the brunt of *domesticities* of which he was ever utterly impatient —M.A.D.Howe *b*1864⟩

do·mes·ti·cize \də'mestə,sīz, dō'-\ *vt* -ED/-ING/-S [*domestic* + *-ize*] : DOMESTICATE

domestic relations court *n* : COURT OF DOMESTIC RELATIONS

domestic science *n* : instruction and training in domestic management and the household arts (as cooking and sewing) — compare HOME ECONOMICS

domestic ship *n* : a ship whose owner is resident in the country considered as one's own

domestic system *n* : a system of manufacturing based upon work done at home on materials supplied by merchant employers — contrasted with *factory system*; compare COTTAGE INDUSTRY

do·met *or* **do·mett** \dō'met, 'dämə̇t\ *n* -S [origin unknown] : a cotton or cotton and wool flannel similar to outing flannel

domey *var of* DOMY

do·mey·kite \dō'mā,kīt\ *n* -S [G *domeykit*, fr. Ignacio *Domeyko* †1889 Polish mineralogist in Chile + G *-it* -ite] : a mineral Cu_3As (sp. gr., 7.2–7.75) of tin-white or steel-gray color consisting of copper arsenide

dom·ic \'dōmik, 'däm-\ *or* **dom·i·cal** \-mə̇kəl\ *adj* [¹*dome* + *-ic, -ical*] : relating to, shaped like, or having a dome — **dom·i·cal·ly** \-mə̇k(ə)lē\ *adv*

dom·i·cil·able \'däməˌsiləbəl, 'dōm-, ,==s'===\ *adj* : eligible to be domiciled

¹**dom·i·cile** \'däməˌsīl, 'dōmə,sīl, 'däməsəl, 'däm(,)sil\ *also* **dom·i·cil** \'däməsəl, -(,)sil\ *n* -S [MF, fr. L *domicilium*, fr. *domus* house — more at TIMBER] **1** : the place of residence either of an individual or of a family : ABODE **2 a** : the place with which a person has a settled connection for important legal purposes (as determination of his civil status, jurisdiction to impose personal judgments or taxes on him, or determination of the succession to his personal property on his death) : the place of his permanent and principal home or of his last such home if he has not yet acquired a new one or the place assigned by law to him as his home if he has no legal capacity to choose his own (as in the case of a minor or insane person) **b** : an actual dwelling place that is one's permanent and principal home **c** : the state in which a corporation or business concern is created or incorporated : the principal place of doing business or maintaining an office of a corporation or business concern as registered in accordance with law

²**domicile** \"\ *vt* -ED/-ING/-S **1** : to settle in or provide with a domicile ⟨benefits extended to veterans *domiciled* in hospitals⟩ **2** : to make (a bill of exchange or promissory note) payable at a designated place other than that of the residence of the drawee

domiciled *adj* : having an established domicile

domicile of choice : a domicile that a person acquires by an exercise of his own will while he has legal capacity to change his domicile

domicile of origin : the domicile assigned to a person at his birth; *esp* : the domicile of a child's father at the time of the child's birth

¹**dom·i·cil·iary** \,dämə'silē,erē, ,dōm-, -lyərē, -ri\ *also* **dom·i·cil·i·ar** \-lē·ə(r), -ē,är, -ē,á(r\ *adj* [F *domiciliaire*, fr. MF, fr. ML *domiciliarius*, fr. L *domicilium* domicile + *-arius* -ary — more at DOMICILE] : relating to a domicile: **a** : serving as a domicile ⟨~ mounds⟩ **b** : including or regarding the domicile of the person under consideration ⟨jeopardizing his ~ status⟩ **c** : provided or attended in the home rather than in an institution ⟨~ obstetrics⟩ **d** : providing, constituting, or provided by a rest home for chronically ill or permanently disabled war veterans requiring minimal medical attention ⟨~ care available⟩ ⟨state ~ facilities⟩

²**domiciliary** \"\ *n* -ES : a domiciliary establishment (as for disabled veterans) : BARRACKS

domiciliary visit *n* : a visit to a private dwelling (as for searching it) under authority

dom·i·cil·i·ate \-lē,āt\ *vb* -ED/-ING/-S [L *domicilium* domicile + E *-ate*] *vt* **1** : DOMICILE **2** : DOMESTICATE 3, 4 ~ *vi* : to establish residence : RESIDE — **dom·i·cil·i·a·tion** \,==,==-'āshən\ *n* -S

domify *vt* -ED/-ING/-ES [ME *domifyen*, fr. ML *domificare* to build a house, fr. *domi-* (fr. L *domus* house) + L *-ficare* -fy — more at TIMBER] **1** *obs* : to divide (the zodiac) into 12 houses **2** *obs* : to specify the position of (a planet) in one of the houses of the zodiac

domina *n, pl* **dominae** *often cap* [L, mistress, lady — more at DAME] *obs* : a woman of rank; *specif* : a woman holding a barony in her own right

do·mi·na li·tis \'dämənə 'lēd·əs, -'lī\ *n, pl* **domi·nae litis** \-,nī'lēl, -,nē'lī\ [L, mistress of the suit] : a female client in a law case

dom·i·nance \'dämənən(t)s\ *n* -S **1** : dominant position in an order of forcefulness : ASCENDANCY ⟨the sexes in chimpanzees are about as different from each other dimorphously as human sexes are, but ~ in the band may be by either sex —Weston La Barre⟩ ⟨in total, it would create a situation ultimately favorable to Soviet ~ in the world —Dean Acheson⟩; *specif* : the relative position of an animal in the social hierarchy of its kind — compare PECK ORDER **2** : position or exercise of dominant authority, leadership, or influence ⟨the ~ of government in the field of labor relations⟩ ⟨even boards of directors, the theoretical representatives of the stockholders, have more and more come under managerial ~ —*Fortune*⟩ **3** : dominant position in space ⟨the ~ of the towers of the cathedral over the city⟩ **4** : highest or superior prevalence : PREPONDERANCE ⟨on a continent where the rural life is predominant, Argentina is notable for the ~ of its big cities —P.E. James⟩ ⟨the area provides a ~ of effusive igneous rocks⟩ **5 a** : the quality of one of a pair of alleles that suppresses the expression of the other member of the pair when both are present; *also* : the suppression so exerted **b** : the influence or control over ecological communities exhibited by dominants **c** : functional asymmetry between a pair of bodily structures ⟨~ of the right hand over the left in right-handedness⟩

¹**dom·i·nant** \-mənənt\ *adj* [MF or L; MF, fr. L *dominant-, dominans*, pres. part. of *dominari* to rule, govern — more at DOMINATE] **1 a** : commanding, controlling, or having supremacy or ascendancy over all others by reason of superior strength or power ⟨the emperors were the ~ members of the papal-imperial partnership which claimed universal rule over all Christendom —W.K.Ferguson⟩ ⟨considered as a subordinate and inferior class of beings, who had been subjugated by the ~ race —R.B.Taney⟩ ⟨in spite however of this rapid recovery of its strength by Mercia, Northumberland remained the ~ state in Britain —J.R.Green⟩ ⟨during the latter part of this period Islam was ~ over the greater part of India —Seymour Vesey-Fitzgerald⟩ **b** *astrology* : exercising chief influence ⟨having Saturn ~ in his horoscope⟩ **2 a** : superior to all others in guiding and directive influence : most determinative ⟨an archaistic movement running counter to the ~ historical movement —Bernard Smith⟩ ⟨I will not say that money has ceased to be the ~ force in American life —Max Lerner⟩ ⟨this society has been the ~ influence in the city's musical life⟩ **b** : having authority or prestige or compelling character such as to subordinate others ⟨during the middle ages, for example, the feudal family was ~ over business and frequently ignored government —Herbert Agar⟩ ⟨a ~ individuality refuses to be subdued to what it works in —J.L. Lowes⟩ ⟨he occupied a ~ position in the Republican party counsels —H.W.H.Knott⟩ **3 a** : overlooking and commanding from a superior elevation ⟨the dome of the state capitol ~ on the skyline⟩ ⟨the ~ hill⟩ **b** *of a forest tree* : sufficiently taller than surrounding trees as to have the crown exposed to sunlight from the sides as well as above **4** : prevailing over all others in number, frequency, or distribution or in productivity or fecundity : PREDOMINANT, PREPONDERANT, CHIEF ⟨the ~ industry⟩ ⟨the four principal eras of geological time may be identified by the names given to the ~ form of animal life in each —R.W.Murray⟩ ⟨cotton and corn are the ~ crops in the section⟩ **5 a** : prevailing over all others in extent and firmness of acceptance ⟨why a complex of beliefs is ~ at one time and subordinate at another —Irving Howe⟩ ⟨prolonged economic depression will invariably be accompanied by a loss of confidence in the ~ system —L.S.Feuer⟩ : surpassing or overshadowing others in prominence ⟨melancholy was the ~ note of his temperament —James Joyce⟩ ⟨the ~ hue of the glass should be sage green —H.G.Armstrong⟩ **b** : holding the foremost position or rank or the preeminence in fulfilling a function or role ⟨and certainly the least debatable fact in terms of American myth is that Abraham Lincoln became our ~ folk hero —E.H.Eby⟩ ⟨the ~ theme in the first book is the splendor of life —E.K.Brown⟩ **6** : having a right of servitude or easement attached or enjoying such a right ⟨a ~ estate⟩ ⟨a ~ owner⟩ **7** : relating to the dominant of the musical scale **8** : of or relating to an ecological dominant : exerting ecological dominance **9** : *of paired bodily structures* : being the one that is more effective or predominant in action ⟨~ eye⟩ ⟨~ hand⟩ ⟨~ hemisphere⟩ **10** *of an allele* : predominating over a contrasting allele in its manifestation — opposed to *recessive* ⟨tallness is ~, dwarfness recessive⟩ ⟨many apparently ~ characters are actually examples of multifactorial determination⟩; compare MENDEL'S LAW **11** : growing more vigorously than other parts of the same embryo and exerting a controlling influence on adjacent tissues

syn PREDOMINANT, PARAMOUNT, PREPONDERANT, PREPONDERATING, SOVEREIGN: DOMINANT connotes swaying, ruling, or commanding ⟨a *dominant* economic group which calls itself an aristocracy —V.L.Parrington⟩ ⟨the *dominant* tendency of thought in the nineteenth century as expressed by Darwin —H.J.Mackinder⟩ ⟨the emigration to America had fortunately taken place in a way which made the English language and English institutions everywhere *dominant* —Allan Nevins & H.S.Commager⟩ PREDOMINANT stresses commanding influence and occas. may suggest recent ascendancy ⟨the Catholic Church must prosper by the French energy and with the French Crown at least strong and independent; better yet, *predominant* —Hilaire Belloc⟩ ⟨the emotional elements (and they were the *predominant* and overwhelming) of the Christian *vita contemplativa* —H.O.Taylor⟩ PARAMOUNT indicates supremacy in power, rank, or importance ⟨Napoleon was master of the whole continent .... In the Europe of 1808 every State had been brought into a defined relation to the *paramount* power, by annexation, by vassalage, or by alliance on terms of submission —G.M.Trevelyan⟩ ⟨certainly all those who have framed written constitutions contemplate them as forming the fundamental and *paramount* law of the nation —John Marshall⟩ ⟨as the *paramount* question in the life of a bird is the question of food —John Burroughs⟩ PREPONDERANT and PREPONDERATING describe influence or power that outweighs everything else ⟨some contact of some human individuals must necessarily happen if anything cultural is to spread. But the contact need by no means be the migration of whole populations; and the evidence is *preponderant* that mostly it is not —A.L.Kroeber⟩ ⟨through its banking and financial affiliations it also exercises a *preponderating* control over the money and credit of the country —*Current History*⟩ Every other thing is clearly subordinate or inferior to that which is SOVEREIGN ⟨forced to defend their contention that Parliament, although *sovereign* in the empire, did not have control over the internal affairs of the colonies —S.E.Morison & H.S.Commager⟩ ⟨the older superstition of medieval medicine that bloodletting is the only and the *sovereign* remedy for all bodily ills —M.R.Cohen⟩

²**dominant** \"\ *n* -S **1** : something that is dominant ⟨elimination of undesirable ~s in color films⟩ ⟨the deeper-lying psychic elements are the least readily brought into consciousness, while they are the constant unrealized ~s of the mind —A.G. Tansley⟩ : one that is dominant ⟨to the urban ecologist the central business district is considered a ~, maintaining the control of certain environmental characteristics —*Social Forces*⟩ ⟨among the more traditional painters Dufy on the one hand and Van Gogh on the other seem to be the ~s —R.M. Coates⟩ **2 a** : the principal reciting note in the ecclesiastical modes usu. a fifth above the final in the authentic modes and a third above in the plagal **b** : the fifth note of the scale ⟨G is the ~ of the key of C⟩ **3** *biol* **a** : a dominant character or factor **b** : an organism possessing one or more dominant characters **4 a** : any of one or more kinds of organism (as a species or variety) in an ecological association that by reason of size, number, or habits exerts a controlling influence on the environment and thereby largely determines what other kinds of organisms share in the association **b** : any of one or more kinds of organism that constitutes the bulk or most conspicuous element of an ecological community **5** : a dominant forest tree

dom·i·nant·ly *adv* **1** : to a surpassing extent or degree : for the most part : PREVAILINGLY **2** : in a dominant position

dominant seventh chord *n* : a seventh chord comprising a major triad and a minor seventh and occurring on the dominant of a major or a minor scale — see SEVENTH CHORD illustration

dominant term *n* : the mathematical term greater in absolute value than any other (as in a set) or than the sum of the others

dominant wavelength *n* : wavelength of the spectrum light that when combined in suitable proportions with the specified achromatic light yields a match with the light being considered — see COLOR 1c

dom·i·nate \'dämə,nāt, *usu* -ād.+V\ *vb* -ED/-ING/-S [L *dominatus*, past part. of *dominari* to rule, govern, fr. *dominus* lord, master — more at DAME] *vt* **1 a** : to hold supremacy or mastery over by reason of superior power, strength, authority, or prowess ⟨it has been said that whoever ~s Germany controls

Europe⟩ ⟨regional blocs *dominated* by the great powers might well defy the decisions of the Security Council —Vera M. Dean⟩ ⟨the Cabinet ∼s the government of a province in much the same way and to the same extent as the federal Cabinet ∼s the government of Canada —R.M.Dawson⟩ ⟨the family financial houses that *dominated* prewar Japan's industry⟩ ⟨a racketeer-*dominated* union⟩ **b :** to hold in subjection through force of personality or other intangible force ⟨the emotions of the prima donna in the hour when she ∼s her audience must be unique —Arnold Bennett⟩ ⟨the resentment of subordination and the tendency to ∼ others are both grounded in fear —G.S.Blum⟩ ⟨the power to alter and so to ∼ much of his environment —W.E.Swinton⟩ **2 a :** to determine decisively the course or aim or the direction of development of ⟨the Nile ∼s all life in Egypt for good and for bad —Herbert Moller⟩ ⟨two other leaders ∼ that dynamic age: Innocent III and Frederick II —Will Durant⟩ ⟨the highest efficiency cannot be produced in any human being unless his whole character and his whole activity be *dominated* by some sentiment or passion —C.W.Eliot⟩ **b :** to exert the supreme determining or guiding influence upon ⟨I have been criticized for "being *dominated*" by ideas rather than *dominating* them while composing —J.D.Cook⟩ ⟨painting, essentially a two-dimensional art, was for centuries *dominated* by the effort to achieve tridimensionality —Herbert Read⟩ ⟨Brown was well over 50 years of age before the idea of freeing the slaves by force *dominated* his mind⟩ **3 :** to overlook from a superior elevation or command because of superior height ⟨the once fiery volcano ∼s the land for a hundred miles around —G.W. Long⟩ ⟨the Presidentials ∼ the other mountain ranges —Bernard DeVoto⟩ ⟨a war-memorial tower ∼s the campus⟩ ⟨the meetinghouse which ∼s the square —R.M.Hodesh⟩ **4 a :** to overspread or permeate so as to push all else into the background **:** PREDOMINATE ⟨the cypress, gum, and white cedar which ∼ this swamp forest⟩ ⟨Easterners early fixed the culture pattern *dominating* this section⟩ ⟨this dream pervades the life of a culture as the fantasies of night ∼ the mind of a sleeper —Lewis Mumford⟩ ⟨the idea of inescapable illness and operations *dominated* his life some years before he died —R.T. Hopkins⟩ **b :** to occupy in respect to prevalence or prominence the foremost position in ⟨cotton manufacture ∼s the city⟩ ⟨name brands ∼ the market⟩ ⟨in Congress law ∼s the professions⟩ ⟨national security expenditures continue to ∼ the budget⟩ ⟨Egyptian art is *dominated* by religion⟩ **5 a :** to prevail or be paramount in by virtue of superior or significant quality ⟨he is one of those figures that ∼ an age —Clive Bell⟩ ⟨collecting rather than creating man ∼s the art scene at the moment —Emily Genauer⟩ ⟨his eyes were closed and no longer *dominated* his face with their fierce pride —T.B.Costain⟩ **b :** to hold a preeminence in or over esp. so as to submerge all else in obscurity ⟨in his interiors . . . color so ∼s the canvas that the composition dissolves into a series of lights —Denys Sutton⟩ ⟨budgetary developments so drastic as to ∼ the economic outlook —R.A.Musgrave⟩ ∼ *vi* **1 :** to hold superiority or mastery in power or strength ⟨it was necessary for her to ∼ and enslave, all her virtues — her strong lust to serve, to give, and to nurse, to amuse — came from the imperative need for dominance over almost all she touched —Thomas Wolfe⟩ ⟨his lust for power, his craving to ∼, his burning sense of a historical mission given to him by God —W.L.Shirer⟩ **2 :** to provide directive control **:** constitute governing or determining influence ⟨at times such material considerations as oil are allowed to ∼ —Karl Baehr⟩ ⟨the application by the courts of the method of sociology . . . . Even when it does not seem to ∼, it is always in reserve —B.N.Cardozo⟩ ⟨a *dominating* factor in industrial growth⟩ **3 :** to occupy a more elevated or superior position ⟨a village nestled under a *dominating* crag⟩ **4 :** to prevail over or exceed all others in number, proportion, or frequency ⟨flimsy temporary structures ∼ —P.S.Fritz⟩ ⟨the *dominating* rocks are granitic⟩ ⟨the *dominating* winds are westerly⟩ **5 :** to surpass or overshadow all others in prominence, recognition, prestige ⟨let one color ∼, using it in the largest areas —Betty Fisk⟩ ⟨the *dominating* theme in all this avant-garde fiction —G.A.Wagner⟩

dominating *adj* **1 :** having an air of command ⟨a great many women, brave in mannish clothes, ∼ and active in manner —Louis Bromfield⟩ **2 :** given to exercising an autocratic or otherwise unwarranted ascendancy over another ⟨because the boy remains fixed in an outmoded dependency relationship with his ∼ and overprotective mother and does not dare the rewards of a more dangerous manhood —Weston La Barre⟩

dom·i·nat·ing·ly *adv* **:** in a dominating manner

dom·i·na·tion \ˌdäməˈnāshən\ *n* -S [ME, *dominacioun*, fr. MF *domination*, fr. L *domination-, dominatio*, fr. *dominatus*, + *-ion-, -io* -ion] **1 :** supremacy or ascendancy over another or others **2 a :** exercise of mastery or ruling power ⟨looking out for one's own today is rapidly taking the form of attempted global ∼ —Norman Cousins⟩ ⟨the only alternative to complete ∼ in Southeast Asia —Hugh Gaitskell⟩ **b :** DOMINION, SUZERAINTY ⟨named during the French and Spanish ∼ of Louisiana⟩ **3 :** exercise of preponderant influence **4 a :** compelling political and economic influence ⟨with the empire going, the establishment of British ∼ has to take a new direction: in the field of technology —Jean Hills⟩ **b :** governing or controlling influence ⟨the long period of Chinese ∼ in Japanese art —Laurence Binyon⟩ ⟨perhaps not marry, for she was under the ∼ of her creed which did not permit divorce —Donn Byrne⟩ ⟨what varies surprisingly little is the efficacy of his personal ∼ of both orchestra and public —Virgil Thomson⟩ **c :** the dominating by an employer of a labor organization **5 dominations** *pl* **:** DOMINION 4

dom·i·na·tive \ˈdäməˌnād·iv, -ˌnət\ *adj* [ML *dominativus*, fr. L *dominatus* + *-ivus* -ive] **:** GOVERNING, DOMINATING, DETERMINING

dom·i·na·tor \-ˌnād·ə(r), -ātə-\ *n* -S [ME *dominatoure*, fr. MF *dominateur*, fr. L *dominator*, fr. *dominatus* (past part. of *dominari* to rule, govern) + *-or* — more at DOMINATE] **1 :** a dominating person or power **:** RULER, MASTER **2** *obs* **:** a planet or sign supposed in astrology to have a commanding influence **3 :** a brightness receptor in the retina of the eye that is supposedly a group of cones linked to the terminals of a single nerve fiber

do·mi·ne *like* DOMINIE\ *n* -S [L, voc. of *dominus* lord, master — more at DAME] **1** *obs* **:** MASTER — used as a title of respect **2** [D *dominee*, fr. L *domine*] *archaic* **:** DOMINIE 3

dom·i·neck \ˈdäməˌnek\ *or* **dom·i·neck·er** \-kə(r)\ *n* -S *often cap* [fr. *Dominique* (Dominica), one of the Windward islands, West Indies] **:** DOMINIQUE

¹dom·i·neer \ˌdäməˈni(ə)r, -iə\ *vb* -ED/-ING/-S [D *domineren*, fr. F *dominer*, fr. L *dominari* to rule — more at DOMINATE] *vi* **1 :** to exercise or to attain despotic mastery **:** rule with arbitrariness or with insolence **2** *obs* **a :** REVEL **b :** SWAGGER **3 :** to be prevalent ⟨tetanus is no longer a very ∼*ing* menace —Berton Roueché⟩ **4 :** to tower dominantly ∼ *vt* **1 :** to rule over with arbitrariness or with insolence **:** tyrannize over **2 :** to tower above

²domineer \"\ *n* -S **:** a domineering air ⟨one recognizes a ∼ about him before he speaks⟩

domineering *adj* **:** disposed to exercise or to flaunt dictatorial authority in a way to override any protestation **:** OVERBEARING, TYRANNICAL ⟨then, and ever, she felt humbly about herself at heart, however arrogant and ∼ she could be on the surface —Havelock Ellis⟩ ⟨like ∼ mothers, the states refuse cities the right to run their own lives —T.C.Desmond⟩ ⟨the self-pride of the merchant that sustained him in his encounters with a ∼ aristocracy —V.L.Parrington⟩ **syn** see MASTERFUL

dom·i·neer·ing·ly *adv* **:** in a domineering manner

dom·i·neer·ing·ness *n* -ES **:** the quality or state of being domineering

doming *pres part of* DOME

domini *pl of* DOMINUS

dom·i·ni·ca cedar \ˌdäməˈnēkə-, -ˈnikə-\ *n, usu cap D* [fr. *Dominica*, one of the Windward islands, West Indies] **:** a tropical American tree (*Tabebuia bahamensis*)

¹do·min·i·cal \dəˈminəkəl, -nēk-\ *adj* [in sense 1, fr. ML *dominicalis*, fr. L *dominicus* of a master or lord (fr. *dominus* master, lord + *-icus* -ic) + *-alis* -al; in sense 2, fr. LL *dominicalis*, fr. *dominicus (dies)* Sunday (fr. L *dominicus* of a master or lord) + L *-alis* -al — more at DAME] **1 :** given by or closely associated with Jesus Christ as Lord ⟨the ∼ prayer⟩ ⟨the ∼ supper⟩ **2 :** belonging or relating to the Lord's day

²dominical \"\ *n* -S **1 :** DOMINICAL LETTER **2** [by shortening] **:** one who observes Sunday but not as representing the Sabbath of the Old Testament — compare SABBATARIAN

dominical altar *n* **:** an ecclesiastical high altar

dominical letter *n* **:** the letter designating Sundays in a given year esp. for use in determining the date of Easter (as when the first seven letters of the alphabet are applied consecutively to the days of the year beginning with *A* on Jan. 1 and skipping the intercalary day in leap year) — called also *Sunday letter;* see EASTER table

¹do·min·i·can \dəˈminəkən, -nēk-\ *n* -S *cap* [after St. *Dominic* (Domingo de Guzmán) †1221 Span. Roman Catholic priest who founded it + E *-an*] **:** a member of an order of mendicant preaching friars founded in Languedoc in 1215 under the rule of St. Augustine with many borrowings from the Premonstratensian statutes — called also *friar preacher*

²dominican \"\ *adj, usu cap* **1 :** of or relating to St. Dominic **2 :** of or relating to the Dominicans

³dominican \"\ *adj, usu cap* [*Dominican* Republic, Hispaniola island, West Indies] **:** of or from the Dominican Republic **:** of the kind or style prevalent in the Dominican Republic

⁴dominican \"\ *n* -S *cap* **:** a native or inhabitant of the Dominican Republic

dom·i·ni·ca oak \ˌdäməˈnēkə-, -ˈnikə-\ *n, usu cap D* [*Dominica*, one of the Windward islands, West Indies] **:** a West Indian holly (*Ilex sideroxyloides*)

dominica rosewood *n, usu cap D* **:** SPANISH ELM

dom·i·nick \ˈdämə(ˌ)nik\ *or* **dom·i·nick·er** \-ˌnikə(r)\ *n* -S *often cap* [fr. *Dominque* (Dominica)] **:** DOMINIQUE

dom·i·nie \ˈdämənē, ˈdōm-, -ni *sometimes* -mn-; ˈdäm- *is more frequent in senses 1 & 2*, ˈdōm- *in sense 3*\ *n* -S [alter. of *domine*] **1** *chiefly Scot* **:** PEDAGOGUE, SCHOOLMASTER **2** *archaic* **:** the master of a boardinghouse for oppidans at Eton **3** [D *dominee* — more at DOMINE] **a :** a pastor of the Reformed Dutch Church **b** *dial* **:** MINISTER

do·min·i·gene \dəˈminəˌjēn, ˈdämən-\ *n* [*domin*ance + *-i-* + *gene*] **:** a gene that modifies the dominance of another gene

do·min·ion \dəˈminyən\ *n* -S [ME *dominioun*, fr. MF *dominion* modif. of L *dominium* — more at DOMAIN] **1 a :** a supremacy in determining and directing the actions of others or in governing politically, socially, or personally **:** acknowledged ascendancy over human or nonhuman forces such as assures cogency in commanding or restraining and being obeyed **:** SOVEREIGNTY ⟨the federal government's claim of ∼ over the resources of the marginal sea⟩ ⟨I became profoundly conscious of the ∼ of unalterable law —John Buchan⟩ ⟨theorists who suggested that man had ∼ over the environment through his intellect —S.F.Mason⟩ **b :** the exercise of such supremacy or ascendancy **:** RULE ⟨little people striving to free themselves from the ∼ of their oppressors⟩ ⟨of the way young people should look, and of the things they should do, under the ∼ of the passion —George Meredith⟩ **c :** preponderant or overriding influence **:** DOMINANCE ⟨the fact is that the free ∼ of the mind and of art has never been achieved in capitalist democracy —J.T. Farrell⟩ ⟨neither in their lives nor their work were they able to escape the dream's ∼ —Leo Marx⟩ ⟨he possessed, superlatively, that air of ∼ by which it is possible to single out the stage favorite —Osbert Sitwell⟩ **2 :** something that is subject to sovereignty or control **3 a :** the estate or domain of a feudal lord **b :** a territory or country subject to a ruler or under the control of a particular government ⟨the ∼s of a king⟩ **c :** the special realm of activity or influence of a particular branch of art or knowledge **:** DOMAIN **4 dominions** *pl* **:** an order of angels — see CELESTIAL HIERARCHY **5** *often cap* **:** one of the self-governing, autonomous states within the British Commonwealth equal in status with the United Kingdom and with each other ⟨as far as the world of states is concerned, *Dominion* status is tantamount to statehood —H.M.Clokie⟩ ⟨born in reaction against colonial inferiority, *Dominion* nationalism was promptly stimulated by the advances in autonomy and in turn furthered these advances —Alexander Brady⟩ **6 :** absolute ownership **:** DOMINIUM **syn** see POWER

dominion day *n, usu cap both Ds* **1 :** July 1 observed in Canada as a legal holiday commemorating the anniversary of the proclamation of dominion status in 1867 **2 :** Sept 26 observed in New Zealand as a statutory bank holiday celebrating the anniversary of the coming into dominion status in 1907

do·min·ion·hood \-ˌhu̇d\ *n* **:** status as a dominion

do·min·ion·ite \-yəˌnīt\ *n* -S *often cap* **:** an advocate of dominion status for his community

dom·i·nique \ˈdämə(ˌ)nik, -ˌnēk, ˌdäməˈnēk\ *n* [fr. *Dominique* (Dominica), one of the Windward islands, West Indies] **1** *usu cap* **:** an American breed of domestic fowls with rose combs, yellow legs, and barred plumage **2** -S **:** any bird of the Dominique breed; *sometimes* **:** any barred fowl

do·min·i·um \dəˈminēəm\ *n* -S [L — more at DOMAIN] **1** *Roman law* **:** absolute ownership of corporeal property by a person subject only to the power of the state and including the right to use and enjoy, the right to take profit therefrom, and the right of disposal **2** [ML, fr. L] *in medieval Europe & England* **a :** any of various property rights; *esp* **:** OWNERSHIP **b :** political power (as through lordship, sovereignty, suzerainty)

dominium di·rec·tum \-dəˈrektəm, -ˌdīˈ-\ *n* [L, direct ownership] *Roman & feudal law* **:** the general ownership of property of one holding the title — called also *superiority;* contrasted with *dominium utile*

dominium uti·le \-ˈyüdᵊl(ˌ)ē\ *n* [L, ownership of use] *Roman & feudal law* **:** the right of one not having title (as a vassal) of using property (as for enjoyment, improvement, or profit) **:** beneficial tenancy or ownership — compare DOMINIUM DIRECTUM

¹dom·i·no \ˈdäməˌnō\ *n, pl* **dominoes** *or* **dominos** [F, prob. fr. L *domino* (in the prayer formula *benedicamus Domino* let us bless the Lord), dat. of *dominus* lord, master — more at DAME] **1 a :** a hood worn by cathedral canons **:** AMICE **b :** a hooded cape worn by members of certain religious sisterhoods **2 :** a long loose lightweight cloak with a hood usu. worn with a half mask as a masquerade costume **3 :** a half mask that is worn with a masquerade costume and formerly was used by women when traveling **4 :** a person wearing a domino **5** [F, fr. It, prob. fr. *domino* master, lord (exclamation of the winner), fr. L *dominus*] **a :** a flat rectangular block of bone, ivory, wood, or plastic the face of which is divided into two equal parts called ends which are blank or bear from one to usu. six dots arranged as on dice faces **b** *dominoes pl but usu sing in constr* **:** any of several games played with a set of usu. 28 pieces of dominoes and characterized generally by the matching of the end of a domino in the hand with an unmatched end of a domino already played **c** (1) **:** the matching by a player of the last domino in his hand ⟨the player who makes ∼ wins the hand⟩ — often used interjectionally in the game (2) **:** an act or moment of completion or irrevocable finality ⟨I felt sure it was ∼ for me and my prospects⟩

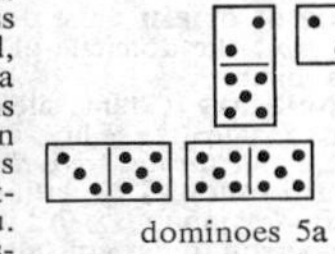

dominoes 5a

²domino \"\ *vi* -ED/-ING/-ES **:** to match the last domino in one's hand with one already played and thereby win the hand

domino bridge *n* **:** DRAWBRIDGE

dom·i·nule \ˈdäməˌnyül\ *n* -S [²*dominant* + *-ule*] **:** an ecological dominant in a microhabitat

do·mi·nus \ˈdämənəs\ *n, pl* **domi·ni** \-ˌnē, -ˌnī\ [L, lord, master — more at DAME] **1 :** an owner as distinguished from a user **2 :** a principal as distinguished from an agent

dominus di·rec·tus \-dəˈrektəs, -ˌdīˈ-\ *n, pl* **domini direc·ti** \-məˌnēdəˈrekˌtē, -məˌnīdəˈrekˌtī, -ˌdīˈ-\ [L, direct master] **:** the person having the dominium directum

dominus li·tis \-ˈlēˌdəs, -ˈlīˌ\ *n, pl* **domini litis** \-ˌnēˈlēˌ, -ˌnīˈlī\ [L, master of the suit] **:** a male client in a law case

dom·i·ta·ble \ˈdäməd·əbəl\ *adj* [L *domitare* to tame (freq. of *domare*) + E *-able* — more at TAME] **:** TAMABLE

do·mi·tae na·tu·rae \ˈdäməˌtīnəˈtu̇ˌrī, -məˌtēnəˈtu̇ˌrē\ *adj* [L, of a tamed nature] **:** DOMESTICATED

do·mi·tian \dəˈmishən, dōˈ- *sometimes* -shēən\ *or* **do·mi·ti·an·ic** \-ˌmishēˈanik\ *adj, usu cap* [after *Domitian* (Domitianus Augustus) †A.D.96 Roman emperor] **:** peculiar to or relating to the Roman emperor Domitian or his reign ⟨two documents emanating from the *Domitian* terror —M.H.Shepherd⟩

dom·nei \ˈdämˈnā\ *n* [OProv, fr. *domna* lady, fr. L *domina* — more at DAME] **:** the Provençal ideal or cult of courtly love prevalent among the troubadours

dom nut \ˈdōm-\ *n* [³*dom*] **:** the ivory nut as produced under cultivation in eastern Africa usu. consisting of the seed plus the endocarp

dom palm \"-\ *n* [F *doum* — more at DOOM PALM] **:** DOOM PALM

¹dom pe·dro \dəmˈpē(ˌ)drō\ *n, usu cap D&P* [prob. fr. Pg *dom* master, sir (as in *Dom Pedro* II †1891 emperor of Brazil) + E *pedro*] **:** pedro in which the 3, 5, and 9 of trumps are counted at face value and a joker is added which ranks as the lowest trump but counts 15 points when taken in a trick

²dom pedro \"\ *n* [after *Dom Pedro* II †1891] **:** a stout work shoe having one buckle and a bellows tongue.

dompt \ˈdäm(p)t\ *vt* **dompted; dompted; dompting; dompts** \-m(p)(t)s\ [F *dompter* to tame, fr. L *domitare*, fr. *domare* to tame — more at TAME] **:** to hold (as a lion) at bay

dom·ra \ˈdämrə, ˈdȯm-\ *n* -S [Russ *domra, dombra*, of Turkic origin; akin to Turk *tambura*, a kind of guitar, Kirghiz *dombra*] **:** a Russian instrument like a lute

doms *pl of* DOM

-doms *pl of* -DOM

dom·siek·te \ˈdämˌsēktə\ *n* -S [Afrik, lit., stupid disease, fr. *dom* stupid (fr. MD) + *siekte* disease, fr. MD *siecte*, fr. *siec* ill, sick; akin to OHG *tumb* inexperienced, foolish and OHG *sioh* sick, ill — more at DUMB, SICK] **:** a pregnancy disease of sheep in southern Africa

do·mus \ˈdōməs\ *n, pl* **domus** [L — more at TIMBER] **:** a dwelling of ancient Roman or medieval times

domy *or* **dom·ey** \ˈdōmē\ *adj* [¹*dome* + *-y*] **1 :** having a dome **2 :** like a dome

¹don \ˈdän\ *n* -S [Sp, fr. L *dominus*, master, lord — more at DAME] **1 a :** LORD, SIR — prefixed to the Christian name of a Spaniard of high rank **b** (1) **:** SENOR — used among Spanish-speaking people prefixed to the Christian name as a courtesy title (2) **:** MASTER — used as a form of address for an Italian priest **2** *often cap* **:** a Spaniard or man of Spanish descent ⟨he played on Jackson's obsession against the Spanish by promising to drive the ∼s from America —C.G.Bowers⟩ **3 a** *archaic* **:** a great or famous person **:** a person of consequence **:** GRANDEE ⟨the great ∼s of wit —John Dryden⟩ **b :** a head, tutor, or fellow in an English university ⟨she didn't want to be a ∼'s wife and live in Oxford forever —Virginia Woolf⟩; *broadly* **:** a college or university teacher

²don \"\ *vt* **donned; donned; donning; dons** [contr. of *do* + *on*] **1 a :** to put on (an article of wear) **:** dress in ⟨*donned* the robes of his office⟩ **b :** to apply (as greasepaint) to the face or body **c :** to insert (a cone) in the holder in a textile machine **2 :** to clothe or envelop oneself in **:** ASSUME ⟨able to ∼ the personality of another person⟩ ⟨perhaps the truest understanding would come from the *donning* of new and more tyrannous moralities —Edward Sapir⟩

¹do·ña \ˈdōnyə\ *n* -S [Sp, fr. L *domina* — more at DAME] **:** a Spanish or Spanish-American woman — used esp. as a title prefixed to the Christian name of a married woman of rank

²do·na \ˈdōnə\ *n* -S [Pg, fr. L *domina*] **:** a Portuguese or Brazilian woman — used esp. as a title prefixed to the Christian name of a married woman of rank

do·na·ble \ˈdōnəbəl\ *adj* [L *donabilis*, fr. *donare* to present, grant + *-abilis* -able — more at DONATION] **:** capable of being donated ⟨army surplus declared ∼ to educational institutions⟩

do·nac·i·dae \dōˈnasəˌdē\ *n pl, cap* [NL, fr. *Donac-, Donax*, type genus + *-idae*] **:** a family of marine bivalve mollusks (suborder Tellinacea) comprising the wedge shells that are esp. abundant in warm shallow seas — see DONAX

do·nac·i·form \-səˌfȯrm\ *adj* [NL *Donac-, Donax* + E *-iform*] **:** shaped or formed like a mollusk of the genus *Donax*

donack *n* -S [by alter.] **:** ²DORNICK 1

do·nah \ˈdōnə\ *n* -S [perh. fr. It *donna* woman, wife, lady, fr. L *domina* lady — more at DAME] *slang Brit* **:** WOMAN; *esp* **:** SWEETHEART

do·na·ry \ˈdōnərē\ *n* -ES [L *donarium* place in a temple where an offering is made, offering, fr. *donum* gift + *-arium* -ary — more at DONATION] *archaic* **:** a gift to a sacred, charitable, or educational use

do·na·tary \ˈdōnəˌterē, ˈdän-\ *n* -ES [ML *donatarius*, fr. L *donatus* (past part. of *donare* to present, grant) + *-arius* -ary — more at DONATION] *Scots law* **:** the receiver of a donation; *specif* **:** the receiver of any right bestowed by the king after its forfeiture to the crown

do·nate \ˈdōˌnāt *also* dōˈn-; *usu* -ād·+V\ *vb* -ED/-ING/-S [back-formation fr. *donation*] *vt* **1 a :** to make a free gift or a grant of **:** contribute esp. to a charitable cause or toward a public-service institution ⟨a retired manufacturer *donated* a site for a park⟩ ⟨city physicians ∼ part-time services⟩ ⟨magazines *donated* space⟩ **b :** SUPPLY, LOAN ⟨*donated* property for the theatrical performance⟩ **2 :** EMIT, TRANSFER ⟨∼ electrons⟩ ∼ *vi* **:** to donate something

donated stock *n* **:** stock that is returned to a corporation by promoters or stockholders who have received it as full-paid stock in exchange for property in order that it may be sold to provide capital

do·na·tee \ˌdōnāˈtē, -ˌnāˈ-\ *n* -S **:** a recipient of a free gift

do·na·tio \dōˈnäd·ēˌō, -nāshēˌō\ *n, pl* **donati·o·nes** \-ˌnäd·ēˈōˌnās, ˌnāshēˈōˌnēz\ [L] *law* **:** GIFT; *esp* **:** DONATION

donatio in·ter vi·vos \-ˌintərˈwēˌwōs, -ˈvīˌvōs\ [L, gift between living people] **:** a voluntary gratuitous alienation of property by one person to another not made in contemplation of death that constitutes in the civil law an executed gift that takes effect and becomes irrevocable on acceptance by the donee but in the common law requires delivery

donatio mor·tis cau·sa \-ˌmȯrd·əˈskau̇ˌsä, -ˈskȯzə\ [L, gift because of death] **:** a gift of personal property made by one believing himself near to death and to take effect only in case the giver dies, being valid if there is an actual delivery of the gift

do·na·tion \dōˈnāshən *sometimes* dəˈ-\ *n* -S [ME *donatyowne*, fr. L *donation-, donatio*, fr. *donatus* (past part. of *donare* to give as a gift, present, grant, fr. *donum* gift, fr. *dare* to give) + *-ion-, -io* -ion — more at DATE] **1** *archaic* **:** a formal grant of sovereignty or dominion **2 :** the action of making a gratuitous gift or free contribution esp. to a charity, humanitarian cause, or public institution or utility ⟨yearly ∼ of prizes for scholastic and athletic achievement⟩ **3 :** voluntary alienation of property **:** gratuitous transfer of property from one to another **4 a :** assignment of public land on liberal terms under act of Congress to settlers **b :** a portion of land so assigned ⟨owner of the ∼ land claim on which the town was built⟩ **5 :** a free contribution **:** GIFT ⟨the money value of ∼s to needy applicants⟩

donation party *n* **:** a party at which some gift is brought to the host by each guest ⟨a *donation party* for the minister⟩

donatio prop·ter nup·ti·as \-ˌprȯptərˈnüptēˌäs, -ˌpräptərˈnəpshēəs\ [L, gift because of marriage] **:** a marriage gift or settlement required by law of the husband or his family early during the later Roman Empire and that was required by Justinian to be equal to the wife's dowry but permitted to be made after and used for expenses of the marriage — formerly called when made before the marriage *donatio ante nuptias*

don·a·tism \ˈdänəˌtizəm, ˈdōn-\ *n* -S *usu cap* [*Donatus* + E *-ism*] **:** the doctrines or beliefs peculiar to the Donatists

don·a·tist \-ˌtəst\ *n* -S *usu cap* [ML *Donatista*, fr. *Donatus*, 4th cent. bishop of Carthage + L *-ista* -ist] **:** a member of a schismatic party of Christians in No. Africa from 311 to the 7th century who held that the validity of the sacraments depends on the spiritual state of the minister, that sanctity is essential for church membership, and that all who joined their group should be rebaptized

don·a·tis·tic \ˌ==ˈtistik\ *adj, usu cap* **:** of or referring to Donatists or Donatism

¹do·na·tive \ˈdōnəd·iv, ˈdän-\ *n* -S [L *donativum*, fr. neut. of *donativus*, adj., fr. *donatus* (past part. of *donare* to give as a gift, present, grant) + *-ivus* -ive — more at DONATION] **1 :** a special compensation or donation **:** PREMIUM, BOUNTY ⟨the doles and ∼s which kept the populace and the army in good temper —R.M.French⟩ **2 :** a donative benefice

2donative \"\ *adj* [L *donativus*] **1 :** having the character or object of or being subject to donation ⟨at the time of the transfer the deceased had full ~ capacity⟩ ⟨~ disposition of land⟩ **:** vested or vesting by donation ⟨a ~ advowson⟩ — opposed to *presentative* **2 :** conferred upon a bishop or priest of the Church of England by the founder or patron without either presentation or institution by the ordinary or induction by his orders ⟨~ benefices were abolished in 1898⟩ — **do·na·tive·ly** \-d.əvlē, -li\ *adv*

1do·na·tor \'dō,nād·ə(r), -ātə- *also* dō'n-\ *n* -s [L, fr. *donatus* + *-or*] **:** DONOR

2do·na·tor \'dōnətər, 'dän-, -nə,tȯr\ *n* -s [ML *donatorius*, fr. L *donatus* + *-orius* -ory] *Scots law* **:** DONEE

do·nax \'dō,naks\ *n* [NL, fr. L, a shellfish, fr. Gk] **1** *cap* **:** a genus of small marine bivalve mollusks that is the type of the family Donacidae and that includes forms having long separate siphons, a well-developed foot, and an equivalve somewhat triangular shell **2** -ES **:** COQUINA 1

don·cel·la \dän'selə\ *n* -s [AmerSp, fr. Sp, girl, virgin, housemaid, fr. (assumed) VL *domnicilla*, dim. of L *domina* lady — more at DAME] **1 :** any of several brightly colored wrasses of the West Indies and Florida: **a :** the slippery dick and closely related fishes **b :** LADYFISH b **2 :** either of two West Indian timber trees (*Byrsonima spicata* and *B. cuneata*) valued for their hard wood — compare SURETTE

don·cy \'dän(t)sē\ *var of* DONSIE

don·dom \'dändəm\ *n* -s [1*don* + *-dom*] **:** the office or position of an academic don

1done [ME *doon*, *ydoon* (past part. of *don*, *doon* to do), fr. OE *gedōn*, past part. of *dōn* to do; akin to OHG *gitān* done — more at DO] *past part & substand past of* DO

2done \'dən\ *adj* [ME *doon*, *ydoon*, fr. *doon*, *ydoon*, past part.] **1 :** conformable to social convention or the proprieties of a sport, profession, or system of protocol **;** according with good breeding or the amenities **:** DECOROUS ⟨you know it isn't ~ to hold hands in public places —Louis Auchincloss⟩ ⟨at table there are cases where there is now the ~ thing to use the fingers⟩ **2 :** arrived at the finish or the very end of a course or of one's concern **:** having reached adequate accomplishment or the limit of one's need, use, or endurance **:** THROUGH ⟨just one more question and I'm ~⟩ ⟨certain to make history before he's ~⟩ ⟨will you never get ~ with that scraping⟩ **3 :** having strength or energy depleted **:** quite exhausted **:** suffering collapse **:** SPENT ⟨the camels were too ~ to carry our weight —T.E.Lawrence⟩ — often used with *up* ⟨are you ~ up, or would you like to take me up the ladder and show me the sights —Elmer Davis⟩ **4** *of time* **:** brought to an end **:** gone by ⟨he said the day of the circus big top is ~⟩ **5 :** doomed to failure, defeat, or death ⟨industry in this section is ~⟩ **6 :** cooked or roasted sufficiently (as for serving) ⟨the meat is ~⟩ **7 :** fitted out or dressed esp. in flawless or in elaborate fashion **:** given finishing touches ⟨his clothes in press, his shoes perfectly ~ —Emily Post⟩ — sometimes used with *up*

3done \"\ *adv* **1** *dial* **:** ALREADY **2** *dial* **:** ACTUALLY, EXCEEDINGLY

do·nee \(')dō¦nē\ *n* -s [*donor* + *-ee*] **1 :** a recipient of a gift **2 a :** one on whom a power to transfer property by will or deed is conferred for execution — called also *appointor* **b :** the recipient of a blood transfusion or of tissue or an organ for grafting

done for \'dən,fō(ə)r, -ȯ(ə)\ *adj* **1 :** irretrievably lost or mortally stricken **:** DOOMED ⟨when we saw the explosion we thought he was *done for*⟩ **2 :** left with no effective power and no capacity or opportunity for recovery **:** DOWN-AND-OUT ⟨defeat in this election would mean he was *done for*, his career at an end⟩ **3 :** sunk in defeat **:** WASHED-UP, BEATEN ⟨you know, it may come out any day, and then we're *done for* —George Meredith⟩ ⟨if this country ever runs out of people who don't like to be pushed around, we are *done for* —Elmer Davis⟩ **4 :** relegated to the discard ⟨the impression that the old, great, simple books are declassed, passé, dated, outmoded, *done for* —J.C.Powys⟩

don·e·gal \'dänē,gȯl, 'dən-, -nō,-, ¦==¦=\ *adj, usu cap* [fr. *Donegal* county, Ireland] **:** of or from County Donegal, Ireland **:** of the kind or style prevalent in County Donegal

donegal tweed *n, usu cap D* **:** a heavy woolen homespun of Irish origin characterized by colorful slubs in the weft yarn and a neutral color in the warp; *also* **:** a tweed of similar character woven plain or twill from wool or other fibers

done in \,də'nin\ *adj* **:** physically exhausted

do·netsk \də'netsk\ *adj, usu cap* [fr. *Donetsk*, city in eastern Ukraine, U.S.S.R.] **:** of or from the city of Donetsk **:** of the kind or style prevalent in Donetsk

done with \'dən,with, -th\ *adj* **:** brought to an end **:** decisively abandoned or dismissed ⟨but killing was *done with* except for predators that molested him —Stuart Cloete⟩ ⟨in my craft a thing done is a thing *done with* —Katharine F. Gerould⟩ — **have done with :** to bring to an end **:** have no further concern with **:** ABANDON, DISMISS ⟨he was soon to *have done with* calendared time, and it had already ceased to count for him —Willa Cather⟩ ⟨let us *have done with* character assassination⟩

1do·ney \'dōnē\ *n* -s [alter. of ME *donek*, *dunoke* — more at DUNNOCK] *dial Brit* **:** HEDGE SPARROW

2doney \"\ *n* -s [by alter.] **:** 2DORNICK 1

3doney \"\ *n* -s [prob. alter. of *donah*] *chiefly Midland* **:** GIRL FRIEND, SWEETHEART

1dong \'dȯŋ, 'däŋ\ *vb* -ED/-ING/-S [imit.] *vi* **:** to give a deep-toned sound of or as if of a large bell ~ *vt, chiefly Austral* **:** HIT, STRIKE

2dong \"\ *n* -s **1 :** a sound of donging **2** *chiefly Austral* **:** a heavy blow (as with the fist) **3 :** PENIS — usu. considered vulgar

3dong \"\ *n, pl* **dong** [Annamese] **1 :** SAPEQUE **2 a :** PIASTER 4 **b** (1) **:** the basic monetary unit of Vietnam — see MONEY table (2) **:** a coin or note representing this

don·ga \'däŋgə, 'dȯŋ-\ *n* -s [Afrik, fr. Zulu] *chiefly Africa* **:** a narrow steep-sided ravine formed by water erosion but usu. dry except in the rainy season

don·go·la kid \'däŋ¦gələ-, 'dȯŋ¦-; ÷(')dän¦'gōlə-, ÷(')däŋ¦-, ÷(')dȯŋ¦-\ *n, usu cap D* [fr. *Dongola*, region of Sudan] **:** a leather made by a process of tanning goatskin, calfskin, or sheepskin so that it resembles kid

don·go·lese \,däŋgə¦lēz, ¦dȯŋ-, -ēs\ *n, pl* **dongolese** *cap* [*Dongola* + E *-ese*] **:** a native or inhabitant of Dongola

dong·on \'dȯŋ,ȯn\ *n* -s **:** DUNGON

dong-son \'däŋ,sän, 'dȯŋ-\ *adj, usu cap D&S* [fr. *Dong-Son*, site in northern Annam, Indochina, where artifacts were found] **:** of or relating to a culture of northern Indochina of not later than 300 B.C. characterized by bronze drums and weapons including the kris

doni *var of* DHONI

don·ick \'dänik\ *n* -s [by alter.] **:** 2DORNICK 1

don·ick·er \'dänikə(r)\ *n* -s [E dial. *dunnekin*, *donnick* privy, open cesspool] *slang* **:** PRIVY, TOILET

don·jon \'dänjən, 'dən-\ *n* -s [ME *donjon*, *dongeoun* — more at DUNGEON] **:** a massive chief tower in ancient castles — see CASTLE illustration

donjon keep *n* **:** DUNGEON

don juan \(')dän'(h)wän, dän'jüən, ,dänə'wän — *usu* -'jüən *with reference to Byron's poem, where such a pronunc is required by rhymes*\ *n, pl* **don juans** *usu cap D&J* [after *Don Juan*, legendary Spanish nobleman featured in many works of literature, esp. *El Burlador de Sevilla* by Gabriel Téllez (Tirso de Molina) †1648 Span. dramatist, and *Don Juan*, by George Gordon, Lord Byron †1824 Eng. poet] **:** a man that pursues women **:** LIBERTINE

don·juan·esque \,¦dän,(h)wä¦nesk, (,)dän¦jüə¦n-, ¦dänə,wä¦n-\ *adj* **:** resembling a Don Juan **:** of or relating to a Don Juan

don juan·ism \-,nizəm\ *n, pl* **don juanisms** *usu cap D&J* **:** male sexual promiscuity attributable to feelings of impotence or inadequate masculinity

1donk \'däŋk, -ə-, -ȯ-\ *n* -s [by shortening] **:** DONKEY 1

2donk \'däŋk, 'dəŋk\ *dial var of* DANK

don·key \'däŋkē, -ki *also* 'dəŋ- *or* 'dȯŋ-\ *n* -s [perh. fr. *dun* + *-key* (as in *monkey*)] **1 :** the domestic ass **2 :** a stupid or obstinate person **3 :** a workbench fitted with a frame on which is mounted a fine saw for cutting marquetry veneers; *also* **:** a machine for this operation

donkeyback \'==,=\ *adv* **:** on a donkey

donkey boiler *also* **donkey** *n* -s **:** an auxiliary boiler (as one carried aboard ship for use in port)

donkey boy *n* **1 :** a driver of donkeys **2 :** an operator of a donkey engine

donkey cart *n* **:** a cart with an underslung axle and two lengthwise seats — called also *pony cart*, *tub-cart*; compare GOVERNESS CART

donkey doctor *n* **:** a logging mechanic who maintains and repairs a donkey engine

donkey engine *also* **donkey** *n* -s **1 :** a small usu. portable auxiliary steam, diesel, compressed-air, or other engine; *esp* **:** one used to power a windlass on shipboard or in logging **2 :** a small locomotive used in switching

don·key·ish \-ish\ *adj* **:** showing the stupidity or obstinacy of a donkey **:** ASININE

don·key·ism \-,izəm\ *n* -s **:** ASININITY

donkey-lick \'==,=\ *vt, Austral* **:** to beat so easily as to humiliate

don·key·man \-mən\ *n, pl* **donkeymen :** an operator of a donkey engine ⟨the second engineer and the ~ were firing up —Joseph Conrad⟩

donkey party *n* **:** a parlor game in which blindfolded players try to attach a tail to the right place on a picture of a donkey

donkey pump *also* **donkey** *n* -s **:** an auxiliary pump

donkey puncher *n* **:** a donkeyman in a logging camp

donkey's breakfast *n, slang* **:** a straw mattress

donkey sled *n* **:** a heavy foundation frame for a donkey engine

donkey stack *n* **:** an auxiliary smokestack on a steamship

donkey's years *n pl* **:** a very long time

donkeywork \'==,=\ *n* **:** plodding and toilsome work **:** DRUDGERY ⟨electronic brains are taking over the ~ of mathematics —Edwin Colston Shepherd⟩; *also* **:** heavy work

dön·meh *or* **dun·meh** \'dən¦mā, (')dən¦-\ *n pl, usu cap* [Turk *dönme*, lit., convert, renegade] **:** crypto-Jewish descendants of the followers of the professed messiah Sabbatai Zebi (1626–1676) now centered chiefly in Turkey and professing Islam — compare SABBATIAN

don·na \'dänə, *It* 'dȯnnä\ *n, pl* **don·ne** \'dä,nā, 'dȯnnā\ [It, fr. L *domina* lady — more at DAME] **:** an Italian woman — used esp. as a title prefixed to the Christian name of a married woman of rank

don·nan equilibrium \'dänən-\ *n, usu cap D* [after Frederick G. *Donnan* †1956 Brit. chemist and physicist] **:** the ionic equilibrium reached in a solution of an electrolyte whose ions are diffusible through a semipermeable membrane but are distributed unequally on the two sides of the membrane because of the presence of a nondiffusible colloidal ion (as a protein ion) on one side of the membrane

don·né \(')dȯ¦nā, ¦də¦-\ *n, pl* **donnés** \-ā(z)\ [F, fr. past part. of *donner* to give, fr. L *donare* to give as a present, present, grant — more at DONATION] **:** one who has dedicated himself to missionary work

don·ne·an *or* **don·ni·an** \'dänēən, 'dän-\ *adj, usu cap* [John *Donne* †1631 Eng. poet + E *-an* or *-ian*] **:** of or relating to John Donne or his metaphysical poetry

donned *past of* DON

don·née \(')dȯ¦nā, ¦də¦-\ *n, pl* **données** \-ā(z)\ [F, fr. fem. past part. of *donner*] **1 :** the main assumption or set of assumptions (as a social situation or set of personal relationships) upon which a work of literature or drama proceeds **2 :** a basic fact, condition, or notion offering the chief source of dependence in shaping an action at a particular moment or juncture

donne·ish \'dənish, 'dän-\ *adj, usu cap* [John *Donne* + E *-ish*] **:** having characteristics of John Donne or his poetry

don·nered \'dänərd\ *also* **don·nert** \-rt\ *adj* [fr. past part. of Sc *donner*, *dunner* to stupefy, make a noise like thunder, perh. fr. D *donderen* to thunder, fr. *donder* thunder, fr. MD; akin to OHG *thonar* thunder — more at THUNDER] *chiefly Scot* **:** DAZED, STUPEFIED

don·nesque \'də¦nesk, (')dä¦-\ *adj, usu cap* [John *Donne* + E *-esque*] **:** like or suggestive of John Donne's poetry esp. in manner or style

don·nick \'dänik\ *n* -s [by alter.] **:** 2DORNICK 1

don·nick·er *var of* DONICKER

donning *pres part of* DON

don·nish \'dänish, -nēsh\ *adj* [1*don* + *-ish*] **:** relating to or characteristic of a university don **:** ACADEMIC, PEDANTIC ⟨a certain ~ carefulness of speech —L.P.Smith⟩ — **don·nish·ly** *adv* — **don·nish·ness** *n* -ES

don·nism \'dä,nizəm\ *n* -s [1*don* + *-ism*] **:** donnish attitude or manner

don·not \'dänət\ *n* -s [by alter.] *dial* **:** DONOUGHT

don·ny·brook \'dänē,brük, -ni,-\ *also* **donnybrook fair** *n*, *often cap D* [fr. *Donnybrook Fair*, an annual event known for its brawls held in Donnybrook, suburb of Dublin, Ireland] **1 :** an uproarious brawl **:** FREE-FOR-ALL **2 :** a rowdy contention between rival forces carried on in public (as in legislative halls and public print)

do·nor \'dōnə(r) *also* 'dō,nō(ə)r *or* 'dō,nȯ(ə) *sometimes* 'dän(ə)r *or* dō'nō-\ *n* -s [MF *doneur*, fr. L *donator* — more at DONATOR] **1 :** one that gives, donates, or presents ⟨a ~ of funds to research foundations⟩ ⟨a list of paintings and the ~*s*⟩: **a :** one that confers a power for execution — opposed to *donee* **b :** one used as a source of biological material ⟨a ~ of blood for transfusion⟩ ⟨a ~ of a chromosome complex to a hybrid⟩ ⟨a ~ of a tissue for transplantation⟩ **2** *chem* **:** a substance capable of giving up part of itself (as an atom, radical, or elementary particle) for combination with another substance ⟨water may act as a hydrogen ~⟩ ⟨adenosine triphosphate is a phosphate ~⟩ ⟨an amine with its unshared electrons is an electron ~⟩ — compare ACCEPTOR 3 **3 :** an impurity that yields a limited supply of mobile electrons that contribute to the conductivity of a semiconducting material — compare ACCEPTOR 4c

do·nor·ship \-,ship\ *n* **:** presentation by or relation of a donor ⟨of unavowed ~⟩

1do-nothing \'=,==\ *n* **:** a shiftless or habitually slothful person

2do-nothing \"\ *adj* **:** marked by slothful inactivity or minimal activity; *specif* **:** marked by lack of initiative, disinclination to disturb the status quo and attack problems, or failure to make positive progress esp. toward reform of public policy ⟨the alleged *do-nothing* record of that session of Congress⟩ — compare LAISSEZ-FAIRE — **do–noth·ing·ness** *n* -ES

do–noth·ing·ism \-,izəm\ *n* -s **:** commitment to a do-nothing policy

do·nought \'=,=\ *n* [1*do* + *nought*] *archaic* **:** DO-NOTHING 1

don·o·van body \'dänəvən-, 'dən-\ *n, usu cap D* [after Charles *Donovan* †1951 Brit. physician] **:** an organism of the genus *Calymmatobacterium* characterized by one or two opposite polar chromatin masses

don qui·xote \,dänkē'(h)ōd·|ē, -äŋk-, -ōt|, |i, -ō,tā; *sometimes* dän'kwiksə|t *or* -,sō|t *or* (+V) |d·\ *n* -s *usu cap D&Q* [Sp (now spelled *Quijote*), after *Don Quixote*, foolishly idealistic and anachronistically chivalric hero of *Don Quijote de la Mancha* by Miguel de Cervantes Saavedra †1616 Span. writer] **:** an impractical idealist and quixotic enthusiast bent on righting wrongs

dons *pl of* DON, *pres 3d sing of* DON

don·ship \'dän,ship\ *n* -s [1*don* + *-ship*] **1 :** possession of the title or rank of a don **2 :** position as a university don

don·sie *or* **don·sy** \'dän(t)sē\ *adj* [perh. fr. ScGael *donas* evil, harm, hurt + E *-ie*, *-y*] **1** *dial Brit* **:** inclined to misfortune **:** UNLUCKY **2** *dial* **:** neat and tidy; *often* **:** FASTIDIOUS **3** *Scot* **4 :** QUICK-TEMPERED, TESTY, UNMANAGEABLE **b :** SAUCY, PERT **4** *dial* **:** slightly ill **:** SICKLY, FEEBLE

1don't \(ˌ)dō|n(t), *before a pause* |nt; *before* p, b, m: |n(t) *or* |m(p) *or* (*before* m) (ˌ)dō; *before* k, g: |n(t) *or* |ŋ(k); *before* n: |n(t) *or* |(ˌ)dō *or* (*in* "don't know") (ˌ)də *or* ˌdᵊ\ [contr. of *do not*] **1 :** do not **2 :** does not — often used with a singular subject by cultivated speakers though the construction is sometimes objected to

2don't \'dōnt\ *n* -s **:** a command or entreaty not to do something **:** PROHIBITION ⟨a long list of ~*s*⟩

do·num \'dänəm, 'dōn-\ *n* -s [Turk *dönüm*, lit., turn] **:** a land measure used in regions included in the former Ottoman Empire and of varying size but usu. less than one acre

do·nut *n* [by alter.] **:** DOUGHNUT

don·zel \'dänzəl\ *n* -s [It *donzello*, fr. OIt, fr. OProv *donzel*, fr. (assumed) VL *domnicillus*, dim. of L *dominus* master — more at DAME] *archaic* **:** a young gentleman in training for knighthood **:** SQUIRE, PAGE

don·zel·la \dän'zelə, dȯnt'selə\ *n* -s [It, fr. OIt, fr. OProv *donsela*, fr. (assumed) VL *domnicilla*, dim. of L *domina* lady — more at DAME] **:** DAMSEL

doo \'dü\ *n* -s [ME (Sc dial.) *dow*, var. of *douve*, *dove*, *doufe* — more at DOVE] *Scot* **:** DOVE

doob \düb\ *n* -s [Hindi *dūb*, fr. Skt *dūrvā* — more at TARE] *India* **:** BERMUDA GRASS

doo·cot \'dükət\ *n* -s [ME *dowcot*, *dowecote* — more at DOVECOT] *Scot* **:** DOVECOT

doo·dad *also* **do·dad** \'dü,dad, -aa(ə)d\ *or* **doo·dab** \-ab, -aa(ə)b\ *n* -s [origin unknown] **1 :** a small unrecognizable or nondescript article: as **a :** an accessory implement or device **:** GADGET, JIGGER, THINGUMBOB ⟨a newfangled ~ for peeling potatoes⟩ **b :** a fancy article for wear about the person **:** TRINKET ⟨from its crown sprang a number of wired ~*s* that tinkled like wind bells when they shook —Cornelia O. Skinner⟩ **c :** an ornamental attachment or decoration ⟨an angler catching nothing despite his array of pretty ~*s*⟩ ⟨a mantelpiece cluttered up with all kinds of ~*s*⟩ **d :** a fancy food item **e :** a decorative detail or design (as a printer's ornament) ⟨star, asterisk, or other ~ at the margin —M.J.Adler⟩

doo·dah \'dü,dä\ *n* -s [origin unknown] *Brit* **:** a state of tremulous excitement ⟨opening night — all of a ~ —J.B.Priestley⟩

doodeen *or* **doodheen** *var of* DUDEEN

doo·dia \'düdēə\ *n* [NL, fr. Samuel *Doody* †1706 Eng. botanist + NL *-ia*] **1** *cap* **:** a small genus of Asiatic and Australasian ferns (family Polypodiaceae) with curved sori in rows between the margin and midrib of the frond segments **2** *pl* **doo·diae** \-ē,ē\ **:** any plant of the genus *Doodia*

1doo·dle \'düd'l\ *n* -s [perh. fr. LG *dudeldopp*] **:** a foolish or frivolous person

2doodle \"\ *vt* -ED/-ING/-S *dial* **:** to make a fool of **:** CHEAT

3doodle \"\ *vt* -ED/-ING/-S [G *dudeln*, fr. *dudel* bagpipe, fr. Czech or Pol *dudy*; akin to Russ *dudá* fife, shawm, Lith *daudýtė* shawm] *dial Brit* **:** to play on (the bagpipe)

4doodle \"\ *n* -s [short for *haydoodle*, perh. fr. 2*hay* + *doodle* (in *cock-a-doodle-do*), euphemism for *-cock* (associated with 1*cock* penis)] *dial* **:** a small pile of hay in the field **:** HAYCOCK

5doodle \"\ *n* -s [by shortening] **:** DOODLEBUG 1

6doodle \"\ *vb* **doodled; doodled; doodling** \-üd(ᵊ)liŋ\ **doodles** [perh. fr. 2*doodle*] *vi* **1 :** to make a doodle ⟨the chairman during the questioning continued to ~ with a red pencil⟩ **2 :** to engage in aimless, haphazard, or inconsequential activity **:** DAWDLE, TRIFLE, TOY ⟨acquired the habit of mental *doodling* that went through life with him —Florence B. Lennon⟩ ⟨for the last six years he has been *doodling* at an autobiography —J.K.Hutchens⟩ ~ *vt* **1 :** to mark or overspread with doodles **2 :** to expend in doodling ⟨he *doodled* the hours away⟩ **3 :** to trace in the manner of a doodle ⟨he reread the stack of invoices and *doodled* dollar signs on the blank edges —David Wagoner⟩

7doodle \"\ *n* -s **:** an aimless more or less automatic scribble, outline, design, or improvised sketch traced while one is mentally occupied with something else

1doodlebug \'==,=\ *n* [prob. fr. 1*doodle* + *bug*] **1 :** the larva of an ant lion; *broadly* **:** any of several other insects **2 :** one who does not stand up for his convictions **3 a** (1) **:** an unscientific device (as a divining rod) for locating underground gas, water, oil, or ores (2) *also* **doo·dle·bug·ger** \"+ə(r)\ **:** one professing skill with such a contrivance (3) **:** a seismograph, gravimeter, or other scientific device for the location of minerals **b :** a small tractor used in lumbering or farming **c** (1) **:** a rail motorcar used by railroad employees in construction and maintenance-of-way work (2) **:** a small local train **d** (1) **:** a small military tank (2) **:** an army utility truck **e :** ROBOT BOMB **f :** a magnetic detecting device; *specif* **:** an airborne magnetometer used for spotting submarines **g :** a midget racing automobile **h :** a very small airplane

2doodlebug \"\ *vi* **:** to use a doodlebug in a search

doo·dler \'düd(ᵊ)lə(r)\ *n* -s [6*doodle* + *-er*] **1 :** one that practices doodling **2 :** one that dillydallies

doo·dle·sack \'düdᵊl,sak\ *n* [G *dudelsack*, fr. *dudel* bagpipe + *sack* bag, fr. OHG *sac* — more at DOODLE, SACK] *dial Brit* **:** BAGPIPE

doodling *n* -s [fr. gerund of 6*doodle*] **:** a doodle or a plot or sequence of doodles ⟨collected his random ~*s* from his wastebasket, inked over the penciled lines, submitted the pictures to the art editor —Russell Maloney⟩

doods·kop \'düt,skäp\ *n* -s [Afrik, fr. *doods* (gen. of *dood* death, fr. MD *doot*) + *kop* head, fr. MD *cop*, *coppe* drinking vessel, skull, head; akin to OE *dēath* death — more at DEATH, CUP] **:** a southern African shallow-water edible chimaera (*Callorhynchus capensis*) having the snout prolonged into a fleshy lobe which is used in rooting up mollusks and crabs from sandy bottoms

doofunny *var of* DOFUNNY

doo·hick·ey \'dü,hikē, -ki\ *n* [prob. fr. *doodad* + *hickey*] **:** DINGUS, THINGUMBOB

1dook \'dük\ *Scot var of* DUCK

2dook \"\ *n* -s [prob. fr. 1*dook*] **:** a haulage incline at a mine

dool \'dül\ *Scot var of* DOLE

dool·fu \'dülfə\ *chiefly Scot var of* DOLEFUL

doo·ly *or* **doo·lie** \'dülē\ *n, pl* **doolies** [Hindi *dolī*, fr. Skt *dolikā*, fr. *dola* swinging] *India* **:** a litter borne on men's shoulders **:** PALANQUIN

1doom \'düm\ *n* -s [ME, fr. OE *dōm*; akin to OHG *tuom* condition, state, dignity, ON *dōmr* judgment, court, sentence, Goth *doms* sentence, fame; all fr. a prehistoric Gmc verb represented by OE *dōn* to do — more at DO] **1 a :** a law established by custom and judicial interpretation **b :** ORDINANCE, DECREE **2** *obs* **a :** rectitude and just dealing **b :** JUDGMENT, DISCRIMINATION ⟨with . . . unerring ~ he sees what is —John Dryden⟩ **3 a :** a judgment or decision pronounced ⟨whose ~ discording neighbors sought —Sir Walter Scott⟩ ⟨there are no such things as rules or principles: there are only isolated ~*s* —B.N.Cardozo⟩; *esp* **:** a condemnation or penal decree ⟨the inspired teaching of the ~ of men to excruciation in endlessness —George Meredith⟩ ⟨the guilty person who excessively fears death, anticipating it as a punishment and unconsciously acknowledging the justice of such a ~ can now be reassured —Weston La Barre⟩ **b :** God's final judgment of mankind **:** LAST JUDGMENT ⟨we thought the day of ~ had come⟩ **c** *obs* **:** the end of one's life **4** *archaic* **:** the process of judging **:** legal trial ⟨awaiting the opening of the ~⟩ **5 :** something that is inevitably destined to befall: **a :** a state or end to which one is inexorably bound to come; *esp* **:** a final unhappy or calamitous fate, destiny, or lot ⟨they were glad he was going West at once, to fulfill his ~ where they would not be onlookers —Willa Cather⟩ ⟨luminous organs for attracting other creatures to their ~ —J.L.B.Smith⟩ **b :** inevitable ending in frustration, desolation, or tragedy **:** predestined calamity or extinction ⟨feverish enterprise, as if everyone was aware of approaching ~ and was in a hurry to get somewhere before the thunderbolt fell —Harrison Smith⟩ ⟨the sense of ~ that infects many contemporary poets —C.I.Glicksberg⟩ **c :** inescapable penalty **:** unavoidably attendant or consequent ill fortune ⟨his proud spirit sank under the ~ of prison life —Thomas Barbour⟩ **syn** see FATE

2doom \"\ *vb* -ED/-ING/-S [ME *domen*, fr. *doom*, n.] *vt* **1** *archaic* **:** to weigh or assess and pass judgment on **2 :** to render judgment against **:** pronounce sentence on **:** CONDEMN ⟨absolves the just and ~*s* the guilty souls —John Dryden⟩ ⟨sometimes a ~*ed* book published in England reaches the Irish market in large quantities ahead of the censorship ban —Paul Blanshard⟩ **3** *archaic* **:** to ordain as penalty or sentence ⟨have I tongue to ~ my brother's death —Shak.⟩ **4 a :** to force irresistibly or inexorably, consign irrevocably, relegate irretrievably, or constrain inescapably **:** destine or predestine ineluctably — used with *to* ⟨some people will say that the world ~*s* itself to war because man is still aggressive at heart —J.B.Priestley⟩ ⟨pity for one inexorably ~*ed* to die for his people at the hands of a brutal mob —Alan Paton & Liston Pope⟩ ⟨I was of those ~*ed* to imperfect achievement —W.B. Yeats⟩ ⟨its vitality was ~*ed* to wane before the rivalry of the vernacular tongue —H.O.Taylor⟩ **b :** to render certain of failure, defeat, or nullification **:** set on a fixed course to elimination, destruction, or other disastrous conclusion **:** inflict impending ruin, disaster, or death upon ⟨if the blowoff comes it may forever ~ the efforts of Europe to undo peacefully the colonial harm she has done —Emory Ross⟩ ⟨life is a risk and all individual plans precarious, all human achievements transient, and all individual lives ~*ed* —Irwin Edman⟩ ⟨once the horrors that lay in the background of Calvinism were disclosed to common view, the system was ~*ed* —V.L. Parrington⟩ ⟨experiments which were from the outset plainly ~*ed* —Osbert Sitwell⟩ **5** *archaic* **:** to assess a tax upon (one not making return of his taxable property) by estimate or at discretion **~** *vi, archaic* **:** to pronounce judgment ⟨who's to ~ when the judge himself is dragged to the bar —Herman Melville⟩

doom·age \-ij\ *n* -S **:** an assessing on default

doombook \ˈ=,=\ *n* [trans. of OE *dōmbōc*] **:** an ancient code of laws; *specif* **:** a code of laws of West Saxon kings

doom·er \-mə(r)\ *n* -S [²*doom* + -*er*] **1** *archaic* **:** one that pronounces sentence **2 :** a prognosticator of doom

doom·ful \-mfəl\ *adj* **1 :** presaging or betokening doom **:** FATEFUL, PORTENTOUS, OMINOUS ⟨the ~ drums of jungle tragedy —*Newsweek*⟩ **2** *obs* **:** appointed for pronouncing judgment — **doom·ful·ly** \-fəlē\ *adv*

doomlike \ˈ=,=\ *adj* **:** suggestive of impending doom **:** PORTENTOUS, FATEFUL

doom palm \ˈdüm-\ *n* [F *doum*, fr. Ar *dawm*] **:** a large African fan palm (*Hyphaene thebaica*) that is important as a soil stabilizer in desert areas and that has fibrous leafstalks used for ropes and a fruit with a gingerbread-flavored pulp and a rind which is used in making a beverage

doom ring *n* [trans. of ON *dōmhringr*, fr. *dōmr* court, judgment + *hringr* ring — more at DOOM, RING] **:** a stone circle of Norway marking the limits of an ancient Norse court of justice

¹**dooms** *pl of* DOOM, *pres 3d sing of* DOOM

²**dooms** \ˈdümz\ *adv* (*or adj*) [euphemism] *Scot* **:** DAMNED

doom·say·er \ˈdüm,sāər, -,se(ə)r\ *n* **:** one given to forebodings and predictions of impending calamity **:** a prophet of doom

dooms·day \ˈdümz,dā\ *n* [ME *domesday*, fr. OE *dōmes dæg*, fr. *dōmes* (gen. of *dōm* judgment) + *dæg* day — more at DOOM, DAY] **1 :** a day of final judgment ⟨from now until ~⟩ ⟨a profound sense of irony enables him to distill savage comedy and atrocious farce out of his ~ vision of the world —C.J. Rolo⟩ **2** *archaic* **a :** a day of judgment **b :** a day of death or dissolution

dooms·man \-.mən\ *n, pl* **doomsmen** [ME *domesman*, fr. *domes* (gen. of *doom* judgment) + *man* — more at DOOM] *archaic* **:** DOOMSTER

doom·ster \-mztə(r), -mst-\ *n* -S [alter. (influenced by ¹*doom*) of *dempster*] **:** one invested with authority as a judge

doom tree *n* **:** a tree used for hanging the condemned

¹**doon** \(ˈ)dün\ *Scot var of* DOWN

²**doon** \ˈdün\ *n* -S [Sinhalese *dun*-gaha doon tree] **:** a large tree (*Doona zeylanica*) of the family Dipterocarpaceae of Ceylon that yields a colorless varnish resin and wood that is very durable

doo·put·ty \düˈpəd·ē\ *var of* DOPATTA

door \ˈdō(ə)r, -ó(ə)r,-ōə,-ó(ə)\ *n* -S [ME *dor*, fr. OE, door, gate & ME *dure*, fr. OE *duru*; akin to OHG *tor* & *turi* door, gate, ON *dyrr*, Goth *daur*, L *fores*, Gk *thyra*, Skt *dvār*] **1 a :** a movable piece of firm material or a structure supported usu. along one side and swinging on pivots or hinges, sliding along a groove, rolling up and down, revolving as one of four leaves, or folding like an accordion by means of which an opening may be closed or kept open for passage into or out of a building, room, or other covered enclosure or a car, airplane, elevator, or other vehicle — see KALAMEIN DOOR, PANEL DOOR **b :** a similar part by which access is prevented or allowed to the contents of a repository, cabinet, vault, or refrigeration or combustion chamber **2 a :** an opening in a wall of a building, room, or a side or rear of a vehicle by which to go in or out **:** DOORWAY **b :** one of two openings 3½ ft. wide in the wall of a court-tennis court between the first and second gallery **3 a :** a means of access, admittance, participation, or enjoyment ⟨the opening of our ~*s* to all the distressed peoples of Asia —M.R.Cohen⟩ ⟨leaving the ~ open for a settlement⟩ ⟨opening with the magic of storytelling the ~*s* to the world's great treasure-house of literature —Nancy K. Hosking⟩ **b :** an opening or route that suggests or resembles a door in giving physical access, entrance, or exit ⟨this pass was the ~ through which the invaders poured into the doomed country⟩ ⟨slipped into Switzerland by almost the last remaining ~ out of France —Robert Payne⟩ **4 a :** one of the entranceways to buildings in a row; *esp* **:** one facing on a street ⟨he resides three ~*s* beyond the church⟩ ⟨living next ~ to you⟩ **b :** one's home and immediate family or one's personal knowledge and experience ⟨striving to keep scandal from his ~⟩ ⟨this fact was not left to Japanese research to discover: it was brought to their ~ —A.M.Young⟩ **5 :** a gateway at the threshold of some supernatural realm or giving escape from the normal human state ⟨the old statesman lingered for several weeks at death's ~⟩ **6 :** OTTER BOARD — **a foot in the door :** an assurance of a continuing chance of eventual accomplishment of one's purpose ⟨those connections . . . would at best enable him only to get his *foot in the door* —Hamilton Basso⟩ — **at door** *or* **at doors** *obs* **:** at the door — **at one's door 1 :** very close and accessible to one or to one's place of residence or business **:** in closest proximity **2 :** as a charge against one as being accountable **:** to one's responsibility ⟨it is hard to consider it aright and know *at whose door* to lay it —John Locke⟩ ⟨errors as well as omissions in it, which, however, he lays mainly *at the door* of the Constantinopolitan excerpter —Benjamin Farrington⟩ — **in doors :** inside, within, or into the house or any covered building **:** INDOORS — **next door 1 :** very close in position or relation **2 :** nearly equivalent **:** nearest thing ⟨*next door* to starving —Daniel Defoe⟩ ⟨it must be *next door* to impossible to rise to power in a democratic community unless you can catch the ears of the public —W.S.Maugham⟩ — **open the doors 1 :** to accept enrollments **2 :** to initiate business operations; *esp* **:** to begin to make sales — **out of doors 1 :** outside or out of the house or any covered building **:** in or into the open air **:** OUTDOORS **2** *obs* **:** out of consideration **:** beside the point — **within doors :** INDOORS — **without doors :** OUTDOORS

door 1a: *a* stile, *b* rail, *c* mullion

doora *var of* DURRA

door badge *n* **:** a floral spray hung at the door of a house as a sign that a death has occurred within

door bed *n* **:** a form of recess bed designed to be hung on a door

doorbell \ˈ=,=\ *n* **1 :** a bell, gong, or set of chimes to be rung usu. by a push button at an outer door **2 :** a push button connected with a doorbell **3 :** the sound of a ringing doorbell **4 :** a bell so connected to a door as to ring automatically when the door is opened

door bolt *n* **:** a sliding bolt for locking a door

doorboy \ˈ=,=\ *n* **:** a boy who tends a door esp. in a mine

door·brand \ˈ=,brand\ *n* [alter. of earlier *doorband*, fr. ME *dorband*, fr. *dor* door + *band*] **:** STRAP HINGE; *esp* **:** one securing the boards composing the door

door buck *n* **:** ¹BUCK 6b

door butt *n* **:** a door hinge

doorcase \ˈ=,=\ *n* **:** the visible frame of a door — compare CASING 1a, DOORFRAME

door chain *n* **:** a chain serving as an inside lock for preventing a door from opening more than a few inches until one end is withdrawn from a slide fitting

door check *or* **door closer** *n* **:** a device to check a door; *specif* **:** an attachment that is used to close a door and prevent its slamming

doorcheek \ˈ=,=\ *n, dial Brit* **:** the jamb or sidepiece of a door; *also* **:** DOOR, DOORWAY

do-or-die \ˌ==ˈ=\ *adj* **1 :** inflexibly, doggedly, or desperately determined to reach one's objective **:** unyielding and unwavering **:** INDOMITABLE ⟨*do-or-die* revolutionaries⟩ **2 :** presenting as the only alternatives complete success or complete ruin ⟨a *do-or-die* conflict⟩

doored \ˌdō(ə)rd, -ó(ə)rd,-ōəd,-ó(ə)d\ *adj* **:** having a door ⟨a dresser with ~ compartments⟩ ⟨a wide-*doored* entrance⟩

door face *n* **1** *also* **door facing :** DOORCASE **2 :** a papier-mâché mask for masqueraders

doorframe \ˈ=,=\ *n* **:** the jambs and top of a doorway and usu. supporting a door; *also* the jambs and upper transverse member enclosing the sides and top of a doorway and usu. supporting a door

door grass *n* **:** KNOTGRASS 1

door handle *n, chiefly Brit* **:** DOORKNOB

doorhead \ˈ=,=\ *n* **:** the upper transverse member of a doorframe; *esp* **:** one of ornamental woodwork often with ogive or pediment in 18th century style

door holder *n* **:** a device for holding a door open

doorjamb \ˈ=,=\ *n* **:** an upright piece forming the side of a door opening

doorkeeper \ˈ=,==\ *n* **1 a :** one that tends the door of an establishment and admits only those qualified to enter **b :** an officer of a legislative chamber who has charge of the furniture and equipment and enforces the rules regulating admission to the floor and galleries **2** *Roman Catholicism* **:** a member of the lowest of the minor orders — called also *ostiary*, *porter*

door-key child *n* **:** a child who because his parents are absent from home all day carries the door key of the home to school and goes home to an empty house or roams the streets

doorknob \ˈ=,=\ *n* **:** a knob that when turned releases a door latch

door·less \ˈ=ləs\ *adj* [ME *dorless*, fr. *dor* door + -*less*] **:** having no door

door·man \ˈ=,man, -mən, -,maa(ə)n\ *n, pl* **doormen 1 :** one that tends a door: as **a :** one that tends the door of a hotel, apartment house, or other building and assists people by calling taxis and helping in and out of cars — called also *footman* **b :** a theater barker or ticket taker **2 :** one that solicits business for tobacco-warehouse auctions, arranges display space for patrons, and attempts to attract the goodwill of customers **3** *Brit* **:** a farrier's assistant

doormat \ˈ=,=\ *n* **1 :** a mat placed before or just inside a door for wiping mud and dirt from the shoes **2 :** a constant and unprotesting sufferer from the impositions and ill-treatment of another **:** one that submits supinely or spinelessly to abuse or indignities ⟨becomes a despised ~ or an overworked drudge or both —Agnes M. Miall⟩ **3** *slang* **:** a team that usu. finishes hopelessly last

door money *n* **:** money collected for admission to an entertainment at the time of entering

doornail \ˈ=,=\ *n* [ME *dornail*, fr. *dor* door + *nail*] **:** a large-headed nail easily clinched for nailing doors through the battens — used chiefly in the phrase *dead as a doornail*

doorn·boom \ˈdůrn,bùm\ *n* -S [obs. Afrik (now *doringboom*), fr. obs. Afrik *doorn* thorn (now *doring*) (fr. MD *dorn*) + Afrik *boom* tree, fr. MD; akin to OHG *dorn* thorn & to OHG *boum* tree — more at THORN, BEAM] **:** a southern African thorny shrub or small tree (*Acacia horrida*) whose bark is used in tanning

door opener *n* **1 :** a device to open a door: as **a :** a tool used by firemen to jimmy a locked door **b :** a release mechanism attached to a door lock and activated by a pushbutton or electric eye **2 :** an inexpensive gift or premium offered to a prospect by a door-to-door salesman in order to get inside the house and present his sales talk

doorplate \ˈ=,=\ *n* **1 :** a plate on a door of a house or apartment giving the name of the occupant **2 :** FINGER PLATE

doorpost \ˈ=,=\ *n* **:** DOORJAMB

door prize *n* **:** a prize awarded to a holder of one of the winning coupons passed out at the door of an entertainment

door rock *n, archaic* **:** DOORSTONE

door roller *n* **:** a wheel or roller supporting a sliding door usu. running on a door track

doors *pl of* DOOR

doorsill \ˈ=,=\ *n* **:** ¹SILL c

doors·man \ˈdō(ə)zmən\ *Brit var of* DOORMAN

door starter *n* **:** a device for helping to start a door of a railroad boxcar to open

door·stead \ˈdōr,sted, ˈdůr-, -,stēd, -.stəd\ *n* [*door* + *stead* place] *now dial Eng* **:** DOORWAY

doorstep \ˈ=,=\ *n* **:** a step or one of several steps before an outer door — **at one's doorstep :** at one's door

doorstone \ˈ=,=\ *n* **:** a flat-topped stone used as a threshold or doorstep

doorstop \ˈ=,=\ *n* **1 :** a device for holding a door open to any degree or preventing it from opening beyond a particular point **2 :** a projection usu. covered with rubber used to prevent damaging contact between an opening door and a wall or piece of furniture

doorstops 2

door strap *n* **:** a metal part fastened to the top of a door (as of a garage or barn) and suspended from a hanger

door-to-door \ˌ==ˈ=\ *adj* **1 :** HOUSE-TO-HOUSE ⟨a *door-to-door* salesman⟩ **2 :** providing delivery to the specified house address ⟨direct *door-to-door* service⟩

door track *n* **:** a usu. overhead track for door rollers

door trap *n* **:** a trap with a closing door for taking birds or animals alive

door·ward \ˈ=wə(r)d\ *or* **door·wards** \-dz\ *adv* **:** toward a door

doorway \ˈ=,=\ *n* **1 :** the passageway or opening that a door closes **:** the entranceway into a building or a room **:** PORTAL **2 :** a means of gaining access to or enjoyment of (as some desirable condition) ⟨these studies brought the inquirer only to the ~ of a rich country of spiritual truth invisible to the superficial observer —R.W.Southern⟩ ⟨the Asians actually regard freedom and national independence as the ~ to international order — just as we do —A.E.Stevenson †1965⟩

doorweed \ˈ=,=\ *n* **:** KNOTGRASS 1

door window *n* **:** a casement window reaching to the floor and opening like a pair of folding doors

dooryard \ˈ=,=\ *n* **:** a yard about the door of a dwelling

dooryard grass *n* **:** KNOTGRASS 1

dooryard plantain *n* **:** BROAD-LEAVED PLANTAIN 1

doos *pl of* DOO

doot \ˈdüt\ *Scot var of* DOUBT

doot·ed \ˈdütəd\ *var of* DOTED

do-over \ˈ=,==\ *n* -S [fr. *do over*, v.] **1 :** a reprocessing or a product of reprocessing (as a garment returned by an inspector in a dry-cleaning establishment for recleaning or refinishing) **2 :** a beauty-shop transformation treatment for women

doo·zer \ˈdüzə(r)\ *or* **doo·zy** \-zē\ *n, pl* **doozers** *or* **doozies** [perh. alter. of *daisy*] *slang* **:** an extraordinary one of its kind **:** HUMDINGER ⟨it made one of those ~*s* that yank the long arm of probability right out of its socket —E.J.Abbott⟩

¹**dop** *vi* **dopped; dopped; dopping; dops** [ME *doppen*; akin to OE *dūfedoppa* pelican, *doppettan* to plunge in, immerse, MD *doppen* to dip into, *dop*, *doppe* shell, goblet, pot, MHG *topf* pot, OHG *topfo* dot, OE *dyppan* to dip — more at DIP] **1** *obs* **:** to sink abruptly beneath the surface of water **:** DIVE **2** *obs* **:** to duck the head or suddenly lower the body **:** CURTSY

²**dop** *n* -S *obs* **:** a dip esp. of head or body **:** CURTSY

³**dop** *also* **dopp** \ˈdäp\ *n* -S [D, fr. MD *dop*, *doppe* shell, goblet, pot — more at ¹DOP] **:** a device in which a diamond or other gemstone is held while being cut

⁴**dop** \"\ *vt* **dopped; dopped; dopping; dops :** to fasten (as a diamond) in a dop usu. with a cement

⁵**dop** \"\ *n* -S [Afrik, lit., husk, fr. MD *dop*, *doppe* husk, shell, goblet, pot — more at ¹DOP] **:** a brandy of southern Africa similar to French marc and made from the distilled residue of grapes after pressing

DOP *abbr* developing-out paper

do·pa \ˈdōpə\ *n* -S [*d*ihydr*o*xy*p*henyl*a*lanine] **:** a crystalline amino acid $(HO)_2C_6H_3CH_2CH(NH_2)COOH$ found in various fruits and vegetables and formed as an intermediate product in the oxidation of tyrosine by oxidases to dark pigments (as melanins); B-(3,4-dihydroxyphenyl)=alanine

do-pas-so \ˌdō,paˈsō\ *n* -S [blend of *do-si-do* and *pass*] **:** a square-dance variation of do-si-do for three or four couples in which the man with right arm around his partner's waist turns her around counterclockwise into starting position

do·pat·ta \dōˈpəd·ə\ *n* -S [Hindi *dopaṭṭā*] *India* **:** a scarf of silk or muslin often with gold or silver threads

dop·chick \ˈdäp+,-\ *archaic var of* DABCHICK

¹**dope** \ˈdōp\ *n* -S [D *doop* sauce, fr. *dopen* to dip, baptize, fr. MD *dōpen*; akin to OHG *toufen* to baptize, Goth *daupjan* to baptize, dip into, ON *deypa* to dive, OE *dyppan* to dip — more at DIP] **1 a :** any of various thick liquid or pasty preparations (as formerly of pan drippings or gravy and more recently of grease for use as a lubricant) ⟨pipe ~ should be applied to the male end in making up a screwed joint⟩ ⟨coated the water pipelines with a corrosive-resisting ~⟩ **b :** a lubricant for the bottoms of skis **c :** any of various cosmetic or medicinal preparations or insect repellents ⟨~ for dry skin⟩ **2 :** any of various additive substances or liquid preparations introduced into a substance or applied to a surface to contribute a desired quality: as **a :** a food adulterant **b :** a coating (as a cellulose lacquer) applied esp. to a fabric (as of airplanes to produce tautness and increase strength or of balloons to increase gastightness) **c** (1) **:** a syrupy liquid consisting chiefly of cellulose derivatives in solution from which the transparent support or backing of a sensitive film is made (2) **:** a liquid preparation or varnish used to facilitate retouching, to block out parts of a negative, or to reduce reflection from the surface of a print **d :** a material (as an antiknock agent) added in small quantities to an internal-combustion fuel (as gasoline) to improve engine performance — called also *fuel dope* **e :** a light varnish added to lithographic ink to reduce the tack **3 a :** absorbent or adsorbent material (as wood pulp or kieselguhr) used in certain manufacturing processes ⟨active ~ for dynamite⟩ — compare ¹BASE 2b(1) **b :** absorbent material used in packing to reduce the effects of friction or to provide lubrication (as the oil-soaked cotton waste packed in the journal boxes of freight cars) **4 a :** a preparation of opium or other narcotic or habit-forming drug (as cocaine, heroin, marihuana) esp. as used for a certain initially pleasurable stimulating or stupefying effect **b** *slang* **:** a preparation (as of opium) given to a horse to depress or stimulate it temporarily (as before a race) **c** *slang* **:** an opium or narcotic addict **d :** a dull-witted, obtuse, or stupid person **:** NITWIT **5** *slang* **a :** information, factual data, details, or comment concerning a particular subject esp. when purporting to come from an informed source ⟨the British Travel Association has a great deal of ~ on this subject —Richard Joseph⟩ **b :** information or prediction concerning the progress or outcome of a situation or coming event ⟨advance ~ on military purchasing policies⟩ **6** *South & Midland* **:** a cola beverage **7 :** a solution (as of cellulose acetate in acetone) for spinning synthetic fibers **:** a spinning bath — called also *spinning dope*

²**dope** \"\ *vb* -ED/-ING/-S *vt* **1 a :** to smear or lubricate with dope ⟨ready with snowshoes thoroughly *doped*⟩ **b :** to apply dope to (as the fabric of an airplane or balloon) **2 a :** to introduce an adulterant into (a food) or an additive into (a fluid) ⟨a compound for *doping* the fluid of a battery⟩ **b :** to treat or impregnate with a foreign substance to impart a desired appearance or property **:** DOCTOR ⟨prepare leather for tanning by *doping* it with fatty compounds⟩ ⟨ways of *doping* a used car to hide its faults⟩ ⟨samples of germanium *doped* with iron and cobalt⟩ **3 a :** to give a stupefying or exhilarating drug to **:** DRUG **b :** to put a stupefying drug into ⟨knocked out by *doped* wine⟩ **c :** to administer a drug to (a horse) to increase or decrease speed in a race **d :** to induce inaction, apathy, or submissiveness in by a mental diet designed to produce such qualities or attitudes ⟨keep them in submissive slavery by *doping* them with promises of bliss after death —G.B.Shaw⟩ **4** *slang* **:** to work out from one's interpretation of available information a forecast about the outcome of (a competition) or the performance or placing of (competitors) ⟨busy *doping* the day's horses⟩ **~** *vi* **:** to indulge in or be addicted to a narcotic

dope fiend *n, slang* **:** a habitual user of a narcotic

dopehead \ˈ=,=\ *n, slang* **:** an opium addict

dope off *vi, slang* **:** to drowse stupidly or doze as if under the effect of a narcotic ⟨the way you *doped off* on that ditchdigging detail yesterday —L.M.Uris⟩

dope out *vt* **1** *slang* **:** to figure out from one's interpretation of what information is available ⟨lists of football games around the country which he had been *doping out* —T.H.White b.1915⟩ **a :** to devise by system ⟨then some practical guy came along later and *doped out* how it could be sold —Theodore Morrison⟩ **b :** to puzzle out, solve, or discover by mental effort or ingenuity ⟨the specifications are there . . . could you *dope* them *out* and build the boat without blueprints —K.M.Dodson⟩ **c :** to reason or infer by guess ⟨anyone with half an eye could *dope out* from this that there's a big deal, that it's a back-door deal —Claud Cockburn⟩ **d :** to discern the identity and intentions of ⟨I could see him stare as he tried to *dope* us *out* —Saul Bellow⟩ **2** *slang* **:** to plan out or arrange in advance ⟨we are to *dope out* a full year's schedule of major and minor sports⟩

dop·er \ˈdōpə(r)\ *n* -S **:** one that dopes: as **a** *also* **dope puller :** a railroad employee who packs the journal boxes of freight cars with dope — called also *greaser* **b :** a worker who applies dope to airplane fabric **c** *also* **dope·man** \-p,man, -pmən\ *pl* **dopemen :** one that applies a protective dope (as to airplane fabric, pipelines, automobiles)

dope ring *n* **:** a gang conspiring to import or distribute opium or other narcotic

dopesheet \ˈ=,=\ *n* **1** *also* **dopebook** \ˈ=,=\ **:** a circular of information for bettors listing entries of racehorses and their past records **2 :** a circular of up-to-date information, reports, and analyses on any special activity or personnel ⟨reports on keys by locksmiths over the country are tabulated in a ~⟩ ⟨a stock exchange ~⟩ ⟨every district attorney comes to the task of jury selection with a special ~ on all members of the panel —H.M.Robinson⟩

dope·ster \ˈdōpstə(r)\ *n* -S [¹*dope* + -*ster*] **:** one that makes a practice of publicly forecasting the outcome of sports contests, political elections, or like events marked by a high degree of uncertainty

dope story *n* **:** a background story presenting explanatory, interpretative, and evaluative material designed to make more understandable some news event — compare THINK PIECE

dop·ey *also* **dopy** \ˈdōpē, -pi\ *adj* **dopier; dopiest** [¹*dope* + -*y*] **1 :** having the mind and senses dulled and responses slowed from the effects of alcohol or a narcotic **:** FUDDLED, BEMUSED **2 :** feeling and acting in a benumbed or dazed state **:** sluggish and listless ⟨I am still ~ from amazement —L.L.Rice⟩ **3 :** mentally dull **:** fatuous and rather ridiculous or contemptible ⟨its theme, I gather, is that men are all dopes, and the biggest of us would be just that much *dopier* if it weren't for the women in our lives —Richard Joseph⟩

dop·i·ness *also* **dop·ey·ness** \ˈdōpēnəs, -pin-\ *n* -ES **:** a dopey state ⟨prepare ourselves . . . to face courageously the rising curve of ~ —*Wall Street Jour.*⟩

dop·ing·ly *adv* **:** in such a manner as to lull one as does a narcotic ⟨when they have nothing to say their music ticks over ~ —Charles Reid⟩

doping rod *n* **:** a long steel rod used by dopers to pack freight car journal boxes with dope

dopp *var of* DOP

dopped *past of* DOP

dop·pel·flö·te \ˈdäpəl,flād·ə, -lōd·ə, *G* ˈdȯpəl,flœtə\ *n* -S *usu cap* [G, fr. *doppel*- double (fr. MHG *dobbel*, fr. OF *doble*) + *flöte* flute, fr. earlier *floete*, fr. MHG *vloite*, *floute*, fr. MD *flûte*, *fleute*, *floyte*, fr. OF *flaute*, *fleute* — more at DOUBLE, FLUTE] **:** an 8-foot flute pipe-organ stop each pipe of which has two mouths

dop·pel·gäng·er *or* **dop·pel·gang·er** *also* **dop·pel·gaeng·er** \ˌdäpəlˈgaŋə(r), -geŋ-, ˈ==,==, *G* ˈdȯpəl,geŋər\ *n* -S [G *doppelgänger*, fr. *doppel*- double + -*gänger* goer, fr. MHG *gengære*, fr. OHG -*gengeri*, fr. *gangan* to go + -*eri*, -*āri* -er — more at GANG] **:** a ghostly counterpart and companion of a person; *esp* **:** a ghostly double of a live person that haunts him through life and is usu. visible only to himself

¹**dop·per** \ˈdäpə(r)\ *n* -S [ME, fr. *doppen* to dop, dive + -*er* — more at DOP] **:** any of certain diving birds (as a dabchick or bufflehead)

²**dopper** \"\ *n* -S *usu cap* [Afrik, fr. 16th cent. D, fr. *dop*, a kind of hat, lit., shell, pot (fr. MD *dop*, *doppe* shell, goblet, pot) + -*er* — more at DOP] **:** a member of a rigidly Calvinistic sect of Afrikaners

dop·pia \ˈdäpēə, ˈdōp-, ˈdȯp-, It ˈdȯppyä\ *n* -S [It, fr. fem. of *doppio* double, fr. L *duplus* — more at DOUBLE] **:** any one of several old gold coins of Italian states constituting the double

of some unit (as the sequin or scudo); *also* : a unit of value equal to a doppia coin ⟨an 8-*doppia* coin⟩ ⟨¼-*doppia* coin⟩
dopping *pres part of* DOP
dop·pio \'däpē,ō, 'dōp-,'dōp-, *It* 'dȯppyō\ *adj (or adv)* [It, fr. L *duplus* — more at DOUBLE] : DOUBLE, TWICE — used as a direction in music
doppio mo·vi·men·to \-,mōvə'men·(,)tō\ *adv (or adj)* [It, double movement] : twice as fast as the preceding — used as a direction in music
doppio pe·da·le \-pā'dä(,)lā\ *adv (or adj)* [It, double pedal] : using both feet simultaneously in parallel octaves or independent parts — used as a direction in organ music
doppio più lento \-,pyü'len·(,)tō, -,pē,ü-\ *adv (or adj)* [It *doppio più lento* twice as slow] : twice as slow as the preceding — used as a direction in music
dopp·ler broadening \'däplə(r)-\ *n, usu cap D* [after Christian J. *Doppler* †1853 Austrian physicist] : a lack of sharpness in the spectrum lines of gases due to the Doppler effect of the random thermal motion of the molecules
doppler effect *n, usu cap D* [after C. J. *Doppler*] : a change in the frequency with which waves (as sound, light, or radio waves) from a given source reach an observer, the frequency decreasing with the speed at which source and observer move away from each other and increasing with the speed at which they move toward each other so that the pitch of a sound is apparently raised or lowered as the source and the observer move toward or away from each other or the spectral lines of a star are shifted toward red or violet as the star recedes or approaches the earth
dopp·ler·ite \'däplə,rīt\ *n* -s [G *dopplerit*, fr. C. J. *Doppler* + G *-it* -ite] : a brownish black elastic acid substance occurring in peat beds that is composed of carbon, hydrogen, oxygen, and possibly calcium
doppler navigation *n, usu cap D* : navigation (as of an airplane) in which the change of frequency of reflected radar waves due to the Doppler effect is utilized by automatic devices to give information on velocity and position
doppler shift *n, usu cap D* [after C. J. *Doppler*] **1** : a change in frequency of an electromagnetic radiation caused by the motions of the atoms, molecules, or nuclei in the line of sight **2** : the slight displacement in the positions of the spectrum lines of light from a star or other celestial body due to the Doppler effect
dops *pres 3d sing of* DOP, *pl of* DOP
dop·ster \'däpstə(r)\ *n* -s [origin unknown] : a clerk who uses the measurer's notes to make out order tickets for custom-made clothing
dop stick *n* [³*dop*] : a short handle for a dop; *also* : the dop with its handle or stem or other means for holding or for fastening to a tang
¹**dopy** *var of* DOPEY
²**dopy** \'dōpē, -pi\ *n* -ES [¹*dopy*] *slang* : a narcotic addict
¹**dor** *or* **dorr** \'dȯ(ə)r, -ō(ə)\ *also* **dor bug** *n* -s [ME *dorre, dore*, fr. OE *dora* bumblebee; akin to MLG *dorte* drone, OE *drān* — more at *drone*] : any of various insects that fly with a buzzing noise — used often in combination ⟨~ fly⟩
²**dor** \"\ *also* **dorre** \"\ *n* -s [prob. of Scand origin; akin to ON *dār* mockery, fr. *dāra*] *archaic* : TRICK, DECEPTION : MOCKERY — **give one the dor** *archaic* : to make a fool of one
³**dor** \"\ *also* **dorre** \"\ *vt* **dorred; dorred; dorring; dors** *also* **dorres** [prob. of Scand origin; akin to ON *dāra* to mock, scoff, fr. MLG *bedōren* to make a fool of, fr. *dōre* fool, lunatic; akin to MD *dōr* fool, MHG *tōre* fool, lunatic, deaf person, *dōsen* to be quiet, doze, L *fumus* smoke — more at FUME] *obs* : to make a fool of : MOCK
⁴**dor** \"\ *n, pl* **dor** *or* **dors** *usu cap* : ¹BONGO
do·rab \'dōr,ab, də'rab\ *n* -s [origin unknown] : the common wolf herring (*Chirocentrus dorab*) of the tropical Indian and Pacific oceans
do·rad \'dōr,ad\ *n* -s [NL *Doradidae*] : a catfish of the family Doradidae
do·rad·i·dae \də'radə,dē\ *n pl, cap* [NL, fr. *Dorad-, Doras*, type genus + *-idae*] : a family of So. American armored catfishes (type genus *Doras*) having a series of bony plates along the sides that are reputed to journey overland in search of water during dry seasons
do·ra·do \də'rä(,)dō\ *n* -s [Sp *dorado*, fr. past part. of *dorar* to gild, fr. L *deaurare*, fr. *de-* + *-aurare* (fr. *aurum* gold) — more at ORIOLE] **1** *also* **dou·ra·de** \dō'rädə\ *or* **dou·ra·do** \-ä(,)dō\ **a** : DOLPHIN 2 **b** [AmerSp, fr. Sp] : a large golden characin (*Salminus maxillosus*) of the Rio Plata drainage of So. America and sometimes related species that resemble salmons and are outstanding sport and food fishes **2** : a light yellowish brown that is redder, lighter, and stronger than khaki, lighter and stronger than walnut brown, and lighter, stronger, and slightly yellower than cinnamon — called also *cuir, honey beige*
do·ra·pho·bia \,dōrə'fōbēə\ *n* -s [NL, fr. Gk *dora* hide, skin + NL *-phobia*] : a dread of touching the skin or fur of an animal
do·ras \'dōrəs\ *n, cap* [NL] : the type genus of the family Doradidae
dorbeetle \'=,==\ *n* [¹*dor* + *beetle*] : any of various beetles that fly with a buzzing sound; *specif* : a common European dung beetle (*Geotrupes stercorarius*)
dor·cas gazelle \'dȯrkəs-\ *n* [NL *dorcas* (specific epithet of *Gazella dorcas*), fr. L, gazelle, fr. Gk *dorkas, dorkos, dorx*, alter. of *zorkas, zorx* gazelle, deer; akin to W *iwrch* roebuck, Corn *yorch*, Bret *yourc'h*] : a common gazelle (*Gazella dorcas*) of northern Africa and parts of southwestern Asia
dor·cas·try \'dȯrkəstrē\ *n* -ES [*Dorcas*, Christian woman of Joppa celebrated in the early church for her good works (Acts 9:36) + E *-try* (as in *deviltry*)] : a church auxiliary organized to plan and execute benevolent work
dor·ca·the·ri·um \,dȯrkə'thirēəm\ *n, cap* [NL, fr. Gk *dorkas* gazelle, deer + NL *-therium*] : a genus of extinct chevrotains related to the water chevrotain
dor·cop·sis \dȯr'käpsəs\ *n, cap* [NL, fr. Gk *dorkas* + NL *-opsis*] : a genus of marsupials comprising the gazelle-faced wallabies of New Guinea
¹**do·ré** \də'rā, dō'-\ *n* -s [CanF, fr. F, past part. of *dorer*] *chiefly Canad* : WALLEYED PIKE
²**do·ré** \də'rā, (')dō'rā\ *adj* [F, fr. past part. of *dorer* to gild, fr. L *deaurare* — more at DORADO] **1** : golden in color **2** : containing gold ⟨~ silver⟩
³**doré** *or* **doré bullion** *n* -s : unparted gold and silver in bars
doree *var of* ¹DORY
doré furnace *n* : a furnace in which doré bullion is refined
do-re-mi \,dō,rā'mē\ *n* -s [fr. *do, re, mi*, the first three notes of the major musical scale, influenced in meaning by *dough* (money)] *slang* : MONEY
dorey *var of* ²DORY
dorhawk \'=,=\ *n* [¹*dor* + *hawk*; fr. its diet] : the common European nightjar (*Caprimulgus europaeus*)
do·ria \'dōrēə\ *n* -s [Hindi *ḍoriyā*, fr. *ḍor* line, cord] : a striped Indian muslin
¹**do·ri·an** \'dōrēən, 'dȯr-\ *adj, usu cap* [L *dorius* Dorian (fr. Gk *dōrios*, fr. *Dōris*, region in the central part of ancient Greece that included the cities of Sparta and Corinth) + E *-an*] **1** : belonging to a racial and linguistic division of classical Greece ⟨the stark severity of *Dorian* shrines⟩ **2** : peculiar to or having characteristics of the people of the Dorian division of Greece ⟨she was a *Dorian* girl . . . who had undergone a training as severe as a boy's —Van Wyck Brooks⟩ ⟨a *Dorian* festival in honor of Apollo⟩
²**dorian** \"\ *n, pl* **dorian** *or* **dorians** *usu cap* : one of a Hellenic race that about the 12th century B.C. completed the overthrowing of Mycenaean civilization and settled in Doris, Megaris, Argolis, Laconia, and Messenia, in Crete and other islands, and on the coast of Asia Minor
dorian mode *n, usu cap D* [trans. of Gk *dōria harmonia*] **1** : a Greek mode consisting of two disjunct tetrachords represented on the white keys of the piano by a descending diatonic scale from E to E — see GREEK MODE illustration **2** : an authentic ecclesiastical mode consisting of a pentachord and an upper conjunct tetrachord represented on the white keys of the piano by an ascending diatonic scale from D to D — see MODE illustration
dorian tetrachord *n, usu cap D, in Greek music* : a descending tetrachord consisting of two whole steps followed by a half step
¹**dor·ic** \'dȯrik, 'där-,'dōr-\ *adj, usu cap* [L *doricus*, fr. Gk *dōrikos*, fr. *Dōris*, region of ancient Greece + Gk *-ikos* -ic] **1** : DORIAN 1 ⟨the *Doric* idiom⟩ **2** : peculiar to the institutions and culture of the Dorians ⟨the *Doric* trend was martial⟩; *specif* : belonging to the oldest and simplest of the ancient Greek architectural orders characterized by a fluted column shaft with no base and with a capital consisting of an echinus separated from the shaft by one or more annulets and supporting a square unmolded abacus **3** : having the characteristics of the Dorians (as boldness, rugged masculine strength) ⟨could be capable of a fierce rage if not a *Doric* manner — Rolfe Humphries⟩ **4** *of a dialect of English* : UNCOUTH, UNREFINED, BROAD ⟨the *Doric* dialect of the lake district —*Athenaeum*⟩
²**doric** \"\ *n* -s **1** *usu cap* : a dialect of ancient Greek spoken in southern and eastern Peloponnesus, the Isthmus of Corinth, some of the southernmost Aegean islands, Crete, Rhodes, the southwest coast of Asia Minor, and several colonial areas esp. in Sicily and southern Italy and used in literature esp. by the Greek poets Pindar †443 B.C. and Theocritus 3d cent. B.C. **2** *cap* : a rustic dialect of English ⟨her nervous northern *Doric* —Charlotte Brontë⟩ **3** *usu cap* **a** : SANS SERIF **b** : a boldface type with strokes of fairly even weight and rather wide set

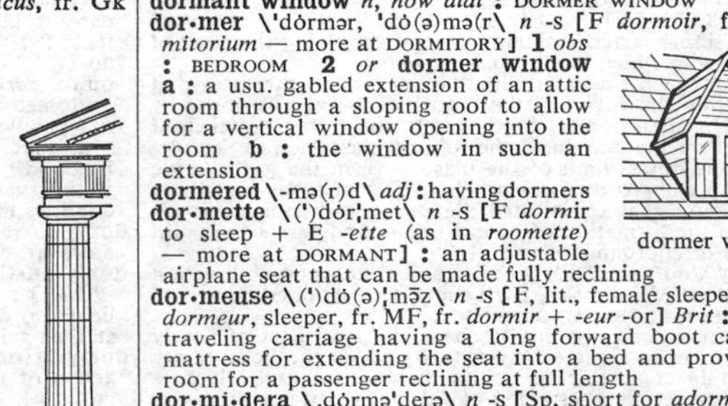

Doric order: Greek, *A;* Roman *B*

dor·i·cism \-rə,sizəm\ *n* -s *usu cap* : a Doric phrase or idiom
doric mode *n, usu cap D* : DORIAN MODE
doric tetrachord *n, usu cap D* : DORIAN TETRACHORD
do·rid·i·dae \də'ridə,dē\ *n pl, cap* [NL, fr. *Dorid-, Doris*, type genus + *-idae*] : a large family of gastropods including the genus *Doris*
dories *pl of* DORY
do·rip·pid \də'ripəd\ *n* -s [NL *Dorippidae*] : a crab of the family Dorippidae
do·rip·pi·dae \-pə,dē\ *n pl, cap* [NL, fr. *Dorippe*, type genus (prob. fr. *Dorippa*, a L & Gk feminine name) + *-idae*] : a nearly cosmopolitan family (type genus *Dorippe*) of small deep-water oxystomatous crabs
dor·is \'dōrəs\ *n, cap* [NL, fr. *Doris*, the daughter of Oceanus, fr. L, fr. Gk *Dōris*] : a cosmopolitan genus (the type of the family Dorididae) of the suborder Nudibranchia consisting of nudibranchs or sea slugs having a depressed body, two oral lobes, and a retractile tuft of pinnate branchiae around the anus
dor·ism \'dō,rizəm, 'dä,ri-, 'dōr,i-\ *n* -s *usu cap* [Gk *dōrismos*, fr. *dōrios* Dorian + *-ismos* -ism — more at DORIAN] **1** : Dorian character, manners, or speech **2** : a Doric phrase or idiom
dor·king \'dȯrkiŋ, -ō(ə)k-, -kēŋ\ *n* [fr. *Dorking*, Surrey, England] **1** *usu cap* : an English breed of large domestic fowls having five toes or the hind toe double **2** -s *often cap* : a bird of the Dorking breed that was developed as a general-purpose fowl, but is now largely a fancier's breed
dor·lach \'dȯrlək, -lək\ *n* -s [ScGael *dōrlach*, lit., handful] **1** *obs Scot* : a quiver for arrows **2** *Scot* **a** : BUNDLE, PACKAGE **b** : SUITCASE
¹**dorm** \'dȯ(ə)rm\ *vi* [prob. fr. MF *dormir* — more at DORMANT] *now dial Eng* : SLEEP, DOZE
²**dorm** \"\ *n* -s [by shortening] : DORMITORY
dor·man·cy \'dȯ(r)mənsē, -si\ *n* -ES : the quality or state of being dormant : QUIESCENCE, LATENCY, ABEYANCE ⟨~ in bacterial spores⟩ ⟨some volcanoes have eruptive cycles followed by stretches of ~⟩ ⟨Egypt is just awakening from centuries of ~; she and her neighbors are gradually adopting western techniques of farming and industry —Keith Wheelock⟩
dor·mant \'dȯrmənt, 'dȯ(ə)m-\ *adj* [ME *dormaunt*, fr. MF *dormant*, fr. pres. part. of *dormir* to sleep, fr. L *dormire*; akin to Gk *edrathon, erdathon* I slept, Skt *drāti, drāyati* he sleeps, OSlav *drěmati* to doze, Arm *tartam* slow, sleepy] **1 a** *archaic* : fixed in position ⟨a ~ timber across a foundation⟩ **b** : relaxed or immobile ⟨one of the ancient's hoary eyebrows seemed to go up a few millimeters but otherwise his face remained ~ —Earle Birney⟩ **2** : INACTIVE: **a** *heraldry* : lying down with the head resting on the forepaws — distinguished from *couchant* **b** (1) : sleeping or drowsing ⟨the preacher, who would interrupt his discourse to denounce a ~ worshiper —*Amer. Guide Series: Mich.*⟩ (2) : having the faculties suspended or as if suspended : SLUGGISH, LETHARGIC ⟨he lay there ~ with his eyes closed but waiting for a chance to escape⟩ **c** : having growth, development, or other biological activity suspended; *esp* : being in a state of suspended animation (as in hibernation) ⟨when the surrounding water gets too hot mollusks become ~⟩ **d** (1) : RESTING, INACTIVE — used of buds or other plant parts (2) : associated with, carried out, or applied during dormancy ⟨~ grafting⟩ ⟨a 5 percent ~ oil is used to control fruit-tree leaf roller⟩ **e** *of a volcano* : passing a considerable period in a state of repose yet still eruptive **3 a** *archaic* : written with name or particulars blank to be filled in when put to use **b** : of no effect or unevoked or unenforced during an interval of time ⟨reviving a long-*dormant* statute⟩ **c** : vacant or neglected by the rightful holder yet heritable ⟨a peerage said to be ~⟩ **4** : temporarily devoid of discernible activity, energy, power, or effect: **a** : existing in latent form or in a minimum degree but capable of bursting into full activity ⟨it seemed to him that crime was a seed in the whole of humanity . . . it lay ~ everywhere —Ben Hecht⟩ ⟨that native musical talent lay ~ in the mountain folk⟩ ⟨feeling between the two girls which had for some time been reasonably ~ flared up again —Ernest Beaglehole⟩ ⟨thoughts lie ~ for ages; and then, almost suddenly as it were, mankind finds that they have embodied themselves in institutions —A.N.Whitehead⟩ **b** : waiting only to be called into play ⟨his imaginative powers will for the most part lie ~ —C.S. Kilby⟩ ⟨which power can never be exercised by the people themselves but must be placed in the hands of agents or lie ~ —John Marshall⟩ **c** : having natural or normal functions suspended yet capable of resumption ⟨the Church of England was, indeed, if anything more ~ than the Catholic Church in France —Stringfellow Barr⟩ ⟨a ~ corporation⟩ **d** (1) : marked by or giving an appearance of inactivity or stagnation : slow-moving : DROWSY ⟨the mouse-chewed papers of an old family in a ~ English hamlet —R.D.Altick⟩ (2) : tending to stagnate socially, intellectually, or artistically : failing to make strides : UNPROGRESSIVE ⟨where science had been ~ since the days of Kepler —S.F.Mason⟩ **5** : neglected or allowed to lapse into disregard or obscurity yet revocable or revivable ⟨the controversy lay ~ through 1873 and 1874 and might have expired altogether —J.A.Cassidy⟩ **6** : discarded or unused but of potential utility ⟨methods of salvaging ~ metals in the printing industry⟩ **7** *of stock* : moving imperceptibly in the market **8** *of a period of time* : marked by suspension of activity : covering the extent of dormancy ⟨war all over again after five ~ years —Robert Sherrod⟩ **syn** see LATENT, PRONE
dormant account *n* : a deposit account in which there has been no deposit or withdrawal for a number of years
dormant bolt *n* : a concealed door bolt movable only by a special contrivance (as a key or knob)
dormant lock *n* : a lock with no self-closing bolt
dormant partner *n* : SLEEPING PARTNER
dormant spray *n* : a spray applied to trees and shrubs when they are in an inactive state at any time between leaf fall and the beginning of bud swelling at the start of the next growing season
dormant table *n* [ME *table dormant, dormaunt table*, fr. MF *table dormant*] *archaic* : a table that is fixed to the floor or forms a stationary piece of furniture
dormant window *n, now dial* : DORMER WINDOW
dor·mer \'dȯrmər, 'dȯ(ə)mə(r\ *n* -s [F *dormoir*, fr. L *dormitorium* — more at DORMITORY] **1** *obs* : BEDROOM **2** *or* **dormer window** **a** : a usu. gabled extension of an attic room through a sloping roof to allow for a vertical window opening into the room **b** : the window in such an extension
dormered \-mə(r)d\ *adj* : having dormers
dor·mette \(')dȯr¦met\ *n* -s [F *dormir* to sleep + E *-ette* (as in *roomette*) — more at DORMANT] : an adjustable airplane seat that can be made fully reclining

dormer window

dor·meuse \(')dȯ(ə)¦məz\ *n* -s [F, lit., female sleeper, fem. of *dormeur*, sleeper, fr. MF, fr. *dormir* + *-eur* -or] *Brit* : a private traveling carriage having a long forward boot carrying a mattress for extending the seat into a bed and providing leg room for a passenger reclining at full length
dor·mi·dera \,dȯrmə'derə\ *n* -s [Sp, short for *adormidera*, fr. *adormir* to put to sleep, fr. *a-* (fr. L *ad-*) + *dormir* to sleep, fr. L *dormire*; fr. the narcotic properties of the seeds — more at DORMANT] : CALIFORNIA POPPY
dor·mie *or* **dor·my** \'dȯr¦mē, -ō(ə)¦, ¦mi\ *adj* [origin unknown] *golf* : being up as many holes as remain to be played ⟨he stood ~8 — 8 up and 8 holes to play⟩ — used of a player or side
dormie house \"-\ *n* [*dormie* prob. short for *dormitory*] *Brit* : a building with dormitory accommodations operated by a golf club for lodging members overnight
dor·mi·ent \'dȯrmēənt\ *adj* [L *dormient-, dormiens*, pres. part. of *dormire* to sleep — more at DORMANT] *archaic* : SLEEPING
dor·mi·tion \dȯr'mishən\ *n* -s [MF, fr. LL *dormition-, dormitio*, fr. L, act of sleeping, fr. *dormitus* (past part. of *dormire* to sleep) + *-ion-, -io* -ion — more at DORMANT] : death resembling falling asleep
dor·mi·tive \'dȯrməd·iv\ *adj* [MF *dormitif*, fr. L *dormitus* + MF *-if* -ive] : inducing sleep
dor·mi·to·ry \'dȯ(ə)rmə,tōrē, -tōr-, -ri\ *n* -ES *often attrib* [L *dormitorium*, fr. *dormitus* + *-orium* -ory] **1** : a room intended primarily to be slept in; *esp* : a large room providing sleeping quarters for many persons and sometimes divided into cubicles **2** : a residence hall providing separate rooms or suites for individuals or for groups of two, three, or four with common toilet and bathroom facilities but usu. without housekeeping facilities ⟨most of the students of the college live in *dormitories*⟩ ⟨reading in the ~ of the fire station⟩ — called also *hostel* **3** *archaic* : a retreat for taking rest **4** *obs* : a place for repose of the dead **5** : a residential community consisting of homes for sleeping and personal activities from which the majority of the working population commute to places of employment, trade, and recreation ⟨brings the millions from their ~ suburbs to their benches and desks and takes them home again at night —Sam Pollock⟩
dormitory car *n* : a passenger-train car equipped with sleeping and toilet facilities for members of dining-car and other service crews
dormitory ship *n* : a ship equipped with dormitory accommodations (as for round-trip student tours)
dor·mouse \'dȯr,maùs\ *n, pl* **dor·mice** \-mīs\ [ME *dormowse*, perh. fr. F *dormir* to sleep + ME *mowse, mous* mouse; fr. its cold-weather torpidity — more at DORMANT, MOUSE] : any of numerous small Old World rodents of the family Gliridae that resemble small squirrels, live in trees, feed on nuts and acorns, become torpid in cold weather, and yield a velvety fur used in trimming — see LEROT, LOIR
dormouse opossum *or* **dormouse phalanger** *n* : any of several small phalangers (genus *Cercaertus* syn. *Dromicia*) that resemble mice with long nearly naked prehensile tails, that are chiefly nocturnal, and that feed on insects and fruit
dorms *pl of* DORM
¹**dor·nick** *also* **dor·neck** \'dȯrnik\ *or* **dar·nick** \'där-\ *n* -s [ME *dornewick*, fr. *Doornik* (Tournai), city in Belgium where such fabrics were first manufactured] : a coarse damask of wool and silk formerly used for hangings and vestments
²**dor·nick** \'dȯrnik, 'dän-\ *n* -s [prob. fr. IrGael *dornōg* handful, small stone, fr. *dorn* hand, fist] **1** *dial* : a roundish stone or chunk of rock usu. of a size suitable for throwing by hand **2** : a boulder of iron ore found in limonite mines
do·ro·bo \də'rō(,)bō\ *n, pl* **dorobo** *or* **dorobos** *usu cap* **1** : a people of southern and central Kenya that speak Nandi and that were formerly dependent on hunting **2** : a member of the Dorobo people
do·ron \'dōr,än\ *n* -s *usu cap* [Brig. Gen. Georges F. *Doriot* b1899 Am. business executive army officer + E *-on* (as in *nylon*)] : a layered glass cloth impregnated with a hard plastic that is used for body armor
do·ron·i·cum \də'ränəkəm\ *n* [NL, fr. Ar *darūnaj, darūnaj*] **1** *cap* : a genus of Eurasian perennial herbs (family Compositae) having alternate often clasping stem leaves and long peduncled yellow flower heads and comprising the leopard's-banes several of which are cultivated for their flowers **2** -s : any plant of the genus *Doronicum*
do·ro·so·ma \,dōrə'sōmə\ *n, cap* [NL, fr. *doro-* (fr. Gk *dory* wood, trunk of a tree, spear) + *-soma* — more at TREE] : a genus (sometimes the type of the family Dorosomidae or Dorosomatidae) of fishes that includes the gizzard shad and is now usu. placed among the Clupeidae
dor·o·thy bag \'dȯr¦əthē-, 'där¦, -thi-\ *n, usu cap D* [fr. the name *Dorothy*] *Brit* : a woman's handbag hung from the wrist
dorothy dix \¦==='diks\ *n, pl* **dorothy dixes** *usu cap both Ds* [after *Dorothy Dix*, pseudonym of Elizabeth M. Gilmer †1951 Am. journalist and conductor of a syndicated advice-to-the-lovelorn column] : a counselor esp. of women on personal adjustment, etiquette, or other intimate matters
dorp \'dȯ(ə)rp\ *n* -s [D, fr. MD; akin to OHG *dorf* village — more at THORP] **1** *archaic* : a village esp. in the Netherlands **2** [Afrik, fr. MD] *Africa* : VILLAGE, TOWNSHIP
dor·per \'dȯrpər\ *n* [*Dorset* Horn + *Persian* (sheep)] **1** *usu cap* : a breed of mutton-type sheep with white body and black face and a pelt of mingled wool and hair developed in So. Africa by crossing the blackhead Persian and the Dorset Horn breeds **2** -s *often cap* : any sheep of the Dorper breed
¹**dorr** *var of* DOR
²**dorr** \'dȯ(ə)r, 'dō(ə)\ *n* -s [fr. the name *Dorr*] : a glacial trough crossing a ridge or mountain range
dorre *var of* DOR
dorred *past of* DOR
dorring *pres part of* DOR
dors *pl of* DOR, *pres 3d sing of* DOR
dors- *or* **dorsi-** *or* **dorso-** *comb form* [LL *dors-* back, fr. L *dorsum*] **1** : back ⟨*dors*ad⟩ : dorsal ⟨*dorsi*flexion⟩ : dorsally ⟨*dorsi*fixed⟩ **2** : dorsal and ⟨*dorso*lateral⟩
dorsa *pl of* DORSUM
dor·sad \'dȯr,sad\ *adv* [*dors-* + *-ad*] : toward the back : DORSALLY — used chiefly of anatomic relations
¹**dor·sal** \'dȯrsəl, 'dȯ(ə)s-\ *adj* [LL *dorsalis*, fr. L *dorsum* back + *-alis* -al] **1 a** : belonging to or situated near or on the back of an animal or of one of its parts — opposed to *ventral* **b** *chiefly Brit* : THORACIC **c** *of echinoderms and coelenterates* : ABORAL **d** : having or forming an elongated ridge suggestive of an animal's back : situated on such a part ⟨a ~ gun turret⟩ **e** : placed or worn on a human back **2** *bot* **a** : ABAXIAL **b** : belonging to the upper surface of a creeping dorsiventral structure (as a thallus) **3** : articulated with a part of the tongue posterior to the tip; *specif* : articulated with a part of the tongue posterior to that employed in a palatal articulation
²**dorsal** \"\ *n* -s **1** : a dorsally located part; *esp* : THORACIC VERTEBRA **2** : a dorsal sound **3** [ML *dorsale*, fr. neut. of LL *dorsalis*, adj.] : DOSSAL
dorsal carpal ligament *n* : a broad flat ligament at the back of the wrist serving to hold in place the tendons of the extensor muscles
dorsal column *n* : a column lying dorsally in each lateral half of the spinal cord and receiving terminals from certain afferent fibers of the dorsal roots of the spinal nerves
dor·sa·le \dȯr'sa(,)lē, -sā-,-sä-\ *n* -s [ML] : DOSSAL
dorsal fin *n* **1** : a median longitudinal vertical fin on the back of a fish or other aquatic vertebrate — see FISH illustration **2** : a vertical fin on the upper side of the after end of an airplane fuselage to provide greater directional stability

dor·sa·lis \dȯrˈsāləs, -sal-,-säl-\ *n, pl* **dorsa·les** \-a(,)lēz, -ā(,)lēz, -ä,lās\ [NL, fr. LL, adj., dorsal — more at DORSAL] **:** any of several arteries situated in and supplying the back of the parts with which they are associated
dorsal lamina *n* **:** a longitudinal membrane in tunicates that projects into the cavity of the branchial sac and is borne by the large median dorsal blood vessel; *also* **:** that vessel itself
dorsal lip *n* **:** the margin of the fold of blastula wall that delineates the dorsal limit of the blastopore in the gastrulating amphibian embryo or corresponds to this in other vertebrate embryos and that constitutes the primary organizer, is essential to the formation of neural tissue, and forms the point of origin of chordamesoderm
dor·sal·ly \ˈdȯ(r)səlē, -li\ *adv* **:** in a dorsal situation or direction
dor·sal·most \ˈ⁼⁼səl,mōst\ *adj* **:** most nearly dorsal
dorsal nerve *n* **:** THORACIC NERVE
dorsal pore *n* **:** an opening in the mid-dorsal part of nearly every segment in many earthworms by which the body cavity is placed in communication with the exterior and which is believed to permit moistening of the body surface with coelomic fluid for lubrication and to facilitate respiration
dorsal root *n* **:** the one of the two roots of a spinal nerve that passes dorsally to the spinal cord and consists of sensory fibers — compare VENTRAL ROOT
dorsal-root ganglion *n* **:** SPINAL GANGLION
dorsal suture *n* **:** the outer suture of a pod or other monocarpellary fruit that is the midrib of the carpellary leaf from which the fruit is formed
dorsal vertebra *n* **:** THORACIC VERTEBRA
dorsal vessel *n* **:** the elongated dorsally situated heart of insects and other arthropods
dor·sal·ward \ˈdȯ(r)səlwərd\ *or* **dor·sal·wards** \-dz\ *adv* **:** toward the dorsal surface **:** DORSAD
d'or·say \(ˈ)dȯrˈsā, -ˈzā\ *or* **d'orsay pump** *n, often cap D&O* [after Count Alfred G.G. d'Orsay †1852 Fr. society leader and arbiter of fashion] **:** a pump-type shoe or slipper made with a circular vamp and a quarter that curves to meet the vamp at the shank line

d'orsay

dorse \ˈdȯ(ə)rs\ *n* -s [L *dorsum* back] *archaic* **:** the back of a book or folded document
dorser *var of* DOSSER
¹dor·set \ˈdȯrsət, -ȯ(ə)s-, *usu* -əd.+V\ *n* -s *often cap* [fr. the county of *Dorset*, England, where it was first made] **:** BLUE VINNY
²dorset \"\ *n, usu cap* [fr. Cape *Dorset* near Baffin island, Franklin district, Northwest Territories, Canada] **:** an Eskimo culture of northeastern Canada and northern Greenland about A.D. 100-1000 characterized by the hunting of caribou and seals and by microlithic flake tools and harpoon heads having gouged rather than drilled holes
dorset down \ˈ⁼⁼ˈdau̇n\ *n* [fr. the county of *Dorset*, England, where it was originally bred] **1** *usu cap both Ds* **:** an English breed of short-wooled mutton-type sheep derived from the Hampshire Down **2** *pl* **dorset downs** *often cap both Ds* **:** a sheep of the Dorset Down breed
dorset horn \ˈ⁼⁼ˈ⁼\ *also* **dorset** *n* [fr. the county of *Dorset*, England] **1** *usu cap D&H* **:** an English breed of sheep with very large and in the ram much-coiled horns that has a close-textured fleece of medium-length wool and that has been much used for hothouse lamb production because of the early breeding of the ewes and the high percentage of twin lambs **2** -s *often cap D&H* **:** a sheep of the Dorset Horn breed
dor·set·shire \ˈ⁼⁼,shi(ə)r, -iə, -,shə(r)\ *or* **dorset** *adj, usu cap* [fr. *Dorsetshire* or *Dorset*, England] **:** of or from the county of Dorset, England **:** of the kind or style prevalent in Dorset
dorsi- — see DORS-
dor·sian \ˈdȯrzhən, -rshən\ *n, usu cap* [blend of *Dorset* (*Horn*) and *Persian* (sheep)] **:** DORPER
dor·si·branchiate \ˌdȯ(r)sə+\ *adj* [*dors-* + *branchiate*] **:** having branchiae along the back
dor·si·col·lar \ˌdȯ(r)səˈkälə(r)\ *adj* [*dors-* + L *coll*um neck + E -*ar* — more at COLLAR] **:** belonging or relating to the back and neck
dor·si·duct \ˈdȯ(r)sə,dəkt\ *vt* -ED/-ING/-S [*dors-* + L *ductus*, past part. of *ducere* to lead — more at TOW] *physiol* **:** to turn or draw toward the back
dor·sif·er·ous \(ˈ)dȯ(r)ˈsif(ə)rəs\ *adj* [*dors-* + *-ferous*] **1 :** bearing the sori on the back of the frond — used of various ferns **2 :** carrying the eggs or young upon the back
dor·si·fixed \ˈdȯ(r)sə,fikst\ *adj* [*dors-* + *fixed*] **:** attached by the back — used esp. of anthers
dor·si·flex \-,fleks\ *vb* [*dors-* + *flex*] *vi* **:** to flex in a dorsal direction ⟨the toe will ~⟩ ~ *vt* **:** to cause to flex in a dorsal direction ⟨various central lesions both ~ and supinate the foot⟩ — **dor·si·flex·ion** \ˌ⁼⁼ˈflekshən\ *n*
dor·si·flex·or \ˈ⁼⁼,fleksə(r)\ *n* [NL, fr. *dors-* + *flexor*] **:** a muscle causing flexion in a dorsal direction
dor·si·grade \ˈ⁼⁼,grād\ *adj* [*dors-* + *-grade*] **:** walking on the back of the toes ⟨~ armadillos⟩
dor·si·spinal \ˌdȯ(r)sə+\ *adj* [*dors-* + *spinal*] **:** of or relating to the back and spine
dor·si·ventral \"+\ *adj* [*dors-* + *ventral*] **1 :** having distinct dorsal and ventral surfaces ⟨~ leaves⟩ **2 :** DORSOVENTRAL 1 — **dor·si·ven·tral·i·ty** \ˌdȯ(r)səven·ˈtraləd·ē\ *n* -ES — **dor·si·ventrally** \ˌ⁼⁼+\ *adv*
dorso- — see DORS-
dor·so·caudad \ˌdȯ(r)(,)sō+\ *adv* [*dors-* + *caudad*] **:** to or toward the dorsal surface and caudal end of the body
dor·so·lateral \"+\ *also* **dor·si·lateral** \ˌdȯ(r)sə+\ *adj* [*dors-* + *lateral*] **:** of, relating to, or involving both the back and sides
dor·so·lumbar \ˌdȯ(r)(,)sō+\ *also* **dor·si·lumbar** \ˌdȯ(r)sə+\ *adj* [*dors-* + *lumbar*] **:** of or involving structures in the region occupied by the dorsal and lumbar vertebrae ⟨~ myelitis⟩
dorso·lumbar nerve *n* **:** a small nerve connecting the last thoracic nerve with the lumbar plexus
dor·so·medial \ˌdȯ(r)(,)sō+\ *or* **dor·so·median** \"+\ *also* **dor·si·median** \ˌdȯ(r)sə+\ *adj* [*dors-* + *medial* or *median*] **:** located toward the back and near the midline
dor·so·posteriad \ˌdȯ(r)(,)sō+\ *adv* [*dors-* + *posteriad*] **:** to or toward the dorsal surface and posterior end of the body
dor·so·ulnar \"+\ *adj* [*dors-* + *ulnar*] **:** of or relating to the inner side of the back of the forearm or hand
dor·so·ventral \"+\ *adj* [ISV *dors-* + *ventral*] **1 :** extending from the dorsal toward the ventral side ⟨the ~ axis of an animal⟩ **2 :** DORSIVENTRAL 1 — **dor·so·ventrally** \"+\ *adv*
dor·ste·nia \dȯ(r)ˈstēnēə\ *n* [NL, fr. Theodor *Dorsten* †1552 Ger. botanist + NL *-ia*] **1** *cap* **:** a large genus of tropical herbs (family Moraceae) having basal leaves and small monoecious flowers crowded upon a fleshy receptacle at the end of a long naked peduncle — see CONTRAYERVA **2** *pl* **dorstenias** *also* **dor·steni·ae** \-ē,ē\ **:** any plant of the genus *Dorstenia*
dor·sum \ˈdȯrsəm, -ȯ(ə)s-\ *n, pl* **dor·sa** \-sə\ [L] **1 :** BACK; *esp* **:** the entire dorsal surface of an animal or the upper surface of an appendage or part (as of the nose, tongue, or foot) ⟨the ~ of a segment⟩ **2** [NL, fr. L] **:** the upper side of the tongue behind the tip; *specif* **:** the part opposite the velum when the tongue is at rest
dors·umbonal \(ˌ)dȯ(r)s+\ *adj* [*dors-* + *umbonal*] **:** dorsal and umbonal **:** being one of the accessory valves of mollusks of the family Pholadidae
dort \ˈdȯrt\ *vi* -ED/-ING/-S [origin unknown] *Scot* **:** to take offense **:** SULK
dor·ter *or* **dor·tour** \ˈdȯrd·ər\ *n* -s [ME, fr. OF *dortoir*, fr. L *dormitorium* — more at DORMITORY] **:** a dormitory esp. in a religious house
dort·mund \ˈdȯrt,mu̇nt, -nd, -,mənd\ *adj, usu cap* [fr. *Dortmund*, Germany] **:** of or from the city of Dortmund, Germany **:** of the kind or style prevalent in Dortmund
dorts \ˈdȯrts\ *n pl* [origin unknown] *chiefly Scot* **:** a mood of bad temper **:** SULKS
dorty \ˈdȯrtī\ *adj* [*dort* + *-y*] *Scot* **:** PEEVISH, SULKY
¹do·ry *also* **do·ree** \ˈdōrē, ˈdȯr-, -ri\ *n, pl* **dories** *also* **dorees** [ME *dorre, dorray*, fr. MF *dorée*, fr. fem. of *doré*, past part. of *dorer* to gild — more at DORÉ] **1 :** the John Dory or a related fish **2 :** WALLEYED PIKE
²do·ry \"\ *also* **do·rey** \"\ *n, pl* **dories** *also* **doreys** [Mosquito *dóri, dúri* dugout] **:** a flat-bottomed boat with high flaring sides, sharp bow, and deep V-shaped transom that is used esp. on the New England coast and by American fishing vessels and is noted for its qualities in riding seas

dory

dory- *comb form* [NL, fr. Gk *dory* — more at TREE] **:** spear ⟨*Dory*anthes⟩
dor·y·an·thes \ˌdȯrēˈan(ˌ)thēz\ *n, cap* [NL, fr. *dory-* + *-anthes*] **:** a small genus of Australian plants (family Amaryllidaceae) with a basal rosette of large leaves and a large long-stalked spike of red flowers — see SPEAR LILY
dor·y·lai·mi·na \ˌdȯrəˈlīmənə\ *n pl, cap* [NL, fr. *Dorylaimus*, genus of nematode worms (fr. *dory-* + Gk *laimos* throat, gullet) + *-ina*] **:** a suborder of Enoplida including free-living and parasitic nematodes lacking setae but having a buccal stylet — compare DIOCTOPHYMATINA, ENOPLINA
¹dor·y·line \ˈdȯrə,līn\ *adj* [NL *Dorylinae*, subfamily of ants, fr. *Dorylus*, type genus (fr. Gk *dory* wood, trunk of a tree, spear) + *-inae* — more at TREE] **:** of or relating to dorylines
²doryline \"\ *n* **:** any of various large specialized migratory tropical ants that are blind except for the functional males **:** ARMY ANT
do·ry·man \ˈdōrēmən, ˈdȯr-, -rim-\ *n, pl* **dorymen :** a fisherman working from or handling a dory
dor·y·mouse \ˈdäri,mau̇s\ *n* [by alter.] *dial Eng* **:** DORMOUSE
dory trawler *n* [²*dory*] **:** a trawler with several dories working for her
¹dos *or* **do's** *pl of* DO
²dos \ˈdōs, ˈdäs\ *n* -ES [L — more at DOWER] **1** *Roman law* **:** the property contributed by the wife or by someone else on her behalf to the husband for sustaining the burdens of matrimony, orig. becoming the husband's absolutely but by the time of Justinian required to be surrendered to the original donor on the termination of the marriage by death or divorce **2** *English law* **:** the property settled by a husband upon his wife at the time of the marriage
do-sa-do *or* **dos-a-dos** *var of* DO-SI-DO
¹dos-à-dos \ˌdōzəˈdō *or like* DO-SI-DO\ *adv* [F] *archaic* **:** back to back ⟨passing *dos-à-dos* in a quadrille⟩
²dos-à-dos \"\ *n, pl* **dos-à-dos** [F, fr. *dos-à-dos* back to back] **:** a dogcart having four wheels and seats set back to back
³dos-à-dos \"\ *adj* [F, lit., back to back] *of two books* **:** bound back to back with one common board between and the fore edge of one next to the backbone of the other ⟨a psalter and a New Testament in a *dos-à-dos* style⟩
dos·age \ˈdōsij, -sēj\ *n* -s **1 a :** the amount of medicine or other therapeutic agent (as X rays) prescribed or proper for a given patient or illness ⟨the ~ of the vitamins and of calcium received through the diet and in other ways will be determined by the doctor —Morris Fishbein⟩ **b :** the administration of such dosages by any means **c :** a dose of radiation encountered other than in medical treatment **2 a :** addition of some ingredient or application of or treatment with some agent in one or more measured doses ⟨yeast ~s of sewage⟩ ⟨the recommended spraying ~ for controlling codling moth⟩ ⟨even heavy ~s of antioxidant do not prolong the life of polyethylene to more than one or two years —B.S.Biggs⟩ **b :** a mixture of sweet syrup and aged wine added to bottle-fermented sparkling wines after secondary fermentation and disgorgement **c :** the presence and relative representation or strength of some factor or agent ⟨the effects of six rather than the usual three levels of gene ~ —*Genetics*⟩ **3 a :** regulation or determination of doses ⟨an old practitioner's expertness in ~⟩ ⟨research in radiation ~⟩ **b :** a dealing out of or an exposure to (some experience) in or as if in measured portions ⟨he had a nice sense of ~, spicy but not obtrusive, in dealing with the percussion section —Virgil Thomson⟩ ⟨minute portions of melodrama every day, a fragmentation of suspense into endless daily anxiety — with a special ~ on Friday to carry over the weekend —Gilbert Seldes⟩ ⟨education as the only antidote for a ~ of propaganda⟩ ⟨for dramatic sopranos and contraltos a moderate ~ of unhappiness is splendid forcing ground for the emotional side of their temperaments —*N.Y. Times*⟩
dosage meter *n* **:** DOSIMETER
dosage response *n* **:** the effect of a biologically active agent (as a chemical) upon a disease organism
¹dose \ˈdōs\ *n* -s [F, fr. LL *dosis*, fr. Gk, lit., act of giving, gift, fr. *didonai* to give — more at DATE] **1 a :** the measured quantity of a medicine or other therapeutic agent to be taken at one time or in a period of time ⟨the same amount daily in divided ~s until the temperature remains normal⟩ **b :** the quantity of radiation administered to (as in radiotherapy) or absorbed accidentally by a given volume or mass of tissue at one time, measured in terms of the intensity of radiation, the distance from the source, and the length of exposure **2 :** a portion of an additive admitted during a process ⟨a faulty champagne can be hidden rather conveniently under a strong ~ of sugarcane —Barrett McGurn⟩ **3 a :** a measure or portion of some experience to which one is exposed or subjected ⟨schools where reluctant youths are being exposed to a heavy ~ of book learning unrelated to their interests and their ambitions —J.B.Conant⟩ ⟨so we gave him a large ~ of squash and track work —Harry Gordon⟩ ⟨I had a long ~ of Spinoza with far more admiration than previously —H.J. Laski⟩ ⟨after I saw my first burst damaged him I flew in closer and gave him a second ~⟩ ⟨taken in easy ~s, a chapter at a time because of its close-packed variety, this book is a treasure-house of marvelous reading —Hal Lehrman⟩ ⟨feeding them immense ~s of propaganda⟩ **b** *nonstand* **:** a gonorrheal infection **4 :** a standard increment of labor and capital conceived as being applied to land to measure changes in its productiveness at different intensities of cultivation
²dose \"\ *vb* -ED/-ING/-S *vt* **1 :** to proportion (a medicine or other therapeutic agent) properly with reference to the patient or illness **2 :** to give a dose to: **a :** to give medicine to **b :** to subject to an experience by way of correction or instruction ⟨*dosed* the jeering lads with a bucket of water⟩ ⟨*dosed* him with a stiff course of reading in the Greek and Latin⟩ **3 :** to treat with an application or agent ⟨a powerful ray that *dosed* the paint for a long period⟩ ⟨his dark mustache . . . was liberally *dosed* with bear grease —R.W.Thorp⟩ **4 :** to apply a dose of labor or capital to ~ *vi* **:** to take medicine ⟨he is forever *dosing*, but he gets worse⟩
dos gris \(ˈ)dōˈgrē\ *n, pl* **dos gris** [LaF, lit., gray back] *chiefly South* **:** SCAUP DUCK
do-si-do *or* **do-se-do** *also* **do-sa-do** *or* **dos-a-dos** \ˌdō(,)sēˈdō *sometimes* -ōt(,)sēˈ- *or* -ō,sīˈ- *or* -ō(,)chēˈ- *or* -ōsəˈ- *or* -ōzəˈ-\ *n, pl* **do-si-dos** *or* **do-se-dos** [¹*dos-à-dos*] **:** a square-dance figure in which the dancers passing by right shoulder circle each other back to back
do·sim·e·ter \dōˈsimәd·ә(r)\ *also* **dose·me·ter** \ˈdōs,mēd·ə(r)\ *n* [*dosimeter*, ISV *dosi-* (fr. L *dosis* dose) + *-meter*; *dosemeter* fr. ¹*dose* + *-meter* — more at DOSE] **:** an instrument or device for measuring doses of X rays or of radioactivity — **do·sim·e·try** \dōˈsimə·trē\ *n* -ES
do·si·met·ric \ˌdōsəˈme·trik\ *adj* [ISV *dosimetry* + *-ic*] **:** devoted or relating to dosimetry
dosing tank *n* **:** a tank in which sewage is collected and later discharged at the rate required by subsequent treatment processes
do·sin·ia \dōˈsinēə\ *n, cap* [NL, fr. *dosin*, native name in Senegal for a species of this genus + NL *-ia*] **:** a genus of bivalve mollusks (family Veneridae) having a flattened rounded shell, large foot, and united siphons
do·sith·e·an \dōˈsithēən\ *n* -s *usu cap* [*Dositheus*, 1st cent. A.D. Jewish heretic + E *-an*] **:** a member of a Samaritan sect believing in the heretic Dositheus as the Messiah and stressing esp. the precepts of the law concerning the Sabbath
dos no·mi·na·ta \-,nämәˈnād·ə, -nād·ə\ *n* [L, specified dower] *English law* **:** a dos consisting of certain specified lands
dos ra·ti·o·na·bi·lis \-,räd·ēōˈnäbələs, -,rashəˈnab-\ *n* [L, reasonable dower] *English law* **:** a dos consisting of one third of the lands of which the husband is seised at the time of the espousals
¹doss \ˈdäs\ *vt* -ED/-ING/-ES [perh. alter. of *toss*] *dial Eng* **:** to toss with the horns
²doss \"\ *n* -ES [origin unknown] **1** *chiefly Brit* **:** a makeshift bed **2** *or* **doss house** *chiefly Brit* **:** a cheap rooming house **3** *chiefly Brit* **:** SLEEP
³doss \"\ *vi* -ED/-ING/-ES *chiefly Brit* **:** to sleep or bed down in any convenient place ⟨pea pickers sometimes ~*ed* under the straw stack —Thomas Wood †1950⟩ — often used with *down* ⟨never mind, we can ~ down in the car —Joyce Cary⟩
dos·sal *or* **dos·sel** \ˈdäsəl\ *n* -s [ML *dossale, dorsale* — more at DORSAL] **1** *archaic* **:** an ornamental cloth for the back of a throne or chair **2 :** an ornamental cloth hung back of and above the altar or beside the chancel
dos·sen·nus \dəˈsenəs\ *n* -ES [L *Dossennus, Dossenus*] **:** a stock character of Roman comedy representing a sharp-witted hunchback
¹dos·ser \ˈdäsər\ *also* **dor·ser** \ˈdȯrsər\ *n* -s [ME *dosser, dorser*, fr. MF & ML; MF *dossier*, fr. ML *dorsarium*, fr. L *dorsum* back + *-arium* -ary] **1** *archaic* **:** DOSSAL **2 :** a basket to be carried on a person's back or, in pairs, by a horse or other beast of burden **:** PANNIER
²dos·ser \ˈdäsə(r)\ *n* -s [*doss* (*house*) + *-er*] *chiefly Brit* **:** one that frequents doss houses
dos·se·ret \ˌdäsəˈret\ *n* -s [F, fr. MF, small dosser, dim. of *dossier*] **:** a clearly defined block resting on the capital of a column and serving as an extra impost in Byzantine and Romanesque architecture

dosseret

dos·sier \ˈdōs,yā *also* ˈdäs- *or* ˈ⁼ˈ⁼; ˈdäsē,ā *also* ˌ⁼⁼ˈ⁼\ *n* -s [F, bundle of documents with a label on the back, dossier, fr. *dos* back (fr. L *dorsum*) + *-ier*] **1 :** an accumulation of records, reports, miscellaneous pertinent data, and documents bearing on a single subject of study or investigation **:** FILE ⟨a ~ of criminal acts of occupation troops⟩ ⟨a numbered ~ is kept on each patient containing a full history of his physical condition⟩ ⟨a year ahead of production of the film researchers began a ~ on the locale and period⟩ ⟨no censorship of written or spoken words, no tapping of telephones, opening of letters, compiling of ~s —*Horizon*⟩ ⟨methods of the police state that run the gamut from wire tapping to the maintenance of the ~ —G.B.Oxnam⟩ **2 :** an author's accumulation of items toward the creation of a projected fictional character
doss·i·ly \ˈdäsəlē, -li\ *adv, chiefly Brit* **:** in a dossy manner
dossy \ˈdäsē, -si\ *adj* -ER/-EST [Sc *dossie* sprucely dressed person, fr. *doss* neat (fr. *doss* to dress, fr. D *dossen*, fr. *dos* clothes, fr. MD, perh. fr. OF *dos* back, fr. L *dorsum*) + *-ie*] *chiefly Brit* **:** pretentiously fashionable
¹dost *archaic pres 2d sing of* DO
²dost \ˈdōst\ *dial var of* DOSE
dos·to·ev·ski·an \ˌdästəˈyefskēən, ˌdȯs-, -stō̇ye-, -stēˈe-, -(,)stō̇ˈ(y)e-, -stȯiˈ(y)e-, -evzk-,-evsk-, -kiən *sometimes* ˌdəs- *or* -stəˈe- *or* -,stō̇ˈe-\ *adj, usu cap* [Fedor *Dostoevski* †1881 Russ. novelist + E *-an*] **:** of, relating to, or typical of Fedor Dostoevski or his writings ⟨the *Dostoevskian* milieu seemed barbaric, lawless, Eastern, an enemy of the "sanity and method" he clung to —Irving Howe⟩
¹dot \ˈdät, *usu* -äd.+V\ *n* -s [fr. (assumed) ME, fr. OE *dott* head of a boil; akin to OHG *tutta* nipple, D *dot* knot, tuft, Norw *dot* lump, small knot, OE *dyttan* to stop up] **1 :** a minute particle of a substance or liquid or a spot of color visible on a surface ⟨spin appear as ~s on a fertile fern frond⟩ ⟨the telltale ~s of measles⟩ ⟨watching the wagon as it grew smaller and smaller until it was only a ~ on the horizon —O.E.Rölvaag⟩ ⟨islands show as mere ~s on the ocean⟩ **2 :** a small round mark made on a surface with or as if with a pointed instrument ⟨the ~ on the chart represents the ship's position⟩ ⟨put a ~ before the name of each as he pays⟩: **a :** such a mark written or printed as a sign or part of a sign of spelling or orthography or punctuation: as (1) **:** PERIOD ⟨a colon consists of one ~ on the base line with another directly above⟩ ⟨a row of printed ~s denoting the omission of words⟩ ⟨*W.A.C.* written with ~s or without⟩ (2) **:** the topmost element of a lower-case letter *i* or *j* (3) **:** a centered period as a divider of syllables **b :** such a mark as an integral part of certain letters (as *ṁ* in Sanskrit) in various forms of the Roman alphabet or in phonetics used above, below, or after a symbol with any of various values **c** (1) **:** DECIMAL POINT (2) **:** a sign of multiplication **d :** one of the points used in braille or other raised-point system of writing for the blind **e** *in music notation* (1) **:** a point placed immediately after a note or rest indicating augmentation of its time value by one half (2) **:** a point placed over a note indicating a moderate staccato — compare DASH 3d **f :** one of the spots constituting the printing surface of a halftone **g** *logic* (1) **:** a sign for "and" — compare CONJUNCTION (2) **:** a sign used to indicate the beginning or end of a group of statements belonging together **3 :** something very small; *esp* **:** a very small portion or specimen ⟨a ~ of a child⟩ **4 :** a precise point in time or space; *esp* **:** a moment exactly appointed ⟨arriving and departing on the ~⟩ ⟨correct to a ~⟩ **5 a :** a striking of a pointed object or the sound of its striking on a hard surface ⟨we knew him far off by the ~ of his crutch⟩ **b :** a short click on a telegraph sounder forming a letter or part of a letter (as in the Morse code) — compare DASH 8a **c :** a flash of a beam from a momentary opening of the shutter of a signal light representing a letter or part of a letter in a communication system (as the Morse code) — compare DASH 8c **d :** a wave of a flag through an arc of 90 degrees to the right from vertical as an element of a code alphabet in flag signaling — compare WIGWAG **6 :** a small circle of solid color used as a design motif ⟨a broadcloth print with big coin ~s⟩ — compare POLKA DOT — **in the year dot** *Brit* **:** in the year one **:** as long ago as anyone can count ⟨says that he used this system *in the year dot* —*Motor*⟩ — **off one's dot** *slang Brit* **:** disordered in mind **:** DOTTY
²dot \"\ *vb* **dotted; dotted; dotting; dots** *vt* **1 a :** to mark with a dot ⟨a *dotted* 32d note⟩ **b :** to put a dot over (a letter *i* or *j*) **c :** JOT — used with *down* ⟨~ down these notes⟩ **2 a :** to mark or diversify with numerous dots or objects scattered at random **:** INTERSPERSE ⟨of one of those enigmas that ~ the literary landscape in every period —J.G.Keller⟩ ⟨a curious type of formal English *dotted* with sudden colloquialisms —J.J.Espey⟩ ⟨*dotted* across the country are pressure groups which complain loudly that education has gotten away from the fundamentals —E.O.Melby⟩ ⟨pictures of animals which are *dotted* about in the text of the bestiaries —O. Elfrida Saunders⟩ **b** (1) **:** to cause a scattering of marks resembling dots to appear on ⟨a rising southeast wind that *dotted* the lake with whitecaps —Joseph Millard⟩ (2) **:** to make a dot or dots upon ⟨*dotted* the canvas with infinitely small specks of paint⟩ **3** *cookery* **:** to dab here and there with small bits of a soft substance (as butter) **:** scatter small bits of an ingredient over **4** *slang Brit* **:** HIT ~ *vi* **:** to make a dot ⟨a pen point that ~s without blotting⟩ — **dot and carry one 1** *archaic* **:** to set down, point, and carry the figures as in elementary arithmetic **2** *archaic* **:** DOT AND GO ONE — **dot and go one 1** *archaic* **:** to walk with a limp or with the aid of a crutch **2** *archaic* **:** to progress jerkily — **dot the i :** to fill in details **:** make explicit statement ⟨the chairman *dotted no i's* but everyone present knew the man he meant⟩ ⟨Henry James suggests the dissolute vulgarity of the malignant janitor without *dotting the i* as much as he might be expected to —Henry Hewes⟩
³dot \ˈdä|t, ˈdȯ|, *usu* |d.+V\ *n* -s [F, fr. L *dot-, dos* dowry — more at DOWER] **:** a woman's marriage portion
dot·age \ˈdōd·|ij, -ōt|, |ēj\ *n* -s [ME, fr. *doten* to dote + *-age*] **1 a :** feebleness or impairment of understanding and reason **:** mental infirmity ⟨I may venture to assert, without exposing myself to the charge of ~ —William Cowper⟩ **b :** advanced age attended by enfeebled mentality and childishness — called also *second childhood* **2 :** an utterance or a work showing a writer's or artist's feebleness of mind or execution from old age ⟨more important than Galsworthy's increasingly desiccated social propaganda and the ~s of Bernard Shaw —F.B. Millett⟩ **3** *archaic* **a :** a weak and foolish or silly doting

: a blind fondness or affection **b :** the object of such fondness or affection

do·tal \'dōd·ᵊl\ *adj* [L *dotalis,* fr. *dot-, dos* dowry + *-alis* -al — more at DOWER] **:** relating to a woman's marriage portion

¹dot-and-dash \ˌ**=**ˌ**=**\ *or* **dot-dash** \'**=**ˌ**=**\ *adj* **1 :** formed of or as if of alternating dots and dashes ⟨run a *dot-and-dash* line across the sheet⟩ **2 :** consisting of or using an alphabet made up of dots and dashes as signals for communicating ⟨secret conversations by means of long and short muscular movements in the Morse *dot-and-dash* system⟩

²dot-and-dash \"\ *or* **dot-dash** \"\ *vt* **1 :** to mark with a succession of dots and dashes **2 :** to convey by means of a dot-and-dash system

dotant *n* -s [¹*dote* + *-ant*] *obs* **:** DOTARD 1a

do·tard \'dōd·ə(r)d, -ōtə-\ *n* -s [ME, fr *doten* to dote + *-ard*] **1 a** *obs* **:** IMBECILE **b :** one in his dotage **2 :** HARBOR SEAL **3** *obs* **:** a tree stump that has lost its branches by decay

¹dote *also* **doat** \'dōt, *usu* -ōd·+V\ *vb* -ED/-ING/-S [ME *doten;* akin to MLG *dotten, dutten* to be foolish, MD *dutten* to be enraged, be mad, Icel *dotta* to nod from fatigue, Norw *dudra* to tremble — more at DODDER] *vi* **1 a** *archaic* **:** to be or become foolish or imbecile or deranged ⟨a sword is upon the liars and they shall ~ —Jer 50:36 (AV)⟩ **b :** to be weak-minded or mentally deficient by reason of old age **2 :** to show strong, excessive, or fatuous fondness or affection — used with *on* or *upon* ⟨those who hate him seem to agree in certain respects with those who ~ on him⟩ ⟨I ~ on the serene pleasures of marvelous landscapes —Vance Locke⟩ ⟨here are two peoples both of whom love palaver and ~ on uproar —Elizabeth Monroe⟩ **3** *of a tree or lumber* **:** to begin to decay or to become partly decayed ⟨an old *doting* oak —O.W.Holmes †1894⟩ ~ *vt, obs* **:** to cause to dote **syn** see LIKE

²dote \"\ *n* -s [ME, fr. *doten,* v.] **1** *now dial* **:** IMBECILE, DOTARD **2 :** decay in timber **:** ROT

³dote *n* -s [MF or L; MF *dot* dowry, fr. L *dot-, dos* dowry, gift — more at DOWER] **1** *obs* **:** ³DOT **2 dotes** *pl* [L *dot-, dos*] **:** natural endowments

dot·ed *also* **doat·ed** \'dōtəd\ *adj* [ME *doted,* fr. past part. of *doten*] **1** *now Scot* **:** weak-minded from age **2** *obs* **:** extravagantly fond

do tell \'**=**'**=**\ *interj* — used esp. to express mild or polite surprise

dot·er *also* **doat·er** \'dōd·ə(r), -ōtə-\ *n* -s **1 :** a man whose understanding is enfeebled by age **:** DOTARD **2 :** one that is foolishly or excessively fond ⟨a ~ on fried clams⟩

dot etching *n* **:** a method in printing of correcting the color or tones of a halftone negative or positive usu. utilizing the chemical reduction of halftone dots

dot figure *n* **:** a collection of dots arranged regularly or irregularly that on being steadily examined seem to fall successively into different groupings

doth *archaic pres 3d sing of* DO

doth·er \'däthə(r)\ *dial Eng var of* DODDER

do·thid·e·ace·ae \(ˌ)dōˌthidē'āsēˌē\ *n pl, cap* [NL, fr. *Dothidea,* type genus (fr. Gk *dothiēn* small abscess, boil) + *-aceae*] **:** a family of saprophytic or parasitic fungi (order Dothideales) with a plurilocular stroma that is erumpent and superficial at maturity — **do·thid·e·aceous** \(ˌ)dōˌthidē'āshəs\ *adj*

do·thid·e·ales \-'ā(ˌ)lēz\ *n pl, cap* [NL, fr. *Dothidea* + *-ales*] **:** an order of ascomycetous fungi (subclass Euascomycetes) having the mycelium embedded in the substrate and a stroma with a hard dark rind and soft pale inner layer that is divided into cavities resembling perithecia within which asci are produced in tufts or hymenial layers

doth·i·del·la \ˌdäthə'delə, ˌdōth-\ *n, cap* [NL, fr. Gk *dothiēn* + NL *-ella*] **:** a genus of fungi (family Dothideaceae) having hyaline, unequally 2-celled ascospores, and including a fungus (*D. ulmi*) that attacks the leaves of elm

do·thid·i·a·ce·ae \(ˌ)dōˌthidē'āsēˌē\ *syn of* DOTHIDEACEAE

do·thid·i·a·les \-ˌā(ˌ)lēz\ *syn of* DOTHIDEALES

do·thi·o·rel·la \ˌdōthēō'relə\ *n, cap* [NL, irreg. fr. Gk *dothiōn, dothiēn* small abscess, boil + NL *-ella*] **:** a form genus of imperfect fungi (family Sphaeriopsidaceae) characterized by single-celled hyaline spores (grouped in superficial stromata) of the pycnidia

dotier *comparative of* DOTY

dotiest *superlative of* DOTY

doting *also* **doating** *adj* [fr. pres. part. of ¹*dote, doat*] **1 :** IMBECILE, FOOLISH; *esp* **:** weak-minded from old age **2 :** excessively or foolishly fond **:** OVERINDULGENT ⟨deceiving her preoccupied and ~ husband with a young captain⟩ ⟨~ mothers end by ruining their children —Hallam Tennyson⟩ — **dot·ing·ly** *adv* — **dot·ing·ness** *n* -ES

dot·ish *also* **doat·ish** \'dōd·ish\ *adj* [²*dote* + *-ish*] *archaic* **:** IMBECILE

dotkin *var of* DODKIN

dot·let \'dätlət\ *n* -s [¹*dot* + *-let*] **:** a small dot

do·to \'dōd·(ˌ)ō\ *n, cap* [NL, fr. L *Doto,* a sea nymph, fr. Gk *Dōtō*] **:** a genus of nudibranch mollusks with tuberculated cerata

dot product *n* [¹*dot;* fr. its being commonly written *A·B*] **:** the scalar product of two vectors

do·tri·a·con·tane \ˌdōˌtrīə'känˌtān\ *n* -s [ISV *dotriacont-* (fr. *do-* — as in *dodeca-* — + *triacont-* — fr. Gk *triakonta* thirty) + *-ane*] **:** a paraffin hydrocarbon of the formula $C_{32}H_{66}$; *esp* **:** the crystalline normal isomer $CH_3(CH_2)_{30}CH_3$

dots *pl of* DOT, *pres 3d sing of* DOT

¹dotted *adj* [fr. past part. of ²*dot*] **1 :** made of or executed with dots **:** STIPPLED ⟨~ leaders in the table of contents⟩ ⟨the ~ manner of engraving⟩ **2 :** marked or covered with dots or small spots ⟨the ~ scad called cigarfish⟩ **3 :** strewn with scattered objects resembling dots ⟨a vast plain ~ with infrequent settlements⟩ **4 :** relating to a musical note or rest increased in length by one half of its value by the addition of a dot

dotted line *n* **1 :** a row of dots on a paper indicating the place for a signature **2 :** a succession of dots as a guide for cutting or partial perforations resembling dots for easy detachment — **on the dotted line :** in full acceptance of a written statement or agreement; *esp* **:** in unquestioning acceptance of the binding terms of an engagement ⟨your signature *on the dotted line* guarantees freedom from worries about heat⟩

dotted manner *n* **:** MANIÈRE CRIBLÉE

dotted smartweed *n* **:** WATER SMARTWEED

dotted swiss *n* **:** a sheer muslin with open weave and crisp finish characterized by small evenly spaced dots woven in by the use of extra filling yarns and used esp. for clothing or curtains

¹dot·ter \'däd·ə(r)\ *vi* [ME *doteren,* perh. alter. of *toteren* to totter — more at TOTTER] *dial Brit* **:** to walk shakily **:** TOTTER

²dot·ter \'däd·ə(r), -ätə-\ *n* -s [²*dot* + *-er*] **1 :** one that makes dots **2 :** a worker who by means of a centering machine locates the optical and focal centers, axis, and terminal points of ground lenses to guide workers who will cut, edge, trim, and mount the lenses — called also *spotter* **3 :** a device for training gun pointers without using ammunition consisting of a vertically oscillating paper target close to the gun's muzzle that is dotted by an electrically operated pencil at the point at which the sights are directed when the pointer presses the firing key

dot·ter·el *or* **dot·trel** \'däd·ərəl, -ätərəl, -ä·trəl\ *n* -s [ME *dotrelle,* fr. *doten* to dote + *-erelle* (as in *cokerelle* cockerel) — more at DOTE, COCKEREL] **1** *sometimes pl* **dotterel** *or* **dotterel :** a plover (*Charadrius morinellus*) of Europe and Asia formerly common in England; *also* **:** any of various congeners chiefly of eastern Asia, Australia, and So. America that are highly regarded as table birds **2** *Brit* **:** a stupid foolish person **:** DOTARD

dot·ti·ly \'däd·ᵊlē, -ätᵊl, |ōlē, -i\ *adv* [²*dotty* + *-ly*] **1 :** with a feeble or unsteady gait **2 :** in a crazy manner

dot·ti·ness \|ēnəs, |in-\ *n* -ES [²*dotty* + *-ness*] **1 :** unsteadiness of gait **2 a :** FEEBLEMINDEDNESS, CRAZINESS ⟨was already showing such symptoms of future ~ as . . . greeting oak trees as old friends —*Time*⟩ **b :** droll eccentricity

dotting *pres part of* DOT

¹dot·tle *also* **dot·tel** \'däd·ᵊl, -ätᵊl\ *n* -s [ME *dottel, dotelle,* fr. (assumed) ME *dot* lump, dot — more at ¹DOT] **1** *obs* **:** PLUG **2 :** unburnt and partially burnt tobacco caked in the bowl of a pipe **:** HEEL

²dottle \"\ *adj* [Sc, fool, fr. ME *dotel,* fr. *doten* to dote — more at DOTE] *Scot* **:** FOOLISH, FEEBLEMINDED

³dottle \"\ *vt* -ED/-ING/-S [*dottle (pin)*] **:** to keep apart by dottle pins or by thimbles (as in glost firing)

dottle pin *n* [¹*dottle*] **:** a small plug or pin of burned fireclay used to separate articles during firing

dot·to·re \dō'tōrē, -ōr,ā\ *n, usu cap* [It, doctor, fr. L *doctor* teacher — more at DOCTOR] **:** a stock character in the commedia dell' arte represented as a windy pedantic jurist, philosopher, or physician ridiculed by the other characters

¹dot·ty \'däd·|ē, -ät|, |i\ *adj* -ER/-EST [¹*dot* + *-y*] **:** composed of or characterized by dots

²dotty \"\ *adj* -ER/-EST [alter. of ²*dottle*] **1 :** unsteady in gait **2 :** obsessed or infatuated with ⟨if your friend is so ~ about Judith, he'd better ask her to marry him —Edith Wharton⟩ **3 :** slightly unbalanced mentally **:** touched in the head **:** FEEBLEMINDED, ECCENTRIC ⟨her deliciously ~ Aunt Elinor, at the moment incarcerated in an expensive sanitarium —Florence Bullock⟩ **4 :** ABSURD, RIDICULOUS

doty \'dōd·|ē, -ōt|, |i\ *adj* -ER/-EST [¹*dote* + *-y*] **1** *of timber* **:** affected by incipient or partial decay often with discoloration **2** *South* **:** WEAK-MINDED; *esp* **:** having the mentality impaired in old age

douane \dwän\ *n, pl* **douanes** \-n(z)\ [F, fr. MF, fr. OIt *doana,* fr. Ar *dīwān,* fr. Per, account book — more at DIVAN] **:** CUSTOMHOUSE

doua·nier \dwänyā\ *n, pl* **douaniers** \-ā(z)\ [F, fr. MF, fr. *douane*] **:** a customs officer

dou·ar \dü'är, də'wär\ *n* -s [Ar *dawwār*] **:** an Arabian village consisting typically of a group of tents or huts that encircle an open space

¹dou·ble \'dəbəl\ *adj* [ME, fr. OF *doble, duble,* fr. L *duplus,* fr. *du-* (fr. *duo* two) + *-plus* multiplied by; akin to OFris *twīfil* doubt, OHG *zwīval,* Goth *tweifls* doubt, MIr *dīabul* double, Gk *diploos* double, OE *fealdan* to fold — more at TWO, FOLD] **1 :** having a twofold relation or character **:** combining two often dissimilar things or qualities **:** DUAL ⟨the wonderful ~ gift of seeing and saying —Carlos Baker⟩ ⟨a discussion of verbs with ~ function . . . verbs used both transitively and intransitively —A.M.Sturtevant⟩ **2 :** consisting of two usu. combined members, things, or sets **:** having two parts joined together **:** forming a pair ⟨~ balconies running around three sides of a grassy courtyard —Tom Marvel⟩ ⟨an egg with a ~ yolk⟩ **3 :** being two times as great or as many **:** multiplied by two **:** TWOFOLD ⟨the college had ~ the number of expected applicants⟩ ⟨was produced in quantities ~ the prewar output⟩ **4 :** characterized by duplicity **:** acting two parts or in two ways, one usu. being praiseworthy and the other blameworthy **:** DECEITFUL, HYPOCRITICAL, INSINCERE ⟨never speaks with a ~ tongue —T.B.Costain⟩ ⟨a ~ agent . . . pretending to serve the Nazis while actually working for the British —*N. Y. Herald Tribune*⟩ **5 :** folded in two **:** DOUBLED ⟨letters written on ~ sheets of stationery⟩ **6 :** made, being, or having parts twice as large, strong, or valuable: as **a** *of a coin* **:** worth two of the specified unit ⟨~ ducat⟩ ⟨~ taler⟩ **b** *printing* **:** of twice or almost twice the belly-to-back size of — used only of pre-point-system type names ⟨~ great primer⟩ ⟨~ paragon⟩ ⟨~ pica⟩; compare TWO-LINE **c :** having the shorter dimension doubled — used of a paper size ⟨crown is 15 x 20 and ~ crown is 30 x 20⟩; compare QUAD **7 a :** of extra size, strength, or value ⟨a mighty mug of . . . ~ ale —Lord Byron⟩ **b :** having more than the normal number of floral leaves often at the expense of the sporophylls ⟨~ stamens⟩ — used esp. of cultivated plants **8** *music* **a :** DUPLE 2a **b :** sounding an octave lower than the single or normal instrument **9 a** *of meter* **:** DUPLE 2b **b** *of rhyme* **:** having two syllables **10** *of a card game* **:** played with two full packs of cards mixed together ⟨~ pinochle⟩

²double \"\ *n* -s [ME, fr. *double,* adj.] **1 :** something twice the ordinary size, strength, speed, quantity, or value: as **a** (1) **:** an old French billon coin worth about two deniers (2) **:** a copper or bronze coin of Guernsey worth about ⅛ English penny **b :** any of various feasts in the Roman Catholic church ranking above a simple in order of precedence **c :** a 16-foot organ stop **d doubles** *pl* **:** a game between two pairs of players ⟨played three sets of ~*s*⟩ ⟨his ~*s* partner⟩ **e :** a two-base hit in baseball ⟨led the league in ~*s*⟩ **f** *Brit* **:** a double count made with a single stroke in billiards (as by pocketing both cue ball and object ball) **g :** the catching of two fish on one line at the same cast **h :** DOUBLE TIME — usu. used with *on* or *at* ⟨marched back again on the ~ —Earle Birney⟩ ⟨began to march at the ~ —Francis Hackett⟩ **i doubles** *pl* **:** sheet metal having a thickness of approximately $\frac{1}{32}$ inch **2 :** one that is the counterpart of another **:** COPY, DUPLICATE: as **a** (1) **:** a living person that closely resembles another living person ⟨thought I saw you on the street yesterday but it turned out to be your ~⟩ (2) **:** the apparition of a living person **:** WRAITH ⟨the appearance of a ~ or fetch has ever been held . . . to signify approaching death —R.A.Procter⟩ **b :** one who resembles an actor and who performs in his stead typically when the script requires special talent that the actor does not possess **c :** one (as an actor or singer) prepared to substitute for another in his absence **:** UNDERSTUDY **3 :** a twofold or repeated action: as **a** (1) **:** a sharp turn or reversal (as in running) (2) **:** an evasive shift (as in argument) **b** (1) **:** a 16th century court-dance step consisting of three steps and a close (2) **:** a folk-dance sequence of four running steps forward or backward **c** (1) **:** a musical variation (as in a classical suite) (2) **:** a repeated version of a movement of a musical composition (as a suite) with variation **d doubles** *pl* **:** the changes rung or capable of being rung on a set of five bells **e :** a twofold victory or defeat (as in two races on the same day or in a match and a return match) **4 :** something consisting of two paired members: as **a :** something doubled over or together **:** FOLD ⟨hit the horse with the ~ of his rope⟩ **b** *printing* (1) **:** DOUBLET (2) **:** a sheet inadvertently printed twice on one side **c :** DOUBLE STAR **d :** a letter occurring twice in succession in a word or in adjoining words of connected text **e :** a two-horse parlay **f :** DOUBLE JUMP 1 **g :** a double-barreled shotgun **h :** a domino with the same number of pips on each half **i :** two consecutive strikes in bowling **j :** two targets thrown simultaneously in skeet shooting **k :** a cricketer's feat of scoring 1000 runs and taking 100 wickets in one season **l doubles** *pl* **:** two fishing hooks fastened together at the shank so as to form a double hook **5 a** (1) **:** an act of doubling in card games (2) **:** the announcement by which a player in such games signifies that he doubles **b** (1) **:** a call in bridge that has the effect of increasing the points scored for odd tricks if the declarer fulfills his contract and for undertricks if he does not (2) **:** a hand strong enough to justify making such a call **c :** an act of doubling the stakes in backgammon

³double \"\ *vb* **doubled; doubled; doubling** \-b(ə)liŋ\ **doubles** [ME *doublen,* fr. OF *dobler, doubler,* fr. L *duplare,* fr. *duplus* double — more at ¹DOUBLE] *vt* **1 :** to increase by adding an equal quantity **:** multiply by two **:** make twice as great or as many ⟨his brother was *doubling* in this new will his posthumous provision for her —F.M.Ford⟩: as **a :** to be twice as great or as many as **:** amount to twice the number of ⟨births *doubled* deaths in the state last year⟩ **b** (1) **:** to line or cover (a wooden ship) with an additional layer of planking (2) **:** to line or trim (a garment) with additional material — now used chiefly in heraldry **c** (1) **:** to combine (as two slivers of yarn) by compressing or twisting into a single unit (2) *chiefly Brit* **:** PLY ⟨~ yarns⟩ **d** (1) **:** to add a note an octave above or below to (a specified note) (2) **:** to reinforce (a musical part) with an additional part having the same notes either at the same pitch or at the octave **e** (1) **:** to make a call in bridge that increases the value of odd tricks or undertricks at (an opponent's bid) (2) *Brit* **:** RAISE ⟨he *doubled* my poker bet⟩ **f** (1) **:** to advance (a base runner in baseball) by a two-base hit ⟨the batter walked and was *doubled* to third base⟩ (2) **:** to bring about the scoring of (a run in baseball) by a two-base hit ⟨*doubled* in two runs in the third inning⟩ **g :** to put out (a base runner in baseball) in completing a double play ⟨was *doubled* off second base when the batter lined to the shortstop⟩ ⟨forced the runner at second and was *doubled* at first base⟩ — sometimes used with *up* ⟨was *doubled up* at first⟩ **2 a :** to make of two thicknesses by turning or bending usu. in the middle **:** FOLD **b :** to close tightly (the hand or fist) **:** CLENCH ⟨he turned swiftly, *doubling* his fists —Hamilton Basso⟩ — often used with *up* **c :** to cause to stoop **:** BEND ⟨hit him in the stomach and *doubled* him over⟩ — often used with *up* ⟨*doubled* him up⟩ **3 a :** to avoid by doubling **:** ELUDE **b** *of a ship* **:** to sail around (as a cape) by reversing the direction of motion ⟨had *doubled* so many capes and run before the wind and brought back news of faraway men —Van Wyck Brooks⟩ **c** *Brit* **:** to cause (a billiard ball) to rebound **4** [trans. of F *doubler*] **a :** to replace in a dramatic role ⟨he was *doubling* the hero in a sword fight —Niven Busch⟩ **b :** to play (dramatic roles) by doubling ⟨~*s* the part of leader or squire with that of clown or entertainer —Douglas Kennedy⟩ **c :** to prepare (a talking part in a motion picture) for audiences speaking different languages ~ *vi* **1 :** to become increased to twice the ordinary size, strength, speed, quantity, or value **:** increase or grow to twice as much ⟨the population *doubled* in 10 years⟩: as **a :** to march at double time **b** (1) **:** to reread a line inadvertently ⟨lines sufficiently separated to prevent *doubling* —Stanley Morison⟩ (2) **:** to set a doublet **c** (1) **:** to double a bid (as in bridge) (2) **:** to propose that the stake be doubled (as in backgammon) **d :** to make a two-base hit in baseball ⟨*doubled* off the left-field fence⟩ **e :** to fire both rounds in a double-barreled shotgun with a single trigger pull **f :** to use an additional layer of planking on a wooden ship **2 a :** to turn sharply and suddenly in running; *esp* **:** to turn back on one's course — often used with *back* ⟨the rabbit *doubled* back on his tracks⟩ **b :** to follow a circuitous course ⟨a road . . . *doubled* round the hollow in a long sweep —H.E.Bates⟩ **c :** to enclose an enemy's fleet between two fires **d** *Brit* **:** REBOUND — used of a billiard ball **e** *archaic* **:** to make evasive shifts **:** act deceitfully ⟨if thy tongue ~*s* with me —Sir Walter Scott⟩ **3 :** to become bent or folded usu. in the middle **:** bend over — often used with *up* ⟨she *doubled* up with pain⟩ **4 a :** to serve an additional purpose or perform an additional duty ⟨a big gymnasium that ~*s* as an auditorium —C.B.Palmer b.1910⟩ ⟨court's switchboard operator was *doubling* as a receptionist —Katherine T. Kinkead⟩ **b :** to play an additional instrument — usu. used with *on* ⟨the guitarist *doubled* on piano⟩ **c :** to play two parts esp. in a dramatic production ⟨she *doubled* as the maid in the first act and the secretary in the third⟩ **d :** to play a dramatic role as a double ⟨*doubled* for the hero in the fencing match⟩ — **double in balk :** to leave the object ball and the cue ball in balk at the end of one's turn in billiards when the opponent's ball is not yet in play — **double in brass 1 :** to perform on a musical instrument other than one's regular instrument **2 :** to serve an additional purpose or perform an additional duty ⟨the jeep *doubled in brass* as a snowplow⟩ ⟨the announcer *doubled in brass* as the station's music librarian⟩ — **double the hill :** to cut a railroad train in half and take it over a hill in two sections because of the steep grade

⁴double \"\ *adv* [ME, fr. *double,* adj.] **1 a :** to twice the extent or amount **:** DOUBLY ⟨bright eyes were ~ bright —John Keats⟩ **b :** two together **:** in a pair ⟨some people sleep better ~ and some single —Morris Fishbein⟩ **2** *archaic* **:** with duplicity **:** DECEITFULLY ⟨if you should deal ~ with her —Shak.⟩ **3 :** downward and forward from the usual position ⟨he was bent ~ with pain⟩

⁵dou·blé \(')dü¦blā\ *adj* [F, past part. of *doubler* to line, fr. MF, to line, double — more at ³DOUBLE] *of a book cover* **:** made with a doublure

double account *n* **:** a system of accounting prescribed by British law for railway and public utility enterprises whereby permanent capital is offset against fixed assets purchased with monies contributed from permanent capital

double-acting \¦**=**¦**==**\ *adj* **:** acting or operating in two directions or with two motions ⟨a *double-acting* engine⟩ ⟨a *double-acting* pump⟩

double-action \¦**=**¦**==**\ *adj* **1 :** DOUBLE-ACTING **2** *of a firearm* **:** capable of being cocked and fired by a single pull of the trigger ⟨a fairly accurate *double-action* shot —Harry Reeves⟩

double-action harrow *n* **:** DOUBLE-DISC HARROW

double-and-twist \¦**==**¦**=**\ *n* **:** a two-ply yarn with contrasting colors

double appoggiatura *n* [trans. of It *appoggiatura doppia*] **1 :** two disjunct appoggiaturas above and below the principal note — see APPOGGIATURA illustration **2 :** two appoggiaturas occurring simultaneously in different voices or parts

double-aspect theory *n* **1 :** a philosophical theory that takes mind and body or the mental and the material to be related aspects of a single more ultimate reality — compare NEUTRAL MONISM **2 :** a philosophical theory that holds the conscious processes and the neural processes in the brain to be aspects of the same real series of events — compare INTERACTIONISM, PSYCHOPHYSICAL PARALLELISM

double assurance *n* [trans. of G *doppelte sicherung*] **:** dual control of differentiation resulting from synergistic interaction of a specific organizer and a competent embryonic tissue capable of self-differentiation in the absence of the organizer

double ax *n* **:** an ax with a 2-edged blade; *specif* **:** such an ax used as a sacred symbol in the art of prehistoric Crete and later associated with the worship of Zeus

double ballade *n* **:** a ballade having six stanzas and usu. an envoi

double-banked \¦**==**¦baŋkt, -aiŋ-\ *adj* **1 a** *of a rowboat* **:** having two banks of rowers sitting side by side **b** *of an oar* **:** manned by two rowers **2 :** having two tiers ⟨the bireme was a *double-banked* galley⟩ ⟨a *double-banked* frigate⟩ ⟨a *double-banked* organ⟩

double bar *n* **:** two adjacent vertical lines or a heavy single line separating principal sections of a musical composition — see BAR illustration

double-barrel \¦**==**¦**==**\ *n* **:** a double-barreled gun

double-bar·reled *or* **double-bar·relled** \¦**==**¦barəld *also* -ber-\ *adj* **1** *of a firearm* **:** having two barrels mounted side by side — compare OVER-AND-UNDER **2 :** TWOFOLD; *esp* **:** having a double purpose ⟨our *double-barreled* desire to make things profitable as well as attractive —Louis Kronenberger⟩

double-base powder *n* **:** an explosive powder or propellant that contains nitrocellulose and nitroglycerin as the essential components — compare SINGLE-BASE POWDER

double bass *n* [¹*double* + *bass*] **:** CONTRABASS

double bassoon *n* **:** CONTRABASSOON

double bed *n* **:** a bed designed for two persons

double-bed·ded \¦**==**¦bedəd\ *adj* **1 :** having two beds **2 :** furnished with a double bed

double bill *n* **:** a bill (as at a theater) offering two principal features

double-bit ax *n* **:** an ax having a head with two cutting edges

double-bitt \¦**==**¦\ *vt* [⁴*double* + *bitt,* v.] **:** to secure (a cable) by passing it around a pair of bitts

double-bit·ted \¦**==**¦bid·əd-\ *adj* **:** having two sharp edges ⟨a *double-bitted* ax⟩ — see AX illustration

double blossom *n* **:** a disease of dewberry and blackberry caused by a fungus (*Fusarium rubi*) and characterized by witches'-brooms and enlargement and malformation of the flowers

double boiler *n* **:** a cooking utensil consisting of two vessels, one fitting into the other, the contents of the upper being cooked by boiling water in the lower

double boiler

double bond *n* **:** a chemical bond consisting of two covalent bonds between two atoms in a molecule, usu. represented in chemical formulas by two lines, two dots, or four dots denoting two pairs of electrons (as in the formulas for ethylene $H_2C{=}CH_2$, $H_2C{:}CH_2$, or $H_2C{::}CH_2$) — compare TRIPLE BOND, UNSATURATED

double bottom *n* **1 :** the space in a ship between the inner bottom and the shell plating **2 :** a market decline on the stock exchange characterized by two successive low points and regarded by chart readers as a prelude to a recovery — compare DOUBLE TOP

double-breasted \¦**==**¦**==**\ *adj* **1** *of a coat or jacket* **:** having one half of the front lapped over the other and usu. a double row of buttons and a single row of buttonholes **2** *of a suit* **:** having a double-breasted coat

double brilliant *n* **:** a brilliant with 72 facets, 40 above and 32 below the girdle — called also *split brilliant, trap brilliant*

double-brood·ed \¦**==**¦brüdəd\ *adj* **:** producing two broods each year **:** BIVOLTINE

double buggy *n* **:** a buggy having two seats

double cabin *n* **:** a log cabin consisting of two rooms connected by a roofed passage

double canon *n* **:** a musical canon with two subjects

double capital *n* **1 :** a capital so carved as to suffice for two shafts **2 :** a capital having a dosseret

double carom *n* **:** a shot in certain table games (as pool) in which the cue ball strikes each of three object balls

double centner *n* **:** METRIC CENTNER

double chair *n* **1 :** a light chaise having two seats **2 :** a chair for two persons with the back formed by two chair backs joined together

double chant *n* **:** an Anglican chant 14 measures long and covering 2 verses

double check *n* [¹*double* + *check*] **1 :** a situation in chess in which the move of a checking piece discovers a check by another piece **2 :** a careful examination, investigation, or inspection designed esp. to determine accuracy, condition, or progress

double-check \ˈ=ˌ=\ *vb* [*double check*] *vt* **:** to subject to a double check ⟨the final version was *double-checked* for accuracy —*Time*⟩ ~ *vi* **:** to make a double check ⟨send his accountant to a publisher's office to *double-check* against the possibility of error —*Saturday Rev.*⟩

double chin *n* **:** a fleshy or fatty fold under the chin — **double-chinned** \ˈ=ˌ=\ *adj*

double chorus *n* **1 :** a musical composition for a divided choir **2 :** the two choirs singing a double chorus

double circulation *n* **:** a circulatory system in which the blood makes two distinct circuits — compare PULMONARY CIRCULATION, SYSTEMIC CIRCULATION

double-claw \ˈ=ˌ=\ *n* **:** UNICORN PLANT

double cloth *n* **1 :** a compound cloth consisting of two distinct fabrics united at regular intervals by having a thread of warp or filling passing from one to the other and used esp. for coating, blankets, and upholstery **2 :** a backed cloth

double-clutch \ˈ=ˌ=\ *vi* [¹*double* + *clutch*, n.] **:** to shift gear in an automotive vehicle usu. to a lower speed by shifting first into neutral and then to the speed required with the clutch being released each time

double coat *n* **:** a pelt (as of various dogs) consisting of a dense soft or woolly undercoat and a long coarse outer coat

double-coat·ed \ˈ=ˌ=ˈkōd·əd\ *adj, of paper* **:** having two coatings or a single heavy coating on one side

double coconut *n* **:** SEA COCONUT 1b

double column *n* **1 :** an advertisement covering the width of two columns (as of a newspaper) **2 :** a newspaper article having a headline and sometimes its body set two columns wide

double concerto *n* **:** a composition for two solo instruments with orchestra

double cone *n* **:** a complete cone formed by straight lines through the vertex, the straight lines being indefinitely extended in both directions — opposed to *half cone*

double consciousness *n* [prob. trans. of F *double conscience*] **:** the presence of two apparently unconnected streams of consciousness in one individual

double consonant *n* **1 :** a consonant letter occurring twice in succession in a word (as *nn* in *tunnel*) **2 a :** an acoustic impression apprehended or functioning as two consonants, produced by prolonging an articulation (as of \s\ in *bus seat*), by repeating an articulation (as of \r\ in Spanish *parra*, or by prolonging the interval between successive components of an articulation (as between the occlusion and the release of \t\ in *coattail*) **b :** a consonant produced by a simultaneous double articulation (as a \p\ pronounced with release of both lips and glottis) **c :** two different consonant sounds occurring in succession (as \mp\ in *stamp*)

double contraoctave *n* **:** SUBCONTRAOCTAVE

double contrast enema *n* **:** BARIUM ENEMA

double corner *n* **:** one of the two diagonally opposed corners of a checkerboard that have a light square flanked by two dark playing squares

double counterpoint *n* **:** 2-part counterpoint so constructed that either part may be above or below the other — called also *invertible counterpoint*

double couplers *n pl* **:** two coupling grabs united by a short chain or cable and used for fastening logs together

double-coursed \ˈ=ˌ=ˈkō(ə)rst, -ō(ə)rst,-ōəst,-ó(ə)st\ *adj* **:** having building cover (as shingles) placed so that all areas are covered with no less than two thicknesses of material

double-crested cormorant \ˈ=ˌ=ˌ=-\ *n* **:** a large long-tailed cormorant (*Phalacrocorax auritus*) with a tuft of feathers on each side of the head, present on both coasts of No. America and on inland waters north to Hudson Bay

double-crop \ˈ=ˌ=\ *vb* [⁴*double* + *crop*, v.] *vi* **:** to grow two or more crops on the same land in the same season or at the same time ⟨the land is so fertile that most ranchers *double-crop* —*Time*⟩ ~ *vt* **:** to cultivate for double-cropping ⟨part of the land is *double-cropped* —Royall Brandis⟩

double cross *n* [¹*double* + *cross*] **1 :** an act of treachery **:** BETRAYAL ⟨politics is too full of stories of *double crosses* and sellouts —D.D.McKean⟩ ⟨master of the art of the *double cross* —D.G.Haring⟩: **a :** an act of winning or trying to win a fight or match after agreeing to lose it **b :** an act of betraying a person with whom one is associated in an enterprise **2 :** a cross between first-generation hybrids of four separate inbred lines (as in the production of hybrid seed corn)

double-cross \ˈ=ˌ=\ *vt* [*double cross*] **:** to deceive by double-dealing **:** BETRAY ⟨don't go out on a limb for a man who may *double-cross* you tomorrow —Stanley Walker⟩ **syn** see DECEIVE

double-crosser \ˌ=ˈ=ˌ=\ *n* **:** one that double-crosses

Double-Crostic \ˌ=ˈkrȯstik, -räs-, -tēk\ *trademark* — used for a puzzle whose object is to fill in with words guessed from definitions a column of numbered dashes and then copy each letter in the correspondingly numbered square of a diagram so that words in the diagram form a quotation and the initial letters of the words in the column spell the author and title from which the quotation is taken

double-current signaling *n* **:** a system of telegraphy using both direct and inverse electric currents

double-cut file *n* **:** a file with a surface cut into two series of parallel ridges crossing each other usu. at less than a right angle, both ridges being diagonal to the center line of the file

double-cut saw *n* **:** a saw having teeth that cut during both the pushing and pulling strokes

doubled *past of* DOUBLE

double dagger *n* **:** the character ‡ used commonly as the third in the series of reference marks — called also *diesis*

double dash *n* **:** a graphic character consisting of two long parallel horizontal dashes of which the top one is heavy and the bottom one light that is sometimes used to mark page or column divisions in printed matter — called also *oxford dash*

double date *n* [¹*double* + *date*] **:** a date participated in by two couples

double-date \ˈ=ˌ=\ *vi* [*double date*] **:** to participate in a double date

double daylight saving time *n* **:** daylight saving time that is two hours in advance of standard time

double-dealer \ˌ=ˈ=ˌ=\ *n* **:** one who practices double-dealing

¹double-dealing \ˌ=ˈ=ˌ=\ *n* [¹*double* + *dealing*, fr. gerund of *deal*] **:** deception by action contradictory to an attitude professed or a role assumed **:** DUPLICITY ⟨incompetence in many places, ignorance in others, and downright *double-dealing* in still others —F.V.W.Mason⟩ **syn** see DECEPTION

²double-dealing \ˈ=ˌ=\ *adj* [⁴*double* + *dealing*, fr. pres. part. of *deal*] **:** given to or marked by duplicity

double-deck \ˈ=ˌ=\ *or* **double-decked** \ˈ=ˌ=ˈdekt\ *adj* **:** having two stories, decks, or levels ⟨a *double-deck* bus⟩ ⟨a *double-deck* bed⟩

double-decker \ˌ=ˈ=ˌ=\ *n* [*double deck* (fr. ¹*double* + *deck*) + *-er*] **1 :** a ship with two decks above the waterline **2 :** a conveyance with one level over another level for additional passengers, stock, or freight (as a railway car, bus, or airplane) **3 :** a house or building (as a 2-family tenement) having two stories **4 :** BIPLANE **5 :** something having two horizontal layers like decks: as **a :** a large machine having upper and lower operating platforms (as a printing press) **b :** two single beds one above the other **c :** a sandwich made of three layers of bread and two of filling **d :** an outdoor advertising stand with one billboard built on top of another **6 :** a long novel in two volumes

double decomposition *n* **:** a chemical reaction between two compounds in which part of the first compound becomes united with part of the second and the remainder of the first compound becomes united with the remainder of the second (as in AB + CD → AD + BC) — called also *metathesis*

double descent *n* **:** descent through both the patrilineal and the matrilineal group with attendant rights and obligations

double detection *n* **:** superheterodyne reception

double diapason *n* **:** a large open organ pipe yielding characteristic diapason tone at 16-foot or 32-foot pitch

double-disc \ˈ=ˌ=\ *vt* [⁴*double* + *disk*, v.] **:** to cultivate (soil) twice with a disc harrow either with a tandem disc or by lapping half of the width of a single disc on each round to provide a more even seedbed

double-disc harrow *n* [*double-disc* fr. ¹*double* + *disk*, n.] **:** a harrow with two sets of discs so arranged that one set throws soil outward and the other throws it inward — called also *double-action harrow*

double-distilled \ˈ=ˌ=ˌ=\ *adj* **:** being without any qualification or reservation **:** ABSOLUTE, THOROUGHGOING ⟨a *double-distilled* fool⟩

double-dog dare *vt, chiefly South & Midland* **:** to challenge defiantly

double-dome \ˈ=ˌ=\ *n* **:** EGGHEAD ⟨had demonstrated his machine to scores of scientific *double-domes* —W.M.Swann⟩

double door *n* **:** an opening provided with two vertical doors which meet in the middle of the opening when closed — compare DUTCH DOOR

double dot *n* **:** two points placed immediately after a musical note or rest to indicate augmentation of its time value by three-quarters

double dribble *n* **:** a dribble made in violation of the rules by a basketball player who has already completed a legal dribble

double drift *n* **:** a method of determining the speed and direction of the wind by measuring the drift angle on each of two aircraft headings at a known airspeed

double drum *n* **:** KETTLEDRUM 1

double drummer *n, Austral* **:** any of several noisy cicadas; *esp* **:** a large red and black form (*Thopha saccata*)

double dummy *n* **:** bridge or whist played by two players, each having a dummy and from observation of the two exposed hands and his own knowing the exact location of every card

double dutch *n, usu cap 2d D* **:** something that is unintelligible; *esp* **:** unintelligible speech

double-duty \ˈ=ˌ=\ *adj* **:** designed for two purposes or performing two duties

double-dyed \ˈ=ˌ=\ *adj* **1 :** dyed twice **:** thoroughly or intensely colored **2 :** confirmed esp. in habits or opinions **:** THOROUGHGOING ⟨a *double-dyed* villain⟩

double eagle *n* **1 :** a 20-dollar gold piece of the U.S. first issued in 1849 and last issued in 1933 — see EAGLE **2 :** a score of three under par made on a hole in golf

double edge *n* **:** FLAT 14b

double-edged \ˈ=ˈejd\ *adj* **1 :** having two cutting edges ⟨a *double-edged* sword⟩ **2 a :** having a dual purpose or effect ⟨fighter-bombers often carried out *double-edged* missions —*Coast Artillery Jour.*⟩ **b :** capable of being understood or interpreted in two ways **:** AMBIGUOUS, EQUIVOCAL ⟨the old-timers gave the new arrival a *double-edged* welcome —*Time*⟩

double-end·ed \ˈ=ˈendəd\ *adj* **:** similar at both ends ⟨a *double-ended* bolt⟩

double-end·er \ˌ=ˈendə(r)\ *n* [*double end* (fr. ¹*double* + *end*) + *-er*] **1 a :** a ship with bow and stern of similar shape **b :** a self-propelled vehicle (as a streetcar) constructed and equipped to permit normal operation in either direction **2** *or* **double-ender file** \ˈ=ˌ=ˌ=-\ **:** a file with teeth cut from both ends toward the middle

double englishman's knot *n, usu cap E* [¹*double* + *englishman's knot*] **:** BARREL KNOT b

dou·ble en·ten·dre \ˌdübəˌläⁿ(n·)ˈtäⁿ(n)dr(ᵊ), ˌdəbəˌlä-, ˌdüˌblä-, -län·ˈtän, \dr(rə)\ *n, pl* **double entendres** [obs. F, lit., double meaning] **1 :** ambiguity of meaning arising from language that lends itself to more than one interpretation ⟨rooted mainly in the basic humor of insult, malapropism, and *double entendre* —Wolcott Gibbs⟩ **2 :** a word or expression capable of two interpretations, one of them often having a risqué connotation ⟨a kind of old-fashioned bedroom farce with many of the *double entendres* that go with that form of entertainment —John McCarten⟩

double entry *n* **:** a method or system of bookkeeping that recognizes both the receiving and the giving sides of a business transaction by debiting the amount of the transaction to one account and crediting it to another account, the total debits in the system always equaling the total credits — compare SINGLE ENTRY

double envelopment *n* **:** simultaneous attack on both flanks of an enemy

double exposure *n* **:** two photographic exposures on the same sensitized surface

double-faced \ˈ=ˌ=\ *adj* **1 :** having two faces or sides designed for use ⟨*double-faced* clocks⟩: as **a** *of cloth* **:** finished on both sides **:** REVERSIBLE **b** *of corrugated paperboard* **:** having liners attached on both sides **c** *of a disc record* **:** having a recording on each side **2 a :** having two aspects **:** AMBIGUOUS ⟨these facts, as facts so often do, prove *double-faced* —Virginia Woolf⟩ **b :** given to duplicity **:** HYPOCRITICAL, INSINCERE ⟨a *double-faced* infernal traitor and schemer —W.M.Thackeray⟩

double fault *n* **:** two consecutive faults made while serving in tennis and resulting in the loss of a point

double feature *n* **:** a movie program consisting of two main pictures

double fertilization *n* **:** fertilization that is characteristic of most seed plants and that involves a fusion between the egg nucleus and a sperm nucleus, which results in the production of the embryo, and a fusion between the second sperm nucleus and the two separate or fused polar nuclei, which gives rise to the endosperm — compare XENIA

double first *n* **1 :** first-class honors in two different subjects esp. at Cambridge and Oxford universities **2 :** a student who takes a double first

double fisherman's knot *n* [¹*double* + *fisherman's knot*] **:** BARREL KNOT b

double flageolet *n* **:** a musical instrument of the flute family composed of two tubes connected to a single mouthpiece

double flaming *n* **:** the burning off of weeds with oil-burning equipment that throws flames on both sides of a row of plants

double flat *n* **:** a character ♭♭ placed after a note in musical notation that lowers its pitch by a whole step

double floor *n* **:** a floor in which binding joists support flooring joists above and ceiling joists below

double-fold \ˈ=ˌ=\ *adj* [ME, fr. ¹*double* + *-fold*] *archaic* **:** TWOFOLD

double foul *n* **:** two personal fouls in basketball committed by opponents against each other at the same time

double-framed floor \ˈ=ˌ=-\ *n* **:** a double floor having girders into which the binding joists are framed

double fugue *n* **:** a musical fugue with two subjects

dou·ble·gang·er \ˌdəbəlˈgaŋə(r), ˈ=ˌ=ˌ=\ *n* -s [part trans., part modif. of G *doppelgänger* — more at DOPPELGÄNGER] **:** DOPPELGÄNGER

double genitive *n* **:** DOUBLE POSSESSIVE

double glazing *n* **:** two layers of glass set in a window to reduce heat flow in either direction

double gown *n* **:** a heavy dressing gown usu. of reversible material

double-graft \ˈ=ˌ=\ *vt* **:** DOUBLE-WORK

double gun *n* **:** a double-barreled gun

¹doublehanded \ˈ=ˌ=\ *adj* [¹*double* + *handed*] **1 :** adapted for use with both hands (as by having two handles) **2 :** capable of double use, interpretation, or action

²doublehanded \"\ *adv* [¹*double* + *-handed* (as in *singlehanded*)] **:** with each of two persons helping the other ⟨captured an . . . admiral ~ —R.L.Taylor⟩

double-head \ˈ=ˌ=\ *vb* [back-formation fr. *doubleheader*] *vi* **:** to run powered by two locomotives ⟨the train *double-headed* up the mountain⟩ ~ *vt* **:** to pull (a train) with two locomotives ⟨the heavy coal trains were *double-headed*⟩

double-headed \ˈ=ˌ=\ *adj* **1 :** having two heads ⟨a *double-headed* muscle⟩ **:** BICIPITAL **2** *of a railroad rail* **:** having a dumbbell-shaped cross section keyed into chairs spiked to the ties

dou·ble·head·er \ˌ=ˈhedə(r)\ *n* [*double head* (fr. ¹*double* + *head*) + *-er*] **1 :** a railroad train pulled by two locomotives **2 a :** two games (as of baseball) played consecutively on the same day by the same teams **b :** two games (as of basketball) played consecutively on the same day by two different pairs of teams

double header \"\ *n* [*doubleheader*] **:** a door or window lintel made from two pieces of lumber placed upright next to each other and usu. nailed or bolted together

doublehearted \ˈ=ˌ=\ *adj* **:** having a dissembling heart

double house *n* **1 :** a house with rooms on each side of an entrance hall **2 :** a house divided vertically by a party wall and designed for two families living side by side

double-hung \ˈ=ˌ=\ *adj, of a window sash* **:** supported on each side by a counterweighted sash cord or a spring tension device for easy raising and lowering and holding position

double hyphen *n* **:** a punctuation mark = used in place of a hyphen at the end of a line to indicate that a word so divided is normally hyphenated

double indemnity *n* **:** a provision in a life-insurance or accident policy whereby the company agrees to pay twice the face of the contract in case of accidental death

double insurance *n* **:** several policies of insurance covering at least part of the same subject, having the same insurable interest, and subject to the same hazards

double jeopardy *n* **:** the putting of a person on trial for an offense for which he has previously been put on trial under a valid charge **:** two adjudications for one offense

double-jointed \ˈ=ˌ=\ *adj* **:** having joints that permit exceptional degrees of freedom of motion of the parts joined

double jump *n* **1 :** the action of capturing two checkers in successive jumps by the same man in one move **2 :** a double hurdle consisting typically of two fences set at such a distance that a horse must jump each in turn **3 :** a bid in bridge of two tricks more than necessary to overcall (as three spades over one club)

double-key cipher *n* **:** polyalphabetic substitution; *esp* **:** a Vigenère cipher with a key-word-mixed alphabet

double killing *n* **:** DOUBLE PLAY

doubleleaf \ˈ=ˌ=\ *n, pl* **doubleleaves :** a plant of the genus *Listera*; *esp* **:** TWAYBLADE

double letter *n* **1 :** LIGATURE **2 :** a letter written on two sheets and requiring double postage

double liability *n* **:** the liability of the owner of stock (as of a bank) that is subject to assessment up to its face value although orig. full-paid

double-lock \ˈ=ˌ=\ *vt* **:** to lock with two bolts or by two turns of the key **:** fasten doubly

double long *n* **:** LARGE 4

double-mate \ˈ=ˌ=\ *vt* **:** to practice breeding from distinctive matings of (poultry) to produce males and females of exhibition type esp. when the standards adopted for color for the two sexes differ (as in barred Plymouth Rocks)

double meaning *n* **:** DOUBLE ENTENDRE ⟨the men and girls strained to anticipate the *double meanings* —Charles Jackson⟩

double-minded \ˈ=ˌ=\ *adj* **1 :** wavering in mind **:** UNDECIDED, VACILLATING ⟨a *double-minded* man unstable in all his ways —Jas 1:8 (RSV)⟩ **2 :** marked by hypocrisy **:** INSINCERE

double monastery *n* [trans. of ML *monasterium duplex*, trans. of LGk *diploun monastērion*] **:** a religious community of men and women living in adjacent establishments, using the same church, governed by one superior, and usu. obeying the same rule

double mordent *n* **:** a melodic ornamentation consisting of four grace notes or tones preceding a principal note or tone and executed by a rapid alternation of a principal tone with its lower auxiliary tone

double-name paper *n* **:** TWO-NAME PAPER

double negative *n* **1 :** a now substandard syntactic construction containing two negatives and having a negative meaning (as in *I didn't hear nothing* meaning "I didn't hear anything") **2 :** a reiterated denial that equals an affirmative — compare NEGATION

double nelson *n* **:** FULL NELSON

dou·ble·ness *n* -ES [ME *doublenesse*, fr. ¹*double* + *-nesse* -ness] **:** the quality or state of being double or doubled

double-nose \ˈ=ˌ=\ *or* **double-nosed** \ˈ=ˈnōzd\ *adj* **:** having more than one growing point and usu. producing more than one flower stalk — used of narcissus and various other bulbs

double note *n* **:** BREVE 4b

double numeration *n* **:** the numbering of the pages of a book with one or more sets of numbers in addition to or in place of page numbers so that the first number in one representative system denotes chapter or section and the second number denotes page or numbered paragraph

double-o \ˌ=ˈ=\ *n* -s *often cap O* [so called fr. the two *O*'s in *once-over*] **:** a close examination or inspection ⟨gave the two strangers the well-known *double-o* —Walker Matheson⟩

double octave *n* **:** a musical interval of two octaves **:** FIFTEENTH

double or nothing *also* **double or quits** *of a bet or chance* **:** with the result being the cancellation or the doubling of a debt

double oxer *n* **:** an oxer with a guardrail on each side

double paddle *n* **:** a canoe paddle with a blade at each end used esp. with kayaks

double-page spread *n* **:** DOUBLE-SPREAD

double pair royal *n* **:** FOUR OF A KIND

double paper *n* **:** a paper composed of a thin surface layer and a thicker backing layer used in the printing of postage stamps esp. to prevent the removal of cancellation marks

double-park \ˈ=ˌ=\ *vb* **:** to park in a street next to automobiles parked parallel to the curb

double pedal point *or* **double pedal** *n* **:** two pedal points sustained through a succession of musical harmonies (as tonic and dominant)

double pedro *n* **:** ³CINCH

double-pitch \ˈ=ˌ=\ *adj* **:** pitched in two planes **:** sloping in two directions **:** GABLED ⟨a *double-pitch* roof⟩

double play *n* **:** a defensive play in baseball by which two players are put out ⟨grounded into a *double play* short to second to first⟩

double plea *n* **:** a plea in law alleging two or more distinct matters in answer to the declaration where either of such matters alone would be a sufficient bar to the action

double plow *n* **:** a plow with two different shares or discs: as **a :** a two-way plow that turns the soil in one direction while moving in the opposite direction **b :** a deep tiller that turns soil at two depths simultaneously

double pneumonia *n* **:** pneumonia involving both lungs

double point *n* **:** a point on a curve at which there are two tangents

double-pole switch *n* **:** an electrical switch having two blades with their contacts for simultaneous opening or closing both sides of a circuit

double ponceau R *n, usu cap D&P* **:** an organic pigment — SEE DYE table I (under *Pigment Red 54*)

double-pored tapeworm \ˈ=ˌ=-\ *n* **:** DOG TAPEWORM

double possessive *n* **:** a syntactic construction in English consisting of the preposition *of* followed by a noun in the possessive case (as *of Bill's* in *a friend of Bill's*) or by a possessive pronoun (as *of mine* in *this brain of mine*) and having the same meaning as if the idea of possession were expressed only once

double postal card *n* **:** a double-size postal card having two halves one of which is to be torn off and used for making reply to a communication on the other half with postage for the reply being paid by the original sender

double predestination *n* **:** the theological doctrine that God has chosen some to be saved and some to be lost — compare ELECTION, REPROBATION

double prime *n* **:** a symbol ″ suffixed to distinguish one character from a related character (as *a*″ from *a*′) or to indicate a relative unit (as a second of angle or an inch)

double-print \ˈ=ˌ=\ *vt* **:** to produce two images from two negatives in a fixed position on (a photoengraving plate)

double procession *n* **:** the theological doctrine of the procession of the Holy Spirit from the Father and the Son

double quartet *n* **1 :** a musical composition for eight voices or instruments **2 :** eight musicians performing a double quartet

double quatrefoil *n* **:** an ornamental foliation with eight foils used as the cadency mark of a ninth son

double–queued \ˌ¦=¦kyüd\ *adj* [¹*double* + F *queue* tail + E *-ed* — more at QUEUE] **:** having a double tail — used of a lion in heraldry

¹**double–quick** \ˈ==ˌ=, ˌ==ˈ=\ *n* [⁴*double* + *quick*, adj.] **:** DOUBLE TIME

²**double–quick** \"\ *vi* **:** DOUBLE-TIME

double–quirked bead \ˈ=ˌ=-\ *n* **:** a bead set off by two quirks — see BEAD illustration

¹**dou·bler** \ˈdübl(ə)r\ *n* -s [ME *dobler*, fr. MF *doblier*, *doublier*, fr. *doblier*, *doublier*, adj., double, fr. LL *duplarius*, fr. L *duplus* double + *-arius* -ary — more at DOUBLE] *dial Eng* **:** a large plate or bowl

²**dou·bler** \ˈdəb(ə)lə(r)\ *n* -s [³*double* + *-er*] **1 :** one that doubles: as **a :** a textile worker who doubles thread or folds cloth usu. by machine **b :** a textile machine for doubling yarn **2 a :** an instrument for so increasing a small initial quantity of electricity that it may be detected by the electroscope or the appearance of sparks **b :** an amplifier circuit whose output has twice the frequency of the input when the plate circuit is tuned to oscillate twice to each cycle of grid potential ⟨frequency ∼⟩ **c :** a rectifier circuit in which each blocked half cycle of input voltage charges a capacitor so connected as to add its discharge to the next forward cycle and thus double the rectified output voltage ⟨voltage ∼⟩ **3 :** a part of a distilling apparatus for intercepting the heavier fractions and returning them to be redistilled **4 :** either of a pair of mating crabs **5 :** a usu. fabric interlining that reinforces the lining of a shoe at vamp and tip

double raise *n* **:** a bid in bridge in the same suit as but two tricks higher than one's partner's bid and at least one trick more than is necessary to overcall any intervening bid

double reed *n* **:** two cane reeds bound together to form an air passage so that one can vibrate against the other and used as the mouthpiece of musical instruments of the oboe family

double–reef \ˌ==¦=\ *vt* **:** to reduce the spread of (a sail) by taking in two reefs

double–refined iron \ˌ===¦=-\ *n* **:** newly wrought iron made from iron rolled into bars that have been twice piled and rerolled

double refraction *n* **:** the refraction of light (as in most crystals) in two slightly different directions to form two rays — called also *birefraction*, *birefringence*

double rhyme *n* **:** end rhyme involving two syllables (as in *ceases* and *releases* or *inviting* and *exciting*) — compare FEMININE RHYME

double rhythm *n* **:** rhythm in which the thesis is twice as long as the arsis

double rifle *n* **:** a rifle having two barrels mounted side by side

double–ripper \ˌ==ˈ=\ *n*, *NewEng* **:** BOBSLED 2

double–rivet \ˌ==ˈ=\ *vt* **:** to rivet (a joint) in such a manner that all the rivets used are arranged in two rows if a lap joint or four rows if a butt joint

double root *n* **:** a root that appears twice in the solution of an algebraic equation

double rose *n* **:** a gem (as a diamond) cut so that it has 48 facets and the shape of two ordinary roses placed base to base

double round *n* **:** an archery round shot twice and the scores added

double rum *n* [¹*double* + *rum* (var. of *rummy*)] **:** COONCAN

double–runner \ˌ==ˈ=\ *n* **1** *NewEng* **:** BOBSLED 2 **2 :** a child's skate with two parallel blades

doubles *pl of* DOUBLE, *pres 3d sing of* DOUBLE

double salt *n* **1 :** a salt (as an alum) yielding on hydrolysis two different cations or anions **2 :** a salt regarded as a molecular combination of two distinct salts rather than as a coordination complex

double scull *vi*, *of a skater* **:** to move backward by weighting the inner edge of each skate and moving the feet alternately apart and together

double seamer *n* **:** a closing machine that rolls together the rims and lids of metal cans to make a hermetic seam

double–seater \ˌ==ˈ=\ *n* [*double seat* (fr. ¹*double* + *seat*) + *-er*] **:** TWO-SEATER

double series *n* **:** a mathematical series made up of terms each of which is itself a series

double–set trigger *n* **:** a set-trigger mechanism employing two triggers one in front of the other by means of which a very light trigger pull may be obtained

double sharp *n* **:** a character × or ※ placed after a note in musical notation that raises its pitch by a whole step

double shear *n* **:** simultaneous shear across two usu. parallel planes (as when a rivet passes through three thicknesses of metal)

double–shear steel *n* **:** shear steel that has been cut into shorter lengths, heated to a welding heat, piled, and rehammered into a single bar

double shuffle *n* **1 :** a clog dance characterized by fast syncopated taps of the feet **2 :** the characteristic step in the double shuffle

double–sided \¦==¦==\ *adj* **:** having two sides or aspects ⟨every stage of the process has a *double-sided* result —J.H. Muirhead⟩

double–sighted \¦==¦==\ *adj* **:** having double sight or two sights; *specif* **:** having unusual clearness of vision

double snipe *n* **:** GREAT SNIPE

double sole *n* **:** the foot of fine single-thread hosiery reinforced by knitting in an extra thread

double solitaire *n* **:** a card game for two in which each player plays his own game of Klondike or Canfield but can build upon his opponent's as well as his own aces, the winner being the one who has played the greater number of cards to the center

double–space \¦==¦=\ *vt* **:** to type (copy) leaving alternate line spaces blank ∼ *vi* **:** to type on every second line space

double spanish burton *n*, *usu cap S* **:** a tackle having one double block and two single blocks

double–spread \¦==¦=\ *n* **:** an advertisement that covers two facing pages (as in a newspaper) — called also *double-page spread*

double spruce *n* **1 :** BLACK SPRUCE 1 **2 :** WHITE SPRUCE 1a **3 :** FRASER FIR

double square *n* **:** ADJUSTABLE SQUARE

double standard *n* **1 :** BIMETALLISM **2 :** a set of principles that applies differently and usu. more rigorously to one group of people or circumstances than to another; *specif* **:** a code of morals that applies different and more severe standards of sexual behavior to women than to men — compare SINGLE STANDARD

double star *n* **1 :** BINARY STAR **2 :** two stars in very nearly the same line of sight but seen as physically separate by means of a telescope — called also *optical double star*

double–starred \¦==¦=\ *adj* **:** marked with a double star to indicate more than usual interest or excellence ⟨the places *double-starred* on my educational program —Hamlin Garland⟩

double steal *n* **:** a play in baseball in which each of two base runners steals a base

double stitch *n* **:** a stitch (as in a pamphlet) made by fastening two loops of a single thread in the center of the fold

¹**double–stop** \¦==¦=\ *vt* **:** to produce two or more tones simultaneously on (a stringed instrument)

²**double–stop** \"\ *n* **:** an instance of double-stopping ⟨his famous silken tone, his equally famous *double-stops* —Virgil Thomson⟩

double–strength \¦==¦=\ *adj*, *of glass* **:** having a thickness of 0.118 to 0.133 inch

double–struck \¦==¦=\ *adj*, *of a coin* **:** bearing a double impression as a result of having shifted between the dies

double substitution *n* **:** DOUBLE-KEY CIPHER

double summer time *n*, *Brit* **:** daylight saving time two hours ahead of standard time — abbr. *DST*

double–surfaced \¦==¦==\ *adj* **:** having two finished surfaces — used of airplane wings covered on both sides with fabric

double–swing door *n* **:** a door with hinges that permit it to swing either in or out

dou·blet \ˈdəblət, *usu* -əd+V\ *n* -s [ME, fr. MF, fr. OF, fr. *doble*, *double* double + *-et* — more at DOUBLE] **1 a :** a man's close-fitting garment for the upper body made with or without long sleeves and with or without short skirts, usu. padded, quilted, and decorated with slashes, embroidery, and jewels, and worn in western Europe esp. during the 16th and 17th centuries **b :** a quilted undergarment reinforced by rings of mail and worn under armor **2 :** something consisting of two identical or similar parts: as **a** (1) **:** a gem composed of two pieces of crystal or semiprecious stone sometimes with a layer of colored glass between them (2) **:** a piece of paste or glass covered by a veneer of real stone **b :** a lens consisting of two components (as for reducing aberration or increasing power); *specif* **:** a small magnifying hand lens consisting of two single lenses mounted in a metal cylinder and often with an attached metal carrying case **c :** a spectrum line having two close components **d :** a radio antenna of two wires pointing in opposite directions from the point where the power is supplied and usu. having dimensions that are small compared to the wavelength of the signal being used **e :** DOUBLE 4 h **3 :** a set of two identical or similar things **:** PAIR, COUPLE: as **a :** the result of a cast of two dice when each has the same number of spots on the face lying uppermost — usu. used in pl. **b :** two birds killed in the air at one time with a double-barreled gun **4 :** one of a pair **:** one of two identical or similar things: as **a :** one of two or more words in the same language derived by different routes of transmission from the same source (as English *dais* from Middle English *deis* from Old French *deis* from Latin *discus*, English *dish* from Middle English *dish* from Old English *disc* from Latin *discus*, and English *discus* from Latin *discus*) **b :** one or more characters or words typeset or typed twice by mistake — called also *double* **c :** material (as a news item) unintentionally repeated in an issue of a newspaper

doublet 1a

double take *n* **1 :** a delayed reaction to a surprising or significant situation after initial failure to recognize anything unusual — usu. used in the phrase *do a double take* ⟨we all did a *double take* at the sight of two housewives hanging out the family wash in a pouring rain —E.J.Moran⟩; *specif* **:** a technique of comic acting in which an actor at first reacts inappropriately (as if from absentmindedness) to a line of dialogue or to a situation and then quickly reacts appropriately **2 :** a second look ⟨bypassers sometimes gave the lawn a quick *double take* and went on —R.M.Yoder⟩

¹**double–talk** \ˈ==ˌ=\ *n* **1 :** language that appears to be earnest and meaningful but in fact is a mixture of sense and nonsense **:** GIBBERISH ⟨*double-talk* .. produces in the victim upon whom it is worked a strong suspicion that he is either hard of hearing or slowly going mad —*Life*⟩ **2 :** inflated, involved, and often deliberately ambiguous language **:** GOBBLEDYGOOK, JARGON ⟨lost in the miasma of *double-talk*, hypocrisy, and shortsightedness —R.E.Lauterbach⟩ ⟨writes the sort of *double-talk* which is all things to everybody —Max Lerner⟩

²**double–talk** \"\ *vi* **:** to use double-talk ⟨go on *double-talking* with him, always skirting the main subject but never touching it —Philip Barry⟩

double taxation *n* **:** the imposition by the same taxing body of two taxes on what is essentially the same thing (as in the case of taxing the income of corporations under the corporate income tax and taxing the part of corporate income distributed to stockholders as dividends under the personal income tax)

double–team \¦==¦=\ *vi* **1 :** to use two teams in hauling ⟨a steep sandy hill up which the wagons must be got by *double-teaming* —D.L.Morgan⟩ **2 :** to bring double force to bear — used with *on* or *upon* ⟨we *double-teamed* on one section of his army —T.E.Watson⟩ **3 :** to use two players to block or guard an opponent (as in football) ∼ *vt* **:** to block or guard (an opponent) with two players ⟨the center and left tackle *double-team* the guard —*Athletic Jour.*⟩

double ten *also* **double tenth** *n*, *usu cap D&T* [trans. of Chin *shuang¹ shih²*; fr. its being the tenth day of the tenth month] **:** October 10th celebrated by Nationalist China as the anniversary of the 1911 revolution against the Manchu dynasty

doublethink \ˈ==ˌ=\ *n* -s **:** the keeping of two contradictory ideas or opinions in one's mind at the same time and the conscious belief in both of them ⟨his mind slid away into the labyrinthine world of ∼ —George Orwell⟩

double thread *n* **:** two parallel threads of equal dimensions on the same screw one of which is 180° ahead of the other

double–threaded \¦==¦==\ *adj* **:** consisting of two threads twisted together **:** having or using two threads

double three *n* **:** a fancy skating figure resembling a cloverleaf and consisting of two threes executed in one circle

double–throw switch *n* **:** an electric switch having moving blades that may engage either of two different sets of fixed contacts

double time *n* [¹*double* + *time*] **1 :** a marching cadence of 180 36-inch steps per minute — called also *double-quick* **2 :** payment of a worker at twice his regular wage rate (as on holidays)

double–time \ˈ==ˌ=\ *vb* [*double time*] *vi* **:** to move at double time ⟨he reached the crest of the hill and *double-timed* over the top —A.C.Fields⟩ ∼ *vt* **:** to cause to move at double time ⟨they could *double-time* him forever and work him till he dropped —James Jones⟩

dou·ble·ton \ˈdəbəltən, -tᵊn\ *n* -s [¹*double* + *-ton* (as in *singleton*)] **:** an original holding (as in bridge) of two cards in any suit — compare SINGLETON

doubletone \ˈ==ˌ=\ *n* **:** a printing ink producing the effect of one hue in the parts printed in full color and another hue in parts printed less solidly

¹**double–tongue** \ˈ==ˌ=\ *n* [¹*double* + *tongue*, n.; fr. the foliose bract that grows from the cladophyll] **:** a dwarf shrub (*Ruscus hypoglossum*) of southern Europe

²**double–tongue** \¦==¦=\ *vi* [⁴*double* + *tongue*, v.] **:** to play a wind musical instrument by using the tongue in rapidly alternating articulations to produce enunciation of fast or repeated notes in groups of two

double–tongued \¦==¦=\ *adj* [ME *double tonged*, fr. ¹*double* + *tonged* tongued] **:** characterized by hypocrisy **:** INSINCERE

double–tongue graft *n* **:** a graft similar to a whip graft except that two clefts instead of one are made in both stock and scion

double–tooth \ˈ==ˌ=\ *n* -s [prob. trans. of NL *Bidens*, genus name] **:** a bur marigold (*Bidens cernua*)

double top *n* **:** a market rise on the stock exchange chart terized by two successive high points and regarded by chart readers as a prelude to a decline — compare DOUBLE BOTTOM

double topsails *n pl* **:** two sails used in square-rigged ships and made in the same width as but half the height of the old-fashioned topsail

double touch *n* **:** a mechanism in a pipe organ for causing one effect when keys or pistons are fully depressed and another when they are depressed only partly

double–track \¦==¦=\ *vt* **:** to furnish (a railroad) with two parallel lines of track

double transfer *n* **:** a double impression on a lithographed postage stamp produced in the transfer of the design to the stone

double transposition *n* **:** encipherment by successive transpositions usu. with different keys

dou·ble·tree \ˈdəbəl·(ˌ)trē,-l·tri\ *n* **:** an evener for use with a two-horse team

double–trip \¦==¦=\ *vi* **:** to tie up to the shore some of the barges in a tow, proceed through a difficult stretch of river with the others, tie them up, and return to pick up the barges left behind

double–trouble \¦==¦==\ *n* **:** a step in a rustic dance originated by plantation Negroes

double truck *n* [prob. fr. ¹*double* + *truck* (vehicle)] **:** a 2-page editorial or advertising layout (as in a newspaper) made up as a single unit

doublets *pl of* DOUBLET

dou·blette \düˈblet, ˌdəˈ-\ *n* -s [F, fr. *double* + *-ette*] **1 :** a 2-foot stop in a French pipe organ **:** FIFTEENTH 4a **2 :** MIXTURE STOP

double–u *also* **double–you** *same pronunc as at* w\ *n*, *sometimes cap U* **:** the letter *w*

double up *vi* **1 :** to share accommodations typically designed for one person or family ⟨you wouldn't mind *doubling up* with your brother —Marcia Davenport⟩ **2 :** to bet double the amount of the previous bet **3 :** to increase the mooring lines of a ship by putting out bights on lines already run

double vision *n* **:** DIPLOPIA

double wall *n* **1 :** a composite paperboard of two corrugations and three attached liners **2 :** a bag of two separate plies used for packaging — called also *duplex bag*

double weighing *n* **:** a method of weighing in which the object is balanced first on one pan and then on the other in order to eliminate any possible error from inequality in the balance

double whip *n* **:** a purchase consisting of two single blocks and a standing part not secured to one of the blocks

double whole note *n* **:** BREVE 4b

double window *n* **:** a window having two sets of glazed sashes with an air space between them

double wingback formation *or* **double wing** *n* **:** an offensive football formation in which two halfbacks play approximately one yard outside the offensive ends and one yard behind the line of scrimmage

double–work \¦==¦=\ *vt* **:** to propagate (a plant) by grafting or budding a scion to an intermediate piece of one variety grafted on a stock of another variety (as for overcoming incompatibility between scion and stock or for providing a superior trunk) — **double–working** *n*

double–woven \¦==¦==\ *adj* **1** *of cloth* **:** woven as a double cloth **2** *of pile cloth* **:** woven face to face and later cut apart **3** *of a single cloth* **:** having two finished sides

double zero *n* **:** a compartment on roulette wheels used in the U.S. that is colored green, marked 00, and equal in effect to the zero

doubling *n* -s [ME *doublinge*, fr. *doublen* to double + *-inge* -ing] **1 :** the act or process of one that doubles: as **a :** a sudden unexpected turn (as in running) **b :** the process of redistilling spirits to improve the strength and flavor **c :** a process for the treatment of antimony sulfide or crude antimony containing the sulfide by fusing it with iron or other antimony containing iron so as to form an iron sulfide the removal of which eliminates both iron and sulfur **d** (1) **:** the process of combining by machine two or more laps, slivers, or rovings into one lap, sliver, roving, or yarn (2) **:** the process of plying two or more yarns **e :** a reduplication of chromosomes **2 :** something used to make a second layer or thickness: as **a :** the lining of a garment — used esp. in heraldry **b :** DOUBLURE 1 **c :** a second thickness of planks or plates in a ship **3 :** something that is doubled: as **a doublings** *pl* **:** redistilled liquor **b :** the doubled border of a sail **c :** the overlapping part of each of two masts esp. of a lower mast and topmast — see SHIP illustration

doubling cube *n* **:** a cube used in backgammon to indicate the current value of the stake as a result of doubling

dou·bloon \ˌdəˈblün\ *n* -s [Sp *doblón*, aug. of *dobla*, old Spanish gold coin, fr. L *dupla*, fem. of *duplus* double — more at DOUBLE] **1 :** an old gold coin of Spain and Spanish America worth 8 gold escudos or 16 pieces of eight **2 :** OCHER BROWN

dou·blure \ˌdəˈblü(ə)r, düˈ-\ *n* -s [F, fr. MF, lining of a garment, fr. *doubler* to line, double + *-ure* — more at DOUBLE] **1 :** the lining of a book cover; *esp* **:** an ornamental lining (as of tooled leather, painted vellum, or rich brocade) **2 :** the reflexed margin of a trilobite's carapace

dou·bly \ˈdəb(ə)lē, -li\ *adv* [ME, fr. ¹*double* + *-ly*] **1 a :** to twice the degree **:** in twice the quantity ⟨this responsibility is ∼ heavy —Hunter Mead⟩ ⟨would now be ∼ certain to investigate —T.B.Costain⟩ **b :** in a twofold manner **:** in two degrees — used chiefly in botany ⟨∼ crenate⟩ ⟨∼ dentate⟩ **2** *obs* **:** in a deceitful manner **:** DISHONESTLY ⟨they lay a man under a necessity to deal ∼ with them —Samuel Richardson⟩

doubly ruled surface *n*, *math* **:** a ruled surface with two systems of rulings or generators; *specif* **:** a quadric surface

¹**doubt** \ˈdau̇t, *usu* -au̇d·+V\ *vb* -ED/-ING/-S [ME *douten* to fear, doubt, fr. OF *douter*, fr. L *dubitare* to doubt; akin to L *dubius* doubtful — more at DUBIOUS] *vt* **1** *archaic* **a :** to be afraid of **:** FEAR — used with an infinitive phrase or a clause as object ⟨I ∼ I have been beguiled —Sir Walter Scott⟩ **b :** to be apprehensive of (something feared or not desired) ⟨fear nought — nay, that I need not say — but ∼ not aught from mine array —Sir Walter Scott⟩ **2 :** to be in doubt about; *specif* **:** to be uncertain or undecided in opinion of or belief in ⟨begins to ∼ all the maxims he has hitherto accepted —Bertrand Russell⟩ **3 a :** to lack confidence in **:** DISTRUST, SUSPECT ⟨find myself ∼*ing* him even when I know that he is honest —H.L.Mencken⟩ **b :** to be inclined not to believe or accept **:** consider unlikely or improbable ⟨I ∼ that they would have helped me —George Santayana⟩ ⟨I ∼ whether the facts bear him out —Adelaide Hahn⟩ ⟨I ∼ if he ever wrote a single paragraph that was not carefully planned —Deems Taylor⟩ ⟨ready to fight anyone who dared to ∼ its success —Sherwood Anderson⟩ ∼ *vi* **1 :** to be in doubt; *specif* **:** to be uncertain or undecided in opinion or belief ⟨its obvious elements are willingness to hold belief in suspense, ability to ∼ until evidence is obtained —John Dewey⟩ **2** *archaic* **:** HESITATE, SCRUPLE ⟨hath not ∼*ed* to assert that you may see a spirit in open daylight —Henry Fielding⟩

²**doubt** \"\ *n* -s [ME *doute* fear, doubt, fr. OF, fr. *douter*] **1 a :** uncertainty of belief or opinion; *specif* **:** the subjective state of being uncertain of the truth of a statement or the reality of an event as a result of incomplete knowledge or evidence ⟨like one that prayed in sorrow, under some extremity of ∼, for light that should guide him to the better choice —Thomas De Quincey⟩ **b :** a deliberate suspension of judgment or withholding of belief ⟨took his point of departure in something deeper than an abstract intellectual ∼, namely, in a concrete personal despair —D.F.Swenson⟩ — compare CARTESIANISM, SKEPTICISM **c :** a systematic weighing of the reasons for holding a belief or opinion ⟨∼ is the beginning and the end of our efforts to know —William Hamilton †1856⟩ **2 :** the condition of being objectively uncertain **:** a state of affairs giving rise to uncertainty, hesitation, or suspense ⟨there were four states whose votes were in ∼ —Carol L. Thompson⟩ **3 :** a feeling of uncertainty ⟨had already fallen a prey to those ∼*s* and misgivings which are ever the result of a lack of decision —Theodore Dreiser⟩ **4** *obs* **:** an uncertain or unsettled point or matter **:** DIFFICULTY ⟨and I have heard of thee, that thou canst make interpretations and dissolve ∼*s* —Dan 5:16 (AV)⟩ **5 a :** a lack of confidence **:** DISTRUST, SUSPICION ⟨the ∼ everyone felt concerning his past —Sherwood Anderson⟩ ⟨their mutual ∼*s* and suspicions . . have been enhanced rather than alleviated by the war —Vera M. Dean⟩ **b :** an inclination not to believe or accept **:** QUESTION ⟨there can be little ∼ that in matters of literary style the sovereign virtue . . . is clearness —B.N. Cardozo⟩ **syn** see UNCERTAINTY — **no doubt :** DOUBTLESS

doubt·able \ˈdau̇d·əbəl, -au̇tə-\ *adj* [ME *doutable*, fr. MF, causing doubt, doubting, fr. LL & L; LL *dubitabilis* doubting, fr. L, capable of being doubted, fr. *dubitare* to doubt + *-abilis* -able] **:** capable of being doubted **:** QUESTIONABLE

doubtedly *adv* [*doubted* (fr. past part. of ¹*doubt*) + *-ly*] *obs* **:** DOUBTFULLY, QUESTIONABLY

doubt·er \ˈdau̇d·ə(r), -au̇tə-\ *n* -s **:** one that doubts **:** SKEPTIC, UNBELIEVER

¹**doubt·ful** \ˈdau̇tfəl\ *adj* [ME *douteful*, fr. *doute* doubt + *-ful*] **1 :** giving rise to doubt **:** open to question **:** not obvious, clear, or certain **:** not easily defined, classed, or named ⟨a method of investigation whose object is the establishment of truth about ∼ propositions —R.M.Weaver⟩ ⟨it is ∼ whether the captain had ever had so much fun —John Steinbeck⟩ **2** *archaic* **a :** giving rise to apprehension **:** PERILOUS ⟨reported the ∼ and dangerous situation of the empire —Edward Gibbon⟩ **b :** full of apprehension **:** FEARFUL ⟨I hear things which make me ∼ and anxious —Edmund Burke⟩ **3 a :** lacking settled opinion, conviction, or determination **:** unsure

about beliefs, observations, or decisions : WAVERING, HESITATING ⟨even after they had been assured . . . they looked ~ —Harold Griffin⟩ ⟨some were ~ how the law would hold —Alfred Tennyson⟩ **b** : uncertain in outcome, issue, or result : UNDECIDED ⟨were fighting a ~ battle in which victory was not assured —D.W.Brogan⟩ **c** : not certain or easily predictable in regard to political preferences : likely to be carried by either political party ⟨concentrated on winning the electoral votes of the ~ states⟩ **4** : characterized by qualities that impugn and raise often well-founded doubts about worth, honesty, or validity : of uncertain worth or soundness : of equivocal character ⟨the only difference between themselves and others is that they are nice men and the others of very ~ repute —T.S.Eliot⟩ ⟨she wrote rather ~ grammar —W.M.Thackeray⟩

syn DUBIOUS, PROBLEMATICAL, PROBLEMATIC, QUESTIONABLE: DOUBTFUL and DUBIOUS indicate uncertainty and indecision in reference to persons or uncertainty, undeterminedness, or unpredictability in reference to events and situations. DOUBTFUL simply indicates lack of certainty or conviction; DUBIOUS stresses lack of these qualities to somewhat greater degree ⟨she takes me in, telling me there's nobody there. I'm *doubtful*, but she swears she's alone —Dashiell Hammett⟩ ⟨there is the defense of Egypt and the Canal, against greatly superior numbers of the enemy, which six months ago, at all events, looked rather a difficult affair, a *doubtful* affair —Sir Winston Churchill⟩ ⟨the president-elect had expressed the opinion that government, after all, was a pretty simple business. He is now to put that hopeful theory to the test. Friendly counselors thought the prospect more *dubious* —S.H.Adams⟩ In reference to value judgments, PROBLEMATICAL and PROBLEMATIC describe something of the nature of a problem or refer to a situation with a quite unpredictable outcome ⟨at present it is easy to make rash predictions. Publishing is now in a very *problematic* state —J.T.Farrell⟩ ⟨effect of the union endorsement on the labor vote is *problematical* —*New Republic*⟩ Often DOUBTFUL so strongly questions worth, honesty, or validity that it implies their absence or lack ⟨in very many interpretations where words play no recognizable part, introspection, unless excessively subtle and therefore of *doubtful* value as evidence, fails to show the imagery is present —C.K.Ogden & I.A.Richards⟩ ⟨the builder, on the other hand, who had spent a long life of constant industry, but *doubtful* honesty, in scraping up a decent fortune —Anthony Trollope⟩ Not so strong, DUBIOUS stresses suspicion or mistrust, perhaps well grounded ⟨all sorts of dogmatic standards have been set up by which to measure the degree of a people's civilization . . . Yet the more carefully we look into the nature of these standards the more *dubious* they become —Havelock Ellis⟩ ⟨millions were stolen outright, and additional millions . . . poured into *dubious* railroads and business ventures which rarely repaid ten cents on the dollar —Allan Nevins & H.S.Commager⟩ QUESTIONABLE may mean simply open to question ⟨the detailed study of history should be supplemented by brilliant outlines, even if they contained *questionable* generalizations —Bertrand Russell⟩ It often describes falsity, unsoundness, or immorality to such a degree that it may be commonly believed in but may be asserted only in guarded statements or hints ⟨the virtues that feed on suffering are very *questionable* virtues —G.B.Shaw⟩

²**doubtful** \"\ *n* -s : one that is doubtful

doubt·ful·ly \-fəlē, -li\ *adv* [ME *doutefully*, fr. *douteful* + *-ly*] : in a doubtful manner ⟨looking ~ at it two or three times as if to be sure that it was really there —Charles Dickens⟩

doubt·ful·ness \-fəlnəs\ *n* -ES : the quality or state of being doubtful : UNCERTAINTY

doubting *pres part of* DOUBT

doubt·ing·ly *adv* : in a manner that indicates doubt

doubting mania *n* [prob. trans. of F *folie du doute*] : compulsive doubt and indecision permeating the entire personality

doubt·ing·ness *n* -ES : the quality or state of one that doubts

doubting thom·as \-'täməs\ *n*, *usu cap T* [after *Thomas*, one of Jesus' twelve apostles, who according to Jn 20:24–29 doubted Jesus' resurrection until he had proof of it] : an incredulous or habitually doubtful person : DOUBTER ⟨even the *doubting Thomases* . . . were forced to admit the fertility of the black soil —R.H.Brown⟩

¹**doubt·less** \'dau̇tləs\ *adv* [ME *douteles*, fr. *doute* doubt + *-les* (adv. suffix), fr. *-lees* (adj. suffix) -less] **1** : without doubt : UNQUESTIONABLY ⟨was ~ the smartest girl in her class⟩ **2** : in all probability : PRESUMABLY

²**doubtless** \"\ *adj* [ME *douteles*, fr. *doute* doubt + *-lees* -less] **1** : free from doubt : CERTAIN ⟨one of the ~ sources of many Shakespearean quotations —*Notes & Queries*⟩ **2** *obs* : free from fear or suspicion ⟨pretty child, sleep ~ and secure —Shak.⟩ — **doubt·less·ly** *adv*

doubt·less·ness *n* -ES : the quality or state of being doubtless

doubts *pres 3d sing of* DOUBT, *pl of* DOUBT

doubt·some \'dau̇tsəm, 'düt-\ *adj*, *dial Brit* : DOUBTFUL

douc \'dük\ *n* -s [native name in Cochin China] : a monkey (*Presbytis nemaea*) of Cochin China remarkable for its variegated colors

douce \'düs\ *adj* [ME, fr. MF, fr. OF, fem. of *douz*, fr. L *dulcis* — more at DULCET] **1** *obs* : SWEET, PLEASANT ⟨the ~ sound of harps —Patrick Forbes⟩ **2** *dial Brit* **a** : HOSPITABLE, GENIAL, CHEERFUL **b** : MODEST **c** : NEAT, TIDY **3** *chiefly Scot* : DECOROUS, RESPECTABLE, SEDATE ⟨the ~ faces of the mourners —L.J.A.Bell⟩ **4** [F (fem. of *doux* sweet), fr. OF, fem. of *douz*] : DOLCE — used as a direction in music — **douce·ly** *adv*

douce·pere \'düs(ə),pi(ə)r, -pe(-\ *n* -s [ME *dosepers*, back-formation fr. *doseperes*, pl., the twelve peers of Charlemagne, fr. OF *doze pers*, *doze per*, lit., twelve peers] *archaic* : an illustrious noble; *specif* : one of the twelve peers of Charlemagne's guard of honor

doucets *var of* DOWSETS

dou·ceur \(')dü¦sər\ *n* -s [F, sweetness to the sense of taste, pleasantness, fr. LL *dulcor*, fr. L *dulcis* sweet] **1** *archaic* : gentleness and sweetness of manner : AMIABILITY ⟨answered with all his accustomed ~ and politeness —Fanny Burney⟩ **2** *archaic* : an amiable remark : COMPLIMENT ⟨such elaborate ~s . . . look too much like adulation —*Edinburgh Rev.*⟩ **3** : a conciliatory gift : GRATUITY, PRESENT ⟨would not give permission for the train to go out until he received a substantial ~ —*N.Y.Times*⟩

¹**douche** \'düsh\ *n* -s [F, fr. It *doccia*, fr. *docciare* to gush, pour, fr. *doccia* water pipe, prob. back-formation fr. *doccione* conduit pipe, fr. L *duction-*, *ductio* action of leading or conducting, fr. *ductus* (past part. of *ducere* to lead) + *-ion-*, *-io* -ion — more at TOW] **1 a** : a jet or current (as of water) directed against a part or into a cavity of the body **b** : a bath taken by means of a douche **2** : a device (as a syringe) for giving douches

²**douche** \"\ *vb* -ED/-ING/-S *vt* : to administer or apply a douche to : DRENCH ~ *vi* : to take a douche

dou·cine \(')dü¦sēn\ *n* -s [F, fr. MF *doulcine*, prob. fr. *doulz*, *doux* sweet, fr. OF *douz*] : a molding that is convex and concave in continuous curve : CYMA

doudle *var of* ³DOODLE

douf \'dau̇f\ *var of* DOWF

doug \'dau̇g\ *Scot var of* DOG

¹**dough** \'dō\ *n* -s [ME *dogh*, fr. OE *dāg*; akin to OHG *teic* dough, ON *deig*, Goth *daigs* dough, *digan* to mold, shape, L *fingere* to shape, Gk *teichos* wall, Skt *degdhi* he smears] **1** : a mixture of flour and other ingredients stiff enough to knead or roll — compare BATTER **2** : something resembling dough esp. in consistency: as **a** : a soft mass of rubber and other ingredients produced during the mixing and vulcanizing processes **b** : the material from which puppies used by bookbinders are made **3** : MONEY, CASH ⟨bright young graduate students who needed to pick up a little ~ on the side —Dwight Macdonald⟩ **4** : DOUGH STAGE ⟨grain in the ~⟩ **5** [short for *doughboy*] : INFANTRYMAN

²**dough** \"\ *vb* -ED/-ING/-S *vi* : to make dough : become dough or like dough ~ *vt* : to make (a mixture) into or like dough; *specif* : to mix (malt) with water to form mash — usu. used with *in*

dough–baked \'=,=\ *adj* **1** *obs* : imperfectly baked : DOUGHY **2** *dial Eng* : HALF-WITTED, STUPID

doughball \'=,=\ *n* **1** : a small lump of dough usu. cooked with meat or vegetables **2** : a small quantity of dough used as bait for fishing

doughbelly \'=,==\ *n*, *West* : a pail-fed calf

doughbird \'=,=\ *n* : ESKIMO CURLEW

doughboy \'=,=\ *n* **1 a** *chiefly Brit* : a flour dumpling **b** : a piece of bread dough fried in deep fat and served as a hot bread **2** [prob. so called fr. the large round brass buttons on the U.S. infantry uniform in the Civil War] : INFANTRYMAN **3** : a small flattish brightly colored edible scallop (*Mimachlamys asperrimus*) common off the southern coast of Australia and about Tasmania

dough·er·ty wagon \'dō|ərd·ē-, 'dä|, 'dȯ|, 'däg|, 'dȯg|; ÷'dȯrəd·ē-, ÷'därəd·ē-\ *n*, *often cap D* [prob. fr. the name *Dougherty*] : a four-wheeled covered wagon with side doors, two or three transverse seats for passengers, and canvas side curtains

doughface \'=,=\ *n* **1** : FALSE FACE, MASK **2 a** : a congressman from a northern state who did not oppose slavery **b** : a northerner sympathetic to the South during the Civil War

dough–faced \'=¦=\ *adj* : having the traits of a doughface

doughfoot \'=,=\ *n*, *pl* **doughfeet** *or* **doughfoots** *slang* : INFANTRYMAN

dough god \'=,=\ *n*, *North & West* : a fried biscuit

doughhead \'=,=\ *n*, *slang* : BLOCKHEAD, FOOL

dough·i·ness \'dōēnəs, -ōin-\ *n* -ES : the quality or state of being doughy

doughlike \'=,=\ *adj* : resembling dough

dough·nut \'dō(,)nət, *usu* -əd·+V\ *n* -s **1** : a small cake fried in deep fat: as **a** : one typically ring-shaped made of rich dough leavened usu. with baking powder **b** : one shaped like a ring or a ball and made of yeast-leavened dough — called also *raised doughnut* **2** : something resembling a doughnut esp. in shape

doughnut tire *n* : a balloon tire extra large in annular section and requiring very low air pressure

dough stage *n* : a stage in the development of cereal grains when the interior of the kernel is of doughlike consistency

dought \'däkt\ [ME *doughte*, fr. OE *dohte*; akin to OHG *tohta* had worth — more at DOW] *chiefly Scot past of* ¹DOW

dough·ti·ly \'dau̇d·ᵊlē, -au̇t|, |ᵊlē, -li\ *adv* [ME, fr. *doughty* + *-ly*] : in a doughty manner

dough·ti·ness \|ēnəs, |in-\ *n* -ES [ME *doughtinesse*, fr. *doughty* + *-nesse* -ness] : the quality or state of being doughty

dough tray *or* **dough trough** *n* : a piece of kitchen furniture consisting of a trough for holding rising dough and a removable flat top on which the dough is kneaded — called also *kneading table*

dough·ty \|ē, |i\ *adj* -ER/-EST [ME, fr. OE *dohtig*, prob. alter. (influenced by *dohte* dought) of *dyhtig*; akin to MD *duchtich* strong, MHG *tühtec* good for something, OE *dēah*, *dēag* have worth, OHG *toug*, Goth *daug* have worth, Gk *teuchein* to make, build, Lith *daug* much, and perh. to Skt *dogdhi* he milks] : marked by fearless resolution and by stoutness in contest or struggle : ABLE, STRONG, VALIANT ⟨the ~ little man had not a hand's breadth on head or arm without its scar —Charles Kingsley⟩ ⟨he was a soldier's soldier — rough, tough, and ~ —Frederick Nebel⟩ **syn** see BRAVE

doughy \'dōē, -ōi\ *adj*, *usu* -ER/-EST [¹*dough* + *-y*] : having the characteristics of dough esp. in appearance or consistency: as **a** : not thoroughly baked ⟨~ bread⟩ **b** : unhealthily pale ⟨his face had gone a little ~ but his voice was almost normal —Dashiell Hammett⟩ **c** : heavy and formless ⟨the radio was still sending forth the ~ music of the organ —Irwin Shaw⟩ **d** : soft and lifeless ⟨all that ~, woolly, anodyne writing that exists merely to fill a gap of leisure —Aldous Huxley⟩

doug·las fir *also* **douglas spruce** *or* **douglas pine** *or* **douglas hemlock** \'dəgləs-\ *n*, *usu cap D* [after David *Douglas* †1834 Scot. botanist in America] : a tall evergreen timber tree (*Pseudotsuga menziesii* or *P. taxifolia*) of the western U. S. having thick bark, pitchy wood, and pendulous cones, with bracts that protrude conspicuously beyond the cone scales — called also *Oregon pine*, *red fir*

douglas–fir beetle *also* **douglas fir bark beetle** *n*, *usu cap D* : a bark beetle (*Dendroctonus pseudotsugae*) very destructive to Douglas fir and sometimes to western larch

douglas–fir tussock moth *n*, *usu cap D* : a dull-colored moth (*Hemerocampa pseudotsugata*) with a red-spotted hairy larva that feeds on and may seriously defoliate Douglas fir and sometimes other firs

doug·la·site \'dəglə,sīt, 'dùg-\ *n* -s [G *douglasit*, fr. *Douglashall*, near Stassfurt, Germany, its locality + G *-it* -ite] : a mineral $K_2[FeCl_4.2H_2O]$(?) consisting of a hydrated potassium iron chloride

douglas's cul–de–sac *or* **douglas's fossa** *or* **douglas's pouch** *n*, *usu cap D* [after James *Douglas* †1742 Scot. anatomist] : POUCH OF DOUGLAS

doug·las squirrel \'dəgləs-\ *n*, *usu cap D* [after David *Douglas* †1834] : a large ground squirrel (*Tamiasciurus douglasii*) of the western coastal area of No. America typically grizzled gray with a wedge-shaped black mark on the nape

dou·kho·bor *or* **du·kho·bor** \'dükə,bȯ(ə)r\ *n*, *pl* **doukhobors** *or* **doukhobors** \-rz\ *also* **dukho·bor·tsy** \,dükə'bȯrtsē\ *usu cap* [Russ *dukhoborets*, fr. *dukho-* (fr. *dukh* spirit) + *borets* wrestler, fr. *borot'* to overcome; akin to Lith *dvasas* spirit breath and to L *ferire* to strike — more at DUST, BORE] : a member of a Russian sect originating in the 18th century that emphasizes the supreme authority of inner experience, that believes in the embodiment of the Spirit in different persons whom it follows as prophets and leaders, and that rejects all external ecclesiastical and civil authority (as by refusing to do military service or pay taxes)

doum \'düm, 'dau̇m\ *also* **doum palm** *n* -s [F *doum* — more at DOOM PALM] : DOOM PALM

douma *var of* DUMA

doun·da·ké \dün'däkē\ *or* **doundaké bark** *n* -s [Wolof *dundaké*, a creeper] : the bark of the country fig formerly used as an astringent and febrifuge

doup \'dau̇p, 'dəu̇p\ *n* -s [modif. of D *dop* eggshell, fr. MD; akin to MLG *dop* pot, MHG *topf*, and prob. to OE *dyppan* to dip — more at DIP] **1** *Scot* : the end or bottom of something: as **a** : the rounded end of an egg **b** : the end of a burned-down candle **c** : BUTTOCKS **2** : a special heddle used in leno weaving

do up *vt* **1 a** : to clean and make ready for use or wear : LAUNDER ⟨the only laundress left who knew how to *do up* damask —Josephine Pinckney⟩ **b** : to put in order : straighten up ⟨one of the girls was sick and I had to help to *do up* the rooms —Henry Lapham⟩ **c** : REPAIR, RENOVATE ⟨for years no one . . . had their houses *done up* —John Galsworthy⟩ **2 a** : to wrap up ⟨are now *done up* in neat bundles —Creighton Peet⟩ **b** : to put up : CAN ⟨*did up* two bushels of peaches⟩ **3 a** : to arrange and fasten (the hair) in place ⟨her golden hair was *done up* on the top of her head —John Steinbeck⟩ **b** : to deck out : CLOTHE ⟨the waitresses are *done up* in abbreviated bloomers and net stockings —Horace Sutton⟩ **4** : to wear out : EXHAUST ⟨this contact with righteousness has about *done me up* —Sinclair Lewis⟩ — **do up brown** : to make a thorough job of : do thoroughly ⟨set out to *do* the romantic historical novel *up brown* once and for all —*N.Y.Times*⟩

doup·er \-pər\ *n* -s : a textile worker who replaces broken doups

doup·pi·o·ni *or* **dou·pi·o·ni** *also* **du·pi·o·ni** \,düpē'ōnē\ *or* **dou·pi·on** *or* **du·pi·on** \'düpē,ōn\ *n* -s [F & It; F *doupion*, fr. It *doppione* (pl. *doppioni*) double cocoon made by two silkworms, aug. of *doppio* double, fr. L *duplus* — more at DOUBLE] **1** : a usu. large and uneven double silk thread reeled usu. from two united cocoons and used in various fabrics (as shantung and pongee) **2** : a fabric of douppioni yarn

dour \'dau̇(ə)r, 'dü|, |ə, *Scot* 'dür\ *adj*, *usu* -ER/-EST [ME, prob. fr. L *durus* hard — more at DURE (hard)] **1** : marked by sternness or severity : HARSH, FORBIDDING ⟨a literary mode that had slowly percolated through the crust of Puritan provincialism and imparted a certain sprightliness to a ~ temper —V.L.Parrington⟩ ⟨an imposing composition, somewhat ~ and ascetic in character but full of theatrical thunder and loud declamation —Winthrop Sargeant⟩ **2** : marked by obstinacy or stubbornness : UNYIELDING, DOGGED ⟨an insistent hunger for learning and a ~ and often sacrificial determination to achieve it —Walter Moberly⟩ ⟨resisted change with a ~ persistence —Russell Kirk⟩ **3** : marked by gloomy silence or ill humor : SULLEN ⟨an independent individual, suspicious of strangers and frequently ~ in disposition —Pamela Gulliver & P.H.Gulliver⟩ ⟨in camp . . . he was silent, gloomy and ~, frequently irritable, unfriendly and hostile to everybody —C.W.M.Hart⟩ **4** *chiefly Scot* **a** *of weather* : bleak and gloomy **b** *of land* : barren and infertile **syn** see SULLEN

doura *or* **dourah** *var of* DURRA

dourade *or* **dourado** *var of* DORADO

dou·rine \'dü,rēn, 'dü,-, =¦=\ *n* -s [F, perh. fr. Ar *darin* filthy, scabby] : a contagious disease esp. of horses and asses that is caused by a trypanosome (*Trypanosoma equiperdum*) transmitted from host to host during copulation and that commonly assumes a chronic course marked by inflammation of the genitals, subcutaneous edematous plaques, low-grade fever, progressive paralysis, emaciation, and death

dour·lach \'dürlək, -ləḵ\ *var of* DORLACH

dour·ly *adv* [ME, fr. *dour* + *-ly*] : in a dour manner

dour·ness *n* -ES [ME *dournes*, fr. *dour* + *-nes* -ness] : the quality or state of being dour

dou·rou·cou·li *also* **dou·ro·cou·li** *or* **du·ru·ku·li** \,dürə'külē\ *n* -s [native name in So. America] : any of certain small roundheaded stocky-bodied bushy-tailed nocturnal monkeys (genus *Aotes*) of tropical America distinguished by their very large eyes

¹**douse** \'düs, 'dau̇s\ *also* **dowse** \'dau̇s\ *n* -s [origin unknown] *Brit* : BLOW, STROKE

²**douse** *also* **dowse** \'dau̇s\ *vt* -ED/-ING/-S **1 a** : to take in : LOWER, STRIKE ⟨~ a sail⟩ ⟨~ a mast⟩ **b** : SLACKEN ⟨~ a rope⟩ **2** : to take off : DOFF

³**douse** *also* **dowse** \'dau̇s, 'dau̇z\ *vb* -ED/-ING/-S [prob. fr. ²*douse* (in obsolete sense "to smite"), after E *souse* to strike: *souse* to immerse] *vt* **1** : to plunge into water : IMMERSE ⟨begin your washing by *dousing* curtains in clear water to remove surface dust —Mary B. Picken⟩ **2 a** (1) : to throw water on : DRENCH ⟨she leaned over the basin and began to ~ her face with the cold water —W.V.T.Clark⟩ ⟨the monsoon . . . ~s the hillsides —Christopher Rand⟩ (2) : to cover with water or another liquid ⟨picking a little mess of red raspberries for her breakfast . . . she *doused* them good with cream —Jean Stafford⟩ **b** : THROW ⟨*doused* water at each other⟩ : SLOSH ⟨still use their native bathhouse . . . in which they ~ water on a heated rock fireplace —*Amer. Guide Series: Minn.*⟩ **3** : to put out (as a light or fire) : EXTINGUISH ⟨his wife *doused* the candle —S.H.Holbrook⟩ ~ *vi* **1** : to fall or become plunged into water ⟨no jesting trivial matter to swing in the air or ~ in water —Samuel Butler †1680⟩ **2** : to lie in water : BATHE ⟨I *doused* pleasantly in the cool fresh water for an hour or two every day —F.N.Souza⟩

⁴**douse** *also* **dowse** \"\ *n* -s : DOWNPOUR, DRENCHING ⟨his voice came to the crew like a ~ of ice water —T.O. Heggen⟩

dous·er *also* **dows·er** \-sə(r), -zə-\ *n* -s : one that douses; *specif* : a fireproof shutter that controls or intercepts the light reaching the film aperture of a motion-picture mechanism (as a projector) or of a stereopticon

dousing chock *or* **dowsing chock** *n* [*dousing* prob. fr. gerund of ²*douse*] : a piece of curved timber laid across the apron and secured to the knightheads at the upper deck of a ship

dous·ti·o·ni \,düstē'ōnē\ *n*, *pl* **doustioni** *or* **doustionis** *usu cap* [F, of AmerInd origin] **1** : a Caddo people of the Natchitoches confederacy **2** : a member of the Doustioni people

dout \'dau̇t, 'düt\ *vt* -ED/-ING/-S [¹*do* + *out*] *dial* : to put out : EXTINGUISH

do ut des \,dō,ùt'dās\ *n* [NL, I give in order that you may give] : a commutative contract whereby something is given so that something may be received in return

dout·er \'dau̇tər, 'düt-\ *n* -s *now dial Eng* : EXTINGUISHER; *specif* : CANDLESNUFFER

do ut fa·ci·as \,dō,ùt'fäkē,äs\ [NL, I give in order that you may do] : a commutative contract whereby something is given so that something may be done in return

doux \'dü\ *adj* [F, lit., sweet, fr. OF *douz* — more at DOUCE] *of champagne* : containing at least seven percent sugar by volume : sweeter than demi-sec : very sweet

dou·zaine \(')dü¦zān\ *n* -s [F, lit., dozen, fr. OF *dozaine* — more at DOZEN] : a body of 12 men representing a Guernsey parish

dou·zai·nier \¦dü,zān¦yā\ *n* -s [F, fr. *douzaine*] : a member of a douzaine

do·vap \'dō,vap\ *n* -s *usu* DOVAP [Doppler velocity *and* position] : a method of tracking long-range missiles that utilizes continuous radio waves and the Doppler effect

¹**dove** \'dəv\ *n* -s [ME *douve*, *dove*, *doufe*, fr. (assumed) OE *dūfe* (in *Dūfe*, fem. prop. name); akin to OHG *tūba* dove, ON *dūfa*, Goth hraiwadūbo turtledove, and prob. to OE *dēaf* deaf — more at DEAF] **1** : any of numerous birds of the family Columbidae: **a** : any of various smaller wild pigeons (as the turtledove or mourning dove) **b** : PIGEON **2 a** : pure and gentle woman or child — used esp. as a term of endearment ⟨come little ~, don't be afraid⟩ **3 a** : PELICAN 4 **b** : DOVE GRAY

²**dove** *past of* DIVE

dove·cote \'dəv,kō|t *sometimes* -,kä| *or* -kə|; *usu* |d·+V\ *or* **dove·cot** \-,kät *sometimes* -kə|\ *n* -s [ME *dowecote*, *doufecot*, fr. *douve*, *doufe* dove + *cote* or *cot* — more at COTE (coop), COT (cottage)] **1** : a small compartmented raised house or box for domestic pigeons **2** : a settled or harmonious group or organization ⟨his determined aggressiveness caused a real flutter in the ~⟩

dove dock *n* [¹*dove* + *dock* (plant)] : COLTSFOOT a

dove–eyed \'=¦=\ *adj* : having soft gentle eyes

doveflower \'=,==\ *n* **1** : a tropical American orchid (*Peristeria elata*) having a tall scape with numerous fragrant white flowers and a column in the center of the flower suggesting a dove **2** : the blossom of the doveflower

dovefoot \'=,=\ *n* -s [so called fr. the shape of the leaf] : SPOTTED CRANESBILL

dove gray *n* : a purplish gray that is redder, lighter, and stronger than crane, lighter than granite, slightly stronger than cinder, and redder and deeper than zinc

dovehouse \'=,=\ *n* [ME *dowfhows*, fr. *dowf*, *douve* dove + *hows*, *hous* house] : DOVECOTE 1

dove·kie *also* **dove·key** \'dəvkē\ *n* -s [dim. of ¹*dove*] **1** : BLACK GUILLEMOT **2** : a small short-billed auk (*Plautus alle*) breeding on arctic coasts and ranging south in winter

dove·let \'dəvlət\ *n* -s [¹*dove* + *-let*] : a small or immature dove

dovelike \'=,=\ *adj* : mild as a proverbial dove : pure and lovable : GENTLE ⟨our host introduced us to his two daughters, beautiful and ~ creatures⟩

dove pox *n* : PIGEON POX

do·ve prism \'dōvə-\ *n*, *usu cap D* [prob. after Heinrich W. *Dove* †1879 Ger. physicist] : a prism that reverts an image but does not produce deviation or displacement of the beam, the rotation of the prism about the axis of the beam rotating the beam at twice the rate of rotation of the prism

¹**do·ver** \'dōvər\ *vi* -ED/-ING/-S [freq. of (assumed) E dial. (16th cent. Sc) *dove* to be stupid, fr. (assumed) ME *doven*, fr. OE *dofian*; akin to OHG *tobōn*, *tobēn* to be insane, ON *dofinn* benumbed, OE *dēaf* deaf — more at DEAF] *Scot* : to doze off or lose consciousness for a moment — often used with *over*

²**dover** \"\ *n* -s **1** *chiefly Scot* : a drowsy state **2** *chiefly Scot* : NAP

³**dover** \'dōvə(r)\ *adj*, *usu cap* **1** [fr. *Dover*, England] : of or from Dover, England : of the kind or style prevalent in Dover **2** [fr. *Dover*, Delaware] : of or from Dover, the capital of Delaware ⟨a *Dover* merchant⟩ : of the kind or style prevalent in Dover

dover beater *n* [fr. *Dover*, a trademark] : ROTARY BEATER

dover catchfly *n*, *usu cap D* [perh. fr. *Dover*, port city in southeastern England] : NODDING CATCHFLY

dover gray *n*, *often cap D* [prob. fr. *Dover*, England] : a dark gray that is darker than pelican and lighter than fashion gray or Oxford gray

dover sole *n*, *often cap D* [prob. fr. *Dover*, England] **1** : a common European sole (*Solea solea* or *S. vulgaris*) that is highly esteemed as a food fish **2 :** a brownish blotched flatfish (*Microstomus pacificus*) of the Pacific coast of No. America that attains a length of about two feet and is becoming an important market fish in California

do·ver's powder \'dōvə(r)z,-\ *n, usu cap D* [after Thomas *Dover* †1742 Eng. physician] **:** a powder of ipecac and opium that is now compounded in the U.S. with lactose and in England with potassium sulfate and that is used as an anodyne and diaphoretic

doves *pl of* DOVE

dove's-foot \'=,=\ *n, pl* **dove's-foots** [so called fr. the shape of the leaf] **:** any of several chiefly European plants of the genus *Geranium* (esp. *G. molle*)

dove shell *n* [so called fr. the color of the shell] **:** any of numerous small marine gastropod mollusks (family Columbellidae) with oval to conical shells that have a high luster and brilliant coloring

[1]**dovetail** \'=,=\ *n* -s **:** something (as a flaring tenon, tongue, or machine part) felt to resemble a dove's tail in shape ⟨cutting ~*s* in the end of a timber⟩; *esp* **:** DOVETAIL JOINT

[2]**dovetail** \"\ *vb* -ED/-ING/-S *vt* **1 a :** to join (as timbers) by means of dovetails **b :** to cut to a dovetail or into dovetails ⟨~*ing* the end of the board with a special device⟩ **2 a :** to fit, connect, or combine skillfully or exactly to form a continuous or harmonious whole **:** fit ingeniously or precisely ⟨the manner in which he ~*s* his investigations into their sociological framework is unique —*New Statesman & Nation*⟩ **b :** to fit together with **:** interlock with ⟨my discoveries ~ those made by others⟩ **~** *vi* **:** to fit together into a unified or coordinated whole ⟨the way the laws of chemistry and physics ~⟩ ⟨corn growing and hog raising ~ into a practical efficient enterprise in parts of the Middle West⟩

dovetail cramp *n* **:** a dovetailed cramp used to hold masonry

dovetailed \'=,tāld\ *adj* [[1]*dovetail* + *-ed*] **1 :** having a tail like a dove's **2 :** joined with or as if with dovetails **:** having a dovetail or a dovetailed part ⟨carefully ~ air and land operations made the attack successful⟩ **3** *heraldry* **:** partitioned or bounded by a line broken into a series of dovetails ⟨per chevron ~ gules and argent⟩ ⟨gules a chevron ~ ermine⟩

dove·tail·er \'=,tālə(r)\ *n* -s **:** one that dovetails; *specif* **:** an operator of a machine for cutting dovetails in wood

dovetail hinge *n* **:** BUTTERFLY HINGE

dovetail joint *n* **:** a flaring tenon and a mortise into which it fits tightly making an interlocking joint between two pieces that resists pulling apart in all directions except one

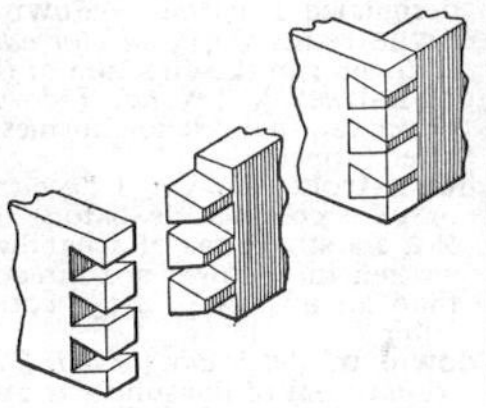

dovetail molding *n* **:** an architectural molding of any convex section that is zigzag like a series of dovetails

dovetail plane *n* **:** a woodworking plane specially adapted for forming the tongue and grooves of dovetail joints

dovetail saw *n* **:** a small backsaw with thin blade, fine teeth, and straight handle used for accurate work (as in cabinetmaking and patternmaking)

dovetail joints

dove tree *n* [so called fr. the appearance of the flowers] **:** a Chinese deciduous tree (*Davidia involucrata*) of the family Cornaceae that has flower heads with two large unequal creamy-white bracts and alternate leaves which sometimes release a nauseous odor

doveweed \'=,=\ *n* **1 :** any of several New World plants of the genus *Croton* **2 :** TURKEY MULLEIN

[1]**dow** \'daů, 'dō, *Scot* 'dəů\ *vi* -ED/-ING/-S [ME *dow, deih* have worth, am good for something (1st & 3d sing. pres. indic. of assumed *dowen*, pl. pres. *dowen*, past *doughte*), fr. OE *dēah*, *dēag* (infin. assumed *dugan*, pl. pres. *dugon*, past *dohte*); akin to OHG *toug* have worth (infin. assumed *tugan*, 3d pl. pres. *tugun*), Goth *daug* have worth (infin. assumed *dugan*, 3d pl. pres. assumed *dugun*), ON *duga* (infin.) to help — more at DOUGHTY] **1** *obs* **:** to have worth, value, validity, availability, or suitableness **2** *chiefly Scot* **:** to be able or capable **3** *dial Brit* **a :** to thrive and prosper **b :** to recover from illness **c :** to feel sufficiently concerned to take action — usu. used with a negative

[2]**dow** \'daů\ *vt* -ED/-ING/-S [ME *dowen*, fr. OF *doer*, *douer*, fr. L *dotare*, fr. *dot-*, *dos* gift, dower — more at DOWER] *archaic* **:** to endow or give as an endowment ⟨he . . . ~*ed* her with all the virtues in the Bible —Rudyard Kipling⟩

[3]**dow** \'dü\ *dial Brit var of* DOVE

[4]**dow** \'dəů\ *vi* [origin unknown] *chiefly Scot* **:** to fade away **:** become dull or withered

[5]**dow** *var of* DHOW

[6]**dow** \'daů\ *n* -s [Hindi *dāo*, fr. Skt *dātra* crooked knife, fr. *dāti* he cuts; akin to Skt *dayate* he apportions — more at TIDE] **:** [1]DAH

dow·able \'daůəbəl\ *adj* [AF, fr. OF *doer*, *douer* to endow + *-able*] **:** capable of being endowed; *esp* **:** legally entitled to dower

dow·a·ger \'daůəjə(r), 'daůēj-\ *n* -s *often attrib* [MF *douagiere*, fr. *douage* dower, fr. *douer* to endow (fr. OF *doer*, *douer*) + *-age*] **1 :** a widow in the enjoyment of some property or a title that has come to her from her deceased husband — often added to a title so enjoyed esp. when there is a wife of the new incumbent of the title of the deceased husband ⟨the empress's seal as ~⟩ ⟨the ~ duchess⟩ ⟨countess ~ of Rimrock⟩ **2 :** an elderly woman of imposing appearance or dominant personality; *often* **:** one of the elder women of assured position who tend to set the tone of an assembly, social group, or community ⟨the ~*s* shook their heads over the younger generation⟩ ⟨appealing to the ~ trade⟩

dowd \'daůd\ *n* -s [ME *doude*] **:** a dowdy person; *esp* **:** a dowdy woman

dowd·i·ly \'daůdᵊlē, -dəlē, -li\ *adv* **:** in a dowdy manner

dowd·i·ness \'daůdēnəs, -din-\ *n* -ES **:** dowdy state; *esp* **:** drab slovenly dress

[1]**dowdy** \'daůdē, -di\ *n* -ES [*dowd* + *-y* (diminutive suffix)] **1 :** a dowdy woman **2 :** PANDOWDY

[2]**dowdy** \"\ *adj* -ER/-EST **1** *of feminine appearance or apparel* **:** lacking neatness and charm; *often* **:** slovenly or slatternly **:** untidily shabby ⟨an old woman bedraggled and ~⟩ ⟨a ~ gray dress⟩ **2 a :** lacking in smartness or taste ⟨a clean sunny but completely ~ room⟩ ⟨expensive ~ country tweeds⟩ **b :** not modern in style **:** OLD-FASHIONED **:** out of date ⟨two ~ meandering novelettes —*New Yorker*⟩ **syn** see SLATTERNLY

dowdy·ish \-dēish, -di·ish\ *adj* **:** somewhat dowdy

[1]**dow·el** \'daů(ə)l\ *n* -s [ME *dowle*, prob. fr. MLG *dövel;* akin to OHG *tubili* plug, MLG *dövicke* plug, LGk *typhos* wedge] **1 :** a headless smooth or barbed pin usu. of circular section fitting into corresponding holes in abutting pieces to act as a temporary fastening or to keep them permanently in their proper relative position; *also* **:** a round rod or stick used esp. for cutting up into dowels **2 :** a piece of wood driven into a wall so that other pieces may be nailed to it **3 :** DOVETAIL CRAMP

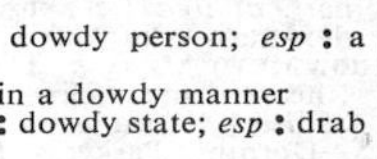

a dowels

[2]**dowel** \"\ *vt* **doweled** *or* **dowelled**; **doweled** *or* **dowelled**; **doweling** *or* **dowelling**; **dowels :** to fasten or locate (a part with reference to another part) by dowels **:** furnish with dowels

dow·el·er \'daů(ə)lə(r)\ *n* -s **1 :** a worker who inserts dowels by hand or by machine **2 :** an operator of a dowel-making machine

dowel jig *or* **doweling jig** *n* **:** a jig for holding material to be doweled

dowel screw *n* **:** a dowel threaded on both ends

[1]**dow·er** \'daů(ə)r, 'daůə\ *or* **dow·ry** \'daů(ə)rē, -ri\ *n, pl* **dowers** *or* **dowries** [*dower* fr. ME *dowere*, *dowaire*, fr. MF *douaire*, fr. OF *doaire*, *douaire*, modif. (influenced by OF *doer*, *douer* to endow, fr. L *dotare*, fr. *dot-*, *dos*) of ML *dotarium*, fr. L *dot-*, *dos* gift, dower + *-arium* -ary; *dowry* fr. ME *dowarie*, fr. AF, irreg. fr. ML *dotarium;* akin to Gk *dōs* gift, L *dare* to give — more at DATE] **1** *usu dower* **:** the portion of or interest in the real estate of a deceased husband that is given by law to his widow during her life **2 a** *usu dowry* **:** the money, goods, or estate that a woman brings to her husband in marriage **:** a bride's portion **:** DOT **b** *usu dowry* **:** a gift of property by a man to or for his bride ⟨ask me never so much *dowry* and gift, and I will give . . .; but give me the damsel to wife —Gen 34:12 (AV)⟩ **c :** a sum of money or its equivalent required of postulants by some religious communities (as of cloistered nuns) **3 :** gift of nature **:** TALENT, ENDOWMENT

[2]**dower** \"\ *vt* -ED/-ING/-S **:** to supply with a dower or dowry **:** ENDOW ⟨nature had so richly ~*ed* him —J.A.Symonds⟩

dower chest *n* **:** HOPE CHEST

dow·er·ess \'daů(ə)rəs\ *n* -ES *archaic* **:** a dowered widow **:** DOWAGER

dower house *n, Brit* **:** a residence forming part of the dower of or intended for the use of a widow and usu. being a less pretentious dwelling on the same grounds as the family residence

dow·er·less \'daů\|(ə)rləs, \|əl-\ *or* **dow·ry·less** \\|(ə)rēl-, -ril-\ *adj* **:** lacking a dower or dowry

dowf *also* **dowff** \'dəůf\ *adj* [perh. fr. ON *daufr* deaf — more at DEAF] **1** *chiefly Scot* **:** lacking in force and energy **:** LISTLESS, APATHETIC **2** *chiefly Scot* **:** dismal and gloomy **3** *chiefly Scot, of sound* **:** lacking resonance **:** HOLLOW

dowg \'dəůg\ *Scot var of* DOG

dow·ie *also* **dowy** \'dəůi\ *adj* [alter. of earlier *dolly*, fr. ME (Sc), perh. fr. ME *dol*, *dul* dull + *-y*, adj. suffix — more at DULL] **1** *chiefly Scot* **:** dreary and dispirited **:** DOLEFUL **2** *chiefly Scot* **:** dull and oppressive — **dow·i·ly** \'dəůəli\ *adv*

dow·ie·ism \'daůē,izəm\ *n, usu cap* [John A. *Dowie* †1907 + E *-ism*] **:** the principles and practices of Dowieites

dow·ie·ite \-ē,īt\ *n* -s *usu cap* [John A. *Dowie* †1907 Scot. religious leader in the U.S. + E *-ite*] **:** a member of the Christian Catholic Apostolic Church in Zion, a religious organization chiefly centered in Zion City near Chicago, Ill., formed in 1896 by John Alexander Dowie and devoted orig. to the practice of a religious communal life, faith healing, and abstinence

dowing *pres part of* DOW

dow·itch \'daůich\ *n* -ES [by shortening] *dial* **:** DOWITCHER

dow·itch·er \'daůəchə(r)\ *n, pl* **dowitchers** *also* **dowitcher** [of Iroquoian origin; akin to Mohawk & Cayuga *tawis* dowitcher, Onondaga *tawish*] **:** a long-billed snipe (*Limnodromus griseus*) that is intermediate in characters between the typical snipes (genus *Capella*) and the sandpipers and that breeds in northern No. America and winters largely in Central America or So. America — called also *brownback*, *grayback*, *red-breasted snipe*

do with \'=(,)=\ *vt* **1 :** to deal with **:** MANAGE ⟨I can't *do with* a man of his age who never speaks the truth —Archibald Marshall⟩ **2 :** to get along on **:** manage with ⟨have *done with* very little sleep throughout their lives —Geoffrey Jefferson⟩ **3 :** to make use of **:** profit from ⟨I could *do with* a cup of coffee —Frances P. Keyes⟩ ⟨they could *do with* some typographical improvement —J.E.Gloag⟩

do without \¦==¦=\ *vt* **:** to dispense with **:** get along without ⟨limiting the production of goods that we could *do without* —M.R.Cohen⟩

dow-jones average *also* **dow-jones index** \'daů¦jōnz-\ *n, usu cap D&J* [after Charles H. *Dow* †1902 and Edward D. *Jones* †1920 Am. financial statisticians] **:** an index of the relative price of securities based on the daily average price of selected lists of industrial, railroad, and utility common stocks

dowl *or* **dowle** \'daů(ə)l\ *n* -s [ME *doule*] *now dial Eng* **:** feathery or woolly down **:** FILAMENT a (4)

dow·las \'daůləs\ *n* -ES [alter. (influenced by *Daoulas*) of ME *douglas*, by folk etymology (influence of name *Douglas*) fr. *Daoulas*, Brittany, France] **1 :** a coarse linen cloth used widely in the 16th and 17th centuries and manufactured orig. in Brittany but later esp. in northern England and Scotland **2 :** a cotton imitation of dowlas

dow·ly \'daůlē, 'dōlē\ *adj* [ME, dull, miserable, perh. fr. ON *dauflígr* dull, lonely, fr. *daufr* deaf — more at DEAF] *dial* **:** DULL, LOWERING

[1]**down** \'daůn\ *n* -s [ME *doun* hill, fr. OE *dūn;* akin to MD *dūne* dune, OIr *dūn* fortress, Skt *dhūnoti* he shakes — more at DOWN (feathers)] **1** *archaic* **:** HILL; *often* **:** a hillock of sand thrown up by the wind on or near a shore **:** DUNE **2 a :** an undulating generally treeless upland with sparse soil — usu. used in pl. **b downs** *pl, often cap* **:** treeless chalk uplands along the south and southeast coast of England **3** *often cap* **:** a sheep of any breed originating in the downs of southern England typically being of good mutton conformation and producing moderately fine wool of medium length — compare SOUTHDOWN

[2]**down** \"\ *adv* [ME *doun*, fr. OE *dūne*, short for *adūne*, *of dūne*, fr. *a-* (fr. *of*) or *of* off, from + *dūne*, dat. of *dūn* hill — more at OF] **1 a :** in the direction of gravity or toward the center of the earth ⟨~ beneath the solid crust of the earth⟩ **:** from a higher point to or toward the earth's surface ⟨the wind blew all the apples ~⟩ **:** to the ground or other base ⟨the house burned ~ during the night⟩ ⟨planning to tear ~ the old shed⟩ **b :** from a higher to a lower place or position ⟨pull ~ the blind⟩ ⟨then we turned ~ toward the valley⟩ ⟨looking ~ over the face of the cliff⟩ **c :** from an upright position to or toward a surface regarded as a base in respect to which something is normally oriented ⟨the roof sagging, the chimney tumbling ~⟩ or to or into a state more relaxed or more humble ⟨do sit ~⟩ ⟨let slaves bow ~ when freemen pass⟩ **d :** out of one's hands or charge ⟨put the cake ~ on the table⟩ ⟨lay ~ your book for a minute⟩; *often* **:** into such a position as to free or relieve one ⟨put ~ your load and rest⟩ ⟨laying ~ the burdens of state⟩ **e :** in or into a recumbent position ⟨lie ~ and go to sleep⟩ ⟨knocked his opponent ~ with a sudden blow⟩ **f :** toward or below the horizon ⟨the sun far ~ in the west⟩ ⟨the moon went ~ an hour ago⟩ **g :** to or toward the bottom of a body of water ⟨sank ~ before they could reach him⟩ **h :** from an upper to a lower floor in a building esp. to meet or join companions ⟨I'll come ~ in a minute⟩ ⟨all of us hurried ~ to dinner⟩ **i :** toward the bottom of a sheet or page of paper ⟨here your hand, guiding your rapid pen, moved up and ~ —Edna S.V.Millay⟩ — in most senses opposed to or contrasted with *up;* often used as a function word to intensify a modified verb esp. of action or motion; sometimes used with the force of a verb in command or exclamation ⟨~ before he sees who you are⟩ ⟨~ on your knees, ungrateful girl, and pray for forgiveness⟩ **2 a :** in a direction that is conventionally or temporarily the opposite of *up* **b :** from an outlying part to or toward a center of activity (as a business district, a metropolis, or a terminal point); *often* **:** to or toward the lower part of town **:** DOWNTOWN **c :** from a center of activity to or toward an outlying part or remote place ⟨going ~ to the country for a rest⟩; *often* **:** to a place other than one's regular or urban abode to which one has a right to issue invitations ⟨come ~ to our camp on the river anytime⟩ ⟨grandma would love to have you run ~ some weekend⟩ **d** *Brit* **:** away from a university or other seat of learning ⟨sent ~ for misconduct without his degree⟩ ⟨he got a job in advertising shortly after he came ~ and has stayed with the firm ever since⟩ **e :** in a southerly direction ⟨they went ~ to Florida for Christmas⟩ **f :** to a source or a place of concealment ⟨tracking ~ a wounded deer⟩ ⟨run ~ this vile rumor⟩ ⟨I'm not sure how you can track ~ that quotation⟩ **g :** in or into the stomach ⟨he eats but the food won't stay ~⟩ ⟨get your drink ~, we're late already⟩ **3 a :** to or into a lower or inferior state (as of humility, defeat, disgrace, or restraint) ⟨held ~ by his lack of education⟩ ⟨a man come ~ in life⟩ **b :** to a point of complete control, stoppage, or quiet ⟨tie ~ the load⟩ ⟨now calm ~, my dear⟩ ⟨they had to strap the patient ~⟩ ⟨shouting ~ the opposition⟩ **c :** to a great or the utmost degree **:** very heavily ⟨burdened ~ with the cares of a family⟩ **d :** to completion **:** FULLY **:** from top to bottom ⟨I dusted ~ the whole house⟩ ⟨wash ~ the car⟩ **e :** under a perennial crop ⟨it is sometimes profitable to leave land ~ to hay for several years⟩ **4 a :** with forcible or abrupt descent ⟨fell ~ and cut his lip⟩ **b :** ACTIVELY, SERIOUSLY, VIGOROUSLY ⟨finally settled ~ to work⟩ **5 :** from a past time **:** from remoter times or people ⟨tales handed ~ by word of mouth⟩ ⟨these spoons have passed ~ in our family since the 17th century⟩ **6 a :** from a greater to a lesser amount, bulk, or strength ⟨don't forget to water ~ the wine⟩ **b :** from a thinner to a thicker consistency ⟨boiled ~ the sap into syrup⟩ **:** from a larger dilute volume to a smaller more concentrated one ⟨finally got his report ~ to three pages⟩ **c :** from a higher to a lower value ⟨most stocks went ~ last week⟩ **d :** in descending order of rank — used of a series of plays or discards from the same suit in certain card games **7 :** in or into symbols (as written letters) that can be preserved for future reference ⟨write ~ everything she says⟩ ⟨put ~ the following figures⟩ **8 a :** in or into a position indicative of an intent to bet (as on a particular number) ⟨he put his money ~ on the red⟩ **:** at hazard ⟨the chips are ~, the result is in the hands of fate⟩ **b :** immediately in cash ⟨I can't pay more than $10 ~⟩ **9 :** into defeat — used chiefly in relation to the scoring of games ⟨we went ~ two tricks⟩ **10 a :** in lower case or with a lower-case initial letter **b :** on a verso page and with its head next to the binding edge — used of the facing of an illustration **11 :** to press or the pressroom — used of newspaper copy or an edition of a newspaper ⟨the edition has already gone ~⟩ **12 :** toward the front of a theatrical stage — compare DOWNSTAGE **13 :** in or into a perfected or thoroughly understood state ⟨had the subject ~ pat⟩ — **down to the ground :** COMPLETELY, EXCELLENTLY, PERFECTLY ⟨that suits me *down to the ground*⟩ — **down with** \'=(,)=\ **1 :** in the direction of gravity or toward the center of the earth **:** from a higher point to or toward the earth's surface — often used interjectionally to express a wish, exhortation, or command that someone or something should be moved in such a direction ⟨*down with* the flag that is flying yonder⟩ ⟨*down with* him into the pit⟩ **2 :** to or into a lower or inferior state (as of humility, defeat, disgrace, or restraint) — often used interjectionally to express a wish, exhortation, or command that someone or something should be brought into such a state ⟨*down with* the government!⟩

[3]**down** \(¦)daůn\ *prep* **1 a :** in a descending direction along ⟨swiftly rolling ~ the hill⟩ **b :** from a higher to a lower point upon or within ⟨sweat trickling ~ his neck⟩ **c :** at a lower level on or in ⟨we keep the butter ~ the well⟩ **2 a :** along the course of ⟨children running ~ the street⟩ **b :** from the source toward the mouth of ⟨a rapids three miles further ~ the stream⟩ **:** toward the outlet or southerly end of ⟨we wandered ~ the valley⟩ **c :** along the margin of ⟨steaming ~ the coast⟩ **d :** in the same course as **:** WITH ⟨clouds blowing ~ the wind⟩ **3** — used as a function word to indicate movement in the opposite direction to a direction arbitrarily designated *up* without regard to actual ascent or descent ⟨pacing up and ~ the room⟩ **4 :** down into the ⟨he went ~ town⟩ ⟨he went ~ cellar⟩ **:** down in the ⟨they had some canned goods ~ cellar⟩ — often used in combination with a following noun to form adverbs and adjectives ⟨the *down*river end of town⟩

[4]**down** \'daůn\ *adj* **1 a :** going or directed down **b :** declining from a previous or normal level ⟨new construction is sharply ~⟩ **c :** conveying or for conveying downward **d :** running vertically ⟨~ lines on a ledger page⟩ **2 a :** reduced temporarily to a state of inactivity, inoperativeness, or depression ⟨the wind is ~⟩ **b :** low in spirits **:** DOWNCAST ⟨I'm completely ~ and out of sorts today⟩; *also* **:** fallen from a better to a worse or from a higher to a lower state ⟨don't kick a man when he's ~⟩ **c :** suffering from ill health ⟨my wife is ~ with malaria⟩; *sometimes* **:** off the feet esp. because of illness ⟨always try to get a ~ horse on his feet⟩ ⟨half the herd was ~ before morning⟩ **d :** closed down (as for repairs, remodeling, reorganization) ⟨the shop will be ~ while the new machines are installed⟩ ⟨it's unlikely that most of the ~ watermills will reopen⟩ **e** *of an electric battery* **:** not adequately charged **f** *of a football* **:** not being in play because its progress is wholly stopped or the officials stop the play for any reason **3 :** occupying or returned to a low or a lower position or state ⟨the window is ~ from the top⟩ **:** on or toward the ground, floor, or any surface regarded as a base with respect to which something is oriented ⟨the shades are ~⟩ ⟨all the vines are ~⟩: as **a :** below the horizon ⟨the moon is ~⟩ **b :** lower in price or characterized by lower prices ⟨wheat is ~ over 10 per cent⟩ **c** *of grass* **:** fallen to the ground after being mowed **d** *of timber* **:** lying on the ground esp. as the result of being blown over or cut **e** *of a boxer* **:** having any part of the body other than the feet in contact with the floor; *also* **:** in a position of helplessness if so recognized by the referee **f** *of a team or contestant* **:** defeated or behind an opponent (as in points scored) ⟨he was ~ on all cards at the middle of the 10th round⟩ ⟨the honors broke badly and they were ~ two tricks⟩ **g :** retired from play **:** OUT — used chiefly in baseball **h** *of a cricket wicket* **:** broken so that a batsman is out **i :** written or printed with a lower-case letter or initial letter; *also* **:** partial to lower-case rather than capital initial letters ⟨a ~ style⟩ **4 a :** directed to or forming part of the traffic to a place (as a business section, metropolis, or terminal) conventionally regarded as lower ⟨you can take a ~ train at the local station⟩ ⟨~ traffic is heavy this morning⟩ **b :** of, relating to, or intended for the use of down traffic or transportation ⟨go to the ~ platform in the subway station⟩ **5** *of a payment* **:** being that part of a price that is paid at the time of purchase or delivery when the entire price is not then paid ⟨a ~ payment of $10⟩ **6 :** gone to press — used of an item of news copy or of an edition of a newspaper ⟨the paper was ~ in the late afternoon⟩ **7 :** FINISHED, CONSUMED, PROCESSED ⟨eight ~ and two to go⟩ — **down on** \'=,=\ **:** full of dislike for **:** with a grudge against

[5]**down** \'daůn\ *n* -s **1 a :** a descent, decline, depression, or dwindling — used esp. in the phrase *ups and downs* ⟨emotional ups and ~*s*⟩ ⟨the recurrent ups and ~*s* of the business cycle⟩ ⟨the erratic ups and ~*s* of livestock production⟩ **b :** a reverse in fortune; *often* **:** a period of depressed activity (as in business) ⟨certain industries are esp. subject to seasonal ~*s*⟩ **c :** an alteration in the quality of a speaker's voice (as in radio acting) designed to distinguish narration from dialogue in matter he is reciting **2 a :** an instance of putting down (as an opponent in wrestling) **b** (1) **:** the termination of an attempt to advance the ball in football occurring when the referee blows his whistle or declares the ball dead (2) **:** a complete play to advance the ball or its duration **c :** failure to score on a badminton serve — called also *handout* **3 :** a firm and persistent dislike **:** GRUDGE — used with the indefinite article and with *on* ⟨why should she have such a ~ on me?⟩

[6]**down** \"\ *vb* -ED/-ING/-S *vt* **:** to cause to come or go down: as **a :** SWALLOW ⟨quickly ~*ing* his drink⟩ **b :** to relegate to obscurity or forgetfulness **:** SUPPRESS ⟨he could not ~ his regrets⟩ **c :** to get the better of **:** DEFEAT ⟨the coalition ~*ed* the bill after a lengthy fight⟩ ⟨do our best to protect the one and ~ the other —John Buchan⟩ **d** (1) **:** to bring to a stop (as a game animal or an adversary) by a shot or blow ⟨market hunters ~*ing* geese by the hundreds⟩; *often* **:** KILL (2) **:** to bring to the ground (a football opponent) by tackling (3) **:** to shoot from the air (an aircraft) ⟨accidentally ~*ed* a British airliner⟩ **e** (1) **:** to put (the helm) down (2) **:** to lower (as a signal or sail) (3) **:** to decrease the rate or speed of (the revolutions of a propeller) **f :** to lay aside **:** put down ⟨he ~*ed* his ax and sat on a stump to rest⟩; *often* **:** to cease to employ or engage in — usu. used with a material object that may be taken as a symbol of an activity or occupation ⟨the boys ~*ed* their bats and fishing rods at vacation's end and went back to school⟩ ⟨the union will certainly ~ tools if no settlement is reached⟩ **~** *vi* **:** to go down or be put down: as **a :** to become swallowed; *sometimes* **:** to appeal to the taste ⟨a drink that really ~*s* on a wintry evening⟩ **b :** to become brought to nothing or suppressed ⟨his regret may never ~⟩

[7]**down** \"\ *n, pl* **down** *also* **downs** *often attrib* [ME *doun*, fr. ON *dūnn;* akin to ON *daunn* odor, *dȳja* to shake, Goth *dauns* odor, L *suffire* to fumigate, Gk *thyein* to rage, Skt *dhūnoti* he shakes, L *fumus* smoke — more at FUME] **1 a :** a covering of soft fluffy feathers somewhat resembling fur that clothes young precocial birds before they acquire true feathers **b :** the small fluffy feathers that lie next to the body of adult birds, that are esp. prominent over the abdomen, and that are notably developed and fine in texture in ducks, geese, and other water birds from which they are often collected and used for stuffing (as in pillows, sleeping bags, or bedcovers) because of their light weight and good insulating quality ⟨a ~ comforter⟩ ⟨pluck the ~ from a hundred geese⟩ **c** *pl downs* **:** one of the feathers making up the down of a bird **2 :** something felt to resemble down esp. in soft fluffy quality: as **a :** the first growth of

beard on the human face ⟨a slender lad with just a trace of ~ on his cheeks⟩; *also* **:** fine soft hair elsewhere on the body ⟨tanned arms lightly covered with a silvery ~⟩ **b :** the pubescence of a plant ⟨wipe the ~ off the peaches⟩; *also* **:** a soft tuft (as a coma or pappus) on some plant part **c :** soft fur fiber usu. from the undercoat of an animal **d :** a fine powdery coating or surface ⟨a ~ of crystals⟩ — **in the down** *of a young bird* **:** covered with down

[8]**down** \"\ *vt* -ED/-ING/-S **:** to cover, ornament, line, or stuff with down **:** make downy ⟨a mouse ~*ed* in its winter coat —Herbert Gold⟩

[9]**down** \"\ *adj, usu cap* [fr. *Down,* county of Northern Ireland] **:** of or from County Down, Northern Ireland **:** of the kind or style prevalent in County Down

dow·na \'dau̇nə\ [[1]*dow* + *na*] *chiefly Scot* **:** CANNOT

down-along \ˌ-ˌ-ˈ-\ *adv, dial* **:** down the length of something (as a coast or road) **:** to or at a point in the distance

[1]**down-and-out** \ˌ-ˌ-ˈ-\ *adj* [[4]*down* + *and* + *out,* adj.] **1 :** so weakened, disabled, or incapacitated as to be ineffective **:** broken in health **2 :** suffering irrecoverably from financial losses or deficiencies **3** *of a boxer* **:** so broken down by past beatings as to be incompetent as a pugilist

[2]**down-and-out** \"\ *n* -S [[1]*down-and-out*] **1** *also* **down-and-out·er** \-ə(r)\ [*down-and-outer* fr. [1]*down-and-out* + *-er*] **:** a person who is down-and-out **2 :** the play or discard in bridge of a high card of a nontrump suit followed by a lower card of the same suit to indicate ability to trump if a third round of the suit is led

down-at-heel \ˌ-ˌ-ˈ-\ *or* **down-at-the-heel** \ˌ-ˌ-ˌ-ˈ-\ *also* **down-at-heels** \ˌ-ˌ-ˈ-\ *or* **down-at-the-heels** \ˌ-ˌ-ˌ-ˈ-\ *adj* **:** marked by a slovenly slipshod condition or having a threadbare faded appearance **:** SHABBY ⟨loneliness gnawed at the lives of all the guests in . . . a *down-at-the-heel* private hotel in an English seaside town —Pamela Taylor⟩ ⟨occurred to him that he was *down-at-heel,* dingy —Martha Gellhorn⟩ ⟨should have to pass the hat round or try (dressed like a *down-at-heels* corner boy) to get some sort of job —Nicholas Monsarrat⟩

downbear \(')-ˈ-\ *vt* [ME *dounberen,* fr. *doun* down + *beren* to bear, carry — more at DOWN, BEAR] *archaic* **:** to bear down **:** DEPRESS **:** press upon

[1]**downbeat** \'-ˌ-\ *n* **1 :** the downstroke of the conductor indicating the first stressed beat of a musical composition; *also* **:** any first beat **:** THESIS **2 :** an ictus or arsis **:** STRESS **3 :** a decline in activity or prosperity **:** depressed condition

[2]**downbeat** \"\ *adj* **:** PESSIMISTIC, GLOOMY, UNHAPPY ⟨a movie with a ~ ending⟩

down-beater \'-ˌ--\ *n* [[2]*down* + *beater*] **:** a rotating device used on a combine to beat down the moving grain and help to feed it uniformly to the cylinder

downbend \'-ˌ-\ *n* **:** a depression (as in the bed of the sea) due to downward bending of the earth's crust

downbent \'-ˌ-\ *adj* **:** bowed or drawn downward ⟨~ trees marked the path of the storm⟩ ⟨a tired ~ old man⟩

downbound \'-ˌ-\ *adj* **:** heading or leading in any direction that is conventionally down ⟨a ~ channel⟩ ⟨~ traffic⟩

down-bow \'-ˌbō\ *n* **:** a stroke in playing a bowed instrument (as a violin) from the heel toward the point of the bow — contrasted with *up-bow;* symbol ∧ or ⊓

downbuckle \'-ˌ--\ *n* **:** a generally long and relatively narrow portion of the earth's crust that has been bent sharply downward — **downbuckling** \'-ˌ-(-)-\ *n*

down-budding \'-ˌ--\ *n* **:** a method of budding in which the scion is inserted in an inverted position

downbye *also* **downby** \(')dün¦bī\ *adv* [[2]*down* + *by,* adv.] *Scot* **:** down that way **:** down below

down calver *n* [[2]*down* + *calve* + *-er*] *Brit* **:** a down-calving cow

down-calving \'-ˌ--\ *adj* [[2]*down* + *calving,* fr. pres. part. of *calve*] *Brit* **:** nearly ready to calve

down card \'-ˌ-\ *n* **1 :** a card dealt face down in any card game in which certain other cards are dealt face up **2 :** a card that is part of a player's hand but is left face down on the table while other of his cards are exposed **3 :** HOLE CARD

[1]**downcast** \(')-ˈ-\ *vt* [ME *douncasten,* fr. *doun* down + *casten* to cast — more at DOWN, CAST] *archaic* **:** OVERTHROW, DEMOLISH; *also* **:** DEJECT

[2]**downcast** \'-ˌ-\ *n* [ME *douncast,* fr. *douncasten,* v.] **1 :** a casting down **:** OVERTHROW **2 :** a downcast or melancholy glance or appearance **3 :** a ventilating shaft down which fresh air passes in circulating (as through a mine or the hold of a ship); *also* **:** the current of air through the shaft

[3]**downcast** \'-ˌ-\ *adj* [fr. past part. of [1]*downcast*] **1 :** low in spirit **:** DEPRESSED, DISPIRITED, DEJECTED **2** *of looks* **:** cast downward **:** directed to the ground (as from bashfulness modesty, dejection, or guilt) **3 :** having a downward draft ⟨a ~ mine shaft⟩

syn DISPIRITED, DEJECTED, DEPRESSED, DISCONSOLATE, WOEBEGONE: DOWNCAST suggests utter lack of cheer, confidence, and hope, perhaps accompanied by shame, chagrin, or bashfulness ⟨their smiling faces became *downcast,* their eyes held a look of furtiveness and uneasiness —Francis Birtles⟩ DISPIRITED indicates low-spiritedness and discouragement, usu. after failure or disappointment ⟨they could make no impression, and fell back at daybreak beaten and *dispirited* —J.A.Froude⟩ ⟨a fragile, *dispirited* gentlewoman who appeared to find everything in the world immeasurably sad and who spoke mostly in the past tense —Jean Stafford⟩ DEJECTED may imply more utter lowering of spirits and remarkable loss of hope, courage, and strength ⟨timorous and *dejected,* apprehending themselves to be haunted and possessed with vengeful spirits —William Bartram⟩ DEPRESSED implies a sinking under heavy burdens, often economic ones; it may describe chronic underprivilege or indicate psychological incapacity for hope, gladness, or even purposive activity ⟨the *depressed* populations of the ghettos of the Middle East and North Africa —John Hersey⟩ ⟨*depressed* by his failures and contemplating suicide⟩ ⟨*depressed* and stolid after the manic phase⟩ DISCONSOLATE describes one so utterly dispirited that he cannot be consoled, comforted, or encouraged ⟨the Jews sat *disconsolate* on the poop; they complained much of the cold they had suffered —George Borrow⟩ ⟨the *disconsolate* frown of a hunter who has seen nothing but warblers all day —James Thurber⟩ WOEBEGONE describes the appearance of dejection and defeat, sometimes lugubrious ⟨officers, seamen, and prisoners alike, we were as gaunt and *woebegone* a crowd as had ever been cast ashore from a shipwrecked vessel —C.B.Nordhoff & J.N.Hall⟩

down·cast·ness *n* -ES **:** the quality or state of being downcast

down·come \'dau̇nˌkəm\ *n* -S [ME (Sc) *douncome,* fr. ME *doun* down + *come* action of coming, alter. (influenced by *comen* to come) of *kime,* fr. OE *cyme,* fr. *cuman* to come — more at DOWN, COME] **1** *archaic* **:** a coming down **:** DESCENT **:** sudden fall **:** DOWNFALL **:** OVERTHROW **2 :** DOWNCOMER a

downcomer \'-ˌ--\ *n* [[2]*down* + *comer*] **:** a pipe to conduct something downward: as **a :** a pipe for leading the hot gases from the top of a blast furnace downward to the dust collectors and flue system — see BLAST FURNACE illustration **b :** a tube larger in diameter than the water tubes in some watertube boilers to conduct water from each top drum to a bottom drum under the influence of thermal circulation

downcountry \'-¦--\ *adv (or adj)* [[3]*down* + *country*] **:** in, toward, or of the seaboard or peripheral regions of an area

downcourt \'-¦-\ *adv (or adj)* **:** in or into the direction of the goal (as in basketball)

downcry \(')-ˈ-\ *vt* **:** to cry down **:** DISPARAGE

downcurved \'-ˌ-\ *adj* **:** curved downward esp. at the end — used of projecting parts ⟨the long ~ bill of the curlew⟩

downcut \(')-ˈ-\ *vb* **:** to cut down or downward by or as if by erosion — used chiefly as a present participle and esp. in distinguishing between downward and lateral stream erosion

downdale \'-¦-\ *adv* **:** DOWNHILL

downdraft \'-ˌ-\ *n* -S *often attrib* **:** a downward current of air or other gas (as in a mine shaft, kiln, or carburetor or during a thunderstorm)

down east \(')-¦-\ *adv (or adj), often cap D&E* **:** in or into the northeast coastal section of the U. S. and parts of the Maritime Provinces of Canada; *specif* **:** in or into coastal Maine

down east·er \dau̇'nēstə(r)\ *n, often cap D&E* **1 :** one born or living down east **2 :** a ship built down east; *esp* **:** a sailing ship from Maine

downed *past of* DOWN

down·er \'dau̇nə(r)\ *n* -S [[6]*down* & [4]*down* + *-er*] **:** one that downs or that takes, brings, gets, or puts down; *esp* **:** a weak, sick, or crippled animal in a shipping load that is down and unable to rise

downface \(')-ˈ-\ *vt* [[2]*down* + *face,* v.] **:** CONTRADICT

down-faced \'-ˌ-\ *adj* **:** having a continuous slope from forehead top to end of muzzle or bill with little or no stop — used of domestic mammals and birds; compare DISH-FACED

downfall \'-ˌ-\ *n* -S [ME *dounfal,* fr. *doun* down + *fal* fall — more at DOWN, FALL (noun)] **1 a :** a sudden fall from high estate, power, reputation, or happiness **:** DESTRUCTION, RUIN ⟨the ~ of the government⟩ **b :** a fall (as of snow or rain) esp. when sudden or heavy **:** DESCENT **2 a** *archaic* **:** a precipitous descent **:** ABYSS **b :** a trap having some device that falls and imprisons or injures the prey when the trap is sprung — compare DEADFALL **c :** something that causes a downfall (as of a person) ⟨drink was his ~⟩

downfallen \'-ˌ--\ *adj* [[2]*down* + *fallen*] **:** FALLEN, RUINED

downfalling \'-ˌ--\ *adj* [[2]*down* + *falling,* adj.] *archaic* **:** falling down **:** DECAYING

downfaulted \'-ˌ--\ *adj* [[2]*down* + *faulted,* fr. past part. of *fault*] *of a geological formation* **:** lowered by faulting

downfield \'-¦-\ *adv (or adj)* [[3]*down* + *field*] **:** in or into the part of a football field beyond the line of scrimmage toward the opposing team's goal ⟨a play should be planned to allow the ends to get ~ if needed⟩ ⟨effective ~ blocking⟩

downflow \'-ˌ-\ *n* **:** a downward flow or something that flows down; *esp* **:** a downward flowing current of air

downflowing \'-ˌ--\ *adj* **:** running or cascading down

downfold \'-ˌ-\ *n* **:** SYNCLINE — **downfolded** \'-ˌ--\ *adj*

down·gone \'dau̇nˌgȯn *also* -gän\ *adj* [prob. alter. (influenced by [2]*down* and *gone,* past part. of go) of [2]*doggone*] *dial* **:** in poor condition **:** DISTRESSED; *often* **:** DARNED, DOGGONE

[1]**downgrade** \'-ˌ-\ *n* [[4]*down* + *grade,* n.] **1 :** a downward grade (as of a road) **2 :** a descent toward an inferior state **:** DETERIORATION — used esp. in the phrase *on the downgrade*

[2]**downgrade** \'-ˌ-\ *adv (or adj)* **:** DOWNHILL ⟨the road dips ~⟩ ⟨the crossing where the ~ freights hit so many buggies and teams —Wright Morris⟩

[3]**downgrade** \(')-ˈ-\ *vt* [[2]*down* + *grade,* v.] **1 :** to minimize or depreciate in grade ⟨the folly of *downgrading* Soviet technology⟩ ⟨those countries preparing to ~ their commitments to NATO⟩ **2 a :** to lower the market class of (as grain or produce) esp. because of impurities or defects ⟨several carlots of wheat were *downgraded* for excessive cockle⟩ **b :** to alter the status of (a workman or his job) so as to lower the rate of pay ⟨older workers may often be kept employed by *downgrading* them to jobs that they are still able to handle⟩ ⟨any major shift in production or methods is likely to require extensive *downgrading* of jobs⟩ **3 :** to assign (as a document) to a less restricted classification of security

downgrowth \'-ˌ-\ *n* **:** the growing downward of a structure; *also* **:** the product of such growth

down-gyved *adj* [[2]*down* + *gyved,* fr. past part. of *gyve*] *obs* **:** hanging down like gyves

downhand \'-ˌ-\ *adj* [prob. fr. [3]*down* + *hand,* n.] *of welding* **:** performed from the upper side of the joint with the face of the weld approximately horizontal

downhaul \'-ˌ-\ *n* [[2]*down* + *haul,* v.] **:** a rope or line for hauling down or holding down a sail or spar ⟨a staysail ~⟩

downhearted \'-¦--\ *adj* **:** DEJECTED — **down·heart·ed·ly** \(')-¦---\ *adv*

down·heart·ed·ness *n* -ES **:** the quality or state of being downhearted

[1]**downhill** \'-ˌ-\ *n* [[4]*down* + *hill*] **1 a** *archaic* **:** the slope toward the bottom of a hill **:** DECLIVITY, DESCENT **b :** a descending gradient (as in circumstances or human existence) ⟨the tragic ~*s* that bring many promising careers to an end⟩ **2** [[2]*downhill*] **:** a competitive ski event consisting of skiing down a trail against time

[2]**downhill** \'-¦-\ *adv* [[3]*down* + *hill*] **1 :** toward the bottom of a hill ⟨traveling ~ we really got up speed⟩ **2 :** toward a lower, poorer, or inferior state or level — used esp. in the phrase *go downhill* < the town has gone ~ since the mill closed⟩ ⟨after he retired he went ~ very rapidly⟩

[3]**downhill** \'-ˌ-\ *adj* [[2]*downhill*] **1 :** sloping downhill **2** [[1]*downhill* 2] **:** of, relating to, or designed for use in skiing downhill ⟨a leading ~ contestant⟩ ⟨attractive ~ trousers⟩

downhill turn *n* **:** any skiing turn down the slope from a traverse run

downhold \'-ˌ-\ *n* **:** an act of minimizing (as of expenses) ⟨a stringent ~ on cable tolls⟩

down-house \'-¦-\ *adv* [[3]*down* + *house*] *dial Brit* **:** DOWNSTAIRS

downier *comparative of* DOWNY

downiest *superlative of* DOWNY

down·i·ly \'dau̇nᵊlē, -nəlē\ *adv* **:** in a downy manner **:** ARTFULLY

down·i·ness \'dau̇nēnəs, -au̇nin-\ *n* -ES **:** the quality or state of being downy

downing *pres part of* DOWN

dow·nin·gia \dau̇'niŋ(g)ēə\ *n, cap* [NL, fr. Andrew J. *Downing* †1852 Am. horticulturist + NL *-ia*] **:** a small genus of annual dwarf American herbs (family Lobeliaceae) with alternate leaves and showy sessile flowers having an unsplit corolla tube

down-in-the-mouth \ˌ-ˌ-ˌ-ˈ-\ *adj* **:** DEPRESSED, DOLOROUS

down-land \'-ˌland\ *n* [1]DOWN 2

down-lead \'-ˌlēd\ *n* **:** a radio lead-in

down·less \'-ləs\ *adj* **:** having or growing no down ⟨a ~ chick⟩

downlight \'-ˌ-\ *n* **:** a small spotlight set in the ceiling and directed downward

downline \'-¦-\ *adv* [[3]*down* + *line,* n.] **:** down the railway line

down lock *n* **:** a device in an airplane that locks the landing gear in the down position after it has been lowered

down·looked \'-ˌlu̇kt\ *adj* [[4]*down* + *look,* n. + *-ed*] *archaic* **:** downcast in countenance as or as if from guilt **:** SHEEPISH

downlying \'-ˌ--\ *n* -S [[2]*down* + *lying,* fr. gerund of *lie*] **1** *now dial Eng* **:** the time or act of going to bed **:** time of repose **2** *also* **down·lig·ging** \'-ˌligən, -giŋ\ [*downligging* fr. [2]*down* + *ligging,* fr. gerund of *lig*] *chiefly Scot* **:** LYING-IN

down milling *n* [[4]*down* + *milling*] **:** CLIMB MILLING

down·most \'-ˌmōst *sometimes chiefly Brit* -ˌməst\ *adv (or adj)* **:** farthest down

down·ness \'dau̇nnəs\ *n* -ES **:** the state or condition of being down

downpipe \'-ˌ-\ *n, Brit* **:** DOWNSPOUT

downpour \'-ˌ-\ *n* **:** a pouring or streaming downward (as of sunlight); *esp* **:** a heavy drenching

[1]**downright** \'-ˌ-\ *adv (or adj)* [ME *dounright,* fr. *doun* down + *right,* adv. — more at DOWN] **1** *archaic* **:** straight down **:** in a perpendicular course **2 :** OUT-AND-OUT, PLAIN, OUTRIGHT ⟨I was ~ ashamed of our party⟩ ⟨a ~ liar⟩; *sometimes* **:** VERY **:** to the utmost degree ⟨the sunset was ~ lovely⟩ **3 :** without ceremony **:** with plain blunt honesty **:** FORTHRIGHT ⟨a ~ answer⟩ ⟨so ~ a moralist⟩ ⟨he was kind but ~⟩ ⟨went ~ to his task⟩ — **down·right·ness** \'-ˌ-nəs\ *n*

[2]**downright** \"\ *n* **:** an inferior short-staple wool — usu. used in pl.

down·right·ly \'-ˌ-lē, -li\ *adv* [[1]*downright* + *-ly*] **:** in a straightforward or forthright manner **:** without hesitation

downriver \'-¦--\ *adv (or adj)* [[3]*down* + *river*] **:** from, toward, or at a point near the mouth of a river ⟨drifted ~ on a raft⟩ ⟨important ~ markets⟩

downs *pl of* DOWN, *pres 3d sing of* DOWN

down·set \'dünˌset\ *n* [[2]*down* + *set,* v.] *Scot* **:** a provision of money or an establishment; *specif* **:** MARRIAGE SETTLEMENT

down-sexed \'dau̇nˌsekst\ *adj* [[2]*down* + *sexed*] **:** having sex appeal minimized ⟨*down-sexed* illustrations⟩

[1]**downshift** \'-ˌ-\ *vi* [[2]*down* + *shift,* v.] **:** to shift an automotive vehicle into a lower gear ⟨~ into low or second gear⟩

[2]**downshift** \"\ *n* **:** a shift into a lower automotive gear

downside \'-ˌ-\ *n* **1 :** the under or lower side ⟨a gaily tilted hat with a decorative clasp on the ~⟩ **2 :** a trend downward (as of prices) — used chiefly in the phrase *on the downside*

downside up *adv* **:** TOPSY-TURVY

downsitting \'-ˌ--, *Scot* 'dün-\ *n* [[2]*down* + *sitting,* fr. gerund of *sit*] **1 :** the action of sitting down **:** REPOSE **2** *Scot* **:** DOWNSET

downslide \'-ˌ-\ *n* **:** a decline to a lower level (as of prices or business)

[1]**downslope** \'-¦-\ *adv* [[3]*down* + *slope*] **:** in a downward direction **:** DOWNHILL ⟨khaki-clad figures . . . sliding ~ toward him —Walt Sheldon⟩

[2]**downslope** \"\ *adj* **:** DOWNHILL, DESCENDING ⟨~ winds⟩ ⟨~ movement of ice⟩

[3]**downslope** \'-ˌ-\ *n* [[4]*down* + *slope*] **:** DOWNHILL ⟨he had only to remember to keep the ~ on his right —W.T.Clark⟩

downs·man \'dau̇nzmən\ *n, pl* **downsmen** [*downs* (pl. of [1]*down*) + *man*] **:** a dweller on the downs

down·some \'dau̇n(t)səm\ *adj* **:** DISPIRITED, DEPRESSED

down south \'-¦-\ *adv, often cap S* **:** in or into a more southerly location ⟨learned about the ways of fish in Canadian waters before he came *down south* —*Sydney* (*Australia*) *Bull.*⟩; *esp* **:** in or into the southeastern part of the U.S.

downspout \'-ˌ-\ *n* **:** a pipe leading downward; *esp* **:** a pipe to carry off rain water from a roof

down's syndrome \'dau̇nz-\ *n, cap D* [after J.L.H. *Down* †1896 Eng. physician, who first described it] **:** MONGOLISM

[1]**downstage** \'-¦-\ *adv (or adj)* [[3]*down* + *stage,* n.] **:** toward or at the front of a theatrical stage ⟨swept her train ~⟩ ⟨bent the ~ knee⟩ — compare UPSTAGE

[2]**downstage** \'-ˌ-\ *n* **:** the front of a stage immediately behind the footlights

[1]**downstairs** \(')-¦-\ *adv* [[3]*down* + *stairs,* pl. of *stair*] **1 :** down the stairs **:** on or to a lower floor **2** *aeronautics* **:** on, near, or to the ground

[2]**downstairs** *also* **downstair** \'-ˌ-\ *adj* **1 :** situated on the main, lower, or ground floor of a building **2 :** placed at or occupying a lower level ⟨the ~ television channels⟩

[3]**downstairs** \(')-¦-\ *n pl but sing or pl in constr* **1 :** the part of the house belowstairs **:** the lower floor or floors **2 :** persons occupying the lower part of a building; *often* **:** the servants of a household ⟨~ were shocked at such goings on⟩

downstart \'-ˌ-\ *n* [[2]*down* + *-start* (as in *upstart*)] **:** an Irishman of good birth and upbringing but with little fortune; *often* **:** a younger son of good family

[1]**downstate** \'-¦-\ *adv (or adj)* [[3]*down* + *state,* n.] **1 :** into or in a part of a state designated as downstate ⟨the voting was light ~⟩ **2 :** characteristic of a part of a state designated as downstate ⟨peculiarities of ~ pronunciation⟩

[2]**downstate** \"\ *n* **:** the more southerly part of a state of the U.S. as distinguished from a northerly part conventionally designated as *upstate* — **down·stat·er** \'-ˈstād·ə(r)\ *n* -S

downstream \'-¦-\ *adv (or adj)* [[3]*down* + *stream,* n.] **:** down a stream **:** in the direction of flow of a stream

downstreet \'-¦-\ *adv* [[3]*down* + *street,* n.] **:** to, toward, or in the main retail business section of a town ⟨going ~ after supper⟩

downstroke \'-ˌ-\ *n* **1 :** a stroke (as of a piston in a cylinder or of a conductor's baton) made in a downward direction **2 a :** a stroke (as of a handwritten cursive letter) commonly written in a downward direction and in some styles heavier than an upstroke **b :** a corresponding stroke of a printed letter

downsun \'-¦-\ *adv (or adj)* [[3]*down* + *sun,* n.] **:** in a direction from or out of the sun ⟨a ~ attack by an aircraft⟩

downswing \'-ˌ-\ *n* **1 :** a swing downward; *esp* **:** the forward and downward sweep of a golf club following the backswing **2 :** a downward or depressed trend ⟨the ~ in interest in politics⟩ ⟨in the ~ of a cyclic mania⟩; *esp* **:** the contraction phase of a business cycle

downtake \'-ˌtāk\ *n* [[2]*down* + *-take* (as in *intake*)] **:** a pipe, duct, or flue (as for air, gas, or water) that leads downward

down-the-line \ˌ-ˌ-ˈ-\ *adj (or adv)* **:** all the way **:** to the end ⟨supporting the party ticket right *down-the-line*⟩ ⟨a *down-the-line* union man⟩

down the river *n, often cap D&R* **:** SEVEN-CARD STUD

downthrow \'-ˌ-\ *n* **1 :** the act or process of throwing down **:** state of being overthrown **:** OVERTHROW ⟨the sudden ~ of a reputation⟩ **2 :** the side of a geologic fault that moved downward relative to the other side — compare THROW

downthrown \'-ˌ-\ *adj* [[2]*down* + *thrown,* fr. past part. of *throw*] **:** thrown down **:** DEPRESSED

downthrust \'-ˌ-\ *n* **:** downward movement of an object under impact or steady pressure; *also* **:** an impact or pressure tending to cause downthrust

downtime \'-ˌ-\ *n* [[4]*down* + *time*] **1 :** time during which a machine, department, or factory is inactive during normal operating hours (as for repairs or setting up or from lack of materials) **2 a :** a period during which an incentive worker is unable to produce because of plant factors beyond his control and therefore receives payment at an agreed base rate **b :** money paid a worker for downtime

down-to-date \ˌ-ˌ-ˈ-\ *adj* **:** UP-TO-DATE

down-to-earth \ˌ-ˌ-ˈ-\ *adj* **:** practical and straightforward **:** having no frills or foibles **:** REALISTIC

down·to·ni·an \(')dau̇n-¦tōnēən\ *adj, usu cap* [*Downton,* town in Wiltshire, England + E *-ian*] **:** of, relating to, or constituting a subdivision of the European Silurian — see GEOLOGIC TIME table

[1]**downtown** \(')-¦-\ *adv (or adj)* [[3]*down* + *town*] **1 :** to, toward, or in the lower part or business center of a city ⟨this bus goes ~⟩ ⟨delinquents roaming the ~ streets⟩ **2 :** relating to or characteristic of the business center of a city ⟨always patronizes the ~ stores⟩

[2]**downtown** \"\ *n* **:** the business center of a city ⟨the ~*s* of a hundred cities dressed and lighted for Christmas⟩ — **down·town·er** \'-ˈtau̇nə(r)\ *n* -S

down tree *n* [[7]*down* + *tree;* fr. the thick cottony fibers surrounding the seeds] **:** BALSA 1

downtrend \'-ˌ-\ *n* **:** a tendency downward esp. in economic matters ⟨a persistent ~ in sales⟩

downtrod *obs var of* DOWNTRODDEN

down·trod·den \(')-¦trädᵊn\ *adj* [[2]*down* + *trodden,* fr. past part. of *tread*] **:** abused by superior power — **down·trod·den·ness** \-ᵊn(n)əs\ *n* -ES

downturn \'-ˌ-\ *n* **1 :** an act or instance of turning down ⟨the ~ of an anticlinal fold —W.Y.Westervelt⟩; *also* **:** the state of being turned down ⟨the ~ of her mouth became a habit —Dorothy Parker⟩ **2 :** DECLINE, DECREASE ⟨a sharp ~ in new construction⟩; *usu* **:** a downward trend in economic matters ⟨the ~ of prices⟩ ⟨business began to show a ~⟩

down-twister \'-ˌ--\ *n* **:** a textile manufacturing machine with downward feeds for plying yarn while adding some twist — compare UP-TWISTER

[1]**down under** *adv* [[2]*down* + *under,* adv.; fr. the conception of the antipodes as being located beneath one's feet] **:** into or in Australia or New Zealand

[2]**down under** *n, sometimes cap D&U* **:** ANTIPODE 2

[1]**down·ward** \'dau̇nwə(r)d\ *also* **down·wards** \-dz\ *adv* [*downward* fr. ME *dounward,* fr. *doun* down + *-ward; downwards* fr. ME *dounwardes,* fr. *dounward* + *-es* (adverbially functioning gen. sing. ending of nouns) — more at DOWN, -S] **1 :** from a higher place to a lower **:** in a descending course ⟨looking ~ to the grass⟩ ⟨the streams roll ~ to the sea⟩ **2 :** from a higher to a lower condition ⟨revised his estimate ~⟩ **:** toward misery, humility, disgrace, or ruin ⟨fell from grace and went ~ in life⟩ **3 :** from a remote or earlier time **:** from an ancestor or predecessor **:** from one to another in a descending line ⟨prophets from Elijah ~ who preached repentance⟩

[2]**downward** \"\ *adj* [ME *dounward,* fr. *dounward,* adv.] **1 :** moving or extending from a higher to a lower place **:** tending toward the earth or its center or toward a lower level ⟨the ~ pull of gravity⟩ **2 :** descending from a head, origin, or source ⟨a ~ line of descent⟩ ⟨the ~ course of a stream⟩ **3 a** *archaic* **:** tending to a lower state **:** DEJECTED **b :** directed toward or leading to ruin, destruction, or damnation ⟨a man on the ~ path⟩ ⟨took her ~ way⟩ **c :** DEBASING ⟨the scripture contains many ~ comparisons of man and his ways⟩ **4** *archaic* **:** being below **:** LOWER — **down·ward·ly** *adv* — **down·ward·ness** *n* -ES

[1]**downwarp** \(')-ˈ-\ *vb* [[2]*down* + *warp,* v.] *vt* **:** to cause or produce a downwarp in ~ *vi* **:** to undergo downwarping

[2]**downwarp** \'-ˌ-\ *n* **:** a broad generally shallow geological downfold

downwash \'-ˌ-\ *n* **1 :** material washed downward (as from a mountainside) **2** *aeronautics* **:** the airstream which is deflected downward by an airfoil and the momentum of which gives rise by its reaction on the airfoil to the lift

1downwind \'=¦=\ adv (or adj) [1down + wind, n.] : in the direction that the wind is blowing : LEEWARD ⟨problems involved in making a safe ~ landing⟩ ⟨the smell of her cooking traveled ~ to where we were working⟩

2downwind \'=,=\ n [4down + wind, n.] : a wind blowing in or along one's course

down·with \'dün(,)=\ adj [ME (Sc) dounwith, fr. dounwith (adv.) downward, fr. ME doun down + with (adv.) together, fr. OE, fr. with (prep.) with, against — more at DOWN, WITH (prep.)] Scot : DOWNWARD

down wool n [1down + wool] : wool produced by Down sheep

1downy \'daunē, -ni\ adj -ER/-EST [2down + -y] 1 : like the down of a bird esp. in softness and fluffiness ⟨the ~ milkweed seeds⟩ 2 a : having or covered with down, pubescence, or soft hairs ⟨a downy-cheeked lad⟩ ⟨the ~ surface of a ripe peach⟩ b of a young bird : not yet having developed feathers other than down 3 a : made of down ⟨a ~ quilt⟩ b : soft or quiet : SOOTHING ⟨the ~ touch of her hand⟩ 4 [obs. E slang down in a state of awareness (fr. E 2down) + E -y] slang : CUNNING, WARY, KNOWING

2downy \"\ adj -ER/-EST [1down + -y] : being or characterized by downs ⟨a rolling ~ landscape⟩

downy ash n [1downy] : RED ASH 1

downy brome or **downy bromegrass** or **downy cheat** or **downy chess** n : an annual or winter annual grass (Bromus tectorum) with softly pubescent leaves and leaf sheaths

downy false foxglove n : a false foxglove (Gerardia virginica) with gray downy oak-shaped leaves

downy grape n : a wild grape (Vitis cinerea) of the central U.S. with downy foliage and black acid fruit

downy haw also **downy hawthorn** n : RED HAW

downy mildew n 1 : a fungus of the family Peronosporaceae that is parasitic on higher plants (as grapes, potatoes, and various cucurbits) and that produces whitish masses of sporangiophores or conidiophores on the undersurface of the leaves of the host — called also false mildew 2 : a plant disease caused by a downy mildew — compare POWDERY MILDEW

downy myrtle n : an evergreen shrub (Rhodomyrtus tomentosa) of the family Myrtaceae that is native to tropical Asia and the Philippines and is sometimes cultivated for its pink flowers and edible berrylike fruits

downy oat grass n : an erect grass (Trisetum spicatum) with a spikelike panicle that is a valuable forage grass in many alpine and northern parts of the northern hemisphere

downy poplar n : SWAMP COTTONWOOD

downy woodpecker n : a small black-and-white woodpecker (Dendrocopos pubescens) of No. America

downy yellow violet n : a spring-flowering violet (Viola pubescens) having clear yellow flowers with brown-purple veins near the base of the petals and softly pubescent leaves and stems

1dowp var of DOUP

2dowp \'daup, 'dōp\ n -s [origin unknown] dial Eng : CARRION CROW

dowry var of DOWER

dows pres 3d sing of DOW, pl of DOW

dow·sa·bel n -s [Dowsabel, fem. proper name] obs : SWEETHEART

1dowse var of DOUSE

2dowse \'dau̇|z sometimes |s\ vb -ED/-ING/-S [origin unknown] vi 1 : to use the divining rod (as in search of water or ore) 2 : to seek something with meticulous care esp. with the aid of a mechanical device ⟨electrical devices for use in dowsing for cable⟩ ~ vt : to find (as water) by dowsing

1dows·er \|zə(r) sometimes |sə(r)\ n -s [2dowse + -er] : a divining rod for dowsing; also : a person who uses it

2dowser var of DOUSER

dow·sets \'dau̇sə̇ts\ n pl [ME doucette (pl. doucettes), a sweet dish, fr. MF doucette (fem. of doucet), fr. OF doucete, fem. of doucet sweet, pleasant, fr. douz sweet, fr. L dulcis — more at DULCET] archaic : the testes of a deer

dowsing rod n [dowsing fr. gerund of 2dowse] : a dowser's divining rod

dowst \'deu̇st\ dial Eng var of DUST

dow·ter \'dōtə(r)\ dial Eng var of DAUGHTER

dow theory \'dau̇- also **dow's theory** \'dau̇z-\ n, usu cap D [after Charles H. Dow †1902 — more at DOW-JONES AVERAGE] : a system of stock-market forecasting based on the observed swings of the market itself

dowy var of DOWIE

dox·ic \'däksik\ also **dox·i·cal** \-sə̇kəl\ adj [Gk doxa opinion + E -ic, -ical] : of, relating to, or based on such intellectual processes as belief or opinion

dox·og·ra·pher \däk'sägrəfə(r)\ n -s [modif. (influenced by E -grapher) of NL doxographus, fr. doxo- (fr. Gk doxa opinion) + -graphus writer, fr. Gk -graphos — more at -GRAPH] : a collector and compiler of extracts from and commentator on ancient Greek philosophers — **dox·o·graph·i·cal** \ˌdäksə'grafə̇kəl\ or **dox·o·graph·ic** \-fik\ adj — **dox·og·ra·phy** \däk'sägrəfē\ n -ES

dox·o·log·i·cal \ˌdäksə'läjə̇kəl, -jēk-\ adj [doxology + -ical] 1 : relating to doxology or a doxology 2 : giving praise to God — **dox·o·log·i·cal·ly** \-jə̇k(ə)lē, -jēk-, -li\ adv

dox·ol·o·gize \däk'säləˌjīz\ vb -ED/-ING/-S [doxology + -ize] vi : to give glory to God (as in a doxology) ~ vt : to praise (God) with doxologies

dox·ol·o·gy \-ləjē, -ji\ n -ES [ML doxologia, fr. LGk, fr. Gk doxa glory, opinion (fr. dokein to seem good, seem, think) + -logia -logy — more at DECENT] 1 a obs : praise to the Deity : thanksgiving for divine protection b : an utterance expressing pleasure in or thanksgiving for some event or occurrence 2 : a commonly short hymn or formula expressing praise to God and usu. designed to be sung, chanted, or said by the choir or the congregation; esp : one used in Christian worship

1doxy also **dox·ie** \'däksē, -si\ n, pl doxies [perh. modif. of obs. D docke doll, fr. MD; akin to OHG tocka doll — more at DOCK] 1 : a loose wench : TROLLOP, PROSTITUTE; sometimes : MISTRESS 6a 2 dial : GIRL FRIEND, SWEETHEART

2doxy \"\ n -ES [by shortening fr. orthodoxy & heterodoxy] : OPINION, DOCTRINE; esp : religious opinion — compare ISM

dox·yl·a·mine \däk'siləˌmēn, -ˌmə̇n\ n [prob. fr. d- (fr. dimethyl) + oxy- + -l (fr. -yl) + amine] : an antihistamine $C_{17}H_{22}N_2O$ derived from pyridine and usu. administered in the form of its succinate

doyen \'dȯiən, 'dȯi,(y)en, 'dwä,yaⁿ(n)\ n -s [F, fr. LL decanus chief of ten — more at DEAN] 1 a : the senior male member of a body or group (as of a diplomatic corps) — called also dean; esp : one specifically or tacitly allowed to speak for the body or group ⟨the ambassador as ~ objected strenuously to the foreign office on behalf of his colleagues⟩ b : a person uniquely skilled by long experience in some field of endeavor ⟨rightly regarded as the ~ among English and American specialists on Japan —K.S.Latourette⟩ ⟨the ~ of the Arlberg ski instructors —Joseph Wechsberg⟩ 2 a : the oldest example of some category ⟨the ~ of the country's papers⟩ b : something outstanding of its kind ⟨some fanciers think dried ant's eggs the ~ of fish food⟩ ⟨among the few virtues to which I lay vigorous claim, punctuality is the ~ —Jerome Weidman⟩

doyenne \(')dȯi|(y)en, -ȯ|yen; (')dwä|yen, -wä|-; (')dwī|en\ n -s [F, fem. of doyen] : a female doyen ⟨feasted on the haute cuisine served up by the ~ of America's kitchens —Gail Jennes⟩

doy·ley or **d'oy·ley** or **doy·ly** \'dȯili\ Brit var of DOILY

doylt \'dȯilt\ var of DOILED

doz abbr dozen

1doze \'dōz\ vb -ED/-ING/-S [prob. of Scand origin; akin to ON dūsa to doze, dūs lull, calm; akin to MLG dōre fool, MHG dōsen to be quiet, doze — more at DOR] vt 1 archaic : to make dull : STUPEFY, MUDDLE, CONFUSE 2 : to pass (as time) drowsily — usu. used with away ⟨dozing his life away⟩ ~ vi 1 a : to sleep lightly or intermittently b : to fall into a light sleep — often used with off ⟨dozed off in the middle of her reading⟩ 2 : to be in a dull or stupefied condition as if half asleep : be drowsy **syn** see SLEEP

2doze \"\ n -s 1 : a light sleep : DROWSE 2 : decay in timber

3doze \"\ vt -ED/-ING/-S [prob. back-formation fr. dozer (bulldozer)] : BULLDOZE 3

dozed \-zd\ adj [prob. fr. past part. of 1doze] of timber : unsound from decay

1doz·en \'dəzᵊn\ n, pl **dozens** or **dozen** often attrib [ME dozeine, fr. OF dozaine, fr. doze twelve, fr. L duodecim, fr. duo two + -decim (fr. decem ten) — more at TWO, TEN] 1 a : a group of 12 ⟨oranges sold by the ~⟩ ⟨a ~ eggs⟩ ⟨three ~ bottles of ale⟩ ⟨~s of people⟩ b : any of the three columns respectively representing the numbers 1 to 12, 13 to 24, and 25 to 36 on which one may bet at roulette 2 a : a group containing an indefinite small number ⟨a ~ years ago⟩ ⟨scribbled a ~ words on a scrap of paper⟩ b : a larger number than one might expect — usu. used in pl. ⟨I've ~s of things to do⟩ ⟨she had ~s of chances to marry⟩ 3 archaic : coarse woolen cloth formerly made in England and commonly woven in lengths of approximately 12 yards each — usu. used in pl.

2dozen \"\ vt -ED/-ING/-S : to make up into lots of a dozen ⟨~ed the load of apples⟩

do·zened \'dōzᵊnd, 'däz-\ adj [ME (Sc) dosnyt, dosinnit, perh. of Scand origin; akin to ON dūsa to doze] chiefly Scot : STUPEFIED ⟨~ with drink —R.L.Stevenson⟩

do·zent \dōt'sent\ n, pl **dozen·ten** \-ntᵊn\ [G — more at DOCENT] : a docent in a German university

doz·enth \'dəzᵊn(t)th\ adj [dozen + -th] 1 : TWELFTH 2 : being about the twelfth ⟨I'm telling you for the ~ and last time⟩

1doz·er \'dōzə(r)\ n -s [1doze + -er] : one that dozes

2dozer \"\ n -s [by shortening] : HOPPERDOZER

3dozer \"\ n -s [by shortening] : BULLDOZER 3

dozy \'dōzē, -zi\ adj -ER/-EST [1doze + -y] 1 : DROWSY : inclined to doze : SLEEPY, SLUGGISH ⟨a tired ~ child⟩ 2 : in a state of decay : DOTY ⟨~ flawed wood⟩ : somewhat dozed ⟨a ~ post⟩

DP abbr 1 dew point 2 direct port 3 displaced person 4 documents against payment; documents for payment 5 double play 6 double pole 7 duty paid

DPB abbr deposit passbook

DPDT abbr double pole, double throw

DPh \ˌdē(ˌ)pē'ach\ or **DPhil** \'dē'fil\ abbr or n -s : a doctor of philosophy

DPH \ˌdē(ˌ)pē'āch\ abbr or n -s : a doctor of public health

dpl abbr diploma

DPN \ˌdē(ˌ)pē'en\ abbr or n -s diphosphopyridine nucleotide

DPST abbr double pole, single throw

dpt abbr 1 department 2 deponent 3 depth

dpty abbr deputy

DQ abbr 1 developmental quotient 2 direct question

dr abbr 1 debit; debtor 2 often cap doctor 3 door 4 drachma 5 dram 6 drawer; drawing; drawn 7 drive 8 drum

DR abbr 1 dead reckoning 2 deposit receipt 3 differential rate 4 dining room 5 district registry 6 dock receipt

1drab \'drab, -aa(ə)b\ n -s [perh. of Celt origin; akin to ScGael drabag dirty woman, IrGael drabog slattern, slut, fr. & akin to IrGael drab spot, stain, dirt, fr. MIr, grape husks, dregs — more at DRAFF] 1 : a slatternly woman 2 : PROSTITUTE, HARLOT

2drab \"\ vi **drabbed; drabbed; drabbing; drabs** : to associate with strumpets : WENCH ⟨a waster, an idler; drinking and drabbing —Aldous Huxley⟩

3drab \"\ n -s [MF drap cloth, fr. LL drappus, prob. of Celt origin; akin to Celt personal names Drappō, Drappus; akin to Gk drepein to pluck, Skt drāpi mantle, garment, OE teran to tear — more at TEAR] 1 : any of various cloths of a dull brown or gray color ⟨the carpet was an ancient ~ —Ethel Wilson⟩; esp : a thick woolen coating or a heavy cotton 2 [4drab] a : a light olive brown that is slightly less strong than sponge, less strong and slightly redder than average mustard tan, and darker than the color dust — called also mode beige, rustic drab, sand dune b : a dull, lifeless, or faded hue or appearance ⟨the silks with which the figures are embroidered have mostly faded to a general ~, but it is still possible to make out some red and green —O. Elfrida Saunders⟩ 3 : the quality or state of being drab : DULLNESS ⟨for this slight relief from the intolerable ~ of his life story one may be grateful —V.L.Parrington⟩

4drab \"\ adj **drabber; drabbest** 1 a : of the dull brown color of drab cloth b : of the color drab 2 : characterized by dullness and monotony : COLORLESS, CHEERLESS ⟨a ~ pile of masonry⟩ ⟨a usually ~ and lifeless subject —R.T.Hoober⟩ ⟨the writer's ~ vision of life⟩ — **drab·ly** adv — **drab·ness** n -ES

5drab \"\ vt **drabbed; drabbed; drabbing; drabs** [4drab] : to dull or tone down (color)

6drab \"\ n -s [origin unknown] : a wooden box used in saltworks for holding the salt taken out of the pans used in boiling

dra·ba \'drābə, -äbə\ n [NL, fr. Gk drabē, a kind of cress] 1 cap : a very large genus of low tufted herbs (family Cruciferae) of temperate and arctic regions with small flowers and oblong or linear siliques 2 -s : any plant of the genus Draba — compare WHITLOW GRASS

drab·bet \'drabə̇t\ n -s [3drab + -et] dial Eng : a coarse unbleached linen fabric usu. in twill weave

drab·ble \'drabəl\ vb **drabbled; drabbled; drab·bling** \-b(ə)liŋ\ **drabbles** [ME drabelen — more at DRIVEL] vt : to wet and befoul by draggling : DRAGGLE ⟨~ a gown or cloak⟩ ~ vi 1 : to be or become wet and muddy : dabble in or go through wet or miry places 2 : to fish with a rod and a long line that is drawn along through the water ⟨~ for barbels⟩

drab·bler or **drab·ler** \'drablə(r)\ n -s : a piece of canvas laced to the bonnet of a sail to give it more drop

dra·bi \'dräbē\ n -s [fr. various languages of India, modif. of E driver] India : DRIVER

dra·cae·na \drə'sēnə\ n [NL, fr. LL, she-serpent, fr. Gk drakaina, fem. of drakōn serpent — more at DRAGON] 1 cap : a genus of shrubs or trees (family Liliaceae) native to the Old World tropics that have branches terminated by clusters of sword-shaped leaves, that bear panicles of small greenish white flowers, and that yield a dragon's blood — see DRAGON TREE 2 or **dracaena palm** or **dracena** -s : any plant of the genus Dracaena or of the related genus Cordyline

drachm \'dram, -aa(ə)m\ n -s [alter. (influenced by L drachma) of ME dragme, drame — more at DRAM] 1 : DRACHMA 2 : DRAM

drach·ma \'drakmə\ n, pl **drachmas** \-məz\ also **drach·mae** \-ˌmē, -ˌmī\ or **drach·mai** \-ˌmī\ [L, fr. Gk drachmē — more at DRAM] 1 a : any of various ancient Greek units of weight; specif : the Attic unit equal to about 66.4 grains or 4.30 grams b : any of various modern units of weight: (1) : DRAM 1 (2) : a Greek unit equal to 15.432 grains or 1 gram 2 a : an ancient Greek silver coin equivalent to 6 obols and according to the Attic standard weighing 4.37 grams or 67.5 grains; also : a unit of value equivalent to a drachma coin being the basic unit of the silver coinage b : the basic monetary unit of modern Greece; also : a coin representing this unit — see MONEY table

drach·mal \'drakməl, -a(a)məl\ adj : of or relating to a drachm

dra·co \'drā(ˌ)kō\ n [in sense 1, fr. LL, fr. L, serpent; in sense 2, NL, fr. L, serpent — more at DRAGON] 1 pl **dra·co·nes** \drā'kō(ˌ)nēz, drə'-\ : a flag in the form of a serpent-shaped or dragon-shaped bag made open at one end so as to be inflated by the wind when carried and used in the later imperial period of Rome as the standard of a cohort and in armies in medieval Europe 2 cap : a genus of agamid lizards — see DRAGON 7

dra·co·ceph·a·lum \ˌdrākō'sefələm\ n, cap [NL, fr. L draco + NL -cephalum (neut. of cephalus); fr. the form of the corolla] : a genus of American mints comprising the dragonheads and having opposite serrate leaves and bracted bilabiate flowers

dra·co·ni·an \(')drā|kōnēən, drə'k-\ adj, often cap [L Dracon-, Draco fl 621 B.C. Athenian lawgiver (fr. Gk Drakōn) + E -ian] 1 : of, relating to, or suggestive of the lawgiver Draco or the severe code of laws that is said to have been framed by him as thesmothete 2 : marked by extreme severity or cruelty : HARSH, RIGOROUS ⟨emancipation at the price of a ruinous war and a Draconian peace —G.W.Johnson⟩ ⟨by ~ labor laws . . . the regime makes life harder than it need be —F.C.Barghoorn⟩

1dra·con·ic \drə'kānik\ adj [L dracon-, draco serpent + E -ic] : of, relating to, or like a dragon

2dra·con·ic \(')drā|känik, drə'k-\ adj [L Dracon-, Draco, Athenian lawgiver (fr. Gk) + E -ic] adj, sometimes cap : DRACONIAN — **dra·con·i·cal·ly** \-nə̇k(ə)lē\ adv

draconic period n [L Dracon-, Draco, a northern circumpolar constellation (fr. Gk Drakōn, fr. drakōn serpent) + E -ic — more at DRAGON] : NODICAL MONTH

drac·on·ti·a·sis \ˌdraˌkän'tīəsə̇s\ n [NL, fr. Gk drakontiasis, fr. drakontion Guinea worm (dim. of drakont-, drakōn serpent) + -iasis] : DRACUNCULOSIS

dra·con·ti·um \drə'känchēəm\ n, cap [NL, fr. L, a kind of arum, fr. Gk drakontion, dim. of drakont-, drakōn serpent] : a genus of tropical American herbs (family Araceae) with compound leaves and hooded spathes

drac·u·la \'drakyələ\ n -s usu cap [after Count Dracula, a vampire depicted in the novel Dracula (1897) by Bram Stoker †1912 Brit. writer] : one who maintains a relationship like that of a vampire toward another by sapping his physical or emotional strength ⟨I wish I could find a truly cruel, fiendish woman, a sheer vicious Dracula —Calder Willingham⟩

dra·cun·cu·li·a·sis \drəˌkaŋkyə'līəsə̇s\ n [NL, fr. 1Dracunculus + -iasis] : DRACUNCULOSIS

dra·cun·cu·lo·sis \-'lōsə̇s\ n [NL, fr. 1Dracunculus + -osis] : infestation with or disease caused by the Guinea worm

1dra·cun·cu·lus \drə'kaŋkyələs\ n, cap [NL (trans. of Gk drakontion Guinea worm), fr. L, small serpent, dim. of draco dragon — more at DRAGON] : a genus (the type of the family Dracunculidae) of greatly elongated nematode worms including the Guinea worm

2dracunculus n [NL, fr. L, tarragon, small serpent] 1 cap : a genus of herbs (family Araceae) with compound leaves — see GREEN DRAGON 2 pl **dracuncu·li** \-ˌlī\ : any plant of the genus Dracunculus

drae·ger·man \'drāgə(r)mən\ n, pl **draegermen** [Alexander B. Dräger †1928 Ger. scientist and inventor of a combined gas mask and oxygen inhalator worn in underground rescue work + E man] : one of a crew of miners trained in underground emergency and rescue work

draff \'draf, -aa(ə)-,-ai-\ n -s [ME draf dregs, draff, fr. (assumed) OE dræf or ON draf; akin to OHG trebir grape husks, draff, MIr drab dregs, OE deorc dark — more at DARK] : the damp remains of malt after brewing often used as an appetizer or supplement in animal rations

draffsack \'=,=\ n [ME draf sak, fr. draf draff + sak sack — more at SACK (bag)] 1 Scot : a sack for draff 2 Scot : a lazy glutton 3 Scot : PAUNCH ⟨celebrated his son's arrival by filling his ~ with ale —T.B.Costain⟩

draffy \-fē\ adj, often -ER/-EST : resembling draff : WORTHLESS

1draft or **draught** \'draft, -aa(ə)-, -ai-, -a\ n -s [ME draht, draght, draught; akin to OHG traht, trahta act of carrying, ON dráttr act of pulling; derivatives fr. the root of OE dragan to draw — more at DRAW] 1 : the act of drawing a net : a sweeping of the water for fish; also : the quantity of fish taken at one drawing ⟨but not a single fish of all the ~ —S.T. Coleridge⟩ 2 a : the act of moving loads by drawing or pulling : PULL, TRACTION ⟨these animals make poor beasts of ~ or burden⟩ b : the harness for work animals c : a team of animals together with what they draw 3 a : the force required to pull a plow or other implement ⟨the effect on plow ~ of 5 factors was tested by means of a hydraulic dynamometer —Biol. Abstracts⟩ b : load or load-pulling capacity ⟨the ~ . . . of a typical draft horse working at about 2½ miles per hour has been given as the order of 150 lb. —F.D.Smith & Barbara Wilcox⟩ 4 a : the act of drawing into the mouth and throat liquor, smoke, vapor, or air : the act or an instance of drinking or inhaling ⟨inhaled the smoke in long luxurious ~s⟩ ⟨swallowed the beer at one ~⟩; also : the portion or quantity that is drunk or inhaled at a single swallow or inhalation ⟨breathing in great ~s of invigorating . . . air —Hugh Walpole⟩ b : a portion of liquid (as medicine) poured out or mixed for drinking : DOSE, POTION ⟨thought himself well enough at night to omit the opium ~ —J.B.Holroyd⟩ ⟨a ~ whose ingredients included the juice of willow bark was esteemed . . . as an antipyretic —Berton Roueché⟩ 5 : a portion of some particular kind of experience to which one is exposed or subjected ⟨the criminal of old was given copious ~s of exhortation and homily —B.N. Cardozo⟩ ⟨the officeholder is refreshed by periodic ~s of opposition —S.B.Chrimes⟩ 6 a : a delineation or representation (as a drawing, painting, sculpture, map, plan, sketch); specif : the plan of something to be constructed ⟨it is usual . . . for any person before he begins to erect a building, to have designs or ~s made —Joseph Moxon⟩ b : SCHEME, DESIGN, PLOT c : a preliminary or tentative sketch, outline, or version (as of a document or picture) ⟨asked him to prepare a ~ of the proposed law⟩ ⟨carefully revised the first ~ of the poem⟩ 7 archaic : INCLINATION, ATTRACTION, TENDENCY 8 : the act, result, or plan of drawing out or stretching: as a : the act in spinning of drawing or attenuating fiber webs, slivers, or rovings b : the amount of such attenuation expressed as a ratio between length of material produced and length of material fed in or as a ratio between surface speeds of rollers effecting that result c : the act in shoe manufacturing of stretching fabric or leather or the placing of paper to determine the pattern shape and contours of a last d : a plan of drawing the warp through the heddles to produce a desired pattern in weaving 9 a : the act of drawing (liquid) from a cask, barrel, or other container b : a portion of liquid that is so drawn ⟨a ~ of ale⟩ 10 a : a drawing down of the pan or platform of a balance or scale b : the material weighed at one time esp. when a quantity is ascertained in several weighings c Brit : any of a number of measures of weight of fish ⟨their cod brought only $1.80 a ~ (238 lbs.) —Time⟩ d : a slight deduction in weight to offset the amount by which something being weighed must overbalance the weights of a scale e : an allowance granted a buyer for loss in weight (as that due to drying or repacking); specif : an allowance of one pound per hundredweight deducted with the tare from the gross weight of any package of wool 11 obs : SINK, SEWER, DRAIN, PRIVY 12 : the depth of water a ship draws esp. when loaded ⟨a ship of 12 feet ~⟩ ⟨found the fleet too deep of ~ to enter small rivers and inlets —S.E. Morison⟩ 13 a : the detaching or selecting of an individual from a group or mass for some special purpose ⟨a ~ of cattle for branding⟩ : the condition of being so drafted ⟨the ex-governor accepted his ~ as candidate with misgivings⟩; specif : a selecting of persons for compulsory military service ⟨the ~ has affected some industries⟩ b : a group of individuals so selected ⟨in a normal year 25 lambs per acre are fattened, the first ~ being taken between February 20 and 25 —T.A.Sellwood⟩ c : a group of men drafted for compulsory military service ⟨discipline when our own new ~s first hit the field left a lot to be desired —J.W.Bellah⟩ d Brit : a group of soldiers or sailors moved or assigned on a particular occasion as a body 14 a : a drawing of money from a fund or stock: as (1) : a written order drawn by a creditor directing a debtor to pay a sum of money to a third party or to bearer — used chiefly of a domestic order or one directed to a person in the country of its origin; compare BILL OF EXCHANGE (2) : CHECK 10b b : the act or an instance of drawing from or making demands upon something : DEMAND, CLAIM ⟨a serious ~ on national resources⟩ 15 a : a current of air in a closed-in space (as a room, ventilator, furnace, or chimney) b : the difference in pressure between the air outside (as of a furnace or chimney) and the gases inside that is responsible for a flow of air c : a contrivance for regulating the flow of air (as in a fireplace, stove, or furnace) 16 a chiefly Midland : GULLY, GORGE b Midland : a small stream : CREEK 17 a : the taper given to a pattern so that it can be easily withdrawn from a mold b : the taper given to a die so that the work can be easily withdrawn from it c : the slant that is given to the furrows of a millstone 18 : a narrow border worked to a plane surface along the edge of a stone or across its face esp. as a guide to the stonecutter 19 : 2DRAW 2f 20 : a system whereby exclusive rights to selected new players are apportioned among teams of a professional baseball, football, or hockey league — **on draft** *adj, of a liquid* **:** ready to be drawn (as from a cask or other container) ⟨the little drugstore with cologne *on draft* like beer —Claudia Cassidy⟩ — **on draft** *adv* **:** from a cask ⟨beer or ale to be served *on draft* —*Brewing in Brief*⟩

²**draft** *or* **draught** \"\ *adj* [ME *draght*, fr. *draht, draght*, n.] **1 :** used for drawing loads ⟨~ animals⟩ — see DRAFT HORSE **2 :** SELECTED — used chiefly of animals selected from a herd or flock (as for branding or classification) **3 :** constituting a preliminary or tentative version, sketch, or outline (as of a literary composition or other document) ⟨Pope . . . proposed to write a history of English poetry, and the ~ scheme of that history has been preserved —A.T.Quiller-Couch⟩ ⟨a ~ treaty⟩ ⟨~ conventions submitted to member nations for their approval⟩ **4 :** on draft; *also* **:** DRAWN ⟨~ beer⟩ — distinguished from *bottled*

³**draft** *or* **draught** \"\ *vb* **drafted** *or* **draughted; drafted** *or* **draughted; drafting** *or* **draughting; drafts** *or* **draughts** [¹*draft, draught*] *vt* **1 a :** to detach or select (an individual) for some special purpose with or without the element of compulsion being present ⟨the convention ~*ed* and nominated the popular attorney general⟩ ⟨his friend . . . was ~*ed* to paint prepared areas —Robert Berkelman⟩ ⟨she had no call to the religious life but was ~*ed* into it by her family —Anthony West⟩ ⟨all able-bodied men were ~*ed* to work on the levee⟩; *specif* **:** to conscript (a person) for service in the armed forces ⟨~*ed* all able-bodied youths⟩ **b** *Austral* **:** to separate into flocks **:** select and detach (an animal) from a herd for a special purpose ⟨~ sheep and take them to sale⟩ **2 a :** to make a draft of **:** draw the preliminary sketch or plan of **:** OUTLINE ⟨~*ing* speeches to be polished and styled by his resourceful secretary⟩ **b :** to draw up **:** COMPOSE, PREPARE, FRAME ⟨at once ~*ed* a telegram, signing it with the code word which he employed in emergencies —John Buchan⟩ ⟨~*ing* plans to meet the anticipated emergency⟩ **3 :** to draw up, off, or away ⟨all pumpers should be capable of ~*ing* water where necessary —*Fire Manual (Mass.)*⟩ ⟨her rents had been ~*ed* to London —Henry Fielding⟩ **4 :** to reduce (fiber webs, slivers, or rovings) in bulk in the processes between loose fiber and spun yarn **5 :** to design (a pattern) in weaving for drawing in warp threads **6 :** to mark (as a stone) with a draft in masonry **7 :** to draw or stretch (leather) in the lasting of shoes ~ *vi* **:** to engage in drafting (as of documents) **:** practice draftsmanship ⟨if anyone thinks that he can ~ more simply . . ., I advise him to try his hand —Ernest Gowers⟩

draft·able \-təbəl\ *adj* **:** qualified for or subject to draft into the armed forces

draft allowance *n* **:** DRAFT 10d, 10e

draft chair *n* **:** WING CHAIR

draft·ee \(')draf¦tē, -raaf-,-raif-,-räf-\ *n* -s [³*draft* + *-ee*] **:** one that is drafted into the armed forces **:** CONSCRIPT

draft·er \'⸗tə(r)\ *n* -s **1 :** one that drafts **2 :** DRAFT HORSE

draft gear *n* **:** a mechanism for transmitting the pull from one railroad car to another

draft horse *n* **:** a horse adapted for or used in drawing heavy loads; *specif* **:** such a horse over 1600 pounds in weight and over 16 hands high — compare CARRIAGE HORSE, CART HORSE, CHUNK, SADDLE HORSE

draft·i·ly \⸗tə̇lē, -li\ *adv* **:** in the manner of a draft **:** in such a manner as to cause a draft ⟨a brakeman came ~ into the dirty plush coach —Thomas Wolfe⟩

draft·i·ness \'tēnə̇s, -tin-\ *n* -ES **1 :** the condition of being exposed to or abounding in drafts ⟨complained of the ~ of her room⟩ **2 :** the condition of being drafty esp. in conformation of body

drafting *pres part of* DRAFT

drafting board *n* **:** DRAWING BOARD

drafting machine *n* **:** a drafting instrument consisting of linked parts that perform the functions of the T square, triangle, linear scale, and protractor

drafting race *n, Austral* **:** a race used for dividing sheep into groups

drafting table *n* **:** DRAWING TABLE

drafting yard *n, Austral* **:** a yard divided into compartments where cattle may be separated into groups

draft·man \-f(t)mən\ *n, pl* **draftmen** [by alter.] **:** DRAFTSMAN — **draft·man·ship** \-,ship\ *n* -s

draft mark *n* **:** one of various marks required by law to be painted at the bow and stern of a ship to show how much water she draws — compare PLIMSOLL MARK

draft net *n* **:** a hauling net **:** SEINE

draft off *vt* **:** ³DRAFT 1b

draft rein *n* **:** the long outer rein of a harness

draft rod *n* **:** a hooked rod attachment on a planter for raising and lowering the marker

drafts *pl of* DRAFT, *pres 3d sing of* DRAFT

drafts·man \-f(t)smən\ *n, pl* **draftsmen** [*drafts* (gen. of ¹*draft*) + *man*] **1 :** one who draws pleadings or other writings **2 :** one who makes drawings; *specif* **:** one who draws plans and sketches (as of machinery or structures) **3 :** an artist who excels in drawing ⟨his genius as a ~ has obscured his talent as a colorist⟩

drafts·man·ship \-,ship\ *n* -s **:** the art or practice of drawing or drafting ⟨the forms of his earliest documents show that the clerks of his chapel included men trained in English conventions of ~ —F.M.Stenton⟩ ⟨though the subjects of these paintings are different . . ., they are similar in their free ~ and their decorative motifs —*Technical Studies*⟩

draft stop *n* **:** CURTAIN BOARD

draft tube *n* **:** an airtight pipe or channel extending downward into the tailrace from a turbine wheel located above it to make the whole fall available

drafty \-ftē, -ti\ *adj* -ER/-EST **1 :** relating to or exposed to a draft ⟨a ~ room⟩ **2 :** resembling or characteristic of a draft horse esp. in conformation

¹**drag** \'drag, -aa(ə)g,-aig\ *n* -s *often attrib* [ME *dragge*, prob. fr. *draggen*, v.] **1 :** something that is dragged, pulled, or drawn along or over a surface **:** as **a :** HARROW 1 **b** *chiefly NewEng* **:** a sledge for conveying heavy bodies ⟨a stone ~⟩ **c :** a steel instrument for completing the dressing of soft stone **d :** an apparatus (as a wooden or metal frame) drawn over ground (as a road) to smooth it — see DRAG SCRAPER **e :** CONVEYANCE; *esp* **:** a private coach that has seats on its top and that is usu. drawn by four horses **f :** the bottom part of a foundry molding flask, mold, or pattern — called also *nowel* **g :** FLOAT 5d (1) **h :** a railroad car or set of cars moved usu. by a switching engine from one part of a yard to another or from one yard to another **i :** crushed and broken ore found in and along a fault zone **2 :** something that is used to drag with **:** as **a :** a device (as a wire, grapnel, net, or scoop) for dragging under water along the bottom or through the water below the surface to detect the presence of, dislodge, obtain, or recover objects **b :** the log carriage in a veneer sawmill **c** [by shortening] **:** DRAGROPE **a 3 a :** something that retards motion **:** as (1) *also* **drag anchor :** something towed in the water to retard a ship's progress or to keep her head up to the wind **:** SEA ANCHOR; *esp* **:** a canvas bag with a hooped mouth used in this manner — compare DRAG SAIL (2) **:** a skid for retarding the motion of a carriage wheel — called also *shoe, dragshoe, skidpan* (3) **:** any of several adjustable devices attached to a fishing reel to prevent the spool from spinning too freely (4) [by shortening] **:** DRAGBAR 1 (5) **:** the retarding force acting on a body (as an airfoil or airplane) moving through a fluid (as air) parallel and opposite to the direction of motion **:** the component of the total aerodynamic force on a body parallel to the relative wind (6) **:** friction esp. between engine parts; *also* **:** retardation due to friction **b :** something that hinders or obstructs nonphysical movement or progress ⟨material . . . unrelated to the running narrative and a considerable ~ on it —Bernard DeVoto⟩ ⟨considered them a ~ on humanity —L.G.Dernisseau⟩ **:** STRAIN, DRAIN, BURDEN ⟨sustained the ~ and turmoil of an active career in the deserts and marshes of Hindustan —Humphrey Bullock⟩ ⟨counted on the continued ~ of occupation costs and manpower to bring the Western Powers around —*Collier's Yr.Bk.*⟩ **4 a** (1) **:** the scent left by a fox or by other game **:** TRAIL (2) **:** an object (as a bag of aniseed) drawn over the ground to leave a scented trail for hounds to follow (3) **:** the hunting with hounds upon an artificial scent **b** (1) **:** a log or other heavy object fastened to a trap as a clog to prevent the escape of the trapped animal (2) **:** a scented bait drawn over the area adjacent to a trap to attract a desired kind of animal to the trap **5 a :** the act or an instance of dragging or drawing **:** as (1) **:** a drawing along or over a surface with considerable effort or pressure ⟨the ~ of chalk on blackboard slate —Lee Anderson⟩ **:** PULL, TUG ⟨the beat and ~ of the wind⟩ (2) **:** motion effected with slowness or difficulty ⟨it was a long ~ up the hill⟩; *also* **:** the condition or appearance of painful slowness or impeded movement ⟨there was a ~ in his walk⟩ ⟨no torture was comparable with the ~ of that single hour after luncheon —Osbert Sitwell⟩ (3) **:** a draw on a pipe, cigarette, or cigar **:** PUFF ⟨the professor took a long, deliberate ~ on his five-cent cigar —O.W.Butz⟩; *also* **:** a draft of liquid **:** DRINK ⟨he took a ~ from the glass —R.P.Warren⟩ **b :** a movement, inclination, or retardation caused by or as if by dragging **:** as (1) *Brit* **:** backspin imparted to a cue ball by striking it somewhat below the center so as to cause it perceptibly to slide along the cloth and to stop dead or nearly so on striking the object ball; *also* **:** a shot so played (2) **:** an excess of draft at the stern of a ship as compared with the bow (3) **:** a downward portamento in lute playing (4) **:** a stroke used in playing the snare drum usu. consisting of 3 or 4 grace notes preceding the beat (5) **:** a bending of rock strata adjacent to a fault (6) **:** a drooping or sagging **:** INCLINATION, HANG ⟨an habitual ~ of the lips⟩ **c** (1) **:** pull exerted by the knife that causes a sliding movement of the lower sheets in a book or pile of sheets being cut typically in the direction of travel of the knife (2) **:** the resistance of cotton fibers to being pulled apart **d** *slang* **:** influence securing special favor or partiality **:** PULL ⟨he must have lots of ~⟩ **6 :** something characterized by slow retarded motion **:** as **a :** a slow freight train **b** *West* (1) **:** the rear section of a herd or flock; *also* **:** a weak or footsore animal in such a herd or flock (2) **:** the men assigned to trail the drag portion of a herd ⟨it was . . . hell for swing and flank and double hell for ~ —A.B.Guthrie⟩ **c** (1) **:** a popular dance in slow rhythm originating in New Orleans; *also* **:** the music for such a dance (2) *or* **dragging step :** a dance step involving the dragging of one foot after the other **7** *slang* **:** STREET, ROAD ⟨strolling up and down this bustling ~ —J.P.O'Donnell⟩ ⟨the main ~⟩ **8** *slang* **a :** woman's dress worn by a man ⟨the first to perform were three queer boys who were completely in ~, with wigs, false eyelashes, high-heeled pumps and beautiful evening gowns —Polly Adler⟩ **b :** a homosexuals' party **9** *slang* **:** a girl that one is escorting **:** GIRL FRIEND, DATE ⟨cadets strolling down the walk with their ~*s*⟩ **10** *or* **drag race** *slang* **:** an acceleration contest between automobiles, esp. hot rods

drag 1e

²**drag** \"\ *vb* **dragged** \-gd\ *or dial* **drug** \'drəg\ **dragged** *or dial* **drug; dragging; drags** [ME *draggen*, fr. ON *draga* to drag, draw, pull or OE *dragan* to drag, draw — more at DRAW] *vt* **1 a** (1) **:** to pull along by main force **:** draw slowly or heavily **:** HAUL ⟨~ stone⟩ ⟨~ a net in fishing⟩ (2) **:** to move (as oneself) with painful slowness or difficulty ⟨the tired man *dragged* himself home⟩ ⟨~ one foot after the other⟩ ⟨the negotiations *dragged* their interminable length along⟩ **b :** to force (a person or group) by nonphysical means into or out of some situation, condition, or course of action ⟨*dragged* me into a fruitless discussion⟩ ⟨*dragging* his friends down to ruin with him⟩ ⟨his infectious humor *dragged* me out of my black musings⟩ ⟨did not want his country *dragged* into a useless war⟩ **c** (1) **:** to pass (a space of time) in lingering pain, tedium, or unhappiness — used chiefly with *out* ⟨*dragged* out his remaining years in bitter loneliness⟩ (2) **:** to protract (as a narrative or musical passage) unduly or tediously — often used with *out* ⟨*dragged* out his anecdote to an intolerable length⟩ ⟨*dragged* out the florid run to impress her audience⟩ **2 a** (1) **:** to pass a drag over (as a field or dirt road) (2) **:** to explore with a drag ⟨*dragged* the river for the drowned boy⟩ (3) **:** SEARCH **:** RANSACK ⟨even when she *dragged* her mind for an excuse or even an idea, she could not unearth one —Ellen Glasgow⟩ **b :** to catch with a dragnet or trawl **3 :** to smooth and pulverize (soil) by the use of a drag or harrow **4 :** to retard by or as if by a drag ⟨the singer continually *dragged* his tempi⟩ **5** *Midland* **:** RALLY, TEASE **6 :** to dress the surface of (a stone) with a drag **7 :** to apply (pigment) by drawing a loaded brush over a tacky surface so that the pigment adheres in irregular spots allowing the ground color to appear between them **8 :** to hit (a bunt) esp. by pulling the bat back at the moment of impact and without being squared around toward the pitcher **9 :** to fly low over (an area) for the purpose of observing the surface conditions esp. if an emergency landing is to be made ~ *vi* **1 :** to hang or lag behind ⟨suddenly noticed that one of the climbers was beginning to ~⟩; *specif* **:** to lag behind in singing or playing ⟨a singing comedienne, she has an effective way of *dragging* behind the beat —*New Yorker*⟩ **2 :** to fish or search with a drag **3 a :** to trail along on the ground ⟨her silken gown *dragged* behind her⟩ **b** (1) **:** to yield or give way along the ground or along the bottom of the sea (as of an anchor that does not hold) (2) *of a ship* **:** to drag anchor **4 a :** to move onward heavily, laboriously, or slowly **:** advance with weary effort ⟨a rheumy old man, crumpled together, bent at the shoulders, feet *dragging* —Elizabeth M. Roberts⟩ **:** go on lingeringly ⟨the negotiations *dragged*, without any prospect of an early solution⟩ **:** cause tedium esp. because of length or lack of interest ⟨the last act ~*s* terribly, and is enough to kill any play —Arnold Bennett⟩ — often used with *on* or *along* ⟨the ride homeward *dragged* on indefinitely —Sherwood Anderson⟩ **b** (1) **:** to move with friction over a surface ⟨the overturned car *dragged* along the street for some distance before stopping⟩ (2) *of brakes* **:** to fail to release **5 :** to make a plucking or pulling movement **:** TUG — used chiefly with *at* ⟨he plucked his thin linen trousers and *dragged* at his collar —Rudyard Kipling⟩ **6 :** DRAW ⟨~ on a cigarette⟩ **7** *slang* **:** to race with a drag ⟨anybody's got the bug to ~ can use the strip long as they have a driver's license —J.M.Flagler⟩ **syn** see PULL — **drag anchor :** to have the anchor fail to hold on the bottom — **drag one's feet** *or* **drag one's heels :** to fail to act with the necessary promptness or vigor **:** be deliberately slow, dilatory, or ineffective in action **:** do less than required or expected ⟨at times local organizations may knife the presidential candidate or at least *drag their feet* in the campaign —V.O.Key⟩

dra·gade \drə'gäd\ *vt* -ED/-ING/-S [origin unknown] **:** to break up (glass) by pouring while melted into water

drag anchor *n* **:** DRAG 3a (1)

dragbar \'⸗,⸗\ *n* [¹*drag* + *bar*] **1 :** a hinged or pivoted bar or yoke attached to the back of a mine car on inclines to prevent its backing if the cable breaks — called also *drag* **2** *Brit* **:** DRAWBAR 2a

dragboat \'⸗,⸗\ *n* **:** DRAGGER

dragbolt \'⸗,⸗\ *n* **:** COUPLER 1a

drag bunt *n* **:** a slow bunt made by pulling the bat back at the moment of impact and without being squared around toward the pitcher

drag cart *n* **:** BUMMER 3

drag chain *n* **:** a chain that drags: as **a :** a chain for coupling freight cars **b :** a metal conveyor belt for removing the clinker from a cement kiln **c :** a chain that is attached to the chassis of a motor vehicle (as a gasoline tank truck) and drags on the roadway to ground the chassis and prevent accumulation of static electricity

drag chute *n* **:** DRAG PARACHUTE

drag coefficient *n* **:** a factor representing the ratio of the aerodynamic drag acting esp. on an airfoil to the product of the airspeed and the area of the airfoil

drag conveyor *n* **:** a conveyor consisting of wooden or steel plates attached to endless chains and running in a trough through which the material is dragged

drag down *vt* **1** *slang* **:** to earn as a wage or salary **:** bring in (a certain sum of money) ⟨two hundred dollars . . . means a lot when you're just *dragging down* an ensign's pay —Land Kaderli⟩ ⟨the super show . . . *dragged down* good money and continued to do so —F.B.Gipson⟩ **2 :** to remove part of (one's craps winnings) and leave the rest as one's next bet

dra·gée \(')dra¦zhā\ *n* -s [F, fr. MF *dragie*, prob. fr. L *tragemata* sweetmeats, fruits eaten as dessert, fr. Gk *tragēmata*, fr. *trōgein* to gnaw, eat fruits; akin to OE *thurh* through — more at THROUGH] **1 a :** a sweetmeat in the form of a sugar-coated nut **b :** a small round usu. silvered confection often used for decorating cakes **2 :** a sugar-coated medicated confection

drag fold *n* **:** a minor geological fold produced in soft or thinly laminated beds lying between harder or more massive beds in the limbs of a major fold

dragged *past of* DRAG

drag·ger \'dragə(r), -raag-,-raig-\ *n* -s **:** one that drags; *specif* **:** a fishing boat operating a trawl or dragnet

dragger-down \¦⸗⸗¦⸗\ *n, pl* **draggers-down :** one who draws heated billets from furnaces

drag·ger·man \-mən\ *n, pl* **draggermen :** one that operates or works on a dragger

dragger net *n* **:** DRAGNET 1a

dragger-out \¦⸗⸗¦⸗\ *n, pl* **draggers-out :** one that drags out; *specif* **:** a worker who withdraws bars from a roughing furnace

dragging *adj* [fr. pres. part. of ²*drag*] **1 :** used in dragging, hauling, or dredging ⟨searched the bottom of the lake with a ~ rope⟩ **2 :** marked by a painfully slow, tired, or sluggish manner (as of movement or speech) ⟨it was a strange ~ approach, half a walk and half a slide —J.P.Marquand⟩ ⟨a soft and ~ voice —Carson McCullers⟩ **:** painfully or tediously protracted **:** LINGERING ⟨two years of ~, ruinous war and military control —Giorgio de Santillana⟩ **:** TEDIOUS ⟨do not . . . prevent the play from being a ~ riddle —Marya Mannes⟩ — **drag·ging·ly** *adv*

dragging beam *or* **dragging piece** *or* **dragging tie** *n* **:** DRAGON BEAM

dragging step *n* **:** DRAG 6c(2)

drag·gle \'dragəl, -raig-\ *vb* **draggled; draggled; draggling** \-g(ə)liŋ\ **draggles** [²*drag* + *-le*] *vt* **:** to make thoroughly wet **:** make limp and sodden by wetting **:** drag or trail (as through dirt or mire) **:** DRABBLE, BESMIRCH ⟨a bough of brier rose whose pale blossoms sweet were *draggled* in the dust —William Morris⟩ ~ *vi* **1 :** to trail on the ground **:** become wet or dirty by being dragged or trailed ⟨her long gown *draggling* on the ground⟩ **2 :** to straggle in the rear **:** trail along with a slovenly or dragging gait **:** SHUFFLE ⟨the girl ~*s* about in sneakers and a short cotton frock —Frank Swinnerton⟩ ⟨most of the actors ~ through their paces —*Time*⟩

draggled *adj* **1 :** thoroughly wet and limp **:** SOAKED, SODDEN ⟨the ~ ends of her hair⟩ ⟨gave him that bright-hued shirt she wore, sadly ~ and muddy now —B.A.Williams⟩ **2 :** soiled esp. by dragging through mud or dirt ⟨scarecrows in battered hats or ~ skirts —Israel Zangwill⟩ ⟨dresses . . . yet gorgeous in color . . . but ~, torn, and untidy —Osbert Sitwell⟩ ⟨grimy, haggard men and a few ~ women —Kenneth Roberts⟩ **:** DIRTY, UNKEMPT, UNTIDY

draggle-tail \'⸗⸗,⸗\ *n* **1 :** a woman who lets her skirt trail along the ground **2 :** SLATTERN

draggletailed \'⸗⸗,⸗\ *adj* **:** UNTIDY, SLUTTISH, SLATTERNLY — **drag·gle·tailed·ness** \¦⸗⸗¦tālədnə̇s, -l(d)n-\ *n* -ES

drag·gly \'drag(ə)lē, -raig-\ *adj* -ER/-EST **:** DRAGGLED, UNTIDY ⟨wagging her old ~ tail —P.E.Green⟩

drag·gy \'dragē, -raag-,-raig-\ *adj* -ER/-EST **:** inclined to drag **:** SLUGGISH, DULL ⟨a bleak, ~ little picture —*Time*⟩ ⟨~ sales are attributed to a . . . psychology of caution —*Nation's Business*⟩

draghound \'⸗,⸗\ *n* **:** a hound trained to follow a scent made with a drag

drag hunt *or* **drag hunting :** DRAG 4a(3)

drag in *vt* **:** to bring in or inject esp. into an argument irrelevantly or inappropriately ⟨the speaker's references to his political opponent were only *dragged in* out of spite⟩ ⟨a ballet that, for once, isn't *dragged in*, that is a perfectly legitimate part of the scene —Deems Taylor⟩

drag iron *n* **:** an attachment for the bottom of a lister to steady the implement and keep a uniform depth

dragline \'⸗,⸗\ *n* **1 :** a line used in or for dragging **2 :** an excavating machine in which the bucket is attached only by cables and is drawn toward the machine during the filling operation — compare BACKHOE **3 :** a glacial stria formed on the lee side of older grooves

drag link *n* **1 :** a link joining the cranks of two shafts **2 :** a rod connecting the steering-gear lever to the steering knuckle in automotive vehicles

drag·man \'dragmən, -raag-,-raig-\ *n, pl* **dragmen :** a man who drags something: as **a :** a fisherman who uses a dragnet **b :** the man who trails the drag in hunting **c :** one who operates a drag conveyor to load metal ore into cars or chutes **d :** an operator of a system of drag chains that convey cement clinker from burning kiln to storage pile

dragnet \'⸗,⸗\ *n* **1 a :** a net that is specially designed to be drawn along the bottom of a body of water **:** TRAWL **b :** a similar net used on the ground (as to capture small game) **2 a :** a device for gathering objects usu. of a certain kind in the mass ⟨do not send out wholesale ~*s* to collect opinions and data —A.T.Weaver⟩ **b :** a network of measures for apprehension (as of criminals) ⟨suspects caught in the police ~⟩

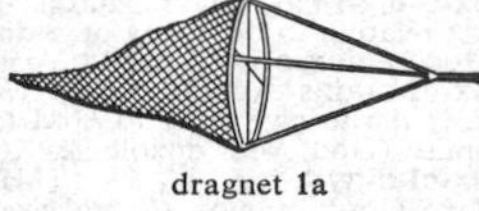
dragnet 1a

dragnet clause *n* **:** a clause in a tariff law that imposes a certain rate of duty on articles not enumerated as free from duty or as subject to any other duty

dra·go \'drä(,)gō\ *n* -s [MexSp, fr. Sp, dragon tree, fr. L *draco* dragon, serpent — more at DRAGON] **:** a Mexican tree (*Pterocarpus acapulcensis*) with large yellow flowers and a red juice that forms a resin similar to kino

drag·o·man \'dragəmən, -raig-\ *n, pl* **dragomans** \-mənz\ *or* **drago·men** \-mən\ [ME *drogman*, fr. MF *drogman, drogoman, dragoman*, fr. OIt *dragomanno*, fr. MGk *dragomanos*, fr. Ar *tarjumān*, fr. Aram *tūrgĕmānā*] **:** an interpreter chiefly of Arabic, Turkish, or Persian employed as official interpreter by an embassy or consulate or as a guide by tourists

drag·on \'dragən, -raig-\ *n* -s [ME *dragun, dragoun*, fr. OF *dragun, dragon*, fr. L *dracon-, draco* serpent, dragon, fr. Gk *drakōn* serpent; akin to OE *torht* bright, splendid, noble, OHG *zoraht* bright, clear, Goth *gatarhjan* to mark, Gk *derkesthai* to see clearly, look at, *drakos* eye, MIr *derc* eye, Skt *darśayati* he causes to see; basic meaning: seeing] **1** *archaic* **:** a huge serpent **2 :** a fabulous animal generally represented as a monstrous winged and scaly serpent or saurian with a crested head and enormous claws **3 a :** the heraldic representation of a monster with a griffin's head, a scaly winged body with four legs and claws, and a long barbed tail and tongue borne as a charge or used as a supporter **b** *dial Brit* **:** a paper kite of dragon form **c :** a beneficent supernatural creature in Chinese mythology connected with rain and floods **4 :** a violent, combative, or very strict person; *esp* **:** a woman that watches fiercely and vigilantly over the welfare of her charges ⟨jealous and touchy, but a very faithful old ~ with the family —Ngaio Marsh⟩ **5 :** any of several arums popularly associated with dragons: as **a :** GREEN DRAGON **b :** JACK-IN-THE-PULPIT 1 **c :** WATER ARUM **d :** a plant of the genus *Dracontium* **6 a :** a short musket formerly carried hooked to a soldier's belt; *also* **:** a soldier carrying such a musket **b :** an armored tractor for artillery **7** [trans. of NL *Draco*] **a :** any of numerous small brilliantly colored arboreal agamid lizards (genus *Draco*) of the East Indies and southern Asia having five or six of the hind ribs on each side prolonged and covered with a web of skin forming a sort of wing and aiding them in making long gliding leaps from tree to tree — called also *flying dragon* **b :** any of certain other lizards of related genera: as (1) **:** JEW LIZARD (2) **:** WATER DRAGON 1

dragon 3a

dragon arum *n* **1 :** a plant of the genus *Arisaema* **2** *Brit* **:** GREEN DRAGON 1

dragon beam *or* **dragon piece** *n* **:** a beam in a hip roof that runs horizontally into the angle of the wall plate and is framed to the hip rafter above — called also *dragon tie*

dragon boat festival *n, usu cap D&B&F* **:** a Chinese festival held just before the summer solstice that has as its chief event a race among long narrow boats resembling dragons

dragon–bushes \ˈ≈,≈\ *n pl but sing or pl in constr, dial Eng* **:** a toadflax (*Linaria vulgaris*)

drag·on·et \ˌ≈≈ˈet, ˈ≈≈ət\ *n* -s [ME, fr. *dragon, dragoun* dragon + *-et*] **1 :** a little dragon **2** [trans. of NL *dracunculus*] **:** any of various small often brightly colored scaleless marine fishes having flattened heads, sharp spines on the gill covers, and marked sexual dimorphism, constituting the family Callionymidae, and including a well-known European fish (*Callionymus lyra*) sometimes used as food

dragonfish \ˈ≈≈,≈\ *n* **1 :** DRAGONET **2 :** a fish of the genus *Pegasus* **3 :** any of various elongated black deep-sea stomiatoid fishes constituting *Idiacanthus* and related genera, having luminous organs of the cheeks and in rows along the sides, and exhibiting strong sexual dimorphism with the males neotenic and greatly reduced in size

dragonfly \ˈ≈≈,≈\ *n* **1 :** any of numerous large predaceous insects constituting the order Odonata, having a large freely movable head with enormous compound eyes, minute antennae, long slender abdomen, four long narrow finely net-veined wings, strong jaws, and legs adapted for grasping their prey, being entirely harmless and among the most useful of insects, the adults feeding on insects which they capture on the wing and destroying vast numbers of flies, gnats, and mosquitoes, and the aquatic predaceous nymphs destroying mosquito larvae — compare DAMSELFLY **2 :** a strong greenish blue that is bluer and duller than grotto and greener and duller than cobalt blue

dragonfly

dragonhead *or* **dragon's–head** \ˈ≈≈,≈\ *n, pl* **dragonheads** *or* **dragon's–heads** [trans. of NL *Dracocephalum*] **:** a mint of the genus *Dracocephalum; esp* **:** a No. American plant (*D. parviflorum*)

drag·on·ish \ˈ≈≈ish\ *adj* **:** being or resembling a dragon in character or temper ⟨it needs . . . ~ duennas to inflame desire to passion —Aldous Huxley⟩

dragon lizard *n* **:** an Indonesian monitor lizard (*Varanus komodoensis*) that is the largest of all known lizards and reaches 11 feet in length

dragon plant *n* **:** a tree or other plant of the genus *Dracaena*

dragonroot \ˈ≈≈,≈\ *n* **:** a jack-in-the-pulpit or green dragon

dragons *pl of* DRAGON

dragon's blood *n* **1 :** any of several resinous mostly dark red substances derived from various trees; *specif* **:** the resin from the fruit of several palms of the genus *Daemonorops* (esp. *D. draco*) that yields the true dragon's blood of commerce which is used for coloring varnish and in photoengraving for preventing undercutting of the printing surface during etching **2 :** the thickened juice of the dragon tree of the Canary islands or a related tree of Socotra **3 :** a synthetic powder used in photoengraving similarly to true dragon's blood **4** *or* **dragon's–blood red :** POMPEIAN RED

dragon's–claw *also* **dragon claw** \ˈ≈≈,≈\ *n, pl* **dragon's–claws** *also* **dragon claws :** either of two coralroots (*Corallorhiza odontorhiza* or *C. maculata*)

dragon's–mouth \ˈ≈≈,≈\ *n, pl* **dragon's–mouths 1 :** SNAPDRAGON 1a **2 :** an orchid (*Arethusa bulbosa*) with a wide-gaping corolla

dragon's teeth *n pl* **1** [so called fr. the story in Greek mythology that Cadmus, the founder of Thebes in Boeotia, sowed the teeth of a dragon that sprang into armed men who fought each other until only five survived] **:** seeds of mutual strife **2 :** wedge-shaped concrete antitank obstacles laid in multiple rows

dragon's–tongue \ˈ≈≈,≈\ *n, pl* **dragon's–tongues :** SPOTTED WINTERGREEN

dragon tie *n* **:** DRAGON BEAM

dragon tree *n* **:** a tree of the Canary islands (*Dracaena draco*) notable for reaching great age

dragon worm *n* **:** GUINEA WORM

¹dra·goon \drəˈgün, draˈ-,draiˈ-\ *n* -s [F *dragon* dragon, military standard, dragoon, fr. MF — more at DRAGON] **1 a :** a mounted infantryman of the 17th and 18th centuries; *esp* **:** one armed with a carbine **b :** CAVALRYMAN **2** *obs* **:** an ancient carbine **:** DRAGON **3 :** a variety of medium-sized blocky wattled domestic pigeons

²dragoon \ˈ"\ *vt* -ED/-ING/-S **1 :** to reduce to subjection by dragoons **:** persecute by the harsh use of troops **2 :** to compel or attempt to compel submission by violent measures **:** HARASS, PERSECUTE ⟨they ~*ed* him into working⟩

dragoon bird *n* [so called fr. its crest that suggests the headdress of a dragoon] **:** a brightly colored Australian pitta (*Pitta versicolor*) that feeds on snails — called also *noisy pitta*

dragooner *n* -s [prob. fr. G *dragoner*, fr. F *dragon* — more at DRAGOON] *obs* **:** DRAGOON 1a

dragos *pl of* DRAGO

drag parachute *n* **:** a parachute released from the rear of an airplane to help slow it down during the ground run in landing

drag race *n* **:** DRAG 10

drag rake *n* **1 :** a heavy rake used for harvesting **2 :** a rake with curved teeth used for digging clams

dragrope \ˈ≈,≈\ *n* **:** a rope with which something is dragged or that drags from a thing: as **a :** a rope with a short chain and a hook that is attached to an artillery carriage and used in emergencies in dragging it or locking its wheels **b :** a rope dropped from an aerostat for use as a variable ballast, as a brake, or as a mooring line

drags *pl of* DRAG, *pres 3d sing of* DRAG

drag sail *or* **drag sheet** *n* **:** a sea anchor made from a sail or piece of canvas

dragsaw \ˈ≈,≈\ *n* **:** a saw with teeth that are slanted so as to cut on the pulling stroke; *specif.* **:** a large power-operated saw for sawing felled trees

drag scraper *n* **1 :** an earth-digging and transporting device consisting of a crescent-shaped bottomless bucket operated along the ground by a cable between a mast and an anchor **2 :** a bottomless tractor-towed earth scraper

drag seine *n* **:** BEACH SEINE

dragshoe \ˈ≈,≈\ *n* **:** DRAG 3a(2)

dragshovel \ˈ≈,≈≈\ *n* **:** BACKHOE

drags·man \ˈdragzmən, -raag-,-raig-\ *n, pl* **dragsmen** [*drags* (gen. of ¹*drag*) + *man*] **:** a driver of a drag; *also* **:** one who works with a drag

dragstaff \ˈ≈,≈\ *n* **:** a trailing pole pivoted on the rear of a vehicle to check any backward movement

drag·ster \-gztə(r), -gst-\ *n* -s [¹*drag* + road*ster*] **:** an automobile rebuilt or stripped down esp. for use in a drag race **:** HOT ROD

drag–stone mill *n* **:** a mill in which ores are ground by means of a heavy stone dragged around on a circular or annular stone bed

drag strip *n* **:** the site of a drag race

drag strut *n* **:** a fore-and-aft compression member of the internal bracing system of an airplane

drag through *vt* **:** to test the fit of (a probable word, a segment of key, or another message) everywhere throughout a cipher-text

drag tooth *n* **:** RAKER 1f

drag truss *n* **:** a horizontal truss between the wing spars for stiffening the structure and resisting the drag forces acting on the wing of an airplane

drag wire *n* **:** a member of a truss in the wing and also in the wing support of an airplane for sustaining the backward reaction due to the drag of the wing

draht·haar \ˈdrät,här\ *n* -s [G, lit., wire hair, fr. *draht* wire (fr. OHG *drāt* thread) + *haar* hair (fr. OHG *hār*) — more at THREAD, HAIR] **:** a dog of a German breed of wire-haired pointers

drai·gle \ˈdrāgəl\ *Scot var of* DRAGGLE

drai·gon \ˈdrāgən\ *Scot var of* DRAGON

¹drail \ˈdrāl, *esp before pause or consonant* -āəl\ *n* -s [fr. obs. E *drail* to drag or trail along, perh. alter. (influenced by *draw* & *drag*) of *trail*] **1 :** a hook with a lead-covered shank used in trolling for fish (as bluefish) **2 :** a perforated iron projecting from the beam of a plow to which the horses are hitched

²drail \ˈ"\ *vb* -ED/-ING/-S **:** to fish by trolling with a drail

¹drain \ˈdrān\ *vb* -ED/-ING/-S [ME *draynen*, fr. OE *drēahnian, drēhnian*; perh. akin to ON *drangr* dry log, Fris *drūgen* to strain, OE *drȳge* dry — more at DRY] *vt* **1** *obs* **:** to pass (liquid) through some permeable substance **:** FILTER **2 a :** to draw off (liquid) by degrees **:** cause to flow gradually out or off **:** draw off completely (as by means of a drain or trench) ⟨~ the water from a tank⟩ ⟨waterspouts to ~ off the rain⟩ **b** (1) **:** to cause the gradual disappearance or extinction of ⟨fright had ~*ed* all color from his face⟩ ⟨the urge to conform was slowly ~*ing* the boy's individuality⟩ **:** EXHAUST ⟨war had ~*ed* the country's treasure and best manhood⟩ (2) **:** VENT, DISCHARGE ⟨~ an undesirable emotion⟩ ⟨enabling the patient to ~ his deeply repressed anxieties⟩ (3) **:** to exhaust physically or emotionally ⟨~*ed* as he was by his session . . ., he did not feel up to it —Hamilton Basso⟩ ⟨matinee days are tough: two shows a day ~ a girl —Ethel Merman⟩ **3 a :** to exhaust of liquid contents by drawing them off **:** make gradually dry or empty ⟨~ a flooded mine⟩ ⟨~ a marsh⟩ **:** receive or carry away the surface water or discharge of ⟨~*ing* mountains of everlasting snow, the river twists for nineteen hundred miles —J.F.Dobie⟩ ⟨this lake ~*s* the numerous small streams of the area⟩ **b** (1) **:** EMPTY ⟨~ of wealth or resources⟩ ⟨~*ed* the country of its gold⟩ (2) **:** to drink (a liquid) to the last drops ⟨took the drink out of the drawer and ~*ed* it —Barnaby Conrad⟩ **:** empty (a glass or other container) by drinking ⟨allow you a respectable interlude in which to ~ your glass —Richard Joseph⟩ **~** *vi* **1 a :** to flow off gradually ⟨blood ~*ing* from a wound⟩ **b :** to disappear gradually **:** DWINDLE — often used with *away* ⟨his nervousness ~*ed* away, as it always did —H.A.Sinclair⟩ ⟨all his wealth had ~*ed* away⟩ **2 :** to become emptied or freed of liquid by its flowing or dropping ⟨put the umbrella on the porch to ~⟩ **3 :** to discharge surface or surplus water or streams in a given direction or to an outlet ⟨the middle western states ~ into the Gulf of Mexico⟩ **syn** see DEPLETE

²drain \ˈ"\ *n* -s *often attrib* **1 a :** an artificial channel by means of which liquid or other matter is drained or carried off **:** SEWER, SINK, TRENCH **b :** a watercourse esp. when narrow **2 a :** the act of draining or drawing off liquid **:** gradual outflow or withdrawal ⟨~ from a wound⟩ ⟨~ from a leaky faucet⟩ **b** (1) **:** a gradual outflow or withdrawal of something nonliquid **:** depletion or the amount of such depletion ⟨a ruinous ~ of dollars⟩ ⟨a net ~ from the East of five million souls —G.W.Pierson⟩ (2) **:** something that causes depletions (as of resources) **:** BURDEN, STRAIN ⟨indebtedness is apt to be one of the great ~*s* upon the income of peasant families —*Notes & Queries on Anthropology*⟩ ⟨the medical and social care of old people . . . constitutes a heavy ~ on the economic resources of society —M.A.Abrams⟩ ⟨the office worker emerged as a major ~ on business profits —Gabriel Kolko⟩ **3 drains** *pl* **a :** DREGS ⟨as though . . . I had emptied some dull opiate to the ~*s* —John Keats⟩ **b** *brewing, Brit* **:** the grain from the mash tun **4 a :** the liquid or other matter that is drained off or away ⟨the ~ had collected at the foot of the spout, forming a small pool⟩ **b :** a small remaining amount of liquid ⟨they still had a tiny ~ of petrol for the works car for station trips —Nevil Shute⟩ **c :** a drink esp. of some alcoholic beverage ⟨she thought a ~ of gin and peppermint . . . would do most good —William Heath⟩ ⟨his cigar going and a ~ of brandy . . . before him —A.J.Cronin⟩ **5 :** a tube or a cylinder usu. of absorbent material for drainage of a wound — compare CIGARETTE DRAIN

drain·age \-nij,-nēj\ *n* -s **1 a :** the act or an instance of draining ⟨by this ~ of colonial wealth the empire financed its costly wars⟩ ⟨~ of the marshy lands was completed in a short time⟩ **b :** DRAINING **:** a gradual flowing off or dropping down ⟨complained of ~ of rain water into the cellar⟩ ⟨gold ~ and gold hoarding . . . were feared —F.L.Paxson⟩; *also* **:** something that is drained off ⟨this lake receives the ~ of many mountain streams⟩ **c** *chiefly Brit* **:** SEWAGE; *also* **:** the sewage system of a building **2 :** the manner in which the waters of a country pass off (as by streams and rivers) ⟨subsurface ~⟩ **3 a :** the removal of excess water from land by means of surface or subsurface conduits; *also* **:** a system of such conduits **b :** AERIAL DRAINAGE **4 a :** area or district drained (as by a river) **b** *or* **drainage system :** the streams or other waterways by which a region is drained **5 :** the act, process, or means of drawing off fluids from a cavity or wound by means of suction or gravity **6 :** a process or means of release of internal conflicts or pent-up feelings (as hostility or guilt)

drainage basin *n* **:** BASIN 2d

drainage district *n* **:** a governmental corporation or quasi corporation created by a state for the drainage of a specified territory

drainage line *n* **:** the course of a major stream in a drainage system

drainageway \ˈ≈≈,≈\ *n* **:** a route or course along which water moves or may move to drain a region

drainboard \ˈ≈,≈\ *n* **:** a sloping shelf beside and draining into a sink

drained *adj* [fr. past part. of ¹*drain*] **1 :** emptied or freed of excess water or other liquid; *also* **:** drawn off (as by pouring or flowing) ⟨a ~ marsh⟩ **2 :** exhausted physically or emotionally **:** emptied of emotion **:** DULL ⟨leaving him ~ and apathetic, an old man . . . not caring any longer about anything —Angus Mowat⟩

drain·er \-nə(r)\ *n* -s **:** one that drains: as **a :** a worker who tends to the filling and emptying of vats of bleached wood pulp **b :** a kitchen device used in draining ⟨a wire mesh ~ for vegetables⟩ **c :** DRAINING VAT

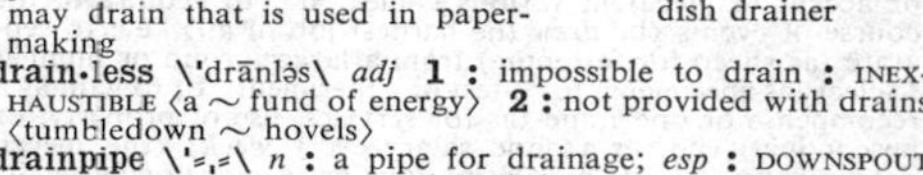
dish drainer

drain·er·man \-mən\ *n, pl* **drainermen :** a worker who attends to draining vats in papermaking

draining *pres part of* DRAIN

draining board *n, Brit* **:** DRAINBOARD

draining vat *n* **:** a tank with a porous bottom through which water may drain that is used in papermaking

drain·less \ˈdrānləs\ *adj* **1 :** impossible to drain **:** INEXHAUSTIBLE ⟨a ~ fund of energy⟩ **2 :** not provided with drains ⟨tumbledown ~ hovels⟩

drainpipe \ˈ≈,≈\ *n* **:** a pipe for drainage; *esp* **:** DOWNSPOUT

drainpipe trousers *n pl* **:** tight-fitting trousers that taper to the ankles

drains *pres 3d sing of* DRAIN, *pl of* DRAIN

drai·sine \drāˈzēn, drāˈzēnə, drīˈzēnə\ *n* -s [F & G; F *draisine, draisienne*, fr. G *draisine*, fr. Baron Karl von *Drais* †1851 Ger. forester, its inventor + G *-ine* (as in *maschine* machine)] **:** DANDY HORSE

¹drake \ˈdrāk\ *n* -s [ME, fr. OE *draca*; akin to OHG *trahho* dragon, MLG & MD *drake*, ON *dreki*; all fr. a prehistoric WGmc-NGmc word borrowed fr. L *draco* dragon, serpent — more at DRAGON] **1** *archaic* **:** DRAGON **2 :** a small piece of artillery of the 17th and 18th centuries **3** [by shortening] **:** DRAKE FLY

²drake \ˈ"\ *n* -s [ME; akin to G dial. *drache, trech* drake, OHG *antrahho, antrehho*, LG *drake*] **1 :** the male of a wild or domestic duck **2 a :** the flat stone used in the game of duck on a rock **b :** DRAKESTONE **3** *or* **drake green :** a dark greenish blue that is bluer and stronger than average teal, bluer, lighter, and stronger than average teal blue, and greener, lighter, and stronger than teal duck — called also *drake's-neck green*

drake fly *n* [ME *drake flye*, fr. ¹*drake* + *flye* fly — more at FLY] **:** MAYFLY

drake foot *n* [²*drake*] **:** a furniture foot carved with three lobes so as to suggest the contracted toes of a male duck — compare DUTCH FOOT; see FOOT illustration

drake·let \-lət\ *also* **drake·ling** \-liŋ\ *n* -s [²*drake* + *-let, -ling*] **:** a young drake

drake's–neck green *n* **:** ²DRAKE 3

drakestone \ˈ≈,≈\ *n* [²*drake* + *stone*] **:** a flat stone used for skipping in the game of ducks and drakes

¹dram \ˈdram, -aa(ə)m\ *n* -s [ME *drame, dragme*, fr. MF & LL; MF *drame, dragme* dram, drachma, fr. LL *dragma*, fr. L *drachma*, fr. Gk *drachmē*, lit., handful, fr. *drassesthai* to grasp — more at TARGET] **1 a :** either of two units of weight: (1) **:** an avoirdupois unit equal to 27.343 grains (2) **:** an apothecaries' unit equal to 60 grains — see MEASURE table **b :** FLUIDRAM **2 a :** a small portion of something to drink (as of distilled alcoholic liquor) ⟨a ~ of brandy⟩ **b :** a small amount **:** MITE ⟨a ~ of well-doing —John Milton⟩

²dram \ˈ"\ *vb* **drammed; drammed; dramming; drams** *vi, archaic* **:** to drink liquor **:** TIPPLE **~** *vt, archaic* **:** to give a drink of liquor to

dra·ma \ˈdrämə, -amə, -ȧmə\ *n* -s [LL, fr. Gk, deed, action on the stage, drama, fr. *dran* to do, act; akin to Gk *drainein* to be ready to do and prob. to Lith *daryti* to do, make, Latvian *darīt*] **1 :** a composition in verse or prose arranged for enactment (as by actors on a stage) and intended to portray life or character or to tell a story through the actions and usu. dialogue of the enactors **:** PLAY **2 :** dramatic art, literature, or affairs ⟨a person skilled in ~⟩ ⟨a devotee of the ~⟩ ⟨the highlights of English ~⟩ **3 a :** a condition, situation, or series of events involving interesting or intense conflict of forces suggesting that characteristic of a play ⟨whatever happens in the ~ of today, the future lies with freedom —J.T. Shotwell⟩ ⟨between fantasy and exact knowledge, between ~ and technology, there is an intermediate station: that of magic —Lewis Mumford⟩ **b :** dramatic state, effect, or quality ⟨the ~ of New York's skyline⟩ ⟨why not use candles sometimes for a bit of ~ at the family table⟩

dramage *var of* DRAMMAGE

dra·ma·logue \-,lȯg *also* -,läg\ *n* -s [*drama* + *-logue*] **:** a reading of a play to an audience

Dram·a·mine \ˈdramə,mēn\ *trademark* — used for dimenhydrinate

¹dra·mat·ic \drəˈmad·ik, -atǀ, ǀēk\ *adj* [MF & LL; MF *dramatique*, fr. LL *dramaticus*, fr. Gk *dramatikos*, fr. *dramat-, drama* deed, drama + *-ikos* -ic — more at DRAMA] **1 a :** of or relating to or for the drama ⟨exquisitely staged ~ performances⟩ ⟨something is achieved by way of drama which we of the ~ stage could never attempt —*New Republic*⟩ **b :** of, relating to, devoted to, or concerned specifically or professionally with current drama or the contemporary theater ⟨a ~ critic⟩ ⟨one of the outstanding ~ events of the current theatrical season⟩ **2 a :** suitable to or characteristic of the drama esp. in being expressed with or as if with action ⟨a highly ~ appeal⟩ ⟨his ~ attempt to escape⟩ **b :** striking in appearance or effect ⟨continued after a ~ pause⟩ ⟨there could be no more ~ reminder of this fact than the contrast between the subsequent career of Sir Winston Churchill and his school record —F.C.James⟩ ⟨~ floral prints were popular⟩ **3** *of a singing voice* **:** having expressive power and a ringing quality and capable of a declamatory or theatrical style ⟨a ~ soprano⟩ ⟨a ~ tenor⟩ — compare LYRIC

²dramatic *n* -s *obs* **:** DRAMATIST

dra·mat·i·cal \drəˈmad·əkəl, -atǀ, ǀēk-\ *adj, archaic* **:** DRAMATIC 1

dra·mat·i·cal·ly \-k(ə)lē, -li\ *adv* **:** in a dramatic manner **:** so as to have striking effect **:** VIVIDLY

dramatic irony *n* **:** irony produced by incongruity between a situation developed in a drama and accompanying or preceding words or actions whose inappropriateness it reveals

dra·mat·i·cism \ə,sizəm\ *n* -s **:** dramatic character

dramatic monologue *n* **:** a literary work (as a poem) in which the character of a protagonist is vividly revealed in a monologue addressed to another person or a group of persons usu. with interplay of speaker and audience

dra·mat·i·co–musical \drəˌmad·iǀ(,)kō, -atǀ, ǀē(,)kō+\ *adj* [¹*dramatic* + *-o-* + *musical*] **:** consisting of drama and music ⟨*dramatico-musical* works⟩

dramatic overture *n* **:** the orchestral prelude to or as if to an opera

dramatic present *n* **:** HISTORICAL PRESENT

dramatic reading *n* **:** a public reading or recitation of a work of literature (as a poem or play) with an interpretative or dramatic use of the voice and often of gestures

dra·mat·ics \drəˈmad·iks, -atǀ, ǀēks\ *n pl but sing or pl in constr* **1** *obs* **:** dramatic writings **2 a :** theatricals esp. as an extracurricular activity in school or college — usu. construed as pl. **b :** theatrical technique ⟨studied ~ under one of the best coaches in New York⟩ **3 :** dramatic behavior or expression ⟨I hoped she would go without any ~ —Hartley Howard⟩ ⟨a flair for ~ in his painting⟩

dra·mat·i·cule \ˌ≈ˈ≈ə,kyül\ *n* -s [LL *dramat-, drama* drama + E *-i-* + *-cule* (fr. L *-culus*, dim. suffix)] **:** a little or insignificant drama

dramatic unities *n pl* **:** the unities of time, place, and action observed in classical drama

dram·a·tism \ˈdramə,tizəm, -räm-,-ram-\ *n* -s [LL *dramat-, drama* + E *-ism* — more at DRAMA] **1 :** dramatic manner or form (as of speech or writing) **2 :** a technique of analysis of language and thought as basically modes of action rather than as means of conveying information

dra·ma·tis per·so·nae \ˌdramad·əspərˈsō(,)nē, -äm-, -,nī, ÷ drəˌmad·-\ *n pl* [NL, lit., people of a drama] **1 a :** the characters or actors in a drama or in a novel or poem **b :** a descriptive list of the characters in a drama; *esp* **:** one printed at the beginning of the text of a drama **2 :** the participants in an actual event or series of events

dram·a·tist \ˈdramad·əst, -äm-,-ȧm-, -mətə-\ *n* -s [LL *dramat-, drama* + E *-ist*] **1 :** PLAYWRIGHT **2 :** one that dramatizes ⟨a man of moods . . . both a poet and a ~ of his instrument who gave to everything he played . . . a unique coloring —Duncan MacDougald⟩

dram·a·tis·tic \ˌ≈≈ˈtistik\ *adj* **:** of, relating to, or by the methods of dramatism ⟨a ~ analysis of the poem⟩ **— dram·a·tis·ti·cal·ly** \-stək(ə)lē\ *adv*

dram·a·ti·za·tion \ˌdramad·əˈzāshən, -ətəˈz-, -ə,tīˈz- *also* -äm- *or* -ȧm-\ *n* -s **1 :** an act, process, or product of dramatizing ⟨the ~ of ideas⟩ ⟨his conscious ~ of his troubles⟩ ⟨a ~ of a problem⟩; *esp* **:** a dramatized version (as of a novel) **2 :** the transformation which in psychoanalytic theory the underlying dream thoughts undergo into dramatic and pictorial form before they can take part in the actual dream

dram·a·tize \ˈ≈mə,tīz\ *vb* -ED/-ING/-S *see -ize in Explan Notes* [LL *dramat-, drama* drama, play + E *-ize* — more at DRAMA] *vt* **1 a :** to rewrite (as a novel) or adapt (as an incident or account) for theatrical presentation ⟨several of his short stories were later *dramatized*⟩ ⟨one of the shows for which he *dramatized* episodes of colonial history⟩ **b :** to act out (material usu. read or presented in writing) ⟨*dramatizing* commercials on television⟩ **2 a :** to recount in a dramatic manner ⟨she often seems to be *dramatizing* her material according to the methods of painting rather than those of literature —*New Republic*⟩ ⟨a long epic that ~*s* the gradual dissolution of a family⟩ **b :** to present or represent in a dramatic manner: as (1) **:** to make a dramatic scene of ⟨she never fails to ~ her entries and exits⟩ (2) **:** to display (oneself or one's problems or motives) to advantage as if playing a part on a stage ⟨he lost votes because of his inability to ~ himself to his constituents⟩; *often* **:** to display outwardly and often flauntingly one's own conception of (oneself or one's virtues) ⟨compensating for lack of real ability by consciously *dramatizing* her appearance⟩ (3) **:** to exhibit graphically in such a manner as to show forth qualities, attributes, or aspects likely to be overlooked ⟨wartime shortages *dramatized* the importance of foreign trade⟩ ⟨the new vaccine ~*s* the need for continued medical research⟩ (4) **:** to make (as an article of apparel) strikingly attractive esp. by careful attention to detail ⟨a brocade wrap *dramatized* by huge sleeves⟩ **~** *vi* **1 :** to be suitable for dramatization ⟨the story would ~ well⟩ **2 :** to dramatize oneself **:** put on an act

dram·a·tiz·er \-zə(r)\ *n* -s **:** one that dramatizes

dram·a·turge \ˈdramə,tərj, -äm-,-ȧm-\ *n* -s [G *dramaturg* & F *dramaturge*, fr. Gk *dramatourgos* dramatist, fr. *dramat-, drama* deed, drama + *-ourgos* (fr. *ergon* work) — more at

DRAMA, WORK] : a person skilled in the writing or revision of plays; *also* : a functionary of certain European theaters who is responsible esp. for selecting and arranging the repertoire and often cooperates with and advises the producer in the course of rehearsal

dram·a·tur·gic \¦==¦tərjik\ *or* **dram·a·tur·gi·cal** \-jəkəl\ *adj* **1 :** relating to dramaturgy, esp. to the technical aspects of play construction ⟨~ theory⟩ ⟨modification of ~ techniques to the peculiar needs of the motion picture⟩ **2 :** DRAMATIC, THEATRICAL ⟨the ~ heights attained by some of the older Shakespearean actors⟩

dram·a·tur·gy \'==,=jē\ *n* -ES [G *dramaturgie* (in *Die hamburgische Dramaturgie*, critical work by Gotthold E. Lessing †1781 Ger. dramatist and critic), fr. Gk *dramatourgia* dramatic composition, action of a play, fr. *dramatourgos* + *-ia* -y] **1 :** the art or technique of writing drama ⟨a professor of ~⟩ **2 :** the technical devices that are used in writing drama and that tend to distinguish it from other literary forms ⟨a play with sound ~ and excellent acting⟩ ⟨a first-rate clinical example of ~ but a second-rate "show" —G.J.Nathan⟩; *often* : use of or the product of the use of such technical devices ⟨reviewers . . . neglecting honest ~ for incandescent performing — *N.Y. Herald Tribune*⟩

drame \'dräm, -åm\ *n* -S [F (also, drama), fr. LL *drama* — more at DRAMA] : TRAGICOMEDY 1a

dram equivalent *n* : the weight of a smokeless shotgun powder that gives the same shot velocity and the same approximate gas pressure as a given weight in drams of black powder

dram·mage *or* **dram·age** \'dramij\ *n* -S : a measure of silk size based on the weight in drams of a 1000-yard skein

dram·ma per mu·si·ca \¦drämə,per'müzēkə\ *n* [It, lit., drama for music] : early lyric drama that was a precursor of opera

dram·ma·ti·co \drə'mäd·ē,kō\ *adv* (*or adj*) [It, dramatic, fr. LL *dramaticus* — more at DRAMATIC] : in a dramatic manner — used as a direction in music

drammed *past of* DRAM

dram·mer \'dramə(r), -aam-\ *n* -S : one that drinks : TIPPLER

dramming *pres part of* DRAM

dram·mock \'dramək\ *n* -S [ScGael *dramag* foul mixture, crowdy] **1** *chiefly Scot* : raw oatmeal mixed with cold water **2** *chiefly Scot* : an unpalatable mixture

dram pers *abbr* dramatis personae

drams *pl of* DRAM, *pres 3d sing of* DRAM

dramseller \'=,==\ *n, archaic* : a seller of distilled liquors by the drink

dramshop \'=,=\ *n, archaic* : BARROOM

drang \'draŋ\ *var of* DRONG

drank *past of* DRINK

drant \'drant, -å-\ *vi* -ED/-ING/-S [Sc *drant, draunt* droning or drawling tone, modif. of ScGael *dranndan, draundan* hum, buzzing, complaint, growl; akin to IrGael *dranntan* hum, buzzing, growl] *chiefly Scot* : to speak in a tiresome whining drawl

[1]drap \'drå\ *n, pl* **draps** \"\ [F — more at DRAB (cloth)] : CLOTH

[2]drap \'drap\ *dial var of* DROP

drap·able *also* **drape·able** \'drāpəbəl\ *adj* : fit for draping : capable of being draped ⟨heavy ~ satins⟩

drap–de–ber·ry \,drädə,be'rē\ *n, usu cap B* [F, lit., cloth from Berry (region in France)] : a woolen cloth formerly made in Berry, France

drap d'é·té \,drä(,)dā'tā\ *n* [F *drap d' été*, lit., summer cloth] : a thin woolen or blended fabric that has a twill weave and is used esp. for summer clothing

[1]drape \'drāp\ *vb* -ED/-ING/-S [ME *drapen*, fr. MF *draper*, fr. *drap* cloth — more at DRAB (cloth)] *vt* **1** *obs* : to make into cloth : WEAVE **2 :** to cover or adorn with or as if with or swathe in or as if in folds of cloth ⟨great cypress trees *draped* with Spanish moss⟩ ⟨*draping* the building fronts with bunting⟩: as **a :** to cover following the contours of ⟨dark chestnuts ~ the mountainside —F.L.Lucas⟩ **b :** ENFOLD ⟨the child was *draped* in expensive linens⟩ ⟨*draping* himself in abstruse thought⟩ **c :** to hang or put on (as a garment) casually or loosely **d :** to let (as oneself) sprawl ⟨*draping* garlands about the singer's neck⟩ ⟨*draped* her furs over her arm⟩ ⟨several of the regulars had *draped* themselves around the bar⟩ **e :** to shroud or enclose with surgical drapes ⟨~ a patient for operation⟩ **3 :** to arrange in flowing lines or folds or according to a pattern or design ⟨*draping* a satin dress to minimize heavy hips⟩ ⟨a cleverly *draped* suit⟩ ~ *vi* : to fall in or into folds, esp. into graceful folds ⟨this silk ~*s* beautifully⟩; *often* : to become arranged in decorative folds ⟨a full skirt that ~*s* to a huge bow⟩

[2]drape \"\ *n* -S [partly fr. F *drap* cloth; partly fr. [1]*drape*] **1** *archaic* : CLOTH, TEXTILES **2 a :** a drapery esp. for a window; *esp* : OVERDRAPE **b :** a sterile covering used in an operating room (as about the operative site or between the anesthetist and the surgical team) to decrease the chance of contamination — usu. used in pl. **3 a :** arrangement in or of folds ⟨the classic ~ of her gown⟩; *often* : decorative fold or folds in a garment or hanging ⟨a soft ~ in front flattered her flat chest⟩ **b :** the property of falling in graceful folds ⟨a silk with excellent ~⟩ **4 a :** the cut or hang of clothing (as of a man's double-breasted suit jacket) **b** *slang* (1) : a man's suit with jacket of unusual length and exaggerated cut sometimes popular with adolescents — compare ZOOT SUIT (2) : a wearer of a drape

[1]drap·er \-pə(r)\ *n* -S [in sense 1, fr. ME, maker of cloth, fr. MF *drapier*, fr. OF, fr. *drap* cloth + *-ier* -er; in sense 2, fr. [1]*drape* + *-er*] **1** *Brit* : a dealer in cloth and sometimes also in clothing and dry goods **2 :** one that drapes (as cloth) or arranges draperies (as on a stage setting)

[2]dra·per \"\ *n* -S [origin unknown] **1 :** a machine for cleaning sugar-beet seed **2 :** the canvas conveyor of a header, binder, or combine

drap·er·ied \'drāp(ə)rēd, -rid\ *adj* [[1]*drapery* + *-ed*] : covered or supplied with drapery or draperies

draper's cap *n* : thin brown wrapping paper that is glazed on one side

draper's teasel *n* [[1]*draper;* fr. its being formerly used to raise a nap on cloth] : FULLER'S TEASEL

[1]drap·ery \'drāp(ə)rē, -ri\ *n* -ES [ME *draperie* (also, manufacture of cloth, dealing in cloth), fr. MF, fr. OF, fr. *drap* cloth + *-erie* -ery — more at DRAB (cloth)] **1** *Brit* : DRY GOODS **2** *Brit* : the occupation of a draper **3 :** a piece of material (as cloth, lace, or plastic) used for decorative purposes and usu. hung in loose folds arranged in a graceful design: as **a :** clothing or a piece of cloth arranged in graceful folds and worn or represented in art as worn on the human body **b :** CURTAIN 1a; *esp* : a curtain of heavy fabric often used over sheer curtains **c :** loose coverings for furniture; *also* : an arrangement of cloth for use in interior decoration esp. as a wall covering : HANGINGS **4 :** something that serves to cover, adorn, or conceal ⟨facts buried under the *draperies* of his turgid prose⟩ **5 :** the draping or arranging of materials or their representation ⟨great skill in ~⟩

[2]drapery \"\ *vt* -ED/-ING/-ES : to furnish or adorn with or as if with drapery — used chiefly as a past participle ⟨she was *draperied* in soft flowing velvet⟩

drapet *n* -S [It *drappetto*, dim. of *drappo* cloth, fr. LL *drappus* — more at DRAB (cloth)] *obs* : CLOTH, COVERING

drap·ey \'drāpē, -pi\ *adj* **1 :** of, relating to, or characterized by drape ⟨a soft ~ fabric⟩ **2 :** depending on drape for effect ⟨a ~ lace dress⟩

drapped *past of* DRAP

drap·pie *or* **drap·py** \'drapē, -pi\ *n, pl* **drappies** [[2]*drap* + *-ie, -y*] **1** *chiefly Scot* : a small amount of liquid **2** *chiefly Scot* : intoxicating drink ⟨was unco fond o' the ~ —James Ballantine⟩

drapping *pres part of* DRAP

draps *pl of* DRAP, *pres 3d sing of* DRAP

drash \'drash\ *dial var of* THRASH

[1]dras·tic \'drastik, -aas-,-ais-, -tēk *sometimes* -ås-\ *adj* [Gk *drastikos*, fr. (assumed) *drastos* (verbal of *dran* to do, act) + *-ikos* -ic] **1 :** acting rapidly and violently — used chiefly of purgatives **2 a :** acting with violence or harshness : extreme or radical in effect : RIGOROUS ⟨~ measures⟩ ⟨~ repressive laws⟩ **b :** notably severe or vigorous ⟨~ alterations in the national economy⟩ ⟨a ~ wave of pain⟩ — **dras·ti·cal·ly** \-tək(ə)lē, -tēk-, -li\ *adv*

[2]drastic \"\ *n* -S : a powerful medicinal agent; *esp* : a strong purgative

drat \'drat, *usu* -ad·+V\ *vb* **dratted; dratted; dratting; drats** [prob. euphemistic alter. of *God rot*] : DAMN — used as a mild oath ⟨~ their interference⟩

dratch·ell \'drachəl\ *n* -S [origin unknown] *dial Eng* : a loose slatternly woman : SLUT

draught *var of* DRAFT

draughtboard \'=,=\ *n* [*draughts* + *board*] *Brit* : CHECKERBOARD

draught·house \'=,=\ *n* [[1]*draft* (privy) + *house*] *archaic* : PRIVY

draughts \'dråfts\ *n pl but sing or pl in constr* [ME *draghtes*, fr. pl. of *draght, draught* act of moving, move in chess — more at DRAFT] *Brit* : the game of checkers

draughts·man \'dråf(t)smən\ *n, pl* **draughtsmen** [*draughts* + *man*] *Brit* : one of the pieces used in the game of draughts

draunt \'drånt, -a-\ *var of* DRANT

[1]drave *archaic past of* DRIVE

[2]drave \'drāv\ *n* -S [ME (northern dial.) *drave* act of driving, var. of *drove* — more at DROVE] **1** *Scot* : the season in which herring are fished **2** *Scot* : a herring fishing expedition

draves test \'drāvz-\ *n, usu cap D* [after Carl Z. *Draves* b1894 Am. chemist, its deviser] : a test of the efficiency of a wetting agent based on the time required for a standard skein of cotton yarn carrying a standard weight to sink in a water solution of that wetting agent

dra·vi·da \'drävədə\ *n, pl* **dravidas** *also* **dravida** *usu cap* [Skt *Drāviḍa, Draviḍa*, of Dravidian origin; akin to Tamil *tamiṛ* Tamil] **1 :** DRAVIDIAN 1 **2 :** any of several Dravidian languages **3 :** one of the basic styles of medieval Indian architecture

[1]dra·vid·i·an \drə'vidēən\ *n* -S *usu cap* [Skt *Drāviḍa, Draviḍa* + E *-ian*] **1 :** an individual of an ancient Australoid race in India that forms the bulk of the population of southern India except on the west coast which is occupied by Scytho-Dravidians **2 :** the speech of the Dravidians — see DRAVIDIAN LANGUAGE

[2]dravidian \"\ *also* **dra·vid·ic** \-dik\ *adj, usu cap* : of or relating to the Dravidians or their languages

dra·vid·i·an·ist \-dēənəst\ *n* -S *usu cap* : a specialist in Dravidian languages

dravidian language *n, usu cap D* : a language of a family of languages that are used in southern India, northern Ceylon, and in the isolated case of Brahui in West Pakistan, that have no established genetic relationship to any other family, and that are classified into a Dravida group comprising Tamil, Malayalam, Kanarese, Kurukh, and Malto, an Andhra group comprising Telugu, Gondi, and Khond, and a Brahui group containing only Brahui

dra·vite \'drä,vīt\ *n* -S [G *dravit*, fr. the *Drave* or *Drava* river, Austria and Yugoslavia, its locality + G *-it* -ite] : a magnesium-containing tourmaline that is often brown in color

[1]draw \'drȯ\ *vb* **drew** \'drü\ *also archaic or substand* **drawed** \'drȯd\ **drawn** \'drȯn\ **drawing** \'drȯiŋ\ **draws** [ME *dragen, drawen*, fr. OE *dragan* to pull, draw, drag; akin to OHG *tragan* to carry, ON *draga* to pull, draw, Goth ga*dragan* to accumulate, Russ *doroga* way, trip and perh. to L *trahere* to pull, draw, drag] *vt* **1 :** to cause to move toward or after a compelling force, forward or in another indicated or implied direction, or toward a surface : PULL, DRAG ⟨the horse *drew* us along at a smart pace⟩ ⟨we *drew* up our nets full of fishes⟩ ⟨using a poultice to ~ inflammation to a head⟩: as **a :** to haul (as a load) usu. in a cart or wagon ⟨he *drew* over 100 cords of wood that winter⟩ **b :** to drag (a criminal) to the place of execution (as at a horse's tail or on a hurdle) **c :** to cause (as a sail or drawbridge) to be raised **d :** to pull (as a curtain) over so as to cover or conceal or aside so as to uncover or reveal ⟨*drew* the bedcovers over her⟩ ⟨~ the blinds and light the lamps⟩ **e :** to bring out or cause to come out (as from a setting or receptacle) ⟨~ the cork gently and decant the wine⟩ ⟨the dentist *drew* the abscessed tooth⟩ ⟨the blow *drew* blood⟩ ⟨~ me a glass of ale⟩ **f :** to remove (a weapon) from a sheath ⟨now ~ your swords and fall to it⟩ **g :** to promote suppuration in (as a wound); *broadly* : to cause (an unwanted element) to depart (as from the body or a lesion) ⟨this will help ~ the poison⟩ **h :** to cause (a bow) to bend; *also* : to pull back (an arrow) on the bowstring **i :** to pull off (as a tablecloth after a meal); *also* : to remove a tablecloth from (a table) **j :** to remove (as coals) from a grate ⟨the furnaces are *drawn* during a strike⟩; *also* : to remove a fire from (a grate) **k :** to pull (warp threads) through the heddles in proper order to produce a desired pattern in weaving — often used with *in* ⟨~*ing* warps in by hand⟩ **l :** to cause (the ball or other mobile piece used in certain sports) to move in a particular direction or toward a particular objective usu. by applying a specialized stroke or imparting a specialized movement (as of spinning) — used in golf, billiards, bowls, cricket, and curling **m :** to remove (seedlings) from a plant bed preparatory to transplanting **2 a :** to cause (as a person) to move, proceed, or act (as by leading, conducting, or diverting) ⟨~*ing* his cousin to one side⟩ ⟨tried to ~ her thoughts from her troubles⟩ **b :** ATTRACT ⟨the accident *drew* a great crowd⟩ ⟨like iron filings *drawn* by a magnet⟩ : ENTICE, ALLURE ⟨~*ing* him with an unspoken promise in her eyes⟩ **c :** to influence toward or away from a particular course (as of action) ⟨kindness and understanding will often ~ a boy to unburden his conscience⟩; *often* : to influence to do something undesirable : SEDUCE ⟨he was *drawn* from his family and religion by selfish interests⟩ ⟨don't let me ~ you away from your work⟩ **d :** to force (a hunted animal) from cover ⟨using dogs to ~ the game⟩ **e :** to rouse (as a person) to action or response ⟨the final taunt *drew* him⟩ ⟨her insolence *drew* him to say things he knew he would regret⟩ **f :** to force the playing of (a particular card or suit) in a card game ⟨lead the king to ~ her opponent's ace⟩ ⟨won with the queen and then *drew* three rounds of spades⟩ **3 :** TAKE, GAIN; as **a :** to take (breath) into the lungs ⟨she *drew* a deep breath of clean pine-scented air⟩ **b :** to require (a specified depth) of a supporting medium in which to float ⟨a ship that ~*s* 12 feet of water⟩ **c** (1) : to take or accept at random (one from a number of things) esp. in order to decide something by chance ⟨let's ~ straws to see who gets dinner⟩ (2) : to receive (as a prize) from a lottery ⟨he *drew* one of the favored horses in the sweepstakes and sold his ticket profitably long before the race was run⟩ (3) : to obtain by luck or chance : gain by fortune : WIN ⟨a man who seemed to ~ money⟩ (4) : to select by the drawing of lots ⟨the jury panel was *drawn*⟩ (5) : to take or accept (a card) in a card game according to some arbitrary or randomizing system and usu. after an initial deal (as to improve a poker hand) (6) : to similarly take or accept (a piece) in various games **d :** to acquire in the course of events ⟨he *drew* the hardest job of all⟩ **e :** to separate (as sheep for fattening) from a larger group or number : select (as specimens) for a test or experiment **f :** to gain as a recompense or one's due (as for services, use of property, or misconduct) ⟨he ~*s* a good salary every week⟩ ⟨the speech *drew* a round of applause⟩ ⟨let your extra money stay in the bank and ~ interest⟩ ⟨if he keeps on chasing married women he's likely to ~ a punch in the jaw⟩ ⟨~ rations for three days⟩ **g :** EXTRACT, ELICIT, DERIVE ⟨you'll never ~ a compliment from her⟩ **h :** to infer from evidence or reasons : deduce from premises ⟨let the future ~ lessons from the past⟩ ⟨~ your own conclusions from what you have seen⟩ **i :** to take (as money) from a place of deposit ⟨*drew* several hundred dollars from the bank⟩ **4 :** to alter esp. in form or content: as **a :** to tear to pieces ⟨condemned to be *drawn* asunder by wild horses⟩ **b :** CONTRACT, PUCKER, WRINKLE ⟨persimmons ~ the mouth unless thoroughly ripened⟩ ⟨her face *drawn* with pain⟩; *also* : to cause to swell ⟨rubber soles ~ my feet⟩ **c** (1) : to extend in length or lengthwise : PROTRACT, STRETCH ⟨*drew* out her call interminably⟩ ⟨a rubber band *drawn* to its greatest length⟩ (2) *obs* : to build or cause to extend (as a ditch or wall) lengthwise from one place to another (3) : to cause (a plant) to become spindly and etiolated (as from lack of light) — used chiefly as a participial adjective **d :** to shave (stonework) to shape **e** (1) : to stretch, spread, or shape (metal) by passing through dies or by stamping successively (as with a series of dies or by hammering); *specif* : to make a metal rod into (wire) by pulling it through a series of holes of diminishing size thus decreasing the sectional area and increasing the length at each stage (2) : to shape by stretching (as plastic) or by drawing (as plastic filaments) through dies (3) : to shape (as a shingle) or smooth (as a spoke) with a drawknife or comparable tool (4) : to shape (glass) by guiding molten glass from the furnace over a series of automatic rollers **f :** TEMPER *vt* 4a(1) **g :** to attenuate (textile slivers or rovings) by passing successively through rollers each pair of which revolves slightly faster than its predecessor thereby causing the fibers to be straightened **h** *of honeybees* : to build up (foundation) into comb — often used with *out* **i :** to make (candles) by passing a length of wick repeatedly through molten wax and successively larger circular holes **5 a** (1) : to produce by or as if by tracing a pen or other instrument of delineation over a surface ⟨~ a line⟩ ⟨~*ing* pictures in the sand⟩ (2) : to represent by lines drawn : make a picture of in this manner ⟨he ~*s* the scene from memory⟩ **b :** to represent by words: (1) : to write in due form : prepare a draft of : INDITE ⟨*drew* a memorial to the queen⟩ ⟨~ a check for the whole amount⟩ (2) : to express graphically in words : DELINEATE ⟨~*ing* acid pen-portraits of her neighbors⟩ ⟨the novelist *drew* his characters precisely and believably⟩ **c :** to set forth in due and proper form or formally : FORMULATE ⟨it is often necessary to ~ fine distinctions⟩ ⟨have a lawyer ~ up your will if your plans are at all complicated⟩ **6 :** to remove the contents of: as **a :** to remove the viscera of : EVISCERATE ⟨fowls come to market plucked and *drawn*⟩ **b :** to extract or drain the essence of ⟨that final climb seemed to ~ his strength away⟩ ⟨some people ~ their tea too long⟩ **c :** to force or draw something from (as a place of security) : drive game out of (as a covert) ⟨they *drew* the open fields with beaters, the rugged hills with dogs⟩ : fish by dragging a net through (as a pond) ⟨they *drew* the river above the weir⟩ **d :** to remove (as fired brick) from a kiln **7 :** to bring (an existing relation or situation) to an end: as **a** *archaic* : to withdraw (as a horse) from a race **b :** to finish (a contest) in a draw : bring (as a game) to a conclusion without having established the superiority (as in skill or scoring) of any contestant ~ *vi* **1 :** to come or go; MOVE : draw oneself — now used only with prepositions and adverbs of direction ⟨he *drew* away from the smoldering wall⟩ ⟨night ~*s* near⟩ ⟨as we *drew* toward the town⟩ **2** *obs* : to approach or tend esp. to a particular state **3 :** to perform the act of drawing something: as **a :** move something by pulling ⟨*drew* continuously without emptying the well⟩ ⟨there's nothing like a team of oxen for ~*ing* in really rugged country⟩ **b :** to exert an attractive force : act as an inducement or enticement ⟨the play is still ~*ing* well⟩ **c :** to pull back the string of a bow preparatory to releasing the arrow **d :** to perform the act or practice the art of delineation : form figures or pictures by tracing lines; *often* : SKETCH **e :** to make a written demand for payment of money deposited or due; *often* : to make demands (as on a person or a resource) — usu. used with *on* or *upon* ⟨he *drew* on his savings account for a down payment⟩ ⟨~ on me for any help you need⟩ ⟨~*ing* on his last reserve of energy⟩ **f :** to search for game; *often* : to track game by the scent — used chiefly of a sporting dog **g** (1) : to cause local congestion : induce blood or other body fluid to localize at a particular point : be effective as a blistering agent or counterirritant — used of a poultice and comparable means of medication (2) *of a lesion* : to become localized — used in the phrase *draw to a head* **h :** to leave a game or contest undecided : end a contest in a draw ⟨our team *drew* three times this year⟩ **: i** to draw one or more cards in a card game **4 :** to sink in water : require a depth for floating ⟨greater hulks ~ deep —Shak.⟩ **5 :** to alter in form or content: as **a :** to change shape by or as if by pulling : STRETCH, WRINKLE, CONTRACT ⟨she shivered and her skin seemed to ~ with the cold⟩ ⟨the spring *drew* longer and longer with the strain⟩ **b** *of a sail* : to swell out with the wind **c :** STEEP, INFUSE ⟨the tea may ~ a bit longer⟩ **d** *of curing tobacco* : to become uniformly moist — used of the hand of leaves after petuning **6 a :** to become subjected to drawing or suitable for being drawn ⟨the new cart ~*s* easily⟩ **b** *of liquid* : to drain away **c :** RISE **d :** to produce a draft whereby a current (as of hot gases) is drawn ⟨the chimney ~*s* well since it was cleaned⟩; *sometimes* : to pass in a current ⟨breezes *drew* through the room⟩ **e :** to pull a pattern from a mold in an indicated manner (as hard, easily, cleanly) **7 :** to obtain information, supplies, or other matters ⟨~*ing* from a common fund of knowledge⟩ ⟨*drew* heavily on their supply of food⟩ **8 :** to perform a draw in dancing **syn** see PULL — **draw a bead on :** to bring into line with the front sight and rear sight of a rifle : take aim at; *broadly* : use as a target ⟨always ready to *draw a bead on* an errant public official⟩ — **draw a blank** *also* **draw blank 1 :** to draw a loser : obtain something without value **2 :** to fail to find what one seeks — **draw a line** *or* **draw the line :** to fix an arbitrary boundary between things that tend to intermingle ⟨the courts must *draw a line* between the right of free speech and genuinely subversive utterance⟩; *often* : to fix a boundary excluding what one will not tolerate or engage in ⟨I'm not intolerant but one must *draw the line* somewhere⟩ — **draw a longbow** *or* **draw the longbow :** to exaggerate or overstate the truth — **draw blood :** to wound in body or spirit; *often* : to subject to distress and embarrassment ⟨he *drew blood* when he guyed us about our failure⟩ — **draw in one's horns :** to act more conservatively or cautiously than at some former time ⟨he'd better *draw in his horns* if he wants to keep out of trouble⟩ — **draw it fine :** to be very precise (as in making distinctions) — **draw it mild** [so called fr. its original use in reference to beer] *chiefly Brit* : to express or tell (something) without exaggerating — usu. used imperatively ⟨*draw it mild*, after all, we saw the whole thing happen⟩ — **draw lots :** to decide or assign by or as if by the drawing of lots — **draw on 1 :** to order (as a bank or business firm) to pay out money held to the credit of the drawer **2 :** to withdraw (money) from one's account ⟨*drew on* his savings for the whole amount⟩ **3** *or* **draw upon :** to use or depend on as a base or as source material : exploit the resources of ⟨she has *drawn on* her mother's old notebooks for some excellent recipes⟩ ⟨*drawing on* the Bible for authority⟩ — **draw one's time :** to quit a job esp. under pressure ⟨get to work or *draw your time* right now⟩ ⟨he *drew his time* and went south⟩ — **draw rein :** to check one's speed (as in riding) : stop short : STOP — **draw straws :** to draw lots using straws of uneven length for lots — **draw the fangs :** to render harmless or ineffective — used with *of* ⟨this forthright answer *drew the fangs* of his criticism⟩ — **draw the temper :** to reduce or impair the hardness of tempered steel by heating ⟨he tried to sharpen his ax on an emery wheel and completely *drew the temper*⟩ — **draw together 1 :** to draw into unity : render whole : UNITE, UNIFY ⟨I'll just *draw together* this snag in your cuff⟩ ⟨only hatred shared *drew* them *together*⟩ **2 :** to come to accord : UNITE ⟨sensible people will *draw together* to face a common danger⟩

[2]draw \"\ *n* -S *often attrib* **1 :** an act or process of drawing (as of metals, loads, lots, or a bow) : PULL: as **a :** one complete outward and inward run of a mule carriage in spinning **b :** DRAWING-IN **c :** a sucking pull on something (as a sipping straw or cigarette) held with the lips ⟨took a long ~ on his pipe before answering⟩; *sometimes* : a drawing (as of vapor or liquid) into the system **d** (1) : the removing of a revolver or automatic pistol from its holster ⟨a cross ~ with the left hand⟩; *esp* : near simultaneous drawing of such weapons by individuals proposing to shoot at one another — used with *the* ⟨the sheriff was quicker on the ~⟩ (2) : advantage esp. when gained by superior alertness or skill : EDGE — usu. used with *the* ⟨the senator's experience gives him the ~ on his opponents⟩ **e :** a stroke or play in certain games or sports involving drawing (as of a ball) **f :** a competition in which the pulling ability of draft animals is tested under standardized conditions ⟨the ox ~*s* at New England fairs⟩ **g** *or* **draw step :** a dance step in which one foot is drawn on the floor to meet the other **2 :** something that draws or serves as a means of drawing: as **a** [by shortening] *dial* : DRAWER 2 **b** *archaic* : something designed to draw out, entrap, or mislead **c** (1) *also* **drawspan** : the movable part of a drawbridge (2) : the opening through it **d :** a stroke or blow given in drawing metal **e :** a natural drainageway or gully generally shallower or more open than a ravine or gorge : a dry stream bed : COULEE 1a ⟨a small stream that cuts through a large ~ in which deer like to winter —Robert Crichton⟩ **f :** the angle given to the locking faces of the pallets in a lever-escapement watch that when acted upon by the force of the escape-wheel teeth draws the lever to the banking pins and ensures freedom of the roller **g :** an influence that draws attention or a crowd ⟨a dogfight has a powerful ~ for small boys⟩ : ATTRACTION; *often* : a theatrical event or personality that draws patronage **h** : the weaving pattern formed by drawing-in **3** : the product or state of drawing or of being drawn: as **a** : a lot or chance drawn **b** : a contest that ends without a clear-cut victory for either side ⟨the battle was a ~⟩: (1) : a sporting event (as a boxing or wrestling match) in which each contestant receives equal scores : TIE (2) : a sporting event or game in which there is no winner because some impasse precludes carrying the contest to a decisive end (as in a cricket match with the batting team behind and time expiring before the innings is complete) **c** : the essence or strength of tea **d** : a young shoot or sprout; *specif* : one of the young spring shoots of the sweet potato **e** : ANGLE, TAPER, DRAFT; *specif* : the taper of a leaf spring **f** : the distance from the string to the back of a drawn bow; *often* : the force required to draw a bow fully ⟨a bow with a 50-pound ~⟩ **g** : a list of contestants in a sports event arranged in an order obtained by drawing lots **4** : something that is or can be drawn: as **a** : DRAWER PULL **b** (1) : a card or piece drawn in certain games (as for replacement of one expended); *also* : the deal in draw poker to improve the hands after players have discarded (2) : DRAW POKER **c** : the distance that a camera bellows may be extended **d** : a number, allocation, or amount (as of money or goods) that is available at regular or particular intervals: (1) : DRAWING ACCOUNT 2 (2) : the part of a seaman's pay that he has a right to draw while in port in the course of a voyage (3) : the number of each issue of a periodical (as a magazine or newspaper) regularly consigned to a particular vendor

draw away *vt* : WITHDRAW, REMOVE ⟨*drew* his hand *away* from her touch⟩ ⟨*drawing* her *away* from the window⟩ ~ *vi* : to move away (as from one's opponent in a race) ⟨we started even but he soon *drew away* from me⟩

draw back *vt* **1** : to receive back (as duties paid on goods for exportation); *broadly* : to cause to return **2** : DISCOUNT, DEDUCT ~ *vi* : RETREAT, SHRINK, WITHDRAW — usu. used with *from* ⟨*drew back* from the scorching heat⟩ ⟨*drawing back* slowly⟩

drawback \ˈ⸗ˌ⸗\ *n* -s [*draw back*] **1** : money remitted after being collected : REFUND: as **a** : customs or other duties refunded on (1) an imported product subsequently exported, (2) an imported product used in the production of a product for export, or (3) on the part of an imported product (as tobacco) which becomes scrap in the manufacturing process **b** : a refund of excise or other tax on a product used for some favored purpose (as alcohol used for nonbeverage purposes) **c** : money refunded as compensation (as for damages) or as a special often secret favor or inducement — compare KICKBACK **2** : an objectionable feature : DEFECT, HINDRANCE ⟨the ~*s* of country living⟩ ⟨slow drying is the chief ~ of this paint⟩ **3** : a part of a mechanical device that can be drawn back: as **a** (1) : a part of a foundry mold that can be drawn back to permit the removal of a pattern from the mold (2) : a plate or comparable structure on which this part of the mold may be lifted out **b** : a door bolt that can be released by drawing back on a knob on the inside

drawback lock *n* **1** : a door lock that can be opened from the inside by a handle and from the outside by a key **2** : a lock that can ordinarily be opened by hand (as by turning a knob) except when locked with a key

drawband \ˈ⸗ˌ⸗\ *n* : a metal or woven fabric strip that connects the mainspring and carriage of a typewriter to provide motive power — called also *carriage band*

drawbar \ˈ⸗ˌ⸗\ *n* **1** : a removable bar in a fence **2 a** (1) : a bar that is used to connect a steam locomotive and tender and is secured in the drawhead of the locomotive by a pin (2) : a railroad coupler — not used technically **b** : a beam across the rear of a tractor to which implements are hitched **3** : a clay block submerged in molten glass in a tank furnace for controlling the position of sheet glass during drawing

drawbar pull *n* : the pulling power exerted at the drawbar (as by a locomotive or tractor)

drawbench \ˈ⸗ˌ⸗\ *n* : a machine for drawing strips of metal through dies; *esp* : one used in making wire

drawboard \ˈ⸗ˌ⸗\ *n* : a movable board or assembly of boards for bridging an open space (as between railroad cars and platforms or boats and docks)

drawbolt \ˈ⸗ˌ⸗\ *n* **1** : COUPLER 1a **2** : a bolt with washer and nut used to draw parts of an assembly tightly together **3** : BOLT 2a

¹drawbore \ˈ⸗ˌ⸗\ *n* [¹*draw* + *bore*] : a bore for a mortise pin placed so as to draw the tenon and thus make the joint tighter

²drawbore \"\ *vt* **1** : to make a drawbore in (as a tenon) **2** : to enlarge the bore of (a tube, as a gun barrel) by drawing through with the working tool instead of thrusting

drawbore

drawboy \ˈ⸗ˌ⸗\ *n* : a boy who operates the harness cords of a hand loom; *broadly* : a part of a power loom that performs the same task

drawbridge \ˈ⸗ˌ⸗\ *n* [ME *drawebrigge*, fr. *drawen* to draw + *brigge* bridge — more at DRAW, BRIDGE] : a bridge of which either the whole or a part is made to be raised up, let down, or drawn aside so as to permit or hinder passage

draw bridge *n* : a two-handed bridge game in which each player is dealt 13 cards and draws one of the undealt cards after each trick — called also *domino bridge, strip bridge*

drawcard *var of* DRAWING CARD

draw cock *n* : PET COCK

drawcord \ˈ⸗ˌ⸗\ *n* : a cord so arranged as to draw draperies across or back from an opening in a single operation

drawbridge of a medieval castle

draw curtain *n* **1** : a curtain in front of a stage that meets or overlaps in the middle and is drawn back on both sides when open **2** : one of a pair or set of domestic curtains usu. of rather substantial and more or less opaque material that may be drawn together or apart by a mechanical device (as a traverse rod)

drawcut \ˈ⸗ˌ⸗\ *n* : a cut toward the machine or operator (as in shaping a part)

drawcut shaper *n* : a shaper that cuts toward the column of the machine

draw down *vt* **1** : to be the cause of : ATTRACT ⟨their behavior *drew down* a storm of protest⟩ **2** : EARN, RECEIVE ⟨*drew down* full pay⟩ **3** : EXPEND, DEPLETE ⟨*drawing down* gold reserves⟩ ⟨*drew down* his balance in the checkbook⟩

drawdown \ˈ⸗ˌ⸗\ *n* -s [*draw down*] **1** : the distance by which the fluid surface level (as in a well or reservoir) is lowered (as by pumping or gate opening) **2** : the curving downward of the water surface near the edge of a weir notch

drawed *archaic or substand past of* DRAW

draw·ee \(ˈ)drȯ¦ē\ *n* -s [¹*draw* + *-ee*] : the person on whom an order or bill of exchange is drawn — contrasted with *drawer*

draw·er *R* ˈdrȯ(ə)r; *-R before pause or consonant* -ȯə *also in senses 2 & 3* -ȯ, *before vowel* " *or* -ȯ(ə)r\ *n* -s [ME, fr. *drawen* to draw + *-er* — more at DRAW] **1** : one that draws: as **a** : a person who draws liquor for guests in a place of public resort : a waiter in a taproom **b** : a person who delineates or depicts : DRAFTSMAN ⟨a clever ~ of animals⟩ **c** (1) : a textile worker who operates a drawing frame (2) : DRAWER-IN **d** : a worker who forms wire, rod, or tubing by drawing metal through a series of successively smaller dies **e** : a worker who assists in the removal of firebrick or other wares from kilns **f** (1) : an individual who draws or issues a bill of exchange or order for payment — contrasted with *drawee* (2) : the maker of a promissory note **2** : something that is drawn: as **a** (1) : a sliding box or receptacle (as one of a number enclosed in a case or frame) that is opened by pulling out and closed by pushing in ⟨a desk ~⟩ ⟨a bureau ~⟩; *sometimes* : a post-office box in the form of a drawer (2) **drawers** *pl* : a chest made up of several drawers with a suitable cabinet and base **b drawers** *pl* : an undergarment enclosing the lower trunk and having independent sheaths for all or part of each leg **3** : level of social or professional status, accomplishment, worth

drawer-down \ˈ⸗(⸗)¦⸗\ *n, pl* **drawers-down** : one that draws down; *esp* : a worker in a rolling mill who draws hot billets down to rolls

drawer-in \ˈ⸗(⸗)¦⸗\ *n, pl* **drawers-in** : a textile worker who does drawing-in

drawer-off \ˈ⸗(⸗)¦⸗\ *n, pl* **drawers-off** : one that draws something off esp. as an occupation ⟨got work as a *drawer-off* at the brewery⟩

drawer-out \ˈ⸗(⸗)¦⸗\ *n, pl* **drawers-out** : one that draws out; *esp* : a worker who draws metal bars or blooms from furnaces

drawer pull *n* : a handle for pulling open a drawer

drawfile \ˈ⸗ˌ⸗\ *vt* : to file by pushing the file held with its length transverse to the direction of its motion

draw frame *var of* DRAWING FRAME

draw game *n* : a domino game in which a player having no playable piece is forced to draw from the stock until he gets one

draw gang *n* : the group of workers that cuts and handles glass as it comes from the lehr

drawgear \ˈ⸗ˌ⸗\ *n, Brit* : a device used to connect adjoining railroad carriages or cars : COUPLER

drawhead \ˈ⸗ˌ⸗\ *n* : the socket or base on the ends of locomotives and cars to which the drawbar or other coupling device is secured

draw in *vt* **1** : to induce to participate or enter : ENTICE, INVEIGLE ⟨was asked to participate but he refused to be *drawn in*⟩ **2** : to draw roughly or as part of a whole : SKETCH ⟨*drew in* the background⟩ **3** : to shape (as the toe of a sock) so that the area of each succeeding section along a longitudinal axis will be smaller than that of the section preceding it ~ *vi* **1** : to draw quickly toward an end ⟨as day *drew in* and twilight deepened⟩ : shorten in a seasonally normal manner ⟨the evenings are *drawing in* and it will soon be winter⟩ **2** : to be or become more economical or conservative ⟨we've spent too much lately, we'll have to *draw in* for a while⟩ ⟨when I read him his own words he *drew in* and admitted he had gone too far⟩

draw-in bolt \ˈ⸗ˌ⸗\ *n* : a bolt for tightening collets in the headstock of a lathe

drawing *n* -s *often attrib* [ME, fr. gerund of *drawen* to draw — more at DRAW] **1** : an act or instance of drawing; *specif* : an occasion when something is decided by a drawing of lots ⟨there being 607 applications for 81 parcels of land a ~ will be held to determine the recipient of each parcel⟩ **2 a** : the projection of an image or a series of points by the forming of lines on a surface (as by use of a pencil, pen, or etchers' point) ⟨neat careful ~⟩; *broadly* : formation of a representation in which delineation plays a determining part **b** : the art or technique of representing an object or outlining a figure, plan, or sketch by means of lines ⟨a professor of ~⟩ **3** : something that is drawn or subject to drawing: as **a** : money taken in (as by a business or for a particular purpose) **b** : a figure or representation formed by drawing : SKETCH, PLAN ⟨a ~ of his sister⟩ ⟨a magnificent scale ~⟩ **c** : a portion of tea for steeping — **in drawing** : correctly drawn or delineated — **out of drawing** : incorrectly drawn; *broadly* : INAPPROPRIATE : out of keeping (as with surrounding elements)

drawing account *n* **1** : CURRENT ACCOUNT **2** : an account showing usu. periodic cash payments to an employee in advance of actual earnings or for expenses to be incurred; *esp* : one showing advances to a salesman against commissions on future sales or for traveling expenses **3** : an account showing the withdrawals of a proprietor or partner from his business; *esp* : one showing withdrawals against current or anticipated profits — called also *personal account*

drawing awl *n* : an awl with an eye for pulling a thread through the hole bored

drawing block *n* **1** : a block of drawing paper **2** : ¹BLOCK 1h

drawing board *n* **1** : a board that has at least one straight edge against which a T square may be placed and that is used as a base for paper to be drawn on **2** : a heavy bond or bristol board with hard smooth surface that is used for drawing or lettering

drawing card \ˈ⸗⸗ˌ⸗\ *also* **drawcard** \ˈ⸗ˌ⸗\ *n* : something (as a feature or performer) that attracts a great deal of attention or patronage

drawing chamber *n* [short for obs. E *withdrawing chamber*, fr. ME *withdrawyng chambre*] *archaic* : DRAWING ROOM

drawing cloth *n* : TRACING CLOTH

drawing die *n* : a die used to shape cuplike articles out of sheet metal that is pushed into it by a punch and prevented from wrinkling by a blank holder which holds the outer edge of the metal firm

drawing frame *or* **draw frame** *n* : a machine for combining and drawing slivers of a textile fiber (as of hemp for rope manufacture or cotton for spinning)

drawing-in \ˈ⸗⸗¦⸗\ *n, pl* **drawings-in** : the action or operation of drawing warp yarns through the eyes of the heddles of a loom

drawing knife *var of* DRAWKNIFE

drawing paper *n* : a paper specially prepared for the use of drawers (as draftsmen or sketchers)

drawing pen *n* : a pen designed for use in drawing: as **a** : RULING PEN **b** : a freehand artist's pen that varies the width of strokes according to the pressure applied

drawing pin *n, Brit* : THUMBTACK

drawing pliers *n pl but sing or pl in constr* : DRAWTONGS

drawing point *n* : ANCHOR POINT

drawing power *n* : the capacity for drawing; *esp* : the ability to attract business or customers

drawing press *or* **draw press** *n* : a punch press that performs a drawing and cutting operation (as in forming hollow vessels from sheet metal)

drawing punch *n* : the punch that operates with a drawing die

drawing right *n* : a grant of credit from one nation to another that is a condition for the granting of funds or credit to the first nation from a third and is intended to stimulate and facilitate international trade

drawing room *n* [short for *withdrawing room*] **1 a** *archaic* : a room to which one may retire for privacy or rest : CLOSET; *esp* : one adjacent to public apartments **b** *obs* : a room or apartment forming a private part of the suite of a person (as a king) living in state and being often the setting of various informal activities or gatherings **c** : a more or less formal reception room (as in a home or hotel); *esp* : the room to which ladies withdraw from the dining room — compare PARLOR, SITTING ROOM **d** : a private room on a railroad passenger car with three berths and an enclosed toilet **2** : a formal or ceremonial reception; *esp* : one that is an official function of a royal court ⟨made her curtsy at the queen's last *drawing room*⟩ **3 a** : persons gathered in a drawing room ⟨disturbed the *drawing room* with his radical talk⟩ **b drawing rooms** *pl* : people of substance and position accustomed to formal living : polite society ⟨the report of her elopement shocked the *drawing rooms*⟩

drawing-room \ˈ⸗⸗ˌ⸗\ *adj* [*drawing room*] **1** : of, relating to, characteristic of, or suitable for a drawing room ⟨*drawing-room* manners⟩ ⟨a new *drawing-room* rug⟩ **2** : dealing with or representing the drawing room; *esp* : concerned with life in polite society ⟨a *drawing-room* comedy⟩ **3** *of a railroad car* : equipped with drawing rooms

drawing string *var of* DRAWSTRING

drawing table *n* : a table with a surface adjustable for elevation and angle of incline

draw into *vt* : to draw in

drawk \ˈdrȯk\ *vt* -ED/-ING/-S [ME (Sc dial.) *drawken*, perh. of Scand origin; akin to ON *drukna* to drown — more at DROWN] *dial Brit* : to saturate with moisture

drawknife \ˈ⸗ˌ⸗\ *also* **drawing knife** *n* : a woodworker's tool having a blade with a handle at each end used to shave off surfaces by drawing it toward one — called also *drawshave*

drawing table

draw-knob \ˈ⸗ˌ⸗\ *n* : a knob in a pipe organ for admitting wind to a set of pipes or in a reed organ to a set of reeds

drawknot \ˈ⸗ˌ⸗\ *n* **1** : SLIPKNOT **2** : a half bowknot

¹drawl \ˈdrȯl\ *vb* -ED/-ING/-S [prob. freq. of ¹*draw*] *vi* **1** : to speak slowly esp. as a matter of habit with vowels greatly prolonged so that vowels monophthongal in other styles of speech are often diphthongized (as in *bin, web, bad, knob, talk, good*) **2** *archaic* : to move slowly : LOITER ~ *vt* **1** : to utter in a slow lengthened tone ⟨~*ed* out the hymn⟩ **2** *archaic* : to cause to pass or move sluggishly : drag out — **drawl·er** \-lə(r)\ *n* -s

drawknot

²drawl \"\ *n* -s : a drawling manner of speaking; *often* : something spoken in a drawling manner

¹drawl·ing \ˈdrȯliŋ, -lēŋ\ *adj* [fr. pres. part. of ¹*drawl*] **1** : slow-moving : LAGGING **2** *of speech* : uttered with a drawl — **drawl·ing·ly** *adv*

²draw·ling \"\ *n* -s [¹*draw* + *ling* (plant); prob. fr. the belief that sheep seize the plant and draw up a long underground part] : COTTON GRASS

drawlink \ˈ⸗ˌ⸗\ *n* [¹*draw* + *link*] : a drawbar on a railroad car

drawloom \ˈ⸗ˌ⸗\ *n* [¹*draw* + *loom*] : a hand loom formerly used for figure weaving and operated by a drawboy

drawly \ˈdrȯlē\ *adj* -ER/-EST [²*drawl* + *-y*] : characterized by drawling

draw·man \ˈdrȯmən\ *n, pl* **drawmen** : a worker who draws precut plastic materials to desired shapes in a hand or power press

draw-moss \ˈ⸗ˌ⸗\ *n* [so called fr. the fact that sheep pull out its leaf bases] : a cotton grass (esp. *Eriophorum vaginatum*)

drawn *past part of* DRAW

drawn bond *n* : a bond called for redemption before maturity

drawn butter *n* : melted butter often with chopped herbs or other seasoning

drawn edge *n* : COMB MARBLING

drawnet \ˈ⸗ˌ⸗\ *n* [¹*draw* + *net*] : a net formerly used for catching large wild birds

drawn glass *n* : glass (as window glass or fiber glass) that is made by continuous drawing of the molten glass by a series of rolls on automatic machinery

drawn grain *n* : a shrunken wrinkled condition of leather usu. due to improper handling of hides during tanning

drawn-out \ˈ⸗¦⸗\ *adj* : stretched to great or greater length ⟨the story of a simple-minded girl whose sweetness manages to survive *drawn-out* brutality —*Newsweek*⟩; *esp* : made to seem or be longer than desirable or normal (as by monotony) ⟨that lecture was long and *drawn-out*⟩

drawn teind *n, Scots law* : the part of a crop selected by the church as its tithe from the whole crop after reaping but before removal from the land

drawnwork \ˈ⸗ˌ⸗\ *n* **1** : decoration on fabric articles (as clothing and household linens) made by drawing out threads according to a pattern and usu. grouping and stitching the exposed threads in lacy designs **2** : plastering in which a brown coat is applied over the scratch coat before it is dry

draw off *vt* : to remove esp. from an environment or container : WITHDRAW, ABSTRACT; *often* : to extract by distillation ~ *vi* : to move away esp. to allow oneself room for action, regrouping, or reconsideration ⟨the enemies' losses forced them to *draw off*⟩ ⟨we *drew off* from that approach and reexamined the situation⟩

drawoff \ˈ⸗ˌ⸗\ *n* -s [*draw off*] **1** : something (as a liquid) that is drawn off **2** : a device (as a tap or valve) by which something is drawn off

draw on *vi* : APPROACH ⟨winter *draws on* apace⟩ — often used with *toward* ⟨*drawing on* toward destruction⟩ ~ *vt* **1** : to occasion as a consequence : bring on : CAUSE ⟨their folly *drew on* their disgrace⟩ **2** : to lead (one) on : INDUCE ⟨their encouragement *drew* him *on* to speak freely⟩ **3** : to pull or put on (as clothes) ⟨he *drew on* his boots⟩

draw out *vt* **1 a** : REMOVE, EXTRACT ⟨it might have been worthwhile to *draw out* these resemblances —W.R.Inge⟩ ⟨*drawing out* the fundamental meaning of his work⟩ **b** : to cause or lead (a person) to speak out freely ⟨your calm interest may serve to *draw* him *out*⟩ **c** : to call upon : demand the full expression of ⟨the new responsibilities *drew out* his latent talents⟩ **2** : to cause to become longer ⟨*drawing out* glass tubing⟩ : LENGTHEN, PROLONG ⟨he refused to *draw out* the interview⟩ ~ *vi* **1** : to become longer ⟨the days are *drawing out*⟩ **2** : to pull away : get ahead of companions or rivals ⟨at the head of the stretch the horse *drew out* from the field and won by six lengths⟩

drawout \ˈ⸗ˌ⸗\ *n* -s [*draw out*] : something that is drawn out; *esp* : a small portion of colored paste spread out in a thin layer on a sheet of white paper to show its color characteristics

draw pin *n* : a mortise pin used in a drawbore

drawplate \ˈ⸗ˌ⸗\ *n* **1** : a die with holes through which wires are drawn **2** : BAR PLATE

drawpoint \ˈ⸗ˌ⸗\ *n* : a pointed tempered steel tool used to scratch in transferred pencil lines or to stitch and pierce holes (as a mandrel for making small rings)

draw poker *n* : a game of poker in which each player is dealt five cards face down and after preliminary betting may discard unwanted cards and receive other cards to replace them prior to further betting

draw press *var of* DRAWING PRESS

drawrod \ˈ⸗ˌ⸗\ *n* : a rod that unites the drawgear at opposite ends of adjoining railroad cars in the European type of coupling

drawrope \ˈ⸗ˌ⸗\ *n* : a large heavy drawstring

draw runner *or* **draw slip** *n* : either of a pair of small pieces of wood that may be pulled out to support the drop front of certain desks or secretaries

draws *pres 3d sing of* DRAW, *pl of* DRAW

drawshave \ˈ⸗ˌ⸗\ *n* : DRAWKNIFE

drawsheet \ˈ⸗ˌ⸗\ *n* : a sheet drawn tight over a surface: as **a** : the outside or top sheet that holds the makeready on the platen or the impression cylinder of a printing press **b** : a narrow sheet used chiefly in hospitals and stretched across the bed lengthwise often over a rubber sheet underneath the patient's trunk

draw shot *n* : a pool stroke in which a player applies backspin to the cue ball to cause it to draw back from the object ball after hitting it — compare FOLLOW SHOT

drawspan \ˈ⸗ˌ⸗\ *n* : ²DRAW 2c(1)

drawspring \ˈ⸗ˌ⸗\ *n* : the spring to which a drawbar between railroad cars is attached in the European type of coupling

draw step *n* : ²DRAW 1g

drawstring \ˈ⸗ˌ⸗\ *also* **drawing string** *n* : a string, cord, or tape inserted into hems or casings or laced through eyelets for use in closing a bag or controlling fullness in garments or curtains

drawstroke \ˈ⸗ˌ⸗\ *n* : a canoeing stroke executed by reaching the paddle out to the side and pulling it toward the canoe with the blade flattened

draw table *n* : a table whose top is extendible by pulling out leaves from under each end

bag with drawstring

draw taper *n* : draft as given to a foundry pattern

drawtongs \ˈ⸗ˌ⸗\ *n pl but sing or pl in constr* : a tool for handling wire in wiredrawing

drawtube \ˈ⸗ˌ⸗\ *n* : a telescoping tube (as that containing the eyepiece of certain optical instruments)

drawtwister \ˈ⸗ˌ⸗⸗\ *n* : a machine used to stretch synthetic textile yarns (as nylon) soon after extrusion

draw up *vt* **1** : to arrange (as a body of troops) in order **2** : to draft in due form: **a** : to formulate and produce ⟨*drew up* a plan for more equitable taxation⟩ **b** : to write out ⟨a list *drawn up* in a strange handwriting⟩ **3** : to straighten (oneself) to an erect posture esp. as an assertion of dignity or resentment ⟨she *drew herself up* indignantly⟩ **4** : to bring to a halt ⟨he *drew up* his horse and came in⟩ ~ *vi* : to come to a halt : STOP ⟨the car *drew up* at the door⟩

draw well *n* : a relatively deep well from which water is drawn (as by a bucket and chain) rather than dipped up with a container held in the hand

draw works *n pl but sing or pl in constr* : an oil-well drilling apparatus that consists of a countershaft and drum and that is used for supplying driving power and lifting heavy objects

1dray \ˈdrā\ *n* -s [ME *draye,* fr. OE *dræge* dragnet; akin to ON

dray 2

draga timber carried on horseback and trailing on the ground; derivative fr. the root of E *draw*] **1 :** any of several wheelless land vehicles used for haulage: as **a :** STONEBOAT **b :** TRAVOIS 1 **c :** a single bobsled used to support the forward end of a log in skidding on bare or rough ground — compare ALLIGATOR 6b **2 :** a strong low cart or wagon without permanent sides used for carrying heavy loads esp. locally and for hire; *broadly* **:** any vehicle (as a motortruck) that serves the purposes of a dray
2dray \"\ *vb* -ED/-ING/-S *vt* **:** to carry or transport on a dray **:** CART ~ *vi* **1 :** to drive a dray esp. for a livelihood **2 :** to haul goods usu. locally
3dray *var of* DREY
dray·age \ˈdrāij, -āēj\ *n* -s [*1dray* + *-age*] **1 :** the draying of goods **2 :** the charge or sum paid for draying (as of goods)
dray horse *n* **1 :** DRAFT HORSE; *esp* **:** one used for draying **2 :** DRUDGE
draying *n* -s [fr. gerund of *2dray*] **:** the action or business of hauling with drays or hauling (as goods) locally ⟨engaged in ~ for over 20 years⟩
dray·man \-āmən\ *n, pl* **draymen :** a man who drives a dray or drays goods
DRE *abbr* director of religious education
1dread \ˈdred\ *vb* -ED/-ING/-S [ME *dreden,* fr. OE *drǣdan;* akin to OS *antdrādan* to fear, dread, OHG *intrātan*] *vt* **1 a :** to fear greatly **:** be in terror of ⟨a burned child ~s the fire⟩ **b** *archaic* **:** to stand in awe of **:** REVERENCE **2 :** to anticipate with fear of evil, pain, or trouble **:** look forward to with apprehensiveness **:** feel great anxiety about ⟨they ~ change, lest it should make matters worse —G.B.Shaw⟩ ~ *vi* **:** to be very apprehensive or fearful ⟨~ not, neither be afraid of them —Deut 1:29 (AV)⟩
2dread \"\ *n* -s [ME *drede, dred,* fr. *dreden,* v.] **1 a :** great fear esp. in the face of impending evil **:** fearful apprehension of danger **:** anticipatory terror ⟨looked forward with ~ to the night alone in the dark farmhouse —Sherwood Anderson⟩ ⟨~ of insecurity⟩ **b** *archaic* **:** reverential or respectful fear **:** AWE **2 :** a person or thing regarded with fear or awe ⟨the days of wooden ships and wooden homes, when fire was an omnipresent ~ —F.W.Saunders⟩ **3** [trans. of Dan & G *angst*] **:** ANXIETY 3 **syn** see FEAR
3dread \"\ *adj* [ME *dred,* fr. past part. of *dreden,* v.] **1 :** causing great fear or apprehensiveness **:** FRIGHTENING ⟨~ "secret" weapons which are evaluated solely by their capacity to kill —B.M.Baruch⟩ ⟨a ~ disease⟩ **2 :** inspiring reverential fear or awe ⟨most ~ lord⟩ — **dread·ly** *adv*
dreaddour *var of* DREDDOUR
1dread·ful \ˈdredfəl\ *adj* [ME *dredful,* fr. *drede, dred* + *-ful*] **1 a :** full of dread or terror **:** FEARFUL **b** *obs* **:** full of reverence or awe **2 a :** inspiring dread **:** causing great fear **:** FRIGHTENING ⟨a ~ storm⟩ ⟨that snake provided me with one of the most ~ experiences of my life —Jack McLaren⟩ **b :** inspiring awe or reverence ⟨out from the portico there gleamed a god, Apollon . . . all his shape one ~ beauty —Robert Browning⟩ **3 a :** exciting repugnance or loathing **:** REVOLTING, HORRIBLE ⟨no more ~ horror through the whole story than the bloody sack of Limoges —H.O.Taylor⟩ ⟨the ~ theory that if a teacher has studied education, he does not have to have a real mastery of the subject he is teaching —Oliver La Farge⟩ **b :** arousing great pity or sympathy **:** TRAGIC ⟨when she's alone and humiliated and broken it would be ~ if she had nowhere to go —W.S.Maugham⟩ **c :** arousing feelings of disapproval or dissatisfaction: as (1) **:** of poor quality ⟨a ~ road⟩ ⟨~ acoustics⟩ (2) **:** socially unacceptable **:** UNREFINED ⟨to prevent her marrying ~ people —Edith Wharton⟩ (3) **:** offensive to good taste ⟨~ furniture⟩ ⟨a ~ sight in her country clothes —R.H. Sampson⟩ **d :** unpleasant to experience, remember, or contemplate ⟨the ~ conclusion that the date 1869 . . . marks definitely the hour at which Latin . . . became a dead language —A.T.Quiller-Couch⟩ **4 :** EXTREME **:** very great ⟨a lady in a long skirt . . . was making ~ havoc with the standing grass —F.M.Ford⟩ ⟨boats and tackle were in ~ disrepair —Arthur Rucker⟩ **syn** see FEARFUL
2dreadful \"\ *adv, chiefly North* **:** VERY, EXTREMELY ⟨~ sick⟩ ⟨a ~ good man⟩
3dreadful \"\ *n* -s **:** a cheap and sensational story or periodical; *esp* **:** a story of crime or desperadoes such as was popular in late Victorian England ⟨a shilling ~⟩ — compare DIME NOVEL, SHOCKER
dread·ful·ly \-f(ə)lē, -li\ *adv* [ME *dredfully,* fr. *dredful* + *-ly*] **1 :** with dread ⟨he looked ~ over his shoulder to see if he were followed —Eric Linklater⟩ **2 :** in such a way as to cause dread **:** FRIGHTENINGLY ⟨the war whoop ripped ~ through the dewy greenness and freshness —Marjory S. Douglas⟩ **3 :** in such a manner or to such a degree as to excite repugnance, pity, disgust, dissatisfaction, or unpleasantness ⟨her response to all her varied experiences strikes the reader as ~ deficient in both thought and feeling —A.S.P.Woodhouse⟩ **4 :** EXTREMELY, EXCEEDINGLY ⟨I'm ~ tired, ~ stupid, nervy, worked up —Walter de la Mare⟩
dread·ful·ness \-fəlnəs\ *n* -ES [ME *dredfulnesse,* fr. *dredful* + *-nesse* -ness] **:** the quality or state of being dreadful
dread·ing·ly *adv* **:** in the manner of one that dreads ⟨approached the task fearfully, ~⟩
dread·less \-ləs\ *adj* [ME *dredelees,* fr. *drede, dred* + *-lees* -less] *archaic* **:** free from dread **:** INTREPID, DAUNTLESS — **dread·less·ly** *adv, archaic*
dreadnought *also* **dreadnaught** \ˈ=,=\ *n* -s **1 :** FEARNOUGHT 1 **2** [fr. *Dreadnought,* Brit. battleship finished 1907, the first of this type] **:** a battleship of the 20th century that has its main armament entirely of big guns all of one caliber
1dream \ˈdrēm\ *n* -s [ME *dreem,* fr. OE *drēam* noise, joy, music, prob. influenced in meaning by ON *draumr* dream; prob. akin to OHG *troum* dream, ON *draumr,* Gk *thrylos* noise, din, Latvian *duñduris* gadfly, wasp — more at DRONE] **1 a :** a series of thoughts, images, or emotions occurring during sleep **:** a semblance of reality or events occurring to one asleep **b** *psychoanalysis* **:** condensed, elaborated, symbolized, or otherwise distorted images of memories or of unconscious impulses experienced esp. during sleep but also during other lapses in attention the meaning of which is concealed from the ego; *also* **:** the verbal or written report of such images or experiences **2 :** an experience of waking life having the characteristics of a dream: as **a :** a visionary creation of the imagination **:** DAYDREAM ⟨the ~s of youth⟩ **b :** a state of mind marked by abstraction or release from the sense of reality **:** REVERIE ⟨lives in a ~, oblivious of all practical concerns⟩ **c :** an object seen in a dreamlike state **:** VISION ⟨if you be what I think you, some sweet ~ —Alfred Tennyson⟩ **3 :** something that is notable for its beauty, excellence, or enjoyable quality ⟨she wore a ~ of a dress⟩ ⟨it was a ~ of a trip⟩ ⟨the food is marvelous . . . and the setting is an absolute ~ —T.H. Fielding⟩ **4 :** a major aim, goal, or purpose the attainment of which is ardently desired or longed for **:** IDEAL ⟨the shore thou foundest verifies thy ~ —Walt Whitman⟩ ⟨the ~ of . . . an empire stretching to the Pacific —R.W.Van Alstyne⟩ ⟨achieved her ~ of becoming a professional writer —*Current Biog.*⟩ **syn** see FANCY
2dream \"\ *vb* **dreamed** \ˈdrem(p)t, -ēmd\ *or* **dreamt** \-em(p)t\ **dreamed** *or* **dreamt; dreaming** \-ēmiŋ\ **dreams** \-ēmz\ [ME *dremen,* fr. *dreem,* n.] *vi* **1 :** to have a dream **:** have ideas or images in the mind while asleep ⟨there are very normal people who ~ nightly —Otto Fenichel⟩ ⟨she ~*ed* of taking a trip and awoke with a feeling of excitement⟩ **2 :** to let the mind run on in idle reverie **:** give oneself over to effortless thought esp. of a fanciful nature ⟨the tendency of the population to ~ about their ancient glory rather than struggle with contemporary facts —Samuel Van Valkenburg & Ellsworth Huntington⟩ ⟨~*ing* of renown to come —Charles Kingsley⟩ **3 :** to wish for something ardently or yearningly **:** LONG **:** scheme, plan, or aspire for the attainment of some object — usu. used with *of* ⟨she ~*ed* of becoming a language teacher —Gertrude Samuels⟩ ⟨those powers who ~ of further aggrandizement in the East⟩ **4 :** to appear tranquil or dreamy **:** be suggestive of or give an impression of tranquility or dreaming ⟨quaint historic villages where pre-Revolutionary houses ~ in leafy shadows —Gladys Taber⟩ ⟨the pale ~*ing* sky —Dorothy C. Fisher⟩ ~ *vt* **1 :** to have a dream of **:** imagine in sleep **:** think of or seem to have a sensory impression of while asleep ⟨your old men shall ~ dreams —Acts 2:17 (RSV)⟩ ⟨according to Descartes a dreamer supposes that what he ~s are real objects and incidents —Margaret Macdonald⟩ ⟨I *dreamt* that I dwelt in marble halls —Alfred Bunn⟩ **2 :** to consider as a possibility **:** conceive of **:** IMAGINE ⟨little ~*ing* that I could park my car, climb down the bank, set up my rod and catch big trout —Joseph Novick⟩ ⟨the great new country whose expanse they did not ~ —Meridel Le Sueur⟩ **3 :** to pass (time) in reverie or inaction — usu. used with *away* ⟨he ~*ed* his life away⟩ — **dream of :** to think of as possible, fitting, or proper **:** give serious consideration to ⟨inventions that our grandfathers never *dreamed of*⟩ ⟨they would never *dream of* building a cumbersome railway . . . when the cableway is so much less expensive to build and to operate —M.L.Hoffman⟩ ⟨only a madman would *dream of* attempting to drive at that speed in such places —Priscilla Hughes⟩
3dream \"\ *adj* [*1dream*] **1 :** of, relating to, involved in, or resembling a dream **2 :** experienced in a dream ⟨~ myths of the Mohave, that are sung by the person who has dreamt the myth —Edward Sapir⟩ **3 :** appropriate to a pleasant dream **:** marked by as desirable qualities as can be imagined **:** approaching perfection or the ideal ⟨win a ~ holiday in Europe⟩ ⟨he is the ~ competitor — the one in 10,000 who has the temperament to match the talent —*Time*⟩ ⟨a display of ~ cars⟩
dreamboat \ˈ=,=\ *n* **1** *slang* **:** the embodiment of what one imagines or thinks to be highly desirable ⟨the local college student who declared . . . he'd rather have a 1934 Ford than any other car he has finally found his ~ —*Springfield (Mass.) Daily News*⟩ ⟨black Alaska seal, the new ~ for not only daytime but cocktails and evening —Lois Long⟩ **2** *slang* **a :** the person that most nearly fulfills one's idea of what a member of the opposite sex should be like ⟨brought to movie stardom a lady who, after 25 years, is still my ~ —S.J.Perelman⟩ **b :** SWEETHEART ⟨waiting for her ~ to finish his 21-month hitch in gaol —*Police Detective*⟩
dream book *n* **:** a book claiming to interpret the significance of dreams esp. as omens of the future
dream·er \ˈdrēmə(r)\ *n* -s [ME *dremere,* fr. *dremen* to dream + *-ere* -er] **1 :** one that dreams: as **a :** one who has ideas or images in the mind while asleep ⟨the ~ apparently moves about at will in the past, as in the present —Weston La Barre⟩ **b :** one that engages in daydreaming or idle reverie **:** one that builds castles in the air ⟨~s who yearned for things that are not . . . or things that have been —Norman Douglas⟩ **c :** one that conceives and usu. attempts to achieve a major objective (as of social change or scientific or geographic discovery) that is regarded by most of his contemporaries as impracticable or fanciful ⟨the great ~s, seers, and visionaries of history⟩ **2** *usu cap* **:** an adherent of a No. American Indian religious sect originated by the Wanapûm chief Smohalla about 1850-60 and extending to many of the Oregon, Washington, and Idaho tribes **3 :** one who claims to select lucky policy-game numbers or horse-race tips by occult means and sells them to bettors
dream·ery \ˈdrēmərē\ *n* -ES **:** impractical fancies
dream·ful \-mfəl\ *adj* **:** full of dreams **:** DREAMY ⟨awake after ~ sleep —Max Steele⟩ ⟨various peculiarities and faults of my writings are due to this mechanical and ~ way of composing them —George Santayana⟩ — **dream·ful·ly** \-fəlē\ *adv* — **dream·ful·ness** \-lnəs\ *n* -ES
dream·i·ly \-məlē, -li\ *adv* **:** as if in a dream **:** in a dreamy manner **:** VAGUELY
dream·i·ness \-mēnəs, -min-\ *n* -ES **:** the quality or state of being dreamy
dream·ing·ly *adv* [*dreaming* (pres. part. of *2dream*) + *-ly*] **:** as if dreaming **:** DREAMILY
dream·land \-m,land, -aa(ə)nd\ *n* **:** an unreal delightful country existing only in imagination or in dreams **:** NEVER-NEVER ⟨a charming fantasy set in a ~ filled with desirable girls and prime wine⟩
dream·less \-mləs\ *adj* **:** having no dreams ⟨a ~ sleep⟩ — **dream·less·ly** *adv* — **dream·less·ness** *n* -ES
dreamlike \ˈ=,=\ *adj* **:** like that seen or occurring in a dream ⟨the old castle stood there in all its ~ loveliness⟩ **:** resembling a dream (as in transitoriness or unreal quality) ⟨that fast furious ride across the moor he remembered only as a frightening ~ experience⟩ **:** VAGUE, NEBULOUS, SHADOWY ⟨night invested the quiet lake with a ~ charm⟩
dreams *pl of* DREAM, *pres 3d sing of* DREAM
dreamt *past of* DREAM
dreamtime \ˈ=,=\ *n* [prob. trans. of Australian *alchera, alcheringa*] **:** the aboriginal time of creation in the mythology of the Australian natives **:** the mythical beginning time when all things were created, including the first human ancestors, and to which myths are generally traceable ⟨a patriarchal or ~ father —Daisy Bates⟩
dream up *vt* **:** to invent, devise, or concoct esp. in an outburst of artistic improvisation or an unbridled flight of fancy ⟨the most fantastic rumors he could *dream up* —Joseph Millard⟩ ⟨all the magnificent plans they're *dreaming up* —Bennett Cerf⟩
dream vision *n* **1 :** a poetic framework esp. popular in medieval literature in which the poet pictures himself as falling asleep and envisioning in his dream a series of allegorical people and events **2 :** a poem utilizing the dream vision
dreamwork \ˈ=,=\ *n* [trans. of G *traumarbeit*] **:** the process of concealing the latent content of dreams from the conscious mind
dreamworld \ˈ=,=\ *n* **1 :** DREAMLAND; *also* **:** a world of illusion or fantasy ⟨his struggle to grow out of the ~ of childhood —J.W.Aldridge⟩ **2 :** a state of intense preoccupation with or absorption in intellectual or unworldly concerns ⟨musicians are pictured as tempestuous characters . . . lost in a ~ of creation —Gretchen Finletter⟩
dreamy \ˈdrēmē, -mi\ *adj* -ER/-EST [*1dream* + *-y*] **1 a :** VAGUE, IDLE, HAZY ⟨the drone of the greenfinch lulls me into ~ meditations —L.P.Smith⟩ **b :** given to dreaming or fantasy ⟨the child was ~ and introverted, playing with imaginary playmates and having visions⟩ ⟨you're frightfully ~ and unpractical and unbusinesslike —Christopher Isherwood⟩ **2 :** having the quality or characteristics of a dream **:** DREAMLIKE **3 a :** INDISTINCT ⟨the mountains growing softer in outline and ~ looking —John Muir †1914⟩ **b :** quiet and soothing ⟨~ waltzes⟩ **c :** DELIGHTFUL, PLEASING, IDEAL ⟨own and run a hotel and ski resort in a perfectly ~ spot in Utah —Carl Jonas⟩ ⟨he's so handsome . . . real ~ —Greg Foley⟩ **4 :** suggestive of a dream or a dreamlike state ⟨her eyes were ~ and great, as of one who looketh afar —William Morris⟩ ⟨she walked home that night in a ~ silence —Robert Fawcett⟩
drean \ˈdrēn\ *dial var of* DRAIN
1drear \ˈdri(ə)r, -iə\ *n* -s [back-formation fr. *dreary*] *archaic* **:** DREARINESS
2drear \"\ *adj* [short for *dreary*] **1 :** cheerless and depressing **:** uninteresting and dull **:** DREARY ⟨though the setting is ~ and circumstances oppressive, this is not a degrading story —E.A. Weeks⟩ ⟨a barren and ~ existence⟩ **2 :** SAD ⟨I had taken a hot whisky punch to the master, poor creature, he seemed so lone and ~ —James Reynolds⟩ — **drear·ly** *adv* — **drear·ness** *n* -ES
drear·i·head *pronunc at* DREARY +,hed\ *or* **drear·i·hood** \-,hu̇d\ *n* [*drearihead* fr. ME *drerihed,* fr. *drery* dreary + *-hed, -hede* (akin to ME *-hod* -hood); *drearihood* fr. *dreary* + *-hood*] *archaic* **:** DREARINESS
drear·i·ly \ˈdrirəlē, -rēr-, -li\ *adv* [ME *drerily,* fr. OE *drēoriglice,* fr. *drēorig* sad, bloody + *-līce* -ly] **:** in a dreary way
drear·i·ment \-rēmənt, -rim-\ *n* -s **:** the quality or state of being dreary
drear·i·ness \-rēnəs, -rin-\ *n* -ES [ME *drerinesse,* fr. OE *drēorignys,* fr. *drēorig* sad, bloody + *-nys, -nes* -ness] **1** *archaic* **:** SADNESS **2 a :** the quality or state of being dull and uninteresting **:** MONOTONY, GLOOMINESS ⟨the occasional ~ of being dutiful —Claudia Cassidy⟩ **b :** something that is dull, monotonous, and uninteresting ⟨the concert was one of those fragmentary ~es that people endure because they are fashionable —Mark Twain⟩
drear·i·some \-rēsəm, -ris-\ *adj, archaic* **:** characterized by dreariness
dreary \ˈdrir|ē, -rēr|, |i\ *adj* -ER/-EST [ME *drery,* fr. OE *drēorig* sad, bloody, fr. *drēor* gore, falling blood; akin to OE *drēosan* to fall, OHG *trūrēn* to be sad, MHG *trōr* dripping liquid, ON *dreyri* flowing blood, Goth *driusan* to fall, Gk *thrauein* to shatter] **1** *obs* **:** CRUEL, DIRE, GRIEVOUS **2 :** feeling, displaying, or reflecting a settled mood of listlessness or discouragement **:** without liveliness, cheer, joy, or hope ⟨she would fix her eyes on the distance in ~ contemplation, and her mind would follow her eyes in a vacant and wistful regard —G.D.Brown⟩ ⟨restore a crazy constitution and cheer a ~ mind —George Berkeley⟩ **3 :** not having anything likely to cheer, comfort, encourage, interest, or enliven **:** making for gloomy dullness **:** DEPRESSING, DISCOURAGING, ENERVATING ⟨~ sketches of people in breadlines —R.H.Rovere⟩ ⟨abandoned farms alone remained as ~ reminders of former prosperity —*Amer. Guide Series: Mass.*⟩ ⟨life in a perfectly sensible, utilitarian community would be intolerably ~ —Aldous Huxley⟩ **syn** see DISMAL
dreck \ˈdrek\ *n* -s [Yiddish *drek* & G *dreck,* fr. MHG *drec;* akin to OE *threax* rubbish, ON *threkkr* excrement, L *stercus* excrement, LGk *sterganos* privy, Gk *tryg-, tryx* dregs, and prob. to Russ *sterva* carrion] **1 :** FILTH, LITTER, TRASH, JUNK ⟨your food is ~, it is fit only for pigs —Michael Gold⟩ ⟨the ~ of the cities⟩ **2 :** a garment badly made or of inferior materials
dred·dour \ˈdredər\ *n* -s [ME (Sc) *dredour,* fr. ME *drede* dread + *-our* (as in *horrour* horror) — more at DREAD] *chiefly Scot* **:** DREAD, TERROR
1dredge \ˈdrej, ˈdrəj\ *n* -s [alter. of ME *dragge, draggeye,* fr. MF *dragie* mixture of grains grown as a forage crop, fr. (assumed) VL (of Gaul) *dravocata,* fr. Gaulish *dravoca* darnel; akin to ME *tare* vetch — more at TARE] *dial Brit* **:** mixed grains sown together; *esp* **:** a mixture of oats and barley grown together for making malt
2dredge \ˈdrej, *chiefly dial* ˈdrəj\ *n* -s *often attrib* [prob. alter. of Sc *dreg-* (in the compound *dregbot* dredge boat), fr. ME (Sc) *dreg-,* perh. irreg. fr. the root of OE *dragan* to pull — more at DRAW] **1 :** an implement or machine for scooping or digging objects or earth from the bed of a body of water: **a :** an oblong iron frame with a bag net attached or a similar apparatus for gathering fish, shellfish, or natural history specimens **b :** a machine for scooping up or removing earth (as in excavating or deepening stream or harbor channels, building levees, or digging ditches) usu. by a series of buckets on an endless chain, a pump or suction tube, or a single bucket or grab at the end of an arm — see DIPPER DREDGE, HYDRAULIC DREDGE; compare DRAGLINE 2 **2 :** a boat or barge used in dredging
3dredge \"\ *vb* -ED/-ING/-S *vt* **1 a :** to catch, gather, or pull out with a dredge — often used with *up* ⟨silt and old refuse were *dredged* up from the river bottom —Green Peyton⟩ **b :** to bring to light or gather by deep searching as if with a dredge — often used with *up* ⟨facts *dredged* from the records⟩ ⟨I tried to ~ up a little of that deep, involuntary wisdom that tells you what to do in a critical situation —Anne S. Mehdevi⟩ **c :** to make a search of or dig into deeply with or as if with a dredge ⟨the harbor still is being *dredged* for boats sunk —*Springfield (Mass.) Union*⟩ ⟨*dredging* his memories and finding them intolerable —*Time*⟩ **2 :** to deepen with a dredging machine **:** excavate with a dredge ⟨*dredged* a cutoff three blocks long . . . where the river swings eastward in a wide semicircle —Green Peyton⟩ ~ *vi* **:** to use a dredge **:** to search with or as if with a dredge ⟨*dredging* for oysters⟩ ⟨he *dredged* into himself for words —Oliver La Farge⟩
4dredge \"\ *vt* -ED/-ING/-S [obs. *dredge,* n., sweetmeat, fr. ME *drege,* alter. of *drage,* fr. MF *dragie, dragee,* modif. of L *tragemata* (pl.) sweetmeats, fr. Gk *tragēmata,* pl. of *tragēmat-, tragēma* sweetmeat, dried fruit] **:** to sprinkle with a powdered substance: as **a :** to coat (food) by sprinkling (as with flour or sugar) **b :** to dust (hot ware) with dry enamel powder in dry process enameling
5dredge \"\ *n* -s **:** a box or package attachment with holes for sprinkling or sifting the contents
dredge corn *n* [*1dredge*] **:** a mixed crop of oats and barley used in Great Britain for stock feed
dredge·man \-mən\ *n, pl* **dredgemen** [*2dredge*] **1 :** DREDGER 1 **2 :** one who is in charge of the operation of a dredge used to mine metal-bearing sands from the bottom of a body of water
1dredg·er \-jə(r)\ *n* -s [*3dredge* + *-er*] **:** one that dredges; *esp* **:** 2DREDGE
2dredger \"\ *n* -s [*4dredge* + *-er*] **1 :** a shaker for condiments used at the table **2 :** 5DREDGE
dredger master *n* **:** DREDGEMAN 2
dred·gie \ˈdrejē\ *n* -s [by alter.] **:** DIRGIE 2
dredging *n* -s [fr. gerund of *3dredge*] **:** the act or operation of one who dredges; *also* **:** something that is dredged up
dredging bucket *n* **:** a bucket (as an orange-peel or clamshell bucket) used in dredging

dredgers 1

1dree \ˈdrē\ *vb* **dreed; dreed; dreeing; drees** [ME *dreen, drien,* fr. OE *drēogan* to perform, endure — more at DRUDGE] *vt* **1** *chiefly Scot* **:** ENDURE, SUFFER ⟨the slighted maids my torments see and laugh at a' the pangs I ~ —Robert Burns⟩ **2** *archaic Scot* **:** to pass (time) or spend (one's life) usu. unhappily **3** *chiefly Scot* **:** DREAD, FEAR ~ *vi, dial Brit* **:** ENDURE — **dree one's weird** *chiefly Scot* **:** to endure one's fate
2dree \"\ *n* -s *chiefly Scot* **:** MISFORTUNE, SUFFERING
3dree \"\ *var of* DREICH
dreed \ˈdrēd\ *dial Brit var of* DREAD
dreel \ˈdrēl\ *Scot var of* DRILL
dreen \ˈdrēn\ *dial var of* DRAIN
dreep \ˈdrēp\ *dial Brit var of* DRIP
dreepy \-pi\ *adj* -ER/-EST [*dreep* + *-y*] *dial Brit* **:** spiritless and ineffective **:** DROOPY
dreg \ˈdreg\ *n* -s [ME, fr. ON *dregg;* akin to L *fraces* dregs of oil, Gk *taratein, tarassein* to disturb, stir, Alb *dia* dregs of oil, OE *deorc* dark — more at DARK] **1 :** sediment contained in a liquid or precipitated from it **:** LEES — usu. used in pl. ⟨the night-porter took a tankard from a hook and emptied all the ~s from the glasses into it —George Bellairs⟩ **2 :** the poorest or most undesirable part of anything — usu. used in pl. ⟨the ~s of society⟩ **3 :** the last remaining part **:** VESTIGE ⟨with some ~s of timidity still in his soul —John Buchan⟩
dreg·gy \-gē\ *adj* -ER/-EST [ME, fr. *dreg* + *-y*] **:** full of dregs **:** MUDDY, FOUL
d region *n, usu cap D* **:** the lowest part of the ionosphere occurring between 25 and 40 miles above the surface of the earth and capable of reflecting radio waves of very low frequency but absorbing energy of radio waves of high frequencies that are reflected by higher ionosphere layers
dregs of wine : a dark red to deep reddish brown that is less strong than Malaga — called also *wine dregs, wine lees*
dreich *or* **dreigh** \ˈdrēk\ *adj* [ME *dregh, dreich,* of Scand origin; akin to ON *drjūgr* substantial, lasting; akin to OE *drēogan* to perform, endure — more at DRUDGE] **1** *chiefly Scot* **a :** long and drawn out **:** PROTRACTED ⟨a ~ job hoeing potatoes⟩ **b :** tedious and uninteresting **:** TIRESOME ⟨a ~ sermon⟩ **2** *chiefly Scot* **:** slow or tardy esp. in paying debts **3** *chiefly Scot* **:** dismal and gloomy **:** DREARY ⟨~ damp days —D.B. Forrester⟩
dreid \ˈdrēd\ *Scot var of* DREAD
drei·del \ˈdrād°l\ *n, pl* **dreidels** *or* **dreidel** [Yiddish *dreidl,* fr. *drehen* to turn, fr. MHG *dræjen, dræhen,* fr. OHG *drāen* — more at THROW] **1 :** a 4-sided die that revolves like a spinning top, that is marked on each side with a different Hebrew letter, and that is used as a toy esp. during the Hanukkah festival **2 :** a children's game of chance similar to put-and-take that is played with the dreidel
drei·kan·ter \ˈdrī,käntə(r), -kan-\ *n, pl* **dreikanters** *or* **dreikanter** [G, lit., one having three edges, fr. *drei* three (fr. OHG *drī*) + *kante* edge (fr. LG *kant, kante,* fr. MLG, fr. MD *cant*) + *-er* (fr. OHG *-āri*) — more at THREE, CANT, -ER] **:** a

3-faced pebble faceted by wind-blown sand; *broadly* : VENTIFACT

dreis·sen·sia \drī'sen(t)sēə, -nch(ē)ə\ *n, cap* [NL, irreg. fr. *Dreyssen*, 19th cent. Belg. physician + NL *-ia*] : a genus of Old World bivalve mollusks (suborder Tellinacea) somewhat resembling the true mussels

¹drench \'drench\ *n* -ES [ME, fr. OE *drenc;* akin to OHG *trank* drink, Goth *dragk;* derivative fr. the root of OE *drincan* to drink — more at DRINK] **1 a :** DRINK, DRAFT **b :** a poisonous or medicinal drink; *specif* **:** a large dose of medicine mixed with liquid and put down the throat of an animal **2 a :** something that drenches ⟨this alternance of sun and ~ proliferates plant and beast —Waldo Frank⟩ **b :** a quantity sufficient to drench or saturate ⟨the heather of the bogs, the hill turf, and the gravel of the road had lost their color under a ~ of dew —John Buchan⟩ ⟨few men have subjected all their borrowings to so strong a ~ of personability —H.S.Canby⟩ **c :** a solution usu. of fermenting bran used for drenching hides

²drench \"\ *vb* -ED/-ING/-ES [ME *drenchen* to cause to drink, drown, fr. OE *drencan;* akin to OHG *trenken* to cause to drink, ON *drekkja* to drown, Goth *drankjan* to cause to drink; causative fr. the root of OE *drincan* to drink] *vt* **1 a** *archaic* **:** to force to drink **b :** to administer a drench to (an animal) **2** *obs* **a :** to submerge in water **b :** DROWN **3 :** to steep or saturate by immersion in liquid ⟨desserts ~*ed* in brandy —Dwight Macdonald⟩; *specif* **:** to soak (hides) in a weak acid bath to remove lime left by the liming process **4 :** to soak or cover thoroughly with liquid that falls or is precipitated ⟨within five minutes the daily downpour of tropical rain would ~ the jungle —William Beebe⟩ ⟨the sweat poured down his body until he was ~*ed* —Pearl Buck⟩ **5 :** to fill completely as if by soaking or precipitation **:** SATURATE, STEEP, PERVADE ⟨ominous iridescences ~ every paragraph —Frederic Morton⟩ ⟨familiar with the Hebrides and ~*ed* in Highland lore —J.W.Krutch⟩ ⟨klieg lights snapped on, ~*ing* rostrum and orchestra floor with hot light —F.L.Allen⟩ ⟨sun-*drenched* Italy —G.C. Sellery⟩ ~ *vi* **:** to fall heavily and cause saturation ⟨driving snow and sleet, which ~*ed* cruelly down on little townships that already . . . had had too much of water —Mollie Panter-Downes⟩

drench·er \-chə(r)\ *n* -S **:** one that drenches; *specif* **:** a delimer who uses bran drench

drench·ing·ly *adv* **:** in a manner that drenches

dreng *also* **drengh** \'dreŋ\ *n* -S [ME *dreng, dring,* fr. OE *dreng* warrior, fr. ON *drengr* young man, valiant man; akin to MIr *dringid* he steps, Russ *derzhat'* to hold, L *firmus* firm — more at FIRM] *old English law* **:** a free tenant esp. in ancient Northumbria who held under a partly military and partly servile form of tenure antedating the Norman conquest

dren·gage \'dreŋ(g)ij\ *n* -S [ML *drengagium,* fr. ME *dreng* + ML *-agium* -age (fr. OF -age)] *old English law* **:** the tenure or service of a dreng

drep·a·nas·pis \ˌdrepə'naspə̇s\ *n, cap* [NL, fr. Gk *drepanē* sickle (fr. *drepein* to pluck) + NL *-aspis* — more at DRAB] **:** a genus of Devonian ostracoderms (class Heterostraci)

drep·a·ne \'drepə(ˌ)nē\ *n* [NL, fr. Gk *drepanē* sickle; prob. fr. the shape of its pectoral fins] **1** *cap* **:** a genus (coextensive with a family Drepanidae) of compressed percoid food fishes comprising a single species (*D. punctata*) and having a protrusible mouth that when extended forms a tubular downward projection **2** -S **:** any fish of the genus *Drepane*

drep·a·nid \-ˌnə̇d\ *n* -S [irreg. fr. NL *Drepanididae*] **:** a bird of the family Drepanididae **:** a Hawaiian honeycreeper

dre·pan·i·dae \drə'panəˌdē\ *n pl, cap* [NL, fr. *Drepana,* type genus (fr. Gk *drepanē* sickle) + *-idae;* fr. the shape of the forewings] **:** a family of small slender moths usu. having the tips of the forewings hooked — see HOOKTIP

drep·a·nid·i·dae \ˌdrepə'nidəˌdē\ *n pl, cap* [NL, fr. *Drepanid-, Drepanis,* type genus (fr. L *drepanis,* a bird, perh. the swift, fr. Gk *drepanid-, drepanis,* fr. *drepanē* sickle) + *-idae*] **:** a family of Hawaiian passerine birds having the bill precisely adapted in curvature and length for the obtaining of nectar from various plants of the family Lobeliaceae — see MAMO

dre·pan·i·form \drə'panəˌfȯrm, 'drepən-\ *adj* [Gk *drepanē* sickle + E *-iform*] *biol* **:** shaped like a sickle **:** FALCATE

drep·a·no·cy·to·sis \ˌdrepə(ˌ)nōˌsī'tōsə̇s\ *n, pl* **drepanocytoses** \-ōˌsēz\ [NL, fr. *drepano-* (fr. Gk *drepanē* sickle) + *cyt-* + *-osis*] **1 :** SICKLE-CELL ANEMIA **2 :** SICKLE-CELL TRAIT

drep·a·noid \'drepəˌnȯid\ *adj* [Gk *drepanoeidēs,* fr. *drepan-* (fr. *drepanē, drepanon* sickle) + *-oeidēs* -oid] **:** shaped like a sickle

drep·a·no·phy·cus \ˌdrepənō'fīkəs\ *n, cap* [NL, prob. fr. *drepano-* (fr. Gk *drepanē, drepanon* sickle) + *-phycus* (fr. Gk *phykos* seaweed) — more at FUCUS] **:** a genus of very large Devonian fossil plants resembling and prob. closely related to the psilophytons but distinguished by spiny verticellate or spiral appendages resembling leaves and sometimes having sporangia in their axils

¹dres·den \'drezdən\ *adj, usu cap* [fr. *Dresden,* industrial city of Saxony, Germany] **:** of or from the city of Dresden, Germany **:** of the kind or style prevalent in Dresden

²dresden \"\ *n* -S *usu cap* **:** DRESDEN CHINA

dresden blue *n, often cap D* **:** a moderate blue that is greener and duller than average copen, redder, lighter, and stronger than azurite blue or pompadour, and greener and paler than bluebird

dresden brown *n, often cap D* **:** FOX 5

dresden china *or* **dresden ware** *n, usu cap D* [*Dresden,* Germany] **:** hard-paste porcelain (as Meissen) made in the vicinity of Dresden and typically characterized by daintiness of design and ornate decoration

dresden–china \ˌ=ˌ==\ *adj, usu cap D* [*Dresden china*] **:** having a delicate or insipid prettiness ⟨proud of his *Dresden-china* doll of a wife⟩

¹dress \'dres\ *vb* -ED/-ING/-ES [ME *dressen,* fr. MF *dresser,* fr. OF *drecier,* fr. (assumed) VL *directiare,* fr. L *directus* direct, past part. of *dirigere* to direct, fr. *di-* (fr. *dis-* apart) + *-rigere* (fr. *regere* to rule) — more at DIS-, RIGHT] *vt* **1 :** to make or set straight **:** put in proper position: as **a** *now dial* **:** ERECT, PRICK ⟨the cat ~*ed* up her ears at the sound⟩ **b :** to arrange (troops, equipment) in a straight line and at proper intervals **:** ALIGN ⟨~ the ranks⟩ **c :** to place the actors on (a stage) so as to create a pleasing and well-balanced scene **2** *archaic* **:** to dress down **3 :** to put clothes on **:** provide with clothing **:** CLOTHE ⟨she ~*ed* the child in a snowsuit⟩ ⟨she ~*es* her family on a small budget⟩ **4 :** to cover with, array in, or add something that improves the appearance or heightens the effectiveness of **:** add decorative details or accessories to **:** EMBELLISH ⟨the ruins, which are ~*ed* by the moon in even more compelling mystery —P.E.Deutschman⟩ ⟨then I ~ my hair with the little chrysanthemums —Amy Lowell⟩ — often used with *up* ⟨she ~*ed up* her black dress with rhinestone clips⟩ ⟨cars ~*ed* up with chrome⟩ ⟨needlessly rebinding old manuscripts and incunabula in order to *dress* up books —Edith Diehl⟩ **5 a :** to provide with the suitable furnishings for a particular purpose or occasion **:** make ready **:** OUTFIT ⟨~*ed* the table for supper —George Meredith⟩ ⟨besides doubling and tripling as performers, everyone took a turn ~*ing* the ring for the other acts —Bill Ballantine⟩ — compare WINDOW DRESSING **b :** to cover (the hooped curd) with cloth in cheese making **6 a :** to apply dressings, bandages, or therapeutic materials to (as wounds) **b** (1) **:** to arrange (the hair) by combing, brushing, curling (2) **:** to groom and curry (an animal) **c :** to make ready for use or for cooking or for use or service: as (1) **:** to prepare (a fishhook) for fishing; *also* **:** prepare (flies or bait) for use on a hook (2) **:** to prepare (food animals) for market usu. by bleeding and cleaning — often used with *out* ⟨bleed and ~ out the animal so that no meat would be wasted —Frances Judge⟩ (3) **:** CULTIVATE, TEND ⟨~ a crop⟩ ⟨~ a field⟩; *specif* **:** to apply manure or fertilizer to — compare TOP-DRESS (4) *chiefly Brit* **:** PACK ⟨~ the impression cylinder of a printing press⟩; *also* **:** to attach the printing surface to (the plate cylinder of a press) **d** (1) **:** to free (as grain or ore) of impurities or irregularities; *specif* **:** to sift (flour) so as to remove bran flakes and insure even granulation (2) **:** to remove worn-out abrasive from (an abrasive wheel) **7 :** to put through a finishing operation or process: as **a :** to cure (fur skins) by softening, fleshing, oiling, and drumming; *sometimes* **:** TAN 1 **b :** to give a smooth or glossy finish to (as leather, textiles, pottery) **c :** to make trim and smooth (lumber, stone, a gem) **d :** to shape (as a tool) by grinding **e :** to impart a surface finish to (a racetrack) esp. by scraping ~ *vi* **1 a :** to put on clothing ⟨he ~*ed* quickly⟩ ⟨she ~*ed* warmly for skiing⟩ **b :** to put on or wear one's best clothes or formal clothes ⟨she is ~*ing* for the opera⟩ — often used with *up* ⟨he ~*es* up only when guests are coming⟩ **c :** to dress elaborately or bizarrely ⟨~*ing* up for a masquerade ball⟩ **d :** to wear clothes ⟨she always ~*es* in good taste⟩ **2** *of a food animal* **:** to weigh after being dressed ⟨the chicken ~*ed* four pounds⟩ — often used with *out* ⟨the steer ~*ed* out to 70 percent of his weight⟩ **3 :** to align oneself with the next soldier in a line to make the line straight — **dress one's droddum** *Scot* **:** to give a thrashing or beating — **dress ship 1 :** to ornament a ship while in port by hoisting national ensigns at the mastheads and running a line of signal flags and pennants from bow to stern by way of the mastheads in honor of a special occasion (as a national holiday) or as a courtesy to a foreign nation or a distinguished person **2 :** to ornament a ship in the U.S. Navy by hoisting national ensigns at the mastheads, the ship's largest ensign at the flagstaff, and the jack at the jackstaff

²dress \"\ *n* -ES **1** *obs* **:** the action of making right or setting straight **:** REDRESS **2 :** utilitarian or ornamental covering for the human body: as **a :** clothing and accessories suitable to a specific purpose or occasion ⟨a soldier in battle ~⟩ ⟨in pilgrimage ~ on his way to Mecca —R.C.Doty⟩ **b :** clothing characteristic of a particular period, geographic area, or nation ⟨18th century ~⟩ ⟨Oriental ~⟩ ⟨Arab ~⟩ **c :** style of clothing **:** manner of wearing clothes ⟨conservative in ~⟩ ⟨thoughtless about his ~⟩ **3 a :** an outer garment for females or small children usu. made in a one-piece style of bodice and skirt **b :** a two-piece garment consisting of blouse and skirt or jacket and skirt **4 :** covering, adornment, or appearance that is appropriate or peculiar to a particular time or season ⟨mountains, proud and glistening in full winter ~ —Marcia Davenport⟩: as **a :** a particular state of plumage of a bird ⟨breeding ~⟩ ⟨summer ~⟩ **b :** the style of makeup and typography of a newspaper or periodical **c :** the particular form under which something is presented ⟨routine love story in pioneer ~ —Joan S. Bishop⟩ ⟨the whole Bible appeared in English ~ —I.M. Price⟩ ⟨no one will object to ornateness if it is the proper ~ for your thoughts and feelings —A.T.Weaver⟩

³dress \"\ *adj* [²*dress*] **1 :** relating to or used for a dress ⟨~ material⟩ ⟨~ pattern⟩ ⟨~ buttons⟩ **2 a :** suitable for a ceremonial or formal occasion ⟨~ clothes⟩ ⟨~ shoes⟩ — compare DRESS SUIT, DRESS UNIFORM **b :** suitable for wear or use with ceremonial or formal clothing ⟨a ~ sword⟩ ⟨a ~ watch⟩ **3 :** requiring or permitting formal dress ⟨the graduation will be a ~ affair⟩ — compare DRESS PARADE, DRESS REHEARSAL

dres·sage \drə'säzh, dre'-, -säzh\ *n* -S [F, preparation, straightening, training, fr. *dresser* to prepare, make straight, train + *-age* — more at DRESS] **:** the execution by a horse of maneuvers involving changes of gait, pace, and airs in response to barely perceptible movements of a rider's hands, legs, and weight; *also* **:** the systematic training of a horse in obedience and deportment

dress cap *n* **:** a cap of a specified design to be worn with any of the dress uniforms of the military services

dress circle *n* [so called because dress clothes were once commonly worn there] **:** the first or lowest curved tier of seats in a theater or opera house; *also* **:** a corresponding section of seats in a motion-picture theater

dress coat *n* **1 :** TAILCOAT **2 :** the coat of a dress uniform

dress down *vt* **:** to reprove severely **:** REBUKE, REPRIMAND ⟨he is *dressed down* for violating the code of the regiment —E.A. Weeks⟩

dressed *adj* [fr. past part. of ¹*dress*] *of poultry* **:** killed, bled, and more or less completely prepared for cooking — compare FULL-DRESSED, NEW YORK DRESSED

dressed and matched *adj, of a board* **:** planed and shaped at the edges to make intimate joints (as by tongue and groove)

dressed masonry *n* **:** masonry faced and smoothed

dressed overall *adj, Brit* **:** FULL-DRESSED 2

¹dress·er \'dresə(r)\ *n* -S [ME *dressore, dresser,* fr. MF *dresseur,* fr. OF *dreçor,* fr. *drecier* to arrange, make straight — more at ¹DRESS] **1** *obs* **:** a table or sideboard on which meat and other things were prepared for use or from which food was served **2 :** a cupboard or set of shelves to hold dishes and cooking utensils **3 :** a piece of bedroom furniture (as a chest of drawers or bureau) with a mirror

dresser 3

²dresser \"\ *n* -S [¹*dress* + *-er*] **1 :** one that dresses commercial articles in preparation for their use: as **a :** one that finishes leather **b :** one that smooths and polishes pottery **c :** one that cleans fish **d :** one that sets up machinery (as well-drilling rigs) for operation **e :** one that takes care of growing plants (as fruit trees or fruiting vines) by performing operations (as cultivating, pruning, thinning) required to insure a crop — usu. used in combination ⟨a vine*dresser*⟩ **2 a :** one that assists another in dressing; *specif* **:** one that cares for the wardrobe of an actor and helps with costume changing **b** (1) **:** one that dresses in a particular way ⟨a careful ~⟩ ⟨a careless ~⟩ (2) **:** one that is noted for the use of careful or stylish dress ⟨look well enough for anybody, though he will never be much of a ~ —Thomas Hughes⟩ **3 :** one that serves as a doctor's assistant esp. in the dressing of wounds or other lesions **4 :** a tool or machine for dressing something: as **a :** a pick for shaping large coal **b :** a mallet for working sheet lead **c :** a machine for facing millstones **d :** a flour bolter **e :** a smith's tool which fits into the hardie hole and over which the work is finished to shape **f :** a device for removing worn-out abrasive from abrasive wheels **g :** a textile machine used in preparing warp (as of wool) for the loom

dres·ser coupling \'dresə(r)-\ *n, usu cap D* [after Solomon R. *Dresser* †1911 Am. congressman, its inventor] **:** a pipe coupling for unthreaded pipe

dresser set *n* [¹*dresser*] **:** a set for use on a dresser or dressing table consisting of comb, hairbrush, and mirror and sometimes including such other personal items as manicure articles and cosmetics containers

dresser tray *n* **:** a tray (as of glass, ceramic, or plastic) for holding small objects on the top of a dresser

dresses *pres 3d sing of* DRESS, *pl of* DRESS

dress form *n* **:** a paper, cloth, or wire representation of a woman's figure from shoulder to thighs but minus arms that is mounted on a stand and used for fitting garments

dress goods *n pl but sometimes sing in constr* **:** fabrics suitable for lightweight clothing (as women's dresses)

dressier *comparative of* DRESSY

dressiest *superlative of* DRESSY

dress in *vt* **:** to outfit (a new prisoner) with prison clothes; *also* **:** to admit to prison

dress·i·ness \'dresēnə̇s, -sin-\ *n* -ES **:** the quality or state of being dressy

dressing *n* -S [ME *dressinge,* fr. *dressen* to dress + *-inge* -ing] **1 a :** the act or process of one who dresses **b :** an instance of such act or process **2 :** something added to a basically complete article or object to decorate, enhance, or lend character or interest: as **a :** a sauce or similar mixture (as mayonnaise) for adding to a certain dish (as a salad) **b :** a seasoned mixture (as of bread, potato, nuts, oysters) used as a stuffing for poultry, meat, or fish or baked separately **c :** an ornamental finish ⟨reconstructed in brick with stone ~*s* —Nikolaus Pevsner⟩ **3 :** something used as a cleaning or conditioning agent: as **a :** material (as ointment, gauze) applied to cover a sore, wound, or other lesion — compare PRESSURE DRESSING **b :** manure, compost, or other material used as a fertilizer — see SIDE-DRESSING, TOPDRESSING **c :** sizing applied to yarns and fabrics usu. to make them smooth and firm during manufacturing processes or sometimes to improve their weight and appearance when finished **d :** a substance used to soften, clean, polish, or waterproof leather **4 :** DRESSING DOWN

dress form

dressing case *n* **1 :** a small piece of hand luggage containing or fitted with makeup and toilet articles **2** *archaic* **:** BUREAU, DRESSER

dressing down *n, pl* **dressing downs** [fr. gerund of *dress down*] **:** a severe reprimand ⟨gave him a *dressing down* for lying⟩

dressing glass *n* **:** a small mirror set to swing in a standing frame for use on a dresser or chest

dressing gown *n* **:** an ankle-length or knee-length loose or tailored robe usu. of silk or other fine material that is worn informally (as at home) esp. while dressing or resting ⟨enveloped . . . in a man's *dressing gown* of silk brocade —C.G. Norris⟩ ⟨a thin *dressing gown* over her nightdress —*Scribner's*⟩

dressing line *n* **:** a line to which flags are attached for dressing ship

dressing room *n* **:** a room used primarily for dressing and making one's toilet; *esp* **:** a room backstage in a theater where a performer changes costumes and makeup

dressing sack *or* **dressing sacque** *n* **:** a woman's loose jacket worn while dressing or lounging

dressing station *n* **:** AID STATION

dressing table *n* **:** a low table often fitted with drawers and a mirror in front of which one sits while making a toilet — called also *vanity*

dressmake \'=ˌ=\ *vi* [back-formation fr. *dressmaker*] **:** to make dresses

¹dressmaker \'=ˌ==\ *n* [²*dress* + *maker*] **:** one that does dressmaking; *sometimes* **:** COUTURIER

²dressmaker \"\ *adj, of women's clothes* **:** having softness, rounded lines, and intricate detailing in contrast with the straight-lined simplicity of tailored clothes ⟨a ~ suit⟩

dressmaking \'=ˌ==\ *n* [²*dress* + *making*] **:** the process or occupation of making clothes, esp. dresses

dress parade *n* **:** a formal ceremonial parade in dress uniform

dress rehearsal *n* **:** a full rehearsal of a play in costume and with stage properties shortly before the first performance

dress shield *n* **:** SHIELD 2h

dress shirt *n* **:** a man's white shirt; *specif* **:** a white shirt with a starched or pleated front for wear with evening dress

dress suit *n* **:** a suit worn for full dress — compare EVENING DRESS

dress uniform *n* **1 :** a uniform for formal wear; *specif* **:** a blue uniform worn by U.S. Army personnel for formal occasions **2 :** a dark blue U.S. Navy uniform regularly worn in cool seasons or climates — compare FULL-DRESS UNIFORM, UNDRESS

dress up *vt* [¹*dress* + *up*] **1 a :** to attire in best or formal clothes ⟨*dressed* the child *up* for the birthday party⟩ **b :** to attire in clothes suited to a particular role ⟨*dressed* him *up* for the part of Othello⟩ **2 :** to present or cause to appear in a certain light (as by distortion, exaggeration, or padding) **:** DISGUISE, CAMOUFLAGE ⟨some conservative newspapers have tried to *dress up* the delegation as treachery to democracy —*New Republic*⟩ ⟨accounting devices for *dressing up* the balance sheet —Albert Lepawsky⟩; *esp* **:** to embellish or enhance the interest of (an event or account) with supplementary usu. fanciful details ⟨a remarkable feat of bodily exertion, which . . . he should be able to *dress up* and magnify —George Eliot⟩

dress–up \'=ˌ=\ *n* [*dress up*] **:** a situation or time requiring the wearing of good clothes ⟨a *dress-up* occasion⟩

dressy \'dresē, -si\ *adj* -ER/-EST [²*dress* + *-y*] **1 a :** habitually wearing or fond of wearing elaborate or formal dress ⟨his wife's friends were too ~ to suit him⟩ **b :** requiring or characterized by fancy or formal dress ⟨a ~ affair⟩ **2 :** having more or less fancy or formal details: as **a :** suitable for social or festive occasions ⟨a ~ handbag⟩ ⟨a ~ blouse⟩ **b :** ELABORATE, ORNATE ⟨she appeared in an outfit that was much too ~ for the occasion⟩ ⟨a ~ office⟩

drew *past of* DRAW

drey *or* **dray** \'drā\ *n* -S [origin unknown] **:** a squirrel's nest

drey·fu·sard \ˌdrīfə'särd, ˌdrāf-, -f(y)ü'-, -ˈzä-\ *n* -S *usu cap* [F, fr. Alfred *Dreyfus* †1935 Fr. army officer + F *-ard*] **:** a defender or partisan of Captain Dreyfus

drg *abbr* drawing

dri·as \'drīəs\ *n* -ES [origin unknown] **:** DEADLY CARROT

¹drib \'drib\ *vb* **dribbed; dribbed; dribbing; dribs** [prob. alter. of *drip*] *vi* **:** DRIBBLE ⟨a jokester's *dribbing* glass with inconspicuous holes near the top⟩ ~ *vt* **1** *obs* **:** to utter bit by bit **2** *obs* **:** to shoot (an arrow) aside from the mark

²drib \"\ *n* -S [prob. back-formation fr. *dribble* & *driblet*] *chiefly dial* **1 :** a drop of liquid ⟨as the tide draws away, the ~*s* and dregs of water left behind —Thomas Wood⟩ **2 :** a small amount **:** FRAGMENT ⟨various lesser ~*s* for my side endeavors —I.S.Cobb⟩ ⟨the word-by-word reader brings the thought from the printed page in ~*s* —P.D.Leedy⟩

¹drib·ble \'dribəl\ *vb* **dribbled; dribbled; dribbling** \-b(ə)liŋ\ **dribbles** [freq. of ¹*drib*] *vi* **1 a :** to fall or flow in drops or in a quick succession of drops or in a thin intermittent stream **:** TRICKLE ⟨to prevent *dribbling* of fuel from an injection nozzle⟩ ⟨uncontrollable *dribbling* of urine⟩ **b :** to issue like a trickling liquid slowly and sporadically in a succession of tiny portions ⟨the *dribbling* sands of an hourglass⟩ ⟨allowing the seeds to ~ along the ground⟩ ⟨letting smoke ~ through his chiseled nostrils —John Galsworthy⟩ **2 :** to let saliva drip, trickle, or ooze from a corner of the mouth (as of a teething infant or an imbecile) **:** DROOL, DRIVEL ⟨picnickers *dribbling* in anticipation of the barbecue⟩ **3 :** to drift, sift, issue, or dwindle slowly, little by little, or one by one in a sluggish succession ⟨replies to the questionnaire are *dribbling* in⟩ ⟨words, like ideas, were *dribbling* back into her mind —Ellen Glasgow⟩ ⟨he saw the people *dribbling* out by twos and threes —Mary Austin⟩ ⟨the piano and the singing *dribbled* away —Berton Roueché⟩ **4 a :** to dribble a ball or puck **b :** to proceed by dribbling ⟨the guard *dribbled* down the sideline⟩ ~ *vt* **1 :** to let or cause to fall in drops or slowly little by little ⟨the chief *dribbled* wine on the ground⟩ ⟨~ in the cereal and boil⟩ ⟨the young couple ~ rice from their clothes⟩ **2 a :** to dispense or disperse sporadically and in small bits ⟨*dribbled* out funds in small grants-in-aid to individual scientists —J.P.Baxter⟩ ⟨a very famous informer *dribbled* out his revelations over a period of ten years —John Steinbeck⟩ **b :** FRITTER — used with *away* ⟨why had they *dribbled* away (yes, and sold out) their gifts for such trifling gains —Samuel Yellen⟩ ⟨as they ~ away their days in futility, hoping vainly for a miracle —*Time*⟩ **c :** to daub or press (paint) straight from the tube onto canvas ⟨~ his paint instead of using brushes —R.M.Coates⟩ **3 :** to propel and maintain control of (a ball or puck) by successive slight taps or bounces with hand, foot, or stick

²dribble \"\ *n* -S **1 a** *archaic* **:** a small quantity of a liquid ⟨burghers husbanded their ~*s* of brandy —Sir Walter Scott⟩ **b :** liquid dripping in a small stream (as from the mouth or a leak) ⟨a brown ~ at the corner of his mouth⟩ **2 a :** a descent of liquid in drops or a thin stream: (1) **:** a drizzling shower (2) **:** a falling or leaking in drops ⟨need we call a plumber for these few ~*s*⟩ **b :** an inconsiderable and fitful flow **:** TRICKLE ⟨on the roads a monotonous ~ of gray army lorries, jeeps, motorcycles —Earle Birney⟩ ⟨the export of private capital is a ~, not a flow —R.R.Nathan⟩ **3 a :** a tiny or insignificant bit of something that appears sporadically ⟨they come in ~*s* from Shanghai —Han Suyin⟩ ⟨news material issued in ~*s*⟩ **b :** a trifling or insignificant sum of money ⟨until I can begin to send you a ~ now and then —Booth Tarkington⟩ **4 :** an act or instance of dribbling a ball or puck **5 :** dregs of molten glass remaining in the melting pot after pouring

drib·bler \-b(ə)lə(r)\ *n* -S **1 :** one that dribbles ⟨damned ~ . . . you need a bib —C.S.Barry⟩ ⟨a violation for a ~ to step on or outside a boundary line⟩ **2 :** a worker who removes dribble after molten glass has been poured

dribblet *obs var of* DRIBLET

drib·let \'driblə̇t\ *n* -S [¹*drib* + *-let*] **1 :** a trifling sum ⟨do not like having money doled out to me in ~*s* —D.G.Gerahty⟩ **2 :** one of a succession of small or insignificant quantities, amounts, portions, or bits ⟨~*s* of information that drifted in⟩ ⟨withdrew his army in ~*s*⟩ **3 :** a falling drop **:** DRIBBLE 1b ⟨~*s* came through the bedroom ceiling⟩

driblet cone *n* **:** a miniature lava cone formed by the accretion of drops of lava projected from gas vents or blowholes and falling on one spot

dribs and drabs *n pl* **:** miserably small or paltry amounts, portions, or fragments usu. scattered over a period of time ⟨taxes collected in *dribs and drabs*⟩ ⟨set to *dribs and drabs* of Meyerbeer's music —Douglas Watt⟩

drid·der \'dridər\ *var of* DREDDOUR

drid·dle \'drid°l\ *vi* -ED/-ING/-S [origin unknown] **1** *chiefly Scot* **:** to proceed in an unsteady or feeble manner **2** *chiefly Scot* **:** to lag behind **:** DAWDLE

drie *obs var of* ¹DREE

driech *var of* DREICH

dried *past of* DRY

dried alum *n* **:** BURNT ALUM

dried beef *n* **:** beef preserved by being pickled in brine, dried, and smoked

dried-fruit beetle *n* **:** a very small broad brown beetle (*Carpophilus hemipterus*) with pale-spotted elytra which do not cover the abdomen that is a cosmopolitan pest on stored products and is esp. destructive to dried fruit and cereals

dried milk *n* **:** milk dehydrated to about 5 percent of moisture by evaporation — called also *milk powder, powdered milk;* compare EVAPORATED MILK

dried-up \'≡,≡\ *adj* [fr. past part. of *dry up*] **:** WIZENED

driegh *var of* DREICH

¹**dri·er** *also* **dry·er** \'drī(ə)r, -īə\ *comparative of* DRY

²**drier** *also* **dryer** \"\ *n* -S [*dry*, v. + *-er*, n. suffix] **1 a :** something that extracts or absorbs moisture **b** *or* **dri·er·man** \-mən\ **:** a worker who attends to the drying of a material or a product in process of manufacture **c :** a piece of blotting paper used in drying herbarium specimens **2 :** a liquid or solid substance (as a metallic soap) that accelerates the drying of drying oils and of paints, varnishes, and printing inks containing such oils **3** *usu dryer* **:** a device for drying esp. by heat, forced ventilation, centrifugal action, or a vacuum or freezing process: as **a :** a furnace or revolving kiln for drying raw material (as ore, stone, sand) **b :** a rack on which laundry is hung to dry or a machine in which laundry is dried by a current of heated air **c :** a blower for drying hair **d :** any of the heated drums on which paper is dried on a paper-making machine

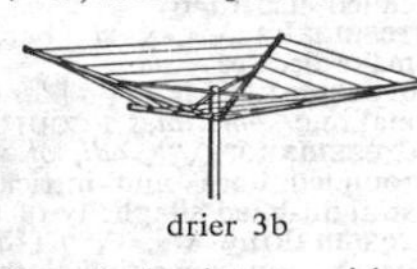

drier 3b

drier-down \'≡,≡\ *n* -S **:** TAKER-DOWN

dries *pres 3d sing of* DRY, *pl of* DRY

driest *also* **dryest** *superlative of* DRY

¹**drift** \'drift\ *n* -S *often attrib* [ME; akin to MD *drift* herd, ford, MHG *trift* driving, pasturage, ON *drift* snowdrift; derivative fr. the root of OE *drīfan* to drive — more at DRIVE] **1 :** the act of driving something along: as **a :** the driving together of the cattle in a forest to determine ownership — used in British forest law **b :** the horizontal thrust of an arch **c :** continued movement of a machine due to inertia after the shutoff of power **d :** a skid of a motor vehicle **:** SIDESLIP **e :** the flow or the velocity of the current of a river or ocean stream **2 :** something driven, propelled, or urged along or drawn together in a clump by or as if by a natural agency: as **a :** wind-driven snow, rain, cloud, dust, or smoke usu. at or near the ground surface ⟨watched the ~*s* of rain moving up the valley —E.L.Thomas⟩ **b** (1) **:** a mass of matter driven or forced onward together in a body or deposited together by or as if by wind or water ⟨scudding over ~*s* on skis⟩ ⟨harbor ~ collects in streaks⟩ (2) **:** a helter-skelter accumulation of something appearing as if windblown ⟨a ~ of newspapers around his feet⟩ (3) **:** something filmy or fleecy fluttering or undulating lightly in masses or folds as if afloat in a breeze or on water ⟨as the beach plums dapple our dunes and fields with snowy ~*s* —*Christian Science Monitor*⟩ ⟨putting away the ~*s* of muslin and curd-soft silk —Edith Sitwell⟩ **c** *dial* **:** DROVE, FLOCK ⟨a ~ of coyotes cried at moonrise⟩ ⟨a ~ of hogs⟩ ⟨a steady ~ of terns could be seen on a northeasterly course —Llewellyn Howland⟩; *also, West* **:** a casual assemblage or swarm of persons ⟨some of the newly arrived ~ were smooth-spoken gentry —Julian Dana⟩ **d :** a volley of arrows esp. when aimed high in air **e :** something (as driftwood or seaweed) that has been washed ashore by waves and tide and left stranded ⟨hauled himself out on a dry bit of ~ —Frederick Way⟩ ⟨strolling the sands . . . searching for ~ that he might turn to a profit —Morris Markey⟩ **f :** a set of fishnets; *also* **:** DRIFT NET **g** (1) **:** rock debris moved by natural agents from one place and deposited in another (2) **:** a deposit of clay, sand, gravel, and boulders transported by a glacier and deposited unstratified or more or less stratified by running water emanating from the glacier — compare ⁹TILL 2 **h :** something wafted by gentle air currents to be caught by the senses ⟨a ~ of woodsmoke curled up —Ellen Glasgow⟩ ⟨it submerged entirely the ~ of far-off band music —J.G.Cozzens⟩ ⟨a faint ~ of the clean, light scent that she had always used —Robert Murphy⟩ **3 :** observable course or direction taken toward an effect: as **a :** a general underlying and inferable design and intent (as of thought, policy, or program) ⟨we see the ~ of his thought in the manuscripts —R.I.Aaron⟩ ⟨the whole ~ of his social philosophy —W.L.Miller⟩ ⟨in agreement with the temper and main ~ of his naturalism —J.E.Smith⟩ **b :** tendency discernible in the past and present course ⟨until the time the upward ~ in the propensity to spend should level off⟩ ⟨in this survey of the ~ of 20th century poetry —Herbert Read⟩; *often* **:** development, progress, or evolution whose general course is assumed to be impersonally determined and continuous into the future ⟨while reasoning on this matter is somewhat a priori, the ~ of history and archaeology confirms it —A.L.Kroeber⟩ ⟨to combat disease, pestilence, prolong the span of life — all these mean a fight against the ~ of Nature —Mildred Gilman⟩ **c :** prevalent leaning or dominant inclination in the current thought and opinion **:** SLANT ⟨the ~ being on the whole away from the home toward the church —W.L.Sperry⟩ **d :** the meaning, import, or purport to be gathered from what is spoken or written ⟨made out the ~ of a conversation going on round me —A.W.Long⟩ ⟨maybe they understand you better in the town you come from, but I don't get your ~ —Maxwell Anderson⟩ **e :** trend (as of a rate) esp. when fluctuating ⟨the upward ~ of respiration in a germinating seed⟩ **4 :** something driven down upon or forced into a body: as **a :** a tool used for ramming down or driving something (as a metal wedge used in tightening hoops on a barrel) **b** *obs* **:** piles sunk in an interlocking row **c :** the difference between the size of a bolt and the hole into which it is driven or between the circumference of a hoop and that of a mast on which it is to be driven **d :** a place in an old-fashioned deep-waisted ship where the sheer was raised and the rail was cut off and usu. terminated by a scroll **e** *or* **driftpin** \'≡,≡\ **:** a broach or reamer of square section and with one or more cutting faces for cleaning out holes too small to be drilled and slotted — called also *cutting drift, square drift* **f :** a tool used in charging the case of a firework (as a rocket) **g** *or* **driftpin :** a smooth tapered pin resembling a punch for stretching rivet holes and bringing them into alignment — called also *smooth-taper drift* **h :** a punch with the point inclined to the shank for knocking out keys — called also *key drift* **5 :** the motion or action of drifting spatially usu. under external influence ⟨distal ~ of all lower teeth to the right of the lower central incisor —H.M.Lang⟩: as **a :** the deviation of a ship from its set course caused by currents; *also* **:** a voyage of a ship allowed to drift ⟨the icebreaker carried out its three regular annual ~*s*⟩ **b :** the length of a seaman's rope from a point where it is made fast whether stretching to another point of fastening, remaining loose or coiled as an extra length, or running from the fixed block to the movable block of a tackle **c :** one of the slower movements of oceanic circulation **:** a general tendency of surface water subject to diversion or reversal by the wind ⟨the easterly ~ of the North Pacific⟩ — see CURRENT table **d :** a deviation of a missile out of a rifled gun from the vertical plane of fire due to rotation and the resistance of the air **e :** the lateral motion of an airplane due to air currents; *also* **:** DRIFT ANGLE **f :** tendency to alter and esp. to decrease in weight during shipment; *also* **:** the amount by which the weight is altered **g :** CREEP 8b **h :** the distance cargo in the hold of a ship has to be dragged to a hatch **i :** an easy moderate more or less steady flow, sweep, or shifting along a spatial course ⟨aerial ~ of pollen⟩ ⟨the general ~ of population from country to city —H.C.Laxson⟩ ⟨the industrial ~ southward⟩ ⟨any ~ of our solar system in our galaxy —N.E.Nelson⟩ **j :** a slow onward, upward, or downward course (as an advance, transition, or withdrawal) proceeding usu. by inconspicuous steps **:** a gradual shift in attitude, opinion, or position not pronounced in process but unmistakable in direction ⟨a ~ to war⟩ ⟨the ~ toward centralization of power⟩ ⟨the gradual ~ of wealth from farm to industry —S.A.Spiller⟩ ⟨this steady ~ away from the conception of a divine Will that dwarfed the human will —V.L. Parrington⟩ ⟨signs he sees of a dangerous ~ in American life away from standards of excellence in politics —William Barrett⟩ **k :** an aimless directionless course; *often* **:** a foregoing of any attempt at direction or control letting events and developments take their own course **:** abdication of control to a blind flow of circumstances ⟨vigorous local action, moreover, can reverse the policy of ~ which has seen local government denuded of function after function, largely by default —R.V.Presthus⟩ ⟨to continue the policy of ~, of blind stumbling from crisis to crisis —*Time*⟩ **l :** a deviation or veering off from a true reproduction, representation, or reading ⟨frequency ~ is merely the inability of the set to remain exactly tuned to the frequency for which you have adjusted it —*Pilots' Radio Handbook*⟩ **6 :** a passage driven or for driving in a particular direction: as **a :** a nearly horizontal mine passageway driven on or parallel to the course of a vein or rock stratum — compare LEVEL 8 **b :** a small crosscut in a mine connecting two larger tunnels; *also* **:** an exploratory mine tunnel **c** [Afrik, fr. D, fr. MD] *Africa* **:** a ford in a river **7 :** a slow gradual change in character, aspect, or some attendant phenomenon: as **a :** an assumed trend toward a general change in the structure of a language over a period of time underlying or revealed by various specific changes ⟨the ~ toward loss of final syllables in the Germanic languages⟩ **b :** change in genotypes of small populations due to random loss or multiplication of certain gene groups **c :** a gradual change in the zero reading of an instrument or more generally in any quantitative characteristic of a given piece of equipment that is supposed to remain constant **d :** a gradual change in some aspect of culture deriving from an accumulated variation in behavior or belief and resulting in a new pattern or institutional form ⟨a cultural ~ away from spiritual values to materialistic ones⟩ **syn** see TENDENCY — **on the drift** *West* **:** roving about the country without or seeking employment ⟨restless unsettled youths *on the drift*⟩

drift 4g: driftpin for stretching rivet holes

²**drift** \"\ *vb* -ED/-ING/-S *vi* **1 a :** to become driven or carried along by a current of water, wind, or air ⟨can ~ in a canoe the 30 miles from the falls —*Amer. Guide Series: Minn.*⟩ ⟨with the tide at the ebb he was ~*ing* in those dark depths out through the Golden Gate —P.B.Kyne⟩ ⟨a wisp of smoke ~*ing* from the chimney⟩ ⟨rain fell at intervals from ~*ing* shreds of clouds —O.E.Rölvaag⟩ ⟨an evasive and delicate fragrance ~*ed* from her person —Agnes S. Turnbull⟩; *also* **:** to move gently and silently without propulsion often floating or gliding along through the air with slight quivering motions ⟨a solitary leaf ~*s* down⟩ **b :** to wander or stray lightly, gently, effortlessly offering no resistance as if suspended and floating in the air and usu. seeming to leave the choice of direction to the drift of the air ⟨let my eyes ~ around the room —R.Y.Thurman⟩ ⟨a very faint smile ~*ed* across his face —Raymond Chandler⟩ ⟨it is only by ~*ing* with the wind that I have found myself —John Reed⟩; *also* **:** to float through the air in mild and soothing or vibrant waves of sound ⟨the corporal's voice sounded deceptively kind ~*ing* in from away across the North Parade Ground —Earle Birney⟩ ⟨street noises that ~ through closed windows and doors⟩ **c :** to move smoothly and unhurriedly with little or no apparent effort or unobtrusively a few at a time in a manner suggestive of floating on water — usu. followed by a directional word ⟨strikers began to ~ back to work⟩ ⟨the orchestra stopped playing and dancers ~*ed* off the floor⟩ ⟨he'd ~ with the play and make the quarterback commit himself, then make the tackle either way —H.R.Sanders⟩; *also* **:** to migrate in a slow stream ⟨other roving soldiers . . . ~*ed* out to Colorado, Wyoming, Montana —Dixon Wecter⟩ **d :** to pass without contributory effort or serious resistance or become borne slowly by imperceptible degrees toward or away from an association or into or out of some state ⟨he ran with a gang and ~*ed* into petty crime —S.L.A.Marshall⟩ ⟨those dreamy spells of hers, the way she used to go ~*ing* off into space —Hamilton Basso⟩ ⟨the chances are that Asia will gradually ~ toward Communism —K.S.Latourette⟩ ⟨written and spoken languages tend to ~ ever further apart —Frank Denman⟩ **e :** to retain momentum for a time after shutoff of power **2 a :** to wander without hurry and without clear purpose or goal esp. moving along the line of least resistance ⟨he ~*ed* around for eight years without a trace of his whereabouts —Liam O'Flaherty⟩ ⟨loved best to ~, elusive as a skeleton leaf, along the streets of Rome —Elinor Wylie⟩ **b** *West, of cattle* **:** to bunch up and wander from the home range in a storm **c :** to travel about in a random way as an itinerant workman or in search of work **d :** to become carried along subject to no guidance or control ⟨whether this conversation was ~*ing* or aimed, certain that it was out of his hands —Edmund Fuller⟩; *often* **:** to relinquish planning, decision, initiative, and conscious direction leaving control to chance or circumstances ⟨allowing students to ~ through four years without developing sufficient incentive or goal —*Bull. of Bates Coll.*⟩ **3 a :** to accumulate in a mass or be piled up in heaps by action of wind or water ⟨~*ing* snow banked in the side of the house up to the windowsills⟩ ⟨miles of fence had already been buried under ~*ed* dust —K.S.Davis⟩ ⟨an old hulk far out on the beach fast filling with ~*ing* sand at every high tide⟩ **b :** to become covered with a drift ⟨the streets ~*ed* level with the marquees of the buildings —William Fifield⟩ **4** *mining* **:** to make a drift **:** DRIVE **5 :** to fish with drift nets **6 a :** to vary or deviate from a set course or adjustment ⟨some television sets ~ during warmup and require retuning⟩ **b :** to vary sluggishly usu. without establishing a definite trend — used esp. of prices or income ⟨its freight revenues ~*ed* down more than 14 percent last year —R.E.Bedingfield⟩ ⟨the market has been ~*ing* the last few days, probably because of the approaching holidays⟩ ⟨grain futures ~*ed* in a narrow range⟩ **c :** SKID **7** *of a language* **:** to develop in the direction characteristic of its drift ~ *vt* **1 a :** to cause to be driven in a current ⟨the tide turning began ~*ing* back the ship helplessly seaward —Herman Melville⟩ ⟨a smudge ~*ing* smoke across their beds to keep insects away —B.A.Williams⟩ **b** *West* **:** to drive (livestock) slowly esp. to allow grazing ⟨leaving orders for the outfit to ~ the herd into it and water —Andy Adams⟩ **2 a :** to drive by the force of the wind and deposit in heaps ⟨heavy clay when granulated is readily ~*ed* —A.F.Gustafson⟩ **b :** to cover with drifts ⟨southwestern slopes were deeply ~*ed*⟩ **3 :** to use a drift in or upon (as for enlarging holes, forcing holes into alignment, driving out pins and keys) **4 :** to cant (as a pole) over at the top

drift·age \'driftij, -tēj\ *n* -S [²*drift* + *-age*] **1 :** a drifting of some object esp. through action of wind or water **2 :** deviation from a set course (as from a ship's course due to leeway or currents) **3 :** something that is drifting or has drifted ⟨I sell them stuff: bait and lobsters, and sometimes an interesting bit of ~ —Erle Stanley Gardner⟩

drift alarm *n* **:** a device that indicates when the anchor of a ship is dragging

drift anchor *n* **:** SEA ANCHOR

drift angle *n* [prob. trans. of F *angle de dérive*] **1 :** the angle between the axis of a ship when turning and the tangent to the path on which it is turning **2 :** the horizontal angle between the longitudinal axis of an airplane and its path relative to the ground **:** the angle between the heading and the track — called also *leeway*

drift avalanche *n* **:** an avalanche composed of dry powdery snow initially set in motion by wind

drift boat *n* **:** DRIFTER 2b

driftbolt \'≡,≡\ *n* **1 :** a bolt for driving out other bolts or pins **2 :** a metal rod for securing timbers resembling a spike but with or without point or head

drift bottle *n* **:** a bottle containing a record of the time and place at which it was set adrift in the ocean for supplying when recovered data to aid in determining the circulation of surface waters in the ocean — called also *floater*

drift copper *n* **:** fragments of native copper carried from their source by glaciers

drift current *n* **:** a slowly moving current in a lake or ocean

drift dam *n* **:** a deposit of glacial drift that dams or has dammed a stream

drift·er \-tə(r)\ *n* -S **1 a :** a living being that travels or moves about aimlessly ⟨there were about 40 in the family and usu. a dozen ~*s* —W.D.Wyman⟩ ⟨these ~*s* vary in size from the bacteria and the minute yellowish microscopic plants . . . to copepods —R.E.Coker⟩ **b :** a worker who moves from job to job without remaining long at any one place of employment **c :** a person of passive spiritless character lacking aim, ambition, and initiative and given to roving from one diversion to another without any steady interest **:** TEMPORIZER **d :** a fierce and driving snowstorm (as in the far north) **2 a** *also* **drift·er·man** \-tə(r)mən\ *pl* **driftermen :** a person who fishes with a drift net — called also *drift netter* **b :** a boat equipped for and employed in drift-net fishing — called also *drift boat* **3 a :** an excavator of mine drifts **b :** a rock drill used for driving mine drifts and crosscuts **c :** an operator of a heavy drill for drilling through rock in tunnel construction, mining, or quarrying

drift fence *n, West* **:** a stretch of fence strung by ranchers across the open range for preventing grazing cattle from drifting from their home range

drift float *n* **:** a float dropped from an aircraft flying over water as a marker for determining the drift angle or the direction of surface wind

drift ice *n* **:** sea or lake ice broken apart by winds and currents **:** fragments of a floe

driftier *comparative of* DRIFTY

driftiest *superlative of* DRIFTY

drift indicator *or* **drift meter** *or* **drift sight** *n* **:** a flight instrument used for measuring the angle of drift of an aircraft and equipped with a hairline or sight wire that may be rotated until objects on the ground appear to travel parallel with it so that from the position of the wire the drift angle may then be read directly from a calibration chart

¹**drifting** *adj* [fr. pres. part. of ²*drift*] **1 :** disposed to drift or move aimlessly **:** PUSILLANIMOUS, AMBITIONLESS ⟨seemed gentle, affectionate, ~ —W.B.Yeats⟩ ⟨we see weak, neurotic, helpless, ~, unhappy people —J.C.Powys⟩ **2 :** constantly shifting or floating about ⟨a ~ double-dealer has appeared . . . and chiseled himself in as top man —Hoffman Birney⟩

²**drifting** *n* -S [fr. gerund of ²*drift*] **:** the act or motion of one that drifts; *specif* **:** the act of driving a mine drift

drift·ing·ly *adv* [¹*drifting* + *-ly*] **:** in an unguided or random manner

drift·land \'drift,land\ *n* [¹*drift* + *land*] **:** DROFLAND

drift lead \-,led\ *n* **:** a heavy lead put overboard when a ship is at anchor with a line attached and left slack so that its tautening will indicate any drift or dragging

drift·less \'driftlə̇s\ *adj* [¹*drift* + *-less*] **1 :** having no aim or direction **:** being without purpose ⟨to the rookie, military directives seem ~⟩ **2 :** free from glacial drift ⟨a section ~ except for loess deposits⟩

driftless area *n* **:** an area (as in Wisconsin and parts of Minnesota, Illinois, and Iowa) that is free from glacial drift and seems not to have been covered by the Pleistocene ice

drift·less·ness *n* -ES **:** the quality or state of being driftless ⟨the ~ of the play's characters⟩

drift·man \'driftmən\ *n, pl* **driftmen** [¹*drift* + *man*] **:** a worker who drives drifts in a coal mine

drift mine *n* [¹*drift* + *mine*] **:** a placer or gravel deposit worked by underground-mining methods

drift mining *n* **:** mining gold-bearing gravel deposits by shafts and drifts instead of by hydraulic methods

drift net *n* **:** a large net that is arranged to drift with the tide or current and that is either buoyed up by floats or attached to a drift boat

drift netter *n* [*drift net* + *-er*] **:** DRIFTER 2a

drift period *n, often cap D* **:** GLACIAL EPOCH

driftpiece \'≡,≡\ *n* **1 :** an upright or curved piece of timber connecting the plank sheer with the gunwale of a ship **2 :** a scroll terminating a rail at the drift — compare DRIFT 4d

driftpin *n* **:** ¹DRIFT 4e, 4g

drift plain *n* **:** a plain underlain with glacial drift

drift plug *n* [¹*drift* + *plug*] **:** a hardwood plug that is conical or has rounded ends to be driven into or through a lead pipe to flare it or to straighten a buckle

drift punch *n* **:** a blunt-ended punch of long taper used to align holes (as for bolts, pins, rivets)

drift sail *n* **:** DRAG SAIL

drift sheet *n* **:** a widespread deposit of glacial drift

drift slide *n* **:** a device on the rear sight of a gun to permit making compensation for the drift of the projectile

driftway \'≡,≡\ *n* [¹*drift* + *way;* so called fr. its use as a passage for herds or flocks] *dial* **:** a sometimes private lane or narrow country road **:** DRIVEWAY 1

driftweed \'≡,≡\ *n* **1 :** seaweed or other aquatic vegetation drifted ashore **2 :** any of various seaweeds (as members of the genus *Laminaria*) that tend to break free and drift ashore

driftwind \'≡,≡\ *n* **:** wind that drifts snow, sand, or other material

driftwood \'≡,≡\ *n* **1 :** wood drifted or floated by water **2 :** useless or worthless scraps cast off by a social or cultural activity ⟨that 12th century temperament which loved to gather ~ from the wreckage of the ancient world of thought —H.O. Taylor⟩; *specif* **:** social parasites or human idlers drifting along with the current of civilized life **:** FLOTSAM 2, WRECKAGE 3 ⟨the unemployed were the political ~ of the revolution —*Political Science Quarterly*⟩

drifty \'driftē, -ti\ *adj* -ER/-EST [¹*drift* + *-y*] **1 :** full of drifts **:** tending to form drifts **2** [²*drift* + *-y*] **:** giving the effect of drifting or floating ⟨dress collection . . . has a ~ quality which immediately evokes resort backgrounds —*Women's Wear Daily*⟩

driki *var of* DRY-KI

¹**drill** \'dril\ *vt* -ED/-ING/-S [ME *drillen* to delay] **1** *now dial Brit* **a :** to waste (time) idly **:** DAWDLE **b :** to let (something) continue — used with *out* or *on* **2** *now dial Brit* **:** LURE, DRAW ⟨easily ~*ed* on to vote yea⟩ ⟨they soon ~*ed* him into the plot⟩

²**drill** \"\ *vi* -ED/-ING/-S [perh. alter. of *trill* — more at TRILL (to trickle)] *obs* **:** TRICKLE, DRIP

³**drill** \'dril\ *n* -S *archaic* **:** a small trickling stream **:** RILL

⁴**drill** \"\ *vb* -ED/-ING/-S [D *drillen*, fr. MD; akin to MHG *drillen* to turn, round off, OHG *drāen* to turn — more at THROW] *vt* **1 a :** to make (a rounded hole or cavity in a solid) by removing bits with a rotating drill — compare BORE 1 **b :** to make or excavate a hole in (a solid material) with a drill ⟨they ~*ed* boulders for inserting dynamite sticks⟩ ⟨bones ~*ed* for insertion of a pin⟩ ⟨~*ing* a tooth for a filling⟩ **c :** to drive a hole in, puncture, or perforate as if with a drill **:** pierce, penetrate, or drive deep into the interior of ⟨the lightning ~*ing* the hills to the east and upriver —Frederick Way⟩ **d :** to open or sink (a well) in the earth by striking a spot repeatedly with a sharp pointed instrument or by using a rotary drill **e :** to shoot through the head or body ⟨would haul out a gun and indiscriminatingly ~ them both —Marjorie Brace⟩; *also* **:** to penetrate or puncture like a bullet ⟨we are ~*ed* by about 100 cosmic rays every minute of our lives —Stuart Chase⟩ **2** *archaic* **:** to whirl or twirl like a drill ⟨~ a stick into a pit containing tinder to kindle fire⟩ **3 a :** to instruct thoroughly in the rudiments and methods of any skill or branch of knowledge **:** DISCIPLINE **b :** to impart or communicate (ideas) in this way ⟨~ knowledge or sense into a pupil⟩ ⟨trade secrets ~*ed* into a man's subconscious⟩ **c :** to train or exercise (as a soldier) in military evolutions and in servicing and using weapons and other equipment **4 :** to remove (a railroad car) from among others on the same track by switching ⟨the diner to be added to number 41 had already been ~*ed*⟩ ~ *vi* **1 a :** to pierce or sink a hole with a drill ⟨reaming, ~*ing*, and honing are also considered boring operations —H.D. Burghardt & Aaron Axelrod⟩ ⟨intending to ~ for oil⟩ ⟨painless dental ~*ing*⟩ **b :** to penetrate in a straight line as if driven with a drill ⟨he sensed that the eyes of the men were ~*ing* into the back of his neck —Fred Majdalany⟩ ⟨the violent daylight ~*ing* into the room —Brendan Gill⟩ **2 :** to practice an exercise **:** engage in a drill **3 :** to give forth a series of metallic percussive sounds or tones ⟨the sharp ~*ing* of the telephone had sounded from the hall —F.M.Ford⟩ **4** *of a motor vehicle* **:** SKID, SIDESLIP **syn** see PERFORATE, PRACTICE

5drill \"\ *n* -s [in sense 1, prob. fr. D *dril*, fr. MD, fr. *drillen* to drill; in other senses, fr. *4drill*] **1 a :** an instrument with an edged or pointed end used for making holes in hard substances; *specif* **:** a tool that cuts with its end by revolving (as in drilling metals) or by a succession of blows (as in drilling stone) — see CROSS BIT, TWIST DRILL; compare AUGER, 1BIT 3a **b :** a drill with the appliance or machine for operating it or the appliance or machine alone (as a drill press or a portable drill) **2 :** the act or exercise of training soldiers in the execution of evolutions and the using and servicing of weapons and other equipment; *specif* **:** a kind or method of military exercise ⟨infantry *drill*⟩ **3 a :** repetitive instruction and strictly supervised exercise in methods (as of business, sport, education) ⟨we build up habits by ~, but we build up intelligent capacities by training —Gilbert Ryle⟩ **b :** a physical or mental exercise aimed at perfecting facility and skill in a particular operation esp. by regular practice ⟨the methods were largely lecture and ~*s* for memory, with daily and monthly reviews —H.R.Douglass⟩ **c :** a formal exercise by a team of marchers consisting of strictly timed figures and evolutions as part of a ritual or as an exhibition of skill ⟨the competition will continue until each drum corps has completed its ~⟩ **d** *chiefly Brit* **:** the approved or correct procedure for accomplishing something efficiently ⟨two people who knew the ~ perfectly and could easily mount an expedition in the given time —L.J.Van Der Post⟩ **4 a :** a marine snail (*Urosalpinx cinerea*) that is very destructive to oysters on the Atlantic coast of the U.S. by boring through their shells and feeding on the soft parts **b :** any of several other mollusks of the family Muricidae (as *Thais floridana*) **5 :** sharp closely repeated taps or insistent moderately percussive tones ⟨tried to shut his ears against the sharp ~ of his voice —Hamilton Basso⟩ ⟨the prolonged ~ of cicadas⟩ ⟨counted the separate, muffled ~*s* on the wire —Kay Boyle⟩

1 2 3 4 5

drills 1a: *1* flat, *2* straight-flute, *3* single-twist, *4* two-groove, *5* star

6drill \"\ *n* -s [prob. native name in West Africa] **:** a West African baboon (*Mandrillus leucophaeus*) closely related to the typical mandrills but smaller and lacking the bright facial coloring of the latter

7drill \"\ *n* -s [perh. fr. *3drill*] **1 a :** a shallow furrow or trench into which seed is sown **b :** a row of seed sown in such a furrow **2 :** a planting implement that makes holes or furrows, drops in the seed and sometimes fertilizer, and covers them with earth ⟨tractor-drawn ~*s* used to sow wheat⟩ ⟨a ~ adjusted to four rows at one time of forest-tree seeds⟩ — see HOE DRILL, PLOW DRILL, PRESS DRILL

8drill \"\ *vt* -ED/-ING/-S **1 :** to sow (seeds) by dropping along a shallow furrow ⟨he ~*s* soybeans in the same rows with corn to be cut together for silage⟩ **2 a :** to sow with seed or set with seedlings inserted in drills ⟨we've ~*ed* a whole hill with slash pine —Kathleen L. Sutton⟩ **b :** to distribute seed or fertilizer in by means of a drill ⟨compare the yields of a ~*ed* acre and a broadcast acre⟩

9drill \"\ *n* -s [back-formation fr. *drilling* — more at DRILLING (fabric)] **:** a strong durable cotton fabric in twill weave made in various weights for clothing, interior decoration, and industrial uses

drill·able \-ləbəl\ *adj* **:** capable of or fit for being drilled ⟨an alloy not readily ~⟩ ⟨recruits scarcely ~⟩ ⟨mixed fertilizers granulated in order to make a more ~ product⟩

drill barrow *n* **:** a wheeled machine for planting in drills

drill bit *n* **:** 5DRILL 1a

drill block *n* **:** a steel block containing one or more V-shaped grooves in which cylindrical pieces may be held while being drilled

drill bow *n* **:** a small bow used for turning a bow drill by giving the string a turn about the drill

drill chuck *n* **:** a chuck for holding a drill on a spindle usu. by means of adjustable jaws — see CHUCK illustration

drill corps *n* **:** DRILL TEAM

drill drift *n* **:** a wedge-shaped drift for knocking loose a drill or drill socket from a receiving member

drilled *past of* DRILL

drill·er \-lə(r)\ *n* -s **:** one that drills something, drills others, engages in drill, or is employed to carry out drilling operations

drill file *n* [*5drill*] **:** a small fine-toothed flat file having square or round edges and teeth on the edges only

drill hall *n* **:** a spacious hall suitable for drilling: as **a :** such a hall for drill by military or other drill teams (as in an armory) **b** *Brit* **:** a building containing such a hall

drill head *n* **:** DRILL CHUCK; *esp* **:** one that holds and drives two or more drills at once

drill in *vt* **:** to complete (an oil or gas well) by penetrating the producing formation

1drilling \'driliŋ, -lēŋ\ *n* -s [fr. gerund of *4drill*] **:** material removed by a drill in making a hole — usu. used in pl. ⟨brushed aside the ~*s* from about the hole⟩

2dril·ling \"\ *n* -s [by folk etymology fr. G *drillich*, fr. MHG *drilich* fabric woven with a threefold thread, fr. *drilich* threefold, fr. OHG *drilīh* made up of three threads, by folk etymology (influence of OHG *dri-* — akin to OHG *drī* three — & OHG *-līh* -ly) fr. L *trilic-, trilix*, fr. *tri-* + *-lic-, -lix* (fr. *licium* thread); perh. akin to L *liquis* oblique — more at OBLIQUE, THREE, -LY (adj. suffix)] **:** 9DRILL

3drill·ing \"\ *adj* [fr. pres. part. of *4drill*] **1 :** appearing to see far into **:** PIERCING ⟨sharp ~ eyes —Olive H. Prouty⟩ **2 :** deeply penetrative **:** BITING ⟨~ sarcasm about money —Marcia Davenport⟩

drilling cable *n* [*drilling* fr. gerund of *4drill*] **:** a cordage product made of three ropes twisted together with a left lay, having the surface treated with lubricant to resist abrasion, heat, and water, and used as the line to which drilling tools are attached in well drilling and quarry drilling

drilling fluid *or* **drilling mud** *n* **:** a preparation of water, clays, and chemicals circulated in oil-well drilling for lubricating and cooling the bit, flushing the rock cuttings to the surface, and plastering the side of the well to prevent cave-ins

drilling hammer *n* **:** a stonecutter's hammer having a flat square face at each end of the head for striking rock drills

drilling machine *n* **:** a machine for drilling, reaming, counterboring, and tapping holes; *esp* **:** a power machine for drilling holes in metal (as a drill press or radial drill)

drill-like \'dril,līk\ *adj* **:** like a drill in form or action ⟨pointed *drill-like* shells⟩ ⟨an evolution *drill-like* in its precision⟩

drill·man \-ilmən, -,man\ *n, pl* **drillmen :** one who operates a drill or drilling machine

drillmaster \'=,==\ *n* [trans. of G *drillmeister*] **:** one who teaches or coaches drill or by drilling: **a :** an instructor in military drill or of an exhibition drill corps or lodge team **b :** a police officer who instructs, drills, and trains members of the force in military tactics, marksmanship, and discipline **c :** an instructor or director who maintains severe discipline stressing method, formalities, minutiae ⟨the expert ~*s* whose only concern was to see that I mastered the contents of textbooks —H.N.Fairchild⟩ ⟨marshals notes before us like a ~, making them execute intricate formations with almost incredible precision and high style —Edward Cushing⟩

drill pin *n* **:** the pin in a lock which enters the key stem

drill pipe *or* **drill rod** *n* **:** a pipe or rod that drives a rotary drill bit (as in drilling wells)

drill plow *n* **:** a combination of plow and drill

drill press *n* **:** an upright drilling machine the drill of which is pressed to the work by a hand lever or by power

drills *pres 3d sing of* DRILL, *pl of* DRILL

drill sergeant *n* **:** a noncommissioned officer who instructs soldiers in military exercises and evolutions

drill steel *or* **drill rod** *n* **:** steel usu. with 0.85 percent or more carbon content used for rock drills, pins, and dowels

drill stem *n* **:** the string of drill pipe that transmits power from the surface down to the drill bit in well drilling

drill-stem test *n* **:** a test for determining productivity of an oil or gas well by means of sampling the flow while the drill stem is still in the bore

drillstock \'=,=\ *n* **:** a frame or head for holding a drill spindle or a drill

drill team *n* **:** an exhibition marching team for demonstrating precision in drill — called also *drill corps*

drill tower *n* **:** a structure resembling the side of a building used in fire-fighting drill, to practice ladder raising and jumping into life nets

dril·vis \'dril,fis\ *n* -ES [Afrik, fr. *dril* to shake, vibrate, drill (fr. D *drillen*) + *vis* fish; akin to OE *fisc* fish — more at DRILL, FISH] *Africa* **:** ELECTRIC RAY

drily *var of* DRYLY

dri·mys \'drīməs\ *n* [NL, fr. Gk, sharp, acrid; fr. the taste of the bark; akin to Latvian *drīsme* crack, split, Gk *derein* to skin — more at TEAR] **1** *cap* **:** a genus of chiefly Australian shrubs or trees (family Magnoliaceae) having evergreen aromatic foliage — see WINTER'S BARK **2** -ES **:** any plant of the genus *Drimys*

d ring *n, cap D* **:** a metal ring having the shape of a capital D through which straps or ropes are passed (as one to which the suspension ropes of a parachute are attached)

1drink \'driŋk\ *vb* **drank** \'draŋk, -aiŋk\ *or dial* **drunk** \'drəŋk\ *or substand* **drinked** \'driŋ(k)t\ **drunk** *or* **drank** *or substand* **drinked** *or archaic* **drunk·en** \'drəŋkən *sometimes* -k°ŋ\ **drinking; drinks** [ME *drinken*, fr. OE *drincan*; akin to OHG *trinkan* to drink, ON *drekka*, Goth *drinkan*] *vt* **1 a :** SWALLOW, IMBIBE ⟨~ liquid⟩ ⟨don't sip it . . . but ~ it like the divine draught it is —Margery Allingham⟩ ⟨other animals and birds stand by to ~ its blood —*Interpreter's Bible*⟩ ⟨not a drop left. Who *drank* it up⟩ ⟨hurry, child, ~ it down so that we can start⟩ ⟨ordered a Scotch and *drank* it off —Polly Adler⟩ **b :** to take in or suck up **:** ABSORB ⟨~ up moisture⟩ ⟨the hot surface of the porous rock *drank* water like a sponge⟩; *broadly* **:** to take in (something intangible) or cause to vanish in a way suggestive of a liquid being swallowed ⟨~*ing* the thin sharp air⟩ ⟨atmospheric pressure then pushes air in, and your lungs can ~ their fill —A.C.Fisher⟩ ⟨*drank* in eagerly the latest version of the news⟩ **c** *obs* **:** SMOKE ⟨~ tobacco⟩ **2 :** to salute and wish health and honor to (a person) or success to (some prospect or wish) or to give or join in (a toast) or give a toast to (another's health) by raising and then drinking from a vessel ⟨will you ~ our good luck⟩ **3 a :** to spend in or expend or waste on consumption of alcoholic beverages — often used with *away* ⟨they *drank* the hours away⟩ ⟨a son-in-law who'd hit her and take her pension off her and ~ it to the last penny —Ruth Park⟩ **b :** to bring to a specified state by taking drink ⟨don't ~ that fountain dry⟩ ⟨had *drunk* himself into the poorhouse or the grave —Ellen Glasgow⟩ ⟨how we love the unexpected turn, like ~*ing* the devil under the table —Coulton Waugh⟩ **4 :** to take into one's mind or consciousness pleasurably through one or more of the senses — usu. used with *in* ⟨I just wanted to ~ in all those monumental buildings, dynamic streets full of hurrying people —Dong Kingman⟩ ⟨while his ears *drank* in the wonderful story of the great mare —Gerald Beaumont⟩ ⟨young men passed his door, *drank* the enchantments of his conversation —Van Wyck Brooks⟩ ⟨as I walked along the river ~*ing* in its beauty my soul expanded —Alexander MacDonald⟩ **5** *archaic* **:** to accommodate with drink by way of refreshment **~** *vi* **1 a :** to take liquid into the mouth for swallowing ⟨we saw baby elephants ~*ing* from their mothers —Stuart Cloete⟩ **b :** to receive into one's mind or consciousness a portion of something refreshing or pleasurable ⟨a desire to seek this inspiration at its source and ~ from the living waters —V.L.Parrington⟩ ⟨Ben Franklin who *drank* deep from the stream in Europe and then democratized his knowledge —Roger Burlingame⟩ ⟨students can hardly be blamed for ~*ing* deep of the culture which surrounds them —L.R.Ward⟩ **2 :** to partake of alcoholic beverages esp. habitually ⟨he ~*s* but does not smoke⟩; *specif* **:** to indulge in alcoholic beverages with disagreeable effect ⟨to say that a man ~*s* means that he ~*s* too much —Joyce Cary⟩ ⟨began to ~ in childhood and was an alcoholic by the time he was 18 —*Times Lit. Supp.*⟩ ⟨obvious that he had been ~*ing* —Louis Auchincloss⟩ **3 :** to make or join in a toast ⟨~ to the prosperity of the newest state⟩ **4** *obs* **:** TASTE

2drink \"\ *n* -s [ME *drink, drinke*, fr. OE *drinc, drinca*, fr. *drincan*, v.] **1 a :** liquid suitable for swallowing by man or beast esp. to quench thirst or to provide nourishment or refreshment ⟨I was thirsty and you gave me ~ —Mt 25:35 (RSV)⟩ ⟨natives satisfied my demands for food and ~⟩ ⟨the only available ~ was the milk of coconuts⟩ ⟨for centuries before a very light beer was the common ~ —G.E.Fussell⟩ **b** *archaic* **:** liquid taken in or absorbed (as by a plant) **c :** a source of mental and emotional refreshment or stimulation ⟨it was meat and ~ to him to be the guardian of a secret —John Buchan⟩ **2 a :** any particular natural or prepared usu. agreeable liquid for swallowing **:** BEVERAGE, POTABLE, BREW, LIQUOR ⟨able to make a palatable ~ from seawater⟩ ⟨a fermented ~ made of water and honey⟩ ⟨my favorite among the carbonated soft ~*s* is ginger ale⟩ **b :** alcoholic liquor ⟨excessive indulgence in ~ and tobacco —A.A.Bogomolets⟩ ⟨a *drink*-sodden derelict⟩ ⟨we speak of ~ as if it were synonymous with alcoholic beverages and use such phrases as the ~ traffic —O.A.Mendelsohn⟩ **3 :** a draft or portion of liquid (as water or a prepared beverage) taken or to be taken by or served to an individual at one time ⟨taking a long ~ from the spring⟩ ⟨it requires a barium ~, fluoroscopic examination, and several radiographs — *X Rays & You*⟩ ⟨give the dog a ~ of water⟩ ⟨the plant needs a ~⟩ **4 a :** the consuming of or habit of consuming alcoholic beverages liberally or to excess ⟨that the old doctor is befuddled with ~ all the time —Ellen Glasgow⟩ ⟨~ will be his ruination⟩ ⟨he took to ~ when his business failed⟩ ⟨her didos will drive me to ~⟩ **b** *Brit* **:** a convivial get-together **:** DRUNK, SPREE **5 :** a sizable body of water or a broad stream ⟨slipped off the rock and into the ~⟩; *esp* **:** OCEAN ⟨my regiment embarked, leaving me on this side of the ~⟩ ⟨off West Palm Beach, Fla., an air force crash boat pulled a pilot from the ~ —*Time*⟩ ⟨burst into flames and went headlong into the ~ —J.S.Childers⟩ — **in drink :** DRUNK ⟨the poor monster's *in drink* —Shak.⟩

1drink·able \-kəbəl\ *adj* **:** suitable or safe for drinking **:** POTABLE ⟨a barely ~ substitute for coffee⟩ ⟨the sulfur gives the water an unpleasant flavor and odor but it is perfectly ~⟩ — **drink·ably** \-blē, -li\ *adv*

2drinkable \"\ *n* -s **:** a liquid suitable for drinking **:** POTABLE, BEVERAGE

drink·er \-kə(r)\ *n* -s [ME *drinkere*, fr. OE *drincere*, fr. *drincan* to drink + *-ere* -er] **1 a :** one that drinks ⟨all the ~*s* of the toast⟩ **b :** one that drinks alcoholic beverages ⟨a bar that stays open for the lone ~⟩ ⟨a problem ~⟩ **2** *or* **drinker moth** [so called fr. its long suctorial proboscis] **:** a large brownish European moth (*Cosmotriche potatoria*) with a larva that feeds on grasses **3 :** a vessel or device used to provide water for domestic animals or poultry

drink·ery \-kərē, -ri\ *n* -ES **:** BARROOM, SALOON

drink hail *n* [ME *drinkhayl*, fr. *drink* (imper. sing. of *drinken* to drink) — *hayl* healthy, being in good health, fr. ON *heill* healthy — more at WHOLE] *obs* **:** an early English bidding to drink to good health or good luck made in reply to a pledge of wassail

1drinking *n* -s [fr. gerund of *1drink*] **1 :** a drinking party **:** CAROUSAL **2** *dial Eng* **:** a light lunch eaten between meals

2drinking *adj* [fr. pres. part. of *1drink*] **1 :** addicted to or marked by immoderate consumption of alcoholic beverages ⟨traffic accidents caused by ~ drivers⟩ ⟨not a ~ woman⟩ **2 :** ABSORBENT, BIBULOUS — used of paper or other materials **3** [fr. *drinking*, gerund of *1drink*] **:** used or designed to be used in drinking ⟨a ~ room⟩; *esp* **:** used to contain an individual portion of beverage ⟨a ~ glass⟩

drinking fountain *n* **:** a fixture with nozzle delivering a stream or jet of water for drinking esp. one with an upward jet enabling one to drink directly without use of a cup — called also *bubbler*

drinking fountain

drinking song *n* **:** a song on a convivial theme composed usu. for singing in accompaniment to drinking

drink·less \'driŋkləs\ *adj* [ME *drinkelees*, fr. *drinke* drink + *-lees* -less] **:** being without or deprived of drink ⟨with liquor flowing freely he forced himself to go ~⟩

drink money *n, archaic* **:** a gratuity orig. for drink **:** POURBOIRE

drink offering *n* **:** a libation of wine, milk, or oil often in biblical times made with other sacrifices and required with every public offering

drink·om·e·ter \driŋ'kämǝd·ǝ(r), 'driŋkǝ,mē\ *n* [*2drink* + *-o-* + *-meter*] **:** an apparatus for recording fluid consumption (as of an experimental animal)

drinky \'driŋkē\ *adj, sometimes* -ER/-EST [*2drink* + *-y*] **:** partially inebriated **:** DRINKING

drinn \'drin\ *n* -s [Ar *darīn* dry herbage] **:** a coarse prickly weedy grass (*Aristida pungens*) of northern Africa; *broadly* **:** a stretch of country overgrown with this grass

1drip \'drip\ *vb* **dripped** *or* **dript; dripped** *or* **dript; dripping; drips** [ME *drippen*, fr. OE *dryppan*; akin to MD *druppen* to drip, trickle, OE *dropa* drop — more at DROP] *vt* **1 a :** to let fall in drops ⟨the rain fell in a steady drizzle, and the air was so damp that [her] hair *dripped* moisture —Laura Krey⟩ ⟨*dripping* paint direct from the tube onto their canvases —W.C. Smith⟩ ⟨each word she said *dripped* acid on the Italian woman's heart —Donn Byrne⟩ **b :** to spill or emit (something likened to a copiously dropping liquid) in an overflow or enveloping shower ⟨the honey locusts ~ their golden scent —Mary A. Taylor⟩ ⟨their crimes have increased in violence and often ~ horror —*Time*⟩ ⟨*dripping* invective from every sentence⟩ **2 :** to provide (a pipe) with a cock for draining condensate **3 :** to prepare (the beverage coffee) by letting boiling water seep slowly through finely ground coffee **~** *vi* **1 a :** to let fall drops of moisture or liquid ⟨trees *dripping* after the rain⟩ ⟨icicles *dripping* on the roof⟩ ⟨allowing the paint to ~ evenly upon the ground color —H.A.Helverston⟩ **b :** to become so saturated as to overflow in drops ⟨toast *dripping* with butter⟩ **c :** to exude or become enveloped in a shower of something likened to a dropping liquid ⟨tunic *dripping* with gold braid and lace —Marcia Davenport⟩ ⟨she beamed, she seemed fairly to ~ with the milk of human kindness —P.B.Kyne⟩ ⟨the latest ballads *dripping* with sentiment —Carl Wittke⟩ **d** *obs, of weather* **:** DRIZZLE, MIST **2 a :** to fall in drops ⟨water ~*s* from the eaves⟩ **b :** to hang or appear to hang suspended like a drop about to fall ⟨a brown, handmade cigarette forever *dripped* from his lower lip —Harold Sinclair⟩ **c :** to seem to drift down or to overflow slowly and gently like drops of a light rain ⟨the music ~*s* from saxophones —Maxwell Anderson⟩ ⟨pale moonlight, *dripping* through the leaves, spilled down in splashes —Hamilton Basso⟩ ⟨the most abject sentimentality ~*s* from every page —Pamela Taylor⟩

2drip \"\ *n* -s **1 a :** a falling in drops ⟨the woods by day and by night were full of nothing but solitude . . . and ~ —John Collier b. 1884⟩ ⟨an overflow of the wax called guttering but more commonly known as ~ —W.W.Klenke⟩; *also* **:** a letting something fall in drops or blobs ⟨a water clock — a ~ affair on the order of an hourglass —A.L.Kroeber⟩ ⟨the first application of the ~ technique to painting —*Time*⟩ **b :** liquid that falls, leaks, overflows, or is extruded in drops ⟨the jungle was exuding its fog ~ —Norman Mailer⟩ ⟨a pan for catching the ~ from wet umbrellas —J.E.Gloag⟩ ⟨the ~ of frozen foods exuded during thawing⟩ ⟨gripping the ~ gutters of a car⟩ ⟨postnasal ~ into the trachea⟩ ⟨gobs here, ~*s* there, the palette knife always more active than the brush —R.M.Coates⟩ **c :** an accumulation formed by descending or extruded drops: (1) *Brit* **:** DRIPPING 2b ⟨bread and ~⟩ (2) **:** a collection of drops (as of paint or varnish) at the bottom edge of an article that has been coated by dipping **d :** a manner of hanging suggestive of something dripping wet or having been dripping wet ⟨a tricolor or two hung in a dry ~ from an occasional balcony —Bruce Marshall⟩ ⟨the long ~ of her straight hair —Edith Sitwell⟩ **2 :** the sound made by or as if by falling drops ⟨a faint ~ of oars⟩ ⟨the stiff, tinny ~ of the banjos on the lawn —Scott Fitzgerald⟩ **3** *also* **drip pipe :** a small pipe or outlet for draining condensate (as from a main or a heating-system radiator) **4 :** a part of a cornice, sill course, window head, or other horizontal architectural member that projects beyond the rest and is of such section as to throw off the rainwater; *also* **:** an overlapping lead or strip of tin or copper serving the same purpose **5 :** a device for the slow continued administration of a fluid at a steady rate esp. into a vein of the body; *also* **:** any material so administered ⟨a glucose ~⟩ **6** *slang* **:** a trickle or weak stream of senseless fatuous talk or writing **:** sloppy sentiment **:** DRIVEL ⟨the daily ~ I have to listen to —Thorne Smith⟩ ⟨just the sort of ~ one has come to expect from the author⟩ **7** *slang* **:** someone looked on as tiresomely or annoyingly dull from lack of personality, animation, or social amenability; *also* **:** a rather simple or stupid person

drip cap *n* **:** a drip or head flashing installed over a window or door

drip coffee *n* **:** coffee made by letting boiling water drip slowly through finely ground coffee

drip culture *n* **:** a method of hydroponic plant culture in which a nutrient solution drips slowly onto sand or other inert medium in which the plants are growing — compare SLOP CULTURE

drip-drip \'=,=\ *n* [redupl. of *2drip*] **:** a continued dripping

1drip-dry \'=;=\ *vi* **:** to dry with few or no wrinkles when hung dripping wet ⟨nylon *drip-dries* in seconds, takes little ironing —*advt*⟩

2drip-dry \'=,=\ *adj* [*1drip-dry*] **:** made of a washable fabric that will drip-dry ⟨a *drip-dry* suit⟩

drip loop *n* **:** a downward loop (as in a wire entering a building to permit rainwater to drip off or in a pipe to collect water condensed in the pipe system)

drip mold *n* **:** a drip (as along an eaves) formed of wooden molding

drip oil *n* **:** a liquid by-product of the manufacture of illuminating gas that condenses from the gas stream and contains styrene, indene, and related compounds

drip·page \'dripij\ *n* -s **1 :** a dripping esp. of water from the eaves of a house **2 :** something accumulated by dripping ⟨had to clean the ~ from the sump pit⟩

drip pan *or* **dripping pan** *n* [*drip pan* fr. *2drip* + *pan; dripping pan* fr. ME *drepyngpanne*, fr. *drepyng* dripping + *panne* pan] **1** *usu drip pan* **:** a container for catching material that drips (as from above or from the burners of a gas range or a piece of oily machinery) **2** *usu dripping pan* **:** a usu. shallow rectangular metal pan used esp. for baking and roasting

drip·per \-ipə(r)\ *n* -s **:** one that drips **:** something from which a liquid is allowed to drip

1dripping *n* -s [ME *drippinge, drepyng*, fr. *drippen* to drip + *-inge, -ing* -ing] **1 :** the sound made by falling drops **2 a :** liquid waste that drips (as from machines) — often used in pl. **b :** fat and juices drawn from meat during cooking esp. when used as shortening or a spread — often used in pl.

2dripping *adv* [fr. pres. part. of *1drip*] **:** to a high degree **:** THOROUGHLY — usu. used in the phrase *dripping wet*

drip·ple \'dripəl\ *vi* **drippled; drippled; drippling** \-p(ə)liŋ\ **dripples** [prob. blend of *1drip* and *1dribble*] **1 :** to dribble briskly **2 :** to drip with wet

drip pot *n* **:** a pot for making drip coffee

drip primrose *n* **:** MISTASSINI

drip·py \'dripē\ *adj* -ER/-EST [*2drip* + *-y*] **1 :** characterized by drips **:** RAINY, DRIZZLY ⟨a ~ climate⟩ **2 :** nauseatingly emotional **:** MAWKISH ⟨a lot of ~ endearments —H.L.Spinner⟩

drips *pres 3d sing of* DRIP, *pl of* DRIP

dripstone \'=,=\ *n* **1 :** a drip (as along an eaves) made of stone **2 :** calcium carbonate in the form of stalactites or stalagmites

dript *past of* DRIP

dri·sheen \drə'shēn\ *n* -s [IrGael *drisīn*] **:** a sausage prepared with sheep's blood, milk, and seasonings chiefly in the vicinity of Cork in Ireland

drisk \'drisk\ *n* -s [origin unknown] *NewEng* **:** a drizzling mist

drite \'drīt\ *vi* [ME *driten*, fr. OE *drītan* — more at DIRT] *Scot* **:** DEFECATE

driv·able *also* **drive·able** \'drīvəbəl\ *adj* **:** capable of being driven ⟨as soon as the colt is ~⟩ ⟨the road is not ~ in winter⟩; *specif* **:** suitable for floating logs

driv·age \'drīvij\ *n* -s **:** a driving of a mine passage

1drive \'drīv\ *vb* **drove** \'drōv\ *or archaic* **drave** \'drāv\ *or dial* **driv** \'driv\ *or* **druv** \'drəv\ **driv·en** \'drivən *also* -iv°m *or* -ib°m\ *or archaic* **drove** *or dial* **driv** *or* **druv; driv·ing** \'drīviŋ\ **drives** \'drīvz\ [ME *driven*, fr. OE *drīfan*; akin to OHG *trīban* to drive, ON *drīfa* to dash (said of spray), Goth *dreiban* to drive, and perh. to Lith *dribti* to fall in mushy flakes (said of snow)] *vt* **1 :** to set and keep in motion or in action through application of some amount of force: **a :** to impart an onward or forward motion to by expenditure of physical force **:** PROPEL ⟨he slammed the door and *drove* the bolt home⟩ ⟨cheerily *drove* his pen afresh —George Meredith⟩ ⟨as white as the *driven* snow⟩ ⟨the trade winds ~ the equatorial currents⟩ ⟨*driving* his canoe onto the beach⟩ **b :** to impart violent motion or great impetus to **:** hurl, thrust, plunge, or press irresistibly — used with a following preposition or adverb indicating the direction ⟨a tackler should ~ his body so as to hit the ball-carrier just above the knees⟩ ⟨he *drove* the muzzle hard into the man's face —Max Peacock⟩; *specif* **:** VAPORIZE — used with *off* ⟨heat will ~ off the quicksilver⟩ **c :** to urge along (as cattle) guiding and often goading ⟨cowboys *drove* herds north⟩ ⟨prisoners were *driven* onto barges⟩ **d :** to cause to penetrate with force ⟨as a man would ~ a nail —J.G.Frazer⟩ **:** plunge forcibly ⟨I *drove* my sword through his heart —Padraic Colum⟩ **e :** to direct hostile force or a strong offensive movement against **:** exert strong effective pressure against — used with a separative expression ⟨many attempts to ~ the British out of Egypt⟩ ⟨the task of *driving* the invaders back across the border⟩ ⟨with the German eagle *driven* from the seas —R.W.Van Alstyne⟩ ⟨the noise would ~ you out of the place —Ellwood Kirby⟩ **f :** to constrain to go or to remove by reason of superior authority or influence or because of circumstantial pressure (as political or economic) ⟨engaged in a long attempt to ~ Burr from public life —Nathan Schachner⟩ ⟨this wetback competition annually ~*s* thousands of Texans as far north as Oregon in search of work —D.L.Graham⟩; *also* **:** to force the removal or banishment of ⟨radio has *driven* the newspaper extra from the streets⟩ **g :** to supply with motive power ⟨machines *driven* by clockwork⟩ ⟨whether it was being *driven* as a generator or was running as a motor —F.A.Annett⟩ **:** set or keep in operation ⟨*drove* their mills with water power⟩ **2 a :** to direct the motions and course of (a draft animal) **b :** NAVIGATE ⟨~ a watercraft⟩ **c :** to operate the controls of (a locomotive) or to operate the mechanism and controls and direct the course of (as a motor vehicle or speedboat) **d :** to convey in a vehicle ⟨he had to ~ his produce to market before daylight⟩ **e :** to guide a vehicle along or through ⟨*drove* the river road in all kinds of weather⟩ ⟨*drove* creek beds and side-hills to reach his backcountry patients⟩ **f :** to own and use (as an automobile of an indicated kind) ⟨he always *drove* a sedan⟩ **g :** to float (logs) down a stream **3 a :** to carry on or carry through energetically ⟨shipowners were *driving* a roaring trade in oriental ports⟩ **b :** to carry through to a conclusion or to completion in spite of hindrances ⟨they will not give up their bargaining advantage without *driving* a hard bargain politically —Cecil Hobbs⟩; *specif* **:** to lay out and construct by the methods of engineering ⟨superhighway being *driven* across the state⟩ **c :** to build (a highway, canal, railroad) along a projected course **4 :** to subject to effective pressure or compulsion to act in a certain way or to submit to a certain condition: as **a :** to exert inescapable or coercive pressure on (a person) **:** motivate or incite irresistibly **:** COERCE, CONSTRAIN, OBLIGE — used often with a following preposition or infinitive indicating the direction of constraint ⟨hunger *drove* him to steal⟩ ⟨to make us believe that his characters are fellow beings *driven* by their own passions and idiosyncracies —Virginia Woolf⟩ ⟨he used only persuasion, for he knew she could not be *driven*⟩ ⟨a wayward genius who is *driven* to incredible writing feats by pressure of debts —Leslie Rees⟩ ⟨economic insecurity that ~*s* young people into vocational training —A.W.Griswold⟩ **b :** to oblige to suffer or have recourse to a mood or mental state ⟨to what depths of bitterness she had been *driven* —Herbert Read⟩ ⟨continuing pressure of the unsolved problem ~*s* the society . . . to a precipitate and spurious defense mechanism —Weston La Barre⟩; *specif* **:** to compel to undergo or suffer a change of state ⟨*driven* desperate by the pressures of drab life —Evelyn Eaton⟩ ⟨a stupid cocotte who has begun by *driving* him mad with jealousy —Edmund Wilson⟩ **c :** to urge relentlessly to continuous exertion ⟨he ~*s* them hard with five-mile runs before breakfast —Harry Gordon⟩ ⟨I have been ruthlessly *driven* — hence this silence —H.J.Laski⟩ **:** press or spur to greater intensity of determined striving ⟨a tired spirit *driving* body and nerves to an effort they were crying to avoid —Fred Majdalany⟩ ⟨believed men were *driven* hardest by ambition —M.A.Kline⟩ ⟨he lacked the will that *drives* one to disregard human factors, to crush all who opposed him⟩ **d :** to press or force (something) inflexibly into a certain activity, course, direction, or state ⟨forces which had *driven* the tide of population across the Alleghenies —R.A. Billington⟩ ⟨discipline required to ~ the bill through congress⟩ ⟨advised against *driving* the party underground⟩; *specif* **:** to subject to pressure to bring about change either up or down ⟨going to try to ~ interest rates down which meant *driving* up the capital value of existing loans —Harold Wincott⟩ **e :** to project, inject, or impress incisively ⟨only a few are willing to ~ this doctrine straight through to its logical conclusion —Clinton Rossiter⟩ ⟨the basic point at last is *driven* solidly home in a 56-page booklet —R.D.Darrell⟩ ⟨the laconic or sententious phrase to ~ home and imbed what might otherwise be lost or scattered —B.N.Cardozo⟩ **f :** to cause (something intangible) to dissipate or vanish decisively through the pressure of some moving power or influence ⟨as the corroborative detail *drove* doubts from his mind —T.B.Costain⟩ ⟨a sad day for the U.S. if the tradition of dissent were *driven* out of the universities —J.B.Conant⟩; *specif* **:** to dispel and replace ⟨resolved that sound Latin . . . should ~ out, for literary purposes, the Italian vernaculars and medieval Latin —G.C. Sellery⟩ **5** *archaic* **:** BRING ⟨~ bad luck⟩ **:** CAST ⟨~ not the fault on him —Robert Bridges †1930⟩ **6 a** *obs* **:** to cause to pass ⟨~ the tedious hours away —John Dryden⟩ **b :** PROTRACT, DEFER ⟨~ bedtime⟩ **7** *obs* **:** to conclude from premises **:** DEDUCE **8 a** *obs* **:** to pursue (game) as a hunter **b :** to cause (as game animals) to move in a desired direction (as toward waiting hunters) ⟨beaters *drove* the birds toward the guns⟩; *also* **:** to drive game in (a particular place) ⟨we will ~ the small woods by the stream tomorrow⟩ — compare STALK, WALK UP **c** *obs* **:** to clear or strip (as a region) of animals or other property; *also* **:** to drive off **:** SEIZE ⟨~ animals⟩ **9 a :** to advance (as a tunnel or a horizontal or upwardly inclined mine passage) by cutting and excavating **b :** PRODUCE ⟨~ a well⟩ **10 :** to propel (an object of play) swiftly (as by a powerful stroke or throw): **a :** to strike (a bowled cricket ball) with the bat so as to propel in a forward direction **b :** to send (a croquet ball) to some desired position by striking another ball held in contact **c :** to play (a golf ball) from the tee esp. with a full stroke made with a driver **d :** to hit (a tennis ball) on the bounce with a below-shoulder-level swing and with top spin — distinguished from *chop*, *slice*, and *volley* **e :** to return (a shuttlecock) with a low hard shot parallel to the ground — compare SMASH **f :** to cause (a run or runner) to be scored in baseball esp. by making a hit — usu. used with *in* **g :** to force (a billiard ball) to strike one or more cushions and return to the desired position for the next shot ~ *vi* **1 a :** to dash, plunge, or surge ahead rapidly or violently ⟨the halfback *drove* through the line⟩ ⟨he *drove* rudely past her into the room —E.F.McGuire⟩ **b :** to rush along thrusting or striking with force against any obstruction ⟨he crossed the river in the midst of *driving* ice⟩ ⟨a meteor *driving* toward the earth⟩ ⟨the slanting rain, which *drove* faster every minute —Ellen Glasgow⟩ **c :** to press a hostile attack ⟨the division *drove* some 400 miles⟩ **d :** to penetrate with force ⟨the harpoon *drove* deep⟩ **2 :** to move to leeward or with the tide out of control by rudder, sail, or engines; *also* **:** to carry excessive sail **3 :** to launch a blow or missile or discharge a bullet — often used with a following *at* and a preceding *let* ⟨just as a snarling Queen's Ranger *drove* at him —F.V.W.Mason⟩ ⟨he then seized the shotgun and let ~ with both barrels⟩ **4 a :** to strive determinedly on a course or toward an objective ⟨try to ~ toward a generalization and a hypothesis —Lionel Trilling⟩ ⟨*driving* through obstacles —*Time*⟩ ⟨the decision to ~ ahead with all speed for the manufacture of the hydrogen bomb —W.H. Chamberlin⟩; *also* **:** to make a strong effort ⟨the justices are *driving* hard to clean up pending cases —*Christian Science Monitor*⟩ **b :** to spur oneself or others to strenuous effort or to greater intensity of physical or mental exertion ⟨even after reaching the top he continues to ~⟩ **5 a :** to guide a horse-drawn vehicle **b :** to operate and steer a motor vehicle ⟨road signs warning motorists to ~ slow⟩ **c :** to have oneself carried in a vehicle ⟨I *drove* there with a friend and flew back by myself⟩ **6** *archaic* **:** to levy a distress to obtain satisfaction of a claim for rent **:** DISTRAIN **7 :** to drive a mine passage **8 :** to drive an object of play (as a golf ball) **9 :** to perform music with a strong rhythmic impulse **:** play with momentum **syn** see MOVE — **drive at :** to aim or intend to express ultimately often despite initial failure to achieve clarity or to reveal the full implications ⟨many of their statements are so qualified as to make it difficult to know what they are *driving at* —L.A.White⟩ — usu. used with the pronoun *what* as inverted object

²**drive** \"\ *n* -s **1 :** an act of driving: **a :** a short trip in a vehicle (as a carriage or automobile) wholly or partly under one's control as distinguished from a vehicle (as a train) under the control of another ⟨an afternoon ~ along the lakefront⟩ ⟨a 2-hour ~ to the next city⟩ **b :** an overland journey in a vehicle esp. along a highway for a long distance ⟨a cross-state ~⟩ ⟨the third day's ~ became wearisome⟩ **c :** an urging and gathering together of animals (as cattle or sheep) from a wide area; *also* **:** the animals gathered for capture, slaughter, or branding **d :** a driving of cattle or sheep overland ⟨the long ~ lingered only in the memories and imaginations of old cowhands —D.B.Davis⟩ **e :** a hunt or shoot in which the game is driven within range past the weapons of hunters; *also* **:** the mass of animals so driven **f :** the guiding of logs downstream to a mill; *also* **:** the floating logs amassed in a drive **g** (1) **:** the act or an instance of driving an object of play (as a ball) ⟨the ~ is called the basic scoring shot in cricket⟩ ⟨a low ~ that hit the net⟩ (2) **:** the flight of a hard-hit ball or shuttlecock ⟨his solid ~*s* range between 220 and 240 yards⟩ **h :** the forward thrust or propulsive force of a boat under way **i** *Brit* **:** a stately or ceremonious public procession **2 a :** a private road for vehicles affording access to a residence or other buildings ⟨the house stands at the end of a long ~ surrounded by spacious lawns and gardens —*Amer. Guide Series: Fla.*⟩ **:** DRIVEWAY 2 **b :** a road for leisure driving esp. in a park or along a scenic route ⟨the highway now skirts the lakeshore with all the fresh beauty of a seacoast ~ —*Amer. Guide Series: Vt.*⟩ **c :** an urban street or boulevard ⟨Morningside *Drive* overlooking the Hudson⟩ **3 :** a tract over which game is driven **:** the site of an organized hunt **4 :** an offensive, aggressive, or expansionist move ⟨in the path of the Soviet ~ toward the Adriatic —H.C.Wolfe⟩ ⟨both touchdowns capped long ~*s*⟩; *esp* **:** a strong military attack against enemy-held terrain ⟨a swift nine-month ~ from the Normandy bridgehead . . . across France and Germany and into Austria —*Current Biog.*⟩ **5 :** the state of being hurried and under pressure ⟨elude the ruthless ~ of work and worry —S.H.Adams⟩ ⟨I am in such a ~ that I can't expatiate —H.J.Laski⟩ **6 :** a driven mine passage or tunnel **7 :** STRIKE 14 **8 :** a systematic effort strenuously participated in by a group or organized by a group and insistently urged upon a community or a nation toward attainment of a certain objective or furtherance of some special design **:** an intensive campaign ⟨an annual ~ for membership in the league⟩ ⟨a propaganda ~ aimed at undermining our prestige abroad⟩ ⟨sparked ~*s* that raised many hundreds of thousands of dollars for veterans' hospitals and . . . relief —J.A.Morris b. 1904⟩ ⟨the ~ for national independence has had a long history in Indochina —Cecil Hobbs⟩ **9 :** a progressive game (as of whist or bridge) **10 :** inciting or impelling character or quality: **a :** an urgent basic or instinctual need pressing for satisfaction **:** a physiological tension, lack, or imbalance (as a state of hunger or thirst) impelling the organism to activity ⟨those sexual ~*s* which are such a fertile source of conflict among most vertebrates —Ralph Linton⟩ ⟨habits attached to the hunger ~⟩; *also* **:** a tendency or disposition to act following or as a result of a deprivation or need **b :** a powerfully impelling culturally acquired concern, interest, or longing that incites one to unremitting action ⟨possessed with a ~ for perfection —*Time*⟩ ⟨the integrating ~ or disposition that gives a life history its continuity or a personality its consistency and integrity —H.J.Muller⟩ ⟨a prisoner of the old national and imperialist ~*s* —*Partisan Rev.*⟩ ⟨"Asia for the Asians" . . . represents the ~ of millions upon millions of people —W.O.Douglas⟩ **c :** dynamic quality marked by initiative, promptness of decision, abundance of concentrated energy, and indomitable persistence in carrying through an undertaking toward accomplishment **:** vigorous enterprise **:** the amount of energy and persistence evidenced in a given activity **:** ÉLAN, PUSH ⟨his ~ and enthusiasm overcame all obstacles —*Times Lit. Supp.*⟩ ⟨a tremendous energy ~ that keeps him in a constant state of high gear —Martin Gardner⟩ ⟨the city had lost . . . the surging ~ that supposedly was so characteristically American —Harold Sinclair⟩ ⟨concerned with the dynamic core of a society, its central impulse and ~ —Charles Maughan⟩ **d :** a quality of sustained vitality and intensity of expression in intellectual or artistic composition or performance ⟨he developed irresistible ~ in the performance of plays —Sheldon Cheney⟩ ⟨a stronger ~ in the big climaxes —Irving Kolodin⟩ **e :** dramatic intensity and suspensiveness that captures attention **f :** a strong rhythmic impulse communicated in musical performance **11 a :** the means for giving motion to a machine or machine part ⟨belt ~⟩ ⟨electric ~⟩; *also* **:** a method of driving machines ⟨a group ~⟩ **b :** the means by which the propulsive power of an automobile is applied to the road ⟨front-wheel ~⟩ ⟨four-wheel ~⟩ **c :** the means by which the propulsion of an automotive vehicle is controlled and directed ⟨a left-hand ~⟩; *also* **:** the place where the operator sits to drive ⟨an enclosed ~⟩ **12 :** the pressure that causes oil or other fluid to enter a well from the surrounding rock strata ⟨water ~⟩ ⟨gas-cap ~⟩ **13 :** an offering of goods at a low price (as in reducing inventory) **syn** see VIGOR

³**drive** \"\ *adj* **:** used in or for driving **:** serving to drive **:** IMPELLING ⟨a ~ chain⟩

driveaway \'==,=\ *n* -s [*drive away*, v., fr. ¹*drive* + *away*] **:** the delivery of an automobile by driving it under its own power from the factory to a purchaser or dealer ⟨organized a ~ service⟩ ⟨a ~ of 60 cars⟩

driveboat \'=,=\ *n* **:** a rowboat used in menhaden fishing to drive the fish into the nets

drivehead \'=,=\ *n* **:** a plug, ring, or cap for screwing into or fitting over the end of a mechanical part so that it can be driven with minimum deformation or bruising

drive-in \'drī,vin\ *n* -s *often attrib* [*drive in*, v., fr. ¹*drive* + *in*] **:** a place of business (as a motion-picture theater, bank, or refreshment stand) laid out and equipped so as to allow its patrons to be served or accommodated while remaining in their automobiles ⟨a new *drive-in* business⟩ ⟨the convenient *drive-in* window at the bank⟩ ⟨let's eat at the *drive-in* tonight⟩

¹**driv·el** \'drivəl\ *vb* **driveled** *or* **drivelled**; **driveled** *or* **drivelled**; **driveling** *or* **drivelling** \-v(ə)liŋ\ **drivels** [ME *drivelen*, alter. of *drevelen*, fr. OE *dreflian;* akin to ME *draf* draff — more at DRAFF] *vi* **1 :** to let saliva drip or run in a thin stream from the mouth or mucus from the nostrils (as of an infant or imbecile) **:** SLAVER ⟨the panting dog ~*ed* on my hand⟩ **2 :** to talk stupidly and carelessly without due thought, knowledge, or consideration **:** be silly in manner or content of speech ⟨while the idiots on the platform were ~*ing*, the people kept calling for Lincoln —Winston Churchill⟩ ⟨he ~*ed* on about his family, his influence, his properties⟩ **3** *archaic* **:** TRICKLE, DRIBBLE ⟨water ~*ing*⟩ ~ *vt* **1** *obs* **:** to let trickle like saliva from the mouth ⟨the wound is ~*ing* blood⟩ **2 :** to utter in an infantile or imbecilic way ⟨he ~*ed* a few words of apology then left at once⟩ **3 :** to waste or fritter in a childish fashion

²**drivel** \"\ *n* -s [ME *drivil, drevel*, fr. *drivelen, drevelen*, v.] **1** *archaic* **:** saliva trickling from the mouth **2 :** inarticulate or foolish utterance ⟨phrases which on the face of them may be platitudinous to a degree approaching ~ —C.E.Montague⟩ ⟨writes endless narcissistic ~ in a stream-of-consciousness and disorganized manner —Albert Deutsch⟩

driv·el·er *or* **driv·el·ler** \-v(ə)lə(r)\ *n* -s **:** one that drivels **:** one who talks in a silly, foolish, or babyish way

driveling *or* **drivelling** *adj* [ME *drivelinge* talking stupidly, fr. *drivelen* to let saliva drip from the mouth, talk stupidly + *-inge, -ing* -ing] **1 :** feeble like an infant in thought or action ⟨reduced to a ~ idiot⟩ **2 :** inane in an infantile or feeble-minded way ⟨a ~ and idiotic and superficial travesty of the Italian culture —Ezra Pound⟩ — **driv·el·ing·ly** *or* **driv·el·ling·ly** *adv*

¹**driven** *adj* [fr. past part. of ¹*drive*] **:** evidencing marked strenuousness of effort or a compelling sense of urgency ⟨even his Beethoven performances . . . were sometimes too ~ and sleek for my taste —Winthrop Sargeant⟩ ⟨then his own ~ sense of obligation would rear up —Norman Kelman⟩

²**driven** *n* -s **:** a gear wheel or pulley that takes its motion from another **:** FOLLOWER

driven note *n, obs* **:** DRIVING NOTE

drive nozzle *n* **:** a high-pressure spraying nozzle the stream from which breaks at about 30 feet in the air into a coarse mist for spraying tall trees

driven well *n* **:** a well made by driving a tube into the earth to a water-bearing stratum

drive out *vt* **:** to space (typeset matter) widely

drivepipe \'=,=\ *n* **:** a pipe with a sharp edge for driving short distances into the solid ground (as to reach a water-bearing stratum or to insert concrete piles)

driv·er \'drīvə(r)\ *n* -s *often attrib* [ME *drivere*, fr. *driven* to drive + *-ere* -er] **1 :** one that drives something: as **a :** one that drives cattle, sheep, or beasts of burden **b :** a person in actual physical control of a vehicle (as an automobile) ⟨~ for the colonel⟩ ⟨hundreds of ~*s* parked their cars by the shore⟩ ⟨Sunday ~*s*⟩ — compare OPERATOR **c :** one that dispels or expels ⟨a pianist is my surest ~ away of worry⟩ ⟨a dedicated ~ out of superstition⟩ **d :** a beater, drover, or other individual engaged in driving animals toward a destination **e :** one competent to carry projects to execution or completion ⟨a ~ of bargains⟩ **f :** one skilled or adept at driving an object in flight, into desired shape, or so as to penetrate ⟨he proved the longest ~ in the tournament⟩ ⟨a ~ of rivets⟩ ⟨the steam driller was taking work from ~*s*⟩ **g :** an overseer of a gang of workers responsible for their working at a satisfactory pace; *broadly* **:** a harsh and exacting taskmaster **h :** a workman who guides logs being floated down a stream **i :** the operator or tender of a machine that drives ⟨a pile ~⟩ **j :** a member of a purse-seiner crew who goes out ahead in a small boat to determine the direction and size of schools of fish and helps to keep fish from escaping while the net is being set **k :** an individual with executive ability and the tense and rigorous disposition to spur others to maintain a high level of well-directed exertion — used often with an implication of pushing relentlessly and ruthlessly ⟨almost invariably he is a tense or intense person, enthusiastic, conscientious, more or less of a perfectionist, a go-getter, a real ~ —C.M.Jones⟩ ⟨a great man is a leader of men, not a ~ —S.McC.Crothers⟩ ⟨every steel company needs at least one hard-boiled ~ of men —*Current Biog.*⟩ **2 :** any of certain implements or tools used for driving: as **a :** MALLET **b :** a tamping iron **c :** a hammer for driving on barrel hoops **d :** any of various sporting implements (as a bat, racket, or club) esp. adapted for driving (as by shape); *esp* **:** a golf club with a wooden head and nearly straight face used in driving a ball from the tee — see WOOD illustration **e :** an electrical device (as an electron tube) that produces and sustains oscillations or pulses in a circuit **f :** the magnetic device that actuates a loudspeaker diaphragm to produce sound **3 a** *obs* **:** a square sail set on a yard at the end of a spanker boom with the wind aft **b :** SPANKER 2 **c :** the sixth mast on a many-masted schooner; *also* **:** the lower sail set on this mast **4 :** a piece for imparting motion to another piece either directly or indirectly: as **a :** the first of a train of wheels giving motion to the rest **b :** a locomotive driving wheel **c :** a dog in the faceplate of a lathe for driving a straight-tailed dog **d :** a crossbar on a grinding-mill spindle for driving the upper stone **5 :** DOWITCHER

driver ant *also* **driver** *n* **:** ARMY ANT; *specif* **:** any of various African and Asian ants of *Dorylus* and related genera that move in vast armies and devour insects and small animals

driver boom *n, obs* **:** SPANKER BOOM

driv·er·less \'drīvə(r)ləs\ *adj* **:** having no driver

driver salesman *n* **:** a salesman (as of beverages, ice cream, cigars) who calls on customers along a regular route carrying samples of new products and combining sales activities with deliveries and collection of empties

driv·er·ship \-,ship\ *n* -s **1 :** skill in driving vehicles **2 :** attitude and method in overseeing and supervising men at work or study; *esp* **:** hard driving and exacting method

driver's license *n* **:** a license issued under governmental authority that permits the holder to operate a motor vehicle

driver's seat *n* **1 :** the position of top authority and governing power ⟨whether a czar or a commissar sits in the *driver's seat* is immaterial —L.A.White⟩ **2 :** the position of dominance or of tight control (as of a situation) ⟨the feeling that the occupation authorities unwittingly assisted the Nazis back into the *driver's seat*⟩ ⟨with cars no longer scarce the buyer seemed firmly in the *driver's seat*⟩

drives *pres 3d sing of* DRIVE, *pl of* DRIVE

drivescrew \'=,=\ *n* **:** a screw that is driven home or nearly home with a hammer

drive shaft *n* **:** a shaft that transmits mechanical power — see JET ENGINE illustration

drive shoe *n* **:** the sharp edge of a drivepipe

drive-volley \'=,==\ *n* **:** a tennis volley executed in the manner of a forehand drive

driveway \'=,=\ *n* **1 :** a road or way along which animals (as stock or game) are driven **2 :** a private road giving access from a public thoroughfare to a building or buildings on abutting grounds **3 :** a way leading to an upper level (as of a barn) for passage of vehicles

drivewell \'=,=\ *n* **:** DRIVEN WELL

drive wheel *n* **:** DRIVING WHEEL

drive-yourself \'==,=\ *adj* [¹*drive*] **:** of or constituting a service providing automobiles for hire to be driven by the hirer

¹**driving** *adj* [fr. pres. part. of ¹*drive*] **1 :** acting with vigor **:** ENERGETIC ⟨responsibility turned the spoiled playboy into a ~ young executive⟩ **2 :** prone to urge or goad others (as subordinates or employees) to stepped-up or unreasonable exertion ⟨a ~ supervisor⟩ **3 :** being of such character as to produce or effect and sustain consistently directed, progressive, or constructive action ⟨the ~ force was not academic training but his innate enthusiasm for constructive and creative work —John Bradford⟩ ⟨the ~ energy required of an executive⟩ ⟨in the 1860s and 1870s the irresistible ~ power of the American trek westward —*Amer. Guide Series: Texas*⟩ **4 :** exercising an inescapable pressure or compulsive influence in inciting and stimulating thoughts or actions in mounting sequence **:** DYNAMIC ⟨little by little the pleasure of opiates gives way to the ~ necessity to take drugs in order to avoid withdrawal distress —D.W.Maurer & V.H.Vogel⟩ ⟨the stirring and ~ quality of all truly spiritual leaders who are in the world but not of it —M.R.Cohen⟩ ⟨the ~ concern of the book to expose actual conditions in the institution⟩ ⟨a ~ personal ambition⟩ **5 :** having a dramatic and suspensive quality stimulative to readers or hearers ⟨he gives us a quick and ~ narrative of a tired and indomitable and angry man —*Saturday Rev.*⟩

²**driving** *n* -s [fr. gerund of ¹*drive*] **:** management of an automobile or other vehicle on the road ⟨clever at ~ in heavy traffic⟩

driving axle *n* **:** the axle of a driving wheel (as of a locomotive)

driving box *n* **:** the journal box of a locomotive driving axle

driving clock *n* **1 :** a mechanism for turning an equatorial telescope or a coelostat around its polar axis at the proper rate to keep a celestial body in the field of view **2 :** a driving mechanism for a chronograph or other recording mechanism

driving face *n* **:** BLADE FACE

driving horse *n* **:** a light horse suitable for hauling a passenger vehicle

driving iron *n* **1 :** a sharp-pointed steel rod for driving holes (as for subsoil blasting, stump blasting, tree planting) **2 :** an iron golf club with little loft that is used sometimes in making the drive — called also *number one iron;* see IRON illustration

driv·ing·ly *adv* **:** with driving force or energy

driving mashie *n* **:** MASHIE IRON

driving note *n, obs* **:** a syncopated note in music

driving park *n* **:** an area with a racetrack for harness racing

driving range *n* **:** an area or field equipped with distance markers, clubs, balls, and tees for practicing the golf drive and iron shots

driving spring *n* **:** a supporting spring resting upon a locomotive driving box to minimize shock
driving wheel *n* **:** a wheel that communicates motion: as **a :** one of the large wheels of a locomotive to which the side rods are attached and which are driven by the engine connecting rods **:** DRIVER **b :** the main wheel of a watch or clock that transmits the driving power of the spring, weight, or electromagnetic impulse to the succeeding parts of the train
¹driz·zle \'drizəl\ *vb* **drizzled; drizzled; drizzling** \-z(ə)liŋ\ **drizzles** [perh. alter. of ME *drysnen* to fall, fr. OE *-drysnian* to disappear; akin to OE *drēosan* to fall — more at DREARY] *vi* **1 :** to rain in very small drops ⟨a raw *drizzling* rain⟩ ⟨it *drizzled* off and on all day⟩; *sometimes* **:** to rain lightly **:** SPRINKLE ⟨come on, it's only *drizzling* now⟩ **2 :** to shed minute drops or particles like fine rain ⟨the *drizzling* eyes to eat her beauty —Robinson Jeffers⟩ **~** *vt* **1 :** to shed or let fall in minute drops or particles ⟨the aphids *drizzled* honeydew on our heads⟩ ⟨the air doth ~ dew —Shak.⟩ ⟨after four minutes turn roe and mushrooms . . . then slowly ~ on wine, sprinkle with parsley —*Ford Times*⟩ **2 :** to make wet with minute drops ⟨the dew on the branches disturbed by our passage *drizzled* our hair and shoulders⟩
²drizzle \"\ *n* -s **1 :** a fine misty rain; *specif* **:** a light rain of very small drops falling at a velocity of between 144 feet per hour and 2¼ feet per second — compare SHOWER **2 a :** a slow dribble or trickle of a liquid ⟨a lukewarm ~ from the faucet⟩ **b :** a slow steady issue of hints or bits (as of an idea or attitude) ⟨a ~ of sensationalism —Elizabeth Janeway⟩
driz·zle-droz·zle \'drizəl,dräzəl\ *n* -s [redupl. of ²*drizzle*] **:** a gentle continuous rainfall
driz·zling·ly *adv* [*drizzling* (fr. pres. part. of ¹*drizzle*) + *-ly*] **:** in a drizzle ⟨it rained ~, disappointing the farmers in the drought area who were praying for a good hard rain⟩
driz·zly \-z(ə)lē, -li\ *adj* -ER/-EST [²*drizzle* + *-y*] **:** characterized by fine rain ⟨this section of the country is unpleasant and ~ in the winter⟩
drod·dum \'drädəm\ *n* -s [origin unknown] *Scot* **:** BUTTOCKS
drof·land \'drōflənd\ *also* **dryf·land** \'drif-\ *n* [alter. of ¹*drove* + *land*] **:** land held in early England by the service of driving the lord's cattle from place to place
drog \'dräg, 'drōg\ *n* [ME *drogge* — more at DRUG] *Scot* **:** DRUG
dro·gher \'drōgə(r)\ *n* -s [D *droger* (formerly spelled *drogher*), lit., drier (i.e., of herring), fr. *drogen* to dry (fr. *droog* dry, fr. MD *drōge*) + *-er* — more at DRY] **1 :** a sailing barge used in the West Indian coastal trade esp. in the Gulf of Paria **2 :** a clumsy cargo boat esp. of coasting type ⟨a pulpwood ~ lumbering up the tide-torn river —S.W.Dean & Marguerite Marshall⟩ **3 :** CARRIER, PORTER ⟨one of our best and most reliable ~s had brought his woman along to carry rations and dunnage —P.A.Zahl⟩
drogue \'drōg\ *n* -s [prob. alter of ¹*drag*] **1 :** a device attached to the end of a harpoon line to retard or tire out a whale when running or sounding **2 a :** a sea anchor (as a canvas bag with a hooped mouth) used to reduce the speed of a boat and keep her head into the wind **b** (1) **:** a sea anchor trailed from the stern of a seaplane to reduce yawing (2) **:** a cylindrical cloth target towed by an airplane for air-to-air firing practice (3) **:** a towed aerodynamic drag device used to maintain tension in a refueling hose; *also* **:** a small parachute for deceleration or stabilization of something **3 :** a device shaped like a funnel or cone with a wide mouth which is attached to the end of a long flexible hose suspended from a tanker airplane in flight and into which the probe of another airplane in flight is fitted so as to receive fuel from the tanker airplane
droich \'drȯik\ *n* -s [ScGael] *Scot* **:** DWARF
¹droil *or* **droile** *n* -s [origin unknown] *obs* **:** DRUDGE
²droil *or* **droile** *vi* **droiled; droiled; droiling; droils** *or* **droiles** *obs* **:** DRUDGE
droit \'drȯit\ *n* -s [origin unknown] **:** a former moneyers' unit of weight equal to ¹⁄₂₄ mite or ¹⁄₄₈₀ grain
droit ad·mi·nis·tra·tif \drwäädmēnēsträtēf\ *n* [F] **1** *French law* **:** ADMINISTRATIVE LAW **2 :** the rules of continental European administrative law exempting governmental agents from liability in other than administrative tribunals
droit d'au·baine \drwädōbān\ *n* [F, right of escheat] **:** the right formerly possessed by the crown or state in France of confiscating all the property, real and personal, of which a domiciled alien died possessed
droit du sei·gneur \drwädüsānʸœr\ *n* [F, right of the lord] **:** a supposed legal or customary right at the time of a marriage whereby a feudal lord had sexual relations with a vassal's bride on her wedding night
droits ci·vils \drwäsēvēl\ *n pl* [F] *French law* **:** private rights
droits of admiralty \'drȯits-\ *usu cap A* [MF *droit* law, right, fr. ML *directum*, fr. neut. of LL *directus* just, fr. L, straight, direct — more at DRESS] *English law* **:** certain rights or perquisites (as the proceeds of enemies' ships seized in port or taken by uncommissioned captors or from wrecks and derelicts) that formerly belonged to the Court of Admiralty but are now allowed to the captor
droi·tu·ral \'drȯichərəl\ *adj* [F *droiture* straightforwardness, honesty (fr. *droit* straight, upright — fr. L *directus* straight, direct — + -ure) + E *-al* — more at DRESS] **:** relating to right or title of property as distinguished from right of possession ⟨~ actions at law⟩
droke \'drōk\ *n* -s [origin unknown] *Canad* **:** THICKET, COPSE ⟨put my camp in a ~ of spruce —J.G.Millais⟩
drokpa *usu cap, var of* DRUPA
drô·le·rie \ˌdrōlə'rē, (')drōl,rē\ *n* -s [F — more at DROLLERY] **:** DROLLERY
¹droll \'drōl\ *adj, usu* -ER/-EST [F *drôle*, fr. *drôle* scamp, rascal, fr. MF *drolle*, fr. MD, imp, elf, sprite] **:** causing or capable of causing mirth or amusement by funny, whimsical, or odd speech or conduct ⟨a ~ little man⟩ **:** having a humorous, whimsical, or odd character ⟨says things so ~ I can't answer him for laughing —Kenneth Roberts⟩ ⟨a book of ~ stories for the invalid⟩ **syn** see LAUGHABLE
²droll \"\ *n* -s [F *drôle*] **1 a :** one that habitually amuses or diverts by droll speech or behavior **:** WAG, JESTER ⟨played the ~ with his quips and sallies⟩ **b :** an actor in comedy ⟨an out-of-work comedian, an old ~ of the halls —May L. Becker⟩ **2 a :** a short dramatic composition or stage presentation of a comic or farcical character **:** BURLESQUE ⟨incipient circuses, ~s, and puppet shows all had a share in clearing the way for the stage in New England —Katharine L. Bates⟩; *also* **:** PUPPET SHOW **b :** a farcical folktale — compare FABLIAU
³droll \"\ *vb* -ED/-ING/-S *vi* **1** *archaic* **:** to jest or sport **:** make fun — often used with *on, upon* or *at* ⟨~*ing* a little upon the corporal —Laurence Sterne⟩ **2 :** to speak monotonously **:** DRONE ⟨~*s* on plaintively about the *Last Rose of Summer* —*Belfast (Ireland) Telegraph*⟩ **~** *vt, archaic* **:** to decline or put away in a jesting manner **:** influence (a person) toward or away from some action or opinion by jesting or raillery
droll·ery \'drōl(ə)rē, -ri\ *n* -ES [F *drôlerie*, fr. *drôle* droll + *-erie* -ery] **1 :** something that is droll: as **a :** a comic picture or drawing ⟨for thy walls, a pretty slight ~ —Shak.⟩ **b :** DROLL 2a **c :** an amusing story or manner **:** JEST ⟨could not keep his *drolleries* out of the pulpit —H.E.Starr⟩ **d :** an artistic or intellectual production of a light and humorous character ⟨the delightful *drolleries* of Gilbert and Sullivan⟩ ⟨produced some excellent verse, *drolleries*, and children's books —H.E. Starr⟩ **2 :** the act or an instance of making jest of or burlesquing ⟨a notable talent for ~⟩ **3 :** the quality of being droll **:** whimsical humor ⟨stories that amuse not by their wit but by their ~⟩
droll·ing·ly *adv* **:** in the manner of one that drolls
droll·ness *n* -ES **:** the quality or state of being droll ⟨the lecturer's ~ endeared him to his listeners⟩
drol·ly \'drōl(l)ē, -)i\ *adv* [¹*droll* + *-ly*] **:** in a droll manner **:** HUMOROUSLY, QUIZZICALLY ⟨looked at me ~ as if only half believing what I said⟩ ⟨spoke ~ and cleverly⟩
drom- *or* **dromo-** *comb form* [Gk, fr. *dromos*] **1 :** course **:** racecourse **:** running ⟨*Dromornis*⟩ **2 :** speed ⟨*dromometer*⟩
drome \'drōm\ *n* -s [short for *airdrome*] **:** AIRPORT
¹-drome \ˌdrōm\ *n comb form* -s [MF, fr. L *-dromos*, fr. Gk *dromos;* akin to Gk *dramein* to run] **1 :** racecourse ⟨*motordrome*⟩ **2 :** large specially prepared place ⟨*aerodrome*⟩ ⟨*picturedrome*⟩
²-drome \"\ *adj comb form* [Gk *-dromos*, fr. *dromos* course, racecourse, act of running] **:** running ⟨*homodrome*⟩

drom·e·dary \'drämə,derē, -ri *sometimes* 'drəm-\ *n* -ES [ME *dromedarie*, fr. MF *dromedaire*, fr. LL *dromedarius* (*camelus*), fr. Gk *dromad-, dromas* running (as in *dromas kamēlos* dromedary, lit., running camel) + L *-arius* -ary; akin to Gk *aramein* to run, *dromos* racecourse, Skt *dramati* he runs, OE *treppan* to tread, trap — more at TRAP] **1 a :** a camel of unusual speed bred and trained esp. for riding **b :** the Arabian camel (*Camelus dromedarius*) as distinguished from the Bactrian camel **2** *obs* **:** a stupid or clumsy person **3 :** a trailer truck in which the tractor unit itself has a short freight compartment

dromedary

dro·mi·a·cea \ˌdrōmē'āsh(ē)ə\ *n pl, cap* [NL, fr. *Dromia*, genus of crabs (fr. Gk *dromias* a kind of crab) + NL *-acea*] **:** a group of crabs (suborder Brachyura) in which the last pair of thoracic legs are modified, dorsal, and often chelate and are used for placing sponges, shells, and other objects on the carapace — **dro·mi·a·ceous** \ˌ¦=ˌ=¦āshəs\ *adj*
drom·ic \'drämik\ *also* **drom·i·cal** \-məkəl\ *adj* [*dromic* fr. Gk *dromikos*, fr. *dromos* course, racecourse, running + *-ikos* -ic; *dromical* fr. *dromic* + *-al*] **1 :** of, relating to, or in the form of a racecourse **2** [MGk *dromikos*, fr. Gk] *archit* **:** having a long and narrow ground plan
dro·mi·cia \drō'mish(ē)ə\ [NL, fr. Gk *dromikos* swift (fr. *dromos* + *-ikos* -ic) + NL *-ia*] *syn of* CERCAERTUS
drom·o·ma·nia \ˌdrämə'mānēə\ *n* [NL, fr. *drom-* + *-mania*] **:** an exaggerated desire to wander
drom·ond \'drämənd, 'drəm-\ *n* -s [ME *dromond, dromoun, dromon*, fr. MF *dromont, dromon*, fr. LL *dromon-, dromo*, fr. Gk *dromōn* light ship, fr. *dramein* to run] **:** a large medieval fast-sailing galley or cutter
dro·mor·nis \drə'mȯrnəs\ *n, cap* [NL, fr. *drom-* + *-ornis*] **:** a genus of ratite birds of Queensland related to the cassowaries and emus
drom·os \'drä,mäs, 'drō,-, -məs\ *n, pl* **dromi** \-ˌmī, -ˌmē\ *or* **drom·oi** \-ˌmȯi\ [Gk *dromos*, racecourse, course, public walk — more at -DROME] **:** the passage to an ancient Egyptian or Mycenaean subterranean tomb
drom·o·trop·ic \¦drämə¦träpik, -rōm-\ *adj* [*drom-* + *-tropic*] **:** affecting the conductivity of cardiac muscle — used of the influence of cardiac nerves
-dro·mous \ˌdrəməs\ *adj comb form* [NL *-dromus*, fr. Gk *-dromos* — more at -DROME] **:** running ⟨*catadromous*⟩
¹drone \'drōn\ *n* -s *often attrib* [ME *drane, drone*, fr. OE *drān, drǣn;* akin to OS *dreno, dran* drone, OHG *treno*, MLG *drone* drone, ON *drynja* to roar, Goth *drunjus* sound, OE *drēam* joy, mirth, music, LGk *thrōnax* drone, Gk *thorybos* confused noise, Latvian *dun̦duris* wasp, Skt *dhranati* it sounds; basic meaning: buzzing, murmuring] **1 :** a male bee; *esp* **:** the male of the honeybee that develops from an unfertilized egg, is larger and stouter than the worker, lacks a sting, takes no part in honey gathering or care of the hive, and is of use to the colony only if a virgin queen requires insemination — see DRONE CELL **2 :** one that lives on the labors of others **:** IDLER, PARASITE ⟨a new Utopia in which robots . . . do all the work while human ~s recline in pneumatic bliss —John Diebold⟩ **3 a :** a pilotless airplane remote-controlled by radio signals (as from another airplane) **b :** a seagoing ship remote-controlled by radio
²drone \"\ *vb* -ED/-ING/-S *vi* **1 a :** to make a sustained deep murmuring, humming, or buzzing sound ⟨threshing machine was *droning* like a gigantic swarm of June beetles —Ellen Glasgow⟩ **b :** to talk in a persistently dull or monotonous tone ⟨eyes closed and heads nodded as he *droned* on and on⟩ **2 :** to live in idleness like a drone bee ⟨who would ~ when he might live by honest labor⟩ **:** be inactive; *also* **:** DROWSE ⟨found him *droning* by the fire —*Western Rev.*⟩ **3 :** to pass or proceed in a dull, drowsy, or uneventful manner ⟨the chill November days *droned* by —Earle Birney⟩ **:** act or perform in a drowsy, routine, or indifferent manner ⟨*droned* through Bryce's two fat volumes —H.J.Laski⟩ **~** *vt* **1 :** to utter or pronounce with a drone ⟨*droning* out dull papers on dull subjects⟩ **2 :** to pass or spend in idleness ⟨*droned* away the precious years of youth⟩ or in dull or monotonous activity ⟨*droned* away the years in the dust of musty libraries⟩
³drone \"\ *n* -s [²*drone*] **1 a :** BAGPIPE **b** (1) **:** one of the usu. three pipes on a bagpipe that sound fixed continuous tones as accompaniment to the melody played by the chanter (2) **:** one or more strings on a medieval bowed instrument playing a drone accompaniment to the melody **c :** the sound emitted by the drone of a bagpipe **2 :** any deep sustained or monotonous sound **:** HUM ⟨a sleepy ~ of well-wheels across the fields —Rudyard Kipling⟩ **:** a monotonous tone of voice ⟨the steady ~ of some tiresome old bore⟩ **3 a** *or* **drone bass :** an unvarying sustained bass note in a musical composition (as a pastoral) **:** PEDAL POINT **b :** one who speaks monotonously (as with a drawl)
drone bee *n* **:** ¹DRONE 1
drone cell *n* **:** one of the larger cells of a honeycomb in which the larvae of drones are reared
drone fly *n* **:** a nearly cosmopolitan two-winged fly (*Eristalis tenax*) of the family Syrphidae superficially resembling the drone bee — see RAT-TAILED LARVA
drone layer *n* **:** a queen bee capable only of producing drones
dron·er \'drōnə(r)\ *n* -s **:** one that drones
drong \'dräŋ\ *n* -s [prob. akin to OE *thringan* to press, compress — more at THRONG] *dial Eng* **:** a passageway or lane esp. between walls or hedges ⟨as if this homely ~ had been transformed to a royal path in some greenwood —Llewelyn Powys⟩
dron·go \'dräŋ(ˌ)gō\ *n* -s [native name in Madagascar] **1** *also* **drongo-shrike :** a bird of the family Dicruridae native to Asia, Africa, and Australia **2** *slang Austral* **:** ROOKIE, NOVICE
drongo cuckoo *n* **:** a cuckoo of India (*Surniculus lugubris*) resembling the black drongo
dron·ing·ly *adv* **:** in a droning manner
dron·ish \'drōnish\ *adj* [¹*drone* + *-ish*] **:** like a drone **:** INDOLENT, SLOW
dronk·grass \'dräŋk+,-\ *n* [Afrik *dronkgras*, lit., intoxication grass, fr. *dronk-* intoxication (fr. *dronken* drunk, fr. MD) + *gras* grass; akin to OHG *gras* — more at DRUNK, GRASS] **:** a southern African grass (*Melica decumbens*) the eating of which causes cattle to become semidelirious
drony \'drōnē\ *adj, usu* -ER/-EST [¹*drone* + *-y*] **1 :** like a drone **:** SLUGGISH, LAZY **2 :** characterized by or producing a drone ⟨the drowsy ~ hum of bees⟩
drook \'drük\ *var of* DROUK
¹drool \'drül\ *vb* -ED/-ING/-S [perh. alter. of *drivel*] *vi* **1 a :** to secrete saliva in anticipation of food **:** water at the mouth ⟨three hungry men . . . ~*ed* at the thought of fresh chops —G.G.Carter⟩ **b :** to let saliva or some other substance flow from the mouth **:** SLAVER ⟨most babies begin to ~ at about four months —Louise Zabriskie⟩ **2 :** to make a profuse display of pleasure or delight **:** show enthusiasm ⟨a work for the ages, one that nature-lovers have ~*ed* over since 1925 —Alfred Stefferud⟩ **3 :** to talk nonsense **:** speak in a pointless manner **:** DRIVEL ⟨I won't keep on ~*ing* on this same old subject —E.A. Robinson⟩; *esp* **:** to fill up allotted time on a radio or television program with improvised and trivial talk or activity **~** *vt* **1 :** to let (saliva or some other substance) flow from the mouth ⟨~*ed* his food and displayed other senile traits⟩ **2 :** to utter or phrase unctuously or sentimentally ⟨political candidates ~*ing* reform measures and promises of a Utopian way of life⟩ **:** perform with cloying sentimentality ⟨every movie pianist ~*ed* out its saccharine phrases —Irving Lowens⟩

²drool \"\ *n* -s **1 :** saliva flowing from the mouth **2 :** NONSENSE, DRIVEL
drooly \-lē,-li\ *adj* -ER/-EST **:** that drools **:** tending to drool ⟨~ infants⟩
droon \'drün\ *Scot var of* DROWN
¹droop \'drüp\ *vb* -ED/-ING/-S [ME *drupen, droupen*, fr. ON *drūpa;* akin to OE *dropian* to drip, MLG *drūpen* to drip, ON *drjūpa* — more at DROP] *vi* **1 :** to have or assume a slouched or bent posture (as from exhaustion or grief) **:** hang, bend, or incline downward ⟨a tree that ~*s* gracefully as if inviting to its shade —H.A.Overstreet⟩ ⟨his heavy eyelids ~*ed* —Kenneth Roberts⟩ **2 :** to fall, sink, or go down ⟨~*s* the soaring youth with slackened wing —S.T.Coleridge⟩ ⟨as night drew near the crimson sun ~*ed* slowly in the west⟩ **3 a :** to become depressed **:** decline in spirit or courage ⟨let not your spirits ~ too low when the decision is adverse —B.N. Cardozo⟩ **b** (1) **:** to lack strength or energy **:** pine away **:** LANGUISH ⟨who ~*s* far off on a sick bed —S.T.Coleridge⟩ (2) **:** to show signs of exhaustion **:** FLAG ⟨her thoughts ~*ed* with fatigue —Ellen Glasgow⟩ **~** *vt* **:** to let droop or sink ⟨the bird ~*ed* his wings⟩
syn WILT, FLAG, SAG: DROOP may indicate either a literal or a figurative hanging or bending downward through exhaustion after a period of thriving or flourishing ⟨he shrank, *drooped*, sank heavily into his chair, and once more his face folded into its lines of despair —G.W.Brace⟩ ⟨"He knows it", the trainer said to himself with a *drooping* of the heart —Donn Byrne⟩ WILT often applies to the loss of freshness and firmness of flowers and leaf or stalk vegetables deprived of water; it is often used of enervation, discouragement, and loss of spirit, force, and resolution ⟨flowers *wilting* in the sun⟩ ⟨I fear it's a feeble and sickly patriotism that *wilts* before such dreadful hardships —Kenneth Roberts⟩ FLAG indicates a dwindling into forcelessness or vacuity of interest or energy ⟨for a couple of hours he wrote with energy, and then his energy *flagged* —H.G. Wells⟩ ⟨these devices succeed, every time, in stimulating our interest afresh just at the moment when it was about to *flag* —T.S.Eliot⟩ ⟨to keep him up to his duties when he showed signs of *flagging*, he was made much of by his superiors and told what a fine fellow he was —Rudyard Kipling⟩ SAG may indicate a sinking out of line at one point; more figuratively it indicates a drooping or decline accompanying loss of strength, determination, spirit, resiliency, or power ⟨the *sagging* floor of the old house⟩ ⟨in places the rail level may *sag* out of true —O.S.Nock⟩ ⟨his heart *sagged* with disappointment —Van Wyck Mason⟩ ⟨stared out of the window, his face *sagging* once more —Gertrude Atherton⟩
²droop \"\ *n* -s **1 :** downward deflection ⟨the ~ of a gun⟩ **:** the condition or appearance of drooping ⟨her figure had a listless ~ —A.J.Cronin⟩ **2 :** a downward drift in the value of a variable quantity or in the indication of a measuring instrument
drooped ailerons *n pl* **:** hinged trailing-edge flag-type ailerons so rigged that both right and left ailerons have a positive downward deflection of 10 to 15 degrees with the control column in the neutral position
drooping *adj* **1 :** inclining downward **2 :** NODDING — used specif. of inflorescence — **droop·ing·ly** *adv* — **droop·ing·ness** *n* -ES
droopy \-pē,-pi\ *adj* -ER/-EST [ME *drupy*, fr. *drupen* to droop + *-y* — more at DROOP] **1 :** drooping or tending to droop ⟨a bent posture or a ~ position while at work —Morris Fishbein⟩ **2 :** GLOOMY, DEJECTED ⟨looking ~ and miserable⟩
¹drop \'dräp\ *n* -s *often attrib* [ME *drope, drop*, fr. OE *dropa;* akin to OS *dropo* drop, OHG *tropfo, troffo*, ON *dropi*, OIr *drucht* drop, OE *drēopan* to drip, OS *driopan*, OHG *triofan*, ON *drjūpa* to drip, Goth *driusan* to fall — more at DREARY] **1 a** (1) **:** the quantity of fluid which falls in one spherical or spheroidal mass **:** a liquid globule (2) **drops** *pl* **:** a medicine the dose of which is measured by drops; *specif* **:** a solution (as of atropine) for dilating the pupil of the eye **b** (1) **:** a minute quantity or degree of something nonmaterial or intangible ⟨wrings the last ~ of meaning from the word⟩ ⟨has not a ~ of kindness in him⟩ (2) *obs* **:** an old Scottish unit of weight equal to ¹⁄₁₆ oz. (3) **:** a small quantity or portion of drink esp. of an alcoholic beverage ⟨obviously had had a ~ too much⟩ (4) **:** the smallest practical unit of liquid measure varying in size according to the specific gravity and viscosity of the liquid and to the conditions under which the drop is formed — compare MINIM (5) **:** a minute quantity of some nonliquid substance ⟨a mere ~ of animated jelly —*Encyc. Americana*⟩ **c :** something that hangs like or resembles a liquid drop: as (1) **:** a pendent jewel or ornament attached to a piece of jewelry or jeweled decoration; *also* **:** an earring with such a pendant (2) **:** GUTTA (3) **:** PENDANT 2a (3) (4) **:** a small candy approximately globular in form ⟨chocolate ~*s*⟩ (5) **:** a small pear-shaped figure occas. borne as a heraldic charge but more often borne bestrewed in an indefinite number over the field — called also *goutte;* see GUTTÉE **2** [²*drop*] **a** (1) **:** the act or an instance of dropping **:** a fall or descent in space ⟨the slow ~ of idle tears⟩ (2) **:** a decline in quantity ⟨a relatively mild ~ in farm prices⟩ or quality ⟨his reputation took a sudden ~⟩ (3) **:** a curve in which a baseball breaks down and usu. away from a right-handed batter (4) [by shortening] **:** DROPKICK (5) **:** the act of giving birth to young; *also* **:** the young so born ⟨the entire ~ of lambs for the year⟩ (6) **:** a descent by parachute; *also* **:** the men or equipment dropped by parachute — compare AIRDROP (7) **:** a central point or depository to which something is brought for distribution or transmission; *specif, slang* **:** a place used for the deposit and distribution of stolen goods **b** (1) **:** the distance from a higher to a lower level ⟨a ~ of 2000 feet from mountain to sea⟩ **:** the distance through which something drops ⟨made a ~ of 15 feet⟩ **:** a slope or incline often steep or precipitous ⟨a steep ~ of 300 feet on the mountain face⟩ (2) **:** the depth of a course measured at mid-spread from headrope to foot — compare HOIST (3) **:** the fall in pressure of the steam in a compound steam engine between the high-pressure cylinder and the receiver, or between receiver and low-pressure cylinder (4) **:** a fall of electric potential due to resistance of the circuit or other causes (5) **:** the distance of the axis of a shaft in a mechanical device below the base of a hanger (6) **:** the space through which an unrestrained escape wheel moves while disengaged from the pallets (7) **:** the distance of the comb of the butt of a rifle or shotgun below the line of the top of the barrel (8) *music* **:** a fall or reduction in pitch ⟨the octave ~*s* are conspicuous⟩ **c :** a slot or other opening into which something is to be dropped ⟨mail ~⟩; *also* **:** the receptacle into which the dropped object falls **3** [²*drop*] **:** something that drops, hangs, or falls: as **a :** a movable plate serving to cover the keyhole of a lock **b :** an unframed piece of cloth scenery in a theater; *also* **:** DROP CURTAIN **c :** a hinged platform or trapdoor on a gallows on which a condemned person stands; *also* **:** the gallows itself **d :** an immature usu. unfertilized or diseased fallen fruit; *also* **:** a fallen but normal ripe fruit ⟨a peach ~⟩ **e :** a drop hammer or punch press **f :** a shutter in an electric annunciator that drops when the circuit is closed **g :** the group of wires used to extend a power circuit or telephone circuit from a pole to a building ⟨a telephone ~⟩ **h :** a structure built in an open drainage channel having excess grade that permits the water to go abruptly from one level to a lower level without injury to the channel **4 :** a destructive wilt and stem rot of various garden vegetables (as lettuce) caused by a fungus (*Sclerotinia sclerotiorum*) or a closely related fungus **5 :** the advantage of having an opponent covered with a firearm; *also* **:** any kind of advantage or superiority over an opponent — usu. used in the phrase *get the drop on* ⟨kept my eyes open for fear he'd get the ~ on me⟩ or *have the drop on* ⟨the nation enjoying industrial supremacy has the ~ on all the others⟩ — **at the drop of a hat :** as soon as the slightest occasion is given **:** readily or promptly ⟨he would blush *at the drop of a hat*⟩ — **drop in the bucket :** a part so small as to be negligible
²drop \"\ *vb* **dropped** *or archaic* **dropt; dropped** *or archaic* **dropt; dropping; drops** [ME *droppen*, fr. OE *dropian;* akin to OE *drēopan* to drip — more at ¹DROP] *vi* **1 a :** to fall in drops ⟨a gentle rain *dropped*⟩ **b** *archaic* **:** to let drops fall **:** be so wet that moisture falls in drops ⟨~ with sweat and blood⟩ **c** *of an animal* **:** DEFECATE **2 a** (1) **:** to fall in any

manner ⟨the book *dropped* from his hand⟩ ⟨tunes . . . *dropped* into my mind unbidden —Noel Coward⟩ (2) **:** to descend from one line or level to another ⟨the river ~*s* some 850 feet to virtually sea level —Tom Marvel⟩ **:** incline downward ⟨the road ~*s* into the valley⟩ **b** (1) **:** to fall or sink to the ground ⟨under that withering fire men *dropped* like flies⟩ ⟨*dropped* dead from a heart attack⟩ **:** fall in a state of collapse (as from exhaustion) ⟨so tired she felt she would ~⟩ (2) **:** DIE — sometimes used with *off* ⟨*dropped* off peacefully in his sleep⟩ (3) **:** to let oneself down ⟨she *dropped* gratefully into the chair⟩ **:** let oneself fall ⟨*dropped* safely from a third-story window⟩ (4) **:** to alight or descend from a vehicle — used with *off* ⟨*dropped* off at the square and changed to a suburban bus⟩ (5) *of a card* **:** to become played by reason of the obligation to follow suit ⟨the king *dropped* under the ace⟩ ⟨all the trumps *dropped*⟩ (6) **:** to withdraw from participation in a poker pot by discarding one's hand or announcing refusal to call the preceding bet — often used with *out* **c** (1) **:** to move (as down a river) with a favoring wind or current — usu. used with *down* ⟨we *dropped* down the harbor and were soon steering south⟩ (2) **:** RETREAT, WITHDRAW — usu. used with *back* ⟨order the troops to ~ back⟩ (3) **:** to fail to maintain a proper or desired pace — usu. used with *behind* ⟨*dropped* behind in his work⟩ **d** *of a dog* **:** CROUCH **3 :** STOP *vi* 4d — used with *around, by, in, over, up* ⟨an old friend just *dropped* in⟩ **4 :** to enter as if without conscious effort of will into some state, condition, or activity ⟨*dropped* into a troubled sleep —Margaret A. Barnes⟩ ⟨*dropped* into reminiscence about old military campaigns⟩ **5 a :** to come to an end **:** cease to be of concern **:** CEASE, LAPSE ⟨resolved to let the matter ~⟩ **:** VANISH, DISAPPEAR **b** (1) **:** to become less, diminish, or decline in any way (as in force, degree, level, amount) ⟨world production of bauxite *dropped*⟩ ⟨her voice *dropped*⟩ — often used with *off* ⟨business ~*s* off in the stores⟩ (2) **:** FALL *vi* 3b(4) **c :** to withdraw from participation or membership **:** QUIT, LEAVE **:** pass or become lost (as from view or notice) ⟨one man *dropped* from the group⟩ — often used with *out* ⟨forced to ~ out of amateur athletics —Gilbert Millstein⟩ **~** *vt* **1 a :** to let fall or cause to fall in any way ⟨stumbled and *dropped* the vase⟩ ⟨pulled a lever and *dropped* the missile⟩ ⟨a few species of trees ~ their leaves in the dry season —P.E.James⟩ ⟨*dropped* anchor in a spacious harbor⟩ **b** (1) **:** to lower or cause to descend from one line or level to another ⟨the dress would look better if you ~ the hem two inches⟩ ⟨*dropped* the water level eight or nine feet⟩ (2) **:** to lower (wheels) in preparation for landing an airplane (3) **:** to cause to lessen or decrease ⟨*dropped* his speed by three knots⟩ **:** reduce in quality or degree (4) **:** to set down from a ship or vehicle ⟨asked him to ~ me at the hotel⟩ **:** UNLOAD, DEPOSIT ⟨*dropping* groceries and beer casks at the port of Louth —C.E.W.Bean⟩ ⟨new hotels to care for the 150 passengers that each jet will ~ at the big airports —P.J.C. Friedlander⟩; *also* **:** AIR-DROP (5) **:** to unhitch and drive away from (a trailer or trailing implement) ⟨~ the harrow before driving onto the highway⟩ (6) **:** to cause (the voice) to be less loud ⟨*dropped* his voice as he saw strangers approaching⟩ ⟨we ~ our voice at the end of a sentence⟩ **c :** CURTSY ⟨she learned . . . to ~ a graceful curtsy —Max Peacock⟩ **d** (1) **:** to bring down with a shot ⟨leaden slugs *dropped* his Indians as they worked —Julian Dana⟩; *also* **:** to knock down (as in boxing) **:** FLOOR ⟨as he had *dropped* the great champion —Donn Byrne⟩ (2) **:** to force another player to play (a high card) by leading a card to which he must follow suit ⟨he led the ace and *dropped* the king⟩ (3) *sports* **:** to cause (a ball) to fall into a hole or basket ⟨*dropped* a 3-foot putt⟩ ⟨raced down the floor to ~ a shot⟩ **2 a :** to pour or let fall in drops ⟨~ a tear⟩ **b** *archaic* **:** to cover with drops **:** BESPRINKLE ⟨their waved coats *dropped* with gold —John Milton⟩ **3 a :** to abandon or give up (as an activity, idea, or concern) **:** cease to hold, use, or concern oneself with ⟨advised him to ~ the matter⟩ ⟨permission to ~ the course⟩ **:** leave incomplete ⟨~ a sentence in the middle⟩ **:** not take into account ⟨~ the four poorest years in computing the average⟩ **b :** to break off an association or connection (as friendship, employment) with ⟨~ a failing student⟩ ⟨his clubs *dropped* him⟩ **:** DISMISS ⟨a number of stations and sponsors *dropped* him —Gilbert Seldes⟩ **c** (1) **:** to leave behind (as in sailing) **:** LEAVE ⟨that day they *dropped* the last of the islands⟩ (2) **:** to take leave of or dismiss (as a pilot or escort) after a mission is accomplished ⟨the submarine zone left behind, the convoy *dropped* her destroyer escorts⟩ **d :** to use a variant pronunciation that is less accurately represented by (a letter present in the standard orthography, esp. *g, h,* or *r*) than is another variant pronunciation: as (1) **:** to omit the sound of (as *r* in \wȯ\ instead of \wȯr\ for *war* or *h* in \yüj\ instead of \hyüj\ for *huge*) (2) **:** to substitute another sound for (as *r* in \wȯə\ instead of \wȯr\ for *war* or *ng* for \n\ instead of \ŋ\ in *going*) (3) **:** to omit and compensate for (as *r* in \fäːm\ instead of \färm\ for *farm*, with compensatory lengthening of \ä\) **e :** to leave off (an ending) in inflecting a word ⟨a tendency to ~ the *-ly* of certain adverbs⟩ **f :** to leave out (as a letter, line, or paragraph) in writing ⟨~ a whole line in copying⟩ **4 a :** to utter or mention in a casual or offhand way ⟨a foreman ~*s* a suggestion⟩ or with pretended casualness ⟨obtained his release by *dropping* a word in the right quarter⟩ **b :** to send (as a letter or postcard) by mail — often used in the phrase *drop a line* ⟨expected he would ~ me a line by now⟩ **5** *of an animal* **:** to give birth to ⟨lambs *dropped* in June⟩ **6 :** to lose (money or a contest) ⟨he was *dropping* money every day at the track —Ernest Hemingway⟩ ⟨the team *dropped* five straight games⟩ **:** SPEND ⟨*dropped* $200 on her new spring outfit⟩ **7 :** SINK *vt* 13 **8 :** to draw from an external point (as from a point to a line or plane) ⟨~ a perpendicular⟩ **syn** see DISMISS, FALL — **drop a brick** *slang* **:** to do or say something indiscreet **:** make a blunder — **drop into :** to pitch into **:** SCOLD, REPROVE — **drop one's lines :** to forget or misquote one's lines in a play or other theatrical performance ⟨a state of confusion before curtain time caused the actor to *drop his lines*⟩

drop arch *n* **:** a two-centered blunt pointed arch drawn from centers within the span

drop ball *n* **:** a method of putting a soccer ball in play by dropping it between two players after a temporary suspension or when a free kick is not called for

drop band *also* **drop bunch** *n, West* **:** a group of ewes about ready to lamb

drop bar *n* **1 :** a bar or roller that guides a sheet into a printing press or folding machine — called also *drop roller* **2 :** any of the vertical bars in a suspension bridge connecting the roadway and the chain or cable

drop batter *n* **:** batter of such consistency as to drop from a bowl or spoon without running usu. made in a proportion of two parts flour to one part liquid — compare POUR BATTER

drop black *n* **:** any of several black pigments sometimes in the form of drops or pellets: as **a :** FRANKFORT BLACK **b :** bone black esp. when reclaimed after use as a decolorizing agent

drop bolt *n* **1 :** a bolt designed to drop into a socket **2 :** a bolt whose withdrawal releases the drop of a gallows

drop bottom *n* **:** a bottom opening downward ⟨a railroad freight car with a *drop bottom*⟩

drop-bottom bucket *n* **:** a bucket with a bottom that can be opened and used esp. in excavating earth and in placing concrete under water

drop bow *or* **drop compass** *n* **:** a bow compass that permits the center leg to remain stationary while the pen or pencil rotates around the center shaft and that is used esp. for drawing small circles

drop box *n* **:** a box on a loom containing two or more shuttles with filling yarns of different colors or types that can be brought into action as required by the weaving pattern

drop chalk *n* **:** PREPARED CHALK

drop cloth *n* **:** a sheet of cloth or paper used esp. by house painters and laid over floors, furniture, and fixtures to protect them during painting or decorating

drop cord *n* **:** an electric-light cord used to suspend a lamp usu. from an overhead outlet

drop crop *n* **:** PENDULOUS CROP

drop curtain *n* **:** a stage curtain that is lowered instead of drawn

drop ear *n* **:** BUTTON EAR — **drop-eared** \ˈ=ˌ=\ *adj*

drop elbow *n* **:** an elbow made with ears or lugs for attachment to a wall and used for joining pipes

drop fence *n* **:** a fence on one side of which the ground is lower than on the other side

drop flare *n* **:** a flare capable of being dropped from an airplane to illumine an area or target

drop fly *n* **:** DROPPER 1a

drop folio *n* **:** a page number at the bottom of a page

drop-forge \ˈ=ˌ=\ *vt* **:** to forge between dies by a drop hammer or punch press — **drop forger** *n*

drop forging *n* **:** a forging made by the force of a dropped weight (as in a drop hammer)

drop frame *n* **:** a machine for stamping sheets of candy and cutting them into pieces or figures

drop-frame \ˈ=ˌ=\ *adj* **:** having most or all of the floor at an unusually low level — used esp. of the chassis of a motor truck or a trailer

drop front *n* **:** a hinged cover on the front of a desk or secretary that may be lowered to form a writing table — **drop-front** \ˈ=ˌ=\ *adj*

drop front

drop glass *n* **:** DROPPER, PIPETTE

drop goal *var of* DROPPED GOAL

drop hammer *n* **1 :** a power hammer (as for forging or striking metal) that is raised and then released to drop on the metal resting on an anvil or die **2 :** PILE HAMMER — **drop hammerman** *n*

drop handle *n* **:** a pendent handle; *specif* **:** a door handle or drawer pull that hangs like a pendant when not in use

drop hanger *n* **:** an adjustable frame for attaching a shaft bearing to the ceiling; *also* **:** the frame and bearing combined

¹drophead \ˈ=ˌ=\ *n* **1 :** a device for a desk or table that enables an attached typewriter or sewing machine to be swung or dropped down to leave a flat table top **2** [²*drophead*] *Brit* **:** a convertible automobile

²drophead \ˈ"\ *adj, Brit, of an automobile* **:** CONVERTIBLE

drop head *n* **:** a newspaper headline that accompanies but is subordinate to a banner head **:** DROPLINE

drop initial *n* **:** DROP LETTER 3

drop keel *n, Brit* **:** CENTERBOARD

dropkick \ˈ=ˌ=\ *n* **1 :** a kick made by dropping a football to the ground and kicking it at the moment it starts to rebound **2 :** an attempt to floor a wrestling opponent by diving at him feetfirst

drop-kick \ˈ=ˌ=\ *vb* [*dropkick*] *vi* **:** to make a dropkick **~** *vt* **:** to score (a goal) with a dropkick — **dropkicker** \ˈ=ˌ==\ *n*

drop kip *n* **:** a kip on the high or parallel bars in which the leg kick is executed as the body swings backward

drop leaf *n* **:** a table leaf hinged to the side or end of a table and folded down when not in use

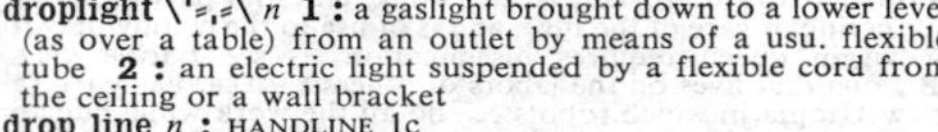

drop leaf

drop·let \ˈdräplət\ *n* **-s :** a tiny drop (as of water)

droplet infection *n* **:** infection by means of contact with airborne droplets of sputum containing infectious organisms

drop letter *n* **1 :** a letter mailed at a post office not having carrier service and addressed locally to someone who is to call for it at the same office **2** *Canad* **:** a letter mailed at or in the delivery area of the same post office from which it will be delivered **3 :** an initial letter (as at the beginning of a chapter in a book) that extends downward to a depth of two or more text lines

droplight \ˈ=ˌ=\ *n* **1 :** a gaslight brought down to a lower level (as over a table) from an outlet by means of a usu. flexible tube **2 :** an electric light suspended by a flexible cord from the ceiling or a wall bracket

drop line *n* **:** HANDLINE 1c

dropline \ˈ=ˌ=\ *n* **:** a newspaper headline employing lines of equal length with each lower line indented a consistent number of spaces more than the line above

drop lock *n* **:** the spot on the locking surface of a timepiece pallet upon which the escape tooth first makes contact after drop

drop manhole *n* **:** a shaft in which sewage is dropped from a higher to a lower level

drop off *vi* **:** to fall asleep

drop-off \ˈ=ˌ=\ *n* **-s** [fr. *drop off,* v.] **:** a very steep or perpendicular drop or descent ⟨shoals here at the *drop-off* are referred to as the outer reefs —P.A.Zahl⟩ ⟨a climb of many short turns and dizzy *drop-offs* —C.F.Saunders⟩

drop out *vi* **:** to make a dropout in rugby football **~** *vt* **:** to mask or etch away (the highlight dots of a halftone negative or plate) in order to increase the highlights

dropout \ˈ=ˌ=\ *n* **-s** [*drop out*] **1 :** a dropkick in rugby football made from within a defending player's 25-yard line after the ball has crossed a touch-in-goal line or has been touched down **2 a :** one who drops out before achieving his goal (as from school or a program of training) **b :** the act or an instance of dropping out **3 a :** a halftone having a dropped-out area; *also* **:** a print made from it — called also *highlight halftone* **b :** the dropped-out area of a dropout

drop-out voltage *n* **:** the voltage at which the contacts of an electromagnetic cutout open under normal conditions

drop·pa·ble \ˈdräpəbəl\ *adj* **:** capable of being dropped ⟨early hydrogen devices . . . became ~ bombs —*Time*⟩

drop·page \-pij\ *n* **-s 1 :** a portion of a quantity of material that is dropped in the process of its use or application (as of mortar while laying brick) **2 :** a portion of a fruit crop that falls from the tree before it is ready for picking ⟨warm weather, which caused much tree ~ —*Wall Street Jour.*⟩

dropped *past of* DROP

dropped egg *n* **:** POACHED EGG

dropped goal *also* **drop goal** *n* **:** a goal scored in rugby by a dropkick that is not a free kick or penalty kick and that counts 3 points or formerly 4 points

dropped seat *n* **:** a chair seat made slightly concave in the center

dropped shoulder *n* **:** the shoulder line of a garment extended beyond the top of the upper arm

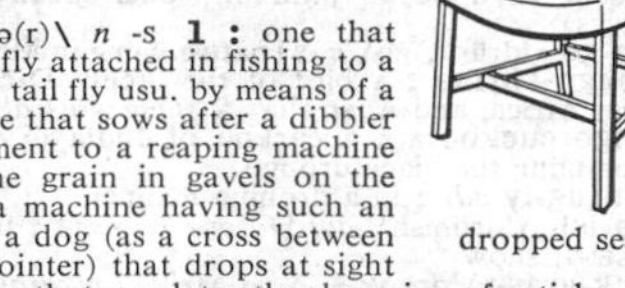

dropped seat

drop·per \ˈdräpə(r)\ *n* **-s 1 :** one that drops: as **a :** a fly attached in fishing to a leader above the tail fly usu. by means of a snell **b** (1) **:** one that sows after a dibbler (2) **:** an attachment to a reaping machine for dropping the grain in gavels on the ground; *also* **:** a machine having such an attachment **c :** a dog (as a cross between a setter and a pointer) that drops at sight of game **d :** one that regulates the dropping of articles into receptacles in the process of manufacture **e :** a heavy vertical wire on the horizontal wires of a fence to maintain the vertical spacing **2 :** a branch vein in a mine which drops off from or leaves the main lode on the footwall side **3 :** a vegetative shoot that grows downward and develops a new bulb at its apex in certain bulbous plants (as the tulip) **4 a :** a short glass tube with one end constricted and the other fitted with a small rubber bulb used to measure liquids by drops — called also *eyedropper, medicine dropper* **b :** a similar tube having the external diameter of the outlet three millimeters and adjustable to deliver at 15°C 20 drops of distilled water weighing one gram — called also *normal dropper, standard dropper* **5 :** a mechanical attachment on a loom or warper for stopping the machine when a warp yarn breaks — called also *drop wire* **6 :** a worker who runs cars down the inclined haulageways of a mine by riding or pushing or lowering by cable — called also *car dropper, load dropper* **7** *Africa* **:** a fence post

dropper fly *n* **:** DROPPER 1a

dropping *n* **-s** [ME, fr. gerund of *droppen* to drop — more at DROP] **1 :** something dropped ⟨the ground was littered with ~*s* from the trees⟩ ⟨~*s* from a candle⟩ ⟨gulls screaming and diving after the galley ~*s* at the stern —Katherine Mansfield⟩ **2 :** the dung of animals — now usu. used in pl. **3 droppings** *pl* **:** wool or other fiber cast off from the different cylinders in carding **:** ²FLY 7d **4 :** LETTING-OUT

dropping angle *n* **:** RANGE ANGLE

dropping board *also* **droppings board** *n* **:** a surface directly under the roost in a poultry house on which droppings accumulate

dropping bottle *n* **1 :** a small pitcher-shaped bottle with a curved or tapered neck used to supply liquids in small amounts (as to test tubes) — compare BURETTE **2 a :** a small bottle with a grooved glass stopper and neck permitting the contents to be poured out in drops **b :** a bottle furnished with a dropper or a glass rod applicator

dropping fire *n* **:** a continuous desultory discharge of firearms

dropping ground *n* **:** DROP ZONE

drop·ping·ly *adv* [ME, fr. *dropping* (pres. part. of *droppen* to drop) + *-ly* — more at DROP] **:** in the manner of something that drops **:** drop by drop **:** in drops

dropping plate *n* **:** an attachment to a hill planter (as for corn or cotton) regulating the dropping of seeds at intervals

dropping system *n* **:** a brewing process in which wort having passed through the first stage of fermentation is dropped or run down into a lower vessel for skimming off the yeast

drop pit *n* **:** a pit built crosswise of the tracks in an engine-house; *esp* **:** one designed to give access for removing the wheels of a locomotive

drop pod *n* **:** a detachable part (as a fuel tank) of an airplane designed to be dropped in flight

drop press *n* **1 :** PUNCH PRESS **2 :** DROP HAMMER

drop roller *n* **1 :** DROP BAR 1 **2 :** a printing-press roller that drops at intervals to carry ink to the distributing table and rollers — called also *ductor*

drops *pl of* DROP, *pres 3d sing of* DROP

drop scene *n* **:** a drop curtain on which a scene is painted

drop scone *n, Brit* **:** GRIDDLE CAKE

drop seat *n* **1 :** a hinged seat (as in a vehicle) that may be dropped down **2 :** a seat (as in an undergarment) that falls down when unbuttoned

dropseed \ˈ=ˌ=\ *n* **:** a grass of the genus *Sporobolus*

drop shipment *n* **:** a shipment of goods made by a manufacturer directly to a retailer and not by the wholesaler who made the sale

drop shipper *n* **:** a wholesaler who deals in drop shipments — called also *desk jobber*

drop shot *n* **1 :** a delicately hit ball or shuttlecock that drops quickly after crossing the net or dies after hitting the front wall — used in racket games (as tennis, rackets, badminton) **2 :** shot made by dropping molten shot metal from a height

drop shutter *n* **:** an early form of camera shutter consisting of a plate which when released falls vertically and carries an aperture in its center past the opening of the lens

drop·si·cal \ˈdräpsəkəl, -sēk-\ *adj* [*dropsy* + *-ical*] **1 :** of, relating to, characterized by, or affected with dropsy **2 :** PUFFY, SWOLLEN ⟨her pretty face became ~ and red —Jean Stafford⟩ **:** excessively large **:** INFLATED, TURGID ⟨cast-off clothes that gave Sam a ~ look —Dixon Wecter⟩ — **drop·si·cal·ly** \-sək(ə)lē, -sēk-, -li\ *adv* — **drop·si·cal·ness** \-kəlnəs\ *n* **-ES**

drop siding *n* **:** building siding with a tongue-and-groove edge joint or a rabbeted or shiplap joint — called also *matched siding, novelty siding*

drop·sied \ˈdräpsēd, -sid\ *adj* [*dropsy* + *-ed*] **:** DROPSICAL

drop·sonde \ˈdräpˌsänd\ *n* **-s** [*drop* + *radiosonde*] **:** a radiosonde dropped by parachute from a high-flying airplane to obtain pressure, temperature, and moisture measurements of the air below

drop stitch *n* **:** a pattern in machine knitting made by disengaging certain needles at regular intervals

dropstone *n* [¹*drop* + *stone*] *obs* **:** a stalactite or stalagmite

drop strake *n* **:** a strake that terminates toward the stem or stern of a ship because of the hull's decreasing girth

drop·sy \ˈdräpsē, -si\ *n* **-ES** [ME *dropesie*, short for *ydropesie*, fr. OF *idropisie, ydropesie*, fr. L *hydropisis*, modif. of Gk *hydrōps*, fr. *hydōr* water — more at WATER] **1 :** EDEMA 1; *specif* **:** ANASARCA **2 :** EDEMA 2

dropsy plant *also* **dropsywort** \ˈ==ˌ=\ *n* [so called fr. its being reputed to cure dropsy] **:** LEMON BALM

dropt *archaic past of* DROP

drop table *n* **:** a hinged tabletop that folds against a wall when not in use

drop-tank \ˈ=ˌ=\ *n* **:** an auxiliary gas tank for airplanes that is usu. attached to the underside of the wing and can be jettisoned when empty

drop test *n* **:** an instance of drop-testing

drop-test \ˈ=ˌ=\ *vt* [*drop test*] **:** to test by dropping under trial conditions ⟨*drop-testing* parachutes with dummies⟩

drop the handkerchief *n* **:** a game in which one player runs behind the other players as they stand in a circle and drops a handkerchief behind one of them who then must pick up the handkerchief and run around the circle after the first player and try to tag, catch, or kiss him before he gets to the vacant place in the circle left by the second player

drop weight *n* **:** the weight of a drop of a liquid falling from a given opening used as a measure of the surface tension

drop window *n* **:** a window usu. double hung and with a single sash that is opened by lowering it into a concealed pocket or slot

drop wire *n* **:** DROPPER 5

dropwise \ˈ=ˌ=\ *adv* [¹*drop* + *-wise*] **:** drop by drop ⟨add a 5 percent solution of the chemical ~⟩

dropwort \ˈ=ˌ=\ *n* [¹*drop* + *wort*] **1 :** a Eurasian herb (*Filipendula hexapetala*) with pinnate incised leaves and panicles of white or reddish flowers **2 :** a plant of the genus *Oenanthe* — usu. used with an attributive ⟨hemlock ~⟩

drop zone *n* **:** the area on which troops, supplies, or equipment are to be air-dropped

dros·era \ˈdräsərə\ *n* [NL, fr. Gk, fem. of *droseros* dewy, watery, fr. *drosos* dew, water] **1** *cap* **:** the type genus of Droseraceae comprising numerous low perennial or biennial bog-inhabiting insectivorous plants generally with leaves in a basal tuft and flowers in a one-sided racemose inflorescence on a naked scape — see SUNDEW **2 -s a :** any plant of the genus *Drosera* **b :** the air-dried flowering plant of either of two droseras (*D. rotundifolia* and *D. longifolia*) formerly used in the medication of chest disorders

dros·er·a·ce·ae \ˌdräsəˈrāsēˌē\ *n pl, cap* [NL, fr. *Drosera*, type genus + *-aceae*] **:** a small family of insectivorous plants (order Sarraceniales) comprising the sundews and having flat to filiform circinate leaves with the blade covered by long glandular hairs — see DROSERA — **dros·er·a·ceous** \ˌdräsəˈrāshəs\ *adj*

drosh·ky \ˈdräshkē, -ki\ *also* **dros·ky** \-sk-\ *n* **-ES** [Russ *drozhki*, fr. *droga* pole of a wagon; akin to OE *dragan* to draw — more at DRAW] **:** a low 4-wheeled open carriage used esp. in Russia and consisting of a long bench on which the passengers ride sideways or astride as on a saddle with their feet on bars near the ground; *also* **:** any of various 2-wheeled or 4-wheeled public carriages used in Russia and other countries

dro·som·e·ter \drōˈsäməd·ə(r)\ *n* [F *drosomètre*, fr. Gk *drosos* dew + F *-mètre* -meter] **:** an instrument for measuring the weight of dew deposited on a body

dro·soph·i·la \drōˈsäfələ\ *n* [NL, fr. Gk *drosos* + NL *-phila*] **1** *cap* **:** a genus (the type of the family Drosophilidae) of small two-winged flies that have been used extensively in breeding experiments to study basic mechanisms of inheritance **2 -s :** any fly of the genus *Drosophila* (as fruit fly)

dro·soph·i·list \-ləst\ *n* **-s** [NL *Drosophila* + E *-ist*] **:** one who uses the vinegar fly (genus *Drosophila*) in the study of genetics

dros·o·phyl·lum \ˌdräsəˈfiləm\ *n* [NL, fr. Gk *drosos* + NL *-phyllum*] **1** *cap* **:** a genus of insectivorous plants (family Droseraceae) having narrow leaves arranged like those of plants of the genus *Drosera* and yellow flowers with 10 stamens — compare SUNDEW **2** *pl* **drosophyl·la** \-lə\ **:** any plant of the genus *Drosophyllum* — called also *flycatcher*

¹dross \ˈdräs, ˈdrȯs\ *n* **-ES** [ME *dros, drosse*, fr. OE *drōs* filth, dregs, sediment; akin to OE *drōsna, drōsne* filth, dregs, sediment, OHG *truosana* dregs, lees, ON *dregg* dreg — more at DREG] **1 :** the solid scum that forms on the surface of a metal (as lead, antimony) when molten or melting largely as a result of oxidation but sometimes of the rising of dirt and impurities to the surface **2 :** waste or foreign matter mixed with a substance or left as a residue after that substance has been used or processed **:** IMPURITY ⟨every bushel of corn contains a quantity of ~) **3 :** something that is base, gross, or commonplace ⟨the riches of this world are mere ~⟩ **:** the base, unworthy, or trivial part or element in something that is otherwise good or admirable ⟨less ~ in *Hamlet* than in other Shakespeare plays —G.W.Stone⟩

2dross \"\ *vt* -ED/-ING/-ES **1 :** to make dross of (lead) **:** convert into massicot by calcining **2 :** to free from dross

dross·er \-sə(r)\ *n* -S **:** a furnaceman who makes red lead from litharge or who recovers spelter from dross

drossy \-sē,-si\ *adj* -ER/-EST [ME, fr. *dros, drosse* + *-y*] **:** of, relating to, or resembling dross **:** full of dross **:** WORTHLESS ⟨a wise man . . . can gather gold out of the *drossiest* volume —John Milton⟩

drost·dy \drȯ'stā, -ȯs'dā\ *n* -S [Afrik (now *drosdy*), fr. *drost* sheriff (fr. MD *drossāte*, fr. *dros-* retinue + *-sāte* commander) + *-y* (fr. MD *-ie*, fr. OF *-ie* fr. OE *dryht* retinue and to OE *-sæta* commander, OHG *-sazzo*, derivatives fr. the root of E *sit* — more at DRUDGE, SIT] *southern Africa* **1 :** the office or residence of a landdrost **2 :** the jurisdiction of a landdrost

drott-kvaett \'drȯt,kfät\ *n* -S [modif. of ON *drōttkvæthr, drōttkvæthi*, fr. *drōtt* retinue + *-kvæthr, kvæthi* poem, fr. *kvetha* to say, speak, recite — more at QUOTH] **:** an Old Icelandic verse consisting of a stanza of eight regular lines with a complex pattern of internal and terminal rhyme, alliteration, and esp. alternation of consonance with full rhyme at the ends of lines

drought *or* **drouth** \'drau̇|th, |t, *or* +V |d·; *sometimes* -rō|\ *n* -S [ME *drought, drouth*, fr. OE *drūgath, drūgoth*, fr. *drūgian* to dry up, wither, fr. the root of *drȳge* dry — more at DRY] **1** *archaic* **:** the condition or quality of being dry **:** DRYNESS **:** lack of moisture ⟨the ~ of the sun-baked ground⟩ ⟨crickets sing at the oven's mouth . . . the blither for their ~ —Shak.⟩ **2 :** a period of dryness esp. protracted and causing extensive damage to crops or preventing their successful growth **3** *now dial* **:** a thirst usu. for alcoholic drink ⟨there's a great ~ on me, and the night is young —J.M.Synge⟩ **4 a :** a prolonged or chronic shortage or lack of something that is needed or desired ⟨behind the candy scarcity lies the sugar ~ —*Wall Street Jour.*⟩ ⟨suffering from a ~ of intellect and sensitivity⟩

drought·i·ness \-th|ēnəs, -d·|, -t|, -in-\ *n* -ES **:** the quality or state of being droughty **:** lack of rain **:** ARIDITY

drought spot *n* **:** an external physiological disorder of fruits caused by a boron deficiency

droughty *or* **drouthy** \|ē, |i\ *adj* -ER/-EST **1 :** DRY, ARID **:** lacking moisture ⟨the ~ desert —A.D.Carruthers⟩ **2 :** of, relating to, or afflicted by a prolonged drought ⟨we look into a ~ sky —I.R.Tannehill⟩ ⟨over most of the area ~ conditions still prevail⟩ **3 :** THIRSTY

drouk \'drük\ *vt* **drouk·it** *or* **drouk·et** \-kət\ **droukit** *or* **drouket; drouking; drouks** [perh. of Scand origin; akin to ON *drukna* to drown — more at DROWN] *dial Brit* **:** to wet through and through **:** SOAK, DRENCH

1drove \'drōv\ *n* -S [ME, fr. OE *drāf*, fr. *drīfan* to drive — more at DRIVE] **1** *dial Eng* **:** an unimproved road used mainly for driving cattle **2 a :** a crowd or group of people esp. when acting, following, or moving in concert or in a docile manner as if in a herd ⟨they repaid him by voting in ~*s* as he directed —Paul Blanshard⟩ **b :** a large group of animals esp. when moving or being driven in a body ⟨bees . . . flew in ~*s* about her head —Sherwood Anderson⟩; *also* **:** a group of things moving in this manner ⟨icebergs . . . often came in large ~*s* —Valter Schytt⟩ **3 :** a flock or herd of livestock esp. when being driven **4 a** *also* **drove chisel :** a stonecutter's chisel about two inches wide used in forming a grooved surface or a roughly shaped finish in preparation for the finer work to follow — called also *boaster* **b** *also* **drove work :** the grooved surface of stone finished by the drove chisel

2drove \"\ *vb* -ED/-ING/-S [prob. back-formation fr. *drover*] *vi, Brit* **:** to follow the occupation of a drover ⟨he learnt to ride while *droving* on the plains —A.B.Paterson⟩ ~ *vt* **1** *Brit* **:** to drive (as cattle or sheep) to pasture or to market **2** *Brit* **:** to finish (as stone) with a drove

3drove *past & archaic past part of* DRIVE

dro·ver \'drōvə(r)\ *n* -S [ME *drovare*, fr. *drove* + *-are* -er] **1 :** one that drives cattle or sheep to pasture or to market **:** a cattle herder; *specif* **:** a person in charge of taking a large number of cattle to market by rail **2** *archaic* **:** DRIFTER 2b

drove road *or* **drove way** *n* [*1drove*] *chiefly Scot* **:** a public cattle road not kept up for motor traffic

1drow \'drau̇\ *n* -S [origin unknown] *Scot* **:** a cold mist or drizzle

2drow \"\ *n* -S [origin unknown] *Scot* **:** a momentary illness; *esp* **:** a fainting spell

drown \'drau̇n\ *vb* **drowned** \-nd\ *or substand* **drownd·ed** \-ndəd\ **drowned** *or substand* **drownded; drown·ing** \-niŋ\ *or substand* **drownd·ing** \-ndiŋ\ **drowns** \-nz\ *or substand* **drownds** \-n(d)z\ [ME *drunen, drounen*, prob. alter. of *drunknen*, fr. OE *druncnian*; akin to ON *drukna* to drown; inchoatives fr. the root of E *drink* — more at DRINK] *vi* **1 a :** to suffocate in water or some other liquid ⟨fell in the water and ~*ed*⟩ **b :** to suffocate because of excess of body fluid that interferes with the passage of oxygen from the lung to the tissues (as in pulmonary edema) **2** *of things* **:** to sink in water or some other liquid and become submerged ⟨the boat ~*ed* but we were saved⟩ **:** become flooded **:** lie under water impounded by a dam ⟨many towns ~ —A.W.Baum⟩ **3 a :** to become overpowered by or come completely under the influence of something (as an emotion or idea) ⟨~*ing* in bliss—Ellen Glasgow⟩ ⟨~*ing* in self-condemnation —Marcia Davenport⟩ **b :** to swoon or have the senses reel (as under the influence of strong emotion) ⟨stare on beauty till his senses ~ —Edna S. V. Millay⟩ ⟨a passionate, knowing, ~*ing* experience —Irwin Shaw⟩ **c :** to experience extreme difficulty or perplexity ⟨~*ed* in extracurricular paperwork⟩ ⟨~*ing* in the intricacies of calculus⟩ ~ *vt* **1 a :** to suffocate by submersion in water or some other liquid ⟨~*ed* three kittens⟩ ⟨~*ed* himself in the river⟩ **b :** to submerge esp. by a rise of the water level or by a sinking of the land ⟨the river overflowed, ~*ing* whole villages⟩ ⟨a movement of the sea ~*ed* the lower ends of the valleys⟩ **c :** to sink (an object) in water or some other liquid **:** send to the bottom ⟨deeper than ever did plummet sound I'll ~ my book —Shak.⟩ **:** immerse in water ⟨~ the nitrated sheets in water at 40°C⟩ **d :** to wet thoroughly **:** cover with moisture **:** SOAK, DRENCH ⟨a heavy rain, soaking cartridges and ~*ing* powder horns⟩ ⟨~*ed* the fish in a rich sauce⟩ **2 :** to engage (oneself) deeply or strenuously ⟨~*ed* himself in work⟩ — used with *in* **3 :** to cause (a sound) not to be heard by making a loud noise —often used with *out* ⟨a clamor of denials ~*ed* out the landlord —T.B.Costain⟩ **4 a :** to drive out (as a sensation or an idea) **:** EXTINGUISH ⟨the smell of coffee ~*ed* the spruce smell and the sea smell —Willa Cather⟩ ⟨their system tends to ~ initiative —Andrew Buchanan⟩ **:** REPRESS ⟨try to ~ their fundamental instincts —Paul Blanshard⟩ **:** extinguish by merging in something else ⟨~*ed* the main issue in a general debate⟩ **b :** to tower over **:** OVERWHELM **:** reduce to insignificance ⟨a personality that ~*ed* all who stood beside him⟩ **:** STUN, DAZZLE ⟨vistas that ~ the imagination⟩ **c :** to drive from the memory or consciousness — often used in the phrase *drown one's sorrows* ⟨tried to ~ his sorrows in liquor⟩ — **drown the shamrock :** to drink on St. Patrick's day

drownd \'drau̇nd\ *substand var of* DROWN

drown out *vt* **:** to drive (a person or an animal) from home by flooding **:** force (as a mine) to shut down by inundation

1drowse \'drau̇z\ *vb* -ED/-ING/-S [prob. akin to OE *drūsan, drūsian* to sink, become low, inactive, *drēosan* to fall — more at DREARY] *vi* **1 :** to be half asleep **:** fall into a light slumber — often used with *off* ⟨*drowsed* off and awoke with a start⟩ **2 :** to be inactive or present an appearance of peaceful inactivity or isolation ⟨villages *drowsing* in the sun⟩ ~ *vt* **1 :** to make drowsy or inactive ⟨the spells that ~ my soul —S.T. Coleridge⟩ **2 :** to pass (time) drowsily or in drowsing — usu. used with *away* ⟨~ away the afternoon⟩ **syn** see SLEEP

2drowse \"\ *n* -S **:** the act or an instance of drowsing **:** a light slumber **:** DOZE ⟨nudged papa who was just falling into a ~ —J.T.Farrell⟩

drow·si·head \-zē,hed\ *also* **drow·si·hood** \-hu̇d\ *n* [*drowsy* + *-head* or *-hood*] *archaic* **:** DROWSINESS

drows·i·ly \'drau̇zəlē, -li\ *adv* **:** in a drowsy manner

drows·i·ness \-zēnəs, -zin-\ *n* -ES **1 :** the state of being drowsy ⟨an exquisite ~ had spread through him —Stephen Crane⟩ **2** *archaic* **:** LETHARGY, SLOTH

drowsy \-zē, -zi\ *adj* -ER/-EST [*1drowse* + *-y*] **1 a :** ready to fall asleep **:** SLEEPY ⟨made ~ by the long ride⟩ **b :** tending to induce sleep ⟨that ~ undertone with which men talk in the dark —Washington Irving⟩ **c :** INDOLENT, LETHARGIC ⟨his ~ slow-moving mode of life⟩ **2 :** giving the appearance or impression of peaceful inactivity ⟨a ~ village⟩ ⟨~ cornlands and solemn forests —John Buchan⟩

1drub \'drəb\ *vb* **drubbed; drubbed; drubbing; drubs** [perh. fr. Ar *daraba* to beat] *vt* **1 :** to beat severely (as with a cudgel or stick) **:** PUMMEL, THRASH **2 :** to drive as if by cudgeling or pummeling ⟨he *drubbed* those silly notions out of his son's head⟩ ⟨constantly *drubbed* the state legislature for money —*Time*⟩ **3 :** to abuse with words **:** BERATE, CENSURE ⟨the book was *drubbed* by every critic⟩ **4 :** to defeat decisively ⟨*drubbed* her opponent in the tennis match⟩ ⟨*drubbed* in the election by a heavy margin⟩ ~ *vi* **:** STAMP, TAP **:** DRUM, POUND ⟨*drubbing* with their heels —Thomas Hughes⟩ ⟨the blood *drubbed* in his old man's veins —Audrey Barker⟩

2drub \"\ *n, archaic* **:** a heavy blow (as with a cudgel) **:** THUMP

druck·en \'drükən, -rək-\ *chiefly Scot var of* DRUNKEN

1drudge \'drəj\ *vb* -ED/-ING/-S [ME *druggen*; prob. akin to OE *drēogan* to work, perform, endure, Goth *driugan* to do service as a soldier, OE *dryht* retinue, armed followers, OHG *trukt*, ON *drōtt* retinue, Goth *gadraubts* warrior, OSlav *drugŭ* companion, L *firmus* firm — more at FIRM] *vi* **:** to perform hard, menial, or monotonous work ⟨~ all day doing wasteful work badly —Bertrand Russell⟩ ⟨*drudging* over the translation of a Japanese history —K.C.Lamott⟩ ~ *vt* **:** to force to do hard and monotonous work ⟨wouldn't like to have a daughter of mine dragged and *drudged* all her life —Michael McLaverty⟩

2drudge \"\ *n* -S **1 :** one who is obliged to work at hard, unpleasant, or menial tasks **:** SLAVEY ⟨the lodging-house ~ bustled in and out —Oscar Wilde⟩ **2 :** a routine and boring task **:** GRIND ⟨reporters on a daily ~ through the Surrogate's Court —*Time*⟩ **3 :** one whose work is routine and boring; *also* **:** one who through lack of imagination allows his life to become centered around and limited by the physical tasks that he must perform **:** HACK ⟨men of originality and spirit became docile ~*s* —Virginia Woolf⟩

3drudge \"\ *dial var of* DREDGE

drudg·ery \-j(ə)rē, -ri\ *n* -ES **:** dull, fatiguing, and unrelieved work or expenditure of effort **:** work of an irksome or menial nature done through necessity ⟨day-in, day-out ~ —G.S.Perry⟩ ⟨the mechanical and uninspired ~ of a scrivener —Newton Arvin⟩ **syn** see WORK

drudging *adj* **:** marked by drudgery **:** MONOTONOUS, TIRING ⟨the waiting, ~ side of war —William Gilman⟩ ⟨a ~ but indispensable chore —A.C.Spaulding⟩

drudg·ing·ly *adv* **:** in the manner of one that drudges **:** with drudgery

1drug \'drəg\ *n* -S *often attrib* [ME *drogge*, perh. fr. MD *drōge* (*vat*) dry barrel — more at DRY] **1 a** *obs* **:** something used in dyeing or chemical operations **b :** a substance used as a medicine or in making medicines for internal or external use **c** *according to the Food, Drug, & Cosmetic Act* (1) **:** a substance recognized in an official pharmacopoeia or formulary (2) **:** a substance intended for use in the diagnosis, cure, mitigation, treatment, or prevention of disease in man or other animal (3) **:** a substance other than food intended to affect the structure or function of the body of man or other animal (4) **:** a substance intended for use as a component of a medicine but not a device or a component, part, or accessory of a device **2 :** a commodity that lies on hand or is not salable **:** something for which there is little or no demand — now used only in the phrase *drug on the market* or *drug in the market* **3 a :** a narcotic substance or preparation ⟨~ addict⟩ ⟨~ user⟩ **b :** something that is narcotic in its effect ⟨power is sweet; it is a ~, the desire for which increases with habit —Bertrand Russell⟩ ⟨with his ~ of study, in his closed-in, precarious world —Edmund Wilson⟩ **4 drugs** *pl* **:** stocks or bonds of drug companies

2drug \"\ *vb* **drugged; drugged; drugging; drugs** *vt* **1 :** to poison with or as if with a drug ⟨the very air was *drugged* with the long-festering animosity —L.C.Douglas⟩ **2 :** to administer a drug to ⟨his wife, *drugged* against pain —Victor Canning⟩ **3 :** to lull or stupefy as if with a drug ⟨the kind of overly familiar music that delights most audiences and ~*s* most critics —*Time*⟩ ⟨her mind was still *drugged* by the stupor of exhaustion —Ellen Glasgow⟩ ⟨the strong aromatic sunlight *drugged* him into cheerfulness —John Buchan⟩ ~ *vi* **:** to take drugs for narcotic effect ⟨he neither drinks nor ~*s*⟩ ⟨it wouldn't surprise me if they *drugged!* They've got a very queer look in their eyes —Osbert Sitwell⟩

3drug \", 'drüg\ *vt* **drugged; drugged; drugging; drugs** [prob. by alter.] *dial Brit* **:** DRAG

4drug \'drəg\ *n* -S **:** a low heavy horse-drawn truck used esp. in moving timber

5drug \"\ *dial past of* DRAG

drug-fast \'≈,≈\ *adj* **:** resistant to the action of a drug

drugger *n* -S [*1drug* + *-er*] *obs* **:** DRUGGIST

drug·gery \'drəgərē\ *n* -ES [MF *droguerie*, fr. *drogue* drug (fr. MD *drōge*) + *-erie* -ery — more at DRUG] **1** *obs* **:** DRUGS, MEDICINE **2 :** the practice of giving drugs

drug·get \'drəgət\ *n* -S [MF *droguet*, dim. of *drogue* trash, stuff, drug] **1 :** a fabric of wool or wool mixed with linen or silk formerly used for clothing **2 :** a coarse durable cloth usu. of wool mixed with linen, jute, or cotton used chiefly as a lining or protective covering for carpets **3 :** a rug having a cotton warp and a wool filling made from fleece of wire-haired sheep of India — called also *India drugget*

drug·gist \'drəgəst\ *n* -S [prob. fr. F *droguiste*, fr. *drogue* drug + *-iste* -ist] **1 :** one who sells drugs wholesale or retail **2 :** PHARMACIST — compare APOTHECARY **3 :** one who owns or manages a drugstore

drug·gist·er \'drəg(ə)stə(r), 'drüg-\ *n* [F *droguiste* + E *-er*] *dial Eng* **:** DRUGGIST

drug ice *n* [*3drug*] **:** soft ice that slows up the stone in curling

drug·less \'drəgləs\ *adj* **:** not using drugs ⟨~ therapy⟩

drugs \'drəgz\ *dial var of* DREGS

drugster *n* -S [*1drug* + *-ster*] *obs* **:** DRUGGIST

drugstore \'≈,≈\ *n* **1 :** PHARMACY 3; *also* **:** a retail shop where medicines and miscellaneous articles (as candy, magazines, cosmetics) and usu. refreshments (as at a soda fountain) are sold **2 :** a place in Europe where medicines are sold but no compounding or dispensing is done

drugstore beetle *or* **drugstore weevil** *n* **:** a small light-brown beetle (*Stegobium paniceum*) of the family Anobiidae that infests stored products (as tobacco and drugs) and old books

drugstore cowboy *n* **1 :** one who wears cowboy clothes but has had no experience as a cowboy **2 :** a loafer who loiters on street corners or in drugstores

drugstore fold *n* **:** a multiple folding over of the lapped parts of a hand-formed small packet or wrapper

dru·id \'drüəd\ *n* -S [L *druides, druidae*, pl., fr. Gaulish *druides*; akin to OIr *druí* (pl. *druid*) wizard, *daur* oak tree, W *derwen* oak tree, OE *trēow* tree — more at TREE] **1 a** *often cap* **:** a member of a priesthood in ancient Gaul, Britain, and Ireland who are said to have studied the natural sciences, prophesied through priestly sacrifices, and acted as judges and teachers but who later appeared in Irish and Welsh sagas and Christian legends as magicians and wizards **b :** BARD, PROPHET **2 :** an officer of the Welsh bardic assembly — compare GORSEDD

dru·id·ess \-dəs\ *n* -ES **:** a female druid

dru·id·i·cal \(')drü'idəkəl, -dēk-\ *or* **dru·id·ic** \(')drü'idik, -dēk\ *also* **druid** *adj* **1 :** of or relating to the druids **2 :** resembling a druid ⟨groves of ~ trees —J.M.Brinnin⟩

druidical bead *n* **:** ADDER STONE

druidical circle *n* **:** STONE CIRCLE

dru·id·ism \'drüə,dizəm\ *n* **:** the system of religion, philosophy, and instruction of the druids consisting of early Celtic and perhaps pre-Celtic beliefs and including belief in the immortality of the soul

druids' altar *n* **:** a dolmen or cromlech of Great Britain sometimes ascribed to the druids

druid stone *n* **:** one of the sarsen stones of Great Britain often found in ancient stone circles

drukpa *usu cap, var of* DRUPA

1drum \'drəm\ *n* -S *often attrib* [prob. fr. D *trom*, fr. MD *tromme*; akin to MLG & MHG *trumme*, prob. of imit. origin] **1 a :** a musical instrument of percussion usu. consisting of a hollow cylinder with a skin head stretched over each end which is beaten with a stick or pair of sticks in playing; *broadly* **:** a hollow instrument or device of any nonmetallic material beaten in any manner to produce a deep-toned rumbling or booming sound **b :** DRUMMER 1 **2 a :** TYMPANUM 1a(1) **b :** the timbal of a sound-producing insect **3 a :** the sound of a drum **b :** a repetitious action similar to the beating of a drum ⟨woodpeckers' ~*s*⟩; *also* **:** the sound made by such an action ⟨heard the swooping ~ of the racer's hooves —Eve Langley⟩ **4 :** something resembling a drum in shape: as **a** (1) **:** one of the cylindrical or nearly cylindrical blocks of which the shaft of a column is composed (2) **:** a vertical wall that is circular or polygonal and carries a cupola or dome **b :** a revolving cylinder in which hides are tumbled during processing into leather (as for washing, pickling, tanning, dyeing) or in which furs are cleaned (by tumbling with fine sawdust) **c :** a hollow revolving cylinder for containing something to be acted upon: as (1) **:** a cask in which the colors of fabrics are fixed by steaming (2) **:** a drum washer in paper making (3) **:** a perforated cylinder for sorting ore (4) *also* **drum barker :** a long open-ended cylinder in which logs are tumbled in water to loosen and remove the bark **d :** a hollow or solid revolving cylinder or barrel that acts or is acted upon by something exterior to itself: as (1) **:** the winding part of a capstan or hoisting machine (2) **:** a doffer in a carding machine (3) **:** the roller for an autographic record (4) **:** a long pulley for several belts (5) **:** BRAKE DRUM **e :** the barrel of a clock upon which the weight cord is wound **f :** the circular housing of a banjo-clock movement **g :** a straight-sided cylindrical shipping container of metal, plywood, or paperboard with flat or slightly bowed ends one of which may be removable; *specif* **:** a metal container for liquids having a capacity between 12 and 110 gallons or a fiber container with a capacity up to 10 cubic feet **h :** a small paper tube with a paper or transparent film covering one end ⟨face-powder ~⟩ **i :** a cylindrical or rounded attachment for hot water, steam, or gases (as for a radiator or a reservoir) **j :** any of several disk-shaped magazines for feeding ammunition to automatic arms **5 :** any of various fishes of the family Sciaenidae that are capable of making a drumming noise — compare CROAKER 2; see BLACK DRUM, CHANNEL BASS, FRESHWATER DRUM **6** *Austral* **:** a bundle of personal possessions carried by a swagman

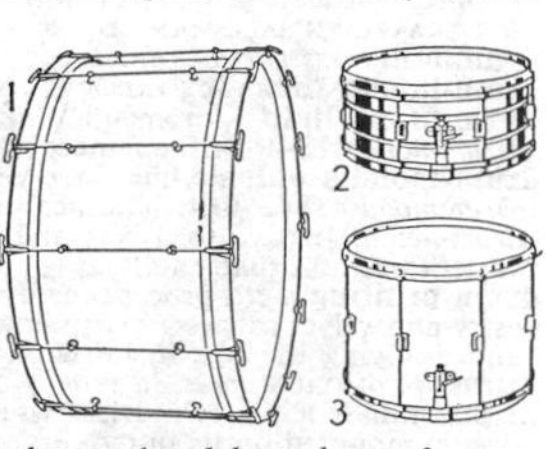

drums, 1a: *1* bass drum, *2* snare drum (for orchestra), *3* snare drum (for parades)

2drum \"\ *vb* **drummed; drummed; drumming; drums** *vi* **1 :** to beat a drum **2 :** to make a succession of strokes or vibrations that produce sounds like drumbeats ⟨his fingers *drummed* on the table⟩; *specif, of a bird* **:** to produce such vibrations esp. by beating the wings ⟨the male grouse *drumming* in the distance⟩ **3 :** to throb or sound rhythmically with or as if with drumbeats ⟨the spring freshet ~*s* in the narrow brooks —S.V.Benét⟩ ⟨a plane ~*s* in the sky overhead —Coulton Waugh⟩ **4 :** to stir up interest **:** SOLICIT, CANVASS ⟨gangsters who fear peace and ~ for war —*Newsweek*⟩ ⟨*drumming* for business⟩ ~ *vt* **1 a :** to summon, gather, or enlist by or as if by beating a drum ⟨to confound such time that ~*s* him from his sport —Shak.⟩ ⟨to make the detective appear a figure of power the police . . . are *drummed* into his service —W.O.Aydelotte⟩ ⟨*drumming* up talent —*New Republic*⟩ **b :** to arouse or further interest in by repeated promotional efforts ⟨cheered on by poets *drumming* the new struggle with Spartan despotism —E.R.May⟩ **2 :** to drive or dismiss ignominiously as if with accompaniment of drumbeats **:** EXPEL — now used with *out* ⟨a beggar being *drummed* out of town —J.H. Allen⟩ ⟨*drummed* out of military school —*Springfield (Mass.) Republican*⟩ **3 :** to drive or force by unremitting effort or reiteration ⟨~*s* into the girls two mottoes of her own —*Time*⟩ ⟨my father *drummed* the idea out of my head⟩ ⟨two issues almost daily *drummed* into the ears of Californians —M.F. A.Montagu⟩ **4 a :** to strike or tap repeatedly ⟨began to ~ her heels against the wall —T.B.Costain⟩ ⟨*drummed* the table with his fingers⟩ **b :** to produce (rhythmic sounds) by such action ⟨rain *drummed* an accompaniment to the words —Christine Weston⟩ **5 a :** to treat (a hide) in a drum **b :** to clean (a fur) by prolonged shaking with fine sawdust in a revolving drum **6 :** to put into a drum

3drum \"\ *n* -S [ScGael *druim* back ridge; akin to OIr *druimm* back ridge, W *trum*] **1** *chiefly Scot* **:** a long narrow hill or ridge **2 :** DRUMLIN

drum armature *n* **:** an armature having drum winding

drumbeat \'≈,≈\ *n* **:** a stroke on a drum or its sound; *also* **:** the measured beat of a percussion section of an orchestra

drumbeater \'≈,≈≈\ *n* **:** one that beats the drum for an idea, doctrine, or policy **:** a vociferous supporter of a cause ⟨~ for U.S. intervention in World War II —Ralph de Toledano⟩

drumbeating \'≈,≈≈\ *n* **:** vociferous advocacy of a cause

drum·ble-drone \'drəm(b)əl,drōn, 'drùm-\ *n* [*drumble* to buzz (of imit. origin) + *drone*] **1** *dial Eng* **:** a drone bee **2** *dial Eng* **:** a stupid or useless person

drum controller *n* **:** a rotary contactor mechanism for manual control of motors and electrically propelled vehicles

drumfire \'≈,≈\ *n* **1 :** artillery firing so continuous as to sound like a drum **2 :** something suggestive of drumfire in its disquieting continuance **:** BARRAGE ⟨conservative politicians kept up a ~ of warnings —Roy Lewis & Angus Maude⟩ ⟨an incessant ~ of lies and hatred —Barry Bingham⟩

drumfish \'≈,≈\ *n* **:** 1DRUM 5

drum gate *n* **:** a hinged gate at the top of a dam consisting of a horizontal cylindrical sector that can be raised from its compartment to increase the height of the spillway

1drumhead \'≈,≈\ *n* [*1drum* + *head*] **1 :** the skin stretched over either end of a drum **2 :** TYMPANIC MEMBRANE **3 :** the top of a capstan which is pierced with sockets for levers used in turning it **4** *also* **drumhead cabbage :** a cabbage having a rounded flattened head

2drumhead \"\ *adj* **:** taking place at or having the characteristics of a drumhead court-martial; *often* **:** taking place on the spot **:** SUMMARY ⟨~ judgment⟩ ⟨~ procedure⟩ ⟨~ trial⟩

drumhead court-martial *n* [fr. its having been held around a drumhead as table] **:** a court-martial to try offenses on the battlefield or the line of march

drumheads \'≈,≈\ *n pl but sing in constr* **:** a milkwort (*Polygala cruciata*) of the eastern U.S. with a thick cylindrical raceme of flowers

drum·lie *also* **drum·ly** \'drəmlē\ *adj* [alter. of ME *drubly*] **1** *chiefly Scot, of water* **:** turbid and muddy **2** *chiefly Scot, of weather* **:** dark and gloomy ⟨~ winter, dark and drear —Robert Burns⟩ **3 :** in a muddle **:** CONFUSED, TROUBLED

drumlike \'≈,≈\ *adj* **:** like the head of a drum **:** attached peripherally but free to vibrate centrally — used chiefly of various plant and animal membranes

drum·lin \'drəmlən\ *n* -S [IrGael *druim* ridge, back (fr. OIr) + E *-lin* (alter. of *-ling*) — more at DRUM] **:** an elongate or oval hill of glacial drift

drum major *n* **1** *archaic* **:** the first drummer of a regiment **2 :** the marching leader of a band or drum corps

drum majorette \,drəm,mājə'ret\ *n* [*drum major* + *-ette*] **:** a female baton twirler who accompanies a marching band or drum corps; *also* **:** a female drum major

drummed *past of* DRUM

drum·mer \'drəmə(r)\ *n* -S **1 :** one who plays a drum **2 a :** a large cockroach (*Blaberus giganteus*) of Central America, the West Indies, and tropical So. America that drums on woodwork as a sexual call; *also* **:** any of several related insects of similar habits **b :** any of various fishes that make a sound when caught: as (1) **:** WEAKFISH (2) **:** a member of the family Kyphosidae; *esp* **:** a common Australian fish (*Kyphosus syd-*

neyanus) little regarded for food or sport **3** : SWAGMAN **4** : TRAVELING SALESMAN **5** : a workman who tends a drum
drumming *pres part of* DRUM
drum·mock \'drəmək\ *var of* DRAMMOCK
drum·mond light \'drəmənd-\ *n, usu cap D* [after Thomas *Drummond* †1840 Brit. engineer] : LIMELIGHT 1a, 1b
drum·mond's phlox \-mən(d)z-\ *n, usu cap D* [after James *Drummond* †1863 Brit. botanical collector] : a phlox (*Phlox drummondii*) native to Texas and widely cultivated in many varieties as an ornamental
drum printing *n* : a process for dyeing woolen yarns for tapestry and velvet carpets by winding the yarns on a large drum and applying the dye in horizontal bands of varying width
drums *pl of* DRUM, *pres 3d sing of* DRUM
drum sander *n* : a cylindrical wheel with abrasive (as sandpaper) mounted on its outer curved surface and used for sanding flat surfaces of decorative stones
drum saw *n* : BARREL SAW
drum scale *n* : CYLINDER SCALE
drum sieve *n* : a sieve in a box like a drum used for fine powders
drumskin \'⸗,⸗\ *n* : TYMPANIC MEMBRANE
drumslade *n* -s [D *trommenslager, trommelslager*, fr. *tromme, trommel* drum + *slager* beater, fr. *slagen* to beat (fr. MD *slaen*) + *-er;* akin to OE *slēan* to beat, slay — more at DRUM, SLAY] *obs* : DRUMMER
drum slide *n* : a drawing of the backs of the fingers across the strings of a banjo to produce an arpeggio chord
drumstick \'⸗,⸗\ *n* **1** : a stick for beating a drum — see DRUM illustration **2** : something resembling a drumstick in form; *specif* : the segment of a fowl's leg between the thigh and tarsus **3** : a capsule of the horseradish tree
drumstick tree *n* [so called fr. the shape of the pods] **1** : an East Indian tree (*Cassia fistula*) having pods whose pulp is used medicinally — called also *pudding-pipe tree, purging cassia;* see CASSIA FISTULA **2** : HORSERADISH TREE 1
drum-stretch \'⸗,⸗\ *vt, bookbinding* **1** : to fasten (as fabric) to another material by drawing taut and securing at the edges **2** : to flatten and dry out (pasted or wet materials) by fastening clamps or weights to the edges
drum stuffing *n* : a rapid method of stuffing a leather by rotating it in a heated drum until warm, adding liquid grease to the drum, and then rotating again for a short time
drum switch *n* : an electric switch in which the connecting parts are held by spring pressure against contact surfaces in a revolving cylinder or sector
drum table *n* : a round-topped table supported on a central pedestal with a deep apron often containing drawers
drum up *vt* : to arouse by persistent effort : SOLICIT ⟨tried to *drum up* sentiment against the commission —A.H.Raskin⟩ ⟨*drum up* trade⟩ ⟨*drum up* support⟩; *also* : ORIGINATE, INVENT ⟨when the campaign was over, he told himself, he was going to *drum up* some way of making liquor —Norman Mailer⟩
drum washer *n* : a drum for washing paper pulp
drum winding *n* : an armature winding in which the coils are arranged upon the outer surface of a cylinder with those under consecutive poles being united by end connections — distinguished from *ring winding*

drum table

drungar *n* -s [ML *drungarius*, fr. LL *drungus* body of soldiers (of Gmc origin; akin to OE *thrang* crowd, throng) + L *-arius* -ary, -ar — more at THRONG] *obs* : a military commander
¹**drunk** \'drəŋk\ *adj* -ER/-EST [ME *drunke, dronke*, alter. of *drunken*] **1** : being in a condition caused by alcoholic drink in which control of the faculties is impaired and inhibitions are broken and in later stages of which one tends toward or reaches insensibility ⟨he came home ~⟩ ⟨~ folks were never quiet —Truman Capote⟩ **2** : dominated as if under the influence of alcohol by some feeling (as fanatic zeal, imperious pride, or passionate love) so that calm, judicious, realistic reflection is impossible ⟨if ~ with sight of power, we loose wild tongues —Rudyard Kipling⟩ ⟨he was ~, not with wine, but with joy —Maurice Samuel⟩ **3** *obs* : DRUNKEN 2 ⟨arrows ~ with blood —Deut 32:42 (RSV)⟩ **4** : relating to, caused by, or attended by intoxication ⟨a ~ and fitful sleep⟩ ⟨convicted of ~ driving —*Time*⟩
syn DRUNKEN, INTOXICATED, INEBRIATED, TIPSY, TIGHT: DRUNK and DRUNKEN are plainspoken rather blunt words which do not imply either censure or apology and do not suggest exact degrees of intoxication. The former is generally postposed or predicative, the latter often preposed ⟨"you think I am *drunk*?" "I think you have been drinking" —Charles Dickens⟩ ⟨he had seen front yards littered with empty bottles, and three *drunken* boys sprawling on the grass after a dance at a club —Ellen Glasgow⟩ DRUNKEN may suggest habitual excessive use of alcohol ⟨a *drunken* sot⟩ INTOXICATED does not indicate an exact degree of drunkenness, but, since its suggestions are learned and polite, it may indicate relatively slighter effects ⟨and *intoxicated* as he was . . . he knew enough to charge the steward . . . with the present safety of the ship —Herman Melville⟩ INEBRIATED and the less common INEBRIATE suggest more noisy, hilarious, or roistering indulgence ⟨volunteering to sing a song (which he did in that maudlin high key peculiar to gentlemen in an *inebriated* state) —W.M.Thackeray⟩ All of these preceding words may be used to describe the effects of any dominating feelings, emotions, or thoughts ⟨England was *drunk* with her glory and with the hope of plunder —J.R.Green⟩ ⟨he was no longer conscious of his emotions. He had become demented, *drunk* with the fury of his hatred —Liam O'Flaherty⟩ ⟨*drunken* with blood and gold —P.B.Shelley⟩ ⟨I dream that at Naples, at Rome, I can be *intoxicated* with beauty —R.W.Emerson⟩ ⟨he drank in the natural influences of the scene, and was *intoxicated* as by an exhilarating wine —Nathaniel Hawthorne⟩ ⟨intellects *inebriate* with summer —Emily Dickinson⟩ TIPSY, mild and venial in suggestion, implies difficulty with muscular coordination and unsteadiness ⟨drinking steadily, until just manageably *tipsy*, he contrived to continue so —Herman Melville⟩ TIGHT implies rather pronounced intoxication almost to the point of loss of muscular control, discretion, or judgment ⟨He was *tight*, and, as was characteristic of him, he soon dropped any professional discretion that he might have been supposed to exercise —Edmund Wilson⟩
²**drunk** \"\ *n* -s **1** : a period of excessive drinking : SPREE ⟨after a week's ~ and a week to sober himself —F.M.Ford⟩; *also* : a condition of drunkenness ⟨old men sleeping off ~s in the gutters —*Wisconsin Idea Theatre Quarterly*⟩ **2** : a drunken person : DRUNKARD ⟨the great cost of jailing and hospitalizing ~s⟩
drunk·ard \-kə(r)d\ *n* -s [¹*drunk* + *-ard*] **1** : one who habitually becomes drunk : one suffering from or subject to acute or chronic alcoholism **2 drunkards** *pl, NewEng* : CHECKERBERRY
drunkard's chair *n* : a wide upholstered armchair popular in 18th century England
¹**drunk·en** \-kən *sometimes* -kᵊŋ\ *adj* [ME, fr. OE *druncen*, fr. past part. of *drincan* to drink — more at DRINK] **1** : DRUNK 1 ⟨when he was ~, he was vulgar and silly —Katherine A. Porter⟩ ⟨reeled like a ~ giant —H.G.Wells⟩ **2** *obs, of a person* : saturated with liquid or moisture : DRENCHED ⟨let the earth be ~ with our blood —Shak.⟩ **3 a** : given to habitual excessive use of alcoholic drinks ⟨we can not afford to have poor people anyhow, whether they be lazy or busy, ~ or sober —G.B.Shaw⟩ **b** : of, relating to, attended by, or characterized by intoxication ⟨they come from . . . broken homes, ~ homes —P.B. Gilliam⟩ ⟨a ~ cry⟩ ⟨not in a ~ triumph but with awe —S.T. Coleridge⟩ **c** : resulting from or as if from alcoholic intoxication ⟨~ stupor⟩ ⟨the diver is subject to wild, ~ delusions —Rachel L. Carson⟩ **4** : unsteady or lurching as if from alcoholic intoxication ⟨insects which have walked on films of DDT soon begin to stagger in a ~ manner —*Atlantic Monthly*⟩ **5** : DRUNK 2 ⟨still ~ with hope and despair —Eve Langley⟩ **6** *of a screw thread* : having inequalities of pitch : WOBBLY
syn see DRUNK
²**drunken** *vi* -ED/-ING/-S *obs* : to become drunk
drunk·en·ly *adv* : in a drunken manner
drunk·en·ness \-kən(n)əs\ *n* -ES [ME *drunkennesse*, fr. OE *druncenness*, fr. *druncen* + *-nesse* -ness] **1** : the condition of being drunk with or as if with alcohol : INTOXICATION **2** : ALCOHOLISM **3** : mental or emotional extravagance suggestive of the disorders caused by alcohol ⟨the ~ of factious animosity —T.B.Macaulay⟩
drunken saw *n* : a circular saw fixed askew on its spindle so as to cut a groove whose width is determined by the angle of tilt of the saw — called also *wobble saw*
drunker *comparative of* DRUNK
drunk·ery \'drəŋkərē\ *n* -ES *archaic* : a place for drinking liquor : SALOON
drunkest *superlative of* DRUNK
drunk·om·e·ter \,drəŋ'kämə|d·ə(r), 'drəŋkə,mē|\ *n* [¹*drunk* + *-o-* + *-meter*] : a device for measuring the alcohol content of the blood through a chemical analysis of the breath
dru·pa \'drüpə\ *also* **drok·pa** \'dräkpə\ *or* **druk·pa** \-rük-\ *n, pl* **drupa** *or* **drupas** *usu cap* **1** : a mountain-dwelling nomadic people of Tibet **2** : a member of the Drupa people
dru·pa·ceous \(')drü¦pāshəs\ *adj* [*drupe* + *-aceous*] : of or relating to a drupe : bearing drupes ⟨~ fruits⟩ ⟨~ trees⟩
drupe \'drüp\ *n* -s [NL *drupa*, fr. L *drupa, druppa* overripe olive, fr. Gk. *dryppa* olive] : a one-seeded indehiscent fruit having a hard bony endocarp, a usu. fleshy mesocarp, and a thin epicarp like a skin (as in the cherry, plum, and peach) or dry and almost leathery (as in the almond) — called also *stone fruit;* see DRUPELET

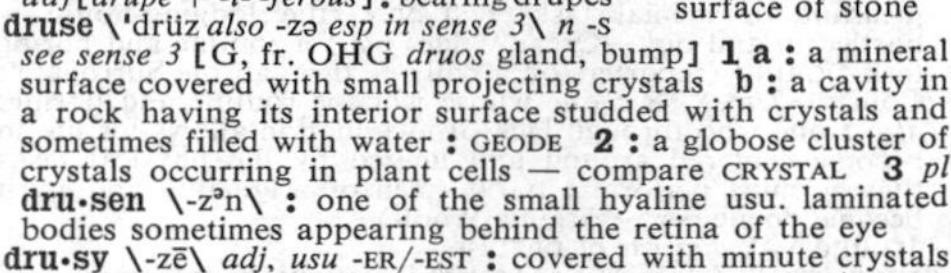

drupe of peach showing section of skin and flesh and surface of stone

drupe·let \-plət\ *also* **drup·el** \-pəl\ *n* -s [*drupelet* fr. *drupe* + *-let; drupel* fr. NL *drupella*, fr. *drupa* + *-ella*] : a small drupe; *specif* : one of the individual parts of an aggregate fruit (as the raspberry)
dru·pif·er·ous \(')drü¦pif(ə)rəs\ *adj* [*drupe* + *-i-* + *-ferous*] : bearing drupes
druse \'drüz *also* -zə *esp in sense 3*\ *n* -s *see sense 3* [G, fr. OHG *druos* gland, bump] **1 a** : a mineral surface covered with small projecting crystals **b** : a cavity in a rock having its interior surface studded with crystals and sometimes filled with water : GEODE **2** : a globose cluster of crystals occurring in plant cells — compare CRYSTAL **3** *pl* **dru·sen** \-zᵊn\ : one of the small hyaline usu. laminated bodies sometimes appearing behind the retina of the eye
dru·sy \-zē\ *adj, usu* -ER/-EST : covered with minute crystals : containing cavities lined with crystals ⟨a ~ surface⟩ ⟨a ~ vein⟩
druth·ers \'drəthə(r)z\ *n pl but sing in constr* [*druther* (dial. alter. of *would rather*) + *-s*] *dial* : free choice : PREFERENCE ⟨if I had my ~ I'd go fishing⟩
druv *dial past of* DRIVE
druxy \'drəksē\ *adj, usu* -ER/-EST [alter. of earlier *dricksie*, fr. obs. *drix* decayed part of timber + *-y*] *of timber* : having decayed spots in the heartwood
druze *or* **druse** \'drüz\ *n* -s *cap* [Ar *Durūz*, pl., fr. Muḥammed ibn- Ism'aīlal- *Darazīy* †1019 Muslim religious leader, one of the founders] : a member of a tightly organized independent religious sect dwelling chiefly in the mountains of Syria and Lebanon since the 11th century, whose founder advanced the claim that Hakim the sixth Fatimid caliph was the final incarnation of God, and whose other beliefs including the unity of God, the transmigration of souls, and final perfection are drawn from various religions (as Judaism, Christianity, and Islam) — **druz·ean** *or* **drus·ian** \-üzēən,-üzhən\ *adj, cap*
¹**dry** \'drī\ *adj* **dri·er** *also* **dry·er** \-ī(ə)r, -īə\ **dri·est** *also* **dry·est** \-īəst\ [ME *drie, dry*, fr. OE *drȳge;* akin to OHG *truckan, truchan* dry, MLG *drœge, drēge*, MD *drōge* and perh. to ON *draugr* dry wood] **1** : free or relatively free from water or liquid : not wet or moist: as **a** *obs* : naturally having no moisture — used in ancient and medieval sciences to describe one of the qualities of the four elements; opposed to *moist* **b** *of a sign of the zodiac* : having a dry complexion **2** : characterized by loss of water or of life-giving moisture: as **a** : lacking or comparatively free from precipitation and humidity ⟨the path is dusty on a ~ day⟩ ⟨a ~ summer⟩ **b** : lacking freshness : WITHERED **c** : ANHYDROUS **3 a** : not being in or under water : beneficially not having undue moisture or water ⟨~ land⟩ ⟨~ clothes⟩ **b** : employing no liquid or as little as possible ⟨the ~ method of assaying gold⟩ ⟨portland cement may be manufactured by ~ process or wet process⟩ — compare WET 8 **c** : built or constructed without the use of any process that requires water: (1) : using no mortar ⟨~ masonry⟩ ⟨a ~ stone wall⟩ (2) : using prefabricated plaster board, composition board, or wood paneling rather than a construction involving plaster or mortar bonding ⟨a ~ wall⟩ ⟨~ wall construction⟩ **d** *of breadstuff* : served or eaten without butter or milk — now used chiefly of toast without butter **e** *of a foodstuff* : having the water removed by evaporation : DEHYDRATED; *often* : reduced to powder or flakes **f** *of natural gas* : containing little or no recoverable gasoline or other liquid hydrocarbon **g** *of a friction clutch* : intended to function without lubrication **4 a** (1) : harmfully devoid of water or lubricant ⟨the garden is ~ from lack of rain⟩ ⟨the machine automatically stops when it runs ~⟩ (2) : THIRSTY ⟨he felt ~ after his walk⟩ **b** : marked by the absence of or abstention from alcoholic beverages ⟨it was a ~ party but the food was good⟩ ⟨a man who had been ~ for a dozen years —*N.Y. Times Bk. Rev.*⟩ **c** (1) : containing no uncombined water — used esp. of a paint or pigment (2) : wholly solidified : no longer liquid or sticky — used esp. of a coating (as paint) or ink applied to a surface or of the surface so treated; opposed to *wet* **d** : exclusive of accessories and operating fluids (as lubricant and coolant) — used of the weight of an engine **5** : characterized by exhaustion of a supply of water or other liquid: as **a** *of a container or receptacle* : depleted of liquid contents : EMPTY ⟨a ~ well⟩ ⟨the fountain pen ran ~ in the middle of a sentence⟩ **b** : devoid of running water ⟨a ~ ravine⟩ **6** *of an animal or its udder* : not giving milk : not lactating ⟨a ~ cow⟩ **7 a** (1) : not shedding tears ⟨hardly a ~ eye at the funeral⟩ (2) : not accompanied by tears ⟨a ~ sob⟩ **b** : continent of urine ⟨some children learn to stay ~ much earlier than others⟩ **c** (1) : marked by the absence or scantiness of secretions, effusions, or other forms of moisture ⟨a ~ pleurisy⟩ (2) *of a cough* : not accompanied by the raising of mucus or phlegm **8 a** *obs* : free from bloodshed : not causing or accompanied by an effusion of blood ⟨~ war⟩ ⟨~ death⟩ **b** : designed or executed in practice or planning for the future and lacking some essential (as live ammunition) of the situation being simulated : intended for practice only ⟨~ rehearsal⟩ ⟨~ firing⟩ **9 a** : solid as opposed to liquid ⟨~ groceries⟩ ⟨~ provisions⟩ ⟨~ cargo⟩ **b** : SLACK 6 **10 a** : not manifesting or communicating warmth, responsiveness, sympathy, enthusiasm, or tender feeling whether through natural indifference or studied unconcern : IMPASSIVE, UNEMOTIONAL, MATTER-OF-FACT ⟨under that peculiar sort of ~, blunt manner, I know you have the warmest heart —Jane Austen⟩ ⟨she sat there looking ~ and indifferent —Lionel Trilling⟩ **b** *fine art* : exhibiting a sharp frigid preciseness of execution : lacking delicate contour in form or easy transition in coloring **11 a** : not yielding what is expected or desired : not giving satisfaction : BARREN, STERILE, UNPRODUCTIVE ⟨a poet who is going through a ~ period which he finds frustrating —Rosemary Benét⟩ **b** *obs, of a person* : STINGY **c** *dial* : RESERVED, ALOOF **12** : marked by a matter-of-fact manner of expression that seems unconscious or unintentional but is actually ironic, caustic, keen, shrewd, terse — used esp. of humor or the person expressing it ⟨his ~ humor which made him say the most amusing things and keep his face so absolutely solemn —Eleanor Roosevelt⟩ **13** : having no personal inclination, bias, or emotional concern : having clear impartial perception or judgment ⟨ought . . . to have used the ~ light of reason in discussing matters of high morality, politics and religion —*Times Lit. Supp.*⟩ ⟨a certain ~ spirit of detachment and analysis —Aldous Huxley⟩ **14** : dull because lacking in inherent interest and adornment : lacking elements that would lend attractiveness and appeal : UNINTERESTING, WEARISOME, INSIPID ⟨in the *dryest* passages of her historical summaries these delightful descriptions come running to the rescue —Robert Payne⟩ ⟨his ~ schoolmaster temperament, the hurdy-gurdy monotony of him —William James⟩ **15 a** : having nothing superfluous : lacking embellishment : consisting of essentials only : UNADORNED, PLAIN, BARE ⟨~ simplicity⟩ ⟨~ fact⟩ ⟨~ formality⟩ **b** *archaic* : paid in actual coin — used of money or fees **c** *of a dog* : having the skin close fitting esp. about the neck and mouth **16 a** (1) *of beverages* : lacking sweetness (2) *of wines and other fermented beverages* : having all or most sugar fermented to alcohol : SUGARLESS ⟨~ champagne⟩ ⟨~ sauterne⟩ — see SEC **b** *of mixed drinks* : containing only ingredients low or lacking in sugar content ⟨a ~ martini⟩ **c** : marked by a harsh, rasping, or jarring tone : lacking smooth or liquid sound qualities ⟨a ~ rasping voice⟩ ⟨a chipping sparrow gives a ~, unmusical trill —W.P.Smith⟩ ⟨the ~ whisper of winter leaves —Edith Sitwell⟩ ⟨this recording of the piano solo is ~ and harsh⟩ **17** : relating to or favoring the prohibition or drastic regulation and limitation of the manufacture or distribution of alcoholic beverages ⟨~ law⟩ ⟨~ agent⟩ ⟨~ sentiment⟩ ⟨a ~ state⟩
syn ARID: ARID is usu. more extreme than DRY. DRY suggests freedom from moisture or deficiency of moisture, ARID destitution or deprivation of moisture and extreme dryness ⟨not a drop of water could we find, and the *arid* aspect of the valley as a whole showed only too plainly that the rainfall, on this side of the island at least, must be scant indeed —C.B. Nordhoff & J.N.Hall⟩ DRY suggests lack of qualities compelling interest, ARID absence of worthwhile, fruitful, or significant, as well as interesting, qualities ⟨a very *dry* book⟩ ⟨the frank elucidation of such a principle, with an aesthetic near to a moral obligation, might imply only bleak and *arid* results —Holbrook Jackson⟩ Applied to persons, their manner or sayings, DRY implies loss of warmth, responsiveness, enthusiasm, or emotion, ARID an absence of or incapacity for these ⟨this structural defect might have been overcome — and may still be overcome — if the intellectual leadership were less *arid* —Barbara Ward⟩ **syn** see in addition SOUR
— **not dry behind the ears** : IMMATURE, NAIVE
²**dry** \"\ *vb* **dried; dried; drying; dries** [ME *drien, dryen*, fr. OE *drȳgan*, fr. *drȳge*, adj.] *vt* **1** : to make dry : to rid of moisture or liquid (as by wiping, rubbing, draining, squeezing) — often used with *up, out, off; specif* : to remove or reduce the moisture content of by exposure to heat or air : DESICCATE — compare DEHYDRATE, EVAPORATE **2** : to take up (moisture or liquid) by absorption — usu. used with *up* ⟨the sun will ~ up the dew quickly⟩ **3** : to cause (a female mammal) to stop giving milk — used with *off* or *up* ~ *vi* **1** : to become dry : become free from wetness or moisture — often used with *off, out* ⟨nylon *dries* rapidly⟩ ⟨I *dried* at the electric blower —Saul Bellow⟩ **2 a** *of moisture or a liquid* : to evaporate, become absorbed, or drain away — often used with *up* ⟨the ~*ing* up during the summer of the shallow ponds —W.H.Dowdeswell⟩ **b** : to become hard, tough, and elastic as a result of oxidation and polymerization : SOLIDIFY — used esp. of various oils, paints, and varnishes applied as thin films **3** *of a female mammal* : to stop giving milk — used with *off* or *up*
syn DESICCATE, DEHYDRATE, BAKE, PARCH: DRY is a general term applicable to any process, natural or artificial, whereby moisture is extracted from something ⟨clothes *drying* on the line⟩ ⟨to *dry* up a swamp⟩ ⟨*drying* the dishes with a towel⟩ DESICCATE indicates a complete exhaustion of moisture, with resultant shriveling or withering; in reference to persons it indicates loss of animation, vitality, capacity to interest ⟨*desiccated* fish⟩ ⟨*desiccated* coconut meat⟩ ⟨the spur of an imagination not yet *desiccated* by a too strict adhesion to those so-called 'laws' —Eric Partridge⟩ ⟨achieves her dream of gentility by marrying a stockbroker and settles into a mold of *desiccated* snobbery —C.J.Rolo⟩ DEHYDRATE, like DESICCATE, indicates complete elimination of water but usu. lacks additional suggestion ⟨*dehydrated* fruits⟩ It may refer to a condition of the body resulting from loss or deprivation of fluids ⟨he may develop fever from becoming *dehydrated* —Benjamin Spock⟩ BAKE in the meaning here involved may indicate not only drying by heat or fire but also hardening, sometimes with resulting cracking ⟨clay tablets on which all three types were present — that is, tablets on which the wedges had been impressed while they were still soft and then *baked* in —Fletcher Pratt⟩ ⟨the sun-*baked* mud flats⟩ PARCH suggests drying by dry heat or drought; it may imply effects comparable to thirst and suggest that water will restore and refresh ⟨record heat waves which have *parched* mid-America's usually productive plains —*N.Y. Times Mag.*⟩ ⟨we had drunk all our water and so were *parched* and all done in when we finally espied a small, scattered Bedouin camp —*Nat'l Geographic*⟩
³**dry** \"\ *n* -ES *see sense 6* [ME *drie, dry*, fr. *drie, dry*, adj.] **1** : the condition of being dry : DRYNESS **2** : something dry: as **a** *chiefly Austral* (1) : the rainless season of the year (2) : a desert area **b** : a place that is dry (as a piece of dry land) **3** [by shortening] : DRYHOUSE **4** : a natural seam constituting a flaw in stone **5** : THIRST; *esp* : a craving for intoxicating liquor **6** *pl* **drys** : PROHIBITIONIST **7** : the action of becoming dry ⟨speed of ~ of printing inks⟩
⁴**dry** \"\ *adv* [¹*dry*] : in a dry way ⟨"what a thrilling life you have!" "Yeah," I says, ~ —Bant Singer⟩
dry- *or* **dryo-** *comb form* [NL, fr. Gk, fr. *drys* tree, oak — more at TREE] : tree — in generic names (*Dryopithecus*)
dry·ad \'drīəd, -ī,ad\ *n* -s [L *dryad-, dryas*, fr. Gk. *drys*] : WOOD NYMPH 1
dry·as \'drīəs\ *n* [NL, fr. L] **1** *cap* : a small genus of arctic and alpine tufted plants (family Rosaceae) with simple leaves and white or yellow solitary flowers **2** *pl* **dryas** : any plant of the genus *Dryas*
¹**dryasdust** \'⸗⸗,⸗\ *n* -s *often cap* [after Dr. Jonas *Dryasdust*, fictitious person to whom Sir Walter Scott †1832 Scottish author dedicated some of his novels] : one that is uninteresting because of concentration upon minutiae : PEDANT ⟨the researches of a *Dryasdust* —C.E.Montague⟩
²**dryasdust** \"\ *adj* : marked by characteristics that bring about lack of interest or boredom : UNINSPIRED, PEDANTIC, PROSAIC ⟨~ presentation⟩ ⟨~ scholarship⟩ ⟨a ~ teacher⟩
dry-ash \'⸗¦⸗\ *vt* : to convert (a sample) to ash in chemical analysis
dry band *or* **dry bunch** *n* : a flock of sheep not including gravid or lactating ewes
dry bark *n* : a phase of shell bark of citrus in which the outstanding symptoms are yellowing and some defoliation, loss of vigor, and death of tissues nearly down to the cambium of trunk and large branches with checking but little or no shelling of the bark
dry battery *n* : a battery of dry cells; *also* : DRY CELL
dry bible *or* **dry bible disease** *n* [¹*bible* (omasum)] *Austral* : botulism of cattle
dry bone *or* **dry-bone ore** *n* : SMITHSONITE
dry bridge *n, NewEng* : a bridge over a dry way (as a railroad)
drybrush \'⸗¦⸗\ *n* : a method of ink or watercolor painting in which most of the pigment has been removed from the brush before application
dry budding *n* **1** : PLATE BUDDING **2** : CHIP BUDDING
dry-bulb temperature *n* : temperature indicated by a dry-bulb thermometer that is the actual temperature of the air — contrasted with *wet-bulb temperature;* compare PSYCHROMETER
dry-bulb thermometer *n* : an ordinary thermometer; *specif* : the thermometer with unmoistened bulb in a psychrometer
dry camp *n* : a camp made where there is no source of water
dry cell *n* : a voltaic cell whose contents are made nonspillable by the use of some absorbent (as sawdust or gelatin); *esp* : a cell of the Leclanché type in which a mixture of plaster of paris, flour, and sal ammoniac with water takes the place of the solution
dry-clean \'⸗¦⸗\ *vt* [back-formation fr. *dry cleaning*] : to subject to dry cleaning
dry cleaner *n* : one whose business is the dry cleaning of textiles
dry cleaning *n* : the cleansing of fabrics with substantially nonaqueous organic solvents (as petroleum naphtha or chlorinated hydrocarbons) to which special detergents or soaps are often added — compare WET CLEANING
dry coal *n* : coal containing little volatile matter
dry color *n* : a pigment in powder form — compare FLUSH COLOR, PULP COLOR
dry course *n* : a starter course in roofing consisting of roofing felt or paper laid over insulation and not bedded in tar or asphalt
dry-cure \'⸗¦⸗\ *vt* : to cure (as meat) by drying : DRY-SALT — compare PICKLE
dry dash *n* : ROCK DASH

dry·de·ni·an \(ˈ)drīˈdēnēən, -ˈden-\ *adj, cap* [John *Dryden* †1700 Eng. poet + E *-ian*] **:** of or in the manner of the poet Dryden

dry digging *n* **:** an alluvial mine in an arid region — usu. used in pl.; called also *dry placer*

dry–dip \ˈ=,=\ *n* **:** a tanning solution into which sole leather is dipped to increase firmness and restore color

dry–disk rectifier *n* **:** a rectifier cell of the barrier-layer type

dry distillation *n* **:** the distillation of substances in a dry condition; *esp* **:** DESTRUCTIVE DISTILLATION

dry dock *n* **:** a dock that can be kept dry for use during the construction or repairing of ships — see FLOATING DOCK, GRAVING DOCK; compare MARINE RAILWAY

dry–dock \ˈ=ˌ=\ *vt* [*dry dock*] **:** to place in a dry dock

dry–dye \ˈ=ˌ=\ *vt* **:** to dye (a fabric) by using a nonaqueous solvent (as petroleum naphtha)

dry end *n* **:** the section of a papermaking machine extending from the place where the wet web is first subjected to the drying process to the place where the finished paper is reeled — compare WET END

dryer *var of* DRIER

dryest *var of* DRIEST

dry face *n* **:** a chipped or tapped area on a turpentine tree that fails to produce a flow of oleoresin

dry farm *n* **:** a nonirrigated farm on dry land

dry–farm \ˈ=ˌ=\ *vt* [*dry farm*] **:** to farm without irrigation — **dry farmer** *n*

dry farming *n* **:** production of crops on dry land without irrigation principally by tillage methods conserving soil moisture and by the use of drought-enduring or drought-evading crops — called also *dryland farming*

dry–fine \ˈ=ˌ=\ *vt* **:** to repolish (metals) on a dry fine-grained wheel when an esp. smooth surface is required

dry finish *n* **:** a finish given to paper or board by calendering dry — compare WATER FINISH — **dry–finished** \ˈ=ˌ=\ *adj*

dryfist *n* [ˡ*dry* + *fist*] *obs* **:** NIGGARD, MISER

dryfland *var of* DROFLAND

dry fly *n* **:** an artificial fly designed to float upon the surface of the water

dry fog *n* **1 :** a haze caused by dust or smoke in the air **2 :** a fog occurring above the dew point and caused by some substance (as coal-tar vapor) that prevents evaporation of the water droplets

dryfoot \ˈ=ˌ=\ *adv* [ME *drie foot*] **1 :** with dry feet **2** *obs* **:** by the scent of the foot

dry foot *n* **:** the bottom of a piece of pottery when unglazed

dry fruit *n* **:** a fruit (as a capsule or achene) in which the pericarp is not succulent or pulpy

dry gangrene *n* **:** gangrene that develops in the presence of pure arterial obstruction, is sharply localized (as in an extremity or an udder), and is characterized by dryness of the dead tissue which is of a dark brown or black color and sharply demarcated from adjacent tissue by a line of inflammation

dry goods \ˈ=ˌ=\ *n pl but sometimes sing in constr* **:** textiles, ready-to-wear clothing, and notions as distinguished from hardware, jewelry, groceries, and wet goods

dry–grind \ˈ=ˌ=\ *vt* **:** to grind without using liquid

dry grins *n pl* **:** smiling caused by a feeling of embarrassment

dry–gulch \ˈ=ˌ=\ *vt* **:** to kill from ambush

dry–handed \ˈ=ˌ==\ *adj* **:** without weapons

dry hole *n* **1 :** a hole drilled (as through rock in a quarry) without using water **2 :** a well that does not yield oil or gas in commercial quantities — called also *dry well, duster*

dry hopping *n* **:** the addition of hops to beer in the cask

dryhouse \ˈ=ˌ=\ *n* **1 :** CHANGE HOUSE **2 :** a drying room (as in a factory)

dry ice *n* **:** a substance that consists of solidified carbon dioxide usu. in the form of blocks, that at −78.5° C changes directly to a gas as it absorbs heat, and that is used chiefly as a refrigerant and coolant

drying *adj* [ME, fr. the pres. part. of *dryen, drien* to dry — more at DRY] **:** capable of rapidly becoming dry and hard by absorbing oxygen on exposure to air — see DRYING OIL

drying loft *n* **:** a loft in which paper is dried under carefully regulated atmospheric conditions

drying oil *n* **:** a natural or synthetic unsaturated fatty oil (as linseed oil or dehydrated castor oil) that changes readily to a hard, tough, elastic substance when exposed in a thin film to the air and may serve as a vehicle in paints, varnishes, and printing inks — compare BLOWN OIL, BODIED OIL, BOILED OIL

drying oven *n* **:** a heated chamber for drying; *specif* **:** one for drying clay ware or glazed ware before firing

dry·i·nid \ˈdrīənəd, -ˌnid\ *n* -S [NL *Dryinidae*] **:** one of the Dryinidae

dry·in·i·dae \drīˈinəˌdē\ *n pl, cap* [NL, fr. *Dryinus*, type genus + *-idae*] **:** a family of small broad-headed wasps parasitic as larvae on the nymphs of leafhoppers and related insects

dry–ki *or* **dri·ki** \ˈ=ˌkī\ *n* -S [origin unknown] **:** standing or fallen weather-beaten timber (as of trees killed by flooding)

dry kiln *n* **:** a heated chamber for drying and seasoning cut lumber

dry labor *n* **:** childbirth characterized by premature escape of the amniotic fluid

dry lake *n* **:** a tract of salt-encrusted land in a region of slight rainfall which may occas. be covered by a temporary lake **:** PLAYA

dry land *n* **1** \ˈ=ˌ=\ **:** a region of low or inadequate rainfall **2** \ˈ=ˈ=\ **:** TERRA FIRMA ⟨eager to set foot on *dry land* again⟩

dry–land \ˈ=ˌ=\ *adj* [*dry land*] **1 :** of, relating to, or found on terra firma ⟨where the toad is called a *dry-land* frog⟩ ⟨*dry-land* rice⟩ **2** *usu* **dryland :** of or relating to arid regions or to dry farming ⟨*dryland* wheat⟩ ⟨typical *dryland* genera⟩

dryland blueberry *n* **1 :** a low shrub (*Vaccinium pallidum*) of eastern No. America **2 :** the sweet blue berry borne by the dryland blueberry

dryland farming *n* **:** DRY FARMING

dry lodging *n, obs* **:** lodging without board

dry loft *n* **:** a tannery area where leather is hung to dry

drylot \ˈ=ˌ=\ *n* **:** an enclosure of limited size that is usu. bare of all vegetation and is used for feeding and fattening livestock

dry·ly *or* **dri·ly** \ˈdrīlē, -li\ *adv* [ME *dryely*, fr. *drye, dry* + *-ly*] **:** in a dry manner: as **a :** without moisture **b :** with caustic or sardonic humor **:** SARCASTICALLY **c :** without emotion **:** INDIFFERENTLY, COLDLY ⟨freely, if ~, advised lady guests on the respective qualities of moire and surah —Margery Sharp⟩ **d :** in a plain unadorned style **:** in a dull uninteresting manner ⟨he is never ~ didactic —*Manchester Guardian Weekly*⟩; *also* **:** in a clear, forthright, and unbiased manner ⟨~ academic and methodical —*Nation*⟩

dry·man \ˈ=mən, -ˌman\ *n, pl* **drymen :** one in charge of a dryhouse

dry measure *n* **1 :** a series of units of capacity for dry commodities — see MEASURE table **2 :** a measure for dry commodities

dry milk *n* **:** whole or skim milk from which the water has been removed

dry milk solids *n pl* **:** the constituents of milk (as protein, lactose, minerals, vitamins, ash) remaining after the removal of water

dry mop *n* **:** a long-handled duster for use on floors — called also *dust mop*

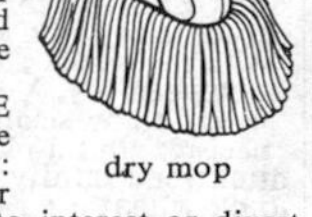
dry mop

dry mounting *n* **:** a method of attaching photographic prints to a support by means of a thermoplastic tissue treated with shellac and the application of heat and pressure

dry multure *n, Scots law* **:** a yearly tax payable in money or grain to a mill owner for the grinding of grain grown on land subject to thirlage or for the right to have that grain ground elsewhere

dry·ness *n* -ES [ME *drynesse*, fr. OE *drȳgnes*, fr. *drȳge* dry + *-nes* -ness — more at DRY] **:** the quality or state of being dry: as **a :** lack of emotional warmth or imaginative quality **b :** lack of power to interest or divert **:** MONOTONY **c :** quiet or sardonic humor **d :** sobriety esp. in a person previously suffering from alcoholism

dry nurse *n* **1 :** a nurse who cares for but does not suckle an infant — compare WET NURSE **2 :** one who aids or instructs another usu. unnecessarily

dry–nurse \ˈ=ˌ=\ *vt* [*dry nurse*] **:** to act as dry nurse to; *esp* **:** to give unnecessary supervision to ⟨I have gone round the world alone and do not need to be *dry-nursed* through a tour in Ireland —G.B.Shaw⟩

dryo- — see DRY-

dry·o·bal·a·nops \ˌdrīōˈbaləˌnäps\ *n* [NL, fr. *dry-* + *balan-* + *-ops*] **1** *cap* **:** a small genus of resin-producing trees (family Dipterocarpaceae) having flowers with a cup-shaped calyx the limb of which is divided into leafy segments — see BORNEO CAMPHOR **2** -ES **:** any tree of the genus *Dryobalanops*

dry·ob·a·tes \drīˈäbəˌtēz\ [NL, fr. *dry-* + *-bates*] *syn of* DENDROCOPOS

dry off *vt* **:** to develop dormancy in (a plant) by withholding water

dry offset *n* [so called fr. the fact that no water is used] **:** offset printing in which the inked impression from letterpress or relief is etched on a thin metal surface, then printed on an intermediate rubber surface (as a blanket), and then offset onto the paper

dry·o·phyl·lum \ˌdrīōˈfiləm\ *n, cap* [NL, fr. *dry-* + *-phyllum*] *bot* **:** a genus of widely distributed Upper Cretaceous and Tertiary fossil trees (family Fagaceae) considered to be ancestors of modern oaks and beeches

dry·o·pi·the·cid \ˌdrīōpəˈthēsəd, -ēkəd, -ˈpithəˌsid, -əˌkid\ *n* -S [NL *Dryopithecus* + E *-id*] **:** an ape of the subfamily Dryopithecinae

dry·o·pith·e·ci·nae \-ˌpithəˈsī(ˌ)nē, -ˈkī-\ *n pl, cap* [NL *Dryopithecus*, type genus + *-inae*] **:** a subfamily of Pongidae comprising Miocene and Pliocene Old World anthropoid apes regarded by some as common ancestors of man and modern anthropoids and including the genera *Dryopithecus, Proconsul, Sivapithecus*, and less-known related forms — **dry·o·pith·e·cine** \-ˈpithəˌsīn, -ˌkīn\ *adj or n*

dry·o·pi·the·cus \ˌ==pəˈthēkəs, -ˈpithəkəs\ *n, cap* [NL, fr. *dry-* + *-pithecus*] **:** a genus of generalized Miocene and Pliocene Old World apes sometimes regarded as common ancestral forms of the anthropoid apes and man

dry·op·te·ris \drīˈäptərəs\ *n, cap* [NL, fr. L, a kind of fern, fr. Gk, fr. *dry-* + *pteris*, a kind of fern, fr. *pteron* feather — more at FEATHER] **:** a large cosmopolitan genus of ferns (family Polypodiaceae) having the indusium reniform or orbicular with a deep sinus and comprising the shield ferns

dry·op·te·roid \-əˌrȯid\ *adj* [NL *Dryopteris* + E *-oid*] **:** resembling or relating to the genus *Dryopteris*

dry ore *n* **:** an ore valuable for gold or silver but containing little lead and much silica and so requiring additions of lead and fluxes for successful treatment

dry painting *n* **:** SAND PAINTING

dry pan *n* **:** a grinder for ceramic materials consisting of a rotating perforated metal pan containing revolving mullers

dry–pick \ˈ=ˌ=\ *vt* **:** to remove the feathers from (fowl) without scalding

dry–pipe system *n* **:** a sprinkler system in which water is admitted to the system upon the release of air pressure that the pipes normally contain and which is used where there is danger of freezing

dry–pipe valve *also* **dry valve** *n* **:** a valve admitting water to a dry-pipe sprinkler system upon the release of air pressure in the system

dry placer *n* **:** DRY DIGGING

dry plate *n* **:** a photographic plate coated with a sensitized silver halide emulsion (as in gelatin) and dried before exposure — called also *plate*

dry pleurisy *n* **:** pleurisy in which the exudation is mainly fibrinous

drypoint \ˈ=ˌ=\ *n* **1 :** an engraving made with a needle or other pointed instrument instead of a burin directly into the metal plate without the use of acid as in etching, the burr made by the point being retained to produce the characteristic soft line in the print **2 :** a print made from such an engraving

dry–press \ˈ=ˌ=\ *vt* **:** to mold (clayware) by compressing moist powdered clay in metal dies

dry rendering *n* **:** a process of cooking animal tissues in the absence of water for extraction of the fat

dry rent *n, old English law* **:** RENT SECK

dry rice *n* [so called fr. its being grown without irrigation] **:** UPLAND RICE

dry rot *n* **1 :** a decay of seasoned timber caused by certain fungi (as the house fungi and some polypores) that consume the cellulose of wood leaving a mere soft skeleton that is readily reduced to powder **2 :** a rot of plant tissue in which the affected areas are not soft and wet but dry and often firmer than normal or more or less mummified: as **a :** decay of standing timber involving such rot and caused chiefly by polypores **b :** any of various fungous diseases of cultivated plants involving such rot esp. of roots, tubers, and fruits and caused usu. by fungi of the genera *Fusarium, Diaporthe, Diplodia*, or *Volutella* **3 :** a fungus causing dry rot **4 :** deterioration and decay from within caused by apathy or by resistance to new and vitalizing forces; *also* **:** the cause of such decay ⟨warned against the *dry rot* which infects art when it becomes more interested in itself than in what it is saying —*Saturday Rev.*⟩ ⟨in a representative democracy lack of strong conviction in the electorate is a form of *dry rot* capable of eventually destroying the whole fabric —G.W.Johnson⟩

dry–rot \ˈ=ˌ=\ *vb* [*dry rot*] *vt* **:** to affect with dry rot ~ *vi* **:** to become affected with dry rot ⟨what counted inside you *dry-rotted* if you pretended it wasn't there —Hugh MacLennan⟩

dry rubble *n* **:** rubble masonry laid without mortar

dry run *n* **1 :** a practice exercise or rehearsal without ammunition (as of a military combat operation) **2 :** a practice exercise **:** REHEARSAL, TEST, TRIAL ⟨after 17 *dry runs*, using paid actors as the quizzees, the kinks were ironed out and the show went on the air —*Newsweek*⟩

drys *pl of* DRY

dry–salt \ˈ=ˌ=\ *vt* **:** to treat with salt in the dry state **:** cure (as meat or hides) by salting and drying

drysalter \ˈ=ˌ==\ *n* [ˡ*dry* + *salter*] *Brit* **:** a dealer in crude dry chemicals and dyes

drysaltery \ˈ=ˌ===\ *n* **1** *Brit* **:** the articles kept by a drysalter **2** *Brit* **:** the business of a drysalter

dry sand *n* **1 :** foundry sand artificially dried after being made into a mold — distinguished from *greensand* **2 :** a sand not producing oil or gas

dry sausage *n* **:** SUMMER SAUSAGE

dry–shave \ˈ=ˌ=\ *vt, slang* **:** DEFRAUD, CHEAT

dry–shod \ˈ=ˌ=\ *adj* **:** having dry shoes on **:** not wetting the shoes or feet ⟨a land bridge over which men and animals could have crossed *dry-shod* —*Scientific American*⟩

dry shrinkage *n* **:** shrinkage occurring in kiln-dried lumber after removal of the surface crust (as by planing)

dry–sickness \ˈ=ˌ==\ *n* **:** pine of sheep and cattle caused by cobalt deficiency

dry skin *n* **:** skin or hide preserved by air drying after slaughter

dry socket *n* **:** a tooth socket in which after tooth extraction a blood clot fails to form or disintegrates without undergoing organization; *also* **:** a condition that is marked by the occurrence of such a socket or sockets and that is usu. accompanied by neuralgic pain but without suppuration

dry spot *n* **:** GRAY SPECK

dry steam *n* **:** steam containing no free water particles — compare WET STEAM

dry storage *n* **:** cold storage (as for milk and cream) in which refrigeration is by a current of cooled air

dry stove *n* **:** a hothouse with low relative humidity for xerophytic plants

dry suit *n* **:** a close-fitting waterproof rubber suit used esp. by a skin diver

dryth \ˈdrīth\ *n* -S [ˡ*dry* + *-th* (as in *warmth*)] *now dial Eng* **:** DRYNESS, DROUGHT

dry trust *n* **:** PASSIVE TRUST

dry up *vt* **:** to end the existence of by or as if by cutting off at the source or exhausting the supply ⟨fear *dried up* the words —E.T.Thurston⟩ ⟨closure of the Mediterranean *dried up* commerce in Western Europe⟩ ⟨the finance-ministry project to *dry up* . . . their purchasing power by compulsory saving —George Axelsson⟩ ~ *vi* **1 :** to disappear as if by evaporation, absorption, or draining **:** become exhausted (as of a supply) **:** cease to exist because of the cutting off of a source of supply or of vital elements ⟨without intellectual enterprise, economic enterprise *dries up* —H.S.Commager⟩ ⟨they are filling the vacuum left by the virtual *drying up* of immigration from Europe —Hal Burton⟩ ⟨is not the only one whose power of expression *dries up* —*Times Lit. Supp.*⟩ **2 :** to wither or die through gradual loss of vitality ⟨the skin keeps the body from *drying up* through evaporation of fluid —Morris Fishbein⟩ ⟨under tyranny individual men *dry up* for lack of spiritual exercise —Lyman Bryson⟩ **3 a :** to stop talking **:** be at a loss for words ⟨he was so surprised and angry that he just *dried up*⟩ ⟨"*Dry up!*" advised the grizzled old-timer —S.E.White⟩ **b** *of an actor* **:** to forget one's lines

dry valve *var of* DRY-PIPE VALVE

dry wash *n* **1 :** laundry washed and dried but not ironed **2** *West* **:** WASH 3d

dry–waxed \ˈ=ˌ=\ *adj, of waxed paper* **:** so made that the wax is almost all driven into the paper — compare WET-WAXED

dry well *n* **1 :** DRY HOLE 2 **2 :** a hole excavated in porous ground and usu. covered and filled with loose gravel or rubble or walled (as with stone, brick, or cinder blocks) to receive water (as drainage from a roof) and allow it to percolate away

dry whiskey *n* [so called fr. the fact that eating the tops of the tubercles causes intoxication] **:** MESCAL BUTTON

dry–wood termite *n* **:** any of various termites (family Kalotermitidae) that live and feed in dry wood without a soil connection and include some which are destructive pests in domestic construction — see CRYPTOTERMES

ds *abbr* decistere

DS *abbr* **1** [It *dal segno*] from the sign **2** days after sight **3** day's sight **4** detached service **5** document signed **6** double stitch

d's *or* **ds** *pl of* D

DSc *abbr or n* -S **:** doctor of science

dsgn *abbr* design

d sharp \ˈ=ˈ=\ *n, usu cap D* **1 :** the keynote of D-sharp minor **2 :** the tone a half step above D

d–sharp minor \ˈ=ˌ=ˈ==\ *n, usu cap D* **:** the minor musical key having a signature of six sharps

DSP *abbr* [L *decessit sine prole*] he died without issue

DST *abbr* **1** daylight saving time **2** double summer time

dstn *abbr* destination

dstspn *abbr* dessertspoon

DT *abbr* **1** daylight time **2** double throw **3** double time

DTP *abbr* diphtheria, tetanus, pertussis (vaccines)

dt's \ˈdēˈtēz\ *also Brit* **dt** \ˈdēˈtē\ *n pl, often cap D&T* [by abbr.] **:** DELIRIUM TREMENS

du *dial Brit var of* DO

du *abbr* **1** dual **2** duke

du·ad \ˈd(y)üˌad\ *n* -S [irreg. fr. Gk *dyad-, dyas* two (n.), pair — more at DYAD] **:** a union of two **:** PAIR

ˡ**du·al** \ˈd(y)üəl, \üəl *also* \ül\ *adj* [L *dualis*, fr. *duo* two + *-alis* -al — more at TWO] **1** *of an inflectional form or grammatical number* **:** denoting reference to two ⟨Gothic *wit* "we two" is a first person ~ pronoun⟩ — compare PLURAL, QUADRUAL, SINGULAR, TRIAL **2 a :** consisting of two parts or elements **:** DOUBLE, TWOFOLD ⟨the ~ tones of an American toad's song —W.P.Smith⟩ ⟨that the work of a painter who looks important in England . . . has stood up to the ~ test of international competition and the Adriatic sun —David Sylvester⟩ **b :** having two aspects **:** having a double character or nature ⟨the man had a ~ nature, one half positive and passionate to yearning, one half negative, satirical, and really perverse —H.S.Canby⟩ ⟨immigrants, as a rule, retain a ~ patriotism —Bertrand Russell⟩ **c :** containing two or being one of two often identical parts **:** TWIN ⟨high-compression heads complete with a ~ exhaust system —Gregor Felsen⟩ **d :** consisting of or used on a pair of wheels (as automotive driving wheels) joined together side by side (as by bolting or welding) on a common axle ⟨~ tires⟩ **3 :** characterized by a division of controlling agents or factors: as **a :** consisting of two sets of authorities having mutually exclusive spheres of power ⟨a ~ federalism⟩ ⟨a ~ form of government⟩ **b :** fitted for operation by either or both of two agents ⟨driving lessons given on *dual*-control cars⟩ ⟨*dual*-fuel engines that run on oil or oil and gas⟩

²**dual** \ˈ"\ *n* -S **1 :** the dual number of a language or a form in it **2 :** the result obtained in consequence of interchanging conjunction and alternation throughout a formula in the propositional calculus **3 :** a chess problem for which two solutions exist **4 :** a pair of dual wheels or dual tires

dua·la \düˈ(w)älə\ *n, pl* **duala** *or* **dualas** *usu cap* **1 a :** a Bantu-speaking people of the coastal area of Cameroun **b :** a member of such people **2 :** the Bantu language of the Duala people used as a language of trade and education in Cameroun

dual banking *n* **:** banking in which both state and national banks operate in the same state or community

dual citizenship *n* **1 :** the citizenship of a citizen of a state that is organized under a constitution with other states into a national state (as the U. S.) recognized as a nation by the family of nations **2 :** DUAL NATIONALITY

dual highway *n* **:** DIVIDED HIGHWAY

dual ignition *n* **:** automobile ignition by two independent currents from a battery and from a magneto

du·al·ism \ˈd(y)üəˌlizəm, -üə-\ *n* -S [F *dualisme*, fr. L *dualis* + F *-isme* -ism] **1 :** a theory that divides the world or a given realm of phenomena or concepts into two mutually irreducible elements or classes of elements: as **a :** an ontological theory that divides reality into (1) subsistent forms and spatiotemporal objects or into (2) mind and matter ⟨Cartesian *dualism*⟩ — compare MONISM, PLURALISM **b :** an epistemological theory that objective reality is known by means of subjective ideas, representations, images, or sense data — contrasted with *monism* **2 :** the quality or state of being dual **:** twofold division ⟨all our policies . . . have been plagued by ~; we have too often tried to straddle the fence of expediency —H.W.Baldwin⟩ **3 a :** the doctrine that the universe is under the dominion of two opposing principles one of which is good and the other evil **b :** a view of man as constituted of two original and independent elements (as matter and spirit) **4 :** the theory originated by Lavoisier and developed by Berzelius that all definite chemical compounds are binary and consist of two distinct constituents, themselves simple or complex, and possess opposite electrical properties — compare UNITARY THEORY **5 :** a theory in hematology holding that the blood cells arise from two kinds of stem cells one of which yields lymphatic elements and the other myeloid elements — compare HEMATOPOIESIS

du·al·ist \-ˌləst\ *n* -S **:** an adherent or advocate of dualism or a dualism

du·al·is·tic \ˌ==ˈlistik\ *also* **du·al·ist** \ˈ==ˌləst\ *adj* **1 :** consisting of two **:** DUAL **2 :** characterized by dualism **:** having reference to dualism or duality — **du·al·is·ti·cal·ly** \ˌ==ˈlistək(ə)lē\ *adv*

dualistic formula *n* **:** a chemical formula written in accordance with the theory of dualism ⟨$CaO.SO_3$ is the *dualistic formula* for calcium sulfate ($CaSO_4$)⟩ — called also *Berzelian formula*

du·al·i·ty \d(y)üˈalədē, -ətē, -i\ *n* -ES [ME *dualite*, fr. MF *dualité*, fr. LL *dualitat-, dualitas*, fr. L *dualis* dual + *-itat-, -itas* -ity — more at DUAL] **1 :** the quality or state of being dual or of being made up of two elements or aspects **:** DOUBLENESS, DICHOTOMY ⟨he was amused by the eternal ~ of truth and fiction —John Fountain⟩ ⟨a deep ~ was introduced between morality and the life of impulse —Bertrand Russell⟩ — see PRINCIPLE OF DUALITY

du·al·ize \ˈd(y)üəˌlīz, -üə-\ *vt* -ED/-ING/-S **:** to make dual ⟨*dualized* into a four-lane highway —Richard Thruelsen⟩

du·al·ly \-əlē, -li\ *adv* **:** in a double capacity **:** in two ways

dual nationality *n* **:** the status of an individual when two or more nations each claim sole allegiance from him — called also *multiple nationality*; compare DUAL CITIZENSHIP

dual organization *n* **:** division (as of a tribe or society) into moieties

dual pay *n* **:** wages determined on that one of two alternative bases of computation which is more advantageous to the employee (as on a mileage or hourly basis in the transportation industry)

dual–purpose \ˌ==ˈ==\ *adj* **1 :** intended for or serving two purposes **2 :** bred for two purposes (as to provide milk and meat or eggs and meat)

dual-rotation propeller *n* **:** an assembly of two airplane propellers mounted one behind the other on coaxial shafts and rotating in opposite directions

duals *pl of* DUAL

dual union *n* **:** a labor union claiming jurisdiction over workers organized by another union — **dual unionism** *n*

du·an \ˈdüən, ˈthü-\ *n* -s [ScGael] **:** a division of a Gaelic poem corresponding to a canto **:** POEM, SONG

du·ant \ˈd(y)üənt\ *n* -s [L *duo* two + E *-ant* — more at TWO] **:** DEE

du·ar \dü'är\ *n* -s [Hindi *duār, dvār*, lit., door, fr. Skt *dvār* — more at DOOR] *India* **:** a tract of land leading to a mountain pass

du·ar·chy \ˈd(y)ü,ärkē\ *n* -ES [irreg. fr. LGk *dyarchia*, fr. Gk *dy-* + *-archia* -archy] **:** a government by two rulers having equal power

¹dub \ˈdəb\ *vb* **dubbed; dubbed; dubbing; dubs** [ME *dubben*, fr. OE *dubbian* to dub a knight; akin to ON *dubba* to dub a knight, EFris *dubben* to strike against, push, MLG *dobbel* die, MHG *toppel* die, Norw *dubb* peg, plug, OHG *tubili* plug — more at DOWEL] *vt* **1 a :** to confer knighthood upon by the ceremonial tapping of the shoulder with a sword ⟨the king *dubbed* his son a knight⟩ **b :** to dignify or give new character to by a name, title, or description ⟨a man of wealth is *dubbed* a man of worth —Alexander Pope⟩ ⟨*dubbed* him a "born actor" —*Time*⟩ ⟨a region *dubbed* the Switzerland of America⟩ **c :** to call by a descriptive name or epithet **:** NICKNAME ⟨people *dubbed* his enterprise a folly⟩ ⟨if a man persists in advancing views that are contradicted by all available evidence . . . he will rightfully be *dubbed* a crank by his colleagues —Martin Gardner⟩ **2** *Brit* **:** DRESS ⟨~ a line for fly fishing⟩ **3 :** to thrust or make a thrust at **4 a :** to trim or remove the comb and wattles of (as a cockerel) — compare CROP 1b (2) **b :** to trim or make smooth with an adz (as a timber) **5 :** to rub with grease (as in stuffing leather) **6 a :** to hit (a golf ball or a golf shot) poorly **b :** to execute poorly ⟨he *dubbed* his first attempt at a sale⟩ ⟨he *dubbed* the exam⟩ ~ *vi* **:** to thrust or make a thrust **:** POKE

²dub \"\ *n* -s **:** one who is unskillful (as at a game, a trade, politics) because of inexperience or lack of talent **:** a clumsy or stupid person **:** DUFFER

³dub \"\ *n* -s [ME (Sc dial.) *dubbe*; akin to MLG *dobbe* pool, puddle, Fris *dobbe* pit, hole] **1** *chiefly Scot* **:** a pool of water: as **a :** a water hole or stagnant pond **b :** a deep pool in a river **c :** a pool of rainwater **:** MUD PUDDLE **2** *Scot* **:** BOG, MIRE

⁴dub \"\ *n* -s [Telugu *ḍabbu* & Marathi *ḍhabbū*] **:** a small copper coin formerly current in parts of India

⁵dub \"\ *vt* **dubbed; dubbed; dubbing; dubs** [by shortening & alter. fr. *double*] **1 :** to provide (a motion-picture film) with a new sound track (as for substituting dialogue in a foreign language) **2 :** to add (sound effects) to a motion-picture film or to a radio or television production — usu. used with *in* **3 :** to transpose (sound already recorded) to a new record **:** RERECORD; *also* **:** to combine (two or more sources of sound at least one of which is a recording) into one record

⁶dub \"\ *n* -s **:** DUBBING

dub-a-dub \ˌdəbəˈdəb\ *n* -s [imit.] **:** the sound of drum beating

¹du bar·ry \d(y)üˈbarē\ *n*, *often cap D&B* [prob. after Marie Jean Bécu, Comtesse *du Barry* †1793 mistress of King Louis XV of France] **:** BITTERSWEET PINK

²du barry \(ˈ)=ˌ==\ *adj, usu cap D&B* [after Comtesse *du Barry*] *of a soup or sauce* **:** made with cauliflower

du·bash \düˈbäsh\ *n* -ES [Hindi *dubhāṣiyā*, fr. *du-* two (fr. Skt *dvi*) + *-bhāṣiyā* (fr. Skt *bhāṣā* language); akin to Skt *bhāṣate* he talks — more at TWO, BELLOW] *India* **:** INTERPRETER

dub·bel·tje \ˈdəbəlchə\ *n* -s [D, fr. *dubbel* double (fr. MD *dubbel, dobbel*, fr. OF *doble*) + *-tje* (dim. suffix) — more at DOUBLE] **:** a former silver coin of the Netherlands equivalent to two stivers or ⅒ of a gulden

¹dub·ber \ˈdəbə(r)\ *n* -s [¹*dub* + *-er*] **:** one that dubs

²dubber \"\ *or* **dup·per** \ˈdəpə(r)\ *also* **dub·ba** \ˈdəbə\ *n* -s [Per *dabba*] **:** a large globular leather bottle used in India to hold ghee, oil, or other liquid

¹dub·bin \ˈdəbən\ *also* **dub·bing** \", -biŋ\ *n* -s [fr. gerund of ¹*dub* (to dress leather)] **:** a mixture of oil and tallow for dressing leather

²dubbin \"\ *vt* -ED/-ING/-S **:** to apply dubbin to

¹dubbing *n* -s [fr. gerund of ¹*dub* (to dress a fly)] **:** the materials tied to a fishhook in making the body of an artificial fly

²dubbing *n* -s [fr. gerund of ⁵*dub*] **:** a record made by dubbing

¹dub·by \ˈdəbi\ *adj* -ER/-EST [¹*dub* + *-y*] *dial Brit* **:** DULL, BLUNT

²dubby \"\ *adj* -ER/-EST [³*dub* + *-y*] *Scot* **:** MUDDY

du·ber·some \ˈd(y)übə(r)səm\ *adj* [alter. of *dubious* + *-some*] *dial* **:** DOUBTFUL

du·bi·e·ty \d(y)üˈbīəd·ē, -ətē, -i\ *n* -ES [LL *dubietas*, fr. L *dubius* + *-etas* (fr. *-itas* -ity)] **1 :** the quality or state of being doubtful or skeptical **:** DUBIOUSNESS, UNCERTAINTY ⟨there was ~ in his voice and a hint of uncertainty in his eye —John Buchan⟩ **2 :** a doubt or matter of doubt ⟨the problems and *dubieties* of an average individual⟩ **syn** see UNCERTAINTY

du·bi·os·i·ty \ˌd(y)übēˈäsəd·ē, -ətē, -i\ *n* -ES [fr. *dubious*, after such pairs as E *curious: curiosity*] **:** DOUBT, UNCERTAINTY, DUBIETY **syn** see UNCERTAINTY

du·bi·ous \ˈd(y)übēəs\ *adj* [L *dubius*, fr. *dubare* to doubt, vacillate, fr. *duo* two — more at TWO] **1 :** occasioning doubt **:** EQUIVOCAL, UNCERTAIN, UNDETERMINED ⟨what one finds certain and indubitable in the situation, the other finds ~ or downright false —S.C.Pepper⟩ **2 a :** being in doubt **:** unsettled in opinion **:** DOUBTFUL, QUESTIONING, UNDECIDED ⟨he had never heard of me and was a little ~ about signing his name —Henry Miller⟩ ⟨she was nervous and ~ about the project⟩ **b :** expressive of doubt or uncertainty ⟨this loyalty . . . does not become shaky or ~ as the years pass —D.F. Miller⟩ **3 :** of doubtful promise or uncertain outcome **:** UNPROMISING, UNLIKELY ⟨seemed the most promising of all the ~ solutions presented⟩ ⟨a ~ and potentially dangerous gift —Vera M. Dean⟩ ⟨I was a ~ scholastic risk —Sidney Lovett⟩ **4 :** characterized by qualities that occasion suspicion, mistrust, disparaging suggestion, or hesitation **:** questionable as to value, quality, origin, or character **:** open to question ⟨spies, traitors, or others of ~ reliability and patriotism —R.E. Cushman⟩ ⟨rhetorically effective, but of ~ value scientifically —M.R.Cohen⟩ ⟨if not actually disreputable, was at best a ~ figure —S.H.Adams⟩ **syn** see DOUBTFUL

du·bi·ous·ly *adv* **:** in a manner expressive of doubt, hesitation, or suspicion **:** DOUBTFULLY, UNCERTAINLY

du·bi·ous·ness *n* -ES **:** the quality or state of being dubious

du·bi·ta·ble \ˈd(y)übəd·əbəl, |tə-\ *adj* [L *dubitabilis*, fr. *dubitare* to doubt + *-abilis* -able — more at DOUBT] **:** open to doubt or question ⟨on what grounds would my thesis be ~? —S.M.Brown⟩ ⟨it was more than ~ whether the friend was as influential as she thought —Karen Horney⟩

du·bi·tan·cy \|d·ənsē, |tən-\ *n* -ES [ML *dubitantia*, fr. L *dubitant-, dubitans* + *-ia* -y] **:** DOUBT, UNCERTAINTY

du·bi·tant \-nt\ *adj* [L *dubitant-, dubitans*, pres. part. of *dubitare* to doubt — more at DOUBT] **:** DOUBTING

¹du·bi·tan·te \ˌdübəˈtänˌtā\ *adj* [L, abl. sing. masc. of *dubitant-, dubitans*] **:** DOUBTING — used of a judge who expresses doubt about a decision reached by the court

²dubitante \"\ *n* -s **1 :** DOUBTER — used of a judge **2 :** the expression of doubt of a dubitante

du·bi·tate \ˈd(y)übəˌtāt\ *vi* -ED/-ING/-S [L *dubitatus*, past part. of *dubitare* — more at DOUBT] *archaic* **:** DOUBT

du·bi·ta·tion \ˌd(y)übəˈtāshən\ *n* -s [ME *dubytacion*, fr. MF *dubitation*, fr. L *dubitation-, dubitatio*, fr. *dubitatus* + *-ion-, -io* -ion] *archaic* **:** the quality or state of doubting **:** an instance of doubting **:** DOUBT ⟨I am in some ~ whether it ever existed at all —T.A.Guthrie⟩

du·bi·ta·tive \ˈd(y)übəˌtād·iv\ *adj* [F *dubitatif*, fr. LL *dubitativus*, fr. L *dubitatus* + *-ivus* -ive] **1 :** tending or given to doubt **:** DOUBTING **2 :** expressing doubt ⟨the ~ mood of a verb⟩ — **du·bi·ta·tive·ly** \-d·əvlē\ *adv*

dub·lin \ˈdəblən\ *adj, usu cap* [fr. *Dublin*, city & county in Ireland] **1 :** of or from Dublin, the capital of the Republic of Ireland **:** of the kind or style prevalent in the city of Dublin **2 :** of or from county Dublin, Ireland **:** of the kind or style prevalent in county Dublin

dub·lin·er \-nə(r)\ *n* -s *cap* [*Dublin*, Ireland + E *-er*] **:** a native or resident of Dublin, Ireland

du·boi·sia \d(y)üˈbȯizēə\ *n, cap* [NL, fr. F. N. *Dubois* †1824 Fr. botanist + NL *-ia*] **:** a genus of soft-wooded Australian shrubs or small trees (family Solanaceae) having white flowers in axillary clusters and yielding an alkaloid having an action similar to atropine

du bois-rey·mond's law \(ˈ)d(y)übˈwä|rāˈmōⁿz-, -ü|bȯi|\ *or* **du bois-reymond principle** *n, usu cap D&B&R* [after Emil *du Bois-Reymond* †1896 Ger. physiologist] **:** a statement in physiology: a nerve is stimulated only by a change in electric current and not by a steady flow of electricity

du·bon·net \ˌd(y)übəˈnā\ *n* -s [*Dubonnet*] **:** very dark purplish red

Dubonnet \"\ *trademark* — used for a sweet purplish red aromatized wine used as an aperitif or as a cocktail ingredient

dubonnet cocktail *n, cap D* **:** a cocktail consisting of approximately equal parts of Dubonnet wine and gin chilled and usu. garnished with a twist of lemon peel

¹dubs *pres 3d sing of* DUB, *pl of* DUB

²dubs \ˈdəbz\ *interj* [short for *doubles*] — a call by a player in the game of marbles invoking a special privilege according to the rules of the game

du·cal \ˈd(y)ükəl\ *adj* [MF, fr. LL *ducalis* of a leader, fr. L *duc-, dux* leader + *-alis* -al — more at DUKE] **1 :** of, belonging to, or befitting a duke or dukedom ⟨a ~ palace⟩ **2 :** having the rank of a duke ⟨a mere ~ husband —*Time*⟩ — **du·cal·ly** \-əlē, -li\ *adv*

ducal coronet *n* **1** *heraldry* **:** a coronet ornamented with three strawberry leaves and often used as a crest coronet **2 :** DUKE'S CORONET

ducal crest coronet *n* **:** a ducal coronet borne as a crest coronet

du·cape \(ˈ)d(y)üˈkāp\ *n* -s [origin unknown] **:** a heavy corded silk dress fabric popular chiefly in the 18th century

duc·at \ˈdəkət, *usu* -əd·+V\ *n* -s [ME *ducat, doket*, fr. MF *ducat*, fr. OIt *ducato* coin with a portrait of the doge on it, fr. *duca* doge, guide, fr. MGk *douk-, doux* leader, fr. LGk, fr. L *duc-, dux* — more at DUKE] **1 :** any one of a number of gold coins of European countries copied from a coin issued by Roger II of Sicily about 1150, 20th century issues of which include a coin of Austria issued 1901–15 and one of Czechoslovakia issued 1923–38 **2 :** a unit of value equivalent to the value of one gold ducat ⟨many fractional and multiple ~ pieces have been coined⟩ **3** *also* **duck·et** \"\ *slang* **:** TICKET

duc·a·toon \ˌdəkəˈtün\ *or* **duc·a·ton** \-tän\ *n* -s [F *ducaton*, dim. of *ducat*] **:** a silver crown-sized coin of the Netherlands first struck in 1598; *also* **:** a similar coin of Italy

du·ce \ˈdü(ˌ)chā\ *n* -s [after Il *Duce* (It, lit., the leader), title of Benito Mussolini †1945 Italian dictator] **:** DICTATOR

duces *pl of* DUX

duces tecum *n* -s **:** SUBPOENA DUCES TECUM

duchan *var of* DUKAN

du·ches·nea \d(y)üˈkānēə\ *n, cap* [NL, after Antoine N. *Duchesne* †1827 Fr. botanist] **:** a small genus of perennial Asiatic herbs (family Rosaceae) comprising two species of plants that resemble strawberries but have yellow flowers and spongy dry fruits — see INDIAN STRAWBERRY

duch·ess \ˈdəchəs\ *n* -ES [ME *duchesse*, fr. MF, fr. *duc* duke + *-esse* -ess — more at DUKE] **1 :** the wife of a duke **2 :** a woman who holds a ducal title in her own right

du·chesse \(ˈ)d(y)üˈshes\ *n* -s [F, lit., duchess] **1 :** a chaise longue with arms that was popular in 18th century France **2** *also* **duchess :** a fine lustrous rayon or silk satin for clothing **3 :** a very small cream puff with sweet or savory filling used as dessert or served with cocktails

duchesse lace *also* **duchess lace** *n* [part trans. of F *dentelle duchesse*] **:** a fine bobbin lace of Flemish origin having delicate floral and foliage designs joined by bobbin-made brides

duchesse potato *n* [F *duchesse*, lit., duchess] **:** potato mashed and mixed with raw egg used as a garnish or made into patties and oven-browned

duchy \ˈdəchē, -chi\ *n* -ES [ME *duche, duchie*, fr. MF *duché*, fr. *duc* duke — more at DUKE] **:** the territory or dominions of a duke or duchess **:** DUKEDOM

¹duck \ˈdək\ *n* -s *often attrib* [ME *doke*, fr. OE *dūce* — more at ²DUCK] **1** *or pl* **duck a :** any of various swimming birds of the family Anatidae which have the neck and legs short, the body more or less depressed, the bill often broad and flat, the tarsi scutellate in front, and the sexes almost always differing from each other in plumage and which are distinguished by these characteristics and by their comparatively small size from the swans and geese **b :** the flesh of any of these birds used as food **2 :** a female duck as distinguished from a male — compare DRAKE **3** *Brit* **a** *or* **ducks** *pl but sing in constr* **:** PET, DARLING — often used as a term of address **b :** something or someone attractive or charming ⟨a ~ of a car —*Everybody's Magazine*⟩ ⟨she was a nice old ~, and very fond of her —Margery Sharp⟩ **4 :** one that cannot act effectively because of disablement or other cause — compare DEAD DUCK, LAME DUCK, SITTING DUCK **5 :** DUCK ON A ROCK; *also* **:** one of the players' stones **6** *slang* **a :** a person with peculiar mental or physical characteristics ⟨a little old ~ with waxed mustache, you say, and a cane? —Frank King⟩ ⟨he's a queer ~⟩ **b :** RASCAL **7** *Brit* **:** a score of nothing **:** GOOSE EGG ⟨the batsman was bowled first ball for a ~⟩ **8 :** MIG **9** [so called fr. its shape] *slang* **:** URINAL

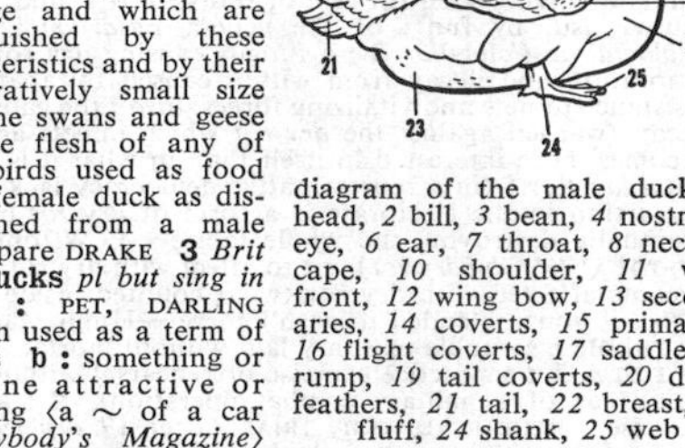

diagram of the male duck: *1* head, *2* bill, *3* bean, *4* nostril, *5* eye, *6* ear, *7* throat, *8* neck, *9* cape, *10* shoulder, *11* wing front, *12* wing bow, *13* secondaries, *14* coverts, *15* primaries, *16* flight coverts, *17* saddle, *18* rump, *19* tail coverts, *20* drake feathers, *21* tail, *22* breast, *23* fluff, *24* shank, *25* web

²duck \"\ *vb* -ED/-ING/-S [ME *douken, duken*; akin to OE *dūce* duck, MLG & MD *düken* to dive, OHG *tūhhan*] *vt* **1 :** to plunge under water; *specif* **:** to plunge the head of (a person or animal) under water **2 :** to lower (as the head or body) quickly **:** BOW ⟨~*ed* her head to everyone on the platform, and ran down the steps —Hodding Carter⟩ ⟨~*ing* her head against the rain, hastened on —Pearl Puckett⟩ **3 :** AVOID, EVADE ⟨he tried to ~ the blame⟩ ⟨most of the Senate wanted to ~ the issue —T.R.Ybarra⟩ ⟨much evidence that administrators, faculties, and trustees ~ their separate responsibilities —Albert Lumley⟩ ~ *vi* **1 a :** to go quickly under the surface of water and reappear **b :** to descend suddenly **:** DIVE, DIP ⟨the trail ~*ed* into a narrow gulch —Wallace Stegner⟩ **2 a :** to lower the head or body suddenly ⟨the batteries he fired at promptly ceased their fire as the gunners ~*ed* behind cover —C.S.Forester⟩ ⟨she would ~ through the low entrance of her hut —Jacquetta & Christopher Hawkes⟩ **b :** BOW, BOB **3 :** to try to seize an apple with the teeth as it floats in a tub of water — used with *for;* compare BOB vi 1c **4 a :** to move quickly and often surreptitiously (as to escape danger or observation) **:** disappear suddenly **:** DODGE ⟨at sight of the officer he ~*ed* around the corner and into an alley⟩ — often used with *out* ⟨I ~*ed* out of the convention hall half a dozen times to watch the TV —E.D.Canham⟩ **b :** to avoid a duty, question, or responsibility **:** back out ⟨some grocery bills that a little hole-in-the-wall lunch counter was trying to *duck* out on —H.L. Davis⟩ **5 :** to play a low card rather than cover a card previously played or try to win a trick **syn** see DIP, DODGE

³duck \"\ *n* -s **:** a sudden lowering of the head or stooping of the body **:** a dip or quick plunge

⁴duck \"\ *n* -s [D *doek* cloth, linen, canvas, fr. MD *doec;* akin to OS *dōk* cloth, OHG *tuoh*, and perh. to Skt *dhvaja* flag, Av *dvazh-* to flutter] **1 :** a durable plain closely woven fabric now usu. of cotton made in various weights and used in the gray (as for sails, bags, belting) or with various finishes (as for tents, awnings, clothing) — compare CANVAS **2 ducks** *pl* **:** light clothes made of duck; *esp* **:** trousers made of such material

⁵duck \"\ *n* -s *sometimes cap* [alter. (influenced by ¹*duck*) of *DUKW*, its code designation] **:** a 2½-ton 6-wheel-drive truck equipped with a propeller and watertight hull for ferrying, lighter service, or amphibious landing of troops

duck acorn *n* **:** WATER CHINQUAPIN

¹duck and drake *var of* DUCKS AND DRAKES

²duck and drake *n* **:** DUCK ON A ROCK

¹duckbill \ˈ=ˌ=\ *n* [¹*duck* + *bill*] **1** *or* **duckbill platypus :** PLATYPUS **2** *or* **duckbill cat :** PADDLEFISH a **3 :** DUCK-BILLED DINOSAUR **4 :** a metal flange welded to a tank tread for giving increased traction in muddy terrain **5 :** a power shovel with a flat round nose for loading coal in a mine

²duckbill \"\ *or* **duckbilled** \ˈ=ˌ=\ *adj* **1 :** having a bill shaped like that of a duck **:** shaped like or terminating in something shaped like a duck's bill **2** *of a cap or hat* **:** having a visor in the shape of a duck's bill

duck-billed dinosaur *n* **:** any of numerous herbivorous ornithischian dinosaurs having flattened side teeth resembling blades, no incisors, and the fore part of the jaws covered by a horny birdlike bill and constituting *Trachodon* and related genera — see HADROSAUR

duckbill gar *n* **:** SHORTNOSE GAR

duck blue *n* **:** INDIGO CARMINE 2

duckboard \ˈ=ˌ=\ *n* **:** a boardwalk or slatted flooring laid on a wet, muddy, or cold surface for the ease and safety of people crossing or standing on it — usu. used in pl. ⟨the ~*s* are down for students to cross the muddy green —Corey Ford⟩; see TRENCHBOARD

duckboat \ˈ=ˌ=\ *n* **:** a low-lying flat-bottomed boat used by duck hunters

duck bumps *n pl, dial* **:** GOOSE PIMPLES

duck call *n* **:** a device like a whistle for imitating the calls of ducks

duck disease *n* **:** DUCK SICKNESS

ducked *past of* DUCK

duck egg *or* **duck's egg** *n, Brit* **:** GOOSE EGG, ZERO ⟨an opening batsman ignominiously dismissed for a ~⟩

duck·er \ˈdəkə(r)\ *n* -s [²*duck* + *-er*] **:** one that scalds carcasses in a slaughterhouse

ducket *var of* DUCAT

duck fit *n* **:** FIT 4

¹duckfoot \ˈ=ˌ=\ *n, pl* **duckfoots** *or* **duckfeet** *see numbered senses* [¹*duck* + *foot*] **1** *pl* **duckfeet :** DUTCH FOOT **2** *pl* **duckfoots :** a gastropod mollusk (*Aporrhais occidentalis*) of offshore waters of the western No. Atlantic that has a long vertical aperture and a much-expanded somewhat triangular outer lip — called also *duck's-foot shell* **3 :** a triangular cultivator blade or shovel used as an attachment to a cultivator

²duckfoot \"\ *vt* -ED/-ING/-S **:** to till land with a duckfoot cultivator

¹duckfooted \ˈ=ˌ==\ *adj* **:** having the hind toe directed more or less forward — used of domestic fowls

²duckfooted \"\ *adv* **:** with feet pointed outward **:** FLAT-FOOTED

duck grass *n* **1 :** a submerged aquatic plant (*Potamogeton pectinatus*) with filamentous leaves and hard bony fruits that are relished by ducks **2 :** FOWL MEADOW GRASS

duck green *n* **:** a dark bluish green that is greener and duller than average teal green and greener and slightly stronger than invisible green (sense 2) — called also *bluegrass, pine tree, vagabond*

duck hawk *n* **1 :** the American falcon that is a variety of the peregrine falcon **2** *Brit* **:** MARSH HARRIER

duckie *var of* DUCKY

duckier *comparative of* DUCKY

duckies *pl of* DUCKY

duckiest *superlative of* DUCKY

¹duck·ing \ˈdəkiŋ, -kēŋ\ *n* -s [¹*duck* + *-ing*] **:** the sport of hunting wild ducks ⟨a good gun for ~⟩

²ducking \"\ *n* -s [⁴*duck* + *-ing*] **:** ⁴DUCK

ducking stool *n* [fr. pres. part. of ²*duck*] **:** a seat attached to the end of a plank overhanging a pond used as a means of punishment in the 15th to 18th centuries the culprit being tied to the seat and plunged into the water — compare CUCKING STOOL

duck-legged *US usu* ˈ=ˌlegəd, *Brit usu* -gd\ *adj* **:** having short legs — used of a person or animal

duck·let \ˈdəklət\ *n* -s **:** DUCKLING 1

duck·ling \-liŋ, -lēŋ\ *n* -s [ME *dookelynge*, fr. *dooke*, duck + *-lynge, -ling*] **1 :** a young duck **2 :** a dark greenish blue that is bluer and duller than average teal and darker and slightly bluer and stronger than average teal blue

duck malaria *n* **:** a destructive febrile disease of wild and domestic ducks caused by a blood protozoan (*Leucocytozoon anatis*) that is transmitted by a blackfly of the genus *Simulium*

duckmole \ˈ=ˌ=\ *n* **:** PLATYPUS

duck moss *n* **:** DUCK GRASS 1

duck oak *n* **:** WATER OAK 1

duck on a rock *or* **duck on the rock** *also* **duck on drake :** a game in which each player has a stone that he places on a rock for other players to try to knock off before retrieving their own stones without getting tagged by the first player

duck pass *n* **:** an aerial path used by wild waterfowl usu. over a narrow strip of land between two lakes

duckpin \ˈ=ˌ=\ *n* [so called fr. its short squat appearance] **1 :** a small bowling pin shorter than a tenpin but proportionately wider at mid-diameter **2 duckpins** *pl but sing in constr* **:** a bowling game using duckpins and differing from tenpins in that a smaller ball is used and three balls per frame are bowled

duck potato *n* **:** WAPATOO

duck river baptist *n, cap D&R&B* [fr. *Duck river*, Tenn.] **:** a member of a Baptist body founded in Tennessee in 1807 holding Calvinistic doctrines and observing the practices of close communion and foot washing

ducks *pl of* DUCK, *pres 3d sing of* DUCK

ducks and drakes *also* **duck and drake** *n* **:** the pastime of skimming flat stones or shells along the surface of calm water — **play ducks and drakes with** *also* **make ducks and drakes of :** to throw away heedlessly **:** SQUANDER

duck's bill brachiopod *n* **:** an elongated more or less oblong dorsoventrally flattened inarticulate brachiopod (genus *Lingula*) somewhat resembling the bill of a duck

duck's egg *var of* DUCK EGG

duck's-foot \ˈ=ˌ=\ *n, pl* **ducks'-foots** *or* **ducks'-feet :** MAYAPPLE

duck's-foot shell *n* **:** DUCKFOOT

duck shot *n* **:** a medium-heavy lead shot used in duck hunting

duck sickness *n* **:** a highly destructive form of botulism affecting esp. wild ducks in areas of the western U.S. in which drought has caused decay of aquatic vegetation thereby permitting excessive multiplication of botulinus bacteria (*Clostridium botulinum* type C) and spreading of their characteristic toxin in feeding areas — compare LIMBERNECK

duck's-meat \ˈ=ˌ=\ *n, pl* **duck's-meats :** DUCKWEED

duck soup *n* **:** something requiring little effort **:** something easy to do and often remunerative

duck stamp *n* **:** the federal migratory-bird hunting stamp first issued in 1934 that is required on the hunting licenses of wildfowl hunters over 16 years of age and that is sold to raise funds for the protection of migratory birds (as by the purchase of sanctuary areas)

duckstone \ˈ=ˌ=\ *n* **:** DUCK ON A ROCK; *also* **:** the stone on which the duck is placed

ducktail \ˈ=ˌ=\ *n, often attrib* **:** a teen-age boy's haircut in which the sides are kept long and brushed to meet at the back of the head

duckwalk \ˈ=ˌ=\ *n* **:** DUCKBOARD

duck walk *vi* **:** to walk with a waddle or with turned-out toes; *specif* **:** to walk as a hazing stunt while grasping the ankles with the hands

duckweed \ˈ=ˌ=\ *n* [ME *dockewede*, fr. *docke*, duck + *wede*, weed] **:** any small floating aquatic plant of the family Lemnaceae; *esp* **:** a plant of the genus *Lemna*

duckweed family *n* **:** LEMNACEAE

duck wheat *n* **:** TARTARIAN BUCKWHEAT

duckwing \ˈ=ˌ=\ *n* **:** Modern Game fowl having wing coverts that form a bluish black bar across the wing

¹ducky *also* **duck·ie** \ˈdəkē, -ki\ *n, pl* **duckies** [¹*duck* + *-y, -ie*

(n. suffix)] 1 : a young duck 2 *chiefly Brit* : PET, DARLING — usu. used as a term of address

²ducky \"\ *adj* -ER/-EST [¹duck + -y (adj. suffix)] 1 : very satisfactory : FINE, PLEASANT ⟨everything is just ~ for you to do, but all wrong for everybody else —Mark Reed⟩ ⟨everybody has a ~ time at a cost of about $300 per camper —*Reader's Digest*⟩ 2 : DARLING, CUTE ⟨a ~ little restaurant⟩

¹duct \ˈdəkt\ *n* -s [L *ductus* act of leading, shape (of a letter), fr. past part. of *ducere* to lead — more at TOW] 1 *obs* a : action of leading : GUIDANCE b : DIRECTION c : PASSAGE d : a stroke of a letter 2 [NL *ductus*, fr. ML, aqueduct, fr. L] *anat* : a tube or vessle — used esp. of those that carry off the secretion of a gland but used also of lymphatic vessels, certain blood vessels, and other canals ⟨thoracic ~⟩ ⟨acoustic ~⟩ 3 a : a pipe, tube, or channel by which a substance (as water, gas, air) is conveyed b : a usu. underground pipe or tubular runway for carrying an electric power line, telephone cables, or other conductors 4 *bot* a : a continuous tube formed by a row of elongated cells which have lost their intervening end walls — compare TRACHEA, VESSEL b : an elongated cavity formed by disintegration or separation of cells (as a resin canal of a conifer) 5 : INK FOUNTAIN 6 : an atmospheric condition which usu. obtains when warm dry air is resting on cool moist air and by which radio waves are confined to the neighborhood of the earth's surface with resulting abnormally long transmission ranges

²duct \"\ *vt* -ED/-ING/-S : to convey (as a gas) through a duct

duc·tal \-tᵊl\ *adj* : of or belonging to a duct : made up of ducts

duct·ed \-təd\ *adj* [¹duct + -ed] : situated or operating in a duct ⟨a ~ fan⟩ ⟨a ~ radiator⟩

duc·ti·ble \-təbəl\ *adj* [ME, fr. MF, fr. ML *ductibilis*, fr. L *ductus* (past part.) + -*ibilis* -ible] *archaic* : DUCTILE

duc·tile \ˈdəktᵊl *also* -ˌtīl *or* -(ˌ)til\ *adj* [MF & L; MF, fr. L *ductilis*, fr. *ductus* (past part. of *ducere* to lead) + -*ilis* -ile — more at TOW] 1 : capable of being fashioned into a new form 2 a : capable of being permanently drawn out without breaking ⟨a ~ metal⟩; *specif* : capable of being drawn out into wire or thread — compare MALLEABLE b : capable of being molded or worked : PLIANT, FLEXIBLE 3 : capable of being conveyed in channels — used of water 4 : easily led or influenced : TRACTABLE, COMPLIANT ⟨a vast portion of the public feels rather than thinks, a ~ multitude drawn easily by the arts of the demagogue —Amy Loveman⟩ **syn** see PLASTIC

duc·tile·ly \-ᵊl(l)ē, -ītlē, -il(l)ē, |iˌ\ *adv* : in a ductile manner

duc·til·i·ty \ˌdəkˈtiləd·ē, -ətē, -i\ *n* -ES : the quality or state of being ductile

duct·ing \ˈdəktiŋ\ *n* -s [¹duct + -ing] : a system of ducts; *also* : the material composing a duct

duct·less \ˈdəktləs\ *adj* : being without a duct

ductless gland *n* : ENDOCRINE GLAND

duct of bo·tal·lus \-bōˈtaləs\ *usu cap B* [trans. of NL *ductus Botalli*, fr. *Botallus* (Leonardo Botallo), 16th cent. Ital. physician] : DUCTUS ARTERIOSUS

duct of cu·vier \-ˈk(y)üvēˌā, -kǖevyā\ *usu cap C* [after Baron Georges *Cuvier* †1832 Fr. naturalist] : either of a pair of large transverse venous sinuses that conduct blood from the cardinal veins to the sinus venosus of the vertebrate embryo — called also *common cardinal vein*

duct of gart·ner \-ˈgertnər\ *usu cap G* [after Hermann T. *Gärtner* †1827 Dan. anatomist] : the remains in the female mammal of a part of the wolffian duct of the embryo

duct of mül·ler \-ˈmyüla(r), -ˈmil-,-ˈmul-,-ˈməl-\ *usu cap M* [after Johannes P. *Müller* †1858 Ger. anatomist] : MÜLLERIAN DUCT

duct of ri·vi·nus \-rəˈvēnəs\ *usu cap R* [after Augustus Q. *Rivinus* †1723 Ger. physiologist] : any of several small inconstant efferent ducts of the sublingual gland

duct of san·to·ri·ni \-ˌsantəˈrēnē, -ˌsän-\ *usu cap S* [after Giovanni D. *Santorini* †1737 Ital. anatomist] : an accessory pancreatic duct branching from the duct of Wirsung and opening into the duodenum above the main duct

duct of steno *usu cap S* [after Nicolaus *Steno* (Niels Stensen) †1687 Dan. anatomist] : STENO'S DUCT

duct of wharton *usu cap W* [after Thomas *Wharton* †1673 Eng. anatomist] : WHARTON'S DUCT

duct of wir·sung \-ˈvir(ˌ)zuŋ, -rzəŋ\ *usu cap W* [after Johann G. *Wirsung* †1643 Ger. anatomist] : the chief duct of the pancreas conducting its secretions to the duodenum — compare DUCT OF SANTORINI

duc·tor \ˈdəktə(r)\ *n* -s [L *ductor* leader (fr. *ducere* to lead + -*or*) — more at TOW] : DROP ROLLER 2

ductor blade *n* : DOCTOR 6a

ducts *pl of* DUCT, *pres 3d sing of* DUCT

duc·tule \ˈdək,t(y)ül\ *n* -s [¹duct + -ule] : a small duct

duc·tus \ˈdəktəs\ *n, pl* ductus [in sense 1, NL; in sense 2, fr. L — more at DUCT] 1 : DUCT 2 2 : HANDWRITING : the general shape of manuscript letters ⟨a bold monumental ~ formed of straight lines and circles — H.A.R.Gibb⟩

ductus ar·te·ri·o·sus \-(ˌ)ärˌtirēˈōsəs\ *n* [NL, arterial duct] : a short broad vessel conducting blood from the pulmonary artery and descending aorta of the fetus — called also *duct of Botallus, ductus Botalli*

ductus cho·le·do·chus \-kəˈledəkəs\ *n* [NL, choledoch duct] : COMMON BILE DUCT

ductus de·fer·ens \-ˈdefəˌrenz, -ˌrənz\ *n* [NL, deferent duct] : VAS DEFERENS

ductus ve·no·sus \-vəˈnōsəs, -vē-\ *n* [NL, venous duct] : a vein passing through the liver and connecting the left umbilical vein with the inferior vena cava of the fetus, losing its circulatory function after birth, and persisting as one of the supporting ligaments of the liver

ductwork \ˈ≈ˌ≈\ *n* : a system of ducts (as in hot-air heating or air conditioning)

ducu·la \ˈdəkyələ, ˈd(y)ük-\ *n, cap* [NL] : a genus of large coppery brown or black and white Asiatic pigeons — see NUTMEG PIGEON

¹dud \ˈdəd\ *n* -s [ME *dudde*] 1 : an article of clothing — now usu. used in pl. ⟨another thing you can scratch off the vacation budget is a heavy outlay for resort ~s —*Christian Science Monitor*⟩ 2 **duds** *pl, slang* : personal belongings ⟨pack up yer ~s an' get off'n my land —Hamlin Garland⟩ 3 **duds** *pl, chiefly dial* : ragged or cast-off clothes : RAGS, TATTERS 4 a : person or thing that proves to be ineffective : a flat failure ⟨the convention . . . is turning out to be a ~ as far as business is concerned —Lucille Eddinger⟩ 5 : an explosive-filled missile that fails to explode when it should

²dud \"\ *adj* : of little or no worth : INEFFECTIVE, FAKE, BAD ⟨issued ~ checks and then committed suicide —James Agate⟩

du·daim \ˈd(y)üˌdīm, ≈ˈ≈\ *n* -s [Heb *dūdhā'īm* mandrake] 1 : MANDRAKE 2 *also* **dudaim melon** : a melon (*Cucumis melo dudaim*) probably orig. of central Asia with small fragrant fruit grown chiefly for ornament

dud·die *or* **dud·dy** \ˈdədē\ *adj* [¹dud (rag) + -*ie*, -*y*] *Scot* : RAGGED, TATTERED

dude \ˈd(y)üd\ *n* -s [origin unknown] 1 : a man who is overfastidious in dress and manner : an ultrafashionable man : FOP, DANDY 2 a : a city man : TENDERFOOT; *esp* : an easterner touring or staying in the West b : a guest at a dude ranch

du·deen *also* **du·dheen** *or* **doo·deen** *or* **doo·dheen** \(ˈ)düˌdēn\ *n* -s [IrGael *dūidīn*, dim. of *dūd* pipe] : a short tobacco pipe made of clay

du·del·sack \ˈdüdᵊlˌsak, *G* -ˌzäk\ *n* -s [G — more at DOODLESACK] : a German bagpipe

dude ranch *n* : a ranch or resort for vacationers offering primarily horseback riding and other activities typical of western ranches

dude up *vi, slang* : to dress up ⟨he *duded up* for the dance⟩

dude wrangler *n* : one employed as a guide and host on a dude ranch

dudgen *adj* [origin unknown] *obs* : HOMELY, RUDE, COARSE

¹dud·geon \ˈdəjən\ *n* -s [ME *dogeon, dugion*, fr. AF *digeon*] 1 *obs* : a wood perhaps boxwood used esp. for the handles of daggers 2 *archaic* : a dagger or other implement having a handle of dudgeon 3 *obs* : a haft made of dudgeon

²dudgeon \"\ *n* -s [origin unknown] : aggrieved or angered feeling : ILL HUMOR, RESENTMENT — usu. used with *in* and a qualifier ⟨fuming, he stalked off in high ~⟩ **syn** see OFFENSE

dud·ine \(ˈ)d(y)üˌdēn\ *n* -s [dude + -ine] : a female dude

dud·ish \ˈd(y)üdish\ *adj* [dude + -ish] : having the appearance of a dude : like a dude — **dud·ish·ly** *adv*

dud·ism \-üˌdizəm\ *n* -s [dude + -ism] : the quality or state of being a dude

dud·ley \ˈdədlē\ *adj, usu cap* [prob. fr. the name *Dudley*] *of a dog's nose* : having a flesh or pink color undesirable in some breeds

dud·ley·ite \-ˌīt\ *n* -s [*Dudley*ville, Ala. + E -*ite*] : a variety of vermiculite

¹due \ˈd(y)ü\ *adj* [ME *dewe, due*, fr. MF *deu* (past part. of *devoir* to owe), fr. L *debitus*, past part. of *debēre* to owe — more at DEBT] 1 : owed or owing as a debt 2 *obs* : owed or owing as a necessity : FATED, INEVITABLE 3 a : owed or owing in accordance with natural or moral right ⟨every character gets the reward or the punishment ~ to his wit and address or his lack of both —J.W.Krutch⟩ ⟨such awe is ~ to the high name of God —P.B.Shelley⟩ b : requisite or appropriate in accordance with accepted notions of what is right, reasonable, fitting, or necessary ⟨representatives . . . who have exhibited their full powers found to be in good and ~ form —*Charter of the United Nations*⟩ ⟨will exercise this right with ~ respect to their obligations —Gilbert Seldes⟩ ⟨he has written with care and skill, with ~ regard for beauty and suitability of style — L.R.McColvin⟩ 4 a : satisfying or capable of satisfying a need, requirement, obligation, or duty : ADEQUATE, SUFFICIENT ⟨education for adults is receiving ~ attention⟩ ⟨walking all the while in ~ fear of the Lord —Guy McCrone⟩ ⟨seafaring activities which in ~ course came to be so vital a part of English life —Kemp Malone⟩ b : REGULAR, LAWFUL ⟨indemnity for loss will be paid subject to ~ proof of loss⟩ — see DUE PROCESS OF LAW 5 : owing or attributable : ASCRIBABLE — used with *to* ⟨this advance is partly ~ to a few men of genius —A.N.Whitehead⟩ ⟨his success was ~ to his persistence⟩; compare DUE TO 6 : having reached the date at which payment is required : PAYABLE — used esp. of a note or obligation in which the time for payment is specified 7 : required or expected in the prescribed, normal, or logical course of events : SCHEDULED ⟨tax legislation that Congress is ~ to consider⟩ ⟨the train is ~ at noon⟩; *specif* : about to bring forth young

syn RIGHTFUL, CONDIGN: DUE applies to what is owing or obligatory in accordance with legal agreements, formal procedure, or sanctioned ways or with what is just, right, or reasonable ⟨driving fast but with *due* caution⟩ ⟨tried according to *due* processes of law⟩ ⟨with *due* religious rites⟩ ⟨the parishes sent their *due* contingent of armed men —J.R.Green⟩ ⟨the characteristically Greek love of moderation, proportion, harmony, and *due* measure —Lucius Garvin⟩ ⟨so painful a scandal may well be allowed to die out. With *due* discretion the incident itself may, however, be described —A.C.Doyle⟩ RIGHTFUL applies to what is right, just, equitable, fair, or fitting; it is commonly used in situations in which these characteristics have been, or are in danger of being, ignored, lost sight of, or flouted ⟨looked askance, jealous of an encroacher on his *rightful* domain —Nathaniel Hawthorne⟩ ⟨the disloyal subject who had fought against his *rightful* sovereign —T.B.Macaulay⟩ ⟨happy the man at such a period, who enjoys a bedroom which he can secure with a key — for without such precaution the *rightful* possessor is not at all unlikely, on entering his own premises, to find three or four somewhat rough-looking strangers —Anthony Trollope⟩ ⟨years of neglect followed, but it finally acquired its *rightful* place among the nation's hallowed relics —*Amer. Guide Series: Pa.*⟩ CONDIGN indicates what is exactly or fitly deserving or meriting; it now applies more frequently to punishments than to anything else ⟨trembled with rage as he lay, and he resolved on *condign* revenge —Arthur Morrison⟩ ⟨to defy those papal laws which protected clerical sinners from *condign* punishment —G.G.Coulton⟩

²due \"\ *n* -s [ME *dewe, due*, fr. *dewe, due* adj.] 1 a : something that is due or owed : something that rightfully belongs to a person or thing ⟨was denied the promotion which his scientific colleagues thought his ~ —Anthony Harris⟩ ⟨those advanced in culture and in wealth longed to have their ~ in social recognition —Oscar Handlin⟩ ⟨the southern talent for government has won the recognition which is its ~ —Adlai Stevenson b. 1900⟩ b : a payment or obligation required by custom, law, morality, ethics : DEBT ⟨revenue . . . from the feudal ~s of his vassals and towns —Hilaire Belloc⟩ c **dues** *pl* : the fee or charge required for membership, affiliation, initiation, use, subscription ⟨~s are five dollars a year⟩ 2 *obs* : just title or claim : RIGHT 3 : POSTAGE-DUE STAMP

syn DESERT, MERIT: DUE in this sense is likely to suggest a quite apt or fitting reward decided upon judiciously and with consideration ⟨giving each man his *due* . . . impartial as the rain from Heaven's face —Vachel Lindsay⟩ ⟨this qualified respect, the old man's *due*, is paid without reluctance —William Wordsworth⟩ DESERT is likely to suggest a reward rightly owed in view of ethics, fairness, moral right ⟨the manly desire to exercise the talents which are given us by Heaven and reap the prize of our *desert* —W.M.Thackeray⟩ ⟨but families of less illustrious fame whose chief distinction is their spotless name must shine by their true *desert* —William Cowper⟩ MERIT stresses the existence of qualities or actions worth consideration in connection with rewards or punishments rather than the fact of their being considered or judged ⟨had this latter part of the charge been true, no *merits* on the side of the question which I took could possibly excuse me —Edmund Burke⟩ ⟨but originality, as it is one of the highest, is also one of the rarest, of *merits* —E.A.Poe⟩

³due \"\ *adv* [¹due] 1 *obs* : DULY 2 : DIRECTLY, EXACTLY ⟨the road runs ~ north⟩

⁴due *vt* [ME *duen*, fr. MF *douer*, fr. L *dotare*, fr. *dot-, dos* dower — more at DOWER] *obs* : ENDUE : ENDOW

due bill *n* : a written acknowledgment of a debt not made payable to order used esp. to make payment in services rather than cash (as by hotels for advertising) 2 : a bill for the balance due where the first bill was insufficient

due care *n* : the care that an ordinarily reasonable and prudent person exercises under all circumstances for his own protection

due cor·de \ˌdü(ˌ)āˈkȯrˌdā\ [It, two strings] — used as a direction in music (1) to play the same tone on two strings (as of the violin) simultaneously or (2) to release the una corda or soft pedal of the piano; compare TRE CORDE

due date *n* : the date on which a debt becomes payable : the maturity date of a bill, note, bond, or other evidence of debt

dueful *adj* [²due + -ful] *obs* : FIT, BECOMING

¹du·el \ˈd(y)üəl, -ü̇əl *also* -ü̇l, *chiefly Brit* |(ˌ)il\ *n* -s [ML *duellum* (influenced in meaning by folk etymological association with L *duo* two), fr. L, war (poetical variant of *bellum*), fr. OL; perh. akin to Gk *daiein* to ignite, burn up — more at TWO, TEEN] 1 : a combat between two persons: a *obs* : personal combat to determine a trial by battle b : a prearranged formal combat with deadly weapons fought between two persons in the presence of witnesses usu. as a result of an injury done or an insult given by one to the other — compare ²PRINCIPAL, ²SECOND 2 : a conflict between persons, ideas, or forces that are antagonistic ⟨when the long-drawn-out ~ . . . ended in a war —W.J.Hail⟩ ⟨artillery ~⟩ ⟨a ~ between the two emotions of repugnance and duty —Hilaire Belloc⟩

²duel \"\ *vb* **dueled** *or* **duelled**; **dueled** *or* **duelled**; **dueling** *or* **duelling**; **duels** *vi* : to fight a duel ~ *vt* : to encounter (an opponent) in a duel

dueling *or* **duelling** *n* -s : the fighting of duels

dueling pistol *n* : a long-barreled pistol designed esp. for dueling and with cases, made in pairs

du·el·ist *or* **du·el·list** \ˈd(y)üələst, -ü̇ə-\ *n* -s : one who engages in duels

du·el·is·tic *or* **du·el·lis·tic** \ˌ≈≈ˈlistik\ *adj* : having reference to dueling or a duelist

du·el·lo \d(y)üˈe(ˌ)lō\ *n* -s [It, fr. ML *duellum* — more at DUEL] 1 : DUELING 2 : the rules of dueling 3 : DUEL

due·ness *n* -ES : the quality or state of being due

du·en·na \d(y)üˈenə\ *n* -s [Sp *dueña*, fr. L *domina* lady — more at DAME] 1 : an elderly woman serving as governess and companion to the younger ladies in a Spanish or a Portuguese family 2 : GOVERNESS, CHAPERON

due process of law *or* **due course of law** : a course of proceedings at law or carried out through agency rules or other devices that is in accordance with the law of the land — called also *due process*

dues *pl of* DUE, *pres 3d sing of* DUE

duesseldorf *usu cap, var of* DÜSSELDORF

due stamp *n* : POSTAGE-DUE STAMP

¹du·et \(ˈ)d(y)üˈet, *usu* -ed·+V\ *n* -s [It *duetto*, dim. of *duo* duet — more at DUO] 1 a : a musical composition or movement for two singers or two instrumentalists with or without accompaniment b : a performance of such a composition c : two musicians performing such a composition 2 : a dance by two people : PAS DE DEUX 3 : an action participated in by two parties ⟨the birds which continue ~s of "mouth opening" and other dual rites and mutual displays —E.A.Armstrong⟩

²duet \"\ *vi* **duetted**; **duetted**; **duetting**; **duets** : to perform a duet

due to *prep* : because of ⟨the number and influence of investors are increasing, *due to* several causes —*Mag. of Wall Street*⟩ ⟨when German power was at its peak, *due to* the unpreparedness of her neighbors —Joseph Rosenfarb⟩ ⟨the event was canceled *due to* inclement weather⟩ — compare ¹DUE 5

du·et·tist \d(y)üˈed·əst, -etə-\ *n* -s : a participant in a duet

du·et·to \düˈed·(ˌ)ō\ *n, pl* **duet·tos** \-d·ˌōz\ *or* **duet·ti** \-d·(ˌ)ē\ [It] : DUET

due vol·te \ˌdü(ˌ)āˈvȯlˌtā\ *adv* [It] : two times — used as a direction in music to repeat a passage

¹duff \ˈdəf\ *n* -s [E dial. *duff*, var. of ¹*dough*] 1 : a stiff flour pudding usu. containing raisins and currants and boiled in a bag or steamed ⟨plum ~⟩ — compare PLUM PUDDING 2 : the partly decayed organic matter on the forest floor ⟨scratchings of dirt and twigs and forest ~ —Verne Athanas⟩ — compare HUMUS, LITTER, MOR 3 : fine coal : SLACK

²duff \"\ *vt* -ED/-ING/-S [back-formation fr. *duffer*] 1 *slang* a : to treat or manipulate so as to give a specious appearance to : FAKE b : CHEAT 2 *Austral* : to alter the brand on (stolen cattle or horses) : steal and alter the brand on (cattle or horses) 3 *Brit* : to misplay (a golf ball) esp. by striking the ground back of the ball before the club strikes the ball

³duff \"\ *n* -s [origin unknown] *slang* : BUTTOCKS

duffadar *var of* DAFADAR

duf·fel *or* **duf·fle** \ˈdəfəl\ *n* -s [D *duffel*, fr. *Duffel*, town near Antwerp, Belgium] 1 : a coarse heavy woolen blanketing or overcoating with a thick nap 2 *usu duffle* : transportable personal belongings, equipment, and supplies ⟨a car that bulged with people, suitcases, and assorted *duffle* —F.L.Allen⟩ ⟨soldiers stowing *duffle* and rifles into hard canvas bunks —K.M.Dodson⟩

duffel bag *n* : a large cylindrical canvas or rubberized fabric bag for transporting personal belongings ⟨with tents, a camping outfit, and *duffel bags* —Van Wyck Brooks⟩

duf·fer \ˈdəfə(r)\ *n* -s [origin unknown] 1 *slang* a : a peddler or hawker esp. of cheap flashy articles (as sham jewelry) b : something counterfeit or worthless 2 a : a stupid, dense, or stubbornly unreasonable person b : one that is incompetent or clumsy (as at a game or a trade) ⟨horsemen, both skilled and ~s —Gladwin Hill⟩ c : an elderly and ineffectual man ⟨he was quite used to having people set him down as a harmless, worn-out old ~ —Dorothy C. Fisher⟩ 3 *Austral* : a cattle rustler 4 *Austral* : SHICER

duffle coat *or* **duffel coat** *n* : a heavy woolen coat usu. knee-length and hooded worn for protection against cold and stormy weather

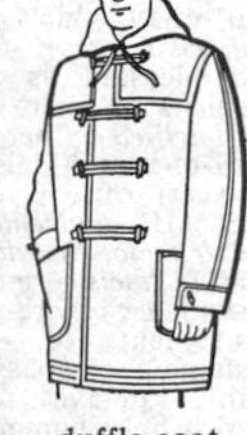
duffle coat

duf·fy \ˈdəfē, -i\ *adj, usu cap* [after Richard *Duffy* †1956 Brit. hemophiliac] : relating to, characteristic of, or being a system of blood groups determined by the presence or absence of any of several antigens in red blood cells ⟨*Duffy* blood group system⟩ ⟨*Duffy* antigens⟩

du·fre·nite \d(y)üˈfrāˌnīt\ *n* -s [F *dufrénite*, fr. O.P.A. Petit-*Dufrénoy* †1857 Fr. mineralogist + F -*ite*] : a blackish green mineral $Fe_5(PO_4)_3(OH)_5.2H_2O$ consisting of hydrous iron phosphate commonly massive or in nodules

du·fre·noy·site \ˌd(y)üfrəˈnȯiˌzīt\ *n* -s [F *dufrénoysite*, irreg. fr. O.P.A. Petit-*Dufrénoy* + F -*ite*] : a lead-gray mineral $Pb_2As_2S_5$ consisting of a compound of lead arsenic sulfide occurring in orthorhombic crystals or massive

duf·ter \ˈdəftə(r)\ *var of* DAFTAR

dufterdar *var of* DAFTARDAR

duf·tery *or* **duf·try** \ˈdəft(ə)rē\ *n* -ES [Hindi *daftarī* record keeper, office keeper, fr. Per, fr. *daftar* book, record — more at DAFTAR] *India* : a servant in an office whose duty is to dust and bind records, rule paper, make envelopes : OFFICE BOY

duft·ite \ˈdəfˌtīt\ *n* -s [G *duftit*, fr. G. *Duft*, 20th cent. director of mines at Tsumeb, South-West Africa + G -*it* -ite] : a mineral $PbCu(AsO_4)(OH)$ consisting of a basic arsenate of lead and copper

¹dug \ˈdəg\ *past of* DIG

²dug \"\ *n* -s [perh. of Scand origin; akin to OSw *dæggia* to suckle, Dan *dægge*; akin to Goth *daddjan* to suckle — more at FEMININE] : an udder or breast; *also* : a teat or nipple — usu. used of a suckling animal but vulgar when used of a woman

dug·dug \ˈdəgˌdəg\ *n* -s [native name in Guam] : the fertile form of the breadfruit tree

du·ge·sia \d(y)üˈjēzh(ē)ə\ *n, cap* [NL, fr. Antoine-Louis *Dugès* †1838 Fr. physician and zoologist + NL -*ia*] : a genus of widespread No. American triclad flatworms including a common brown freshwater planarian (*D. tigrina*)

du·gong \ˈdüˌgäŋ, -gȯŋ *also* ˈdyü-\ *n* [NL modif. of Malay & Tag *duyong*] 1 *cap* : a monotypic genus (the type of a family Dugongidae) of aquatic herbivorous mammals that with the manatees constitute the order Sirenia, that are distinguished from the manatees by a bilobate tail resembling that of a whale, fewer molar teeth and less deeply cleft upper lip, and upper incisors which are altered into tusks in the male, and that commonly attain a length of 8 feet or more 2 *pl* **dugongs** *also* **dugong** : any mammal of the sole species (*Dugong dugon*) of the genus *Dugong* — called also *sea cow*

dugout \ˈ≈ˌ≈\ *n* -s 1 : a canoe or boat made by hollowing out a large log 2 : a shelter or primitive dwelling excavated in a hillside or dug in the ground and roofed with sod : ABRI; *specif* : a cave in the side of a trench for quarters, storage, or protection from gunfire 3 : a low shelter facing the baseball diamond and containing the players' bench

dugway \ˈ≈ˌ≈\ *n* 1 : a road constructed along a hillside by using for the fill on the downhill side material excavated immediately above it 2 : an excavated road

dug well *n* : a well made by excavating with hand tools or power machinery instead of by drilling or driving

du·hat \ˈdüˌhät\ *n* -s [Tag] *Philippines* : JAVA PLUM

dui·ker *also* **duy·ker** \ˈdīkə(r), ˈdāk-\ *n, pl* **duikers** *also* **duiker** [Afrik *duiker* (formerly spelled *duyker*), lit., diver, fr. *duik* to dive (fr. MD *dūken*) + -*er* — more at DUCK] 1 : any of several small African antelopes of *Cephalophus* and related genera having short straight horns and commonly regarded as forming a subfamily of the Bovidae — compare BLUE DUIKER 2 *Africa* : CORMORANT

dui·ker·bok \-(r)ˌbäk\ *also* **dui·ker·buck** \-ˌbək\ *n, pl* **duikerbok** *or* **duikerboks** [Afrik, fr. *duiker* diver + *bok* male antelope; akin to OHG *boc* male goat — more at BUCK] : DUIKER 1

duis·burg-ham·born \ˌdüsˌbu̇rgˈhamˌbȯrn, -üz-, -ˌbərg-, -ˌhamˈbō(ə)rn, -häm-; *G* ˈdüesbu̇rkhämˈbȯrn *or* -u̇rk- *or* -ˈhäm-ˌb-\ *adj, usu cap D&H* [fr. *Duisburg-Hamborn*, Germany] : of or from the city of Duisburg-Hamborn, Germany : of the kind or style prevalent in Duisburg-Hamborn

duit \ˈdȯit, ˈdīt\ *n* -s [D — more at DOIT] : DOIT 1

du jour \dəˈzhu̇(ə)r, dü'-\ *adj* [F, of the day] : as cooked or prepared on a particular day ⟨potatoes *du jour*⟩ ⟨the soup *du jour* is onion⟩

du·kan *or* **du·chan** \dü'kän, -ˈk̲-, ˈ≈ˌ≈; ˈdükən\ *n* -s [Heb *dūkhān* platform] 1 : the platform on which the priest of the Hebrew Temple stood to pronounce the benediction 2 : PRIESTLY BLESSING

duk-duk \ˈdu̇kˌdu̇k\ *n* -s [native name in New Britain] 1 : a native secret society of islands of the Pacific ocean certain of whose members form a self-constituted judiciary and pose as sorcerers 2 : a member of a duk-duk

duke \ˈd(y)ük\ *n* -s [ME *duc, duke*, fr. OF *duc*, fr. L *duc-, dux* leader, commander, fr. *ducere* to lead — more at TOW] 1 *obs* : LEADER, CHIEF 2 : a sovereign prince or ruler of a duchy on the continent of Europe 3 a : a nobleman of the highest hereditary rank in certain continental European countries **b** : a member of the first and highest grade of the peerage in Great Britain **4** *slang* **a** : FIST; *also* : HAND — usu. used in pl. **b** : the raised fist as a symbol of victory (as in a prizefight) ⟨the winner was given the ~ at the end of the fight⟩ **c** : a player's hand of cards **5** *also* **duke cherry** : any of several cultivated cherries that are intermediate in characteristics between sweet cherries and sour cherries and are usu. considered to have originated by hybridization of these — compare BIGARREAU CHERRY, HEART CHERRY

duke·dom \ˈk-dəm\ *n* -S [ME *ducdom*, fr. *duc*, duke + -*dom*] **1** : the state or territory ruled by a duke or duchess : DUCHY **2** : the rank or dignity of a duke

duked up *adj* : dressed up ⟨chips . . . *duked up* with the master's initials or his whole name —*Mademoiselle*⟩

duke·ling \ˈd(y)üklin\ *n* -S **1** *archaic* : the child of a duke **2** : a petty or insignificant duke

duke·ly \-lē\ *adj* : of or suitable to a duke

duke's coronet *n* : the coronet of a British or Irish duke having eight conventional strawberry leaves upon the rim of the circlet — compare DUCAL CORONET

duk·ey rider \ˈd(y)ükē,-, ˈdükē,-\ *n* [alter. of ²*dook* + -*ey* (var. of -*ie*)] : BRAKEMAN 1a(2)

dukhn \ˈdükən\ *n* -S [Ar] *Sudan* : PEARL MILLET 1

dukhobor *usu cap, var of* DOUKHOBOR

du·ku \ˈdü(,)kü\ *n* -S [Malay] : a lanseh tree having nearly round dark-colored fruit

dukw *n* -S *sometimes cap* [fr. *DUKW*, its code designation] : ⁵DUCK

du·lat \ˈdü,lat\ *also* **du·lan** \-an\ *n* -S *usu cap* : one of the major divisions of the Great Horde

dul·bert \ˈdəlbə(r)t, ˈdül-\ *n* -S [prob. fr. ¹*dull* + -*bert* (fr. ¹*beard*)] *dial Brit* : BLOCKHEAD, DULLARD

dul·ca·ma·ra \,dəlkəˈmärə, -ma(a)rə\ *n* -S [NL, fr. ML *dulcis* sweet + *amara*, fem. sing. of *amarus* bitter — more at DULCET, AMARINE] **1** : BITTERSWEET 2a **2** : dried stems of dulcamara formerly used as a diuretic and sedative

¹**dulce** *adj* [L *dulcis*] *obs* : sweet to the taste : SOOTHING, AGREEABLE

²**dul·ce** \ˈdül(,)sā\ *n* -S [Sp, fr. *dulce*, adj., sweet, fr. L *dulcis*] **1** *Southwest* : SWEETMEAT, CANDY **2** : a sweet Spanish wine

³**dulce** *var of* DULSE

¹**dul·cet** \ˈdəlsət, *usu* -əd·+V\ *adj* [alter. (influenced by L *dulcis*) of ME *doucet*, fr. MF, fr. *douz* sweet (fr. L *dulcis*) + -*et* (dim. suffix); perh. akin to Gk *glykys* sweet] **1** : sweet to the taste : LUSCIOUS ⟨Catawba wine . . . ~, delicious, and dreamy —H.W.Longfellow⟩ **2** : pleasing to the ear : MELODIOUS ⟨~ symphonies and voices sweet —John Milton⟩ **3** : extremely pleasant or soothing ⟨the most beautiful and remote beaches, the most ~ bathing —Edward Weeks⟩ **syn** see SWEET

²**dulcet** \"\ *n* -S : a pipe-organ stop like the dulciana but an octave higher

dul·cet·ly *adv* : in a dulcet manner

dulcian *var of* DOLCIAN

dul·ci·ana \,dəlsēˈanə, -ˈänə\ *n* -S [NL, fr. ML, bassoon, fr. L *dulcis* + -*ana* (fem. sing. of -*anus* -an)] : a labial pipe-organ stop having metal pipes and a tone of soft sweet string quality of 8-foot pitch in the manual organ but 16-foot in the pedal organ

dul·ci·fy \ˈdəlsə,fī\ *vt* -ED/-ING/-ES [LL *dulcificare*, fr. L *dulcis* sweet + -*ficare* -fy — more at DULCET] : to make sweet or pleasant: as **a** : to free from saltness or acidity ⟨*dulcified* spirits of niter⟩ **b** : to make agreeable : MOLLIFY, APPEASE ⟨*dulcified* by a fresh-lit pipe of tobacco —Nathaniel Hawthorne⟩

dul·ci·mer \ˈdəlsəmə(r)\ *n* -S [alter. (influenced by L *dulcis* sweet) of ME *dowcemere*, fr. MF *doulcemer*, fr. OIt *dolcimelo*, fr. *dolce* sweet, fr. L *dulcis* — more at DULCET] **1** : a wire-stringed instrument of trapezoidal shape encompassing two to three octaves and played with light hammers held in the hands : CIMBALOM **2** *or* **dul·ci·more** \-,mō(ə)r, -,mȯ(ə)r\ : an American folk instrument that has three or four strings stretched over an elongate fretted soundbox and that is held on the lap and played by plucking or strumming

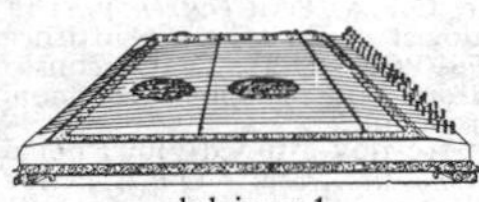
dulcimer 1

Dul·cin \ˈdəlsən\ *trademark* — used for a sweet crystalline compound used as a sweetening agent

dul·ci·nea \,dəlsəˈnēə, ,dəlˈsinēə\ *n* -S [Sp. after *Dulcinea* del Toboso, the beloved of Don Quixote — more at DON QUIXOTE] : MISTRESS, SWEETHEART

dul·ci·tol \ˈdəlsə,tȯl, -ōl\ *n* -S [obs. *dulcite* (fr. L *dulcis* sweet + E -*ite*) + -*ol* — more at DULCET] : a white faintly sweet crystalline hexahydric alcohol $HOCH_2(CHOH)_4CH_2OH$ occurring in various plants, obtained from a manna from Madagascar, and made from galactose by reduction

Dul·ci·tone \-tōn\ *trademark* — used for a keyboard instrument similar to the celesta in which hammers strike a set of tuning forks for sound production

dul·ci·tude \ˈdəlsə,tüd, -sə-,tyüd\ *n* -S [L *dulcitudo*, fr. *dulcis* + connective -*t*- + -*udo* -ude] : SWEETNESS

dulcorate *vt* [L *dulcoratus*, fr. (assumed) *dulcor* sweetness (whence LL; fr. L *dulcis* + -*or*) + -*atus* -ate] *obs* : DULCIFY

dulcoration *n, obs*

dül·fer rappel \ˈdilfə(r)-, ˈdül\ *n, usu cap D* [after *Dülfer*, 20th cent. Ger. alpinist] : BODY RAPPEL

du·lia \d(y)üˈlīə\ *n* -S [ML, fr. LGk *douleia* service, work done, business, fr. Gk, slavery, fr. *doulos* slave (prob. of non-IE origin) + -*eia* -y] *Roman Catholicism* : veneration or respect paid to the saints and angels as the servants and friends of God — compare LATRIA

¹**dull** \ˈdəl\ *adj* -ER/-EST [ME *dul, dulle*; akin to OE *dol* foolish, OHG *tol* foolish, ON *dul* concealment, conceit, Goth *dwals* foolish, OIr *dall* blind, Gk *tholeros* muddy, troubled, and prob. to L *fumus* smoke — more at FUME] **1** : mentally slow : somewhat lacking in intelligence : STUPID, DOLTISH, THICKHEADED ⟨although ~ at classical learning, at mathematics he was uncommonly quick —W.M.Thackeray⟩ ⟨be ~ and soulless, like a beast of the field — a brainless animal, with listless eye, unlighted by any ray of fancy, or of hope, or fear, or love, or life —J.K.Jerome⟩ **2 a** : slow or blunted in perception or sensibility : UNFEELING, INSENSIBLE ⟨she was worn out; so exhausted that she was ~ to what went on about her —Willa Cather⟩ **b** *dial Brit* : HARD-OF-HEARING **3** : lacking zest or vivacity : depressed in spirits : DISHEARTENED, LISTLESS, HOPELESS ⟨you must not fall back into any of your ~ moods —William Black⟩ ⟨~ apathy of despair —Oscar Wilde⟩ **4 a** : slow in action, motion, or response : SLUGGISH, INERT, LIFELESS, PONDEROUS ⟨the ~ heaviness in his heart —Agnes S. Turnbull⟩ ⟨his ~ brain⟩ **b** : marked by inactivity esp. in business ⟨talk of further curtailment by mills because of the ~ market in cotton goods —*Wall Street Jour.*⟩ ⟨lay off some of their staff in the ~ season —*Jour. of Accountancy*⟩ **5** : lacking sharpness of edge or point : BLUNT **6** : lacking brilliance or luster ⟨*dull*-finish aluminum⟩ : MUFFLED, MUTED : not clear : INDISTINCT, DIM : lacking in force or intensity ⟨the kerosene lamp gave a ~ light⟩ ⟨the ~ boom of the breaking waves —John Cooke⟩ ⟨~, rankling anger —Rudyard Kipling⟩ **7** *of a color* : low in saturation and low in lightness **8** *of the weather* : CLOUDY, OVERCAST, GLOOMY **9** *of paper or its finish* : smooth but relatively low in gloss **10** : furnishing little delight, spirit, or variety : TEDIOUS, UNINTERESTING ⟨eating ~ food and wearing shabby clothes —J.E.Evans⟩ ⟨I find the book long-winded, incredibly boring, heavy to the last degree, and deadly ~ —*John o' London's Weekly*⟩ ⟨a ~ speaker⟩

syn BLUNT, OBTUSE: DULL may refer to an edge or point that has lost its sharpness ⟨a *dull* knife⟩ It may apply to lack or loss of keenness, pungency, interest, poignancy, or intensity ⟨a *dull* pain⟩ ⟨a *dull* diet⟩ ⟨transferred from the *dull* pages of the textbook to the livelier writing of romance —T.C.Chubb⟩ ⟨compared with her, other women were heavy and *dull;* even the pretty ones seemed lifeless —Willa Cather⟩ BLUNT may refer to an edge or point not intended or designed to be sharp ⟨the *blunt* edge of a table knife⟩ BLUNT may indicate lack of keenness in perception, sensitivity, or discrimination ⟨*blunt* in perception and feeling and quite destitute of imagination —A.C.Bradley⟩ ⟨*blunt*, unemotional, completely lacking in subtlety, Mr. Strydom accepts and proclaims without question —James Gray⟩ OBTUSE may apply in technical or mathematical writing to an angle or convergence of more than 90 degrees. Otherwise OBTUSE suggests more-or-less stupid lack of perception or sensitivity ⟨carelessly egotistical as she was, she was not really *obtuse;* she had realized from the outset that she was being allowed to come on this expedition as a favor —Ann Bridge⟩ ⟨there was, one vaguely feels, something a little *obtuse* about Dr. Burney. The eager, kind, busy man, with his head full of music and his desk stuffed with notes, lacked discrimination —Virginia Woolf⟩ **syn** see in addition STUPID

²**dull** \"\ *vb* -ED/-ING/-S [ME *dullen*, fr. *dul, dulle*, adj.] *vt* : to make dull: **a** : to make less clear, distinct, or bright ⟨the painting's original warm colors have been greatly ~*ed* by age⟩ ⟨grime ~*ed* his brown skin —Audrey Barker⟩ **b** : to make less keen or acute : make less active or forceful : STUPEFY, DEVITALIZE ⟨fear ~*s* the sense of adventure —Mary E. Chase⟩ ⟨~*ed* by routine and sunk in apathy —John Dewey⟩ ⟨old age is ~*ing* my taste for books —O.W.Holmes †1935⟩ **c** : to deprive of sharpness (as of edge or point) : BLUNT ⟨~*ed* somewhat the cutting edge of popular resentment —Cabell Phillips⟩ ⟨believes tighter credit has done its job and ~*ed* the inflation threat —*Newsweek*⟩ **d** : to lessen the sensitivity of (as the physical senses) ⟨eyes and ears ~*ed* by age⟩ **e** : to reduce the luster of (as rayon) : DELUSTER, BLIND ~ *vi* : to be or become dull

¹**dul·lard** \ˈdələ(r)d\ *n* -S [MF *dullarde*, fr. *dul, dulle* + -*arde* -ard] : a stupid person

²**dullard** \"\ *adj* : characterized by dullness or insensitivity

dull emitter *n* : an electron tube in which the cathode is a filament which does not glow brightly

¹**duller** *comparative of* DULL

²**dull·er** \ˈdələ(r)\ *n* -S [²*dull* + -*er*] : one that produces a dull or clouded effect on furniture by a mildly abrasive rubbing of or action on the finish

dullest *superlative of* DULL

dull gold *n* : a light olive color that is redder and deeper than citrine or grape green and redder and slightly darker than old moss green

dullhead \ˈ=,=\ *n* : BLOCKHEAD, DULLARD

dull·ish \ˈdəlish, -lēsh\ *adj* [ME *dullisshe*, fr. *dul, dulle* + -*isshe* -ish] : somewhat dull

dull·ness *or* **dul·ness** *n* -ES [ME *dulnesse*, fr. *dul, dulle* + -*nesse* -ness] **1** : the quality or state of being dull : STUPIDITY, APATHY, DROWSINESS, BLUNTNESS : a lack of luster, vividness, or brightness : MONOTONY ⟨the village street is well shaded by elms, with flower beds brightening the general ~ —*Amer. Guide Series: Vt.*⟩ ⟨exports . . . underwent a quick recovery after the seasonal ~ of the summer months —*Paper Trade Jour.*⟩ ⟨the men were getting freshened up from the day's monotonies and ~*es* —Mark Twain⟩ **2** : something that is dull ⟨checkbooks and columns of figures and rent bills and grocer's bills and light bills and telephone bills and other awful ~*es* —J.L.Street †1947⟩

¹**dull-normal** \ˈ=¦==\ *adj* : having an intelligence level on the borderline between normal intelligence and mental deficiency

²**dull-normal** \"\ *n* [¹*dull-normal*] : one who is dull-normal

dul·ly \ˈdəl(l)ē, -)i\ *adv* : in a dull manner : STUPIDLY, SLOWLY, DIMLY, SLUGGISHLY : without life or spirit

du·long and pe·tit's law \ˌd(y)ü,lȯnənpəˈtēz-, d(y)üˈl\ *n, usu cap D&P* [after Pierre L. *Dulong* †1838 and Alexis T. *Petit* †1820 Fr. physicists] : a law in physics and chemistry: the atomic heats of most solid elements are nearly the same averaging a little over 6 calories per degree C per gram atom

du·lo·sis \d(y)üˈlōsəs\ *n, pl* **dulo·ses** \-ō,sēz\ [NL, fr. Gk *doulōsis* slavery, fr. *douloun* to enslave (fr. *doulos* slave) + -*sis* — more at DULIA] : enslavement by an insect (as some ants of the genera *Formica* and *Polyergus*) that captures and rears the larvae or pupae of another species — **du·lot·ic** \(ˈ)d(y)ü¦läd·ik\ *adj*

dulse *also* **dulce** \ˈdəls *also* -lts\ *n* -S [ScGael & IrGael *duileasg*; akin to W *delysg* dulse] : any of several coarse red seaweeds (esp. *Rhodymenia palmata*) found principally in northern latitudes and used as a food condiment

dult \ˈdəlt\ *or* **dult·ie** \-tē\ *n* -S [*dult* alter. of *dolt; dultie* fr. *dult* + -*ie*] *Scot* : DOLT, DUNCE

du·luth \dəˈlüth\ *adj, usu cap* [fr. *Duluth*, Minn.] : of or from the city of Duluth, Minnesota : of the kind or style prevalent in Duluth : DULUTHIAN

¹**du·luth·ian** \-thēən\ *adj, usu cap* [*Duluth*, Minn. + E -*ian*] **1** : of, relating to, or characteristic of Duluth, Minnesota **2** : of, relating to, or characteristic of the people of Duluth

²**duluthian** \"\ *n* -S *cap* : a native or resident of Duluth

du·ly \ˈd(y)ülē, -li\ *adv* [ME *dueliche, duly*, fr. *dewe, due* + -*liche, -ly* — more at DUE] : in a due manner, time, or degree : as is right and fitting : PROPERLY, REGULARLY, SUFFICIENTLY ⟨any infringements must be clearly recognized and their authors ~ punished —J.S.Pictet⟩ ⟨~ authorized representatives⟩ ⟨all pertinent factors should be ~ considered⟩

dulzian *var of* DOLCIAN

dum *or* **dumb** \ˈdəm\ *adj (or adv)* [euphemism] : DAMN

du·ma *also* **dou·ma** \ˈdümə, -,mä\ *n* -S [Russ *duma*, of Gmc origin; akin to Goth *doms* judgment — more at DOOM] **1** : an elective council in Russia ⟨Catherine II introduced elective municipal ~*s* —F.A.Ogg & Harold Zink⟩ **2** *often cap* : a legislative assembly functioning primarily as a council of state in czarist Russia ⟨an unsatisfactory bill was presented by the government for the consideration of the Third *Duma* —Valentine Ughet & Eleanor Davis⟩

du·ma·gat \ˈdümə,gät\ *n, pl* **dumagat** *or* **dumagats** *usu cap* [Tag, fr. *dagat* sea] **1** : any of several Negroid pagan peoples inhabiting the eastern coast of central Luzon, Philippines **2** : a member of any of the Dumagat peoples

¹**dumb** \ˈdəm\ *adj* -ER/-EST [ME, fr. OE; akin to OHG *tumb* mute, inexperienced, stupid, ON *dumbr* mute, Goth *dumbs* mute, OE *dēaf* deaf — more at DEAF] **1** : destitute of the power of speech ⟨he must have been ~, for never a word did he utter —Herman Melville⟩ **2 a** : by nature incapable of speech like that of human beings ⟨~ animals⟩ **b** *of an animal* : having no capacity to make sounds : MUTE **c** : having no voice — used of inanimate things ⟨the great ~ trees —Anton Vogt⟩ **3** : temporarily unable to speak (as from astonishment, grief, shock) ⟨one pictures newspaper reporters going about, struck ~ with amazement at every smallest incident in this amazing life we lead —Rose Macaulay⟩ **4 a** : not expressed in uttered words : not communicated verbally — used of feelings, emotions, ideas ⟨how terrible is that ~ grief which has never learned to moan —John Galsworthy⟩ ⟨let the world wail! . . . my sorrow shall be ~! —Edna S. V. Millay⟩ **b** : incapable of being expressed or communicated verbally ⟨the expression of loss and loneliness and ~ desire on his face —Irwin Shaw⟩ **5** : SILENT, QUIET: as **a** : saying little or nothing usu. through lack of desire to speak : TACITURN, UNCOMMUNICATIVE ⟨if they had nothing to say, they were capable of sitting for hours, ~ and unabashed, over their pipes or their plugs of tobacco —Ellen Glasgow⟩ ⟨I beg that you remain ~, that you write no more poems —Amy Lowell⟩ **b** : not having the usual accompaniment of speech or sound ⟨with frantic ~ play Anton signaled to Vincent —Basil Thomson⟩ ⟨legend and tradition demand that bells be ~ until they are blessed —P.D.Peery⟩ **6** : having little or no meaning : INEXPRESSIVE ⟨his work is infantile, ~ with botched detail, wooden scenes, and collapsed characterizations —J.S.Shrike⟩ **7** : lacking some usual attribute or concomitant; *esp, of a boat* : having no means of self-propulsion ⟨~ barge⟩ ⟨~ lighter⟩ **8** [influenced in meaning by D *dom* stupid, G & PaG *dumm*] : STUPID, FOOLISH: **a** *of a person* : lacking perception or understanding : UNRESPONSIVE ⟨too ~ to do things in the right way —W.J.Reilly⟩ ⟨blind to Galileo on his turret, ~ to Homer, ~ to Keats —Robert Browning⟩ **b** *of an action or thing* : resulting from or characterized by stupidity ⟨must learn to disregard the ~ advice . . . of relatives and friends —R.V.Seliger⟩ ⟨bad weather, youthful recklessness, carelessness, and plain ~ flying —*Time*⟩

syn MUTE, SPEECHLESS, INARTICULATE: DUMB and MUTE are often interchangeable, but some differences may be noted. In reference to animals, MUTE implies an inability to make sounds, DUMB an incapacity for speech ⟨must I live all my life as *mute* as a mackerel? —L.P.Smith⟩ ⟨yon *dumb* patient camel —Robert Browning⟩ In reference to persons, DUMB may imply some physical defect, MUTE an insensibility to speech brought about through deafness ⟨the other was a wretch from infancy made *dumb* by poison —P.B.Shelley⟩ ⟨like the *mute* dwarfs which wait upon a naked Indian queen —Robert Browning⟩ In reference to persons normally able to speak, DUMB may suggest a quite short deprivation of ability to utter sounds ⟨I was bewildered and *dumb* until Livilla gave me a good pinching, at which I burst into tears —Robert Graves⟩ ⟨he made despairing gestures with his hands, but still no words came from his mouth. He might have been struck *dumb* —W.S. Maugham⟩ MUTE may be used when an inner compulsion to stay silent is suggested ⟨but every man was *mute* for reverence —Alfred Tennyson⟩ ⟨as the conversation took fire, she hadn't so much as a chip to throw in. She sat *mute* —Sinclair Lewis⟩ SPEECHLESS, although it often has the same suggestions of DUMB or MUTE, commonly indicates momentary loss of power to speak ⟨overcome with *speechless* gratitude —William Wordsworth⟩ ⟨I can remember, across the years, standing there with that paper in my hand; dumb, *speechless* and probably tearful —W.A.White⟩ INARTICULATE implies either lack of satisfactory speech functions or an inability to speak coherently, clearly, or purposefully ⟨his jaws opened, and he muttered some *inarticulate* sounds —Mary W. Shelley⟩ ⟨but when Richard, *inarticulate* at first, in his haste, cried out: "My dear, dear father!" —George Meredith⟩ ⟨his rage was a madness. His lips were flecked with a soapy froth, and sometimes he choked and became *inarticulate* —Jack London⟩ ⟨as shyly *inarticulate* as a schoolgirl on this theme so vital to her —Rose Macaulay⟩ **syn** see in addition STUPID

²**dumb** \"\ *vb* -ED/-ING/-S *vi* : to become dumb or silent — used with *up* ~ *vt* : to make silent : DEADEN ⟨the sight of the great assembly that ~*ed* the words in his mouth —Donn Byrne⟩ ⟨would lie around, ~*ed* by the drugs —Norman Mailer⟩

dum·ba \ˈdəmbə, ˈdüm-\ *n* -S [Per, fr. *dumb* tail; akin to OHG *zumpho* penis, Ar *duma*- tail, OE *tæppa* tap — more at TAP] : a fat-tailed sheep of Bokhara and the Kirghiz steppe that furnishes astrakhan

dumb act *n* : an act (as in vaudeville) without dialogue

dumb ague *n* : malarial fever with no well-defined chill and with slight periodicity

dumbartonshire *or* **dumbarton** *usu cap, var of* DUNBARTONSHIRE

dumb barter *also* **dumb commerce** *n* : a primitive system of barter in which the parties avoiding personal contact leave goods at accepted locations in return for others

dumbbell \ˈ=,=\ *n* **1** : an apparatus similar to that formerly used in ringing a church bell that is used in learning bell ringing or for bodily exercise **2** : a weight (as of wood or metal) that consists of two identical spheres connected by a short bar serving as a handle and that is used usu. in pairs for calisthenic exercise **3** : something shaped like a calisthenic dumbbell **4** : one that is dull and stupid : DUMMY ⟨if we don't give him a shove the poor ~ never will propose —Sinclair Lewis⟩ ⟨every time I opened the chicken-house door . . . the ~*s* would fly up in the air —Betty MacDonald⟩

dumbbell 2

dumbbell tenement *n* [so called fr. its resemblance in shape to a dumbbell] : a tenement building formerly common in New York City and having a long narrow plan characterized by two narrow air wells at each side

dumb bet·ty \-ˈbed·|ē, -et|, |i\ *n* [fr. the name *Betty*] *n* : a primitive mechanical household contrivance (as a washing machine or dumbwaiter) used to lighten the work of early American housewives

dumb bid *n* : the owner's undisclosed limit below which no bid shall avail as a purchase in an auction

dumb-bird \ˈ=,=\ *n* : RUDDY DUCK

dumb cane *n* : a tropical American herb (*Dieffenbachia seguine*) that when chewed causes the tongue to swell — called also *mother-in-law plant*

dumb cluck *or* **dumb bunny** *n, slang* : DUMBBELL 4

dumb compass *n* [so called fr. its having no magnets or directive force] : PELORUS

dumb crambo *n* : a game in which one team chooses a word to be guessed and gives a rhyming word as a clue to the other team which then pantomimes its guess as to the original word

dumb do·ra \¦=ˈdōrə\ *n, usu cap 2d D* [fr. the name *Dora*] : a stupid and often naive woman

dum be·ne se ges·se·rit \(,)düm¦benē,sāˈgesərət\ *adv* [L, as long as he behaves well] : during his good behavior — used of an appointment that is not for a period of time or at the pleasure of the appointer but that ends only at the appointee's death or misconduct

dumber *comparative of* DUMB

dumbest *superlative of* DUMB

dumbfish \ˈ=,=\ *n* : DUNFISH

dumb·found *or* **dum·found** \ˌdəmˈfaund\ *vt* -ED/-ING/-S [¹*dumb* + -*found* (as in *confound*)] : to strike dumb : confuse with astonishment : AMAZE ⟨he was ~*ed* by the rebuke⟩ **syn** see PUZZLE

dumbfounded *or* **dumfounded** *adj* : CONFUSED, BEWILDERED, AMAZED — **dumb·found·ed·ly** *adv*

dumb·found·er *or* **dum·found·er** \-də(r)\ *vt* : DUMBFOUND ⟨she takes possession of it and by her action ~*s* and antagonizes the family and the countryside —*Spectator*⟩

dumbhead \ˈ=,=\ *n, slang* : BLOCKHEAD

dumb iron *n* **1** : a caulking iron used to open up and straighten close seams prior to caulking esp. in new work **2** : a rigid connecting piece between the frame of an automotive vehicle and the spring shackle

dumb jockey *n* : a contrivance for bitting and training colts that consists of a saddle to the lower part of which sidechecks are fastened and two arms with elastic ends extending upward to which adjustable reins and crupper strap are fastened

dum·ble \ˈdəm(b)əl, ˈdüm-\ *var of* DIMBLE

dum·ble·dor *also* **dum·ble·dore** \ˈdəmbəl,dō(ə)r, -ȯ(ə)r\ *n* -S [*dumble* + *dor*] **1** *dial* : BUMBLEBEE **2** *dial* : COCKCHAFER

dumb·ly \ˈdəmlē, -li\ *adv* : in a dumb manner : VAGUELY

dumb·ness *n* -ES [ME *dumbnesse*, fr. *dumb* + -*nesse* -ness] **1** : the quality or state of being dumb : MUTENESS, SILENCE : inability to speak **2** : STUPIDITY, DULLNESS

dumb piano *n* : a portable keyboard for soundless piano practice and finger exercising

dumb rabies *n* : rabies marked by sluggishness and by early paralysis esp. of the muscles of jaw and throat — compare FURIOUS RABIES

dumbs *pres 3d sing of* DUMB

dumb sheave *n* : a block with a sheaveless hole or a groove in a spar for a rope to be rove through

dumb show *n* **1** : a part of a dramatic representation presented by actions unaccompanied by speech **2** : a presentation that communicates solely by signs and gestures : PANTOMIME ⟨the art of conveying a story by *dumb show* —W.P.Frith⟩ ⟨in fables that might be acted by puppets or in a *dumb show* and yet be tragical —W.P.Ker⟩

dumb struck *also* **dumb stricken** *adj* : struck dumb : made silent by astonishment : surprised and confused

dumbwaiter \ˈ=ˈ==\ *n* **1** : a portable serving table or stand often with revolving shelves arranged in tiers **2** : a small elevator used for conveying food and dishes or small goods from one story of a building to another

dumb watches *n pl* [so called fr. the disk-shaped style] : PITCHER PLANT a

dum cas·ta \düm'kästə\ *adv* [L] : while chaste — used as a proviso in limiting a bequest or devise to a widow or in conditioning the payment of alimony

dum·dum \ˈdəm,dəm\ *n* -S [fr. *Dum-Dum*, town near Calcutta, India, where dumdum bullets were once made] : a soft-nosed bullet or a standard bullet with vertical cuts made in its point so that it expands upon hitting an object

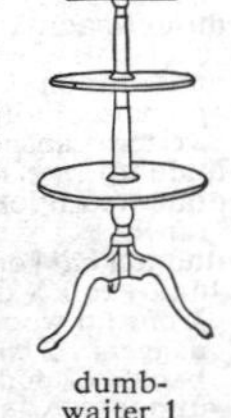
dumbwaiter 1

dumdum fever *n* [fr. *Dum-Dum*, India, where it was once prevalent] : KALA-AZAR

dum·fries·shire \,dəmˈfrēs(h),shi(ə)r, -(h)shər *also* ,də-\ *or* **dum·fries** \-ēs\ *adj, usu cap* [fr. *Dumfriesshire* or *Dumfries* county, Scotland] : of or from the county of Dumfries, Scotland : of the kind or style prevalent in Dumfries

dum fu·it in·fra ae·ta·tem \ˌdu̇m'füəd·ˌinfrə,ī'täd·əm\ *adv* [L, while he was under age] **:** while under age — used of an old writ for enabling a man after coming of age to recover lands he alienated while an infant

dum·ka \'du̇mkə, -üm-\ *n, pl* **dum·ky** \-kē\ [Czech, elegy, of Gmc origin; akin to Goth *dōms* judgment — more at DOOM] *music* **:** a slow movement of melancholy character

dum·mel \'dəməl, 'du̇m-\ *adj* [prob. fr. [1]*dumb* + *-el* (var. of *-le*)] **:** slow and stupid

dum·mi·ness \'dəmēnəs, -min-\ *n* -ES **:** the condition of being a dummy — used esp. of a horse

dumm·kopf \'du̇m,kȯf *also* 'dəm- *or* -ȯpf\ *n* -S [G, fr. *dumm* stupid (fr. OHG *tumb* mute, inexperienced, stupid) + *kopf* head, fr. OHG, drinking vessel — more at DUMB, CUP] *slang* **:** BLOCKHEAD

[1]**dum·my** \'dəmē, -mi\ *n* -ES [[1]*dumb* + *-y*] **1 :** one that is dumb: as **a :** one that is incapable of speaking **b :** one that is habitually silent **c :** one that is stupid **:** DOLT, DUMBBELL **2 a :** the exposed hand in bridge played by declarer in addition to his own hand **b :** a player in bridge who lays his cards face up on the table to be so played by declarer **3 :** an imitation, copy, or likeness of something intended for use as a substitute **:** EFFIGY: as **a** (1) **:** a form representing part or all of the human figure used for displaying or fitting clothes — compare LAY FIGURE (2) **:** a stuffed figure representing the trunk and legs of a man and supported by a rope or frame that is used by football players for practice in tackling and blocking (3) **:** a large puppet usu. having movable head, jaws, and arms and held on the knees of a ventriloquist entertainer **b :** a sham package or one that does not contain what its exterior indicates; *esp* **:** an empty package used for display **c** *chiefly Brit* **:** a false nipple **:** PACIFIER **4 :** one (as a person, body of people, corporation) that although seeming to act for itself is in reality acting for another usu. with little or no freedom of action or with fraudulent intent ⟨the directors, being controlled by one man, are only *dummies*⟩ ⟨if a woman appears as the owner of a business, it should be ascertained that she is not a ~ for the real owner . . . who for legal or other reasons may not be able to hold property —A.F.Chapin⟩ **5 a :** a block (as of wood) put on a library shelf to replace a missing book and marked with title, call number, and indication of the book's whereabouts **b :** a card in a file or catalog indicating location of material filed elsewhere or temporarily missing from the file **6 :** something usu. mechanically operated that serves to replace or aid a human being in the performance of a task: as **a :** DUMBWAITER **b :** a glassblower's device operated by foot pedals for wetting, raising, opening, and shutting a paste mold **c :** a device having lights on four sides placed at a street intersection to control traffic **7 :** one that plays a part (as in a play) intended merely to fill in (as in a group or scene) or fulfill an expectation and having no essential significance **8 :** a piece that serves as a model in a profiling machine **9 :** DRIFT PLUG **10 a :** a pattern volume (as of a book, magazine, or newspaper) projected or in process with blank pages or pasted-in examples of type or illustrative material **b :** LAYOUT **11 a :** an early comparatively quiet locomotive made with condensing engines and no blast pipe and sometimes used in city transit service **b :** a switching locomotive having the boiler and running gear entirely housed **12 :** a horse lacking the ability to respond to ordinary stimuli because of cerebral damage esp. following encephalomyelitis

[2]**dummy** \"\ *adj* **1 :** marked by sham or deception: as **a :** having the appearance of being real but lacking capacity to function **:** ARTIFICIAL ⟨~ foods in the shop windows —*Times Lit. Supp.*⟩ ⟨~ hinges⟩ **b :** existing in name only **:** FICTITIOUS ⟨a specialist in secretly buying up the stock of companies under ~ names —*Newsweek*⟩ ⟨pack the ballot with ~ candidates to split the vote —*New Republic*⟩ **2 :** having the appearance of acting independently or for oneself while really acting at the instruction of another ⟨issued patents for sixty thousand acres to ~ holders, who deeded the land to him after he had retired from office —V.L.Parrington⟩

[3]**dummy** \"\ *vb* -ED/-ING/-ES *vt* **1** *Austral* **:** to take up (land) for another in one's own name **2 :** to make a dummy of (as a book or page of a publication) ⟨the book was *dummied* and ready to go to press⟩ — often used with *up* ⟨the editor is now *~ing* up the editorial page⟩ **~** *vi* **1** *Austral* **:** to dummy land **2** *slang* **:** to refuse to talk — used with *up* ⟨when I mentioned his name they *dummied* up⟩

dummy duck *n* **:** RUDDY DUCK

dummy index *n* **:** UMBRAL SYMBOL

dum·my·ism \-,izəm\ *n* -S *Austral* **:** the act or practice of dummying land

dummy share *or* **dummy stock** *n* **:** a share or stock issued to a person to qualify him for election or for a vote

dummy whist *n* **:** whist played by three players with a fourth hand that is dealt opposite the dealer, turned face up before play begins, and managed by the dealer

du·mont·ite \'d(y)ü,mänt·,īt, ='=,=\ *n* -S [F *dumontite*, fr. André *Dumont* †1857 Belgian geologist + F *-ite*] **:** a hydrated phosphate $Pb_2(UO_2)_3(PO_4)_2(OH)_4.3H_2O$ of uranium and lead occurring in yellow orthorhombic crystals

du·mont's blue \'d(y)ü,män(t)s-, ='=-\ *n, often cap D* [fr. the name *Dumont*] **:** SMALT 2

du·mor·ti·er·ite \d(y)ü'mȯrd·ēə,rīt, ,d(y)ü(,)mȯr'ti,rīt\ *n* -S [F *dumortiérite*, fr. Eugène *Dumortier*, 19th cent. Fr. paleontologist + F *-ite*] **:** a bright blue or greenish blue mineral perhaps $Al_8BSi_3O_{19}OH$ consisting of basic aluminum borosilicate

[1]**dump** \'dəmp\ *n* -S [prob. fr. D *domp* exhalation, haze, fr. MD *damp, domp* — more at DAMP] **1** *obs* **:** a state of reverie or perplexity **2 :** a dull gloomy state of mind **:** low spirits **:** DESPONDENCY — now used in the pl. chiefly in the phrase *in the dumps* ⟨doleful *~s* the mind oppress —Shak.⟩ ⟨she will be there to cuddle him, praise him, help him out of his occasional *~s* —H.A.Overstreet⟩ ⟨she gets easily discouraged and down in the *~s*⟩ **3** *obs* **a :** a slow mournful melody or song **b :** a dance to such music **syn** see SADNESS

[2]**dump** \"\ *vb* -ED/-ING/-S *vi* **1** *obs* **:** MUSE **2** *obs* **:** to be downcast and sad **~** *vt, obs* **:** to cast into melancholy **:** GRIEVE, SADDEN

[3]**dump** \"\ *n* -S [perh. back-formation fr. *dumpling*] **1** *dial Brit* **:** something thick, ill-shaped, or shapeless ⟨*~s* of soft paper . . . to arrest bleeding —B.H.Chamberlain⟩; *specif* **:** a small leaden counter used in such games as chuck-farthing **2 a :** a coin that is small and very thick **b :** a small Australian silver coin bearing the words *fifteen pence* made from a piece cut from the center of a holey dollar **3** *archaic* **:** a short stout person

[4]**dump** \"\ *vb* -ED/-ING/-S [perh. fr. D *dompen* to immerse, tumble, topple; akin to MLG *dumpeln* to duck, OHG *tumpfilo* whirlpool, OE *dyppan* to dip — more at DIP] *vt* **1 a :** to let fall in a heap or mass **:** cast down or away ⟨had proceeded to the wharf and had *~ed* the first shipload of tea into the harbor —C.G.Bowers⟩ ⟨she *~ed* the contents of her purse onto the table⟩ ⟨uncork the bottle and ~ the stuff out —D.B. Chidsey⟩ ⟨a hydraulic hoist to tip the truck body and ~ the coal out⟩ ⟨the conveyor *~ed* the dirt into self-discharging barges —N.M.Clark⟩ **b :** to get rid of unceremoniously (as if by dumping) **:** dispose of somewhat irresponsibly **:** JETTISON ⟨France *~ed* her third government in a few months⟩ ⟨captains of industry speedily *~ed* labor from their payrolls, and the breadlines grew —Stringfellow Barr⟩ ⟨the indenture system offered huge profits to the masters of the vessels which *~ed* their human cargo on American shores —A.D.Graeff⟩ ⟨the biggest problem that was ever *~ed* into his lap⟩ **2** *slang* **:** to hit hard **:** knock down **:** BEAT ⟨*~ed* their attackers, who scrambled to their feet and fled⟩ **3** *Austral* **:** to compress and secure (wool) into bales **4 :** to sell (commodities or securities) in quantity at a very low price; *specif* **:** to sell (surplus goods) abroad at less than the market price at home ⟨some factory owners fear that the military will ~ surplus goods on the market at cut-rate prices —*N.Y.Times*⟩ ⟨the union complained that foreign residual oil, *~ed* into this country with low import taxes, had displaced more than 30 million tons of coal production —*Wall Street Jour.*⟩ **5 :** to transfer (typeset matter) from stick to galley or galley to form or (as slugs) to bank; *often* **:** to lay aside (dead matter) for distribution **~** *vi* **1 :** to fall abruptly **:** PLUNGE, DROP **2 :** to dump goods or refuse ⟨no *~ing* allowed⟩

[5]**dump** \"\ *n* -S *often attrib* **1 a :** an accumulation of refuse or other discarded materials ⟨the city ~ caught fire⟩ ⟨is now a resort town, but its former greatness shows in the tremendous *~s* and the sprawling buildings of the Argo mine —G.R. Stewart⟩ **b :** a place where such materials are dumped **2 a :** a quantity of supplies or reserve materials accumulated at one conveniently located but safe place ⟨we have laid out *~s* of food and petrol across the polar plateau —Edmund Hillary⟩ **b :** the place where such materials are stored: as (1) **:** a place for the temporary storage of military supplies in the field ⟨ammunition ~⟩ (2) **:** the place in a composing room where dead matter is placed before it is distributed **3 :** a disorderly, slovenly, or dilapidated place indoors or outdoors ⟨instead of working in such a ~ he could have been in his comfortable hotel room —Morley Callaghan⟩ **4 :** something that has been dumped or deposited in a pile ⟨fresh avalanche *~s* contain large quantities of snow and ice, with occasional rock inclusions —R.L.Ives⟩ **5 :** DUMP TRUCK **6 :** DEFECATION — often considered vulgar

dum palm \'düm-\ *n* [F *doum* — more at DOOM PALM] **:** DOOM PALM

dump body *n* **:** a motor-truck or trailer body that can be manipulated to discharge its contents by gravity

dump car *n* **:** a railroad car whose body can be tilted for the dumping out of its contents

dumpcart \'=,=\ *n* **:** a cart having a body that can be tilted or a bottom opening downward for emptying the contents without handling

dumpcart in position for dumping

dump·er \'dəmpə(r)\ *n* -S **1 :** one that dumps: as **a :** DUMPCART, DUMP TRUCK **b :** a device that is used for unloading freight cars by tilting or dumping **c :** a worker who tips up the body and releases the gates of loaded cars to dump the contents (as coal, ore, rock) — called also *dumpman, tipman, tipper* **d :** a worker who empties materials or products from the molds in which they are formed or the containers in which they are stored or transported **2 :** a textile worker who examines cloth before it is printed in order to cut out and reverse any pieces that have been sewed in face down

dump hook *n* **:** a chain grabhook with a lever attachment for releasing it (as in unhitching a team in loading logs)

dump·i·ly \'dəmpəlē, -li\ *adv* **:** in a dumpy manner **:** shortly and thickly **:** PUDGILY ⟨a girl rather ~ constructed⟩

dump·i·ness \'dəmpēnəs, -pin-\ *n* -ES **:** the quality or state of being dumpy

dumping *n* -S [fr. gerund of [4]*dump*] **:** the selling of goods in quantity at below market price (as to dispose of a surplus or to break down competition) esp. in international trade

dumping duty *n* **:** a duty imposed by an antidumping law

dumping syndrome *n* **:** a condition characterized by weakness, dizziness, flushing and warmth, nausea, and palpitation immediately or shortly after eating and produced by abnormally rapid emptying of the stomach in persons who have had part of the stomach removed or in hypersensitive or neurotic individuals

dump·ish \'dəmpish, -pēsh\ *adj* [[1]*dump* + *-ish*] **1** *obs* **:** DULL, STUPID **2 :** SAD, MELANCHOLY, DEJECTED — **dump·ish·ly** *adv*

dump·ler \-plə(r)\ *n* -S [D *dompelaar*, fr. *dompelen* to immerse (freq. of *dompen* to immerse, tumble, topple) + *-aar* -er — more at DUMP] *archaic* **:** DUNKER

dump·ling \'dəmpliŋ, -lēŋ\ *n* -S *often attrib* [perh. alter. of [1]*lump* + *-ling*] **1 a :** a small mass of leavened dough cooked by boiling or steaming (as with soup, stew, or fruit with which it is to be served) **b :** a dessert made by wrapping fruit (as a whole apple) in biscuit dough and baking **2 :** something that has a somewhat rounded shapelessness like a dumpling ⟨a large, evenly terraced red mass, topped by a ~ of buff sandstone, rises above symmetrical outlying buttes —*Amer. Guide Series: Ariz.*⟩; *specif* **:** a short fat person or animal **3 :** APPLEBERRY — usu. used in pl. **4 :** something precious **:** DARLING — used as a term of endearment ⟨a new doll for your ~ daughter —*Wall Street Jour.*⟩

dump·man \'=,man, -mən\ *n, pl* **dumpmen** [[4]*dump* + *man*] **1 :** BANKMAN **2 a :** DUMPER 1c **b :** one that operates cable machinery for drawing cars of raw materials to a crane for dumping in a cement storage yard

dump power *n* [[5]*dump*] **:** surplus electric power that is in excess of existing local load requirements and that is made available because of overabundance of stored water in a hydroelectric plant

dump rake *n* **:** a hay rake mounted on two wheels consisting of a set of long curved steel teeth and equipped with a device for raising the teeth to dump the hay

dumps *pl of* DUMP, *pres 3d sing of* DUMP

dump shot *n* **:** DUNK SHOT

dump trailer *n* **:** a truck trailer with a dump body

dump truck *n* **:** a motor or hand-propelled truck for transporting and dumping loose materials; *esp* **:** a motor-driven truck that has a dump body and is designed esp. for the transportation of heavy bulk material (as sand, rock, or coal)

dump valve *n* **:** a large emergency valve at the bottom of a container (as an airplane fuel tank) by which it may be emptied much more quickly than by the ordinary drain cock (as in emergency jettisoning of fuel)

dump wagon *n* **1 :** DUMPCART **2 :** DUMP TRUCK

[1]**dumpy** \'dəmpē, -pi\ *adj* -ER/-EST [[1]*dump* + *-y*] **:** DUMPISH 2

[2]**dumpy** \"\ *adj* -ER/-EST [[3]*dump* + *-y*] **1** *also* **dump·ty** \-m(p)tē, -ti\ **:** lacking graceful height, length, or stature **:** being short and thick in body **:** SHAPELESS ⟨a *dumpy*-looking bunch of women . . . beefy and sturdy —Joseph Bennett⟩ ⟨fitting ~ concrete columns into the balustrade —Harold Brodkey⟩ **2** *of a coin* **:** small and thick **syn** see STOCKY

dumpy level *n* [[2]*dumpy*] **:** a surveyor's level with a short usu. inverting telescope that is rigidly fixed to a table and capable only of rotatory movement in a horizontal plane — called also *Troughton level*; compare Y LEVEL

dum so·la \ˌdu̇m'sōlə\ *adv* [L] **:** while unmarried — used of the status of a woman either maiden, widow, or divorced

[1]**dun** \'dən\ *adj, often* **dunner; dunnest** [ME, fr. OE *dunn* — more at DUSK] **1 a :** having a dun color **b** *of a horse* **:** exhibiting reduced hair pigmentation usu. accompanied by black points and dorsal stripe so that a basically black coat becomes pale grayish, a bay becomes yellowish, or a sorrel becomes pale and drab **2 :** marked by dullness and drabness **:** DARK, GLOOMY ⟨the ~ and dreary prairie —Laura Krey⟩ ⟨when ~ clouds flooded the naked plains with foul remorseless rains —Edmund Blunden⟩ ⟨the ~ professorial period of his life —V.L.Parrington⟩ — **dun·ness** \'dənnəs\ *n* -ES

[2]**dun** \"\ *vt* **dunned; dunned; dunning; duns** [ME *dunnen*, fr. OE *dunnian*, fr. *dunn*, adj.] **1 :** to make dun colored **:** DARKEN **2 :** to cure (as codfish) by the method formerly common in New England of salting, laying in a pile in a dark place, and covering (as with salt grass)

[3]**dun** \"\ *n* -S [ME, fr. *dun*, adj.] **1 :** a dun horse **2 :** a variable color averaging a nearly neutral slightly brownish dark gray and ranging from red to yellow in hue **3 a :** the subimago of a mayfly; *also* **:** an artificial fly tied to imitate such an insect **b :** CADDIS FLY

[4]**dun** \"\ *vt* **dunned; dunned; dunning; duns** [origin unknown] **1 :** to make persistent demands upon (as for money) **:** ask for repeatedly ⟨the grocer *dunned* that customer monthly by mail and by telephone for payment of his bill⟩ ⟨some organizations are always *dunning* their members for contributions⟩ **2 :** to plague or pester constantly ⟨*dunned* by troubles literary and monetary —*Irish Digest*⟩ ⟨hear her ~ him for a secret —Edith Sitwell⟩

[5]**dun** \"\ *n* -S **1 :** DUNNER 1 **2 :** an urgent request; *esp* **:** a demand for payment

[6]**dun** \'dün\ *n* -S [ScGael & IrGael. *dūn*, fr. OIr — more at DOWN] **:** a fortified residence in Scotland and Ireland surrounded by two or more concentric circular earthen mounds with a deep moat filled with water between them or a wall and a circular mound fortified with palisades

dun·al \'d(y)ün^əl\ *adj* [*dune* + *-al*] **:** of or relating to a dune

du·nam *also* **du·num** \'dünəm\ *n* -S [NHeb *dunam*, fr. Turk *dönüm*] **:** a unit of land area used esp. in the state of Israel equal to 1000 sq. meters or about ¼ acre

dun·bar·ton·shire \ˌdən'bärt^ən,shi(ə)r, -ˌshər\ *or* **dun·bar·ton** \-t^ən\ *also* **dum·bar·ton·shire** *or* **dum·bar·ton** \ˌdəm'-\ *adj, usu cap* [fr. *Dunbartonshire, Dumbartonshire* or *Dunbarton, Dumbarton* county, Scotland] **:** of or from the county of Dunbarton, Scotland **:** of the kind or style prevalent in Dunbarton

dunbird \'=,=\ *n* [[1]*dun* + *bird*] **:** any of several ducks: as **a** *Brit* **:** POCHARD **b :** RUDDY DUCK

dun·can phyfe \ˌdəŋkən'fīf *sometimes* -k^ən-\ *adj, usu cap D&P* [after *Duncan Phyfe* †1854 Scot.-Am. cabinetmaker] **1 :** of, relating to, being, or imitative of furniture designed and built by or in the style of Duncan Phyfe who used modified Hepplewhite, Sheraton, Directoire, and Empire forms characterized in chairs by turned and reeded legs, lyre-backs, and scrolled arms, in sofas by turned legs and back and arm rails carved in low relief and later by outward-sweeping cornucopia legs and rolled arms, in tables by turned or lyre-shaped pedestal bases with outflaring feet, and generally by decorative carvings of cornucopias, wheat sprays, plumes, and drapery swags **2 :** EMPIRE b

a Duncan Phyfe chair

dunce \'dən(t)s\ *n* -S *often attrib* [alter. of earlier *duns*, after John *Duns* Scotus †*ab*1308 Scot. scholastic theologian, whose once widely accepted writings were strongly ridiculed in the 16th cent.] **1** *obs* **a :** a copy of writings by Duns Scotus **b :** a textbook, comment, or gloss containing his teachings or written after his manner **2** *obs* **a :** SCOTIST **:** a sophist who cavils or splits hairs **b :** PEDANT **3 :** a dull-witted and stupid person **:** DUMBBELL, DULLARD

dunce cap *or* **dunce's cap** *n* **:** a conical cap slowe marked with a D formerly used as a punishment for slow learners at school

dunc·ery \'dən(t)s(ə)rē\ *n* -ES **1** *obs* **:** something characteristic of a Scotist **2** *archaic* **:** intellectual dullness **:** STUPIDITY

[1]**dunch** \'dənch, 'du̇nch\ *vt* -ED/-ING/-ES [ME *dunchen*; prob. akin to Icel, Sw & Norw *dunka* to strike, ON *dynkr* noise, *dynr* din — more at DIN] *dial chiefly Brit* **:** to nudge or bump esp. with the elbow

[2]**dunch** \'dənch\ *n* -ES [ME *dunche*, fr. *dunchen*, v.] *chiefly Scot* **:** BLOW, PUSH

[3]**dunch** \'dənch, 'du̇nch\ *adj* [origin unknown] **1** *dial Eng* **:** HARD-OF-HEARING **2** *dial Eng* **:** slow in recognition or comprehension

dun·ci·cal \'dən(t)səkəl\ *adj* **1** *obs* **:** having the characteristics of a dunce **2 :** marked by the qualities of a dunce **:** STUPID, DUNCISH

dun·ci·fy \-sə,fī\ *vt* -ED/-ING/-ES **:** to cause to appear stupid **:** make a dunce of

dunc·ish \-sish\ *adj* **:** like a dunce — **dunc·ish·ly** *adv*

dun crow *n* **:** the European hooded crow

dun·das·ite \'dəndə,sīt, ˌdən'da,s-\ *n* -S [*Dundas*, Tasmania + E *-ite*] **:** a mineral $PbAl_2(CO_3)_2(OH)_4.2H_2O$ consisting of a basic lead aluminum carbonate occurring in white spherical aggregates

dun·dathu pine \ˌdən'da(ˌ)thü-\ *also* **dun·dath·ee pine** \-athē-\ *n* [native name in Queensland, Australia] **:** an Australian timber tree (*Agathis robusta*) resembling the kauri pine but having wood much lighter in weight and softer — called also *Queensland kauri*

dun·dee \ˌdən¦dē\ *adj, usu cap* [fr. *Dundee*, Scotland] **:** of or from the city of Dundee, Scotland **:** of the kind or style prevalent in Dundee

[1]**dun·der** \'dən(d)ər\ *n* -S [perh. fr. D *donderen* to thunder — more at DONNERED] *chiefly Scot* **:** a noise like thunder **:** a noisy blow

[2]**dun·der** \'dəndə(r)\ *n* -S [origin unknown] **:** the lees of cane juice used to promote fermentation in the distillation of rum

dun·der·funk \'dəndə(r),fəŋk\ *n* -S [origin unknown] **:** broken sea biscuits or crackers mixed with molasses and baked

dun·der·head \-,hed\ *n* [perh. fr. D *donder* thunder (used as an intensifier in compound; fr. MD) + E *head*; akin to OHG *thonar* thunder — more at THUNDER] **:** DUNCE, NUMSKULL, BLOCKHEAD

dun·der·head·ed \¦==¦=əd\ *adj* **:** being a dunderhead — **dun·der·head·ed·ness** *n* -ES

dun·der·pate \-,pāt\ *n* [prob. fr. D *donder* + E *pate*] **:** DUNDERHEAD

dun diver *n* **:** a female or immature merganser

dun·drear·ies \ˌdən'drirēz\ *or* **dun·dreary whiskers** \(')dən-¦drirē-\ *n pl, often cap D* [after Lord *Dundreary*, character in the play *Our American Cousin* (1858), by Tom Taylor †1880 Eng. dramatist, as portrayed by Edward A. Sothern †1881 Eng. actor] **:** long flowing side whiskers

dune \'d(y)ün\ *n* -S *often attrib* [F, fr. OF, fr. MD *dune* — more at DOWN] **1 :** a hill or ridge of sand piled up by the wind commonly found along shores, along some river valleys, and generally where there is dry surface sand during some part of the year **2 :** TWINE 5

dun·edin \ˌdə¦nēd^ən, -dən\ *adj, usu cap* [fr. *Dunedin*, New Zealand] **:** of or from the city of Dunedin, New Zealand **:** of the kind or style prevalent in Dunedin

dune heath *n* **:** a treeless area of low heathlike vegetation found on sand dunes and sand plains

dune plant *n* **:** a plant (as beach heather, certain bayberries, and many grasses) adapted to growth on a sand dune esp. by its ability to resist drought

dunfish \'=,=\ *n* [[1]*dun* + *fish*] **:** fish cured by dunning

[1]**dung** \'dəŋ\ *n* -S [ME, fr. OE, dung, prison; akin to OE *dyncge* manure, manured land, OHG *tunga* manuring, *tung* cellar roofed with manure, ON *dyngja* manure pile, women's workroom, OIr *dingid* he suppresses, Lith *deñgti* to cover; basic meaning: pressing, covering] **1 :** MANURE **2 :** the excrement of an animal **3 :** something vile or loathsome

[2]**dung** \"\ *vb* -ED/-ING/-S [ME *dungen*, fr. *dung*, n.] *vt* **1 :** to fertilize or dress with dung **2 :** to immerse or steep (printed cloth) in a dung bath **~** *vi* **:** DEFECATE — used of an animal

dungan *usu cap, var of* TUNGAN

dun·ga·ree \ˌdəŋgə'rē, '=,=\ *n* -S [Hindi *dūgrī*] **1 :** a heavy coarse durable cotton twill woven from colored yarns; *specif* **:** blue denim **2 dungarees** *pl* **:** heavy cotton work clothes (as pants or overalls) made usu. of blue dungaree

dun·ga-run·ga \ˌdəŋgə¦rəŋgə\ *n* -S [native name in Australia] **:** a small Australian tree (*Notelaea ovata*) yielding a very hard wood used for tool handles — compare AXBREAKER

dung bath *n* **:** a bath orig. made with dung but now with chemicals for removing acid and thickening from printed cloth so that it will receive dye

dung beetle *also* **dung chafer** *n* **:** a scarabaeid beetle (as a dorbeetle or tumblebug) that rolls balls of dung in which the eggs are laid and on which the larvae feed

dun·ge·ness crab \ˌdənjə¦nes-\ *n, usu cap D* [fr. *Dungeness*, village on Juan de Fuca strait, northwest Washington] **:** a large edible crab (*Cancer magister*) of the Pacific coast of No. America from Alaska to San Francisco that is the chief commercial crab of the region

[1]**dun·geon** \'dənjən\ *n* -S *often attrib* [ME *donjon, dongeoun, dungeon*, fr. MF *donjon*, fr. ML *dominion-, dominio*, fr. L *dominus* lord, master + *-ion-, -io* -ion — more at DAME] **1 :** DONJON **2 :** a close dark prison or vault commonly underground; *esp* **:** a lower room in the keep of a castle **3** *chiefly Scot* **:** a person having a notable talent or ability ⟨a ~ of wit⟩

[2]**dungeon** \"\ *vt* -ED/-ING/-S **:** to shut up in or as if in a dungeon ⟨*~ed* in the human breast doubtless secrets lie —Emily Dickinson⟩

dung·er \'dəŋə(r)\ *n* -S **:** an operator of a machine for chemically removing acetic acid and thickening from printed cloth so that it will receive mordant dye

dung fly *n* **:** any of numerous small two-winged flies (family Scatophagidae) that breed in dung and decaying vegetable matter; *broadly* **:** any fly of similar habits

dunghill \'=,=\ *n* [ME, fr. [1]*dung* + *hill*] **1 :** a heap of dung **2 :** a vile or degraded situation, condition, or thing ⟨He . . . lifteth up the beggar from the ~ —1 Sam 2:8 (AV)⟩ **3** *also* **dunghill fowl :** the common domestic fowl — opposed to *game fowl*

dung·on \'dün,ōn\ *n* -s [Tag] **1 :** a valuable Philippine timber tree (*Tarrietia sylvatica*) **2 :** the hard pale reddish wood of the dungon

dungs *pl of* DUNG, *pres 3d sing of* DUNG

dung worm *n* **1 :** any of certain earthworms living in dung heaps; *esp* **:** a common pink worm (*Eisenia foetida*) sometimes used as bait **2 :** an insect larva (as of a two-winged fly) that develops in dung

dungy \'dəŋē\ *adj* -ER/-EST [ME, fr. [1]*dung* + *-y*] **:** like dung **:** FILTHY

du·nic \'d(y)ünik\ *adj* **:** of, relating to, or resembling a dune

dunier *comparative of* DUNY

duniest *superlative of* DUNY

du·nie·was·sal \ˌdünē¦wäsəl\ *or* **dun·nie·was·sel** \ˌdən-\ *n* [ScGael *duine-uasal*, lit., noble man] **1** *Scot* **:** a Highland gentleman **2** *Scot* **:** a cadet of a family of rank

du·nite \'dü,nīt, 'də,-\ *n* -s [Mt. *Dun*, near Nelson, New Zealand, its locality + E *-ite*] **:** a granitoid igneous rock belonging to the peridotites and consisting chiefly of olivine with a little chromite or other spinel — **du·nit·ic** \(ˈ)dü¦nid·ik, ¦də¦-\ *adj*

[1]**dunk** \'dəŋk\ *vb* -ED/-ING/-S [PaG *dunke* to dip, fr. MHG *dunken, tunken*, fr. OHG *dunkōn, thunkōn* — more at TINGE] *vt* **1 :** to dip (as a piece of bread, cake, or doughnut) into liquid (as coffee, milk, or tea) while eating **2 :** to dip or submerge temporarily in liquid ⟨a varnish that can be ~*ed* in acid without ill effect⟩ ⟨the old man ~*ed* the two plates up and down in a bucket of water and wiped them —Shirley A. Grau⟩ ~ *vi* **:** to submerge oneself in water (as by swimming or falling in) ⟨an outdoor, glass-protected pool to ~ in —Horace Sutton⟩ ⟨aviators who had ~*ed* signaled for rescue —O.O.Jensen⟩ **syn** see DIP

[2]**dunk** \"\ *n* -s **:** DIP 7

dun·ka·doo \ˌdəŋkə¦dü\ *n* -s [imit.] *dial* **:** AMERICAN BITTERN

dun·ker \'dəŋkə(r)\ *or* **dun·kard** \-(r)d\ *also* **tun·ker** \'təŋkə(r)\ *n* -s *usu cap* [*dunker* fr. PaG, fr. *dunke* to dip + *-er; dunkard, tunker* alter. of *dunker*] **:** a member of one of the denominations (as the Church of the Brethren) deriving from an orig. German Baptist group that practice trine immersion, love feasts, simplicity of life, and avoidance of oaths, lawsuits, and military service — called also *Dipper*

dunking *n* -s **:** IMMERSION ⟨shrinks after each ~ in hot water⟩

[1]**dun·kirk** *also* **dun·kerque** \'dən,kərk *also* ,=ˈ= *sometimes* -əŋ-\ *n* -s *usu cap* [fr. *Dunkirk* or *Dunkerque*, seaport in northern France, scene of the evacuation of allied troops in World War II after the fall of France, May 29–June 2, 1940] **1 :** a desperate evacuation under bombardment of remnants of a defeated army **2 :** a serious crisis demanding decisive action ⟨the immediate effect would plainly be a *Dunkirk* for U.S. foreign policy —*Time*⟩

[2]**dunkirk** \"\ *vt* -ED/-ING/-S **:** to force to execute a Dunkirk

dunk·irk·er \-kərkə(r)\ *n* -s *usu cap* [*Dunkirk*, France + E *-er*] **:** a 17th century privateer from Dunkirk; *also* **:** one of its crew

dunk shot *n* **:** a basketball shot made usu. by a tall player who jumps up and drops the ball over the rim and into the basket

dun·lin \'dənlən\ *n, pl* **dunlins** *or* **dunlin** [[1]*dun* + *-lin* (alter. of *-ling*)] **:** RED-BACKED SANDPIPER

dun·lop \'dən,läp, *chiefly Scot* ,dən'l-\ *or* **dunlop cheese** *n* -s *usu cap D* [fr. *Dunlop*, Ayr co., Scotland] **:** a rich white pressed Scotch cheese

dunmeh *usu cap, var of* DÖNMEH

[1]**dun·nage** \'dənij\ *n* -s [origin unknown] **1 a :** mats, boughs, pieces of wood, or other loose materials placed under or among goods carried as cargo in the hold of a ship to keep them dry and to prevent their motion and chafing **b :** temporary blocking or bracing installed by the shipper in the hold of a ship, in a railroad car, or in a truck to protect freight during shipment **c :** cushioning or padding used in a shipping container to protect fragile articles against shock and breakage **2 :** baggage or personal effects ⟨mules would pack our ~ from this jump-off point to the various camps we would pitch along our route —D.R.Brower⟩ **3 :** lumber below the recognized merchantable grades

[2]**dunnage** \"\ *vt* -ED/-ING/-S **:** to stow or secure with dunnage

dunned *past of* DUN

[1]**dunner** *comparative of* DUN

[2]**dun·ner** \'dənə(r)\ *n* -s [[4]*dun* + *-er*] **1 :** one that duns; *esp* **:** one that solicits payment of debts **2 :** [5]DUN 2

[3]**dunner** \"\ *var of* [1]DUNDER

dunnest *superlative of* DUN

dunniewassel *var of* DUNIEWASSAL

dunning *pres part of* DUN

dunning draft *n* [fr. pres. part. of [4]*dun*] **:** a draft drawn on a delinquent customer and deposited with a bank for payment

dun·nish \'dənish\ *adj* [[1]*dun* + *-ish*] **:** somewhat dun

dun·nock \'dənək, 'dún-\ *n* -s [ME *donek, dunoke*, fr. [1]*dun* + *-ek, -oke* *-ock*] *dial Eng* **:** HEDGE SPARROW

[1]**dunny** *adj* [[1]*dun* + *-y*] *obs* **:** DUNNISH

[2]**dun·ny** \'dəni, 'düni\ *adj* [origin unknown] *dial Brit* **:** slow to perceive **:** DULL

duns *pres 3d sing of* DUN, *pl of* DUN

dun·siek·te \'dən,sēktə\ *also* **dun·ziek·te** \-,zē-\ *n* -s [Afrik *dunsiekte* (formerly spelled *dunziekte*), fr. *dun* thin (fr. MD *dunne*) + *siekte* disease, fr. MD *siecte*, fr. *siec* ill; akin to OHG *dunni* thin and to OHG *sioh* sick, ill — more at THIN, SICK] **:** a serious intoxication of animals (as horses) of southern Africa that is caused by eating plants of the genus *Senecio* and is marked by emaciation, liver degeneration, and sometimes by nervous symptoms — compare WALKABOUT DISEASE

dunst \'dənzt, -n(t)st\ *n* -s [origin unknown] **:** the finest middlings usu. still containing some bran

dun·sta·ble \'dənztəbəl, -n(t)st-\ *adj* [fr. the *Dunstable* way, a road from London to the municipal borough of Dunstable, Bedfordshire, England, known for its straightness] *archaic* **:** PLAIN, DIRECT

[1]**dunt** \'dənt\ *n* -s [ME *dount, dunt*, var. of *dint* — more at DINT] **1** *chiefly Scot* **:** a heavy blow or stroke **2** *chiefly Scot* **:** BRUISE, WOUND **3** *chiefly Scot* **:** a quickened beat of the heart **:** THROB **4** *Scot* **:** a sizable lump

[2]**dunt** \"\ *vb* -ED/-ING/-S *vt, chiefly Scot* **:** to strike heavily **:** BEAT ~ *vi* **1** *chiefly Scot* **:** to fall with a heavy sound **2** *chiefly Scot, of the heart* **:** THROB

[3]**dunt** \"\ *vi* -ED/-ING/-S [origin unknown] *ceramics* **:** to crack while firing or afterward by temperature change or by inversion of crystals to greater volume

dunum *var of* DUNAM

duny \'d(y)ünē\ *adj* -ER/-EST **:** having many dunes

duo \'d(y)ü(,)ō\ *n, pl* **du·os** \-ü,ōz\ [It, fr. L *duo* two — more at TWO] **1 :** DUET; *also* **:** the participants in a duet **2 :** a group of two **:** PAIR

duo- *comb form* [L *duo* — more at TWO] **:** two ⟨*duo*secant⟩ ⟨*duo*machy⟩

duo *abbr* duodecimo

du·o·decennial \¦d(y)ü(,)ō+\ *adj* [LL *duodecennium* period of 12 years (fr. L *duodecim* twelve — fr. *duo* two + *-decim*, fr. *decem* ten — + *-ennium*, fr. *annus* year) + E *-al* — more at TWO, TEN, ANNUAL] **:** occurring once in 12 years

du·o·decillion \"+\ *n, often attrib* [L *duodecim* twelve + E *-illion* (as in *million*)] — see NUMBER table

[1]**du·o·dec·i·mal** \ˌdüə¦desəməl, -üō;-\ *adj* [L *duodecim* twelve + E *-al*] **:** of or relating to twelve or twelfths **:** proceeding in computation by twelves **:** expressed in the scale of twelves — **du·o·dec·i·mal·i·ty** \ˌ==ˌ==ˈmaləd·ē\ *n* -ES — **du·o·dec·i·mal·ly** \ˌ==ˈdesəməlē\ *adv*

[2]**duodecimal** \"\ *n* -s **:** a twelfth part

du·o·dec·i·mo \ˌ==ˈdesə,mō\ *n* -s [L, abl. of *duodecimus* twelfth, fr. *duodecim* twelve] **1 :** TWELVEMO — symbol *D;* see BOOK tables **2** [modif. of It *duodecima*, fr. fem. of *duodecimo* twelfth, fr. L *duodecimus*, fr. *duodecim* twelve] **:** the musical interval of a twelfth

du·o·dec·i·mole \ˌ==ˈ==,mōl\ *n* -s [It, fr. *duodecimo*] **:** DODECUPLET

duo·decyl \¦d(y)üə, -üō+\ *n* [*duo-* + *decyl*] **:** DODECYL

duoden- *or* **duodeno-** *comb form* [NL, fr. ML *duodenum*] **1 :** duodenum ⟨*duoden*itis⟩ ⟨*duodeno*gram⟩ **2 :** duodenal and ⟨*duodeno*jejunal⟩

du·o·de·nal \ˌd(y)üə¦dēnᵊl, (ˈ)d(y)ü¦ädᵊnəl\ *adj* [NL *duodenalis*, fr. ML *duodenum* + L *-alis* -al] **:** of or relating to the duodenum

duodenal gland *n* **:** BRUNNER'S GLAND

duodenal juice *n* **:** an alkaline protein-containing fluid of weak digestive power that is secreted by the duodenum, aids in neutralizing the acid chyme of the stomach, and contains invertase, maltase, lactase, erepsin, and enterokinase

duodenal tube *n* **:** a long flexible rubber tube that can be passed through the esophagus and stomach into the duodenum

duodenal ulcer *n* **:** a peptic ulcer situated in the duodenum

du·o·den·a·ry \ˌd(y)üə¦denərē, -dēn-\ *adj* [L *duodenarius*, fr. *duodeni* twelve each (fr. *duodecim* twelve) + *-arius* -ary — more at DUODECENNIAL] **1 :** containing 12 ⟨a ~ cycle of years⟩ **2 :** based on the number 12 ⟨a ~ system of computation⟩

du·o·de·ni·tis \ˌd(y)üə,dēˈnīd·əs, (ˌ)d(y)ü,ädᵊnˈī-\ *n* -ES [NL, fr. *duoden-* + *-itis*] **:** inflammation of the duodenum

du·o·de·num \ˌd(y)üəˈdēnəm, d(y)üˈädᵊn-\ *n, pl* **duode·na** \-ēnə,-ᵊnə\ *or* **duodenums** \-ēnəmz,-ᵊnəmz\ [ME, fr. ML, fr. L *duodeni* twelve each; fr. its length, about 12 fingers' breadth] **:** the first, shortest, and widest part of the small intestine that in man is about 10 inches long and that extends from the pylorus to the undersurface of the liver where it descends for a variable distance and receives the bile and pancreatic ducts and then bends to the left and finally upward to join the jejunum near the second lumbar vertebra — see DIGESTION illustration

duo·drama \'d(y)üə+,-\ *n* [*duo-* + *drama*] **:** a drama for two performers in which the dialogue is spoken with an instrumental accompaniment

duo·graph \'d(y)üə,graf, -râf\ *n* [*duo-* + *-graph*] **:** DUOTONE

du·o·logue \-,lȯg *also* -,läg\ *n* -s [*duo-* + *-logue*] **1 :** dialogue confined to two **2 :** a dramatic or musical piece for two participants

duo·mo \'dwȯ(,)mō\ *n* -s [It — more at DOME] **:** CATHEDRAL

duo–pianist \¦d(y)ü(,)ō+\ *n* [*duo*] **:** one of two pianists that play duets each at a separate piano

du·op·o·ly \d(y)üˈäpəlē\ *n* -ES [*duo-* + mono*poly*] **:** a market situation in which two competing sellers hold the controlling power of determining the amount and price of a product or service offered to a large number of buyers — compare DUOPSONY, MONOPOLY, OLIGOPOLY

du·op·so·ny \-psənē\ *n* -ES [*duo-* + Gk *opsōnia* purchase of victuals, catering, fr. *opsōnein* to purchase victuals (fr. *opson* prepared food, relish) + *-ia* -y] **:** a market situation in which two rival buyers hold the controlling power of determining the demand for a product or service from a large number of sellers — compare MONOPSONY, OLIGOPSONY

duos *pl of* DUO

[1]**duo·tone** \'d(y)üə,tōn\ *or* **duo·toned** \-nd\ *adj* [*duo-* + *tone* or *-toned*] **:** having or yielding two tones or colors

[2]**duotone** \"\ *n* -s **:** a process for making prints typically in two shades of the same color or in black and one tint by the use of two halftone plates made with the screen set at two different angles ⟨~ plates⟩ ⟨~ illustrations⟩; *also* **:** a print made by this process

duo·type \-,tīp\ *n* [*duo-* + *type*] **:** a process for making prints in two colors by the use of two halftone plates made from the same negative but etched differently; *also* **:** a print made by this process

dup \'dəp\ *vt* [contr. of *do up*] *now dial Brit* **:** OPEN

dup *abbr* **1** duplex **2** duplicate

dup·able \'d(y)üpəbəl\ *adj* **:** that can be duped

[1]**dupe** \'d(y)üp\ *n* -s [F, fr. MF *duppe*, prob. fr. a dial. word meaning "hoopoe", alter. (resulting fr. false word division of *de huppe*) of *huppe* hoopoe — more at HOOPOE] **1 :** one that is easily deceived (as by flattering promises) because lacking power to discriminate **:** FOOL **2 :** a puppet or tool esp. of a powerful person or idea **:** SLAVE ⟨he that hates truth shall be the ~ of lies —William Cowper⟩ ⟨with the same mental rigidity that made him a ~ to communism —Bradford Smith⟩

[2]**dupe** \"\ *vt* -ED/-ING/-S [F *duper*, fr. *dupe*] **:** to make a dupe of **:** mislead or trick by imposing on one's credulity **:** DECEIVE, FOOL ⟨refuses to be *duped* by his foiled lover's frenzies —Karl Polanyi⟩

syn DUPE, GULL, BEFOOL, TRICK, HOAX, HOODWINK, and BAMBOOZLE mean, in common, to delude by underhanded or deceptive means esp. for one's own ends. DUPE stresses the unwariness of the one deluded and his unsuspecting acceptance of the false as true, the worthless as genuine, and so on ⟨men in high positions are as gullible and as easily *duped* as the rest of us —*New Statesman & Nation*⟩ ⟨hunters bent on *duping* a wild turkey gobbler —Allen Rankin⟩ GULL implies the great credulousness of the one imposed upon and generally made a laughingstock of ⟨"good people" they call them, because they are easily *gulled* in the matter of weights and measures —Norman Douglas⟩ ⟨Barnum knew the American public loved to be *gulled*. It was a shame not to take the money. His genius consisted in knowing how to swindle them —W.L.Phelps⟩ ⟨could not tell . . . whether he was enlightened by fact or *gulled* by pretense —F.L.Paxson⟩ BEFOOL usu. stresses no weakness in the victim nor does it suggest very strongly an intent to delude on the part of the agent, stressing rather the victim's being made foolish ⟨innocent philosophic critics, too easily *befooled* by words —Havelock Ellis⟩ ⟨a world long *befooled* by false messiahs and enslaved by false loyalties —John Bright †1889⟩ ⟨pictures supplant one another so swiftly as to *befool* the eye with the illusion of continuity —S.H.Adams⟩ TRICK stresses an intent to delude or deceive, by strategem, ruse, wiles, or fraud, not necessarily implying a base end, suggesting strongly the use of craft or cunning ⟨it enables some lawyers to *trick* us into bringing in the wrong verdict —W.J.Reilly⟩ ⟨his accidental abandonment, which Sam never forgot, but which his recollection *tricked* him into placing at the earlier date of 1839, as if to heighten the pathos —Dixon Wecter⟩ ⟨never recommended it to my students because I knew they would suspect me of trying to *trick* them into reading it —A.W.Long⟩ HOAX in one sense implies the use of trickery for fun or as a demonstration of someone else's gullibility; in another it suggests a fraud, often on a large scale, intended to deceive even the most skeptical, usu. to one's own advantage ⟨he was flawed with impish faults. He *hoaxed* poor Rafinesque into solemn belief in the "red-headed swallow", concocted for his benefit, and even got him to accept drawings of imaginary fishes and publish them as new species —D.C.Peattie⟩ ⟨a get-rich-quick scheme intended to *hoax* the public⟩ HOODWINK often stresses a deliberate confusing of another so as to blind him to the truth, and often a self-delusion arising from an inability to distinguish false from true ⟨injures the interests of whatever nation is *hoodwinked* by the lie —Lucius Garvin⟩ ⟨since she'd *hoodwinked* your uncle, she thought she could pull the wool over my eyes, too —Kenneth Roberts⟩ ⟨*hoodwinked* by a simple political trick⟩ BAMBOOZLE usu. implies the use of out-and-out humbug or illusion or a transparent cajolery, though it may often be interchanged with TRICK, HOAX, or HOODWINK, being generally less fixed in its implications ⟨we circus people are scoundrels, we do all sorts of tricks to *bamboozle* the world —Eduard Bass⟩ ⟨is it not a technique for persuading people that they themselves have chosen what has been dexterously palmed off on them? And that is to add insult to injury; you not only manipulate people but also *bamboozle* them —Walter Moberly⟩

[3]**dupe** \"\ *n or vb* [by shortening] **:** DUPLICATE

dup·ery \-pərē\ *n* -ES [F *duperie*, fr. *dupe* + *-erie* -ery] **1 :** the act or practice of duping **:** DECEPTION ⟨when Maximilian's ~ could no longer be hidden —Francis Hackett⟩ **2 :** the condition of being duped ⟨the ~ and weakness of the sufferers —Adam Smith⟩

dupioni *or* **dupion** *var of* DOUPPIONI

du·pla·tion \d(y)üˈplāshən\ *n* -s [LL *duplation-, duplatio* act of doubling, fr. *duplatus* (past part. of *duplare* to double, fr. L *duplus* double) + *-ion-, -io* -ion] **:** multiplication by repeated doubling (as done formerly esp. in Egypt)

du·ple \'d(y)üpəl\ *adj* [L *duplus* — more at DOUBLE] **1 a :** consisting of two **:** TWOFOLD, DOUBLE **b :** taken by twos or in groups of two **2 a** *music* **:** having two or a multiple of two beats per measure ⟨~ time⟩ **b** *of meter* **:** consisting of feet of two syllables **c** *of rhythm* **:** consisting of cadences that rise and fall within a span of two syllables

du·plet \-plət\ *n* -s [*duple* + *-et*] **:** two musical notes played in the time of three of the same value — compare TRIPLET

[1]**du·plex** \'d(y)ü,pleks\ *adj* [L, fr. *duo* two + *-plex* (akin to Gk *diplax* double) — more at TWO, SIMPLE] **1 :** having two parts or elements **:** DOUBLE, TWOFOLD: as **a** *of a machine tool or other device* **:** having two parts that operate at the same time or in the same way where the simpler form has but one **b** *of paper or paperboard*: (1) **:** consisting of two or more plies (2) **:** having two surfaces that differ in color, texture, or finish **c** *of an electric cable* **:** having two insulated conductors **2 :** having or distinguished by two homologous dominant genes — used chiefly of autotetraploids; compare SIMPLEX **3 :** allowing telecommunication in opposite directions simultaneously ⟨~ system⟩ ⟨~ telephony⟩ — distinguished from *diplex*

[2]**duplex** \"\ *n* -ES **:** something duplex: as **a :** DUPLEX APARTMENT **b :** TWO-FAMILY HOUSE

[3]**duplex** \"\ *vt* -ED/-ING/-ES **:** to make duplex: as **a :** to arrange (as a telegraph line) so that two messages may be transmitted simultaneously **b :** to use in dual combination in a specific metallurgic process (as two furnaces in a duplex process) **c :** BORROW 8

duplex apartment *n* **:** a suite in an apartment house that includes rooms on two floors

duplex bag *n* **:** DOUBLE WALL 2

duplex dahlia *n* **:** any of various dahlias having open centered flowers with only two rows of rays

du·plex·er \-sə(r)\ *n* -s **:** a switching device that utilizes two electron tubes to permit alternate transmission and reception with the same radar antenna

duplex house *n* **:** TWO-FAMILY HOUSE

duplex iron *n* **:** cast iron that has been heated in an electric furnace after being melted in the usual manner in a cupola

du·plex·ite \'d(y)ü,plek,sīt\ *n* -s [S. *Duplex*, 20th cent. Australian quarry manager who found it + E *-ite*] **:** a mineral perhaps $Be_4Ca_8Al_2Si_{14}O_{41}.2H_2O$ consisting of hydrous beryllium calcium aluminosilicate

du·plex·i·ty \d(y)üˈpleksəd·ē\ *n* -ES [[1]*duplex* + *-ity*] **:** DUPLICITY 2

duplex lock *n* **:** a cylinder lock with two pin-tumbler cylinders acting independently on the same bolt, one for an ordinary key and the other for a master key

duplex process *n* **:** a process for making steel in which the material is partially treated in a furnace of one type, orig. a Bessemer, and then transferred without interruption to a furnace of another type, orig. an open-hearth furnace

duplex pump *n* **:** a pump with two cylinders; *esp* **:** one whose plungers are driven directly by the piston rods of a compound steam engine

duplex querela *n* [L, double complaint] **:** a complaint in the nature of an appeal from the ordinary to his immediate superior (as from a bishop to an archbishop)

duplex steel *n* **:** steel made by a duplex process

du·pli·ca·ble \ˌd(y)üpləkəbəl, -lēk-\ *or* **du·pli·cat·able** \'d(y)üplə,kād·əbəl, -ātə-, ˌ==ˈ===\ *adj* [*duplicate* + *-able*] **:** capable of being duplicated

du·pli·cand \ˌd(y)üplə¦kand\ *also* **du·pli·can·do** \-n(,)dō\ *n* -s [L *duplicando*, abl. of *duplicandum*, gerund of *duplicare*] *Scots law* **:** the doubling of a feu-duty; *also* **:** the double duty itself

[1]**du·pli·cate** \'d(y)üpləkə|t, -lēk- *sometimes* -lə,kā|; *usu* |d·+V\ *adj* [ME, fr. L *duplicatus*, past part. of *duplicare* to double, fr. *duplic-, duplex* double, twofold — more at DUPLEX] **1 :** consisting of or existing in two corresponding or identical parts or examples ⟨the firm always made out ~ invoices, one for its own records and one for the customer⟩ **2 :** being exactly the same as one or more others of its kind ⟨in eleven years he has not made a ~ prayer —*N.Y.Times*⟩ ⟨make six ~ copies of the memo⟩ **3 :** of, relating to, or being a card game in which all players play identical hands in order to allow a comparison of scores — compare DUPLICATE BRIDGE

[2]**duplicate** \"\ *n* -s **1 :** either of two things that exactly resemble or correspond to each other — usu. used of a copy or transcript made at the same time or by the same pattern as its original **2 :** something that is like another thing in content or appearance but is not derived from the same source or made in the same manner **:** COUNTERPART ⟨doll carriages that are ~*s* of baby carriages⟩; *specif* **:** an additional copy of a book, periodical, or pamphlet already in a library **3 :** a duplicate game; *specif* **:** DUPLICATE BRIDGE **4** *law* **:** an original instrument repeated **:** a document the same as another in essential particulars and differing from a copy in that it is valid as an original **5 a :** a photographic negative prepared from another negative by printing first a master positive from which the later negative is printed **b :** a positive print either black and white or color that is made by reversal development of a print from a positive — **in duplicate** *adv* **:** with an original and one copy

[3]**du·pli·cate** \-lə,kāt, *usu* -ād·+V\ *vb* -ED/-ING/-S *vt* **1 :** to make double or twofold ⟨the walls should be *duplicated* . . . in order to have a second line of defense if the outer wall is breached —J.A.Steers⟩ **2 :** to be or make a duplicate, copy, or transcript of ⟨the furnishings ~ those used by Washington —*Amer. Guide Series: Pa.*⟩ ⟨we are totally unable, after decades of experiment, to ~ Attic glazed pottery —W.F. Albright⟩ ⟨small firms may ~ their own business forms⟩ ~ *vi* **:** to celebrate mass twice in a day

duplicate board *n* **:** BOARD 5 f(1)

duplicate bridge *n* **:** bridge (as contract bridge) in which each contestant, pair, or team of four players plays the same hands as other contestants and each deal of which is scored independently of each other deal with match-point or cumulative-point scoring — see BOARD 5 f(1)

duplicate factor *or* **duplicate gene** *n, biol* **:** any of two or more nonallelic factors having the same expression

duplicate stitch *n* **:** a hand-sewn stitch that imitates a knitted stitch and that is used for working patterns on finished knitted garments

duplicating machine *n* **1 :** a machine or attachment that shapes an exact copy of a given sample (as of a die or key) or shapes two or more identical parts at once **2 :** DUPLICATOR 1a

du·pli·ca·tion \ˌd(y)üpləˈkāshən\ *n* -s [ME *duplicacioun*, fr. MF *duplication*, fr. L *duplication-, duplicatio*, fr. *duplicatus* + *-ion-, -io* -ion] **1 :** the action or process of duplicating or doubling or the quality or state of being duplicated or doubled ⟨save time and money by avoiding ~ of effort⟩ ⟨after his initial success, the author's successive novels were marked mainly by ~⟩ **2 :** DUPLICATE, COPY, COUNTERPART **3 :** CHORISIS **4 :** celebration of mass by the same priest twice in a day **5** [L *duplication-, duplicatio*, lit., action of doubling] **:** a rebuttal pleading in Roman, canon, and civil law by which a party to litigation avoids the legal effect of matter just pleaded by his adversary

duplication of the cube : the mathematical problem of finding the edge of a cube having twice the volume of a given cube

du·pli·ca·tive \'d(y)üplə,kād·iv, -lək-, -lēk-, |tiv\ *adj* **1 :** able to duplicate ⟨~ memory⟩ **2 :** marked by duplication ⟨the two agencies working in this area are not ~⟩

duplicato- *comb form* [prob. fr. NL, fr. L *duplicatus* duplicate — more at DUPLICATE] **:** doubly ⟨*duplicato*-dentate⟩

du·pli·ca·tor \'d(y)üplə,kād·ə(r), -ātə-\ *n* -s **1 :** one that duplicates: **a :** a machine for making one or more copies of typed, drawn, and often printed matter **b :** a device (as an attachment on a cash register or meter) for recording particular readings or for recording and duplicating the recording (as on a customer invoice or other separate slip) **2 :** LAYOUT MAN

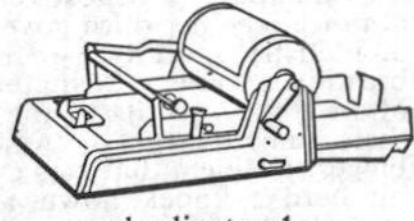

duplicator 1a

du·pli·ca·ture \-ləkə,chù(ə)r, -ləkəchər, -lə,kāchər\ *n* -s [F, fr. MF, fr. L *duplicatus* + F *-ure*] **:** a doubling or fold esp. of a membrane

du·plici·den·ta·ta \d(y)ü,plisə,denˈtäd·ə, -ād·ə\ *n pl, cap* [NL, fr. L *duplic-, duplex* double, twofold + *-i-* + *dentata*, neut. pl. of *dentatus* toothed — more at DUPLEX, DENTATE] *in former classifications* **:** a suborder of Rodentia coextensive with the order Lagomorpha

du·plic·i·tous \(ˈ)d(y)ü¦plisəd·əs, -sətəs\ *adj* **:** showing duplicity

du·plic·i·ty \d(y)ü'plisəd·ē, -ətē, -i\ *n* -ES [ME *duplicite*, fr. MF *duplicité*, fr. LL *duplicitat-, duplicitas*, fr. L *duplic-, duplex* + *-itat-, -itas* -ity] **1 :** doubleness of heart, thought, speech, or action **:** deception by pretending to entertain one set of feelings and acting under the influence of another **:** bad faith **:** DOUBLE-DEALING ⟨the simplicity and openness of their lives brought out for him the ~ that lay at the bottom of ours —Mary Austin⟩ **2 :** the quality or state of being double or twofold ⟨these double stars . . . show a doubling of the spectral lines that must be caused by a ~ in the source of light —*New Internat'l Encyc.*⟩ **3 a :** the use of two or more distinct allegations or answers where one is sufficient **:** pleading double **b :** the union of two incompatible offenses in an indictment **syn** see DECEIT

duplicity theory *or* **duplicity principle** *n* **:** a theory in physiology: the normal retina in man and other vertebrates contains a dual receptor mechanism consisting of (1) organs of achromatic low-intensity vision and (2) organs of chromatic high-intensity vision — compare CONE, ROD; PHOTOPIA, SCOTOPIA

du·ply \'dü'plī\ *n* -ES [ML *duplica*, fr. L *duplic-, duplex* double, twofold — more at DUPLEX] **:** a defendant's answer to a plaintiff's reply in Scots law

du·pon·di·us \d(y)ü'pändēəs\ *n, pl* **dupon·dii** \-ē,ī\ [L, fr. *duo* two + *-pondius* (fr. *pondus*, a weight) — more at POUND] **:** an ancient Roman bronze or under the Empire brass coin worth two asses

dupper *var of* DUBBER

dup·py \'dəpē\ *n* -ES [Bube *dupe* ghost] **:** a haunting spirit of the dead conceived in folklore of West Indian Negroes as a usu. malevolent shadow or immaterial body

du·puy·tren's contracture \də¦pwē·¦tranz-, də'pwē·trənz-\ *n, usu cap D* [after Guillaume *Dupuytren* †1835 Fr. surgeon and anatomist] **:** a condition marked by fibrosis with shortening and thickening of the palmar fascia resulting in flexion contracture of the fingers into the palm of the hand

dur \'dú(ə)r\ *adj* [G, fr. MHG *bedūre*, fr. ML *b durum* b natural, fr. L *b* + *durum*, neut. of *durus* hard — more at DURE] **:** MAJOR ⟨C ~⟩

¹du·ra \'d(y)ürə\ *n* -S [by shortening] **:** DURA MATER

²dura *var of* DURRA

du·ra·bil·i·ty \,d(y)ürə'biləd·ē, -ətē, -i\ *n* -ES [ME *durabilite*, fr. MF *durabilité*, fr. LL *durabilitat-, durabilitas*, fr. L *durabilis* durable + *-itat-, -itas* -ity] **:** the quality or state of being durable

du·ra·ble \'d(y)ürəbəl\ *adj* [ME, fr. MF, fr. L *durabilis*, fr. *durare* to last, endure + *-abilis* -able — more at DURE] **:** able to exist for a long time with retention of original qualities, abilities, or capabilities **:** LASTING, ENDURING, UNCHANGEABLE, STRONG ⟨traditional controversies between member nations . . . must be settled before there can be created the general goodwill that makes economic union ~ —Alan Valentine⟩ ⟨the ~ Michelangelo who lived to be 89 —*Time*⟩ ⟨the less ~ rocks were gradually worn away to form the valley⟩ ⟨the small body of ~ poetry written in our time —T.S.Eliot⟩ — compare PERDURABLE

du·ra·ble·ness *n* -ES **:** the quality or state of being durable **:** DURABILITY

durables *or* **durable goods** *n pl* **:** consumer goods or producer goods (as household appliances, automobiles, or machinery) whose usefulness continues for a number of years and is not consumed or destroyed in single usage — called also *hard goods;* sometimes used in sing. ⟨since television became a mass market *durable* —*Wall Street Jour.*⟩

du·ra·bly \-blē, -li\ *adv* **:** in a lasting manner **:** LASTINGLY, STRONGLY ⟨~ bound in buckram⟩

du·rain \'d(y)ü,rān\ *n* -S [L *durus* hard + *-ain* (as in *fusain*)] **:** one of two dull constituents of banded bituminous coal forming lenses or layers and composed of finely comminuted woody debris only partly decomposed — compare CLARAIN, FUSAIN, VITRAIN

¹du·ral \'d(y)ürəl\ *adj* [¹*dura* + *-al*] **:** of or relating to the dura mater

²du·ral \'d(y)ü,ral\ *n* **:** a Duralumin alloy

Du·ral·u·min \d(y)ə'ralyəmən, d(y)ü'-; ,d(y)ürə'lümən *sometimes* ,d(y)ürəl'yü-\ *trademark* — used for an alloy consisting of 95.5 parts of aluminum to 3 parts of copper, 1 of manganese, and 0.5 of magnesium that after age-hardening is comparable in strength and hardness to soft steel

du·ra ma·ter \'d(y)ürə,mā|d·ə(r), -ür-, -mäl|, -mā|, |tə-, ˌ==ˈ==\ *also* **dura** *n* -S [ME, fr. ML, lit., hard mother] **:** the tough fibrous membrane lined with endothelium on the inner surface that envelops the brain and spinal cord external to the arachnoid and pia mater, in the cranium closely lining the bone and not dipping down between the convolutions though certain large supporting folds (as the falx cerebri and tentorium cerebelli) are derived from it and containing numerous blood vessels and venous sinuses and in the spinal canal being separated from the bone by a considerable space and containing no venous sinuses

du·ra·men \d(y)ə'rāmən, -)ü'-\ *n* -S [NL, fr. L, hardness, fr. *durare* to harden, fr. *durus* hard — more at DURE] **:** HEARTWOOD

du·rance \'d(y)ürən(t)s, -ür-\ *n* -S [MF, fr. *durer* to last, endure + *-ance* — more at DURE] **1 a** *obs* **:** CONTINUANCE, DURATION **b** *archaic* **:** DURABILITY **c** *archaic* **:** ENDURANCE **2 :** restraint by or as if by physical force **:** CONFINEMENT, IMPRISONMENT ⟨he has not, certainly, been cramped . . . there has been no ~ within the four walls of the House of Commons —Max Beerbohm⟩ — often used in the phrase *durance vile* ⟨after ~ vile of ten days he was released —J.E.Davies⟩ **3 :** an obsolete strong felted cloth of woolen or worsted usu. made in imitation of buff leather

du·ran·gite \d(y)ə'raŋ,gīt, -)ü'-\ *n* -S [*Durango*, state in Mexico + E *-ite*] **:** an orange-red mineral $NaAlFAsO_4$ consisting of a fluoride and arsenate of sodium and aluminum

du·ran·go \-ŋ(,)gō\ *n* -S *often cap* [fr. *Durango*, Mexico] **:** CARTOUCHE 6

du·ra·ni \dü'ränē\ *n, pl* **durani** *or* **duranis** *usu cap* [Pashto] **1 :** a people of mixed Semitic and Iranian stock that comprise the most dominant group of Afghans **2 :** a member of the Durani people

dur·ant \'d(y)ürənt\ *n* -S [by alter.] **:** DURANCE 3

du·ran·ta \d(y)ə'rantə, -)ü'-\ *n, cap* [NL, after C. *Durante* †1590 Ital. herbalist] **:** a genus of tropical American shrubs (family Verbenaceae) with long terminal racemes of small flowers

du·ran·te \-tē\ *prep* [L, abl. of *durant-, durans*, pres. part. of *durare* to last — more at DURE] *law* **:** DURING

durante ab·sen·tia \-(,)ab'sench(ē)ə, -,əb-\ *adv* [L] **:** during absence

durante be·ne·pla·ci·to \-,benə'plasə,tō, -nē'-\ *adv* [L] **:** during the pleasure or at the discretion (as of a king) — usu. used of a tenure of office

durante fu·ro·re \-fyə'rōrē, -yü'-\ *adv* [L] **:** during madness

durante mi·no·re ae·ta·te \-mə'nōrē,ī'täd·ē\ *adv* [L] **:** during minority

durante vi·du·i·ta·te \-,vijəwə'täd·ē\ *adv* [L] **:** during widowhood

durante vi·ta \-'vīd·ə; dü'rän,tä'wē,tä\ *adv* [L] **:** during life

duras *pl of* DURA

du·ra·tion \d(y)ə'rāshən, -)ü'-\ *n* -S [ML *duration-, duratio*, fr. L *duratus* (past part. of *durare* to last) + *-ion-, -io* -ion — more at DURE] **1 :** the quality or state of lasting for a period of time **:** continuation in time or existence **:** LASTINGNESS ⟨a play of short ~⟩ **2 :** a portion of time which is measurable or during which something exists, lasts, or is in progress ⟨gave up all worries for the ~ of the holiday⟩ ⟨the ~ of a meal⟩ ⟨the ~ of life⟩ ⟨the ~ of the world⟩ ⟨the ~ of the play⟩; *specif* **:** the period of time during which something that almost totally obstructs or prevents normal activities (as a war) or that engages virtually all one's efforts or attention is in progress — used with *the* ⟨universities had to be persuaded to scrap their scientific and educational responsibilities for the ~ and take on war work —J.B.Conant⟩ ⟨once you were in the theater, and the lights were dimmed, you were there for the ~ —Burns Mantle⟩ **3** *obs* **:** durableness or endurance in use — **du·ra·tion·al** \-shən°l, -shnəl\ *adj* — **du·ra·tion·al·ly** \-ē\ *adv*

¹du·ra·tive \'d(y)ürəd·iv\ *sometimes* d(y)ə'rād·- *or* -)ü'-\ *adj* [ISV *durat-* (fr. L *duratus*, past part. of *durare* to last) + *-ive*] **1 a :** not completed **:** CONTINUING **b :** implying duration or continuance ⟨a ~ prefix⟩ **2 :** IMPERFECTIVE

²durative \"\ *n* -S [ISV, fr. *durative*, adj.] **1 :** CONTINUANT a **2 :** the durative aspect in a language **:** a durative verb form

dur·azol blue 8G \'d(y)ürə,zōl-, -zōl-\ *n, usu cap D&B* [origin unknown] **:** a direct dye — see DYE table I (under *Direct Blue 86*)

¹dur·ban \'dùrbən\ *n* **:** DURBEN OIRAT

²dur·ban \'dərbən\ *adj, usu cap* [fr. *Durban*, Union of So. Africa] **:** of or from the city of Durban, Union of So. Africa **:** of the kind or style prevalent in Durban

dur·bar \'dər,bär, (,)dər'b-\ *n* -S [Hindi *darbār*, fr. Per, fr. *dar* door + *bār* door, admission, audience] **1 a :** court held by a native Indian prince **b :** a festive reception given by a maharajah for his subjects at which they pledge their fealty to him **c :** a formal reception of native Indian princes given by the British governor-general **2** *India* **:** an audience hall **3 :** the governing body of a native Indian state; *also* **:** a member of such a body

dur·ben oi·rat \,dùrbən'òirət\ *n, pl* **durben oirat** *or* **durben oirats** *usu cap D&O* **:** a Mongol people found in the western part of the Mongolian plateau and in the lake region of Tsinghai province in China

durch·kom·po·niert \'dùrk,kòmpō¦ni(ə)rt\ *adj* [G, fr. past part. of *durchkomponieren* to create through-composed music, fr. *durch* through (fr. OHG *duruh*) + *komponieren* to compose, fr. L *componere* — more at THROUGH, COMPOSE] **:** THROUGH-COMPOSED

dur·dum \'dərdəm\ *var of* DIRDUM

¹dure \'d(y)ü(ə)r\ *vb* -ED/-ING/-S [ME *duren*, fr. OF *durer*, fr. L *durare* to last, endure, prob. fr. *durare* to harden, fr. *durus* hard] *vi, archaic* **:** ENDURE **~** *vt, obs* **:** SUSTAIN, ENDURE

²dure \"\ *adj* [ME, fr. MF *dur*, fr. L *durus* hard, rough; perh. akin to Skt *dāruṇa* hard, rough, *dāru* wood — more at TREE] *archaic* **:** HARD, SEVERE ⟨the winter is severe, and life is ~, and rude —W.H.Russell⟩

du·rene \'d(y)ü,rēn\ *n* -S [ISV *dur-* (fr. L *durus* hard) + *-ene*] **:** a colorless crystalline hydrocarbon $C_6H_2(CH_3)_4$ having an odor like camphor and occurring in coal tar and in petroleum; 1,2,4,5-tetramethyl-benzene

dü·rer·esque *or* **du·rer·esque** \¦d(y)ürə¦resk, ¦düerə¦-\ *adj, usu cap* [Albrecht *Dürer* †1528 German painter and engraver + E *-esque*] **:** resembling in style or manner the work of the artist Dürer noted for his accurate and delicate drawing and his delineation of character esp. in his engravings which are characterized by profuse and literal detail

du·ress \d(y)ə'res, -)ü'- *sometimes* 'd(y)ü,res *or*)ü,-\ *n* -ES [ME *duresse* hardness, severity, oppression, restraint, confinement, fr. MF *duresce, durece* hardness, hardheartedness, fr. L *duritia*, fr. *durus* hard — more at DURE] **1 :** restraint or check by force (as arrest or imprisonment) **:** DURANCE ⟨while the German army was still held in ~ by the Versailles treaty —S.L.A.Marshall⟩ **2 :** stringent compulsion by threat of danger, hardship, or retribution **:** distress arising from such compulsion **:** COERCION ⟨a population working under the ~ of dictatorship —*Science*⟩ ⟨ordinary clergymen subscribe them under ~ because they cannot otherwise obtain ordination —G.B.Shaw⟩ **3 :** compulsion or constraint by which a person is illegally forced to do or forbear some act by actual imprisonment or physical violence to the person or by threat of such violence, the violence or threat being such as to inspire a person of ordinary firmness with fear of serious injury to the person (as loss of liberty or of life or limb), reputation, or fortune **syn** see FORCE

du·rez·za \dü'retsə\ *n* -S [It, lit., hardness, fr. L *duritia*] *music* **:** HARSHNESS

dur·fee grass \'dərfē,-\ *n* [origin unknown] **:** COUCH GRASS 1a

dur·gan *or* **dur·gen** \'dərgən\ *n* -S [perh. fr. ME *dwerg* dwarf — more at DWARF] *dial Eng* **:** an undersized person or animal

¹dur·ham \'dər·əm, 'də·rəm, 'dùrəm\ *adj, usu cap* [fr. *Durham* county, England] **:** of or from the county of Durham, England **:** of the kind or style prevalent in Durham

²durham \"\ *n* -S *usu cap* **:** SHORTHORN

durham boat *n, usu cap D* [after Robert *Durham*, 18th cent. Am. boat builder] **:** a long narrow flat-bottomed boat used to transport freight on the rivers of No. America in the 18th and early 19th centuries

du·ri·an \'dùrēən, ¦dùrē¦än\ *also* **du·ri·on** \'dùrēən\ *n* -S [Malay *durian*, fr. *duri* thorn] **1 :** the large oval or globose fruit of a tree (*Durio zibethinus*) of the East Indian islands having a hard prickly rind, a soft cream-colored pulp, a most delicious flavor, an offensive odor, and seeds that are roasted and eaten like chestnuts **2 :** the tree that bears durians

du·ri·crust \'d(y)ürə,krəst\ *n* [L *durus* hard + E *-i-* + *crust* — more at DURE] **:** a hard crust formed at or near the surface of the ground as a result of the upward migration and evaporation of mineral-bearing ground water — compare CALICHE

¹dur·ing \'d(y)üriŋ, -ür-, -rēŋ\ *prep* [ME, fr. pres. part. of *duren* to last — more at DURE] **1 :** throughout the continuance or course of ⟨no attainder of treason shall work corruption of blood or forfeiture except ~ the life of the person attainted —*U.S.Constitution*⟩ **2 :** at some point in the course of ⟨been away for a couple of weeks ~ the summer —J.M.Barzun⟩

²during \"\ *adj* [ME, fr. pres. part. of *duren* to last] *archaic* **:** ENDURING, LASTING

du·rio \'d(y)ürē,ō\ *n* [NL, fr. Malay *durian*] **1** *cap* **:** a small genus of tall Asiatic and Indian trees (family Bombacaceae) with tapering leaves and small greenish flowers **2** -S **:** any tree of the genus *Durio*

durity *n* -ES [L *duritas*, fr. *durus* hard + *-itas* -ity — more at DURE] *obs* **:** HARDNESS

durk \'dərk\ *Scot var of* DIRK

durk·hei·mi·an \'(')d(y)ùr¦kemēən, -kām-,-kīm-\ *adj, usu cap* [Émile *Durkheim* †1917 Fr. sociologist + E *-ian*] **:** of or relating to Émile Durkheim or his sociological theory esp. that social science must be made an objective statistical study

dur·mast \'dər,mast\ *also* **durmast oak** *n* [perh. alter. of *dun mast*, fr. ¹*dun* + *mast* (acorns)] **:** a European oak (*Quercus sessiliflora* or *Q. petraea*) that is valued esp. for its dark heavy tough elastic wood

¹durn \'dərn\ *n* -S [ME *dyrne*, of Scand origin; akin to OSw *dyrni* doorpost, Norw *dyrn;* akin to ON *dyrr* door — more at DOOR] **1** *dial Eng* **:** GATEPOST, DOORPOST **2** *dial Eng* **:** the wooden framework of a door — usu. used in pl.

²durn *var of* DARN

durned *var of* DARNED

du·ro \'dü(,)rō\ *n* -S [Sp, short for *peso duro*, lit., hard peso] **:** a Spanish or Spanish American peso or silver dollar

du·roc \'d(y)ü,räk, -ü,-\ *n* [after *Duroc*, 19th cent. Am. stallion living on the farm where the Duroc breed of swine was developed] **1** *usu cap* **:** a breed of large vigorous red lard-type hogs of American origin **2** -S *often cap* **:** any animal of the Duroc breed

duroc-jersey \'=,=ˈ==\ *n, usu cap D&J* **:** DUROC

du·rom·e·ter \d(y)ə'rämǝd·ə(r)\ *n* [ISV *duro-* (fr. L *durus* hard) + *-meter* — more at DURE] **:** an instrument for measuring hardness that consists essentially of a small drill or blunt indenter point working under pressure (as that exerted by a spring)

du·roy \d(y)ə'rôi\ *n* -S [origin unknown] **:** a coarse woolen cloth made in England in the 18th century and used chiefly for men's wear

dur·ra *also* **du·ra** *or* **dhur·ra** *or* **doo·ra** *or* **dou·ra** *or* **dou·rah** \'dùrə\ *n* -S [Ar *dhurah*] **:** any of several grain sorghums that are of medium size with dry pithy stalks and narrow leaves and are widely grown in warm dry parts of southern Asia and northern Africa and to a limited extent in the southwestern U.S. — called also *guinea corn, Indian millet*

durrin *var of* DHURRIN

durst *archaic & dial past of* DARE

durukuli *var of* DOUROUCOULI

du·rum wheat \'d(y)ürəm-, -)ər|\ *also* **durum** *n* -S [NL *durum* (specific epithet of *Triticum durum*), fr. L, neut. of *durus* hard — more at DURE] **:** a wheat (*Triticum durum*) that occurs in several cultivated varieties, is grown esp. in southern Russia, No. Africa, and north central No. America as a spring wheat, has slender compact spikes with spikelets containing two to four very hard translucent white or red kernels, and yields a flour which is high in gluten-producing proteins and is chiefly used in making semolina, macaroni, and spaghetti

dur·wan \də(r)'wän, -wón\ *n* -S [Per *darwān*, fr. *dar* door (fr. MPer, fr. OPer *duvar-*) + Per *-wān* keeping, guarding, fr. MPer *-pān;* akin to Skt *dvār* door — more at DOOR] *India* **:** PORTER, DOORKEEPER

dur·yl \'d(y)ürəl\ *n* -S [ISV *durene* + *-yl*] **:** a univalent radical $C_6H(CH_3)_4$ derived from durene; 2,3,5,6-tetramethyl-phenyl

dur·za·da \də(r)'zädə\ *n, pl* **durzada** *or* **durzadas** *usu cap* **1 :** a Persian people extending throughout Makran and similar to the Dehwar **2 :** a member of the Durzada people

dur·zee \dər'zē, '=,=\ *var of* DARZI

¹dusk \'dəsk\ *adj* [ME *dosk, duske*, alter. of OE *dox;* akin to OE *dunn* dun, OHG *tusin* yellow, OS *dosan* chestnut brown, ON *dunna*, a kind of duck, MIr *doun* dark, L *fuscus* dark brown, blackish, Skt *dhūsara* dust colored, L *fumus* smoke — more at FUME] **:** DUSKY ⟨the dim, ~ yard —Thomas Williams⟩ ⟨~ faces with white silken turbants wreathed —John Milton⟩ ⟨called the children in when it grew ~⟩ **syn** see DARK

²dusk \"\ *vb* -ED/-ING/-S [ME *dosken, dusken*, fr. *dosk, duske*, n.] *vi* **:** to become dusky or dark ⟨in the ~*ing* room —Walter Karig⟩ **~** *vt* **1 :** to make dark or dim ⟨a gray light ~*ed* the room —William Sansom⟩ **2 :** to darken in mood or spirit **:** cast gloom upon ⟨his national formality ~*ed* by the saturnine mood of ill health —Herman Melville⟩

³dusk \"\ *n* -S [¹*dusk*] **1 :** the darker part of twilight or of dawn **2 a :** darkness or semidarkness caused by the shutting out of light ⟨the cool ~ of ancient tombs⟩ ⟨the ~ of the great forest⟩ **b :** the condition of being dark or darkish in color ⟨ivory skin framed in the silken ~ of her tresses —Kay Rogers⟩ **3 a :** a variable color averaging a bluish gray that is redder and deeper than clair de lune, redder, lighter, and stronger than Medici blue, and redder and deeper than puritan gray **b :** a dark purplish gray that is bluer and duller than slate, redder, lighter, and slightly stronger than charcoal, and bluer and darker than pigeon

dusk blue *n* **:** a pale purplish blue to pale violet that is darker than average twilight blue

dusk dark *also* **dusky dark** *n, chiefly South & Midland* **:** TWILIGHT

dusk·i·ly \'dəskəlē, -li\ *adv* **:** in a dusky manner **:** OBSCURELY

dusk·i·ness \-kēnəs, -kin-\ *n* -ES **:** the quality or state of being dusky **:** DUSK

dusk·ish \-kish\ *adj* **:** rather dark or black **:** partially obscured — **dusk·ish·ly** *adv* — **dusk·ish·ness** *n* -ES

dusk·ly \-klē, -li\ *adv* [¹*dusk* + *-ly*] **:** DUSKILY

dusk·ness \-knəs\ *n* -ES **:** DUSKINESS

¹dusky \'dəskē, -ki\ *adj* -ER/-EST [¹*dusk* + *-y*] **1 :** somewhat dark in color **:** of low lightness **:** BLACKISH ⟨a ~ brown⟩ ⟨a ~ blush rose to her cheek —Edith Wharton⟩; *specif* **:** having dark skin — used of a colored person **2 :** characterized by slight or deficient light **:** somewhat dark **:** DIM ⟨the room was already ~ . . . and one of the boys switched on the light —Willa Cather⟩ ⟨in that ~ firelight —Ellen Glasgow⟩ **3 :** GLOOMY, DEPRESSING ⟨a ~ frown settled on his face⟩ **4 :** not clear **:** partially hidden **:** OBSCURE ⟨through all the winding corridors of literary history to the ~ regions of folklore —Newton Arvin⟩ ⟨the records of his life . . . are ~ and brief —Carl Van Doren⟩ **syn** see DARK

²dusky \"\ *n* -ES **:** a dusky color ⟨a white bird barred with ~⟩

dusky duck *n* **:** BLACK DUCK a

dusky-footed rat \'==,==-\ *n* **:** an Australian water rat (*Rattus lutreolus*)

dusky grouse *n* **:** a large grouse (*Dendragapus obscurus*) of the mountains of the western U.S.

dusky salamander *n* **1 :** a dark color phase of the red-backed salamander

a dusky salamander 2

2 : any of several common No. American plethodontid salamanders (genus *Desmognathus*) typically mottled or marked with dull browns or grayish black

dusky shark *n* **:** a shark (*Carcharias obscurus*) of the No. Atlantic similar to the cub shark but darker

dusky wing *n* **:** any of numerous skipper butterflies (genus *Erynnis*) having dark wings with inconspicuous patterns — compare SKIPPER

düs·sel·dorf *or* **dues·sel·dorf** *or* **dus·sel·dorf** \'düsəl,dòrf, 'dyü-, *G* 'dʊs-\ *adj, usu cap* [fr. *Düsseldorf*, Germany] **:** of or from the city of Düsseldorf, Germany **:** of the kind or style prevalent in Düsseldorf

dusserah *usu cap, var of* DASEHRA

dus·sert·ite \'dəsə(r),tīt\ *n* -S [F, fr. D. *Dussert*, 20th cent. Fr. mining engineer + F *-ite*] **:** a mineral $BaFe_3(AsO_4)_2(OH)_5.H_2O$ consisting of hydrous basic arsenate of barium and iron

dus·su·mie·ri·idae \,dəsəmə'rīə,dē\ *n pl, cap* [NL, fr. *Dussumieria*, type genus (fr. the name *Dussumier* + NL *-ia*) + *-idae*] **:** a family of marine fishes (order Isospondyli) comprising the round herrings — see ETRUMEUS

¹dust \'dəst\ *n* -S *often attrib* [ME, fr. OE *dūst;* akin to OHG *tunst, tunist* storm, breath, Dan *dyst* flour dust, Norw *dysja* to drizzle, L *furere* to rage, Gk *thyein* to rage, seethe, sacrifice, *thymos* breath, life, spirit, soul, Lith *dvasas* spirit, breath, Skt *dhvaṁsati* he perishes, falls to dust, L *fumus* smoke — more at FUME] **1 :** fine dry pulverized particles of earth or other matter **:** something reduced to minute portions **:** fine powder ⟨the floors were deep in the ~ of spring sandstorms —Willa Cather⟩ ⟨a huge cloud of snow spray and snow ~ —Carl Jonas⟩: as **a :** VOLCANIC DUST **b :** meteoric dust **c :** GOLD DUST **d :** finely divided or ground food ⟨asparagus, dipped in egg and cracker ~ —H.H.Huff⟩ **e :** a material (as an insecticide or fungicide) used in a dry form resembling dust to control pests **2 a :** the particles into which a thing disintegrates **:** the earthy remains of a body (as a human corpse) once alive ⟨the repository of the ~ of many of those illustrious men —C.B.Fairbanks⟩ **b :** something that is left after the substance of a thing is gone ⟨stirring up the ~ of history —Richard Joseph⟩ **c :** something that beclouds or dulls ⟨yes, I know, . . . though he tried to throw ~ in my eyes —Kathleen Freeman⟩ ⟨society can do something for itself . . . by blowing out of the museums and galleries the ~ of erudition and the stale incense of hero worship —Clive Bell⟩ **3 :** the mortal body of a human being ⟨the troubles of our proud and angry ~ are from eternity, and shall not fail —A.E.Housman⟩ **4 a :** something worthless ⟨vile gold, dross, ~ —Shak.⟩ **b :** a state of humiliation ⟨her spirit is contrite to the ~ —Eden Phillpotts⟩ **5 a :** the earth esp. as a place of burial ⟨for now shall I sleep in the ~ —Job 7:21 (AV)⟩ **b :** the surface of the ground ⟨he railed at me and made to fight me, I took off my hat, and there I laid him in the ~ —Gilbert Parker⟩ — compare *bite the dust* at ¹BITE **6** *archaic* **:** MONEY **7 :** a small quantity (as of a fine or powdered substance) ⟨add a ~ of flour⟩ ⟨a cherry sundae with a ~ of nuts over the top —Hugh MacLennan⟩ **8 a :** a cloud of dust ⟨the wagon, with a thin ~ rising from the hooves, went on into the lazy afternoon —H.V.Morton⟩ **b :** CONFUSION, DISTURBANCE ⟨let us kick up what ~ we will over "Imperial ideals" —A.T.Quiller-Couch⟩ **c :** DUSTUP **9** *now dial* **:** a single particle (as of earth) ⟨to touch a ~ of England's ground —Shak.⟩ **10** *Brit* **:** sweepings or other refuse ready for collection **11 :** a light olive brown that is lighter than drab, paler than sponge, and paler and slightly redder than average mustard tan — called also *antelope* **12** *slang Austral* **:** FLOUR — **in dust and ashes 1 :** with dust and ashes put on the head as a sign of grief or humiliation **2 :** with repentance and sorrow **:** in sackcloth and ashes

²dust \"\ *vb* -ED/-ING/-S [ME *dustyn*, fr. *dust*, n.] *vt* **1 a :** to reduce to dust **b :** to reduce to a fine powder **:** LEVIGATE **2** *archaic* **:** to make dusty **:** soil with dust **3 a :** to make free of dust **:** brush, wipe, or sweep away dust from ⟨~ the table⟩ — often used with *off* **b :** to brush away like dust ⟨~*ed* the moths out of the furs —Meridel Le Sueur⟩ **c :** to prepare to use again **:** refurbish or renovate for use ⟨something that has long been neglected or disused) — used with *off* ⟨standards are ~*ed* off again and reappraised, reassessed —L.H.Bristol⟩ **d :** to free (raw wool) of loose dirt by shaking in a machine **4 :** to sprinkle with or as if with dust, powder, or other fine particles ⟨whipped cream ~*ed* with cinnamon —S.H.Delaplane⟩ ⟨a face . . . covered with little freckles as if it had been ~*ed* over with gold motes of the light —Edith Sitwell⟩ ⟨~*ing* crops with insecticide⟩ ⟨~*ed* the table for fingerprints⟩; *specif* **:** to spread or distribute a coating of finely ground rock or shale dust in (coal-mine workings) in order to reduce the explosion hazard **5 :** to give a beating to **:** THRASH, WHIP ⟨I will ~ their backsides for them —T.B.Costain⟩ **6 a :** to strew or sprinkle in the form of dust **:** SIFT ⟨sulfur ~*ed* into shoes and clothes —*Girl Scout Handbook*⟩ ⟨airplanes ~ insecticides over the crops⟩ **b :** to sow (a crop) in dry soil — used with *in* ⟨*dusted*-in rye⟩ **7 :** to dupe or confuse as if by throwing dust in the eyes **~** *vi* **1 a :** to disintegrate into dust **b :** to give off or produce dust — used of a concrete floor **2** *slang* **:** HURRY; *esp* **:** to leave in a hurry **3** *of a bird* **:** to sprinkle itself with dust **4 :** to remove dust (as from furniture) ⟨I went in now and then to ~ and clean —B.A.Williams⟩ — **dust a dam :** to fill up the interstices between the planks in a splash-dam gate with earth or gravel — **dust one's jacket :** to give one a beating

dust bag *n* **:** the part of a vacuum sweeper in which dust and other sweepings are collected

dust ball *n* **:** a concretion composed of vegetable or mineral matter found in the intestines (as of the horse) and varying in size from a few ounces to several pounds — called also *intestinal calculus;* compare HAIR BALL

dustband *n* **:** a metal ring inserted between the upper and lower plates of a watch to exclude dust

dustbin \ˈ=,=\ *n* **1** *Brit* **a :** a usu. metal receptacle for rubbish **:** TRASH CAN **b :** a garbage can **2 :** a place of neglect or oblivion ⟨the ~ of public indifference⟩

dust·blu \ˈ=ˌblü\ *n* -s [¹*dust* + *blu*, alter. of *blue*] **:** a pale blue that is redder and darker than average powder blue, redder and duller than Sistine, and redder, stronger, and slightly darker than average cadet gray

dust board *also* **dust bottom** *n* **:** a horizontal board that separates one drawer from another (as in a chest of drawers)

dust bowl *n* **:** a region that suffers from prolonged droughts and dust storms

dust bowler *n* **:** an inhabitant of a dust bowl

dustbox \ˈ=,=\ *n* **1 :** a box used to hold or collect dust: as **a :** a box containing sand or powder (as for drying ink) **b :** DUSTBIN **c :** DUST CHAMBER **2 :** the part of a box strike that encloses the opening thus concealing the jamb

dust cap *n* **:** a protecting cover for the lens of a telescope sight

dust cart *n, Brit* **:** a vehicle used for rubbish collection

dust cell *n* **:** a pulmonary histiocyte that takes up and eliminates foreign particles introduced into the lung alveoli with inspired air

dust chamber *n* **:** a chamber through which gases are passed to permit them to deposit solid particles (as in connection with a lead or copper smelting furnace)

dustcloth \ˈ=,=\ *n* **1 :** a cloth for dusting **2 :** DUST COVER 1

dustcoat \ˈ=,=\ *n, chiefly Brit* **:** DUSTER 2

dust counter *n* **:** an instrument for determining the number of dust particles or condensation nuclei per unit volume of a sample of air

dust cover *n* **1 :** a piece of cloth (as sheeting) used to protect furniture and other articles when not in use from soil, fading, wear **2 :** JACKET 3f(1)

dust devil *n* **:** a whirlwind containing sand or dust seen esp. in arid and semiarid regions — called also *dust whirl, sand column*

dust disease *n* **:** PNEUMOCONIOSIS

dusted target *n* **:** a target in trapshooting that is struck by the shot but not broken and thus not scored as a hit

dust·er \ˈdəstə(r)\ *n* -s **1 :** one that removes dust and dirt: as **a :** a cloth or brush for dusting (as furniture) **b :** a machine typically employing a rotating wire-cloth cylinder for removing dust from raw material (as rags) prior to pulping — called also *willow* **c :** a machine for brushing and sifting the flour from bran or shorts **2 a :** a lightweight washable overgarment usu. made like a coat and worn to prevent clothing from becoming soiled **b :** a woman's lightweight dress-length housecoat **c :** a woman's loose-fitting unlined summer coat made of lightweight material **3 :** one that scatters dustlike material: as **a :** a container with a perforated lid for sifting or sprinkling ⟨a sugar ~⟩ **b :** an implement or machine for applying insecticidal or fungicidal dusts to crops **4 :** one whose work is removing dust or sprinkling with a dusting of some substance **5 :** a nonproductive oil well **6** *South & Midland* **:** DUST STORM **7** *slang Brit* **:** a ship's flag **8 :** a baseball pitched at or near the batter

duster 3b

dust exhaust *n* **:** a device for drawing off dust (as that produced in dry grinding)

dust furrow *n* **:** a furrow or trench around a field used to check migrating insects (as chinch bugs)

dust gun *n* **:** a hand device used for applying dust to a surface (as an insecticide to crops or calcium cyanide in the burrows of rodents to destroy them by gas)

dustheap \ˈ=,=\ *n* **1 :** a pile of refuse **2 :** the status to which something unimportant, unwanted, or forgotten is relegated ⟨ferreting out from the ~ of time the half-obliterated data of circumstance and events —*Manchester Guardian Weekly*⟩

dust·i·ly \ˈdəstəlē, -li\ *adv* **:** in a dusty condition **:** with much dust

dust·i·ness \-tēnəs, -tin-\ *n* -ES **:** the quality or state of being dusty

dusting *n* -s [fr. gerund of ²*dust*] **1 :** a small quantity lightly applied to or sprinkled on or appearing as if sprinkled on a surface (a ~ of powder over her distressing freckles —Elizabeth Goudge) ⟨the wing is much overlaid with olivaceous ~ —A.B. Klots⟩ **2** *slang* **a :** BEATING **b** *of a boat* **:** a buffeting in stormy weather **3 :** the formation of dust by the wearing away of concrete floor surfaces under traffic

dusting brush *n* **:** a brush used for dusting

dusting powder *n* **:** a powder used esp. on the skin or on wounds (as for allaying irritation or absorbing moisture)

dust jacket *n* **:** JACKET 3f(1)

dust·less \ˈdəstləs\ *adj* **:** free from dust

dustlike \ˈ=,=\ *adj* **:** as fine and powdery as dust

dust louse *n* **:** BOOK LOUSE

dust·man \ˈdəs(t)mən\ *n, pl* **dustmen 1** *Brit* **:** a trash collector or a garbage collector **2** *Brit* **:** SANDMAN

dust mop *n* **:** DRY MOP

dust mulch *n* **:** a fine loose dry layer of surface soil maintained by cultivation under the assumption that it will prevent evaporation of soil moisture

dust off *vt* **1 :** to intentionally pitch a baseball directly at or near (the batter) **2** *slang* **:** KILL

dus·toor *or* **dus·tour** \dəˈstü(ə)r\ *var of* DASTUR

dus·too·ree *or* **dus·too·ri** \-ürē\ *var of* DASTURI

dustpan \ˈ=,=\ *n* **:** a shovel-shaped pan usu. with a short handle for receiving and conveying away dirt swept from the floor

dust pearl *n* **:** a very small seed pearl

dust process *n* **:** the process of molding ceramic ware by dry pressing

dustproof *or* **dust-tight** \ˈ=ˌ=\ *adj* **:** impervious to dust **:** so tight as to exclude dust

dustpan

dustrag \ˈ=,=\ *n* **:** DUST CLOTH 1

dust remover *n* **:** a filter for the air intake of an internal-combustion engine

dust ruffle *n* **1 :** a ruffle on the lower edge of a woman's skirt; *esp* **:** one on the inside to keep the skirt clean **2 :** a decorative ruffle attached to the rails or springs of a bed and reaching the floor; *also* **:** a wide ruffle on the edge of a bedspread

dusts *pl of* DUST, *pres 3d sing of* DUST

dust sheet *n* **:** DUST COVER 1

dust shot *n* **:** the smallest size of shot

dust storm *n* **1 :** a violent dust-laden whirlwind that moves across an arid region and that is usu. associated with very hot excessively dry air and attended by high electrical tension **2 :** strong winds bearing clouds of dust

dus·tuck *or* **dus·tuk** \ˈdə(ˌ)stək\ *n* -s [Hindi *dastak*, fr. Per] *India* **:** a passport or customs permit

dustup \ˈ=,=\ *n* -s [fr. *dust up*, v.] **:** QUARREL, ROW, ARGUMENT ⟨another literary ~ . . . has been raging between publishers and authors —Mollie Panter-Downes⟩

dust well *n* **:** a pit in a glacier formed by the more rapid melting of the ice beneath a deposit of dust or earth

dust whirl *n* **:** DUST DEVIL

dust wrapper *n* **:** JACKET 3f(1)

dusty \ˈdəstē, -ti\ *adj* -ER/-EST [ME, fr. ¹*dust* + *-y*] **1 :** marked by the presence of dust **:** filled with dust **:** covered or clouded with dust ⟨the table is ~⟩ ⟨two thirsty travelers . . . came upon the lake after a ~ trek —*Amer. Guide Series: Calif.*⟩ **2 :** consisting of dust **:** POWDERY ⟨two acres of stony, ~ ground —Bernard Gutteridge⟩ **3 :** WORTHLESS, CONTEMPTIBLE, MISERABLE, SORDID ⟨he who is born on the steps of a throne and never ascends them has a ~ fate —*Times Lit. Supp.*⟩ **4 :** DIM, CLOUDED ⟨in the moonlight grows a smile mid its rays of ~ pearl —G.W.Russell⟩ ⟨your splendor is ~ —Max Beerbohm⟩ **5** *of the weather* **:** STORMY, BLOWY **6 :** dry and lifeless (as from age or disuse) **:** BARREN, UNPRODUCTIVE, STALE, UNSATISFYING; *also* **:** lacking in interest **:** DULL ⟨the old man will suck a little of her sweetness to prolong his ~ life —Elinor Wylie⟩ ⟨while the work of his contemporaries today seems ~ and dated, his drawings still retain their freshness and vigor —L.R.Sander⟩ ⟨ah, what a ~ answer gets the soul when hot for certainties in this our life —George Meredith⟩ — **not so dusty** *Brit* **:** pretty good **:** not bad

dusty aqua *n* **:** a pale blue that is greener and duller than average powder blue, greener and less strong than Sistine, and greener and slightly lighter than average cadet gray

dusty aqua blue *n* **:** a pale blue that is greener and duller than average powder blue and greener and less strong than Sistine

dusty aqua green *n* **:** a pale green that is bluer and deeper than celadon gray, bluer and stronger than bayberry gray, and bluer and darker than spray green

dusty blue *n* **:** a variable color averaging a pale blue that is redder and darker than average powder blue, redder and less strong than Sistine, and greener and stronger than average cadet gray — called also *mist blue, misty blue*

dusty cedar *n* **:** a variable color averaging a grayish red that is paler and very slightly bluer than bois de rose and yellower and paler than blush rose or appleblossom

dusty clover *n* **:** a bush clover (*Lespedeza capitata*) with silvery foliage

dusty copen blue *n* **:** a deep blue that is greener and much paler than Yale blue and greener and much paler than royal (sense 8b)

dusty coral *n* **:** a variable color averaging a dark pink that is yellower and paler than wild rose and yellower and lighter than average colonial rose

dustyfoot \ˈ==,=\ *n, pl* **dustyfeet** *or* **dustyfoots** [ME *dustiefute*, fr. *dustie, dusty* dusty + *fute, fot* foot; trans. of AF *piepowdrous*] *Scot* **:** a wayfaring peddler — compare COURT OF PIEPOUDRE

dusty green *n* **1 :** a variable color averaging a pale green that is yellower and deeper than spray green and bluer, stronger, and slightly darker than aloes green **2 :** a light grayish olive that is darker than Quaker gray and greener and less strong than hemp

dusty jade green *n* **:** a pale green that is bluer, lighter, and stronger than celadon gray or bayberry gray and bluer, lighter, and stronger than spray green

dusty lavender *n* **:** a pale violet that is deeper than old lavender (sense 1) and redder and deeper than dusty periwinkle blue

dusty lilac *n* **:** a grayish purple that is redder, lighter, and stronger than telegraph blue, bluer and stronger than mauve gray or average orchid gray, and bluer, lighter, and stronger than average rose mauve

dusty mauve *n* **:** a pale purple that is redder and duller than average lavender or wistaria (sense 2a) and redder and deeper than flossflower blue

dusty miller *n* **1 :** any of several plants having ashy-gray or white tomentose leaves: as **a :** a stiff perennial (*Senecio cineraria*) with very white woolly pinnatifid leaves **b :** SNOW-IN-SUMMER a **c :** MULLEIN PINK **d :** either of two plants of the genus *Centaurea* (*C. cineraria* and *C. gymnocarpa*) with white tomentose foliage **e :** BEACH WORMWOOD **2 :** MILLER 2a

dusty olive *n* **:** a variable color averaging a light olive that is greener and stronger than citrine, deeper and slightly redder than grape green, and stronger and slightly redder than old moss green

dusty orange *n* **:** a moderate orange that is yellower, darker, and slightly stronger than honeydew and yellower and duller than Persian orange

dusty orchid *n* **:** a variable color averaging a pale reddish purple that is bluer and duller than anemone

dusty peach *n* **:** a grayish to moderate yellowish pink

dusty periwinkle blue *n* **:** a pale violet that is bluer, lighter, and stronger than old lavender (sense 1) and bluer and paler than dusty lavender

dusty pink *n* **:** a moderate yellowish pink that is yellower and duller than coral pink, redder and duller than peach pink, and redder and duller than average peach

dusty rose *n* **:** a variable color averaging a light grayish purplish red

dusty turquoise *n* **:** a moderate greenish blue that is greener and paler than average peacock blue and greener and less strong than Brittany

dusty turquoise blue *n* **:** a variable color averaging a light greenish blue that is bluer and duller than average turquoise blue or average aqua and bluer, less strong, and very slightly lighter than average turquoise (sense 2a)

dusty turquoise green *n* **:** a variable color averaging a moderate bluish green that is bluer and paler than porcelain green or sea blue

dusty wing *n* **:** CONIOPTERYGID

dusty yellow *n* **:** a grayish greenish yellow that is redder, lighter, and stronger than yellow stone or hay and redder, lighter, and slightly stronger than absinthe yellow

du·sun \ˈdüsᵊn\ *n, pl* **dusun** *or* **dusuns** *usu cap* [Malay (*orang*) *dusun* country people] **1 :** a Dayak people in British North Borneo **2 :** a member of the Dusun people

¹dutch \ˈdəch\ *adj, usu cap* [ME *Duch, Duche*, fr. MD *duutsch, dūtsch*, fr. a prehistoric EGmc-WGmc compound (represented also by OE *thēodisc* gentile, OS *thiudisk*, OHG *thiutisc, diutisc* German, Goth *thiudisko* gentile) whose components are akin to OS *thioda* people and OS *-isk* -ish; akin to OE *thēod* people, retainers, gentiles, OHG *diot* people, Goth *thiuda*, ON *thjōth*, OIr *tuath* people, Oscan *touto* city, OPruss *tauto* land, Latvian *tauta* people] **1 a** *archaic* **:** of or relating to the Germanic peoples of Germany, Austria, Switzerland, and the Low Countries **b :** of or relating to the Netherlands or its inhabitants **c** [influenced in meaning by G *deutsch*, fr. OHG *thiutisc, diutisc*] *slang* **:** GERMAN 1b **2 a** *archaic* (1) **:** of, relating to, or in any of the Germanic languages of Germany, Austria, Switzerland, and the Low Countries (2) **:** GERMAN 2 **b :** of, relating to, or in the Dutch language **c :** of, relating to, or in Afrikaans **3** [influenced in meaning by PaG *deitsch* German, fr. OHG *thiutisc, diutisc*] **:** of or relating to the Pennsylvania Dutch or their language **4** *of a meal* **:** served buffet style

²dutch \"\ *n* [ME *Duche*, fr. *Duche*, adj.] **1** -ES *cap* **a** *archaic* (1) **:** any of the Germanic languages of Germany, Austria, Switzerland, and the Low Countries — compare HIGH GERMAN, LOW GERMAN (2) **:** GERMAN 2 **b :** the Germanic language of the majority of the inhabitants of the Netherlands and the northern half of Belgium — see FLEMISH **c :** AFRIKAANS **2** *pl in constr, cap* **a** *archaic* **:** the Germanic peoples of Germany, Austria, Switzerland, and the Low Countries **b** *archaic* **:** GERMAN 1 **c :** the people of the Netherlands, principally of Frankish, Frisian, and Saxon origin **3** -ES *cap* [PaG *deitsch* German, fr. OHG *thiutisc, diutisc*] **:** PENNSYLVANIA DUTCH **4** -ES *usu cap, slang* **:** DANDER ⟨the fighting tone he used indicated that the President's *Dutch* is up —*Newsweek*⟩ **5** -ES *usu cap* **:** DISFAVOR, WRONG, TROUBLE — used with *in* ⟨the story is accurate, but its publication put me in *Dutch* with the composer in question —Nicolas Slonimsky⟩ ⟨every time he got in *Dutch* —J.T.Farrell⟩ **6** *usu cap* **:** a breed of small rabbits developed in the Netherlands with white blaze, collar, chest, and feet

³dutch \"\ *vt* -ED/-ING/-ES *sometimes cap* [¹*Dutch*] **1 :** to clean and harden (a quill) for use as a pen esp. by plunging in hot sand **2 :** to miscalculate in placing (a series of bets) so as to have a mathematical expectancy of losing rather than winning ⟨the man had ~*ed* his book, as clumsy operators sometimes did in their haste to take bets —*Newsweek*⟩

⁴dutch \"\ *adv, sometimes cap* [¹*Dutch*] **:** with each person treating himself or paying his own way ⟨they went ~ on the check —Truman Capote⟩ ⟨a candidate may drink ~ or even accept drinks from constituents —*Time*⟩

⁵dutch \"\ *n* -ES [prob. by shortening & alter. fr. *duchess*] *slang Brit* **:** WIFE — now used as a term of affection

dutch auction *n, usu cap D* **:** the public offer of property at a high price and then at gradually lowering prices until someone buys it

dutch backgammon *n, usu cap D* **:** a variation of backgammon in which a player's men must all be entered before any can be moved and a blot cannot be hit by a player until at least one of his men has reached home table

dutch bargain *n, usu cap D* **:** a bargain made and sealed while drinking — called also *wet bargain*

dutch barn *n, usu cap D* **:** a roofed farm shelter closed in only on the weather side and often used for storing and curing hay or tobacco

dutch bath *n, usu cap D* **:** a mordant composed of hydrochloric acid and potassium chlorate used in etching

dutch beech *n, usu cap D* **:** WHITE POPLAR 1a

dutch belted *n, usu cap D&B* **:** a breed of medium-sized dairy cattle originating in Holland, the cattle being black with a broad band of white around the body

dutch blue *n, often cap D* **1 :** a variable color averaging a moderate blue that is redder and darker than average copen, redder, lighter, and stronger than azurite blue, and redder and deeper than Dresden blue **2 :** a grayish blue that is redder and paler than electric or copenhagen and lighter than Gobelin

dutch bob *also* **dutch cut** *n, usu cap D* **:** a bob with straight bangs across the front and the rest of the hair cut evenly about earlobe length

dutch bond *n, usu cap D* **:** ENGLISH CROSS BOND

dutch brass *n, usu cap D* **:** LOW BRASS

dutch bulb *n, usu cap D* **:** a bulb or bulbous plant imported from Holland (as the hyacinth, tulip, and daffodil) — compare CAPE BULB

dutch cap *n, usu cap D* **:** a woman's cap with a triangular piece rolled back at each side

dutch cheese *n, usu cap D, North* **:** COTTAGE CHEESE

dutch clinker *also* **dutch brick** *n, usu cap D* **:** a long, narrow, and very hard yellowish brick made in Holland

dutch clover *n, usu cap D* **:** WHITE CLOVER a

dutch colonial *adj, usu cap D* [so called fr. the style prevailing in New York during the Dutch colonial period] *of a style of architecture* **:** characterized by the gambrel roof with widely overhanging eaves

dutch courage *n, usu cap D* **:** courage due to intoxicants or other artificial stimulation ⟨had to nerve himself with *Dutch courage* to face a skilled gunfighter —W.S.Campbell⟩ ⟨singing and crooning old Irish airs to give myself *Dutch courage* —S.J. Roche⟩

dutch curse *n, usu cap D* **:** DAISY 1b

dutch door *n, usu cap D* **:** a door divided horizontally so that the lower part can be shut while the upper remains open — compare DOUBLE DOOR

Dutch door

dutch elm *n, usu cap D* **:** a hybrid European shade tree (*Ulmus hollandica major*) planted for ornament

dutch elm disease *n, usu cap D* **:** a vascular disease of elms caused by a fungus (*Ceratostomella ulmi*) which is transmitted by bark beetles (genera *Scolytus* and *Hylurgopinus*) and which produces destructive toxic substances that are largely responsible for wilting and yellowing of the foliage, defoliation, and death first of local areas then of the entire plant

dutch engine *n, usu cap D* **:** HOLLANDER 3b

dutches *pl of* DUTCH, *pres 3d sing of* DUTCH

dutch flax *n, usu cap D* **:** GOLD OF PLEASURE

dutch foot *n, usu cap D* **:** a foot found on cabriole legs suggesting a hoof in its outward turn and in its thick disklike formation — called also *duck foot;* compare CLUB FOOT, DRAKE FOOT, SNAKE FOOT

dutch frill *n, usu cap D & often cap F* **:** a domestic canary of a variety distinguished by large size, upright carriage, and crimped and ruffled feathers

dutch-ga·bled \ˈ=ˌ==\ *adj, usu cap D* **:** having gables like those of Dutch houses

dutch grass *n, usu cap D* **1 :** COUCH GRASS **2 :** PARA GRASS 1

dutch guianese *also* **dutch guianan** *adj or n, usu cap D&G* [*Dutch Guiana* (older name for Surinam) + E *-ese* or *-an*] **:** SURINAMESE

dutch hoe *n, usu cap D* **:** SCUFFLE HOE

dutchier *comparative of* DUTCHY

dutchies *pl of* DUTCHY

dutchiest *superlative of* DUTCHY

dutch·i·fy \ˈdəchə,fī\ *vt* -ED/-ING/-ES *often cap* **:** to make Dutch in quality or traits

dutching *pres part of* DUTCH

dutch iris *n, usu cap D* **:** any of certain beardless bulbous irises derived primarily from the species irises (*Iris tingitana* and *I. filifolia*)

dutch lap *n, usu cap D* **:** the lapping of roof shingles not only at their butts but also at their sides

dutch light *n, usu cap D* **:** a removable glazed sash used in the erection of greenhouses

dutch lottery *n, usu cap D* **:** a lottery in which tickets are drawn in certain classes or series for each of which certain prizes increasing in number and value with each class are fixed — called also *class lottery*

dutch lunch *n, usu cap D* **:** an individual serving of assorted sliced cold meats and cheeses — compare COLD CUTS

dutch·ly *adv, often cap* **:** in the manner of the Dutch ⟨streets, concrete and *Dutchly* clean —Bill Redgrave⟩

dutch·man \ˈ=mən\ *n, pl* **dutchmen** [ME *Ducheman*, fr. *Duche* Dutch + *man*] **1** *cap* **a** *archaic* **:** a member of any of the Germanic peoples of Germany, Austria, Switzerland, and the Low Countries **b :** a native or inhabitant of the Netherlands **:** HOLLANDER **c :** a person of Dutch descent born in southern Africa — compare AFRIKANER **d** *slang* **:** GERMAN 1 **2 a :** a contrivance to hide or counteract defective work (as an odd piece inserted to fill an opening) **b :** a short prop for supporting a log esp. to prevent pinching during sawing or to keep logs from falling from a load **c :** a strip of cloth used in the theater to conceal the crack between two scenery flats **d :** a piece of pipe or duct used to replace temporarily a piece of equipment (as a heating unit in a ventilation duct)

dutchman's-breeches \ˈ=='=ˌ==\ *n pl but sing or pl in constr, usu cap D* [so called fr. the shape of the blossoms] **:** a delicate spring-flowering herb (*Dicentra cucullaria*) of the eastern U.S. having finely divided leaves and cream-white double-spurred flowers

dutchman's log *n, usu cap D* **:** a method of estimating the speed of a boat in which an object that will float (as a piece of wood) is thrown over the bow and calculations are made based on the time that elapses before the stern passes

dutchman's-pipe \ˈ=='=ˌ=\ *n, pl* **dutchman's-pipes** *usu cap D* **:** a vine (*Aristolochia durior*) with large leaves and early summer flowers having the tube of the calyx curved like the bowl of a pipe

dutch metal *or* **dutch leaf** *or* **dutch gold** *n, usu cap D* **:** low brass esp. in the form of foil **:** imitation gold leaf

Dutchman's-breeches

dutch myrtle *n, usu cap D* **:** SWEET GALE

dutch orange *n, often cap D* **:** a moderate to strong orange yellow that is slightly darker than Indian yellow — called also *Florida gold, orpiment red, realgar orange, yellow carmine*
dutch oven *n, usu cap D* **1 :** a metal utensil for baking fitted with shelves and having one open side that is placed close to the fire **2 :** a brick oven in which cooking is done by the preheated walls **3 a :** a cast-iron usu. three-legged kettle with a tight cover on which coals may be heaped that is used for baking in an open fire **b :** a heavy pot with a tight-fitting domed cover used for braising, steaming, or baking on top of a stove **4 :** a furnace or other heating equipment in which the temperature is stabilized by indirect application of heat

Dutch oven 3b

dutch pink *n, often cap D* **1 :** a yellow lake prepared usu. from Persian berries or from quercitron and used chiefly as an artist's pigment **2 :** a light yellow that is greener and slightly darker than jasmine and greener and stronger than average maize or popcorn — called also *English pink, Italian pink, madder yellow, stil-de-grain yellow, yellow madder*
dutch–process \ˈ⁼ˌ⁼\ *adj, usu cap D* **:** treated with an alkaline substance — used of cocoa and chocolate
dutch process *n, usu cap D* **:** a method of manufacturing white lead in which metallic lead gratings or plates are placed in the upper part of pots containing dilute acid and the pots stacked in fermenting tanbark or manure and left for about three months
dutch quill *also* **dutch pen** *n* **:** a pen made of a quill that has been dutched
dutch rabbit *n, usu cap D* **1 :** a genetic variety of the domestic rabbit characterized by more or less extensive white spotting typically forming a white belt on a dark ground **2 :** DUTCH 6
dutch reformed *adj, usu cap D&R* **:** of or referring to the Reformed Church in America that traces its beginnings to the Dutch communities of New York state as early as 1614 and that took its present name in 1867
dutch roll *n, usu cap D* **1 :** CROSS ROLL **2 :** a combination directional-lateral oscillation of an airplane
dutch rose *n, usu cap D* **:** a cut (as of a diamond or other gem) having 24 triangular facets — see ROSE illustration
dutch rush *n, often cap D* **:** a scouring rush (*Equisitum hyemale*)
dutch scarlet *n, often cap D* **:** CASTILIAN RED
dutch settle *n, usu cap D* **:** a wooden bench whose back may be tipped forward to form a table
dutch straight *n, usu cap D* **:** SKIP STRAIGHT
dutch treat *n, sometimes cap D* **:** a meal, entertainment, or trip for which each person present pays his own way ⟨a *dutch treat* was better than no date at all⟩
dutch 200 *n, pl* **dutch 200s :** a bowling score of exactly 200 made by rolling alternate strikes and spares
dutch uncle *n, usu cap D* **:** one who admonishes or reprimands with great severity and directness **:** a severe mentor ⟨I got mad and talked like a *Dutch uncle* —Joseph Hergesheimer⟩
dutch vermilion *n, often cap D* **:** a vivid reddish orange that is redder and lighter than international orange and redder and deeper than chrome orange — called also *toreador*
dutchware blue \ˈ⁼,⁼-\ *n, often cap D* **:** DELFT 2
dutch wife *n, usu cap D* **:** a long round bolster or an open frame of rattan or cane used in beds in tropical countries as a rest for the limbs and an aid in keeping cool
dutch woodbine *n, usu cap D* **:** a purplish variety (*Lonicera periclymenum belgica*) of the common European honeysuckle
¹dutchy \ˈdəchē, -chi\ *adj* -ER/-EST *usu cap* [²*Dutch* + *-y*] **:** characteristically Dutch
²dutchy \"\ *n* -ES *usu cap* **1 :** DUTCHMAN **2 :** GERMAN
du·te·ous \ˈd(y)üd-ēəs, -ütēəs *chiefly Brit* -ü·tyəs\ *adj* [irreg. fr. *duty* + *-ous*] **1 :** marked by a sense of duty **:** DUTIFUL ⟨his chaste and ∼ wife —Andrew Lang⟩ **2** *obs* **:** OBSEQUIOUS ⟨many a ∼ and knee-crooking knave that . . . wears out his time . . . for naught but provender —Shak.⟩ — **du·te·ous·ly** *adv* — **du·te·ous·ness** *n* -ES
du·ti·able \-ēəbəl, -yəb-\ *adj* **:** subject to a duty ⟨∼ imports⟩
du·tied \ˈd(y)üd-ēd\ *adj, archaic* **:** subjected to a duty (as when imported)
du·ti·ful \ˈd(y)üd-ə̇fəl, -üt|, |ēf-\ *adj* **1 :** filled with or motivated by a sense of duty to one's natural or legal superiors **:** having due respect for one's own moral obligations **:** willingly obedient ⟨a ∼ son⟩ ⟨a ∼ servant⟩ ⟨she's a wonderfully ∼ girl. Her father's wish would be sacred to her —G.B.Shaw⟩ **2 :** proceeding from or expressive of a sense of duty **:** DEFERENTIAL ⟨the tender and ∼ manner in which she had supported her parents —W.M.Thackeray⟩ ⟨∼ attendance at church⟩ — **du·ti·ful·ness** *n* -ES
du·ti·ful·ly \-f(ə)lē, -li\ *adv* **:** in a dutiful manner **:** from a sense of duty ⟨a promise of secrecy was . . . ∼ given —Jane Austen⟩ ⟨a group of sailor boys . . . all ∼ saluted —H.A. Chippendale⟩
du·tu·bu·ri \ˌdüd-əˈbu̇rē\ *n* -S [MexSp] **:** a women's ceremonial circle dance of the Tarahumara Indians of Chihuahua, Mexico
¹du·ty \ˈd(y)üd-ē, -ütē, -i\ *n* -ES [ME *duete, dewte,* fr. AF *dueté, duité,* fr. OF *deu* due + *-té* -ty — more at DUE] **1 a :** conduct due parents and superiors **:** respectful or obedient behavior **:** RESPECT ⟨every prince that has parents owes them as much filial ∼ and obedience —John Locke⟩ **b :** conduct or activities showing respect **:** expression of respect ⟨addressed the king with humble ∼⟩ **2 a :** obligatory tasks, conduct, service, or functions enjoined by order or usage according to rank, occupation, or profession ⟨*duties* that he knew he would have to do —Joseph Conrad⟩ **b :** service, ministration, or performance enjoined on a clergyman **c :** active military or naval service **:** assigned participation in activity **:** service under orders **d :** responsibility for maintaining continued operation or status **:** supervision of a post, ship, or installation in the interest of normal operation — used with *the* ⟨the commander had the ∼ on Monday⟩ **3 a :** behavior required by moral obligation, demanded by custom, or enjoined by feelings of rightness or fitness — compare CATEGORICAL IMPERATIVE **b :** the force of moral obligation **:** feeling for or sense of such obligation ⟨the call of ∼⟩ **c :** the conduct or acts of a person motivated by pure goodwill **:** conduct that produces the greatest good — used in axiological philosophy **4 a :** a payment or service imposed by law or custom; *esp* **:** a charge payable to a government **b :** a sum paid as a tax on import, export, manufacture, or consumption of goods ⟨no tax or ∼ shall be laid on articles exported from any state —*U.S. Constitution*⟩ **5 a :** work done by a particular machine under certain conditions (as of time or energy) ⟨the ∼ of a stamp may be stated as the number of tons of ore crushed to a given degree of fineness in a given time⟩ **b :** a measure of the overall efficiency (as of a machine, engine, pump, power plant, but esp. of a water pump) expressed in terms of the amount of work delivered for a certain quantity of input energy **6** *also* **duty of water :** the quantity of irrigation water required to satisfy the requirements of the area of a particular crop expressed in acre-inches or acre-feet per acre or as acres per second per foot of water **7 a :** service required (as of a machine) under specified conditions of load and rest (intermittent ∼) ⟨continuous ∼⟩ **b :** USE, SERVICE, FUNCTION ⟨if one chain, one rope, or one bolt was strong enough for a particular ∼ —O.S.Nock⟩; *esp* **:** service as a replacement or substitute ⟨a big book doing ∼ as a doorstop⟩ ⟨making the word do ∼ for the thing —Edward Sapir⟩ **syn** see FUNCTION, OBLIGATION, TASK — **in line of duty :** within the scope of one's duties **:** in accordance with assigned duties ⟨feeling that he had acted *in line of duty*⟩ — **off duty :** not assigned to any specific task or duty **:** free from assignment or responsibility ⟨men *off duty* loafing around the barracks⟩ — **on duty :** assigned to a task or duty **:** engaged in or responsible for some specific performance
²duty \"\ *adj* **1 :** done as a duty ⟨paying ∼ calls on his elderly relatives⟩ **2 :** being on duty **:** having the responsibility for certain assigned tasks or functions ⟨he was ∼ officer the night of the raid⟩ ⟨a ∼ doctor to take care of emergencies⟩
duty mark *n* **:** a punch mark in the form of the sovereign's head which had to be placed on all British wares made of silver or gold from 1784 to 1890 to show that duty had been paid
duty plate *n* **:** the plate that prints the frame, denomination, and sometimes also (as on certain British colonial stamps) the name of the country on a bicolor postage stamp
duty roster *n* **:** a roster of a military unit showing what duties (as guard and kitchen police) each man has performed
du·um·vir \d(y)üˈəmvər, -ˌvi(ə)r\ *n, pl* **duumvirs** \-rz\ *also* **duumvi·ri** \-ˌvəˌrī, -ˌrē\ [L, fr. *duum* of two (gen. of *duo* two) + *vir* man — more at TWO, VIRILE] **1 :** one of two Roman officers or magistrates constituting a board, commission, or court appointed for a specific function **2 :** one of two men jointly holding power or associated in some official position
du·um·vi·rate \-vərə̇t, -ˌrāt\ *n* -S [L *duumviratus,* fr. *duumvir* + *-atus* -ate] **1 :** the office or government of the Roman duumvirs **2 :** two people associated in high office or position **:** a coalition of two people
du·vet \(ˈ)d(y)ü¦vā\ *n* -S [F, lit., down, fr. MF, alter. of (assumed) *dumet* (whence later MF *dumet* & Bret *dumed*), dim. of *dum* down, fr. OF, alter. (prob. influenced by *plume* feather) of *dun,* fr. ON *dūnn* — more at DOWN (feathers)] **:** a downy growth characteristic of some fungus cultures
du·ve·tyn \ˈd(y)üvətə̇n, ˈdəvt-\ *also* **du·ve·tyne** \", ˈd(y)üvəˌtēn\ *n* -S [F *duvetine,* fr. *duvet* down + *-ine*] **:** a smooth lustrous velvety fabric that has a napped surface which obscures the twill weave and that is made usu. in solid colors from wool, silk, rayon, cotton, or various combinations
du·wa·mish \dəˈwämish, ˈdwä-\ *n, pl* **duwamish** *or* **duwamishes** *usu cap* [fr. the *Duwamish* river, Wash.] **1 :** a Salishan people of the valley of the Duwamish river and its tributaries in the state of Washington **2 :** a member of the Duwamish people
dux \ˈdəks, ˈdu̇ks\ *n, pl* **du·ces** \ˈd(y)üˌsēz, ˈdüˌkās\ *also* **duxes** \ˈdəksə̇z, ˈdu̇k-\ [L, lit., leader — more at DUKE] **1 :** a military commander stationed in a province of the later Roman Empire **2** *Brit* **:** the pupil at the academic head of his class or of his school **3 :** the theme of a fugue or canon — compare COMES
d'ux·elles *or* **dux·elles** \(ˈ)du̇k¦sel, (ˈ)dək-, (ˈ)d(y)ük-, *F* dü̇sel\ *n, pl* **d'uxelles** \-lz, *F* -l\ *or* **duxelles** *often cap U in the apostrophized form* [after the Marquis *d'Uxelles,* 17th cent. Fr. nobleman, patron of the Sieur de la Varenne, famous 17th cent. Fr. chef] **:** a garnish or sauce whose principal ingredients are minced mushrooms and tomato puree
duyker *var of* DUIKER
DV *abbr* **1** [L *Deo volente*] God willing **2** distinguished visitor **3** *often not cap* double vibration
dvan·dva \ˈdvänˌ(ˌ)dvä, dəˈv-, -vəndvə\ *n, pl* **dvandvas** *or* **dvandva** [Skt *dvandva,* lit., a pair, couple, redupl. of *dva* two — more at TWO] **:** a class of compound words having two immediate constituents that are equal in rank and related to each other as if joined by *and* **:** a compound word belonging to this class (as *bittersweet, secretary-treasurer, sociopolitical*) — see ²COPULATIVE 2
dva·pa·ra yu·ga \ˌdväpərəˈyu̇gə\ *n, usu cap D&Y* [Skt *dvāparayuga,* fr. *dvāpara* third best throw at dice (that of the two) (fr. *dva* two + *para* further) + *yuga* yoke, age of the world — more at TWO, PEREION, YOKE] **:** the third age of a Hindu world cycle
dvi- *comb form* [Skt *dvi-* two — more at TWI-] **:** standing or assumed to stand in the second place beyond (a specified element) in the same family of the periodic table — in names of chemical elements esp. when not yet discovered ⟨*dvi*-manganese (now called *rhenium*)⟩; compare EKA-
dvr *abbr* driver
DW *abbr* **1** deadweight **2** delayed weather **3** distilled water **4** dock warrant **5** dust wrapper
dwai·ble \ˈdwābəl\ *also* **dwai·bly** \-bli\ *adj* [origin unknown] *chiefly Scot* **:** feeble and shaky **:** UNSTABLE ⟨I would just be a hindrance with my ∼ legs —John Buchan⟩
dwale \ˈdwā(ə)l\ *n* -S [ME, stupefying drink, belladonna, perh. of Scand origin; akin to OSw *dvala* trance, lethargy, delay, Dan *dvale* trance, lethargy, ON *dvöl* short stay, delay — more at DWELL] **:** BELLADONNA 1
dwall \ˈdwal\ *Scot var of* DWELL
¹dwalm *or* **dwam** \ˈdwäm\ *n* -S [akin to OE *dwolma* chaos, OHG *twalm* bewilderment, stupefaction, ON *dylminn* careless, indifferent, Goth *dwalmon* to be foolish, insane — more at DWELL] **1** *chiefly Scot* **:** a fainting spell or sudden attack of illness **2** *chiefly Scot* **:** DAYDREAM, REVERIE
²dwalm *or* **dwam** \"\ *vi* -ED/-ING/-S *chiefly Scot* **:** to fall in a faint **:** become dazed
¹dwarf \ˈdwȯ(ə)r|f, -ō(ə)|\ *n, pl* **dwarfs** \|fs\ *or* **dwarves** \|vz\ [ME *dwerg, dwerf,* fr. OE *dweorg, dweorh;* akin to OFris *dwerch* dwarf, OHG *twerg,* ON *dvergr,* and perh. to Skt *dhvaras* demon, *dhvarati* he bends, injures — more at FRAUD] **1 a :** an abnormally small person; *esp* **:** one of markedly atypical proportions **b :** a person of small or negligible powers or endowments ⟨a literary ∼ . . . writing in something that resembles, however inadequately, your style —Osbert Sitwell⟩ **2 :** an animal or plant much below the normal size of its species or kind: as **a :** a small fruit tree reaching a height at maturity of as little as four or five feet and bearing early but normal fruit **b :** a plant of abnormally small size developed by root pruning, starving, pruning of leaders, or other measures that restrict growth **3 :** a legendary manlike being of small stature usu. misshapen and ugly and skilled as an artificer **4** *also* **dwarf star :** a star (as the sun) of ordinary or low luminosity and relatively small mass and size
²dwarf \"\ *vb* -ED/-ING/-S *vt* **1 a :** to make dwarf in size **:** stunt in growth ⟨malnutrition had ∼*ed* these children⟩ ⟨an arid climate ∼*ing* oaks into mere shrubs⟩; *specif* **:** to make (a plant) dwarf by grafting a scion of standard size to a dwarf stock **b :** to cause the intellectual or moral development of (a person) to be hindered or stunted ⟨incessant repetition of the same handwork ∼*s* the man —R.W.Emerson⟩ **2 :** to cause to appear smaller or inferior in any way in relation to some other individual or thing ⟨∼*ed* the chair in which he sat⟩ ⟨∼ the achievements of his predecessors⟩ ∼ *vi* **:** to become dwarf
³dwarf \"\ *adj* -ER/-EST **1** *of a plant or animal* **:** extremely small as contrasted with related species or varieties **2 :** resembling a dwarf **:** characterized by smallness or insignificance of size, proportion, scope, strength, or power **:** DIMINUTIVE ⟨the farmer on a ∼ holding . . . must supplement his income by working off his own land —J.M.Mogey⟩ ⟨what is man but a species . . . dominant over other species on a ∼ planet —W.R.Inge⟩
⁴dwarf \"\ *also* **dwarf disease** *n* -S **:** any of various diseases of plants characterized by shortened internodes and generally reduced size of the plants ⟨rice ∼ is a virus disease known chiefly from Japan⟩
dwarf agave *n* **:** a lechuguilla (*Agave lecheguilla*)
dwarf alder *n* **1 :** a small American buckthorn (*Rhamnus alnifolia*) with leaves resembling those of the alder **2 :** a shrub (*Fothergilla gardeni*) of the southeastern U.S. with white flowers
dwarf apple *n* **1 :** a small apple tree produced by grafting a scion of a standard variety onto a dwarfing rootstock **2 :** any of several horticultural apple varieties marked by trees of low stature
dwarf ash *n* **1 :** GOUTWEED **2 :** SINGLE-LEAF ASH
dwarf banana *n* **:** a low-growing banana (*Musa nana* or *M. cavendishii*) cultivated esp. in the West Indies and distinguished by its compact growth habit and its six-angled curved fragrant fruit — called also *Canary banana, Cavendish banana, Chinese banana*
dwarf bean *n* **:** any of various beans that form a comparatively small plant; *esp* **:** BUSH BEAN
dwarf bilberry *or* **dwarf blueberry** *n* **:** a low-growing tufted blueberry (*Vaccinium caespitosum*) of northern and alpine No. America with deep pink to coral red flowers followed by light blue primrose edible berries
dwarf birch *n* **:** any of several low shrubs of the genus *Betula* (esp. *B. pumila, B. glandulosa,* and *B. nana*)
dwarf box *n* **1 :** any of several Australian eucalypts (as *Eucalyptus bicolor*) **2 :** SAND MYRTLE **3 :** a dwarf variety (*Buxus sempervirens suffruticosa*) of the box with small leaves
dwarf buckeye *n* **:** BOTTLEBRUSH BUCKEYE
dwarf buffalo *n* **1 :** ANOA **2 :** CONGO BUFFALO
dwarf bunt *n* **:** a bunt disease of wheat that causes dwarfing
dwarf buttercup *n* **:** any of several small or low-growing buttercups; *esp* **:** a weak-stemmed buttercup (*Ranunculus pygmaeus*) that is native to Europe but widely distributed in moist rocky northern and alpine parts of America and that usu. has several stems each bearing a single flower
dwarf canadian primrose *n, usu cap C* **:** MISTASSINI
dwarf cassia *n* **:** SENSITIVE PEA
dwarf cherry *n* **:** any of several small usu. shrubby cherries: as **a :** the wild sour cherry **b :** any of certain sand cherries (esp. *Prunus cuneata*)
dwarf chestnut *n* **:** a low-growing shrubby chestnut; *esp* **:** CHINQUAPIN 1a
dwarf chestnut oak *n* **:** a low shrubby chestnut oak (*Quercus prinoides*)
dwarf chinquipin oak *n* **:** CHINQUAPIN OAK b
dwarf cornel *n* **:** either of two red-berried perennial herbs of the genus *Cornus:* **a :** a creeping plant (*C. canadensis*) having whorled leaves and white floral bracts **b** *or* **dwarf honeysuckle :** a closely related plant (*C. suecica*) with opposite leaves and purple bracts
dwarf crab *n* **:** a tiny pear-shaped hairy crab (*Pelia tumida*) found among seaweeds along the west coast of Central America and Mexico
dwarf cudweed *n* **:** a white-tomentose alpine or circumboreal perennial herb (*Gnaphalium supinum*) with mostly basal leaves and yellowish flowers
dwarf cypress *n* **:** an alpine and circumboreal club moss (*Lycopodium alpinum*)
dwarf dandelion *n* **:** KRIGIA 2
dwarf eggplant *n* **:** a small straggling herb (*Solanum melongena depressum*) with thin scarcely lobed leaves, small flowers, and obovoid to pyriform dark purple fruit
dwarf elder *n* **1 :** DANEWORT **2 :** GOUTWEED **3 :** BRISTLY SARSAPARILLA
dwarf elm *n* **:** SIBERIAN ELM
dwarf false musk *n* **:** a low tufted perennial figwort (*Mazus pumilio*) with small bluish white flowers
dwarf fan palm *n* **:** any of several usu. low-growing fan palms; *esp* **:** a hemp palm (*Chamaerops humilis*)
dwarf forest *n* **:** a low usu. deciduous forest — compare CHAPARRAL, KRUMMHOLZ
dwarf french pink *n, usu cap F* **:** DEPTFORD PINK
dwarf ginseng *n* **:** a small herbaceous perennial (*Panax trifolius*) having stalkless leaves and a globular root — called also *groundnut*
dwarf goldenrod *n* **:** a dyer's-weed (*Solidago nemoralis*)
dwarf gourami *n* **:** a small Indian anabantid fish (*Colias lalia*) the male of which is light blue and barred with orange-red stripes and the female less brilliant
dwarf gray willow *n* **:** SAGE WILLOW
dwarf horse chestnut *n* **:** BOTTLEBRUSH BUCKEYE
dwarf houseleek *n* **:** a prostrate European herb (*Sedum reflexum*) with yellow flowers that is sparingly adventive in the eastern U.S.
dwarf huckleberry *n* **:** BUSH HUCKLEBERRY
dwarfing *pres part of* DWARF
dwarfing stock *n* **:** a stock used in budding or grafting that produces a dwarf tree
dwarf iris *n* **:** any of several low-growing American irises (as *Iris verna* and *I. cristata*); *also* **:** any of several exotic irises common in cultivation (as *I. pumila*)
dwarf·ish \ˈdwȯrfish, -ō(ə)f-, -fēsh\ *adj* **:** of or like a dwarf ⟨a bewhiskered, button-faced ∼ man —R.S.Harper⟩ **:** very small ⟨sounded in the distance like an elf upon his ∼ drum —G.K.Chesterton⟩ — **dwarf·ish·ly** *adv* — **dwarf·ish·ness** *n* -ES
dwarf·ism \-ˌfizəm\ *n* -S **:** the condition of stunted growth **:** NANISM ⟨∼ results from a recessive gene —Merrill Gregory⟩
dwarf japanese quince *n, usu cap J* **:** a low Japanese shrub (*Chaenomeles japonica*) cultivated chiefly for its early blooming orange-scarlet flowers
dwarf juniper *n* **:** any of several low-growing or prostrate shrubs of the genus *Juniperus:* as **a :** SAVIN 1 **b :** a horticultural variety (*J. communis depressa*) of the common juniper
dwarf larkspur *n* **:** a No. American larkspur (*Delphinium tricorne*) with blue or white flowers
dwarf laurel *n* **1 :** SHEEP LAUREL **2 :** MEZEREON 1
dwarf lemur *n* **:** any of several very small Malagasy lemurs constituting the genus *Microcebus*
dwarf·ling \-ȯrfliŋ, -ō(ə)f-\ *n* -S **:** a little dwarf
dwarf lupine *n* **:** a low-growing plant of the genus *Lupinus; esp* **:** an alpine (*L. minimus*) of the Rocky mountains
dwarf male *n* **1 :** a small plant of algae of the family Oedogoniaceae that consists of a few cells, develops from an androspore near the oogonium, is usu. attached to the cell below it, and produces only spermatozoids — called also *nannander* **2 :** COMPLEMENTAL MALE
dwarf mallow *n* **:** a prostrate European weedy plant (*Malva rotundifolia*) having long-stalked roundish leaves, blue flowers, and small flat fruits — called also *blue mallow;* compare CHEESE 4
dwarf maple *n* **:** a low shrubby maple (*Acer glabrum*) of the Rocky mountain region
dwarf milkweed *n* **:** WHORLED MILKWEED
dwarf mistletoe *n* **:** AMERICAN MISTLETOE 1
dwarf mountain fir *or* **dwarf mountain pine** *n* **:** MUGHO PINE
dwarf mulberry *n* **1 :** CLOUDBERRY 1 **2 :** a low-growing mulberry that is a variety of the white mulberry (*Morus alba*) used for silkworm culture
dwarf·ness *n* -ES **:** the quality or state of being a dwarf **:** DWARFISM
dwarf nettle *n* **:** SMALL NETTLE
dwarf nipplewort *n* **:** LAMB SUCCORY
dwarf oak *n* **1 :** any of various trees of the genus *Teucrium* **2 :** a shrubby tree of the genus *Quercus; esp* **:** CHINQUAPIN OAK b
dwarf palmetto *n* **1 :** BLUE PALMETTO **2 :** a low-growing palm (*Sabal minor*) of the southeastern U.S. with subterranean rootstock and a short underground trunk from which flat-bladed leaves project in a crown
dwarf partition *n* **:** a partition that does not extend up to the ceiling
dwarf pea *n* **:** CHICK-PEA 2
dwarf phlox *n* **:** MOSS PINK
dwarf pine *n* **1 :** MUGHO PINE **2** *in California* **:** BISHOP PINE
dwarf pocket rat *n* **:** any of several small No. American pouched rats (genus *Microdipodops*)
dwarf rafter *n* **:** JACK RAFTER
dwarf raspberry *n* **:** any of several low prostrate or trailing plants of the genus *Rubus; esp* **:** a No. American plant (*R. pubescens*) with reddish purple fruit
dwarfs *pl of* DWARF, *pres 3d sing of* DWARF
dwarf salamander *n* **:** a small tailed amphibian (*Manculus quadridigitatus*) of the southern U.S.
dwarf salmon *n* **:** a landlocked salmon of western No. America
dwarf senna *n* **:** SENSITIVE PEA
dwarf signal *n* **:** a low home signal for railroad trains — called also *backup signal*
dwarf solomon's seal *n, usu cap 1st S* **:** FALSE LILY OF THE VALLEY
dwarf spurge *n* **:** a European erect or depressed annual spurge (*Euphorbia exigua*) adventive in the northeastern U.S.
dwarf star *n* **:** DWARF 4
dwarf sumac *n* **:** a common nonpoisonous shrub (*Rhus copallina*) of eastern No. America having green paniculate flowers, red fruit, and compound leaves — called also *black sumac*
dwarf tapeworm *n* **:** the common hymenolepidid tapeworm (*Hymenolepis nana*) of man — compare HYMENOLEPIS
dwarf tiger lily *n* **:** BLACKBERRY LILY
dwarf upland willow *n* **:** SAGE WILLOW
dwarf wall *n* **:** a low toe wall built to retain the slope of an excavation or embankment
dwarf water plantain *n* **:** a low aquatic or marsh plant (*Helianthium parvulum*) of the family Alismataceae common in No. America and having long-stalked lanceolate leaves and white flowers
dwarf weasel *n* **:** LEAST WEASEL
dwarf whin *n* **:** a low spiny almost leafless furze (*Ulex nanus*) of western Europe with yellow flowers
dwarf willow *n* **:** any of several low-growing willows: as **a :** a widely distributed alpine or boreal shrubby willow (*Salix*

herbacea) with partially underground creeping stems and bright green lustrous reticulate-veined leaves **b :** SAGE WILLOW

dwarf yew *n* **:** GROUND HEMLOCK

dwarves *pl of* DWARF

DWC *abbr* deadweight capacity

dwee·ble \'dwēbəl\ *var of* DWAIBLE

1**dwell** \'dwel\ *vb* **dwelt** \-lt\ *also* **dwelled** \-lt, -ld\ **dwelt** *also* **dwelled; dwelling; dwells** [ME *dwellen*, fr. OE *dwellan* to lead astray, go astray; akin to OHG *twellen* to tarry, hesitate, ON *dvelja* to delay, *dvöl* delay, Goth *dwalmōn* to be mad, OE *dol* foolish — more at DULL] *vi* **1 a :** LIVE, RESIDE ⟨~ for years in the same town⟩ **b :** to be or continue in some state or condition ⟨*dwelt* in bondage to his mother —Edmund Fuller⟩ **c :** to exist or be present ⟨wisdom must ~ in a mind so honest⟩ **d :** CONSIST, LIE ⟨the poem's main interest ~*s* in its unusual imagery⟩ **2 a :** to linger over something (as with the mind or eyes) — used with *on* or *upon* ⟨sights on which the eyes may ~ with pleasure⟩ ⟨her mind *dwelt* on his good qualities —Ellen Glasgow⟩ **b :** to speak or write with emphasis or at length — used with *on* or *upon* ⟨~*ing* eloquently on the power of Milton's prose style⟩ ~ *vt, obs* **:** to inhabit or occupy as a place of residence **syn** see RESIDE

2**dwell** \"\ *n* -s **1 :** a short interruption or intermission in the motion of a part of a machine that gives time for its own proper operation or for the operation of another part **2 :** the time during which material is subjected to a particular operation (as in a manufacturing process) ⟨the ~ during heat sealing of plastic⟩; *specif* **:** the time during which material to be printed is in contact with the printing surface

dwell·er \-lə(r)\ *n* -s [ME, fr. *dwellen* to dwell + *-er*] **:** one that dwells **:** INHABITANT, RESIDENT ⟨a vast number of services available for city and town ~*s* — J.B.Conant⟩

dwell·ing \'dweliŋ, -lēŋ\ *n* -s [ME, fr. gerund of *dwellen* to dwell — more at DWELL] **:** a building or construction used for residence **:** ABODE, HABITATION

dwelling house *n* **:** a house or sometimes part of a house that is occupied as a residence in distinction from a store, office, or other building and that may legally include associated or connected buildings within the same curtilage

dwg *abbr* **1** drawing **2** dwelling

dwight–lloyd \'dwīt¦lȯid \ *adj, usu cap D&L* [after A.S.*Dwight* †1946 and R.L.*Lloyd* *b*1870 Am. mining engineers] **:** relating to a process for roasting and sintering fine ores whereby the ore is ignited in a thin layer on a traveling grate which passes over a suction box

1**dwin·dle** \'dwindᵊl, ÷-nᵊl\ *vb* **dwindled; dwindled; dwindling** \-(ᵊ)liŋ\ **dwindles** [prob. freq. of *dwine*] *vi* **:** to become steadily less **:** diminish in size, amount, or quality **:** SHRINK ⟨the boat gradually *dwindled* to a speck⟩ ⟨population is *dwindling*⟩ ⟨the novel ~*s* away to a most unsatisfactory ending⟩ ~ *vt* **:** to make steadily less **:** reduce in any way ⟨~*s* all other developments to insignificance⟩ **syn** see DECREASE

2**dwindle** \"\ *n* -s **:** DECREASE, DECLINE

dwine \'dwīn\ *vi* -ED/-ING/-S [ME *dwinen*, fr. OE *dwīnan;* akin to MD *dwīnen* to disappear, languish, faint, ON *dvīna* to dwindle or pine away, OIr *dīth* end, death, Arm *di* corpse, ON *deyja* to die — more at DIE] *now chiefly dial* **:** to waste or pine away **:** LANGUISH

dwt *abbr* [*denarius* + *weight*] pennyweight

DWT *abbr, often not cap* deadweight ton

DX \(')dē¦eks\ *abbr or n* -ES distance — used of long-distance radio transmission

dy- *or* **dyo-** *comb form* [LL *dy-* & G *dyo-*, fr. Gk *dy-*, *dyo-*, fr. *dyo* — more at TWO] **:** two ⟨*dy*archy⟩ ⟨*dy*aster⟩ ⟨*dyo*theism⟩

dy *abbr* **1** delivery **2** [L *denarius* + E *penny*] penny **3** deputy

Dy *symbol* dysprosium

dyable *var of* DYEABLE

1**dy·ad** *also* **di·ad** \'dī,ad, -īəd\ *n* -s [LL *dyad-*, *dyas* two (n.), fr. Gk, fr. *dyo* two — more at TWO] **1 :** two units treated as one **:** COUPLE, PAIR; *specif* **:** a pair of individuals (as husband and wife, teacher and pupil) maintaining a sociologically significant relationship **2 :** a bivalent element, atom, or radical **3 :** a meiotic chromosome after separation of the two homologous members of a tetrad **4** *math* **:** an operator indicated by writing the symbols of two vectors without a dot or cross between (as AB)

2**dy·ad** *var of* DIAD

1**dy·ad·ic** *also* **di·ad·ic** \(')dī¦adik\ *adj* [*dyad*, *diad* + *-ic*] **:** of, having reference to, or concerning a dyad **:** being of two parts or elements **:** involving two in its formation ⟨a ~ relation between the spectator and the experience —Daniel Bell⟩ ⟨~ arithmetic⟩ ⟨cultural importance, intimate nature, and ~ character of the family —J.G.March⟩ ⟨a ~ relation between a sign and an object —R.S.Wells⟩

2**dyadic** \"\ *n* -s **:** a sum of mathematical dyads

dyak *usu cap, var of* DAYAK

dy·a·kis·dodecahedral \¦dīəkəs, dī¦akəs+\ *adj* **:** having the shape or the symmetry of a diploid

dy·a·kis·dodecahedron \"+\ *n* -s [ISV *dyakis* (fr. Gk *dyakis* twice, fr. *dyo* two) + *dodecahedron*] **:** DIPLOID

dy·ar·chic \(')dī¦ärkik\ *also* **dy·ar·chi·cal** \-rkəkəl\ *or* **dy·ar·chal** \-rkəl\ *adj* **:** of or having reference to a dyarchy

dy·ar·chy *also* **di·ar·chy** \'dī,ärkē\ *n* -ES [*dy-* or *di-* + *-archy*] **:** a government in which power is vested in two rulers or authorities; *specif* **:** a dual form of government established first in the provinces of India and now used in some British colonies in which the British government shares power and responsibility with native ministers responsible to a locally elected legislature

dy·as·sic \(')dī¦asik\ *adj* [NL *Dyas* Permian system (fr. LL, two, n.) + E *-ic* — more at DYAD] **:** PERMIAN

dyaster *n* -s [*dy-* + *-aster* (star)] **:** DIASTER

dyb·buk *or* **dib·buk** \'dibək\ *n, pl* **dybbu·kim** *or* **dibbu·kim** \¦dibu̇¦kēm, di'bu̇kim\ *also* **dybbuks** *or* **dibbuks** \'dibəks\ [Heb *dibbūq*, fr. *dābhaq* to cling, cleave] **:** an evil spirit or the wandering soul of a dead person believed in Jewish folklore to enter the body of a man and control his actions until exorcised by a religious rite

1**dye** \'dī\ *n* -s [ME *dehe*, fr. OE *dēah, dēag;* akin to OE *dīegol* secret, hidden, OS *dōgalnussi* secret, hiding place, OHG *tugōn* to become variegated, *tougan* dark, hidden, secret, L *fumus* smoke — more at FUME] **1 :** color produced by dyeing **2 :** a natural or esp. a synthetic coloring matter whether soluble or insoluble that is used to color materials (as textiles, paper, leather, or plastics) usu. from a solution or fine dispersion and sometimes with the aid of a mordant — called also *dyestuff;* compare PIGMENT, STAIN, TINT; see DYE table — **of deepest dye** *or* **of the deepest dye :** of the worst kind ⟨a scoundrel *of the deepest dye*⟩ **:** of the most pronounced kind ⟨an intellectual *of the deepest dye*⟩

DYES

The dyes listed include most of the synthetic dyes and pigments manufactured in the U.S., a very few domestic natural dyes that continue to be important, and six representative foreign-made fiber-reactive dyes. The American-made dyes have been taken from the *Technical Manual of the American Association of Textile Chemists and Colorists* (AATCC), in which all American dye manufacturers voluntarily list their domestic products. Only synthetic dyes and pigments have been selected whose compositions have been disclosed in the *Colour Index* (CI), 2d ed., compiled and published jointly by the Society of Dyers and Colourists of Great Britain and the American Association of Textile Chemists and Colorists.

The dyes in the table are arranged in the first column in accordance with the names assigned to them in part I of the *Colour Index*, 2d ed. These names are derived from the use classes described after the table, and within each use class the dyes are arranged coloristically in the following order: yellow, orange, red, violet, blue, green, brown, and black. Within each use class and color, dyes are differentiated from one another by serial arabic numbers, which are a part of the name. For example, Methylene Blue 2B becomes Basic Blue 9 in the new system of nomenclature, and that dye can be unequivocally designated by that name instead of by one of the commercial names, many of which contain a trademark.

In the second (double) column the small number to the left indicates the type of chemical structure to which the dye on that line belongs, the number referring to one of the 31 structure types given at the end of this paragraph. Each number to the right, which always has 5 digits, indicates the structural formula—if known—that is shown for the dye in part II, volume III, of the *Colour Index*. Structure Types:

1 nitroso	17 indamine
2 nitro	18 indophenol
3 monoazo	19 azine
4 disazo	20 oxazine
5 trisazo	21 thiazine
6 polyazo	22 sulfur
7 azoic diazo component	23 lactone
8 azoic coupling component	24 amino ketone
9 stilbene	25 hydroxy ketone
10 diphenylmethane	26 anthraquinone
11 triarylmethane	27 indigoid
12 xanthene	28 thioindigoid
13 acridine	29 phthalocyanine
14 quinoline	30 natural organic
15 methine or polymethine	31 oxidation base
16 thiazole	

In the third column is given at least one commercial or common name for each dye under which the dye may be defined in the body of the dictionary. This name has been selected because it may be the one given to it by the first manufacturer (and may thus often be reflected in the names given by other manufacturers) or because it may be considered as most used in old literature. However, United States trademarks are usually replaced by other appropriate names. Final letters often indicate shade (as R for reddish and G for greenish or yellowish, the latter from the German *gelb*). Numbers with the letters or doubled letters indicate the extent of redness, greenness, and so on; thus "Blue 5R" indicates a very reddish blue.

Each number given in the last column is either the old *Colour Index* number (CI No.) of the first edition or the Prototype number (Pr No.) assigned to the dye in question by the AATCC.

The uses of the various dyes are given in general under the descriptions of each use class after the table.

DYE TABLE I

Part I Colour Index Generic Name	Chemical Structure Type	Part II Colour Index No.	Commercial Name	Old Colour Index No. or Prototype No.
ACID				
Yellow 1	2	10,316	Naphthol Yellow S Ext D&C Yellow No. 7	CI 10
Yellow 2	14	47,010	Quinoline Yellow KT	CI 802
Yellow 3	14	47,005	Quinoline Yellow D&C Yellow No. 10	CI 801
Yellow 7	24	56,205	Brilliant Sulpho Flavine FF	Pr 224
Yellow 9	3	13,015	Fast Yellow	CI 16
Yellow 11	3	18,820	Fast Light Yellow Ext D&C Yellow No. 3	CI 636
Yellow 17	3	18,965	Xylene Light Yellow	CI 639
Yellow 23	3	19,140	Tartrazine D&C Yellow No. 5 FD&C Yellow No. 5	CI 640
Yellow 29	3	18,900	Acid Yellow 3 GL	Pr 474
Yellow 34	3	18,890	Fast Light Yellow	CI 636
Yellow 36	3	13,065	Metanil Yellow Ext D&C Yellow No. 1	CI 138
Yellow 38	4	25,135	Milling Yellow O	Pr 139
Yellow 40	3	18,950	Acid Yellow 2G	CI 642

Part I Colour Index Generic Name	Chemical Structure Type	Part II Colour Index No.	Commercial Name	Old Colour Index No. or Prototype No.
ACID—*Continued*				
Yellow 42	4	22,910	Acid Yellow R	Pr 187
Yellow 44	4	23,900	Milling Yellow H5G	Pr 138
Yellow 54	3	19,010	Acid Fast Yellow ELN	Pr 330
Yellow 63	3	13,095	Azo Yellow	CI 146
Yellow 73	12	45,350	Fluorescein, Uranine Ext D&C Yellow Nos. 10 and 11	CI 766
Yellow 99	3	13,900	Acid Yellow GR	Pr 316
Orange 1	3	13,091	Azo Flavine RR	CI 145
Orange 3	2	10,385	Amido Yellow E	CI 11
Orange 7	3	15,510	Orange II D&C Orange No. 4	CI 151
Orange 8	3	15,575	Orange R	CI 161
Orange 10	3	16,230	Orange G D&C Orange No. 3	CI 27
Orange 11	12	45,370	Eosine H8G	
Orange 12	3	15,970	Croceine Orange G	CI 26
Orange 20	3	14,600	Orange I Ext D&C Orange No. 3	CI 150
Orange 24	4	20,170	Resorcin Brown D&C Brown No. 1	CI 234
Orange 45	4	22,195	Acid Orange R	Pr 152
Orange 49	4	23,260	Acid Orange GS	Pr 151
Orange 50	3	13,150	Milling Orange G	Pr 137
Orange 51	4	26,550	Acid Brown 5R	Pr 562
Orange 52	3	13,025	Methyl Orange	CI 142
Orange 56	4	22,895	Acid Orange G	Pr 186
Orange 74	3	18,745	Acid Fast Orange GN	Pr 315
Orange 76	3	18,870	Acid Orange R	Pr 146
Red 1	3	18,050	Amido Naphthol Red G Ext D&C Red No. 11	CI 31
Red 4	3	14,710	Azo Eosine G	CI 114
Red 12	3	14,835	Diamond Blue 3B	CI 180
Red 14	3	14,720	Azo Rubine Ext D&C Red No. 10	CI 179
Red 17	3	16,180	Fast Red B	CI 88
Red 18	3	16,255	Cochineal Red A	CI 185
Red 25	3	16,050	Croceine Scarlet 3BX	CI 183
Red 26	3	16,150	Ponceau R D&C Red No. 5	CI 79
Red 27	3	16,185	Amaranth FD&C Red No. 2	CI 184
Red 29	3	16,570	Chromotrope 2R	CI 29
Red 32	3	17,065	Fast Light Rubine BL	Pr 188
Red 33	3	17,200	Fast Acid Fuchsine B Ext D&C Red No. 23	CI 30
Red 34	3	17,030	Guinea Fast Red 8BL	Pr 102
Red 35	3	18,065	Acid Red 3B	Pr 193
Red 37	3	17,045	Guinea Fast Red BL	Pr 101
Red 51	12	45,430	Erythrosine Bluish FD&C Red No. 3	CI 773
Red 52	12	45,100	Sulpho Rhodamine B	CI 748
Red 66	4	26,905	Ponceau 3RB	CI 280
Red 73	4	27,290	Brilliant Croceine M Ext D&C Red No. 13	CI 252
Red 80	26	68,215	Alizarine Rubinol R	CI 1091
Red 85	4	22,245	Acid Red G	CI 430
Red 87	12	45,380	Eosine G or Y D&C Red Nos. 22 and 23	CI 768
Red 88	3	15,620	Fast Red A Ext D&C Red No. 8	CI 176
Red 89	4	23,910	Milling Scarlet 4R	CI 487
Red 92	12	45,410	Phloxine B D&C Red No. 28	CI 778
Red 94	12	45,440	Rose Bengal B	CI 779
Red 95	12	45,425	Erythrosine Yellowish D&C Orange No. 11	CI 772
Red 97	4	22,890	Acid Anthracene Red G	CI 443
Red 99	4	23,285	Acid Red	CI 430
Red 106	3	18,110	Brilliant Acid Red	CI 32
Red 115	4	27,200	Cloth Red B	CI 262

Part I Colour Index Generic Name	Chemical Structure Type	Part II Colour Index No.	Commercial Name	Old Colour Index No. or Prototype No.
ACID—*Continued*				
Red 133	3	17,995	Acid Chrome Red B	Pr 360 and 649
Red 134	4	24,810	Acid Bordeaux B	CI 430
Red 137	3	17,755	Paper Red A	Pr 148
Red 151	4	26,900	Cloth Scarlet G	CI 275
Red 179	3	19,351	Acid Bordeaux R	Pr 145
Red 182	—	—	Acid Red B	Pr 591
Red 183	3	18,800	Acid Red GRE	Pr 391
Red 186	3	18,810	Acid Fast Pink BN	Pr 326
Violet 1	3	17,025	Victoria Fast Violet RR	Pr 197
Violet 3	3	16,580	Victoria Violet 4BS	CI 53
Violet 6	3	16,600	Chromotrope 6B	CI 56
Violet 7	3	18,055	Amido Naphthol Red 6B Ext D&C Red No. 1	CI 57
Violet 9	12	45,190	Fast Acid Violet R	CI 758
Violet 12	3	18,075	Guinea Carmine B	Pr 100
Violet 13	3	16,640	Chromotrope 10B	CI 90
Violet 14	3	17,080	Acid Fast Red 6BL	Pr 453
Violet 17	11	42,650	Formyl Violet S4B	CI 698
Violet 19	11	42,685	Acid Fuchsine Acid Magenta	CI 692
Violet 34	26	61,710	Anthraquinone Violet	CI 1080
Violet 43	26	60,730	Alizarine Acid Violet R Ext D&C Violet No. 2	CI 1073
Violet 49	11	42,640	Acid Violet 6B FD&C Violet No. 1	CI 697
Violet 56	3	16,055	Acid Fast Violet 3RN	Pr 328
Violet 58	3	16,260	Acid Fast Violet 5RN	Pr 329
Blue 1	11	42,045	Azure Blue VX	CI 672
Blue 5	11	42,052	Patent Blue A	CI 714
Blue 7	11	42,080	Azure Blue Z	CI 673
Blue 9	11	42,090	Azure Blue AEG FD&C Blue No. 1	CI 671
Blue 13	11	42,571	Fast Acid Violet 10B	CI 696
Blue 15	11	42,645	Brilliant Milling Blue B	Pr 37
Blue 20	19	50,405	Induline	CI 861
Blue 22	11	42,755	Soluble Blue	CI 707
Blue 23	26	61,125	Alizarine Light Blue 4GL	Pr 485
Blue 25	26	62,055	Alizarine Supra Blue A	Pr 12
Blue 27	26	61,530	Alizarine Starry Blue B	CI 1075
Blue 40	26	62,125	Alizarine Direct Blue A2G	Pr 10
Blue 41	26	62,130	Alizarine Direct Blue AR	Pr 11
Blue 43	26	63,000	Alizarine Saphirol SE	CI 1053
Blue 45	26	63,010	Alizarine Saphirol B Ext D&C Blue No. 4	CI 1054
Blue 47	26	62,085	Cyananthrol R	CI 1076
Blue 59	19	50,315	Wool Fast Blue BL	CI 833
Blue 74	27	73,015	Indigotine IA Indigo Carmine FD&C Blue No. 2	CI 1180
Blue 75	11	42,576	Acid Cyanine A	CI 699
Blue 78	26	62,105	Alizarine Sky Blue B	CI 1088
Blue 81	26	64,515	Anthraquinone Blue SR	CI 1089
Blue 83	11	42,660	Brilliant Indocyanine 6B	Pr 222
Blue 89	3	13,405	Acid Blue B	CI 209
Blue 90	11	42,655	Brilliant Indocyanine G	Pr 223
Blue 92	3	13,390	Acid Blue R	CI 208
Blue 93	11	42,780	Methyl Cotton Blue	CI 706
Blue 102	19	50,320	Wool Fast Blue GL	CI 833
Blue 104	11	42,735	Brilliant Wool Blue FFR	Pr 40
Blue 109	11	42,740	Brilliant Wool Blue FFB	Pr 39
Blue 110	11	42,750	Alkali Blue	CI 704
Blue 113	4	26,360	Acid Cyanine 5R	CI 289

Part I Colour Index Generic Name	Chemical Structure Type	Part II Colour Index No.	Commercial Name	Old Colour Index No. or Prototype No.
ACID—*Continued*				
Blue 118	4	26,410	Acid Cyanine G	CI 288
Blue 120	4	26,400	Acid Cyanine GR	CI 289
Blue 158	3	14,880	Acid Fast Blue GGN	Pr 144
Blue 158A	3	15,050	Acid Blue 2G	Pr 144
Blue 161	3	15,076	Acid Fast Blue BN	Pr 318
Green 1	1	10,020	Naphthol Green B Ext D&C Green No. 1	CI 5
Green 3	11	42,085	Guinea Green B Acid Green B FD&C Green No. 1	CI 666
Green 5	11	42,095	Light Green SF Yellowish FD&C Green No. 2	CI 670
Green 7	11	42,055	Acid Green A	Pr 688
Green 9	11	42,100	Brilliant Milling Green B D&C Green No. 7	CI 667
Green 11	11	42,038	Fast Green Extra Bluish	CI 691
Green 12	3	13,425	Acid Fast Green BLN	Pr 321
Green 16	11	44,025	Naphthalene Green V	CI 735
Green 20	4	20,495	Amido Black Green B	CI 247
Green 22	11	42,170	Alkali Fast Green 10G	Pr 131
Green 25	26	61,570	Alizarine Cyanine Green G D&C Green No. 5	CI 1078
Green 35	3	13,361	Acid Dark Green B	Pr 560
Green 50	11	44,090	Wool Green S	CI 737
Brown 13	2	10,410	Acid Brown 3GL	Pr 579
Brown 14	4	20,195	Resorcin Dark Brown	CI 235
Black 1	4	20,470	Naphthol Blue Black Naphthylamine Black 10B D&C Black No. 1	CI 246
Black 2	19	50,420	Nigrosine	CI 865
Black 7	4	26,300	Naphthylamine Black D	CI 308
Black 24	4	26,370	Acid Cyanine Black B	CI 307
Black 26B	4	26,690	Nerol 2B	CI 304
Black 31	3	17,580	Acid Black BR	Pr 189
Black 35	4	26,320	Acid Black R	CI 271
Black 41	4	20,480	Naphthol Blue Black S	Pr 141
Black 47	24	56,055	Acid Gray G	Pr 705
Black 48	26	65,005	Alizarine Fast Gray BBLW	Pr 206
Black 52	3	15,711	Acid Black WA	Pr 143
AZOIC				
Yellow 1		37,610+37,090	Azoic Yellow G	Pr 171
Yellow 2		37,610+37,120	Azoic Yellow GG	Pr 353
Yellow 3		37,610+37,558	Azoic Golden Yellow R	Pr 345
Orange 2		37,520+37,005	Azoic Orange G	Pr 348
Orange 3		37,558+37,010	Azoic Orange R	Pr 349
Red 1		37,558+37,090	Azoic Scarlet RS	Pr 170
Red 2		37,530+37,120	Azoic Red R	Pr 169
Red 6		37,520+37,090	Azoic Red GS	Pr 168
Red 12		37,550+37,150	Azoic Red ITR	Pr 402
Red 16		37,520+37,100	Azoic Bordeaux R	Pr 165
Violet 1		37,505+37,165	Azoic Violet B	Pr 351
Violet 3		37,540+37,160	Azoic Corinth IB	Pr 511
Blue 6		37,505+37,175	Azoic Blue B	Pr 163
Blue 7		37,505+37,155	Azoic Blue R	Pr 342
Green 1		37,585+37,175	Azoic Green B	Pr 347
Brown 2		37,545+37,010	Azoic Brown IR	— —
Brown 10		37,550+37,605	Azoic Black Brown IT	Pr 340
Black 1		37,235+37,175	Azoic Black MG	Pr 339
Coupler 2	8	37,505	Naphthol AS	Pr 302
Coupler 3	8	37,575	Naphthol AS-BR	Pr 304
Coupler 4	8	37,560	Naphthol AS-BO	Pr 303
Coupler 5	8	37,610	Naphthol AS-G	Pr 309
Coupler 7	8	39,565	Naphthol AS-SW	Pr 313
Coupler 8	8	37,525	Naphthol AS-TR	Pr 314
Coupler 9	8	37,625	Naphthol AS-L4G	Pr 647
Coupler 10	8	37,510	Naphthol AS-E	Pr 308
Coupler 11	8	37,535	Naphthol AS-RL	Pr 312
Coupler 12	8	37,550	Naphthol AS-ITR	Pr 310
Coupler 13	8	37,595	Naphthol AS-SG	Pr 388
Coupler 14	8	37,558	Naphthol AS-PH	Pr 557
Coupler 15	8	37,600	Naphthol AS-LB	Pr 387
Coupler 16	8	37,605	Naphthol AS-DB or AS-BT	Pr 307
Coupler 17	8	37,515	Naphthol AS-BS	Pr 305
Coupler 18	8	37,520	Naphthol AS-D	Pr 306
Coupler 19	8	37,545	Naphthol AS-BG	Pr 385
Coupler 20	8	37,530	Naphthol AS-OL	Pr 311
Coupler 21	8	37,526	Naphthol AS-KB	Pr 604
Coupler 22	8	37,511	Naphthol AS-MCA	Pr 693
Coupler 23	8	37,555	Naphthol AS-LC	Pr 460
Coupler 24	8	37,540	Naphthol AS-LT	Pr 506
Coupler 25	8	37,590	Naphthol AS-SR	Pr 558
Coupler 27	8	37,516	Naphthol AS-AN	Pr 692
Coupler 29	8	37,527	Naphthol AS-MX	Pr 556
Coupler 30	8	37,559	Naphthol AS-RP	Pr 694
Coupler 31	8	37,521	Naphthol AS-RT	Pr 695
Coupler 33	8	37,620	Naphthol AS-L3G	Pr 555
Coupler 34	8	37,531	Naphthol NEL	Pr 559
Coupler 35	8	37,615	Naphthol AS-LG	Pr 505
Coupler 36	8	37,585	Naphthol AS-GR	Pr 386
Diazo 1	7	37,135	Fast Bordeaux GP Base or Salt	Pr 260
Diazo 2	7	37,005	Fast Orange GC Base or Salt	Pr 264
Diazo 3	7	37,010	Fast Scarlet 2G Base or Salt	Pr 94
Diazo 4	7	37,210	Fast Garnet GBC Base or Salt	CI 17

Part I Colour Index Generic Name	Chemical Structure Type	Part II Colour Index No.	Commercial Name	Old Colour Index No. or Prototype No.
AZOIC—*Continued*				
Diazo 5	7	37,125	Fast Red B Base or Salt	CI 117
Diazo 6	7	37,025	Fast Orange GR Base or Salt	Pr 265
Diazo 7	7	37,030	Fast Orange R Base or Salt	CI 38
Diazo 8	7	37,110	Fast Red GL Base or Salt	CI 69
Diazo 9	7	37,040	Fast Red 3GL Base or Salt	Pr 269
Diazo 10	7	37,120	Fast Red RC Base or Salt	Pr 271
Diazo 11	7	37,085	Fast Red TR Base or Salt	Pr 273
Diazo 12	7	37,105	Fast Scarlet G Base or Salt	CI 68
Diazo 13	7	37,130	Fast Scarlet R Base or Salt	CI 118
Diazo 20	7	37,175	Fast Blue BB Base or Salt	Pr 258
Diazo 22	7	37,240	Diazo Blue Salt RT	Pr 358
Diazo 23	7	37,205	Fast Black LB Base	Pr 257
Diazo 24	7	37,155	Fast Blue RR Base or Salt	Pr 498
Diazo 27	7	37,215	Fast Garnet GC Base or Salt	Pr 501
Diazo 28	7	37,151	Fast Red PDC Base or Salt	Pr 501
Diazo 32	7	37,090	Fast Red KB Base or Salt	Pr 270
Diazo 33	7	37,075	Fast Red FR Base or Salt	Pr 671
Diazo 34	7	37,100	Fast Red RL Base or Salt	Pr 272
Diazo 35	7	37,255	Diazo Blue Salt B	Pr 357
Diazo 36	7	37,275	Fast Red AL Salt	Pr 267
Diazo 37	7	37,035	Fast Red 2G Base or Salt	CI 44
Diazo 38	7	37,190	Fast Black K Salt	Pr 256
Diazo 39	7	37,220	Fast Corinth V Salt	Pr 261
Diazo 40	7	37,170	Fast Bordeaux BD Salt	Pr 259
Diazo 41	7	37,165	Fast Violet B Base or Salt	Pr 274
Diazo 42	7	37,150	Fast Red ITR Base or Salt	Pr 378
Diazo 44	7	37,000	Fast Yellow GC Base or Salt	Pr 275
Diazo 46	7	37,080	Fast Scarlet TR Base	Pr 442
Diazo 48	7	37,235	Fast Blue B Base or Salt	CI 499
BASIC				
Yellow 1	16	49,005	Thioflavine T	CI 815
Yellow 2	10	41,000	Auramine	CI 655
Yellow 9	13	46,040	Euchrysine GG	CI 797
Yellow 11	15	48,055	Methine Basic Yellow 3G	— —
Orange 1	3	11,320	Chrysoidine R	CI 21
Orange 2	3	11,270	Chrysoidine G	CI 20
Orange 10	13	46,035	Brilliant Phosphine G	CI 789
Orange 14	13	46,005	Acridine Orange NO	CI 788
Orange 15	13	46,045	Phosphine	CI 793
Orange 21	15	48,035	Methine Basic Orange G	— —
Red 1	12	45,160	Rhodamine 6G	CI 752
Red 2	19	50,240	Safranine	CI 841
Red 9	11	42,500	Para Fuchsine Para Magenta Para Rosaniline	CI 676
Violet 1	11	42,535	Methyl Violet B	CI 680
Violet 2	11	42,520	New Fuchsine	CI 678
Violet 3	11	42,555	Crystal Violet Gentian Violet	CI 681
Violet 4	11	42,600	Ethyl Violet	CI 682
Violet 5	19	50,205	Methylene Violet 3R	CI 842
Violet 10	12	45,170	Rhodamine B Ext D&C Red No. 21	CI 749
Violet 13	11	42,536	Benzyl Violet	CI 683
Violet 14	11	42,510	Fuchsine Magenta Rosaniline	CI 677
Blue 1	11	42,025	Basic Blue 6G	CI 658
Blue 5	11	42,140	Brilliant Basic Blue 5B	CI 663
Blue 6	20	51,175	Meldola's Blue New Blue R	CI 909
Blue 7	11	42,595	Victoria Pure Blue B	Pr 198
Blue 9	21	52,015	Methylene Blue B Ext D&C Blue No. 1	CI 922
Blue 11	11	44,040	Victoria Blue R	CI 728
Blue 12	20	51,180	Basic Blue A	CI 913
Blue 26	11	44,045	Victoria Blue B	CI 729
Green 1	11	42,040	Brilliant Green	CI 662
Green 4	11	42,000	Malachite Green	CI 673
Green 5	21	52,020	Methylene Green B	CI 924
Brown 1	4	21,000	Bismarck Brown G	CI 331
Brown 2	4	21,030	Phoenix Brown Leather Brown 5RT	Pr 552
Brown 4	4	21,010	Bismarck Brown R	CI 332
DEVELOPER				
1	—	—	Developer Z	Pr 597
5	8	37,500	Beta Naphthol	Pr 586
8	—	—	Beta Oxy Naphthoic Acid 3-Hydroxy-2-naphthoic Acid Developer BON	Pr 587
14	31	76,035	Developer MTD	Pr 602
DIRECT				
Yellow 1	4	22,250	Chrysamine G	CI 410
Yellow 4	4	24,890	Brilliant Yellow	CI 364
Yellow 5	14	47,035	Direct Quinoline Yellow	Pr 533
Yellow 6	9	40,001	Mikado Yellow G	CI 622
Yellow 7	16	49,010	Thioflavine S	CI 816

Part I Colour Index Generic Name	Chemical Structure Type	Part II Colour Index No.	Commercial Name	Old Colour Index No. or Prototype No.
DIRECT—*Continued*				
Yellow 8	3	13,920	Direct Yellow 5G	Pr 249 and 492
Yellow 9	3	19,540	Naphthamine Pure Yellow G	CI 813
Yellow 11	9	40,000	Curcumin S	CI 620
Yellow 12	4	24,895	Chrysophenine G	CI 365
Yellow 19	9	40,030	Diphenyl Chrysoine G	CI 631
Yellow 20	4	22,410	Cresotine Yellow G	CI 411
Yellow 26	4	25,300	Cotton Yellow G Benzo Fast Yellow 5GL	CI 346
Yellow 27	3	13,950	Direct Supra Yellow 5GL	Pr 99
Yellow 28	3	19,555	Direct Yellow	CI 814
Yellow 29	3	19,556	Direct Supra Yellow RT	CI 814
Yellow 41	4	29,005	Direct Fast Yellow RL	Pr 54
Yellow 50	4	29,025	Direct Supra Yellow R	Pr 582
Yellow 59	16	49,000	Primuline	CI 812
Yellow 62	6	36,900	Diazo Fast Yellow GG	Pr 251
Orange 1	4	22,375/430	Direct Fast Orange G	CI 653
Orange 6	4	23,375	Toluylene Orange G	CI 478
Orange 8	4	22,130	Benzo Orange R	CI 415
Orange 10	4	23,370	Alkali Orange RT	CI 446
Orange 15	9	40,002/3	Mikado Orange	CI 621
Orange 18	4	20,216	Diamine Orange B	CI 409
Orange 26	4	29,150	Benzo Fast Orange S	CI 326
Orange 29	4	29,155	Benzo Fast Orange WS	CI 326
Orange 37	9	40,265	Diamine Fast Orange ER	Pr 73
Orange 39	9	40,215	Direct Supra Orange GGL	Pr 276
Orange 41	9	40,235	Direct Supra Orange RRL	Pr 576
Orange 73	4	25,200	Direct Orange R	Pr 173
Orange 74	4	28,255	Direct Orange RR	Pr 435
Orange 75	3	17,840	Diazo Brilliant Orange GR	Pr 376
Red 1	4	22,310	Diamine Fast Red F	CI 419
Red 2	4	23,500	Benzopurpurine 4B	CI 448
Red 4	4	29,165	Benzo Fast Scarlet GS	CI 326
Red 7	4	24,100	Benzopurpurine 10B	CI 495
Red 10	4	22,145	Congo Corinth G	CI 375
Red 13	4	22,155	Diamine Bordeaux B	Pr 67
Red 16	4	27,680	Benzo Bordeaux 6B	Pr 19
Red 17	4	22,150	Congo Rubine	CI 376
Red 20	3	15,075	Diamine Pink BD	CI 128
Red 23	4	29,160	Benzo Fast Scarlet 4BS	CI 327
Red 24	4	29,185	Benzo Fast Scarlet S	CI 326
Red 26	4	29,190	Benzo Fast Scarlet 8BS	CI 326
Red 28	4	22,120	Congo Red	CI 370
Red 31	4	29,100	Benzo Rose Red B	Pr 31
Red 32	4	28,395	Direct Fast Rubine B	Pr 539
Red 37	4	22,240	Diamine Scarlet B	CI 382
Red 39	4	23,630	Diamine Scarlet 3B	CI 382
Red 43	4	22,205	Benzo Fast Red 9BL Diamine Brilliant Bordeaux R	CI 400
Red 44	4	22,500	Bordeaux COV	CI 385
Red 45	3	14,780	Thiazine Red R	CI 225
Red 46	4	23,050	Acetopurpurine 8B	CI 436
Red 47	3	14,985	Erica GGN	CI 126
Red 51	3	14,990	Erica B	CI 130
Red 53	4	22,405	Oxamine Brilliant Red B	Pr 393
Red 75	4	25,380	Benzo Fast Pink 2BL	CI 353
Red 76	9	40,270	Direct Supra Scarlet GG	Pr 577
Red 79	4	29,065	Direct Fast Red 6BLL	Pr 428
Red 80	6	35,780	Direct Fast Red 5BRL	Pr 246
Red 81	4	28,160	Benzo Fast Red 8BL	CI 278
Red 83	4	29,225	Direct Fast Violet 2RLL	Pr 491
Red 84	6	35,760	Direct Supra Brown 3RL	Pr 575
Red 120	4	25,275	Diazo Rubine B	Pr 89
Red 121	4	28,250	Diazo Fast Bordeaux FBL	Pr 438
Red 122	4	29,210	Diazo Brilliant Scarlet BBL	Pr 79
Red 123	3	17,820	Diazo Brilliant Scarlet ROA	Pr 80
Red 148	4	25,005	Direct Bordeaux B	Pr 404
Red 149	4	29,110	Diazo Bordeaux 7B	Pr 77
Red 152	4	28,360	Diazo Fast Red 8BL	Pr 84
Red 153	4	28,210	Diazo Fast Red 7BL	Pr 85
Red 155	4	25,210	Diazo Brilliant Scarlet 5BLN	Pr 377
Red 189	4	28,400	Direct Rubine G	Pr 681
Violet 1	4	22,570	Diamine Violet N	CI 394
Violet 9	4	27,885	Brilliant Benzo Violet B	Pr 35
Violet 12	4	22,550	Oxamine Violet	CI 393
Violet 14	4	29,105	Benzo Direct Red 3B	Pr 32
Violet 22	4	22,480	Direct Violet B	CI 387
Violet 47	4	25,410	Direct Supra Red Violet RL	Pr 277
Violet 51	4	27,905	Brilliant Benzo Fast Violet BL	Pr 367
Blue 1	4	24,410	Chicago Blue 6B Diamine Sky Blue FF	CI 518
Blue 2	4	22,590	Diamine Black BH	CI 401
Blue 3	4	23,705	Oxamine Blue 3R	CI 471
Blue 4	4	24,380	Chicago Blue B	CI 516
Blue 6	4	22,610	Benzo Blue BB	CI 406

Part I Colour Index Generic Name	Chemical Structure Type	Part II Colour Index No.	Commercial Name	Old Colour Index No. or Prototype No.
DIRECT—*Continued*				
Blue 8	4	24,140	Benzo Azurine C	CI 502
Blue 14	4	23,850	Diamine Blue 3B	CI 477
Blue 15	4	24,400	Diamine Pure Blue	CI 520
Blue 21	4	23,710	Diamine Blue BX	CI 472
Blue 22	4	24,280	Chicago Blue RW Benzo Blue RW	CI 512
Blue 25	4	23,790	Direct Blue B	CI 466
Blue 26	5	31,930	Benzo Chrome Black Blue B	Pr 20
Blue 27	4	23,750	Direct Blue R	CI 464
Blue 30	5	31,955	Congo Fast Blue B	CI 576
Blue 41	11	42,700	Brilliant Sky Blue 5G Cotton Pure Blue B	CI 710
Blue 55	4	27,940	Brilliant Congo Blue BFL	Pr 417
Blue 63	5	31,910	Congo Fast Blue R	CI 567
Blue 64	4	22,595	Benzo Cyanine R	CI 405
Blue 71	5	34,140	Benzo Supra Blue FFL	Pr 71
Blue 81	5	34,215	Direct Supra Blue BL	Pr 594
Blue 86	29	74,180	Durazol Blue 8G	Pr 278
Blue 98	4	23,155	Direct Supra Blue FBGL	Pr 443
Blue 120	5	34,085	Diazo Indigo Blue BR	Pr 74
Blue 120A	5	34,090	Diazo Indigo Blue M	Pr 74
Blue 126	5	34,010	Diaminogen Blue NA	Pr 529
Blue 127	5	34,080	Diazo Indigo Blue 4GL	—
Blue 130	4	27,110	Diazo Brilliant Blue BBL	Pr 436
Blue 133	5	34,005	Diazo Indigo Blue 4RL	Pr 87
Blue 136	4	24,065	Diazo Sky Blue B	Pr 90
Blue 138	4	26,650	Diazo Sky Blue 3GL	Pr 91
Blue 175	6	35,465	Direct Blue BB	Pr 675
Green 1	5	30,280	Diamine Dark Green N	CI 583
Green 6	5	30,295	Diamine Green B	CI 593
Green 8	5	30,315	Diamine Green G	CI 594
Green 11	4	27,540	Brilliant Benzo Green B	Pr 368
Green 12	5	30,290	Direct Green B	CI 589
Green 26	5	34,045	Direct Fast Green BLL	Pr 425
Green 28	3	14,155	Direct Fast Green 5GLL	Pr 616
Green 38	4	28,280	Diazo Brilliant Green 3G	Pr 78
Green 39	5	30,220	Diazo Olive G	CI 595
Green 51	5	34,260	Diazo Fast Green GF	Pr 530
Brown 1	5	30,045	Benzo Chrome Brown G Benzamine Brown 3GO	CI 596
Brown 2	4	22,311	Diamine Brown M	CI 420
Brown 6	5	30,140	Congo Brown G	CI 598
Brown 21	5	30,155	Congo Brown R	CI 601
Brown 27	5	31,725	Benzo Chrome Brown G	Pr 364
Brown 29	9	40,505	Diphenyl Catechine G	CI 628
Brown 30	3	17,630	Direct Brown B	Pr 208
Brown 33	6	35,520	Diamine Catechine B	Pr 68
Brown 57	5	31,705	Cotton Dark Brown T Direct Brown B	CI 560
Brown 58	4	22,340	Diphenyl Brown BBN	CI 422
Brown 59	4	22,345	Diamine Brown B	CI 423
Brown 74	6	36,300	Diamine Catechine 3G	Pr 70
Brown 95	5	30,145	Direct Supra Brown BRS	Pr 47
Brown 101	5	31,740	Benzo Chrome Brown G	Pr 365
Brown 106	6	36,200	Direct Supra Brown G	Pr 28
Brown 112	4	29,166	Direct Fast Brown 8RLL	Pr 423
Brown 132	5	31,505	Diazo Brown 3RB	Pr 83
Brown 138	5	31,500	Diazo Brown 3R	Pr 250
Brown 151	5	31,685	Para Brown V	Pr 397
Black 3	4	27,710	Neutral Gray G	CI 267
Black 4	5	30,245	Direct Deep Black RW	CI 582
Black 9	5	31,560	Columbia Black FF	CI 539
Black 17	4	27,700	Zambesi Black D	Pr 201
Black 19	6	35,255	Naphthamine Fast Black RF	CI 619
Black 22	6	35,435	Cotonerol A	Pr 372
Black 29	4	22,580	Diamine Black RO	CI 395
Black 38	5	30,235	Direct Deep Black EW Columbia Black EAW	CI 581
Black 41	5	30,260	Chrome Leather Fast Black S	Pr 371
Black 51	4	27,720	Benzo Fast Black L	Pr 24
Black 56	5	34,170	Diphenyl Fast Gray B	CI 403
Black 71	4	25,040	Direct Supra Gray VGL	Pr 379
Black 74	5	34,180	Benzo Fast Gray BL	Pr 416
Black 75	6	35,870	Direct Supra Gray R	Pr 96
Black 78	5	30,015	Zambesi Black V	Pr 202
Black 80	5	31,600	Oxydiaminogen OB	Pr 147
Black 83	5	31,850	Diazo Blue Black RS	CI 552
DISPERSE				
Yellow 1	2	10,345	Disperse Fast Yellow RR	Pr 243
Yellow 3	3	11,855	Disperse Fast Yellow G	Pr 242
Yellow 5	3	12,790	Disperse Yellow 5G	Pr 245
Yellow 11	24	56,200	Disperse Brilliant Yellow FF	Pr 369
Yellow 23	—	—	Disperse Fast Yellow 4RL	Pr 583

Part I Colour Index Generic Name	Chemical Structure Type	Part II Colour Index No.	Commercial Name	Old Colour Index No. or Prototype No.
DISPERSE—*Continued*				
Yellow 31	15	48,000	Disperse Fast Yellow 7G	Pr 420
Yellow 33	—	—	Disperse Fast Yellow GLF	Pr 537
Orange 1	3	11,080	SRA Orange I	Pr 637
Orange 3	3	11,005	Disperse Orange GR	Pr 43
Orange 5	3	11,100	Disperse Fast Brown 3R	Pr 230
Orange 11	26	60,700	SRA Orange II	Pr 638
Orange 13	4	26,080	Disperse Golden Orange I	Pr 635
Orange 15	2	10,350	SRA Fast Golden Orange III	Pr 636
Red 1	3	11,110	Disperse Scarlet B	Pr 244
Red 4	26	60,755	Disperse Fast Pink RF	Pr 370
Red 5	3	11,215	Disperse Fast Rubine 3B	Pr 239
Red 9	26	60,505	SRA Red VI–X	Pr 639
Red 11	26	62,015	Disperse Fast Pink FF3B	Pr 235
Red 13	3	11,115	Disperse Fast Rubine B	Pr 238
Red 15	26	60,710	SRA Fast Red VII	Pr 234
Red 17	3	11,210	SRA Red VIII	Pr 236
Red 31	3	11,250	Disperse Scarlet G	Pr 63
Red 32	3	11,190	Disperse Fast Brown 5R	Pr 231
Violet 1	26	61,100	Disperse Fast Red Violet RN	Pr 237
Violet 4	26	61,105	Disperse Fast Violet 6B	Pr 241
Violet 6	26	61,140	SRA Fast Red FSI	Pr 640
Violet 8	26	62,030	Disperse Fast Violet B	Pr 240
Violet 13	3	11,195	Disperse Violet R	Pr 641
Blue 1	26	64,500	Disperse Sapphire Blue G	Pr 62
Blue 3	26	61,505	Disperse Fast Blue FFR	Pr 228
Blue 7	26	62,500	Disperse Fast Blue Green B	Pr 229
Blue 9	26	61,115	Disperse Fast Blue FR	Pr 227
Blue 19	26	61,110	Disperse Direct Blue RS	Pr 642
Black 1	3	11,365	Disperse Diazo Black STN	Pr 630
Black 2	3	11,255	Disperse Diazo Black B	Pr 58
Black 6	7	37,235	Disperse Diazo Navy B (Fast Blue B Base)	CI 499
Black 7	3	11,035	Disperse Diazo Black NS	Pr 41
FIBER-REACTIVE				
Red	—	—	Cibacron Brilliant Red 3B	—
Red	—	—	Procion Brilliant Red H3B	—
Red	—	—	Remazol Red 3B	—
Blue	—	—	Cibacron Blue 3G	—
Blue	—	—	Procion Brilliant Blue R	—
Blue	—	—	Remazol Brilliant Blue R	—
FLUORESCENT				
Brightener 1	9	40,630	Brightener BVA	Pr 698
Brightener 5	6	36,900	Diazo Fast Yellow GG	Pr 251
Brightener 30	9	40,600	Brightener R	Pr 690
Brightener 34	9	40,605	Direct White 2GT	—
Brightener 41	16	49,015	Brightener RS	Pr 710
Brightener 74	12	45,550	Fluorol 5G (Solvent Green No. 4)	Pr 542
FOOD				
Yellow 3	3	15,985	FD&C Yellow No. 6	Pr 674
Red 1	3	14,700	FD&C Red No. 4	Pr 673
Red 6	3	16,155		CI 80
Green 3	11	42,053	FD&C Green No. 3	Pr 672
INGRAIN				
Blue 1	29	74,240	Alcian Blue 8GX	—
Blue 2	29	74,160	Phthalogen Brilliant Blue IF3G	—
MORDANT				
Yellow 1	3	14,025	Alizarine Yellow 2G	CI 36
Yellow 3	3	14,095	Chrome Yellow D	CI 195
Yellow 5	3	14,130	Chrome Flavine A	CI 219
Yellow 8	3	18,821	Acid Alizarine Flavine R	Pr 1
Yellow 10	3	14,010	Chrome Yellow G	Pr 56
Yellow 14	3	14,055	Azo Alizarine Yellow GP	CI 52
Yellow 16	4	25,100	Anthracene Yellow C	CI 343
Yellow 20	3	14,110	Crumpsall Yellow	CI 197
Yellow 26	4	22,880	Chromocitronine R	CI 441
Yellow 30	3	18,710	Chrome Yellow ME	Pr 317
Yellow 36	3	14,135	Diamond Flavine G	CI 110
Yellow 38	3	14,080	Alizarine Yellow 5G	CI 122
Orange 1	3	14,030	Alizarine Yellow R	CI 40
Orange 4	3	18,940	Chrome Fast Orange 3RL	Pr 247
Orange 6	4	26,520	Acid Alizarine Orange GR Milling Orange	CI 274
Red 3	26	58,005	Alizarine Red S	CI 1034
Red 5	3	14,290	Acid Alizarine Garnet R	CI 168
Red 7	3	18,760	Chrome Red B	CI 652
Red 8	4	23,095	Anthracene Red	CI 431
Red 9	3	16,105	Acid Alizarine Red B	CI 216

Part I Colour Index Generic Name	Chemical Structure Type	Part II Colour Index No.	Commercial Name	Old Colour Index No. or Prototype No.
MORDANT—*Continued*				
Red 11	26	58,000	Alizarine VI D&C Orange No. 15	CI 1027
Red 19	3	18,735	Metachrome Red G Metachrome Red 5G	Pr 135
Red 21	3	17,995	Acid Chrome Red B	Pr 360
Violet 1	11	43,565	Naphthochrome Violet R	Pr 461
Violet 5	3	15,670	Acid Alizarine Violet N	CI 169
Violet 11	11	43,550	Mordant Brilliant Violet B	Pr 484
Blue 1	11	43,830	Chrome Azurol B	CI 720
Blue 3	11	43,820	Chrome Cyanine R	CI 722
Blue 7	3	17,940	Chrome Cyanine BLL	Pr 603
Blue 8	26	58,805	Anthracene Blue WGG	CI 1060
Blue 9	3	14,855	Acid Chrome Blue RR	Pr 7
Blue 10	20	51,030	Gallocyanine	CI 883
Blue 13	3	16,680	Fast Mordant Blue B	Pr 93
Blue 32	26	58,605	Anthracene Blue WR	CI 1062
Blue 51	21	52,055	Brilliant Alizarine Blue G	CI 931
Blue 54	3	16,685	Acid Chrome Blue 3G	Pr 408
Blue 56	20	51,120	Delphine Blue B	CI 878
Green 9	3	19,515	Acid Chrome Green G	Pr 527
Green 12	4	27,520	Diamond Green B	CI 302
Green 17	3	17,225	Chrome Fast Green G	CI 99
Green 26	3	18,180	Metachrome Olive BL	Pr 254
Brown 1	4	20,110	Anthracene Chromate Brown EB	Pr 14
Brown 4	3	11,335	Metachrome Brown B	CI 101
Brown 13	3	13,225	Acid Alizarine Brown B	CI 167
Brown 15	3	14,870	Acid Anthracene Brown KE	Pr 203
Brown 18	4	20,150	Anthracene Acid Brown G	CI 238
Brown 19	3	14,250	Chrome Brown DKL	Pr 253
Brown 21	3	19,600	Acid Anthracene Brown TBL	Pr 584
Brown 22	3	14,235	Acid Anthracene Brown WSG	Pr 205
Brown 33	3	13,250	Acid Anthracene Brown RH	CI 98
Brown 35	3	14,765	Acid Anthracene Brown V	Pr 3
Brown 40	3	17,590	Acid Anthracene Brown PG	Pr 4
Brown 42	26	58,200	Anthracene Brown Anthragallol	CI 1035
Brown 61	3	16,070	Chrome Fast Brown V	Pr 634
Black 1	3	15,710	Chrome Black A	CI 204
Black 3	3	14,640	Chrome Blue Black B	CI 201
Black 5	4	26,695	Diamond Black F	CI 299
Black 9	3	16,500	Diamond Black PV	CI 170
Black 10	4	21,720	Acid Alizarine Black SE	CI 336
Black 11	3	14,645	Chrome Black T	CI 203
Black 13	26	63,615	Alizarine Blue Black B	CI 1085
Black 17	3	15,705	Chrome Blue Black R	CI 202
Black 38	3	18,160	Metachrome Black Blue G	Pr 299
NATURAL				
Yellow 8	30	75,660	Osage Orange	—
Yellow 10	30	75,720	Quercitron, Flavine	CI 1233
Yellow 11	30	75,240	Fustic, Old Fustic	CI 1232
Red 4	30	75,470	Carmine, Cochineal	CI 1239
Red 24	30	75,280	Extract of Brazilwood	CI 1243
Brown 1	30	75,620	Young Fustic	CI 1231
Brown 3	30	75,250	Cutch, Gambier, Catechu	CI 1249
Black 1	30	75,290	Hematine, Logwood	CI 1246
Black 4	30	75,291	Steam Black Logwood Printing Black	CI 1253
OXIDATION				
Base 1	19	50,440	Aniline Oil, Aniline Salt, Aniline Black	CI 870
Base 2	31	76,085	Diphenyl Black Base	CI 871
PIGMENT				
Yellow 1	3	11,680	Pigment Yellow G Ext D&C Yellow No. 5	Pr 103
Yellow 3	3	11,710	Pigment Yellow 10G	Pr 105
Yellow 10	3	12,710	Pigment Yellow R	—
Yellow 12	4	21,090	Benzidine Yellow	Pr 518
Yellow 13	4	21,100	Vulcan Fast Yellow GR	Pr 479
Yellow 14	4	21,095	Vulcan Fast Yellow G	Pr 478
Yellow 16	4	20,040	Permanent Fast Yellow NCG	—
Orange 1	3	11,725	Pigment Yellow 3R Ext D&C Orange No. 1	Pr 280
Orange 2	3	12,060	Ortho Nitraniline Orange	Pr 697
Orange 5	3	12,075	Permanent Red GG Ext D&C Orange No. 6	Pr 657
Orange 13	4	21,110	Vulcan Fast Orange G	Pr 475
Orange 14	4	21,165	Vulcan Fast Orange GG	—
Orange 16	4	21,160	Diane Orange Pulp Y-25	Pr 663
Red 1	3	12,070	Paranitraniline Red	CI 44
Red 2	3	12,310	Permanent Red FRR	—
Red 3	3	12,120	Toluidine Red Toner D&C Red No. 35	CI 69
Red 4	3	12,085	Permanent Red R D&C Red No. 36	Pr 541
Red 5	3	12,490	Permanent Carmine FB	Pr 398

Part I Colour Index Generic Name	Chemical Structure Type	Part II Colour Index No.	Commercial Name	Old Colour Index No. or Prototype No.
PIGMENT—*Continued*				
Red 7	3	12,420	Permanent Red F4RH	—
Red 10	3	12,440	Permanent Red FRL	—
Red 12	3	12,385	Permanent Bordeaux FRR	—
Red 15	3	12,465	Romanesta Red MT-2544	Pr 701
Red 18	3	12,350	D&C Red No. 38	Pr 661
Red 22	3	12,315	Pigment Orange R	CI 68
Red 23	3	12,355	Textile Red WD-263	Pr 708
Red 32	3	12,320	Vulcan Fast Rubine BF	—
Red 38	4	21,120	Vulcan Fast Red B	Pr 476
Red 40	3	12,170	Pigment Bordeaux N	CI 82
Red 41	4	21,200	Vulcan Fast Red BBE	Pr 664
Red 48	3	15,865	Permanent Red 2B	Pr 563
Red 49	3	15,630	Lithol Red R Toner Ext D&C Red Nos. 17, 18, 19, and 20	CI 189
Red 50	3	15,500	Lake Red D	CI 214
Red 51	3	15,580	Pigment Red RMT	Pr 112
Red 52	3	15,860	Lithol Red 2G	CI 166
Red 53	3	15,585	Lake Red C Ext D&C Red Nos. 15 and 16	CI 165
Red 54	3	14,830	Double Ponceau R	CI 84
Red 55	3	15,820	Cabarine Red MB	Pr 651
Red 57	3	15,850	Lithol Rubine B D&C Red Nos. 6 and 7	CI 163
Red 60	3	16,105	Pigment Scarlet 3B Acid Alizarine Red B	CI 216
Red 63	3	15,880	Lake Bordeaux B D&C Red No. 34	CI 190
Red 64	3	15,800	Brilliant Lake Red R D&C Red No. 31	CI 35
Red 81	12	45,160	Rhodamine 6G Toner	CI 752
Red 83	26	58,000	Madder Lake Alizarine Lake D&C Orange No. 15	CI 1027
Red 84	26	58,210	Pigment Fast Rubine RL	Pr 407
Red 87	28	73,310	Indo Red MV-6632	Pr 686
Red 100	3	13,058	D&C Red No. 39 Alba Red	Pr 662
Violet 1	12	45,170	Rhodamine B Lake	CI 749
Violet 3	11	42,535	Methyl Violet B Lake Gentian Violet Lake	CI 680
Violet 5	26	58,055	Pigment Fast Rubine 4BL	Pr 406
Violet 12	26	58,050	Quinizarin	CI 1028
Blue 1	11	42,595	Victoria Pure Blue BO Lake	Pr 198
Blue 2	11	44,045	Victoria Blue B Lake	CI 729
Blues 5 and 14	11	42,600	Ethyl Violet Lake	CI 682
Blue 9	11	42,025	Basic Blue 6G Lake	CI 658
Blue 15	29	74,160	Phthalocyanine Blue B	Pr 481
Blue 16	29	74,100	Phthalocyanine Blue G	Pr 482
Blue 21	26	69,835	Pigment Blue BCS	CI 1114
Blue 24	11	42,090	Peacock Blue Lake D&C Blue No. 4	CI 671
Blue 25	4	21,180	Diane Blue Pulp B-34 Pigment Blue WNL	Pr 699
Green 1	11	42,040	Brilliant Green Lake	CI 662
Green 4	11	42,000	Malachite Green Lake	CI 657
Green 7	29	74,260	Phthalocyanine Green G	Pr 483
Green 8	1	10,006	Pigment Green B	Pr 149
Green 10	3	12,775	Pigment Fast Yellow GD Virescent Gold	Pr 691
Brown 2	3	12,071	Paratone Brown ZUS	Pr 709
Brown 3	4	21,010	Bismarck Brown Lake	CI 332
Brown 5	3	15,800	Ginger Brown T-5902	CI 35
Black 1	19	50,440	Pigment Black B (Aniline Black)	CI 870
SOLVENT				
Yellow 1	3	11,000	Aminoazobenzene Oil Yellow B Spirit Yellow G	CI 15
Yellow 2	3	11,020	Butter Yellow O Oil Yellow	CI 19
Yellow 3	3	11,160	Aminoazotoluene Spirit Yellow R	CI 17
Yellow 5	3	11,380	Oil Yellow AB Ext D&C Yellow No. 9	CI 22
Yellow 6	3	11,390	Oil Yellow OB Ext D&C Yellow No. 10	CI 61
Yellow 14	3	12,055	Sudan I Sudan Orange R	CI 24
Yellow 19	3	13,900A	Solvent Fast Yellow GR Zapon Fast Yellow GR	Pr 216
Yellow 29	4	21,230	Sudan Yellow GRN	Pr 472
Yellow 30	4	21,240	Sudan Yellow GR Conc	Pr 703
Yellow 33	14	47,000	Quinoline Yellow Spirit-Soluble D&C Yellow No. 11	CI 800
Yellow 34	10	41,000B	Auramine Base	CI 655
Orange 2	3	12,000	Ext D&C Orange No. 4	—
Orange 3	3	11,270B	Chrysoidine G Base	CI 20
Orange 5	3	18,745A	Solvent Fast Orange G Zapon Fast Orange G	Pr 211
Orange 7	3	12,140	Sudan II Ext D&C Red No. 14	CI 73
Orange 18	12	45,371	D&C Orange No. 16	Pr 656
Red 1	3	12,150	Sudan R Pigment Purple A	CI 113
Red 8	3	12,715	Zapon Fast Red BE Solvent Fast Red BE	Pr 488
Red 22	4	21,250	Sudan Red GG	Pr 471

Part I Colour Index Generic Name	Chemical Structure Type	Part II Colour Index No.	Commercial Name	Old Colour Index No. or Prototype No.
SOLVENT—*Continued*				
Red 23	4	26,100	Sudan III D&C Red No. 17	CI 248
Red 24	4	26,105	Sudan IV	CI 258
Red 26	4	26,120	Oil Red OB	Pr 696
Red 27	4	26,125	Oil Red O D&C Red No. 18	Pr 658
Red 35	3+12	16,260+45,170	Zapon Fast Red 3B	Pr 213
Red 41	11	42,510B	Fuchsine Base Magenta Base Rosaniline Base	CI 677
Red 42	12	45,366	D&C Red No. 24	Pr 659
Red 43	12	45,380A	D&C Red No. 21	CI 768
Red 48	12	45,410A	Phloxine B D&C Red No. 27	CI 778
Red 49	12	45,170B	Rhodamine B Base Ext D&C Red No. 22	CI 749
Red 52	26	68,210	Alizarine Rubinol G Base Solvent Oil Red R	CI 1091
Red 72	12	45,370A	Dibromofluorescein Ext D&C Orange No. 5	—
Red 73	12	45,425A	Erythrosine G D&C Orange No. 10	CI 772
Violet 8	11	42,535B	Methyl Violet Base	CI 680
Violet 9	11	42,555B	Crystal Violet Base	CI 681
Violet 10	12	45,190A	Solvent Violet R Base Ext D&C Red No. 3	CI 758
Violet 13	26	60,725	Alizarine Violet IR Spirit-Soluble D&C Violet No. 2	CI 1073
Blue 3	11	42,775	Spirit Blue B	CI 689
Blue 4	11	44,045B	Victoria Blue B Base	CI 729
Blue 5	11	42,595B	Victoria Pure Blue B Base	Pr 198
Blue 6	11	44,040B	Victoria Blue R Base	CI 728
Blue 7	19	50,400	Induline Spirit-Soluble	CI 860
Blue 11	26	61,525	Alizarine Sky Blue B Base	CI 1075
Blue 12	26	62,100	Alizarine Pure Blue B Base	CI 1088
Green 1	11	42,000	Victoria Green Base Malachite Green Base	CI 657
Green 3	26	61,565	Alizarine Cyanine Green G Base D&C Green No. 6	CI 1078
Green 4	12	45,550	Fluorol 5G	Pr 542
Brown 12	4	21,010B	Bismarck Brown Base	CI 332
Black 3	4	26,150	Sudan Black BT	Pr 610
Black 5	19	50,415	Nigrosine Spirit-Soluble	CI 864
Black 7	19	50,415B	Nigrosine Base B	CI 864
SULFUR				
Yellow 1	22	53,040	Thiochem Sulfur Yellow R	CI 950
Yellow 2	22	53,120	Sulfur Yellow G	CI 951
Yellow 3	22	53,125	Kryogen Yellow G	CI 952
Yellow 4	22	53,160	Sulfur Yellow GG	CI 955
Red 1	22	53,721	Sulfur Bordeaux G	CI 1012
Red 5	22	53,830	Sulfur Red Brown CL3R	Pr 702
Red 6	22	53,720	Sulfur Red Brown 3B	CI 1012
Blues 1, 5, and 11	22	53,235	Sulfur Direct Blue RL	CI 956
Blue 7	22	53,440	Sulfur Indone R	CI 959
Blue 9	12	53,430	Sulfur Pure Blue Sulfur Brilliant Blue CLB	CI 957
Blue 10	22	53,470	Sulfur New Blue FBL	Pr 285
Blue 13	22	53,450	Sulfur Indigo	CI 961
Blue 15	22	53,540	Sulfur Green Blue CV	Pr 65 and 129
Green 1	22	53,166	Sulfur Dark Green B	Pr 707
Green 2	22	53,571	Sulfur Green BB	CI 1006
Green 3	22	53,570	Sulfur Green GG	CI 1006
Green 8	22	53,175	Sulfur Olive B	Pr 706
Green 11	22	53,165	Italian Green Sulfur Olive G	CI 1002
Brown 1	22	53,000	Cachou de Laval	CI 933
Brown 2	22	53,060	Sulfur Brown B	CI 937
Brown 10	22	53,055	Sulfur Orange C	CI 949
Brown 12	22	53,721	Sulfur Bordeaux G	CI 1012
Brown 14	22	53,246	Sulfur Black Brown A	Pr 545
Brown 26	22	53,090	Sulfur Yellow D	CI 948
Black 1	22	53,185	Sulfur Black T	CI 978
Black 2	22	53,195	Cross Dye Black RX	CI 978 and 983
Black 6	22	53,295	Sulfur Black CLG	Pr 126
Black 10	22	53,190	Sulfur Black 3G	CI 978
Black 11	22	53,290	Sulfur Black CLS	Pr 126
VAT				
Yellow 1	26	70,600	Vat Yellow G	CI 1118
Yellow 2	26	67,300/1	Anthraflavone GC	Pr 9
Yellow 3	26	61,725	Vat Yellow GK	CI 1132
Yellow 4	26	59,100/1	Vat Golden Yellow GK	Pr 291
Yellow 5	24	56,006	Vat Ester Yellow HCG	CI 1176
Yellow 9	26	66,510	Vat Yellow GF	Pr 451
Yellow 12	26	65,405	Vat Yellow 3GF	Pr 549
Yellow 13	26	65,425	Vat Yellow 4G	—
Yellow 21	26	69,705	Vat Yellow R	CI 1170
Yellow 28	26	69,000	Vat Yellow FFRK	Pr 450
Orange 1	26	59,105/6	Vat Golden Yellow RK	Pr 292
Orange 2	26	59,705/6	Vat Orange RRT	CI 1098
Orange 3	26	59,300	Vat Brilliant Orange RK	Pr 116
Orange 4	26	59,710	Vat Orange 4R	Pr 381
Orange 5	28	73,335/6	Thioindigo Orange RF	CI 1217
Orange 7	26	71,105	Vat Brilliant Orange GR	—

Part I Colour Index Generic Name	Chemical Structure Type	Part II Colour Index No.	Commercial Name	Old Colour Index No. or Prototype No.
VAT—*Continued*				
Orange 9	26	59,700	Vat Golden Orange G	CI 1096
Orange 11	26	70,805	Vat Yellow 3R	Pr 452
Orange 15	26	69,025	Vat Golden Orange 3G	Pr 290
Orange 16	26	69,540	Vat Orange F3R	Pr 446
Orange 21	26	69,700	Vat Orange R	CI 1169
Red 1	28	73,360/1	Thioindigo Pink R D&C Red No. 30	Pr 109
Red 10	26	67,000/1	Vat Red FBB	Pr 296
Red 13	26	70,320	Rubine R	Pr 124
Red 14	26	71,110	Vat Scarlet GG	—
Red 15	26	71,100	Vat Bordeaux RR	—
Red 29	26	71,140	Vat Scarlet R	Pr 449
Red 32	26	71,135	Vat Scarlet B	Pr 409
Red 35	26	68,000	Vat Red RK	CI 1162
Red 41	28	73,300	Thioindigo Red B Vat Red 5B	CI 1207
Red 45	28	73,860	Thioindigo Scarlet G	CI 1228
Violet 1	26	60,010/1	Vat Brilliant Violet RR	CI 1104
Violet 2	28	73,385/6	Thioindigo Red Violet RH	CI 1212
Violet 3	28	73,395/6	Thioindigo Red Violet RRN	Pr 503
Violet 9	26	60,005	Vat Brilliant Violet 3B	Pr 288
Violet 13	26	68,700	Vat Violet BN or FFBN	CI 1163
Violet 14	26	67,895	Vat Red Violet RRK	CI 1161
Violet 17	26	63,365	Vat Brilliant Violet RK	CI 1135
Blue 1	27	73,000	Indigo D&C Blue No. 6	CI 1177
Blue 1	27	73,001	Indigo White (leuco)	CI 1178
Blue 1	27	73,002	Solubilized Indigo O	CI 1178
Blue 4	26	69,800	Indanthrone Vat Blue RS	CI 1106
Blue 5	27	73,065	Brilliant Indigo 4B	CI 1184
Blue 5	27	73,066	Solubilized Indigo O4B	CI 1184
Blue 6	26	69,825/6	Vat Blue BCS D&C Blue No. 9	—
Blue 7	26	70,305/6	Vat Blue 3G	CI 1173
Blue 9	27	73,071	Solubilized Indigo O6B (ester)	CI 1185
Blue 12	26	69,840	Vat Blue 3G	CI 1109
Blue 14	26	69,810	Vat Blue GCD	—
Blue 16	26	71,200	Vat Dark Blue G	Pr 522
Blue 18	26	59,815	Alizanthrene Navy Blue R	CI 1100
Blue 20	26	59,800	Vat Dark Blue BO Violanthrone	CI 1099
Blue 29	29	74,140	Vat Brilliant Blue 4G	Pr 623
Blue 35	27	73,060	Indigo Blue B Indigo Blue R	CI 1182/3
Blue	30	75,800	Tyrian Purple (natural isomer of Vat Blue 35)	CI 1182/3
Blue 41	27	73,040	Brilliant Indigo BASF/B	Pr 528 CI 1190
Blue 43	22	53,630	Carbazole Blue R	CI 969
Green 1	26	59,825/6	Vat Jade Green	CI 1101
Green 2	26	59,830/1	Vat Brilliant Green GG	Pr 632
Green 3	26	69,500/1	Vat Olive Green B	Pr 293
Green 7	26	58,825	Vat Olive G	CI 1167
Green 8	26	71,050	Vat Khaki GG	Pr 122
Green 9	26	59,850	Anthra Green B Vat Black B	CI 1102
Brown 1	26	70,800/1	Vat Brown BR	Pr 118
Brown 3	26	69,015/6	Vat Brown R	CI 1151
Brown 5	28	73,410/1	Thioindigo Brown RRD	Pr 121
Brown 25	26	69,020	Vat Red Brown 5RF	Pr 448
Brown 31	26	70,695	Vat Red Brown R	Pr 447
Black 1	28	73,671	Solubilized Thioindigo Gray IBL (ester)	Pr 295
Black 9	26	65,230	Vat Direct Black RB	Pr 289
Black 25	26	69,525	Vat Olive T	Pr 547
Black 27	26	69,005	Vat Olive R	CI 1150

The dyes on the market may be classified as follows with respect to the properties that determine their use:

Acid dyes (as Naphthol Blue Black) dye wool and silk directly in an acid bath; the degree of acidity necessary for effective dyeing and the resultant fastness (as to light and washing) vary widely with the type of dye. *Milling acid dyes* are simple acid dyes fast to fulling on wool. The acid dyes that give the best washfastness on wool and silk and in many cases are also very fast to light are the premetallized acid dyes. Acid dyes are also dyed on acrylic, nylon and other polyamide, and regenerated protein fibers. They are employed for economical shades of poor wetfastness on bast fibers (as jute) and other lignocellulosic fibers (as coir). Acid dyes may likewise be printed on fibers on which they can be dyed. Other important uses include the dyeing of leather, paper, and anodized aluminum and the coloring of wood stains, varnishes, inks, plastics, foods, drugs, and cosmetics. A few serve as biological stains and as chemical indicators. Some acid dyes are made into pigments.

Azoic compositions contain both an azoic coupling component and an azoic diazo component in a stabilized condition of such a nature that the two do not couple to form an insoluble azoic dye in situ until printed onto the fabric and steamed in an atmosphere of organic acid. The fastness properties are the same as those of the azoic dyeings produced from azoic coupling components and azoic diazo components.

Azoic coupling components (as Naphthol AS) are water-insoluble but dissolve in dilute alkali and couple with diazotized azoic diazo components after being padded or exhausted on cotton to form azoic dyes in situ in and on the fiber. These ingrain azoic dyeings are known for very good wetfastness and for economy in deep shades, especially among red, scarlet, and orange hues, in which vat dyes appear to less advantage than in other colors. Although azoic dyeings have very good fastness to washing, they vary widely in fastness to chlorine and light, and the color, esp. when badly applied, tends somewhat to crock. Azoic dyeings are employed mostly on cotton, rayon, linen, and other cellulosic textiles, but are employed also to some extent on silk, acetate, nylon and other polyamide fibers, polyester fibers, and even on wool, fur, and leather.

Azoic diazo components (fast color bases or salts) are aromatic amines that require diazotization with nitrite and acid for use or that are stabilized diazo salts of those amines. A diazo component in the diazotized state couples with an azoic coupling component to produce an azoic dye in situ on the fiber.

Basic dyes (as Methylene Blue B) dye wool and silk directly and cotton if the cotton is first mordanted with tannin and tartar emetic. Basic dyes display very high tinctorial value and brightness of color rather than good fastness. They now find very little use on cotton but are still used on jute, coir, raffia, and other lignocellulosic fibers, which they dye directly without mordanting. Basic dyes are used to some extent on silk, esp. for colored discharges printed on a colored ground or colored patterns printed on white. They are printed also on acetate, nylon, and polyester textiles. Basic dyes are applied to a slight extent on wool yarns but virtually not at all on wool piece goods. Newer basic dyes (as the polymethine types) and a few of the better older ones are used on acrylic fibers, on which they have adequate lightfastness and wetfastness. Although of minor importance for textiles, basic dyes have a greater variety of other uses than any other dye type. They are applied directly on leather, furs, sheepskin, and paper. The free bases or oleates of basic dyes are used as solvent dyes. Basic dyes are employed for coloring hectograph papers, spirit inks, varnishes, aqueous and spirit wood stains, carbon paper, and typewriter ribbons; as biological stains, chemical indicators, and food colors; and for medicinal and photographic purposes. Many basic dyes are manufactured into pigments.

Developers (as Developer Z, which is methyl-phenyl-pyrazolone, or Developer BON, which is 3-hydroxy-2-naphthoic acid) couple with a diazotized direct dye on cotton or other cellulosic fiber or with a diazotized disperse dye on acetate for improvement of wetfastness and other fastness properties and for deepening of the color.

Direct cotton dyes (as Direct Deep Black EW) dye cotton directly in the presence of a suitable quantity of common salt. They vary widely in lightfastness but most are poor in washfastness. Aftertreatment with developers, formaldehyde, copper or chromium salts, or diazotized *para*-nitroaniline improves the lightfastness, washfastness, or both of some direct dyes on cotton. Besides dyeing cotton, direct dyes are employed for dyeing and printing rayon, linen, and other cellulosic fibers, jute and other lignocellulosic fibers, silk, wool, and nylon, and for dyeing paper and leather. Some direct dyes are converted into pigments, and some are useful as chemical indicators and biological stains.

Disperse dyes (as Disperse Fast Blue FFR) are only slightly soluble in water but are readily dispersed in water with the aid of sulfated oil. Disperse dyes partition themselves in a solubility equilibrium between water and certain fibers (as acetate and nylon) in the dyeing process. Some disperse dyes on acetate are subject to acid fading in air containing traces of nitrogen oxides (as in combustion gases). Disperse dyes are used on nylon knit goods (as hosiery and sweaters) rather than acid dyes in spite of poorer fastness to washing because they do not show up knitting streaks as acid dyes do. Disperse dyes are used also to dye polyester fibers in the presence of a carrier, acrylic fibers, cellulose triacetate fiber, and vinylidene chloride polymer. Disperse dyes are also printed on acetate and nylon. Some disperse dyes are employed for dyeing pastels on wool, sheepskins, and furs, some for the surface dyeing of thermoplastic resins, and a few for coloring oils, fats, and waxes when in a pure state.

Fiber-reactive dyes have the ability to combine with cellulose by covalent bonds to form esters or ethers. Derivatives of cyanuric chloride and of vinyl sulfone have been utilized for this purpose. As fiber-reactive dyes are applied by hydrolysis in alkaline solution, a considerable proportion of the activated dye reacts with water before it can react and combine with cellulose, and thus is wasted. Fiber-reactive dyes are employed mostly on cotton, rayon, and other cellulosic fibers but are also suggested for use on wool and even silk.

Fluorescent brighteners are colorless water- or solvent-soluble aromatic compounds with affinity for fibers of various kinds. They have the property of transforming ultraviolet radiation into radiation of 400 to 500 millimicrons visible as violet, blue, and blue-green colors and are capable of increasing both the blueness and the brightness of a substrate with a resulting marked whitening effect. Brighteners are used on white papers and on wool and silk as well as cellulosic textiles; they are especially useful for improving white discharges and the brightness of tints. Brighteners are incorporated into detergents of all kinds for washing textiles to enhance the apparent cleansing action of the detergent and to obviate the need for bluing.

Food colors in the *Colour Index*, 2d ed., are those dyes and pigments that find important use in foods throughout the world where food colors are under regulation. Because all but a very few of these are also classified in the *Colour Index* under other names (as Acid Blue 74 and Solvent Yellow 5) only those are listed under *Food* in the first Column of table I that are not given under another use type. See table II.

Ingrain dyes taken as a separate subgroup are those that form water-insoluble dyes in situ upon being suitably printed or dyed on cellulosic textiles and properly fixed, respectively, in subsequent steaming or by treatment in solution. Those that belong to the azoic class are entered under *Azoic* in the table.

Mordant dyes (as Alizarine) dye wool, silk, and cotton that have been mordanted with compounds of polyvalent metals (as chromium or tin). This kind of mordant dye is no longer of importance in America for dyeing or printing textiles and is fast losing importance throughout the world. Most mordant dyes now in use are mordant acid dyes (as Chrome Black T) which dye wool and silk in an acid bath after, during, or before treatment of the fiber with a mordanting salt like sodium dichromate or chromium fluoride to give dyeings with better wetfastness and also lightfastness than most dyeings of acid dyes on wool or silk. Chrome dyeings in general are faster to fulling on wool than either metallized or simple acid dyes. Mordant acid dyes are used also for dyeing nylon, leather, and anodized aluminum and for Vigoureux printing as well as for the ordinary printing of wool, silk, and cellulosic fabrics. Some mordant dyes are used to some extent for coloring paper and furs, for the manufacture of pigments, and as indicators, biological stains, cosmetics, and food dyes.

Natural dyes are organic substances of plant or animal origin that are used mainly for dyeing and printing textiles and for dyeing leather. Many natural dyes could be classified also among the other use types described here or among the chemical structures listed in the second column of the table.

Oxidation bases (as Aniline Black) are in most cases aromatic amines but in some cases amino phenols or aromatic diols. When suitably oxidized after being applied mainly on furs and to some extent on textiles they yield various shades of black, gray, and brown of good wetfastness and lightfastness.

Organic pigments are water-insoluble azo, vat, and other dye types that are usu. insoluble in some organic solvents or are lakes prepared from acid, basic, direct, mordant, or mordant acid dyes or from other dye types by precipitation with a suitable precipitant. Some water-soluble dyes that are more important for the preparation of lakes than for dyeing textiles are listed under Pigments though they are often sold to the lake manufacturer in water-soluble form. Toners are full-strength organic pigments that have not been extended with a solid diluent. Pigments have a great many uses, all of which depend upon the incorporation of the pigment into a medium in which it is usu. rather insoluble. They are employed in coating compositions of many kinds, including oil paints, emulsion paints, lacquers of many types, enamels, leather finishes, poster colors, and water colors. Pigments are esp. important in the manufacture of letterpress and intaglio inks and many inks for special purposes (as for wallpaper and metal foil). In the printing of textiles the pigment is bonded to the fabric with synthetic resins. Viscose-rayon, acetate, and other man-made fibers can be colored in the mass with pigments before being spun through a spinneret. Paper is colored in the beater with pigments and is also coated with compositions containing pigments. Detergents, soap, candles, wax compositions, modeling clay, chalk, wax crayons, and colored pencils are all often colored with pigments. Builders' items colored with pigments include cement for concrete, roofing granules, linoleum, and tiles of asphalt, rubber, or vinyl. Rubber, other elastomers, plastics, molding powders, and casting resins are also colored with pigments, and foods, drugs, and cosmetics are permitted to be colored with selected pigments.

Solvent dyes are generally insoluble in water but dissolve in varying degree in different organic media in liquid, molten, or solid form, including alcohols, esters, ketones, aliphatic or aromatic hydrocarbons, chlorinated hydrocarbons, oils, fats, and waxes. Solvent dyes do not normally contain a sulfonic or carboxylic group unless the dye has been combined with an organic base that imparts solubility in organic solvents. Basic dyes become somewhat solvent-soluble when prepared as the free base, but generally the free base is melted in about two parts of oleic acid before commercial use as a solvent-soluble dye. The uses of a particular solvent dye depend not only upon fastness to light and adequate solubility in a required solvent but often also on other properties (as stability to heat, acid, or alkali, or freedom from bleeding in water). Solvent dyes are used in spirit and oil wood stains and varnishes, in transparent lacquers of various kinds, in shellac, in inks, on copying paper and typewriter ribbons, in printing inks, in ball-point inks, in candles and sealing waxes, and in polishes for shoes and other purposes. Gasoline, soap, cosmetics, foods, drugs, fuel oil, and signaling smokes are other materials colored with solvent dyes. Molding powders and various resinous and plastic materials are also colored with solvent dyes.

Sulfur dyes are usu. dissolved and then dyed on cotton and also on rayon and other cellulosic fibers in a hot dilute solution containing sodium sulfide and sodium carbonate. Salt is required for exhaustion. Sulfur dyes are occasionally dyed on silk and less often on wool, and sometimes on leather and paper. Sulfur dyeings are limited in brightness, the oranges, reds, and violets being quite dull, while the yellows are less fast than the other colors. The blacks, browns, blues, and greens display fair to good and very good fastness to light, esp. when aftertreated with copper sulfate and acetic acid. Sulfur dyeings have reasonably good fastness to washing, which is also often improved considerably by aftertreatment with dichromate and acetic acid. *Solubilized sulfur dyes* are ordinary sulfur dyes that have been prepared in strong prereduced leuco form either as a liquid or as a powder or that have been premixed with a suitable alkaline reducing mixture that dissolves them when they are placed in hot water. They are not listed separately in table I from the sulfur dyes from which they are derived and which they yield in dyeing.

Vat dyes are water-insoluble aromatic organic compounds containing at least two symmetrically located carbonyl groups in the molecule. They dissolve in water when vatted with an alkaline solution of the reducing agent sodium hydrosulfite; many require salt for good exhaustion on cotton from such an aqueous solution. In the printing of textiles reduction and dyeing in the areas of the printed pattern take place in the steam atmosphere of a neutral vat ager by the reducing action of sodium formaldehydesulfoxylate and potash printed on the cloth with the dye in a printing paste also containing gums. Upon subsequent oxidation and soaping the vat dye is regenerated in the fiber. Many vat dyeings, but not those from indigo, display excellent fastness to light, washing, and dilute hypochlorite and peroxide and thus are among the fastest dyes for cotton, rayon, linen, and other cellulosic fibers. Some vat dyes are applied by special methods on silk, wool, nylon, and acrylic textiles. Some are now finding increasing use as lightfast pigments, and a few as food, drug, and cosmetic colors. *Solubilized vat dyes* are the sodium salts of the sulfuric monoesters of the leuco compounds of vat dyes, are more expensive than ordinary vat dyes, and hence are used mainly for dyeing pastels on cotton, rayon, and linen when the best possible levelness and penetration in addition to fastness are demanded. Bright blue or green solubilized vat dyes are often printed on cotton alongside azoic dyes, which are deficient in brightness in the blue-green range. Solubilized vat dyes are occasionally applied on silk, wool, acetate, acrylic, polyester, and polyamide fibers when the very best fastness properties are required. An advantage of these dyes for fibers that are sensitive to alkali is that they are applied in neutral or slightly acid solution. Dyeings on all fibers must finally be oxidized and hydrolyzed, for example with sodium nitrite and dilute sulfuric acid. Only a few are listed in table I because all of the solubilized vat dyes have *Colour Index* names and structural numbers closely related to those of the dyes from which they are derived and yield those vat dyes on the fiber upon development in dyeing. Thus Solubilized Vat Blue 6 with the structural formula 69,826 is the leuco ester of Vat Blue 6 with the structural formula 69,825.

COLORS PERMITTED FOR FOODS, DRUGS, AND COSMETICS

In the U.S. only selected acid, mordant acid, direct, basic, and solvent dyes and selected pigments are permitted by the Food and Drug Administration for use in foods, drugs, and cosmetics that enter into interstate commerce. Further, each batch of permitted color must be analyzed and certified as free from certain deleterious impurities. There are three separate categories of these permitted colors: (1) Food, Drug, and Cosmetic Colors (FD&C); (2) Drug and Cosmetic Colors (D&C); and (3) External Drug and Cosmetic Colors (Ext D&C). The colors of group 3 may be used in drugs and cosmetics for external parts of the body, but not on mucous membranes. For example, colors of group 3 may not be used in lipstick.

In the first column are listed the permitted dyes and pigments by the names that have been assigned to them by the Food and Drug Administration, and in the second column the *Colour Index* generic names of the corresponding dyes from which batches of permitted colors are purified.

DYE TABLE II

Permitted Color	Colour Index Generic Name
FD&C	
Yellow No. 5	Acid Yellow 23
Yellow No. 6	Food Yellow 3
Red No. 2	Acid Red 27
Red No. 3	Acid Red 51
Red No. 4	Food Red 1
Violet No. 1	Acid Violet 49
Blue No. 1	Acid Blue 9
Blue No. 2	Acid Blue 74
Green No. 1	Acid Green 3
Green No. 2	Acid Green 5
Green No. 3	Food Green 3
D&C	
Yellow No. 5	Acid Yellow 23
Yellow No. 10	Acid Yellow 3
Yellow No. 11	Solvent Yellow 33
Orange No. 3	Acid Orange 10
Orange No. 4	Acid Orange 7
Orange No. 10	Solvent Red 73
Orange No. 11	Acid Red 95
Orange No. 15	Mordant Red 11 Pigment Red 83
Orange No. 16	Solvent Orange 18
Red No. 5	Acid Red 26
Red Nos. 6 and 7	Pigment Red 57
Red No. 17	Solvent Red 23
Red No. 18	Solvent Red 27
Red No. 21	Solvent Red 43
Red Nos. 22 and 23	Acid Red 87
Red No. 24	Solvent Red 42
Red No. 27	Solvent Red 48
Red No. 28	Acid Red 92
Red No. 30	Vat Red 1
Red No. 31	Pigment Red 64
Red No. 34	Pigment Red 63
Red No. 35	Pigment Red 3
Red No. 36	Pigment Red 4
Red No. 38	Pigment Red 18
Red No. 39	Pigment Red 100
Violet No. 2	Solvent Violet 13
Blue No. 4	Pigment Blue 24
Blue No. 6	Vat Blue 1
Blue No. 9	Vat Blue 6
Green No. 5	Acid Green 25
Green No. 6	Solvent Green 3
Green No. 7	Acid Green 9
Brown No. 1	Acid Orange 24
Black No. 1	Acid Black 1
EXT D&C	
Yellow No. 1	Acid Yellow 36
Yellow No. 3	Acid Yellow 11
Yellow No. 5	Pigment Yellow 1
Yellow No. 7	Acid Yellow 1
Yellow No. 9	Solvent Yellow 5
Yellow No. 10	Solvent Yellow 6
Yellow Nos. 11 and 12	Acid Yellow 73
Orange No. 1	Pigment Orange 1
Orange No. 3	Acid Orange 20
Orange No. 4	Solvent Orange 2
Orange No. 5	Solvent Red 72
Orange No. 6	Pigment Orange 5
Red No. 1	Acid Violet 7
Red No. 3	Solvent Violet 10
Red No. 8	Acid Red 88
Red No. 10	Acid Red 14
Red No. 11	Acid Red 1
Red No. 13	Acid Red 73
Red No. 14	Solvent Orange 7
Red Nos. 15 and 16	Pigment Red 53
Red Nos. 17, 18, 19, and 20	Pigment Red 49
Red No. 21	Basic Violet 10
Red No. 22	Solvent Red 49
Red No. 23	Acid Red 33
Violet No. 2	Acid Violet 43
Blue No. 1	Basic Blue 9
Blue No. 4	Acid Blue 45
Green No. 1	Acid Green 1

[2]**dye** \"\ *vb* **dyed**; **dyed**; **dyeing**; **dyes** [ME *dyen*, fr. OE *dēagian*, *dēgian*, fr. *dēag*, *dēah*] *vt* **1 :** to color throughout **:** impart a new and often permanent color to esp. by impregnating with a dye — compare DYEING 1; STAIN, TINT **2 a :** to impart (a color) by dyeing ⟨~ a blue over a yellow⟩ **b :** to cause (a dye) to be applied **3 :** to color or tinge in any way ⟨a warm flush *dyed* her cheeks —Ellen Glasgow⟩ **:** STAIN ⟨*dyed* his hands in the blood of innocents⟩ **~** *vi* **:** to take up or impart color in dyeing ⟨wool *~s* readily with acid dyes⟩ ⟨level *~ing* properties of acid dyes⟩

dye·able *also* **dy·able** \ˈdīəbəl\ *adj* **:** capable of being dyed

dye base *n* **:** an organic base that is itself a dye or that with acids forms salts which are dyes — called also *color base;* compare LEUCO BASE

dyebath \ˈ=¦=\ *n* **:** a solution containing a dye used in dyeing

dyebeck \ˈ=,=\ *n* [[1]*dye* + *beck* (vat)] **:** a large shallow dye vat equipped with a winch and used for dyeing pieces of fabric in rope form

dye–bleach process *n* **:** any of several processes of color photography in which dyes are destroyed in the presence of a metallic image by the application of chemical agents — distinguished from *bleach-out process*

dye·crete process \ˈdī,krēt-\ *n* [[2]*dye* + con*crete*] **:** a process for coloring cement and concrete with organic dyes which are insoluble in water and fast to light, moisture, and atmospheric effects

dyed–in–the–wool \¦===¦=\ *adj* **1 :** dyed before spinning **2 :** DEVOTED ⟨a *dyed-in-the-wool* fisherman⟩ **:** firm and uncompromising in principle ⟨a *dyed-in-the-wool* conservative⟩

dyehouse \ˈ=,=\ *n* **:** a building, department, or plant in which dyeing and related processes or operations are carried out

dyeing *n* -s **1 :** the process or art of applying (as to textile fibers or leather) a coloring matter usu. in a solution or fine dispersion in a liquid (as water) so that the coloring matter is taken up from the dyebath and the color imparted is not readily removed by washing **2 :** a product of dyeing **:** a substance colored with a dye or a color produced by dyeing ⟨this red ~ is fast⟩

dye intermediate *n* **:** an organic compound (as aniline or a naphthol) that is prepared for use in synthesizing dyes

dyeleaves \ˈ=,=\ *n pl* **1 :** SWEETLEAF **2 :** INKBERRY 1

dyer \ˈdī(ə)r, -īə\ *n* -s [ME, fr. *dighere*, *dyere*, fr. *dyen* to dye + *-ere* -er] **:** one that dyes (as fabrics, leather, hats, fur, or wooden articles)

dyer·ma *also* **djer·ma** \dēˈermə, ˈdyer-\ *n, pl* **dyerma** *or* **dyermas** *usu cap* **1 a :** a Negroid people of the middle Niger valley **b :** a member of such people **2 :** the Songhai language of the Dyerma people

dyer's alkanet *n* **:** ALKANET 1

dyer's barberry *n* **:** an Indian barberry (*Berberis aristata*) yielding a yellow dye

dyer's–broom \¦==¦=\ *n, pl* **dyer's–brooms :** WOODWAXEN

dyer's broom *n* **:** a light to moderate greenish yellow that is less strong than acacia and redder and less strong than liqueur green — called also *broom*, *dyewood*, *genestrole*, *genet*

dyer's buckthorn *n* **:** any of several shrubs of the genus *Rhamnus* (esp. *R. infectoria*) yielding a yellow dye

dyer's cleavers *n* **:** MADDER

dyer's furze *or* **dyer's genista** *or* **dyer's greenweed** *or* **dyer's greenwood** *n* **:** WOODWAXEN

dyer's grape *n* **:** POKEWEED

dyer's mulberry *n* **:** FUSTIC

dyer's oak *n* **1 :** an Asiatic tree (*Quercus infectoria*) the galls of which yield a dye **2 :** a black oak (*Quercus velutina*)

dyer's rocket *also* **dyer's mignonette** *n* **:** a European mignonette (*Reseda luteola*) cultivated for its yellow dye and naturalized in No. America

dyer's saffron *n* **:** SAFFLOWER 1

dyer's–weed \ˈ==,=\ *n, pl* **dyer's–weeds 1 :** any of several dye-yielding plants (as the dyer's rocket, the woodwaxen, the dyer's woad) **2 :** any of certain plants of the genus *Solidago* (esp. *S. nemoralis* and *S. rugosa*) whose yellow flowers are occas. used in dyeing

dyer's whin *n* **:** WOODWAXEN

dyer's woad *n* **:** a woad (*Isatis tinctoria*) that yields an indigo

dyer's woodruff *n* **:** a perennial woodruff (*Asperula tinctoria*) having a creeping rootstock that is sometimes used as a substitute for madder

dyes *pl of* DYE, *pres 3d sing of* DYE
dye shell *n* : DOG WHELK b
dyestuff \ˈ=,=\ *n* [prob. trans. of G *farbstoff*] : DYE 2
dye toning *n* : the process of altering the color of a developed image by converting it into a mordant and then bathing in a suitable dye solution
dye transfer *n* **1** : a color printing process in which dyed images (cyan, magenta, and yellow) on three matrices are transferred successively in register onto a paper surface **2** : a print made by the dye transfer process
dyeweed \ˈ=,=\ *n* **1** : WOODWAXEN **2** : a small American weedy herb (*Eclipta alba*) of the family Compositae with yellowish white flowers
dyewood \ˈ=,=\ *n, often attrib* **1** : a wood (as logwood or fustic) from which coloring matter is extracted for dyeing ⟨~ extract⟩ **2** : DYER'S BROOM
dying *adj* [ME, fr. pres. part. of *dien* to die — more at DIE] **1 a** : passing from life : being about to die ⟨a ~ man⟩ : gradually ceasing to be : EXPIRING ⟨the ~ day⟩ ⟨a ~ fire⟩ **b** : having reached an advanced or ultimate stage of decay or disuse ⟨a ~ civilization⟩ ⟨a ~ tradition⟩ **2** : of or relating to death or dying ⟨recorded his ~ words⟩ ⟨promised to fulfill his ~ wishes⟩ ⟨the ~ crisis of a decadent culture⟩
dying declaration *n* : a declaration made by a person in the immediate prospect of death and having no hope of recovery : an antemortem statement
dykage *var of* DIKAGE
dyke *var of* DIKE
-dym·ia \ˈdimēə\ *n comb form* -s [NL, fr. *-dymus* + *-ia*] : condition of being a pair of twin terata joined at (a specified body part) ⟨cephalo*dymia*⟩
-dy·mus \dəməs\ *n comb form* -ES [NL, irreg. fr. Gk *didymos* twin, fr. *dyo* two — more at TWO] : pair of twin terata joined at (a specified body part) ⟨sterno*dymus*⟩
dyn *abbr* **1** dynamics **2** dynamo
dy·na·graph \ˈdīnə,graf, -ráf\ *n* -s [Gk *dyna*mis power + E *-graph*] : an apparatus in a railroad car for recording the condition of a line of track, the resistance of a train, its speed, and other features of its performance
dynam- *or* **dynamo-** *comb form* [prob. fr. F, fr. Gk, fr. *dynamis*] : power ⟨*dynam*ism⟩ ⟨*dynamo*graph⟩
-dy·nam·ia \,dīˈnamēə, ˌdəˈ-, -nām-\ *n comb form* -s [NL, fr. Gk, fr. *dynamis* + *-ia* -y] : strength : condition of having (such) strength ⟨a*dynamia*⟩ ⟨myo*dynamia*⟩
¹dy·nam·ic \(ˈ)dīˌnamik, -mēk *sometimes* dəˈn-\ *also* **dy·nam·i·cal** \-mə̇kəl, -mēk-\ *adj* [F *dynamique*, NL *dynamicus*, & G *dynamisch*, fr. Gk *dynamikos* powerful, fr. *dynamis* power (fr. *dynasthai* to be able) + *-ikos* -ic, -ical] **1** *in Kantianism* : relating to the grounds or reasons for the existence of a sense presentation ⟨the ~ categories of relation⟩ **2 a** : of or relating to power : relating to physical force or energy ⟨the ~ theory of heat⟩ **b** : of or relating to dynamics : of or relating to forces producing motion : ACTIVE — compare POTENTIAL, STATIC **3** : FUNCTIONAL 1b (1) ⟨a ~ disease⟩ **4 a** : characterized by continuous movement, advance, or expansion ⟨a ~ economy⟩ ⟨a ~ population⟩ : characterized by continuous change ⟨an unstable ~ age⟩ or tending to produce change ⟨the ~ force of technology⟩ : having or relating to a nonphysical force or energy ⟨every social behavior pattern . . . contains a ~ component —S.F.Nadel⟩ : FORCEFUL, ENERGETIC ⟨a ~ personality⟩ **b** : having reference to change or behavior ⟨the ~ relationship between man and institutions —Abram Kardiner⟩; *specif* : relating to a system or culture marked by continuous alteration and a resulting lack of equilibrium of its elements ⟨a ~ system like a human individual or social group —H.V.Dicks⟩ **c** : characterized by a concern with or interest in cultural change or process and the patterns of cultural change ⟨wrote social history of the static sort, as opposed to the ~ interpretative variety —J.B.Hedges⟩ **5 a** : producing an effect of energetic movement or progression ⟨a ~ line⟩ ⟨~ brushwork⟩ **b** : characterized by an aesthetic equilibrium of parts which considered separately are unstable **6** : taking time into account as an explicit factor in economic processes so that variables at different points in time are functionally related **7** : characterized by variations of accent dependent on variation in force of expiration or stress — compare EXPIRATORY, STRESS ACCENT **8** : relating to volume of musical sound or to relative loudness and softness ⟨the ~ range of the piano⟩ — **dy·nam·i·cal·ly** \-mə̇k(ə)lē, -mēk-, -li\ *adv*
²dynamic \"\ *n* -s [prob. fr. F *dynamique*, fr. *dynamique*, adj.] **1 a** : DYNAMICS 2 a ⟨convert its ~ of grievance and discontent into revolutionary class struggle —A.L.Locke⟩ **b** : a particular dynamic force ⟨the generative force, the historical ~ of their country —Archibald MacLeish⟩ **2** : DYNAMICS 3
dynamical parallax *n* : the parallax of a binary star determined by the use of the relation between mass and absolute magnitude
dynamic augment *n* : the force produced by centrifugal action of the incompletely balanced weight of reciprocating parts of a steam locomotive
dynamic brake *n* : a brake operating by dynamic braking
dynamic braking *n* : a system of braking (as in electric trains or machinery) in which the driving motor is converted into a generator and is driven by the kinetic energy of the vehicle thus exerting a retarding force
dynamic factor *n* : the ratio between the load carried by any part of an aircraft when accelerating or otherwise subjected to abnormal conditions and the load carried in normal flight
dynamic geology *n* : a branch of geology that deals with the causes and processes of geological change
dynamic head *n* : VELOCITY HEAD
dynamic isomerism *n* : TAUTOMERISM
dynamic load *n* : a live load (as a motor vehicle in motion) on a structure (as a bridge)
dynamic metamorphism *n, geol* : metamorphism characterized by shear movements as well as elevated temperature — compare CONTACT METAMORPHISM
dynamic meteorology *n* : a branch of meteorology that deals with motions of the atmosphere and the forces that cause them
dynamic microphone *n* : a microphone in which the sound waves cause a movable wire or coil to vibrate in a magnetic field and thus induce a current
dynamic model *or* **dynamic scale model** *n* : a copy (as of an airplane) usu. smaller than the original and having linear dimensions, weight, and moments of inertia reproduced to scale in proportion to those of the original
dynamic monarchianism *n, usu cap D&M* : the doctrine that Christ was a mere man who was made son of God by adoption — called also *dynamistic monarchianism*
dynamic oceanography *n* : the science that deals with ocean waves, currents, and tides
dynamic pressure *n* **1** : the pressure on a surface at which a flowing fluid is brought to rest in excess of the pressure on it when the fluid is not flowing **2** : the quantity of air measured by most airspeed instruments and equal to the product $\frac{1}{2}\rho V^2$ where ρ is the density of the air and V is the relative speed of the air
dynamic psychology *n* : a psychological approach or system affirming that human acts are understandable and predictable only through an analysis of the previous experiences and motivational states of the organism rather than through a simple description of the objective stimuli temporally preceding human acts — compare PSYCHOANALYSIS
dynamic range *n* : the ratio of the loudest to the weakest sound intensity which can be transmitted or reproduced by a recording or broadcasting system
dynamic refraction *n* : the reciprocal of the near-point distance of the eye — compare STATIC REFRACTION
dynamic reproducer *n* : a phonograph pickup whose electrical output is produced when the stylus moves a coil in a magnetic field
dy·nam·ics \dīˈnamiks, -mēks *sometimes* dəˈ-\ *n pl but often sing in constr* [F *dynamique*, fr. *dynamique*, adj., dynamic — more at DYNAMIC] **1** : a branch of mechanics that deals with forces and their relation primarily to the motion but sometimes also to the equilibrium of bodies of matter — compare KINEMATICS, KINETICS, STATICS **2 a** : the driving physical, moral, or intellectual forces of any kind or the laws that relate to them ⟨the principal ~ of climatic change is the sun —Gerard Piel⟩ ⟨the ~ of an acquisitive society⟩ **b** : PSYCHODYNAMICS **3 a** : the pattern of any process of sociocultural growth and change ⟨the study of population ~⟩ : the pattern of response or adaptation to environment by an individual or group ⟨insights into cultural ~ can be obtained . . . why certain common elements of Spanish culture were accepted by one group, rejected by a second, and profoundly modified by a third —G.M.Foster⟩ **b** : the pattern of change or growth of any object or phenomenon ⟨the ~ of these storms⟩ **c** : economic analysis that stresses the sequence of phenomena, the rate at which phenomena occur, and the functional relationships of variables at different points in time **4** : variation and contrast in force or intensity (as in music, in the use of color, or in the execution of a dance)
dynamic speaker *n* : ELECTRODYNAMIC SPEAKER
dynamic viscosity *n* : COEFFICIENT OF VISCOSITY
dy·na·mis \ˈdīnəmə̇s\ *n, pl* **dyna·mes** \-,mēz\ [Gk — more at DYNAMIC] : the state of that which is not yet fully realized : POWER, POTENTIALITY — contrasted with *energeia*
dy·na·mism \ˈdīnə,mizəm\ *n* -s [prob. fr. F *dynamisme*, fr. *dynam-* + *-isme* -ism] **1 a** : a theory or doctrine that explains the universe in terms of forces and their interplay (as immanent forces that are irreducible to matter and its motion) — used esp. of ancient hylozoistic doctrines and Leibnizianism; contrasted with *mechanism*; compare ENERGETICS **b** : a theory that considers becoming, change, motion, or energy as fundamental to the constitution of the universe **2 a** : a dynamic or expansionist quality ⟨a ~ threatening the balance of power in Europe⟩ : a quality of insistent restless drive or movement esp. in a particular direction ⟨found in the 12th century an escape from the ~ of the 20th⟩ : FORCE, ENERGY ⟨a passionate person filled with an incredible ~⟩ **b** : a quality in artistic representation that conveys (as to the observer or auditor) an impression of dynamic movement ⟨the ~ of the Gothic architectural style⟩ ⟨his readings of Beethoven have never been surpassed in fluency and ~⟩ **c** : DYNAMICS 3
dy·na·mist \-,mə̇st\ *n* -s [prob. fr. F *dynamiste*, fr. *dynam-* + *-iste* -ist] : an adherent of dynamism — **dy·na·mis·tic** \ˌdīnəˈmistik, -tēk\ *adj*
dynamistic monarchianism *n, usu cap D&M* : DYNAMIC MONARCHIANISM
dy·na·mi·tard \ˌdīnəmə̇ˈtärd\ *n* -s [¹*dynamite* + *-ard*] : one that uses dynamite for anarchistic or other political acts of violence
¹dy·na·mite \ˈdīnə,mīt, *usu* -īd·+V\ *n* -s [ISV *dynam-* + *-ite*; orig. formed as Sw *dynamit*] **1** : a solid blasting explosive used esp. in mining, quarrying, and engineering that contains nitroglycerin incorporated with a base which increases the safety of handling: as **a** : an explosive in which the base (as kieselguhr) is inert **b** : an explosive in which the base is active and consists essentially of a carbonaceous combustible material (as wood pulp) and an oxidizing material (as sodium nitrate) — called also *straight dynamite* **c** : a strong explosive similar to a straight dynamite but containing ammonium nitrate in place of part of the nitroglycerin and often part of the oxidizing material — called also *ammonia dynamite* **d** : GELATIN DYNAMITE **2** : a blasting explosive used similarly to dynamite but containing an essential constituent (as nitrostarch) other than nitroglycerin **3** : one that is characterized by notable vitality, power, or effectiveness ⟨box-office ~ —Steve McNeil⟩ ⟨not only is he tough and ruthless; he is also ~ with the ladies —*Saturday Rev.*⟩; *also* : something that has great potential (as for causing strife or trouble) ⟨devaluation is ~ and politicians don't like its sound —M.A.Heilperin⟩ ⟨this letter is ~ —Erle Stanley Gardner⟩
²dynamite \"\ *vt* -ED/-ING/-S **1** : to charge with dynamite **2** : to blow up or shatter with dynamite **3** : to cause the utter failure or destruction of ⟨it is easy to ~ an industrial system —M.R.Cohen⟩ ⟨the board has *dynamited* its own findings in two particulars —B.H.Kizer⟩
dy·na·mit·er \-īd·ə(r), -ītə-\ *n* -s **1** : one that blasts with dynamite **2** : DYNAMITARD
dy·na·mit·ic \ˌdīnəˈmid·ik\ *also* **dy·na·mit·i·cal** \-mid·ə̇kəl\ *adj* : of, like, or relating to dynamite
dy·na·mi·za·tion \,dīnəmə̇ˈzāshən, -,mīˈz-\ *n* -s : the act or an instance of dynamizing
dy·na·mize \ˈdīnə,mīz\ *vt* -ED/-ING/-S [*dynam-* + *-ize*] **1** : to make (a drug) effective (as by comminution or dilution) **2** : to make dynamic : endow with force
dy·na·mo \ˈdīnə,mō\ *n* -s [short for *dynamo machine* & *dynamoelectric machine*; trans. of G *dynamomaschine* & *dynamoelektrische maschine*] **1** : GENERATOR 3; *esp* : a direct-current generator **2** : an individual possessing great or unusual force or energy ⟨this stubby ~ of thirty-four organizes unions, writes poetry —George Weller⟩

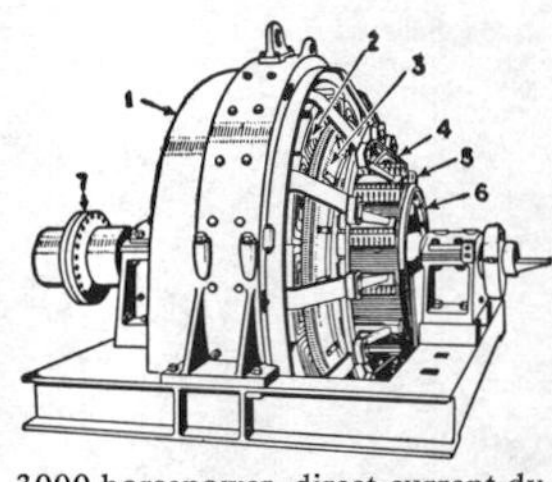

3000 horsepower, direct-current dynamo: *1* frame, *2* field, *3* armature, *4* brush rigging, *5* brushes, *6* commutator, *7* coupling

dynamo- — see DYNAM-
dy·na·mo·electric \ˌ==,=+\ *adj* [ISV *dynam-* + *electric*; orig. formed as G *dynamoelektrisch*] : relating to the conversion by induction of mechanical energy into electrical energy or vice versa
dy·na·mo·genesis \,===+\ *n, pl* **dynamogeneses** [NL, fr. *dynam-* + *-genesis*] : an increase of mental and motor activity resulting from stimulation of any sense organ
dy·na·mo·gen·ic \ˌdīnəmōˈjenik\ *also* **dy·na·mog·e·nous** \-ˈmäjənəs\ *adj* [*dynam-* + *-genic, -genous*] : relating to or instrumental in dynamogenesis
dy·na·mog·e·ny \,dīnəˈmäjənē\ *n* -ES [ISV *dynam-* + *-geny*] : DYNAMOGENESIS
dy·na·mo·metamorphic \ˌdīnə(,)mō+\ *adj* [*dynam-* + *metamorphic*] : of or belonging to dynamometamorphism
dy·na·mo·metamorphism \ˌdīnə(,)mō+\ *n* [*dynam-* + *metamorphism*] *geol* : metamorphism in which mechanical energy (as exerted in pressure and movement) is the principal agent — contrasted with *hydrometamorphism*, and *pyrometamorphism*
dy·na·mom·e·ter \,dīnəˈmäməd·ə(r)\ *n* -s [F *dynamomètre*, fr. *dynam-* + *-mètre* -meter] **1** : an instrument for measuring mechanical forces or torques usu. by the elastic deformation produced (as a machine for testing the strength of materials or of a man's grip) **2** : an apparatus for measuring mechanical power (as of an engine, an electric motor, or a draft animal) : ERGOMETER — see TRANSMISSION DYNAMOMETER **3** : ELECTRODYNAMOMETER
dynamometer car *n* : a laboratory car with equipment for measuring and recording drawbar pull, horsepower, brake-pipe pressure, and other information on locomotive performance and train operation
dy·na·mo·met·ric \ˌdīnəmōˈme·trik\ *or* **dy·na·mo·met·ri·cal** \-rə̇kəl\ *adj* : of, belonging to, or measured by dynamometry
dy·na·mom·e·try \-ämə·trē\ *n* -ES [ISV *dynam-* + *-metry*] : an art or process of measuring forces doing work; *specif* : measurement of the strength of muscular contraction
dy·na·mo·static \ˌdīnəmō+\ *adj* [*dynam-* + *static*] *adj* : of or relating to a machine for producing static electricity by the use of a direct or alternating current
dy·na·motor \ˈdīnə+,-\ *n* [*dynamo* + *motor*] : a motor generator combining the motor and generator in a single machine with one field magnet and with two armatures or with one armature with two windings one of which receives current as a motor and the other of which generates current as a dynamo
-dy·na·mous \dīnəməs\ *adj comb form* [prob. fr. NL *-dynamus*, fr. Gk *-dynamos* having (such) power, fr. *dynamis* power — more at DYNAMIC] *bot* : having developing power of a (specified) type ⟨andro*dynamous*⟩
dy·nast \ˈdī,nast, \nəst, |,naa(ə)st *sometimes* ˈdi|\ *n* -s [L *dynastes*, fr. Gk *dynastēs*, fr. *dynasthai* to be able] **1** : a ruler over a state; *esp* : a hereditary ruler : one of a line of kings or princes **2** : a person that founds or belongs to a family powerful in a particular field ⟨a ~ in the field of international finance⟩
dy·nas·tes \dīˈna(,)stēz, dəˈ-\ *n, cap* [NL, fr. L, dynast] : a genus (the type of the family Dynastidae) of large chiefly tropical lamellicorn beetles having large mandibles and commonly greatly elongated pointed processes on the head and prothorax of the males — see RHINOCEROS BEETLE
dy·nas·tic \(ˈ)dīˌnastik, dəˈn-, -naas-, -tēk\ *also* **dy·nas·ti·cal** \-tə̇kəl, -tēk-\ *adj* [Gk *dynastikos*, fr. *dynastēs* + *-ikos* -ic, -ical] : of or belonging to a dynasty ⟨ended two centuries of ~ rule⟩ ⟨debated Europe's tangled ~ relations⟩ — **dy·nas·ti·cal·ly** \-tə̇k(ə)lē, -tēk-, -li\ *adv*
dy·nas·ti·cism \dīˈnastə,sizəm, dəˈ-, -naas-\ *n* -s : the theory, practice, or an instance of dynastic government ⟨nationalism . . . lost the implication of liberalism which it had had so long as it figured as the opponent of ~ —G.H.Sabine⟩
dy·nas·ty \ˈdī|nastē, -ti *also* |,nas- *or* |,naas- *sometimes* ˈdi|\ *n* -ES [Gk *dynasteia*, fr. *dynastēs* + *-eia* -y] **1** : a succession of rulers of the same line of descent **2 a** : a group or class of individuals having power or authority in some sphere of activity and able to choose their successors ⟨a literary ~, dictating to the country in matters of taste⟩ ⟨a tightly knit ~ of industrialists and bankers⟩ **b** : a family that establishes and maintains predominance in a particular field of endeavor for generations ⟨a famed theatrical ~⟩
dy·na·tron \ˈdīnə·,trän\ *n* -s [Gk *dynamis* power + E *-tron* — more at DYNAMIC] : a four-electrode vacuum tube in which the secondary emission of electrons from the plate results in a decrease in the plate current as the plate voltage increases
dyne \ˈdīn\ *n* -s [F, fr. Gk *dynamis* power — more at DYNAMIC] : the unit of force in the cgs system equal to the force that would give a free mass of one gram an acceleration of one centimeter per second per second
Dy·nel \(ˈ)dīˌnel\ *trademark* **1** — used for a fiber made in staple form from vinyl chloride and acrylonitrile and characterized by great resistance to burning **2** : a yarn or fabric made of Dynel fiber
dy·node \ˈdī,nōd\ *n* -s [Gk *dynamis* power + E *-ode*] : one of the electrodes in an electron multiplier each of which in turn increases by its secondary emission the total flux of electrons
dyo- — see DY-
dy·oph·y·site \dīˈäfə,sīt\ *n* -s *usu cap* [LGk *Dyophysitai*, *Diphysitai*, pl., fr. *dyo-* dy- or *di-* + *-physitai* (fr. *physis* nature) — more at PHYSIC] : one who maintains the Chalcedonian doctrine that full deity and full humanity exist in the person of Jesus Christ as two natures without confusion or change — compare MONOPHYSITE — **dy·oph·y·sit·ic** \(ˌ)dīˌäfəˌsid·ik\ *adj, usu cap*
dy·o·the·ism \ˈdīə(,)thē,izəm, ,==ˈ=,==\ *n* -s [*dy-* + *-theism*] : a doctrine or system recognizing two gods
dy·oth·e·lite \dīˈäthə,līt\ *or* **dy·oth·e·lete** \-lēt\ *n* -s *usu cap* [*dy-* + *-thelite*, *-thelete* (as in *Monothelite*, *Monothelete*)] : an adherent of Dyothelitism
dy·oth·e·lit·ism \-līd·,izəm\ *or* **dy·oth·e·let·ism** \-lēd-\ *n* -s *usu cap* : the theological doctrine that in Christ there were two wills, the human and the divine — opposed to *Monothelitism*
dyp·none \ˈdip,nōn\ *n* [*di-* + *hypnone*] : a liquid ketone $C_6H_5COCH{:}C(CH_3)C_6H_5$ formed by the condensation of two molecules of acetophenone and used as a plasticizer
dys- *prefix* [alter. (influenced by L & Gk *dys-*) of ME *dis-*, fr. MF & L; MF *dis-*, fr. L *dys-*, fr. Gk; akin to OE *tō-*, *te-* apart, to pieces, OHG *zi-*, *zir-* apart, to pieces, ON *tor-* difficult, Goth *tuz-* (in *tuzwerjan* to doubt), Skt *dus-* difficult, bad] **1 a** : abnormal : diseased ⟨*dys*hidrosis⟩ ⟨*dys*plasia⟩ **b** : difficult ⟨*dys*menorrhea⟩ ⟨*dys*uria⟩ : with difficulty ⟨*dys*oxidize⟩ : poorly ⟨*dys*crystalline⟩ — sometimes opposed to *eu-* **c** : faulty : impaired ⟨*dys*function⟩ ⟨*dys*pepsia⟩ **d** : bad : unfavorable ⟨*dys*pathy⟩ ⟨*dys*phemism⟩ — sometimes opposed to *eu-* **2** : absence or reverse of ⟨*dys*teleology⟩
dys·acou·sia \,disəˈküzh(ē)ə\ *also* **dys·acou·sis** \-üsə̇s\ *n, pl* **dysacousias** \-üzh(ē)əz\ *also* **dysacou·ses** \-ü,sēz\ [NL, fr. *dys-* + *-acousia* or Gk *akousis* act of hearing — more at -ACOUSIA] : a condition in which ordinary sounds produce discomfort or pain
dys·adaptation \dəs, (ˌ)dis+\ *n* [*dys-* + *adaptation*] : an impaired ability of the iris and retina to adapt properly to variations in light intensities that is often indicative of vitamin-A deficiency
dys·ar·thria \dəˈsärthrēə\ *n* -s [NL, fr. *dys-* + *arthr-* + *-ia*] : difficulty in articulating words due to disease of the central nervous system — compare DYSPHASIA — **dys·ar·thric** \dəˈsärthrik, (ˈ)diˌs-\ *adj*
dys·arthrosis \ˌdis+\ *n, pl* **dysarthroses** [NL, fr. *dys-* + *arthr-* + *-osis*] **1** : a condition of reduced joint motion due to deformity, dislocation, or disease **2** : DYSARTHRIA
dys·che·zia *also* **dys·che·sia** \dəˈskē|zēə, -kē|, |zh(ē)ə\ *n* -s [NL, fr. *dys-* + Gk *chezein* to defecate + NL *-ia* — more at GATE] : constipation associated with a defective reflex for defecation and accompanied by accumulation of feces in the rectum — **dys·che·zic** \dəˈskēzik, (ˈ)diˌs-, -kez-\ *adj*
dys·chon·dro·pla·sia \dəˌskändrōˈplāzh(ē)ə, (ˌ)di,s-\ *n* -s [NL, fr. *dys-* + *chondr-* + *-plasia*] : CHONDRODYSPLASIA
dys·chromatopsia \dəs, (ˌ)dis+\ *n* [NL, fr. *dys-* + *chromatopsia*] : incomplete color blindness — **dys·chromatoptic** \"+\ *adj*
dys·cra·sia \dəˈskrāzh(ē)ə\ *n* -s [NL, fr. ML, mixture of the humors in bad proportions, fr. Gk *dyskrasia*, fr. *dys-* + *-krasia* (fr. *krasis* mixing, combination, temperature, temperament) — more at CRASIS] : an abnormal condition of the body : an imbalance of physiologic or constitutional elements esp. of the blood — opposed to *eucrasia*
dys·cra·site \ˈdiskrə,sīt\ *n* -s [alter. of F *discrase* (fr. *dis-* dys- + *crase*, fr. Gk *krasis* mixing, combination) + E *-ite*] : a native compound Ag_3Sb of antimony and silver usu. massive and silver-white
dys·crystalline \dəs, (ˈ)dis+\ *adj* [*dys-* + *crystalline*] : poorly crystallized — used of rocks
dys·der·cus \dəsˈdərkəs\ *n, cap* [NL, prob. fr. Gk *dysderkēs* ugly, hard to see, fr. *dys-* + *-derkēs* (fr. *derkesthai* to see, flash)] : a genus of long-legged slender-bodied usu. brightly colored bugs (family Pyrrhocoridae) that feed chiefly in the developing seed of cotton causing discoloration of the lint — see COTTON STAINER
dys·en·ter·ic \ˌdisᵊnˈterik\ *adj* [L *dysentericus*, fr. Gk *dysenterikos*, fr. *dysenteria* + *-ikos* -ic] : of or relating to dysentery : having dysentery ⟨a ~ patient⟩ ⟨~ symptoms⟩
dys·en·ter·i·form \-erə,fȯrm\ *adj* [*dysentery* + *-form*] : resembling that of dysentery ⟨~ stool⟩ ⟨~ symptoms⟩
dys·en·tery \ˈdisᵊn,terē, -,teri *also* -ˌt(ə)r-\ *n* -ES [ME *dissenterie*, fr. L *dysenteria*, fr. Gk, fr. *dys-* + *enteron* intestine + *-ia* -y — more at INTER-] **1** : an often epidemic or endemic disease characterized by severe diarrhea with passage of mucus and blood and often with intestinal ulceration and generalized toxemia, marked by abdominal pain and tenesmus, and usu. caused by infection with pathogenic bacteria or protozoans that are spread chiefly through contaminated food or water — see AMEBIC DYSENTERY; compare SHIGELLOSIS **2** : DIARRHEA; *esp* : severe diarrhea of domestic animals **3** : any of various infectious or nutritive disorders of insects (as honeybees or silkworms) characterized by the passage of excessive amounts of usu. atypical frass
dys·er·gia \dəˈsərj(ē)ə\ *also* **dys·er·gy** \ˈdi,sərjē, dəˈs-\ *n, pl* **dysergias** *also* **dysergies** [NL *dysergia*, fr. Gk, difficulty in working, inability to exert oneself, fr. *dys-* + *-ergia* -ergy] : lack of muscular coordination due to defect in innervation
dys·esthesia \ˌdis+\ *n* -s [NL, fr. *dys-* + *esthesia*] : impairment of sensitivity esp. to touch — **dys·esthetic** \"+\ *adj*
dys·function *also* **dis·function** \dəs, (ˈ)dis+\ *n* [*dys-* or ¹*dis-* + *function*] **1** : impaired or abnormal functioning (as of an organ of the body) **2** : a nonadaptive trait or condition; *esp* : one failing to serve a useful or adjustive purpose in society — **dys·functional** \dəs, (ˈ)dis+\ *adj*
dys·genesis \dəs, (ˈ)dis+\ *n, pl* **dysgeneses** [NL, fr. *dys-* + *genesis*] : infertility esp. between hybrids that remain fertile with either parent but not with one another
dys·gen·ic *also* **dis·gen·ic** \dəsˈjenik, (ˈ)disˌj-\ *adj* [*dys-* or ¹*dis-* + *-genic*] : detrimental to the hereditary qualities of a stock (as of man) or tending to counteract racial improvement through an influence bearing on reproduction : biologically

defective or deficient — contrasted with *eugenic* — **dys·gen·i·cal·ly** \-nək(ə)lē\ *adv*

dys·gen·ics \dəs'jeniks\ *n pl but sing in constr* : the study of racial degeneration

dys·ger·mi·no·ma \dəs,jərmə'nōmə, (,)dis-\ *n, pl* **dysgerminomas** *or* **dysgerminomata** [NL, fr. *dys-* + L *germin-, germen* sprout, bud, germ + NL *-oma* — more at GERM] : a malignant tumor of the ovary arising from undifferentiated germinal epithelium

dys·gonic \dəs'gänik, (')dis¦g-\ *adj* [*dys-* + *gon-* + *-ic*] : growing with difficulty on artificial media — used chiefly of certain strains of tubercle bacilli; opposed to *eugonic*

dys·hi·dro·sis \¦dis,hī¦drōsəs, -s·hə¦\ *or* **dys·idro·sis** \-s,ī¦-, -sə¦-\ *n, pl* **dyshidro·ses** *or* **dysidro·ses** \-ō,sēz\ [NL, fr. *dys-* + *hidrosis*] : an abnormality of sweat production

dys·keratosis \dəs, (¦)dis+\ *n, pl* **dyskeratoses** [NL, fr. *dys-* + *kerat-* + *-osis*] : faulty development of the epidermis with abnormal keratinization — **dys·ker·a·tot·ic** \-,kerə¦täd·ik\ *adj*

dys·ki·ne·sia \,diskə'nēzh(ē)ə, -,kī'-\ *n* -s [NL, fr. Gk *dyskinēsia* difficulty in moving, fr. *dys-* + *-kinēsia* (fr. *kinēsis* motion + *-ia*) — more at KINESIS] : impaired or abnormal motion of voluntary or involuntary muscle — **dys·ki·net·ic** \¦=(,)=¦ned·ik\ *adj*

dys·la·lia \də'slālēə, -lal-\ *n* -s [NL, fr. *dys-* + *-lalia*] : defect in articulative power caused by malformation of or imperfect distribution of nerves to the organs of articulation

[1]**dys·lec·tic** \də'slektik, (')di¦s-\ *adj* [fr. NL *dyslexia*, after such pairs as LL *apoplexia* apoplexy : E *apoplectic*] : suffering from dyslexia

[2]**dyslectic** \"\ *n* -s : a dyslectic person

dys·lex·ia \də'sleksēə\ *n* -s [NL, fr. *dys-* + *-lexia*] : a disturbance of the ability to read — **dys·lex·ic** \də'sleksik, (')di¦s-\ *adj*

dys·lex·i·ac \də'sleksē,ak\ *n* -s [NL *dyslexia* + E *-c* (as in *maniac*)] : one affected with dyslexia

dys·lo·gia \də'slōj(ē)ə\ *n* -s [NL, fr. *dys-* + *-logia*] : difficulty in expressing ideas through speech caused by impairment of the power of reasoning (as in certain psychoses and feeblemindedness)

dys·lo·gis·tic *also* **dis·lo·gis·tic** \¦dislə¦jistik\ *adj* [*dys-* or [1]*dis-* + *-logistic* (as in *eulogistic*)] : UNCOMPLIMENTARY, DISPARAGING ⟨~ terms like *nitwit* and *scalawag*⟩ — opposed to *eulogistic* — **dys·lo·gis·ti·cal·ly** \-tək(ə)lē\ *adv*

dys·lu·ite \'di(,)slü,īt, də's-\ *n* -s [irreg. fr. *dys-* + Gk *lyein* to loosen, dissolve + E *-ite* — more at LOSE] : a brown variety of gahnite

dys·men·or·rhea *also* **dys·men·or·rhoea** \(¦)di,smenə¦rēə, də,==''==\ *n* -s [NL, fr. *dys-* + *meno-* + *-rrhea*, *-rrhoea*] : painful menstruation — **dys·men·or·rhe·al** \(¦)di¦smenə¦rēəl, də¦s-\ *or* **dys·men·or·rhe·ic** \-ēik\ *adj*

dys·met·ria \də'sme·trēə\ *n* -s [NL, fr. *dys-* + Gk *metron* measure + NL *-ia* — more at MEASURE] : impaired ability to estimate distance in muscular action

dys·o·dile \'disə,dīl\ *n* -s [F, fr. Gk *dysōdēs* ill-smelling (fr. *dys-* + *-ōdēs*, fr. *ozein* to smell) + F *-ile* — more at ODOR] : a hydrocarbon mineral occurring in thin flexible folia and emitting a highly fetid odor when burning

dys·o·don·ta \,disə'däntə\ [NL, fr. *dys-* + *-odonta*] *syn of* ANISOMYARIA

dys·ontogenetic \dəs, (¦)dis+\ *adj* [*dys-* + *ontogenetic*] : involving abnormal growth and differentiation of cells or tissues (as in the formation of certain cysts or tumors)

dys·ostosis \¦dis+\ *n, pl* **dysostoses** [NL, fr. *dys-* + *-ostosis*] : defective formation of bone

dys·pareunia \¦dis+\ *n* [NL, fr. *dys-* + *pareunia*] : difficult or painful coitus

dys·pa·thy \'dispəthē\ *n* -ES [prob. fr. obs. F *dispathie*, fr. *dis-* dys- + *-pathie* -pathy] : lack of sympathy : ANTIPATHY

dys·pep·sia \də'spepshə, -epsēə\ *n* -s [L, fr. Gk, fr. *dyspeptos* hard to digest (fr. *dys-* + *peptos* cooked, fr. *peptein*, *pessein* to cook) + *-ia* — more at COOK] : a condition of disturbed digestion characterized by nausea, heartburn, pain, gas, and a sense of fullness due to local causes or to disease elsewhere in the body : INDIGESTION — opposed to *eupepsia*

dys·pep·sy \-epsē\ *n* -ES [F or L; F *dyspepsie*, fr. L *dyspepsia*] *now chiefly dial* : DYSPEPSIA

[1]**dys·pep·tic** \də'speptik, (')di¦s-\ *also* **dys·pep·ti·cal** \-təkəl, -tēk-\ *adj* [Gk *dyspeptos* + E *-ic*, *-ical*] **1** : relating to dyspepsia : having dyspepsia ⟨a ~ symptom⟩ — opposed to *eupeptic* **2 a** : gloomy or negative ⟨took a ~ view of the whole affair⟩ **b** : ILL-TEMPERED, MOROSE

[2]**dyspeptic** \"\ *n* -s : a person having dyspepsia

dys·pha·gia \də'sfāj(ē)ə\ *n* -s [NL, fr. *dys-* + *-phagia*] : difficulty in swallowing — **dys·phag·ic** \də'sfajik, (')di¦s-\ *adj*

dys·pha·sia \də'sfāzh(ē)ə\ *n* -s [NL, fr. *dys-* + *-phasia*] : loss of or deficiency in the power to use or understand language caused by injury to or disease of the brain — **dys·pha·sic** \-āzik\ *n or adj*

dys·phe·mia \də'sfēmēə\ *n* -s [NL, fr. *dys-* + *-phemia*] : STAMMERING

dys·phe·mism \'disfə,mizəm\ *n* -s [*dys-* + *-phemism* (as in *euphemism*)] : substitution of a disagreeable, offensive, or disparaging word or expression for an agreeable or inoffensive one (as of *axle grease* for *butter*, *old man* for *father*, or *heap* for *car*); *also* : a word or expression so substituted — contrasted with *euphemism*

dys·pho·nia \də'sfōnēə\ *n* -s [NL, fr. *dys-* + *-phonia*] : impairment of the voice manifested by hoarseness or other defects of phonation due to organic, functional, or psychic causes — **dys·phon·ic** \də'sfänik, (')di¦s-\ *adj*

dys·pho·ria \də'sfōrēə\ *n* -s [NL, fr. Gk, malaise, vexation, fr. *dysphoros* hard to bear (fr. *dys-* + *-phoros*, fr. *pherein* to bear) + *-ia* — more at BEAR] : a generalized state of feeling unwell or unhappy — opposed to *euphoria* — **dys·phor·ic** \də'sfórik, (')di¦s-\ *adj*

dys·pho·tic \də'sfōd·ik, (')di¦s-\ *adj* [*dys-* + Gk *phōt-*, *phōs* light + E *-ic* — more at FANCY] : having feeble illumination : occurring where the light is very limited (as at marine depths)

dys·phra·sia \dəs'frāzh(ē)ə\ *n* -s [NL, fr. *dys-* + *-phrasia*] : defective speech due to impairment of intellect

dys·pla·sia \də'splāzh(ē)ə\ *n* -s [NL, fr. *dys-* + *-plasia*] : abnormal growth or development (as of organs, tissues, or cells); *broadly* : anatomic structure that presents some abnormality as a result of such growth — **dys·plas·tic** \də'splastik, (')di¦s-\ *adj*

dysp·nea *also* **dysp·noea** \'dis(p)nēə *also* dəs(p)'nēə\ *n* -s [L *dyspnoea*, fr. Gk *dyspnoia*, fr. *dyspnoos*, *dyspnous* short of breath (fr. *dys-* + *-pnoos*, *-pnous*, fr. *pnoē* breathing, fr. *pnein* to breathe) + *-ia* — more at SNEEZE] : difficult or labored respiration — distinguished from *eupnea* — **dysp·ne·ic** *or* **dysp·noe·ic** \(')dis(p)¦nēik, dəs(p)'n-\ *adj*

dys·pro·si·um \də'sprōzēəm\ *n* -s [NL, fr. Gk *dysprositos* hard to get at (fr. *dys-* + *prositos* approachable) + NL *-ium*] : a trivalent metallic element of the rare-earth group that forms compounds which are among the most highly magnetic known, and of which the oxide is white and the salts yellowish — symbol *Dy*; see ELEMENT table

dys·rhyth·mia \dəs'rithmēə *sometimes* -th-\ *n* -s [NL, fr. *dys-* + L *rhythmus* rhythm + NL *-ia* — more at RHYTHM] : abnormal rhythm; *specif* : disordered rhythm in the brain waves as disclosed by an electroencephalogram — **dys·rhyth·mic** \(')dis¦rithmik, dəs'r- *sometimes* -th-\ *adj*

dys·se·ba·cia \,dis(s)ə'bāsh(ē)ə\ *n* -s [NL, fr. *dys-* + ISV *sebaceous* (*gland*) + NL *-ia*] : a disorder of the sebaceous glands marked by reddening and accumulation of greasy flaky scales on affected areas and often indicative of vitamin deficiency

dys·so·dia \də'sōdēə\ *n, cap* [NL, modif. of Gk *dysōdia* foul smell, fr. *dysōdēs* ill-smelling + *-ia* — more at DYSODILE] : a small genus of prairie herbs (family Compositae) found in the central part of No. America with fetid finely dissected leaves and small yellow heads of tubular and ray flowers

dys·synergia \¦di(s)+\ *also* **dys·synergy** \(¦)di(s), də+\ *n, pl* **dyssynergias** *also* **dyssynergies** [NL *dyssynergia*, fr. *dys-* + *syn-* + *-ergia*] : DYSKINESIA — **dys·synergic** \¦di(s)+\ *adj*

dys·teleological \dəs, (¦)dis+\ *adj* : of or relating to dysteleology : PURPOSELESS

dys·teleology \"+\ *n* [G *dysteleologie*, fr. *dys-* + *teleologie* teleology] **1** : absence of purpose in nature esp. as manifested in rudimentary or nonfunctional structures; *also* : the doctrine of purposelessness in nature — compare TELEOLOGY **2 a** : frustration or evasion of a normal functional end **b** : a vestigial organ

dys·thy·mia \də'sthīmēə\ *n* -s [NL, fr. Gk, despondency, fr. *dysthymos* despondent (fr. *dys-* + *-thymos*, fr. *thymos* spirit, mind, courage) + *-ia* -y — more at FUME] : morbid anxiety and depression accompanied by obsession — **dys·thy·mic** \-mik\ *adj*

dys·to·cia \də'stōsh(ē)ə\ *or* **dys·to·kia** \-ōkēə\ *n* -s [NL, fr. Gk *dystokia*, fr. *dys-* + *tokos* childbirth, parturition + *-ia*; akin to Gk *teknon* child — more at THANE] : slow or difficult labor or delivery — opposed to *eutocia* — **dys·to·cial** \də'stōsh(ē)əl\ *adj*

dys·to·nia \də'stōnēə\ *n* -s [NL, fr. *dys-* + *-tonia*] : a state of disordered tonicity of tissues (as of muscle) — **dys·ton·ic** \də'stänik, (')di¦s-\ *adj*

dys·trophic \dəs, (')dis+\ *adj* **1** : relating to or caused by faulty or imperfect nutrition **2** *of a lake* : brownish in color with much dissolved humic matter, a small bottom fauna, and a notably high oxygen consumption — compare EUTROPHIC, OLIGOTROPHIC

dys·tro·phy \'distrəfē, -fi\ *also* **dys·tro·phia** \də'strōfēə\ *n, pl* **dystrophies** *also* **dystrophias** [NL *dystrophia*, fr. *dys-* + *-trophia* -trophy] : imperfect or faulty nutrition; *specif* : any of several neuromuscular disorders — see MUSCULAR DYSTROPHY

dys·uria \də'shůrēə, dəs'yů-\ *n* -s [NL, fr. Gk *dysouria*, *dysouriē*, fr. *dys-* + *-ouria*, *-ouriē* -uria] : difficult or painful discharge of urine — **dys·uric** \də'shůrik, dəs'yů-, (')dis¦yů-\ *adj*

dy·syn·tri·bite \də'sin·trə,bīt\ *n* -s [*dys-* + Gk *syntribein* to rub together, shatter, crush (fr. *syn-* + *tribein* to rub) + E *-ite* — more at THROW] : a variety of pinite

-dy·tes \,də,tēz\ *also* **-dy·ta** \,dəd·ə, ,dətə\ *n comb form* [NL, fr. Gk *dytēs*, fr. *dyein* to enter, dive in, sink — more at ADYTUM] : diver — in generic names chiefly of birds ⟨Aptenodytes⟩

dy·tis·cid \dī'tisəd, də'-\ *n* -s [NL *Dytiscidae*] : one of the Dytiscidae : DIVING BEETLE

dy·tis·ci·dae \-sə,dē\ *n pl, cap* [NL, fr. *Dytiscus*, type genus + *-idae*] : a family of predacious aquatic beetles of oval flattened form with filamentous antennae comprising the diving beetles, being notably voracious, and feeding on aquatic insects, worms, and even young fish — see WATER DEVIL

dy·tis·cus \-skəs\ *n, cap* [NL, irreg. fr. Gk *dytikos* able to dive, fr. (assumed) Gk *dytos* (verbal of Gk *dyein* to enter, dive in, sink) + Gk *-ikos* -ic — more at ADYTUM] : the type genus of Dytiscidae including many of the larger and better-known American diving beetles

dyu·la \dē'ülə, 'dyü-\ *n, pl* **dyula** *or* **dyulas** *usu cap* **1 a** : a Negro people who live widely scattered among other peoples in the Ivory Coast, Upper Volta, and neighboring parts of West Africa, many of whom are active traders **b** : a member of such people **2** : a Mande language of the Dyula people that is widely used as a trade language in the Ivory Coast and Upper Volta — compare MANDINGO

dy·vour \'dīvər\ *n* -s [ME (Sc dial.) *dyour*] *Scot* : a man in debt : BANKRUPT

dz *abbr* dozen

dzau·dzhi·kau \(d)zaů'jē,kaů\ *adj, usu cap* [fr. *Dzaudzhikau*, U.S.S.R.] : of or from the city of Dzaudzhikau, U.S.S.R. : of the kind or style prevalent in Dzaudzhikau

dzeggetai *var of* CHIGETAI

dze·ren \(d)zə'ren, '(d)zerən\ *or* **dze·ron** \(d)zə'rän, '(d)zerən\ *also* **dze·rin** \(d)zə'rin, '(d)zerən\ *n* -s [Russ *dzeren*, fr. Kalmuck *zērn*] : a gregarious fawn-colored black-tailed gazelle (*Procapra gutturosa*) of Central Asia, Tibet, and China

dzer·zhinsk \d(y)ə(r)'zhinzk, (d)zə-, -n(t)sk\ *adj, usu cap* [fr. *Dzerzhinsk*, U.S.S.R.] : of or from the city of Dzerzhinsk, U.S.S.R. : of the kind or style prevalent in Dzerzhinsk

dzo \'(d)zō\ *or* **zho** \'zhō\ *n, pl* **dzos** *also* **dzo** *or* **zhos** *also* **zho** [Tibetan *wdzo*] : a hybrid between the yak and the domestic cow

dzun·gar \'(d)zůŋ,gär, -zəŋ-\ *n* -s *cap* : a native of Dzungaria

¹e \ˈē\ *n, pl* **e's** *or* **es** *also* **ees** \ˈēz\ *often cap, often attrib* **1 a :** the fifth letter of the English alphabet **b :** an instance of this letter printed, written, or otherwise represented **c :** a speech counterpart of orthographic *e* (as long *e* in *equal*, short *e* in *let*, or *e* in German *mehl*) **2 a :** the keynote of E major or E minor **b :** the tone E **3 :** a printer's type, a stamp, or some other instrument for reproducing the letter e **4 :** someone or something arbitrarily or conveniently designated *e* esp. as the fifth in order or class **5 a :** a grade assigned by a teacher or examiner rating a student's work as falling in the fifth highest class in a scale of 5 or 6 classes and usu. constituting a conditional pass ⟨received an *E* in Latin⟩ **b :** one graded or rated with an E ⟨one of the *E's* in the class⟩ **6 :** the base of the natural system of logarithms being the *x*th root of the expression $1+x$ as *x* approaches the limit 0 and having the approximate numerical value 2.71828 **7 :** the second-class Lloyd's rating for the quality of a merchant ship **8 :** something having the shape of the letter E **9 :** an award usu. in the form of a pennant bearing a symbolic E for excellence or exceptional merit (as in performance, production, or product) given usu. to an industrial organization by an agency of the U. S. government (as one of its armed forces)

²e *abbr, often cap* **1** earl **2** early **3** earth **4** easily **5** east; easterly; eastern **6** Easter **7** eccentricity **8** edge **9** educated **10** efficiency; efficient **11** Egyptian **12** elasticity **13** eldest **14** ell **15** empty **16** end **17** energy **18** engine; engineer; engineering **19** English **20** entrance **21** equatorial **22** erg **23** error **24** escudo **25** estimate; estimated **26** excellence; excellency; excellent **27** export **28** exposure

³e *symbol* **1** *cap* Elohistic or Ephraimitic — used in biblical criticism ⟨the *E* source in the Hexateuch⟩ ⟨an *E* psalm⟩ **2** *cap* Young's modulus of elasticity **3** *cap* electric intensity **4** *cap* illumination **5** the charge of an electron **6** *cap* oxidation-reduction potential

e- *prefix* [ME, not, out, forth, away, fr. OF & L; OF, out, forth, away, fr. L, fr. *ex-* — more at EX-] **1 a :** not ⟨*e*carinate⟩ ⟨*e*rostrate⟩ **b :** missing **:** absent ⟨*E*cardines⟩ ⟨*e*dental⟩ **2 :** out **:** on the outside ⟨*e*scribe⟩ **3 :** thoroughly ⟨*e*vaporize⟩ **4 :** forth ⟨*e*radiate⟩ **5 :** away ⟨*e*luvium⟩

ea \ˈē(ə)\ *n* -s [ME *æ, ee,* fr. OE *ēa* — more at ISLAND] *dial Eng* **:** RIVER, STREAM

ea *abbr* each

EA *abbr* **1** economic adviser **2** educational age **3** enemy aircraft

eace·worm \ˈēs,=\ *n* [E dial. *eace, easse* earthworm (fr. ME *ees* bait, carrion, fr. OE *ǣs*) + E *worm;* akin to OHG *ās* carrion, L *esca* food, bait, Lith *edesis* food, OE *etan* to eat — more at EAT] *NewEng* **:** EARTHWORM

¹each \(ˌ)ēch\ *adj* [ME *ech,* fr. OE *ǣlc;* akin to OHG *iogilīh* each; both fr. a prehistoric WGmc compound whose first and second constituents respectively are represented by OE *ā* always and by OE *gelīc* alike — more at AYE, LIKE] **:** being one of two or more distinct individuals having a similar relation and often constituting an aggregate **:** this as well as that or the next or any other of two or more separate but similar individuals ⟨a boat . . . hung from the ceiling by ropes attached at ~ end —J.G.Frazer⟩ ⟨the little chipmunk . . . with a piñon nut in ~ cheek pouch —*Nature Mag.*⟩ ⟨~ day was like every other one —H.D.Skidmore⟩ ⟨~ year the Cape has a summer inundation of people —R.W.Hatch⟩ ⟨a program flexible enough to be tailored to ~ individual employee —A.J.Nickerson⟩ ⟨giving to ~ syllable an equal stress —Max Beerbohm⟩ ⟨some publishers . . . will have books to show in ~ category —James Britton⟩

²each \"\ *pron* [ME *ech,* fr. OE *ǣlc,* fr. *ǣlc,* adj.] **1 :** each one — usu. used with reference to a preceding substantive or followed by *of* ⟨shot after shot, ~ missing by inches⟩ ⟨~ of them is to pay his own fine⟩ ⟨~ of them are to pay their own fine⟩ **2 :** each person **:** EVERYBODY — used with indefinite or vaguely implicit reference ⟨whatever their faults ~ believes in the gods of his father⟩ **3 :** all considered one by one — used following a series ⟨your songs, your thoughts, your doings, ~ divide this perfect beauty —Amy Lowell⟩

³each \"\ *adv* **:** to or for each **:** APIECE ⟨allow two helpings ~⟩ ⟨the reports cost a dollar ~⟩

each and every *pron, Midland* **:** EVERYBODY

each other *pron* [ME *ech other,* fr. OE *ǣlc ōther,* fr. *ǣlc* each + *ōther* other] **:** each of two or more in reciprocal action or relation **:** ONE ANOTHER — used esp. in the possessive case or as the object of a verb or preposition to indicate that of the two or more persons or things referred to by two or more substantives or by a plural or collective substantive any particular one performs the same action upon or stands in the same relation to one or more of the others as one or more of the others do to him ⟨army officers salute *each other*⟩ ⟨when he and I saw *each other's* faces⟩ ⟨the two are now writing to *each other* daily⟩; sometimes used with only *other* in the possessive case or as the object of a verb or preposition and with *each* in a different construction typically as subject of a verb or in apposition with the subject of a verb ⟨*each* at *other* looked —John Keats⟩ ⟨*each* for *other* they were born —R.W.Emerson⟩

ead *abbr* [L *eadem*] the same

-e·ae \ˌē,ē, ˈē,ē\ *n pl suffix* [NL, fr. L (fem. pl. of *-eus* -eous)] **:** those belonging to (such a group) — in biological taxonomic names of groups (as tribes) larger than the genus ⟨Diatom*eae*⟩ ⟨Florid*eae*⟩ ⟨Ured*ineae*⟩

¹ea·ger \ˈēgə(r)\ *adj, sometimes* -ER/-EST [ME *egre* sharp, sour, eager, fr. OF *aigre,* fr. L *acer* sharp, sour, spirited, zealous; akin to Gk *akros* highest, extreme, Skt *aśri* corner, edge — more at EDGE] **1 :** marked of its kind by reason of notable development of some quality (as sourness, savor, fierceness, violence, chill, or vigor) — obs. except of weather phenomena ⟨an ~ breeze ruffled the lake⟩ ⟨a nipping and an ~ air —Shak.⟩ **2 :** having or characterized by strong and urgent interest, desire, ardor, enthusiasm, or impatience ⟨an ~ lad determined to make his mark⟩ ⟨they were ~ to get on their way before the storm broke⟩ **3** *obs, of metal* **:** BRITTLE **:** lacking in ductility or temper

syn AVID, KEEN, ANXIOUS, AGOG, ATHIRST: EAGER is likely to imply ardor, enthusiasm, and impatient reluctance at delay ⟨the parent, moreover, is likely to be too *eager* and too much interested in his child's progress —Bertrand Russell⟩ ⟨when the boys saw one another taking their seats, they were as *eager* as before they had been slow; and they hustled each other at the bottom of the table —Anthony Trollope⟩ AVID may have suggestions of intense desire or insatiability ⟨the westward-moving settlers, *avid* for land —D.E.Clark⟩ ⟨outward satiety such as follows a too *avid* thirst for pleasure —G.W.Russell⟩ ⟨she watched him eagerly, *avid* for any gleam of surprise or disapproval —Margery Allingham⟩ KEEN suggests sharp and lively interest marked by lasting intensity and ready responsiveness ⟨I was making the acquaintance of my shipmates, and so *keen* on learning my new duties that the days were all too short —C.B.Nordhoff & J.N.Hall⟩ ⟨she was a *keen* horticulturist, and won prizes at all the local flower shows —John Buchan⟩ ANXIOUS may suggest deep desire intermixed with worry and fear of frustration or disappointment ⟨the average immigrant was pathetically *anxious* to become an American —Allan Nevins & H.S.Commager⟩ ⟨the schoolmasters may be pathetically *anxious* to guide boys right, and to guard them from evil —A.C.Benson⟩ ⟨I am particularly *anxious* in this lecture not to assume the role of Christian apologist —W.R. Inge⟩ AGOG suggests excited or impatient expectancy ⟨awaiting him impatiently, *agog* with curiosity —Fred Majdalany⟩ ⟨a greenhorn who arrives in Australia, all *agog* to begin life as a station owner —Leslie Rees⟩ ATHIRST may suggest yearning or longing ⟨on naturalism and materialism a constant war is waged by one or two great souls *athirst* for pure aesthetic rapture —Clive Bell⟩ ⟨older boys and girls eager for the universities, all of them *athirst* for experience —*Saturday Rev.*⟩

²eager *var of* EAGRE

eager beaver *n* **:** one who is overzealous, overdiligent, and impatient not only to perform his part with promptness but to volunteer for more ⟨was an *eager beaver,* always doing more than he was told, always studying — Joseph Wechsberg⟩

ea·ger·ly *adv* [ME *egrely,* fr. *egre* + *-ly*] **:** in an eager manner **:** with urgent desire or enthusiasm

ea·ger·ness *n* -ES [ME *egrenesse,* fr. *egre* + *-nesse* -ness] **1 :** the quality or state of being eager **:** ARDOR, ENTHUSIASM **2 :** an act or instance of being eager

¹ea·gle \ˈēgəl\ *n* -s [ME *egle,* fr. OF *egle, aigle,* fr. L *aquila*] **1 :** any of various large diurnal birds of prey (family Accipitridae) noted for their strength, size, graceful figure, keenness of vision, and powers of flight — see AQUILA, BALD EAGLE, GOLDEN EAGLE, HARPY EAGLE, IMPERIAL EAGLE, SEA EAGLE **2 :** any of various figures or representations of an eagle esp. when used as an emblem or symbol: as **a :** the standard of the ancient Romans **b :** the seal or standard of any nation having an eagle as emblem (as the U.S. or France under the Bonapartes) **c** *or* **eagle lectern :** a lectern whose brass or wooden book support is shaped like an eagle with outspread wings **d :** one of a pair of silver insignia of rank worn by a colonel in the army, marine corps, or air force and by a captain in the navy or coast guard **e :** a green conventionalized figure of an eagle that is used as the identifying symbol of the fifth suit in 5-suit packs of playing cards manufactured in the U. S. **f** *or* **eaglebird** \ˈ==,=\ **:** a compartment on some roulette wheels marked with an eagle and equivalent to the zero and double zero of other wheels **3 :** a gold coin of the U. S. bearing an eagle on the reverse and worth 10 dollars, first issued 1795, last issued 1933 **4 :** CLOVE BROWN 2 **5 :** a golf score of two strokes less than par on any hole but a par-three hole

eagle 2d

²eagle \"\ *adj* **:** like that of an eagle ⟨hooked ~ nose⟩ ⟨a bright ~ glance⟩; *esp, of the eye* **:** keen-sighted, bright, and piercing

³eagle \"\ *vt* -ED/-ING/-S **:** to shoot (a hole in golf) in two strokes under par ⟨*eagled* the 510-yard par five 13th hole —*United Press International*⟩

eagle boat *n* **:** an antisubmarine warship smaller than a destroyer

eagle dance *n* **:** a widespread American Indian ritual dance esp. for rain among the Pueblos and for cure and peace among the Iroquois that is derived from the calumet dance and is performed by two or four men commonly with artificial wings bound to their arms and with movements which are imitative of eagles

eagle eye *n* **1 :** the ability to see or observe with exceptional keenness **2 :** one that sees or observes with exceptional keenness ⟨her sewing would never pass that *eagle eye* without stern criticism —Flora Thompson⟩

eagle-eyed \ˈ==ˌ=\ *adj* **:** keen of vision or insight ⟨the *eagle-eyed* scout watched the distant dust cloud⟩ ⟨an *eagle-eyed* appraisal of the situation⟩

eagle fern *n* **:** a common brake (*Pteridium aquilinum*)

eagle-hawk \ˈ==,=\ *n* **1 :** any of numerous tropical American birds of prey (family Accipitridae) intermediate in size between the typical hawks and eagles and often crested **2** *Austral* **:** WEDGE-TAILED EAGLE

eagle-kite \ˈ==,=\ *n* **:** BRAHMINY KITE; *also* **:** any of several closely related birds

eagle owl *n* **:** any of numerous large horned owls constituting the genus *Bubo; specif* **:** a very large Old World owl (*B. bubo*) that is widely distributed in Europe and northern Asia

eagle ray *n* **:** any of several large active stingrays of the family Myliobatidae having broad pectoral fins like wings and being represented by several species that are widely distributed esp. in warm seas — see SPOTTED EAGLE RAY

eagle scout *n* **:** a boy scout who has been awarded 21 merit badges — compare STAR SCOUT

eaglestone \ˈ==,=\ *n* **:** a concretionary nodule of clay ironstone about the size of a walnut that the ancients believed an eagle takes to her nest to facilitate egg-laying

ea·glet \ˈēglət\ *n* -s [MF *aiglet,* fr. *aigle* eagle + *-et*] **:** a young eagle

eagle vulture *n* **:** a large black-and-white western African bird (*Gypohierax angolensis*) intermediate in some respects between eagles and vultures and feeding on the fruit of oil palms and on carrion (as fish) — called also *vulturine sea eagle*

eaglewood \ˈ==,=\ *n* [prob. trans. of F *bois d' aigle,* prob. trans; (influenced by Pg *águia* eagle) of Pg *pao d'águila,* lit., agalloch wood] **:** AGALLOCH

ea·gre *or* **ea·ger** *also* **ae·gir** \ˈēgə(r), ˈāg-\ *n* [alter. of earlier *higre,* fr. (assumed) ME *higre* (whence ML *higra*)] **:** a tidal flood or flow **:** BORE

eal·der·man *or* **eal·dor·man** *archaic var of* ALDERMAN

ea·ling \ˈēliŋ\ *adj, usu cap* [fr. *Ealing,* municipal borough in England] **:** of or from the municipal borough of Ealing, England **:** of the kind or style prevalent in Ealing

ean \ˈēn\ *vb* -ED/-ING/-S [ME *enen,* fr. OE *ēanian* — more at YEAN] *dial Eng* **:** YEAN

-ean — see -AN

E and OE *abbr* errors and omissions excepted

E and P *abbr* extraordinary and plenipotentiary

eanling *n* -s [*ean* + *-ling*] *obs* **:** YEANLING

EAON *abbr* except as otherwise noted

¹ear \ˈi(ə)r, ˈiə\ *n* -s [ME *ere,* fr. OE *ēare;* akin to OHG *ōra* ear, ON *eyra,* Goth *auso,* L *auris,* Gk *ous,* Lith *ausis*] **1 a :** the characteristic vertebrate organ of hearing and equilibrium consisting in the typical mammal of a sound-collecting outer ear separated by a membranous drum from a sound-transmitting middle ear which in turn is separated from a sensory inner ear by membranous fenestrae, the whole being variously simplified in lower vertebrates in which the outer ear is frequently absent, the middle often modified or absent, and the inner in some cases reduced to the structures concerned with equilibrium **b :** any of various organs (as an otocyst or a chordotonal organ) capable of detecting vibratory motion esp. of frequencies higher than several vibrations per second that is taking place in the surrounding medium whether this detection takes the form of hearing as commonly understood or not — compare HEARING, LABYRINTHINE SENSE; ORGAN OF CORTI **2 :** the external ear of man and most mammals **3 a :** the sense or act of hearing ⟨a keen ~⟩ **:** perception of sound **b :** refinement or acuity of the sense of hearing ⟨a nice ~ for pitch⟩ **c :** the ability to catch and retain or reproduce music by hearing it ⟨to play by ~⟩; *often* **:** the ability to imagine aurally a tone or group of tones with correct relative pitch ⟨a violinist must have a good ~⟩ **4 :** something resembling in shape or position a mammalian ear: as **a :** a projecting part (as a lug, plate, or handle) or either of a pair of such parts that is suitable for lifting, transporting, adjusting, or fixing in position the object of which it is a part (as the handle of a pitcher or platter or tub, the cannon of a bell, or the leather pull for tightening the cord of a drum) **b (1) :** a process on an animal body **:** AURICLE (2) **:** either of a pair of tufts of lengthened feathers on the head of certain birds (3) **:** the tuft of specialized feathers associated with the ear opening in some birds **c :** CROSSETTE 1 **d :** either of the lateral scrolled ends of the cresting of a Chippendale chair or mirror **e :** a projecting tag inadvertently formed during deep-drawing of sheet metal **f :** a device usu. in the form of a grooved bronze casting for supporting a trolley wire **g :** a projection on certain printed letters (as the right-hand projection of the upper part of *g*) **h :** the projecting part of a typesetter's composing rule — called also *neb* **i :** either of two right-angled projections at the uppermost edge of a linotype matrix **j :** one of the boxes or spaces in the upper corners of the front page of a newspaper usu. containing advertising of the paper itself or a weather forecast **5 a :** HEARING, AUDIENCE; *esp* **:** compassionate and favorable attention ⟨give ~ to my plea⟩ ⟨I seek the merciful ~ of our Lord⟩ **b :** AWARENESS, ATTENTION ⟨when her kindness came to the ~ of her enemies, they were bowed with shame⟩ ⟨it has come to my ~ that you have missed several classes⟩ **6 :** the stiff reflexed end of an oriental composite bow — **by the ears** *adv* **:** in or into discord ⟨set the whole neighborhood *by the ears*⟩ — **in one ear and out the other** *or* **in at one ear and out at the other :** through the mind without making an impression ⟨everything you say to him goes *in one ear and out the other*⟩ — **on one's ear 1** *slang* **:** into a state of irritation or rage ⟨his insults really put me *on my ear*⟩ **2 :** head over heels **:** UNCEREMONIOUSLY ⟨if you ever made that mistake you went out *on your ear* — Nicholas Monsarrat⟩ — **to the ears** *adv* **:** to the limit of capacity ⟨drunk *to the ears*⟩ — **up to the ears** *or* **up to one's ears :** heavily or deeply involved **:** implicated or concerned to a greater degree than is safe or proper ⟨*up to his ears* in the conspiracy⟩ ⟨*up to the ears* in debt⟩

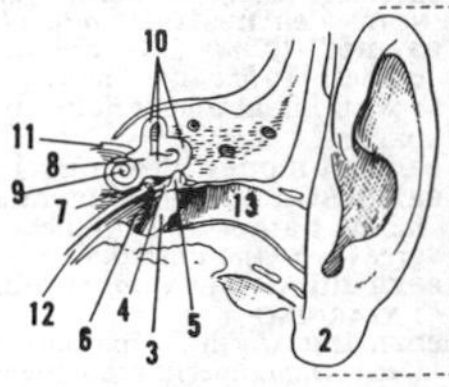

ear: *1* pinna, *2* lobe, *3* tympanic membrane, *4* incus, *5* malleus, *6* tympanum, *7* stapes, *8* vestibule, *9* cochlea, *10* semicircular canals, *11* auditory nerve, *12* eustachian tube, *13* auditory meatus

²ear \"\ *vt* -ED/-ING/-S [ME *eren,* fr. OE *erian;* akin to OHG *erien* to plow, ON *erja,* Goth *arjan,* L *arare,* Gk *aroun,* Lith *arti*] *now dial Eng* **:** to plow or till **:** CULTIVATE

³ear \"\ *n* -s [ME *ere, er,* fr. OE *ēar;* akin to OHG *ahir* ear, ON *ax,* Goth *ahs* ear, L *acus* chaff, Gk *achnē* chaff, OE *ecg* edge — more at EDGE] **:** the fruiting head of a cereal (as Indian corn, wheat, or rye) including both the kernels of grain and protective and supporting structures ⟨plump golden ~*s* of wheat rustling in the breeze⟩

⁴ear \"\ *vi* -ED/-ING/-S [ME *eren,* fr. *ere, er,* n.] **:** to form ears in the course of growing ⟨this corn ~*s* well⟩ — often used with *up* ⟨the rye should soon be ~*ing up*⟩

⁵ear \(ˌ)ār, (ˌ)er, ər\ *var of* ¹ERE

⁶ear \ˈi(ə)r, ˈiə\ *dial var of* YEAR

earache \ˈ=,=\ *n* **:** an ache or pain in the ear **:** OTALGIA

ear·age \ˈirij\ *n* -s **:** length of ears measured from tip to tip across the top of the head — used of certain dogs and rabbits

ear banger *n* [so called fr. the practice of talking as much as possible to someone who is influential or has rewards at his disposal] *slang* **:** a person who is overanxious to please his superiors or seniors

earbash \ˈ=,=\ *vt* -ED/-ING/-ES *Austral* **:** HARANGUE, LECTURE ⟨a treat to have an authentic account after having been ~*ed* by those other blowhards —*Sydney (Australia) Bull.*⟩

earbob \ˈ=,=\ *n* -s **:** EARRING

ear-brisk \ˈ=,=\ *adj, of a horse* **:** carrying the ears pricked forward

ear canker *n* [¹*ear*] **:** CANKER 7a

earclip \ˈ=,=\ *n* **:** an earring with a clip fastener

earcockle \ˈ=,==\ *n* **:** a disease of wheat caused by a nematode (*Anguina tritici*) that invades the developing ear and causes galls to form

ear conch *n* [¹*ear*] **:** PINNA 2b

ear covert *n* [¹*ear*] **:** EAR 4b(3)

ear crystal *n* [¹*ear*] **:** OTOLITH, OTOCONIUM

ear defender *n* **:** a device (as an earplug) designed to lessen the transmission of excessive or damaging sound to the auditory receptors of the inner ear

eardrop \ˈ=,=\ *n* **1** *also* **eardropper** \ˈ=,=\ **:** EARRING; *esp* **:** one with a pendant **2 eardrops** *pl but sing or pl in constr* **a :** a plant of the genus *Dicentra* (esp. *D. spectabilis*) — called also *bleeding heart* **b :** FUCHSIA 2 **c :** BUCKWHEAT VINE **3 eardrops** *pl* **:** medicine in liquid form to be instilled by drops into the external auditory meatus

eardrop tree *n* **:** CONACASTE

eardrum \ˈ=,=\ *n* [¹*ear*] **:** TYMPANUM 1a(1)

ear dust *n* [¹*ear*] **:** OTOCONIA

¹eared \ˈi(ə)rd, ˈiəd\ *adj* [ME *ered,* fr. *ere* ear + *-ed* — more at ¹EAR] **1 :** having ears; *usu* **:** having external ears esp. of a specified character — often used in combination ⟨long-*eared*⟩ ⟨pink-*eared*⟩ ⟨flop-*eared*⟩ **2 :** having projecting processes: as **a :** having tufts of feathers resembling ears in form or position ⟨an ~ owl⟩ **b** *of a heraldic shield* **:** having small triangular projections at the two upper corners

²eared \"\ *adj* [ME *ered,* past part. of *eren* to ear — more at ⁴EAR] **1** *of cereal plants* **:** having ears usu. of a specified character ⟨~ wheat stalks bending in the breeze⟩ — used chiefly in combination ⟨golden-*eared* grain⟩ ⟨full-*eared* corn⟩ **2 :** being in ear **:** come into ear ⟨an ~ field of corn⟩

eared grebe *n* **:** a rather small grebe (*Podiceps nigricollis*) having yellow ear tufts of fan shape and a black neck and being represented by various subspecies in Europe, Asia, southern Africa, and western No. America — called also *black-necked grebe*

eared pheasant *n* **:** any of several pheasants (genus *Crossoptilon*) having a tuft of bright feathers projecting from each side of the head and being native to eastern and central Asia but now often bred as ornamentals

eared seal *n* **:** any of various seals comprising the family Otariidae, including the sea lions and fur seals, having the hind limbs independent and mobile so that they are able to move with some facility on land, and being distinguished from other seals by small but well-developed external ears

earflap \ˈ=,=\ *n* [¹*ear*] **1 :** PINNA 2b **2 :** a warm covering for the ear; *esp* **:** an extension on the lower edge of a cap that may be folded up or down

earflap 2

earflower \ˈ=,==\ *n* [¹*ear*] **:** SACRED EARFLOWER

ear fly *n* [¹*ear*] **:** DEERFLY

ear·ful \ˈi(ə)r,fu̇l, ˈiə,-\ *n* -s **1 a :** an astonishing and usu. unexpected oral response ⟨the probers got an ~ —Vance Packard⟩ **b :** an outpouring of news or gossip often unwanted **2 :** a sharp reprimand **:** TALKING-TO

ear fungus *n* [¹*ear* + *fungus;* fr. the shape of the sporophores] **:** a fungus of the order Auriculariales; *esp* **:** JEW'S-EAR

earhead \ˈ=,=\ *n* **:** the ear of grain — used esp. of millets and sorghums

earhole \ˈ=,=\ *n* [¹*ear*] **:** the orifice of the external auditory meatus; *broadly* **:** the meatus itself

ear·ing *or* **ear·ring** \ˈir(,)iŋ, ˈirēŋ\ *n* -s [perh. fr. ¹*ear* + *-ing*] **1 :** a line used to fasten the upper corners of a sail to the yard or gaff — called also *head earing* — see SAIL illustration **2 :** a line for hauling the reef cringle to the yard — called also *reef earing* **3 :** a line fastening the corners of an awning (as on a ship) to the rigging or stanchions

earjewel \ˈ=,==\ *n* [¹*ear*] **:** JEWELWEED

earl \ˈər(-ə)l, ˈəl, ˈəil\ *n* -s [ME *erl,* fr. OE *eorl* warrior, nobleman; akin to OS *erl* man, ON *jarl* warrior, nobleman ranking next to a king, and perh. to OE *rīsan* to rise — more at RISE] **1** *in Anglo-Saxon England* **a :** a man of noble rank **b :** the governor of one of the great divisions of England established by Canute **2** *obs* **:** a feudal noble or prince **:** COUNT **3 :** a member of the third grade of the peerage in Great Britain ranking below a marquess and above a viscount — compare COUNTESS

ear·land·ite \ˈirlən,dīt, ˈər-\ *n* -s *often cap E* [Arthur *Earland* †1958 Eng. civil servant + E *-ite*] **:** a mineral $Ca_3(C_6H_5O_7)_2 \cdot 4H_2O$ consisting of a hydrous citrate of calcium found in ocean-bottom sediments from the Weddell sea

earlap \ˈi(ə)r,lap, ˈiə,-\ *n* [ME *erelappe,* fr. OE *ēarlæppa,* fr. *ēar-* (fr. *ēare* ear) + *læppa* lap — more at ¹EAR, LAP] **:** EARFLAP

earl·dom \ˈərldəm, ˈəl-, ˈəil-\ *n* -s [ME *erldom,* fr. OE *eorldōm,* fr. *eorl* earl + *-dōm* -dom] **1 :** the domain or territory of an earl or countess **2 :** the rank or dignity of an earl or countess

ear-leaved umbrella tree \ˈ=,=-\ *n* **:** a slender tree (*Magnolia fraseri*) having oblong spatulate leaves that are auriculate at the base

ear·less \ˈi(ə)rləs, ˈiəl-\ *adj* **1 :** lacking ears **2 :** deficient in auditory acuity esp. in respect to music

earless seal *n* **:** a seal of the family Phocidae — compare EARED SEAL

ear·let \-lət\ *n* -s [¹*ear* + *-let*] **1 :** a small ear (as of a plant leaf) **2 :** the tragus esp. when exceptionally large (as in the ears of some bats)

earlier on *adv* **:** PREVIOUSLY, BEFORE ⟨I told you yes *earlier on*⟩

earlike \ˈ=,=\ *adj* **:** projecting like or otherwise like an ear

earlily *adv* [*early,* adj. + *-ly*] *obs* **:** EARLY

ear·li·ness \ˈərlēnəs, ˈəl-, ˈəil-, -lin-\ *n* -ES **:** the quality or state

E F

of being early; *esp* **:** the ability of a plant to produce the product (as flowers or fruit) for which it is cultivated at an earlier period in the growing season than is usual of related plants ⟨a sweet corn of superior ~ and good flavor⟩

earl marischal *n, pl* **earls marischals** *or* **earl marischals** *or* **earls marischal :** a marshal of Scotland from the 15th century to 1716 — compare EARL MARSHAL; see MARISCHAL

earl marshal *n, pl* **earls marshals** *or* **earl marshals** *or* **earls marshal** [ME *erl marshal,* fr. *erl* earl + *marshal*] **1 :** a marshal of England who since 1194 has always been at least an earl in rank, who in medieval times was a principal military officer of the crown, but who in more recent times has been chiefly an attendant upon the sovereign at the opening and closing of Parliament arranging the order of state processions (as for coronations and royal marriages and funerals) and as head of the College of Arms appointing kings of arms, heralds, and pursuivants **2 :** a former marshal of Scotland or of Ireland when either office was held by an earl — compare EARL MARISCHAL

earl marshal's court *n, usu cap E&M, often cap C* **:** the English court of chivalry since the time when it has been held before the earl marshal alone — called also *Marshal's court;* compare COURT OF THE CONSTABLE AND MARSHAL

earlobe \ˈ=,=\ *n* **1 :** the pendent part of the pinna of the ear of man or certain apes **2 :** a fleshy appendage below the ear of a fowl

earlock \ˈ=,=\ *n* **:** a lock or curl of hair hanging in front of the ear ⟨with ~*s* down to the collarbone —I.M.Lask⟩

earl of coventry *n, usu cap E&C* **:** SNIPSNAPSNORUM

earl palatine *n* **:** COUNT PALATINE 2

earl·ship \ˈərl,ship, ˈə̄l-,ˈəil-\ *n* **:** the rank or dignity of an earl

¹ear·ly \ˈərlē, ˈə̄l-, ˈəil-\ *adv* -ER/-EST [ME *erly,* fr. OE *ǣrlīce,* fr. *ǣr* early, soon + *-līce* -ly — more at ERE] **1 a :** near the beginning of a period of time ⟨this great and salutary reaction began ~ in the present century —H.T.Buckle⟩ ⟨awoke ~ in the morning⟩ **b :** near the beginning of a course, process, or series ⟨is too ~ to guess the outcome⟩ ⟨~ in his senatorial career⟩ **c :** in a distant past time ⟨were men of education and business experience and their stamp on the village gave it a degree of culture that ~ eliminated many frontier crudities —*Amer. Guide Series: Minn.*⟩ ⟨~ discovered the use of fire⟩ **2 a :** before the expected or usual time ⟨retired from business quite ~ for a lawyer⟩ ⟨the train arrived ~⟩ **b** *archaic* **:** in the near future **:** SOON ⟨that from these may grow a hundredfold, who, having learnt thy way, ~ may fly the Babylonian woe —John Milton⟩ **c :** at a time sooner than related forms ⟨these apples bear ~ and heavy⟩

²early \"\ *adj* -ER/-EST [ME *erly,* fr. *erly,* adv.] **1 :** of, relating to, or occurring near the beginning of a period of time ⟨in the ~ Renaissance⟩ ⟨the ~ morning⟩ **b :** of, relating to, or occurring near the beginning of a development, movement, or series ⟨work on the thymus gland is still in an exceedingly ~ experimental stage —Morris Fishbein⟩ ⟨the ~ days of the West⟩ **c (1) :** distant in past time ⟨the ~ character of the state⟩ **(2) :** PRIMITIVE ⟨~ art forms⟩ ⟨~ tools found in recent excavations⟩ **2 a :** occurring before the expected or usual time ⟨taking an ~ walk before breakfast —W.F.De Morgan⟩ ⟨planned an ~ dinner before the concert⟩ ⟨an ~ death⟩ **b :** occurring in the near future ⟨other commitments making it impossible for him to schedule an ~ production of the play —*Current Biog.*⟩ ⟨hope for an ~ improvement in international relations⟩ **c :** maturing or producing sooner than related forms ⟨~ flowers and vegetables —Geoffrey Boumphrey⟩ ⟨an ~ sweet corn⟩

³early \"\ *n* -ES **:** one that arrives, produces, or is ready early; *esp* **:** a plant that matures its economic part (as flowers or fruit) more rapidly than the average

early ambulation *n* **:** a technique of postoperative care in which a patient gets out of bed and engages in light activity (as sitting, standing, or walking) as soon as possible after an operation

early american *adj, usu cap E&A* **1 :** built or produced during the colonial period in the American colonies — used chiefly of buildings, furniture, and domestic articles **2 :** of the type built, produced, or used in the American colonies

early bird *n* [so called fr. the proverb "the early bird catches the worm"] **1 :** an early riser **2 :** one that arrives beforehand esp. before possible competitors ⟨a bargain sale for *early birds*⟩

early bite *n, Brit* **:** pasturage adapted to or in condition for grazing early in the season

early blight *n* **:** any of several blights of plants in which symptoms appear early in the season: as **a :** a leaf spot esp. of the potato and tomato that is caused by a fungus (*Alternaria solani*) — compare LATE BLIGHT **b :** a leaf spot of celery caused by a fungus (*Cercospora apii*) — see CELERY BLIGHT

early coralroot *n* **:** a small parasitic orchid (*Corallorhiza trifida*) of the eastern U. S. having flowers with a 3-lobed lip

early-day \ˈ==ˈ=\ *adj* **:** of an earlier or former period ⟨the *early-day* settlers of New England⟩

early english style *or* **early english** *n, usu cap both E's* **:** the first of the pointed Gothic architectural styles used in England (as from 1180 to about 1250) — see ARCHITECTURE table

early foot *n* **:** a vigorous start (as in a race or contest) — used esp. of racehorses

early germ *n* **:** a cleaving zygote up to the completion of blastulation

early goldenrod *n* **:** a smooth early flowering No. American goldenrod (*Solidago juncea*) with oval lanceolate toothed leaves and yellow flower heads in branched clusters

early hawkweed *n* **:** RATTLESNAKE WEED 1

ear·ly·ish \ˈərlēish, ˈə̄l-,ˈəil-, -li-ish\ *adj* **:** somewhat early; *often* **:** early enough ⟨don't go; it's ~ yet⟩

early meadow parsnip *or* **early parsnip** *n* **:** GOLDEN MEADOW PARSNIP

early meadow rue *n* **:** a delicate No. American spring-flowering meadow rue (*Thalictrum dioicum*) with greenish to purple apetalous flowers

early on *adv* **1** *Brit* **:** at or during an early stage (as in a process) ⟨the reasons were obvious *early on* in the experiment⟩ **2** *Brit* **:** SOON ⟨he could see very *early on* that it would be impossible⟩

early saxifrage *n* **:** a small sticky white-flowered herb (*Saxifraga virginiensis*) common on rocky ledges in eastern No. America

early scorpion grass *n* **:** a small dry-land forget-me-not (*Myosotis virginica*) of eastern No. America with hairy foliage and white flowers

early wake-robin *n* **:** a low perennial white-flowered trillium (*Trillium nivale*) of the southeastern U. S.

early-warning radar *n* **:** a set or line of radar sets operating in air defense on the perimeter or outward from the defended area to give the earliest possible warning of approaching airplanes

early winter cress *also* **early cress** *n* **:** a biennial European weedy cress (*Barbarea verna*) that is naturalized widely in No. America, has pinnatifid leaves and deep yellow flowers, and is sometimes used for a salad plant or potherb

earlywood \ˈ==,=\ *n* **:** SPRINGWOOD

ear mange *n* **:** canker of the ear esp. in cats and dogs usu. caused by a rather large long-legged strictly parasitic ear mite (*Otodectes cynotes*)

¹earmark \ˈ=,=\ *n* [ME *ere mark,* fr. *ere* ear + *mark* — more at ¹EAR, MARK] **1 :** a mark of identification (as a cropping or slitting) on the ear esp. of a domestic animal **2 :** a distinguishing or a characteristic mark **:** an indicative sign ⟨all the ~*s* of poverty⟩ ⟨a book with the ~*s* of a doctoral dissertation⟩ — **under earmark :** EARMARKED ⟨gold *under earmark* for a foreign account⟩

common earmarks of cattle: *1* crop, *2* oversquare, *3* undersquare, *4* swallow fork, *5* steeple fork, *6* overslope, *7* underslope, *8* split, *9* underbit, overbit

²earmark \"\ *vt* **1 a :** to mark (as livestock) with an earmark **b :** to mark (something) in a distinguishing manner esp. as one's property ⟨dissipation ~*s* a man⟩ ⟨Satan ~*s* his own⟩ **2 a :** to designate or set aside (funds) for a specific use or owner ⟨the part of income that is ~*ed* for financing expansion⟩ ⟨a gift ~*ed* for a new dormitory⟩ — used esp. of gold held by one central bank for a new dormitory⟩ — used esp. of gold held by one central bank for and as the property of another central bank or government **b :** to designate, hold, or recognize as the property of another ⟨the postmastership is traditionally ~*ed* for a leading politician⟩ ⟨goods ~*ed* for future delivery⟩

ear-minded \ˈ=ˈ==\ *adj* **:** having one's mental imagery predominantly auditory **:** inclined to remember and think of things in terms of their sounds **:** AUDILE — compare EYE-MINDED

ear mite *n* **:** any of various mites attacking the ears of mammals — compare CANKER 7a

ear mold *n* **1 :** any of various fungi (as *Diplodia zeae*) that resemble molds and attack ears of grain; *esp* **:** fungus of the genus *Fusarium* that causes diseases of Indian corn **2 :** a disease caused by an ear mold

earmuff \ˈ=,=\ *n* **:** one of a pair of ear coverings connected by a strip of cloth, elastic band, or flexible metal strap and worn as protection against cold **2 :** EARFLAP

earmuff

¹earn \ˈərn, ˈə̄n,ˈəin\ *vb* -ED/-ING/-S [ME *ernen,* fr. OE *earnian;* akin to OHG *arnōn* to reap, ON *önn* working season, Goth *asans* harvest, OSlav *jesenĭ* autumn] *vt* **1 a :** to receive as equitable return for work done or services rendered **:** have accredited to one as remuneration **b :** to come to be duly worthy of or entitled to as remuneration for work or services ⟨he has ~*ed* his promotion, but we cannot give it to him now⟩ **c :** to bring in by way of return — used of income-producing property ⟨money in bonds may ~ less but it is more secure⟩ ⟨this block of stocks should ~ $5000 a year⟩ **2 a :** to come to be duly worthy of or entitled or suited to by way of reward, praise, penalty, or censure ⟨she had once ~*ed* a scolding from her nurse by filling her stockings with mud —G.B.Shaw⟩ ⟨his wasteful heedless ways ~*ed* him the name of a spendthrift⟩ **b :** to receive as ostensibly due by way of praise or blame **c :** to obtain (as a degree or a number of credits) at an educational institution by fulfilling the requirements and meeting definite standards **d :** to play in such a way as to score (as a point or run) in a sports contest; *esp* **:** to score (a run in baseball) without benefit of error by the opponent ~ *vi* **:** to obtain income by labor or as a return on capital ⟨so many students must now ~ in order to attend school⟩ ⟨stocks that do not ~ regularly are rarely a good investment⟩ **syn** see DESERVE

²earn *vb* -ED/-ING/-S [prob. alter. of *yearn*] *obs* **:** to yearn or grieve

earn *abbr* earnings

earned income *n* [*earned* fr. past part. of ¹*earn*] **:** income (as wages, salary, professional fees, or commissions) that results from the personal labor or services of an individual — compare UNEARNED INCOME

earned premium *n* **:** the pro rata share of a total insurance premium for the expired portion of a policy term

earned run average *n* **:** the average number of earned runs per game scored off a pitcher determined by dividing the total of earned runs scored against him by the total number of innings pitched and multiplying by nine

earned surplus *n* **:** the net accumulated balance of earnings of a corporation that remains after deducting losses, distributions to stockholders, and transfers to capital stock accounts and that includes appropriated surplus (as reserve for contingencies) as well as unappropriated surplus — called also *retained income*

earn·er \ˈərnər; ˈə̄nə(r, ˈəin-\ *n* -S **:** one that earns esp. money ⟨however trite they may be Westerns are among the motion-picture industry's best ~*s*⟩ — often used in combination ⟨wage *earners*⟩

¹ear·nest \ˈərnə̇st, ˈə̄n-,ˈəin-\ *n* -S [ME *ernest,* fr. OE *eornost;* akin to OHG *ernust* seriousness, ON *ern* vigorous, Goth *arniba* safely and prob. to OE *rīsan* to rise — more at RISE] **1 :** a serious and intent mental state; *usu* **:** grave and intense attention, interest, or purpose **:** SERIOUSNESS — usu. used with *in* and often contrasted with *jest* ⟨and given in ~ what I begged in jest —Shak.⟩ ⟨are you sure you're in ~ about this⟩ **2** *archaic* **:** serious matter or expression

²earnest \"\ *adj* [ME *ernest,* fr. OE *eornoste,* fr. *eornost,* n.] **1 :** characterized by or proceeding from an intense and serious state of mind **:** not light, flippant, playful, or jesting ⟨~ attention⟩ ⟨an ~ plea⟩ **2 :** of a grave or important nature **:** not trivial ⟨life is real, life is ~ —H.W.Longfellow⟩ **syn** see SERIOUS

³earnest \"\ *adv, obs* **:** EARNESTLY

⁴earnest \"\ *n* -S [ME *ernest,* prob. by folk etymology (influence of ME *ernest* seriousness) fr. *ernes,* modif. of OF *erres,* pl. of *erre* earnest, fr. L *arra,* short for *arrabon-, arrabo,* fr. Gk *arrhabōn,* fr. Heb *'ērābōn*] **1 :** something of value given by a buyer to a seller to bind a bargain — compare EARNEST MONEY, GOD'S PENNY **2 :** a token or installment of what is to come **:** PLEDGE ⟨the Resurrection which was an ~ of the coming redemption of the world —G.W.H.Lampe⟩ ⟨his whole expression was an ~ of his good intentions⟩ **syn** see PLEDGE

earnestful *adj* [ME *ernestful,* fr. *ernest,* n. + *-ful*] *obs* **:** EARNEST — **earnestfully** *adv, obs*

ear·nest·ly *adv* [ME *ernestly,* fr. OE *eornostlīce,* fr. *eornoste* earnest + *-līce* -ly — more at ²EARNEST] **:** in an earnest manner **:** with intent and serious mind **:** not lightly, casually, or flippantly

earnest money *n* [⁴*earnest*] **:** money paid as earnest

ear·nest·ness *n* -ES **:** intent and serious state or quality (as of mind) **:** ardor and firmness (as of purpose) ⟨he worked with great ~⟩ ⟨the unshakable ~ of their outlook⟩

earn·ful \ˈərnfəl\ *adj* [prob. alter. of *yearnful*] *now dial Eng* **:** YEARNING

earn·ing \ˈərniŋ, ˈə̄n-,ˈəin-, -nēŋ\ *n* -S [ME *erning* merit, fr. OE *earnung* merit, recompense, fr. *earnian* to earn + *-ung* -ing — more at ¹EARN, -ING] **1 earnings** *pl* **a :** something (as wages or dividends) earned as compensation for labor or the use of capital ⟨his ~*s* never amounted to more than $2000 a year⟩ ⟨corporation ~*s* are up⟩ **b :** the balance of revenue for a specific period that remains after deducting related costs and expenses incurred — compare PROFIT **2 :** the act or process of acquiring (as a reward or honor) or of fitting oneself to receive (as a commendation or rebuke) ⟨the ~ of his high position was not easy⟩ ⟨he seemed to set himself doggedly to the ~ of his degree⟩

earning asset *n* [*earning* fr. pres. part. of ¹*earn*] **:** an asset (as a loan or security) of a bank on which interest is received — usu. used in pl.

earning power *n* [*earning* fr. gerund of ¹*earn*] **:** the relative ability of an individual or an organization to command earnings in return for services or goods ⟨a corporation with good *earning power*⟩ ⟨the general rise in all *earning power* has tended to divorce the worker from the specific job by minimizing the importance of wage differentials —*Management Rev.*⟩

earns *pres 3d sing of* EARN

ea·rock \ˈē,räk, ˈērək\ *n* -S [ScGael *eireag* & IrGael *eireog*] *Scot & Irish* **:** PULLET

earphone \ˈ=,=\ *n* -S **:** any device that converts electrical energy into sound waves and is worn over or inserted into the auditory opening

earpick \ˈ=,=\ *n* [ME *erepik,* fr. *ere* ear + *pik* pick — more at ¹EAR, PICK] **:** a device often of precious metal for removing wax or foreign bodies from the ear

earpiece \ˈ=,=\ *n* **1 :** a piece (as of a helmet or cap) intended to cover and protect the ear **2 :** a part of an instrument (as a stethoscope or hearing aid) to which the ear is applied; *esp* **:** EARPHONE **3 :** one of the two sidepieces that support eyeglasses by passing over or behind the ears

ear piercer *n* [¹*ear*] **:** one that pierces the ear

ear-piercing \ˈ=ˈ==\ *adj* **:** shrill and irritating to the ear ⟨an *ear-piercing* shriek⟩

earplug \ˈ=,=\ *n* **1 :** an ornament often of spool shape inserted in the lobe of the ear esp. to distend it **2 :** a device of pliable material for insertion into the outer opening of the ear (as for protection against water or to deaden sound)

¹earring \ˈi(,)riŋ, ˈirēŋ, ˈir,riŋ\ *n* -S [ME *erering,* fr. OE *ēarhring,* fr. *ēar-* (fr. *ēare* ear) + *hring* ring — more at ¹EAR, RING] **:** an ear ornament with or without a pendant attached to a pierced earlobe by a loop of wire or to an unpierced earlobe by a screw or a clip

earrings: *1* for pierced ears, *2* screw type, *3* clip type

²earring *var of* EARING

earringed \-ŋd\ *adj* [¹*earring* + *-ed*] **:** wearing earrings

ear rot *n* **:** a condition marked by decay or molding of ears of Indian corn and caused usu. by fungi of the genera *Diplodia, Fusarium,* or *Gibberella*

ears *pl of* EAR, *pres 3d sing of* EAR

earscrew \ˈ=,=\ *n* **:** an earring with a screw fastener

ear shell *n* [so called fr. the shape] **:** ABALONE

earshot *also* **earreach** \ˈ=,=\ *n* **:** the range within which the unaided voice may be heard

ear snail *or* **ear shell** *n* [so called fr. the shape] **:** any gastropod mollusk of the family Ellobiidae

ear snail

earsplitting \ˈ=,==\ *adj* **:** distressingly or intolerably loud or shrill **:** DEAFENING ⟨the ice let go with an ~ roar⟩ **syn** see LOUD

earspool \ˈ=,=\ *n* **:** a spool-shaped earplug worn buttoned through a hole in the earlobe esp. by the ancient Hopewell and Copena people

ear stone *n* [¹*ear*] **:** OTOLITH

eartab \ˈ=,=\ *n* [¹*ear*] **:** EARFLAP 2

ear tag *n* [¹*ear* + *tag*] **:** a metal identification tag attached to the ear of an animal

ear-tag \ˈ=,=\ *vt* [*ear tag*] **:** to mark (an animal) for future identification with an ear tag

¹earth \ˈərth, ˈə̄th,ˈəith\ *n* -S *often attrib* [ME *erthe,* fr. OE *eorthe;* akin to OHG *erda* earth, ON *jörth,* Goth *airtha,* OHG *ero* earth, Gk *eraze* to earth, W *erw* acre] **1 a :** the fragmental material composing part of the surface of the globe **:** SOIL, GROUND ⟨give him a little ~ for charity —Shak.⟩ — usu. distinguished from *bedrock* **b :** soil for cultivating ⟨good ~ in a sheltered valley⟩ ⟨a clayey ~ difficult to drain⟩ **c :** one of the four elements of the alchemists **2 :** the sphere of mortal life comprising the world with its lands and seas as distinguished from spheres of spirit life — compare HEAVEN, HELL **3 a :** areas of land uncovered by water **b :** the solid footing formed of earth ⟨good to feel the ~ under his feet again⟩ **c :** the solid materials that make up the physical globe **4** *archaic* **:** a particular region of the world **:** COUNTRY, LAND ⟨would I had never trod this English ~ —Shak.⟩ **5** *often cap* **:** the planet upon which we live and which being about 93 million miles from the sun is the third in order of distance from the sun and which having a diameter at the equator of 7927 miles is the fifth in size among the planets **6 a :** the people of the planet earth **b :** the mortal body of man — distinguished from *soul, spirit* **c :** the pursuits, interests, and allurements of earthly life **:** worldly as distinguished from spiritual concerns **7 :** the burrow of a burrowing animal **8 a :** a difficultly reducible metallic oxide (as alumina, zirconium oxide, yttrium oxide) formerly classed as an element — see ALKALINE EARTH, RARE EARTH **b :** EARTH COLOR ⟨red ~⟩ **c :** a clay or substance resembling clay used chiefly as an adsorbent ⟨active ~*s*⟩ — see BLEACHING CLAY, FULLER'S EARTH **9** *chiefly Brit* **:** GROUND 7 — **on earth :** among numberless possibilities **:** EVER — used as an intensive ⟨where *on earth* can he be?⟩ ⟨I can't imagine who *on earth* would do such a thing⟩ ⟨what *on earth* shall we do?⟩

²earth \"\ *vb* -ED/-ING/-S [ME *erthen,* fr. *erthe,* n. — more at ¹EARTH] *vt* **1** *now dial Brit* **:** BURY, INTER **2 :** to hide (as oneself) or cause to hide (as an animal) in the earth or in a burrow or den **3 :** to draw soil about (plants) **:** cultivate so as to throw soil toward (as a row crop) **:** BANK, RIDGE — often used with *up* ⟨potatoes should be ~*ed* up before blooming⟩ ⟨soil should be kept out of the heart when ~*ing* celery⟩ **4** *chiefly Brit* **:** GROUND *vt* 6 ~ *vi* **:** to hide in the ground (as in an earth or den) **:** go to ground — used esp. of a hunted animal

³earth \", ˈi(ə)rth, ˈiəth\ *n* -S [ME *erth, erthe,* fr. OE *eorth, yrth,* fr. *erian* to plow — more at ²EAR] *now dial Brit* **:** an act of plowing **:** a stirring or tilling of soil in preparation for planting

earth almond *n* **:** CHUFA

earth apple *n* **1 :** POTATO **2 :** JERUSALEM ARTICHOKE

earth-ball \ˈ=,=\ *n* **:** any of certain usu. tuberous subterranean fruiting bodies of fungi (as a truffle or the hard-skinned fruit of members of the family Sclerodermataceae)

earthborn \ˈ=,=\ *adj* **1 :** coming into life by emergence from the ground — used chiefly of certain mythological persons ⟨the ~ sons of the dragon's teeth⟩ **2 :** born on this earth **:** of mortal race **:** HUMAN — compare ANGELIC, IMMORTAL **3 :** associated with earthly life or occasioned by earthly objects ⟨~ cares and sorrows⟩; *broadly* **:** arising from or typical of earth ⟨~ storms⟩

¹earthbound \ˈ=,=\ *adj* [¹*earth* + *bound* (fastened)] **1 a :** fast in or to the soil ⟨~ roots⟩ **b :** restricted to land or to the surface of earth ⟨armies are no longer ~⟩ **c :** restricted to the planet Earth ⟨man is still an ~ creature⟩ **2 :** lacking in freedom (as of expression) or in imagination ⟨a competent but ~ performance⟩; *sometimes* **:** EARTHY, HOMELY ⟨~ peasant speech⟩ **3 :** bound by earthly interests **:** lacking in spiritual quality ⟨an ~ outlook⟩ ⟨the ~ soul of man⟩

²earthbound \"\ *adj* [¹*earth* + *bound* (going)] **:** on the way to or toward earth ⟨an ~ meteor⟩ ⟨~ cosmic rays⟩

earth bread *n* **:** MANNA LICHEN 1; *often* **:** a food prepared from one of these lichens (esp. *Lecanora esculenta*)

earthbred \ˈ=,=\ *adj* **1 :** bred in or on the earth **2 :** lacking in elevated or spiritual quality; *often* **:** EARTHY, LOW, VULGAR

earth closet *n, chiefly Brit* **:** a privy in which earth is used as a covering or as an absorbing or deodorizing agent

earth club *n* [¹*earth* + *club* (staff)] **:** SQUAWROOT 1

earth coal *n, obs* **:** COAL 3a — distinguished from *charcoal*

earth color *n* **:** a colored mineral (as an ocher) used as a pigment

earth current *n* **:** an electric current flowing through the ground that is set up by either natural or man-made differences of potential — called also *ground current*

earth eating *n* **:** GEOPHAGY

earth·en \ˈərthən, ˈə̄th|, ˈəith|, -th|\ *also* **earth·ern** \|ə(r)n\ *adj* [*earthen* fr. ME *erthen,* fr. *erthe* earth + *-en; earthern* alter. of *earthen* — more at ¹EARTH] **1 a :** made of earth ⟨an ~ dam⟩ ⟨~ walls rammed firm⟩ **b :** made of fired clay ⟨glazed ~ tiles⟩ ⟨an ~ jug⟩ **2 :** characteristic of earth esp. in human or mortal quality **:** EARTHLY

earthenware \ˈ==,=\ *n, often attrib* **:** vessels and other utensils or ornaments made of low-fired clay that is slightly porous, opaque, and lacking sonority and commonly covered with a nonporous glaze — compare CHINA, PORCELAIN

earthfall \ˈ=,=\ *n* **:** LANDSLIDE

earthfast \ˈ=,=\ *adj* **:** EARTHBOUND

earth flax *n* **:** AMIANTHUS

earthflow \ˈ=,=\ *n* **:** a landslide consisting of unconsolidated surface material that moves down a slope when saturated with water — compare MUDFLOW

earth foam *n* [trans. of F *écume de terre*] **:** soft or earthy aphrite

earth god *n* **:** a deity concerned with vegetation and fertility and usu. with the underworld

earth goddess *n* **:** a goddess concerned with vegetation and fertility and usu. with the underworld

earth hog *n* [trans. of obs. Afrik *aardvark*] **:** AARDVARK

earth house *n* [ME *erthehous,* fr. OE *eorthhūs,* fr. *eorth-* (fr. *eorthe* earth) + *hūs* house] **:** a dwelling built into or covered with earth: as **a :** PICTS' HOUSE **b :** EARTH LODGE

earth hunger *n* **:** a desire or craving to possess or control land

earth·ian \-thēən, -th-\ *n* -S **:** an inhabitant of the earth

earthier *comparative of* EARTHY

earthiest *superlative of* EARTHY

earth·i·ly \-thəlē, -li *sometimes* -th-\ *adv* **:** in an earthy manner

earth inductor *n* **1 :** an inclinometer (sense 1) whose indications depend on the current generated in a coil revolving in the earth's magnetic field **2** *or* **earth inductor compass** : INDUCTION COMPASS

earth·i·ness \-thēnəs, -thin- *sometimes* -t͟h-\ *n* -ES [ME *erthynesse,* fr. *erthy* earthy + *-nesse* -ness] **:** the quality or state of being earthy: as **a :** a realistic or matter-of-fact or human quality (as of a literary or dramatic production) **b :** an anomalous or off flavor (as of wines or certain foods) suggestive of soil

earthing *pres part of* EARTH

earth lichen *n* **:** a lichen growing in soil; *esp* **:** any of various ascolichens (genus *Baeomyces*) with fruiting bodies filled with cottony hairs or nearly solid

earthlight *var of* EARTHSHINE

earthlike \'=,=\ *adj* **:** resembling earth or something earthly ⟨an ~ atmosphere⟩ ⟨drab ~ coloring⟩

earth·li·ness \-thlēnəs, -lin-\ *n* -ES **:** the quality or state of being earthly ⟨the deep original materialism or ~ of human nature itself —Walter Pater⟩

earth·ling \-thliŋ, -lēŋ\ *n* -S **1 :** an inhabitant of the earth; *esp* **:** a mortal human **2 :** a worldly-minded person **:** WORLDLING

earth-lit \'=,=\ *adj* **:** illuminated by earthshine

earth lodge *n* **:** a dwelling (as a hogan) constructed of earth or sod, often supported on a wooden frame, and often placed partially below the surface of the ground

earth louse *n* [trans. of L *pediculus terrae*] **:** any of numerous aphids that feed on the roots of plants

earth·ly \-thlē, -li\ *adj* [ME *erthely, erthly,* fr. OE *eorthlīc,* fr. *eorth-* (fr. *eorthe* earth) + *-līc* -ly] **1 a :** characteristic of or belonging to this earth — often distinguished from *heavenly* ⟨no ~ sovereign can do what he pleases —M.R. Cohen⟩ ⟨there could be a new order based on vital harmony and the ~ millenium might approach —E.M.Forster⟩ **b :** relating to man's actual life on this earth **:** REALISTIC, FACTUAL, WORLDLY **:** not ideal, spiritual, or utopian **2** *archaic* **:** EARTHEN **3 :** existing, living, or occurring on or in the ground ⟨airplane travel would have remained a merely minor quantitative improvement over ~ locomotion —Maya Deren⟩ **4 :** conceivable according to actualities and facts **:** POSSIBLE ⟨there is no ~ doubt that men degenerate —J.B.Cabell⟩ ⟨not an ~ chance to win⟩

syn TERRESTRIAL, TERRENE, EARTHY, MUNDANE, WORLDLY, SUBLUNARY: EARTHLY is generally an opposite for *heavenly* or *spiritual* ⟨the high gods, who dwell remote from the fret and fever of this *earthly* life —J.G.Frazer⟩ ⟨we felt that the holy calm that lay like sunshine over the wasted face and form was only an *earthly* token and symbol of the calm that was to reign forever —Bram Stoker⟩ TERRESTRIAL, sometimes a sonorous or scientific close synonym for EARTHLY, is often an opposite for *celestial.* It may be used to designate land in contrast to water or air or to indicate planets nearer the sun in contrast to those more distant ⟨it was probably not the first time that struggles for *terrestrial* power were carried on in terms of celestial ideology; it certainly has not been the last —L.A.White⟩ ⟨strictly *terrestrial,* being from the nature of its claws unable to climb trees—James Stevenson-Hamilton⟩ TERRENE is an uncommon synonym for EARTHLY and for TERRESTRIAL in general nonscientific applications ⟨and so the empyrean element, lying smothered under the *terrene,* and yet inextinguishable there, made sad writings —Thomas Carlyle⟩ ⟨all that was mixed and reconciled in Thee . . . of high with low, celestial with *terrene* —William Wordsworth⟩ EARTHY differs from EARTHLY in centering attention on the soil or ground of the earth rather than on the earth as a planet or as the habitat of mankind; it may imply grossness, crudeness, concern with material things, and lack of anything exalted ⟨he smelled the *earthy* fragrance rising up out of the furrows —Pearl Buck⟩ ⟨these native passion plays are more *earthy* than religious, are enlivened with a good many broadly comic touches —Green Peyton⟩ ⟨with much *earthy* dross in her, she was yet preeminently a creature of "fire and air" —John Buchan⟩ MUNDANE is opposed to *spiritual, lofty, exalted,* or *elevated;* it centers attention on practical affairs and concerns, immediate objectives, base or basic needs and pleasures, and occas. routine or humdrum activity ⟨she did not allow them to talk of *mundane* affairs on these expeditions to and from church —Archibald Marshall⟩ ⟨the real meaning of the play is evidently the triumph of the spiritual over the *mundane* —Grenville Vernon⟩ ⟨such *mundane* activities as washing dishes or driving an automobile —Ralph Linton⟩ WORLDLY may suggest indifference to and obliviousness about matters spiritual and attention to success, pleasure, sophistication, and gain ⟨the obvious thing to say of her was that she was *worldly;* cared too much for rank and society and getting on in the world—which was true in a sense —Virginia Woolf⟩ ⟨our medieval universities were founded not for laymen but for monks and clerics whose business was primarily not with *worldly* affairs but with the eternal hereafter —M.R.Cohen⟩ SUBLUNARY is a rather literary synonym for TERRESTRIAL or, sometimes, for EARTHLY ⟨the quakes and *sublunary* conflicts of this negligible earth —L.P.Smith⟩ ⟨the contrast between the transcendental, immutable, and eternal heavens, the home of the blest, on the one hand, and the *sublunary* sphere of the earth, the scene of birth, change, decay, and death on the other —G.C.Sellery⟩

earthly-minded \'==!==\ *adj, archaic* **:** WORLDLY-MINDED

earth·man \-th,man, -mən\ *n, pl* **earthmen :** a human native or resident of the planet Earth

earth metal *n* **:** a metal whose oxide is classed as an earth

earth mother *n, often cap E&M* **:** the earth viewed (as in primitive theology) as the divine source of terrestrial life **:** the female principle of fertility

earth movement *n* **:** differential movement of the earth's crust **:** elevation or subsidence of the land **:** DIASTROPHISM, FAULTING, FOLDING

earthmover \'=,==\ *n* **:** a machine (as a bulldozer or power shovel) for excavating, pushing, or transporting large quantities of earth (as in road building)

earthnut \'=,=\ *n* [ME *erthenote,* fr. OE *eorthnutu,* fr. *eorth-* (fr. *eorthe* earth) + *nutu, hnutu* nut — more at NUT] **1 :** any of various roots, tubers, or subterranean pods: as **a :** the tuber of a common southern European plant (*Conopodium denudatum*) of the family Umbelliferae having the flavor of roasted chestnuts **b :** CHUFA **c :** PEANUT **d** *also* **earthnut pea :** the root of the heath pea **2 :** any plant producing earthnuts **3 :** TRUFFLE

earthnut oil *n* **:** PEANUT OIL

earth oil *n, archaic* **:** PETROLEUM

earth people *n, usu cap E&P* **:** the living humans and the witches and ghosts who according to Navaho religion inhabit the profane world — called also *Earth Surface People;* contrasted with *Holy People*

earth physics *n pl but sing or pl in constr* **:** GEOPHYSICS

earth pig *n* [trans. of obs. Afrik *aardvark*] **:** AARDVARK

earth pillar *also* **earth pyramid** *n* **:** a column of unconsolidated earth materials that is formed by differential erosion and that typically tapers upward and is often capped by a stone — called also *demoiselle*

earth pitch *n* [trans. of G *erdpech*] **:** MALTHA 2a

earth plate *n* **:** GROUND PLATE 2

earth plum *n* **1 :** any of several leguminous plants (genera *Astragalus* and *Geoprumnon*) of the southwestern U.S. and adjacent Mexico with pods which suggest plums and are edible when unripe **2 :** the pod of an earth plum

earth quadrant *n* **:** a fourth of the earth's circumference

earthquake \'=,=\ *n, often attrib* [ME *erthequake,* fr. *erthe* earth + *quake*] **:** a shaking or trembling of the earth that accompanies mountain building or other crustal movements including those caused by deposition of heavy loads of sediment on the sea bottom; that usu. has an actual double amplitude of vibration of less than one millimeter, though a range of 76 millimeters is on record and the amplitude is commonly increased in unconsolidated surface material; and that is divisible into the two major classes volcanic and tectonic according to the major precipitating factor — see AFTERSHOCK, FOCUS 7, FORESHOCK

earth·quaked \-kt\ *or* **earth·quak·en** \-kən\ *adj* [*earthquaked* fr. *earthquake* + *-ed; earthquaken* fr. *earthquake* + *-en* (as in *shaken*)] **:** shaken by earthquakes **:** subject to earthquakes

earthquake insurance *n* **:** insurance against loss resulting from damage to buildings and their contents by earthquake, volcanic eruption, or both

earthquake-proof \'==,=\ *adj* **:** designed to withstand the shattering effect of an earthquake ⟨an *earthquake-proof* building⟩

earthquake sea wave *n* **:** TSUNAMI

earthquake wave *n* **:** a seismic wave

earthquaking \'=,==\ *adj* [partly fr. [1]*earth* + *quaking,* pres. part. of *quake;* partly fr. *earthquake* + *-ing*] **1 :** causing the earth to shake ⟨an ~ roar⟩ **2 :** EARTHQUAKED

earthquaky \'=,==\ *adj* [*earthquake* + *-y*] **:** suggesting the effects or the characteristic movement of an earthquake

earths *pl of* EARTH, *pres 3d sing of* EARTH

earth science *n* **1 :** a science (as geology, geography, geophysics, geomorphology, geochemistry, meteorology, or oceanography) that deals with the earth or with one or more of its parts — often used in pl. **2 :** any one of the earth sciences

earthshaker \'=,==\ *n* **:** something outstanding in merit, importance, or stature

earthshaking \'=,==\ *adj* **:** of fundamental importance ⟨~ proposals⟩

earthshine *or* **earthlight** \'=,=\ *n* **:** sunlight reflected by the earth that faintly illuminates the dark part of the moon and is best seen during the moon's crescent phases

earthshock \'=,=\ *n* **:** an earthquake esp. when sharply localized ⟨the ~ following a heavy explosion⟩

earth-smoke \'=,=\ *n* [trans. of ML *fumus terrae*] **:** FUMITORY

earth sounds *n pl* **:** audible deep-pitched vibrations accompanying an earthquake that are prob. caused by the transmission of earth vibrations to the air

earth spirit *n* [prob. trans. of G *erdgeist*] **1 :** the earth personified either poetically or as a deity supposed to live in or under the earth **2 :** a humanoid long-lived or immortal entity (as a gnome)

earthstar \'=,=\ *n* **:** a fungus of the genus *Geastrum* in form suggesting a puffball with a double peridium the outer layer of which splits into the shape of a star and the inner one forms a ball containing the dustlike spores

earth stopper *n* **:** one that stops up fox holes prior to a hunt

earth surface people *n, usu cap E&S&P* **:** EARTH PEOPLE

earth table *n* **:** the course of stones in a building next above the ground — called also *ground table*

earth tide *n* **:** a periodic alteration in the conformation of the earth's crust caused by the same forces that produce ocean tides

earth tilting *n* **:** a change in attitude of any portion of the earth's surface whether temporary or undulatory (as in some earthquakes) or permanent (as in areas of block faulting); *esp* **:** one in which the inclination of the surface is increased

earthtongue \'=,=\ *n* [trans. of NL *Geoglossum*] **:** any fungus of a genus *Geoglossum* having ascomata that resemble the sporophores of the simpler club fungi and grow on decaying logs or damp soil

earth tremor *n* **:** an earthquake esp. of low or moderate intensity

earth·ward \'=wə(r)d\ *or* **earth·wards** \-dz\ *adv* [ME *ertheward,* fr. *erthe* earth + *-ward*] **:** toward the earth

earth wave *n* **1 a :** an elastic vibration of the material of the earth **b :** a visible undulation of alluvial or unconsolidated material at the surface of the earth that has been reported to occur in severe earthquakes **2 :** an immobile undulation on the earth's surface

earth wax *n* [trans. of G *erdwachs*] **:** OZOKERITE

earth wire *n* **:** GROUND WIRE 1

earth wolf *n* [trans. of Afrik *aardwolf*] **:** AARDWOLF

earthwork \'=,=\ *n* **1 :** a field fortification made chiefly of earth **2 a :** the operations connected with excavations and embankments of earth (as in preparing foundations of buildings or in constructing canals, railroads) **b :** an embankment or other construction made of earth

earthworm \'=,=\ *n* [ME *ertheworm,* fr. *erthe* earth + *worm*] **1 :** any terrestrial annelid worm of the class Oligochaeta; *esp* **:** any of numerous widely distributed tapering segmented hermaphroditic worms that constitute the family Lumbricidae and that lack true appendages but move through the soil by means of setae, feed on decaying organic matter, and are an important factor in loosening and aerating the upper layers of soil in which they dwell — called also *angleworm* **2** *archaic* **:** a mean sordid person **:** WORM

earthy \'ərthē, 'ōth-,'əith-, -thi *sometimes* -t͟h-\ *adj* -ER/-EST [ME *erthy,* fr. *erthe* earth + *-y*] **1 :** consisting of or resembling earth **:** having a property or properties characteristic of soil: as **a :** suggesting or resembling earth in a manner directly perceptible by the senses ⟨a stale ~ smell⟩ ⟨wine with an ~ flavor⟩ ⟨clad in dull ~ hues⟩ **b** *of a mineral* **:** without luster or dull and roughish to the touch **c :** containing earthlike impurities **2 a** *archaic* **:** of or relating to the earth **:** TERRESTRIAL; *esp* **:** WORLDLY — distinguished from *spiritual, heavenly* **b :** characteristic of or associated with mortal life on the earth **:** not predominantly spiritual, ideal, or ethereal ⟨a vigorous ~ woman⟩ **3 :** characterized by realistic material attitudes ranging from the matter-of-fact and practical to the unrefined, gross, and low ⟨my anger and disgust at his gross ~ egoism —W.H.Hudson †1922⟩ **4 :** having a cold and dry complexion **:** predominating in the elements earth and water — used with reference to phenomena and bodies as understood by the old natural philosophers and of signs of the zodiac; compare HUMOR **5 :** relating to an earth oxide **syn** see EARTHLY

earthy cobalt *n* **:** ASBOLITE

ear tick *n* **:** any of several ticks infesting the ears of mammals, including man; *esp* **:** SPINOSE EAR TICK

ear tree *n* [prob. trans. of Nahuatl *cuauhnacaztli*] **:** CONACASTE

ear trumpet *n* **:** a trumpet-shaped instrument used for collecting and intensifying sounds to aid a person with defective hearing

ear tuft *n* **:** EAR 4b(2)

ear wagon *n* **:** a wagon having a bangboard

ear warden *n* [[1]ear] **:** EARPLUG

earwax \'=,=\ *n* [ME *erewax,* fr. *ere* ear + *wax* — more at [1]EAR] **:** CERUMEN

[1]**ear·wig** \'i(ə)r,wig, 'iə,-\ *n* -S [ME *erwigge,* fr. OE *ēarwicga,* fr. *ēar-* (fr. *eare* ear) + *wicga* insect; prob. fr. a belief that the insect creeps into the human ear — more at [1]EAR, VETCH] **1 a :** any of numerous insects of the order Dermaptera having slender many-jointed antennae, a pair of large forceps at the end of the body the use of which is unknown, the fore wings when wings are present modified into elytra, and nymphs that are very similar to the adults **b :** any of various small centipedes (as those of the genus *Geophilus*) **2 a** *archaic* **:** a whispering busybody **:** TOADY, FLATTERER **b :** EAVESDROPPER

[2]**earwig** \"\ *vt* **earwigged; earwigged; earwigging; earwigs :** to annoy or attempt to influence by private talk

ear·wig·gy \-wigē\ *adj* [[1]*earwig* + *-y*] **:** full of earwigs ⟨an ~ hostelry on the outskirts of the town —W.J.Locke⟩

earwitness \'=!==\ *n* **:** a person who does or can testify to something heard by himself

earworm \'=,=\ *n* **:** any of certain larval insects (as the corn earworm) that feed in the developing maize ear

eas *pl of* EA

[1]**ease** \'ēz\ *n* -S [ME *ese,* fr. OF *aise* comfort, opportunity, fr. L *adjacent-, adjacens* neighboring place, fr. *adjacent-, adjacens,* pres. part. of *adjacēre* to lie near — more at ADJACENT] **1 :** the state of being comfortable: as **a :** freedom from pain or discomfort ⟨with all the ~ of wearing an old, comfortable . . . dressing gown —H.V.Gregory⟩ ⟨a special seat mounting for ~ in riding —*Motor Transportation in the West*⟩ **b :** freedom from care or worry **:** TRANQUILLITY, SECURITY ⟨~ of mind⟩ ⟨there is ~ in the family and in the village —Abram Kardiner⟩ **c :** freedom from labor, effort, inconvenience, or burden **:** RELAXATION ⟨shallow waters where she could swim with ~ —Agnes Repplier⟩ ⟨she took her ~ on Sunday⟩ **d :** freedom from embarrassment, constraint, or formality **:** NATURALNESS ⟨he experiences ~ among his friends⟩ ⟨with an ~ of manner sportsmen are apt to have —A.W.Long⟩ **2 :** relief from or mitigation of discomfort, pain, constraint, or obligation ⟨the medicine brought almost instant ~⟩ ⟨there seemed to him to be no ~ from the burdens of life⟩ **3 :** FACILITY, EFFORTLESSNESS ⟨she rides a horse with ~⟩; *esp* **:** stylistic smoothness in literary or artistic expression ⟨the ~ and polish of the best 18th century English prose⟩ **4 a :** EASEMENT 3 **b :** an allowance of fullness that is usu. placed across the back shoulders, over the bust, and about the hips in a garment to permit free motion of the body **5 :** an act of easing (as of a restriction) or state of being eased (as of a market) ⟨credit ~ tends to promote buying⟩; *esp* **:** a lowering trend in prices ⟨the grain market showed considerable ~ last week⟩ — **at ease 1 :** free from pain or discomfort ⟨after the doctor's visit, the patient felt more *at ease*⟩ **2 a** *or* **at one's ease :** free from restraint or formality **:** RELAXED ⟨the quiet and the solitude of the place put the visitor *at his ease*⟩ **b** (1) *of a man in military ranks* **:** standing silently with the right foot in place — often used as a command to assume this position (2) *of a man marching* **:** silent but relaxed from attention and free to break step — often used as a command to proceed in this manner **3** *or* **at one's ease :** as and when one wishes ⟨he was allowed to complete the task *at his ease*⟩ **syn** see REST

[2]**ease** \"\ *vb* **eased; eased; easing; eases** [ME *esen,* fr. OF *aaisier* & *aisier;* OF *aaisier* fr. *a-* (fr. L *ad-*) + *aisier,* fr. *aise,* n.] *vt* **1 a :** to free from something that pains, disquiets, or burdens **:** relieve esp. from toil or care ⟨*eased* and comforted the sick⟩ — usu. used with *of* ⟨let him ~ you of your troubles⟩ **b** *obs* **:** to provide with food and lodging **:** ENTERTAIN **c :** to take something away from easily **:** ROB ⟨a pickpocket slipped up and *eased* him of his purse⟩ **2 :** to take away **:** LESSEN, ALLEVIATE ⟨took an aspirin to ~ the pain⟩ ⟨we cannot ~ taxes while every special interest demands more money⟩ **3 a :** to lessen the pressure or tension of (as by slackening, lifting, or shifting) ⟨~ the spring gently⟩ **:** adjust by gradual movements so as to relieve strain or avoid injury or damage ⟨*easing* himself into his chair⟩ **:** maneuver gently or carefully ⟨they *eased* the heavy block into position⟩ — often used with a directional word ⟨~ in that line⟩ ⟨~ your clutch in slowly⟩ ⟨he *eased* the bolt in carefully⟩ **b :** to moderate or reduce esp. in amount, intensity, or rate of performance ⟨*easing* the flow from the faucet until he could hear what she said⟩ **:** make more gentle, gradual, or slow ⟨*eased* his climb with a brief rest by the side of the path⟩; *often* **:** to cause to slow down or stop ⟨~ the car down to 20 miles an hour on this curve⟩ **c :** to adjust (fullness in a garment) by pulling, gathering, or pleating so that a longer and a shorter part join smoothly; *broadly* **:** to provide (a garment) with requisite ease **4 :** to make less difficult **:** FACILITATE **5 a :** to bring (a ship) into position to meet a wave bow on (as by putting the helm alee or by regulating the sails) **b :** to let (a helm or rudder) come back a little after having been put hard over **~** *vi* **1 :** to give freedom or relief (as from pain or discomfort) **:** lessen pain or oppressiveness ⟨a hot bath often ~s and relaxes⟩ **2 :** to move or pass with freedom from abruptness or awkwardness or with little resistance — sometimes used with a directional word (as *along, over*) **3 :** MODERATE, SLACKEN, DIMINISH; *also* **:** STOP, DESIST — now usu. used with an expletive (as *off, up*)

eased-up \'=!=\ *adj* **1 :** relieved from strain or tension **:** RELAXED ⟨she looked comfortable and *eased-up*⟩ **2** *of a racehorse* **:** not running all out

ease·ful \'ēzfəl\ *adj* [ME (Sc) *esful,* fr. ME *es, ese* ease + *-ful* — more at [1]EASE] **1 :** suitable for affording ease or rest **:** RESTFUL ⟨a quiet ~ corner⟩ ⟨~ plenty⟩ **2 :** characterized by or full of ease ⟨a poised ~ manner⟩ ⟨a placid ~ life⟩ — **ease·ful·ly** \-fəlē\ *adv*

ea·sel \'ēzəl\ *n* -S *often attrib* [D *ezel* ass, donkey, fr. MD *esel;* akin to OE *esol* ass, OS & OHG *esil,* Goth *asilus;* all fr. a prehistoric Gmc word borrowed with modification fr. L *asinus* ass — more at ASS] **:** a frame for supporting something at a desired angle: as **a :** a wooden, metal, or plastic frame to hold a canvas upright or inclined at a proper level for the painter's convenience in working **b :** a display frame for advantageous exhibition (as of a painting, a piece of china, or a poster) **c :** a frame for holding photographic paper flat in enlarging or copying **d :** the sheet of plain glass on which the constituent pieces of a work of stained glass are first assembled

easel a

easelback \'==,=\ *n* **:** a back by which a flat object (as a framed picture) may be made to stand upright or suitably inclined usu. by means of a tab or prop made fast with the back above and pulled out at an angle below — **easel-backed** \'==!=\ *adj*

ea·seled \'ēzəld\ *adj* **:** mounted on an easel

ease·less \'ēzləs\ *adj, archaic* **:** subject to no relief or rest **:** UNCEASING

easel painting *n* **1** *or* **easel picture :** a painting of a size and on a material suitable for framing — often distinguished from *mural* **2 :** the practice of painting easel paintings

ease·ment \'ēzmənt\ *n* -S [ME *esement,* fr. MF *aaisement* & *aisement;* MF *aaisement* fr. *aaise-* (fr. *aaisier*) + *-ment;* MF *aisement* fr. *aise-* (fr. *aisier*) + *-ment*] **1 :** an act or means of easing or relieving (as from pain, discomfort, or burdens) ⟨a long needed ~ of taxation⟩ ⟨an ~ of international tension⟩ **2** *obs* **:** food and lodging **:** ENTERTAINMENT **3 :** a curved structural member used to prevent abrupt change of direction (as in a baseboard or handrail) **4 :** an incorporeal usu. nonprofitable interest granted by deed or created by will, deed, or prescription that is held by one person in land owned by another and that entitles its holder to a specific limited use or enjoyment (as the right to cross the land or to have a view continue unobstructed over it) — compare SERVITUDE

easement appurtenant *n* **:** an easement that is intended to and does benefit the possessor of a particular tract of land in the physical use and enjoyment made of that land and that is described as appurtenant to that land

easement curve *n* **:** a curve (as on a highway) whose degree of curvature is varied either uniformly or according to a definite pattern to give a gradual transition between a tangent and a simple curve which it connects or between two simple curves

easement in gross : an easement (as the right to take or sell water from another's land) that exists for the benefit of the holder independently of his possession of any land and that does not benefit any particular land possessed by the holder

ease off *vt* **:** to lessen the tension of **:** SLACKEN ⟨*eased off* the rope⟩ **~** *vi* **:** to become less tense, vigorously active, or engaged **:** decrease in intensity ⟨she lowered the flame and the boiling *eased off*⟩ ⟨as I grow older I find I have to *ease off* now and then⟩ ⟨the weather bureau said the storm . . . would *ease off* today —*Associated Press*⟩

eas·er \'ēzə(r)\ *n* -S **:** one that eases: as **a :** a bar for slackening threads in a loom **b** *or* **easer rail :** a railroad rail placed close to the running rail to provide a bearing for the overhang of worn wheel treads

eases *pl of* EASE, *pres 3d sing of* EASE

easied *past of* EASY

easier *comparative of* EASY

easies *pres 3d sing of* EASY

easiest *superlative of* EASY

eas·i·ly \'ēz(ə)lē, -li\ *adv* [ME *esily,* fr. *esy* easy + *-ly*] **1 :** in an easy manner **:** without difficulty, discomfort, or reluctance **:** READILY, SMOOTHLY, GENTLY **2 :** without question **:** by far ⟨~ the most original thinker of his generation⟩ ⟨this is ~ the best course⟩

eas·i·ness \'ēzēnəs, -zin-\ *n* -ES [ME *esinesse,* fr. *esy* easy + *-nesse* -ness] **1 :** freedom from difficulty or hardship ⟨the ~ of the trip astonished them⟩ ⟨the ~ of the earlier puzzles⟩ **2 a :** freedom from harshness **:** gentle indulgent quality **:** KINDNESS ⟨a certain ~ of temper⟩ **b :** relaxed easy poise (as of manner or style) ⟨entered the room with a quiet ~ of bearing⟩ ⟨a pleasant ~ of style marks his presentation⟩ **c :** casual unconcern or indifference **:** indolent disregard ⟨his losses were largely due to his foolish ~⟩ **d** *archaic* **:** susceptibility to influence **:** CREDULITY **3 :** a state of economic weakness characterized by declining prices and usu. by reduced volume of trade ⟨rubber futures closed slightly steadier after ~ —*Wall Street Jour.*⟩

eas·ing *n* -S [ME *esing,* fr. *esen* to ease + *-ing*] **1 a :** the act or process of an easer **b :** an instance of such act or process **2 :** EASEMENT 3

ea·sings \'ēzᵊnz, 'āz-, -zənz\ *n pl* [pl. of obs. & E dial. *easing* eaves of a building, fr. ME *esing*, contr. of *evesing*, fr. *eves* eaves + *-ing* — more at EAVE] *dial Brit* **:** the eaves of a building

ea·sing sparrow \'ēzᵊnz-, 'āz|, |zən-\ *n* [E dial. *easing* eaves of a building + E *sparrow*] *dial Brit* **:** HOUSE SPARROW

eas·sel \'ēsəl, 'ās-\ *adv* [irreg. fr. *east*] *Scot* **:** EASTWARD

1**east** \'ēst\ *adv* [ME *est*, fr. OE *ēast;* akin to OHG *ōstar* to the east, ON *austr* to the east, L *aurora* dawn, Gk *ēōs*, Skt *uṣas*] **:** to, toward, or in the east **:** EASTWARD

2**east** \"\ *adj* [ME *est*, fr. OE *ēast-*, fr. *ēast*, adv.] **1 a :** situated toward or at the east ⟨the ~ gate⟩ **b** [ME *est*, fr. OE *ēastan-*, fr. *ēastan*, adv; akin to OHG *ōstana* from the east, ON *austan;* derivative fr. the root of E 1*east*] **:** coming from the east ⟨the ~ wind⟩ **2 :** situated in the direction of the altar from the nave of a church **:** being or situated in that part of a church containing the chancel

3**east** \"\ *n* -s [ME *est*, fr. *est*, adv.] **1 a :** the general direction of sunrise **:** the direction toward the right of one facing north **b :** the part of the sky in which celestial bodies rise; *specif* **:** the place on the horizon where the sun rises when it is near one of the equinoxes **c :** the cardinal point directly opposite to west — abbr. *E;* see COMPASS CARD **d :** the point of the horizon having an azimuth or bearing of 90° and marking one intersection of the horizon and the celestial equator **:** the direction of the earth's daily rotation **:** the direction on the celestial sphere opposite to its apparent rotation **:** the direction of increasing right ascension or celestial longitude **:** the direction of revolution around the sun of the earth and the principal planets when seen from the north side of their orbits **2** *usu cap* **a :** regions or countries lying to the east of a specified or implied point of orientation ⟨the worn mountains of the *East*⟩ **b :** something (as people, culture, or institutions) characteristic of the East ⟨the *East* is strongly opposed to these innovations⟩ ⟨the *East* has produced some of our most original thinkers⟩ **3 :** the east wind **4** *often cap* **:** the one of four positions at 90-degree intervals that lies toward the east; *often* **:** a person (as a bridge player or a Masonic officer) occupying this position in the course of a specific activity

4**east** \"\ *vb* -ED/-ING/-S [1*east*] **:** to move or veer toward the east **:** ORIENT

5**east** \"\ *n* -s [by alter.] *dial* **:** YEAST

eastabout \'ˌ=ˌ=\ *adv (or adj)* **:** about in tacking so as to head east; *broadly* **:** toward the east **:** EASTWARD

east african cedar *n, usu cap E&A* **:** a tropical African timber tree (*Juniperus procera*) with fragrant wood

east african hunting dog *n, usu cap E&A* **:** AFRICAN HUNTING DOG

east african yellowwood *or* **east african pine** *n, usu cap E&A* **:** a tropical African timber tree (*Podocarpus gracilior*) that is related to the yews and is sometimes cultivated as a greenhouse ornamental

1**east anglian** *adj, usu cap E&A* **1 :** of or relating to the Anglo-Saxon kingdom of East Anglia, its people, or their language **2 :** of or belonging to the modern region of East Anglia, England, corresponding to Norfolk and Suffolk counties

2**east anglian** *n, cap E&A* **1 :** a native or resident of East Anglia **2 :** the speech of East Anglia; *esp* **:** the Middle English dialect characteristic of this region

eastbound \'ˌ=ˌ=\ *adj* **:** traveling or headed in an easterly direction; *broadly* **:** headed east or north — used of freight cars in railroad accounting

1**east by north :** a compass point that is one point north of due east **:** N 78° 45′ E — abbr. *E b N, E by N;* see COMPASS CARD

2**east by north** *adv (or adj)* **1 :** toward east by north **2 :** from east by north

1**east by south :** a compass point that is one point south of due east **:** S 78° 45′ E — abbr. *E b S, E by S;* see COMPASS CARD

2**east by south** *adv (or adj)* **1 :** toward east by south **2 :** from east by south

east coast fever *n* **:** an acute highly fatal febrile disease of cattle esp. of eastern and southern Africa that is caused by a protozoan (*Theileria parva*) transmitted by ticks (genus *Rhipicephalus*) and is marked by intense fever, labored breathing, gastrointestinal hemorrhage, swelling of the lymph glands, and generalized weakness and emaciation

1**eas·ter** \'ēstə(r)\ *n* -s *usu cap, often attrib* [ME *ester*, *estre*, fr. OE *ēaster*, *ēastre;* akin to OHG *ōstarun* (pl.) Easter; both fr. the prehistoric WGmc name of a pagan spring festival, derived fr. the root of E 1*east*] **1 :** an annual church celebration that commemorates Christ's resurrection and is observed with variations of date due to different calendars on the first Sunday after the paschal full moon on or next after March 21 **2 :** the Easter season **:** EASTERTIDE

EASTER DATES[1]

YEAR	GOLDEN NUMBER	EPACT	DOMINICAL LETTER	PASCHAL FULL MOON[2]	ASH WEDNESDAY	EASTER
1985	10	8	F	Apr 5	Feb 20	Apr 7
1986	11	19	E	Mar 25	Feb 12	Mar 30
1987	12	0	D	Apr 13	Mar 4	Apr 19
1988	13	11	CB	Apr 2	Feb 17	Apr 3
1989	14	22	A	Mar 22	Feb 8	Mar 26
1990	15	3	G	Apr 10	Feb 28	Apr 15
1991	16	14	F	Mar 30	Feb 13	Mar 31
1992	17	25	ED	Apr 17	Mar 4	Apr 19
1993	18	6	C	Apr 7	Feb 24	Apr 11
1994	19	17	B	Mar 27	Feb 16	Apr 3
1995	1	29	A	Apr 14	Mar 1	Apr 16
1996	2	10	GF	Apr 3	Feb 21	Apr 7
1997	3	21	E	Mar 23	Feb 12	Mar 30
1998	4	2	D	Apr 11	Feb 25	Apr 12
1999	5	13	C	Mar 31	Feb 17	Apr 4
2000	6	24	BA	Apr 18	Mar 8	Apr 23
2001	7	5	G	Apr 8	Feb 28	Apr 15
2002	8	16	F	Mar 28	Feb 13	Mar 31
2003	9	27	E	Apr 16	Mar 5	Apr 20
2004	10	8	DC	Apr 5	Feb 25	Apr 11
2005	11	19	B	Mar 25	Feb 9	Mar 27
2006	12	0	A	Apr 13	Mar 1	Apr 16
2007	13	11	G	Apr 2	Feb 21	Apr 8
2008	14	22	FE	Mar 22	Feb 6	Mar 23
2009	15	3	D	Apr 10	Feb 25	Apr 12
2010	16	14	C	Mar 30	Feb 17	Apr 4

[1]As established by the first Nicene Council, Easter is always the first Sunday after the paschal full moon on or next after the vernal equinox, fixed as March 21 for this calculation. If the paschal full moon falls on Sunday, Easter is observed one week later.

[2]The paschal full moon is determined according to certain calendar rules and may differ from that of the astronomical full moon.

2**east·er** \"\ *n* -s [2*east* + *-er*] **:** a strong east wind

easter anemone *n, usu cap E* **:** PASQUEFLOWER

easter bell *n, usu cap E* **:** GREATER STITCHWORT

easter cactus *n, usu cap E* **:** a So. American cactus (*Schlumbergera gaertneri*) with oblong joints and coral-red flowers

easter candle *n, usu cap E* **:** PASCHAL CANDLE

easter daisy *n, usu cap E* **:** a low-growing ash-gray perennial herb (*Townsendia exscapa*) of western No. America with linear or linear-oblanceolate leaves arranged in a rosette and sessile white flower heads that appear at about Easter season

easter duty *n, usu cap E* **:** the obligation in the Roman Catholic Church of receiving Communion during Easter time

easter egg *n, usu cap 1st E* **:** an egg given as a present at or used to celebrate Easter and often dyed with bright colors or otherwise decorated; *broadly* **:** a symbolic representation of an egg (as in confectionery or the jeweler's art) similarly used

easter even *n, usu cap both Es* [ME *ester even*, fr. *ester* Easter + *even* eve — more at EVEN (eve)] **:** the 24-hour period preceding Easter

easter flower *n, usu cap E* **1 :** PASQUEFLOWER **2 :** DAFFODIL 1

easter lily *n, usu cap E* **1 :** any of certain predominantly white cultivated lilies that bloom or can be forced into bloom in early spring: as **a :** MADONNA LILY **b :** BERMUDA LILY **2 :** any of several native or cultivated spring-flowering plants (as the daffodil, the atamasco lily, or the dogtooth violet)

eas·ter·li·ness \-ēnəs, -in-\ *n* -ES **:** the situation of being easterly

1**east·er·ling** \'ēstərliŋ -təl-,-tᵊl-\ *n* -s [ME *esterling*, fr. *ester*, *estern* eastern + *-ling*] **:** a native of a country eastward of another — used esp. of German merchants from Baltic cities who traded in England or competed with the English in foreign ports

2**easterling** \"\ *n* -s [alter. (influenced by 1*easterling*) of *sterling;* fr. a belief that it was coined by German merchants from Baltic cities] **1** *or* **easterling penny :** a medieval English silver coin **2 :** the weight of an easterling **:** PENNYWEIGHT **:** ¹⁄₂₀ ounce

1**east·er·ly** \'ēstərlē, -li; *-R* -təl- *sometimes* -tᵊl-\ *adj* [obs. E *easter* eastern (fr. ME *ester*, *estern*) + E *-ly*] **1 :** situated toward the east ⟨the ~ shore⟩ **2 :** blowing from the east

2**easterly** \"\ *adv* **1 :** from the east **2 :** toward the east

3**easterly** \"\ *n* -ES **:** a wind from the east

easter mackerel *n, usu cap E* **:** CHUB MACKEREL

easter monday *n, usu cap E&M* [ME *ester monday* Monday after Easter, fr. *ester* Easter + *monday* Monday] **:** the Monday after Easter observed as a legal holiday in North Carolina, England, Wales, Northern Ireland, the Republic of Ireland, Canada, Australia, New Zealand, and the Republic of So. Africa

east·er·most \'ēstə(r),mōst, *esp Brit also* -ˌməst\ *adj* [obs. E *easter* eastern + E *-most*] *archaic* **:** EASTERNMOST

1**east·ern** \'ēstə(r)n, *-R also* -tᵊn\ *adj* [ME *estern*, fr. OE *ēasterne;* akin to OHG *ōstrōni* eastern, ON *austrœnn;* derivative fr. the root of E 1*east*] **1** *often cap* **:** of, relating to, originating or dwelling in, or characteristic of any region conventionally designated East (as the Orient, the more easterly or northeasterly part of the U. S., or the predominantly Slavic part of Europe) ⟨proposals for settling the ~ question⟩ ⟨~ beef⟩ **2** *usu cap* **a :** of, relating to, or being the totality of Christian churches originating in the church of the Eastern Roman Empire and comprising various Eastern Orthodox, Uniate, Monophysite, and Nestorian churches **b :** Eastern Orthodox **3 a :** lying toward the east ⟨dawn breaking in the ~ sky⟩ ⟨the ~ boundary of the state⟩ **b :** coming from the east ⟨an ~ wind⟩ **4** *often cap* **:** being or characterizing the native speech of eastern New England and of the r-dropping population of New York City and its suburbs

2**eastern** \"\ *n* -s *usu cap* **1 :** an inhabitant of the East; *esp* **:** ORIENTAL **2 :** a member of the Eastern Church **3 :** eastern American speech

eastern apple box *n, sometimes cap E* **:** a wooden box with protective pads that is used esp. for apples from eastern orchards of the U.S.

eastern bluestem *n* **:** BLUESTEM 2b

eastern brook trout *n* **:** BROOK TROUT

eastern crow *n* **:** the common crow (*Corvus brachyrhynchos brachyrhynchos*) of northeastern No. America

eastern crown *or* **eastern coronet** *n* **:** ANTIQUE CROWN

east·ern·er *R* -tə(r)nər, *-R* -tənə(r *also* -tᵊnə(r\ *n* -s *usu cap* **:** a native or inhabitant of the East; *esp* **:** a native or resident of the eastern part of the U.S.

eastern gall rust *n, usu cap E* **:** a disease of various hard pines (as shortleaf and scrub pine) that is caused by a rust fungus (*Cronartium quercuum*) and characterized by formation of globose galls on the stems

eastern hemisphere *n* **:** the vertical half of the earth that lies chiefly to the east of the Atlantic ocean and includes Europe, Asia, Africa, and minor landmasses

eastern hemlock *n* **:** a common forest tree (*Tsuga canadensis*) of the eastern U.S. and Canada that has leaves narrowed toward the apex and with pale stomatal lines beneath, yields a soft, splintery, but moisture-resistant lumber, and is largely used for pulp production

eastern hindi *n, cap E&H* **:** a group of Indic dialects in northern India including Awadhi

east·ern·ism \-ˌnizəm\ *n* -s *usu cap* **:** ORIENTALISM

east·ern·ize \-ˌnīz\ *vt* -ED/-ING/-S *sometimes cap* **1 :** to imbue with qualities native to or sometimes associated with residents of eastern U.S. **2 :** ORIENTALIZE

eastern kingbird *n* **:** a common American kingbird (*Tyrannus tyrannus*) that breeds in much of No. America from coast to coast and winters in tropical America and is distinguished from related birds by a wide white band on the tip of the tail and an orange-red crest which is usu. obscured

eastern larch *n* **:** a tamarack (*Larix laricina*)

east·ern·ly \-nlē, -li\ *adv (or adj)* **1 :** EASTERLY **2** *often cap* **:** in the Eastern manner **:** ORIENTALLY

eastern mermaid *n* **:** a fake stuffed animal usu. consisting of the foreparts of a monkey sewed to the hindpart of a fish

east·ern·most \-n,mōst *esp Brit also* -ˌməst\ *adj* **:** farthest to the east **:** most eastern

eastern orthodox *adj, usu cap E&O* **:** of, relating to, or being the body of Eastern churches in communion with the ecumenical patriarch of Constantinople that includes the churches of the ancient patriarchates of Constantinople, Alexandria, Antioch, and Jerusalem and a number of autocephalous often national churches (as the Greek and Russian Orthodox churches) and that adheres to the Niceno-Constantinopolitan Creed and to a rite having the same liturgies in different languages, Communion under both kinds, an ecclesiastical year including days for Old Testament saints and based on the Julian calendar, and a married parish clergy

eastern phoebe *n* **:** a common phoebe (*Sayornis phoebe*) of eastern No. America that is grayish brown above with darker head and grayish white breast

eastern pickerel *n* **:** CHAIN PICKEREL

eastern red cedar *n* **:** RED CEDAR 1a

eastern roll *n, usu cap E* **:** a method of high jumping in which the jumper approaches the bar at right angles, kicks off from his outside foot while flinging the leading leg forward and upward, and lands on the outside foot — compare BARREL ROLL, WESTERN ROLL

eastern spruce *n* **1 :** WHITE SPRUCE 1a **2 :** RED SPRUCE **3 :** BLACK SPRUCE 1

eastern sudanic *n, usu cap E&S* **:** a language group containing the Nilotic and Nubian languages and constituting a subfamily of the Chari-Nile language family

eastern tent caterpillar *n* **:** the gregarious web-building larva of a reddish brown American moth (*Malacosoma americanum*) hatching in spring, feeding on the young foliage of apple, wild cherry, and related trees, and building community nests of silk in crotches of the trees invaded

eastern time *or* **eastern standard time** *n, often cap E* **:** the time of the 5th time zone west of Greenwich that is based on the 75th meridian, is used in the eastern parts of Canada and the U.S., and is five hours slower than Greenwich time — abbr. *ET, EST*

eastern white pine *n* **:** WHITE PINE 1a

easters *pl of* EASTER

easter sepulcher *n, usu cap E* **1 :** a shallow recess in the north side of the chancel in some churches in which formerly the sacred elements were reserved from Maundy Thursday to Easter **2 :** a tomb in medieval churches in which the altar crucifix was buried from Good Friday to Easter Sunday

easter sunday *n, usu cap E&S* **:** the Sunday on which Easter falls

easter term *n, usu cap E* **1 :** the term from April 15 to May 8 during which the superior courts of England were formerly open — compare HILARY TERM, TRINITY TERM **2** *also* **easter sitting :** the sitting of the High Court of Justice of England between April 21 and May 29

eastertide \'ēstə(r),tīd\ *also* **easter time** *n, usu cap E* [*Eastertide* fr. ME *estertide* Easter season, fr. OE *ēastertīd*, fr. *ēaster* Easter + *tīd* time; *Easter time* fr. ME *ester time* period from Easter to Whitsunday, fr. *ester* Easter + *time* — more at TIDE] **:** a period extending from Easter to Ascension Day, to Whitsunday, or to Trinity Sunday

easter water *n, usu cap E* **:** water blessed with special ceremonies on Holy Saturday (as in the Roman Catholic Church) a part of which is set aside for use as a sacramental in the church and at home, the remainder being ceremonially mixed with consecrated oils and used for baptisms in the church

east germanic *n, cap E&G* [prob. trans. of G *ostgermanisch*] **:** a now extinct division of the Germanic languages containing Gothic and prob. also certain languages of which no connected written records survive, esp. those of the Burgundians and Vandals — see INDO-EUROPEAN LANGUAGES table

east goth *n, cap E&G* **:** OSTROGOTH

east ham \'ēst¦ham, 'ē¦stam, -aa(ə)m\ *adj, usu cap E&H* [fr. *East Ham*, county borough in England] **:** of or from the former county borough of East Ham, England **:** of the kind or style prevalent in East Ham

east india company *n, usu cap E&I&C* [*East India*, collective name applied loosely and vaguely to India, Indochina, and the Malay archipelago] **:** any of several companies organized chiefly during the 17th and 18th centuries for carrying on trade with the East Indies

east india kino *or* **east indian kino** *n, usu cap E&I* **:** KINO 1a

east indiaman *n, usu cap E&I* [*East India* + E *man*] **:** a sailing ship formerly running to the East Indies; *esp* **:** a large fast sailing ship used on this run

1**east indian** *adj, usu cap E&I* [*East India* + E *-an*] **1 :** of, relating to, or characteristic of the East Indies **2 :** of, relating to, or characteristic of India or Pakistan

2**east indian** *n, cap E&I* **1 :** a native or inhabitant of the East Indies; *sometimes* **:** EURASIAN **2 :** a native or inhabitant of India or Pakistan; *also* **:** a person of East Indian ancestry

east indian arrowroot *n, usu cap E&I* **:** INDIAN ARROWROOT 2b

east indian lotus *n, usu cap E&I* **:** INDIAN LOTUS

east indian rhubarb *n, usu cap E&I* **:** CHINESE RHUBARB

east indian rosewood *n, usu cap E&I* **:** BLACKWOOD b

east indian satinwood *n, usu cap E&I* **:** SATINWOOD 1

east indian sumbul *n, usu cap E&I* **:** BOMBAY SUMBUL

east indian walnut *n, usu cap E&I* **1 :** LEBBEK **2 :** the wood of the lebbek that resembles and is used similarly to walnut

east india resin *also* **east india** *n, usu cap E&I* **:** any of several pale to black hard semifossil dammar resins

east india root *n, usu cap E&I* **:** the rhizome of a galingale (*Alpinia officinarum*)

east indies *adj, usu cap E&I* [fr. *East Indies*, the former Netherlands Indies (in some usage, the entire Malay archipelago; in some usage, India, Indochina, and the Malay archipelago)] **:** of or from the East Indies **:** of the kind or style prevalent in the East Indies **:** EAST INDIAN

east·ing \'ēstiŋ\ *n* -s [1*east* + *-ing*] **1 :** difference in longitude to the east from the last preceding point of reckoning **2 :** easterly progress **:** a going eastward ⟨weeks of snow . . . and not for anything can you keep an ~ —Joseph Hergesheimer⟩

east·lake \'ēst,lāk\ *adj, usu cap* [after Sir Charles L. *Eastlake* †1865 Eng. painter and art critic] *of furniture* **:** being machine-made after a style characterized by sturdy rectangular lines

east·lin \'ēstlən\ *or* **east·ling** \-liŋ\ *adv (or adj)* [1*east* + *-ling*] *Scot* **:** EASTERLY

east·lins \-nz\ *or* **east·lings** \-nz,-ŋz\ *adv* [1*east* + *-lings*] *Scot* **:** to the east

east london boxwood *n, usu cap E&L* [after *East London*, city in the Republic of So. Africa] **1 :** a box (*Buxus macowani*) that grows in nearly pure stands at East London, Republic of South Africa **2 :** the wood of East London boxwood

east lo·thi·an \-'lōthēən, -thyən\ *adj, usu cap E&L* [fr. *East Lothian*, county in Scotland] **:** of or from the former county of East Lothian, Scotland **:** of the kind or style prevalent in East Lothian

east midland *n, cap E&M* **:** the branch of the Midland dialect of Middle English that is the basis of modern standard English

east·most \'ēs(t),mōst, *esp Brit also* -ˌməst\ *adj* [ME *estmest*, fr. OE *ēastemest*, *ēastmest*, fr. *ēast-* east + *-mest* -most — more at 2EAST] **:** EASTERNMOST

east·ness \'ēs(t)nəs\ *n* -ES **:** the quality or state of being east

1**east-northeast** \(ˌ)ˌ=¦=ˌ=\ *adv (or adj)* [ME *est northest*, fr. *est* east + *northest* northeast — more at 1EAST] **1 :** toward east-northeast **2 :** from east-northeast

2**east-northeast** \"\ *n* **:** a compass point that is two points north of due east **:** N 67°30′ E — abbr. *ENE;* see COMPASS CARD

eas·ton·ite \'ēstəˌnīt\ *n* -s *often cap* [*Easton*, city in eastern Pennsylvania, its locality + E *-ite*] **:** a mineral $K_2Mg_5AlSi_5Al_3O_{20}(OH)_4$ consisting of basic silicate of potassium, aluminum, and magnesium and being an end-member of the biotite system

easts *pl of* EAST, *pres 3d sing of* EAST

eastside \'=¦=\ *adj, often cap* [fr. the *East Side*, the eastern part of Manhattan] **:** of, relating to, or situated in the eastern part of Manhattan ⟨~ tenements⟩

east-sid·er \'ēs(t)¦sīdə(r)\ *n, often cap E&S* [*East Side*, the eastern part of Manhattan borough, New York City + E *-er*] **:** a native or resident of the East Side of New York City

east slavic *n, cap E&S* **:** a subdivision of the Slavic languages that includes Russian, Ukrainian, and Belorussian — see INDO-EUROPEAN LANGUAGES table

1**east-southeast** \(ˌ)ˌ=¦=ˌ=\ *adv (or adj)* [ME *est southest*, fr. *est* east + *southest* southeast — more at 1EAST] **1 :** toward east-southeast **2 :** from east-southeast

2**east-southeast** \"\ *n* **:** a compass point that is two points south of due east **:** S 67° 30′ E — abbr. *ESE;* see COMPASS CARD

1**east·ward** \'ēstwə(r)d\ *adv (or adj)* [ME *estward*, fr. OE *ēastweard*, fr. *ēast* east + *-weard* -ward — more at 1EAST] **:** toward the east ⟨turned ~ down the slope⟩ ⟨~ movement of the herd⟩

2**eastward** \"\ *n* -s **:** eastward direction or part ⟨sail to the ~⟩

east·ward·ly *adv (or adj)* **:** toward or from the east **:** EASTERLY

east·wards \-dz\ *adv* [*eastward* + *-s* (fr. ME *-es*, adverbially functioning gen. sing. ending of nouns) — more at -s] **:** EASTWARD

east-west \'=¦=\ *adv (or adj)* **:** from east to west **:** from or along a line of geographic latitude ⟨the first *east-west* railroad⟩

east-windy \'=¦==\ *adj* [*east wind* (fr. 2*east* + *wind*) + *-y*] **:** BLEAK, UNPLEASANT

1**easy** \'ēzē, -zi\ *adj* -ER/-EST [ME *esy*, fr. OF *aaisié* (past part. of *aaisier* to ease) & *aisié* (past part. of *aisier* to ease) — more at 2EASE] **1 :** causing, exacting, or involving little difficulty, exertion, hardship, or discomfort to execute or cope with **:** performed, accomplished, achieved, solved, coped with, taken, acted on, or cared for with ready ease ⟨it was ~ to sit on a camel's back without falling off but very difficult to get the best out of her —T.E.Lawrence⟩ ⟨ritual is not ~ compliance with detailed and punctilious rule —W.G.Sumner⟩ ⟨an ~ victim . . . of this good-natured diplomatist —W.M. Thackeray⟩ ⟨feeding this outfit would have been ~ for an old hand —*Amer. Guide Series: Ariz.*⟩ ⟨the St. Lawrence route is . . . ~ of navigation —B.K.Sandwell⟩ **2 a :** not severe, not stern, not harsh **:** readily assuaged or placated **:** MILD, LENIENT, COMPLAISANT ⟨you are . . . so ~ that every servant will cheat you —Jane Austen⟩ ⟨we really ought to be ~ on him because everybody makes mistakes —V.G.Heiser⟩ **b :** marked by gentle gradual change or variation making for ease in traversing or following **:** not steep, not abrupt, not sharp ⟨this is the ~ country of the pass where the stream flows gently —Ernest Hemingway⟩ ⟨terraced steps rise in ~ flights —*Amer. Guide Series: Mich.*⟩ ⟨a pleasant ~ angle —Richard Jefferies⟩ **c :** marked by ease and convenience in going from one place to another usu. by short distances at a time ⟨brought him back by ~ stages —Willa Cather⟩ **d :** not difficult to endure or undergo **:** not burdensome or onerous **:** complied with or fulfilled without marked discomfort ⟨an ~ penalty⟩ ⟨an ~ contract⟩ ⟨William Pitt . . . condemned the Peace of Paris as too ~ —Stringfellow Barr⟩ **e :** readily prevailed on **:** overcome without difficulty: as (1) **:** yielding quickly to sexual importunities ⟨women of the ~ kind, the lusty kind, the ardent and the impudent —T.H.Raddall⟩ (2) **:** not difficult to trick, deceive, or take advantage of ⟨fell an ~ prey to her wiles⟩ (3) **:** especially susceptible (as to disease or predation) ⟨in winter upland game birds are ~ victims to predators where cover is poor⟩ ⟨exhausted by overwork he was an ~ victim to infection⟩ **f** (1) **:** obtained or obtainable with ease **:** not involving especial effort, inconvenience, or anguish ⟨he won an ~ victory⟩ (2) *of money, credit, or commodities* **:** available in such large quantities that interest rates or prices are depressed ⟨farmers generally want *easier* money⟩ ⟨the hog market has been irregular and ~ for several days⟩ — compare EASY-MONEY **g :** clear and without complexity or difficulty **:** very readily understood although often without challenge or reward ⟨~ language — no strain upon either adult or youthful reader —J.D.Hart⟩ **3 a :** marked by ease, by peace, comfort, and placid rest ⟨retired and living an ~ life⟩ ⟨the ~ warmth of most southern cities —Green Peyton⟩ **b** : not hurried, not ruffled, not strenuous : marked by or suited to placid calm or mild, slow, or gentle activity ⟨an ~ walk through the meadow⟩ ⟨the ~ climate of the island⟩ ⟨a stretch of ~ water —C.S.Forester⟩ **4 a** : free from pain, distress, annoyance, discomfort ⟨the patient was *easier* after the sedative⟩ **b** : marked by social ease : constituting or facilitating ready natural sociability : calm, smooth, and without restraint, formality, embarrassment, or harshness ⟨~ and familiar manners of men who had worked for years together —Sir Winston Churchill⟩ ⟨the ~ carriage of a man born to a dignified place in life —Jack London⟩ **c** : marked by or arising from a complaisant desire for ease or by an attitude of careless casual acquiescence : showing a disinclination to energetic individual action or resolute independent thought ⟨his ~ disposition made him fall in unresistingly with the family courses —George Eliot⟩ ⟨the ~, irreligious gay society which jumped the life to come —H.O.Taylor⟩ **d** : free from mental or emotional agitation : unruffled and not harassed by discontent, anxiety, doubt, or fear : TRANQUIL ⟨an ~ and dignified calm, far removed from the intensity of life —Thomas Hardy⟩ ⟨men who fish for a living must have an ~ courage —Mary H. Vorse⟩ **e** : enjoying or showing comfortable assured tranquillity about money and expenses : rich enough for comfort or luxury ⟨he married an heiress and found himself in ~ circumstances —*Times Lit. Supp.*⟩ **f** : marked by ready facility at smooth composition or performance without labored effort : EFFORTLESS ⟨he wrote in an ~, rapid, flowing style —H.S.Robinson⟩ **g** : felt, experienced, or attained to readily, naturally, and spontaneously without guided or forced effort : not conscious, purposive, or factitious ⟨an ~ familiarity with his subject⟩ ⟨~ emotions⟩ **h** : no less than — used with the indefinite article and terms denoting quantity (as of years of age) ⟨looking an ~ 35 in the harsh light⟩ ⟨an ~ two hours' work⟩ ⟨weighs an ~ 200⟩ **5 a** : conducive to or facilitating ease, comfort, relaxation, or surcease from discomfort, inconvenience, or vexation ⟨~ furniture⟩ ⟨an ~ arrangement of the room⟩ **b** (1) : supportable with ease : not onerous or burdensome ⟨got very ~ terms from his creditors⟩ (2) *of payments* : designed to be made in installments over a period of time and from regular income ⟨furnished his house on an easy-payment plan⟩ **c** *of a garment* : fitting comfortably with due allowance for motion of the body : not tight or constricting ⟨an ~ shoe⟩ ⟨an ~ fit⟩ **6 a** : evenly divided — used of the aces in a no-trump contract in auction bridge when each partnership holds two **b** *Austral* : willing to consider or participate but not enthusiastic

syn FACILE, SIMPLE, LIGHT, EFFORTLESS, SMOOTH: EASY applies to persons and to things making demands answerable without much effort or difficulty ⟨he found his studies too *easy* to require serious attention, and, being very large and strong, he devoted his energies to athletics —E.S.Bates⟩ ⟨the English owe more to their national home than do most nations. Its insular situation made it readily accessible in time of peace and *easy* to defend in time of war —Kemp Malone⟩ FACILE, sometimes a close synonym of EASY, now applies to execution, accomplishment, or performance seemingly without effort or with very little effort; sometimes it is derogatory in implying undue haste or careless execution ⟨full of *facile* theories, with glib explanations of everything —Bertrand Russell⟩ ⟨Chrétien is a *facile* narrator, with little sense of the significance that might be given to the stories —H.O.Taylor⟩ SIMPLE stresses ease in comprehending and freedom from complexity or intricacy ⟨feeding this outfit would have been easy for an old hand, but it was far from *simple* to me —*Amer. Guide Series: Ariz.*⟩ ⟨the English mother or the English nurse has a *simpler* job. She must teach her charge to start as few fights as possible and that there are rules. That is enough —Margaret Mead⟩ LIGHT involves freedom from the onerous or burdensome ⟨college teaching job — preferably where your formal duties are as *light* as you can decently make them —W.G.Carleton⟩ ⟨it was no *light* thing to encounter the rage and despair of fifty thousand fighting men —T.B.Macaulay⟩ EFFORTLESS suggests appearance of ease and often implies perfected artistry or mastery ⟨so that attention became concentration, and concentration became at first *effortless*, then involuntary —Charles Morgan⟩ ⟨that *effortless* grace with which only a true poet can endow his work —Martha O. Smith⟩ SMOOTH suggests absence of obstacles, hindrances, unevennesses, interruptions ⟨the *smooth* advance of the German Army into France in 1940 —S.L.A.Marshall⟩ ⟨by the time he had warmed up his motors, the sky had cleared and it was day. The takeoff was *smooth* as cream —John Dos Passos⟩ **syn** see in addition COMFORTABLE

²easy \"\ *adv* -ER/-EST [ME *esy*, fr. *esy*, adj.] **1** : EASILY ⟨~ come, ~ go⟩ ⟨take it ~⟩ ⟨my boots went on ~⟩ **2** : without undue speed : SLOWLY ⟨go ~ here, the road is very rough⟩ ⟨worked ~ until his muscles loosened up⟩ : without undue excitement — often used interjectionally to suggest proceeding with caution ⟨~, the road's washed out just ahead⟩ or calming down ⟨~, there's nothing to be afraid of now⟩

³easy \"\ *vb* -ED/-ING/-ES [¹*easy*] : EASE

⁴easy \"\ *vb* -ED/-ING/-ES [²*easy*] *vi* : to stop rowing ⟨the crew *easied* on approaching the dock⟩ — often used as a command, sometimes with *all* ⟨~ all⟩ ~ *vt* : to command (an oarsman or crew) to stop rowing

⁵easy \"\ *usu cap* — a communications code word for the letter *e*

easy chair *n* : a roomy usu. upholstered chair designed for comfortable relaxation

easy-does-it \ˌēzēˈdəzət, -zi-, *usu* -əd·+V\ *adj* : free from strain and tension : comfortable and pleasantly relaxing ⟨an *easy-does-it* approach to a problem⟩

easygoing \ˌ==ˈ==\ *adj* **1** *of a horse* : having a comfortable gait **2** : taking life easily : PLACID, CALM ⟨an ~ man, rarely stirred to anger⟩: as **a** : indolent and careless ⟨those ~ slipshod ways would not do today⟩ **b** : not bound by rigid standards of conduct or morals ⟨a country that, for all its reputation of being ~, has often set a moral example to the rest of Europe —*Manchester Guardian Weekly*⟩ **3** : free from onerous demands or exactions : casually pleasant and comfortable ⟨the ~ way of 19th century cultured living⟩ ⟨an ~ unhurried tempo⟩ ⟨the ~ demands of the present public taste —Kenkichi Yoshida⟩ — **easy·go·ing·ness** *n* -ES

easylike \ˈ==ˌ=\ *adv* : with ease : GENTLY, CAUTIOUSLY ⟨leaned ~ against the fence⟩ ⟨crept forward ~ until we could hear what was said⟩

easy mark *n* [so called fr. the similarity to a target that can easily be hit] : one easily imposed upon, duped, or overcome

easy money *n* : money obtained without especial hardship or effort; *often* : money obtained unfairly or improperly (as by trickery or crime)

easy-money \ˌ==ˈ==\ *adj* [*easy money*] : devoted to or concerned with increasing the availability of money and credit ⟨the present *easy-money* policy of the government⟩ — compare ¹EASY 2f(2)

easy-osey or **easy-osie** \ˌēziˈōzi\ *adj* [redupl. of ¹*easy*] *Scot* : EASYGOING, CASUAL

easy rider *n, slang* : a parasitical hanger-on; *esp* : PIMP

easy street *n, sometimes cap E&S* : a situation marked by financial independence — usu. used with *on* ⟨if I get that contract I'll be on *easy street* for months⟩

easy virtue *n* : sexually promiscuous behavior or habits

¹eat \ˈēt, *usu* ˈēd·+V\ *vb* **ate** \ˈā|t *chiefly in substand speech* ˈe|t, *usu* |d·+V; *Brit* ˈet *sometimes* ˈāt\ *or dial* **eat** \ˈe|t, ˈē|t, *usu* |d·+V\ *also* **et** \ˈet, *usu* ˈed·+V\ **eat·en** \ˈētᵊn\ *or dial* **eat** \ˈe|t, ˈē|t, *usu* |d·+V\ *also* **et** \ˈet, *usu* ˈed·+V\ **eat·ing** \ˈēd·iŋ, ˈētiŋ\ **eats** \ˈēts\ [ME *eten*, fr. OE *etan*; akin to OHG *ezzan* to eat, ON *eta*, Goth *itan*, L *esse*, *edere*, Gk (Homeric) *edmenai* to eat, Skt *atti* he eats, *admi* I eat] *vt* **1 a** : to take in through the mouth as food ⟨sat *eating* a ripe plum⟩ : ingest, chew, and swallow (food) — used of solids and then contrasted with *drink* ⟨he *ate* his sandwich and drank a glass of milk⟩ or broadly of both solids and liquids ⟨he ~*s* dinner at noon⟩ ⟨~ your soup⟩ **b** : to use as food : make a food of : obtain nourishment from ⟨the carnivores ~ meat⟩ ⟨~ whatever is put before you⟩ **2** : destroy, use up, or waste by or as if by eating : DEVOUR, CONSUME, RAVAGE ⟨time ~*s* the strongest walls⟩ ⟨the wooded hills were *eaten* by fire⟩ ⟨locusts *ate* the country bare⟩ ⟨an inheritance *eaten* up by debt⟩ **3** : to take in in order to obtain some benefit (as nourishment, wisdom, or comfort) ⟨Thy words were found, and I *ate* them —Jer. 15:16 (RSV)⟩ **4 a** : to consume gradually ⟨waves ~*ing* the cliffs⟩ : waste or wear away ⟨*eaten* by a high fever⟩ : CORRODE ⟨acid ~*ing* the surface of a metal plate⟩ **b** *slang* (1) : to consume with vexation ⟨what's ~*ing* her now⟩ (2) : to defeat decisively ⟨our team can ~ those chumps⟩ **5 a** *obs* : to submit tamely to (as insult or abuse) : accept as one's portion — compare EAT CROW, EAT DIRT **b** *slang* : to accept unquestioningly : believe uncritically — usu. used with *up* ⟨he *ate* up the stories of our journeys⟩ **6 a** : to gnaw, perforate, or bore into ⟨the timber was so *eaten* by termites as to be useless⟩ **b** : to bring (as oneself) to a particular state by eating ⟨he *ate* himself sick⟩ ⟨the peach was *eaten* hollow by Japanese beetles⟩ ⟨he'll ~ us out of house and home⟩ ~ *vi* **1** : to take food or a meal ⟨where shall we ~ this evening⟩; *broadly* : BOARD ⟨I ~ at the little café around the corner⟩ **2** : to present a specified quality or characteristic when eaten ⟨crackers alone ~ very dry⟩ ⟨the beef *ate* surprisingly tender⟩ **3 a** : to affect something by a gradual destructive action — used with *into* ⟨the acid *ate* into the metal⟩ ⟨an ulcer *ate* into the flesh⟩ **b** : to use up in part esp. over a period of time — used with *into* ⟨smokers ~ greedily into dollar reserves —*English Digest*⟩ ⟨his extravagances *ate* into his inheritance⟩ **4** *slang* : to annoy or irritate someone — used with *on* ⟨what's ~*ing* on her⟩

syn SWALLOW, INGEST, DEVOUR, CONSUME: EAT is a general term, often without especial connotation; figuratively, it may indicate a wasting or wearing away, often gradual ⟨the river has been *eating* away its west bank rather than east —*Amer. Guide Series: La.*⟩ ⟨poor Mother, the farm has *eaten* away her life —Ellen Glasgow⟩ SWALLOW may focus attention on passage down the throat without chewing or without much chewing ⟨chewing pemmican and *swallowing* army bread —F.V.W.Mason⟩ Figuratively, it implies a seizing, taking in, engulfing, encompassing, or dominating so that existence or identity of the object concerned is threatened or lost ⟨in opera the music *swallows* the words and the other arts of the theater —Susanne K. Langer⟩ ⟨Detroit burst its bounds, *swallowed* other sizable cities —*Amer. Guide Series: Mich.*⟩ INGEST indicates with comprehensiveness and indefiniteness any process of taking through the mouth and into the stomach ⟨does a man dine well because he *ingests* the requisite number of calories? —Walter Lippmann⟩ ⟨anyone who accidentally *ingests* some of the fluid should not go untreated —H.G. Armstrong⟩ Figuratively, it likewise stresses the fact of reception, absorption, or assimilation without more specific suggestion ⟨*ingested* the statement slowly, thought, and then began to express surprise—Elizabeth Bowen⟩ ⟨the U.S.S.R. wants to annex and *ingest* as many satellite nations as possible —B.A. Javits⟩ DEVOUR indicates an eating up wholly, typically with force, intemperance, greed, or rapacity ⟨it is only when an object in the water is still that a shark can *devour* it —H.A. Chippendale⟩ ⟨crossties are of steel, since the customary wooden ties would be quickly *devoured* by insects —Tom Marvel⟩ Figuratively, it implies greedy or very avid seizing or using ⟨an omnivorous reader, *devouring* history, biography, philosophy, science, and fiction —A.F.Harlow⟩ CONSUME may stress the fact of using up entirely by eating or drinking or otherwise employing or assimilating ⟨taking a piece of asparagus in her hand, she was deeply mortified at seeing her hostess *consume* the vegetable with the aid of a knife and fork —G.B.Shaw⟩ ⟨one famous class of British locomotives *consumed* about 52 pounds of coal per mile on ordinary express duty —O.S.Nock⟩ It may indicate utter consumption accomplished forcefully, fiercely, or wastefully ⟨the first two buildings occupying this site were destroyed by fire, the last being *consumed* in the flames that swept the city in 1794 —*Amer. Guide Series: La.*⟩

— **eat crow** : to accept what one has fought against : recede from a position taken — **eat dirt** : to be or become grovelingly submissive — **eat high on the hog** : to live well — **eat one's head off 1** : to eat excessively or gluttonously **2** *slang* : to nag or grumble at one : scold or pick at one ⟨she *ate his head off* when he came in late⟩ — **eat one's heart out** : to grieve bitterly and without hope — **eat one's words** : to retract what one has said — **eat out of one's hand** : to accept habitually and supinely the domination of another — **eat someone's salt** : to partake of someone's hospitality — **eat stick** : to suffer a beating (as with a rod or bastinado) — **eat the air** *obs* : to have vain hopes

²eat \ˈēt\ *n* -S [ME *et*, fr. OE *ǣt*; akin to OHG *āz* food, ON *āt*, Russ *eda*; derivative fr. the root of E ¹*eat*] : something to eat : FOOD — usu. used in pl. ⟨saw the jolly bunch come waltzing in for ~*s* —Sinclair Lewis⟩

¹eat·able \ˈēd·əbəl, ˈētəb-\ *adj* [ME *etable*, fr. *eten* to eat + *-able* — more at ¹EAT] : fit to be eaten: **a** : such as can be taken as food without risk or utter revulsion though usu. without pleasure ⟨a piece of bread, stale and slightly moldy but ~⟩ **b** : pleasant to eat ⟨her cherry cobbler is very ~⟩

²eatable \"\ *n* -S **1** : something to eat **2 eatables** *pl* : FOOD

eat·age \ˈēd·ij\ *n* -S [prob. by folk etymology (influence of ¹*eat* and *-age*) fr. *eddish*] **1** : eatable growth of grass for horses and cattle esp. after a second mowing **2** : right of using grassland for pasturage

eat away *vt* : to consume by eating : ERODE ⟨wind *eating away* the dunes⟩ ~ *vi* : to eat heartily or to repletion ⟨they *ate away* with right good will⟩ ⟨*eat away*, children, you're welcome to all you want⟩

eaten *past part of* EAT

eaten-out \ˈ==ˌ=\ *adj, of grazing land* : grazed beyond capacity for recovery : rendered barren by overgrazing ⟨the miles of *eaten-out* range attest our incapacity to manage natural resources⟩

eat·er \ˈēd·ə(r), ˈētə-\ *n* -S [ME *etere*, fr. OE, fr. *etan* to eat + *-ere* -er — more at ¹EAT] : one that eats or is accustomed to eat (as a heavy ~) ⟨careless ~*s*⟩ ⟨the dog is basically a meat ~⟩

eat·ery \ˈēd·ərē, ˈētə-, -ri\ *n* -ES : LUNCHROOM, RESTAURANT

eath or **eith** \ˈēth\ *adv (or adj)* [ME *eth*, *ethe*, fr. OE *ēath*, *ēathe*; akin to OHG *ōdi* easy, *ōdo* perhaps, ON *auth-* easily, and perh. to L *avēre* to long for — more at AVID] *Scot* : EASY

eath·ly or **eith·ly** \-li\ *adv* [ME *etheliche*, fr. OE *ēathelīce*, fr. *ēathelīc* (adj.) easy, fr. *ēathe* + *-līc* (adj. suffix) -ly] *Scot* : EASILY

¹eating *n* -S [ME *etinge*, fr. OE *etting*, fr. *etan* to eat + *-ing*] **1** : the act of one that eats ⟨the daintiness of her ~⟩ **2** : food to eat ⟨there's no better ~ than fried chicken and fresh green peas⟩ ⟨lobster makes hard ~ for a young child⟩

²eating \"\ *adj* [ME *eting*, fr. *eten* to eat + *-ing*] **1** : CONSUMING, DEVOURING, GNAWING, CORROSIVE, FRETTING ⟨~ cares⟩ **2** [¹*eating*] **a** : used for eating ⟨an ~ room⟩ ⟨~ utensils⟩ **b** : suitable for eating; *often* : being for or of the kind used for human food ⟨~ corn is sweeter than field corn⟩ **c** : fit to be eaten raw — distinguished from *cooking* ⟨these are excellent mild ~ apples but I like something a little tarter for pie⟩

eating house *n* [ME *etinge house*, fr. *etinge* eating + *hous* house — more at ¹EATING] : a place where cooked food is served; *often* : a cheap or inferior restaurant

eat out *vt* **1** : to consume the herbage from esp. to excess ⟨the marsh was badly *eaten out* by muskrats⟩ **2** *slang* : to reprimand (a person) severely ~ *vi* : to eat away from home, esp. at a restaurant ⟨we usually *eat out* on Thursdays⟩

eat-out \ˈ=ˌ=\ *n* -S [*eat out*] : an area of marsh denuded of vegetation by the feeding of an excessive population (as of muskrats or waterfowl)

eats *pres 3d sing of* EAT, *pl of* EAT

eat up *vt* [ME *eten up*, fr. *eten* to eat + *up*] **1** : to eat completely and without delay ⟨*eat up* your dinner before it gets cold⟩ ⟨the locusts *ate up* the bean crop⟩ **2** : DISTRESS, STRAIN, EXHAUST ⟨a tedious monotonous job *eats* a person *up*⟩ **3** : to consume entirely ⟨her savings were *eaten up* by illness⟩ ⟨a man so *eaten up* with vanity as to be scarcely human⟩ **4** *slang* : to exhibit avid interest in or enjoyment of ⟨the crowd *ate up* the maudlin scene⟩ ⟨the jury will *eat up* the lurid testimony⟩ ⟨even sensible men *ate up* the chance to get in on such a good thing⟩

eau \ˈō\ *n, pl* **eaux** \ˈō(z)\ [F, lit., water, fr. L *aqua* — more at ISLAND] : a watery solution (as of perfume); *esp* : a liqueur of moderate density and sweetness

eau de co·logne \ˌōdəkəˈlōn\ *n, pl* **eaux de cologne** \ˌō(z)d-\ *sometimes cap E&C* [F, lit., Cologne water, fr. *Cologne*, Germany, where it was manufactured] : COLOGNE 1

eau de ja·vel green \ˌōdəˌzhaˈvel-, -ˌzhǝ-\ *n, often cap J* : JAVEL GREEN

eau de javelle \ˌ==(ˌ)=ˈ=\ or **eau de javel** \"\ *n, pl* **eaux de javelle** \ˌō(z)d-\ *usu cap J* [F, lit., Javel water, fr. *Javel*, former town now included in Paris, France] : JAVELLE WATER

eau de nile \ˌōdəˈnē(ə)l, -nī(-\ *n, pl* **eaux de nile** \ˌō(z)d-\ *often cap N* [F *eau de Nil*, lit., Nile water, fr. *Nil* Nile, river in northeast Africa] : NILE

eau-de-vie \ˌōdəˈvē\ *n, pl* **eaux-de-vie** \ˌō(z)d-\ [F, lit., water of life, trans. of ML *aqua vitae*] : a spirit distilled from grape wine or other fermented fruit juice : BRANDY

eau-de-vie de marc \ˌōdəˌvēdəˈmärk\ *n* [F] : MARC 2

eave \ˈēv\ *n* -S *often attrib* [back-formation fr. *eaves* (taken as a plural), fr. ME *eves*, fr. OE *efes*; akin to OHG *obasa* portico, ON *ups* eaves, Goth *ubizwa* portico, Goth *uf* under — more at UP] **1** *usu* **eaves** *pl but sing or pl in constr* **a** : the lower border of a roof that overhangs the wall ⟨worn by the dripping from the ~⟩ ⟨the ~*s* are neatly boxed⟩ **b** : the corresponding overhang of thatch (as on a stack of fodder) **2** *usu* **eaves** *pl but sing or pl in constr* : a projecting edge (as of a hill or a hat)

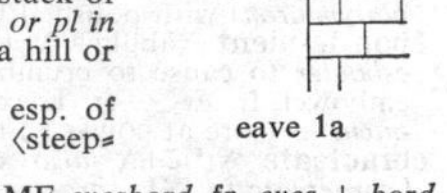

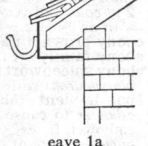

eave 1a

eaved \-vd\ *adj* : having eaves esp. of an indicated kind ⟨deep-*eaved*⟩ ⟨steep-*eaved*⟩

eaves board *also* **eave board** *n* [ME *evesbord*, fr. *eves* + *bord* board] : an arris fillet nailed across the rafters at the eaves of a building in order to raise the starter course of slates or tiles

¹eaves·drop \ˈēvzˌdräp *sometimes* -vˌd-\ *vb* [prob. back-formation fr. *eavesdropper*] *vi* : to listen secretly to what is said in private — usu. used with *on* ⟨*eavesdropping* on the senate conference⟩ ⟨he hid under the table and *eavesdropped* on his sister and her sweetheart⟩ ~ *vt* **1** *archaic* : to learn or overhear by eavesdropping **2** : to eavesdrop on (as a conversation) ⟨I've just *eavesdropped* two demographers or geopoliticians —Christopher Morley⟩

²eavesdrop \"\ *also* **eaves·drip** \-ˌdrip\ *n* [*eavesdrop* fr. ME *evesdrop*, fr. *eves* + *drop*; *eavesdrip* fr. *eaves* + *drip*] **1** : the water that falls in drops from the eaves of a house **2** : the ground on which the water falls from the eaves **3** : a servitude formerly required in England before one could build so that water from one's eaves could fall directly on the land of another

eaves·drop·per \-pə(r)\ *n* [ME *evesdropper*, fr. *evesdrop*, n. + *-er*] : one that eavesdrops

eaves lath *also* **eave lath** *n* [ME *eveslath*, fr. *eves* + *lath*] : EAVES BOARD

eaves molding *also* **eave molding** *n* : a molding below the eaves of a building that acts as a cornice or part of a cornice

eaves swallow *also* **eave swallow** *n* : a swallow that nests under the eaves of buildings (as the cliff swallow or the common European martin)

eaves tile *also* **eave tile** *n* : roofing tile used for the row along the eaves of a building — called also *starter*

eaves trough *also* **eave trough** *n* : a gutter along the eaves

EB *abbr* eastbound

éba·no \ˈäbəˌnō, ˈeb-\ *n* -S [AmerSp, fr. Sp, ebony, fr. L *ebenus* — more at EBON] : any of several Mexican and Central American timber trees of the genus *Caesalpinia* (esp. *C. sclerocarpa*)

ébauche \āˈbōsh\ *n* -S [F, fr. *ébaucher* to rough out, outline, roughhew, fr. MF *esbocher*, fr. *es-* (fr. L *ex-*) + *-bocher* (fr. OF *-bauchier*, fr. *bauch*, *bauc* beam) — more at DEBAUCH] : an incomplete watch movement consisting of plates, bridges, wheels, and barrels to be finished and fitted with jewels, escapement, mainspring, hands, and dial

ébau·choir \ˌā(ˌ)bōshˈwär\ *n* -S [F, fr. *ébaucher*] : a chisel used to roughhew sculpture

¹ebb \ˈeb\ *n* -S [ME *eb*, *ebbe*, fr. OE *ebba*; akin to OFris *ebba* ebb, MD *ebbe*, OS *ebbia* ebb, ON *efja* river bend in which the current flows backwards, OE *of* from — more at OF] **1** : the reflux or flowing back of the tide : return of the tidal wave toward the sea ⟨the boats will go out on the ~⟩ — opposed to *flood* **2** : a point or condition of gradual decline from a higher to a lower level (as of activity) or from a better to a worse state — often used in the phrase *at the ebb* ⟨faith in the possibilities of mankind . . . is at the ~ —B.R.Redman⟩ or *at a low ebb* ⟨Federalism in New York was at a low ~ —L.B.Mason⟩

²ebb \"\ *vb* -ED/-ING/-S [ME *ebben*, fr. OE *ebbian*, fr. *ebba*, n.] *vi* **1** : to recede from its flood (as of the water of a tide toward the ocean) — opposed to *flow* **2 a** : to fall gradually from a higher to a lower level (as of activity) or from a better to a worse state : DECLINE ⟨his energy seemed to ~⟩ : draw to a close : DIMINISH, LESSEN ⟨capacity to resist ~*ed* away —Oscar Handlin⟩ **b** : RETURN, REVIVE — used with *back* ⟨his courage ~*ed* back again —O.E.Rölvaag⟩ ~ *vt* : to dry by the recession of the tide ⟨an ~*ed* beach⟩

³ebb \"\ *adj* [ME *eb* being at ebb, fr. *eb*, *ebbe*, n.] *dial Brit* : SHALLOW

ebb and flow *n* **1** : the alternate ebb and flood of the tide **2** : a condition or rhythm of alternate forward and backward movement or of alternate decline and renewed advance ⟨the *ebb and flow* of battle⟩ ⟨the *ebbs and flows* of business⟩

ebb-and-flow structure *n* : stratified rock structure characterized by alternating horizontal and cross-bedded layers thought to be produced by tidal ebb and flow

eb·bet \ˈebət\ *n* -S [alter. of earlier *evat*, *evet* newt, fr. ME *evete* — more at EFT] : the common green newt (*Triturus viridescens*) of the eastern U.S.

ebb tide *n* **1** : the tide while ebbing or at ebb — opposed to *flood tide* **2** : a period or state of decline ⟨civilization at its *ebb tide*⟩

eb·e·na·ce·ae \ˌebəˈnāsēˌē\ *n pl, cap* [NL, fr. L *ebenus* ebony + NL *-aceae* — more at EBON] : a family of plants (order Ebenales) comprising trees and shrubs (as the ebony and persimmon) with very hard wood, entire leaves, and dioecious or rarely perfect flowers succeeded by fleshy berries — **eb·e·na·ceous** \ˌ==ˈnāshəs\ *adj*

eb·e·na·les \ˌ==ˈnā(ˌ)lēz\ *n pl, cap* [NL, fr. L *ebenus* + NL *-ales*] : an order of dicotyledonous shrubs or trees having flowers with united petals and superior ovary and stamens borne on the corolla tube and constituting the families Ebenaceae, Sapotaceae, Styracaceae, and Symplocaceae

eb·e·ne·zer \ˌebəˈnēzə(r)\ *n* -S [Heb *ebhen hā-'ezer* stone of help; fr. the application of this name by Samuel to the stone which he set up in commemoration of God's help to the Israelites in their victory over the Philistines at Mizpah (1 Sam 7:12)] **1** *usu cap* : a commemoration of divine assistance ⟨here I raise mine *Ebenezer*; hither by Thy help I'm come —Robert Robinson⟩ **2** *dial* : ANGER, TEMPER ⟨he must have had a tempestical time of it for she had got her ~ up —T.C. Haliburton⟩

eber·hard effect \ˈebərˌhärd-, ˈābərˌhärt-\ *n, usu cap 1st E* [after Gustav *Eberhard* †1940 Ger. astronomer] : an effect observed in developed photographic images in which the density of small equally exposed areas varies with their size — compare ADJACENCY EFFECT

eb·er·thel·la \ˌebə(r)ˈthelə\ *n, cap* [NL, fr. Karl J. *Eberth* †1926 Ger. bacteriologist + NL *-ella*] *in many classifications* : a genus of motile aerobic gram-negative bacteria (family Enterobacteriaceae) forming acid but no gas on many carbohydrates, including certain pathogens (as *E. typhosa* which causes typhoid fever in man), and being sometimes replaced by *Salmonella* or *Bacterium*

ebi·o·nism \ˈēbēəˌnizəm, ˈeb-\ *n* -S *cap* [*ebion-* (fr. *Ebionite*) + *-ism*] : the principles and practices of the Ebionites

ebi·o·nite \-ˌnīt\ *n, usu cap* [ME, fr. ML *ebionita*, fr. Heb *ebyōn* poor + L *-ita* -ite] : one of a Judaistic Christian Gnostic sect of the 2d century A.D. that observed the Jewish law in part, rejected St. Paul, accepted only the Gospel of Matthew, and held an adoptionist Christology — **ebi·o·nit·ic** \ˌ===ˈnid·ik\ *adj, usu cap*

ebi·o·nit·ism \ˈ⸗⸗⸗,nīd·,izəm\ *n* -s *cap* : EBIONISM
ebo *or* **eboe** \ˈē(,)bō\ *n, pl* **ebo** *or* **ebos** *or* **eboe** *or* **eboes** *usu cap* : IBO
¹eb·on \ˈebən\ *n* -s [ME *eban*, fr. L *ebenus*, fr. Gk *ebenos*, fr. Egypt *hbnj*] *archaic* : ¹EBONY
²ebon \ˈ"\ *adj* : ²EBONY
eb·on·ite \-,nīt\ *n* -s [¹*ebon* + *-ite*] : hard rubber esp. when left black — sometimes used only of unfilled compositions
eb·on·ize \-,nīz\ *vt* -ED/-ING/-S : to make black or stain black in imitation of ebony
¹eb·o·ny \ˈebənē, -ni\ *n* -ES [prob. alter. of ME *hebenyf*, modif. of LL *hebeninus*, *ebeninus* of ebony, fr. Gk *ebeninos*, fr. *ebenos* ebony] **1** : a hard heavy durable wood yielded by various trees of the genus *Diospyros* in tropical Asia and Africa **2** : a tree from which ebony is obtained **3** : any of several trees yielding wood resembling ebony (as green ebony) **4** : a variable color averaging a dark grayish olive that is almost black — called also *teak*
²ebony \ˈ"\ *adj* **1** : made of or like ebony ⟨an ~ handle⟩ **2** *of color* : of very low lightness : BLACK, DARK ⟨a lanky man with an ~ face —R.G.Hubler⟩
ebony brown *n* : a reddish black
ebony family *n* : EBENACEAE
ebony spleenwort *n* : a common No. American fern (*Asplenium platyneuron*) with polished black stipes
ébou·le·ment \ābülmäⁿ\ *n* -s [F, fr. MF *esboulement*, fr. *esbouler* to cause to crumble down (fr. OF *esboeler* to disembowel, fr. *es-* — fr. L *ex-* — + *-boeler*, fr. *boel* bowel) + *-ment* — more at BOWEL] : LANDSLIDE
ebracteate \(ˈ)ē+\ *also* **ebrac·te·at·ed** \-ktē,ād·əd\ *adj* [*ebracteate* fr. NL *ebracteatus*, fr. *e-* + *bracteatus* bracteate; *ebracteated* fr. NL *ebracteatus* + E *-ed*] : being without bracts
ebracteolate \(ˈ)ē+\ *adj* [NL *ebracteolatus*, fr. *e-* + *bracteolatus* bracteolate] : being without bracteoles
ebri·e·ty \əˈbrīəd·ē, ē'-, -ətē, -i\ *n* -ES [ME *ebriete*, fr. MF or L; MF *ebrieté*, fr. L *ebrietat-*, *ebrietas*, fr. *ebrie-* (fr. *ebrius* drunk) + *-tat-*, *-tas* -ty — more at SOBER] : INEBRIETY
ébril·lade \ˌābrēˈyäd\ *n* -s [obs. F *ébrillade*, *esbrillade*, fr. It *sbrigliata*, fr. *sbrigliare* to jerk the rein, unbridle, fr. *s-* (fr. L *ex-*) + *-brigliare*, fr. *briglia* bridle, prob. of Gmc origin; akin to OE *brigdils* bridle, OHG *brittil* rein — more at BRIDLE] : a checking of a horse by means of jerking one rein when he refuses to turn
ebri·os·i·ty \ˌēbrēˈäsəd·ē, -ətē, -i\ *n* -ES [L *ebriositat-*, *ebriositas*, fr. *ebriosus* addicted to drink (fr. *ebrius* drunk + *-osus* -ose) + *-itat-*, *-itas* -ity] : habitual intoxication
ebul·lience \əˈbu̇lyən(t)s, ē'-,e'- *also* -ˈbəl- *or* -lēə-\ *n* -s [fr. *ebullient*, after such pairs as E *confluent*: *confluence*] : the quality of lively or animated expression of thoughts or feelings : high spirits : ENTHUSIASM, EXUBERANCE ⟨exhorted with his characteristic ~ and bluntness —G.H.Bolsover⟩
ebul·lien·cy \-nsē, -si\ *n* -ES [*ebullient* + *-cy*] : EBULLIENCE
ebul·lient \-nt\ *adj* [L *ebullient-*, *ebulliens*, pres. part. of *ebullire* to come bubbling out, fr. *e-* + *bullire* to bubble, boil, fr. *bulla* bubble — more at POLL (head)] **1** : BOILING, AGITATED ⟨indicates the presence of ~ internal energy —E.A.Armstrong⟩ **2** : characterized by ebullience ⟨three acts of ~ breezy music —C.M.Smith⟩ — **ebul·lient·ly** *adv*
ebul·li·om·e·ter \ə,bu̇lēˈäməd·ə(r), ē,-, e,- *also* -,bəl-\ *n* -s [ISV *ebullio-* (fr. L *ebullire*) + *-meter*] : an instrument for the usu. precise determination of either the absolute or the differential boiling points of liquids used esp. for determining the molecular weight of a solute dissolved in a liquid, the purity of liquids, and the alcoholic content of beverages
ebul·li·o·met·ric \⸗ˌ⸗lēəˈme·trik\ *adj* [*ebulliometry* + *-ic*] : relating to or by means of ebulliometry
ebul·li·om·e·try \⸗,⸗lēˈäm·ə·trē\ *n* -ES [ISV *ebullio-* + *-metry*] : the determination of boiling points of liquids or the change of boiling point of a liquid owing to the presence of dissolved material
ebul·lio·scope \⸗ˈ⸗lēə,skōp, -lyə-\ *n* [ISV *ebullio-* + *-scope*; orig. formed as F *ébullioscope*] : EBULLIOMETER
ebul·li·o·scop·ic \⸗ˌ⸗(⸗)⸗ˈskäpik\ *adj* [ISV *ebullioscope* + *-ic*] : EBULLIOMETRIC
ebul·li·os·co·py \⸗,bu̇lēˈäskəpē, -,bəl-\ *n* -ES [ISV *ebullio-* + *-scopy*] : EBULLIOMETRY
eb·ul·li·tion \,ebəˈlishən, ,ēb-\ *n* -s [LL *ebullition-*, *ebullitio*, fr. L *ebullitus* (past part. of *ebullire*) + *-ion-*, *-io* -ion] **1** : the act, process, or state of boiling or bubbling up **2** : a sudden and violent outburst or display ⟨an ~ of chivalry, indignation, and racial solidarity —Douglas Stewart⟩
eb·ur·nat·ed \ˈebər,nād·əd, ˈē(,)bər-; əˈbər-, ē'-,e'-\ *adj* [fr. *eburnation*, after such pairs as E *creation*: *created*] : hard and dense like ivory ⟨~ bone⟩ ⟨~ cartilage⟩
eb·ur·na·tion \,ebərˈnāshən, ,ē(,)bər-\ *n* -s [fr. (assumed) NL *eburnation-*, *eburnatio*, fr. L *eburnus*, *eburneus* of ivory (fr. *ebur* ivory) + *-ation-*, *-atio* -ation — more at IVORY] : a diseased condition in which bone or cartilage is eburnated
ebur·ne·an \əˈbərnēən, ē'-,e'-\ *or* **ebur·ne·ous** \-ēəs\ *adj* [*eburnean* fr. L *eburneus* + E *-an*; *eburneous* fr. L *eburneus*] : resembling ivory in color
¹ec- *prefix* [ME, fr. OF, fr. L, fr. Gk *ek*, fr. *ex* — more at EX-] : out of : outside of : outside ⟨*ec*cyesis⟩
²ec- *or* **eco-** *also* **oec-** *or* **oeco-** *or* **oiko-** *comb form* [earlier also *yco-*, fr. MF & LL; MF *yco-*, fr. LL *oeco-*, *oiko-*, fr. Gk *oik-*, *oiko-*, fr. *oikos* house, habitation — more at VICINITY] **1 a** : household ⟨*eco*nomy⟩ **b** : economic and ⟨*eco*-cultural⟩ **2** : habitat or environment esp. as a factor significantly influencing the mode of life or the course of development ⟨*eco*species⟩ ⟨*eco*system⟩ ⟨*ec*ad⟩
ec *abbr* economics
EC *abbr* **1** east central **2** error corrected **3** established church **4** [L *exempli causa*] for example
ecad \ˈē,kad, ˈe,-\ *n* -s [²*ec-* + *-ad*, n. suffix] **1** : an organism or kind of organism (as a species) modified by environment **2** : a nonheritable somatic modification induced by environment : an acquired character
ecalcarate \(ˈ)ē+\ *adj* [*e-* + L *calcar* spur + E *-ate* — more at CALCAR] *biol* : being without a spur
ecan·da \əˈkandə\ *n* -s [prob. fr. Umbundu *ekanda*] : a tropical African vine (*Raphionacme utilis*) of the family Asclepiadaceae that yields rubber
ecardinal \(ˈ)ē+\ *adj* [*e-* + L *cardin-*, *cardo* hinge + E *-al* — more at CARDINAL] : being without a hinge — used of inarticulate brachiopods or their shells
ecardines \(ˈ)ē+\ [NL, fr. *e-* + *-cardines* creatures having (such) a hinge, fr. L *cardines*, pl. of *cardin-*, *cardo* hinge] *syn of* INARTICULATA
ecarinate \(ˈ)ē+\ *adj* [*e-* + *carinate*] *biol* : being without a carina or keel
¹écar·té \ˌā,kärˈtā, āˈkär,tā\ *n* -s [F, fr. past part. of *écarter* to discard, fr. *é-* (fr. L *ex-*) + *-carter* (fr. *carte* card) — more at CARD] : a two-handed card game which is played with a 32-card pack and in which each player is dealt 5 cards and has the right to replace any or all of them before play can begin, the object being to win at least 3 tricks in a given hand
²écarté \ˈ"\ *adj* [F, past part. of *écarter* to separate, spread apart, fr. OF *escarter*, fr. (assumed) VL *exquartare* to divide into four parts, fr. L *ex-* + (assumed) VL *-quartare*, fr. L *quartus* fourth — more at QUART] *ballet, of the legs* : held wide apart with an oblique side extension of one foot and the same arm
ecaudata \ˌē+\ [NL, fr. neut. pl. of *ecaudatus*] *syn of* SALIENTIA
ecaudate \(ˈ)ē+\ *adj* [NL *ecaudatus*, fr. *e-* + ML *caudatus* having a tail — more at CAUDATE] : having no tail
ec·bol·ic \ekˈbälik\ *n* -s [ISV *ecbol-* (fr. Gk *ekbolē* expulsion, fr. *ekballein* to throw out, fr. *ek* out of, out — fr. *ex* — + *ballein* to throw) + *-ic* — more at EX-, DEVIL] : a drug (as ergot) that tends to increase uterine contractions and that is used esp. to facilitate delivery
ec·ce \ˈ⸗(,)⸗ — *see* ECCE HOMO\ *interj* [L, see, behold, fr. *ec-* (prob. akin to Gk *ekeinos* that one, Russ *eto* this, Skt *adaḥ* that, L *iterum* again) + *-ce* (akin to L *cis* on this side) — more at ITERATE, HE] — used to call attention often to one persecuted unjustly
ec·ce ho·mo \ˌe(,)chāˈhō(,)mō (*usu in the Catholic Church*), ˌe(,)kā-, ˌek(,)sē-\ *n* [LL, behold the man; fr. the Vulgate version of the words spoken by Pilate in presenting Christ wearing the crown of thorns to the Jews (Jn 19:5)] : a picture in which the central figure is Christ crowned with thorns

¹ec·cen·tric \ikˈsentrik, (ˈ)ekˈs-, -rēk\ *n* -s [ME *excentryke*, fr. MF & ML; MF *excentrique*, fr. ML *excentricus*, *eccentricus*, fr. *eccentricus*, adj.] **1** *in the Ptolemaic system of astronomy* : the circular orbit of the sun around the earth, the latter not being at the center of the circle; *also* : the orbit or deferent of the epicycles of the moon or a planet **2** : a mechanical device consisting of a disk through which a shaft is keyed eccentrically and a circular strap which works freely round the rim of the disk for communicating its motion to one end of a rod the other end of which is compelled to move in a straight line so as to produce reciprocating motion **3 a** : a person that deviates from conventional or accepted conduct esp. in odd or whimsical ways ⟨an ~ who cluttered his estate with statues of himself⟩ **b** : a person or thing that varies from some established type, pattern, or rule in any way ⟨Milton seems to me . . . the greatest of all ~*s* —T.S.Eliot⟩
²eccentric \ˈ"\ *or* **ex·cen·tric** \ˈ"\ *adj* [ML *eccentricus*, fr. Gk *ekkentros* not having the earth as center, eccentric (fr. *ek* out of, out — fr. *ex* — + *-kentros*, fr. *kentron* center of a circle) + L *-icus* -ic — more at CENTER] **1** : not having the same center — used of circles, cylinders, spheres, and certain other figures; opposed to *concentric* **2** : deviating from some established type, pattern, or rule ⟨his goods were so ~ that only he could ever sell them —Wolf Mankowitz⟩ : deviating from conventional or accepted usage or conduct esp. in odd or whimsical ways ⟨famed for his ~ spelling⟩ ⟨~ behavior made him the butt of many jokes⟩ **3 a** : deviating or departing from the center or from the line of a circle ⟨an ~ orbit⟩ : relating to deviation from the center or from circular motion **b** : located elsewhere than at the geometrical center : having its axis or support so located ⟨~ wheel⟩ **4** : being away or remote from a center ⟨their ~ location makes it . . . costly to get oil from there —Ellsworth Huntington & Samuel Van Valkenburg⟩ : OFF-CENTER ⟨~ loading occurs when force on a member such as a column is not applied at the center of the column —*Army Tech. Manual 5-230*⟩ **5** : of or relating to an eccentric : driven by an eccentric ⟨an ~ strap⟩ ⟨an ~ rod⟩
syn see STRANGE
ec·cen·tri·cal \-rəkəl\ *archaic var of* ECCENTRIC
ec·cen·tri·cal·ly \-rək(ə)lē, -rēk-, -li\ *adv* : in an eccentric way
ec·cen·tric·i·ty \,ek,senˈtrisəd·ē, -ətē, -i *sometimes* ,eksən- *or* ik,sen- *or* ek,sen-\ *n* -ES [ML *eccentricitat-*, *eccentricitas*, fr. *eccentricus* + L *-itat-*, *-itas* -ity] : the condition, degree, or an instance of being eccentric: as **a** *in machinery* : the distance of the center of figure of a body from an axis about which it turns : THROW — compare ¹ECCENTRIC 2 **b** : deviation from an established pattern, rule, or norm ⟨speaking French with an ~ that could not be ignored —F.M.Ford⟩ : odd or whimsical behavior ⟨mild and retiring to the point of ~ —C.B. Forcey⟩ **c** : the ratio of the distances from any point of a conic section to a focus and the corresponding directrix, being less than one in the ellipse, greater than one in the hyperbola, equal to one in the parabola, and equal to zero in the circle
eccentric-shaft press *n* : a punch press in which pressure is applied to the slide by means of an eccentric shaft
ec·chy·mosed \ˈekə,mōzd, -ōst\ *adj* [*ecchymosis* + *-ed*] : affected with ecchymosis
ec·chy·mo·sis \,ekəˈmōsəs\ *n, pl* **ecchymo·ses** \-ō,sēz\ [NL, fr. Gk *ekchymōsis*, fr. *ekchymousthai* to extravasate blood (fr. *ek* out of, out — fr. *ex* — + *-chymousthai*, fr. *chymos* juice) + *-osis* — more at EX-, CHYME] : the escape of blood into the tissues from ruptured blood vessels marked by a livid black-and-blue or purple spot or area; *also* : the discoloration so caused — compare PETECHIA — **ec·chy·mot·ic** \ˌ⸗⸗ˈmäd·ik\ *adj*
eccl *abbr* **1** ecclesiastical **2** ecclesiology
ec·cle \ˈekəl\ *n* -s [alter. of *hickwall*] *dial Eng* : GREEN WOODPECKER
ec·cles cake \ˈekəlz-\ *n, usu cap E* [*Eccles*, municipal borough in Lancashire, England] *Brit* : a rich cake with fruit filling (as currants)
ecclesi- *or* **ecclesio-** *comb form* [ME *ecclesi-*, fr. LL, fr. *ecclesia* church, fr. L, assembly of citizens of a Greek state, fr. Gk *ekklēsia* church, assembly of citizens of a Greek state, fr. *ekkalein* to call forth, summon, fr. *ek* out of, out (fr. *ex*) + *kalein* to call — more at EX-, LOW (moo)] : church ⟨*ecclesi*arch⟩ ⟨*ecclesio*graphy⟩
ec·cle·sia \əˈklēzēə, e'-, -lēzh(ē)ə\ *n, pl* **ecclesi·ae** \-lēz(h)ē,ē, -lāzē,ī\ [in sense 1, fr. L, fr. Gk *ekklēsia*; in other senses, fr. LL, church, fr. L] **1** : a political assembly of citizens of ancient Greek states; *esp* : the periodic meeting of the Athenian citizens for conducting public business and for considering affairs proposed by the council **2** : CHURCH 4 d, 4 e **3** : one of the local organizations of the Christadelphians
ec·cle·si·arch \-lēzē,ärk\ *n* -s [*ecclesi-* + *-arch*] **1** : a high church official or ruling prelate **2** [MGk *ekklēsiarchēs*, fr. Gk *ekklēsia* church + *-archēs* -arch] : a sacristan in the Eastern Church
ec·cle·si·ast \-zē,ast, -ēəst, -ē,aa(ə)st\ *n* -s [ME *ecclesiaste*, fr. LL *ecclesiastes*, fr. Gk *ekklēsiastēs*, lit., member of a Greek ecclesia, fr. *ekklēsia* church, ecclesia + *-astēs* -ast] **1** : ECCLESIASTIC **2** : a member of the Athenian ecclesia
ec·cle·si·as·tic \ə,klēzēˈastik, e,-, -ˈaas-, -tēk\ *n* -s [LL *ecclesiasticus*, fr. *ecclesiasticus*, adj.] : a person in holy orders or consecrated to the service of the church : CLERGYMAN, PRIEST
ec·cle·si·as·ti·cal \⸗ˌ⸗⸗ˈ⸗tәkəl, -tēk-\ *or* **ec·cle·si·as·tic** \-tik,-tēk\ *adj* [*ecclesiastical* fr. ME, fr. LL *ecclesiasticus* ecclesiastical + ME *-al*; *ecclesiastic* fr. MF *ecclesiastique*, fr. LL *ecclesiasticus*, fr. Gk *ekklēsiastikos*, lit., of an ecclesia, fr. *ekklēsiastēs* + *-ikos* -ic] **1 a** : of or relating to a church esp. as a formal and established institution ⟨whether tried in an ~ or a civil court⟩ ⟨~ history⟩ **b** : belonging to, suggestive of, or suitable for use in a church building or service of worship ⟨roofing material ideal for ~ work⟩ ⟨~ music⟩ : CHURCHLY ⟨spoke with an ~ solemnity⟩ **2** : of or relating to the formal and established institutions or government of any religion ⟨the festivals of the ~ year in ancient Athens⟩ ⟨the Jewish board that gives ~ endorsement to chaplaincy candidates⟩ — **ec·cle·si·as·ti·cal·ly** \-tәk(ə)lē, -tēk-, -li\ *adv*
ecclesiastical calendar *n* : a lunisolar calendar used in Roman Catholic and many Protestant countries for determining the times of Easter and other movable feasts
ecclesiastical corporation *n* : a corporation concerned only with religious matters and consisting wholly of ecclesiastics (as the dean and chapter of a cathedral church) — contrasted with *lay corporation*
ecclesiastical court *n* : a court having jurisdiction in ecclesiastical affairs : a tribunal in an ecclesiastical body — called also *Court Christian*
ecclesiastical law *n* : the law established by a church or religious denomination and administered in its courts : CANON LAW : the law whether of ecclesiastical or civil law origin applied to a church
ecclesiastical mode *n* : an ascending diatonic musical scale of eight notes or tones comprising an octave and consisting of a pentachord and a tetrachord of which the highest tone of one is the lowest tone of the other — called also *Gregorian mode, medieval mode*; see DORIAN MODE, HYPODORIAN MODE, HYPOMIXOLYDIAN MODE, HYPOPHRYGIAN MODE, LYDIAN MODE, MIXOLYDIAN MODE, PHRYGIAN MODE; MODE illustration
ec·cle·si·as·ti·cism \ə,klēzēˈastə,sizəm, e,-, -ˈaas-\ *n* -s : excessive attachment to ecclesiastical forms, methods, and practices ⟨the struggle between religion and ~⟩
ec·cle·si·ast·ry *pronunc at* ECCLESIAST + rē\ *n* -ES : ecclesiastical matters
ec·cle·si·ol·a·try \ə,klēzēˈälə·trē, -e,-\ *n* -ES [*ecclesi-* + *-latry*] : excessive devotion to the church
ec·cle·si·o·log·i·cal \⸗ˌ⸗zēəˈläjəkəl\ *also* **ec·cle·si·o·log·ic** \-jik\ *adj* [*ecclesiology* + *-ical*, *-ic*] : of or relating to ecclesiology — **ec·cle·si·o·log·i·cal·ly** \-jәk(ə)lē\ *adv*
ec·cle·si·ol·o·gist \⸗,⸗⸗ˈäləjəst\ *n* -s [*ecclesiology* + *-ist*] : a specialist in ecclesiology
ec·cle·si·ol·o·gy \-jē\ *n* -ES [*ecclesi-* + *-logy*] **1** : the science or study of ecclesiastical art and antiquities esp. with reference to the adornment and equipment of churches **2** : the study of the doctrine of the church **3** : church policy ⟨a venture in practical ~ in southern India⟩
ec·co·pro·ti·co·phor·ic \,ekō,prōd·əkōˈfórik, -präd·-\ *adj* [obs. E *eccoprotic*, n., laxative (fr. assumed NL *eccoproticum*, fr. neut. of assumed NL *eccoproticus*, adj., laxative, fr. Gk *ekkoprōtikos*, fr. assumed Gk *ekkoprōtos* — verbal of *ekkoproun* to empty of excrement, fr. *ek* out of, out, fr. *ex* + *-koproun*, fr. *kopros* excrement, dung — + Gk *-ikos* -ic) + E *-o-* + *-phoric* — more at EX-, COPR-] : exhibiting the properties of a laxative
ec·cri·na·les \,ekrəˈnā(,)lēz\ *n pl, cap* [NL, fr. *Eccrina*, genus of fungi + *-ales*] : an order of fungi (class Phycomycetes) containing lower fungi that occur as parasites in the alimentary canals of arthropods, that have slender coenocytic hyphae with funnel-shaped attachment disks, and that reproduce by endospores
ec·crine \ˈekrən; -,krin, -īn,-ēn\ *adj* [ISV ¹*ec-* + *-crine* (fr. Gk *krinein* to separate) — more at CERTAIN] : producing a fluid secretion without removing cytoplasm from the secreting cells : produced by an eccrine gland — compare APOCRINE, MEROCRINE
eccrine gland *n* : any of the rather small sweat glands that produce an eccrine secretion, are restricted to the human skin, and are lined with cuboidal epithelium surrounded by contractile myoepithelial cells — compare APOCRINE GLAND
ec·cri·nid \ˈekrənəd, -,nid\ *n* -s [NL *Eccrina* + E *-id*] : a fungus of the order Eccrinales
ec·cri·nol·o·gy \,ekrəˈnäləjē\ *n* -ES [F *eccrinologie*, fr. *eccrino-* (fr. Gk *ekkrinein* to secrete, fr. *ek* out of, out + *krinein* to separate) + *-logie* -logy] : a branch of physiology that deals with secretion and secretory organs
ec·cy·cle·ma \,eksəˈklēmə\ *n* -s [Gk *ekkyklēma*, fr. *ekkyklein* to wheel out, fr. *ek* out of, out + *kyklein* to wheel, revolve, fr. *kyklos* wheel — more at WHEEL] : a machine used to display an interior scene (as dead bodies after a murder) in the classic theater
ec·de·mite *or* **ek·de·mite** \ekˈdē,mīt, ˈekdə,m-\ *n* -s [Sw *ekdemit*, fr. Gk *ekdēmos* being away from home (fr. *ek* + *dēmos* deme, populace) + Sw *-it* -ite — more at DEM-] : a yellow or green lead arsenate and chloride of uncertain composition occurring in crystals, masses, and crusts
ec·dys·i·al \(ˈ)ekˈdizēəl, -izh(ē)əl\ *adj* [*ecdysis* + *-al*] : of, relating to, or functioning in ecdysis ⟨an ~ gland⟩
ec·dys·i·ast \ekˈdizē,ast, -ēəst\ *n* -s [*ecdysis* + *-ast*] : STRIPTEASER
ec·dy·sis \ˈekdəsəs\ *n, pl* **ecdy·ses** \-ə,sēz\ [NL, fr. Gk *ekdysis* act of getting out, escape, fr. *ekdyein* to take off, strip off (fr. *ek* out of, out + *dyein* to dive in, put on, don) + *-sis* — more at ADYTUM] : the act of molting or shedding an outer cuticular layer (as in insects and crustaceans) — opposed to *endysis*
ece \ˈēs\ *n* -s [Gk *oikos* house, habitation — more at VICINITY] : HABITAT
ECE *abbr* extended coverage endorsement
ece·sic \əˈsēsik, ē'-\ *adj* [*ecesis* + *-ic*] : of, relating to, or engaging in ecesis
ece·sis \-ēsəs\ *n* -ES [Gk *oikēsis* act of inhabiting, fr. *oikein* to inhabit (fr. *oikos*) + *-sis*] : ESTABLISHMENT 5
ECG *abbr* electrocardiogram
ec·go·nine \ˈekgə,nēn, -,nən\ *n* -s [ISV *ecgon-* (fr. Gk *ekgonos* born of, sprung from, fr. *ek* out of, out + *gonos* child) + *-ine*; akin to Gk *gignesthai* to be born — more at KIN] : a crystalline alkaloid $C_9H_{15}NO_3$ obtained by hydrolysis of cocaine; tropine-carboxylic acid
ech *abbr* echelon
échap·pé \ˌā,shaˈpā, āˈsha,pā\ *adj* [F, fr. past part. of *échapper* to escape, fr. (assumed) VL *excappare* — more at ESCAPE] *ballet, of the legs* : opened from closed position
échappée \ˈ"\ *n* -s [F, fr. fem. of *échappé*, past part. of *échapper* to escape] : ESCAPE NOTE
ech·ard \ˈe,kärd\ *n* -s [Gk *echein* to hold, withhold + *ardein* to water — more at SCHEME, ARDELLA] : the soil water that is unavailable to plant organisms — compare CHRESARD, HOLARD
eche *vt* -ED/-ING/-S [ME *echen* — more at EKE (to increase)] *obs* : INCREASE, ENLARGE
eche·lette \ˌeshəˈlet, ˌāsh-\ *n* -s [F *échelette* small rack, fr. MF *eschelette* small ladder, fr. *eschele*, *eschiele* ladder + *-ette*] : a reflection grating made by ruling parallel V-shaped grooves in a polished metal plate so that light is reflected from the corresponding faces of successive grooves
echel·i·dae \əˈkelə,dē, ē'-\ *n pl, cap* [NL, prob. fr. *Echelus*, type genus (prob. modif. of Gk *enchelys* eel) + *-idae* — more at ANGUIS] : a family of small tropical eels comprising the worm eels
¹echelle \āˈshel\ *n* -s [F *échelle* ladder] : a lacing of ribbons on the stomacher of a 17th century costume
²echelle \ˈ"\ *n* -s [F *échelle* ladder, fr. OF *eschiele*, fr. LL *scala* — more at SCALE] : a diffraction grating made by ruling narrow flat steps on a plane metallic mirror and having a grating space and resolving power intermediate between an echelette and an echelon
¹ech·e·lon \ˈeshə,län\ *n* -s *often attrib* [F *échelon*, lit., rung of a ladder, fr. OF *eschelon*, fr. *eschele*, *eschiele* ladder] **1 a** : an arrangement of a body of troops with its units each somewhat to the left or right of the one in the rear like a series of steps; *also* : any similar formation of units or individuals ⟨a long ~ of wild geese —H.L.Davis⟩ — often used with *in* ⟨long staggering line of north canoes turned in ~ —Walter O'Meara⟩ **b** : a flight formation in which each airplane flies at a certain elevation above or below and at a certain distance behind and to the right or left of the airplane ahead **c** : one of a number of military units in echelon formation; *also* : any military or nonmilitary unit or group of individuals acting or appearing to act in a disciplined, organized, or united manner ⟨the first ~*s* in an amphibious assault —*Aero Digest*⟩ **2 a** : a group of individuals having a particular responsibility or occupying a particular level or grade (as of command, authority, or leadership) in an organization, profession, or field of activity ⟨the financial, supply, and training ~*s* of the European Army —*Newsweek*⟩ ⟨the lower ~*s* of the bureaucracy⟩ ⟨the higher ~*s* of the Social Register —Alva Johnston⟩ **b** : one of a series of levels or grades (as of leadership or responsibility) in an organization or field of activity ⟨permits employees on every ~ to participate in the development of policy⟩ **3** : a diffraction grating giving spectra of very high order and dispersion and used mainly in the study of fine structure that consists of a series of plane-parallel glass plates of exactly equal thickness each wider than its neighbor by the same small amount and thus forms a miniature stairway, light normally entering at the widest plate and emerging at the successive risers of the stairway **4** : an arrangement of geologic features (as mountains, folds, fractures) in a pattern resembling that of a military echelon

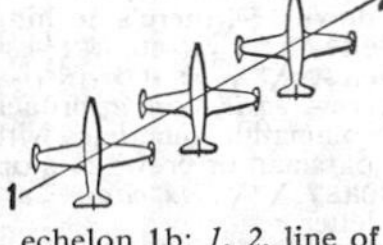

echelon 1b: *1, 2*, line of bearing

²echelon \ˈ"\ *vb* -ED/-ING/-S [F *échelonner*, fr. *échelon*] *vt* : to place (as troops or fortifications) in echelon ~ *vi* : to take position in echelon
ech·e·lon·ment \-nmənt, ,⸗⸗ˈ⸗⸗\ *n* -s [F *échelonnement*, fr. *échelonner* + *-ment*] : the timing or positioning of troops or supplies to provide uninterrupted flow to the front
ech·e·ne·id \,ekəˈnēəd\ *n* -s [NL *Echeneid-*, *Echeneis*] : a fish of the genus *Echeneis*; *broadly* : REMORA
ech·e·ne·is \-ēəs\ *n, cap* [NL, fr. L, remora, fr. Gk *echenēis*, fr. *echenēis* that detains ships, fr. *eche-* (fr. *echein* to hold) + *-nēis* (fr. *naus* ship); fr. a supposed ability to slow down ships — more at SCHEME, NAVE] : a genus (the type of the family Echeneididae or Echeneidae) of marine fishes comprising the typical remoras
ech·e·ve·ria \,echəvəˈrēə, -rīə\ *n* [NL, after *Echeveria*, 19th cent. Mex. botanical illustrator] **1** *cap* : a large genus of tropical American succulent plants (family Crassulaceae) having flowers with erect petals that spread only at the tips and axillary flower clusters **2** -s : any plant of *Echeveria* or of the closely related genus *Cotyledon*
¹echid·na \əˈkidnə, ē'-,e'-\ *n* [NL, fr. L, viper, fr. Gk — more at ANGUIS] **1** -s **a** : an oviparous burrowing nocturnal mammal (*Tachyglossus aculeatus*) of the order Monotremata native to Australia, Tasmania, and New Guinea that is somewhat larger than a hedgehog and has the hair of the skin

mingled with spines on the upper part of the body, the snout long and tapering, the mouth wholly toothless with a long extensile tongue adapted for feeding on ants, the salivary glands enlarged, and the claws long and heavy **b :** a member of a related New Guinea genus (*Zaglossus*) having three claws on each foot **2** *cap* **:** a genus of moray eels that are usu. rather small with strikingly marbled and reticulated patterns on the body surface

²echidna \"\ [NL, fr. L, viper] *syn of* TACHYGLOSSUS

³echidna \"\ [NL, fr. L, viper] *syn of* BITIS

¹echid·ni·dae \-nə,dē\ [NL, fr. *Echidna* genus of moray eels + *-idae*] *syn of* MURAENIDAE

²echidnidae \"\ [NL, fr. *²Echidna* + *-idae*] *syn of* TACHYGLOSSIDAE

echid·noph·a·ga \,ē,kid'näfəgə, ,e,-\ *n, cap* [NL, prob. fr. *echidno-* (fr. Gk, fr. *echidna*) + *-phaga* (fem. of *-phagus* -phagous, fr. Gk *-phagos*)] **:** a genus comprising fowl fleas (as the sticktight flea) of which the female remains attached to the host

echim·y·ine \ə'kimē,īn, ē'-,e'-, -mēən\ *adj* [NL *Echimys* + E *-ine*] **:** of or relating to *Echimys*

echi·mys \-'kīməs, 'ekə,mis\ *n, cap* [NL, irreg. fr. Gk *echinos* hedgehog + *mys* mouse — more at ANGUIS, MOUSE] **:** a genus (the type of the family Echimyidae) of hystricomorph rodents of So. and Central America comprising various spiny rats or urares

echin- *or* **echino-** *comb form* [L *echin-* prickle, fr. *echinus* sea urchin, fr. Gk *echinos* hedgehog, sea urchin] **1 :** prickle **:** prickly ⟨*Echino*cactus⟩ **2 a :** sea urchin ⟨*echin*al⟩ ⟨*echino*chrome⟩ **b :** echinoderm ⟨*echin*ology⟩

ech·i·na·cea \,ekə'nāshēə\ *n* [NL, fr. *echin-* + *-acea* (fem. of *-aceus* -aceous)] **1** *cap* **:** a small genus of coarse herbs (family Compositae) having thick rough leaves and long-stalked flower heads with showy purplish, crimson, or yellow rays **2 :** the dried rhizome and roots of either of two herbs (*Echinacea pallida* and *E. angustifolia*) formerly used in the treatment of ulcers and boils

echi·nal \ə'kīnᵊl, ē'-,e-; 'ekənᵊl\ *adj* [*echin-* + *-al*] **:** relating to a sea urchin

echi·nate \-nət, -,nāt\ *also* **echi·nat·ed** \-,nād·əd\ *adj* [*echinate* fr. L *echinatus*, fr. *echin-* + *-atus* -ate; *echinated* fr. L *echinatus* + E *-ed*] **:** densely covered with stiff bristles or spines **:** prickly like a hedgehog — compare ECHINULATE, MURICATE

eching *pres part of* ECHE

echini *pl of* ECHINUS

echi·nid \ə'kīnəd, ē'-,e'-\ *n* -s [NL *Echinidae*] **:** SEA URCHIN

echin·i·dae \-'kinə,dē\ *n pl, cap* [NL, fr. *Echinus*, type genus + *-idae*] **:** a family (order Centrechinoida) including a large number of widely distributed sea urchins a few of which are used as food — see ECHINUS

ech·i·nid·ea \,ekə'nidēə\ [NL, fr. *Echinus* + *-idea*] *syn of* ECHINOIDEA

ech·i·nite \'ekə,nīt; ə'kī,-, ē'-,e'-\ *n* -s [NL *echinita*, fr. L *echinus* sea urchin + *-ita* -ite] **:** a fossil sea urchin

echi·no- *in pronunciations below*, ≈≈≈ = ə¦kīnō *or* ē¦- *or* e¦ *or* -nə *or* ¦ekə(,)nō\ — see ECHIN-

echi·no·cactus \≈≈≈ *at* ECHINO- + \ *n* [NL, fr. *echin-* + *Cactus*] **1** *cap* **:** a large genus of globular or cylindrical strongly ribbed and usu. very spiny cacti that occur from the southwestern U.S. to Brazil **2 :** any plant of the genus *Echinocactus*

echi·no·car·is \" + 'ka(a)rəs\ *n, cap* [NL, fr. *echin-* + *-caris*] **:** a genus of extinct crustaceans (order Nebaliacea) the tail spines of which are common in various Devonian rocks

echi·no·ce·re·us \" + 'sirēəs\ *n* [NL, fr. *echin-* + *Cereus*] **1** *cap* **:** a genus of low ribbed cacti **2** *pl* **echinoce·rei** \-ē,ī\ **:** any plant of the genus *Echinocereus* having single or few usu. short joints and spiny ovaries and flower tubes

ech·i·noch·loa \,ekə'näkləwə\ *n, cap* [NL, fr. *echin-* + Gk *chloa, chloē* young verdure, fr. *chloos* light green color; fr. the prickly awns — more at GLOW] **:** a genus of succulent grasses found in warm regions — see BARNYARD GRASS, JAPANESE MILLET

echi·no·chrome \≈≈≈ *at* ECHINO- + ,krōm\ *n* -s [*echin-* + *-chrome*] **:** any of several red to brown respiratory pigments found in certain sea urchins

echi·no·coc·cic \"+¦käk(s)ik\ *adj* [ISV *echinococc-* (fr. NL *Echinococcus*) + *-ic*] **:** of, relating to, or involving *Echinococcus* or hydatids

echi·no·coc·co·sis \"+(,)kä'kōsəs\ *n, pl* **echinococco·ses** \-ō,sēz\ [NL, fr. *Echinococcus* + *-osis*] **:** infestation with or disease caused by a small tapeworm (*Echinococcus granulosus*); *esp* **:** HYDATID DISEASE

echi·no·coc·cus \"+'käkəs\ *n* [NL, fr. *echin-* + *-coccus*] **1** *cap* **:** a genus of tapeworms (family Taeniidae) that alternate a minute adult usu. having no more than three proglottids and living as a harmless commensal in the intestine of dogs and other carnivores with a hydatid larva invading tissues esp. of the liver of cattle, sheep, swine, and man, and acting as a serious often fatal pathogen **2** *pl* **echinococ·ci :** any worm of the genus *Echinococcus; sometimes* **:** HYDATID

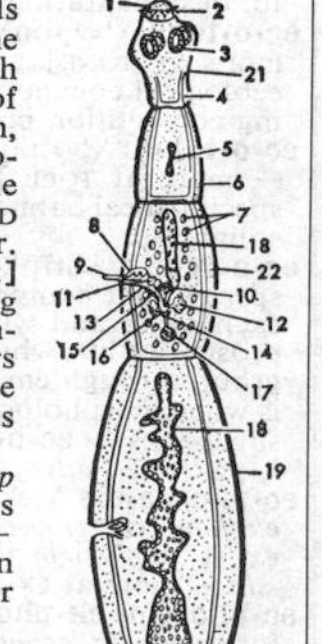

echinococcus: *1* rostellum, *2* hooklets, *3* sucker, *4* neck, *5* germinal mass, *6* immature proglottid, *7* testes, *8* cirrus pouch, *9* cirrus, *10* vas deferens, *11* genital pore, *12* ovary, *13* vagina, *14* vitelline duct, *15* seminal receptacle, *16* ootype, *17* vitelline gland, *18* uterus, *19* gravid proglottid, *20* eggs

echi·no·cys·tis \"+'sistəs\ *n* [NL, fr. *echin-* + *-cystis*; fr. the spiny globular fruit] **1** *cap* **:** a genus of prostrate or climbing American herbaceous plants (family Cucurbitaceae) with greenish white flowers followed by densely spiny oblong to ovate fruits **2** -ES **:** any plant of the genus *Echinocystis*

echi·no·cys·toi·da \"+sə'stȯidə\ *n pl, cap* [NL, irreg. fr. *Echinocystites*, fossil genus of Echinodermata (fr. *echin-* + *-cystis* + *-ites* -ite) + *-oida*] **:** an order of Silurian fossil echinoids having small irregular spheroidal or flattened tests

echi·no·der \"+,de(ə)r\ *n* -s [NL *Echinodera*] **:** KINORHYNCH

ech·i·nod·era \,ekə'nädərə\ [NL, fr. *Echinoderes*] *syn of* KINORHYNCHA

ech·i·nod·er·es \-,rēz\ *n, cap* [NL, fr. *echin-* + *-deres* (fr. Gk *derē, deirē* neck) — more at DER-] **:** a genus (the type of the family Echinoderidae) of minute segmented spinous marine worms that is the first-known and best-known representative of the class Kinorhyncha

ech·i·nod·er·id \-rəd, -rid\ *n* -s [NL *Echinoderidae* (family including the genus *Echinoderes*), fr. *Echinoderes*, type genus + *-idae*] **:** KINORHYNCH

echi·no·derm \≈≈≈ *at* ECHINO- + ,dərm\ *n* -s [NL *Echinodermata*] **:** one of the Echinodermata

echi·no·der·ma \"+'dərmə\ [NL, fr. *echin-* + *-derma* (fr. Gk *derma* skin) — more at DERM-] *syn of* ECHINODERMATA

echi·no·der·ma·ta \-məd·ə\ *n pl, cap* [NL, fr. *echin-* + *-dermata*] **:** a phylum of radially symmetrical coelomate marine animals consisting of the starfishes, sea urchins, and their related forms all having a calcareous exoskeleton, a blood-vascular system, a nervous system, and a water-vascular system that through small tubular appendages of the body connecting with these vessels provides tentacles and organs of locomotion — compare TUBE FOOT — **echi·no·der·ma·tous** \-¦dərməd·əs\ *adj*

ech·i·nod·o·rus \,ekə'nädərəs\ *n, cap* [NL, fr. *echin-* + Gk *doros* leather bag, fr. *derein* to skin; fr. the form of the ovary — more at TEAR] **:** a genus of chiefly American aquatic or marsh herbs (family Alismataceae) having long-stalked often spotted leaves, delicate white flowers in racemes or panicles, and spiny clusters of beaked fruits

echi·noid \ə'kī,nȯid, ē'-,e'-, 'ekə,-\ *n* -s [NL *Echinoidea*] **:** SEA URCHIN

ech·i·noi·dea \,ekə'nȯidēə\ *n pl, cap* [NL, fr. *echin-* + *-oidea*] **:** a class of motile bottom-dwelling echinoderms comprising the sea urchins and related forms having a disk-shaped shell formed of regular and usu. united plates studded with tubercles bearing spines and with pedicellariae and pores through which the tube feet emerge and most having a characteristic complicated system of pentamerous jaws in the mouth — compare ARISTOTLE'S LANTERN, CENTRECHINOIDA, CIDAROIDA, EXOCYCLOIDA

ech·i·nol·o·gy \,ekə'näləjē\ *n* -ES [*echin-* + *-logy*] **:** a branch of zoology that deals with echinoderms

echi·no·mys \≈≈≈ *at* ECHINO- + ,mis\ [NL, alter. (influenced by Gk *echinos* hedgehog) of *Echimys*] *syn of* ECHIMYS

ech·i·nop·a·nax \,ekə'näpə,naks\ *n, cap* [NL, fr. *echin-* + *Panax*] **:** a small genus of prickly shrubs of the family Araliaceae

echi·no·pa·ryph·i·um \≈≈≈ *at* ECHINO- + pə'rifēəm\ *n, cap* [NL, fr. *echin-* + *-paryphium* (fr. Gk *paryphē* border woven along a robe, fr. *para-* + *hyphē* web); akin to Gk *hyphainein* to weave — more at WEAVE] **:** a genus of digenetic trematodes (family Echinostomatidae) infesting the small intestine of waterfowl and domestic poultry and sometimes carnivorous mammals or man

echi·no·pluteus \"+\ *n* [NL, fr. *echin-* + *pluteus*] **:** the pluteus larva of an echinoid

ech·i·nops \'ekə,näps; ə'kī,näps, ē'-,e'-\ *n, cap* [NL, fr. *echin-* + *-ops*] **:** a large genus of Mediterranean herbs (family Compositae) comprising the globe thistles that have one-flowered heads aggregated in dense globular clusters

ech·i·nop·sine \,ekə'näp,sēn, -sən\ *n* -s [ISV *echinops-* (fr. NL *Echinops*) + *-ine*] **:** a crystalline alkaloid $C_{10}H_9NO$ derived from quinoline occurring in the seeds of globe thistles and having a physiological effect like that of strychnine and brucine

echi·no·rhin·i·dae \≈≈≈ *at* ECHINO- + 'rinə,dē *or* 'rīn-\ [NL, fr. *Echinorhinus* + *-idae*] *syn of* SQUALIDAE; see ECHINORHINUS

echi·no·rhi·nus \-'rīnəs\ *n, cap* [NL, fr. *echin-* + Gk *rhinos* skin; akin to OE *wrītan* to write — more at WRITE] **:** a genus of sharks (family Squalidae) comprising the bramble sharks and sometimes being made type of a separate family Echinorhinidae

echi·no·rhyn·chus \-'riŋkəs\ *n, cap* [NL, fr. *echin-* + *-rhynchus*] **:** a genus (the type of the family Echinorhynchidae) of small cylindrical acanthocephalan worms that are parasitic in various vertebrates

echi·no·so·rex \-'sōr,eks\ *n, cap E* [NL, fr. *echin-* + *Sorex*] **:** a genus of ratlike southern Asiatic insectivores including only the moonrat

echi·no·sto·mat·i·dae \,stō'mad·ə,dē\ *n pl, cap* [NL, fr. *Echinostomat-, Echinostoma*, type genus (fr. *echin-* + *-stoma*) + *-idae*] **:** a family of digenetic trematode worms (type genus *Echinostoma*) that are rare in man but common and widely distributed as parasites of birds and lower vertebrates and armed with spines

echi·no·stome \≈≈≈ *at* ECHINO- + ,stōm\ *n* -s [NL *Echinostoma*] **:** one of the Echinostomatidae — **ech·i·nos·to·moid** \¦ekə¦nästə,mȯid\ *adj*

echi·no·sto·mi·a·sis \"+stə'mīəsəs; *or* ,ekə,nästə'-\ *n, pl* **echinostomia·ses** \-ə,sēz\ [NL, fr. *Echinostoma* + *-iasis*] **:** infestation with or disease caused by worms of the family Echinostomatidae

echi·no·zoa \≈≈≈ *at* ECHINO- + 'zōə\ *n pl, cap* [NL, fr. *echin-* + *-zoa*] *in some classifications* **:** a major division of Echinodermata consisting of the Echinoidea and Holothurioidea

echin·u·late \ə'kinyələt, ē'-,e'-, -'kin-, -,lāt\ *also* **echin·u·lated** \-,lād·əd\ *adj* [*echinulate* prob. fr. (assumed) NL *echinulatus*, fr. (assumed) NL *echinulus* small prickle (fr. L *echinus* prickle + *-ulus* -ule) + L *-atus* -ate; *echinulated* fr. (assumed) NL *echinulatus* + E *-ed* — more at ECHIN-] **:** set with small spines or prickles — compare ECHINATE — **echin·u·la·tion** \≈,≈≈'lāshən\ *n* -s

echi·nus \ə'kīnəs, ē'-,e'-\ *n* [ME, fr. L, fr. Gk *echinos* hedgehog, sea urchin — more at ANGUIS] **1 a** *pl* **echi·ni** \-,nī\ **:** SEA URCHIN **b** *cap* [NL, fr. L] **:** the type genus of Echinidae that comprises numerous sea urchins including the common edible European urchin (*E. esculenta*) **2** [L, echinus of a capital, sea urchin; prob. fr. its shape] **a :** the rounded molding forming the bell of the capital in the Greek Doric order and having in profile a peculiar elastic curve; *also* **:** a similar member in other orders, the Ionic having the egg-and-dart ornament **b :** a quarter-round molding **c :** EGG AND DART

ech·is \'ekəs, 'ēk-\ *n, cap* [NL, fr. Gk, viper; akin to Gk *echidna* viper — more at ANGUIS] **:** a genus of vipers found in India, Arabia, and No. Africa

ech·ites \-'kīd·ēz\ *n, cap* [NL, irreg. fr. Gk *echis* viper; fr. the coiling stem of some species] **:** a large genus of woody vines (family Apocynaceae) chiefly of tropical America having a 5-lobed disk in the flowers and a glandular or fine-scaled calyx

ech·i·um \'ekēəm\ *n* [NL, fr. Gk *echion* echium, fr. *echis* viper] **1** *cap* **:** a genus of bristly herbs and some shrubs (family Boraginaceae) having an irregular corolla and unequal exserted stamens **2** -s **:** any plant of the genus *Echium*

ech·i·u·ri·da \,ekē'yürədə\ [NL, fr. *Echiurus* + *-ida*] *syn of* ECHIUROIDEA

¹ech·i·u·roid \-ü,rȯid\ *n* -s [NL *Echiuroidea*] **:** one of the Echiuroidea

²echiuroid \¦≈≈;≈,≈\ *adj* **:** of or relating to the Echiuroidea

ech·i·u·roi·dea \,ekēyə'rȯidēə\ *n pl, cap* [NL, fr. *Echiurus* + *-oidea*] **:** a group of marine worms of obscure position though commonly classed as a division of Gephyrea and distinguished by a sensitive but nonretractile proboscis overlying the mouth which in some forms (as some worms of the genus *Bonellia*) may attain great size

ech·i·u·rus \,ekē'yürəs\ *n, cap* [NL, fr. Gk *echis* viper + NL *-urus*] **:** a common genus (the type of the family Echiuridae) of echiuroid worms — compare ECHIUROIDEA

¹echo \'e(,)kō\ *n* -ES [ME *ecco*, fr. MF & L; MF *echo*, fr. L, fr. Gk *ēchō*; akin to L *vagire* to cry (said of a child), Gk *ēchē*, *ēchos* sound, and perh. Skt *vagnu* sound, cry] **1 :** the repetition of a sound caused by reflection of sound waves **:** the sound due to such reflection **2 a :** a repetition or imitation (as of the style or ideas) of another **:** REFLECTION ⟨you catch the ~ everywhere of this strong sense of purpose —Joseph Alsop⟩ ⟨containing strong ~*es* from the work of older and greater poets⟩ **:** REPERCUSSION, RESULT ⟨the economic collapse had dangerous political ~*es*⟩ **:** SURVIVAL, TRACE, VESTIGE ⟨~*es* of an older culture linger in the area⟩ **:** RESPONSE ⟨his appeal would find a sympathetic ~ in most minds —Roger Fry⟩ **b :** one who closely imitates or repeats another's words, ideas, or acts ⟨the minister may . . . become a pious ~ of their opinions —W.L.Sperry⟩ **3 :** the repetition of a sound, syllable, word, or phrase for rhetorical or poetic purposes; *esp* **:** repetition in imitation of an echo popular in 16th and 17th century poetry at the end of a line or stanza — see ECHO VERSE **4 a :** a soft repetition of a musical phrase **b :** ECHO ORGAN **c :** ECHO STOP **d :** a mute used to soften and modify the tone of brass wind instruments **5 a :** a signal in whist play in response to a signal given by one's partner; *specif* **:** the trump signal by a player whose partner has previously given the trump signal **b :** the play or discard in bridge of an unnecessarily high card followed by a lower one — compare HIGH-LOW **6 a :** the repetition of a received radio signal a perceptible time after the signal is first received due to the travel of the radio waves over a path (as the indirect path when the waves are reflected from an ionized layer of the atmosphere) other than the most direct path between transmitter and receiver **b** (1) **:** the reflection of transmitted radar signals by an object (2) **:** the visual indication of this reflection as seen on a radarscope **:** BLIP, PIP — **to the echo** *adv* **:** to the point of causing an echo **:** LOUDLY ⟨cheered him *to the echo* —Henry Irving⟩

²echo \", *in pres part* " *or* 'ekəw\ *vb* -ED/-ING/-ES *vi* **1 a :** to resound with echoes ⟨woods ~*ing* with the chopping of axes⟩ **:** produce echoes or become repeated by echoes ⟨the sound of battle ~*ed* over all the hills —Farley Mowat⟩ **b :** to repeat like an echo ⟨"a fine life", he said . . . "a fine life", he ~*ed*, drowsily —Laura Krey⟩ **2 :** REPEAT ⟨a theme which ~*es* throughout the novel —Ruth Suckow⟩ **:** become reflected or find renewed expression ⟨the effects of this revolutionary change still ~ throughout human anatomy and physiology —Weston La Barre⟩ **3 :** to make an echo in a game of cards (as bridge) **~** *vt* **1 :** REPEAT, IMITATE ⟨~*ing* the words and ideas of his famous father⟩ ⟨cushions in faint colors that ~ the carpet —Rumer Godden⟩ **2 :** to send back or repeat (a sound) by the reflection of sound waves

³echo \'e(,)kō\ *usu cap* — a communications code word for the letter *e*

echo box *n* **:** CAVITY RESONATOR

echo chamber *n* **:** a room with sound-reflecting walls used for producing hollow or echoing sound effects

echo·gram \'ekō,gram\ *n* -s [¹*echo* + *-gram*] **:** the record made by an echograph

echo·graph \-raf, -rȧf\ *n* -s [¹*echo* + *-graph*] **:** a sonic depth finder that automatically records depths

echo·ic \ə'kōik, e'-\ *adj* [¹*echo* + *-ic*] **:** of, relating to, or being an echo; *specif* **:** formed in imitation of some natural sound **:** IMITATIVE, ONOMATOPOEIC

echo·ing·ly *adv* **:** in the manner of something echoing

echo·ism \'ekō,izəm, -kə,wi-\ *n* -s [¹*echo* + *-ism*] **1 :** the formation of echoic words **:** ONOMATOPOEIA **2 :** the phonetic assimilation of a following to a preceding sound (as a vowel)

echo·ki·ne·sia \,e(,)kōkə'nēzh(ē)ə, -,kī'-\ *or* **echo·ki·ne·sis** \-nēsəs\ *n, pl* **echokinesias** *or* **echokineses** [NL, fr. L *echo* + NL *-kinesia* or *kinesis*] **:** ECHOPRAXIA

echo·la·lia \,ekō'lālēə, -lal-\ *n* -s [NL, fr. L *echo* + NL *-lalia*] **:** the often pathological repetition of what is said by other people as if echoing them — **echo·lal·ic** \¦≈≈¦lalik, -lāl-\ *adj*

echo·less \'ekōləs\ *adj* **:** having or producing no echo ⟨the hollow and ~ darkness —K.L.Patton⟩

echolocation \¦≈(,)≈≈¦≈≈\ *n* [¹*echo* + *location*] **1 :** a process that is used by an animal (as a bat) to orient itself and avoid obstacles esp. in darkness and that involves emission of high-frequency sounds which are reflected back from environing surfaces and thus indicate the relative distance and direction of such surfaces **2 :** a technical process (as in sounding or seismography) for locating a distant object by measuring the time a wave takes to travel to and from the object

echo·me·ter \'ekō,mēd·ə(r)\ *n* -s [¹*echo* + *-meter*] **:** an apparatus for measuring depths of objects in water or underground by timing the echoes of sound reflected from them

echo·mim·ia \,ekō'mimēə\ *n* -s [NL, fr. L *echo* + *mimus* mime + NL *-ia* — more at MIME] **:** ECHOPRAXIA

echo organ *n* **:** a division of a pipe organ situated at a distance from the rest of the instrument and containing soft stops suitable for echo effects

echoppe \ā'shäp, -shȯp\ *n* -s [F *échoppe*, by folk etymology (influence of F *échoppe* booth, fr. OF *escope*, fr. MD *schoppe*) fr. obs. F *eschople*, alter. of MF *eschalpre* scraping or graving tool, fr. L *scalprum* chisel, knife — more at SCALPEL, SHOP] **:** an engraver's needle beveled to an oval facet at the end and used to reopen previously incised lines

echo·prac·tic \,ekō¦praktik\ *adj* [fr. *echopraxia*, after such pairs as E *ataxia: atactic*] **:** of or relating to echopraxia **:** suffering from echopraxia

echo·prax·ia \,ekō'praksēə\ *n* -s [NL, fr. L *echo* + NL *-praxia*] **:** pathological repetition of the actions of other people as if echoing them

echo ranging *n* **:** determination of the distance and direction of an object (as under water) by means of an echo (as of sound) returned by the object — compare ECHO SOUNDING, SONAR

echo sounder *n* **:** SONIC DEPTH FINDER

echo sounding *n* **:** sounding a body of water by means of a sonic depth finder or of a radar device

echo stop *n* **1 :** a stop on a harpsichord for producing the soft effect of distant sound **2 :** an organ stop having its pipes enclosed for echoic effects

echo verse *n* **:** poetry that uses the device of an echo

¹echt \'äkt, 'ekt\ *adj* [ME *eghte*, *eighte* — more at EIGHT] *Scot* **:** EIGHT

²echt \'ekt\ *adj* [G, fr. LG, fr. MLG *echt*, *echte* lawful; akin to OFris *aft* lawful, OHG *ēhaft*; all fr. a prehistoric WGmc compound whose first constituent is represented by OE *ǣ*, *ǣw* law, OFris *ēwa*, *ā*, *ē*, OS *ēo*, OHG *ēwa* and whose second constituent is represented by OE *hæft*, adj., captive, OHG *haft* captive, bound, Goth *hafts* united; first constituent prob. akin to Goth *aiws* time, eternity, second constituent akin to OHG *heffen*, *hevan* to raise — more at AYE, HEAVE] **:** GENUINE, AUTHENTIC ⟨as performances these are ~ masterpieces —*Metronome*⟩

eciliate \(')ē+\ *adj* [*e-* + *ciliate*] **:** having no cilia

ec·i·ton \'esə,tän\ *n, cap* [NL] **:** a genus of blind polymorphic ants comprising the American army ants

ecize \'ē,sīz\ *vi* -ED/-ING/-S [*²ec-* + *-ize*] *of a migrant organism* **:** to become established in and adjusted to a new habitat **:** COLONIZE

eck·er·mann·ite \'ekə(r)mə,nīt\ *n* -s [Sw *eckermannit*, fr. Claes W. H. von *Eckermann* b1886 Swed. professor + Sw *-it* -ite] **:** a mineral $Na_3(Mg,Li)_4(Al,Fe)Si_8O_{22}(OH,F)_2$ consisting of an amphibole containing magnesium, lithium, iron, and some fluorine

eck·ert projection \'ekə(r)t-\ *n, usu cap E* [after Max *Eckert* †1938 Ger. cartographer] **:** any of several projections developed by Max Eckert in which the poles are parallel straight lines half the length of the equator

eck fistula \'ek-\ *n, usu cap E* [after N.V.*Eck*, 19th cent. Russ. physiologist] **:** an artificial anastomosis between the portal vein and inferior vena cava by which blood from the intestinal region is diverted from the liver to flow directly to the heart

ecl *abbr* **1** eclectic **2** eclogue

éclair \(')ā¦kla(a)|(ə)r, -le|, |ə, ə'k-\ *n* -s [F, lit., lightning, fr. OF *esclair* lightning, light, fr. *esclairier* to light, shine, flash, fr. (assumed) VL *exclariare*, alter. of L *exclarare* to light up, illuminate, fr. *ex-* + *clarare* to make clear, make bright, fr. *clarus* clear, bright — more at CLEAR] **:** a usu. chocolate-frosted oblong cream puff with whipped cream or custard filling

éclair·cisse·ment \āklersēsmäⁿ\ *n, pl* **éclaircissements** \-äⁿ(z)\ [F, fr. MF *esclaircissement*, alter. (influenced by MF *cler*, *clair* clear, bright) of OF *esclarcissement*, fr. *esclarciss-* (stem of *esclarcir* to light up, illuminate, fr. — assumed — VL *exclaricire*, alter. of — assumed — VL *exclaricare*, fr. L *ex-* + *claricare* to glow, gleam, fr. *clarus*) + *-ment*] **:** the clearing up of something obscure **:** ENLIGHTENMENT

ec·lamp·sia \e'klampsēə, ə'-\ *n* -s [NL, modif. (influenced by NL *-ia*) of Gk *eklampsis* brightness, shining forth, fr. *eklampein* to shine forth (fr. *ek* out of, out, forth — fr. *ex* — + *lampein* to shine) + *-sis* — more at EX-, LAMP] **:** a convulsive state **:** an attack of convulsions: as **a :** toxemia of pregnancy esp. when severe and marked by convulsions and coma — compare PREECLAMPSIA **b :** a condition comparable to milk fever of cows occurring in domestic animals (as dogs and cats) — **ec·lamp·tic** \(')e¦klam(p)tik, ə'k-\ *adj*

éclat \(')ā¦klä, -lȧ\ *n* -s [F, splinter, fragment, explosion, ostentation, fr. OF *esclat* splinter, fr. *esclater* to splinter, burst, prob. fr. (assumed) VL *exclapitare*, fr. L *ex-* + (assumed) VL *clapitare*, prob. of imit. origin] **1 :** dazzling effect **:** BRILLIANCE ⟨the stern imagery and rhetorical ~ of the first stanza —Robert Lowell⟩ **:** display of pomp or pageantry ⟨arrived with much ~, entering the capital in a coach of state drawn by eight milk-white horses —C.G.Bowers⟩ **:** DASH, ENERGY ⟨the croupiers . . . spin the wheel with ~ —Joseph Wechsberg⟩ **2 a :** public display or ostentation **:** PUBLICITY ⟨this letter was sprung . . . with great ~ . . . in public hearing —*New Republic*⟩ **b** *archaic* **:** NOTORIETY, SCANDAL ⟨with the object of saving an ~ —Lord Byron⟩ **3 :** brilliant or conspicuous success ⟨dominated the House of Commons with ~ —C.H.Driver⟩ **:** FAME, RENOWN ⟨handed down to posterity with all the ~ of a proverb —Jane Austen⟩ **:** APPLAUSE ⟨gave me more ~ than my efforts merited —S.H.Adams⟩ **syn** see FAME

¹ec·lec·tic \(')e¦klektik, ə'kl-,ē'kl-\ *adj* [Gk *eklektikos*, fr. *eklektos* picked out, select (verbal of *eklegein* to pick out, select, fr. *ek* out of, out + *legein* to pick up, gather) + *-ikos* -ic — more at LEGEND] **1 :** selecting what appears to be best or true in various and diverse doctrines or methods **:** rejecting a single, unitary, and exclusive interpretation, doctrine, or method **:** of or relating to eclecticism **:** SELECTIVE ⟨an ~ painter, mirroring the restlessness of his times, on a constant search for varied experience —H.D.Walker⟩ ⟨her taste was ~ in music as in persons —Osbert Sitwell⟩ **2 :** composed of elements drawn from various sources ⟨a party with an ~ program —*Time*⟩ ⟨an ~ liturgy . . . incorporating such usages of . . . other churches as he might consider most profitable —F.M.Stenton⟩ — **ec·lec·ti·cal·ly** \-tək(ə)lē, -tēk-, -li\ *adv*

²**eclectic** \"\ *n* -s [Gk *eklektikos*, fr. *eklektikos*, adj.] **:** one who uses an eclectic method or approach in any field of thought or activity ⟨~*s* who derive most of their theory from Freud but add a little of Jung or Adler —*Time*⟩

ec·lec·ti·cism \ə'ˌtə,sizəm\ *n* -s [¹*eclectic* + *-ism*] **1 :** the theory or practice of an eclectic method **:** the selection of doctrines or elements from various and diverse sources according to their presumed utility or validity usu. for the purpose of combining them into a satisfying or acceptable style, system of ideas, or set of practices; *also* **:** the eclectic style, system of ideas, or method formed in this manner **2 :** a system of medicine once popular in the U.S. that depended primarily on plant remedies

eclectic resinoid *n* **:** RESINOID 2a

ec·lec·tus parrot \(')eˌkl|ektəs-, ə'kl|, ē'kl|\ *n* [NL *Eclectus*, fr. Gk *eklektos* picked out, select] **:** any of certain parrots of the southwest Pacific constituting a genus (*Larius*, formerly *Eclectus*) and being distinguished by having males predominantly green and females predominantly red

ec·leg·ma \e'klegmə\ *n* -s [NL, alter. of L *ecligma* electuary, fr. Gk *ekleigma*, fr. *ekleichein* to lick up — more at ELECTUARY] *archaic* **:** a syrup on licorice root sucked for the relief of cough

¹**eclipse** \ə'klips, ē'k- *sometimes* 'ē,k-\ *n* -s [ME, fr. OF, fr. L

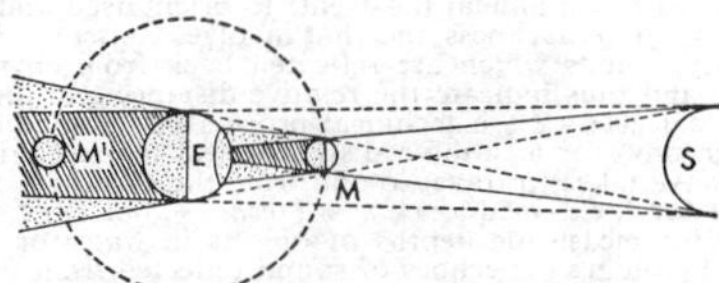

diagram of eclipse: sun, *S;* earth, *E;* moon in a solar eclipse, *M;* moon in a lunar eclipse, *M*¹

eclipsis, fr. Gk *ekleipsis*, lit., abandonment, cessation, fr. *ekleipein* to leave out, abandon, cease, fr. *ek* out of, out (fr. *ex*) + *leipein* to leave — more at EX-, LOAN] **1 a :** the obscuration of one celestial body by another ⟨an ~ of the sun by the moon⟩ **:** the passing into the shadow of a celestial body ⟨an ~ of the moon in the earth's shadow⟩ **:** the cutting off of some or all of the light from one celestial body by another (as in an eclipsing variable) — compare ANNULARITY, APPULSE, CONTACT, OCCULTATION, SHADOW TRANSIT, TOTALITY, TRANSIT **b :** the period or phase of darkness of an occulting light **2 :** the act or process or an instance of falling into obscurity, disuse, or disgrace **:** a temporary or permanent disappearance **:** DECLINE, DOWNFALL ⟨mourned the ~ of the hereditary upper class⟩ ⟨the ~ of the familiar essay will be slow —Clifton Fadiman⟩ **:** a period or condition of obscurity or disgrace ⟨returned to Versailles after a temporary ~ at court —Evelyn G. Cruickshanks⟩ or of decline or decay ⟨in the seventeenth century science came out of a long ~ —R.W.Livingstone⟩ **3 :** the assuming of dull eclipse plumage after the mating season (as by the normally brilliantly colored males of certain ducks); *also* **:** the state of a bird in such plumage

²**eclipse** \"\ *vb* -ED/-ING/-S [ME *eclipsen*, fr. *eclipse*, n.] *vt* **1 :** to cause the obscuration of **:** darken by or as if by an eclipse ⟨the moon ~*s* the sun⟩ ⟨when the sun is artificially *eclipsed* in a special telescope —Hugh Odishaw⟩ **2 a :** to reduce esp. in importance or repute **:** cast down (as into obscurity or disgrace) ⟨this . . . monocled military order was only *eclipsed* but never eliminated by the Versailles Treaty —G.W.Speyer⟩ **:** EXTINGUISH ⟨whose sudden death . . . *eclipsed* the gaiety of so many of his faithful readers —*Times Lit. Supp.*⟩ **b :** to make insignificant by comparison **:** throw into the shade ⟨whose history ~*s* that of the English colonies as a stirring and fascinating romance —A.L.Burt⟩ **:** SURPASS, EXCEL ⟨a new quarterly aluminum-production record . . . *eclipsing* the previous record —*Wall Street Jour.*⟩ **3 :** to cause eclipsis of (a sound) ~ *vi* **:** to suffer an eclipse **syn** see OBSCURE

eclipse plumage *n* **:** comparatively dull plumage usu. of seasonal occurrence in birds that exhibit a distinct nuptial plumage; *specif* **:** dull plumage developed in the adult male following a postnuptial molt — compare NUPTIAL PLUMAGE

eclips·er \-sə(r)\ *n* -s **:** one that eclipses; *specif* **:** the occulting screen for a lighthouse light

eclipse series *n* **:** SAROS SERIES

eclipse year *n* **:** the interval of 346.62 sidereal days between two successive conjunctions of the sun with the same node of the moon's orbit

eclipsing variable *also* **eclipsing double star** *or* **eclipsing binary** *n* [*eclipsing* fr. pres. part. of ²*eclipse*] **:** a binary star in which the orbit plane lies near the line of sight so that one or both of the stars may eclipse the other as they revolve and produce rhythmic fluctuations in the total light of the system

eclip·sis \ə'klipsəs, ē'-,e'-\ *n, pl* **eclip·ses** \-p,sēz\ *or* **eclip·sises** [Gk *ekleipsis* omission, eclipse, abandonment — more at ¹ECLIPSE] **:** an omission or suppression of words or sounds

¹**eclip·tic** \ə'kliptik, (')ē'k-, -tēk\ *adj* [ME *ecliptik*, fr. LL *eclipticus*, fr. L, of an eclipse, fr. Gk *ekleiptikos*, fr. *ekleipsis* eclipse] **1 :** of or relating to the ecliptic **2** [L *eclipticus*] **:** of or relating to an eclipse

²**ecliptic** \"\ *n* -s [ME *ecliptik*, fr. ML *ecliptica*, fr. LL, fem. of *eclipticus*, adj.; fr. the fact that eclipses occur on this circle] **1 :** the great circle of the celestial sphere that is the apparent path of the sun among the stars or of the earth as seen from the sun **:** the plane of the earth's orbit extended to meet the celestial sphere — see OBLIQUITY **2 :** a great circle drawn on a terrestrial globe making an angle of about 23° 27′ with the equator and used for illustrating and solving astronomical problems

eclip·ti·cal \-tәkәl\ *adj* [¹*ecliptic* + *-al*] **:** ECLIPTIC

ecliptic coordinate *n* **:** one of the coordinates in the ecliptic system of coordinates

ecliptic pole *n* **:** either of the poles in the ecliptic system of coordinates

ecliptic system of coordinates : a system of celestial coordinates based on the ecliptic — compare CELESTIAL LATITUDE, CELESTIAL LONGITUDE

ec·lo·gite \'eklə,jīt\ *n* -s [F *éclogite*, fr. Gk *eklogē* selection + F *-ite*] **:** a metamorphic rock consisting of soda-rich pyroxene and magnesia-rich garnet as essential minerals

ec·logue \'e,klȯg *also* -läg\ *n* -s [partly alter. (influenced by L *ecloga*) of earlier *eglog*, fr. MF *eglogue*, fr. L *ecloga* eclogue, short poem, choice extract or group of extracts from a literary work, fr. Gk *eklogē* selection, choice extract or group of extracts from a literary work, fr. *eklegein* to pick out, select; partly fr. ME *eclog*, fr. L *ecloga* — more at ECLECTIC] **:** a poem in which shepherds are introduced conversing **:** BUCOLIC, IDYL

eclose \ē'klōz\ *vi* -ED/-ING/-S [back-formation fr. *eclosion*] *of an insect* **:** to emerge from the eggshell or pupal case

eclo·sion \-ōzhən\ *n* -s [F *éclosion*, fr. *éclore* to hatch, fr. (assumed) VL *exclaudere* to hatch out (transitive), alter. (influenced by L *claudere* to close) of L *excludere* to hatch out (transitive), exclude — more at EXCLUDE, CLOSE] **1** *of a full-grown insect* **:** the act of emerging from the pupal case **2** *of an insect larva* **:** the act of hatching from the egg

eco- — see ²EC-

ECO *abbr* electron-coupled oscillator

eco·bi·ot·ic \'ekō, ¦ēkō+\ *adj* [²*ec-* + *-biotic*] **:** tending to produce or associated with adjustment to a particular mode of life ⟨~ adaptation⟩

eco·climate \'ekō, 'ēkō+,-\ *n* [²*ec-* + *climate*] **:** climate as an ecological factor; *specif* **:** the actual climatic condition of a habitat ⟨the ~ of a coniferous forest⟩ — **eco·climatic** \¦==+\ *adj*

eco·clinal \¦ekō¦klīnᵊl, ¦ēk-\ *adj* [*ecocline* + *-al*] **:** of, relating to, or inducing an ecocline ⟨~ variation⟩

eco·cline \'==,klīn\ *n* [²*ec-* + *cline*] **:** a series of intergrading forms produced within a group in a zone of intergradation between two distinctive ecological niches — compare GENOCLINE

ecod \ē'käd, i'-\ *interj* [by alter.] *archaic* **:** EGAD

ec·o·deme \'ekō,dēm, 'ēk-\ *n* [²*ec-* + *deme*] **:** a population occupying a particular ecological niche

ecog·ra·phy \ē'kägrəfē, ə'-\ *n* -ES [²*ec-* + *-graphy*] **:** the descriptive phase of ecology

ecoid *or* **oe·coid** \'ē,kȯid\ *n* -S [ISV *ec-* (fr. Gk *oikos* house) + *-oid* — more at VICINITY] **:** the colorless stroma of a red blood cell

ec·o·log·i·cal \¦ekə¦läjəkəl, ¦ēk-, -jēk-\ *also* **ec·o·log·ic** \-jik\ *adj* [*ecology* + *-ical*, *-ic*] **1 :** of or relating to the science of ecology **2 :** of or having to do with the environments of living things or with the pattern of relations between living things and their environments ⟨these then are the ~, the environmental diseases —*Science*⟩ **3 :** relating to or characterized by the interdependence of organisms ⟨departure from sound ~ principles in labeling hawks as good or bad . . . without any recognition of their essential role in all wildlife communities —I.R.Barnes⟩ — **ec·o·log·i·cal·ly** \-jək(ə)lē, -jēk-, -li\ *adv*

ecological subspecies *n* **:** PHYSIOLOGIC RACE

ecol·o·gist \ē'käləjəst, ə'-\ *n* -s [*ecology* + *-ist*] **:** a specialist in ecology

ecol·o·gy *also* **oe·col·o·gy** *or* **ae·col·o·gy** \-jē,-ji\ *n* -ES [G *ökologie*, fr. *ök-* ²*ec-* + *-logie* -logy] **1 :** a branch of science concerned with the interrelationship of organisms and their environments esp. as manifested by natural cycles and rhythms, community development and structure, interaction between different kinds of organisms, geographic distributions, and population alterations — see AUTECOLOGY, GENECOLOGY, SYNECOLOGY; compare BIOGEOGRAPHY, PHYTOSOCIOLOGY **2 :** the totality or pattern of relations between organisms and their environment ⟨the ~ of a mountain pine⟩ ⟨assist the peasants . . . in improving their ~ and technology —R.A. Hall *b*.1911⟩ **3 :** HUMAN ECOLOGY

econ *abbr* economic; economics; economy

econ·o·met·ric \ē¦känə¦me·trik, ə¦k-\ *adj* [*economy* + *-metric* (as in *barometric*)] **:** of or relating to econometrics

econ·o·me·tri·cian \=,==mə'trishən\ *n* -s **:** a specialist in econometrics

econ·o·me·trics \-'me·triks\ *n pl but sing in constr* [fr. *econometric*, after such pairs as E *economic: economics*] **:** the application of mathematical form and statistical techniques to the testing and quantifying of economic theories and the solution of economic problems — **econ·o·met·rist** \-trəst; ˌekə'nämə-tr-, ˌēk-\ *n* -s

ec·o·nom·ic \¦ekə¦nämik, ¦ēk-, -mēk\ *also* **ec·o·nom·i·cal** \-məkəl, -mēk-\ *adj* [*economic* fr. LL *oeconomicus* of or relating to a divine dispensation, fr. LGk *oikonomikos*, fr. Gk, skilled in the management of a household, frugal, fr. *oikonomos* steward + *-ikos* -ic; *economical* fr. LL *oeconomicus* + E *-al* — more at ECONOMY] **1** *usu economical, archaic* **:** of or relating to a household or its management **:** of or relating to a divine dispensation or system of government **2** *usu economical* **:** given to thrift ⟨a sturdy, handsome, high-colored woman . . . *economical* and sensible —Carl Van Doren⟩ **:** productive of saving ⟨sea power is the . . . most *economical* form of military power —*Time*⟩ **:** sparing in quantity (as of words) ⟨a style as *economical* and exact as a theorem in geometry —Richard Harrity⟩ **3 a :** of or relating to the science of economics ⟨rejected the ~ doctrines of Ricardo⟩ **:** of, relating to, or concerned with the production, distribution, and consumption of commodities ⟨a program to prevent inflation and ~ collapse⟩ ⟨a council of ~ advisers⟩ **:** MATERIAL ⟨moved exclusively by ~ motives⟩ **b :** having practical or industrial significance, uses, or application ⟨the ~ plants of a region⟩ **:** affecting or liable to affect material resources or welfare ⟨two ~ pests were intercepted by . . . inspectors during recent weeks —*Farm Chemicals*⟩ **c :** operated or produced on a profitable basis **:** producing an excess of returns over expenditures ⟨reactor types which might be developed to produce ~ power —*U.S. Code*⟩ **:** capable of or liable to profitable exploitation ⟨~ beds of phosphate are found only under marine conditions —A.M.Bateman⟩ **:** PROFITABLE ⟨barely ~, since she paid a nurse almost as much as she made herself —Elizabeth Janeway⟩ **syn** see SPARING

ec·o·nom·i·cal·ly \-mək(ə)lē, -mēk-, -li\ *adv* **:** in an economic or economical way or manner

economic botany *n* **:** a division of botany that deals with the utilization of plants

economic council *n* **:** a body that is composed of representatives of all economic groups including both management and labor and that acts as an advisory governmental body or has direct governing power

economic cycle *n* **:** BUSINESS CYCLE

economic determinism *n* **:** ECONOMIC INTERPRETATION OF HISTORY

economic geography *n* **:** a branch of geography that deals with the relations of physical and economic conditions to the production and distribution of commodities

economic geology *n* **:** a branch of geology that deals with geological materials of economic utility — see MINING GEOLOGY, PETROLEUM GEOLOGY

economic good *n* **:** a commodity or service that is useful to man but that must be paid for — usu. used in pl.

economic interpretation of history : the theory that in the last analysis economic factors including esp. the level of technology attained by a particular society and the economic relations into which men enter on the basis of that technology exert a decisive influence on the course of political, social, and intellectual evolution — compare HISTORICAL MATERIALISM

economic life *n* **:** the period during which an economic good retains its utility

economic man *n* **:** an imaginary individual created in classical economics and conceived of as behaving rationally, regularly, and predictably in his economic activities with motives that are egoistic, acquisitive, and short-term in outlook

economic poison *n* **:** a substance or mixture of substances (as an insecticide, fungicide, rodenticide, or herbicide) for control of plants or animals that have economic significance as pests (as in agriculture, industry, or households) **:** PESTICIDE

economic rent *n* **:** the return for the use of a factor in excess of the minimum required to bring forth its service — compare CONSUMER SURPLUS, RENT

ec·o·nom·ics \ˌekə'nämiks, ˌēk-, -mēks\ *n pl but usu sing in constr* [modif. (influenced by E *-s*, pl. ending) of NL *oeconomica*, fr. Gk *oikonomika*, fr. neut. pl. of *oikonomikos* skilled in the management of a household — more at ECONOMIC] **1** *obs* **:** a science or art of managing a house or household **2 a :** a social science that studies the production, distribution, and consumption of commodities **b :** economic aspect or significance ⟨the ~ of the tideland issue was relatively simple —T.H.White *b*1915⟩ **:** considerations of cost and return ⟨standards by which the ~ of electric vs. manual typewriters could be evaluated —H.B.Averill⟩

economic science *n* **:** ECONOMICS

economic strike *n* **:** a strike by employees over wages, hours, or working conditions as opposed to one called in protest against unfair practices by an employer

econ·o·mism \ē'känə,mizəm, ə'-\ *n* -S [F *économisme*, fr. *économie* economy (alter. — influenced by such forms as ML *economus* steward — of MF *yconomie*) + *-isme* -ism] **:** a theory or viewpoint that attaches decisive or principal importance to economic goals or interests

econ·o·mist \-məst\ *n* -s [*economy* + *-ist*] **1** *archaic* **a :** one who manages household affairs **:** HOUSEKEEPER **b :** one who practices or advocates economy ⟨~*s* even to parsimony —Edmund Burke⟩ **2** [F *économiste*, fr. *économie* economy + *-iste* -ist] *archaic* **:** PHYSIOCRAT **3 :** a specialist in or student of economics

econ·o·mite \-,mīt\ *n* -s *cap* [*Economy* (now Ambridge), Pennsylvania + E *-ite*] **:** one of a group of Harmonites who in 1803 settled in Pennsylvania, who in 1825 formed the settlement of Economy, Pennsylvania, and whose religious community came to an end in 1903 following the introduction of celibacy in 1807

econ·o·mize \-,mīz\ *vb* -ED/-ING/-S *see -ize in Explan Notes* [*economy* + *-ize*] *vi* **:** to practice economy: **a :** to use more sparingly ⟨it was necessary to ~ in the running of diesel engines —G. de Q.Robin⟩ **b :** to effect a saving — usu. used with *on* ⟨the larger animal . . . can ~ on brain, eyes, and certain other organs —J.B.S.Haldane⟩ ~ *vt* **1 :** to use more economically **:** SAVE ⟨regenerators which ~ fuel —E.B.Shand⟩ **2 :** to give economic value to **:** utilize to the best advantage ⟨they learned how to ~ the soil —Richard Koebner⟩

econ·o·miz·er \-zə(r)\ *n* -s **:** an apparatus for utilizing heat otherwise wasted; *specif* **:** a system of water tubes in the breeching of a boiler to heat the feedwater — compare REGENERATOR

econ·o·my \ē'känəmē, ə'-, -mi\ *n* -ES *often attrib* [alter. (influenced by such forms as ML *economus* steward, fr. LL *oeconomus*, fr. Gk *oikonomos*) of earlier *yconomie*, fr. MF, fr. ML *oeconomia*, fr. Gk *oikonomia*, fr. *oikonomos* steward (fr. *oikos* house + *-nomos* manager, fr. *nemein* to distribute, manage) + *-ia* -y — more at VICINITY, NIMBLE] **1 a** *obs* **:** an art of managing a household **b** *archaic* **:** the management of the affairs of a group, community, or establishment with a view to insuring its maintenance or productiveness **c :** God's plan or system for the government of the world ⟨the Incarnation would be no accident in the divine ~ —P.E.More⟩; *also* **:** a special divine dispensation suited to the needs of a nation or period **d :** the management of a person's household or private affairs **2 a :** thrifty or economical use or administration of material resources **:** frugality in expenditures sometimes verging on parsimony ⟨the great cathedrals after 1200 show ~, and sometimes worse —Henry Adams⟩; *also* **:** an instance or a means of economizing **:** SAVING ⟨a small ~ if achieved at the expense of quality⟩ **b** (1) **:** cautious, selective, or partial exposition of facts or principles esp. to avoid causing displeasure — used chiefly in the phrase *economy of truth* ⟨either suffering from a lapse of memory or practicing an official ~ of truth —*Times Lit. Supp.*⟩ (2) **:** the efficient and sparing use of nonmaterial resources ⟨~ of effort⟩ ⟨~ of motion⟩ **:** the reduction to a minimum of the steps or processes required to achieve some end or reach some conclusion (as in logical reasoning); *also* **:** the saving achieved thereby (3) **:** conciseness in verbal or artistic expression **:** elimination of all unnecessary details so as to produce the maximum artistic effect ⟨every device of ~ known to musical expression —Virgil Thomson⟩ ⟨the incidents are treated with dramatic ~ —Hector Chevigny⟩ **3 a :** the system of arrangement or mode of operation or functioning of anything **:** ORGANIZATION ⟨the individual's psychic ~⟩ ⟨the place of the university in the educational ~ of the state⟩ **b** (1) **:** the natural ordering or system of operation of the processes of anabolism and catabolism in living bodies ⟨the ~ of the cell⟩ (2) **:** the body of an animal or plant as an organized whole ⟨disorganizing wide segments of the body ~ —Leonard Engel⟩ **4 a :** the structure of economic life in a country or area **:** an economic system ⟨the ~ was rising to new peaks of production and employment —F.B.Wilde⟩; *also* **:** a segment of an economic system ⟨sweeping changes in our farm ~⟩ **b :** a particular type of economic system or stage of economic development ⟨a money ~⟩ ⟨a pastoral ~⟩ **syn** see SYSTEM

economy coil *n* **:** a high-inductance coil shunted around series lamps to prevent an open circuit in case a lamp burns out

ec·o·phene \'ekō,fēn, 'ēk-\ *n* -s [²*ec-* + *-phene* (fr. *phenotype*)] **:** ECAD

eco·phenotype \¦ekō, ¦ēkō+\ *n* [²*ec-* + *phenotype*] **:** a phenotype modified by specific adaptive response to environmental factors **:** ECAD

écor·ché \¦ā,kȯr¦shā, ā'kȯr,shā\ *n* -s [F, fr. past part. of *écorcher* to skin, peel, fr. OF *escorchier* to skin, peel, fr. LL *excorticare* to peel, fr. L *ex-* + LL *-corticare* (fr. L *cortic-*, *cortex* bark) — more at CUIRASS] **:** an anatomical figure or manikin showing the muscles and bones that are visible with the skin removed

ecorticate \(')ē+\ *adj* [*e-* + *corticate*] **:** being without a cortex; *specif* **:** being without an external tough investment ⟨~ lichens⟩

eco·species \'ekō, 'ēkō+ ,-\ *n* [²*ec-* + *species*] **:** a subdivision of a cenospecies that is capable of free gene interchange between its members without impairment of fertility but is less capable of fertile crosses with members of other subdivisions of the cenospecies and that is typically more or less equivalent to the taxonomic species

eco·specific \¦==+\ *adj* **:** of, relating to, or like an ecospecies

ecos·saise \¦ā kȯ¦säz, -,kō¦, -ˌkə¦-\ *n* -s [F *écossaise*, fr. fem. of *écossais* Scottish, fr. *Écosse* Scotland] **1 :** an old-fashioned dance in slow three-quarter time **2 :** a lively dance tune in duple rhythm

ecostate \(')ē+\ *adj* [*e-* + *costate*] *of a leaf* **:** having no midvein

eco·system \'ekō, 'ēkō+ ,-\ *n* [²*ec-* + *system*] **:** an ecological community considered together with the nonliving factors of its environment as a unit

ec·o·ton·al \¦ekə¦tōnᵊl, ¦ēk-\ *adj* [*ecotone* + *-al*] **:** of, relating to, or constituting an ecotone

ec·o·tone \'==,tōn\ *n* [²*ec-* + *-tone* (fr. Gk *tonos* tension) — more at TONE] **:** a transition area between two adjacent ecological communities (as forest and grassland) usu. exhibiting competition between organisms common to both

ec·o·top·ic \¦==¦täpik\ *adj* [²*ec-* + *-topic* (fr. Gk *topos* place) — more at TOPIC] **:** tending to or involving adjustment to specific local habitat conditions ⟨~ divergence among common songbirds⟩

ec·o·type \'==,tīp\ *n* [²*ec-* + *type*] **:** a subdivision of an ecospecies that comprises individuals which are interfertile with each other and with members of other ecotypes of the same ecospecies but which maintain their individuality as a distinct group through environmental selection and isolation and that is when morphologically distinct comparable with a taxonomic subspecies — **ec·o·typ·ic** \¦==¦tipik\ *adj* — **ec·o·typ·i·cal·ly** \-pək(ə)lē\ *adv*

ec·pho·ne·sis \ˌekfə'nēsəs\ *n, pl* **ecphone·ses** \-ē,sēz\ [Gk *ekphōnēsis*, fr. *ekphōnein* to cry out (fr. *ek* out of, out — fr. *ex* — + *phōnein* to speak, sound, fr. *phōnē* sound, voice) + *-sis* — more at EX-, BAN] **:** EXCLAMATION

ec·phore *or* **ek·phore** \'ek,fō(ə)r\ *vt* -ED/-ING/-S [prob. back-formation fr. *ecphoria*, *ecphorize*] **:** ECPHORIZE

ec·pho·ria \ek'fōrēə\ *n, pl* **ecphorias** \-ēəz\ *or* **ecpho·riae** \-ē,ē\ [G *ekphorie*, fr. *ek-* ¹*ec-* + *-phorie* (fr. Gk *-phoria* action of bearing) — more at -PHORIA] **:** the rousing of an engram or system of engrams from a latent to an active state (as by repetition of the original stimulus or by mnemic excitation)

ec·pho·rize \'ekfə,rīz\ *vt* -ED/-ING/-S [*ecphoria* + *-ize*] **:** to revive or rouse (an engram or system of engrams) from latency

ecra·se *or* **écra·sé** \¦ā(,)krä¦zā, -,krə¦-\ *adj* [F *écrasé*, past part. of *écraser* to crush, fr. MF *escraser*, fr. *e-* (fr. L *ex-*) + *-craser* (prob. fr. E ¹*craze*)] **:** CRUSHED, FLATTENED — used esp. of fabrics or leather

écre·visse \ākrəvēs\ *n* -s [F, fr. OF *escrevice*, *crevice* — more at CRAYFISH] **:** CRAYFISH

ecri·bel·la·tae \ˌēkrəbə'lā,tē\ *n pl, cap* [NL, fr. *e-* + *cribellum* + L *-atae* (fem. pl. of *-atus* -ate)] *in some classifications* **:** a group of arachnomorph spiders comprising those which lack a cribellum

¹**ecribellate** \(')ē+\ *adj* [NL *cribellum* + E *-ate*] **:** lacking a cribellum **:** of or relating to the Ecribellatae

²**ecribellate** \"\ *n* -s **:** an ecribellate spider

ec·ru \'e(,)krü, 'ā(-, =¦=\ *n* -s [F *écru* unbleached, fr. OF *escru*, fr. *es-* completely — fr. L *ex-* — + *cru* raw, fr. L *crudus* — more at RAW] **1 :** a grayish yellow that is greener and paler than chamois or old ivory **2** *of a textile* **:** a light grayish yellowish brown that is yellower and lighter than gravel

ecru silk *n* **:** a partially degummed silk with little luster and some harshness

ec·sta·si·ate \ek'stāz(h)ē,āt\ *vb* -ED/-ING/-S [F *extasier* to cause to go into an ecstasy (fr. MF, fr. *extasie* ecstasy) + E *-ate*] **:** ECSTASIZE

ec·sta·size \'ekstə,sīz\ *vb* -ED/-ING/-S [*ecstasy* + *-ize*] *vt* **:** to cause to go into an ecstasy ⟨*ecstasizing* her audience⟩ ~ *vi* **:** to go into an ecstasy

¹**ec·sta·sy** *also* **ec·sta·cy** \'ekstəsē, -si\ *n* -ES [ME *extasie*, fr. MF, fr. LL *extasis*, *ecstasis*, fr. Gk *ekstasis*, fr. *existanai* to put out of place, derange, fr. *ex* out of, out + *histanai* to cause to stand — more at EX-, STAND] **1 :** a state of being beyond reason and self-control through intense emotional excitement, pain, or other sensation **:** obsession by powerful feeling ⟨in an ~ of pain —Ludwig Bemelmans⟩ ⟨whose eyes kept sweeping in an ~ of fear from side to side —Irwin Shaw⟩

2 : a state of exaltation or rapturous delight manifested either demonstratively ⟨sending their shrill, diamond-hard cries of ~ streaming across the streets —Kay Cicellis⟩ or in a profound calm or abstraction of mind ⟨a state of quiet ~ which illuminated his whole being —E.S.Bates⟩ **3 :** a trance state in which intense absorption in divine or cosmic matters is accompanied by loss of sense perception and voluntary control ⟨at the sight of a crucifix . . . she would at once fall into an ~ —Norman Douglas⟩

syn ECSTASY, RAPTURE, and TRANSPORT agree in designating a feeling or state of intense, often extreme, mental and emotional exaltation. ECSTASY in one sense signifies an exalted state resembling a trance in which contemplation of what inspires the exaltation makes one oblivious of all else, and in another sense signifies an overmastering exalting joy or similar intense emotion ⟨this picture of Fra Angelico in a state of religious *ecstasy* —*Time*⟩ ⟨these were thrilling words, and wound up Catherine's feelings to the highest points of *ecstasy* —Jane Austen⟩ ⟨such a success threw us into a perfect *ecstasy* of hilarity —Ben Riker⟩ ⟨their faces were fixed in a calm *ecstasy* of malevolence —Elinor Wylie⟩ ⟨a drunken *ecstasy*, compounded of superstition, greed, bloodlust, seized upon the hundreds of servitors of the goddess —Maurice Samuel⟩ RAPTURE implies intense bliss or beatitude, sometimes connoting an accompanying ecstasy ⟨he was familiar with the passionate *rapture* of lovers on the stage, in books, and in pictures —William Black⟩ ⟨he put little of this personal *rapture* of holiness into his published works —P.E.More⟩ ⟨continual ups and downs of *rapture* and depression —Edith Wharton⟩ TRANSPORT applies to any violent or powerful emotion that lifts one out of oneself and usu. provokes vehement expression ⟨thronged about him and embraced and kissed him, with such joy and *transport*, as he said, that he always looked upon that moment as the happiest of his life —Van Wyck Brooks⟩ ⟨a periodical that is weekly moved to *transports* of delight about contemporary America —Bruce Bliven b.1889⟩ ⟨the first *transports* of love⟩

²ecstasy \"\ *vt* -ED/-ING/-ES **:** to fill with ecstasy or rapture **:** ENRAPTURE ⟨the most *ecstasied* order of holy . . . spirits —Jeremy Taylor⟩

¹ec·stat·ic \(ˈ)ekˌstad·|ik, ək's-, -at|, |ēk\ *adj* [ML *ecstaticus*, fr. Gk *ekstatikos*, fr. *existanai*] **1 :** of or relating to ecstasy ⟨the ~ element in medieval religion⟩ **2 :** caused by, expressing, or causing ecstasy ⟨the first taste of the water in his mouth was ~ —Norman Mailer⟩ ⟨looked at her with an ~ stare⟩ **:** in a state of ecstasy ⟨~ at his new possession —Nevil Shute⟩

²ecstatic \"\ *n* -S **:** a person who is subject to states resembling trances

ecstatical *adj* [ML *ecstaticus* + E *-al*] *obs* **:** ECSTATIC

ec·stat·i·cal·ly \|ək(ə)lē, |ēk-, -li\ *adv* **:** in an ecstatic manner

ect- *or* **ecto-** *comb form* [NL, fr. Gk *ekto-* outside, fr. *ektos*, fr. *ex* out of, out — more at EX-] **1 :** outside **:** external ⟨*ectos*-tosis⟩ ⟨*ecto*plasm⟩ — compare END-, EXO- **2 :** out of place ⟨*ecto*cardia⟩

ECT *abbr* electroconvulsive therapy

ec·tad \ˈek,tad\ *adv* [*ect-* + *-ad*, adv. suffix] *anat* **:** OUTWARD

ec·ta·de·ni·um \,ektəˈdēnēəm\ *n, pl* **ectade·nia** \-nēə\ [NL, fr. *ect-* + Gk *aden-*, *adēn* gland + NL *-ium* — more at ADEN-] **:** one of the ectodermal accessory reproductive glands of male insects — compare MESADENIUM

ec·tal \ˈektᵊl\ *adj* [*ect-* + *-al*] *anat* **:** EXTERIOR, OUTER — opposed to *ental* — **ectal·ly** \-ᵊlē\ *adv*

ec·ta·sia \ekˈtāzh(ē)ə\ *n* -S [NL, modif. (influenced by NL *-ia*) of Gk *ektasis*] **:** the expansion of a hollow or tubular organ

ec·ta·sis \ˈektəsəs\ *n, pl* **ecta·ses** \-ə,sēz\ [LL, fr. Gk *ektasis* extension, stretching, lengthening of a short syllable, fr. *ekteinein* to stretch out, fr. *ek* out of, out (fr. *ex*) + *teinein* to stretch — more at EX-, THIN] **1 :** the lengthening of a short syllable **2** [NL, fr. Gk] **:** DILATATION, ECTASIA

ec·tat·ic \(ˈ)ekˌtad·ik\ *adj* [fr. (assumed) NL *ectaticus*, fr. Gk *ektatos* capable of extension (verbal of *ekteinein*) + L *-icus* -ic] **:** of, relating to, or involving ectasia

ectene *var of* EKTENE

ect·epicondylar \(ˌ)ekˌt+ˌ-\ *adj* [*ect-* + *epicondyle* + *-ar*] **:** relating to the external condyle of the distal end of the humerus

¹ect·ethmoid \(ˈ)ekˌt+ˌ-\ *n* [*ect-* + *ethmoid*, n.] **:** either of two lateral parts of the ethmoid bone lying on either side of the mesethmoid and forming part of the anterior wall of the orbit

²ectethmoid \"\ *also* **ect·ethmoidal** \(ˌ)ekˌt+ˌ-\ *also* **ec·to·ethmoid** \ˌektō+\ *adj* **:** lateral or external to the ethmoid

ec·thlip·sis \ekˈthlipsəs\ *n, pl* **ecthlip·ses** \-p,sēz\ [LL, fr. Gk *ekthlipsis* loss of a sound or letter in a word, squeezing out, fr. *ekthlibein* to squeeze out (fr. *ek* out of, out — fr. *ex* — + *thlibein* to squeeze, alter. — influenced by Gk *thlan* to crush, bruise — of Gk — Aeol & Ion — *phlibein* to squeeze) + *-sis*; Gk *thlan* akin to Czech *dlasmati* to press and perh. to Skt *dṛṣad*, *dhṛṣad* millstone — more at EX-, PROFLIGATE] *Latin prosody* **:** the elision of a final *m* with a preceding short vowel before a word beginning with *h* or a vowel

ec·thy·ma \ekˈthīmə\ *n* -S [NL *ecthymat-*, *ecthyma*, fr. Gk *ekthymat-*, *ekthyma* pimple, fr. *ekthyein* to break out, fr. *ek* + *thyein* to rage, seethe; akin to L *fumus* smoke — more at FUME] **1 :** a cutaneous eruption marked by large flat pustules that have a hardened base surrounded by inflammation, heal with pigmented scar formation, and occur esp. on the lower legs **2 :** sore mouth of sheep — **ec·thym·a·tous** \(ˈ)ekˈthimədəs, -thīm-\ *adj*

ec·to·blast \ˈektə,blast\ *n* [ISV *ect-* + *-blast*] **:** EPIBLAST — **ec·to·blas·tic** \ˌ≠≠ˈblastik\ *adj*

ec·to·can·thi·on \,ektōˈkan(t)thēən\ *n* -S [*ect-* + *-canthion* (irreg. fr. LL *canthus* corner of the eye) — more at CANTHUS] **:** the point at which the outer ends of the upper and lower eyelids meet — compare ENDOCANTHION

ec·to·car·dia \-ˈkärdēə\ *n* -S [NL, fr. *ect-* + *-cardia*] **:** abnormal position of the heart

ec·to·car·pa·ce·ae \-,kärˈpāsē,ē\ *n pl, cap* [NL, fr. *Ectocarpus*, type genus + *-aceae*] **:** a cosmopolitan family of chiefly epiphytic marine brown algae (order Ectocarpales) that includes algae with a thallus of erect branching filaments arising from a creeping filament or layer or sometimes being compacted into a pseudoparenchymatous thallus — see ECTOCARPUS — **ec·to·car·pa·ceous** \ˌ≠≠ˌ≠ˈpāshəs\ *adj*

ec·to·car·pa·les \ˌ≠≠ˌ≠ˈpā(ˌ)lēz\ *n pl, cap* [NL, fr. *Ectocarpus* + *-ales*] **:** a large order of rather simple heterotrichous brown algae that lack true oogamy — see ECTOCARPACEAE

ec·to·car·pic \ˌektōˈkärpik\ *adj* [NL *Ectocarpus* + E *-ic*] **:** of or relating to algae of the genus *Ectocarpus*

ec·to·car·pous \-pəs\ *adj* [*ect-* + *-carpous* having such fruit — more at -CARPOUS] **:** having reproductive organs developed from the ectoderm — used of hydromedusae

ec·to·car·pus \ˌ≠≠ˈ≠pəs\ *n, cap* [NL, fr. *ect-* + *-carpus*] **:** the type genus of Ectocarpaceae containing numerous more or less branched filamentous brown algae that are esp. abundant in cold seas and are sometimes considered the most primitive of living brown algae

ec·to·chon·dral \ˌ≠≠ˈkändrəl\ *adj* [*ect-* + *chondr-* + *-al*] **:** on the surface of cartilage ⟨an ~ lesion⟩ ⟨~ bone formation⟩

ec·to·commensal \ˌek(ˌ)tō+\ *n* [*ect-* + *commensal*] **:** an organism that lives as a commensal on the surface of the body of another organism

ec·to·condyle \ˌektō+\ *n* [*ect-* + *condyle*] **:** the lateral condyle of a bone — **ec·to·condyloid** \"+\ *adj*

ec·to·co·nus \,ektəˈkōnəs\ *n, cap* [NL, fr. *ect-* + L *conus* cone — more at CONE] **:** a genus of primitive ungulate mammals (order Condylarthra) of the Paleocene of No. America thought to have been forest-dwelling browsers

ec·to·cornea \ˌektō+\ *n* [NL, fr. *ect-* + ML *cornea*] **:** the external layer of the cornea

ec·to·cranial \"+\ *adj* [*ect-* + *cranial*] **:** of or relating to the exterior of the skull

ec·to·cyst \ˈektə,sist\ *n* [ISV *ect-* + *cyst*] **:** the external layer of the walls of a zooecium

ec·to·derm \-tə,dərm\ *n* -S [ISV *ect-* + *-derm*] **1 :** the outer cellular membrane of a medusa or other diploblastic animal **2 :** the outermost of the three primary germ layers of an embryo **:** the source of neural tissue and sense organs, of the outer layer of the skin, and of minor adult structures **:** EPIBLAST; *also* **:** any tissue wherever located derived from this germ layer — compare EPIDERMIS — **ec·to·der·mal** \ˌ≠≠ˈdərməl\ *or* **ec·to·der·mic** \-mik\ *adj*

ec·to·der·moi·dal \ˌ≠≠(ˌ)dərˌmȯidᵊl\ *adj* [*ectoderm* + *-oidal*] **:** resembling ectoderm

ec·to·dynamomorphic *or* **ek·to·dynamomorphic** \ˌektō+\ *adj* [*ect-* + *dynam-* + *-morphic*] *of a developing soil* **:** characterized by changes brought about by external (as climatic) forces or agencies — opposed to *endodynamomorphic*

ec·to·entad \"+\ *adv* [*ect-* + *entad*] *anat* **:** from without inward

ectoethmoid *var of* ECTETHMOID

ec·to·gen·e·sis \,ektō+\ *n* [NL, fr. *ect-* + L *genesis*] **:** development outside the body; *esp* **:** development of a mammalian embryo in an artificial environment — **ec·to·genetic** \ˌ≠≠+\ *adj*

ec·to·gen·ic \ˌ≠≠ˈjenik\ *adj* [prob. fr. G *ektogen* ectogenic (fr. *ekt-* ect- — fr. NL — + *-gen* -genic, -genous, fr. Gk *-genēs* born) + E *-ic* — more at -GEN] **1** *of disease* **:** EXOGENOUS **2** *of an organism* **:** ECTOGENOUS

ec·tog·e·nous \(ˈ)ekˈtäjənəs\ *adj* [prob. fr. G *ektogen* + E *-ous*] **:** capable of development apart from the host — used chiefly of pathogenic bacteria

ec·tog·na·thous \(ˈ)ekˈtägnəthəs\ *adj* [*ect-* + *-gnathous*] **:** having the mouthparts exserted; *sometimes* **:** THYSANURAN — compare ENTOGNATHOUS

ec·to·lecithal \ˌektō+\ *adj* [ISV *ect-* + *lecith-* + *-al*] **:** CENTROLECITHAL

ec·to·loph \ˈektə,läf\ *n* -S [*ect-* + *-loph*] *zool* **:** one of the principal crests of a lophodont molar extending from the paracone to the metacone — compare METALOPH, PROTOLOPH

-ec·tome \ˈek,tōm\ *n comb form* -S [NL *-ectomus*, fr. *-ectomia*, after NL *-tomia* -tomy: *-tomus* -tome] **:** instrument used in surgical removal of (a specified organ or part) ⟨neur*ectome*⟩ ⟨tonsill*ectome*⟩

ec·to·meninx \ˌektō+\ *n, pl* **ectomeninges** [NL, fr. *ect-* + Gk *mēninx* membrane — more at MEMBER] **:** the layer of mesoderm from which the dura mater and much of the membrane bone of the skull develop in the higher vertebrate embryo

ec·to·mere \ˈektə,mi(ə)r\ *n* -S [*ect-* + *-mere*] **:** a blastomere destined to form ectoderm — **ec·to·mer·ic** \ˌ≠≠ˈmerik\ *adj*

ec·to·mesenchyme \ˌektō+\ *n* [*ect-* + *mesenchyme*] **:** mesenchyme derived from ectoderm

ec·to·mesoblast \"+\ *n* [*ect-* + *mesoblast*] **:** an undifferentiated layer of cells destined to produce both epiblast and mesoblast

ec·to·mesoderm \"+\ *n* [*ect-* + *mesoderm*] **1 :** ECTOMESENCHYME **2 :** ECTOMESOBLAST — **ec·to·mesodermal** \"+\ *adj*

ec·to·mo·lare \ˌektōmōˈla(a)rē\ *n* -S [*ect-* + *-molare* (irreg. fr. L *molaris* molar) — more at MOLAR] *anthrop* **:** the most lateral point on the exterior surface of the alveolar border

ec·to·morph \ˈektə,mȯrf\ *n* -S [*ectoderm* + *-morph*] **:** an ectomorphic individual

ec·to·mor·phic \ˌ≠≠ˈmȯrfik\ *adj* [*ectoderm* + *-morphic*] **:** characterized by predominance of the structures developed from the ectodermal layer of the embryo, the skin, nerves, sense organs, and brain **:** of a light or asthenic type of body build — compare ENDOMORPHIC, MESOMORPHIC — **ec·to·mor·phy** \ˈ≠≠,≠fē\ *n* -ES

-ec·to·my \ˈektəmē, -mi\ *n comb form* -ES [NL *-ectomia*, fr. *ec-* + *-tomia* -tomy] **:** cutting out **:** surgical removal ⟨gastr*ectomy*⟩

ec·to·nephridium \ˌek(ˌ)tō+\ *n* [NL, fr. *ect-* + *nephridium*] **:** a nephridium of ectodermal origin (as that of certain mollusks)

ec·to·parasite \ˌektō+\ *n* [ISV *ect-* + *parasite*] **:** a parasite that lives on the exterior of its host — opposed to *endoparasite* — **ec·to·parasitic** \"+\ *adj*

ec·toph·a·gous \(ˈ)ekˈtäfəgəs\ *adj* [*ect-* + *-phagous*] **:** feeding from without: **a** *of a parasitoid insect larva* **:** developing external to and feeding on the surface of the host — compare ENDOPHAGOUS **b :** consuming vegetation or plant debris by ingestion (as by browsing) rather than by disintegrating it from within

ec·to·phlo·ic \ˌektəˈflōik\ *adj* [*ect-* + *phloem* + *-ic*] *bot* **:** having phloem only external to the xylem — used of the siphonostele of certain vascular plants; compare AMPHIPHLOIC

ec·to·phyte \ˈ≠≠,fīt\ *n* -S [ISV *ect-* + *-phyte*] **:** an ectoparasitic plant — **ec·to·phyt·ic** \ˌ≠≠ˈfid·ik\ *adj*

ec·to·pia \ekˈtōpēə\ *n* -S [NL, fr. Gk *ektopos* away from a place (fr. *ek* out of, out — fr. *ex* — + *topos* place) + NL *-ia* — more at EX-, TOPIC] **:** an abnormal congenital or acquired position of an organ or part ⟨~ of the heart⟩

ec·top·ic \(ˈ)ekˈtäpik, -tōp-\ *adj* [ISV *ectopia* + *-ic*] **:** exhibiting ectopia ⟨an ~ kidney⟩ **:** occurring in an unusual position ⟨~ lesions⟩ or in an unusual manner or form ⟨~ heartbeat⟩ — compare ENTOPIC

ectopic pregnancy *n* **:** gestation elsewhere than in the uterus (as in a fallopian tube or in the peritoneal cavity)

ec·to·placenta \ˌektō+\ *n* [NL, fr. *ect-* + *placenta*] **:** TROPHOBLAST — **ec·to·placental** \"+\ *adj*

ec·to·plasm \ˈektə,plazəm\ *n* -S [ISV *ect-* + *-plasm*] **1 :** the outer relatively rigid granule-free layer of the cytoplasm usu. held to be a thixotropic gel — compare ENDOPLASM **2 :** the emanation from a spiritualistic medium that is believed to effect telekinesis and similar phenomena — **ec·to·plasmatic** \ˌ≠≠+\ *or* **ec·to·plasmic** \"+\ *adj*

ec·to·plast \ˈ≠≠,plast\ *n* -S [*ect-* + *-plast*] **1 :** PLASMA MEMBRANE 1 **2 :** the ectoplasmic content of a cell

ec·to·proct \-,präkt\ *n* -S [NL *Ectoprocta*] **:** a bryozoan of the group Ectoprocta

ec·to·proc·ta \ˌ≠≠ˈpräktə\ *n pl, cap* [NL, fr. *ect-* + ¹*-procta*] *in some classifications* **:** an order or subclass coextensive with Bryozoa — used by those who use Bryozoa as a division of Molluscoidea —**ec·to·proc·tous** \ˌ≠≠ˈ≠təs\ *adj*

ec·to·pterygota \ˌektō+\ *n pl, cap* [NL, fr. *ect-* + Gk *pterygōta*, neut. pl. of *pterygōtos* winged — more at PTERYGOTA] *syn of* HEMIMETABOLA

ec·to·rhinal \"+\ *adj* [*ect-* + *rhinal*] **:** of, related to, or located on the outside of the nose ⟨the ~ fissure⟩

ec·to·sarc \ˈektə,särk\ *n* -S [*ect-* + *-sarc*] **:** the semisolid external layer of protoplasm in some unicellular organisms (as the ameba) **:** ECTOPLASM — **ec·to·sar·cous** \ˌ≠≠ˈsärkəs\ *adj*

ec·to·som·al \ˌ≠≠ˈsōməl\ *adj* **:** of or relating to the ectosome

ec·to·some \ˈ≠≠,sōm\ *n* -S [*ect-* + *-some*] **:** the cortical part of a sponge

ec·to·sphenotic \ˌek(ˌ)tō+\ *adj* [*ect-* + *sphenotic*] **:** of or relating to the external part of the sphenotic bone

ec·to·sphere \ˈektə,sfi(ə)r\ *n* [*ect-* + *sphere*] **:** the cortical zone of the attraction sphere

ect·osteal \(ˈ)ekˌt+ˌ-\ *adj* [*ect-* + *osteal*] **1 :** of, produced by, or relating to ectostosis **2 :** of or relating to the surface of a bone — **ect·osteally** *adv*

ect·os·to·sis \ˌek,tä+\ *n, pl* **ectostoses** [NL, fr. *ect-* + *-ostosis*] **:** bone formation beginning immediately beneath the perichondrium and surrounding or replacing the underlying cartilage — compare ENDOSTOSIS

ec·to·symbiont *or* **ec·to·symbiote** \ˌek(ˌ)tō+\ *n* [*ect-* + *symbiont* or *symbiote*] **:** a symbiont dwelling on the surface of or physically separate from its host — **ec·to·symbiosis** \"+\ *n* — **ec·to·symbiotic** \"+\ *adj*

ec·to·therm \ˈektə,thərm\ *n* -S [*ect-* + *-therm*] **:** a cold-blooded animal **:** POIKILOTHERM

ec·to·ther·mic \ˌ≠≠ˈthərmik\ *adj* **:** deriving heat from without the body **:** COLD-BLOODED

ec·to·thrix \ˈ≠≠,thriks\ *adj* [NL, fr. *ect-* + Gk *thrix* hair — more at TRICHINA] **:** occurring on the surface of hair ⟨~ fungi⟩ — compare ENDOTHRIX

ec·to·trophic *also* **ec·to·tropic** \ˌektō+\ *adj* [*ect-* + *-trophic* or *-tropic*] *of a mycorrhiza* **:** growing as a close web on the surface of the associated root — opposed to *endotrophic*

ec·to·zoa \ˌ≠≠ˈzōə\ *n pl, often cap* [NL, fr. *ect-* + *-zoa*] **:** external animal parasites — often used as if a taxon — **ec·to·zo·an** \ˌ≠≠ˈzōən\ *adj or n*

ec·to·zo·ic \ˌ≠≠ˈzōik\ *adj* [NL *ectozoa* + E *-ic*] **:** living on the surface of an animal **:** ECTOZOAN

ec·to·zo·on \ˌ≠≠ˈzō,än\ *sing of* ECTOZOA

ectro- *comb form* [NL, fr. Gk *ektrōsis* miscarriage, fr. *ektitrōskein* to miscarry, fr. *ek* out of, out (fr. *ex*) + *titrōskein* to wound, damage; akin to Gk *tribein* to rub — more at EX-, THROW] **:** congenitally absent — in teratological terms chiefly indicating absence of a particular limb or part ⟨*ectro*dactylism⟩

ec·tro·dactylism *also* **ec·tro·dactylia** *or* **ec·tro·dactyly** \ˌektrō+\ *n, pl* **ectrodactylisms** *also* **ectrodactylias** *or* **ectrodactylies** [*ectrodactylism* fr. *ectro-* + *-dactylism*; *ectrodactylia* & *ectrodactyly* fr. NL *ectrodactylia*, fr. *ectro-* + *-dactylia*] **:** congenital complete or partial absence of one or more digits — **ec·tro·dac·ty·lous** \ˌ≠≠ˈdaktələs\ *adj*

ec·tro·me·lia \ˌektrōˈmēlēə\ *n* -S [NL, fr. *ectro-* + *-melia*] **1 :** congenital absence or imperfection of one or more limbs **2 :** MOUSEPOX

ec·tro·mel·ic \ˌ≠≠ˈmelik, -mēl-\ *adj* [*ectromelia* + *-ic*] **:** marked by or having ectromelia

ec·tro·pi·on \ekˈtrōpē,än, -ēən\ *n* -S [NL, fr. Gk *ektropion*, fr. *ek* out of, out (fr. *ex*) + *-tropion* (fr. *trepein* to turn) — more at TROPE] **:** an abnormal turning out of a part (as an eyelid)

ec·tro·pi·um \-ēəm\ *n* -S [NL, fr. Gk *ektropion*] **:** ECTROPION

ec·typ·al \ˈek,tīpəl, -ˌtəp-\ *adj* **:** having the characteristics of an ectype

ec·type \ˈek,tīp\ *n* [*ec-* coming from something else, derivative (fr. Gk *ek* out of, out, fr. *ex*) + *-type* (as in *archetype*) — more at EX-] **1 :** a copy from an original **:** an imitation or reproduction (as an impression of a seal) **2 a :** something in the world of external reality as distinguished from its eternal and ideal archetype or prototype **b** *Lockeanism* **:** an idea or impression more or less corresponding to some external reality

ecu \(ˈ)āˌkyü, ākˈü\ *n* -S [MF *ecu*, *escu* ecu, shield, fr. OF *escu* shield, fr. L *scutum* — more at ESQUIRE] **1 :** an old French coin having a shield as part of the design: **a :** a gold coin worth three livres issued from the 14th century until the introduction of the louis d'or in 1640 **b :** a silver crown-sized coin first issued in 1642 as equivalent to three livres but later varied arbitrarily esp. under Louis XIV between five, six, and eight livres **2 :** a silver piece worth five francs after introduction of the franc in 1795; *also* **:** the 20-franc silver piece issued 1929–38 **3 :** a unit of value equivalent to one ecu coin ⟨the captain's pay was one thousand ~s⟩ ⟨a ½-ecu coin⟩

ec·ua·dor \ˈekwə,dȯ(ə)r, -ō(ə)\ *adj, usu cap* [fr. *Ecuador*, republic in So. America] **:** of or from the Republic of Ecuador **:** of the kind or style prevalent in Ecuador **:** ECUADORIAN

¹ec·ua·dor·i·an \ˌekwəˈdōrēən, -dȯr-\ *also* **ec·ua·dor·an** \-ˈdōrən\ *or* **ec·ua·dor·e·an** \-ˈdōrēən, -dȯr-\ *adj, usu cap* **1 :** of, relating to, or characteristic of Ecuador **2 :** of, relating to, or characteristic of the people of Ecuador

²ecuadorian \"\ *also* **ecuadoran** \"\ *or* **ecuadorean** \"\ *n* -S *cap* **:** a native or inhabitant of Ecuador

ecuelle \āˈkwel\ *n* -S [F *écuelle*, fr. (assumed) VL *scūtella* drinking bowl, alter. of L *scūtella* — more at SCUTTLE] **:** a 2-handled bowl used for soup

ec·u·mene \ˈekyə,mēn, eˈkyüm(ˌ)nē\ *n* -S [Gk *oikoumenē*, fr. fem. of *oikoumenos* inhabited, pres. part. middle of *oikein* to inhabit, fr. *oikos* house, habitation — more at VICINITY] **1 a :** the permanently inhabited portion of the earth as distinguished from the uninhabited or temporarily inhabited area ⟨but that the southern limit of the ~ should be pushed southward, to about latitude 68° S. in Graham Land —*Geog. Rev.*⟩ **b :** the nuclear area or center of maximum activity of a state having the densest population and the closest network of transportation routes ⟨Russia's ~ is on the same grand scale as that of the U.S. —Derwent Whittlesey⟩ **2** *anthrop* **:** a nuclear area of high culture to which neighboring regions stand in a relation of cultural backwardness and dependence **:** CIVILIZATION

ec·u·men·ic *also* **oec·u·men·ic** \ˌekyəˈmenik, -nēk *sometimes* ˈēk-\ *adj* [LL *oecumenicus*, fr. LGk *oikoumenikos*, fr. Gk *oikoumenē* + *-ikos* -ic] **:** ECUMENICAL

ec·u·men·i·cal *also* **oec·u·men·i·cal** \-nəkəl, -nēk-\ *adj* [LL *oecumenicus* ecumenical + E *-al*] **1 :** worldwide, general, or universal in extent or influence ⟨dreamed of re-creating an ~ church⟩ or in application ⟨the shrewdest political and ~ comment of our time —Christopher Morley⟩ **2 a :** of, relating to, representing, or governing the whole of a body of churches ⟨an ~ council⟩ **b :** of or relating to the ecumenical movement ⟨~ leaders⟩ ⟨~ discussions⟩ **c :** promoting or tending toward worldwide Christian unity ⟨~ thinking⟩ ⟨~ activity⟩ **d :** of, relating to, or being a chiefly 20th century movement toward worldwide interconfessional Christian unity originating in Protestantism and now focused in a world council of churches that is supported by many Protestant, Eastern Orthodox, and other church bodies and that promotes through functional organizations cooperation on such common tasks as missions and work among students and through conferences mutual understanding on fundamental issues in belief, worship, and polity and a united witness on world problems **syn** see UNIVERSAL

ec·u·men·i·cal·ism \ˌ≠≠ˈ≠kə,lizəm\ *n* -S **:** the principles and practices of ecumenical Christianity; *esp* **:** those underlying the ecumenical movement

ec·u·men·i·cal·ly \ˌ≠≠ˈ≠nək(ə)lē, -nēk-, -li\ *adv* **:** in an ecumenical manner **:** in a manner that demonstrates ecumenical principles

ecumenical patriarch *n* **:** the patriarch of Constantinople who is the acknowledged highest ecclesiastical official in the Eastern Orthodox Church by virtue of a primacy of honor

ecumenical patriarchate *n* **:** the office of the ecumenical patriarch

ec·u·men·i·cism \ˌ≠≠ˈ≠nə,sizəm\ *n* -S **:** ECUMENICALISM

ec·u·men·i·cist \-nəsəst\ *n* -S **:** one who favors ecumenicity esp. as expressed through the ecumenical movement

ec·u·me·nic·i·ty \ˌekyəməˈnisəd·ē, ˌēk-, -(ˌ)meˈ-\ *n* -ES [*ecumenic* + *-ity*] **:** the quality or state of being ecumenical; *esp* **:** the condition of being ecumenically united in a worldwide interconfessional and interdenominational Christian fellowship **:** ecumenical Christianity

ec·u·men·ics \ˌ≠≠ˈmeniks, -nēks\ *n pl but sing in constr* [fr. *ecumenic*, after such pairs as *economic: economics*] **:** the study of the nature, mission, problems, and strategy of the Christian church from the perspective of its ecumenical character as a worldwide Christian fellowship, often including within its scope an emphasis on the contributions of Christian mission work to the rise of the ecumenical movement

ec·u·me·nism \ˈekyəmə,nizəm, eˈkyüm- *sometimes* ˈēkyəm-\ *n* -S [ISV *ecumenic* + *-ism*] **:** ecumenical principles and practices particularly as exemplified in the ecumenical movement

ec·u·me·nist \-ˌnəst\ *n* -S [ISV *ecumenic* + *-ist*] **:** an advocate of ecumenism

ecus *pl of* ECU

ec·ze·ma \ˌ÷igˈzēmə, ˈeksəmə, ˈegzəmə, egˈzēmə\ *n* -S [NL *eczemat-*, *eczema*, fr. Gk *ekzemat-*, *ekzema*, fr. *ek* out of, out (fr. *ex*) + *-zemat-*, *-zema* fermentation, boiling, fr. *zein* to boil — more at EX-, YEAST] **:** an acute or chronic noncontagious inflammatory condition of the skin that is characterized by redness, itching, and oozing vesicular lesions which become scaly, crusted, or lichenified and that is often associated with exposure to chemical or other irritants

eczematization \igˌzēmədˌəˈzāshən, eg-, -zem-\ *n* -S [ISV *eczemat-* (fr. NL *eczemat-*, *eczema*) + *-ize* + *-ation*] **:** an eczematous skin lesion complicating a noneczematous dermatitis

ec·ze·ma·to·gen·ic \igˌzēmədˌōˈjenik, eg-, -zem-\ *or* **ec·ze·ma·tog·e·nous** \-məˈtäjənəs\ *adj* [NL *eczemat-*, *eczema* + E *-o-* + *-genic* or *-genous*] **:** giving rise to eczema

ec·ze·ma·toid \ˈ≠≠mə,tȯid\ *adj* [ISV *eczemat-* + *-oid*] **:** resembling eczema

ec·ze·ma·tous \igˈzēməd·əs, (ˈ)egˈz-, -zem-, -mətəs\ *adj* [ISV *eczemat-* + *-ous*] **:** relating to eczema ⟨~ dermatitis⟩ **:** having the characteristics of eczema ⟨~ eruption⟩ **:** affected with eczema ⟨an ~ skin⟩

¹-ed \d *after infinitive forms ending in a vowel or in* b, g, j, ŋ, t͟h, v, z, zh, *or* r (r *in such position is usually regarded as a vowel*); t *after infinitive forms ending in* ch, f, k, p, s, sh, *or* th; əd *sometimes* (ˌ)ed *after infinitive forms ending in* d *or* t; *after a few infinitives ending in* l, m, *or* n, *the pronunciation* d *is alternative to* t *and the spelling -ed to -t (dwell, kneel, spell, dream, burn, lean, learn); some forms that are -d or -t when used as verbs are alternatively, sometimes only,* -əd *or* -(ˌ)ed *when used* *as adjectives* (*blessed, cursed, forked, striped, learned*); *adjectivally used forms in which -ed* (*often written -èd*) *follows infinitival terminals other than* d *and* t *are sometimes* -əd *or* -(,)ed *in poetry for the sake of the meter; -ed forms that are regularly* -d *or* -t *are often alternatively* -əd *or* -(,)ed *when -ly or -ness is added, the tendency to the latter pronunciations being in general in proportion to the difficulty of the consonantal cluster of which* l *or* n *is the final member*\ *vb suffix or adj suffix* [ME, fr. OE *-ed, -od, -ad*, fr. *-e-, -o-, -a-* (thematic vowels of various classes of weak verbs) + *-d*, past part. ending of weak verbs; akin to OHG *-t*, past part. ending of weak verbs, ON *-thr*, Goth *-ths*, L *-tus*, past part. ending, Gk *-tos*, suffix forming verbal adjectives, Skt *-ta*, past part. ending] **1** — used to form the past participle of regular weak verbs ⟨*ended*⟩ ⟨*followed*⟩ ⟨*dressed*⟩; regularly accompanied by coalescence with final *e* of the base word ⟨*faded*⟩, change of final postconsonantal *y* of the base word to *i* ⟨*tried*⟩, or doubling of the final consonant of the base word immediately after a short stressed vowel ⟨*patted*⟩ **2** — used to form adjectives of identical or nearly identical meaning from Latin-derived adjectives ending in *-ate* ⟨*crenulated*⟩ ⟨*pinnated*⟩ **3 a :** having **:** provided or furnished with **:** characterized by — in adjectives formed from nouns ⟨*balconied*⟩ ⟨*cultured*⟩ ⟨*moneyed*⟩ ⟨*winged*⟩ or from combinations having a noun as final constituent ⟨two-*legged*⟩ ⟨deep-*chested*⟩ ⟨three-*storied*⟩ **b :** having the characteristics of — in adjectives formed from nouns ⟨*bigoted*⟩ ⟨*dogged*⟩

²-ed \"\ *vb suffix* [ME *-ede, -de*, fr. OE *-ode, -ede, -ode, -ade*, past ending (1st pers. sing. indic.) of weak verbs, fr. *-e-, -o-, -a-* (thematic vowels of various classes of weak verbs) + *-de*, past ending (1st pers. sing. indic.) of weak verbs; akin to OHG *-ta*, past ending (1st pers. sing. indic.) of weak verbs, ON *-tha*, Goth *-da*, and prob. to OE *-d*, past part. ending of weak verbs] — used to form the past tense of regular weak verbs; regularly accompanied by coalescence with final *e* of the base word ⟨*judged*⟩, change of final postconsonantal *y* of the base word to *i* ⟨*denied*⟩, or doubling of the final consonant of the base word immediately after a short stressed vowel ⟨*dropped*⟩

ed *abbr* **1** edited; edition; editor **2** educated; education

ED *abbr* **1** election district **2** ex dividend **3** extra duty

eda·cious \ə'dāshəs, ē'-\ *adj* [L *edac-, edax* (fr. *edere* to eat) + E *-ious* — more at EAT] **:** relating to eating **:** VORACIOUS, DEVOURING ⟨time may have its ~ way even with those who deal in . . . absolute truths —Clifton Fadiman⟩

edac·i·ty \-'dasəd-ē\ *n* -ES [L *edacitas*, fr. *edac-, edax* + *-itas* -ity] **:** the quality or state of being edacious **:** APPETITE, VORACITY ⟨the ~ of vultures⟩

edam \'ēdəm, 'ē,dam, 'ē,daa(ə)m\ *or* **edam cheese** *n* -S *usu cap E* [fr. *Edam*, Netherlands] **:** a Dutch pressed cheese of yellow color and mild flavor made in balls weighing up to 10 pounds and usu. colored dark red outside

edaph·ic \ə'dafik, ē'-\ *adj* [ISV *edaph-* (fr. Gk *edaphos* bottom, ground, soil) + *-ic*; prob. akin to Gk *hezesthai* to sit — more at SIT] **1 :** of or relating to the soil ⟨~ relations⟩ ⟨~ factors in forest development⟩ **2 a** *of ecological formations* **:** resulting from or influenced by factors inherent in the soil (as salinity, alkalinity, or drainage) — opposed to *climatic; see* EDAPHIC CLIMAX **b :** AUTOCHTHONOUS 1 — **edaph·i·cal·ly** \-fək(ə)lē\ *adv*

edaphic climax *n* **:** an ecological climax resulting from soil factors and commonly persisting through cycles of climatic and physiographic change — compare PHYSIOGRAPHIC CLIMAX

ed·a·phol·o·gy \,edə'fäləjē\ *n* -ES [Gk *edaphos* + E *-logy*] **:** PEDOLOGY

ed·a·phon \'edə,fän\ *n* -S [ISV *edaph-* (fr. Gk *edaphos*) + *-on* (as in *plankton*); orig. formed in G] **:** the animal and plant life present in soils — compare PLANKTON

ed·a·pho·sau·ria \,edəfō'sȯrēə\ *n pl, cap* [NL, fr. Gk *edaphos* bottom, ground, soil + NL *-sauria*] **:** a suborder of Pelycosauria that includes Edaphosauridae and certain related families of extinct reptiles — compare EDAPHOSAURUS

¹ed·a·pho·sau·rid \;===;sȯrəd\ *adj* [NL *Edaphosauridae* family of reptiles, fr. *Edaphosaurus*, type genus + *-idae*] **:** of or relating to Edaphosauria or to reptiles of this group

²edaphosaurid \"\ *n* -S **:** a reptile or fossil of the suborder Edaphosauria

ed·a·pho·sau·rus \,===='sȯrəs\ *n, cap* [NL, fr. Gk *edaphos* + NL *-saurus*] **:** a genus (the type of the family Edaphosauridae) of heavy-bodied prob. herbivorous late Paleozoic reptiles having a bony dorsal sail or crest resembling that characteristic of the genus *Dimetrodon*

edd *abbr* editions; editors

ed·dic \'edik\ *also* **ed·da·ic** \(')e¦dāik\ *adj, usu cap* [ON *Edda* (prob. fr. *edda* great-grandmother) + E *-ic*; prob. akin to MHG *eide* mother, ON *eitha*, Goth *aithei*] **1 :** of or relating to the Old Norse *Edda* which is a 13th century collection of mythological, heroic, and gnomic poems many of which were composed at a much earlier date **2 :** having the characteristics of the alliterative strophic poetry of the *Edda* that is relatively simple in syntax and imagery — compare SKALDIC

ed·dish \'edish\ *n* -ES [ME *eddysche*, prob. fr. OE *edise* enclosed pasture; perh. akin to OE *ed-* again — more at EDDY] **1** *now dial Brit* **:** second-growth hay **:** AFTERMATH **2** *dial Eng* **:** STUBBLE ⟨a field of wheat ~⟩

ed·do \'e(,)dō\ *n* -ES [of African origin; akin to Twi *o¹de³* yam, Fanti *o¹do³*] **1 :** TARO **2 :** the edible root or stem of any of several aroids; *esp* **:** the root of taro

¹ed·dy \'edē, -di\ *n* -ES [alter. of ME (Sc dial.) *ydy*, prob. fr. ON *itha*; akin to OE & OS *ed-* again, OHG & ON *ith-* again, Goth *ith* but, L *et* and, Gk *eti* yet, still, Skt *ati* beyond, very; basic meaning: beyond] **1 :** a current of air or water running contrary to the main current; *esp* **:** one moving circularly **:** WHIRLPOOL **2 a :** a movement or school (as of thought or policy) that is static and unprogressive or that runs counter to the main trend ⟨this was merely an ~ in the stream of American foreign policy —P.C.Jessup⟩ ⟨shows a minute acquaintance with the minor *eddies* of the periodical literature —P.B. Rice⟩ **b :** a stagnant provincial region **:** a region that is remote from the main center of life and activity — often used with *back* ⟨when civilization moved northward and westward, Rome became a back ~ in European affairs —C.L.White & G.T.Renner⟩ **c :** an agitated or spasmodic movement (as of controversy or conflict); *esp* **:** one that is haphazard, aimless, or unproductive ⟨*eddies* and flurries of tribal strife ruled out the possibility of a topographical survey —J.V.Harrison⟩ **3 :** a material substance or group of individuals moving in a swirling or circular manner within a relatively limited area ⟨a constant wind whined through the tunnels, whipping *eddies* of coal dust into our eyes —Franc Shor⟩ ⟨little *eddies* of people were dancing with each other in the streets —L.C.Stevens⟩

²eddy \"\ *vb* -ED/-ING/-ES *vt* **:** to cause to move in an eddy ~ *vi* **:** to move in an eddy or in the manner of an eddy ⟨at the base of which the river swirls and *eddies* in a manner dangerous to small craft —Tom Marvel⟩ ⟨a crowd of blue-gowned men ~*ing* as starlings do about a tree —Patrick O'Donovan⟩ **syn** see TURN

eddy chamber *n* **:** a chamber where a fluid is caused to whirl in eddies

eddy current *n* **:** an electric current induced by an alternating magnetic field in a massive conductor (as the core of an armature or a transformer) — called also *Foucault current*

eddy-current brake *n* **:** a speed-control dynamometer in which the resistance to rotation is produced by eddy currents generated by the relative rotation of copper disks and magnets **:** an electromagnetic brake — compare MAGNETIC DAMPING

eddy-current loss *n* **:** loss of energy (as in electrical machinery or transformers) due to eddy currents in cores or conductors — compare CORE LOSS

ed·dy·root \'edē,=, -di,=\ *n* [by folk etymology fr. *eddo* + *root*] **:** TARO

ede- *or* **edeo-** *comb form* [NL *aedoe-, aedoeo-*, fr. Gk *aidoi-* & LGk *aidoio-*, fr. Gk *aidoia* genitals, fr. neut. pl. of *aidoios* worthy of reverence or compassion, fr. *aidōs* reverence, shame; prob. akin to OE *ār* honor, reverence, OHG *ēra* honor, reverence, ON *eir* clemency, Goth *aistan* to respect, Skt *īḍe* I praise] **:** genitals ⟨*edeitis*⟩ ⟨*edeoscopy*⟩

edel·e·a·nu process \ə,delē'ä(,)nü-\ *n, usu cap E* [after L. *Edeleanu* †1941 Romanian chemist] **:** a process for refining petroleum fractions (as kerosine or heavier oils) by extraction with liquid sulfur dioxide

edel·weiss \'ād°l,wīs, -,vīs\ *n* -ES [G, fr. *edel* noble (fr. OHG *edili*) + *weiss* white (fr. OHG *hwīz, wīz*); akin to OE *æthelu* nobility — more at ATHELING, WHITE] **1 :** a small perennial herb (*Leontopodium alpinum*) having a dense woolly white pubescence and growing high in the Alps **2 :** a New Zealand herb (*Leucogenes leontopodium*) related to and closely resembling the European edelweiss **3 :** any of various plants of the genus *Gnaphalium*

ede·ma *also* **oe·de·ma** \ə'dēmə, ē'-\ *n, pl* **edemas** \-məs\ *also* **edem·a·ta** \-'demədə, -'dēm-, -ətə\ *or* **oedemas** *or* **oedemata** [NL, fr. Gk *oidēma* swelling, tumor, fr. *oidein, oidan* to swell; akin to Gk *oidos* swelling, tumor — more at ATTER] **1 :** an abnormal accumulation of serous fluid in connective tissue causing puffy swelling or in a serous cavity (as the peritoneal or pleural) causing distention and compression of the contents that is usu. associated with defective circulation either primary or secondary to other conditions (as nephritis) **2 a :** extended swelling of plant organs or parts of organs from an overdevelopment of cells induced by an excess of water combined with unfavorable light and temperature relations **b :** any of various specific diseases of plants (as the tomato) characterized by such swellings — compare INTUMESCENCE

edem·a·tous \-'demədəs, -'dēm-, -ətəs\ *adj* [NL *edemat-, edema* + E *-ous*] **:** relating to, affected by, or having edema

eden \'ēd°n\ *n* -S *usu cap* [fr. *Eden*, the garden where Adam and Eve resided before the Fall (Gen 2:8), fr. LL, fr. Heb *'Ēdhen*] **:** PARADISE 2

eden·ic \(')ē¦denik\ *adj, usu cap* **:** of or relating to an Eden **:** PARADISIACAL

eden·ite \'ēd°n,īt\ *n* -S [G *edenit*, fr. *Edenville*, N.Y. + G *-it* -ite] **:** a light-colored variety of aluminous amphibole

eden·tal \(')ē¦dent°l\ *or* **eden·ta·lous** \-°ləs\ *adj* [*edental* fr. *e-* + *dent-* + *-al*; *edentalous* fr. *edental* + *-ous*] **:** EDENTATE

eden·ta·ta \,ē,den'tädə, -tād-ə\ *n pl, cap* [NL, fr. L, neut. pl. of *edentatus*, past part. of *edentare* to make toothless, fr. *e* out of (fr. *ex*) + *dent-, dens* tooth — more at EX-, TOOTH] **:** an order of Eutheria comprising mammals with teeth if present few and small, a small unconvoluted cerebrum, and the skin hairy or covered with bony plates and including the sloths, armadillos, and New World anteaters and formerly also the pangolins, the aardvark, and sometimes other forms

¹eden·tate \(')ē¦den,tāt\ *adj* [in sense 1, fr. L *edentatus*; in sense 2, fr. NL *Edentata*] **1 :** lacking teeth ⟨an ~ animal⟩ ⟨an ~ leaf⟩ **2 :** belonging to the Edentata

²edentate \"\ *n* -S **:** one of the Edentata

eden·tu·late \(')ē¦denchələt, -,lāt\ *adj* [L *edentulus* + E *-ate*] **:** lacking teeth **:** EDENTATE — used esp. of animals

eden·tu·lous \-,ləs\ *adj* [L *edentulus*, fr. *e-* out of + *dent-, dens* tooth + *-ulus* -ulous] **:** lacking teeth; *esp* **:** having lost teeth previously present

edeo- — see EDE-

edes·san \ə'des°n, ē'-\ *also* **edes·sene** \-,sēn\ *adj, usu cap* [*Edessa*, Mesopotamia + E *-an* or *-ene*] **:** of or relating to Edessa (modern Urfa), a city of ancient Mesopotamia

edes·tin \ə'destən, ē-\ *n* -S [ISV *edest-* (fr. Gk *edestos* eatable, fr. *edein* to eat) + *-in* — more at EAT] **1 :** a crystalline globulin found in many edible seeds (as in oats or rye) — not used technically **2 :** a crystalline globulin obtained esp. from hempseed that contains all of the essential amino acids

ed·gar \'edgə(r)\ *n* -S *usu cap* [after *Edgar* Allan Poe †1849 Am. poet and story writer known as the father of the detective story] **:** any of several small busts of Edgar Allan Poe awarded annually by a professional organization of writers to authors in various branches of mystery writing

¹edge \ 'ej\ *n* -S *often attrib* [ME *egge*, fr. OE *ecg*; akin to OS *eggia* edge of a blade, edge, OHG *ecka*, ON & OFris *egg*, L *acies* sharp edge, point, *acer* sharp, Gk *akmē* point, edge, LGk *akē* point, Skt *aśri* corner, angle, edge] **1 a :** the cutting side of the blade of an instrument ⟨the ~ of an ax⟩ **b** *archaic* **:** an edged weapon or tool **c :** the sharpness or degree of sharpness of a blade ⟨the sickle has no ~⟩ **d** (1) *obs* **:** ardor or inclination esp. for battle (2) **:** FORCE, EFFECTIVENESS ⟨local resistance blunted the ~ of radical legislation at Washington⟩ **:** vigor or energy esp. of mind and body ⟨he looked and acted flabby; the ~ of him was gone —Carleton Beals⟩ **:** incisive or penetrating quality (as of thought or expression) ⟨the cutting ~ of Machiavelli's irony —E.R.Bentley⟩ **:** a quality of hardness, harshness, or bite ⟨his voice had an ~ like ice —John Buchan⟩ ⟨your goodness must have an ~ in it — else it is none —R.W. Emerson⟩ (3) **:** keenness or intensity esp. of desire or enjoyment ⟨when they'd taken the ~ off their own hunger —Kenneth Roberts⟩ **:** RELISH, ZEST, SAVOR ⟨flying bombs . . . gave a brilliant ~ of chance to homely days and nights —Audrey Barker⟩ **:** SPUR, STIMULUS ⟨to give more ~ to the contest, he felt for his rival the bitter hate that . . . was typically Venetian —T.B.Costain⟩ **2 a :** the extreme verge or brink (as of a cliff or precipice) **b :** the crest of a ridge of hills **:** the escarpment of a plateau **3 a :** the line or point where a material object or area begins or ends **:** BORDER ⟨the town stands on the ~ of a plain⟩ ⟨a smoldering hulk, burned to the water's ~ —H.A.Chippendale⟩; *also* **:** the portion of the surface of an object or area that is adjacent to its border ⟨walked on the ~ of the deck⟩ **b :** a point near the beginning or the end (as of an era, condition, subject, or action) **:** a dividing line or line of transition from one state or condition to another **:** MARGIN — often used in the phrase *on the edge* ⟨science stood on the ~ of a major theoretical advance⟩ ⟨her body hovered delicately on the last ~ of childhood —Scott Fitzgerald⟩ ⟨many of the ranches . . . are on the ~ of bankruptcy —H.W. Baldwin⟩ ⟨was on the ~ of screaming⟩ **4** *obs* **:** EDGING, BORDER **5 :** a terminating border ⟨the ~ of a tablecloth⟩ **:** a line that is the intersection of two plane faces of a solid object ⟨the ~*s* of a pyramid⟩ **:** the relatively thin surface or side of any object bounded by plane surfaces ⟨the ~ of a book⟩ **6 a :** the inside or outside verge of the blade of a skate **b :** a skating stroke including appropriate body lean made on one edge of the blade of a skate ⟨a forward inside ~⟩; *also* **:** the resultant pattern cut in the ice **7 :** the privilege in poker of betting last after the other players have revealed their intentions — called also *age* **8 :** a favorable margin **:** ADVANTAGE ⟨had the ~ on top speed —A.S.Kramer⟩ ⟨the open spaces that gave the suburb . . . an ~ over the city — Lewis Mumford⟩ ⟨a decisive ~ in military strength⟩ **9** *slang* **:** a condition of being intoxicated **:** degree of intoxication ⟨got a good ~ on —Ernest Hemingway⟩ **syn** see BORDER — **on edge :** NERVOUS, ANXIOUS, UNEASY ⟨as a conductor . . . he kept the singers uncomfortably *on edge* —*Time*⟩

²edge \"\ *vb* -ED/-ING/-S [ME *eggen*, fr. *egge*, *n.*] *vt* **1 :** to give an edge to ⟨asked him to ~ the ax⟩ ⟨hurt resentment *edged* his wife's voice —G.G.Carter⟩ **2** *obs* **:** to set (one's teeth) on edge **3 a** (1) **:** to finish (an edge) with a binding, band, strip, or trimming ⟨~ a blouse with lace⟩ ⟨~ a plywood counter⟩ (2) **:** to decorate an edge of (as a book) (3) **:** to level an edge of (a rafter); *also* **:** to square an edge of **b :** to serve as a border to **:** FRINGE ⟨warehouses and terminals ~ the 25-mile waterfront —L.A.Borah⟩ **:** be on an edge of ⟨grew up in a community still *edging* the wilderness —H.M.Kallen⟩ ⟨now *edging* sixty, he retains all his vigor⟩ **4** *archaic* **:** to urge or egg on **5 :** to move gradually or by pressing forward edgewise ⟨*edged* his master out of hearing —George Meredith⟩ ⟨~ him off the road⟩ **:** force (as from a position) by the application of pressure ⟨*edging* his foes out of every position of influence⟩ **:** DISPLACE ⟨machine-made muslins and calicoes have been *edging* out native-made muslins —John Murra⟩ **6 a :** to strike (a bowled ball) in cricket with the edge of the bat **b :** to incline (a ski) sideways so that one edge cuts into the surface of the snow ~ *vi* **:** to move in one direction by degrees ⟨*edged* over the open plains toward the western extremities of the country —Oscar Handlin⟩ ⟨~ away from his responsibilities⟩ **:** move edgeways ⟨began to ~ along the front of the bureau —Berton Roueché⟩

edgebone *var of* AITCHBONE

edged \'ejd *sometimes* 'ejəd\ *adj* **1 :** having a specified kind of edge, boundary, or border ⟨black-*edged*⟩ ⟨rough-*edged*⟩ ⟨scalloped-*edged*⟩ or number of edges ⟨two-*edged*⟩ **2 :** SHARP, CUTTING ⟨an ~ knife⟩ **:** TRENCHANT ⟨an ~ remark⟩ ⟨~ satire⟩

edge effect *n* **1 :** the result of the presence of two adjoining plant communities (as in an ecotone) on the numbers and kinds of animals present in the immediate vicinity **2 :** a special physical condition (as of electric surface density or turbulence) existing at the edge of an area (as a charged metal plate) or region

edge-grain \'=,=\ *or* **edge-grained** \'=;=\ *adj* **:** QUARTERSAWED

edge in *vt* **:** to work in **:** INTERPOLATE ⟨with difficulty *edging in* a word of his own⟩

edge iron *n* **:** a gardener's tool for cutting turf along a border (as of a walk or flower bed)

edge joint *n* **:** a joint formed by uniting two edges or two surfaces (as by welding) esp. making a corner

edge·less \'ejləs\ *adj* **:** lacking an edge **:** DULL, BLURRED

edge lighting *n* **:** the ability of a transparent substance (as plastic) to transmit light (as from the edge of a sheet or the end of a rod) so that it remains invisible until it emerges at the far edge or end regardless of bends or turns in the substance

edge mill *n* **1 :** an ore-grinding machine of the Chile-mill type **2 :** a narrow plain milling cutter

edge on *adv* **:** EDGEWAYS **:** on an edge ⟨receive a blow *edge on*⟩

edge out *vt* **:** to defeat or surpass by a small margin ⟨coming from behind to *edge out* the opposing team by one point⟩ ⟨*edged* his opponent *out* by 367 votes in a total vote of 40,000⟩

edge protector *n* **:** a right-angle piece of metal or hard fiber placed over the edge (as of a shipping case, crate, box, or bale) to prevent cutting by metal strapping or wire

edg·er \'ejə(r)\ *n* -S **1 a :** a worker who stitches or finishes the edge of a garment **b :** an operator of a burnishing machine for finishing the skived edge of a shoe upper to make it appear rolled or for setting the edge of the forepart of a sole **c :** a person who bevels or grinds the edge of optical glass **d :** STRANDER 2 **e :** an operator of a lumber-edging machine **2 a :** a machine for edging lumber; *esp* **:** one with feed rolls, press rolls, and several circular saws **b :** a wood-sanding machine adapted to work around an edge (as of a floor) **c :** a tool used to trim an edge (as of a lawn) along a sidewalk or curb **3 :** BREAKDOWN 5

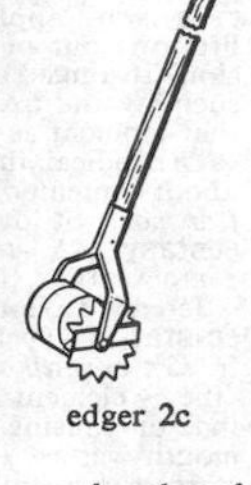

edger 2c

edge rail *n* **1 :** a railroad rail set on edge with which a flanged wheel with a conoidal tread is used — contrasted with *tram rail* **2 :** a guardrail laid alongside the main rail at a switch

edg·er·man \'==mən\ *n, pl* **edgermen :** EDGER 1

edge roll *n* **1 a :** a tool for rolling in decoration on the edge of a book cover **b :** decoration made with an edge roll **2 :** a molding of semicircular section replacing the arris at the edge of a member

edge roll 2

edge runner *n* **1 :** a stone or metal wheel in an edge mill **2 :** a machine consisting of one or more heavy steel rolls or grindstones set on a horizontal shaft rotating round a pan or trough that is used for crushing stone, fibrous matter for papermaking, or other material

edges *pl of* EDGE, *pres 3d sing of* EDGE

edgeshot \'=,=\ *adj* [¹*edge* + *shot*, past part. of *shoot* (to plane)] **:** having an edge planed

edgestitch \'=;=\ *vt* **:** to seam or stitch for decoration along a fold line of (a piece of cloth)

edgestone \'=,=\ *n* **1 :** CURBSTONE **2 :** a stone roller in an edge mill

edge strip *n* **:** a strap for a butt joint in riveted plate work esp. when used for a fore-and-aft joint in a ship's hull

edge tone *n* **:** a tone produced by an air stream deflected by a sharp edge (as in a flute)

edge tool *n* **1 :** a tool with a sharp cutting edge (as a chisel, plane, knife, or gouge) **2 :** a tool for forming or dressing an edge **:** an edging tool

edge trim *n* **:** a contour (as bevel or round) given in finishing the edge of a sole

edgewater \'=,==\ *n* **:** water underlying petroleum in an oil-bearing sand — compare EDGE WELL

edgeways *or* **edgewise** \'=,=\ *adv* **:** with the edge toward or foremost **:** on, by, or with the edge ⟨saw a plank ~⟩; *also* **:** as if by an edge **:** BARELY — chiefly used in the phrase *get a word in edgeways* ⟨had to raise his voice to get a word in ~ —George Bellairs⟩

edge well *n* **:** a well on the edge of an oil or gas pool

edg·i·ly \'ejəlē, -li\ *adv* **:** in an edgy manner

edg·i·ness \'ejēnəs, -jin-\ *n* -ES **1 :** sharpness or angularity of outline ⟨the ~ of a fresh-cut gem —R.C.B.Brown⟩ **2 :** the condition of being on edge **:** NERVOUSNESS

edging *n* -S [¹*edge* + *-ing*] **1 :** something that forms an edge or border: as **a :** a narrow piece of lace, fringe, or braid usu. with one straight edge used to finish or decorate an edge or joining on clothing, upholstery, or curtains **b :** a border of plants, wood, metal or bricks used to define an edge (as of a bed or lawn) or the material used for such a border **c :** small solid wood squares set into the edge of a veneered top to protect the veneer **d :** a narrow rounded or right-angled strip (as of metal) on the edge of a flat surface (as a table top or ski) for decoration or protection **2 :** a piece of waste wood produced in edging

edging box *n* **:** a dwarf box (*Buxus sempervirens* var. *suffruticosa*) that is used esp. for edging (as around a bed in a garden)

edging grinder *n* **:** a cutting machine for grinding up refuse wood

edg·ing·ly *adv* **:** little by little **:** GRADUALLY

edgy \'ejē, -ji\ *adj* -ER/-EST **1 :** SHARP, EDGED ⟨often displayed a perceptive, ~ wit —*New Yorker*⟩ ⟨the vocal quality on this occasion was raw and ~ —Irving Kolodin⟩ **:** hard or angular in line or outline **2 :** being on edge **:** TENSE, NERVOUS, IRRITABLE ⟨looked well, though a little tired and ~ —H.L.Davis⟩ ⟨the ~ days before World War I —*Saturday Rev.*⟩ ⟨tempers became ~ —Gordon Webber⟩

edh *or* **eth** \'eth\ *n* -S [Icel *eth*] **:** a letter ð formed with a stroke across the simple *d* used in Old English and in Icelandic writing to represent an interdental fricative and in the International Phonetic alphabet to represent the voiced interdental fricative (as in *then*) — compare THORN 3

ed·i·bil·i·ty \,edə'biləd-ē, -ətē, -i\ *n* -ES **:** the quality or state of being edible

¹ed·i·ble \'edəbəl\ *adj* [LL *edibilis*, fr. L *edere* to eat + *-ibilis* -ible — more at EAT] **:** suitable by nature for use as food esp. for human beings **:** NONPOISONOUS, EATABLE — **ed·i·ble·ness** *n* -ES

²edible \"\ *n* -S **:** something that is edible ⟨state police rushed food to stricken families . . . only cold ~*s* were transported —*N.Y.Times*⟩

edible bird's nest *n* **:** the nest of various small swifts (genus *Collocalia*) of southern Asia and neighboring islands that is made chiefly of the dried glutinous secretion of the salivary glands of the birds and is used in making soup

edible canna *n* **:** an Asiatic herb (*Canna edulis*) cultivated for its starchy rootstocks — see TOUS-LES-MOIS

edible dormouse *n* **:** any of various common European dormice (genus *Glis*) esp. of the Mediterranean region

edible frog *n* **:** a European frog (*Rana esculenta*)

edible galingale *n* **:** CHUFA

edible-podded pea \'===,=-\ *or* **edible pod pea** \'===,=-\ *n* **:** a pea of a variety (*Pisum sativum macrocarpon*) with edible pods

edible snail *n* **:** a snail used as food (as *Helix pomatia* and *H. aspersa* of Europe)

edict \'ē(,)dikt, 'ēdēkt, *archaic* ='=\ *n* -S [L *edictum*, fr. neut. of *edictus*, past part. of *edicere* to declare, decree, fr. *e-* + *dicere* to say — more at DICTION] **1 a :** a public notice issued by official ecclesiastical or state authority **:** a public command or ordinance by the sovereign power **:** the proclamation of a law or rule of conduct made by competent authority — compare DECREE, RESCRIPT **b :** an order or command esp. when suggesting such an official public notice ⟨so the wife won't notice it and issue bitter ~*s* about slovenliness —*Fortnight*⟩ **2 :** the order of the court in Scots and Roman Dutch law commanding that notice of a pending civil or criminal suit be given to an absent or nonresident defendant by citation and specifying in what manner it should be given — compare EDICTAL CITATION

edic·tal \(ˈ)ēˈdiktᵊl, ēˈd-\ *adj* [LL *edictalis*, fr. L *edictum* + *-alis* -al] **:** relating to or consisting of an edict **:** announced by an edict

edictal citation *n* **:** a citation or summons in Scots and Roman Dutch law proclaimed, published, or deposited in a public place and summoning nonresident or absent defendants to court in civil or criminal cases

edic·tal·ly \-ᵊlē\ *adv* **:** by means of an edict

ed·i·cule \ˈedə,kyül\ *var of* AEDICULA

ed·i·fi·ca·tion \,edəfəˈkāshən\ *n* -s [ME *edificacioun*, fr. LL & L; LL *aedification-, aedificatio* spiritual improvement, fr. L, construction, fr. *aedificatus* (past part. of *aedificare* to construct) + *-ion-, -io* -ion — more at EDIFY] **1 a :** a building up of the mind, character, or faith **:** intellectual, moral, or spiritual improvement ⟨images of ~ are offered to our eyes —E.R. Bentley⟩ **b :** ENLIGHTENMENT ⟨examples of good quality in our public museums for the ~ of the man off the street —S.L. Faison⟩ **2** *archaic* **:** construction esp. of a building ⟨the assured ~ of his church —Joseph Hall⟩

edif·i·ca·to·ry \əˈdifəkə,tōrē, ēˈdif-, edəf-; ˈedəfə,kād·ərē\ *adj* [LL *aedificatorius*, fr. *aedificatus* (past part. of *aedificare* to edify) + L *-orius* -ory — more at EDIFY] **:** intended or suitable for edification ⟨a minister given to the writing of ~ epistles to his congregation⟩; *also* **:** EDIFYING ⟨the ~ force of an oration⟩

ed·i·fice \ˈedəfəs\ *n* -s [ME, fr. MF, fr. L *aedificium*, fr. *aedificare* to construct — more at EDIFY] **1 :** BUILDING; *esp* **:** a large or massive structure (as a church or government building) **2 :** something built up in a manner analogous to the erection of an architectural structure ⟨on this argument he based his ~ of faith —A.N.Whitehead⟩ ⟨does not feel that the whole ~ of science has collapsed and crumbled —G.B. Shaw⟩

ed·i·fi·cial \ˌedəˈfishəl\ *adj* [LL *aedificialis*, fr. L *aedificium* + *-alis* -al] **1 :** relating to an edifice **:** STRUCTURAL **2 :** IMPOSING

ed·i·fi·er \ˈedə,fī(ə)r, -īə\ *n* -s [ME, fr. *edifien* + *-er*] **:** one that edifies

ed·i·fy \ˈedə,fī\ *vb* -ED/-ING/-S [ME *edifien, edefien*, fr. MF *edifier, edefier*, fr. LL & L; LL *aedificare* to instruct or improve spiritually, fr. L, to erect a house, construct, fr. L *aedes* temple, house, building (prob. orig. "hearth") + *-ficare* -fy; akin to OE *ād* funeral pyre, fire, OHG *eit* funeral pyre, fire, G dial. *aitel*, a kind of bright fish, Sw *id* ide (fish), L *aestas* summer, Gk *aithein* to ignite, burn, Skt *inddhe* he ignites] *vt* **1** *archaic* **a :** BUILD ⟨a holy chapel *edified* —Edmund Spenser⟩ ⟨*edified* fourteen hundred mosques —Edward Gibbon⟩ **b :** ORGANIZE, ESTABLISH **2 :** to instruct and improve esp. in moral and religious knowledge **:** ENLIGHTEN, ELEVATE, UPLIFT ⟨the object of these paintings . . . was to instruct and ~ all who came into the church, even if they could not read —O. Elfrida Saunders⟩ ⟨believe myself to be *edified* by the old liturgy —D.W.Brogan⟩ ~ *vi* **1** *obs* **:** GROW, PROSPER **2 a** *obs* **:** to profit spiritually **:** IMPROVE **b** *archaic* **:** to gain knowledge **:** LEARN

ed·i·fy·ing·ly \ˈ==,==, ,==ˈ===\ *adv* **:** so as to edify **:** in an edifying manner

ed·i·fy·ing·ness \ˈ==,===, ,==ˈ===\ *n* -ES **:** the quality or state of being edifying

edile *var of* AEDILE

ed·in·burgh \ˈedᵊn,bər·ə, -,bə·r|, |ō *also* -,bərg *or* -,bəg *or* -,bəig\ *adj, usu cap* [fr. *Edinburgh*, Scotland] **:** of or from Edinburgh, the capital of Scotland **:** of the kind or style prevalent in Edinburgh

ed·ing·ton·ite \ˈediŋtə,nīt\ *n* -s [after *Edington*, 19th cent. Scot who found it] **:** a grayish white zeolitic mineral $BaAl_2Si_3O_{10}.4H_2O$ consisting of hydrous aluminum barium silicate (hardness 4–4.5, sp. gr. 2.69)

ed·i·son battery \ˈedəsən-\ *or* **edison storage battery** *n* [fr. *Edison*, a trademark] **:** a storage battery employing a solution of caustic potash as the electrolyte, nickel hydroxide and iron as the active agents of the plates, and nickel-plated steel as the framework and container

edison cell *n* [fr. *Edison*, a trademark] **:** a cell of an Edison battery

edison effect *n, usu cap E* [after Thomas A. *Edison* †1931 Am. inventor] **:** the thermionic current observed when an additional electrode is introduced into an incandescent-lamp bulb and connected externally with the positive terminal through a galvanometer

ed·it \ˈedət, *usu* -əd·+V\ *vt* -ED/-ING/-S [back-formation fr. *editor*] **1 a :** to prepare an edition of **:** select, emend, revise, and compile (as literary material) to make suitable for publication or for public presentation ⟨~*ed* the complete poetic works⟩ ⟨the newsroom staff ~*s* the bulletins for radio broadcasts⟩ ⟨this old opera was recently revived and ~*ed*⟩ ⟨~*s* his thoughts before speaking⟩ **b :** to assemble (a photographic film sequence or tape recording) by cutting, rearranging, and combining its component parts ⟨the ~*ed* film is a selected assembly of many "bits and pieces" of all kinds . . . the result is a smooth-flowing continuity —W.H.Offenhauser⟩ ⟨~*ed* the tape recording to fit a 15-minute program⟩ **c :** to alter, adapt, or refine esp. to bring about conformity to a standard or to suit a particular purpose ⟨~*s* the finished creations with an architect's eye for line and proportion —*Fashion Digest*⟩ ⟨famous last words are usually ~*ed* after the fact —John Hersey⟩ ⟨took the liberty of ~*ing* the information that was presented to the committee at the hearing⟩ **2 :** to superintend or direct the publication of ⟨~*ed* the daily paper⟩ ⟨~*ed* scientific journals⟩ **3 :** OMIT, DELETE, ELIMINATE — usu. used with *out* ⟨~*ing* clichés out of other people's writing —Max Ascoli⟩ ⟨has mistakenly ~*ed* out of his book a wealth of characterization and anecdote that his original research must have provided —R.N.Denney⟩ ⟨~ out undesirable film⟩

edi·tion \əˈdishən, ēˈ-\ *n* -s [MF & ML; MF *edition*, fr. ML *edition-, editio*, fr. L, act of bringing forth, fr. *editus* (past part. of *edere* to bring forth, produce, proclaim, publish, fr. *e-* + *-dere* to put or *-dere*, fr. *dare* to give) + *-ion-, -io* -ion — more at DO, DATE] **1** *obs* **a :** the action of publishing **b :** the action or result of bringing into existence: (1) **:** EXTRACTION, ORIGIN (2) **:** CREATION ⟨can we treat the absolute ~ of the world as a legitimate hypothesis? —William James⟩ **2 :** the form in which a literary work (as an edited text) or group of works (as the works of several poets) is published: as **a :** the whole number of bound copies printed from a single setting of type or from plates made therefrom **b :** PRINTING **c :** a printed production the same as an earlier one in title but with substantial changes in or additions to the text **d :** a set of copies differing in some way from others of the same published text ⟨a thumb-indexed ~⟩ ⟨an india-paper ~⟩ **e :** an arbitrarily limited number of copies or complete sheets of an impression **3 a :** one of the forms in which something is issued or otherwise presented to the public ⟨most of the standard ~*s* of the older music contain few staccato marks —Warwick Braithwaite⟩ ⟨the Spanish Civil War ~ of the Goya etchings —H.L.Matthews⟩ ⟨this year's ~ of the annual charity ball⟩ **b :** the whole number of articles of one style put out at one time ⟨a limited ~ of custom-made radiophonographs⟩; *specif* **:** the number of stamps or of items of a particular piece of postal stationery in one issue **c :** something that resembles another in its main characteristics **:** REPRODUCTION, COPY, VERSION ⟨the Southern Uplands form a softer and kindlier ~ of the Highlands —L.D.Stamp⟩ ⟨her younger sister, a weaker ~ of Octavie —Dorothy C. Fisher⟩ **4 :** all the copies printed in a single pressrun of a newspaper — see CITY EDITION, FINAL EDITION, FIRST EDITION, MAIL EDITION

edition bindery *n* **:** a plant specializing in machine binding of complete editions or large quantities of books as distinguished from a plant doing job binding or hand binding

edition binding *n* **:** the binding of books in uniform style usu. by mass-production methods and in relatively large quantities esp. as contrasted with hand binding or library binding; *also* **:** a book so bound — called also *publisher's binding, trade binding*

edi·tio prin·ceps \əˌdid·ē,ōˈpriŋ,keps; əˌdishē,ōˈprin,seps, ēˈ-\ *n, pl* **edi·ti·o·nes prin·ci·pes** \əˌdid·ēˈō,nāˈspriŋkə,pās; ə,dishēˈō(,)nēzˈprin(t)sə,pēz, ē,d-\ [NL, lit., first edition] **:** the first printed edition esp. of a work that circulated in manuscript before printing became common ⟨the *editio princeps* of the Greek New Testament —*Times Lit. Supp.*⟩

ed·i·tor \ˈedəd·ə(r), -ətə(r)\ *n* -s [LL, publisher, fr. L *editus* (past part. of *edere* to bring forth, produce, proclaim, publish) + *-or* — more at EDITION] **1 a :** one who revises, corrects, or arranges the contents and style of the literary, artistic, or musical work of others for publication or presentation ⟨the ~ of some early English ballads⟩ ⟨an ~ of Aristotle⟩ ⟨the ~ of a film⟩ **b :** one who alters or revises another's work to make it conform to some standard or serve a particular purpose ⟨some ~ had bowdlerized th letter before publishing it⟩ **c :** one who directs or supervises the expressive policies or the preparation of a publication (as a newspaper, periodical, reference work) **d :** one who has contextual supervision of a section, special department, or feature of a publication ⟨the sports ~ of the evening paper⟩ ⟨the fiction ~ of a magazine⟩ **e :** one who handles the written product as distinct from other matters (as sales) in many publishing concerns ⟨the ~*s* and the sales and business personnel of the magazine stayed on friendly terms⟩ **2 :** a device usu. consisting of a splicer and viewer and used in editing film

¹ed·i·to·ri·al \ˌedəˈtōrēəl, -ȯr-\ *adj* [*editor* + *-ial*] **1 a :** being an editor or consisting of editors ⟨an ~ staff⟩ **b :** of or relating to an editor or his functions ⟨an ~ job⟩ ⟨the ~ desk⟩ ⟨the punctuation is ~ —R.H.Robbins⟩ **2 a :** of, befitting, or resembling an editorial **:** expressive of an opinion ⟨an ~ broadcast⟩ ⟨an ~ statement⟩ **b :** of, relating to, or constituting the literary contents of a publication ⟨the ~ content of a woman's magazine sandwiched in among the ads⟩

²editorial \"\ *n* -s **:** a newspaper or periodical article that is usu. given a special or significant place and that intentionally expresses the views of those in control of the publication on a matter of current interest; *also* **:** an expression of opinion that resembles such an article

ed·i·to·ri·al·ist \,==ˈ==ələst\ *n* **:** a writer of editorials

ed·i·to·ri·al·i·za·tion \,==,==əlˈzāshən, -,līˈz-\ *n* -s **:** the action of editorializing

ed·i·to·ri·al·ize \,==ˈ==ə,līz\ *vi* -ED/-ING/-S **1 :** to express an opinion in the form of an editorial ⟨all the local papers *editorialized* on the subject⟩ **2 :** to introduce opinion into the reporting of facts (as by overt comment or by slanting the report) ⟨the interpretative function of a newspaper or a radio news program need entail no *editorializing*⟩ **3 :** to express an opinion (as on a controversial issue) ⟨the advertisement did not so much sell goods as ~ on local issues⟩

ed·i·to·ri·al·iz·er \-zə(r)\ *n* -s **:** one that editorializes

ed·i·to·ri·al·ly \,==ˈ==əlē, -li\ *adv* **1 :** in editorials or in an editorial manner ⟨the evening paper commented ~ on his appointment⟩ **2 :** in the capacity of editor ⟨he was ~ connected with the publication for many years⟩

editor in chief \ˌ====ˈ=\ *n, pl* **editors in chief :** an editor who is the head of the entire editorial staff of a publication

ed·i·tor·ship \ˈ===,ship\ *n* **1 a :** the position and functions of an editor ⟨he had the ~ of the magazine⟩ **b :** the tenure of such a position ⟨the publication thrived during his ~⟩ **2 :** editorial revision or alteration ⟨it was hard to tell the extent of the Russian ~ of the reports⟩

ed·i·tress \ˈedə·trəs\ *n* -ES [*editor* + *-ess*] **:** a female editor

edits *pres 3d sing of* EDIT

EDL *abbr* edition deluxe

ed·mon·ton \ˈedməntən, -ntᵊn\ *adj, usu cap* **1** [fr. *Edmonton*, England] **:** of or from the municipal borough of Edmonton, England **:** of the kind or style prevalent in Edmonton, England **2** [fr. *Edmonton*, Alberta, Canada] **:** of or from Edmonton, the capital of Alberta **:** of the kind or style prevalent in Edmonton, Alberta

edn *abbr* **1** edition **2** education

ednl *abbr* educational

edo \ˈe(,)dō\ *n, pl* **edo** *or* **edos** *usu cap* **1 a :** a Negro people of the province of Benin in southern Nigeria **b :** a member of such people **2 :** a Kwa language of the Edo people

edom·ite \ˈēdə,mīt\ *n* -s *usu cap* [*Edom* (Esau), eponymous ancestor of the Edomites (Gen 36) + E *-ite*] **:** a member of an ancient people who were descended from Esau and who lived southeast of the Dead sea — **edom·it·ic** \ˌēdəˈmid·ik\ *adj*

ed·reo·benthos \ˌedrēō+\ *n* [*edreo-* (fr. Gk *hedraios* sedentary, fr. *hedra* seat, sitting) + *benthos*; akin to Gk *hezesthai* to sit — more at SIT] **:** obligatorily sedentary organisms of the benthos (as mussels and rock oysters)

ed·ri·as·ter·oi·dea \,edrē,astəˈrȯidēə\ *syn of* EDRIOASTEROIDEA

¹ed·rio·as·ter·oid \ˌedrēō,astə,rȯid\ *adj* [NL *Edrioasteroidea*] **:** of or relating to the Edrioasteroidea

²edrioasteroid \"\ *n* -s **:** an echinoderm of the class Edrioasteroidea

ed·rio·as·ter·oi·dea \,===,==ˈrȯidēə\ *n pl, cap* [NL, fr. *edrio-* (fr. Gk *hedraios* sedentary, stationary) + *Asteroidea*] **:** a class of extinct echinoderms (subphylum Pelmatozoa) with a plated but flexible body resembling a sac

ed·ri·oph·thal·ma \ˌedrē,äfˈthalmə\ *n pl, cap* [NL, fr. *edri-* (fr. Gk *hedraios*) + *-ophthalma*] *in some classifications* **:** a superorder of Malacostraca that includes forms with sessile eyes and is coextensive with the orders Isopoda and Amphipoda — compare ARTHROSTRACA — **ed·ri·oph·thal·ma·tous** \ˌ==,=ˈmad·əs\ *or* **ed·ri·oph·thal·mous** \-məs\ *adj*

ed·ri·oph·thal·ma·ta \ˌedrē,äfˈthalməd·ə\ [NL, irreg. fr. *edri-* + Gk *ophthalmos* eye] *syn of* EDRIOPHTHALMA

¹ed·ri·oph·thal·mi·an \,==,=ˈmēən\ *n* -s [NL *Edriophthalma* + E *-ian*] **:** a crustacean of the superorder Edriophthalma

²edriophthalmian \ˈ==,=ˈ==\ *adj* **:** of or relating to the Edriophthalma

EDTA *abbr* ethylenediaminetetraacetic acid

educ *abbr* **1** educated **2** education

ed·u·ca·bil·ia \,ejəkəˈbilyə, -lēə\ *n pl, cap* [NL, fr. L *educare* to bring up, rear, educate + *-abilia* (neut. pl. of *-abilis* -able) — more at EDUCATE] *in former classifications* **:** a superorder of placental mammals having the large cerebrum overlapping the cerebellum and optic lobes and including the higher mammals (as the Primates, Carnivora, Ungulata) — **ed·u·ca·bil·ian** \,==ˈ==lēən\ *adj*

ed·u·ca·bil·i·ty \,ejəkəˈbiləd·ē, -ətē, -i\ *also* **ed·u·cat·abil·i·ty** \-,kād·əˈb-, -,kātə-\ *n* -ES **:** the quality or state of being educable

ed·u·ca·ble \ˈejəkəbəl\ *also* **ed·u·cat·able** \-,kād·əbəl, -,kātə-, ,==ˈ===\ *adj* [*educate* + *-able*] **:** capable of being educated ⟨molders of young, still ~ Americans —Austin Warren⟩

ed·u·cand \ˌejəˈkand\ *n* -s [L *educandus*, gerundive of *educare*] **:** one that is to be educated **:** STUDENT

ed·u·cate \ˈejə,kāt, *usu* -ād·+V\ *vb* -ED/-ING/-S [ME *educaten*, fr. L *educatus*, past part. of *educare* to rear, bring up, educate, fr. *e-* + *-ducare* (fr. *ducere* to lead) — more at TOW] *vt* **1** *obs* **:** to bring up (as a child or animal) **:** REAR **2 a :** to develop (as a person) by fostering to varying degrees the growth or expansion of knowledge, wisdom, desirable qualities of mind or character, physical health, or general competence esp. by a course of formal study or instruction **:** provide or assist in providing with knowledge or wisdom, moral balance, or good physical condition esp. by means of a formal education ⟨more things than a formal schooling serve to ~ a man⟩ ⟨~ their children by tutors⟩ ⟨*educated* rather by wide experience than by books⟩ ⟨the poverty of the institutions which ~ her mind and her body —Virginia Woolf⟩ **:** provide with formal schooling ⟨*educated* at a prep school and then at college⟩ **b :** to train by formal instruction and supervised practice esp. in a trade, skill, or profession ⟨~*s* physically handicapped children for useful work —*Amer. Guide Series: Mich.*⟩ ⟨~ a dog to sit up and beg⟩ ⟨felt that he needed to ~ himself more before he could understand the larger machines the factory operated⟩ **c :** to provide with information **:** INFORM ⟨can . . . ~ himself as to the most desirable attributes of the good field-trial dog —W.F.Brown b. 1903⟩ **d :** to bring about an improvement in or refinement of ⟨one of the most important arenas for the exercise of intelligence, in purging and *educating* our values —P.W.Bridgman⟩ ⟨psychoanalysis has *educated* our sensibilities —Abram Kardiner⟩ **3 a :** ACCUSTOM ⟨the absence of an accustomed stimulant to which she had *educated* his nerves —Francis Hackett⟩ **b** (1) **:** to condition or persuade to feel, believe, or react in a particular way by providing with often selective information or knowledge ⟨spent some time trying to ~ the club membership to place more responsibility and trust in the club officers⟩ ⟨~ stockholders and keep them eager to support the companies they own —*Time*⟩ ⟨~ people to call the police without hesitation —V.A.Leonard⟩ ⟨furniture manufacturers . . . put on a national drive to ~ people to desire homes that are more attractive and livable —N.C. Brown⟩ (2) **:** to make willing to accept (as by providing with knowledge, information, or experience) — used with *in* or *to* ⟨*educating* the leaders in the wisdom of a change —L.S.B. Leakey⟩ ⟨people of the world are more *educated* to international organization —André Schenker⟩ ⟨~ the Filipinos to the necessity of giving blood —Irene Kuhn⟩ **4 :** to make (as a person) competent in the handling of or in dealing with by preparation, discipline, or expansion of knowledge or competence — used with *to* and a secondary object ⟨a greater moral perceptiveness and a will *educated* to a new social responsibility —Lucius Garvin⟩ **5 a :** to remove (as from a person's makeup) by education — used with *out of* ⟨the fundamental preference for one's own race and breed neither is wholly educated into one nor can be wholly *educated* out of one —Katharine F. Gerould⟩ ⟨~ bad manners out of a child⟩ **b :** to raise (as to a higher social or cultural level) by education ⟨*educating* underprivileged children up to a better level of opportunity⟩ ~ *vi* **:** to educate a person, a thing, or a group ⟨the belief that a teacher should confine himself to *educating* and avoid proselytizing⟩ **syn** see TEACH

educated *adj* **1 :** possessing an education; *esp* **:** having information or knowledge beyond the average **2 a :** marked by perfection of performance that is the result of training and practice **:** SKILLED ⟨Doc worked over him with his ~ fingers —Budd Schulberg⟩ **b :** befitting one that is educated esp. by much formal schooling ⟨colorless voices of ~ conversation —Thomas Munro⟩ **c :** based on some knowledge of fact ⟨the precise results to be attained by modern aerial warfare could only be an ~ guess —G.C.Marshall⟩ **d :** consisting of people of education ⟨in ~ circles⟩

ed·u·cat·ee \ˌejə,kād·ˈē, -āˈtē, -,kəˈtē\ *n* -s [*educate* + *-ee*] **:** a recipient of education

ed·u·ca·tion \,ejəˈkāshən\ *n* -s [L *education-, educatio*, fr. *educatus* (past part. of *educare*) + *-ion-, -io* -ion] **1 :** the act or process of educating or of being educated: as **a** *obs* **:** the act or process of rearing or bringing up (as a child or animal) or developing physically from childhood or of being reared, brought up, or developed in this way **b :** the act or process of providing with knowledge, skill, competence, or usu. desirable qualities of behavior or character or of being so provided esp. by a formal course of study, instruction, or training ⟨the child received his ~ at home from a governess until he was nearly 10⟩ ⟨a prominent man whose ~ ended in grade school⟩ ⟨devoting himself to the ~ of adults who never got any formal schooling⟩ ⟨an ~ in dealing with his fellowmen⟩ ⟨an ~ in the handling of farm machinery⟩ **c :** a conditioning, strengthening, or disciplining esp. of the mind or faculties ⟨the ~ of the will⟩ ⟨the ~ of an audience to appreciate modern music⟩ ⟨the ~ of the muscles to respond faster⟩ **2 a :** a process or course of learning, instruction, or training that educates or is intended to educate ⟨a man too busy to give any time to an ~ other than hard experience⟩; *esp* **:** a formal course of instruction or training offered by an institution (as a college) primarily designed to provide an education ⟨~ in the high school⟩ ⟨a college ~⟩ — often used with a modifier specifying the type or field of instruction or training ⟨physical ~⟩ ⟨health ~⟩ ⟨driver ~⟩ — see ADULT EDUCATION, HIGHER EDUCATION; GENERAL EDUCATION, LIBERAL EDUCATION **b :** a system of formal education as a whole (as in a particular area) ⟨investigating ~ in several states⟩ **3 :** the product of an education **:** the totality of the knowledge, skill, competence, or qualities of character gained by education ⟨these groups acquired a great deal of their ~ by discussion, talking over and analyzing all aspects of life —H.R.Douglass⟩ ⟨formerly most of the child's ~ was obtained in the home —H.C.McKown⟩ ⟨he obtained his ~ in the local schools and college⟩ **4 :** the field of study that concerns itself primarily with the principles and methods of teaching or of learning esp. in formal education ⟨a professor of ~ in a small college⟩

ed·u·ca·tion·al \ˌejəˈkāshənᵊl, -shnəl\ *adj* **1 :** of, relating to, or concerned with education or the field of education ⟨~ concept⟩ ⟨~ TV⟩ ⟨~ adviser⟩ ⟨~ theorists⟩ **2 :** serving to further education ⟨the documentary subject is really an ~ film for pupils of all ages —Andrew Buchanan⟩

educational age *n* **:** ACHIEVEMENT AGE

ed·u·ca·tion·al·ly \-ᵊlē, -əlē, -li\ *adv* **:** with reference to education ⟨backward and ~ subnormal children —*Brit. Book News*⟩

educational psychology *n* **:** a field of study that deals with the application of objective psychological methods and esp. of standardized tests to such problems as the selection of students for advanced or specialized training, the assessment of a student's progress, and the development of more effective methods of instruction

educational quotient *n* **:** ACHIEVEMENT QUOTIENT 1

educational sociology *n* **:** the sociology of education **:** study of educational objectives and organization in the light of an analysis of the group life as a whole

educational test *n* **:** a test that measures achievement in subjects of study

ed·u·ca·tion·ist \,ejəˈkāsh(ə)nəst\ *also* **ed·u·ca·tion·al·ist** \-shənᵊləst, -shnəl-\ *n* -s **1** *chiefly Brit* **:** EDUCATOR ⟨~*s* are agreed that the medium of instruction in schools must be the local language —*Times Lit. Supp.*⟩ ⟨if progress is to be not only rapid but of a high standard many more *educationalists* are needed —Harold Ingrams⟩ **2 :** an educational theorist ⟨pragmatism was foisted on the American people by the ~*s* —F.M.Hechinger⟩ — usu. used disparagingly

ed·u·cat·ive \ˈejə,kād·|iv, -āt|, |ēv *also* |əv\ *adj* **1 :** having to do with education **:** EDUCATIONAL ⟨the problem is also an ~ one —John Dewey⟩ **2 :** tending to educate **:** INSTRUCTIVE ⟨much that is ~ occurs outside the school —Paul Woodring⟩ ⟨the able editor . . . makes his paper a real ~ force in community and nation —F.L.Mott⟩

ed·u·ca·tor \-kād·ə(r), -ātə- *sometimes* ,==ˈkā,tȯ(ə)r *or* -ō(ə)\ *n* -s [L, fr. *educatus* + *-or*] **1 :** one skilled in teaching **:** TEACHER **2 a :** a student of the theory and practice of education **:** EDUCATIONIST 2 **b :** an administrator in education

ed·u·ca·to·ry \ˈejəkə,tōrē, -ȯr-, -ri, *chiefly Brit* ˌ==ˈkātəri *or* -ā·tri\ *adj* **:** EDUCATIVE

educe \ēˈd(y)üs, iˈ-\ *vt* -ED/-ING/-S [L *educere* to lead forth, draw out, fr. *e-* + *ducere* to lead — more at TOW] **1 :** to bring into manifestation (as a form, quality, or law conceived to be present in a latent, potential, or undeveloped state) **:** ELICIT, EVOLVE ⟨they want to ~ and cultivate what is best and noblest in themselves —Matthew Arnold⟩ ⟨*educing* power from confusion —H.O.Taylor⟩; *sometimes* **:** EVOKE ⟨from the reader, he can only ~ pity, not respect or interest —V.A.Young⟩ **2 :** to arrive at (as from reasoning) ⟨seem to be able to ~ from common sense a more or less clear reply to the questions raised —Henry Sidgwick⟩ ⟨~ the conclusion —O.W.Holmes †1935⟩

syn EDUCE, EVOKE, ELICIT, EXTRACT, and EXTORT agree in meaning to draw out what is hidden, latent, or reserved. EDUCE usu. implies the bringing out of something potential or latent, often by inference but usu. by means of development ⟨polls rarely *educe* future attitudes —E.L.Bernays⟩ ⟨constantly straining on to *educe* further salutary meaning from the text —H.O.Taylor⟩ ⟨aimed to *educe* the innate capabilities of the student —Reyner Banham⟩ EVOKE now implies some strong agency that can produce a particular effect, usu. immediately, or that serves as a stimulus in arousing (as an emotion, a passion, or an interest) ⟨choose the right words to *evoke* the right mood⟩ ⟨there was melody in it, such as a woodpecker knows how to *evoke* from a smooth dry branch —John Burroughs⟩ ⟨words *evoking* concrete imagery —Alice Bensen⟩ ⟨there is much in this volume to *evoke* a smile —*N.Y.Herald Tribune Bk. Rev.*⟩ ⟨*evoke* the hope that you were going to see more —O.W.Holmes †1935⟩ ELICIT, often interchangeable with EVOKE, usu., however implies care, trouble, or skill in drawing something forth or out, often against resistance ⟨which *elicited* alternate jeers and applause from the shilling audience below —G.B.Shaw⟩ ⟨no subject *elicits* a more animated response than some question about a woman's work —A.R.Williams⟩ ⟨to make a study of blank verse alone would be to *elicit* some curious conclusions —T.S.Eliot⟩ ⟨the inductive method of *eliciting* general laws —A.N.Whitehead⟩ ⟨*elicit* information by cross-examination⟩ EXTRACT, in this context, implies an action, force, or effort resembling the physical use of pressure or suction ⟨we journeyed on, fed by food *extracted* from the peasants —Bertrand Russell⟩ ⟨eke out her personal adornment by gifts which she managed to *extract* from her admirers —Mary Austin⟩ ⟨in spite of incessant questioning, all he had been able to *extract* from this young girl was the story that the admiral had offered to lend her his house —Edith Sitwell⟩ EXTORT implies a wringing or wresting, esp. from someone reluctant or resisting ⟨*extort* money by blackmail⟩ ⟨his perfect command of all his faculties *extorted* praise from those who neither loved nor esteemed him —T.B. Macaulay⟩ ⟨whose income is ample enough to *extort* obsequiousness from the vulgar of all ranks —Arnold Bennett⟩

educ·ible \-səbəl\ *adj* : capable of being educed

educt \'ē,dəkt\ *n* -s [L *eductus*, past part. of *educere* to lead forth, draw out — more at EDUCE] : something that is educed: **a** *chem* : a substance separated from material in which it already existed — distinguished from *product* **b** : INFERENCE

educ·tion \ē'dəkshən, i'-\ *n* -s [LL *eduction-, eductio* act of leading forth, drawing out, fr. L *eductus* + *-ion-, -io* -ion] **1** : the action or process of educing, eliciting, or directly inferring **2** : the result of the process of educing : INFERENCE **3** : the action or process of conducting a fluid away from a container (as oil from a tank car)

educ·tive \-ktiv\ *adj* [L *eductus* + E *-ive*] : relating to eduction

educ·tor \-ktə(r)\ *n* -s [LL, one that leads forth, fr. L *eductus* + *-or*] : one that educes: as **a** : EJECTOR 2 **b** : a device similar to an ejector for mixing two fluids (as air and water)

edul·co·rate \ə'dəlkə,rāt, ē'-\ *vt* -ED/-ING/-S [NL *edulcoratus*, past part. of *edulcorare*, blend of LL *edulcare* to sweeten (fr. L *e-* + LL *dulcare* to sweeten, fr. L *dulcis* sweet) and *dulcorare* to sweeten, fr. *dulcor* sweetness, fr. L *dulcis* — more at DULCET] **1** *obs* : to make (food) sweet **2** *archaic* : to free from acids, salts, or other soluble substances by washing **3** : to free from harshness (as of attitude) : make pleasant ⟨cozened and flattered and *edulcorated* the Turks —Vincent Sheean⟩ — **edul·co·ra·tion** \⸗,⸗⸗'rāshən\ *n* -s

¹ed·war·de·an *or* **ed·war·di·an** \(')e¦dwärdēən, -wȯd-, -wȯ(r)d-\ *adj, usu cap* [Jonathan *Edwards* †1758 Am. Congregational clergyman and theologian + E *-ean* or *-ian*] : of or relating to the Calvinistic theological doctrines of Jonathan Edwards : derived from such doctrines : accepting such doctrines

²edwardean *or* **edwardian** \"\ *n* -s *usu cap* : an adherent of the theology of Jonathan Edwards

¹edwardian \"\ *adj, usu cap* [*Edward* VII †1910 king of England + E *-ian*] : of, relating to, or having the characteristics of the era of Edward VII of England (1901–10): as **a** : characterized by opulence and a complacent sense of material security **b** : marked by a socially analytical and critical frame of mind **c** *of clothing* : marked by the hourglass silhouette for women and the long narrow fitted suits for men that were popular during this period

²edwardian \"\ *n* -s *usu cap* : one belonging to or as if to the Edwardian era

ed·ward·ine \'edwə(r),dīn, -dēn\ *adj, usu cap* [*Edward* VII + E *-ine*] : EDWARDIAN

ed·ward·sia \e'dwärdzēə, -wȯd-, -wȯ(r)d-\ *n, cap* [NL, fr. Henri Milne-*Edwards* †1885 Fr. zoologist + NL *-ia*] : a genus (the type of the family Edwardsiidae) of sea anemones having eight mesenteries and living in tubes in the sand

ed·ward·si·an \(')⸗¦⸗zēən\ *adj, usu cap* [Jonathan *Edwards* + E *-ian*] : EDWARDEAN

ee \'ē\ *n, pl* **een** \'ēn\ [ME (northern dial.), fr. OE *ēage* — more at EYE] *Scot* : EYE

¹-ee \(¦)ē\ *n suffix* -s [ME *-e*, fr. MF *-é*, fr. OF, fr. *-é*, past part. ending of some verbs, fr. L *-atus*, past part. ending of 1st conj. verbs — more at -ATE (adj. suffix)] **1** : animate and usu. human undergoer, recipient, or beneficiary of (a specified action) ⟨appointee⟩ ⟨draftee⟩ ⟨grantee⟩ ⟨trainee⟩ ⟨trustee⟩ **2** : person furnished with (a specified thing) ⟨patentee⟩ **3** : person that performs (a specified action) ⟨escapee⟩ ⟨standee⟩

²-ee \"\ *n suffix* -s [prob. alter. of *-ie*] **1** : one associated with ⟨bargee⟩ ⟨goalee⟩ ⟨townee⟩ **2** : a particular esp. small kind of ⟨bootee⟩ ⟨coatee⟩ **3** : one resembling or suggestive of ⟨goatee⟩

EE \(')⸗¦⸗\ *abbr or n* -s electrical engineer

EE *abbr* **1** envoy extraordinary **2** errors excepted

ee·bree \'ē,brē\ *n* -s [*ee* + *bree*] **1** *chiefly Scot* : EYEBROW **2** *chiefly Scot* : EYELASH — usu. used in pl.

EEG *abbr* electroencephalogram

¹eel \'ēl, *esp before pause or consonant* 'ēəl\ *n, pl* **eels** *also* **eel** [ME *ele*, fr. OE *ǣl*; akin to OS & OHG *āl* eel, ON *āll*] **1 a** : any of numerous voracious elongate snakelike teleost fishes that constitute the order Apodes and that have a smooth slimy skin often without scales, are destitute of pelvic and sometimes of pectoral fins, and have the median fins confluent around the tail — see ANGUILLA, CONGER EEL, LEPTOCEPHALUS, MORAY **b** : any of numerous elongate fishes more or less resembling the true eels (as those of the order Symbranchii) — see ELECTRIC EEL, SAND EEL, SNAKE EEL **2** : any of various nematodes or eelworms ⟨the vinegar ~⟩ **3** : a person or thing that is slippery or elusive

²eel \"\ *vi* -ED/-ING/-S **1** : to fish for eels **2** : WORM 2

eel-back flounder *n* : a small flounder (*Liopsetta putnami*) of the coasts of northern New England and the Maritime Provinces

eelboat \'⸗,⸗\ *n* : SCHUYT

eel cat *n* : a broad-headed catfish (*Ictalurus anguilla*) of the lower Mississippi and Ohio valleys — compare CHANNEL CAT

eel·ery \'ēlərē\ *n* -ES [¹*eel* + *-ery*] : a place for catching eels

eelfare \'⸗,⸗\ *n* [¹*eel* + *fare* (journey)] : the migration of young eels up a stream

eelgrass \'⸗,⸗\ *n* **1** : a submerged marine plant (*Zostera marina*) with very long narrow leaves that is found in abundance along the No. Atlantic coast — called also *grass wrack* **2** : TAPE GRASS

eelgrass family *n* : ZOSTERACEAE

eel·like \'ē(ə)l,līk\ *adj* : like an eel in sinuosity, swimming ability, or evasiveness

eelpot \'⸗,⸗\ *n* : a trap like a box with funnel-shaped openings for catching eels

eelpout \'⸗,⸗\ *n* [¹*eel* + *pout* (fish)] **1** : any of various marine fishes resembling blennies and constituting the family Zoarcidae: as **a** : a viviparous blenny (*Zoarces viviparus*) of Northern Europe **b** : MUTTONFISH 2 **2** : BURBOT

eelspear \'⸗,⸗\ *n* : a barbed spear for spearing eels

eelworm \'⸗,⸗\ *n* : a nematode worm; *esp* : any small free-living or plant-parasitic roundworm, some of which are serious pathogens of cultivated plants — see BULB EELWORM

eely \'ēlē, -li\ *adj* -ER/-EST : resembling an eel (as in being wriggly or slippery)

¹een \(¦)ēn\ *Scot var of* ONE

²een \'ēn\ *pl of* EE

¹e'en \(¦)ēn\ *adv* [by contr.] : EVEN

²e'en *or* **een** \'ēn\ *n* -s [contr. of ¹*even*] *chiefly Scot* : EVENING

¹-een \¦ēn\ *n suffix* -s [prob. partly fr. the *-een* of *ratteen* and partly alter. of the *-ine* of *armozine, bombazine*] : inferior fabric resembling (a specified fabric) : imitation ⟨sateen⟩ ⟨velveteen⟩

²-een \"\ *n suffix* -s [IrGael *-īn*] *chiefly Irish* : small one : dear one : petty or contemptible one — in diminutive nouns ⟨birdeen⟩ ⟨buckeen⟩ ⟨squireen⟩

een·a·most \¦ēnə,mōst\ *adv* [¹*e'en* + *amost*, alter. of *almost*] : even almost : NEARLY

eence \'ēn(t)s\ *Scot var of* ONCE

eend \'ēnd\ *dial var of* END

-eer \¦i(ə)r, ¦iə\ *n suffix* -s [MF *-ier*, fr. L *-arius* — more at -ARY (n. suffix)] **1** : one that deals in, is concerned with professionally, manages, conducts, or produces ⟨auctioneer⟩ ⟨pamphleteer⟩ — often in words with derogatory meaning or connotation ⟨profiteer⟩ **2** : contemptible one ⟨patrioteer⟩

e'er \(')e(ə)r, (')a(ə)l, ¦ə\ *adv* [by contr.] : EVER

ee·rie *also* **ee·ry** \'irē, 'ēr-, -ri\ *adj* -ER/-EST [ME (northern dial.) *eri*, fr. OE *earg* cowardly, lazy, slow, wretched — more at ARGH] **1** *dial Brit* : affected with fear esp. of the supernatural : FRIGHTENED ⟨when I sleep I dream, when I wake I'm ~ —Robert Burns⟩ **2** : unusual, unexpected, or unnatural to such a degree as to inspire fear : WEIRD, FRIGHTENING ⟨it is an ~ experience to drive for miles through ghostly ranks of . . . cypress woods —*Amer. Guide Series: Fla.*⟩ ⟨an uncomfortable and ~ stillness had settled over the piazza —Alan Moorehead⟩; *also* : STRANGE, MYSTERIOUS, UNCANNY ⟨blue and yellow flames that at night cast an ~ glow over the landscape —*Amer. Guide Series: Pa.*⟩ ⟨the *eeriest* mystery in modern court records—a persistent riddle —*Life*⟩ ⟨the clarinet sings, in its ~, plaintive tone —Sara R. Watson⟩ **3** *Scot* : GLOOMY, DISMAL **syn** see WEIRD

ee·ri·ly \-rəlē, -li\ *adv* : in an eerie manner : MYSTERIOUSLY, WEIRDLY ⟨the sea moaned ~ as if in anticipation of what was to come —G.G.Carter⟩

ee·ri·ness \-rēnəs, -rin-\ *n* -ES **1** : inexplicable fear ⟨private distresses, a streak of ~, dark moods —*Times Lit. Supp.*⟩ **2** : the quality or state of being eerie

ees *pl of* E *or of* EE

-ees *pl of* -EE

¹ef *also* **eff** \'ef\ *n* -s : the letter *f*

²ef \(¦)ef, əf\ *dial var of* IF

ef- — see EX-

EF *abbr* **1** English finish **2** expeditionary force **3** extra fine; extremely fine

ef·a·tese \¦efə¦tēz, e'fä,t-, -ēs\ *n, pl* **efatese** *usu cap* [*Efate*, one of the New Hebrides islands in the So. Pacific + E *-ese*] **1 a** : a Melanesian people of Efate in the New Hebrides islands **b** : a member of such people **2** : the language of the Efatese people

efe \'ā,fā, 'e,-\ *n* -s *cap* : the central Sudanic language of the Mbuti pygmies of the Belgian Congo

eff *abbr* **1** effect; effective **2** efficiency; efficient

ef·fa·ble \'efəbəl\ *adj* [L *effabilis*, fr. *effari* to speak out, fr. *ex-* + *fari* to speak, say — more at BAN] : capable of being uttered or expressed

¹ef·face \ə'fās, e'-, ē'-\ *vt* -ED/-ING/-S [MF *effacer*, fr. *ef-* (fr. L, fr. *ex-*) + *face* — more at FACE] **1 a** : to eliminate clear evidence of (something written, painted, or otherwise marked upon a surface) by abrasive or leveling action ⟨the "murals" have long since been *effaced* by rock slides and the weathering of the cliff's wall —*Amer. Guide Series: Pa.*⟩ **b** : to cause to disappear : eliminate completely : wipe out : DESTROY, ERADICATE ⟨his year . . . of peace had *effaced* all the ill effects of his previous suffering —Samuel Butler †1902⟩ ⟨fire suppression . . . and a comprehensive program of reforestation have *effaced* the worst of the scars —*Amer. Guide Series: Mich.*⟩ **2** : to remove from cognizance, consideration, or memory ⟨he had left a mark on the affairs of the church which would not easily be *effaced* —R.W.Southern⟩; *also* : to make insignificant : OVERSHADOW ⟨the bloodthirsty aspect of the tyrant is becoming *effaced* —Norman Douglas⟩ **3** : to withdraw (oneself) entirely from attention : make (oneself) inconspicuous and modestly or shyly unnoticeable ⟨the wife of a man who had done anything disgraceful in business had only one idea: to ~ herself, to disappear with him —Edith Wharton⟩ **syn** see ERASE

²ef·fa·cé \¦efə¦sā\ *adj* [F, fr. past part. of *effacer* to stand apart, stand sideways, fr. *ef-* (fr. L, fr. *ex-*) + *face*] *ballet* : facing the audience obliquely, sometimes with opposite arm and leg raised

ef·face·able \ə'fāsəbəl, e'-,ē'-\ *adj* : capable of being effaced

ef·face·ment \-smənt\ *n* -s : the act or process of effacing : the state of being effaced; *esp* : reduction to insignificance

ef·fac·er \-sə(r)\ *n* -s : one that effaces

¹ef·fect \ə'fekt, e'-,ē'-\ *n* -s [ME, fr. MF & L; MF, fr. L *effectus*, fr. *effectus*, past part. of *efficere* to bring about, accomplish, effect, fr. *ex-* + *-ficere* (fr. *facere* to make, do) — more at DO] **1** : something that is produced by an agent or cause : something that follows immediately from an antecedent : a resultant condition : RESULT, OUTCOME ⟨low mortality, the ~ of excellent social services available in every village —William Petersen⟩ ⟨as tolerance develops, the addict needs more and more of the drug to give him the same ~ he originally obtained from a small dose —D.W.Maurer & V.H.Vogel⟩ ⟨his feet in the most appalling state from the ~*s* of porcupine quills —James Stevenson-Hamilton⟩ **2 a** : PURPOSE, INTENTION, END ⟨as a boy he had gone to work early to the ~ that he might help out his parents⟩ **b** : the result of purpose or intention : ADVANTAGE ⟨employed his knowledge to little ~ in the development of his organization⟩ **3** : an outward sign : MANIFESTATION, APPEARANCE ⟨the sky ~*s* by day and night are grander —Wilfrid Eggleston⟩ **4** *obs* : ACCOMPLISHMENT, FULFILLMENT **5** *obs* : something acquired as the expected result of an action **6** : REALITY, FACT — now used only in the phrase *in effect* ⟨the guilder became in ~ convertible with other currencies in free Continental Europe —Alan Valentine⟩ **7** : power to bring about a result : operative force : INFLUENCE ⟨the ~ of wind in changing tide levels —*Geog. Rev.*⟩ ⟨the ~ of great demand upon supply⟩ ⟨all of the children in the schoolroom felt the ~ of her happiness —Sherwood Anderson⟩ **8 effects** *pl* : movable property : GOODS ⟨her household ~*s* were sold at auction but her clothing, jewelry, and other personal ~*s* were given away⟩ **9 a** : a distinctive impression upon the human senses ⟨a concentration on detail at a cost to total ~ —Irving Kolodin⟩ ⟨achieves amazing ~*s* with his woodcuts —José Gómez-Siere⟩ ⟨decorated in yellow, which increased the ~ of lightness —Sheila Kaye-Smith⟩; *also* : the creation of a desired impression ⟨her sobs were purely for ~⟩ **b** : something designed to produce such an impression ⟨never have we been so bombarded with trick ~*s*—3-D, cinemascope, panoramic screens —John Baker⟩ ⟨the technique of sound ~*s* was extremely limited and used only . . . for such things as doorbells —Richard Hubbell⟩ **10** : the quality or state of being operative ⟨the subcommittee's recommendations were quickly given ~ —W.R.Langdon⟩ ⟨the court will not give ~ to a judgment based on unfair proceedings⟩; *specif* : OPERATION ⟨a commission was set up to carry the new proposals into ~⟩ ⟨the agreement will have to be approved by a majority before it can go into ~⟩ ⟨the same excises and corporate tax rates that are now in ~ —William Fellner⟩ — compare *take effect* at TAKE **11** : basic meaning : TENOR, ESSENCE **12** : a specific scientific phenomenon named usu. for its discoverer ⟨Faraday ~⟩ **13** : one in a series of evaporators

syn RESULT, CONSEQUENCE, UPSHOT, AFTEREFFECT, AFTERMATH, SEQUEL, ISSUE, OUTCOME, EVENT: these ten nouns are similar in signifying something, usu. a condition, situation, or occurrence, ascribable to a cause or combination of causes. EFFECT is the correlative of the word *cause* and in general use implies something necessarily and directly following upon or occurring by reason of the cause, generally applying to intangibles such as bodily or social conditions or states of mind or feeling ⟨the *effect* of the medicine was an intermittent dizziness⟩ ⟨the *effect* of the speech was immediate governmental reform⟩ ⟨tanning is the *effect* of exposure to sunlight⟩ ⟨the *effects* of the hurricane were visible in roofless houses and uprooted trees⟩ RESULT, close to EFFECT in meaning, implies a direct relationship with an antecedent action or condition though possibly less direct than EFFECT, usu. suggesting an effect in the character of a termination of the operation of a cause, and applying more commonly than EFFECT to tangible objects ⟨the *result* of the investigation was a scandalous exposure of corruption⟩ ⟨his limp was the *result* of an automobile accident⟩ ⟨the *result* of the marriage was a family of seven children⟩ ⟨the subsiding flood or surface waters cause mineral deposits and the *result* is a mound —Alice Duncan-Kemp⟩ CONSEQUENCE may suggest a direct but looser or more remote connection with a cause than either EFFECT or RESULT, usu. implying an adverse or calamitous effect and often suggesting a chain of intermediate causes or a complexity of effect ⟨one of the *consequences* of his ill-advised conduct was a loss of prestige⟩ ⟨his poor health is a *consequence* of early privation⟩ ⟨both good and bad *consequences* can follow upon the acquisition of much leisure⟩ UPSHOT often implies a climax or conclusion in a series of consequent occurrences, or the most conclusive point of a single complex gradual consequence ⟨we spent the time swimming at Glenelg and dancing at the Palais Royal in the city. The *upshot* was that, before we left . . . we were engaged —Rex Ingamells⟩ ⟨they won the battle, and the *upshot* was a short-lived bourgeois republic —Roy Lewis & Angus Maude⟩ ⟨the *upshot* of the whole matter was that there was no wedding —Padraic Colum⟩ AFTEREFFECT and AFTERMATH both usu. designate secondary rather than direct or immediate effects. AFTEREFFECT besides designating a secondary effect sometimes suggests a side effect but more generally implies an effect ascribable to a previous effect that has become a cause ⟨the *aftereffects* of an atomic-bomb explosion —*Current Biog.*⟩ ⟨although the pioneer effort had reached a dead end, its *aftereffects* were all too apparent —Dayton Kohler⟩ ⟨to the left of the highway the blackened appearance is the *aftereffect* of a fire that has recently swept across the flat —G.R. Stewart⟩ ⟨the *aftereffects* of the war were a general disorder and confusion⟩ AFTERMATH, often suggesting a more complex effect or generalized condition than AFTEREFFECT, usu. carries the notion of belated consequences that appear after the effects, esp. disastrous effects, seem to have passed ⟨the serious dislocations in the world as an *aftermath* of war —*U.S.Code*⟩ ⟨the *aftermath* of the epidemic in Memphis was worse than the dismal days of Reconstruction —*Amer. Guide Series: Tenn.*⟩ ⟨asbestos dust has the same effect as silica, the resulting disease being known as "asbestosis", with pulmonary tuberculosis as the *aftermath* —V.M.Ehlers & E.W.Steel⟩ SEQUEL is usu. used to signify a result that follows after an interval ⟨spinal curvature . . . may be a symptom or a *sequel* to many different diseases —Morris Fishbein⟩ ⟨she lay rigid experiencing the *sequel* to the pain, an ideal terror —Jean Stafford⟩ ISSUE, the way something, for example an argument, comes out, carries strongly the notion of result as a solution or resolution ⟨a contest of wits between the criminal and the police—usually aided in fiction by a quicker-witted private detective—a contest in which the *issue* is still the greatest and gravest of all, life or death —A.C.Ward⟩ ⟨the war was by then obviously proceeding toward a successful *issue* —F.M.Ford⟩ OUTCOME, interchangeable with RESULT or with ISSUE, possibly carries the notion of less finality than does ISSUE ⟨the *outcome* of the presidential election⟩ ⟨the enduring organisms are now the *outcome* of evolution —A.N.Whitehead⟩ ⟨one *outcome* of this report was the formation of the Southern Conference for Human Welfare —*Current Biog.*⟩ ⟨his book is the *outcome* of two years' travels in India, China, and Siam —*Geog. Jour.*⟩ EVENT, rare and somewhat archaic in the sense pertinent here, of *outcome* or *result*, usu. carries the notion of an unpredictable or unforeseeable outcome ⟨the happiness of Rome appeared to hang on the *event* of a race —Edward Gibbon⟩ ⟨he employed himself at Edinburgh till the *event* of the conflict between the court and the Whigs was no longer doubtful —T.B.Macaulay⟩ ⟨the calm assumption that I should live long enough to carry out my extensive plan at leisure . . . has in the *event* been justified —Havelock Ellis⟩ — **in effect** *adv* : in substance : VIRTUALLY ⟨these tribal bodies included the entire soldiery of the tribe; *in effect*, the nation in arms —W.J.Shepard⟩ ⟨though stated in polite terms his reply was, *in effect*, a flat refusal⟩ — **to the effect** : with the meaning ⟨speculations *to the effect* that Shakespeare did the grand tour —D.W.Brogan⟩ ⟨his comments about the incident were less coherent but *to the* same *effect*⟩

²effect \"\ *vt* -ED/-ING/-S **1** : to cause to come into being : PRODUCE ⟨specific genes ~ specific bodily characters⟩ **2 a** : to bring about esp. through successful use of factors contributory to the result : ACCOMPLISH, EXECUTE ⟨passage could be ~*ed* only by way of certain transverse valleys and high passes —W.G.East⟩ ⟨the Romans who, with superb political skill, ~*ed* the unification of Italy —Benjamin Farrington⟩ ⟨minor repairs to the road were ~*ed* during the summer⟩ — compare ³AFFECT 1 **b** : to put into effect ⟨consistently taken the position that the function of the president is to ~ the public will —R.H.Rovere⟩ **syn** see PERFORM

effecter *var of* EFFECTOR

ef·fect·ful \-tfəl\ *adj* : creating effects : EFFECTUAL

ef·fect·ible \-təbəl\ *adj, archaic* : capable of being effected

¹ef·fec·tive \ə'fektiv, e'-,ē'-, -tēv *also* -təv\ *adj* [ME, fr. MF or LL; MF *effectif*, fr. LL *effectivus*, fr. L *effectus* (past part. of *efficere* to bring about, accomplish, effect) + *-ivus* -ive — more at EFFECT] **1 a** : capable of bringing about an effect : productive of results ⟨an air-cooled motor was more ~ than a witch's broomstick for rapid long-distance transportation —Lewis Mumford⟩ ⟨a new organization which would be strong where the league had been weak, . . . ~ where the league had been fumbling —G.L.Kirk⟩ ⟨his arm was too badly injured to deliver an ~ blow —L.C.Douglas⟩ **b** : capable of having its normal effect : able to function normally ⟨at 26,000 feet none are able to retain ~ consciousness . . . without oxygen —C.H.Best & N.B.Taylor⟩ **2** : marked by the quality of being influential or exerting positive influence: **a** : exerting authority : carrying weight ⟨the countries represented had virtually all the ~ power in the world —M.W.Straight⟩ ⟨his ~ career began inauspiciously⟩ **b** : able to accomplish a purpose : EFFICIENT ⟨persons who will do nothing unless they get something out of it for themselves are often highly ~ persons of action —G.B.Shaw⟩ **c** : IMPRESSIVE, COGENT, TELLING ⟨an ~ if not eloquent preacher —E.W.Knight⟩ ⟨equally ~ in portraiture, landscape, and still life —*Current Biog.*⟩ **d** : PLEASING, SATISFYING ⟨a most ~ substitute for the conventional Christmas tree —*Amer. Guide Series: La.*⟩ **3 a** : capable of being used to a purpose ⟨his handwriting was still so bad he couldn't take ~ notes —Sloan Wilson⟩ ⟨the ~ value of our annual income for scholarship endowment has been diminished —J.B.Conant⟩ **b** : equipped and ready for service — used esp. of military forces ⟨the fort was held by about 100 ~ soldiers⟩ **4** : ACTUAL ⟨committed the blunder of confusing the increased load of equipment and the increased expenditure with the quantity of ~ work done —Lewis Mumford⟩ ⟨the number of ~ wage earners, excluding workers absent for the whole of one week, fluctuated —*Collier's Yr. Bk.*⟩ ⟨a gain in housing units in response to ~ demand⟩ **5** *of a verb form or aspect* : expressing the final point of an action or state or a result attained **6** : taking effect : VALID, OPERATIVE ⟨the following resignations were accepted ~ during the academic year under review —J.B.Conant⟩ ⟨the order was ~ as of June 7⟩ **7** *of the publication of a taxon* : accompanied by sale, exchange, or other distribution of printed matter containing a new taxon or new combination — see VALID 5b **8** *of a natural population* : INTERBREEDING

syn EFFECTUAL, EFFICIENT, EFFICACIOUS: EFFECTIVE may indicate the power to produce an effect or the actual production of an effect ⟨we are calling on men and women and property and money to join in making our defense *effective* —F.D. Roosevelt⟩ ⟨Bob had rebuked him after all, and his rebuke, though less hurtful than Sir James's, had been even more *effective* —Archibald Marshall⟩ EFFECTUAL may apply to what has accomplished an intended result and may approach the connotations of *decisive* ⟨the powers of sovereignty and the eminent domain were ceded with the land. This was essential, in order to make it *effectual*, and to accomplish its objects —R.B.Taney⟩ ⟨an appeal to the emotions is little likely to be *effectual* before luncheon —W.S.Maugham⟩ EFFICIENT may designate that which is actually operative; it may apply to smooth operation with a maximum of work or output accomplished with a minimum of effort ⟨it should be obvious that it is the conditions producing the end effects which must be regarded as the *efficient* causes of them —M.F.A.Montagu⟩ ⟨a strong tendency to break up cumbersome estates into small, *efficient* farms —Allan Nevins and H.S.Commager⟩ ⟨since the steam engine requires constant care on the part of the stoker and engineer, steam power was more *efficient* in large units than in small ones: instead of a score of small units, working when required, one large engine was kept in constant motion —Lewis Mumford⟩ EFFICACIOUS may suggest possession of potent, powerful, or proper qualities productive of effective power ⟨in their opinion, the flesh and blood of an enemy killed in battle is the most *efficacious* of all charms and makes a first-rate drug —J.G.Frazer⟩ ⟨the pained expression that he had long since found to be much more *efficacious* than anger —Edith Wharton⟩

²effective \"\ *n* -s : one that is effective: as **a** : a soldier equipped, fit, and ready for active service ⟨the troop figure includes quartermasters, MPs, and signal, transportation, and medical corpsmen to a total of perhaps half its ~*s* —T.H. White b. 1915⟩ **b** : an effective aspect of a verb or an effective verb form

effective aperture *n* **:** the diameter of the entrance pupil of an optical system; *specif* **:** the apparent diameter of the diaphragm opening in a camera lens as seen through the front of the lens
effective current *n* **:** the value of an alternating or otherwise variable current that would result in the same heat production in a circuit as that of a direct current in the same length of time **:** the square root of the means of the squares of the instantaneous values of an alternating current
effective horsepower *n* **:** the net horsepower required to move a vehicle or boat that is the part of the total propelling engine horsepower that remains after deducting losses due to engine friction and propeller and other inefficiencies
ef·fec·tive·ly \-təvlē, -li\ *adv* [ME, fr. *effective* + *-ly*] **:** in an effective manner **:** with great effect ⟨he knows how to communicate his ideas ~⟩; *also* **:** COMPLETELY ⟨rain . . . blotting out the landscape as ~ as a fog would do —C.S.Forester⟩
ef·fec·tive·ness \-tivnəs, -tēv- *also* -təv-\ *n* -ES **1 :** the quality or state of being effective ⟨declining public interest caused laws to lose ~ —J.W.McConnell⟩ **2 :** power to be effective **:** EFFICACY
effective pitch *n* **:** the distance an airplane advances along its flight path for one revolution of the propeller **:** PITCH
effective range *n* **:** the range of an airplane under the specific requirements of a specific mission
effective rate *n, of interest* **:** the excess over unity of the accumulation factor for a year, furnishing the rate at simple interest which would yield in one year the same amount as the actual or nominal rate at compound interest
effective resistance *n* **:** ALTERNATING-CURRENT RESISTANCE
effective value *n* **:** the value of an alternating current or voltage equal to the square root of the arithmetic mean of the squares of the instantaneous values taken throughout one complete cycle
ef·fec·tiv·i·ty \ˌe,fek'tivəd·ē, ə,-, ē,-\ *n* -ES **:** EFFECTIVENESS
ef·fect·less \ə'fektləs, e'-,ē'-\ *adj, archaic* **:** lacking effect **:** FECKLESS
ef·fec·tor \ə'fektə(r), e'-,ē'-\ *n* -S **1** *also* **ef·fect·er** \"\ **:** one that effects ⟨sheer force of personality as an ~ of discipline —Nathaniel Burt⟩ **2 :** a bodily organ that becomes active in response to stimulation — distinguished from *receptor*
effects *pl of* EFFECT, *pres 3d sing of* EFFECT
ef·fec·tu·al \-'fekch(əw)əl, -ksh-\ *adj* [ME *effectuel, effectual,* fr. MF & ML; MF *effectuel,* fr. ML *effectualis,* fr. L *effectus* effect + *-alis* -al — more at EFFECT] **1 :** characterized by adequate power to produce an intended effect **:** productive of a result or effect **:** EFFECTIVE ⟨a man to whom painting was but another and less ~ way of writing dramas, novels, or history —Aldous Huxley⟩ ⟨no Oriental veil could be more ~ than her beautiful Catholic quiet —H.G.Wells⟩ **2** *obs* **:** impressively earnest or pertinent ⟨the ~ fervent prayer of a righteous man availeth much —Jas 5:16 (AV)⟩ **3 :** ACTUAL ⟨the ~ truth of the matter⟩ ⟨sufficient to supply the ~ demand and no more —Adam Smith⟩ **syn** see EFFECTIVE
effectual calling *n* **:** the action of the Holy Spirit in producing conviction of sin and bestowing the gift of faith in Christ according to Calvinist theology
ef·fec·tu·al·i·ty \-ˌfekchə'waləd·ē, -ksh-, -ətē, -i\ *n* -ES **:** EFFECTUALNESS
ef·fec·tu·al·ly \-'fekch(əw)əlē, -ksh-, -li\ *adv* [ME *effectuelly, effectually,* fr. *effectuel, effectual* + *-ly*] **:** in an effectual manner **:** with great or decisive effect; *also* **:** COMPLETELY
ef·fec·tu·al·ness \-lnəs\ *n* -ES **:** the quality or state of being effectual
ef·fec·tu·ate \ə'==ˌwāt, *usu* -ād·+V\ *vt* -ED/-ING/-S [ML *effectuatus,* past part. of *effectuare,* fr. L *effectus* effect] **:** EFFECT 2 ⟨strove successfully to ~ a settlement not by force but by reason —F.D.Roosevelt⟩ ⟨the question was still open as to the extent to which the courts would ~ the change —B.N.Cardozo⟩
ef·fec·tu·a·tion \əˌfekchə'wāshən, (ˌ)e,f-, ē,f-, -ksh-\ *n* -S **:** the action of putting into effect **:** ACCOMPLISHMENT ⟨the court did not enjoin the ~ of the plan absolutely —*Corporation Jour.*⟩
ef·feir \ə'fēr\ *Scot var of* AFFAIR
ef·fem·i·na·cy \ə'femənəsē, e'-,ē'-, -si\ *n* -ES [*effeminate* + *-cy*] **:** the quality or state of being effeminate **:** a womanlike delicacy, weakness, or softness in a man, in a thing produced by a man (as a painting), or in something generally classified as male
¹ef·fem·i·nate \-nət, *usu* -əd·+V\ *adj* [ME *effeminat,* fr. L *effeminatus,* past part. of *effeminare* to make effeminate, fr. *ex-* + *femina* woman — more at FEMININE] **1 :** marked by qualities more characteristic of and suited to women than to men **:** lacking manly strength and purpose **:** exhibiting or proceeding from delicacy, weakness, emotionalism **:** marked by luxuriousness or voluptuousness ⟨such men practiced extravagances and affectations, and are generally described as ~ —W.G.Sumner⟩ ⟨had found in his nature strange depths of love for the little mite . . . and thought the exhibition of it ~ —Ruth Park⟩ ⟨blessed with all good things, these godchildren soon became ~ and suffered all manner of misfortunes —*Amer. Guide Series: La.*⟩ **2** *obs* **:** TENDER, SOFT, DELICATE **3** *of wool* **:** overdelicate or oversoft **syn** see FEMALE
²ef·fem·i·nate \-ˌnāt, *usu* -ād·+V\ *vt* -ED/-ING/-S [L *effeminatus*] **:** to make effeminate **:** WEAKEN ⟨it will not corrupt or ~ children's minds —John Locke⟩
³ef·fem·i·nate \-ˌnət, *usu* -əd·+V\ *n* -S [¹*effeminate*] **:** an effeminate person
ef·fem·i·nate·ly \-nətlē, -li\ *adv* **:** in an effeminate manner
ef·fem·i·nate·ness *n* -ES **:** the quality or state of being effeminate
ef·fem·i·na·tion \əˌfemə'nāshən, (ˌ)e,f-, ē,f-\ *n* -S [LL *effemination-, effeminatio,* fr. L *effeminatus* + *-ion-, -io* -ion] **:** the act or process of making or becoming effeminate; *specif* **:** the taking on by a man of the mental characteristics of a woman
ef·fem·i·nize \ə'==ˌnīz\ *vt* -ED/-ING/-S [¹*effeminate* + *-ize*] **:** to make effeminate ⟨he has become *effeminized,* without having the virtues of being frankly feminine —Sinclair Lewis⟩
ef·fen·di \ə'fendē, e'-, -di\ *n* -S [Turk *efendi,* fr. NGk *aphentēs,* alter. of Gk *authentēs* murderer, master, doer — more at AUTHENTIC] **1 :** MASTER, SIR — used in Turkey until 1935 as a title of respect esp. for a state official but often as a courtesy title for an educated man or a man of the upper classes **2 a :** one of a class of feudal landowners in an eastern Mediterranean country; *esp* **:** an Arab landowner **b :** a member of the upper classes or an educated man in such a country **3 :** a white-collar worker in an eastern Mediterranean or esp. an Arab country
ef·fer·ence \'ef(ə)rən(t)s\ *n* -S **:** efferent activity
¹ef·fer·ent \-nt\ *adj* [F *efférent,* fr. L *efferent-, efferens,* pres. part. of *efferre* to carry outward, fr. *ex-* + *ferre* to carry — more at BEAR] **:** bearing or conducting outward from a part or an organ; *specif* **:** conveying nervous impulses from a nerve center to an effector **:** CENTRIFUGAL, MOTOR — opposed to *afferent* — **ef·fer·ent·ly** *adv*
²efferent \"\ *n* -S **:** an efferent part (as a blood vessel or nerve fiber)
ef·fer·vesce \ˌefə(r)'ves\ *vi* -ED/-ING/-S [L *effervescere,* fr. *ex-* + *fervescere* to begin to boil, incho. of *fervēre* to boil — more at BURN] **1 :** to bubble and hiss (as of fermenting liquors or carbonated water); *also* **:** to issue in bubbles (as of the escaping gas from carbonated water) **2 :** to exhibit (as in speech or action) almost unrestrainable enthusiasm or happy emotion **:** bubble over ⟨I was full and *effervescing* with joy of creation —Mary Austin⟩ ⟨the honeymooners hectically *effervesced* into small talk — Owen Wister⟩
ef·fer·ves·cence \ˌ==='ves³n(t)s\ *n* -S [L *effervescere* + E *-ence*] **1 :** the action or process of effervescing **:** the commotion of a liquid produced by effervescing **2 :** inner excitement or turmoil usu. finding expression in lively action **:** the quality or state of being effervescent ⟨London today, even with all the grimness, has a sort of early New Deal intellectual ~ —J.R.Chamberlain⟩ ⟨continued in a state of ~ —Edith Wharton⟩
ef·fer·ves·cent \ˌ==='ves³nt\ *adj* [L *effervescent-, effervescens,* pres. part. of *effervescere*] **1 :** marked by or expressing a state of effervescence **:** impossible or difficult to restrain or suppress **:** BUBBLING, EXUBERANT ⟨his fertile ~ mind never ceased thinking of new and more effective ways to organize workers and win strikes —C.A.Madison⟩ **2 :** having the property of effervescing ⟨~ wine⟩ ⟨~ salts⟩ **syn** see ELASTIC
ef·fer·ves·cent·ly *or* **ef·fer·vesc·ing·ly** *adv* **:** in an effervescent manner
ef·fer·vesc·ible \ˌ==='vesəbəl\ *adj* **:** able or ready to effervesce
ef·fete \ə'fēt, e'-\ *adj* [L *effetus,* fr. *ex-* + *fetus* pregnant, breeding, fruitful — more at FEMININE] **1 :** exhausted of fertility **:** no longer able to produce young or fruit **:** UNFRUITFUL ⟨eroded ~ earth⟩ **2 :** marked by lack or deprivation of some inherent characteristic **:** ENERVATED: **a** *of a substance* **:** having lost its unique quality (as flavor) **b :** exhausted of physical energy **:** worn out **:** SPENT ⟨~, weary, burned-out revolutionists —H.F.Mooney⟩ **c :** having lost character, courage, strength, stamina, or vitality ⟨~ literary critics and dogmatic professors —J.T.Farrell⟩ **:** DEGENERATE ⟨a soft, ~, and decadent race —R.P.Parsons⟩ **d :** totally devoid of an original positive drive or purposiveness ⟨vaguely educated for minor diplomatic or other governmental posts in an ~ struggle to maintain position —Janet Flanner⟩ **e :** soft or decadent as a result of overrefinement of living conditions or laxity of mental or moral discipline ⟨the ~ householder who wants things done for him —*New Yorker*⟩ ⟨the ~ gentility that lay like a blight on the critical writing of the nineties —C.I.Glicksberg⟩ **f :** OUT-OF-DATE, OUTMODED ⟨an old but by no means ~ statute —Edward Jenks⟩ — **effetely** *adj* — **effeteness** *n* -ES
ef·fi·ca·cious \ˌefə'kāshəs\ *adj* [L *efficac-, efficax* (fr. *efficere* to bring about, accomplish, effect) + E *-ious* — more at EFFECT] **:** characterized by qualities giving power to bring about an intended result ⟨written propaganda is less ~ than the habits and prejudices, the class loyalties . . . of the readers —Aldous Huxley⟩ ⟨an ~ law⟩ **syn** see EFFECTIVE
ef·fi·ca·cious·ly *adv* **:** in an efficacious manner **:** EFFECTIVELY
ef·fi·ca·cious·ness *n* -ES **:** the quality of being efficacious **:** EFFECTIVENESS
ef·fi·cac·i·ty \ˌefə'kasəd·ē, -ətē, -i\ *n* -ES [ME *efficacite,* fr. L *efficacitas,* fr. *efficac- efficax* + *-itas* -ity] **:** EFFICACY, EFFECTIVENESS
ef·fi·ca·cy \'efəkəsē, -fēk-, -si\ *n* -ES [L *efficacia,* fr. *efficac-, efficax* + *-ia* -y] **:** the power to produce an effect **:** EFFECTIVENESS ⟨the ~ of prayer⟩ ⟨~ of medicine⟩ ⟨the ~ of the Security Council in safeguarding world security —Vera M. Dean⟩
efficience *n* -S [L *efficientia*] *obs* **:** efficient action; *also* **:** EFFICACY
ef·fi·cien·cy \ə'fishənsē, e'-,ē'-, -si\ *n* -ES [L *efficientia,* fr. *efficient-, efficiens* (pres. part. of *efficere* to bring about, accomplish, effect) + *-ia* -y — more at EFFECT] **1 :** the power, characteristic quality, or manner of operation of an efficient cause ⟨it is absurd to credit inert mass with ~ —James Ward⟩ **2 a :** EFFECTIVENESS; *esp* **:** capacity to produce desired results with a minimum expenditure of energy, time, money, or materials ⟨increasing recognition of the unfairness of such scales of pay is corroding the ~ of the economic system —J.A.Hobson⟩ ⟨the despairing conclusion that their evil ~ knows no limits —S.L.A.Marshall⟩ **b :** suitability for a task or purpose ⟨the ~ of the drawing board is in no way impaired —*Gadgets Annual*⟩ **3 :** efficient operation as measured by a comparison of actual results with those that could be achieved with the same expenditure of energy ⟨structural changes may take place to render the respiratory organs to remain in a state of ~ —W.H.Dowdeswell⟩ ⟨the invention of instruments for assessing degrees of ~ in communication —Barbara Wootton⟩: as **a :** the ratio of the useful energy delivered by a dynamic system (as a machine, engine, or motor) to the energy supplied to it over the same period or cycle of operation **b :** performance of a task with little or no waste effort **c :** economic productivity **:** YIELD — used esp. of the average number of times a unit of money serves to effect an exchange in a specified period **d :** the relative effective operation of a biological system as measured by the ratio of energy released in product (as milk, muscular effort, or wool) to the energy consumed (as in food) — called also *feed efficiency* **4** *or* **efficiency apartment :** a small usu. furnished apartment having minimal kitchen and bath facilities
efficiency engineer *also* **efficiency expert** *n* **:** one who analyzes methods, procedures, and jobs in order to devise means for securing maximum efficiency of equipment and personnel
¹ef·fi·cient \-nt\ *adj* [ME, fr. MF or L; MF *efficient,* fr. L *efficient-, efficiens*] **1 :** serving as or characteristic of an efficient cause **:** causally productive **:** OPERANT ⟨the ~ action of heat⟩ **2 :** marked by ability to choose and use the most effective and least wasteful means of doing a task or accomplishing a purpose **:** COMPETENT ⟨her education made it likely that she would be a typist more ~ than the average —W.S.Maugham⟩ ⟨the ~ housewife takes the best possible care of her utensils⟩ **3 :** marked by qualities, characteristics, or equipment that facilitate the serving of a purpose or the performance of a task in the best possible manner **:** eminently satisfactory in use **:** effective to an end ⟨the most ~ kind of phrase for the purpose of communicating these subtle, complex impressions —H.J.Muller⟩ ⟨the new barn is more ~ —S.H.Holbrook⟩ **syn** see EFFECTIVE
²efficient *n* -S *obs* **:** EFFICIENT CAUSE ⟨the great ~ of the world —Joseph Hall⟩
efficient cause *n* **:** the immediate agent in the production of an effect ⟨I have a free morning, and this is the *efficient cause* of the chance for talk with you —H.J.Laski⟩
ef·fi·cient·ly *adv* **:** in an efficient manner **:** with success, competence, or adequate effect ⟨a church where he considered the mass ~ performed —T.S.Eliot⟩ ⟨failed to meet the requirements of his position ~⟩
ef·fig·ial \ə'fij(ē)əl, e'-\ *adj* [*effigy* + *-al*] **:** of or resembling an effigy
ef·fig·i·ate \-jēˌāt\ *vt* -ED/-ING/-S [LL *effigiatus,* past part. of *effigiare,* fr. L *effigies*] **:** to form or represent in or as if in an effigy — **ef·fig·i·a·tion** \ˌ===='āshən\ *n* -S
ef·fi·gi·es \ə'fijēˌēz, e'-, -jēz\ *n, pl* **effigies** [L] **:** EFFIGY
ef·fig·u·rate \(')e, ə +\ *adj* [*ex-* + *figurate*] *bot* **:** having a definite form ⟨~ lichens⟩ — **ef·fig·u·ra·tion** \(ˌ)e, ə +\ *n* -S
¹ef·fi·gy \'efəjē, -ji\ *n* -ES [MF *effigie,* fr. L *effigies,* fr. *effingere* to form, fashion, portray, fr. *ex-* + *fingere* to form, shape — more at DOUGH] **:** a full or partial representation esp. of a person: as **a :** a sculptured likeness ⟨the old man himself sits in bronze ~ on a cornerstone —Lawrence Constable⟩ **b :** a portrait on a coin ⟨in those distant days when the only representation of the sovereign was a rough-drawn ~ on coin or seal —R.T.B.Fulford⟩ **c :** a crude figure often in the form of a stuffed dummy that is tortured or disposed of (as by burning or hanging) to represent treatment felt to be due to a person who is the object of hatred — see ⁴GUY 1

sculptured effigy on a tomb

²effigy \"\ *vt* -ED/-ING/-ES **:** to represent by an effigy
effigy mound *n* **:** a prehistoric American Indian burial mound shaped like an animal (as a bird or serpent)
ef·fleu·rage \ˌeflə'räzh, -(ˌ)flü'-\ *n* -S [F, fr. *effleurer* to stroke lightly (fr. *ef-* — fr. L *ex-* — + *fleur* flower, surface, fr. OF *flour, flur, flor*) + *-age* — more at FLOWER] **:** a light stroking movement used in massage
ef·flo·resce \ˌeflə'res\ *vi* -ED/-ING/-S [L *efflorescere,* fr. *ex-* + *florescere* to begin to blossom — more at FLORESCENCE] **1 a** *obs* **:** BLOSSOM **b :** to burst forth or become manifest as if flowering **2** *chem* **a :** to change on the surface or throughout to a whitish mealy or crystalline powder from the loss of water of crystallization on exposure to the air ⟨Glauber's salt ~*s*⟩ **b :** to become covered with a powdery crust or hard coating ⟨bricks may ~ owing to the deposition of soluble salts⟩
ef·flo·res·cence \ˌ==='res³n(t)s\ *n* -S [F, fr. MF, fr. L *efflorescere* + MF *-ence*] **1 :** the period or state of flowering **:** ANTHESIS **2 a :** the action or process of developing and unfolding as if coming into flower **:** BLOSSOMING ⟨his concern for the organic roots of architecture and its eventual ~ in beauty —Lewis Mumford⟩ ⟨periods of higher prosperity and intellectual and artistic ~ —Julian Huxley⟩ **b :** an instance or example of developmental growth ⟨that amazing ~ of genius —DeLancey Ferguson⟩ ⟨perhaps the most astonishing ~ of intellectual adventure in the history of mankind —Lancelot Hogben⟩ **c :** the result or culminating feature of a developmental process **:** OUTGROWTH, FLOWER ⟨the change in art is merely the ~ of certain long prepared and anticipated effects —Roger Fry⟩ ⟨shows how the rich ~ of civilization in the West was achieved —*Times Lit. Supp.*⟩ **3** *chem* **a :** the process of efflorescing **b :** the powder or crust thus formed **4 :** a redness of the skin **:** eruption (as in a rash)
ef·flo·res·cent \ˌ==='res³nt\ *adj* [F or L: F, fr. L *efflorescent-, efflorescens,* pres. part. of *efflorescere*] **:** forming or resembling an efflorescence **:** EFFLORESCING
ef·flu·ence \'eˌflüən(t)s, 'eflәwən-\ *n* -S [L *effluere* to flow out + E *-ence*] **1 :** the action or process of flowing out **:** EMANATION, EFFLUX ⟨the ~ of power rather than the conscious application of it —John Burroughs⟩ **2 :** something that flows out (as from a person or substance) — usu. used of something having an effect ⟨some ~ from its ageless hills and waters laid a spell upon me which has never been broken —John Buchan⟩
¹ef·flu·ent \-nt\ *adj* [L *effluent-, effluens,* pres. part. of *effluere* to flow out, fr. *ex-* + *fluere* to flow — more at FLUENT] **:** flowing out **:** EMANATING, OUTGOING ⟨the Pigeon river, whose blackened waters are flecked with white foam, ~ from the mill —*Amer. Guide Series: N.C.*⟩ ⟨~ vein⟩ ⟨~ stream⟩
²effluent \"\ *n* -S **:** something that flows out: as **a :** an outflowing branch of a main stream or lake — compare AFFLUENT **b :** liquid discharged as waste (as water used in an industrial process or sewage)
ef·fluve \'eˌflüv; e'-,ə'f-\ *n* -S [F, fr. L *effluvium*] **:** a feeble electric discharge due to convection in a fluid dielectric under high voltage
ef·flu·vi·um \e'flüvēəm, ə'-\ *also* **ef·flu·via** \-vēə\ *n, pl* **ef·flu·via** \-vēə\ *or* **effluviums** *also* **effluvias** [L, act of flowing out, outlet, fr. *effluere* to flow out — more at EFFLUENT] **1 :** something esp. subtle and invisible that flows out or issues forth **:** EMANATION: as **a :** EFFLUX 1b(1) **b :** a hypothetical imponderable formerly believed to be manifest as an efflux from electrified bodies and magnets and to be responsible for their powers of attraction and repulsion **c :** an exhalation or smell esp. when unpleasant ⟨emerging from the barbershop, his jowls gray with powder, moving in an ~ of pomade —William Faulkner⟩ ⟨the mingled *effluvia* of rotting leaves and manure heaps . . . drifted toward her —Ellen Glasgow⟩; *also* **:** gaseous waste **:** EXHAUST ⟨carbon monoxide is generously present in the *effluvia* of all internal-combustion engines, most industrial plants, and many mines, mills, or workshops —Berton Roueché⟩ **2 :** a by-product usu. in the form of waste ⟨the big rum distillery just below the town sweetens the air with a luscious smell of molasses when the *effluvia* are being run off into the river —Francis Ratcliffe⟩ ⟨most of the most admired literature . . . has been to all appearance the ~ of a sick society —Elmer Davis⟩
ef·flux \'eˌfləks\ *n* -ES [L *effluxus,* past part. of *effluere*] **1 a :** something that emanates in or as if in a stream **:** EFFUSION ⟨many wished to touch the relics and so absorb their healing ~*es* —E.H.Short⟩ ⟨used secretly to think ourselves the Wordsworth and Coleridge of an endless ~ of lyrical ballads —Christopher Morley⟩ **b** (1) **:** an emanation supposed by Empedocles and the Sophists to be continually given off by external objects and to be the cause of our perception of them (2) **:** EMANATION 1b **2 :** the action or process of flowing or seeming to flow out ⟨large underground ~ of salt water from the lake —*Geog. Jour.*⟩ ⟨the influx and ~ of gold —R.F.Harrod⟩ ⟨the annual ~ of men and women for work —V.G.J.Sheddick⟩ **b :** a lapse or passing of time ⟨the influx and ~ of life, which we call the seasons —A.C.Benson⟩ ⟨for a brief second, for an inexpressibly curtailed ~ of time —Anthony Powell⟩; *also* **:** END, EXPIRATION
ef·flux·ion \e'fləkshən, ə'-\ *n* -S [LL *effluxion-, effluxio* act of flowing out, fr. L *effluxus* + *-ion-, -io* -ion] **:** EFFLUX — used esp. of time ⟨mere ~ of time has given him a long range of observation⟩ ⟨his term of office expired by ~ of time previously fixed⟩
ef·fo·di·en·tia \(ˌ)eˌfōdē'ench(ē)ə, ə,-\ *n pl, cap* [NL, fr. L neut. pl. of *effodient-, effodiens,* pres. part. of *effodere* to dig out, fr. *ex-* + *fodere* to dig — more at BED] *in former classifications* **:** the Edentata as most broadly conceived excepting only the sloths; *sometimes* **:** an order or other group comprising the pangolins and the aardvark
efforce *vt* [MF *efforcer,* fr. OF *esforcier,* fr. *es-* (fr. L *ex-*) + *forcier* to force — more at FORCE] *obs* **:** FORCE
ef·form \(')ə¦fȯ(ə)rm\ *vt* [LL *efformare,* fr. L *ex-* + *formare* to form — more at FORM] *archaic* **:** FORM, SHAPE — **efformation** *n, obs*
ef·fort \'efə(r)t *also* -ˌfȯr| *or* -ˌfȯ(ə)| *sometimes* -ˌfȯr| *or* -ˌfōə|; *usu* |d·+V\ *n* -S [MF, fr. OF *esfort, esforz,* fr. OF *esforcier* to force (as in *s'esforcier* to exert oneself) — more at EFFORCE] **1 a :** conscious exertion of physical or mental power ⟨the constant ~ of the dreamer to attain his ideal —Henry Adams⟩ ⟨the church was built through community ~⟩ ⟨the speech of the Southerner appears to ignore ~ in its slow, carelessly articulated syllables —*Amer. Guide Series: N.C.*⟩ **b :** expenditure of energy toward a particular end **:** forceful attempt ⟨his clumsy ~*s* at certain rural tasks —A.C.Cole⟩ ⟨made one last ~ to obtain Negro suffrage in the South —Carol L. Thompson⟩ ⟨the company's ~*s* to improve working conditions⟩ **c :** hard work ⟨an A for ~⟩ ⟨the work is highly skillful . . . one feels, what was absent from the previous work, a distinct sense of ~ —F.J.Mather⟩ **2 :** the product or result of expenditure of energy — used esp. of a literary or artistic creation ⟨their magnificent churches being justly ranked among the most wonderful ~*s* of the human hand —H.T.Buckle⟩ ⟨one of his television ~*s* —J.P.Shanley⟩ **3 a :** active or effective force ⟨muscular ~⟩ **b :** the force applied to a simple machine (as a lever) as distinguished from the force exerted by it against the load **4 :** the total energy expended and work done to achieve a particular purpose or result **:** UNDERTAKING ⟨the war ~⟩ ⟨an unsuccessful rescue ~⟩

syn EFFORT, EXERTION, PAINS, and TROUBLE can signify in common the active expenditure of physical or mental power in producing or attempting to produce a desired result. EFFORT implies conscious attempt or a toiling or straining to achieve ⟨to divorce the worker's income from any dependence on the *efforts* he makes —*Time*⟩ ⟨modern science, with infinite *effort,* has discovered and announced that man is a bewildering complex of energies —Henry Adams⟩ ⟨made an *effort* to increase his income⟩ EXERTION stresses the active, often vigorous, exercise of a power or faculty ⟨his work was done with remarkable grace, but with *exertions* which it was painful to witness —Margaret Deland⟩ ⟨prodigious *exertions* were made to bring in the cargoes and to protect the ships —Sir Winston Churchill⟩ ⟨by a violent *exertion* of his powers of self-command he reassumed his tranquillity —Elinor Wylie⟩ PAINS implies toilsome or solicitous effort ⟨taken unusual *pains* to inform himself beforehand concerning the subject matter of the conference —Vera M. Dean⟩ ⟨exercising great *pains* to improve one's speech⟩ TROUBLE implies exertion that inconveniences ⟨a lazy man's expedient for ridding himself of the *trouble* of thinking and deciding —B.N.Cardozo⟩ ⟨no need to go to all the *trouble* of pushing through a constitutional amendment —Zechariah Chafee⟩ ⟨for the *trouble* of looking, . . . you will acquire the warm and palpitating facts of life —R.L.Stevenson⟩
ef·fort·ful \'efə(r)tfəl\ *adj* **:** marked by the presence of or necessity for an expenditure of effort **:** LABORED ⟨a dry subject that makes for ~ reading⟩ ⟨he answered with an ~ smile⟩ ⟨~ reporting of fact⟩ — **ef·fort·ful·ly** \-fəlē, -li\ *adv*
ef·fort·less \-tləs\ *adj* **1 :** requiring no effort ⟨a style the layman and the immature reader can absorb with ~ pleasure —*Saturday Rev.*⟩ **2 :** having the effect by virtue of ease, mastery, artistry, or smoothness of performance of being or having been accomplished without effort ⟨even the swallows, the restless swallows, glided in an ~ way through the busy air —Richard Jefferies⟩ ⟨she walked with ~ grace⟩ ⟨this writer of ~, almost casual, verses —Arna W. Bontemps⟩ **syn** see EASY
ef·fort·less·ly *adv* **:** in an effortless manner
ef·fort·less·ness *n* -ES **:** the quality of being effortless **:** absence of strain or apparent difficulty
effort syndrome *n* **:** CARDIAC NEUROSIS
ef·frac·tion \e'frakshən, ə'-\ *n* -S [F, modif. (influenced by F *-ion*) of LL *effractura,* fr. L *effractus* (past part. of *effringere* to break open, fr. *ex-* + *-fringere,* fr. *frangere* to break) + *-ura*

-ure — more at BREAK] **:** the action of making forcible entry ⟨criminal ~ of a house⟩ ⟨~ into a store⟩

ef·fron·tery \ə'frəntərē, e'-,ē'-, -ri\ *n* -ES [F *effronterie*, fr. MF, fr. *effronté* shameless (fr. LL *effront-, effrons* — fr. L *ex-* + *front-, frons* forehead — + MF *-é*, fr. L *-atus* -ate) + *-erie* -ery — more at FRONT] **:** flagrant boldness that is offensive or insolent in its crass discourtesy or utter presumption **:** GALL ⟨the ~ to propound three such heresies —*Times Lit. Supp.*⟩ **syn** see TEMERITY

effs *pl of* EFF

ef·fulge \e'fʊlj, ə'-,ē'-, -'fəlj\ *vi* -ED/-ING/-S [L *effulgēre*, fr. *ex-* + *fulgēre* to shine, flash — more at FULGENT] **:** to shine forth **:** RADIATE

ef·ful·gence \-jən(t)s\ *n* -S [LL *effulgentia*, fr. L *effulgent-, effulgens* + *-ia* -y] **:** strong radiant light **:** glorious splendor **:** BRILLIANCE ⟨that crimson flow, that ~ at the solemn twilight hour —Willa Cather⟩

ef·ful·gent \-nt\ *adj* [L *effulgent-, effulgens*, pres. part. of *effulgēre*] **:** marked by or as if by brightly shining light **:** impressive in resplendence **:** extremely radiant **:** BRILLIANT ⟨her ~ beauty —Arnold Bennett⟩ ⟨the same little ~ flash of intuition —J.D.Salinger⟩ **syn** see BRIGHT

ef·fund \e'fənd\ *vt* -ED/-ING/-S [ME *effunden*, fr. L *effundere*] *archaic* **:** EFFUSE

¹ef·fuse \e'fyüz, ə'-,ē'-\ *vb* -ED/-ING/-S [L *effusus*, past part. of *effundere*, fr. *ex-* + *fundere* to pour — more at FOUND] *vt* **1 :** to pour out (a liquid) **2 :** to give off **:** SHED, RADIATE ⟨the drawing room . . . *effused* an atmosphere of unhappiness and discontent —I.V.Morris⟩ ~ *vi* **:** to flow out **:** EMANATE

²ef·fuse \(')e¦fyüs, ə'f-,ē'f-\ *adj* [L *effusus*, past part.] **1 :** poured out freely **:** overflowing without restraint **:** PROFUSE ⟨so should our joy be very ~ —Isaac Barrow⟩ **2** *bot* **:** DIFFUSE; *specif* **:** spread out flat without definite form ⟨~ lichens⟩ — compare EFFIGURATE **3 :** having the lips separated by a gap — used of certain shells

³effuse *n* -S [¹*effuse*] *obs* **:** EFFUSION

ef·fu·si·om·e·ter \ə,fyüzē'äməd·ə(r)\ *n* [*effusion* + *-meter*] **:** an apparatus for determining the effusion velocities of gases and hence their densities

ef·fu·sion \ə'fyüzhən, e'-,ē'-\ *n* -S [ME *effusioun*, fr. MF or L; MF *effusion*, fr. L *effusion-, effusio*, fr. *effusus* + *-ion-, -io* -ion] **1 :** the action or process of effusing or of being poured out ⟨desirous to stop the ~ of British blood —C.G.Bowers⟩: as **a :** escape of a fluid into a tissue or part (as the pleural cavity) by rupture of a vessel or by exudation through the walls **:** EXTRAVASATION **b :** the flow of a gas through an aperture whose diameter is small as compared with the distance between the molecules of the gas ⟨~ through a plug of unglazed porcelain⟩ **2 :** unrestrained expression of feelings ⟨greeted her with great ~ —Olive H. Prouty⟩ ⟨in the first ~ of self-admiration —J.A.Froude⟩ **3 a :** something that is poured out with little or no restraint — used esp. of evidences of self-expression ⟨she bore with the ~*s* of his endless conceit —Jane Austen⟩ ⟨literary and critical ~*s* —Rex Ingamells⟩ **b :** the liquid that escapes in extravasation

ef·fu·sive \-üsiv, -üz|, |ēv *also* |əv\ *adj* **1** *archaic* **:** pouring freely ⟨washed with the ~ wave —Alexander Pope⟩ **2 :** expressing or marked by unrestrained emotion **:** unduly demonstrative **:** GUSHING ⟨at the sight of the stranger he sprang to his feet and darted forward, his hands outstretched, smiling with all his teeth, ~ —Aldous Huxley⟩ ⟨insincere and ~ demonstrations of sentimental friendship —Dean Acheson⟩ **3 :** characterized or formed by a nonexplosive outpouring of lava ⟨~ volcano⟩ ⟨~ eruption⟩ ⟨~ rock⟩ — **ef·fu·sive·ly** \|əvlē, -li\ *adv* — **ef·fu·sive·ness** \|ivnəs |ēv- *also* |əv-\ *n* -ES

ef·ik \'efik\ *n, pl* **efik** *or* **efiks** *usu cap* **1 a :** a Negro people of southeastern Nigeria **b :** a member of such people **2 :** a dialect of Ibibio that is used as the literary language throughout the Ibibio area and in some neighboring areas and by the Efik people as their language

e flat \'ē¦-\ *n, usu cap E* **1 :** the keynote of E-flat major or E-flat minor **2 :** the tone a half step below E

e–flat major \'ē-¦-'--\ *n, usu cap E* **:** the major musical key having a signature of three flats

e–flat minor *n, usu cap E* **:** the minor musical key having a signature of six flats

efoveolate \(')ē+\ *adj* [*e-* + *foveolate*] **:** not foveolate

ef·reet *var of* AFREET

efs *pl of* EF

¹eft \'eft\ *n* -S [ME *evete, ewte*, fr. OE *efete*] **1** *obs* **:** LIZARD **2 :** NEWT; *esp* **:** the terrestrial phase of a predominantly aquatic newt

²eft \"\ *adv* [ME, fr. OE *eft, æft*; akin to OE *æfter* after — more at AFTER] **1** *archaic* **:** AGAIN **2** *archaic* **:** AFTER, AFTERWARD

ef·ter \'eftər\ *chiefly Scot var of* AFTER

eft·soons \(')eft¦sünz\ *also* **eft·soon** \-ün\ *adv* [ME *eftsones* (fr. *eft* + *sone* immediately, soon + *-s*, adverbial suffix) & *eftsone*, fr. *eft* + *sone* — more at SOON, -S] **1** *archaic* **:** a second time **:** AGAIN **2** *archaic* **:** soon afterward **:** QUICKLY **3** *archaic* **:** from time to time **:** OFTEN

ef·wa·ta·ka·la grass \,efwə'täkələ-\ *n* [Kongo *efwatakala*] *Africa* **:** MOLASSES GRASS

eg *abbr* [L *exempli gratia*] for example

EG *abbr* edge grain

egad \ē'gad, i'-, -gaa(ə)d\ *interj* [prob. euphemism for *oh God*] — used as a mild oath

egal \'ēgəl\ *adj* [ME, fr. MF, fr. L *aequalis* — more at EQUAL] *obs* **:** EQUAL

¹egal·i·tar·i·an \(')ē¦galə¦terēən, ə¦g-, -taar-,-tär-\ *adj* [F *égalitaire* (fr. *égalité* equality — fr. L *aequalitat-, aequalitas* — + *-aire* -ary) + E *-ian* — more at EQUALITY] **:** marked by or believing in egalitarianism **:** DEMOCRATIC ⟨an ~ age can have no place for the snobbish and feudal notion that one occupation can be of greater worth than another —Christopher Hollis⟩

²egalitarian \"\ *n* -S **:** one who believes in egalitarianism

egal·i·tar·i·an·ism \(,)ē¦--'--ə,nizəm, ə,-\ *n* -S **1 :** a belief in human equality: **a :** a belief that all men are equal in intrinsic worth and are entitled to equal access to the rights and privileges of their society; *specif* **:** a social philosophy advocating the leveling of social, political, and economic inequalities ⟨the theory of English ~ has . . . postulated a process of leveling up, not down; of increasing, not diminishing, the middle classes —Roy Lewis & Angus Maude⟩ **b :** the belief that men are born equal in aptitudes and capacities ⟨Plato's view of human nature was such as to be clearly opposed to ~. . . . Men are naturally unequal —H.E.Barnes & H.P.Becker⟩ **2 :** the suppression of all distinctions between individuals and groups as inherently unjust **:** an extreme social and political leveling ⟨the Tiv people of Nigeria . . . are nurtured in a "fierce and rather brutal ~", and dislike anything that singles anybody out for special attention —Barbara Wootton⟩ **3 :** social, political, or economic equality ⟨the ~ of the early Christian communities, where distinctions of class were disregarded and even a slave could hold an important position —H.E.Barnes & H.P.Becker⟩

éga·li·té \āgälētā\ *also* **egal·i·ty** \ē'galəd·ē, ə'-\ *n* -S [F *égalité* equality] **:** social or political equality; *esp* **:** an extreme social and political leveling

egally *adv* [ME, fr. *egal* equal + *-ly* — more at EGAL] *obs* **:** EQUALLY

eg·ba \'egbə\ *n, pl* **egba** *or* **egbas** *usu cap* **1 :** a Yoruba-speaking people of southwestern Nigeria primarily concentrated in the vicinity of Abeokuta **2 :** a member of the Egba people

eger·an \'āgərən, -,ran\ *n* -S [G, fr. *Eger* (Cheb), Czechoslovakia, its locality + *-an*] **:** a brown idocrase

ege·ria \ə'jirēə, ē'-\ *n* -S *usu cap* [after *Egeria*, mythical adviser of Numa Pompilius, legendary 2d king of Rome, fr. L] **:** a woman adviser or companion ⟨listening to the promptings of his *Egeria* —*Encyc. Britannica*⟩ ⟨the most highly esteemed as an *Egeria* by old friends —Janet Flanner⟩

egest \(')ē¦jest, ə'j-\ *vt* -ED/-ING/-S [L *egestus*, past part. of *egerere* to carry outside, discharge, fr. *e-* + *gerere* to carry, bear — more at CAST] **:** to cast out (indigestible matter) from the digestive tract; *broadly* **:** to rid the body of (waste matter) by any normal route (as the skin, lungs, or kidneys)

eges·ta \ə'jestə\ *n pl* [NL, fr. L, neut. pl. of *egestus*] **:** something egested from the body **:** DEJECTA, EXCRETA — opposed to *ingesta*

eges·tion \ə'jes(h)chən\ *n* -S [ME *egestioun*, fr. MF or L; MF *egestion*, fr. L *egestion-, egestio*, fr. *egestus* + *-ion-, -io* -ion] **:** the act or process of egesting

¹egg \'eg, 'āg\ *vt* -ED/-ING/-S [ME *eggen*, fr. ON *eggja*, fr. *egg* edge of a blade, edge — more at EDGE] **:** to provoke or goad to action **:** INCITE, TEMPT, ENCOURAGE — usu. used with *on* ⟨his vanity ~*ed* him on —O.S.J.Gogarty⟩ ⟨~ their governments on to spend hundreds of millions —G.B.Shaw⟩ **syn** see URGE

²egg \"\ *n* -S *often attrib* [ME *egge*, fr. ON *egg*; akin to OE *ǣg* egg, OHG *ei*, Crimean Goth *ada*, L *ovum*, W *wy*, Gk *ōion*, OPer *xāya* and perh. to L *avis* bird — more at AVIARY] **1 a** (1) **:** the hard-shelled reproductive body produced by a bird, esp. by domestic poultry ⟨a dozen new-laid ~*s*⟩ (2) **:** the content of such an egg used as food ⟨I like an ~ for breakfast⟩ **b :** an animal reproductive body (as of reptiles, birds, and most insects) consisting of an ovum together with its nutritive and protective envelopes and being capable of development that results in the production and release of a new individual capable of independent existence — used esp. of such bodies when enclosed in a firm membrane or shell and able to withstand exposure to air **c :** OVUM 1 **d :** the pupa of certain insects — not used technically **2 :** something resembling an egg: as **a :** an incipient idea ⟨that a handful of men . . . carry in their brains the ovarian ~*s* of the future —Van Wyck Brooks⟩ **b** *slang* **:** a military explosive; *esp* **:** an aerial bomb ⟨the fighter-bombers . . . dropped their ~*s* —G.S. Patton⟩ **3** *slang* **:** FELLOW, GUY ⟨a good ~⟩ ⟨a bad ~⟩ **4 :** ACID EGG

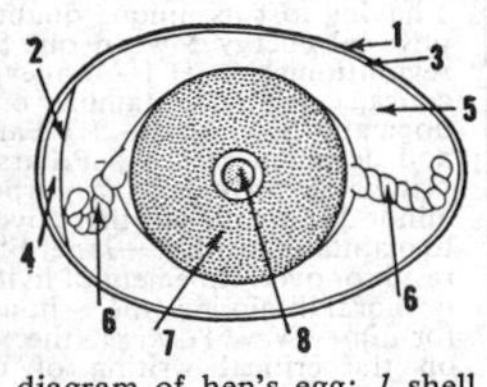

diagram of hen's egg: *1* shell, *2* inner shell membrane and *3* outer shell membrane enclosing air space *4*, *5* albumen or white, *6* chalazas, *7* yolk, *8* blastodisc

³egg \"\ *vb* -ED/-ING/-S *vt* **1 :** to cover with egg ⟨slices of meat, ~*ed*, crumbed, and fried⟩ **2 :** to pelt with eggs **:** break eggs on ⟨pranksters had ~*ed* his car⟩ ~ *vi* **:** to gather the eggs of wild birds

egg albumin *n* **1 :** the albumin of eggs; *esp* **:** OVALBUMIN 1 **2 :** dried whites of eggs (as of hen's eggs) obtained usu. as yellowish lumps or powder and containing ovalbumin and other proteins

egg and dart *also* **egg and tongue** *or* **egg and anchor** *n* **:** a carved ornamental design in relief consisting of an ovoid figure and a roughly triangular figure usu. approximating a somewhat elongated javelin or arrow head repeated alternately (as along a molding or cornice)

egg and dart

egg apparatus *n* **:** a group of three cells at the micropylar end of the embryo sac in seed plants consisting of the egg and two sterile cells

egg apple *n* **:** EGGPLANT

egg·ar *also* **egg·er** \'egə(r), 'āg-\ *n* -S [*eggar* alter. of *egger*; *egger* fr. ²*egg* + *-er*; fr. the shape of the cocoon] **:** any of various moths of the family Lasiocampidae (as many members of the genera *Eriogaster* and *Lasiocampa*) that have nonfunctional mouthparts as adults and plumose antennae in the males and produce larvae that feed on the foliage of trees

egg axis *n* **:** an embryonic axis passing through the animal and vegetal poles of an egg

eggbeater \'-,--\ *n* **1 :** a rotary beater operated by hand for beating eggs or cream and other liquids **2 :** HELICOPTER

egg bed *n* **:** an area where many grasshoppers have deposited egg pods

eggberry \'-- — *see* BERRY\ *n* [alter. of *hagberry*] **:** EUROPEAN BIRD CHERRY

egg bird *n* **:** any of various sea birds whose eggs are used for food; *esp* **:** SOOTY TERN

egg bonnet *n* **:** WATER SHIELD 1

¹egg-bound \'-,-\ *adj* [²*egg* + *bound*] **:** unable to expel eggs in the normal manner — used of a fowl or a fish

²egg-bound \"\ *n* -S **:** the condition of being egg-bound

eggbox \'-,-\ *adj, Brit* **:** EGGCRATE ⟨~ screening⟩

egg bread *n, Midland* **:** SPOON BREAD

egg burster *n* **:** a ridge, group of teeth, or other prominence on the body of an insect embryo by which it ruptures the egg membranes in hatching

egg case *n* **1 a** *or* **egg capsule :** a protective case enclosing eggs (as of certain insects and mollusks) **:** OOTHECA — see SEA NECKLACE **b** *or* **egg sac :** a pouch of spun silk in which many spiders carry their eggs **c :** a highly specialized outer envelope that encloses an egg and that is either soft and gelatinous (as in certain amphibians) or strong and horny with special adaptations for the escape of the young (as in skates) — see SEA PURSE **2 :** a container (as of cardboard) for marketing eggs

egg cell *n* **:** the female germ cell — contrasted with *sperm cell*

egg cement *or* **egg glue** *n* **:** a secretion by which eggs (as those of many crustaceans) are fastened together or to some object

egg coal *n* **:** anthracite coal of a large size — see ANTHRACITE table

egg cowry *n* **:** a large smooth spindle-shaped cowrie (*Amphiperas ovum*) of the Indian and southwest Pacific oceans that is pure white without and deep brown within the shell and is prized by natives of the area for ornament and as a fertility symbol — called also *shuttle shell*

eggcrate \'-,-\ *adj* **:** having rectangular cells that direct and diffuse light ⟨an ~ ceiling shuts out direct view of fluorescent lamps⟩

eggcup \'-,-\ *n* **:** a cup made to hold an egg that is to be eaten from the shell

egg dance *n* **:** an old English dance performed by a blindfolded dancer among eggs

eggeater \'-,--\ *also* **egg-eating snake** \'-,---\ *n* **:** a snake living entirely on eggs: as **a :** a small aglyphous snake (*Dasypeltis scaber*) of Africa **b :** a related Indian snake (*Elachistodon westermanni*) — compare DASYPELTIDAE

eggcup

¹egger *var of* EGGAR

²egg·er \'egə(r), 'āg-\ *n* -S [³*egg* + *-er*] **:** one that collects the eggs of wild birds esp. for gain

egg flat *n* **:** a partition used between layers in egg crates to prevent breakage

eggfruit \'-,-\ *n* **1 :** any of several edible fruits of plants of the genus *Pouteria*; *esp* **:** CANISTEL **2 :** EGGPLANT

egghead \'-,-\ *n* **1 :** one with intellectual interests or pretensions **:** INTELLECTUAL ⟨an can be considered an ~ himself (he boned up for covering the Korean war by reading Thucydides) —*Newsweek*⟩ **:** HIGHBROW ⟨radio programming so sophisticated that it appeals only to ~*s*⟩ **2 :** a highly educated person ⟨the know-nothing at the expense of the ~ —William Barrett⟩ **:** THEORIST ⟨a kind of McCarthy ~ not because he is liberal . . . but because he is the theoretician —Harvey Breit⟩ ⟨was a creation of the longhairs, the do-gooders, the ~*s* —Malcolm Cowley⟩

egghot \'-,-\ *n* -S **:** a hot drink consisting of beer and eggs sweetened and seasoned with nutmeg

egging *pres part of* EGG

egg·ler \'eglə(r)\ *n* -S [¹*egg* + *-ler* (as in *higgler, peddler*)] *dial Brit* **:** an egg dealer

egg·less \'egləs, 'āg-\ *adj* **:** lacking or deprived of eggs

egg membrane *n* **:** a membrane enveloping an egg; *esp* **:** VITELLINE MEMBRANE

eggnog \'-,-\ *n* -S [²*egg* + *nog*] **:** a drink consisting of eggs beaten up with sugar, milk or cream, and often rum, brandy, or other liquor or sometimes a wine usu. served cold and flavored with grated nutmeg

egg nucleus *n* **:** FEMALE PRONUCLEUS

egg parasite *n* **:** any of numerous small hymenopterons that develop within the eggs of other insects

egg picking *n* **:** a game in which two contestants strike boiled Easter eggs together until one egg is cracked

eggplant \'-,-\ *n* **1 a :** a hairy upright somewhat woody perennial herb (*Solanum melongena*) that is prob. native to southeastern Asia but is widely cultivated in many horticultural varieties usu. as an annual for its edible purple, white, or occas. yellow or striped fruits which are commonly used as a vegetable — called also *aubergine, brinjal, garden egg* **b :** the usu. smooth ovoid fruit of the eggplant **2 :** a variable color averaging a blackish purple that is bluer and stronger than burgundy (sense 2b) — called also *aubergine*

eggplant

egg powder *n* **:** a powder made from dried eggs

egg raft *n* **:** a floating mass of eggs produced by certain fishes and mosquitoes

egg receptor *n* **:** a hypothetical substance in the egg cell that in conjunction with fertilizin and the sperm receptor is held to play a part in the fertilization of the egg

egg roll *n* **:** an egg-dough casing filled with minced vegetables fried in deep fat

egg rolling *n* **1 :** an old European folk custom of rolling eggs down a hill as part of a spring festival **2 :** a frolic for children usu. held during the Easter season

eggs *pres 3d sing of* EGG, *pl of* EGG

egg sac *n* **1 :** EGG CASE 1b **2 :** one of a pair of egg masses that project into the water from the first abdominal segment of certain crustaceans (as most copepods)

eggs–and–bacon \¦--'--\ *n* -S **:** TOAD FLAX 1

egg sauce *n* **:** any of various sauces containing eggs: as **a :** a sauce made of fish or meat stock and beaten eggs **b :** a drawn butter sauce with beaten egg yolks or minced hard-boiled eggs

eggs ben·e·dict \-'benə,dikt\ *n pl but sing or pl in constr, usu cap B* [prob. fr. the name *Benedict*] **:** poached eggs placed on broiled ham laid on toasted halves of English muffin and topped with hollandaise sauce

¹eggshell \'-,-\ *n* [ME, fr. *egge* + *shell*] **1 a :** the hard exterior covering of an egg **b :** something resembling an eggshell esp. in fragility ⟨the old carrier was hardly in the ~ class —*Newsweek*⟩ **2** *usu* **egg shell :** any of various smooth somewhat oval gastropod shells of *Ovula* and related genera **3 :** a paper with a relatively rough finish finer than antique and rougher than vellum **4 a :** any of the colors exhibited by the shells of birds' eggs; *esp* **:** those of the hen's egg **b** *of textiles* **:** a variable color averaging a pale yellow that is redder, slightly lighter, and very slightly stronger than ivory and redder and darker than cream

²eggshell \"\ *adj* **1 :** like an eggshell: **a :** thin and fragile ⟨~ china⟩ ⟨~ porcelain⟩ **b :** having semimat luster ⟨~ paint⟩ ⟨~ enamel⟩ **:** SEMIGLOSS ⟨~ finish⟩ ⟨~ black⟩ **2 :** GENTLE ⟨the helicopter . . . came down to an ~ landing —*Time*⟩

eggshell blue *or* **eggshell green** *n* **:** ROBIN'S-EGG BLUE 2

eggshell nail *n* **:** a thin fingernail turning up at the outer edge seen in some diseases and nutritional disorders

egg timer *n* **:** a small sandglass running about three minutes for timing the boiling of eggs — compare HOURGLASS

egg tooth *n* **:** a hard sharp prominence on the tip of the beak or nose of embryo birds and oviparous reptiles with which they break through the eggshell; *also* **:** an analogous chitinous prominence on the head of an insect

egg tray *n* **:** a usu. square paperboard tray shaped to hold and protect eggs in a shipping case or crate

egg tube *n* **1 :** OVIDUCT **2 :** OVARIOLE

egg urchin *n* **:** a globular thin-shelled sea urchin

egg white *n* **:** the white of an egg (as of a hen or duck) used beaten or unbeaten in cookery ⟨beat an *egg white* until stiff⟩ ⟨separate the *egg whites* from the yolks⟩

egg–white injury *also* **egg–white disease** *n* **:** a vitamin-deficiency disease induced by feeding upon an excess of raw egg white — see AVIDIN, BIOTIN

egis *var of* AEGIS

eg·lan·tine \'eglən·,tīn, -tēn\ *n* -S [ME *eglentyn*, fr. MF *aiglent* (fr. — assumed — VL *aculentum*, fr. L *acus* needle, fr. *acer* sharp) + ME *-yn* -ine — more at EDGE] **1 :** SWEETBRIER **2 :** AUSTRIAN BRIER **3 :** DOG ROSE

eg·la·tere \'eglə,ti(ə)r\ *n* -S [ME *eglenter*, fr. MF *eglentier*, *aiglentier*, fr. *aiglent* + *-ier* -er] *archaic* **:** EGLANTINE

eg·le·ston·ite \'egəlztə,nīt, -lst-\ *n* -S [Thomas *Egleston* †1900 Am. mineralogist + E *-ite*] **:** a mineral Hg_4Cl_2O consisting of mercury oxychloride occurring in brownish yellow isometric crystals

eglo·mi·se *or* **églo·mi·sé** \¦āglə(,)mē¦zā, ¦eg-\ *adj* [F *églomisé*, past part. of *églomiser* to decorate a glass panel by painting on its back, fr. *é-* (fr. L *e-*) + *Glomy*, 18th cent. Fr. decorator + F *-iser* -ize] **:** made of glass on the back of which and showing through is a painted or gilded picture ⟨a mahogany banjo clock with ~ panel⟩

eg·mont buttercup \'eg,mänt-\ *n, usu cap E* [fr. Mt. *Egmont*, New Zealand] **:** a New Zealand crowfoot (*Ranunculus nivicola*) with yellow flowers

ego \'ē(,)gō *sometimes* 'e(- *or* 'ā(-\ *n* -S [NL, fr. L, I — more at I] **1 :** the self esp. as inside one as contrasted with something outside (as another self or the world): as **a** *metaphysical philos* (1) *in Descartes* **:** the soul or an underlying mental or spiritual substance (2) *in Kant* **:** a transcendentally postulated unity either of apperception or of the morally free person — called also *pure ego* (3) *in Fichte* **:** pure self-determining activity positing itself — called also *pure ego* **b** *empirical philos* (1) *in Hume* **:** a complex of ideas or a system of successive mental states (2) *in Kant* **:** the conscious subject of experience (3) **:** the consciousness of an individual's being in distinction from other selves **c :** SELF 3 **2 a :** SELF-ESTEEM ⟨few things are more soothing to a battered ~ than an afternoon's shopping —Ralph Linton⟩ **:** EGOTISM ⟨nice boy . . . not a speck of ~ in him —Clifford Odets⟩ **b :** WILL ⟨Stalin chose Malenkov as the most faithful projection of his own political ~ —*Reporter*⟩ **3** [trans. of G *ich*] *psychoanalysis* **:** the largely conscious part of the personality that is derived from the id through contacts with reality and that mediates the demands of the id, of the superego, and of external everyday reality in the interest of preserving the organism **4** *ethnol* **:** an individual person taken as a point of reference in a particular framework (as a kinship system)

¹ego·cen·tric \¦ēgō¦sen·trik, -gə¦-, -trēk *sometimes* ¦eg-\ *adj* [NL *ego* + E *-centric*] **1 :** concerned with the individual person rather than society **:** INDIVIDUALISTIC ⟨this literature reveals two main attitudes, the one, ~ . . . , stresses the horror, waste, and futility of war; the other, ethnocentric, is aware of the comradeship between soldier and soldier —*Canadian Forum*⟩ **2 :** taking the ego as the necessary starting point in philosophy **:** viewed from one's own mind as a center ⟨the new realist revolutionizes philosophic thought by abandoning the ~ position —May Sinclair⟩ **3 a :** limited in outlook or concern to one's own activities or needs or to those of one's group **:** wrapped up in oneself ⟨~ . . . speech shows no concern for the audience —G.A.Miller⟩ ⟨the ~ policy of France . . . bears the germs of a new war —*Nation*⟩ **b :** tending to self-assertion or self-satisfaction **:** SELFISH ⟨~ personalities, lacking in conscience and feeling for others —E.J.Coventry⟩

²egocentric \"\ *n* -S **:** an egocentric person ⟨~*s* grappling glibly with the world's most ponderous problems —*Saturday Rev.*⟩

ego·cen·tric·i·ty \,--(,)sen'trisəd·ē, -sən-, -ətē, -i\ *n* -ES **:** the quality or state of being egocentric ⟨he sees himself as the hub of the wheel and all of the rest of the people in the world revolve about him and everything leads to him . . . this is the classic formula of ~ —Rudolf Hirschberg⟩

egocentric predicament *n* **:** the epistemological predicament of apparently being unable to get outside one's own mind because all that the knower can know will be what is present to his own mind

ego·cen·trism \,--'sen,trizəm\ *n* -S **1 :** EGOCENTRICITY **2 :** the effort to get personal recognition esp. by socially unacceptable behavior **:** psychic overcompensation

egoc·er·us \ē'gäsərəs, ə'-\ [NL, fr. Gk *aigo-, aix* goat + NL *-cerus* — more at AEGIS] *syn of* HIPPOTRAGUS

ego–defense \ˌ≈(ˌ)≈≈ˌ≈, ˌ≈(ˌ)≈'≈ˌ≈\ *n* **:** a psychological mechanism designed consciously or unconsciously to protect one's self-image or self-esteem

ego–expansion \ˌ≈(ˌ)≈≈¦≈≈\ *n* **:** broadening, fulfillment, or realization of the self

ego·hood \'ēgō,hu̇d *sometimes* 'eg- *or* 'äg-\ *n* [NL *ego* + E *-hood*] **:** SELFHOOD

ego ideal *n* **:** the group of positive standards, ideals, goals, and ambitions assimilated from the superego that a person consciously entertains **:** an idealized picture of what one would like to be; *broadly* **:** CONSCIENCE

ego–identity \ˌ≈(ˌ)≈(ˌ)≈¦≈≈\ *n* **:** perception of continuity and coherence in one's self-picture and in one's social relations

ego–involve \ˌ≈(ˌ)≈≈¦≈\ *vt* **:** to involve (a person) by investing a situation or object with a component that arouses feelings of pride or its opposite **:** MOTIVATE

ego–involvement \ˌ≈(ˌ)≈≈¦≈≈\ *n* **:** an involvement of one's self-esteem in the performance of a task or in an object

ego·ism \'ē|gə,wizəm, -(ˌ)gō,iz- *sometimes* 'e|\ *n* -S [F *égoïsme*, fr. NL *egoismus*, fr. L *ego* I + *-ismus* -ism — more at I] **1 a** (1) **:** the philosophic doctrine of some Cartesians and Fichteans that all the elements of knowledge are in the ego and the relations that it implies or provides for (2) **:** SOLIPSISM **b :** the philosophic doctrine (as that held by Fichte) that identifies ultimate reality with an absolute ego **2 a :** the ethical doctrine that individual self-interest is the actual motive of all conscious action — called also *psychological egoism* **b :** the ethical doctrine that individual self-interest is the valid end of all action — called also *ethical egoism;* compare ALTRUISM **3** [by alter.] **:** EGOTISM **4 :** excessive libidinization of the ego — compare NARCISSISM **syn** see CONCEIT

ego·ist \|gəwəst, |(ˌ)gō·ə-\ *n* -S [F *égoïste*, fr. L *ego* I + F *-iste* -ist] **1 :** a believer in egoism ⟨the psychological ~'s view that every voluntary action is determinately motivated by the agent's desire to benefit himself —C.A.Baylis⟩ **2 :** a person who is egocentric or egotistic ⟨to a selfish or proud man, triumph is pleasant and defeat painful, but to an ~, both are equally interesting, for what matters is not the content of the experience but the fact that it is his —W.H.Auden⟩

ego·is·tic \ˌ≈gə¦wistik, -gō¦is-, -tēk\ *also* **ego·is·ti·cal** \-təkəl, -tēk-\ *adj* **1 :** EGOCENTRIC, EGOTISTIC **2 :** of or relating to the ego or egoism ⟨the interior ~ relations of a single subject —James Martineau⟩ ⟨an ~ interpretation of social behavior, a denial of the existence of altruistic conduct —F.W. Znaniecki⟩ — **ego·is·ti·cal·ly** \-tək(ə)lē, -tēk-, -li\ *adv*

egoistic hedonism *n* **:** the ethical theory that the valid aim of right conduct is one's own happiness — contrasted with *universalistic hedonism*

ego·ity \ē'gōəd·ē, e'-, ə'-\ *n* -ES [NL *ego* + E *-ity*] **1 :** SELFHOOD **2 :** EGO 1a(3)

ego–libido \ˌ≈(ˌ)≈≈¦≈≈\ *n* **:** the part of the libido attached to the self — compare OBJECT LIBIDO

ego·ma·nia \ˌēgō'mānēə, -gə'-, -nyə *sometimes* ˌeg-\ *n* [NL, fr. *ego* + *-mania*] **:** extreme egocentricity **:** abnormally developed egotism ⟨religious individualism degenerating into egoism and producing even ~ —W.B.Selbie⟩

ego·ma·ni·ac \-nē,ak\ *n* [*ego* + *maniac*] **:** one characterized by egomania ⟨~s of incredible selfishness and utter callousness —*Atlantic*⟩ — **ego·ma·ni·a·cal** \ˌ≈≈mə¦nīəkəl\ *adj*

ego–oriented \ˌ≈(ˌ)≈¦≈≈¦≈≈\ *adj* **:** arousing ego-involvement

egoph·o·ny *also* **ae·goph·o·ny** \ē'gäfənē\ *n* -ES [ISV *ego-* (fr. Gk *aig-, aix* goat) + *-phony* — more at AEGIS] **:** a modification of the voice resembling bleating heard on auscultation of the chest in certain diseases (as in pleurisy with effusion)

ego psychology *n* **:** the study of the ego esp. with regard to mechanisms of defense, transference, reality-testing, and attainment of the ego ideal

egos *pl of* EGO

ego–satisfaction \ˌ≈(ˌ)≈ˌ≈≈¦≈≈\ *n* **:** SELF-SATISFACTION

ego–syntonic \ˌē(ˌ)gō *sometimes* ¦e(- *or* ¦ä(-+\ *adj* **:** compatible with or acceptable to the ego ⟨the *ego-syntonic* profanity of a Rabelais —George Devereux⟩

ego·tism \'ēgə,tizəm, -gō| *sometimes* 'eg-\ *n* -S [L *ego* I + E *-tism* (as in *idiotism*) — more at I] **1 a :** the practice of speaking or writing of oneself esp. in excess **:** BOASTFULNESS; *specif* **:** the frequent use of the words *I, my,* and *me* ⟨banish the ~ out of your conversation —Earl of Chesterfield⟩ **b :** a sense of self-importance **:** SELF-CENTEREDNESS, SELFISHNESS **2 :** a sense of superiority often accompanied by contempt toward others **:** PRIDE ⟨this ~, this arrogance, this complete indifference to what the rest of the world thinks of him —James Stern⟩ **3** [by alter.] **:** EGOISM 1a **syn** see CONCEIT

ego·tist \|_təst, |d·ə-\ *n* -S **:** one characterized by egotism **:** one marked by boastfulness or arrogance or egocentricity ⟨an atrocious ~ in his disregard of others —G.B.Shaw⟩ — **ego·tis·tic** \ˌ≈gə¦tistik, -gō¦-\ *or* **ego·tis·ti·cal** \-stəkəl, -tēk-\ *adj* — **ego·tis·ti·cal·ly** \-stək(ə)lē, -stēk-, -li\ *adv*

ego·tize \'≈gə,tīz, -gō-\ *vi* -ED/-ING/-S **:** to refer unduly to oneself

egre·gious \ə'grējəs, ē'- *sometimes* -jēəs\ *adj* [L *egregius*, fr. *e* out of (fr. *ex*) + *greg-, grex* flock, herd — more at EX-, GREGARIOUS] **1** *archaic* **:** remarkable for good quality **:** DISTINGUISHED, STRIKING **2 :** conspicuous for bad quality or taste **:** NOTORIOUS ⟨the ~ epicure who condescended to take only one bite out of the sunny side of a peach —J.G.Lockhart⟩ ⟨a bilious combination of brummagem melodrama and synthetic seascapes . . . the picture is ~ —John McCarten⟩ **3 a :** EXTRAORDINARY, EXTREME ⟨a published story which seemed too ~ to be believed —*Economist*⟩ **b :** FLAGRANT ⟨~ errors⟩ ⟨some Germans, conditioned by experience to ~ behavior on the part of their rulers —E.J.Kahn⟩ **4 :** ASOCIAL ⟨it is rather a gregarious instinct to keep together by minding each other's business . . . we must be preserved from becoming ~ —Robert Frost⟩ — **egre·gious·ly** *adv* — **egre·gious·ness** *n* -ES

¹egress \'ē,gres\ *n* -ES [L *egressus*, fr. *egressus*, past part. of *egredi* to go out, come out, fr. *e-* + *-gredi* (fr. *gradi* to step, go) — more at GRADE] **1 :** the act or right of going or coming out (as from a place of confinement) ⟨provided that reasonable means of ingress and ~ be allowed to the livestock —*Farmer's Weekly (So. Africa)*⟩; *specif* **:** the emergence of a celestial object from eclipse, occultation, or transit **2 :** a place or means of going out **:** EXIT, OUTLET ⟨a small room whose only ~ . . . was . . . a mammoth rat hole —Agnes M. Cleaveland⟩

²egress \(')ē¦gres\ *vi* -ED/-ING/-ES [L *egressus*, past part.] **:** to go out **:** ISSUE

egres·sion \ē'greshən\ *n* -S [ME *egressioun*, fr. L *egression-, egressio* act of going out, fr. *egressus* (past part.) + *-ion-, -io* -ion] **1 :** an act of emergence or emigration **2** *obs* **:** OUTBURST

egres·sive \-esiv\ *adj* [L *egressus*, past part. + E *-ive*] **:** of or relating to egress **:** OUTGOING

egret \'ēgrə|t, ē'gre|, 'egrə| *also* 'ē,gre| *or* ə'gre|, *usu* |d.+V\ *n* -S [ME, fr. MF *aigrette*, fr. OProv *aigreta*, of Gmc origin; akin to OHG *heigaro* heron — more at HERON] **1 :** any of various herons that bear long plumes on the lower back during the breeding season and commonly have pure white plumage — see AMERICAN EGRET, CATTLE EGRET, SNOWY EGRET **2 :** an egret plume or a plume resembling it **:** AIGRETTE

egret monkey *n* [F *aigrette;* fr. the tuft on top of its head] **:** an East Indian macaque (*Macaca cynomolga*)

egual·men·te \ˌāgwäl'mān·tā\ *adv* [It, equally, even, adv. of *eguale* equal, even, fr. L *aequalis* equal — more at EQUAL] **:** EVENLY — used as a direction in music

eguei·ite \e'gwā,īt\ *n* -S [F *egueïite*, fr. *Egueï* region, Chad territory, French Equatorial Africa + F *-ite*] **:** a mineral that consists of a hydrous basic ferric iron phosphate with a little calcium and aluminum and that occurs in nodules in clay

egypt \'ējəpt\ *adj, usu cap* [fr. *Egypt*, country in northeastern Africa] **:** of or from Egypt **:** of the kind or style prevalent in Egypt **:** EGYPTIAN

egyp·ti·ac \ə'jiptē,ak, (')ē¦j-\ *adj, usu cap* [L *Aegyptiacus*, fr. Gk *Aigyptiakos*, fr. *Aigyptos* Egypt] **:** of or relating to ancient Egypt ⟨*Egyptiac* society . . . became extinct in the 5th century of the Christian era —A.J.Toynbee⟩

¹egyp·tian \-pshən\ *adj, usu cap* [ME *Egipcian*, fr. OF *egipcien*, adj. & n., fr. *Egipte* Egypt (fr. L *Aegyptus*, fr. Gk *Aigyptos*) + OF *-ien* -ian] **1 :** of or relating to Egypt, the Egyptians, or the Egyptian language ⟨*Egyptian* architecture⟩ ⟨*Egyptian* conquest⟩ **2** [fr. the reference in Exod 10:22 to a plague of darkness visited upon Egypt] **:** EXTREME, INTENSE — usu. used in the phrase *Egyptian darkness*

²egyptian \"\ *n* -S *cap* [ME *Egipcien, Egipcian*, fr. MF *egipcien*] **1 :** a native or inhabitant of Egypt **2 :** the Afro-Asiatic language of the ancient Egyptians from earliest times to about the 3d century A.D. — compare COPTIC, DEMOTIC EGYPTIAN, MIDDLE EGYPTIAN, NEW EGYPTIAN, OLD EGYPTIAN; see AFRO-ASIATIC LANGUAGES table **3 :** the ancient Egyptian system of writing in any of its forms — see DEMOTIC, HIERATIC, HIEROGLYPHIC **4** *obs* **:** GYPSY **5** [so called fr. the fact that Cairo is a principal city] **:** a native or inhabitant of southern Illinois — used as a nickname **6** *often not cap* **:** a heavy typeface having little contrast between thick and thin strokes and thick squared serifs

egyptian alfalfa weevil *n, usu cap E* **:** an Old World weevil (*Hypera brunneipennis*) related to the alfalfa weevil and established in western No. America where it feeds on alfalfa and various clovers

egyptian architecture *n, usu cap E* **:** the architecture of ancient Egypt from approximately 5000 B.C. to early Christian times — see ARCHITECTURE table

egyptian bean *n, usu cap E* **1 a :** INDIAN LOTUS **b :** the seed of the Indian lotus resembling a bean **2 :** HYACINTH BEAN

egyptian black *n, usu cap E* **:** BASALT 2

egyptian blue *n, usu cap E* **:** a blue silicate of copper and calcium used as a pigment by the ancient Egyptians and Romans

egyptian clover *n, usu cap E* **:** BERSEEM

egyptian corn *n, usu cap E* **:** SORGHUM; *esp* **:** DURRA

egyptian cotton *n, usu cap E* **:** a fine long-staple often somewhat brownish cotton grown chiefly in Egypt and believed to be a derivative of sea island cotton from which it is distinguished by shorter fiber length or of Peruvian cotton or possibly a hybrid between these or between one of these and unknown African cottons — see PIMA

egyptian cross *n, usu cap E* **:** TAU CROSS 1

egyptian ginger *n, usu cap E* **:** the root of the taro

egyptian goose *n, usu cap E* **:** a brightly colored bird (*Alopochen aegypticus*) of Africa and Palestine that is related to the sheldrakes but popularly regarded as a true goose and is often bred as an ornamental waterfowl

egyptian grass *n, usu cap E* **1 :** a creeping grass (*Dactyloctenium aegypticum*) with spikes like fingers — called also *crab grass, crowfoot grass* **2 :** JOHNSON GRASS

egyptian green *n, often cap E* **:** a moderate green that is yellower, lighter, and stronger than sea green (sense 1a) and bluer, lighter, and stronger than myrtle green (sense 3a) or average laurel green (sense 1)

egyptian gum *n, usu cap E* **:** GUM ARABIC

egyptian hallel *n, usu cap E&H* **:** HALLEL

egyptian henbane *n, usu cap E* **:** the leaves of an herb (*Hyoscyamus muticus*) used as a source of hyoscyamine

egyptian henna *n, usu cap E* **:** HENNA 1

egyptian indigo *n, usu cap E* **1 :** an indigo yielded by a shrub (*Tephrosia apolinea*) of southern Europe **2 :** the shrub that yields Egyptian indigo

egyp·tian·ism \-shə,nizəm\ *n* -S *usu cap* **:** a quality or group of qualities characteristic of Egypt, its people, or its language

egyp·tian·i·za·tion \≈ˌ≈shənə'zāshən, -ˌnī'z-\ *n* -S *usu cap* **:** the act or process of Egyptianizing or the state of being Egyptianized ⟨decreed the *Egyptianization* of British and French banks —*Newsweek*⟩

egyp·tian·ize \≈'≈≈,nīz\ *vt* -ED/-ING/-S *usu cap* [*Egyptian* + *-ize*] **:** to make Egyptian (as in quality, traits, or ownership)

egyptian jackal *n, usu cap E* **:** a large wild dog (*Canis anthus lupaster* or *C. lupaster*) of northern Africa that resembles a wolf in size and proportions

egyptian lotus *n, usu cap E* **1 :** either of two water lilies held sacred by the Egyptians: **a :** a white lily (*Nymphaea lotus*) **b :** a blue lily (*N. caerulea*) **2 :** INDIAN LOTUS

egyptian lupine *n, usu cap E* **:** an erect hairy annual legume (*Lupinus termis*) orig. of the eastern Mediterranean but introduced into certain dry regions of the U.S. that has white flowers tinged with blue on the standard and bluish green on the keel apex

egyptian millet *n, usu cap E* **:** JOHNSON GRASS

egyptian onion *n, usu cap E* **:** TREE ONION

egyptian ophthalmia *n, usu cap E* **:** TRACHOMA

egyptian privet *n, usu cap E* **:** HENNA 1

egyptian red *n, often cap E* **:** a dark red to strong reddish brown

egyptian soaproot *n, usu cap E* **:** a European herb (*Gypsophila struthium*) having a 5-angled inflated calyx

egyptian thorn *n, usu cap E* **:** BABUL 1a — used esp. of the tree as it occurs in the Sudan where it is a source of high-grade gum arabic; compare AMRAD GUM

egyptian vulture *n, usu cap E* **:** a small vulture (*Neophron percnopterus*) with largely white plumage that is widely distributed over much of Africa, southern Europe, and southern Asia — called also *Pharaoh's chicken*

egyptian wheat *n, usu cap E* **1 :** any of certain bearded branching wheats cultivated since ancient times **2 :** PEARL MILLET **3 :** a grain sorghum resembling kafir corn

egyp·tic·i·ty \(ˌ)ē,jip'tisəd·ē, ˌējəp-, ə,jip-\ *n* -ES *usu cap* [*Egypt* + *-icity* (as in *eccentricity*)] **:** EGYPTIANISM

egypt·ize \'ējəp,tīz, ē'jip-\ *vi* -ED/-ING/-S *often cap* [*Egypt* + E *-ize*] **:** to become Egyptian (as in quality or traits)

egypto- *comb form, cap* [prob. fr. F *égypto-*, fr. Gk *aigypto-*, fr. *Aigyptos* Egypt] **1 :** Egypt ⟨*Egypto*logy⟩ **2 :** Egyptian and ⟨*Egypto*-Arabic⟩ ⟨*Egypto*-Greek⟩

egyp·to·log·i·cal \(¦)ē¦jiptə¦läjəkəl, ə¦jip-, ¦ējəp-, -¦äjēk-\ *adj, usu cap* **:** of or relating to Egyptology ⟨~ studies⟩

egyp·tol·o·gist \(ˌ)ē,jip'täləjəst, ə,jip-, ˌējəp-\ *n* -S *usu cap* **:** a specialist in Egyptology

egyp·tol·o·gy \-ləjē, -ji\ *n* -ES *usu cap* [*Egypto* + *-logy*] **:** the study of Egyptian antiquities

eh \'(h)ā(ⁿ), '(h)ai(ⁿ), '(h)e(e)(ⁿ)(?), '(h)a(a)(ⁿ)(?), '(h)ȧ(ȧ)(ⁿ)(?), *all with interrogatory intonation*\ *interj* [ME *ey*] — used to invite confirmation or to express inquiry or slight surprise

Eh \(')ē¦āch\ *symbol* standard oxidation-reduction potential

ehat·i·saht \ā'hädə,sät\ *n, pl* **ehatisaht** *or* **ehatisahts** *usu cap* **1 :** an Indian people of Vancouver Island **2 :** a member of the Ehatisaht people

EHF *abbr, often not cap* extremely high frequency

EHP *abbr* **1** effective horsepower **2** electric horsepower

eh·re·tia \e'rēsh(ē)ə\ *n* [NL, fr. George D. *Ehret* †1770 Ger. botanical illustrator + NL *-ia*] **1** *cap* **:** a large genus (family Boraginaceae) of tropical or subtropical shrubs and trees having cymose usu. white flowers succeeded by fleshy drupes **2** -S **:** any plant of the genus *Ehretia*

eh·rings·dorf man \'eriŋz,dȯrf-, 'ār-\ *n, usu cap E* [fr. *Ehringsdorf*, village near Weimar, Germany] **:** an early Neanderthal man known from skeletal remains found associated with Acheulean and pre-Mousterian artifacts near Weimar

ehr·lich's 606 \'erlik(s)¦sik(ˌ)sō'siks, 'ār-, -lik(-\ *n, usu cap E* [after Paul *Ehrlich* †1915 Ger. bacteriologist] **:** ARSPHENAMINE

EHT *abbr* extra high tension

ehu·a·wa \ˌā(ˌ)hü'äwə\ *n* -S [Hawaiian] **:** a sedge (*Cyperus laevigatus*) cultivated as a fiber plant in Hawaii

-ei *pl of* -EUS

EI *abbr* **1** endorsement irregular **2** extra-illustrated

eich·hor·nia \ī'kȯrnēə, īk'hȯ-\ *n, cap* [NL, fr. Johann A. F. *Eichhorn* †1856 Prussian official + NL *-ia*] **:** a genus of chiefly tropical floating aquatic herbs (family Pontederiaceae) having rounded or broad clustered leaves with inflated petioles — see WATER HYACINTH

eicosa- *or* **eicos-** *comb form* [ISV, fr. Gk *eikosa-, eikos-* twenty, fr. *eikosi* — more at VICENARY] **:** containing 20 atoms (as of carbon) ⟨*eicos*ane⟩

ei·co·sane \'īkə,sān\ *n* -S [ISV *eicosa-* + *-ane*] **:** any of the isomeric hydrocarbons $C_{20}H_{42}$ of the methane series; *esp* **:** normal eicosane $CH_3(CH_2)_{18}CH_3$ obtained as a colorless solid from paraffin wax

ei·co·sa·no·ic acid \ˌīkəsə¦nōik-\ *n* [ISV *eicosane* + *-o-* + *-ic*] **:** ARACHIDIC ACID

eid- *or* **eido-** *comb form* [Gk, form, fr. *eidos* — more at IDOL] **:** image **:** figure ⟨*eid*optometry⟩

eide *pl of* EIDOS

ei·dent \'īdᵊnt\ *adj* [ME (northern dial.) *ithen, ithand*, fr. ON *ithinn, īthen*, fr. *ith, īth* work, activity; akin to OE *īdig* busy] *chiefly Scot* **:** diligent and conscientious **:** HARDWORKING ⟨~ in Scotland's cause⟩ — **ei·dent·ly** *adv*

ei·der \'īdə(r)\ *n* -S [D, G, or Sw, fr. Icel *æthur*, fr. ON *æthr;* akin to Sw dial. *åd, åda* eider duck] **1** *or* **eider duck :** any of several large northern sea ducks constituting *Somateria* and related genera and being distinguished by the profuse fine soft down that forms an insulating layer protecting the body from cold, that is used by the female for lining the nest, and that is eagerly sought by man resulting in near extinction of the birds in some areas **2 :** EIDERDOWN 1

eiderdown \'≈≈,≈\ *n* [prob. fr. G *eiderdaune*, fr. Icel *æthardūnn*, fr. *æthar* (gen. of *æthur*) + *dūnn* down, fr. ON — more at DOWN] **1 :** the down of the eider valued for its lightness, softness, resiliency, and warmth **2 :** a quilt or comforter; *esp* **:** one filled with eiderdown **3 :** a soft lightweight clothing fabric knitted or woven of wool, cotton, or man-made fibers and napped on one or both sides

¹ei·det·ic \(')ī¦ded·ik\ *adj* [Gk *eidētikos*, fr. *eidos* + *-ētikos* -etic] **1 a :** of, relating to, or having the characteristics of eide, essences, forms, or images **b :** INTUITIONIST ⟨phenomenology . . . attempts the construction of a priori sciences on the basis of concrete intuition — pure grammar, pure logic, pure law, the ~ science of the world intuitively apprehended —Maurice Natanson⟩ **2 :** of or relating to voluntarily producible visual images having almost photographic accuracy **:** VIVID, LIFELIKE ⟨perhaps the artists have a greater ~ power than most adults —Franz Boas⟩ — **ei·det·i·cal·ly** \ed·ək(ə)lē\ *adv*

²eidetic \"\ *n* -S **:** one that experiences eidetic images

eidolo- — see IDOLO-

ei·do·lon \ī'dōlən\ *n, pl* **eidolons** \-lənz\ *or* **eido·la** \-lə\ [Gk *eidōlon* phantom, image, idol — more at IDOL] **1 :** an unsubstantial image ⟨free from her troubles among the ~s of sleep —J.C.Powys⟩ **:** PHANTOM **2 a :** an ideal figure ⟨he had created in the Boss an ~ a half century before this machine-age man became triumphant in history —H.S.Canby⟩ or idealized person ⟨Lincoln . . . the ~ of democracy —G.W. Johnson⟩ **:** EXEMPLAR **b :** IDEAL ⟨psychiatry's ~ of the personality completely . . . at home in the world —Bernard DeVoto⟩ **3 :** a small winged figure human or combining human with animal elements found in Greek vase painting

ei·dos \'ī,däs, 'ā,-\ *n, pl* **ei·de** \'ī,dē, 'ā,dā\ [Gk, lit., shape, form — more at IDOL] **1 :** something that is seen or intuited: **a** *in Platonism* **:** IDEA **b** *in Aristotelianism* (1) **:** FORM, ESSENCE (2) **:** SPECIES **c :** an appearance, conception, or form of intuition **2 :** the cognitive part of cultural structure made up of the criteria of credibility, the logic used in thinking and acting, and the basic ideas by which the members of a culture organize and interpret experience **:** logical structure ⟨the ~ is visible wherever group behavior is characterized by intellectual efforts of a similar kind —S.F.Nadel⟩ — contrasted with *ethos*

ei·fe·li·an \(')ī¦fēlēən\ *adj, usu cap* [*Eifel*, region in western Germany + E *-ian*] **:** of, relating to, or constituting a subdivision of the European Devonian — see GEOLOGIC TIME table

ei·gen·frequency \'īgən+,-\ *n* [part trans. of G *eigenfrequenz*, fr. *eigen-* peculiar to, characteristic (fr. *eigen* own, fr. OHG *eigan*) + *frequenz* frequency — more at OWN] **:** one of the frequencies with which a given oscillatory system is capable of vibrating

ei·gen·function \"+,-\ *n* [part trans. of G *eigenfunktion*, fr. *eigen-* + *funktion* function] **:** the solution of a differential equation (as the Schrödinger wave equation) satisfying specified conditions

ei·gen·state \"+,-\ *n* [part trans. of G *eigenstand*, fr. *eigen-* + *stand* state, condition] **:** a state of a quantized dynamic system (as an atom, molecule, or crystal) in which one of the variables defining the state (as energy or angular momentum) has a determinate fixed value

ei·gen·tone \"+,-\ *n* [part. trans. of G *eigenton*, fr. *eigen-* + *ton* tone] **:** a tone or one of several tones produced by and characteristic of a vibrating body or system

ei·gen·value \"+,-\ *n* [part trans. of G *eigenwert*, fr. *eigen-* + *wert* value] **:** any of the permissible values of a parameter in an eigenfunction (as the discrete values of the energy in the solution of the Schrödinger wave equation)

¹eight \'āt, *usu* 'ād.+V\ *adj* [ME *eighte*, fr. OE *eahta;* akin to OHG *ahto* eight, ON *ātta*, Goth *ahtau*, L *octo*, Gk *oktō*, Skt *aṣṭā*] **:** being one more than seven in number ⟨~ years⟩ — see NUMBER table

²eight \"\ *pron, pl in constr* [ME *eighte*, fr. OE *eahte*, fr. *eahta*, adj.] **:** eight countable persons or things not specified but under consideration and being enumerated ⟨~ are here⟩

³eight \"\ *n* -S [ME *eighte*, fr. *eighte*, adj. & pron.] **1 :** twice four **:** four times two **:** the cube of two **2 a :** eight units or objects ⟨a total of ~⟩ **b :** a group or set of eight ⟨arranged by ~s⟩ **3 a :** the numerable quantity symbolized by the arabic numeral 8 **b :** the figure 8 **4 :** eight o'clock — compare BELL table, TIME illustration **5 :** the eighth in a set or series: as **a :** a playing card marked to show that it is eighth in a suit **b :** an article of clothing of the eighth size ⟨wears an ~⟩ **6 :** FIGURE EIGHT e **7 :** something having as an essential feature eight units or members: as **a :** an octosyllabic usu. iambic line of verse — usu. used in pl. ⟨a poem in ~s⟩ **b eights** *pl* **:** OCTAVO ⟨a book printed in ~s⟩ **c** (1) **:** an 8-oared racing boat (2) **:** the crew of such a boat **d :** an 8-cylinder engine or automobile **8 eights** *pl but sing in constr* **:** a game in which each successive player must play a card either of the same suit or of the same rank as that played by the preceding player or may play an eight and call for any suit and in which the object is to get rid of all one's cards first — called also *crazy eights*

eight ball *n* **1 :** a black pool ball numbered 8 **2 :** a game of pool played with a cue ball and 15 object balls in which a player or side must pocket either the balls numbered from one to seven or nine to 15 and in which the winner is the player or side that first pockets its numerical group and then legally pockets the eight ball **3 :** a round black nondirectional microphone **4** *slang* **:** NEGRO — usu. used disparagingly **5** *slang* **:** a soldier often in trouble **:** MISFIT, SAD SACK ⟨for . . . a chronic *eight ball* in perpetual flight from life, going AWOL is an easy decision —Taliaferro Boatwright⟩ — **behind the eight ball :** in a highly disadvantageous position or baffling situation ⟨finds himself *behind the eight ball*, unable to buy the things his family needs —Philip Murray †1952⟩

¹eigh·teen \(')ā(t)¦tēn *sometimes* (')ād¦ēn\ *adj* [ME *eightetene, eightene*, fr. OE *eahtatīene, eahtatȳne, eahtatēne* (akin to OHG *ahtozehan* eighteen, ON *āttjān, ātjān*), fr. *eahta* eight + *-tīene, -tȳne, -tēne* (fr. *tīen, tȳn, tēn* ten) — more at EIGHT, TEN] **:** being one more than 17 in number ⟨~ years⟩ — see NUMBER table; used prepositively to designate certain years of the 19th century ⟨the *eighteen-eighties*⟩ ⟨the early *eighteen*-hundreds⟩

²eighteen \"\ *pron, pl in constr* [ME *eightetene, eightene*, fr. OE *eahtatīene, eahtatȳne, eahtatēne*, fr. *eahtatīene, eahtatȳne, eahtatēne*, adj.] **:** 18 countable persons or things not specified but under consideration and being enumerated ⟨~ are here⟩

³eighteen \"\ *n* -S **1 :** 10 and eight **:** twice nine **:** nine times two **:** three times six **2 a :** 18 units or objects ⟨a total of ~⟩ **b :** a group or set of 18 **3 :** the numerable quantity symbolized by the arabic numerals 18 **4 :** the 18th in a set or series; *esp* **:** an article of clothing of the 18th size ⟨wears an ~⟩ **5 :** EIGHTEENMO — usu. used in pl. ⟨a book printed in ~s⟩ **6 :** something having as an essential feature 18 units or members

eigh·teen·mo \≈'≈,mō\ *n* -S [*eighteen* + *-mo* (as in *duodecimo*)] **:** the size of a piece of paper cut 18 from a sheet; *also* **:** paper or a page of this size — abbr. *18mo;* symbol *18°;* see BOOK tables

eighteen-one balkline *n* **:** a carom billiards game in which balklines are 18 inches from the cushions and a player may score only one point when balls are in balk — usu. written *18.1 balkline;* compare EIGHTEEN-TWO BALKLINE

¹eigh·teenth \(')ā(t)¦tēn(t)th *sometimes* (')ād-¦ē-\ *adj* [ME *eightetenthe, eightenthe*, adj. & n., alter. (influenced by *eightetene, eightene*) of *eightetethe, eightethe*, fr. OE *eahtatēotha, eahtēotha* (akin to ON *āttjāndi, ātjāndi* eighteenth), fr. *eahtatīene, eahtatȳne, eahtatēne* eighteen + *-otha, -tha* -th] **1 :** being number 18 in a countable series ⟨the ~ day⟩ — see NUMBER table **2 :** being one of 18 equal parts into which something is divisible ⟨an ~ share of the money⟩

²eighteenth \"\ *n, pl* **eighteenths** \-n(t)s,-n(t)ths\ [ME *eightetenthe, eightenthe*] **1 :** number 18 in a countable series

⟨the ~ of the month⟩ **2 :** the quotient of a unit divided by 18 **:** one of 18 equal parts of something ⟨one ~ of the total⟩
eighteen-two balkline *n* **:** a carom billiards game in which the balklines are 18 inches from the cushions and a player may score two points when the balls are in balk — usu. written *18.2 balkline;* compare EIGHTEEN-ONE BALKLINE
eight·er from de·ca·tur \ˌād·ə(r)f(r)əmdə'kād·ə(r), -mdē'k-\ *usu cap D* [rhyming slang: *Decatur* prob. fr. *Decatur*, Ill.] *slang* **:** the throw of eight in craps
eightfoil \'=,=\ *n* **:** DOUBLE QUATREFOIL
¹eight·fold \'āt¦fōld\ *adj* [ME *eightefold*, fr. OE *eahtafeald*, fr. *eahta* eight + *-feald* -fold] **1 :** having eight parts or aspects **2 :** being eight times as large, as great, or as many as some understood size, degree, or amount ⟨an ~ increase⟩
²eightfold \"\ *adv* **:** to eight times as much or as many **:** by eight times ⟨increased ~⟩
eightfold path *n, usu cap E & P* **:** the Buddhist teaching of the means of attaining Nirvana through rightness of belief, resolve, speech, action, livelihood, effort, thought, and meditation — see FOUR NOBLE TRUTHS
eight-foot octave *n* **:** GREAT OCTAVE
eight-foot pitch *n* **:** the pitch of an 8-foot stop on a pipe organ
eight-foot stop *n* **:** a pipe-organ stop sounding the pitches indicated by the notes, the lowest pipe of such a stop being approximately eight feet in length — compare FOUR-FOOT STOP, SIXTEEN-FOOT STOP
eight-four \'=¦=\ *adj* **:** of or relating to a plan of school organization with eight elementary and four secondary grades — compare SIX-THREE-THREE
eight-gauge \'=¦=\ *adj, of a shotgun* **:** having a bore 0.835 inch in diameter
¹eighth \'ātth, ÷'āth\ *adj* [ME *eightethe, eighthe*, adj. & n., fr. OE *eahtotha* (akin to OHG *ahtodo* eighth, ON *āttandi*, Goth *ahtudin*, dat. sing. masc.) fr. *eahta* eight + *-otha, -tha* -th — more at EIGHT] **1 :** being number eight in a countable series ⟨the ~ day⟩ — see NUMBER table **2 :** being one of eight equal parts into which something is divisible ⟨an ~ share of the money⟩
²eighth \"\ *n, pl* **eighths** \'āts, 'ātths, ÷'āths\ [ME *eightethe, eighthe*] **1 :** number eight in a countable series ⟨the ~ of the month⟩ **2 :** the quotient of a unit divided by eight **:** one of eight equal parts of something ⟨one ~ of the total⟩ **3 a :** OCTAVE **b :** EIGHTH NOTE
³eighth \"\ *adv* **1 :** in the eighth place **2 :** with seven exceptions ⟨the nation's ~ largest city⟩
eighth cranial nerve *or* **eighth nerve** *n* **:** AUDITORY NERVE
eighth·ly \'ātthlē, ÷'āth-\ *adv* **:** in the eighth place ⟨the search is . . . , ~, a search for ideals —R.G.F.Robinson⟩
eighth note *n* **:** a musical note with the time value of one eighth of a whole note — called also *quaver*

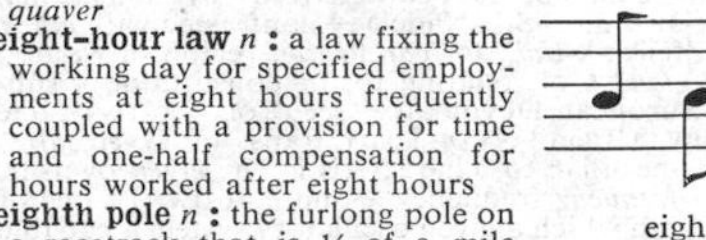
eighth notes

eight-hour law *n* **:** a law fixing the working day for specified employments at eight hours frequently coupled with a provision for time and one-half compensation for hours worked after eight hours
eighth pole *n* **:** the furlong pole on a racetrack that is ⅛ of a mile from the finish
eighth rest *n* **:** a musical rest corresponding in value to an eighth note
¹eight·i·eth \'ād·ēəth, 'āt¦, ¦iəth\ *adj* [ME *eightetithe, eightithe*, adj. & n., fr. OE *hundeahtatigotha*, fr. *hundeahtatig* eighty + *-otha -tha* -th — more at EIGHTY] **1 :** being number 80 in a countable series ⟨the ~ day⟩ — see NUMBER table **2 :** being one of 80 equal parts into which something is divisible ⟨an ~ share of the money⟩
²eightieth \"\ *n* -s [ME *eightetithe, eightithe*] **1 :** number 80 in a countable series **2 :** the quotient of a unit divided by 80 **:** one of 80 equal parts of something ⟨one ~ of the total⟩
eight·ling \'ātliŋ\ *n* -s **:** a compound or twin crystal made up of eight individuals
eight·pen·ny nail \'āt,penē-, -ni-\ *n* [so called fr. the former price per hundred nails] **:** a nail typically 2½ inches long
eight-pointed cross \'=,==-\ *n* **:** MALTESE CROSS 1b
eights *pl of* EIGHT
eight·some \'ātsəm\ *n* -s *often attrib* [¹*eight* + *-some*] **:** a Scottish reel for eight dancers
eight-spotted forester \'=,==-\ *n* **:** a familiar day-flying moth (*Alypia octomaculata*) of the eastern U.S. that is black with eight conspicuous pale spots on the wings and has humped and transversely striped larvae which often defoliate ornamental vines and grapevines
eight-square \'=¦=\ *adj* **:** OCTAGONAL ⟨an *eight-square* rifle barrel⟩
¹eighty \'ād·|ē, 'āt|, |i\ *adj* [ME *eightety, eighty*, fr. OE *eahtatig*, short for *hundeahtatig*, fr. *hundeahtatig*, n., group of 80, fr. *hund* hundred + *eahta* eight + *-tig* group of ten; akin to OHG *-zug* group of ten, ON *tigr*, Goth *-tigjus;* all derivatives fr. the root of OE *tīen, tȳn, tēn* ten — more at HUNDRED, EIGHT, TEN] **:** being one more than 79 in number ⟨~ years⟩ — see NUMBER table
²eighty \"\ *pron, pl in constr* [ME *eightety, eighty*, fr. *eightety eighty* adj.] **:** 80 countable persons or things not specified but under consideration and being enumerated ⟨~ are here⟩ ⟨~ were found⟩
³eighty \"\ *n* -ES **1 :** eight tens **:** twice 40 **:** five times 16 **:** four twenties **:** FOURSCORE **2 a :** 80 units or objects ⟨a total of ~⟩ **b :** a group or set of 80 **3 :** the numerable quantity symbolized by the arabic numerals 80 **4 :** the 80th in a set or series **5 :** something having as an essential feature 80 units or members **6 :** an 80-acre tract of land **7 eighties** *pl* **a :** the numbers 80 to 89 inclusive ⟨a golf score in the *eighties*⟩ ⟨all his grades in that subject are in the *eighties*⟩ **b :** the members of a series or set of successive numbers that end in 80 to 89 inclusive ⟨the *eighties* of the preceding century⟩ ⟨lives in the *eighties* in the next block⟩ **c :** the portion of a continuum lying between 80 and 90 on a scale of measurement or segmentation ⟨temperatures in the high *eighties* tomorrow⟩ ⟨a man still vigorous in his *eighties*⟩
¹eighty-eight \¦==¦=\ *adj* **:** being one more than 87 in number ⟨*eighty-eight* years⟩ — see NUMBER table
²eighty-eight \"\ *pron, pl in constr* **:** 88 countable persons or things not specified but under consideration and being enumerated ⟨*eighty-eight* are here⟩ ⟨*eighty-eight* were found⟩
³eighty-eight \"\ *n* **1 :** eight and 80 **:** four times 22 **:** eight times 11 **2 a :** 88 units or objects ⟨a total of *eighty-eight*⟩ **b :** a group or set of 88 **3 :** the numerable quantity symbolized by the arabic numerals 88 **4 :** the 88th in a set or series **5** [so called fr. the standard number of keys] *slang* **:** PIANO **6 :** an 88 millimeter gun
eighty-eighter \ˌād·ē'ād·ə(r)\ *n, slang* **:** PIANIST
¹eighty-eighth \¦==¦=\ *adj* **1 :** being number 88 in a countable series ⟨the *eighty-eighth* day⟩ — see NUMBER table **2 :** being one of 88 equal parts into which something is divisible ⟨an *eighty-eighth* share of the money⟩
²eighty-eighth \"\ *n* **1 :** number 88 in a countable series **2 :** the quotient of a unit divided by 88 **:** one of 88 equal parts of something ⟨one *eighty-eighth* of the total⟩
¹eighty-fifth \¦==¦=\ *adj* **1 :** being number 85 in a countable series ⟨the *eighty-fifth* day⟩ — see NUMBER table **2 :** being one of 85 equal parts into which something is divisible ⟨an *eighty-fifth* share of the money⟩
²eighty-fifth \"\ *n* **1 :** number 85 in a countable series **2 :** the quotient of a unit divided by 85 **:** one of 85 equal parts of something ⟨one *eighty-fifth* of the total⟩
¹eighty-first \¦==¦=\ *adj* **1 :** being number 81 in a countable series ⟨the *eighty-first* day⟩ — see NUMBER table **2 :** being one of 81 equal parts into which something is divisible ⟨an *eighty-first* share of the money⟩
²eighty-first \"\ *n* **1 :** number 81 in a countable series **2 :** the quotient of a unit divided by 81 **:** one of 81 equal parts of something ⟨one *eighty-first* of the total⟩
¹eighty-five \¦==¦=\ *adj* **:** being one more than 84 in number ⟨*eighty-five* years⟩ — see NUMBER table
²eighty-five \"\ *pron, pl in constr* **:** 85 countable persons or things not specified but under consideration and being enumerated ⟨*eighty-five* are here⟩ ⟨*eighty-five* were found⟩
³eighty-five \"\ *n* **1 :** five and 80 **:** five times 17 **2 a :** 85 units or objects ⟨a total of *eighty-five*⟩ **b :** a group or set of 85 **3 :** the numerable quantity symbolized by the arabic numerals 85 **4 :** the 85th in a set or series
¹eighty-four \¦==¦=\ *adj* **:** being one more than 83 in number ⟨*eighty-four* years⟩ — see NUMBER table
²eighty-four \"\ *pron, pl in constr* **:** 84 countable persons or things not specified but under consideration and being enumerated ⟨*eighty-four* are here⟩ ⟨*eighty-four* were found⟩
³eighty-four \"\ *n* **1 :** four and 80 **:** three times 28 **:** four times 21 **:** six times 14 **:** seven times 12 **:** seven dozen **2 a :** 84 units or objects ⟨a total of *eighty-four*⟩ **b :** a group or set of 84 **3 :** the numerable quantity symbolized by the arabic numerals 84 **4 :** the 84th in a set or series
¹eighty-fourth \¦==¦=\ *adj* **1 :** being number 84 in a countable series ⟨the *eighty-fourth* day⟩ — see NUMBER table **2 :** being one of 84 equal parts into which something is divisible ⟨an *eighty-fourth* share of the money⟩
²eighty-fourth \"\ *n* **1 :** number 84 in a countable series **2 :** the quotient of a unit divided by 84 **:** one of 84 equal parts of something ⟨one *eighty-fourth* of the total⟩
¹eighty-nine \¦==¦=\ *adj* **:** being one more than 88 in number ⟨*eighty-nine* years⟩ — see NUMBER table
²eighty-nine \"\ *pron, pl in constr* **:** 89 countable persons or things not specified but under consideration and being enumerated ⟨*eighty-nine* are here⟩ ⟨*eighty-nine* were found⟩
³eighty-nine \"\ *n* **1 :** nine and 80 **2 a :** 89 units or objects ⟨a total of *eighty-nine*⟩ **b :** a group or set of 89 **3 :** the numerable quantity symbolized by the arabic numerals 89 **4 :** the 89th in a set or series
eighty-niner \ˌād·ē'nīnə(r)\ *n* -s **:** one that entered Oklahoma when it was opened to settlement in 1889
¹eighty-ninth \¦==¦=\ *adj* **1 :** being number 89 in a countable series ⟨the *eighty-ninth* day⟩ — see NUMBER table **2 :** being one of 89 equal parts into which something is divisible ⟨an *eighty-ninth* share of the money⟩
²eighty-ninth \"\ *n* **1 :** number 89 in a countable series **2 :** the quotient of a unit divided by 89 **:** one of 89 equal parts of something ⟨one *eighty-ninth* of the total⟩
¹eighty-one \¦==¦=\ *adj* **:** being one more than eighty in number ⟨*eighty-one* years⟩ — see NUMBER table
²eighty-one \"\ *pron, pl in constr* **:** 81 countable persons or things not specified but under consideration and being enumerated ⟨*eighty-one* are here⟩ ⟨*eighty-one* were found⟩
³eighty-one \"\ *n* **1 :** one and 80 **:** three times 27 **:** nine nines **:** the square of nine **2 a :** 81 units or objects ⟨a total of *eighty-one*⟩ **b :** a group or set of 81 **3 :** the numerable quantity symbolized by the arabic numerals 81 **4 :** the 81st in a set or series
¹eighty-second \¦==¦==\ *adj* **1 :** being number 82 in a countable series ⟨the *eighty-second* day⟩ — see NUMBER table **2 :** being one of 82 equal parts into which something is divisible ⟨an *eighty-second* share of the money⟩
²eighty-second \"\ *n* **1 :** number 82 in a countable series **2 :** the quotient of a unit divided by 82 **:** one of 82 equal parts of something ⟨one *eighty-second* of the total⟩
¹eighty-seven \¦==¦==\ *adj* **:** being one more than 86 in number ⟨*eighty-seven* years⟩ — see NUMBER table
²eighty-seven \"\ *pron, pl in constr* **:** 87 countable persons or things not specified but under consideration and being enumerated ⟨*eighty-seven* are here⟩ ⟨*eighty-seven* were found⟩
³eighty-seven \"\ *n* **1 :** seven and 80 **:** three times 29 **2 a :** 87 units or objects ⟨a total of *eighty-seven*⟩ **b :** a group or set of 87 **3 :** the numerable quantity symbolized by the arabic numerals 87 **4 :** the 87th in a set or series
¹eighty-seventh \¦==¦==\ *adj* **1 :** being number 87 in a countable series ⟨the *eighty-seventh* day⟩ — see NUMBER table **2 :** being one of 87 equal parts into which something is divisible ⟨an *eighty-seventh* share of the money⟩
²eighty-seventh \"\ *n* **1 :** number 87 in a countable series **2 :** the quotient of a unit divided by 87 **:** one of 87 equal parts of something ⟨one *eighty-seventh* of the total⟩
¹eighty-six \¦==¦=\ *adj* **:** being one more than 85 in number ⟨*eighty-six* years⟩ — see NUMBER table
²eighty-six \"\ *pron, pl in constr* **:** 86 countable persons or things not specified but under consideration and being enumerated ⟨*eighty-six* are here⟩ ⟨*eighty-six* were found⟩
³eighty-six \"\ *n* **1 :** six and 80 **:** 43 times two **2 a :** 86 units or objects ⟨a total of *eighty-six*⟩ **b :** a group or set of 86 **3 :** the numerable quantity symbolized by the arabic numerals 86 **4 :** the 86th in a set or series
¹eighty-sixth \¦==¦=\ *adj* **1 :** being number 86 in a countable series ⟨the *eighty-sixth* day⟩ — see NUMBER table **2 :** being one of 86 equal parts into which something is divisible ⟨an *eighty-sixth* share of the money⟩
²eighty-sixth \"\ *n* **1 :** number 86 in a countable series **2 :** the quotient of a unit divided by 86 **:** one of 86 equal parts of something ⟨one *eighty-sixth* of the total⟩
¹eighty-third \¦==¦=\ *adj* **1 :** being number 83 in a countable series ⟨the *eighty-third* day⟩ — see NUMBER table **2 :** being one of 83 equal parts into which something is divisible ⟨an *eighty-third* share of the money⟩
²eighty-third \"\ *n* **1 :** number 83 in a countable series **2 :** the quotient of a unit divided by 83 **:** one of 83 equal parts of something ⟨one *eighty-third* of the total⟩
¹eighty-three \¦==¦=\ *adj* **:** being one more than 82 in number ⟨*eighty-three* years⟩ — see NUMBER table
²eighty-three \"\ *pron, pl in constr* **:** 83 countable persons or things not specified but under consideration and being enumerated ⟨*eighty-three* are here⟩ ⟨*eighty-three* were found⟩
³eighty-three \"\ *n* **1 :** three and 80 **2 a :** 83 units or objects ⟨a total of *eighty-three*⟩ **b :** a group or set of 83 **3 :** the numerable quantity symbolized by the arabic numerals 83 **4 :** the 83d in a set or series
¹eighty-two \¦==¦=\ *adj* **:** being one more than 81 in number ⟨*eighty-two* years⟩ — see NUMBER table
²eighty-two \¦==¦=\ *pron, pl in constr* **:** 82 countable persons or things not specified but under consideration and being enumerated ⟨*eighty-two* are here⟩ ⟨*eighty-two* were found⟩
³eighty-two \"\ *n* **1 :** two and eighty **:** 41 times two **2 a :** 82 units or objects ⟨a total of *eighty-two*⟩ **b :** a group or set of 82 **3 :** the numerable quantity symbolized by the arabic numerals 82 **4 :** the 82d in a set or series
eigne \'ān\ *adj* [modif. of MF *ainé, aisné, ainsné*, fr. OF, fr. *ainz* before (fr. L *ante*) + *né* born — more at ANTE-, NEE] **:** ELDEST, FIRSTBORN
eijk·man test \'īk|mən-, 'āk|\ *n, usu cap E* [after Christiaan *Eijkman* †1930 Dutch physiologist] **:** a test for the identification of coliform bacteria from warm-blooded animals on the basis of their ability to produce gas or glucose media at 46° C
eik \'ēk, 'āk, 'əik\ *var of* EKE
eikon *var of* ICON
eikon- *or* **eikono-** — see ICON-
ei·ko·nom·e·ter \ˌīkə'nämәd·ə(r)\ *n* [*icon-* + *-meter*] **1 :** ICONOMETER **2 :** a device to detect aniseikonia or to test stereoscopic vision
¹eild \'ē(ə)ld\ *var of* ELD
²eild \'ē(ə)l(d)\ *adj* [ME *yeld*, fr. OE *gelde* barren, sterile — more at GELD] **1** *Scot, of an animal* **:** BARREN **2** *Scot, of a cow* **:** DRY
eil·ding \'ēldən, -diŋ\ *var of* ELDING
ei·me·ria \ī'mirēə\ *n, cap* [NL, fr. Theodor *Eimer* †1898 Ger. zoologist + NL *-ia*] **:** a genus of coccidia that invade the intestinal wall or other visceral epithelia of many vertebrates and some invertebrates and include serious pathogens — see EIMERIIDAE — **ei·me·ri·al** \(')ī¦mirēəl\ *adj* — **ei·me·ri·an** \-ēən\ *adj or n*
ei·me·ri·idae \ˌīmə'rīə,dē\ *n pl, cap* [NL, fr. *Eimeria*, type genus + *-idae*] **:** a family of coccidia that includes several genera (as *Eimeria* and *Isospora*) of medical or veterinary importance and with minor families constitutes a suborder of the order Coccidia
-ein *or* **-eine** *n suffix* -s [ISV, alter. of *-in, -ine*] **:** a compound distinguished from a compound with a name ending in *-in* or *-ine* — usu. *-eine* in names of bases and *-ein* in names of nonbases ⟨nicoteine⟩ ⟨phthalein⟩
eind·ho·ven \'īnt,hōvən, 'änt-\ *adj, usu cap* [fr. *Eindhoven*, Netherlands] **:** of or from the city of Eindhoven, Netherlands **:** of the kind or style prevalent in Eindhoven
ein·kan·ter \'īn,käntə(r)\ *n* -s [G, lit., something having one edge, fr. *ein* one (fr. OHG) + *kante* edge + *-er* — more at ONE, DREIKANTER] **:** a stone with a single sharp edge worn by wind-driven sand — compare DREIKANTER, VENTIFACT
ein·korn \'īn,kȯrn\ *n* -s [G, fr. OHG, fr. *ein* one + *korn* grain — more at CORN] **:** a one-grained wheat (*Triticum monococcum*) that has a short flat spike like barley, is regarded by some as the most primitive wheat, and is grown esp. in poor soils in central Europe
ein·stein \'īnz,tīn, 'īn,st- *sometimes* 'īn,sht-\ *n* -s [after *Albert Einstein* †1955 Am. physicist and mathematician] **1** *often cap* **:** the radiant energy of a given frequency required to effect the complete photochemical transformation of one mole of a photosensitive substance being equal to about 0.004 erg second times the frequency in question **2** *usu cap* **:** a mathematical genius ⟨the statistics . . . would give pause to an *Einstein —Official Guide to the Army Air Forces*⟩
einstein-bose statistics *n, usu cap E&B* **:** BOSE-EINSTEIN STATISTICS
einstein-de haas effect \-də'häs-\ *n, usu cap E&H* [after Albert *Einstein* and Arthur E. *de Haas* †1941 Austrian physicist] **:** a rotational impulse imparted to a body upon sudden magnetization — compare BARNETT EFFECT
einstein equation *n, usu cap E* [after Albert *Einstein*] **:** any of several equations in physics: as **a :** MASS-ENERGY EQUATION **b :** EINSTEIN'S PHOTOELECTRIC EQUATION **c :** a formula expressing the diffusion coefficient of suspended colloidal particles as the product of the Boltzmann's constant, the Kelvin temperature, and the particle mobility
ein·stein·ian \'=,=ēən, ='===\ *adj, usu cap* [Albert *Einstein* + E *-ian*] **:** of or relating to Albert Einstein or his theories
ein·stein·ium \'=,=ēəm, ='===\ *n* -s [NL, fr. Albert *Einstein* + NL *-ium*] **:** a radioactive element artificially produced (as by bombardment of plutonium with neutrons) — symbol *Es* or *E;* see ELEMENT table
einstein law of photochemical equivalence *usu cap 1st E* [after Albert *Einstein*] **:** a law in quantum theory: each molecule activated in any photochemical process absorbs one photon of radiant energy — compare EINSTEIN 1
einstein shift *or* **einstein effect** *n, usu cap 1st E* [after Albert *Einstein*] **:** a slight displacement of the lines in the spectra of very dense stars from their normal wavelength positions toward the red — compare RED SHIFT
einstein's photoelectric equation *n, cap 1st E* [after Albert *Einstein*] **:** an equation in physics giving the kinetic energy of a photoelectron emitted from a metal as a result of the absorption of a radiation quantum: $E_k = h\nu - \omega$ where E_k is the kinetic energy of the photoelectron, *h* is the Planck constant, ν is the frequency associated with the radiation quantum, and ω the work function of the metal
einstein temperature *n, usu cap E* [after Albert *Einstein*] **:** DEBYE TEMPERATURE
einstein theory *n, usu cap E* [after Albert *Einstein*] **:** the theory of relativity
ei·rann \'a(a)rən, 'er-,'ār-\ *adj, usu cap* [IrGael *Ēireannach*, fr. *Ēire*] **:** IRISH
ei·re \'a(a)rə, 'er-,'ār-,'īr-, -rē,-ri\ *adj, usu cap* [fr. *Eire* Republic of Ireland, fr. IrGael *Ēire*] **:** IRELAND 2
eirenic *var of* IRENIC
ei·ren·i·con *also* **iren·i·con** \ī'renə,kän, -əkən, *chiefly Brit* -rēn-\ *n* -s [LGk *eirēnikon*, fr. neut. of Gk *eirēnikos* of peace — more at IRENIC] **:** a statement that attempts to harmonize conflicting doctrines (as in a church) **:** RECONCILIATION ⟨can a new ~ be enforced on rival sects by making them share a common ping-pong table —J.E.MacColl⟩
eis·e·ge·sis \ˌīsə'jēsəs\ *n, pl* **eisege·ses** \-ē,sēz\ [NL, fr. Gk *eisēgēsis* act of proposing, advising, introducing, fr. *eisēgeisthai* to bring in, introduce, propose, advise (fr. *eis* into + *hēgeisthai* to lead) + *-sis;* akin to Gk *en* in — more at IN, SEEK] **:** the interpretation of a text (as of the Bible) by reading into it one's own ideas — compare EXEGESIS — **eis·e·get·i·cal** \¦==¦jed·əkəl\ *adj*
ei·sen·how·er jacket \'īz°n,hau̇|(ə)r, |ə *sometimes* -z°n,al|\ *n, usu cap E* [after Dwight D. *Eisenhower* *b*1890 Am. general and 34th U.S. president] **:** a short jacket fitting snugly at the waist and cuffs; *specif* **:** one used as a part of a military uniform
ei·se·nia \ī'sēnēə, ī'-, -nyə\ *n, cap* [NL, fr. Gustav A. *Eisen* †1940 Am. zoologist and archaeologist + NL *-ia*] **:** a widely distributed genus of small earthworms (family Lumbricidae) including the common pink dung worm (*E. foetida*)
ei·stedd·fod \ī'steth(,)vȯd, (i)'s-\ *n* -s [W, lit., session, fr. *eistedd* to sit, sitting (derivative fr. the root of W *sedd* seat) + *bod* to be, being; akin to L *sedēre* to sit and to OIr *brith* to be, being, OE *bēon* to be — more at SIT, BE] **:** a Welsh competitive festival of the arts esp. in singing ⟨adjudicating at a local ~ in Wales where there were three male voice choirs competing in the final —Warwick Braithwaite⟩ — compare FEIS 2, MOD — **ei·stedd·fod·ic** \ˌī,steth¦vȯdik\ *adj*
eith \'ēth\ *var of* EATH
¹ei·ther \'ēthə(r), *sometimes* 'īth-; *Eng & Wales* 'īth-; *Ireland & Scot* 'āth-\ *adj* [ME *either, aither*, adj. & pron., fr. OE *ǣghwæther, ǣgther* both, each (akin to OHG *iogihwedar* each of two), fr. *ā* always + *ge-*, collective prefix + *hwæther* which of two, whether — more at AYE, CO-, WHETHER] **1 :** the one and the other of the two **:** EACH ⟨flowers blooming on ~ side of the walk⟩ **2 :** the one or the other of the two ⟨use ~ foot, no matter which⟩ ⟨you may take ~ fork of the road⟩
²either \"\ *pron* [ME *either, aither*] **1** *archaic* **a :** each of two or more ⟨at ~ of the three corners is an exquisite . . . bust —W.D.Howells⟩ **b :** each other ⟨as two yoke devils sworn to ~'s purpose —Shak.⟩ **2 :** one of two or more: as **a :** the one or the other ⟨take ~ of the two routes⟩ **b :** any one (of more than two) ⟨three famous talkers . . . ~ of whom would illustrate what I say —O.W.Holmes †1935⟩ — usu. sing. in constr. except when a plural (usu. after *of*) intervenes between *either* and the verb form in which circumstance the verb is often plural in form ⟨of the two forms of address ~ is appropriate to the situation⟩ ⟨~ of them is satisfactory⟩ ⟨~ of them are satisfactory⟩
³either \"\ *conj* [ME *either, aither*, fr. OE *ǣghwæther (ge), ǣgther (ge)* both, fr. *ǣghwæther, ǣgther*, pron.] **1 —** used as a function word before two or more coordinate words, phrases, or clauses joined usu. by *or* to indicate that what immediately follows is the first of two or more alternatives that are equally applicable ⟨that voice, which could be used ~ as a glaive or as an organ stop —Victoria Sackville-West⟩ ⟨the man did not kill himself ~ physically or spiritually —E.C.Wagenknecht⟩ ⟨unready, ~ politically, economically, or militarily —H.E. Gaston⟩ or mutually exclusive ⟨the statement as originally worded must be ~ true or false⟩ ⟨the population will ~ die, migrate, or plunge into economic chaos —Herbert Hoover⟩ **2** *obs* **:** OR
⁴either \"\ *adv* [ME *either, aither*, fr. *either, aither*, adj., pron., & conj.] **1 :** at all **:** LIKEWISE, MOREOVER — used for emphasis after a negative ⟨they are the best available and are not expensive ~⟩ esp. one contradicting a previous affirmation ⟨it's raining. It isn't ~⟩ or agreeing with a previous negative statement ⟨I didn't see it. Nor I ~⟩ or supplementing one ⟨you'll not go far in life and you won't be happy ~ —W.J.Reilly⟩ — compare TOO **2 :** for that matter — used for emphasis after an alternative following a question or conditional clause esp. where negation is implied ⟨who answers for the Irish parliament? or army ~? —Robert Browning⟩ ⟨if his father had come or his mother ~ all would have gone well⟩
¹either-or \¦=thə'(r) ȯ(ə)r, -ȯ(ə)\ *adj* **:** of or marked by either-or **:** BLACK-AND-WHITE ⟨has written an *either-or* book in which the good are totally good and the wicked are totally bad⟩
²either-or \"\ *n* -s **:** an unavoidable choice or exclusive division between only two alternatives **:** DICHOTOMY ⟨the problem of specialized versus general courses is not one of *either-or* —*Science*⟩ ⟨no *either-or* between nature and . . . culture —C.K. Kluckhohn⟩
¹ejac·u·late \ə'jakyə,lāt, ē'-, *usu* -ād·+V\ *vb* -ED/-ING/-S [L *ejaculatus*, past part. of *ejaculari* to throw out, hurl, fr. *e-* + *jaculari* to throw, fr. *jaculum* dart, javelin, fr. *jacere* to throw — more at JET] *vt* **1 a** *obs* **:** to throw out (as a dart) suddenly and swiftly **:** EJECT **b :** to eject (a fluid) from a living body; *specif* **:** to eject (semen) in orgasm **2 :** to blurt out (as in anger or surprise) ⟨angry and *ejaculating* unfinished sentences —Jean Stafford⟩ ~ *vi* **1 a :** to dart out suddenly and swiftly

b : to eject a fluid (as semen) **2 :** to utter an ejaculation **:** cry out ⟨the seagull flapped away . . . *ejaculating* from time to time as seagulls do —Ethel Wilson⟩ **syn** see EXCLAIM

²**ejac·u·late** \-ˌlə̇t, -ˌlāt, *usu* ǀd·+V\ *n* -s **1 :** the semen released by one ejaculation **2 :** EJACULATION 1

ejac·u·la·tion \=ˌ==ˈlāshən\ *n* -s [L *ejaculatus* + E *-ion*] **1 a :** the act or process of ejaculating; *specif* **:** the sudden or spontaneous discharging of a fluid (as semen in orgasm) from a duct **b :** an instance of such an act or process **2 :** something ejaculated: as **a :** a short sudden emotional utterance **b :** a short urgent prayer ⟨he received a birthday spiritual bouquet from the children advising him that they had offered . . . 10,705 *ejaculations*, 340 sacrifices, and 270 acts of charity in his behalf —E.J.Kahn⟩

ejac·u·la·tio prae·cox \=ˌ==ˈlāshēˌōˈprēˌkäks\ *n* [NL] **:** premature ejaculation in coitus

ejac·u·la·tive \=ˈ==ˌlā‖d·ǀiv, -ˌlə̇|, ‖t|, ǀēv *also* ǀəv\ *adj* **:** EJACULATORY

ejac·u·la·tor \-ˌlād·ə(r), -ātə-\ *n* -s **:** one that ejaculates

ejac·u·la·to·ry \-ˌlə̇ˌtōrē, -ȯr-, -ri\ *adj* **1 :** casting or throwing out; *specif* **:** associated with or concerned in physiological ejaculation ⟨~ vessels⟩ **2 :** marked by or given to ejaculation ⟨an ~ prayer⟩ ⟨a breathless ~ hotelkeeper who is forcing a traveling salesman to hear her story —*Times Lit. Supp.*⟩

ejaculatory duct *n* **:** a duct through which semen is ejaculated; *specif* **:** either of the paired ducts in man that are formed by the junction of the duct from the seminal vesicle with the vas deferens, pass through the prostate, and open into the upper part of the urethra

ejac·u·lum \-ˌləm\ *n, pl* **ejacu·la** \-lə\ [NL, fr. L *ejaculari* to throw out — more at EJACULATE] **:** EJACULATE 1

¹**eject** \ə̇ˈjekt, ēˈ-\ *vt* -ED/-ING/-S [ME *ejecten*, fr. L *ejectus*, past part. of *eicere*, fr. *e-* + *-icere* (fr. *jacere* to throw) — more at JET] **1 a :** to drive (as a person) out esp. by physical force **:** EXPEL ⟨he was being *~ed* for taunting the pianist —Brooks Atkinson⟩ **b :** to deprive of membership or of a position or office **:** OUST ⟨the membership *~ed* the chairman by acclamation⟩ **c :** to evict from property **:** DISPOSSESS ⟨*~ed* for nonpayment of rent⟩ **2 a :** to throw or force out from within ⟨a mechanism that *~s* the empty cases from the gun⟩ **b :** to throw off ⟨an electron *~ed* from an atom of copper⟩ **c** *obs* **:** EMIT ⟨every look . . . mine eyes *~s* —Ben Jonson⟩

syn EJECT, EXPEL, OUST, EVICT, and DISMISS can mean, in common, to force or thrust (a thing or person) out. EJECT carries the strongest implication of throwing out from within ⟨cones of material *ejected* from the volcanoes —W.E.Swinton⟩ ⟨the solar system had been formed out of matter *ejected* from the sun —S.F.Mason⟩ ⟨into solid bank of smoke *ejected* itself from the breastworks —Kenneth Roberts⟩ ⟨a roaring fire *ejecting* sparks —T.S.Eliot⟩ ⟨cowboys forcibly *eject* the farmers from their places in line —*Amer. Guide Series: Texas*⟩ EXPEL, stressing a thrusting out or driving away, implies more generally a voluntary compulsion than EJECT, indicating more generally an intent to get permanently rid of ⟨*expel* the air from the lungs⟩ ⟨the fish and the bird, which *expel* the egg from the body —H.M.Parshley⟩ ⟨he was arrested . . . then *expelled* from the city with the warning never to come back —*Current Biog.*⟩ ⟨*expelled* from his seat in the Senate for plotting with the British —R.B.Morris⟩ OUST implies removal or dispossession by the power of a law or the exercise of force or compulsion ⟨to *oust* squatters from his property —*Amer. Guide Series: Pa.*⟩ ⟨the first explorers were the Genoese, who had been *ousted* from the Levant trade by the Venetians —S.F.Mason⟩ ⟨Ferdinand . . . *ousted* the local king from Navarre —Francis Hackett⟩ EVICT now means to turn out (of house and home, one's place of business, or the like) by legal or equally effective means, commonly for nonpayment of rent ⟨after two months the landlord had the tenants *evicted* for rowdyism and destruction of property besides nonpayment⟩ ⟨Roger Williams, rebel against the Puritans and *evicted* by them from the sacred confines of Massachusetts —R.W.Hatch⟩ ⟨thousands of crofters were *evicted* to make way for large sheep farms —*London Calling*⟩ DISMISS stresses a getting rid of (something) by refusing it further consideration, ejecting it from the thoughts, or taking steps to ensure its no longer annoying one ⟨nonviolence as a political weapon . . . should not be *dismissed* lightly —*African Abstracts*⟩ ⟨a very downright sort of Yankee, given to *dismissing* people who disagreed with him —Charlton Laird⟩ ⟨*dismiss* an enemy by having him deported⟩

²**eject** \ˈēˌjekt\ *n* -s **:** PROJECTION 8

ejec·ta \ə̇ˈjektə, ēˈ-\ *n pl but sing or pl in constr* [NL, fr. L, neut. pl. of *ejectus*] **:** material thrown out (as from a volcano)

ejec·ta·men·ta \ə̇ˌjektəˈmentə, (ˌ)ēˌj-\ *n pl* [NL, fr. L, pl. of *ejectamentum* something thrown out, fr. *ejectare* to throw out (freq. of *eicere*) + *-mentum* -ment] **:** EJECTA

ejec·tion \ə̇ˈjekshən, ēˈ-\ *n* -s [ME *ejeccioun*, fr. L *ejection-*, *ejectio*, fr. *ejectus* + *-ion-*, *-io* -ion] **1 :** the act or process of ejecting **:** EXPULSION ⟨automatic ~ of empty cartridge cases from revolvers —C.S.Comeaux⟩ **2** *Scots law* **:** EJECTMENT 2 **3 :** EJECTA

ejection capsule *n* **:** a pressurized cockpit designed to be ejected from airplanes in an emergency and equipped with an automatic parachute, survival gear, rations, and radio transmitter

ejection port *n* **:** an opening in the receiver of a firearm through which the expended cases are thrown from the piece after firing

ejection seat *or* **ejector seat** *n* **:** an emergency escape seat designed to propel its occupant out and away from an airplane by means of an explosive charge

¹**ejec·tive** \-ktiv, -tēv *also* -təv\ *adj* [¹*eject* + *-ive*] **1 :** causing ejection ⟨the ~ force is supplied by an explosive charge under the seat⟩ **2** *of a voiceless consonant* **:** uttered with simultaneous glottal stop ⟨an ~ explosive is heard when the mouth closure and glottis are released almost simultaneously⟩ — **ejec·tive·ly** \-təvlē, -li\ *adv*

²**ejective** \"\ *n* -s **:** an ejective consonant

eject·ment \-k(t)mənt\ *n* -s **1 :** DISPOSSESSION ⟨the ~ of tenants from their homes⟩ **2 a :** a mixed action admissible for the recovery of possession of property and for damages and costs for the wrongful withholding of it **b :** the writ by which this action is commenced

ejec·tor \-ktə(r)\ *n* -s **1 :** one that ejects: as **a :** the mechanism of a firearm that ejects the empty cartridge **b :** a device that ejects finished work (as a cast slug) from the mold of a typecasting mechanism or the die of a die-casting mechanism or hydraulic press ⟨the casting is removed by pressure from ~ pins fastened to the ~ plate behind the movable die —David Basch⟩ **2 :** a jet pump for withdrawing a gas, fluid, or powdery substance (as air, water, or sand) from a space

ejects *pres 3d sing of* EJECT, *pl of* EJECT

eji·dal \eˈkēthəl, ehē-\ *adj* [MexSp, fr. *ejido* + *-al*] **:** of or relating to an ejido or the ejido system **:** COMMUNAL ⟨~ lands⟩ ⟨~ procedure⟩ ⟨~ agriculture⟩

eji·da·ta·rio \-ˌthäˈtäryō\ *n, pl* **ejidatarios** \-yōs\ [MexSp, fr. *ejido*] **:** a member of an ejido

eji·do \eˈkēthō, eˈhē-\ *n, pl* **ejidos** \-ōs\ [MexSp, fr. Sp, common land in a village used for pasturage or threshing, fr. L *exitus* departure, way out — more at EXIT] **1 :** a tract of land held in common by the inhabitants of a Mexican village and farmed cooperatively or individually **:** COMMON **2 :** a Mexican village having an ejido **3 :** a system of communal land tenure in Mexico — compare HACIENDA

ejoo \ˈē(ˌ)jü\ *n* -s [Java *ijo*] **:** GOMUTI 2

ejus·dem ge·ne·ris \ēˌyüs(ˌ)demˈgenərə̇s, ēˌjəs(ˌ)demˈje-\ *adj* [L] **:** of the same kind or class ⟨the articles here imported are not *ejusdem generis* with the class of articles specifically named in said paragraph 217 —*U.S. Daily*⟩ — usu. used in law to limit the application of a broad term to a specific class of things

eka- \ˌekə, ˈākə\ *comb form* [Skt *eka* one — more at ONE] **:** standing or assumed to stand next in order beyond (a specified element) in the same family of the periodic table — in names of chemical elements esp. when not yet discovered ⟨*eka*cesium (now called francium)⟩; compare DVI-

eka·iodine \"+\ *n* [*eka-* + *iodine*] **:** ASTATINE

eka·ri \āˈkärē\ *n, pl* **ekari** *or* **ekaris** *usu cap* **1 :** a Papuan people of western New Guinea **2 :** a member of the Ekari people

ekdemite *var of* ECDEMITE

¹**eke** \ˈēk\ *adv* [ME, fr. OE *ēac*; akin to OHG *ouh* also, ON & Goth *auk*, L *aut* or, Gk *au* again, Skt *u* and, but] *archaic* **:** in addition **:** ALSO, MOREOVER ⟨the most entertaining, ~ the most learned —H.J.Laski⟩

²**eke** *or* **eik** \ˈēk, ˈāk, ˈaik\ *n* -s [ME *eke*, fr. OE *ēaca*; akin to OE *ēacian* to increase] *now chiefly Scot* **:** an addition or extension: as **a :** a piece added to increase the size or length of a garment **b :** an additional drink ⟨an ~ before I go⟩

³**eke** \ˈēk, *Scot* " *or* ˈāk *or* ˈaik\ *vb* -ED/-ING/-S [ME *eken*, *echen*, fr. OE *ēacian* (v.i.) to increase and *ēacan* (v.i.) to increase and *īecan*, *ēcan* (v.t.) to increase, augment, carry out; akin to OHG *ouhhōn* to add, ON *auka* to increase, Goth *aukan*, L *augēre*, Gk *auxein* to increase, Skt *oja* strength] *vt* **1** *or* **eik** *chiefly Scot* **a :** ADD, INCREASE ⟨*eked* a few words fit for the occasion⟩ ⟨the memory *eked* her sadness⟩ **b :** to repair by adding material **:** PATCH, LENGTHEN ⟨let out and ~ the petticoat⟩ **2 a :** to supplement or fill (what is felt to be deficient) esp. by a laborious, inferior, or scanty addition — used with *out* ⟨to ~ out his meager pay . . . he turned to writing —*English Digest*⟩ ⟨~ out the information given in the native chronicles and so to reconstruct . . . the society of the first centuries —G.B.Sansom⟩ **b :** to make (a supply) last by economy ⟨~ out the stores by strict rationing⟩ or partial use of a substitute ⟨this wool could be obtained only in small and uncertain quantities and was often *eked* out as a facing to a core of cedar bark —C.D.Forde⟩ **:** STRETCH — used with *out* **3 a :** to obtain, maintain, or achieve with effort usu. in small quantity **:** SQUEEZE ⟨he asked about the living conditions . . . and I tried to ~ out the little knowledge I had collected —Christopher Isherwood⟩; *specif* **:** to make (a living) meagerly and laboriously — used with *out* ⟨from . . . unproductive cutover land many farmers have *eked* out a precarious living —*Amer. Guide Series: Minn.*⟩ **b :** to live from day to day esp. with boredom or with difficulty — used with *out* ⟨on this, with £1 a month from his father, the boy *eked* out his year —*Sydney (Australia) Bull.*⟩ **~** *vi, chiefly Scot* **:** ADD ⟨it *eked* to her woe⟩ **:** AUGMENT

eke·name \ˈēkˌnām\ *n* [ME — more at NICKNAME] *archaic* **:** NICKNAME

EKG *abbr, often not cap* electrocardiogram

ekhi·mi \eˈkēmē\ *n* -s [native name in Africa] **:** the grayish brown coarse-grained wood of a tropical African tree (*Piptadenia africana*) used for structural work and inexpensive furniture

ek·ka \ˈe(ˌ)kä, ˈekə\ *n* -s [Hindi *ekā*, *ekkā*, lit., unit, fr. Skt *ekatā*, fr. *eka* one — more at ONE] **:** a light 2-wheeled one-horse one-passenger carriage used in India

ek·ki \ˈekē\ *n* -s [native name in Africa] **1 :** a tropical African timber tree (*Lophira alata* or *L. procera*) of the family Ochnaceae yielding a heavy hard durable reddish brown wood that is used esp. for wharves, railway ties, and flooring **2 :** the wood of the ekki

ekoi \ˈāˌkȯi\ *n, pl* **ekoi** *or* **ekois** *usu cap* **1 a :** a Negro people of southeastern Nigeria noted for their carved masks **b :** a member of such people **2 :** the language of the Ekoi people belonging to the Central branch of the Niger-Congo language family

ekphore *var of* ECPHORE

ek·te·ne *or* **ec·te·ne** \ˌektəˈnē\ *n* -s [MGk *ektenē*, fr. Gk *ektenēs* assiduous, prolonged, fr. *ekteinein* to stretch out, fr. *ek*, *ex* out + *teinein* to stretch — more at EX-, THIN] **:** SYNAPTE

ektodynamomorphic *var of* ECTODYNAMOMORPHIC

¹**el** \ˈel\ *n* -s **:** the letter *l*

²**el** \"\ *n* -s *often cap, often attrib* [by shortening] **:** ELEVATED RAILROAD ⟨the Third Avenue ~⟩

-el \ˌel, əl\ *n suffix* -s [ME, fr. OF *-el*, *-ele*, fr. L *-ellus*, *-ella*, *-ellum*] **:** small one ⟨cormel⟩

el *abbr* **1** eldest **2** elected **3** electric; electricity **4** element **5** elevated; elevation

¹**elab·o·rate** \ə̇ˈlab(ə)rə̇t, ēˈ-, *usu* -rəd·+V\ *adj* [L *elaboratus*] **1** *archaic* **:** produced by labor **2 a :** planned or carried out with great care and exactness **:** worked out in detail **:** COMPLEX ⟨the ~ register of the inhabitants prevented tax evasion —John Buchan⟩ ⟨he began an ~ calculation on his fingers —Dorothy Sayers⟩ **b :** marked by complexity, fullness of detail, or ornateness **:** INTRICATE, COMPLICATED ⟨~ wood decorations, mansard roofs, and long porches —Fred Zimmer⟩ **c :** PAINSTAKING, DILIGENT ⟨an ~ collector of etchings⟩ — **elab·o·rate·ly** *adv* — **elab·o·rate·ness** *n* -ES

²**elab·o·rate** \-bəˌrāt, *usu* -ād·+V\ *vb* -ED/-ING/-S [L *elaboratus*, past part. of *elaborare* to work out, labor diligently, acquire by labor, fr. *e-* + *laborare* to labor — more at LABOR] *vt* **1 :** to produce by labor **:** fashion with care **2** *of a living organism* **:** to alter the chemical makeup of (as a foodstuff) to one more suited to bodily needs (as of assimilation or excretion); *esp* **:** to build up (complex organic compounds) from simple ingredients ⟨some neoplasms ~ abnormal proteins⟩ ⟨green plants ~ organic compounds from inorganic by means of photosynthesis⟩ **3 a :** to work out in detail **:** DEVELOP ⟨requested all nations to meet to ~ a code of international law⟩ **b :** to expand, develop, or perfect esp. by analysis or reasoning ⟨the idea of mechanical energy was . . . inherent in Newton's work and was *elaborated* by those who followed him —W.V.Houston⟩ **~** *vi* **1 :** to become elaborate ⟨this particular area seems a point where such influences have flowered and *elaborated* —Ruth Underhill⟩ **2 :** to expand something in detail **:** discuss something at length ⟨he never *elaborated* on that remark —Irving Kristol⟩ ⟨declined to ~ in spite of strong hints that he tell all⟩ **:** dwell on a subject ⟨and then *elaborated* in response to questions —*N.Y.Times*⟩ **syn** see UNFOLD

elab·o·rat·er *or* **elab·o·ra·tor** \-ād·ə(r), -ātə-\ *n* -s **:** one that elaborates

elab·o·ra·tion \=ˌ==ˈrāshən\ *n* -s [L *elaboration-*, *elaboratio*, fr. *elaboratus* + *-ion-*, *-io* -ion] **1 a :** the act or process of elaborating ⟨scholars were mainly concerned in translation and ~ of texts —H.J.J.Winter⟩ **b :** the quality or state of being elaborated ⟨reached an extravagant degree of ~ in the 'seventies and 'eighties —James Laver⟩ **2 :** something produced by elaborating ⟨can be used to solicit suggestions, to obtain *~s*, to elicit reasons —S.L.Payne⟩ **3 :** psychic interpretation or amplification of the content of dreams and other unconscious processes

elab·o·ra·tive \=ˈ=bəˌrā‖d·ǀiv, -b(ə)rə|, ‖t|, ǀēv *also* ǀəv\ *adj* **:** capable of elaborating **:** tending to elaborate — **elab·o·ra·tive·ly** \ǀəvlē, ǀēv-, -li\ *adv*

elab·o·ra·to·ry \-b(ə)rəˌtōrē, -ȯr-, -ri\ *n* -ES [L *elaboratus* + E *-ory*] *archaic* **:** LABORATORY

el·a·chis·ta·ce·ae \ˌeləkə̇ˈstāsēˌē\ *n pl, cap* [NL, fr. *Elachista*, type genus (fr. Gk *elachistē*, fem. superl. of *elachys* small) + *-aceae* — more at LIGHT (in weight)] **:** a family of brown algae (order Ectocarpales) found on other marine algae esp. of the family Fucaceae — **el·a·chis·ta·ceous** \ˌ=ˌ===ˈstāshəs\ *adj*

el·a·chis·to·don·ti·dae \ˌeləˌkistəˈdäntəˌdē\ *n pl, cap* [NL, fr. *Elachistodont-*, *Elachistodon*, type genus (fr. Gk *elachistos* — superl. of *elachys* — + NL *-odont-*, *-odon*) + *-idae*] **:** a small family of Indian egg-eating snakes comprising a single genus that is sometimes placed with the egg-eating snakes of southern Africa in the family Dasypeltidae

el·ae·ag·na·ce·ae \ˌeləˌagˈnāsēˌē\ *n pl, cap* [NL, fr. *Elaeagnus*, type genus + *-aceae*] **:** a family of trees or shrubs (order Myrtales) having silvery, scurfy, or stellate-pubescent foliage, small perfect or dioecious flowers, and baccate fruit — **el·ae·ag·na·ceous** \ˌeleˌagˈnāshəs\ *adj*

el·ae·ag·nus \ˌeleˈagnəs\ *n, cap* [NL, fr. Gk *elaiagnos*, a kind of willow, fr. *elaia* olive, olive tree + *agnos* chaste tree — more at OLIVE, AGNUS CASTUS] **:** a genus (the type of the family Elaeagnaceae) of chiefly Asiatic shrubs or trees having alternate leaves and perfect flowers with four stamens — see GOUMI, RUSSIAN OLIVE, SILVERBERRY

elae·is \ə̇ˈlēə̇s\ *n, cap* [NL, prob. modif. of Gk *elais* olive tree, fr. *elaia* olive] **:** a genus of pinnate-leaved palms having very dense clusters of crowded flowers and bright red fruits — see AFRICAN OIL PALM

elae·nia \ə̇ˈlēnēə\ *n* [NL, modif. of Gk *elainea*, fem. of *elaineos* of the olive, of olivewood, fr. *elaia* olive; fr. the color of the plumage] **1** *cap* **:** a genus of small crested insectivorous birds (family Tyrannidae) of tropical America and the West Indies **2** -s **:** any bird of the genus *Elaenia*

elae·o·blast \ə̇ˈlēəˌblast\ *n* [*elaio-* + *-blast*] **:** an outgrowth at the posterior end of the embryo of certain tunicates believed to contain nutritive material — **elae·o·blas·tic** \=ˌ==ˈblastik\ *adj*

elae·o·car·pa·ce·ae \ə̇ˌlēō(ˌ)kärˈpāsēˌē\ *n pl, cap* [NL, fr. *Elaeocarpus*, type genus + *-aceae*] **:** a widely distributed family of trees and shrubs (order Malvales) closely related to Tiliaceae — **elae·o·car·pa·ceous** \=ˌ==(ˌ)=ˈpāshəs\ *adj*

elae·o·car·pus \=ˌ==ˈkärpəs\ *n, cap* [NL, fr. *elaio-* + *-carpus*] **:** a genus (the type of the family Elaeocarpaceae) of Indian and Australian trees and shrubs having simple leaves and small racemose flowers and including some species valuable as timber trees — see BRISBANE QUANDONG

el·ae·od·o·chon \ˌeleˈädəˌkän\ *n* -s [NL, fr. Gk *elaiodochon*, neut. of *elaiodochos* holding oil, fr. *elaio-* + *dochos* containing, able to hold — more at CHOLEDOCH] **:** the oil gland of a bird situated near the base of the tail

elaeolite *var of* ELEOLITE

el·ae·om·e·ter \ˌeleˈäməd·ə(r)\ *n* [prob. fr. F *élaiomètre*, fr. *élaio-* elaio- + *-mètre* -meter] **:** OLEOMETER

el·ae·oph·o·ra \ˌeleˈäf(ə)rə\ *n, cap* [NL, fr. *elaio-* + *-phora*] **:** a genus of filarioid nematode worms which infest the arteries of sheep and other ruminants and whose larvae move into the subcutaneous tissues and cause lesions esp. about the head and feet

elaeoptene *var of* ELEOPTENE

elaeostearic acid *var of* ELEOSTEARIC ACID

el·a·id·ic acid \ˌeləˌidik-\ *n* [*elaio-* + *-ide* + *-ic*] **:** a white crystalline unsaturated acid $C_{17}H_{33}COOH$ obtained from oleic acid by isomerization; the trans isomer of oleic acid

ela·i·din \ə̇ˈlāəd°n, -dən\ *n* -s [ISV *elaidic* + *-in*] **:** a glycerol ester of elaidic acid

ela·i·din·i·za·tion \ə̇ˌlāəˌdinə̇ˈzāshən\ *n* -s **:** the process of elaidinizing

ela·i·din·ize \ə̇ˈlāəd°nˌīz, -dəˌnīz\ *vt* -ED/-ING/-S **:** to isomerize (as an unsaturated fatty acid or ester) from the cis form to the trans form (as from oleic acid to elaidic acid)

elaidin reaction *n* **:** elaidinization used as a test for unsaturated glycerides (as olein) in fatty oils

elaio- *or* **elaeo-** *or* **eleo-** *comb form* [G *elaio-* & NL *elaeo-*, fr. Gk *elaio-* olive oil, oil, fr. *elaion*, fr. *elaia* olive — more at OLIVE] **:** oil ⟨*elaio*plast⟩ ⟨*elaeo*blast⟩ ⟨*eleo*cyte⟩

elai·o·plast \ə̇ˈlīəˌplast, -lāə-\ *n* -s [ISV *elaio-* + *-plast*; orig. formed as G *elaioplast*] **:** a leucoplast that secretes oil

elam·ite \ˈēləˌmīt\ *n* -s *usu cap* [*Elam*, ancient kingdom east of Babylonia + E *-ite*] **1 :** one of an ancient people living northeast of Babylonia whose civilization goes back to the fifth millennium B.C. **2** *also* **elam·it·ic** \ˌēləˈmid·ik\ **:** a language of unknown affinities used in Elam and known from texts ranging in date approximately from the 25th to the 4th centuries B.C. and mostly in cuneiform characters — called also *Anzanite*, *Susian*

élan \āˈlä^n, (ˈ)āˈlän, -ˈlan\ *n* -s [F, fr. MF *eslan* dash, rush, fr. *(s')eslancer* to rush] **:** vigor, spirit, or enthusiasm typically revealed by assurance of manner, brilliance of performance, or liveliness of imagination **:** ARDOR, ZEST ⟨a man of the world of considerable dash and ~ —Frank Sullivan⟩ ⟨performed with great ~ in a sophisticated style —*Dance Observer*⟩ ⟨the ~ that went into the writing of the great novels of the twenties —Perry Miller⟩ **syn** see VIGOR

elance \ē+\ *vt* -ED/-ING/-S [F *élancer*, fr. MF *(s')eslancer* to rush, fr. *es-* (fr. L *ex-*) + *lancer* to hurl, launch — more at EX-, LANCE] *archaic* **:** THROW ⟨~ a spear⟩ **:** LAUNCH

eland \ˈēlənd, -ˌland, -laa(ə)nd\ *n, pl* **eland** *or* **elands** [Afrik, elk, eland, fr. D, elk, fr. obs. G *elen*, *elend*, fr. Lith *elnis*; akin to OHG *elaho* elk — more at ELK] **:** either of two large African antelopes of the genus *Taurotragus* bovine in form and having short spirally twisted horns in both sexes: **a :** the common dark fawn-colored eland (*T. oryx*) of southern and eastern Africa the male of which sometimes attains six feet in height and weighs 1500 pounds **b :** the larger dark-striped giant eland (*T. derbianus*) restricted to western equatorial Africa

el·a·nus \ˈelənəs\ *n, cap* [NL, fr. LGk *elanos* kite] **:** a genus of small kites of both the Old and New Worlds that have the tail unforked and the plumage black, white, and gray

élan vi·tal \āˈlä^nvēˈtäl\ *n* [F] **:** the vital force or impulse of life ⟨became a firm believer in electricity's curative powers because he regarded it as a kind of *élan vital* —J.H.Plumb⟩; *specif* **:** the creative principle and fundamental reality held by Bergson to be immanent in all organisms and responsible for evolution — compare CREATIVE EVOLUTION

el·a·phe \ˈeləfē\ *n, cap* [NL, prob. fr. Gk *elaphē* deerskin, fr. *elaphos* deer — more at ELK] **:** a large genus of colubrid snakes comprising the rat snakes that are widely distributed in the northern hemisphere where they are valuable as destroyers of rodents — see CORN SNAKE, FOX SNAKE, LEOPARD SNAKE

el·a·phine \ˈeləˌfīn, -ˌfən\ *adj* [Gk *elaphos* deer + E *-ine*] **:** of, relating to, or resembling the red deer

elaph·o·dus \ə̇ˈlafədəs\ *n, cap* [NL, fr. Gk *elaphos* deer + NL *-odus*; fr. the large upper canines of the male] **:** a genus of mammals (family Cervidae) comprising the tufted deer of China which is related to the muntjacs but lacks frontal glands and has antlers greatly reduced

el·a·pho·glos·sum \ˌeləfōˈgläsəm\ *n, cap* [NL, fr. Gk *elaphos* deer + NL *-glossum* (fr. Gk *glōssa* tongue) — more at ELK, GLOSS] **:** a large genus of tropical ferns (family Polypodiaceae) having shaggy stipes and firm or thick oblong to paddle-shaped fronds entire or forked, the fertile fronds being covered beneath with a felty layer of sporangia lacking indusia — see ELEPHANT-EAR FERN

el·a·pho·my·ces \-ˈmīˌsēz\ *n, cap* [NL, fr. Gk *elaphos* deer + NL *-myces*] **:** a genus (the type of the family Elaphomycetaceae) of subterranean ascomycetous fungi resembling the truffles but having sessile ascocarps which are about the size of walnuts and are often rooted up by animals for food

el·a·phure \ˈeləˌfyu̇(ə)r\ *n* -s [NL *Elaphurus*, genus of deer, fr. Gk *elaphos* deer + NL *-urus*] **:** PÈRE DAVID'S DEER — **el·a·phu·rine** \ˌeləˈfyu̇ˌrīn, -rən\ *adj*

¹**el·a·pid** \ˈeləpə̇d\ *adj* [NL *Elapidae*] **:** of or relating to the Elapidae

²**elapid** \"\ *n* -s **:** one of the Elapidae

elap·i·dae \ə̇ˈlapəˌdē\ *n pl, cap* [NL, fr. *Elap-*, *Elaps*, type genus + *-idae*] **:** a family of front-fanged venomous snakes found in the warmer parts of both hemispheres and including the cobras and mambas, the coral snakes of the New World, and the majority of Australian snakes (as the death adder, black snake, and tiger snake) — see ELAPINAE

el·a·pi·nae \ˌeləˈpīˌnē\ *n pl, cap* [NL, fr. *Elap-*, *Elaps*, type genus + *-inae*] **:** the Elapidae when considered as a subfamily of Colubridae — **el·a·pine** \ˈeləˌpīn, -ˌpən\ *adj*

¹**el·a·poid** \ˈeləˌpȯid\ *adj* [NL *Elap-*, *Elaps* + E *-oid*] **:** of, relating to, or resembling the Elapidae

²**elapoid** \"\ *n* -s **:** one of the Elapidae

elaps \ˈēˌlaps\ *n, cap* [NL *Elap-*, *Elaps*, fr. MGk *elaps*, a fish, alter. of Gk *ellops*, *elops* — more at ELOPS] **:** a genus (the type of the family Elapidae) of venomous snakes formerly including many of the groove-fanged snakes (as those now placed in *Micrurus*) but now usu. restricted to a few garter snakes of southern Africa

¹**elapse** \ə̇ˈlaps, ēˈ-\ *vb* -ED/-ING/-S [L *elapsus*, past part. of *elabi* to slip away, escape, fr. *e-* + *labi* to fall, slide — more at SLEEP] *vi* **:** to slip by **:** glide away **:** PASS — usu. used of time ⟨after 1330, a whole generation *~s* before there is another recorded demand for annual parliaments —J.G.Edwards⟩ **~** *vt, obs* **:** to permit (time) to pass **:** OUTLAST, OVERSTAY

²**elapse** \"\ *n* -s **1** *archaic* **:** a flowing out **:** EMANATION **2** *of time* **:** PASSAGE, EXPIRATION ⟨after the ~ of five years the screen is now permitted to dramatize the greatest news event of the modern age —Louise Mace⟩

elapsed time *n* **:** the actual time taken by a boat to sail over a course in yacht racing — see CORRECTED TIME

elasm- *or* **elasmo-** *comb form* [F *élasm-* & NL *elasmo-*, fr. Gk *elasmos* metal plate; akin to Gk *elaunein* to drive — more at ELASTIC] **:** plate ⟨*Elasmo*branchii⟩

¹**elas·mo·branch** \ə̇ˈlazməˌbraŋk\ *also* **elas·mo·bran·chi·an** \=ˌ==ˈbraŋkēən\ *or* **elas·mo·bran·chi·ate** \-kēə̇t, -kēˌāt\ *adj* [*elasmobranch* fr. NL *Elasmobranchii*; *elasmobranchian*, *elasmobranchiate* fr. NL *Elasmobranchii* + E *-an*, *-ate*] **:** of or relating to the Chondrichthyes

²**elasmobranch** \"\ *also* **elasmobranchian** \"\ *or* **elasmobranchiate** \"\ *n* -s **:** one of the Chondrichthyes

¹**elas·mo·bran·chii** \=ˌ==ˈbraŋkēˌī\ [NL, fr. *elasm-* + *-bran-*

chii (fr. L *branchia* gill) — more at BRANCHIA] *syn of* CHONDRICHTHYES

²**elasmobranchii** \"\ [NL, fr. *elasm-* + *-branchii*] *syn of* EUSELACHII

elas·mo·saur \ə'==,sȯ(ə)r\ *n* -S [NL *Elasmosaurus*] **:** a reptile of the genus *Elasmosaurus*

elas·mo·sau·rus \=,=='sȯrəs\ *n, cap* [NL, fr. *elasm-* + *-saurus*] **:** a genus of gigantic long-necked marine reptiles (order Sauropterygia) from the Cretaceous of Kansas related to *Plesiosaurus*

elas·mo·there \ə'==,thi(ə)r\ *n* -S [NL *Elasmotherium*] **:** a rhinoceros of the genus *Elasmotherium*

elas·mo·the·ri·um \=,=='===\ *n, cap* [NL, fr. *elasm-* + *-therium;* fr. the enamel plates of the molars] **:** a genus of rhinoceroses of the Pleistocene of Russia

elast- *or* **elasto-** *comb form* [NL *elast-*, fr. LGk *elastos* ductile] **1 :** elasticity ⟨*elastin*⟩ **2 :** elastic and ⟨*elastoviscous*⟩

elas·tase \ə'la,stās, ē'-, -āz\ *n* -S [*elastin* + *-ase*] **:** an enzyme that decomposes elastin and collagen and has been obtained in crystalline form from the pancreas

¹**elas·tic** \ə'lastik, ē'-, -laas-, -tēk *sometimes chiefly Brit* -lȧs-\ *adj* [NL *elasticus* expansive, impulsive, fr. LGk *elastos* ductile, beaten (fr. Gk *elaunein* to drive, beat out) + L *-icus* -ic; akin to Gk *elan* to drive, OIr *luid* went, and perh. to Arm *elanim* I become] **1 a** *of a solid* **:** capable of recovering size and shape after deformation **b** *of a liquid* **:** capable of resisting compression **c** *of a gas* **:** capable of indefinite expansion **2 :** capable of recovering quickly from low spirits, disappointment, or misfortune ⟨a very cheerful and ~ gentleman —T.L. Peacock⟩ **:** marked by buoyancy **:** RESILIENT ⟨one called the young Indians "boys", perhaps because there was something youthful and ~ in their bodies —Willa Cather⟩ **3 :** capable of being easily stretched or expanded and of snapping back or resuming former shape **:** FLEXIBLE ⟨a brave old Panama hat ... so ~ that upon rolling it up it sprang into perfect shape again —Herman Melville⟩ **4 a :** capable of ready change or easy expansion ⟨left as ~ as possible the constitution of the new institutions —P.J.Noel-Baker⟩ **:** not rigid or constricted ⟨the word *democratic* is doubtless one of the most ~ in the language —D.D.McKean⟩ **b :** receptive to new ideas and willing to modify previous judgments **:** ADAPTABLE ⟨the French mind is ~ and French public opinion tolerant to a degree which shames the prejudice of other peoples —W.C. Brownell⟩ **5 :** enlarging or decreasing readily in demand in response to changes in price ⟨the market is a fixed one in certain ways and quite ~ in other ways —Charles Yerkow⟩

syn EXPANSIVE, RESILIENT, BUOYANT, VOLATILE, EFFERVESCENT: ELASTIC may indicate an ability to recover quickly from discouragement or dejection and enjoy optimism or elation again ⟨the buoyant and *elastic* temper of the French trouveur —J.R. Green⟩ ⟨an *elastic* faculty of throwing off such recollections as would be too painful for endurance —Nathaniel Hawthorne⟩ ⟨to him whose *elastic* and vigorous thought keeps pace with the sun, the day is a perpetual morning —H.D. Thoreau⟩ EXPANSIVE may imply high spirits, optimism, benevolence, geniality, and communicativeness ⟨an *expansive* mood is one of the most familiar and sometimes costly first responses to a Florida winter sun. The person noted for taciturnity in his home community often becomes loquacious —*Amer. Guide Series: Fla.*⟩ RESILIENT may stress speed of return to accustomed good or high spirits after stress, tribulation, or depression ⟨already the shock and horror of it was fading from her *resilient* mind —Ruth Park⟩ ⟨good fighters, outspoken and tenacious of opinion, unsparing in attack, refusing to be browbeaten, *resilient* and tough as seasoned hickory —V.L. Parrington⟩ BUOYANT may indicate a temperamental lightness of spirit incapable of lasting dejection or depression ⟨in the dark days of the Revolution there was a *buoyant* American spirit —*Encyc. Americana*⟩ ⟨no such immaterial burden could depress that *buoyant*-hearted young gentleman for many hours together —George Eliot⟩ VOLATILE suggests lightness, levity, gaiety, or flightiness overcoming the sedate, serious, sober, or downcast ⟨how different from the *volatile* Polynesian in this, as in all other respects, is our grave and decorous North American Indian —Herman Melville⟩ ⟨was suspected of levity, irreverence, disregard, and affectation. He was too *volatile*; he talked too much —*John o' London's Weekly*⟩ EFFERVESCENT suggests a bubbling liveliness and boisterousness over which restraint or suppression is unlikely or impossible ⟨an *effervescent* sort of chap with an enthusiasm that takes off like a rocket —Richard Joseph⟩ **syn** see in addition FLEXIBLE

²**elastic** \"\ *n* -S **1 a :** ELASTIC WEB **b :** a fabric that is woven usu. of yarns containing rubber and that is used esp. for girdles and elastic hose **c :** something made from such fabric; *esp* **:** GARTER 1 — usu. used in pl. **2 :** easily stretched rubber usu. prepared in cords, strings, or bands: as **a :** RUBBER BAND **b :** a band of elastic placed around a tooth at the gum line in effecting its nonsurgical extraction

elas·ti·ca \-tȯkə\ *n* -S [NL, fr. fem. of *elasticus*] **1 :** either of two layers of elastic tissue present in the walls of most arteries: **a :** an inner layer between the intima and media **b :** an outer layer between the media and adventitia **2 :** ELASTIC CURVE

elastic afterwork *or* **elastic afterworking** *n* **:** the plastic yielding or creep of certain crystals of a metal on recovery after the release of a stress that has previously caused plastic deformation

elastical *obs var of* ¹ELASTIC

elas·ti·cal·ly \-tȯk(ə)lē, -tēk-, -li\ *adv* **:** in an elastic manner **:** utilizing an elastic quality ⟨could be bent ~ —E.F.Riebling & W.W.Webb⟩

elastic bitumen *n* **:** ELATERITE

elastic cartilage *n* **:** a yellowish flexible cartilage having the matrix infiltrated in all directions by a network of elastic fibers and occurring chiefly in the external ear, eustachian tube, and certain cartilages of the larynx and epiglottis

elastic collision *n* **:** a collision in which the total kinetic energy of the colliding pair remains unchanged and the total momentum is conserved although usu. reapportioned between them

elastic constant *n* **:** one of the constants that express the elastic behavior of a given material — compare BULK MODULUS, ELASTIC LIMIT, POISSON'S RATIO, SHEAR MODULUS, YIELD POINT, YOUNG'S MODULUS

elastic currency *n* **:** a currency that automatically increases and decreases in volume with the demands of business

elastic curve *n* **:** the curve assumed by the longitudinal axis of an originally straight elastic strip or bar bent within its elastic limits by any system of forces

elastic deformation *n* **:** deformation that disappears upon removal of the external forces causing the alteration and the stress associated with it

elastic fiber *n* **:** a thick very elastic smooth yellowish connective tissue fiber that contains elastin and that branches and anastomoses with other similar fibers — see ELASTIC CARTILAGE, ELASTIC TISSUE

elastic glue *n* **:** FLEXIBLE GLUE

elastic hysteresis *n* **:** HYSTERESIS 1b

elas·tic·i·ty \ə,la'stisəd-ē, (,)ē,l-, -laa'-, -ətē, -i *sometimes chiefly Brit* -,lȧ'- *or* ,e(,)l- *or* -,lȧ'-\ *n* -ES **1 :** the quality or state of being elastic: as **a :** the capability of a strained body to recover its size and shape after deformation in any way **:** SPRINGINESS **b :** RESILIENCE ⟨with the ~ of youth she quickly recovered⟩ **c :** ADAPTABILITY ⟨they do not always perceive that the ~ of democracy is its strength —*New Yorker*⟩ **2 :** the property in paint or varnish that enables the film to follow without breaking changes in the surface to which it is applied **3 :** the responsiveness of a dependent variable to changes in a causal factor ⟨the price ~ of exports and imports may not be adequate to bring about equilibrium —A.H.Hansen⟩ ⟨~ of demand⟩

e·las·ti·cized \ə'==stə,sīzd\ *adj* **1 :** woven or knitted with elastic or rubber thread ⟨~ fabrics⟩ **2 :** stitched with elastic thread or made with inserts of elastic ⟨an ~ belt⟩ ⟨~ shoes⟩

elastic limit *n* **1 :** the greatest stress that an elastic solid can sustain without undergoing permanent deformation **2 :** the greatest stress for which the strain of an elastic body is proportional to the stress

elastic membrane *n* **:** a membrane consisting of or containing elastic tissue

elastic modulus *n* **:** MODULUS OF ELASTICITY

elastic scattering *n* **:** a scattering of material particles or photons as the result of elastic collision

elastic stocking *n* **:** STOCKING 2a

elastic tissue *n* **:** tissue consisting chiefly of elastic fibers that is found esp. in certain ligaments and tendons

elastic wave *n* **:** a wave in which the propagated disturbance is an elastic deformation of the medium

elastic web *or* **elastic webbing** *n* **:** a narrow fabric woven of various textile fibers and typically rubber threads and used esp. for garters and suspenders

elas·tin \ə'==stən\ *n* -S [ISV *elast-* + *-in;* orig. formed in G] **:** a protein that is similar to collagen and forms the chief constituent of elastic fibers

elas·tique \ā,la'stēk\ *n* -S [F *élastique* elastic (adj. and n.), fr. NL *elasticus* expansive, impulsive — more at ELASTIC] **:** a firm fabric resembling cavalry twill that is usu. made of wool or worsted and is used for uniforms and sportswear

elasto- — see ELAST-

elas·to·mer \ə'lastəmə(r), ē'-\ *n* -S [*elast-* + *-mer*] **:** an elastic rubberlike substance (as a synthetic rubber or a plastic having some of the physical properties of natural rubber) ⟨polyvinyl ~s⟩ — **elas·to·mer·ic** \=,=='merik\ *adj*

elas·tom·e·ter \ə,la'stäməd-ə(r), (,)ē,l-\ *n* [*elast-* + *-meter*] **:** an instrument for measuring elasticity (as of body tissues or rubber) — **elas·tom·e·try** \-mə·trē\ *n* -ES

Elas·to·plast \ə'lastə,plast, ē'l-\ *trademark* — used for an elastic adhesive bandage used as a dressing or support (as a cast or a corset)

¹**elas·to·plas·tic** \ə'lastə,plastik, ē'l-\ *n* [*elast-* + *plastic* (n.)] **:** a substance having both elastic and plastic properties **:** a rubberlike plastic

²**elastoplastic** \"\ *adj* [*elast-* + *plastic* (adj.)] **:** relating to the state of stress between the elastic limit of a material and its breaking strength in which the material exhibits both elastic and plastic properties — **elas·to·plas·tic·i·ty** \=,==,plas'tisəd-ē\ *n* -ES

elas·to·sis \ə,la'stōsəs, (,)ē,l-\ *n, pl* **elasto·ses** \-ō,sēz\ [NL, fr. *elast-* + *-osis*] **:** a condition marked by loss of elasticity of the skin in elderly people due to degeneration of the connective tissue

elas·tra·tion \-'strāshən\ *n* -S [blend of ²*elastic* and *castration*] **:** bloodless castration (as of a lamb) by fitting a strong rubber band about the scrotum

¹**elate** \ə'lāt, ē'-, *usu* -ād·+V\ *adj* [ME *elat*, fr. L *elatus*] **1** *archaic* **:** of high position **:** LOFTY, PROUD **2 :** in high spirits ⟨who can be alone ~ while the world lies forlorn —Matthew Arnold⟩ **:** EXALTED ⟨the poet's eyes ... careworn, not ~ —Hugh McCrae⟩

²**elate** \"\ *vt* -ED/-ING/-S [L *elatus* (suppletive past part. of *efferre* to carry out), fr. *e-* + *latus*, suppletive past part. of *ferre* to bear — more at EFFERENT, BEAR, TOLERATE] **1** *archaic* **:** to raise up **:** LIFT ⟨~ his shady forehead —George Chapman⟩ **2 a :** to raise the spirits of **:** EXCITE, INSPIRE ⟨it was a fine sunny day, the sort of day that ~s the heart of young and old —W.S. Maugham⟩ **b :** to flush with triumph or success **:** puff up (as with pride) ⟨*elated* over his great bargain —M.M.Musselman⟩

elated *adj* **:** elevated in spirit **:** excited esp. with pride **:** EXULTANT ⟨I felt at once tranquil and ~ —John Galsworthy⟩ — **elat·ed·ly** *adv* — **elat·ed·ness** *n* -ES

elate·ment \-ātmənt\ *n* -S **:** ELATION

el·a·ter \'eləd-ə(r)\ *n* [NL, fr. Gk *elatēr* driver, fr. *elaunein* to drive, beat out — more at ELASTIC] **1** -S *obs* **:** ELASTICITY **2** [NL, fr. Gk *elatēr*] **a** *cap* **:** the type genus of Elateridae **b** -S **:** any beetle of the family Elateridae **:** CLICK BEETLE **3** -S **:** a filamentous plant structure functioning in the distribution of some product (as spores): as **a :** one of the elongated filaments among the spores in the capsule of a liverwort **b :** a filament of the capillitium of a slime mold **c :** one of the filamentous appendages of the spores in the scouring rushes

¹**elat·er·id** \ə'lad-ərəd\ *adj* [NL *Elateridae*] **:** of or relating to the Elateridae

²**elaterid** \"\ *n* -S **:** a beetle of the family Elateridae **:** CLICK BEETLE

el·a·ter·i·dae \,elə'terə,dē\ *n pl, cap* [NL, fr. *Elater*, type genus + *-idae*] **:** a large family of elongated tapering beetles that commonly have the ability when overturned to flip into the air by a sudden movement of the prothorax and so produce a distinct clicking — compare CLICK BEETLE, WIREWORM

elat·er·in \ə'lad-ərən\ *n* -S [ISV *elaterium* + *-in*] **:** a bitter white crystalline poisonous cathartic substance obtained esp. from elaterium and colocynth

elat·er·ite \-,rīt\ *n* -S [G *elaterit*, fr. Gk *elatēr* driver + G *-it* -ite] **:** a mineral consisting of a dark brown elastic resin occurring in soft flexible masses — called also *elastic bitumen, mineral caoutchouc*

el·a·te·ri·um \,elə'tirēəm\ *n* -S [L, fr. Gk *elatērion* (also, squirting cucumber), fr. neut. of *elatērios* driving, driving away, purgative, fr. *elatēr* driver] **:** a purgative substance precipitated as a fine powder from the juice of the squirting cucumber on spontaneous evaporation and used in the form of yellowish cakes

elat·i·na·ce·ae \ə,latᵊn'āsē,ē, ,elətᵊ'nā-\ *n pl, cap* [NL, fr. *Elatine*, type genus + *-aceae*] **:** a widely distributed family of aquatic or marsh plants (order Parietales) having opposite leaves and small axillary flowers — **elat·i·na·ceous** \ə;latᵊn-'āshəs, ;elətᵊ;nā-\ *adj*

elat·i·ne \ə'latᵊn,ē\ *n, cap* [NL, fr. L, a kind of plant, fr. Gk *elatinē*, fr. fem. of *elatinos* of the silver fir, fr. *elatē* silver fir; perh. akin to Arm *elevin* cedar, Russ *yalovets* juniper] **:** a genus (the type of the family Elatinaceae) of aquatic or amphibious creeping herbs having dimerous to tetramerous flowers

elating *pres part of* ELATE

ela·tion \ə'lāshən, ē'-\ *n* -S [ME *elacioun*, fr. MF *elation*, fr. L *elation-, elatio*, fr. *elatus* (suppletive past part. of *efferre* to carry out) + *-ion-, -io* -ion — more at EFFERENT, ELATE] **1 :** the quality or state of being elated: **a :** SELF-EXALTATION, VAINGLORY ⟨when Lincoln was reelected in 1864 he felt no ~, only humility —Ruth P. Randall⟩ **b :** high spirits **:** BUOYANCY, JOY ⟨and within us, tramping over the valley meadows, was the incredible ~ of those who set out before the sun has risen —John Galsworthy⟩ **2 :** pathological euphoria sometimes accompanied by intense pleasure

¹**ela·tive** \'ēləd·iv, 'el-\ *adj* [L *elatus* + E *-ive*] *of a grammatical case* **:** denoting motion away from

²**elative** \"\ *n* -S [L *elatus* + E *-ive*] **1** *linguistics* **:** the absolute superlative **2** [¹*elative*] **a :** the elative case of a language **b :** a form in the elative case

e layer *n, cap E* **:** the lowest well-defined layer of the ionosphere regularly occurring during the daytime at about 60 miles above the earth's surface and capable of reflecting radio waves of medium frequency — compare E REGION

¹**el·bow** \'el,bō\ *n* -S [ME *elbowe*, fr. OE *elboga, elnboga;* akin to OHG *elinbogo* elbow, ON *olbogi, ölnbogi*, MD *ellenboge;* all fr. a prehistoric Gmc compound whose constituents are akin to OE *eln* ell and *boga* bow — more at ELL, BOW] **1 a :** the joint between the human forearm and upper arm that supports the outer curve of the arm when bent **b :** a joint in the anterior limb of a vertebrate animal corresponding to the human elbow — see DOG illustration **c :** the portion of the sleeve of a garment that encloses this joint; *esp* **:** the portion that covers the outer bend when the arm is flexed ⟨wearing a tattered coat with holes in the ~s⟩ **2 :** something felt to resemble an elbow: as **a :** a sharp bend in a river or coast ⟨north to south through the ~ of the Minnesota river —Meridel Le Sueur⟩ **b** (1) **:** a bend or projection (as in a wall or building) ⟨her starboard quarter ... hit with a solid thump against the ~ of the brick-faced canal side —C.S. Forester⟩ (2) **:** CROSSETTE 1 **c** *archery* **:** the part of the limb of a reflexed bow that bends sharply away from the string **d :** an angular pipe fitting **:** ELL **3 :** an arm of a chair ⟨he sat leaning backward obliquely in an easy chair with his leg thrown over the ~ of it —*Punch*⟩ — **at one's elbow** *or* **at the elbow :** at one's side **:** close at hand **:** NEARBY, ALONGSIDE ⟨with him *at her elbow*, she became a fine draftsman and a compositional designer of enviable talent —J.T.Soby⟩ — **bend an elbow** *also* **crook an elbow** *or* **lift an elbow :** to drink intoxicating liquor **:** have a drink ⟨don't *bend elbows* with strangers in bars —*Wall Street Jour.*⟩ — **out at elbows 1 :** shabbily dressed **:** RAGGED, SHABBY ⟨the wretched little *out at elbows* youngster with ink smudges on his face —Mary S. Watts⟩ **2 :** in financial straits **:** short of funds ⟨if he is a trifle *out at elbows*, so is the empire itself —G.W.Johnson⟩

pipe elbows

²**elbow** \"\ *vb* -ED/-ING/-S *vt* **1 :** to shove aside by jabbing with or as if with the elbow **:** press upon **:** PUSH, JOSTLE, NUDGE ⟨they ~*ed*, punched, and insulted each other —Wirt Williams⟩ ⟨little bazaars and shops ~*ed* one another for standing room —L.C.Douglas⟩ **2 a :** to make (one's way) by elbowing people ⟨the boy ~*ed* his way through the crowd⟩ **b :** to force (one's way) forwardly and impudently ⟨a habit of ~*ing* her way into the best social circles⟩ ~ *vi* **1 :** to elbow one's way **:** push or jostle along ⟨~*ing* through the crowd —Robert Westerby⟩ **2 :** to make an angle **:** TURN ⟨the passage ~*ed* and we were in an enormous cellar —Merle Considine⟩

elbow bending *n* **:** the drinking of beer or liquor

elbowboard \'=(,)=,=\ *n* **:** the inside ledge formed by the projecting board covering the bottom of a window frame

elbow chair *n* **:** ARMCHAIR ⟨he was seated before a large fire in an *elbow chair* —*Encore*⟩

el·bowed \'el,bōd\ *adj* [¹*elbow* + *-ed*] **:** GENICULATE ⟨~ antennae of certain weevils⟩

elbow grease *n* **:** energy vigorously exerted in the performance esp. of manual labor **:** strenuous application of oneself **:** SWEAT ⟨this was the first such expedition not powered solely by the *elbow grease* of oarsmen —*New Yorker*⟩

elbow in hawse : a foul hawse resulting from a 360 degree turn made by a ship riding at two anchors — compare ROUND TURN

elbow of capture : an abrupt turn in the course of a river attributable to stream piracy

elbowroom \'=(,)=,=\ *n* **1 a :** ample room for moving the elbows freely ⟨stepped back to give them ~ —John Fountain⟩ **b :** adequate space for comfortable existence or development **:** sufficient room for work or operation ⟨this plane needs ~ to fly⟩ **2 :** freedom of movement or opportunity **:** LIBERTY ⟨more ~ for interpreting the party line⟩ **syn** see ROOM

elbow stand *n* **:** an acrobatic position in which the body is balanced on the forearms and the legs are held in the air

elbow stone *n* **:** a prehistoric curved stone artifact found in Puerto Rico and the Dominican Republic

el·buck \'el(,)bək\ *Scot var of* ELBOW

eld \'eld\ *n* -S [ME *elde*, fr. OE *yldo, eldo, ældo;* akin to OHG *altī, eltī* old age, eld, ON *elli;* derivative fr. the root of E *old*] **1 a** *dial Brit* **:** period of life **:** AGE **b** *archaic* **:** OLD AGE **2** *archaic* **:** old times **:** ANTIQUITY ⟨a spirit of immemorial ~ pervades this tavern —Norman Douglas⟩ **3** *archaic* **:** an old person

eld *abbr* eldest

el de·bab \el'de,bab\ *n* [Ar *al-dhubāb* the flies (the source of the disease)] **:** a trypanosomiasis of northern African camels resembling surra but caused by a distinct parasite (*Trypanosoma soudanense*)

¹**el·der** \'eldə(r)\ *n* -S [ME *eldre, eller, ellern*, fr. OE *ellærn, ellen;* prob. akin to OE *alor* alder — more at ALDER] **:** a shrub or tree of the genus *Sambucus; esp, Brit* **:** BOURTREE

²**el·der** \'eldə(r)\ *adj* [ME, fr. OE *yldra, ieldra, eldra*, compar. of *ald, eald* old — more at OLD] **1 :** of earlier birth ⟨much the ~ of the two —Norman Demuth⟩ **:** of greater age ⟨the ~ service flag was a ... cobwebby bunting —MacKinlay Kantor⟩ **:** OLDER ⟨great, rich, established ~ nations —Joseph Alsop⟩ **2 :** of or relating to earlier times **:** FORMER ⟨his poems are of the ~ New England tradition —H.V.Gregory⟩ **3** *obs* **:** of or relating to a more advanced time of life **:** LATER ⟨I tender you my service raw and young; which ~ days shall ripen —Shak.⟩ **4 :** of greater experience **:** SENIOR ⟨an ~ educator⟩

³**elder** \"\ *n* -S [ME *eldre*, fr. OE *yldra, ieldra, eldra*, fr. *yldra, ieldra, eldra*, adj.] **1 :** one who lived at an earlier period — usu. used in pl. ⟨rules and standards passed down from the ~s —Paul Woodring⟩ **2 a :** one who is older **:** SENIOR — usu. used in pl. ⟨young people ski and their ~s golf —S.H.Holbrook⟩ **b** *archaic* **:** an aged person ⟨the wither'd ~ hath his Poll claw'd like a Parrot —Shak.⟩ **3** [ME, trans. of LL *senior*] **:** a member of a governing body or ruling class made up of those whose age or experience confers a special dignity on them **:** SUPERIOR — usu. used in pl. ⟨hereditary village ~s governing by common consent ... held political authority beyond the courts —J.M. Van der Kroef⟩ **4** [trans. of LL *presbyter* & Gk *presbyteros*] **:** any of certain church officers or leaders: as **a :** PRESBYTER 1 ⟨at first the Christian churches followed the precedent of the synagogues in their organization and the ~s were the official leaders —E.H.Sugden⟩ **b :** a permanent officer elected by a Presbyterian congregation and ordained to serve on the session and assist the pastor at communion **c :** a fully ordained Methodist minister ⟨made a deacon in 1790 and ordained ~ in 1793 —H.E.Starr⟩ **d :** one ordained to the Melchizedek priesthood in the Mormon Church

⁴**elder** \"\ *n* -S [Flem; prob. akin to OE *ūder* udder — more at UDDER] *dial* **:** UDDER

elderberry \'==- — *see* BERRY\ *n* [ME *eldreberye*, fr. *eldre* elder (bush) + *berye* berry] **1 a :** the edible berrylike drupe of an elder, (as the European bourtree or the No. American elder blow) that is eaten raw or processed into preserves or wines **b :** an elder bush or tree **2 :** DERBY BLUE

elder blow *n* [¹*elder* + *blow* (blossom)] **:** an elder plant; *esp* **:** the No. American elder (*Sambucus canadensis*)

elder fungus *n* **:** JEW'S-EAR

el·der·li·ness \'eldə(r)lēnəs, -lin-\ *n* -ES **:** the quality or state of being elderly

el·der·ly \-lē, -li\ *adj* [²*elder* + *-ly*] **1 :** somewhat old: **a :** rather advanced in years **:** past middle age ⟨we must face the problems of an aging population, i.e., where a much larger proportion of the citizens is ~ —Alan Gregg⟩ **b :** OLD-FASHIONED, OUT-OF-DATE, OUTMODED ⟨an ~ office building on lower Fifth Avenue —Dwight Macdonald⟩ **2 :** of, relating to, or characteristic of one past the prime of life ⟨the Frate carried his doctrine rather too far for ~ ears —George Eliot⟩

el·dern \'eldərn\ *adj* [ME (Scot dial.), fr. ²*elder* + ¹*-en*] *chiefly Scot* **:** ELDERLY

elder statesman *n* **:** an eminent senior member of a group or organization ⟨a much honored *elder statesman* of the geographic profession —*Economic Geog.*⟩; *esp* **:** a retired statesman who unofficially advises national leaders ⟨may hand over the premiership to his younger second-in-command after a year or two in office and stay on in the role of *elder statesman* —*New Yorker*⟩

el·dest \'eldəst\ *adj* [ME, fr. OE *yldest, ieldest, eldest*, superl. of *eald, ald* old — more at OLD] **:** of the greatest age or seniority: **a** *archaic* **:** most ancient **:** EARLIEST ⟨let us pay heed to our ~ scientific brothers and shrewdest symbolists, the mathematicians —Weston La Barre⟩ **b :** FIRSTBORN, OLDEST ⟨when their ~ child was arriving at school age —F.L.Allen⟩

eldest born *n* **:** FIRSTBORN

eldest hand *n* **:** the card player who first receives cards in the deal; *specif* **:** the player to the left of the dealer

el·ding \'eldən, -diŋ\ *n* -S [ME, fr. ON *elding*, fr. *eldr* fire + *-ing* (n. suffix) — more at ANNEAL] *chiefly Scot* **:** FUEL, FIREWOOD

el·do·ra·do \,eldə'rä|(,)dō, -rā|, -ra|, -rá|, |də\ *n* -S *often cap* [after *El Dorado*, fabulously wealthy city or country that 16th cent. explorers thought existed in So. America, fr. Sp, lit., the gilded one] **:** a place of fabulous wealth, abundance, or opportunity ⟨in the ~ of the New World they quickly amassed wealth and power⟩ ⟨the town is a composer's ~ —Aaron Copland⟩ ⟨orchards which in blossoming time offer an ~ of color —Samuel Van Valkenburg & Ellsworth Huntington⟩

el·dress \'eldrəs\ *n* -ES [³*elder* + *-ess*] **:** a female church elder

el·dritch *also* **el·drich** *or* **el·ritch** \'el(d)rich\ *adj* [perh. fr. (assumed) OE *ælfrīce* fairyland, fr. OE *ælf* elf + *rīce* kingdom, power; akin to OE *rīce* powerful, rich — more at ELF, RICH] **:** WEIRD, EERIE, UNCANNY ⟨the ~ screech of hunting horns swelled louder —F.V.W.Mason⟩ ⟨its ~ comedy captivated audiences around the world —Lincoln Barnett⟩

elds *pl of* ELD

¹**el·e·at·ic** \;elē;ad·ik\ *adj, usu cap* [L *Eleaticus* (also, of Elea), fr. Gk *Eleatikos*, fr. *Eleatēs* of Elea (fr. *Elea* — Velia — ancient town in southern Italy) + *-ikos* -ic] **:** of or relating to a school of Greek philosophers founded by Parmenides and developed by Zeno who principally asserted the unity of being and the unreality of motion or change — compare PARMENIDEAN

2eleatic \"\ *n* -s *usu cap* **:** an Eleatic philosopher

el·e·at·i·cism \-d·ə,sizəm\ *n* -s *usu cap* **:** Eleatic doctrine

elec *abbr* **1** electric; electrical; electrician; electricity; electrified **2** electuary

el·e·cam·pane \,eləˌkam'pān, -ˌkəm-, -lē(,)-; -ˈkam,pān\ *n* -s [ME *elena campana*, fr. ML *enula campana*, lit., field inula, fr. *enula* inula (alter. of L *inula* elecampane) + *campana*, fem. of *campanus* of the field, fr. L *campus* field + *-anus* -an — more at INULA, CAMP] **:** a large coarse European herb (*Inula helenium*) having yellow ray flowers and being naturalized in the U.S.

1elect \ə'lekt, ē'l- *sometimes* 'ē,l-\ *adj* [ME, fr. LL & L; LL *electus* chosen of God, fr. L, choice, excellent, selected, fr. past part. of *eligere*] **1 :** chosen esp. by preference or for excellence **:** carefully selected **:** EXCLUSIVE, CHOICE ⟨considered themselves a very ~ group⟩ **2 a :** chosen for office or position but not yet installed — usu. used after the noun ⟨president-*elect*⟩ ⟨delegate-*elect*⟩ **b :** chosen for marriage at some future time to a specified person ⟨bride-*elect*⟩ **3 :** chosen as an object of divine mercy or favor **:** set apart for eternal life — used in theology ⟨to ~ souls a Redeemer comes down who reveals the secret knowledge —W.F.Howard⟩

2elect \ə'l-,ē'l-\ *n, pl* **elect** [ME, fr. LL & L *electus*, adj. & n.] **:** one chosen or set apart: **a :** one chosen by God as the object of mercy or favor ⟨the emperor was the ~ of God —R.M. French⟩ ⟨they were of the ~, those chosen by God —J.C. Brauer⟩ **b :** a select or exclusive group of people ⟨her status changed from that of "outsider" to one of the ~ when her classmates discovered that she could sing F above high C —*Current Biog.*⟩

3elect \"\ *vb* -ED/-ING/-S [ME *electen*, fr. L *electus*, past part. of *eligere* to pick out, choose, select, fr. *e-* + *-ligere* (fr. *legere* to gather, pick out, choose) — more at LEGEND] *vt* **1 :** to make a selection of **:** CHOOSE ⟨having ~*ed* deliberately . . . that stern land and weather —William Faulkner⟩ ⟨concentrators in geological sciences ~ either geology or geography —*Official Register of Harvard Univ.*⟩ **2 :** to choose (a person) for an office, position, or membership ⟨~ a chairman⟩ ⟨~ a leader⟩ ⟨~ a member of a board⟩; *esp* **:** to select (a person) for political office by vote ⟨~ the president of the U.S.⟩ **3 :** to choose (a course of action) esp. by preference **:** decide upon ⟨~*ed* suicide as a preferable fate —*Sydney (Australia) Bull.*⟩ ⟨received the opening kickoff and ~*ed* to punt —Harry Molter⟩ **4 :** to designate or choose as an object of divine mercy or favor ⟨Wyclif argued that the true Church is made up only of those ~*ed* by God —K.S.Latourette⟩ ~ *vi* **:** to make a selection **:** CHOOSE ⟨what is worse still is the power of the big company to ruin the individual as capriciously as it ~*s* —Robert Lekachman⟩ **syn** see DESIGNATE

elect *abbr* **1** electric; electrical; electrician; electricity **2** electuary

elec·tion \ə'lekshən, ē'-\ *n* -s [ME *eleccioun*, fr. MF *election*, fr. LL & L; LL *election-, electio* election to divine favor, fr. L, choice, selection, fr. *electus* (past part. of *eligere* to pick out, choose) + *-ion-, -io* -ion] **1 a :** the act or process of electing **:** CHOICE ⟨the faculty of ~, or the power of free choice —Frank Thilly⟩ ⟨our income-tax system is replete with ~*s* —*Jour. of Accountancy*⟩ **b :** the act or process of choosing a person for office, position, or membership by voting ⟨they had an ~ last week⟩ **c :** an instance of the electorate's exercising its function ⟨the ~ of 1936 was rather uneventful⟩ **d :** divine choice; *specif* **:** predestination of individuals as objects of divine mercy and salvation **e :** the choice of an astrologically favorable time **f :** the selection of a site for or method of surgery **2 :** the fact or status of being elected ⟨an open convention . . . to ratify his ~ to party chief —*Time*⟩ **syn** see CHOICE

election cake *n* **:** a fruitcake usu. made of bread dough, raisins, figs, sugar, egg, and butter and baked in a bread pan

election day *n* **:** a day legally established for the election of public officials; *specif, often cap E&D* **:** the first Tuesday after the first Monday in November in an even year designated for national elections in the U.S. and observed as a legal holiday in most states

election district *n* **1 a :** a district that is created for the administration of elections ⟨all party organization rests ultimately upon the "unit cell" of the precinct or *election district* —W.S.Sayre⟩ **b :** PRECINCT 1c **2 :** a political division of a county in certain states (as Alabama, Florida, Wyoming) in the U.S. — compare JUDICIAL TOWNSHIP

1elec·tion·eer \ə,lekshə'ni(ə)r, ē,-\ *vi* -ED/-ING/-S [*election* + *-eer* (as in *auctioneer*, v.)] **:** to take an active part in an election campaign: as **a :** to campaign for one's own election ⟨the senator ~*ed* vigorously in his opponent's home county⟩ **b :** to try to sway public opinion esp. by the use of propaganda ⟨skillful, amateur ~*ing* all over the country —*New Republic*⟩ ⟨whip up public feeling for ~*ing* purposes or to launch smear attacks —A.E.Norman⟩

2electioneer \"\ *n* -s **:** one who electioneers

election pink *n* **:** PINXTER FLOWER

election posies *n pl* **:** INDIAN PAINTBRUSH

1elec·tive \ə'lektiv, -tēv *also* -təv\ *adj* [MF & ML; MF *electif*, fr. ML *electivus*, fr. L *electus* (past part. of *eligere* to pick out, choose) + *-ivus* -ive — more at ELECT] **1 a** (1) **:** chosen by popular election ⟨an ~ legislature⟩ (2) **:** assigned or filled by popular election ⟨first ~ position was as county probate judge —*Current Biog.*⟩ **b :** of or relating to election ⟨all other ~ functions can only be exercised by the General Assembly —Herbert Weinschel⟩ ⟨the ~ franchise⟩ **c :** based on the right or principle of election ⟨governments may be described . . . as either hereditary or ~ —F.L.Windolph⟩ **2 :** that may be elected **:** permitting a choice (as between alternatives) ⟨a law is ~ if the employer is allowed to accept or reject the act —G.W.Miller⟩ **:** OPTIONAL ⟨for the other half day ~ courses are followed in heterogeneous groups — music, art . . . and physical education —Elise Martens⟩ **3 a :** tending to operate on one substance rather than another ⟨~ fermentation⟩ ⟨~ absorption⟩ ⟨~ attraction⟩ **b :** tending toward one object rather than another **:** sympathetically inclined toward ⟨we Southerners lack . . . an ~ affinity with that book —Norman Douglas⟩ — **elec·tive·ly** \-təvlē, -li\ *adv* — **elec·tive·ness** \-tivnəs, -tēv- *also* -təv-\ *n* -ES

2elec·tive \"\ *n* -s **:** an elective course or subject (as in a college curriculum) ⟨in the late seventies, when I was an undergraduate, ~*s* were still unknown in the smaller New England colleges —John Dewey⟩ ⟨his ~*s* included English 136 and Philosophy 101⟩

elec·tor \-tə(r) *also* -,tō(ə)r *or* -,tȯ(ə)r\ *n* -s [ME *electour*, fr. MF *electeur*, fr. L *elector* one that chooses, fr. *electus* (past part. of *eligere* to pick out, choose) + *-or*] **:** one who is entitled to vote esp. in a political election ⟨the numerous unthinking ~*s* who cast ballots in response to superficial and emotional appeals —Alexander Brady⟩: as **a** [MF or ML; MF *electeur*, fr. ML *elector*, fr. L, one that chooses] **:** one of the German princes entitled to take part in choosing the sovereign head of the Holy Roman Empire ⟨the ~ of Hanover⟩ **b :** a member of the electoral college that elects the president and vice-president of the U.S. ⟨in 1860 he was presidential ~ on the Douglas ticket —H.E.Nettles⟩

elec·tor·al \ə'lekt(ə)rəl, ē'l; ÷ˌlek'tōr-, ÷-ˌtȯr-\ *adj* **1 :** belonging to or holding rank as a German elector ⟨the vendors did not enter ~ Saxony —R.H.Bainton⟩ **2 a :** of or relating to an elector ⟨an ~ district⟩ ⟨the ~ vote⟩ **b :** of or relating to election ⟨the ~ system was modified through the Twelfth Amendment —W.S.Sayre⟩

electoral college *n, sometimes cap E&C* **:** a body of electors ⟨the Prussian House of Representatives was chosen by *electoral colleges* —F.A.Magruder⟩; *esp* **:** the group of presidential electors representing the states in the U.S. ⟨the *Electoral College* is composed of as many representatives as there are senators and representatives in Congress —*Voter's Guide*⟩

elec·tor·al·ly \-rəlē, -li\ *adv* **:** in a manner relating to or involving electors or elections

elec·tor·ate \ə'lekt(ə)rə̇t, ēl- *sometimes* -tə,rāt; *usu* |d·+V\ *n* -s [F *électorat*, fr. ML *elector* + F *-at* -ate] **1 :** the territory, jurisdiction, or dignity of a German elector **2 :** a body of people entitled to vote ⟨the president appealed directly to the ~⟩

elec·to·ri·al \ə'lek'tōrēəl, ē'-, ˌēˌeˌ-, -tȯr-\ *adj* **:** ELECTORAL

electr- *or* **electro-** *comb form* [NL *electr-*, fr. L *electrum* amber] **1 a :** electricity ⟨*electro*meter⟩ **b :** electric ⟨*electrize*⟩ ⟨*electro*magnet⟩ **:** electric and ⟨*electro*medical⟩ **:** electrically ⟨*electro*positive⟩ **2 :** electrolytic ⟨*electro*analysis⟩ **3 :** electromagnetic ⟨*electro*chronograph⟩ **4 :** electron ⟨*electro*philic⟩

elec·tra complex \ə'lektrə-, ē'l\ *n, usu cap E* [after *Electra*, Greek mythological personage who urged her brother Orestes to slay their mother Clytemnestra in revenge for her murder of their father Agamemnon, fr. L, fr. Gk *Ēlektra*] **:** the female counterpart of the Oedipus complex

elec·tress \-rəs\ *n* -ES [fr. earlier *electoress*, fr. *elector* + *-ess*] **:** the wife or widow of a German elector

elec·tret \-rət\ *n* -s [*electricity* + *magnet*] **1 :** a dielectric body in which a permanent state of electric polarization has been set up **2 :** the material of which an electret is composed

1elec·tric \ə'lektrik, ē'-, -rēk\ *or* **elec·tri·cal** \-rəkəl, -rēk-\ *adj* [NL *electricus* produced from amber by friction, electric, fr. ML, of amber, fr. L *electrum* amber, alloy of gold and silver (fr. Gk *ēlektron*) + *-icus* -ic, -ical; akin to Gk *ēlektōr* beaming sun, Skt *ulkā* fiery phenomenon in the sky, meteor] **1 a :** of, relating to, or produced by electricity ⟨~ supply⟩ ⟨~ output⟩ ⟨*electrical* industry⟩ ⟨*electrical* shock⟩ **b :** of, relating to, or produced by a method of reproducing sound in which the cutting stylus is electrically vibrated — compare ACOUSTIC 3a(2) **2 a :** operated by an electric motor ⟨an ~ refrigerator⟩ **b :** heated by an electric current ⟨an ~ stove⟩ **c :** charged by an electric potential **3 :** charged with or as if with an electric current ⟨black hair . . . which went out in all directions in a wild, ~ way —R.P.Warren⟩; *esp* **:** marked by or producing intense excitement ⟨when the people are Irishmen and the town is Dublin, the possibilities are fairly ~ —Harry Levin⟩ ⟨a part in which she gave an ~ performance —Brooks Atkinson⟩ ⟨the effect upon the jurors was *electrical* —Erle Stanley Gardner⟩ ⟨two hours later, before an audience ~ with expectation, the President began his speech —*N.Y. Times*⟩ — **elec·tri·cal·ly** \-rək(ə)lē, -rēk-, -li\ *adv*

2electric \"\ *n* -s **1** *archaic* **:** a nonconductor of electricity (as amber, glass, resin) used to excite or accumulate electricity **2** [*electric (lamp)* or *electric (light)*] **:** an electric light — usu. used in pl. ⟨the church was lit with little ~*s* —Richard Llewellyn⟩ **3 :** an electrically operated vehicle: **a** [*electric (motorcar)*] **:** an electric automobile ⟨nice old ladies driving down . . . Broad Street in their elegant Baker ~*s* —James Thurber⟩ **b** [*electric (railway)*] **:** an electric train or streetcar ⟨~*s* and diesels do not have side rods —John Page⟩ **4** *dial* **:** ELECTRICITY **5** *or* **electric blue** *or* **electric green :** a grayish blue that is greener and deeper than copenhagen, Saxe blue, or old china, redder and deeper than Gobelin, and greener and duller than Quimper

electrical degree *n* **1 :** one 360th of a cycle of an alternating current **2 :** one 360th of the angle subtended at the axis of an alternating current by two consecutive field poles of like polarity

electrical drainage *n* **:** diversion of electric currents from underground pipes to prevent damage by electrolysis

electrical engineer *n* **:** one trained in electrical engineering

electrical engineering *n* **:** a branch of engineering that deals with the practical application of electricity esp. as related to communications, the distribution of power, and the design and operation of machinery and equipment

electrical interlock *n* **:** an interlock operating by the combined action of mechanical and electrical means

electrical precipitation *n* **:** ELECTROSTATIC PRECIPITATION

electrical sheet *n* **:** flat-rolled silicon steel used in electric motors, generators, and transformers

electrical storm *var of* ELECTRIC STORM

electrical transcription *n* **1 :** a phonograph record esp. designed for use in radiobroadcasting **2 :** a radio program broadcast from an electrical transcription

electric board *n* **:** a hard fiberboard used (as in electric switches) for insulation

electric brain *n* **:** COMPUTER a

electric calamine *n* [so called fr. its strong pyroelectric properties] **:** HEMIMORPHITE

electric catfish *n* **:** a catfish (*Malapterurus electricus*) of northern and tropical Africa attaining a length of about 30 inches and having an electric organ of epidermal origin capable of giving a strong shock — called also *raad*

electric cell *n* **:** CELL 6

electric chair *n* **1 :** a chair used in carrying out the death penalty by electrocution **2 :** the penalty of death by electrocution

electric charge *n* **:** a definite quantity of electricity, either negative or positive, usu. regarded as a more or less localized population of electrons separated or considered separately from their corresponding protons or vice versa **:** the quantity of electricity held by a body and construed as an excess or deficiency of electrons

electric clock *n* **:** any of various clocks operated by electricity: **a :** a clock having a spring or weighted arm that is wound at regular intervals by an electric motor **b :** a clock whose pendulum is kept in vibration by electromagnetic impulse **c :** one of a system of electrically operated clocks consisting of a master clock and a number of sympathetic clocks **d :** a clock connected with an electromagnetic recording apparatus **e :** a clock having neither pendulum nor balance, consisting simply of a small alternating-current motor that drives the clock hands through a reducing train of gearing, and telling time by current controlled at the generator to a definite rate of alternations per second

electric current *n* **:** a movement of positive or negative electric particles (as electrons) accompanied by such observable effects as the production of heat, of a magnetic field, or of chemical transformations — compare ALTERNATING CURRENT, DIRECT CURRENT, DISPLACEMENT CURRENT

electric displacement *n* **:** DISPLACEMENT 3a

electric double layer *n* **:** a region existing at the boundary of two phases and assumed to consist of two oppositely charged layers (as a layer of negative ions adsorbed on colloidal particles that attracts a layer of positive ions in the surrounding electrolytic solution) — called also *Helmholtz double layer*

electric ear *n* **1 :** a microphone with accessories adapted to the measurement of sound intensity **2 :** an apparatus resembling an electric ear used for the automatic control of machinery

electric eel *n* **:** an eel-shaped cyprinoid fish (*Electrophorus electricus*) of the rivers of the Orinoco and Amazon basins often attaining a length of six feet and said to disable large animals by its shocks produced by electric organs that consist of modified muscle tissue situated along the ventral part of the body

electric eraser *n* **:** a hand-sized machine with an erasing head driven by an electric motor used esp. in drafting and library work

electric eye *n* **1 :** a photoelectric cell with accessories adapted to the automatic performance of a process (as color selection or lighting control) **2 :** a miniature cathode-ray tube that indicates determination of a condition (as the proper tuning of a radio receiver) — called also *electron-ray tube*

electric fence *n* **:** a wire fence electrically charged to give animals touching it a slight warning shock

electric field *n* **:** a region established by the proximity of electric charges or the variation of surrounding magnetic intensity resulting in the application of mechanical force to an electric charge introduced into the region, the direction of the field at any point being that of the force on a small positive charge placed at that point — compare ELECTRIC INTENSITY

electric fire *n, Brit* **:** a small electric space heater for rooms

electric fish *n* **:** any of several fishes (as the electric eel, electric catfish, electric ray) able to communicate an electric shock by means of special organs

electric fluid *n* **:** a hypothetical imponderable fluid to the presence of which electrical phenomena were formerly attributed — compare EFFLUVIUM 1b

electric furnace *n* **:** a furnace that is heated usu. to very high temperatures by an electric current and used esp. in industry for fusing alloys and refractory materials — see ARC FURNACE, INDUCTION FURNACE

electric green *n* **:** ELECTRIC 5

electric guitar *n* **:** a guitar whose tone is magnified electrically by a microphone or pickup device that is built into the instrument or attached externally, by an audio-frequency amplifier, and by a loudspeaker, the volume and resonance being controlled by the player

electric hammer *n* **:** an electrically driven hammer used esp. in riveting or caulking

electric hygrometer *n* **:** a hygrometer that utilizes changes in electrical resistance (as of a film of salt) to indicate changes in atmospheric humidity

elec·tri·cian \ə,lek'trishən, ē,l- *sometimes* ,ē,l-, *chiefly Brit* ,e,lek- *or* ,elik-\ *n* -s [*electr-* + *-ician* (as in *technician*)] **1 :** a specialist in the field of electricity **2 :** one who installs, maintains, operates, or repairs electrical equipment; *specif* **:** a warrant officer in the U.S. Navy whose specialty is supervision of the installation, maintenance, operation, and repair of electrical equipment

electric intensity *n* **:** the strength of an electric field at any point as measured by the force exerted upon a unit positive charge placed at that point

electric iron *n* **:** an electrically heated smoothing or pressing iron

elec·tric·i·ty \ə,lek'trisəd·ē, ē,l-, -s(ə)t|ē, |i *sometimes* ,ē,l-, *chiefly Brit* ,e,lek- *or* ,elik-\ *n* -ES [NL *electricus* electric + E *-ity* — more at ELECTRIC] **1 :** a fundamental entity of nature consisting of negative and positive kinds composed respectively of electrons and protons or possibly of electrons and positrons, usu. measured in electrostatic units (as the statcoulomb) or electromagnetic units (as the coulomb), observable in the attractions and repulsions of bodies electrified by friction and in certain natural phenomena (as lightning or the aurora borealis), and usu. utilized in the form of electric currents — see NEGATIVE ELECTRICITY, POSITIVE ELECTRICITY, STATIC ELECTRICITY **2 :** a science that deals with the phenomena and laws of electricity **3 :** a contagious feeling of keen excitement or inspiration **:** ENTHUSIASM ⟨you can feel the ~ in the crowd and the band —Bill Simon⟩ **4 :** ELECTRIC CURRENT ⟨heating by ~⟩

electric knife *n* **:** an electrode in the form of a needle that simultaneously cuts and sears tissue

electric lamp *n* **:** a lamp in which electricity is the source of light — compare ARC LAMP, FLUORESCENT LAMP, INCANDESCENT LAMP, NEON LAMP, NERNST LAMP

electric light *n* **:** light produced by an electric lamp; *also* **:** ELECTRIC LAMP

electric light bug *n* [so called fr. the fact that adult bugs are often attracted by bright lights] **:** GIANT WATER BUG

electric lobes *n pl but sing or pl in constr, zool* **:** the part of the medulla of an electric ray that controls the electric organs

electric lock *n* **:** a device to prevent or restrict the movements of a lever, switch, or drawbridge unless the locking member is withdrawn by an electrical device

electric locking *n* **:** the locking by electricity of a railroad mechanism (as a signal or switch) to prevent a change which might endanger an approaching or passing train

electric locomotive *n* **:** an electrically operated locomotive that obtains electric power from an overhead wire, a third rail, or storage battery or that generates its own electric power — compare DIESEL-ELECTRIC LOCOMOTIVE, TURBINE-ELECTRIC LOCOMOTIVE

electric log *n* **1 :** a device for determining the nature of geological strata (as in well digging) by electrical means usu. through resistivity measurements **2 :** the record of tests made by an electric log — compare 1LOG 3b(3)

electric moment *n* **:** the product of the distance between the centers of the charges composing an electric dipole and the magnitude of either charge

electric organ *n* **1 :** a pipe organ with an electric action **2 :** a specialized tract of tissue in which electricity is generated and which consists of closely packed prisms typically of modified muscle tissue separated by sheaths of connective tissue and abundantly supplied with nerves, each prism in turn being composed of many layers of disklike electroplaxes separated from one another by a layer of gelatinous material into which the nerve fibers enter and from which they are distributed to one surface of an adjacent electroplax

electric oscillation *n* **:** OSCILLATION 3

electric pen *n* **:** a hand pen for making stencils that consists essentially of a puncturing needle and a small magnetoelectric device for making it reciprocate

electric plate *n* **:** ELECTROPLAX

electric potential *n* **:** a quantity that in an electric field is roughly analogous to elevation or level in a gravity field and that is measured at any point by the potential energy of a unit positive charge placed at that point and reckoned with reference to some arbitrary zero of potential (as that at an infinite distance from all electric charges or for practical purposes that of the earth or any well-grounded conductor)

electric railroad *or* **electric railway** *n* **:** a railroad on which the trains are drawn by electric locomotives

electric ray *n* **:** any of numerous bottom-dwelling rays (family Torpedinidae) that are widely distributed in warm seas and have the anterior part of the body round and disklike, a short tail terminating in a rayed fin, and a pair of electric organs composed of modified pectoral muscles and occupying the lateral part of each side between the head and the pectoral fin: as **a :** a ray (*Tetranarce occidentalis*) of the eastern coast of No. America that attains a length of about five feet and is capable of giving a severe shock **b :** a somewhat smaller fish (*T. californica*) of the Pacific coast

electric refrigeration *n* **:** refrigeration by means of a compression machine driven by an electric motor

electrics *pl of* ELECTRIC

electric seal *n* **:** hare or rabbit fur clipped and dyed to simulate sealskin

electric shock *n* **:** 3SHOCK 5

electric shocker *n* **:** a device for stunning freshwater fishes by passing a current of electricity through the water of a stream or pond (as for collecting fishes for transport from one body of water to another or for studying fish population)

electric shock therapy *or* **electric shock treatment** *also* **electric shock** *or* **electric therapy** *n* **:** ELECTROSHOCK THERAPY

electric shovel *n* **:** a power shovel using electric power

electric steel *n* **:** steel refined in an electric furnace — called also *electrosteel*

electric storm *or* **electrical storm** *n* **:** a sudden and violent storm usu. accompanied by rain and characterized by electrical phenomena (as thunder and lightning) that often interfere with communications and electric light systems **:** THUNDERSTORM

electric strength *n* **:** DIELECTRIC STRENGTH

electric switch *n* **:** SWITCH 5

electric tape *n* **:** FRICTION TAPE

electric torch *n, Brit* **:** FLASHLIGHT d

electric varnish *n* **:** a varnish having good insulating properties

electric wave *n* **1 :** ELECTROMAGNETIC WAVE **2 :** a high-frequency alternating-current cycle considered as a wave propagated with definite velocity in a conductor

elec·tri·fi·ca·tion \ə,lektrəfə'kāshən, ē,-\ *n* -s **:** the act or process of electrifying or the state of being electrified: as **a :** the act or process of charging, equipping, or supplying with or operating by electricity or the state of being so charged, equipped, supplied, or operated ⟨the ~ of cloud droplets⟩ ⟨the ~ of rural areas⟩ ⟨the ~ of the railroads⟩ **b :** the act or process of markedly exciting or thrilling or the state of being markedly excited or thrilled ⟨the strange pure ecstasy was not a transient ~ —George Meredith⟩ ⟨his charm wrought a positive ~ of the audience⟩

elec·tri·fi·er \-ˌēˌ,fī(ə)r, -īə\ *n* -s **:** one that electrifies

elec·tri·fy \-,fī\ *vt* -ED/-ING/-S [*electric* + *-fy*] **1 :** to charge with electricity ⟨~ a glass rod⟩ **2 :** to excite suddenly and markedly as if by an electric shock **:** startle, jar, or thrill into total attention or concern ⟨a hunger strike that *electrified* all Egypt —*Holiday*⟩ ⟨the boys cooked up a hair-raising piece of news . . . to ~ the girls —Dixon Wecter⟩ esp. pleasurably ⟨the blue-eyed girl whose silvery tones and immense vitality had *electrified* audiences —Alan Tomkins⟩ **3 :** to equip, operate, or supply with electricity ⟨in Minnesota, where the number of *electrified* farms has risen . . . to 90 percent —A.E. Stevenson †1965⟩ ⟨there is waterpower enough to ~ the continent —Waldo Frank⟩

elec·tro \ə'lek(,)trō, e'-\ *n* -s [short for 1*electrotype*] **1 :** ELEC-

TROTYPE **2 :** a reproduction of a coin made by the electrotype process ⟨an ~ of a 1793 cent⟩
elec·tro- *in pronunciations below,* =ˈ== = ə̇ˈlek(ˌ)trō *or* ēˈ- *or* -ˌtrə\ — see ELECTR-
elec·tro·acous·tic *also* **elec·tro·acous·ti·cal** \=ˈ==+\ *adj* [*electr-* + *acoustic, acoustical*] **:** of or relating to electroacoustics
elec·tro·acous·tics \"+\ *n pl but sing in constr* **:** a science that deals with the transformation of acoustic energy into electric energy or vice versa
elec·tro·anal·y·sis \"+\ *n* [NL, fr. *electr-* + *analysis*] **:** chemical analysis by electrolytic methods involving the use of significant amounts of electrical energy (as for electrodeposition) in distinction from electrical methods (as potentiometry or conductometric methods) that use negligible amounts — **elec·tro·an·a·lyt·ic** \"+\ *or* **elec·tro·an·a·lyt·i·cal** \"+\ *adj*
electrobiological \"+\ *adj* **:** of or relating to electrobiology
electrobiologist \"+\ *n* **:** a specialist in electrobiology
electrobiology \"+\ *n* [*electr-* + *biology*] **:** a branch of biology that deals with the electrical phenomena of living organisms
electrocapillarity \"+\ *n* [ISV *electr-* + *capillarity;* orig. formed as F *électrocapillarité*] **:** a change in the surface tension between two immiscible liquids when an electric current passes through the interface from one to the other (as in capillary tubes) — **electrocapillary** \"+\ *adj*
electrocardiogram \"+\ *n* [*electr-* + *cardiogram*] **:** the tracing made by an electrocardiograph used to determine abnormality in the heart muscle
electrocardiograph \"+\ *n* [*electr-* + *cardiograph*] **:** an instrument for recording the changes of electrical potential occurring during the heartbeat (as by photographing vibrations of a string galvanometer connected with the right and left hands or with one hand and one foot) used esp. in diagnosing irregularities of heart action — **electrocardiographic** \"+\ *adj* — **electrocardiographically** \"+\ *adv* — **electrocardiography** \"+\ *n*

electrocardiogram: *P*, first upward deflection due to contraction of auricles; *Q, R, S, T*, deflections due to action of ventricles

electrocautery \"+\ *n* [*electr-* + *cautery*] **1 :** a cautery operated by an electric current **2** *also* **electrocauterization** \"+\ **:** the cauterization of tissue by means of an electrocautery **:** ELECTROCOAGULATION
electrochemical \"+\ *adj* [*electr-* + *chemical*] **:** of or relating to electrochemistry ⟨~ corrosion⟩ — **electrochemically** \"+\ *adv*
electrochemical equivalent *n* **:** the weight of a substance (as an element) deposited or evolved during electrolysis by the passage of a specified quantity of electricity and usu. expressed in grams per coulomb, the value for silver as the usual standard being 0.001118 gram
electrochemical series *n* **:** ELECTROMOTIVE SERIES
electrochemical telegraph *n* **:** CHEMICAL TELEGRAPH
electrochemist \"+\ *n* [*electr-* + *chemist*] **:** a specialist in electrochemistry
electrochemistry \"+\ *n* [*electr-* + *chemistry*] **:** a science that deals with the relation of electricity to chemical changes and with the interconversion of chemical and electrical energy (as in electric cells or in electrolysis) and that has many applications in industry (as in the production of aluminum, alkalies, and chlorine or in electroplating)
electrochromatography \"+\ *n* [*electr-* + *chromatography*] **:** chromatography involving differential electrical migration produced by application of an electric potential
electroclean \"+\ *vt* [*electr-* + *clean*] **:** to clean (a metal surface) by immersion in the form of an electrode in the alkaline bath of an electrolytic cell
electrocoagulate \"+\ *vt* [back-formation fr. *electrocoagulation*] **:** to cause the electrocoagulation of
electrocoagulation \"+\ *n* [*electr-* + *coagulation*] **:** the coagulation of tissue by surgical diathermy; *also* **:** the operation of coagulating tissue in this way **:** ELECTROCAUTERY
electrocoma \"+\ *n* [*electr-* + *coma* (unconsciousness)] **:** the coma induced in electroshock therapy
electroconductive \"+\ *adj* [*electr-* + *conductive*] **:** capable of conducting electricity
electroconization \"+\ *n* [*electr-* + *conization*] **:** CONIZATION
electrocontractility \"+\ *n* [*electr-* + *contractility*] **:** contractility (as of a muscle) in response to electric stimulation
electroconvulsive \"+\ *adj* [*electr-* + *convulsive*] **:** of, relating to, or involving convulsive response to electroshock
electroconvulsive therapy *or* **electroconvulsive shock** *n* **:** ELECTROSHOCK THERAPY
electrocorticogram \"+\ *n* -S [*electr-* + *cortico-* + *-gram*] **:** an electroencephalogram made with electrodes in direct contact with the brain
electrocortin \"+\ *n* [*electr-* + *cortin*] **:** ALDOSTERONE
elec·troc·u·lo·gram \ə̇ˌlekˈträkyəlōˌgram, ēˌl-\ *n* -S [*electr-* + *ocul-* + *gram*] **:** a record of eye movement **:** a recording of the moving eye
elec·tro·cute \ə̇ˈlektrəˌkyüt, ēˈ-, *usu* -üd.+V\ *vt* -ED/-ING/-S [*electr-* + *-cute* (as in *execute*)] **1 :** to put to death as a legal punishment by causing a fatally large electric current to pass through the body ⟨~ a criminal⟩ ⟨a person may be *electrocuted* for treasonable activities in some states⟩ **2 :** to kill by electric shock ⟨the lineman was *electrocuted* when he happened to touch a power wire⟩
elec·tro·cu·tion \=ˌ==ˈkyüshən\ *n* -S **:** the act of killing or putting to death by electric current — **elec·tro·cu·tion·al** \=ˌ==ˈkyüshənᵊl, -shnəl\ *adj*
electrocutor trap *n* **:** an insect trap that kills the insects attracted to it by electric energy
elec·trode \-ˌtrōd\ *n* -S [*electr-* + *-ode*] **:** a conductor (as a metallic substance or carbon) used to establish electrical contact with a nonmetallic portion of a circuit (as in an electrolytic cell, a storage battery, an electron tube, or an arc lamp) — see ANODE, CATHODE
electrodecantation \=ˈ== *at* ELECTRO-+\ *n* [*electr-* + *decantation*] **:** an electrophoretic process utilizing two vertical membranes for concentrating and separating colloidal dispersions by stratification, the layers so formed being separable by decantation into the dispersed particles and the liquid dispersion medium
elec·trode·less discharge \ə̇ˈlekˌtrōdlə̇s-, ēˈ\ *n* **:** a discharge produced in the neighborhood of a high-frequency alternating current under certain conditions through a gas contained in a closed tube without electrodes
[1]**electrodeposit** \=ˈ== *at* ELECTRO-+\ *n* [*electr-* + *deposit* (n.)] **:** a deposit (as metal or rubber) formed on or at an electrode by electrolysis (as in electroplating or electroforming)
[2]**electrodeposit** \"\ *vt* **:** to deposit (as nickel, copper, or rubber) by electrical action, esp. electrolysis
electrodeposition \=ˈ== *at* ELECTRO-+\ *n* [*electr-* + *deposition*] **:** the process of electrodepositing
electrode potential *n* **:** the difference in electric potential between an electrode and the electrolyte with which it is in contact
electrodesiccation \=ˈ== *at* ELECTRO- +\ *n* [*electr-* + *desiccation*] **:** the drying up of tissue by use of a high-frequency electric current applied with a needle electrode
electrodialysis \"+\ *n* [NL, fr. *electr-* + *dialysis*] **:** dialysis accelerated by an electromotive force applied to electrodes adjacent to the membranes and useful esp. in removing electrolytes from naturally occurring colloids (as proteins) — compare ELECTROOSMOSIS
electrodialyze \"+\ *vt* [*electr-* + *dialyze*] **:** to subject to electrodialysis
electrodisintegration \"+\ *n* [*electr-* + *disintegration*] **:** the disintegration of atomic nuclei due to bombardment with electrically charged particles — compare PHOTODISINTEGRATION
elec·tro·dot·ic \"+ˈdäd·ik\ *adj* [*electr-* + Gk *dotikos* inclined to give, giving freely, fr. *dotos* (verbal of *didonai* to give) + *-ikos* -ic — more at DATE] **:** NUCLEOPHILIC
electrodynamic \"+\ *adj* [F *électrodynamique,* fr. *électro-* electr- + *dynamique* dynamic — more at DYNAMIC] **:** of or relating to electrodynamics ⟨signal voltage . . . obtained from ~ velocity-sampling transducers —B.S.Melton⟩
electrodynamics \"+\ *n pl but usu sing in constr* [F *électrodynamique,* fr. *électrodynamique,* adj.] **:** a branch of physics that deals with the effects arising from the interactions of electric currents with magnets, with other currents, or with themselves
electrodynamic speaker *n* **:** a loudspeaker in which the voice coil is attached to and vibrates with the diaphragm — called also *dynamic speaker*
electrodynamometer \"+\ *n* [ISV *electr-* + *dynamometer;* prob. orig. formed as G *elektrodynamometer*] **:** an ammeter or galvanometer in which the torque due to the reaction between two coils in series with each other is balanced by a spiral spring
electroencephalogram \"+\ *n* [ISV *electr-* + *encephalogram;* orig. formed as G *elektrenkephalogramm*] **:** the tracing of brain waves made by an electroencephalograph
electroencephalograph \"+\ *n* [ISV *electr-* + *encephalograph*] **:** an apparatus for detecting and recording brain waves — **electroencephalographic** \"+\ *adj* — **electroencephalographically** \"+\ *adv* — **electroencephalography** \"+\ *n*
electroendosmosis \"+\ *also* **electroendosmose** \"+\ *n, pl* **electroendosmoses** [NL *electroendosmosis,* fr. *electr-* + *endosmosis*] **:** ELECTROOSMOSIS — **electroendosmotic** \"+\ *adj*
electroextraction \"+\ *n* [*electr-* + *extraction*] **:** extraction (as of metals from ores) by electrochemical processes
electrofiltration \"+\ *n* [*electr-* + *filtration*] **:** ELECTROSTATIC PRECIPITATION
electroform \=ˈ==+ˌ-\ *vt* [*electr-* + *form*] **:** to form (shaped articles) by electrodeposition on a mold (as in making electrotypes) — compare ELECTROPLATE
electrogalvanize \=ˈ==+\ *vt* [*electr-* + *galvanize*] **:** to electroplate with zinc
elec·tro·gram \=ˈ==+ ˌgram\ *n* [*electr-* + *-gram*] **:** a tracing of the electric potentials of a tissue (as the brain) made by means of electrodes placed directly in the tissue instead of on the surface of the body
elec·tro·graph \-ˌgraf, -ˌgrȧf\ *n* [*electr-* + *-graph*] **1 :** a phototelegraphic apparatus for the electrical transmission of pictures **2 :** a device used for the etching or transfer of pictures or designs by electrolytic means
elec·tro·graph·ic \=ˈ==+ˈgrafik\ *adj* **1 :** relating to an electrograph **2** [*electr-* + *-graphic*] **:** relating to a method for the analysis of minerals and metals whereby a minute amount of the sample is transferred by electrical means to a suitable surface (as treated paper) where ions are then identified
electrographite \=ˈ== *at* ELECTRO- +\ *n* [ISV *electr-* + *graphite*] **:** artificial graphite produced by heating carbon (as petroleum coke) in an electric furnace — called also *graphitized carbon*
elec·trog·ra·phy \ə̇ˌlekˈträgrəfē, ēˌl- *sometimes* ˌēˌl- *or* (ˌ)eˌl-\ *n* -ES [*electr-* + *-graphy*] **:** the art or process of using an electrograph
electrohysterograph \=ˈ== *at* ELECTRO- +\ *n* [*electr-* + *hyster-* + *-graph*] **:** an instrument for recording changes in electric impulses in the contracting uterine muscle during labor and used esp. in the detection of deviations from the normal progress of labor — **electrohysterography** \"+\ *n*
electrojet \=ˈ==+ˌ-\ *n* [*electr-* + *jet*] **:** an overhead concentration of electric current that is restricted laterally so that in its effects it resembles a line current, that is found in the regions of strong auroral displays and along the magnetic equator, and that is sensitive to changes in the sun's emission of gases and radiation
electrokinetic \=ˈ==+\ *adj* [*electr-* + *kinetic*] **:** relating to the motion of particles or liquids that results from or produces a difference of electric potential (as in electrophoresis, electroosmosis, or the production of a streaming potential) — **electrokinetically** \"+\ *adv*
electrokinetic potential *n* **:** ZETA POTENTIAL
electrokinetics \"+\ *n pl but sing in constr* [*electr-* + *kinetics*] **:** a branch of physics that deals with the motion of electricity esp. as governed by the laws of steady currents in circuits and networks or with the motion of electrified particles in electric and magnetic fields
electrokinetograph \"+\ *n* [*electr-* + *kinet-* + *-graph*] **:** an instrument for measuring velocities of ocean currents by means of electrical effects of their movement in the earth's magnetic field
electrokymogram \"+\ *n* [*electr-* + Gk *kymo-* cym- + E *-gram*] **:** the tracing made by an electrokymograph
electrokymograph \"+\ *n* [*electr-* + Gk *kymo-* cym- + E *-graph*] **:** an instrument for recording graphically the motion of the heart as seen in silhouette on a fluoroscopic screen — **electrokymographic** \"+\ *adj* — **electrokymographically** \"+\ *adv* — **electrokymography** \"+\ *n*
electro–lethaler \"+ˈlēthələ(r)\ *n* -S [*electr-* + *lethal* + *-er*] *Brit* **:** an electrically operated device for shocking a slaughter animal into insensibility before killing it
elec·tro·lier \ə̇ˌlektrəˈli(ə)r, ēˈ-\ *n* -S [*electr-* + *-lier* (as in *chandelier*)] **:** a support for electric lamps; *esp* **:** one like a chandelier
Electrolimit Gage \=ˈ== *at* ELECTRO-+ . . .\ *trademark* — used for a gauge in which contact with the work is indicated by an electric signal
elec·trol·o·gist \ə̇ˌlekˈträlə̇jə̇st, (ˌ)ēˌ-\ *n* -S [blend of NL *electrolysis* (sense 2) and E *-logist*] **:** one that removes hair, warts, moles, and birthmarks by means of an electric current applied to the body with a needle-shaped electrode
electroluminescence \=ˈ== *at* ELECTRO-+\ *n* [*electr-* + *luminescence*] **:** luminescence resulting from a high-frequency discharge through a gas or from application of an alternating current to a layer of phosphor — **electroluminescent** \"+\ *adj*
elec·trol·y·sis \ə̇ˌlekˈträlə̇sə̇s, ēˌl- *sometimes* ˌēˌl-, *chiefly Brit* ˌeˌlek- *or* ˌelik-\ *n* [NL, fr. *electr-* + *-lysis*] **1 :** the process of producing chemical changes by passage of an electric current through an electrolyte (as in a cell), the ions present carrying the current by migrating to the electrodes where they may form new substances (as in the deposition of metals or the liberation of gases) — compare ELECTRODEPOSITION, ELECTROFORM, ELECTROPLATE; see FARADAY'S LAW a **2 :** the destruction of hair roots with an electric current
elec·tro·lyte \ə̇ˈlektrəˌlīt, ēˈ-, *usu* -īd.+V\ *n* -S [*electr-* + Gk *lytos* that may be untied, soluble, verbal of *lyein* to loosen, dissolve — more at LOSE] **1 :** a nonmetallic electric conductor (as a solution, liquid, or fused solid) in which current is carried by the movement of ions instead of electrons with the liberation of matter at electrodes **:** a liquid ionic conductor — see ELECTROLYSIS 1 **2 :** a substance (as an acid, base, or salt) that when dissolved in a suitable solvent (as water) or when fused becomes an ionic conductor
electrolyte acid *n* **:** BATTERY ACID
[1]**elec·tro·lyt·ic** \=ˌ==ˈlid·ik, ˈ=(ˌ)==-, -lit|, |ēk\ *adj* [*electr-* + Gk *lytikos* able to loose — more at LYTIC] **:** of or relating to electrolysis or an electrolyte ⟨an ~ solution⟩ **:** produced or brought about by electrolysis ⟨~ copper⟩ ⟨~ oxidation and reduction⟩ — **elec·tro·lyt·i·cal·ly** \|ə̇k(ə)lē, |ēk-, -li\ *adv*
[2]**electrolytic** \"\ *n* -S **1 :** ELECTROLYTE **2 :** a device utilizing an electrolyte; *specif* **:** ELECTROLYTIC CONDENSER
electrolytic cell *n* **:** a cell for use in electrolysis
electrolytic condenser *n* **:** a capacitor in which one plate is formed of a metal (as aluminum) and the other plate by an electrolyte, the separating dielectric consisting of a film of gas deposited on the metal when the metal is used as an anode in a suitable electrolyte
electrolytic interrupter *n* **:** an electrical interrupter consisting of a cell containing two electrodes in an electrolytic solution in which bubbles formed at frequent intervals by application of current to one of the electrodes continually interrupt the passage of current
electrolytic polishing *n* **:** ELECTROPOLISHING
electrolytic rectifier *n* **:** a rectifier having electrodes that are immersed in an electrolyte and permitting the passage of a current in only one direction
electrolytic refining *n* **:** ELECTROREFINING
elec·tro·lyze \ə̇ˈlektrəˌlīz, ēˈ-\ *vt* -ED/-ING/-S [*electr-* + *-lyze*] **:** to subject to electrolysis
electromagnet \=ˈ== *at* ELECTRO-+\ *n* [*electr-* + *magnet*] **:** a core of magnetic material (as soft iron) that is surrounded wholly or in part by a coil of wire, that is magnetized when an electric current is passed through the wire, and that retains its power of attraction only while the current is flowing
electromagnetic \"+\ *adj* [*electr-* + *magnetic*] **:** of, relating to, or produced by electromagnetism — **electromagnetically** \"+\ *adv*
electromagnetic field *n* **:** a field of force that is made up of associated electric and magnetic components, that results from the motion of an electric charge, and that possesses a definite amount of electromagnetic energy

electromagnet: *1, 1* current-carrying coils, *2* armature, *3* load

electromagnetic induction *n* **:** the induction of an electromotive force in a circuit by varying the magnetic flux linked with the circuit
electromagnetic mass *n* **:** the mass that is equivalent to the kinetic energy of a moving charge
electromagnetic radiation *n* **:** a succession of electromagnetic waves
electromagnetics \"+\ *n pl but sing in constr* **:** ELECTROMAGNETISM 2
electromagnetic spectrum *n* **:** the entire range of wavelengths or frequencies of electromagnetic radiation from the shortest gamma rays to the longest radio waves, visible light comprising only a small part of the range
electromagnetic theory of light : a theory in physics: light consists of electromagnetic oscillations perpendicular to the direction of travel of the wave motion
electromagnetic unit *n* **:** any of a system of electrical units based primarily upon the magnetic properties of electric currents, the fundamental cgs unit being the abampere
electromagnetic wave *n* **:** one of the waves that are propagated by simultaneous periodic variations of electric and magnetic field intensity, the two kinds of oscillation being perpendicular to each other, and that include radio waves, infrared, visible light, ultraviolet, X rays, and gamma rays in ascending order of frequency
electromagnetism \"+\ *n* [*electr-* + *magnetism*] **1 :** magnetism developed by a current of electricity **2 :** a branch of physical science that deals with the physical relations between electricity and magnetism (as the development of magnetism by an electric current or the effect of magnets upon currents)
electromechanical \"+\ *adj* [*electr-* + *mechanical*] **1 :** of, relating to, or being a mechanical process, device, or assembly of parts actuated or controlled electrically **2 :** of or relating to electromechanics
electromechanics \"+\ *n pl but sing in constr* [ISV *electr-* + *mechanics*] **:** a branch of electrodynamics that deals with the mechanical forces involved in electric circuits
elec·tro·mer \ə̇ˈlektrəmə(r), ēˈ-\ *n* -S [*electr-* + *-mer*] **:** one of two or more substances that differ only in the distribution of electrons — compare RESONANCE — **elec·tro·mer·ic** \=ˈ==-ˈmerik\ *adj*
electrometallurgical \=ˈ== *at* ELECTRO-+\ *adj* **:** of or relating to electrometallurgy
electrometallurgist \"+\ *n* **:** a specialist in electrometallurgy
electrometallurgy \"+\ *n* [*electr-* + *metallurgy*] **:** a branch of metallurgy that deals with the application of electric current either for electrolytic deposition or as a source of heat (as in smelting or refining)
elec·trom·e·ter \ə̇ˌlekˈträməd·ə(r), (ˌ)ēˌ-\ *n* [*electr-* + *-meter*] **:** any of various instruments for detecting or measuring electric-potential differences or ionizing radiations by means of the forces of attraction or repulsion between charged bodies — compare CAPILLARY ELECTROMETER, ELECTROSCOPE
electrometer tube *n* **1 :** an amplifier tube of extremely high sensitivity used in a vacuum-tube measuring instrument (as a voltmeter) **2 :** a vacuum tube having high impedance in the grid circuit so as to minimize the undesirable control-grid current
electrometric \=ˈ== *at* ELECTRO-+\ *adj* [*electr-* + *-metric*] **:** of or relating to electrical measurements esp. of differences of potential **:** measured by an electrometer — **electrometrically** \"+\ *adv*
electromigratetics \=ˈ== *at* ELECTRO-+\ *n pl but usu sing in constr* [*electr-* + *migratetics*] **:** ELECTRONOGRAPHY
electromigration \"+\ *n* [*electr-* + *migration*] **:** migration (as of ions or colloidal particles) in an electric field; *specif* **:** an electrolytic process of separating isotopes or ionic species on the basis of their different ionic mobilities
electromotive \"+\ *adj* [*electr-* + *motive* (adj.)] **:** of, relating to, or tending to produce an electric current
electromotive force *n* **:** something that moves or tends to move electricity **:** the amount of energy derived from an electrical source per unit quantity of electricity passing through the source (as a cell or generator)
electromotive series *or* **electromotive force series** *n* **:** an arrangement of metallic elements or ions usu. in a column or table according to their electrode potentials determined under specified conditions, the order showing the tendency of one metal to reduce the ions of any other metal below it in the series; *also* **:** a similar arrangement including nonmetallic elements or ions as well as metallic elements — called also *electrochemical series*
electromyogram \"+\ *n* [*electr-* + *myogram*] **:** a tracing made by an electromyograph
electromyograph \"+\ *n* [*electr-* + *myograph*] **:** an instrument for the simultaneous recording of a visual and sound record of electric waves associated with activity of skeletal muscle that is used in the diagnosis of neuromuscular disorders — **electromyographic** \"+\ *adj* — **electromyographically** \"+\ *adv* — **electromyography** \"+\ *n*
elec·tron \ə̇ˈlekˌträn *sometimes* -ˌtrən\ *n* -S [*electr-* + *-on*] **:** one of the constituent elementary particles of an atom being a charge of negative electricity equal to about 1.602×10^{-19} coulomb, having a mass when at rest of about 9.109×10^{-28} gram or $\frac{1}{1837}$ that of a proton, being the least massive known charged particle, and having a magnetic moment of about 1 Bohr magneton associated with its one half quantum unit of spin
electron affinity *n* **1 :** the degree to which an atom or molecule attracts additional electrons **2 :** the minimum energy required to remove an electron from a negative ion to produce a neutral atom or molecule **3 :** the negative of the energy required to introduce an additional initially free electron into a crystal
elec·tro·nar·co·sis \=ˈ== *at* ELECTRO-+\ *n* [NL, fr. *electr-* + *narcosis*] **:** unconsciousness induced by passing a weak electric current through the brain and used in treating certain mental disorders
electron ballistics *n* **:** a branch of electronics that deals with the motions of free electrons or other electric particles in electric or magnetic fields
electron cloud *n* **1 :** the system of electrons surrounding the nucleus of an atom **2 :** an electronic space charge in a vacuum tube
electron diffraction *n* **:** an effect due to the wavelike nature of electrons and observed when a narrow beam of them upon passing through a very thin layer of a material (as a metal crystal) is deflected in particular directions and if allowed to fall on a fluorescent screen produces a pattern of light and dark areas, the pattern formed by these areas being characteristic of the material traversed
electronegative \=ˈ== *at* ELECTRO-+\ *adj* [*electr-* + *negative*] **1 a :** charged with negative electricity **:** having a tendency to pass to the anode in electrolysis **b :** capable of acting as the positive electrode of a voltaic cell **:** CATHODIC — used esp. in electrical engineering **2 a :** having a tendency to attract electrons esp. in the formation of an electrovalent bond **:** ELECTROPHILIC ⟨fluorine is the most ~ of the elements⟩ **b :** capable of acting as the negative electrode of a voltaic cell **:** ANODIC
electronegativity \"+\ *n* **:** the quality, state, or degree of being electronegative; *specif* **:** the power of an atom or radical in a compound to attract electrons esp. in the formation of an electrovalent bond

electron emission *n* **1 :** the issuing of electrons from a substance (as in photoelectric, thermionic, or radioactive processes) **2 :** the rate of electron emission
electroneutral \ˌ=ˈ== *at* ELECTRO-+\ *adj* [*electr-* + *neutral*] **:** NEUTRAL 3e — **electroneutrality** \"+\ *n*
electron gas *n* **:** a population of free electrons either in a vacuum or in a metallic conductor whose distribution and motions are subject to laws somewhat analogous to those of gas molecules
electron gun *n* **:** the electron-emitting cathode and its surrounding assembly in a cathode-ray tube for directing, controlling, and focusing the stream of electrons to a spot of desired size
elec·tron·ic \əˌlekˈtränik, ēˌl- *sometimes* eˌl- *or* ˌēˌl- *or* ˌeˌl-\ *adj* [*electron* + *-ic*] **1 :** of or belonging to an electron ⟨an ~ rectifier⟩ **2 :** of or relating to electronics; *esp* **:** utilizing devices constructed or working by the methods or principles of electronics ⟨an ~ circuit⟩ ⟨an ~ organ⟩ ⟨an ~ clock⟩ ⟨~ control⟩ — **elec·tron·i·cal·ly** \-nək(ə)lē, -nēk-, -li\ *adv*
electronic brain *n* **:** a large computing machine that depends primarily on electronic devices for its operation
electronic carillon *n* **:** CARILLON 1c
electronic heating *n* **:** DIELECTRIC HEATING
elec·tron·ics \əˌlekˈträniks, ēˌl- *sometimes* ˌēˌl- *or* (ˌ)eˌl-\ *n pl but sing in constr* **:** a branch of physics that deals with the emission, behavior, and effects of electrons in vacuums and gases and with the utilization of electronic devices
electronic tube *n* **:** ELECTRON TUBE
electron lens *n* **:** a device for converging or diverging a beam of electrons by means of either an electric or a magnetic field
electron micrograph *n* **:** a micrograph made with an electron microscope — **electron micrography** *n*
electron microscope *n* **:** an electron-optical instrument in which a beam of electrons focused by means of an electron lens is used to produce an enlarged image of a minute object on a fluorescent screen or photographic plate in a manner analogous to that in which light is used to form the image in a compound microscope — **electron microscopy** *n*
electron multiplier *also* **electron multiplier tube** *n* **:** an electronic device (as an electron tube or a component of an electron tube) that amplifies a corpuscular or photon emission by means of the secondary electron emission produced by it
elec·tron·o·graph·ic \əˌlekˌtränəˈgrafik, (ˌ)ēˌl-\ *adj* **:** done by or designed for electronography ⟨an ~ press⟩ ⟨~ printing⟩
elec·tro·nog·ra·phy \əˌlektrəˈnägrəfē, ēˌl-\ *n* -ES [*electron* + *-o-* + *-graphy*] **:** a printing process in which the ink is transferred by electrostatic action across a gap between printing plate and impression cylinder — called also *onset*
elec·tron–optical \əˈlekˌträn, -ˌtran+\ *adj* **:** of or relating to electron optics
electron optics *n* **:** a branch of electronics that deals with those properties of beams of electrons that are analogous to the properties of rays of light
electron pair *n* **:** a group of two electrons belonging to one atom or shared by two atoms as a chemical bond
electron–ray tube *n* **:** ELECTRIC EYE 2
electron telescope *n* **:** an electron-optical instrument that penetrates obstacles to vision (as fog, smoke, darkness, or distance) by means of infrared rays, the image being focused on a photosensitive cathode that in turn produces the final enlarged electron image on a fluorescent screen
electron tube *n* **:** an electronic device in which conduction by electrons takes place through a vacuum or a gaseous medium within a sealed glass or metal container and which has various common uses (as amplification of electrical energy and the conversion of alternating current to direct current and vice versa) that are based on the controlled flow of electrons
electron volt *n* **:** a unit of energy equal to the energy gained by an electron in passing from a point of low potential to a point one volt higher in potential: 1.60×10^{-12} erg
electrooptic \ˌ=ˈ== *at* ELECTRO-+\ *or* **electrooptical** \"+\ *adj* [*electr-* + *optic, optical*] **:** of or relating to electrooptics — **electrooptically** \"+\ *adv*
electrooptics \"+\ *n pl but sing in constr* [ISV *electr-* + *optics*] **:** a branch of optics that deals with the effects of an electric field upon light traversing it
electrosmosis \"+\ *also* **electroosmose** \"+\ *or* **elec·tros·mo·sis** \əˈ|lektr, ē|+\ *n, pl* **electroosmoses** [NL *electroosmosis, electrosmosis*, fr. *electr-* + *osmosis*] **:** the movement of a conducting liquid (as water in clay) through a porous diaphragm under the action of an electromotive force applied to electrodes on opposite sides of the diaphragm — called also *electroendosmosis* — **electroosmotic** \ˌ=ˈ== *at* ELECTRO-+\ *adj* — **electroosmotically** \"+\ *adv*
electrooxidation \ˌ=ˈ== *at* ELECTRO-+\ *n* [*electr-* + *oxidation*] **:** oxidation at the anode in an electrolytic cell
elec·tro·phil·ic \"+ˈfilik\ *adj* [*electr-* + *-philic*] **:** having an affinity for electrons **:** electron-seeking **:** CATIONOID — contrasted with *nucleophilic* ⟨~ reagents⟩ ⟨~ attack on a double bond⟩ — **elec·tro·phil·i·cal·ly** \-lək(ə)lē\ *adv*
elec·tro·phone \ə=ˌ=ˌfōn\ *n* [*electr-* + *-phone*] **:** an instrument (as a theremin) that produces musical tones by means of oscillating electric circuits — **elec·tro·phon·ic** \ˌ=ˌ=ˈfänik\ *adj* — **elec·tro·phon·i·cal·ly** \-nək(ə)lē\ *adv*
elec·tro·pho·re·sis \ˌ=ˌ==ˌfəˈrēsə̇s\ *n* [NL, fr. *electr-* + *-phoresis*] **:** the movement of suspended particles through a fluid under the action of an electromotive force applied to electrodes in contact with the suspension, important applications being in the separation of colloids (as proteins, clay, humus) and the deposition on one of the electrodes of coatings (as of oxides on cathodes for electron tubes and of rubber and synthetic polymers) — called also *cataphoresis* — **elec·tro·pho·ret·ic** \ˌ==fəˈred·ik\ *adj* — **elec·tro·pho·ret·i·cal·ly** \-d·ək(ə)lē\ *adv*
[1]**elec·troph·o·rus** \əˌlekˈträf(ə)rəs, ēˌl- *sometimes* ˌēˌl- *or* (ˌ)eˌl-\ *n, pl* **electropho·ri** \-fəˌrī, -ˌrē\ [NL, fr. *electr-* + *-phorus* (fr. Gk *-phoros* -phore)] **:** an instrument for the production of electric charges by induction consisting of a disk (as of resin, shellac, or ebonite) that is negatively electrified by friction and a metal plate that becomes charged by induction when placed upon the disk, the repelled negative charge being conducted away by momentary contact (as of the operator's finger) after which the plate with its remaining positive charge is removed by its insulating handle
[2]**electrophorus** \"\ *n, cap* [NL, fr. *electr-* + *-phorus*] **:** a genus of cyprinoid fishes comprising the electric eel and being included in the family Gymnotidae or sometimes made the type of a separate family
electrophotographic \ˌ=ˈ== *at* ELECTRO-+\ *adj* **:** of, relating to, or used in electrophotography
electrophotography \"+\ *n* [*electr-* + *photography*] **:** photography in which images are produced by electrical means (as in xerography)
electrophrenic \"+\ *adj* [*electr-* + *phrenic*] **:** relating to or induced by electrical stimulation of the phrenic nerve ⟨~ respiration⟩
electrophrenic respiration *n* **:** artificial respiration by means of an electrophrenic respirator used esp. in poliomyelitis and other conditions in which the nervous control of breathing is impaired
electrophrenic respirator *n* **:** a device for the regular recurrent electrical stimulation of the phrenic nerve or nerves to induce respiratory movements artificially and induce breathing
electrophysiologic \ˌ=ˈ== *at* ELECTRO- +\ *or* **electrophysiological** \"+\ *adj* [ISV *electrophysiology* + *-ic, -ical*] **1 :** of or relating to electrophysiology ⟨~ methods⟩ **2** [*electr-* + *physiologic, physiological*] **:** of, relating to, or involving the electrical aspects of physiological processes ⟨~ phenomena⟩ — **electrophysiologically** \"+\ *adv*
electrophysiologist \"+\ *n* **:** a specialist in electrophysiology
electrophysiology \"+\ *n* [ISV *electr-* + *physiology*] **1 :** a branch of physiology that is concerned with the electric phenomena associated with living bodies and involved in their functional activity **2 :** electric phenomena (as of a body part or organ) ⟨the ~ of synaptic transmission⟩
elec·tro·pism \əˈlektrəˌpizəm, ēˈ-\ *n* [blend of *electr-* and *-tropism*] **:** ELECTROTROPISM
[1]**elec·tro·plate** \-ˌplāt\ *n* [*electr-* + *plate*, n.] **:** something electroplated; *specif* **:** [1]ELECTROTYPE 1
[2]**electroplate** \"\ *vt* **1 :** to plate with an adherent continuous coating by electrodeposition; *esp* **:** to plate (a metal or metal-coated or graphite-coated nonmetal serving as cathode during the electrolysis) with a metal ⟨~ a wax recording disc⟩ — compare ELECTROFORM **2 :** ELECTROTYPE
elec·tro·plat·er \-ād·ə(r)\ *n* **:** one that electroplates **:** PLATER
elec·tro·plax \-ˌplaks\ *n* -ES [NL, fr. *electr-* + Gk *plax* anything flat and broad — more at PLANK] **:** one of the flattened plates of modified muscle constituting the typical structural element of the electric organ of some fishes
elec·tro·plexy \-ˌpleksē\ *n* -ES [*electr-* + *-plexy* (as in *apoplexy*)] *Brit* **:** ELECTROSHOCK THERAPY
elec·tro·pneu·mat·ic \ˌ=ˈ== *at* ELECTRO- +\ *adj* [*electr-* + *pneumatic*] **:** of or relating to a combination of electrical and pneumatic effects **:** operated by electric and pneumatic power ⟨an ~ signal⟩ — **electropneumatically** \"+\ *adv*
electropolish \"+\ *vt* [*electr-* + *polish*] **:** to produce a smooth bright surface on (metal) by immersion as an anode in an electrolytic bath
electropositive \"+\ *adj* [*electr-* + *positive*] **1 a :** charged with positive electricity **:** having a tendency to pass to the cathode in electrolysis **b :** capable of acting as the negative electrode of a voltaic cell **:** ANODIC — used esp. in electrical engineering **2 a :** having a tendency to release electrons esp. in an oxidation-reduction reaction **:** NUCLEOPHILIC ⟨sodium is a highly ~ element⟩ **b :** capable of acting as the positive electrode of a voltaic cell **:** CATHODIC
electroprecipitation \"+\ *n* [*electr-* + *precipitation*] **:** ELECTROSTATIC PRECIPITATION
elec·tro·pult \əˈlektrəˌpəlt, -pu̇lt\ *n* -S [*electr-* + *-pult* (as in *catapult*)] **:** an electrical catapult for accelerating airplanes to takeoff speed on a short runway that consists of a car and a track which react with each other as the stator and rotor of an induction motor to give the car great acceleration when enormous electrical power is supplied for a short time
electropyrexia \ˌ=ˈ== *at* ELECTRO- +\ *n* [NL, fr. *electr-* + *pyrexia*] **:** artificial fever induced by electrical means for therapeutic purposes
electroreduction \"+\ *n* [*electr-* + *reduction*] **:** reduction at the cathode in an electrolytic cell
electrorefining \"+\ *n* [*electr-* + *refining*] **:** refining of a metal (as copper) by electrolysis, the crude metal being used as the anode going into solution and the pure metal being deposited upon the cathode — called also *electrolytic refining*
electroresection \"+\ *n* [*electr-* + *resection*] **:** resection by electric means **:** ELECTROSURGERY
elec·tro·ret·i·no·gram \"+ˈret°nəˌgram\ *n* [*electr-* + *retina* + *-o-* + *-gram*] **:** a graphic record of the electric activity of the retina used esp. in the diagnosis of conditions of the retina
electros *pl of* ELECTRO
elec·tro·scope \əˈ==+ˌskōp\ *n* [prob. fr. F *électroscope*, fr. *électro-* electr- + *-scope*] **:** any of various instruments for detecting the presence of an electric charge on a body, for determining whether the charge is positive or negative, or for indicating and measuring intensity of radiation by means of the motion imparted to charged bodies (as strips of gold leaf) suspended from a metal conductor within an insulated chamber — compare ELECTROMETER
electroshock \ˌ=ˈ=+\ *n* [*electr-* + *shock*] **1 :** [3]SHOCK 5 **2 :** ELECTROSHOCK THERAPY
electroshock therapy *n* **:** the treatment of mental disorder by the induction of coma through use of an electric current
electrosmosis *var of* ELECTROOSMOSIS
electrostatic \ˌ=ˈ== *at* ELECTRO- +\ *adj* [ISV *electr-* + *static*] **1 :** of or relating to static electricity or electrostatics **2 :** of, relating to, or characterized by a special type of spray painting utilizing electrically charged paint particles to insure complete coating of an object — **electrostatically** \"+\ *adv*
electrostatic bond *n* **:** a chemical bond (as an electrovalent bond or a hydrogen bond) characterized by electrostatic attraction between ions or molecules
electrostatic field *n* **:** ELECTRIC FIELD
electrostatic generator *n* **:** an apparatus for the production of heavy electrical discharges at very high voltage commonly consisting of an insulated hollow conductor (as a sphere) that accumulates in its interior the charge continuously conveyed from a source of direct current (as a high-voltage rectifier-transformer) by an endless belt of flexible nonconducting material (as silk, rayon, or paper) revolving on insulated motor-driven drums, the voltage thus generated being used esp. for accelerating charged particles in nuclear bombardment
electrostatic induction *n* **:** induction of an electric charge in a conductor due to the proximity of another charged body
electrostatic lens *n* **:** an electron lens that utilizes an electric field
electrostatic precipitation *n* **:** removal of suspended particles (as dust and acid mists) from a gas (as air or blast-furnace gas) by charging the particles and precipitating them by applying a strong electric field (as by passing the gas between collecting and discharge electrodes in a precipitator) — compare COTTRELL PROCESS
electrostatics \ˌ=ˈ== *at* ELECTRO- +\ *n pl but sing in constr* **:** a branch of physics that deals with phenomena due to attractions or repulsions of electric charges but not dependent upon their motion
electrostatic unit *n* **:** any of a system of electrical units based primarily upon forces of interaction between electric charges with the fundamental cgs unit being the statcoulomb — abbr. *esu*
electrostatic voltmeter *n* **:** an electrometer of the electrostatic type graduated to read directly in volts or kilovolts
electrosteel \ə=ˈ=+ˌ-\ *n* [*electr-* + *steel*] **:** ELECTRIC STEEL
electrostimulation \ˌ=ˈ=+\ *n* [*electr-* + *stimulation*] **:** electroshock administered in nonconvulsive doses
electrostriction \"+\ *n* [*electr-* + *-striction* (as in *constriction*)] **:** deformation of a dielectric body as the result of an applied electric field — compare MAGNETOSTRICTION — **elec·tro·stric·tive** \"+ˌstriktiv\ *adj*
electrosurgery \"+\ *n* [*electr-* + *surgery*] **:** diathermy for surgical purposes
electrosurgical \"+\ *adj* [*electr-* + *surgical*] **:** of, relating to, or performed by means of electrosurgery
electrosynthesis \"+\ *n* [NL, fr. *electr-* + *synthesis*] **:** synthesis accomplished with the aid of electricity; *esp* **:** synthesis of an organic compound by electrolysis — **electrosynthetic** \"+\ *adj* — **electrosynthetically** \"+\ *adv*
electrotactic \"+\ *adj* [*electr-* + *-tactic*] **:** of or relating to electrotaxis
electrotaxis \"+\ *n* [NL, fr. *electr-* + *-taxis*] **:** movement in which an electric current constitutes the directive factor **:** GALVANOTAXIS
electrotechnic \"+\ *or* **electrotechnical** \"+\ *adj* [*electr-* + *technic, technical*] **:** of or relating to electrotechnology
electrotechnician \"+\ *n* [*electr-* + *technician*] **:** a specialist in electrotechnology
electrotechnics \"+\ *n pl but sing in constr* [*electr-* + *technics*] **:** ELECTROTECHNOLOGY
electrotechnology \"+\ *n* [*electr-* + *technology*] **:** a science that deals with the practical application of electricity
electrotherapist \"+\ *n* **:** one that practices electrotherapy
electrotherapy \"+\ *n* [*electr-* + *therapy*] **:** treatment of disease by means of electricity (as by diathermy or by means of electrically generated heat) — compare ELECTROSHOCK THERAPY
electrothermal \"+\ *or* **electrothermic** \"+\ *adj* [*electr-* + *thermal or thermic*] **:** relating to both electricity and heat **:** combining electricity and heat ⟨~ bath⟩; *specif* **:** relating to the generation of heat by electricity — compare THERMOELECTRIC
electrotin \"+ˌtin\ *vt* [*electr-* + *tin*] **:** to electroplate with tin
elec·tro·tome \əˈ==+ˌtōm\ *n* [*electr-* + *-tome*] **:** an electric cutting instrument used in electrosurgery
electrotone \"+ˌ-\ *n* [*electr-* + *tone*] **:** ELECTROPHONE
electrotonic \ˌ=ˈ=+\ *adj* [NL *electrotonus* + E *-ic*] **1 :** of, induced by, relating to, or constituting electrotonus ⟨the ~ condition of a nerve⟩ ⟨~ induction of depolarization⟩ **2 :** ELECTROPHONIC — **electrotonically** \"+\ *adv*
electrotonicity \"+\ *n* **:** ELECTROTONUS
elec·trot·o·nus \əˌlekˈträt°nəs, ēˌl- *sometimes* ˌēˌl- *or* (ˌ)eˌl-\ *n* [NL, fr. *electr-* + *tonus*] **:** the altered sensitivity of a nerve when a constant current of electricity passes through any part of it — see ANELECTROTONUS, CATELECTROTONUS
electrotropic \ˌ=ˈ== *at* ELECTRO- +\ *adj* [*electr-* + *-tropic*] **:** of or relating to electrotropism
elec·trot·ro·pism \əˌlekˈträ·trəˌpizəm, ēˌl- *sometimes* ˌēˌl- *or* (ˌ)eˌl-\ *n* [*electr-* + *-tropism*] **:** bodily orientation in relation to an electric current **:** GALVANOTROPISM
[1]**elec·tro·type** \əˈlektrəˌtīp, ēˈ-\ *n* [*electr-* + *type*] **1 :** a duplicate printing surface made by pressure molding in wax, lead, or other plastic material the surface to be reproduced, dusting the mold with graphite when necessary to make it electroconductive, and electrodepositing on it a thin shell (as of copper) which is then backed up with lead and sometimes given an extra facing of a harder metal (as nickel or chromium) — compare NICKELTYPE **2 :** a print made from an electrotype
[2]**electrotype** \"\ *vt* **:** to make an electrotype from (a printing surface) ~ *vi* **:** to be reproducible by electrotyping
elec·tro·typ·er \-pə(r)\ *n* **:** one that makes electrotypes
electro–ultrafiltration \ˌ=ˈ== *at* ELECTRO- +\ *n* [*electr-* + *ultrafiltration*] **:** ultrafiltration brought about by electroosmosis
electrovalence \"+\ *or* **electrovalency** \"+\ *n* [*electr-* + *valence, valency*] **:** valence characterized by the transfer of one or more electrons from one atom to another with the formation of ions (as in sodium chloride and other simple salts); *also* **:** the number of positive or negative charges acquired by an atom by the loss or gain of electrons — called also *ionic valence;* distinguished from *covalence* — **electrovalent** \"+\ *adj* — **electrovalently** \"+\ *adv*
electrovalent bond *n* **:** a chemical bond formed between ions of opposite charge — called also *ionic bond;* distinguished from *covalent bond*
electroviscosity \"+\ *n* [*electr-* + *viscosity*] **:** the effect of the presence of ions upon the viscosity of a solution or suspension — **electroviscous** \"+\ *adj*
electroviscous effect *n* **:** the increase in viscosity due to an electric charge on solid particles in a solution
electrowinning \"+\ *n* [*electr-* + *winning*] **:** the recovery esp. of metals from solutions by electrolysis
elec·trum \əˈlektrəm, ēˈ-\ *n* -S [ME, fr. L — more at ELECTRIC] **1** *archaic* **:** AMBER 2 **2 :** a natural pale yellow alloy of gold and silver
elects *pres 3d sing of* ELECT
elec·tu·ary \əˈlekchəˌwerē, ēˈ-, -ri\ *n* -ES [ME *electuarie*, fr. L *electuarium, electarium*, prob. by folk etymology (influence of *electus*, past part. of *eligere* to elect and *-arium* -ary) fr. Gk *ekleikton*, fr. *ekleichein* to lick up, fr. *ek*, *ex* out + *leichein* to lick — more at ELECT, EX-, LICK] **:** CONFECTION 1b; *esp* **:** a medicated paste prepared with honey or other sweet, used in veterinary practice, and administered by smearing on the teeth, gums, or tongue
el·ee·mos·y·nar \ˌeləˈmäsᵊnə(r) *also* -lē(ə)ˈm- *sometimes* -ˈmäzᵊn-\ *n* -S [ML *eleemosynarius*, fr. LL *eleemosyna* alms + L *-arius* -ary, -ar (n. suffix) — more at ALMS] **:** one that distributes charity or doles out relief **:** ALMONER
el·ee·mos·y·nary \-ᵊnˌerē, -ri\ *adj* [ML *eleemosynarius*, fr. LL *eleemosyna* + L *-arius* -ary (adj. suffix)] **1 :** of or relating to charity **:** CHARITABLE, PHILANTHROPIC ⟨a rich man given to many ~ activities⟩ ⟨~ relief⟩ **2 a :** nonprofit and receiving all or a great part of sustaining funds from donations or gifts ⟨about 90 percent of the hospitals are of a governmental, charitable, or ~ and nonprofit character —*U.S. Code*⟩ ⟨churches, lodges, and other ~ institutions —*Sat. Eve. Post*⟩ **b :** provided by an institution of this nature ⟨an ~ education⟩
eleemosynary corporation *n* **:** a corporation organized for charitable purposes — contrasted with *civil corporation*
el·e·gance \ˈeləgən(t)s, -lēg-\ *n* -S [MF *elegance*, fr. L *elegantia*, fr. L *elegant-, elegans* + *-ia* -y] **1 a :** refined grace or dignified propriety that expresses good breeding or good taste **:** URBANITY ⟨never looked more radiant, moved with greater ~, ease, or grace, or acted with truer style —John Mason Brown⟩ ⟨waltzes performed with great delicacy and ~ to the music of eight guitars —C.L.Jones⟩ **b :** tasteful richness of design or ornamentation **:** refined luxury ⟨householders who demand ~ in the chambers they sleep in, no matter what the price tags say —*New Yorker*⟩ **c :** dignified gracefulness or restrained beauty of style **:** POLISH ⟨a cultivated man should express himself by tongue or pen with some accuracy and ~ —C.W.Eliot⟩ **d :** scientific precision, neatness, and simplicity ⟨the ~ of a mathematical equation —Lewis Mumford⟩ **2 :** something that is elegant **:** REFINEMENT ⟨I flatter myself that we've always preserved the ~s, the finer graces —Elmer Davis⟩ **3** *pharmacy* **:** the quality or state of being elegant or of having elegant characteristics
el·e·gan·cy \-nsē, -si\ *n* -ES [ME *elegancie*, fr. L *elegantia*] **:** ELEGANCE — usu. used in pl. ⟨Lord Chesterfield . . . that arbiter of *elegancies* —P.E.More⟩ ⟨*elegancies* such as silk, porcelain, fans, and screens —Victor Purcell⟩
[1]**el·e·gant** \-nt\ *adj* [MF or L; MF *elegant*, fr. L *elegant-, elegans;* akin to L *eligere* to choose, select — more at ELECT] **1 a :** characterized by refined grace or dignified propriety esp. in appearance or manner **:** tastefully correct and refined ⟨she is not conventionally beautiful . . . but she is charming to look at and ~ to her fingertips —John Martin⟩ **b :** characterized by tasteful richness esp. of design or ornamentation **:** luxurious or sumptuous in a refined way ⟨carrying his briefcase, an ~ piece of luggage of excellent leather and the best bronze hardware —Lionel Trilling⟩ ⟨in the glade, still standing in it, many of them after two hundred years, are thirty-nine ~ white houses —*New Yorker*⟩ **c :** characterized by dignified gracefulness and restrained beauty esp. in style or performance **:** POLISHED ⟨an ~ novel, one with the richness, restraint, and subtle obliquity which belong properly to elegance —*Saturday Rev.*⟩ **d :** characterized by scientific precision, neatness, and simplicity ⟨mathematicians say of a problem, a demonstration, or a solution in their science, when it exhibits perfect lucidity and form, that it is ~ —Isabel Paterson⟩ **2** *pharmacy* **:** pleasant in taste, attractive in appearance, and free from objectionable odor ⟨an ~ nontoxic emulsion⟩ **3 :** of a high grade or quality **:** EXCELLENT, FINE, SPLENDID ⟨he agreed with her that it must be an ~ place and he didn't wonder she wanted to go there —J.C.Lincoln⟩ **syn** see CHOICE
[2]**elegant** *or* **élé·gant** \ālāgäⁿ\ *n, pl* **elegants** *or* **élégants** \-äⁿ(z)\ [F *élégant*, fr. *élégant*, adj., fr. MF *elegant*] **:** a fashionable man **:** DANDY
ele·gante *or* **élé·gante** \ālāgäⁿt\ *n, pl* **elegantes** *or* **élégantes** \-t(s)\ [F *élégante*, fr. fem. of *élégant*, adj.] **:** a fashionable woman
el·e·gant·ly \ˈeləgəntlē, -lēg-, -li\ *adv* **:** in an elegant manner
[1]**el·e·gi·ac** \ˌeləˈjīək, -lēˈ- *also* -īˌak; *also* əˈlējēˌak *or* ēˈlē-\ *also* **el·e·gi·a·cal** \ˌeləˈjīəkəl, -lēˈ-\ *adj* [LL *elegiacus*, fr. Gk *elegeiakos*, fr. *elegeion* elegiac couplet, elegy] **1 a :** consisting of two dactylic hexameter lines the second of which is often felt to be pentameter and is made up of two hemistichs each containing two dactyls and a long syllable **:** consisting of two dactylic hexameter lines the second of which has the short elements omitted in the third and sixth feet — usu. used of classical Greek couplets **b :** comprising or metrically similar to the second line of such a couplet **c** (1) **:** written in or consisting of such couplets (2) **:** noted for having written poetry in such couplets **d :** of or relating to the period in Greece around the seventh century B.C. when poetry written in such couplets flourished **2 :** of, relating to, befitting, or comprising elegy or an elegy ⟨an ~ poem on the death of a friend⟩; *esp* **:** expressing sorrow or lamentation often for something now past **:** PLAINTIVE, NOSTALGIC, MELANCHOLY ⟨an ~ regret for departed youth⟩ ⟨an ~ lament for a long-lost tradition⟩ ⟨~ poignance, excruciating nostalgia —Peggy Bennett⟩ **3 :** being the meter characteristic of a kinah — compare KINAH METER
[2]**elegiac** \"\ *n* -S **:** an elegiac couplet, verse, or poem
elegiac pentameter *n* **:** an elegiac hexameter verse
elegiac stanza *n* **:** a quatrain in iambic pentameter with alternate lines rhyming
ele·gi·am·bus \ˌeləˌjīˈambəs, əˌlējēˈam-\ *n, pl* **elegiam·bi** \-ˌbī\ [LL, fr. LGk *elegiambos*, fr. Gk *elegeion* + *iambos* iamb — more at IAMB] **:** a verse in classical Greek or Latin poetry composed of half an elegiac pentameter and four iambic feet
el·e·gi·ast \ˌeləˈjīəst, -lēˈ-, -īˌast; əˈlējēˌast, ēˈlē-, -jēəst\ *n* -S [by alter.] **:** ELEGIST
el·e·gist \ˈeləjəst\ *n* -S [*elegy* + *-ist*] **:** a composer of an elegy

ele·git \ə'lējət, ā'lāgət\ *n* -s [L, he has chosen, perf. indic. 3d sing. of *eligere* to choose — more at ELECT] **:** a judicial writ of execution no longer legal in England by which a defendant's goods and if necessary his lands are delivered for debt to the plaintiff until either the debt is paid by the rents and profits or the defendant's interest has expired

el·e·gize \'eləˌjīz\ *vb* -ED/-ING/-S [*elegy* + *-ize*] *vi* **:** to lament or celebrate in elegy ~ *vt* **:** to write an elegy upon

el·e·gy \'eləjē, -ji\ *n* -ES [L *elegia*, fr. Gk *elegeia*, *elegeion*, fr. *elegos* song of mourning or lamentation accompanied by the flute, prob. of non-IE origin] **1 a :** a song or poem expressing sorrow or lamentation esp. for one who is dead **2 :** a poem in elegiac couplets **3 a :** a pensive or reflective poem typically highly subjective and usu. sorrowful, nostalgic, or melancholy **b :** a musical composition in pensive or mournful mood

ele·i·din \ə'lēədən\ *n* -s [F *eleidine*, fr. *eleo-* elaio- + *-ide* -ide + *-ine* -in] **:** a substance related to keratin and occurring in small granules that stain deeply with hematoxylin and are located in the cells of the stratum lucidum of the epidermis

elem *abbr* **1** element **2** elementary

el·e·me figs *or* **el·e·mi figs** \'eləmē-\ *n pl* [Turk *eleme* selected, sifted] **:** Smyrna figs of superior quality packed flat

[1]**el·e·ment** \'eləmənt\ *n* -s [ME, fr. OF & L; OF, fr. L *elementum*] **1 a :** one of the simple substances air, water, fire, and earth of which according to early natural philosophers the physical universe was composed **b :** one of these substances in its natural form or occurrence ⟨the ~ of the fire is quite put out —John Donne⟩ ⟨drank of the pure and limpid ~⟩ **c** (1) **:** one of the celestial spheres of ancient astronomy **:** one of the celestial bodies (2) **:** HEAVENS, SKY **d elements** *pl* **:** weather conditions viewed as activities of the elements; *esp* **:** violent or severe weather ⟨attacked by the full fury of the ~*s*⟩ **e** (1) **:** one of the four elements viewed as a natural habitat ⟨water is the ~ of fishes⟩ (2) **:** the state or sphere natural or suited to any person or thing ⟨in that cloistered academic atmosphere he was in his ~⟩ ⟨mystery was his mental ~ —T.L.Peacock⟩ **2 :** one of the constituent parts, principles, materials, or traits of anything **:** one of the relatively simple forms or units that enter variously into a complex substance or thing ⟨bricks are ~*s* of a wall⟩ ⟨cells are ~*s* of living bodies⟩ **:** one of the simplest parts or principles of which anything consists or into which it may be analyzed: as **a elements** *pl* **:** the bread and wine used in the Eucharist **b elements** *pl* **:** the simplest principles of any art, science, or subject of study **:** RUDIMENTS ⟨mastered the ~*s* of this abstruse and subtle doctrine⟩ ⟨taught him the ~*s* of geometry⟩ **c :** one of a number of distinct or disparate units, parts, traits, or characteristics of which something tangible or intangible is composed ⟨the constitution was oddly compounded of democratic and feudal ~*s*⟩ ⟨there was an ~ of gravity in his appearance⟩; *specif* **:** one of a number of distinct or different groups or classes of which a human community is composed ⟨the criminal ~ in this city⟩ ⟨he obtained the solid support of the laboring ~⟩ **d** (1) **:** a part of a geometric magnitude (as of an area) (2) **:** a generator of a geometric figure (as of a cone) (3) **:** one of a set of numbers (as in a progression) or of symbols (as in a matrix) **e** (1) **:** one of the necessary data or values upon which a system of calculations depends or general conclusions are based ⟨the ~*s* of a planet's orbit⟩ (2) **:** one of the factors or conditions playing a part in or determining the outcome of some process or activity ⟨fine teamwork and hard hitting were key ~*s* in the team's pennant victory⟩ **f :** any of more than 100 fundamental metallic and nonmetallic substances that consist of atoms of only one kind and that either singly or in combination constitute all matter, most of these substances lighter in weight than and including uranium being found in nature and the rest being produced artificially by causing changes in the atomic nucleus (as by bombardment) **:** a substance that is composed exclusively of atoms having the same atomic number and that cannot be separated into simpler substances by ordinary chemical means — compare [3]COMPOUND 2a, ELEMENTARY PARTICLE; see ISOTOPE, PERIODIC TABLE, RADIOELEMENT **g :** a distinct part of a composite device (as the cathode, grid, and plate of a triode, the individual lenses of an objective, or the two metals of a thermocouple) ⟨circuit ~*s* of a doorbell installation⟩ ⟨heating ~ of an electric iron⟩ **h :** one of the basic constituent units of a tissue (as a cell or fiber) **i :** any of the modified cells often lacking the protoplast and with end walls lacking wholly or in part that make up the vessels of xylem or the sieve tubes of phloem; *also* **:** a young protoxylem cell before it has differentiated into a trachea or tracheid **j :** one of the subdivisions of a military unit (as a squad, company, or battalion) **k :** a part of a biota (as a fossil biota) that is usu. associated with a different region or environmental situation ⟨an extrazonal ~ from Moravia —*Biol. Abstracts*⟩ **l :** one of the physical properties or states of the atmosphere (as temperature, humidity, pressure, clouds, wind, or precipitation) **m** (1) **:** a simple component of perception **:** a sensation or sense datum (2) **:** a member of a class in logic

CHEMICAL ELEMENTS

ELEMENT	SYMBOL	ATOMIC NUMBER	ATOMIC WEIGHT[1]	SPECIFIC GRAVITY[2]	MELTING POINT[3]	BOILING POINT[3]	DISCOVERY DATE[4]
actinium	Ac	89	[227]	—	1050	—	1899
aluminum	Al	13	26.9815	2.702	660	2057	1754
americium	Am	95	[243]	11.7	<1100	—	1944
antimony	Sb	51	121.75	6.684	630.5	1380	ancient
argon	Ar or A	18	39.948	1.784g/l	−189.2	−185.7	1894
arsenic	As	33	74.9216	5.727	814 (36 atm.)	615 (subl.)	1649
astatine	At	85	[210]	—	—	—	1940
barium	Ba	56	137.34	3.5	850	1140	1774
berkelium	Bk	97	[247]	—	—	—	1949
beryllium	Be	4	9.0122	1.85	1278	2970	1798
bismuth	Bi	83	208.980	9.80	271.3	1560	1737
boron	B	5	10.811	3.33	2300	2550	1702
bromine	Br	35	79.909	2.928	−7.2	58.78	1826
cadmium	Cd	48	112.40	8.642	320.9	767	1817
calcium	Ca	20	40.08	1.55	845	1240	1808
californium	Cf	98	[251]	—	—	—	1949
carbon	C	6	12.01115	2.25(gr.)	3700 (subl.)	4200	ancient
cerium	Ce	58	140.12	6.90	640	1400	1803
cesium	Cs	55	132.905	1.873	28.5	670	1860
chlorine	Cl	17	35.453	3.214g/l	−103	−34.6	1810
chromium	Cr	24	51.996	7.20	1890	2200	1797
cobalt	Co	27	58.9332	8.9	1495	2900	1737
columbium	Cb	(see niobium)					
copper	Cu	29	63.54	8.92	1083	2336	ancient
curium	Cm	96	[248]	7 (?)	—	—	1944
dysprosium	Dy	66	162.50	8.56	—	—	1886
einsteinium	Es or E	99	[254]	—	—	—	1952
erbium	Er	68	167.26	9.16	1250	—	1843
europium	Eu	63	151.96	5.24	1150	—	1901
fermium	Fm	100	[253]	—	—	—	1952
fluorine	F	9	18.9984	1.70g/l	−223	−188	1768
francium	Fr	87	[223]	—	—	—	1939
gadolinium	Gd	64	157.25	7.95	—	—	1886
gallium	Ga	31	69.72	5.904(s)	29.78	1983	1875
germanium	Ge	32	72.59	5.35	958.5	2700	1886
gold	Au	79	196.967	19.3	1063	2600	ancient
hafnium	Hf	72	178.49	13.3	2207	<3200	1923
helium	He	2	4.0026	0.1785g/l	−272.2 (26 atm.)	−268.9	1895
holmium	Ho	67	164.930	8.76	—	—	1879
hydrogen	H	1	1.00797	0.0899g/l	−259.14	−252.8	1671
indium	In	49	114.82	7.30	156.4	2000	1863
iodine	I	53	126.9044	4.93	113.7	184.35	1811
iridium	Ir	77	192.2	22.42	2454	>4800	1804
iron	Fe	26	55.847	7.86	1535	3000	ancient
krypton	Kr	36	83.80	3.708g/l	−156.6	−152.9	1898
lanthanum	La	57	138.91	6.15	826	1800	1839
lawrencium	Lr	103	[257]	—	—	—	1961
lead	Pb	82	207.19	11.344	327.4	1620	ancient
lithium	Li	3	6.939	0.534	186	1336	1817
lutetium	Lu	71	174.97	9.74	—	—	1907
magnesium	Mg	12	24.312	1.74	651	1107	1755
manganese	Mn	25	54.9380	7.20	1260	1900	1774
mendelevium	Md or Mv	101	[256]	—	—	—	1955
mercury	Hg	80	200.59	13.55	−38.87	356.58	ancient
molybdenum	Mo	42	95.94	10.2	2620	5560	1777
neodymium	Nd	60	144.24	6.9	840	—	1885
neon	Ne	10	20.183	0.9002g/l	−248.7	−245.9	1898
neptunium	Np	93	[237]	19.5	640	—	1940
nickel	Ni	28	58.71	8.90	1455	2900	1751
niobium	Nb	41	92.906	8.55	1950	2900	1801
nitrogen	N	7	14.0067	1.2506g/l	−209.9	−195.8	1772
nobelium	No	102	[253]	—	—	—	1957
osmium	Os	76	190.2	22.48	2700	>5300	1804
oxygen	O	8	15.9994	1.429g/l	−218.4	−182.96	1774
palladium	Pd	46	106.4	11.40	1549	2540	1803
phosphorus	P	15	30.9738	1.82 (yell.)	44.1 (yell.)	280	1669
platinum	Pt	78	195.09	21.45	1773	4300	1748
plutonium	Pu	94	[244]	19.82	639.5	3508	1940
polonium	Po	84	[210]	—	—	—	1898
potassium	K	19	39.102	0.86	62.3	760	1702
praseodymium	Pr	59	140.907	6.5	940	—	1885
promethium	Pm	61	[145]	—	—	—	1947
protactinium	Pa	91	[231]	15.37	—	—	1917
radium	Ra	88	[226]	5	960	1140	1898
radon	Rn	86	[222]	9.73g/l	−110	−61.8	1900
rhenium	Re	75	186.2	20.53	3160	—	1925
rhodium	Rh	45	102.905	12.4	1985	>2500	1803
rubidium	Rb	37	85.47	1.532	38.5	700	1861
ruthenium	Ru	44	101.07	12.6	>1950	—	1844
samarium	Sm	62	150.35	6.93	1350	—	1879
scandium	Sc	21	44.956	2.5	1200	2400	1879
selenium	Se	34	78.96	4.82	220	688	1818
silicon	Si	14	28.086	2.42	1420	2600	1824
silver	Ag	47	107.870	10.5	960.8	1950	ancient
sodium	Na	11	22.9898	0.97	97.5	880	1702
strontium	Sr	38	87.62	2.6	757	1150	1790
sulfur	S	16	32.064	2.07(rh)	112.8	444.6	ancient
tantalum	Ta	73	180.948	16.6	3027	4100	1802
technetium	Tc	43	[99]	11.49	—	—	1937
tellurium	Te	52	127.60	6.25	452	1390	1783
terbium	Tb	65	158.924	8.33	—	—	1843
thallium	Tl	81	204.37	11.85	302	1457	1861
thorium	Th	90	232.038	11.2	1750	>3000	1828
thulium	Tm	69	168.934	9.35	—	—	1879
tin	Sn	50	118.69	7.28	231.9	2270	ancient
titanium	Ti	22	47.90	4.5	1800	>3000	1791
tungsten	W	74	183.85	19.3	3370	5900	1783
uranium	U	92	238.03	18.7	1133	3818	1789
vanadium	V	23	50.942	5.96	1710	3000	1831
wolfram	W	(see tungsten)				—	
xenon	Xe	54	131.30	5.851g/l	−112	−107	1898
ytterbium	Yb	70	173.04	7.01	1800	—	1907
yttrium	Y	39	88.905	5.51	1490	2500	1794
zinc	Zn	30	65.37	7.14	419.5	907	1742
zirconium	Zr	40	91.22	6.4	1900	>2900	1789

[1]International chemical atomic weights (C=12) are given which for most elements are those of a naturally occurring mixture of isotopes. Numbers in square brackets are mass numbers of the isotopes of longest known life.
[2]For gases density in grams per liter is given instead of specific gravity.
[3]Temperatures are given in centigrade degrees.
[4]"Ancient" indicates that the element has been known since ancient times and that there is no record of date of discovery. A dash means that data are not known.

Abbreviations (designations of allotropic forms under SPECIFIC GRAVITY apply to all physical constants):

atm.	=atmospheres	s	=solid
g/l	=grams per liter	subl.	=sublimes
gr.	=graphite	yell.	=yellow
rh	=rhombic		

syn COMPONENT, CONSTITUENT, INGREDIENT, INTEGRANT, FACTOR: ELEMENT applies to anything, tangible or intangible, making up a part of a complex or compound whole ⟨the *elements* of a house are the walls, roof, and floors —*Military Engineer*⟩ ⟨the *elements* in an electrical circuit are electrical resistance, inductance, and electrical capacitance —H.F.Olson⟩ ⟨another *element* common to all novels is characterization —R.D.Jacobs⟩ ⟨another useful *element* in the theories of Paracelsus was the doctrine that diseases were highly specific in their action —S.F.Mason⟩ It sometimes indicates irreducible simplicity ⟨resolving the problem into its various *elements*⟩ COMPONENT and CONSTITUENT are often interchangeable in applying to any parts comprising a compounded or complex thing or intangible system, although the first may occas. call attention to the fact of existing as a separate entity, the second to the fact of comprising as a part ⟨he employed numerous workmen to make the lock *components* by hand —S.F.Mason⟩ ⟨in addition to the music-minded who will shop and combine *components* with view entirely to end results, there are those who prefer the convenience of an assembled unit —Irving Kolodin⟩ ⟨the *components* of knowledge can never be harmonized until all the relevant facts are in —Bernard De Voto⟩ ⟨to discover the structure of a chemical molecule it was necessary to know the combining numbers of its *constituent* atoms —S.F.Mason⟩ ⟨the *constituent* elements in the great monopolies found other ways to maintain a community of interest —Allan Nevins & H.S.Commager⟩ ⟨rhythm is a property of words, character a product that needs analysis before a satisfactory account of its effect can be given in terms of its *constituents*, and a product, moreover, that invites extraliterary scrutiny —C.H.Rickword⟩ INGREDIENT is more likely to stress notions of tangible substances that one combines together to form something else than the preceding words are ⟨the *ingredients* of a cake⟩ ⟨the *ingredients* of concrete⟩ ⟨electric power is one of the basic *ingredients* of the nation's industrial and economic welfare —K.W.Hamilton⟩ ⟨using the word "philosophic" to cover the unscientific *ingredients* of philosophy —T.S.Eliot⟩ INTEGRANT may apply to a binding essential component. FACTOR, often not a synonym for other words in this group, may apply to an element or component that exerts effectuating force toward composition, operation, or direction ⟨the mechanical engineer became a dominant *factor* in a civilization based on the utilization of the energy in coal —Waldemar Kaempffert⟩ ⟨only recently has the original Darwinian bias toward an overemphasis of the *factor* of natural selection yielded to the proper evaluation of other factors —Edward Sapir⟩

[2]**element** *vt* -ED/-ING/-S [back-formation fr. *elemented*, fr. ME, fr. [1]*element* + *-ed*] *obs* **:** to compose of elements

[1]**el·e·men·tal** \ˌelə'mentᵊl\ *adj* [ME *elementall*, fr. ML *elementalis*, fr. L *elementum* + *-alis* -al] **1 a :** of, relating to, or caused by a great force of nature ⟨~ forces important to those engaged in a struggle with the soil —Frank Thilly⟩ ⟨the rains come with ~ force, scourging the earth wrathfully each day —Gertrude Diamant⟩ ⟨and over all the ancient ~ smell of the sea —Al Hine⟩ ⟨a race against hail, cold rains, or some other ~ catastrophe —J.K.Howard⟩ **b** *obs* **:** MATERIAL, PHYSICAL **c :** representing or personifying a force of nature ⟨the worship of ~ spirits⟩ **:** of or relating to a natural force or object conceived as a supernatural power or being ⟨~ religion⟩ **d :** comparable to a force or object of nature (as in power or breadth) **:** characterized by stark simplicity, naturalness, or unrestrained or undisciplined vigor or force **:** not complex or refined **:** CRUDE, PRIMITIVE, FUNDAMENTAL, BASIC, ⟨his roughhewn ~ poetry —*Key Reporter*⟩ ⟨the ~ simplicity of his mind that baffled me —Jack London⟩ ⟨the real Highland world . . . is . . . something raw, stark, and ~ —Richard Joseph⟩ ⟨a creature of flesh and ~ feelings —Nicola Chiaromonte⟩ ⟨had a shrewd knowledge of all those predicaments in which ~ human nature comes to the surface —John Erskine⟩ ⟨the smell was ~, farmyards and manure and sweat —Laura H. Mackenzie⟩ **2 a** (1) **:** of, relating to, or being an element (2) **:** consisting of a single chemical element **:** UNCOMBINED ⟨~ sulfur⟩ (3) **:** of, relating to, or being the ultimate or basic constituent of anything ⟨the ~ stuff . . . out of which the many forms of life have been molded —Jack London⟩ **b :** ELEMENTARY, INTRODUCTORY, RUDIMENTARY ⟨in the new nations they lacked ~ political and civic rights —Oscar Handlin⟩ ⟨this ~ recital of what your Government is doing —F.D. Roosevelt⟩ **c :** forming an integral part **:** INHERENT ⟨such self-assurance is so ~ that it is not even tinged with conceit —Albert Dasnoy⟩ ⟨possessed an ~ sense of rhythm⟩ — **el·e·men·tal·ly** \-ᵊlē, -ᵊli\ *adv*

[2]**elemental** \"\ *n* -s **1 :** SPIRIT, SPECTER, WRAITH ⟨a frightening ~ which appears as a pillar of whirling darkness —G.G.Carter⟩ **2 :** an elementary concern **:** a first principle **:** RUDIMENT — usu. used in pl. ⟨sorrow, deprivation, and dread—those constant ~*s* among the very poor —Sylvia Berkman⟩ ⟨not too much I can teach him . . . but I guess I still remember the ~*s* —Agnes S. Turnbull⟩

el·e·men·tal·ism \ˌ==ˈ=ᵊlˌizəm\ *n* -s **:** a tendency to postulate a separation into independent entities or elements of things (as mind and body, space and time) that can be only verbally so separated — **el·e·men·tal·is·tic** \ˌ==ˌ=ᵊlˈistik\ *adj* — **el·e·men·tal·is·ti·cal·ly** \-tək(ə)lē, -tēk-, -li\ *adv*

el·e·men·tar·i·ly \ˌelə(ˌ)menˈterəlē, -'men·trəlē, -li\ *adv* **:** in an elementary manner

el·e·men·ta·ri·ness \ˌelə'mentərēnəs, -n·trē-, -rin-\ *n* -ES **:** the quality or state of being elementary

el·e·men·ta·ry \ˌelə'mentərē, -n·trē, -ri\ *adj* [ME *elementare*, fr. MF or L; MF *elementaire*, fr. L *elementarius*, fr. *elementum* element + *-arius* -ary — more at ELEMENT] **1 a** *obs* **:** MATERIAL,

PHYSICAL **b** : ELEMENTAL 1 ⟨these stark ~ powers . . . this wind, this earth, this sea, this forest —J.C.Powys⟩ **2** : of, relating to, or treating of the elements, rudiments, or first principles of any subject or thing : INTRODUCTORY, RUDIMENTARY, SIMPLE, FUNDAMENTAL, PRIMITIVE ⟨an ~ text in geology⟩ ⟨an ~ precaution of historical research —M.R.Cohen⟩ ⟨the play has a very ~ plot⟩ ⟨the serf had the ~ security of the land itself —Lewis Mumford⟩ ⟨look at those hippopotami —how ~ is their . . . appearance —Llewelyn Powys⟩ : BEGINNING ⟨a concise aid to ~ students of Irish literature —G.B. Saul⟩; *specif* : of or relating to an elementary school ⟨Alaska's public schools had 765 teachers serving 100 ~ departments —*Americana Annual*⟩ ⟨a skilled craftsman has always . . . been able to earn more than an ~ schoolmaster —Roy Lewis & Angus Maude⟩ **3 a** : ELEMENTAL 2a(2) ⟨an ~ substance⟩ **b** : of, relating to, or being the nuclear family **4** *of a hand* : coarse and clumsy with the palm large and heavy and with short fingers and short nails usu. held by palmists to indicate low or animal characteristics and very little mental capacity or self-control ⟨the ~ hand rarely rises above the most menial occupations —Alice D. Jennings⟩

elementary algebra *n* : the part of algebra dealing with the simple properties (as the fundamental operations, factoring, simple equations)

elementary analysis *n* : the detection or determination of the elements composing a substance

elementary body *n* : one of the distinguishable units making up an inclusion body and believed to be or to contain the actual infective particles of certain viruses

elementary charge *n* : an apparently fundamental constant that is the smallest known quantity of electricity, is either positive or negative (as the positron or the electron), and has a value of about 4.802×10^{-10} statcoulomb or 1.602×10^{-19} absolute coulomb

elementary geometry *n* : the part of Euclidean geometry dealing with the simpler properties of straight lines, circles, planes, polyhedrons, the sphere, the cylinder, and the right circular cone

elementary particle *n* : any of the subatomic units of matter and energy (as the electron, pion, proton, and photon) formerly held to be indivisible entities that are distinguished by a characteristic mass and by quantum properties (as charge and spin)

elementary school *n* : a school in which elementary subjects (as reading, writing, spelling, and arithmetic) are taught to children from about six to about twelve years of age which in the U.S. covers the first six or eight grades — compare SECONDARY SCHOOL

elementary species *n* : SUBSPECIES

elements *pl of* ELEMENT, *pres 3d sing of* ELEMENT

elements of an orbit : a set of numerical quantities that define the orbit of a member of the solar system or of a binary star and permit computation of the body's position at any given time

el·e·mi \ˈeləmē\ *n* -s [alter. of earlier *elimi*, fr. NL, prob. fr. Ar *al-lāmi* the elemi] : any of certain fragrant oleoresins obtained from tropical trees of the family Burseraceae and used chiefly in varnishes, lacquers, and printing inks and formerly in medicinal plasters: as **a** : a soft yellowish plastic resin from several African, Asiatic, and Philippine trees of the genus *Canarium*; *esp* : MANILA ELEMI — compare BREA 1a(2) **b** : a resin obtained from certain trees of the genus *Protium* and used as incense

elem·i·cin \əˈleməsən\ *n* -s [ISV *elemic* (fr. *elemi* + *-ic*) + *-in*; orig. formed as G *elemizin*] : a liquid ether $C_{12}H_{16}O_3$ found in some essential oils (as oil of Manila elemi)

elemi figs *var of* ELEME FIGS

el·e·mol \ˈeləˌmōl, -ōl\ *n* -s [*elemi* + *-ol*] : a crystalline alcohol $C_{15}H_{25}OH$ obtained from oil of Manila elemi and citronella oil

elench *n* -s [L *elenchus*] **1** *obs* : ELENCHUS **2** *obs* : SOPHISM

elen·chus \əˈleŋkəs, ēˈ-\ *n, pl* **elen·chi** \-ˌkī, -ˌkē\ [L, fr. Gk *elenchos* cross-examination, refutation, fr. *elenchein* to shame, cross-examine, refute; perh. akin to MIr *lang* shame, Latvian *langāt* to scold, Hitt *link-* to swear] : REFUTATION; *esp* : one cast in syllogistic form — compare IGNORATIO ELENCHI

elenc·tic *or* **elench·tic** \-ŋtik\ *also* **elenc·ti·cal** *or* **elench·ti·cal** \-təkəl\ *adj* [Gk *elenktikos*, fr. *elenktos* (verbal of *elenchein*) + *-ikos* -ic, -ical] : serving to refute — used of indirect modes of proof; opposed to *deictic*

el·enge \ˈelənj\ *adj* [ME, fr. OE *ǣlenge*, fr. *ǣ-* (var. of *ā-*, *ar-*, perfective & intensive prefix) + *-lenge* (fr. *lang* long) — more at ABEAR, LONG] *archaic* : TEDIOUS, REMOTE, MISERABLE, DREARY

eleo- — see ELAIO-

el·e·och·a·ris \ˌelēˈäkərəs\ *n, cap* [NL, fr. Gk *hele-*, *helos* marsh + *charis* grace, beauty — more at HELODES, CHARISMA] : a genus of sedges (family Cyperaceae) with dense spikes of flowers and leaves reduced to basal sheaths

ele·o·cyte \əˈlēəˌsīt\ *n* -s [*elaio-* + *-cyte*] : a coelomocyte containing numerous fat globules

ele·o·lite *or* **elae·o·lite** \-ˌlīt\ *n* -s [G *eläolith*, fr. *eläo-* elaio- + *-lith* -lite] : NEPHELINE

el·e·op·tene *or* **el·ae·op·tene** \ˌelēˈäpˌtēn\ *n* -s [ISV *elaio-* + Gk *ptēnos* winged; akin to Gk *petesthai* to fly — more at FEATHER] : the liquid portion of any natural essential oil that partly solidifies in the cold — distinguished from *stearoptene*

el·eo·stearic acid *or* **el·aeo·stearic acid** \ˌelē(ˌ)ō, əˌlē(ˌ)ō+ . . .\ *n* [ISV *elaio-* + *stearic*] : a crystalline unsaturated fatty acid $C_4H_9(CH{:}CH)_3(CH_2)_7COOH$ that exists in two stereoisomeric forms, (1) the alpha acid occurring as the glycerol ester esp. in tung oil and (2) the beta acid obtained from the alpha acid by irradiation; 9, 11, 13-octa-deca-trien-oic acid

¹**el·e·o·trid** \ˌelēˈōtrəd\ *adj* [NL *Eleotridae*] : of or relating to the Eleotridae

²**eleotrid** \"\ *n* -s : a member of the Eleotridae

el·e·o·tri·dae \ˌelēˈōtrəˌdē\ *n pl, cap* [NL, fr. *Eleotris*, type genus (fr. Gk *eleōtris*, a fish of the Nile river) + *-idae*] : a large widely distributed family of chiefly small fishes comprising the sleepers that are closely related to and sometimes included among the gobies from which they are distinguished by pelvic fins that are separate and do not form a cup or disk

el·e·paio \ˌeləˈpī(ˌ)ō\ *n* -s [Hawaiian *ʼelepaio*] : a flycatcher (*Chasiempis sandwichensis*) found on several of the Hawaiian islands

el·e·phant \ˈeləfənt\ *n* -s [ME *olifaunt*, *elephant*, fr. OF & L; OF *olifant* elephant, ivory, fr. L *elephantus*, fr. Gk *elephant-*, *elephas*, perh. of Hamitic origin; akin to Egypt ³*b(w)* elephant, ivory] **1 a** : any of certain thickset mostly very large nearly hairless four-footed mammals of the family Elephantidae esp. of the genera *Elephas* and *Loxodonta* having the snout prolonged into a muscular trunk, two incisors in the upper jaw developed esp. in the male into long curved tusks which furnish ivory, the head large with much diploic tissue and a well-developed brain, and the feet short and rounded with five toes **b** : an animal of the order Proboscidea — see MAMMOTH, MASTODON **2** : one that is an uncommonly large specimen of its kind ⟨he was an ~ of a man⟩ **3** : a size of paper ranging from 20x27 to 23x30 inches **4** : a grooving and rabbeting machine

Indian elephant

el·e·phan·ta \ˌeləˈfantə\ *n* -s [Pg *elefante*, lit., elephant, fr. L *elephantus*; fr. the fact that the elephant is a symbol of the Hindu 13th lunar mansion, when such storms occur] : a violent East Indian storm either at the close or at the setting in of the monsoon

elephant apple *n* **1** : WOOD APPLE 1 **2** : BEL

elephant beetle *n* **1** : any of several very large chiefly tropical lamellicorn beetles that bear a forked upwardly curved horn on the front of the head **2** *also* **elephant bug** : WEEVIL

elephant bird *n* : AEPYORNIS 2

elephant creeper *n* : an East Indian vine (*Argyreia speciosa*) of the family Convolvulaceae that has large cordate leaves with silvery lower surface and funnel-shaped rose-colored flowers and is widely cultivated as an ornamental in tropical areas

elephant-ear fern *n* : a tropical American fern (*Elaphoglossum crinitum*) with large simple fronds

elephant-ear sponge *n* : a fine soft durable fan-shaped or cup-shaped commercial sponge (*Spongia officinalis lamella*) occurring in the Mediterranean sea

elephant fish *n* : a chimaeroid fish (*Callorhynchus callorhynchus*) with an elongated mobile projection of the snout; *broadly* : any of various other chimaeras

elephant folio *n* : a publication (as a book or atlas) of the largest size

elephant grass *n* **1** : an Old World cattail (*Typha elephantina*) ranging from southern Europe to the East Indies and having leaves that are used in making baskets and pollen that is used in India for making bread **2** : NAPIER GRASS

elephant green *n* : HUNTER GREEN

elephant gun *n* : a rifle of large caliber (as .400 or above) designed primarily for hunting the largest of African or Indian game animals

el·e·phan·ti·as·ic \ˌeləˌfantēˈasik; -fənˌtīəˌsik, -ˌfan-\ *adj* [NL *elephantiasis* + E *-ic*] : affected with or characteristic of elephantiasis

el·e·phan·ti·a·sis \ˌeləfənˈtīəsəs, -ˌfan-\ *n, pl* **elephantia·ses** \-īəˌsēz\ [NL, fr. L, a kind of leprosy in which the skin takes on the appearance of an elephant's hide, fr. Gk, fr. *elephant-*, *elephas* elephant + *-iasis* — more at ELEPHANT] **1** : enlargement and thickening of tissues; *specif* : the enormous enlargement of a limb or the scrotum resulting from obstruction of lymphatics by filarial worms — compare FILARIASIS **2** : an undesirable enormous growth, enlargement, or overdevelopment ⟨dislikes ~ in labor and in government as much as in industry —Robert Lekachman⟩ ⟨his obsession for self-expression . . . resulted in verbal ~ —*Saturday Rev.*⟩

el·e·phan·tic \ˌeləˈfantik\ *adj* : ELEPHANTINE

el·e·phan·ti·dae \ˌeləˈfantəˌdē\ *n pl, cap* [NL, fr. *Elephant-*, *Elephas*, type genus + *-idae*] : a family of bulky mammals (order Proboscidea) comprising the recent elephants and related extinct forms (as the mammoths) that differ from these chiefly in respect to their dentition and in former classifications including also the mastodons

el·e·phan·tine \ˌeləˈfanˌtēn, -ˌtēn, -faan- *also* -ˈfa(a)n·ˌtīn *or* ˈeləfən·ˌtēn *or* ˈeləfən·ˌtīn\ *adj* [L *elephantinus* of an elephant, of ivory, fr. Gk *elephantinos* of ivory, fr. *elephant-*, *elephas* elephant, ivory + *-inos* -ine — more at ELEPHANT] **1** : of or relating to an elephant **2 a** : of enormous size or weight : uncommonly large : IMMENSE, MASSIVE ⟨all his limbs . . . were ~ —George Meredith⟩ **b** : lacking in grace or ease : PONDEROUS, CLUMSY, HEAVY-FOOTED ⟨wrote some ~ light verse⟩ ⟨they chat with . . . raucous malevolence and ~ facetiousness —Warren Beck⟩ **syn** see HUGE

elephantine tortoise *n* : ELEPHANT TORTOISE 1

elephant iron *n* : iron in large semicylindrical sheets of corrugated steel used in roofing (as of dugouts or other military installations)

el·e·phan·toid \ˌeləˈfan·ˌtȯid, ˈeləfən-\ *adj* **1** : of or resembling an elephant **2** [NL *elephantiasis* + E *-oid*] : resembling or relating to elephantiasis

el·e·phan·to·pus \ˌeləˈfantəpəs\ *n* [NL, fr. *elephanto-* (fr. L *elephantus* elephant) + *-pus* — more at ELEPHANT] **1** *cap* : a genus of alternate-leaved perennial American herbs (family Compositae) with agglomerate bracted heads of blue or purple flowers **2** -ES : any plant of the genus *Elephantopus*

elephant seal *n* **1** : a very large seal (*Mirounga leonina*) formerly abundant along many coasts of the southern hemisphere but hunted nearly to extermination for its oil and having a male that attains a length of 20 feet and has a long inflatable proboscis **2** : a very similar smaller seal (*Mirounga angustirostris*) formerly abundant along the California and Lower California coast but now restricted to a single herd protected by the Mexican government on the island of Guadalupe

elephant's ear *also* **elephant ear** *n* : any of several plants having large one-sided leaves: as **a** : BEGONIA **b** : a plant of the genus *Colocasia; esp* : TARO

elephant's-foot \ˈ═══ˌ═\ *n, pl* **elephant's-foots** **1 a** : a plant of the genus *Elephantopus* **b** : a southern African vine (*Dioscorea elephantipes*) having a massive rootstock covered with a deeply fissured bark — called also *tortoise plant*; see HOTTENTOT BREAD **2** : a ram with a foot for holding the work to the block in a flanging machine

elephant's grass *n* : ELEPHANT GRASS

elephant shark *n* **1** : BASKING SHARK **2** : ELEPHANT FISH

elephant's-head *or* **elephant head** \ˈ═══ˌ═\ *n, pl* **elephant's heads** [so called fr. the shape of the corolla] : a lousewort (*Pedicularis groenlandica*) of arctic and western alpine No. America with spikes of crimson flowers

elephant shrew *n* : any of several leaping African shrews comprising a family (Macroscelididae) remotely related to both the true shrews and the hedgehogs and having the nose long and flexible like a proboscis

elephant's-tooth \ˈ═══ˌ═\ *n, pl* **elephant's-tooths** : TOOTH SHELL

elephant's-trunk plant \ˈ═══ˌ═-\ *n* : UNICORN PLANT

elephant's-tusk \ˈ═══ˌ═\ *or* **elephant's-tusk shell** *n, pl* **elephant's-tusks** *or* **elephant's-tusk shells** : TOOTH SHELL

elephant thorn *n* : an East Indian tree (*Acacia tomentosa*) with large spreading brown spines

elephant tortoise *n* **1** : a giant tortoise (*Testudo gigantea*) of the Aldabra islands **2** : a tortoise (*Testudo elephantopus*) of the Galápagos islands that is now extinct

elephant tree *n* : a spicy-odored small tree or shrub (*Bursera microphylla*) of the southwestern U.S. having a light-gray outer bark, slender zigzag twigs, and white flowers in mostly 3-flowered clusters

elephant trunk *n* : a flexible chute used to direct coal onto a pile with limited blowing of dust or to direct concrete with minimum spatter

elephant wood *n* : a shrub or small tree (*Pachycormus discolor*) of the family Anacardiaceae found only in Lower California and having a large swollen trunk, a low crown, and clusters of small red flowers

el·e·phas \ˈeləfəs, -ˌfas\ *n, cap* [NL, fr. Gk, elephant — more at ELEPHANT] : the type genus of the family Elephantidae comprising the Asiatic elephant and extinct related forms and formerly being nearly coextensive with Elephantidae

elepidote \(ˈ)ē+\ *adj* [*e-* + *lepidote*] *bot* : lacking small scurfy scales

el·et·tar·ia \ˌeləˈta(a)rēə\ *n, cap* [NL, prob. fr. a native name like Jav *ela-ela* cardamom, prob. redupl. of Skt *elā*] : a genus of East Indian herbs (family Zingiberaceae) having lanceolate sheathing leaves and small purple-striped flowers in a long spike — see CARDAMOM

el·eu·sin·e \ˌelyüˈsī(ˌ)nē\ *n* [NL, fr. Gk *Eleusinē*, a name for Demeter, goddess of grain] **1** *cap* : a genus of grasses with digitate or rarely scattered spikes consisting of many-flowered spikelets — see RAGI, YARD GRASS **2** -S : any plant of the genus *Eleusine*

¹**el·eu·sin·i·an** \ˌelyüˈsinēən\ *adj, usu cap* [L *Eleusinius* (fr. Gk *Eleusinios*, fr. *Eleusis*, city of ancient Greece) + E *-an*] : of or relating to the ancient city of Eleusis in Attica

²**eleusinian** \"\ *n* -s *cap* : a citizen or inhabitant of the city of Eleusis in ancient Greece

el·e·ut *also* **el·e·uth** \ˈeləˌüt\ *n* -s *usu cap* : KALMUCK

eleuther- *or* **eleuthero-** *comb form* [Gk, free, fr. *eleutheros* — more at LIBERAL] **1** : freedom ⟨*eleutheromania*⟩ **2** : free ⟨*Eleutherozoa*⟩

eleu·thera bark \əˈlüthərə-\ *n* [fr. Eleuthera Island, Bahamas] : CASCARILLA 1

el·eu·the·ria \ˌelyəˈthirēə\ *n, cap* [NL, fr. Gk, freedom, fr. *eleutheros* + *-ia* -y] : a genus of atypical hermaphroditic hydrozoan jellyfishes

eleu·thero·dac·ty·lus \əˌlüthə(ˌ)rōˈdaktələs\ *n, cap* [NL, fr. *eleuther-* + Gk *daktylos* finger, toe] : a large genus of small chiefly tropical New World frogs (family Bufonidae or Leptodactylidae) that commonly complete metamorphosis within the egg

eleu·ther·o·zoa \-thərəˈzōə\ *n pl, cap* [NL, fr. *eleuther-* + *-zoa*] : a subphylum or other division of Echinodermata including the Asteroidea, Ophiuroidea, Echinoidea, and Holothurioidea — **eleu·ther·o·zo·an** \ˌ═ˌ═══ˈzōən\ *adj or n* — **eleu·ther·o·zo·ic** \-ˈōik\ *adj*

¹**el·e·vate** \ˈeləˌvāt, -ˌvət\ *adj* [ME *elevat*, fr. L *elevatus*, past part.] *archaic* : ELEVATED

²**el·e·vate** \ˈeləˌvāt, *usu* -ād·+V\ *vb* -ED/-ING/-S [ME *elevaten*, fr. L *elevatus*, past part. of *elevare* to raise up, lighten, fr. *e-* + *levare* to raise, lighten — more at LEVER] *vt* **1 a** : to lift up in space : RAISE ⟨materials are *elevated* to the top floor by a hoist⟩ **b** : to lift up (the Host) at Mass **c** : to cause (a structure) to be built : ERECT, REAR ⟨*elevated* a palace⟩ **d** : to cause to rise ⟨the gas, being lighter than air, ~*s* the balloon⟩ **e** : to turn, aim, or direct upward ⟨*elevated* his eyebrows, and looked at him in amazement —Oscar Wilde⟩ **f** : to increase markedly the degree or level of ⟨~ the temperature⟩ **2 a** (1) : to raise (a person) in rank, station, or dignity ⟨the appeal of the frontier democracy which had *elevated* Andrew Jackson to the presidency —A.C.Cole⟩ (2) : to advance (as an idea or activity) to a higher level of importance or significance ⟨~ an automatic movement of history to the position of supreme arbiter —John Dewey⟩ **b** : to improve or tend to improve (as in morality, taste, culture, or quality) : ENNOBLE, EXALT, REFINE ⟨~ backward peoples⟩ ⟨~ the art of reedworking into something more . . . wonderful than it really is —Ben Riker⟩ ⟨claims the artist should not only entertain but ~ his audience⟩ **3** *obs* : to mitigate or lessen by depreciation or extenuation **4** : to cause (the voice) to rise **5** : to raise the spirits of : EXHILARATE, ELATE ⟨the morning air of heaven refreshed and *elevated* me —W.H.Hudson †1922⟩ : inspire fervor or excitement in ⟨the subject *elevated* him to more than usual solemnity of manner —Jane Austen⟩ ~ *vi* : to raise the moral or intellectual faculties ⟨contended that art and music not only entertain but ~⟩ **syn** see LIFT

¹**elevated** *adj* **1 a** : raised esp. above the ground or other surface : situated at a high level ⟨the house stood on an ~ site⟩ ⟨after the skin becomes ~ and lumpy, pus forms —Morris Fishbein⟩ **b** : increased esp. abnormally (as in degree or amount) ⟨the pulse rate is ~ slightly —D.W.Maurer & V.H. Vogel⟩ ⟨an ~ temperature⟩ **2 a** : morally or intellectually on a high plane : aloof from what is mean or ignoble : marked by nobility of thought or feeling : NOBLE, REFINED, EDIFYING ⟨his ~ mind abominated the luxuries of an effete civilization —Elinor Wylie⟩ ⟨~ ideas⟩ **b** : FORMAL, DIGNIFIED, EXALTED, LOFTY ⟨we must not smile at the ~ diction of this letter —H.S.Canby⟩ ⟨by prose I mean . . . plain, workaday prose, not artistic or ~ prose —J.L.Lowes⟩ **3 a** : exalted in mood or feeling : EXHILARATED, EXCITED ⟨she was in one of those moods of ~ feeling, when the soul is upheld by a strange tranquillity —Nathaniel Hawthorne⟩ **b** : TIPSY, INTOXICATED ⟨he drinks much champagne and becomes ~ —Joyce Cary⟩ — **el·e·vat·ed·ly** *adv* — **el·e·vat·ed·ness** *n* -ES

²**elevated** \"\ *n* -s : ELEVATED RAILROAD

elevated pole *n* : the one of the two celestial poles that is above the observer's horizon

elevated railroad *or* **elevated railway** *n* : a railroad usu. for local transit in urban or interurban areas all or part of which is raised (as on trestlework) above the ground level

elevating *adj* : tending to improve morally or intellectually : EDIFYING ⟨the discovery that to borrow books and ideas from Europe was . . . ~ in itself —G.W.Pierson⟩ ⟨exercised an ~ influence on society —Wilmot Harrison⟩ ⟨the theory . . . is that a taste for music is an ~ passion —H.L.Mencken⟩ — **el·e·vat·ing·ly** *adv*

elevating arc *n* : a vertical graduated arc on a gun or its carriage used in elevating or depressing the gun

ele·va·tio \ˌäləˈvädˌē(ˌ)ō, -ätsē,ō\ *n, pl* **elevati·o·nes** \ˌ══ˌ══-ˈō,nās\ [ML, fr. L, elevation] : the rising of a melody beyond the ambitus of the mode in medieval music

el·e·va·tion \ˌeləˈvāshən\ *n* -s [ME *elevacioun*, fr. L *elevation-*, *elevatio*, fr. *elevatus* + *-ion-*, *-io* -ion] **1** : the height to which something is elevated: as **a** : the angular distance of a celestial object above the horizon ⟨computing the ~ of the pole⟩ **b** (1) : the vertical pointing of an artillery piece; *also* : ANGLE OF ELEVATION (2) : the height of an arrow's head in relation to the nock in the act of aiming **c** : the height above sea level : ALTITUDE **d** (1) : a ballet dancer's or skater's leap and illusory suspension in the air (2) : the ability of a dancer or skater to attain height in the air (3) : the height in the air attained by a dancer or skater; *usu* : the distance between the pointed toes and the ground **2 a** : the act or an instance of elevating : the act of raising something from a lower to a higher level ⟨the ~ of second-rate . . . scientists to posts of authority —Martin Gardner⟩ ⟨an ~ of the eyebrows⟩ **b** *often cap* : a portion of an Eastern or Western Christian liturgy in which the priest solemnly raises one or both of the eucharistic elements for the people to view with homage or adoration **c** : something that is elevated: as (1) : an elevated place or station : HILL ⟨an ~ of the ground⟩ (2) : a swelling esp. on the skin **3** : the condition or quality of being elevated: as **a** : the condition of being raised in rank, dignity, or importance ⟨overjoyed at his ~ to that honorable post⟩ **b** : the state or an instance of being piously exalted or uplifted ⟨he can never hear the Ave-Mary bell without an ~ —Douglas Bush⟩; *also* : a lifting of spirits : a state of marked cheerfulness or gaiety : EBULLIENCE ⟨he was subject to periods of ~ and wretched depression⟩ **c** (1) : dignity or sublimity of style, mood, or thought : loftiness of tone ⟨epics, like Greek tragedies, must be rendered with ~ —Dudley Fitts⟩ ⟨the English translation is not good; its failure to convey the very slight ~ of tone is a fundamental failure —Allen Tate⟩ ⟨he is always impressive, and . . . the foreign policy speech reaches an admirable ~ —*Nation's Business*⟩ (2) : nobility of character or spirit ⟨he had too much ~ of mind to save himself by informing against others —T.B.Macaulay⟩ **d** : a usu. abnormal increase (as in degree or amount) ⟨an ~ of the pulse rate⟩ ⟨an ~ of temperature⟩ **4** : a grace used in old English music : SLIDE **5** : a geometrical projection (as of a building) on a plane perpendicular to the horizon : orthographic projection on a vertical plane

elevation head *n* : head (sense 14b) that corresponds to the potential energy of elevation of a flowing liquid

elevation meter *n* : an instrument that combines both odometer and inclinometer features and that when drawn along a hilly road automatically computes and records the net change in elevation as the vehicle proceeds

ele·va·to \ˌeləˈväd·(ˌ)ō\ *adj (or adv)* [It, fr. L *elevatus*] : elevated in tone : SUBLIME — used as a direction in music

el·e·va·tor \ˈeləˌvād·ə(r), -ātə-\ *n* -s **1** : one that raises or lifts up anything: as **a** : an endless belt or chain conveyor with cleats, scoops, or buckets for raising material **b** : a cage or platform and its hoisting machinery (as in a building or mine) for conveying persons or goods to or from different levels — see HYDRAULIC ELEVATOR **c** : a building for elevating, storing, discharging, and sometimes processing grain **d** : a compressed-air lift or pump for raising acids **e** : a tool or device for raising or lowering pipe or rods out of or into a well **2** : a movable auxiliary airfoil usu. attached to the tail plane the function of which is to impress a pitching moment on an airplane thus producing rotation about its lateral axis, positive or downward deflection of the elevator causing the airplane to dive, and negative or upward deflection causing it to climb **3** : a dental instrument for removing the roots of teeth **4** : a surgical instrument for raising a depressed part (as of a bone) or for separating contiguous parts **5** *printing* : either of two mechanisms in keyboard slugcasting machines for raising set matrices, one used for casting and the other for distribution

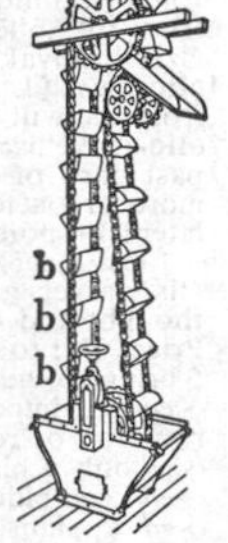

one form of elevator 1a: *b*, *b*, *b*, buckets

elevator dredge *n* : a dredge operating by means of a bucket conveyor

el·e·va·tor·ing \-ād·əriŋ, -ātr-\ *n* -s : passenger elevators

elevator liability insurance *or* **elevator insurance** *n* : insurance against loss due to legal liability for bodily injury or property damage resulting from ownership, maintenance, or use of elevators, escalators, lifts, or hoists

elevator shoe *n* [fr. *Elevators*, a trademark] : a shoe having a specially constructed raised insole intended to make the wearer look taller

el·e·va·to·ry \'eləvə,tōrē, *chiefly Brit* -,vāt(ə)ri *or* -,vā·tri\ *adj* **:** tending to elevate ⟨~ forces⟩

¹elev·en \ə'levən, ē'-, -lev°m, -leb°m, *rapid* 'le-\ *adj* [ME *enleven, elleven,* fr. OE *endleofan;* akin to OHG *einlif* eleven, OS *ēlleban,* ON *ellifu,* Goth *ainlibim* (dat.); all fr. a prehistoric Gmc compound whose first constituent is represented by OE *ān* one, and whose second constituent is prob. akin to Lith *-lika* (as in *vēnūlika* eleven), OHG *līhan* to lend — more at ONE, LOAN] **:** being one more than 10 in number ⟨~ years⟩ — see NUMBER table

²eleven \"\ *pron, pl in constr* [ME *enleven, elleven,* fr. OE *endleofane,* fr. *endleofan,* adj.] **:** 11 countable persons or things not specified but under consideration and being enumerated ⟨~ are here⟩ ⟨~ were found⟩

³eleven \"\ *n* -s [ME *enleven, elleven,* fr. *enleven, elleven,* adj. & pron.] **1 :** 10 and one **2 a :** 11 units or objects ⟨a total of ~⟩ **b :** a group or set of 11 **3 :** the numerable quantity symbolized by the arabic numerals 11 **4 :** a playing team of 11 members; *esp* **:** a football team **5 :** 11 o'clock — compare BELL table, TIME illustration

eleven rule *n* **:** RULE OF ELEVEN

elev·ens·es \-ənziz,-°mziz\ *n pl* [irreg. pl. of ³*eleven* (o'clock)] *Brit* **:** a light lunch or sometimes only coffee or tea taken around the middle of the morning

¹elev·enth \-ən(t)th,-°mth\ *adj* [ME *enlefte, ellefte, enleventhe, elleventhe,* adj. & n., fr. OE *endleofta, endlyfta* (akin to OHG *einlifto* eleventh, ON *ellifti*), fr. *endleofan* eleven + *-tha* -th] **1 :** being number 11 in a countable series — see NUMBER table **2 :** being one of 11 equal parts into which something is divisible ⟨an ~ share of the money⟩

²eleventh \"\ *n, pl* **elevenths** \-ən(t)s,-°m(p)s,-ən(t)ths, -°mths\ [ME *enlefte, ellefte, enleventhe, elleventhe*] **1 :** number 11 in a countable series ⟨the ~ of the month⟩ **2 :** the quotient of a unit divided by 11 **:** one of 11 equal parts of anything ⟨one ~ of the total⟩ **3 a :** the musical interval made up of an octave and a fourth **b :** a tone at this interval

eleventh cranial nerve *or* **eleventh nerve** *n* **:** ACCESSORY NERVE

eleventh hour *n* [so called fr. the parable of the vineyard (Mt 20:1–16) where laborers hired at the "eleventh hour" are paid the same wage as those hired early in the day] **:** the latest possible time ⟨perceived the danger of it at the *eleventh hour* —Louis Eisenmann⟩

el·e·von \'elə,vän\ *n* -s [*elevator* + *-on* (as in *aileron*)] **:** an airplane control surface that combines the functions of elevator and aileron — called also *ailavator*

elf \'elf, 'eu̇lf\ *n, pl* **elves** \lvz\ *also* **elfs** [ME, fr. OE *ælf;* akin to MLG *alf* incubus, MHG *alp* incubus, ON *alfr* elf, and prob. to OE *ælbitu, ielfetu* swan, OHG *alba* insect larva, *albiz, elbiz* swan, ON *elptr, ölpt* swan, L *albus* white, Gk *alphos,* a white skin disease, W *elfydd* earth, world, Russ *lebed'* swan; basic meaning: white] **1 :** a mythical diminutive being in human form endowed with magical powers and given to beneficial or mischievous interference in human affairs **:** FAIRY, SPRITE, PIXIE **2 a :** a small being or creature **:** DWARF; *esp* **:** a small usu. playful or prankish child ⟨the school yard teemed with running, shouting, laughing *elves*⟩ ⟨a little child, a limber ~ —S.T.Coleridge⟩ **b :** a mischievous, sly, or malicious person **3** *also* **elft** \lft\ *Africa* **:** BLUEFISH 1

ELF *abbr, often not cap* extremely low frequency

elf arrow *also* **elf bolt** *or* **elf dart** *n* **:** a flint arrowhead or similarly shaped stone supposed in some parts of Great Britain to be arrows shot by elves esp. at cattle and to possess magical powers

elf child *n* **:** CHANGELING

elf cup *n* **:** the apothecium of a fungus of the family Pezizaceae

elf dock *n* **:** ELECAMPANE

¹elf·in \'elfən\ *adj* [irreg. fr. *elf*] **1 a :** of, relating to, or produced by an elf ⟨~ bells⟩ ⟨all the little creatures joined in the ~ dance⟩ **b :** of or relating to a small child or to childhood ⟨the ~ and adventurous time when tall weeds closed over us like woods —G.K.Chesterton⟩ **2 a :** small, slight, and delicately made or proportioned **:** DWARFISH ⟨a little ~ man whose reddish hair was beginning to thin and gray —W.A. White⟩ ⟨apparently was obsessed by things ~ and small —Green Peyton⟩ **b :** quick, agile, and delicate (as in movement or thought) ⟨unfailingly shows poetic insight and ~ liveliness of fancy —*Amer. Guide Series: Ind.*⟩ ⟨his touch was light, crisp, and somehow deliciously comic; he could start the keys into ~ life —J.B.Priestley⟩ **c :** good-naturedly or slyly mischievous **:** PLAYFUL, PUCKISH ⟨with ~ delight he perpetuated a successful practical joke —J.A.Morris b. 1904⟩ **d :** having an otherworldly, unearthly, or magical quality **:** FEY ⟨a strange ~ creature⟩ ⟨thunderheads quivered with the ~ flares of the heat lightning —Edwin Granberry⟩

²elfin \"\ *n* -s **1 :** ELF; *also* **:** CHILD, URCHIN **2 :** any of several delicate grayish brown or orange-brown hairstreak butterflies (genus *Incisalia*) flying in early spring

elfinwood \'ˌ=,=\ *n* **:** KRUMMHOLZ

elfin woodland *n* **:** stunted forest growing at higher elevation in warm moist regions and characterized by gnarled stumpy trees heavily burdened with epiphytes and abundant growth of mosses — compare KRUMMHOLZ

elf·ish \'elfish, -fēsh\ *adj* [alter. of *elvish*] **1 :** of or relating to an elf **:** resembling an elf **:** ELFIN ⟨~ figures⟩ **2 :** MISCHIEVOUS, IMPISH, ELVISH ⟨~ pranks⟩ — **elf·ish·ly** *adv*

elf·land \'el,fland\ *n* **:** FAIRYLAND ⟨where earth and ~ meet —Walter de la Mare⟩

elflock \'=,=\ *n* **:** hair matted as if by elves — usu. used in pl.

el fo *abbr* elephant folio

elf owl *n* **:** a very small insectivorous owl (*Micropallas whitneyi*) living in or about the giant cacti of desert areas of the southwestern U. S. and northern Mexico

¹elf-shot \'=,=\ *n* [*elf* + *shot,* n.] **:** ELF ARROW

²elf-shot \"\ *adj* [*elf* + *shot,* past part. of *shoot*] *Scot* **:** afflicted with a disease supposed to result from a wound by an elf arrow

elfwort \'=,=\ *n* **:** ELECAMPANE

el·gin·shire \'elgən,shi(ə)r, -,shər\ *or* **el·gin** \'elgən\ *adj, usu cap* [*Elginshire, Elgin* (Moray), county in northeast Scotland] **:** MORAY

eliad *obs var of* OEILLADE

elian \'ēlēən, -lyən; *sometimes* 'el-, *which appears to have been the pronunc used by Lamb*\ *adj, usu cap* [*Elia,* pseudonym of Charles Lamb †1834 English essayist and critic + E *-an*] **:** of, relating to, or like the essayist Lamb or his writing ⟨*Elian* technique —W.H.Gardner⟩

eli·as·ite \ə'līə,sīt, -līə\ *n* -s [G *eliasit,* fr. the *Elias* mine in Czechoslovakia + G *-it* -ite] **:** GUMMITE

¹elicit *adj* [L *elicitus,* past part.] *obs, of an act* **:** proceeding from the will — contrasted with *imperate*

²elic·it \ē'lisət, ə'-, *usu* -əd·+V\ *vt* -ED/-ING/-S [L *elicitus,* past part. of *elicere,* fr. *e-* + *-licere* (fr. *lacere* to allure) — more at DELIGHT] **1 a :** to draw or bring out (something latent or potential) ⟨~ a flame by the friction of the word —J.G.Frazer⟩ ⟨~*ed* harmonious sounds from his instrument⟩ ⟨the larger gatherings may have ~*ed* more aspects of his thought and revealed more sides of his personality —Lucien Price⟩ **b :** to derive (as a truth or principle) by logical process **:** bring to view (as by reason or argument) ⟨the controversy ~*ed* one important truth⟩ **2 :** to call forth or draw out (a response or reaction) **:** EVOKE, PROVOKE, CAUSE ⟨his question ~*ed* only a blank stare⟩ ⟨best quality cauliflowers and carrots ~*ed* keen bidding —*Farmer's Weekly (So. Africa)*⟩ ⟨his antics ~*ed* applause and laughter⟩ ⟨his ability to ~ support from subordinates⟩ **syn** see EDUCE

elic·it·able \-ədəbəl, -ətə-\ *adj* **:** capable of being elicited

elic·i·tate \-sə,tāt\ *vt* -ED/-ING/-S [L *elicitus* + E *-ate*] **:** ELICIT

elic·i·ta·tion \(,)ē,lisə'tāshən, ə,l-\ *n* -s **:** a drawing forth **:** EVOCATION, EXTRACTION ⟨the ~ of the true story took time⟩

elic·i·tor \ə'=səd·ə(r), -sətə(r), -sə,tó(ə)r, -ó(ə)\ *n* -s **:** one that elicits ⟨a skillful ~ of confidential information⟩

elide \ə'līd, ē'-\ *vt* -ED/-ING/-S [L *elidere,* fr. *e-* + *-lidere* (fr. *laedere* to hurt, damage) — more at LESION] **1** *archaic* **:** DESTROY ⟨~ the force of his argument⟩ **:** ANNUL **2 a :** to suppress or alter (as a vowel or syllable) by elision **b :** to strike out (as a written figure, word, or passage) ⟨I write very slowly and ~ a good deal —A.N.Whitehead⟩ ⟨these figures should be *elided* wherever possible, the minimum being used to give the sense —P.G.Burbidge⟩ ⟨sternly *elided* the reference to the fact that he had laughed —John Gunther⟩ **c :** to leave out of consideration **:** pass over **:** IGNORE, OMIT, SUPPRESS ⟨he ~*s,* as much as possible, the incest motif —Francis Fergusson⟩ ⟨it may seek to ~, instead of recognizing, the high and solemn function of parliament —Ernest Barker⟩ **d :** CURTAIL, ABRIDGE, SHORTEN, REDUCE, DIMINISH ⟨the two worlds often have the power of mutually *eliding* . . . their effectiveness —Pier-Maria Pasinetti⟩ ⟨the circulating exhibitions are not *elided* versions of the Museum of Modern Art's own shows —Roger Angell⟩

elid·ible \-dəbəl\ *adj* **:** capable of being elided ⟨~ vowels⟩

el·i·gi·bil·i·ty \,eləjə'biləd·ē, -lēj-, -ləte, -i\ *n* -ES **1** *archaic* **:** the quality of being advantageous or preferable **:** ADVANTAGE ⟨this was his plan . . . and he thought it an excellent one, full of ~ —Jane Austen⟩ **2 :** the quality or state of being eligible **:** FITNESS, SUITABILITY, QUALIFICATION ⟨determine the ~ of various nations for loans —*Current Biog.*⟩ ⟨~ of prisoners for repatriation⟩ ⟨~ of a candidate for office⟩

¹el·i·gi·ble \'===,bəl\ *adj* [ME, fr. MF & LL; MF, fr. LL *eligibilis,* fr. L *eligere* to choose + *-ibilis* -ible — more at ELECT] **1 :** fitted or qualified to be chosen or used **:** entitled to something ⟨only native-born citizens are ~ to the office of president⟩ ⟨~ for benefits⟩ ⟨the book is not ~ for copyright in this country⟩ ⟨not ~ to play in the championship game⟩ ⟨anyone with an ~ craft . . . is invited to enter —Geneva J. Yockey⟩ **2 :** worthy to be chosen or selected **:** ADVANTAGEOUS, PREFERABLE, DESIRABLE ⟨recorded his wonder that so ~ a spot was not finally chosen —A.T.Quiller-Couch⟩ ⟨commenting upon the ~ circumstances of the paupers —G.E.Fussell⟩ ⟨had chosen this bright Sunday morning as ~ for churchgoing —George Eliot⟩; *specif* **:** suitable or desirable for marriage ⟨flirted with . . . all the bachelor squires who seemed ~ —W. M.Thackeray⟩ ⟨disappointed mothers of other more ~ damsels —Florence Bullock⟩ **3** *archaic* **:** subject to choice or adoption **:** capable of being adopted **:** POSSIBLE ⟨the villainy and shallowness of rulers . . . are just as ~ to these states as to any foreign despotism —Walt Whitman⟩

²eligible \"\ *n* -s **:** one that is eligible ⟨I hope all the rest of the ~*s* register too —A.E.Stevenson †1965⟩

el·i·gi·ble·ness *n* -ES **:** ELIGIBILITY

eligible paper *n* **:** notes and bills designated as proper for rediscount by the Federal Reserve banks

el·i·gi·bly \-blē, -li\ *adv* **:** in an eligible manner

eli·jah's chair \ə|'lījəz-, ē|\ *n, usu cap E* [after *Elijah,* 9th cent. B.C. Hebrew prophet] **:** an empty chair that is traditionally reserved among Jews for the prophet Elijah during the circumcision ceremony

elijah's cup *n, usu cap E* **:** a cup of wine set on the table at the celebration of the seder on Passover and reserved for the precursor of the Messiah, the prophet Elijah, who according to Jewish tradition may come anytime as a guest

elim·i·na·bil·i·ty \ə,limənə'biləd·ē, ē,-, -ləte, -i\ *n* -ES **:** the quality or state of being eliminable

elim·i·na·ble \ə'==nəbəl\ *adj* [*eliminate* + *-able*] **:** capable of being eliminated

elim·i·nant \-nənt\ *n* -s [L *eliminant-, eliminans,* pres. part. of *eliminare*] **1 :** a function of the coefficients of *n* equations connecting *n* symbols, whose vanishing is the necessary and sufficient condition that the equations are consistent — called also *resultant* **2 :** an agent that promotes bodily elimination

elim·i·nate \-,nāt, *usu* -ād·+V\ *vt* -ED/-ING/-S [L *eliminatus,* past part. of *eliminare,* fr. *e-* + *limin-, limen* threshold — more at LIMB] **1** *archaic* **:** to put out of doors **:** thrust out **2 a :** to cast out **:** REMOVE, EXPEL, EXCLUDE, DROP, OUST ⟨the resultant cabinet change *eliminated* twelve ministers —*Current Biog.*⟩ ⟨~ gangster elements from the organization⟩ ⟨the two teams losing two games in succession will be *eliminated* —*N.Y. Times*⟩ ⟨a number of candidates were *eliminated* for poor flying technique⟩ **b :** to cause the disappearance of esp. as a factor or element in a process or situation **:** get rid of **:** ERADICATE ⟨to ~ surprise, the theory goes, is to ~ nuclear war —W.R.Frye⟩ ⟨seek to ~ the odium attaching to the word *materialism* —William James⟩ ⟨succeeded in *eliminating* the city's debt⟩ ⟨~ a distracting noise⟩; *sometimes* **:** to get rid of by killing or destroying ⟨*eliminated* his opponents with ruthless cruelty⟩ **3 :** to expel from the living body **:** EXCRETE, EGEST ⟨*eliminating* toxins from the intestine⟩ ⟨the kidneys ~ urea⟩ **4** *archaic* **:** to isolate (as a principle) from surrounding or confusing details **:** DEDUCE **5 :** to cause to disappear by combining two or more equations ⟨~ an unknown quantity⟩ **syn** see EXCLUDE

elim·i·na·tion \=,=='nāshən\ *n* -s *often attrib* **:** the act, process, or an instance of eliminating or discharging: as **a (1) :** the act of discharging or excreting waste products or foreign substances from the body **(2) eliminations** *pl* **:** bodily discharges **:** urine, feces, and vomitus **b :** the act of making a quantity disappear from an equation; *esp* **:** the operation of deducing from several equations containing several unknowns a less number of equations containing a less number of unknowns **c :** the removal of logical terms or their symbols by combining or transforming logical equations **d :** the act or process of excluding from a match, tournament, or other contest the losers of any round or heat ⟨~ race⟩ **e :** the removal from a molecule of a simpler molecule in the form of atoms and groups that can combine ⟨the ~ of water from ethyl alcohol in the form of hydrogen and hydroxyl produces ethylene⟩ — compare ADDITION 6 **f** *or* **elimination play :** a process in bridge by which the declarer removes from his hand and dummy all cards of each suit that an opponent might safely lead so as to gain a trick when next an opponent leads — called also *strip, stripping play;* compare END PLAY 2, THROW-IN

elim·i·na·tive \ə'==,nād·iv, -,nəl, |t|, |ēv *also* |əv\ *adj* **:** serving or tending to eliminate; *specif* **:** relating to, operating in the process of, or carrying on bodily elimination ⟨citrous foods aid the ~ organs in their work⟩

elim·i·na·tor \-,nād·ə(r), -ātə-\ *n* -s **:** one that eliminates — **elim·i·na·to·ry** \-,nə,tōrē, -ȯr-, -ri, *chiefly Brit* -,nātəri *or* -,nā·tri\ *adj*

el·in·var \'elən,vär\ *n* -s [F *élinvar,* fr. *élasticité invariable* invariable elasticity] **:** an alloy that contains about 50 percent iron, 36 percent nickel, and 12 percent chromium, that has low thermal expansivity and a modulus of elasticity virtually unaffected by changes in temperature, and that is used for springs for watches and other precise instruments

eli·quate \ē'lī,kwāt, ə'-; 'elə,k-\ *vt* -ED/-ING/-S [L *eliquatus,* past part. of *eliquare* to strain, clarify, cause to flow freely, fr. *e-* + *liquare* to strain, liquefy, melt — more at LIQUATE] **1** *obs* **:** to cause to flow freely **:** LIQUEFY **2 a :** LIQUATE, SMELT **b :** to part by liquefaction

eli·qua·tion \(,)ē,lī'kwāshən, ə,lī'-, ,elə'-, -āzhən\ *n* -s [LL *eliquation-, eliquatio* act of liquefying, fr. L *eliquatus* + *-ion-, -io* -ion] *obs* **:** LIQUEFACTION **2 :** LIQUATION

eli·sion \ə'lizhən, ē'-\ *n* -s [LL *elision-, elisio,* fr. L *elisus* (past part. of *elidere* to elide) + *-ion-, -io* -ion — more at ELIDE] **1 :** the use of a speech form that lacks a final or initial sound that a variant speech form has (as the use of *l'* and not *le* in French *l'été* or the use of *'s* instead of *is* in English *there's*); *specif* **:** the deliberate syllable-reducing suppression or consonantalization of a final proclitic vowel in poetry for the sake of the meter (as in \th(y)ə'presiv'chānz\ for *the* (or *th'*) *oppressive chains* or in \t(w)ə'mēlyə'zīz\ for *to* (or *t'*) *Amelia's eyes*) **2 :** the act or an instance of dropping out or omitting something **:** OMISSION, CUT ⟨~ of false scenery, explanatory essays, useless subplots —V.S.Pritchett⟩ ⟨makes a few ~*s* in the ballet . . . but preserves all the solos —Arthur Knight⟩

¹elite \ā'lēt *also* ə'- *sometimes* e'- *or* ē'-; *usu* -lēd·+V\ *n* -s [F *élite,* fr. OF *eslite* choice, fr. fem. of *eslit,* past part. of *eslire* to choose, fr. (assumed) VL *exligere,* alter. (influenced by L *ex-*) of L *eligere* — more at ELECT] **1 :** the choice part or segment **:** FLOWER, CREAM, ARISTOCRACY ⟨an intellectual ~⟩ ⟨the ~ of coffees⟩: as **a :** a segment or group regarded as socially superior ⟨a store catering only to the ~⟩ **b :** highly trained soldiers ⟨threw the ~ of his army at the enemy's weakened flank⟩ **c :** a minority group or stratum that exerts influence, authority, or decisive power ⟨a power ~⟩ ⟨party managers and the leaders of the control groups within the parties are the ~*s* —B.J.Loewenberg⟩ **2 :** a size of typewriter type providing 12 characters to the linear inch and 6 lines to the vertical inch

²elite \"\ *adj* **1 :** of, relating to, or constituting an elite ⟨seeking to attain ~ status⟩ ⟨it cannot . . . be argued that the ~ principle means necessarily a dictatorship —F.G.Wilson⟩ ⟨he has . . . denied holding the ~ theory —G.A.Wagner⟩ ⟨~ troops⟩ **2 :** CHOICE, SUPERIOR, SELECT ⟨it places easily in the ~ class of historical fiction —Edmund Fuller⟩ ⟨an ~ brand of coffee⟩ ⟨all the officers are dressed in most ~ uniforms —Johnny Johnson & P.E.Green⟩

elite seed *n* **:** foundation stock of pure selected seed of a certain crop variety

elit·ism \-lēd·,izəm, -lē,tiz-\ *n* -s **1 :** belief in and advocacy of leadership or rule by an elite ⟨in other recent writers . . . one can find a similar ~ and a similar concern with . . . strong leadership —David Riesman⟩; *also* **:** leadership or rule by an elite ⟨will . . . be charged . . . with being undemocratic, or, worse, of advocating ~ —Cormac Philip⟩ **2 :** consciousness of being an elite or one of the elite ⟨they escape the ~ which is characteristic of the administrative class in the national government —C.J.Friedrich⟩ ⟨the new liberalism enjoyed its taste of ~, of being in the know —Louis Filler⟩

¹elit·ist \-lēd·əst, -lētə-\ *n* -s [*elite* + *-ist*] **1 :** one who is an adherent of elitism ⟨the few may rule for the logical reason that they do rule, as some ~*s* maintain —C.E.Merriam⟩ **2 :** one who is or regards himself as a member of an elite ⟨he was an ~, who esteemed himself better than Americans from most classes of the population —Louis Filler⟩

²elitist \"\ *adj* **:** of or relating to elitism **:** characterized by or favorable to elitism ⟨there is a good deal of ~ thinking among those neoliberals —C.J.Friedrich⟩ ⟨these new ~ and totalitarian regimes —F.G.Wilson⟩

elix·ate \ə'lik,sāt\ *vt* -ED/-ING/-S [L *elixatus,* past part. of *elixare,* fr. *elixus* thoroughly boiled, fr. *e-* + *-lixus* (fr. *lixa* water, lye) — more at LIQUID] *archaic* **:** BOIL, SEETHE

elix·a·tion \ə,lik'sāshən\ *n* -s [L *elixatus* + E *-ion*] *archaic* **:** the action of boiling or seething

elix·ir \ə'liksə(r), ē'-\ *n* -s [ME *elixir, elixer,* fr. ML *elixir,* fr. Ar *al-iksīr* the elixir, fr. *al* the + *iksīr* elixir, prob. fr. Gk *xērion* desiccative powder, fr. *xēros* dry — more at SERENE] **1 a :** a substance held esp. in the middle ages to be capable of transmuting metals into gold; *also* **:** a substance or concoction held to be capable of prolonging life indefinitely — used esp. in the phrase *elixir of life* **b :** CURE-ALL, PANACEA ⟨do we have to be persuaded that it is a panacea, an ~, before we take any of it? —Glenway Wescott⟩ **c** *archaic* **:** a strong extract or tincture **d (1) :** the quintessence of a thing **:** its driving force or principle ⟨injected one way or another with the élan or ~ of the poet's dominant attitudes —Allen Tate & J.P.Bishop⟩ **(2) :** something (as an experience or idea) that acts potently upon one, invigorating or filling with exuberant energy or cheer ⟨the distant sound of music . . . the bright flash of colored skirts . . . was like a strong ~ —Victor Canning⟩ ⟨an ~ was at work on American colonials . . . they saw life full of opportunities and believed they were alive under a new sky —Adrienne Koch⟩ **2 :** any of a class of sweetened aromatic preparations that contain variable percentages of alcohol and are used either for their medicinal ingredients or in prescriptions for their flavoring quality

elixirate *vt* -ED/-ING/-S [*elixir* + *-ate*] *obs* **:** DISTILL, PURIFY

eliz·a·beth \ə'liz(ə)bəth, ē'-, *rapid* 'li-\ *adj, usu cap* [fr. *Elizabeth,* N. J.] **:** of or from the city of Elizabeth, N. J. ⟨*Elizabeth* refineries⟩ **:** of the kind or style prevalent in Elizabeth

¹eliz·a·be·than \ə¦lizə'bēthən, ē¦- *sometimes* -beth-\ *adj, usu cap* [*Elizabeth* I †1603 queen of England + E *-an*] **1 a :** of or relating to Queen Elizabeth I or her reign ⟨the *Elizabethan* age⟩ ⟨*Elizabethan* policy⟩ **b :** of or relating to the Elizabethan age or its culture (as its literature) ⟨studies of *Elizabethan* idiom —C.W.Shumaker⟩ ⟨*Elizabethan* sea power⟩ ⟨an *Elizabethan* lyric⟩ ⟨the *Elizabethan* climate of opinion⟩ **c :** of or relating to a style in women's clothing characterized esp. by long pointed waists and standing collars **2** [*Elizabeth* II b1926 queen of England + E *-an*] **:** of or relating to Queen Elizabeth II or her reign

²elizabethan \"\ *n* -s *usu cap* **:** an Englishman of the age of Elizabeth I; *specif* **:** an Elizabethan poet or dramatist ⟨the intimate lyrics of the *Elizabethans* —George Steiner⟩

elizabethan collar *n, usu cap E* **:** a broad circle of stiff cardboard or other material placed about the neck of a cat or dog to prevent it from licking or biting an injured part

elizabethan style *n, usu cap E* **1 :** an early Renaissance architectural style combining Tudor and Italian features, common in English country houses of Elizabeth's reign, and characterized by large windows, long galleries, tall decorated chimneys, and a profusion of ornamental strapwork **2 :** the Renaissance style of furniture esp. as developed in the Elizabethan era, characterized by massive structure and elaborate carving

¹elk \'elk, 'eu̇k\ *n, pl* **elk** *or* **elks** [ME, prob. fr. OE *eolh;* akin to OHG *elaho* elk, ON *elgr,* Gk *elaphos* deer, OIr *elit* roe deer, Arm *eln* deer, Skt *ṛśya* male of a species of antelope] **1** *pl usu* **elk a :** the largest existing deer (*Alces alces*) of Europe and Asia resembling the moose of No. America but not so large and found in parts of Scandinavia, Germany, Russia, and Siberia **b :** WAPITI **c :** any of various large Asiatic deer (as the sambar) **2 :** soft tanned rugged cattlehide leather used for work shoes, sport shoes — called also *smoked elk* **3** *pl* **elks,** *usu cap* **:** a member of one of the major benevolent and fraternal orders **4 :** LAMA 2

²elk \"\ *n* -s [origin unknown] *dial Eng* **:** a wild goose or swan

elk bark *n* **:** LARGE-LEAVED MAGNOLIA

el·ke·saite \'elkə,sīt, ,elkə'sā,īt, -'sī,īt\ *n* -s *usu cap* [*Elkesai,* semilegendary author of a 2d or 3d cent. work of religious inspiration + E *-ite*] **:** a member of an Ebionite sect in whose system magic and astrology played a conspicuous role

elkhorn fern \'=,=-\ *n* **:** STAGHORN FERN; *esp* **:** the Australian staghorn fern (*Platycerium alcicorne*)

elkhound \'=,=\ *n* **:** NORWEGIAN ELKHOUND

elk kelp *n* **:** a large marine brown alga of the genus *Pelagophycus* (order Laminariales) sometimes reaching a length of 100 feet or more and characterized by blades that are split, the whole structure being somewhat like a tree in shape

elk nut *n* **:** BUFFALO NUT

elk·slip \'elk,slip, 'eu̇k-\ *n* **:** a marsh marigold (*Caltha rotundifolia*) of the northwestern U. S.

elk tree *n* **:** SOURWOOD

elkwood \'=,=\ *n* **1 :** SOURWOOD **2 a :** the soft wood of the umbrella tree (*Magnolia tripetala*) **b :** UMBRELLA TREE

¹ell \'el\ *n* -s [ME *eln, ellen, elle,* fr. OE *eln;* akin to OHG *elina* ell, ON *eln, öln, alin* forearm, ell, Goth *aleina,* L *ulna* elbow, arm, ell, Gk *ōlenē* elbow, Skt *āṇi* linchpin, part of the leg immediately above the knee] **1 :** an English unit of length chiefly for cloth equal to 45 inches but no longer used **2 :** any of various units of length similar in use to the English ell (as the old Dutch or Flemish unit of about 27 inches, the Scotch unit of about 37 inches, or the modern unit of the Netherlands equal to 1 meter) **3 :** CUBIT

²ell \"\ *n* -s **1 :** ¹EL **2 :** an extension at right angles to the length of a main building **3 :** an elbow in a pipe or conduit

-el·la \'elə\ *n suffix, pl* **-ellae** *or* **-ellas** [L — more at -EL] **1 :** little one resembling — often in generic names ⟨*Capsella*⟩ **2 :** little one ⟨squam*ella*⟩ **3 :** little one belonging to ⟨*Moluccella*⟩

el·la·chick \'elə,chik\ *n* [Nisqualli] **:** a freshwater tortoise (*Clemmys marmorata*) of California used as food

el·lag·ic acid \ə|¦lajik-, e|\ *n* [F *ellagique,* fr. *ellag* (anagram of *galle* gallnut, gall) + *-ique* -ic — more at GALL (excrescence)] **:** a crystalline phenolic dilactone $C_{14}H_6O_8$ obtained from bezoar stones, oak galls, and many tannins by oxidation of gallic acid

el·lagi·tannin \ə¦lajə, e'-+\ *n* [ISV *ellagic* + *tannin*] **:** a tannin occurring in various tanning extracts (as those from myrobalans and divi-divi) and yielding ellagic acid on hydrolysis

el·leck \'elik\ *n* -s [origin unknown] **:** RED GURNARD 1

el·ler \'elə(r)\ *dial var of* ²ELDER

el·le·stad·ite \'elə,sta,dīt, ,=='=,=\ *n* -s [Reuben B. *Ellestad* b1900 Am. chemist + E *-ite*] **:** a variety of apatite $Ca_5(F,Cl,OH)[(P,Si,S,C)O_4]_3$ containing silicon, carbon, and sulfur replacing some of the phosphorus

el·liot's pheasant \'elēəts-, -lyəts-\ *n, usu cap E* [prob. after Daniel G. *Elliot* †1915 Am. zoologist] **:** a large brilliantly colored barred pheasant (*Syrmaticus ellioti*) native to southeastern China where it is highly regarded as a game bird and extensively bred elsewhere as an ornamental

el·lipse \ə'lips, e'-,ē'-\ *n* -s [alter. of *ellipsis*] **1 :** an elongated circle **:** a regular oval; *specif* **:** a closed plane curve generated by a point so moving that its distance from a fixed point divided by its distance from a fixed line is a positive constant less than 1 **2 :** ELLIPSIS

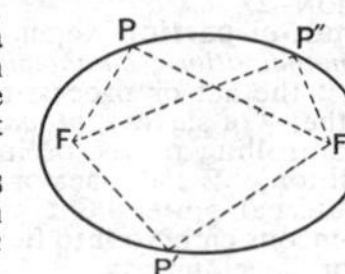

ellipse 1: *F, F′* foci; *P, P′, P″* any point on the curve; $FP + PF' = FP'' + P''F' = FP' + P'F'$

el·lip·sis \-psəs\ *n, pl* **ellip·ses** \-p,sēz\ [Gk *elleipsis*, lit., condition of falling short, defect, fr. *elleipein* to leave in, leave out, fall short (fr. *el-* — fr. *en* in — + *leipein* to leave) + *-sis* — more at IN, LOAN] **1 :** ELLIPSE **2** [L, fr. Gk *elleipsis*] **a** (1) **:** omission of one or more words that are obviously understood but must be supplied to make a construction grammatically complete (as in "all had turned out as expected" for "all had turned out as had been expected") ⟨fine examples of Shakespearean compression and ~ —F.R.Leavis⟩ ⟨a writer . . . whose very syntax is warm with the ~ of spoken speech —Robert Phelps⟩ ⟨uses ~ for poetic and comic effects —*Times Lit. Supp.*⟩ (2) **:** an instance of such omission **:** a grammatical construction marked by ellipsis ⟨the poem's striking *ellipses* offer no impediment to the reader's ear⟩ ⟨a crisp spare style abounding in *ellipses*⟩ (3) **:** the practice or use of ellipsis ⟨a writer much given to ~⟩ **b :** omission of an element (as from a train of thought or a speech) either fortuitously or for artistic effect **:** a leap or sudden passage without logical connectives, from one topic to another ⟨a complicated recital . . . full of grunts and *ellipses* —Hamilton Basso⟩ ⟨~ of both syntax and sense —Robert Browning⟩ **3 :** marks or a mark (as . . . or * * * or ——) showing omission of letters, words, or other material — compare SUSPENSION PERIODS

el·lip·so·graph \-psə,graf, -äf\ *n* [*ellipse* + *-o-* + *-graph*] **:** an instrument used for drawing ellipses

el·lip·soid \-p,sȯid\ *n* -s [F *ellipsoïde*, fr. *ellipse* + *-oïde* -oid] **:** a surface all plane sections of which are ellipses or circles; *also* **:** the corresponding solid

ellipsoid

el·lip·soi·dal \ə;lip'sȯid°l, e;-, ē;-; ;e(,)lip;s-\ *adj* **1 :** resembling an ellipsoid **2 :** having a shape like a round pillow — used esp. of lava

ellipsoidal spotlight *n* **:** a spotlight used in theatrical lighting that contains an ellipsoidal reflector and that is particularly designed for long throws and is more efficient than conventional spotlights, reflecting rays that others waste

ellipsoid of revolution *math* **:** a figure generated by the revolution of an ellipse about one of its axes **:** SPHEROID

el·lip·som·e·ter \ə,lip'sämət·ə(r), e,-, ē,-, ,e(,)-\ *n* [*ellipse* + *-o-* + *-meter*] **:** a polarimeter designed esp. for determining the ellipticity of polarized light

el·lip·tic \ə'liptik, (')e;l-, ē'l-, -tēk\ *or* **el·lip·ti·cal** \-təkəl, -tēk-\ *adj* [Gk *elleiptikos* defective, elliptic (grammatical sense), fr. (assumed) *elleiptos* (verbal of *elleipein* to leave out, fall short) + *-ikos* -ic, -ical — more at ELLIPSIS] **1 :** of, relating to, or shaped like an ellipse ⟨an ~ mirror⟩ ⟨an ~ orbit⟩ — see LEAF illustration **2 a** (1) **:** of, relating to, or marked by grammatical ellipsis ⟨the clause of comparison is often *elliptical* —G.O. Curme⟩ (2) **:** of or relating to a statement that is grammatically complete but lacks an element needed to assert a definite proposition ("the car moves now" is *elliptical* for "the car moves now relatively to the earth" —Arthur Pap⟩ (3) **:** of or relating to a mark showing omission (as of words) ⟨many authors use brief phrases, separated by three *elliptical* dots —L.E.Bowling⟩ **b** (1) **:** of, relating to, or marked by a manner of speech or writing characterized by extreme economy of expression or omission of superfluous elements **:** SUMMARY, BRIEF, CONCISE, CONDENSED ⟨the author in her *elliptical* four-page introduction —B.S.Myers⟩ ⟨concise, even *elliptical* to the verge of obscurity —H.O.Taylor⟩ ⟨listened to them talk, in tight, exclusive groups, with their own peculiar, *elliptical* language —Irwin Shaw⟩ (2) **:** of, relating to, or marked by a literary style that cultivates a studied obscurity for artistic effect **:** ENIGMATIC, CRYPTIC, OBLIQUE, OBSCURE ⟨the dialogue between them is stately, ~, and full of dark hints of the metaphysical —Wolcott Gibbs⟩

elliptical galaxy *n* **:** a galaxy of a generally elliptical shape, from round to lenticular, differing chiefly from other types in having no apparent internal structure or spiral arms — called also *spheroidal galaxy*

el·lip·ti·cal·ly \-tək(ə)lē, -tēk-, -li\ *adv* **1 :** in an elliptic manner **:** in the shape or manner of an ellipse ⟨moves ~ about its orbit⟩ **2 a :** with omission of an element (as one needed to complete a train of thought or speech) **:** without transition or logical connectives **:** CRYPTICALLY, ENIGMATICALLY ⟨one might go ~ . . . from talk of toothache to talk of ships storm-tossed at sea —K.D.Burke⟩ **b :** with great economy of expression **:** CONCISELY ⟨this whole earlier empire-building clan . . . is described so eloquently and so ~ —M.D.Geismar⟩ **c :** in a passing or tangential way ⟨even in the pieces upon which he impinges most ~ —Richard Watts⟩

el·lip·ti·cal·ness \-kəlnəs\ *n* -ES **:** the quality or state of being elliptical

elliptical projection *n* **:** a map of the earth's surface upon the interior of an ellipse

elliptical stern *n* **:** an overhanging ship's stern in which the part above the knuckle line (as the bulwark) is of conical form with a rake aft

elliptic arch *n* **:** an arch whose intrados is or approximates an ellipse

elliptic compass *n* **:** ELLIPSOGRAPH

elliptic gear *n* **:** a change gear consisting of a pair of equal gear wheels which are elliptical in shape and each of which rotates around one of its foci

elliptic arch

elliptic geometry *n* **:** geometry that adopts all of Euclid's axioms except the parallel axiom which is replaced by the axiom that through a point in a plane there pass no lines that do not intersect a given line in the plane

elliptic integral *n* **:** the integral as to *x* of a function rational in *x* and the square root of a polynomial of third or fourth degree in *x*

el·lip·tic·i·ty \ə,lip'tisəd·ē, e,-, ē,-, ,e(,)-\ *n* -ES **1 :** deviation of an ellipse or a spheroid from the form of a circle or a sphere **2 :** the difference between the equatorial and polar semidiameters, divided by the equatorial or occas. by the polar — used esp. in ref. to the figure of the earth ⟨the ~ of the earth is approximately $\frac{1}{300}$⟩

elliptic-lanceolate *adj, bot* **:** intermediate between elliptic and lanceolate

elliptic spring *or* **elliptical spring** *n* **:** a spring composed of laminated steel plates and having an elliptical shape

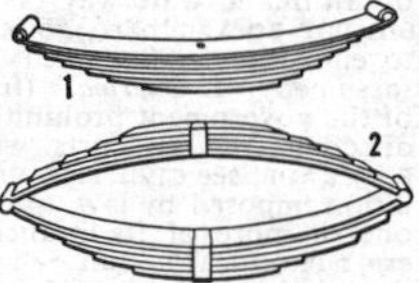

elliptic springs: *1* half elliptic, *2* elliptic

el·lip·to·cyte \ə'liptə,sīt, e'-, ē'-\ *n* -s [ISV *elliptic* + *-o-* + *-cyte*] **:** an elliptical red blood cell **:** OVALOCYTE

el·lip·to·cy·to·sis \-,-,sī'tōsəs\ *n, pl* **elliptocyto·ses** \-ō,sēz\ [NL, fr. ISV *elliptocyte* + NL *-osis*] **:** OVALOCYTOSIS

el·lo·bi·idae \,elə'bīə,dē\ *n pl, cap* [NL, fr. *Ellobium*, type genus + *-idae*] **:** a family of pulmonate snails that have a conoidal shell with a strongly toothed ear-shaped aperture and that are widely distributed in salt marshes chiefly along tropical and subtropical shores

el·lo·bi·um \ə'lōbēəm, e'-\ *n, cap* [NL, fr. Gk *ellobion* that which is in the lobe of the ear, earring, fr. *el-* (fr. *en* in) + *lobos* lobe + *-ion* (dim. suffix) — more at IN, LOBE] **:** the type genus of Ellobiidae

el·lops \'e,läps\ *n, pl* **ellops** *or* **ellopses** [Gk *ellops*, *elops*, a fish — more at ELOPS] **:** ELOPS

ells *pl of* ELL

ellul *usu cap, var of* ELUL

ell·wand \'elwän(d)\ *n* [ME *elenwand*, *elle wande*, *el wande*, fr. *eln*, *ellen*, *elle* ell + *wand* — more at ELL] *Scot* **:** a measuring rod one ell long

elm \'elm, 'eùm, *dial or substand* 'eləm\ *n* -s *often attrib* [ME, fr. OE; akin to OHG *elme*, *elm* elm, ON *almr*, L *ulmus*, MIr *lem* elm, and perh. to L *alnus* alder — more at ALDER] **1 a :** a tree of the genus *Ulmus* — see ROCK ELM, SIBERIAN ELM, SLIPPERY ELM — see TREE illustration **b :** the hard tough wood of this tree used extensively for implements, furniture, and barrel hoops **2 :** any of various chiefly Australian and West Indian trees or shrubs having foliage resembling that of members of the genus *Ulmus*

el man·su·ra \;el,man;sùrə\ *adj, usu cap E&M* [fr. *El Mansura*, Egypt] **:** of or from the city of El Mansura, Egypt **:** of the kind or style prevalent in El Mansura

elm bark *n* **:** SLIPPERY ELM 1c

elm bark beetle *n* **:** either of two beetles that are vectors of the fungus which causes Dutch elm disease: **a :** a native beetle (*Hylurgopinus rufipes*) of eastern No. America **b :** a smaller European beetle (*Scolytus multistriatus*) that has become established in the same part of the New World

elm blight *n* **:** DUTCH ELM DISEASE

elm borer *n* **:** any of several beetles having larvae that bore into the elm; *esp* **:** a rather large hairy longicorn beetle (*Saperda tridentata*) of the eastern U.S.

elm calligrapha *n* **:** a coppery green and yellow calligrapha (*Calligrapha scalaris*) that often feeds on the foliage of elm

elm·en \'elmən\ *adj* [ME *elmyn*, fr. *elm* + *-yn* -en] *dial Eng* **:** relating to or made of wood from an elm tree

el·men·dorf test \'elmən,dȯrf-\ *n, usu cap E* [after Armin *Elmendorf* b1890 Am. mechanical engineer, its inventor] **:** a standard test for the tearing strength of paper

el·men·tei·tan \;elmən·;tāt°n\ *adj, usu cap* [*Elmenteita* Lake, Kenya + E *-an*] **:** of or relating to an early Neolithic or Mesolithic culture of eastern Africa characterized by obsidian microliths

elm family *n* **:** ULMACEAE

elm green *n* **:** a moderate olive green that is slightly lighter than forest green (sense 2), yellower, lighter, and stronger than cypress, and greener and stronger than Lincoln green

el·min·i·us \el'minēəs\ *n, cap* [NL] **:** a genus of acorn barnacles native to the southern hemisphere but including one form (*E. modestus*) that has recently become established on the English coast where it is a pest of oyster beds

el·mi·ra system \el'mīrə-\ *n, usu cap E* [fr. *Elmira*, N.Y., where the system was adopted in a reformatory in 1876] **:** a system of penology based on the indeterminate sentence with possible commutation

elm leaf beetle *n* **:** a small orange-yellow black-striped Old World chrysomelid beetle (*Pyrrhalta luteola*) that is long established in eastern No. America and is both as adult and larva a leaf-eating pest on elm

elm phloem necrosis *n* **:** PHLOEM NECROSIS C

elm sawfly *n* **:** a large American sawfly (*Cimbex americana*) that has knobbed antennae, orange-tinged tarsi, black head and thorax with somewhat lighter, spotted abdomen, and smoke brown wings, and produces yellowish or greenish white larvae with a dorsal black stripe which are vigorous defoliators chiefly of elm and willow

elm scale *or* **elm scurfy scale** *n* **:** any of several scales that feed on elm trees; *esp* **:** a widely distributed scale (*Chionaspis americana*) of eastern No. America that feeds on elm and hackberry and has the female covered by a dull white scale often darkened anteriorly by secretion

elm tea *n* **:** an infusion prepared from slippery-elm bark that is used as a demulcent

elm water *n* **1 :** a decoction of slippery-elm bark **2 :** a watery exudation from the galls of the English elm

elmy \'elmē, 'eùmē\ *adj, sometimes* -ER/-EST **:** characterized by or abounding in elms

elocular \(')ē+\ *adj* [*e-* + *locular*] **:** having but one cavity **:** not divided by a septum **:** lacking loculi

el·o·cute \'elə,kyüt\ *vb* -ED/-ING/-S [back-formation fr. *elocution*] **:** DECLAIM ⟨the senator ranted and *elocuted* but made little impression on the crowd⟩ ⟨a frail drama superbly acted, and excellently *elocuted* —*N.Y. Times*⟩

el·o·cu·tion \,elə'kyüshən\ *n* -s [ME *elocucioun*, fr. L *elocution-*, *elocutio*, fr. *elocutus* (past part. of *eloqui* to speak out, orate) + *-ion-*, *-io* -ion — more at ELOQUENT] **1** *archaic* **a :** literary style or expression **b :** impressive writing or style **:** ELOQUENCE ⟨to express these thoughts with ~ —John Dryden⟩ **2 a :** oratorical, dramatic, or expressive oral delivery ⟨an expert user of ~⟩ **b :** style or manner of speaking ⟨clear concise ~⟩; *sometimes* **:** an affected or overembellished style or manner of speaking **3 :** the art of oratorical or expressive public speaking

el·o·cu·tion·ary \-shə,nerē, -ri\ *adj* **:** of, relating to, or exhibiting elocution ⟨~ recitals⟩ ⟨an ~ Oxonian delivery —E.R.Bentley⟩

el·o·cu·tion·ist \-sh(ə)nəst\ *n* -s **:** a person adept in elocution: as **a :** a teacher of elocution **b :** a professional reciter or reader

elo·dea \ə'lōdēə, ,elə'dēə\ *n* [NL, irreg. fr. Gk *helōdēs* marshy — more at HELODES] **1** *cap* **:** a small genus of submerged aquatic herbs (family Hydrocharitaceae) that are native to No. and So. America and that have leafy stems and small dioecious or polygamous flowers arising from a 2-cleft spathe — see WATERWEED **2** -s **:** any plant of the genus *Elodea*

eloge \ā'lōzh, ālōözh\ *n, pl* **elog·es** \-ōzhəz,-ōözh\ [MF, fr. ML *elogium* (influenced in meaning by ML *eulogium* eulogy), fr. L, maxim, saying, inscription on a tombstone, prob. by folk etymology (influence of L *e-* and Gk *logos* word) fr. Gk *elegeion* elegy — more at EULOGY, LOGIC, ELEGY] **1** *archaic* **:** ENCOMIUM, EULOGY **2 :** a panegyrical funeral oration

el·o·gy \'eləjē, -ləjē\ *also* **elo·gium** \ə'lōj(ē)əm, ē'-,e'-\ *n, pl* **elogies** *also* **elogiums** [in sense 1, fr. L *elogium*; in sense 2 & 3, fr. ML *elogium*] **1** *obs* **:** an inscription esp. on a tombstone **2** *archaic* **:** a characterization or biographical sketch esp. in praise **3** *obs* **:** a funeral oration

elo·him \,elō'hēm, -lō'-, -'him; e'lō,him, ə'-\ *n* [Heb *ĕlōhīm*, pl. of *ĕlōah* god] **1** *cap* **:** God esp. as conceived of in the Old Testament or in those Old Testament passages where he is designated in the Hebrew text by the word *ĕlōhīm* **2 elohim** *pl, usu cap* **:** local or minor divinities of the ancient Canaanites and Hebrews

el·o·him·ic \;elō;himik\ *adj, cap* **:** ELOHISTIC 2

elo·hism \'elō,hizəm, -lō,-; e'lō,-, ə'-\ *n* -s *cap* **:** the religion and worship of Elohim — compare YAHWISM

¹elo·hist \-,(h)əst\ *n* -s *usu cap* [*elohim* + *-ist*] **1 :** an author of an Elohistic document **2** *archaic* **:** a priestly writer

²elohist \"\ *adj, usu cap* **:** ELOHISTIC

el·o·his·tic \;elō;histik\ *adj, usu cap* **1 :** of, relating to, or characteristic of one of the supposed ancient biblical sources ⟨*Elohistic* document⟩ **2 :** characterized by use in Hebrew of the word *ĕlōhīm* rather than *yahweh* as a designation of God ⟨Psalms 42–83, the *Elohistic* Psalter⟩ **3 :** of, or characteristic of, or characterized by worship of God as Elohim rather than as Yahweh

eloign \ə'lȯin, ē'-\ *vt* -ED/-ING/-S [ME *eloynen*, *esloignen*, fr. MF *esloigner*, fr. OF *esloignier*, fr. *es-* (fr. L *ex-*) + *loing* far, fr. L *longe* long, far, adv., fr. *longus* long — more at LONG] **1** *archaic* **:** to take (oneself) far away **2** *archaic* **a :** to convey to a distance or beyond a legal jurisdiction **b :** CONCEAL ⟨~ goods liable to distress⟩

Elon \'ē,län, ≠'≠\ *trademark* — used for a white soluble powder used as a photographic developer

¹elon·gate \ē'lȯŋ,gāt, ə'- *also* -läŋ- *sometimes* 'ē,≠,≠; *usu* -ād+V\ *vb* -ED/-ING/-S [LL *elongatus*, past part. of *elongare*, fr. L *e-* + *longus* long] *vt* **:** to increase the length of **:** stretch out **:** LENGTHEN ⟨he *elongated* his face as he heard their story⟩ ⟨the British *elongating* their defense program —*Economist*⟩ ~ *vi* **:** to grow in length **:** LENGTHEN — used esp. of plants and their parts ⟨rapidly *elongating* internodes⟩ **syn** see EXTEND

²elongate \"\ *adj* [LL *elongatus*, past part.] **:** stretched out **:** LENGTHENED; *esp* **:** having a form notably long in comparison to its width ⟨an ~ tail that tapers to a point —R.E.Coker⟩

³elongate \"\ *vi* -ED/-ING/-S [LL *elongatus*, past part. of *elongare*, fr. L *e-* + *longe* far — more at ELOIGN] **1** *archaic* **:** to go away **:** DEPART, RECEDE **2** *archaic, of a celestial body* **:** to appear to recede from its primary or from a particular point in the sky — compare ELONGATION

elongated *adj* **:** ELONGATE

elongate nut shell *n* **:** BEAKED COCKLE

¹elon·ga·tion \(,)ē,lȯŋ'gāshən, ə,- *also* -läŋ-\ *n* -s [ME *elongacioun*, fr. ML *elongation-*, *elongatio*, fr. LL *elongatus* (past part. of *elongare* to withdraw) + L *-ion-*, *-io* -ion] **1 a :** the angular distance of a celestial body from another around which it revolves or from a particular point in the sky ⟨the ~ of a planet from the sun⟩ ⟨the ~ of an eclipsing variable⟩ — see GREATEST ELONGATION **b :** the daily extreme east or west position of a star with reference to the north celestial pole ⟨the ~s of the North Star⟩ **2** *obs* **:** removal to a distance **:** REMOTENESS

²elongation \"\ *n* -s [¹*elongate* + *-ion*] **1 a :** a lengthening or state of being lengthened **:** PROTRACTION, EXTENSION ⟨the ~ of a muscle under tension⟩ ⟨~ of the apex of a plant⟩ **b :** the total deformation in the direction of load or per unit of length caused by a tensile force; *sometimes* **:** the maximum permanent stretch per unit of original length induced in a body by a force that causes it to break **2 :** something that is elongated **:** PROLONGATION, CONTINUATION ⟨the arm may be considered a specialized ~ of the earlier fin⟩

elongato- *comb form* [*elongate* + *-o-*] **:** elongated and ⟨*elongato*-ovate⟩

elope \ə'lōp, ē'-\ *vi* -ED/-ING/-S [AF *aloper*, perh. fr. *a-* (fr. OF *es-*, fr. L *ex-*) + MD *lōpen* to run; akin to OE *hlēapan* to leap, jump, run — more at LEAP] **1 a** *of a married woman* **:** to run away from one's husband with a lover **b** *of an unmarried woman* **:** to run away from one's home with the unannounced intention of getting married ⟨she *eloped* with her second cousin and they were married in the next state⟩ **c** *of two persons of opposite sex* **:** to go away secretly with the intention of marrying or establishing a more or less permanent relation of cohabitation ⟨her mother wanted a big wedding but the young people decided to ~⟩ **2 :** to run or slip away (as from a mental institution or training school) **:** ESCAPE, FLEE ⟨he *eloped* from his creditors⟩ — **elope·ment** \-pmənt\ *n* -s

elop·er \-pə(r)\ *n* -s **:** one that elopes

elops \'e,läps, 'ē,-\ *n* [L, fr. Gk *ellops*, *elops*, a fish; perh. akin to Gk *lepis* scale — more at LEPID-] **1** *pl* **elops** *or* **elopses** *obs* **:** a marine animal sometimes identified as the sturgeon; *also* **:** SEA SERPENT **2** *cap* [NL, fr. L] **:** a genus (the type of the family Elopidae) of fishes of the order Isospondyli that are related to the tarpons and contain the ten-pounder (*E. saurus*)

el·o·quence \'eləkwən(t)s *sometimes* -lēk- *or* -lik-\ *n* -s [ME, fr. MF, fr. L *eloquentia*, fr. *eloquent-*, *eloquens* + *-ia* -y] **1 a :** discourse marked by force and persuasiveness suggesting strong feeling or deep sincerity; *esp* **:** discourse marked by apt and fluent diction and imaginative fervor ⟨the poetry of western nations is ~ in meter —George Santayana⟩ **b :** the art or power of using such discourse ⟨Plato's ~ and moral fervor —G.R.Morrow⟩ **2 :** forceful or persuasive usu. oral expressiveness ⟨he convinces himself by the sheer ~ of his own voice —H.J.Laski⟩ ⟨the ~ of the photographs —*Times Lit. Supp.*⟩ **3** *archaic* **:** RHETORIC

el·o·quent \-nt\ *adj* [ME, fr. MF, fr. L *eloquent-*, *eloquens*, fr. pres. part. of *eloqui* to speak out, fr. *e-* + *loqui* to speak] **1 :** adept at skilled easy pleasing communication of a thought, idea, or feeling usu. in a fluent, moving, vivid, or forceful manner ⟨but he was no Emerson, of the grave ~ voice, the noble presence —H.S.Canby⟩ **2 :** clearly and forcefully indicative of some feeling, condition, or character ⟨that paternal pressure on his hand was ~ to him how warmly he was beloved —George Meredith⟩ ⟨a tremulous little man in greenish black broadcloth, ~ of continued depression in some village retail trade —A.T.Quiller-Couch⟩ **syn** see EXPRESSIVE, VOCAL

el·o·quent·ly *adv* [ME, fr. *eloquent* + *-ly*] **:** with eloquence **:** in an eloquent manner

el·o·quent·ness *n* -ES **:** the quality or state of being eloquent

el·o·the·ri·um \,elə'thirēəm\ [NL, irreg. fr. Gk *helos* marsh + NL *-therium* — more at HELODES] *syn of* ENTELODON

elo·ti·llo \,elō'tē(,)(y)ō\ *n* -s [MexSp, dim. of *elote* ear of green corn, fr. Nahuatl *elotl*] **:** SQUAWROOT 1

el paso \el'pa(,)sō\ *adj, usu cap E&P* [fr. *El Paso*, Texas] **:** of or from the city of El Paso, Texas **:** of the kind or style prevalent in El Paso

el paso·an \el'pasəwən\ *n* -s *cap E&P* [*El Paso*, Texas + E *-an*] **:** a native or resident of El Paso, Texas

el·paso·lite \el'pasō,līt\ *n* -s [*El Paso* co., Colo. + E *-lite*] **:** a mineral K_2NaAlF_6 consisting of sodium potassium aluminum fluoride

el·pi·dite \'elpə,dīt\ *n* -s [Sw *elpidit*, fr. Gk *elpid-*, *elpis* hope + Sw *-it* -ite; fr. the expectation of finding other minerals in the same locality — more at VOLUPTUOUS] **:** a mineral $Na_2ZrSi_6O_{15}.3H_2O$ consisting of a hydrated sodium zirconium silicate

elritch *var of* ELDRITCH

els *pl of* EL

-els *pl of* -EL

el sal·va·dor \el'salvə,dȯ(ə)r, (,)≠,≠≠'≠\ *adj, usu cap E&S* [fr. *El Salvador*, republic of Central America] **:** of or from the Republic of El Salvador **:** of the kind or style prevalent in El Salvador **:** SALVADORAN

¹else \'els, -lts\ *adv* [ME *elles*, fr. OE; akin to OHG *elles* otherwise, ON *elligai* otherwise, Goth *aljis* other, L *alius* other, *alter* other of two, Gk *allos* other, Arm *ail* other, OE *eall* all — more at ALL] **1 a :** in a different manner ⟨how ~ could he act under the circumstances⟩ **:** in a different place ⟨here and nowhere ~⟩ **:** at a different time ⟨Friday isn't convenient for me so when ~ can we meet⟩ **b :** in an additional manner ⟨how ~ can buildings be heated⟩ **:** in an additional place ⟨where ~ is gold found⟩ **:** at an additional time ⟨Friday is convenient for one of the two weekly lessons but when ~ can we get together⟩ **2 a :** if the facts are different **:** if the facts were different **:** if not **:** OTHERWISE — often preceded by *or* ⟨do what I tell you, or ~ you will be sorry⟩ and used absolutely without a following clause to express a threat of unspecified but presumably dire consequences ⟨do what I tell you or ~⟩ **b :** whether it is not so ⟨house, land, money are things obtainable . . . by clever headwork: ask my father ~ —Robert Browning⟩ **c :** apart from that **:** with the exception of that ⟨a tower of refuge built for the forlorn —William Wordsworth⟩

²else \"\ *adj* [ME *elles*, fr. *elles*, adv.] **:** OTHER: **a :** being different in identity ⟨nothing ~ but the best will do⟩ ⟨such decisions are to be made by the commanding officer and no one ~⟩ **b :** being in addition ⟨what ~ did he say⟩ ⟨did you meet anyone ~⟩ — now usu. used with a preceding pronoun; followed by the possessive ending *'s* when the combination of the pronoun and *else* is in the possessive case dependent on an immediately following noun ⟨somebody ~'s house⟩ ⟨I don't know who ~'s hat it could be⟩ and usu. also when not dependent on an immediately following noun ⟨it couldn't be anybody ~'s⟩ ⟨I don't know who ~'s it could be⟩ ⟨I don't know whose ~ it could be⟩

elseways \'≠,≠\ *adv* [¹*else* + *-ways*] *dial* **:** OTHERWISE

elsewhence \'≠,≠, ≠'≠\ *adv* [¹*else* + *whence*] **:** from another quarter

else·where \'el(t)s,(h)we(ə)r, -wa(ə)r, |ə, ≠'≠\ *also* **elsewheres** \|(ə)rz, |ez\ *adv* [ME *elleswher*, fr. OE *elles hwǣr*, fr. *elles* else + *hwǣr* where — more at ELSE, WHERE] **:** in or to some or any other place ⟨it is found in town and ~⟩ ⟨we went ~ for dinner⟩ ⟨~ he mentions his dependence on his mother⟩

elsewhither \'≠,≠,≠, ≠'≠≠\ *adv* [ME *elleswhider*, fr. OE *elles hwider*, fr. *elles* else + *hwider* whither — more at WHITHER] **:** to some or any other place in a different direction or toward a different objective ⟨his soul aimed ~⟩

elsewise \'≠,≠, ≠'≠\ *adv* [¹*else* + *-wise*] **:** OTHERWISE

el·sholt·zia \el'shōltsēə\ *n, cap* [NL, fr. Johann S. *Elsholtz* †1688 Ger. physician and botanist + NL *-ia*] **:** a genus of chiefly Asiatic aromatic herbs (family Labiatae) with blue or purple flowers in one-sided spikes

el·sin *or* **el·shin** *or* **el·son** \'els(h)ən\ *n* -s [ME *elsen*, prob.

fr. MD *elsene, else;* akin to OHG *alunsa, alansa* awl, G dial. (Swiss) *alesne,* (assumed) Goth *alisna* (whence OSp *alesna*), ON *alr* — more at AWL] *dial Brit* **:** a shoemaker's awl

el·sin·oë \el'sinə,wē\ *n, cap* [NL] **:** a genus of ascomycetous fungi that have a flat stroma with a gelatinous interior and a crustose rind and that cause various anthracnose and scab diseases of higher plants

el·u·ate \'elyəwət, -,wāt\ *n* -s [L *eluere* to wash out (fr. *e-* + *-luere,* fr. *lavere* to wash) + E *-ate* — more at LYE] **:** the washings obtained by eluting (as a solution containing a formerly adsorbed substance)

elu·ci·date \ə'lüsə,dāt, ē'- *also* əl'yü- *or* ēl'yü-; *usu* -ād·+V\ *vb* -ED/-ING/-S [LL *elucidatus,* past part. of *elucidare,* fr. L *e-* + *lucidus* clear, bright — more at LUCID] *vt* **:** to make clear; *esp* **:** to make intelligible by clear explanation or careful analysis ⟨*elucidated* the pattern of ancient roadways⟩ ⟨served to ~ the policy of the government⟩ ⟨critical notes that ~ the text⟩ ~ *vi* **:** to provide a clarifying explanation ⟨well, ~, my boy; you know all the answers⟩

elu·ci·da·tion \=,==ˈdāshən\ *n* -s **:** the act, process, or means of elucidating **:** EXPLANATION; *sometimes* **:** identification or determination esp. of the nature of something ⟨~ of the chemical structure of an antibiotic⟩

elu·ci·da·tive \=ˈ==,dād·|iv, -,dəl, |t|, |ēv *also* |əv\ *or* **elu·ci·da·to·ry** \-,də,tōrē, -ōr-, -ri, *chiefly Brit* -,dātəri *or* -,dā·tri\ *adj* **:** tending or serving to elucidate **:** EXPLANATORY ⟨~ comments on a difficult passage⟩

elu·ci·da·tor \-,dād·ə(r), -ātə-\ *n* -s **:** one that elucidates

eluctation *n* -s [LL *eluctation-, eluctatio,* fr. L *eluctatus* (past part. of *eluctari* to struggle out, fr. *e-* + *luctari, luctare* to struggle, wrestle) + *-ion-, -io* -ion — more at LOCK (ringlet of hair)] *obs* **:** a bursting or struggling forth

elucubrate \ē, ə+\ *vt* -ED/-ING/-S [L *elucubratus,* past part. of *elucubrare* to compose by lamplight, fr. *e-* + *lucubrare* to work by lamplight — more at LUCUBRATE] **:** to work out or express by studious effort — **elucubration** \(,)ē, ə+\ *n* -s

elude \ē'lüd, ə'- *also* ēl'yüd *or* əl'y-\ *vt* -ED/-ING/-S [L *eludere,* fr. *e-* + *ludere* to play — more at LUDICROUS] **1** *obs* **:** TRICK, DELUDE; *also* **:** BAFFLE, FRUSTRATE **2 :** to avoid slyly or adroitly (as by artifice, stratagem, or dexterity) **:** EVADE ⟨~ a blow⟩ ⟨he ~s law by piteous looks aloft —Robert Browning⟩ ⟨*eluding* their responsibilities⟩ **3 :** to escape the notice or perception of ⟨the reality of human nature is bound to ~ us if we look only at a momentary cross section of it —Walter Lippmann⟩; *esp* **:** to baffle or evade by reason of recondite or inconspicuous character ⟨a sense that ~s definition⟩ **syn** see ESCAPE

elud·er \-də(r)\ *n* -s **:** one that eludes

el·u·ent *or* **el·u·ant** \'elyəwənt\ *n* -s [L *eluent-, eluens,* pres. part. of *eluere* to wash out — more at ELUATE] **:** the solvent used in eluting

elul *or* **el·lul** \e'lül\ *n* -s *usu cap* [Heb *ĕlūl*] **:** the 12th month of the civil year or the 6th month of the ecclesiastical year in the Jewish calendar — see MONTH table

elu·sion \ē'lüzhən, ə'- *also* ēl'yü- *or* əl'y-\ *n* -s [ML & LL; ML *elusion-, elusio* evasion, fr. LL, deception, fr. L *elusus* (past part. of *eludere* to elude) + *-ion-, -io* -ion — more at ELUDE] **1** *obs* **a :** the act of deluding **b :** deceptive quality **c :** ILLUSION **2 :** an instance or act of eluding: as **a :** adroit escape (as by artifice) **b :** an evasion esp. of a problem or an order

elu·sive \=ˈ=s|iv, |ēv *also* -z| *or* |əv\ *adj* [*elusion* + *-ive*] **:** tending to elude **:** EVASIVE: as **a :** tending to avoid or evade grasp or pursuit ⟨shy ~ denizens of the deep woods⟩; *often* **:** incapable of being prolonged ⟨~ pleasures of a sunny afternoon in childhood⟩ **b :** not easily comprehended or defined **:** BAFFLING ⟨that ~ thing, the soul⟩ ⟨an ~ person⟩ **c :** hard to pin down, isolate, or identify ⟨use of egg cultures to isolate certain hitherto ~ viruses⟩ ⟨a haunting ~ odor⟩ ⟨the ~ atomic particles called mesons —John Pfeiffer⟩ — **elu·sive·ly** \|əvlē, -li\ *adv*

elu·sive·ness \|ivnəs, |ēv- *also* |əv-\ *n* -ES **:** the quality or state of being elusive ⟨the author's ~ may at times be construed . . . as evasiveness —J.W.Chase⟩ ⟨brings vividly before us the ~ of the eternal objects of sense —A.N.Whitehead⟩ ⟨resented charges of rough tactics in his base running, maintaining that he developed ~ by his fall-away or fadeaway slide —*Current Biog.*⟩

elu·so·ry \-üs(ə)rē, -üz(-, -ri\ *adj* [ML *elusorius,* fr. L *elusus* + *-orius* -ory] **:** EVASIVE, ELUSIVE

elute \ē'lüt, ə'- *also* ēl'yüt *or* əl'y-\ *vt* -ED/-ING/-S [L *elutus,* past part. of *eluere* to wash out — more at ELUATE] **:** to wash out **:** EXTRACT; *specif* **:** to remove (adsorbed material) from an adsorbent by means of a solvent (as in chromatography)

elu·tion \-üshən\ *n* -s [LL *elution-, elutio* act of washing out, fr. L *elutus* + *-ion-, -io* -ion] **:** the process or action of eluting

elu·tri·ate \-ü·trē,āt\ *vt* -ED/-ING/-S [L *elutriatus,* past part. of *elutriare* to wash out, decant, prob. fr. (assumed) *elutor* one that washes out, fr. *elutus* + *-or*] **:** to subject to elutriation

elu·tri·a·tion \=,==ˈāshən\ *n* -s [L *elutriatus* + E *-ion*] **1 :** the removal of substances from a mixture by washing and decanting ⟨the ~ of liquid sludge⟩ **2 :** the separation of finer lighter particles from coarser heavier particles in a mixture by means of a usu. slow upward stream of fluid so that the lighter particles are carried upward **3 :** the washing away of the lighter or finer particles (as of humus or clay) in a soil esp. by the splashing of raindrops

elu·tri·a·tor \=ˈ==,ād·ə(r)\ *n* -s **:** an apparatus for separating particles (as of clay) according to size by elutriation

elu·vial \(')ē¦lüvēəl, -vyəl *also* (')el¦yü-\ *adj* [NL *eluvium* + E *-al*] **1 :** of, relating to, or composed of eluvium **2 :** of or relating to eluviation or to eluviated materials or areas (as soils or soil horizons)

elu·vi·ate \=ˈ=vē,āt\ *vi* -ED/-ING/-S [NL *eluvium* + E *-ate*] **:** to undergo eluviation

elu·vi·a·tion \(,)=,=vēˈāshən\ *n* -s **:** the transportation of dissolved or suspended soil material within the soil by the downward or lateral movement of water when rainfall exceeds evaporation — compare ILLUVIATION

elu·vi·um \=ˈ=vēəm\ *n* -s [NL, fr. L *eluere* to wash out, after such pairs as L *alluere* to wash against: LL *alluvium* — more at ELUATE, ALLUVION] **1 :** rock debris produced by the weathering and disintegration of rock in situ — compare ALLUVIUM **2 :** fine soil or sand deposited by wind (as in dunes)

el·vel·la·ce·ae \,elvə'lāsē,ē\ *syn of* HELVELLACEAE

el·ver \'elvə(r)\ *n* -s [alter. of *eelfare*] **:** a small cylindrical young eel that is more advanced in development than a leptocephalus and that is found chiefly along shores or about estuaries — called also *glass eel*

elves *pl of* ELF

el·vish \'elvish, -vēsh\ *adj* [ME *elvissh,* fr. *elf* + *-issh* -ish] **1 :** of or relating to elves **:** being or like elves ⟨~ tricks disturbed the cattle⟩ ⟨ugly shrunken ~ men⟩ **2 :** characteristic of or like that of elves ⟨~ laughter⟩: as **a :** MISCHIEVOUS **b :** SPITEFUL **c :** IRRITATING — **el·vish·ly** *adv*

el·y·mi \'elə,mī\ *n pl, usu cap* [L, fr. Gk *Elymoi*] **:** an ancient people of northwest Sicily

el·y·mus \-,məs\ *n, cap* [NL, fr. Gk *elymos* millet] **:** a genus of tall tufted perennial grasses comprising the lyme grasses, having closely flowered terminal flower spikes, and being sometimes used as fodder and to bind loose sandy soil — see WILD RYE

ely·sia \ə'lizh(ē)ə, ē'-,e'-, -lēzh-\ *n, cap* [NL, prob. fr. L *Elysium*] **:** the type genus of Elysiidae comprising sea slugs that lack both cerata and gills

ely·sian \-zh(ē)ən\ *adj, often cap* [L *Elysius* (fr. Gk *Ēlysios*) + E *-an*] **1 :** relating to Elysium **2 :** sweetly blissful **:** BEATIFIC ⟨~ peace⟩

elysian fields *n pl, often cap E* **:** ELYSIUM

el·y·si·idae \,elə'sīə,dē\ *n pl, cap* [NL, fr. *Elysia,* type genus + *-idae*] **:** a family of slender creeping sea slugs with distinct head, tapering tail, auriculate tentacles, and lateral body folds functioning as fins when the animal swims

ely·si·um \ə'liz(h)ēəm, ē'-,e'-, -lēz(h)-, -zhəm\ *n, pl* **elysiums** \-z(h)ēəmz,-zhəmz\ *or* **ely·sia** \-z(h)ēə,-zhə\ *often cap* [L, fr. Gk *Ēlysion,* fr. neut. of *Ēlysios* Elysian] **1 :** the dwelling place of happy souls after death as conceived by the ancient Greeks and Romans either as a concrete physical region or a state of existence **2 :** abode or state of ideal delight and happiness **:** PARADISE ⟨lovers sitting cheek by jowl for an hour of idle ~ —John Galsworthy⟩

elytr- *or* **elytri-** *or* **elytro-** *comb form* [prob. fr. NL, fr. *elytron*] **1 :** elytron ⟨*elytroid*⟩ ⟨*elytriferous*⟩ **2 :** vagina ⟨*elytropolypus*⟩

elytra *pl of* ELYTRON

el·y·tral \'elətrəl\ *adj* [NL *elytron* + E *-al*] **:** of or relating to an elytron

el·y·trif·er·ous \¦elə¦trif(ə)rəs\ *adj* [*elytr-* + *-ferous*] **:** bearing elytra — used esp. of segments of certain polychaetes

elyt·ri·form \ə'li·trə,fȯrm, e'li·t-,'elə·t-\ *adj* [*elytr-* + *-form*] **:** resembling or shaped like an elytron **:** SHIELD-SHAPED

el·y·trig·er·ous \¦elə¦trij(ə)rəs\ *adj* [*elytr-* + *-gerous*] **:** ELYTRIFEROUS

el·y·troid \'elə·,trȯid\ *adj* [*elytr-* + *-oid*] **:** resembling an elytron

el·y·tron \'elə·,trän\ *or* **elytrum** \'elə·trəm\ *n, pl* **ely·tra** \-,trə\ [NL, fr. Gk *elytron* sheath, wing cover] **1 :** one of the thickened sclerotized anterior wings in beetles and some other insects that serve only to protect the posterior pair — called also *wing cover* **2 :** one of the shielding dorsal scales of various polychaete worms

elyt·ro·phore \ə'li·trə,fō(ə)r, e'li·t-,'elə·t-\ *n* -s [*elytr-* + *-phore*] **:** a modified cuticular prominence to which an elytron of a polychaete worm is attached

el·y·troph·o·rous \¦elə¦träf(ə)rəs\ *adj* [*elytr-* + *-phorous*] **:** having elytra

el·y·trous \'elə·trəs\ *adj* [*elytr-* + *-ous*] **:** resembling or suggestive of an elytron

[1]**el·ze·vir** \'elzə,vi(ə)r, -lsə-\ *adj, usu cap* [after the *Elzevir* (Elzevier) family, Dutch printers and publishers that flourished in the 16th & 17th centuries] **:** of, relating to, or being books or editions esp. of the Greek New Testament and the classics printed and published by the Elzevir family at Amsterdam or Leiden from about 1583 to 1680

[2]**elzevir** \"\ *n* -s *usu cap* **:** an Elzevir publication

[1]**em** \'em\ *n* -s **1 :** the letter *m* **2 :** the set dimension of an em quad used as a unit of measure **3 :** PICA

[2]**em** \"\ *adj* **1 :** having the form of capital M ⟨an ~ fold⟩ **2 :** of the size of an em ⟨an ~ dash⟩ ⟨a 24 ~ line of type⟩

em- — see EN-

em *abbr* **1** emanation **2** eminence

EM *abbr* **1** earl marshal **2** electromagnetic **3** end matched **4** enlisted man **5** [L *episcopus et martyr*] bishop and martyr

Em *symbol* emanation

'em \əm; *after* p, b, f, *or* v, ᵊm *or* əm; *an immediately preceding* v *may become* b *by assimilation; thus "save 'em" may be* 'sāvᵊm *or* 'sābᵊm *or* 'sāvəm\ *pron* [ME *hem,* fr. OE *heom, him,* dat. pl. of *hē* he — more at HE] **:** THEM

emacerate \ē, ə+\ *vb* [L *emaceratus,* fr. *e-* + *maceratus,* past part. of *macerare* to soften, macerate — more at MACERATE] *archaic* **:** EMACIATE

[1]**ema·ci·ate** \ə'māshē,āt, ē'-, *usu* -ād·+V\ *vb* -ED/-ING/-S [L *emaciatus,* past part. of *emaciare,* fr. *e-* + *macies* leanness, thinness, fr. *macer* lean, thin — more at MEAGER] *vt* **1 :** to cause to lose flesh so as to become very lean ⟨his sickness *emaciated* him⟩ **2 :** to make poor and weak or unattractive **:** ATTENUATE ⟨all extraneous light *emaciated* and shattered by the flare of gas and electricity —William Beebe⟩ ⟨consistency . . . is the hobgoblin of foolish nations. It ~s a people's life —M.Y.Buch⟩ ~ *vi* **:** to waste away in body **:** become very lean

[2]**ema·ci·ate** \-ē,ā|t, -ēə|t, *usu* |d·+V\ *adj* [L *emaciatus*] **:** EMACIATED

ema·ci·at·ed \-ē,ād·əd, -ātəd\ *adj* **1 :** made lean by impairment (as from hunger) ⟨~ bony hands⟩; *also* **:** MEAGER, NARROW ⟨an ~ outlook on life⟩ ⟨the succession of ~ parsonages —Ellery Sedgwick⟩ **2 :** ENFEEBLED, ATTENUATED ⟨failed to pass even this ~ version of the original bill⟩ ⟨the ~ state of the controversy⟩

ema·ci·a·tion \-,māshē'āshən *also* -āsē- *by sh-dissimilation*\ *n* -s **1 :** the process of making or becoming emaciated **2 :** the state of being emaciated; *esp* **:** a wasted condition of the body

em·a·gram \'emə,gram\ *n* -s [[1]*em* + *-agram* (as in *diagram*)] **:** a thermodynamic chart on which temperature is shown on a linear scale as abscissa and pressure on a logarithmic scale as ordinate

email \ā'mī, āmȧȧy\ *n, pl* **emails** \-īz,-ȧȧy\ [F *émail,* fr. OF *esmail, esmal* — more at ENAMEL] **1 :** ENAMEL **2 :** a moderate bluish green to greenish blue that is lighter than gendarme, deeper than cyan blue, and duller than parrot blue — called also *bleu Louise*

ema·ja·gua \,emə'hägwə\ *n* -s [AmerSp, alter. of *demajagua, damajagua* — more at MAJAGUA] **1 :** MAJAGUA **2 :** MOUNTAIN MAHOE **3 :** a small tree (*Daphnopsis philippiana*) of the family Thymelaeaceae that is endemic in Puerto Rico

e major *n, usu cap E* **:** the major musical key having a signature of four sharps

em·a·nant \'emənənt\ *adj* [L *emanant-, emanans,* pres. part. of *emanare*] **:** issuing or flowing forth **:** emerging from or as if from a source ⟨water ~ from the earth⟩ — used esp. of mental acts ⟨an ~ volition⟩

em·a·nate \-,nāt, *usu* -ād·+V\ *vb* -ED/-ING/-S [L *emanatus,* past part. of *emanare,* fr. *e-* + *manare* to flow] *vi* **:** to come out from a source ⟨fragrance ~s from flowers⟩ ⟨much of the criticism against him *emanated* from defeated candidates⟩ ⟨transitory powers *emanating* from an editor's desk —Horace Gregory⟩ ~ *vt* **:** to give out **:** spread abroad as or as if an emanation **:** EMIT ⟨the serenity she *emanated* touched him so warmly —Jean Stafford⟩ ⟨some radioactive substances can ~ dangerous radiations for many years⟩ **syn** see SPRING

em·a·na·tion \,emə'nāshən\ *n* -s [LL *emanation-, emanatio,* fr. L *emanatus* + *-ion-, -io* -ion] **1 a :** the action of emanating **:** a flowing forth ⟨experiencing our consciousness as an ~ of the creative impulse that rules the world —Albert Schweitzer⟩ ⟨the ~ of light from a candle⟩ **b :** the origination of the world conceived in Neoplatonism not as a creation out of nothing but as a series of hierarchically descending radiations from the Godhead to nous and other intermediate stages and ultimately to matter **c :** the procession (as of Jesus Christ or the Holy Spirit) directly from the Godhead — distinguished from *creation* as used of mortal beings **2 :** something that emanates or is produced by emanation **:** EFFLUX: as **a :** a quality or property issuing from a source ⟨the dark ~s of the unconscious —Herbert Read⟩ ⟨the soul may be considered an ~ of divinity lodged in man⟩ **b :** something impalpable (as light, odor, or effluvium) that arises from a material source ⟨the air was tainted with musky ~s from the alligator pens⟩; *esp* **:** a heavy gaseous element produced by radioactive disintegration ⟨radium ~⟩ — symbol *Em;* compare ACTINON, RADON, THORON **c :** CONSEQUENCE, OUTCOME; *esp* **:** any of the specific products of a particular social milieu or cultural level **:** a cultural aspect ⟨the stylized art of the Egyptians was as definite an ~ of their culture as was the heroic naturalism of the Greeks⟩ — **em·a·na·tion·al** \¦emə¦nāshənᵊl, -shnəl\ *adj*

em·a·na·tion·ism \,==ˈ=shə,nizəm\ *or* **em·a·na·tism** \'emənə,tiz-\ *n* -s **:** a theory of the origination of the world by emanation

em·a·na·tion·ist \,emə'nāsh(ə)nəst\ *n* -s **1** *or* **em·a·na·tist** \'emənətəst\ **:** an adherent of the philosophical theory of emanationism **2 :** a sociologist that seeks to derive all human action and belief from the existing cultural orientation

em·a·na·tive \'emə,nād·|iv, -,nə|, |t|, |ēv *also* |əv\ *adj* [*emanation* + *-ive*] **1 :** tending to emanate or cause to emanate **2 :** resulting from or relating to emanation — **em·a·na·tive·ly** \|əvlē, -li\ *adv*

em·a·na·tor \-,nād·ə(r), -ātə-\ *n* -s **:** one that emanates

em·a·na·tory \'emənə,tōrē, -ōr-, -ri, *chiefly Brit* -,nātəri *or* -,nā·tri\ *adj* [*emanation* + *-ory*] **1 :** being an emanation ⟨~ matter⟩ **2 :** of or relating to emanation ⟨an ~ theory of the origin of matter⟩

[1]**eman·ci·pate** \ə'man(t)sə,pāt, ē'-, -maan-, *usu* -ād·+V\ *vt* -ED/-ING/-S [L *emancipatus,* past part. of *emancipare,* fr. *e-* + *mancipare* to deliver as property, transfer, sell — more at MANCIPATE] **1 :** to release (a child) from the parental power, making the person released sui juris — used chiefly in ancient Roman and civil law **2 :** to set free from the power of another **:** LIBERATE; *specif* **:** to free from bondage ⟨*emancipated* the slaves⟩ **3 :** to free from any controlling influence **4** *obs* **:** to deliver into bondage **:** ENSLAVE **syn** see FREE

[2]**eman·ci·pate** \-,pāt, -,pət\ *adj* [L *emancipatus*] **:** EMANCIPATED

eman·ci·pat·ed \-,pād·əd, -ātəd\ *adj* **:** at liberty **:** FREE, UNTRAMMELED; *often* **:** not bound or formulated by or adherent to currently accepted mores, techniques, or beliefs ⟨those ~ spirits who demand the right to live their lives in their own way⟩

eman·ci·pa·tio \(,)ā,män(t)sə'päd·ē,ō\ *n* -s [L] **:** EMANCIPATION 2

eman·ci·pa·tion \ə,man(t)sə'pāshən, (,)ē,-, -maan-\ *n* -s [L *emancipation-, emancipatio,* fr. *emancipatus* + *-ion-, -io* -ion] **1 :** the act or process of setting or making free **:** LIBERATION ⟨the ~ of slaves⟩; *broadly* **:** deliverance from any onerous and controlling power or influence ⟨~ of the mind from superstition⟩ **2 :** the act or procedure of legally freeing from the paternal power **3 :** gradual segregation of an orig. homogeneous embryo into fields with different specific potentialities for development

eman·ci·pa·tion·ist \-sh(ə)nəst\ *n* -s **:** an advocate of emancipation

eman·ci·pa·tor \=ˈ==,pād·ə(r), -ātə-\ *n* -s [LL, fr. L *emancipatus* + *-or*] **:** one that emancipates or advocates emancipation

eman·ci·pa·to·ry \-,pə,tōrē, -ōr-, -ri, *chiefly Brit* -,pātəri *or* -,pā·tri\ *adj* **:** designed or tending to produce emancipation ⟨~ efforts⟩ ⟨~ laws⟩

eman·ci·pist \-'man(t)səpəst\ *n* -s [*emancipate* + *-ist*] **:** a former convict in Australia who has served out the term of his sentence

emandibulate \¦ē+\ *adj* [*e-* + *mandibulate*] **:** being without functional or well-developed mandibles

emane \ē'mān\ *vb* -ED/-ING/-S [F *émaner,* fr. L *emanare* — more at EMANATE] *archaic* **:** EMANATE

em·a·nom·e·ter \,emə'nämәd·ə(r)\ *n* [*emanation* + *-o-* + *-meter*] **:** any of various devices designed to measure quantities or intensity of emanation — **em·a·no·met·ric** \¦emənō¦me·trik\ *adj* — **em·a·nom·e·try** \,emə'nämə·trē\ *n* -ES

emarginate \(')ē+\ *or* **emarginated** \"+\ *adj* [*emarginate* fr. L *emarginatus,* past part. of *emarginare* to deprive of a margin, fr. *e-* + *margin-, margo* edge, margin; *emarginated* fr. L *emarginatus* + E *-ed* — more at MARGIN] **:** having the margin notched: **a :** having a shallow marginal notch (as at the apex of a leaf or in the caudal fin of a fish) — compare OBCORDATE, RETUSE **b** *of a crystal* **:** having truncated edges — **emar·gi·nate·ly** *adv*

emargination \(,)ē+\ *n* -s **:** a notching at the margin (as of a crustacean's carapace)

emar·gin·ula \,ē,mär'jinyələ\ *n, cap* [NL, fr. ISV *emarginate* + NL *-ula*] **:** a genus of small keyhole limpets

[1]**emas·cu·late** \ə'maskyə,lāt, ē'-, *sometimes chiefly Brit* -mȧs-; *usu* -ād·+V\ *vt* -ED/-ING/-S [L *emasculatus,* past part. of *emasculare,* fr. *e-* + *masculus* male — more at MALE] **1 :** to deprive of virile or procreative power **:** CASTRATE, GELD **2 :** to deprive of masculine vigor or spirit **:** weaken or attenuate by removal or alteration of potent qualities: as **a :** to divest (language) of vigor and freedom (as by excision, euphemism, or weakening of sense) **b :** to deprive (a law) of force or effectiveness (as by amendment or interpretation) **3 :** to remove the androecium of (a flower) in the process of artificial cross-pollination **syn** see UNNERVE

[2]**emas·cu·late** \-,lə|t, -,lā|t, *usu* |d·+V\ *adj* [L *emasculatus*] **:** EMASCULATED

emas·cu·lat·ed \-,lād·əd, -ātəd\ *adj* **:** deprived of or lacking virility, vigor, or characteristic flavor **:** IMPOTENT, INEFFECTIVE, ATTENUATED

emas·cu·la·tion \(,)=,==ˈlāshən\ *n* -s [L *emasculatus* + E *-ion*] **:** the act or process of emasculating **:** the state of being emasculated

emas·cu·la·tome \=ˈ==,lə,tōm\ *n* -s [blend of [1]*emasculate* and *-tome*] **:** a pair of double-hinged pincers for castrating domestic animals bloodlessly by crushing the spermatic cord through the unbroken skin — compare EMASCULATOR

emas·cu·la·tor \-,lād·ə(r), -ātə-\ *n* -s **:** one that emasculates; *specif* **:** an instrument often with a broad surface and a cutting edge used in castrating livestock — compare EMASCULATOME

emb *abbr* **1** embankment **2** embargo **3** embark; embarkation **4** embassy **5** embossed **6** embroidered **7** embryo; embryology

em·ba·dom·o·nas \,embə'dämənəs\ *n, cap* [NL, fr. *embado-* (fr. Gk *embad-, embas* slipper, coarse shoe, fr. *embainein* to step in, go on, fr. *em-* [2]*en-* + *bainein* to go) + *-monas;* fr. the shape — more at IN, COME] **:** a genus of small flagellates with two unequal flagella commensal in the intestines of various vertebrates including man

em·bale \əm, em+\ *vt* [[1]*en-* + *bale* (n.)] *archaic* **:** BALE, WRAP

em·ball \"+\ *vt* [[1]*en-* + *ball* (n.)] *archaic* **:** ENCIRCLE

em·bal·lo·nu·ri·dae \(,)em,balə'n(y)ürə,dē\ *n pl, cap* [NL, fr. *Emballonura,* type genus (fr. Gk *emballōn* — pres. part. of *emballein* to throw in — + NL *-ura*) + *-idae;* fr. the loose appearance of the tail — more at EMBLEM] **:** a family of insectivorous bats having the face obliquely truncated, no nose leaf, and the tail partly free

em·balm \əm'bä|m, em-, -bȧ| *also* |lm; *archaic* -bam\ *vt* -ED/-ING/-S [ME *enbaumen, embaumen, embalmen,* fr. MF *embaumer, embalmer,* fr. OF *embasmer, embausmer,* fr. *em-* [1]*en-* + *basme* balm — more at BALM] **1 :** to treat (a dead body) so as to protect from decay or to sterilize: **a :** to prepare for burial by soaking in brine or bitumen often together with packing the body cavities with spices and aromatic substances (as in the preparation of the mummies of ancient Egyptians) **b :** to prepare for burial by injecting into the arterial system and body cavities a preservative and disinfectant fluid (as a solution of formaldehyde) **2 :** to fill with odors ⟨[drying] codfish which had ~*ed* the air for blocks around —Mary H. Vorse⟩; *usu* **:** to make sweet or pleasing with odors **:** PERFUME ⟨spring ~s the woods and fields⟩ **3 a :** to protect from decay or oblivion ⟨his memory is ~*ed* in the hearts of his people⟩ **b :** to preserve (as food) by chemical or other agencies — often used disparagingly ⟨reduced to eating weeviled biscuit and ~*ed* beef⟩ **4 :** to fix in a static condition **:** leave with no opportunity to grow or develop ⟨make them think of it as something living on the stage, not as something ~*ed* in a book —Dorothy De Huneeus⟩ ⟨big fortunes ~*ed* in bank deposits or in tax-exempt bonds —H.E.Stassen⟩

em·balm·er \-mə(r)\ *n* -s **:** one that embalms; *esp* **:** a person whose work is to embalm the dead

em·balm·ment \-mmənt\ *n* -s **1 :** the act or process of embalming **2 :** a preparation used in embalming

em·bank \əm, em+\ *vt* [[1]*en-* + *bank* (n.)] **:** to enclose (as a marsh) or confine (as a stream) by means of embankments

em·bank·ment \"mənt\ *n* -s **1 :** the action or process of embanking **2 :** a structure (as of earth or gravel) raised usu. to prevent water from overflowing a level tract of country, to retain water in a reservoir or a stream in its bed, or to carry a roadway or railroad

em·bar \əm, em+\ *vt* [ME *enbarren,* fr. MF *embarrer,* fr. *em-* [1]*en-* + *barre* bar] **:** to stop, check, or hinder by or as if by enclosing with bars: as **a** *obs* **:** to interrupt or impede (as commerce) by an embargo **b** *archaic* **:** ENCLOSE, IMPRISON **c** *obs* **:** to put a stop to by legal means **:** BAR ⟨~ a claim⟩

em·bar·ca·de·ro \(,)em,bärkə'de(,)rō\ *n* -s [Sp, fr. *embarcado* (past part. of *embarcar* to embark, fr. *em-* — fr. L *im-* [2]*in-* — + *barca* bark, fr. LL) + *-ero* -er — more at BARK (ship)] *West* **:** a landing place **:** WHARF, QUAY; *esp* **:** a landing place on an inland waterway (as a navigable stream)

[1]**em·bar·go** \əm'bär(,)gō, em-, -bȧ(\ *n* -ES [Sp, fr. *embargar* to embargo, fr. (assumed) VL *imbarricare,* fr. L *im-* [2]*in-* + (assumed) VL *-barricare* (fr. *barra* bar)] **1 :** an edict or order of the government prohibiting the departure or entry of ships of commerce at ports within its dominions — compare BLOCKADE; see CIVIL EMBARGO, HOSTILE EMBARGO **2 :** a prohibition imposed by law upon commerce either in general or in one or more of its branches **3 :** STOPPAGE, IMPEDIMENT; *esp* **:** PROHIBITION ⟨an ~ against employment of union labor was notoriously one of the chief obstructions to collective bargaining —Felix Frankfurter⟩ **4 :** an order that is issued by a common carrier or public regulatory agency and that prohibits the acceptance of all or of specified kinds of freight for transportation on its lines or between specified points or areas because of traffic congestion, labor difficulties, or other reasons

[2]**embargo** \"\, *in pres part* " *or* -gəw\ *vt* -ED/-ING/-ES **1 :** to lay or put an embargo on (as ships or commerce); *often* **:** to

prevent the movement of (as diseased plants or animals) in commerce **2 :** to retain or seize for state purposes or under state authority ⟨~*ing* all batches of vaccine until the source of contamination could be identified⟩ **:** REQUISITION

em·bark \əm'bärk, em-, -bȧk\ *vb* -ED/-ING/-S [MF *embarquer*, fr. OProv *embarcar*, fr. *em-* (fr. L *im-* ²in-) + *barca* bark — more at BARK (ship)] *vt* **1 :** to cause to go on board a boat or airplane **2 :** to engage, enlist, or invest (as persons or money) in an enterprise ⟨he ~*ed* his fortune in trade⟩ ~ *vi* **1 :** to go on board a boat or airplane for transportation ⟨the troops ~*ed* at midnight⟩ **2 :** to make a start **:** COMMENCE — usu. used with *on* or *upon* ⟨after the war the company ~*ed* on a program of expansion⟩ ⟨she had no hesitation about ~*ing* on a new career⟩ ⟨ready to ~ upon any new adventure⟩

em·bar·ka·tion *also* **em·bar·ca·tion** \,em,bär'kāshən, -,bȧ'k-, -bə(r)'k-\ *n* -S **1 a :** the action or process of embarking ⟨the ~ of troops⟩ **b :** something (as a body of troops) that is embarked **2** *archaic* **:** SHIP, BOAT

em·bark·ment \əm'bärkmənt, em-, -bȧk-\ *n* -S [MF *embarquement*, fr. *embarquer* + *-ment*] **:** EMBARKATION 1a

em·bar·ras *n* [F, obstacle, trouble, embarrassment, fr. *embarrasser* to hinder, embarrass] **1** *like* EMBARRASS\ -ES *archaic* **:** EMBARRASSMENT **2** \ˌäⁿbə'rä\ *pl* **embarras** [LaF, fr. F] **:** snags or packed masses of tree trunks or driftwood (as in a Louisiana bayou)

em·bar·rass \əm'barəs, em- *also* -ber-\ *vt* -ED/-ING/-ES [F *embarrasser*, fr. Sp *embarazar*, fr. Pg *embaraçar*, prob. fr. *em-* (fr. L *im-* ²in-) + *baraça* noose, rope] **1 a :** to place in doubt, perplexity, or difficulties ⟨the Government was again ~*ed* from within party ranks by a political speech —*Current Biog.*⟩ ⟨too often preciosity and aimless verbiage ~ the thought and confuse the emotion —Mathurin Dondo⟩ **b :** to involve (as a person or his affairs) in difficulties concerning money matters ⟨we believe the company will be seriously ~*ed* if it does not get this loan⟩ ⟨heavy gambling losses ~*ed* him for years⟩ ⟨the estate was ~*ed* by the prospect of heavy death duties⟩ **c :** to cause to experience a state of self-conscious distress **:** ABASH ⟨their frank discussion of his looks ~*ed* the boy⟩ ⟨it ~*es* many people to walk into a room full of strangers⟩ **d :** to impair the activity of (a bodily function) ⟨his digestion was ~*ed* by overeating and irregular hours⟩ or the function of (a bodily part) ⟨the congestion of pneumonia ~*es* the lungs⟩ **2 :** to hamper or impede the movement or freedom of movement of (as a person) ⟨a man who refused to let physical handicaps ~ him⟩; *often* **:** HAMPER, IMPEDE ⟨~*ed* our freedom of movement⟩ ⟨our progress was ~*ed* by mountains of baggage⟩ ⟨they counted on the spring rains to ~ the advance of the enemy⟩ **3 :** to make intricate **:** COMPLICATE ⟨a course of legislation had prevailed . . . which weakened the confidence of man in man, and ~*ed* all transactions between individuals —John Marshall⟩ ⟨the courts . . . were not established to . . . enable a few to harass and ~ sovereign action by the government —F.D.Roosevelt⟩

syn DISCOMFIT, ABASH, DISCONCERT, RATTLE, FAZE: EMBARRASS is likely to implicate an agency or influence checking and hampering free choice or action, often with accompanying chagrin, confusion, and loss of face ⟨in immense flood of litigation, which seriously *embarrassed* the courts —T.F.T. Plucknett⟩ ⟨the problems of food, shelter, and sanitation for the impoverished veterans *embarrassed* Washington, and there was latent danger of disorder —J.M.Hanson⟩ ⟨the southern housewife is not unduly *embarrassed* by an unexpected guest —*Amer. Guide Series: N.C.*⟩ DISCOMFIT implies hampering or frustrating and also chagrining, causing loss of self-possession, and confusing ⟨Bradley's polemical irony and his obvious zest in using it, his habit of *discomfiting* an opponent with a sudden profession of ignorance, of inability to understand, or of incapacity for abstruse thought —T.S.Eliot⟩ ⟨she may heckle the dealer, add a running commentary to the demonstrations, or just assume a *discomfiting* smugness —*Fortune*⟩ ABASH suggests the calling up of feelings of shyness, unworthiness, diffidence, shame, and loss of self-pride through some vexation or check ⟨she would feel *abashed* before any woman who had not been rejected like herself —Rebecca West⟩ ⟨as *abashed* as a child interrupted in his game of make-believe —Rudyard Kipling⟩ DISCONCERT implies a bringing about of confused uncertainty and hesitation in proceeding or of loss of composure and assurance ⟨I was *disconcerted* to find that they were locked. I stood there irresolute and uneasy like a baffled thief —Joseph Conrad⟩ ⟨watched the beautiful young man with her solemn unwinking stare that *disconcerted* self-conscious people —Rose Macaulay⟩ RATTLE suggests an utter loss of poise, composure, and accustomed control of a situation, along with disorganization of wonted mental powers ⟨that means that Freddy is *rattled* out of his senses —John Buchan⟩ ⟨*rattled* by hypothetical eyes spying upon her —Jean Stafford⟩ ⟨when other advisers became *rattled*, Mr. Adams was calm —Tris Coffin⟩ FAZE applies to loss of assurance, face, and confidence brought about by a check, retort, sudden difficulty ⟨it hit Marciano flush on the right side of the jaw, but it didn't seem to *faze* him a bit —A.J.Liebling⟩ ⟨he had ice water in his veins. Nothing *fazed* him, not insult or anger or violence or getting his face beat into a hamburger —R.P. Warren⟩

em·bar·rassed·ly \-stlē, -sədlē, -li\ *adv* **:** in an embarrassed manner **:** with embarrassment ⟨he spoke ~⟩

embarrassingly *adv* **:** to an embarrassing degree **:** so as to cause embarrassment ⟨her ~ plain speech⟩

em·bar·rass·ment \-smənt\ *n* -S [F *embarrassement*, fr. *embarrasser* + *-ment*] **1 a :** the state of being embarrassed **:** PERPLEXITY **:** confusion or discomposure of mind ⟨his ~ when he dropped the cake in his lap was pitiful to see⟩ ⟨the ~ of dull minds faced by the complexities of modern life⟩; *often* **:** difficulty or perplexity arising from the want of money to pay debts ⟨financial ~ was chronic in our family⟩ **b :** difficulty in functioning as a result of disease ⟨cardiac ~⟩ ⟨respiratory ~⟩ **2 a :** something that embarrasses **:** IMPEDIMENT, ENCUMBRANCE ⟨a shrill harsh voice is a serious ~ in business and social life⟩ **b :** an excessive quantity from which a selection must be made ⟨an ~ of choices things to see —*N.Y. Times*⟩ — used esp. in the phrase *embarrassment of riches* ⟨an age that builds whole libraries to house the papers of presidents, an ~ of riches —Leon Edel⟩ ⟨the unprejudiced observer would have some difficulty saying just which details might best be dropped, so many wryly devastating moments crop up at every turn — a real ~ of riches —*Saturday Rev.*⟩

em·barren \əm, em+\ *vt* [¹*en-* + *barren* (adj.)] *archaic* **:** to make barren

em·base \"+\ *vt* [¹*en-* + *base* (adj.)] *archaic* **:** to lower esp. in rank, dignity, or quality **:** DEBASE

embassade *var of* AMBASSADE

embassador *var of* AMBASSADOR

em·bas·sage \'embəsij\ *n* -S [ME *ambassage*, prob. alter. of *ambassade* — more at AMBASSADE] **1** *archaic* **:** a sending of an ambassador **:** EMBASSY; *also* **:** status as ambassador **2** *archaic* **:** message, errand, business, or charge of an ambassador

em·bas·sy \'embəsē, -si\ *n* -ES *often attrib* [MF *ambassee*, modif. of OIt *ambasciata*, fr. OProv *ambaisada*, fr. (assumed) *ambaisa* mission, of Gmc origin; akin to OE *ambiht* office, service, OHG *ambaht*, ON *embætti*, Goth *andbahti*; all fr. a prehistoric Gmc word of Celt origin; akin to Gaulish *ambactos* vassal, W *amaeth* farmer; both fr. a prehistoric Celt compound whose constituents are akin respectively to W *am-* around, Gk *amphi*, and to OIr *ad-aig* to drive — more at BY, AGENT] **1 a :** the function or position of an ambassador ⟨held the ~ in that country for over nine years⟩ **b :** a journey or stay away from one's homeland or accustomed place undertaken in the character of an ambassador or other envoy ⟨an expeditionary force, or official visit abroad, such as *embassies* or other necessary missions —K.R.Popper⟩ **2 :** the message, charge, or business of an ambassador or other envoy **3 :** an ambassador or other envoy usu. together with his suite **4 :** the official residence and offices of an ambassador

em·bathe \əm, em+\ *vt* [¹*en-* + *bathe*] **:** to wash freely **:** BATHE, IMMERSE, DRENCH

em·batholithic \(¦)em+\ *adj* [²*en-* + *batholithic*] **:** relating or belonging to or constituting ore deposits formed among closely spaced outcrops of the projecting parts of a batholith where the invaded rocks predominate

¹em·battle \əm, em+\ *vb* [ME *embatailen*, fr. MF *embatailler*, fr. *em-* ¹en- + *batailler* to battle — more at BATTLE] *vt* **1 :** to arrange (as an army) in order of battle **:** array for battle ⟨the English are *embattled*, you French peers. To horse, you gallant princes —Shak.⟩ **2 :** to make (as oneself) ready for conflict **:** be prepared to fight ⟨let them gather themselves, and be scattered; let them ~ themselves, and be broken —John Milton⟩ **3 :** FORTIFY ⟨~ a building⟩ ⟨~ a city⟩ ~ *vi, obs* **:** to prepare for battle

²embattle \"\ *vt* [ME *embatailen*, fr. ¹*en-* + *batailen* to fortify with battlements — more at BATTLE] **:** to furnish with battlements ⟨received royal permission to ~ [his residence] —Sam Boal⟩

embattled *adj* [ME *embatailed*, fr. past part. of *embatailen* to furnish with battlements] **1 :** having battlements **:** CASTELLATED **2 :** having the edge broken with indentations like the crenels of battlements — used esp of a heraldic device (as a fess or bend)

em·battlement \əm, em+\ *n* [ME *embatailment*, fr. *embatailen* to furnish with battlements + *-ment*] **:** BATTLEMENT

¹em·bay \əm'bā, em-\ *vt* -ED/-ING/-S [¹*en-* + *bay* (body of water)] **1 a :** to shut in or shelter esp. in a bay ⟨an ~*ed* fleet⟩ **b :** ENCIRCLE, SURROUND **2 :** to form into a bay ⟨an ~*ed* shore⟩

²embay *vt* [prob. fr. ¹*en-* + *-bay* (alter. of *bathe*)] *obs* **:** BATHE, SUFFUSE

embayed mountain *n* **:** a mountain depressed so that sea water enters the valleys

em·bay·ment \əm'bāmənt, em-\ *n* -S **1 a :** formation of a bay (as by depression of the land about a river mouth so that the sea overflows it) — compare ESTUARY 1 **b :** a bay or a conformation resembling a bay **2 :** an irregular corrosion of a crystal by the magma in which it occurs as a foreign inclusion or as a previously crystallized mineral

emb·den *or* **em·den** \'emdən\ *n* [fr. *Emden*, Germany] **1** *usu cap* **:** a breed of large white domestic geese with an orange-colored bill and deep orange shanks and toes **2** -S *often cap* **:** a goose of the Embden breed

em·bed *or* **im·bed** \əm'bed, em-\ *vb* [¹*en-* or ²*in-* + *bed* (n.)] *vt* **1 a :** to enclose closely in or as if in a matrix ⟨pebbles *embedded* in silt⟩ ⟨~ brick firmly in mortar⟩ **b :** to introduce as an integral part ⟨~*s* Latin constructions in a passage of Italian —*Publ's Mod. Lang. Assoc. of Amer.*⟩ ⟨the tales of his prowess that have become *embedded* in folklore⟩ **c :** to prepare (material for microscopic examination) for sectioning (as with a microtome) by infiltrating with and enclosing in a supporting substance (as paraffin or celloidin) **2 :** to surround closely **:** ENCLOSE ⟨a sweet edible pulp ~*s* the seed of plums and related fruits⟩ ~ *vi* **:** to become embedded ⟨dirt ~*s* under their fingernails⟩ ⟨the great bulk of the tree slowly *embedded* into the soft soil⟩

em·bed·ment \-dmənt\ *n* -S **:** the act, process, or product of embedding

em·be·lia \em'bēlyə, -ēlēə\ *n* [NL, prob. fr. native name in Ceylon] **1** *cap* **:** a large genus of Old World tropical woody vines (family Myrsinaceae) with alternate leaves and racemose flowers **2** -S **:** the dried powdered fruit of an Indian vine (*Embelia ribes*) used locally as a tapeworm remedy

¹em·be·lif \ˌembə'lif\ *adj* [ME, fr. MF *en belif*] *heraldry* **:** OBLIQUE

²embelif \"\ *adv* [ME, fr. MF *en belif*] *heraldry* **:** OBLIQUELY

em·be·lin \'embələn\ *also* **em·bel·ic acid** \(')em'belik-\ *n* -S [NL *Embelia* (genus name of *Embelia ribes*) + E *-in* or *-ic*] **:** an orange phenolic quinone $C_{17}H_{26}O_4$ obtained esp. from embelia and used formerly as an anthelmintic

em·bel·lish \əm'belish, em-, -lēsh, *esp in pres part* -ləsh\ *vt* -ED/-ING/-ES [ME *embelisshen*, fr. MF *embeliss-*, stem of *embelir*, fr. *em-* ¹en- + *bel* beautiful — more at BEAUTY] **1** *obs* **:** to make beautiful **2 :** to make beautiful or elegant with ornaments or ornamentation **:** DECORATE, ADORN ⟨~*ed* a book with pictures⟩ ⟨the faults with which nature has generously ~*ed* us all —Henry Adams⟩ **3 :** to enhance, amplify, or garnish (an account) by elaboration with inessential but decorative or fanciful details ⟨speech . . . ~*ed* with felicitous classical quotations —H.W.H.Knott⟩ ⟨~*ed* his story, distorting and inventing detail to suit himself —Rex Ingamells⟩ **syn** see ADORN

em·bel·lish·er \-shə(r)\ *n* -S **:** one that embellishes

em·bel·lish·ment \-shmənt\ *n* -S **1 :** the act or process of embellishing **:** ORNAMENTATION ⟨money provided for the ~ of the new cathedral⟩ **2 :** something serving to embellish ⟨~ of a literary work⟩ ⟨similes and metaphors as poetical ~*s* —J.L. Lowes⟩ ⟨the graces and ~*s* of the exterior man —Isaac Taylor⟩ ⟨a style stripped of all hyperbole and ~ —H.D.Aiken⟩ **3 :** ORNAMENT 5

em·ber \'embə(r)\ *n* -S [ME *eymere*, *eymbre*, modif. of ON *eimyrja*; akin to OE *ǣmerge* ashes, OHG *eimuria* ember; all fr. a prehistoric NGmc-WGmc compound whose first and second constituents respectively are akin to E *oam*, ON *eimr* steam, vapor and to OE *ysle* spark, ash, ON *ysja* fire, L *urere* to burn, Gk *heuein* to singe, Skt *oṣati* he burns] **1 a :** a lighted coal **:** a glowing fragment of coal, coke, wood, or other solid fuel from a fire; *esp* **:** such a coal smoldering in ashes **b :** the smoldering remains of a fire — usu. used in pl. **2 embers** *pl* **:** slowly cooling emotions, memories, ideas, or responses from past experience that are still capable of being enlivened ⟨~*s* of an old love⟩ ⟨generals . . . who kept alive the ~*s* of resistance —Telford Taylor⟩ **3 :** a moderate red that is yellower and duller than cerise, claret (sense 3a), average strawberry (sense 2a), or Turkey red and yellower and less strong than Harvard crimson (sense 1)

em·ber day \"+ˌ\ *n* [ME *ymber day*, *embyr day*, fr. OE *ymbrendæg*, fr. *ymbryne*, *ymbrene* circuit, course, anniversary (fr *ymb*, *ymbe* around + *ryne* course, running, period of time) + *dæg* day; akin to OHG *umbi* around, ON *um*, *umb*, Gk *amphi*, and to OE *rinnan* to run — more at BY, RUN, DAY] **:** a Wednesday, Friday, or Saturday in any of the four weeks commencing on the first Sunday in Lent or on Whitsuntide or including or immediately following September 14 or December 13 set apart for fasting and prayer and observed esp. by the Anglican and Roman Catholic Churches

em·ber·goose \"+ˌ\ *n, pl* **embergeese** [*ember* (by folk etymology fr. Norw *ymbre*, *imbre*, *hymber* embergoose, fr. ON *himbrin*) + *goose*] **:** COMMON LOON

em·be·ri·za \ˌembə'rēzə, -rīzə\ *n, cap* [NL, fr. G dial. (Alemannic) *emberitze*, *emmeritz* yellowhammer, fr. MHG *ameriz*, fr. OHG *amarzo*, *amirzo*, dim. of *amaro* — more at YELLOWHAMMER] **:** a genus of passerine birds that includes numerous typical buntings and is made the type of a separate family or included with the finches and related birds in Fringillidae — **em·ber·i·zine** \-ˌzīn, -ˌzən\ *adj*

embetter *vt* [¹*en-* + *better* (adj.)] *obs* **:** BETTER

em·bez·zle \əm'bezəl, em-\ *vt* **embezzled**; **embezzled**; **embezzling** \-z(ə)liŋ\ **embezzles** [ME *embesilen*, fr. AF *embeseiller* to destroy, embezzle, fr. MF *em-* ¹en- + *besillier* to destroy] **1** *obs* **a :** to make away with **b :** to cause (as a document) to be destroyed, mutilated or falsified **2** *obs* **:** LESSEN; *sometimes* **:** WEAKEN, SQUANDER, DISSIPATE **3 :** to appropriate fraudulently to one's own use (as property entrusted to one's care) ⟨*embezzled* a trust fund⟩ ⟨succeeded in *embezzling* several thousand dollars⟩

em·bez·zle·ment \-zəlmənt\ *n* -S **:** the act of embezzling; *specif* **:** fraudulent appropriation of property by a person to whom it has been entrusted (as of an employer's money by his clerk or of public funds by the officer in charge) — compare LARCENY

em·bez·zler \-z(ə)lə(r)\ *n* -S **:** one that embezzles

em·bi·ar·ia \ˌembē'a(a)rēə\ *n* [NL, fr. *Embia* genus of insects (fr. Gk *embiē*, fem. of *embios* having life, fr. *em-* ²en- + *bios* mode of life) + *-aria* — more at QUICK] *syn of* EMBIODEA

em·bi·id \'embēəd\ *n* -S [NL *Embiidae*] **:** one of the Embiodea **:** WEB SPINNER

em·bi·idae \em'bīəˌdē\ *n pl, cap* [NL, fr. *Embia*, type genus + *-idae*] **:** a major family of Embiodea

em·bi·idi·na \ˌembēə'dīnə\ [NL, fr. *Embiidae* + *-ina*] *syn of* EMBIODEA

em·bind \əm, em+\ *vt* [¹*en-* + *bind*] **:** BIND

em·bi·o·dea \ˌembē'ōdēə\ *n pl, cap* [NL, fr. *Embia* + *-odea*] **:** a small order of slender elongated chiefly tropical insects with large head and 10-segmented abdomen having males that are usu. winged and both nymphs and adults that live in silken webs which they spin with glands in the fore tarsi — see WEB SPINNER

em·bi·op·tera \ˌembē'äpt(ə)rə\ [NL, fr. *embio-* (fr. *Embia*) + *-ptera*] *syn of* EMBIODEA

em·bi·ot·o·cid \-ē'ädəsəd; -ēə'täsəd, -tōs-\ *n* -S [NL *Embiotocidae*] **:** a fish of the family Embiotocidae

em·bi·o·toc·i·dae \ˌembēə'täsəˌdē, -tōs-\ *n pl, cap* [NL, fr. *Embiotoca*, type genus (fr. Gk *embios* having life + *-toca*, fr. *tokos* offspring, fr. *tiktein* to bear, beget) + *-idae* — more at EMBIARIA, THANE] **:** a family of viviparous percoid fishes comprising the surf fishes

em·bi·ra \em'bērə\ *n* -S [Pg, fr. Tupi] **:** any of several Brazilian bast fibers that are derived from trees of the genera *Daphnopsis* (family Thymelaeaceae) and *Xylopia* and are used for making nets

em·bit·ter \əm'bid·|ə(r), em-, -it|\ *also* **im·bit·ter** \əm-\ *vt* -ED/-ING/-S [¹*en-* or ²*in-* + *bitter* (adj.)] **1 :** to make bitter or more bitter ⟨hops serve to ~ beer⟩ **2 :** to excite bitter feelings or animosities in **syn** see EXACERBATE

em·bit·ter·er \|ərə(r)\ *n* -S **:** one that embitters

em·bit·ter·ment \|ə(r)mənt\ *n* -S **:** the act of embittering or state of being embittered ⟨the ~ that followed his father's needless death persisted for years⟩

¹em·blaze \əm'blāz, em-\ *vt* -ED/-ING/-S [¹*en-* + *blaze* (to blazon)] **1** *archaic* **:** to set forth in or adorn with heraldic devices **:** EMBLAZON **2 :** to adorn sumptuously **:** EMBELLISH ⟨with gems and golden luster rich *emblazed* —John Milton⟩ **3** *obs* **:** to place among the honored or noteworthy

²emblaze \"\ *vt* [¹*en-* + *blaze* (fire)] **1 :** to illuminate esp. by a blaze **:** cause to blaze with light **2 :** to set in a blaze **:** KINDLE

em·blaz·er \-zə(r)\ *n* -S **:** one that emblazes

em·bla·zon \əm'blāzᵊn, em-\ *vt* **emblazoned**; **emblazoned**; **emblazoning** \-z(ᵊ)niŋ\ **emblazons** [¹*en-* + *blazon*] **1 :** to inscribe or adorn with heraldic bearings or devices **2 a :** to deck in bright colors **:** set off conspicuously (as by rich or brilliant decorations) **:** display sumptuously ⟨many banners, ~*ed* with the emblem of the cross —G.W.Benson⟩ **b :** to depict or delineate with brightness and approbation **:** CELEBRATE, EXTOL ⟨this subjects ~*ed* the good king's fame to all the world⟩ — **em·bla·zon·er** \-(ᵊ)nə(r)\ *n* -S

em·bla·zon·ment \-ᵊnmənt\ *n* -S **:** heraldic emblazonry — usu. used in pl.

em·bla·zon·ry \-ᵊnrē, -ri\ *n* -ES **1 :** the act or art of emblazoning **2 :** emblazoned figures **:** brilliant decoration ⟨the glowing ~ of the coronation setting⟩

¹em·blem \'embləm *also* -blim *or* -ˌblem\ *n* -S [ME, fr. L *emblema* inlaid work, tesselated work, fr. Gk *emblēma*, lit., insertion, fr. *emballein* to throw in, put in, insert, fr. *em-* ²en- + *ballein* to throw — more at DEVIL] **1 :** a picture with a motto or set of verses intended as a moral lesson or a subject of meditation that was common in the 17th century **2** *obs* **:** inlaid or mosaic work **3 a :** a visible sign of an idea **:** an object or the figure of an object symbolizing and suggesting another object or an idea by natural aptness or by association ⟨a balance is an ~ of justice⟩ ⟨a scepter, ~ of sovereignty⟩ **b :** a typical representative **:** SYMBOL ⟨evening cooling is an ~ of autumn chill⟩ ⟨trying to find out enough about eagles to keep our national ~ from dying out —Caroline Bird⟩ **4 a :** a symbolic object used as a heraldic device or badge **b :** a device, symbol, design, or figure adopted and used as an identifying mark (as a publisher's colophon) **syn** see SYMBOL

²emblem \"\ *vt* -ED/-ING/-S **:** to represent by or as if by an emblem **:** IMAGE ⟨~*ed* with the state seal⟩

em·ble·ma \em'blēmə, -lämə,-lemə\ *n, pl* **emblema·ta** \-mədə\ [L] **1 :** a featured picture or ornament in mosaic work used frequently by the ancients for decorating pavement or wall **2 :** separate ornament done in relief and often in precious metal that was attached as decoration (as to a ship or piece of furniture) esp. by the ancient Romans — usu. used in pl.

em·blem·at·ic \ˌemblə'mad·|ik, -at|, |ēk\ *also* **em·blem·at·i·cal** \|əkəl, |ēk-\ *adj* [Gk *emblēmatikos*, fr. *emblēmat-*, *emblēma* + *-ikos* -ic, -ical] **:** relating to, containing, or constituting an emblem **:** SYMBOLIC, REPRESENTATIVE ⟨a crown is ~ of royalty⟩ ⟨the free discussion that is ~ of the democratic process⟩ — **em·blem·at·i·cal·ly** \|ək(ə)lē, |ēk-, -li\ *adv* — **em·blem·at·i·cal·ness** \|əkəlnəs, |ēk-\ *n* -ES

em·blem·a·tist \em'blemədəst\ *also* **em·blem·ist** \'embləməst\ *n* -S [*emblematist* fr. L *emblemat-*, *emblema* + E *-ist*; *emblemist* fr. ¹*emblem* + *-ist*] **:** a writer, designer, or inventor of emblems

em·blem·a·tize \em'blemə,tīz\ *or* **em·blem·ize** \'emblə,mīz\ *vt* -ED/-ING/-S [*emblematize* fr. L *emblemat-*, *emblema* + E *-ize*; *emblemize* fr. ¹*emblem* + *-ize*] **1 :** to represent by or by an emblem **:** SYMBOLIZE **2 :** to be or to serve as an emblem of

emblem book *n* **:** a book consisting of emblems

em·ble·ment \'embləmənt, -bəlm-\ *n* -S [ME *emblayment*, *embloyment*, fr. MF *emblaement*, fr. *emblaer* to sow a field with grain (fr. *em-* ¹en- + *-blaer*, fr. *blee* grain) + *-ment*] **:** the growing crop or vegetable growth resulting from annual manurage and cultivation as distinguished from the produce from old roots (as pasturage) or from trees (as timber or fruit) **:** the profits from such a crop

em·blic \'emblik\ *n* -S [NL *emblica*, fr. Ar *amlaj*, fr. Per *āmlah*] **1 :** an East Indian tree (*Phyllanthus emblica*) used with other myrobalans for tanning **2 :** the fruit of emblic — called also *Indian gooseberry*

em·blossom \əm, em+\ *vt* [¹*en-* + *blossom* (n.)] **:** to cover or adorn with blossoms ⟨trees ~*ed* by the warmth of spring⟩

em·bod·i·er \əm'bädēə(r), em- -diə-\ *n* -S **:** one that embodies

em·bod·i·ment \-dēmənt, -dəm-\ *n* -S **1 :** the act of embodying or state of being embodied ⟨worked for years toward the ~ of a set of rules that would solve all philosophical problems mathematically⟩ **2 :** a thing in which something (as a soul, idea, principle, or type) is embodied **:** INCARNATION ⟨the ~ of courage⟩ ⟨the ~ of all our hopes⟩ **3 :** organization in an aggregate **:** INCORPORATION ⟨log tables and their immediate ~ in slide rules —Bryan Morgan⟩

em·body \-dē, -di\ *vb* [¹*en-* + *body* (n.)] *vt* **1 :** to give a body to (a spirit) **:** invest with a body **:** INCARNATE **2 a :** to cause to become material or sensual **:** deprive of spirituality **b :** to make concrete by expression in perceptible form (as in words, acts, institutions, or works of art) ⟨attempted to ~ basic democratic principles in the treaty⟩ ⟨a dictatorship *embodied* in a triumvirate⟩ **3 :** to cause to become a body or part of a body **:** INCORPORATE, ORGANIZE ⟨*embodied* a revenue provision in the new law⟩ ⟨they must ~ their ideas in substantial institutions if they are to survive⟩ **4 :** to represent in human or animal form ⟨*embodied* virtue⟩ **:** PERSONIFY ⟨~*ing* love as Cupid⟩ ~ *vi* **1** *obs* **:** to become embodied or materialized — used esp. of the soul **2 :** to unite in a body or mass **:** COALESCE ⟨fat globules *embodied* into butter⟩

em·bog \əm, em+\ *vt* [¹*en-* + *bog* (n.)] **:** to sink into or as if into a bog **:** bog down **:** MIRE ⟨the meeting became *embogged* in arguments over precedent⟩

em·boî·té \äⁿbwȧtā\ *adj* [F, fr. past part. of *emboîter* to put in a box, encase, fit together, fr. *em-* ¹en- + *boîte* box, fr. OF *boiste* — more at BOIST] *of a ballet step* **:** joined with the feet interlocked

em·boî·te·ment \äⁿbwȧtmäⁿ\ *n* -S [F, fr. *emboîter* + *-ment*] **:** ENCASEMENT 1b

embol- *or* **embolo-** *comb form* [NL *embol-*, fr. ML (in *embolismus* intercalation) — more at EMBOLISM] **1 :** embolus ⟨*embolectomy*⟩ ⟨*emboliform*⟩ **2 :** wedge ⟨*Embolomeri*⟩

em·bold·en \əm'bōldən, em-\ *vt* -ED/-ING/-S [¹*en-* + *bold* + *-en*] **:** to impart boldness or courage to **:** instill with boldness, bravery, or resolution enough to overcome timidity or misgiving ⟨~*ed* by the weakness of the royal governor, an irresponsible mob . . . set upon a squad of ten soldiers —R.W.G. Vail⟩ **syn** see ENCOURAGE

embole *var of* EMBOLY

em·bo·lec·to·my \ˌembə'lektəmē\ *n* -ES [*embol-* + *-ectomy*] **:** surgical removal of an embolus

em·bo·le·mia *also* **em·bo·lae·mia** \-lēmēə\ *n* -S [NL, fr. *embol-* + *-emia*, *-aemia*] **:** an abnormal state characterized by the presence of emboli in the blood

emboli *pl of* EMBOLUS

em·bol·ic \(')em'bälik, im'b-\ *adj* [*embol-* + *-ic*] **1 :** of or relating to an embolus or embolism **2 :** of, relating to, or produced by emboly

em·bo·lism \'embə,lizəm\ n -s [ME *embolisme*, fr. ML *embolismus*, fr. *embolismus* intercalary, fr. LL, modif. of Gk *embolimos*, fr. *embolos* stopper, fr. *emballein* to throw in, put in, insert — more at EMBLEM] **1 :** INTERCALATION 1 **2 :** a liturgical expansion of the last two petitions of the Lord's Prayer that is found in many Eastern and Western liturgies with the exception of the Byzantine and Ethiopic **3** [NL *embolismus*, fr. ML] **a :** the sudden obstruction of a blood vessel by an embolus **b :** EMBOLUS — not used technically

em·bo·lis·mic \¦==¦lizmik\ *also* **em·bo·lis·mi·cal** \-məkəl\ *adj* : relating to, formed by, or including a temporal embolism ⟨any doubt as to when the ~ terms are to be applied must be solved by the calendar Easter new moon —Peter Archer⟩ ⟨an ~ year⟩; *often* : inserted as an intercalation ⟨an ~ lunation completing the 13-month Anglo-Saxon year⟩

em·bo·lite \'embə,līt\ n -s [G *embolit*, fr. Gk *embolion* + G *-it* -ite] : a mineral Ag(Cl, Br) consisting of native silver chloride and bromide and resembling cerargyrite

em·bo·li·um \em'bōlēəm\ n, pl **embo·lia** \-ēə\ [NL, fr. Gk *embolion* insertion, embossed ornament, dim. of *embolos*] : a narrow piece on the costal margin of the corium of the wings of certain true bugs

em·bo·li·za·tion \,embələ'zāshən, -,lī'z-\ n -s : the condition of being embolized ⟨pulmonary ~⟩ or of embolizing ⟨~ of a thrombus⟩

em·bo·lize \'embə,līz\ vb -ED/-ING/-S [*embol-* + *-ize*] vt, *of an embolus* : to lodge in and obstruct (as a blood vessel or organ) ~ vi : to break up into emboli or become an embolus ⟨marrow fragments *embolized* and were swept to the lung from the site of the fracture⟩

em·bo·lo \'embə,lō\ n -s [native name in Africa] : the edible bluish fleshy fruit of the Cape ebony

em·bo·lo·la·lia \,embəlō'lālēə, ¦'lal-\ *also* **em·bo·la·lia** \,embə¦\ n -s [*embololalia*, NL, fr. *embol-* + *-lalia*; *embolalia*, NL, blend of *embol-* and *-lalia*] : the interpolation of meaningless sounds or words into speech

em·bo·lo·mere \'embəlō,mi(ə)r\ n -s [NL *Embolomeri*] : an animal or fossil of the order Embolomeri

em·bo·lom·eri \,embə'lämə,rī\ n pl, cap [NL, fr. *embol-* + *-meri* (fr. Gk *meros* part) — more at MERIT] : an order of primitive labyrinthodonts including most of the larger Carboniferous amphibians and having vertebrae in which both intercentra and pleurocentra are complete disks

em·bo·lom·er·ism \-,rizəm\ n -s [*embolomerous* + *-ism*] : the condition of being embolomerous

em·bo·lom·er·ous \¦==¦lämərəs\ *adj* [ISV *embol-* + *-merous*] **1 :** having both centrum and intercentrum present and pierced for passage of the persistent notochord : DIPLOSPONDYLIC — used of the vertebrae of various primitive fishes and amphibians **2 :** having embolomerous vertebrae

em·bo·lo·phra·sia \,embəlō'frāzh(ē)ə\ n -s [NL, fr. *embol-* + *-phrasia*] : EMBOLOLALIA

em·bo·lus \'embələs\ n, pl **embo·li** \-,lī, -,lē\ [NL, fr. L, piston of a pump, fr. Gk *embolos* stopper] **1** *archaic* : something inserted (as a wedge or the piston of a syringe) **2 :** a foreign or abnormal particle circulating in the blood (as a bubble of air or a blood clot) — see EMBOLISM; compare THROMBUS **3 :** a complex chitinous structure that forms the apex of the digital joint of the palpus of a male spider, that contains the terminal portion of the receptacle in which sperm is stored prior to insemination, and that assists in transferring sperm to the female

em·bo·ly *also* **em·bo·le** \'embəlē\ n, pl **embolies** *also* **emboles** [Gk *embolē* act of putting into, insertion, fr. *emballein* to throw in, put in, insert — more at EMBLEM] : a process of gastrula formation by simple invagination or infolding of the blastula wall that is typical of embryos with holoblastic and approximately equal cleavage

em·bon·point \ä^{n}bō^{n}pwa^n\ n [F, fr. MF, fr. *en bon point* in good condition] : plumpness of person : STOUTNESS ⟨firmly corseted ~⟩ ⟨an elderly gentleman of dignified ~⟩ ⟨an actress better known for her ~ than her artistic skill⟩

emborder vt [1*en-* + *border* (n.)] *obs* : to enclose with a border : EDGE

em·bosk \əm, em+\ vt -ED/-ING/-S [1*en-* + *bosk*] : to shroud or conceal esp. with plants or greenery ⟨the summerhouse all ~*ed* with vines⟩

em·bosom *also* **im·bosom** \əm, em+\ vt [1*en-* or 2*in-* + *bosom* (n.)] **1** *archaic* : to take into or place in the bosom; *broadly* : CHERISH, FOSTER **2 :** to shelter closely : ENCLOSE, SURROUND ⟨his house ~*ed* in the grove —Alexander Pope⟩

1em·boss \əm'bäs, em-, -bȯs\ vt [ME *embosen* to become exhausted from being hunted, perh. fr. 1*en-* + MF *bos, bois* forest, of Gmc origin; akin to OHG *busc* bush — more at BUSH] **1** *obs* : to drive (as a hunted animal) to bay or to exhaustion **2** *obs* : to cause (as an animal) to foam at the mouth with exhaustion or sometimes with rage or other emotion **3** *archaic* : to cover or spatter with foam

2emboss \"\ vt [ME *embosen*, fr. MF *emboccer*, fr. *em-* 1*en-* + *boce* boss — more at BOSS (protuberance)] **1** *obs* : to cause to swell or protrude : INFLATE **2 a :** to raise in relief from a surface (as an ornament, a head on a coin, or a device on a letterhead) either by carving or handiwork or now more commonly by mechanical means (as by embossing dies) — opposed to *deboss* **b :** to raise the surface of into bosses or protuberances esp. by pressure against a steel die roller cut or engraved with a pattern **c :** to mark (a postage stamp) with a grill **3 :** to adorn (as leather or metal) with raised work **4 a :** to produce (as braille characters or a notary's seal) in relief usu. by stamping on paper or other impressionable surface **b :** to record (sounds) on a disc record by pushing material to either side without actually removing the material from the disc

3emboss vt [origin unknown] *obs* : ENCLOSE, ENSHEATHE

embossed *adj* [fr. past part. of 2*emboss*] : prepared, ornamented, or finished by embossing; *esp, of cloth* : having a permanent raised design usu. produced by pressure ⟨an ~ satin blouse⟩ ⟨washable, ~, taffetized cotton sundress —*advt*⟩

embossed book n : a book with embossed text (as one in braille)

embossed stamp n : an imprinted stamp with raised lettering and design

em·boss·er \-sə(r)\ n -s [2*emboss* + *-er*] : one that embosses: as **a :** a punch used in repoussé work for striking metal on the reverse side to raise the relief **b :** an operator of a machine for forming raised designs (as on leather, book covers, textiles, or stationery) **c :** a writer of braille; *esp* : one whose work is embossing braille by stereotyping

embossing n -s [ME *embosing*, fr. gerund of *embosen* to emboss] **1 :** a product of embossing : an embossed figure or design; *sometimes* : 1GRILLE 3 **2 :** the act of or process used by one that embosses; *esp* : a calendering process for finishing textiles with a raised, moiré, or other ornamental pattern produced by passing the cloth under heat and pressure between a pair of correspondingly engraved rollers

embossing press n : a punch press used for embossing (as of book covers)

embossing stylus n : a stylus that is used in disc recording and that has a rounded tip which pushes the disc material to either side in forming the groove

em·boss·ment \-smənt\ n -s [2*emboss* + *-ment*] **1 :** the process of embossing **2 :** BOSS, PROTUBERANCE **3 :** embossed work; *specif* : embossed ornamentation

em·both·ri·um \em'bäthrēəm\ n, cap [NL, fr. 2*en-* + Gk *bothrion* small pit, dim. of *bothros* pit] : a genus of shrubs or small trees (family Proteaceae) with long willowy branches, leathery entire leaves, and showy reddish flowers in terminal racemes

em·bouche·ment \äm'büshmənt\ n -s [F, fr. *emboucher* + *-ment*] : EMBOUCHURE 1

em·bou·chure \,ämbü¦shů(ə)r, -bə¦-\ n -s [F, fr. (s')*emboucher* to flow into, fr. *em-* 1*en-* + *bouche* mouth, mouth of a river, fr. L *bucca* cheek — more at POCK] **1 :** the mouth of a river; *also* : expansion of a river valley into a plain **2 a :** the position and use of the lips in producing a musical tone on a wind instrument — called also *lip, lipping* **b :** the mouthpiece of a musical instrument **3 :** BOUCHE 2

em·bound *also* **im·bound** \əm, em+\ vt [1*en-* or 2*in-* + *bound* (n.)] : BIND

em·bow \əm'bō, em-\ vt [ME *embowen*, fr. 1*en-* + *bowe* bow — more at BOW (arch)] *archaic* : to form into an arch or vault

em·bowed \-ōd\ *adj* [ME, fr. past part. of *embowen*] : bent like a bow: as **a :** ARCHED, VAULTED ⟨an ~ ceiling⟩ **b** *heraldry, of the arm or leg* : represented with the elbow or knee bent to the dexter **c :** curved outward to form a projecting recess ⟨an ~ window bay⟩

em·bowel \əm, em+\ vt [1*en-* + *bowel* (v.)] **1 :** DISEMBOWEL **2** [1*en-* + *bowel* (n.)] *obs* : to hide in the inward parts : ENCLOSE, ENCOMPASS ⟨deep ~*ed* in the earth —Edmund Spenser⟩

em·bower *also* **im·bower** \"+\ vt [1*en-* or 2*in-* + *bower* (n.)] : to shelter or enclose in or as if in a bower ⟨a house ~*ed* with shrubs⟩

em·box \"+\ vt [1*en-* + *box* (n.)] : to enclose in or as if in a box

embr *abbr* **1** embroidered **2** embryo; embryology

1em·brace \əm'brās, em-\ vb -ED/-ING/-S [ME *embracen*, fr. MF *embracer*, fr. OF *embracier*, fr. *em-* 1*en-* + *brace* two arms — more at BRACE] vt **1 a :** to clasp in the arms usu. as a gesture of affection : HUG **b :** to copulate with **c** *archaic* : to greet or salute by clasping in the arms **2 :** ENCIRCLE, ENCLOSE, ENCOMPASS ⟨a quiet valley *embraced* by dark forests⟩ ⟨the strong walls that ~ the city⟩ **3** *archaic* : to take in hand or under consideration : UNDERTAKE **4 :** to receive or take up esp. readily or gladly: as **a :** to come to believe in and seek to further, defend, support, or join willingly ⟨a cause which is *embraced* and cherished by so vast a portion of American society —Kenneth Roberts⟩ ⟨finally he *embraced* his father's religion and politics and settled down to be a country gentleman⟩ **b :** to welcome or accept eagerly : attach oneself to : avail oneself of readily ⟨this life secured for the mind of him who *embraced* it the inestimable advantages of solitude and silence —Joseph Conrad⟩ ⟨an instructor should ~ every opportunity to prepare himself —C.H.Grandgent⟩ ⟨ready to ~ the hard life of a pioneer⟩ **5 :** to attempt to or act so as to influence (as a jury or court) corruptly **6 :** to take in : ENFOLD, INCLUDE, COVER : treat as part, item, or phase of a larger whole; *sometimes* : to be equal or equivalent to : total to ⟨called *Summae*, as their scope *embraced* the entire contents of the faith —H.O.Taylor⟩ ⟨my financial assets which *embraced* a few hundred dollars . . . as my immediate assets —Herbert Hoover⟩ ~ vi : to participate in an embrace ⟨*embracing* tearfully before they parted⟩ **syn** see ADOPT, INCLUDE

2embrace \"\ n -s **1 a :** a close encircling with the arms and pressure to the bosom esp. as a mark of affection or passion ⟨rushed to the comforting ~ of his mother's arms⟩ ⟨a quick ~ full of love and despair⟩ **b :** COPULATION; *broadly* : any close physical relation designed to ensure fertilization of eggs ⟨the amplectic ~ of amphibians⟩ **c :** a clasping with the forelimbs when in conflict — used esp. of an animal ⟨the grim ~ of the grizzly bear⟩ **2 :** ENCIRCLEMENT, ENCLOSURE, GRIP ⟨helpless in the ~ of terror⟩ ⟨a valley lying in the ~ of wooded hills⟩ **3 :** acceptance esp. with favor or approbation ⟨his ready ~ of Communist doctrine⟩

3embrace vt -ED/-ING/-S [1*en-* + *brace* (n.)] *obs* : to fasten (as armor) with or as if with a brace or buckle

em·brace·able \əm'brāsəbəl, em-\ *adj* : suitable for embracing or capable of being embraced; *sometimes* : such as may be comprehended and accepted — **em·brace·ably** \-blē\ *adv*

em·brace·ment \-smənt\ n -s : EMBRACE; *esp* : ready or cheerful acceptance (as of an idea, point of view, or method)

em·brace·or \-sə(r)\ n -s [AF, fr. OF, MF *embracer* to embrace + *-eor* -or] : one guilty of embracery

em·brac·er \"\ n -s [ME, fr. *embracen* + *-er*] : one that embraces; *esp* : EMBRACEOR

em·brac·ery \-s(ə)rē\ n -ES [ME *embracerie*, fr. *embracen* + *-erie* -ery] : the act of one who attempts to or acts so as to influence a court, jury, or other office or officer corruptly (as by promises, entreaties, money, entertainments, or threats)

embracing *adj* : ENCIRCLING, ENCLOSING: as **a** *of a leaf* : having the base clasped about the supporting stem of the plant **b :** COMPREHENSIVE, INCLUSIVE ⟨an all-*embracing* glance⟩ — **em·brac·ing·ly** *adv* — **em·brac·ing·ness** n -ES

em·brac·ive \-siv\ *adj* **1 :** disposed to embrace **2 :** INCLUSIVE, COMPREHENSIVE

em·brail \əm, em+\ vt [1*en-* + *brail* (n.)] : BRAIL 1

em·branch·ment \əm'branchmənt, em-, -raan-,-rain-,-rän-\ n -s [F *embranchement*, fr. (s')*embrancher* to branch out (fr. *em-* 1*en-* + *branche* branch) + *-ment* — more at BRANCH] **1 :** a branching off or out (as of a valley or a mountain range) **2 :** BRANCH, RAMIFICATION

em·bran·gle *also* **im·bran·gle** \əm'braŋ(g)əl, em-\ vt [1*en-* or 2*in-* + *brangle*] : CONFUSE, ENTANGLE ⟨all *embrangled* with this election squabble⟩ ⟨the outside snares and commitments which so *embrangled* him in his first two years —*Isis*⟩ — **em·bran·gle·ment** \-lmənt\ n -s

em·bra·sure \əm'brāzhə(r), em-\ n -s [F, fr. obs. *embraser* to widen an opening + *-ure*] **1 :** a recess of a door or window; *esp* : one sloped or beveled to give an effect of largeness from one side **2 :** an opening with sides flaring outward in a wall or parapet of a fortification usu. for allowing the firing of cannon **3 :** the sloped valley between adjacent teeth (as in the human mouth)

em·bra·sured \-(r)d\ *adj* : having or furnished with embrasures ⟨an ~ fort⟩

em·brave \əm, em+\ *also* **en·brave** \ən, en+\ vt [1*en-* + *brave* (adj.)] **1** *archaic* : to make fine or impressive : BRIGHTEN **2** *archaic* : to inspire with courage : make brave or daring

embreathe vt [ME *embrethen*, fr. 1*en-* + *brethen* to breathe — more at BREATHE] : INHALE

embrasure 1

embrew *obs var of* IMBRUE

embright vt -ED/-ING/-S [1*en-* + *bright* (adj.)] *obs* : to make bright : ILLUMINATE

em·brighten \əm, em+\ vt [1*en-* + *brighten*] : to make brighter : BRIGHTEN

embrion *obs var of* EMBRYO

em·bri·thop·o·da \,embrə'thäpədə\ n pl, cap [NL, fr. *embritho-* (fr. Gk *embrithēs* weighty) + NL *-poda*] : a small order of extinct African ungulate mammals possibly related to the Hyracoidea

em·brittle \əm, em+\ vb -ED/-ING/-S [1*en-* + *brittle* (adj.)] vt : to make (as metal or plastic) brittle ~ vi : to become brittle — **em·brit·tle·ment** \"mənt\ n -s

em·bro·cate \'embrə,kāt, -rō,-\ vt -ED/-ING/-S [LL *embrocatus*, past part. of *embrocare*, fr. Gk *embrochē* embrocation, lotion, fr. *embrechein* to bathe with a lotion, fr. *em-* 2*en-* + *brechein* to wet — more at BRECHITES] : to moisten and rub (a part of the body) with a lotion

em·bro·ca·tion \,==¦kāshən\ n -s [LL *embrocatus* + E *-ion*] : LINIMENT

embroche n -s [Gk *embrochē*] *obs* : EMBROCATION

embroglio *var of* IMBROGLIO

em·broi·der \əm'brȯidə(r), em-\ vb **embroidered; embroidered; embroidering** \-d(ə)riŋ\ **embroiders** [ME *embroden, embroderen*, fr. MF *embroder*, fr. *em-* 1*en-* + *broder* to embroider — more at BROIDER] vt **1 a :** to ornament with needlework ⟨~*ed* a sampler⟩ **b :** to form with needlework ⟨~*ing* tiny flowers on a scarf⟩ **2 a :** EMBELLISH, ORNAMENT; *esp* : to present (as an account) with florid language or fictitious details **b :** EXAGGERATE ⟨~*ed* the story of his adventures in the jungle —Rudyard Kipling⟩ ~ vi **1 :** to make embroidery **2 :** to provide embellishments or ornamentation (as fictitious details) : ELABORATE — used with *on* or *upon* ⟨he would take a theme and ~ upon it with . . . drollery —W.S.Maugham⟩ ⟨he develops his subject . . . ~*ing* on rather than deepening its significance —C.D.Lewis⟩

em·broi·der·er \-dərə(r)\ n -s [ME *embrawderer*, fr. *embrawderen, embrouderen* to embroider + *-er*] : one that embroiders

em·broi·der·ess \-d(ə)rəs\ n -ES : a woman who embroiders

em·broi·dery \-d(ə)rē, -ri\ n -ES *often attrib* [ME *embrouderie*, fr. *embrouderen, embroderen* + *-erie* -ery] **1 a :** the art or process of forming decorative designs in plain or fancy stitches by hand or machine (as on cloth, leather, or paper) **b :** any such design or decoration ⟨enlivened by ~ on the collar and cuffs⟩ ⟨a neckline accented by ~⟩ **c :** an object decorated with embroidery ⟨made a modest living by sale of her *embroideries*⟩ **2 :** elaboration of decorative often fictitious detail : EMBELLISHMENT ⟨the succinct statement of economic facts and principles, without ~ —W.B.Shaw⟩ ⟨little time and breath to waste on long speeches, ~, and trivialities —Robert Moses⟩ ⟨a classic case of ~ on fact —*Reporter*⟩ **3 :** diversified ornamentation esp. by contrasts ⟨fields in spring's ~ are dressed —Joseph Addison⟩ **4 :** something pleasing or desirable but superficial and nonessential ⟨most of the content of all cultures consists of *embroideries* which, although they possess use and function, cannot be regarded as direct responses to the basic needs of the society —Ralph Linton⟩ ⟨those who consider the humanities mere educational ~⟩

embroidery hoop n : either of two hoops fitting snugly one over the other for holding fabric taut while embroidering

embroidery hoops

1em·broil \əm'brȯil, *esp before pause or consonant* -ȯiəl\ vt [F *embrouiller*, fr. MF, fr. *em-* 1*en-* + *brouiller* to mix, confuse — more at BROIL (mix)] **1 a :** to cause (as a person or affairs) to fall into disorder or confusion ⟨political complications which ~*ed* the whole policy of the great oceanic expeditions —C.P.Fitzgerald⟩ : CONFUSE, DISORDER, DISTRACT ⟨her emotions were forever ~*ing* her intellect —V.L.Parrington⟩ ⟨the city was ~*ed* in gigantic traffic bottlenecks —*New Yorker*⟩ **b :** to throw into physical uproar or disorder ⟨the wind ~*ing* the sea⟩ **2 :** to involve esp. in conflict or with a problem, adversaries, or the law ⟨~*ed* in ideological arguments⟩ ⟨found himself ~*ed* with the group investigating the union's finances⟩ ⟨an opinionated and litigious lady who . . . was forever ~*ed* with landlords, travel agencies, and shops —Louis Auchincloss⟩ ⟨often ~*ed* in federal criminal proceedings⟩ ⟨his drinking often ~*s* him with the law⟩

2embroil \"\ n -s *archaic* : EMBROILMENT

em·broil·er \-ȯilə(r)\ n : one that embroils; *esp* : TROUBLEMAKER

em·broil·ment \-ȯi(ə)lmənt\ n -s [F *embrouillement*, fr. *embrouiller* + *-ment*] **1 :** the act of embroiling or state of being embroiled; *often* : UPROAR, COMMOTION, QUARREL ⟨an ~ that led to a crowded police court the next morning⟩ **2 :** ENTANGLEMENT, PERPLEXITY, INVOLVEMENT ⟨trying to avoid ~ in continental quarrels⟩

em·brown \əm'braůn, em-\ vt [1*en-* + *brown* (adj.)] **1** *archaic* : DARKEN **2** *archaic* : to cause to turn brown

embrue *var of* IMBRUE

embrute *var of* IMBRUTE

embry- *or* **embryo-** *comb form* [LL, fr. Gk, fr. *embryon*] : embryo ⟨*embry*ectomy⟩ ⟨*embryo*logy⟩

em·bryo \'embrē,ō\ n -s *often attrib* [ML *embryon-, embryo*, modif. of Gk *embryon*, fr. (assumed) Gk *embryein* to swell inside, fr. Gk *em-* 2*en-* + *bryein* to swell — more at SAUERKRAUT] **1 a** *archaic* : a human or other animal offspring at any stage of development prior to birth or hatching as a young individual fundamentally similar to the adult **b :** an animal organism in the early stages of growth and differentiation that are characterized by cleavage, the laying down of fundamental tissues, and the formation of primitive organs and organ systems and that in higher forms (as mammals) merge insensibly into fetal stages but in lower forms are terminated by commencement of larval life, often with a form markedly different from that of the adult — compare FETUS, ZYGOTE **c :** the developing human individual from the time of implantation to the end of the eighth week after conception — compare FETUS, OVUM **2 :** the young sporophyte of a seed plant, resulting from union of the egg and one of the two sperm nuclei, sometimes consisting of only a few cells (as in orchids) but usu. comprising a rudimentary plant with plumule, radicle, and cotyledons, and typically embedded in endosperm that provides nutriment for the developing plant upon germination — called also *germ* **3 :** something as yet undeveloped and lacking final form and differentiation : a conception precedent to realization; *often* : the state characteristic of such a thing : a state of incipience — used esp. in the phrase *in embryo*

em·bryo·car·dia \,embrēō'kärdēə\ n [NL, fr. *embry-* + *-cardia*] : a symptom of heart disease in which the heart sounds resemble those of the fetal heart

em·bryo·gen·e·sis \-ō'jenəsəs\ n [NL, fr. *embry-* + L *genesis*] : EMBRYOGENY

em·bryo·gen·ic \¦===¦jenik\ *also* **em·bry·o·ge·net·ic** \¦==(,)=jə¦ned·ik\ *adj* : of, relating to, or involved in embryogeny

em·bry·og·e·ny \,embrē'äjənē\ n -ES [*embryo-* + *-geny*] : the formation and development of the embryo whether direct or indirect — compare HETEROBLASTIC, HOMOBLASTIC

em·bry·oid \'embrē,ȯid\ *adj* [ISV *embry-* + *-oid*] : resembling an embryo

em·bry·o·log·ic \,embrēə¦läjik, -jēk\ *or* **em·bry·o·log·i·cal** \-jəkəl, -jēk-\ *adj* : of, relating to, used in, or involving the methods of embryology ⟨~ development⟩ ⟨~ apparatus⟩ ⟨an ~ approach to a problem⟩ — **em·bry·o·log·i·cal·ly** \-jək(ə)lē, -jēk-, -li\ *adv*

em·bry·ol·o·gist \,embrē'äləjəst\ n -s : a specialist in embryology

em·bry·ol·o·gy \-jē, -ji\ n -ES [F *embryologie*, fr. *embry-* + *-logie* -logy] **1 :** a branch of biology that relates to embryogeny in animals and plants : the study of the development of the individual from the egg to birth or hatching ⟨a student of ~⟩ — compare ONTOGENY **2 :** the features and phenomena exhibited in the formation and development of an embryo ⟨certain peculiarities of the ~ of the brook trout⟩ **3 :** a treatise on embryology

em·bry·o·ma \,embrē'ōmə\ n, pl **embryomas** \-məz\ *or* **embryoma·ta** \-məd·ə\ [NL, fr. *embry-* + *-oma*] : a tumor derived from embryonic structures : TERATOMA

em·bry·on \'embrē,än\ n -s [ML *embryon-, embryo* — more at EMBRYO] : EMBRYO — not used technically

embryon- *or* **embryoni-** *comb form* [ML *embryon-, embryo*] : embryo ⟨*embryon*ic⟩ ⟨*embryoni*form⟩

em·bry·o·nal \em'brīənəl\ *adj* : EMBRYONIC 1 — **em·bry·o·nal·ly** \-ənəlē\ *adv*

em·bry·o·nary \'embrēə,nerē\ *adj* [*embryon-* + *-ary*] : EMBRYONIC

em·bry·o·nate \-,nāt\ vi -ED/-ING/-S [*embryon-* + *-ate*] *of an egg or zygote* : to produce or differentiate into an embryo

em·bry·o·nat·ed \-,nād·əd\ *also* **em·bry·o·nate** \-,āt\ *adj* [*embryon* + *-ated, -ate*] : having an embryo; *esp* : far-enough developed to have a perceptible living embryo ⟨growing viruses on ~ hen's eggs⟩

em·bry·o·na·tion \,embrēə'nāshən\ n -s : the formation of an embryo within an egg

em·bry·on·ic \,embrē¦änik, -nēk\ *adj* [*embryon-* + *-ic*] **1 :** of or relating to an embryo **2 :** incipient and rudimentary — **em·bry·on·i·cal·ly** \-nək(ə)lē, -nēk-, -li\ *adv*

embryonic disk n **1 a :** BLASTODISC **b :** BLASTODERM **2** *or* **embryonic shield :** the part of the inner cell mass of a blastocyst from which the embryo of a placental mammal develops

embryonic knob n : INNER CELL MASS

embryonic layer n : GERM LAYER

embryonic membrane n : a structure that derives from the fertilized ovum but does not form a part of the embryo, including true membranes (as the amnion and chorion) and other structures (as the placenta and umbilical cord) not usu. considered membranes

embryonic vesicle n : EGG 1b

em·bry·o·ny \'embrēənē, em'brīə-\ n -ES [*embryon-* + *-y*] : the condition of having or the production of an embryo — compare MONEMBRYONY, POLYEMBRYONY

em·bry·op·a·thy \,embrē'äpəthē\ n -ES [*embry-* + *-pathy*] : a congenital but usu. not hereditary malformation

em·bry·o·phore \'embrēə,fō(ə)r\ n -s [*embry-* + *-phore*] : the outer cellular covering of the hexacanth embryo of a tapeworm; *broadly* : the covering and included embryo

em·bry·oph·y·ta \,embrē'äfəd·ə\ n pl, cap [NL, fr. *embry-* + *-phyta*] *in some classifications* : a primary division or subkingdom of Plantae that comprises all plants producing an embryo and developing vascular tissues and including all plants except the Myxophyta and Thallophyta — **em·bry·o·phyte** \'embrēə,fīt\ n -s

embryos *pl of* EMBRYO

embryo sac *n* **:** the female gametophyte of a seed plant consisting of a thin-walled sac within the nucellus that typically develops from a single functional megaspore and contains several meiotically reduced nuclei which lack separating cell walls and which include the egg nucleus and others that give rise to endosperm on fertilization

em·bry·ot·ic \ˌembrēˈäd·ik\ *adj* [*embryo* + *-tic* (as in *patriotic*)] **:** EMBRYONIC 2

em·bry·o·tome \ˈembrēəˌtōm\ *n* -s [*embry-* + *-tome*] **:** an instrument used in embryotomy

em·bry·ot·o·my \ˌembrēˈäd·əmē\ *n* -ES [F *embryotomie*, fr. *embry-* + *-tomie* -tomy] **1 :** mutilation of a fetus for removal from the uterus when natural delivery is impossible **2 :** dissection of embryos for examination

em·bry·o·troph \ˈembrēəˌträf, -rȯf\ *or* **em·bry·o·trophe** \-rōf\ *n* -s [F *embryotrophe*, fr. *embry-* + *-trophe* (fr. Gk *trophos* one that feeds or rears, fr. *trephein* to nourish) — more at ATROPHY] **:** the pabulum of uterine tissue fluids and cellular debris that nourishes the embryo of a placental mammal prior to the establishment of the placental circulation — **em·bry·ot·ro·phy** \ˌembrēˈä·trəfē\ *n* -ES

em·bry·ous \ˈembrēəs\ *adj* [*embry-* + *-ous*] **:** EMBRYONIC

embue *var of* IMBUE

embuia *var of* IMBUIA

em·bus \ə̇m, em+\ *vi* [1*en-* + *bus* (n.)] **:** to get aboard a bus

em·bus·qué \ˌämˌ(ˌ)büˌskā, äⁿbüeskā\ *n* -s [F, fr. past part. of (*s'*)*embusquer* to lie in ambush, shirk, fr. OF *embuschier* to place in ambush — more at AMBUSH] **:** a person seeking to avoid military service (as by working in a government office) **:** SHIRKER, SLACKER

1em·cee \(ˈ)emˌsē\ *n* -s [1*em* + *cee* (letter); fr. the initials *M.C.*] **:** MASTER OF CEREMONIES; *esp* **:** a person who conducts a program (as on television) introducing numbers, introducing and interviewing speakers, and usu. providing the continuity

2emcee \"\ *vb* **emceed**; **emceed**; **emceeing**; **emcees** *vt* **:** to act as master of ceremonies of ⟨~*ing* a nightly show⟩ ~ *vi* **:** to act as master of ceremonies ⟨a leading comedian will ~⟩

em dash *n* [1*em*] **:** a dash that is one em wide

emden *usu cap, var of* EMBDEN

eme \ˈēm\ *n* -s [ME, fr. OE *ēam* — more at UNCLE] **1** *chiefly Scot* **:** UNCLE **2** *chiefly Scot* **:** FRIEND

-eme \ˌēm\ *n suffix* -s [F *-ème* thing, unit (in *phonème* speech sound), fr. Gk *-ēmat-*, *-ēma* (in *phōnēmat-*, *phōnēma* utterance), fr. *-ē-* (stem vowel of *phōnein* to sound) + *-mat-*, *-ma* (noun suffix) — more at -MENT] **:** significantly distinctive unit of structure of a (specified) kind in a language or dialect ⟨morph*eme*⟩ ⟨ton*eme*⟩ — compare ALLO-

emeer *var of* EMIR

emend \ēˈmend, ə̇ˈ-\ *vt* -ED/-ING/-S [ME *emenden*, fr. L *emendare* — more at AMEND] **1** *archaic* **:** to free from faults or defects **:** BETTER, IMPROVE **2 a :** to correct (as a literary work) usu. by textual alterations ⟨will ~ a chapter here or a verse there —*London Calling*⟩ **b :** to alter (as a literary work) to serve a purpose different from the original ⟨the Roman Paul borrowed Plato's image and ~*ed* it to suit his needs —Henry Silverstein⟩ **syn** see CORRECT

emend·able \-dəbəl\ *adj* **:** capable of being emended **:** RECTIFIABLE; *esp, of offenses against early English law* **:** such as may be forgiven in return for a payment of money or goods

emen·dan·dum \(ˌ)ēˌmenˈdan|dəm, ˌēmən-, ˌeˌmen-, ˌemən-, ə̇ˌmen-\ *n, pl* **emendan·da** \|də\ [L, neut. of *emendandus*, gerundive of *emendare*] **:** CORRIGENDUM

emen·date \ˈēˌmenˌdāt, ˈēmən-, ˈeˌmen-, ˈemən-, ēˈmen-, ə̇ˈmen-, *usu* -ād·+V\ *vt* -ED/-ING/-S [L *emendatus*, past part. of *emendare*] **:** EMEND 2a

emen·da·tion \(ˌ)ēˌmenˈdāshən, ˌēmən-, ˌeˌmen-, ˌemən-, ə̇ˌmen-\ *n* -s [ME *emendatioun*, fr. L *emendation-*, *emendatio*, fr. *emendatus* + *-ion-*, *-io* -ion] **1 :** the act of emending **:** CORRECTION **2 a :** corrections or alterations made in the emending (as of a text) ⟨a manuscript full of ~*s*⟩ **b :** the word or the matter substituted for incorrect or unsuitable matter in an emended work ⟨I have retained all such ~*s* —Bernard De Voto⟩ **3** *obs* **:** COMPENSATION **4 a :** an alteration of the spelling of a taxonomic name ⟨*Agchylostoma* is an invalid ~ of *Ancylostoma*⟩ **b :** a redefinition of a taxon that alters the composition of that taxon ⟨many taxonomists reject any ~ of Compositae that puts the thistles in a separate family⟩

emen·da·tor *pronunc at* EMENDATE + ə(r)\ *n* -s [L, fr. *emendatus* + *-or*] **:** one that emends

emen·da·to·ry \ēˈmendəˌtōrē, ə̇ˈ-, -ȯr-, -ri\ *adj* [LL *emendatorius*, fr. *emendatus* + *-orius* -ory] **:** of or relating to emendation **:** CORRECTIVE

emer *abbr* **1** emergency **2** emeritus

1em·er·ald \ˈem(ə)rəld\ *n* -s [ME *emeraude*, *emerallde*, fr. MF *esmeragde*, *esmeraude*, *esmeralde*, fr. (assumed) VL *smaragda*, *smaralda*, fr. L *smaragdus*, fr. Gk *smaragdos*, *maragdos*, prob. of Sem origin; akin to Heb *bāreqet* emerald] **1 a :** a variety of beryl distinguished by a rich green color caused by the presence of chromium and highly prized as a gemstone **b :** any of various green gemstones (as synthetic corundum or demantoid) — used chiefly in combination **2** *or* **emerald green a :** a brilliant green that is the color of emerald green pigment — called also *Mitis green*, *Vienna green* **b** *of textiles* **:** a strong yellowish green approximating the color of the emerald — called also *emeraude* **c :** a variable color averaging a strong bluish green **3** *Brit* **:** MINIONETTE **4 :** any of various tropical American hummingbirds more or less marked with emerald green

2emerald \"\ *adj* **1 :** brightly or richly green ⟨the ~ fields of spring⟩; *sometimes* **:** of the color emerald ⟨an ~ scarf⟩ **2** *of a mineral* **:** gemmy and richly green in color ⟨~ spodumene⟩ **3** *of a jewelry setting* **:** square or rectangular — compare EMERALD CUT

emerald copper *n* **:** DIOPTASE

emerald cuckoo *n* **1 :** a small brilliant green African cuckoo (*Chrysococcyx smaragdineus*) with yellow breast **2 :** a small bright green cuckoo (*Chrysococcyx maculatus*) found from the Himalayas to southern China

emerald cut *n* **:** a step cut in which the contour of the gem is square or rectangular — see CUT illustration

emerald feather *n* **:** a commonly cultivated ornamental asparagus (*Asparagus sprengeri*) with long slender wiry or drooping stems bearing flat slender pointed cladophylls, tiny stellate pink blossoms in axillary inflorescences, and bright red berries

emerald green *n* **1 a :** a clear bright green resembling that of the emerald **b :** EMERALD 2 **2 a :** Paris green for use as a pigment **b :** GUIGNET'S GREEN **c :** BRILLIANT GREEN

1em·er·al·dine \-lˌdēn, -dīn\ *adj* [1*emerald* + *-ine*] **:** EMERALD 1

2em·er·al·dine \-dēn\ *n* -s **:** a blue basic compound yielding bottle-green salts with acids that is formed as an intermediate in the production of aniline black

emerald tint *n* **:** a very pale green that is yellower and lighter than tourmaline, bluer, lighter, and stronger than celadon tint, and yellower, lighter, and slightly stronger than microcline green

emerald whip snake *n* **:** WHIP SNAKE a

em·er·ant \ˈem(ə)rənt\ *dial var of* EMERALD

em·er·aude \ˈeməˌrōd\ *or* **emeraude green** *n* -s [F *émeraude* emerald, fr. OF *esmeragde*, *esmeraude*, *esmeralde* — more at EMERALD] **1 :** EMERALD 2b **2 :** VIRIDIAN 2

emerge \ēˈmərj, ə̇ˈ-, -mə̄j, -məij\ *vi* -ED/-ING/-S [L *emergere*, fr. *e-* + *mergere* to dip, plunge — more at MERGE] **1 :** to rise from or as if from an enveloping fluid **:** come out into view ⟨when land first *emerged* from the sea⟩ ⟨the sun ~*s* from eclipse⟩ ⟨rays *emerging* from a prism⟩ ⟨a road *emerging* from the park⟩ **2 :** to become revealed **:** become manifest **:** become known ⟨a new problem then *emerged*⟩ ⟨it ~*s* that her past behavior was far from irreproachable⟩ ⟨after long study there *emerged* an overall picture of conditions that was extremely disheartening⟩ **3 :** to come forth or rise from an inferior, obscure, or unfortunate position or condition into one of superiority, prominence, or success ⟨as the common people *emerged* from illiteracy⟩ ⟨someone must ~ as a leader⟩ ⟨*emerged* the unchallenged head of the state⟩ ⟨the youngest runner *emerged* the victor⟩ **4 a :** to arise by emergent evolution **b :** to come into being through evolution ⟨certain new viruses appear to have *emerged* in recent years⟩ ⟨there is no certainty as to the ancestors from which vertebrates *emerged*⟩

emer·gence \-jən(t)s\ *n* -s [*emerge* + *-ence*] **1 :** the act or an instance of emerging **:** a coming forth or rising into view ⟨slow ~ from barbarism⟩ ⟨the cold weather delayed the ~ of the apple blossoms⟩: as **a :** the appearance of an emergent or the process of emerging — compare EMERGENT EVOLUTION **b :** the recovering of consciousness (as after anesthesia) **c** *often cap* **:** the issuing forth from an underworld abode of the original ancestors of the human race — used in various No. American Indian mythologies **2** [ML *emergentia*] *archaic* **a :** EMERGENCY **b :** urgent need **3 :** any of various outgrowths (as the prickle of a rose) from superficial layers of plant tissue usu. from both the epidermis and immediately underlying layers — compare ENATION, TRICHOME

emer·gen·cy \-nsē, -si\ *n* -ES *often attrib* [ML *emergentia*, fr. L *emergent-*, *emergens*, (pres. part. of *emergere*) + *-ia* -y] **1 :** an unforeseen combination of circumstances or the resulting state that calls for immediate action ⟨they were far from help when the ~ overtook them⟩: as **a :** a pressing need **:** EXIGENCY ⟨a state of ~ existed during which any help was acceptable⟩ **b :** a sudden bodily alteration such as is likely to require immediate medical attention (as a ruptured appendix or surgical shock) **c :** a usu. distressing event or condition that can often be anticipated or prepared for but seldom exactly foreseen ⟨wait until the ~ is over, prices will go down then⟩ ⟨an ~ water supply⟩ ⟨~ docking facilities⟩ ⟨~ crews working to clear the roads⟩ **2** [*emerge* + *-ency*] *archaic* **:** the act or an instance of emerging **:** EMERGENCE 1 **3 :** the theory of emergent evolution **syn** see JUNCTURE

emergency barrage *n* **:** a standing barrage for which an artillery battery has prepared data and to which it can shift on call

emergency brake *n* **:** a hand brake (as on an automobile) that can be set so that it continues to hold in the driver's absence and is commonly used as a parking brake — compare SERVICE BRAKE

emergency landing field *n* **:** a surface either of water or land that is adapted but not equipped for the landing and taking off of aircraft

emergency money *n* **:** NECESSITY MONEY

emergency power *n* **:** power granted to or used or taken by a public authority to meet the exigencies of a particular emergency (as of war or disaster) whether within or outside a constitutional frame of reference

1emer·gent \-nt\ *adj* [ME, fr. L *emergent-*, *emergens*, pres. part. of *emergere* to emerge — more at EMERGE] **1 :** emerging out of a fluid or something that covers or conceals **:** issuing forth **:** rising into notice ⟨like the lovely goddess ~ from the waves⟩ ⟨~ coastal islands⟩ ⟨the ~ vegetation along the shore⟩ **2 :** suddenly appearing **:** arising unexpectedly; *often* **:** calling for prompt action **:** URGENT ⟨~ danger⟩ ⟨an ~ state in a hemophiliac⟩ **3 :** arising as a natural or logical consequence or outcome ⟨political issues ~ from war⟩ **4 :** appearing as or involving the appearance of something novel in a process of evolution — compare EMERGENT EVOLUTION — **emer·gent·ly** *adv*

2emergent \"\ *n* -s **1** *obs* **:** EMERGENCY **2 :** an emergent quality, character, or individual **3 :** a plant (as a tall tree with its crown above the level of the forest) that emerges from its substrate; *esp* **:** any of various plants (as a bulrush) rooted in shallow water and having most of the vegetative growth above water

emergent evolution *n* **:** evolution conceived as characterized by the appearance at different levels of wholly new and unpredictable characters or qualities (as life and consciousness) through a rearrangement of preexistent entities — compare CREATIVE EVOLUTION

emer·gent·ist \-ntə̇st\ *n* -s **:** an adherent of the theory of emergent evolution

emer·gent·ness *n* -ES **:** the quality or state of being emergent

emerges *pres 3d sing of* EMERGE

emerging *pres part of* EMERGE

emeried *past of* EMERY

emeries *pl of* EMERY, *pres 3d sing of* EMERY

emeril *obs var of* EMERY

emer·il·lon \āˈmerəˌlän, -əˌyän\ *n, pl* **emerillon** *or* **emerillons** *usu cap* **1 a :** a Tupian people living along the north Brazilian coast from the mouth of the Amazon into French Guiana **b :** a member of such people **2 :** the language of the Emerillon people

1emer·i·ta \ə̇ˈmerəd·ə, ēˈ-, -rətə\ *n, cap* [NL, fr. L, fem. of *emeritus*] **:** a genus of anomuran decapod crustaceans (suborder Reptantia) widely distributed along sandy shores of both coasts of No. America and the western coast of So. America — see BAIT BUG

2emerita \"\ *adj* [L, fem. of *emeritus*] **:** EMERITUS — used only of the female and esp. in titles ⟨Professor *Emerita* Mary Smith⟩

emer·it·ed \-d·ə̇d, -tə̇d\ *adj* [L *emeritus* + E *-ed*] *archaic* **:** retired from a service or occupation

1emer·i·tus \ə̇ˈmerəd·əs, ēˈ-, -rətəs\ *adj* [L, past part. of *emerēre* to obtain by service, to complete one's term, fr. *e-* + *merēre* to earn, serve one's time — more at MERIT] **1 :** holding after retirement (as from professional or academic office) an honorary title corresponding to that held last during active service ⟨he is ~ professor of English at a women's college⟩ ⟨a red-faced ~ cook⟩ **2 :** retired from an office or position esp. after gaining public or professional recognition ⟨an ~ dramatic critic —*N. Y. Times Book Rev.*⟩ — often used postpositively ⟨professor ~⟩ and sometimes converted to *emeriti* after a plural substantive ⟨professors *emeriti*⟩

2emeritus \"\ *n, pl* **emeri·ti** \-rəˌtī, -ˌtē\ **:** one retired from professional life but permitted to hold the rank of his last office as an honorary title ⟨joining the ranks of the *emeriti* —W.W.Sweet⟩

em·er·ize \ˈeməˌrīz\ *vt* -ED/-ING/-S [1*emery* + *-ize*] **:** to nap (fabric) with emery rollers for a surface resembling suede

em·er·od \ˈeməˌräd\ *n* -s [ME *emeroidea*, *emerodes*, pl., fr. MF *emorroides*, fr. L *haemorrhoidae* — more at HEMORRHOID] *archaic* **:** HEMORRHOID

emer·sal \(ˈ)ēˌmərsəl, ə̇ˈm-\ *adj* [L *emersus* (past part. of *emergere* to emerge) + E *-al* — more at EMERGE] **:** rising toward or floating at the surface of water — used esp. of aquatic plants or animals or their products ⟨the ~ eggs of many marine fishes⟩; contrasted with *demersal*

emersed \ēˈmərst\ *adj* [L *emersus* + E *-ed*] **:** standing out of or rising above a surface (as of a fluid) ⟨an aquatic plant with flower stalk ~⟩

emer·sion \ēˈmər|zhən, -mə̄|, -məi| *also* |sh-\ *n* -s [L *emersus* + E *-ion*] **1** *archaic* **:** an act of emerging **:** EMERGENCE **2 :** the reappearance of a celestial body after eclipse or occultation or a conjunction with the sun

em·er·so·nian \ˌemə(r)ˌsōnēən, -ōnyən\ *adj, usu cap* [Ralph W. *Emerson* †1882 Am. writer + E *-ian*] **:** like or relating to Ralph Waldo Emerson, his writings, or his theories — see TRANSCENDENTALISM 1b — **em·er·so·nian·ism** \-ēəˌnizəm, -yəˌ-\ *n* -s *usu cap*

1em·ery \ˈem(ə)rē, -ri\ *n* -ES *often attrib* [ME, fr. MF *emeri*, fr. OIt *smiriglio*, fr. ML *smiriglum*, fr. Gk *smyrid-*, *smyris* powdered emery — more at SMEAR] **1 :** a common dark granular corundum that contains varying amounts of magnetite or hematite and that on account of its great hardness is used in the form of powder, grains, or larger masses for grinding and polishing **2 a :** a natural abrasive used in modern gem grinding that is composed of an impure mixture of corundum and magnetite **b :** a hard abrasive powder — not used technically **3** *or* **emery bag :** a small cloth bag filled with powdered emery and used for polishing and sharpening needles **4** *or* **emery board :** a nail file made of cardboard covered with powdered emery

2emery \"\ *vt* -ED/-ING/-ES **1 :** to cover with emery (as in the preparation of abrasive papers) **2 :** to roughen or smooth by rubbing with emery

emery ball *n* **:** a baseball illegally roughened by powdered emery or by a piece of emery cloth or emery paper

emery cake *n* **:** powdered emery or a synthetic substitute caked in a binding material

emery stone *n* **1 :** a mixture of powdered emery and a suitable binder that can be molded into grinding wheels and other devices **2 :** WHETSTONE

emery wheel *n* **:** a wheel made of consolidated emery powder or having a surface of emery and used esp. for abrading, grinding, or polishing

emes *pl of* EME

-emes *pl of* -EME

em·e·sa \ˈeməsə\ [NL, fr. *Emesa* (now Homs), ancient city in Syria, fr. L, fr. Gk] *syn of* PLOIARIA

eme–sal \ˌeməˌsäl\ *n, usu cap* [Sumerian] **:** a form or dialect of Sumerian in which many religious texts were written

em·e·sis \ˈeməsə̇s\ *n, pl* **eme·ses** \-əˌsēz\ [NL, fr. Gk, fr. *emein* + *-sis*] **:** VOMITING

1emet·ic \ə̇ˈmed·|ik, ēˈ-, -et|, |ēk\ *n* -s [L *emetica*, fr. Gk *emetikē*, fr. fem. of *emetikos*] **:** an agent that induces vomiting

2emetic \"\ *also* **emet·i·cal** \|ə̇kəl, |ēk-\ *adj* [LL *emeticus*, fr. Gk *emetikos*, fr. *emetos* vomiting (fr. *emein* to vomit) + *-ikos* -ic, -ical — more at VOMIT] **:** inducing to vomit — **emet·i·cal·ly** \|ə̇k(ə)lē, -|ēk-, -li\ *adv*

emetic holly *n* **:** a yaupon (*Ilex vomitoria*)

emetic mushroom *n* **:** a mushroom (*Russula emetica*) with a deep-red or rarely white pileus that grows usu. in the woods and is violently emetic and poisonous

emetic root *n* **:** FLOWERING SPURGE

emetic weed *n* **:** INDIAN TOBACCO

em·e·tine \ˈeməˌtēn, -ətᵊn\ *n* -s [F *émétine*, fr. *émétique* emetic (fr. L *emetica*) + *-ine*] **:** an amorphous alkaloid $C_{29}H_{40}N_2O_4$ extracted from ipecac root and used as an emetic, expectorant, and amebicide

emeu *archaic var of* EMU

émeute \āmœ̄œ̄t\ *n* -s [F, fr. OF *esmuete* act of starting up, motion, fr. fem. of *esmuet*, past part. of *esmovoir* to start out, incite — more at EMOTION] **:** an outbreak of disorder or violence; *esp* **:** a popular uprising

EMF *abbr, often not cap* **:** electromotive force

em·gal·la \emˈgalə\ *n* -s [native name in Africa] **:** the southern African wart hog

-e·mia *or* **-ae·mia** \ˈēmēə, *esp Brit* ˈēmyə\ *also* **-hemia** *or* **-haemia** *n comb form* -s [NL *-emia*, *-aemia*, fr. Gk *-aimia*, fr. *haima* blood + *-ia* -y — more at HEM-] **1 :** condition of having (such) blood ⟨leuk*emia*⟩ ⟨septic*emia*⟩ **2 :** condition of having (a specified thing) in the blood ⟨chol*emia*⟩ ⟨ur*emia*⟩

1em·i·grant \ˈemə̇grənt, -mēg- *sometimes* -ˌgrant *or* -ˌgraa(ə)nt\ *n* -s [L *emigrant-*, *emigrans*, pres. part. of *emigrare* to depart, emigrate, fr. *e-* + *migrare* to depart, migrate — more at MIGRATE] **1 :** a person who leaves a country or region to establish permanent residence elsewhere; *esp* **:** a pioneer moving esp. during the 19th century from the settled lands of the eastern U.S. to unsettled lands to the west — compare IMMIGRANT **2 :** a plant or animal that is a migrant

2emigrant \"\ *adj* [L *emigrant-*, *emigrans*] **1 :** departing from a country or region to settle permanently elsewhere **2 :** of, relating to, concerned with, or for the use of emigrants ⟨~ cars⟩ ⟨~ agents⟩

em·i·grate \ˈeməˌgrāt, *usu* -ād·+V\ *vb* -ED/-ING/-S [L *emigratus*, past part. of *emigrare*] *vi* **:** to leave a place of abode (as a country) for life or residence elsewhere **:** be or behave as an emigrant — usu. used with *from* or *to* ⟨*emigrated* to Texas⟩ ⟨*emigrated* from England⟩ ~ *vt* **:** to cause, force, or help to emigrate

em·i·gra·tion \ˌeməˈgrāshən\ *n* -s [LL *emigration-*, *emigratio*, fr. L *emigratus* + *-ion-*, *-io* -ion] **1 :** an act or instance of emigrating **:** departure from a place of abode, natural home, or country for life or residence elsewhere ⟨several separate Oregon ~*s*⟩ ⟨considered the advantage of ~⟩ **2 :** a body of emigrants ⟨the ~ set out in early spring⟩ **3 :** DIAPEDESIS 1

em·i·gra·tion·al \ˌ==ˌgrāshənᵊl, -shnəl\ *adj* **:** concerned with emigration ⟨~ agencies⟩

em·i·gra·to·ry \ˈemə̇grəˌtōrē, -mēg-, -ȯr-, -ri\ *adj* **:** relating to or engaged in emigration; *usu* **:** MIGRATORY

émi·gré *or* **emi·gré** *also* **emi·gre** \ˌeməˌgrā, ˌām-, -mēˌ-\ *or* **emi·gree** \", ˌeməˌgrē\ *n* -s *often attrib* [F *émigré* (masc.) & *émigrée* (fem.), fr. past part. of *émigrer* to emigrate, fr. L *emigrare*] **:** EMIGRANT; *esp* **:** a person forced to emigrate (as from France or Russia during their revolutions or from Germany under the Nazis) by political or other circumstances beyond his control

emi·lia \ə̇ˈmēlyə, ēˈ-, -lēə *also* -mil-\ *n, cap* [NL, prob. fr. the name *Emilia*] **:** a genus of tropical Asiatic and African herbs (family Compositae) resembling *Senecio* but having a simple involucre and fruits with fine acute angles and being widely naturalized in So. America — see TASSEL FLOWER

emim \ˈēˌmim\ *n pl, usu cap* [Heb *ēmīm*, lit., terrible ones] **:** Rephaim orig. inhabiting Moab ⟨like the Anakim they are known as Rephaim, but the Moabites call them *Emim* —Deut 2:11 (RSV)⟩

em·i·nence \ˈemənən(t)s\ *n* -s [ME, fr. MF, fr. L *eminentia*, fr. *eminent-*, *eminens* + *-ia* -y] **1 :** a condition or station of prominence or superiority by reason of rank or office or of personal attainments ⟨her sons have attained the pinnacle of literary ~⟩ ⟨sent her climbing to ~ as an embezzler —R.T. Moriarty⟩ ⟨New York owes its ~ primarily to its natural advantages —Robert Moses⟩ ⟨the ~ of the presidency⟩ **2** *obs* **a :** superiority or superior quality; *esp* **:** UPPER HAND **b :** consideration due an eminent person **:** HOMAGE **3 :** something eminent, outstanding, or lofty: as **a :** a protuberance or projection esp. on a bone **b :** a person of high rank or attainments ⟨the theatrical ~*s* of New York⟩ ⟨a gathering of literary ~*s*⟩ — used as a title or in a mode of address usu. for a cardinal and then usu. cap. **c :** a natural elevation **:** a piece of high ground ⟨built his home on an ~ overlooking the city⟩ ⟨reached the ~ of the cliff⟩ **4 :** a dark purple that is bluer, stronger, and slightly lighter than average prune, redder and deeper than mulberry (sense 2a), redder and stronger than mulberry purple, and stronger than plum (sense 6b)

émi·nence grise \āmēnäⁿsəgrēz\ *n, pl* **éminences grises** \"\ [F, lit., gray eminence, nickname of Père Joseph (François Le Clerc du Tremblay) †1638 French monk and diplomat who was confidant of Cardinal Richelieu †1642 Fr. statesman and cardinal who was styled *Éminence Rouge* red eminence; fr. the colors of their respective habits] **:** a confidential agent; *esp* **:** one exercising unsuspected or unofficial power

em·i·nen·cy \ˈemənənsē, -si\ *n* -ES [L *eminentia*] **1 :** *obs* **:** EMINENCE **2 a :** a point in which one excels **:** FORTE ⟨his *eminencies* were kindness and understanding⟩ **b :** outstanding quality **:** PROMINENCE ⟨men of scientific ~⟩

em·i·nent \-nənt\ *adj* [ME, fr. MF or L; MF, fr. L *eminent-*, *eminens*, pres. part. of *eminēre* to stand out, be prominent, fr. *e-* + *-minēre* (akin to L *mont-*, *mons* mountain) — more at MOUNT] **1 :** standing out so as to be readily perceived or noted **:** CONSPICUOUS, EVIDENT, NOTEWORTHY ⟨his ~ services to the party⟩ ⟨a man of ~ fairness⟩ ⟨churches of ~ beauty⟩ **2 :** PROJECTING, PROTRUDING ⟨a house standing ~ near the top of a hill⟩; *sometimes* **:** LOFTY, TOWERING **3 :** exhibiting eminence esp. in standing above others in some quality or position (as birth, office, professional attainment, talent, or virtue) **:** high in public estimation **:** PROMINENT, OUTSTANDING ⟨the ~ conductor of the civic orchestra⟩ ⟨a man ~ in scholarship⟩ ⟨several of our most ~ military authorities⟩ **4** *obs* **:** IMPORTANT, VALUABLE **5** *of a geologic cleavage* **:** capable of complete or perfect division (as into layers)

eminent domain *n* **1 :** superior dominion exerted by a sovereign state over all property within its boundaries that authorizes it to appropriate all or any part thereof to a necessary public use, reasonable compensation being made **2 :** a right wider than angary sometimes considered to exist in international law for one nation to appropriate the territory or property of another as a necessary measure of self-protection

em·i·nen·ter \ˌeməˈnentə(r), ˌāməˈnenˌte(ə)r\ *adv* [LL, adv. fr. *eminent-*, *eminens*] **:** EMINENTLY 3

em·i·nen·tia \ˌeməˈnench(ē)ə\ *n* -s [NL, fr. L] **:** EMINENCE 3a

emi·nen·tis·si·mo \ˌeməˌnen·ˈtisəˌmō, ˌām-, -tēs-\ *n* -s [It, fr. superl. (used as a title for cardinals) of *eminente* eminent, fr. L *eminent-*, *eminens*] **:** a person of superlative eminence

em·i·nent·ly \ˈemənəntlē, -li\ *adv* [ME, fr. *eminent* + *-ly*] **1** *obs* **:** in a high or conspicuous position **:** so as to be readily observed **2 :** to a high degree **:** NOTABLY, EXTREMELY, VERY ⟨an ~ competent workman⟩ ⟨~ practical studies⟩ ⟨did an ~ satisfactory job⟩ ⟨an ~ pleasing state of affairs⟩; *sometimes* **:** WHOLLY, COMPLETELY ⟨a man ~ sane and competent⟩ **3** *philos* **:** in a manner reflecting an overplus of reality or of power

emi·nen·to \ˌemə'nen·ˌtō\ *n* -s [modif. of It *eminente*] **:** an eminent person

e minor *n, usu cap E* **:** the minor musical key having a signature of one sharp

emir *or* **amir** *also* **ameer** *or* **emeer** \ə'mi(ə)r, (')ā¦m-\ *n* -s [Ar *amīr* commander] **:** a nobleman, independent chieftain, or native ruler esp. in Arabia and Africa — often used as a title ⟨the *Emir* of Kano attended the coronation of Elizabeth II⟩

emir·ate *or* **amir·ate** *also* **ameer·ate** *or* **emeer·ate** \ə'mirət, ā'm-, -ˌrāt\ *n* -s **:** the state or jurisdiction of an emir

em·is·sar·i·um \ˌemə'sa(a)rēəm\ *n, pl* **emissar·ia** \-ēə\ [L, fr. *emissus* (past part. of *emittere* to send out) + *-arium* — more at EMIT] **:** a subterranean channel used by the ancient Romans for the drainage of a lake lacking a natural outlet

¹em·is·sary \'eməˌserē, -ri\ *n* -ES [L *emissarius,* fr. *emissus* + *-arius* -ary] **1 a :** an agent or representative usu. empowered to act more or less independently (as in collecting or conveying information or in negotiating) ⟨sent a special ~ to discuss possible peace terms⟩ ⟨acted as the president's personal ~ to the union leaders⟩ **b :** a spy or other undercover agent ⟨was reported to be nothing but a Communist ~⟩ **c :** MESSENGER ⟨sent an ~ backstage to order quiet⟩ **2 a** *archaic* **:** an outlet esp. of a lake or river **b** *obs* **:** an emissary duct or vessel

²emissary \"\ *adj* **1** *obs* **:** relating to or acting as an emissary **2 :** leading outward — used esp. of certain veins that pass through apertures in the skull and connect the venous sinuses of the dura mater with veins external to the skull

emis·sile \ē'misəl, ə'-\ *adj* [L *emissus* + E *-ile*] *archaic* **:** capable of being protruded — used esp. of the oral structures of certain worms

emis·sion \ē'mishən, ə'-\ *n* -s [L *emission-, emissio,* fr. *emissus* + *-ion-, -io* -ion] **1** *obs* **:** an act of sending forth (as on a mission) **2 a :** an act or instance of emitting (as heat or light) **:** EMANATION ⟨the ~ of the sun's rays⟩ ⟨slow ~ of warmth from a banked fire⟩ **b :** a putting into circulation (as of a coinage) ⟨the ~ of bank notes unbacked by specie⟩ **c** *archaic* **:** publication esp. of a writing **d :** a flow of electrons out of the heated filament or cathode of an electron tube **3 a :** something that is sent forth by or as if by emitting **:** a discharge esp. of electrons **b** (1) **:** a discharge of fluid from the living body (2) **:** EJACULATE 1 — called also *emissio seminis* **c :** EFFLUVIUM, EMANATION ⟨any ~ from the person of the medium such as ectoplasm or odor⟩ ⟨an evil-smelling sticky ~ from the cut surface⟩

emission spectrum *n* **:** an electromagnetic spectrum that derives its characteristics from the material of which the emitting source is made and from the way in which the material is excited — compare ABSORPTION SPECTRUM

emis·sive \-isiv\ *adj* [L *emissus* + E *-ive*] **1 :** sending out **:** EMITTING **2 :** sent out **:** EMITTED

emissive power *n* **:** the energy of thermal radiation emitted in all directions per unit time from each unit area of a surface at any given temperature

emis·siv·i·ty \ˌemə'sivəd·ē, ˌēm-, -(ˌ)mi's-\ *n* -ES **:** the relative emissive power of a radiating surface expressed as a fraction of the emissive power of a black-body radiator at the same temperature

emit \ē'mit, ə'-, *usu* -id·+V\ *vb* **emitted; emitted; emitting; emits** [L *emittere,* fr. *e-* + *mittere* to send — more at SMITE] *vt* **1 :** to send out **:** DISCHARGE, RELEASE: as **a :** to throw or give off or out (as effluvia, light, heat, gases, or charged particles) ⟨a fire *emitting* heat and smoke⟩ ⟨gamma rays may continue to be *emitted* for years⟩ **b :** EJECT, EXUDE, LOOSE ⟨some puffballs ~ myriads of spores⟩ ⟨aphids ~ a sweet fluid attractive to ants⟩ ⟨a cloudy sky *emitting* occasional drops of rain⟩ **c :** TRANSMIT 2b **2 a :** to cause to be issued (as an order or decree); *esp* **:** to put (as money or bills) into circulation **b** *obs* **:** PUBLISH **3 a :** to give utterance to (as words, ideas, or emotions) **:** EXPRESS ⟨they *emitted* constant complaints over the lack of conveniences⟩ ⟨*emitting* a stream of angry words⟩ ⟨in this book she ~*s* her inmost thoughts concisely and lucidly⟩ **b :** to give voice to (sound) ⟨the cricket *emitting* his shrill chirp⟩ ⟨sound cannot be *emitted* in a complete vacuum⟩ ~ *vi* **:** to come forth **:** ISSUE ⟨a sharp odor *emitting* from a broken gas line⟩

syn EMIT, EXUDE, OOZE, VENT, EXHALE, and REEK agree in meaning to discharge something such as moisture, vapor, or fumes. EMIT is the most inclusive in carrying the base meaning ⟨a small hose *emitting* a dribble of water⟩ ⟨a chimney *emitting* smoke⟩ ⟨to *emit* a groan⟩ ⟨to *emit* a stench⟩ ⟨a boat *emitting* a stream of passengers⟩ EXUDE usu. implies an emitting (as of a liquid) through pores, interstices, cracks, and so on, or an action resembling this ⟨to *exude* a cold perspiration⟩ ⟨the resin is made plastic and *exuded* through a nozzle —J.C.Tarr⟩ ⟨to *exude* confidence —*Newsweek*⟩ ⟨sickened at the evil that a crocodile seems to *exude* —F. Tennyson Jesse⟩ OOZE implies a slow passing (as of a liquid or of gas) through pores or interstices, or a slowness of movement suggesting this ⟨the steam *oozing* out of the leaky joints —C.S.Forester⟩ ⟨the dirt *oozes* out between the flags of the floor —Donat O'Donnell⟩ ⟨a trickle of blood *oozing* down his face —F.V.W.Mason⟩ VENT implies discharge through a relatively small outlet; it stresses the idea of release of what presses for release from within ⟨an exhaust pipe *venting* a blue smoke⟩ ⟨a factory outlet *vents* warm water into the Miami river —G.X.Sand⟩ ⟨the Norman woman would not dare *vent* her hatred on him —T.B. Costain⟩ ⟨*vented* an impatient snort —Cameron Hawley⟩ EXHALE implies a breathing out, often of something delicate or subtle ⟨the pans . . . *exhaled* a sulphurous stench —T.B. Macaulay⟩ ⟨their wet macintoshes . . . *exhaled* a smell of rubber —Rebecca West⟩ ⟨she *exhaled* a style and distinction of her own —Osbert Sitwell⟩ REEK stresses the emission of smoke, fumes, or strong odors, esp. offensive ones ⟨a pipe along a barge was gasping and *reeking* —Frederick Way⟩ ⟨the players, *reeking* of dirt and sweat —J.J.Godwin⟩ ⟨the waiter, a man, was *reeking* with rose water or musk —Ralph Knight⟩

emit·tance \-it^ən(t)s\ *n* -s **:** EMISSIVITY

emittent *adj* [L *emittent-, emittens,* pres. part. of *emittere*] *obs* **:** EMISSIVE

emit·ter \-id·ə(r), -itə-\ *n* -s **:** one that emits; *often* **:** a substance or electrode that emits particles ⟨radium is an alpha ~⟩ ⟨thermionic ~*s*⟩

em·ma \'emə\ *usu cap* [fr. Brit. signalmen's pron. of *M* (as in A.M.)] — a communications code word for the letter *m* — see ACK EMMA, PIP EMMA

em·marble \e, ə+\ *also* **en·marble** \en, ən+\ *or* **im·marble** \ə+\ *vt* [¹*en-* or ²*in-* + *marble* (n.)] **1 :** to change into or embody in marble **2 :** to make like marble

em·marvel \e, ə+\ *vt* [¹*en-* + *marvel*] *archaic* **:** to cause to marvel

em·me·leia \ˌemə'līə\ *n* -s [Gk, lit., harmony, fr. *emmelēs* harmonious, suitable + *-ia* -y] **:** a solemn and stately dance used in ancient Greek tragedy

em·men·a·gog·ic \ə¦menə¦gäjik, (ˌ)e,=ˈ==, -mēn-, -ägik\ *adj* **:** acting as an emmenagogue **:** promoting menstruation

¹em·men·a·gogue \=ˈ==,gäg\ *adj* [Gk *emmēna* menses (fr. neut. pl. of *emmēnos* monthly, fr. *em-* ²*en-* + *mēn* month) + E *-agogue* (fr. LL *-agogus* promoting the expulsion of) — more at MOON, *-agogue*] **:** EMMENAGOGIC

²emmenagogue \"\ *n* -s **:** an agent that promotes the menstrual discharge

em·men·ta·ler *or* **em·men·tha·ler** \'emən,tälə(r)\ *or* **em·men·tal** *or* **em·men·thal** \-äl\ *or* **emmentaler cheese** *or* **emmenthaler cheese** *n* -s *usu cap E* [G *Emmentaler* (formerly spelled *Emmenthaler*) *käse,* lit., Emmental cheese, fr. Emmental, region in Switzerland] **:** SWISS CHEESE

em·mer \'emə(r)\ *n* -s [G, fr. OHG *amari* — more at YELLOWHAMMER] **:** a hard red wheat (*Triticum dicoccum*) having spikelets with two kernels that remain in the glumes after threshing and being grown in several varieties in Russia and Germany and to a limited extent in the U.S. as a stock feed; *broadly* **:** any tetraploid wheat — compare SPELT

em·met \'emət\ *n* -s *now chiefly dial* [ME *emete* — more at ANT] **:** ANT

em·me·trope \'emə·ˌtrōp\ *n* -s [ISV *emmetr-* (fr. Gk *emmetros* in measure, proportioned, suitable) + *-ope*] **:** a person having emmetropic eyes

em·me·tro·pia \ˌemə'trōpēə\ *n* -s [NL, fr. Gk *emmetros* + NL *-opia*] **:** the normal refractive condition of the eye in which with accommodation relaxed parallel rays of light are all brought accurately to a focus upon the retina — distinguished from *astigmatism* and *myopia*

em·me·trop·ic \¦==¦träpik, -rōp-\ *adj, of the eye* **:** having normal refraction **:** exhibiting emmetropia

em·mons·ite \'emən,zīt\ *n* -s [Samuel F. *Emmons* †1911 Am. geologist + E *-ite*] **:** a mineral $Fe_2Te_3O_9.2H_2O$ consisting of a hydrous oxide of iron and tellurium

em·my \'emē, -mi\ *n, pl* **emmys** *or* **emmies** *usu cap* [fr. alter. of *Immy,* nickname for *Image Orthicon*] **:** a statuette awarded annually by a professional society for outstanding cultural, educational, or technological achievement in television

an Emmy

em·o·din \'emədən, -d^ən\ *n* -s [ISV *emodi-* (fr. NL *emodi,* specific epithet of *Rheum emodi*) + *-in*] **:** an orange crystalline phenolic compound $C_{14}H_4O_2(OH)_3CH_3$ derived from anthraquinone and obtained esp. from plants (as rhubarb, cascara buckthorn, and senna) yielding cathartic substances — called also *frangula emodin*

emol·li·ate \ə'mälē,āt, ē'-\ *vt* -ED/-ING/-S [L *emollire* to soften + E *-ate*] **:** to make weak, ineffective, or effeminate

emol·lience \-lyən(t)s, -lēə-\ *n* -s **:** the quality or state of being emollient

¹emol·lient \-nt\ *adj* [L *emollient-, emolliens,* pres. part. of *emollire* to soften, fr. *e-* + *mollire* to soften, fr. *mollis* soft — more at MELT] **:** making soft or supple; *also* **:** soothing esp. to the skin or mucous membrane ⟨an ~ cream for the hands⟩ ⟨an ~ preparation to apply to the membranes of the nose⟩ **:** MOLLIFYING ⟨soothe us in our agonies with ~ words —H.L.Mencken⟩ ⟨had an ~ effect on the man's exasperation⟩

²emollient \"\ *n* -s **:** an emollient agent ⟨an ~ added to a rubber compound to give pliability⟩ ⟨an ~ for the hands⟩

emollition *n* -s [L *emollitus* (past part. of *emollire*) + E *-ion*] *obs* **:** the act, process, or effect of softening

emo·loa \ˌāmə'lōə, ˌem-\ *n* -s [Hawaiian] **:** a rough tufted tall Hawaiian grass (*Eragrostis variabilis*)

emol·u·ment \ə'mälyəmənt, ē'-\ *n* -s [ME, fr. L *emolumentum* profit, gain, lit., sum paid to have grain ground up, fr. *emolere* to grind up (fr. *e-* + *molere* to grind) + *-mentum* -ment — more at MEAL] **1 :** profit or perquisites from office, employment, or labor **:** FEES, SALARY ⟨~ in the form of a wage and tips⟩ ⟨a goose . . . raised to the dignity and ~*s* of a household pet, and carried about in a basket —Agnes Repplier⟩; *also* **:** COMPENSATION ⟨was telling this sympathetic American all about how the coup d'etat had been pulled off, and what territorial ~*s* had been promised his native land —Upton Sinclair⟩ **2** *archaic* **:** ADVANTAGE, BENEFIT ⟨the idol of the people . . . how surprisingly he exerted himself for the ~, convenience, and pleasure of his fellow-citizens —Tobias Smollett⟩ **syn** see WAGE

em·o·ny \'emənē\ *n* -ES [by shortening & alter. (resulting from incorrect word division of *anemone,* taken as *an emone*)] *dial Eng* **:** ANEMONE

em·o·ry oak \'em(ə)rē-\ *n, usu cap E* [after W.H.*Emory* †1887 Am. soldier and engineer] **:** a low shrubby black oak (*Quercus emoryi*) of the southwestern U.S. with evergreen leaves and very heavy wood

emote \ə'mōt, ē'-, *usu* -ōd·+V\ *vi* -ED/-ING/-S [back-formation fr. *emotion*] **:** to give expression to emotion ⟨June is the month when more Americans ~ than at any other time of year —E.A.Weeks⟩ ⟨knowledge about how man ~*s* and about what structures in the brain and what physiological devices therein produce emotions —*Jour. Amer. Med. Assoc.*⟩ esp. in or as if in a play or movie ⟨the producers, realizing that picture audiences unconsciously yearn for a little more expression than is common on the lacquered faces of the contemporary screen stars, make Miss Swanson ~ with a physical abandon —H.E.Clurman⟩ often falsely or in a manner befitting a ham actor ⟨but more often she assaults her readers with rhetoric . . . ~*s,* postures, harangues —*Time*⟩

emot·er \-d·ə(r), -tə-\ *n* -s **:** one that emotes

emo·tion \ə'mōshən, ē'-\ *n* -s [MF, fr. *emouvoir* to start out, incite, stir up (after MF *mouvoir* to move: *motion*), fr. OF *esmovoir,* fr. L *exmovēre, emovēre* to move out, move away, fr. *ex-* ¹ex-, *e-* + *movēre* to move — more at MOVE] **1 a** *obs* **:** a physical or social agitation, disturbance, or tumultuous movement **b :** turmoil or agitation in feeling or sensibility ⟨the nerveless dreamer, who spends his life in a weltering sea of sensibility and ~ —William James⟩ ⟨love between men and women . . . is such a hot, stupid, middling thing, all ~ and no thought —Rose Macaulay⟩ **c :** a physiological departure from homeostasis that is subjectively experienced in strong feeling (as of love, hate, desire, or fear) and manifests itself in neuromuscular, respiratory, cardiovascular, hormonal, and other bodily changes preparatory to overt acts which may or may not be performed — often used in pl. ⟨how can I describe my ~*s* at this catastrophe —Mary W. Shelley⟩ **d :** an instance of such a turmoil or agitation in feeling or sensibility **:** state of strong feeling (as of fear, anger, disgust, grief, joy, or surprise) ⟨he felt a sudden rage but quickly controlled the ~⟩ ⟨overcome with the ~ of grief when he heard of his friend's death⟩ ⟨the girl hardly knew what love was since she had never before experienced so tender an ~⟩ **2 a :** the affective aspect of consciousness **:** FEELING ⟨we are not men of reason, we are creatures of ~ —C.C.Furnas⟩ **b :** a reaction of or effect upon this aspect of consciousness ⟨the essential ~ of the play is the feeling of a son toward a guilty mother —T.S.Eliot⟩ ⟨the ~ of beauty, like all our emotions, is certainly the inherited product of unimaginably countless experiences in an immeasurable past —P.E.More⟩ ⟨reason rather than ~ forms the main basis for his marriage —Nellie Maher⟩ ⟨the mind must have its share in deciding these important matters, not merely the ~*s* and desires —Rose Macaulay⟩ **3 :** the quality (as of a song or painting) that arouses an emotion, esp. a pleasant one ⟨the melody of the song voices the ~, the appeal —Anatole Chujoy⟩ **4 :** an expression of feeling, esp. strong feeling ⟨the king moves anonymously among his men . . . listening to their ~*s* about the war —Delmore Schwartz⟩ **syn** see FEELING

emo·tion·able \-sh(ə)nəbəl\ *adj* **:** capable of being moved by feeling

emo·tion·al \-shən^əl, -shnəl\ *adj* **1 :** of or relating to emotion, esp. to more than usual emotion: as **a :** dominated chiefly by emotion ⟨a highly ~ condition of mind⟩ **b :** expressing more than usual emotion ⟨~ language used in the heat of argument⟩ ⟨an ~ expression of friendship⟩ **c :** prone to arousal of the emotions ⟨he is intensely ~, is sometimes moved to tears by the pathos of his own words —*Time*⟩ **d :** motivated chiefly by the emotions as opposed to the intellect ⟨an ~ act⟩ ⟨an ~ drive⟩ **:** largely lacking a rational justification ⟨an ~ judgment⟩ **e :** appealing to or arousing the emotions ⟨~ art⟩ **f :** involving emotion ⟨verbal rather than ~ acceptance of social precepts —M.S.Gurvitz⟩ **g :** having particular impact or bearing upon the emotions ⟨the ~ shock of war⟩ ⟨~ security⟩ **2 :** markedly aroused or agitated in feeling or sensibilities ⟨he has been known to get ~ over a . . . piece of costume jewelry —*Time*⟩ — **emo·tion·al·ly** \-^əlē, -əlē, -li\ *adv*

emotional insanity *n* **:** PSYCHOPATHIC PERSONALITY

emo·tion·al·ism \-shən^əl,izəm, -shnə,lizəm\ *n* -s **1 a :** undue indulgence in or display of emotions ⟨it is . . . not a curtsy to sentimentality, not a maudlin ~ —C.S.Kilby⟩ **b :** a disposition to indulge in or display emotion unduly ⟨the ~ of adolescent girls⟩ **2 a :** a tendency to regard things emotionally or to respond emotionally as opposed to rationally ⟨a critic whose judgments are marked by ~⟩ **b :** a tendency to overvalue the emotions esp. as expressed in the arts ⟨the romantic ~ characteristic of much early 19th century writing⟩

emo·tion·al·ist \-shən^əlәst, -shnəl-\ *n* -s **1 :** one that tends to rely upon emotion as opposed to reason; *esp* **:** one who bases a theory or policy (as in artistic matters) upon an emotional conviction or justifies it by setting up a certain emotional condition as its end **2 :** one given to emotionalism ⟨an austere and rational way of life hardly palatable to an ~⟩ — **emo·tion·al·is·tic** \=¦mōshən^əl¦istik, -shnə¦li-, -tēk\ *adj*

emo·tion·al·i·ty \=ˌmōshə'naləd·ē, -ətē, -i\ *n* -ES **:** the quality or state of being emotional esp. unduly emotional ⟨the ~ inspired by barefoot soldiers —N.W.Stephenson & H.W.H.Knott⟩

emo·tion·al·ize \=ˈmōshən^əl,īz, -shnə,līz\ *vt* -ED/-ING/-S **:** to make emotional: as **a :** to express in a way that arouses emotion ⟨concerned to get his idea across, not to ~ it —Edith Hamilton⟩ **b :** to place in inseparable association with feeling ⟨the birth of his son affected him little until some years later when it suddenly in memory became a highly *emotionalized* experience⟩ **c :** to cause to react emotionally ⟨the various devices of humor furnish convenient ways of *emotionalizing* an audience —A.T.Weaver⟩ **:** cause to be moved or dominated by emotion ⟨trying to handle an extremely *emotionalized* woman⟩ **d :** to motivate by feeling ⟨this firm and highly *emotionalized* touch —F.J.Mather⟩ ~ *vi* **:** to express oneself in a way inspired by or expressive of emotion rather than reason **:** pour forth one's feeling esp. in a disordered way ⟨vagueness or confusion or loose *emotionalizing* —R.H.Pearce⟩

emo·tion·less \=ˈmōshənləs\ *adj* **:** unmoved by feeling ⟨he kept his ~ objectivity and his faith in the cause he served —Vincent Sheean⟩ **:** giving no evidence of emotion ⟨grimly lord of himself, he stood ~ before the world —George Meredith⟩ **:** expressing no emotion ⟨the colonel's words were short and ~ —*Infantry Jour.*⟩ — **emo·tion·less·ness** *n* -ES

emo·tive \ə'mōd·|iv, ē'-, -ōt|, |ēv *also* |əv\ *adj* [*emotion* + *-ive*] **1 :** marked by special bearing upon, reference to, or involvement with the emotions ⟨the ~ side of her nature⟩ ⟨an ~ concept of art⟩ ⟨~ associations⟩ **2 a :** evocative of or appealing to the emotions ⟨an ~ utterance⟩ ⟨the ~ use of language⟩; *esp* **:** HORTATORY **b :** expressive of feeling ⟨the rudimentary language of the lower animals seems to be purely ~ —Aldous Huxley⟩ — **emo·tive·ly** \|əvlē, -li\ *adv*

emotive theory *n* **:** a theory according to which value judgments or normative ethical statements are exhortatory rather than cognitive

emo·tiv·ism \|ə,vizəm, |ē,v-\ *n* -s **:** an emotive theory of ethics or the advocacy of such a theory — **emo·tiv·ist** \-,vəst\ *n* -s

emo·tiv·i·ty \ˌē(ˌ)mō'tivəd·ē, ə,mō, ē,mō-, -ətē, -i\ *n* -ES **:** the quality or state of being emotive ⟨a musical rendition marked by great ~⟩

emp *abbr* **1** emperor; empire; empress **2** employment

empale *var of* IMPALE

em·pa·na·da \ˌempə'nädə, -ä*th*ə\ *n* -s [AmerSp, fr. Sp, fem. of *empanado,* past part. of *empanar* to put a crust of dough around, fr. *em-* (fr. L, ¹en-) + *pan* bread, fr. L *panis* — more at FOOD] **:** a turnover filled with meat

empanel *var of* IMPANEL

em·panoply \əm, em+\ *vt* [¹*en-* + *panoply* (n.)] **:** to enclose in a full suit of armor

emparadise *var of* IMPARADISE

emparl *var of* IMPARL

em·pa·thet·ic \ˌempə¦thed·|ik, -et|, |ēk\ *adj* [fr. *empathy,* after such pairs as *sympathy: sympathetic*] **:** EMPATHIC — **em·pa·thet·i·cal·ly** \|ək(ə)lē, |ēk-, -li\ *adv*

em·path·ic \(')em¦pathik, əm'p-, -thēk\ *adj* **:** involving, characterized by, or based on empathy ⟨an ~ understanding of others⟩ — **em·path·i·cal·ly** \-thək(ə)lē, -thēk-, -li\ *adv*

em·pa·thize \'empə,thīz\ *vb* -ED/-ING/-S *vt* **:** to regard with empathy ~ *vi* **:** to experience empathy

em·pa·thy \'empəthē, -thi\ *n* -ES [²*en-* + *-pathy;* trans. of G *einfühlung*] **1 :** the imaginative projection of a subjective state whether affective, conative, or cognitive into an object so that the object appears to be infused with it **:** the reading of one's own state of mind or conation into an object (as an artistic object) ⟨without ~ an artistic emotion is purely intellectual and associative —W.H.Wright⟩ **2 :** the capacity for participating in or a vicarious experiencing of another's feelings, volitions, or ideas and sometimes another's movements to the point of executing bodily movements resembling his ⟨the goal of all reading is ~ with the content and the spirit of the material read —Stella Center⟩ ⟨an example of ~ is a feeding situation in which a fright experienced by the mother results in eating disturbances on the part of the child —G.S.Blum⟩ **syn** see SYMPATHY

empearl *var of* IMPEARL

¹em·ped·o·cle·an \əm¦pedə¦klēən, em-¦, em,==ˈ==\ *adj, usu cap* [*Empedocles,* 5th cent. B.C. Greek philosopher and statesman + E *-an*] **:** of, relating to, or befitting the philosopher Empedocles or his philosophy according to which change takes place through the uniting and dividing forces of love and hate upon the elements earth, air, fire, and water

²empedoclean \"\ *n* -s *usu cap* **:** one whose philosophy is Empedoclean

em·pei·ne \em'pā(ˌ)nā\ *n* -s [MexSp, fr. Sp, impetigo, fr. ML *impedigin-, impedigo,* alter. of L *impetigin-, impetigo* — more at IMPETIGO] **:** PINTID

em·pen·nage \¦ämpə¦näzh, ¦em-\ *n* -s [F, feathers of an arrow, empennage, fr. *empenner* to put feathers on an arrow (fr. *em-* ¹en- + *penne* feather, fr. L *pinna*) + *-age* — more at PEN] **:** the tail assembly of an aircraft

empeople *vt* [¹*en-* + *people* (n.)] *obs* **:** POPULATE, PEOPLE

em·per·or \'emp(ə)rə(r)\ *n* -s [ME *emperour,* fr. OF *empereor,* fr. L *imperator,* fr. *imperatus* (past part. of *imperare* to command, fr. *im-* ²in- + *-perare,* fr. *parare* to prepare, order) + *-or* — more at PARE] **1 :** the sovereign or supreme monarch of an empire ⟨George VI was the last British king to be called *Emperor* of India⟩ **2** *obs* **:** COMMANDER, IMPERATOR **3 :** the largest size of handmade paper, commonly 48×72 inches **4 :** EMPEROR BUTTERFLY **5 :** EMPEROR MOTH

emperor boa *n* **:** a Central American boa (*Constrictor constrictor imperator*)

emperor butterfly *n* **:** any of several large richly colored butterflies of the family Nymphalidae (as the purple emperor)

emperor fish *n* **:** a large brilliantly colored edible butterfly fish (*Holacanthus imperator*) of the Japanese seas

emperor goose *n* **:** a medium-sized goose (*Philacte canagica*) of the coast of Alaska and adjacent islands having ashen gray plumage barred with black and white, a white head and nape, black foreneck, and yellow-orange feet

emperor moth *n* **:** a moth of the family Saturniidae; *esp* **:** a large European moth (*Saturnia pavonia*)

emperor penguin *n* **:** the largest known penguin (*Aptenodytes forsteri*) occurring only south of the antarctic circle and noted for its habit of brooding the egg or young between the feet and a fold of abdominal skin resembling a pouch

em·pery \'emp(ə)rē, -ri\ *n* -ES [ME *emperie,* fr. OF, fr. *emperer* to command, fr. L *imperare*] **1 a** *obs* **:** the position or the dominion of an emperor **b** *archaic* **:** the territory of an emperor or of an absolute ruler **2 :** SOVEREIGNTY, EMPIRE; *also* **:** CONTROL, DOMINION

em·pest \əm, em+\ *vt* -ED/-ING/-S [¹*en-* + *pest* (n.)] **:** to infect with or as if with a contagion ⟨sleeping in an ~*ed* atmosphere —Aldous Huxley⟩

em·pe·tra·ce·ae \ˌempə'trāsē,ē\ *n pl, cap* [NL, fr. *Empetrum,* type genus + *-aceae*] **:** a small family of heathlike shrubs (order Sapindales), having small diclinous flowers and drupes that resemble berries — compare CROWBERRY 1a — **em·pe·tra·ceous** \¦==¦=shəs\ *adj*

em·pe·trum \'empə·trəm\ *n, cap* [NL, fr. Gk *empetron,* neut. of *empetros* growing on rock, fr. *em-* ²en- + *-petros* (fr. *petra* rock)] **:** a genus (the type of the family Empetraceae) of low shrubs having flowers scattered and solitary or few in the axils — see CROWBERRY

em·pha·sis \'em(p)fəsəs\ *n, pl* **empha·ses** \-fə,sēz\ [L, fr. Gk, exposition, significance, implied meaning, fr. *emphainein* to exhibit, display, indicate (fr. *em-* ²en- + *phainein* to show) + *-sis* — more at FANCY] **1 a :** a forcefulness of expression that gives special impressiveness, calls to special attention, or gives special significance ⟨writing with commendable ~ on the need for reform⟩ **b :** a particular prominence given in reading or speaking to one or more words or syllables (as by voice stress or pitch) to attract attention to or focus attention on their special emotional or logical importance (as when words or the things they represent are contrasted) ⟨the speaker's ~ was on the word *conciliation*⟩ **c :** stress or relative importance given to a certain part or feature of a literary work (as by its prominent position in the whole or its fullness of presentation) ⟨the biography gave considerable ~ to his early life⟩ **2** *obs* **:** an implied meaning in a word **3 a :** special consideration of or stress or insistence upon something ⟨his father's ~ had always been on discipline⟩ ⟨the ~ of the campaign was to be on the elimination of graft⟩ ⟨he disliked the school's ~ on classics —*Current Biog.*⟩ ⟨the first congress at which special ~ is laid on tropical forestry —Hilary Phillips⟩ **b :** something given such emphasis ⟨good citizenship, another chief ~ in the Camp Fire program —*Collier's Yr. Bk.*⟩ **4 :** PROMINENCE, DISTINCTNESS, VIVIDNESS ⟨the altering of the colors in the painting caused the main figure to lose all ~⟩

em·pha·size \ˈfə,sīz\ *vt* -ED/-ING/-S *see -ize in Explan Notes* [*emphasis* + *-ize*] **:** to give emphasis to or place emphasis upon **:** STRESS ⟨which is to be *emphasized* — morale or efficiency —W.H.Whyte⟩ ⟨I ~ that many of the figures quoted in the succeeding paragraphs . . . are little more than estimates —W.B. Fisher⟩ ⟨*emphasizing* the importance and desirability of fairness in the conduct of congressional investigations —J.D. Morris⟩ ⟨he had swung one knee above the other, *emphasizing* the trimness of his fur-topped boots —T.B.Costain⟩

em·phat·ic \əm'fad·ik, em'-, -at|, |ēk\ *adj* [Gk *emphatikos* forcible, expressive, var. of *emphantikos*, fr. (assumed) *emphantos* (verbal of Gk *emphainein*) + *-ikos* -ic] **1 a :** marked by emphasis **:** uttered with emphasis **:** made prominent by stress ⟨an ~ word⟩ ⟨an ~ argument⟩ **b :** commanding attention by prominence, forcefulness, or insistence ⟨even more ~ is the chapter . . . which comes out frankly for rescuing the Adirondack country from destruction at the hands of eager tourists —C.L.Carmer⟩ ⟨unfolding a still more vast and ~ display in blue and yellow —Dorothy L. Sayers⟩ ⟨this document, which may be termed New Jersey's first constitution, contained a particularly ~ guarantee of religious liberty —*Amer. Guide Series: N.J.*⟩ **c :** INSISTENT ⟨the point is one worth being rather ~ about —A.A.Hill⟩ **2 a :** tending to express oneself in emphatic speech or to take habitually brusque or decisive action ⟨a little ~ man —Charles Dickens⟩ ⟨I wish I were unflinching and ~, and had big, bushy eyebrows and a Message for the Age —L.P.Smith⟩ **b :** markedly forceful ⟨used an ~ blue pencil freely —W.L.McAtee⟩ **3 a :** attracting special attention **:** strikingly conspicuous ⟨some ~ feather or brooch —John Galsworthy⟩ ⟨government of the U.S. had been so commonly on dead center, with not even a party able to enact its wish, that its contrast to government by parliament and cabinet was ~ —F.L.Paxson⟩ **b :** clearly delineated **:** definite in outline or features ⟨the line of tall fir trees at the lake's edge casting their ~ shadows on the ice —Jean Stafford⟩ **4** *of a linguistic form* **:** expressive of special emphasis ⟨the ~ article in Samoan⟩; *esp* **:** constituting or belonging to a set of tense forms in English that consist of the auxiliary *do* followed by an infinitive without *to* and are used to facilitate rhetorical inversion (as *did see* in "only then did he see the danger"), to take the place of a simple verb form normally in negative or interrogative sentences (as *did believe* in "he did not believe it" or *do think* in "what do you think?"), or to emphasize (as *does work* in "but I tell you he does work hard") **5** *of some Semitic consonants* **:** differing from the other member of a pair through being velarized and alveolar rather than dental or being pharyngeal rather than velar — **em·phat·i·cal·ly** \|ək(ə)lē, |ēk-, -li\ *adv* — **em·phat·i·cal·ness** \|əkəlnəs, |ēk-\ *n* -ES

em·phat·i·cal \|əkəl, |ēk-\ *archaic var of* EMPHATIC

emphatic pronoun *n* **:** INTENSIVE PRONOUN

emphatic state *n* **:** the state or form of a noun in Syriac and Aramaic that makes it determinate or definite — compare ABSOLUTE STATE, CONSTRUCT STATE

em·phy·se·ma \,em(p)fə'zēmə, -'sē-\ *n* -S [NL, fr. Gk *emphysēma* inflation or swelling of a part of the body, fr. *emphysan* to inflate, fr. *em-* ²en- + *physan* to blow — more at FOG] **:** a condition characterized by air-filled expansions like blisters in interstitial or subcutaneous tissues; *specif* **:** a local or generalized condition of the lung marked by distention, progressive loss of elasticity, and eventual rupture of the alveoli and accompanied by labored breathing, a husky cough, and frequently by impairment of heart action

em·phy·sem·a·tous \¦==¦z|emədəs, ¦==¦s|, |ēm-\ *adj* [NL *emphysemat-*, *emphysema* + E *-ous*] *adj* **1 :** relating to, being, or resembling emphysema **:** SWELLED, BLOATED **2** *bot* **:** inflated like a bladder **:** BLADDERY

emphysematous anthrax *or* **emphysematous gangrene** *n* **:** BLACKLEG 1

em·phy·teu·sis \,em(p)fə'tüsəs, -fə·'tyü-\ *n, pl* **emphyteuses** \-ü,sēz\ [LL, fr. LGk, fr. Gk *emphyteuein* to implant (fr. *em-* ²en- + *phyteuein* to plant, fr. *phyton* plant) + *-sis* — more at PHYT-] **:** a Roman and civil law contract by which a grant is made of a right either perpetual or for a long period to the possession and enjoyment of orig. agricultural land subject to the keeping of the land in cultivation or from depreciation, the payment of a fixed annual rent, and some other conditions; *also* **:** the heritable and alienable right so granted or the tenure by which it is held

em·phy·teu·ta \-üd·ə\ *n, pl* **emphyteu·tae** \-d·,ē\ [LL, fr. LGk *emphyteutēs*, fr. Gk *emphyteuein*] **:** one holding land by emphyteusis

em·phy·teu·tic \¦==¦tüd·ik, ¦==¦tyü-\ *adj* [LL *emphyteuticus*, fr. *emphyteuta* + L *-icus* -ic] **:** being or in tenure by an emphyteusis

em·pid \'empəd\ *n* -S [NL *Empidae*] **:** one of the Empididae

em·pi·dae \'empə,dē\ [NL, fr. *Empis* + *-idae*] *syn of* EMPIDIDAE

em·pid·i·dae \em'pidə,dē\ *n pl, cap* [NL, fr. *Empid-*, *Empis*, type genus (fr. Gk *empid-*, *empis* mosquito, gnat) + *-idae*] **:** a large family of small predaceous brachycerous flies that fly in swarms with a dancing movement in the mating season, the males of many species courting the females with prey captured in silken balloons or webs produced from silk glands on their forelegs

em·pi·do·nax \,empə'dō,naks, em'pidə,naks\ *n, cap* [NL, irreg. fr. Gk *empid-*, *empis* + *anax* lord, master] **:** a genus of small olivaceous American flycatchers comprising several familiar birds (as the least flycatcher and the Acadian flycatcher)

em·piece·ment \əm'pēsmənt, em-\ *n* -S [¹*en-* + *piece* + *-ment*] **:** a piece of material inserted in a garment usu. as trimming or ornamentation

em·pierce \əm, em-+\ *vt* [¹*en-* + *pierce*] *archaic* **:** PIERCE, PENETRATE

¹em·pire \'em,pī(ə)r, -īə; *sense 4 &* ²EMPIRE *are more often* (')äm¦pi(ə)r *or* (')öm- *or* -iə\ *n* -S [ME, fr. OF *empire*, *empirie*, fr. L *imperium*, fr. *imperare* to command — more at EMPEROR] **1 a :** an extended territory usu. comprising a group of nations, states, or peoples under the control or domination of a single sovereign power: as (1) **:** a state comprising a dominating conquering people and the conquered people dominated ⟨the Babylonian ~⟩ ⟨the Aztec ~⟩ (2) **:** a state comprising a confederacy in which one strong member dominates its confederates or its confederates, conquests, and colonies ⟨the Athenian ~⟩ ⟨the Roman ~⟩ (3) **:** a state that has a great extent of territory and a great variety of peoples under one rule and often has a ruler with the title of emperor ⟨the former Japanese ~⟩ **b :** the territory or peoples under such control or domination ⟨the former large colonial ~ of Spain⟩ ⟨the colonial ~ proper numbers some 60,000,000 in Asia, America, and Africa —*New Republic*⟩ **c :** REALM, PROVINCE, TERRITORY ⟨fish in their watery ~⟩ ⟨the ~ of gnats and midges⟩ ⟨primarily an inland ~, Texas nevertheless has the third longest coastline of the States —*Amer. Guide Series: Texas*⟩ ⟨a whole ~ of enjoyment is yours to command —*N.Y.Times*⟩ **2 a :** supreme or absolute power esp. of an emperor **:** imperial dominion, sway, or sovereignty ⟨the problems of a colonial administration in retreat from ~ —*N.Y.Times Book Rev.*⟩ ⟨the first Ptolemies were consolidating their ~ over Egypt —Benjamin Farrington⟩ **b :** DOMINATION, CONTROL ⟨reckless revolt against the ~ of business and convention —E.K.Brown⟩ ⟨even as a child her ~ over her two sisters and her half-brothers . . . was complete —*Times Lit. Supp.*⟩ ⟨the ~ of strong emotion —C.W.Cunnington⟩ **3 :** an extended territory or an extensive enterprise or group of related enterprises dominated or significantly controlled by a single person, family, or group of interested persons ⟨a cattle ~ of several thousand acres⟩ ⟨a fabulous ~, with no strings attached, was given to the railroads, to encourage the construction of transportation facilities —J.E. Lawrence⟩ ⟨state officials . . . nor competitors had been able to halt the growth of his branch-banking ~ —*Newsweek*⟩ ⟨the breakup of the former . . . utilities ~ —*Wall Street Jour.*⟩ ⟨a motion-picture ~ that at one time included a leading film-producing company, hundreds of theaters, and a newsreel organization —*Americana Annual*⟩ ⟨one of the world's greatest industrialists, a man who created a billion-dollar ~ —Paul Marcus⟩ **4** *often cap* [²*empire*] **:** CADMIUM GREEN — distinguished from *Empire green* and *Empire blue*

²empire *see* ¹EMPIRE\ *adj, usu cap* [F *Empire*, fr. (*le premier*) *Empire*, the First Empire of France (1804–1814)] **:** of, relating to, or befitting the style popular in France in the early 19th century: as **a** *of clothing* **:** having the characteristics of the French Directoire style but usu. with richer fabrics, greater formality, and elaborate accessories **b** *of furniture* **:** characterized by classic and oriental motives, long curving lines, some carving, and ornamentation in brass and ivory — see DIRECTOIRE b

empire blue *n, often cap E* [²*empire*] **:** a moderate blue that is greener and duller than average copen or Dresden blue, redder and deeper than azurite blue, and redder and darker than pompadour

empire builder *n* **:** one whose aim or achievement is the formation of an empire: as **a :** one whose aim and activities are chiefly designed to and usu. do notably increase the territory of or controlled by a country or notably enhance a country's authority and dominion **b :** one whose aim and achievement is the extension of his control (as financial or political) over a large territory or an extensive enterprise or set of related enterprises

empire building *n* **:** the activities of an empire builder ⟨our forefathers were often too busy with *empire building* to worry about their souls⟩

empire cloth *n* **:** a cloth treated with oxidized oil for use as an electrical insulator

empire day *n, usu cap E&D* [fr. (*British*) *Empire*] **1 :** COMMONWEALTH DAY — used before the official adoption of *Commonwealth Day* in 1958 **2 :** formerly the last school day before Victoria Day in Canada commemorated by special patriotic observances in the schools

empire green *n, often cap E* [²*empire*] **:** a dark grayish green to dark yellowish green that is yellower than Danube green

empire red *n, often cap E* [²*empire*] **:** vermilion or a color resembling it

empire wine *n, usu cap E* [fr. (*British*) *Empire*] **:** a wine produced within the British Empire and shipped to England for sale

empire yellow *n, often cap E* [²*empire*] **:** a light to brilliant yellow that is lighter than orpiment

em·pir·ic \əm'pirik, em-, -rēk\ *n* -S [L *empiricus*, fr. Gk *empeirikos*, fr. *empeirikos* experienced, fr. *empeiros* (fr. *em-* ²en- + *-peiros*, fr. *peiran* to try, attempt, experiment) + *-ikos* -ic — more at FEAR] **1 a :** a member of an ancient sect of physicians who based their practice on experience alone disregarding all theoretical and philosophic considerations **b** *archaic* **:** one that in any walk of life disregards or deviates from the rules of science or accepted practice **:** QUACK, CHARLATAN **2 :** one who follows an empirical method **:** one who relies upon practical experience

em·pir·i·cal \əm'pirəkəl, (')em¦p-, -rēk-\ *or* **em·pir·ic** \-rik,-rēk\ *adj* **1** *archaic* **a :** following or used in the practice of the empirics **b :** relying on experience or observation alone without proper regard for considerations of system, science, and theory **c :** being or befitting a quack or charlatan **2 a :** originating in or relying or based on factual information, observation, or direct sense experience usu. as opposed to theoretical knowledge ⟨~ law⟩ ⟨an ~ equation⟩ ⟨an ~ basis for an ethical theory⟩; *also* **:** relying on or proceeding on the information to be derived from experience and observation for lack of other knowledge **:** proceeding strictly experimentally or by the trial and error method ⟨an ~ treatment of a disease about which little is known⟩ ⟨much medical lore had had an ~ origin . . . centuries of trial-and-error gropings after remedies —R.H.Shryock⟩ ⟨agriculture from its primitive beginnings has been an individualistic, unorganized, ~ business —*Yrbk. of Agriculture*⟩ **b :** EXPERIENTIAL; *broadly* **:** OBSERVATIONAL, FACTUAL ⟨~ data⟩ ⟨the psychoanalysts have had no trouble in finding ~ confirmation for their theories —H.M.Parshley⟩ ⟨an immense mass of evidence, gathered by ~ investigation —*Newsweek*⟩ **3 :** capable of being confirmed, verified, or disproved by observation or experiment ⟨~ statements or laws⟩ — **em·pir·i·cal·ly** \-rək(ə)lē, -rēk, -li\ *adv* — **em·pir·i·cal·ness** \-rəkəlnəs, -rēk-\ *n* -ES

empirical formula *n* **:** a chemical formula based on analysis but not on molecular weight and showing merely the simplest ratio of elements in a compound rather than the total number of atoms in the molecule ⟨CH_2O is the *empirical formula* of formaldehyde, acetic acid, methyl formate, and glucose⟩ — compare MOLECULAR FORMULA

empirical truth *n* **:** exact conformity as learned by observation or experiment between judgments or propositions and externally existent things in their actual status and relations — called also *actual truth, contingent truth*

em·pir·i·cism \əm'pirə,sizəm, em-\ *n* -S **1 a :** a former school of medical practice founded on experience without the aid of science or theory **b :** QUACKERY, CHARLATANRY **2 a :** the practice of emphasizing experience esp. of the senses or the practice or method of relying upon observation, experimentation, or induction rather than upon intuition, speculation, deduction, dialectic, or other rationalistic means in the pursuit of knowledge ⟨most research into forecasting over the past forty years has been directed at avoiding ~ and replacing it with some sort of theory —B.W.Atkinson⟩ **b :** a tenet arrived at empirically **3 a :** the theory associated esp. with the British philosophers John Locke, George Berkeley, and David Hume that all knowledge originates in experience **b :** logical empiricism, radical empiricism, or scientific empiricism — compare PHENOMENALISM, POSITIVISM, PRAGMATISM, SENSATIONALISM

em·pir·i·cist \-səst\ *n* -S **:** one that advocates or practices empiricism **:** EMPIRIC ⟨remained a stubborn ~, one whose theories were always open to revision in the light of fresh experience —*Times Lit. Supp.*⟩

em·pir·ics \-'piriks\ *n pl but sing in constr* **:** empirical practices or beliefs; *broadly* **:** the science of empirics

empirio- *also* **empirico-** *comb form* [*empirio-* fr. G, fr. Gk *empeiria* experience (fr. *empeiros* experienced + *-ia* -y) + G *-o-*; *empirico-* fr. *empiric*, adj. + *-o-*] **1 :** experience **:** experiment ⟨*empirio*genic⟩ ⟨*empirio*symbolist⟩ **2 :** empirical and ⟨*empirico*inductive⟩

em·pir·io·critical \əm¦pirē(,)ō, em-+\ *adj* [*empirio-* + *critical*] **:** of, relating to, or advocating empiriocriticism

em·pir·io·criticism \"+\ *n* [part trans. of G *empiriokritizismus*, fr. *empirio-* + *kritizismus* criticism] **:** a scientifically oriented phenomenalistic form of empiricism that endeavors to reduce knowledge to a description of pure experience and eliminate all aspects of apriorism, metaphysics, and dualism

em·pir·io·logical \"+\ *adj* [F *empiriologique*, fr. *empirio-* + *logique* logical, fr. L *logicus* — more at LOGICAL] **:** emphasizing or based on procedures that are both logical and empirical (as those employing mathematics and experiments) ⟨~ in contrast to ontological methods⟩

em·pi·rism \'empə,rizəm\ *n* -S [*empiric* + *-ism*] **:** EMPIRICISM 2, 3 — **em·pi·ris·tic** \¦==¦ristik\ *adj*

em·place \əm'plās, em-\ *vt* [back-formation fr. *emplacement*] **:** to put into position ⟨where thick glacial deposits were *emplaced* by ice moving —W.R.Hansen⟩ ⟨the deeply *emplaced*, presbytic eyes, peering out from under the dark brows —A.J.Liebling⟩ ⟨two artificial harbors to be *emplaced* off the beaches —G.C.Marshall⟩ ⟨a smooth sea enabled us to get more troops ashore and to ~ some artillery —*Time*⟩ ⟨an area where the annoying guns were evidently thought to be *emplaced* —E.J.Kahn⟩

em·place·ment \-smənt\ *n* [F, fr. obs. F *emplacer* to put in place (fr. MF, fr. *em-* ¹en- + *place*) + F *-ment* — more at PLACE] **1 :** the situation or location of something (as of a building) ⟨a pile of embers marking the ~ of the fort and the little village —*Amer. Guide Series: Mich.*⟩ ⟨the clue to the genesis of the continents must lie in the origin and ~ of granite —C.M.Nevin⟩ ⟨took his flock of llamas to a sheltered ~ . . . for the night —*Springfield (Mass.) Union*⟩ **2 :** a prepared position for weapons (as a gun or group of guns) or military equipment from which they can operate effectively ⟨a concealed gun ~⟩ **3** [*emplace* + *-ment*] **:** a putting into position **:** PLACEMENT ⟨~ of the panels on the steel frames of the buildings involves little more than lifting the panels into position and inserting bolts —*Civil Engineering*⟩ ⟨the ore ~ has been chiefly by cavity filling —A.M.Bateman⟩

emplane *var of* ENPLANE

emplant *var of* IMPLANT

¹em·plas·tic \(')em¦plastik, əm'p-\ *adj* [Gk *emplastikos*, fr. *emplastos* (verbal of *emplassein* to plaster up, make stick, fr. *em-* ²en- + *plassein* to mold, form, plaster — more at PLASTER] **:** ADHESIVE

²emplastic \"\ *n* **:** an emplastic substance

emplead *archaic var of* IMPLEAD

em·plec·tite \əm'plek,tīt, em-\ *n* -S [G *emplektit*, fr. Gk *emplektos* inwoven + G *-it* -ite] **:** a grayish or white metallic-looking mineral consisting of a compound of copper, bismuth, and sulfur $CuBiS_2$ occurring in thin prisms

em·ple·o·ma·nia \,emplēō'mānēə, em,plēə'-\ *n* [Sp *empleomanía*, fr. *empleo* employment, use, public office (fr. *emplear* to employ, use, fr. OSp, fr. OF *empleoir*, *emploiier*) + *-mania* (fr. NL *-mania*)] **:** a mania for holding public office

¹em·ploy \əm'plȯi, em-\ *vt* -ED/-ING/-S [ME *emploien*, fr. MF *emploier* fr. OF *empleoir*, *emploiier*, fr. L *implicare* to infold, involve, implicate, engage, fr. *in-* ²in- + *plicare* to fold — more at PLY] **1 a :** to make use of ⟨~ a pen for sketching⟩ ⟨~ metal girders in building construction⟩ ⟨~ questionable methods in business⟩ ⟨craftsmen were finding in the new land raw materials on which they could ~ all their artistry —*Amer. Guide Series: Pa.*⟩ ⟨atomic energy could be ~*ed* for military purposes —*Current Biog.*⟩ ⟨office buildings are beginning to ~ whole banks of elevators which . . . run without operators or starters —John Lear⟩ **b :** to use or occupy (as time) advantageously ⟨~ your leisure in reading⟩ ⟨possible fields where the capacities and interests of the student might best be ~*ed* —Bates Boyle⟩ **c :** to use or engage the services of ⟨~ a lawyer to straighten out a legal tangle⟩; *also* **:** to provide with a job that pays wages or a salary or with a means of earning a living ⟨he is ~*ed* by a local plumbing concern⟩ **d :** to devote to or direct toward a particular activity or person ⟨~ all his talent to the creation of frivolities⟩ ⟨all his caddishness was ~*ed* against her —J.F.Gore⟩ **e :** OCCUPY, BUSY ⟨~ oneself in charitable activities⟩ ⟨~ the child at cutting out paper dolls⟩ **2** *obs* **a :** COMPRISE, INCLUDE, ENCLOSE **b :** SIGNIFY, IMPLY **3** *obs* **:** to dispatch (a person) with a commission **syn** see USE

²employ \" *sometimes* 'em,p-\ *n* -S **1** *archaic* **a :** something on which one is employed or with which he is occupied; *also* **:** USE, PURPOSE ⟨that war chest . . . which had been accumulated by the late king for the proposed Spanish war, and which had now no ~ —Hilaire Belloc⟩ **b :** BUSINESS, OCCUPATION, TRADE, PROFESSION **2 :** the state of being employed esp. for wages or a salary by someone or something (as an employer or a business firm) ⟨in the ~ of a trucking company⟩ ⟨professors of science, though not actually in the government's ~ —Waldemar Kaempffert⟩ **3** *archaic* **:** an official public position

em·ploy·abil·i·ty \əm,plȯiə'biləd·ē, (,)em-, -ətē, -i\ *n* -ES **:** the quality or state of being employable

em·ploy·able \əm'plȯiəbəl, em-\ *adj* **:** capable of being employed; *specif* **:** physically and mentally capable of earning a wage at a regular job and available for hiring

em·ploy·ee *or* **em·ploye** \əm,plȯ(i)'ē, (,)em,=ˈ=, əm'plȯi(,)ē, -'plȯ,ē, -'plȯi, em'=(,)=, *sometimes* (,)äm- *or* -ȯi'ä *or* -ȯi(,)ä\ *n* -S [F *employé*, fr. past part. of *employer* to employ, fr. OF *empleoir*, *emploiier*] **1 :** one employed by another usu. in a position below the executive level and usu. for wages **2** *in labor relations* **:** any worker who is under wages or salary to an employer and who is not excluded by agreement from consideration as such a worker

em·ploy·er \əm'plȯi(y)ə(r), em'-, -ȯyə-\ *n* -S **:** one that employs something or somebody: as **a** (1) **:** the owner of an enterprise (as a business or manufacturing firm) that employs personnel for wages or salaries (2) **:** such an enterprise itself **b :** an agent acting for such an enterprise in employing persons

employers' association *n* **:** an organization of owners of business or manufacturing enterprises employing personnel or of their agents for the purpose of concerted action (as in labor negotiations)

employer's liability insurance *n* **:** insurance against loss an employer may suffer from his common-law liability for injury to an employee excluding liability imposed by a workmen's compensation act

em·ploy·ment \-ȯimənt\ *n* -S [ME *employement*, fr. *emploien* to employ + *-ment* — more at EMPLOY] **1 :** USE, PURPOSE **2 a :** activity in which one engages and employs his time and energies ⟨her baby will give her ~ enough now —Rachel Henning⟩ ⟨those in public office usually had to attend to their private ~*s* —C.L.Jones⟩: as (1) **:** work (as customary trade, craft, service, or vocation) in which one's labor or services are paid for by an employer ⟨~ as a mechanic⟩ ⟨in the ~ of the contractor⟩ (2) **:** temporary or occasional work or service for pay ⟨went from town to town, working when I could get ~ —Oliver Goldsmith⟩ (3) **:** occasional activity engaged in as an avocation, pastime, habit, or expedient **b :** an instance of such activity ⟨no sooner did he get an ~, however lowly, than his employer turned out to be a Communist —F.M.Ford⟩ ⟨in blitz war, the tactical ~*s* of the airplane are many and varied —S.L.A.Marshall⟩ **3 a :** the act of employing someone or something or the state of being employed ⟨the ~ of a pen in sketching⟩ ⟨the ~ of all means to an end⟩ ⟨the ~ of new workers⟩ ⟨walk to a distant table, and, leaning there in pretended ~, try to subdue the feelings —Jane Austen⟩ ⟨the routine ~ of blood transfusion —*Current Biog.*⟩ ⟨the next four essays examine the way in which the ~ of myth, belief, or even manners give meaning and form to the novel —W.V. O'Connor⟩ **b :** the degree or extent to which the persons needing employment or available for employment are provided with it or lack it because of the prevailing economic conditions ⟨~ in the particular area is likely to increase or decrease with the economic condition of the country as a whole⟩ ⟨efforts to increase ~ by stimulating local industry⟩ **syn** see WORK

employment agency *n* **:** an agency whose business is to find jobs for those seeking them or people to fill jobs that are open

employment agent *n* **:** one that runs an employment agency or as a business finds jobs for those seeking them or people to fill jobs that are open

employment bureau *n* **1 :** EMPLOYMENT AGENCY **2 :** an office (as in a school) that places applicants in jobs or gets and makes available information on job opportunities

employment certificate *n* **:** an authorization issued by school authorities for a child of school age to work at a job paying wages or salary

employment exchange *n* **:** any of the offices established in England for the collection of labor statistics, for the placing of employees, and for handling part of the system of unemployment insurance

emplume *var of* IMPLUME

em·po·as·ca \,empō'askə\ *n, cap* [NL] **:** a cosmopolitan genus of leafhoppers (family Cicadellidae) having the ocelli vestigial or wanting and including numerous serious pests of cultivated plants (as the potato leafhopper)

em·pocket \əm, em+\ *vt* [¹*en-* + *pocket* (n.)] **:** to put into one's pocket

em·po·di·um \əm'pōdēəm, em-\ *n, pl* **empo·dia** \-ēə\ [NL, fr. ²*en-* + *-podium*] **:** a small median appendage between the claws of the tarsi of many insects and arachnids

em·poison \əm, em+\ *vt* [ME *empoysonen*, fr. MF *empoisoner*, fr. OF, fr. *em-* ¹en- + *poison* — more at POISON] **1** *archaic* **:** POISON **2 :** EMBITTER ⟨a look of ~*ed* acceptance —Saul Bellow⟩ — **em·poi·son·ment** \"mənt\ *n* -S

em·poisoner *n* [ME *empoysoner*, fr. *empoysonen* + *-er*] *obs* **:** POISONER

em·polder *or* **im·polder** \əm, em +\ *vt* -ED/-ING/-S [D *inpolderen*, fr. *in-* ¹in- (akin to OE *in-*) + *polder* — more at IN-,

POLDER] **:** to make (land that is underwater or periodically flooded) cultivable by the erection of banks or levees to prevent or control inundation and by adequate drainage

em·po·ri·um \əmˈpōrēəm, em-, -ȯr-\ *n, pl* **emporiums** \-ēəmz\ *also* **empo·ria** \-ēə\ [L, fr. Gk *emporion*, fr. *emporos* traveler, trader, fr. *em-* ²en- + *-poros* (fr. *poros* path, road, journey — more at FARE] **1 a :** a place of trade **:** MARKETPLACE, MART; *esp* **:** a commercial center ⟨the ~ of the innumerable kinds of merchandise which are exchanged between China, Central Asia, and Europe —W.H.G.Kingston⟩ ⟨it has been primarily an industrial city rather than a commercial ~ —Lewis Mumford⟩ **b :** an esp. sizable place of business or center of activity that serves customers ⟨earning his living at the local furniture ~ —William McFee⟩ ⟨he has built and equipped two eating ~*s* with a combined capacity of more than 200 food consumers at a sitting —Fred Hawthorne⟩ ⟨a hardware ~⟩ **c :** a store, shop, or similar enterprise making claim to fanciness or special commercial significance ⟨drinking and gambling ~ —*Amer. Guide Series: Oregon*⟩ ⟨found his once sedate carriage shop transformed into a sort of Hollywood hot-rod ~ —Hugh Humphrey⟩ ⟨the dresses in the windows of the dry-goods ~ —Hamilton Basso⟩ ⟨one of the shiny movie ~*s* —P.E.Deutschman⟩ ⟨a Chinese chop-suey ~ —Bennett Cerf⟩ **2 :** a store carrying a great diversity of merchandise ⟨that general ~ which catered to a variety of human needs —Della Lutes⟩ ⟨an air-conditioned news, candy, and soda-fountain ~ —J.P.Marquand⟩

empory *obs var of* EMPORIUM

em·power \əm, em+\ *vt* [¹*en-* + *power* (n.)] **1 :** to give official authority to **:** delegate legal power to **:** COMMISSION, AUTHORIZE ⟨~*ed* the Supreme Court and the district courts of the U.S. to issue writs of habeas corpus in circumstances involving the exercise of jurisdiction by Federal authorities —C.B.Swisher⟩ ⟨these courts of appeal are also ~*ed* to review and enforce orders of federal administrative bodies —W.S. Sayre⟩ ⟨the department was ~*ed* by the legislature to begin courses in medicine —*Amer. Guide Series: Minn.*⟩ **2 :** to give faculties or abilities to **:** ENABLE ⟨the emotion which ~*s* artists to create significant form —Clive Bell⟩ ⟨~*ed* by long training, the young priest blotted himself out of his own consciousness and meditated upon the anguish of his Lord —Willa Cather⟩ — **em·pow·er·ment** \ˈ"mənt\ *n* -S

em·pre·sa·rio \ˌemprəˈsärēˌō, -sa(a)r-, -ser-, -sär-\ *n* -S [Sp, contractor, manager, prob. fr. It *impresario* — more at IMPRESARIO] **:** one who before Texas became part of the U.S. entered into a contract with the Spanish or Mexican government to settle a certain number of families in Texas in exchange for sizable grants of land

¹**em·press** \ˈemprə̇s\ *n* -ES [ME *emperesse*, fr. OF, fem. of *empereor* emperor — more at EMPEROR] **1 :** the wife or widow of an emperor **2 :** a woman who holds an imperial title in her own right ⟨in 1876 Parliament conferred the title *Empress of India* on Queen Victoria⟩

²**empress** *obs var of* ⁷IMPRESS

em·presse·ment \äⁿpresmäⁿ\ *n, pl* **empressements** \-mäⁿ(z)\ [F, fr. (*s'*)*empresser* to hurry, be eager (fr. *em-* ¹en- + *presser* to hurry) + *-ment* — more at PRESS] **:** emotional interest or involvement **:** FERVOR ⟨lively, too lively, fond of showing off, exhibiting abundance of ~ in everything —W.G.Hammond⟩ ⟨if I hear anything very sinister and dramatic related with great ~ —Ngaio Marsh⟩ **:** WARMTH, CORDIALITY ⟨came forward to welcome her with considerable ~ —Agatha Christie⟩ ⟨his manner lacked ~ —Elizabeth Bowen⟩

em·press·ite \ˈemprəˌsīt\ *n* -S [*Empress* Josephine mine, Kerber creek dist., Colorado + E *-ite*] **:** a mineral AgTe consisting of telluride of silver

empress tree *n* [ˈ*empress;* after Anna Pavlovna, after whom the genus *Paulownia* was named — more at PAULOWNIA] **:** a paulownia (*Paulownia tomentosa*)

em·prise \emˈprīz\ *n* -S [ME, fr. MF, fr. OF, fr. fem. of *empris*, past part. of *emprendre* to undertake, fr. (assumed) VL *imprehendere*, fr. L *im-* ²in- + *prehendere* to seize — more at GET] **1 :** UNDERTAKING, ENTERPRISE ⟨when a nation of men starts making literature it invariably starts on the difficult ~ of verse, and goes on to prose as by an afterthought —A.T. Quiller-Couch⟩; *esp* **:** adventurous, daring, or chivalric enterprise ⟨the deep-breathed glory of high ~ —S.E.White⟩ **2 :** an instance of esp. adventurous or daring emprise ⟨in a high ~ that to the rest of us is at once a challenge and a solace —R.M.Neal⟩

em·pros·thot·o·nos \ˌemˌpräsˈthätᵊnəs\ *n* -ES [NL, fr. Gk drawn forward and stiffened, fr. *emprostho-* (fr. *emprosthen* before, in front) + *-tonos* (fr. *teinein* to stretch)] **:** a tetanic spasm which bends the body ventralward

empt \ˈem(p)t\ *vb* -ED/-ING/-S [ME *empten, emptien*, fr. OE *ǣmtian, ǣmettigian* to empty, be at leisure, fr. *ǣmtig, ǣmettig* empty, unoccupied — more at EMPTY] *now dial* **:** EMPTY

emptied *past of* EMPTY

¹**emptier** *comparative of* EMPTY

²**emp·ti·er** \ˈem(p)tē(r)\ *n* -S **:** one that empties

empties *pres 3d sing of* EMPTY, *pl of* EMPTY

emptiest *superlative of* EMPTY

emp·ti·ly \ˈem(p)tə̇lˌē, -tᵊl|, |i\ *adv* **:** in an empty manner ⟨gazing ~ at television —Perry Miller⟩ ⟨the play after that ~ thins down —Stark Young⟩

emp·ti·ness \-tēnə̇s, -tin-\ *n* -ES [ME *emptinesse*, fr. *empty* + *-nesse* -ness] **1 a :** the quality or state of being empty **b :** the quality or state of lacking or being devoid of contents (as typical or customary) ⟨the ~ of the coal bin⟩ ⟨the ~ of the garage⟩ **c :** the quality or state of being uninhabited, unfrequented, or containing no human beings ⟨the ~, the blankness of great solitudes —Laurence Binyon⟩ ⟨the peculiar ~ of the green meadows and the tiny hidden lanes —Margery Allingham⟩ **2 a :** BARRENNESS ⟨a life . . . ghastly in its ~ and sterility —Aldous Huxley⟩; *esp* **:** lack of imagination or creative ability ⟨paintings marked by simplicity but not ~⟩ **b :** lack of something necessary to spiritual growth or sustenance ⟨the vulgarity, the cheapness, the showy pretentiousness, the dreadful ~ of life for the middle classes during the uneasy peace —W.L. Shirer⟩ ⟨the spiritual ~ of army life will have deeply affected the thinking habits of many men —B.B.Seligman⟩ **c :** INANITY, FOOLISHNESS, SENSELESSNESS ⟨he realized the ~ of mere opposition to the U.S. on such questions —A.F.Buchan⟩ **d :** lack of significant purposefulness **:** an engaging in purposeless or inane activity ⟨life without a customary companion was ~, ennui, restiveness and fidget —Francis Hackett⟩ **3 :** HUNGER ⟨the family had sat down, ill-humored from ~, to dinner at four o'clock —Ellen Glasgow⟩ **4 a :** LACK ⟨they were glad to overlook its frequent ~ of content —Van Wyck Brooks⟩ **b :** lack of warmth, love, or affection ⟨with her children she feels affectionate and at the same time has an impression of ~, which she gloomily interprets as complete indifference —H.M.Parshley⟩ **c :** marked unhappiness deriving from the loss of something loved ⟨the ~ of utter loss —F.R.Leavis⟩ **d :** sense of loss esp. of something desirable ⟨only an ~, a feeling that something was over —Stuart Cloete⟩ **5 :** uninhabited or unknown territory ⟨stood on the shores of this nameless lake at last . . . saying that we should turn back from the ~ which stretched ahead —Farley Mowat⟩ ⟨appears as a sort of outpost, standing almost on the edge of ~ —Green Peyton⟩ **6 :** something lacking significant content **:** FRIVOLITY 2 ⟨a play that was nothing more than a competent piece of ~⟩ **7** *Buddhism* **:** NIRVANA

emp·tins \ˈem(p)tə̇nz\ *or* **emp·tings** \",-tiŋz\ *n pl* [alter. of *emptyings*, pl. of *emptying*, fr. gerund of ²*empty*] *dial* **:** a liquid leavening usu. made at home from potatoes or hops and kept from one baking to the next

emp·tion \ˈem(p)shən\ *n* -S [L *emption-, emptio*, fr. *emptus* (past part. of *emere* to buy) + *-ion-, -io* -ion — more at REDEEM] **1 :** the act of buying **:** PURCHASE ⟨relieved both of the ~ of stuffs and of the payment of tailors and property-makers —E.K.Chambers⟩ **2 :** RIGHT OF EMPTION — **emp·tion·al** \-shənᵊl\ *adj*

emp·tio·ven·di·tio \ˈem(p)tēˌōˌwenˈdid·ēˌō\ *or* **emptio et venditio** \-tēˌō(ˌ)et(ˌ)w-\ *n* [L *emptio et venditio* buying and selling] **:** the consensual contract between two parties for the purchase of something by one party and its sale by the other at an agreed price

emp·tor \ˈem(p)tər, -ˌtȯ(ə)r\ *n* -S [L, fr. *emptus* + *-or*] **:** PURCHASER, BUYER

¹**emp·ty** \ˈem(p)tē, -ti\ *adj* -ER/-EST [ME, fr. OE *ǣmtig, ǣmettig* empty, unoccupied, fr. *ǣmetta* leisure, rest (fr. *ǣ-* not, without + *-metta*, fr. *mōtan* to have to) + *-ig* -y — more at MUST] **1 a :** containing nothing **:** devoid of contents **:** not filled ⟨an ~ box⟩; *esp* **:** lacking typical, expected, or former contents ⟨a cold ~ stove⟩ ⟨an ~ pantry⟩ ⟨an ~ purse⟩ ⟨an ~ chair⟩ ⟨shows the ~ cross and the distant rising sun —T.A. Stafford⟩ **b :** VACANT, UNOCCUPIED ⟨an ~ house⟩ ⟨an ~ lot⟩ ⟨~ factory space⟩ **c :** devoid of people ⟨an ~ theater⟩ ⟨along the road that had been so quiet and ~ the night before, but was now crowded with people —Archibald Marshall⟩ **:** UNINHABITED ⟨colonize ~ lands where the Red Indian nomad would be the only person aggrieved —G.M.Trevelyan⟩ ⟨most of the northeast coast is ~ except for the villages —P.E.James⟩ **:** UNFREQUENTED ⟨seemed less disagreeable when one could walk in quiet, ~ places after dark —W.B.Yeats⟩ ⟨the muddy waters are ~, except for an occasional small ship such as the one taking me away —H.W.Carter⟩ **d** *of a female domestic animal* **:** not bearing a fetus **:** not pregnant ⟨an ~ heifer⟩ **e** *logic, of a class* **:** having no members **:** NULL **2 :** having nothing to carry or transport **:** not loaded or burdened ⟨an ~ truck⟩ ⟨an ~ mail pouch⟩ **:** lacking cargo ⟨an ~ freighter⟩ ⟨an ~ camel train⟩ **3 a :** destitute of reality or substance ⟨an ~ dream⟩ ⟨~ lip service⟩ **b :** destitute of value **:** HOLLOW, VAIN ⟨an ~ pleasure⟩ ⟨confirmation of appointments by the senate is anything but an ~ form —*Amer. Guide Series: N.J.*⟩ ⟨~ bragging and all the playacting that springs from insincerity —H.M.Parshley⟩ ⟨an ~ display of erudition —Benjamin Farrington⟩ ⟨unless our party is reunited . . . the nomination for presidency will be purely an ~ honor —F.D.Roosevelt⟩ ⟨the idle or ~ use of God's name —*Interpreter's Bible*⟩ **c :** destitute of effect or force ⟨~ threats⟩ **d :** devoid of sense **:** MEANINGLESS, FOOLISH ⟨a speech made up of ~ and platitudinous ideas⟩ ⟨if all that cannot be understood or satisfactorily explained is to be dismissed as impossible or unreal, life will be an ~ thing indeed —W.F.Hambly⟩ **e :** devoid of knowledge, intelligence, or sense ⟨where a member of the aristocracy may be as husky of body and as ~ of mind as the most menial of the working caste —W.C.Allee⟩ **f :** devoid of expression or of any sign of intelligence ⟨an ~ face⟩ **4 :** HUNGRY ⟨after missing lunch the children were very ~ by suppertime⟩ **5 a :** lacking meaningful occupation or activity ⟨she wakened in the morning with a slight feeling of anticipation, a faint stirring of hope, instead of the horror and dread of another ~ day —Dorothy Witton⟩ ⟨summer in the city was an ~ season —Nancy Cardozo⟩ **:** not occupied with any purposeful activity **:** IDLE ⟨to fill the ~ hours, her daughter asked her to embroider a worsted picture —*Current Biog.*⟩ ⟨she enjoys turning her ~ leisure into a bountiful offering —H.M.Parshley⟩ **b :** having no purpose **:** USELESS ⟨a certain amount of ~ mileage is unnecessarily run —*Brit. Transport Rev.*⟩ **c :** yielding no return ⟨it was tedious work and involved following a lot of ~ leads —*Best True Fact Detective*⟩ **6 a :** marked by the absence of human life or activity or anything providing comfort or human warmth ⟨the ~ silence of the night⟩ ⟨a cold and ~ wasteland⟩ ⟨blank and ~ fields —Pearl Buck⟩ **b :** lacking human affection, warmth, or love ⟨it had been an acrid ~ home with everyone growing alien to one another —Norman Mailer⟩ **7 :** DESTITUTE, DEVOID ⟨~ of all purpose or meaning⟩ ⟨the streets are ~ of automobiles —Jean Stafford⟩ ⟨did the roads look peculiarly ~ of traffic —Meridel Le Sueur⟩ ⟨the air was never ~ of their sweet, sad calling —Mary Webb⟩ ⟨~ of meaning⟩ **8 a :** marked by a strong sense of loss or unhappy purposelessness ⟨the weeks after his wife's death were ~ and desolate⟩ **:** experiencing a marked and unsatisfied emotional need ⟨one evening you are lonely and ~ because the moon is shining and there is a strange beauty over the land —Charlton Laird⟩ **b :** incapable of experiencing further emotion **:** emotionally dulled or exhausted ⟨his outburst had left him completely ~, like a shaken sack —Liam O'Flaherty⟩

syn VACANT, BLANK, VOID, VACUOUS: EMPTY is a general term describing something lacking content; its usual antonyms are *full* or *filled* ⟨an *empty* basket⟩ ⟨an *empty* room from which the furniture had been moved⟩ ⟨the dark and *empty* auditorium of a theater in the morning when only one or two cleaners are moving about —Alan Moorehead⟩ Figuratively, EMPTY indicates lack of content or significance ⟨when words came they did not break the silence. The wall remained. The words that came were *empty*, meaningless words —Sherwood Anderson⟩ ⟨the unthinking mind is not necessarily dull, rude, or impervious; it is probably simply *empty* —C.W.Eliot⟩ VACANT describes what is without an occupant, incumbent, tenant, inmate, or person or thing appropriately settled or fixed within ⟨a *vacant* room ready for a new tenant⟩ ⟨the nook among the brambles where his van had been standing was as *vacant* as ever the next morning —Thomas Hardy⟩ ⟨a *vacant* throne⟩ ⟨a *vacant* professorship⟩ Figuratively, VACANT may indicate lack of an agency or attribute considered as a usual occupant ⟨her partner, the poor snail, was a *vacant* creature, scarcely more than half-witted — and the hard work, of course, was put off on her —Willa Cather⟩ ⟨his *vacant* eye, his lack of interest in what went on about him, and his strange gestures and mutterings were symptoms of a failing mind —C.B. Nordhoff & J.N.Hall⟩ BLANK describes what is free from writing or marking ⟨a *blank* book⟩ ⟨a *blank* page⟩ In more figurative uses it may indicate lack of signs of expression, comprehension, or meaning ⟨she had not a word to say, and in *blank* astonishment she beheld the carriage drive off —William Black⟩ ⟨their utterances are more or less seriously taken because the public, equally ignorant, is just as *blank* and undiscriminating —C.H.Grandgent⟩ VOID intensifies the notions of EMPTY ⟨*void* barren desert⟩ ⟨a large smooth shining face, *void* of a sign of mustache or whiskers —Henry James †1916⟩ ⟨*void* of human interest or poetic quality, as yet unstirred by a breath of life —H.O.Taylor⟩ VACUOUS may suggest the emptiness of a vacuum; in figurative applications to persons and their notions, it is a synonym of *inane* ⟨the substances are dried in a bell jar or desiccator over concentrated sulfuric acid. The drying takes place more rapidly if the containing vessel is rendered *vacuous* —J.F.Thorpe & Martha A. Whiteley⟩ ⟨to see whether he could detect any surprise or suspicion. There was nothing to be read in the *vacuous* face, blank as a school notice-board out of term —Graham Greene⟩

syn see in addition VAIN

²**empty** \"\ *vb* -ED/-ING/-ES *vt* **1 a :** to make empty, devoid of content, or vacant **:** deprive of contents, furnishings, or inhabitants ⟨~ a box⟩ ⟨~ a truck⟩ ⟨~ a house⟩ ⟨~ a city⟩ **b :** DEPRIVE, DIVEST ⟨~ a phrase of all meaning⟩ ⟨*emptied* himself of all power to control⟩ ⟨the Christ who *emptied* Himself of His glory and accepted humiliation and suffering —R.M. French⟩ ⟨his eyes *emptied* themselves of light and intelligence —R.H.Newman⟩ ⟨a style *emptied* of human content —Anthony Blunt⟩ ⟨the curriculum can be *emptied* of all the studies and the disciplines which relate to faith and to morals —Walter Lippmann⟩ **c :** to discharge (itself) of contents ⟨the stream *empties* itself into the river⟩ ⟨the water pipe *emptied* itself into the rain barrel with a gurgling sound⟩ **d :** to fire (a repeating firearm) until empty ⟨he leaped to his feet and *emptied* his gun through the broken window —S.H.Holbrook⟩ **2 :** to remove from what holds, encloses, or contains (as by carrying, pouring, or leading out) ⟨~ the grain from a sack⟩ ⟨~ the money from a purse⟩ ⟨~ the furniture from a house⟩ ⟨~ the cattle from a stable⟩ **3 :** to place, deposit, carry, dump, or pour by emptying from what holds, encloses, or contains ⟨~ grain into a bin⟩ ⟨~ his armful of packages onto the table⟩ ⟨~ the sacks from the truck onto the porch⟩ ⟨no waste, garbage, or refuse may be *emptied* on highways —*Amer. Guide Series: N. H.*⟩ ~ *vi* **1 :** to become empty ⟨the theater *emptied* rapidly after the show ended⟩ **2 :** to empty or discharge its contents ⟨the river *empties* into the ocean⟩ **3 :** to defecate or urinate **:** EVACUATE

³**empty** \"\ *n* -ES **:** something that is empty; *esp* **:** an empty container (as a box, bottle, cask) or vehicle (as a cab or car) ⟨an engine pulling five full boxcars, one coal car, and several *empties*⟩ ⟨always drunk two quarts of wine a day on the job, tossing his *empties* into the basement —Clifford Aucoin⟩

empty-cell process *or* **empty-cell treatment** *n* **:** a method of treating wood so that the chemical preservative coats the cell walls, the cell cavities remaining nearly or quite empty — compare FULL-CELL PROCESS

empty glume *n* **:** GLUME

empty-handed \ˌ==ˈ==\ *adj* **:** being without gain or acquisition **:** having acquired or gained nothing ⟨went out to win a fortune but came home *empty-handed*⟩ ⟨lack of mining equipment and geological data forced him to sail home *empty-handed* —*Amer. Guide Series: Mich.*⟩

empty-headed \ˌ==ˈ==\ *adj* **:** uninformed and scatterbrained ⟨an *empty-headed* wriggle-hipped blonde —*Time*⟩

emptyhearted \ˌ==ˈ==\ *adj* **:** having an empty heart ⟨hardly consistent with the levity of that society, alike ~ and empty-headed —James Martineau⟩

empty out *vt* **:** EMPTY ⟨*empty out* the water barrel to clear it of sediment⟩ ⟨*empty* a boat *out* by beaching it and turning it over⟩

empty weight *n* **:** the weight of the structure, power plant, and fixed equipment of an airplane in flying condition

empty word *n* **:** FUNCTION WORD

em·purple \əm, em+\ *vb* [¹*en-* + *purple* (adj.)] *vt* **1 a :** REDDEN ⟨blood from a deep cut *empurpling* the leg⟩ **b :** to make flushed (as with effort or embarrassment) ⟨broke off, his red face *empurpled*, mouthing speechlessly —J.E.Macdonnell⟩ **2 :** to make purple (as with cold or anger) ⟨a dying sun *empurpling* the distant hills⟩ ⟨a face *empurpled* by exposure⟩ ~ *vi* **:** to become red or flushed ⟨face *empurpled*, and the sweat poured down as she toiled away with the cranky thing —C.S. Forester⟩

empurpled *adj* **:** marked by purple passages ⟨a lush and ~ prose⟩ ⟨a writer of ~ literature⟩

em·pu·sa \emˈpyüsə, -üzə\ [NL, fr. Gk *empousa* hobgoblin, specter] *syn of* ENTOMOPHTHORA

em·py·e·ma \ˌemˌpīˈēmə, -pēˈē-\ *n, pl* **empyema·ta** \-ˈēməd·ə, -ˈem-\ *or* **empyemas** [LL, fr. Gk *empyēma*, fr. *empyein* to suppurate] **:** the presence of pus in a bodily cavity (as the pleural cavity) **:** purulent pleurisy — **em·py·e·mic** \ˌ=ˌ=ˈēmik -ˈem-\ *adj*

em·py·re·al \ˌemˌpīˈrēəl, -pə-; (ˈ)emˈpirēəl, -ˈpīr-\ *adj* [LL *empyreus, empyrius* (fr. LGk *empyrios*, fr. Gk *empyros* fiery, fr. *em-* ²en- + *-pyros*, fr. *pyr* fire) + E *-al* — more at FIRE] **1 :** of or relating to the empyrean **:** CELESTIAL **2 :** SUBLIME ⟨well-meaning ineptitude, that rises to ~ absurdity —M.S. Dworkin⟩

¹**em·py·re·an** \-ēən\ *adj* [LL *empyreus, empyrius* + E *-an*] **:** EMPYREAL ⟨the earthly perfection of the individual to a height no less ~ than Luther's ideal of religious salvation —Helen Sullivan⟩ ⟨~ aplomb —Hamilton Basso⟩

²**empyrean** \"\ *n* -S **1 a :** the highest heaven or heavenly sphere in ancient and medieval cosmology usu. described as a sphere of fire or light — compare ELEMENT 1; ETHER, HEAVEN **b :** the true and ultimate heavenly paradise — used chiefly by certain Christian writers (as John Milton) **2 :** FIRMAMENT **:** HEAVENS ⟨an inhabitant of Mars guiding his spaceship through the ~ —Lucius Garvin⟩ ⟨the blue and cloudless ~ —F.L. Allen⟩ **3 :** a transcendentally sublime or lofty otherworldly place esp. from which lofty ideas may be thought to derive ⟨forever to inhabit an ~ of blithe intellectual play, of charming fancies and biting good sense —Edmund Wilson⟩ ⟨he alone stands still while the whole ~ of Greek life circles about him —J.J.Chapman⟩ ⟨the social theorist high in the ~ of pure ideas uncontaminated by mundane facts —R.K.Merton⟩

empyreum *n* -S [ML, fr. neut. of LL *empyreus*] *obs* **:** EMPYREAN 2

em·py·reu·ma \ˌempəˈrümə, -pēˈ-, -ˌpīˈ-\ *n, pl* **empyreuma·ta** \-məd·ə\ [Gk, live coal covered with ashes, fr. *empyreuein* to light a fire, fr. *em-* ²en- + *pyreuein* to light, fr. *pyr*] **:** the peculiar odor of the products of organic substances burned in closed vessels

em·py·reu·mat·ic \ˌ=(ˌ)=ˌrüˈmad·ik\ *also* **em·py·reu·mat·i·cal** \-d·ə̇kəl\ *adj* [Gk *empyreumat-, empyreuma* + E *-ic, -ical*] **:** being or having an odor of burnt organic matter as a result of decomposition at high temperatures ⟨creosote and other ~ oils⟩

em quad *n* [¹*em*] **:** a quad whose point dimension and set dimension are the same or very nearly the same **:** a quad with a square or almost square body

ems *pl of* EM

emu \ˈē(ˌ)myü *sometimes* -mü\ *n* -S [modif. of Pg *ema*] **1 :** a large Australian ratite bird (*Dromiceius novae-hollandiae*) now almost wholly restricted to northern and western Australia and being the largest existing bird next to the closely related ostrich, inhabiting open forests and plains, and having rudimentary wings and plumage of slender drooping feathers with greatly developed aftershafts and a head and neck feathered and without wattles **2 :** any of various tall flightless birds (as the rhea and cassowary)

EMU *abbr, usu not cap* electromagnetic unit

emu apple *n* **:** an Australian tree (*Owenia acidula*); *also* **:** its subacid fruit that is about as large as a small nectarine

emu bush *n* **1 :** an Australian tree of the genus *Pholidia* of the family Myoporaceae (esp. *P. longifolia*) **2 :** an Australian tree (*Heterodendron oleaefolium*) of the family Sapindaceae

emul *abbr* emulsion

¹**em·u·late** \ˈemyəˌlāt, *usu* -ād·+V\ *vb* -ED/-ING/-S [L *aemulatus*, past part. of *aemulari*, fr. *aemulus* rivaling, envious, akin to Gk *aitia* cause — more at ETIOLOGY] *vt* **1 a :** to strive to equal or excel **:** imitate with the intention of equaling or outdoing ⟨a simplicity *emulated* without success by numerous modern poets —T.S.Eliot⟩ **b :** IMITATE ⟨book-covering materials which one way or another ~ leather —*Book Production*⟩ ⟨some of the early Protestant congregations *emulated* this custom, but soon gave up the practice —*Amer. Guide Series: La.*⟩ **2** *obs* **:** to be jealous of **:** ENVY **3 :** to equal or approach equality with **:** RIVAL ⟨her companions she loved and admired, but could not ~, for they were wise about things she knew not of —Rose Macaulay⟩ ⟨modern watercolor in the West, when it tries, as it often does, to ~ the force and solidity of oil painting, only succeeds in sacrificing its own special felicities —Laurence Binyon⟩ ⟨he became president . . . at the age of 32, *emulating* his father's election to the post when he was 34 —H.T.Brundidge⟩ ~ *vi, obs* **:** STRIVE, ENDEAVOR

²**emulate** *adj* [L *aemulatus*, past part.] *obs* **:** EMULOUS

em·u·la·tion \ˌemyəˈlāshən\ *n* -S [L *aemulation-, aemulatio*, fr. *aemulatus* + *-ion-, -io* -ion] **1 a :** a striving by imitation to equal others in accomplishment or quality ⟨earlier there was rivalry and even antagonism between the two nations of British culture but there was little ~ —Edward Shils⟩ ⟨creating manufacturing industries in ~ of the U.S. —George Wythe⟩; *also* **:** IMITATION ⟨slavish ~ of the elite —M.D.Geismar⟩ ⟨native military traditions tolerated no blind ~ of a foreign prototype —Hajo Holborn⟩ **b :** a striving to excel others in accomplishment or quality **:** RIVALRY ⟨the spirit of ~ enters into the majority of games, and usually the contest element masks other features of the games —*Notes & Queries on Anthropology*⟩ **c** *archaic* **:** the ambition to equal or excel in accomplishment or quality **d** *obs* **:** contentious rivalry **2** *archaic* **:** JEALOUSY, ENVY

em·u·la·tive \ˈemyəˌlād|iv, -ˌlə|, |t|, |ēv *also* |əv\ *adj* **:** characterized by emulation ⟨a son's ~ drive to achieve the same success as his father⟩ **:** tending to emulation ⟨a man's character marked by strong ~ qualities⟩ **:** deriving from emulation or the impulse or drive to emulation ⟨the exploitation of materialistic drives and ~ anxieties —D.M.Potter⟩ — **em·u·la·tive·ly** \|ə̇vlē, -li\ *adv*

em·u·la·tor \-ˌlād·ə(r), -ātə-\ *n* -S [L *aemulator*, fr. *aemulatus* + *-or*] **:** one that emulates **:** IMITATOR, RIVAL

em·u·la·to·ry \ˈemyələˌtōrē, -ōr-, -ri, *chiefly Brit* -ˌlātəri *or* -ˌlā·tri\ *adj* **:** EMULATIVE

emulge \ə̇ˈməlj, ēˈ-\ *vt* -ED/-ING/-S [L *emulgēre* to milk out] *archaic* **:** to draw off the fluid from (a bodily organ)

emul·gent \-jənt\ *adj* [L *emulgent-, emulgens*, pres. part. of *emulgēre* to milk out, fr. *e-* + *mulgēre* to milk — more at MILK] **:** that provides a drain for or strains out the product of something (as the kidneys)

em·u·lous \ˈemyələs\ *adj* [L *aemulus* rivaling, envious — more at EMULATE] **1 a :** ambitious or eager to emulate **:** striving for an accomplishment or quality equal or superior to that of another **:** marked by a desire to imitate or rival ⟨~ suitors⟩ **b :** inspired by or deriving from a desire to emulate ⟨~ fervor⟩ **2** *obs* **:** JEALOUS, ENVIOUS **3** *archaic* **:** ZEALOUS — **em·u·lous·ly** *adv* — **em·u·lous·ness** *n* -ES

emul·si·fi·abil·i·ty \-ˌməlsəˌfīəˈbilədē\ *or* **emul·si·bil·i·ty** \-səˈbil-\ *n* -ES **:** capacity for being emulsified

emul·si·fi·able \ə'məlsə,fīəbəl, ē'-, ˌ=ˌ=='===\ *or* **emul·si·ble** \ə'=səbəl\ *adj* **:** capable of being emulsified ⟨~ oils⟩

emul·si·fi·ca·tion \-səfə'kāshən\ *n* -s **:** the process of emulsifying

emul·si·fi·er \-'məlsə,fī(ə)r, -īə\ *n* -s **1 :** an emulsifying agent **:** a surface-active agent (as a soap) for promoting the formation and stabilization of an emulsion **2 :** a machine (as a mixer) for emulsifying — compare HOMOGENIZER

emul·si·fy \-,fī\ *vt* -ED/-ING/-ES [*emulsion* + *-ify*] **:** to convert (as an oil) into an emulsion — compare HOMOGENIZE

emul·sin \-'məlsən\ *n* -s [G, fr. L *emulsus* + G *-in*] **:** any of various enzyme preparations that are obtained usu. from plants (as almonds and mold fungi) as white amorphous powders and that contain glycosidases active on beta-glycosides (as amygdalin or cellobiose)

emul·sion \ə'məlshən, ē'-\ *n* -s [NL *emulsion-, emulsio,* fr. L *emulsus* (past part. of *emulgēre* to milk out) + *-ion-, -io* -ion — more at EMULGENT] **1 a :** a milky fluid made by rubbing almonds or other seeds with water and used as a demulcent **b :** any of various milky liquids **2 a** (1) **:** an intimate mixture of two incompletely miscible liquids (as oil and water) in which one of the liquids in the form of fine droplets is dispersed in the other usu. with the aid of an emulsifier **:** a disperse system in which both phases are liquids ⟨milk is an oil-in-water ~⟩ (2) **:** an intimate mixture consisting of a semisolid or solid (as a resinous or bituminous material) dispersed in a liquid ⟨an ~ of asphalt in water⟩ — compare FOAM 1, SUSPENSION 2b (3) **b :** an emulsion of a liquid or solid substance in an aqueous liquid with an emulsifier (as a gum or gelatin) used esp. to improve the palatability of a medicine ⟨~ of cod-liver oil⟩ **3 :** a suspension of a finely divided sensitive silver salt (as silver bromide) or a mixture of silver halides in a viscous medium (as a gelatin solution) used for coating photographic plates, films, and paper; *also* **:** the resultant coating when dried

emulsion paint *n* **:** a paint having water usu. as the volatile phase with various nonvolatile substances (as a linseed-oil varnish) in emulsion as the binder — compare LATEX PAINT

emul·sive \-lsiv\ *adj* [*emulsion* + *-ive*] **:** constituting or yielding an emulsion ⟨~ insecticidal spray oils⟩

emul·soid \-,sȯid\ *n* -s [ISV *emulsion* + *-oid*] **1 :** a colloidal system consisting of a liquid dispersed in a liquid — not used scientifically; compare SUSPENSOID **2 :** a lyophilic sol (as a gelatin solution) — used esp. in biology — **emul·soi·dal** \ə'məl,sȯidᵊl, ē'-; ¦e,məl¦s-\ *adj*

emul·sor \ə'məlsə(r), ē'-\ *n* -s [*emulsion* + *-or*] **:** EMULSIFIER 2 ⟨centrifugal ~s⟩

emunc·to·ry \ə'məŋ(k)t(ə)rē, ē'-\ *n* -ES [NL *emunctorium,* fr. L *emunctus* (past part. of *emungere* to blow or wipe the nose, fr. *e-* + *-mungere,* akin to *mucus*) + *-orium* -ory — more at MUCUS] *archaic* **:** an organ or part of the body (as the kidneys or skin) that serves to carry off body wastes

emundation *n* -s [LL *emundation-, emundatio,* fr. L *emundatus* (past part. of *emundare* to clean out, fr. *e* + *mundare* to clean, fr. *mundus* clean) + *-ion-, -io* -ion — more at MOTHER (membrane)] *obs* **:** ceremonial cleansing

emus *abbr* [L *eminentissimus*] most eminent

emu wren *n* **:** any of several small Australian warblers (genus *Stipiturus*) that resemble wrens but have the tail feathers long and loosely barbed like emu feathers

emyd·ea \ə'midēə, ē'\ *n pl, cap* [NL, fr. *Emyd-, Emys*] *in former classifications* **:** a group of turtles nearly coextensive with the family Emydidae

em·y·did \'emə,did; ə'midəd, ē'-\ *adj* [NL *Emydidae*] **:** of or relating to the Emydidae

emyd·i·dae \ə'midə,dē, ē'-\ *n pl, cap* [NL, fr. *Emyd-, Emys,* type genus + *-idae*] **:** a family of chelonians comprising most of the freshwater aquatic tortoises and terrapins and closely related to Testudinidae in which it has often been included as a subfamily

em·y·do·sau·ria \,emədō'sȯrēə\ [NL, fr. Gk *emyd-, emys* + NL *-o-* + *-sauria*] *syn of* LORICATA

¹**em·y·do·sau·ri·an** \¦===¦sȯrēən\ *adj* [NL *Emydosauria* + E *-an*] **:** of or relating to the Loricata **:** CROCODILIAN

²**emydosaurian** \"\ *n* -s **:** LORICATE

emys \'ēməs, 'em-\ *n, cap* [NL, fr. Gk *emys* freshwater tortoise] **:** a small genus of turtles (family Emydidae) including the common European pond tortoise (*E. orbicularis*) and a No. American tortoise (*E. blandingii*)

¹**en** \'en\ *n* -s **1 :** the letter *n* **2 :** the set dimension of an en quad used esp. in Great Britain as a unit of measure of a typesetter's production

²**en** \ən, ᵊn, ˌēn\ *dial Eng var of* HIM

³**en** \'en, 'ān, 'ai(ə)n\ *Scot var of* END

⁴**en** \(¦)äⁿ(n), (¦)ān, (¦)en, (¦)in\ *prep* [F, lit., in, fr. L *in*] **:** in the form or manner of — see EN BLOC, EN BROSSE, EN CABOCHON

¹**en-** *also* **em-** *prefix* [ME, fr. OF, fr. L *in-, im-,* fr. *in* — more at IN] **1 :** put into ⟨*en*cradle⟩ **:** put on to ⟨*en*throne⟩ **:** cover or surround with ⟨*en*verdure⟩ **:** go into or on to ⟨*em*bus⟩ — in verbs formed from nouns **2 :** cause to be ⟨*en*glad⟩ ⟨*en*slave⟩ — sometimes in verbs that also have the suffix *-en* ⟨*em*bolden⟩; in verbs formed from adjectives or nouns **3 :** provide with ⟨*en*collar⟩ ⟨*em*power⟩ — in verbs formed from nouns **4 :** so as to cover or surround ⟨*en*wrap⟩ **:** thoroughly ⟨*en*tangle⟩ — often in verbs differing little or not at all in meaning from the corresponding verb without prefix ⟨*en*tame⟩; in verbs formed from verbs; in all senses usu. *em-* before *b, m,* or *p* and *en-* in other circumstances

²**en-** *also* **em-** *prefix* [ME, fr. L, fr. Gk, fr. *en* in — more at IN] **:** in **:** within **:** inside ⟨*en*dermic⟩ ⟨*en*gram⟩ ⟨*en*zootic⟩ — usu. *em-* before *b, m,* or *p* ⟨*em*batholithic⟩ and *en-* in other circumstances

³**en-** — see OEN-

⁴**en-** *comb form* [ISV, fr. *-ene*] **:** chemically unsaturated; *esp* **:** having one double bond ⟨*en*amine⟩

¹**-en** \ən, ᵊn *sometimes* ᵊm *after* p, b, f, *or* v *sometimes* ᵊŋ *after* k *or* g\ *also* **-n** \n\ *adj suffix* [ME, fr. OE; akin to OHG *-īn* made of, ON *-inn,* Goth *-eins* made of, of or belonging to, L *-inus* (with long *ī*) of or belonging to, Gk *-inos* made of, of or belonging to, Skt *-īna* of or belonging to] **:** made of **:** consisting of ⟨earth*en*⟩ ⟨wool*en*⟩ — now relatively infrequent because of the widespread attributive use of nouns or of adjectives formed from nouns without the addition of a suffix (as in *gold* cup, *wheat* cake) and to be found chiefly in adjectives which are obsolete ⟨tinn*en*⟩ or archaic ⟨oak*en*⟩ or in which a sense other than the literal one has become prominent ⟨gold*en*⟩ ⟨wood*en*⟩; usu. *-n* after *-er* ⟨silver*n*⟩

²**-en** \"\ *vb suffix* -ED/-ING/-S [ME *-nen,* fr. OE *-nian* (as in *fæstnian* to fasten); akin to OS *-nōn,* final segment of certain transitive infinitives (as in *fastnōn* to fasten), OHG *-inōn* (as in *festinōn* to fasten), ON *-na* (as in *fastna* to pledge, betroth)] **1 a :** cause to be ⟨sharp*en*⟩ — sometimes in verbs that also have the prefix *en-* ⟨*em*bold*en*⟩; in transitive verbs formed from adjectives **b :** cause to have ⟨length*en*⟩ — in transitive verbs formed from nouns **2 a :** come to be ⟨steep*en*⟩ — in intransitive verbs formed from adjectives **b :** come to have ⟨length*en*⟩ — in intransitive verbs formed from nouns

en *abbr* enemy

en *symbol* ethylenediamine — in chemical formulas ⟨$[Co(en)_3]Br_3$⟩

EN *abbr* exception noted

en·able \ə'nābəl, e'-\ *vt* **enabled; enabled; enabling** \-b(ə)liŋ\ **enables** [ME *enablen,* fr. ¹*en-* + *able,* adj.] **1 a :** to render able ⟨~ a person to earn a living⟩ **:** give power, strength, or competency ⟨his particular theology *enabling* him to overcome some of the difficulties —S.F.Mason⟩ **b :** to make possible, practical, or easy ⟨*enabled* passage of the anti-poll-tax law —H.F. & Katharine Pringle⟩ **2 a** *archaic* **:** to give authority or sanction to **:** ENDOW **b :** to give legal capacity to **3 :** to give the opportunity to **:** ALLOW ⟨examinations so designed that high-school graduates are *enabled* to pass⟩

en·abler \-b(ə)lə(r)\ *n* -s **:** one that enables

enabling *adj* [fr. pres. part. of *enable*] **:** giving or providing legal power or sanction esp. beyond usual bounds in order to meet the demands of an unusual or anomalous situation ⟨an ~ act⟩ ⟨~ resolution⟩

¹**en·act** \ə'nakt, e'-\ *vb* [ME *enacten,* fr. ¹*en-* + *acte* act, formal record — more at ACT] *vt* **1** *obs* **:** to enter into the public records **:** CHRONICLE **2 :** to establish by legal and authoritative act **:** make into a law; *esp* **:** to perform the last act of legislation upon (a bill) that gives the validity of law **3 :** to act out **:** REPRESENT, PLAY ⟨a lot of history has been ~*ed* within my view —Douglas Carruthers⟩ ⟨this scene being ~*ed* in the courtroom —Beatrice Griffith⟩ ~ *vi* **:** to act on or as if on the stage **:** PERFORM

²**enact** *n* [ME *enacte,* fr. *enacten,* v.] *obs* **:** ENACTMENT

enacting clause *n* [*enacting* fr. pres. part. of ¹*enact*] **:** the clause of an act that formally expresses the legislative sanction and that usu. appears after the title or preamble of the act

en·ac·tion \ə'nakshən, e'-\ *n* [¹*enact* + *-ion*] **:** ENACTMENT

en·act·ment \-k(t)mənt\ *n* -s **1 :** the act or action of enacting **:** PASSING ⟨the ~ of a bill by the legislature to aid private industry⟩ **2 :** something that has been enacted (as a law, bill, or statute)

en·ac·tor \-ktə(r)\ *n* **:** one that enacts ⟨the new laws . . . fulfilled the fondest hopes of their ~s —Oscar Handlin⟩

enacture *n* -s *obs* **:** ENACTMENT, RESOLUTION

en·a·lid \'enᵊləd\ *n* -s [ISV *enal-* (fr. Gk *enalios* of the sea, fr. *en-* ²*en-* + *halios* of the sea, fr. *hal-, hals* sea) + *-id;* akin to Gk *hals* salt — more at SALT] **:** a submerged marine plant (as eelgrass)

en·al·i·or·nis \ə,nalē'ȯrnəs\ *n, cap* [NL, fr. *enali-* (fr. Gk *enalios* of the sea) + *-ornis*] **:** a genus comprising Cretaceous swimming birds from the Greensand formations of England and related to *Hesperornis*

en·al·i·o·saur \ə'nalēə,sȯ(ə)r\ *n* -s [NL *Enaliosauria*] **:** a marine reptile of the division Enaliosauria

en·al·i·o·sau·ria \ˌ=ˌ===\'sȯrēə\ *n pl, cap* [NL, fr. *enalio-* (fr. Gk *enalios* of the sea) + *-sauria*] *in some classifications* **:** a division of extinct marine reptiles comprising the Ichthyosauria and the Plesiosauria and other forms — **en·al·i·o·sau·ri·an** \ˌ=¦===¦sȯrēən\ *adj or n*

en·a·lite \'enᵊl,īt\ *n* -s [*Ena,* town in central Honshu, Japan + E *-lite*] **:** a uraniferous thorite

enam \ə'näm\ *n* -s [Hindi *in'ām* enam, gift, favor, fr. Per, gift, favor, fr. Ar] *Hindu law* **:** a grant of land to be held rent free or on favorable rent; *specif* **:** such a grant in perpetuity — compare JAGIR

enam·dar \-,där\ *n* -s [Hindi *in'āmdār,* fr. Per, fr. *in'ām* + *-dār* holder — more at BHUMIDAR] **:** the holder of an enam

¹**enam·el** \ə'naməl, e'-\ *vt* **enameled** *or* **enamelled; enameled** *or* **enamelled; enameling** *or* **enamelling** \-m(ə)liŋ\ **enamels** [ME *enamelen,* fr. MF *enameler, enamailler,* fr. *en-* ¹*en-* + *esmaillier, amaillier* to enamel, fr. OF *esmaillier,* fr. *esmail, esmal* enamel, of Gmc origin; akin to OHG *smelzan* to melt — more at SMELT] **1 :** to cover or inlay with enamel **2 :** to beautify or adorn with or as if with a colorful bright surface ⟨sun . . . ~*ed* the whole scene —*London Calling*⟩ **3 :** to form or produce a glossy surface upon (as paper, leather, or cloth) **4 :** to apply enamel to (the face or nails)

²**enamel** \"\ *n* -s [ME, fr. *enamelen,* v.] **1 :** a usu. opaque or semiopaque vitreous composition applied by fusion to the surface of metal, glass, or pottery for ornament or protection or as a basis for decoration — see CHAMPLEVÉ, CLOISONNÉ; compare GLAZE **2 :** a surface, exterior, or outer covering that resembles or suggests enamel **3 :** a paint that flows out to a smooth hard coat when applied, that contains a specially prepared vehicle instead of raw oil, and that usu. dries with a glossy appearance **4 :** something that is enameled **:** enameled ware **5 :** a cosmetic intended to give the appearance of a smooth and beautiful complexion or to produce a glossy appearance **6 :** the intensely hard calcareous substance that forms a thin layer capping or partly covering the teeth of most mammals (as man) and many other vertebrates, being the hardest substance of the animal body and consisting of minute prisms that are secreted by ameloblasts, are arranged at right angles to the surface, and are bound together by a cement substance — see TOOTH illustration **7 a :** the coating of carbonized glue or shellac that forms the acid-resisting portion of a metal photoengraving plate **b :** the facing material of coated paper

enamel cell *n* **:** AMELOBLAST

enameled brick *n* [*enameled* fr. past part. of ¹*enamel*] **:** a brick having a smooth impervious easily cleaned surface secured by coating with a special wash before burning and used in bathrooms, hotel kitchens, and swimming pools

enameled leather *n* **:** leather having a hard varnished surface; *specif* **:** PATENT LEATHER

enam·el·er *or* **enam·el·ler** \-m(ə)lə(r)\ *n* -s **:** one that applies enamel: as **a :** one that fuses enamel into jewelry settings **b :** one that coats cast-iron sanitary units with enamel

enameling *or* **enamelling** *n* -s [ME *enamelinge,* fr. *enamelen* to enamel + *-inge* -ing] **1 :** ENAMEL; *specif* **:** enamel ornamentation **2 a :** the application of enamel **b :** the process or technique of applying enamel

enam·el·ist *or* **enam·el·list** \-məlәst\ *n* -s **:** ENAMELER

enamel kiln *n* **:** a muffle kiln used by enamelers in which colors and gold applied over the glaze are fired **:** a decorating kiln

enamel organ *n* **:** an ectodermal ingrowth from the dental ridge that forms a cap with two walls separated by a reticulum of stellate cells, encloses the anterior part of the developing dental papilla and the cells of the inner enamel layer adjacent to the papilla, and differentiates into columnar ameloblasts which lay down the enamel rods of the tooth

enamel painting *n* **:** painting with enamel colors that are fixed with heat usu. upon a surface of fired enamel

enamel rod *n* **:** one of the elongated prismatic bodies making up the enamel of a tooth

enamelware \ə'==,=\ *n* **:** ware (as iron cooking utensils) coated with enamel for protection (as from rust or the action of acids)

en·am·or \ə'namə(r), e'-\ *vt* **enamored; enamored; enamoring** \-m(ə)riŋ\ **enamors** *see -or in Explan Notes* [ME *enamouren,* fr. OF *enamourer, enamorer,* fr. *en-* ¹*en-* + *amour, amor* love — more at AMOUR] **:** to inflame with love **:** CHARM, CAPTIVATE — usu. used in the passive with *of* ⟨tourists were ~*ed* of the town⟩ and sometimes with *with* ⟨a beautiful Indian girl with whom he was ~*ed* —Walter Havighurst⟩

en·am·ored·ness \-mə(r)dnəs\ *n* -ES **:** the state of being enamored

enan·thal·de·hyde *or* **oe·nan·thal·de·hyde** \,ē,nan'thaldə,hīd\ *n* [ISV *enanth-, oenanth-* (as in *enanthic acid*) + *aldehyde*] **:** a pungent oily compound $CH_3(CH_2)_5CHO$ obtained by pyrolysis of castor oil and used esp. in making artificial cognac — called also *heptaldehyde, heptanal*

enan·thate *or* **oe·nan·thate** \ə'nan,thāt, ē'-\ *n* -s [ISV *enanth-, oenanth-* + *-ate*] **:** a salt or ester of enanthic acid

en·an·them \ə'nan(t)thəm, e'-\ *or* **en·an·the·ma** \,e,nan'thēmə\ *n, pl* **enanthems** \-thəmz\ *or* **enanthe·ma·ta** \-'thēməd·ə, -'them-\ [NL *enanthema,* fr. ²*en-* + *-anthema*] **:** an eruption upon a mucous surface — **en·an·them·a·tous** \¦=ˌ=¦themədˑəs, -¦thēm-\ *adj*

enan·thic acid *or* **oe·nan·thic acid** \ə¦nan(t)thik-, ē¦\ *n* [ISV *enanth-, oenanth-* (fr. L *oenanthe* wild grape, fr. Gk *oinanthē* grape blossom, fr. *oinē* grapevine + *anthē* blossom) + *-ic;* akin to Gk *oinos* wine and to Gk *anthos* flower — more at WINE, ANTHOLOGY] **:** an oily fatty acid $CH_3(CH_2)_5COOH$ usu. made by oxidizing enanthaldehyde and used chiefly in making esters for flavoring materials — called also *heptanoic acid*

enantio- *comb form* [NL, fr. Gk, fr. *enantios,* fr. *enanti* in the presence of, fr. *en* in + *anti* against — more at IN, ANTE-] **1 :** opposite ⟨*enantio*tropy⟩ **2 :** antagonistic ⟨*enantio*biosis⟩

en·an·ti·o·bi·o·sis \ə,nantēō,bī'ōsəs, e,-\ *also* **en·an·to·bi·o·sis** \-tō,b-\ *n, pl* **enantiobioses** *also* **enantobioses** [NL, fr. *enantio-* + *-biosis*] **:** antagonistic symbiosis

en·an·ti·o·blas·tic \ə¦nantēō¦blastik, e¦-\ *also* **en·an·ti·o·blas·tous** \-stəs\ *adj* [*enantio-* + *-blastic* or *-blastous* (fr. *-blast* + *-ous*)] **:** originating at the end of a seed opposite the hilum — used of an embryo

en·an·ti·o·mer \ə'nantēōmər, e'-, -,me(ə)r\ *n* -s [*enantio-* + *-mer*] **:** ENANTIOMORPH 2

en·an·ti·o·mer·ic \-¦nantēō¦merik\ *adj* [*enantio-* + *-meric*] **:** ENANTIOMORPHOUS

en·an·ti·o·morph \ə'=ˌ==,mȯrf\ *n* -s [ISV *enantio-* + *-morph;* orig. formed as G] **1 :** either of two enantiomorphous crystals **2 :** either of two crystalline forms or compounds exhibiting enantiomorphism — called also *optical antipode;* distinguished from *diastereoisomer;* compare RACEMIC

en·an·ti·o·mor·phism \ˌ=ˌ==='mȯr,fizəm\ *n* -s [*enantio-* + *-morphism*] **:** the phenomenon of mirror-image relationship exhibited by right-handed and left-handed crystals (as of quartz) or by the molecular structures of two stereoisomeric compounds (as *dextro*-tartaric acid and *levo*-tartaric acid) — distinguished from *diastereoisomerism;* compare ASYMMETRIC CARBON ATOM, OPTICAL ISOMERISM

en·an·ti·o·mor·phous \=¦===¦mȯrfəs\ *or* **en·an·ti·o·mor·phic** \-fik\ *adj* [*enantio-* + *-morphous* or *-morphic*] **:** of, relating to, or exhibiting enantiomorphism

en·an·ti·o·trop·ic \=¦===¦träpik\ *adj* [*enantio-* + *-tropic*] **:** of, relating to, or exhibiting enantiotropy

en·an·ti·ot·ro·py \ˌ=ˌ=='ä·trəpē\ *n* -ES [ISV *enantio-* + *-tropy*] **:** the relation of two different forms of the same substance (as two allotropic forms of tin) that have a definite transition point and can therefore change reversibly each into the other — compare MONOTROPY

en·arched \ə'närcht, e'-\ *adj* (fr. past part. of obs. *enarch* to provide with an arch or arches, fr. ME *enarchen,* fr. ¹*en-* + *arche,* n., arch] *heraldry* **:** bent into a curve or arch ⟨an ~ fess⟩

en·ar·gite \ə'när,jīt, 'enər-\ *n* -s [G *enargit,* fr. Gk *enargēs* visible (fr. *en* in + *argēs* bright) + G *-it* -ite; fr. its cleavage; akin to Gk *argos* white — more at ARGENT] **:** a grayish black or iron-black copper arsenic sulfide (Cu_3AsS_4) of metallic luster occurring in small orthorhombic crystals or massive and often containing antimony

en·arm \ə'närm, e'-\ *vt* [ME *enarmen,* prob. fr. ¹*en-* + *armen* to arm] *archaic* **:** to equip with arms or armor

en·arme \"\ *n* -s [obs. F, fr. OF, fr. *enarmer* to provide (a shield) with straps through which an arm may be passed, fr. (assumed) VL *inarmare,* fr. L *in* + (assumed) VL *-armare* (fr. L *armus* shoulder) — more at IN, ARM] **:** the strap or the set of straps by which a shield was held on the arm — usu. used in pl.

enar·ra·tion \,ē,na'rāshən, ,e,n-\ *n* -s [L *enarration-, enarratio* detailed exposition, fr. *enarratus* (past part. of *enarrare* to explain in detail, fr. *e-* + *narrare* to narrate) + *-ion-, -io* -ion — more at NARRATE] *archaic* **:** a detailed exposition or description

en ar·rière \äⁿnäryeer\ *adv (or adj)* [F, behind, backward, in arrears] **1** *heraldry* **:** from the back ⟨an eagle proper *en arrière*⟩ **2** *ballet* **:** toward the back **:** BACKWARD — used of a movement or of the execution of a step ⟨a glissade *en arrière*⟩

en·ar·thro·di·al \¦e,när¦thrōdēəl\ *adj* [NL *enarthrodia* enarthrosis (fr. ²*en-* + *arthrodia*) + E *-al*] **:** of, relating to, or having the form of an enarthrosis

en·ar·thro·sis \ˌ=ˌ='thrōsəs\ *n, pl* **enarthro·ses** \-ō,sēz\ [NL, fr. Gk *enarthrōsis,* fr. *en-* ²*en-* + *arthrōsis* arthrosis] **:** an articulation in which the rounded head of one bone fits into a cuplike cavity of the other and admits movement in any direction **:** a ball-and-socket joint (as the hip joint)

enas·cent \ē, ə+\ *adj* [L *enascent-, enascens,* pres. part. of *enasci* to spring up, sprout, fr. *e-* + *nasci* to be born — more at NATION] *archaic* **:** NASCENT

¹**enate** \'ē,nāt\ *adj* [L *enatus,* past part. of *enasci*] **1 :** growing out **2 :** ENATIC

²**enate** \"\ *n* -s [L *enatus,* past part. of *enasci*] **:** one related on the mother's side — compare AGNATE

enat·ic \(')ē¦nad·ik\ *adj* [L *enatus* (past part. of *enasci*) + E *-ic*] **:** descended from the same mother **:** related on the mother's side ⟨~ clans⟩

ena·tion \ē'nāshən\ *n* -s [L *enatus* (past part. of *enasci*) + E *-ion*] **1 :** an outgrowth from the surface of an organ ⟨a plant virus forming ~s on leaves⟩ **2 :** kinship on the mother's side

enation mosaic *n* **:** mosaic (as of tobacco, potato, and tomato) in which raised pin-shaped corrugated outgrowths appear chiefly on the lower surface of the leaves

en avant \äⁿnávaⁿ\ *adv (or adj)* [F, in front, forward] *ballet* **:** in front **:** FORWARD — used of a movement or of the execution of a step

en axe \äⁿnäks\ *adj* [F, on the axis] **:** placed symmetrically in or upon the axis — used with *with* ⟨pillars *en axe* with the central aisle⟩

en banc \äⁿbäⁿ\ *adv (or adj)* [F, on the bench] **:** in full court **:** with full judiciary authority ⟨in the recent . . . case all seven circuit judges sat *en banc* —Archibald Cox⟩

en bas \äⁿbä\ *adv (or adj)* [F, below, down] *ballet* **:** in a low position — used of the arms

en bloc *pronunc at* ⁴EN + 'bläk\ *adv (or adj)* [F] **1 :** as a body or whole **:** in a lump or mass ⟨forced the islanders . . . to move *en bloc* —D.B.Forrester⟩ ⟨one escape for harassed editors is to buy a group of strips *en bloc* from some syndicate —Coulton Waugh⟩ **2 :** in one piece **:** as a unit ⟨an engine with cylinders cast *en bloc*⟩

enbrave *var of* EMBRAVE

en bro·chette \äⁿbrō¦shet\ *adv (or adj)* [F] **:** on a skewer ⟨broiled kidney *en brochette*⟩

en brosse \äⁿbrȯs\ *adv (or adj)* [F, lit., in the manner of a brush] **:** in a manner resembling the short erect bristles of a brush — used of a man's hair style ⟨his black hair . . . stood up *en brosse* —Hugh Walpole⟩ ⟨his very thick graying hair *en brosse* added an extra inch to his stature —Kathryn Grondahl⟩

enc *abbr* **1** enclosed; enclosure **2** encyclopedia

en cab·o·chon \en'kabə,shän\ *adv* [F, in the manner of a cabochon] **:** in convex form but not faceted ⟨a ruby cut *en cabochon*⟩

en·cae·nia \en'sēnyə, in'-, -nēə\ *n pl but sing or pl in constr, sometimes cap* [NL, fr. L, dedication festival, fr. Gk *enkainia,* fr. *en* in + *-kainia* (fr. *kainos* new) — more at IN, RECENT] **:** an annual university ceremony (as at Oxford University) of commemoration with recital of poems and essays and conferring of degrees

en·cage \ən, en+\ *vt* [¹*en-* + *cage,* n.] **:** CAGE 1

en·camp \ən, en+\ *vb* [¹*en-* + *camp,* n.] *vt* **:** to form into or place in a camp ⟨~ soldiers⟩ ~ *vi* **:** to form or occupy a camp **:** prepare and settle in temporary habitations (as tents or huts)

en·camp·ment \"mənt\ *n* -s **1 a :** the action of encamping **b :** the state of being encamped **2 a :** the place where a body of troops or campers is encamped **:** CAMP ⟨was not enthusiastic over the choice of Valley Forge as a winter ~ —F.V.W. Mason⟩ ⟨a well-fortified ~⟩ ⟨the ~ of migratory workers outside the city⟩ **b :** the individuals that make up an encampment ⟨the whole ~ was in an uproar⟩ **3 :** COMMANDERY 3 **4 :** a convention of a national association of ex-servicemen

en·cap·su·late \ən'kapsə,lāt, en- *also* -syə-\ *also* **en·capsule** \ən, en+\ *vb* -ED/-ING/-S [*encapsulate* fr. ¹*en-* + *capsule,* n. + *-ate,* vb. suffix; *encapsule* fr. ¹*en-* + *capsule,* n.] *vt* **:** to surround, encase, or protect in or as if in a capsule **:** CAPSULE ⟨the tissues of the body surround the [trichina] organisms and ~ them —Morris Fishbein⟩ ⟨in his youth he was *encapsulated* in affection —H.L.Mencken⟩ ~ *vi* **:** to become encapsulated ⟨a bacillus that ~s in the human body⟩ ⟨some very small poikilotherms desiccate and ~ for protection —Samuel Brody⟩ — **en·capsulation** \ən, (,)en+\ *n*

encapsulated *adj* [fr. past part. of *encapsulate*] *biol* **:** surrounded by a gelatinous or membranous envelope ⟨~ water bacteria⟩

encaptive *vt* [¹*en-* + *captive,* n. or adj.] *obs* **:** to make captive

encarnadine *var of* INCARNADINE

en·carnalize \ən, en+\ *vt* [¹*en-* + *carnalize*] **:** to make carnal ⟨grossness *encarnalizing* a conversation⟩

en·car·pus \en'kärpəs\ *n, pl* **encar·pi** \-,pī, -,pē\ [alter. (influenced by Gk *enkarpos*) of earlier *encarpa* festoons as an architectural ornament, fr. L, fr. Gk *enkarpa,* neut. pl. of *enkarpos* containing fruit, fr. *en-* ²*en-* + *-karpos* -carpous] **:** an ornament on a frieze or capital consisting of festoons (as of fruit or flowers)

en car·ré \äⁿkärā\ *adv* [F, lit., in the form of a square] **:** on the intersection of four numbers in roulette so as to include all four — used of a bet

en·case *also* **in·case** \ən'kās, en-\ *vt* [¹*en-* or ²*in-* + *case,* n.] **1 :** to enclose in, place in, or provide with a case ⟨each product *encased* in leatherette⟩ **2 :** to cover or surround with or as if with something solid, impermeable, or confining ⟨the neurotic loneliness of a woman *encased* in her ambition —*Saturday Rev.*⟩

encased knot *n* [*encased* fr. past part. of *encase*] **:** a dead or loose knot or portion of a branch partially or entirely embedded in the bole of a tree

encased postage stamp *n* **:** a postage stamp mounted in a metal case with a transparent face (as of mica) for use as a piece of money

en·case·ment *also* **in·case·ment** \-mənt\ *n* **1 a :** the act or process of encasing or the state of being encased **b :** the supposed enclosure in a living germ of the germs of all future generations that might develop from it — compare PREFORMATION **2 :** CASE, COVERING

en·cash \ən, en+\ *vt* [¹*en-* + *cash*, n.] *Brit* **:** CASH — **en·cash·able** \"əbəl\ *adj, Brit* — **en·cash·ment** \-mənt\ *n* -S *Brit*

en casserole *pronunc at* ⁴EN+\ *adv (or adj)* [F] **:** in a casserole — used of foods so cooked and served ⟨chicken *en casserole*⟩ ⟨ham cooked *en casserole*⟩

en·cas·tage \äⁿkästäzh\ *n* -S [F, action of placing pieces of pottery in saggers, fr. *encaster* to place (pieces of pottery) in saggers (irreg. fr. *en-* ¹en- + *casette* sagger, fr. *case* compartment, square of a chessboard — fr. Sp *casa* square of a chessboard, house, fr. L, hut, cabin — + *-ette*) + *-age* — more at CASA] **:** the placing of pottery in a kiln for firing

en·cas·tre \äⁿkästrā\ *adj* [F *encastré*, past part. of *encastrer* to embed, fit into a recess, fr. It *incastrare*, fr. LL, fr. L *in* + *castrare* to trim, cut off, castrate — more at CASTRATE] **:** built in at the supports ⟨an ~ beam⟩

¹**en·caus·tic** \ən'kȯstik, (')en¦k-, -tēk\ *adj* [L *encausticus*, fr. Gk *enkaustikos*, fr. *enkaustos* painted in encaustic (fr. *enkaiein* to burn in, paint in encaustic, fr. *en-* ²en- + *kaiein* to burn) + *-ikos* -ic — more at CAUSTIC] **:** of or relating to encaustic ⟨the ~ method⟩ ⟨an ~ picture⟩ — **en·caus·ti·cal·ly** \-tək(ə)lē, -tēk-, -li\ *adv*

²**encaustic** \"\ *n* **1 :** a paint mixed with melted beeswax and after application fixed by heat **2 :** the method involving the use of encaustic; *also* **:** a picture produced by this method

encaustic tile *n* **1 :** a tile decorated with colored clays inlaid and fired **2 :** colored tile laid in a wall or floor to form a pattern — usu. used in pl.

en·cave \ən'kāv, en-\ *vt* [¹*en-* + *cave*, n.] **:** to hide in or as if in a cave

-ence \ən(t)s, ᵊn(t)s, *in some words* " *or* -,en(t)s; "*-erence*" *is often* ərn(t)s\ *n suffix* -S [ME, fr. OF, fr. L *-entia*, fr. *-ent-*, *-ens* -ent + *-ia* -y] **1 :** action or process ⟨abstin*ence*⟩ ⟨emerg*ence*⟩ ⟨confluen*ce*⟩ **:** instance of an action or process ⟨refer*ence*⟩ ⟨reminisc*ence*⟩ **2 :** quality or state ⟨condescend*ence*⟩ ⟨depend*ence*⟩ **:** one having a (specified) quality or being in a (specified) state ⟨standing on an emin*ence*⟩

¹**en·ceinte** \(')äⁿ¦sant, (')än¦-, -sent,-sänt, *F* äⁿsaaⁿt\ *adj* [MF, fr. (assumed) VL *incienta*, alter. of L *incient-*, *inciens* being with young, fr. *in* + *-cient-*, *-ciens* (akin to Gk *kyein* to be pregnant) — more at CAVE] **:** being with child **:** PREGNANT

²**enceinte** \"\ *n* -S [F, enclosed area, fr. OF, enclosing wall or fence, fr. fem. of *enceint*, past part. of *enceindre* to enclose, fr. L *incingere* to gird, surround, fr. *in* + *cingere* to gird — more at CINCTURE] **1 :** a line of fortification enclosing a castle or town **2 :** the area or town enclosed by an enceinte

en·ce·lia \ən'sēlēə\ *n* [NL] **1** *cap* **:** a genus of shrubs (family Compositae) of the southwestern U.S. and northern Mexico having linear leaves, radiate flower heads, and flat achenes — see BRITTLEBUSH **2** -S **:** any plant of the genus *Encelia* — see INCIENSO

encephal- *or* **encephalo-** *comb form* [F *encéphal-*, fr. Gk *enkephal-*, fr. *enkephalos* brain] **1 :** brain ⟨*encephal*itis⟩ ⟨*encephalo*cele⟩ **2 :** of or belonging to the brain and ⟨*encephalo*spinal⟩

encephala *pl of* ENCEPHALON

en·ceph·a·lar·tos \ən,sefə'lärd·əs\ *n* [NL, fr. Gk *enkephalos* heart of the date palm, brain + *artos* bread — more at ARTO-] **1** *cap* **:** a genus of arborescent African cycads (family Cycadaceae) having stout cylindrical trunks and a terminal crown of mostly long spiny pinnate leaves — see KAFFIR BREAD **2** -ES **:** any plant of the genus *Encephalartos*

-encephali *pl of* -ENCEPHALUS

-en·ce·pha·lia \,ensə'fālyə, -lēə\ *n comb form* -S [NL, fr. *-encephalus* + *-ia* -y] **:** condition of having (such) a brain ⟨scler*encephalia*⟩

en·ce·phal·ic \¦ensə¦falik, -lēk\ *adj* [F *encéphalique*, fr. *encéphal-* encephal- + *-ique* -ic] **:** of or relating to the brain; *also* **:** lying within the cranial cavity

-encephalies *pl of* -ENCEPHALY

en·ceph·a·lit·ic \ən¦sefə¦lid·|ik, (,)en, -it|, |ēk\ *adj* [ISV *encephalit-* (fr. NL *encephalitis*) + *-ic*] **:** relating to, affected with, or characteristic of encephalitis

en·ceph·a·li·tis \=,=='līd·əs, -ītəs\ *n, pl* **encephalit·i·des** \-'lid·ə,dēz, -itə-\ [NL, fr. *encephal-* + *-itis*] **:** inflammation of the brain esp. when due to infectious agents or their toxins; *specif* **:** any of several diseases of man in which a virus of any of several related strains normally parasites of lower vertebrates and commonly transmitted by biting arthropods invades the brain causing inflammatory and degenerative lesions commonly accompanied by apathy, muscular weakness, and lethargy passing into more or less profound somnolence — see SLEEPING SICKNESS

encephalitis le·thar·gi·ca \-lə'thärjəkə, -le'-\ *n* [NL, lethargic encephalitis] **:** epidemic virus encephalitis in which somnolence is marked

en·ceph·a·li·to·gen·ic \=¦==¦līd·ə¦jenik\ *also* **en·ceph·a·li·tog·e·nous** \=¦==,lī¦täjənəs\ *adj* [*encephalito-* (fr. NL *encephalitis*) + *-genic* or *-genous*] **:** tending to cause encephalitis ⟨an ~ strain of virus⟩

en·ceph·a·li·to·zo·on \=,==,līd·ə'zō,än, -ōən\ *n* [NL, fr. *encephalito-* (fr. *encephalitis*) + *-zoon*] **1** *cap, in some classifications* **:** a genus of microorganisms of uncertain systematic position that are known from intracellular bodies in neural and visceral structures of various mammals (as the rabbit) in which they are associated with an encephalitis and sometimes a nephritis **2** *pl* **encephalito·zo·a** \-ōə\ **:** an organism or intracellular body assigned to the genus *Encephalitozoon*

en·ceph·a·lo·cele *also* **en·ceph·a·lo·coele** \=¦==fəlō,sēl\ *n* -S [*encephalocele* ISV *encephal-* + *-cele*; *encephalocoele* alter. (influenced by *-coele*) of *encephalocele*] **:** hernia of the brain either congenital or due to trauma

encephalocoele \"\ *n* -S [*encephal-* + *-coele*] **:** the ventricles of the brain

en·ceph·a·lo·gram \,gram\ *n* -S [ISV *encephal-* + *-gram*] **:** an X-ray picture of the brain made by encephalography

en·ceph·a·lo·graph \-,graf, -àf\ *n* -S [*encephal-* + *-graph*] **1 :** ENCEPHALOGRAM **2 :** ELECTROENCEPHALOGRAPH

en·ceph·a·lo·graph·ic \=¦===¦grafik\ *adj* [*encephalography* + *-ic*] **:** of, relating to, or by means of encephalography — **en·ceph·a·lo·graph·i·cal·ly** \-fək(ə)lē\ *adv*

en·ceph·a·log·ra·phy \=,=='lägrəfē\ *n* -ES [ISV *encephal-* + *-graphy*] **:** roentgenography of the brain after the cerebrospinal fluid has been replaced by air or other gas

en·ceph·a·loid \=¦==,lȯid\ *adj* [ISV *encephal-* + *-oid*; prob. orig. formed as F *encéphaloïde*] **:** resembling the material of the brain

en·ceph·a·lo·malacia \=¦==(,)lō+\ *n* [NL, fr. *encephal-* + *malacia*] **:** softening of the brain due to degenerative changes in nervous tissue (as in crazy chick disease) — **en·ceph·a·lo·ma·lac·ic** \"+mə¦lasik\ *adj*

en·ceph·a·lo·meningitis \"+\ *n* [NL, fr. *encephal-* + *meningitis*] **:** MENINGOENCEPHALITIS

en·ceph·a·lo·mere \=¦===,mi(ə)r\ *n* -S [*encephal-* + *-mere*] **:** a segment of the embryonic brain — **en·ceph·a·lo·mer·ic** \=¦===¦merik\ *adj*

en·ceph·a·lo·myelitic \=¦===+\ *adj* [*encephalomyelitis* + *-ic*] **:** of, relating to, or of the nature of encephalomyelitis

en·ceph·a·lo·myelitis \"+\ *n* [NL, fr. *encephal-* + *myelitis*] **:** concurrent inflammation of the brain and spinal cord; *specif* **:** any of several severe enzootic arthropod-transmitted virus diseases of horses characterized by fever, sluggishness, incoordination, and damage to the central nervous system and represented in the U.S. by a severe eastern and a milder western form caused by distinct viruses either of which may produce encephalitis in man — called also *infectious equine encephalomyelitis, sleeping sickness*

en·ceph·a·lon \ən'sefə,län, en-, -lən\ *n, pl* **encepha·la** \-lə\ [NL, modif. of Gk *enkephalos* brain, fr. *en* in + *kephalē* head — more at IN, CEPHALIC] **:** the vertebrate brain

en·ceph·a·lop·a·thy \=,=='läpəthē\ *n* -ES [NL *encephalopathia*, fr. *encephal-* + *-pathia* -pathy] **:** a disease of the brain; *esp* **:** one involving alterations of brain structure

en·ceph·a·lo·phone \=¦===+,fōn\ *n* -S [*encephal-* + *-phone*] **:** an apparatus that emits a continuous hum whose pitch is changed by interference of brain waves transmitted through oscillators from electrodes attached to the scalp and that is used to diagnose abnormal brain functioning

en·ceph·a·lo·sis \-'lōsəs\ *n, pl* **encephalo·ses** \-ō,sēz\ [NL, fr. *encephal-* + *-osis*] **:** ENCEPHALOPATHY

-en·ceph·a·lous \(,)en¦sefələs, ən-,ᵊn-\ *adj comb form* [Gk *-enkephalos*, fr. *enkephalos* brain] **:** having (such) a brain ⟨micr*encephalous*⟩

-en·ceph·a·lus \=¦===\ *n comb form, pl* **-encepha·li** \-,lī\ [NL, fr. Gk *-enkephalos* -encephalous] **1 :** fetus having (such) a brain ⟨pseud*encephalus*⟩ **2 :** condition of having (such) a brain ⟨micr*encephalus*⟩

-en·ceph·a·ly \=¦==lē, -li\ *n comb form* -ES [NL *-encephalia*] **:** condition of having (such) a brain ⟨an*encephaly*⟩

-ences *pl of* -ENCE

en·chafe \ən'chāf, en-\ *vt* [ME *enchaufen*, fr. ¹*en-* + *chaufen* to chafe] *archaic* **:** CHAFE, HEAT, EXCITE

en·chain \ən'chān, en-\ *vt* [ME *encheynen*, fr. MF *enchaëner*, *enchainer*, fr. OF, fr. *en-* ¹en- + *chaeine* chain] **1 :** to bind with or put in chains **:** restrain with or as if with chains **:** FETTER ⟨men *~ed* by reason of their greed⟩ **2 :** to attract and hold (as the attention or emotions) ⟨a speaker hoping to ~ the attention of the audience⟩ **3** *obs* **:** to link together **:** CONNECT

en·chaîne·ment \äⁿshānmäⁿ, -shen-\ *n* -S [F, enchainement, series, action of binding with chains, fr. MF *enchainement* chain, fr. *enchainer* + *-ment*] **:** a short series of steps in ballet comprising a phrase which can be repeated or varied

en·chain·ment \ən'chānmənt, en-\ *n* -S [*enchain* + *-ment*] **1 :** the act or action of linking together **2 :** the quality or state of being linked together

en·chant \ən'chant, en-, -aa(ə)-,-ai-,-à-\ *vb* [ME *enchanten*, fr. MF *enchanter*, fr. L *incantare*, fr. *in* in, against + *cantare* to sing — more at IN, CHANT] *vt* **1 :** to influence by or as if by charms and incantation **:** BEWITCH ⟨a princess *~ed* by a cruel sorcerer⟩ ⟨the scene *~ed* her to the point of tears —Elinor Wylie⟩ **2 :** to thrill or enrapture **:** DELIGHT ⟨new talent to ~ viewers this coming television season —Goodman Ace⟩ **3 :** to endow with charm **:** infuse, permeate, or transfix with allure, fascination, or attraction ⟨the rare smile that *~ed* her whole face —Edith Wharton⟩ **~** *vi* **1 :** to employ or practice magic or sorcery **2 :** to be charming **:** create delight **syn** see ATTRACT

en·chant·er \-tə(r)\ *n* -S [ME, alter. (influenced by ME *-er*) of *enchantour*, fr. OF *enchanteor*, fr. LL *incantator*, fr. L *incantatus* (past part. of *incantare*) + *-or*] **1 :** one that practices sorcery **:** WITCH, MAGICIAN **2 :** one that fascinates or delights

enchanter's nightshade *n* **:** any plant of the genus *Circaea* (esp. *C. lutetiana*) of the family Onagraceae characterized by inconspicuous white flowers and bristly fruit

en·chant·ing *adj* [fr. pres. part. of *enchant*] **:** CHARMING, FASCINATING ⟨~ dinner dresses —*New Yorker*⟩ — **en·chant·ing·ly** *adv* — **en·chant·ing·ness** *n* -ES

en·chant·ment \-tmənt\ *n* -S [ME *enchantement*, fr. OF, fr. L *incantamentum* incantation, fr. *incantare* + *-mentum* -ment] **1 a :** the act or action of enchanting **:** BEWITCHMENT **b :** the quality or state of being enchanted **:** FASCINATION ⟨having missed almost everything that lent ~ to a normal childhood —L.C.Douglas⟩ **2 :** something that fascinates, bewitches, or charms ⟨the dangers and *~s* of mountainous country⟩

en·chant·ress \-ntrəs\ *n* -ES [ME *enchaunteresse*, fr. MF *enchanteresse*, fr. OF, fr. *enchanteor* enchanter + *-esse* -ess] **1 :** a woman who practices magic **:** SORCERESS **2 :** a fascinating or bewitching woman

en·charge \ən, en+\ *vt* [ME *enchargen*, fr. MF *enchargier*, fr. (assumed) VL *incarricare*, fr. L *in* + LL *carricare* to charge, load — more at IN, CHARGE] **1** *archaic* **:** to give into the charge of a person ⟨*encharging* him the custody and defense thereof —Robert Barret⟩ **2 :** to give a responsibility, duty, or task to **:** ENTRUST — usu. used with *with* ⟨found himself *encharged* with the bringing up of a young nobleman —R.H. Quick⟩

en·chase \ən'chās, en-\ *vt* [ME *enchasen* to emboss, fr. MF *enchasser* to enshrine (as a holy relic), set (as a jewel), fr. OF, fr. *en-* ¹en- + *chasse* reliquary, fr. L *capsa* box, case — more at CASE] **1 :** ENCASE, ENCLOSE ⟨~ a gem⟩ **:** SET ⟨a diamond *enchased* in a gold ring⟩ **2 :** ORNAMENT, DECORATE: as **a :** to cut or carve (as figures or designs) in relief **:** ENGRAVE **b :** INLAY ⟨a table *enchased* with ivory⟩ **3** *obs* **:** to enclose solemnly **:** ENSHRINE

en·chas·er \-sə(r)\ *n* **:** one that enchases

encheason *n* -S [ME *enchesoun*, fr. OF *enchaison*, alter. (influenced by OF *en-* ¹en-) of *achaison*, modif. (influenced by OF *a-*, fr. L *ad-*) of L *occasion-*, *occasio* — more at OCCASION] *obs* **:** OCCASION, CAUSE, REASON

en·cheer \ən, en+\ *vt* [¹*en-* + *cheer*] *archaic* **:** CHEER

en·chel·y·ceph·a·li \(,)en,kelə'sefə,lī\ *n pl, cap* [NL, fr. Gk *enchelys* eel + NL *-cephali* (pl. of *-cephalus*) — more at ANGUIS] *in some classifications* **:** a suborder of Apodes including the common eels

en·chi·la·da \,enchə'lädə, -ladə\ *n* -S [AmerSp, fr. fem. of *enchilado*, past part. of *enchilar* to season with chili, fr. Sp *en-* ¹en- (fr. L *in-*) + *chile* chili] **:** a tortilla topped or rolled up with a highly seasoned meat or other filling and served with tomato sauce seasoned with chili

en·chi·rid·i·on *also* **en·chei·rid·i·on** \,en|,kī'ridēən, ,eŋ|, |,kə'-, -ē,än\ *n* -S [LL *enchiridion*, fr. Gk *encheiridion*, fr. *en* in + *cheir* hand + *-idion* -idium — more at IN, CHIR-] **:** HANDBOOK, MANUAL ⟨a bulky ~ for pious women —Israel Zangwill⟩

¹**en·cho·don·tid** \¦eŋkə¦däntəd\ *or* **en·cho·don·toid** \-n-,tȯid\ *adj* [*enchodontid* fr. NL *Enchodontidae*, fr. *Enchodont-*, *Enchodus*, type genus + *-idae*; *enchodontoid* fr. NL *Enchodont-*, *Enchodus* + E *-oid*] **:** of or relating to the genus *Enchodus* or the Enchodontidae

²**enchodontid** *or* **enchodontoid** \"\ *n* -S **:** an enchodontid fish

en·cho·dus \'eŋkədəs\ *n, cap* [NL, fr. Gk *enchos* spear + NL *-odus*] **:** a genus (the type of the family Enchodontidae) of large-mouthed Cretaceous stomiatoid fishes with spear-shaped teeth

en·chondral \(')en (')eŋ+\ *adj* [ISV ²*en-* + *chondral*] **:** ENDOCHONDRAL

en·chon·dro·ma \,en,kän'drōmə, ,eŋ,k-\ *n, pl* **enchondromas** *or* **enchondroma·ta** \-məd·ə\ [NL, fr. ²*en-* + *chondr-* + *-oma*] **:** a tumor consisting of cartilaginous tissue; *esp* **:** one arising where cartilage does not normally exist — **en·chon·drom·a·tous** \¦=,=¦drämәd·əs, -rōm-\ *adj*

en·chon·dro·sis \¦=,='drōsəs\ *n, pl* **enchondro·ses** \-ō,sēz\ [NL, fr. ²*en-* + *chondr-* + *-osis*] **:** a cartilaginous outgrowth; *also* **:** CHONDROMA

en·cho·ri·al \(')en¦kōrēəl, (')eŋ¦k-\ *adj* [Gk *enchōrios* of the country, native, domestic (fr. *en-* ²en- + *-chōrios*, fr. *chōra* place, land, country) + E *-al*; akin to Gk *chēros* left, bereaved — more at HEIR] **:** DEMOTIC 2 a

en·chy·le·ma \,en,kī'lēmə, ,eŋ,k-\ *n* -S [ISV ²*en-* + *chyle* + *-ma* (as in *-oma*); in sense 1 prob. orig. formed as G *enchylem*; in sense 2 prob. orig. formed as F *enchylème*] **1 :** HYALOPLASM **2 :** KARYOLYMPH — **en·chy·lem·a·tous** \¦=¦=¦lemәd·əs, -lēm-\ *adj*

-en·chy·ma \'eŋkəmə, 'enk-\ *n comb form, pl* **-enchymata** *or* **-enchymas** [NL, fr. *-enchyma* (in *parenchyma*)] **:** cellular tissue of a (specified) type ⟨coll*enchyma*⟩ ⟨cyst*enchyma*⟩

en·chym·a·tous \en'kimәd·əs, eŋ'k-\ *adj* [NL *enchymat-*, *enchyma* infusion (fr. Gk, fr. *enchein* to pour in, infuse, fr. *en* in + *chein* to pour) + E *-ous* — more at IN, FOUND] *of gland cells* **:** distended with secretion

-en·chyme \ən,kīm, 'eŋ,k-, 'en,k-\ *n comb form* -S [NL *-enchyma*] **:** -ENCHYMA ⟨coll*enchyme*⟩

en·chy·trae \'eŋkə·,trē, 'enk-\ *n pl* [irreg. fr. NL *Enchytraeus*] **:** worms belonging to the genus *Enchytraeus* and used as food for aquarium fishes

¹**en·chy·trae·id** \¦=¦=¦trēəd\ *adj* [NL *Enchytraeidae*] **:** of or relating to the genus *Enchytraeus* or to the Enchytraeidae

²**enchytraeid** \"\ *n* -S **:** a worm of the genus *Enchytraeus*

en·chy·trae·idae \,=¦=¦trēə,dē\ *n pl, cap* [NL, fr. *Enchytraeus*, type genus + *-idae*] **:** a family of oligochaete worms including the genus *Enchytraeus*

en·chy·trae·us \-ēəs\ *n, cap* [NL, fr. ²*en-* + Gk *chytraios* of earthenware, fr. *chytra* earthen pot, fr. *chein* to pour] **:** a genus of small white worms (family Enchytraeidae) comprising both terrestrial and aquatic forms, often found in sewage filters, and widely propagated as food for aquarium fishes

-encies *pl of* -ENCY

en·ci·na \ən'sēnə, en-\ *n* -S [AmerSp, fr. Sp, holm oak, modif. of LL *ilicina*, fem. of *ilicinus* of holm oak, fr. L *ilic-*, *ilex* holm oak + *-inus* -ine — more at ILEX] **1 :** COAST LIVE OAK **2 :** LIVE OAK a

en·ci·nal \¦en(t)sə¦nal, -näl\ *n* -S [AmerSp, fr. Sp, grove of holm oak, fr. *encina*] **:** an oak grove or an area marked primarily by the growth of oaks

en·cincture \ən, en+\ *vt* [¹*en-* + *cincture*, n.] **:** to encircle with or as if with a girdle **:** GIRD ⟨a lake *encinctured* with a belt of forest⟩

en·ci·ni·llo \,en(t)sə'nē(,)(y)ō\ *n* -S [AmerSp, dim. of Sp *encina* holm oak] **:** an endemic Puerto Rican shrub (*Drypetes ilicifolia*) of the family Euphorbiaceae with leathery leaves, inconspicuous flowers, and drupaceous fruit

en·cipher \ən, en+\ *vt* [¹*en-* + *cipher*, n.] **:** to convert (a message) into cipher

en·cipherer \"+\ *n* -S **:** one that enciphers

enciphering alphabet *n* [*enciphering* fr. gerund of *encipher*] **:** a substitution alphabet with its plain component in normal alphabetic order — see ALPHABET 1j, CONJUGATE ALPHABET

en·ci·pher·ment \"mənt\ *n* -S **1 :** the act or process of enciphering **2 :** the result of enciphering **:** CIPHERTEXT

en·circle \ən, en+\ *vt* [¹*en-* + *circle*, n.] **1 :** to form a circle about ⟨insert each comma in your shorthand notes and ~ it —L.A.Leslie⟩ **:** enclose within a circle **:** SURROUND ⟨a ring *encircled* her finger⟩ ⟨a camp *encircled* by enemies⟩ **2 :** to make a circuit about **:** go around ⟨as a hungry wolf might have *encircled* . . . the firelit camp of a hunter —Sherwood Anderson⟩ **syn** see SURROUND

en·cir·cle·ment \"mənt\ *n* -S **:** the act or action of encircling, surrounding, or encompassing ⟨the ~ of the globe by an airplane⟩ ⟨the ~ of a wound by scar tissue⟩; *specif* **:** the policy of one or more countries of gradually enveloping or isolating another country ⟨ridden by the nightmare of ~ —*Yale Rev.*⟩

encl *abbr* enclosed; enclosure

en clair \äⁿ'kle(ə)r\ *adv (or adj)* [F, lit., in clear] **:** in plain language ⟨the message was in cipher, not *en clair* —E.O. Hauser⟩ — used esp. of diplomatic messages sent by telegraph

en·clasp *also* **in·clasp** \ən, en+\ *vt* [¹*en-* or ²*in-* + *clasp*] **:** to seize and hold **:** CLASP ⟨he *~ed* her waist in his arm⟩

¹**en·clave** \'e|n,klāv, 'ä| *also* |ŋ,k- *sometimes* 'ä . . . läv *or* 'ä . . . làv\ *n* -S [F, fr. MF, fr. *enclaver*, v.] **1 :** a tract or territory enclosed within foreign territory; *also* **:** a district or region (as in a city) inhabited by a particular race or set apart for a special purpose — compare EXCLAVE **2 a :** something enclosed in an organ or tissue but not a continuous part thereof **b :** a small often relict community of one kind of plant in an opening of a larger plant community

²**enclave** \"\ *vt* -ED/-ING/-S [F *enclaver*, fr. OF, fr. (assumed) VL *inclavare* to enclose, lock up, fr. L *in* + (assumed) VL *-clavare* (fr. *clavis* key); akin to L *claudere* to close — more at CLOSE] **:** to enclose within or encircle or surround by alien or foreign territory

en·cli·sis \'eŋkləsəs, 'enk-\ *n, pl* **encli·ses** \-ə,sēz\ [LL, fr. Gk *enklisis*, fr. *enklinein*] **:** pronunciation as an enclitic

¹**en·clit·ic** \(')en¦klid·|ik, in'k-, -lit|, |ēk *also* (')eŋ¦- *or* iŋ¦-\ *adj* [LL *encliticus*, fr. Gk *enklitikos*, fr. *enklinein* to cause to incline, pronounce as an enclitic, fr. *en* in + *klinein* to lean — more at IN, LEAN] **1 :** leaning or dependent with reference to accent: **a** *of a word or particle in Greek or Latin grammar* **:** being without independent accent and being attached in pronunciation to a preceding word in which it may cause certain accentual changes (as Greek *te* in *anthrōpoi te*, Latin *-ne* in *videsne*) **b** *of a word or particle in the grammar of languages other than Greek and Latin* **:** treated in pronunciation as forming a part of the preceding word (as English *thee* in *prithee* and *not* in *cannot*) — compare PROCLITIC **2 :** INCLINED — used of the relation of the planes of the fetal head to those of the maternal pelvis — compare SYNCLITIC

²**enclitic** \"\ *n* -S **:** an enclitic word or particle

enclog *vt* [¹*en-* + *clog*, v.] *obs* **:** CLOG

encloister *vt* [¹*en-* + *cloister*, n.] *obs* **:** to immure esp. in a cloister **:** CONFINE

en·close *or* **in·close** \ən'klōz, en-\ *vt* [ME *enclosen*, *inclosen*, prob. fr. *enclos*, *inclos*, adj., enclosed, fr. MF *enclos*, past part. of *enclore* to enclose, fr. (assumed) VL *inclaudere*, alter. (influenced by L *claudere* to close) of L *includere* to enclose, include — more at INCLUDE, CLOSE] **1 a :** to close in ⟨~ a porch with glass⟩ **:** SURROUND ⟨~ a yard with a fence⟩; *specif* **:** to fence off or in (common land) in order to appropriate to individual use **b :** ENVELOP, ENFOLD ⟨mountains *enclosed* the town⟩ ⟨*enclosed* in a circle of candlelight —Stuart Cloete⟩ **c :** to hem in **:** CONFINE ⟨a convict *enclosed* within walls for life⟩ **:** subject (a religious or a building or an area) to the rules of enclosure ⟨an *enclosed* order of nuns⟩ ⟨~ the chapel⟩ **d :** to complete the shell of (a building under construction) so as to make weatherproof and secure from intrusion **2 :** to place (as a document, note, or bill) in a parcel or envelope ⟨a check *enclosed* with a letter⟩ **3 :** to seize or grasp securely **:** HOLD ⟨his fingers *enclosed* the money⟩

syn ENVELOP, FENCE, PEN, COOP, CORRAL, CAGE, WALL: ENCLOSE is a general word without rich or specific connotation or definite limitation ⟨their prey *enclosed* within a ring —William Wordsworth⟩ ⟨the study of the history of ideas and their *enclosing* words —C.A.Beard⟩ ENVELOP implies complete enclosure on all sides, esp. one opaque or translucent but yielding and penetrable ⟨the sweet, often incense-laden atmosphere . . . *enveloped* her like a warm and healing garment —Rose Macaulay⟩ ⟨the great chilly unused drawing room whose spacious ceremoniousness seemed to embrace and *envelop* her —J.C.Powys⟩ The remaining words in this set are closely connected with cognate nouns and may show regional variations. In general, FENCE is to close off as if with a fence; it suggests an area barred to entrance or exit and somewhat protected. It is wide and often figurative in use ⟨a Kirghiz tent, with all its muffled walls . . . would not suffice to *fence* out that insistent sunlight —Sacheverell Sitwell⟩ ⟨*fencing* off a corner of the sea with dikes —*N.Y.Times*⟩ PEN is to enclose in a pen esp. to prevent straying. It expresses irksome restriction, but ideas of confinement are stronger in the following words ⟨pigs and geese are *penned* up for the night⟩ ⟨practically the whole of the population is *penned* in on a narrow coastal strip —W.A. Lewis⟩ COOP reinforces notions of prevention of straying, stresses structure rather than area, and more strongly implies narrow and cramped limitation inhibiting activity ⟨poultry *cooped up*⟩ ⟨they feel themselves in a state of thralldom, they imagine that their souls are *cooped* and cabined in —Edmund Burke⟩ ⟨sent their whole army over here onto this island and *cooped* it up so it couldn't get away —Kenneth Roberts⟩ CORRAL suggests prevention of straying or escape by enclosing in larger, less cramping, but stronger and more secure quarters ⟨to *corral* rodeo broncos⟩ It usu. connotes difficulty in driving or controlling whatever is corralled and is often figurative ⟨the vitamins are being *corralled* one by one and the proteins are being brought under control —C.C.Furnas⟩ ⟨to *corral* as many different and mutually hostile groups of voters as he can —*New Republic*⟩ CAGE connotes prevention of escape by confinement in a strong small structure; it suggests more inexorable confinement ⟨*caged* eagles⟩ ⟨as sullen as a beast new-*caged* —Alfred Tennyson⟩ ⟨the feeling of *caged* muscular tightness has provoked a fairly widespread desire to emigrate from Britain —J.R.Chamberlain⟩ WALL suggests strong impenetrable construction barring entrance or exit and guaranteeing confinement or security ⟨when towns were so small that they were *walled* in as gardens are now —G.B.Shaw⟩ ⟨an artificial universe . . . *walled* off from the world of nature —Aldous Huxley⟩

enclosed arc lamp *n* [*enclosed* fr. past part. of *enclose*] **:** an arc lamp having electrodes protected from the atmosphere by a close-fitting globe that much reduces their rate of consumption

enclosed rhyme *or* **enclosing rhyme** *n* [*enclosing* fr. pres. part. of *enclose*] **:** the rhyming pattern *a b b a* found in certain quatrains

en·clos·er \-zə(r)\ *n* **:** one that encloses

en·clo·sure *or* **in·clo·sure** \ən'klōzhə(r), en-\ *n* -s [ME *enclosure*, fr. MF, fr. OF, fr. *enclos* + *-ure*] **1 :** the act or action of enclosing: as **a :** the separation of land from common ground by a fence or barrier **b :** separation (as for fire protection) of one part of a building from others **2 :** the quality or state of being encompassed or shut up ⟨books musty and damp from long ~⟩ **3 :** something that encloses (as a barrier) **4 a :** something enclosed in a package or letter ⟨each envelope contained miscellaneous ~*s*⟩ **b :** an enclosed or fenced-in area ⟨a ranch and its outlying ~*s*⟩ **c :** the part of a monastery or convent strictly reserved for the religious of the community to the exclusion of outsiders or of certain outsiders (as those of the opposite sex) **5 :** the regulation that establishes and is designed to preserve the enclosure of a monastery or convent ⟨an order with a very strict ~⟩

enclosure wall *n* **:** CURTAIN WALL 2

en·clothe \ən, en+\ *vt* [¹*en-* + *clothe*] **:** to cover with or as if with clothing

en·code \ən'kōd, en-\ *vt* [¹*en-* + *code*, n.] **:** to transfer (as a body of information) from one system of communication into another ⟨~ chemical data on punched cards⟩; *esp* **:** to convert (a message) into code

en·code·ment \-mənt\ *n* -s **:** the process or result of encoding

en·cod·er \-də(r)\ *n* **:** one that encodes; *esp* **:** CIPHER MACHINE

en·coffin \ən, en+\ *vt* [¹*en-* + *coffin*, n.] **:** to shut up in or as if in a coffin

en·coi·gnure \ən'känyər, än'k-, -kȯin-, *F* äⁿkônyǖr\ *n* -s [F, fr. MF, corner formed by the junction of two walls, fr. *encoigner* to put into a corner (fr. OF *encoignier*, fr. *en-* ¹en- + *coing* corner) + *-ure* — more at COIN] **:** a small piece of furniture (as a cabinet) made to fit into a corner

en·col·pion *or* **en·kol·pion** \eŋ'kȯlp,yōn\ *n, pl* **encol·pia** *or* **enkol·pia** \-,yä\ [MGk *enkolpion*, fr. Gk, neut. of *enkolpios* in or on the bosom, fr. *en* in + *-kolpios* (fr. *kolpos* bosom) — more at IN, GULF] **:** a medallion bearing a sacred picture that is worn on the breast of a bishop of the Eastern Orthodox Church

en·co·lure \¦äŋkə¦lu̇(ə)r\ *n* -s [F, neck of an animal, fr. MF, fr. *en* in (fr. L *in*) + *col* neck + *-ure* — more at COL] **:** the mane of a horse

en·co·men·de·ro \(,)en,kōmən'de(,)rō, -kăm-\ *n* -s [Sp, fr. *encomienda*] **:** the holder of an encomienda

en·co·mi·ast \ən'kōmē,ast, en-, -ē,aa(ə)st, -ēəst\ *n* -s [Gk *enkōmiastēs*, fr. *enkōmiazein* to praise, fr. *enkōmion* laudatory ode, eulogy] **:** one that praises **:** PANEGYRIST ⟨he was not a true mystic . . . but rather an ~ of piety —A.J.Arberry⟩

¹**en·co·mi·as·tic** \ən¦==¦astik, (,)en,==¦==, -tēk\ *also* **en·co·mi·as·ti·cal** \-təkəl, -tēk-\ *adj* [*encomiastic* fr. Gk *enkōmiastikos*, fr. *enkōmiastēs* + *-ikos* -ic; *encomiastical* fr. Gk *enkōmiastikos* + E *-al*] **:** of, belonging to, or bestowing praise **:** EULOGISTIC ⟨~ remarks⟩ — **en·co·mi·as·ti·cal·ly** \-tək(ə)lē, -tēk-, -li\ *adv*

²**encomiastic** \"\ *n* -s *archaic* **:** PANEGYRIC

en·co·mic \(')en¦kōmik\ *adj* [²*en-* + *coma* + *-ic*] *of human hair* **:** KINKY, CRINKLED

en·co·mi·en·da \(,)en,kōmē'endə, -,kăm-; ,enkəm'yen-\ *n* -s [Sp, fr. *encomendar* to entrust, fr. *en-* ¹en- (fr. L *in-*) + obs. Sp *comendar* to entrust, fr. L *commendare* — more at COMMEND] **:** an estate of land and the inhabiting Indians formerly granted to Spanish colonists or adventurers in America for purposes of tribute and evangelization — compare REPARTIMIENTO

en·co·mi·o·log·ic \ən¦kōmēə¦läjik\ *adj* [LL *encomiologicus*, fr. Gk *enkōmiologikos*, lit., of a laudatory ode, fr. *enkōmion* + *-logikos* -logic] **:** of or having to do with a compound verse in Greek and Latin prosody that is made up of a dactylic penthemimer followed by an iambic penthemimer

encomion *n, pl* **encomia** *or* **encomions** [Gk *enkōmion*] *obs* **:** ENCOMIUM

en·co·mi·um \ən'kōmēəm, en-\ *n, pl* **encomiums** \-ēəmz\ *or* **enco·mia** \-ēə\ [L, fr. Gk *enkōmion* laudatory ode, fr. *en* in + *-kōmios* (fr. *kōmos* revel, celebration) — more at IN, COMEDY] **:** an often formal expression of warm or high praise **:** EULOGY, PANEGYRIC ⟨an unstinted ~ of a national hero⟩

en·compass \ən, en+\ *vt* [¹*en-* + *compass*, n.] **1 a :** to form a circle about **:** ENCIRCLE ⟨with the rising of ~*ing* mountain ranges the Mojave became a cooped-in desert —*Amer. Guide Series: Calif.*⟩ **b** *obs* **:** to make a circuit around **:** go completely around **2 a :** ENVELOP, ENWRAP ⟨a thick fog ~*ed* the building⟩ ⟨have ~*ed* him with every protection —Charles Dickens⟩ **b :** to hem or box in **:** CONFINE ⟨~*ed* by hostile natives⟩ **c :** to bring within **:** INCLUDE, COMPREHEND ⟨in the telling are ~*ed* . . . the philosophy, the traditions, and the ritual beauty of that ancient land —*Saturday Rev.*⟩ **3** *obs* **:** to get the better of **:** OUTWIT **4 :** to bring to completion, fruition, or perfection **:** ACCOMPLISH ⟨a difficult dramatic part few actors can ~⟩ **syn** see SURROUND

en·com·pass·ment \"mənt\ *n* -s **1 :** the act or action of encompassing ⟨the president's adroit ~ of each difficulty⟩ **2 :** the quality or state of being encompassed ⟨had a feeling of complete ~ by unfriendly forces⟩

en·cop·re·sis \,en(,)kä'prēsəs, ,kə'-\ *n, pl* **encopre·ses** \-ē,sēz\ [NL, fr. *en-* (as in *enuresis*) + *copr-* + *-esis*] **:** involuntary defecation of psychic origin

en co·quille \¦äⁿkō¦kē\ *adv (or adj)* [F] **:** in the shell — used esp. of oysters baked in their shells

en·cor·bel·ment *or* **en·cor·bell·ment** \ən'kȯ(r)bəlmənt, en-\ *n* -s [F *encorbellement*, fr. MF *encorbelement*, fr. *en* in (fr. L *in*) + *corbel* + *-ment* — more at CORBEL] **:** projection of each course of masonry over the one below it

¹**en·core** \'än,kō(ə)r, -ȯ(ə)r,-ōə,-ȯ(ə) *sometimes* 'äŋ,k-\ *n* -s *often attrib* [F, still, yet, in addition, prob. fr. (assumed) VL *hinc ad horam*, fr. L *hinc* from here (fr. *hic* this) + *ad* to + *horam* (accus. of *hora* hour) — more at AT, HOUR] **1 :** a request usu. indicative of approbation made by an audience (as by clapping or calls of *encore*) for the further appearance of a performer or the repetition of a particular performance — often used interjectionally **2 :** the further appearance of a performer or an additional performance requested by an audience

²**encore** \"\ *vt* -ED/-ING/-S **:** to request (as by clapping or calls of *encore*) a repetition or the further appearance of ⟨~ a song⟩

¹**en·coun·ter** \ən'kau̇ntə(r), en'-\ *vb* **encountered; encountered; encountering** \-ntəriŋ *also* -n·triŋ\ **encounters** [ME *encountren*, fr. OF *encontrer*, fr. ML *incontrare*, fr. LL *incontra* toward, against, fr. L *in* + *contra* against — more at COUNTER (adv.)] *vt* **1 a :** to meet in the role of an adversary or enemy **:** CONFRONT **b :** to engage in conflict with ⟨enemy raiding parties were ~*ed* and driven back⟩ **2 :** to come upon face to face **:** MEET ⟨~ an old acquaintance on the street⟩ **3 :** to come upon accidentally or unexpectedly ⟨~ difficulties⟩ ~ *vi* **1** *obs* **:** to meet in a hostile manner **2 :** to come together by chance **syn** see MEET

²**encounter** \" *sometimes* 'en,k-\ *n* -s [ME *encountre*, fr. OF *encontre*, fr. *encontrer*, v.] **1 a :** a meeting between hostile factions or persons **b :** a sudden often violent clash **:** BATTLE ⟨a bloody ~⟩ **2 a :** a chance meeting **:** an unexpected often direct coming upon **b :** a direct often momentary meeting **:** momentary or temporary contact **3 :** the coming of one molecule within the sphere of action of another with consequent change of direction or velocity of motion — see COLLISION 2d

encounterer *n* -s *obs* **:** OPPONENT, ADVERSARY

en·cour·age \ən'kər|ij, en-, -kə·r|, |ēj, *chiefly in pres part* |əj\ *vt* -ED/-ING/-S [ME *encoragen*, fr. MF *encoragier*, fr. OF, fr. *en-* ¹en- + *corage* courage — more at COURAGE] **1 :** to give courage to **:** inspire with courage, spirit, or hope **:** HEARTEN ⟨an example that *encouraged* struggling peoples to fight for liberty⟩ **2 :** to spur on **:** STIMULATE, INCITE ⟨the conversation was . . . skillfully *encouraged* by host and hostess —Lucien Price⟩ **3 :** to give help or patronage to **:** FOSTER ⟨government grants designed to ~ conservation⟩ **4 :** to call forth **:** PRODUCE, CREATE ⟨sharp competition among newsmen . . . tends to ~ sensationalism —F.L.Mott⟩

syn INSPIRIT, CHEER, HEARTEN, EMBOLDEN, NERVE, STEEL: ENCOURAGE suggests generally instilling with courage, confidence, and purpose or fostering enough of these characteristics by advice, inducement, or similar influence to perform or endure as indicated ⟨so much is she overshadowed by her husband, who, indeed, did little himself to *encourage* her personality beyond the home —H.S.Canby⟩ ⟨the treatment should begin by *encouraging* him to utter freely even his most shocking thoughts —Bertrand Russell⟩ INSPIRIT, a rather literary word, indicates imparting of a spirit, esp. one of courageous or optimistic resolution ⟨the marches [of Sousa] were most *inspiriting* . . . and so patriotic —Osbert Sitwell⟩ ⟨an astonishing and *inspiriting* record of what human ingenuity can accomplish —Basil Davenport⟩ CHEER indicates lifting up in spirit, either from a degree of sadness or discouragement or to a degree of courage, optimism, and hope needed to continue or persevere ⟨doctored the sick, *cheered* the downhearted . . . and by sheer force of character made himself their indispensable leader —G.H.Genzmer⟩ HEARTEN suggests imparting new or renewed courage, ardor, energy, and optimism ⟨gifts . . . which both strengthen our resources and *hearten* our endeavors —J.B.Conant⟩ ⟨*heartened* by the arrival of three great soldiers —Kenneth Roberts⟩ EMBOLDEN is likely to suggest overcoming timidity, reticence, or reservation and imparting sufficient boldness for whatever is under consideration ⟨on seeing a carriage drive up to the Abbey, she was *emboldened* to descend and meet him under the protection of visitors —Jane Austen⟩ ⟨the government, *emboldened* by this first victory, now aimed a blow at an enemy of a very different class —T.B. Macaulay⟩ NERVE and STEEL are likely to indicate an imparting or collecting of qualities of moral strength, resolution, and courage for some special occasion, accomplishment, task, or duty; they may differ in that STEEL may be stronger in indicating an inflexible resolution or utter insensibility to what would enervate or mollify ⟨this commercial opportunity *nerved* the Ottawas to an unaccustomed doing —Bernard De Voto⟩ ⟨*nerving* myself with the thought that if I got crushed by the fall I should probably escape a lingering and far more painful death, I dropped into the cloud of foliage —W.H.Hudson †1922⟩ ⟨the aspirant must school and *steel* himself to sniffs and sneers —H.L.Mencken⟩ ⟨it taught them to *steel* their wills, to discipline their habits, to work intensively —A.R.Williams⟩ **syn** see in addition FAVOR

en·cour·age·ment \-mənt\ *n* -s **1 :** the act or action of encouraging ⟨the government's ~ of new industries⟩ **2 :** the quality or state of being encouraged **3 :** something that encourages **:** INCENTIVE ⟨gifts of money and other ~*s*⟩

en·cour·ag·er \-jə(r)\ *n* -s **:** one that encourages

encouraging *adj* [fr. pres. part. of *encourage*] **:** giving hope or promise **:** INSPIRITING, FAVORING — **en·cour·ag·ing·ly** *adv*

en·cra·tism \'eŋkrə,tizəm, 'enk-\ *n* -s *usu cap* [*encratite* + *-ism*] **:** the doctrines or tenets of the Encratites

en·cra·tite \-,tīt\ *n* -s *usu cap* [LL *encratita*, fr. LGk *enkratitēs*, fr. Gk *enkratēs* self-disciplined (fr. *en* in + *-kratēs*, fr. *kratos* strength) + *-itēs* -ite — more at IN, HARD] **:** a member of certain 2d century ascetic sects that condemned sexual intercourse, clericalism, and the use of animal food and strong drink — compare APOSTOLICI

en creux \äⁿ'krə̄, -rər(·), *F* -rœ̄\ *adj* [F, lit., in the hollow] **:** being in intaglio **:** sunk below the surface ⟨an engraving *en creux*⟩

en·cri·nal \(')en¦krīnᵊl, (')eŋ¦-\ *adj* [NL *Encrinus* + E *-al*] **:** of, relating to, or made up of encrinites

en·crin·ic \(')en¦krinik, (')eŋ¦-\ *or* **en·cri·nit·al** \¦eŋkrə¦nīdᵊl, ¦enk-\ *adj* [*encrinic* fr. NL *Encrinus* + E *-ic*; *encrinital* fr. *encrinite* + *-al*] **:** ENCRINAL

en·cri·nite \'eŋkrə,nīt, 'enk-\ *n* -s [NL *encrinites*, fr. *Encrinus* + *-ites* -ite] **:** CRINOID; *esp* **:** a fossil crinoid (as one belonging to or like one belonging to the genus *Encrinus*) — **en·cri·nit·ic** \¦==¦nid·ik\ *or* **en·cri·nit·i·cal** \-d·əkəl\ *adj*

en·cri·noid \'eŋkrə,nȯid, 'enk-; en'krī,n-, eŋ'k-\ *adj* [NL *Encrinus* + E *-oid*] **:** ENCRINAL

en·cri·nus \en'krīnəs, eŋ'-\ *n* [NL, fr. ²*en-* + *-crinus* (fr. Gk *krinon* lily)] **1** *cap* **:** a genus (the type of the family Encrinidae) of extinct stalked crinoids whose remains are abundant in some Triassic formations (as in beds of limestone formed chiefly of fragments of their stalks) **2** *pl* **encri·ni** \-,nī\ **:** a crinoid of the genus *Encrinus*

¹**en·croach** \ən'krōch, en-\ *vi* -ED/-ING/-ES [ME *encrochen* to get, seize, fr. MF *encrochier* to seize, hang up, set aloft, fr. OF, fr. *en-* ¹en- + *croc* hook, of Scand origin; akin to ON *krōkr* hook — more at CROOK] **1 :** to enter by gradual steps or by stealth into the possessions or rights of another **:** TRESPASS, INTRUDE — usu. used with *on* or *upon* ⟨~ on the territory of a neighboring country⟩ **2 :** to advance beyond desirable or normal limits **:** take undue liberties — usu. used with *on* or *upon* ⟨a governor ~*ing* upon the liberties of his people⟩ **syn** see TRESPASS

²**encroach** \"\ *n* -ES **:** ENCROACHMENT ⟨the ~ of fungi into crevices⟩

en·croach·ment \-mənt\ *n* -s [ME *encrochement*, fr. AF, fr. MF *encrochier* + *-ment*] **1 :** the act or action of encroaching ⟨the gradual ~ of the white people upon the Indian territories⟩ **2 :** an instance of encroaching (as the building of a structure in a public park or a fence that projects over a neighbor's land)

en·crust *also* **in·crust** \ən'krəst, en-\ *vb* [*encrust* prob. alter. (influenced by ¹*en-*) of *incrust*, fr. L *incrustare*, fr. *in* + *crustare* to encrust, fr. *crusta* crust — more at CRUST] *vt* **1 :** to form a crust on the surface of **:** crust over ⟨the rust of ages ~*ed* the hull⟩ ⟨ice ~*ed* the edges of the pool⟩ **2 a :** COVER, OVERLAY ⟨~ a wall with marble⟩ ⟨~ glass with gold leaf⟩ **b :** to inlay esp. jewels into the surface of **3 :** to conceal or obscure as if with a layer or crust ⟨words that are so heavily ~*ed* with images and feelings that we forget that after all they are only words —J.C.Powys⟩ ~ *vi* **:** to form a crust ⟨salt had ~*ed* on the bottom of the kettle⟩

¹**en·crust·ant** *also* **in·crust·ant** \-stənt\ *adj* **:** forming a crust

²**encrustant** *also* **incrustant** \"\ *n* -s **:** something that forms a crust

encrustation *var of* INCRUSTATION

en·crypt \ən'kript, en-\ *vt* -ED/-ING/-S [¹*en-* + *-crypt* (fr. *cryptogram*, *cryptograph*)] **:** to encipher or encode

en·cryp·tion \-pshən\ *n* -s [*encrypt* + *-ion*] **1 :** the act or process of encrypting **2 :** the result of encrypting

en·cul·tu·rate \ən'kəlchə,rāt, en-\ *vt* -ED/-ING/-S [prob. back-formation fr. *enculturation*] **:** to modify or condition by enculturation ⟨*enculturated* to the established norms of behavior —M.J.Herskovits⟩

en·cul·tu·ra·tion \ən,kəlchə'rāshən, (,)en-\ *n* -s [¹*en-* + *-culturation* (as in *acculturation*)] **:** the process by which an individual learns the traditional content of a culture and assimilates its practices and values — compare SOCIALIZATION — **en·cul·tu·ra·tive** \=¦==,rā|d·iv, -,rə|\ *adj*

en·cum·ber *also* **in·cum·ber** \ən'kəmbə(r), en-\ *vt* **encumbered; encumbered; encumbering** \-b(ə)riŋ\ **encumbers** [ME *encombren*, fr. MF *encombrer* to obstruct, burden, fr. OF, fr. *en-* ¹en- + (assumed) *combre* abatis (whence MF *combre* barrier constructed in the bed of a river to hold back fish or protect the banks), perh. of Celt origin; akin to the source of ML *combrus* abatis and to MIr *commar* confluence; both these fr. a prehistoric Celt compound whose first constituent is represented by OIr *com-* together and whose second constituent is akin to L *ferre* to carry — more at CO-, BEAR] **1 a :** to weigh down ⟨a man ~*ed* with parcels⟩ ⟨shock troops ~*ed* with mortars and flamethrowers⟩ **b :** to load to excess **:** OVERBURDEN ⟨a summer resort . . . ~*ed* with great clapboard-and-stucco hotels —A.J.Liebling⟩ **2 :** to impede or hamper the natural or requisite function or activity of ⟨elaborate ritual ~*ing* international diplomacy⟩ **:** HINDER ⟨a project ~*ed* by lack of funds⟩ **3 :** to load with debts or other legal claims ⟨~ an estate with mortgages⟩ **syn** see BURDEN

en·cum·ber·ing·ly *adv* [*encumbering* (pres. part. of *encumber*) + *-ly*] **:** in a manner to encumber

en·cum·brance \-brən(t)s *also* -bər-\ *n* -s [ME *encombraunce*, fr. OF *encombrance*, fr. *encombrer* + *-ance*] **1** *obs* **:** the quality or state of being encumbered **:** PERPLEXITY, TROUBLE **2 :** something that encumbers **:** a burden that impedes action or renders it difficult **:** IMPEDIMENT **3** *or* **in·cum·brance** \"\ **a :** a burden or charge upon property **:** a claim or lien upon an estate that may diminish its value; *specif* **:** any interest or right in land existing to the diminution of the value of the fee but not preventing the passing of the fee by conveyance **b :** a dependent person (as a child)

en·cum·branc·er \-nsə(r)\ *n* -s **:** one that holds an encumbrance

-en·cy \ənsē, ᵊn-, -si\ *n suffix* -ES [ME *-encie*, fr. L *-entia* — more at -ENCE] **1 :** quality or state ⟨efficiency⟩ ⟨expediency⟩ **2 :** one having a (specified) quality or being in a (specified) state ⟨His Excell*ency*⟩ **3 :** instance of a (specified) quality or state ⟨repeated inadvert*encies*⟩

ency *or* **encyc** *abbr* encyclopedia

¹**en·cyc·li·cal** \ən'sikləkəl, en-, -lēk-\ *also* **en·cyc·lic** \-klik, -lēk\ *adj* [*encyclical* fr. LL *encyclicus* + E *-al*; *encyclic* fr. LL *encyclicus*, modif. (influenced by L *-icus* -ic) of Gk *enkyklios* circular, general, fr. *en* in + *kyklos* circle, wheel — more at IN, WHEEL] **:** sent to many persons or places **:** intended for many or for a whole order **:** GENERAL ⟨an ~ letter⟩

²**encyclical** \"\ *also* **encyclic** \"\ *n* -s **:** an encyclical letter (as sent by a bishop or high church official) that treats a matter of grave or timely importance and is intended for extensive circulation; *specif* **:** such a letter issued by a pope

en·cy·clo·pe·dia *also* **en·cy·clo·pae·dia** \ən,sīklə'pēdēə, (,)en-, *in rapid speech sometimes* -dē *in some contexts, as in "Encyclopaedia Britannica"*\ *n* -s [ML *encyclopaedia* course of general education, fr. a supposed Gk *enkyklopaideia* (in MSS of the Roman rhetorician Quintilian), fr. Gk *enkyklios paideia* general education, fr. *enkyklios* general + *paideia* education, rearing of a child, fr. *paid-*, *pais* child — more at FOAL] **:** a work that treats comprehensively all the various branches of knowledge and that is usu. composed of individual articles arranged alphabetically; *also* **:** such a work treating only a particular branch of knowledge ⟨an ~ of agriculture⟩ ⟨an ~ of religion⟩

en·cy·clo·pe·di·ast *also* **en·cy·clo·pae·di·ast** \-dē,ast, -,əst\ *n* -s [*encyclopedia*, *encyclopaedia* + *-ast*] **:** ENCYCLOPEDIST

en·cy·clo·pe·dic *also* **en·cy·clo·pae·dic** \ən¦==¦pēdik, (¦)en-, -dēk\ *also* **en·cy·clo·pe·di·cal** *also* **en·cy·clo·pae·di·cal** \-dəkəl, -dēk-\ *adj* [*encyclopedia*, *encyclopaedia* + *-ic*, *-ical*] **:** of, relating to, resembling, or suggestive of an encyclopedia or its methods of treating or covering a subject: as **a :** embracing or informed in a wide range of subjects ⟨an ~ mind⟩ **b :** comprehensive in treatment or knowledge of a subject ⟨an ~ article on Egyptian religion⟩ — **en·cy·clo·pe·di·cal·ly** *also* **en·cy·clo·pae·di·cal·ly** \-dək(ə)lē, -dēk-, -li\ *adv*

en·cy·clo·pe·dism *also* **en·cy·clo·pae·dism** \=,==¦pē,dizəm\ *n* -s [*encyclopedia*, *encyclopaedia* + *-ism*] **1 :** possession of a wide range of knowledge **2** *often cap* **:** the writings, views, and influence on thought of the encyclopedists

en·cy·clo·pe·dist *also* **en·cy·clo·pae·dist** \-ēdəst\ *n* -s [*encyclopedia*, *encyclopaedia* + *-ist*] **1 :** one who compiles or assists in the compilation of an encyclopedia **2** [F *encyclopédiste*, fr. *encyclopédie* encyclopedia (fr. ML *encyclopaedia*) + *-iste* -ist] **a** *often cap* **:** one of the writers of the French *Encyclopédie ou Dictionnaire raisonné des Sciences, des Arts, et des Métiers* (1751-80) who were identified with the Enlightenment and advocated deism and scientific rationalism **b :** one who adheres to or displays affinities with 18th century rationalism

¹**en·cyr·tid** \ən'sərd·əd, (')en¦s-\ *adj* [NL *Encyrtidae*] **:** of or relating to the Encyrtidae

²**encyrtid** \"\ *n* -s **:** a fly of the family Encyrtidae

en·cyr·ti·dae \ən'sərd·ə,dē, en-\ *n pl, cap* [NL, fr. *Encyrtus*, type genus (fr. Gk *enkyrtos* curved, crooked, fr. *en* in + *kyrtos* convex, bulging) + *-idae*; akin to L *curvus* curved — more at IN, CROWN] **:** a large cosmopolitan family of small chalcid wasps parasitic in the eggs or later stages of many insects

en·cyst \ən'sist, en-\ *vb* -ED/-ING/-S [¹*en-* + *cyst*, n.] *vt* **:** to enclose in or as if in a cyst or capsule ⟨an ~*ed* tumor⟩ ~ *vi* **:** to form or become enclosed in a cyst or capsule ⟨protozoans ~*ing* in order to resist desiccation⟩

en·cys·ta·tion \,en,si'stāshən, ən-\ *n* -s **:** ENCYSTMENT

en·cyst·ment \ən'sis(t)mənt, en-\ *n* -s **:** the process of forming a cyst or becoming enclosed in a capsule

¹**end** \'end\ *n* -s [ME *ende*, fr. OE; akin to OHG *enti* end, ON *endir*, Goth *andeis* end, L *ante* before, Gk *anti* against, Skt *anta* end, Hitt *hanz* front] **1 a** (1) **:** the portion of an area or territory that lies at or by the termination and that often serves as a delimitation or boundary; *specif* **:** a section of a city not within the center portion ⟨the East *End* of London⟩ (2) **:** the extreme, ultimate, or most remote section or area ⟨a criminal hunted to the very ~*s* of the earth⟩ **b** (1) **:** a point that marks the extent of something **:** LIMIT ⟨no ~ of good things⟩ ⟨gifts without ~ showered upon the newcomers⟩ (2) **:** the point where something possessed of or exhibiting temporal progression ceases to exist ⟨the ~ of the fiscal year⟩ ⟨the ~ of a bullet's flight⟩ **c** (1) **:** a narrow, sharp, or pointed part of something longitudinal or slender ⟨the ~ of a pencil⟩ ⟨the ~*s* of a pole⟩ ⟨the dangerous ~ of a knife⟩ (2) **:** the extreme or last part lengthwise ⟨the ~ of a board⟩ ⟨~ of a garden⟩ ⟨~ of a rope⟩ ⟨the rear ~ of an automobile⟩ **d** (1) **:** the terminal unit of something spatial that is marked off by or exhibits a progression of units ⟨the ~ of a series⟩ (2) **:** the portion of a distillate (as from petroleum) at either extremity of its distillation range ⟨the light or low ~*s* are the most volatile portions⟩ (3) **:** END MAN (4) **:** a player stationed at the extremity of a line or team (as in football) **e** (1) **:** the heading of a barrel or the lid of a metal can or drum (2) **:** either half of a domino face (3) **:** either extremity of a cricket pitch ⟨batsmen changing ~*s* after a run⟩ **2 a :** cessation of a course of action, pursuit, or activity ⟨the ~ of a war⟩ ⟨working and never seeing the ~ in sight⟩ **b** (1) **:** termination of being **:** DEATH ⟨an opponent of taxation until his very ~⟩ (2) **:** the dissolution of structural or functional existence **:** DESTRUCTION, DEMOLITION ⟨a freighter that met its ~ in a hurricane⟩ **c** (1) **:** the ultimate state **:** final condition ⟨the ~ being utter oblivion⟩ (2) **:** the result of an activity **:** ISSUE ⟨the ~ of the matter being general agreement⟩ **d :** the complex of events, parts, or sections that forms an extremity, termination, or finish ⟨the frontal attacks that marked the ~ of the war⟩ **3 :** something incomplete, fragmentary, or undersize: as **a :** a leftover or scrap **:** REMNANT ⟨the ~*s* of meat⟩ — see ODDS AND ENDS **b :** a short or half piece of cloth — see MILL END **c :** a deal or batten of timber less than eight feet long **4 a :** an outcome worked toward esp. with forethought, deliberate planning, and organized effort **:** PURPOSE ⟨the ~ being complete mastery of the subject⟩ ⟨a politician working to the ~ that all debts be paid off⟩ **b** (1) **:** the goal, ultimate intention, or purpose for the attainment of which an agent does something or ought to be acting (2) **:** the object by virtue of which or the objective for the sake of which an event or a series of events happens or is said to take place **:** a final cause **5 a :** a particular duty **:** share in an undertaking — used with *keep* and *up* ⟨he was able to keep his ~ up⟩ **b :** a department or particular phase of an undertaking, business, or organization ⟨the advertising ~ of insurance⟩ **6 a :** a unit or turn in shooting (as in archery) **b :** an inning in a game played from one limit of a course toward the other (as in bowls) **7 a** (1) **:** a warp thread or yarn (2) **:** a single sliver, roving, or yarn while in the process of manufacture on a textile machine **b :** WAXED END **8 :** the number of arrows (as three in England and six in America) shot by an archer during his turn

syn TERMINATION, ENDING, TERMINUS: END, the most common and most inclusive of the terms, may apply to the finish or the final limit in nearly any application ⟨the *end* of a meal⟩ ⟨the *end* of a book⟩ ⟨the *end* of a road⟩ ⟨the *end* of a life⟩ ⟨the *end* of a play⟩ ⟨the *end* of a journey⟩ ⟨the *end* of a friendship⟩ ⟨the *end* of one's endurance⟩ TERMINATION or ENDING usu. applies to an end in time or, less often, in space, of something that is brought to a close as by having set bounds or by being completed or no longer purposeful, ENDING often also including a portion prior to the exact terminal point ⟨the *termination* of a lease⟩ ⟨the *termination* of a moratorium⟩ ⟨the *ending* of a play⟩ ⟨the *ending* of vacation⟩ ⟨to change the *ending* of a song⟩ ⟨a long *ending* to a symphony⟩ TERMINUS applies to an end, usu. a definite point or place, to which something moves or progresses or beyond which it does not go ⟨the modern city hall is the *terminus* of the tour⟩ ⟨an airline *terminus*⟩ ⟨the northern *terminus* of the natural-gas pipeline⟩ ⟨the eighth grade is for many the *terminus* of religious teaching —C.T.H. Sherlock⟩ **syn** see in addition INTENTION

— **end for end** *adv* **:** with the ends reversed **:** upside down ⟨it will fit if you turn it *end for end*⟩ — **end of one's rope :** the limit of one's endurance, patience, or resources — **in the end** *adv* **:** after all **:** ULTIMATELY — **no end** *adv* **:** AWFULLY, EXCEEDINGLY ⟨the whole crowd was *no end* put out by the poor spirit of the home team⟩ — **on end** *adv* **1 :** with the end down or on the bottom ⟨a box standing *on end*⟩ **2 :** without a break or stop **:** with no letup ⟨rained for days *on end*⟩

²end \" \ *vb* -ED/-ING/-S [ME *enden*, fr. OE *endian;* akin to OHG *entōn* to end, ON *enda;* denominative fr. the root of E ¹end] *vt* **1** *obs* **:** to carry out **:** perform fully **2 a :** to bring to an end **:** TERMINATE ⟨the speech ~*ed* the ceremonies⟩ **b :** to bring about the death of **:** KILL ⟨if he love another, may panthers ~ him —W.B.Yeats⟩ **3 :** to make up the end of **:** constitute the last element of ⟨*k* ~*s* the word *back*⟩ ⟨a brass band ~*ed* the parade⟩ **4 :** to place on end **:** UPEND **5 :** to stand as the supreme example of — usu. used in the infinitive ⟨a novel to ~ all novels⟩ **6 :** to attach the top and bottom pieces of (a set-up paper box) ⟨containers ~*ed* by hand⟩ ~ *vi* **1 a :** to come to an end **:** reach a final or ultimate point ⟨the song ~*ed* on a high note⟩ — often used with *up* ⟨the party ~*s* up with dancing⟩ or *in* ⟨his efforts ~*ed* in failure⟩ **b :** to come to a conclusion or ultimate state or situation ⟨the poem stops rather than ~*s*⟩ — often used with *up* ⟨the whole gang ~*ed* up in jail⟩ **2 :** DIE ⟨his parents ~*ed* in the . . . gas ovens —Joseph Alsop⟩ — sometimes used with *up* **syn** see CLOSE

³end \" \ *vt* [prob. alter. of ³*in*, v.] *now dial Eng* **:** to put (grain or hay) into a barn or stack

end *abbr* endorsed; endorsement

end- *or* **endo-** *comb form* [F, fr. Gk, fr. *endon* within, at home, fr. *en* in + *-don* (perh. akin to L *domus* house) — more at IN, TIMBER] **1 a :** within **:** inside ⟨*End*amoeba⟩ ⟨*endo*scope⟩ **b :** taking in **:** requiring ⟨*end*ergonic⟩ — opposed to *exo-* **2** *endo-* **a :** forming a bridge between two atoms in a cyclic system or having a bond or bivalent radical regarded as a bridge ⟨*endo*ethylenic bridge⟩ ⟨1,4-*endo*methylene-cyclohexane⟩ **b** *sometimes ital* **:** having one or more substituents directed inward — in names of stereoisomeric compounds containing a 6-membered ring in its boat form ⟨2,5-methylene-*endo*-cyclohexyl-amine⟩; compare EXO- b **3 :** endocardium and ⟨*endo*pericarditis⟩

end–all \ˈ=,=\ *n* -S **:** something that stands as the ultimate goal or conclusion ⟨elucidating . . . may not be the *end-all* of philosophical activity —Morris Weitz⟩

en·damage \ən, en+\ *vt* [ME *endamagen*, prob. fr. ¹*en-* + *damage*, n.] **:** to cause loss or damage to **:** HARM, INJURE ⟨testimony sufficient to ~ a reputation⟩ — **en·dam·age·ment** \"mənt\ *n* -S

end·amebiasis *or* **end·amoebiasis** \ˌend+\ *n* [NL *endamoebiasis*, fr. *Endamoeba* + *-iasis*] **:** infection with or disease caused by amoebas of the genus *Endamoeba* **:** AMEBIASIS

end·amoeba \ˌend+\ *n* [NL, fr. *end-* + *amoeba*] **1** *cap* **:** the type genus of the family Endamoebidae comprising amoebas parasitic in the intestines of insects and in some classifications various parasites of vertebrates including the amoeba (*E. histolytica*) that causes amebic dysentery in man — see ENTAMOEBA **2** *also* **end·ame·ba** \"+\ **:** any amoeba of the genus *Endamoeba* including *Entamoeba* — **end·amoebic** *also* **end·amebic** \"+\ *adj*

end·amoe·bi·dae \ˌendəˈmēbəˌdē\ *n pl, cap* [NL, fr. *Endamoeba*, type genus + *-idae*] **:** a large family of endoparasitic amoebas (order Amoebina) that invade the digestive tract of vertebrates and invertebrates and are typically passed from host to host in a resistant cyst through the medium of contaminated food or drink — compare ENDAMOEBA, ENTAMOEBA

end–and–end \ˈ=,=ˈ=\ *adj, of textiles* **:** woven with warp threads of alternating white and color and filling threads of one color or alternating white and color for a striped or checked effect

en·dan·ger \ənˈdānjə(r), en-\ **endangered; endangered; endangering** \-j(ə)riŋ\ **endangers** *vt* [ME *endaungeren*, fr. ¹*en-* + *daunger* power, jurisdiction — more at DANGER] **1** *obs* **:** to subject to another's power; *also* **:** to make liable to punishment or arrest **2 :** to bring into danger or peril of probable harm or loss **:** imperil or threaten danger to ⟨he condemned the abolitionists as agitators who actually ~*ed* the cause of freedom —A.C.Cole⟩ ~ *vi* **:** to create a dangerous situation ⟨driving to ~⟩ **syn** see VENTURE

en·dan·ger·ment \-jə(r)mənt\ *n* -S **:** the act of placing in danger or the state of being placed in danger ⟨an act that constituted an ~ of the state⟩ ⟨had never been in a position of ~ before⟩

end·aortic \ˌend+\ *adj* [*end-* + *aortic*] **:** of or relating to the interior of the aorta or to its lining membrane

en·darch \ˈenˌdärk\ *adj* [*end-* + *-arch*] **:** formed or taking place from the center outward — used of the primary xylem (as of a root) or its development; compare EXARCH, MESARCH — **en·dar·chy** \-kē\ *n* -ES

endark *or* **endarken** *vt* [*endark* fr. ME *endarken*, fr. ¹*en-* + *derk*, *dark* dark; *endarken* fr. ¹*en-* + *darken* — more at DARK (adj.)] *obs* **:** DARKEN

end around *n* **:** a football play in which an offensive end comes behind the line of scrimmage to take a hand-off and attempts to carry the ball around the opposite flank

end·arterial \ˌend+\ *adj* [*end-* + *arterial*] **:** of or relating to the intima of an artery

end·arteritis \ˌend+\ *n* [NL, fr. *end-* + *arteritis*] **:** inflammation of the intima of one or more arteries

endarteritis ob·lit·er·ans \-əˈblidəˌranz\ *n* [NL, obliterating endarteritis] **:** endarteritis in which the intimal tissue proliferates and ultimately plugs the lumen of an affected artery

end·ar·te·ri·um \ˌendärˈtirēəm\ *n, pl* **endarte·ria** \-ēə\ [NL, fr. *end-* + L *arterium* artery, alter. of *arteria* — more at ARTERY] **:** the intima of an artery

endartery \ˈ=,=(=)=\ *n* [¹*end* + *artery;* trans. of G *endarterie*] **:** a terminal artery supplying all or most of the blood to a body part without significant collateral circulation

en dash *n* [¹*en*] **:** a dash that is one-half the length of an em dash

endball \ˈ=,=\ *n* [¹*end* + *ball*] **:** a game played with a basketball on a divided court with one third of each team standing in its own end zone and the remaining players occupying the opposite playing area and attempting to score by tossing the ball over the opponents to their teammates in the end zone

end batter *n* **:** the mashing and wear of a rail at a rail joint caused by the repeated passing of railroad-car wheels

endboard \ˈ=,=\ *n* **:** TAILBOARD

endbrain \ˈ=,=\ *n* [trans. of NL *telencephalon*] **:** the anterior subdivision of the forebrain **:** TELENCEPHALON

end brush *n* **:** END PLATE

end bud *n* **1 :** END BULB 1 **2 :** the knob of tissue undifferentiated into germ layers that forms the primitive knot and later forms posterior portions of the body of an embryo

end bulb *n* **1** *also* **end corpuscle :** one of the bulbous bodies in which some of the sensory nerve fibers end in certain parts of the skin and mucous membranes **2 :** BOUTON

end cell *n* **:** one of those cells of a storage battery which may be switched in or out of the circuit to adjust the voltage

end construction *n* **:** hollow structural blocks or tiles laid with the cells running vertically — compare SIDE CONSTRUCTION

end–cut brick *n* **:** brick having the end surfaces wire-cut — compare SIDE-CUT BRICK

end–dump \ˈ=,=\ *adj* **:** having a truck body that tips up and discharges its contents from the rear end ⟨an *end-dump* truck⟩

en·dear \ənˈdi(ə)r, en-, -iə\ *vt* -ED/-ING/-S [¹*en-* + *dear*, adj.] **1** *obs* **:** to make higher in cost, value, or estimation **2** *obs* **:** to value highly or hold in affection or love **3 :** to make dear, beloved, or esteemed ⟨his humor ~*ed* him to the public⟩ ⟨they ~*ed* themselves to the whole town⟩

endearing *adj* [fr. pres. part. of *endear*] **:** arousing affection, tenderness, or admiration ⟨~ smile⟩ ⟨~ qualities⟩ — **en·dear·ing·ly** *adv* — **en·dear·ing·ness** *n* -ES

en·dear·ment \-di(ə)rmənt, -diəm-\ *n* -S **1 :** the act or process of endearing ⟨the passionate embrace, the joy in personal ~ —H.A.Overstreet⟩ **2 :** something that endears or manifests affection ⟨a term of ~⟩ ⟨peculiarly lavish of the ~*s* —D.H.Lawrence⟩ **:** CARESS **3** *obs* **a :** ENHANCEMENT **b :** attachment through love or gratitude

¹en·deav·or *also* **en·deav·our** \ənˈdevə(r), en-\ *vb* **endeavored; endeavored; endeavoring** \-v(ə)riŋ\ **endeavors** [ME *endeveren*, fr. ¹*en-* + *dever* duty — more at DEVOIR] *vt* **1 a** *obs* **:** to exert (oneself) strenuously **b :** TRY 6 ⟨she walked up and down the room, ~*ing* to compose herself —Jane Austen⟩ **2** *obs* **:** to strive to achieve or reach **3** *obs* **:** to make an attack against ~ *vi* **1** *obs* **:** to exert oneself **:** STRIVE **2 :** to work with set purpose **:** make an effort ⟨however much he ~*ed*, the goal stayed unattained⟩ **syn** see TRY

²endeavor *also* **endeavour** \" \ *n* -S [ME *endevour*, fr. *endeveren*, v.] **:** a serious determined effort ⟨an ~ to bring about national economic stabilization —B.F.Fairless⟩

endeavor river pear *n, cap E&R* [fr. *Endeavour river*, Queensland, Australia] **:** an Australian plant (*Eugenia eucalyptoides*) having fruit used in jam

endecasyllabic *var of* HENDECASYLLABIC

en·de·cha \enˈdächa\ *n* -S [Sp, prob. fr. L *indicta*, neut. pl. of *indictus*, past part. of *indicere* to proclaim, announce, fr. *in* + *dicere* to say — more at DICTION] **:** a short mournful Spanish song usu. having four lines of six or seven syllables

ended *past of* END

en de·dans \äⁿd(ə)däⁿ\ *adv (or adj)* [F, inside] **:** INWARD — used of a circular ballet movement of arms or legs leading toward the body or of the position in which the toes are turned in

en de·hors \äⁿdə(h)ȯr\ *adv (or adj)* [F, outside] **:** OUTWARD — used of a circular ballet movement of arms or legs leading away from the body or of the position in which the toes are turned out

en·dek \ˈenˌdek\ *n* -S *usu cap* [Pol, fr. *en* (name of the letter *n*, here standing for the initial letter of the first word of *Narodowa Demokracja* National Democratic party, lit., National Democracy) + *-dek* (irreg. fr. the *d* and *k* in *Demokracja*)] **:** a member of the fascist anti-Semitic National Democratic party of Poland

en·del·lion·ite \enˈdelyəˌnīt\ *n* -S [G *endellionit*, fr. *Endellion*, Cornwall, England, its locality + G *-it* -ite] **:** BOURNONITE

en·dell·ite \ˈendəˌlīt\ *n* -S [fr. Kurd *Endell* †1946 Ger. ceramic engineer + E *-ite*] **:** a clay mineral consisting of hydrous silicate of aluminum with varying amounts of water and being more hydrous than halloysite

en·de·mi·al \(ˈ)enˈdēmēəl\ *adj* [Gk *endēmios* native, endemic (fr. *en* in + *dēmos*) + E *-al*] **:** ENDEMIC

¹en·dem·ic \(ˈ)enˈdemik, -mēk *sometimes* -dēm-\ *also* **en·dem·i·cal** \-məkəl, -mēk-\ *adj* [*endemic* fr. F *endémique*, fr. *endémie*, n., endemic (fr. Gk *endēmia* action of dwelling or staying, fr. *endēmos*, adj., native, endemic — fr. *en* in + *dēmos* deme, populace — + *-ia* -y) + *-ique* -ic; *endemical* fr. F *endémique* + E *-al* — more at DEM-] **1 :** belonging or native to a particular people or country **:** not introduced or naturalized ⟨the many shades of radicalism ~ in Spain —*Harper's*⟩ **2 :** restricted to or native to a particular area or region **:** INDIGENOUS — used of kinds of organisms ⟨the islands have a number of interesting ~ species⟩; compare EXOTIC **3 :** peculiar to a locality or region — used of a disease that is constantly present to a greater or less extent in a particular place; distinguished from *epidemic, sporadic* **syn** see NATIVE

²endemic \" \ *n* -S **1 :** an endemic disease or an instance of its occurrence **2 :** an organism or kind of organism (as a species) that is endemic **:** INDIGENE

en·dem·i·cal·ly \-mək(ə)lē, -mēk-, -li\ *adv* **:** in an endemic manner **:** natively and not by introduction from outside or by naturalization **:** as a phenomenon peculiar to a locality

en·de·mic·i·ty \ˌendəˈmisədē\ *n* -ES [ISV ¹*endemic* + *-ity*] **:** ENDEMISM

en·de·mism \ˈendəˌmizəm\ *n* -S [ISV *endem-* (fr. ¹*endemic*) + *-ism*] **:** the quality or state of being endemic

en·den·i·za·tion \ənˌdenəˈzāshən, (ˌ)enˌd-\ *n* -S [¹*en-* + *denize* + *-ation*] *archaic* **:** the act or process of naturalizing **:** DENIZATION

endenize *vt* [¹*en-* + *denize*] *obs* **:** ENDENIZEN

en·denizen \ən, en+\ *vt* [¹*en-* + *denizen*, n.] **:** to admit to the privileges of a denizen **:** NATURALIZE

end·er·gon·ic \ˌen(ˌ)dərˈgänik\ *adj* [*end-* + Gk *ergon* work + E *-ic* — more at WORK] **:** requiring work or the expenditure of energy — opposed to *exergonic;* used of a chemical reaction occurring in biological processes

en·der·mat·ic \ˌendə(r)ˈmad·ik\ *adj* [²*en-* + *dermat-* + *-ic*] **:** ENDERMIC

en·der·mic \(ˈ)enˈdərmik\ *adj* [ISV ²*en-* + *derm-* + *-ic*] **:** acting through the skin or by direct application to the skin ⟨~ ointment⟩ or applied in the skin ⟨~ injection⟩ **:** INTRADERMAL — **en·der·mi·cal·ly** \-mək(ə)lē, -mēk-, -li\ *adv*

en dés·ha·bil·lé \äⁿdāzàbēyā\ *adv (or adj)* [F] **:** in a state of undress

en·dew *obs var of* ENDUE

end–fire array *n* **:** a radio antenna with strong directional properties consisting of a number of antenna elements arranged in a line

end fly *n* **:** TAIL FLY

end fold *n* **:** the portion of a wrapper that is folded and adhered to the bottom of the package

end foot *n* **:** BOUTON

end game *n* **1 :** the last stage (as the last three tricks) in playing a bridge hand **2 :** the final phase of a board game; *specif* **:** the stage of a chess game following serious reduction of forces

endgate \ˈ=,=\ *n* **:** TAILBOARD

endgate seeder *n* **:** a seeding machine attached to the rear of a wagon or truck and used to broadcast seeds

endgate spreader *n* **:** a 2-wheeled machine attached to the rear of a truck or wagon that distributes ground limestone or fertilizer by means of gears activated by the wheels

end–grain \ˈ=,=\ *adv (or adj)* **:** with the end of the wood grain outward **:** across the grain

end–grain nailing *n* **:** nailing in which the nail shanks run parallel to the grain of the wood

end group *n* **:** a group at the end of a chain of a molecule; *esp* **:** a functional group at the end of the chain of a linear polymer ⟨the amino and carboxyl *end groups* in a polypeptide⟩

endhand \ˈ=,=\ *n* [trans. of G *hinterhand*] **:** the last skat player in turn to bid — called also *hinterhand*

end hardening *n* **:** the treating by heat of the upper part of a railhead at the end to minimize end batter

end·ing \ˈendiŋ, -dēŋ\ *n* -S [ME *ending, endinge*, fr. OE *endung*, fr. *endian* to end + *-ung* -ing — more at ²END] **:** something that constitutes an end: as **a :** CONCLUSION **b :** death or destruction **c** (1) **:** one or more letters or syllables added to a word base (as in inflection) (2) **:** a sound or class of sounds peculiar to or found in final syllables **syn** see END

¹en·dite \enˈdīt\ *archaic var of* INDITE

²en·dite \ˈenˌdīt\ *n* -S [*end-* + *-ite*] **1 :** one of the appendages of the inner side of the limb of an arthropod **2 :** the chewing ridge on the inner surface of the pedipalpus or maxilla of many arachnids

end–item \ˈ=,==\ *n* **:** a manufactured product that can be put to use without further work being done on it ⟨military *end-items*⟩

en·dive \ˈenˌdīv *sometimes* ˈänˌdēv *or* änˈdēv\ *n* -S [ME, fr. MF, fr. LL *endivia*, alter. of L *intubus, intibus*, perh. of Sem origin; akin to Ar *hindab* endive] **1 :** an annual or biennial herb (*Cichorium endivia*) probably native to India but widely cultivated as a salad plant and occurring in cultivation in two forms distinguished by one having deeply lobed and laciniate leaves and the other having much-curled but entire leaves — called also *escarole* **2 :** the developing crown of chicory when blanched for use as salad — called also *French endive, witloof*

endive blue *n* **:** ²IRIS 3

end lap *n* **1** *or* **end lap joint :** a joint (as of two boards) made by cutting away half the thickness of each member so that each overlaps the other — called also *half lap* **2 :** the overlapping parts of successive aerial photographs of contiguous areas in a line of flight

endleaf \ˈ=,=\ *n* **:** ENDPAPER

end·less \ˈen(d)ləs\ *adj* [ME *endelees*, fr. OE *endelēas*, fr. *ende* end + *-lēas* -less — more at ¹END, -LESS] **1 :** having no end **:** BOUNDLESS, INFINITE ⟨~ duration⟩ ⟨an ~ line⟩ ⟨~ praise⟩ **2 :** extremely numerous **:** very many ⟨~ waves⟩ ⟨~ scraps⟩ **3 :** united at the ends so as to form a continuous whole ⟨an ~ chain⟩ — **end·less·ly** *adv*

endless belt *n* **:** a conveyor in the form of a continuous belt traveling around a set of pulleys

end·less·ness *n* -ES [ME *endelesnesse*, fr. *endeles, endelees* endless + *-nesse* -ness] **:** the quality or state of being endless **:** PERPETUITY

end·lich·ite \ˈen(d)liˌkīt, ˈentl-\ *n* -S [fr. F. M. *Endlich*, 19th cent. American + E *-ite*] **:** a mineral $Pb_5Cl[(As,V)O_4]_3$ in composition falling between mimetite and vanadinite and consisting of lead arsenate, vanadate, and chloride

end line *n* **:** a line marking an end or boundary: as **a :** a line at either end of a football field 10 yards beyond and parallel with the goal line — see FOOTBALL illustration **b :** either of the lines running at right angles to the sidelines and marking the two ends of a basketball court — see BASKETBALL illustration

end loader *n* **:** a pneumatic or hydraulic platform elevator that lifts loads to the level of the rear of a truck

endlong \ˈ=,=\ *adv* [ME *endelong*, by folk etymology (influence of *ende* end) fr. *andlong*, fr. OE *andlang*, adv., along, fr. *andlang*, prep., along — more at ALONG] *archaic* **:** LENGTHWISE

end man *n* **:** the last man in a row; *esp* **:** the man at each end of the line of performers who with the interlocutor creates the comic repartee of a minstrel show

end–match \ˈ=,=\ *vt* **:** to finish (as flooring) at the end with a tongue and groove

end matter *n* **:** BACK MATTER

end–member \ˈ=,==\ *n* **:** a pure chemical compound in some cases hypothetical but regarded as a component entering into solid solution with other pure chemical compounds to form an isomorphous series of minerals ⟨fayalite Fe_2SiO_4 and forsterite Mg_2SiO_4 are *end-members* of the olivine series $(Mg,Fe)_2SiO_4$⟩

end mill *n* **:** a milling cutter having cutting teeth on the end of a cylindrical shank and usu. spiral blades on the lateral surface — see MILLING CUTTER illustration

end moraine *n* **:** a moraine deposited by a glacier at its end — compare TERMINAL MORAINE

end·most \ˈen(d)ˌmōst\ *adj* **:** situated at the very end **:** FARTHEST

endnote \ˈ=,=\ *n* **:** a note placed at the end of the text (as of an article or chapter) — compare FOOTNOTE

en·do \ˈen(ˌ)dō\ *adj* [*end-*] **:** being, having, or characterized by valence bonds of a 6-membered ring in its boat form that are directed inward ⟨the ~ form of dicyclopentadiene⟩ — compare END- 2b

endo- — see END-

en·do·adaptation \ˌen(ˌ)dō+\ *n* [*end-* + *adaptation*] **:** modification of an organism resulting in more effective interaction between its various parts — compare EXOADAPTATION

en·do·basal body \ˌendō+ . . . -\ *n* [*end-* + *basal*] **:** an intranuclear body serving as a centrosome (as in protozoans)

en·do·basion \ˌendō+\ *n* [*end-* + *basion*] **:** the most anterior point of the edge of the foramen magnum at the level of its smallest diameter

en·do·batholithic \ˌen(ˌ)dō+\ *adj* [*end-* + *batholithic*] **:** of or relating to ore deposits formed in and near the roof pendants of a large batholith where the intrusive rock predominates

en·do·biotic \"+\ *adj* [ISV *end-* + *-biotic*] **:** dwelling within the tissues of a host as parasite or symbiont

en·do·blast \ˈendəˌblast\ *n* -S [ISV *end-* + *-blast*] **:** HYPOBLAST — **en·do·blas·tic** \ˌ==ˈblastik\ *adj*

en·do·bronchial \ˌen(ˌ)dō+\ *adj* [*end-* + *bronchial*] **:** located within a bronchus ⟨~ tuberculosis⟩ — **en·do·bronchially** \"+\ *adv*

en·do·cannibalism \"+\ *n* [ISV *end-* + *cannibalism;* orig. formed as G *endokannibalismus*] **:** cannibalism of members of one's own family or tribe — contrasted with *exocannibalism*

en·do·can·thi·on \ˌendōˈkan(t)thēən, -ēˌän\ *n* -S [*end-* + *-canthion* (irreg. fr. LL *canthus* corner of the eye) — more at CANTHUS] **:** the point at which the inner ends of the upper and lower eyelid meet — compare ECTOCANTHION

en·do·cardiac \ˌen(ˌ)dō+\ *adj* [ISV *end-* + *cardiac*] **:** ENDOCARDIAL

en·do·car·di·al \ˌendōˈkärdēəl\ *adj* [*end-* + Gk *kardia* heart + E *-al* — more at HEART] **:** situated within the heart **:** of, relating to, or involving the endocardium

en·do·carditis \ˌendō+\ *n* [NL, fr. *endocardium* + *-itis*] **:** inflammation of the lining of the heart and its valves produced by bacterial infection or other causes

en·do·car·di·um \ˌendōˈkärdēəm\ *n, pl* **endocar·dia** \-ēə\ [NL, fr. *end-* + *-cardium*] **:** a thin serous membrane lining the cavities of the heart

en·do·carp \ˈendəˌkärp\ *n* -S [F *endocarpe*, fr. *end-* + *-carpe* -carp (fr. NL *-carpium*)] **:** the inner layer of the pericarp when it consists of two or more layers of different texture or consistency (as in the apple or orange) — compare EPICARP, MESOCARP — **en·do·car·pal** \ˌ==ˈkärpəl\ *or* **en·do·car·pic** \-pik\ *adj*

vertical section of a cherry, showing *1* epicarp, *2* mesocarp, *3* endocarp, *4* seed. *1*, *2*, and *3* together form the pericarp

en·do·car·poid \-ˌpȯid\ *adj* [NL *Endocarpon* genus of lichens having the apothecia immersed in the thallus (fr. *end-* + *-carpon*, fr. Gk *-karpon*, neut. of *-karpos* -carpous) + E *-oid*] *of lichens* **:** having the apothecia immersed in the thallus

en·do·cellular \ˌen(ˌ)dō+\ *adj* [ISV *end-* + *cellular*] **:** INTRACELLULAR

en·do·centric \ˌendō+\ *adj* [*end-* + *-centric*] **:** having the same grammatical function as one of its immediate constituents that does not modify the other immediate constituent — used of a compound or construction (as *blackbird*, which is like *bird* in function, or *my little Mary*, which is like *Mary* in function); compare EXOCENTRIC

en·doc·er·as \enˈdäsərəs\ *n, cap* [NL, fr. *end-* + *-ceras*] **:** a genus (the type of the family Endoceratidae) of Ordovician and Silurian nautiloid cephalopods with a straight shell having a very large siphuncle and endocones and reaching a length of 12 feet — **en·do·cer·a·tid** \ˌendōˈserəd·əd\ *adj or n*

en·do·cer·a·tite \ˌ==ˈserəˌtīt\ *n* -S [NL *Endocerat-, Endoceras* + E *-ite*] **:** a fossil of the genus *Endoceras* — **en·do·cer·a·tit·ic** \ˌ==,==ˈtid·ik\ *adj* — **en·do·cer·a·toid** \ˌ==ˈ==,tȯid\ *n* -S

en·do·cervical \ˌen(ˌ)dō+\ *adj* [NL *endocervic-, endocervix* + E *-al*] **:** of, relating to, or affecting the endocervix

en·do·cervicitis \"+\ *n* [NL, fr. *end-* + *cervicitis*] **:** inflammation of the lining of the uterine cervix

en·do·cervix \"+\ *n, pl* **endocervices** [NL, fr. *end-* + *cervix*] **:** the epithelial and glandular lining of the uterine cervix

en·do·chondral \ˌen(ˌ)dō+\ *adj* [ISV *end-* + *chondr-* + *-al*] **:** occurring within the substance of cartilage — used chiefly of bone and bone formation; compare PERICHONDRAL

endochondral ossification *n* **:** ossification taking place from centers arising in cartilage and involving deposition of lime salts in the cartilage matrix followed by secondary absorption and replacement by true bony tissue — compare INTERMEMBRANOUS OSSIFICATION

en·do·chorion \ˌ==+\ *n* [NL, fr. *end-* + *chorion*] **:** the inner of the two layers usu. making up the chorion of an insect egg

en·do·chrome \ˈendəˌkrōm\ *n* [ISV *end-* + *-chrome*] **:** coloring matter within a cell; *specif* **:** coloring matter other than chlorophyll in plant cells

en·do·coele *or* **en·do·coel** \-ˌsēl\ *n* -S [*end-* + *-coele*] **:** the space between a pair of mesenteries in certain anthozoans — **en·do·coel·ic** \ˌ==ˈsēlik\ *adj*

en·do·commensal \ˌen(ˌ)dō+\ *n* [*end-* + *commensal*] **:** a commensal dwelling within the body of its host

en·do·condensation \"+\ *n* [*end-* + *condensation*] **:** condensation occurring within a molecule

en·do·cone \ˈendəˌkōn\ *n* [*end-* + *cone*] **:** one of the concentric conical structures developed within the calcareous siphuncle of certain cephalopod shells (as of the genus *Endoceras*)

en·do·conidium \ˌen(ˌ)dō+\ *n, pl* **endoconidia** [NL, fr. *end-* + *conidium*] **:** an endogenous conidium

en·do·corpuscular \"+\ *adj* [*end-* + *corpuscular*] **:** located within a corpuscle; *specif* **:** located within a red blood cell ⟨~ parasites of malaria⟩

en·do·cranial \ˌendə+\ *adj* [*endocranium* + *-al*] **:** of or belonging to the endocranium

endocranial cast *n* **:** a cast of the cranial cavity showing the approximate shape of the brain

en·do·cranium \"+\ *n, pl* **endocrania** [NL, fr. *end-* + *cranium*] **1 :** the processes of the inner surface of the cranium of certain insects **:** TENTORIUM **2 a :** DURA MATER **b :** the inner surface of the cranium

en·do·cri·nal \ˌendəˈkrīnᵊl, -rēn-, -rin-\ *adj* **:** ENDOCRINE

¹en·do·crine \ˈendəkrən; -ˌkrin, -ˌrīn, -ˌrēn\ *adj* [ISV *end-* +

-*crine* (fr. Gk *krinein* to separate) — more at CERTAIN] **1 :** secreting internally; *specif* **:** producing secretions that are distributed in the body by way of the blood stream rather than discharged through ducts — used of glands (as the thyroid, suprarenal, and pituitary) that secrete hormones **2 :** of, relating to, or associated with a hormone **3 :** of or belonging to an endocrine gland **:** like that of an endocrine gland

²**endocrine** \"\ *also* **en·do·crin** \-ˌkrən, -ˌkrin\ *n* -S **1 :** a secretion leaving the gland producing it by way of the circulatory system **:** HORMONE **2 :** ENDOCRINE GLAND

endocrine gland *n* **:** a gland that produces an endocrine secretion — called also *gland of internal secretion*

endocrine system *n* **:** the glands and parts of glands that produce endocrine secretions

en·do·crin·ic \ˌendəˈkrinik, -nēk\ *adj* **:** ENDOCRINE

en·do·crin·o·log·ic \ˌ==ˌkrinᵊlˈäjik, -rīn-, -rēn-\ *also* **en·do·crin·o·log·i·cal** \-jəkəl\ *adj* [*endocrinology* + *-ic, -ical*] **:** involving or relating to the endocrine glands or secretions or to endocrinology

en·do·cri·nol·o·gist \ˌ==krəˈnäləjəst, -ˌkrī'-, -ˌkrē'-\ *n* -S [*endocrinology* + *-ist*] **:** one specializing in endocrinology

en·do·cri·nol·o·gy \-jē\ *n* -ES [ISV *endocrine* + *-o-* + *-logy*] **:** a science or study of the internal secretions and endocrine glands and their physiology and pathology as related to each other and to the organism as a whole

en·do·crin·o·path \ˌ==ˈkrinəˌpath, -rīn-, -rēn-\ *n* -S [ISV *endocrine* + *-o-* + *-path*] **:** one suffering from endocrinopathy

en·do·crin·o·path·ic \ˌ==ˌ==ˈpathik\ *adj* [ISV *endocrine* + *-o-* + *-pathic*] **:** involving endocrinopathy

en·do·cri·nop·a·thy \ˌ==krəˈnäpəthē, -ˌkrī'-, -ˌkrē'-\ *n* -ES [ISV *endocrine* + *-o-* + *-pathy*] **:** a disease marked by disorder in action or function of one or more of the endocrine organs

en·doc·ri·nous \(ˈ)enˈdäkrənəs\ *adj* **:** ENDOCRINE

en·do·cuticle \ˈendō+\ *n* [*end-* + *cuticle*] **:** the inner layer of a cuticle; *specif* **:** the colorless flexible highly chitinized inner layer of the exoskeleton of an insect — compare EPICUTICLE — **en·do·cuticular** \"+\ *adj*

en·do·cu·tic·u·la \ˌ==kyüˈtikyələ\ *n, pl* **endocuticu·lae** \-ˌlē\ [NL, fr. *end-* + L *cuticula*] **:** ENDOCUTICLE

en·do·cyclic \ˈendō+\ *or* **endocyclical** *adj* [*endocyclic* fr. NL *Endocyclica; endocyclical* fr. NL *Endocyclica* + E *-al*] **:** of or relating to the Regularia

en·do·cyc·li·ca \ˌ==ˈsiklәkə\ [NL, fr. *end-* + *-cyclica* (fr. Gk *kyklika*, neut. pl. of *kyklikos* circular, cyclic) — more at CYCLIC] *syn of* REGULARIA

en·do·cyst \ˈendəˌsist\ *n* [ISV *end-* + *-cyst*] **1 :** the soft layer of the body wall of a bryozoan lining the ectocyst and consisting of ectoderm with a layer of mesoderm **2 :** the lining membrane of a hydatid cyst from which larvae are budded off

en·do·derm \-ˌdərm\ *n* -S [F *endoderme*, fr. *end-* + Gk *derma* skin, fr. *derein* to skin — more at TEAR] **:** the innermost of the three primary germ layers of an embryo and the source of the epithelium of the digestive tract and its derivatives **:** HYPOBLAST; *also* **:** any tissue wherever located that is derived from this germ layer

en·do·der·mal \ˌ==ˈdərməl\ *or* **en·do·der·mic** \-mik\ *adj* **:** of or derived from endoderm or from endodermis

endoderm disk *n* **:** an unpaired thickening on the posterior ventral surface of the crayfish embryo

en·do·der·mis \ˌ==ˈ==məs\ *n* [NL, fr. *end-* + *-dermis*] **:** the innermost tissue of the cortex in the majority of roots and some stems consisting usu. of a single layer of living cells with no intercellular spaces and with walls in part at least suberized or cutinized and often thickened in bands radially and transversely and supposedly functioning as a controlling element in the movement of water and other substances into and out of the stele — called also *starch sheath;* compare CASPARIAN STRIP

en·do·der·mi·za·tion \ˌ=ˌ=məˈzāshən\ *n* -S [*endoderm* + *-ize* + *-ation*] **:** excessive formation of endoderm due to experimental modification of the course of development

endoderm lamella *n* **:** a thin sheet of endoderm extending from the gastric cavity to the circular canal between adjacent radial canals in a medusa and separated from the ectoderm on either side by mesoglea

en·do·don·tia \ˌ==ˈdänch(ē)ə\ *n* -S [NL, fr. *end-* + *-odontia*] **:** a branch of dentistry concerned with the diagnosis and treatment of diseases of the pulp — **en·do·don·tic** \ˌ==ˈdäntik\ *adj* — **en·do·don·tist** \ˌ==ˈdäntəst\ *n* -S

en·do·don·tics \ˌ==ˈdäntiks\ *n pl but sing in constr* [by alter. (influence of *-ics*)] **:** ENDODONTIA

en·do·dynamomorphic \ˌen(ˌ)dō+\ *adj* [*end-* + *dynam-* + *-morphic*] *of a developing soil* **:** characterized by changes brought about by inherent properties of the parent rock rather than by external forces or agencies — opposed to *ectodynamomorphic*

en·do·ectothrix \ˌendō+\ *adj* [NL, fr. *end-* + *ectothrix*] **:** occurring in and on hair

en·do·enzyme \ˈendō+\ *n* [ISV *end-* + *enzyme*] **:** an enzyme that acts within the cell (as in most higher plants) **:** an intracellular enzyme — distinguished from *exoenzyme*

en·do·epithelial \ˌen(ˌ)dō+\ *adj* [*end-* + *epithelial*] **:** occurring within epithelial cells ⟨~ parasites⟩

en·do·er·gic \ˌendōˈərjik\ *adj* [*end-* + *erg-* + *-ic*] **:** absorbing energy **:** ENDOTHERMIC ⟨~ nuclear reactions⟩ — opposed to *exoergic*

en·do·erythrocytic \ˌen(ˌ)dō+\ *adj* [*end-* + *erythrocytic*] **:** occurring within red blood cells — used chiefly of stages of malaria parasites

en·do·form \ˈendō+ˌ-\ *n* [*end-* + *form*] **:** a rust producing spores in the aecia which have the appearance of aeciospores but which germinate like teliospores by a promycelium — compare EU-FORM

en·do·gam·ic \ˌendōˈgamik\ *adj* [*endogamy* + *-ic*] **:** ENDOGAMOUS

en·dog·a·mous \(ˈ)enˈdägəməs\ *adj* [*end-* + *-gamous*] **:** of, relating to, or characterized by endogamy

en·dog·a·my \=ˈ==mē\ *n* -ES [*end-* + *-gamy*] **1 :** marriage within a specific group as required by custom or law — contrasted with *exogamy* **2 a :** sexual reproduction between near relatives; *esp* **:** pollination of a flower by pollen from another flower of the same plant — compare AUTOGAMY, EXOGAMY **b :** fertilization by union of two female gametes

en·do·gastric \ˌen(ˌ)dō+\ *adj* [*end-* + *gastric*] **:** of or relating to the inside of the stomach — **en·do·gastrically** \"+\ *adv*

en·do·gen \ˈendəjən, -ˌjen\ *n* -S [F *endogène*, fr. *endogène* endogenous, fr. *end-* + *-gène* (fr. Gk *-genēs* born) — more at -GEN] **:** a plant that develops by endogenous growth (as most monocotyledons)

en·do·genesis \ˌendə+\ *n* [NL, fr. *end-* + L *genesis*] **:** ENDOGENY

en·do·genetic \ˌ==+\ *adj* [*end-* + *genetic*] **1 :** of or having to do with rocks formed by solidification from fusion, precipitation from solution, or sublimation — compare CLASTIC **2 :** ENDOGENOUS

en·do·gen·ic \ˌ==ˈjenik\ *adj* [modif. (influenced by E *-ic*) of G *endogenisch*, fr. *end-* + *-genisch* (fr. Gk *-genēs* born + G *-isch* -ish, fr. OHG *-isc, -isk*)] **:** of or having to do with the processes of metamorphism taking place within the earth — compare EXOGENOUS e

en·do·ge·nic·i·ty \ˌ==jəˈnisədē\ *n* -ES [*endogenous* + *-ic* + *-ity*] **:** endogenous quality or origin

en·dog·e·nous \(ˈ)enˈdäjənəs\ *adj* [F *endogène* endogenous + E *-ous*] **1 a :** growing from or on the inside ⟨~ tissues⟩ **:** developing within the cell wall ⟨~ spores⟩ **b :** originating within the body ⟨an ~ disease⟩ **:** arising from internal structural or functional causes ⟨~ malnutrition⟩ ⟨~ mental deficiency⟩ **c :** constituting or relating to metabolism of the nitrogenous constituents of cells and tissues — compare EXOGENOUS **2 :** of, relating to, or resembling an endogen **3 :** originating in the individual's own psychodynamics rather than through external causes — **en·dog·e·nous·ly** *adv*

en·dog·e·ny \enˈdäjənē\ *n* -ES [*end-* + *-geny*] **:** growth from within or from a deep-seated layer

en·dog·nath \ˈendəgˌnath, -ˌdäg-\ *n* -S [*end-* + Gk *gnathos* jaw; akin to Gk *genys* jaw — more at CHIN] **:** the inner and principal branch of an oral appendage of a crustacean

en·dog·na·thal \(ˈ)enˈdägnəthəl\ *adj* [*end-* + Gk *gnathos* + E *-al*] **1 :** of or relating to the endognath **2 :** situated within the jaw

en·do·gnathion \ˌendō+\ *n* [NL, fr. *end-* + *gnathion*] **:** the medial segment of the premaxilla situated on each side of the midline of the palate and bearing the medial incisor

en·do·li·max \ˌendəˈlīˌmaks\ *n, cap* [NL, fr. *end-* + L *limax* slug, snail — more at LIMAX] **:** a genus of amoebas commensal in vertebrate intestines including a species (*E. nana*) found in man

en·do·lith·ic \ˌendəˈlithik\ *adj* [ISV *end-* + *lithic*] **:** living within rocks or other stony substance (as mollusk shells or coral) ⟨~ algae⟩

en·do·lymph \ˈendə+\ *n* [ISV *end-* + *lymph*] **:** the watery fluid in the membranous labyrinth of the ear

en·do·lym·phat·ic \ˌendəˌlimˈfad·ik\ *adj* [fr. *endolymph*, after E *lymph: lymphatic*] **:** of or containing endolymph ⟨~ duct⟩

en·do·meninx \ˈendō+\ *n, pl* **endomeninges** [NL, fr. *end-* + Gk *mēninx* membrane — more at MEMBER] **:** the layer of embryonic mesoderm from which the arachnoid coat and pia mater of the brain develop

en·do·mere \ˈendəˌmi(ə)r\ *n* -S [*end-* + *-mere*] **:** a blastomere forming endoderm

en·do·mesoderm \ˈendō+\ *n* [*end-* + *mesoderm*] **:** MESENDODERM — **en·do·mesodermal** \"+\ *adj*

en·do·me·tri·al \ˌendəˈmē·trēəl\ *adj* [ISV *endometri-* (prob. fr. NL *endometrium*) + *-al*] **:** of, belonging to, or consisting of endometrium

en·do·me·tri·o·ma \ˌ==ˌmē·trēˈōmə\ *n, pl* **endometriomas** *or* **endometrioma·ta** \-məd·ə\ [NL, fr. *endometri-* (fr. *endometrium*) + *-oma*] **1 :** a tumor containing endometrial tissue **2 :** ENDOMETRIOSIS — used chiefly of isolated foci of endometrium outside the uterus

en·do·me·tri·o·sis \-ˈōsəs\ *n, pl* **endometrioses** [NL, fr. *endometri-* + *-osis*] **:** the presence of functioning endometrial tissue in places where it does not belong esp. where (1) invading the myometrium or (2) forming multiple foci and invading any organ within the pelvic cavity — called also respectively (1) *internal endometriosis, adenomyosis;* (2) *external endometriosis*

en·do·me·tri·tis \ˌ==məˈtrīd·əs\ *n* [NL, fr. *endometr-* (prob. fr. *endometrium*) + *-itis*] **:** inflammation of the endometrium

en·do·me·tri·um \ˌ==ˈmē·trēəm\ *n, pl* **endome·tria** \-rēə\ [NL, fr. *end-* + *-metrium*] **:** the mucous membrane lining the uterus

en·do·mic·tic \ˌendəˈmiktik\ *adj* [fr. *endomixis*, after such pairs as E *apomixis: apomictic*] **:** of or relating to endomixis

en·do·mitosis \ˌendə+\ *n* [ISV *end-* + *mitosis*] **1 :** division of chromosomes in a nucleus without subsequent nuclear division resulting in duplication of the chromosome complex **2 :** PROMITOSIS — **en·do·mitotic** \"+\ *adj* — **en·do·mitotically** \"+\ *adv*

en·do·mix·is \ˌendəˈmiksəs\ *n* -ES [NL, fr. *end-* + *-mixis*] **:** a periodic nuclear reorganization in certain ciliated protozoans marked by degeneration of the macronucleus and its replacement by a product of micronuclear origin; *broadly* **:** any of several nuclear reorganization activities (as autogamy or hemixis) in ciliates that are distinct from conjugation

en·do·mo·lare \ˌendōmōˈla(a)rē\ *n* -S [*end-* + *-molare* (irreg. fr. L *molaris* molar) — more at MOLAR] **:** the most lateral point on the lingual aspect of the alveolar process of the jaw

en·do·morph \ˈendəˌmȯrf\ *n* -S [ISV *end-* + *-morph*] **1 a :** a crystal of one species enclosed in one of another **2** [*endoderm* + *-morph*] **:** an endomorphic individual

en·do·mor·phic \ˌ==ˈmȯrfik\ *adj* [*end-* + *-morphic*] **1 a :** of or relating to an endomorph **b :** of, relating to, or produced by endomorphism — opposed to *exomorphic* **2** [*endoderm* + *-morphic*] **:** characterized by predominance of the structures (as the internal organs) developed from the endodermal layer of the embryo **:** of a pyknic type of body build — compare ECTOMORPHIC, MESOMORPHIC — **en·do·mor·phy** \ˈ==ˌ=fē\ *n* -ES

en·do·mor·phism \ˌ==ˈ=ˌfizəm\ *n* -S [ISV *end-* + *-morphism;* orig. formed as F *endomorphisme*] **:** a change (as in texture or in chemical composition by assimilation of foreign material) produced in an intrusive rock by reaction with the wall rock

en·do·my·ces \ˌendəˈmīˌsēz\ *n, cap* [NL, fr. *end-* + *-myces*] **:** a genus (the type of the family Endomycetaceae) of fungi having very simple structure with spirally wound gametangia which fuse apically

en·do·my·ce·ta·ce·ae \-ˌmīsəˈtāsēˌē\ *n pl, cap* [NL, fr. *Endomycet-, Endomyces*, type genus + *-aceae*] **:** a family of fungi (order Endomycetales) having the characteristics of the genus *Endomyces* and the asci 4-spored and borne directly on the hyphae

en·do·my·ce·ta·les \-ˈtā(ˌ)lēz\ *n pl, cap* [NL, fr. *Endomycet-, Endomyces* + *-ales*] **:** an order of ascomycetous fungi (subclass Hemiascomycetes) having a zygote or a single cell developing directly into an ascus

en·do·my·si·um \ˌendəˈmiz(h)ēəm\ *n, pl* **endomy·sia** \-ēə\ [NL, fr. *end-* + Gk *mys* muscle, mouse + NL *-ium* — more at MOUSE] **:** the delicate connective tissue surrounding the individual muscular fibers within the smallest bundles — compare EPIMYSIUM

end on *adv* **:** with an end pointing in a given direction or toward the eye of an observer — opposed to *broadside*

end–on \ˈ=ˈ=\ *adj* [*end on*] *of a coal working* **:** parallel in direction to the course of the main cleavage planes

en·do·neu·ri·al \ˌendōˈn(y)u̇rēəl\ *adj* [*endoneurium* + *-al*] **:** of or consisting of endoneurium

en·do·neu·ri·um \ˌ==ˈ=rēəm\ *n, pl* **endoneu·ria** \-ēə\ [NL, fr. *end-* + *neur-* + *-ium*] **:** the delicate connective tissue network holding together the individual fibers of a nerve trunk

en·do·parasite \ˌen(ˌ)dō+\ *n* [ISV *end-* + *parasite*] **:** a parasite that lives in the internal organs or tissues of its host — opposed to *ectoparasite* — **en·do·parasitic** \"+\ *adj* — **en·do·parasitism** \"+\ *n*

en·do·peptidase \"+\ *n* [*end-* + *peptidase*] **:** any of a group of enzymes that hydrolyze peptide bonds inside the long chains of protein molecules **:** PROTEINASE — distinguished from *exopeptidase*

en·do·pericardial \"+\ *adj* [*end-* + *pericardi-* + *-al*] **:** of or involving the endocardium and pericardium ⟨~ infection⟩

en·do·peridial \ˌen(ˌ)dō+\ *adj* [*endoperidium* + *-al*] **:** of or relating to the endoperidium

en·do·peridium \"+\ *n, pl* **endoperidia** [NL, fr. *end-* + *peridium*] **:** the inner peridium when consisting of two layers (as in the puffballs) — compare EXOPERIDIUM

en·doph·a·gous \(ˈ)enˈdäfəgəs\ *adj* [*end-* + *-phagous*] **:** feeding from within: **a** *of a parasitoid insect larva* **:** developing within and feeding on the internal organs and tissues of the host — compare ECTOPHAGOUS **b :** consuming vegetation or plant debris by burrowing in and disintegrating plant structures (as in the tunneling of leaves by leaf miners)

en·do·pha·sia \ˌendəˈfāzh(ē)ə\ *n* -S [It *endofasia*, fr. *end-* + *-fasia* -phasia] **:** speech that is not audible or visible **:** implicit speech — contrasted with *exophasia*

en·do·phragm \ˈ==ˌfram\ *n* -S [ISV *end-* + *-phragm* (as in *diaphragm*)] **:** SEPTUM; *specif* **:** one formed by the apodemes of the crustacean thorax — **en·do·phrag·mal** \ˌ==ˈfragməl\ *adj*

en·do·phyl·lum \ˌ==ˈfiləm\ *n, cap* [NL, fr. *end-* + *-phyllum*] **:** a genus (type of the family Endophyllaceae) of rusts producing teliospores in chains in cuplike spore fruits

en·do·phyte \ˈ==ˌfīt\ *n* -S [ISV *end-* + *-phyte;* prob. orig. formed in F] **:** a plant living within another plant but not necessarily parasitic upon it

en·do·phyt·ic \ˌ==ˈfid·ik\ *adj* [ISV *endophyte* + *-ic*] **1 :** of, relating to, or being an endophyte ⟨an ~ plant⟩ **2 :** situated or occurring within plant tissues ⟨oviposition in Odonata is often ~⟩ ⟨~ development⟩ **3 :** tending to grow inward into tissues in fingerlike projections from a superficial site of origin — used of certain tumors; opposed to *exophytic* — **en·do·phyt·i·cal·ly** \-d·ək(ə)lē\ *adv*

en·doph·y·tous \(ˈ)enˈdäfəd·əs\ *adj* [*endophyte* + *-ous*] **:** living within the tissues of plants ⟨~ insects⟩ ⟨~ fungi⟩

en·do·plasm \ˈendəˌplazəm\ *n* [ISV *end-* + *-plasm*] **:** the inner relatively fluid part of the cytoplasm — compare ECTOPLASM — **en·do·plas·mic** \ˌ==ˈplazmik\ *adj*

en·do·plas·ma \ˌ==ˈplazmə\ *n* [prob. fr. G, fr. *end-* + *-plasma* -plasm] **:** ENDOPLASM

en·do·plast \ˈ==ˌplast\ *n* -S [ISV *end-* + *-plast*] **1 :** ENDOPLASM **2 :** NUCLEUS 2a — **en·do·plas·tic** \ˌ==ˈplastik\ *adj*

en·do·plastron \ˌen(ˌ)dō+\ *n* [*end-* + *plastron*] **:** ENTOPLASTRON

en·do·pleu·ra \ˌendəˈplu̇rə\ *n* [NL, fr. *end-* + *-pleura*] **:** the inner coating or integument of a seed — called also *tegmen* — **en·do·pleu·ral** \ˌ==ˈ=rəl\ *adj*

en·do·pleu·rite \ˌ==ˈ=ˌrīt\ *n* -S [ISV *end-* + *pleurite*] **1 :** the portion of an apodeme of a crustacean developed from the interepimeral membrane **2 :** one of the lateral infoldings on the thorax of an insect which extend into the body cavity — **en·do·pleu·rit·ic** \ˌ=(ˌ)plüˈrid·ik\ *adj*

en·do·pod \ˈendəˌpäd\ *n* -S [*end-* + *-pod*] **:** ENDOPODITE

en·dop·o·dite \enˈdäpəˌdīt\ *n* [ISV *end-* + *-podite*] **:** the mesial or internal branch of a typical limb of a crustacean that is borne upon the protopodite and that in the thoracic limbs of the higher Decapoda forms the entire limb — **en·dop·o·dit·ic** \(ˌ)=ˌ==ˈdid·ik\ *adj*

en·do·polyploid \ˌendō+\ *adj* [*end-* + *polyploid*] **:** of or relating to endopolyploidy

en·do·pol·y·ploi·di·za·tion \ˌ=(ˌ)=ˌpäləˌplȯidəˈzāshən\ *n* -S [*endopolyploid* + *-ize* + *-ation*] **:** the act or process of becoming endopolyploid

en·do·polyploidy \ˌ==(ˌ)=+\ *n* [*end-* + *polyploidy*] **:** the polyploid state characteristic of cells, tissues, or individuals in which the chromosomes have divided repeatedly without mitosis or subsequent cell division

en·do·proct \ˈendəˌpräkt\ *n or adj* [NL *Endoprocta*] **:** ENTOPROCT

en·do·proc·ta \ˌ==ˈ=tə\ [NL, fr. *end-* + *-procta*] *syn of* ENTOPROCTA

en·do·proc·tous \ˌ==ˈ=təs\ *adj* [NL *Endoprocta* + E *-ous*] **:** ENTOPROCTOUS

en·do·psychic \ˌendō +\ *adj* [*end-* + *psychic*] **:** arising or existing within the mind

en·do·pterygota \ˌen(ˌ)dō+\ [NL, fr. *end-* + Gk *pterygōta*, neut. pl. of *pterygōtos* winged — more at PTERYGOTA] *syn of* HOLOMETABOLA

en·do·pterygote \"+\ *adj* [NL *Endopterygota*] **:** HOLOMETABOLOUS

end·oral \(ˈ)enˈd+ˌ-\ *adj* [ISV *end-* + *oral*] **:** situated within a mouth or stoma ⟨~ groove⟩

end organ *n* **:** a structure forming the peripheral terminus of a path of nerve conduction and consisting of an effector or a receptor with its associated nerve terminations

en·do·rhe·ic *or* **en·do·re·ic** \ˌendəˈrēik\ *adj* [ISV *end-* + *-rheic, -reic* (fr. Gk *rhein* to flow + ISV *-ic*)] **:** relating to or characterized by endorheism

en·do·rhe·ism *or* **en·do·re·ism** \ˌ==ˈrēˌizəm\ *n* -S [ISV *end-* + *-rheism, -reism* (fr. Gk *rhein* to flow + ISV *-ism*) — more at STREAM] **:** interior drainage **:** the condition of a region in which little or none of the surface drainage reaches the sea

en·dors·able \ənˈdȯ(r)səbəl, en-\ *adj* **:** that can be endorsed

¹**en·dorse** *or* **in·dorse** \ənˈdȯ(ə)rs, en-, -ō(ə)s\ *vt* -ED/-ING/-S [*endorse* alter. (influenced by *indorse*) of *endoss*, fr. ME *endosen*, fr. MF *endosser*, fr. OF, to put on one's back, fr. ¹*en-* + *dos* back, fr. L *dorsum; indorse* fr. ME *indorsen*, fr. ML *indorsare*, fr. L *in* in, on + ML *-dorsare* (fr. L *dorsum* back)] **1 a :** to write on the back of (a commercial document): as (1) **:** to sign one's name as payee on the back of (a check) in order to obtain the cash or credit represented on the face (2) **:** to register payments of interest on (as a note or bill) by writing the amounts on the back with the signature of the one receiving the payment **b :** to inscribe (one's signature) on a check, bill, note, or other commercial document **:** SIGN ⟨he *endorsed* his name on the check⟩ **c :** to inscribe (as an official document) with a title, direction, memorandum, or explanation ⟨mail not delivered at the original address must be *endorsed* to show the next address —*Postal Term Glossary*⟩; *specif* **:** to write an endorsement on (a letter) in military communication **d :** to make over to another (the value represented in a check, bill, or note) by inscribing one's name on the document sometimes with specific directions for transfer **e :** to acknowledge receipt of (all or part of a sum specified in a note or bill) by one's signature on the document with proper notation **2** *obs* **:** to load upon the back **3 :** to express definite approval or acceptance of ⟨*endorsed* happiness, parenthood, and babies —Jack Gould⟩ **:** support or aid explicitly by or as if by signed statement **:** vouch for **:** UNDERWRITE ⟨a lot of people will ~ a good idea, but . . . few will fight for it —Owen Lattimore⟩ ⟨all of these measures had been *endorsed* by the governor —G.C. Wright⟩ **syn** see APPROVE — **endorse in blank :** to write one's name on the back of (a note or bill) without adding restrictions as to endorsee or manner of payment

²**endorse** \"\ *n* -S [perh. fr. ¹*endorse*] *heraldry* **:** a cotise paralleling a pale

endorsed *adj* [perh. fr. past part. of ¹*endorse*] **1 :** ADDORSED **2** *of a heraldic pale* **:** enclosed between two endorses

endorsed bond *n* [*endorsed* fr. past part. of ¹*endorse*] **:** a bond the payment of which is guaranteed by endorsement

en·dors·ee \ənˌdȯrˈsē, ˌenˌd-, -dō(ə)ˈ-\ *n* -S **:** one to whom a note or bill is endorsed or assigned by endorsement

en·dorse·ment \ənˈdȯrsmənt, en-, -ō(ə)s-\ *n* -S **1 :** the act or process of writing on the back of a note, bill, or other written instrument **2 a :** something that is written (as a name or an order for or a receipt of payment) on the back of a note, bill, or other document; *esp* **:** a writing usu. on the back but sometimes on the face of a negotiable instrument by which the property therein is assigned and transferred **b :** a provision added to an insurance contract altering its scope or application that takes precedence over printed portions of the policy in conflict therewith **3 a :** SANCTION, SUPPORT, APPROVAL ⟨the president's wholehearted ~ of a policy⟩ ⟨against his father's judgment but with his mother's sympathetic ~, he decided to be a missionary —K.S.Latourette⟩ **b :** RECOMMENDATION **4 :** a reply, comment, or forwarding note added to a letter by an officer or headquarters staff in military communication

en·dors·er \-sə(r)\ *n* -S **:** one that endorses: as **a :** a holder or payee who transfers title to a bill or note by endorsement **b :** one who signs a negotiable instrument (as a check or note) as an accommodation to enable another to obtain money or credit — compare COMAKER

en·dors·ing·ly *adv* [*endorsing* (pres. part. of ¹*endorse*) + *-ly*] **:** so as to endorse

en·do·salpinx \ˌen(ˌ)dō+\ *n, pl* **endosalpinges** [NL, fr. *end-* + *salpinx*] **:** the mucous membrane lining the fallopian tube

en·do·sarc \ˈendəˌsärk\ *n* -S [*end-* + *-sarc*] **:** the central usu. semifluid part of the protoplasm of some unicellular organisms (as amoebas) **:** ENDOPLASM — **en·do·sar·cous** \ˌ==ˈsärkəs\ *adj*

en·do·sclerite \ˌen(ˌ)dō+\ *n* [*end-* + *sclerite*] **:** a sclerite that is part of the internal skeleton of an insect or other arthropod

en·do·scope \ˈendəˌskōp\ *n* [ISV *end-* + *-scope;* prob. orig. formed in F] **1 :** an instrument for visualizing the interior of a hollow organ or part (as the rectum or urethra) — compare BRONCHOSCOPE, CYSTOSCOPE, OTOSCOPE **2 :** an optical instrument for examining the interior surface of a hole drilled through a pearl and used to distinguish between cultured and natural pearls

en·do·scop·ic \ˌ==ˈskäpik\ *adj* [*endoscope* + *-ic*] **1 :** of, relating to, or by means of the endoscope or endoscopy **2** [*end-* + *-scopic*] *bot* **:** having the apex of the embryo pointing toward the base of the archegonium — compare EXOSCOPIC

en·dos·co·pist \enˈdäskəpəst\ *n* -S **:** a physician specializing in the use of the endoscope

en·dos·co·py \-pē, -pi\ *n* -ES [ISV *endoscope* + *-y*] **:** examination with the endoscope

en·do·sep·sis \ˌendəˈsepsəs\ *n, pl* **endosep·ses** \-pˌsēz\ [NL, fr. *end-* + Gk *sēpsis* putrefaction, decay] **:** an internal rotting of figs caused by a fungus (*Fusarium moniliforme fici*) introduced by the fig wasp during pollination

en·do·siphon \ˌen(ˌ)dō+\ *n* [*end-* + *siphon*] **:** ENDOSIPHUNCLE — **en·do·siphonal** \"+\ *adj* — **en·do·siphonate** \"+\ *adj*

en·do·siphuncle \"+\ *n* [*end-* + *siphuncle*] **:** an inner tube in the calcareous siphuncle of certain fossil cephalopods

en·do·skeletal \"+\ *adj* [*endoskeleton* + *-al*] **:** of or belonging to an endoskeleton

en·do·skeleton \"+\ *n* [*end-* + *skeleton*] **:** an internal skeleton or supporting framework in an animal (as the system of apodemes in an insect or the internal system of articulated bones in a vertebrate) — compare EXOSKELETON

end·osmometer \ˌen,d+\ *n* [ISV *endosmo-* (fr. F *endosmose*) + *-meter*] : an instrument for measuring endosmosis — **end·osmometric** \"+\ *adj*

end·osmosis \ˌen,d+\ *n, pl* **endosmoses** [alter. (influenced by Gk *-sis*) of earlier *endosmose*, fr. F, fr. *end-* + Gk *ōsmos* action of thrusting or pushing, fr. *ōthein* to push; akin to Skt *vadhati* he strikes, kills] **1** : passage (as of a surface-active substance) through a membrane from a region of lower to a region of higher concentration — used chiefly in biology; compare EXOSMOSIS 2 **2** : osmotic diffusion toward the inside of a cell or vessel **3** : infiltration or permeation of one cultural group by members of another — **end·osmotic** \"+\ [fr. *endosmosis*, after such pairs as E *narcosis: narcotic*] *adj* — **end·osmotically** \"+\ *adv*

en·do·some \ˈendə,sōm\ *n* -s [*end-* + *-some*] **1** : the central body of a vesicular nucleus whether a karyosome or a plasmosome (as in various protozoan nuclei) **2** : the inner part of the body of various higher sponges that contains flagellated chambers and few if any supporting spicules

en·do·sperm \-,spərm\ *n* [F *endosperme*, fr. *end-* + *sperme* sperm] **1** : a nutritive tissue in seed plants formed around the embryo within the embryo sac by proliferation of the endosperm nucleus to form a mass of thin-walled triploid cells rich in carbohydrates which may be absorbed by the developing embryo or may remain until the seed germinates **2** : any storage tissue within the seed regardless of its origin (as the female gametophyte tissue in gymnospermous seeds) — **en·do·sper·mic** \ˌ==ˈspərmik\ *adj* — **en·do·sper·mous** \-məs\ *adj*

endosperm nucleus *n* : the triploid nucleus formed in the embryo sac of a seed plant by fusion of a sperm nucleus with the two polar nuclei or with a nucleus produced by their prior fusion — compare DOUBLE FERTILIZATION

en·do·sphae·ra·ce·ae \ˌen(,)dōsfəˈrāsē,ē\ *n pl, cap* [NL, fr. *end-* + *sphaer-* + *-aceae*] : a family of irregularly shaped unicellular green algae (order Chlorococcales) living as endophytes or parasites within other algae, mosses, or seed plants

en·do·spore \ˈendə+,-\ *n* [ISV *end-* + *spore*] **1** : an asexual spore developed within the cell esp. in bacteria — compare EXOSPORE **2** : INTINE **3** : the thin inner layer surrounding the protoplast of a sporozoan spore — **en·do·spor·ous** \ˌ==ˈspōrəs, (ˈ)enˈdäspərəs\ *adj* — **en·do·spor·ous·ly** *adv*

en·do·spo·ri·um \ˌendəˈspōrēəm\ *n, pl* **endospo·ria** \-ēə\ [NL, fr. *end-* + *-sporium*] : INTINE

en·do·sporulation \ˌendə+\ *n* [fr. *endospore*, after E *spore: sporulation*] : the production of endospores

en·doss \ənˈdäs, en-, -dȯs\ *vt* [ME *endosen* — more at ¹ENDORSE] *archaic* : ENDORSE

end·osteal \(ˈ)en¦d+,-\ *adj* [*endosteum* + *-al*] **1** : of, relating to, or involving the endosteum **2** : located within bone or cartilage ⟨~ bone formation⟩ — **end·osteally** \"+\ *adv*

end·osteitis \ˌen,d+\ *or* **end·ostitis** \"+\ *n* -ES [NL, fr. *endosteum* + *-itis*] : inflammation of the endosteum

en·do·sternite \ˌen(,)dō+\ *n* [ISV *end-* + *sternite*] : a part of the endoskeleton of an arthropod: **a** : the part of one apodeme of a crustacean derived from the membrane between sternal plates **b** : ENTOSTERNITE **c** : one of the ventral segmental parts of the insect endoskeleton

end·os·te·um \enˈdästēəm\ *n, pl* **endos·tea** \-ēə\ [NL, fr. *end-* + Gk *osteon* bone — more at OSSEOUS] : the layer of vascular connective tissue lining the medullary cavities of bone

en·dos·to·ma \ˌenˈdästəmə\ *n, pl* **endosto·ma·ta** \ˌen,däˈstōmədə, ˌendəˈs-\ *or* **endostomas** \enˈdästəməz\ [NL, fr. *end-* + *stoma*] : a plate which supports the labrum in some crustaceans

en·do·stome \ˈendə,stōm\ *n* -s [ISV *end-* + *-stome*; prob. orig. formed in F] **1 a** : the opening in the inner integument of an ovule having two integuments **b** : the inner part of the peristome of a moss **2** [NL *endostoma*] : ENDOSTOMA

end·ostosis \ˌen,d+\ *n, pl* **endostoses** [NL, fr. *end-* + *-ostosis*] : ossification beginning in the substance of a cartilage — compare ECTOSTOSIS

end·os·tra·cal \(ˈ)en¦dästrəkəl\ *adj* [*endostracum* + *-al*] : consisting of or involving an endostracum

end·os·tra·cum \ˌ=ˈ==kəm\ *n, pl* **endostra·ca** \-kə\ [NL, fr. *end-* + Gk *ostrakon* hard shell; akin to Gk *osteon* bone] : the inner layer of a shell esp. of a crustacean

en·do·style \ˈendə,stīl\ *n* [ISV *end-* + *-style*] : a pair of parallel longitudinal folds projecting into the pharyngeal cavity and bounding a furrow lined with glandular ciliated cells in lower chordates (as amphioxus and the tunicates) that is believed to be morphologically equivalent to the thyroid of higher forms — **en·do·sty·lic** \ˌ==ˈstīlik\ *adj*

en·do·symbiont *or* **en·do·symbiote** \ˌen(,)dō+\ *n* [*end-* + *symbiont* or *symbiote*] : a symbiont dwelling within the body of its symbiotic partner

en·do·symbiosis \"+\ *n, pl* **endosymbioses** [NL, fr. *end-* + *symbiosis*] : symbiosis involving a member which is living as an endosymbiont

en·do·symbiotic \"+\ *adj* [*end-* + *symbiotic*] : of, relating to, or engaged in endosymbiosis

en·do·tergite \ˌen(,)dō+\ *n* [*end-* + *tergite*] : a dorsal phragma of the insect skeleton to which muscles are attached

en·do·theca \ˈendə+\ *n, pl* **endothecae** [NL, fr. *end-* + *theca*] : the tissue that partly fills the interior of the interseptal chambers of most madreporarian corals — **en·do·thecal** \"+\ *adj* — **en·do·thecate** \"+\ *adj*

en·do·the·ci·al \ˌ==ˈthēsh(ē)əl, -sēəl\ *adj* [*endothecium* + *-al*] **1** : of or belonging to an endothecium **2** : having asci enclosed in an ascocarp

en·do·the·ci·um \ˌ==ˈthēs(h)ēəm\ *n, pl* **endothe·cia** \-ēə\ [NL, fr. *end-* + *-thecium*] **1** : the middle of the three layers making up the young anther wall of a flowering plant that becomes the innermost layer in the mature anther upon disintegration of the original inner wall cells **2** : the central mass of cells within the young sporophyte in mosses and liverworts that develops into sporogenous tissue — compare AMPHITHECIUM

endotheli- *or* **endothelio-** *comb form* [ISV, fr. NL *endothelium*] : endothelium ⟨*endothelio*cyte⟩ ⟨*endothelio*ma⟩

en·do·the·li·al \ˌendəˈthēlēəl\ *adj* [ISV *endotheli-* + *-al*] : of, relating to, or produced from endothelium

en·do·the·lio·chorial \ˌendə¦thēlē(,)ō+\ *adj* [*endotheli-* + *chorial*] *of a placenta* : having fetal epithelium enclosing maternal blood vessels (as in carnivores and some insectivores) — compare EPITHELIOCHORIAL, HEMOCHORIAL, SYNDESMOCHORIAL

en·do·the·li·o·cyte \ˌ==ˈ=lēə,sīt\ *n* -s [*endotheli-* + *-cyte*] **1** : MONOCYTE **2** : HISTIOCYTE

en·do·the·li·o·ma \ˌ==ˌ=lēˈōmə\ *n, pl* **endotheliomas** *or* **endothelioma·ta** \-məd·ə\ [NL, fr. *endotheli-* + *-oma*] : a tumor developing from endothelial tissue

en·do·the·li·um \ˌ==ˈ=lēəm\ *n, pl* **endothe·lia** \-ēə\ [NL, fr. *end-* + *-thelium* (as in *epithelium*)] **1** : an epithelium of mesoblastic origin composed of a single layer of thin flattened cells that lines internal body cavities (as the serous cavities or the interior of the heart) **2** : the inner layer of the seed coat of certain plants whose cells upon disorganization of the nucellus elongate radially and form a nutritive layer around the embryo sac — **en·do·the·loid** \ˌ==ˈ=,lȯid\ *adj*

en·do·therm \ˈendə,thərm\ *n* [*end-* + *-therm*] : a warm-blooded animal

end·o·thermal \ˌ==+\ *adj* [*end-* + *thermal*] : ENDOTHERMIC 1

en·do·thermic \"+\ *adj* [ISV *end-* + *thermic*] **1** : characterized by or formed with absorption of heat : ENDOERGIC ⟨~ chemical reactions⟩ — opposed to *exothermic* **2** [*endotherm* + *-ic*] : WARM-BLOODED, HOMOIOTHERMIC — **en·do·ther·mi·cally** \"+\ *adv* — **en·do·ther·mism** \"+ˈthər,mizəm\ *n* -s

en·do·ther·my \ˈendə,thərmē\ *n* -ES [ISV *end-* + *-thermy*] : DIATHERMY

en·doth·ia \enˈdäthēə, -dōth-\ *n, cap* [NL, fr. Gk *endothen* within, from within (fr. *endon* within) + NL *-ia*; fr. the immersed perithecia — more at END-] : a genus of ascomycetous fungi (family Melogrammataceae) having ellipsoid 2-celled ascospores and including the fungus (*E. parasitica*) that causes chestnut blight

endothia canker *n, cap E* : CHESTNUT BLIGHT

en·do·thoracic \ˌendə+\ *adj* [fr. *endothorax*, after E *thorax: thoracic*] : of or relating to an endothorax

en·do·thorax \"+\ *n* [ISV *end-* + *thorax*] : the system of apodemes in the thorax or cephalothorax of an arthropod

¹en·do·thrix \ˈendə,thriks\ [NL, fr. *end-* + *-thrix*] *syn of* TRICHOPHYTON

²endothrix \"\ *n, pl* **endothrixes** \-sə̇s\ *or* **endothri·ces** \ˌ==ˈthrī,sēz\ [NL *Endothrix*] : TRICHOPHYTON 2

³endothrix \"\ *adj* [NL, fr. *end-* + Gk *thrix* hair — more at TRICHINA] : occurring within a hair — compare ECTOTHRIX

en·do·toxic \ˌen(,)dō+\ *adj* [*endotoxin* + *-ic*] : of, relating to, or acting as an endotoxin

en·do·toxin \"+\ *n* [ISV *end-* + *toxin*] : a toxin of internal origin; *specif* : any of a class of poisonous substances present in bacteria (as of typhoid fever) but separable from the cell body only on its disintegration — compare EXOTOXIN

en·do·toxoid \"+\ *n, often attrib* [*endotoxin* + *-oid*] : a toxoid derived from an endotoxin

en·do·tracheal \ˌen(,)dō+\ *adj* [*end-* + *tracheal*] **1** : placed within or passed inside of the trachea ⟨an ~ tube⟩ **2** : applied or effected through the trachea ⟨~ anesthesia⟩ ⟨~ aspiration⟩

en·do·tro·phi \ˌen(,)dōˈtrō,fī\ [NL, fr. *end-* + *trophi*] *syn of* ENTOTROPHI

en·do·troph·ic \ˌendə¦träfik, -rōf-\ *also* **en·do·trop·ic** \-räpik\ *adj* [*end-* + *-trophic* or *-tropic*] *of a mycorrhiza* : penetrating into the associated root and ramifying between the cells — opposed to *ectotrophic*

en·do·venous \ˌen(,)dō+\ *adj* [ISV *end-* + *venous*] : INTRAVENOUS

en·dow \ənˈdau̇, en-\ *vb* -ED/-ING/-S [ME *endowen*, fr. AF *endouer*, fr. MF *en-* ¹en- + *douer* to endow, fr. L *dotare*, fr. *dot-*, *dos* gift, dower — more at DOWER] *vt* **1** *obs* : to furnish with a dower **2** : to furnish (as an institution) with an income ⟨a millionaire who ~*ed* several hospitals⟩ **3 a** : to provide or equip gratuitously — usu. used with *with* ⟨nature ~*ed* him with good eyesight⟩ **b** : ENRICH, HEIGHTEN, ENHANCE — usu. used with *with* ⟨Shakespeare took these words . . . and ~*ed* them with new significance —C.S.Kilby⟩ **c** : to consider usu. favorably as the possessor of a quality : CREDIT 5a — usu. used with *with* ⟨during the 19th century the ether was ~*ed* with some very remarkable properties —W.V.Houston⟩ ~ *vi, of an insurance policy* : to mature or become payable

en·dow·ment \-mənt\ *n* -s [ME *endowement*, fr. AF *endouement*, fr. *endouer* + MF *-ment*] **1** : the act or process of bestowing a dower, endowing, or permanent provision for support **2** : something that is endowed; *specif* : the portion of an institution's income usu. in the form of dividends from invested funds that is derived from donations **3** : natural capacity, power, or ability ⟨a duty for men of great ~s . . . to sow the seed of the mind freely and lavishly —A.C.Benson⟩ **4** : a course of instruction given only in a Mormon temple concerning past and present dispensations and their associated ordinances **5** : PURE ENDOWMENT

endowment insurance *n* : life insurance that promises to pay a stated amount to a designated beneficiary if the insured dies within a stipulated time or to the insured himself if he survives

en·do·xerosis \ˌen(,)dō+\ *n, pl* **endoxeroses** [NL, fr. *end-* + *xer-* + *-osis*] : a physiological disease of citrus causing the juice sacs esp. in the stylar end of the fruit to collapse and leave a hollow region — **en·do·xerotic** \"+\ *adj*

en·do·zoa \ˌendəˈzōə\ *n pl* [NL, fr. *end-* + *-zoa*] : ENTOZOA

en·do·zo·ic \ˌ==ˈzōik\ *adj* [ISV *end-* + *-zoic*] : living within or involving passage through an animal ⟨~ distribution of weeds⟩

endpaper \ˈ=,=\ *n* : a folded sheet of paper in books being plain or printed and having one leaf that forms a pastedown and another that forms a flyleaf — called also *endleaf, endsheet*

endpiece \ˈ=,=\ *n* : a piece at or forming an end

end pin *n* **1** : the button of a violin **2** : the usu. adjustable peg on which a cello or contrabass in use rests on the floor

end plate *n* : a flat plate or structure at the end of something: as **a** : a complex terminal arborization of a motor nerve fiber — called also *end brush* **b** : one of the main end timbers of a shaft set in a mine **c** : a surface attached approximately perpendicular to and near the end of an airfoil in order to produce an effective increase in the aspect ratio of the airfoil

¹end play *n* **1** : slight endwise movement (as of a shaft or axle); *also* : room for such movement **2 a** : any of various plays in bridge usu. made on the eleventh trick and occurring when a declarer forces an opponent to make a lead favorable to the declarer and after the declarer has first eliminated all cards not essential to the play — compare COUP, ELIMINATION, SQUEEZE, THROW-IN **b** : THROW-IN 2 **c** : END GAME

²end play *vt* **1** : to execute a throw-in when playing (a bridge hand) **2** : to force (a bridge opponent) to win a trick and make a subsequent lead unfavorable to him

endpleasure *n* : pleasurable excitement that results from the release of tensions at the culmination of an act — compare FOREPLEASURE

end point *n* : a point marking the completion of a process or stage of a process : a final point : RESULTANT: as **a** : a point in a titration at which a definite effect is observed (as the change of color of an indicator in the neutralization of an acid by a base) **b** (1) : the highest temperature observed in a distillation esp. in the analysis of various petroleum products (as gasoline) (2) : the temperature at which liquid ceases to distill over **c** : the greatest dilution (as of a virus or a vitamin) that will produce a specified effect in a biological system (as the production of a disease or the alleviation of an avitaminosis) and that is usu. determined in bioassay as the 50 percent end point at which the specified effect appears in one half of the test subjects

end post *n* : a piece of nonconducting material used to provide electrical insulation between adjoining rail ends

end product *n* **1** : the final product of a series of changes, processes, or operations ⟨industry whose *end product* — yarns and fabrics — has been Britain's bread and butter for centuries —Sam Pollock⟩ **2** : the ultimate result of a series of activities, experiences, or tendencies ⟨every culture . . . is the *end product* of a long series of events occurring mostly in other cultures —A.L.Kroeber⟩

end-rack \ˈ=,=\ *vt* : to stack (as lumber) on end esp. for drying

end reaction *n* : a reaction that occurs only at the end of a process or as the final stage of a series of reactions

end rhyme *n* : rhyme of terminal syllables of verses

en·drin \ˈendrən\ *n* -s [blend of *end-* and *dieldrin*] : an insecticide $C_{12}H_8Cl_6O$ that is a stereoisomer of dieldrin and resembles dieldrin in toxicity and other properties

end ring *n* : the ring at either end of an induction motor rotor to which the copper or aluminum bars are connected

end rot *n* : a disease of the cranberry caused by an imperfect fungus (*Fusicoccum putrefaciens*) and characterized by decay starting at either end of the fruit

end·rumpf \ˈent·,ru̇m(p)f; ˈen,drəm-, -drüm-\ *n* -s [G, fr. *ende* end (fr. OHG *enti*) + *rumpf* trunk, torso (fr. MHG *rumph*) — more at END, RUMP] : PENEPLAIN

end run *n* **1** *or* **end sweep** : a football play in which the ball carrier attempts to run wide around his own left or right flank **2** : an evasive trick : an artful move

ends *pl of* END, *pres 3d sing of* END

end scraper *n* : a prehistoric flint scraper with scraping edge at one or both ends

ends down *n pl* : breaks in sliver, roving, or yarn during manufacture

endseal \ˈ=,=\ *n* : an adhesively applied label placed over the folded ends of a wrapper to increase durability and make a smooth closure

endsheet \ˈ=,=\ *n* : ENDPAPER

end-shrink \ˈ=,=\ *vi* : to shrink in length (as of lumber)

end stone *n* : a polished flat unpierced jewel in a timepiece that limits a pivot's end play and acts as a bearing

end-stopped *adj* : marked by a grammatical pause at the end — used of verse, esp. of blank verse; compare RUN-ON

end table *n* : a small table used beside a larger piece of furniture

end thrust *n* : THRUST 3b

end-to-end \ˌ==ˈ=\ *adj* **1** : characterized by having the end of one object placed against the end of another ⟨an *end-to-end* position⟩ **2** : effected by suturing one severed end (as of intestine) to the other **3** : END-AND-END

en·due *or* **in·due** \ənˈd(y)ü, en-\ *vt* -ED/-ING/-S [ME *endewen, enduen, induen* (in sense 1 influenced in meaning by ME *endowen* to endow), fr. MF *enduire* to bring in, introduce, digest, fr. L *inducere* to bring in, introduce, induce — more at INDUCE] **1 a** (1) : PROVIDE, SUPPLY — usu. used with *with* (2) : INVEST — usu. used with *with* ⟨the court *endued* him with the full rights of a citizen⟩ **b** : IMBUE, TRANSFUSE — usu. used with *with* ⟨~ an object with life⟩ **2** [ME *induen* to take upon oneself, clothe, fr. L *induere* to put on, don, fr. *ind-* (fr. OL *indu, endo* in) + *-uere* (as in *exuere* to take off) — more at INDIGENOUS, EXUVIAE] **a** : to put on : DON **b** : CLOTHE — usu. used with *with* ⟨*endued* with gorgeous robes⟩ **3** *obs* : DIGEST — used chiefly of hawks

en·due·ment \-mənt\ *n* -s [*endue* + *-ment*] **1** : the act of enduing **2** : something that is endued

en·du·ra \ənˈd(y)u̇rə, en-\ *n* -s [ML, fr. OProv, fast, fr. *endurar* to fast, endure, fr. (assumed) VL *indurare* to last, continue] : a hunger strike against evil carried out by the Cathari and usu. leading to death

en·dur·able \ənˈd(y)u̇rəbəl, en-\ *adj* : capable of being endured : BEARABLE, TOLERABLE ⟨~ burdens⟩ ⟨our table manners were reasonably ~ —W.A.White⟩ — **en·dur·a·ble·ness** \-bəlnə̇s\ *n* -ES — **en·dur·a·bly** \-blē, -li\ *adv*

en·dur·ance \-rən(t)s\ *n* -s *often attrib* **1** : PERMANENCE, DURATION ⟨a political confederacy of variable ~ —Fredrik Barth⟩ **2 a** (1) : the ability to withstand hardship or tribulation ⟨the great physical ~ of mountain troops⟩ (2) : the ability of a person or thing to continue to perform esp. under adverse conditions ⟨the five-mile cross-country stretch . . . becomes under these conditions a supreme test of ~ —Frank Weldon⟩ ⟨~ swimming⟩ **b** (1) : the power of holding out : STAMINA ⟨a hike beyond the ~ of most of us⟩ (2) : the capability of acting with moral courage and strength : FORTITUDE ⟨the indescribable look of high ~, which used to mark the sailing-ship seamen —John Masefield⟩ **3** : SUFFERING ⟨the ~ of the inequalities of life by the poor is the marvel of human society —J.A.Froude⟩ **4** : an instance of enduring (as hardship or tribulation) : TRIAL ⟨all these grim sights of tragic birth and tragic death, and the deep solitary ~s among the beasts of the field —J.C.Powys⟩ **5** : the maximum time of performance, function, or operation esp. at an efficient level; *specif* : the maximum length of time an aircraft can remain in the air under given conditions without refueling

endurance limit *n* : FATIGUE LIMIT

endurance ratio *n* : FATIGUE RATIO

endurance strength *n* : FATIGUE STRENGTH

en·dur·ant \-rənt\ *adj* : capable of enduring adversity, severity, or hardship ⟨an ~ animal⟩

en·dure \ənˈd(y)u̇(ə)r, en-, -u̇ə\ *vb* -ED/-ING/-S [ME *enduren*, fr. MF *endurer*, fr. (assumed) VL & L; (assumed) VL *indurare* to last, continue, fr. L *indurare* to harden, fr. *in* + *durare* to harden, fr. *durus* hard — more at DURE] *vi* **1** : to continue in essentially the same state : LAST ⟨laws that have *endured* for centuries⟩ **2** : to attain to or retain position or stature : maintain permanent recognition ⟨the question of why one novel ~s and another does not⟩ **3 a** : to remain firm under adversity : bear up (as under tribulation) without yielding ⟨*enduring* despite criticism⟩ **b** : to continue to act or function esp. under adverse conditions ⟨~ to the bitter end⟩ ~ *vt* **1** *obs* : to make hard, callous, or tough : STRENGTHEN **2** : to undergo (as a hardship or difficulty) esp. without faltering, giving in, or breaking : SUFFER ⟨~ tension⟩ ⟨we must try to ~ all this in the fashion of philosophers —Louis Bromfield⟩ **3** : to be compatible with : ALLOW, PERMIT ⟨a poem that will not ~ a facile interpretation⟩ **4 a** : to allow to stand : COUNTENANCE, TOLERATE — often used with a negative ⟨a century ago hospitals were charnel houses, presenting a spectacle no one could ~ today —*Saturday Rev.*⟩ **b** : to face with equanimity or tolerance : put up with — often used with a negative ⟨unable to ~ jazz⟩ **syn** see BEAR, CONTINUE

en·dur·er \-u̇rə(r)\ *n* -s : one that endures

¹en·dur·ing \-riŋ, -rēŋ\ *prep* [ME *enduringe*, fr. *enduringe* (pres. part. of *enduren*), fr. *enduren* + *-inge* -ing (pres. part. suffix)] *dial* : through the course of : DURING ⟨keep track of him ~ the holidays —Maristan Chapman⟩

²enduring \"\ *adj* [fr. *enduring* (pres. part. of *endure*), fr. ME *enduringe* (pres. part. of *enduren*)] **1** : LASTING, PERMANENT ⟨an ~ novel⟩ **2** : capable of existing without deterioration : DURABLE ⟨an ~ substance⟩ **3** : PATIENT, LONG-SUFFERING ⟨an ~ disposition⟩ **4** *dial* : LIVELONG, ENTIRE — often used with *whole* ⟨he stayed the whole ~ day⟩

en·dur·ing·ly *adv* : LASTINGLY, PERMANENTLY

en·dur·ing·ness *n* -ES : lasting quality : PERMANENCE

enduring of *prep, dial* : ENDURING

end use *n* : the ultimate specific use to which a manufactured product (as paper) is put or restricted

endways \ˈ=,=\ *adv (or adj)* **1** : with the end forward (as toward the observer) : END ON ⟨with houses built ~⟩ **2** : in or toward the direction of the ends : LENGTHWISE ⟨~ pressure⟩ **3** : at or on the end ⟨poles leaning ~ against a wall⟩ **4** *chiefly Scot* : well along : AHEAD ⟨couldn't get ~ with the job⟩

endwise \ˈ=,=\ *adv (or adj)* : ENDWAYS

en·dy·ma \ˈendəmə\ *n* -s [NL, fr. Gk *endyma* garment, fr. *endyein*] : EPENDYMA — **en·dy·mal** \-məl\ *adj*

en·dy·sis \ˈendəsə̇s\ *n, pl* **endy·ses** \-ə,sēz\ [NL, fr. Gk, act of putting on, fr. *endyein* to put on, dive in, fr. *en* in, on + *dyein* to dive in, put on, don) + *-sis* — more at IN, ADYTUM] : the act or process of developing a new coat of hair or a new set of feathers — opposed to *ecdysis*

end zone *n* **1** : the area at each end of a football field bounded by the end line, the goal line, and the side lines — see FOOTBALL illustration **2** : the part of an ice-hockey rink between each zone line and the nearer end of the rink — see ICE HOCKEY illustration

-ene \ˌēn *sometimes* ˈēn\ *n suffix* -s [ISV, fr. Gk *-ēnē* (fem. patronymic suffix)] : unsaturated carbon compound ⟨ben*zene*⟩; *esp* : carbon compound characterized by the presence of one double bond ⟨prop*ene*⟩ — in names of straight-chain hydrocarbons; distinguished from *-ane, -yne*; compare -YLENE

ENE *abbr* east-northeast

en echelon \äⁿ+\ *adv (or adj)* [F *en échelon*] : in the arrangement or order of an echelon ⟨*en echelon* faults⟩

-ened *past of* -EN

ene·di·ol \ˌēnˈdī,ōl, -ōl, =ˈ=,=\ *n* -s *often attrib* [ISV *ene-* (fr. *-ene*) + *diol*] : an organic compound characterized by the grouping >C(OH)—C(OH)< containing 2 hydroxyl groups adjacent to a double bond ⟨a reducing sugar can form an ~⟩

en·e·ma \ˈenəmə\ *n, pl* **enemas** *also* **enem·a·ta** \ˌenəˈmäd·ə, ˈenəmə-; əˈnemədə, eˈ-, ēˈ-; -tə\ [LL, fr. Gk, fr. *enienai* to send in, inject, fr. *en* in + *hienai* to send — more at JET] **1** : the injection of liquid into the intestine by way of the anus for cleansing, examination, or other purpose **2** : material for injection or injected as an enema — see BARIUM ENEMA

en·e·my \ˈenəmē, -mi\ *n, pl* **enemies** *often attrib* [ME *enemi*, fr. OF *enemi, inimi*, fr. L *inimicus*, fr. *in-* not + *amicus* friend — more at UN-, AMIABLE] **1** : one that seeks the injury, overthrow, or failure of a person or thing to which he is opposed : ADVERSARY, OPPONENT ⟨the two brothers were political *enemies*⟩ **2** : something injurious, harmful, or deadly ⟨drink was his greatest ~⟩ **3 a** : a military foe ⟨the ~ was driven off⟩ ⟨meet the ~ on equal terms⟩ — sometimes pl. in constr. ⟨the ~ were in large force⟩ **b** : a hostile unit, ship, tank, or aircraft ⟨after a running battle the ~ was sunk by a direct hit at 1000 yards⟩ **c** *pl* **enemy** : a member of a hostile force ⟨30 to 40 ~ engaged a friendly patrol —*N.Y. Times*⟩

syn ENEMY and FOE both signify a thing, person, or group that is hostile to one. ENEMY usu. stresses antagonism manifest in a desire to harm or destroy although it may suggest only an active dislike or habit of preying upon ⟨to amass adequate air power to deter our *enemies* from immediate attack⟩ ⟨let the teacher appear always the ally of the pupil, not his natural *enemy* —Bertrand Russell⟩ ⟨time is at once the *enemy* and the ally of life and of love —F.B.Millett⟩ ⟨the mortal *enemies* of man are . . . the aspects of the physical world that limit or challenge his control —W.C.Allee⟩ ⟨germ-bearing insects and other *enemies* of mankind⟩ FOE generally implies active warfare, usu. figurative ⟨the intransigent *foe* of hypocrisy and false standards —Gene Baro⟩ ⟨laughter is by no means a *foe* of reason —H.A.Overstreet⟩ ⟨the representative from Michigan has a reputation as a *foe* of waste, particularly in the armed services —*Current Biog.*⟩ In application to an opponent in war, ENEMY is the common word and FOE is chiefly poetic or rhetorical ⟨he had fresh troops and superior numbers and forced the *enemy* back until they abandoned the field —C.H. Lanza⟩ ⟨donning his sword and buckler to fight the *foe*⟩

enemy alien *n* **:** a foreigner resident in a country with which his country is at war

eneolithic *usu cap, var of* AENEOLITHIC

en•epidermic \(ˌ)en+\ *adj* [²*en-* + *epidermic*] **:** applied to the unbroken skin for medicinal purposes

ener•geia \ˌenərˈjīə, -rˈgī, |āə, |ē(y)ə; eˈnerˌgāˌä\ *n* -s [Gk, activity, operation — more at ENERGY] **:** ENERGY 4a — contrasted with *dynamis*

en•er•get•ic \ˌenə(r)ˈjed·|ik, -et|, |ēk\ *adj* [Gk *energētikos* active, fr. (assumed) *energētos* (verbal of *energein* to be in action, effect, fr. *energos* active, effective) + *-ikos* -ic] **1 :** exhibiting energy **:** STRENUOUS ⟨an ~ administration of business affairs⟩ **:** marked by energy ⟨an ~ walk⟩ ⟨an ~ campaigner⟩ **2 :** operating with force, vigor, or effect ⟨~ laws⟩ ⟨an ~ oxidizing agent for the creation of high temperatures⟩ **3 :** possessing energy **:** having the capacity for action or exerting force ⟨the volcanoes that raised the islands are still ~ in places⟩ **4 :** of, relating to, based on, or in terms of energy ⟨~ stability⟩ ⟨~ equation⟩ **syn** see VIGOROUS

en•er•get•i•cal \|əkəl, |ēk\ *adj* [Gk *energētikos* + E *-al*] **:** ENERGETIC — **en•er•get•i•cal•ly** \|ək(ə)lē, |ēk-, -li\ *adv*

en•er•get•i•cist \ˌ==ˈjed·|əsəst, -et|\ *n* -s [fr. *energetics*, after such pairs as E *physics: physicist*] **:** a specialist in energetics

en•er•get•ics \|iks, |ēks\ *n pl but sing in constr* **:** a branch of mechanics that deals primarily with energy and its transformations ⟨nuclear ~⟩

en•er•ge•tis•tic \ˌenə(r)ˌjed·ˈistik, -jeˈtis-, -tēk\ *adj* [*energetics* + *-ist* + *-ic*] **:** relating to energetics

ener•gic \(ˈ)eˈnərjik, əˈn-,ēˈn-\ *adj* [*energy* + *-ic*] **:** ENERGETIC

en•er•gid \ˈenə(r)jəd, -(ˌ)jid\ *n* -s [ISV *energ-* (fr. Gk *energos* active) + *-id;* orig. formed as G *energid*] **:** a nucleus and the body of cytoplasm with which it interacts — called also *protoplast*

en•er•gism \ˈenə(r)ˌjizəm\ *n* -s [G *energismus*, fr. *energie* energy (fr. LL *energia*) + *-ismus* -ism] **1 :** a doctrine that certain phenomena (as mental states) are explicable in terms of energy **2 :** an ethical theory that the supreme good consists in the efficient exercise of normal human faculties rather than in happiness or pleasure **:** SELF-REALIZATIONISM

en•er•gist \-jəst\ *n* -s **:** an adherent of energism

en•er•gize *also* **en•er•gise** \-ˌjīz\ *vb* [*energy* + *-ize*] *vi* **:** to put forth energy **:** ACT ~ *vt* **1 :** to impart energy to **:** make active ⟨~ the will⟩ **2 :** to make energetic or vigorous ⟨~ the administration of an office⟩ **3 :** to make an electric circuit alive electrically by applying voltage to ⟨allow current to flow from the battery to ~ the windings —Joseph Heitner⟩ **syn** see STRENGTHEN, VITALIZE

en•er•giz•er \-zə(r)\ *n* -s **:** one that energizes; *specif* **:** a metal carbonate (as barium carbonate) mixed with charcoal in a carburizing compound to increase carburizing speed

en•er•gu•men \ˌenə(r)ˈgyümən\ *n* -s [LL *energumenus* one possessed by an evil spirit, fr. LGk *energoumenos*, fr. Gk, worked on, being the object of an action, pres. middle part. of *energein* to be in action, effect, fr. *energos* active, effective] **1 :** a person possessed by or as if by an evil spirit **:** DEMONIAC; *specif* **:** one belonging to a Christian church in the first centuries and placed in a special class ministered to by exorcists and allowed limited participation in common worship **2 :** a fanatical devotee, adherent, or enthusiast ⟨military ~*s*⟩

en•er•gy \ˈenə(r)jē, -ji\ *n* -ES [LL *energia*, fr. Gk *energeia* activity, operation, fr. *energos* active, effective, fr. *en* in + *ergon* work — more at IN, WORK] **1** *of language or style* **:** imaginative or affective force **:** VITALITY **2 :** the capacity of acting, operating, or producing an effect **:** inherent power ⟨an individual of great intellectual ~⟩ ⟨he expended his *energies* in useless tasks⟩ **3 :** power efficiently and forcefully exerted **:** vigorous or effectual operation **:** VIGOROUSNESS ⟨the ~ and success of an argument⟩ **4 a :** the realized state of potentialities as opposed to their unrealized state — compare ENTELECHY **b** (1) **:** ACTIVITY; *esp* **:** psychical activity (2) **:** the product of activity **:** EFFECT **5 :** an entity rated as the most fundamental of all physical concepts and usu. regarded as the equivalent of or the capacity for doing work either being associated with material bodies (as a coiled spring or speeding train) or having an existence independent of matter (as light or X rays traversing a vacuum), its physical dimensions being the same as those of work $ML^2 \div T^2$ where M is mass, L length, and T time, usu. being expressed in work units (as foot-pounds or ergs), and in any form being endowed with the properties of mass (as inertia, momentum, gravitation) by relativity which assigns to the energy E an equivalent mass m by the equation $m = E \div c^2$ where c is the speed of light — see CONSERVATION OF ENERGY, KINETIC ENERGY, POTENTIAL ENERGY **6 :** MUZZLE ENERGY **syn** see POWER

energy balance *n* **:** the relation between intake of food and output of work (as in muscular or secretory activity) that is positive when the body stores extra food as fats and negative when the body draws on stored fat to provide energy for work

energy density *n* **:** the amount of energy (as in a beam of radiation) per unit volume

energy level *or* **energy state** *n* **:** one of the stable states of constant energy that may be assumed by a physical system — used esp. of the quantum states of electrons in atoms or molecules, of nuclei, or of other systems of interacting elementary particles

energy spectrum *n* **:** an arrangement of particle energies (as of alpha particles or photoelectrons) in a heterogeneous beam that is analogous to the arrangement of frequencies in an optical spectrum

¹ener•vate \ēˈnərvət, əˈn-,eˈn-\ *adj* [L *enervatus*, past part. of *enervare*] **:** ENERVATED

²en•er•vate \ˈenə(r)ˌvāt, *usu* -ād·+V\ *vt* -ED/-ING/-S [L *enervatus*, past part. of *enervare* to make weak or effeminate, fr. *e* out of, out + *nervus* sinew, nerve) — more at E-, NERVE] **1** *obs* **:** to cut the nerves or tendons of; *specif* **:** HAMSTRING **2 :** to lessen the nerve, vitality, or strength of **:** ENFEEBLE ⟨heat ~*s* people⟩ **3 :** to reduce the mental or moral vigor of **:** WEAKEN ⟨a government *enervated* by corruption⟩ **syn** see UNNERVE

en•er•vat•ed \ˈenə(r)ˌvād·əd, -ātəd\ *adj* [fr. past part. of ²*enervate*] **:** lacking physical, mental, or moral vigor **:** ENERVATE **syn** see LANGUID

en•er•va•tion \ˌenə(r)ˈvāshən\ *n* -s [LL *enervation-, enervatio*, fr. L *enervatus* + *-ion-, -io* -ion] **1 :** the act or action of enervating **2 :** the quality or state of being enervated

en•er•va•tor \ˈenə(r)ˌvād·ə(r), -ātə-\ *n* -s **:** one that enervates

enerve *vt* [F *énerver*, fr. L *enervare*] *obs* **:** ²ENERVATE

-enes *pl of* -ENE

eneuch *or* **eneugh** \əˈn(y)ük, -ˈ(y)ük, -ˈ(y)ək\ *Scot var of* ENOUGH

enew *vt* -ED/-ING/-S [ME *enewen*, fr. AF *enewer* to moisten, fr. OF *en-* ¹en- + *ewe, eve, aigue* water (fr. L *aqua*) — more at ISLAND] *obs, of a hawk* **:** to drive or plunge (a fowl) into the water

en face \äⁿfäs\ *adj* [F, opposite] **1 :** facing forward **:** having face or front forward ⟨a portrait *en face*⟩ **2 :** OPPOSITE ⟨a collection of French poems with English translation *en face*⟩

en•face \ənˈfās, en-\ *vt* [*en-* (as in *endorse*) + *face*, n.] *Brit* **:** to write or print on the face of (a draft or bill) ⟨~ drafts with memoranda⟩; *also* **:** to write or print (a memorandum or direction) on the face of a draft or bill

en•face•ment \-mənt\ *n* -s *Brit* **:** the act of enfacing; *also* **:** something (as a note or bill) that is enfaced — compare ENDORSEMENT

en•fant ter•ri•ble \äⁿfäⁿterēbl(ᵊ), -b(lə)\ *n, pl* **enfants terribles** \"\ [F, terrible child] **1 :** a child whose inopportune remarks cause embarrassment **2 :** a person who compromises his cause or party by rash actions

en•fa•ti•co \ämˈfätē(ˌ)kō\ *adj* [It, fr. LL *emphaticus* forcible, expressive, fr. Gk *emphatikos* — more at EMPHATIC] **:** EMPHATIC, FORCEFUL — used as a direction in music

en•fee•ble \ənˈfēbəl, en-\ *vt* **enfeebled; enfeebled; enfeebling** \-b(ə)liŋ\ **enfeebles** [ME *enfeblen*, fr. MF *enfeblir*, fr. OF, fr. *en-* ¹en- + *feble, foible* feeble — more at FEEBLE] **:** to make feeble ⟨a man *enfeebled* by hunger⟩ **:** deprive of strength **:** reduce the strength of ⟨a country *enfeebled* by civil war⟩ **syn** see WEAKEN

en•fee•ble•ment \-bəlmənt\ *n* -s **1 :** the action of enfeebling **2 :** the quality or state of being enfeebled

en•fee•bler \-b(ə)lə(r)\ *n* -s **:** one that enfeebles

en•feoff \ən, en +\ *vt* -ED/-ING/-S [ME *enfeffen, enfeoffen*, fr. AF *enfeffer, enfeoffer*, fr. OF *en-* ¹en- + *fief*, n., fee — more at FEE] **1 :** to invest with a fief or fee **:** invest (a person) with a freehold estate by feoffment ⟨the holdings in which a baron ~*ed* his leading tenants —F.M.Stenton⟩ **2** *obs* **:** to give into vassalage

en•feoff•ment \"mənt\ *n* -s [ME *enfeffement*, fr. AF, fr. *enfeffer* + MF *-ment*] **1 :** the act of enfeoffing **2 :** the instrument or deed by which one is enfeoffed

en fête \äⁿfāt\ *adj* [F, in festival] **:** being in festal dress **:** making a holiday showing

en•fetter \ən, en +\ *vt* [¹*en-* + *fetter*, n.] **:** to bind in fetters

¹en•field \ˈenˌfēld\ *adj, usu cap* [fr. *Enfield*, urban district in Middlesex, England] **:** of or from the urban district of Enfield, England **:** of the kind or style prevalent in Enfield

²enfield \"\ *or* **enfield rifle** *n* -s *usu cap E* [fr. *Enfield*, Middlesex, Eng., where it was orig. manufactured] **1 :** a muzzle-loading rifled musket of .577 caliber used by the British during the Crimean War and by U.S. troops in the Civil War **2 :** a .303 caliber magazine rifle of bolt type used by the British **3 :** a .30 caliber rifle used by U.S. troops in World War I — see RIFLE illustration

¹en•fi•lade \ˈenfəˌlād, -ˌäd,-ˌad *also* ˈän...äd *or* ˈän...ˌäd; ˌ==ˈ=\ *n* -s [F, series, row, military enfilade, fr. *enfiler* to thread, string, rake with gunfire in a lengthwise direction (fr. OF, to thread, fr. *en-* ¹en- + *fil*, n., thread) + *-ade* — more at FILE] **1 :** arrangement (as of rooms, doors, trees) in opposite and parallel rows **2 a :** a condition permitting the delivery of fire at an objective (as a trench or line of troops) from a point on or near the prolongation of its longest axis **b :** a position favorable for enfilade firing

²enfilade \"\ *vt* -ED/-ING/-S **1 :** to arrange (as trees or rooms) to form an enfilade **2 :** to rake or be in a position to rake (as a fortification or column of troops) with gunfire in a lengthwise direction

en•file \ənˈfīl, en-\ *vt* [ME *enfilen*, fr. MF *enfiler*] *archaic* **:** to put on a string **:** THREAD

enfiled *adj* [fr. past part. of *enfile*] *heraldry* **:** passed or thrust through — used with *with* or *of* ⟨two branches ~ with a baron's coronet⟩ ⟨~ with a chaplet of roses —Edward Almack⟩

en•fire \ən, en +\ *vt* [ME *enfiren*, fr. *en-* ¹en- + *fir*, n., fire — more at FIRE] *archaic* **:** KINDLE

enflame *var of* INFLAME

en•flesh \ən, en +\ *vt* [¹*en-* + *flesh*, n.] **:** to clothe with or as if with flesh ⟨~ the idea of spirit —H.O.Taylor⟩

en•fleu•rage \ˌäⁿflüˈräzh\ *n* -s [F, fr. *enfleurer* to saturate with the perfume of flowers (fr. *en-* ¹en- + *fleur*, n., flower, fr. L *flor-, flos*) + *-age* — more at BLOW (to bloom)] **:** a process of obtaining fragrant oils for perfumes by exposing successive batches of freshly picked flowers to layers of fat (as a mixture of lard and tallow) coated on stacked glass plates and finally extracting usu. with alcohol the resulting pomade

en•fold \ənˈfōld, en-\ *vt* **enfolded; enfolded** *or archaic* **enfolden enfolding; enfolds** [alter. (influenced by ¹*en-*) of *infold*] **1 a :** to surround with a covering **:** CONTAIN ⟨gilded tombs do worms ~ —Shak.⟩ ⟨~*ed* within the covers of this volume —*N.Y.Herald Tribune Bk. Rev.*⟩ **b :** to cover with or as if with folds **:** ENVELOP ⟨the new atmosphere that seemed to ~ her —Helen R. Martin⟩ ⟨blackness moved up the walls till night ~*ed* the pass —Zane Grey⟩ ⟨she lay *enfolden* in the warm shadow of her loveliness —P.B.Shelley⟩ **2 a :** to clasp within or within the arms **:** EMBRACE ⟨arms ~*ing* bunches of flowering branches —Angélica Mendoza⟩ **b :** to take in and hold ⟨either ~ them as respectable . . . members of a commercial society or drive them on —Russell Lord⟩ **3 :** to make or put a fold in **:** fold over or back ⟨~*ed* margins⟩

en•fold•er \-də(r)\ *n* **:** one that enfolds

enfolding *n* **:** a folding in **:** FOLD, CREASE

en•fold•ment \-l(d)mənt\ *n* -s **:** an action of enfolding

en•force \ənˈfō(ə)rs, en-, -ō(ə)rs,-ōəs,-ō(ə)s\ *vt* [ME *enforcen*, fr. MF *enforcier* to strengthen, force, fr. OF, fr. *en-* ¹en- + *force*, n., strength & *forcier*, v., to attack — more at FORCE (n.), FORCE (v.)] **1 :** to give force to **:** REINFORCE ⟨his comment is enough to confirm and ~ the significance attributed to a free ballot⟩ **2 a :** to urge with energy ⟨~ arguments⟩ **b** *obs* **:** ENCOURAGE, INSPIRE **3** *obs* **:** to use force upon **:** ASSAIL, ASSAULT **4** *obs* **:** to fling or drive forcibly **5 :** CONSTRAIN, COMPEL ⟨~ obedience from children⟩ **6** *obs* **:** to make or obtain by force ⟨~ a passage⟩ **7 :** to put in force **:** cause to take effect **:** give effect to esp. with vigor ⟨~ laws⟩ ⟨a government unable to ~ its national interests⟩ ⟨*enforced* his rule by cruel methods —C.S.Forester⟩

syn IMPLEMENT: ENFORCE refers to requiring operation, observance, or protection of laws, orders, contracts, and agreements by authority, often that of a whole government or of its executive or legal branches ⟨this law is seldom *enforced*⟩ ⟨in order to make the papal bureaucracy disciplined and fit for such duties he *enforced* the hated rule of celibacy upon his clergy —Herbert Agar⟩ ⟨the mediator's request for troops to back up its resolutions and *enforce* the truce —*Collier's Yr. Bk.*⟩ IMPLEMENT suggests performance of such acts as are necessary to bring into actual effect or operation some agreed-on plan or measure ⟨the estimates of public accountants that the actual cost of *implementing* the bill would be about double the amount the president forecast —*Current Biog.*⟩ ⟨he also urged that military equipment be given to the nations of Western Europe to *implement* the Brussels pact —*Current Biog.*⟩ ⟨to *implement* the prison's group activities by providing films, books, and pamphlets —*Saturday Rev.*⟩

en•force•abil•i•ty \=ˌ=ˈbiləd·ē, -ətē, -i\ *n* -ES **:** the quality or state of being enforceable

en•force•able \=ˈ=əbəl\ *adj* **:** capable of being enforced

en•forced \-st\ *adj* [fr. past part. of *enforce*] **:** COMPELLED, FORCED ⟨~ obedience⟩ ⟨~ idleness⟩ — **en•forc•ed•ly** \-sədlē, -stlē, -li\ *adv*

en•force•ment \-smənt\ *n* -s [MF *enforcement*, fr. OF, fr. *enforcier* + *-ment*] **:** the act of enforcing: as **a :** compulsion esp. by physical violence **b :** forcible urging or argument ⟨the ~ of a reasonable claim⟩ **c :** the compelling of the fulfillment (as of a law or order)

en•forc•er \=ˈ=ə(r)\ *n* -s **:** one that enforces; *specif* **:** a gunman used to enforce discipline within a gang

en•forc•ive \=ˈ=iv\ *adj, obs* **:** tending to enforce

enforest *vt* [¹*en-* + *forest*, n.] *obs* **:** AFFOREST

enfouldred *adj* [¹*en-* + obs. E *foudre* thunderbolt, lightning (fr. ME *fouldre, foudre*, fr. MF, fr. L *fulgur*) + E *-ed;* akin to L *flagrare* to burn — more at BLACK] *obs* **:** mixed with or emitting lightning

en•frame \ənˈfrām, en-\ *vt* [¹*en-* + *frame*, n.] **:** FRAME — **en•frame•ment** \-āmmənt\ *n* -s

enfranch *vt* [prob. by shortening] *obs* **:** ENFRANCHISE

en•fran•chise \ənˈfranˌchīz, en-, -raar- *sometimes* -īs\ *vt* [ME *enfraunchisen*, fr. MF *enfranchiss-*, stem of *enfranchir*, fr. OF, fr. *en-* ¹en- + *franc* free — more at FRANK] **1 :** to set free (as from slavery, prison, or obligation) **2 a :** to endow with a franchise **:** admit to the privileges of a freeman or citizen **b :** NATURALIZE **3 :** to admit (a town or city) to political privileges **:** give political rights to (a town or city) **4 :** to make (lands) freehold under feudal law **syn** see FREE

en•fran•chise•ment \-mənt, -chəzmənt *sometimes* -chəsm- *or* ənˌfra(a)nˈchī- *or* (ˌ)enˌfra(a)nˈchī- *or* ˌenfrənˈchī-\ *n* **:** the act of enfranchising: as **a :** the releasing from slavery or custody **b :** admission to the freedom of a corporation or body politic **c :** the making of lands (as copyhold) freehold under feudal law

en•fran•chis•er \=ˈ=ˌchīzə(r) *sometimes* -īsə- *n* -s **:** one that enfranchises

enfume *vt* [F & L; F *enfumer*, fr. L *infumare*, fr. *in* + *fumus* smoke — more at FUME] *obs* **:** to envelop in smoke

¹eng \ˈeŋ\ *n* -s [native name in Burma] **:** a large timber tree (*Dipterocarpus tuberculatus*) of Burma and parts of India that produces a hard strong heavy straight-grained reddish brown timber

²eng \"\ *n* -s **:** the symbol ŋ that is widely used in pronunciation alphabets for the velar nasal consonant which is the sound of *ng* in English *thing* and of *n* in English *think*

eng *abbr* **1** engine; engineer; engineering **2** engraved; engraver; engraving

en•gage \ənˈgāj, en-\ *vb* -ED/-ING/-S [ME *engagen*, fr. MF *engager, engagier*, fr. OF *engagier*, fr. *en-* ¹en- + *gage* pledge, pawn — more at GAGE] *vt* **1 a** *obs* **:** MORTGAGE, PAWN, PLEDGE **b :** to offer (as one's life or word) as backing to a cause or aim **:** expose to risk for the attainment or support of some end ⟨*engaged* his all in the king's cause⟩ ⟨I would like to drop out of this undertaking but my word is *engaged*⟩ **2 a** *obs* **:** to involve or entangle (as a person) in some affair or enterprise **b** *obs* **:** to entangle or entrap in or as if in a snare or bog **c :** to attract and hold ⟨*engaged* his attention by a series of sprightly comments⟩ **d :** to make (an architectural member) fast; *esp* **:** to partially incorporate (a column) in a wall **e :** to come into contact or interlock with **:** MESH ⟨the teeth of one gear wheel *engaging* those of another to transmit power⟩; *also* **:** to cause (parts) to engage ⟨~ the gears, then slowly let in your clutch⟩ **3 a** *obs* **:** to commit (as a person) as surety (as for the payment of a debt or performance of an obligation) **b :** to bind (as oneself) to do or to forbear doing something by or as if by a formal promise or contract ⟨he *engaged* himself not to call on his father for help⟩; *esp* **:** to bind (as oneself) by a pledge to marry ⟨a girl who *engaged* herself to three different men in as many months⟩ — usu. used passively ⟨they had been *engaged* for over six years⟩ **c :** to pledge or commit (as oneself) to participate in some social or business activity ⟨*engaged* herself to attend the meeting⟩; *often* to bind by a previous commitment ⟨I would like to go with you but I am *engaged* that evening⟩ ⟨a popular hairdresser whose time is *engaged* weeks in advance⟩ **4 a :** to provide occupation for (as a person, his interest, or labor) **:** require the use of ⟨it *engaged* all their strength to budge the stone⟩ ⟨to fix the attention, but not to ~ the mind, is a precise statement of the advertiser's formula —D.M.Potter⟩ ⟨subsistence farming ~*s* the major efforts of the settlers⟩ ⟨his family had been *engaged* in trade for generations⟩ **b :** to arrange to obtain the services of usu. for a wage or fee ⟨she was *engaged* to play the leading role in the new opera⟩ ⟨you will need to ~ a cook and two extra maids if you take that house⟩; *also* **:** to enter (oneself) into an agreement to serve ⟨he *engaged* himself with the new company for two years⟩ **c :** to secure or arrange to secure (as accommodations, goods, or aid) ⟨we will ~ a suite at the hotel⟩ ⟨have your agent ~ wheat for fall delivery⟩ ⟨I have *engaged* the help of the local chief in order to recruit enough porters⟩ **d :** to gain over **:** win and attach **:** ATTRACT ⟨his gentle persistence gradually *engaged* all the neighbors⟩ ⟨she ~*s* everyone with her pretty girlish ways⟩ **5 a** *archaic* **:** to call upon **:** EXHORT, INDUCE, PERSUADE **b :** to hold the attention of **:** ENGROSS, OCCUPY ⟨the puzzle *engaged* him all evening⟩ ⟨we were *engaged* in cleaning the cottage until just before you came⟩ **c :** to induce to participate **:** draw out ⟨I *engaged* him in conversation⟩ **6 a :** to enter into contest with **:** bring to conflict ⟨ordered to seek out and ~ the enemy fleet⟩ **b :** to bring together or interlock (weapons) ⟨*engaged* their foils after a preliminary pass or two⟩ ⟨the battling stags ~ their heavy antlers and strive for mastery⟩ ~ *vi* **1 a :** to promise or pledge oneself ⟨*engaged* to free the Holy Land⟩ **:** enter into or take on an obligation ⟨they *engaged* to sell our grain at the best possible price⟩ ⟨the Indians *engaged* to keep the peace⟩ **b :** to become pledged or answerable **:** GUARANTEE, PROMISE — usu. used with *for* ⟨he'll be there on time but that's all I can ~ for⟩ ⟨he ~*s* for the honesty of his brother⟩ **2 a :** to begin and carry on an enterprise, esp. a business or profession ⟨he *engaged* in trade for several years⟩ **b :** to employ or involve oneself ⟨he *engaged* in one long round of pleasure as long as his money lasted⟩ **c :** to take part **:** PARTICIPATE ⟨he *engaged* in a long-winded dispute⟩ ⟨*engaging* in a hog-calling contest⟩ **3 a :** to enter into conflict **:** join battle **b :** to bring together or interlock weapons — used esp. of fencers **4** *archaic* **:** to become involved or entangled **5** *of machinery* **:** to be or become in gear (as of two gear wheels working together) **:** interlock and interact **syn** see PROMISE

en•gaged \-jd\ *adj* [fr. past part. of *engage*] **1 :** OCCUPIED, EMPLOYED **2 :** pledged or promised esp. in marriage **:** BETROTHED **3 :** greatly interested **:** EARNEST **4 :** involved esp. in a hostile encounter ⟨the ~ ships continued the fight⟩ **5** *of an architectural member* **a :** partly embedded or bonded (as in a wall) ⟨an ~ column⟩ **b :** FITTED, FRAMED **6 a** *of machinery* **:** being in gear **b** *of gears* **:** MESHED — **en•gaged•ly** \-jədlē, -jdlē, -li\ *adv* — **en•gaged•ness** \-jədnəs, -j(d)n\ *n* -ES

en•gage•ment \-jmənt\ *n* -s **1 a :** the act of engaging or state of being engaged **:** a pledging or pledged state **:** INVOLVEMENT, ATTACHMENT **b :** BETROTHAL **2 a :** something that engages (as an engrossing occupation, an obligation) ⟨his ~*s* kept him very busy⟩ **b :** PREPOSSESSION, BIAS **:** favorable attachment ⟨religion, which is the chief ~ of our league —John Milton⟩ **3 a :** a promise to be present at a specified time and place **:** APPOINTMENT ⟨a previous ~⟩ **b :** employment esp. by contract for a stated time ⟨an ~ as leading lady⟩ **4 engagements** *pl* **:** pecuniary liabilities **:** OBLIGATIONS **5 :** the act of crossing fencing blades in any of the eight positions **6 :** the state of being in gear or in such contact that motion may be transmitted ⟨one part of a clutch is brought into ~ with the other part⟩ **7 :** the phase of parturition in which the fetal head passes into the pelvic canal **8 a :** hostile encounter between military forces ⟨forces . . . reported small patrol ~*s* during the day —*N.Y.Times*⟩ **b :** a duel or other single combat

syn ENGAGEMENT, APPOINTMENT, RENDEZVOUS, TRYST, ASSIGNATION, DATE can apply, in common, to an agreement or commitment to be in a specific place at a specific time for a specified purpose. ENGAGEMENT is the general term interchangeable in basic meaning with any of the rest ⟨his *engagement* with the duke —F.M.Stenton⟩ ⟨an *engagement* with the doctor at 2 p.m.⟩ ⟨an *engagement* to meet secretly after dark⟩ APPOINTMENT applies chiefly to an engagement with someone, as a doctor or executive, who must apportion his time in order to meet all commitments ⟨an *appointment* with the dentist⟩ ⟨an *appointment* to see the governor⟩ ⟨an *appointment* with fate⟩ RENDEZVOUS, now commonly an agreed-upon meeting or meeting place, can still signify a pledge, often implicit, to meet someone or something usu. at a specific place and time which honor makes inescapable ⟨I have a *rendezvous* with Death —Alan Seeger⟩ ⟨this generation of Americans has a *rendezvous* with destiny —F.D.Roosevelt⟩ TRYST, now chiefly poetic, applies generally to a lovers' agreement to meet at a particular place or time ⟨young women kept *trysts* with their beaux here —*Amer. Guide Series: N.C.*⟩ An ASSIGNATION is commonly a tryst but is usu. illicit or clandestine ⟨make *assignations* for them with ladies of the street —G.B.Shaw⟩ DATE is interchangeable with but more current in speech than ENGAGEMENT, often suggesting a more casual agreement esp. between young men and women ⟨remembering suddenly he had a riding *date* with the major's wife at 12:30 —James Jones⟩ ⟨she has a *date* with a boy⟩

engagement ring *n* **:** a ring given in token of betrothal; *esp* **:** a diamond solitaire so given by a man to his fiancée

engagement ring

en•gag•er \-jə(r)\ *n* -s **:** one that engages: as **a** *obs* **:** a person who acts as a guarantor **:** SURETY **b :** one that engages in an activity or occupation **c :** a person who engages another's service **:** EMPLOYER

engaging *adj* [fr. pres. part. of *engage*] **:** tending to draw favorable attention or the affections **:** ATTRACTIVE ⟨~ manners⟩ **syn** see SWEET

en•gag•ing•ly *adv* **:** in an engaging manner **:** CHARMINGLY

en•gag•ing•ness *n* -ES **:** the quality of being engaging

en•garland \ən, en+\ *vt* [¹*en-* + *garland*, n.] **:** to deck or encircle with or as if with a garland

engastrimyth *n* -s [MF *engastrimythe*, fr. Gk *engastrimythos*, fr. *en* in + *gastr-* + *mythos* speech — more at IN, MYTH] *obs* **:** VENTRILOQUIST

en•gas•tri•myth•ic \ənˌgastrəˈmithik, en-\ *adj* **:** relating to or like ventriloquism

en•gaud \ən, en+\ *vt* -ED/-ING/-S [¹*en-* + *gaud*, n.] **:** to make showy; *esp* **:** to lend a false glamor to ⟨lowly occupations ~*ed* by pompous names⟩

en•gel•man•nia \ˌeŋgəlˈmanēə\ *n, cap* [NL, fr. George *Engelmann* †1884 Am. botanist born in Germany + NL *-ia*] **:** a genus of No. American herbs (family Compositae) resembling sunflowers and having pinnatifid leaves and large yellow flower heads

en·gel·mann ivy \ˈeŋgəlmən-\ *n, usu cap E* **:** a Virginia creeper (*Parthenocissus quinquefolia engelmannii*) that is distinguished by small thick leathery leaves

engelmann spruce *also* **engelmann's spruce** *n, usu cap E* **:** a large mountain spruce (*Picea engelmanni*) of the Rocky mountain region and British Columbia that yields a light-colored wood used chiefly as rough lumber and for boxes

engelmann spruce beetle *n, usu cap E* **:** a very destructive reddish brown or blackish bark bettle (*Dendroctonus obesus*) that feeds in the cambium of Engelmann spruce

en·gel's law \ˈeŋ(g)əlz-\ *n, usu cap E* [after Ernst *Engel* †1896 Ger. statistician and economist] **:** a generalization in economics: as family income increases, the percentage spent for food decreases, that spent for clothing, rent, heat, and light remains the same, while that spent for education, health, and recreation increases

en·gen·der \ənˈjendə(r), en-\ *vb* **engendered; engendered; engendering** \-d(ə)riŋ\ **engenders** [ME *engendren*, fr. MF *engendrer*, fr. L *ingenerare*, fr. *in* + *generare* to beget — more at GENERATE] *vt* **1 :** to produce by the union of the sexes **:** BEGET, PROCREATE, PROPAGATE **2 :** to cause to exist or to develop **:** bring forth **:** sow the seeds of **:** PRODUCE ⟨angry words ~ strife⟩ ⟨the class struggle tends to ~ fear and hatred⟩ ~ *vi* **1** *archaic* **a** *of disease* **:** ORIGINATE, STEM **b :** COPULATE **c :** to breed, multiply, or develop **2 :** to assume form **:** come gradually into being ⟨a storm was ~*ing* in the mountains⟩

en·gen·der·er \-d(ə)rə(r)\ *n* -s [ME *engendrer*, alter. (influenced by ME *-er, -ere* -er) of *engendrour*, fr. MF *engendreur*, fr. OF *engendreor*, fr. *engendrer* to engender + *-eor* -or] **:** one that engenders **:** PRODUCER, PRECURSOR ⟨flies are often ~*s* of disease⟩

en·gen·drure\ -drər, -ˌdrü(ə)r\ *also* **en·gen·dure** \-dyər, -ˌdyü(ə)r\ *n* -s [*engendrure* fr. ME, fr. MF, fr. OF *engendreure*, fr. *engendrer* to engender + *-ure*; *engendure* fr. ME, alter. of *engendrure*] **1** *obs* **:** the act of engendering **2** *archaic* **:** DESCENT, PARENTAGE; *also* **:** ORIGIN, SOURCE

engg *abbr* engineering

en·gild \ən, en+\ *vt* [ME *engilden*, fr. ¹*en-* + *gilden* to gild] **1** *archaic* **:** GILD **2** *obs* **:** to make bright with or as if with light

engin *abbr* **1** engineer **2** engineering

¹en·gine \ˈenjən\ *n* -s [ME *engin*, fr. OF, skill, trick, mechanical contrivance, fr. L *ingenium* natural capacity, natural disposition, fr. *in* + *-genium* (akin to L *gignere* to beget) — more at KIN] **1** *obs* **a :** natural capacity **:** ABILITY, SKILL **b :** ingenuity or an instance or product of it; *often* **:** cunning or evil contrivance **:** ARTIFICE, WILE ⟨all the ~*s* of her wit —Edmund Spenser⟩ **2** *archaic* **:** something that is used to effect a purpose **:** AGENT, MEANS, METHOD ⟨all these ~*s* of lust —Shak.⟩ **3 a :** a mechanical contrivance or tool: as (1) **:** an instrument or machine of war (2) *obs* **:** a torture implement; *esp* **:** RACK (3) *obs* **:** a net, trap, or similar device (4) *obs* **:** MACHINE 1e **b :** MACHINERY, APPARATUS **c :** any of various mechanical appliances — often used in combination; see FIRE ENGINE, ROSE ENGINE, RULING ENGINE **4 :** a machine for converting energy (in such forms as heat, chemical energy, nuclear energy, radiation energy, and the potential energy of elevated water) into mechanical force and motion **5 :** a railroad locomotive **6 :** ENGINE COMPANY **syn** see MACHINE

²engine \"\ *vt* -ED/-ING/-S [ME *enginen* to contrive, deceive, fr. OF *engignier*, fr. *engin*] **1** *obs* **:** CONTRIVE, PLAN **2** [¹*engine*] **:** to equip with an engine ⟨such planes were not *engined* for high-altitude combat⟩ ⟨a 4-*engined* bomber⟩

engine bell *n* **1 :** a bell on a locomotive used in signaling train and locomotive movements **2 :** a part of the engine-room telegraph of a ship

engine burn fracture *n* **:** a progressive fracture in a rail that originates at spots where the driving wheels of a locomotive have slipped or spun

engine company *n* **:** a fire-department company having charge of one or more fire engines

engine control *n* **:** a device used by the pilot of an airplane in controlling or modulating the power output of an engine

engine driver *n, Brit* **:** ENGINEER 4; *esp* **:** one in charge of a railroad locomotive

¹en·gi·neer \ˌenjəˈni(ə)r, -iə\ *n* -s [alter. (influenced by *-eer*) of earlier *enginer*, fr. ME, alter. (influenced by ME *-er, -ere* -er) of *enginour*, fr. MF *engigneur*, fr. OF *engigneor*, fr. OF *engignier* to contrive + *-eor* -or] **1 a** *obs* **:** a builder of military engines **b** *obs* **:** a designer or builder of military works (as fortifications) **c** (1) *obs* **:** ARTILLERYMAN (2) **:** a member of a military group devoted to engineering work (as in building bridges or roads, removing land mines, or preparing airfields) **2** *obs* **a :** a person who designs, invents, or contrives **b :** a crafty schemer **:** PLOTTER **3 a :** a designer or builder of engines, esp. steam engines or heavy machinery **b :** a person who is trained in or follows as a calling or profession a branch of engineering (as civil, military, electrical, mining, structural, or sanitary engineering) — in some jurisdictions legally restricted in technical use to a person who has completed a prescribed course of study and complied with requirements concerning registration or licensing **c :** a person who carries through an enterprise or brings about a result esp. by skillful or artful contrivance ⟨a political ~ of some note⟩ ⟨the ~ of the compromise that settled the dispute⟩ ⟨a skilled ~ of the economy of the nation —Frank Paddock⟩ **d :** a person who is trained or skilled in the technicalities of some field (as sociology or insurance) not usu. considered to fall within the scope of engineering and who is engaged in using such training or skill in the solution of technical problems **e :** a person with or without technical training who affects technical knowledge to further his endeavors (as in selling) **4 :** a person who runs or supervises engines or other complex technical machinery or apparatus: as **a :** a person in charge of the engines of a ship **b :** the driver of a locomotive **c :** STATIONARY ENGINEER **5 :** a person engaged in any of various occupations commonly regarded as requiring little skill or special knowledge — often used with a qualifying word ⟨the white-coated ~*s* who sweep the streets of the city⟩

²engineer \"\ *vb* -ED/-ING/-S *vi* **1 :** to perform the work of an engineer **2 :** CONTRIVE, MANEUVER ~ *vt* **1 a :** to act as an engineer in the laying out, construction, or management of ⟨he ~*ed* some great dams⟩ **b :** to design or produce by the methods of engineering ⟨with the day approaching when fabrics can be ~*ed* for any desired purpose —Henry Lesesne⟩ ⟨~*ing* bigger and faster ships and longer and wider docks⟩ **2 a :** to contrive or plan out usu. with more or less subtle skill or craft ⟨~*ed* a daring jailbreak⟩ ⟨Roosevelt skillfully ~*ed* events —Louis Morton⟩ ⟨a hundred men could carry out such a plan for one who could ~ it⟩ **b :** to guide the course of **:** manage or supervise during production or development ⟨~*ing* a bill through congress⟩ ⟨~*ed* a corner in grain futures⟩ ⟨the prenatal health clinic was ~*ed* by the joint effort of local physicians and philanthropists⟩ **syn** see GUIDE

engineer boot *n* **:** a boot with a supporting strap across the instep and a strap-adjusted gusset on the outer side

en·gi·neer·ing \ˌenjəˈniriŋ, -rēŋ\ *n* -s [fr. gerund of ²*engineer*] **1 :** the activities or the function of an engineer; *esp* **:** the art of managing engines **2 :** the science by which the properties of matter and the sources of energy in nature are made useful to man in structures, machines, and products — see CHEMICAL ENGINEERING, CIVIL ENGINEERING, ELECTRICAL ENGINEERING, HYDRAULIC ENGINEERING, INDUSTRIAL ENGINEERING, MECHANICAL ENGINEERING, MUNICIPAL ENGINEERING, SANITARY ENGINEERING

engineer boot

engineering geology *n* **:** a branch of geology that deals with the application of geology to engineering

en·gi·neer·ing·ly *adv* **:** from the point of view of the engineering problems involved ⟨an ~ feasible project⟩

engineer's brake valve *n* **:** a valve in the cab of a locomotive for operating the air brake

engineer's chain *n* **:** a chain (sense 1c(1)) 50 or 100 feet long consisting of one-foot links

engineer's hammer *n* **:** any of various hand hammers used by engineers and metalworkers and resembling a machinist's hammer but heavier

engineer's level *n* **:** SURVEYOR'S LEVEL

engineer's scale *also* **engineer's rule** *n* **:** a scale that is commonly of triangular cross section and has different decimal scales on its edges

enginehouse \ˈ⸗⸗ˌ⸗\ *n* **:** a building for housing an engine (as a fire engine, a railroad locomotive, or a stationary engine)

engine lathe *n* **:** a screw-cutting lathe equipped with a back-geared cone-driven headstock or with a headstock of the geared-head type

en·gine·less \ˈ⸗⸗ləs\ *adj* **:** lacking an engine

en·gine·man \ˈenjənˌman, -ˌmaa(ə)n, -ˌmən\ *n, pl* **enginemen** **1 :** a man who supervises, operates, tends, or tests an engine (as a locomotive engineer or fireman) **2 :** ENGINE DRIVER

engine mount *n* **:** a framework that is usu. of steel tubing, is used to mount the engine of an airplane, and is attached to the airplane in such a manner as to be readily detachable

engine room *n* **:** a room (as on a steamer) in which an engine is located

engine-room telegraph *n* **:** a signaling device for transmitting orders from an officer on the bridge of a ship to the engineer in charge relating to the direction and speed of the engine

en·gine·ry \ˈenjənrē, -ri\ *n* -ES [¹*engine* + *-ery, -ry*] **1** *obs* **:** the art of constructing or managing engines, esp. military engines **2 a :** instruments of war **b :** machines, tools, and mechanical devices (as of a plant or an industry or for the carrying out of a process) ⟨the complex ~ of a modern refining plant⟩; *broadly* **:** PLANT 3a ⟨the physical elements of this marvelous ~ for multiplying man's powers and possibilities are three — tracks, trains, locomotive power —R.S.Henry⟩ **c :** things that underlie and form a basis for the functioning of something **:** MACHINERY 4 ⟨Keats was beginning . . . to bring forward the vast ~ of his mind to attack the riddle of life in its deeper aspects, when death cut him short —G.M.Trevelyan⟩ ⟨the subtler and cruder ~ of threat —H.A.Overstreet⟩ ⟨a ponderous ~ of statistics, graphs, and mathematical devices⟩

engines *pl of* ENGINE, *pres 3d sing of* ENGINE

engine sand *n* **:** TRACTION SAND

engine-size \ˈ⸗⸗ˌ⸗\ *vt* **:** BEATER-SIZE

engine-turn \ˈ⸗⸗ˌ⸗\ *vt* **:** to ornament or finish with engine turning

engine turning *n* [fr. gerund of *engine-turn*] **1 :** a method of ornamentation of a surface (as of a watch) by means of a rose engine or lathe **2 :** ornamentation in the form of a pattern of fine lines produced by engine turning

engining *pres part of* ENGINE

enginous *adj* [ME *enginous*, fr. MF *engigneus*, fr. L *ingeniosus* ingenious, talented — more at INGENIOUS] *obs* **:** contrived with care **:** INGENIOUS, CRAFTY

en·gird \ən, en+\ *vt* [¹*en-* + *gird*, v.] **:** GIRD, ENCOMPASS

en·gir·dle \ən, en+\ *vt* [¹*en-* + *girdle*, n.] **:** GIRDLE

engirt *vt* [¹*en-* + *girt*, v.] *obs* **:** ENVELOP, ENCIRCLE, ENGIRD

en·gla·cial \ən, (ˈ)en+\ *adj* [²*en-* + *glacial*] **:** embedded in a glacier ⟨~ drift⟩ **:** being within the body of a glacier ⟨an ~ stream⟩ — **en·gla·cial·ly** \"+\ *adv*

en·glam·our \ən, en+\ *vt* -ED/-ING/-S [¹*en-* + *glamour*] **1 :** to surround with or as if with illusions **2 :** to render glamorous

en·gland \ˈiŋglənd *also* ˈiŋl- *sometimes* ˈeŋ\ *adj, usu cap* [fr. *England*, south part of the island of Great Britain, excluding Wales, fr. ME *Engeland*, fr. OE *Engla land*, lit., land of the Angles, fr. *Engla* (gen. of *Engle*, pl., Angles) + *land* — more at ANGLE] **:** of or from England **:** of the kind or style prevalent in England **:** ENGLISH

en·gland·er \-də(r)\ *n* -s *cap* **:** a native of England

en·gler flask \ˈeŋ(g)lə(r)-\ *n, usu cap E* [after Karl *Engler* †1925 Ger. chemist] **:** a standard distilling flask usu. of 100-milliliter capacity used to determine the volatility characteristics of petroleum products (as gasoline, naphtha, or kerosine)

en·gler·o·phoenix \ˌeŋglərō+\ *n, cap* [NL, fr. Adolf *Engler* †1930 Ger. botanist + NL *-o-* + *Phoenix* genus of palms — more at PHOENIX] **:** a genus of tropical American pinnate-leaved palms with linear pinnae

¹en·glish \ˈiŋglish, -lēsh *also* ˈiŋl- *sometimes* ˈeŋ\ *adj, usu cap* [ME, fr. OE *englisc*, fr. *Engle*, pl., Angles + *-isc* -ish] **1 :** of or from England **:** of the kind or style prevalent in England ⟨*English* earth⟩ ⟨fine *English* tailoring⟩ ⟨*English* customs⟩ — often used in English-speaking areas outside the British isles to identify that one of two or more kinds of plant or animal sharing a common vernacular to which the vernacular is applied in England without regard to actual prevalence or origin ⟨*English* catchfly⟩ ⟨*English* cherry wood⟩ **2 :** of, relating to, or characteristic of the English language ⟨beauties of *English* expression⟩ ⟨*English* studies⟩ ⟨a literal *English* translation⟩ ⟨vagaries of the *English* colloquial idiom⟩ **3 :** BRITISH

²english \"\ *n* -ES *see sense 2* [ME, fr. OE *englisc*, fr. *englisc*, adj.] **1** *cap* **a :** the language of the people of England and the U.S. and most of the British colonies and dominions — see ANGLO-SAXON, MIDDLE ENGLISH, OLD ENGLISH, INDO-EUROPEAN LANGUAGES table **b :** a particular variety of English (as that characteristic of a nation, locality, class of people, or an individual) distinguished by peculiarities (as of pronunciation, vocabulary, idiom, syntax, or style) ⟨speaking a beautiful precise *English*⟩ ⟨the archaic *English* that often lingers in isolated communities⟩ ⟨the comparative informality of American *English*⟩ ⟨the *English* of the gutter⟩ **c :** English language, literature, or composition or a part thereof regarded as a field of study or teaching ⟨most colleges require all freshmen to take a course in *English*⟩ ⟨he found *English* a difficult subject⟩ **2** *pl in constr, cap* **:** the people of England; *esp* **:** native Englishmen irrespective of residence ⟨the chill formality of the *English* is no more than a caricaturist's generalization⟩ ⟨the *English* and their tea are matched by the Swedes and their coffee⟩ **3** *usu cap* **a :** an English translation or rendering **:** the English equivalent (as of a foreign word) ⟨tell me the *English* for *gluteus*⟩; *sometimes* **:** CRIB, PONY **b :** idiomatic or intelligible English; *often* **:** the plain sense of something obscure, involved, technical, or pedantic ⟨give me the *English* of it⟩ — compare GREEK 2c **4** *often cap* **:** an old size of type approximately 2 points larger than pica **5** *usu cap* **:** a spinning or rotary motion round the vertical axis given to a ball by striking it to the right or left of its center (as in pool) or by releasing it in such a way as to produce this rotary motion (as in bowling) — called also *side*

³english \", *chiefly in pres part* -ləsh\ *vb* -ED/-ING/-ES *often cap* [ME *englishen*, fr. *english*, adj. & n.] *vt* **1 :** to translate into English ⟨regretfully spent his holiday ~*ing* 500 lines of Virgil⟩ **2** *obs* **:** to interpret or set forth plainly ⟨those gracious acts . . . may be *Englished*, more properly, acts of fear and dissimulation —John Milton⟩ **3 :** to adopt into English **:** ANGLICIZE ⟨our language expands chiefly by coining new words and ~*ing* the words already in other languages⟩ ~ *vi* **:** to be translatable into English

⁴english *adv, usu cap* [¹*english*] *obs* **:** ENGLISHLY

english basement *n, usu cap E* **:** a high basement that is usu. mainly above ground, is often adapted to living quarters or domestic offices, but does not contain the principal entrance of the house

english billiards *n pl but usu sing in constr, usu cap E* **:** billiards which is played on a table with six pockets and in which points are scored by cannons and pocketed balls

english bluebell *n, usu cap E* **:** WOOD HYACINTH

english bluegrass *n, usu cap E* **1 :** WIRE GRASS a **2 :** MEADOW FESCUE

english bond *n, usu cap E* **:** a masonry bond in which courses consist alternately of headers and stretchers

English bond

english breakfast tea *also* **english breakfast** *n, usu cap E* **:** CONGOU; *broadly* **:** a black tea or blend of similar character

english bulldog *or* **english bull** *n, usu cap E* **:** BULLDOG

english camomile *or* **english chamomile** *n, usu cap E* **:** a pleasantly strong-scented European downy perennial herb (*Anthemis nobilis*) that is widely cultivated and often escaped

english cavalry saddle *n, usu cap E* **:** ENGLISH SADDLE

english chop *n, usu cap E* **:** a lamb or mutton chop cut across the undivided loin with the bone removed and usu. the kidney rolled in

english corn *n, usu cap E* **:** wheat or other small grain — contrasted with *Indian corn* and now chiefly of historical interest

english cowslip *n, usu cap E* **:** COWSLIP 1a

english cross bond *n, usu cap E* **:** a modification of English bond in which the stretcher courses break joints with each other

english daisy *n, usu cap E* **:** DAISY 1a

english disease *n, usu cap E, archaic* **:** RICKETS

english elm *n, usu cap 1st E* **:** a broad spreading rough-leaved elm (*Ulmus procera*) common throughout western Europe and planted elsewhere — compare WYCH ELM

english equatorial *n, usu cap 1st E* **:** a telescope with its main tube supported in a split or yoke-type polar axle that rests on north and south pedestals permitting continuous observation across the meridian and eliminating the declination counterweight

en·glish·er \-lishə(r), -lēsh-\ *n* -s [¹*english* + *-er*] **1** *cap* **:** ENGLISHMAN ⟨not in very good humour with the *Englishers* —E.B. Ramsay⟩ **2** *usu cap* [³*english* + *-er*] **:** a person who translates into English

english finish *n, usu cap E* **:** a finish on paper that is smooth but not glossy; *specif* **:** a finish intermediate between machine finish and supercalendered

english flute *n, usu cap E* **:** RECORDER 3a

english foot *n, usu cap E* **:** a hosiery foot that has a seam on each side of the sole — compare FRENCH FOOT

english foxhound *n* **1** *usu cap E & F* **:** a breed of foxhounds developed in England and characterized by a large heavily boned form, rather short ears, and lightly fringed tail **2** *usu cap E* **:** any dog of the English Foxhound breed

English foxhound

english garden wall bond *n, usu cap E* **:** a masonry bond employing three courses of stretchers to one of headers

english gooseberry *n, usu cap E* **:** a stocky Eurasian shrub (*Ribes grossularia*) with greenish flowers and pubescent and glandular fruit that is the source of most of the European cultivated gooseberries and a parent of many of those grown in America and is often an escape in eastern No. America

english grain aphid *n, usu cap E* **:** a pale green aphid (*Macrosiphum avenae*) with dark markings that is native to Europe but widespread in No. America and that feeds on grasses and small grains, being esp. destructive when feeding on the developing heads of grain

english grass *n, usu cap E* **:** any of various hay or forage grasses (as timothy or some bluegrasses) orig. introduced (as into the U. S. or Australia) from England

english green *n, often cap E* **1 :** DEEP BRUNSWICK GREEN **2 :** SCHEELE'S GREEN 2 **3 :** EMERALD 2

english guitar *n, usu cap E* **:** a cittern popular in England in the 18th century

english harvest *n, usu cap E, obs* **:** harvest of wheat

english hawthorn *n, usu cap E* **:** either of two Eurasian hawthorns (*Crataegus oxyacantha* and *C. monogyna*) that have deeply cleft leaves and bright red fruits, that are extensively cultivated as ornamentals and under cultivation have developed varied plant forms and flower form and color, and that are established as escapes in much of eastern No. America

english hay *n, usu cap E* **:** hay from English grass; *broadly* **:** cultivated hay as distinguished from native hay

english herring *n, usu cap E, in Maine* **:** the common herring (*Clupea harengus*) of the No. Atlantic

english holly *n, usu cap E* **:** a Eurasian tree or shrub (*Ilex aquifolium*) with thick glossy spiny-margined leaves, bright red persistent berries, and a fine-grained white wood — compare AMERICAN HOLLY

english horn *n, usu cap E* **1 :** a double-reed woodwind musical instrument similar to the oboe but a fifth lower in pitch with a rich and somber tone quality **2 :** an organ stop with a tone similar to that of the English horn

englishing *n* -s *usu cap* [ME, fr. ³*english* + *-inge, -ing* -ing] **:** the act of translating or a translation into English ⟨the earliest *Englishing* of the Bible⟩ ⟨*Englishings*, in the most original and least second-hand fashion, of the peculiar verse stories —George Saintsbury⟩

english iris *n, usu cap E* **:** a bulbous iris (*Iris xiphioides*) that is native to the Pyrenees but is now widely cultivated for its large delicate flowers which are typically dark purple marked with yellow but in cultivation sometimes white, blue, or wine red but never yellow — compare DUTCH IRIS, SPANISH IRIS

en·glish·ism \-ˌshizəm\ *n* -s *usu cap* **1 :** a quality, characteristic, or mode of procedure peculiar to the English **2 :** a form of expression peculiar to English as spoken in England **:** ANGLICISM **3 :** attachment to that which is English

English horn

en·glish·ite \-ˌshīt\ *n* -s *usu cap* [George L. *English* †1944 Am. mineral dealer and collector + E *-ite*] **:** a mineral perhaps in the relation $K_2Ca_4Al_8(PO_4)_8(OH)_{10}.9H_2O$ consisting of hydrous basic phosphate of potassium, calcium, and aluminum

english ivy *n, usu cap E* **:** IVY 1a

en·glish·ize \-ˌshīz\ *vt* -ED/-ING/-S *often cap* **:** ANGLICIZE

english last *n, usu cap E* **:** a shoe last with a low heel and long tapering toe

english laurel *n, usu cap E* **:** CHERRY LAUREL 1

english loose *n, usu cap E* **:** MEDITERRANEAN RELEASE

en·glish·ly *adv, usu cap* [ME, fr. ¹*english* + *-ly*] **:** in the manner of the English ⟨people whose chief value to the community lay, oddly but *Englishly*, in their sturdy individualism —W.B.Adams⟩

english maidenhair *n, usu cap E* **:** MAIDENHAIR SPLEENWORT

en·glish·man \-shmən\ *n, pl* **englishmen** [ME, fr. OE *englisc-man*, fr. *englisc* English + *man* — more at ENGLISH] **1** *cap* **:** a native or inhabitant of England **2** *usu cap* **:** an English ship **3** *usu cap* **:** a marine percoid food fish (*Chrysoblephus anglicus*) of southern Africa having the snout truncate and suggestive of a forehead

englishman's knot *n, usu cap E* **:** FISHERMAN'S KNOT

english maple *n, usu cap E* **:** HEDGE MAPLE

english muffin *n, usu cap E* **:** bread dough rolled and cut into rounds and baked on a griddle

en·glish·ness *n* -ES *usu cap* **:** the distinctive qualities or characteristics that set apart or are felt to set apart the English people, their works, or institutions ⟨Oxford and Cambridge are the very essence of *Englishness*, on a par with the monarchy, Parliament, the Church of England —*Newsweek*⟩

english oak *n, usu cap E* [ME *english oke*, fr. ¹*english* + *oke, ook* oak] **1 a :** a medium-sized to large tree (*Quercus robur*) having glabrous leaves with very short petioles and rounded lobes **b :** the strong durable hard straight-grained wood of this tree that is used in structural work and cabinetwork and tends to darken with prolonged exposure from pale yellowish brown almost to black **2 :** a moderate brown that is paler and slightly yellower than bay, lighter than auburn, and redder, lighter, and slightly stronger than chestnut brown

english ocher *n, often cap E* **:** YELLOW OCHER

english opera *n, usu cap E* **:** BALLAD OPERA

english pea *n, usu cap E, South & Midland* **:** PEA 1a — used esp. to distinguish this vegetable from the black-eyed pea

english pink *n, often cap E* **:** DUTCH PINK 2

english plantain *n, usu cap E* : a ribgrass (*Plantago lanceolata*)
english pool *n, usu cap E* : a pool game in which each player draws one of the colored balls which he uses as cue ball and must play on the color next in a fixed order, being put out of the game when his ball is pocketed three times — called also *color-ball pool*
english primrose *n, usu cap E* : a low-growing perennial European primrose (*Primula vulgaris*) that is widely cultivated for its early bloom which in the wild is usu. single, solitary, and yellow but has developed many divergent forms and colors under cultivation
english rabbit *or* **english spotted** *n, usu cap E* : a breed of white domestic rabbits having distinctive dark markings
english red *n* **1** *usu cap E* : an iron-oxide pigment **2** *often cap E* **a** : a dark reddish orange to strong brown that is stronger than ferruginous — called also *Forest of Dean red, madder red* **b** : COLCOTHAR 2 **c** : GOYA
english rite *n, usu cap E & often cap R* : YORK RITE
english robin *n, usu cap E* : ROBIN 1a
en·glish·ry \-shrē, -ri\ *n* -ES *usu cap* [ME *englisherie, englishrie*, fr. ¹*english* + *-erie, -rie* -ry] **1** : the state or fact of being of English birth **2** : people of English descent esp. in Ireland **3** : English ways (as of speech or conduct); *also* : bias toward English ways
english ryegrass *n, usu cap E* : PERENNIAL RYEGRASS
english saddle *n, usu cap E* : a saddle with long side bars, steel cantle and pommel, no horn, and a leather seat supported by webbing stretched between the saddlebow and cantle — called also *English cavalry saddle*

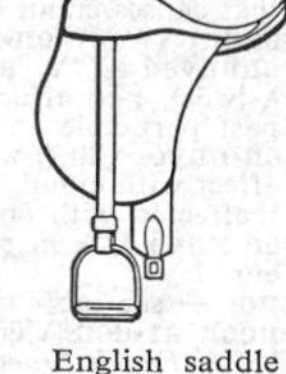
English saddle

english saxon *n, cap E & S, obs* : ANGLO-SAXON
english setter *n* **1** *usu cap E&S* : a breed of bird dogs characterized by a silky coat that is flat, moderately long, and white or white with color (as black, lemon, or orange) and by feathering on the tail and legs, a long moderately domed skull with marked stop, a height of 21 to 23 inches, and a weight when in condition of 35 to 55 pounds **2** *usu cap E* : any dog of the English Setter breed
english shepherd *n* **1** *usu cap E&S* : a breed of vigorous medium-sized working dogs with a long and glossy black coat with tan to brown or sometimes white markings that was developed in England chiefly for herding sheep and cattle **2** *usu cap E* : a dog of the English Shepherd breed
english snipe *n, usu cap E* : WILSON'S SNIPE
english sole *n, usu cap E* **1** : an important pale brown market flatfish (*Parophrys vetulus*) of the Pacific coast of No. America distinguished by a projecting snout **2** : PETRALE SOLE
english sonnet *n, usu cap E* : a sonnet in which the lines are grouped into three quatrains and a couplet and the rhyme scheme is *abab, cdcd, efef, gg*
english sparrow *n, usu cap E* : HOUSE SPARROW
english springer *also* **english springer spaniel** *n, usu cap E* : a springer spaniel of a breed supposed to have originated in Spain characterized by deep-bodied muscular build with weight to 45 pounds when in good condition and a moderately long straight or slightly wavy silky coat of typically black and white hair
english system *n, usu cap E* : BRADFORD SYSTEM
english thistle *n, usu cap E* : WILD TEASEL
english toy spaniel *n* **1** *usu cap E&T&S* : a breed of small blocky spaniels of English origin with well-rounded upper skull projecting forward toward the short turned-up nose — see BLENHEIM SPANIEL, KING CHARLES SPANIEL, RUBY SPANIEL **2** *usu cap E* : any dog of the English Toy Spaniel breed
english turbot *n, usu cap E* : WINDOWPANE 2
english vermilion *n, often cap E* **1** : GOYA **2** : VERMILION 1a; *esp* : a pigment of a light brilliant shade
english violet *n, usu cap E* : SWEET VIOLET
english wallflower *n, usu cap E* : a short-lived perennial wallflower (*Cheiranthus cheiri*) with white, yellow, brown, or reddish to purplish single or double flowers
english walnut *n, usu cap E* **1** : a Eurasian walnut (*Juglans regia*) that is valued for its large edible nut and its hard richly figured wood — called also *Circassian walnut, French walnut, Persian walnut* **2 a** : the fruit of the English walnut **b** : CIRCASSIAN WALNUT 1
english wheat *n, usu cap E* : POULARD WHEAT
english white *n, usu cap E* : whiting used as a pigment
englishwoman \ˈ==,==\ *n, pl* **englishwomen** *usu cap* [ME, fr. ¹*english* + *woman*] : a woman of English birth, nationality, or origin
english yew *n, usu cap E* : a large evergreen tree (*Taxus baccata*) that is native to Eurasia and northern Africa but cosmopolitan in cultivation and is the chief source of yew lumber — called also *European yew*
en·globe \ənˈglōb, en-\ *vt* [¹*en-* + *globe*, n.] **1** : to enclose in or as if in a globe **2** : INGEST ⟨bacteria *englobed* by leukocytes⟩ — **en·globe·ment** \-mənt\ *n* -S
¹**en·glut** \ənˈglət, en-\ *vt* [MF *engloutir*, fr. LL *ingluttire*, fr. L *in* + *gluttire* to swallow — more at GLUTTON] : to gulp down : SWALLOW
²**englut** \"\ *vt* [¹*en-* + *glut*, v.] *archaic* : to satiate or surfeit esp. with food or pleasure
eng·lyn \ˈeŋlən\ *n, pl* **englyns** \-nz\ *also* **englyn·ion** \eŋˈlinˌyōn\ [W] : a usu. epigrammatic quatrain in Welsh poetry consisting of 30 syllables in lines of 10, 6, 7, and 7 syllables, the last three lines rhyming usu. with the 6th syllable of the first line whose final syllable has no rhyme
en·gobe \(ˈ)änˈgōb\ *n* -S [F, fr. *engober* to cover with slip, fr. *en-* ¹en- + *gober* to swallow, gulp down; akin to OF *gobet* mouthful, bite, piece — more at GOBBET] : white or colored slip applied to pottery usu. for decoration or to improve the surface texture
en·gore \ən, en+\ *vt* [¹*en-* + *gore*, n.] : to make bloody : dabble or stain with blood
en·gorge \ən, en+\ *vb* [MF *engorgier* to feed to repletion, devour, fr. OF, to devour, fr. *en-* ¹en- + *gorge* throat — more at GORGE] *vt* **1** : GORGE, GLUT: as **a** : to feed (as oneself or an animal) to repletion ⟨a working horse should not be *engorged* on the weekend⟩ **b** : to fill with blood to the point of congestion — usu. used in passive ⟨the gastric mucosa was greatly *engorged*⟩ **2** : to swallow with greediness : DEVOUR, ENGULF ~ *vi* **1** : to feed with eagerness or voracity **2** *of a bloodsucking invertebrate* : to feed on blood to the limit of body capacity ⟨larvae which had *engorged* . . . previously on an infected guinea pig, transmitted a fatal infection —*Jour. of Infectious Diseases*⟩
en·gorge·ment \"mənt\ *n* -S [obs. F *engorgement* action of devouring & F *engorgement* congestion, fr. MF *engorgement* action of devouring, fr. *engorgier* + *-ment*] **1** : the act of engorging or state of being engorged **2** : overfullness of the vessels of some part of the body ⟨~ of the breast⟩ : CONGESTION, HYPEREMIA
engorgement colic *n* : colic in horses caused by the ingestion of excessive quantities of food, too rapid eating, or the failure of the stomach to pass the food on into the intestines
en·gou·lée *also* **en·gou·lé** \äⁿgüˈlā\ *or* **en·gouled** \(ˈ)änˈgüld\ *adj* [*engoulée* fr. F, fem. of *engoulé*, fr. past part. of *engouler* to swallow up, fr. OF *engoler*, fr. *en-* ¹en- + *gole* throat, mouth, fr. L *gula* throat; *engoulé* fr. F, fr. past part. of *engouler; engouled* modif. (influenced by E *-ed*) of F *engoulé* — more at GLUTTON] *heraldry* : having the extremities issuing from the mouths of animals — used of an ordinary
engr *abbr* **1** engineer **2** engraved; engraver; engraving
en·grace \ən+\ *vt* [¹*en-* + *grace*, n.] : to endue with grace
engraff *vt* [ME *engraffen, ingraffen*, fr. ¹*en-* or ²*in-* + *graffen* to graft, insert (a scion) — more at GRAFT] *obs* : ENGRAFT
en·graft *also* **in·graft** \ən, en+\ *vt* [¹*en-* or ²*in-* + *graft*, v.] **1** : GRAFT 1, 2 **2** : to introduce (infective matter) into a host
en·graf·ta·tion \ˌenˌgrafˈtāshən\ *or* **en·graft·ment** \ənˈgraf(t)mənt, en-, -raaf-,-raif-,-räf-\ *n* -S : the act of engrafting
en·grail \ənˈgrāl, en-, *chiefly before pause or consonant* -āəl\ *vt* -ED/-ING/-S [ME *engrelen*, fr. MF *engresler*, fr. *en-* ¹en- + *gresle, graisle* slender, fr. L *gracilis* — more at GRACILE] **1 a** : to indent (as a heraldic ordinary) with small curves — see ENGRAILED **b** : to ornament esp. with a pattern indented on the edge **2** *obs* : to carve in intaglio **3 a** *obs* : ROUGHEN **b** : to cause to appear serrated ⟨a scene ~*ed* by three tall peaks⟩
engrailed *adj* [ME *engreled*, fr. *engrelen* + *-ed*] **1** : indented at the edge with small concave curves ⟨an ~ heraldic bordure⟩ **2** : made of raised dots ⟨an ~ circle on a coin⟩ : bordered by a circle of raised dots ⟨an ~ coin⟩
en·grain \ənˈgrān, (ˈ)enˈg-\ *vt* [ME *engreinen*, fr. ¹*en-* + *grain, grein* kermes; in senses 2 and 3 influenced in meaning by E *grain* texture — more at GRAIN] **1** *obs* : to dye with kermes or cochineal or a fast color **2** : INGRAIN 2 ⟨his swart forefinger, deeply ~*ed* with gunpowder —Charles Dickens⟩ ⟨Judaism, Catholicism, and Protestantism are too deeply ~*ed* in the habits of men to be superseded by some newfangled religious institution —S.P.Lamprecht⟩ **3** : to color in imitation of the grain of the wood — compare GRAIN *vt* 3
en·grained \-nd\ *adj* [fr. past part. of *engrain*] : deeply incorporated or infused : DEEP-DYED — **en·grained·ly** \-n(ə)dlē, -li\ *adv*
en·gram *also* **en·gramme** \ˈenˌgram, ˈeŋˌg-\ *n* -S [ISV ²*en-* + *-gram*; orig. formed as G *engramm*] : a memory trace; *specif* : a protoplasmic change in neural tissue hypothesized to account for the persistence of memory — **en·gram·mic** \(ˈ)=ˈgramik\ *adj*
en·gran·dize \ənˈgra(a)nˌdīz, en-; ˈengrən-, ˈeŋgrən-\ *or* **in·gran·dize** \ənˈgra(a)n-\ *vt* -ED/-ING/-S [modif. (influenced by *-ize*) of obs. F *engrandiss-*, stem of *engrandir*, fr. OF, fr. *en-* ¹en- + *grant, grand* great, large — more at GRAND] : to make great or grandiose
en·gran·dize·ment \ənˈgra(a)ndəzmənt, en-, -ˌdīz-; ˈen-ˌgra(a)nˌdīz-, ˌenˌgra(a)nˈdīz-\ *n* -S : an act of engrandizing or the state of being engrandized
en·grau·li·dae \enˈgrôləˌdē\ *n pl, cap* [NL, fr. *Engraulis*, type genus (fr. Gk *engraulis* anchovy) + *-idae*] : a family of small fishes related to the herrings and comprising the anchovies
en·grave \ənˈgrāv, en-\ *vb* **engraved** \-vd\ **engraved** \"\ *or archaic* **en·grav·en** \-vən\ **engraving; engraves** [MF *engraver*, fr. *en-* ¹en- + *graver* to engrave, of Gmc origin; akin to OHG *graban* to dig; E *engrave* influenced in inflection (note past part. *engraven*) by *grave*, v. — more at GRAVE (v.)] *vt* **1 a** : to produce (as letters, figures, or devices) by means of incised lines, spaces, or points ⟨~ an inscription on stone⟩ **b** : to impress deeply : infix as if with a graver ⟨~ principles in men's minds —John Locke †1704⟩ **2 a** : to cut upon (as wood, stone, or metal) with a graving instrument in order to form an inscription or pictorial representation either of the incised lines, spaces, or points (as in copperplate engraving) or of the surface left in relief (as in wood engraving) **b** : to incise (a metal plate or wooden surface) for the purpose of printing therefrom ⟨*engraved* the plates for a new series of banknotes⟩ **c** : to print from an engraved plate ⟨an *engraved* calling card⟩ — used esp. when raised printing results **d** : PHOTOENGRAVE **3** *obs* : to represent (as a scene) in sculpture ~ *vi* **1** : to make engravings ⟨busily *engraving* on wood⟩ **2** : to be suitable for engraving ⟨that clear classic profile would ~ well⟩
engraved *adj* [fr. past part. of *engrave*] : having the surface marked or ornamented with impressed lines — used esp. of the hard exterior coverings of certain insects
engraved glass *n* : glass ornamented with intaglio cutting that is usu. left unpolished — compare CUT GLASS
en·grave·ment \-vmənt\ *n* -S : ENGRAVING
engraven *vt* [by alter.] *obs* : ENGRAVE
en·grav·er \ənˈgrāvə(r), en-\ *n* -S **1** : one that engraves; *esp* : one whose work is the production of engraving (as on silverware or on plates for use in printing) by hand or mechanical processes **2 a** : PHOTOENGRAVER **b** : ENGRAVER BEETLE — usu. used in combination ⟨fir ~*s*⟩
engraver beetle *n* : any of numerous bark beetles that make furrows often arranged in specific patterns in the wood of trees under the bark; *esp* : a beetle of *Scolytus* or a related genus that lives chiefly on young trees — compare DENDROCTONUS
engraver's block *n* : a heavy metal turntable with clamps for securing articles to be engraved
engravery *n* -ES [*engrave* + *-ery*] *obs* : ENGRAVING
engraving *n* -S [fr. gerund of *engrave*] **1** : the act or process of one that engraves — compare ANAGLYPTOGRAPH, ANASTATIC, DRYPOINT, MEZZOTINT, XYLOGRAPHY; ETCHING **2** : something that is engraved: as **a** : an engraved printing surface ⟨prepared the ~*s* for the new banknotes⟩ **b** : engraved work ⟨decorated with delicate ~⟩ **3** : a print or impression from an engraved printing surface
engreaten *vt* [¹*en-* + *great*, adj. + *-en*] *obs* : to make great
en·groove \ənˈgrüv, en-\ *vt* [¹*en-* + *groove*, n.] : to fit or form into a groove
en·gross \ənˈgrōs, en-\ *vt* -ED/-ING/-ES [in sense 1, fr. ME *engrossen*, fr. AF *engrosser*, prob. fr. ML *ingrossare*, fr. L *in* + ML *grossa* engrossment (of a document), fr. L, fem. of *grossus* thick; in sense 2, fr. ME *engrosen, engrossen*, fr. MF *en gros* in large quantities, at wholesale, fr. OF, fr. *en* (fr. L *in*) + *gros* whole quantity, fr. *gros* thick, plentiful, fr. L *grossus*; in sense 3, fr. ME *engrossen*, alter. of *ingrossen*, fr. ML *ingrossare*, fr. L *in* + *grossus* thick — more at GROSS] **1 a** : to copy or write in a large hand : write a fair copy of in a hand formerly used in formal documents, derived from the court hand, and nearly illegible to all but experts or now usu. in a distinct and legible hand **b** *obs* : to inscribe the name of : include in a list : NAME **c** : to prepare the text of (a bill, resolution, treaty, or other official document) by whatever process (as handwriting or printing) may be officially permitted or prescribed; *specif* : to prepare the text of (a bill) for the third reading in a legislature — distinguished from *enroll* **2 a** : to purchase either the whole or large quantities of (commodities) so as to control the market, enhance the price, and make a monopoly profit **b** : to obtain control of (a market) in this way — compare FORESTALL, REGRATE **c** *obs* : AMASS, COLLECT **d** : to take or assume to the exclusion of others : concentrate in one's possession : take the whole of ⟨a few families ~*ed* the power of the state⟩ ⟨the new customer ~*ed* his attention⟩ **3 a** *obs* : to make dense, thick, or large : increase in bulk or quantity : THICKEN **b** *archaic* : to render gross in body or mind **syn** see MONOPOLIZE
en·grossed \-st\ *adj* [fr. past part. of *engross*] **1** : completely occupied or absorbed ⟨~ in her humble task⟩ ⟨an ~ look of rapt delight⟩ **2** : PREOCCUPIED ⟨answered briefly without raising her ~ eyes from the book⟩ — **en·grossed·ly** \-sədlē, -stl-, -li\ *adv*
engrossed bill *n* : a bill printed or written in the final form in which it is presented for the third reading in a house or chamber of a legislative body — compare ENROLLED BILL
en·gross·er \-sə(r)\ *n* -S [ME, fr. *engrossen* + *-er, -ere* -er] **1** : a monopolist or a person who attempts to establish a monopoly (as of goods or power) **2** : one that engrosses documents
engrossing *adj* [fr. pres. part. of *engross*] **1** : monopolizing or tending to monopolize **2** : taking up the time or attention completely : ABSORBING, FASCINATING ⟨hidden under the ~ surface of the story —Harrison Smith⟩ **syn** see INTERESTING
en·gross·ing·ly *adv* : so as to engross
en·gross·ing·ness *n* -ES : the quality of being engrossing
en·gross·ment \-smənt\ *n* -S **1 a** : the engrossing of a document **b** : an engrossed document **2 a** : the buying up or hoarding of a commodity esp. for speculative purposes **b** : the taking up of common or public lands (as by enclosure or purchase) often for speculative purposes **3** : the state of being absorbed or occupied ⟨his ~ with the nation's problems⟩
engs *pl of* ENG
en·gulf \ən, en+\ *vt* [¹*en-* + *gulf*, n.] **1 a** : to flow over and enclose : OVERWHELM ⟨a man ~*ed* by fear⟩ ⟨the mounting seas threatened to ~ the island⟩ **b** : to take in (food) by or as if by flowing over and enclosing ⟨the amoeba ~*s* particulate matter with its pseudopodia⟩ ⟨snakes ~ their food whole⟩ **2** : to plunge (as oneself) into something ⟨~*ing* himself in the political mire⟩ ⟨to be ~*ed* in the whirling, curving, backing fleet of cars at the station —Eve Langley⟩ **syn** see OVERPOWER
en·gulf·ment \"mənt\ *n* -S : the act of engulfing or state of being engulfed
en·gys·seismology \ˌenjə̇, ˌeŋg|, |ē +\ *n* [Gk *engys* near + E *seismology*] : a branch of seismology that deals with the records of earthquake shocks registered in or near the region of disturbance — compare TELESEISMOLOGY
en·gys·to·mat·i·dae \(ˌ)enˌjistəˈmadəˌdē, (ˌ)eŋˌgistəˈm-; ˌenj-|əstōˈm, ˌeŋg|, |əstōˈm-\ [NL, fr. *Engystomat-, Engystoma* (prob. influenced in meaning by G *eng* narrow, fr. OHG *engi*), former name of an included genus (fr. Gk *engys* near + NL *-stomat-, -stoma* -stoma) + *-idae* — more at ANGER] *syn of* BREVICIPITIDAE
en·halo \ən, en+\ *vt* [¹*en-* + *halo*, n.] : to honor or surround with or as if with a halo ⟨a figure ~*ed* with misty light⟩ ⟨an enlightened clergyman who . . . ~*es* the ticket collectors, bus conductors, waitresses —E.M.Forster⟩
en·hance \ənˈhan(t)s, en-, -haa(ə)n-,-hain-,-hän-\ *vt* -ED/-ING/-S [ME *enhauncen*, fr. AF *enhauncer*, alter. of OF *enhaucier*, fr. *en-* ¹en- + *haucier* to raise, fr. (assumed) VL *altiare*, fr. L *altus* high — more at OLD] **1** *obs* **a** : RAISE, LIFT **b** : to exalt esp. in rank or spirit; *also* : EXTOL **2** : ADVANCE, AUGMENT, ELEVATE, HEIGHTEN, INCREASE ⟨our pleasure was *enhanced* by our hostess's care⟩ ⟨his gracious courtesy *enhanced* his scholarship⟩ **3 a** : to increase the worth or value of ⟨an estate *enhanced* by careful management⟩ **b** : ORNAMENT, BEAUTIFY ⟨proposed to ~ the paneling with gilt medallions⟩ ⟨a young girl should avoid trying to ~ her looks with heavy makeup⟩ **syn** see INTENSIFY
enhanced *adj* [fr. past part. of *enhance*] *of a heraldic charge* : placed higher than is usual — opposed to *abased*
en·hance·ment \-smənt\ *n* -S : the act of enhancing or state of being enhanced : AUGMENTATION, INTENSIFICATION: as **a** : induced increase in some chemical or physical property ⟨the current ~ by gas filling may be greater by 20 to 30 percent for infrared light —V.K.Zworykin & E.G.Ramberg⟩ ⟨~ of the virulence of a virus by egg passage⟩ **b** : accentuation or exaggeration of tonal or positional characteristics of a sound recording
en·hanc·er \-sə(r)\ *n* -S [ME *enhauncere*, fr. *enhauncen* + *-er -ere* -er] : one that enhances
en·hanc·ive \-siv\ *adj* : tending to enhance
en·harden \ən, en+\ *vt* [¹*en-* + *harden*, v.] *archaic* : HARDEN ⟨nor hath conversation, age or travel been able to . . . ~ me —Sir Thomas Browne⟩
¹**en·harmonic** \ˌen+\ *adj* [F *enharmonique*, fr. MF *enarmonique, enharmonique*, modif. (influenced by MF *-ique* -ic) of Gk *enarmonios*, fr. *en* in + *harmonia* joint, concord, musical scale — more at IN, HARMONY] **1 a** *in ancient Greek music* : relating to that genus or scale employing quarter tones **b** *of a Greek tetrachord* : comprising a major third and two quarter tones — compare CHROMATIC **2** : relating to a written change of notes that sound the same on all instruments using the tempered scale ⟨the ~ change from A flat to G sharp⟩ **3** : relating to the difference in pitch that results from the exact tuning of a diatonic scale and its transposition into another key — **en·harmonically** \ˌen+\ *adv*
²**enharmonic** \"\ *n* : an enharmonic note or chord
enharmonic diesis *n* **1** *in ancient Greek music* : QUARTER TONE **2** : the difference between three conjunct major thirds and an octave (ratio 125:128)
enharmonic modulation *n* : a modulation in which by enharmonically altering one or more notes the harmonic relation of a chord is changed so as to lead to a new key
en haut \äⁿō\ *adv* [F, above, up] *ballet* : in a high position — used of the arms
en·hearten \ən, en+\ *vt* [¹*en-* + *hearten*] : to give or restore strength and courage to ⟨their cheerfulness ~*ed* his saddened spirit⟩
en·hedge \ənˈhej, en-\ *vt* [¹*en-* + *hedge*, n.] : to enclose or surround with or as if with a hedge
enherit *obs var of* INHERIT
en·horror \ən, en+\ *vt* -ED/-ING/-S [¹*en-* + *horror*, n.] : HORRIFY
en·hunger \ən, en+\ *vt* [¹*en-* + *hunger*, n.] : to make hungry ⟨passions . . . ~*ed* to feed on innocence —James Martineau⟩
en·hy·dra \enˈhīdrə\ *n, cap* [NL, irreg. fr. Gk *enydris* otter, fr. *enydros* living in water, fr. *en* in + *hydōr* water — more at IN, WATER] : a genus of carnivorous mammals (family Mustelidae) that contains only the sea otter
en·hy·drite \-ˌdrīt\ *n* -S [ISV *enhydr-* (fr. *enhydrous*) + *-ite*] **1** : ENHYDROS **2** : a mineral or rock containing water — **en·hy·drit·ic** \ˌenˌhīˈdridik\ *adj*
en·hy·dros \-ˈīdrəs\ *n* -ES [NL, fr. L, enhydrous mineral, fr. Gk *enydros*] : a hollow nodule of chalcedony containing water
en·hy·drous \(ˈ)enˈhīdrəs\ *adj* [LL *enhydrus*, fr. Gk *enydros* containing water, living in water] *of certain crystalline minerals* : having water within : containing fluid drops
en·hy·po·sta·sia \ˌenˌhīpəˈstāzh(ē)ə\ *also* **en·hy·pos·ta·sis** \ˌen(ˌ)hīˈpästəsə̇s\ *n* -S [NL, fr. Gk *enypostatos* substantial (verbal of *enyphistasthai* to subsist in, fr. *en* in + *hyphistasthai* to subsist, exist, stand under), after Gk *statos* standing, fixed: *-stasia* and Gk *statos: stasis* condition of standing, stoppage — more at IN, HYPOSTASIS, -STATE, -STASIA, STASIS] : the dependence of the human nature of Christ upon his divine nature in such fashion that the second is the subsistent hypostasis of the first postulated (as in early Orthodox theology) as a doctrine of hypostatic union excluding an independent and impersonal existence of the human nature and emphasizing its subsistence from the beginning in the person of the Logos — **en·hy·po·stat·ic** \ˌenˌhīpəˈstadik\ *adj*
enig·ma *also* **ae·nig·ma** \ə̇ˈnigmə, ē-,e-\ *sometimes* ˈenigmə *or* ˈenēg-\ *n, pl* **enigmas** \-məz\ *also* **enigma·ta** \-mədə, -mətə\ [L *aenigma*, fr. Gk *ainigma*, fr. *ainissesthai* to speak in riddles, fr. *ainos* tale, fable] **1** : an intentionally obscure statement (as a riddle or complex metaphor) that depends for full comprehension on the alertness and ingenuity of the hearer or reader; *broadly* : an obscure speech or writing ⟨the new . . . novel is a brilliant ~ —Mark Schorer⟩ **2** : an inexplicable circumstance, event, or occurrence ⟨the ~ of human reason⟩ : an unsolved problem ⟨the ~*s* of American prehistory⟩ : MYSTERY **3** : a person not readily understood : an inscrutable person; *often* : one that exhibits an incomprehensible mixture of opposed qualities **syn** see MYSTERY
enigma canon *or* **enigmatic canon** *or* **enigmatical canon** *n* : RIDDLE CANON
enig·mat·ic \ˌe(ˌ)nigˈmadˌik, -ˌnēg-, -atˌ, |ek *also* ˌē(- *or* ˌi(-\ *also* **enig·mat·i·cal** \|ə̇kəl, |ek-\ *adj* [*enigmatic* fr. LL *aenigmaticus*, fr. Gk *ainigmatikos*, fr. *ainigmat-, ainigma* enigma + *-ikos* -ic; *enigmatical* fr. LL *aenigmaticus* + E *-al*] : relating to or resembling an enigma : INEXPLICABLE, PUZZLING ⟨know everything possible about our ~ ally —E.J. Simmons⟩ **syn** see OBSCURE
enig·mat·i·cal·ly \|ə̇k(ə)lē, |ek-, -li\ *adv* : in an enigmatic manner
enig·ma·tite *also* **ae·nig·ma·tite** \ə̇ˈnigməˌtīt, ē-,e-\ *n* -S [G *ainigmatit, änigmatit*, fr. Gk *ainigmat-, ainigma* + G *-it* -ite] : an imperfectly known mineral formerly classed with the amphibole group that occurs in black triclinic crystals and is essentially a silicate of iron, titanium, and sodium (sp. gr. 3.74–3.80)
enig·ma·tize \-ˌtīz\ *vt* -ED/-ING/-S [*enigmatic* + *-ize*] : to make enigmatic ⟨it is the very humanity of man that ~*s* him for the true ascetic⟩
enig·ma·tog·ra·pher \=,==ˈtägrəfə(r)\ *n* -S [*enigmato-* (fr. L *aenigmat-, aenigma*) + *-grapher*] : a propounder of enigmas
enig·ma·tog·ra·phy \-fē\ *n* -ES [*enigmato-* + *-graphy*] : the art of composing enigmas
enig·ma·tol·o·gy \-ˈtäləjē\ *n* -ES [*enigmato-* + *-logy*] : the investigation or analysis of enigmas
eni·ma·gá \ˌenəməˈgä\ *n, pl* **enimagá** *or* **enimagás** *usu cap* [Sp, of AmerInd origin] : MACÁ
enin *var of* OENIN
-ening *pres part of* -EN
en·isle \ən, en +\ *vt* [¹*en-* + *isle*, n.] **1** : to place apart (as on an island) **2** : to make an island of
en·jail \ən, en +\ *vt* [¹*en-* + *jail*, n.] *archaic* : to shut up in or as if in prison
en·jambed \ənˈjamd, en-\ *adj* [fr. *enjambment*, after such pairs as E *refinement: refined*] : marked or characterized by enjambment
en·jamb·ment *or* **en·jambe·ment** \-mmənt\ *n* -S [F *enjambement*, fr. MF, encroachment, fr. *enjamber* to encroach, straddle (fr. *en-* ¹en- + *jambe* leg) + *-ment* — more at JAMB]

: continuation in prosody of the sense in a phrase beyond the end of a verse or couplet : the running over of a sentence from one line into another so that closely related words fall in different lines — compare RUN-ON

enjeopard *vt* -ED/-ING/-S [¹*en-* + *jeopard*, v. or *jeopardy*, n.] *obs* : JEOPARDIZE

en·jewel \ən, en +\ *vt* [¹*en-* + *jewel*, n.] : BEJEWEL

en·join \ən'jȯin, en-\ *vt* [ME *enjoinen*, fr. OF *enjoindre*, fr. L *injungere*, fr. *in* + *jungere* to join — more at YOKE] **1** : to direct, prescribe, or impose by order typically authoritatively and compellingly and with urgent admonition ⟨he was bound to avenge his father, the god Apollo had ~*ed* it —G.L. Dickinson⟩ ⟨his leader had sternly ~*ed* him to avoid any weakness —George Meredith⟩ **2** *obs* : to join together **3 a** : FORBID, PROHIBIT ⟨church synods repeatedly ~*ed* the use of the Roman service books —M.H.Shepherd⟩ ⟨a person who found himself attacked — yet ~*ed* by conscience from deliberately taking human life —Lucius Garvin⟩ **b** : to prohibit or restrain by a judicial order or decree : put an injunction on **syn** see COMMAND, FORBID

en·join·der \-ȯində(r)\ *n* -S [*enjoin* + *-der* (as in *rejoinder*)] **1** : an authoritative request : COMMAND **2** : INTERDICTION, PROHIBITION; *often* : INJUNCTION

en·join·ment \-ȯinmənt\ *n* -S *archaic* : PROHIBITION, INJUNCTION

en·joy \ən'jȯi, en-\ *vb* -ED/-ING/-S [ME *enjoien*, fr. MF *enjoir*, fr. OF, fr. *en-* ¹en- + *joir* to derive benefit or pleasure, fr. L *gaudēre* to rejoice — more at JOY] *vi* **1** *obs* : to feel or manifest joy : REJOICE **2** : to have a good time ~ *vt* **1** : to take pleasure or satisfaction in : experience or possess with pleasure ⟨~*ing* a comfortable chat by the fire⟩ ⟨they ~*ed* the beat of the rain on the roof⟩ ⟨foolish men who having wealth do not ~ it⟩ **2 a** : to have in possession for one's use or satisfaction ⟨he ~*ed* a good salary for many years⟩ ⟨the right to ~ liberty and the pursuit of happiness⟩ **b** : to have the benefit of (as a right, a desirable thing or quality, or something profitable) ⟨she ~*s* a life interest in her husband's estate⟩ ⟨they ~*ed* the esteem of their fellows⟩ ⟨~*ed* the income from a nice little family business⟩ **c** : to undergo the experience of (a change for the better) ⟨dried skim milk ~*ed* an enormous rise —Vance Packard⟩ **3 a** : to have sexual intercourse with ... ⟨~*ed* themselves at the party⟩ **b** *chiefly dial* : ENTERTAIN **4** : to copulate with (a woman) **5** : to be immediately aware of (as an emotion or psychic reaction) not as an object of thought but as a phase or ingredient of one's own conscious state or activity — compare CONTEMPLATE 4 **syn** see HAVE, LIKE

en·joy·able \-ȯiəbəl\ *adj* : capable of being enjoyed : being a source of pleasure or enjoyment ⟨an ~ afternoon at the seaside⟩ ⟨those ~ traits of character that make us humanly weak but strongly human⟩ — **en·joy·able·ness** \-bəlnəs\ *n* -ES — **en·joy·ably** \-blē, -li\ *adv*

en·joy·er \-ȯi(ə)r,-ȯiə\ *n* -S : one that enjoys

en·joy·ing·ly *adv* [*enjoying* (pres. part. of *enjoy*) + *-ly*] : with enjoyment or satisfaction

en·joy·ment \-ȯimənt\ *n* -S **1 a** : the action or state of enjoying something : the deriving of pleasure or satisfaction (as in the possession of anything) **b** : possession and use ⟨the ~ of civic rights⟩ **2** : something that gives pleasure or keen satisfaction ⟨the poorest life has its ~*s* and pleasures⟩ **3** : the mind's immediate consciousness of aspects of itself **syn** see PLEASURE

en·ki·an·thus \,eŋkē'an(t)thəs\ *n, cap* [NL, fr. *enki-* (perh. irreg. fr. Gk *enkyos* pregnant, fr. *en* in + *kyos* fetus) + *-anthus*; akin to L *cavus* hollow — more at IN, CAVE] : a genus of erect Asiatic shrubs (family Ericaceae) that have whorled branches, leaves which are mostly clustered at the twig ends, and nodding flowers in terminal clusters and that are often cultivated as ornamentals

en·kindle \ən, en +\ *vb* [¹*en-* + *kindle*] *vt* **1** : to set (as fuel) on fire : cause to ignite **2** : to make bright and glowing ⟨his passionate conviction . . . ~*s* his book —H.L.Shapiro⟩ ~ *vi* : to take fire : FLAME

en·kindler \"+\ *n* -S : one that enkindles

enkolpion *var of* ENCOLPION

enl *abbr* **1** enlarged **2** enlisted; enlistment

en·lace \ən'lās, en-\ *vt* [ME *enlacen*, fr. MF *enlacier*, fr. OF, fr. *en-* ¹en- + *lacier* to lace — more at LACE] **1** : ENCIRCLE, ENFOLD **2** : ENTANGLE, ENTWINE, INTERLACE

en·lace·ment \-mənt\ *n* -S : INTERLACEMENT

en l'air \äⁿ 'l + *pronunc at* AIR\ *adv* (*or adj*) [F, in the air] *ballet* : in the air — opposed to *par terre*

enlard *vt* [¹*en-* + *lard*, n.] *obs* : LARD

¹**en·large** \ən, en +\ *vb* -ED/-ING/-S [ME *enlargen*, fr. MF *enlargier*, fr. OF, fr. *en-* ¹en- + *large*, adj. — more at LARGE] *vt* **1 a** : to make larger : increase in quantity or dimensions : extend in limits : MAGNIFY ⟨the body is *enlarged* by nutrition⟩ ⟨*enlarging* his fortune by speculation⟩ ⟨such an experience ~*s* your point of view⟩ **b** : to reproduce in larger form ⟨~ a picture⟩ **2 a** : to increase the capacity of : give free scope or greater scope to : EXPAND ⟨he *enlarged* his plan as he grew in experience⟩ **b** : to dilate esp. with joy, affection ⟨this sorrow *enlarged* her heart⟩ **3** : to set at large : set free (as a captive) **4 a** : to make an extension of (as the time for a legal action) **b** : to extend the time limit of (as a lease, order, rule) **c** : to increase the scope of (an estate) — usu. used of a release that operates to convert a life interest or an estate for years into a fee ~ *vi* **1** : to grow large or larger : become more extended : EXPAND ⟨as the city *enlarged* its slums came down to the river⟩ ⟨the embryo gradually ~*s* and differentiates⟩ **2** : to speak or write at length: as **a** : to present in detail something previously outlined — often used with *on* or *upon* ⟨let me ~ on this basic theme⟩ ⟨these gentlemen can ~ upon the scheme I mentioned⟩ **b** : to be diffuse in speech or writing : DILATE, EXPATIATE ⟨the preacher *enlarged* interminably in a dull dry voice⟩ **syn** see INCREASE

²**enlarge** \"\ *n* -S *archaic* : ENLARGEMENT

en·large·able \"əbəl\ *adj* : suitable for enlargement

en·larged \-jd\ *adj* [fr. past part. of *enlarge*] : larger or greater than that formerly, usually, or normally present ⟨an ~ joint⟩ ⟨the ~ authority of the committee⟩ — **en·larged·ly** \-j(ə)dlē, -li\ *adv* — **en·larged·ness** \-jədnəs, -j(d)n-\ *n* -ES

en·large·ment \-jmənt\ *n* -S **1** : an act or instance of enlarging or the state of being enlarged: as **a** : increase in bulk or extent : AUGMENTATION, EXPANSION, EXTENSION **b** : expansion or intensification of mental powers : increase or breadth esp. of knowledge or sympathies **c** : a setting at large : release from confinement, servitude, or distress : LIBERATION **d** : diffusive quality or expatiation in discourse; *often* : amplification esp. by copious illustration or detailed description **e** *archaic* : freedom from constraint (as in prayer) **2** : something that enlarges or is enlarged: as **a** *obs* : RIGHT, PRIVILEGE **b** : something added ⟨building an ~ on his new house⟩ **3 a** : a photographic print larger than the negative that is made by projecting through a lens an image of the negative upon a photographic printing surface

en·larg·er \-jə(r)\ *n* -S : one that enlarges; *specif* : an optical projector used to produce a photographic enlargement

¹**enlarging** *adj* [fr. pres. part. of *enlarge*] : making larger : EXTENDING, AUGMENTING — **en·larg·ing·ly** *adv*

²**enlarging** *n* -S [ME, action or process of making larger, fr. *enlargen* + *-inge*, *-ing* -ing] : the process of making photographic enlargements

en·leg·end·ed \ən'lejəndəd, en-\ *adj* [¹*en-* + *legend*, n. + *-ed*] : LEGENDARY, FABULOUS

en·lève·ment \äⁿlevmäⁿ\ *n, pl* **enlèvements** \-mäⁿ(z)\ [F, action of lifting, fr. MF *enlevement*, fr. *enlever* to lift, raise (fr. OF, to raise, fr. *en* from that place — fr. L *inde*, akin to L *is* he and to L *de* from — + *lever* to raise) + *-ment* — more at ITERATE, DE-, LEVER] : the lift into the air of a ballerina by her supporting male dancer

enlight \ən, en+\ *vt* -ED/-ING/-S [¹*en-* + *light*, n.] *archaic* : ENLIGHTEN

en·light·en \ən'līt°n, en-\ *vb* **enlightened; enlightened; enlightening** \-t(°n)iŋ\ **enlightens** [¹*en-* + *light*, n. + *-en*] *vt* **1** *archaic* : to supply with light : ILLUMINATE ⟨His lightnings ~*ed* the world —Ps 97:4 (AV)⟩ **2** *obs* : to cause to shine or give light : make luminous : ENKINDLE **3 a** : to furnish with useful information : INSTRUCT, INFORM ⟨radio should ~ the listener as well as entertain him⟩ **b** : to supply with spiritual insight or light ⟨the divine mercy can ~ the blackest spirit⟩ ~ *vi* : to give information

enlightened \-t°nd\ *adj* [fr. past part. of *enlighten*] : freed from ignorance and misinformation ⟨an ~ people⟩; *often* : based on full comprehension of the problems involved ⟨an ~ judgment⟩ — **en·light·ened·ly** \-t°n(ə)dlē, -li\ *adv* — **en·light·ened·ness** \-t°n(d)nəs\ *n* -ES

enlightened self-interest *n* : behavior based on awareness that what is in the public interest is eventually in the interest of all individuals and groups ⟨polls that are kept honest only by the *enlightened self-interest* of the pollsters⟩

en·light·en·er \-t(°)nə(r)\ *n* -S : one that enlightens

enlightening *adj* [fr. pres. part. of *enlighten*] : tending to dissipate ignorance or increase knowledge and awareness ⟨an ~ glimpse of government in action⟩ — **en·light·en·ing·ly** *adv*

en·light·en·ment \-t°nmənt\ *n* -S **1** : the act or means of enlightening : the state of being enlightened ⟨the gradual attaining of spiritual ~⟩ **2 a** *usu cap* : a philosophic movement of the 18th century characterized by an untrammeled but frequently uncritical use of reason, a lively questioning of authority and traditional doctrines and values, a tendency toward individualism, and an emphasis on the idea of universal human progress and on the empirical method in science — used with *the* **b** : a mental attitude in the spirit of the Enlightenment; *also* : a movement or period resembling the Enlightenment **3** : the ultimate goal of the Taoist and Buddhist religious life: **a** *Taoism* : the state of being in harmony with the laws of the universe **b** *Buddhism* : the realization of ultimate universal truth

en·link \ən'liŋk, en-\ *vt* [¹*en-* + *link*, v.] : to bring together and make fast as if links of a chain : connect by or as if by links

en·list \ən'list, en-\ *vb* [¹*en-* + ⁶*list*] *vt* **1** : to engage (a person) for military or naval service usu. for a definite period **2** : to secure the support and aid of : employ or utilize in advancing some interest ⟨~ you in a good cause⟩ ⟨~ photography for educational purposes⟩; *broadly* : ATTRACT ⟨a compilation of Collects to ~ the interest of busy people —*Philosophic Abstracts*⟩ ⟨personal participation ~*s* belief in the objectivity of an experience⟩ ~ *vi* **1** : to enroll oneself for military or naval service esp. voluntarily and for a definite period ⟨he ~*ed* for three more years of service in the navy⟩ **2** : to participate heartily (as in a cause or effort) ⟨~*ed* in the cause of world peace⟩ ⟨~*ing* in the argument raging between science and theology⟩

enlisted *adj* [fr. past part. of *enlist*] : of, relating to, for, or constituting the part of a military or naval force ranked below commissioned officers, warrant officers, and persons (as cadets or midshipmen) who are in the course of qualifying as commissioned officers ⟨many officers holding temporary commissions reverted to ~ status after the war⟩ ⟨~ men and women⟩ ⟨~ quarters⟩

enlisted specialist *n* : an enlisted person in U. S. armed forces classified as an occupational specialist

en·list·ee \ən,lis'tē, en-; ¦en,lis¦tē\ *n* -S **1** : a person who enlists esp. for military or naval service **2** : a member of the enlisted ranks of a military or naval force

en·list·ment \ən'lis(t)mənt, en-\ *n* -S **1** : the act of enlisting or state of being enlisted **2** : a period of service in a military or naval force for which an individual can volunteer ⟨the 2-year ~ was discontinued⟩

en·live \ən'līv, en-\ *vt* [prob. fr. ¹*en-* + *live*, adj.] : ENLIVEN

en·liv·en \ən'līvən, en-\ *vt* **enlivened; enlivened; enlivening** \-v(ə)niŋ\ **enlivens** [prob. fr. ¹*en-* + *live*, adj. + *-en*] **1** : to give life, action, or motion to : make vigorous or active **2** : to give spirit or vivacity to : make sprightly, gay, or cheerful : ANIMATE ⟨*enlivened* by the music⟩ **syn** see QUICKEN

en·liv·en·er \-v(ə)nə(r)\ *n* -S : one that enlivens

enlivening *adj* [fr. pres. part. of *enliven*] : imparting spirit or vivacity : STIMULATING — **en·liv·en·ing·ly** *adv*

en·lock \ən, en+\ *vt* [¹*en-* + *lock*, v.] : to lock up : ENCLOSE

enmarble *var of* EMMARBLE

en masse \(')äⁿ'mas, -maa(ə)s,-mais *also* (')äⁿ'- *or* (')in'- *or* (')en'-\ *adv* [F] **1** : in a body ⟨the frogs began to die *en masse*⟩ ⟨the convicts were transported *en masse* to the new prison⟩ **2** : in general : as a whole ⟨viewing the new clothes *en masse*⟩

en·matter \ən, en+\ *vt* [¹*en-* + *matter*, n.] : to endue with or confine in matter ⟨the essences treated by physical science may be considered as ~*ed* and formulable⟩

en·mesh \ən'mesh, en-\ *also* **in·mesh** \in'm\ *or* **im·mesh** \i'm-\ *vt* [¹*en-* or ²*in-* + *mesh*, n.] : to catch or entangle in or as if in meshes ⟨he was ~*ed* in a series of boundary disputes with his neighbors⟩ — **en·mesh·ment** \-mənt\ *n* -S

en·mi·ty \'enm|əd·ē, -ətē, -i, *chiefly in substand speech* 'emn|\ *n* -ES [ME *enmite*, *enemite*, fr. MF *enemité*, *enemitié*, fr. OF *enemistié*, *enemistié*, fr. *enemi* enemy, after OF *ami* friend: *amistié* amity (whence MF *amité*, *amitié*) — more at ENEMY, AMI, AMITY] **1 a** : ill will such as actuates a personal enemy ⟨his act only increased the ~ of his rival⟩ **b** : a condition marked by such ill will : hatred or antagonism esp. when mutual ⟨men settled in ~ toward their fellows⟩ **c** : an instance of such ill will or hostility ⟨he had an ~ with man —Lord Dunsany⟩ **2** *obs* : something baneful or prejudicial

syn HOSTILITY, ANTIPATHY, ANTAGONISM, ANIMOSITY, RANCOR, ANIMUS: ENMITY indicates ill will, dislike, or hatred that may be overt or concealed and absence of any friendly spirit ⟨farmers began to arrive, some to remain and conquer the *enmity* of cattlemen —*Amer. Guide Series: Texas*⟩ ⟨France's feud with Germany and her *enmity* with England —A.L. Guérard⟩ HOSTILITY may, but does not always, indicate an enmity manifesting itself in open active attack or aggression ⟨the *hostility* with which bishops and parish priests regarded monks and friars —G.M.Trevelyan⟩ ⟨driven from their old homes because of their loyalty to the British Crown and their consequent *hostility* to the Revolution —B.K.Sandwell⟩ ⟨Richelieu in his own mind determined upon overt *hostilities*, upon national war —Hilaire Belloc⟩ ANTIPATHY may apply to a temperamental dislike, aversion, or desire to avoid and shun ⟨inveterate *antipathies* against particular nations and passionate attachments for others should be excluded —George Washington⟩ ⟨as for cats and Negroes, he was inclined to believe that both species knew instinctively of his pronounced *antipathy* for them —Osbert Sitwell⟩ ANTAGONISM may suggest a natural hatred or ill will marked by quick hostility or bitter rivalry or resistance ⟨an *antagonism* existed between the two brothers⟩ ⟨her fragility aroused the chivalry of men, her modesty precluded the *antagonism* of women —Victoria Sackville-West⟩ ANIMOSITY suggests intense, vindictive ill will capable of culminating in hostility ⟨her hatred of the idea of it was intensified into violent *animosity* —Arnold Bennett⟩ ⟨vicious *animosity* of political opponents kept alive an unfortunate mistake that occurred at the time of the Jackson marriage —*Amer. Guide Series: Tenn.*⟩ RANCOR may indicate bitter malevolence, often accompanied by brooding over an injustice or wrong ⟨his most faithful disciple and his most trusted helper, for a dozen years. There is small wonder at her feeling an unchristian *rancor* against the nation which had caused his death —C.S.Forester⟩ ANIMUS applies to dislike, often prejudiced, and ill will, often malevolent or spiteful ⟨a sense that he had been patronized lay behind the *animus* that made him a "defiant American", when he was minister to England —Van Wyck Brooks⟩

enmove *vt* [¹*en-* + *move*, v.] *obs* : to move inwardly : cause to feel emotion

enmun *often cap, var of* ONMUN

ennea- *comb form* [Gk, fr. *ennea* — more at NINE] : nine ⟨*ennea*gon⟩ ⟨*ennea*petalous⟩

en·ne·ad \'enē,ad, -ēəd\ *n* -S [Gk *ennead-*, *enneas*, fr. *ennea* nine + *-ad-*, *-as* -ad] : a group of nine; *esp* : any of several groups of nine gods that were considered to be associated in the mythology and religion of ancient Egypt

en·ne·ad·ic \¦enē¦adik\ *adj* : of or relating to an ennead

en·nea·style \'enēə,stīl\ *adj* [*ennea-* + *-style*] : marked by columniation with nine columns across the front — compare DISTYLE

en·nea·sty·los \¦enēə¦stīləs\ *n* -ES [*ennea-* + Gk *-stylos* -style] : an enneastyle building

en·nea·syllabic \¦enēə+\ *adj* [Gk *enneasyllabos* enneasyllabic (fr. *ennea-* + *syllabē* syllable) + E *-ic* — more at SYLLABLE] : having or composed of lines having nine syllables

-en·nial \¦enēəl, ¦enyəl\ *adj comb form* [ME *-eniale*, fr. MF *-ennial*, fr. L *-ennium* (as in *biennium* period of two years) + MF *-al* — more at BIENNIAL] : recurring at or marking intervals of (so many) years ⟨*biennial*⟩ ⟨*centennial*⟩

en·no·ble \ə'nōbəl, e'-\ *vt* **ennobled; ennobled; ennobling** \-b(ə)liŋ\ **ennobles** [ME *ennobelen*, fr. MF *ennoblir*, fr. OF, fr. *en-* ¹en- + *noble*, adj.] **1** : to make noble : elevate in degree or excellence ⟨what can ~ sots, or slaves, or cowards —Alexander Pope⟩ ⟨our buildings are thus *ennobled* by the devotion to service which they proclaim —Joseph Hudnut⟩ **2** : to raise to the rank of nobility ⟨was *ennobled* by Charles II⟩ **3** *archaic* : to make noted or conspicuous **4 a** : to transmute (a base metal) into a noble metal ⟨the . . . conception of *ennobling* metals by a process of death and resurrection —S.F. Mason⟩ **b** : to make (a metal, as iron) resistant to corrosion

en·no·ble·ment \-bəlmənt\ *n* -S : an act of ennobling or the state of being ennobled

ennobling *adj* [fr. pres. part. of *ennoble*] : tending to ennoble ⟨the ~ influence of cultured surroundings⟩ — **en·no·bling·ly** *adv*

ennoblish *vt* [MF *ennobliss-*, stem of *ennoblir*] *obs* : ENNOBLE, HONOR, DISTINGUISH

¹**en·nui** \(')än¦wē *sometimes* ¦än(y)ə¦wē\ *n* -S [F, fr. OF *enui* annoyance — more at ANNOY] **1** : a feeling of weariness and dissatisfaction : languor or emptiness of spirit : TEDIUM, BOREDOM ⟨the moment we indulge our affections, the earth is metamorphosed; . . . all tragedies, all ~*s* vanish —R.W. Emerson⟩ **2 a** : an instance or period of ennui **b** : something that causes ennui ⟨the effort she made was itself an ~⟩

²**ennui** \"\ *vt* **en·nuied** *or* **en·nuied** \-¦wēd\ **ennuied** *or* **ennuyed** \"\ **en·nuy·ing** \-¦wēiŋ, -¦wē-ēŋ\ **en·nuies** \-¦wēz\ : to afflict with ennui : BORE — used chiefly in the past participle

¹**en·nu·yé** \¦än(,)wē¦(y)ā\ *adj* [F, past part. of *ennuyer* to affect with ennui, fr. OF *enuier* to annoy — more at ANNOY] : affected with ennui

²**en·nu·yé** \"\ *n, pl* **ennuyés** *or* **ennuyé** : one affected with ennui

eno- — see OEN-

enoch ar·den \¦ēnə¦kärd°n, -nē¦k-, -kəd-\ *n, usu cap E&A* [after *Enoch Arden*, hero of the poem *Enoch Arden* (1864) by Tennyson] : a person missing and believed dead usu. through no fault of his own who subsequently is found alive

enoch arden law *n, usu cap E&A* : a statute providing for divorce or exempting from liability for remarriage on the ground of unexplained absence of husband or wife for a specified number of years, usu. seven

enoch·ic \(')ē¦näkik\ *also* **eno·chi·an** \-nōkēən, -näk-, -nēk-\ *adj, usu cap* [*Enoch*, patriarch mentioned in Gen 5:18–24 + E *-ic* or *-ian*] : of, relating to, or in the manner of any of the various apocryphal or pseudepigraphical books bearing the name of the patriarch Enoch

enol \(')ē¦nȯl, -ōl\ *n* -S [ISV *ene-* (fr. *-ene*) + *-ol*] : an organic compound containing a hydroxyl group adjacent to a double bond and usu. characterized by the grouping >C:C(OH)— — compare ETHYL ACETOACETATE

eno·lase \'ēnə,lās, -āz\ *n* -S [ISV *enol* + *-ase*] : a crystalline enzyme that may be obtained from muscle and yeast and that plays an important role in the metabolism of carbohydrates by promoting a reversible dehydration of phosphoglyceric acid to phosphopyruvic acid

eno·late \-āt\ *n* -S [*enol* + *-ate*] : a metallic derivative of an enol

eno·lic \(')ē¦nōlik, -näl-\ *adj* [ISV *enol* + *-ic*] : of or relating to an enol

eno·liz·able \¦ēnə¦līzəbəl\ *adj* : capable of being enolized

eno·li·za·tion \,ēnələ'zāshən, -,lī'z-\ *n* -S [ISV *enolize* + *-ation*] : the process of enolizing

eno·lize \'ēnə,līz\ *vb* -ED/-ING/-S [ISV *enol* + *-ize*] *vt* : to convert (as a ketone) into an enol : convert (as a carbonyl group) into an enolic hydroxyl group ~ *vi* : to become enolized

enol-keto tautomerism *n* : KETO-ENOL TAUTOMERISM

enol·o·gist \ē'näləjəst\ *n* -S [*enology* + *-ist*] : a specialist in enology

enol·o·gy *or* **oenology** \ē'näləjē\ *n* -S [*enology* alter. of *oenology*; *oenology* fr. *oen-* + *-logy*] : a science that treats of wine making or wine

en·oph·thal·mos *also* **en·oph·thal·mus** \,e,näf'thalməs, -näp'th-, -,mäs\ *n* -ES [NL, fr. ²*en-* + Gk *ophthalmos* eye or NL *-ophthalmus*] : a sinking of the eyeball into the orbital cavity

en·op·la \e'näplə\ *n pl, cap* [NL, fr. Gk, neut. pl. of *enoplos* armed, fr. *en-* ²en- + *-hoplos* (fr. *hoplon* tool, weapon) — more at HOPLITE] : a class or other division of Nemertea including the orders Hoplonemertea and Bdellonemertea and comprising nemertine worms in which the mouth is anterior to the brain and the proboscis is armed with one or more stylets

en·op·li·da \e'näplədə\ *n pl, cap* [NL, fr. *Enoplus*, genus of nematodes (fr. Gk *enoplos* armed) + *-ida*] : an order of Aphasmidia that comprises nematode worms with the esophagus divisible into two regions and the amphids saccular or poriform and that is usu. divided into the suborders Enoplina, Dorylaimina, and Dioctophymatina — compare CHROMADORIDA — **en·op·loid** \(')e¦näplȯid\ *n* -S

en·op·li·na \,e,näp'līnə, -lēnə\ *n pl, cap* [NL, fr. *Enoplus* + *-ina*] : a suborder of Enoplida including free-living nematode worms that usu. lack a buccal stylet but have setae on the head — compare DIOCTOPHYMATINA, DORYLAIMINA

en·op·li·on \e'näplē,än, -ēən\ *n* -S [Gk, neut. of *enoplios* martial, fr. *enoplos* armed] : an acatalectic hemiepes preceded by one or two short syllables or a long — see PROSODIAC

en·op·tro·man·cy \e'näptrə,man(t)sē\ *n* -ES [F *énoptromancie*, fr. Gk *enoptron* mirror (fr. *en-* ²en- + *op-* — as in *optikos* optic — + *-tron*) + F *-mancie* -mancy] : divination by means of a mirror

en·organic \¦en+\ *adj* [²*en-* + *organic*] : arising within or inherent in the organism

enorm \ə'nȯ(ə)rm, ē'-\ *adj* [ME *enorme*, fr. MF, fr. L *enormis*] **1** *obs* : ABNORMAL, EXTRAORDINARY **2 a** *obs* : OUTRAGEOUS, MONSTROUS **b** *archaic* : ENORMOUS, VAST **3** *Scots law* : legally excessive : constituting a legal enormity — used of an injury sustained by one by reason of being party to a contract or deed

enormious *adj* [ME, fr. L *enormis* + ME *-ous*] *obs* : ENORMOUS

enor·mi·ty \ə'nȯ(r)məd·ē, -ətē, -i\ *n* -ES [MF *enormité*, fr. L *enormitat-*, *enormitas*, fr. *enormis* + *-itat-*, *-itas* -ity] **1** : the quality or state of exceeding a measure or rule or of being immoderate, monstrous, or outrageous ⟨the ~ of the offense⟩ **2 a** : a grave offense against order, right, or decency **3** *obs* **2 a** : ABNORMALITY **b** : something abnormal or eccentric **4 a** : HUGENESS, IMMENSITY **b** : a thing of huge size

¹**enor·mous** \-məs\ *adj* [L *enormis* (fr. *e* out of, out + *norma* rule) + E *-ous* — more at E-, NORMAL] **1** *archaic* **a** : exceeding the usual rule, norm, or measure : out of due proportion : INORDINATE ⟨wallowing unwieldy, ~ in their gait —John Milton⟩ **b** : breaking set norms of conduct : exceedingly wicked, monstrous, shocking : extreme in some bad quality or way ⟨these easy terms on which absolution is obtained certainly encourage the repetition of the most ~ crimes —Tobias Smollett⟩ **2** : marked by extraordinarily great size, amount, number, degree, scope, intensity, or significance : exceeding or transcending usual bounds or commonly accepted notions ⟨the ~ size of the Pacific ocean —F.D.Roosevelt⟩ ⟨~ panoramic views of mountain ranges —*Amer. Guide Series: Calif.*⟩ ⟨the big industries with their vast over-capitalization and their ~ overhead —Lewis Mumford⟩ **syn** see HUGE

²**enormous** \"\ *adv* : EXTREMELY, VERY

enor·mous·ly *adv* : to an enormous degree : EXCEEDINGLY, VASTLY

enor·mous·ness *n* -ES : vast or excessive bulk or size — compare ENORMITY

eno·sis \ə'nōsəs, e'-,ē'-\ *n* -ES [NGk *henōsis*, fr. Gk, union, fr. *henoun* to unite (fr. *hen-*, *heis* one) + *-sis* — more at SAME] : UNION; *specif* : a movement designed to secure the political union of Greece and Cyprus — **eno·sist** \-ōsəst\ *n* -S

¹**enough** \ə'nəf, ē'nəf; *after* t, d(·), s, z, ʺ, *or* °n'əf\ *adj* [ME *ynough*, *inough*, fr. OE *genōg*; akin to OHG *ginuog* enough, ON *gnōgr*, Goth *ganohs*; all fr. a prehistoric Gmc compound whose first constituent is represented by OE *ge-* (perfective, associative, and collective prefix) and whose second constitu-

ent is akin to L *nancisci* to get, Gk *enenkein* to carry, Skt *naśati* he attains — more at CO-] **:** marked by or present or occurring in such quantity, quality, or scope as to satisfy fully the demands, wants, or needs of a situation or of a proposed use or end ⟨there is ~ food today for all of us —F.D.Roosevelt⟩ **syn** see SUFFICIENT

2enough \"\ *adv* [ME *ynough, inough,* fr. OE *genōg,* fr. *genōg,* adj.] **1 :** in or to a degree or quantity that satisfies or is sufficient or necessary to satisfaction **:** SUFFICIENTLY ⟨unstable ~ to react with moisture in the air⟩ **2 :** FULLY, QUITE — used to express slight to marked augmentation of the positive degree ⟨he is ready ~ to embrace the offer⟩ **3 :** in a tolerable degree — used to express mere acceptance or acquiescence and usu. implying some degree of derogation ⟨she sang well ~⟩ ⟨this dress is good ~ for that party⟩

3enough \"\ *n* -s [ME *ynough, inough,* fr. OE *genōg,* fr. *genōg,* adj.] **:** a quantity that satisfies desire, is adequate to the want, or is equal to the power **:** SUFFICIENCY ⟨we have ~ for all our needs⟩ ⟨~ is as good as a feast⟩ — often used interjectionally usu. with an implication that what has gone before has exceeded any proper sufficiency ⟨~! how dare you insult our queen⟩

enounce \ē'nau̇n(t)s, i'-\ *vt* -ED/-ING/-S [F *énoncer,* fr. L *enunciare, enuntiare* to report, declare, express — more at ENUNCIATE] **1 :** to set forth or state as a proposition or argument ⟨the principles of criticism first *enounced* by Aristotle —Malcolm Cowley⟩ **:** state formally or publicly ⟨the angel *enounced* the coming of Christ⟩ **2 :** ENUNCIATE 2

1enow \ə'nau̇, ē'nau̇; *after* t, d(•), s, z, " *or* ᵊn'au̇\ *adv (or adj)* [ME *inow, ynow, inowe, ynowe,* partly fr. OE *genōg,* adj & adv. and partly fr. OE *genōge,* pl. of *genōg,* adj.] *archaic* **:** ENOUGH

2enow \ē(n)'nü, i'nü\ *adv* [contr. of *even now*] **1** *dial Brit* **:** just now **2** *Brit* **:** PRESENTLY

en pas·sant \äⁿpäsäⁿ\ *adv* [F] **:** in passing **:** in the course of a procedure **:** INCIDENTALLY ⟨he mentioned *en passant* that his brother was then in Rome⟩ — used in chess of the capture of a pawn as it makes a first move of two squares by an enemy pawn in a position to threaten the first of these squares; abbr. *e. p.*

en pen·sion \äⁿpäⁿsyōⁿ\ *adv (or adj)* [F, lit., on boarding contract] **:** at a fixed rate for board and lodging **:** on the American plan ⟨possible to live quite reasonably *en pension* in many of the smaller hotels⟩ ⟨argued over *en pension* terms⟩

1en·phy·tot·ic \¦en,fī¦täd·ik\ *adj* [2*en-* + *phyt-* + *-otic*] *of a plant disease* **:** occurring regularly among the plants of a district but only in moderate severity

2enphytotic \"\ *n* -s **:** an enphytotic disease or an outbreak of such disease

en pla·card \äⁿpläkàar\ *adj* [F, lit., on the document] *of a seal* **:** affixed directly to the face of a document rather than pendent from a ribbon or other fastener **:** PLAQUÉ

en·plane \ən'plān, en-\ *or* **em·plane** \əm-,em-\ *vi* [1*en-* + *plane* (airplane)] **:** to board an airplane for purposes of travel

en plein \äⁿplaⁿ\ *adv* [F, lit., in full] **:** on a single number, side, or chance — used of a bet (as in roulette)

en prince \äⁿpraaⁿs\ *adv* [F] **:** in a princely manner; *usu* **:** LAVISHLY, LUXURIOUSLY

en prise \äⁿprēez\ *adj* [F] *of a chess piece* **:** exposed to capture

en quad \'en,•\ *n* [en] **:** a quad whose set dimension is one half that of an em quad

enquest *obs var of* INQUEST

enquire *var of* INQUIRE

en·rage \ən'rāj, en-\ *vb* [MF *enrager* to become mad, fr. OF *enragier,* fr. *en-* 1en- + *rage* — more at RAGE] *vt* **1** *obs* **a :** to make (as the sea) violent **:** cause (as a disease) to become more virulent **:** EXACERBATE **b :** to cause to become fevered or swollen **:** produce heat in (as a lesion) **2 :** to cause to become furious **:** fill with rage **:** MADDEN ⟨the child's teasing *enraged* the animal⟩ *sometimes* **:** to make angry **:** EXASPERATE **:** seriously annoy **~** *vi* **1** *obs* **:** to become distracted or maddened (as by pain or distress) **2 a** *archaic* **:** to become furiously angry **b** *obs* **:** to become intense (as of plague, famine, or tyranny) **:** RAGE

en·raged \-jd\ *adj* [ME, fr. past part. of *enragen*] **:** INFURIATED, MADDENED — **en·raged·ly** \-j(ə)dlē, -li\ *adv*

en·rage·ment \-mənt\ *n* -s [MF, fr. *enrager* + *-ment*] **:** the act of enraging or state of being enraged

en·ra·ma·da \,enrə'mädə\ *n* -s [Sp, fr. fem. of *enramado,* past part. of *enramar* to roof with branches, fr. *en-* (fr. L *in-* 2in-) + *ramo* branch, fr. L *ramus* — more at RAMIFY] *Southwest* **:** a roofed open-sided shelter often used for dances

en·rank \ən, en+\ *vt* [1*en-* + *rank* (n.)] **:** to place in ranks or in order

en rap·port \¦äⁿra¦pȯ(ə)r, -ō(ə)r,-ō(ə),-ōə\ *adj* [F] **:** in harmony **:** in a state of mutual accord and sympathetic understanding ⟨the lecturer was completely *en rapport* with his auditors⟩

en·rapt \ən'rapt, en-\ *adj* [1*en-* + *rapt*] **:** absorbed in or as if in ecstatic contemplation **:** ENRAPTURED ⟨fools listen to him, silent, ~, sighing when he is done —Alan Paton⟩

en·rap·ture \ən'rapchə(r), en-, -psh-\ *vt* **enraptured; enraptured; enrapturing** \-pchəriŋ,-psh(ə)r-\ **enraptures** [1*en-* + *rapture*] **:** to fill with delight **:** gratify completely

enraptured *adj* **:** characterized by or full of poetic fancy ⟨the ~ strain of her allegoric prose⟩ — **en·rap·tured·ly** \-ə(r)dlē, -li\ *adv*

en·ravish \ən, en+\ *vt* [1*en-* + *ravish*] **:** to transport with delight **:** ENRAPTURE

en·regiment \ən, en+\ *vt* [1*en-* + *regiment* (n.)] **:** to subject to discipline and orderly control **:** REGIMENT

en·register \ən, en+\ *vt* [MF *enregistrer,* fr. OF, fr. *en-* 1en- + *registre* register — more at REGISTER] **:** to record in a register **:** to put on record — **en·registration** \ən, (,)en+\ *n*

en·rich \ən'rich, en-\ *also* **en·rich·en** \-chən\ *vt* **enriched** *also* **enrichened; enriched** *also* **enrichened; enriching** \-chiŋ\ *also* **enrichening** \-ch(ə)niŋ\; **enriches** *also* **enrichens** [ME *enrichen,* fr. MF *enrichir,* fr. OF, fr. *en-* 1en- + *riche* rich — more at RICH] **1 a :** to make (as oneself) rich or richer ⟨he *~ed* himself at the expense of his brothers⟩ ⟨the expanding economy gradually *~ed* the workers⟩ **b :** to increase the intellectual or spiritual riches of ⟨his life was *~ed* by his charity⟩ ⟨returning home *~ed* by this new experience⟩ **c :** to fill with things of value **:** add to the valuable contents of ⟨sun and rain ~ the harvest⟩ ⟨his several expeditions *~ed* the museum's collections of tropical fauna⟩ **d :** to add to or improve by additions ⟨our language has been *~ed* from many sources⟩ ⟨physical science is constantly being *~ed* by new discoveries⟩ **2 a :** to supply with ornament ⟨a collar *~ed* with embroidery⟩ **:** ADORN, DECK ⟨the plans to ~ the ceiling with frescoes⟩ **b :** to ornament (as an architectural member) with carving ⟨paneling *~ed* with raised garlands of fruits and leaves⟩ **3 a :** to make richer in some quality (as in nutritive value, savor, or beauty) ⟨~ the gravy with a little flour browned in butter⟩ ⟨the blooming laurel *~es* the hill⟩ ⟨*~ing* culture media for fastidious microorganisms⟩ **b :** to make (soil) more productive esp. by increasing the supply of plant nutrients ⟨the desert can be *~ed* and given new life by irrigation⟩; *usu* **:** FERTILIZE ⟨~ the compost with well-rotted manure or bone meal⟩ **c :** to improve (a food) in nutritive value by addition of vitamins and minerals in processing; *esp* **:** to restore part of the thiamine, nicotinic acid, iron, and riboflavin removed in processing (wheat flour or cornmeal) **4 :** to increase the proportion of valuable metal or mineral in (as by concentration or smelting) **5 :** to expand (a course of study) esp. in an elementary or secondary school by increasing the variety of subjects as well as the depth of treatment ⟨bright pupils are given an *~ed* curriculum and are expected to cover much more than the normal amount of material at their grade level —J.D.Russell & C.H.Judd⟩

en·rich·er \-chə(r)\ *n* -s **:** one that enriches

en·rich·ing·ly *adv* **:** so as to enrich ⟨the silt carried by the river spread ~ over the delta⟩

en·rich·ment \-chmənt\ *n* -s **1 a :** the act of enriching or state of being enriched (as by the addition of ornamentation, wealth, or nutrients) ⟨the ~ of soil by green-manuring⟩ **b :** something (as decorations or possessions) that enriches ⟨old oaken panels carved with linenfold *~s*⟩ **2 :** the natural process by which sulfide-ore deposits gain additions of valuable metals through the descent of metalliferous solutions from the zone of oxidation and through their chemical reaction with the original sulfides below the level of underground water or below the depth to which atmospheric oxygen can penetrate

enridged *adj* [1*en-* + *ridged*] *obs* **:** formed into ridges **:** WAVY

en·ring \ən, en+\ *vt* [1*en-* + *ring* (n.)] **1 :** ENCIRCLE **2 :** to put a ring on

en·robe \ən'rōb, en+\ *vt* [1*en-* + *robe* (n.)] **1 :** to invest or adorn with or as if with a robe; *broadly* **:** ATTIRE **2 :** to cover (confections) with a coating (as of chocolate)

en·rob·er \-bə(r)\ *n* **:** one that enrobes

En·rob·er \"\ *trademark* — used for a machine that coats candies and other foods with a coating esp. of chocolate

en·rock·ment \ən'räkmənt, en-\ *n* -s [1*en-* + *rock* + *-ment*] **:** a mass of large stones thrown into water to form a base (as for a pier)

en·roll *or* **en·rol** \ən'rōl, en-\ *vb* **enrolled; enrolled; enrolling; enrolls** *or* **enrols** [ME *enrollen,* fr. MF *enroller,* fr. *en-* 1en- + *rolle* roll, register — more at ROLL] *vt* **1 a :** to insert, register, or enter (as a person or a fact) in a list, catalog, or roll (as of a court) ⟨nearly 10 percent of our population is *~ed* in the elementary schools⟩ ⟨the surprising speed with which men were *~ed* for the draft⟩ ⟨are they likely to ~ a newcomer on the jury list⟩ **b :** to enlist (oneself) for or as if for military service ⟨he *~ed* himself with those who were determined to stamp out ignorance and poverty⟩ **2 :** to write out in formal or legal form; *esp* **:** to prepare in written or printed form a final perfect copy of (a bill passed by a legislature) — distinguished from *engross* **3 :** to roll, coil, or wrap up; *sometimes* **:** ENFOLD **~***vi* **:** to enroll oneself or cause oneself to be enrolled (as in a military organization, on a list of voters, or for a course of study) ⟨*~ing* in the law school⟩ ⟨hundreds *~ed* in the military reserve forces⟩

enrolled bill *n* **:** a copy of a bill enacted by a U.S. governing body that embodies all changes introduced before enactment and that is filed away as evidence of what the law is

en·roll·ee \ən¦rō¦lē, en-\ *n* -s **:** a person who is enrolled (as in a military force or a course of study)

en·roll·ment *or* **en·rol·ment** \-'rōlmənt\ *n* -s [ME *enrollement,* fr. MF *enrollement,* fr. *enroller* + *-ment*] **1 a :** the act or process of enrolling (as at enlistment or registration) ⟨the problems involved in the ~ of millions of men for the draft⟩ **b :** the state of being enrolled ⟨my college ~ was approved yesterday⟩ **c :** the number enrolled ⟨the course will have a maximum ~ of 20⟩ **2 :** a writing or an entry in which something is enrolled **3 :** the enrolling of a boat engaged in the domestic commerce or fisheries of the U.S. or in navigating the waters on the northern, northeastern, and northwestern frontiers otherwise than by sea

en·root \ən, en+\ *vb* [1*en-* + *root* (n.)] *vt* **:** to fix by or as if by roots **:** ESTABLISH ⟨the Negro, an immigrant like the white man and now as *~ed* —*Geographical Rev.*⟩; *often* **:** to implant firmly or deeply (as in the mind or a social milieu) ⟨the concept of the fundamental dichotomy of good and evil is *~ed* in modern European thought⟩ **~** *vi* **:** to take root and grow **:** become established and develop ⟨spots where the free mind can ~ and grow —J.R.MacGillivray⟩

en·rough \ən, en+\ *vt* [1*en-* + *rough* (adj.)] *archaic* **:** to make rough **:** ROUGHEN

enround *vt* [ME *enrounden,* fr. 1*en-* + *round* anything round] *obs* **:** SURROUND

en route \(')än¦rü|t *also* (')en¦rü| *or* ən¦rü| *or* (')äⁿ ¦rü| *sometimes* (')en¦rau̇| *or* ən'rau̇| *or* (')ōn¦rü| *or* (')ōⁿ ¦rü|; *usu* |d·+V\ *adv (or adj)* [F] **:** on or along the way ⟨noticed while *en route* to church⟩ ⟨in spite of various *en route* delays we arrived safe but tired⟩

1ens \'enz, 'en(t)s\ *n, pl* **en·tia** \'enchēə, 'entēə, 'en(t)sēə\ [ML, fr. L, irreg. pres. part. of *esse* to be — more at IS] **1 a (1) :** abstract being **(2) :** the being of a thing — compare ESSE **b (1) :** an existent being **:** ENTITY **(2) :** something that can be conceived **:** a conceptual being **2 :** something supposed by alchemists to condense within itself all the virtues and qualities of a substance from which it is extracted **:** ESSENCE

2ens *pl of* EN

-ens *pres 3d sing of* -EN

ens *abbr* ensign

en·saffron \ən, en+\ *vt* [1*en-* + *saffron* (adj.)] **:** to make strongly or richly yellow

en·saint \ən, en+\ *vt* [1*en-* + *saint* (n.)] **:** to make saintly or make a saint of

en·sa·la·da \,ensə'lädə, -äthə\ *n* -s [Sp, lit., salad, fr. *en-* (fr. L *in-* 2in-) + *sal* salt (fr. L) + *-ada* -ate — more at SALT] **:** a burlesque madrigal consisting of several popular tunes sung as a quodlibet that was cultivated in Spain in the 16th century

en·sample \ən, en+\ *n* [ME *ensaumple,* fr. MF *ensample, essample, exemple* — more at EXAMPLE] **:** a pattern or model for imitation or warning **:** EXAMPLE, INSTANCE

en·sanguine \ən, en+\ *vt* -ED/-ING/-S [1*en-* + *sanguine* (color)] **1 :** to stain or cover with blood **:** make bloody **2 :** to stain or color blood red ⟨the setting sun *ensanguined* the western sky⟩

en·sate \'en,sāt\ *adj* [L *ensis* sword + E *-ate*] **:** ENSIFORM

en·sche·de \¦enz¦ka¦dā, -ns|, |k-\ *adj, usu cap* [fr. *Enschede,* Netherlands] **:** of or from the city of Enschede, Netherlands **:** of the kind or style prevalent in Enschede

en·sconce \ən'skän(t)s, en-, -n'sk-\ *vb* -ED/-ING/-S [1*en-* + *sconce* (n.)] *vt* **1** *obs* **:** to cover or shelter esp. with a fort **2 :** to place or hide (as oneself) securely **:** CONCEAL ⟨he *ensconced* himself behind the sofa to hear what went on⟩ **3 :** to establish or settle firmly, comfortably, or snugly ⟨the statue was finally *ensconced* in its niche⟩ ⟨such foolish customs tend to ~ themselves in the life of a people⟩ ⟨comfortably *ensconced* before the fire⟩ **~** *vi, obs* **:** to take shelter esp. behind a fortification **syn** see CONCEAL

en·scroll *also* **in·scroll** \ən'skrōl, en-, -n'sk-\ *vt* [1*en-* or 2*in-* + *scroll* (n.)] **:** to inscribe in or as if in a scroll; *broadly* **:** RECORD

ense \'en(t)s, 'enz\ *adv* [alter. of Sc *an* than, else (alter. of *than*) + *else*] *Scot* **:** OTHERWISE, ELSE

en·seal \ən, en+\ *vt* [ME *enselen,* fr. MF *enseeler,* fr. *en-* 2en- + *seel* seal — more at SEAL] **1** *obs* **a :** to impress (as a document) with or as if with a seal **b :** RATIFY **2** *archaic* **:** to seal up (as a box or house)

1en·seam \ən'sēm, en-\ *vb* [ME *enseymen,* alter. of MF *essaimer,* fr. *es-* (fr. L *ex-*) + *saim* fat, grease, fr. ML *sagimen,* fr. L *sagina* food, stuffing, fatness] *vt, archaic* **:** to free (as a hawk or horse) of superfluous fat **:** bring into hard condition **~** *vi, obs, of a hawk* **:** to lose excess weight **:** come into condition

2enseam \"\ *vt* [MF *ensaimer,* fr. *en-* 1en- + *saim* fat] *archaic* **:** to fill or cover with grease — usu. used as past part.

3enseam \"\ *vt* [1*en-* + *seam* (n.)] **:** to mark (as a person) with or as if with seams ⟨an old tomcat, his ears *~ed* with scars⟩

en·search \ən, en+\ *vb* [ME *enserchen,* fr. MF *encercher,* fr. OF *encerchier,* fr. *en-* 1en- + *cerchier* to search — more at SEARCH] *vi, archaic* **:** to make search **~** *vt* **1** *archaic* **:** to examine (as a place or document) attentively **:** SEARCH, SCRUTINIZE **2** *obs* **:** to search for **:** seek out

en·seat \ən, en+\ *vt* [1*en-* + *seat* (n.)] **:** ENTHRONE

1en·sem·ble \(')än¦sämbəl, (')äⁿ ¦sämbəl, (')äⁿ ¦säⁿbl(ᵊ), (')äⁿ ¦säⁿb(l)ə\ *sometimes* (')äⁿ ¦säm\ *n, pl* **ensembles** \-bəlz, -bl(ᵊ), -b(lə), -mz\ *often attrib* [F, fr. *ensemble* together, fr. L *insimul,* fr. *in-* 2in- + *simul* together — more at SAME] **1 a :** a system of items that constitute an organic unity **:** a congruous whole: as **a :** AGGREGATE 5 **b :** concerted music of two or more parts (as a quartet) **c (1) :** a complete costume including a basic garment (as a dress or suit) and the accessories (as gloves, shoes, ornaments, and hat) worn with it for a total harmonious effect **(2) :** two or more articles of clothing designed to complement one another when worn together ⟨a dress-and-jacket ~⟩ ⟨her ~ consisted of a smooth fawn wool suit under a darker coat lined with the suit color⟩ **d :** a group of furnishings (as for a room) designed to harmonize when used together; *sometimes* **:** SUITE 3b **2 :** a group of persons acting together to produce some particular effect or result: as **a :** the musicians engaged in the performance of a musical ensemble **b :** a group of supporting players, singers, or dancers; *esp* **:** CORPS DE BALLET **3 a :** the bringing together of items into an ensemble **:** UNIFICATION ⟨the company develops a sense of ~ and the producer can cast his plays better as he comes to know his actors —Martin Feinstein⟩ **b :** distinctive quality imparted by such bringing together; *esp* **:** the quality of a concerted musical performance as such ⟨the quartet's members were individually excellent but the ~ was somewhat inferior⟩

2ensemble \"\ *vt* -ED/-ING/-S **:** to bring together and coordinate (as clothing or furnishings) into a congruous whole

ensemble acting *n* **:** a system of theatrical presentation in which balanced casting, accurate historical reference, and careful integration of the whole performance replace the star system

en·sepulcher \ən, en+\ *vt* [1*en-* + *sepulcher* (n.)] **:** BURY, ENTOMB, ENGULF

en·serf \ən, en+\ *vt* -ED/-ING/-S [1*en-* + *serf*] **:** to force into serfdom **:** deprive of liberty and personal rights — **en·serf·ment** \"mənt\ *n* -s

en·sete \'en(t)sət\ *n* -s [Amharic *ensat*] **:** ABYSSINIAN BANANA

en·sheathe *also* **en·sheath** *or* **in·sheathe** *or* **in·sheath** \ən, en+\ *vt* [1*en-* or 2*in-* + *sheathe* or *sheath*] **:** to cover with or as if with or enclose in or as if in a sheath ⟨bud scales *ensheathing* the growing point⟩ ⟨the bony core is *ensheathed* by horny tissue⟩

en·shield \ən, en+\ *vt* [1*en-* + *shield* (v.)] **:** SHIELD

en·shrine \ən, en+\ *vt* [1*en-* + *shrine* (n.)] **1 a :** to enclose in or as if in a shrine ⟨*enshrined* the cheese in close folds of bright tinfoil⟩ **b :** to preserve or cherish as or as if something sacred ⟨robes of shadowy silver or *enshrining* light —P.B. Shelley⟩ ⟨certain nearly meaningless traditional expressions that are *enshrined* in English usage⟩ **2 :** to serve as a shrine for ⟨my heart *~s* his memory⟩

en·shrine·ment \"mənt\ *n* -s **:** the act of enshrining or the state of being enshrined

en·shroud \ən, en+\ *vt* [1*en-* + *shroud* (n.)] **:** to cover with or as if with or enclose by or as if by a shroud ⟨much of the aura of haziness which still tends to ~ animal ecology is due to the imperfection of our present knowledge —W.H.Dowdeswell⟩ ⟨darkness *~ed* the earth⟩ ⟨his life became *~ed* in legend⟩

en·si·form \'en(t)sə,fȯrm\ *adj* [F *ensiforme,* fr. L *ensis* sword + F *-forme* -form] *biol* **:** having sharp edges and tapering to a slender point **:** having a shape suggesting a sword ⟨the ~ leaf of the gladiolus⟩ — see LEAF illustration

ensiform cartilage *or* **ensiform process** *also* **ensiform appendix** *n* **:** XIPHOID PROCESS

1en·sign \'en(t)sən, 'en,sīn *sometimes* 'enzən; *in the United States & Brit navies* 'en(t)sən *sometimes* 'enzən\ *n* -s [ME *ensigne,* fr. MF *enseigne,* fr. L *insignia,* pl. of *insigne,* fr. neut. of *insignis* having a distinctive mark, outstanding, fr. *in-* 2in- + *-signis* (fr. *signum* mark, sign) — more at SIGN] **1 :** a flag that has been established by a national authority for display as the symbol of nationality by ships or airplanes and that also may be flown sometimes with a distinctive badge added to its design by a military installation, by an organization (as the customs service, a harbor board, or a marine insurance company) having nautical associations, or by an overseas colony or dominion **2 a :** a badge of office, rank, or power; *sometimes* **:** heraldic bearings — usu. used in pl. **b :** EMBLEM, SYMBOL, SIGN ⟨that ~ of tutorial authority, the hickory stick⟩ **3 a** *archaic* **:** STANDARD-BEARER; *esp* **:** a commissioned officer of the British army before 1871 who acted as a standard-bearer **b :** the most junior naval commissioned officer ranking just below a lieutenant junior grade and above a chief warrant officer **c :** a onetime infantry officer of the lowest commissioned rank **4 :** a dark to blackish blue **syn** see FLAG

ensign 1: Royal Air Force

2en·sign \ən'sīn, en'-\ *vt* [MF *enseigner,* fr. ML *insignare,* fr. L *in-* 2in- + *signum* mark, sign] **1 :** to distinguish by a mark or ornament ⟨a sail *~ed* with an ornamental device⟩ **2 :** to distinguish (as a heraldic charge) by a significant mark (as a granted badge or a crown or miter); *specif* **:** to surmount (as a shield) with such a mark

ensign armorial *n, pl* **ensigns armorial :** a heraldic bearing or emblem

ensign bearer *n* **1 :** the bearer of a flag **2** *archaic* **:** ENSIGN 3a

en·sign·cy *pronunc at* 1ENSIGN +(t)sē,(t)si\ *n* -ES **:** the rank or office of an ensign ⟨purchased an ~ in an Indian regiment⟩

ensign fly *or* **ensign wasp** *n* **:** a parasitic wasp (family Evaniidae) having the abdomen carried high on a long pedicel and larvae that live in the oothecae of cockroaches and feed on their eggs

en·sign·ry \-rē,-ri\ *n* -ES **:** ensigns and banners

ensign staff *n* **:** the staff at the stern of a ship from which the national flag is flown

en·sil·abil·i·ty \ən,sīlə'biləd.ē, (,)en-\ *n* -ES **:** fitness or suitability for ensiling ⟨the ~ of lush young growth rich in protein can be increased by adding carbohydrates⟩

1en·si·lage \'en(t)s(ə)lij, -lēj\ *n* [F, fr. *ensiler* + *-age*] **1 :** the process of preserving fodder by ensiling **2 :** SILAGE

2ensilage \"\ *vt* **:** ENSILE

ensilage blower *n* **:** a machine that elevates cut green forage into a silo by an air blast

ensilage cutter *n* **:** a machine that chops green fodder for ensiling and usu. incorporates a device for elevating it into the silo

en·sile \ən'sīl, (')en¦s-, *chiefly before pause or consonant* -īəl\ *vt* -ED/-ING/-S [F *ensiler,* fr. *en-* 1en- + *silo,* fr. Sp *silo* — more at SILO] **:** to prepare (fodder) usu. by chopping and storing so as to exclude air by compression in a tight silo or pit often with additives (as certain acids, preservatives, or carbohydrates) so as to induce conversion to silage

en·sis \'en(t)səs\ *n, cap* [NL, fr. L, sword] **:** a common genus of razor clams

en·sky \ənz'kī, en-, -n'skī\ *vb* **enskied** *or* **enskyed; enskied** *or* **enskyed; enskying; enskies** [1*en-* + *sky* (n.)] *vt* **1 :** to elevate to or as if to heaven ⟨we view George Eliot *enskied* in fame and time —Sylvia T. Warner⟩ ⟨that wonderful voice is forever *~ing* him —Amy Lowell⟩ **2 :** to raise into or toward the skies ⟨leaves that ~ themselves —Padraic Colum⟩ **~** *vi* **:** to become enskied

en·slave \ən'slāv, en-\ *vt* [1*en-* + *slave* (n.)] *vt* **1 :** to reduce to slavery **:** make a slave of ⟨free peasants reduced to serfdom or *enslaved*⟩; *broadly* **:** to hold in an inferior or subject state **:** SUBJUGATE ⟨millions of people held in subjugation, *enslaved* by poverty and illiteracy —W.O.Douglas⟩ ⟨millions of workers . . . pay tribute . . . and their money is being used further to ~ the American people —M.K.Hart⟩ **2 :** to obtain such influence over as to make slavishly subject ⟨drugs that ~ the will⟩ ⟨even the most pleasant indulgences can end by *enslaving* the indulger⟩ **~** *vi* **:** to make a person slavish ⟨declares that sex *~s* —G.A.Chapman⟩ ⟨routine duties that bind but do not narrow or ~ —R.B.Perry⟩

en·slave·ment \-mənt\ *n* -s **1 :** the act or process of enslaving ⟨the gradual ~ of primitive peoples⟩ **2 :** the state of being enslaved **:** BONDAGE, SERVITUDE

en·slav·er \-və(r)\ *n* **:** one that enslaves

ens·len's vine \'enzlənz-, 'en(t)s|\ *n, usu cap E* [after Aloysius Enslen, 19th cent. botanist] **:** SAND VINE

en·snare \ən'sna(a)|(ə)r, en-, -sne|, |ə\ *vt* [1*en-* + *snare* (n.)] **:** to take in or as if in a snare **:** SNARE ⟨birds *ensnared* in a net⟩ ⟨a simplicity which it would be easy to ~ with the romanticism embodied in him —Victor Canning⟩ **syn** see CATCH

en·snare·ment \|rmənt, |əm-\ *n* -s **:** ENTRAPMENT

en·snar·er \-ra(r)\ *n* -s **:** one that ensnares

en·snar·ing·ly *adv* **:** so as to ensnare **:** for the purpose of ensnaring

en·snarl \ən, en+\ *vt* [1*en-* + *snarl* (n.)] **:** to entangle in or into or as if in or into a snarl ⟨trees all *~ed* with vines and bushes —A.J.Liebling⟩ ⟨ended up by ~ing him in a hopeless love affair⟩

en-sof *or* **en-soph** \än'sōf, en'sȯf\ *n, cap E&S* [Heb *ēn sōph* without end] **:** the absolutely infinite God — used in cabalistic doctrine

en·sor·cell \ən'sȯrsəl, en-\ *or* **ensorcel** *vt* **ensorcelled** *or* **ensorceled; ensorcelled** *or* **ensorceled; ensorcelling** *or* **ensorceling** \-rs(ə)liŋ\ **ensorcells** *or* **ensorcels** [MF *ensorceler*, alter. of OF *ensorcerer*, fr. *en-* ¹en- + *-sorcerer*, fr. *sorcier* sorcerer — more at SORCERER] **:** BEWITCH, ENCHANT ⟨she would not do him any hurt or ~ him —Sir Richard Burton⟩; *broadly* **:** to make rapt with delight or interest **:** FASCINATE ⟨the quiet beauty of the hill country will relax and ~ you⟩ — **en·sor·cell·ment** \-rəlmənt\ *n* -s

en·sor·cer·ize \ən'sȯrs(ə),rīz, en-\ *vt* -ED/-ING/-S [¹*en-* + *sorcerize*] **:** ENSORCELL

en·soul *also* **in·soul** \ən, en+\ *vt* -ED/-ING/-S [¹*en-* or ²*in-* + *soul* (n.)] **1 :** to receive, put, or cherish in the soul **2 :** to endow or imbue with a soul ⟨the spirit of man is . . . ~*ed* spirit —W.R.Inge⟩

en·sphere *also* **in·sphere** \ənz'fi(ə)r, en-, -n'sf-, -iə\ *vt* -ED/-ING/-S [¹*en-* or ²*in-* + *sphere* (n.)] **1 :** to place or enclose in or as if in a sphere **:** ENVELOP, ENCIRCLE ⟨his ample shoulders in a cloud *ensphered* —George Chapman⟩ ⟨its very concrete symbolism seems sometimes to ~ the intended truths of spirit —H.O.Taylor⟩ **2 :** to form into a sphere

enspirit *var of* INSPIRIT

ens ra·ti·o·nis \¦enz,rashē'ōnəs; ¦en(t)s,räd·ē'-, -ätsē'-\ *n* [ML, lit., being of the mind] **:** an abstract logical entity usu. having no positive existence outside the mind — compare ENS REALE

ens re·ale \¦enzrē'ā(,)lē, ¦en(t)srā'ä(,)lā\ *n* [ML, lit., real being] **:** an entity that has either actual or potential existence beyond the confines of the finite mind — compare ENS RATIONIS

en·stamp \ənz'tamp, en-, -n'st-, -taa(ə)mp,-taimp\ *vt* [¹*en-* + *stamp* (n.)] *archaic* **:** to imprint or impress with or as if with a stamp

enstar *var of* INSTAR

enstate *var of* INSTATE

en·sta·tite \'enztə,tīt, 'en(t)stə-\ *n* -s [G *enstatit*, fr. Gk *enstatēs* adversary + G *-it* -ite] **:** an orthorhombic mineral $MgSiO_3$ of the pyroxene group consisting of magnesium silicate usu. occurring massive and varying from grayish white to olive green and brown — compare BRONZITE — **en·sta·tit·ic** \¦==¦tid·ik\ *adj*

en·steel \ənz'tē(ə)l, en-, -n'st-\ *vt* [¹*en-* + *steel* (n.)] **:** to make hard and strong ⟨frost ~*ed* the soil⟩

ensteep *obs var of* INSTEEP

en·stool \ənz'tül, en-, -n'st-\ *vt* [¹*en-* + *stool* (seat of a chief)] **:** to install (a ruler of any of several native African groups) in office — contrasted with *destool* — **enstoolment** *n* -s

enstyle *vt* [¹*en-* + *style* (v.)] *obs* **:** STYLE, NAME

en·su·ant \ən'süənt, en-\ *adj* [*ensue* + *-ant*] **:** following as a consequence ⟨the ~ response to his appeal was very satisfying⟩ — often used postpositively and with *on* ⟨the privations and disorders ~ on war⟩

en·sue \ən'sü, en-\ *vb* -ED/-ING/-S [ME *ensuen*, fr. MF *ensivre, ensuivre, ensuire* (3d sing. *ensuit, ensiut*), fr. OF, fr. *en-* ¹en- + *sivre, suivre* to follow — more at SUE] *vt* **1** *obs* **a :** to correspond to **:** to take the place of or be commensurate with **b :** to take after **:** follow the lead of **:** IMITATE **c :** to follow after **:** be subsequent to **:** SUCCEED **d :** to carry through or on (as a train of thought or a profession) **2 :** to pursue or strive to attain ⟨within certain limits he *ensued* and sometimes attained perfection —John Buchan⟩ ~ *vi* **:** to take place afterward: **a :** to follow as a chance, likely, or necessary consequence **:** RESULT ⟨when his mind fails to stay the pace set by its inventions, madness must ~ —C.D.Lewis⟩ **b :** to follow in chronological succession **syn** see FOLLOW

en·su·ing·ly *adv, obs* **:** in an ensuing manner **:** AFTERWARD

en suite \(')äⁿ ¦swēt, *usu* -ēd·+V; *F* äⁿsẅēt\ *adv (or adj)* [F] **:** in a succession, series, or set **: a :** in an integrated functional unit ⟨rooms arranged *en suite*⟩ ⟨a pleasant sewing room with lavatory *en suite*⟩ **b :** in a coordinated set ⟨a Chippendale wing chair with footstool designed *en suite* —*Antiques*⟩ ⟨heavy tray and sugar bowl *en suite*⟩

ensurance *n* -s [ME *ensuraunce*, fr. AF *ensurance*, prob. alter. of MF *assurance* — more at ASSURANCE] *obs* **:** the act or means of ensuring; *specif* **:** INSURANCE

en·sure \ən'shů(ə)r, en-, -ůə\ *vt* -ED/-ING/-S [ME *ensuren*, fr. AF *enseurer*, prob. alter. of OF *aseurer* to assure — more at ASSURE] **1** *obs* **a :** to make (one) sure (as by pledging, guaranteeing, convincing, or declaring) **:** ASSURE **b :** AFFIANCE, BETROTH; *sometimes* **:** MARRY, ESPOUSE **2 :** INSURE 2 **3 :** to make sure, certain, or safe **:** GUARANTEE ⟨good farming practices go far to ~ good crops⟩ ⟨provisions to ~ the rank and file a voice in union policies⟩ ⟨his industry and ability will ~ his success in life⟩

syn INSURE, ASSURE, SECURE: ENSURE, INSURE, and ASSURE all indicate a making of an outcome or event sure, certain, or inevitable as a consequence or concomitant ⟨certain rules of conduct for the purpose of *ensuring* the safety and victory of the absent warriors —J.G.Frazer⟩ ⟨for the remainder of his life he so constrained the expression of his thoughts as to *ensure* safety —H.O.Taylor⟩ ⟨shipbuilders, who wished to *insure* a profitable career for their vessels —*Amer. Guide Series: Mich.*⟩ ⟨the structural division of the buildings, with no more than four apartments opening on any hallway, *insures* privacy and quiet —*Amer. Guide Series: N.Y. City*⟩ ⟨protected by game laws and reared in state hatcheries, this bird is now *assured* a permanent place among the game birds of the state —*Amer. Guide Series: Tenn.*⟩ ⟨policies and plans for *assuring* the necessary labor force for defense and essential civilian production —*Current Biog.*⟩ ASSURE is the usual form to express the notion of removal of doubt, uncertainty, or worry from a person's mind ⟨I *assured* him that I was far from advising him to do anything so cruel —Joseph Conrad⟩ ⟨*assured* the inhabitants that France intended to grant autonomy —*Current Biog.*⟩ INSURE is now the general word for reference to making certain arrangements for indemnification for loss by contingent events ⟨to *insure* the car against theft and fire damage⟩ SECURE implies purposive action to ensure safety, protection, or certainty against adverse contingencies ⟨lock the door to *secure* us from interruption —Charles Dickens⟩ ⟨one other battalion moved up to *secure* the first battalion's flank —Walter Bernstein⟩

en·sur·er \-ůrə(r)\ *n* -s **:** one that ensures

en sur·tout \¦äⁿ(,)sər¦tü, äⁿ 'sər,tü\ *adv (or adj)* [F, lit., as a centerpiece] **:** in a centered position on another as if laid on top of it — used of one coat of arms in respect to another, esp. of that of a wife in respect to that of her husband

en·swathe \ən, en+\ *vt* [¹*en-* + *swathe*] **:** SWATHE, ENVELOP, ENWRAP ⟨swelling buds still *enswathed* in their furry overcoats⟩ ⟨his head *enswathed* in bloody bandages⟩

en·sweep \ən, en+\ *vt* [¹*en-* + *sweep*] *archaic* **:** to sweep over or across

ent- *or* **ento-** *comb form* [NL & Gk; NL, fr. Gk *entos*; akin to L *intus* within, Gk *en* in — more at IN] **:** inner **:** within ⟨*ent*ad⟩ ⟨*ento*blast⟩

¹-ent \ənt, ᵊnt; *in some words chiefly with stress on the antepenult or by syncope on the penult (as "president") sometimes* ,ent; *in common words "-erent" preceded by stressed vowel and consonant (as in "different") often* ərnt\ *n suffix* -s [ME, fr. OF, fr. L *-ent-, -ens*, fr. pres. part. suffix of the 2d & 3d conjugations, fr. *-e-* (vowel of the 2d & 3d conjugations) + *-nt-, -ns*, pres. part. suffix — more at -ANT] **:** one that performs (a specified action) ⟨regent⟩ ⟨resident⟩ ⟨tangent⟩ — compare ¹-ANT

²-ent \"\ *adj suffix* [ME, fr. OF, fr. L *-ent-, -ens*, pres. part. suffix] **:** doing, behaving, existing (in the way specified) **:** -ing ⟨appar*ent*⟩ ⟨rever*ent*⟩ ⟨subsequ*ent*⟩ — with verbs or verbal roots; compare ²-ANT

ent *abbr* **1** entered; entrance **2** entertainment **3** entomology

en·tab·la·ture \ən'tablə,chů(ə)r, en-, -,chůə, -lǝchə(r), -lə,tyů-, -lə,tü-\ *n* [obs. F, modif. of It *intavolatura*, fr. *intavolato* (past part. of *intavolare* to put on a board or table, fr. *in-* ²in- + *tavola* board, table, fr. L *tabula*) + *-ura* -ure — more at TABLE] **:** an architecturally treated wall consisting of the architrave, the frieze, and the cornice that in classical architecture rests upon the capitals of the columns and supports the pediment or roof plate according to its position on the front or flank of the building; *also* **:** a similar part in a post-and-lintel construction **2 :** an elevated support for certain parts of a machine (as the upper portion of a forging press)

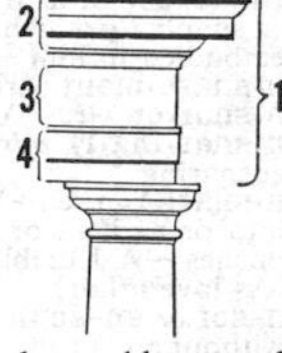

1 entablature, *2* cornice, *3* frieze, *4* architrave

en·tab·la·tured \"+d\ *adj* **:** having an entablature

en·ta·ble·ment \ən'tābəlmənt, en-\ *n* -s [F, fr. OF, fr. *en-* ¹en- + *table* + *-ment* — more at TABLE] **:** a platform supporting a statue and above the dado

en·tad \'en,tad\ *adv* [*ent-* + *-ad*] *anat* **:** INWARD

en·ta·da \en'tädə\ *n, cap* [NL, prob. fr. native name in India] **:** a small genus of tropical woody vines (family Leguminosae) with small flowers in clustered spikes and large woody pealike pods containing large highly polished seeds — see SNUFFBOX BEAN

¹en·tail \ən'tāl, en-, *chiefly before pause or consonant* -āəl\ *vt* -ED/-ING/-S [ME *entailen, entaillen*, fr. ¹*en-* + *taile, taille* limitation — more at TAIL (limitation)] **1 a :** to restrict (property) as to course of descent upon the owner's death by limiting the inheritance to the owner's lineal descendants or to a particular class thereof (as to his male children) **b :** to convert (an estate in certain property) into a fee-tail estate **:** create such an estate in (property) **c :** to settle (land) upon a person in a way designed to preserve for possession in his family as far as legally possible **2 a :** to confer, assign, or transmit as if by entail **:** burden indefinitely with ⟨lament the stupid commonplace and often ribald names ~*ed* upon the rivers and other features of the great West —Washington Irving⟩ **:** FASTEN ⟨blood revenge . . . could be ~*ed* for many generations —A.P. Davies⟩ — often used with *on* or *upon* ⟨~*ed* on them indelible disgrace —Robert Browning⟩ ⟨helped to ~ upon them the ridicule of their neighbors —Tobias Smollett⟩ **b** *obs* (1) **:** to attach inseparably to something **:** TACK (2) **:** to fix (a person) permanently in some status or condition **:** make (a person) the hereditary successor ⟨~ him and his heirs unto the crown —Shak.⟩ ⟨the method ~*ed* upon medieval thought by its scholastic . . . character —H.O.Taylor⟩ **3 a :** to impose, involve, or require as a necessary accompaniment or result ⟨the work ~*s* expense⟩ ⟨political democracy ~*s* a cultural democracy —K.I.L.Lansner⟩ ⟨believed that the wrong faith would ~ hellfire —R.H.Bainton⟩ **b :** to imply with strict logical necessity ⟨a sentence *s* is said to ~ a sentence *t* when the proposition expressed by *t* is deducible from the proposition expressed by *s* —A.J.Ayer⟩

²en·tail \", 'en,t-\ *n* -s [ME *entaile, entaille*, fr. *entailen, entaillen*, v.] **1 a :** an entailing esp. of lands **:** a settling of an estate tail **b :** an estate settled in fee tail or limited in descent to a particular class of issue **c :** the rule by which the descent is fixed **:** the fixed line of devolution **2 a :** irremediable or assured transmission (as of a good or bad quality) ⟨the ~ of ignorance and vice on children born in such surroundings⟩ **b :** something (as a quality) that is transmitted as if by entail **:** LEGACY, INHERITANCE ⟨the doctrine . . . that every child coming into the world is born with an ~ of sin —H.G.Goodykoontz⟩ **c :** logical or necessary consequence or sequence ⟨an evil with a most unfortunate ~ for the future —E.D.Soper⟩

en·tail·er \ən'tālə(r), en-\ *n* -s **:** one that entails

en·tail·ment \-ā(ə)lmənt\ *n* -s **1 :** the act of entailing ⟨~ of property upon a certain heir⟩ **2 :** strict, logical, or analytical implication (as between two statements so that one can be deduced from the other on purely logical grounds)

en·tal \'entᵊl\ *adj* [*ent-* + *-al*] *anat* **:** INNER — opposed to *ectal*

en·tame \ən, en+\ *vt* [¹*en-* + *tame* (adj.)] *archaic* **:** TAME

ent·amebiasis *or* **ent·amoebiasis** \¦en,t+.\ *n* [NL, fr. *Entamoeba* + *-iasis*] **:** endamebiasis esp. of a vertebrate **:** AMEBIASIS

ent·amoeba \¦ent+\ *n* [NL, fr. *ent-* + *Amoeba*] **1** *cap, in some classifications* **:** a genus of parasitic amoebas (family Endamoebidae) that include those members of the genus *Endamoeba* which are parasites of vertebrates — used chiefly in medical literature **2** *also* **entameba :** an endamoeba esp. of a vertebrate — **entamoebic** *also* **entamebic** *adj*

en·tangle \ən, en+\ *vt* [ME *entanglen*, fr. ¹*en-* + *tanglen* to tangle — more at TANGLE] **1 a :** to twist or interweave so as to make separation difficult **:** make tangled and intricate **:** SNARL ⟨~ yarn⟩ **b :** to make complicated or difficult of comprehension **:** CONFUSE ⟨his explanation did not so much clarify as ~ the question⟩ **2 a :** to involve so as to impede physical movement or make extrication difficult **:** ENMESH, ENSNARL ⟨~ a bird in the coils of a net⟩ ⟨*entangled* themselves in a maze of woods and marshes⟩ ⟨*entangled* his feet in the train of her dress⟩ **b :** to involve in a perplexing or troublesome situation from which escape is difficult **:** ENTRAP ⟨*entangling* the country in a vicious circle of wars⟩ ⟨*entangled* himself in a ruinous litigation⟩ ⟨*entangled* his victims in a real-estate scheme that cost them dearly⟩ ⟨had *entangled* the king in a false marriage with her —Edith Sitwell⟩ **c :** to confuse mentally **:** PERPLEX, BEWILDER ⟨*entangled* his listeners in a maze of sophistries⟩ **d** *archaic* **:** ENCUMBER ⟨died . . . leaving an *entangled* estate, due to loans and back rentals —R.J.Porcell⟩

en·tan·gled \-gəld\ *adj* **1 a :** twisted together **:** INTERTWINED, INTERWOVEN, SNARLED ⟨the ropes became ~⟩ ⟨toiled through the ~ growths of scrub oak and mesquite —*Amer. Guide Series: Texas*⟩ **b :** placed in a situation that impedes physical movement or from which extrication is difficult **:** caught fast **:** ENSNARED, ENMESHED ⟨~ in machinery⟩ ⟨one of the hares was ~, and endeavoring to disengage himself —William Cowper⟩ ⟨~ and even lost in the maze of swamps —Frank Debenham⟩ **c :** INTRICATE, COMPLICATED, CONFUSED ⟨moved in a thicker and more ~ machinery of government —Sacheverell Sitwell⟩ ⟨become ~ with still wider social and political problems —J.B.Conant⟩ **2 :** involved in an embarrassing, troublesome, or compromising situation ⟨~ in an affair with another man's wife⟩ ⟨became ~ in a costly litigation⟩ — **en·tan·gled·ly** *adv* — **en·tan·gled·ness** *n* -ES

en·tan·gle·ment \-gəlmənt\ *n* -s **1 a :** the action or an instance of physically entangling **:** the state of being entangled or snarled ⟨walnut legs . . . placed so far under the table that any ~ with the diners' legs is . . . avoided —*New Yorker*⟩ ⟨such waste often causes ~*s* and the breaking of whole batches of threads —J.J.Sussmuth⟩ **b :** something that entangles physically; *specif* **:** an obstacle consisting of specially constructed barbed-wire fences for impeding the advance of foot troops **c :** something that is closely interwoven or tangled ⟨there stand the trees . . . their leafy ~*s* thickly loaded —F.R.Leavis⟩ **2 a :** the condition or an instance of being deeply involved or closely linked usu. in an embarrassing or compromising way ⟨his boy's ~ with . . . the child of a gypsy mother —Edith Sitwell⟩ ⟨a well-known ~ with shady elements seriously injured his chances of reelection⟩ ⟨mistrust of foreign ~*s*⟩ **b** (1) **:** something that involves or preoccupies **:** COMMITMENT, CARE ⟨lamented that the exigencies and ~*s* of business prevented him from giving exclusive attention to chemical research —C.A.Browne⟩ ⟨to Paris she would return whenever she could free herself from the ~*s* of the village —L.C.Powys⟩ (2) **:** something that confuses, complicates, or ensnares **:** ALLURE, COMPLICATION, COMPLEXITY, CONFUSION ⟨contriving many ~*s* to catch the souls of poor sinners⟩ ⟨a plot full of ~*s*⟩ ⟨I cannot look upon the circumstances of this country, without being persuaded that I discern in them an ~ . . . never met with in the history of any other —William Cowper⟩

en·tan·gler \-g(ə)lə(r)\ *n* -s **:** one that entangles

en·tan·gling \-g(ə)liŋ\ *adj* **:** tending to entangle ⟨~ briers⟩; *esp* **:** tending to compromise, involve, or commit in an undesirable way — often used in the phrase *entangling alliance* ⟨~ alliances with foreign powers⟩ ⟨with a boy of eighteen there was always the danger of some ~ alliance —Hamilton Basso⟩

en·ta·sis \'entəsəs\ *n, pl* **enta·ses** \-ə,sēz\ [Gk, lit., distention, stretching, fr. *enteinein* to stretch tight fr. *en-* ²en- + *teinein* to stretch) + *-sis* — more at THIN] **:** a slight convexity (as in the shaft of a column); *esp* **:** one that begins at the base of a shaft and continues to the top and that is greatest a little below the middle point ⟨the ~ of the columns at the corner of the peristyle —Vincent Sheean⟩

entd *abbr* entered

en·té en point *also* **enté en pointe** \¦en,tā,en'pȯint\ *adj* [F] **1** *heraldry* **:** constituting or occupying a point — used of a coat marshaled with two or more others that are conjoined by impalement or quartering ⟨the arms of Spain include León and Castile quartered with those of Granada *enté en point*⟩ **2** *heraldry* **:** including a coat enté en point — used of an escutcheon in which three or more coats are marshaled ⟨the arms of Spain are *enté en point* of the arms of Granada⟩

en·te·lech·i·al \¦entə¦lekēəl\ *adj* **:** being or relating to an entelechy

en·tel·e·chy \en'teləkē, ən-\ *n* -ES [LL *entelechia*, fr. Gk *entelecheia*, prob. fr. *enteles echein* to be complete (fr. *enteles* — neut. of *entelēs* complete, full — + *echein* to have) + *-ia* -y] **1** *in Aristotle* **a :** the full realization of form-giving cause or energeia as contrasted with mere potential existence **b :** the form that actuates this realization **2 a** *in modern philosophy* **:** something that contains or realizes an end or final cause **b :** a supposititious immanent but immaterial agency held by some vitalists to regulate or direct the vital processes of an organism esp. toward the achievement of maturity — compare ÉLAN VITAL

en·tel·lus \en'teləs, ən-\ *n* -ES [NL, prob. fr. L *Entellus*, a Sicilian hero famous as a pugilist] **:** HANUMAN

en·tel·o·don \en'telə,dän\ *n, cap* [NL, fr. Gk *entelēs* complete, full + NL *-odon*] **:** a genus (the type of the family Entelodontidae) of giant pigs widespread in the Oligocene of Europe — compare DINOHYUS

en·tel·o·dont \-änt\ *n* -s [NL *Entelodontidae*, fr. *Entelodont-*, *Entelodon*, type genus + *-idae*] **:** a member of a family (Entelodontidae) of giant pigs that appeared in the Eocene and reached their highest development in the Oligocene of the northern hemisphere — compare DINOHYUS, ENTELODON

en·temple \ən, en+\ *vt* [¹*en-* + *temple* (n.)] *archaic* **:** ENSHRINE

entender *vt* [¹*en-* + *tender* (adj.)] *obs* **:** to make tender in feeling

en·tente \(')än¦tänt, (')äⁿ¦tä(ə)ⁿt\ *n, pl* **ententes** \-änts, -ä(ə)ⁿt(s)\ [F, lit., understanding, fr. OF, intent, effort, understanding, fr. fem. of *entent*, past part. of *entendre* to intend, be attentive, perceive, understand — more at INTEND] **1 :** a written or unwritten international understanding or agreement providing for or marked by a common course of action or policy in foreign affairs but usu. less definite or formally binding than an alliance ⟨it changes the ~ into an alliance, and alliances . . . are not in accordance with our traditions —Edward Grey⟩ **2 :** a coalition of parties to an entente ⟨the three powers formed an extremely powerful ~⟩

entente cor·diale \-,kȯrd'yäl, -yȧl\ *n* [F] **:** cordial understanding esp. between two governments in regard to foreign affairs

¹en·ter \'entə(r)\ *vb* **entered; entered; entering** \'entəriŋ, 'en·triŋ\ **enters** [ME *entren*, fr. OF *entrer*, fr. L *intrare* to enter, fr. *intra* on the inside, within; akin to *inter* between — more at INTER-] *vi* **1 a :** to go or come into a material place **:** make a physical entrance or penetration ⟨knock on the door before you ~⟩ ⟨no evil thing approach nor ~ in —John Milton⟩ **b** (1) **:** to come into the mind or feelings ⟨a strange idea ~*ed* into his head⟩ ⟨a spirit of tenderness ~*ed* into his heart⟩ (2) **:** to come into something intangible ⟨a tone of menace ~*ed* into her voice⟩ **c :** to pass or come into some particular state ⟨by the Lord's favor he ~*ed* into a state of grace⟩ ⟨~*ed* into a deep coma⟩ **d :** to come into a group **:** gain admission **:** become a member **:** JOIN ⟨asked at what school he would ~⟩ ⟨a debutante ~*ing* into society⟩ **2 a :** to make a beginning **:** take the first steps **:** ENGAGE, START ⟨~*ed* into business⟩ ⟨~*ing* upon a career⟩ ⟨~*ed* upon a wearisome account of his travels⟩ ⟨~*ed* into negotiations with the enemy⟩ **b :** to begin to consider a subject ⟨he had barely ~*ed* into the matter when the bell rang⟩ ⟨once he had ~*ed* upon a question, he would never stop⟩ **c :** to make an entrance (as in a fugue) **:** BEGIN **3 :** to go in upon lands as a formal act of ownership **:** take possession **4 :** to come upon the stage — often used as a stage direction in the subjunctive ⟨~ Hamlet⟩ ⟨~ four clowns⟩ **5 :** to play a part **:** be a factor **:** have a bearing **:** CONTRIBUTE ⟨all for the best: . . . sentiment won't ~ in —Elizabeth Bowen⟩ ⟨many processes ~ into the making of this product⟩ ⟨much anxious thought ~*ed* into the framing of this document⟩ ⟨factors other than habitat ~ in this varied adaptation —M.J.Herskovits⟩ **6 :** to register or enroll in a competition **:** become a candidate in a competition ⟨two days before the race he decided not to ~⟩ ⟨candidates may ~ for more than one scholarship⟩ ~ *vt* **1 a :** to come or go into **:** pass into the interior of **:** pass within the outer cover or shell of **:** PENETRATE, PIERCE ⟨~ a house⟩ ⟨rivers ~ the sea⟩ **b :** to come into (the mind) **:** occur to ⟨it never ~*ed* his head that he might be wrong⟩ ⟨a new doubt ~*ed* his mind⟩ **c :** to come into (something intangible) ⟨the shadow of passion ~*ed* her voice —Louis Bromfield⟩ ⟨an extraordinarily beautiful girl who never ~*ed* his life —V.H.Brombert⟩ **2 a** (1) **:** to inscribe or make a record of **:** REGISTER ⟨~ the names of qualified voters⟩ ⟨~ a notation in a journal⟩ ⟨~ a book in a catalog⟩ (2) **:** SKETCH, DEPICT ⟨even ~*ed* these four mountains on the map he sent back —Frank Debenham⟩ **b :** to cause to go into or be received into something **:** cause to be admitted **:** ENROLL ⟨~ a boy at a school⟩ ⟨~ a horse in a race⟩ **c :** to put in **:** INSERT ⟨~ a wedge into a log⟩ ⟨she ~*ed* the key in the door —E.F.McGuire⟩ **d** *of a male animal* **:** to copulate with **3 a :** to make a beginning in **:** take up **:** START, BEGIN ⟨the troops ~*ed* battle⟩ ⟨~ the legal profession⟩ **b :** to pass within the limits of (a particular period of time) ⟨we are ~*ing* a new era⟩ **4 a :** to employ for the first time in actual hunting, racing, hawking **:** exercise initially **:** TRAIN; *specif* **:** to break in (a horse) **b** *archaic* **:** to introduce to a subject **:** INITIATE **5 a :** to become a member of **:** JOIN ⟨~ the army⟩ ⟨~ the university⟩ **b** (1) **:** to become an active participant in ⟨~ a war⟩ ⟨~ a discussion⟩ (2) **:** to become a candidate in (a contest or competition) ⟨~ a race⟩ ⟨~ a short-story contest⟩ **6 :** to go into (a subject) **:** EXAMINE, CONSIDER ⟨for the moment I will not ~ the question of how this decision is to be formulated precisely —M.G.White⟩ **7 a :** to become a part of **:** merge with ⟨the hemlock that killed Socrates . . . is significant only because it ~*s* the context of human cultural history —L.A. White⟩ **b :** to have an intuitive sympathy with **:** identify oneself with **:** UNDERSTAND ⟨few Americans can ~ the poem completely —William Power⟩ ⟨it is hard to ~ the feelings of another⟩ **8 :** to make report of (a ship or her cargo) at the customhouse **:** submit a statement of (imported goods) with the original invoices to the proper officer of the customs for estimating the duties — see ENTRY 6 **9 a :** to put in regular form before a law court usu. in writing **:** put upon record in proper form and order ⟨~ a writ⟩ ⟨~ a judgment⟩ **b :** to file or inscribe upon the records of the land office the required particulars concerning (a quantity of public land) in order to secure the right of preemption **c :** to deposit for copyright the title or description of (as a book, picture, map) ⟨~*ed* according to act of congress⟩ **10 :** to go into or upon and take actual possession of (as lands) **11 :** to put on record (a statement of one's position) **:** present formally or informally **:** ADVANCE, INTERJECT ⟨~*ing* a solemn protest against this forcible intrusion⟩ ⟨~*ed* a caution against excessive haste⟩; *specif* **:** to submit (an offer of a price) in competition with others — used chiefly in the phrase *enter a bid* ⟨~ a bid at an auction⟩ **12 a :** to bring into play (a man that is on the bar) in backgammon **b :** to cause (one's own hand or dummy) to win a trick in bridge in order to lead to the next trick

syn PENETRATE, PIERCE, PROBE: ENTER is a general term without definite implications ⟨one *enters* the apartment through a hallway⟩ ⟨thieves *entered* the apartment and ransacked it⟩ but sometimes, esp. when the object is a thing, it may suggest a pushing through a resisting medium ⟨the bullet *entered* his chest⟩ PENETRATE is applicable to entrance or passage through motivated by an impelling force or facilitated by strength, acuteness, or resolution ⟨a fiber that the ordinary needle will not *penetrate*⟩ ⟨*penetrating* the defense in this sector⟩ ⟨the third attack of the Mexicans succeeded in gaining a breach in the walls. The Mexicans now *penetrated* into the interior of the fortress —*Amer. Guide Series: Texas*⟩ ⟨serving our potential enemies, spreading dissension and confusion; they have *penetrated* to high and sensitive places —Vannevar Bush⟩ ⟨a mind capable of making great and *penetrating* analyses of the nature of the human spirit —William Barrett⟩ PIERCE is likely to suggest the entering, running through, or cutting through of a sharp pointed instrument ⟨to *pierce* the skin with a lancet⟩ ⟨a sword blade that *pierced* me through and through —Vachel Lindsay⟩ ⟨able, with the glittering lance of his

paradoxes, to *pierce* many a weak point in the modernist armor —F.B.Millett⟩ PROBE may suggest exploratory or investigating penetration with or as if with a pointed instrument ⟨a dentist *probing* a cavity⟩ ⟨with surgical objectivity . . . *probes* every detail of his early life and education —Stuart MacClintock⟩ ⟨a squadron of Federal men . . . have been *probing* into his financial affairs —H.H.Martin⟩
— **enter into 1 :** to inquire into (a subject) **:** EXAMINE, CONSIDER ⟨regrettable that the book does not *enter into* the moral aspect of the issue⟩ **2 :** to make oneself a party to or in ⟨*entered into* a solemn treaty and covenant⟩ **3 :** to form a constituent part or element of **:** become a part of ⟨tin *enters into* the composition of pewter⟩ ⟨forbidden . . . to make use of words . . . which *enter into* the names of dead kings —J.G. Frazer⟩ ⟨a combination of brightness, stupidity, and mediocrity probably *enters into* the mental pattern of most children —R.J.Williams⟩ ⟨regarded her with an admiration *into* which awe *entered* —Donn Byrne⟩ **4 a :** to participate or share in ⟨didn't *enter into* the conversation, but lounged . . . haughtily in his chair —Scott Fitzgerald⟩ ⟨cheerfully *entered into* the tasks of the household⟩ **b :** to be in tune or sympathy with **:** identify oneself with **:** UNDERSTAND ⟨*entered into* the festive spirit of the occasion⟩ ⟨to *enter into* the mood of this subtle poem requires both sensitivity and study⟩ ⟨no one can *enter into* an alien culture short of many years' experience —Stuart Chase⟩ ⟨we need to *enter into* the scene imaginatively and sympathetically —J.D.Peter⟩ — **enter into force :** to come to have binding effect or validity ⟨the treaty *enters into force* next month⟩ — **enter the lists :** to accept a challenge **:** engage in contest ⟨*enter the lists* against the forces of corruption⟩

²enter \"\ *n* -s **:** the entrance of a character upon the scene in a play

enter- *or* **entero-** *comb form* [L & Gk; L *entero-*, fr. Gk *enter-, entero-*, fr. *enteron* — more at INTER-] **1 :** intestine ⟨enteritis⟩ ⟨enterocrinin⟩ **2 :** intestinal and ⟨enterohepatic⟩

en·ter·able \ˈentərəbəl\ *adj* **:** capable of being entered ⟨the building is ~ on the street side⟩ **:** suitable or eligible for entry ⟨~ in tomorrow's race⟩ ⟨~ on the books as an allowable charge⟩

en·ter·al \ˈentərəl\ *adj* [*enter-* + *-al*] **:** ENTERIC — **en·ter·al·ly** \-rəlē\ *adv*

en·ter·al·gia \ˌentəˈralj(ē)ə\ *n* -s [NL, fr. *enter-* + *-algia*] **:** pain in the intestines **:** COLIC

en·ter·ec·to·my \ˌentəˈrektəmē\ *n* -ES [ISV *enter-* + *-ectomy*] **:** the surgical removal of a portion of the intestine

entered *past of* ENTER

entered apprentice *n* **1 :** the first degree of Freemasonry **2 :** one who has taken the degree of entered apprentice — compare BLUE LODGE

en·ter·er \ˈentərə(r)\ *n* -s **1 :** one that enters or makes entries **2 :** DRAWER-IN

en·ter·ic \(ˈ)enˈterik, inˈt-\ *adj* [Gk *enterikos*, fr. *enter-* + *-ikos* -ic] **1 :** of or relating to the enteron **:** INTESTINAL **2 :** of, relating to, or being a medicinal preparation treated so that it will pass through the stomach unaltered to be disintegrated in the intestines ⟨an ~ pill⟩

enteric fever *n* **:** typhoid fever or a closely related febrile condition

entering *n* -s [ME *entring* act of entering, fr. gerund of *entren* to enter — more at ENTER] **:** DRAWING-IN

entering port *n* **:** a port cut down to the level of the gun deck (as in old battleships) for convenience in landing or in entering the ship

en·ter·it·i·dis \ˌentəˈridədəs, -ritə-\ *n* -ES [NL, fr. specif. epithet of *Salmonella enteritidis*, fr. *enteritis*] **:** enteritis esp. in young animals that is related to food poisoning in man, is accompanied by diarrhea or scouring, and is caused by the Gaertner bacillus or one of its varieties

en·ter·i·tis \ˌentəˈrīdəs, -ītəs\ *n, pl* **enterit·i·des** \-ˈridəˌdēz, -ˈritə-\ *or* **enteritises** [NL, fr. *enter-* + *-itis*] **1 :** inflammation of the intestines, esp. of the human ileum **:** ILEITIS **2 :** any disease of domestic animals marked by enteritis and diarrhea (as panleukopenia of cats or necrotic enteritis of swine)

enterlude *obs var of* INTERLUDE

en·tero·bacteriaceae \ˌentə(ˌ)rō+\ *n pl* [NL, fr. *enter-* + *Bacteriaceae*] **1** *cap* **:** a large family (order Eubacteriales) of gram-negative straight bacterial rods that ferment glucose with the production of acid or acid and gas and that include the common coliform organisms and other saprophytes as well as a number of serious pathogens of man, lower animals, and plants — see EBERTHELLA, ERWINIA, ESCHERICHIA, SALMONELLA **2 :** members of the family Enterobacteriaceae

en·ter·o·bi·a·sis \ˌentə(ˌ)rōˈbīəsəs\ *n, pl* **enterobia·ses** \-əˌsēz\ [NL, fr. *Enterobius* + *-iasis*] **:** infestation with or disease caused by pinworms of the genus *Enterobius*, common in children and in cases where the infection is heavy marked by toxemic symptoms with wasting, fatigability, irritability, night sweats, feverishness, and often cough and poor appetite **:** human oxyuriasis

en·te·ro·bi·us \ˌentəˈrōbēəs\ *n, cap* [NL, fr. *enter-* + *-bius*] **:** a genus of small nematode worms (family Oxyuridae) including the common pinworm of the human intestine

en·ter·o·cele \ˈentərōˌsēl\ *n* -s [L, fr. Gk *enterokēlē*, fr. *enter-* + *kēlē* tumor, hernia — more at -CELE] **:** a hernia containing a portion of the intestines

en·ter·o·coc·cal \ˌentərōˈkäkəl\ *adj* [NL *enterococcus* + E *-al*] **:** of, relating to, or caused by enterococci

¹en·ter·o·coc·cus \ˌentərōˈkäkəs\ [NL, fr. *enter-* + *-coccus*] *syn of* STREPTOCOCCUS

²enterococcus \"\ *n, pl* **enterococ·ci** \-ˌäˌkī, -ˌäkē, -ˌäkˌsī, -ˌäksē\ **:** STREPTOCOCCUS 2; *esp* **:** a streptococcus (as *Streptococcus faecalis*) normally present in the intestine

en·ter·o·coe·la \ˌentərōˈsēlə\ *n pl, cap* [NL, fr. *enter-* + *-coela* (fr. Gk *koilos* hollow) — more at CAVE] *in some classifications* **:** a group comprising all the invertebrate animals (as echinoderms and coelenterates) in which the sole bodily cavity is the digestive cavity — compare COELOMATA, PSEUDOCOELOMATA; ENTEROCOELE

en·ter·o·coele *or* **en·ter·o·coel** \ˈentərōˌsēl\ *n* -s [*enter-* + *-coele, -coel*] **:** a coelom that originates by outgrowth from the archenteron (as in the echinoderms) — compare SCHIZOCOEL — **en·ter·o·coe·lic** \ˌ=ˌ=ˈsēlik\ *adj* — **en·ter·o·coe·lous** \-ləs\ *adj*

en·tero·colitis \ˌentə(ˌ)rō+\ *n* [NL, fr. *enter-* + *colitis*] **:** enteritis affecting both the small and large intestine

en·ter·o·cri·nin \ˌentərōˈkrīnən *also* -rōˈkrin- *or* -ˈräkrən-\ *n* -s [*enter-* + endo*crine* + *-in*] **:** an intestinal hormone found in several animals that stimulates the digestive glands of the small intestine

en·ter·o·derm \ˈentərōˌdərm\ *n* -s [*enter-* + *-derm*] **:** the endoderm of the alimentary canal

en·ter·o·gas·trone \ˌentərōˈgaˌstrōn\ *n* -s [*enter-* + *gastr-* + hor*mone*] **:** a hormone obtained from the upper intestinal mucosa that has an inhibitory action on gastric motility and secretion

en·ter·og·e·nous \ˌentəˈräjənəs\ *adj* [ISV *enter-* + *-genous*] **:** produced within the intestine

en·ter·o·gram \ˈentərōˌgram\ *n* -s [*enter-* + *-gram*] **:** a graphic representation (as by a tracing) of the motion of the intestine

en·tero·hepatic \ˌentə(ˌ)rō+\ *adj* [*enter-* + *hepatic*] **:** of or involving the intestine and liver

en·tero·hepatitis \"+\ *n* [NL, fr. *enter-* + *hepatitis*] **:** ¹BLACKHEAD 3

en·tero·kinase \"+\ *n* [ISV *enter-* + *kinase*] **:** an enzyme obtained esp. from the upper intestinal mucosa that activates trypsinogen by converting it to trypsin

en·ter·o·lith \ˈentərōˌlith\ *n* -s [ISV *enter-* + *-lith*] **:** a calculus occurring in the intestine

en·ter·o·lo·bi·um \ˌentərōˈlōbēəm\ *n, cap* [NL, fr. *enter-* + Gk *lobos* capsule, pod + NL *-ium*] **:** a small genus of tropical American timber trees (family Leguminosae) with finely dissected compound leaves, globose heads of small flowers with exserted stamens, and spirally coiled pods — see CONACASTE

en·ter·o·mor·pha \-ˈmȯrfə\ *n, cap* [NL, fr. *enter-* + *-morpha*] **:** a genus of green algae (family Ulvaceae) having a hollow tubular thallus with a wall one cell in thickness and often growing on the bottoms of ships

en·ter·on \ˈentəˌrän, -ˌrən\ *n* -s [NL, fr. Gk, intestine — more at INTER-] **:** ALIMENTARY CANAL, ALIMENTARY SYSTEM — used esp. of the incompletely differentiated structures of the embryo or fetus

en·tero·nephric \ˌentə(ˌ)rō+\ *adj* [*enter-* + *nephric*] *of an excretory system* **:** discharging into the intestine (as in certain annelid worms)

en·ter·op·neust \ˈentəˌräpˌn(y)üst\ *or* **en·ter·op·neus·tan** \ˌ=ˌ=ˈn(y)üstən\ *n* -s [*enteropneust* fr. NL ¹*Enteropneusta*; *enteropneustan* fr. NL *Enteropneusta* + E *-an*] **:** an animal of the order Enteropneusta

¹en·ter·op·neus·ta \ˌ=ˌ=ˈn(y)üstə\ *n pl, cap* [NL, fr. *enter-* + *-pneusta*] **:** an order or other division of hemichordate worms consisting of *Balanoglossus* and related genera

²enteropneusta \"\ [NL, fr. *enter-* + *-pneusta*] *syn of* HEMICHORDATA

en·ter·op·to·sis \ˌentəˌräpˈtōsəs\ *n, pl* **enteropto·ses** \-ōˌsēz\ [NL, fr. *enter-* + *ptosis*] **:** an abnormal sagging or downward displacement of the intestines — **en·ter·op·tot·ic** \ˌ=ˌ=ˈtädik\ *adj*

en·ter·or·rha·gia \ˌentərōˈrāj(ē)ə\ *n* -s [NL, fr. *enter-* + *-rrhagia*] **:** bleeding from the intestine **:** intestinal hemorrhage

en·ter·os·to·my \ˌentəˈrästəmē\ *n* -ES [ISV *enter-* + *-stomy*] **:** the surgical formation of an opening into the intestine through the abdominal wall

en·tero·toxemia \ˌentə(ˌ)rō+\ *n* [NL, fr. *enter-* + *toxemia*] **:** a disease attributed to absorption of a toxin from the intestine (as pulpy kidney disease of lambs)

en·tero·toxigenic \"+\ *adj* [*enterotoxin* + *-genic*] **:** producing enterotoxin ⟨an ~ strain of bacteria⟩

en·tero·toxin \ˌentərō+\ *n* [*enter-* + *toxin*] **:** a toxic substance produced by microorganisms (as certain staphylococci) that is responsible for the gastrointestinal symptoms of some forms of food poisoning

en·ter·o·zoa \ˌentərəˈzōə\ *n pl, usu cap* [NL, fr. *enter-* + *-zoa*] **:** ENTOZOA

en·ter·o·zo·an \ˌ=ˌ=ˈzōən\ *adj or n* [NL *enterozoa* + E *-an*] **:** ENTOZOAN

¹en·ter·prise *also* **en·ter·prize** *R* ˈentə(r)ˌprīz, *-R* -təp-\ *n* -s [ME, fr. MF *entreprise*, fr. fem. of *entrepris*, past part. of *entreprendre* to undertake, fr. *entre-* inter- (fr. L *inter-*) + *prendre* to take, fr. L *prehendere* to seize, grasp — more at GET] **1 a :** a plan or design for a venture or undertaking ⟨his friends judged his novel ~ to be impractical and urged him to forget it⟩ **b :** VENTURE, UNDERTAKING, PROJECT; *esp* **:** an undertaking that is difficult, complicated, or has a strong element of risk ⟨indicate the . . . important ~*s* in which he had been engaged, probably battles, expeditions, or treaties of peace —W.A.Mason⟩ ⟨his new ~, a restaurant on Fifth avenue, met with complete failure⟩ ⟨exploring the English character has long been a favorite ~ of literary men —H.S. Commager⟩ ⟨a military ~ of major scope⟩ **c :** a unit of economic organization or activity (as a factory, a farm, a mine); *esp* **:** a business organization **:** FIRM, COMPANY ⟨an old ~ specializing in scientific textbooks —*Current Biog.*⟩ ⟨proposed to encourage the growth of small independent ~*s*⟩ **d :** any systematic purposeful activity or type of activity ⟨agriculture is the principal economic ~ among these people⟩ ⟨history, more than any other literary ~, puts the writer in the debt of other people —J.K.Galbraith⟩ ⟨the . . . problem of the nature of philosophy and the philosophical ~ itself —J.E.Smith⟩ **2 :** readiness to attempt or engage in what requires daring or energy **:** a bold energetic questing spirit **:** independence of thought **:** INITIATIVE, ENERGY ⟨the public rarely shows ~ when in search of entertainment —Tyrone Guthrie⟩ ⟨complained of his lack of ~⟩

²enterprise \"\ *vb* -ED/-ING/-S *vt* **:** to venture upon **:** UNDERTAKE, LAUNCH ⟨new churches are being *enterprised* in every area in America —*Time*⟩ ~ *vi, archaic* **:** to undertake an enterprise

en·ter·prise·less \-ləs\ *adj* **:** lacking enterprise **:** UNAMBITIOUS

en·ter·pris·er \-zə(r)\ *n* -s **:** one who undertakes an enterprise; *specif* **:** ENTREPRENEUR

enterprising *adj* **:** characterized by a bold daring energetic spirit or by independence or originality of thought **:** prompt or ready to undertake or experiment **:** ENERGETIC ⟨distrusted ~ thinkers who . . . can never be satisfied with the status quo —*Britain Today*⟩ ⟨~ peasants who . . . added to their land by purchase or lease —Hans Nabholz⟩ **:** reflecting or attesting to a daring or energetic spirit ⟨there is no question but that he made a number of ~ journeys —*Geog. Jour.*⟩ — **en·ter·pris·ing·ly** *adv*

enters *pres 3d sing of* ENTER, *pl of* ENTER

¹en·ter·tain \ˌentə(r)ˈtān\ *vb* -ED/-ING/-S [ME *entertinen*, fr. MF *entretenir*, fr. *entre-* inter- + *tenir* to hold, fr. (assumed) VL *tenire*, alter. of L *tenēre* to hold — more at THIN] *vt* **1 a** *archaic* **:** to keep up **:** cause (as a custom) to be maintained ⟨~ a friendly correspondence with his brother⟩ ⟨wished to ~ peace with all his neighbors⟩ **b** *obs* **:** to treat in a specified manner **c** *obs* **:** to give reception to (a person) **:** RECEIVE **d** *obs* **:** to enter upon **:** take upon oneself **:** engage in **2 :** to show hospitality to **:** provide for the needs of (a guest) ⟨~ your in-laws over the weekend⟩ ⟨~ a friend at lunch⟩ — often used with *to* in England ⟨~*ed* to dinner by the entire Bench and Bar —E.M.Lustgarten⟩ **3 a** *obs* **:** to maintain or support in one's service ⟨you, sir, I ~ for one of my hundred —*Shak.*⟩ **b** *archaic* **:** HIRE, ENGAGE **c** *obs* **:** to meet in battle **4 a :** to keep, hold, or maintain in the mind with favor **:** keep in the mind **:** HARBOR, CHERISH ⟨~*s* the friendliest sentiments toward him⟩ ⟨~ hopes of a peaceful settlement⟩ ⟨~*s* no grievance against her⟩ **b** (1) **:** to receive and take into consideration (as an idea or proposal) ⟨if it had not been for that woman you would never have ~*ed* this teaching scheme at all —Thomas Hardy⟩ ⟨the chairman will ~ nominations⟩ ⟨refused to ~ her plea⟩ (2) **:** TREAT, CONSIDER ⟨~ a subject⟩ ⟨I am not here going to ~ so large a theme as the philosophy of Locke —Thomas De Quincey⟩ **5 :** to cause the time to pass pleasantly for (someone) **:** AMUSE, DIVERT ⟨fortunately he was able to ~ his nurses as well as provoke them —Virginia D. Dawson & Betty D. Wilson⟩ ⟨~*ed* troops overseas with songs and skits⟩ ~ *vi* **:** to provide entertainment esp. for guests ⟨even the smallest child is accustomed to ~ without self-consciousness —Nora Waln⟩ **syn** see AMUSE

²entertain *n* -s *obs* **:** ENTERTAINMENT

en·ter·tain·er \ˌentə(r)ˈtānə(r)\ *n* -s **:** one that entertains ⟨the rest of the stories are mostly well-written slick-magazine ~*s* —Taliaferro Boatwright⟩; *specif* **:** one who entertains professionally ⟨sent a troupe of ~*s* to the fighting front⟩

entertaining *adj* **:** providing entertainment **:** DIVERTING ⟨an ~ and instructive volume⟩ ⟨an ~ speaker⟩ ⟨spent an ~ evening⟩ — **en·ter·tain·ing·ly** *adv* — **en·ter·tain·ing·ness** *n* -ES

en·ter·tain·ment \ˌentə(r)ˈtānmənt\ *n* -s **1 :** the act of entertaining: as **a :** the act of receiving as a guest **:** hospitable reception ⟨delighted in ~ of friends and relatives⟩ **b :** the act of receiving or considering (as an idea or proposal) ⟨his serious ~ of angelology . . . reveals the complications of a too strictly biblical theology —L.W.Norris⟩ **c :** the act of diverting, amusing, or causing someone's time to pass agreeably **:** AMUSEMENT ⟨engaged a concert pianist for the ~ of her guests⟩ ⟨started a brisk argument for the ~ of the company⟩ **2 a** *archaic* **:** the manner or means of providing for the needs of someone (as a guest or lodger) **:** PROVISION ⟨ten pounds is the usual pension in these convents; but nothing can be more wretched than their ~ —Tobias Smollett⟩ **b** *obs* **:** the condition of being in someone's service **:** EMPLOYMENT **c** *obs* **:** provision for the support of persons in service **:** PAY **3 :** something that diverts, amuses, or occupies the attention agreeably ⟨this book is first-rate ~⟩ ⟨provide ~ for his guests, whimsical as well as culinary —O.S.J.Gogarty⟩ ⟨a serious novel as opposed to an ~ —*Times Lit. Supp.*⟩ ⟨the stream of life is the most permanently available of free ~*s* —Fred Majdalany⟩: as **a :** a social gathering or reception ⟨last night another of these pleasant social ~*s* was given . . . at her home —D.D.Martin⟩ **b :** a public performance designed to divert or amuse ⟨Negro orchestras are in demand at white ~*s* —*Amer. Guide Series: Fla.*⟩ ⟨still frequently produced at school or Sunday-school ~*s* —H.H.Reichard⟩

en·thal·py \ˈenˌthalpē, enˈth-, ənˈth-\ *n* -ES [Gk *enthalpein* to warm in (fr. *en-* ²en- + *thalpein* to heat, warm) + E *-y*] **:** a thermodynamic quantity that is the sum of the internal energy of a body and the product of its volume multiplied by the pressure: $H = U + pV$ — called also *heat content*

en·thrall *also* **en·thral** \ənˈthrȯl, en-\ *vt* **enthralled; enthralled; enthralling; enthralls** *also* **enthrals** [ME *enthrallen*, fr. ¹*en-* + *thral* thrall (n.) — more at THRALL] **1 :** to hold in slavery **:** reduce to the condition of a slave ⟨the bars survive the captive they ~ —Lord Byron⟩ **2 :** to hold spellbound **:** CHARM, CAPTIVATE ⟨his ringing laugh and humorous anecdotes ~*ed* his companions —T.S.Lovering⟩

en·thrall·ing *adj* **:** capable of holding spellbound **:** intensely absorbing or interesting **:** ENGROSSING, THRILLING ⟨it was the most ~ race . . . I've seen all season —G.F.T.Ryall⟩ ⟨this . . . painful little tale of failure and futility is ~ —David Cecil⟩ ⟨music is the most ~ . . . phenomenon in the world —Susanne K. Langer⟩ — **en·thrall·ing·ly** *adv*

en·thrall·ment *also* **en·thral·ment** \-lmənt\ *n* -s **:** the act of enthralling **:** the state of being enthralled ⟨mourned the ~ of his country by a foreign foe⟩ ⟨gazed at her with delight and ~⟩

en·throne \ənˈthrōn, en-\ *vt* [¹*en-* + *throne* (n.)] **1 a :** to seat on a throne **:** exalt to the seat of royalty or high authority ⟨~ a king⟩; *specif* **:** to install a high ecclesiastic in office **b :** to seat in a place associated with some position of authority or influence ⟨*enthroned* at the end of the table as moderator of the evening —Louis Auchincloss⟩ **c :** to seat on a high object or in a high commanding place ⟨old salts . . . *enthroned* on mackerel barrels —Van Wyck Brooks⟩ ⟨prompters are *enthroned* in the loft —*Amer. Guide Series: Conn.*⟩ **2 :** to assign supreme virtue or value to **:** EXALT ⟨the frontiersman *enthroned* work as a god and worshiped it —W.P.Webb⟩

en·throne·ment \-mənt\ *n* -s **:** an act or instance of enthroning; *esp* **:** the ceremony of installing a high ecclesiastic in office ⟨the service for the ~ of the archbishop of Canterbury⟩

en·thron·i·za·tion \ənˌthrōnəˈzāshən, (ˌ)enˌthrō|, ˌenthrə|, |ˌnīˈz-\ *n* -s **:** ENTHRONEMENT

en·thron·ize \ənˈthrōˌnīz, enˈthrō-, ˈenthrə-\ *vt* -ED/-ING/-S [ME *entronizen, intronisen*, fr. MF *entroniser*, fr. LL *enthronizare*, fr. Gk *enthronizein*, fr. *en-* ²en- + *thronos* throne + *-izein* -ize — more at THRONE] **:** ENTHRONE

en·thuse \ənˈth(y)üz, en-\ *vb* -ED/-ING/-S [back-formation fr. *enthusiasm, enthusiast, enthusiastic*] *vt* **1 :** to make enthusiastic ⟨~ her with the potential pleasing power of the merchandise at her disposal —*Fashion Accessories*⟩ **2 :** to express (as an opinion) with enthusiasm ⟨"a sweet little town", he *enthused* —Lawrence Constable⟩ ~ *vi* **:** to grow enthusiastic **:** express enthusiastic sentiments ⟨they are always ready to ~ over arms, the romance of heraldry and the family —L.G.Pine⟩

en·thu·si·asm \-üzēˌazəm *sometimes* -zēəzəm\ *n* -s [Gk *enthousiasmos*, fr. *enthousiazein* to be inspired, fr. *entheos, enthous* inspired, fr. *en-* ²en- + *-theos, -thous* (fr. *theos* god) — more at THE-] **1** *archaic* **:** inspiration by a god or other superhuman power **:** divine possession or frenzy **2** *archaic* **:** a state of impassioned emotion **:** exaltation of feelings **:** TRANSPORT, ECSTASY; *esp* **:** excessive or extravagant display of religious emotion ⟨conservative churchmen frowned on the ~ and mystical tendency of his sermons⟩ **3 a :** strong excitement of feeling on behalf of a cause or a subject **:** ardent zeal or interest **:** FERVOR ⟨supported the party's candidate with ~⟩ ⟨the play aroused his ~⟩ **b :** something that inspires or is pursued or regarded with ardent zeal or fervor ⟨his ~ is sailing⟩ ⟨the great literary realists were his ~*s*⟩ **syn** see PASSION

en·thu·si·ast \-zēˌast, -zēəst, -zēˌaa(ə)st\ *n* -s [Gk *enthousiastēs*, fr. *enthousiazein*] **1 :** a person who is or believes himself to be inspired or possessed by a divine power or spirit ⟨a society of ~*s* dominated by the conviction that they were spirit-possessed —G.W.H.Lampe⟩ **2 :** a person who is visionary, extravagant, or excessively zealous in his religious views or emotions **:** FANATIC ⟨took to task mystics and ~*s* whose faith transcended the bounds of reasonableness —Andrew Brown⟩ **3 a :** a person who is ardently attached to a cause, object, or pursuit ⟨a former mountain-climbing ~ —*Current Biog.*⟩ ⟨an impassioned ~ for both literature and painting —*Times Lit. Supp.*⟩ **b :** a person of an ardent enthusiastic cast of mind **:** one who tends to give himself completely to whatever engages his interest ⟨we are a nation of ~*s* —Oden Meeker⟩

syn FANATIC, ZEALOT, BIGOT: ENTHUSIAST in early use may designate one claiming inspiration or showing such signs as rapture, madness, or marked emotionalism; now it is likely to indicate a person showing keen, ardent, or devoted interest ⟨was not in the least an *enthusiast*, which literally means "possessed by God". He was a casuist and a theorist —Francis Hackett⟩ ⟨he had been in his youth an *enthusiast* for liberty, and had hailed the dawn of the French Revolution —T.L. Peacock⟩ ⟨a chess *enthusiast*⟩ ⟨a sailing *enthusiast*⟩ FANATIC is often used hyperbolically for ENTHUSIAST ⟨a baseball *fanatic*⟩ It may suggest a mad or irrational devotion and concentration, with resolute determination and uncompromising fixity ⟨a virtuous *fanatic*, regarding all ways as wrong but his own, and thinking all men who would not walk as he prescribed wicked as well as mistaken —J.A.Froude⟩ ⟨a utopia about which he was utterly dogmatic—which he explained to me with *fanatic* zeal—as dogmatic, as undeviating as the most rabid Communist —Carleton Beals⟩ ZEALOT applies to one showing ardent devotion to and vehement activity for protecting or furthering a cause ⟨the reopening of village churches that had been closed by the action of local *zealots* —A.R.Williams⟩ BIGOT applies to one blindly and obstinately devoted to his own creed or belief with stern, stiff-necked, dogged disdain, contempt, and intolerance of others ⟨not that the modern *bigot* is any more tolerant or less cruel than her ancestors —G.B.Shaw⟩

¹en·thu·si·as·tic \ənˌth(y)üzēˈastik, (ˌ)en-, -ēˌaas-, -tēk\ *adj* [Gk *enthousiastikos*, fr. (assumed) Gk *enthousiastos* (verbal of Gk *enthousiazein*) + Gk *-ikos* -ic] **1 :** relating to enthusiasm (senses 1, 2) ⟨~ ministers and their hearers preferred extempore or inspired preaching —Douglas Bush⟩ **2 :** filled with, characterized by, or manifesting enthusiasm **:** ZEALOUS, ARDENT ⟨the chair was received with ~ praise⟩ ⟨an ~ supporter of the president⟩ ⟨an ~ golfer and fisherman⟩ **3 :** having an ardent, receptive, responsive temperament **:** tending to give oneself wholly to whatever engages one's interest or liking ⟨one of the most generous and ~ men I ever met —O.S.J.Gogarty⟩

²enthusiastic *n* -s *archaic* **:** ENTHUSIAST, ZEALOT

en·thu·si·as·ti·cal \-stəkəl, -stēk-\ *archaic var of* ENTHUSIASTIC

en·thu·si·as·ti·cal·ly \-stək(ə)lē, -stēk-, -li\ *adv* **:** in an enthusiastic manner

en·thy·me·mat·ic \ˌen(t)thə(ˌ)mēˈmadik\ *adj* [L *enthymemat-, enthymema* + E *-ic*] **:** relating to or constituting an enthymeme ⟨the ~ form of the conventional syllogism —J.T. Clark⟩

en·thy·meme \ˈen(t)thəˌmēm\ *n* -s [L *enthymema*, fr. Gk *enthymēma*, fr. *enthymeisthai* to keep in mind, consider, fr. *en-* ²en- + *thymos* mind] **1 :** an argument or truncated syllogism in which one of the propositions, usu. a premise, is understood but not stated (as *we are dependent; therefore we should be humble*) **2** *Aristotelianism* **:** a rhetorical syllogism which is probable and persuasive but may not be valid

entia *pl of* ENS

en·tice \ənˈtīs, en-\ *vt* -ED/-ING/-S [ME *enticen*, fr. OF *enticier*, fr. (assumed) VL *intitiare*, fr. L *in-* ²in- + *titio* firebrand] **1** *obs* **:** INCITE, INSTIGATE **2 a :** to draw on by arousing hope or desire **:** ALLURE, ATTRACT ⟨with her . . . high-mindedness she *enticed* him into a sphere of spirituality that was not his native realm —E.L.Stahl⟩ ⟨a vivid dark face that ~*s* attention —Claudia Cassidy⟩ **b :** to draw into evil ways **:** lead astray **:** TEMPT ⟨it was . . . your uncle . . . who *enticed* me, saying that you had good harvests stored up —Pearl Buck⟩ **syn** see LURE

en·tice·ment \-mənt\ *n* -s [ME, fr. OF, fr. *enticier* + *-ment*] **1** *obs* **:** INCITEMENT **2 :** the act of enticing **3 :** something that entices **:** a means or method of enticing

enticing *adj* **:** ALLURING, ATTRACTIVE, BEGUILING ⟨they cannot say no to an ~ advertisement or an excited review —Howard Taubman⟩ ⟨~ opportunities for Christian missionary activity —J.W.Pratt⟩ — **en·tic·ing·ly** *adv* — **en·tic·ing·ness** *n* -ES

en·ti·fi·ca·tion \ˌentəfəˈkāshən\ *n* -s **:** the process of entifying

en·ti·fy \ˈentəˌfī\ *vt* -ED/-ING/-ES [ML *ent-, ens* + E *-i-* + *-fy* — more at ENS] **:** REIFY, HYPOSTATIZE

1en·tire \ən·ˈtī(ə)r, (ˈ)en·ˌt-, -īə *sometimes* ˈin·ˌt-\ *adj* [ME *entere, entier, entire*, fr. MF *entier, entir*, fr. L *integer*, fr. *in-* ¹in- + *-teger* (fr. *tangere* to touch) — more at TANGENT] **1** : with no element or part excepted : WHOLE, COMPLETE ⟨made careful notes on the ~ proceeding⟩ ⟨remained alone the ~ day⟩ ⟨the ~ mechanism of the ship was intact⟩ **2 a** : complete in degree : UNDIMINISHED, UNIMPAIRED, TOTAL ⟨the ~ control of the enterprise rests with the mayor⟩ ⟨his ~ ignorance of the subject⟩ ⟨his ~ devotion to his family⟩ ⟨he was an ~ stranger to her⟩ ⟨~ freedom of choice⟩ **b** *obs* : sincerely and unreservedly devoted : FAMILIAR, INTIMATE **3 a** : consisting of one piece : CONTINUOUS, UNDIVIDED ⟨the diamond was ~ and free from flaws⟩ ⟨here the river is ~, but later it divides into two branches⟩ **b** : wholly of one kind : without mixture or alloy : PURE, HOMOGENEOUS ⟨the book is short, ~ in mood, and gives the impression of a single afternoon's reverie —*Times Lit. Supp.*⟩ ⟨their primitive speech has come down ~, without admixture of any kind⟩ **c** *archaic* : having unimpaired strength or vigor : SOUND, HEALTHY **d** (1) : with no part lacking : INTACT ⟨conveniently passed on his estates to his heir ~⟩ ⟨strove to keep the collection ~ and even to augment it⟩ (2) *heraldry* : without difference or cadency mark : UNDIFFERENCED (3) *heraldry* : extending to the edges of the field : THROUGHOUT **4** *obs* : morally unblemished : BLAMELESS ⟨so ~ are all your deeds and you —John Donne⟩ **5** *of a male animal* : not castrated **6** : having the margin continuous or not broken by divisions, teeth, or serrations ⟨an ~ leaf⟩ **syn** see WHOLE

2entire \ˈ"\ *adv* : in entirety : COMPLETELY ⟨was to shatter our little universe ~ —Deneys Reitz⟩

3entire \ˈ"\ *n* -s **1** *archaic* : the whole : ENTIRETY **2** : an uncastrated male domestic animal; *esp* : an uncastrated male horse **3** *brewing, Brit* : PORTER **4 a** : a whole cover bearing a nonadhesive postage stamp **b** : any cover — **on entire** : on cover

en·tire·ly *adv* [ME *enterely, entierly, entirely*, fr. *entere, entier, entire* + *-ly*] **1** *obs* : EARNESTLY, SINCERELY **2** : WHOLLY, COMPLETELY, FULLY ⟨agreed with me ~⟩ ⟨an ~ noble and disinterested person⟩ ⟨lives ~ in the past⟩ ⟨you are ~ welcome⟩ **3** : EXCLUSIVELY, SOLELY ⟨it is his fault ~⟩

en·tire·ness \ə·ˈnəs\ *n* -ES [ME *enternesse, entiernesse*, fr. *entere, entier* entire + *-nesse* -ness] **1** : the quality or state of being entire : COMPLETENESS ⟨an individual marked by the ~ and passion of his commitment to his cause⟩ **2** *obs* : spiritual wholeness or oneness : UNITY, INTIMACY

entire sanctification *n* : the religious doctrine of perfect holiness in this life that there is no sin

en·tire·ty \ən·ˈtīrəd·ē, en-, |t|, |i *also* -ī(ə)r| *or* -īəl\ *n* -ES [ME *enterte*, fr. MF *entiereté*, fr. L *integritat-, integritas*, fr. *integr-, integer* + *-itat-, -itas* -ity] **1** : the state of being entire or complete ⟨his grasp of the singular ~ of medieval civilization —Henry Adams⟩ ⟨his fortunate ~ which made woman as a complement unnecessary to him —Audrey Barker⟩ **2** : SUM TOTAL, WHOLE ⟨its compelling theme and skillful development are not the ~ of this extraordinary play⟩ — **in its entirety** : as a whole ⟨view the problem *in its entirety*⟩

entirety of contract : the indivisibility of a contract — used esp. of a judicial doctrine that if a holder of a fire-insurance policy has violated the terms of his policy so as to render it void as to any of the property thereunder insured it will be void as to all

entire wheat flour *n* : WHOLE WHEAT FLOUR

en·ti·ta·tive \ˈentəˌtād·iv, -ˌtəl\ *adj* [NL *entitativus*, fr. ML *entitat-, entitas* entity + L *-ivus* -ive — more at ENTITY] **1** : considered as mere entity abstracted from all circumstances or relations **2** : being an entity : having real existence — **en·ti·ta·tive·ly** *adv*

en·title \ən·ˈtīd·ᵊl, en-, -īt·ᵊl\ *vt* **entitled; entitled; entitling** \-īd·ᵊliŋ, -īt(ᵊ)liŋ\ **entitles** [ME *entitlen, entitulen*, fr. MF *entitler, entituler*, fr. LL *intitulare*, fr. L *in-* ²in- + *titulus* title] **1** : to give a title to : affix a name or designation to ⟨his discussion ... was contained in a sermon *entitled* Popular Government by Divine Right —S.W.Chapman⟩ **2** : to give a right or legal title to : qualify (one) for something : furnish with proper grounds for seeking or claiming something ⟨his age ~s him to a pension⟩ ⟨you are *entitled* to your opinion⟩ ⟨the work ~s him to a place among the great novelists⟩ **3** *obs* **a** : to regard or represent as holding title, right, or responsibility **b** : ASSIGN, IMPUTE, ASCRIBE

en·ti·tle·ment \-ᵊlmənt\ *n* -s **1 a** : the act of entitling **b** : NAME, DESIGNATION **2 a** : the condition of being entitled : RIGHT; *specif* : the right to benefits under state unemployment-compensation laws or federal old-age and survivors insurance **b** : an allowance of money due to someone ⟨~s of local school districts came to $30 million —E.J.McGrath⟩

en·ti·ty \ˈentəd·ē, -ətē, -i\ *n* -ES [ML *entitas*, fr. L *ent-, ens* (irreg. pres. part. of *esse* to be) + *-itat-, -itas* -ity — more at IS] **1 a** : BEING, EXISTENCE; *esp* : independent, separate, or self-contained existence ⟨seeking to preserve their ~ and individuality⟩ ⟨successfully maintain their tribal ~⟩ ⟨the policy of the government of the U.S. is to seek ... to preserve Chinese territorial and administrative ~ —G.F.Kennan⟩ **b** (1) : the existence of something as contrasted with its attributes or properties (2) : the essence, fundamental nature, or real being of something ⟨for some philosophers, actual *entities* are the ultimate facts of reality⟩ **2** : something that has objective or physical reality and distinctness of being and character : something that has independent or separate existence : something that has a unitary and self-contained character ⟨whether the common cold is an ~ has been debated —*Yr. Bk. of Med.*⟩ ⟨my thoughts were chiefly occupied with the idea of the train, that luxurious complete ~ —Arnold Bennett⟩ ⟨the individual churches are considered independent and autonomous *entities* —*Current Biog.*⟩ ⟨sees Germany as a unified state, an ~ rather than a regional confederation —*N.Y.Times*⟩ **3** : an abstraction, ideal conception, object of thought, or transcendental object : SUBSISTENT ⟨such *entities* as love, reason, and beauty⟩ ⟨such *entities* as numbers, particularized relations, and chimeras are classified as subsistent but not existent —R.J.Butler⟩

ento- — see ENT-

en·to·blast \ˈentəˌblast\ *n* -s [*ent-* + *-blast*] **1** : HYPOBLAST **2** : a blastomere producing endoderm — **en·to·blas·tic** \ˌ==ˈblastik\ *adj*

en·to·bronchium \ˌen(ˌ)tō+\ *n, pl* **entobronchia** [NL, fr. *ent-* + *bronchium*] : one of the ventral branches of the main bronchi in the lungs of a bird

en·to·coele *or* **en·to·coel** \ˈentəˌsēl\ *n* -s [*ent-* + *-coele, -coel*] : ENDOCOELE — **en·to·coe·lic** \ˌ==ˈsēlik\ *adj*

en·to·commensal \ˌen(ˌ)tō+\ *n* [*ent-* + *commensal*] : ENDOCOMMENSAL

en·to·condyle \ˈ"+\ *n* [*ent-* + *condyle*] : the medial condyle of a bone on the side next the body

en·to·cone \ˈentəˌkōn\ *n* [*ent-* + *cone*] : the posterointernal cusp of the talon of an upper molar tooth

en·to·co·nid \ˌ==ˈkōnəd\ *n* -s [*ent-* + *con-* + *-id*] : the posterointernal cusp of the talon of a lower molar tooth

en·to·cornea \ˌen(ˌ)tō+\ *n* [NL, fr. *ent-* + *cornea*] : DESCEMET'S MEMBRANE

en·to·cyth·ere \ˌentōˈsithə(ˌ)rē\ *n, cap* [NL, fr. *ent-* + *Cythere* genus of crustaceans, fr. *Cythere*, epithet of Aphrodite, fr. L, fr. Gk *Kytherē*, fr. *Kythēra* (Cythera), island in the Aegean] : a genus of parasitic ostracods found in the gill cavities of various No. American crayfishes

en·to·derm \ˈentəˌdərm\ *n* [*ent-* + *-derm*] : ENDODERM

en·to·der·mal \ˌ==ˈdərməl\ *or* **en·to·der·mic** \-mik\ *adj* : ENDODERMAL

en·to·gastric \ˌen(ˌ)tō+\ *adj* [ISV *ent-* + *gastric*] : relating to the interior of the stomach

en·tog·na·thous \(ˈ)enˈtägnəthəs\ *adj* [*ent-* + *-gnathous*] *of an insect* : having the mouthparts sunk below the surface of the head — compare ECTOGNATHOUS

en·to·hy·al \ˌentōˈhīəl\ *adj* [*ent-* + Gk *hyalos* transparent stone, glass] : BASIBRANCHIAL

en·toil \ən, en+\ *vt* [¹*en-* + *toil* (n.)] : ENSNARE, ENTRAP ⟨a last desperate attempt to ~ his love —Anne Green⟩ ⟨~ed by the ... least desirable human emotions —Llewelyn Powys⟩

En·to·le·ter \ˈentəˌlēd·ə(r)\ *trademark* — used for a machine for disinfestation in flour processing in which insect eggs remaining in sifted flour are destroyed on impact as the flour is thrown against the lugs and case of a rotor revolving at a high rate of speed

en·to·lo·ma \ˌentəˈlōmə\ *n, cap* [NL, fr. *ent-* + Gk *lōma* fringe] : a genus of pink-spored agarics lacking both volva and annulus, having the gills notched or separating from the fleshy stem, and including some (as *E. lividum*) that are distinctly poisonous

entom- *or* **entomo-** *comb form* [F, fr. Gk *entomon* — more at ENTOMOLOGY] : insect ⟨*entom*ophagous⟩ ⟨*entomo*stracan⟩

en·tomb \ən·ˈtüm, en-\ *vt* [ME *entoumben*, fr. MF *entomber*, fr. *en-* ¹en- + *tombe* tomb — more at TOMB] **1** : to deposit in a tomb : BURY, INTER, INHUME ⟨sixty men were ~*ed* by the mine explosion⟩ **2** : to serve as a tomb for ⟨a rocky hillside ~s the fallen hero⟩ ⟨the sea ~s the lost schooner and her crew⟩

en·tomb·ment \-ümmənt\ *n* -s **1** : the act or process of entombing : BURIAL ⟨~ services will be held on Friday⟩ **2** : the condition of being entombed ⟨the shell, though ... of chitin, is usually modified by its long ~ —W.E.Swinton⟩

en·to·mere \ˈentəˌmi(ə)r\ *n* -s [*ent-* + *-mere*] : ENDOMERE — **en·to·mer·ic** \ˌ==ˈmerik, -mir-\ *adj*

en·to·mesoderm \ˌen(ˌ)tō+\ *n* [*ent-* + *mesoderm*] : MESENDODERM

en·tom·ic \(ˈ)enˈtämik\ *adj* [*entom-* + *-ic*] : relating to insects

en·to·mi·on \en·ˈtōmēˌän, -ēən\ *n, pl* **ento·mia** \-ēə\ [NL, fr. Gk *entomē* notch (fr. fem. of *entomos*, verbal of *entemnein* to cut in, cut up) + *-ion* (dim. suffix) — more at ENTOMOLOGY] : the tip of the thickened angular part of the parietal bone that articulates with the mastoid portion of the temporal bone — see CRANIOMETRY illustration

entomo- — see ENTOM-

en·to·mo·cecidium \ˌentə(ˌ)mō+\ *n* [NL, fr. *entom-* + *cecidium*] : a gall caused by an insect

en·to·mo·fauna \ˈ"+\ *n* [NL, fr. *entom-* + *fauna*] : a fauna of insects : the insects of an environment or region

en·to·mog·e·nous \ˌentəˈmäjənəs\ *adj* [*entom-* + *-genous*] : growing on or in the bodies of insects ⟨~ fungi⟩

en·to·mo·log·i·cal \ˌentəməˈläjəkəl, -jēk-\ *also* **en·to·mo·log·ic** \-jik,-jēk\ *adj* [F *entomologique*, fr. *entomologie* + *-ique* -ic, -ical] : of or relating to entomology — **en·to·mo·log·i·cal·ly** \-jək(ə)lē, -jēk-, -li\ *adv*

en·to·mol·o·gist \ˌentəˈmäləjəst\ *n* -s [F *entomologiste*, fr. *entomologie* + *-iste* -ist] : one specializing in entomology : a student of insects

en·to·mol·o·gize \-ˌjīz\ *vi* -ED/-ING/-S : to study entomology : collect insects

en·to·mol·o·gy \-jē, -ji\ *n* -ES [F *entomologie*, fr. Gk *entomon* insect (fr. neut. of *entomos* cut up, cut in, fr. *entemnein* to cut in, cut up, fr. *en-* ²en- + *temnein* to cut) + F *-logie* -logy — more at TOME] **1** : zoology that deals with insects **2** : a treatise on insects

en·to·moph·a·gous \ˌentəˈmäfəgəs\ *adj* [*entom-* + *-phagous*] : feeding on insects

en·to·moph·i·lous \-fələs\ *adj* [*entom-* + *-philous*] : normally pollinated by insects — compare ANEMOPHILOUS — **en·to·moph·i·ly** \-lē\ *n* -ES

en·to·moph·tho·ra \ˌ==ˈmäfthərə\ *n, cap* [NL, fr. *entom-* + *-phthora*] : a genus (the type of the family Entomophthoraceae) comprising fungi that are parasitic on insects

en·to·moph·tho·ra·ce·ae \ˌ==ˌ==ˈrāsēˌē\ *n pl, cap* [NL, fr. *Entomophthora*, type genus + *-aceae*] : a family of mostly parasitic lower fungi (order Entomophthorales) that typically develop in the bodies of insects, have a reduced mycelium which tends to break up into hyphal bodies, reproduce asexually by usu. multinucleate conidia and in a few instances sexually with the formation of zygospores, and commonly also produce thick-walled chlamydospores under unfavorable conditions — see ENTOMOPHTHORA

en·to·moph·tho·ra·ceous \ˌ==ˌ==ˈrāshəs\ *adj* [NL *Entomophthoraceae* + E *-ous*] : of or relating to the genus *Entomophthora* or family Entomophthoraceae

en·to·moph·tho·ra·les \-ā(ˌ)lēz\ *n pl, cap* [NL, fr. *Entomophthora* + *-ales*] : an order of phycomycetous fungi (subclass Zygomycetes) coextensive with the family Entomophthoraceae

en·to·moph·tho·rous \-thərəs\ *adj* [NL *Entomophthora* + E *-ous*] : relating to or caused by a fungus of the order Entomophthorales

en·to·mo·spo·ri·um \ˌentə(ˌ)mōˈspōrēəm\ *n, cap* [NL, fr. *entom-* + *-sporium*] : a form genus of imperfect fungi (family Melanconiaceae) having 4-celled spores with slender appendages, thus somewhat resembling insects

en·to·mos·tra·ca \ˌentəˈmästrəkə\ *n pl, cap* [NL, fr. *entom-* + *-ostraca* (fr. Gk *ostrakon* earthen vessel, potsherd, shell) — more at OYSTER] *in some classifications* : a subclass of Crustacea comprising the Branchiopoda, Ostracoda, Copepoda, and Cirripedia, groups regarded by most modern systematists as too diverse for inclusion in a single subclass, the name then being used as a term of convenience without taxonomic implications — **en·to·mos·tra·can** \ˌ==ˈ==kən\ *adj or n* — **en·to·mos·tra·cous** \-kəs\ *adj*

en·to·parasite \ˌen(ˌ)tō+\ *n* [*ent-* + *parasite*] : ENDOPARASITE

ent·op·ic \(ˈ)enˈtäpik\ *adj* [ISV *entop-* (fr. Gk *entopos* in a place, fr. *en-* ²en- + *topos* place) + *-ic*] *anat* : occurring in the usual place — compare ECTOPIC

en·to·plasm \ˈentəˌplazəm\ *n* [ISV *ent-* + *-plasm*] : ENDOPLASM — **en·to·plas·tic** \ˌ==ˈplastik\ *adj*

en·to·plastral \ˌentō+\ *adj* [*entoplastron* + *-al*] : of or relating to an entoplastron

en·to·plastron \ˈ"+\ *n, pl* **entoplastra** [*ent-* + *plastron*] : a median bony plate of the anterior part of the plastron of turtles that is considered homologous with the interclavicle of other reptiles

1en·to·proct \ˈentəˌpräkt\ *adj* [NL *Entoprocta*] : of or relating to the Entoprocta

2entoproct \ˈ"\ *n* -s : an animal of the phylum Entoprocta

en·to·proc·ta \ˌentəˈpräktə\ *n pl, cap* [NL, fr. *ent-* + *-procta*] : a phylum of pseudocoelomate animals resembling the Bryozoa but lacking a true coelom and having the anus adjacent to the mouth — **en·to·proc·tous** \ˌ==ˈpräktəs\ *adj*

ent·op·tic \(ˈ)ent·+\ *adj* [ISV *ent-* + *optic*] : lying or originating within the eyeball — used esp. of visual sensations due to the shadows of retinal blood vessels or of opaque particles in the vitreous humor falling upon the retina

en·to·retina \ˌen(ˌ)tō+\ *n* [NL, fr. *ent-* + *retina*] : the internal or neural portion of the retina

en·to·sarc \ˈentəˌsärk\ *n* -s [*ent-* + *-sarc*] : ENDOSARC

en·to·sclerite \ˌen(ˌ)tō+\ *n* [*ent-* + *sclerite*] : ENDOSCLERITE

en·to·sphe·nal \ˌentōˈsfēnᵊl\ *adj* [*ent-* + *sphen-* + *-al*] : BASISPHENOID

en·to·sternal \ˌen(ˌ)tō+\ *adj* [NL *entosternum* + E *-al*] : relating to the entosternum

en·to·sternite \ˈ"+\ *n* [NL *entosternum* + E *-ite*] : a cartilaginous structure giving attachment to muscles in the cephalothorax of various arachnids and of limuli

en·to·sternum \ˈ"+\ *n, pl* **entosterna** [NL, fr. *ent-* + *sternum*] : an internal process or system of processes of the sternum of an insect or other arthropod

en·to·thorax \ˈ"+\ *n* [NL, fr. *ent-* + *thorax*] : ENDOTHORAX

ent·otic \(ˈ)ent·+\ *adj* [*ent-* + *-otic* (of the ear)] : of or relating to the interior of the ear

en·to·trophi \ˌentə+\ *n pl, cap* [NL, fr. *ent-* + *trophi*] : an order of primitively wingless, eyeless, unpigmented insects that are related to the Symphyla and Thysanura, that have the mouthparts largely concealed within the head and the abdomen ending in a pair of filamentous or forcepslike cerci, and that live in the soil

en·tou·rage \ˌäntəˈräzh, ˌänˌ(ˌ)tüˈ-, ˌän·(ˌ)tüˌ-, -räzh\ *n* -s [F, fr. MF, fr. *entourer* to surround (fr. *entour* around, fr. *en* in — fr. L *in* — + *tour* turn, circuit) + *-age* — more at IN, TURN] **1** : one's attendants or subordinates ⟨each matador's ~ is getting things ready —Claudia Cassidy⟩ ⟨the bridesmaid's ~⟩ ⟨talks over national and international problems ... with members of his ~ —*New Yorker*⟩ **2** : the surroundings of a building (as terraces, steps, or planting) ⟨landscape planting played an important part in the ~ of the attractive clubhouse⟩

en tour·nant \ˌäⁿ,türˈnäⁿ\ *adv* [F] *ballet* : while turning — used of the body or of movement of the leg inward or outward

en-tout-cas \ˌäⁿ,tüˈkä\ *n* -ES [F, lit., in any case] : a combination parasol and umbrella

En-Tout-Cas \ˈ"\ *trademark* — used for burnt clay employed as construction material in tennis courts

en·to·zoa \ˌentəˈzōə\ *n pl, often cap* [NL, fr. *ent-* + *-zoa*] : internal animal parasites; *esp* : the intestinal worms — often used as if a taxon though not a natural group — **en·to·zo·an** \ˌ==ˈzōən\ *adj or n*

en·to·zo·ic \-ōik\ *or* **en·to·zo·al** \-ōəl\ *adj* [*entozoic* fr. *ent-* + *-zoic*; *entozoal* fr. *ent-* + *zo-* + *-al*] : living within an animal : ENTOZOAN

en·to·zo·on \ˌ==ˈzōˌän\ *sing of* ENTOZOA

en·tr'acte \ˈäⁿ(n)·ˌtrakt, -räkt, -råkt, =ˈ=\ *n* -s [F, fr. *entre-* inter- (fr. L *inter-*) + *acte* act] **1** : the interval between two acts of a play **2** : a dance, piece of music, or interlude performed between two acts of a play

en·tra·da \ən·ˈträdə, en-\ *n* -s [Sp, lit., entry, entrance, fr. fem. of *entrado* (past part. of *entrar* to enter), fr. L *intratus*, past part. of *intrare* to enter — more at ENTER] : an expedition or journey into unexplored territory ⟨before beginning the long ~, the trappers killed three deer —R.G.Cleland⟩; *esp* : a Spanish exploring or conquering expedition in America ⟨through the many ~s and colonization attempts, to the final conquest after the great Maya revolt —*Science*⟩ ⟨nothing was left except the deeply engraved routes of their remarkable ~s —Frank Waters⟩

en·trail \ˈen·trəl, -rāl\ *n* -s [ME *entraille*, fr. MF, fr. ML *intralia*, alter. of L *interanea*, pl. of *interaneum* intestine, fr. neut. of *interaneus* interior (akin to L *inter* between) + *-aneus* (as in *extraneus* external) — more at INTER-] **1** *archaic* : an internal part of an animal body **2 entrails** *pl* : BOWELS, GUTS, VISCERA **3 entrails** *pl* : the interior or internal parts of something ⟨hairy ~s of the sofa —Berton Roueché⟩ ⟨whole mountains had their ~s torn out —Wyn Roberts⟩

1en·train \ən·ˈtrān, en-\ *vt* [MF *entrainer*, fr. *en-* ¹en- + *trainer* to draw, drag — more at TRAIN] **1 a** : to draw away with or after oneself ⟨the tribes they had ~*ed* with themselves on their long migrations to the West —K.H.Menges⟩ **b** : to bring on as a result : result in ⟨change embodied in ... inventions ... ~s change in the ways of applying human effort —G.B.Hurff⟩ ⟨~*ed* only my own ruin, my own bankruptcy —Henry Miller⟩ **2** : to carry along or over esp. mechanically (as fine drops of liquid in vapors during distillation or evaporation) **3** : to collect and transport (a substance) by the flow of a fluid moving at high velocity ⟨air is ~*ed* by a stream of water in a jet pump⟩ **4** : to incorporate (air in the form of bubbles) into concrete (as for making resistant to the action of frost or to the effects of chemicals used for the removal of ice and snow)

2entrain \ˈ"\ *vb* [¹*en-* + *train* (n.)] *vt* : to put aboard a railroad train ⟨took the mail to the station to be ~*ed*⟩ ~ *vi* : to board a railroad train ⟨immediately after the game the team ~*ed* for New York⟩

en·train·er \-ānə(r)\ *n* [¹*entrain* + *-er*] : one that entrains; *specif* : a liquid added as a third component to liquid mixtures for aiding their separation by fractional distillation (as by the formation of an azeotrope)

en·train·ment \-ānmənt\ *n* -s : the act or process of entraining; *specif* : the process of carrying along or over (as in distillation or evaporation)

en·trammel \ən·, en·+\ *vt* [¹*en-* + *trammel* (net)] : to entangle or hamper : FETTER ⟨allowed himself to become ~*ed* by convention and society —R.S.Hillyer⟩ ⟨the eternal melancholy of the ~*ed* Irish soul —Liam O'Flaherty⟩

1en·trance \ˈen·trən(t)s\ *n* -s [ME *entraunce*, fr. MF *entrance*, fr. *entrer* to enter + *-ance* — more at ENTER] **1 a** : the act or an instance of physical entering : INGRESS ⟨looked up at her ~ into the room⟩ ⟨the ~ of the army into the city⟩ ⟨made an ~ through the window⟩ ⟨the ~ of air and sunshine is desirable⟩ **b** : the means or place for physical entering (as a door, gate, or passage) ⟨all ~s to the city are guarded by armed men⟩ ⟨ships threaded their way down this narrow ~ into the bay⟩ **c** : a particular mode or manner of entering ⟨so many ... were trying to copy that ~ —Barnaby Conrad⟩ ⟨though he had given no thought to an ~, he could not have perfected a better one —Hamilton Basso⟩ **2 a** : the act or fact of entering (as upon an office or course of action) ⟨made his ~ into office one month after the election⟩ ⟨the ~ of new firms into a highly competitive field⟩ ⟨marked the nation's ~ into the role of a great power⟩ ⟨a country's ~ into war⟩ ⟨~ into college was a great event in his life⟩ **b** : a means of entering (as upon a condition or pursuit) ⟨schools of nursing are the principal ~ to the profession⟩ ⟨books were for the child the ~ to a new and kindlier world⟩ **3** : liberty, power, or permission to enter : ADMISSION ⟨applied for ~ at a number of schools⟩ ⟨he did not have the price ... but figured he could wangle an ~ —H.A.Sinclair⟩ **4** : the first part or commencement of a period of time ⟨at the ~ of the night silence fell upon the village⟩ ⟨at the ~ of the holiday season an unwonted bustle and activity began⟩ **5** *cap* [trans. of LGk *eisodos*] : a solemn procession through the body of the church to the bema in the liturgy of the Eastern Church — see GREAT ENTRANCE, LITTLE ENTRANCE **6 a** : the point at which a voice or instrument part begins in ensemble music esp. after a rest ⟨a difficult ~⟩ **b** : the manner in which such a beginning is made ⟨a ragged ~⟩ **7** : the bow or entire forepart of a ship below the waterline — compare RUN — see SHIP illustration **8 a** : the first appearance of an actor in a scene **b** : an opening at the side or rear of a stage scene by which to enter or exit

2en·trance \ən·ˈtran(t)s, en-, -raa(ə)n-,-rain-,-rån-\ *vt* -ED/-ING/-S [¹*en-* + *trance* (n.)] **1** : to put into a trance ⟨the loud, rapid breathing of the *entranced* medium —A.G.N.Flew⟩ **2** : to overpower or carry away with emotion (as with delight, wonder, or rapture) ⟨the beauty of the land *entranced* them —Joseph Baily⟩ ⟨able to hold an audience *entranced* for 20 minutes at a time —W.S.Maugham⟩

entrance cone *n* **1** : the protuberance of cytoplasm through which the fertilizing sperm enters an egg **2** : the portion of a wind tunnel from which the air flows to the test section

en·trance·ment *pronunc at* ²ENTRANCE + mənt\ *n* -s **1** : the act or process of entrancing **2** : the condition of being entranced

entrance path *n* : the course of the sperm or male pronucleus through the egg cytoplasm toward the female pronucleus

entrance pupil *n* : the stop in an optical instrument or the virtual image of the stop that determines the angular diameter of the bundle of rays traversing the instrument from a given point in the object space — compare EXIT PUPIL

entranceway \ˈ==ˌ=\ *n* : ENTRYWAY

entrancing *adj* [fr. pres. part. of ²*entrance*] : giving or capable of giving delight : DELIGHTFUL ⟨antique papers of the most ~ design —*New Yorker*⟩ ⟨~ shades of pink and yellow⟩ ⟨~ descriptions ... of a happy boyhood and youth —Dorothy C. Fisher⟩ — **en·tranc·ing·ly** *adv*

1en·trant \ˈen·trənt\ *n* -s [F, fr. pres. part. of *entrer* to enter — more at ENTER] : one that enters ⟨an illegal ~ into the country⟩ ⟨new ~s into a highly competitive field⟩ ⟨deficiencies of the ~s in the basic skills needed for college study —I.L. Kandel⟩; *esp* : one that enters a competition ⟨~s include leading athletes from many countries⟩

2entrant \ˈ"\ *adj* : being an entrant

en·trap \ən·ˈtrap, en-\ *vt* [MF *entraper*, fr. *en-* ¹en- + *trape* trap — more at TRAP] **1 a** : to catch in or as if in a trap ⟨the pit had *entrapped* big beetles —William Beebe⟩ ⟨*entrapped* by falling timbers⟩ ⟨*entrapped* by ice floes⟩ **b** : to capture and hold (a substance) ⟨a system for *entrapping* the furnace fumes as a safety measure —*Monsanto Mag.*⟩ ⟨wool's tendency to produce lofty fabrics which ~ air —G.E.Hopkins⟩ **2** : to lure or maneuver into a difficult, hopeless, or compromising situation : bring into one's power by stratagem : ENSNARE ⟨it was now too late to ~ and annihilate the Chinese armies —Owen & Eleanor Lattimore⟩ ⟨some women get married easily; but others ... are driven to every possible trick ... to ~ some man —G.B.Shaw⟩; *specif* : to lure into an erroneous, contradictory, or compromising statement ⟨the whole intent of the questioning was to ~ the defendant⟩ ⟨*entrapped* him into making a very damaging admission⟩ **syn** see CATCH

en·trap·ment \-mənt\ *n* -s **1** : the act or process of entrapping ⟨had the good luck to be witness to the ~ of a species ... not seen in these parts for some years⟩ ⟨the ~ of air contaminated with unwanted gases —*Ceramic Abstracts*⟩; *specif* : the luring by an officer of the law of a person into the commission of a crime in order that he may be prosecuted for the offense ⟨brutality, third degree, duress, and ~ are vigorously condemned —J.E.Hoover⟩ **2 :** the condition of being entrapped ⟨did I have the right to risk the ~ in the ice of our 276 men —Glen Jacobsen⟩ ⟨his ~ into marriage to a Southern girl whom he did not really love —James Hilton⟩

en·trap·ping·ly *adv* [*entrapping* (pres. part. of *entrap*) + *-ly*] **:** so as to entrap

entreasure *vt* [¹*en-* + *treasure* (n.)] *obs* **:** to store in a treasury

¹en·treat \ən·ˈtrēt, en-· *usu* -ēd·+V\ *vb* [ME *entreten*, fr. MF *entraitier* to treat of, fr. *en-* ¹en- + *traitier* to treat — more at TREAT] *vt* **1** *archaic* **:** to treat or conduct oneself toward **:** deal with **:** USE ⟨all those knights . . . she foully doth ~ —Edmund Spenser⟩ **2 :** to ask earnestly **:** petition or supplicate urgently **:** beg for ⟨~ him to hold his revengeful hand —L.M.Montgomery⟩ ⟨~*ed* permission to introduce his friend —Jane Austen⟩ ⟨I must . . . ~ both the patience and attention of the reader —Adam Smith⟩ **3** *obs* **a :** to beseech or supplicate successfully **:** prevail upon by pleading **:** PERSUADE **b :** to make a concern of **:** occupy or be occupied with **~** *vi* **1** *obs* **a :** to negotiate esp. for a treaty **b :** TREAT, DISCOURSE ⟨in those old times of which I do ~ —Edmund Spenser⟩ **2 :** to make an earnest petition or request **:** PLEAD ⟨accustomed to command, not to ~ —Willa Cather⟩ **syn** see BEG

²entreat *n*, *obs* **:** ENTREATY

en·treat·ing·ly *adv* [*entreating* (pres. part. of ¹*entreat*) + *-ly*] **:** in an entreating manner

entreatment *n* **1** *obs* **:** TREATMENT **2** *obs* **:** favor entreated ⟨set your ~*s* at a higher rate than a command to parley —Shak.⟩

en·treaty \ən·ˈtrēd·ē, en-·, -rētē, -i\ *n* [ME *entrety*, fr. *entreten* + *-y*] **1** *obs* **a :** TREATMENT **b :** ENTERTAINMENT **2 :** the act of entreating **:** earnest petition or solicitation **:** PLEA ⟨before she could reply to . . . *entreaties* . . . that she would sing again —Jane Austen⟩

en·tre·chat \ˌäⁿ·trə¦shä, ¦äⁿ·t-, -shä\ *n* -s [F, by folk etymology fr. It (*capriola*) *intrecciata*, lit., intertwined caper, fr. fem. of *intrecciato*, past part. of *intrecciare* to interlace, intertwine, fr. *in-* ²in- (fr. L) + *treccia* tress] **:** a leap during which a ballet dancer repeatedly crosses the legs, sometimes beating them together while crossed

en·tre·cote \äⁿ·trəkōt\ *n*, *pl* **entrecotes** \"\ [F *entrecôte*, fr. *entre-* inter- (fr. L *inter*) + *côte* rib, fr. L *costa* — more at UNDER, COAST] **:** a steak cut from between the ribs; *sometimes* **:** SIRLOIN

en·tre·deux \ˌäⁿ·trə¦də, -dā, -¦dər(·), *F* äⁿ·trədœ\ *n*, *pl* **entre·deux** \-ə(z),-ə(z),-ər·,-ərz,-œ\ [F, fr. *entre-* + *deux* two, fr. L *duos*, acc. of *duo* — more at TWO] **:** something placed between two things; *specif* **:** INSERTION 2b

en·trée *or* **en·tree** \ˈän,trā *also* ⸗ˈ⸗\ *n* -s [F *entrée*, fr. OF *entree* — more at ENTRY] **1 a :** the act or manner of entering **:** ENTRANCE ⟨makes her ~ into society this spring⟩ ⟨making a graceful ~ into the parlor⟩ **b :** freedom of access **:** permission or right to enter ⟨he had ~ into the best society —Ludwig Bemelmans⟩ ⟨commented on the ~ which his son had with the president —J.P.Kennedy b. 1888⟩ **c :** something that qualifies one for entrance **:** means of gaining access ⟨the mere . . . possession of money is no ~ —Bentz Plagemann⟩ ⟨a thief⸗girl . . . who served as an ~ to underworld circles in that city —D.W.Maurer⟩ **2 a :** a dish served between the main courses **b :** a made dish served before the roast in England **c :** the principal dish of the meal in the U. S. ⟨this chicken casserole is an excellent ~⟩ **3 a** *obs* **:** a short musical composition in slow march rhythm, usu. in two repeated parts, often accompanying the entry of a procession in an opera or ballet **b :** the opening movement of an opera or ballet following the overture **c :** an introductory musical movement of any kind **4 :** one of the ballet numbers in a divertissement

en·tre·fer \ˌän·trə¦fe(ə)r\ *n* -s [F, fr. *entre-* + *fer* iron, fr. L *ferrum* — more at FARRIER] **:** an air gap between the armature and the field magnets of a dynamo or motor

en·tre·més \ˌen·trəˈmās\ *n*, *pl* **entreme·ses** \-ˈmā,sās\ [Sp, fr. Catal *entremès*, fr. L *intermissus*, past part. of *intermittere* to intermit — more at INTERMIT] **1 :** an interlude sometimes inserted in Spanish mystery plays of the middle ages **2 :** a short comic piece usu. with music and dancing in the Spanish theater

en·tre·mets *in sing constr* ¦äⁿ·trə¦mā *or* ¦äⁿ·t-, *in pl constr* -mā(z)\ *n pl but sing or pl in constr* [F, fr. OF *entremés*, fr. L *intermissus*, past part.] **:** dishes (as vegetables or savories) served in addition to the main course of a meal ⟨precisely the same dinner, down to the ~ that she provided six months ago —*Time*⟩

en·trench *or* **in·trench** \ən·ˈtrench, en-·\ *vb* [¹*en-* or ²*in-* + *trench* (n.)] *vt* **1 a :** to place within or surround with a trench esp. for defensive purposes ⟨the enemy ~*ed* himself strongly along the river⟩ ⟨~ a town⟩ **b :** to place (oneself) in any position that has strong military defensive advantages ⟨the settlers ~*ed* themselves behind a high stout stockade⟩ ⟨an enemy platoon ~*ed* itself in a half-destroyed factory⟩ **c :** to establish so solidly or strongly as to make dislodgment or change extremely difficult **:** CONFIRM ⟨~*ing* a practice⟩ **:** implant firmly **:** STRENGTHEN ⟨the landed interest ~*ed* itself on the steps of the throne —Ernest Barker⟩ ⟨Caucasian contacts gave the Indians more comforts, but also ~*ed* them more firmly as hunters —A.L.Kroeber⟩ ⟨the presence of Louisiana pirates . . . probably ~*ed* the term *bayou* in the Texas gulf area —R.C.West⟩ ⟨this thought is . . . firmly ~*ed* in the minds of many —Louis Tuft⟩ ⟨an ~*ed* habit⟩ **2 :** to cut into **:** FURROW; *specif* **:** to erode downward so as to form a trench **~** *v* **1 :** to dig a trench for defensive purposes **:** place oneself in a trench ⟨the platoon ~*ed* and awaited the enemy attack⟩ **2 :** to encroach upon or take possession of something reserved for other use or belonging to another person **:** TRESPASS — used with *on* or *upon* ⟨it does not appear that he ~*ed* upon his own or his mother's private fortune —John Buchan⟩ **syn** see TRESPASS

entrenched meander *n* **:** INCISED MEANDER; *specif* **:** one with slopes of about the same steepness on each side of the stream — compare INGROWN MEANDER

en·trench·ment *also* **in·trench·ment** \-chmənt\ *n* -s **1 a :** the act of entrenching ⟨used this delay for the ~ of the town⟩ **b :** the condition of being entrenched **2 a :** a defensive work consisting of a trench and a parapet **b :** any defense or protection ⟨municipal government is usually regarded as one of the great ~*s* of democracy —R.M.Dawson⟩ **3** *obs* **:** ENCROACHMENT, INFRINGEMENT **4 a :** the process whereby streams become incised, ingrown, or entrenched **b :** the results of this process

en·tre nous \ˌän·trə¦nü, ¦äⁿ·t-\ *adv* [F] **:** between us **:** in confidence

en·tre·pôt \-rə¦pō\ *n* -s [F, fr. *entreposer* to put in a warehouse (fr. *entre-* + *poser* to put, place, rest), after F *déposer* to deposit: *dépôt* depot — more at POSE] **:** a place serving as an intermediary center for the collection and distribution of goods **:** a transshipment center or point ⟨upon the free flow of goods through this ~ hung the welfare of every farm in the west —Oscar Handlin⟩

en·tre·pre·neur \ˌän·trəp(r)ə¦nər, +V -nər·, ¦äⁿ·t-, -nə̄(r, -n(y)ů(ə)r, -ůə\ *n* -s [F, fr. OF, fr. *entreprendre* to undertake + *-eur* -or — more at ENTERPRISE] **1 :** the organizer of an economic venture; *esp* **:** one who organizes, owns, manages, and assumes the risks of a business ⟨he aimed at . . . increased opportunities for the small ~ —A.M.Schlesinger b. 1917⟩ **2 :** one that organizes, promotes, or manages an enterprise or activity of any kind **:** PRACTITIONER, PROMOTER ⟨a doctor or lawyer, who, as an independent ~, provides service to a client —Bernard Goldstein⟩ ⟨an ~ of the theater⟩ ⟨alert historical ~*s* —J.D.Hicks⟩ ⟨the Yankee ~ . . . who descended on the desolated South to make his fortune —*Holiday*⟩ **3 :** one who serves as an intermediary **:** MIDDLEMAN, GO-BETWEEN ⟨New York is . . . becoming world-city and ~ between Europe and the American hinterland —Donald Davidson⟩ ⟨they are . . . the ~*s*, the links between the businessmen . . . and the fanatics —Eric Ambler⟩

en·tre·pre·neur·i·al \-nər·ēəl, -n(y)ůr- *also* -nə̄r-\ *adj* **:** of or relating to an entrepreneur ⟨~ history⟩ ⟨~ risks and rewards⟩

en·tre·pre·neur·ship \-nər,ship, -nə̄,sh-, -n(y)ů(ə)r,sh-, -ůə,sh-\ *n* -s **:** the condition of being an entrepreneur **:** the role or function of the entrepreneur **:** entrepreneurial ability or activity ⟨recent American experiences have proved how imaginative private ~ can continue to be —L.M.Hacker⟩ ⟨voices a plea for the study of ~ in history —W.C.Scoville⟩ ⟨it is now generally accepted that ~ consists in the meeting of uncertainty —Donald Dewey⟩

en·tre·pre·neuse \-¦nə(r)z, -¦nə̄z, -¦nəiz, -¦n(y)üz\ *n* -s [F, fem. of *entrepreneur*] **:** a woman entrepreneur

en·tre·sol \ˈentə(r),säl, ˈen·trə,s-, ˈän·trə,s-, ˈäⁿ·trə,s-, -sȯl\ *n* -s [F, fr. *entre-* + *sole* story, floor, alter. of OF *suele*, fr. (assumed) VL *sola*, fr. L *solea* sandal, sole, sill — more at SILL] **:** MEZZANINE

en·tro·pi·on \en·ˈtrōpē,än, -ēən\ *n* -s [NL, fr. Gk *entropē* act of turning toward, turning in + *-ion* (dim. suffix)] **:** inversion or turning inward against the eyeball of the border of the eyelids

en·tro·py \ˈen·trəpē, -pi\ *n* -ES [ISV ²*en-* + *-tropy*] **1** *in thermodynamics* **:** a quantity that is the measure of the amount of energy in a system not available for doing work, numerical changes in the quantity being determinable from the ratio dQ/T where dQ is a small increment of heat added or removed and T is the absolute temperature ⟨the ~ of dry air is proportional to its potential temperature —A.H.Thiessen⟩ **2** *in statistical mechanics* **:** a factor or quantity that is a function of the physical state of a mechanical system and is equal to the logarithm of the probability for the occurrence of the particular molecular arrangement in that state **3** *in communication theory* **:** a measure of the efficiency of a system (as a code or a language) in transmitting information, being equal to the logarithm of the number of different messages that can be sent by selection from the same set of symbols and thus indicating the degree of initial uncertainty that can be resolved by any one message **4 :** the ultimate state reached in the degradation of the matter and energy of the universe **:** state of inert uniformity of component elements **:** absence of form, pattern, hierarchy, or differentiation ⟨cultural diversity and heterogeneity counteracts the tendency to cultural ~ —David Bidney⟩ ⟨~ is the general trend of the universe toward death and disorder —J.R.Newman⟩

en·truck \ən·ˈtrək, en-·\ *vb* [¹*en-* + *truck* (n.)] *vi*, *of troops* **:** to get into a truck **~** *vt* **:** to put (troops) into trucks

en·trust *or* **in·trust** \ən·ˈtrəst, en-·\ *vt* [¹*en-* or ²*in-* + *trust* (n.)] **1 :** to confer a trust upon **:** deliver something to (another) in trust ⟨~*ed* him with responsibility for completing the work⟩ ⟨~*ed* him with my money⟩ **2 :** to commit or surrender to another with a certain confidence regarding his care, use, or disposal of ⟨~*ed* money to him⟩ **syn** see COMMIT

en·trust·ment \-s(t)mənt\ *n* -s **1 :** the act of entrusting or the condition of being entrusted **2 :** something with which one is entrusted **:** TRUST ⟨encouraged and imparted Christian spiritual ~*s* —*Time*⟩

en·try \ˈen·trē, -ri\ *n* -ES [ME *entre*, fr. OF *entree*, fr. fem. of *entré*, past part. of *entrer* to enter — more at ENTER] **1 :** the act of entering **:** ENTRANCE, INGRESS ⟨~ into the conflict disposed of the immediate issue of foreign policy —Oscar Handlin⟩ ⟨helps smooth his ~ into group life —*N.Y. Times*⟩ ⟨the Roman conquest of Britain began by an ~ in the southeast —L.D.Stamp⟩ **2 :** the right or privilege of entering **:** ADMISSION, ENTREE ⟨managed to gain ~ to an exclusive club⟩ ⟨I wandered into Symphony Hall and after some difficulty (for the house was sold out, as usual) obtained ~ —Virgil Thomson⟩ **3 a :** the place or point at which entrance is made ⟨at the ~ to the bridge stand two imposing pillars⟩: as (1) **:** VESTIBULE, PASSAGE, HALLWAY ⟨they had played hide-and-seek dodging . . . in and out of the *entries* of apartment houses —Jean Stafford⟩ (2) **:** DOOR, GATE ⟨the procession entered the church by the south ~⟩ (3) **:** the mouth of a river ⟨the French controlled both the St. Lawrence and the Mississippi *entries* to the great interior plain —B.K.Sandwell⟩ **b :** a section of a building (as a college dormitory) that is divided into several sections each with its own entrance ⟨it was the only bathtub in her ~ —George Santayana⟩ **4** *dial Brit* **:** a short lane or alley **5 a :** the act of making or entering a record ⟨~ of a sale⟩ **b :** something that is entered: as (1) **:** a record or notation (as in a journal, diary, or account book) of a particular day's occurrences or of some transaction or proceeding ⟨made no ~ in his logbook for that day⟩ ⟨the *entries* for that year reveal the growing scale of the firm's operations⟩ ⟨one ~ records a vote of censure against the speaker of the house⟩ (2) **:** a descriptive record in a catalog or listing of a book, periodical, or other item in a library's collection (3) **:** HEADWORD; *also* **:** a headword with its appended definitional and informational matter — see VOCABULARY ENTRY (4) **:** one of various similar objects composing a total or series **:** ITEM, OFFERING ⟨the *entries* in this anthology are of uneven worth⟩ ⟨fortunately, this ~ has little in common with the other stories —James Stern⟩ ⟨the latest ~ of the theater season is a very slight comedy⟩ **6 a :** the exhibition or depositing (as by a ship's officer at the customhouse) of the papers required by law to procure license to land or import goods **b :** the giving an account esp. of a ship's cargo to the officer of the customs and obtaining his permission to land or import it — see ENTER *vt* 8 **c :** BILL OF ENTRY **7 a :** a person or thing entered in a contest (as a race) **b :** the aggregate of persons or things so entered ⟨a large ~ is attracted, with the best men and dogs from England —Roy Saunders⟩ **8 :** a main passageway for haulage and ventilation in a mine **9 a :** the actual taking possession of lands or tenements by entering or setting foot on them **b :** a putting upon record in proper form and order **c :** the act in addition to breaking essential to constitute burglary consisting of the introduction of the least part of the person or of any instrument for the purpose of committing a felony **10 a :** ENTRANCE 6 **b :** the entrance of a voice in a fugue esp. after a rest **c :** ENTRÉE 3 **11 :** ENTRANCE 8a **12 a :** the act or means of winning a trick so as to lead to the next trick in bridge **b** *or* **entry card :** the card with which such a trick is or can be won — compare REENTRY

en·try·man \-mən\ *n*, *pl* **entrymen 1 :** one who enters upon public land with intent to secure an allotment under homestead, mining, or other laws **2 :** a coal miner engaged in driving a haulageway, airway, or passageway

entry table *n* **:** a conveyor that feeds material or objects (as bottles to be capped or labeled) into a processing machine

entryway \ˈ⸗⸗,⸗\ *n* **:** a passage for entrance **:** ENTRY

entry word *n* **:** HEADWORD

-ents *pl of* -ENT

ent·wick·lungs·ro·man \ent·¦vik(ə)lůŋ(k)srō¦mään\ *n*, *pl* **entwicklungsroma·ne** \-nə\ *often cap* [G, fr. *entwicklung* development + *roman* novel] **:** an often autobiographical novel treating of the development of a character from childhood to maturity

en·twine *also* **in·twine** \ən·ˈtwīn, en-·\ *vb* [¹*en-* or ²*in-* + *twine*] *vt* **1 a :** to twine together ⟨flowers and vines solidly *entwined*⟩ **b :** to twine or twist around **:** ENCIRCLE, WREATHE ⟨*entwined* a pretty garland about her arms⟩ ⟨a pillar *entwined* by ivy⟩ **2 :** to interweave, attach, or involve inextricably in sentiment or thought ⟨she knows how to ~ herself in your affections —Henry Miller⟩ ⟨these elements of action are so many and so closely *entwined* —McGeorge Bundy⟩ **~** *vi* **:** to become twisted or twined **syn** see WIND

en·twine·ment \-mənt\ *n* -s **:** the act of entwining **:** the condition of being entwined

en·twist *also* **in·twist** \ən·ˈtwist, en-·\ *vt* [¹*en-* or ²*in-* + *twist*] **:** to twist or wreathe round **:** ENTWINE

en·ty·lo·ma \ˌentᵊlˈōmə\ *n*, *cap* [NL, fr. ²*en-* + Gk *tylōma* callus] **:** a genus of parasitic fungi (family Tilletiaceae) that produce abundant conidia on long conidiophores and that comprise the white smuts

en·ty·py \ˈentəpē\ *n* -ES [²*en-* + *-typy*] **:** a method of amnion formation in certain mammals in which the embryonic knob invaginates into the yolk sac and no amniotic folds are formed — compare AMNION

¹enucleate \(ˈ)ē+\ *vt* [L *enucleatus*, past part. of *enucleare* to remove a kernel from, to clarify, fr. *e-* + *nucleus* kernel — more at NUCLEUS] **1** *archaic* **:** to bring out the meaning or sense of **:** CLARIFY, EXPLAIN **2 :** to deprive of a nucleus **3** *med* **:** to remove without cutting into ⟨~ a tumor⟩ ⟨~ the eyeball⟩ **:** shell out from a capsule — **enucleation** \(¦)ē+\ *n* -s — **enucleator** \(ˈ)ē+\ *n* -s

²enucleate \(ˈ)ē+\ *adj* [L *enucleatus*, past part.] *biol* **:** ENUCLEATED

enu·mer·a·ble \ēˈn(y)üm(ə)rəbəl, əˈ-\ *adj* [*enumerate* + *-able*] **:** DENUMERABLE

enu·mer·ate \əˈn(y)ümə,rāt, ēˈ-, *usu* -ād·+V\ *vt* -ED/-ING/-s [L *enumeratus*, past part. of *enumerare*, fr. *e-* + *numerare* to count, fr. *numerus* number — more at NIMBLE] **1 :** to ascertain the number of **:** COUNT ⟨more gulls than I could ~ —E.A.Weeks⟩ ⟨the census . . . *enumerated* 247,450 persons of Hungarian birth —L.M.Sears⟩ ⟨the bank *enumerated* 57 overseas offices in addition to 71 New York branches —*Investor's Reader*⟩; *specif* **:** to make a census of the population of ⟨the population in 1820 when Mississippi was first *enumerated* as a state —*U. S. Census*⟩ **2 :** to relate one after another **:** LIST, SPECIFY ⟨it is not necessary to ~ all the bitter and factious disputes which marked this unhappy quarter century —B.K.Sandwell⟩ ⟨*enumerated* the advantages of his new position⟩ ⟨*enumerated* the necessary qualities of a good general —Eric Linklater⟩ ⟨the *enumerated* and implied powers of Congress⟩ ⟨the circumstances may be roughly *enumerated* as follows —G.G.Coulton⟩ **syn** see COUNT

enu·mer·a·tion \ə,⸗⸗ˈrāshən, (,)ē,-\ *n* -s [MF or L; MF, fr. L *enumeration-*, *enumeratio*, fr. *enumeratus* + *-ion-*, *-io* -ion] **1 a :** the act of listing one after the other **:** DETAILING ⟨the rebel leader's effective ~ of popular grievances⟩ **:** the act of mentioning as an item in a total or series ⟨not so entwined with the government as to warrant ~ as a separate element of the constitutional system —F.A.Ogg & Harold Zink⟩ **b :** an itemized list or detailed or seriatim account **:** CATALOG ⟨the modern way to learn English . . . is to absorb a phrase⸗by-phrase ~ of all that might be conceivably said in ordinary talk —J.M.Barzun⟩ ⟨a careful ~ of the circumstances that led to the tragedy⟩ ⟨the author provides complete ~*s* . . . of the opinions of Cartesian scholars on disputed questions of interpretation —W.F.Doney⟩ **2 a :** the act of counting **:** NUMBERING ⟨as the faculty of speech developed . . . the art of ~ or counting would begin —J.A.N.Friend⟩ **b :** a count of something (as a population) **:** CENSUS ⟨the decennial ~ is only one of the many censuses it conducts —*Current Biog.*⟩ **3** *logic* **:** examination of the instances falling under a universal ⟨total ~ in perfect induction⟩

enu·mer·a·tive \əˈn(y)ümə,rād·iv, ēˈ-, -m(ə)rə|, |t|, |ēv *also* |əv\ *adj* **:** enumerating or concerned with enumeration

enumerative induction *n* **:** inductive verification of a universal proposition by enumeration and examination of all the instances to which it applies — called also *perfect induction*

enu·mer·a·tor \əˈn(y)ümə,rād·ə(r), -ātə-\ *n* -s **:** one that enumerates; *esp* **:** a census taker

enun·cia·ble \ēˈnən(t)sēəbəl, -nənch(ē)əb- əˈ-\ *adj* [*enunciate* + *-able*] **:** capable of being enunciated

enun·ci·ate \-nən(t)sē,āt *sometimes* -nənchē-, *usu* -ād·+V\ *vb* -ED/-ING/-s [L *enunciatus*, *enuntiatus*, past part. of *enunciare*, *enuntiare* to report, declare, express, fr. *e-* + *nunciare*, *nuntiare* to announce, relate, inform, fr. *nuncius*, *nuntius* messenger, message] *vt* **1 a :** to make a definite or systematic statement of **:** FORMULATE ⟨Descartes was the first to ~ the modern principle of inertia —S.F.Mason⟩ ⟨emphasized . . . and *enunciated* a materialistic theory of the universe —*Encyc. Americana*⟩ **b :** ANNOUNCE, PROCLAIM, DECLARE ⟨he *enunciated* the aims of the paper —*Current Biog.*⟩ ⟨*enunciated* the principles to be followed by his administration⟩ **2 :** UTTER, ARTICULATE, PRONOUNCE ⟨*enunciating* their words with peculiar and offensive clarity —Geoffrey Household⟩ **~** *vi* **:** to utter articulate sounds ⟨should children be taught to ~ correctly —Bertrand Russell⟩

enun·ci·a·tion \(,)ē,⸗⸗ˈāshən, ə,⸗⸗-\ *n* -s [L *enunciation-*, *enunciatio*, *enuntiation-*, *enuntiatio*, fr. *enunciatus*, *enuntiatus* + *-ion-*, *-io* -ion] **1 a :** the act of formulating or stating (as a law or principle) in a definite systematic way ⟨the ~ of the exclusion principle resolved the apparent contradiction within the . . . theory —G.H.Wannier⟩ **b :** the act of producing or declaring publicly ⟨we have a national penchant for ~ of broad, idealistic goals —A.B.Lans⟩ **2 :** manner of uttering, articulating, or pronouncing esp. as regards ease of perceptibility ⟨a region of literacy and slurred ~ —James Thurber⟩ ⟨detected in his ~ some slight influence of the brandy —Glenway Wescott⟩ **3 :** something that is enunciated **:** STATEMENT, ANNOUNCEMENT, EXPRESSION ⟨a tentative ~ to a theme which was to become important —G.J.Becker⟩ ⟨contained an ~ . . . of all the traditional freedoms —J.P.Humphrey⟩

enun·cia·tive \-ˈ⸗⸗,ād·iv, |t|, |ēv *also* |əv *sometimes* -nənch(ē)ə|\ *adj* [L *enunciativus*, *enuntiativus*, fr. *enunciatus*, *enuntiatus* + *-ivus* -ive] **1 :** serving to enunciate **:** DECLARATIVE **2 :** relating to enunciation — **enun·cia·tive·ly** \|əvlē, -li\ *adv*

enun·ci·a·tor \-nən(t)sē,ād·ə(r), -ātə- *sometimes* -nənchē-\ *n* -s [LL *enunciator*, *enuntiator*, fr. L *enunciatus*, *enuntiatus* + *-or*] **:** one that enunciates

enure *var of* INURE

en·u·re·sis \ˌenyəˈrēsəs\ *n* -ES [NL, fr. Gk *enourein* to urinate in, to wet the bed (fr. *en-* ²en- + *ourein* to urinate, fr. *ouron* urine) + NL *-esis* — more at URINE] **:** an involuntary discharge of urine **:** incontinence of urine — called also *bed⸗wetting* — **en·u·ret·ic** \¦⸗⸗red·|ik, -et|, |ēk\ *adj or n*

env *abbr* **1** envelope **2** envoy

envassal *vt* [¹*en-* + *vassal* (n.)] *obs* **:** to reduce to vassalage

enveigle *chiefly Brit var of* INVEIGLE

en·veil *also* **in·veil** \ən, *en* +\ *vt* [¹*en-* or ²*in-* + *veil*, n.] **:** to cover with or as if with a veil

en·vel·op *also* **en·vel·ope** \ənˈveləp, en-\ *vt* **enveloped; enveloped; enveloping; envelops** *also* **envelopes** [ME *envolupen*, fr. MF *envoluper*, *envoleper*, *enveloper*, fr. OF, fr. *en-* ¹en- + *voluper*, *voleper*, *veloper* to wrap up] **1 a :** to enclose completely with a garment or other covering **:** wrap up ⟨a shroud ~*ed* her form —Mary W. Shelley⟩ ⟨drew off his coat and ~*ed* him in a white robe —Laura Krey⟩ ⟨other folks ~ the meat in the leaves —E.J.Banfield⟩ **b :** to enclose or surround with a nonsolid material or medium (as air or darkness) **:** obscure or conceal by covering or shrouding ⟨distant hills ~*ed* in a blue haze⟩ ⟨large black clouds ~*ed* the moon⟩ ⟨flames ~*ed* the building⟩ ⟨a snug . . . warmth ~*ed* him —O.E.Rölvaag⟩ **c :** to surround or enfold with something immaterial (as a mood or atmosphere) **:** POSSESS, DOMINATE ⟨the Presbyterian culture that ~*ed* me when I was a boy —St. Clair McKelway⟩ ⟨the drowsy silence that ~*ed* the yacht —Scott Fitzgerald⟩ ⟨she had been ~*ed* in profound peace —Ellen Glasgow⟩ ⟨then she would . . . ~ me in the great, soft, spicy tide of her affection —R.P.Warren⟩ ⟨a feeling of gloom and self-pity ~*ed* him⟩ ⟨he was ~*ed* by that strange sense of detachment —Walter O'Meara⟩ **2** \" *or* ˈenvə,lōp *or* ˈänvə,lōp\ **:** to put in an envelope ⟨she scrawled across the bottom of the letter the word NO and ~*ed* it for return mailing —E.P.O'Donnell⟩ **3 :** to attack or move to attack (one or both of an enemy's flanks) ⟨there were indications that they intended to ~ the northern wing of Army Group South —W.R.Desobry⟩ **syn** see ENCLOSE

en·ve·lope \ˈenvə,lōp, ˈän-\ *also* **en·vel·op** \ənˈveləp, enˈv-, ˈen,veləp, ˈenv(ə)ləp, ˈänv(ə)ləp\ *n* -s [F *enveloppe*, fr. MF *envelope*, fr. *enveloper*] **1 :** something that envelops **:** WRAPPER, CONTAINER, RECEPTACLE ⟨one of these graves . . . may contain the earthly ~ of some immortal mind —Kathleen Freeman⟩ ⟨the ~ of air around the earth⟩ **2 :** a flat flexible usu. paper container in many sizes and constructions made by die cutting and gluing with an overlapped back seam and with bottom and closure flaps both adhering to the back portion **3 a :** the wrapper or cover for a phonograph record or electrical transcription **b :** ENVELOPE STAMP **4 :** something (as a woman's handbag) shaped like a letter envelope ⟨wistfully fingered her . . . narrow beadwork ~ —Maeve Brennan⟩ **5 a :** the outer covering of an aerostat **b :** the bag which contains the gas in a balloon or airship **6** *biol* **:** any enclosing covering (as a membrane, shell, integument, or surrounding leaves) **7 a :** a curve that is tangent to each one of a family of curves **b :** a surface that is tangent to each one of a family of surfaces **8 :** the suggestion of atmosphere surrounding the subject of a painting or sculpture (as by modulation of tone or by shallow and simplified cutting of the form) **9 :** the

envelope 2

container or housing of glass, quartz, or metal that encloses the working elements of a vacuum tube **10 :** JACKET 3b(2)

envelope stamp *n* **:** an embossed postage stamp on an envelope

envelope table *n* **:** a small table having a triangular drop leaf or leaves

en·vel·op·ment \ən'veləpmənt, en'-\ *n* -s **1 :** the act of enveloping or the state of being enveloped **2 :** an attack directed against one or both flanks or the rear of the enemy's forces and usu. accompanied by an attack against his front **3 :** two consecutive binds in fencing carrying the opponent's blade in a complete circle

envelope table

en·venom \ən, en+\ *vt* -ED/-ING/-S [ME *envenimen*, fr. OF *envenimer*, fr. *en-* [1]en- + *venim* venom — more at VENOM] **1** *obs* **:** to poison esp. by a venomous bite **2 a :** to taint or impregnate with venom or any substance harmful to life **:** make poisonous ⟨thoroughly ~*ed* a whole pound of hamburger —Jean Stafford⟩ **b :** to infuse bitterness, malice, or hatred into **:** EMBITTER ⟨~*ing* the relations between the two countries⟩ ⟨a countenance ~*ed* with jealousy and rage⟩

en ven·tre sa mère \äⁿ,väⁿ·trəsä'me(ə)r\ [AF] *of an infant* **:** in utero and therefore for beneficial purposes legally born

en·verdure \ən, en+\ *vt* -ED/-ING/-S [[1]*en-* + *verdure* (n.)] **:** to clothe or cover with verdure ⟨a country *enverdured* with palms and bamboos —Rose Macaulay⟩

en·vermeil \"+\ *vt* -ED/-ING/-S [[1]*en-* + *vermeil* (adj.)] *archaic* **:** to color with or as if with vermilion

en·vi·able \'envēəbəl, -viə-\ *adj* [[2]*envy* + *-able*] **:** being such as to attract envy or desire to possess or resemble **:** highly desirable ⟨an ~ reputation for integrity⟩ ⟨found himself in an ~ position⟩ — **en·vi·able·ness** \-nəs\ *n* -ES

en·vi·ably \-blē, -li\ *adv* **:** in an enviable manner

envied *past of* ENVY

en·vi·er \-ēə(r), -iə-\ *n* -s [ME, fr. *envien* to envy + *-er*] **:** one that envies

envies *pl of* ENVY, *pres 3d sing of* ENVY

en·vi·ous \'envēəs, -viəs\ *adj* [ME, fr. OF *envieus, envious*, fr. L *invidiosus*, fr. *invidia* envy + *-osis* -ous — more at ENVY] **1 :** characterized by, exhibiting, or reflecting envy **:** feeling or motivated by envy **:** maliciously covetous or resentful of the possessions or good fortune of another ⟨tried to look disappointed and angry but . . . only succeeded in looking ~ —Hervey Allen⟩ ⟨the sterile and ~ principle of artificial equality —*Time*⟩ ⟨examining the tire with ~ appreciation —M.M.Musselman⟩ **2** *archaic* **a :** EMULOUS **b :** ENVIABLE ⟨theirs was an ~ gift, but lightly held —Thomas Cole⟩

syn JEALOUS: ENVIOUS is likely to suggest a grudging of another's possessions and accomplishments, a spiteful desiring of their loss, or, most frequently, a malicious or cankerous coveting of them ⟨his successes were so repeated that no wonder the *envious* and the vanquished spoke sometimes with bitterness regarding them —W.M.Thackeray⟩ JEALOUS may suggest distrustful, suspicious, angry, or malcontent intolerance of the notion of anyone else's coming to possess what is viewed as belonging to or befitting oneself ⟨France, *jealous* as it was of his greatness and covetous of his Gascon possessions, he could hold at bay —J.R.Green⟩ ⟨I know that religion, science, and art are all *jealous* of each other because each of them claims, in a sense, to cover the whole field, that is, to interpret all experience from its own point of view —W.R. Inge⟩ It may be used without derogation to indicate cherishing and vigilantly guarding or maintaining ⟨proud of their calling, conscious of their duty, and *jealous* of their honor —John Galsworthy⟩

en·vi·ous·ly *adv* [ME, fr. *envious* + *-ly*] **:** in an envious manner

en·vi·ous·ness *n* -ES [ME *enviousnes*, fr. *envious* + *-nes* -ness] **:** the quality or state of being envious

en·vi·ron \ən'vīrən, en-, -ī(ə)rn\ *vt* -ED/-ING/-S [ME *environen*, fr. MF *environner*, fr. *environ* around, about, fr. *en* in, (fr. L *in*) + *viron* circle, circuit, fr. *virer* to turn, fr. (assumed) VL *virare*, prob. alter. (influenced by L *vibrare* to shake or *vertere* to turn) of L *gyrare* to turn around — more at IN, VIBRATE, WORTH, GYRATE] **1 a :** ENCIRCLE, ENVELOP **:** form a ring around ⟨the seas ~*ing* the island⟩ ⟨a city ~*ed* by pleasant and extensive plains⟩ **b :** to stand close around **:** cluster or press near ⟨ladies in waiting ~*ed* the queen⟩ **2 :** to surround or enfold with a condition, atmosphere, or other intangible thing **:** surround permeatingly ⟨the heavy pressure of the cultural influences that ~ us⟩ ⟨made light of the dangers that ~*ed* him⟩ **syn** see SURROUND

en·vi·ron·ment \-īrənmənt, -ī(ə)rnmə-, *rapid* -īrəmə-\ *n* -s **1 :** something that environs **:** SURROUNDINGS ⟨relaxed . . . in a cosy ~ of apple-green furniture and art linoleum —*Punch*⟩ ⟨sat at the mahogany table surrounded by the ~*s* of his wealth —E.S.Gardner⟩ **2 :** the surrounding conditions, influences, or forces that influence or modify: as **a :** the whole complex of climatic, edaphic, and biotic factors that act upon an organism or an ecological community and ultimately determine its form and survival — compare HABITAT **b :** the aggregate of social and cultural conditions (as customs, laws, language, religion, and economic and political organization) that influence the life of an individual or community

en·vi·ron·men·tal \ən¦vīrən¦mentᵊl, (,)en-, -ī(ə)rn¦me-, *rapid* -īrə¦me-\ *adj* **:** of, relating to, or produced by environment — **en·vi·ron·men·tal·ly** \-ᵊlē, -ᵊli\ *adv*

en·vi·ron·men·tal·ism \(,)=¦=(=)'mentᵊl,izəm\ *n* -s **:** a theory that views environment rather than heredity as the important factor in the development of the individual or a group — compare HEREDITARIANISM — **en·vi·ron·men·tal·ist** \-ᵊləst\ *n or adj* — **en·vi·ron·men·tal·is·tic** \-,mentᵊl'istik\ *adj*

environmental resistance *n* **:** the sum of the environmental factors (as drought, mineral deficiencies, competition) that tend to restrict the biotic potential of an organism or kind of organism and impose a limit on numerical increase

en·vi·rons \ən'vīrənz, en'-, -'vī(ə)rnz *also* 'en,vī- *or* 'envərənz *or* 'envə,ränz\ *n pl* [F, pl. of *environ*, fr. MF, fr. *environ*, adv. & prep., around, about — more at ENVIRON] **1 :** the enclosing limits or boundaries **:** COMPASS ⟨some 2483 concerns . . . were located within the ~ of the various cities —N.R.Heiden⟩ ⟨subsequent administrative developments have further enlarged the ~ of these towns —A.D.Rees⟩ **2 a :** the suburbs or districts round about a city or other populated place ⟨an adequate system of parks . . . for the national capital and its ~ —*Current Biog.*⟩ **b :** any adjoining or surrounding region or space **:** VICINITY, NEIGHBORHOOD ⟨strange biblical duds being worn by the natives in the ~ of the pyramids —Erskine Johnson⟩ **c :** environing things **:** SURROUNDINGS ⟨foliage . . . serves to give a relief to the tree, to make it stand out from among its ~ —Richard Semon⟩

en·vis·age \ən'vizij, en-, -zēj, *chiefly in pres part* -zəj\ *vt* -ED/-ING/-S [F *envisager*, fr. *en-* [1]en- + *visage* — more at VISAGE] **1** *archaic* **:** to meet squarely **:** CONFRONT, FACE **2 a :** to conceive of **:** grasp mentally **:** view or regard in a particular way ⟨*envisaging* man as simply the locus of a polytheism —Aldous Huxley⟩ ⟨of all the points of view from which we may ~ their brilliant activity —G.L.Dickinson⟩ ⟨in the beginning a science is quantitative . . .; only later does it ~ its problems mathematically —Edward Sapir⟩ **b :** to have a mental picture of in advance of realization **:** look forward to **:** have in view **:** CONTEMPLATE, FORESEE ⟨the plan *envisaged* lavish use of mechanical equipment of all kinds —M.A. Abrams⟩ ⟨*envisaged* a single, centralized state embracing all the former colonies⟩ ⟨men of the . . . mental stature to ~ and carry out so great a work —Yvonne Adamson⟩ ⟨I ~ that in the event of a German collapse the need . . . to undertake this work will be all the more apparent —F.D.Roosevelt⟩ **syn** see THINK

en·vis·age·ment \-mənt\ *n* -s **:** the act or an instance of envisaging **:** CONCEPTION ⟨all the main ~*s* or images of us as a nation . . . had begun at least dimly to emerge —*Amer. Quarterly*⟩

en·vision \ən, en+\ *vt* [[1]*en-* + *vision* (n.)] **:** to have a mental image of esp. in advance of realization **:** picture to oneself **:** look forward to **:** ENVISAGE, FORESEE ⟨~*ed* the perfectibility of man through a long process of . . . evolution —*Amer. Scholar*⟩ ⟨she ~*ed* a career in teaching and research — Leonard Engel⟩ ⟨reading this essay, I automatically ~*ed* some accomplished slick writer —F.O.Baker⟩ ⟨he came to the end his prophetic schoolmaster had ~*ed* —C.B.Driscoll⟩ **syn** see THINK

en·voi \'en,vȯi, 'äⁿ-\ *n* -s [F, fr. OF *envei, envoy*] **1 :** the usu. explanatory or commendatory concluding remarks to a poem, essay, or book; *specif* **:** a short fixed final stanza of a poem (as a ballade) pointing the moral and usu. addressing the person to whom the poem is written **2 :** parting word ⟨each one's ~ to his successors ended on a note of frustration and defeat —Cleve Hallenbeck⟩ ⟨Dick's muttered ~ . . . fell . . . with the effect of a stunning blow —Mary McCarthy⟩

en·voûte·ment \äⁿvütmäⁿ\ *n, pl* **envoûtements** \-mäⁿ(z)\ [F, fr. MF *envoutement*, fr. *envouter* to cast a spell on, practice envoûtement on (fr. OF, fr. *en-* [1]en- + *vout* face, image, fr. L *vultus* face) + *-ment*] **:** the magical practice of using an image or likeness of a person to influence his actions or destiny usu. with malevolent intent

[1]**en·voy** \'en,vȯi, 'äⁿ-\ *n* -s [ME, fr. MF *envei, envoy* message, envoi, fr. *enveier, envoier* to send, fr. (assumed) VL *inviare*, fr. L *in-* [2]in- + *via* way — more at VIA] **:** ENVOI 1

[2]**envoy** \"\ *n* -s [alter. of earlier *envoyée, envoyé*, fr. F *envoyé*, fr. past part. of *envoyer* to send, fr. OF *enveier, envoier*] **1 a** *also* **envoy extraordinary :** a minister plenipotentiary accredited to a foreign government ranking between an ambassador and a minister resident **b :** any person deputed to represent one sovereign or government in its intercourse with another **2 :** MESSENGER, AGENT, REPRESENTATIVE ⟨the mutineers sent an ~ to deal with the captain⟩

[1]**en·vy** \'envē, -vi\ *n* -ES [ME *envie*, fr. OF, fr. L *invidia*, fr. *invidus* envious (fr. *invidēre* to look askance at, envy, fr. *in-* [2]in- + *vidēre* to see) + *-ia* -y — more at WIT] **1** *obs* **a :** MALICE, SPITE **b :** OPPROBRIUM, UNPOPULARITY **2 a :** painful or resentful awareness of an advantage enjoyed by another, accompanied by a desire to possess the same advantage ⟨his lavish style of living . . . provoked half-contemptuous ~ among his brothers —Willa Cather⟩ ⟨I have a wild ~ of the man in the taxi with her —Hollis Alpert⟩ **b envies** *pl* **:** instances of envious feeling ⟨the attack . . . was due not only to the jealousies and *envies* —Hilaire Belloc⟩ **c :** an object of envious notice or feeling ⟨my brother and I were the ~ of all our friends —Margaret Bean⟩

[2]**envy** \"\ *vb* -ED/-ING/-ES [ME *envien*, fr. MF *envier*, fr. *envie*] *vt* **1 :** to feel envy toward or on account of **:** be painfully or resentfully aware of the advantage of (another) with a desire to possess the same advantage **:** be envious of ⟨I often ~ the writer who works in a university —V.S.Pritchett⟩ ⟨she pretended to deplore her compatriots' escapades, which actually she *envied* desperately —Jean Stafford⟩ **2** *obs* **:** BEGRUDGE ~ *vi, obs* **:** to feel or show envy

en·vy·ing·ly *adv* [*envying* (pres. part. of [2]*envy*) + *-ly*] **:** so as to feel or show envy

enweave *var of* INWEAVE

enwheel *vt* [[1]*en-* + *wheel* (n.)] *obs* **:** ENCIRCLE

en·wind *also* **in·wind** \ən, en+\ *vt* **enwound; enwound; enwinding; enwinds** [[1]*en-* or [2]*in-* + *wind* (v.)] **:** to wind in or about **:** encircle with windings **:** ENFOLD ⟨his legs *enwound* with bandages following the accident⟩

en·womb \ən, en+\ *vt* -ED/-ING/-S [[1]*en-* + *womb* (n.)] **1** *obs* **:** to make pregnant **:** carry in the womb **2 :** to bury, hide, or contain in the depths or recesses of something ⟨you may ~ yourself in words —Emery Neff⟩

enwoven *var of* INWOVEN

en·wrap *also* **in·wrap** \ən, en+\ *vt* [ME *enwrappen, inwrappen* (trans. of L *involvere*), fr. [1]*en-* or [2]*in-* + *wrappen* to wrap — more at WRAP] **1 a :** to wrap or enfold in a garment or other covering ⟨a shabby overcoat *enwrapped* his body⟩ ⟨designed to ~ luxury items —*Modern Packaging*⟩ ⟨the little packet *enwrapped* in a faded yellow envelope —Stephen Crane⟩ **b :** to enfold in or closely surround with any physical or material substance or condition **:** ENVELOP ⟨only the coldness of the empty house *enwrapped* her —Edith Sitwell⟩ ⟨a house *enwrapped* in flowers⟩ **2 a :** to wrap in or surround with something immaterial (as a mood or atmosphere) ⟨sat there *enwrapped* in a sullen defiance⟩ ⟨silence *enwrapped* the sleeping town⟩ **b :** to enfold in a trance, slumber, or deep thought **:** engross or absorb mentally ⟨*enwrapped* in fond dreams of a bright future⟩

en·wreathe \ən, en+\ *vt* [[1]*en-* + *wreathe*] **:** WREATHE, ENVELOP

enwrought *var of* INWROUGHT

en·zed \(')en¦zed\ *adj, usu cap* [[1]*en* + *zed*; fr. the initials N.Z.] *Austral* **:** NEW ZEALAND

en·zed·der \-d(ə)r\ *n* -s *cap, Austral* **:** NEW ZEALANDER

[1]**en·zo·ot·ic** \¦enzə¦wäd·ik, -zō¦ä-\ *adj* [[2]*en-* + *zo-* + *-otic*] *of animal diseases* **:** peculiar to or constantly present in a locality — compare ENDEMIC, EPIZOOTIC — **en·zo·ot·i·cal·ly** \|ək(ə)lē\ *adv*

[2]**enzootic** \"\ *n* -s **:** an enzootic disease

enzootic ataxia *n* **:** swayback of lambs

enzootic marasmus *n* **:** cobalt deficiency of sheep and cattle in western Australia — compare [1]PINE 3

en·zygotic \¦en+\ *adj* [[2]*en-* + *zyg-* + *-otic*] *of twins* **:** IDENTICAL

en·zy·mat·ic \¦enzə¦mad·ik *also* -,zī¦- *or* **en·zy·mic** \(')en¦zīmik, -zim-\ *adj* [*enzyme* + *-atic* (as in *automatic*) or *-ic*] **:** of, relating to, or produced by an enzyme ⟨~ activity⟩ ⟨~ digestion⟩ — **en·zy·mat·i·cal·ly** \-məd·ək(ə)lē\ *or* **en·zy·mi·cal·ly** \-mək(ə)lē\ *adv*

en·zyme \'en,zīm\ *n* -s [G *enzym*, fr. MGk *enzymos* leavened, fr. Gk *en-* [2]en- + *zymē* leaven; perh. akin to L *jus* broth, soup — more at JUICE] **1 :** any of a very large class of complex proteinaceous substances (as amylases or pepsin) that are produced by living cells, that are essential to life by acting like catalysts in promoting at the cell temperature usu. reversible reactions (as hydrolysis and oxidation) without themselves undergoing marked destruction in the process but frequently requiring the presence of activators (as metal ions) or of coenzymes, and that can act also outside of living organisms and therefore are useful in many industrial processes (as fermentation, tanning of leather, and production of cheese) — see -ASE; APOENZYME, FERMENT 1, SUBSTRATE **2 :** an active system comprising an enzyme usu. together with a coenzyme **:** HOLOENZYME

en·zy·mol·o·gist \,enzə'mäləjəst, -,zī-\ *n* -s **:** a person trained in or engaged in enzymology

en·zy·mol·o·gy \-jē\ *n* -ES [ISV *enzyme* + *-o-* + *-logy*] **:** a branch of science that deals with enzymes and with their chemical nature, biochemical activity, and biological significance

eo- *comb form* [Gk *ēō-* dawn, fr. *ēōs* — more at EAST] **:** earliest **:** oldest ⟨*Eohippus*⟩ ⟨*eolithic*⟩; *specif* **:** first of two or three subdivisions of geologic time ⟨*Eocene*⟩ — compare MES-, MI-, NE-, PLEIO-

EO *abbr* **1** errors and omissions **2** executive officer **3** executive order **4** ex officio

eo·acanthocephala \¦ē(,)ō+\ *n pl, cap* [NL, fr. *eo-* + *Acanthocephala*] **:** an order of Acanthocephala comprising parasites of aquatic vertebrates having the proboscis hooks in quincuncial arrangement and the cement-producing glands syncytial

eo·an \(')ē¦ōən\ *adj* [L *eous* (fr. Gk *ēōios*, fr. *ēōs* dawn) + E *-an*] **:** of or relating to the dawn or the east

eo·an·thro·pus \,ē(,)ō'an(t)thrəpəs, -,an'thrōpəs\ *n, cap* [NL, fr. *eo-* + *-anthropus*] *in some classifications* **:** a genus of the family Hominidae comprising only the Piltdown man

eo·carboniferous \¦ē(,)ō+\ *adj or n, usu cap* [*eo-* + *carboniferous*] *geol* **:** MISSISSIPPIAN

[1]**eo·cene** \'ēə,sēn\ *adj, usu cap* [*eo-* + *-cene*] **:** of or relating to the second principal subdivision of the Tertiary — used commonly of the epoch following the Paleocene and preceding the Oligocene but sometimes of all the Cenozoic era preceding the Miocene — see GEOLOGIC TIME table

[2]**eocene** \"\ *n* -s *usu cap* **1 :** the Eocene epoch **2 :** the series deposited during the Eocene epoch

eo·dis·cid \,ēō'disəd\ *n* -s [NL *Eodiscida*] **:** a member of *Eodiscus* or a related genus

eo·dis·cus \-skəs\ *n, cap* [NL, fr. *eo-* + *-discus*] **:** a genus of minute Cambrian trilobites that with related forms constitute a distinct order of small-eyed trilobites resembling those of the order Agnostida

EOE *abbr* errors and omissions excepted

eo·hip·pus \,ēō'hipəs\ *n* [NL, fr. *eo-* + *-hippus*] **1** *cap* **:** a genus of small primitive 4-toed horses from the Lower Eocene of the western U.S. that is now often included in the European genus *Hyracotherium* — see EQUIDAE illustration **2** -ES **:** an animal or a fossil of the genus *Eohippus*

EOHP *abbr* except as otherwise herein provided

eo·la·tion \,ēə'lāshən\ *n* -s [*Aeolus* god of the winds (fr. L, fr. Gk *Aiolos*) + E *-ation*] **:** the action of wind on land surfaces

eo·la weed \'ēōlə,-\ *n, usu cap E* [prob. fr. the place name *Eola*] **:** KLAMATH WEED

eo·li·an *also* **ae·o·li·an** \ē'ōlēən, -lyən\ *adj* [*Aeolus* + E *-ian*] **:** borne, deposited, produced, or eroded by the wind ⟨~ sand⟩ ⟨~ rock sculpture⟩

eo·lian·ite \ē'ōlyə,nīt, -lēə-\ *n* -s **:** a sedimentary rock of eolian origin

eol·ic \ē'älik\ *adj* [*Aeolus* + E *-ic*] **:** EOLIAN

eo·li·enne \(,)ā,ōlē'en, (,)ē,ō-\ *n* -s [F *éolienne*, fr. fem. of *éolien* Aeolean (of Aeolus), fr. *Aeolus* + F *-ien* -ian] **:** a lustrous lightweight dress fabric woven with a silk warp and coarser filling threads of wool, rayon, or cotton that make a fine cross rib

eolipile *var of* AEOLIPILE

eo·lith \'ēə,lith\ *n* -s [*eo-* + *-lith*] **:** a very crudely or irregularly chipped flint assumed by some archaeologists to have been used by early man

eo·lith·ic \¦ēə¦lithik, -thēk\ *adj, usu cap* [*eo-* + *-lithic*] **:** of or relating to the earliest period of the Stone Age and the earliest assumed stage of human culture characterized by the use of eoliths

eolotropic *var of* AEOLOTROPIC

EOM *abbr* end of month

eon *var of* AEON

eonian *var of* AEONIAN

eon·ism \'ēə,nizəm\ *n* -s [Chevalier d'*Éon* (Charles Eon de Beaumont) †1810 Fr. political adventurer who for many years posed as a woman + E *-ism*] **:** TRANSVESTISM

eo no·mi·ne \¦ē(,)ō'nämə(,)nē, ¦ā(,)ō'nōmə,nā\ [L] **:** by or under that name

eo·paleozoic *or* **eo·palaeozoic** \¦ē(,)ō+\ *adj, usu cap* [*eo-* + *Paleozoic, Palaeozoic*] **:** being or relating to the early part of the Paleozoic

eo·sin \'ēəsən\ *or* **eo·sine** \", -,sēn\ *n* -s [ISV *eos-* (fr. Gk *ēōs* dawn) + *-in, -ine*; orig. formed as G *eosin*; fr. the color it gives to silk — more at EAST] **1 a :** a red crystalline fluorescent dye $C_{20}H_8Br_4O_5$ made by bromination of fluorescein and used chiefly in cosmetics and as a toner; tetrabromo-fluorescein — called also *bromo acid* **b** *often cap* **:** the red to brown crystalline sodium or potassium salt of this dye used chiefly in making pink or red organic pigments, in microscopy as a biological stain, and in pharmaceutical preparations — called also *Eosine G, Eosine Y, Eosine Yellowish*; see DYE table I (under *Acid Red 87*) **2** *often cap* **:** any of several dyes related chemically to eosin ⟨*Eosine* B or *Eosine* Bluish⟩ ⟨*Eosine* H8G⟩ — see DYE table I (under *Acid Orange 11*)

eo·sin·o·cyte \,ēə'sinə,sīt\ *n* -s [ISV *eosin* + *-o-* + *-cyte*] **:** EOSINOPHIL

eo·sin·o·pe·nia \,ēə,sinə'pēnēə, -pēnyə\ *n* -s [NL, fr. ISV *eosin* + NL *-o-* + *-penia*] **:** an abnormal decrease in the number of eosinophils in the blood — **eo·sin·o·pe·nic** \¦=¦=¦=·¦pēnik\ *adj*

eo·sin·o·phil \,ēə'sinə,fil\ *or* **eo·sin·o·phile** \-fīl\ *n* -s [*eosin-* + *-o-* + *-phil, -phile*] **:** a leukocyte or other granulocyte with cytoplasmic inclusions readily stained by eosin — called also *acidophile* — **eo·sin·o·phil·ic** \-¦sinə¦filik\ *adj*

eosinophile \" *or* **eosinophil** \"\ *adj* **:** staining readily with eosin — used chiefly of cells or cell constituents

eo·sin·o·phil·ia \,=¦=,=·'filēə\ *n* -s [NL, fr. ISV *eosinophile* + NL *-ia*] **:** an abnormal increase in the number of eosinophils in the blood characteristic of allergic states and various parasitic infestations — **eo·sin·o·phil·ic** \¦=¦=¦=¦filik\ *adj*

eosinophilic granuloma *n* **:** a disease of adolescents and young adults marked by the formation of granulomas in bone and the presence in them of histiocytes and eosinophile cells with secondary deposition of cholesterol

eo·sper·ma·top·ter·is \,ē(,)ō,spərmə'täptərəs\ *n, cap* [NL, fr. *eo-* + *spermat-* + *-pteris*] **:** a genus of fossil seed ferns of the Devonian Lavive structure and terminal sporangia similar to those of Psilophyton but lacking the leafiness of the Carboniferous and later ferns

eos·pho·rite \ē'äsfə,rīt\ *n* -s [Gk *heōsphoros* bringer of dawn, morning star (fr. *heōs, ēōs* dawn) + E *-ite*; fr. its pink color — more at EAST] **:** a hydrous aluminum manganese phosphate $(Mn,Fe)Al(PO_4)(OH)_2.H_2O$ occurring in prismatic crystals or massive that is generally rose-pink in color

eo·su·chia \,ēō'sükēə\ *n pl, cap* [NL, fr. *eo-* + Gk *souchos*, a kind of crocodile + NL *-ia*] **:** an order of Reptilia comprising primitive extinct 2-arched reptiles (subclass Lepidosauria) from the Upper Permian that are sometimes considered ancestral to modern lizards and snakes — **eo·su·chi·an** \¦=¦=¦=ən\ *adj or n*

eöt·vös balance \'ət|(,)vəsh-, 'et|, 'ōt,vəsh-, 'ōtvəsh-\ *n, usu cap E* [after Roland *Eötvös* †1871 Hung. physicist] **:** a sensitive torsion balance used for the measurement of variations in the density of the underlying rocks that records the horizontal gradient of gravity

eötvös unit *n, usu cap E* **:** a unit for expressing horizontal gradients of gravity (as in geophysical prospecting) equal to 10^{-9} gal per horizontal centimeter

-eous \ēəs, yəs; *or* əs *when the e influences the pronunciation of the preceding consonant as in "cretaceous"*\ *adj suffix* [L *-eus* composed of, of the nature of or resembling (a specified substance); akin to Gk *-eos* composed of, Skt *-aya*] **:** like **:** resembling **:** of the nature of ⟨aqueous⟩ ⟨vitreous⟩

eo·zo·ic \,ēə¦zōik\ *adj or n, usu cap* [*eo-* + *-zoic*] **1 :** PRE-CAMBRIAN **2 :** Proterozoic or Algonkian

eo·zo·on \,ēə'zō,än\ *n, pl* **eozoons** \-nz\ *or* **eo·zoa** \-ōə\ [NL, fr. *eo-* + *-zoon*] **:** a banded arrangement of various ophicalcites associated with the Grenville series of Canada and formerly regarded as the remains of an animal (*Eozoon canadense*) related to the existing Foraminifera — **eo·zo·on·al** \¦ēə¦zōənᵊl\ *adj*

ep- — see EPI-

ep *abbr* **1** [LL *episcopus*] bishop **2** epistle

EP *abbr or n* -s extended play

EP *abbr* **1** electroplate **2** endpaper **3** endpoint **4** [F *en passant*] in passing **5** estimated position **6** evening prayer **7** excess profits **8** extreme pressure

[1]**ep·a·crid** \'epəkrəd\ *adj* [NL *Epacridaceae*] **:** of or relating to the Epacridaceae

[2]**epacrid** \"\ *n* -s **:** a plant of the family Epacridaceae

ep·a·cri·da·ce·ae \,epəkrə'dāsē,ē\ *n pl, cap* [NL, fr. *Epacrid-, Epacris*, type genus + *-aceae*] **:** a large family of Australasian heathlike shrubs, small trees, and woody vines (order Ericales) having flowers with usu. five stamens adnate to the corolla tube and the ovary surrounded by a hypogynous disk or five free scales — **ep·a·cri·da·ceous** \¦=·=·=¦dāshəs\ *adj*

ep·a·cris \'epəkrəs\ *n* [NL, fr. Gk *epakros* pointed at the end; fr. the sharply pointed leaves] **1** *cap* **:** a genus (the type of the family Epacridaceae) of plants having a disk of five scales around the ovary and as fruit a small globular capsule with numerous minute seeds **2** -ES **:** any plant of the genus *Epacris*

epact \'ē,pakt, 'e,-\ *n* -s [MF *epacte*, fr. LL *epacta*, fr. Gk *epaktē*, fr. fem. of *epaktos*, verbal of *epagein* to bring in, lead on, intercalate, teach by induction, fr. *epi-* + *agein* to lead, drive — more at AGENT] **1 a :** the number of days' difference between a lunar year and a solar year — called also *annual epact* **b :** the number of days' difference between a lunar month and a calendar month — called also *menstrual epact* **2 :** the age in number of days of the moon at the beginning of the calendar year used in determining the date of Easter

epac·tal \(')ē¦paktᵊl, (')e¦p-, ə'p-\ *adj* [prob. fr. F *épactal*, fr. Gk *epaktos* + F *-al*] *of a bone* **:** occurring irregularly in the sutures of the skull — compare WORMIAN BONE

ep·a·go·ge \'epə,gōjē *sometimes* -gäjē *or* ¦=·=¦=\ *n* -s [LL, fr. Gk *epagōgē*, fr. *epagein*] **:** logical induction from all the particulars comprised under the inferred generalization **:** induction by simple enumeration — compare BACONIAN INDUCTION — **ep·a·gog·ic** \¦=·=¦gäjik\ *adj*

ep·a·gom·e·nal \¦epə¦gämənᵊl\ *adj* [Gk *epagomenos* (pres.

part. pass. of *epagein*) + E *-al*] : INTERCALARY — used esp. of certain days of the Egyptian solar calendar
epalpate \(ˈ)ē+\ *adj* [*e-* + *palpate*] : lacking palpi
ep·a·naph·o·ra \ˌepəˈnaf(ə)rə\ *n* [LL, fr. LGk, fr. Gk, reference, act of referring, fr. *epanapherein* to refer to, ascribe, fr. *epi-* + *anapherein* to carry up — more at ANAPHORA] : ANAPHORA 1a
ep·a·nor·thi·dae \ˌepəˈnȯ(r)thəˌdē\ [NL, fr. *epi-* + Gk *anorthos* upright, erect + NL *-idae*] *syn of* CAENOLESTIDAE
ep·a·nor·tho·sis \-ˌnȯ(r)ˈthōsə̇s\ *n* -ES [LL, fr. Gk *epanorthōsis* correction, revision, fr. *epanorthoun* to correct, revise (fr. *ep-* + *anorthoun* to restore, correct, fr. *ana-* + *orthoun* to straighten, fr. *orthos* straight, right — more at ORTH-] : a substitution of a more emphatic word or phrase for one just preceding (as in "Most brave, nay, most heroic act!")
epapillate \(ˈ)ē+\ *adj* [*e-* + L *papilla* nipple + E *-ate* — more at PAPULE] : being without papillae
ep·apophysis \ˌep+\ *n, pl* **epapophyses** [NL, fr. *epi-* + *apophysis*] : a median dorsal process of the centrum of a vertebra
epappose \(ˈ)ē+\ *adj* [*e-* + *pappose*] : not pappose
ep·arch \ˈeˌpärk\ *n* -S [Gk *eparchos*, fr. *epi-* + *archos* ruler — more at ARCHI-] : the chief official of a Greek eparchy **2** : a bishop in the Eastern Orthodox Church
ep·arch·ate \-kə̇t, -ˌkāt\ *n* -S : EPARCHY
ep·ar·chi·al \(ˈ)eˈpärkēəl\ *adj* : of or relating to an eparchy
ep·archy \ˈeˌpärkē\ *n* -ES [Gk *eparchia*, fr. *eparchos* + *-ia* -y] **1** : a subdivision of a nomarchy **2** : a diocese in the Eastern Orthodox Church
ep·arcuale \(ˌ)ep+\ *n, pl* **eparcualia** [NL, fr. *epi-* + *arcuale*] : any of the ossification centers from which the spines of the vertebrae develop — compare ARCUALE
ep·arterial \ˌep+\ *adj* [*epi-* + *arterial*] : situated above an artery; *specif* : of or relating to the first branch of the right bronchus — compare HYPARTERIAL
épau·lé \āpōlā\ *adj* [F, fr. past part. of *épauler* to place the shoulder forward, fr. *épaule*] *ballet* : having one shoulder forward
epaule·ment \āpōlmäⁿ\ *n, pl* **epaulements** \-äⁿ(z)\ [F *épaulement*, fr. *épaule* + *-ment*] **1** : a barricade of earth like a rough parapet used mainly as cover from flanking fire **2** *usu* **épaulement** \"\ [F, fr. *épauler* + *-ment*] *ballet* : a shoulder movement performed by turning the body from the waist upward and bringing one shoulder forward and the other back
ep·au·let *also* **ep·au·lette** \ˌepəˈlet, ˈepəl-, *usu* |d·+V\ *n* -S [F *épaulette*, dim. of *épaule* shoulder, fr. OF *espaule*, fr. LL *spatula*, *spathula* shoulder blade, spoon for stirring, dim. of L *spatha* wooden spoon, sword, fr. Gk *spathē* blade of a loom, oar, or sword — more at SPADE] **1** : something that ornaments or protects the shoulder: as **a** : an ornamental fringed usu. gold-colored shoulder pad on a uniform (as the full-dress uniform formerly worn by military officers) **b** : any one of the small articulated shoulder pieces on a suit of plate armor — compare PAULDRON **c** : an ornamental strip sewn across the shoulder of a dress **d** : a shoulder loop (as on a trench coat) **2** : a 5-sided step cut of a gem

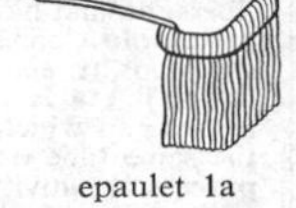
epaulet 1a

epaulet bat *n* : any of several African fruit bats having males distinguished by shoulder glands overlaid with tufts of white hair and constituting *Epomophorus* and related genera
epaulet fish *n* : a highly esteemed percoid food fish (*Glaucosoma scapulare*) of the southern Queensland coast of Australia
epaulette tree *n* : a tree (*Pterostyrax hispida*) of the family Styracaceae having alternate stalked leaves, hanging clusters of white fragrant flowers, and bristly 10-ribbed fruit
épau·lière \ˌāpōlˈye(ə)r\ *n* -S [F, fr. OF *espauliere*, fr. *espaule*] : the part of a suit of armor covering the shoulder : shoulder plate ⟨they were armed to the teeth . . . with heavy ~s on their shoulders and iron morions on their heads —T.B.Costain⟩
ep·ax·i·al \(ˈ)eˈpaksēəl\ *also* **ep·ax·on·ic** \ˌeˌpakˈsänik\ *adj* [*epaxial* fr. *epi-* + *axial*; *epaxonic* fr. *epi-* + Gk *axon-, axōn* axle, axis + E *-ic* — more at AXIS] : located above or on the dorsal side of an axis — **ep·ax·i·al·ly** \(ˈ)eˈpaksēəlē\ *adv*
EPC *abbr* editor's presentation copy
EPD *abbr* excess profits duty
épée \ˈeˌpā, ˈāˌpā, ˌ=ˈ=\ *n* -S [F, fr. L *spatha* wooden spoon, sword — more at EPAULET] **1** : a fencing or dueling sword having a bowl-shaped guard and a rigid 35-inch blade with no cutting edge that has a fluted triangular section tapering to a sharp point blunted with a metal stop for fencing and weighing more than a foil or saber **2** : the art or practice of fencing with the épée that includes the whole body as the target

épée

épée·ist \-ə̇st\ *n* -S [F *épéiste*, fr. *épée* + *-iste* -ist] : one that uses an épée
¹epei·ra \ə̇ˈpīrə\ [NL, fr. *epi-* + *-eira* (fr. Gk *eirein* to fasten in rows, string together) — more at SERIES] *syn of* ARANEA
²epeira \"\ *n* -S : a spider of the genus *Aranea* : GARDEN SPIDER
epei·ric \ə̇ˈpīrik, (ˈ)eˈp-\ *adj* [Gk *ēpeiros* mainland, continent + E *-ic*] *of a shallow sea* : that covers a large part of a continent while remaining connected with the ocean — compare EPICONTINENTAL
¹epei·rid \-rə̇d\ *adj* [NL *Epeiridae*] : of or relating to the Argiopidae
²epeirid \"\ *n* -S : a spider of the family Argiopidae
epei·ri·dae \ə̇ˈpīrəˌdē\ [NL, fr. *Epeira* + *-idae*] *syn of* ARGIOPIDAE
epei·ro·gen·e·sis \ə̇ˌpīrō+\ *n, pl* **epeirogeneses** [NL, fr. Gk *ēpeiro-* (fr. *ēpeiros* mainland, continent) + L *genesis*] : EPEIROGENY — **epei·ro·ge·net·ic** \ə̇ˌpīrō+\ *adj*
epei·ro·gen·ic *also* **epi·ro·gen·ic** \ə̇ˌpīrōˈjenik\ *adj* : of or relating to epeirogeny
ep·ei·rog·e·ny *also* **ep·i·rog·e·ny** \ˌeˌpīˈräjənē\ *n* -ES [Gk *ēpeiro-* + E *-geny*] : the deformation of the earth's crust by which the broader features of relief (as continents, ocean basins, and greater plateaus) are produced — compare DIASTROPHISM, OROGENY
epeirot *var of* EPIROTE
ep·ei·so·di·on \ˌeˌpīˈsōdēˌän\ *n, pl* **epeiso·dia** \-ēə\ [Gk — more at EPISODE] : EPISODE 1a
ep·embryonic \(ˌ)ep+\ *adj* [*epi-* + *embryonic*] : of or relating to biological stages immediately following the embryonic
ep·encephalon \ˌep+\ *n, pl* **epencephala** [NL, fr. *epi-* + *encephalon*] **1** : METENCEPHALON **2** : RHOMBENCEPHALON
ependym- *or* **ependymo-** *comb form* [NL, fr. *ependyma*] : ependyma ⟨*ependym*itis⟩ ⟨*ependymo*epithelium⟩
ep·en·dy·ma \əˈpendəmə\ *n* -S [Gk, upper garment, fr. *epi-* + *endyma* garment, fr. *endyein* to put on, fr. *en-* ²en- + *dyein* to sink, get into (clothes), put on] : an epithelial membrane lining the ventricles of the brain and the canal of the spinal cord — **ep·en·dy·mal** \(ˈ)eˈpendəməl\ *adj* — **ep·en·dy·mary** \-dəˌmerē\ *adj*
ep·en·dy·mo·ma \eˌpendəˈmōmə\ *n, pl* **ependymomas** \-məz\ *also* **ependymoma·ta** \-məd·ə\ [NL, fr. *ependym-* + *-oma*] : a glioma arising in or near the ependyma
ep·en·the·sis \ə̇ˈpen(t)thə̇sə̇s, eˈp-\ *n, pl* **epenthe·ses** \-əˌsēz\ [LL, fr. Gk, fr. *epentithenai* to insert a letter, fr. *epi-* + *entithenai* to put in, fr. *en-* ²en- + *tithenai* to put, place — more at DO] **1** : the occurrence of an intercalated consonant (as a homorganic stop after a nasal consonant) or vowel in a succession of speech sounds without a counterpart in etymon or in orthography (as \t\ in \ˈfents\ *fence;* \ə\ in \ˈathəˌlēt\ *athlete*) **2** : an insertion of a letter in a word to make spelling conform to epenthetic pronunciation (as *b* in *nimble*, earlier *nimel*) — compare ANAPTYXIS
ep·en·thet·ic \ˌepənˈthed·|ik, -et|, |ēk\ *adj* [Gk *epenthetikos*, fr. (assumed) Gk *epenthetos* (verbal of Gk *epentithenai*) + Gk *-ikos* -ic] : inserted by, relating to, or constituting epenthesis — compare INTRUSIVE
epergne \ə̇ˈpərn, ēˈ-,āˈ-, -pən,-pəin\ *n* -S [prob. fr. F *épargne* economy, saving, fr. *épargner* to save, fr. OF *espargnier*, *esparner*, of Gmc origin; akin to OHG *sparōn* to save — more at SPARE] : a composite centerpiece of silver or glass used esp. on a dinner table for serving or decoration: as **a** : a stand holding a large central dish or vase, several smaller dishes or vases, and sometimes candles **b** : a 2-tiered center dish or dish and vase

epergne a

eper·ua \ə̇ˈper(y)əwə\ *n, cap* [NL, of Cariban origin; akin to Galibi *eperu*, a species of *Eperua*] : a small genus of tropical So. American timber trees (family Leguminosae) having leathery leaflets, large white, red, or purple flowers in panicled racemes, and a rather woody 2-valved 2-seeded legume — see WALLABA
ep·eryth·ro·zo·on \ˌepəˌrithrəˈzōˌän\ *n* [NL, fr. *epi-* + *erythr-* + *-zoon*] **1** *cap* : a genus of blood parasites of vertebrates commonly considered to be rickettsiae related to the organism causing Oroya fever in man **2** *pl* **eperythrozoa** \-ōə\ : an organism of the genus *Eperythrozoon*
ep·eryth·ro·zo·on·o·sis \-ˌzōəˈnōsə̇s\ *n* [NL, fr. *Eperythrozoon* + *-osis*] : infection with or disease caused by parasites of the genus *Eperythrozoon* that is esp. severe in young pigs in which it takes the form of an anemia accompanied by jaundice and often terminates fatally
ep·exegesis \(ˌ)eˌp+-\ *n, pl* **epexegeses** [Gk *epexēgēsis*, fr. *epi-* + *exēgēsis* — more at EXEGESIS] : an explanation following a word or larger part of a text that limits its application or clarifies its meaning (as *the great river, the river Euphrates*) : additional information
ep·exegetical *also* **ep·exegetic** \"+\ *adj* [fr. *epexegesis*, after such pairs as E *exegesis: exegetical, exegetic*] : constituting epexegesis ⟨the temptation of . . . piling up *epexegetic* clauses —George Saintsbury⟩
eph- — see EPI-
ephah \ˈēfə, ˈefə\ *also* **ephi** \-ˌfī\ *or* **epha** \-_fə\ *n* -S [Heb *ēphāh*, fr. Egypt *ipt*] : an ancient Hebrew unit of dry measure equal to ¹⁄₁₀ homer or a little over a bushel — compare ³BATH
eph·apse \ˈeˌfaps\ *n* -S [Gk *ephapsis* act of touching, knot, fr. *epi-* + *apsis* loop, wheel — more at APSE] : a point of contact between neurons; *esp* : the lateral contact between parallel fibers in a nerve or fiber tract — **eph·ap·tic** \(ˈ)eˈfaptik\ *adj*
ep·har·mone \(ˈ)epˈhärˌmōn\ *n* -S [back-formation fr. *epharmony*] : an organism that has undergone adaptation to a particular habitat : ECAD
ep·harmonic \ˌep+\ *adj* : of, relating to, or constituting epharmony
ep·harmony \(ˈ)ep+\ *n* [ISV *epi-* + *harmony*; orig. formed in F] : the immediate acquirement by an organism of a morphological or physiological alteration that enables it to exist in an altered environment
ephe·be \ˈeˌfēb; ə̇ˈfēb, eˈ-\ *n* -S [L *ephebus*, fr. Gk *ephēbos*, fr. *epi-* + *hēbē* early manhood, youth] : a young man; *specif* : EPHEBUS
eph·e·be·um \ˌefəˈbēəm\ *n* -S [L, fr. Gk *ephēbeion*, fr. neut. of *ephēbeios* youthful, fr. *ephēbos*] : a place for gymnastic exercises in ancient Greek palaestrae or Roman thermae; *specif* : the exercise court for ephebi
ephe·bic \ə̇ˈfēbik, (ˈ)eˈf-\ *adj* [Gk *ephēbikos*, fr. *ephēbos* + *-ikos* -ic] **1** : of or relating to the ephebi ⟨~ oath⟩ ⟨~ inscriptions⟩ **2** *biol* : being between the neanic and gerontic stages : ADULT
ephe·bus \ə̇ˈfēbəs, eˈ-\ *n, pl* **ephe·bi** \-ˌbī\ [L] : a youth of ancient Greece; *esp* : an Athenian 18 or 19 years old receiving military and gymnastic training in preparation for full citizenship
ephec·tic \ə̇ˈfektik, (ˈ)eˈf-\ *adj* [Gk *ephektikos*, fr. *ephektos*, verbal of *epechein* to hold back, fr. *epi-* + *echein* to hold, have — more at SCHEME] : given to suspense of judgment — used of a school of ancient skeptics; compare EPOCHE
ephed·ra \ə̇ˈfedrə, ˈefədrə\ *n* [NL, fr. L, horsetail, fr. Gk, fr. *ephedros* sitting upon, fr. *epi-* + *hedra* seat — more at SIT] **1** *cap* : a large genus of jointed nearly leafless desert shrubs (family Gnetaceae) having the leaves reduced to opposite or verticillate scales at the nodes — see MAHUANG **2** -S : any plant of the genus *Ephedra*
ephed·rine \ə̇ˈfedrə̇n, eˈf-; ˈefəˌdrēn, ˈefədrən\ *n* -S [ISV *ephedra-* (fr. NL *Ephedra*, genus name of *Ephedra sinica*) + *-ine*] : a white crystalline alkaloid $C_6H_5CHOHCH(CH_3)NHCH_3$ extracted esp. from mahuang or made synthetically and used often in the form of a salt (as the sulfate) chiefly in relieving hay fever, asthma, and nasal congestion
ephe·lis \ə̇ˈfēlə̇s\ *n, pl* **ephe·li·des** \-ləˌdēz, -feləˌ-\ [NL, fr. Gk *ephēlis*] : FRECKLE
¹ephem·era \ə̇ˈfem(ə)rə\ *n* [NL, fr. Gk *ephēmerē*, fem. of *ephēmeros*] **1 a** *cap* : a genus (the type of the family Ephemeridae) of mayflies with shining transparent wings and strong functional legs **b** *pl* **ephemeras** \-rəz\ *or* **ephemer·ae** \-məˌrē\ : MAYFLY, EPHEMERID **2** *pl* **ephemeras** *or* **ephemerae** : ²EPHEMERAL
²ephemera *pl of* EPHEMERON
¹ephem·er·al \ə̇ˈfem(ə)rəl, ēˈf-, (ˈ)eˈf-, *chiefly Brit* -fēm-\ *adj* [Gk *ephēmeros*, lit., lasting a day, daily (fr. *epi-* + *hēmera* day) + E *-al* — more at HEMERA] **1 a** : lasting or existing briefly : TEMPORARY ⟨~ boundaries⟩ ⟨their floors and ceilings . . . thin and ~ in appearance as a card palace —Roderick Cameron⟩ : FLEETING ⟨jazz is perishable, ~, elusive —Whitney Balliett⟩; *specif* : lasting only one day ⟨~ fever⟩ ⟨~ blossom⟩ **b** : of interest or value for only a short time : TOPICAL ⟨were not local and ~ . . . but universal and timeless —J.P.Boyd⟩ **c** : existing in an immaterial form ⟨~ data, the businessman's unrecorded wealth of experiential knowledge of the behavior of consumers⟩ : INTANGIBLE **2** : devoted to what is of temporary interest ⟨a medium so ~ as radio⟩ ⟨prose drama is the most ~ of the arts . . . practically all plays find their resting places on the library shelves after their brief day or few decades in the theater —R.A.Cordell⟩ **syn** see TRANSIENT
²ephemeral \"\ *n* -S : something ephemeral; *specif* : a plant that grows, flowers, and dies in a few days (as many desert and arctic annuals)
ephemeral fever *n* : a three-day fever of cattle
ephem·er·al·i·ty \ə̇ˌfeməˈraləd·ē, ēˌf-, (ˌ)eˌf-, -ətē, -i, *chiefly Brit* -fēm-\ *n* -ES **1** : the quality or state of being ephemeral ⟨a sense of ~, of pale erratic fragility —D.H.Lawrence⟩ **2** : ²EPHEMERAL — usu. used in pl. ⟨"Barrack-Room Ballads" . . . clever *ephemeralities* —Henry Austin⟩
ephem·er·al·ly \ə̇ˈfem(ə)rəlē, ēˈf, (ˈ)eˈf-, -li, *chiefly Brit* -fēm-\ *adv* : in an ephemeral manner ⟨~ popular⟩
ephem·er·al·ness \-əlnə̇s\ *n* -ES : the quality or state of being ephemeral
ephemeral stream *n* : a stream that flows only briefly during and following a period of rainfall in the immediate locality
ephem·er·an \ə̇ˈfem(ə)rən\ *n* -S [Gk *ephēmeros* + E *-an*] : EPHEMERID 1
¹ephem·er·id \-rə̇d\ *adj* [NL *Ephemerida*] : of or relating to the Plectoptera
²ephemerid \"\ *n* -S **1** : one of the Plectoptera : MAYFLY **2** [Gk *ephēmeros* + E *-id*] : ²EPHEMERAL
eph·e·mer·i·da \ˌefəˈmerədə\ [NL, fr. *Ephemera* + *-ida*] *syn of* PLECTOPTERA
eph·e·mer·i·dae \-əˌdē\ *n pl, cap* [NL, fr. *Ephemera*, type genus + *-idae*] : a family of mayflies once made coextensive with the order Plectoptera but now restricted to forms having shining transparent wings as adults and as naiads very large mandibles curved out at the tips, gills extending dorsally over the abdomen, and antennae with long cilia
ephem·er·is \ə̇ˈfem(ə)rə̇s\ *n, pl* **eph·e·mer·i·des** \ˌefəˈmerəˌdēz\ [L, diary, journal, ephemeris, fr. Gk *ephēmeris*, fr. *ephēmeros* daily — more at EPHEMERAL] **1 a** : a publication giving the computed places of the celestial bodies for each day of the year or for other regular intervals and including other data for the astronomer and navigator : an astronomical almanac ⟨the annual ~ —Paul Herget⟩ **b** : any tabular statement of the assigned places of a celestial body for regular intervals — compare SEARCH EPHEMERIS **c** *archaic* : an almanac or calendar ⟨cures plagues, piles and pox by the *ephemerides* —Ben Jonson⟩ ⟨he wrote an ~ of the Irish saints —Thomas Fuller⟩ **2** *archaic* : DIARY, JOURNAL **3** : ²EPHEMERAL
ephemeris time *n* : a uniform measure of time defined by the orbital motions of the planets and determined by correcting mean solar time for the irregularities arising from variations in the rate of rotation of the earth
ephem·er·on \ə̇ˈfeməˌrän\ *n, pl* **ephem·era** \-m(ə)rə\ *also* **ephemerons** \-məˌränz\ [NL, fr. Gk *ephēmeron* May fly, fr. neut. of *ephēmeros* lasting a day, short-lived, daily] **1** : EPHEMERID **2** : ²EPHEMERAL
ephem·er·op·tera \ə̇ˌfeməˈräpt(ə)rə\ [NL, fr. Gk *ephēmeros* + NL *-ptera*] *syn of* PLECTOPTERA
ephem·er·op·ter·an \=ˌ==ˈ=t(ə)rən\ *adj* [NL *Ephemeroptera* + E *-an*] : PLECTOPTERAN
ephem·er·ous \ə̇ˈfem(ə)rəs, ēˈf-, (ˈ)eˈf-, *chiefly Brit* -fēm-\ *adj* [Gk *ephēmeros* — more at EPHEMERAL] : EPHEMERAL
¹ephe·sian \ə̇ˈfēzhən, ēˈ-,eˈ- *sometimes* -zhēən\ *adj, usu cap* [L *Ephesius* (fr. Gk *Ephesios*, fr. *Ephesos* Ephesus, ancient city of Asia Minor) + E *-an*] : of or belonging to Ephesus
²ephesian \"\ *n* -S **1** *cap* : a native or inhabitant of Ephesus **2** *usu cap* : a boon companion ⟨it is thine host, thine *Ephesian*, calls —Shak.⟩
eph·e·sine \ˈefəˌsin, -ˌsēn, -_sə̇n\ *adj, usu cap* [*Ephes*us + *-ine*] : EPHESIAN
ephes·tia \ə̇ˈfestēə\ *n, cap* [NL, fr. Gk, fem. of *ephestios* situated by the hearth, of the house or family, fr. *epi-* + *estia* hearth] : a genus of small dull-colored or mottled moths (family Pyralididae) having larvae that spin silken tunnels in and feed on a variety of stored food products — see ALMOND MOTH, RAISIN MOTH
eph·ete \ˈeˌfēt\ *n, pl* **ephe·tae** \ˈefəˌtē\ *or* **ephe·tai** \-ˌtī\ *usu cap* [Gk *ephetēs*, fr. *ephienai* to command, fr. *epi-* + *hienai* to send] : a member of an ancient Athenian court that tried certain murder cases — compare AREOPAGITE
ephi *var of* EPHAH
eph·i·al·tes \ˌefēˈalˌtēz\ *n, pl* **ephialtes** [Gk *ephialtēs*] *archaic* : NIGHTMARE 1, 2
ephip·pi·al \ə̇ˈfipēəl, (ˈ)eˈf-\ *adj* [NL *ephippium* + E *-al*] : of or relating to an ephippium
ephip·pi·dae \ə̇ˈfipəˌdē, eˈf-\ *n pl, cap* [NL, fr. *Ephippus*, type genus, fr. Gk *ephippos* on horseback, riding, fr. *epi-* + *hippos* horse) + *-idae* — more at EQUINE] : a family of chiefly tropical percoid fishes comprising the spadefishes
ephip·pi·um \-pēəm\ *n, pl* **ephip·pia** \-pēə\ [NL, fr. Gk *ephippion* saddlecloth, saddle, fr. neut. of *ephippios* for putting on a horse, fr. *epi-* + *hippios* of a horse, fr. *hippos* horse] **1** : SELLA TURCICA **2** : a saddlelike chitinous thickening over the brood pouch of various cladocerans that when shed forms a bivalve capsule containing the winter eggs
eph·od \ˈeˌfäd, ˈēˌfäd, ˈefəd\ *n* -S [Heb *ēphōd*] **1** : a linen apron worn by ancient Hebrews in religious ceremonies; *specif* : an ornate vestment of the Jewish high priest consisting of a garment like an apron suspended from the shoulders and fastened with a band ⟨make the ~ of gold, of blue and purple and scarlet stuff, and of fine twined linen, skillfully worked —Exod 28:6 (RSV)⟩ **2** : an Old Testament instrument of priestly divination (as an image of deity or a box)

ephod with breastplate attached

eph·or \ˈefər, ˈeˌfȯ(ə)r, ˈēˌfō-\ *n, pl* **ephors** \-rz\ *also* **epho·ri** \ˈefəˌrī\ [L *ephorus*, fr. Gk *ephoros*, fr. *ephoran* to oversee, fr. *epi-* + *horan* to see — more at WARY] **1** : a magistrate in various ancient Dorian states; *esp* : one of a body of five magistrates chosen by the Spartans to exercise a controlling power over the king **2** : a government official in modern Greece : OVERSEER
eph·or·al·ty \ˈefərəltē\ *n* -ES [*ephor* + *-alty* (as in *mayoralty*)] : EPHORATE
eph·or·ate \ˈefəˌrāt, -_rə̇t\ *n* -S **1** : the office of ephor **2** : the body of ephors
¹ephra·im·ite \ˈēfrēəˌmīt\ *n* -S *usu cap* [*Ephraim*, younger son of Joseph (Gen 41:50–52), the eponymous ancestor of the Ephraimites (Josh 16) + E *-ite*] **1** : a member of the Hebrew tribe of Ephraim — compare MANASSITE **2** : a native or inhabitant of the ancient northern kingdom of Israel
²ephraimite \"\ *adj, usu cap* : EPHRAIMITIC
ephra·im·it·ic \ˌ===ˈmid·ik\ *adj, usu cap* : of or belonging to the Ephraimites or to the northern kingdom of Israel
eph·ra·ta \ˈefrəd·ə\ *adj, usu cap* [fr. *Ephrata*, Pa., where the community was established] : of or relating to a monastic community of German Seventh-Day Baptists founded in Pennsylvania in the early part of the 18th century
eph·rath·ite \ˈefrəˌthīt\ *n* -S *usu cap* [*Ephrath* (Bethlehem), Palestine + E *-ite*] **1** : BETHLEHEMITE **2** : EPHRAIMITE 1
eph·tha·lite \ˈefthəˌlīt\ *also* **heph·tha·lite** \ˈhe-\ *n* -S *usu cap* : a member of the western branch of the Yueh-chi-Tocharians that ruled Russian Turkestan and northwest India in the 5th and 6th centuries A.D. — called also *White Hun*
eph·y·da·tia \ˌefəˈdāsh(ē)ə\ *n, cap* [NL, fr. Gk, fem. of *ephydatios* of the water, in the water, fr. *epi-* + *hydat-, hydōr* water — more at WATER] : a common genus of freshwater encrusting sponges (family Spongillidae) often bright green from included symbiotic algae
¹ephyd·rid \ə̇ˈfidrə̇d, eˈ-; ˈefədrə̇d, -ˌdrid\ *adj* [NL *Ephydridae*] : belonging or relating to the Ephydridae
²ephydrid \"\ *n* -S : one of the Ephydridae
ephyd·ri·dae \ə̇ˈfidrəˌdē, eˈ-\ *n pl, cap* [NL, fr. *Ephydra*, type genus (fr. Gk *ephydrē*, fem. of *ephydros* living on the water, fr. *epi-* + *-hydros*, fr. *hydōr* water) + *-idae*] : a large family of small dark-colored two-winged flies that usu. lack bristles, live in moist places, and have cylindrical larvae having mouth hooks and living in fresh or salt water or occas. in plants — see BRINE FLY
eph·y·ra \ˈefərə\ *n, pl* **eph·y·rae** \-ˌrē\ *or* **ephyras** [NL, fr. *Ephyra*, a nymph, fr. L, fr. Gk] : a free-swimming larva of a scyphozoan jellyfish formed by transverse fission of a scyphistoma and growing into a medusa — compare STROBILA
ephyr·u·la \ə̇ˈfir(y)ələ\ *n, pl* **ephyru·lae** \-ˌlē\ [NL, fr. *Ephyra*, a nymph + NL *-ula*] : EPHYRA
épi \(ˈ)āˈpē\ *n* -S [F, lit., ear of grain, fr. OF *espi*, fr. L *spica*, *spicum* point, head, tuft — more at SPIKE] : a covering for the apex of a sharp-pointed roof usu. in a finial
epi- *or* **ep-** *also* **eph-** *prefix* [*epi-* fr. ME, upon, fr. MF & ML; MF, fr. ML, fr. L, fr. Gk, fr. *epi* on, upon, to; *ep-* fr. MF, fr. L, fr. Gk, fr. *epi*; *eph-* fr. L, fr. Gk, fr. *epi*; akin to OE *eofot* crime, Goth *iftuma* next, following, L *ob* to, before, on account of, Skt *api* besides] **1** : upon ⟨*epi*phyte⟩ : besides ⟨*epen*thesis⟩ : near to ⟨*epen*cephalon⟩ : over ⟨*epi*center⟩ : outer ⟨*epi*dermis⟩ : anterior ⟨*epi*cnemial⟩ : prior to ⟨*epa*cme⟩ : after ⟨*ep*embryonic⟩ — *epi-* before consonants other than *h*, and sometimes *ep-* before vowels and *eph-* before *h* (which is not repeated), but sometimes *epi-* even before *h* or a vowel **2** : chemical compound or group related in some manner to a (specified) chemical compound or group: as **a** : epimer of a (specified) chemical compound ⟨*epi*cholesterol⟩ ⟨*epi*rhamnose⟩ **b** : chemical compound or group distinguished from a (specified) chemical compound or group by having a bridge connection ⟨*epi*chlorohydrin⟩ ⟨9,10-*epi*dioxyanthracene⟩ **3** : altered — in petrographic terms ⟨*epi*diorite⟩ **4** : resting on as a geological stratum : following in time — in names of geological eras, periods, systems, series, or formations ⟨*Ep*archean⟩
ep·i·an·drum \ˌepēˈandrəm\ *n* -S [NL, fr. *epi-* + *-andrum* (fr. neut. of *-andrus* -androus)] : the genital orifice of a male arachnid
epi·basal \ˌepə̇, ˌepē+\ *adj* [ISV *epi-* + *basal*] *bot* : situated anterior to the basal wall ⟨the ~ lower segment of a developing embryo⟩ — compare HYPOBASAL
epi·basidium \"+\ *n* [NL, fr. *epi-* + *basidium*] **1** : a superior prolongation of each cell of the basidium of various heterobasidiomycetous fungi (as members of the order Tremellales) that bears the spore **2** : PROMYCELIUM
epi·batholithic \"+\ *adj* [*epi-* + *batholithic*] *of an ore deposit* : located near the periphery of a batholith
epi·benthos \"+\ *n* [*epi-* + *benthos*] : the fauna and flora of the sea bottom between low-water mark and the mesobenthos down to a lower limit of about 100 fathoms
ep·i·bi·ont \ˌepəˈbīˌänt, ˌepēˈ-\ *n* -S [*epi-* + *-biont*] : an organism that lives on the body surface of another
¹epi·biotic \ˌepə̇, ˌepē+\ *adj* [*epi-* + *biotic*] : living on the surface of plants or living animals usu. parasitically — used esp. of fungi; compare EPIPHYTIC, EPIZOIC

2epibiotic \"\ *adj or n* **:** RELICT

ep·i·blast \ˈepə,blast\ *n* -S [*epi-* + *-blast*] **1 :** the outer layer of the blastoderm **:** ECTODERM — compare GERM LAYER **2 :** a small outgrowth shaped like a claw that lies in front of the plumule and opposite the scutellum in many grasses and has been considered to be a second cotyledon — **ep·i·blas·tic** \ˌepəˈblastik\ *adj*

ep·i·blem \ˈepə,blem\ *or* **ep·i·ble·ma** \,epəˈblēmə\ *n* -S [NL *epiblema*, fr. Gk *epiblēma* covering, fr. *epi-* + *blēma* throw, coverlet, fr. *ballein* to throw — more at DEVIL] **:** the superficial layer of tissue replacing the true epidermis in most roots and in stems of submerged aquatics

ep·i·bol·ic \ˌepəˈbälik\ *adj* **:** of, relating to, produced by, or involving epiboly ⟨~ invagination⟩ ⟨~ growth⟩

epib·o·ly *also* **epib·o·le** \əˈpibəlē, eˈ-\ *n, pl* **epibolies** *also* **epiboles** [Gk *epibolē* act of throwing or laying on, something thrown or laid on, fr. *epiballein* to throw on, fr. *epi-* + *ballein* to throw] **:** the growing of one part about another during embryogenesis, such growth of the dorsal lip area being one of the fundamental movements of gastrulation — compare INVAGINATION, INVOLUTION

1epi·branchial \ˌepə, ˌepē+\ *adj* [*epi-* + *branchial*] **:** of or belonging to the segment next below the pharyngobranchial in a branchial arch

2epibranchial \"\ *n* -S **:** an epibranchial cartilage or bone

1ep·ic \ˈepik, -pēk\ *also* **ep·i·cal** \ˈepəkəl, -pēk-\ *adj* [L *epicus*, fr. Gk *epikos*, fr. *epos* word, speech, epic poem + *-ikos* -ic, -ical — more at VOICE] **1 a :** of, relating to, or befitting an epic ⟨~ poets⟩ ⟨an ~ hero⟩ **:** HEROIC ⟨the ~ period in Greek history⟩ **b :** having the characteristics of, resembling, or suggestive of an epic ⟨they are heroic poems . . . but that they are ~ in any save the most general sense . . . is not quite clear —W.P.Ker⟩ **2 :** extending beyond the usual or ordinary esp. in size or scope ⟨transforms the conventional length of bread into an ~ loaf —Rosamund Frost⟩ ⟨undertaken on a grand scale ⟨the final paragraph of this ~ biography —W.L. Shirer⟩ **:** IMPOSING, IMPRESSIVE ⟨improvisation . . . that ranges from out-and-out burlesque to ~ grandeur of scene and action —Saxe Commins⟩ ⟨a faithful record of an ~ expedition —C.A. Lejeune⟩ ⟨a strange . . . human being of rather ~ proportions —Richard Watts⟩

2epic \"\ *n* -S **1 :** a long narrative poem recounting the deeds of a legendary or historical hero: **a :** a long narrative poem (as Homer's *Iliad*) recounting heroic deeds set against a background of war and the supernatural, having a serious theme developed in a coherent and unified manner, written in a dignified style, and marked by certain formal characteristics (as a beginning in medias res, the invocation to the muse, and the use of extended similes) — called also *classical epic* **b :** a long narrative poem (as Milton's *Paradise Lost*) having the structure, conventions, and tone of the classical epic but dealing with later or different subject matter — called also *literary epic* **c :** a long narrative poem (as *Beowulf*) expressing the early ideals, characteristics, and traditions of a people or nation — called also *folk epic* **d :** the literary genre consisting of epic poems ⟨~ and romance⟩ **2 :** something felt to resemble an epic ⟨an ~ in stone and marble —Samuel Butler †1902⟩: as **a :** a long narrative poem ⟨an ~ . . . every spring —Lord Byron⟩ **b :** a prose narrative (as a novel), play, or motion picture ⟨voluminous ~*s* on the moral conquest of poverty —E.S.Bates⟩ ⟨a Broadway ~ —Wolcott Gibbs⟩ ⟨eager for short features to exhibit along with the full-length Hollywood ~*s* —*Dun's Rev.*⟩; *esp* **:** one embodying a nation's ideals or historical traditions or centering around the adventures or achievements of a single person or character ⟨*Moby Dick* is an American ~ —Richard Chase⟩ **3 :** a series of events or body of legend or tradition felt to form the proper subject of an epic ⟨revives the memories of the great American ~, the winning of the West —William Clark⟩ **4** *usu cap* **:** OLD IONIC

ep·i·cal·ly \-pək(ə)lē, -pēk-, -li\ *adv* **:** in an epic manner

epi·calyx \ˌepə, ˌepē+\ *n* [*epi-* + *calyx*] **:** an involucre resembling the true calyx but consisting simply of a whorl of bracts below the calyx (as in mallows) or resulting from the union of the sepal appendages (as in roses)

epi·can·thic fold \ˌepəˌkan(t)thik-, ˌepē\ *n* [NL *epicanthus* + E *-ic*] **:** a prolongation of a fold of the skin of the upper eyelid over the inner angle or both angles of the eye — called also *eye fold, Mongolian fold*

epi·canthus \ˌepə, ˌepē+\ *n* [NL, fr. *epi-* + *canthus*] **:** EPICANTHIC FOLD

ep·i·car·dia \,epəˈkärdēə\ *n* -S [NL, fr. *epi-* + Gk *kardia* heart — more at HEART] **:** the short part of the esophagus extending from the diaphragm to the stomach

ep·i·car·di·al \ˌ==ˈ=dēəl\ *also* **ep·i·car·di·ac** \-ē,ak\ *adj* [NL *epicardia* & *epicardium* + E *-al* or *-ac* (as in *cardiac*)] **:** of or relating to an epicardium or an epicardia

ep·i·car·di·um \,==ˈ=dēəm\ *n, pl* **epicar·dia** \-ēə\ [NL, fr. *epi-* + *-cardium* (fr. Gk *kardia* heart)] **1 :** the visceral part of the pericardium that closely invests the heart **2 :** a tubular posterior prolongation of the bronchial sac of certain compound ascidians that takes part in the process of gemmation

1ep·i·car·id \ˌepəˈkarəd\ *or* **ep·i·car·i·dan** \-rəd³n\ *adj* [*epicarid* fr. NL *Epicaridea*; *epicaridan* fr. NL *Epicaridea* + E *-an*] **:** of or relating to the Epicaridea

2epicarid \"\ *or* **epicaridan** \"\ *n* -S **:** a crustacean of the suborder Epicaridea

ep·i·ca·rid·ea \,epəkəˈridēə\ *n pl, cap* [NL, fr. *epi-* + *-caridea* (fr. Gk *karid-, karis* shrimp)] **:** a suborder of Isopoda comprising isopods (as those of the family Bopyridae) of which the enlarged and modified females are parasites on other crustaceans while the minute males usu. live attached to the females

ep·i·car·i·des \,epəˈkarə,dēz\ [NL, fr. *epi-* + *-carides* (fr. Gk *karid-, karis* shrimp)] *syn of* EPICARIDEA

ep·i·carp \ˈepə,kärp\ *n* -S [F *épicarpe*, fr. *épi-* epi- + *-carpe* -carp] **:** the outermost layer of the pericarp of a fruit — see ENDOCARP illustration

ep·i·cau·ta \,epəˈkȯd·ə\ *n, cap* [NL, fr. Gk *epikautē*, fem. of *epikautos* burned at the tip, fr. *epikaiein* to burn on the surface, burn at the top, fr. *epi-* + *kaiein* to burn — more at CAUSTIC] **:** a cosmopolitan genus of blister beetles that feed on various cultivated plants as adults and that as larvae are predacious in egg masses or nests of insects

epic caesura *n* **:** a feminine caesura following an extra unstressed syllable intruded into accentual iambic meter under cover of the caesural pause which is there longer than usual (as in Shakespeare's "but how of Cawdor? ‖The Thane of Cawdor lives") — contrasted with *lyric caesura*

epic drama *n* **:** a modern episodic drama that seeks to provoke objective understanding of a social problem through a series of loosely connected scenes that avoid illusion and often interrupt the action to address the audience directly with analysis or argument (as by a narrator) or with documentation (as by a film) — compare LIVING NEWSPAPER

ep·i·cede \ˈepə,sēd\ *or* **ep·i·ce·di·um** \,==ˈsēdēəm\ *n, pl* **epicedes** \ˈ==,sēdz\ *or* **epice·dia** \,==ˈsēdēə\ [L *epicedium*, fr. Gk *epikēdeion*, fr. neut. of *epikēdeios* of a funeral, fr. *epikēdeia* funeral, fr. *epi-* + *kēdeia* funeral, mourning, fr. *kēdos* grief, trouble, sadness + *-eia* -y — more at HATE] **:** a funeral song or ode **:** DIRGE, ELEGY ⟨Lycidas . . . formed a part of a collection of ~*s* on Edward King —George Saintsbury⟩

ep·i·ce·di·al \ˌ==ˈsēdēəl\ *also* **ep·i·ce·di·an** \-ēən\ *adj* **:** of or relating to an epicede **:** ELEGIAC

epicele *var of* EPICOELIA

1ep·i·cene \ˈepə,sēn\ *adj* [ME, fr. L *epicoenus*, fr. Gk *epikoinos*, fr. *epi-* + *koinos* common — more at CO-] **1 :** having but one form to indicate either male or female sex (as Latin *bos* "a bull, ox, or cow") — used of a noun **2 :** having characteristics typical of the other sex **:** INTERSEXUAL ⟨his brothers suspect the ~ wife because of her masculine arms —R.H.Lowie⟩ **:** EFFEMINATE **3 :** lacking the typical characteristics of either sex **:** SEXLESS ⟨perpetual children . . . happy ~ Peter Pans —Dwight Macdonald⟩ **4 :** lacking vigor ⟨recent ~ treatises . . . withdraw from the major task of evaluating significance —Ephraim Fischoff⟩ **:** lacking vigorous masculinity ⟨the hearty sportsman . . . really ~ beneath his tweeds —Wolcott Gibbs⟩ **:** DELICATE ⟨a swift ~ felicity of wit —Evelyn Waugh⟩

2epicene \"\ *n* -S **:** one who is epicene

ep·i·cen·ism \-ē,nizəm\ *n* -S **:** the quality or state of being epicene

epi·center \ˌepə, ˌepē+\ *n* [NL *epicentrum*, fr. *epi-* + L *centrum* center — more at CENTER] **1** *also* **epi·centrum** \"+\ **:** the part of the earth's surface directly above the focus of an earthquake **2 :** CENTER 2 ⟨the White House, that ~ of world power —Stewart Alsop⟩

1epi·central \"+\ *adj* [*epi-* + *central*] **1 :** arising from the centrum of a vertebra **2 :** of or relating to the epicenter of an earthquake ⟨~ area⟩

2epicentral \"\ *n* **:** an epicentral bone or spine

epi·ceratodus \"+\ [NL, fr. *epi-* + *Ceratodus*] *syn of* NEOCERATODUS

ep·i·chei·re·ma *also* **ep·i·chi·re·ma** \,epə,kīˈrēmə\ *n, pl* **epicheiremata** \-ˈrēməd·ə, -rem-\ *also* **epichiremas** [L & Gk; L *epichirema*, fr. Gk *epicheirēma*, fr. *epicheirein* to endeavor, attempt to prove, fr. *epi-* + *cheir* hand — more at CHIR-] **:** a syllogism in which some statement supporting one or both of the premises is introduced with the premises themselves

ep·i·chil·i·um \,epəˈkilēəm\ *also* **ep·i·chil** \ˈepə,kil\ *or* **ep·i·chile** \ˈ==,kīl\ *n, pl* **epichil·ia** \,==ˈkilēə\ [NL *epichilium*, fr. *epi-* + Gk *cheilos* lip + NL *-ium*] **:** the terminal lobe of the labellum in some orchids

epi·chlorohydrin \ˌepə, ˌepē+\ *n* [*epi-* + *chlorohydrin*] **:** a volatile liquid toxic epoxide C_3H_5ClO having an odor like chloroform, made usu. by alkaline hydrolysis of dichlorohydrins, and used chiefly in making epoxy resins

epi·chondrosis \"+\ *n* [NL, fr. *epi-* + *chondrosis*] **:** a cartilaginous growth upon periosteum ⟨an antler arising from an ~⟩ — **epi·chon·drot·ic** \ˌ==ˌkänˈdräd·ik\ *adj*

epi·chordal \ˌepə, ˌepē+\ *adj* [ISV *epi-* + *chordal*; orig. formed in G] **:** located upon or above the notochord — used esp. of vertebrae or elements of vertebrae on the dorsal side of the notochord

ep·i·cho·ric \ˌepəˈkōrik, -kȯr-, -kär-\ *adj* [Gk *epichōrios* of a certain country, in a certain country, local (fr. *epi-* + *-chōrios*, fr. *chōra* land, country, place) + E *-ic*] **:** peculiar to a limited area **:** LOCAL — used of ancient Greek alphabets ⟨every town, certainly every region, had its own ~ script —H.M.Hoenigswald⟩

epi·christian \ˌepə, ˌepē+\ *adj* [*epi-* + *Christian*] **:** of or relating to the period immediately after the lifetime of Christ

ep·i·cist \ˈepəsəst\ *n* -S [*2epic* + *-ist*] **:** an epic poet

epi·clastic \ˌepə, ˌepē+\ *adj* [ISV *epi-* + *-clastic*] *of rocks* **:** formed at the surface of the earth by consolidation of fragments of preexisting rocks

ep·i·cle·sis *or* **ep·i·kle·sis** \,epəˈklēsəs\ *n, pl* **epicle·ses** *or* **epikle·ses** \-ē,sēz\ *often cap* [LGk *epiklēsis*, fr. Gk, surname, title, invocation, fr. *epikalein* to summon, invoke, call by a surname (fr. *epi-* + *kalein* to summon) + *-ēsis* -esis] **:** a liturgical invocation of the Holy Spirit for the purpose of consecrating the eucharistic elements found particularly in Eastern liturgies where it follows the words of institution and is regarded as the point at which the eucharistic bread and wine become the body and blood of Christ

ep·i·cne·mi·al \ˌepə(k)ˈnēmēəl, ˌepē(k)-\ *adj* [*epi-* + Gk *knēmē* tibia + E *-al*] **:** of or belonging to the anterior part of the tibia

epi·coelia \ˌepə, ˌepē+\ *also* **ep·i·coele** *or* **ep·i·cele** \ˈepə,sēl\ *n, pl* **epicoeliae** *also* **epicoeles** *or* **epiceles** [*epicoelia*, NL, fr. *epi-* + *coelia*; *epicoele, epicele* fr. *epi-* + *-coele, -cele*] **:** the cavity of the metencephalon **:** the anterior part of the 4th ventricle of the brain

ep·i·coe·lo·ma \,epəsēˈlōmə\ *also* **epi·coelom** \ˌepə, ˌepē+\ *n* -S [NL, fr. *epi-* + *coelom*] **:** the part of the coelom nearest the notochord

epi·colic \ˌepə, ˌepē+\ *adj* [ISV *epi-* + *colic* (of the colon)] **:** situated upon or over the colon — used esp. of the region of the abdomen adjacent to the colon

epi·condyle \ˌepə, ˌepē+\ *n* [F *épicondyle*, fr. *épi-* epi- + *condyle*] **1 :** the lateral condyle at the distal end of the humerus **2 :** the medial condyle — **epi·con·dyl·i·an** \-ˌkänˈdilēən\ *adj* — **epi·con·dyl·ic** \-lik\ *adj*

epi·continental \ˌepə, ˌepē+\ *adj* [*epi-* + *continental*] **:** found or lying upon a continent or a continental shelf ⟨~ sedimentation⟩ ⟨a partly landlocked ~ sea⟩ ⟨the North sea is ~⟩ — compare EPEIRIC

epi·cor·a·co·humeral \ˌepəˌkȯrə(,)kō, ˌepē+\ *adj* [ˈ*epicoracoid* + *humeral*] **:** of or connecting the epicoracoid and humerus

1epi·coracoid *also* **epi·coracoidal** \ˌepə, ˌepē+\ *adj* [*epi-* + *coracoid, coracoidal*] **:** lying at the sternal end of the coracoid — used of a cartilaginous or bony element lying in the shoulder girdle of some vertebrates (as various reptiles, amphibians, and monotreme mammals)

2epicoracoid \"\ *n* [*epi-* + *coracoid*, n.] **:** an epicoracoid bone or cartilage

ep·i·cor·mic \ˌepəˈkȯrmik\ *adj* [*epi-* + *corm* + *-ic*] **:** growing from a dormant bud exposed to light and air ⟨new ~ branches on thinned forest trees⟩

ep·i·cot·yl \ˈ==,käd·ᵊl, ˌ==ˈ==\ *n* -S [*epi-* + *cotyle*don] **:** the portion of the axis of a plant embryo or seedling above the cotyledonary node — compare HYPOCOTYL, PLUMULE

epi·cotyledonary \ˌepə +\ *adj* [*epi-* + *cotyledonary*] **:** situated above the cotyledons; *often* **:** of or relating to the epicotyl

epi·cranial \ˌepə +\ *adj* [NL *epicranium* + E *-al*] **1 :** situated on the cranium **2 :** belonging to the epicranium

epi·cranium \" +\ *n, pl* **epicrania** [NL, fr. *epi-* + *cranium*] **1 :** the dorsal wall of the head of an insect **2 :** the structures covering the vertebrate cranium

ep·i·cra·ni·us \,epəˈkrānēəs\ *n, pl* **epicra·nii** \-ē,ī\ [NL, fr. *epi-* + *-cranius* (fr. *cranium*)] **:** OCCIPITOFRONTALIS

1epic·ri·sis \əˈpikrəsəs\ *n* [NL, fr. Gk *epikrisis* determination, judgment, fr. *epikrinein* to decide, fr. *epi-* + *krinein* to judge, discern — more at CERTAIN] **:** a critical or analytical summing up esp. of a medical case history

2epi·crisis \ˌepəˈkrīsəs, ˌepē-\ *n* [*epi-* + *crisis*] *med* **:** something that follows a crisis; *specif* **:** a secondary crisis

ep·i·crit·ic \ˌepəˈkrid·ik\ *adj* [Gk *epikritikos* determinative, fr. *epikritos* (verbal of *epikrinein*) + *-ikos* -ic] **1** *of cutaneous reception* **:** marked by accurate discrimination between small degrees of sensation (as of heat, cold, and pain) **2** *of cutaneous sensory receptors* **:** adapted to or subserving epicritic reception **3** *of cutaneous reactivity* **:** dependent on epicritic reception or receptors — compare PROTOPATHIC

epics *pl of* EPIC

epic simile *n* **:** an extended simile often running to several lines used typically in epic poetry to intensify the heroic stature of the subject (as by contrast) and to serve as decoration — called also *Homeric simile*

ep·ic·te·tian \ˌepəkˈtēshən, -pēk-\ *adj, usu cap* [Gk *Epiktētos* (fr. *Epiktētos* Epictetus 1st cent. A.D. Greek Stoic philosopher) + E *-an*] **:** of or relating to Epictetus or to his doctrine that the greatest good lies in independence of external things and in reliance upon the inner life or character

epic theater *n* **:** EPIC DRAMA

ep·i·cure \ˈepə,kyu̇(ə)r, -pē,k-, -u̇ə\ *n* -S [after *Epicurus* (fr. L, fr. Gk *Epikouros*) †270B.C. Greek philosopher] **1** *usu cap, obs* **:** EPICUREAN; *specif* **:** one that disbelieves in any concern of deity with man ⟨were I an ~ I could bate swearing —George Herbert⟩ **2** *archaic* **:** one devoted to sensual pleasure (as eating) **:** SYBARITE ⟨an ~ is for his wine or women or feasts continually —Thomas Traherne⟩ **3 :** one with sensitive and discriminating tastes (as in food, wine, music) **:** CONNOISSEUR ⟨an ~ in many of the delights of the senses —H.S.Canby⟩

syn GOURMET, GOURMAND, GLUTTON, BON VIVANT, GASTRONOME, GASTRONOMER: EPICURE refers to a choice connoisseur of the pleasurable, luxurious, or sensual, esp. in matters of food and drink ⟨the *epicure* is conscious of much more than the taste of the food. Rather, there enter into the taste, as directly experienced, qualities that depend upon reference to its source and its manner of production in connection with criteria of excellence —John Dewey⟩ GOURMET may be close to EPICURE; it may stress delicate taste and steady attempt to savor to the fullest. GOURMAND implies a hearty appetite for good food and drink, not without discernment but with less than a gourmet's ⟨eating habits . . . of a determined *gourmet*, verging at times on those of a *gourmand* —E.J.Kahn⟩ ⟨quality, not quantity, is the source of the attraction; it appeals to the *gourmet* rather than the *gourmand* —C.W.H.Johnson⟩ GLUTTON indicates a voracious eater having a very heavy and quite indiscriminate appetite ⟨skillfully made delicacies from many countries in Europe and Asia . . . in such vast array this season that they threaten to turn the *gourmet* into a *glutton* —Jane Nickerson⟩ BON VIVANT suggests one who takes habitual lively pleasure in dining and drinking with others ⟨somewhat of a *bon vivant*, and his wine was excellent —Sir Walter Scott⟩ GASTRONOME and GASTRONOMER are synonyms for EPICURE; they may suggest undue ritual about the appreciation of fine food ⟨the thing for U.S. *gourmets* to do, of course, would be to wash the illustrious birds down with a full cup of English mead; piment, said *gastronomes*, would go best with grouse —*Time*⟩

epicureal *or* **epicurial** *obs var of* EPICUREAN

1ep·i·cu·re·an \ˌepəkyəˈrēən, -pēk-, -ˌkyu̇rē-\ *adj* [L *Epicureus* (fr. Gk *Epikoureios*, fr. *Epikouros*) + E *-an*] **1** *usu cap* **:** of Epicurus or Epicureanism **2 a :** given to the pursuit of pleasure or to the attainment of sensuous gratification **:** SENSUAL ⟨an ~ family⟩ **b :** stimulating and satisfying to the senses ⟨~ dishes⟩ **c :** of or relating to an epicure **:** LUXURIOUS ⟨an ~ life⟩ **syn** see SENSUOUS

2epicurean \"\ *n* -S **1** *usu cap* **:** a follower of Epicurus **2** *often cap* **:** EPICURE 3 ⟨his adventures . . . had wasted his spirit, leaving him morally languid, a graceful and prudent ~ —Francis Hackett⟩ **3** *usu cap* **:** APIKORES

ep·i·cu·re·an·ism \ˌ==kyəˈrēə,nizəm, -ˈkyu̇rēə-\ *n* -S **1** *usu cap* **a :** the philosophy of Epicurus and his followers who within a framework of modified Democritean atomism subscribed to a hedonistic ethics that considered ataraxy the highest good, held intellectual pleasures superior to others, and advocated the renunciation of momentary in favor of more permanent pleasures **b :** a mode of life in consonance with Epicureanism **2 :** EPICURISM **2 3 :** the attitude or practice of an apikores **:** worldly-mindedness

ep·i·cu·re·ous \ˌ==ˈkyu̇rēəs\ *adj* [L *Epicureus*] *archaic* **:** EPICUREAN 2

ep·i·cur·ism \ˈepə,kyu̇,rizəm, -pē,k-\ *n* -S [prob. fr. F *épicurisme*, fr. *Epicurus* + *-isme* -ism] **1** *usu cap, archaic* **:** EPICUREANISM 1 **2 :** the habits or tastes of an epicure

epicurize *vi* -ED/-ING/-S *obs* **:** to profess or practice Epicureanism

epi·cuticle \ˌepə, ˌepē +\ *n* -S [*epi-* + *cuticle*] **1** *also* **epi·cuticula** \" +\ [*epicuticula*, NL, fr. *epi-* + *cuticula* cuticle] **:** the outermost nonchitinous waxy layer of the insect exoskeleton — compare ENDOCUTICLE **2 :** an outer resistant membrane surrounding various cuticular structures (as wool fibers, animal hairs, or feathers) — **epi·cuticular** \" + \ *adj*

ep·i·cy·cle \ˈepə,sīkəl\ *n* [ME *epicicle*, fr. LL *epicyclus*, fr. Gk *epikyklos*, fr. *epi-* + *kyklos* ring, circle, cycle, wheel — more at WHEEL] **1 a** *in Ptolemaic astron* **:** a circle in which a planet moves and which has a center that is itself carried around at the same time on the circumference of a larger circle **b :** a process or activity going on within the context of a larger one **:** secondary cycle ⟨an ~ of land erosion⟩ **2 :** the circle generating an epicycloid or hypocycloid

ep·i·cy·clic \ˌ==ˈsīklik, -sik-\ *also* **ep·i·cy·cli·cal** \-ləkəl\ *adj* **:** relating to, resembling, or having the motion of an epicycle

epicyclic train *n* **:** a train (as of gear wheels or belt pulleys) designed to have one or more parts travel around the circumference of another fixed or revolving part

ep·i·cy·cloid \,==ˈsī,klȯid\ *n* -S [prob. fr. F *épicycloïde*, fr. *épicycle* (fr. LL *epicyclus*) + *-oïde* -oid] **:** a curve traced by a point on a circle that rolls on the outside of a fixed circle — compare HYPOCYCLOID

ep·i·cy·cloi·dal \ˌ==ˌsīˈklȯid³l\ *adj* **:** relating to or having the properties of the epicycloid

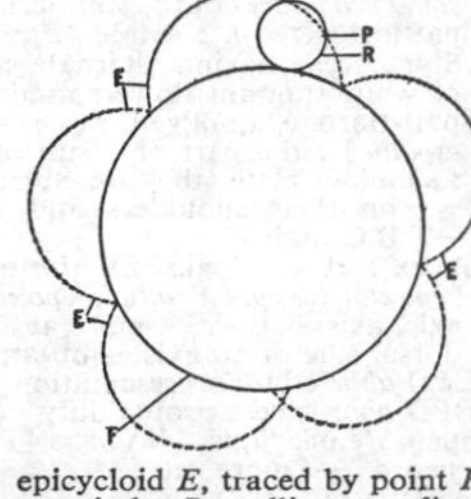

epicycloid *E*, traced by point *P*, on circle *R*, rolling on fixed circle *F*

ep·i·cyte \ˈepə,sīt\ *n* -S [ISV *epi-* + *-cyte*; orig. formed as F *épicyte*] **1 :** the investing membrane of a cell **2 :** an epithelial cell

ep·i·deic·tic \ˌepəˈdīktik\ *adj* [Gk *epideiktikos*, fr. (assumed) Gk *epideiktos* (verbal of Gk *epideiknynai* to exhibit, show off, display, fr. *epi-* + *deiknynai* to show) + Gk *-ikos* -ic — more at DICTION] **:** designed primarily for rhetorical effect **:** DEMONSTRATIVE ⟨~ style of writing⟩ ⟨the Indian speeches are . . . more of the nature of the forensic and, occasionally, ~ or panegyric, than of deliberative oratory —H.J.C.Grierson⟩ — used esp. of ceremonial orations of praise or blame

ep·i·de·mi·al \ˌepəˈdēmēəl\ *adj* [*epidemy* + *-al*] *archaic* **:** EPIDEMIC

1ep·i·dem·ic \ˌepəˈdemik, -mēk\ *also* **ep·i·dem·i·cal** \-məkəl, -mēk-\ *adj* [F *épidémique*, fr. MF *epidemie* epidemic (n.) (fr. LL *epidemia*, fr. Gk *epidēmia* visit, epidemic, fr. *epidēmos* visiting, prevalent, epidemic — fr. *epi-* + *dēmos* deme, populace — + *-ia* -y) + *-ique* -ic, -ical — more at DEM-] **1 a** *of a communicable disease* (1) **:** affecting or tending to affect many persons within a community, area, or region at one time ⟨many children died that winter of ~ fevers⟩ ⟨typhoid was ~⟩; *broadly* **:** PANDEMIC — distinguished from *endemic* (2) **:** epiphytotic or epizootic — not used technically **b :** prevalent esp. to a degree felt to be excessive ⟨padded shoulders became ~ in the late thirties —Lois Long⟩ **:** COMMON; *specif, of economic insects* **:** present in such numbers as to constitute a plague ⟨this defoliator became ~ in 1949⟩ **c :** CONTAGIOUS 3 ⟨an ~ personality⟩ ⟨~ laughter⟩ **2 :** of, relating to, or constituting an epidemic ⟨the outbreak was of ~ proportions⟩ ⟨the ~ phase of the grasshopper cycle⟩ — **ep·i·dem·i·cal·ly** \-mək(ə)lē, -mēk-, -li\ *adv*

2epidemic \"\ *n* -S **1 a :** an outbreak of epidemic disease ⟨the Indonesian malaria ~⟩ ⟨plagues, ~*s*, heat, and other trials⟩ **b :** an outbreak of something felt to resemble an epidemic disease esp. in its rapid spread ⟨harnessed Niagara did not start a hydroelectric ~ —Roger Burlingame⟩ ⟨the ugly ~ of rioting which flared clear across the nation —E.A.Gray⟩ **2 :** a product of epidemic spread, growth, or development; *specif* **:** a natural population (as of insects) suddenly and greatly enlarged

ep·i·de·mic·i·ty \,epə,deˈmisəd·ē, -,dəˈm-, -ətē, -i\ *n* -ES **:** the quality or state of being epidemic; *specif* **:** the relative ability to spread from one host to others ⟨~ of typhoid bacteria⟩

epidemic parotitis *n* **:** MUMPS

epidemic pleurodynia *n* **:** an acute virus infection that is characterized by sudden onset with fever, headache, and acute diaphragmatic pain and that is believed to be caused by the Coxsackie virus

epidemic tremor *n* **:** AVIAN ENCEPHALOMYELITIS

ep·i·de·mi·o·log·ic \ˌepəˌdēmēəˈläjik, -dem-\ *or* **ep·i·de·mi·o·log·i·cal** \-jəkəl\ *adj* **:** of, relating to, or involving epidemiology ⟨characteristic ~ features⟩ — **ep·i·de·mi·o·log·i·cal·ly** \-jək(ə)lē\ *adv*

ep·i·de·mi·ol·o·gist \,==,=mēˈäləjəst\ *n* -S **:** a specialist in epidemiology

ep·i·de·mi·ol·o·gy \-jē\ *n* -ES [ISV *epidemio-* (fr. LL *epidemia*) + *-logy*] **1 :** a science that deals with the incidence, distribution, and control of disease in a population (as of animals or plants) **2 :** the sum of the factors controlling the presence or absence of a disease or pathogen ⟨the ~ of the common cold⟩ **:** the ecology of a disease or pathogen

epidemy *n* -ES [ME *epidemie*, fr. MF & LL; MF, fr. LL *epidemia* — more at EPIDEMIC] *archaic* **:** EPIDEMIC

ep·i·den·drum \,epəˈdendrəm\ *n* [NL, fr. *epi-* + Gk *dendron* tree; akin to Gk *drys* tree — more at TREE] **1** *cap* **:** a very large genus of highly variable chiefly epiphytic American orchids having flowers of which the lip has a spreading and usu. deeply lobed limb and a claw adnate to the column, being chiefly tropical but including a few forms native to the southeastern U.S., and often grown in the greenhouse for their brightly colored flowers **2** *or* **ep·i·den·dron** \-rən\ -S **:** any orchid of the genus *Epidendrum*

ep·i·derm \'epə,dərm\ *n* -s [LL *epidermis*] **:** EPIDERMIS

epiderm- *or* **epidermo-** *comb form* [*epidermis*] **:** epidermis ‹*epidermo*lysis›

ep·i·der·mal \¦epə¦dərməl, -dēm-,-dəim-\ *also* **ep·i·der·mic** \-mik,-mēk\ *or* **ep·i·der·mi·cal** \-məkəl, -mēk-\ *or* **ep·i·der·mous** \-məs\ *adj* **:** of, relating to, or arising from the epidermis ‹~ cells› ‹~ structures›

ep·i·der·mat·ic \¦epə(,)dər¦mad·ik\ *adj* [Gk *epidermat-, epiderma* epidermis (fr. *epi-* + *dermat-, derma* skin) + E *-ic*] **1** *also* **ep·i·der·ma·tous** \-¦dərməd·əs\ [*epidermatous* fr. Gk *epidermat-, epiderma* + E *-ous*] **:** EPIDERMAL **2** *of an ointment* **:** acting only upon the outer surface of the skin — compare DIADERMAL, ENDERMIC

ep·i·der·ma·toid \-¦dərmə,tȯid\ *adj* [Gk *epidermat-, epiderma* + E *-oid*] **:** EPIDERMOID

ep·i·der·mi·cal·ly \¦epə¦dərmək(ə)lē\ *adv* [*epiderm* + *-ical* + *-ly*] **1 :** on the epidermis **:** on the skin **2 :** with regard to kind of skin

ep·i·der·mi·dal·i·za·tion \,epə,dərməd°lə'zāshən\ *n* -s [*epidermidal* epidermal (fr. LL *epidermid-, epidermis* + E *-al*) + *-ization*] **:** the transformation of cuboidal cells derived from the stratum germinativum into flattened cells of the outer horny layer of the skin

ep·i·der·mis \,epə'dərməs, -dēm-,-dəim-\ *n* -ES [LL, fr. Gk, fr. *epi-* + *-dermis* (fr. *derma* skin, fr. *derein* to skin) — more at TEAR] **1 a :** the outer epithelial layer of the external integument of the animal body that is derived from the embryonic epiblast; *specif* **:** the outer nonsensitive and nonvascular layer of the skin of a vertebrate that overlies the corium, consists of numerous layers of squamous epithelial cells of which the outer are progressively more compressed and horny, and is often modified into specialized outgrowths (as hair, feathers, nails, and hoofs) **b :** any of various animal integuments; *esp* **:** PERIOSTRACUM **2 :** a layer of primary tissue in higher plants that is commonly one cell thick, often cutinized on its outer surface, and continuous in young plants except over the stomata, that provides protection to underlying parts against mechanical injury and desiccation, and that is largely replaced (as by periderm or exodermis) in older plants except on leaves and herbaceous stems

ep·i·der·mi·za·tion \-,dərmə'zāshən\ *n* -s [*epiderm* + *-ization*] **:** EPITHELIZATION

ep·i·der·moid \¦epə¦dər,mȯid\ *also* **ep·i·der·moi·dal** \¦==(¦)=¦mȯid°l\ *adj* [*epiderm-* + *-oid, -oidal*] **:** resembling epidermis or epidermal cells **:** made up of elements like those of epidermis ‹~ neoplasms›

epidermoid cyst *or* **epidermoid** *n* **:** a cystic tumor containing epidermal or similar tissue — see CHOLESTEATOMA; compare DERMOID CYST

ep·i·der·mol·y·sis \,epə(,)dər'mäləsəs\ *n, pl* **epidermoly·ses** \-lə,sēz\ [NL, fr. *epiderm-* + *-lysis*] **:** a state of detachment or loosening of the epidermis

ep·i·der·mo·my·co·sis \,epə,dərmō,mī'kōsəs\ *n* -ES [NL, fr. *epiderm-* + *mycosis*] **:** DERMATOMYCOSIS

ep·i·der·moph·y·tid \,epə(,)dər'mäfəd·əd\ *n* -s [NL *Epidermophyton* + E *-id*] **:** a skin eruption accompanying infection with a dermatophyte

ep·i·der·moph·y·ton \-fə,tän\ *n, cap* [NL, fr. *epiderm-* + Gk *phyton* plant] *in some classifications* **:** a genus comprising dermatophytes that are held to be causative agents of athlete's foot and tinea cruris, now usu. being considered to include a single species (*E. floccosum*, syn. *E. inguinale* and *E. cruris*), and sometimes suppressed as a synonym of *Trichophyton*

ep·i·der·moph·y·to·sis \,epə(,)dər,mäfə'tōsəs\ *n, pl* **epidermophyto·ses** \-ō,sēz\ [NL, fr. *Epidermophyton* + *-osis*] **:** a disease of the skin or nails caused by a dermatophyte

ep·i·di·a·scope \,epə'dīə,skōp\ *n* [ISV *epi-* + *dia-* + *-scope*] **1 :** a projector for images of both opaque and transparent objects **2 :** EPISCOPE — **ep·i·di·a·scop·ic** \¦==¦=='skäpik\ *adj*

epididym- *or* **epididymo-** *comb form* [NL, fr. *epididymis*] **:** epididymal and ‹*epididymo*deferential›

ep·i·did·y·mal \¦epə¦didəməl\ *adj* [NL *epididymis* + E *-al*] **:** of or relating to the epididymis

ep·i·did·y·mis \,epə'didəməs\ *n, pl* **epididymi·des** \-'didəmə,dēz; -də'dimə-, -,di'dimə-\ [NL, fr. Gk, fr. *epi-* + *-didymis* (fr. *didymos* twin, testicle) — more at DIDYM-] **:** an elongated mass at the back of the testis composed chiefly of the greatly convoluted efferent tubes of that organ — see VASA EFFERENTIA

ep·i·did·y·mite \,epə-'didə,mīt\ *n* -s [G *epididymit*, fr. *epi-* + *-didymit* (as in *eudidymit* eudidymite)] — more at EUDIDYMITE] **:** a silicate $NaBeSi_3O_7(OH)$ of sodium and beryllium

ep·i·did·y·mi·tis \-,didə'mīd·əs\ *n* -ES [NL, fr. *epididym-* + *-itis*] **:** inflammation of the epididymis

epi·diorite \¦epə, ¦epē +\ *n* -s [ISV *epi-* + *diorite;* orig. formed as G *epidiorit*] **:** a variety of diorite formed by metamorphism from pyroxenic igneous rocks and often being somewhat schistose

ep·i·do·site \,epə'dō,sīt, ə'pidə,s-\ *n* -s [G *epidosit*, fr. Gk *epidosis* free giving, free gift, contribution, advance (fr. *epididonai* to give besides, increase, advance) + G *-it* -ite] **:** a schistose metamorphic rock composed of green epidote with some quartz

ep·i·dote \'epə,dōt\ *n* -s [F *épidote*, fr. (assumed) Gk *epidotos*, verbal of Gk *epididonai* to give besides, increase, fr. *epi-* + *didonai* to give — more at DATE] **:** a yellowish green mineral $Ca_2(Al,Fe)_3Si_3O_{12}OH$ consisting of a silicate of calcium, aluminum, and iron and occurring massive or in grains, columns, and monoclinic crystals (hardness 6–7, sp. gr. 3.25–3.50)

ep·i·dot·ite \'epə,dōd.,īt\ *n* -s **:** a rock composed mostly of epidote

ep·i·dot·i·za·tion \,epə,dōd·ə'zāshən\ *n* -s [*epidote* + *-ization*] **:** metamorphism in which epidote is formed from other minerals

ep·i·dot·ized *or* **ep·i·dot·ised** \'epədōd.,īzd\ *adj* **:** changed by metamorphism into epidote

epi·du·ral \,epə¦d(y)ürəl, ¦epē¦-\ *adj* [*epi-* + *dural*] **:** situated upon or administered outside the dura mater ‹an ~ abscess› ‹~ block› — **epi·du·ral·ly** \-rəlē\ *adv*

epidural anesthesia *n* **:** CAUDAL ANESTHESIA

ep·i·ei·keia \,epē,ī'kīə\ *or* **ep·i·keia** \,epə'kīə\ *n* -s [Gk *epieikeia* reasonableness, equity, fr. *epieikēs* suitable, reasonable + *-ia* -y] **:** interpretation of a law of the Roman Catholic Church that presumes it not applicable in a case of hardship felt to violate natural law (as when a mother presumes she may miss mass rather than leave her baby alone) **:** EQUITY ‹the ~ of the church›

ep·i·fa·gus \,epə'fāgəs\ *n, cap* [NL, fr. *epi-* + L *fagus* beech — more at BEECH] **:** a genus of slender purplish brown leafless herbs (family Orobanchaceae) having whitish flowers and being parasitic on the roots of beech trees — see BEECHDROPS

epi·focal \¦epə, ¦epē +\ *adj* [*epi-* + *focal*] **:** EPICENTRAL 2

epi·folliculitis \"+\ *n* -ES [NL, fr. *epi-* + *folliculitis*] **:** inflammation of hair follicles

ep·i·gaea \,epə'jēə\ *n, cap* [NL, fr. Gk *epigaios* upon the earth, fr. *epi-* + *-gaios* (fr. *gaia* earth)] **:** a genus of half-evergreen creeping or trailing woody plants (family Ericaceae) with white or rose-colored flowers in small axillary and terminal clusters — see ARBUTUS 3

ep·i·gam·ic \¦epə¦gamik\ *adj* [Gk *epigamos* marriageable (fr. *epi-* + *gamos* marriage, wedding) + E *-ic*] **:** tending to attract the opposite sex during the breeding seasons ‹~ colors of birds›

epig·a·mous \ə'pigəməs, (')e¦p-\ *adj* [Gk *epigamos*] **:** EPITOKOUS

ep·i·gas·ter \'epə,gastə(r), ,==¦==\ *n* -s [NL, fr. *epi-* + Gk *gastēr* stomach] **:** the posterior part of the embryonic intestine from which the colon develops

ep·i·gas·tric \¦epə¦gastrik\ *or* **ep·i·gas·tri·cal** \-rəkəl\ *or* **ep·i·gas·tri·al** \-rēəl\ *also* **ep·i·gas·tral** \-rəl\ *adj* [NL *epigastrium* + E *-ic, -ical* or *-al*] **1 :** lying upon or over the stomach **2 a :** of or relating to the anterior walls of the abdomen ‹~ veins› **b :** of or relating to the region of the abdomen lying between the hypochondriac regions and above the umbilical region ‹~ sensation› — see ABDOMINAL REGION illustration

epigastric artery *n* **:** one of three arteries supplying the anterior walls of the abdomen, (1) one being a direct downward continuation of the internal mammary, (2) another arising from the external iliac near Poupart's ligament and ascending along the inner margin of the internal abdominal ring, and (3) a third arising from the femoral, passing through the saphenous opening in the fascia lata, and then ascending upon the lower part of the abdomen — called also respectively (1) *superior epigastric artery*, (2) *inferior epigastric artery* or *deep epigastric artery*, and (3) *superficial epigastric artery*

epigastric fold *n* **:** a fold of peritoneum on the anterior abdominal wall covering the deep epigastric artery

epigastric plexus *n* **:** SOLAR PLEXUS

ep·i·gas·tri·um \,==='gastrēəm\ *also* **ep·i·gas·trae·um** \-,ga'strēəm\ *n, pl* **epigas·tria** \-'gastrēə\ [NL, fr. Gk *epigastrion*, fr. *epi-* + *gastrion*, dim. of *gastr-, gastēr* stomach] **1 :** the epigastric region **2 :** the ventral side of the mesothorax and metathorax of an insect

ep·i·ge·al \¦epə¦jēəl\ *or* **ep·i·ge·ous** \-ēəs\ *also* **ep·i·ge·an** *or* **ep·i·gae·an** \-ēən\ *or* **ep·i·ge·ic** \-ēik, -ēēk\ *adj* [Gk *epigaios* upon the earth + E *-al* or *-ous* or *-an* or *-ic* — more at EPIGAEA] **1 a** *of a plant or a plant part* **:** growing above the surface of the ground ‹green ~ stalks of asparagus›; *esp, of a cotyledon* **:** forced above ground by elongation of the hypocotyl **b** *of plant germination* **:** characterized by the production of epigeal cotyledons **2 :** living near or on the surface of the ground — used esp. of an insect; distinguished from *aericl, hypogeal*

ep·i·gene \¦epə¦jēn\ *adj* [F *épigène*, fr. Gk *epigenēs* growing after, fr. *epigignesthai* to be born after — more at EPIGONE] **1** *of a crystal* **:** not natural to the substance in which it is found **2 :** formed, originating, or taking place on or not far below the surface of the earth — opposed to *hypogene*

ep·i·gen·e·sis \,epə'jenəsəs\ *n* [NL, fr. *epi-* + L *genesis*] **1 a :** development involving gradual diversification and differentiation of an initially undifferentiated entity (as a zygote or spore) — compare PREFORMATION **b :** THEORY OF EPIGENESIS **2 :** change in the mineral character of a rock owing to outside influences — compare METAMORPHISM

ep·i·gen·e·sist \-səst\ *n* -s [irreg. fr. NL *epigenesis* + E *-ist*] **:** an adherent of epigenesis

ep·i·ge·net·ic \¦epəjə¦ned·ik\ *adj* [*epi-* + *genetic*] **1 :** of, relating to, or produced by epigenesis ‹the ~ nature of vertebrate development› **2** *or* **ep·i·gen·ic** \¦epə¦jenik\ *of deposit or structure* **:** formed after the laying down of the enclosing rock **:** POSTDEPOSITIONAL ‹~ structures are formed after deposition of the sediment, as certain concretions . . . and large scaled features as folds and faults —W.C.Krumbein & L.L.Sloss› ‹~ changes — both solution and precipitation —F.J.Pettijohn› — compare SYNGENETIC — **ep·i·ge·net·i·cal·ly** \-jə¦ned·ək(ə)lē\ *adv*

epigenetic drainage *n* **:** drainage by streams whose courses have been determined by the conditions of an older land surface now eroded — compare AUTOGENETIC DRAINAGE

epig·e·nist \ə'pijənəst\ *n* -s [by alter.] **:** EPIGENESIST

epig·e·nite \-,nīt\ *n* -s [G *epigenit*, fr. Gk *epigenēs* growing after + G *-it* -ite — more at EPIGENE] **:** a sulfide perhaps $(Cu,Fe)_5AsS_6$ of copper, iron, and arsenic

epig·e·nous \ə'pijənəs, (')e¦p-\ *adj* [ISV *epi-* + *-genous*] **:** growing upon the surface esp. the upper surface of a leaf or other organ of a plant — compare HYPOGENOUS

ep·i·glot·tal \¦epə¦gläd·°l, -ät|\ *also* **ep·i·glot·tic** \|ik, |ēk\ *adj* [NL *epiglottis* + E *-al* or *-ic*] **:** of, relating to, or produced with the aid of the epiglottis

ep·i·glot·tid·e·an \¦epə(,)glä¦tidēən\ *adj* [NL *epiglottid-, epiglottis* + E *-ean*] **:** EPIGLOTTAL

ep·i·glot·tis \,epə'gläd·əs, -ätəs, '==,==\ *n* [NL, fr. Gk *epiglōttis*, fr. *epi-* + *glōttis* glottis — more at GLOTTIS] **1 :** a thin lamella of yellow elastic cartilage that ordinarily projects upward behind the tongue and just in front of the glottis and that with the arytenoid cartilages serves to cover the glottis during the act of swallowing **2 :** the epistome of a bryozoan **3 :** the epipharynx of an insect

ep·i·glot·ti·tis \,epə,gläd·īd·əs\ *n* -ES [NL, fr. *epiglottis* + *-itis*] **:** inflammation of the epiglottis

epig·o·nal \ə'pigən°l, (')e¦p-\ *adj* **1 :** EPIGONIC **2** *usu cap* **:** of or belonging to a prehistoric culture of coastal Peru and Chile that is part of the Tiahuanaco culture **:** coastal Tiahuanaco

ep·i·go·na·tion \,epēgō'nä-,tyōn\ *n* -s [NGk, dim. of LGk *epigonatis* kneecap, fr. Gk *epi-* + *gonat-, gony* knee — more at KNEE] *Eastern Orthodox Church* **:** a rhombic vestment usu. of stiff material worn by a bishop or certain other ecclesiastical dignitaries on the right hip as a sign of authority and rank

¹ep·i·gone \'epə,gōn\ *also* **ep·i·gon** \-gän\ *n, pl* **epigones** *or* **epigons** [G *epigone*, fr. L *epigonus*, one of the seven sons of seven leaders in Greek legend who were defeated at Thebes and who themselves marched against Thebes, fr. Gk *epigonos*, lit., one born after, fr. *epigonos* born after, fr. *epigignesthai* to be born after, fr. *epi-* + *gignesthai* to be born — more at KIN] **:** an imitative follower; *esp* **:** an inferior imitator of a distinguished writer, philosopher, musician, or artist ‹the obsequious literature of the ~s —Vincent Sheean›

²epigone \"\ *n* -s [NL *epigonium*] **:** EPIGONIUM

ep·i·gon·ic \¦epə¦gänik\ *or* **epig·o·nous** \ə'pigənəs, (')e¦p-\ *adj* **:** of an epigone **:** IMITATIVE ‹the body of ~ poetry which now bulks largest derives from the Georgians —W.V.O'Connor›

ep·i·go·nich·thys \,epəgə'nikthəs\ *n, cap* [NL, fr. *epi-* + *gon-* + *-ichthys*] **:** a genus (the type of the family Epigonichthyidae) of lancelets having gonads only on the right side of the body

epig·o·nism \ə'pigə,nizəm, e'-; 'epə,gō,n-, 'epə,gä,n-\ *n* -s **:** artistic, literary, or intellectual imitation esp. by a later generation than the artist, writer, or thinker imitated ‹your verse . . . supports a primitive traditionalism and ~ —W.R. Benét›

ep·i·go·ni·um \,epə'gōnēəm\ *n* -s [NL, fr. *epi-* + Gk *gonē* seed + NL *-ium*] **:** CALYPTRA; *esp* **:** the cover enclosing the young sporangium of a liverwort

epig·o·nos \ə'pigənəs, e'-, -,näs\ *n, pl* **epigo·noi** \-,nȯi\ [Gk] **:** ¹EPIGONE

epig·o·nus \-,nəs\ *n, pl* **epigo·ni** \-,nī, -,nē\ [L — more at EPIGONE] **:** ¹EPIGONE

ep·i·gram \'epə,gram, -raa(ə)m\ *n* -s [ME *epigrame*, fr. L *epigramma*, fr. Gk, fr. *epigraphein* to write on, inscribe, fr. *epi-* + *graphein* to write — more at CARVE] **1** *obs* **:** EPIGRAPH 1 **2 a :** a short poem treating concisely, pointedly, and often satirically of a single thought or event and often ending with a witticism or ingenious turn of thought ‹the Earl of Rochester's ~ on Charles II: "here lies our sovereign lord the king, whose word no man relies on; he never says a foolish thing nor ever does a wise one"› **b :** a terse, sage, or witty often paradoxical saying ‹speaks in a characteristically paradoxical ~ of the "sacred duty of lawlessness" —G.L.Kline› — compare APHORISM, APOTHEGM **c :** epigrammatic expression ‹his conversation . . . was a cascade of wit, ~, and poetic images —G.H. Genzmer› **3 :** a small piece of meat (as of lamb, game, poultry) usu. breaded and fried and served with a sauce and vegetables as an entree

ep·i·gram·mat·ic \¦epəgrə¦mad·|ik, -pēg-, -at|, |ēk\ *also* **ep·i·gram·mat·i·cal** \|əkəl, |ēk-\ *adj* [LL *epigrammaticus*, fr. L *epigrammat-, epigramma* + *-icus* -ic, -ical] **1 :** having the form of, resembling, or suggestive of an epigram ‹the ~ expression — "some are too foolish to commit follies"› ‹the ~ simplification by means of which fables please and . . . instruct —*Times Lit. Supp.*› **:** PITHY ‹~ style› **2 :** marked by or given to the use of epigrams ‹fairly short, extremely compact, ~ essays —Antonio Iglesias› ‹a jaunty, bulbous, ~ Parisian of eighty —*Holiday*› — **ep·i·gram·mat·i·cal·ly** \|ək(ə)lē, |ēk-, -li\ *adv*

ep·i·gram·ma·tism \,epə'gramə,tizəm\ *n* -s [*epigrammatic* + *-ism*] **:** epigrammatic quality ‹the playfulness and ~ of the general style —Jane Austen›

ep·i·gram·ma·tist \-məd·əst, -mətə-\ *also* **ep·i·gram·mist** \'epə,gramə̇st, -graam-\ *n* -s [*epigrammatist* fr. LL *epigrammatista*, fr. L *epigrammat-, epigramma* + *-ista* -ist; *epigrammist* fr. *epigram* + *-ist*] **:** a maker of epigrams

ep·i·gram·ma·tize \,epə'gramə,tīz\ *vb* -ED/-ING/-S [*epigrammatic* + *-ize*] *vt* **1 :** to express epigrammatically ‹he *epigrammatized* the same thought› **2 :** to make an epigram about (as a person) ~ *vi* **:** to make an epigram ‹*epigrammatizing* on passing events›

ep·i·gram·ma·tiz·er \-zə(r)\ *n* -s **:** EPIGRAMMATIST

ep·i·gramme \'epə,gram, -raa(ə)m\ *n* -s [F *épigramme*, lit., epigram, fr. L *epigramma*] **1 :** EPIGRAM 3 **2 :** a dish of small pieces of one kind of meat (as lamb) prepared in two different ways (as some breaded and fried and others broiled)

ep·i·graph \'epə,graf, -áf\ *n* [Gk *epigraphē*, fr. fem. of *epigraphos* inscribed, fr. *epigraphein* to write on, inscribe — more at EPIGRAM] **1 :** INSCRIPTION; *esp* **:** an inscription engraved in durable material (as on an ancient temple or monument or a coin) **2 :** a quotation set at the beginning of a literary work (as a novel) or a division of it to suggest its theme **:** MOTTO ‹a passage from the *Divine Comedy* provided the ~ of the novel —R.P.Warren›

epig·ra·pher \ə'pigrəfə(r), e'-\ *n* -s **:** EPIGRAPHIST

ep·i·graph·ic \¦epə¦grafik, -fēk\ *also* **ep·i·graph·i·cal** \-fəkəl, -fēk-\ *adj* **1 :** of, consisting of, or bearing inscriptions ‹Syria has begun to produce its ~ wealth of cuneiform tablets —J.H.Iliffe› **2 :** of or relating to epigraphy ‹archaeological, ~, and philological studies› **3 :** of a style characteristically used in inscriptions ‹a block of basalt engraved with a text . . . in Greek ~ characters —M.R.Dobie› — **ep·i·graph·i·cal·ly** \-fək(ə)lē, -fēk-, -li\ *adv*

epig·ra·phist \ə'pigrəfəst, e'-\ *n* -s **:** a specialist in epigraphy

epig·ra·phy \-fē,-fi\ *n* -ES [irreg. (influence of *-graphy*) fr. *epigraph* + *-y*] **1 a :** EPIGRAPHS, INSCRIPTIONS **b :** the style of lettering used in inscriptions ‹on the basis of the ~ and the language this monument has been assigned to the first half of the eighth century —J.H.Fisher› **2 :** a study or science of inscriptions; *esp* **:** the deciphering and interpretation of ancient inscriptions ‹paleography or the decipherment of documents and ~ . . . have been indispensable keys to the history of the alphabet —Edward Clodd›

epig·y·nous \ə'pijənəs, e'-\ *adj* [*epi-* + *-gynous*] **1** *of stamens, petals, and sepals* **:** adnate to the surface of the ovary and appearing to grow from the top of it **2** *of a flower* **:** having epigynous floral parts — compare HYPOGYNOUS, PERIGYNOUS

epig·y·num \-nəm\ *also* **ep·i·gyne** \'epə,jīn\ *n* -s [NL *epigynum*, fr. *epi-* + *-gynum* (fr. Gk *-gynon*, neut. of *-gynos* -gynous)] **:** the female genital opening of an arachnid; *also* **:** a chitinous plate overlying this opening in a spider

epig·y·ny \ə'pijənē, e'-\ *n* -ES [*epi-* + *-gyny*] **:** the condition of being epigynous

epi·hip·pus \,epə'hipəs, ,epē'-\ *n, cap* [NL, fr. *epi-* + *-hippus*] **:** a genus of ancestral horses of the Upper Eocene known only from fragmentary remains and having the middle toe of each foot prominent and the side toes rather slender

epi·hy·al \-'hīəl\ *n* -s [*epi-* + *hyoid* + *-al*] **:** an element of the hyoid arch lying between the stylohyal and the ceratohyal that in man is the stylohyoid ligament and in many vertebrates forms a distinct bone

epi·ianthinite \¦epē+\ *n* [*epi-* + *ianthinite*] **:** a mineral occurring as an alteration product of ianthinite

epikeia *var of* EPIEIKEIA

epiklesis *var of* EPICLESIS

epil *abbr* epilogue

epi·labrum \¦epə, ¦epē+\ *n, pl* **epilabra** [NL, fr. *epi-* + *labrum*] **:** a transverse process at the side of the labrum of certain myriopods

ep·i·lach·na \,epə'laknə\ *n, cap* [NL, fr. *epi-* + *-lachna* (fr. Gk *lachnē* soft woolly hair)] **:** a genus of ladybirds that feed on plants both as larvae and adults — see MEXICAN BEAN BEETLE

epi·lamellar \¦epə, ¦epi+\ *adj* [*epi-* + *lamellar*] *anat* **:** outside the basement membrane

ep·i·lat·ing wax \'epə,lād·iŋ-\ *n* [fr. pres. part. of *epilate* "to remove hair", back-formation fr. *epilation*] **:** a mixture of resins and waxes designed to remove cosmetically undesirable hair by being applied hot to a surface and pulled away with the embedded hairs after cooling

ep·i·la·tion \,epə'lāshən\ *n* -s [F *épilation*, fr. *épiler* to remove hair (fr. *é-* e- + L *pilus* hair) + *-ation* — more at PILE] **:** the loss or removal of hair from any cause or for any reason — compare DEPILATION

ep·i·la·tor \'epə,lād·ə(r)\ *n* -s **:** DEPILATORY; *specif* **:** EPILATING WAX

ep·i·lem·ma \,epə'lemə\ *n* -s [NL, fr. *epi-* + *-lemma*] **:** the sheath covering a terminal nerve fibril — **ep·i·lem·mal** \¦epə¦leməl\ *adj*

ep·i·lep·sy \'epə,lepsē, -si\ *n* -ES [MF *epilepsie*, fr. LL *epilepsia*, fr. Gk *epilēpsia*, fr. *epilēptos* (verbal of *epilambanein* to seize, attack, fr. *epi-* + *lambanein* to take, seize) + *-ia* -y — more at LATCH] **:** a chronic nervous disorder of man and other animals that involves changes in the state of consciousness and of motion and that is due either to an inborn defect which produces convulsions of greater or lesser severity with clouding of consciousness or to an organic lesion of the brain produced by tumor, injury, toxic agents, or glandular disturbances — see GRAND MAL, PETIT MAL; JACKSONIAN EPILEPSY

epilept- *or* **epilepti-** *or* **epilepto-** *comb form* [F *épilept-*, fr. L *epilept-*, fr. Gk *epilēpt-*, fr. *epilēptos*] **:** epilepsy ‹*epilept*oid› ‹*epilepto*genic›

¹ep·i·lep·tic \¦epə¦leptik, -tēk\ *adj* [F *épileptique*, fr. LL *epilepticus*, fr. Gk *epilēptikos*, fr. *epilēptos* + *-ikos* -ic] **1 :** relating to, affected with, or having the characteristics of epilepsy **2 :** suggestive of epilepsy ‹the effect on the public mind was ~ —C.W.Ferguson› **:** CONVULSIVE ‹his dancing was . . . ~ —*Springfield (Mass.) Republican*› — **ep·i·lep·ti·cal·ly** \-tək(ə)lē, -tēk-, -li\ *adv*

²epileptic \"\ *also* **ep·i·lept** \'epə,lept\ *n* -s **:** one affected with epilepsy

ep·i·lep·ti·form \,epə'leptə,fȯrm\ *adj* [*epilept-* + *-form*] **:** resembling that of epilepsy ‹an ~ convulsion›

ep·i·lep·to·gen·ic \¦epə¦leptə¦jenik\ *adj* [*epilept-* + *-genic*] **:** inducing or tending to induce epilepsy

ep·i·lep·toid \-,tȯid\ *adj* [*epilept-* + *-oid*] **:** EPILEPTIFORM ‹an ~ symptom› **:** exhibiting symptoms resembling those of epilepsy ‹an ~ criminal›

ep·i·lim·net·ic \¦epə¦lim¦ned·ik\ *also* **ep·i·lim·ni·al** \-mnēəl\ *adj* [NL *epilimnion* + E *-etic* or *-al*] **:** of, relating to, or constituting an epilimnion

ep·i·lim·ni·on \,epə'limnē,än, -ēən\ *n, pl* **epilim·nia** \-ēə\ [NL, fr. *epi-* + *-limnion*] **:** the layer of water that overlies the thermocline of a lake and is subject to the action of wind — compare HYPOLIMNION

ep·i·lith·ic \¦epə¦lithik\ *adj* [*epi-* + *-lithic*] **:** growing upon stone or stonelike material ‹~ mosses› ‹~ lichens›

ep·i·lo·bi·um \,epə'lōbēəm\ *n* [NL, fr. *epi-* + Gk *lobos* lobe, pod + NL *-ium* — more at SLEEP] **1** *cap* **:** a large genus of widely distributed herbs (family Onagraceae) with pink or rarely yellow flowers, slender lanceolate leaves, and seeds with a silky coma **2** -s **:** any plant of the genus *Epilobium* **:** WILLOW HERB 1

ep·i·lo·bous \¦epə¦lōbəs; ə'piləbəs, e'-\ *adj* [*epi-* + *-lobous* (fr. Gk *lobos* lobe, pod)] *of an annelid prostomium* **:** set off by a groove and overlapping the first true segment

epil·o·gist \ə'piləjəst, e'-; 'epə,lȯgəst *also* -,läg-\ *n* -s [*epilogue* + *-ist*] **:** the writer or speaker of an epilogue

¹ep·i·logue *also* **ep·i·log** \'epə,lȯg *also* -pē-, *or* -pi- *or* -läg\ *n* -s [ME *epiloge*, fr. MF *epilogue*, fr. L *epilogus*, fr. Gk *epilogos*, fr. *epilegein* to say in addition, fr. *epi-* + *legein* to speak, gather — more at LEGEND] **1 :** the final part that serves typically to round out or complete the design of a nondramatic literary work **:** CONCLUSION ‹only in prefaces, ~s and topical interjections . . . did they achieve ease and force —Boris Ford› — called also *afterword;* compare FOREWORD, PREFACE **2 a** (1) **:** a speech often in verse addressed to the audience by one or more of the actors at the end of a play ‹a good play needs no ~ yet . . . good plays prove the better by the help of good ~s —Shak.› — compare PROLOGUE (2) **:** the actor speaking such an epilogue ‹it is not the fashion to see the lady the ~ but it is no more unhandsome than to see the lord the prologue —Shak.› **b :** the final scene of a play whose main action is set within a framework ‹the ~ reassembles the characters of the prologue, their experience enriched by the insight that the main body of the plot has given them —F.H. O'Hara & Margueritte Bro› **3 :** something felt to resemble an epilogue: as **a :** an incident or series of events that completes, rounds out, or gives point to a previous incident or series of events ‹the story can be regarded either as an ~ to the history of Roman Britain or as a prologue to the history of Saxon England —F.M.Stenton› **b :** the concluding section of a musical composition **:** CODA

2epilogue \"\ *vt* -ED/-ING/-S **:** to supply with an epilogue

epiloguize *vi* -ED/-ING/-S *obs* **:** to speak an epilogue

ep·i·loia \ˌepəˈlȯiə\ *n* -S [NL] **:** a dominant genetic anomaly in man marked by mental deficiency and multiple tumor formation of the skin and brain and perpetuated by high mutation rate

ep·i·ma·ni·kion \ˌepēməˈnēkˌyȯn\ *n, pl* **epimani·kia** \-yä\ [MGk, fr. Gk *epi-* + LGk *manikion* sleeve, dim. of *manika*, fr. L *manica* — more at MANCHE] **:** a cuff worn as a liturgical vestment over each sleeve of the sticharion by ecclesiastics of the Eastern Orthodox Church

ep·i·me·di·um \ˌepəˈmēdēəm\ *n, cap* [NL, fr. L *epimedion*, an unknown plant, fr. Gk *epimēdion*, fr. *epi-* + *mēdion*, a species of *Campanula*] **:** a small genus of nearly woody herbs (family Berberidaceae) having pinnately compound leaves and flowers with eight sepals in two whorls and four petals that are mostly transformed into nectaries

ep·i·me·lete \ˌepəˈmēˌlēt\ *n, pl* **epimele·tae** \-ˌməˈlēˌtē\ [Gk *epimelētēs*, lit., curator, fr. *epimelēsthai* to be careful, attentive] **:** an ancient Greek civil or religious official

ep·i·men·i·de·an \ˌepəˌmenəˈdēən\ *adj, usu cap* [*Epimenides*, 7th cent. B.C. Cretan poet and philosopher who according to legend slept for 57 years in a cave + E *-an*] **:** being or resembling that of the Cretan poet and philosopher Epimenides ⟨the *Epimenidean* paradox that "All Cretans are liars"⟩

ep·i·mer \ˈepəmə(r)\ *also* **epim·er·ide** \əˈpiməˌrīd\ *n* -S [*epimer* fr. *epi-* + *-mer*; *epimeride* fr. *epimer* + *-ide*] **:** either of two stereoisomers of a compound containing more than one asymmetric carbon atom that differ in the arrangement of groups around only one of the asymmetric carbons; *specif* **:** either of the stereoisomers of a sugar or sugar derivative that differ in the arrangement around the asymmetric carbon next to the carbonyl or carboxyl group ⟨glucose and mannose are ~s⟩

ep·i·me·ral \ˌ¦epə¦mirəl\ *adj* [NL *epimeron* + E *-al*] **:** of or relating to an epimeron

ep·i·mere \ˈepəˌmi(ə)r\ *n* -S [ISV *epi-* + *-mere*] **:** the dorsal portion of a mesodermal segment of a chordate embryo that functions as the source of myotome and sclerotome

ep·i·mer·ic \ˌ¦epə¦merik\ *adj* [*epimer* + *-ic*] **:** having the relationship of an epimer or epimers ⟨3-α-coprosterol is ~ with 3-β-coprosterol⟩

epim·er·ite \əˈpiməˌrīt, eˈ-\ *n* -S [ISV *epi-* + *mer-* + *-ite*] **:** an anterior prolongation of the protomerite of many gregarines bearing organelles for attachment to the host — **epim·er·it·ic** \ə¦‧‧¦ridik\ *adj*

ep·i·mer·i·za·tion \ˌepəmərəˈzāshən\ *n* -S **:** the process of epimerizing

ep·i·mer·ize \ˈepəməˌrīz\ *vt* -ED/-ING/-S [*epimer* + *-ize*] **:** to change into an epimer

ep·i·me·ron \ˌepəˈmiˌrän\ *n, pl* **epime·ra** \-irə\ [NL, fr. *epi-* + *-meron* (fr. Gk *mēros* thigh) — more at MEMBER] **1 :** a lateral part of the wall of a somite of an arthropod that is situated between the tergum and the insertion of the appendages **2 :** the posterior sclerite of a pleuron of an insect

ep·i·mor·pha \ˌepəˈmȯrfə\ *n pl, cap* [NL, fr. *epi-* + *-morpha*] **:** a division of centipedes commonly considered a subclass, comprising forms having 21 or more leg-bearing segments and young born with the adult number of legs — compare ANAMORPHA

ep·i·mor·phic \ˌ¦epə¦mȯrfik\ *adj* [*epi-* + *-morphic*] **:** having the same form (as the same number of body segments) in successive stages of growth — used of insects and other arthropods undergoing incomplete metamorphosis

ep·i·mor·pho·sis \ˌepəˈmȯrfəsəs *sometimes* -ˌmȯrˈfōs-\ *n* [NL, fr. *epi-* + *-morphosis*] **1 :** regeneration of a part or organism involving extensive cell proliferation followed by differentiation — compare MORPHALLAXIS **2 :** development without fundamental changes of form (as without adding segments) — compare METAMORPHOSIS

epi·myocardium \ˌ¦epə, ¦epē+\ *n* [NL, fr. *epi-* + *myocardium*] **:** the undifferentiated splanchnic mesodermal layer of the embryonic heart that subsequently differentiates into myocardium and epicardium

ep·i·my·si·um \ˌepəˈmiz(h)ēəm\ *n, pl* **epimy·sia** \-ēə\ [NL, fr. *epi-* + Gk *mys* mouse, muscle + NL *-ium* — more at MOUSE] **:** the external connective-tissue sheath of a muscle — compare ENDOMYSIUM, PERIMYSIUM

epi·naos \ˌ¦epə, ¦epē+\ *n, pl* **epinaoi** [*epi-* + *naos*] **:** a room in the rear of the cella of an ancient Greek temple — compare PRONAOS

epi·nard \āpēnäär\ *n, pl* **epinards** \"\ [F *épinard*, alter. (influenced by *-ard*) of MF *espinach* — more at SPINACH] **:** SPINACH

ep·i·nas·tic \ˌ¦epə¦nastik\ *adj* [ISV *epinasty* + *-ic*] **:** of, relating to, or caused by epinasty — **ep·i·nas·ti·cal·ly** \-tək(ə)lē\ *adv*

ep·i·nas·tism \ˌepəˈnaˌstizəm\ *n* -S **:** EPINASTY

ep·i·nas·ty \ˈepəˌnastē\ *n* -ES [ISV *epi-* + *-nasty*; orig. formed as G *epinastie*] **:** a nastic movement by which a plant part is bent outward and often downward (as in the unfolding of a flower petal) ⟨the opening of the bud is brought about by ... ~ —B.S.Meyer & D.B.Anderson⟩

ep·i·ne·phel·i·dae \ˌepənəˈfeləˌdē\ *n, pl, cap* [NL, fr. *Epinephelus*, type genus + *-idae*] *in some classifications* **:** a family of percoid fishes comprising *Epinephelus* and other genera that are usu. placed in Serranidae

ep·i·neph·e·lus \ˌepəˈnefələs\ *n, cap* [NL, fr. Gk *epinephelos* clouded, overcast, fr. *epi-* + *nephelē* cloud — more at NEBULA] **:** a large genus of fishes of warm seas including a number of typical groupers — see SERRANIDAE

ep·i·neph·rine \ˌepəˈneˌfrēn, -ˌfrən\ *also* **ep·i·neph·rin** \-ˌfrən\ *n* -S [ISV *epi-* + *nephr-* + *-ine*, *-in*] **:** a colorless crystalline feebly basic compound $(HO)_2C_6H_3CH(OH)CH_2NHCH_3$ existing in three optically different forms; 1-(3,4-dihydroxy-phenyl)-2-methylamino-ethanol; *esp* **:** the levorotatory form constituting the principal blood-pressure-raising hormone of the medulla of the adrenal glands, prepared from adrenal extracts and also synthetically, and used chiefly as a heart stimulant, as a vasoconstrictor in controlling hemorrhages of the skin and in prolonging the effects of local anesthetics, and as a muscle relaxant in bronchial asthma — called also *adrenaline*, *adrenin*

epi·neritic \ˌ¦epə, ¦epē+\ *adj* [*epi-* + *neritic*] **:** of, relating to, or constituting the upper portion of the neritic zone usu. to a depth of 120 feet — opposed to *infraneritic*

épi·nette \āpēnet\ *n* -S [CanF, dim. of F *épine* thorn, spine, fr. L *spina* — more at SPINE] **1** *dial* **:** any of several No. American spruces; *esp* **:** WHITE SPRUCE 1 **2** *dial* **:** a tamarack (*Larix laricina*)

1epi·neural \ˌ¦epə, ¦epē+\ *adj* [*epi-* + *neural*] **1 :** arising from the neural arch of a vertebra **2 :** overlying nervous tissue; *specif* **:** above the ventral nerve cord of an arthropod

2epineural \"\ *n* **:** a spine or process arising from the neural arch of a vertebra

epineural canal *n, zool* **:** a canal derived from the ambulacral groove and running between the radial nerve and the external epithelium in ophiuroids and echinoids

ep·i·neu·ri·um \ˌepəˈn(y)u̇rēəm\ *n* -S [NL, fr. *epi-* + *neur-* + *-ium*] **:** the external connective-tissue sheath of a nerve trunk

epin·gle \āˈpaŋˌglā; ¦āˌpan¦glā, -paŋ¦-\ *n* -S [F *épinglé*, fr. past part. of *épingler* to pin, fr. *épingle* pin, fr. L *spinula* small thorn, dim. of *spina* thorn, spine — more at SPINE] **:** a silk, rayon, or worsted clothing fabric in plain weave characterized by alternating wide and narrow cross ribs

ep·i·ni·cian \ˌepə¦nishən\ *or* **ep·i·nik·i·an** \-¦nikēən\ *adj* [Gk *epinikios* + E *-an*] **:** celebrating victory ⟨an ancient ~ ode⟩

ep·i·ni·ci·on \ˌepəˈnis(h)ēˌän\ *or* **ep·i·nik·i·on** \-nikē-\ *n, pl* **epini·cia** \-ēə\ *or* **epinik·ia** \-ēə\ [Gk *epinikion*, fr. neut. of *epinikios* of victory, fr. *epi-* + *-nikios* (fr. *nikē* victory)] **:** a song of triumph or a choral ode in honor of a victor in war or games (as in the Olympian or Pythian games)

ep·i·nine \ˈepəˌnēn, -nən\ *n* -S [*epinephrine*] **:** a colorless crystalline compound $(OH)_2C_6H_3CH_2CH_2NHCH_3$ used as a substitute for epinephrine

epinychium *or* **epionychium** *var of* EPONYCHIUM

epi·organism \ˌ¦epē+\ *n* [*epi-* + *organism*] **:** a complex of interacting individuals regarded as a functional entity (as in colonial protozoans or a hive of bees)

1epi·ornithic \ˌ¦epē+\ *adj* [*epi-* + *ornithic*] **:** affecting many birds of one kind at the same time — compare EPIDEMIC

2epiornithic \"\ *n* -S **1 :** an epiornithic disease **2 :** an outbreak of epiornithic disease

1epi·otic \ˌ¦epē+\ *adj* [*epi-* + *-otic* (of the ear)] **:** belonging to or constituting the upper and outer element of the bony capsule of the internal ear that in man forms a part of the temporal bone

2epiotic \"\ *n* -S **:** one of the small cartilage bones of the capsule of the inner ear in birds and lower vertebrates that is represented in mammals by a part of the temporal bone

ep·i·pac·tis \ˌepəˈpaktəs\ *n, cap* [NL, fr. Gk *epipaktis* rupturewort] **:** a genus of orchids with simple stems, plicate clasping leaves, and greenish or purplish irregular flowers in leafy-bracted racemes

epi·paleolithic \ˌ¦epə, ¦epē+\ *adj, usu cap* [ISV *epi-* + *paleolithic*] **:** MESOLITHIC

epiparasite \"+\ *n* [*epi-* + *parasite*] **1 :** ECTOPARASITE **2 :** HYPERPARASITE — **epi·parasitic** \"+\ *adj* — **epi·parasitism** \"+\ *n*

epi·pelagic \"+\ *adj* [*epi-* + *pelagic*] **:** of, relating to, or constituting the part of the oceanic zone into which enough light for photosynthesis penetrates

epi·peripheral \"+\ *adj* [*epi-* + *peripheral*] *of a bodily sensation* **:** originating upon the external surface of the body

epi·petalous \"+\ *adj* [*epi-* + *-petalous*] **:** having stamens inserted on the corolla

ep·i·phan·ic \ˌ¦epə¦fanik\ *adj* [*2epiphany* + *-ic*] **:** of or having the character of an epiphany ⟨~ events⟩

epiph·a·nize \əˈpifəˌnīz, ēˈ-,eˈ-\ *vt* -ED/-ING/-S [*2epiphany* + *-ize*] **:** to represent in a literary epiphany ⟨Joyce once *epiphanized* a whole sermon, audience, theme, and preacher in nine words: 'Pilate! Wy don't you old back that owlin mob?' —Hugh Kenner⟩

1epiph·a·ny \əˈpifənē, ēˈ-,eˈ-, -ni\ *n* -ES *usu cap* [ME *epiphanie*, fr. MF *epiphanie*, fr. LL *epiphania*, fr. LGk *epiphania*, pl., fr. neut. pl. of *epiphanios* manifest, fr. Gk *epiphainein* to display, make manifest, fr. *epi-* + *phainein* to show — more at FANCY] **:** a Christian feast celebrated on Jan. 6 orig. and still in the Eastern Church commemorating the baptism of Christ and secondarily the marriage feast at Cana but since the 5th century in the Western Church commemorating the coming of the Magi as the occasion of the first manifestation of Christ to the Gentiles — called also *Twelfth Day*

2epiphany \"\ *n* -ES [Gk *epiphaneia*, lit., appearance, manifestation, fr. *epiphanēs* coming to light, appearing (fr. *epiphainein*) + *-ia* -y] **1 a :** an appearance or revelatory manifestation of God or of a divine being or a god ⟨the ~ of Jesus at the Transfiguration⟩ ⟨the prophetess of the ancient Greeks prophesied on the day of the god's ~⟩ **b :** an incarnation of God or a god in earthly form ⟨the ~ of God in Christ⟩ ⟨Greek goddesses that had rabbit and pig *epiphanies*⟩ **2 a :** a usu. sudden manifestation or perception of the essential nature or meaning of something ⟨its soul, its whatness leaps to us from the vestment of its appearance ... the object achieves its ~ —James Joyce⟩ **:** an intuitive grasp of reality through something usu. simple and striking (as a commonplace event or person) ⟨Stephen's brothers and sisters, formerly seen as separate entities ... became the essence of childhood; in the performance of his labor, Joyce progressed from things to *epiphanies* of things —J.W. Aldridge⟩ **b :** a literary representation of an epiphany **:** a symbolically revealing work or part of a work ⟨the ~ in *Oedipus*, the final tableau of the blind old man with his incestuous brood ... conveys the moral truth which underlay the action —Francis Fergusson⟩

1epi·pharyngeal \ˌ¦epə, ¦epē+\ *adj* [*epi-* + *pharyngeal*] **1 :** of or relating to the epipharynx **2 :** belonging to the dorsal aspect of the pharynx **:** upon the pharynx; *specif* **:** PHARYNGOBRANCHIAL

2epipharyngeal \"\ *n* **:** PHARYNGOBRANCHIAL

epi·pharynx \"+\ *n* [NL, fr. *epi-* + *pharynx*] **:** a median lobe beneath the labrum of certain insects

ep·i·phe·gus \ˌepəˈfēgəs\ [NL, fr. *epi-* + Gk *phēgos* oak — more at BEECH] *syn of* EPIFAGUS

epi·phenomenal \ˌ¦epə, ¦epē+\ *adj* [*epi-* + *phenomenal*] **:** having the character of or relating to an epiphenomenon **:** DERIVATIVE ⟨social currents of which the war was only an ~ symptom —J.G.Jenkins⟩ — **epi·phenomenally** \"+\ *adv*

epi·phenomenalism \"+\ *n* **:** the doctrine that consciousness or mental processes accompany and are determined by brain processes but cannot influence them — compare INTERACTIONISM

epi·phenomenalist \"+\ *n* **:** one who believes in epiphenomenalism ⟨that behaviorist may ... be also an ~ —*Jour. of Philosophical Studies*⟩ ⟨an ~ view of the mind-body relation⟩

epi·phenomenon \"+\ *n, pl* **epiphenomena** *also* **epi·phenomenons** [*epi-* + *phenomenon*] **1 :** a secondary phenomenon accompanying another phenomenon and thought of as caused by it ⟨fate determines what will happen to us, while ideas, convictions, and intentions are no more than phosphorescent *epiphenomena* —J.W.Krutch⟩ **2 :** an accidental or accessory event or process occurring in the course of a disease but not necessarily related to that disease

ep·i·phloe·dal \ˌ¦epə¦flēdᵊl\ *or* **ep·i·phloe·dic** \-ēdik\ *adj* [irreg. fr. *epi-* + Gk *phloios* bark + E *-al* or *-ic*] **:** growing upon the surface of bark ⟨an ~ lichen⟩

ep·i·pho·ne·ma \ˌepəfōˈnēmə\ *n, pl* **epiphonemas** \-məz\ *or* **epiphone·mae** \-ˌmē\ [L, fr. Gk *epiphōnēma*, fr. *epiphōnein* to mention, fr. *epi-* + *phōnein* to speak, fr. *phōnē* sound — more at FAME] **:** an exclamatory sentence or striking esp. summary comment concluding a discourse

epiph·o·ra \əˈpifərə\ *n* -S [NL, fr. *epi-* + *-phora*] **:** a watering of the eyes due to excessive secretion of tears or to obstruction of the lacrimal passages

ep·i·phragm \ˈepəˌfram\ *n* -S [Gk *epiphragma* covering, lid, fr. *epiphrassein*, *epiphrattein* to block up, stop up, fr. *epi-* + *phrassein*, *phrattein* to enclose, fence in, block — more at FARCE] **1 :** a membranous or calcareous septum with which many inoperculate gastropods close the shell aperture in hibernation or aestivation **2 a :** a taut membrane attached to the tips of the peristome teeth and closing the aperture of the capsule in mosses of the family Polytrichaceae — called also *tympanum* **b :** a delicate membrane closing the cuplike sporophore in fungi of the family Nidulariaceae

ep·i·phyll \ˈepəˌfil\ *n* -S [*epi-* + Gk *phyllon* leaf — more at BLADE] **:** an epiphyte growing on the surface esp. the upper surface of a leaf — see EPIGENOUS

epi·phyllous *also* **epi·phylline** \ˌ¦epə, ¦epē+\ *adj* [*epi-* + *-phyllous* or *phylline*] **:** EPIGENOUS

ep·i·phyl·lum \ˌepəˈfiləm\ *n* [NL, fr. *epi-* + *-phyllum*] **1** *cap* **:** a small genus of tropical American cacti having flattened jointed irregularly branching stems and showy tubular flowers — see ORCHID CACTUS **2** -S **:** any plant of the genus *Epiphyllum*; *esp* **:** CRAB CACTUS

epiph·y·sary \əˈpifəˌserē\ *adj* [NL *epiphysis* + E *-ary*] **:** EPIPHYSEAL

epiph·y·se·al \əˌpifə¦sēəl, -ˈzē- *also* ¦epə¦fizē-\ *also* **ep·i·phys·i·al** \ˌ¦epə¦fizē-\ *adj* [*epiphyseal* alter. of *epiphysial*; *epiphysial* fr. NL *epiphysis* + E *-al*] **:** of or belonging to an epiphysis **:** occurring toward an epiphysis ⟨~ end of a bone⟩ ⟨taking place at an epiphysis ⟨~ formation of bone⟩

epiphyseal arch *n* **:** an arched structure in the embryonic third ventricle marking the site of development of the pineal body

epiphyseal cartilage *n* **:** the cartilage containing an epiphysis and uniting it with the shaft

epiphyseal line *n* **:** the line marking the site of the epiphyseal cartilage

epiphyseal separation *n* **:** EPIPHYSIOLYSIS

epiph·y·si·od·e·sis \əˌpifəsēˈädəsəs, ˌepəˌfizē-\ *n, pl* **epiphysiode·ses** \-dəˌsēz\ [NL, fr. *epiphysio-* (fr. *epiphysis*) + *-desis*] **:** the surgical reattachment of a separated epiphysis to the shaft of its bone

epiph·y·si·ol·y·sis \-ˈäləsəs\ *n, pl* **epiphysioly·ses** \-əˌsēz\ [NL, fr. *epiphysio-* + *-lysis*] **:** abnormal separation of the epiphysis from the bone shaft — called also *slipped epiphysis*

epiph·y·sis \əˈpifəsəs\ *n, pl* **epiphy·ses** \-əˌsēz\ [NL, fr. Gk, fr. *epiphyesthai* to grow on, fr. *epi-* + *phyesthai* to grow, pass. of *phyein* to bring forth) + *-sis* — more at BE] **1 :** a part or process of a bone that ossifies separately and later becomes ankylosed to the main part of the bone; *esp* **:** one of the ends of the long bones of the limbs in higher vertebrates — distinguished from *diaphysis* **2 :** PINEAL BODY **3 :** a movable process of the tibia of certain lepidopterous insects

epiph·y·si·tis \əˌpifəˈsīdəs\ *n* -ES [NL, fr. *epiphysis* + *-itis*] **:** inflammation of an epiphysis

ep·i·phyte \ˈepəˌfīt\ *n* -S [*epi-* + *-phyte*] **1 :** a plant that grows upon another plant (as a tree) nonparasitically or sometimes upon some other object (as a building or telegraph wire), derives its moisture and nutrients from the air and rain and sometimes from debris accumulating around it, and is found in the temperate zone (as many mosses, liverworts, lichens, and algae) and in the tropics (as many ferns, cacti, orchids, and bromeliads) — called also *air plant* **2 :** a plant ectoparasitic on a human or animal body

ep·i·phyt·ic \ˌepə¦fidik\ *also* **ep·i·phyt·al** \-ˈfīdᵊl\ *adj* **1 :** relating to or being an epiphyte **2 :** living on the surface of plants ⟨an ~ marine commensal⟩ ⟨an ~ insect⟩ — **ep·i·phyt·i·cal·ly** \-fidək(ə)lē\ *adv*

ep·i·phy·tol·o·gy \ˌepəˌfīˈtäləjē\ *n* -ES [*epiphyt*otic + *-ology*] **1 :** a science that deals with character, ecology, and causes of outbreak of plant diseases esp. of epiphytotic nature **2 :** the sum of the factors controlling the presence or absence of a disease or pathogen of plants ⟨aspects of ~ and control of tomato fruit rot⟩

1ep·i·phy·tot·ic \ˌ¦epəˌfī¦tädik\ *adj* [*epi-* + *phyt-* + *-otic*] **1** *of an infectious plant disease* **:** tending to recur sporadically usu. over a wide area and to affect large numbers of susceptible plants whenever present ⟨an ~ blight of potatoes⟩ **2 :** of, relating to, or tending to produce an epiphytotic ⟨the disease exhibited an ~ tendency⟩ ⟨~ conditions associated with a single-crop agriculture⟩

2epiphytotic \"\ *n* -S **:** an outbreak of epiphytotic disease

epi·pi·al \ˌepə¦pīəl, ¦epē¦-\ *adj* [*epi-* + *pia* (*mater*) + *-al*] **:** situated upon the pia mater

epi·plankton \ˌ¦epə, ¦epē+\ *n* [*epi-* + *plankton*] **:** the portion of the plankton occurring from the surface of the sea to a depth of about 100 fathoms — **epi·planktonic** \"+\ *adj*

ep·i·plasm \ˈepəˌplazəm\ *n* [ISV *epi-* + *-plasm*] **:** the remnants of cytoplasm left in the ascus of ascomycetous fungi after spore formation — **ep·i·plas·mic** \ˌ¦epə¦plazmik\ *adj*

epi·plastron \ˌ¦epə, ¦epē+\ *n, pl* **epiplastra** *or* **epiplastrons** [*epi-* + *plastron*] **:** one of the first pair of lateral bony plates in the plastron of a turtle sometimes considered homologous with the clavicles of other vertebrates

1epi·pleural \"+\ *adj* [*epi-* + *pleural*] **1 :** arising from or attached to a rib **2** [NL *epipleuron* + E *-al*] **:** of or in the region of the epipleurals or epipleura

2epipleural \"\ *n* **:** a spine or bone arising from the rib of a fish and passing toward the lateral line

epi·pleuron \"+\ *n, pl* **epipleura** [NL, fr. *epi-* + *pleuron*] **:** a part of the outer margin of an elytron of a beetle turned down on the side of the thorax and abdomen

ep·i·plo·ic \ˌ¦epə¦plōik\ *adj* [NL *epiploon* + E *-ic*] **:** of or associated with the epiploon

epiploic foramen *n* **:** the only opening between the omental bursa and the general peritoneal sac — called also *foramen of Winslow*

epip·lo·on \əˈpipləˌwän\ *n, pl* **epip·loa** \-ləwə\ [NL, fr. Gk] **1 :** OMENTUM; *specif* **:** GREATER OMENTUM **2 :** FAT BODY 2

1ep·i·po·di·al \ˌ¦epə¦pōdēəl\ *adj* [NL *epipodium* + E *-al*] **:** of or relating to an epipodium

2epipodial \"\ *adj* [*epipodite* + *-al*] **:** of or relating to an epipodite

3epipodial \"\ *adj* [NL *epipodiale*] **:** of or relating to an epipodiale

ep·i·po·di·a·le \ˌepəˌpōdēˈā(ˌ)lē\ *n, pl* **epipodia·lia** \-ālēə, -ālyə\ [NL, fr. *epi-* + Gk *podion* (dim. of *pod-*, *pous* foot) + L *-ale* (neut. of *-alis* -al) — more at FOOT] **:** any one of the bones of either the forearm or shank

epip·o·dite \əˈpipəˌdīt, eˈ-\ *n* [*epi-* + *-podite*] **:** a branch of the basal joint of the protopodite of the thoracic limbs of many arthropods often highly modified and commonly absent in higher and terrestrial forms — **epip·o·dit·ic** \ə¦‧‧¦didik\ *adj*

ep·i·po·di·um \ˌepəˈpōdēəm\ *n, pl* **epipo·dia** \-ēə\ [NL, fr. *epi-* + *-podium*] **:** a lateral ridge or fold along either side of the foot in various gastropods (as members of the Rhipidoglossa) sometimes bearing appendages, sensory organs, and pigment spots

epi·precoracoid \ˌ¦epə, ¦epē+\ *adj* [*epi-* + *precoracoid*] **:** of, relating to, or constituting a cartilaginous element of the pectoral girdle of some turtles situated at the ventral end of the precoracoid

ep·i·proct \ˈepəˌpräkt\ *n* [*epi-* + Gk *prōktos* anus — more at PROCT-] **:** a plate above the anus of certain insects that is usu. the dorsal part of the 11th segment

ep·i·pter·ic \ˌ¦epə(p)¦terik, ¦eˌpip¦t-, ¦epē¦t-\ *adj* [*epi* + *pter-* + *-ic*] **:** relating to or being a small Wormian bone sometimes present in the human skull between the parietal and the great wing of the sphenoid

1epi·pterygoid \ˌ¦epə, ¦epē+\ *adj* [*epi-* + *pterygoid*] **:** situated above or upon the pterygoid **:** relating to or being a slender bone in the skull of most lizards and some other reptiles that extends between the pterygoid and the parietal or anterior end of the pro-otic

2epipterygoid \"\ *n* -S **:** the epipterygoid bone — called also *columella cranii*

epi·pubic \ˌ¦epə, ¦epē+\ *adj* [*epi-* + *pubic*] **:** borne on the pubis; *specif* **:** relating to or being the epipubis or other cartilage, bone, or pair of bones attached in front of the pubis (as the marsupial bones of marsupials and monotremes)

epipubis \"+\ *n, pl* **epipubes** [NL, fr. *epi-* + *pubis*] **:** an unpaired cartilage or bone in front of the pubis in some amphibians and other vertebrates

epirogeny *var of* EPEIROGENY

epi·rote \əˈpīˌrōt, ēˈ-, ˈepəˌrōt, ˈeˌpī,-\ *also* **epei·rot** \əˈpīrət, ēˈpī-\ *n* -S [L *Epirotes*, fr. Gk *Ēpeirōtēs*, fr. *Ēpeiros* Epirus + *-ōtēs* -ote] **:** a native or inhabitant of ancient or modern Epirus in northwestern Greece

epi·rotulian \ˌ¦epə, ¦epē+\ *adj* [*epi-* + *rotula* + *-ian*] **:** situated upon or superficial to the patella

ep·ir·rhe·ma \ˌepiˈrēmə\ *n* -S [Gk *epirrhēma*, fr. *epi-* + *rhēma* word, saying — more at WORD] **:** an address usu. about public affairs spoken by the coryphaeus after the parabasis in old Greek comedy — **ep·ir·rhe·mat·ic** \ˌ¦epə(ˌ)rē¦madik, -ˌrə¦-\ *adj*

épis *pl of* ÉPI

epis *or* **episc** *abbr* episcopal

epi·scia \əˈpish(ē)ə\ *n* [NL, fr. Gk *episkia*, fem. of *episkios* shaded, dark, fr. *epi-* + *-skios* (fr. *skia* shade, shadow) — more at SHINE] **1** *cap* **:** a genus of tropical American herbs (family Gesneriaceae) having soft hairy foliage and flowers with four stamens and a staminodium **2** -S **:** any plant of the genus *Episcia*

epi·sclera \ˌ¦epə, ¦epē+\ *n* -S [NL, fr. *epi-* + *sclera*] **:** the layer of connective tissue between the conjunctiva and the sclerotic coat of the eye

epi·scleral \"+\ *adj* [*epi-* + *scleral*] **1 :** situated upon the sclerotic coat of the eye **2** [NL *episclera* + E *-al*] **:** of or relating to the episclera

epi·scle·ri·tis \ˌ‧‧skləˈrīdəs\ *n* -ES [NL, fr. *epi-* + *sclera* + *-itis*] **:** inflammation of the superficial layers of the sclera

epis·co·pa·cy \əˈpiskəpəsē, ēˈ-, -si\ *n* -ES [*1episcopate* + *-cy*] **1 :** government of the church by bishops or by a hierarchy (as of bishops, priests, and deacons) ⟨tough Presbyterian Scots who had overthrown the ~ —George Willison⟩ **2 :** the state of being a bishop **:** episcopal rank **3 :** DIOCESE **4 :** EPISCOPATE 3

1epis·co·pal \-pəl\ *adj* [ME, fr. LL *episcopalis*, fr. *episcopus* bishop + L *-alis* -al — more at BISHOP] **1 :** of, being, or suited to a bishop ⟨~ jurisdiction⟩ ⟨~ chairman of the education department⟩ ⟨an ~ voice⟩ ⟨an ~ class⟩ **:** DIOCESAN ⟨~ lands⟩ **2 a :** of, advocating, or governed by an episcopacy ⟨subject to neither presbyterian nor ~ system⟩ ⟨did not save the ~ author from royal displeasure —Douglas Bush⟩ ⟨entertains friendly feelings for the Old Catholic and Lutheran ~ churches —*Sobornost*⟩ **:** HIERARCHICAL ⟨the church of the first few centuries had an ~ type of government —E.A.Nida⟩ **b** *usu cap* **:** of or relating to the Protestant Episcopal Church or the Episcopal Church in Scotland ⟨an ~ rector⟩; *sometimes* : ANGLICAN — **episcopally** *adv*

²**episcopal** \"\ *n* -s *usu cap* : EPISCOPALIAN — not often in formal use

¹**epis·co·pa·lian** \ə,piskə'pālyən, ē,pisk-, -lēən\ *n* -s [¹*episcopal* + *-ian*] **1** : an adherent of the episcopal form of church government **2** *usu cap* : a member of an episcopal church (as the Protestant Episcopal Church)

²**episcopalian** \¦=¦==¦=(=)=\ *adj, usu cap* : EPISCOPAL 2b

epis·co·pa·lian·ism \=,=='pālyə,nizəm, -lēə,-\ *n* -s *cap* : the doctrine and usages of Episcopalians

epis·co·pal·ism \='piskəpə,lizəm\ *n* -s : the theory that in church government supreme authority resides in a body of bishops and not in any one individual — compare GALLICANISM

epis·co·pate \-pə¦t, -,pāt, usu ¦d.+V\ *n* -s [LL *episcopatus*, fr. *episcopus* + L *-atus* -ate] **1 a** : the office of a bishop ⟨he held the ~ for 10 years⟩ **b** : the institution of episcopacy ⟨the abortive effort to introduce the ~ in the colonies —M.H. Shepherd⟩ **2** : DIOCESE ⟨in administrative matters the ~ is an autonomous organization —F.S.Mead⟩ **3** : the body of bishops (as in a country) ⟨the ~ and the nobility⟩ **4** : the period of a bishop's office ⟨he spent almost all his ~ in journeys through his province —S.V.Troitsky⟩

ep·i·scope \'epə,skōp\ *n* -s [ISV *epi-* + *-scope*] : a projector for images of opaque objects — **ep·i·scop·ic** \¦epə¦skäpik\ *adj*

epis·co·pize \ə'piskə,pīz, ē'-\ *vb* -ED/-ING/-S [LL *episcopus* bishop + E *-ize* — more at BISHOP] *vt* **1** : to make a bishop of **2** : to make episcopalian ~ *vi* : to act as bishop

ep·i·sco·tis·ter \,epəskō'tistə(r)\ *n* -s [fr. (assumed) Gk *episkotistēs* (verbal of Gk *episkotizein* to shadow, darken, fr. *epi-* + *skotizein* to darken, fr. *skotos* dark + *-izein* -ize) + E *-er* — more at SHADE] : a device for reducing the intensity of light in known ratio by means of rapidly rotating opaque and transparent sectors

epi·sematic \¦epə, ¦epē+\ *adj* [*epi-* + *sematic*] : serving to assist animals of the same species in recognizing each other — used of colors or structures; compare APOSEMATIC

epi·sepalous \"+\ *adj* [ISV *epi-* + *-sepalous*] *of stamens* : growing on or adnate to the sepals

episio- *comb form* [NL, fr. Gk *epision, epeision* pubic region] : vulva ⟨*episio*tomy⟩ : vulva and ⟨*episio*perineal⟩

ep·i·si·ot·o·my \,epə,sī'ädəmē\ *n* [ISV *episio-* + *-tomy*] : surgical incision of the vulvar orifice for obstetrical purposes during parturition

epi·skeletal \¦epə, ¦epē+\ *adj* [*epi-* + *skeletal*] : above or outside the endoskeleton

ep·i·sode \'epə,sōd *sometimes* -pē| *or* -pi| *or* |,zōd\ *n* -s [Gk *epeisodion*, fr. neut. of *epeisodios* coming in besides, fr. *epi-* + *eisodios* coming in, going in, fr. *eis* in + *-odios* (fr. *hodos* road, way, journey); akin to Gk *en* in — more at IN, CEDE] **1** : a usu. brief unit of action in a dramatic or literary work: as **a** : the part of an ancient Greek tragedy between two choric songs and equivalent to any developed situation in a modern play **b** : a developed situation that is integral to but separable from a continuous narrative (as a novel or play) : INCIDENT ⟨that childhood visit . . . to "dog town" is a perfect little ~ —M.G.Geismar⟩ : SCENE **c** : one of a series of loosely connected stories or scenes ⟨his novels . . . tend to resolve themselves into a series of ~*s* resembling beads on a string —Malcolm Cowley⟩ **d** : the part of a radio, television, or motion-picture serial presented at one performance ⟨a TV film series of 30 ~*s*⟩ **2** : an occurrence or connected series of occurrences and developments which may be viewed as distinctive and apart although part of a larger or more comprehensive series ⟨considers her war work an ~, not equal in quality to her lifework —Christina Baker⟩: as **a** : a distinctive and significant event or series of events in the geological history of a region or feature ⟨fourth glacial ~ of the Quaternary period⟩ ⟨volcanic ~⟩ ⟨two high-water ~*s*⟩ **b** : an occurrence of a usu. recurrent pathological abnormal condition ⟨a febrile ~⟩ ⟨a coronary ~⟩ **3** : a digressive subdivision in a musical composition that is either derived from the chief thematic material (as in a fugue) or is completely new material (as in a rondo) **syn** see OCCURRENCE

ep·i·sod·ic \¦==¦sädik, -dēk *sometimes* -¦zä-\ *also* **ep·i·sod·i·cal** \-dəkəl, -dēk-\ *or* **ep·i·sod·al** \-¦sōdᵊl *sometimes* -¦zō-\ *adj* **1** : made up of separate esp. loosely connected episodes ⟨the book is ~ and the various incidents don't always hang together —Alberta Eiseman⟩ ⟨most of these symphonies are not truly symphonic . . .; their structure is ~ —Winthrop Sargeant⟩ ⟨an ~ life⟩ **2** : having the form of an episode ⟨mixture of ~ adventure, satire, and learned discourses —Douglas Bush⟩ : INCIDENTAL ⟨compresses the five acts of the original into three, eliminates all ~ material —E.H. Zeydel⟩ **3** : of or limited in duration or significance to a particular episode : TEMPORARY, EPHEMERAL ⟨a reform movement that made only an ~ appearance in the life of the city⟩ ⟨the meeting if it is to be historic rather than ~ must usher in an era of peaceful change —J.F.Dulles⟩ ⟨his accounts . . . are more concerned with ~ events such as the succession of rulers and peoples —W.W.Taylor⟩ **4** : occurring, appearing, or changing at usu. irregular intervals : OCCASIONAL, CAPRICIOUS ⟨their ideal of national union was ~ combined resistance to an intruder —T.E.Lawrence⟩ ⟨~ in his affections⟩

ep·i·sod·i·cal·ly \-¦sädək(ə)lē, -dēk-, -li *sometimes* -¦zä-\ *adv* **1** : in an episodic manner **2** : in the form of a series of episodes ⟨would present . . . the man in relation to his work — even if only in facets and perhaps somewhat ~ —*Americas*⟩

ep·i·spa·di·as \,epə'spādēəs\ *n* -ES [NL, fr. *epi-* + *-spadias* (as in *hypospadias*)] : a congenital defect in which the urethra opens upon the upper surface of the penis

¹**ep·i·spas·tic** \¦epə¦spastik\ *adj* [Gk *epispastikos* drawing in, fr. *epispastos* drawn in (fr. *epispan* to draw after, draw in, fr. *epi-* + *span* to draw) + *-ikos* -ic — more at SPAN] : causing a blister or producing a serous discharge by producing inflammation

²**epispastic** \"\ *n* -s : VESICANT 1

ep·i·sperm \'epə,spərm\ *n* [*epi-* + *-sperm*] : TESTA

ep·i·spore \-,spō(ə)r\ *n* [*epi-* + *-spore*] **1 a** : the covering or outer membrane of a spore (as the membrane surrounding the megaspore in heterosporous ferns) **b** : EXOSPORE 2 **2** : the outer layer of a sporocyst

ep·i·spo·ri·um \,epə'spōrēəm\ *n, pl* **epispo·ria** \-ēə\ [NL, fr. *epi-* + *-sporium*] : EXOSPORE 2

epi·stapedial \¦epə, ¦epē+\ *adj* [*epi-* + *stapedial*] : situated on the stapes ⟨the ~ cartilage⟩

epis·ta·sis \ə'pistəsəs\ *n, pl* **epista·ses** \-tə,sēz\ [NL, fr. Gk, act of stopping, stoppage, fr. *ephistanai* to set on, set over, stop, fr. *epi-* + *histanai* to place, set — more at STAND] **1** *med* **a** : suppression of a secretion or discharge **b** : a scum on the surface of urine **2** : suppression of the effect of a gene by a nonallelic gene ⟨the role of ~ in polygenic inheritance⟩

epis·ta·sy \-təsē\ *n* -ES [NL *epistasis* + E *-y*] **1** : EPISTASIS 2 **2** : exhibition of greater phylogenetic modification by one of two related groups

epis·ta·tes \ə'pistə,tēz\ *n, pl* **epista·tae** \-stə,tē, -,tī\ [Gk *epistatēs*, fr. *ephistanai*] : an administrative official in ancient Greece and the Hellenic world

ep·i·stat·ic \¦epə¦stad·ik\ *adj* [after NL *epistasis*, after such pairs as E *emphasis: emphatic*] **1** *of a gene* : exhibiting epistasis toward another gene ⟨the gray coat-color gene is ~ to all other color genes in horses⟩ ⟨~ genes in fruit flies⟩ **2** *of a hereditary character* : induced by epistasis : appearing dominant over another character due to mediation by epistatic genes ⟨pea and rose comb are not dominant to single comb but . . . ~ to it —F.B.Hutt⟩ **3** : serving to suppress a gene or its expression ⟨semidominants whose expression is suppressed by the ~ effect of the genotype —I.L.Dordick⟩

ep·i·stax·is \,epə'staksəs\ *n* -ES [NL, fr. Gk, fr. *epistazein* to drop on, to bleed at the nose again, fr. *epi-* + *stazein* to drop, drip] : NOSEBLEED

ep·i·ste·me \,epə'stē(,)mē\ *n* -s [Gk *epistēmē* understanding, knowledge, fr. fem. of *epistēmōn* understanding, knowing, fr. *epistanai* to understand, know, fr. *epi-* + *histanai* to set, place — more at STAND] : KNOWLEDGE; *specif* : intellectually certain knowledge

ep·i·ste·mic \,epə¦stēmik, -tem-\ *adj* [Gk *epistēmikos* of knowledge, capable of knowledge, fr. *epistēmē* + *-ikos* -ic] : of, having the character of, or relating to episteme, knowledge, or knowing as a type of experience : purely intellectual or cognitive; *also* : SUBJECTIVE ⟨the ~ conditions in our present state of knowledge⟩ ⟨the ~ as contrasted with the phenomenological sense⟩ — **ep·i·ste·mi·cal·ly** \-mək(ə)lē\ *adv*

epis·te·mo·log·i·cal \ə¦pistəmə¦läjəkəl, (,)e¦-, ē¦-\ *adj* **1** : of, relating to, or based on epistemology ⟨the ~ problem⟩ ⟨~ position⟩ ⟨~ type of definition⟩ **2** : EPISTEMIC ⟨to transcend the confines of his own civilization . . . is an ~ impossibility —H.J.Morgenthau⟩ — compare ONTOLOGICAL

epis·te·mo·log·i·cal·ly \-jək(ə)lē\ *adv* : in regard to epistemology ⟨~ he is a dualist⟩

epis·te·mol·o·gist \=,=='mäləjəst\ *n* -s : one devoted to or skilled in epistemology

epis·te·mol·o·gy \-jē\ *n* -ES [*epistemo-* (fr. Gk *epistēmē*) + *-logy*] : the study of the method and grounds of knowledge esp. with reference to its limits and validity; *broadly* : the theory of knowledge — compare GNOSEOLOGY

epis·te·mo·phil·ia \-,mō'filēə\ *n* -s [NL, fr. *epistemo-* + *-philia*] : love of knowledge; *specif* : excessive striving for or preoccupation with knowledge — **epis·te·mo·phil·i·ac** \-lē,ak\ *n* -s — **epis·te·mo·phil·ic** \=¦===¦filik\ *adj*

epi·sternal \¦epə, ¦epē+\ *adj* [*epi-* + *sternal*] **1** : located on or above the sternum **2** : of or relating to the episternum

ep·i·ster·na·lia \,epə,stər'nālēə, -pē,-, -lyə\ *n pl* [NL, fr. *epi-* + *stern-* + *-alia*] : two small centers of ossification sometimes developing between the clavicles and sternum and fusing with the sternum

epi·ster·nite \-'stər,nīt\ *n* -s [NL *episternum* + E *-ite*] : an anterior cuticular sidepiece of a somite of an insect

epi·sternum \¦epə, ¦epē+\ *n, pl* **episterna** [NL, fr. *epi-* + *sternum*] **1 a** : INTERCLAVICLE **b** : any of several other sternal elements of similar origin or position (as the presternum of a mammal or the epiplastron of a turtle) **2** : a lateral division or piece of a somite of an arthropod; *specif* : the anterior sclerite of the pleuron of an insect — compare EPIMERON **3** : MANUBRIUM 1a

epi·stilbite \¦epə, ¦epē+\ *n* [G *epistilbit*, fr. *epi-* + *stilbit* stilbite] : a zeolitic mineral $CaAl_2Si_6O_{16}5H_2O$ consisting of aluminosilicate of calcium and occurring in usu. white prismatic crystals or granular forms

¹**epis·tle** \ə'pisəl, ē'-\ *n* -s [ME *epistel, epistle, epistole*, fr. OF, LL & L; OF *epistle*, fr. LL *epistola, epistula* biblical epistle, fr. L, letter, fr. Gk *epistolē* order, message, epistle, fr. *epistellein* to send to, order, fr. *epi-* + *stellein* to make ready, send — more at STALL] **1** *usu cap* **a** : one of the letters of the New Testament ⟨the General *Epistles* follow Paul's *Epistles* —Madeleine S. & J.L.Miller⟩ **b** : a lection usu. from one of the New Testament Epistles and read or sung as part of a Christian liturgical service (as in Roman Catholic and Anglican churches) ⟨the subdeacon sings the *Epistle* for the day at high Mass⟩ **2 a** : LETTER ⟨flinging the journal into the farthest corners and sitting down to indite ~*s* —H.A.Overstreet⟩ ⟨Pope Gelasius . . . in his ~ mentioning the legend —G.C.Sellery⟩ **b** : a composition in prose or poetry written in the form of a letter to a particular person or group ⟨in spite of Bacon's disclaimer, in a dedicatory ~ to Andrewes —Douglas Bush⟩ ⟨a digressive verse ~⟩

²**epistle** \"\ *vt* -ED/-ING/-S *archaic* : WRITE

epis·tler \-s(ə)lə(r)\ *n* -s [¹*epistle* + *-er*] : EPISTOLER

epistle side *n* : the right side of an altar or chancel as one faces it : south side ⟨the priest goes to the *epistle side*, pours wine into the chalice —C.W.Currier⟩ ⟨one sees the pulpit o' the *epistle side* —Robert Browning⟩ — used esp. of churches in which the Epistle and the Gospel are read or sung from different sides

epistolar *adj* [LL *epistolaris*, fr. L *epistola* + *-aris* -ar] *obs* : EPISTOLARY

¹**epis·to·lary** \ə'pistə,lerē, ē'-, -ri\ *also* **epis·to·la·to·ry** \-tələ,tōrē, -ōr-, -ri\ *adj* [*epistolary* fr. F or LL; F *épistolaire*, fr. LL *epistolarius*, fr. L *epistola* + *-arius* -ary; *epistolatory* alter. of *epistolary*] **1** : of, relating to, or suitable to a letter or epistle ⟨the ordinary Greek ~ salutation is the infinitive of the verb "rejoice" —E.J.Goodspeed⟩ ⟨retain their ~ prowess —*New Republic*⟩ ⟨an ~ style⟩ **2** : contained in or carried on by letters ⟨qualifying statements (chiefly ~) . . . which amount to a confession of polemical overstatement —G.L.Kline⟩ ⟨an endless sequence of . . . ~ love affairs —*Times Lit. Supp.*⟩ **3** : written in the form of a series of letters ⟨the ~ novel⟩ ⟨an ~ short story⟩

²**epistolary** \"\ *or* **epis·to·lar·i·um** \=,=='la(a)rēəm\ *n, pl* **epistolaries** *or* **epistolariums** [ML *epistolarium*, fr. LL *epistola* + L *-arium* -ary] : a lectionary containing the liturgical Epistles

epis·to·ler \=ˈstələ(r)\ *n* -s [LL & L *epistola* + E *-er*] **1** *or* **epis·to·list** \-ləst\ [*epistolist* fr. L *epistola* + E *-ist*] : a writer of epistles **2** : the reader of the Epistle at Holy Communion esp. in Anglican churches

ep·is·tol·ic \¦epə¦stälik\ *or* **ep·is·tol·i·cal** \-ləkəl\ *adj* [L *epistolicus*, fr. Gk *epistolikos*, fr. *epistolē* + *-ikos* -ic] : EPISTOLARY

epis·to·lize \ə'pistə,līz, ē'-\ *vb* -ED/-ING/-S [L *epistola* letter + E *-ize* — more at EPISTLE] *vi* : to write a letter ~ *vt* : to write a letter to ⟨forgive and ~ me —Edward Gibbon⟩

epis·to·liz·er \-zə(r)\ *n* -s : EPISTOLER

epis·to·lo·graph·ic \ə¦pistə(,)lō¦grafik, ē¦p-\ *adj* [LGk *epistolographikos*, fr. Gk *epistolo-* (fr. *epistolē*) + *-graphikos* -graphic] : DEMOTIC 2a

epis·to·log·ra·phy \=,=='lägrəfē\ *n* -ES [Gk *epistolo-* + E *-graphy*] : the art or practice of writing epistles : letter writing ⟨the study of Renaissance ~⟩

ep·i·stom·al \¦epə¦stōməl, ə'pistəm-\ *adj* : of or relating to an epistome

ep·i·stome \'epə,stōm\ *also* **ep·i·sto·ma** \ə'pistəmə\ *n, pl* **ep·i·stomes** \-,stōmz\ *also* **ep·i·sto·ma·ta** \,epə'stōməd·ə\ [NL *epistoma*, fr. *epi-* + *-stoma*] **1 a** : the region between the antennae and the mouth of a crustacean **b** : a plate covering this region **2 a** : the region between the labrum and the epicranium of an insect **b** : CLYPEUS **3** : the region just above the mouth of some two-winged flies **4** : a labiate organ covering the mouth in various bryozoans **5** : an anterior median plate on the doublure of some trilobites

epis·tro·phe \ə'pistrə(,)fē\ *n* [Gk *epistrophē*, lit., turning about, fr. *epi-* + *strophē* turning — more at STROPHE] : repetition of the same word or expression at the end of successive phrases, clauses, or sentences for rhetorical effect (as *government of the people, for the people, and by the people*) — compare ANAPHORA

ep·i·stro·phe·al \¦epə¦strōfēəl\ *adj* [NL *epistropheus* + E *-al*] : of or relating to an axis (sense 3a(1))

ep·i·stro·phe·us \,epə'strōfēəs\ *n* -ES [NL, fr. Gk, fr. *epistrephein* to turn about, fr. *epi-* + *strephein* to turn — more at STROPHE] : AXIS 3a(1)

ep·i·sty·lar \¦epə¦stīlə(r)\ *adj* : of or having the function of an epistyle ⟨~ arcuation⟩

ep·i·style \'epə,stīl\ *also* **ep·i·sty·li·um** \,epə'stīlēəm\ *n, pl* **epistyles** \'==,stīlz\ *or* **episty·lia** \,==ˈstīlēə\ [L *epistylium*, fr. Gk *epistylion*, fr. *epi-* + Gk *stylos* pillar + *-ion* (dim. suffix) — more at STOW] : ARCHITRAVE 1

ep·i·sty·lis \,epə'stīləs\ *n, cap* [NL, fr. *epi-* + *-stylis* (fr. Gk *stylos*)] : a genus (the type of the family Epistylidae) of fixed colonial peritrichous ciliates ectocommensal on aquatic animals and including both solitary and colonial forms

epi·syllogism \¦epə, ¦epē + \ *n* [*epi-* + *syllogism*] : a syllogism one or both of whose premises is the conclusion of a preceding syllogism — compare PROSYLLOGISM

epi·synaloephe \"+\ *n* [LGk *episynaloiphē*, fr. Gk *epi-* + *synaloiphē* synaloepha — more at SYNALOEPHA] *Greek & Latin prosody* **1** : the elision of a vowel at the end of a verse before a vowel beginning the next **2** : SYNERESIS 1a

ep·i·syn·the·ton \,epə'sin(t)thə,tän\ *n* -s [Gk, fr. *epi-* + *syntheton*, neut. of *synthetos* put together, compounded, composed — more at SYNTHETIC] *Greek & Latin prosody* : a meter made up of cola of different kinds of feet

epit *abbr* **1** epitaph **2** epitome

¹**ep·i·taph** \'epə,ta|f, -taa(ə)|, -tä|\ *n, pl* **epitaphs** \|fs *sometimes* |vz\ [ME *epitaphe, epitaphie*, fr. MF & ML; MF *epitaphe*, fr. ML *epitaphium*, fr. L, funeral oration, fr. Gk *epitaphion*, fr. neut. of *epitaphios* being at a tomb or funeral, fr. *epi-* + *-taphios* (fr. *taphos* tomb, funeral); akin to Gk *thaptein* to inter, bury, Arm *damban* grave] **1** : an inscription on or at a tomb or a grave in memory or commendation of the one buried there **2** : something felt to resemble an epitaph: as **a** : a brief statement (as a phrase or sentence) commemorating or epitomizing a deceased person or something past ⟨a book of ~*s* on the death of the knight⟩ ⟨an extemporal ~ on the death of the deer —Shak.⟩ ⟨all over but the recounts: that was the somewhat sardonic American ~ on the mid-term congressional election —Christopher Serpell⟩ **b** : something that commemorates or serves as a final judgment ⟨the abstract style has not replaced representative art; the show . . . must serve more as an ~ than accolade —Lincoln Kirstein⟩

²**epitaph** \"\ *vt* -ED/-ING/-S : to commemorate by an epitaph ⟨the bishop was ~*ed* in a pair of lovely couplets⟩

ep·i·taph·i·al \¦epə¦tafēəl\ *also* **ep·i·taph·ic** \-fik\ *adj* : of or having the character of an epitaph

ep·i·taph·less \'epə,tafləs, -taaf-,-täf-\ *adj* : lacking an epitaph

epit·a·sis \ə'pid·əsəs\ *n, pl* **epita·ses** \-ə,sēz\ [Gk, lit., stretching, increase in intensity, fr. *epiteinein* to stretch upon, stretch over, fr. *epi-* + *teinein* to stretch — more at THIN] : the part of a play developing the main action and leading to the catastrophe — compare CATASTASIS, PROTASIS

ep·i·tax·i·al \¦epə¦taksēəl\ *or* **ep·i·tax·ic** \-sik\ *adj* : having orientation controlled by the crystal substrate — used of crystals and of the relation between them and their substrate

ep·i·taxy \'epə,taksē\ *n* -ES [*epi-* + *-taxy*] : the oriented growth of one crystalline substance on a substrate of a different crystalline substance

ep·i·ten·din·e·um \,epə,ten'dinēəm\ *n* -s [NL, fr. *epi-* + *-tendineum* (fr. F *tendineux* or E *tendinous*) — more at TENDINOUS] : white fibrous tissue covering a tendon

ep·i·tha·lam·ic \¦epəthə¦lamik\ *also* **ep·i·tha·la·mi·al** \-lāmēəl\ *adj* [*epithalamium* + *-ic* or *-al*] : of or being an epithalamium : NUPTIAL ⟨an ~ ode⟩

ep·i·tha·la·mi·um \,epəthə'lāmēəm\ *also* **ep·i·tha·la·mi·on** \-mēən, -ē,ān\ *or* **ep·i·thal·a·my** \-'thaləmē\ *n, pl* **epithalamiums** \-thə'lāmēəmz\ *or* **epithala·mia** \-thə'lāmēə\ *also* **epithalamies** \-'thaləmēz\ [L & Gk; L *epithalamium*, fr. Gk *epithalamion*, fr. neut. of *epithalamios* nuptial, fr. *epi-* + *-thalamios* (fr. *thalamos* room, woman's apartment, bridal chamber)] : a nuptial song or poem in honor or praise of a bride and bridegroom

epi·thalamus \¦epə, ¦epē+\ *n, pl* **epithalami** [NL, fr. *epi-* + *thalamus*] : a dorsal segment of the diencephalon containing the habenula and the pineal body

epi·theca \"+\ *n* [NL, fr. *epi-* + *-theca*] **1** : an external calcareous layer investing the lower portion of the theca of many corals **2** : the outer or upper half or valve of the diatom frustule — compare HYPOTHECA — **epi·thecal** \"+\ *or* **epi·thecate** \"+\ *adj*

epi·thecium \"+\ *n, pl* **epithecia** [NL, fr. *epi-* + *thecium*] : the surface layer of the fruiting body in many fungi and lichens that in fungi is usu. equivalent to the hymenium and in lichens forms a film over the hymenium — compare HYPOTHECIUM

epithel- *comb form* [NL *epithelium*] : epithelium ⟨*epithel*ize⟩ ⟨*epithel*oid⟩

epitheli- *or* **epithelio-** *comb form* [NL *epithelium*] : epithelium ⟨*epitheli*oma⟩ : epithelial and ⟨*epithelio*glandular⟩

ep·i·the·lial \¦epə¦thēlēəl, -thēlyəl\ *adj* [NL *epithelium* + E *-al*] : of or belonging to epithelium

epithelial body *n* : PARATHYROID GLAND

epithelial germ *n* : one of the clusters of embryonic dermal ectoderm cells that are precursors of hairs, sebaceous glands, and apocrine glands of the skin

epithelial pearl *n* : a small firm body that is translucent like a pearl and is formed within an epithelioma

ep·i·the·lio·chorial \,epə¦thēlē(,)ō+\ *adj* [*epitheli-* + *chorial*] *of a placenta* : having maternal and fetal epithelium in contact (as in horses and whales) — compare ENDOTHELIOCHORIAL, HEMOCHORIAL, SYNDESMOCHORIAL

ep·i·the·li·oid \¦epə¦thēlē,ȯid\ *adj* [*epitheli-* + *-oid*] : resembling epithelium : like that of epithelium ⟨~ cells⟩

ep·i·the·li·o·ma \,epə,thēlē'ōmə\ *n, pl* **epitheliomas** \-məz\ *or* **epithelioma·ta** \-məd·ə\ [NL, fr. *epitheli-* + *-oma*] : a benign or malignant tumor derived from epithelial tissue — **ep·i·the·li·om·a·tous** \,epə,thēlē¦ämədəs, -lē¦ōm-\ *adj*

ep·i·the·lio·muscular \,epə¦thēlē(,)ō+\ *adj* [*epitheli-* + *muscular*] : of or being an epithelial cell of coelenterates that is modified to function in contraction and has an elongated fibrillar base that functions in the same manner as a muscle cell

ep·i·the·lio·trop·ic \,epə¦thēlēə¦träpik\ *adj* [*epitheli-* + *-tropic*] : having an affinity for epithelium — used esp. of viruses

ep·i·the·li·um \,epə'thēlēəm\ *n, pl* **epithe·lia** \-lēə\ *also* **epitheliums** [NL, fr. *epi-* + Gk *thēlē* nipple + NL *-ium* — more at FEMININE] **1** : a cellular animal tissue that covers a free surface or lines a tube or cavity, that consists of one or more layers of cells forming a sheet practically unbroken by intercellular substance and either smoothly extended (as in epidermis) or much folded on a basement membrane and compacted (as in glands), and that serves esp. to enclose and protect the other parts of the body, to form the most essential part of the sense organs, to produce secretions and excretions, and to function in assimilation — see ENDOTHELIUM **2** : any of certain layers of plant tissue one or more cells thick consisting of parenchyma that line an internal cavity or tube (as in a resin canal where they excrete the resin into the cavity)

ep·i·the·li·za·tion \,epə,thēlə'zāshən\ *or* **ep·i·the·lial·i·za·tion** \-lēələ'z-, -lyəl-, -,lī'z-\ *n* -s : the process of becoming epithelized ⟨rapid and healthy ~ of wounds⟩ ⟨~ of mesenchyme⟩

ep·i·the·lize \,epə'thē,līz\ *also* **ep·i·the·lial·ize** \-ēlēə,līz, -ēlyə,-\ *vb* -ED/-ING/-S [*epithel-* or *epithelial* + *-ize*] *vt* : to cover (as an open wound) with or convert (another tissue) to epithelium ⟨a completely *epithelized* lesion⟩ ~ *vi* : to become covered with epithelium ⟨the denuded surface rapidly *epithelized*⟩

ep·i·the·loid \¦epə¦thē,lȯid\ *adj* [*epithel-* + *-oid*] : EPITHELIOID

ep·i·them \'epə,them\ *n* -s [ME *epithima, epithime*, fr. L *epithema*, fr. Gk, fr. *epitithenai* to put on, add, fr. *epi-* + *tithenai* to set, place, put — more at DO] **1** *also* **ep·i·theme** \-thēm\ *archaic* : an external local application to the body (as a poultice) **2** : a group of thin-walled loosely arranged cells beneath the epidermis of the leaves of many angiosperms that constitutes an internal hydathode ⟨the ~*s* through which guttation occurs in the tomato leaf⟩

ep·i·the·ma \,epə'thēmə, ə'pithəmə\ *n, pl* **epithe·ma·ta** \-thēməd·ə, -them-\ [NL, fr. Gk *epithema* something put on, fr. *epitithenai*] : a horny excrescence on the bill of some birds (as the casque of a hornbill)

epi·thermal \¦epə, ¦epē + \ *adj* [*epi-* + *thermal*] **1** : deposited from warm waters at rather shallow depth under conditions in the lower ranges of temperature and pressure — used of mineral veins and ore deposits; compare HYPOTHERMAL, MESOTHERMAL **2** : having translational speeds and energies greater than those usu. due to thermal agitation but less than those required for nuclear fission ⟨~ neutrons⟩

¹**ep·i·thet** \'epə,the|t *also* -pē- *or* -pi- *or* -,thə|; *usu* |d.+V\ *n* -s [L *epitheton*, fr. Gk, fr. neut. of *epithetos* added, fr. *epitithenai*] **1 a** *also* **epith·e·ton** \ə'pithə,tän, e'-\ : a characterizing word or phrase ⟨~*s* applied to gorillas by psychologists . . .: cautious, conservative, not skillful mechanically or manually —A.L.Kroeber⟩ ⟨the ~ of "the most unsordid act in history" —*Economist*⟩: as (1) : such a word or phrase joined often by fixed association to the name of a person or thing ⟨identified more familiarly by his ~ as Richard Lionheart than by his number as Richard the First⟩ ⟨such stock ornamental ~*s* in Homer as "wine-dark" that regularly precedes "sea"⟩ (2) : such a word or phrase used as a name for a person or thing ⟨uses the ~ "the Eternal" instead of the usual title "the Lord"⟩ **b** : a disparaging or abusive word or phrase ⟨his sneering tone made "professor" an ~⟩ ⟨hurled the ~*s* "slave-labor law" and "un-American" at the proposed bill⟩ **c** : the part of a scientific name identifying the species, variety, or other subunit within a genus ⟨in the scientific name *Rosa chinensis longifolia*, *chinensis* is the specific ~ and

longifolia is the varietal ~⟩ **2** *obs* **:** EXPRESSION ⟨suffer love! a good ~ . . . for I love thee against my will —Shak.⟩ **3 :** the use of epithets; *esp* **:** NAME-CALLING ⟨loud denunciation, ~, and abuse —A.E.Stevenson †1965⟩

2**epithet** \"\ *vt* -ED/-ING/-S **:** to describe with an epithet ⟨"woeful woman", as he ~*ed* her⟩ ⟨whose appearance she ~*ed* "untimely"⟩

ep·i·thet·ic \¦==¦thed·ik\ *or* **ep·i·thet·i·cal** \-d·ə̇kəl\ *adj* **1 :** using epithets **2 :** of or having the character of an epithet ⟨the poetry . . . was conservatively *epithetical*, containing only about seven adjectives in ten lines —Josephine Miles⟩

ep·i·thet·ize \'epə,thed·,īz, -,thə̇d·-; ə̇'pithə,tīz, e'-\ *vt* -ED/-ING/-S **:** EPITHET ⟨dared ~ him with that insolent character —Miles Davies⟩

ep·i·thu·met·ic \¦epəth(y)ü¦med·ik\ *adj* [irreg. fr. Gk *epithymētikos*, fr. *epithymētos* desired (fr. *epithymein* to long for, desire, covet, fr. *epi-* + *thymos* desire, mind, soul) + *-ikos* -ic — more at FUME] **:** of or relating to appetite or desire **:** SENSUAL ⟨the ~ part of human nature⟩

ep·i·toke \'epə,tōk\ *n* -S [Gk *epitokos* fruitful, fr. *epi-* + *-tokos* (fr. *tiktein* to bear)] **:** the posterior sexual part of various polychaete worms that develops from the anterior sexless part — compare ATOKE — **epit·o·kous** *or* **epit·o·cous** \ə̇'pid·əkəs, (')e¦p-\ *adj*

epit·o·ma·tor \ə̇'pid·ə,mād·ə(r), ē'-,e'-, -itə-, -ātə-\ *n* -S [LL *epitomatus* (past part. of *epitomare* to epitomize, fr. L *epitome*) + E *-or*] **:** EPITOMIST

epit·o·me \ə̇'pid·ə(,)mē, ē'-,e'-, -itə-, -,mi\ *n* -S [L, fr. Gk *epitomē*, fr. *epitemnein* to cut short, abridge, fr. *epi-* + *temnein* to cut — more at TOME] **1 a :** a summary of a written work **:** ABRIDGMENT, ABSTRACT ⟨purporting to be a translation from a French original although it is in fact but a meager ~ of it —Mary D. Anderson⟩ **b :** a brief presentation of a broad topic **:** COMPENDIUM ⟨a convenient ~ of much current knowledge and belief —H.S.Bennett⟩ **c :** a brief statement expressing the essence of something ⟨"five years of fighting and ninety-five of winding up barbed wire" . . . was a fair ~ of war's aftermath —Dixon Wecter⟩ **2 :** a typical representation or ideal expression **:** EMBODIMENT ⟨his manner of receiving my aunt and myself was an ~ of his urbane and appreciative attitude toward the universe —Siegfried Sassoon⟩ ⟨the British monarchy itself is the ~ of tradition —Richard Joseph⟩ ⟨my community . . . considers a man in uniform to be the living ~ of heroism —Lucius Garvin⟩ **3 :** brief or miniature form — used esp. in the phrase *in epitome* ⟨the spectator does in ~ and without halt what the artist did slowly and by process of trial and error —F.J.Mather⟩ **syn** see ABRIDGMENT

ep·i·tom·i·cal \¦epə¦tämə̇kəl\ *or* **ep·i·tom·ic** \-mik\ *adj* **:** of, relating to, or having the characteristics of an epitome ⟨our literature is rich in ballads, a form ~ of the epic and dramatic —Elizabeth B. Browning⟩

epit·o·mist \ə̇'pid·əmə̇st, ē'-,e'-, -itə-\ *n* -S **:** a writer of an epitome

epit·o·mize \-,mīz\ *vt* -ED/-ING/-S **1 :** to make or give an epitome of **:** SUMMARIZE ⟨his personal and political creed is *epitomized* by his own comment —A.C.Gordon⟩ ⟨assertions which ~ one of the richest and boldest metaphysical theories ever invented —Gregory Vlastos⟩ **2** *obs* **:** to reduce in number, size, or degree **3 :** to serve as the typical representation or ideal expression of **:** EMBODY, TYPIFY, SYMBOLIZE ⟨a young, dynamic, aggressive leader who ~*s* many of the self-reliant American virtues —E.D.Raff⟩ ⟨*epitomized* in himself the merits and the defects of the statesmanship of his country —Ernest Barker⟩

epit·o·miz·er \-zə(r)\ *n* -S **:** EPITOMIST

ep·i·to·ni·idae \,epətə'nīə,dē\ *n pl, cap* [NL, fr. *Epitonium*, type genus + *-idae*] **:** a family of marine gastropod mollusks (suborder Taenioglossa) having an elongated conical shell with many whorls and elevated ribs, a horny operculum, and a short siphon and including the wentletraps

ep·i·to·ni·um \,epə'tōnēəm\ *n, cap* [NL, fr. Gk *epitonion* turncock, peg] **:** the type genus of Epitoniidae

epi·toxoid \¦epə̇, ¦epē +\ *n* [*epi-* + *toxoid*] **:** a toxoid weaker in affinity for antitoxin than is the corresponding toxin

ep·i·tra·che·lion \,epētrə'kēlyȯn\ *n* -S [MGk *epitrachēlion*, fr. neut. of *epitrachēlios*, fr. Gk *epi-* + *-trachēlios* (fr. *trachēlos* neck)] **:** a long narrow stole worn by bishops and priests of the Eastern Orthodox Church

ep·i·trich·i·um \,epə'trikēəm\ *n* -S [NL, fr. *epi-* + *trich-* + *-ium*] **:** an outer layer of the epidermis of the fetus of many mammals beneath which the hair develops

ep·i·trite \'epə·,trīt\ *n* -S [LL *epitritos*, fr. Gk, fr. *epitritos* 1⅓, having a ratio of 4:3, having 4 long and 3 short syllables, fr. *epi-* + *tritos* third; akin to Gk *treis* three — more at THREE] **:** a foot in Greek and Latin prosody consisting of three long and one short syllables — **ep·i·trit·ic** \¦epə·¦trid·ik\ *adj*

ep·i·trix \'epə,triks\ *n, cap* [NL, fr. *epi-* + *-trix* (fr. Gk *thrix* hair) — more at TRICH-] **:** a widely distributed genus of flea beetles including pests of various cultivated plants and some that are vectors of virus diseases — see POTATO FLEA BEETLE, TUBER FLEA BEETLE

epi·trochlea \¦epə̇, ¦epē +\ *n* [NL, fr. *epi-* + *trochlea*] *anat* **:** the medial epicondyle at the distal end of the humerus — **epi·trochlear** \"+\ *adj*

epi·trochoid \"+\ *n* [*epi-* + *trochoid*] **:** a plane curve traced by a point on the radius or extended radius of a circle rolling on the outside of a fixed circle — compare EPICYCLOID, HYPOTROCHOID — **epi·trochoidal** \"+\ *adj*

ep·i·troph·ic \¦epə¦träfik, -rōf-\ *adj* **:** characterized by epitrophy

epit·ro·phy \ə̇'pi·trəfē\ *n* -ES [ISV *epi-* + *-trophy*] **:** increased increments of growth upon the upper side of horizontal o ascending branches or roots — opposed to *hypotrophy*

epi·tuberculosis \¦epə̇, ¦epē+\ *n* [NL, fr. *epi-* + *tuberculosis*] **:** an abnormal state of the tissues near a tuberculous lesion that is caused by the spread of products therefrom, occurs usu. in children, and is not associated with severe symptoms — **epi·tuberculous** \"+\ *adj*

epi·tympanic \"+\ *adj* [*epi-* + *tympanic*] **1 :** situated above the tympanic membrane **2 :** HYOMANDIBULAR

epi·tympanum \"+\ *n* [NL, fr. *epi-* + *tympanum*] **:** the upper portion of the middle ear — compare HYPOTYMPANUM

ep·i·typh·li·tis \,epətə̇'flīd·ə̇s\ *n* -ES [NL, fr. *epityphlon* vermiform appendix (fr. *epi-* + Gk *typhlon* cecum) + *-itis*] **:** APPENDICITIS

epiural *var of* EPURAL

ep·i·vag \'epə,vaj\ *n* -S [by shortening] *Africa* **:** EPIVAGINITIS

epi·vaginitis \,epə+\ *n* [NL, fr. *epi-* (as in *epididymitis*) + *vaginitis*] **:** a widespread venereal disease of southern African cattle that is marked by inflammation and discharges from the genital organs and by sterility and that takes the form of an epididymitis in the male

epi·valve \'epə̇, 'epē + ,-\ *n* [*epi-* + *valve*] **1 :** the apical half of the shell of certain dinoflagellates **2 :** the epitheca of a diatom

ep·i·xy·lous \¦epə¦zīləs\ *adj* [*epi-* + *xyl-* + *-ous*] **:** growing on wood ⟨~ fungi⟩

ep·i·zeux·is \,epə'züksə̇s\ *n* -ES [LL, fr. Gk, lit., act of fastening together, fr. *epizeugnynai* to fasten together (fr. *epi-* + *zeugnynai* to join, yoke) + *-sis*] *Greek and Latin prosody* **:** the joining of two successive ionics a minore so that the syllables that come together exchange quantities (as when ◡◡––|◡◡–– becomes ◡◡–◡|–◡––)

ep·i·zoa \,epə'zōə\ *n pl* [NL, fr. *epi-* + *-zoa*] **1 :** ECTOZOA **2** *cap* **:** a group consisting of the fish lice — **ep·i·zo·al** \¦epə¦zōəl\ *adj* — **ep·i·zo·an** \-ōən\ *adj or n*

epi·zoanthus \¦epə̇, ¦epē+\ *n, cap* [NL, fr. *epi-* + *Zoanthus*] **:** a genus of zoanthidean anemones — see CARCINOECIUM

ep·i·zo·ic \¦epə¦zōik\ *adj* [*epi-* + *-zoic*] **:** dwelling upon the body of an animal ⟨an ~ plant parasite⟩ ⟨an ~ commensal⟩ — compare EPIPHYTIC 2 — **ep·i·zo·ism** \,epə'zō,izəm, '==,=-\ *n* -S — **ep·i·zo·ite** \-ō,īt\ *n* -S

ep·i·zo·on \,epə'zō,än\ *n, pl* **epi·zoa** \-ōə\ [NL, fr. *epi-* + *-zoon*] **:** an animal epizoite

1**ep·i·zo·ot·ic** \¦epəzə¦wäd·ik, -zō¦ä-, *in sense 3* -¦züd·-\ *n* -S [*epi-* + *zo-* + *-otic* (fr. *-otic*, adj. suffix)] **1 :** an outbreak of epizootic disease **2 :** an epizootic disease; *specif* **:** EQUINE INFLUENZA **3** *dial* **:** AILMENT, MISERY — often used in pl. ⟨he's not here today — must have the ~*s*⟩

2**epizootic** \"\ *adj, of a disease* **:** affecting many animals of one kind at the same time — compare EPIDEMIC — **ep·i·zo·ot·i·cal·ly** \-d·ə̇k(ə)lē\ *adv*

epizootic abortion *n* **:** CONTAGIOUS ABORTION

epizootic lymphangitis *n* **:** a chronic contagious inflammation chiefly of the superficial lymphatics and lymph nodes of horses, mules, and donkeys that is characterized by enlargement and thickening of the vessels and softening and purulent ulceration of the nodes and is caused by a yeast (*Cryptococcus farciminosus*)

ep·i·zo·oti·o·log·i·cal \¦epə(,)zō¦ōd·ēə¦läjə̇kəl\ *also* **ep·i·zo·oti·o·log·ic** \-jik\ *or* **ep·i·zo·oto·log·ic** \-¦zōəd·ə¦läjik\ *or* **ep·i·zo·olog·i·cal** \¦epə,zōə¦läjə̇kəl\ *adj* **:** of or relating to epizootiology — **ep·i·zo·oti·o·log·i·cal·ly** *or* **ep·i·zo·olog·i·cal·ly** \-jə̇k(ə)lē\ *adv*

ep·i·zo·oti·ol·o·gy \,epə(,)zō,ōd·ē'äləjē\ *or* **ep·i·zo·otol·o·gy** \-,zōə'täləjē\ *or* **ep·i·zo·ol·o·gy** \-,zō'äləjē\ *n* -ES [*epizootio-*, *epizooto-* or *epizoo-* (fr. 1*epizootic*) + *-logy*] **1 :** a science that deals with epizootics and the factors involved in the occurrence and spread of the diseases of animals — compare EPIDEMIOLOGY **2 :** the sum of the factors controlling the presence or absence of a disease or pathogen of animals ⟨the ~, symptoms, and prognosis of fowl cholera⟩

ep·i·zo·oty \,epə'zōəd·ē\ *n* -ES [prob. fr. F *épizootie*, fr. E 1*epizootic* + F *-ie* -y] **:** EPIZOOTIC

EPNS *abbr* electroplated nickel silver

ep·och \'epək *also* 'e,päk *sometimes* 'ē,päk *or* 'epik *or* 'epēk\ *n* -S [ML or NL *epocha*, fr. Gk *epochē* stoppage, cessation, suspension of judgment, position in space or fixed point in time, fr. *epechein* to hold back, pause, fr. *epi-* + *echein* to hold, have — more at SCHEME] **1 a** *obs* (1) **:** the fixed point from which years are numbered in a system of chronology (as in the Greek olympiads) usu. determined by an important event (as the birth of Christ) ⟨a different ~ to account by, . . . the hegira they have from Muhammad —Thomas Herbert⟩ (2) **:** ERA 1 **b** *astron* **:** an instant of time or a date selected as a point of reference for which are given values of the data under consideration ⟨the heliocentric position at a certain zero ~, say 1950.000 —*Popular Astronomy*⟩ **2 a :** an event or a time marked by an event that begins a new period or development **:** a new beginning ⟨we two . . . made an ~ in the criticism of the theater . . . by making it a pretext for a propaganda of our own views of life —G.B.Shaw⟩ **:** TURNING POINT **b :** a memorable event or date ⟨the child's first sight of the circus parade was an ~ in his life⟩ **c :** TIME 8a ⟨the ~ of the completion of a thousand years from the birth of Christ —C.E.Norton⟩ **3 :** an extended period of time usu. characterized by a distinctive development or by a memorable series of events ⟨the feudal ~⟩ ⟨the Napoleonic ~⟩ ⟨Dante's work . . . initiated a new ~ in literature —R.A.Hall b. 1911⟩ ⟨his college years were a happy ~ in his life⟩: as **a :** a division of geologic time **:** EPISODE; *specif* **:** a division of geologic time less than a period and greater than an age ⟨the Niagara ~ of the Silurian period⟩ — see GEOLOGIC TIME table **b :** a period of time during which a particular type of culture is dominant in an area ⟨Magdalenian ~⟩ **4 a :** the value of the phase angle of a periodic process (as an alternating current or small oscillations of a pendulum) at the selected zero of time **b :** TIDAL EPOCH **syn** see PERIOD

ep·o·cha \'epəkə\ *archaic var of* EPOCH

ep·och·al \'epəkəl *also* 'e,päk- *sometimes* (')ē¦päk- *or* 'epik- *or* 'epēk- *or* ə̇¦päk- *or* e'päk-\ *adj* **1 :** of or relating to an epoch **2 a :** bringing about or marking the beginning of a new development or era ⟨the ~ venture of Christopher Columbus —I.M.Price⟩ **b :** uniquely or highly significant (as in a historical development) **:** MOMENTOUS ⟨his fights to advance . . . democracy during his three ~ years in the assembly —C.G. Bowers⟩ **:** UNPARALLELED ⟨the American delegates . . . have fallen for it out of their almost ~ dumbness —J.T.Flynn⟩ — **ep·och·al·ly** \-kəlē, -li\ *adv*

ep·o·che \'epə,kē\ *n* -S [Gk *epochē* — more at EPOCH] **:** suspension of judgment: **a** *in ancient skepticism* **:** the act of refraining from any conclusion for or against anything as the decisive step for the attainment of ataraxy **b :** the methodological attitude of phenomenology in which one refrains from judging whether anything exists or can exist as the first step in the phenomenological recognition, comprehension, and description of sense appearances **:** transcendental reduction

epoch–making \'=(,)=,==\ *adj* **:** EPOCHAL 2

ep·ode \'e,pōd\ *n* -S [L *epodos*, fr. Gk *epōidos*, fr. *epōidos*, sung or said after, fr. *epaidein* to sing to, lit., to sing after, fr. *epi-* + *aidein* to sing — more at ODE] **1 :** a verse form composed of two lines differing in construction and often in meter, the second shorter than the first ⟨the ~*s* of Horace's Fifth Book of Odes⟩ **2 :** the third part of triadically constructed Greek odes following the strophe and the antistrophe

epol·li·cate \(')ē¦päləkə̇t, -lə,kāt\ *adj* [*e-* + L *pollic-*, *pollex* thumb + E *-ate* — more at POLLEX] **1 :** lacking a thumb **2 :** lacking a hind toe — used of certain birds

ep·o·moph·o·rus \,epə'mäfərəs\ *n, cap* [NL, fr. *epi-* + *om-* + *-phorus*] **:** a genus of African fruit bats including several typical epaulet bats

eponge \āpōōⁿzh\ *n* -S [F *éponge*, lit., sponge, fr. L *spongia* sponge — more at SPONGE] **:** a soft fabric of wool, silk, rayon, or cotton loosely woven in a plain weave with one or two sets of nubby ply yarns for a rough uneven appearance

ep·o·nych·i·um *also* **ep·i·nych·i·um** \,epə'nikēəm\ *or* **ep·i·o·nych·i·um** \,epēō'n-\ *n* -S [NL, fr. *epi-* + *-onychium*] **1 :** the thickened layer of epidermal tissue over the developing fetal fingernail or toenail that disappears before birth except over the base of the nail where it persists as the perionychium **2 :** the quick of a nail

ep·o·nym \'epə,nim\ *n* -S [Gk *epōnymos*, fr. *epōnymos* eponymous] **1 :** one for whom or which something is named or supposedly named **:** name giver: as **a :** the usu. mythical ancestor or totem animal or object that a social group (as a tribe) holds to be the origin of its name ⟨it is now the opinion of biblical scholars that . . . the grandchildren of Noah are tribal ~*s* —A.R.Wagner⟩ **b :** an Assyrian official whose name was used in chronology of the period 893–666 B.C. to designate his year of office — called also *limmu* **2** [influenced in meaning by E *-onym*] **:** a name derived from the name of an eponym ⟨taking the name of the totem animal as an ~ —M.J. Herskovits⟩ ⟨the ~ "Weil's disease" assumes that Weil was the first to describe the disease accurately⟩

epon·y·mate \e'pänəmə̇t, -,māt\ *n* -S **:** the year of office of an Assyrian eponym

epon·y·mous \ə̇'pänəməs, (')e¦p-\ *also* **ep·o·nym·ic** \¦epə¦nimik\ *adj* [*eponymous* fr. Gk *epōnymos*, fr. *epi-* + *-ōnymos* (fr. *onyma*, *onoma* name); *eponymic* fr. *eponym* + *-ic* — more at NAME] **:** bearing the name of, being, or relating to an eponym (sense 1) ⟨~ clan⟩ ⟨~ disease⟩ ⟨~ ancestor⟩ ⟨*eponymic* patron saint⟩ ⟨she played the ~ role in the play⟩ ⟨*eponymic* myths which account for the parentage of a tribe by turning its name into the name of an imaginary ancestor —E.B.Tylor⟩ — compare 3NAME, 3TITLE

epon·y·my \='=nəmē\ *n* -ES [Gk *epōnymia*, fr. *epōnymos* + *-ia* -y] **1** *or* **epon·y·mism** \-nə,mizəm\ [*eponymism* fr. *eponym* + *-ism*] **:** the explanation of a proper name (as of a tribe or town) by supposing it to be derived from a fictitious eponym **2 :** EPONYMATE

ep·oophoron \¦ep+\ *n* [NL, fr. *epi-* + *oophoron*] **:** a rudimentary organ homologous with the male epididymis lying in the broad ligament of the uterus and consisting of a number of small tubules that are the remains of the tubules of the wolffian body of the embryo and that open into a larger tube, a remnant of the upper part of the wolffian duct

ep·o·pea \,epə'pēə\ *or* **ep·o·pe·ia** \-'pē(y)ə\ *n* -S [Gk *epopoiia*] **:** EPOPEE

ep·o·pee \'epə,pē\ *n* -S [F *épopée*, fr. Gk *epopoiia*, fr. *epopoios* writer of epics (fr. *epos* + *-poios*, fr. *poiein* to make) + *-ia* -y — more at POET] **:** EPIC; *esp.* **:** an epic poem

ep·opt \'e,päpt\ *n* -S [Gk *epoptēs*, lit., overseer, watcher, fr. *epopteuein* to watch, supervise, be admitted to the highest grade of the Eleusinian mysteries, fr. *epi-* + *opteuein* to see] **1** *pl also* **epop·tae** \e'päp,tē\ *or* **epop·tai** \e'päp,tī\ **:** an initiate in the highest grade of the Eleusinian mysteries **2 :** one instructed in a secret system

epop·tic \(')e¦päptik\ *adj* [Gk *epoptikos*, fr. *epoptēs* + *-ikos* -ic] **1 :** of or designed for an epopt **:** SECRET **2 :** of or being the interference figures exhibited by idiophanous crystals

ep·or·nit·ic \¦e,pȯr¦nid·ik\ *adj or n* [by alter.] **:** EPIORNITHIC — **epor·nit·i·cal·ly** \-d·ə̇k(ə)lē\ *adv*

ep·os \'e,päs\ *n* -ES [Gk, word, speech, epic poem — more at VOICE] **1 :** a body of poetry expressing the tradition of a people; *specif* **:** a number of poems that treat parts of an epic theme but are not formally united ⟨the age of ~ is followed by that of epopee —George Grote⟩ **2 :** EPIC 1 ⟨a wide variety of genre from the simple . . . to the more complex (ceremonial songs and the heroic ~) —T.G.Wiener⟩

ep·oxidation \(¦)e,p+,-\ *n* [*epi-* + *oxidation*] **:** the process of epoxidizing

ep·oxide \(')e¦p+,-\ *n* [*epi-* + *oxide*] **:** an epoxy compound **:** a cyclic ether

ep·oxidize \"+,-\ *vt* [*epi-* + *oxidize*] **:** to convert (as an unsaturated compound) into an epoxide ⟨*epoxidized* oils⟩

ep·oxy \ə̇'päksē, e'p-, (,)ē'p-, -si\ *adj* [*epoxy-*] **:** containing oxygen attached to two different atoms already united in some other way; *specif* **:** containing a 3-membered ring consisting of one oxygen and two carbon atoms (as in ethylene oxide)

epoxy- *comb form* [*epi-* + *oxy-*] **:** epoxy

epoxy resin *also* **epoxy** *n* -ES **:** any of various usu. thermosetting resins that are made by polymerization of an epoxide (as ethylene oxide or epichlorohydrin) esp. with a diphenol, that are characterized by good adhesiveness, flexibility, and resistance to chemicals, and that are used chiefly in coatings and adhesives

epp *abbr* epistles

eprou·vette \¦ā,prü¦vet\ *n* -S [F *éprouvette*, fr. *éprouver* to test, try (fr. OF *esprover*, fr. — assumed — VL *exprobare*, fr. L *ex-* + *probare* to try, approve, prove) + *-ette* — more at PROVE] **:** an apparatus (as a mortar) formerly used for testing the strength of gunpowder

epruinose \(')ē+\ *adj* [*e-* + *pruinose*] *biol* **:** not pruinose

EPs *pl of* EP

ep·si·lon \'epsə,län *also* -,lən, *chiefly Brit* ep'sīlən\ *n* -S [Gk *e psilon*, lit., simple e] **1 :** the fifth letter of the Greek alphabet — symbol Ε or ϵ; see ALPHABET table **2** *in mathematical analysis* **:** an arbitrarily small positive quantity

ep·som·ite \'epsə,mīt\ *n* -S [F, fr. *Epsom*, England, its locality + F *-ite*] **:** a mineral $MgSO_4.7H_2O$ consisting of native Epsom salts usu. occurring massive or in crusts (hardness 2.0–2.5, sp. gr. 1.75)

ep·som salts \'epsəm-\ *n pl but usu sing in constr*, *or* **epsom salt** *usu cap E* [fr. *Epsom*, England] **:** a bitter colorless or white crystalline salt consisting of magnesium sulfate heptahydrate $MgSO_4.7H_2O$, having cathartic qualities, and used esp. in medicine and in the leather and textile industries (as in dyeing and finishing)

EPT *abbr* excess-profits tax

ep·tes·i·cus \ep'tesə̇kəs\ *n, cap* [NL] **:** a nearly cosmopolitan genus of vespertilionid bats that includes the big brown bat and other common forms

ep·thi·a·nu·ra \,epthēə'n(y)u̇rə\ *n* [NL, perh. irreg. fr. Gk *ephthien oura* the tail has wasted away] **1** *cap* **:** a genus of very small short-tailed Australian birds (family Sylviidae) **2** -S **:** any bird of the genus *Epthianura* **:** CHAT 3b

ep·u·la·tion \,epyə'lāshən\ *n* -S [L *epulation-*, *epulatio*, fr. *epulatus* (past part. of *epulari* to feast, fr. *epulum* feast) + *-ion-*, *-io* -ion; akin to L *opus* work — more at OPERATE] **:** FEASTING, BANQUETING

epu·lis \ə̇'pyülə̇s\ *n, pl* **epuli·des** \-lə,dēz\ [NL, fr. Gk *epoulis*, fr. *epi-* + *-oulis* (fr. *oulon* gum)] **:** a tumor or tumorous growth of the gum — **ep·u·loid** \'epyə,lȯid\ *or* **ep·u·loi·dal** \¦epyə¦lȯidᵊl\ *adj*

ep·u·lo \'epyə,lō, 'āpə,-\ *n, pl* **epulo·nes** \-pyə'lō,nēz, -pə'lō,nās\ [L, fr. *epulum*] **:** a member of a college of ancient Roman priests who had charge of the sacrificial banquets

epupillate \(')ē+\ *adj* [*e-* + L *pupilla* pupil + E *-ate* — more at PUPIL] *zool, of a color spot* **:** having no dark central dot

1**ep·ural** \(')e¦pyu̇rəl\ *or* **epi·ural** \¦epē¦y-\ *adj* [*epi-* + Gk *oura* tail + E *-al*] **:** situated on the dorsal side of the tail

2**epural** \"\ *or* **epiural** \"\ *n* -S **:** an epural bone or cartilage on a fish

ep·u·rate \'epyə,rāt\ *vt* -ED/-ING/-S [F *épurer* to purify (fr. OF *epurer*, fr. *e-* + *pur* pure) + E *-ate* — more at PURE] **:** PURIFY

ep·u·ra·tion \,epyə'rāshən\ *n* -S [F *épuration*, fr. *épurer* + *-ation*] **:** PURIFICATION; *specif* **:** the criminal prosecution of French and Italian officials held after World War II to have been fascists or collaborators

epure \(')ā¦pyu̇(ə)r\ *n* -S [F *épure*, fr. *épurer*] *archit* **:** a full-scale pattern of work to be done usu. traced on a wall or floor **:** CARTOON 1

epus *abbr* [LL *episcopus*] bishop

epyl·li·on \e'pilēən, -ē,än\ *n, pl* **epyl·lia** \-ēə\ *or* **epyllions** [Gk, dim. of *epos* word, speech, epic poem — more at VOICE] **:** a relatively short narrative poem resembling an epic in theme, tone, or style ⟨Arnold's emulation of certain Homeric qualities in his ~ *Sohrab and Rustum*⟩

eq *abbr* **1** equal **2** equation **3** equator; equatorial **4** equerry **5** equipment **6** equitable; equity **7** equivalent

EQ *abbr* educational quotient

eqpt *abbr* equipment

eq·ua·bil·i·ty \,ekwə'biləd·ē, -lətē, -i *also* ,ēk-\ *n* -ES [L *aequabilitas*, fr. *aequabilis* + *-itas* -ity] **1 :** the quality or condition of being equable ⟨~ of temperature⟩ **:** EQUANIMITY ⟨they lacked our gusto as surely as we lacked their ~ —John Mason Brown⟩ **2** *archaic* **:** comparability as equals or on equal terms

eq·ua·ble \'ekwəbəl *also* 'ēk-\ *adj* [L *aequabilis*, fr. *aequare* to make level, make equal (fr. *aequus* level, equal) + *-abilis* -able] **1 a :** marked by lack of variation or change **:** UNIFORM **b :** showing regular or consistent movement, occurrence, operation, or character ⟨an ~ stride⟩ **2 :** marked by lack of noticeable, unpleasant, or extreme variation, inequality, or fluctuation ⟨for rest and recreation a warm, ~ climate is doubtless most delightful —Ellsworth Huntington⟩ ⟨my affections tend to be deep and ~ and calm —Havelock Ellis⟩ **syn** see STEADY

eq·ua·ble·ness *n* -ES **:** the quality or condition of being equable

eq·ua·bly \-blē, -li\ *adv* **:** in an equable manner ⟨studied much, slept little, . . . and was ~ cheerful —Charles Dickens⟩

1**equal** \'ēkwəl\ *adj* [ME, fr. L *aequalis*, fr. *aequus* level, equal + *-alis* -al] **1 a** (1) **:** of the same measure, quantity, amount, or number as another or others **:** LIKE ⟨~ quantities of bread for each man⟩ ⟨each placed an ~ distance from the door⟩ ⟨~ pay for ~ work⟩ (2) **:** identical in mathematical value or logical denotation **:** EQUIVALENT — often used with *to* ⟨set each factor ~ to zero⟩ ⟨class *a* is ~ to class *b* if *a* is included in *b* and *b* is included in *a* —M.R.Cohen & E. Nagel⟩ ⟨the temperature there must have been ~ to the freezing point of the sea —Valter Schytt⟩ **b :** like, as great as, or the same as another or others in degree, worth, quality, nature, ability, or status ⟨held men to be ~ in the sight of God⟩ ⟨work ~ to his best⟩ ⟨premature babies . . . eventually . . . become ~ to children born after a normal time —Morris Fishbein⟩ ⟨of ~ interest with the first book⟩; *specif* **:** receiving or entitled to the same treatment or privileges any other individual has or is entitled to ⟨all men are created ~ —*U. S. Declaration of Independence*⟩ **c :** like, as great, or the same for each member of a group or class ⟨failing to provide ~ opportunities⟩ **:** uniform in quantity or quality, measure or degree ⟨an ~ pressure throughout the system⟩ ⟨the song of the birds . . . is not ~ as to melody and force —Richard Semon⟩ **2 :** regarding or affecting all objects in the same way **:** IMPARTIAL ⟨in ~ care to nourish lord in hall or beast in stall —Sidney Lanier⟩ ⟨authors of the past and present should be judged with ~ eyes —F.O.Matthiessen⟩ **:** FAIR, JUST ⟨~ laws⟩ **3 :** free from extremes **:** EQUABLE: as **a :** tranquil of mind or mood **:** showing tranquillity ⟨with ~ mind . . . they fell upon their swords —Philip Murray †1952⟩ **b :** not showing variation in appearance, structure, or proportion ⟨architecture, always hard, logical, and ~ —Osbert Sitwell⟩ **:** LEVEL ⟨the ~ plains of . . . Sicily —Elizabeth B. Browning⟩ **4 a :** capable of meeting the requirements of a situation or a task ⟨neither their financial resources nor their military organization were ~ to the task —A.C.Flick⟩ **:** capable of meeting a demand upon one's ability or resources ⟨he was ~ to extended walks by this time —T.B. Costain⟩ **b :** SUITABLE, COMMENSURATE ⟨work not ~ to his abilities⟩ **5** *archaic* **:** not a matter of concern (as between alternatives) ⟨it was ~ to him whether he fell by his enemies in the field or by his creditors in the city —Oliver Goldsmith⟩ **syn** see SAME

2equal \"\ *n* -s **1 :** one that is equal in status (as social position), achievement, or a particular quality **:** MATCH ⟨humankind as the law views it is a society of ~*s* —B.N.Cardozo⟩ ⟨hardly a man his ~ in the field —Elizabeth M. Roberts⟩ ⟨he has no ~ in common sense and honesty⟩ **2** *obs* **:** CONTEMPORARY ⟨profited in the Jews' religion above many my ~*s* in mine own nation —Gal 1:14 (AV)⟩ **3 :** an equal quantity or number ⟨if ~*s* are taken from ~*s*, the remainders are equal⟩ **4 :** one of two or more playing cards held by one player that are consecutive or equivalent in rank

3equal \"\ *vb* **equaled** *or* **equalled**; **equaled** *or* **equalled**; **equaling** *or* **equalling**; **equals** *vt* **1 a** *archaic* **:** to compare or regard as equal esp. in quality ⟨~*ing* the pleasures of war to social festivity —Sharon Turner⟩ **b** *archaic* **:** to make equal esp. in ability or condition **:** EQUALIZE ⟨the fair democracy of flowers that ~*s* cot and palace —J.G.Whittier⟩ **c** *obs* **:** to make equal in height (as with the ground) **:** LEVEL ⟨cities have been ~*ed* with the ground —Robert Hill⟩ **2 :** to be equal to (as in quantity or quality) ⟨the migrant population ~*ed* the native population⟩ ⟨for sheer relaxation and comfort I don't know anything to ~ it —Keith Munro⟩; *specif* **:** to be identical in value to ⟨two times two ~*s* four⟩ ⟨if the curve *xy* ~*s* the arc *AB*⟩ — symbol = **3 a :** to make or produce something equal to ⟨~ that if you can⟩ **b** *obs* **:** to make equal return to ⟨the ardent passion . . . which if he failed to ~ —Henry Fielding⟩ ~ *vi, obs* **:** to be equal ⟨we are so a body strong enough, even as we are, to ~ with the king —Shak.⟩ **syn** see MATCH

4equal \"\ *adv, obs* **:** EQUALLY ⟨he is ~ ravenous as he is subtle —Shak.⟩

equal–area \¦==¦===\ *adj, of a map projection* **:** maintaining constant ratio of size between quadrilaterals formed by the meridians and parallels and the quadrilaterals of the globe thereby preserving true areal extent of forms represented

equaling file *n* **:** a blunt almost parallel but slightly bulging double-cut file of rectangular section used esp. in fine toolmaking

equal·i·tar·i·an \(,)ē¦kwälə¦terēən, ə̇¦k-, ¦ē,k- *also* -wȯl- *or* -ta(a)r- *or* -tār-\ *adj or n* [*equality* + *-arian*] **:** EGALITARIAN

equal·i·tar·i·an·ism \(,)ē¦==¦==ə,nizəm, ə̇,-\ *n* -s **:** EGALITARIANISM

equal·i·ty \ē'kwälə̇d·ē, ə̇'-, -ətē, -i\ *n* -ES [ME *equalite*, fr. MF *equalité*, fr. L *aequalitat-, aequalitas*, fr. *aequalis* equal + *-itat-, -itas* -ity — more at EQUAL] **:** the quality or state of being equal: as **a :** sameness or equivalence in number, quantity, or measure ⟨~ of size⟩ **b :** likeness or sameness in quality, power, status, or degree ⟨legal ~ of states was accepted in spite of physical inequality —Herbert Weinschel⟩ ⟨master and servant associating in ~⟩ **c :** evenness or uniformity esp. of a surface or of a process or motion **d :** equability of temper **e** *logic* **:** IDENTITY — compare EQUIVALENCE

equality sign *var of* EQUAL-SIGN

equal·i·za·tion \,ēkwələ'zāshən, -,lī'z-\ *n* -s **:** the act of equalizing or the state of being equalized ⟨~ of conditions of employment in agriculture and industry⟩ ⟨~ of brake pressure on all wheels⟩; *specif* **:** the adjustment of the tax valuation of property so as to make the tax burden in different districts proportionate to the value of the taxable property in the district

equalization fund *n* **1 :** a fund for equalizing payments or income to various classes of persons; *specif* **:** a fund raised by tariff duties on certain products and used for equalizing the income of producers of those products in proportion to their respective ratios of production **2** *or* **equalization account :** STABILIZATION FUND

equalization period *n* **:** a period when a previously unmanaged forest will yield regular and continuous crops

equal·ize \'ēkwə,līz\ *vb* -ED/-ING/-S *see -ize in Explan Notes* [*1equal* + *-ize*] *vt* **1** *archaic* **:** EQUAL 1a, 1b, 2 **2 :** to make equal **:** cause to be like in amount or degree **:** make of equal status ⟨extended Roman citizenship to all provincials . . . *equalizing* the conquered peoples with their conquerors —Clyde Pharr⟩ ⟨~ educational opportunities⟩ **3 a :** to reduce or bring up to a normal level **:** compensate for ⟨she has an instinct to ~ an inequality which "nature" may have left —Reinhold Niebuhr⟩ **b :** to make uniform; *specif* **:** to distribute evenly or uniformly ⟨a bar to ~ the pressure on a set of springs⟩ ⟨~ the burden of taxation⟩ **c :** to adjust or correct the frequency characteristics of (an electronic signal) by restoring to their original level high frequencies that have been attenuated in recording or transmission or by other means ~ *vi* **:** to make something equal; *specif, chiefly Brit* **:** to tie the score in a sports match ⟨the score was still 2–1, but then Hofman *equalized* —Jimmy Hogan⟩

equal·iz·er \-zə(r)\ *n* -s **1 :** one that equalizes esp. by equal distribution (as of force): as **a** *or* **equalizing bar** (1) **:** a bar to which the whippletrees of a vehicle are attached to equalize the pull of the draft animals (2) **:** a beam connecting two axle springs of a railway locomotive or car to distribute the weight equally on both axles **b** (1) **:** a device for equalizing the pull of electromagnets (2) **:** a conductor of low resistance joining points of equal potential in the armature winding of a dynamoelectric machine **c :** a device for equalizing an electronic signal **d** *or* **equalizer brake :** a device for distributing braking force between independent brakes of a motor vehicle **e** (1) **:** a machine for sawing wooden stock to uniform lengths (2) **:** an operator of an equalizer **2** *railroading* **:** a straight-arm crank used in interlocking **3** *slang* **:** PISTOL **4 :** a tying score in a sports contest ⟨he scored the ~ with two out in the sixth⟩

equalizer set *n* **:** BALANCER SET 1

equalizing basin *n* **:** a small irrigation reservoir that receives water from a pump and is used to maintain uniform water flow during brief pumping interruptions and to permit temporary water withdrawal in excess of the pump capacity

equalled *past of* EQUAL

equalling *pres part of* EQUAL

equal·ly \'ēkwəlē, -li\ *adv* [ME, fr. *equal* + *-ly*] **1 :** in an equal manner or way: **a :** in equal amounts or shares ⟨divided ~ between girls and boys⟩ **b :** with equal treatment for each **:** JUSTLY, IMPARTIALLY ⟨so to use them as . . . their merits and our safety may ~ determine —Shak.⟩ **c :** UNIFORMLY, EVENLY ⟨distribute the heat ~ through the room⟩ **d :** in the same way **:** LIKEWISE, SIMILARLY ⟨endeavor to encourage learning and ~ to protect students from distracting influences⟩ **2 :** to an equal degree ⟨two ~ undesirable alternatives —Vera M. Dean⟩ **:** ALIKE ⟨respected ~ by young and old⟩ ⟨affecting city governments ~ with states⟩ ⟨~ opposed to Communism as to Fascism —*Ecclesiastical Rev.*⟩

equal·ness \-əlnə̇s\ *n* -ES *archaic* **:** EQUALITY

equals *pres 3d sing of* EQUAL, *pl of* EQUAL

equal–sign \'==,=\ *also* **equals sign** *or* **equality sign** *n* **:** a sign = indicating mathematical or logical equivalence

equal temperament *n* **:** the division of the octave into twelve equal half steps

equa·nim·i·ty \,ēkwə'nimə̇d·ē, ,ek-, -ətē, -i\ *n* -ES [L *aequanimitas*, fr. *aequus* equal + *animus* mind, soul (in the phrase *aequo animo ferre* to bear with equal mind) + *-itas* -ity — more at ANIMATE] **1** *obs* **:** fairness or justness of judgment **:** EQUITY **2 :** evenness of mental disposition **:** emotional balance esp. under stress ⟨the inner life where the rational soul may cultivate ~ in defiance of all outward circumstances —Reinhold Niebuhr⟩ **3 :** right disposition **:** BALANCE ⟨rest restored the strained muscles to physical ~ —Richard Jefferies⟩ ⟨perfection . . . was nothing but perfect ~ and harmony —John Galsworthy⟩

syn COMPOSURE, PHLEGM, SANGFROID: EQUANIMITY suggests a habitual or constitutional emotional balance or poise that is disturbed only by the most trying of circumstances ⟨Stoicism teaches men . . . to accept with proud *equanimity* the misfortunes of life —W.R.Inge⟩ ⟨even direct insult did not disturb his *equanimity*⟩ COMPOSURE usu. suggests the achievement or the maintenance of self-possession or the appearance of self-possession by design or by effort of will, esp. under trying circumstances ⟨we have to call upon our whole people — men, women, and children alike — to stand up with *composure* and fortitude to the fire of the enemy —Sir Winston Churchill⟩ ⟨in the *composure* of his manner, he was unaltered —Charles Dickens⟩ PHLEGM signifies an imperturbability usu. ascribable to a certain sluggishness or slowness of mental or emotional response ⟨to react to terrible news with *phlegm*⟩ ⟨Clare was always restless; she had none of Jane's *phlegm* and stolidity —Rose Macaulay⟩ SANGFROID usu. suggests a constitutional coldness or a preternatural self-possession, esp. under strain ⟨in his feeling that most men were fools, in his *sangfroid* and his scorn of what "folks would say" —Van Wyck Brooks⟩ ⟨Rachmaninoff, who in spite of his apparent *sangfroid* had a very sensitive nervous system —Charles O'Connell⟩

equan·i·mous \(')ē¦kwanəməs, (')e¦k-, ə̇'k-\ *adj* [LL *aequanimus*, back-formation fr. *aequanimitas*] **:** possessing or displaying equanimity ⟨a good-humored, ~ individual —*Current Biog.*⟩ — **equan·i·mous·ly** *adv*

equant \'ēkwənt, -,kwant\ *adj* [L *aequant-, aequans*, pres. part. of *aequare*] **:** of, being, or relating to a crystal having equal or nearly equal diameters in all directions ⟨~ grain⟩ ⟨~ habit⟩

equat·abil·i·ty \(,)ē,kwād·ə'bilə̇d·ē, ə̇,k-\ *n* -ES **:** the quality or state of being equatable

equat·able \(')ē¦kwād·əbəl, ə̇'k-\ *adj* **:** capable of being equated ⟨different but ~ terminologies —Ethel Albert⟩

equate \(')ē¦kwāt, ə̇'k-, *usu* -ād·+V\ *vb* -ED/-ING/-S [ME *equaten*, fr. L *aequatus*, past part. of *aequare* — more at EQUABLE] *vt* **1 a :** to make equal **:** EQUALIZE ⟨Turkey has had difficulties *equating* exports and imports —Welles Hangen⟩ **:** make equal in specific respects ⟨two groups *equated* as to age and sex⟩; *specif* **:** to establish equality with respect to (one or more attributes between colors evoked by different stimuli) ⟨when matching colors in quantitative experiments, hue, brilliance, and saturation must each be *equated*⟩ **b :** to make such an allowance or correction in as will reduce to a common standard or obtain a correct result; *specif* **:** to make allowance for grading or curving (a railroad track or sections of it) by adding a specified distance for each degree of curvature or foot of ascent esp. in obtaining a basis for division of charges between different sections of a through route **c :** to make comparable **:** show the relationship between ⟨~ the production of poetry to the forms of society —J.G. Fletcher⟩ **2 a :** to treat, represent, or regard as equal, equivalent, or comparable ⟨a superior . . . had unbent so far as to ~ her with herself —José Durand⟩ ⟨tend to ~ . . . "good" with "European" —Rosalind Murray⟩; *specif* **:** to put in the form of an equation ⟨not to be . . . *equated* by the mathematician —John Ruskin⟩ **b :** to regard as necessarily or properly associated ⟨they ~ goodness with unhappiness, as some ladies . . . ~ culture with seriousness —O.S.J.Gogarty⟩ ~ *vi* **:** to correspond as equal (as in meaning) ⟨little men from space ~ neatly with our own projected dreams —L.C.Eiseley⟩

equated date *n* **:** AVERAGE DUE DATE

equa·tion \ē'kwāzhən, ə̇'- *also* -āsh-\ *n* -s [ME *equacioun*, fr. L *aequation-, aequatio*, fr. *aequatus* + *-ion-, -io* -ion] **1 a :** the act or process of equating **:** EQUALIZATION ⟨the ~ of service pay and civilian wages⟩ ⟨~ of colors⟩ **:** IDENTIFICATION ⟨the king's ~ of himself with his country⟩ **b** (1) **:** a quantity added or subtracted in equating a computation ⟨~ of the equinoxes⟩ (2) **:** an element affecting a process **:** FACTOR ⟨solely on the merits of their performances on that occasion, and no other ~*s* should enter into his decisions —W.F.Brown b. 1903⟩ (3) **:** a complex of variable factors ⟨sociologists . . . taking into account motives, values, norms, ends — the whole social ~ that fundamentalists in science have considered merely a source of error —H.J.Muller⟩ — compare HUMAN EQUATION, PERSONAL EQUATION **c :** a state of being equated **:** BALANCE ⟨diplomats who work out the delicate ~*s* of power⟩; *specif* **:** a state of association or identification of two or more things ⟨the dreamer . . . can put into symbolic ~ any two diverse things —Weston La Barre⟩ **2 :** a usu. formal statement of equivalence: **a :** a statement of equality between two mathematical expressions (as numbers, functions, magnitudes, operations), the sign = usu. being placed between them **b :** an expression representing a chemical reaction quantitatively by means of chemical symbols, the formulas of the reacting substances being placed on the left and those of the products on the right of the sign → or = or of the sign ⇆ or ⇌ if the reaction is reversible all of which signs should be read "give," not "are equal to" **c** (1) *logic* **:** a formal expression of the sameness of reference of two expressions (2) *symbolic logic* **:** the expression of a proposition or of the relation between propositions in a form analogous to an algebraic equation **d :** the mathematical expression of the proportions in which color stimuli must be mixed for equation of colors

equa·tion·al \-zhənᵊl, -zhnəl *also* -sh-\ *adj* **1 :** of, using, or involving equations **2 a :** dividing into two equal parts — used esp. of the mitotic cell division following reduction in meiosis **b :** occurring in or resulting from an equational division ⟨~ splits appear early in each chromosome⟩ ⟨each ~ half⟩ **3 :** having a subject and predicate not linked by a verb ⟨~ sentence⟩ — **equa·tion·al·ly** \-ᵊl|ē, -əl|; |i\ *adv*

equation clock *n* **:** a timepiece made to exhibit the differences between mean solar time and apparent time

equation of continuity : a partial differential equation whose derivation involves the assumption that matter is neither created nor destroyed

equation of exchange : a formulation in economics: the quantity of money in circulation times its average rate of turnover is equal to the average price level times the quantity of goods exchanged

equation of light : LIGHT-TIME

equation of motion : an equation that enters into the calculation of the position of a point or of a body as a function of time

equation of state : an equation that expresses the relation between the pressure, temperature, and volume of a gas or liquid — compare GAS LAW c

equation of the center : the difference between the place of a planet as supposed to move uniformly in a circle and its place as moving in an ellipse

equation of time : the difference between mean solar time and apparent time usu. expressed as a correction which is to be added to apparent time to give local mean solar time and which never exceeds 16 minutes

1equat·ive \(')ē¦kwād·iv, ə̇'k-\ *adj* [*equate* + *-ive*] **1 :** belonging to or constituting a degree of comparison (as in Welsh) that denotes an equal level of the quality, quantity, or relation expressed by the adjective or adverb compared ⟨the ~ degree⟩ ⟨an ~ form⟩ **2** *of a grammatical case* **:** denoting likeness or identity

2equative \"\ *n* -s **1 :** the equative degree of comparison in a language **:** a form in the equative degree **2 :** the equative case in a language **:** a form in the equative case

equa·tor \ē'kwād·ə(r), ə̇'k- *also* 'ē,k-\ *n* -s [ME, fr. ML *aequator*, fr. L *aequatus* (past part. of *aequare* to make equal) + *-or* — more at EQUABLE] **1 :** the great circle of the celestial sphere whose plane is perpendicular to the axis of the earth **:** CELESTIAL EQUATOR **2 :** the great circle midway between the poles of rotation of a planet, star, or other celestial body; *specif* **:** a great circle of the earth that is everywhere equally distant from the two poles and divides the earth's surface into the northern and southern hemispheres and that is the line from which latitudes are reckoned, its own latitude being everywhere 0 degrees — see ZONE illustration **3 :** a circle or circular band dividing the surface of a body into two usu. equal and symmetrical parts ⟨the rainfall ~⟩; *esp* **:** a circle about a body at the place of its greatest width ⟨~ of a balloon⟩ ⟨~ of an egg⟩ ⟨~ of the eyeball⟩ **4 :** the circle on a surface of revolution that bisects its meridians; *specif* **:** GREAT CIRCLE

equator coordinate *n* **:** a member of the equator system of coordinates

1equa·to·ri·al \¦ēkwə¦tōrēəl, ¦ek-, -tȯr-\ *adj* [*equator* + *-ial*] **1 a :** of, at, or relating to the equator or an equator ⟨~ regions⟩ ⟨~ diameter⟩ **b :** of, in, originating in, or suggesting the region around the geographic equator ⟨~ forests⟩ ⟨~ origin⟩ ⟨~ air masses⟩ ⟨~ heat⟩ **2 :** being or having a support that includes two axles at right angles to each other, one being parallel to the earth's axis of rotation so that motion of the instrument supported in right ascension and declination is possible — used of a telescope or other astronomical instrument **3 :** extending in a direction essentially in the plane of a cyclohexane or similar cyclic structure; *also* **:** characterized by bonds extending in this manner ⟨~ bonds⟩ ⟨~ hydrogen atoms⟩ — distinguished from *axial*

2equatorial \"\ *n* -s **:** a telescope that has an equatorial mounting

equatorial current *n* **1 :** an ocean current flowing westward just north or just south of the equator — called respectively *north equatorial current* and *south equatorial current* **2 :** a tidal current occurring when the moon is over the equator

equatorial guin·ea \-'ginē, -ni\ *adj, usu cap E&G* [fr. *Equatorial Guinea*, country in western Africa] **:** of or relating to Equatorial Guinea **:** of the kind or style prevalent in Equatorial Guinea

equatorial horizontal parallax *n* **:** the geocentric parallax of a celestial body seen on the horizon by an observer at the earth's equator

equa·to·ri·al·ly \-rēəlē, -li\ *adv* **:** in an equatorial manner ⟨a telescope ~ mounted⟩

equatorial plane *n* **:** a plane perpendicular to a mitotic spindle and equidistant from the centrosomes

equatorial plate *n* **1 :** EQUATORIAL PLANE **2 :** METAPHASE PLATE

equatorial tide *n* **:** a tide occurring when the moon is over the equator

equator of heat : THERMAL EQUATOR

equator system of coordinates : the system of celestial coordinates based on the celestial equator, its coordinates being declination and right ascension

1equa·tor·ward *also* **equa·tor·wards** *pronunc at* EQUATOR + wə(r)d(z)\ *adv* [*equator* + *-ward, -wards*] **:** toward the equator ⟨air flowing ~⟩

2equatorward \"\ *adj* **:** lying nearer to or moving toward the equator ⟨~ winds⟩

eq·uer·ry \'ekwərē, -ri; ə̇'kwer-, ē'-,e'-\ *n* -ES [alter. (influenced by L *equus* horse) of earlier *esquiry, escurie*, fr. *esquiry, escurie* stable, fr. MF *escuirie, escurie* collection of squires, office of a squire, stable, fr. *escuier* squire + *-ie* -y — more at ESQUIRE] **1 :** an officer of princes or nobles charged with the care of their horses **2 :** a man usu. of social or military rank in regular attendance upon a member of royalty; *specif* **:** one of the officers of the British royal household in the department of the master of the horse in regular attendance on the sovereign or another member of the royal family (as for carrying messages, receiving formal social correspondence, or announcing guests) — compare LADY-IN-WAITING

eques \'e,kwes, 'ē,kwēz\ *n, pl* **eq·ui·tes** \'ekwə,tās, -,tēz\ [L, lit., horseman, fr. *equus* horse — more at EQUINE] **:** a member of a Roman order between the senatorial order and the ordinary citizen serving orig. as cavalry, having entrance requirements based on wealth, and having during some periods exclusive rights to certain judicial, financial, and military positions — called also *knight*

1eques·tri·an \ə̇'kwestrēən, ē'-,e'-\ *adj* [L *equestr-, equester* of a horseman, of an eques (fr. *eques*) + E *-ian*] **1 a :** of, relating to, or featuring horseback riding **b** *archaic* **:** riding on horseback **:** MOUNTED **c :** representing a person on horseback ⟨an ~ statue⟩ ⟨~ portrait⟩ ⟨~ seal as the reverse of his heraldic seal⟩ **2 :** of, relating to, or composed of knights **:** KNIGHTLY ⟨a 14th century book of Spanish ~ arms⟩

2equestrian \"\ *n* -s **:** one who rides on horseback **:** HORSEMAN, RIDER; *specif* **:** an equestrian acrobat

equestrian director *n* **:** an official of a circus or carnival who is the stage manager and master of ceremonies of the performance and has general responsibility for the performers — compare RINGMASTER

eques·tri·an·ism \-rēə,nizəm\ *n* -s **:** the art or practice of riding a horse **:** HORSEMANSHIP

eques·tri·enne \ə̇¦kwestrē¦en, ē¦k-, e¦k-, ,e,==¦=\ *n* -s [*2equestrian* + *-enne* (as in *tragedienne*)] **:** a female equestrian

equi- *also* **aequi-** *comb form* [ME *equi-*, fr. MF & L; MF *equi-*, fr. L *aequi-*, fr. *aequus* level, equal] **:** equal ⟨*equidistribution*⟩ **:** equally ⟨*equidistant*⟩ ⟨*equisided*⟩

equi·angular \¦ēkwə̇, -wē *sometimes* ¦ekwə̇ *or* ¦ekwē *or* ¦ē,kwī + \ *adj* [*equi-* + *angular*] **:** having all or corresponding angles equal ⟨an ~ triangle⟩ ⟨~ polygons⟩ — **equi·angularity** \,=(,)=+\ *n* -ES

equiangular spiral *n* **:** a plane curve that cuts all its radii vectores at the same angle — called also *logarithmic spiral*

equi·axed \"+,akst\ *adj* [F *équiaxe* (fr. *équi-* equi- + *axe* axis, fr. L *axis*) + E *-ed* — more at AXIS] **:** having approximately equal dimensions in all directions — used esp. of a crystal grain in a metal

equi·caloric \"+\ *adj* [*equi-* + *caloric*] **:** capable of yielding equal amounts of energy in the bodily economy ⟨~ high and low protein diets⟩

equi·cohesive temperature \"+. . .-\ *n* [*equi-* + *cohesive*] **:** the temperature below which fracture of a metal does not occur at crystal boundaries and above which it does occur at such boundaries

equi·crural \"+\ *adj* [LL *aequicrurius* (fr. L *aequi-* equi- + LL *-crurius*, fr. L *crur-, crus* leg) + E *-al* — more at CRUS] *archaic* **:** ISOSCELES

eq·uid \'ekwə̇d, 'ēk-\ *n* -s [NL *Equidae*] **:** one of the Equidae

eq·ui·dae \'ekwə,dē\ *n pl, cap* [NL, fr. *Equus*, type genus + *-idae*] **:** a family of perissodactyl ungulate mammals consisting of the horses, asses, and zebras and various extinct related animals, all recent members being distinguished from the other existing perissodactyls by their comparatively slender and agile build, hypsodont grinding teeth with the grooves between the ridges filled with cement, reduced ulna and fibula fused with the radius and tibia respectively to form in turn a rigid slender forearm and shank, and esp. by the reduction of each foot to a single enlarged functional middle digit upon the tip of which they walk, the other digits being entirely wanting except for rudimentary splint bones of the metapodials of the second and fourth — see EQUUS

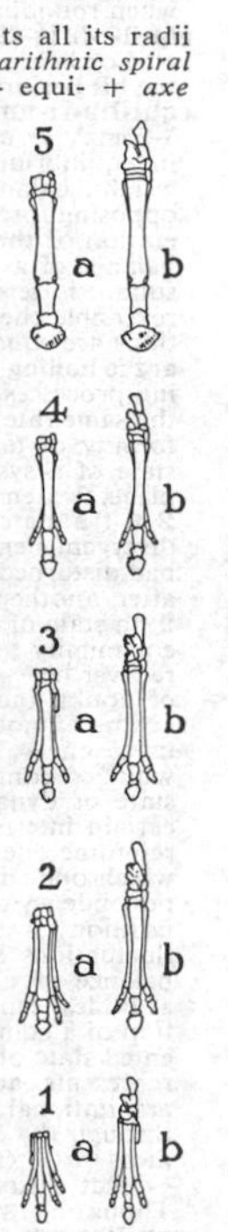

diagram showing evolution of the Equidae: *a* lower fore leg and foot, *b* lower hind leg and foot: *1 Hyracotherium*, Lower Eocene; *2 Eohippus*, Lower Eocene; *3 Mesohippus*, Oligocene; *4 Protohippus*, Miocene; *5 Equus*, Pleistocene to recent

equi·distant *as at* EQUIANGULAR +\ *adj* [MF or LL; MF, fr. LL *aequidistant-, aequidistans*, fr. L *aequi-* + *distant-, distans*, pres. part. of *distare* to stand apart, be distant — more at DISTANT] **1 :** being at an equal distance **:** equally distant — often used with *from* ⟨points on a circle are ~ from its center⟩ ⟨houses ~ from the street⟩ **2 :** representing map distances true to scale in all directions from a given point or along or at right angles to a given meridian or parallel (as the equator) ⟨2-point ~ diagram⟩ ⟨the limited ~ quality of a cylindrical projection⟩ — see AZIMUTHAL EQUIDISTANT PROJECTION — **equidistantly** *adv*

equi·final *as at* EQUIANGULAR +\ *adj* [*equi-* + *final*] **:** having the same effect or outcome from initially different events

equi·finality \,=(,)=+\ *n* [*equi-* + *finality*] **:** the property of allowing or having the same effect or result from different events

equi·form \'ēkwə,fȯrm, 'ek-\ *or* **equi·for·mal** \¦==¦fȯrməl\ *adj* [*equiform* fr. LL *aequiformis*, fr. L *aequi-* equi- + *-formis* -form; *equiformal* fr. LL *aequiformis* + E *-al*] **:** like in shape or function **:** UNIFORM ⟨~ crystals⟩ ⟨~ phonemes⟩ ⟨those plants that radiate from the same center have progressive *equiformal* areas of different size —S.A.Cain⟩ — **equi·for·mi·ty** \,==¦fȯrməd·ē\ *n* -ES

equi·glacial line *as at* EQUIANGULAR +. . .-\ *n* [*equi-* + *glacial*] **:** a line on a map or chart to show coincidence of ice conditions (as in lakes, rivers, or harbors) at a given time — see ISOPAG, ISOPECTIC, ISOTAC

equi·granular *as at* EQUIANGULAR +\ *adj* [*equi-* + *granu-*

lar] **:** having or characterized by crystals of nearly the same size ⟨a rock of ~ texture⟩

equi·lat·er \ˌēkwəˈlad·ə(r), ˌek-\ *adj* [LL *aequilaterus*, fr. L *aequi-* equi- + LL *-laterus* (fr. L *later-, latus* side) — more at LATERAL] **:** EQUILATERAL 1

[1]**equi·lateral** *as at* EQUIANGULAR +\ *adj* [LL *aequilateralis*, fr. L *aequi-* equi- + *lateralis* lateral — more at LATERAL] **1 a :** having all the sides equal ⟨an ~ triangle⟩ ⟨an ~ polygon⟩ **b** *of a polyhedron* **:** having all the faces equal **2 :** bilaterally symmetrical; *specif, of a bivalve shell* **:** divisible into two equal and symmetrical parts by a transverse line drawn through the apex of the umbo

equilateral triangle

[2]**equilateral** \"\ *n* -s **1 :** a side exactly corresponding or equal to others **2 :** a figure of equal sides

equilateral arch *n* **:** a two-centered pointed arch in which the chords of the curves are equal to the span — see TWO-CENTERED ARCH illustration

equilateral cross *n* **:** GREEK CROSS

equilateral hyperbola *n* **:** a hyperbola with its asymptotes at right angles

equi·laterally \"+\ *adv* **:** in an equilateral manner

eq·ui·len·in \ˌekwəˈlenən, əˈkwilənən\ *n* -s [blend of *equilin* and [3]*en-*] **:** a crystalline weakly estrogenic hormone that is a phenolic steroid ketone $C_{18}H_{18}O_2$ and is obtained from the urine of pregnant mares

equil·i·brant \əˈkwiləbrənt, ēˈk- *sometimes* ˌēkwəˈlibrənt *or* ˌekwə- *or* -wəˈlīb-\ *n* -s [equilibrate + -ant] **:** a force or system of forces capable of balancing a given force or system of forces

equil·i·brate \-ˌbrāt, *usu* -ād+V\ *also* **equi·lib·ri·ate** \ˌēkwəˈlibrēˌā- *also* ˌek-\ *vb* -ED/-ING/-S [*equilibrate* fr. LL *aequilibratus*, past part. of *aequilibrare*, fr. L *aequilibris* in equilibrium; *equilibriate* fr. *equilibrium* + *-ate* — more at EQUILIBRIUM] *vt* **:** to bring into or keep in equilibrium **:** BALANCE ⟨the resulting relationship . . . tends to ~ the status of men and women in Hopi society —Laura Thompson⟩ ⟨the gas is measured to ~ the liquid⟩ ~ *vi* **:** to bring about, come to, or be in equilibrium ⟨the forces that ~⟩ ⟨the distribution of the . . . sample will not ~ owing to absorption and excretion —*Science*⟩ ⟨while its weight ~*s* with the other weight⟩

equil·i·bra·tion \əˌkwiləˈbrāshən, ēˌk- *sometimes* ˌēkwələˈb- *or* ˌekwə- *or* -wəˌlīˈb-\ *n* -s [LL *aequilibration-, aequilibratio*, fr. *aequilibratus* + L *-ion-, -io* -ion] **1 :** a bringing into, keeping in, or coming to equilibrium **:** the action of equilibrating ⟨the ~ . . . of solutions of nonvolatile solutes in the same solvent —F.W.Leavitt & Saul Kaye⟩ ⟨an artful ~ . . . of particular interest for the sake of the wider community —Reinhold Niebuhr⟩ **2 :** the state of being equilibrated **:** EQUILIBRIUM ⟨the pilot maintains his ~ in space by controlling the attitude of his machine —H.G.Armstrong⟩

equil·i·bra·tor *pronunc at* EQUILIBRATE + ə(r)\ *n* -s **:** any of various devices for maintaining equilibrium (as in an airplane or on a piece of artillery)

equil·i·bra·to·ry \əˈkwiləbrəˌtōrē, ēˈk-; ˌēkwəˈlib-, ˌekwə-, -wəˈlīb-\ *adj* **:** serving to cause or maintain equilibrium ⟨~ reactions in the form of wing positions that differ from the . . . normal —*Biol. Abstracts*⟩

equilibre *n* -s [F *équilibre*, fr. L *aequilibrium* — more at EQUILIBRIUM] *archaic* **:** EQUILIBRIUM

equi·lib·rio \ˌēkwəˈlibrēˌō *also* ˌek-\ *n* [L *aequilibrio* (as in *in aequilibrio*), ablative of *aequilibrium*] *archaic* **:** EQUILIBRIUM ⟨in uncertain ~ between soberness and its reverse —Herman Melville⟩ — used esp. in the phrase *in equilibrio*

equi·lib·ri·ous \¦==¦librēəs\ *adj* [L *aequilibrium* + E *-ous*] *archaic* **:** characterized by equilibrium **:** BALANCED

equi·lib·rist \ˌ==ˈlibrəst; əˈkwiləb-, ēˈk-\ *n* -s [F *équilibriste*, fr. *équilibre* + *-iste* -ist] **:** one who practices balancing **:** BALANCER; *esp* **:** one who balances himself in unnatural positions and hazardous movements (as in ropedancing)

equi·lib·ri·stat \ˌēkwəˈlibrəˌstat *also* ˌek-\ *n* -s [*equilibrium* + *-stat*] **:** an apparatus consisting essentially of a U-tube with capillary ends designed to test the equilibrium of a railroad car when rounding a curve and measure any deviation therefrom

equil·i·bris·tic \əˌkwiləˈbristik, ēˌk-; ˌēkwəˌlīˈb-, ˌek-\ *adj* **:** of or being an equilibrist ⟨a gravity-defying ~ wonder was the hit performer of the show⟩

equi·lib·ri·um \ˌēkwəˈlibrēəm *also* ˌek-\ *n, pl* **equilibriums** \-ēəmz\ *or* **equilib·ria** \-ēə\ [L *aequilibrium*, fr. *aequilibris* in equilibrium, fr. *aequi-* equi- + *-libris* (fr. *libra* pound, weight, balance)] **1 :** a state of balance between or among opposing forces or processes resulting in the absence of acceleration or the absence of net change: as **a :** a state of static balance of a body or system acted upon by forces whose resultant is zero **b :** a state of dynamic balance attained in a reversible chemical reaction when the velocities in both directions are equal **c :** a state of dynamic balance (as of a liquid at the boiling point) in which two or more simultaneous opposing processes (as vaporization and condensation) proceed at the same rate and thereby cancel each other's effects **d :** uniformity of temperature throughout a body or system **e :** a state of a system in which no spontaneous change can take place, the temperature and pressure being the same throughout **2 a :** a state of adjustment between or among opposing or divergent elements ⟨the introduction of a new and mighty force had disturbed the old ~ and had turned one limited monarchy after another into an absolute monarchy —T.B.Macaulay⟩ **b :** a state of intellectual or emotional balance: (1) **:** a state of equanimity **:** POISE ⟨he was speechless with anger and did not recover his ~ for a week —Sherwood Anderson⟩ (2) **:** a state of doubt, indecision, or indifference resulting from the balancing of motives or reasons ⟨freedom of thought has brought us to an ~, a center of indifference, far removed from the whirl of continental anticlericalism —G.G.Coulton⟩ (3) **:** a state of dynamic stability of mind or temper **:** TENSION ⟨a certain internal ~ of impulsions . . . that mutually excite and reinforce one another —John Dewey⟩ **c** (1) **:** a condition in which opposing economic forces are so balanced that there is no tendency to change in one way or another (2) **:** a normative position toward which economic forces impel or about which fluctuations occur **d :** a state of society characterized by a balance of antagonistic or noncomplementary elements (as attitudes, sentiments, and associations) and the stable operation of a common system of social norms **e :** the normal oriented state of the animal body in respect to the substrate that represents automatic adjustment to changing spatial and gravitational relationships through the labyrinthine sense or through the equivalent static senses in lower forms **3 :** BALANCE 6 a(1) ⟨those constant miracles of precision and of exact ~ that a first-class modern orchestra is capable of —Virgil Thomson⟩ **syn** see BALANCE

equilibrium moisture content *n* **:** the condition of balance with the moisture content of the air, being in wood equivalent to about 15 percent of moisture at which level wood neither takes on nor loses moisture when exposed to air

equilibrium price *n* **:** the price at which supply and demand are equal

equilibrium sense *n* **:** LABYRINTHINE SENSE

equil·i·brize \əˈkwiləˌbrīz, ēˈ-\ *vt* -ED/-ING/-S [*equilibrium* + *-ize*] **:** EQUILIBRATE

eq·ui·lin \ˈekwələn\ *n* -s [L *equi-* horse (fr. *equus*) + connective *-l-* + E *-in* — more at EQUINE] **:** a crystalline estrogenic hormone that is a phenolic steroid ketone $C_{18}H_{20}O_2$ and is obtained from the urine of pregnant mares; dihydro-equilenin

equi·molal *as at* EQUIANGULAR +\ *adj* [*equi-* + *molal*] **1 :** having equal molal concentration **2 :** EQUIMOLAR 1

equi·molar \"+\ *adj* [*equi-* + *molar*] **1 :** of or relating to an equal number of moles ⟨an ~ mixture of chlorine and sulfur dioxide⟩ **2 :** having equal molar concentration

equi·molecular \"+\ *adj* [*equi-* + *molecular*] **1 :** containing an equal number of molecules **2 :** EQUIMOLAR 1

equi·nal \(ˈ)ēˈkwīnᵊl, (ˈ)eˈ-\ *adj* [L *equinus* + E *-al*] *archaic* **:** EQUINE

[1]**equine** \ˈēˌkwīn, ˈeˌ-\ *adj* [L *equinus*, fr. *equus* horse + *-inus* -ine; akin to OE *eoh* horse, OS *ehuskalk* horse servant, ON *jōr* horse, Goth *aihwatundi* thornbush (lit., horse-tooth), Gk *hippos* horse, OIr *ech*, Skt *aśva*] **1 :** resembling a horse **2** [NL *Equus* + E *-ine*] **a :** of or relating to the Equidae **b :** of or being one of the Equidae — **equine·ly** *adv*

[2]**equine** \"\ *n* -s **:** one of the Equidae; *specif* **:** HORSE

equine antelope *n* **:** ROAN ANTELOPE

equine encephalomyelitis *n* **:** either of two virus-induced encephalomyelitides chiefly attacking equines and man in various parts of No. America — called also *eastern equine encephalomyelitis, western equine encephalomyelitis* according to the region of usual occurrence

equine influenza *n* **:** shipping fever of horses

equine plague *n* **:** AFRICAN HORSE SICKNESS

equine syphilis *n* **:** DOURINE

equine variola *n* **:** HORSEPOX

equin·ia \əˈkwinēə, ēˈ-,eˈ-\ *n* -s [NL, fr. L *equinus* equine + NL *-ia* — more at EQUINE] **:** FARCY 1

equin·i·ty \-nəd·ē\ *n* -ES **:** equine nature or character

[1]**equi·noc·tial** \ˌēkwəˈnäkshəl *also* ˌek-\ *adj* [ME *equinoccial, equinoxial*, fr. MF & L; MF *equinoctial*, fr. L *aequinoctialis*, fr. *aequinoctium* equinox + *-alis* -al — more at EQUINOX] **1 :** relating to an equinox or to a state or the time of equal day and night **2 :** relating to the regions or climate of the equinoctial line or equator **:** being in or near that line ⟨~ heat⟩ **3 :** relating to the time when the sun passes an equinoctial point ⟨an ~ storm⟩ **4** *of a sign of the zodiac* **:** beginning at one of the equinoxes

[2]**equinoctial** \"\ *n* -s [ME *equinoccial, equinoxial*, fr. MF & ML; MF *equinocial, equinoctial*, fr. ML *aequinoctialis*, fr. L *aequinoctialis*, adj.] **1 a :** EQUATOR 1 **b** *obs* **:** EQUINOX **c** *archaic* **:** the terrestrial equator **2 :** an equinoctial gale or storm

equinoctial circle *or* **equinoctial line** *n* **:** CELESTIAL EQUATOR

equinoctial colure *n* **:** the circle of 0 and 12 hours right ascension passing through the equinoctial points of the celestial sphere

equinoctial point *n* **:** EQUINOX 2

equinoctial tide *n* **:** a tide that occurs near the time of an equinox

equinoctial year *n* **:** TROPICAL YEAR

equi·nox \ˈēkwəˌnäks *also* ˈek-\ *n* -ES [ME, fr. MF or ML; MF *equinoxe*, fr. ML *equinoxium*, alter. of L *aequinoctium*, fr. *aequi-* equi- + *-noctium* (fr. *noct-, nox* night) — more at NIGHT] **1 :** either of the two times each year when the sun crosses the equator and day and night are everywhere of equal length, being about March 21 and September 23 — called also respectively *vernal equinox, autumnal equinox* **2 :** either of the two points on the celestial sphere where the celestial equator intersects the ecliptic — compare PRECESSION OF THE EQUINOXES

equip \əˈkwip, ēˈ-\ *vt* **equipped**; **equipped** *also* **equipt**; **equipping**; **equips** [MF *equiper*, fr. OF *esquiper, eschiper* to embark, launch a ship, equip a ship, of Gmc origin; akin to OE *scipian* to embark, equip a ship, fr. *scip* ship — more at SHIP] **:** to provide with what is necessary, useful, or appropriate: as **a** (1) **:** to supply with material resources (as implements or facilities) **:** fit out ⟨a ship *equipped* with every mechanical aid to navigation⟩ ⟨a park *equipped* with a playground, ball fields, riding trails, and a historical museum⟩ ⟨he . . . was *equipped* with letters that opened every European door —Van Wyck Brooks⟩ (2) **:** to provide with clothing or ornament ⟨*equipt* in the . . . national dress of the Scottish people —Sir Walter Scott⟩ ⟨the long fitted jacket . . . is *equipped* with a notched cape collar —*New Yorker*⟩ (3) **:** to provide with intellectual or emotional resources (as concepts or traits) ⟨thus *equipped* with a philosophy Emerson was prepared to begin work as a critic —V.L.Parrington⟩ **:** ENDOW ⟨she was *equipped* with an acute business sense —*Current Biog.*⟩ **b :** to make ready or competent for service or action or against a need **:** PREPARE ⟨most junior colleges are well *equipped* to engage . . . in such programs —L.L.Medsker⟩ **:** QUALIFY, FIT ⟨so young and so badly *equipped* to console someone so beset that she could not utter a word —Jean Stafford⟩; *specif* **:** to prepare by training or experience with the necessary skills or knowledge ⟨went back to school to ~ himself for a career as a telegrapher⟩ ⟨his own ordeal *equipped* him to understand and appreciate his friend's suffering⟩ **syn** see FURNISH

[1]**eq·ui·page** \ˈekwəpij, *chiefly in pl* -wəpəj; *also* ÷əˈkwipij *or* ēˈkwip- *sometimes* ˈekwəˌpäzh *or* ˈekwəˌpäj\ *n* -s [MF, fr. *equiper* + *-age*] **1** *obs* **:** EQUIPMENT 1 ⟨hastens the ~ of the galleys —*London Gazette*⟩ ⟨to put himself in ~ for that . . . voyage —James Howell⟩ **2 a** (1) **:** material or articles used in equipping an organized group ⟨the expense of providing arms, ordnance stores, quartermaster stores, and camp ~ —*US Code*⟩ (2) *archaic* **:** a collection of equipment **:** OUTFIT ⟨the queen had ordered a little ~ of all things necessary for me —Jonathan Swift⟩ **:** SET, SERVICE ⟨a complete tea and coffee ~ —*Chelsea Catalog of 1756*⟩ (3) *archaic* **:** ETUI ⟨little ~ of silver gilt containing scissors, thimble, nail trimmer —C.G.D.Roberts⟩ **b** *archaic* **:** a set of clothing and accessories **:** UNIFORM ⟨the ~ of a well-armed trooper of the period —Sir Walter Scott⟩ **:** TRAPPINGS ⟨first strip off all her ~ of pride —Alexander Pope⟩ **3** *archaic* **:** RETINUE ⟨an ~ indeed . . . a hundred servants in ordinary attendance —Thomas Fuller⟩ ⟨Death the crowned phantom with all the ~ of his terrors —Thomas De Quincey⟩ **4** *archaic* **:** ceremonious display **:** STYLE, POMP ⟨kings have their entrance in due ~ —Thomas Heywood⟩ **5** [F *équipage*, fr. MF *equipage*] **a :** an elegant horse-drawn carriage with its retinue of servants **b :** such a carriage without its retinue

[2]**equipage** \"\ *vt* -ED/-ING/-S *archaic* **:** to furnish with an equipage ⟨a goodly train of squires and ladies *equipaged* well —Edmund Spenser⟩

equi·partition *as at* EQUIANGULAR +\ *n* [*equi-* + *partition*] **1 :** EQUIPARTITION OF ENERGY **2 :** distribution of a solute equally between two immiscible solvents

equipartition of energy : an ideal condition postulated as existing among the molecules, atoms, and ions of a gas or vapor wherein the total heat energy is equally apportioned among the various degrees of freedom possessed by those particles, the realization of this ideal at lower temperatures often being impaired by quantum restrictions

eq·ui·pluve \ˈekwəˌplüv, ˈēk-\ *n* -s [*equi-* + *-pluve* (fr. L *pluvia* rain) — more at PLUVIAL] **:** a line on a rainfall map connecting places where the same fraction of their several annual rainfalls occurs during any specified portion of the year (as a given month)

equip·ment \əˈkwipmənt, ēˈ-\ *n* -s **1 a :** the equipping of a person or thing ⟨the development and ~ of a library extension program⟩ **b :** the state of being equipped ⟨the institution did not spring in full maturity and ~ —J.H.Burton⟩ **2 a :** the physical resources serving to equip a person or thing ⟨funds for buildings and ~⟩ ⟨the vocal ~ of a singer⟩ ⟨a new jail became part of the municipal ~ —*Amer. Guide Series: Va.*⟩: as (1) **:** the implements (as machinery or tools) used in an operation or activity **:** APPARATUS ⟨where a tractor is standard ~⟩ ⟨sports ~⟩ (2) **:** all the fixed assets other than land and buildings of a business enterprise ⟨the plant, ~, and supplies of the factory⟩ (3) **:** the rolling stock of a railway **b :** a collection of outfit of clothing ⟨each having its own uniform, flag, and . . . a standardized ~ —S.B.Fay⟩ **c :** a piece of such equipment ⟨manufactured . . . an air-conditioning ~ for beds —*Current Biog.*⟩ ⟨in what a desperate condition the Virginia troops were as regarded clothing and ~*s* —H.E.Scudder⟩ **3 a :** mental or emotional traits or resources ⟨prejudice, intolerance, and bigotry . . . soon become a part of a child's ~ —*Episcopal Churchnews*⟩ **:** PREPARATION ⟨some knowledge of the facts of biology should be an essential part of the ~ of every educated man —*Nineteenth Century & After*⟩ **b :** an aspect of one's mental or emotional makeup **:** ENDOWMENT ⟨a ready repartee is also a valuable ~ for anyone seeking high office —V.L. Albjerg⟩

syn EQUIPMENT, APPARATUS, MACHINERY, PARAPHERNALIA, OUTFIT, TACKLE, GEAR, MATÉRIEL can signify, in common, all the things used in a given work or useful in effecting a given end. EQUIPMENT usu. covers everything, except personnel, needed for efficient operation or service, often applying also to human qualities and skills useful in this way ⟨the marines took with them full combat *equipment*, including tanks, artillery, jeeps, trucks, and flamethrowers —*Time*⟩ ⟨other *equipment* in the park includes tables, benches, and playground apparatus —*Amer. Guide Series: Minn.*⟩ ⟨the only essential *equipment* for softball is a bat and a ball —J.H.Shaw⟩ ⟨innate *equipment* of the child (sensory, neural and glandular) —*Psychological Abstracts*⟩ ⟨the heroine, typically named Virginia, has no *equipment* for life but loveliness and innocence —Carl Van Doren⟩ APPARATUS, a very general term, usu. in this connection covers instruments, tools, machines, and appliances used in a craft or profession, or the equipment used in a sport or recreation, or, more generally, any contrivance or device or set of them commonly used in any activity ⟨a collection of safecracking *apparatus*⟩ ⟨drill, X-ray machine, and other dental *apparatus*⟩ ⟨punitive *apparatus* — bilboes, stocks, pillories, and ducking stools —*Amer. Guide Series: Mass.*⟩ ⟨she had insisted on leaving in his room the materials and *apparatus* for a light meal —Arnold Bennett⟩ MACHINERY covers all devices, means, or agencies which permit a thing to function or accomplish an end ⟨the *machinery* of criminal identification⟩ ⟨the treaty must be given the kind of *machinery* which will permit it to operate efficiently —*New Republic*⟩ ⟨the *machinery* of advertising and propaganda —Jerome Stone⟩ ⟨the *machinery* of recruitment — written examinations, interviews, internal promotions or transfers —*Times Lit. Supp.*⟩ PARAPHERNALIA, sometimes contemptuous in implication, usu. suggests a collection of miscellaneous articles or belongings constituting the usual, often necessary, appurtenances of a particular activity or person engaged in it ⟨a golden chalice, vestments and cruets, all the *paraphernalia* for celebrating Mass —Willa Cather⟩ ⟨family allowances, maternity grants, and all the *paraphernalia* of social security —Roy Lewis & Angus Maude⟩ ⟨little piles of wheels, strips of unworked iron and steel, blocks of wood, the *paraphernalia* of the inventor's trade —Sherwood Anderson⟩ ⟨the chivalric romances . . . are of course replete with adventure of every kind: warlike knight-errantry, magic forests and fountains, enchanted castles, magicians, and all the other *paraphernalia* —R.A.Hall b. 1911⟩ OUTFIT is more colloquially interchangeable with EQUIPMENT but generally is confined to the personal effects necessary for a given occupation, recreation, function, or type of life ⟨a fireman's *outfit*⟩ ⟨a camper's *outfit* consisting of high boots, poncho, sleeping bag, and cooking utensils⟩ ⟨a college girl's *outfit*⟩ ⟨a bride's *outfit*⟩ ⟨a soldier's *outfit*⟩ TACKLE is colloquially interchangeable with APPARATUS ⟨toothbrush and shaving *tackle* in the bedroom —Graham Greene⟩ or EQUIPMENT ⟨fishing *tackle*⟩ GEAR may be interchangeable with EQUIPMENT, often transportable equipment or luggage ⟨housekeeping *gear* —Dorothy C. Fisher⟩ ⟨we had a collapsible stage that broke down into boxes and battens and about a ton of *gear* which travelled with us in a large ancient but very game delivery van —Barry Carman⟩ ⟨we gathered together our *gear* and prepared to make our way back to the railroad station —Thomas Barbour⟩ or with OUTFIT, often in specific reference to wearing apparel ⟨when cowboy *gear* became so popular —D.C.Morrill⟩, or may signify one's belongings collectively ⟨the student immediately stowed all his *gear* in his new room⟩ MATÉRIEL, confined usu. to military or industrial use, is a comprehensive term to designate everything but the personnel ⟨a heavy drain on both the manpower and *matériel* resources —*N.Y. Times*⟩ ⟨the latest developments in artillery *matériel* —*Combat Forces Jour.*⟩

equipment bond *n* **:** a railroad bond that is secured by rolling stock

equipment ground *n* **:** an electrical grounding connection that is required for equipment that may become energized if the winding insulation fails

equipment note *n* **:** a note issued by a railroad to purchase equipment (as locomotives)

equipment obligation *n* **:** a bond, certificate, or share serving as a direct lien on a specific lot of railroad rolling stock

equipment trust *n* **:** a trust established for the ownership and lease of equipment

equipment trust certificate *n* **:** an interest in an equipment trust on which payments are made out of rentals received from lease of the equipment

[1]**eq·ui·poise** \ˈekwəˌpȯiz, ˈēk-\ *n* [*equi-* + *poise*] **1 :** a state of equilibrium or balance ⟨weights in ~⟩ ⟨an ~ of social classes⟩ ⟨the adventure . . . upset the ~ of his sensitive nature —James Joyce⟩ **2 :** COUNTERBALANCE ⟨the aristocracy served as an ~ to the clergy⟩ **syn** see BALANCE

[2]**equipoise** \"\ *vt* **1 :** to serve as an equipoise to ⟨an opposition that nearly *equipoised* the party in power⟩ **2 :** to put or hold in equipoise ⟨an effort to ~ the opposing interests of the two groups⟩

equipoised *adj* **:** lacking lateral dominance **:** neither right-handed nor left-handed ⟨~ children⟩

equi·pol·lence \ˌēkwəˈpälən(t)s, ˌek-\ *also* **equi·pol·len·cy** \-nsē\ *n, pl* **equipollences** *also* **equipollencies** [*equipollence* fr. ME, fr. MF, fr. ML *aequipollentia*, fr. L *aequipollent-, aequipollens* + *-ia* -y; *equipollency* fr. *equipollent* + *-y*] **:** the quality of being equipollent ⟨the ~ of the two propositions⟩

[1]**equi·pol·lent** \¦==¦lənt\ *adj* [ME, fr. MF, fr. L *aequipollent-, aequipollens*, fr. *aequi-* equi- + *pollent-, pollens*, pres. part. of *pollēre* to be strong, be able — more at POLLEX] **1 :** equal in force, power, or validity ⟨our poets put into a foot two ~ syllables —T.S.Omond⟩ ⟨a sea power ~ with France⟩ **2 :** the same in effect or signification ⟨implying that money could be dispensed with if something ~ were provided⟩; *specif* **:** EQUIVALENT 2 b — **equi·pol·lent·ly** *adv*

[2]**equipollent** \"\ *n* -s **:** something that is equipollent (as in signification) ⟨a term having no exact ~ in any European language⟩

equi·pon·der·ant \-ˈpändərənt\ *adj* [ML *aequiponderant-, aequiponderans*, pres. part. of *aequiponderare*] *archaic* **:** of equal weight, force, or power **:** evenly balanced

[1]**equi·pon·der·ate** \ˌ==ˈ==ˌrāt\ *vb* -ED/-ING/-S [ML *aequiponderatus*, past part. of *aequiponderare*, fr. L *aequi-* equi- + *ponderare* to weigh — more at PONDER] *vi, archaic* **:** to be equal in weight or force ⟨the design . . . must be regulated by the art of statics and the duly poising of all parts to ~ —Sir Christopher Wren⟩ ~ *vt, archaic* **:** to equal or make equal in weight **:** COUNTERBALANCE, BALANCE

[2]**equi·pon·der·ate** \¦==¦==rət\ *adj* [ML *aequiponderatus*] *archaic* **:** equiponderant

equi·pon·der·a·tion \ˌ===ˈrāshən\ *n* -s *archaic* **:** a state of being equiponderated **:** BALANCE

equiponderous *adj* [*equi-* + L *ponder-, pondus* weight + E *-ous* — more at PONDER] *obs* **:** having equal weight

equi·potent *as at* EQUIANGULAR +\ *adj* [*equi-* + *potent*] **1 :** having equal effects or capacities ⟨~ genes⟩ ⟨~ doses in different solvents⟩ **2** *of egg protoplasm* **:** potentially capable of developing into any tissue **:** UNDIFFERENTIATED

equi·potential \"+\ *adj* [*equi-* + *potential*] **1 :** having the same potential ⟨~ points⟩ **:** of uniform potential throughout ⟨an ~ surface⟩ **2 :** EQUIPOTENT 2 — **equi·potentiality** \"+\ *n*

equipped *past of* EQUIP

equip·per \əˈkwipə(r), ēˈ-\ *n* -s **:** one that equips a person or thing

equipping *pres part of* EQUIP

equi·probabilism *as at* EQUIANGULAR +\ *n* [fr. *equiprobable*, after E *probable: probabilism*] **:** a theory that in moral questions where certainty is impossible and the arguments for both courses are equiprobable either course may be followed — compare PROBABILIORISM, PROBABILISM

equi·probability \"+\ *n* **:** the state of being equiprobable ⟨determining the ~ of a set of alternatives⟩

equi·probable \"+\ *adj* [*equi-* + *probable*] **:** having the same degree of logical or mathematical probability **:** equally probable ⟨two alternatives are ~ if there is no sufficient reason why one rather than the other should be realized —Arthur Pap⟩ — **equi·probably** \"+\ *adv*

equips *pres 3d sing of* EQUIP

equipt *past part of* EQUIP

equipt *abbr* equipment

eq·ui·se·ta·ce·ae \ˌekwəsəˈtāsēˌē\ *n pl, cap* [NL, fr. *Equisetum*, type genus + *-aceae*] **:** the sole surviving family of the order Equisetales appearing first in the Carboniferous and represented in the recent flora by the single genus *Equisetum*

eq·ui·se·ta·ceous \¦==¦tāshəs\ *adj*

eq·ui·se·ta·les \ˌ===ˈtā(ˌ)lēz\ *n pl, cap* [NL, fr. *Equisetum* + *-ales*] **:** an order of lower tracheophytes (subdivision Sphenopsida) that have the sporangiophores inserted directly on the axis and have existed since the Devonian — see CALAMARIACEAE, EQUISETACEAE; compare ARCHAEOCALAMITES

eq·ui·se·tic \ˌekwəˈsēd·ik, -sed-\ *adj* [NL *Equisetum* + E *-ic*] **:** of or relating to the genus *Equisetum*

eq·ui·se·tin·e·ae \ˌekwəsəˈtinēˌē\ *n pl, cap* [NL, fr. *Equisetum* + *-ineae*] **:** a class of lower tracheophytes coextensive with the subdivision Sphenopsida

eq·ui·se·ti·tes \ˌekwəsəˈtīd·(ˌ)ēz\ *n, cap* [NL, fr. *Equisetum* + L *-ites* -ite] **:** a form genus of fossil pteridophytes closely related and possibly belonging to *Equisetum*

eq·ui·se·tum \ˌekwəˈsēd·əm\ *n* [NL, fr. L *equisaetum* horsetail (plant), fr. *equi-* (fr. *equus* horse) + *-saetum* (fr. *saeta, seta* bristle) — more at EQUINE, SINEW] **1** *cap* **:** the type genus of Equisetaceae comprising perennial plants that spread by creeping rhizomes, are homosporous and asexual, and have leaves reduced to more or less conspicuous nodal sheaths on the hollow jointed grooved shoots that may all bear asexual spores provided with elaters in sporangia arranged on conical spikes or in some cases may be differentiated into sterile and fertile shoots **2** *pl* **equisetums** \-d·əmz\ *or* **equise·ta** \-d·ə\ **:** any plant of the genus *Equisetum*

equi·signal *as at* EQUIANGULAR +\ *adj* [*equi-* + *signal*] **:** of or relating to a radio system used in navigation in which two distinguishable signals of different amplitude emitted by a radio range station merge and become indistinguishable when the receiver is in the on-course region

equi·sonance \"+\ *n* [*equi-* + *sonance*] *music* **:** consonance of the unison or its octaves — **equi·sonant** \"+\ *adj*

eq·ui·ta·ble \ˈekwəd·əbəl, -wətə- *sometimes* (ˈ)eˈkwid·ə- *or* -ˈkwitə-\ *adj* [F *équitable*, fr. MF *equitable*, fr. *equité* equity + *-able* — more at EQUITY] **1 :** characterized by equity **:** fair to all concerned ⟨an ~ pay scale⟩ ⟨an ~ price⟩ **:** without prejudice, favor, or rigor entailing undue hardship ⟨it depended wholly on their individual characters whether their terms of office were ~ or oppressive —John Buchan⟩ **2 :** that can be sustained or made effective in a court of equity or upon principles of equity jurisprudence **:** existing or valid in equity as distinguished from law ⟨~ suits⟩ ⟨~ jurisdiction⟩ **3 :** characterized by evenness (as in temper or climate) **:** EQUABLE **syn** see FAIR

equitable assets *n pl* **:** assets that are charged with or have become a fund for the payment of debts only by operation of equity; *specif* **:** assets charged with the payment of debts by a debtor that would be exempted by law (as real estate of a decedent)

equitable assignment *n* **:** an assignment that is not recognizable at law but will be enforced in equity subject to equities

equitable attachment *n* **:** an attachment of debts, choses in action, or other property that cannot be attached at law or secured under statute, by injunction, or by other equitable process **:** an attachment effected in a suit in equity or by a court of equity

equitable conversion *n* **:** CONVERSION 3d

equitable dower *or* **equitable jointure** *n* **:** a provision made and accepted by a woman (not being an infant) before her marriage in lieu of dower that will generally be enforced in equity as a bar to dower

equitable election *n* **:** the choice that must be made by a party whether he will accept a benefit under an instrument with any burdens imposed by it (as the giving away of property of his own) or remain free of the burden or loss and go without the benefits

equitable estate *n* **:** the estate of one who has a beneficial right in property the legal ownership of which is vested in a trustee or a person treated by equity as a trustee (as in the case of a use, trust, or power) that has under modern statutes some of the characters of a legal estate

equitable fraud *n* **:** FRAUD 1a(2)

equitable garnishment *n* **:** a proceeding under statutory provisions by a judgment creditor to compel discovery of property of, due to, or held in trust for the judgment debtor and to secure payment from it

equitable interest *n* **:** an interest in or with respect to property of the sort recognized by a court of equity (as an interest arising because of fraud)

equitable levy *n* **:** the putting of a lien on a judgment debtor's assets by means of process under a creditor's bill

equitable lien *n* **:** a security interest in real or personal property that does not require possession of the property and that can be reached in an equitable proceeding to prevent unjust enrichment

equitable mortgage *n* **:** a conveyance of or right in property such that it will be treated as a mortgage in equity though not constituting a common-law mortgage (as a deposit of title deeds with a creditor in England or a conveyance nominally absolute but intended merely as a security)

eq·ui·ta·ble·ness *n* -ES **:** the quality or state of being equitable

equitable right *n* **:** a right enforceable in a court having equity jurisdiction or equity powers **:** a right cognizable in a court of equity

equitable title *n* **:** the title or right by which an equitable estate is held

eq·ui·ta·bly \-əblē, -li\ *adv* **:** according to the principle or the system of equity **:** in an equitable manner ⟨the cost of the . . . improvements shall be shared ~ between the participants in proportion to the benefit which each will receive —*U.S. Code*⟩ ⟨property ~ owned⟩

eq·ui·tant \ˈekwəd·ənt, -wətənt *also* -wətᵊnt\ *adj* [L *equitant-, equitans*, pres. part. of *equitare* to ride on horseback, fr. *equit-, eques* horseman — more at EQUES] *of leaves* **:** overlapping each other transversely at the base (as in an iris)

eq·ui·ta·tion \ˌekwəˈtāshən\ *n* -S [MF, fr. L *equitation-, equitatio*, fr. *equitatus* (past part. of *equitare*) + *-ion-, -io* -ion] **:** the act or art of riding on horseback **:** school horsemanship

equites *pl of* EQUES

eq·ui·time point \ˈek|wə,tīm- *also* ˈēk-\ *n* [*equi-* + *time*] **:** the point in the course of a long airplane flight at which the alternatives of returning to base or proceeding to destination involve equal risks and beyond which the pilot must not turn back — see HOWGOZIT CURVE

eq·ui·ty \ˈekwəd·ē, -wətē, -i\ *n* -ES *often attrib* [ME *equite*, fr. MF *equité*, fr. L *aequitat-, aequitas*, lit., equality, fr. *aequus* equal + *-itat-, -itas* -ity] **1 a :** a free and reasonable conformity to accepted standards of natural right, law, and justice without prejudice, favoritism, or fraud and without rigor entailing undue hardship **:** justice according to natural law or right **:** FAIRNESS ⟨prompted by considerations of ~ to honor claims not legally valid⟩; *specif* **:** IMPARTIALITY ⟨tax adjustment for the sake of ~⟩ ⟨presenting both sides of the issue with ~⟩ **b :** something that conforms to the principle of equity (as an equitable act) **:** an instance of equity ⟨the inequities produced by the system being outweighed by the *equities*⟩ **2 a :** a system of law (as in England and the U.S.) originating in the English chancery and comprising a settled and formal body of legal and procedural rules and doctrines that supplement, aid, or override common and statute law and are designed to protect rights and enforce duties fixed by substantive law **b :** trial or remedial justice under or by the rules and doctrines of equity administered in a separate court (as in some states) or in a court of law (as in the federal court system) ⟨a suit or proceeding at law or in ~⟩ **c :** a body of legal doctrines and rules (as the Roman praetorian law) developed to enlarge, supplement, or override a system of law that has become too narrow and rigid in its scope; *specif* **:** a set of rules or treaties accepted or acknowledged in international relations as imposing certain obligations in the mutual conduct of affairs between politically organized peoples **3 a :** a right, claim, or interest existing or valid in equity ⟨the wife's ~ to a settlement of a portion of the property⟩ **b :** the money value of a property or of an interest in a property in excess of claims or liens (as mortgaged indebtedness) against it **c :** a risk interest or ownership right in property; *specif* **:** EQUITY SECURITY ⟨~ investment⟩ ⟨~ finance⟩

equity capital *n* **:** VENTURE CAPITAL

equity of redemption 1 : the right of a mortgagor to redeem his property after the term of the mortgage has expired but before an absolute foreclosure has been authorized **2 :** the interest or estate remaining to the mortgagor in property mortgaged by him or the value of such interest

equity security *also* **equity** *n* -ES **:** a stock issue; *esp* **:** the common stock of a corporation

equiv·a·lence \əˈkwiv(ə)lən(t)s, ēˈ-\ *also* **equiv·a·len·cy** \-nsē, -si\ *n, pl* **equivalences** *also* **equivalencies** [MF & ML; MF *equivalence*, fr. ML *aequivalentia*, fr. LL *aequivalent-, aequivalens* + L *-ia* -y] **1 a :** the state or property of being equivalent **:** EXCHANGEABILITY, CORRESPONDENCE ⟨the ~ of paper money and coins⟩ ⟨the ~ between the hero's career and that of the author⟩ **:** EQUATABILITY ⟨the ~ of mass and energy⟩ **:** geologic contemporaneity ⟨time *equivalency* of the Sly Gap to a portion of the Devonian of Iowa is suggested by new paleological evidence —*Jour. of Geol.*⟩ **b :** an equivalent or an instance of equivalence ⟨a series of logical *equivalences*⟩ **2** *logic* **a :** sameness in truth value; *specif* **:** the logical relationship holding between two statements if they are either both true or both false — called also *material equivalence*; compare BICONDITIONAL **b :** mutual deducibility or reciprocal entailment; *specif* **:** the relationship holding between two statements if to affirm one and to deny the other would result in a contradiction — called also *logical equivalence, strict equivalence* **3 :** equality in metrical value of a regular foot and one in which there are substitutions (as of a long syllable for two short syllables in quantitative verse or of two or more light unaccented syllables for the normal unaccented syllable in accentual or syllabic verse)

equivalence principle *n* **:** PRINCIPLE OF EQUIVALENCE

equivalence zone *n* **:** the part of the range of possible proportions of interacting antibody and antigen in which neither or but small traces of both remain uncombined in the medium

[1]**equiv·a·lent** \-nt\ *adj* [ME, fr. MF or LL; MF, fr. LL *aequivalent-, aequivalens*, pres. part. of *aequivalēre* to have equal power, be equivalent, fr. L *aequi-* equi- + *valēre* to be strong, be worth — more at WIELD] **1 :** equal in force or amount ⟨the misery of such a position is ~ to its happiness⟩ ⟨a new TV film series that has the ~ footage of 13 feature pictures⟩; *specif, of a quantity* **:** equal in area or volume but not admitting of superposition ⟨a square ~ to a triangle⟩ **2 a :** like in signification or import ⟨~ but differently worded statements of the two writers⟩ **:** SYNONYMOUS ⟨substituted a term ~ with it but more familiar⟩ **b** *logic* **:** having equivalence **:** implying each other **3 a :** equal in value **:** COMPENSATIVE, CONVERTIBLE ⟨a person who consumes goods or accepts services without producing ~ goods or performing ~ services in return inflicts . . . injury —G.B.Shaw⟩ ⟨a sum ~ to $250 in our currency⟩ ⟨a vitamin pill ~ to four oranges⟩ ⟨the decimal 0.75 is ~ to the fraction ¾⟩ **b :** corresponding or virtually identical esp. in effect or function ⟨a bureau of the French army ~ to the intelligence division of the American general staff⟩ **:** TANTAMOUNT ⟨where winning the primary is ~ to election⟩ **c :** capable of being placed in one-to-one correspondence ⟨~ mathematical sets⟩ **4** *obs* **:** equal in might or authority ⟨ancestors who stood ~ with mighty kings —Shak.⟩ **5** *chem* **:** having the same combining capacity ⟨~ quantities of two elements⟩ **6 :** contemporaneous in deposition; *sometimes* **:** containing the same fauna or flora — used of strata **7** *of a map projection* **:** EQUAL-AREA **syn** see SAME

[2]**equivalent** \"\ *n* -S **1 :** one that is equivalent (as in value, meaning, or effect) ⟨a price that was the ~ of 10-years rent⟩ ⟨two years of high-school Latin or the ~⟩ ⟨a word with no ~ in the English language⟩ ⟨the prose ~ of a poem⟩ ⟨the secret Australian ballot . . . and its mechanical ~, the voting machine —H.R.Penniman⟩ **:** COUNTERPART ⟨the Chinese ~*s* of Boston, New York, and Philadelphia⟩ ⟨the governor of Jerusalem (the modern ~ of Pontius Pilate) —H.J.Laski⟩ **2** *or* **equivalent weight a :** the relative mass of an element that has the same combining capacity as a given mass of another element, the standard now usu. being eight for oxygen but formerly one for hydrogen **:** the atomic weight divided by the valence — called also *combining weight* **b :** the relative mass of a radical or compound that combines with a given mass of an element, radical, or compound ⟨one ~ of a base reacts with one of an acid to form a normal salt⟩; *esp* **:** the mass of a compound that reacts with one equivalent of a given chemical element **3 :** a psychopathological symptom replacing the usual one in a given disorder ⟨a twilight state may be an epileptic ~⟩

equivalent circuit *n* **:** an electric circuit made up of the basic elements resistance, inductance, and capacitance in a simple arrangement such that its performance would duplicate that of a more complicated circuit or network

equivalent evaporation *n* **:** the rate in pounds per hour at which water would be vaporized in a given steam boiler if supplied and evaporated at the normal boiling point and normal atmospheric pressure

equivalent focal length *or* **equivalent focus** *n* **:** the focal length of a single thin lens that would best duplicate the images formed by a given thick lens, compound lens, or lens system

equiv·a·lent·ly *adv* **:** to an equivalent degree **:** in an equivalent manner **:** EQUALLY ⟨another room ~ bare⟩

equivalent weight *n* **1 :** [2]EQUIVALENT 2 **2 :** ATOMIC WEIGHT — used when atomic weights were more or less conjectural

equi·valve \ˈēkwə, ˈek-+ˌ-\ *adj* [ISV *equi-* + *valve*] *of a bivalve mollusk* **:** having valves equal in size and form — opposed to *inequivalve*; compare EQUILATERAL

equiv·o·ca·cy \əˈkwivəkəsē, ēˈ-\ *n* -ES [*equivocal* + *-cy*] **:** EQUIVOCALITY 1

[1]**equiv·o·cal** \əˈkwivəkəl, ēˈ-\ *adj* [LL *aequivocus* (fr. *aequi-* equi- + *-vocus*, fr. *voc-, vox* voice) + E *-al* — more at VOICE] **1 a :** having two or more significations **:** capable of more than one interpretation **:** of doubtful meaning **:** AMBIGUOUS ⟨an ~ word⟩ ⟨an ~ statement⟩ — compare UNIVOCAL **b :** uncertain as an indication or sign **:** INCONCLUSIVE ⟨the evidence from bacteriologic analysis was ~⟩ **2** *obs* **:** called by the same name but differing in nature or function **:** NOMINAL ⟨they being subject to the oversight of the ephori were but ~ kings —James Ussher⟩ **3 a :** of uncertain nature or classification **:** of a nature that does not admit of definite classification **:** INDETERMINATE ⟨the ~ objects painted by surrealists⟩ **b** (1) **:** of uncertain disposition toward a person or thing **:** UNDECIDED, INSCRUTABLE ⟨the ~ behavior of the officials increased the uneasiness of the riot victims⟩ ⟨something ~ about him contrasting with the other's straightforward manner⟩ (2) **:** characterized by a mixture of opposite feelings **:** AMBIVALENT ⟨an ~ attitude toward the proposal⟩ **c :** open to question regarding advantage, validity, genuineness, or moral rectitude **:** QUESTIONABLE, DUBIOUS ⟨popularity is an ~ crown —A.L.Guérard⟩ ⟨his conscience reproached him with the ~ character of the union into which he had forced his son —Anna Jameson⟩ **syn** see OBSCURE

[2]**equivocal** \"\ *n* -S **:** something equivocal; *esp* **:** an equivocal word or term ⟨regards the term *being* as an analogical ~⟩

equivocal generation *n* **:** ABIOGENESIS

equiv·o·cal·i·ty \ə,==ˈkaləd·ē, -ətē, -i\ *n* -ES **1 :** an equivocal character ⟨the ~ of a law that does not specify the agency having primary authority⟩ **2 :** EQUIVOQUE ⟨unlikely that any reader would see an ~ in the statement⟩

equiv·o·cal·ly \əˈ==vək(ə)lē, -li\ *adv* **:** in an equivocal manner **:** AMBIGUOUSLY ⟨an ~ worded reply⟩

equiv·o·cal·ness \-kəlnəs\ *n* -ES **:** the quality or state of being equivocal **:** AMBIGUITY

equiv·o·cate \-vəˌkāt, *usu* -ād·+V\ *vi* -ED/-ING/-S [ME *equivocaten*, fr. ML *aequivocatus*, past part. of *aequivocare*, fr. LL *aequivocus*] **1 :** to use equivocal language esp. with intent to deceive ⟨avoided both persecution and outright lying by *equivocating* with their questioners⟩ **2 :** to avoid committing oneself in what one says **:** speak evasively ⟨he would anger them with frankness before he would ~⟩ **:** be willfully misleading esp. by the use of double meanings **syn** see LIE

equiv·o·ca·tion \ə,==ˈkāshən\ *n* -S [ME *equivocacioun*, fr. ML *aequivocation-, aequivocatio*, fr. *aequivocatus* + L *-ion-, -io* -ion] **1 :** an equivocal state or character **:** AMBIGUITY; *esp* **:** duplicity of meaning in a word ⟨~ in the word "fallible"⟩ **2 :** an act or instance of equivocating **:** UNCERTAINTY, EVASIVENESS, PREVARICATION ⟨bold and forthright thinking and action are . . . needed; ~, compromise, pussyfooting . . . are no longer to be tolerated —I.M.Ives⟩ **:** confusion of terms or ideas similar in meaning ⟨the evils arising from the ~ between faith and intellectual . . . insight —S.T.Coleridge⟩ ⟨a lie may be told by silence, by ~, . . . by a glance of the eye —John Ruskin⟩ **3 :** a fallacy in logical reasoning arising from an ambiguous use of a word or phrase — contrasted with *amphibology*

equiv·o·ca·tor \əˈ==ˌkād·ə(r), -ātə-\ *n* -S **:** one that equivocates ⟨an ~ who could be quoted on either side of almost any question —John Mason Brown⟩

eq·ui·voc·i·ty \ˌekwəˈväsəd·ē, ˌēk-\ *n* -ES [LL *aequivocus* + E *-ity*] **:** the character of being equivocal in signification or predication

eq·ui·voque *also* **eq·ui·voke** \ˈ==ˌvōk\ *n* -S [F *équivoque*, fr. *équivoque* equivocal, fr. LL *aequivocus*] **1 :** an equivocal word or phrase; *specif* **:** PUN ⟨ready with quip and ~⟩ **2 a :** duplexity or confusion of meaning **:** double meaning **:** the fallacy of equivocation ⟨the ~ in applying indiscriminately to the word *church* the predicates of both the actual and the ideal church⟩ **b :** EQUIVOCATION 2 ⟨an ~ in which the magician offers a choice of right or left without saying whose⟩; *specif* **:** WORDPLAY

eq·uoid \ˈeˌkwȯid, ˈē,-\ *or* **equoi·de·an** \eˈkwȯidēən, əˈk-, ēˈk-\ *adj* [*equoid* fr. NL *Equoidea; equoidean* fr. NL *Equoidea* + E *-an*] **1 :** of or relating to the Hippoidea **2 :** EQUINE

equoi·dea \eˈkwȯidēə, əˈk-, ēˈk-\ [NL, fr. *Equus* + *-oidea*] *syn of* HIPPOIDEA

eq·uus \ˈekwəs, ˈēk-\ *n, cap* [NL, fr. L, horse — more at EQUINE] **:** a genus that comprises the horses, asses, zebras, and related recent and extinct animals and that is the type and only surviving genus of the family Equidae — see EQUIDAE illustration

er \ˈə(ə), ˈə̄(ə̄), ˈä(ä), ˈȧ(ȧ)\ *the* ˈər, *usu prolonged, used by many R speakers when they encounter "er" as they read aloud is not an accurate reproduction of the sound that the spelling, introduced by – R speakers, is intended to convey*\ *interj* — used to express hesitation ⟨said shyly, "I — — don't know"⟩

[1]**-er** \ə(r), *after some vowels* (ə)r *in R speech, after* ŋ gə(r) (*but after* ŋ [2]-ER *is* ə(r))\ *adj suffix or adv suffix* [ME *-er, -ere, -re*, fr. OE *-ra* (in adjectives), *-or* (in adverbs); akin to comparative suffixes OHG *-iro, -ōro* (in adjectives), *-ōr* (in adverbs), ON *-ri, -ari* (in adjectives), *-r, -ar* (in adverbs), Goth *-iza, -oza* (in adjectives), *-is, -os* (in adverbs), L *-ior* (in adjectives), Gk *-iōn* (in adjectives), Skt *-īyas* (in adjectives)] — used to form the comparative degree of adjectives and adverbs of one syllable ⟨hott*er*⟩ ⟨dri*er*⟩ ⟨lat*er*⟩ ⟨soon*er*⟩ ⟨cold*er*⟩ and of certain adjectives and adverbs of two syllables ⟨abl*er*⟩ ⟨complet*er*⟩ ⟨gentl*ier*⟩ ⟨happi*er*⟩ ⟨yellow*er*⟩ and sometimes of longer ones; regularly accompanied by coalescence with final *e* of the base word, change of final postconsonantal *y* of the base word to *i*, or doubling of the final consonant of the base word immediately after a short stressed vowel; compare [2]MORE

[2]**-er** \ə(r) — *compare* [1]-ER\ *also* **-ier** \ēə(r), yə(r)\ *or* **-yer** \yə(r)\ *n suffix* -S [ME *-er, -ere*, fr. OE *-ere*; akin to D & G *-er*, OHG *-āri*, ON *-ari*, Goth *-areis*; all fr. a prehistoric Gmc suffix borrowed fr. L *-arius* [1]-ary; in sense 1, partly fr. ME *-er, -ier, -ere, -iere*, fr. AF *-er, -ere* & OF *-ier, -iere*, fr. L *-arius, -aria, -arium* [1]-ary; in sense 2, partly fr. ME *-er, -ere*, fr. MF *-ere*, fr. L *-ator* (suffix denoting an agent) — more at -ARY, -OR] **1 a :** person occupationally connected with ⟨hatt*er*⟩ ⟨jail*er*⟩ ⟨furri*er*⟩ ⟨hosi*er*⟩ ⟨law*yer*⟩ **b :** person or thing belonging to, related to, or associated with ⟨head*er*⟩ ⟨old-tim*er*⟩ ⟨high school*er*⟩ **c :** native of **:** resident of **:** one coming from ⟨cottag*er*⟩ ⟨London*er*⟩ ⟨Maryland*er*⟩ ⟨New York*er*⟩ **d :** one that has ⟨three-deck*er*⟩ ⟨the baby is a ten-pound*er*⟩ **e :** one that produces or yields ⟨pork*er*⟩ ⟨veal*er*⟩ ⟨wool*er*⟩ **2 a :** one that does or performs (a specified action) ⟨mak*er*⟩ ⟨play*er*⟩ ⟨report*er*⟩ ⟨transform*er*⟩ ⟨range find*er*⟩ — sometimes added to both elements of a compound ⟨build*er*-upp*er*⟩ ⟨try*er*-out*er*⟩ **b :** one that is a suitable object of (a specified action) ⟨broil*er*⟩ ⟨fry*er*⟩ **3 :** one that is ⟨foreign*er*⟩ ⟨gon*er*⟩ ⟨western*er*⟩ ⟨down-and-out*er*⟩ — *-yer* in a small number of words after *w*, *-ier* in a small number of words after other letters, otherwise *-er*; *-er* and *-ier* regularly accompanied by doubling of the final consonant of the base word immediately after a short stressed vowel, *-ier* regularly accompanied by omission of final *e* of the base word, *-er* regularly accompanied by coalescence with final *e* of the base word and sometimes accompanied by change of final postconsonantal *y* of the base word to *i* ⟨fl*ier*⟩ ⟨fl*yer*⟩

ER *abbr* **1** earned run **2** educational ratio **3** en route

Er *symbol* erbium

era \ˈirə, ˈerə, ˈērə\ *n* -S [LL *aera*, fr. L, counters, pl. of *aer-, aes* copper, brass, money — more at ORE] **1 :** a system of chronological notation computed from a given date as basis ⟨the Roman ~ is computed from the date when Rome was supposedly founded⟩ ⟨from the beginnings of history to the 5th century of our ~⟩ **2 a :** a fixed point in time from which a series of years is reckoned **:** the basic date of a chronological era ⟨a hundred years before the Christian ~⟩ **b :** a memorable or important date or event; *esp* **:** one that begins a new period in the history of a person or thing ⟨June 1585 marked an ~ in the foreign policy of Elizabeth —J.A.Symonds⟩ **3 :** a period in the history of a person or thing ⟨the seven years . . . form one of the greatest ~*s* in the annals of British statesmanship —Ernest Barker⟩: as **a :** a period set off or typified by some prominent figure or characteristic feature ⟨a style popular in the Victorian ~⟩ ⟨dates back to the ~ of the horse and buggy⟩ ⟨calls the twenties an ~ of extravagance⟩ **b :** a period of existence or prevalence of something (as a process, quality, or group) ⟨another ~ of rapid expansion in industry⟩ ⟨an ~ of prosperity⟩ ⟨the relatively brief cowboy ~⟩ **:** DAY **c :** a stage in the development of a person or thing (as a nation, institution, or art) ⟨during the first ~ of the nation's existence⟩ ⟨a new ~ in the development of the textbook⟩; *specif* **:** one of the five major divisions of geologic time — see GEOLOGIC TIME table **syn** see PERIOD

ERA *abbr* earned run average

eradiate \(ˈ)ē+\ *vt* -ED/-ING/-S [*e-* + *radiate*] **:** RADIATE 1 — **eradiation** \(ˌ)ē+\ *n* -S

erad·i·ca·ble \əˈradəkəbəl, ēˈr,- -dēk-\ *adj* [*eradicate* + *-able*] **:** that can be eradicated ⟨whether the habit is ~ or ineradicable⟩ — **erad·i·ca·bly** \-blē, -li\ *adv*

[1]**erad·i·cant** \-kənt\ *adj* [*eradicate* + *-ant*] **:** acting or tending to act as a pesticidal eradicant ⟨an ~ spray⟩

[2]**eradicant** \"\ *n* -S **:** an agent of eradication; *esp* **:** a pesticidal spray used to destroy a parasitic organism at its source before it reaches the suscept ⟨an ~ applied to scab-infested apple leaves on the ground⟩ — compare PROTECTANT

erad·i·cate \-dəˌkāt, *usu* -ād·+V\ *vt* -ED/-ING/-S [L *eradicatus*, past part. of *eradicare*, fr. *e-* + *radic-, radix* root — more at ROOT] **1 :** to pull up (as a weed) by the roots **:** UPROOT ⟨perennial creeping rootstocks that are difficult to ~⟩ **2 :** to do away with (something not wanted) **:** root out **:** destroy completely ⟨aerial sprays that ~ weeds, diseases, and insect pests from the wheat fields⟩ ⟨a campaign that virtually *eradicated* illiteracy in the country⟩ **syn** see EXTERMINATE

eradicated *adj, heraldry* **:** depicted with roots exposed as though pulled up ⟨an oak tree ~ vert⟩

erad·i·ca·tion \ə,==ˈkāshən\ *n* -S [LL *eradication-, eradicatio*, fr. L *eradicatus* + *-ion-, -io* -ion] **:** the act or process of eradicating ⟨the ~ of weeds⟩ ⟨the ~ of opposition groups⟩ ⟨the ~ of white pine blister rust depends on destruction of the intermediate host⟩

erad·i·ca·tive \əˈ==ˌkā|d·|iv, -kə|, |t|, |ēv *also* |əv\ *adj* **:** tending or serving to eradicate ⟨~ and preventive measures against trachoma⟩

erad·i·ca·tor \-ˌkād·ə(r), -ātə-\ *n* -S [ML, fr. L *eradicatus* + *-or*] **:** one that eradicates; *specif* **:** a chemical preparation used for removing marks or stains (as of ink or rust)

er·a·gros·tis \ˌerəˈgrästəs\ *n, cap* [NL, fr. Gk *eros* love + *agrōstis*, a kind of grass] **:** a genus of grasses resembling the bluegrasses but having flattened spikelets and deciduous lemmas

eran·the·mum \əˈran(t)thəməm\ *n* [NL, fr. Gk *ēranthemon*, a plant resembling camomile, fr. *ēr*, ear spring + *anthemon* flower, fr. *anthos* — more at ANTHOLOGY, VERNAL] **1** *cap* **:** a small genus of tropical Asiatic shrubs or perennial herbs (family Acanthaceae) having flowers with a 5-parted limb and two stamens **2** -S **:** any plant of the genus *Eranthemum*

eran·this \-thəs\ *n, cap* [NL, fr. Gk *ēr*, ear + NL *-anthis* (fr. Gk *anthos*)] **:** a genus of Eurasian herbs (family Ranunculaceae) with tuberous rootstocks, palmately dissected mostly basal leaves, and solitary yellow flowers — see WINTER ACONITE

eras *pl of* ERA

eras·abil·i·ty \ə,rāsə'bilәd·ē, ē,r-, *chiefly Brit* -āzə-\ *n* -ES **:** the property or degree of being erasable ⟨~ is important in good typing paper⟩ ⟨compared the ~ of different tapes⟩

eras·able \ə'ǝǝbəl\ *adj* **:** capable of being erased esp. without traces or damage that would impair reuse ⟨~ tracing paper⟩ ⟨a signal too loud to be ~ in a single pass through the erase head⟩

erase \ə'rās, ē'-, *chiefly Brit* -āz\ *vb* -ED/-ING/-S [L *erasus*, past part. of *eradere*, fr. *e-* + *radere* to scratch, scrape — more at RAT] *vt* **1 a** (1) **:** to rub or scrape out (as letters or figures written, engraved, or painted) ⟨*erased* the chalk marks⟩ ⟨a typing error neatly *erased*⟩ (2) **:** to remove (recorded matter) from a magnetic storage medium (as magnetic tape) so as to make the surface available for a new magnetic pattern **:** DEMAGNETIZE ⟨the recording can be *erased* and the tape used again⟩; *also* **:** to subject (as a magnetic tape) to erasure **b :** to remove marks, symbols, or other communicating devices from ⟨the school children *erased* the blackboard⟩ **2 a :** to remove from existence or memory as if by erasing **:** wipe out **:** OBLITERATE ⟨a plan to ~ the boundary between the countries⟩ ⟨time had *erased* the bitter memories⟩; *specif* **:** to get rid of (a person) by murder ⟨the efforts of a group of murderers to ~ a blinded man —Anthony Boucher⟩ **b :** to nullify the effect or force of **:** remove from the necessity of consideration **:** make quite insignificant or inconsequential **:** ANNUL ⟨the . . . statement had *erased* in one day months of patient work —W.J.Jordan⟩ **c :** OFFSET, NEUTRALIZE, BALANCE ⟨profit taking *erased* most of these gains —*Wall Street Jour.*⟩ ~ *vi* **1 :** to yield to being erased ⟨marks that ~ easily⟩ ⟨tape that ~*s* when recorded over⟩ **2 :** to remove marks or signals from something ⟨a tape recorder that ~*s* at a higher speed⟩

syn EXPUNGE, BLOT (*out*), EFFACE, OBLITERATE, DELETE, CANCEL: ERASE stresses the fact of removal of symbols or impressions without important damage to the surface involved and may imply a resulting blank usable for a new symbol or impression ⟨*erase* a misspelled word⟩ ⟨a child *erasing* numbers from a slate⟩ ⟨so violently have they hated the soul of the modern man that they have wished to *erase* from the record of history every thought and deed since the Renaissance —J.W.Krutch⟩ EXPUNGE, esp. in relation to tangible and simple action, has been influenced by *sponge* and stresses a complete washing out or off of whatever is affected or indicates its complete removal from consideration ⟨*expunge* a false report⟩ ⟨irrelevant testimony *expunged* from a court proceeding⟩ ⟨a woman's history, you know: certain chapters *expunged* —George Meredith⟩ BLOT (*out*) suggests the complete covering or obscuring of an impression by smearing or blurring over ⟨lines of the manuscript *blotted out* by spilled ink⟩ ⟨the same process by which Communist literature first blackened, and then *blotted out* altogether, Trotsky's exploits in the civil war —*Times Lit. Supp.*⟩ EFFACE suggests complete removal of an impression, sometimes through slow attrition and wear ⟨inscriptions on a pyramid *effaced* by time⟩ ⟨a cliché, a worn counter of a word, with its original meaning all *effaced*, and even its secondary meaning now only just visible —Havelock Ellis⟩ OBLITERATE is perhaps the most forceful of this group in connoting utter, complete, and inexorable removal or elimination of all traces of impressions ⟨a flash of lightning *obliterated* the first letter of 'Caesar' on a statue of Augustus —John Buchan⟩ ⟨the Navajo was careful to *obliterate* every trace of their temporary occupation —Willa Cather⟩ With no suggestion of either the destruction or the preservation of the marks or symbols involved, DELETE now stresses simple exclusion ⟨*delete* a word unnecessarily repeated⟩ ⟨whenever you feel an impulse to perpetrate a piece of exceptionally fine writing, obey it — wholeheartedly — and *delete* it before sending your manuscript to press —A.T.Quiller-Couch⟩ CANCEL, formerly indicating to cross out, now stresses invalidation, nullification, or reduction to insignificance ⟨the laboratory door does not lock behind him and bar his return any more than it swung shut to imprison Darwin and forever *cancel* his status as a naturalist —*Amer. Naturalist*⟩ Many of these words show semantic developments to ideas of destroying, killing, annihilating ⟨the killers may in time succeed in *erasing* me —V.A. Kravchenko⟩ ⟨the few survivors of the brilliant generation of young Englishmen *expunged* by the first World War —Jack Winocour⟩ ⟨they [enemy soldiers] were just *blotted out* —Nevil Shute⟩ and to ideas of balancing, offsetting, equaling, nullifying with equal opposing force ⟨the . . . mixture of races *canceling* each other's beliefs —T.S.Eliot⟩ ⟨a hideous phrase which no amount of palliation can ever quite *obliterate* —P.E.More⟩ These semantic extensions may retain nuances of meaning implied in older uses.

erased *adj, heraldry* **:** depicted with jagged extremities as if torn off — used esp. of the head or leg of an animal ⟨a lion's head ~ proper⟩; compare COUPED

erase head *or* **erasing head** *n* **:** a device mounted on a magnetic recorder that obliterates previous recordings on the magnetic medium by demagnetization just before a new recording is made

erase·ment \-smənt, *chiefly Brit* -zm-\ *n* -S **:** ERASURE

eras·er \-sə(r), *chiefly Brit* -zə-\ *n* -S **:** one that erases: as **a :** an instrument with a handle and sharp blade used to scrape out writing quickly — called also *steel eraser* **b :** a piece of a rubber composition usu. containing vulcanized oil and pumice for erasing pencil, ink, or other marks ⟨a wood-encased ~ of pencil shape⟩ ⟨a ferrule secures the ~ to the pencil⟩ ⟨a typewriter ~ with brush⟩ **c :** a block of absorbent material (as felt strips or sponge rubber) usu. fastened to a hard back and used for removing chalk marks from a slate or blackboard **d :** a wooden instrument with a flat smooth point used to obliterate braille dots by pressure **e :** a chemical solution for removing ink marks **:** ERADICATOR

erasers: *1* typewriter, *2* blackboard, *3* pencil

eraser shield *or* **erasing shield** *or* **erasure shield** *n* **:** a thin plate (as of metal or celluloid) with holes usu. of several sizes used to confine an erasure to a limited area

erases *pres 3d sing of* ERASE

erasing *pres part of* ERASE

era·sion \-āzhən, -āsh-\ *n* -S **1 :** ERASURE 1 ⟨the signatures have been erased . . . not without leaving signs of ~ —Agatha Christie⟩ **2 :** surgical removal of diseased tissue by scraping or curetting

¹**eras·mi·an** \ə'razmēən, -ē'r-\ *adj, usu cap* [Desiderius *Erasmus* (Geert Geerts) †1536 Dutch scholar + E *-ian*] **:** of, relating to, or in the manner of Desiderius Erasmus ⟨the *Erasmian* movement⟩ ⟨*Erasmian* humor⟩ — **eras·mi·an·ism** \-,nizəm\ *n* -S *usu cap*

²**erasmian** \"\ *n* -S *usu cap* **:** a follower of Erasmus

¹**eras·tian** \ə'rastēən, ē'r-, -schən\ *adj, usu cap* [Thomas *Erastus* (Lieber or Liebler) †1583 German-Swiss physician and Zwinglian theologian + E *-ian*] **1 :** of or relating to the physician and theologian Erastus or his doctrines **2 :** of, characterized by, or advocating Erastianism ⟨an ~ doctrine of the relation of church and state⟩ ⟨~ arguments⟩

²**erastian** \"\ *n* -S *usu cap* **:** a supporter of Erastian doctrines; *esp* **:** an upholder of state supremacy in ecclesiastical affairs ⟨the 17th century English *Erastians*⟩

eras·tian·ism \-,nizəm\ *n* -S *usu cap* **:** the doctrine that the state is supreme over the church in ecclesiastical matters — compare BYZANTINISM, CAESAROPAPISM

era·sure \ə'rāshə(r), ē'- *sometimes* -āzh-\ *n* -S [*erase* + *-ure*] **1 :** an act or instance of erasing **:** a rubbing or scratching out **:** OBLITERATION ⟨prevents accidental ~ of the tape⟩ ⟨errors and ~*s* in the typescript⟩ ⟨the bomb spelled ~ of cities —D.D.Eisenhower⟩ **2 :** the place where something has been erased ⟨a feathering of the ink at the ~⟩

erava *var of* YERAVA

er·bi·um \'ərbēəm\ *n* -S [NL, fr. *Ytterby*, Sweden, where gadolinite is found + NL *-ium*] **:** a trivalent metallic element of the rare-earth group that occurs with yttrium (as in gadolinite and fergusonite) and forms a pink oxide and reddish salts — symbol *Er*; see ELEMENT table

er·cles vein \'ər,klēz-\ *n, usu cap E* [*Ercles*, alter. of *Hercules*, ancient Greco-Roman hero, fr. L, fr. Gk *Hēraklēs*] **:** a rousing somewhat bombastic manner of public speaking or writing ⟨could not write in the *Ercles vein* if he would, and he had chosen to give his inaugural address an agreeably quiet tone —*Nation*⟩

erd \'erd\ *dial var of* EARTH

erd shrew *n* **:** the common European shrew (*Sorex vulgaris*)

erdvark *var of* AARDVARK

¹**ere** \'ar, 'er\ *adv* [ME *er*, *ar*, fr. OE *ǣr*, adv. (historically compar. but used as positive and compar.), prep. & conj.; akin to OHG *ēr* earlier, ON *ār* early, Goth *air* early, *airis* earlier, Gk *ēri* early, Av *ayarə* day; basic meaning: day, morning] **1** *chiefly Scot* **:** EARLY **2** *chiefly Scot* **:** SOON

²**ere** \(')e|(ə)r, (')a(ə)|, |ə\ *prep* [ME *er*, *ar*, fr. OE *ǣr*] **:** ²BEFORE 1a ⟨virtues . . . contrived ~ the beginning of the world —Norman Douglas⟩

³**ere** \"\ *conj* [ME *er*, *ar*, fr. OE *ǣr*] **:** ³BEFORE ⟨supersedes it ~ the twentieth century ends —C.H.Moehlman⟩ ⟨I will be thrown into Etna . . . ~ I will leave her —Shak.⟩

⁴**ere** *var of* ²EAR

⁵**ere** *archaic var of* EVER

⁶**ere** \'a(ə)|(ə)r, 'e|, |ə\ *dial var of* THERE

ereb *or* **erev** \'erəv, 'e,rev\ *n* -S [Heb *'erebh*] **:** EVE: **a :** the part of the day or the day immediately preceding the Jewish Sabbath or a Jewish holiday **b :** an indefinite period preceding a Jewish holiday ⟨as busy as a housewife on ~ Yom Kippur⟩

er·ech·ti·tes \,erək'tīd·(,)ēz, ,e,rek-\ *n* [NL, fr. Gk *erechthitis* groundsel, fr. *erechthein* to rend, break] **1** *cap* **:** a genus of coarse herbs (family Compositae) commonly with whitish discoid flower heads and a silky pappus that facilitates their wide distribution as weeds **2** *pl* **erechtites :** any plant of the genus *Erechtites*

¹**erect** \ə'rekt, ē'-\ *adj* [ME, fr. L *erectus*, past part. of *erigere* to erect, fr. *e-* + *-rigere* (fr. *regere* to lead straight, guide, direct) — more at RIGHT] **1 a :** vertical in position **:** UPRIGHT ⟨he is in an ~ position and flying parallel to the earth's surface —H.G.Armstrong⟩ **:** STANDING ⟨buried their dead ~⟩ ⟨a column still ~ amid the ruins⟩ ⟨his armorial crest bore a sword ~ proper⟩; *specif* **:** not spreading or decumbent ⟨an ~ stem⟩ — contrasted with *prone* **b :** standing up or out from the body ⟨hair ~ from fright⟩ **c** *of an image* **:** normal rather than inverted in position **:** right side up ⟨in this device the image is observed ~⟩ **d :** characterized by firm or rigid straightness in bodily posture **:** not leaning or bent **:** not slouching or stooped ⟨the ~ bearing of one . . . accustomed to official uniform —A. Conan Doyle⟩ **2** *archaic* **:** directed upward **:** UPLIFTED ⟨with face ~ against the sun —George Chapman⟩ **3** *obs* **:** characterized by alertness **:** WATCHFUL ⟨bid her well be . . . ~ lest by some fair-appearing good surprised she dictate false —John Milton⟩ **4 :** characterized by aspiration or rectitude **:** NOBLE, UPRIGHT ⟨an ~ mind⟩ ⟨an ~ life⟩ **5 :** being in a state of physiological erection — **erect·ly** *adv*

²**erect** \"\ *vb* -ED/-ING/-S [ME *erecten*, fr. L *erectus*, past part.] *vt* **1 a** (1) **:** to put up (as a building or machine) by the fitting together of materials or parts **:** cause to stand ready for use **:** BUILD ⟨the settlers ~*ed* walls of field stones⟩ ⟨when the state ~*s* a new bridge⟩ ⟨a building ~*ed* in 1920⟩; *specif* **:** to hoist and bolt in place fabricated parts of (a ship's structure) before riveting or welding (2) **:** to fix in an upright position (as a statue, signpost, or plaque) **:** put up ⟨~ a flagpole⟩ ⟨~*ed* a marker over the grave⟩ (3) **:** to cause to stand up or out **:** RAISE ⟨~*ed* himself to full height⟩ ⟨the porcupine ~*s* its quills⟩ ⟨~ the hood of the camera⟩ ⟨an armorial crest bearing a ship at anchor, her oars ~*ed*⟩ **b** *archaic* **:** to direct upward **:** lift up ⟨to stand with their mouths open and ~*ed* —Jonathan Swift⟩ **c :** to change (an image) from an inverted to a normal position ⟨a microscope attachment that ~*s* the image seen⟩ **2 :** to elevate in status **:** raise to a higher office or dignity **:** EXALT, MAGNIFY ⟨~*ed* the worship of nationality into a religion usurping the ancient religion —Hilaire Belloc⟩ ⟨~ methods into dogmas⟩ ⟨has been ~*ed* into a great poet of the 13th century —George Saintsbury⟩; *specif* **:** to hold up as an ideal ⟨the doctrine which ~*s* pleasure as the end of human action —G.D.H. Cole⟩ **3 a :** to bring into existence as if by raising or building **:** set up ⟨~ social barriers along religious lines⟩ **:** ESTABLISH ⟨the attempt to ~ political authority upon the basis of self-interest —John Dewey⟩ **:** build up **:** DEVELOP ⟨~ a complex philosophical system⟩ ⟨~ a civilization⟩ **b :** to give legal existence to (as a unit of civil or church government) by a formal act of authority **:** CONSTITUTE, CREATE ⟨Indiana and Illinois were ~*ed* into territories during Jefferson's first term —H.L.Mencken⟩ ⟨the Holy See alone ~*s* dioceses, cathedral churches, abbeys of monks or nuns, archconfraternities —*Catholic Dict.*⟩ **c :** to set up (a taxonomic category) **4** *obs* **:** to stir up (as the mind or spirits) **:** ALERT, ENCOURAGE, EMBOLDEN ⟨better counsels might ~ our minds and teach us to cast off this yoke —John Milton⟩ **5 a :** to draw or construct (a perpendicular or figure) upon a given base **b :** to calculate (a horoscope) by astrology ~ *vi* **:** to rise to an erect position **:** stand up or out ⟨will make thy hair like . . . bristles to ~ —Robert Burns⟩ **syn** see BUILD

erec·tile \-t°l, -,tīl, -(,)til\ *adj* [F *érectile*, fr. L *erectus* + F *-ile*] **:** capable of being raised to an erect position or state ⟨~ feathers⟩; *esp* **:** CAVERNOUS 3

erec·til·i·ty \ə,rek'tiləd·ē, (,)ē,r-\ *n* -ES **1 :** the state of being erectile **2 :** capacity for erection

erec·tion \ə'rekshən, ē'r-\ *n* -S [ME *ereccioun*, fr. L *erection-*, *erectio*, fr. *erectus* + *-ion-*, *-io* -ion] **1 :** the act or process of erecting **:** CONSTRUCTION ⟨the ~ of a new building⟩ **:** ESTABLISHMENT ⟨the ~ of tariffs⟩ ⟨the ~ of an international economic union⟩ **2 a :** the state of a previously flaccid bodily part containing cavernous tissue when that tissue becomes dilated with blood marked by firm turgid form and erect position **b :** an occurrence of such a state in the penis or clitoris **3 :** something erected; *esp* **:** EDIFICE

erection tower *n* **:** a temporary framework like a tower built to support hoisting equipment for the erection of a building or other structure

erect·ness \-k(t)nəs\ *n* -ES **:** the quality or state of being erect

erec·tor \-ktə(r)\ *n* -S [LL, fr. L *erectus* + *-or*] **:** one that erects or supervises erection: as **a :** a muscle that raises or keeps a part erect — see ERECTOR PILI **b** (1) **:** a workman who works on a structure (as a steel building or bridge) by assembling fabricated parts; *specif* **:** SHIPFITTER (2) **:** a workman who assembles machines, tests the equipment in operation, and makes adjustments (3) **:** a workman who assembles electrical equipment **c :** a machine for erecting (as a derrick)

erector pi·li \-'pī,lī -'pi,lē\ *n* -S [NL, lit., hair-raiser] **:** one of the small fan-shaped smooth muscles associated with the base of each hair that contract when the body surface is chilled and erect the hairs, compress an oil gland above each muscle, and produce the appearance of gooseflesh

erects *pres 3d sing of* ERECT

e region *n, usu cap E* **:** the part of the ionosphere occurring between 40 and 90 miles above the surface of the earth and containing the daytime E layer and the sporadic E layer

erelong \(')ǝ¦ǝ\ *adv* **:** before long **:** SOON ⟨a man . . . following the stag ~ slew him —Edmund Spenser⟩

erem- *or* **eremo-** *comb form* [NL, fr. Gk *erēm-*, *erēmo-*, fr. *erēmos* lonely, solitary and *erēmia* desert, fr. *erēmos* + *-ia* -y — more at RETINA] **:** solitary ⟨*Eremurus*⟩ **:** desert ⟨*eremology*⟩ — chiefly in terms in biology

er·e·ma·cau·sis \,erəmə'kȯsəs\ *n* -ES [NL, fr. Gk *ērema* gently, softly, slowly + *kausis* burning, fr. *kaiein* to burn — more at RIM, CAUSTIC] **:** gradual oxidation of organic matter from exposure to air and moisture

eremeyevite *var of* JEREMEJEVITE

ere·mi·an \ə'rēmēən\ *adj, usu cap* [Gk *erēmia* solitude, desert + E *-an*] **:** of, relating to, or constituting a division of the Palaearctic region including northern Africa, northern Arabia, and Asiatic desert regions

ere·mic \-ēmik, -em-\ *adj* [*erem-* + *-ic*] **:** of or relating to deserts or sandy regions

er·e·mite \'erə,mīt, *usu* -īd·+V\ *n* -S [ME *eremite*, *ermite*, *heremite*, *hermite* — more at HERMIT] **:** HERMIT; *esp* **:** a Christian living for religious reasons in solitary retirement

er·e·mit·ic \¦ǝǝ¦mid·|ik, -it|, |ēk\ *or* **er·e·mit·i·cal** \|əkəl, |ēk-\ *adj* **1 :** of, relating to, or befitting a hermit ⟨the ~ legend⟩ ⟨~ austerities⟩ **2 :** characterized by ascetic solitude in mode of life **:** SOLITARY ⟨~ or corporate monastic life⟩ ⟨the ~ element in the life of the religious colony⟩ — contrasted with *cenobitic*

er·e·mit·ish \'ǝǝ,mīd·ish\ *adj* **:** resembling an eremite **:** suitable to an eremite

er·e·mit·ism \-īd,izəm\ *n* -S **:** the practice of living in solitary retirement ⟨a long tradition of monasticism and ~⟩

er·e·mol·o·gy \,erə'mäləjē\ *n* -S [*erem-* + *-logy*] **:** a science concerned with the desert and its phenomena

er·e·moph·i·la \-'äfələ\ *n* [NL, fr. *erem-* + *-phila* (fem. of *-philus*)] **1** *cap* **:** a genus of shrubs or trees (family Myoporaceae) having large solitary or paired often spotted flowers one species of which (*E. latrobei*) is important in Australia as a stock-poisoning plant **2** -S **:** any plant of the genus *Eremophila*

er·e·mo·phyte \'erəmō,fīt, ə'rēmə,f-\ *n* -S [*erem-* + *-phyte*] **:** DESERT PLANT

er·e·mop·ter·is \,erə'mäptərəs\ *n, cap* [NL, fr. *erem-* + *-pteris*] **:** a form genus of fossil ferns or pteridosperms represented by leaves of Carboniferous age

er·e·mu·rus \-'myürəs\ *n* [NL, fr. *erem-* + *-urus*] **1** *cap* **:** a small genus of Asiatic herbs (family Liliaceae) with leaves in a basal rosette and flowers in racemes at the tops of long naked stalks **2** *pl* **eremu·ri** \-,rī\ **:** any plant of the genus *Eremurus* — called also *desert candle*, *foxtail lily*

erep·sin \ə'repsən\ *n* -S [ISV *er-* (prob. fr. L *eripere* to take away) + *pepsin*; orig. formed in G] **:** a proteolytic enzyme obtained esp. from the intestinal juice and now known to be a mixture of peptidases

ereth·ic \ə'rethik, e'r-\ *adj* [*erethism* + *-ic*] **:** of, relating to, or tending to produce erethism **:** RESTLESS ⟨the most ~ of all its fantasies, wealth —Rebecca West⟩

er·e·thism \'erə,thizəm\ *n* -S [F *éréthisme*, fr. Gk *erethismos* irritation, fr. *erethein*, *erethizein* to provoke, excite, irritate; akin to Gk *ornynai* to urge on, incite, call forth — more at RISE] **:** abnormal irritability or responsiveness to stimulation whether generalized or restricted to a particular body part ⟨cardiac ~⟩ ⟨expressed his view . . . with such an effluence of ~ —*Psychiatry*⟩ — **er·e·this·mic** \¦ǝǝ¦thizmik\ *adj*

er·e·thi·zon \,erə'thīz°n, -,zän\ *n, cap* [NL, fr. Gk *erethizōn*, pres. part. of *erethizein*] **:** the type genus of Erethizontidae comprising the No. American porcupine

er·e·thi·zon·ti·dae \,erəthə'zäntə,dē\ *n pl, cap* [NL, fr. *Erethizont-*, *Erethizon*, type genus + *-idae*] **:** a family of chiefly arboreal hystricomorph rodents comprising the typical New World porcupines with the tail more or less prehensile and the soles of the feet specialized for climbing

er·et·moch·e·lys \,e,ret'mäkələs\ *n, cap* [NL, fr. Gk *eretmon* oar + *chelys* turtle — more at ROW (propel a boat)] **:** a genus of aquatic turtles including only the hawksbill

erev *var of* EREB

erevan *usu cap, var of* YEREVAN

erewhile *also* **erewhiles** \(')ǝ¦ǝ\ *adv* [ME *erwhile*, fr. *er* ere (prep.) + *while*] *archaic* **:** some time ago **:** a little while before **:** HERETOFORE ⟨I am as fair now as I was ~ —Shak.⟩

ere·whon·i·an \¦erə¦(h)wānēən, -wōn-\ *adj, usu cap* [*Erewhon* (anagram of *nowhere*), fictitious land described in the utopian novel *Erewhon* (1872) by Samuel Butler †1902 British writer + E *-ian*] **:** of or suggestive of the utopia described in the book *Erewhon* whose people dealt with disease as a crime and destroyed machinery lest machines destroy them ⟨an *Erewhonian* fear of automation⟩

erf \'e(ə)rf\ *n, pl* **er·ven** \'ervən\ [Afrik, fr. MD *erf*, *erve* plot of ground, inheritance; akin to OHG *erbi* inheritance — more at ORPHAN] *Africa* **:** a plot of land usu. about half an acre in size; *specif* **:** BUILDING LOT

er·furt \'erfərt, -,fürt\ *adj, usu cap* [fr. *Erfurt*, Germany] **:** of or from the city of Erfurt, Germany **:** of the kind or style prevalent in Erfurt

¹**erg** \'ərg, 'ēg, 'əig *sometimes* 'e(ə)rg\ *n* -S [Gk *ergon* work — more at WORK] **:** an absolute cgs unit of work representing the work done by a force of one dyne acting through a displacement of one centimeter in the direction of the force — compare JOULE

²**erg** \'e(ə)rg\ *n, pl* **ergs** \'e(ə)rgz\ [F, of Hamitic origin, akin to Amharic *'ărăgă* rise, ascend] **:** a desert region of shifting sand ⟨the dunes of the Saharan ~*s*⟩

erg- *or* **ergo-** *comb form* [Gk, fr. *ergon*] **:** work ⟨*ergophobia*⟩ ⟨*ergodic*⟩

er·ga·sia \,ər'gāzh(ē)ə\ *n* -S [NL, fr. Gk, work, business, fr. *ergazesthai* to work, labor, fr. *ergon* work] **:** organismic activity **:** BEHAVIOR ⟨held mental illness to involve an ~ of the total organism rather than a physiological function of the brain alone⟩

er·gas·tic \,ər'gastik\ *adj* [Gk *ergastikos* able to work, industrious, fr. (assumed) *ergastos* (verbal of *ergazesthai* to work) + *-ikos* -ic] **:** constituting the nonliving by-products of protoplasmic activity ⟨~ materials⟩ — used chiefly of intracellular deposits (as of starch or fat) or of extracellular secretions; compare METAPLASM

er·gas·to·plasm \,ər'gastə,plazəm\ *n* [ISV *ergasto-* (fr. — assumed — Gk *ergastos*) + *-plasm*; orig. formed as F *ergastoplasme*] **:** ribosome-studded endoplasmic reticulum that is basophilic due to the presence of RNA — **er·gas·to·plas·mic** \¦ǝ¦ǝǝ¦plazmik\ *adj*

er·gas·tu·lum \,ər'gaschələm, -stəl-\ *n, pl* **ergastu·la** \-lə\ [L, prob. modif. of Gk *ergastērion* workshop, fr. *ergazesthai* to work] **:** a dungeon on a large Roman farm in which slave laborers were confined

ergat- *or* **ergato-** *comb form* [ISV, fr. Gk *ergat-*, fr. *ergatēs*, fr. *ergazesthai* to work — more at ERGASIA] **:** worker ⟨*ergatoid*⟩ ⟨*ergatomorphic*⟩

er·ga·tan·dro·morph \,ərgə'tandrə,mȯrf\ *n* -S [*ergat-* + *andr-* + *-morph*] **:** ERGATANER — **er·ga·tan·dro·mor·phic** \¦ǝǝ¦ǝǝ¦mȯrfik\ *adj*

er·ga·tan·drous \¦ǝǝ¦tandrəs\ *adj* [*ergat-* + *andr-* + *-ous*] **:** having wingless males — used of ants — **er·ga·tan·dry** \¦ǝǝ,ǝdrē\ *n* -ES

er·ga·ta·ner \,ərgə'tānər, -tä¦ne(ə)r\ *n* -S [NL, fr. *ergat-* + Gk *anēr* man (male person) — more at ANDR-] **:** a male ant that resembles a worker

er·gate \'ər,gāt\ *n* -S [Gk *ergatēs* worker] **:** an ant of one of the worker castes

¹**er·ga·tive** \'ərgəd·iv\ *adj* [ISV *ergat-* + *-ive*] *of a grammatical case* **:** denoting agency or instrumentality

²**ergative** \"\ *n* -S **1 :** the ergative case of a language **2 :** a form in the ergative case

er·gat·o·gyne \,ər'gad·ə,jīn, 'ərgəd·ō,j-\ *n* -S [ISV *ergat-* + *-gyne*] **1 :** a wingless queen ant resembling a worker **2 :** a worker or soldier ant that develops female characteristics esp. as a result of the attack of parasitic worms — **er·gat·o·gy·nic** \,ǝ¦ǝǝ¦jīnik, ¦ǝǝǝ¦-, -jin-\ *adj* — **er·ga·tog·y·ny** \,ərgə'täjənē\ *n* -ES

¹**er·ga·toid** \'ərgə,tȯid\ *adj* [ISV *ergat-* + *-oid*] **:** having wingless fertile sexual individuals of either sex ⟨~ ants⟩

²**ergatoid** \"\ *n* -S **:** a wingless sexually perfect ant; *specif* **:** ERGATOGYNE 1

er·gat·o·morph \,ər'gad·ə,mȯrf, 'ərgəd·ō,m-\ *n* -S [*ergat-* + *-morph*] **:** an ergatomorphic ant — **er·gat·o·mor·phism** \,ǝ¦ǝǝ'mȯr,fizəm, ¦ǝǝǝ'-,-\ *n* -S

er·gat·o·mor·phic \,ǝ¦ǝǝ¦mȯrfik, ¦ǝǝǝ¦-\ *adj* [*ergat-* + *-morphic*] **:** resembling a worker — used of male and female ants

ergh \'erk\ *Scot var of* ARGH

-ergies *pl of* -ERGY

¹**er·go** \'e(ə)r|(,)gō, 'ər|, 'eə|, 'ō|, 'əi|\ *adv* [L, fr. (assumed) OL *e rogo* from the direction (of)] **:** THEREFORE, HENCE ⟨they fight no battles; ~ in a certain . . . sense they are noncombatant —T.O.Heggen⟩ — often used to emphasize the illogical nature of an inference ⟨if they were not familiar with German theology . . . there just wasn't any; ~, the "Dutch" were just dumb —R.H.Shryock⟩

²**ergo** \"\ *n* -S **:** an inferred conclusion

¹ergo- — see ERG-

²ergo- *comb form* [F, fr. *ergot*] : ergot ⟨*ergo*sterol⟩

er·go·calciferol \ˌər(ˌ)gō+\ *n* -S [²*ergo-* + *calciferol*] : VITAMIN D_2 — used in the system of nomenclature adopted by the International Union of Pure and Applied Chemistry

er·go·cor·nine \ˌərgōˈkȯrˌnēn, -ˌnən\ *n* -S [G *ergokornin*, prob. fr. *ergoxin-* ²*ergo-* + *korn* grain, rye or L *cornu* horn + G *-in*] : a crystalline tripeptide alkaloid $C_{31}H_{39}N_5O_5$ separated from ergotoxine — see DIHYDROERGOCORNINE

er·go·cris·tine \-ˈkriˌstēn, -stən\ *n* -S [G *ergokristin*, fr. *ergo-* ²ergo- + *kristall* crystal + *-in*] : a crystalline tripeptide alkaloid $C_{35}H_{39}N_5O_5$ separated from ergotoxine

er·god·ic \ˌərˈgädik\ *adj* [*erg-* + Gk *hodos* way, journey + E *-ic* — more at CEDE] **1 :** of or relating to a process in which every sequence or sizable sample is the same statistically and therefore equally representative of the whole **2 :** involving or relating to the probability that any state will recur — **er·go·dic·i·ty** \ˌərgəˈdisəd-ē\ *n* -ES

er·go·gen·ic \ˌərgəˈjenik\ *adj* [*erg-* + *-genic*] : increasing capacity for bodily or mental labor esp. by eliminating fatigue symptoms ⟨an ~ drug⟩

er·go·gram \ˈ==ˌgram\ *n* [ISV *erg-* + *-gram*; orig. formed as It *ergogramma*] : a record of muscular work obtained by use of the ergograph

er·go·graph \-ˌraf, -räf\ *n* [ISV *erg-* + *-graph*; orig. formed as It *ergografo*] : an apparatus or instrument with a recording device used to measure the work capacity of a muscle or group of muscles (as when exercised to exhaustion in the study of fatigue) ⟨a weight ~ attached to a finger⟩ — compare DYNAMOMETER — **er·go·graph·ic** \ˌ==ˈgrafik\ *adj*

er·go·ma·nia \ˌ==ˈmānēə\ *n* [NL, fr. *erg-* + *-mania*] : excessive devotion to work esp. as a symptom of mental disorder — **er·go·ma·ni·ac** \-ēˌak\ *n*

er·gom·e·ter \ˌərˈgäməd-ə(r)\ *n* [*erg-* + *-meter*] : an apparatus or instrument with a recording device used to measure the work performed by a group of muscles under control conditions as to time, rate, or resistance (as in comparing the energy yield of different diets) — compare DYNAMOMETER

er·go·met·rine \ˌərgəˈme\|·ˌtrēn, -mē\|, \|·trən\ *n* [²*ergo-* + *metr-* + *-ine*] : ERGONOVINE

er·gone \ˈərˌgōn\ *n* -S[*erg-* + *-one* (as in *hormone*)] : a substance that when present in minute quantities promotes a physiological activity

er·go·nom·ic \ˌərgəˈnämik\ *adj* [*erg-* + *economic*] : of or relating to ergonomics — **er·go·nom·i·cal·ly** \-ik(ə)lē\ *adv*

er·go·nom·ics \ˌ==ˈmiks\ *n pl but sing or pl in constr* [*erg-* + *economics*] : an applied science concerned with the characteristics of people that need to be considered in designing and arranging things that they use in order that people and things will interact most effectively and safely — called also *biotechnology, human engineering*

er·go·no·vine \ˌərgəˈnōˌvēn, -ˌvən\ *n* -S [²*ergo-* + *nov-* + *-ine*] : a crystalline alkaloid $C_{19}H_{23}N_3O_2$ from ergot that has the pharmacological action of ergot and is used chiefly in the form of its maleate — called also *ergometrine*

er·go·phobe \ˈərgəˌfōb\ *n* [*erg-* + *-phobe*] : one suffering from ergophobia

er·go·pho·bia \ˌ==ˈfōbēə\ *n* [NL, fr. *erg-* + *-phobia*] : fear of or aversion to work

er·gos·ter·ol \(ˌ)ərˈgästəˌrōl, -ˌrōl\ *n* [ISV ²*ergo-* + *sterol*] : a crystalline steroid alcohol $C_{28}H_{43}OH$ that occurs esp. in yeast, molds, and ergot and that is converted by ultraviolet irradiation into isomeric products leading to vitamin D_2

er·got \ˈərgə\|t, ˈəg-, ˈəig-, -ˌgä\|, *usu* \|d.+V\ *n* -S [F, lit., cock's spur (which the sclerotium resembles), fr. OF *argos, argoz*, pl., spurs of a horse's hoofs] **1 a :** the black or dark purple sclerotium of fungi of the genus *Claviceps* that occurs as a club-shaped body which replaces the seed of various grasses (as rye) **b :** any fungus of the genus *Claviceps* **2 :** a disease of rye and other cereals caused by fungi of the genus *Claviceps* and characterized by the presence of ergots in the seed heads **3 a :** the dried sclerotial bodies of an ergot fungus grown on rye and containing several alkaloids (as ergonovine, ergotamine) **b :** any of the ergotic alkaloids with pharmacologic effect on peripheral arterioles and esp. on the uterus that are used in therapeutic doses mainly to induce contraction of the uterine muscle after delivery of the fetus and placenta and that may in overlarge doses or from natural sources (as infected rye) produce contraction of peripheral arterioles sometimes leading to gangrene — compare ²ERGOTISM **4 :** a soft horny stub about the size of a chestnut occurring as a normal growth in the tufts of hair on the back of the fetlock in the horse

er·got·a·mine \(ˌ)ərˈgäd-əˌmēn, -mən\ *n* [ISV *ergot* + *amine*] : a crystalline tripeptide alkaloid $C_{33}H_{35}N_5O_5$ from ergot that has the pharmacological action of ergot and is used chiefly in the form of its tartrate in treating migraine

er·go·therapy \ˌərgō+\ *n* [*erg-* + *therapy*] : the treatment of disease by physical work and recreation

er·go·thi·o·ne·ine \ˌər(ˌ)gōˌthīˈōnēˌēn, -ī'än-, -nēən\ *n* [ISV *ergo-* + *thion-* + *-eine*; orig. formed as F *ergothionéine*] : a crystalline betaine $HSC_3H_2N_2CH_2CH[N(CH_3)_3]^+COO^-$ derived from a mercapto-histidine and found esp. in ergot and blood

er·got·ic \ˌərˈgäd·ik, ərˈg-\ *adj* : of, relating to, or produced by ergot

er·got·i·nine \(ˌ)ərˈgätᵊnˌēn, -tᵊnən\ *n* -S [ISV *ergotine*, an extract of ergot (ISV *ergot* + *-ine*) + *-ine*] : a crystalline tripeptide alkaloid $C_{35}H_{39}N_5O_5$ from ergot that is relatively inactive pharmacologically

ergotised *chiefly Brit var of* ERGOTIZED

¹er·go·tism \ˈergəˌtizəm, ˈər-\ *n* -S [F *ergotisme*, fr. *ergoter* to quibble, cavil (fr. OF *argoter*, fr. L *ergo* therefore) + *-isme* -ism — more at ERGO] : logical or sophistical reasoning

²er·got·ism \ˈərgəd·ˌizəm, -ˌgäd-\ *n* -S [*ergot* + *-ism*] : a toxic condition produced by eating grain, grain products (as rye bread), or grasses infected with ergot fungus or by chronic excessive use of the drug ergot and characterized by cramps of the muscles or dry gangrene — see SAINT ANTHONY'S FIRE

er·go·tize \ˈergəˌtīz, ˈər-\ *vi* -ED/-ING/-S [F *ergoter* + E *-ize*] : to argue logically or sophistically

er·got·ized \ˈərgəd·ˌīzd, -ˌgäd-\ *adj* [*ergot* + *-ize* + *-ed*] **1 :** affected by ergotism ⟨~ cattle⟩ **2 :** containing ergot

er·go·tox·ine \ˌərgəˈtäkˌsēn, -sən\ *n*-S [²*ergo-* + *tox-* + *-ine*] **1 :** a crystalline pharmacologically active alkaloid $C_{35}H_{39}N_5O_5$ from ergot that is stereoisomeric with ergotinine **2 :** a mixture of isomorphous pharmacologically active alkaloids from ergot — called also *ergotoxine group*; see ERGOCORNINE, ERGOCRISTINE

ergot poisoning *n* : ²ERGOTISM

ergs *pl of* ERG

-er·gy \ə(r)jē, ˌərj-, ˌəj-, ˌəij-, -ji\ *n comb form* -ES [LL *-ergia*, fr. Gk *-ergeia, -ergia*, fr. *ergon* work + *-eia, -ia* -y — more at WORK] : work ⟨*synergy*⟩ : effect ⟨*allergy*⟩

eri·an \ˈirēən, ˈēr-, -rīən\ *adj, usu cap* [*Erian*, subdivision of the American Devonian, fr. Lake *Erie*, one of the Great Lakes of No. America + E *-an*] : of, relating to, or constituting a subdivision of the American Devonian — see GEOLOGIC TIME table

er·i·an·thus \ˌerēˈan(t)thəs\ *n* [NL, fr. Gk *eri* wool (short for *erion, eirion*, dim. of *eiros* fleece) + NL *-anthus*] **1** *cap* : a genus of reedlike grasses having spikes crowded in a panicle clothed with long silky hairs **2** -ES : any plant of the genus *Erianthus* — called also *plume grass*

er·ic \ˈerik, ˈär-\ *also* **eric fine** *n* -S [IrGael *ēiric*, fr. OIr *ēric*] : a payment imposed for homicide in medieval Irish law upon the slayer and his kin consisting of a fixed price for the life of the slain and the honor price of the slayer : BLOOD FINE — compare CRO, GALANAS, WERGILD

er·i·ca \ˈerəkə; əˈrīkə, əˈrēkə\ *n* [NL, fr. L *erice* heather, fr. Gk *ereikē* — more at BRIER] **1** *cap* : a large genus (the type of the family Ericaceae) of low much-branched evergreen shrubs comprising the true heaths and having whorled scalelike or needlelike leaves and sepals shorter than the petals **2** -S : any plant of the genus *Erica*

er·i·ca·ce·ae \ˌerəˈkāsēˌē\ *n pl, cap* [NL, fr. *Erica*, type genus + *-aceae*] : a family of plants (order Ericales) comprising the heaths and various related plants, being predominantly shrubs, and having usu. distinct stamens borne on a disk and an ovary with four or more locules — **er·i·ca·ceous** \ˌ==ˈshəs\ *adj*

er·i·cad \ˈerəˌkad; əˈrīkəd, əˈrēkəd\ *n* -S [NL *Erica* + E *-ad*] : a plant of the family Ericaceae

erica dye *n, usu cap E* : either of two direct dyes — see DYE table I (under *Direct Red 47* and *51*)

er·i·ca·les \ˌerəˈkā(ˌ)lēz\ *n pl, cap* [NL, fr. *Erica* + *-ales*] : an order comprising chiefly gamopetalous dicotyledonous plants characterized by regular flowers with stamens in two whorls free from the corolla and with a compound ovary and containing the families Ericaceae, Clethraceae, Pyrolaceae, Diapensiaceae, Lennoaceae, and Epacridaceae

er·i·ce·tal \ˌerəˈsēd·ᵊl\ *adj* [NL *ericetum* heath, moorland (fr. L *erice* heather + NL *-etum*) + E *-al*] : composed of or containing heaths ⟨an ~ flora⟩

er·i·ce·tic·o·lous \ˌerəsəˈtikələs\ *adj* [NL *ericetum* + E *-i-* + *-colous*] : inhabiting a heath or similar habitat

erich·thoi·di·na \əˌrikˌthȯiˈdīnə, -dēnə\ *n* -S [NL, fr. ISV *erichthoid* (fr. NL *Erichthus* + ISV *-oid*) + NL *-ina* (fem. of *-inus* -ine)] : a larva of a stomatopod crustacean intermediate between pseudozoea and erichthus

erich·thus \əˈrikthəs\ *n* -ES [NL, fr. Gk *ēri* early + NL *-ichthus* (fr. Gk *ichthys* fish) — more at ERE, ICHTHUS] : a late larva of a stomatopod crustacean

eri·cius \əˈrish(ē)əs\ *n* -ES [L — more at URCHIN] : HEDGEHOG 1 ⟨bittern and ~ shall possess it —Isa 34:11 (NCE)⟩

er·i·coid \ˈerəˌkȯid\ *adj* [NL *Erica* + E *-oid*] : resembling heath; *esp* : narrow and recurved — used of leaves

er·i·co·phyte \ˈerəkōˌfīt, əˈrīkəˌf-\ *n* [*erico-* (fr. L *erice* heather) + *-phyte*] : a plant that grows on a heath or moor

¹erie \ˈirē, ˈēr-, -ri\ *n, pl* **erie** *or* **eries** *usu cap* **1 a :** an Iroquoian people of northern Ohio, northwestern Pennsylvania, and western New York **b :** a member of such people **2 :** the language of the Erie people

²erie \"\ *adj, usu cap* [fr. *Erie*, Pa.] : of or from the city of Erie, Pa. : of the kind or style prevalent in Erie

-eries *pl of* -ERY

erig·er·on \əˈrijərən, -jəˌrän\ *n* [NL, fr. L, groundsel, fr. Gk *ērigerōn*, fr. *ēri-* early + *gerōn* old man; fr. the hoary down of some species — more at ERE, CHURL] **1** *cap* : a widely distributed genus of herbs (family Compositae) having flower heads resembling asters but with fewer and narrower involucral bracts — see DAISY FLEABANE **2** -S **a :** any plant of the genus *Erigeron* **b :** the leaves and tops of plants of the genus *Erigeron* occas. and esp. formerly used as a diuretic and as a hemostatic in uterine hemorrhage **c :** ERIGERON OIL

erig·er·on oil \əˈrijə\|ˌrän-, \|ˌrən-\ *n* : a volatile oil distilled from the horseweed (*Erigeron canadense*) and sometimes used medicinally

er·i·glos·sa \ˌerəˈgläsə, -lȯsə\ *n pl, cap* [NL, fr. Gk *eri-* very much, high + NL *-glossa*] *in some classifications* : a suborder including all the Lacertilia except the chameleons — **er·i·glos·sate** \ˌ==ˈ=sāt, -ˌsāt\ *adj*

erig·na·thus \əˈrignəthəs\ *n, cap* [NL, fr. Gk *eri-* + NL *-gnathus*] : a genus of mammals comprising the bearded seal

er·ik·ite \ˈerəˌkīt\ *n* -S [G or Dan *erikit*, fr. *Erik* (Eric) the Red, 10th cent. Norwegian-Icelandic explorer who organized the first white settlements of Greenland, the mineral's locality + G or Dan *-it* -ite] : a mineral consisting of a silicate and phosphate of the cerium metals that is of uncertain composition and occurs in brown orthorhombic crystals

er·i·na·ceous \ˌerəˈnāshəs\ *adj* [L *erinaceus*, n., hedgehog, fr. *er* hedgehog + *-inaceus* (as in *gallinaceus* cock, fr. *gallinaceus* of a cock) — more at URCHIN, GALLINACEOUS] : like or relating to the hedgehog

er·i·na·ceus \ˌ==ˈ=sēəs, -sh(ē)əs\ *n, cap* [NL, fr. L, hedgehog] : a genus (the type of the family Erinaceidae) of Old World spiny-coated mammals consisting of the true hedgehogs

erin·e·um \əˈrinēəm\ *n, pl* **erin·ea** \-ēə\ *or* **erineums** [NL, fr. Gk *erineon, erineum*, neut. of *erineos, eirineos* woolen, fr. *erion, eirion* wool, dim. of *eiros* fleece] : an abnormal felty growth of hairs from the leaf epidermis of plants caused by various mites

erineum mite *n* : any of various mites chiefly of the family Eriophyidae that feed on plants and induce the formation of erinea

er·in·ite \ˈerəˌnīt\ *n* -S [*Erin* Ireland + E *-ite*] : a mineral $Cu_5(OH)_4(AsO_4)_2$ consisting of emerald-green basic copper arsenate

er·i·nose \ˈerəˌnōs\ *n* -S [NL *erineum* + E *-ose*] **1 :** a disease of plants (as grape, walnut, mountain maple) characterized by the presence of erinea **2 :** ERINEUM

erio- *comb form* [Gk *erio-, eirio-*, fr. *erion, eirion*] : wool ⟨*Eriogonum*⟩ ⟨*eriometer*⟩

er·i·o·bot·rya \ˌerēōˈbäˌtrēə\ *n, cap* [NL, fr. *erio-* + *-botrya* (fr. Gk *botrys* bunch of grapes)] : a small genus of Asiatic evergreen trees (family Rosaceae) having paniculate white flowers and a fruit with large seeds and a thin endocarp — see LOQUAT 1

er·i·o·cau·la·ce·ae \-ōˌkȯˈlāsēˌē\ *n pl, cap* [NL, fr. *Eriocaulon*, type genus + *-aceae*] : a family of chiefly tropical monocotyledonous aquatic or bog herbs (order Xyridales) having clustered or tufted linear leaves and minute flowers in dense heads — **er·i·o·cau·la·ceous** \ˌ===ˈ=shəs\ *adj*

er·i·o·cau·lon \ˌ===ˈkōˌlän\ *n* [NL, fr. *erio-* + *-caulon* (fr. Gk *kaulos* stalk, stem) — more at HOLE] : a genus (the type of the family Eriocaulaceae) of widely distributed acaulescent herbs having flowers with glandular petals and 4 to 6 stamens

er·i·o·chalcite \ˌ===+\ *n* [*erio-* + *chalcite*] : a mineral $CuCl_2.2H_2O$ consisting of hydrous copper chloride

er·i·o·coc·ci·dae \ˌ===ˈkäk(s)əˌdē\ [NL, fr. *Eriococcus* (fr. *erio-* + *Coccus*) + *-idae*] *syn of* PSEUDOCOCCIDAE

er·i·o·dic·ty·ol \ˌ===ˈdiktēˌōl, -ˌȯl\ *n* -S [*eriodictyon* + *-ol*] : a colorless crystalline compound $C_{15}H_{12}O_6$ derived from flavanone and found esp. in the leaves of some resinous shrubs of the genus *Eriodictyon* — see CITRIN, HESPERITIN

er·i·o·dic·ty·on \-ēˌän\ *n* [NL, fr. *erio-* + Gk *diktyon* net, fr. *dikein* to throw; fr. the woolly netlike leaves] **1** *cap* : a small genus of resinous shrubs (family Hydrophyllaceae) of southwestern No. America having finely reticulated leaves often woolly beneath and white or bluish flowers in scorpioid cymes — see YERBA SANTA **2** -S : any plant of the genus *Eriodictyon*

er·i·og·o·num \ˌerēˈägənəm\ *n* [NL, fr. *erio-* + *-gonum* (fr. Gk *gony* knee); fr. the woolly stems of some species — more at KNEE] **1** *cap* : a genus of No. American herbs (family Polygonaceae) with small clustered flowers subtended by an involucre **2** -S : any plant of the genus *Eriogonum*

er·i·om·e·ter \ˌerēˈäməd-ə(r)\ *n* [*erio-* + *-meter*] : an instrument for measuring the diameters of minute particles or fibers from the size of the colored diffraction rings or fringes produced by them in monochromatic light

er·i·o·nite \ˈerēəˌnīt\ *n* -S [Gk *erion* wool + E *-ite* — more at ERINEUM] : a mineral $NaKCaAl_4Si_{12}O_{32}.12H_2O$ consisting of zeolitic aluminosilicate of sodium, potassium, and calcium occurring in aggregates of orthorhombic fibrous white crystals resembling wool (sp. gr. 2)

er·i·oph·o·rum \ˌerēˈäfərəm\ *n* [NL, fr. *erio-* + *-phorum* (neut. of *-phorus*)] **1** *cap* : a genus of bog sedges (family Cyperaceae) characterized by cottony masses of spikelets, the perianth consisting of soft bristles **2** -S : any plant of the genus *Eriophorum* — called also *cotton grass*

er·i·oph·y·es \-fēˌēz\ *n, cap* [NL, fr. *erio-* + *-phyes* (fr. Gk *phyē* growth, stature)] : the type genus of Eriophyidae formerly containing a great number of gall and blister mites most of which are now placed in other genera

¹er·i·oph·y·id \-fēəd\ *adj* [NL *Eriophyidae*] : of or relating to the genus *Eriophyes* or the family Eriophyidae

²eriophyid \"\ *n* -S : an eriophyid mite

er·i·o·phy·i·dae \ˌerēōˈfīəˌdē\ *n pl, cap* [NL, fr. *Eriophyes*, type genus + *-idae*] : a large family of minute wormlike plant-feeding mites with two pairs of legs placed far anterior, lacking a respiratory system, some forming galls, others feeding on leaves and often causing blisters

er·i·o·phyl·lous \ˌerēōˈfiləs\ *adj* [ISV *erio-* + *-phyllous*] : having leaves with a cottony pubescence

er·i·o·so·mat·i·dae \ˌerē(ˌ)ōsəˈmad-əˌdē\ *n pl, cap* [NL, fr. *Eriosomat-, Eriosoma*, type genus (fr. *erio-* + *-somat-, -soma*) + *-idae*] : a family of plant lice having the cornicles reduced or absent and the wing venation simplified and including forms that cause leaf rolling and distortion of host growth and often produce quantities of woolly wax (as the woolly apple aphid)

eris·ma·tu·ra \əˌrizməˈtürə, -məˈtyürə\ *n* -S [NL *Erismatura* former genus of birds containing the ruddy duck, fr. Gk *ereismat-, ereisma* prop, support (fr. *ereisis* propping, supporting, fr. *ereidein* to prop, support) + NL *-ura*] : RUDDY DUCK

eris·ta·lis \əˈristələs\ *n, cap* [NL] : a genus of large syrphid flies having larvae of the rat-tailed type and including the drone fly (*E. tenax*) — compare RAT-TAILED LARVA

¹eris·tic \əˈristik, (ˈ)eˌr-, -tēk\ *also* **eris·ti·cal** \-təkəl, -tēk-\ *adj* [Gk *eristikos* fond of wrangling, fr. *eristos* (verbal of *erizein* to wrangle, vie with, fr. *eris* quarrel, strife) + *-ikos* -ic, -ical] : characterized by disputatious often subtle and specious reasoning (as in argument) ⟨not . . . in any ~ temper, but in order to increase mutual understanding, desiring to get as well as to give —Walter Moberly⟩ — compare APODICTIC, CONTROVERSIAL, DIALECTICAL — **eris·ti·cal·ly** \-tək(ə)lē, -tēk-, -li\ *adv*

²eristic \"\ *n* -S **1 :** a person devoted to logical disputation : CONTROVERSIALIST; *specif* : a Megarian philosopher **2 :** the art or practice of disputation and polemics (as in Aristotelian logic) esp. as based on specious grounds ⟨a kind of ~, training the student to use the processes of thought and their expression . . . to attain an end, commonly argumentative —H.O.Taylor⟩

erith·a·cus \əˈrithəkəs\ *n, cap* [NL, fr. Gk *erithakos*, a bird, probably the robin] : a genus of Old World thrushes including the European robin and various related Asiatic birds

er·i·trea \ˌerəˈtrēə, -trāə\ *adj, usu cap* [fr. *Eritrea*, country in northeastern Africa] : of or from Eritrea : of the kind or style prevalent in Eritrea

er·i·tre·an \ˌ==ˈ=ən\ *adj, usu cap* [*Eritrea* + E *-an*] : of or relating to Eritrea

erivan *usu cap, var of* YEREVAN

eri·zo \əˈrē(ˌ)zō, -ˌsō\ *n* -S [Sp, lit., hedgehog, fr. L *ericius* — more at URCHIN] **1 :** any of several porcupine fishes **2** [AmerSp, fr. Sp] **a :** the strong bast fiber of a So. American timber tree (*Apeiba tibourbou*) of the family Tiliaceae **b :** the tree that yields erizo

erk \ˈərk, ˈək\ *n* -S [alter. of *airc*, short for *aircraftsman*] *Brit* : a member of the lowest rank in the Royal Air Force (as on the ground crew) : AIRCRAFTSMAN

er·len·mey·er flask \ˈərlənˌmī(ə)r-, ˈerl\|\ *n, usu cap E* [after Emil *Erlenmeyer* †1909 Ger. chemist] : a flat-bottomed conical flask whose shape allows the contents to be shaken laterally without danger of spilling

Erlenmeyer flask

erm *abbr* ermine

er·me·lin \ˈərməlǝn\ *n* -S [prob. modif. (influenced by *ermine*) of G *hermelin*, fr. MHG *hermelīn*, fr. OHG *harmilī* weasel, dim. of *harmo* — more at ERMINE] *archaic* : ERMINE

er·mi·line \-ˌlēn, -lən\ *n* -S [alter. of *ermelin*] : white rabbit fur processed to simulate ermine

¹er·mine \ˈərmən, ˈəm-, ˈəim-\ *n* -S *see sense 1* [ME, fr. OF *ermine, hermine*, modif. (influenced by *ermin, hermin* Armenian, fr. L *Armenius*) of a Gmc word akin to OE *hearma* weasel, OS & OHG *harmo* weasel; akin to Rhaeto-Romanic *carmún* weasel, Lith *šarmuõ, šermuõ* weasel, and perh. to OHG *hornunc* February, ON *hjarn* frozen snow, Lith *širvas* gray; basic meaning: gray, white] **1** *or pl* **ermine** : any of several weasels that assume white winter pelage usu. with more or less black on the tail: **a :** a large European weasel (*Mustela erminea*) — called also *stoat* **b :** LEAST WEASEL **c :** any of the more northerly dwelling forms of the long-tailed weasel; *esp* : NEW YORK WEASEL **2 a :** the fine white fur of the ermine in winter pelage prized for ornament (as on the official robes of judges and peers) **b :** a trimming or garment made of ermine **3 :** a rank (as of a king or lord) or office (as of a judge) of which the ceremonial or official robe is ornamented with ermine emblematic of authority and dignity or of purity and honor **4 a :** a heraldic fur consisting of black spots of one of various conventional shapes representing ermine tails set on a white field **b :** any of the heraldic furs having ermine spots — see ERMINES, ERMINITES, ERMINOIS, PEAN

ermine 4a

²ermine \"\ *adj* [ME, fr. MF *ermin, ermine, hermin, hermine*, fr. *ermine, hermine*, n.] **1 a :** of or relating to the ermine or its fur **b :** of the heraldic fur ermine — abbr. *erm.* **2 :** pure white

er·mined \-nd\ *adj* [ME, fr. *ermine* + *-ed*] **1 :** trimmed or lined with ermine ⟨a robe with ~ sleeves⟩ **2 a :** clothed in an ermined robe (as a judge or peer) **b :** made a judge or peer ⟨a newly ~ Labourite⟩ **3 :** having heraldic ermine spots of the tincture specified ⟨a roundel sable ~ argent⟩

ermine moth *n* **1 :** any of several small white moths (genus *Yponomeuta* and esp. *Y. padella*) with black spots suggesting ermine **2 :** any of various rather large moths of the family Arctiidae with markings suggesting ermine

¹er·mines \-nz\ *also* **er·mi·nees** \ˈ=məˌnēz\ *n* [irreg. fr. ¹*ermine*] : a heraldic fur consisting of white ermine spots on a black field

²ermines \"\ *adj* : of the heraldic fur ermines

ermine spot *n* : a heraldic representation of an ermine tail

er·min·ette \ˌ=məˈnet\ *n* -S [¹*ermine* + *-ette*] : rabbit fur processed to simulate ermine

er·min·ites \ˈ=məˌnīts\ *n* [MF *erminite, herminite*, fr. *ermine, hermine*] : a heraldic fur consisting of black ermine spots with a red hair on each side on a white field

¹er·mi·nois \ˌ=məˈnȯiz\ *n* [MF *erminois, herminois*, fr. *ermine, hermine*] : a heraldic fur consisting of black ermine spots on a golden field

²erminois \"\ *adj* : of the heraldic fur erminois

erne *or* **ern** \ˈərn, ˈe(ə)rn\ *n* -S [ME *ern* eagle, fr. OE *earn*; akin to OHG *aro, arn* eagle, ON *ari, ǫrn*, Goth *ara*, OIr *irar* eagle, Gk *ornis* bird, Lith *erēlis* eagle, Arm *oror* seagull] : EAGLE; *esp* : WHITE-TAILED SEA EAGLE

erode \əˈrōd, ēˈ-\ *vb* -ED/-ING/-S [L *erodere* to erode, fr. *e-* + *rodere* to gnaw — more at RAT] *vt* **1 :** to diminish or destroy by degrees : eat into or away: **a :** to eat into or away by slow destruction of substance (as by acid, infection, or cancer) : CORRODE ⟨acids that ~ the teeth⟩ ⟨cancer had *eroded* the bone⟩ **b** (1) : to wear down or away by separation of small particles ⟨friction ~s the moving parts of machinery⟩ : rub or scrape away; *specif* : to remove with an abrasive ⟨a dental tool that quickly ~s the decayed tooth area⟩ (2) : to wear away (as land) by the action of water, wind, or glacial ice ⟨drainage quickly ~s the fine soil of the plowed hillside⟩ ⟨a mountain range that has been *eroded* into low hills⟩ **c :** to cause to deteriorate or disappear as if by eating or wearing away : destroy by degrees ⟨his commitment to a world of conferences . . . and agitation has *eroded* his family life —Anthony West⟩ : WEAR ⟨the institution is *eroded* away . . . person by person —R.T.LaPiere⟩ : IMPAIR ⟨~ the purchasing power of wages⟩ : UNDERMINE ⟨repeated compromises that ~ the basic principle of freedom of worship⟩ **2 :** to produce or form by eroding ⟨glaciers ~ U-shaped valleys⟩ ~ *vi* **1 :** to undergo erosion (as by weathering) ⟨where the land has *eroded* away⟩ **2 :** to deteriorate or disappear as if by eating or wearing away ⟨when the rights of any . . . are chipped away the freedom of all ~s —Earl Warren⟩ ⟨his regional accent has nearly *eroded*⟩

eroded *adj* **1 :** marked by or subject to erosion **2 :** EROSE

erod·ibil·i·ty *also* **erod·abil·i·ty** \ə=ˌrōdəˈbiləd-ē\ *n* -ES : the quality or degree of being erodible; *esp* : rate of soil erosion ⟨the ~ of soils varies with their composition⟩

erod·ible *also* **erod·able** \əˈrōdəbəl\ *adj* : capable of or subject to being eroded (as by action of water and wind) ⟨~ soils⟩ ⟨~ parts of the channel⟩

ero·di·um \-dēəm\ *n* [NL, fr. Gk *erōdios* heron; fr. the long-beaked fruit — more at ARDEA] **1** *cap* : a large genus of herbs (family Geraniaceae) having pinnate or pinnatifid leaves, small flowers, and long bearded twisted tails on the carpels — see ALFILARIA **2** -S : any plant of the genus *Erodium* — called also *heron's-bill, storksbill*

erog·e·ne·i·ty \əˌräjəˈnēəd·ē, ˌerˌr-, (ˌ)eˌr-; ˌerəjə-\ *n* -ES [*erogenous* + *-eity* (as in *homogeneity*)] : the quality of being erogenous ⟨the ~ of the lips⟩

ero·genesis \ˌerə+\ *n* [NL, fr. Gk *erōs* sexual love + NL *-genesis*] : EROTOGENESIS

erog·e·nous \əˈräjənəs, ēˈr-, (ˈ)eˈr-\ *also* **er·o·gen·ic** \ˌerəˈjenik\ *adj* [Gk *erōs* + E *-genous, -genic*] **1 :** producing sexual excitement or libidinal gratification when stimulated **:** sexually sensitive ⟨~ zones of the human skin⟩ **2 :** of or arousing sexual feelings **:** sexually stimulating ⟨~ pleasure⟩ ⟨an ~ quality⟩

erog·e·ny \əˈräjənē, ēˈr-, eˈr-\ *n* -ES [Gk *erōs* + E *-geny*] **:** EROTOGENESIS

eros \ˈeˌräs, ˈiˌ-, ˈēˌ-, ˈāˌ-; ˈirəs\ *n* -ES *see sense 1* [Gk *erōs* sexual love; akin to Gk *erasthai* to love, desire ardently] **1** *pl also* **ero·tes** \əˈrōˌtēz, ēˈr-,eˈr-\ *usu cap* [fr. *Eros*, Greek god of love, fr. Gk *Erōs*, fr. *erōs* sexual love] **:** CHERUB 3, CUPID **2 a** *usu cap* **:** the aggregate of pleasure-directed life instincts whose energy is derived from libido — contrasted with *Thanatos* **b** *often cap* **:** aspiring self-fulfilling love often having a sensuous quality **:** DESIRE, YEARNING ⟨animated by the true scientific ~ . . . for the task of scientific investigation —C.S.Peirce⟩ ⟨~ . . . calculates its relations to others from the standpoint of its own need of others —Reinhold Niebuhr⟩ — compare AGAPE

erose \əˈrōs, ēˈ-\ *adj* [L *erosus*, past part.] **:** IRREGULAR, UNEVEN; *specif, bot* **:** having the margin irregularly notched as if gnawed — **erose·ly** *adv*

ero·si·bil·i·ty \əˌrōzəˈbilədē, ēˌr-\ *n* -ES **:** ERODIBILITY

ero·si·ble \əˈ==zəbəl\ *adj* [*erosion* + *-ible*] **:** ERODIBLE

ero·sion \əˈrōzhən, ēˈ-\ *n* -S [MF, fr. L *erosion-, erosio*, fr. *erosus* (past part. of *erodere* to erode) + *-ion-, -io* -ion — more at ERODE] **1 a** (1) **:** the superficial destruction of a surface area of tissue (as mucous membrane) by inflammation, ulceration, or trauma ⟨~ of the uterine cervix⟩ ⟨gizzard ~ in chicks⟩ (2) **:** progressive loss of the hard substance of a tooth **b :** CORROSION 1a **2 a :** the general process whereby materials of the earth's crust are worn away and removed by natural agencies including weathering, solution, corrasion, and transportation; *specif* **:** land destruction and simultaneous removal of particles (as of soil) by running water, waves and currents, moving ice, or wind ⟨stream ~⟩ ⟨glacial ~⟩ — compare DENUDATION **b :** surface destruction of a metal or refractory material effected by the abrasive or the corrosive and abrasive action of a moving liquid or gas and often accelerated by solid particles in suspension ⟨range errors due to gun ~⟩ ⟨severe ~ of the furnace lining caused by the scouring motion of molten slag⟩ **c :** even disintegration of a paint surface caused by chalking and washing away **3 :** an instance or product of erosion ⟨a circular ~ on the skin half an inch in diameter⟩ ⟨a canyon with red tower-shaped ~*s*⟩ **4 :** progressive impairment or destruction as if by eating or wearing away (as of resources, strength, or effectiveness) **:** DEPLETION, DETERIORATION ⟨~ of real earnings by inflation⟩ ⟨the great ideals of liberty and equality are preserved against . . . the ~ of small encroachments —B.N. Cardozo⟩

ero·sion·al \-zhənᵊl,-zhnəl\ *adj* **:** of, relating to, or produced by erosion ⟨the ~ and depositional work of the ocean⟩ ⟨~ materials on the valley floor⟩

erosion cycle *n* **:** the succession of stages through which a newly uplifted land mass must pass before it is worn down to a peneplain or a surface near sea level including juvenile stages in which the original surface is sharply cut by canyons, mature stages in which the original surface may disappear and the topography be characterized by high steep hills and fairly open valleys, and old-age stages in which the land is so worn down that the streams meander sluggishly across a lowland

ero·sion·ist \-zhənəst\ *n* -S **:** a supporter of the now obsolete theory that the contour of the land is mainly the result of erosion

erosion pavement *n* **:** a surficial concentration of pebbles and rock fragments tending to protect the underlying soil from further erosion

erosion remnant *n* **:** a feature of the landscape standing above the general level to which erosion has reduced its surroundings ⟨as the shoreline is cut landward stacks, caves, islands, and other typical *erosion remnants* may be left standing —P.G. Worcester⟩

erosion surface *n* **:** a surface generally of low relief shaped by erosion — compare PENEPLAIN, UNCONFORMITY

ero·sive \əˈrōs|iv, ēˈ-, -ōz|, |ēv *also* |əv\ *adj* [L *erosus* + E *-ive*] **1 :** tending to erode **:** effecting erosion ⟨nervous fussing and fretting . . . exercise upon the character an ~ effect —Osbert Sitwell⟩ **:** ERODIBLE ⟨dangerously ~ soil⟩ **2 :** soil-exposing ⟨alternate ~ with soil-protecting crops⟩

ero·sive·ness \-vnəs\ *or* **ero·siv·i·ty** \əˌrōˈsivədē, (ˌ)ēˌr-\ *n* -ES **1 :** the quality or degree of effecting erosion **:** the power of eroding ⟨the greater ~ of water on steep slopes⟩ **2 :** ERODIBILITY

erosive stomatitis *n* **:** VESICULAR STOMATITIS

erotes *pl of* EROS

¹erot·ic \əˈräd·|ik, ēˈ-,eˈ-, -ät|, |ēk\ *also* **erot·i·cal** \|əkəl, |ēk-\ *adj* [F & Gk; F *érotique*, fr. Gk *erōtikos*, fr. *erōt-, erōs* sexual love + *-ikos* -ic, -ical — more at EROS] **1 :** of, devoted to, or tending to arouse sexual love or desire: as **a :** treating of or depicting sexual love (as by sensuous or voluptuous description) **:** AMATORY ⟨a poem ~ rather than lyric that delights in feminine beauty and amorous feelings⟩ ⟨~ folk dances depicting courtship with mock teasing and coaxing⟩ **b :** tending to excite sexual pleasure or desire ⟨~ dreams⟩ ⟨the ~ power of perfume⟩ **c :** directed toward sexual gratification ⟨his ~ adventures with prostitutes⟩ ⟨a personality with strong ~ drives⟩ **d :** strongly affected by sexual desire ⟨an ~ person⟩ **2 :** of or relating to eros ⟨the dominance of the ~ over the death instinct⟩ — **erot·i·cal·ly** \|ək(ə)lē, |ēk-, -li\ *adv*

²erotic \"\ *n* -S **1 :** a theory or doctrine of love ⟨developed a mystical ~⟩ **2 :** an erotic person ⟨sex-filled paperbacks suggesting the prevalence of ~*s*⟩

erot·i·ca \|əkə\ *n pl* [NL, fr. Gk *erōtika*, pl. of *erōtikos*] **:** literary or artistic items having an erotic theme; *esp* **:** books treating of sexual love in a sensuous or voluptuous manner — compare PORNOGRAPHY

erot·i·cism \|əˌsizəm\ *also* **er·o·tism** \ˈerəˌtizəm\ *n* -S **1 :** the arousal of or the attempt to arouse sexual feeling by means of suggestion, symbolism, or allusion in an art form **2 a :** a state of sexual arousal or anticipation (as from stimulation of erogenous zones) **3 a :** sexual impulse or desire ⟨the robust *erotisms* that stir deeply in the very autonomic nervous system of the normal individual —Weston La Barre⟩ **b :** abnormally insistent sexual passion

erot·i·cize \əˈräd·əˌsīz, ēˈr-,eˈr-, -ätə-\ *vt* -ED/-ING/-S **:** to render erotic ⟨a film version that ~*s* the original story⟩

er·o·ti·za·tion \ˌerəd·əˈzāshən, -rəˌtīˈz-\ *n* -S **1 :** the act or process of erotizing **2 :** the state of being erotized

er·o·tize \ˈerəˌtīz\ *vt* -ED/-ING/-S **:** to invest with erotic significance or sexual feeling ⟨a highly ambivalent and *erotized* attachment to a mother —Adelaide Johnson & Dora Fishback⟩

eroto- *comb form* [NL, fr. Gk *erōto-*, fr. *erōt-, erōs* sexual love — more at EROS] **:** sexual desire ⟨*erotomania*⟩

ero·to·genesis \əˌrōd·ə, ēˌr-,eˌr-, -räd·ə+\ *n* [NL, fr. *eroto-* + *-genesis*] **:** arousal of sexual feeling

ero·to·gen·ic \ˌ=ˌ==+ˈjenik\ *adj* [*eroto-* + *-genic*] **:** EROGENOUS

ero·to·ge·nic·i·ty \=ˌ===+jəˈnisədē\ *n* -ES **:** EROGENEITY

ero·to·ma·nia \=ˌ==+ˈmānēə\ *n* [NL, fr. *eroto-* + *-mania*] **:** excessive sexual desire esp. as a symptom of mental disorder — **ero·to·ma·ni·ac** \-ēˌak\ *n*

ero·to·path \=ˈ===+ˌpath\ *n* -S [*eroto-* + *-path*] **:** one affected with erotopathy

er·o·top·a·thy \ˌerəˈtäpəthē\ *n* -ES [*eroto-* + *-pathy*] **:** an abnormality of sexual desire

erot·y·lid \əˈräd·ᵊlˌid, -räd-\ *n* -S [NL *Erotylidae*] **:** a beetle of the family Erotylidae

er·o·tyl·i·dae \ˌerəˈtiləˌdē\ *n pl, cap* [NL, fr. *Erotylus*, type genus (fr. Gk *erōtylos* darling, sweetheart, fr. *erōt-, erōs* sexual love) + *-idae* — more at EROS] **:** a family of elongate oval hairy beetles having larvae that live in fungi or bore in higher plants

er·pe·to·ich·thys \ˌərpəˌtōˈikthəs\ *n, cap* [NL, irreg. fr. *herpet-* + Gk *ichthys* fish — more at ICHTHUS] **:** a genus of fishes (order Cladistia) that contains only the African reedfish and is often isolated from the related genus *Polypterus* in a monotypic family

err *R* ˈe(ə)r, ˈər (+V ˈər·) *sometimes* ˈa(ə)r; *–R* ˈeə (+*suffixal vowel* ˈer, +*vowel in a following word* ˈər *or* ˈeə), ə̄ (+*suffixal vowel* ˈər· *also* ˈər, +*vowel in a following word* ˈər· *or* ˈə̄ *also* ˈər)\ *vi* -ED/-ING/-S [ME *erren*, fr. OF *errer*, fr. L *errare*; akin to OE *ierre, yrre* wandering, angry, *iersian* to be angry, OHG *irri* gone astray, angry, *irrōn* to go astray, OS *irri* angry, Goth *airzeis* led astray, deceived, ON *rās* race — more at RACE] **1** *archaic* **a :** to turn aside from the proper path **:** STRAY ⟨all we as sheep ~*ed* —John Wyclif⟩ **b :** to go about aimlessly **:** WANDER, ROAM **2 :** to deviate from a standard (as of wisdom, morality, accuracy) **:** be or do wrong: as **a :** to make a mistake ⟨~*ed* on the side of caution in judging the supplies inadequate⟩ **b :** to violate an accepted standard of conduct **:** SIN, OFFEND ⟨if you ~ and do not observe all these commandments which the Lord has spoken —Num 15:22 (RSV)⟩ **c :** to be inaccurate ⟨a gauge that must not ~ by more than 0.01 mm.⟩

err·abil·i·ty \ˌerəˈbilədē, ˌərə- *sometimes* ˌarə- *or* ˌə̄rə-\ *n* -ES **:** liability to error

err·able \ˈ==bəl\ *adj* **:** liable to error **:** FALLIBLE

er·ran·cy \ˈerənsē, -si *sometimes* ˈərə- *or* ˈarə- *or* ˈə̄rə-\ *n* -ES **:** a state, practice, or instance of erring ⟨denies the ~ of scripture⟩ ⟨the boy's ~ consisted of pranks⟩ ⟨his first ~ from the straight and narrow path —S.H.Adams⟩

er·rand \ˈerənd\ *n* -S [ME *erend* message, business, fr. OE *ǣrend*; akin to OE *ār* messenger, OS *ēr* messenger, OHG *ārunti* message, ON *eyrendi, erendi, ōrendi* message, *ārr* messenger, Goth *airus*] **1** *archaic* **:** an oral message entrusted to a person ⟨tell your king from me this ~ —Richard Stanyhurst⟩ **2 :** a trip made in order to deliver a message or purchase or attend to something ⟨gone to the shopping center on an ~⟩ ⟨run an ~ for his employer⟩ **3 a** *archaic* **:** MISSION, EMBASSY **b :** the object or purpose of a short trip ⟨do several ~*s* of my own in town⟩ **c :** a service, favor, or piece of business undertaken for another ⟨running ~*s* for his mother⟩

¹er·rant \ˈerənt *sometimes* ˈərə- *or* ˈarə- *or* ˈə̄rə-\ *adj* [ME *erraunt*, fr. MF *errant*, pres. part. of *errer* to travel, wander (fr. ML *iterare*, fr. *iter* way, journey) & *errer* to err — more at EYRE, ERR] **1 a :** traveling or given to traveling (as on a mission of chivalry) ⟨an ~ knight⟩ ⟨~ those exiles . . . who with their burden traverse hill and dale —William Wordsworth⟩; *specif* **:** itinerant in an official capacity ⟨~ officials who traveled a quarterly circuit⟩ **b :** quixotically adventurous ⟨her temerity in such an ~ undertaking —Thomas Hardy⟩ **2** *obs* **:** ARRANT 2a ⟨he is so ~ a whig that he strains even beyond his author in his passion for liberty —Henry Cromwell⟩ **3 a :** straying outside the proper path or bounds ⟨in this labyrinth of tunnels the farmer found his ~ pigs —*Amer. Guide Series: Minn.*⟩ **b :** moving about aimlessly or irregularly **:** WANDERING ⟨an ~ breeze⟩; *specif* **:** having an irregular course — used formerly in astronomy to distinguish a planet from a star ⟨seven . . . ~ stars in the lower orbs of heaven —Sir Thomas Browne⟩ **c :** deviating from a standard (as of behavior) **:** ERRING ⟨a parent scolding an ~ child⟩ **d :** liable or inclined to error **:** FALLIBLE ⟨his instincts being basically sound but like those of all natural men somewhat ~ —Gilbert Millstein⟩ **4 :** of or relating to the Errantia — **er·rant·ly** *adv*

²errant \"\ *n* -S **:** one that is errant ⟨separates the one-time ~ from the long-term philanderer —*Time*⟩; *specif* **:** KNIGHT-ERRANT

er·ran·tia \eˈranch(ē)ə, -ntēə\ *n pl, cap* [NL, fr. L, neut. pl. of *errant-, errans*, pres. part. of *errare* to wander, err — more at ERR] *in some classifications* **:** a division of Polychaeta comprising free-swimming worms (as those of the genera *Aphrodite, Nereis*, and *Polynoe*) usu. with well-developed parapodia and sense organs and without special respiratory structures

er·rant·ry \ˈerəntrē, -ri *sometimes* ˈərə- *or* ˈarə- *or* ˈə̄rə-\ *n* -ES **:** WANDERING; *esp* **:** a roving in quest of knightly adventure ⟨set out on their tour with a sense of ~⟩

er·ra·ta \eˈrä|d·ə, əˈr-, -rā|, |tə *also* -ra| *or* -rä|\ *n* -S [fr. pl. of *erratum*] **1 :** ERRATUM **2 :** a list of corrigenda or a page bearing such a list

¹er·rat·ic \əˈrad·|ik, (ˈ)eˈr-, ēˈr-, -at|, |ēk\ *also* **er·rat·i·cal** \|əkəl, |ēk-\ *adj* [*erratic* fr. ME *erratik*, fr. MF or L; MF *erratique*, fr. L *erraticus*, fr. *erratus* (past part. of *errare* to wander, err) + *-icus* -ic; *erratical* fr. *erratic* + *-al* — more at ERR] **1 a :** having no fixed course **:** WANDERING ⟨an ~ comet⟩ **b** *archaic* **:** having no fixed residence **:** NOMADIC ⟨those savages although ~ must remain long enough in one position to cultivate this grain —Z.M.Pike⟩ **2 :** transported by a glacier from an original resting place ⟨~ boulder⟩ ⟨~ block⟩ **3 a :** characterized by lack of consistency, regularity, or uniformity **:** UNPREDICTABLE, CAPRICIOUS ⟨~ as an unroped steer —*New Republic*⟩ **:** FLUCTUATING ⟨the hog market was ~ but pork remained steady⟩ **:** UNEVEN ⟨the pitcher showed ~ control, throwing too many wild pitches⟩; *specif* **:** marked by irregular changes of direction ⟨the ~ course of the river⟩ ⟨streets that run at ~ angles⟩ **b :** deviating from what is ordinary or standard (as in nature, behavior, or opinion) **:** ODD, ECCENTRIC ⟨the key to the code was the ~ punctuation⟩ ⟨he must have been . . . scandalously ~ from the Puritan point of view —*Amer. Guide Series: Mass.*⟩ **syn** see STRANGE

²erratic \"\ *n* -S **:** one that is erratic ⟨we have ~*s*, unscholarly foolish persons —Joseph Cook⟩; *specif* **:** an erratic boulder or block of rock

er·rat·i·cal·ly \|ək(ə)lē, |ēk-, -li\ *adv* **:** in an erratic manner ⟨a tiny spark was glowing ~ upon the river —J.H.Wheelwright⟩

er·rat·i·cism \=ˈrad·əˌsizəm, =ˈratə,-\ *n* -S **:** a state or instance of being erratic; *esp* **:** a wayward act or tendency ⟨what ~*s* mere self-respect can lead to —Edwin Kennebeck⟩

er·ra·tum \eˈrä|d·əm, əˈr-, -rā|, |təm *also* -ra| *or* -rä|\ *n, pl* **erra·ta** \|d·ə, |tə\ [L, fr. neut. of *erratus*, past part.] **1** *archaic* **:** an error (as a misstatement or misprint) in something published or written **2 :** CORRIGENDUM ⟨the ~ directing its deletion was placed on the verso —J.H.Sledd & G.J.Kolb⟩ ⟨incorporating *errata* in text during reprinting —*Library Science Abstracts*⟩

erred *past of* ERR

¹er·rhine \ˈeˌrīn\ *n* -S [Gk *errhinon*, fr. *er-* (fr. *en-* ²en-) + *-rhinon* (fr. *rhin-, rhis* nose) — more at RHIN-] **:** STERNUTATOR

²errhine \"\ *adj* [Gk *errhinos*, fr. *er-* + *-rhinos* (fr. *rhin-, rhis*)] **:** STERNUTATORY

erring *adj* [ME, fr. pres. part. of *erren* to err — more at ERR] **:** that errs (as in behavior) ⟨extend to ~ youth the same legal protection as adult delinquents have⟩; *specif* **:** ADULTEROUS ⟨an ~ wife⟩ — **err·ing·ly** *adv*

er·ro·neous \əˈrōnēəs, eˈr- *also* -nyəs\ *adj* [ME, fr. L *erroneus*, fr. *errare* to err — more at ERR] **1** *archaic* **:** moving about irregularly or aimlessly **:** WANDERING ⟨on the . . . field I fall ~, there to wander —John Milton⟩ **2 :** deviating from what is true, correct, right, or wise: **a :** being or containing an error **:** FALLACIOUS, MISTAKEN, INACCURATE ⟨an ~ doctrine⟩ ⟨received an ~ impression⟩ ⟨a stamp collection of ~ issues⟩ **b :** characterized by error **:** ERRING ⟨our own sad species . . . lapsed and ~ humanity —L.P.Smith⟩ — **er·ro·neous·ly** *adv* — **er·ro·neous·ness** *n* -ES

er·ror \ˈerə(r) *sometimes* ˈeˌrō(ə)r *or* -ō(ə)\ *n* -S [ME *errour*, fr. OF *error, errour*, fr. L *error*, fr. *errare* to err] **1 a :** an act or condition of often ignorant or imprudent deviation from a code of behavior **:** violation of ritual holiness, moral rectitude, or social convention **:** SIN ⟨entice with licentious passions of the flesh men who have barely escaped from . . . ~ —2 Pet 2:18 (RSV)⟩ **:** OFFENSE, FAULT ⟨the official's ~*s* of nepotism and acceptance of large gifts from lobbyists⟩ **b :** an act involving an unintentional deviation from truth or accuracy **:** a mistake in perception, reasoning, recollection, or expression ⟨made an ~ in adding up the bill⟩ ⟨gunnery ~*s*⟩ **c :** an act that through ignorance, deficiency, or accident departs from or fails to achieve what should be done ⟨got lost when he made the ~ of turning left at the fork⟩ ⟨an ~ of judgment⟩ ⟨the ~ of writing last year's date early in January⟩: as (1) **:** a misplay (as a fumble or a wild throw) by a baseball player when normal play would have resulted in an out or prevented an advance by a base runner — not used of a passed ball or wild pitch ⟨an ~ is charged against a fielder at the discretion of the official scorer⟩ (2) **:** a failure in bowling to make a spare when the previous ball left no split (3) **:** a failure in a racket game to return the ball to the opponent's court after touching it with the racket (as in tennis by hitting it into the net or outside the court) **d** (1) **:** a mistake in the proceedings of a court of record in matters of law or of fact (2) **:** WRIT OF ERROR (3) **:** proceedings for a writ of error **2 a :** the quality or state of erring; *esp* **:** the act of believing or of setting forth what is not true ⟨the firm is in ~ as to the facts of the case⟩ ⟨the map is in ~ regarding the junction⟩ **b** *Christian Science* **:** illusion about the nature of reality that is the cause of human suffering **:** the contradiction of truth ⟨~ is a supposition that pleasure and pain, that intelligence, substance, life are existent in matter —Mary B. Eddy⟩ **c :** an instance of false belief **:** a mistaken idea or system of ideas ⟨an opposite ~ . . . is the belief that children are naturally virtuous —Bertrand Russell⟩ **d :** the body of false beliefs **:** FALSEHOOD ⟨hope to reduce ~ by promoting education⟩ **3 :** something (as a misstatement or misprint) produced by mistake ⟨a typographical ~⟩; *specif* **:** a postage stamp released for use that shows flaw in its manufacture (as in differing in color or paper from others of its issue and denomination) **4** *archaic* **:** an irregular course **:** WANDERING ⟨brooks rolling with mazy ~ —John Milton⟩ **5 a** *math* **:** the difference between an observed or calculated value of a quantity and the true value; *specif, statistics* **:** variation in the measurements, calculations, or observations of a quantity due to mistakes or to usu. uncontrollable factors — see PROBABLE ERROR, STANDARD ERROR **b** *in artillery fire* **:** the divergence of a point of impact from the center of impact in a dispersion of shots **:** the distance of a shot from the target **c :** the amount of deviation from a standard or specification ⟨weights used to determine the ~ of a scale⟩ ⟨the allowable ~ in milling a machine part is called its tolerance⟩ **6 :** a deficiency or imperfection in structure or function **:** DEFECT ⟨an ~ in vision may cause headaches⟩

syn MISTAKE, BLUNDER, SLIP, LAPSE, FAUX PAS, BULL, HOWLER, BONER: ERROR indicates a deviation from correct, sanctioned, approved belief, procedure, practice, or course ⟨the *errors* in their beliefs⟩ ⟨an *error* in reasoning⟩ ⟨it is a common *error* to speak of the doctrine of science when what is meant is naturalism —W.R.Inge⟩ ⟨an *error* in addition⟩ ⟨sent by *error* to the wrong department⟩ MISTAKE suggests a misunderstanding, wrong decision, or inadvertent wrong action; it may apply to the unimportant or momentary but does not always do so ⟨a *mistake* in reading the road map⟩ ⟨a *mistake* in admitting these students⟩ ⟨a *mistake* in copying the list⟩ BLUNDER may imply ignorance, stupidity, or culpable lack of foresight and care ⟨fortunate to be acquitted by a court-martial after he had made a tragic *blunder* and lost many of his own men —Peter Forster⟩ ⟨we usually call our *blunders mistakes* and our friends style our *mistakes blunders* —H.B. Wheatley⟩ SLIP may apply to a trivial readily forgivable mistake, inadvertence, or accident ⟨a *slip* of the pen⟩ ⟨a list such as a busy and not very well educated library clerk might make, with many *slips* and grammatical mistakes —R.W. Southern⟩ LAPSE may suggest forgetfulness, inattention, or weakness ⟨you gave natives bits to copy under all possible threats against *lapses* of accuracy, only to discover at the end that they had embroidered the work pleasantly to their own fancy —Mary Austin⟩ FAUX PAS now usu. indicates a social blunder as a violation of etiquette or an instance of tactlessness ⟨John and I, horrified, hustled him out before he could commit any further *faux pas* —S.H.Adams⟩ BULL usu. applies to a blunder marked by stupidity although it is often applied to a remark purposely contrived to contain an amusing incongruity ⟨the well-known *bull* stating that "one man is just as good as another — and sometimes more so"⟩ ⟨"the next train to Dublin has just gone", the stationmaster said and laughed at his own *bull*⟩ HOWLER usu. applies to a ludicrous blunder made through ignorance or dim-wittedness ⟨a schoolboy *howler* that turns the title "Intimations of Immortality" into "Imitations of Immorality"⟩ ⟨refused to go on a quiz show for fear he'd make *howlers*⟩ BONER suggests a blunder made through thoughtlessness as well as dim-wittedness ⟨made the *boner* of inviting his boss to dinner on the night his wife's bridge group was due to meet at his house⟩ ⟨pulled a real *boner* when he said the American Civil War was in the 18th century⟩

er·ror·ist \ˈerərəst\ *n* -S **:** one who holds to and propagates error

er·ror·less \ˈerə(r)ləs\ *adj* **:** done, played, or performed without an error ⟨an ~ baseball game⟩

error-measuring device *n, in automation and feedback controls* **:** the means by which departure is detected and measured for correction in the system

error of closure 1 : the ratio of the distance by which a survey fails to close to the perimeter of the tract surveyed **2 :** the sum of the angles of a traverse as measured minus the true sum required by geometry — called also *closing error*

error of estimate : an error made by using the equation of a regression line to estimate the values of the dependent variable from those of the independent variable

errs *pres 3d sing of* ERR

ers \ˈərs, ˈe(ə)rs\ *n* -ES [MF, fr. OProv, fr. LL *ervor-, ervus*, alter. of L *ervum*, prob. of non-IE origin like OS *erwit* pea, OHG *araweiz, arwiz*, ON *ertr* pea, Gk *orobos* chick-pea] **:** a vetch (*Vicia ervilia*) grown in Mediterranean and Asiatic countries as a forage plant and stock food — called also *kersenneh*

-ers *pl of* -ER

er·sar \erˈsär\ *n, pl* **er·sa·ri** \erˈsärē\ *usu cap* **:** one of a Turkoman people in Bukhara

¹er·satz \ˈerˌz|äts *sometimes* -ˌs| *or* |ats *or* =ˈ=\ *adj* [G *ersatz-*, fr. *ersatz*, n.] **1 :** SUBSTITUTE, SYNTHETIC ⟨~ flour . . . developed from sawdust and vegetable waste —Jackson Martindell⟩ ⟨construction will be largely with ~ materials, iron, steel, and copper being needed for armaments —*Newsweek*⟩ ⟨turn . . . any form of art into an ~ religion —W.K.Wimsatt⟩ **:** SIMULATED ⟨the model . . . nestles on ~ waves —*Newcastle (Australia) Morning Herald*⟩ **:** COUNTERFEIT ⟨since few dared talk about the real issue, there had to be an ~ issue —*New Republic*⟩ **2 :** of, relating to, or marked by the use of substitute products ⟨Germany's wartime ~ economy⟩

²ersatz \"\ *n* -ES [G, substitute, compensation, fr. MHG (Swiss dial.) *ersaz* commensurate punishment, fr. *ersetzen* to replace, fr. OHG *irsezzen*, fr. *ir-* (perfective prefix) + *sezzen* to set — more at ABEAR, SET] **1 :** an artificial replacement for a natural product ⟨rayon is an outstanding example of the ~ become . . . a synthetic textile fiber in its own right —*Economist*⟩ **:** a substitute differing in kind from and often inferior in quality to what it replaces **2 :** something similar in only a superficial or partial way to what it is represented to be **:** something not genuine ⟨a piece of poetic ~ offering sentimentalism for genuine feeling⟩ **3 :** the discovery and use of substitute products **:** SUBSTITUTION ⟨international trade . . . of little importance in a nation skilled in the art of ~ —K.E.Poole⟩

ersatz reserve *n* **:** a reserve of the German army (as in World War II) drawn upon when necessary to fill out regular units and made up of men not qualified for the regular army or the landwehr

¹erse \ˈərs\ *adj, usu cap* [ME (Sc dial.) *Erisch, Ersch*, var. of *Irish* — more at IRISH] **1 a :** of, relating to, or characteristic of the Gaelic-speaking people of Scotland **b :** of, relating to, or characteristic of the language of such people **2 :** Irish Gaelic

²erse \"\ *n* -S *usu cap* [ME (Sc dial.) *Erisch, Ersch*, fr. *Erisch, Ersch*, adj.] **1 :** Scottish Gaelic **2 :** Irish Gaelic

erst \ˈərst\ *adv* [ME *erest* earliest, soonest, first, formerly, fr. OE *ǣrest*, superlative of *ǣr* early, soon — more at ERE] *archaic* **:** FORMERLY

¹erstwhile \(ˈ)=ˈ=\ *adv* [*erst* + *while*] **:** in the past **:** FORMERLY: **a :** in a time past **:** of old **:** ONCE ⟨found an apartment house where ~ stood his childhood home⟩ **:** a short while since **:** of late **:** but now ⟨the school-bound child who it seems ~ wailed in your arms⟩ **b :** till then or now **:** PREVIOUSLY, HERETOFORE ⟨the new cheerfulness of the ~ unhappy man⟩

²erstwhile \ˈ=ˌ=\ *adj* **1 :** having been or existed at some past time **:** of the past **:** ONETIME, SOMETIME, FORMER ⟨the new manager was an ~ machinist who had risen to the top⟩

⟨deserted their ~ friends and allies⟩ **2 :** being, existing, or effective till then or now **:** PREVIOUS ⟨invading the ~ domain of the specialists⟩

er·te·bol·le \ˌertəˈbələ, -ˈbələ, -ˈbələ\ *adj, usu cap* [fr. *Ærtebølle*, town in Jutland, Denmark, where such mounds were found] **:** of or belonging to an Early Neolithic or Late Mesolithic culture in the Baltic region characterized by large kitchen middens, chipped stone tools, and crude pottery

erub *or* **eruv** \āˈrüv, ˈāˌrəv\ *n, pl* **eru·bin** *or* **eru·vin** \ārüˈvēn, āˈrüvin\ [Heb *ʿērūbh*] **:** a means (as a symbolic alteration of a boundary) provided in Jewish law for extending the strict limits anciently placed upon movements of persons and goods on the Sabbath and so accommodating the laws to the needs of daily life

er·u·bes·cent \ˌer(y)əˈbesᵊnt\ *adj* [L *erubescent-, erubescens*, pres. part. of *erubescere* to grow red, fr. *e-* + *rubescere* to grow red — more at RUBESCENT] **:** REDDENING

er·u·bes·cite \ˌ==ˈbeˌsīt\ *n* -S [L *erubescere* + E *-ite*] **:** BORNITE

eruc \əˈrük\ *n* -S [Tag *iruc*] **:** a cordage fiber derived from a Philippine palm (*Corypha elata*)

eru·ca \əˈrükə\ *n* [L, caterpillar, garden rocket, perh. fr. *er* hedgehog — more at URCHIN] **1** -S **:** CATERPILLAR **2** *cap* [NL, fr. L] **:** a small genus of Old World herbs (family Cruciferae) distinguished by a short 4-angled silique — see GARDEN ROCKET

eruci- *comb form* [ISV, fr. L *eruca*] **:** caterpillar ⟨*eruci*form⟩ ⟨*eruci*vorous⟩

eru·cic acid \əˈrüsik-\ *n* [*erucic* ISV *eruc-* (fr. NL *Eruca*) + *-ic*] **:** a crystalline fatty acid $C_8H_{17}CH{=}CH(CH_2)_{11}COOH$ found in the form of glycerides esp. in oils from the seeds of cruciferous plants (as mustard and rape); *cis*-13-docos-enoic acid

eru·ci·form \-səˌfȯrm\ *adj* [ISV *eruci-* + *-form*] *of an insect larva* **:** having a soft cylindrical body with a distinct head and usu. having short thoracic legs **:** like a caterpillar in form

eruct \əˈrəkt, ēˈ-\ *vb* -ED/-ING/-S [L *eructare*, fr. *e-* + *ructare* to belch, fr. (assumed) *ructus*, past part. of (assumed) *rugere* to belch (as in LL *erugere*); akin to L *rugire* to roar — more at BRUIT] *vi* **:** BELCH ~ *vt* **1 :** to bring up (gas) from the stomach by belching **2 :** to eject violently ⟨a volcano that ~*s* noxious fumes⟩

eruc·tate \-kˌtāt, *usu* -ād+V\ *vb* -ED/-ING/-S [L *eructatus*, past part. of *eructare*] **:** ERUCT

eruc·ta·tion \əˌrəkˈtāshən, (ˌ)ēˌr-\ *n* -S [L *eructation-, eructatio*, fr. *eructatus* + *-ion-, -io* -ion] **1 :** the act of belching gas from the stomach **:** BELCH **2 :** a violent belching out or emitting (as of gaseous or other matter from the crater of a volcano) **3 :** something that is emitted by belching

eruc·ta·tive \əˈr-, ēˈr-\ *adj* **:** relating to or given to eructation

eruc·tion \-kshən\ *n* -S **:** ERUCTATION

¹**er·u·dite** \ˈeryəˌdīt *also* ˈerə-; *usu* -īd+V\ *adj* [ME *erudit*, fr. L *eruditus* learned, skilled, experienced, fr. past part. of *erudire* to polish, instruct, fr. *e-* + *rudis* rude, unpolished, unskilled, ignorant — more at RUDE] **1 :** possessing or displaying erudition **:** LEARNED ⟨an ~ lawyer⟩ ⟨an unusually winning prologue . . . ~ but not academic —Louis Untermeyer⟩; *specif* **:** concerned with unduly specialized information **:** PEDANTIC, BOOKISH ⟨contains a vast amount of information without being ~ —*Liturgical Arts*⟩ ⟨knows about . . . sea fighting in a fashion too informed to be ~ —R.J. Purcell⟩ **2 :** characterized by a love of knowledge for its own sake **:** devoted to the pursuit of learning ⟨minutiae that interest only the most ~ scholars⟩

²**erudite** \"\ *n* -S **:** an erudite person ⟨she was a well-known figure among the ~*s* of the area⟩

er·u·dite·ly *adv* **:** in an erudite manner **:** with erudition

er·u·di·tion \ˌ==ˈdishən\ *n* -S [ME *erudicioun*, fr. L *erudition-, eruditio*, fr. *eruditus* + *-ion-, -io* -ion] **1 a :** extensive often profound or recondite knowledge (as of history, literature, or philosophy) acquired chiefly from books **:** command of a large fund of specialized information **:** LEARNING ⟨for this task he requires the aid of taste, not a mass of facts; an active imagination, not the accumulated weight of ~ —C.I.Glicksberg⟩ **b :** the exhibition of thorough sometimes recondite scholarship **:** an erudite quality of writing or speaking **:** LEARNEDNESS ⟨botanical information of great ~ —Bernard DeVoto⟩ ⟨although this book is the product of long . . . study it is not clogged with heavy ~ —Gastón Figueira⟩ **2 :** the practice of scholarly study **:** the pursuit of learning ⟨~ and reflection are complementary in sound scholarship⟩ **syn** see KNOWLEDGE

eruginous *var of* AERUGINOUS

erum·pent \əˈrəmpənt, ēˈ-\ *adj* [L *erumpent-, erumpens*, pres. part. of *erumpere*] **1 :** tending to grow out vigorously from a substrate so as to burst through or rise above its surface ⟨certain ~ fungi that parasitize leaves⟩ **2** *of the fruiting bodies of some fungi and algae* **:** grown or burst through a surface (as of a host's tissue) so as to form a projecting mass ⟨the ~ fruiting bodies of some rusts⟩ ⟨~ acervuli forming black dots on the leaves⟩

erupt \əˈrəpt, ēˈ-\ *vb* -ED/-ING/-S [L *eruptus* past part. of *erumpere* to burst forth, break out, fr. *e-* + *rumpere* to break — more at RUPTURE] *vi* **1 a :** to force out or release suddenly and often violently something pent up (as lava or steam) ⟨a volcano may ~ explosively or quietly⟩ ⟨the man ~*ed* with anger⟩ **b** (1) **:** to burst from or as if from limits or restraint **:** emerge with a sudden often violent rush (as from a volcano or geyser) **:** BURST ⟨towering flames ~ from the oil tank⟩ ⟨steam ~*s* from the geyser⟩ **:** IRRUPT ⟨a new leader ~*s* upon the national scene⟩ ⟨shouting men ~*ed* into the square⟩ (2) *of a tooth* **:** to emerge through the gum **c :** to become active or violent **:** break forth **:** EXPLODE ⟨the village ~*s* into celebration⟩ ⟨the chorus ~*s* into song⟩ ⟨hostility ~*ed* into bloody clashes⟩ ⟨war ~*ed* between the two nations⟩ **2 a :** to break out with or as if with a skin eruption ⟨~*ed* with measles⟩ ⟨the literature of the day ~*ed* with essays on the general depravity of the jazz age —*Esquire's Jazz Bk.*⟩ **b :** to appear in numbers suddenly ⟨pimples ~ all over the skin⟩ **:** BURGEON ⟨the multiplicity of the schemes that seem to ~ all over the place —E.E.Schattschneider⟩ ~ *vt* **:** to force out or release (as something pent up) usu. suddenly and violently **:** cause to erupt **:** throw out **:** EXPEL, EJECT ⟨the volcano ~*ed* lava bombs⟩ ⟨the general ~*ed* orders —Frederic Sondern⟩ ⟨living populations will continue to ~ new biotypes —*American Naturalist*⟩ — **erupt·ible** \-təbəl\ *adj*

erupted *adj* **:** marked by an eruption of the skin or mucous membrane ⟨a badly ~ face⟩

erup·tion \əˈrəpshən, ēˈ-\ *n* -S [ME *erupcioun*, fr. L *eruption-, eruptio*, fr. *eruptus* + *-ion-, -io* -ion] **1 :** an act, process, or instance of erupting ⟨the volcano was in ~⟩ ⟨the ~ of the tooth from the gum⟩ **:** OUTBURST ⟨his loud angry ~*s*⟩ **:** OUTBREAK ⟨the ~ of hostilities⟩ ⟨the ~ of an epidemic⟩ **:** RASH ⟨an ~ of shopping centers has broken out on the countryside —Weare Holbrook⟩; *specif* **:** the breaking out of an exanthem or enanthem on the skin or mucous membrane (as in measles) **2 :** something produced by an act or process of erupting: as **a :** material erupted by a volcano **b :** the condition of the skin or mucous membrane caused by erupting **c :** one of the lesions (as a pustule) constituting this condition **3 :** IRRUPTION d — **erup·tion·al** \-shənᵊl, -shnəl\ *adj*

¹**erup·tive** \-ptiv, -tēv *also* -təv\ *adj* [*eruption* + *-ive*] **1 a :** erupting or tending to erupt **:** bursting forth **:** breaking out ⟨describes a geyser as an intermittently ~ hot spring⟩ ⟨the ~ imagery of the poem⟩ **:** having the character of an eruption ⟨a brawl was the first ~ result of the rising hostility⟩ **b :** characterized by eruption ⟨the ~ stage of smallpox⟩ ⟨~ letters full of outbursts of anger or joking⟩ **2 :** producing eruption ⟨an ~ fever⟩ **3 :** produced by eruption — usu. used of intrusive rocks (as granite, diorite, gabbro) or extrusive rocks (as rhyolite, andesite, basalt) — **erup·tive·ly** \-tə̇vlē, -li\ *adv* — **erup·tive·ness** \-tivnə̇s, -tēv- *also* -təv-\ *n* -ES

²**eruptive** \"\ *n* -S **:** an igneous rock

eruptive evolution *n* **:** the sudden appearance of varied new stocks from a common ancestral strain

erup·tiv·i·ty \əˌrəpˈtivəd·ē, (ˌ)ēˌr-\ *n* -ES **:** the state of being eruptive ⟨return of the geyser from a dormant phase to ~⟩

eruv *var of* ERUB

erven *pl of* ERF

er·vil \ˈərvəl\ *n* -S [L *ervilia*; akin to L *ervum* bitter vetch — more at ERS] **:** ERS

er·win·ia \ˌərˈwinēə\ *n, cap* [NL, fr. *Erwin* F. Smith †1927 Am. bacteriologist + NL *-ia*] **:** a genus of motile bacteria (family Enterobacteriaceae) that comprises numerous pathogens of plants including forms that cause dry necrosis, galls, wilts, and soft rots

-ery \(ə)rē, (ə)ri\ *n suffix* -ES [ME *-erie*, fr. OF, fr. *-ier* -er + *-ie* -y] **1 :** qualities collectively **:** character **:** -NESS ⟨tomfool*ery*⟩ ⟨snobb*ery*⟩ **2 :** art, practice, trade ⟨mountebank*ery*⟩ — compare -RY **3 :** place of doing, keeping, growing, breeding, selling (the thing specified) ⟨pigg*ery*⟩ ⟨rook*ery*⟩ ⟨fish*ery*⟩ ⟨bind*ery*⟩ ⟨bak*ery*⟩ **4 :** collection **:** aggregate ⟨fin*ery*⟩ ⟨green*ery*⟩ — compare -RY **5 :** state **:** condition ⟨slav*ery*⟩ ⟨monk*ery*⟩ — compare -RY

eryn·gi·um \əˈrinjēəm\ *n* [NL, fr. L *eryngion* eryngo, fr. Gk *ēryngion*, dim. of *ēryngos*] **1** *cap* **:** a genus of coarse bristly herbs (family Umbelliferae) having elongate spinulose-margined leaves and flowers in dense bracted heads — see BUTTON SNAKEROOT, SEA HOLLY **2** -S **:** ERYNGO 2

eryn·go \əˈriŋ(ˌ)gō\ *n* -S [modif. of L *eryngion*] **1 :** candied sea-holly root **2** [NL *Eryngium*] **:** a plant of the genus *Eryngium*; *esp* **:** SEA HOLLY 1

ery·on \ˈerēˌän\ *n, cap* [NL, fr. Gk *eryōn*, pres. part. of *eryein* to draw out, drag; fr. the large carapace] **:** a genus of fossil decapod crustaceans (suborder Reptantia) related to the spiny lobsters and found from the Lias to the Cretaceous esp. in lithographic limestones

ery·op·id \ˌerēˈäpə̇d\ *n* -S [NL *Eryop-, Eryops* + E *-id*] **:** an amphibian of *Eryops* or a related genus

ery·ops \ˈerēˌäps\ *n, cap* [NL, fr. Gk *eryein* + NL *-ops*] **:** a genus of large Lower Permian labyrinthodont amphibians (order Rhachitomi) known from Texas and New Mexico

erys·i·mum \əˈrisəməm\ *n, cap* [NL, fr. Gk *erysimon*, a kind of mustard, fr. *erysthai* to defend, protect, save; fr. its use as a medicinal herb] **:** a small genus of Old World herbs (family Cruciferae) including several weeds and having alternate leaves, small yellow flowers, and slender terete pods — see WALLFLOWER, WORMSEED MUSTARD

er·y·sip·e·las \ˌerəˈsip(ə)ləs, ˌir-\ *n* -ES [ME *herisipila, erisipila*, fr. L *erysipelas*, fr. Gk, fr. *erysi-* red (akin to *erythros*) + *-pelas* skin (akin to L *pellis*) — more at RED, FELL (hide)] **1 :** an acute febrile disease that is associated with intense often vesicular and edematous local inflammation of the skin and subcutaneous tissues and that is caused by a hemolytic streptococcus — called also *St. Anthony's fire* **2 :** SWINE ERYSIPELAS — used esp. when the disease affects other hosts than swine

er·y·si·pel·a·tous \ˌ===ˈpelədəs\ *adj* [L *erysipelat-, erysipelas* + E *-ous*] **1 :** of or relating to erysipelas **2 :** ERYSIPELOID

¹**er·y·sip·e·loid** \ˌ==ˈsipəˌlȯid\ *n* -S [ISV *erysipelas* + *-oid*] **:** a localized nonfebrile dermatitis resembling erysipelas, caused by the parasite of swine erysipelas, and occurring esp. about the hands of persons exposed to this organism (as by handling contaminated flesh) — see ERYSIPELOTHRIX

²**erysipeloid** \ˈ==ˈ==ˌ=\ *adj* **:** resembling erysipelas

er·y·sip·e·lo·thrix \ˌ==ˈsipəlōˌthriks\ *n* [NL, fr. L *erysipelas* + *-o-* + *-thrix*] **1** *cap* **:** a genus of microaerophilic, gram-positive, rod-shaped bacteria (family Corynebacteriaceae) forming no spores, tending to produce long filaments, and being usu. considered to include a single form (*E. rhusiopathia*) widespread in nature where nitrogenous matter is disintegrating and the causative agent of swine erysipelas, an arthritis of lambs, and erysipeloid of man **2** -ES **:** a bacterium of the genus *Erysipelothrix*

er·y·si·pha·ce·ae \ˌerəsəˈfāsēˌē\ *n pl, cap* [NL, fr. *Erysiphe*, type genus + *-aceae*] **:** a family of fungi (order Erysiphales) comprising the powdery mildews, being parasitic mostly on leaves, and having delicate hyaline superficial mycelium and perithecia with one to several asci and distinctive appendages — **er·y·si·pha·ceous** \ˌ===ˈfāshəs\ *adj*

er·y·si·pha·les \ˌ===ˈfā(ˌ)lēz\ *n pl, cap* [NL, fr. *Erysiphe* + *-ales*] **:** an order of saprophytic and parasitic ascomycetous fungi (subclass Euascomycetes) that live on plants, have both vegetative and reproductive structures superficial on the host, and include the powdery mildews, many sooty molds, and a few other epiphytic fungi — see ERYSIPHACEAE

er·y·si·phe \ˌerəˈsī(ˌ)fē\ *n, cap* [NL, fr. Gk *erysi-* red + *siphōn* tube — more at ERYSIPELAS, SIPHON] **:** a genus of powdery mildews (family Erysiphaceae) having perithecia with several asci and with usu. unbranched appendages resembling hyphae

er·y·thea \-ˈthēə\ *n* [NL, fr. Gk *Erytheia*, one of the Hesperides] **1** *cap* **:** a genus of Californian and Mexican slender fan palms with smooth trunks and large orbicular leaves whose lobes bear white filaments **2** -S **:** any palm of the genus *Erythea*

er·y·the·ma \-ˈthēmə\ *n* -S [NL, fr. Gk *erythēma*, fr. *erythainein* to redden, fr. *erythros* red — more at RED] **:** abnormal redness of the skin due to capillary congestion (as in inflammation)

er·y·the·mal \ˈ==ˈ==məl\ *adj* [NL *erythema* + E *-al*] **:** relating to or producing erythema ⟨~ radiation⟩

erythema mul·ti·for·me \-ˌməltəˈfȯr(ˌ)mē\ *n* [NL, lit., multiform erythema] **:** a skin disease characterized by papular or vesicular lesions and reddening or discoloration of the skin often in concentric zones about the lesions

erythema no·do·sum \-nōˈdōsəm\ *n* [NL, lit., knotty erythema] **:** a skin condition characterized by small tender reddened nodules under the skin (as over the shin bones) often accompanied by fever and transitory arthritic pains and commonly considered a manifestation of hypersensitivity

erythema so·la·re \-sōˈla(a)(ˌ)rē\ *n* [NL, lit., solar erythema] **:** erythema due to excessive exposure of the skin to ultraviolet rays — compare SUNBURN

er·y·the·ma·to·gen·ic \ˌerəˈthēməd·əˈjenik, -them-\ *adj* [NL *erythemat-, erythema* + E *-o-* + *-genic*] **:** producing erythema

er·y·them·a·tous \ˌerəˈthemədəs, -thēm-\ *also* **er·y·the·mic** \ˌerəˈthēmik\ *or* **er·y·the·mat·ic** \ˌerəthəˈmad·ik\ *adj* [NL *erythemat-, erythema* + E *-ous* or *-ic*] **:** relating to or marked by erythema

erythr- *or* **erythro-** *comb form* [Gk *erythr-, erythro-*, fr. *erythros* — more at RED] **1 :** red ⟨*erythr*ism⟩ ⟨*erythro*phyll⟩ **2 :** related to erythrose ⟨*erythr*onic acid⟩ **3** *erythro-, usu ital* **:** having the same stereochemical arrangement of atoms or groups about two asymmetric carbon atoms as that in erythrose ⟨DL-*erythro*-3-amino-2-butanol⟩ **4 :** erythrocyte ⟨*erythr*emia⟩ ⟨*erythro*poiesis⟩

¹**er·y·thrae·an** \ˌerəˈthrēən\ *adj, usu cap* [*Erythrae*, ancient city of Asia Minor (fr. Gk *Erythrai*) + E *-an*] **:** of or relating to Erythrae, an ancient Ionian city of Asia Minor that claimed to have been the residence of the sibyl Herophile

²**erythraean** *or* **erythrean** \"\ *adj* [L *Erythraeus* (fr. Gk *Erythraios*, lit., red, fr. *erythros*) + E *-an*] **:** of or relating to the sea that in ancient geography comprised the Arabian sea, the Red sea, and the Persian gulf

er·y·thrae·idae \ˌerəˈthrēəˌdē\ *n pl, cap* [NL, fr. *Erythraea*, type genus (fr. Gk *erythraia*, fem. of *erythraios*) + *-idae*] **:** a family of Acarina including active hairy usu. reddish mites of predatory habits having the larvae parasitic on insects or on other arthropods

er·y·thras·ma \-ˈthrazmə\ *n* -S [NL, fr. *erythr-* + Gk *-asma* (n. ending)] **:** a chronic contagious dermatitis caused by an actinomycete (*Nocardia minutissima*) and affecting esp. warm moist areas (as the axilla and groin)

eryth·re·de·ma \əˌrithrəˈdēmə\ *n* [NL, fr. *erythr-* + *edema*] **:** ACRODYNIA

er·y·thre·mia *also* **er·y·thrae·mia** \ˌerəˈthrēmēə\ *n* -S [NL, fr. *erythr-* + *-emia, -aemia*] **:** POLYCYTHEMIA 2

er·y·thri·na \-ˈthrīnə -rēnə\ *n* -S [NL, fr. *erythr-* + *-ina*] **1** *cap* **:** a genus of tropical shrubs or trees (family Leguminosae) often cultivated and having trifoliolate leaves and chiefly reddish flowers in terminal racemes — see CORAL TREE, KAFFIR BOOM **2** -S **:** any plant of the genus *Erythrina*

er·y·thrine \ˈerəˌthrēn, əˈriˌth-, -ˌthrən\ *n* -S [F, fr. *erythr-* + *-ine*] **:** ERYTHRITE 2

er·y·thrin·i·dae \ˌerəˈthrinəˌdē\ *n pl, cap* [NL, fr. *Erythrinus*, type genus (fr. Gk *erythrinos*, a kind of fish, fr. *erythr-* + *-inos* -ine) + *-idae*] **:** a family of carnivorous So. American river fishes that resemble the pikes but are related to and often included in the family Characidae

er·y·thrism \ˈerəˌthrizəm, əˈriˌth-\ *n* -S [ISV *erythr-* + *-ism*] **:** a condition characterized by the exceptional prevalence of red pigmentation (as in skin, hair, or plumage) — **er·y·thris·mal** \ˌerəˈthrizməl\ *adj*

er·y·thris·tic \ˌerəˈthristik\ *adj* **:** of, relating to, or characterized by erythrism

er·y·thrite \ˈerəˌthrīt, əˈriˌth-\ *n* -S [*erythr-* + *-ite*] **1 :** ERYTHRITOL **2 :** a mineral $Co_3(AsO_4)_2.8H_2O$ consisting of a hydrous cobalt arsenate, occurring in monoclinic crystals isomorphous with annabergite and also in globular and reniform masses and in earthy form, and being usu. rose red

eryth·ri·tol \əˈrithrəˌtȯl, -ōl\ *n* -S [ISV *erythr-* + *-itol*] **:** a sweet crystalline tetrahydroxy alcohol $HOCH_2(CHOH)_2CH_2OH$ obtained as the optically inactive meso form from lichens, algae, and yeasts or made by reduction of erythrose and used chiefly in the form of its tetranitrate as a vasodilator

erythro- — see ERYTHR-

eryth·ro·blast \əˈrithrəˌblast\ *n* -S [ISV *erythr-* + *-blast*] **1 :** a polychromatic nucleated cell occurring in red marrow as the first specifically identifiable stage in red blood-cell formation and intermediate in characteristics between hemocytoblast and normoblast **2 :** any of various cells ancestral to red blood cells

eryth·ro·blas·te·mia \-ˌ==ˌblaˈstēmēə\ *n* -S [NL, fr. ISV *erythroblast* + NL *-emia*] **:** the presence of an abnormal number of erythroblasts in the blood

eryth·ro·blas·tic \ˈ=ˈ=ˈblastik\ *adj* **:** of, relating to, or characterized by the presence of erythroblasts

eryth·ro·blas·to·sis \-ˌ==ˌblaˈstōsə̇s\ *n, pl* **erythroblastoses** \-ˌōˌsēz\ [NL, fr. ISV *erythroblast* + NL *-osis*] **:** the abnormal presence of erythroblasts in the circulating blood; *specif* **:** a hemolytic disease of the fetus and newborn that is characterized by destruction of circulating erythrocytes, increase in circulating erythroblasts, and jaundice and that is usu. associated with Rh-factor incompatibility

erythroblastosis fe·ta·lis \-fēˈtaləs\ *n* [NL] **:** erythroblastosis of the fetus

erythroblastosis ne·o·na·to·rum \-ˌnēənəˈtōrəm\ *n* [NL] **:** erythroblastosis of the newborn infant

eryth·ro·blas·tot·ic \əˌrithrəˌblaˈstäd·ik\ *adj* [fr. NL *erythroblastosis*, after such pairs as NL *hypnosis*: E *hypnotic*] **:** of, relating to, or affected by erythroblastosis ⟨an ~ infant⟩

eryth·ro·ce·bus \əˈrithrə+\ *n, cap* [NL, fr. *erythr-* + *Cebus*] **:** a genus of reddish African monkeys including the patas

eryth·ro·cru·o·rin \-ˌ==ˈkrüərə̇n, rüə-\ *n* [*erythr-* + *cruorin* (old name for hemoglobin)] **:** any of various red respiratory pigments that occur in blood, cells, or body fluids of several invertebrate animals and that are or are related to hemoglobins

eryth·ro·cyte \əˈrithrəˌsīt\ *n* -S [ISV *erythr-* + *-cyte*] **1 :** a vertebrate blood cell that contains hemoglobin, functions in the internal transport of oxygen, and in mammals is an enucleated biconcave disk formed from nucleated cells esp. of the red bone marrow and present in numbers up to several millions in each cubic millimeter of blood — compare LEUKOCYTE **2 :** a cell containing a respiratory pigment (as in some marine worms) — **eryth·ro·cyt·ic** \ˈ=ˈ==ˈsid·ik\ *adj*

erythrocyte-maturing factor *n* **:** VITAMIN B_{12}

eryth·ro·cy·the·mia \əˌrithrəˌsīˈthēmēə\ *n* -S [NL, irreg. fr. ISV *erythrocyte* + NL *-emia*] **:** POLYCYTHEMIA 2

eryth·ro·cy·to·gen·e·sis \-ˌ==ˌsīd·ōˈjenəsə̇s\ *n* [NL, fr. ISV *erythrocyte* + NL *-o-* + *-genesis*] **:** ERYTHROPOIESIS

eryth·ro·cy·tom·e·ter \-ˌ==ˌsīdˈämədə(r)\ *n* [*erythrocyte* + *-o-* + *-meter*] **1 :** HEMACYTOMETER **2 :** a device for measuring the diameter of red blood cells

eryth·ro·cy·to·poi·e·sis \-ˌ==ˌsīd·əˌpȯiˈēsə̇s\ *n, pl* **erythrocytopoieses** \-ˌēˌsēz\ [NL, fr. ISV *erythrocyte* + NL *-o-* + *-poiesis*] **:** ERYTHROPOIESIS

eryth·ro·cy·to·sis \-ˌ==ˌsīdˈōsə̇s\ *n, pl* **erythrocytoses** \-ˌōˌsēz\ [NL, fr. ISV *erythrocyte* + NL *-osis*] **:** POLYCYTHEMIA 1

eryth·ro·der·ma \-ˈdərmə\ *n, pl* **erythrodermas** \-məz\ *or* **erythroderma·ta** \-məd·ə\ [NL, fr. *erythr-* + *-derma*] **:** ERYTHEMA

eryth·ro·der·mia \-mēə\ *n* -S [NL, fr. *erythr-* + *-dermia*] **:** ERYTHEMA

eryth·ro·dextrin *also* **eryth·ro·dextrine** \əˈrithrə+\ *n* [ISV *erythr-* + *dextrin, dextrine*] **:** a dextrin that gives a red color with iodine

eryth·ro·gen·e·sis \əˌrithrəˈjenəsə̇s\ *n* [NL, fr. *erythr-* + *-genesis*] **:** ERYTHROPOIESIS

eryth·ro·gen·ic \ˈ=ˈ==ˈjenik\ *adj* [*erythr-* + *-genic*] **1 :** producing a color sensation of redness **2 :** ERYTHROPOIETIC **3 :** inducing reddening of the skin ⟨~ toxins⟩

eryth·ro·gone \əˈ==ˌgōn\ *also* **eryth·ro·go·ni·um** \ˌ=ˌ==ˈgōnēəm\ *n* -S [NL *erythrogonium*, fr. *erythr-* + *gonium*] **:** PROMEGALOBLAST

er·y·throid \əˈriˌthrȯid, ˈerəˌth-\ *adj* [*erythr-* + *-oid*] **:** relating to erythrocytes or their precursors — compare MYELOID

er·y·thro·i·dine \ˌerəˈthrōəˌdēn, -ōədᵊn\ *n* -S [*erythr-* + *-idine*] **:** a crystalline alkaloid $C_{16}H_{19}NO_3$ obtained from plants of the genus *Erythrina* as a mixture of stereoisomers; *esp* **:** the beta stereoisomer that has curariform activity and is a depressant of the central nervous system

er·y·throl \ˈerəˌthrōl, əˈriˌth-, -ōl\ *n* -S [ISV *erythr-* + *-ol*] **1 :** a liquid unsaturated dihydroxy alcohol $CH_2{=}CHCHOHCH_2OH$ formed by decomposition of erythritol **2 :** ERYTHRITOL — used esp. in pharmacy ⟨~ tetranitrate⟩

eryth·ro·leucosis *or* **eryth·ro·leukosis** \əˈrithrō+\ *n* [NL, fr. *erythr-* + *leucosis, leukosis*] **:** LEUKOSIS 2

eryth·ro·mel·al·gia \-ˌ==(ˌ)melˈaljēə\ *n* [NL, fr. *erythr-* + *melalgia* pain in the extremities] **:** a state of excessive dilation of the superficial blood vessels of the feet or more rarely the hands accompanied by hyperemia, increased skin temperature, and burning pain

eryth·ro·my·cin \əˌrithrəˈmīsᵊn\ *n* -S [*erythr-* + *-mycin*] **:** a broad-spectrum antibiotic produced by a bacterium of the genus *Streptomyces* (*S. erythreus*), resembling penicillin in antibacterial activity, and effective also against amoebas, treponemata, and pinworms

er·y·thron \ˈerəˌthrän, əˈriˌth-\ *n* -S [NL, fr. Gk, neut. of *erythros* red — more at RED] **:** a body organ consisting of the red blood cells and their precursors in the bone marrow — compare LEUKON

eryth·ro·neu·ra \əˌrithrəˈn(y)ürə\ *n, cap* [NL, fr. *erythr-* + *-neura*] **:** a widely distributed genus of leafhoppers containing some that have been implicated in the transmission of virus diseases of cultivated plants — see GRAPE LEAFHOPPER

er·y·thro·ni·um \ˌerəˈthrōnēəm\ *n* [NL, fr. Gk *erythronion*, a kind of plant, fr. *erythros* red — more at RED] **1** *cap* **:** a small genus of chiefly No. American herbs (family Liliaceae) having a corm from which arise a pair of usu. mottled basal leaves and one or more scapose flowers **2** -S **:** any plant of the genus *Erythronium*

eryth·ro·phage \əˈrithrəˌfāj\ *n* -S [ISV *erythr-* + *-phage*] **:** a phagocyte that ingests red blood cells of the same body

eryth·ro·pha·gia \ˌ==ˈfāj(ē)ə\ *n* -S [NL, fr. *erythr-* + *-phagia*] **:** ERYTHROPHAGOCYTOSIS

eryth·ro·phagocytosis \əˈrithrə+\ *n* [NL, fr. *erythr-* + *phagocytosis*] **:** consumption of red blood cells by histiocytes and sometimes other phagocytes of the same body

er·y·throph·i·lous \ˌerəˈthräfələs\ *also* **eryth·ro·phile** \əˈrithrəˌfīl\ *adj* [ISV *erythr-* + *-philous, -phile*] *of a tissue or cell* **:** having special affinity for red coloring matter

eryth·ro·phle·ine \əˌrithrəˈflēən, -lēˌēn\ *n* -S [ISV *erythr-* + Gk *phloios* bark + ISV *-ine*] **:** a white crystalline very poisonous alkaloid $C_{24}H_{39}NO_5$ extracted esp. from sassy bark

eryth·ro·pho·bia \-ˈfōbēə\ *n* [NL, fr. *erythr-* + *-phobia*] **1 :** morbid avoidance of the color red **2 :** fear of blushing

eryth·ro·phore \əˈ==ˌfō(ə)r\ *n* -S [*erythr-* + *-phore*] **:** a chromatophore containing a red usu. carotenoid pigment that occurs esp. in some fishes and crustaceans

er·y·thro·pia \ˌerəˈthrōpēə\ *or* **er·y·throp·sia** \-ˈthräpsēə\ *n* -S [NL, fr. *erythr-* + *-opia, -opsia*] **:** a visual disturbance in which all objects appear reddish

eryth·ro·pla·sia \əˌrithrəˈplāzh(ē)ə\ *n* -S [NL, fr. *erythr-* + *-plasia*] **:** a reddened patch with a velvety surface on the oral or genital mucosa that is considered to be a precancerous lesion

eryth·ro·plastid \ə'rithrə+\ *n* [*erythr-* + *-plastid*] **:** a mammalian red blood cell characterized by absence of the nucleus

eryth·ro·poi·e·sis \ə,rithrə,pȯi'ēsəs\ *n* -ES [NL, fr. *erythr-* + *-poiesis*] **:** the production of red blood cells (as from the bone marrow)

eryth·ro·poi·et·ic \ə¦==,=¦ed·ik\ *adj* [*erythr-* + *-poietic*] **:** producing red blood cells

er·y·throp·ter·in \,erə'thräptərən\ *n* -S [*erythr-* + *pterin*] **:** an orange-red pigment $C_9H_9N_5O_5$ found esp. in pierid butterflies

eryth·ro·scope \ə'rithrə,skōp\ *n* [ISV *erythr-* + *-scope;* orig. formed as G *erythroskop*] **:** a device consisting of overlapping yellow and blue glasses through which some shades of green appear red

er·y·throse \'erə,thrōs, ə'ri,th- *also* -ōz\ *n* -S [F *érythrose,* fr. *érythr-* erythr- + *-ose*] **:** a syrupy aldose sugar $HOCH_2(CHOH)_2CHO$ that is the epimer of threose and is obtained by degradation of arabinose

eryth·ro·siderite \ə¦rithrə+\ *n* [ISV *erythr-* + *siderite;* orig. formed as It *eritrosidero*] **:** a mineral $K_2FeCl_5.H_2O$ consisting of hydrous potassium iron chloride and occurring in lavas

eryth·ro·sin *also* **eryth·ro·sine** \ə'rithrəsən, -,sēn\ *n* -S [ISV *erythr-* + *eosin, eosine*] **:** any of several xanthene dyes that are made by iodination of fluorescein and that dye wool, cotton, and silk in reddish shades: as **a :** a brick-red powder $C_{20}H_6I_4Na_2O_5$ that is used esp. in making organic pigments, in coloring foods, as a biological stain, and as a green photographic sensitizer; the sodium salt of tetraiodo-fluorescein — called also *erythrosine bluish;* see DYE table I (under *Acid Red 51*) **b :** a yellowish brown powder $C_{20}H_8I_2Na_2O_5$ used esp. in coloring solutions of drugs and as a biological stain; the sodium salt of diiodo-fluorescein — called also *erythrosine yellowish;* see DYE table I (under *Acid Red 95, Solvent Red 73*)

er·y·thro·sis \,erə'thrōsəs\ *n, pl* **erythro·ses** \-ō,sēz\ [NL, fr. *erythr-* + *-osis*] **1 :** a red or purplish color of the skin (as of the face) resulting from vascular congestion (as in polycythemia) **:** PLETHORA **2 :** a hyperplastic condition of tissues that form red blood cells

er·y·throx·y·la·ce·ae \,erə,thräksə'lāsē,ē\ *n pl, cap* [NL, fr. *Erythroxylon,* type genus + *-aceae*] **:** a family of plants (order Geraniales) having monadelphous stamens, a bifid ligulate appendage or callosity on the inner face of each petal, and drupaceous fruit

er·y·throx·y·lon \,==¦==,län, -lən\ *n, cap* [NL, fr. *erythr-* + *-xylon*] **:** a large genus of chiefly So. American shrubs and small trees (family Erythroxylaceae) with small white or greenish pentamerous flowers — see COCA

er·y·throx·y·lum \-ləm\ [NL, fr. *erythr-* + *-xylum*] *syn of* ERYTHROXYLON

eryth·ro·zincite \ə¦rithrə+\ *n* [ISV *erythr-* + *zincite;* orig. formed as F *érythrozincite*] **:** a manganiferous variety of wurtzite

eryth·ru·lose \ə'rithrə,lōs *also* -ōz\ *n* -S [ISV *erythr-* + *-ule* + *-ose*] **:** a syrupy ketose sugar $HOCH_2CHOHCOCH_2OH$ obtained by bacterial oxidation of erythritol

er·yx \'eriks, 'ir-\ *n, cap* [NL, fr. *Eryx,* a mountain in Sicily, fr. L, fr. Gk] **:** a genus comprising the typical sand snakes — see SAND BOA

er·zah·ler \ert'sālər\ *n* -S [prob. fr. G *erzähler,* lit., narrator, fr. *erzählen* to narrate + *-er*] **:** a gemshorn organ pipe

es *var of* ESS

[1]-es *after letters or letter groups whose pronunc is* s, z, sh, *or* ch: əz, *sometimes* ÷,ēz *in some words in which an unstressed syllable precedes, as "processes"; after* v *or a vowel:* z\ *n pl suffix* [ME *-es, -s* — more at [1]-S] **1** — used to form the plural of most nouns that end in *s* ⟨glass*es*⟩, *z* ⟨fuzz*es*⟩, *sh* ⟨bush*es*⟩, *ch* ⟨peach*es*⟩, or postconsonantal *y* (which changes to *i*) ⟨lad*ies*⟩, of some nouns ending in *o* ⟨hero*es*⟩, and of some nouns ending in *f* (which changes to *v*) ⟨loav*es*⟩ — compare [1]-S 1 **2 :** [1]-S 2 ⟨Christmas*es* we go to grandmother's⟩

[2]-es *after letters or letter groups whose pronunc is* s, z, sh, *or* ch: əz; *after a vowel:* z\ *vb suffix* [ME (Northern & North Midland) — more at [3]-S] **1** — used to form the third person singular present indicative of most verbs that end in *s* ⟨bless*es*⟩, *z* ⟨fizz*es*⟩, *sh* ⟨hush*es*⟩, *ch* ⟨catch*es*⟩, or postconsonantal *y* (which changes to *i*) ⟨def*ies*⟩ — compare [3]-S 1 **2** *substand* **:** [3]-S 2 ⟨then I rush*es* over to him⟩

ES *abbr* **1** eldest son **2** electrostatic **3** engine-sized **4** executive secretary **5** extra series

Es *symbol* einsteinium

e's *or* **es** *pl of* E

-es' \(ə)z\ *n pl suffix* [ME *-es,* fr. *-e,* older gen. pl. ending (fr. OE *-a*) + *-s,* gen. sing. ending — more at -'S] — used to form the plural possessive of most nouns that end in *s, z, sh, ch,* or postconsonantal *y* and of some nouns ending in *f*

esau \'ē,sȯ\ *n* -S *cap* [after *Esau,* son of Isaac and Rebekah and twin brother of Jacob, to whom he sold his birthright (Gen 25, 27)] **:** one that sacrifices a permanent interest for a more immediate but temporary interest; *also* **:** one that may easily be taken advantage of

esc *abbr* **1** escape **2** escudo **3** escutcheon

es·ca \'eskə\ *n* -S [NL, fr. NGk *ischa*] **:** BLACK MEASLES 2

es·ca·drille \'eskə,dril, -drē(y) *also* ,==¦=\ *n* -S [F, flotilla, escadrille, modif. (influenced by F *escadre* squadron) of Sp *escuadrilla,* dim. of *escuadra* squadron, squad — more at SQUAD] **:** a unit of a European esp. French air command containing usu. six airplanes

[1]es·ca·lade \'eskə,lād, -läd, ,==¦=\ *n* -S [F, fr. It *scalata,* fr. fem. of *scalato,* past part. of *scalare* to scale, fr. *scala* ladder, fr. LL — more at SCALE (ladder)] **:** the act of scaling

[2]escalade \"\ *vt* -ED/-ING/-S **:** to climb up or over ⟨forcing them to ~ horrible precipices at midnight on horseback —Norman Douglas⟩ ⟨the storms of rain passed . . . *escalading* the farther bluff —Christina Stead⟩ — **es·ca·lad·er** \-də(r)\ *n* -S

es·ca·la·do \,eskə'lā(,)dō, -lä(-\ *n* -S [modif. of Sp *escalada,* fr. fem. of *escalado,* past part. of *escalar* to scale, fr. *escala* ladder, fr. LL *scala* — more at SCALE (ladder)] *archaic* **:** ESCALADE

es·ca·late \'eskə,lāt, ÷ -kyə-\ *vb* -ED/-ING/-S [back-formation, fr. *escalator*] *vi* **:** to ascend on or as if on a moving staircase or conveyor belt ~ *vt* **:** to carry up on or as if on a moving staircase or conveyor belt

es·ca·la·tion \,==¦lāshən\ *n* -S [*escalator* + *-ion*] **:** an increase (as in the price of an article or in a ship's tonnage) that counteracts an unjust discrepancy (as between the price of a product and the cost of material or between the tonnage of one nation's ships and that of another when both are regulated by the same treaty); *specif* **:** the adjustment of prices proportionally and usu. periodically and automatically to an alteration (as a rise) in the cost of materials or a similar adjustment of wages to an alteration in the cost of living

[1]es·ca·la·tor \'eskə,lād·ə(r), -ātə-, ÷ -kyə-\ *n* -S [fr. *Escalator,* a trademark] **1 :** MOVING STAIRCASE **2 :** a course, means, or agency that carries upward or downward esp. through a series of stages and usu. effortlessly ⟨promised them a place on a never-stopping ~ of economic progress —D.W.Brogan⟩ ⟨rode the ~ right behind him—first to the governorship of his native Veracruz, then to the Ministry of Interior —*Time*⟩ ⟨man had at last found an ~ to heaven . . . had put his foot on the first tread, and time would take care of the rest —*Social Welfare Forum*⟩ **3 :** an escalator clause or provision ⟨many American workers won wage advances, cost-of-living wage ~*s,* various fringe benefits, and strengthening of union security through collective bargaining —*Americana Annual*⟩ ⟨enough to tilt the index into a new high bracket and give a million auto-industry workers a cent-an-hour pay increase under the terms of their ~ —J.A.Loftus⟩

[2]escalator \"\ *adj* **1 :** providing for escalation — used esp. of labor contracts or provisions contained in them ⟨steelworkers whose ~ contracts adjust wages to the government's consumer price index —*Newsweek*⟩ ⟨the introduction of an ~ arrangement tying the base pay of servicemen to living costs and adjustable at one to two-year intervals —*N.Y.Times*⟩ **2 :** providing for periodic and automatic proportionate adjustment similar to escalation ⟨asked for ~ clauses which would enlarge the amount of the loan as prices go up —*Newsweek*⟩ ⟨an ~ plan for state colleges under which one grade will be desegregated each year —Eric Sevareid⟩

es·cal·lo·nia \,eskə'lōnēə\ *n* [NL, fr. *Escallon,* 18th cent. Span. traveler in So. Amer. + NL *-ia*] **1** *cap* **:** a genus that is included among the Saxifragaceae or sometimes made type of the separate family Escalloniaceae and that comprises So. American shrubs and trees with simple glossy leaves having gland-tipped teeth, flowers mostly in terminal racemes, and capsular fruits **2** -S **:** any plant of the genus *Escallonia*

es·cal·lo·ni·a·ce·ae \,eskə,lōnē'āsē,ē\ *n pl, cap* [NL, fr. *Escallonia,* type genus + *-aceae*] *in some classifications* **:** a family of shrubs and mostly small trees (order Rosales) that are widely distributed esp. in the southern hemisphere — see ESCALLONIA — **es·cal·lo·ni·a·ceous** \¦==,==¦āshəs\ *adj*

[1]es·cal·lop \ə'skäləp, e'-, -kal-\ *var of* SCALLOP

[2]escallop \"\ *or* **escallop shell** *n* -S [ME, fr. MF *escalope* shell — more at SCALLOP] **:** a decoration in the form of a scallop shell; *specif* **:** a scallop-shell device in heraldry usu. borne as a charge with the fluted edge downward and the convex side toward the viewer

escallop

es·cal·lo·pi·ne \ə,skälə'pēnē, (,)e,s-\ *n* -S [by alter.] **:** SCALLOPINI

es·ca·lope *also* **es·col·lope** \¦eskə¦lōp\ *n* -S [F *escalope,* fr. MF, shell] **:** SCALLOPINI

es·cam·bio \ə'skambē,ō, e'-\ *n* -S [ML, abl. of *escambium, excambium* exchange, fr. *excambiare* to exchange — more at EXCHANGE] **:** a license formerly required in English law for drawing a bill of exchange on a person overseas

es·cam·bron \¦e,skäm¦brōn\ *n* -S [AmerSp *escambrón,* fr. obs. Sp, hawthorn, buckthorn, perh. modif. of L *crabron-, crabro* hornet — more at HORNET] **:** any of several tropical American thorny shrubs or trees: as **a :** COCKSPUR 2b **b** *Puerto Rico* **:** a shrubby vine (*Drepanocarpus lunatus*) of the family Leguminosae with hooked prickles and showy purple flowers **c :** CAT'S-CLAW

es·ca·mo·tage \eskȧmȯtäzh\ *n* -S [F, fr. *escamoter* to juggle, conjure, make vanish (fr. MF) + *-age*] **:** JUGGLING, SLEIGHT OF HAND, TRICKERY

es·cap·able \ə'skāpəbəl, e'-\ *adj* **:** capable of being escaped **:** AVOIDABLE

es·ca·pade \'eskə,pād, ,==¦=\ *n* -S [F, fr. MF, fr. OIt *scappata,* fr. fem. of *scappato,* past part. of *scappare* to escape, fr. (assumed) VL *excappare*] **1** *archaic* **:** escape from, evasion of, or flight from control or confinement **2 :** an adventure or experience involving action that runs counter to set rules of conservative behavior or approved or orthodox conduct **:** a piece of mischief **:** a daring act or unusual experience ⟨childish ~*s* on Halloween⟩ ⟨the ~*s* of the hero in the wilds of Tibet⟩ ⟨he . . . crossed to Greece, where he was initiated into the Eleusinian mysteries, an odd ~ for one of his character —John Buchan⟩

[1]es·cape \ə'skāp, e'-\ *vb* -ED/-ING/-S [ME *escapen, ascapen,* fr. ONF *escaper, ascaper,* fr. (assumed) VL *excappare,* fr. L *ex-* + LL *cappa* head covering, cloak — more at CAP] *vi* **1 a :** to get away (as by flight or conscious effort) **:** break away, get free, or get clear ⟨the prisoner *escaped* from prison⟩ ⟨~ from boredom by traveling extensively⟩ ⟨eager to ~ from the army and go back to his home town —Dixon Wecter⟩ ⟨the peculiar merit of this book is that it ~*s* from the conventional attitudes towards the conquest of Mexico —*Times Lit. Supp.*⟩ **b :** to issue from confinement or an enclosure esp. by way of a break (as in a waterpipe) ⟨gas *escaping* from a main⟩ ⟨clamp lips firmly so that no air can ~ —Raymond Zauber⟩ ⟨as the fluid runs through the tile lines, it gradually ~*s* through the open joints —J.R.Dalzell⟩ ⟨her hat was jammed onto the back of her head, her hair *escaping* beneath the crumpled brim —William Faulkner⟩ ⟨the eggs develop in this pouch and the young ~ when they hatch —G.E. & Nettie MacGinitie⟩ **c** *of a plant* **:** to run wild from a condition of cultivation or from a cultivated area **2 :** to avoid or elude an evil that threatens **:** evade imminent pain or misfortune ⟨the infection was so widespread that few *escaped*⟩ ⟨the hunters were so thick any game that *escaped* was lucky⟩ ⟨the crew *escaped,* as usual, but the boat was shattered to pieces —Norman Douglas⟩ ⟨he *escaped* momentarily from the heavy humors which had occupied his mind —T.B.Costain⟩; *specif, of an amateur wrestler* **:** to maneuver from a defensive to a neutral position ~ *vt* **1 :** to get free of **:** break away from ⟨*escaped* the jungle to carry forward the struggle —James Atlas⟩ ⟨to ~ the earth's gravitational pull —Edwina Deans et al⟩ **2 a :** to get or be out of the way of (something one wishes to avoid) **:** miss or succeed in averting (pain or misfortune) **:** AVOID, ELUDE, EVADE ⟨~ poverty and unhappiness⟩ ⟨the Greeks *escaped* the evils of priestly government —W.R.Inge⟩ ⟨firstborn babies characteristically ~ the disease —E.W.Page⟩ ⟨set sail hastily to ~ possible punishment for his share in the enterprise —*Amer. Guide Series: Maine*⟩ ⟨our family seems to have *escaped* television addiction —John McNulty⟩ **b :** to be unnoticed by or not obvious, apparent, or recallable to ⟨the more valuable articles *escaped* the eyes of the thieves⟩ ⟨the profounder subtleties of harmony and rhythm more often than not ~ me —Clive Bell⟩ ⟨a veracity that often ~*s* the authors of historical fiction —*Amer. Guide Series: Oregon*⟩ ⟨the myth is a transcendent idea that ~*s* the mental grasp entirely —H.M.Parshley⟩ **3 a :** to issue from ⟨a smile may ~ us in reading Honorius —H.O.Taylor⟩ **b :** to be uttered by (a person) involuntarily ⟨a muffled moan *escaped* the boy —F.V.W.Mason⟩

syn AVOID, EVADE, ELUDE, ESCHEW, SHUN: ESCAPE refers to a getting away from something viewed as imminently or likely to be dangerous, threatening, or otherwise to be feared or disliked ⟨*escaped* serious injury in the accident⟩ ⟨legal maneuvering enabled him to *escape* a prison term⟩ ⟨the fox *escaped* detection by the hounds⟩ ⟨written in secret to *escape* ridicule —Ellen Glasgow⟩ AVOID may be a near synonym of ESCAPE but stresses forethought and caution; it may indicate a keeping well clear of rather than a getting away when exposed to danger ⟨Wang Lung *avoided* them lest some recognize him —Pearl Buck⟩ ⟨by pooling our difficulties, we may at least *avoid* the failures which come from conceiving the problems of government to be simpler than they are —Felix Frankfurter⟩ ⟨life is full of perils, but the wise man ignores those that are inevitable, and acts prudently but without emotion as regards those that can be *avoided* —Bertrand Russell⟩ EVADE suggests cleverness, adroitness, artifice, or occas. subterfuge in avoiding, escaping, or dodging ⟨the king was so far away that his rules might be in large degree *evaded* if not defied —C.L.Jones⟩ ⟨the experience of life shows that people are constantly doing things which must lead to disaster, and yet by some chance manage to *evade* the result of their folly —W.S.Maugham⟩ ELUDE applies to escaping or evading by baffling, shifty, sly, strategic, or abstruse procedure or character ⟨so some biologists, peering into their microscopes, observe remarkable events which somehow *elude* their colleagues —Martin Gardner⟩ ⟨the ruse to which Captain Lyon had resorted to *elude* the writ by transporting his prisoner to Illinois —Winston Churchill⟩ ESCHEW may indicate an avoiding or abstaining from as unwise or distasteful ⟨he says what he has to say in excellent prose, *eschewing* all highflown and arty dithyrambs —*N.Y. Herald Tribune Bk. Rev.*⟩ ⟨*eschewing* melodramatic shortcuts, in spite of the clamor from Rome, he broke the enemy by the only methods possible — starvation, attrition, and a slow, deadly scientific envelopment —John Buchan⟩ ⟨his fundamental respect for human personality makes him instinctively *eschew* the method of authority —M.R.Cohen⟩ SHUN indicates active or pronounced avoidance, usu. with abhorrence, aversion, or contemning as wrong or unwise ⟨a desolate wilderness of maquis, marsh, and coastal swamp, infested with malaria, and *shunned* by people —George Kish⟩ ⟨to *shun* for his health the pleasures of the table —A.T. Quiller-Couch⟩

syn FLY, FLEE, DECAMP, ABSCOND: ESCAPE is the most general in meaning and refers to getting out of confinement, restraint, or captivity or, in the verb's broadest application, out of the clutches or grip of or involvement in anything considered dangerous or unpleasant ⟨*escaped* from jail⟩ ⟨the first action of the war, in which the British ship . . . *escaped* by superior speed after a sharp fight —Edward Breck⟩ ⟨*escape* from his grief and loneliness —Allen Johnson⟩ ⟨*escape* embarrassment⟩ FLY, used in the sense of *escape* only in the present tense, adds to it the idea of haste, as of one in fear ⟨*fly,* father, *fly!* for all your friends are fled—Shak.⟩ ⟨so absolutely flooded by the Hawkesbury and its tributaries, that the farmers are forced to *fly* for their lives —Anthony Trollope⟩ FLEE implies haste and abruptness of escape, often suggesting not only fear but a certain consequent disorder in the departure ⟨make a boy believe that real work is a thing to *flee* from —C.E. Montague⟩ ⟨founded by men who were *fleeing* from something very like this tyranny —Hugh Gaitskell⟩ ⟨the Irish who *fled* in the famine years —Liam Brophy⟩ ⟨everyone *fled* in summer to escape the swarms of mosquitoes —*Amer. Guide Series: N.C.*⟩ DECAMP does not usu. suggest escape as much as mere, although total, removal from one place to another or complete purposeful departure, applying usu. only with a somewhat humorous connotation to the escape of one in confinement or one avoiding confinement or restraint ⟨other tradesmen came to town, took orders, received advances of goods or money, and then *decamped* —C.L.Jones⟩ ⟨the expectation of his *decamping* as fast as he could from such disgraceful companions —Jane Austen⟩ ⟨might play them false and *decamp* with the entire £100,000 —F.W.Crofts⟩ ABSCOND puts emphasis upon the idea of secrecy, esp. criminal secrecy, in an escape, withdrawal, or departure ⟨a promoter with a salted silver mine sold claims to hundreds, at from $50 to $1000 a claim, and *absconded* with the proceeds —*Amer. Guide Series: Texas*⟩ ⟨he *absconded* from college with his clothes and took refuge in a lonely farmhouse —Van Wyck Brooks⟩ ⟨*abscond* with the family silver⟩

[2]escape \"\ *n* -S [ME *escap, escape,* fr. *escapen,* v.] **1 :** the act of escaping or the fact of having escaped: as **a :** evasion of or deliverance from what confines, limits, or holds ⟨an ~ from a mental hospital⟩ ⟨~ from the earth's gravitational pull⟩ ⟨how to make ~ from his tight grasp⟩; *specif* **:** an unlawful departure of a prisoner from the limits of his custody esp. when without prison breach — see NEGLIGENT ESCAPE, VOLUNTARY ESCAPE; compare CONSTRUCTIVE ESCAPE **b :** evasion of or deliverance from what injures, threatens, torments, bores, or is otherwise undesirable ⟨find no method of ~ from pain and suffering⟩ ⟨a gradual ~ . . . from the hideous experiences and whirling ideas of his youth —*Times Lit. Supp.*⟩ ⟨the ~ from this legal confusion —H.O.Taylor⟩ ⟨these islands have symbolized ~ from a world that is too much with us —V.G.Heiser⟩ ⟨comedy is an ~ not from truth but from despair —Christopher Fry⟩ **c :** leakage or outflow esp. of steam or a liquid ⟨trying to stop an ~ of gas from a broken conduit⟩ **d :** distraction or relief from the routine or a burdensome aspect of everyday existence, usu. from its irksome responsibilities or its harsher realities ⟨a miserable life that provided no means of ~ but alcohol⟩ ⟨can't think of anything more genuinely pleasurable these days than the pure ~ offered you by a trip in a luxury liner —Richard Joseph⟩; *esp* **:** such mental distraction or relief achieved by flight into idealizing fantasy or fiction that glorifies the self **2 a** *archaic* **:** BLUNDER, MISTAKE **b** *obs* **:** TRANSGRESSION **3** *obs* **:** OUTBURST **4 a :** a means of escape ⟨his ~ was first constant reading and then, when that did not satisfy, daydreaming⟩ ⟨his moments of intense contemplative vision are not moments of autointoxication or ~ —Douglas Bush⟩ ⟨when he lost all his money there was no ~ left and he finally went to work⟩ **b :** an outlet or gate through which water may be released from a canal or hydraulic structure **c** [by shortening] **:** FIRE ESCAPE; *specif* **:** a wheeled extension ladder used to evacuate a burning building **d :** a maneuver in amateur wrestling that permits a contestant to gain a neutral position from a position of disadvantage **5 :** a commonly cultivated plant that has run wild or has sprung up from self-sown seeds of a cultivated individual **6 :** the action of getting out of a gravitational field ⟨~ by rocket⟩

[3]escape \"\ *adj* [[2]*escape*] **1 :** of or relating to escape or to an escape ⟨asked to explain his ~ methods after he got out of the concentration camp⟩ ⟨his work, for all its fantasy and superreality, was never an ~ world: the threat of war, the dark emanations of the unconscious, the grotesque and the erotic, suffering and death, all find a place in his microcosm —Herbert Read⟩ **2 :** providing a means or opportunity of evading a regulation, claim, agreement, or commitment ⟨an ~ clause⟩ ⟨the contract set the price of steel at a low figure but contained an ~ provision for raising the price $2 a ton if the market went up generally⟩; *specif* **:** providing an opportunity to a new employee in a union shop or to union members following the negotiation of a new union contract for quitting the union without penalty ⟨a union contract with a 30-day ~ period⟩ ⟨forced the union to include an ~ clause in the contract that was finally settled upon⟩

[4]escape \"\ *n* -S [F, fr. MF *escappe,* fr. L *scapus* shaft of a column, stalk — more at SHAFT] **:** APOPHYGE

escape artist *n* **:** one (as a showman) markedly and ingeniously adept at releasing himself from confinement esp. as a stunt ⟨earned a living as a magician and *escape artist*⟩; *specif* **:** a criminal noted for his ability to escape from jail ⟨the life story of the bank robber and *escape artist* —*New Yorker*⟩

escape cover *also* **escape covert** *n* **:** vegetation that by reason of strategic location or natural formation assists the escape of animals from their predators ⟨multiflora rose forms excellent *escape cover* and produces some food for game animals⟩

escaped *past of* ESCAPE

es·cap·ee \¦e,skā¦pē, ə,skā'pē, e,s-; *also* ə'skā(,)pē *or* e's- *or* -,pi; *sometimes* ¦eskə¦pē\ *n* -S [[1]*escape* + *-ee*] **:** one that has escaped; *esp* **:** an escaped prisoner

escape hatch *n* **1 :** a hatch providing an emergency exit from an enclosed space (as the cabin of an airplane) **2 :** a means of evading something that is or may prove burdensome (as a responsibility or regulation) **:** a way out of a dilemma or difficulty ⟨an agreement to negotiate with an *escape hatch* allowing for settlement by a third party in the event of a deadlock⟩ ⟨headaches were an *escape hatch* in a world of insurmountable difficulties⟩

es·cape·less \ə'skāpləs, e'-\ *adj* **:** incapable of being escaped

escape mechanism *n* **:** a mode of behavior or thinking adopted to evade unpleasant facts or responsibilities **:** MECHANISM OF DEFENSE

es·cape·ment \ə'skāpmənt, e'-\ *n* -S **1 a :** the act of escaping **b** *archaic* **:** a way of escape **:** VENT **2 :** something that escapes; *specif* **:** the number of fish that are permitted to survive and spawn (as by adjustment of fishing seasons or provision of fishways) **3** [alter. (influenced by F *échappement*) of earlier *scapement*] **:** the device in a timepiece which controls the motion of the train of wheelwork and through which the energy of the weight, mainspring, or other power source is delivered to the pendulum or balance by means of impulses that keep the latter in regular vibration and thus permit a tooth to escape from a pallet at regular intervals **4 :** the mechanism in the action of a piano that causes the hammer to rebound after striking **5 :** a ratchet device that permits motion in one direction only in successive equal steps with pauses between (as the spacing mechanism of a typewriter carriage) **6 :** the mechanism that releases the matrices from the magazine of a keyboard-operated slug-casting machine

escapement 3

escape note *or* **escape tone** *n* **:** a nonharmonic note or tone approached by a step from a chord tone and left by a skip in the opposite direction — called also *échappée;* compare CHANGING NOTE

escape opening *n* **:** a secondary means of egress (as from a room) for use only in case of fire

es·cap·er \-pə(r)\ *n* -S **:** one that escapes esp. from enemy custody

escape reaction *n* **:** a physiological or psychological response tending to remove the individual from contact with a noxious stimulus

escapes *pres 3d sing of* ESCAPE, *pl of* ESCAPE

escape valve *n* **:** SAFETY VALVE

escape velocity *n* **:** VELOCITY OF ESCAPE

escapeway \ə'=,=\ *n* [*²escape* + *way*] **:** a channel of escape **:** OUTLET; *also* **:** FIRE ESCAPE

escape wheel *n* **:** a wheel that is last in the train of a timepiece and whose teeth are esp. shaped to impart impulses to a pallet or lever

escaping *pres part of* ESCAPE

es·cap·ing·ly *adv* **:** EVASIVELY

es·ca·pism \ə'skā,pizəm, e'-\ *n* -s **1 :** diversion of the mind to purely imaginative activity or entertainment to escape from reality or routine; *esp* **:** habitual diversion of this kind ⟨stigmatized a taste for her books as ~ of the worst variety, headlong flight into vapid unreality —*Times Lit. Supp.*⟩ ⟨the monotony of big-city life and the boredom of an over-regulated existence create a desire for ~, which is the essence of romanticism —Robert Pick⟩ **2 :** an evasion of unpleasant fact or of reality esp. by compensation ⟨it's the old ~ through mockery . . . a hurt pride looking for scapegoats —Ramon Lavalle⟩

¹es·cap·ist \-,pəst\ *n* -s [*¹escape* + *-ist*] **:** one that escapes; *specif* **:** one guilty of or given to escapism ⟨the . . . idyllic ecstasy of a romantic primitivist or ~ —Douglas Bush⟩ ⟨he has been called an ~, a perennial tenant of the ivory tower, a man who writes about life while taking great pains to remain aloof from it —W.M.Kunstler⟩ ⟨a daydreamer, an ~, a lover of peace —William Saroyan⟩

²escapist \"\ *adj* **:** befitting an escapist or escapism ⟨~ visions⟩ ⟨~ literature⟩

es·cap·ol·o·gist \ə,skā'päləjəst, e,-\ *n* -s [*escape* + *-o-* + *-logist*] **:** one who attempts to avoid reality or serious matters by frivolous self-indulgence and merrymaking — not used technically

es·carbuncle \ə's, e's+,-\ *n* [ME, fr. MF *escarbuncle, escarboncle*, modif. (prob. influenced by *esmeraude* emerald) of L *carbunculus* dark red precious stone, small coal — more at CARBUNCLE] **:** a heraldic charge consisting of a center ornament with eight decorated rays to represent the precious stone carbuncle — called also *carbuncle*

es·car·got \eskärgō\ *n, pl* **escargots** \"\ [F, fr. MF *escargot, escargol*, fr. OProv *escaragol*] **:** a snail prepared for use as food

es·car·go·tiere \,e,skärgə'tye(ə)r\ *n* -s [F *escargotière*, lit., snailery, fr. *escargot* snail] **:** an artificial mound or kitchen midden made up primarily of snail shells but containing artifacts (as found in Algeria)

escarmouche *n* -s [MF — more at SKIRMISH] *obs* **:** SKIRMISH

es·ca·role \'eskə,rōl\ *n* -s [F, fr. MF *scariole*, fr. OIt *scariola*, fr. ML, fr. LL *escariola*, fr. L *escarius* of food, for eating (fr. *esca* food — fr. *edere* to eat — + *-arius* -ary) + *-ola* -ole — more at EAT] **:** ENDIVE 1

¹es·carp \ə'skärp, (')e¦s-\ *n* [F *escarpe*, fr. MF, fr. OIt *scarpa* — more at SCARP] **:** SCARP 1

²escarp \"\ *vt* [F *escarper*, fr. MF, fr. *escarpe*] **:** SCARP

es·carp·ment \ə'skärpmənt, e'-\ *n* -s [F *escarpement*, fr. *escarper* to escarp + *-ment*] **1 :** a steep slope in front of a fortification **2 :** a long cliff or steep slope separating two comparatively level or more gently sloping surfaces and resulting from erosion or faulting

escas *pl of* ESCA

-es·cence \'es°n(t)s\ *n suffix* -s [MF, fr. L *-escentia*, fr. *-escent-, -escens* + *-ia*] **:** state or process of becoming ⟨obso*lescence*⟩ ⟨conval*escence*⟩

-es·cent \¦es°nt\ *adj suffix* [MF, fr. L *-escent-, -escens* (pres. part. suffix of inchoative verbs ending in *-escere*), fr. *-esc-*, element forming inchoative verbs + *-ent-, -ens*, pres. part. suffix of the 3d conjugation — more at -ENT] **1 :** beginning, beginning to be, becoming, slightly ⟨obsol*escent*⟩ ⟨arbo*rescent*⟩ ⟨alkal*escent*⟩ **2 :** reflecting or emitting light (in a specified way) ⟨opal*escent*⟩ ⟨fluor*escent*⟩

esch·a·lot \'eshə,lät\ *n* -s [F *échalote*, fr. MF *eschalotte* — more at SHALLOT] **:** SHALLOT

¹es·char \'e,skär, 'eskər\ *n* -s [alter. (influenced by F *eschare* & LL *eschara* eschar) of ME *escare* — more at SCAR] **1 :** a dry crust **:** SCAB; *esp* **:** one formed after a burn **2 :** a lesion covered by an eschar

²eschar *var of* ESKER

es·cha·ra \'eskərə\ *n* [NL, fr. LL, scab, scar — more at SCAR] **1** *cap* **:** a genus of bryozoans (order Cheilostomata) that produce delicate colonies resembling various fragile corals **2** -s **:** any bryozoan of the genus *Eschara*; *also* **:** an erect 2-layered bryozoan colony — **es·cha·rine** \-,rīn, -,rən\ *adj* — **es·cha·roid** \-,rȯid\ *adj*

¹es·cha·rot·ic \¦eskə¦räd·ik\ *adj* [F or LL; F *escharotique*, fr. MF, fr. LL *escharoticus*, fr. Gk *escharōtikos*, fr. (assumed) *escharōtos* (verbal of *escharoun* to form an eschar, fr. *eschara* eschar) + *-ikos* -ic — more at SCAR] **:** producing an eschar

²escharotic \"\ *n* -s **:** an agent (as a chemical) that produces an eschar

es·chat·o·col \e'skad·ə,kȯl *also* -,käl *or* -,kōl *or* -d·əkəl *or* -d·ēkəl\ *n* -s [Gk *eschatos* last, farthest + E *-col* (as in *protocol*)] **:** the concluding part of a protocol

es·chat·o·log·i·cal \¦es,kad·°l'äjəkəl, ¦eskəd·-\ *adj* **:** of, relating to, dealing with, or as regards the ultimate destiny of mankind and the world ⟨~ hope⟩ ⟨~ literature⟩ ⟨~ implications⟩ ⟨~ ideas⟩ — compare ESCHATOLOGY — **es·chat·o·log·i·cal·ly** \-k(ə)lē\ *adv*

es·cha·tol·o·gist \,eskə'täləjəst\ *n* -s **:** one centrally concerned with eschatology or an eschatological belief, teaching, or interpretation (as of scripture)

es·cha·tol·o·gy \-jē\ *n* -ES [Gk *eschatos* last, farthest + E *-logy*; akin to Gk *ex, ek* out of, from — more at EX-] **1 a :** a study or science dealing with the ultimate destiny or purpose of mankind and the world ⟨a theological student with a dominant interest in ~⟩; *also* **:** central concern for such an ultimate destiny or purpose ⟨it was a big step in the movement away from ~ when Luther formulated his doctrine of baptism without reference to the last things —J.R.Coates⟩ **b :** a doctrine or theory or conclusion concerning the ultimate destiny or purpose of mankind and the world ⟨the horrible ~ which hypnotized even the greatest among medieval philosophers and theologians —G.G.Coulton⟩ ⟨it presupposes an ~ or set of assumptions concerning the end events of history —O.J.Baab⟩; *esp* **:** Christian doctrine or theory or a particular Christian doctrine or theory of this kind ⟨one or other of the Protestant *eschatologies* —*Notes & Queries*⟩ **2 :** ultimate destiny or purpose esp. according to Christian doctrine ⟨man's increasing indifference to ~, his crass mistaking of means for ends —W.H.Gardner⟩ ⟨in the apocalyptic writings the ~ of the individual comes to the front, although at first associated with an eternal kingdom on earth —L.E.Fuller⟩ **3 :** a science that deals with or a doctrine or theory about things of final importance to mankind ⟨the Marxian economic ~ —B.B.Seligman⟩

¹es·cheat \əs(h)'chēt, es(-\ *n* -s [ME *eschete*, fr. AF, fr. OF *eschete, escheoite*, fr. *escheoit*, past part. of *escheoir* to fall, happen, fr. (assumed) VL *excadere* to happen, fall to the lot of, fr. L *ex-* + *cadere* to fall — more at CHANCE] **1 a :** the falling back or reversion of lands in English feudal law to the lord of the fee upon the failure of heirs capable of inheriting under the original grant **b :** the lapsing or reverting of land to the crown in England or to the state in the U.S. as original and ultimate proprietor by reason of failure of persons legally entitled to such land — see INQUEST OF OFFICE **c :** the right of taking property that is subject to such reversion **2 :** escheated property **3 a** *Scotland* **:** CONFISCATION, FORFEITURE — see LIFERENT ESCHEAT **b** *obs* **:** an appropriating unfairly or by force **:** PLUNDERING

²escheat \"\ *vb* -ED/-ING/-S [ME *escheten*, fr. *eschete*, n.] *vt* **1 :** to cause to revert, lapse, pass, or come or go into the possession of another by escheat **2** *Scots law* **:** FORFEIT ~ *vi* **:** to revert, fall, lapse, or pass by escheat

es·cheat·able \-chēd·əbəl\ *adj* **:** subject to escheat or capable of being claimed or taken by escheat ⟨since the unpaid dividends are deposited with a New York bank, it may be inferred that they are also ~ by New York —David Fellman⟩

es·cheat·or \-ēd·ər, -ēd·,ȯ(ə)r\ *n* -s [ME *eschetour*, fr. AF, fr. OF *escheoit* (past part. of *escheoir* to fall, happen) + *-our* -or] **:** a legal officer formerly appointed to look after escheats

esch·e·rich·ia \,eshə'rikēə\ *n, cap* [NL, fr. Theodor *Escherich* †1911 Ger. physician + NL *-ia*] **:** a genus of aerobic gram-negative rod-shaped bacteria (family Enterobacteriaceae) that form acid and gas on many carbohydrates (as dextrose and lactose) but no acetoin and that include forms (as members of the type species *E. coli*) normally present in the human or other vertebrate intestines which are occas. pathogenic and indicative of fecal contamination when found in water and other forms which typically occur in soil and water

es·chew \əs(h)'chü, es(-\ *vb* -ED/-ING/-S [ME *eschewen, eschuen*, fr. MF *eschiuver, eschiver* to shun, avoid, fr. OF, of Gmc origin; akin to OHG *sciuhen* to frighten off, make timid — more at SHY] *vt* **1 :** to abstain from (as something wrong, inappropriate, distasteful, or harmful) **:** SHUN ⟨trained to ~ private passions and pursuits —E.A.Mowrer⟩ ⟨some of the millionaires ~*ed* palatial magnificence —F.L.Allen⟩ ⟨despite the engagement to ~ violence, disorders and bloodshed took place —*Collier's Yr. Bk.*⟩ ⟨the normal vegetarian only ~*s* fish, flesh, and fowl —N.C.Wright⟩ **2** *obs* **:** to keep free of **:** ESCAPE ~ *vi, obs* **:** ESCAPE **syn** see ESCAPE, FORGO

es·chew·al \-üəl\ *n* -s **:** SHUNNING, AVOIDANCE ⟨the deliberate ~ of virtuous action —Peter Ure⟩ ⟨an ascetic ~ of female luxury —J.G.Cozzens⟩

esch·scholt·zia \e'shōltsēə\ *n* [NL, fr. J.F.*Eschscholtz* †1831 Ger. naturalist + NL *-ia*] **1** *cap* **:** a genus of showy herbs (family Papaveraceae) of western No. America having leaves ternately dissected several times into linear or oblong segments and sepals coherent into a characteristic pointed hood which is pushed off as the flower buds expand — see CALIFORNIA POPPY **2** -s **:** any plant of the genus *Eschscholtzia*

es·chy·nite *or* **aes·chy·nite** \'eskə,nīt\ *n* -s [G *äschynit*, fr. *äschyn-* (fr. Gk *aischynē* shame) + G *-it* -ite] **:** a mineral $(Ce,Ca,Fe,Th)(Ti,Cb)_2O_6$ consisting of a rare oxide of titanium, columbium, cerium, and other metals isomorphous with priorite and found in nearly black prismatic crystals

es·clandre \esklää^n dr(°), -d(rə)\ *n, pl* **esclandres** \"\ [F, fr. MF, scandal — more at SLANDER] **:** an incident that arouses unpleasant talk or gives rise to scandal **:** a public unpleasant altercation **:** SCENE

es·cla·vage \¦esklä¦väzh\ *n* -s [F, lit., slavery, fr. MF, slavery, fr. OF *esclave* slave + *-age* — more at SLAVE] **:** a necklace having several rows of chains, beads, or jewels

es·co·bi·lla \,eskə'bē(y)ə\ *n* -s [Sp, lit., little broom, dim. of *escoba* broom] **:** a European plant (*Centaurea salmantica*) naturalized as a weed in California

es·co·bi·ta \,eskə'bēd·ə\ *n* -s [AmerSp, lit., little broom, dim. of *escoba* broom, fr. L *scopa, scopae*] **:** any of several Californian plants of the genus *Orthocarpus* (as *O. purpurascens*)

escocheon *n* -s [ME *escochon* — more at ESCUTCHEON] **1 :** ESCUTCHEON **2 :** INESCUTCHEON

es·co·lar \¦eskə¦lär\ *n, pl* **escolar** *or* **escolars** [Sp, lit., scholar; from rings like spectacles around the eyes] **:** a fish of the family Gempylidae; *esp* **:** a large rough-scaled fish (*Ruvettus pretiosus*) that resembles a mackerel, is highly prized for food, and lives at a depth of from 100 to 400 fathoms in the Mediterranean, middle Atlantic, and throughout the southern seas and from whose flesh a purgative oil can be extracted — called also *oilfish*

escollope *var of* ESCALOPE

es·con·son \ə'skän(t)sən\ *n* -s [F *écoinçon, écoinson*, fr. MF *escoinson* — more at SCONCHEON] **:** a jamb shaft in the inside arris of a window jamb

es·co·pe·ta \,eskə'pād·ə, -ped·ə\ *n* -s [Sp, fr. OIt *schioppetto*, lit., small explosion, dim. of *schioppo*, lit., explosion] **:** a short firelock musket

es·co·pette \¦eskə¦pet\ *n* -s [F, fr. MF *eschopette*, fr. OIt *schioppetto*] **:** ESCOPETA

¹es·cort \'e,skȯr|t, -ō(ə)|, *usu* |d·+V\ *n* -s [F *escorte*, fr. MF *escorte, scorte*, fr. OIt *scorta*, lit., act of escorting, fr. *scorgere* to perceive, escort, guide, fr. (assumed) VL *excorrigere* to guide, observe, fr. L *ex-* + *corrigere* to correct, make straight — more at CORRECT] **1 a :** a body of armed men to guard a person or goods on a journey or to accompany as a mark of respect or honor **b :** a protective screen of warships or fighter planes or a single ship or plane attending upon one or more vulnerable craft for fending off enemy attack; *esp* **:** a group of antisubmarine warships accompanying a convoy of merchant ships as protection **c :** protection by an escort ⟨under heavy ~ the big ship made the dangerous trip through the Atlantic and Caribbean to the Panama canal —H.L.Merillat⟩ **2 a :** a body of persons or an individual accompanying another or others as protection or as a mark of honor or courtesy ⟨felt it wise to send an ~ with the group through the more disreputable parts of the city⟩ ⟨included in the Corps of Queen's Messengers is a limited number of ~*s* whose duty it is to accompany and assist the queen's messengers on certain types of journey —*Brit. Information Services*⟩ ⟨I shall give you as many men for an ~ as you think necessary, or you may go entirely alone —Carleton Beals⟩ **b :** the boy or man who goes on a date with a girl or woman ⟨there were many more men in the community than women, and every girl had a choice of ~*s* —David Fairchild⟩ ⟨the older woman left her ~ sitting at the bar⟩ **c :** a man who makes a business of serving as a companion or date for women (as at a restaurant or in attendance at dances or the theater) **3 :** the fact of escorting **:** accompaniment as an escort ⟨he left us, declining our offered ~ —Sheridan Le Fanu⟩ ⟨flying close ~ for the transports —R.L.Scott⟩ **4 :** GUIDE ⟨provide the man with an ~ through the intricate ways of the city⟩; *esp* **:** one who guides visitors to their destination in an industrial establishment

²es·cort \ə'sk-, (')e¦sk-\ *vt* -ED/-ING/-S **1 :** to accompany as an escort ⟨using it as a base, fighters can ~ all kinds of bombers to and from Japan —*Newsweek*⟩ ⟨each spring they lovingly crate dozens of their finest blooms and ~ them by overnight express to the Royal Horticultural Society's Rhododendron Show in London —D.S.Boyer⟩ ⟨the sacred relic is ~*ed* by the saffron-robed priests around the town —Rex Moorfoot⟩ ⟨the great liner and ~*ing* tugs —*This Week Mag.*⟩ **2 a :** CONDUCT ⟨rescued the men and ~*ed* them to a place of safety⟩ ⟨~*ing* that charming young woman across the terrace —Robert Grant †1940⟩ ⟨~*ed* them to their box with a sort of pompous humility —Oscar Wilde⟩ **:** GUIDE ⟨the tours combine the freedom of traveling by private automobile with the advantages of an ~*ed* tour in such tedious matters as baggage and reservations —*Ford Times*⟩ **b :** to take or lead forcibly ⟨was ~*ed* to headquarters, and almost immediately identified as one of the escaped convicts —*Springfield (Mass.) Union*⟩ ⟨two guards assigned to ~ a sailor to the brig⟩

escort carrier *n* **:** a small aircraft carrier (as a converted cargo ship) whose primary mission is usu. antisubmarine warfare — called also *baby carrier*

escort fighter *n* **:** an offensive fighter airplane of maximum fuel capacity for escort to heavy bombers on raids

escort wagon *n* **:** a wagon formerly used in the U.S. Army for general hauling

escot *vt, past part* **escoted** [MF *escoter*, fr. *escot* contribution, of Gmc origin; akin to ON *skot* contribution — more at SCOT] *obs* **:** to provide support for (a child) **:** MAINTAIN

escribed circle \ē,skrībd-, e-\ *n* [*e-* + L *scribere* to write — more at SCRIBE] **:** a circle outside of a triangle that is tangent to one of its sides and also to the other two sides that have been extended

escript *n* [ME, fr. MF — more at SCRIPT] *obs* **:** a written document (as a decree)

es·cri·toire \'eskrə·,twär, -wä(r, ¦==='=\ *n* -s [obs. F *escritoire* (now *écritoire*) writing desk, scriptorium, fr. ML *scriptorium*] **:** a piece of furniture resembling a bureau or combination bureau and bookcase and providing a writing surface (as by a drawer with a hinged front that drops down) or desk area (as behind a hinged front that drops down to form a writing surface) **:** SECRETARY; *also* **:** the writing drawer or desk area of such a piece of furniture

escrod *var of* SCROD

es·crol *also* **es·croll** \ə'skrōl\ *n* -s [modif. (influenced by E *scroll*) of MF *escroele, escrouelle* small piece, bit, dim. of *escroe, escroue* bit, scroll] **:** a heraldic scroll

¹es·crow \'e,skrō, ə's-,e's-\ *n* -s [MF *escroe, escroue* bit, scroll, strip of parchment — more at SCROLL] **1 :** a deed or bond, money, or a piece of property delivered into the keeping of a third party by one party to a contract or sometimes taken from one party to a contract and put in trust to be returned only upon the performance or fulfillment of some condition of the contract or to insure such performance or fulfillment by some other disposition **2 :** a fund or deposit serving as or designed to serve as an escrow ⟨expenses in connection with an ~ established to ensure the payment of the property tax on the house⟩ ⟨the proposed ~ of funds to ensure completion is acceptable —*Veterans Administration Tech. Bull.*⟩ — **in escrow** *adv (or adj)* **:** in trust as an escrow ⟨cash funds will be placed *in escrow* with the trustee to pay interest on and principal of the notes —*U.S. Investor*⟩ ⟨have over $1000 *in escrow* to pay taxes⟩

²es·crow \ə's-, (')e¦s-\ *vt* -ED/-ING/-S **:** to place in escrow ⟨~ a certain amount of money for the payment of taxes⟩ ⟨a certification of loan disbursement showing the loan proceeds which have been ~*ed* —*Veterans Administration Tech. Bull.*⟩

es·crow·ee \¦e,skrō¦ē; e¦skrō¦ē, ə¦s-; ¦eskrə¦wē\ *n* -s **:** the one holding an escrow in trust **:** the depository of an escrow

es·cu·age \'e,skyüij, 'eskyəwij\ *n* -s [MF *escuage*, fr. OF, fr. *escu* shield (fr. L *scutum*) + *-age* — more at ESQUIRE] **1 :** the military service required of a knight incident to his fee **2 :** SCUTAGE

¹es·cu·do \ə'sk(y)ü(,)dō, e'-, -kü(,)t͟hō\ *n* -s [Sp, lit., shield, fr. L *scutum* shield — more at ESQUIRE] **1 a :** an old gold coin of Spain and Spanish America worth two pieces of eight or Spanish dollars **b :** a Spanish silver coin of crown or dollar size **2 :** a unit of value equivalent to one escudo coin

²es·cu·do \ə'sk(y)ü(,)dō, e'-, ish'kü(,)thü\ *n* -s [Pg, lit., shield, fr. L *scutum*] **1 :** an old Portuguese gold coin similar to the Spanish escudo **2 a :** since 1911 the basic monetary unit of Portugal and Portuguese territories — see MONEY table **b :** a coin representing one escudo unit **c :** the basic monetary unit of Cape Verde — see MONEY table

es·cu·lent \'eskyələnt\ *adj or n* [L *esculentus*, fr. *esca* food (fr. *edere* to eat) + *-ulentus* -ulent — more at EAT] **:** EDIBLE

es·cu·le·tin *or* **aes·cu·le·tin** \,eskyə'lēt°n\ *n* -s [ISV, blend of *esculin, aesculin* and *-et-*] **:** a crystalline lactone $C_9H_6O_4$ obtained by hydrolysis of esculin; 6,7-dihydroxycoumarin

es·cu·lin *or* **aes·cu·lin** \'eskyələn\ *n* -s [It *esculina*, fr. NL *Aesculus* (genus name of *Aesculus hippocastanum*, species that produces it) + It *-ina* -in] **:** a crystalline glucoside $C_{15}H_{16}O_9$ from the inner bark of the horse chestnut and roots of the yellow jessamine (*Gelsemium sempervirens*) that absorbs ultraviolet rays

es·cutch·eon *or* **es·cutch·eon** \ə'skəchən, e'-\ *n* -s [ME *escochon*, fr. MF *escuchon, escuçon*, fr. (assumed) VL *scution-, scutio*, fr. L *scutum* shield + *-ion-, -io* -ion — more at ESQUIRE] **1 a :** a defined area on which armorial bearings are depicted, marshaled, or displayed usu. consisting of a shield or something made to resemble a shield — see DEXTER 2, SINISTER; compare BASE, CHIEF, FESS, LOZENGE, NAVEL, NOMBRIL, POINT **b :** the portion of such an area not covered by an armorial bearing **c :** COAT OF ARMS ⟨his haughty, domineering mother, whose family had some claim to an ~ —Theodore Bonnet⟩ **d :** a decorative device or emblem resembling a coat of arms **e :** ²HATCHMENT **2** *or* **escutcheon plate :** a protective or ornamental shield, flange, or border (as around a keyhole or radio dial) **3 :** SHIELD BUDDING **4 :** the part of a vessel's stern on which her name is displayed **5 :** any of certain animal structures shaped somewhat like a shield: **a** (1) **:** an area just above the rear part of the udder of many quadrupeds extending upward and outward to the flanks and being distinguished by the hair which turns upward rather than downward (2) **:** the distinctive hair of such an escutcheon **b :** the mesoscutellum of a beetle or hemipterous insect **c :** the depression behind the beak of certain bivalves

escutcheons 2

es·cutch·eoned \-nd\ *adj* **:** having or decorated with escutcheons

escutcheon of pretense : an inescutcheon on the center of the shield of the husband of an heiress or coheiress

escutcheon pin *n* **:** a small round-headed ornamental usu. brass nail for attaching escutcheon plates

escutellate \(¦)ē+\ *adj* [*e-* + NL *scutellum* + E *-ate*] *of insects* **:** having no visible scutellum

esdragol *var of* ESTRAGOLE

¹-ese \¦ēz, ¦ēs\ *adj suffix* [Pg *-ês* & It *-ese*, adj. & n. suffix, fr. (assumed) VL *-esis*, fr. L *-ensis*] **:** of, relating to, or originating in (a certain place or country) ⟨Japan*ese*⟩ ⟨Vienn*ese*⟩

²-ese \"\ *n suffix, pl* **-ese** [Pg *-ês* & It *-ese*] **1 :** native or resident (of a specified place or country) ⟨Chin*ese*⟩ **2 a :** the language (of a particular place, country, or nationality) ⟨Siam*ese*⟩ ⟨Canton*ese*⟩ **b :** speech, literary style, or diction peculiar to (a specified place, person, or group) — usu. in words applied in dislike or contempt ⟨Carlyl*ese*⟩ ⟨journal*ese*⟩ ⟨Pentagon*ese*⟩ ⟨federal*ese*⟩

ESE *abbr* east-southeast

es·em·plas·tic \¦e,sem¦plastik, ¦esəm-\ *adj* [Gk *es, eis* into (fr. *en* in) + E *em-* (fr. Gk *hen-, heis* one) + E *plastic* — more at IN, HENO-] **:** shaping or having the power to shape disparate things into a unified whole — used of the imagination

eseptate \(')ē+\ *adj* [*e-* + *septate*] **:** having no septa

es·er·ine \'esə,rēn, -,rən\ *n* -s [F *ésérine*, fr. *éséré* Calabar bean (fr. native name in Africa) + *-ine* -in] **:** PHYSOSTIGMINE — used esp. in biology

es·er·in·ize \'esərə,nīz\ *vt* -ED/-ING/-S **:** to treat with physostigmine esp. to enhance the physiologic effect of acetylcholine ⟨proceeded to ~ both eyes of a rabbit —Otto Loewi⟩

es·er·o·line \'esərə,lēn\ *n* -s [ISV, blend of *eserine* and *-ol*] **:** a phenolic nitrogenous base $HOC_6H_3C_7H_{14}N_2$ obtained by hydrolysis of physostigmine

e sharp *n, usu cap E* **:** the tone a half step above E and sounding enharmonically the same as F in the tempered scale

eshi-kongo \,eshē'käŋ(,)gō\ *n pl, usu cap E&K* **:** a division of a Bantu people of Angola descended from the dominant race of the ancient kingdom of Kongo

esh·in \'eshən\ *n* -s [perh. irreg. fr. ¹*ashen*] *dial Eng* **:** PAIL, TUB

e silentio *var of* EX SILENTIO

esill \'ä|səl, 'ē|, |zəl\ *n* -s [ME *eisil, aisil*, fr. OF, vinegar, fr. (assumed) VL *acetulum*, dim. of L *acetum* vinegar, sour wine — more at ACETIC] **1** *archaic* **:** VINEGAR **2** *archaic* **:** a wine made from vinegar

esiphonal \(')ē+\ *adj* [*e-* + *siphon* + *-al*] *of a bivalve mollusk* **:** having no siphon

esiphonate \"+\ *adj* [*e-* + *siphonate*] **:** ESIPHONAL

-e·sis \'ēsəs, ,əsəs\ *n suffix, pl* **-eses** \'ē(,)sēz, ,ə,sēz\ [ME, fr. OE, fr. L, fr. Gk *-esis, -ēsis*, fr. *-e-, -ē-*, derivational element attached to certain verbs + *-sis*, fem. suffix of action] **:** action **:** process ⟨enur*esis*⟩

es·ker *also* **es·kar** *or* **es·char** \'eskə(r)\ *n* -s [IrGael *eiscir* ridge] **:** a long narrow often sinuous ridge or mound of sand, gravel, and boulders deposited between ice walls by a stream flowing on, within, or beneath a stagnant glacier — compare KAME

es·ki·mo \'eskə,mō\ *n* [Dan *Eskimo* & F *Esquimau*, fr. the name applied by the Algonquians to the tribes north of them; akin to Abnaki *esquimantsic* eaters of raw flesh, Cree *askimowew* he eats it raw] **1** *pl* **eskimo** *or* **eskimos** *usu cap* **a :** a group of peoples of northern Canada, Greenland, Alaska, and eastern Siberia **b :** a member of such people **2** -s *cap* **:** the Eskimo-Aleut language of the Eskimo people **3** -s *often cap* **:** RUSTIC BROWN — **es·ki·mo·an** \¦eskə¦mōən\ *adj, usu cap*

eskimo-aleut *n, cap E&A* **:** a language stock consisting of Aleut, Inupik, and Yupik

eskimo curlew *n, usu cap E* **:** a New World curlew (*Numenius borealis*) that breeds in northern No. America and winters in So. America and is now extremely rare

eskimo dog *n, usu cap E* **1 :** a broad-chested powerful dog of a breed native to Greenland and Labrador, where it was developed as a sled dog and hunting dog, and characterized by a heavy double coat, the outer coat long and shaggy and the inner of soft dense wool, by short erect ears, full tail curled across the back, and large hairy paws and averaging 50 to 85 pounds in weight and 20 to 25 inches in height **2 :** any sled dog of American origin

es·ki·moid \'eskə,mȯid\ *adj, usu cap* [*Eskimo* + *-oid*] **:** resembling the Eskimo ⟨their longer, narrower . . . faces were more *Eskimoid* than their successors —H.B.Collins⟩

es·ki·mol·o·gist \ˌeskəˈmäləjəst\ *n* -s *usu cap* **:** a specialist in Eskimology

es·ki·mol·o·gy \-jē\ *n* -ES *usu cap* [*Eskimo* + *-logy*] **:** the study of Eskimo culture or language

Eskimo Pie *trademark* — used for a bar of ice cream enclosed in a chocolate shell and often formed on a stick

eskimo potato *n, usu cap E* **:** SPRING BEAUTY 1; *esp* **:** a plant (*Claytonia tuberosa*) of Alaska and high elevations of more southerly western No. America that has a starchy edible tuberous root and bears rosy flowers in clusters in spring

eskimo purchase *n, usu cap E* **:** a crude tackle of looped rawhide rope devised by Eskimos to haul walrus or seal from the water using holes through the ice and the animal's hide in lieu of pulley sheaves

es·ki·se·hir \ˌeskēˌsheˌhi(ə)r\ *adj, usu cap* [fr. *Eskişehir*, Turkey] **:** of or from the city of Eskisehir, Turkey **:** of the kind or style prevalent in Eskisehir

es·march bandage \ˈeˌsmˌärk, ˈezˌm\ *n, usu cap E* [after J. F. A. von *Esmarch* †1908 Ger. surgeon] **:** a tight rubber bandage for driving the blood out of a limb

es·me·ral·da \ˌezməˈraldə\ *n, pl* **esmeralda** *or* **esmeraldas** *usu cap* [AmerSp, fr. Sp, emerald, fr. (assumed) VL *smaragda*; fr. the emeralds found in its territory — more at EMERALD] **1 :** a now extinct language family of the coast of Ecuador — **es·me·ral·dan** \ˌezməˈraldən\ *adj, usu cap*

es·ne \ˈeznē, -ˌne\ *n* -s [OE; akin to OHG *asni* day laborer, Goth *asneis* day laborer, harvester, *asans* harvest — more at EARN] **:** a laborer or man of the lower classes among the Anglo-Saxons

esnecy *n* -ES [ML *esnescia, aisnecia*, fr. OF *ainsnesse*, fr. *ainsné* eldest, firstborn + *-esse* -ess — more at EIGNE] *Eng law, obs* **:** a prerogative of the eldest coparcener to choose first after an inheritance is divided

eso- *prefix* [Gk *eso-*, fr. *esō* within — more at ESOTERIC] **:** inner ⟨*eso*tropia⟩ ⟨*eso*neural⟩

esoc·i·dae \əˈsäsəˌdē, ēˈ-\ *n pl, cap* [NL, fr. *Esoc-, Esox*, type genus + *-idae*] **:** a family of elongated voracious freshwater fishes (order Haplomi) coextensive with the genus *Esox* and comprising the pikes, pickerels, and muskellunges

esoc·i·form \-äsəˌfȯrm\ *adj* [NL *Esoc-, Esox*, genus name + E *-iform*] **:** resembling the Esocidae

es·od·ic \(ˈ)eˈsädik, (ˈ)ēˈ-\ *adj* [Gk *esodos, eisodos* entrance (fr. *es, eis* into — fr. *en* in — + *hodos* way) + E *-ic* — more at IN, -ODE] *of nerves* **:** AFFERENT

eso·narthex \ˈesō+\ *n* [*eso-* + *narthex*] **:** the inner narthex of a church — compare EXONARTHEX

esophag- *or* **esophago-** *also* **oesophag-** *or* **oesophago-** *comb form* [Gk *oisophagos* gullet — more at ESOPHAGUS] **:** esophagus ⟨*esophag*ectomy⟩ ⟨*esophago*pathy⟩ **:** esophageal and ⟨*esophago*gastroscopy⟩

esoph·a·ge·al \əˈsäfəˈjēəl, ēˈs-, ˈēˌs- *sometimes* ˈēsəˈfaj(ē)əl\ *also* **esoph·a·gal** \əˈsäfəgəl, (ˈ)ēˈs-\ *or* **oe·soph·a·ge·al** *like* ESOPHAGEAL\ *adj* [NL *esophagus, oesophagus* (fr. Gk *oisophagos*) + E *-eal* (as in *tracheal*), *-al*] **:** of or by means of the esophagus

esophageal artery *n* **:** any of several arteries that arise from the front of the aorta, anastomose along the esophagus, and terminate by anastomosis with adjacent arteries

esophageal gland *n* **:** one of the racemose glands in the walls of the esophagus that in man are small and serve principally to lubricate the food but in some birds secrete a milky fluid on which the young are fed

esophageal ring *n* **:** a circle of nerve tissue surrounding the gullet in many invertebrates (as annelids and arthropods) — called also *circumesophageal ring*

esophageal speech *n* **:** a method of speaking which is used by individuals whose larynx has been removed and in which phonation is achieved by expelling swallowed air from the esophagus

esophageal teeth *n* **:** the series of enamel-tipped hypapophyses of the posterior cervical vertebrae of certain snakes (as *Dasypeltis scaber*) that penetrating the esophagus act as teeth to break the shells of eggs

esoph·a·ge·an *also* **oe·soph·a·ge·an** \əˈsäfəˈjēən, eˈs-, ˈēˌs- *sometimes* ˈēsəˈfaj(ē)ən\ *adj* [NL *esophagus, oesophagus* + E *-ean*] **:** ESOPHAGEAL

esoph·a·gi·tis *also* **oe·soph·a·gi·tis** \əˌsäfəˈjīdəs, (ˌ)ēˌs-, -fəˈgī-\ *n* -ES [NL, fr. *esophag-, oesophag-* + *-itis*] **:** inflammation of the esophagus

esoph·a·go·gastrostomy \əˈsäfə(ˌ)gō, ēˈs-+\ *n* [ISV *esophag-* + *gastrostomy*] **:** the surgical formation of an artificial communication between the esophagus and the stomach

esoph·a·go·scope *also* **oe·soph·a·go·scope** \əˈ==gəˌskōp\ *n* [*esophag-, oesophag-* + *-scope*] **:** an instrument for inspecting the interior of the esophagus — **esoph·a·go·scop·ic** \əˌ=ˈ==ˈskäpik\ *adj* — **esoph·a·gos·co·pist** \əˌ==ˈgäskəpəst\ *n* -s

esoph·a·gus *also* **oe·soph·a·gus** \əˈsäfəgəs, ēˈs-\ *n, pl* **esopha·gi** *also* **oesopha·gi** \-ˌgī, -ˌjī, -ˌgē\ [ME *ysophagus*, fr. Gk *oisophagos*, fr. *oiso-* (fr. *oisein*, suppletive future infinitive of *pherein* to carry) + *-phagos*, fr. *phagein* to eat — more at BEAR, BAKSHEESH] **1 :** the tube that leads from the pharynx to the stomach being composed of an outer muscular coat containing both longitudinal and circular fibers, an areolar coat, and an inner mucous coat lined with a stratified pavement epithelium on the surface of which the esophageal glands open, and being in man about nine inches long; passing down the neck between the trachea and the spinal column and behind the left bronchus where it pierces the diaphragm slightly to the left of the middle line and joins the cardiac end of the stomach — see DIGESTION illustration **2 :** PHARYNX 2

es·o·pho·ria \ˌesəˈfōrēə *sometimes* ˌēs-\ *n* -s [NL, fr. *eso-* + *-phoria*] **:** squint in which the eyes tend to turn inward toward the nose **:** LATENT STRABISMUS

¹es·o·ter·ic \ˌesəˈterik, -sōˌ-, -rēk *sometimes* ˈēs-\ *adj* [LL *esotericus*, fr. Gk *esōterikos*, fr. *esōterō* (compar. of *esō* within, fr. *es, eis* into, fr. *en* in) + *-ikos* -ic — more at IN] **1 a :** designed for or understood by the specially initiated alone ⟨types of music . . . that demand special training to be perceived and enjoyed, and its devotees form a cult, so that their art is the most ~ of all arts —John Dewey⟩ ⟨a body of ~ legal doctrine —B.N.Cardozo⟩ ⟨her vocabulary wasn't slimed up with offensive bits of ~ finishing-school slang —R.P.Warren⟩ —opposed to *exoteric* **b :** difficult to understand **:** ABSTRUSE ⟨there are two kinds of classics, the popular and the ~, those that yield their meaning at the first encounter and those that we have to discover by effort and insight —Van Wyck Brooks⟩ ⟨passage involving ~ swordplay —R.L.Taylor⟩ **2 :** holding esoteric doctrines or engaging in esoteric rites ⟨the ~ sects, which guard a mystery known only to the initiated —W.L. Sperry⟩ **:** dealing in or concerned with esoteric matters ⟨an ~ study⟩ ⟨many drivers going through Oak Ridge on their way somewhere else stop to stare at the ~ factories, that, for better or worse, are shaping their futures —Daniel Lang⟩ ⟨the scholarly director of an ~ local research center called the Institute of Jazz Studies —E.J.Kahn⟩ ⟨the museum was an ~, occult place in which a mystic language was spoken —Aline B. Saarinen⟩ **3 a :** confined or limited to a small circle ⟨arctic exploration was an ~ pursuit —F.P.Hanson⟩ ⟨lingers in the twilight of an ~ reputation —H.L.Mencken⟩ **b :** PRIVATE, CONFIDENTIAL ⟨some ~ reason known only to God and himself —Francis Gérard⟩ **4 :** of special, rare, or unusual interest ⟨many are rather ~ items such as aluminum duck presses, mechanical duck pluckers, woolen bands to keep the belly and kidney areas warm when hunting in winter —Bill Wolf⟩ ⟨they would smoke me out and ask me questions, as though I possessed some ~ knowledge of a kind not revealed by the guides —Lawrence Dame⟩ ⟨if the Requiem seems a bit ~ and out of the way for a modern conductor, let us take a symphony —P.H.Lang⟩ ⟨~ colors like taupe or celadon —*New Yorker*⟩ — **es·o·ter·i·cal·ly** \-rək(ə)lē, -rēk-, -li\ *adv*

²esoteric \ˈ"\ *n* -s **1** [LGk *esōterikos*, fr. Gk, adj.] **:** an initiate in esoteric doctrines or rites **2 pl esoterics** *pl* **:** esoteric doctrines or treatises

es·o·ter·i·ca \ˌ==ˈ=rəkə, -rēkə\ *n pl* [NL, fr. Gk *esōterika*, neut. pl. of *esōterikos* esoteric (adj.)] **1 :** esoteric items ⟨such space ~ as the impacts of primary cosmic rays and micrometeorites —*Time*⟩ ⟨persons not familiar with the ~ of maneuvering commands may find the pages of such talk both bewildering and monotonous —Walter Karig⟩ ⟨an American unfamiliar with billabongs, bonzer, and other Australian ~ may find it rough going in spots —Lawrence Griswold⟩ **2 :** PORNOGRAPHY

es·o·ter·i·cism \-rəˌsizəm\ *n* -s **:** esoteric doctrines or practices; *also* **:** the quality or state of being esoteric — **es·o·ter·i·cist** \-rəsəst\ *n* -s

es·o·ter·ism \ˈ==ˌteˌrizəm, ˌ=='=ˌ==\ *n* -s [*esoteric* + *-ism*] **:** ESOTERICISM — **es·o·ter·ist** \ˈ==ˌterəst\ *n* -s

es·o·tery \ˈ==ˌterē\ *n* -ES [*esoteric* + *-y*] **:** ESOTERICISM

es·o·tro·pia \ˌesəˈtrōpēə *sometimes* ˌēs-\ *n* -s [NL, fr. *eso-* + *-tropia*] **:** CROSS-EYE 1 — **es·o·trop·ic** \ˌ==ˈträpik\ *adj*

esox \ˈēˌsäks, ˈeˌ-\ *n, cap* [NL, fr. L, pike (fish), fr. Gk *isox*, a fish, of Celt origin; akin to OIr *eo, eu* salmon, MW *ehawc*] **:** the type and sole genus of Esocidae

esp \ˈesp\ *dial var of* ASP

esp *abbr* **1** especially **2** [It *espressivo*] with expression

ESP *abbr* extrasensory perception

es·pace·ment \əˈspāsmənt, eˈ-\ *n* -s [F, fr. *espacer* to space (fr. MF, fr. *espace* space) + *-ment* — more at SPACE] *Africa* **:** the distance between a series of things that have been or are to be spaced (as in planting) ⟨when should sunflower seeds be planted and what ~ is usual —*Farmer's Weekly (So. Africa)*⟩

es·pa·da \äˈspät̲hä\ *n* -s [Sp, lit., sword, fr. L *spatha* sword — more at EPAULET] **:** SWORDFISH

es·pa·don \ˈespȧdōⁿ\ *n* -s [F (also, two-handed sword), fr. MF, sword, fr. OIt *spadone*, aug. of *spada, spata*, fr. L *spatha*] **:** SWORDFISH

es·pa·drille \ˈespəˌdril, ˌ=='=\ *n* -s [F, alter. of *espardille*, fr. Prov *espardilho*, dim. of *espart* esparto, fr. L *spartum* — more at ESPARTO] **:** a flat sandal usu. having a fabric upper and a flexible often rope sole

espadrille

es·pa·gnole \ˈespənˌyōl, -ˌpan-\ *also* **espagnole sauce** *n* -s [F *sauce espagnol, sauce à l'espagnole*] **:** BROWN SAUCE

es·pa·gno·lette \(ˌ)eˌspanyəˈlet, əˈs-\ *n* -s [F, fr. Prov *espagnouleto*, dim. of OProv *espanhol* Spanish, Spaniard, fr. (assumed) VL *Hispaniolus*, fr. L *Hispania* Spain + *-olus* -ole] **1 :** a fastening for a French door or casement window consisting of a long rod with hooks at the top and bottom of the sash both of which are turned by a single handle to hook around fixed pins in the window frame **2 :** a small metal dome with a nipple used as an ornament (as on the top of a cabinet post) in French 18th century furniture making

¹es·pal·ier \əˈspalyər, eˈs-, -späl-, -spal-; -al(ə)ˌyā, -ill-, -lēˌā; ˈespəˈli(ə)r\ *n* -s [F, fr. MF, trellis, fr. OIt *spalliera*, fr. *spalla* shoulder, fr. LL *spatula* shoulder blade — more at EPAULET] **1 :** a fruit tree or other plant trained to grow flat against a building, wall, railing, trellis, or other support **2 :** a railing or trellis on which fruit trees or shrubs are trained to grow flat

²espalier \ˈ"\ *vt* -ED/-ING/-s **:** to train to grow flat on or as if on an espalier **:** furnish with an espalier

es·pan·toon \ˌeˌspanˈtün\ *n* -s [alter. of *espontoon*] *in Baltimore* **:** a policeman's club

es·par·cet \ˌeˌspärˈsā\ *also* **es·par·sette** \-rˈset\ *n* -s [F *esparcet, esparcette*, fr. Prov *esparcet*, dim. of OProv *espars* pod, fr. *espars* (past part. of *esparser* to scatter), fr. L *sparsus*, past part. of *spargere* to scatter — more at SPARSE] **:** SAINFOIN 1

es·par·to \eˈspärd·(ˌ)ō, əˈ-\ *or* **esparto grass** *n* -s [Sp *esparto*, fr. L *spartum*, fr. Gk *sparton* — more at SPIRE (spiral)] **1 :** either of two Spanish and Algerian grasses (*Stipa tenacissima* and *Lygeum spartum*) of which cordage, shoes, baskets, and paper are made **2 :** the fiber of esparto grass

esparto paper *n* **:** paper made wholly or in large part from esparto fiber

esparto wax *n* **:** a hard brownish wax obtained from esparto grass and used chiefly in polishes

espath·ate \(ˈ)ēˈspāˌt̲hāt, -paˌth-, -pāˌth-\ *adj* [*e-* + *spathe* + *-ate*] **:** lacking a spathe

es·pa·vé \ˌespəˈvā\ *also* **es·pa·vel** \-vel\ *n* -s [AmerSp] **:** a tropical American timber tree (*Anacardium excelsum*) with reddish rather soft wood used for making dugout canoes

es·pe·cial \əˈspeshəl, eˈ-\ *adj* [ME, fr. MF, fr. L *specialis*, fr. *species* + *-alis* -al — more at SPY] **:** SPECIAL: **a :** not general **:** directed toward a specific end **:** designed or intended for a part, purpose, or occasion ⟨gave ~ greetings to his family⟩ ⟨an ~ ceremony for the holiday⟩ ⟨took ~ pains to make himself clear to the young readers⟩ **b :** of special note **:** EXCEPTIONAL, UNUSUAL, NOTABLE ⟨gave ~ attention to the reactions⟩ **c :** PARTICULAR, PECULIAR ⟨he had an ~ aversion to reform —*New Republic*⟩ ⟨several excellent regional orchestras, each with its own ~ character —T.O.Beachcroft⟩ ⟨personal experience with hospital buildings, where I was able to discover that ~ physical and psychological reactions by patients provided good pointers for ordinary housing —*Current Biog.*⟩ ⟨the special temptation of our ~ way of life —*Amer. Guide Series: Vt.*⟩ **d :** CLOSE, DEAR, INTIMATE ⟨he was supposed to be her ~ friend —Bruce Marshall⟩ ⟨his own and most ~ tree shading his borders —C.G.Glover⟩ **e :** capable of being specified **:** SPECIFIC ⟨he drove with no ~ destination in mind⟩ ⟨chose ~ targets for attack⟩ ⟨is there any ~ piece of furniture that you might care to have —Agatha Christie⟩ **syn** see SPECIAL — **in especial** *adv* **:** in particular ⟨the work of the mind and *in especial* of consciousness —J.H.Muirhead⟩ ⟨it would implicate everybody, the councilors *in especial* being unable to evade —Francis Hackett⟩ ⟨*in especial* we shall be able to see whether the individual is training towards cooperation or against it —Alfred Adler⟩

es·pe·cial·ly \-sh(ə)lē, -li\ *adv* [ME, fr. *especial* + *-ly*] **:** in a special way **:** PARTICULARLY, NOTABLY, EXCEPTIONALLY ⟨an ~ cautious approach to the danger⟩ ⟨an ~ devastating assault by the waters in 1874 —*Amer. Guide Series: Ark.*⟩ ⟨the community declined, ~ after Peter Miller's death —*Amer. Guide Series: Pa.*⟩ ⟨vast amounts of ~ treated water are required —E.R.Riegel⟩

es·pe·cial·ness \-shəlnəs\ *n* -ES **:** the quality or state of being especial **:** SPECIALNESS

esperance *n* -s [ME *esperaunce*, fr. MF *esperance*, fr. (assumed) VL *sperantia*, fr. L *sperant-, sperans* (pres. part. of *sperare* to hope) + *-ia* -y — more at DESPAIR] *obs* **:** HOPE, EXPECTATION

¹es·pe·ran·tist \ˌespəˈrantəst, -ˈrän-, -raan-, -rȧn-\ *n* -s *usu cap* **:** a specialist in Esperanto; *also* **:** one enthusiastic about the spread of Esperanto as an international language

²esperantist \ˈ=ˈ==\ *adj, usu cap* **:** of or relating to Esperanto or Esperantists ⟨the *Esperantist* stock of words —Frederick Bodmer⟩

es·pe·ran·to \ˌ=='=(ˌ)tō\ *n* -s [after Dr. *Esperanto*, pseudonym of Dr. L. L. Zamenhof †1917 Pol. philologist and inventor of the language] **1** *cap* **:** an artificial international language based as far as possible upon words common to the chief European languages **2** *often cap* **:** a usu. artificial language or set of symbols common to or designed to be common to a widely diverse and esp. international group ⟨acetylsalicylic acid is the universal comforter known in the *Esperanto* of the laboratory as $CH_3CO_2C_6H_4CO_2H$ and almost everywhere else as aspirin —Berton Roueché⟩ ⟨Russian is a second *Esperanto* taught in all schools of the constituent republics —L.A.Triebel⟩ ⟨the language of vision is a ready-made ~, a lingua franca of supreme universality —Martin James⟩ ⟨reached to all corners of the earth as though broadcast in some kind of *Esperanto* of the senses which was understood by all nations and in all tongues —Sacheverell Sitwell⟩

es·pi·al \əˈspī(ə)l, eˈ-\ *n* -s [ME *espiaille*, fr. MF, fr. *espier* to spy + *-aille* -al — more at SPY] **1 :** the act of spying or watching **:** OBSERVATION ⟨Gabriel withdrew from his point of ~ —Thomas Hardy⟩ **2** *obs* **:** one that espies **:** SPY, SCOUT **:** a scouting party **3 :** an act of espying or being espied **:** NOTICE, DISCOVERY, DETECTION

espied *past of* ESPY

es·piè·gle \ˌespyegl(ᵊ), -g(l)ə\ *adj* [F, after *Ulespiegle* (Till Ulenspiegel or Eulenspiegel), Ger. traditional figure and hero of an early 16th cent. chapbook] **:** ROGUISH, FROLICSOME

es·pi·er \əˈspī(ə)r, -īə\ *n* -s [ME *aspiere, espiere*, fr. *aspien, espien* to espy + *-ere* -er — more at ESPY] **:** one that espies

espies *pres 3d sing of* ESPY, *pl of* ESPY

es·pi·ni·llo \ˌespəˈnē(ˌ)(y)ō\ *n* -s [AmerSp, dim. of Sp *espino* hawthorn] **:** ESPINO 2

es·pi·no \əˈspē(ˌ)nō\ *n* -s [AmerSp, fr. Sp, hawthorn, fr. L *spinus* blackthorn, fr. *spina* thorn — more at SPINE] **1 :** any of numerous tropical So. American thorny or spiny shrubs or trees esp. of the genus *Zanthoxylum* **2 :** a shrubby acacia (*Acacia cavenia*) used as a hedge plant in southern So. America the pod of which is rich in tannin

es·pi·o·nage \ˈespēəˌnäzh, -ˌnij, -ˌnäzh, ˌ==='näzh, ˌ==='näzh *also* ˈ==='ˌnäj *or* ˈ===ˌnäj *or* ˌ==='näj *or* ˌ==='näj *or* əˈspēənij *or* eˈspē- *sometimes* əˈspēəˌnäzh *or* -näj *or* |j *or* -ˈspīənij *chiefly substand* ˈspə(ˌ)n-\ *n* -s [F *espionnage*, fr. MF, fr. *espionner* to spy (fr. *espion* spy, fr. OIt *spione*, aug. of *spia*, of Gmc origin) + *-age*; akin to OHG *spehōn* to spy — more at SPY] **:** the practice of spying **:** the systematic secret observation of words and conduct; *esp* **:** such spying by special agents upon people of a foreign country or upon their activities or enterprises (as war production or scientific advancement in military fields) and the accumulation of information about such people, activities, and enterprises for political or military uses

es·pla·nade \ˈespləˌnäd, -nȧd, -ˌnād, ˌ=='=\ *n* -s [F, fr. MF, fr. OIt *spianata*, fr. fem. of *spaniato*, past part. of *spianare* to level, fr. L *explanare* — more at EXPLAIN] **1 :** a level open stretch of paved or grassy ground; *esp* **:** one designed for walking or driving and often providing a vista (as over water) **2 a :** a clear space between a citadel and the nearest houses of a town **b :** GLACIS **3** *in Conn* **:** a grassed and landscaped median strip on a highway

es·plees \əˈsplēz\ *n pl* [MF *espleiz*, pl. of *espleit* revenue, profit, fr. OF — more at EXPLOIT] **:** the profits or products that land yields (as hay, pasturage, grain, or rents)

espontoon *var of* SPONTOON

es·pous·al \əˈspau̇zəl, eˈ- *also* -au̇səl\ *n* -s [ME *espousaille*, fr. MF *espousailles*, pl., fr. L *sponsalia*, fr. neut. pl. of *sponsalis* of a betrothal or espousal, fr. *sponsus* betrothed, n. (fr. *sponsus*, past part. of *spondēre* to promise solemnly, betroth) + *-alis* -al — more at SPOUSE] **:** the act of espousing: **a :** BETROTHAL ⟨the ~ of the man's son to a neighbor's daughter⟩ **b :** the marriage ceremony **:** NUPTIALS — often used in pl. **c :** MARRIAGE; *also* **:** a union resembling a marriage ⟨the ~ of the soul to Christ⟩ **d :** a taking up or adopting as a cause or belief ⟨his wholehearted ~ of Indian independence —Herrymon Maurer⟩ ⟨values whose ~ has constituted until now the heart of the distinction between human achievement and merely bestial life —Eliseo Vivas⟩

¹es·pouse \əˈspau̇z, eˈ- *also* -au̇s\ *vt* -ED/-ING/-s [ME *espousen*, fr. MF *espouser*, fr. LL *sponsare* to betroth, espouse, fr. L *sponsus*] **1 a :** to take as spouse **:** WED; *usu* **:** to take as wife **b :** to give in marriage **2** *obs* **:** to promise in marriage **:** BETROTH **3 a :** to come to believe in **:** attach oneself to and seek to maintain, support, further, and defend ⟨the causes we ~ elsewhere must be as true to our ideals and character as those we sponsor here —W.O.Douglas⟩ **b :** to adopt usu. as a matter of policy or practicality ⟨will have to work out some better scheme in repertory than it now ~s —*Saturday Rev.*⟩ ⟨Hamlet, the passionate lover of sincerity, has *espoused* insincerity as his weapon and armor —Karl Polanyi⟩ **syn** *see* ADOPT

²espouse *n* -s [ME, fr. MF *espous, espos* (masc.), *espouse, espose* (fem.) — more at SPOUSE] *obs* **:** SPOUSE

es·pous·er \əˈspau̇zə(r), eˈ- *also* -au̇sə-\ *n* -s **:** one that espouses; *esp* **:** SUPPORTER, PARTISAN ⟨an ~ of all good causes⟩

es·pres·si·vo \ˌeˌspreˈsē(ˌ)vō, ˌesprəˈ-\ *adj* (*or adv*) [It, fr. *espresso* declared, evident, pressed out (fr. *espresso* — past part. of *esprimere* to express, declare, press out — fr. L *expressus*, past part. of *exprimere* to express) + It *-ivo* (fr. L *-ivus* -ive) — more at EXPRESS (adj.)] **:** EXPRESSIVE, EXPRESSIVELY — used as a direction in music

es·pres·so \eˈspre(ˌ)sō\ *n* -s [It (*caffè*) *espresso*, lit., pressed out coffee] **1 :** coffee that is brewed by forcing steam through powdered coffee beans **2 :** a device for brewing espresso coffee **3 :** a neighborhood shop where friends gather to drink espresso

es·pring·al \əˈspriŋəl\ *n* -s [MF *espringale*—more at SPRINGALD (military engine)] **:** SPRINGALD

es·prit \əˈsprē, eˈ-\ *n* -s [F, fr. L *spiritus* spirit, breath — more at SPIRIT] **1** *archaic* **:** quick comprehension **:** INTELLIGENCE **2 :** cleverness and vivacity (as of spirit and mind) **:** sprightly wit **:** an inherent and native lively and colorful quality ⟨among so somber and serious a group his small wit passed for full-fledged ~⟩ ⟨had ~ and for us they filled that difficult patch of childhood with color and life —Rumer Godden⟩ **3** [by shortening] **:** ESPRIT DE CORPS ⟨the ~ of the entire regiment dropped considerably at the news of their transfer⟩ ⟨means that the know-how as well as the ~ of the thousands of uncompensated volunteer workers . . . would be lost —*U. S. Code*⟩ **syn** see VIGOR

es·prit de corps \əˌsprēdəˈkō(ə)r, eˌs-, ˌe(ˌ)s-, -kȯ(ə)r, -kōə, -kȯ(ə)\ *n* [F, lit., corps spirit] **:** the usu. selfless and often enthusiastic and jealous devotion of the members of a group or association of persons to the group or to its purposes ⟨the cultivation in the student body of *esprit de corps*, obedience to orders, acceptance of responsibility —*Bull. of Univ. of Ky.*⟩ ⟨an institution must have an *esprit de corps* which induces its members to put the welfare of the institution above their own —P.F.Drucker⟩ ⟨an *esprit de corps* that often unites senators of differing political views, and sometimes of intense personal rivalry, against the world outside the Senate —R.H. Rovere⟩ ⟨though the development of a strong *esprit de corps* is most desirable, within a small and exclusive group it becomes dangerous . . . assumes the form of a closed club, the members of which can, in each other's eyes, do no wrong —*Political Science Quarterly*⟩

es·pun·dia \eˈspündēə, -pu̇n-\ *n* -s [AmerSp, fr. Sp, fr. L *spongia* sponge — more at SPONGE] **:** leishmaniasis of the mouth, pharynx, and nose prevalent in Central and So. America

¹es·py \əˈspī, eˈ-\ *vb* -ED/-ING/-ES [ME *espien, aspien, spien* — more at SPY] *vt* **1 :** SEE, PERCEIVE, DISCOVER ⟨there among the several horses that whistled at her approach she *espied* the white mustang —Zane Grey⟩; *esp* **:** to see and recognize (something distant, obscure, or covert) ⟨in that moment the duke, turning, *espied* us —Rafael Sabatini⟩ **2** *archaic* **:** to inspect closely **:** WATCH ⟨I would fain have *espied* them, but they stopped up the keyhole —W.S.Gilbert⟩; *also* **:** to spy out ~ *vi, obs* **:** to keep a watch **:** observe or look about closely **syn** see SEE

²espy *n* -ES [ME *espie, aspie, spie* — more at SPY] *obs* **:** SPY

esq *or* **esqr** *or* **esqre** *abbr, often cap* esquire

esquamate \(ˈ)ē+\ *adj* [*e-* + *squamate*] **:** being without scales

esquamulose \(ˈ)ē +\ *adj* [*e-* + *squamulose*] **:** not squamulose

¹-esque \ˈesk\ *adj suffix* [F, fr. It *-esco*, of Gmc origin; akin to OHG *-isc* — more at -ISH] **:** in the manner or style of **:** like **:** -ISH ⟨Roman*esque*⟩ ⟨Kipling*esque*⟩ ⟨Lincoln*esque*⟩ ⟨statu*esque*⟩ ⟨Hardy*esque*⟩

²-esque \ˈ"\ *n suffix* -s **:** something in the style of ⟨arab*esque*⟩

es·qui·mau \ˈeskəˌmō\ *n, pl* **esquimau** \-ˌō\ *or* **esqui·maux** \-ˌō(z)\ *usu cap* [F — more at ESKIMO] **:** ESKIMO

¹es·quire \ˈeˌskwī(ə)r, əˈs-, eˈs-, -īə\ *n* -s [ME *esquier, esquier*, fr. MF *escuier, esquier* shield bearer, squire, fr. LL *scutarius*, fr. L *scutum* shield + *-arius* -ary; akin to OHG *sceida* sheath — more at SHEATH] **1 :** a member of the English gentry ranking immediately below a knight **2 a** *archaic* **:** SQUIRE 1 **b :** a candidate for knighthood serving as shield bearer to and attendant upon a knight **c :** an attendant upon a king or nobleman in one of several usu. specified offices ⟨~ of the stable⟩ ⟨~ for the body⟩ **3** — used as a title of courtesy that is usu. placed in its abbreviated form after the surname in written address and that is infrequent and of no precise significance in the U. S. except as sometimes applied to certain public officials (as justices of the peace) but that is applied in British usage to anyone (except a member of the nobility or clergy) considered to have the social position of a gentleman; abbr. *Esq.* **4** *archaic* **:** a landed proprietor

²esquire \ˈ"\ *vt* [ˈ*esquire*] **1** *archaic* **:** to attend as an esquire **2 :** to accompany or escort in public

³esquire \ˈ"\ *n* -s [MF *esquire, esquierre, esquerre* square, carpenter's square — more at SQUARE] **1** *also* **esquire based :** BASE ESQUIRE **2 :** GYRON; *also* **:** a charge resembling a gyron

esquire's helmet *n, heraldry* **:** a helmet represented in profile without grilles, with the visor closed, and unless another tincture is specified with argent to represent steel

es·quisse \(')e¦skēs\ *n* -s [F, fr. MF *esquiche*, fr. OIt *schizzo* — more at SKETCH] **:** a first usu. rough sketch (as of a picture or model of a statue)

esrog *var of* ETHROG

ess \'es\ *n* -ES **1** *also* **es** \"\ **:** the letter *s* **2 :** something resembling the letter *s* in shape ⟨the greater ~*es* the tide left in the estuary —J.M.Brinnin⟩

-ess \əs *sometimes* ¦es\ *n suffix* -ES [ME *-esse*, fr. OF, fr. LL *-issa*, fr. Gk] **:** female ⟨goddess⟩ ⟨giantess⟩ — esp. in agent nouns ⟨actress⟩ ⟨poetess⟩

ess *abbr* essence

essart *var of* ASSART

[1]**es·say** \(')e¦sā, ə'sā\ *vt* -ED/-ING/-S [MF *essaier, assaier*, fr. OF, fr. *essai, assai* (n.)] **1 a** *archaic* **:** to put to a test **:** try out **b** *obs* **:** to find out by making a test **c :** [2]ASSAY 4a **2 a :** to attempt or endeavor esp. by tentative methods or by appraising, probing, or seeking expedients — used with the infinitive ⟨Dick, being carefully installed in the saddle, ~*ed* to descend —Arnold Bennett⟩ ⟨the heavy butler ~*ed* to speak, but the tremendous blow and the baronet's gesture choked him —George Meredith⟩ **b :** to make an effort to do, accomplish, perform, deal with, or venture upon (something difficult or presenting obstacles) ⟨stayed there all day and in the evening again ~*ed* escape —F.Tennyson Jesse⟩ ⟨the medieval men who ~*ed* the paths of natural science —H.O.Taylor⟩ ⟨the ballerina ~*ed* a dramatic role on televison —*Current Biog.*⟩ ⟨the second part ~*s* to give in sixty-four pages an account of our modern knowledge of the universe —*Times Lit. Supp.*⟩ **syn** see TRY

[2]**es·say** *in sense 2* 'e,sā *sometimes* -,sā *or* -,sē *or* -,si *in other senses* (')e¦sā *or* ə'sā\ *n* -s [MF *essai, assai*, fr. OF, fr. LL *exagium* act of weighing, weight, balance, fr. L *ex-* + *-agium*, fr. *agere* to do, drive; influenced by L *exigere* to weigh, test, drive out — more at AGENT, EXACT (adj.)] **1 a :** an effort made to do or perform **:** ATTEMPT, ENDEAVOR ⟨make an ~ to assist a friend⟩ ⟨making an ~ to be gallant, "Present company excepted", he said with a smile and a little bow —Aldous Huxley⟩ ⟨nowhere in the book do we find any systematic ~ to characterize this creative partnership —Lee Strasberg⟩ ⟨politics in England is one long ~ in the gentle art of compromise —W.A.Robson⟩; *esp* **:** an initial and tentative effort ⟨the fledgling bird made a small ~ at flying⟩ **b :** the result or product of the effort to do or perform something (as something difficult or presenting unusual obstacles) ⟨Haydn's final ~ in the symphonic form —*Sydney (Australia) Bull.*⟩ ⟨his first ~*s* in the skyscraper and the industrial building, which paved the way for the successful buildings of the middle nineteen-thirties —Lewis Mumford⟩ ⟨turn . . . the monstrously dull Brahms sonata into the heroic ~ it was undoubtedly meant to be —*N. Y. Herald Tribune*⟩; *esp* **:** a usu. tentative and short intellectual or artistic excursion (as into a new field of endeavor) ⟨a schizoid novel . . . an admirable ~ into the picaresque —*New Yorker*⟩ ⟨concertino for pianoforte and orchestra, a charming ~ in the modernized classical vein —Walter Legge⟩ ⟨Brook's first ~ into politics was in the 1932 state elections campaign —*Current Biog.*⟩ **2 a :** an analytic, interpretative, or critical literary composition usu. much shorter and less systematic and formal than a dissertation or thesis and usu. dealing with its subject from a limited often personal point of view ⟨the thesis must not be a mere ~; it must present evidence of a thorough acquaintance with some limited special field, obtained by recourse to original sources —*Bull. of N. Y. Univ.*⟩ ⟨persuasion is more starkly and simply the purpose of the ~ than of fiction or poetry, since the ~ deals always with an idea —Katharine F. Gerould⟩ ⟨in style and structure the three volumes . . . completed are a thousand-page ~ rather than a systematic treatise —Geoffrey Bruun⟩ **b :** something resembling or suggesting such a composition esp. in its presentation of an extended analytic, interpretative, or critical view of something (as by a series of photographs or a documentary film) ⟨a book he did on Europe's postwar children remains one of the most arresting ~*s* of modern photography —*Newsweek*⟩ ⟨the Shelter drawings made during the war are frankly graphic ~*s* done with no thought of sculpture —R.J.Goldwater⟩ ⟨two young dancers whose evident physical talents have not yet received the polish that this ~ in elegant athletics requires —Winthrop Sargeant⟩ **3 :** TRIAL, TEST ⟨make an ~ of the various methods of removing paint⟩ **4 a** *obs* **:** a trial specimen **:** SAMPLE, EXAMPLE **b :** a proof of an unaccepted design for a stamp or piece of paper money

es·say·er *n* -s **1** \(')e¦sāə(r), ə's-\ **:** one that essays **2** *obs* **:** ESSAYIST

es·say·ette \¦e,sā¦et\ *n* -s [[2]*essay* + *-ette*] **:** a short essay

essay examination *or* **essay test** *n* **:** an examination made up of essay questions or a single comprehensive essay question — compare OBJECTIVE TEST

es·say·ist \'e,sāəst *sometimes* -,sāə- *or* -,sēə- *or* -,siə- *or* e'sāə-\ *n* -s **1 :** one that essays to do something **2 :** a writer of essays

es·say·is·tic \¦=(,)=¦istik\ *adj* **:** of or relating to an essay or an essayist **:** like an essay in quality or character: as **a :** EXPLANATORY ⟨brief ~ statements of overtly moral intent cannot adequately suggest the interplay of emotional struggles —Carl Benson⟩ ⟨the solid ~ style of a historian —Helmut Schoeck⟩ **b :** more informal, discursive, or personal in its exposition of an idea than a dissertation or treatise ⟨the approach is neither philosophical nor purely historical, but ~ —Alfred Neumeyer⟩ **c :** like a piece of formal exposition ⟨all this is kept from seeming too ~ by the high spirits of the author, the piquant element of caricature with which he flavors his personages, and a complicating twist given to the main character —F.C.Flint⟩

essay question *n* **:** an examination question that requires an answer to be framed in a sentence, paragraph, or short composition and usu. calls for individual analysis, assembling of facts, and interpretation by the student — see ESSAY EXAMINATION

es·se \'esē\ *n* -s [ML, fr. L, to be, exist — more at IS] **1** *in scholastic philosophy* **:** actual being **:** EXISTENCE **2 :** essential nature **:** ESSENCE

es·se est per·ci·pi \'e,se,est'perkə,pē\ [NL, lit., to be is to be perceived] *Berkeleianism* **:** a tenet that existence consists in the condition of being perceived

es·se·len \'esələn\ *n, pl* **esselen** *or* **esselens** *usu cap* **1 a :** an Indian people of the California coast near Monterey **b :** a member of such people **2 :** an Esselenian language of the Esselen people **3 :** ESSELENIAN

es·se·le·nian \,esə'lēnyən, -ēnēən\ *n, pl* **esselenian** *or* **esselenians** *usu cap* **:** a language family of the Hokan stock comprising only the Esselen language

es·sen \'esᵊn\ *adj, usu cap* [fr. *Essen*, Germany] **:** of or from the city of Essen, Germany **:** of the kind or style prevalent in Essen

es·sence \'esᵊn(t)s\ *n* -s [ME *essencia, essence*, fr. MF & L; MF *essence*, fr. L *essentia*, fr. *esse* to be + *-ent-, -ens* -ent + *-ia* -y — more at IS] **1 :** a basic underlying or constituting entity, substance, or form: as **a** *archaic* **:** ELEMENT 1a **b** (1) **:** the permanent as contrasted with the accidental and variable and hence phenomenal phases or foundation of being **:** metaphysical substance esp. when a substratum that is distinguished from and that supports attributes (2) **:** something that constitutes the individual, real, or ultimate nature or kind often as opposed to the existence of a being or thing ⟨a picture of a tree should represent the ~ of the tree — its ultimate or basic reality, that which makes it what it is, the thing-in-itself or in its intrinsic nature —Hunter Mead⟩ ⟨succeeds in conveying completely the cruel ~ of loneliness —Arthur Knight⟩ ⟨came to the conclusion that the ~ of heat was motion —S.F.Mason⟩ ⟨everything that one has seen or heard or thought or felt leaves a deposit that never filters entirely through the ~ of mind —Ellen Glasgow⟩ ⟨not life in its humdrum, day-by-day existence, but life in its ~, exciting, meaningful, important —L.D.Rubin⟩; *also* **:** the property, attribute, or element or totality of properties, attributes, or elements indispensable or necessary to the nature of a thing ⟨what is individual, what is the peculiar ~ of the man —T.S.Eliot⟩ ⟨the biographical story of its main character, not in the bulk of its multi-fold detail but in its ~ —Irving Stone⟩ ⟨the ~ of liberalism—freedom of thought and inquiry, freedom of discussion and criticism —M.R.Cohen⟩ ⟨many of our people, . . . have forgotten the ~ of Americanism —George Sokolsky⟩ — see NOMINAL ESSENCE, REAL ESSENCE (3) **:** an immanent form or metaphysical archetype **:** an Aristotelian formal cause **:** a Platonic idea **c** (1) **:** the properties or attributes that every member of a species or class of things must necessarily have in order to belong to that species or class (2) **:** the totality of those properties or attributes that are indispensable to whatever can be named by a certain term or classified as of a certain class **2** *obs* **:** distinguishing nature or character **3 :** condition or fact of being or existing **:** existence considered as a property of a thing **4 :** something by which another is basically motivated or is maintained or by which it subsists ⟨the enthusiasm of its personnel is the ~ and life of any enterprise⟩ ⟨criticism that will keep in mind that the ~ of a performance is the music as it was written —*Saturday Rev.*⟩ ⟨the camera work, which is the ~ of the coverage . . . was a brilliant job —Gilbert Seldes⟩ ⟨a country where controversy is the ~ of politics —Clifton Daniel⟩ ⟨the trend toward a herd state of which the ~ is the denial of supreme value to the human individual —E.A. Mowrer⟩ ⟨the health of our people is the very ~ of our vitality, our strength, and our progress as a nation —D.D. Eisenhower⟩ **5 :** ENTITY; *esp* **:** an abstract entity ⟨the same true characterization which makes each person in the story an ~ with whom spectators will identify themselves —*Current Biog.*⟩ ⟨own little reviews tranquilly engaged in their endless and placid pursuit of poetry as a timeless ~ —William Barrett⟩ **6 a** (1) **:** the volatile matter constituting perfume (2) **:** PERFUME, ODOR, SCENT ⟨the rice and shrimp in Venice, which breathed with the unmistakable ~ of garlic —Horace Sutton⟩ **b** (1) **:** a volatile spirit (as petroleum spirit or gasoline) (2) **:** a substance resembling a volatile spirit ⟨impregnate it with the volatile ~ of their souls —J.G.Frazer⟩ **c :** AURA, CACHET ⟨a special ~ of authority —S.N.Behrman⟩ ⟨captured in words something of the pattern of life, its color or ~ —Ernest Beaglehole⟩ ⟨the drenched condition of the two women seemed to draw into that little room a desolate melancholy ~ composed of fallen leaves, muddy cart ruts, and clammy mist —J.C.Powys⟩ **7 a :** the most significant element, attribute, quality, property, or aspect of a thing ⟨it is the very ~ of Machiavelli that in politics there is neither good nor evil, of a moral kind —Irving Kristol⟩ ⟨the ~ of Scotland—highlands and lowlands, blue lochs and swift brown streams, grouse moors, tidy farmlands and wild sea cliffs —Alice Campbell⟩; *specif* **:** a central focal issue, argument, or point (as in a law case) upon which all other issues, arguments, or points depend or to which they are subordinate ⟨what he could do superbly was to state a case or extract an ~ in a few clear and compelling words —R.H.Rovere⟩ ⟨appellate argument is the most exacting and concentrated work . . . for it involves the presentation of the ~ of a long trial in an hour or less —A.T.Vanderbilt⟩ ⟨the discernment and understanding with which he penetrates to the heart and ~ of the problem —Margaret E. Hall⟩ **b :** a most significant element, attribute, quality, or property of a thing ⟨speak of his paintings in terms of what they consider his Gallic ~*s*—his sensuousness, his economy in putting his pictures into focus, his infinitely civilized feeling for color and the refinement of line —Janet Flanner⟩ **c :** the essential and most characteristic features of a thing ⟨he believes that deceit and mistrust are the ~ of human relationships —Bergen Evans⟩ ⟨attempts to capture the ~ of our twenty-four-dollar island through extreme close-ups of thirty or more representative New York people —James Kelly⟩ ⟨managed to combine the ~ of jazz, mountain music, and New England church music into one —*Saturday Rev.*⟩ **d :** CENTER, CORE, PITH ⟨such attention to appearances and details rather than to true substance went to the very ~ of the struggle —*Time*⟩ ⟨this takes us to the ~ of national strategy —H.H. Arnold & I.C.Eaker⟩ ⟨here is the ethical ~ of the treaty — the common resolve to preserve, strengthen, and make understood the very basis of tolerance, restraint, and freedom —Dean Acheson⟩ **8 a** (1) **:** a substance considered to possess in high degree the predominant qualities or virtues of a plant, drug, or other natural product from which it is extracted (as by distillation or infusion) (2) **:** an extract (as from fruit) used as flavoring in cooking (3) **:** the concentrated juices of foods obtained in the process of cooking **b** (1) **:** ESSENTIAL OIL (2) **:** an alcoholic solution esp. of an essential oil **:** SPIRIT 21 ⟨~ of peppermint⟩ (3) **:** an artificial preparation (as an alcoholic solution of one or more esters) used esp. in flavoring ⟨pineapple ~⟩ (4) **:** ELIXIR 2 ⟨pepsin ~⟩ **9 :** something that resembles or suggests an extract in possessing the quality, virtue, or value of an original larger substance or thing in concentrated form ⟨it is an ~, a distillation, the very best of all our past reduced, not to a list of physical sights, but to a single emotion —Jerome Weidman⟩ ⟨this spot is the heart and ~ of the Green mountains —Carl Brandt⟩ ⟨the heroine who, in the hands of less eminent novelists, appeared to be the ~ of sentimentality —C.W.Cunnington⟩ — **in essence** *adv* **:** ESSENTIALLY, BASICALLY, FUNDAMENTALLY ⟨from that day onward he became *in essence* a painter —E.O.Malley⟩ ⟨art issues . . . were *in essence* political though presented with masks of aesthetics —*Americana Annual*⟩ ⟨the conflicts between labor and capital often give rise to what are *in essence* lynchings —F.W.Coker⟩ — **of the essence** *adj* **:** of unavoidable importance **:** ESSENTIAL, INDISPENSABLE ⟨in politics, personality is very often *of the essence* —R.H.Rovere⟩ ⟨in a revolution, timing is *of the essence:* temporary expedients are apt to congeal into permanent situations —Gladys Delmas⟩ ⟨it is not enough to say that we are trying to equip young women for life in a self-governing country, though that is clearly *of the essence* —*Smith College President's Report*⟩

es·senced \-n(t)st\ *adj, archaic* **:** SCENTED, PERFUMED

es·sence d'ori·ent \¦esᵊn(t)s'dōrēənt, -dȯr-, -ē,ent; esäⁿsdȯryäⁿ\ *n* [F, lit., essence of the Orient] **:** pearl essence esp. from bleak fish

essence peddler *n* **1 :** a peddler of cure-alls and medicinal preparations **2** *slang* **:** SKUNK

es·sene \ə'sēn, e's-, 'e,s-\ *n* -s *usu cap* [Gk *Essēnos*] **:** a member of an ascetic, esoteric, and monastic brotherhood among the Jews of Palestine from the second century B.C. to the second century A.D. who practiced a community of goods and rigorous discipline and for the most part shunned the company of women — **es·se·ni·an** \ə'sēnēən, (')e¦s-\ *adj, usu cap* — **es·sen·ic** \ə'senik, (')e¦s-, -sēn-\ *adj, usu cap* — **es·sen·ism** \ə'sē,nizəm, e's-, 'e,s-\ *n* -s *usu cap*

es·sen·hout \'esᵊn,haut, -hōt\ *n* -s [Afrik, fr. MD *esschenhout* ash wood, fr. *essche* ash + *hout* wood; akin to OHG *ask* ash and to *holz* wood — more at ASH, WOOD] **:** CAPE ASH

es·sen·tia \ə'sench(ē)ə, e'-,ē'-\ *n* -s [L, trans. of Gk *ousia* — more at ESSENCE, OUSIA] **:** ESSENCE 1

[1]**es·sen·tial** \ə'senchəl, e'-,ē'-\ *adj* [ME *essencial*, fr. LL *essentialis*, fr. L *essentia* essence + *-alis* -al] **1 :** of or relating to an essence: as **a :** having or realizing in itself the essence of its kind **:** having or consisting of the basic, most fundamental nature, property, quality, or attribute peculiar to or necessary or indispensable to its kind ⟨the problem is to grasp the ~ man —Carl Bridenbaugh⟩ ⟨the sunshine where it fell was a blinding ~ light without color, so that the grass looked like snowdrifts —John Buchan⟩ **b :** forming or constituting the essence of something **:** making up or being the constituent or intrinsic character or very nature of a thing ⟨his eyes were wide, as one who looks at his ~ self through the mask we wear —George Meredith⟩ ⟨wished his work to have no ornament other than its own ~ beauty, without exterior decoration —Aldous Huxley⟩ ⟨our ~ admixture of matter and spirit, emotions and intelligence —*Word Study*⟩ **c :** belonging to or being part of the essence of something **:** belonging to the constituent fundamental character of a thing **:** not accidental to something ⟨stamens are ~ organs of a flower⟩ ⟨has not shown that the merits of puritan thought are ~ and the defects accidental —M.G.White⟩ ⟨the most ~ characteristic of mind is memory —Bertrand Russell⟩ ⟨the great charm of his personality, his ~ sympathy and kindliness —M.R.Cohen⟩ ⟨did much to direct attention to the ~ immorality of lotteries —J.S.Kendall⟩ — compare ACCESSORY 1 **d :** constituting an indispensable structure, core, or condition of a thing **:** BASIC, FUNDAMENTAL ⟨a little excessive to have to sit through so much frankly nonessential repertory in order to hear two short works from the band's ~ repertory —Virgil Thomson⟩ ⟨there was an ~ soundness in his line of reasoning⟩ **2 a :** NECESSARY, INDISPENSABLE ⟨transporting the heavy ore by rail was difficult and expensive; a water route was ~ —Allan Nevins & H.S. Commager⟩ ⟨international scientific meetings are ~ to scientific progress for the reason that no one nation has a monopoly of either ideas or brains —*Saturday Rev.*⟩ ⟨agreed to request uniform standards for deferment of ~ physicians —*Current Biog.*⟩ ⟨Lutherans from the sixteenth century have regarded choir singing as ~ to their ritual —*Amer. Guide Series: Minn.*⟩ **b :** UNAVOIDABLE ⟨a good many ~ tasks are left until the last minute —Stewart Cockburn⟩ ⟨physicians and lawyers may count their purchases of books as ~ expenses of their profession in computing income tax —*Report: (Canadian) Royal Commission on Nat'l Development*⟩ **c :** important in the highest degree **:** demanding maximum attention **:** unavoidably significant ⟨a great reserve of manpower ~ to the defense of the homeland⟩ **d :** minimal but fundamental to the achievement of an end ⟨make yourself a small pocket map showing the ~ landmarks around camp so that you can find your way back —*Boy Scout Handbook*⟩ **3 :** containing the essence of that portion of a plant or substance which is marked by its characteristic odor or virtue **:** being or relating to an essence (sense 8) ⟨an ~ odor⟩ — see ESSENTIAL OIL **4** *of a musical tone* **:** necessary to or determining the tonality of a piece of music ⟨did not alter the ~ tones but added grace notes⟩ **5 :** having no obvious or known cause **:** IDIOPATHIC, INHERENT ⟨~ disease⟩

syn FUNDAMENTAL, VITAL, and CARDINAL all imply maximum importance, indispensability, and necessary priority in considerations, plans, or discussions. Often the words are interchangeable. When they do differ in implication, these differences are suggested by the etymologies. ESSENTIAL may suggest that the matter in question involves the very essence, or being or real nature, of whatever is concerned ⟨but in the epic, lyric, the dramatic . . . ideality in contrast with actuality plays an intrinsic and *essential* part —John Dewey⟩ ⟨undoubtedly correct in concluding that the *essential* emotion of the play [*Hamlet*] is the feeling of a son toward a guilty mother —T.S. Eliot⟩ FUNDAMENTAL may suggest something of the nature of a foundation, something on which a system or structure rests ⟨such *fundamental* methods as induction and deduction, analysis, synthesis, and comparison are common to all types of systematic knowledge —René Wellek & Austin Warren⟩ ⟨recognition of the importance of *fundamental* skills, since in a democracy citizens must be able to compute, read, write, listen, and speak effectively —*N.Y.Times*⟩ VITAL may suggest that which is necessary to continued life or existence of whatever is in question ⟨nitrate, necessary in fertilizers, but *vital* to the manufacturers of explosives in case of war —A.C.Morrison⟩ ⟨barriers within our own country which stand in the way of bringing to Americans resources *vital* to their own safety and interest —C.E.Odegaard⟩ CARDINAL may refer to the decisive or conclusive since it may suggest that on which an outcome hinges or pivots ⟨to one *cardinal* principle Edwards was faithful—the conception of the majesty and sufficiency of God, and this polar idea provides the clue to both his philosophical and theological systems —V.L.Parrington⟩ ⟨the *cardinal* virtue in the Shavian scale . . . is responsibility; every creed he has attacked Shaw has attacked on the grounds of irresponsibility —E.R.Bentley⟩ **syn** see in addition NEEDFUL

[2]**essential** \"\ *n* -s **:** something essential: as **a :** something basic or fundamental esp. belonging to or forming part of the minimal indispensable body, character, or structure of a thing ⟨the ~*s* of the good life⟩ ⟨the ~*s* of astronomy⟩ ⟨gave only the ~*s* of the story⟩ **b :** something necessary, indispensable, or unavoidable ⟨work was an ~ to survival⟩ ⟨a man considered an ~ in his office⟩ ⟨a job that was both a great chore and an ~ to the success of the enterprise⟩ ⟨all that sort of duplicity is an ~ in any handling of men by methods other than direct authority —Hilaire Belloc⟩

essential amino acid *n* **:** any of usu. ten alpha amino acids that are required for normal health and growth in many vertebrates, are either not manufactured in the body or manufactured in insufficient quantities, are usu. supplied by dietary protein, and in man include arginine, histidine, isoleucine, leucine, lysine, methionine, phenylalanine, threonine, tryptophan, and valine

essential clause *n* **:** RESTRICTIVE CLAUSE

essential hypertension *n* **:** abnormally high blood pressure, both systolic and diastolic, occurring in the absence of any evident cause and resulting typically in marked hypertrophic and degenerative changes in small arteries, hypertrophy of the heart, and often more or less severe kidney damage — see MALIGNANT HYPERTENSION

es·sen·tial·ism \-chə,lizəm\ *n* -s **1 :** a philosophic theory significantly concerned with and esp. based on a conception of essence or essential things: as **a :** a theory subscribing to the idea that metaphysical essences really subsist and are intuitively accessible — compare REALISM **b :** a theory that assigns priority to essence over existence — contrasted with *existentialism* **2 :** an educational theory holding that certain basic ideas and skills or disciplines essential to our culture are formulable and should be taught to all alike by certain time-tested methods — contrasted with *progressivism*

[1]**es·sen·tial·ist** \-ch(ə)ləst\ *n* -s **:** a follower of or believer in essentialism (as in religion, philosophy, or education)

[2]**essentialist** \"\ *adj* **:** of, relating to, subscribing to, or being essentialism **:** of or relating to an essentialist; *also* **:** realist in philosophic theory or point of view — **es·sen·tial·is·tic** \ə¦senchə¦listik, (¦)e¦s-,ē¦s-\ *adj*

es·sen·ti·al·i·ty \ə,senchē'aləd·ē, (,)e,s-,ē,s-, -lətē, -i\ *n* -ES **1 :** the quality or state of being essential ⟨the ~ of certain amino acids in the diet for maximum growth of the tissues —*Jour. Amer. Med. Assoc.*⟩ ⟨the ~ of giving special consideration to the needs of older people —*N. Y. State Legislative Committee on Problems of the Aging*⟩ ⟨are not by tradition fearful or quarrelsome over the ~ of freedom and justice —P.G.Hoffman⟩ **2 a :** the essential nature or character **:** ESSENCE **b :** an essential quality, property, or aspect

es·sen·tial·ize \ə'senchə,līz, e'-,ē'-\ *vt* -ED/-ING/-S **:** to express or formulate in essence or in essential form **:** state or present the essence of **:** distill the essence from **:** reduce to essentials

es·sen·tial·ly \ə'sench(ə)lē, e'-,ē'-, -li\ *adv* [ME *essencially*, fr. *essencial* essential + *-ly*] **:** in an essential manner **:** by its very nature **:** FUNDAMENTALLY ⟨taught her to play golf in the same grave, methodical but ~ encouraging way —Louis Auchincloss⟩ ⟨the species being ~ an inhabitant of southern waters —W.H.Dowdeswell⟩ ⟨government in New Jersey is ~ the same in general pattern as in each of the other 47 States —*Amer. Guide Series: N.J.*⟩ ⟨painting, ~ a two-dimensional art —Herbert Read⟩

es·sen·tial·ness \-chəlnəs\ *n* -ES **:** the quality or state of being essential

essential oil *n* **:** any of a large class of volatile odoriferous oils of vegetable origin that impart to plants odor and often other characteristic properties, that are obtained from various parts of the plants (as flowers, leaves, or bark) by steam distillation, expression, or extraction, that are usu. mixtures of compounds (as terpenoids, aldehydes, or esters), and that are used often in the form of essences in perfumes, flavoring materials, and pharmaceutical preparations — called also *ethereal oil, volatile oil;* distinguished from *fatty oil* and *fixed oil;* see OLEORESIN

essential predication *n* **:** predication in which the predicate is wholly contained in the essence of the subject

essential proposition *n* **:** an analytic proposition

essentiate *vb* [ML *essentiatus*, past part. of *essentiare* to make real or essential, fr. L *essentia* essence — more at ESSENCE] *vt*, *obs* **:** to form or constitute the essence or being of ~ *vi*, *obs* **:** to become essence

esses *pl of* ESS *or of* ESSE

-esses *pl of* -ESS

[1]**es·sex** \'esiks, -sēks *sometimes* -,seks\ *adj, usu cap* [fr. *Essex* co., Eng.] **:** of or from the county of Essex, England **:** of the kind or style prevalent in Essex

[2]**essex** \"\ *n* [fr. *Essex* co., Eng. where it was orig. bred] **1** *usu cap* **:** a British breed of small hardy swine that are black with white markings **2** -ES *often cap* **:** any animal of the Essex breed

es·sex·ite \-,sik,sīt, -sēk-\ *n* -s [*Essex* co., Mass. + E *-ite*] **:** granular intrusive igneous rock of various kinds composed chiefly of hornblende, augite, and labradorite with variable amounts of accessory iron ore, biotite, orthoclase, nepheline, or olivine

¹es·sive \ˈesiv\ *adj* [Finn *essiivi*, fr. L *esse* to be + Finn *-ivi* (fr. L *-ivus* -ive) — more at IS] *of a grammatical case* **:** denoting a state of being — used esp. in Finnish and Hungarian grammar

²essive \"\ *n* -s **:** the essive case of a language **:** a form in the essive case

es·soign *or* **es·soine** \əˈsȯin\ *archaic var of* ESSOIN

¹es·soin \"\ *n* -s [ME *essoine*, fr. MF *essoine*, *essoigne*, fr. ML *essonia*, *essonium*, *exonium*, fr. L *ex-* + LL *sonium* care, worry] **1** *Eng law* **a :** an excuse for not appearing in court at the appointed time **b :** an allegation of an excuse of this kind to the court **2** *obs* **:** EXCUSE, EXEMPTION, DELAY

²essoin \"\ *vt* -ED/-ING/-S [ME *essoinen*, fr. MF *essonier*, *essoignier*, fr. ML *essoniare*, fr. L *ex-* + LL *soniari* to worry, fr. *sonium* care, worry] **:** to offer or allege an essoin **:** excuse or make excuse in behalf of for nonappearance in court

essoin day *n* **:** a day formerly set aside by English law for receiving essoins

es·soin·ee \əˌsȯiˈnē, eˌs-, ˌeˌs-\ *n* -s [AF *essonié*, *essoignié*, past part. of *essonier*, *essoignier*, v.] **:** one whose essoin is allowed

es·soin·er \əˈsȯinə(r)\ *n* -s [AF *essonier*, *essoneour*, fr. *essonier*, v. + *-er*, *-our* -or] **:** one that essoins another

es·so·nite \ˈesᵊnˌīt\ *also* **hes·so·nite** \ˈhe-\ *n* -s [F, fr. Gk *hēssōn* inferior, less + F *-ite*; fr. its being less hard than true hyacinth] **:** a variety of garnet — called also *cinnamon stone*

est \ˈest\ *n* -s [by alter. (resulting from incorrect division of *a nest*)] *Scot* **:** NEST

¹-est \əst\ *adj suffix or adv suffix* [ME, fr. OE *-st*, *-est*, *-ost*; akin to superlative suffixes OHG *-isto*, *-ōsto* (in adjectives), *-ist*, *-ōst* (in adverbs), ON *-str*, *-astr* (in adjectives), *-st*, *-ast* (in adverbs), Goth *-ists*, *-osts* (in adjectives), *-ist* (in adverbs), Gk *-istos* (in adjectives), Skt *-iṣṭha* (in adjectives); prob. fr. the suffix represented by E ¹*-er* + the suffix represented by E ¹*-ed*] — used to form the superlative degree of adjectives and adverbs of one syllable ⟨fatt*est*⟩ ⟨lat*est*⟩ ⟨new*est*⟩, of certain adjectives and adverbs of two syllables ⟨luck*iest*⟩ ⟨oft*enest*⟩ ⟨remot*est*⟩ ⟨simpl*est*⟩, and less often of longer ones ⟨beggarl*iest*⟩; often attached to words (as participles in adjectival use) that rarely if ever show a corresponding comparative formation in *-er* ⟨curs*edest*⟩ ⟨fighting*est*⟩ ⟨lying*est*⟩; regularly accompanied by coalescence with final *e* of the base word, change of final postconsonantal *y* of the base word to *i*, or doubling of the final consonant of the base word immediately after a short stressed vowel; compare ²MOST

²-est \əst\ *or* **-st** \st, *after a voiced consonant* zt *or* st\ *suffix* [ME, fr. OE *-est*, *-ast*, *-st*, 2d sing. pres. endings of various classes of verbs (fr. earlier *-es*, *-as*, *-s* + *-t*, assimilated form of the 2d pers. pron. *thū* thou) & *-est* (fr. earlier *-es* + *-t*), 2d sing. past ending of weak verbs; akin to OHG *-ist*, *-ōst*, *-ēst* (fr. earlier *-is*, *-ōs*, *-ēs* + *-t*, fr. *thū*, *thu* thou), 2d sing. pres. endings, *-ōst* (fr. earlier *-ōs* + *-t*), 2d sing. past ending of weak verbs, Goth *-is*, *-os*, *-ais*, 2d sing. pres. endings, *-es*, 2d sing. past ending of weak verbs, ON *-r*, *-ar*, *-ir*, 2d sing. pres. endings, *-ir*, 2d sing. past ending of weak verbs, L & Gk *-s* (preceded by various thematic vowels), 2d sing. pres. ending, Skt *-si*] — used to form the archaic second person singular indicative of English verbs (with *thou*) ⟨get*test*⟩ ⟨did*st*⟩ ⟨carri*est*⟩ ⟨fail*edst*⟩ ⟨can*st*⟩

est *abbr* **1** established; establishment **2** estate **3** estimate; estimated **4** estuary

EST *abbr* **1** eastern standard time **2** electroshock therapy

es·tab·lish \əˈstablish, eˈ-, -lēsh, *chiefly in pres part* -lәsh\ *vb* -ED/-ING/-ES [ME *establissen*, fr. MF *establiss-*, stem of *establir*, fr. L *stabilire*, fr. *stabilis* firm, stable — more at STABLE] *vt* **1 a :** to make firm or stable **:** fix to prevent or check unsteadiness, wavering, turmoil, or agitation ⟨~ the gun firmly on its base⟩ **b :** to place, install, or set up in a permanent or relatively enduring position esp. as regards living quarters, business, social life, or possession ⟨the family ~*ed* itself in a large house⟩ ⟨~*ed* himself in the community as a grain dealer⟩ ⟨stayed with the team long enough to see it ~*ed* as a member of a major league⟩ ⟨the first day of 1930 saw me ~*ed* in London with a good job on an evening paper —Harold Nicolson⟩ **c :** to found or base securely (as a theory) ⟨~*ed* the moral unity of all people upon the idea of God⟩ ⟨examine critically the foundations of his creed and ~ his theology upon philosophy —V.L.Parrington⟩ **d :** to assist, support, or nurture so that stability and continuance are assured ⟨stayed as principal of the new school until it was well ~*ed*⟩ **e :** to fix or implant (itself) in gaining a firm hold ⟨think of the possibilities if this scourge becomes widely ~*ed* among our eastern oaks —W.H. Camp⟩ ⟨a vice continued until it ~*ed* itself beyond escape⟩ **2 a :** to settle or fix after consideration or by enactment or agreement ⟨a congressional bill ~*ing* duties on a wide range of imports⟩ ⟨an act ~*ing* quota limits on immigration⟩ **b :** APPOINT, ORDAIN, ENTITLE ⟨~*ed* several European correspondents for the newspaper⟩ ⟨~*ed* a new vice-president for the firm⟩ **3** *obs* **:** to settle (as an estate) upon someone **:** secure (as rights) to a group **4 a :** to bring into existence, create, make, start, originate, found, or build usu. as permanent or with permanence in view ⟨~ a factory on the banks of the river⟩ ⟨~*ed* a cranberry bog —*Amer. Guide Series: Oregon*⟩ ⟨the five studies in this volume have the common purpose of ~*ing* a background for an understanding of 18th century English literature —*Univ. of Minn. Press Catalog*⟩ ⟨~ a school for the deaf⟩ ⟨the Italians voted to ~ a republic —*Current Biog.*⟩ ⟨Noah Webster, with his dictionary . . . had ~*ed* American usage in the matter of words —Van Wyck Brooks⟩ **b :** to bring about **:** EFFECT ⟨~*ing* friendly relations with the Indians —*Amer. Guide Series: Maine*⟩ **c** (1) **:** PROVIDE **:** set up ⟨it ~*ed* a fund of $700,000 to open regional offices —*Current Biog.*⟩ (2) **:** to provide for **:** ENDOW ⟨~ a chair of Oriental studies at the university⟩ **5** *obs* **:** to bring (as anger) to a state of calm **:** QUIET **6 a** *archaic* **:** CONFIRM, VALIDATE **b :** to prove or make acceptable beyond a reasonable doubt ⟨the point the speaker was trying to ~ was the imminence of economic collapse⟩ ⟨the impossibility of spontaneous generation was finally ~*ed* as a valuable working principle —J.B.Conant⟩ ⟨~ the fact that he was not there when the murder occurred⟩ **c :** to provide strong evidence for **:** bring unavoidably to the attention ⟨something was said that ~*ed* him as being in the contracting business —Hamilton Basso⟩ **d :** to calculate or determine exactly and with certainty the terms, limits, or identity of ⟨the evidence ~*ed* the motive for the crime⟩ ⟨~ the weight of the planet⟩ **e :** to provide the mind or comprehension with appropriate information about ⟨the opening shot of the movie ~*es* the scene⟩ **7 :** to make a national or state institution of (a church) **8 a :** to provide with a secure reputation esp. as valuable, useful, or certain ⟨screen productions based on ~*ed* novels⟩ ⟨~*ed* as the world's tobacco capital —*Amer. Guide Series: N.C.*⟩ **b :** to place in a position of being accepted, respected, or feared ⟨the British authority had been pretty securely ~*ed*—B.K.Sandwell⟩ ⟨clearly ~*ed* my standing as a man of good character —B.F.Fairless⟩ ⟨upset the ~*ed* order in southeast Asia⟩ **c :** to make a norm, a custom, a convention, or a habit ⟨the ~*ed* way of addressing a clergyman⟩ ⟨~*ed* art styles⟩ ⟨it was his ~*ed* practice to eat an early supper⟩ ⟨an ~*ed* conditioned reflex⟩ **9 a :** to set (as a record) as an achievement **b :** to arrive at (as a result) **10 :** to define and record (as a species) by effective publication in systematic biology **11 :** to make such plays in a card game as will permit (a specified card or all remaining cards of a specified suit) to win tricks ~ *vi* **:** to become naturalized **:** enter and persist without care or cultivation — used chiefly of plants ⟨various xerophytes readily ~ on and stabilize coastal dunes⟩ **syn** see FOUND, SET

es·tab·lish·able \-shəbəl\ *adj* **:** capable of being proved or made acceptable to logic or reason ⟨there are certain laws and generalizations ~ by these means —F.L.Will⟩

established *adj* **1 :** introduced from another region and persisting without aid or cultivation **:** NATURALIZED **2 :** surviving and multiplying on a host or substrate

established church *n* **:** a church that is recognized by law as the official church of a nation, that is supported by civil authority, and that receives in most instances financial support from the government through some system of taxation — called also *state church* ⟨the Church of England is the *established church* in England⟩

es·tab·lish·er \-shə(r)\ *n* -s **:** one that establishes

establishing shot *n* **:** a long shot in movie or television photography to establish a scene or locale before photographing specific action or detail

es·tab·lish·ment \-shmənt\ *n* -s **1 :** something that has been established: **a :** a settled arrangement; *esp* **:** a code of laws **:** RULE, DECREE, LAW **b :** ESTABLISHED CHURCH **c :** a permanent civil or military force or organization **d :** a more or less fixed and usu. sizable place of business or residence together with all the things that are an essential part of it (as grounds, furniture, fixtures, retinue, employees) **e :** a public or private institution (as a school or hospital) **2 :** the act of establishing something or the state of being established: as **a** (1) **:** the act of bringing into existence, creating, founding, originating, or setting up so that a certain continuance is assured ⟨the ~ of a custom⟩ ⟨the ~ of a factory⟩ ⟨the ~ of a new set of laws⟩ (2) **:** the act of setting or achieving (as a record) **b** *obs* **:** a settled or stable condition **:** calm security **c :** the making of a church into an established church **d :** a permanent settled position (as in life or business) **3** *archaic* **:** a regular means of support **:** an assured income **4** *also* **establishment of the port :** VULGAR ESTABLISHMENT **5 :** the naturalization of a plant or sometimes an animal in a new habitat or range typically involving successful growth, survival, and reproduction — called also *ecesis*

¹es·tab·lish·men·tar·i·an \əˌ=ₓₓmən-ˈterēən, -ˌmen-, -ta(a)r-\ *n* -s **:** one who favors the establishment of a state church **:** an adherent of the system by which a government officially recognizes and supports an established church

²establishmentarian \"\ *adj* **:** relating to or favoring religious establishment

es·tab·lish·men·tar·i·an·ism \-ēəˌnizəm\ *n* -s **:** the system of giving official state recognition and support to a particular church **:** the setting up of an established church

es·ta·fette \ˌestəˌfet\ *n* -s [F, fr. It *staffetta*, lit., small stirrup, dim. of *staffa* stirrup, of Gmc origin; akin to OHG *stapfo* step, footstep — more at STEP] **:** a mounted courier

es·ta·fia·ta \ˌestəfēˈäd-ə, -fˈyä-\ *n* -s [MexSp *estafiate*, modif. of Nahuatl *iztauhyatl*] **:** WORMWOOD SAGE

es·tall \əˈstȯl\ *vt* -ED/-ING/-S [MF *estaler* to stop, place — more at INSTALLMENT] *archaic* **:** to arrange to pay (as a debt) in installments

es·ta·min \ˈestəmən\ *or* **es·ta·mene** \ˈestəˌmēn, ˌₓₓˈₓ\ *n* -s [fr. obs. F *estame* (now *étamine*), fr. MF, fr. ML *staminia*, fr. L *staminea*, fem. of *stamineus* made of threads, fr. *stamin-*, *stamen* warp, thread, cloth — more at STAMEN] **:** a worsted twilled fabric with a rough face

es·ta·mi·net \estämēnā\ *n, pl* **estaminets** \-ā(z)\ [F, perh. fr. F dial. (Walloon) *staminet* manger, cow shed, assembly room, fr. *stamon* stake, post, of Gmc origin; akin to OHG *stam* trunk, stem — more at STEM] **:** a small café **:** BISTRO

es·tam·page \ˌeˌstämˈpäzh\ *n* -s [F, fr. *estamper* to stamp, pound (influenced in form by It *stampare* to stamp; F, fr. OF, of Gmc origin; akin to OHG *stampfōn* to crush, pound, stamp) + *-age* — more at STAMP] **:** an impression of an inscription made on inked paper

es·tam·pie \ˌeˌstämˈpē\ *or* **es·tam·pi·da** \-ēdə\ *n* -s [*estampie* fr. F, fr. OF, modif. of OProv *estampida* noise, chatter, dispute, fr. *estampida*, fem. of *estampit*, past part. of *estampir* to resound, repeat, stamp, of Gmc origin; akin to OE *stempan* to stamp — more at STAMP] **1 :** a slow stamping round dance of Provençal origin that was popular in Europe from the 12th to 15th centuries **2 :** music for the estampie typically having repeated sections and refrain somewhat in the manner of the rondeau

es·tan·cia \eˈstän(t)s(ē)yä\ *n* -s [AmerSp, fr. Sp, stay, room, dwelling, fr. (assumed) VL *stantia* — more at STANCHION] **:** a So. American cattle ranch or stock farm

es·tan·cie·ro \ˌeˌstän(t)sēˈe(ˌ)rō\ *n* -s [AmerSp, fr. *estancia* + Sp *-ero* (fr. L *-arius* -er)] **:** the owner or manager of an estancia

¹es·tate \əˈstāt, eˈ-, *usu* -ād·+V\ *n* -s [ME *estat*, fr. MF — more at STATE] **1 :** STATE, CONDITION: **a :** the form of existence or state of being of something; *specif* **:** condition or position in respect to a standard of value or to good repute ⟨he wanted to bring painting back to its original ~ —Henry Miller⟩ ⟨discussing what seem to me to be the primary causes behind the low ~ of the public schools —M.B.Smith⟩ ⟨the Civil War . . . brought our ocean marine insurance to a very low ~ —C.K.Knight⟩ **b :** circumstances or situation in life **:** mental, physical, or material condition ⟨a service which would visualize for womanhood its highest domestic ~ —Edward Bok⟩ ⟨a tonic bitterness in such poems as examine man's ~ —Babette Deutsch⟩ ⟨going to be a field supervisor and later on a district manager, and he must not arrive at his new ~ uninformed —Bernard De Voto⟩ **c** *obs* **:** normal or good condition **2 a** (1) *obs* **:** high social standing or rank (2) **:** social standing or rank ⟨a political platform appealing to people of every ~⟩ **b** *obs* (1) **:** a position or seat of dignity, grandeur, or pomp (2) **:** a canopy, chair, or dais providing this position **c** *obs* **:** a person of high social rank **3 a :** a social or political class or rank **:** a markedly distinguishable class of people in a community or nation esp. when distinguishable by social or political duties or privileges; *specif* **:** one of two or more great classes or orders of a state regarded as part of the body politic who are vested with distinct political powers and whose concurrence is necessary for legislation ⟨generally the three ~*s* of Medieval Europe consisted of the nobility, the clergy, and the merchants of the cities⟩ — called also *estate of the realm* **b estates** *pl* **:** an assembly of the governing classes or of their representatives in a nation or state **:** PARLIAMENT ⟨the levying of taxes was subject to the consent of the ~*s*⟩ **4 a :** the property or a piece or aggregation of property in lands or tenements and sometimes personalty **:** FORTUNE, POSSESSIONS ⟨a man of small ~⟩ **b** (1) **:** the aggregate of property or liabilities of all kinds that a person leaves for disposal at his death ⟨if you don't make a will, the law makes provision for disposing of your ~ for you —*Have You Made a Will?*⟩ (2) **:** such an aggregate considered as a legal entity ⟨the recoverable portion of the debt does not go to the decedent's ~ but to his heirs⟩ **c :** an interest often varying widely in degree, quality, nature, and extent in land or other property ⟨an ~ for life⟩ ⟨an ~ for years⟩ ⟨system of accumulation of funds for the creation of an ~ for old-age security —C.M.Winslow⟩ **5** *obs* **:** form of government **:** governing constitution **6** *obs* **:** body politic **:** COMMONWEALTH, KINGDOM, STATE **7 a :** a usu. large landed property ⟨the proprietor of a large ~ with ponds, woods, and a sizable house to retire to⟩ **b :** a large farm **:** PLANTATION ⟨orange groves and avocado ~*s* lie round about —Aubrey Drury⟩ ⟨European tea ~*s* in Africa⟩ **c** *Brit* **:** PROJECT, DEVELOPMENT ⟨trim housing ~*s* are being built for the workers —Robert Dunnett⟩

²estate \"\ *vt* -ED/-ING/-S **1** *obs* **:** to bestow as an estate — used with *on* or *upon* **2 a :** to endow with — used with *in* ⟨*estated* half his property in his nephew⟩ **b** *obs* **:** to endow or provide with property

estate agent *n, Brit* **:** a real estate broker or manager

estate at sufferance : the interest in a property held by one who remains in possession of or on the property after his tenancy has terminated — compare TENANCY AT SUFFERANCE

estate at will : an interest in a property subject to termination at the will of another person — compare TENANCY AT WILL

estate bottled *adj, of a wine* **:** bottled on and by the vineyard and labeled with the name of the vineyard or its owner ⟨an *estate bottled* claret⟩

estate car *or* **estate wagon** *n, Brit* **:** STATION WAGON

estate duty *n, chiefly Brit* **:** ESTATE TAX

estate in expectancy : an estate either vested or contingent in which one has a present right or interest but of which the possession is postponed or limited to take effect at some future time or upon some future event

estate in possession : a vested estate

estate of inheritance : an estate that descends to an heir and thus endures throughout two or more lives

estates *pl of* ESTATE, *pres 3d sing of* ESTATE

estates general *n* [trans. of F *états généraux*] **:** STATES GENERAL

estate tail *n* **:** an estate of inheritance held in fee tail

estate tax *n* **:** an excise tax levied often at graduated rates upon the privilege of an owner of property often including life insurance proceeds, property held jointly with right of survivorship, and gifts made in contemplation of death or to take effect in enjoyment after death of transmitting his property to others after his death, measured by the value of his total estate after payment of debts and any deductions permitted by law, and payable from the net estate before its distribution

estating *pres part of* ESTATE

estbd *abbr* established

estd *abbr* **1** established **2** estimated

este *abbr* estate

¹es·teem \əˈstēm, eˈ-\ *n* -s [ME *steem*, *extyme*, fr. MF *estime*, fr. *estimer* (v.)] **1 a** *archaic* **:** WORTH, VALUE; *also* **:** estimate of value **:** VALUATION **b** *obs* **:** RANK, STANDING **c** *archaic* **:** REPUTATION — used with *of* **d** *archaic* **:** OPINION, JUDGMENT **2 a :** approval and respect often blended with great liking or fondness because of worthy qualities ⟨an aide rising in his superior's ~⟩ **b :** such approval, respect, or liking held generally **:** FAME, RENOWN ⟨the ~ and prestige which nature attaches to excellence —H.W.Dodds⟩ **syn** see REGARD

²esteem \"\ *vb* -ED/-ING/-S [ME *estemen*, *estimen*, fr. MF *estimer*, fr. L *aestimare*, *aestumare*, prob. a denominative fr. a prehistoric compound whose first constituent is *aes* copper, bronze, money and whose second constituent is akin to Gk *temnein* to cut — more at ORE, TOME] *vt* **1** *obs* **a :** to form a numerical or quantitative estimate of **b :** to set a value on **:** estimate the worth of **:** APPRAISE **2 :** to regard as being or hold to be (of a particular character or status) **:** DEEM ⟨~ the enterprise foolish⟩ ⟨preserve my friend from what I ~*ed* a most unhappy connection —Jane Austen⟩ ⟨he should have ~*ed* it cowardly to hint that he was not happy —Compton Mackenzie⟩ ⟨officials and diplomats . . . likewise ~*ed* this their mighty hour —Harry Hansen⟩ **3 :** to set a high value on **:** hold in high regard **:** RESPECT, PRIZE ⟨~ riches⟩ ⟨two of the most ~*ed* writers of the twenties —Edward Shils⟩ ⟨~*ed* for its antiquity, like a superannuated piece of furniture —C.H.Grandgent⟩ ⟨society knows what it ~*s* and what it despises —W.C.Brownell⟩ **4 a :** to hold in regard to a specified degree ⟨intestines, liver, and other organs are greatly ~*ed* and often eaten —Farley Mowat⟩ ⟨should ~ it highly if I might be permitted to place myself during the journey, under that worthy gentleman's protection —Charles Dickens⟩ **b :** to form or hold an opinion or judgment of **c :** to be of the opinion **:** THINK, BELIEVE — used with a clause as object ⟨she ~*ed* that she knew what life was, and that it was grim —Arnold Bennett⟩ ~ *vi* **1** *obs* **:** to form or have a favorable regard **2** *obs* **:** to form or have a (particular) opinion **:** REGARD, THINK

es·teem·able \-məbəl\ *adj, archaic* **:** ESTIMABLE

es·ter \ˈestə(r)\ *n* -s [G, fr. *essigäther* acetic ether, fr. *essig* vinegar (fr. OHG *ezzīh*, fr. L *acetum*) + *äther* ether, fr. L *aether* — more at ACETIC, ETHER] **:** any of a class of compounds (as ethyl acetate, triphenyl phosphate) that on hydrolysis yield an organic or inorganic acid and an alcohol or phenol and hence may be classified either by their acid constituent (as benzoic esters or nitric esters) or by their alcohol or phenol constituent (as methyl esters or tolyl esters) and that are usu. fragrant liquids if sufficiently volatile, esters of carboxylic acids characterized by the group —COOR being found in essential oils and synthesized esp. for use in artificial fruit essences — see GLYCERIDE, POLYESTER, WAX 2a; compare ACYLAL

es·ter·ase \ˈestəˌrās, -āz\ *n* -s [ISV *ester* + *-ase*] **:** any of a class of enzymes that accelerate the hydrolysis or synthesis of esters (as fats or esters of the lower fatty acids) — compare LIPASE, PHOSPHATASE

ester gum *n* **:** a resinous ester or mixture of esters made by combining a resin of acid nature or resin acids with a polyhydric alcohol; *esp* **:** a hard usu. pale substance made by heating rosin with glycerol and used in varnishes, lacquers, and printing inks

es·ter·i·fi·able \eˈsterəˌfīəbəl, ₌ₓₓˈₓₓₓ\ *adj* **:** capable of being esterified

es·ter·i·fi·ca·tion \eˌsterəfəˈkāshən\ *n* -s **:** the process of esterifying or the state of being esterified

es·ter·i·fy \eˈsterəˌfī\ *vb* -ED/-ING/-ES [*ester* + *-ify*] **:** to convert into an ester (as by the reaction of a carbolic acid with an alcohol)

es·ter·ize \ˈestəˌrīz\ *vb* -ED/-ING/-S **:** ESTERIFY

es·te·ro \eˈste(ˌ)rō\ *n* -s [Sp, fr. L *aestuarium* — more at ESTUARY] **:** an estuary or inlet esp. when marshy; *specif* **:** a tidal channel used as a drainage canal in populated districts

-es·tes \ˈe(ˌ)stēz\ *n comb form* [NL, modif. of Gk *edestēs*, fr. (Homeric) *edmenai* to eat — more at EAT] **:** -eater — in generic names of birds ⟨Sperm*estes*⟩

esth \ˈes(t)th, ˈest\ *n* -s *cap* **:** ESTONIAN

es·tha·cyte *or* **aes·tha·cyte** \ˈesthəˌsīt\ *n* -s [*estha-*, *aestha-* (fr. Gk *aisthanesthai* to perceive) + *-cyte* — more at AUDIBLE] **:** a simple sensory cell (as of a sponge)

es·the·ria \esˈthirēə, eˈsti-\ *n, cap* [NL, prob. fr. the name *Esther* + NL *-ia*] **:** a genus (sometimes made the type of the family Estheriidae) of small branchiopod crustaceans in which the carapace is developed into a bivalve shell not unlike that of some mollusks and enclosing the whole body — **es·the·ri·an** \(ˈ)ₓ¦rēən\ *adj or n*

es·the·sia *also* **aes·the·sia** \esˈthēzh(ē)ə\ *n* -s [NL, backformation fr. *anesthesia*, *anaesthesia*] **:** capacity for sensation and feeling **:** the state of feeling or of being sensible **:** SENSIBILITY — opposed to *anesthesia*

esthesio- *or* **aesthesio-** *comb form* [NL, fr. Gk *aisthēsis* sensation, perception, feeling, fr. *aisthanesthai* to perceive, feel — more at AUDIBLE] **:** sensation ⟨*esthesio*neurosis⟩ ⟨*aesthesiology*⟩

es·the·si·o·blast \esˈthēzēəˌblast, -thēsē-\ *n* -s [*esthesio-* + *-blast*] **:** GANGLIOBLAST

es·the·si·om·e·ter \esˌthēzēˈäməd·ə(r), -thēsē-\ *n* [*esthesio-* + *-meter*] **:** an instrument for measuring sensory discrimination; *esp* **:** one for determining the distance by which two points pressed against the skin must be separated in order that they may be felt as separate

es·the·si·om·e·try \-mə·trē\ *n* -ES [*esthesio-* + *-metry*] **:** the measurement of sensory (as tactile) discrimination

es·the·sio·physiology \esˌthēzē(ˌ)ō, -thēsē-+\ *n* [*esthesio-* + *physiology*] **:** the physiology of sensation and sense organs

es·the·sis *or* **aes·the·sis** \esˈthēsəs\ *n* -ES [NL, fr. Gk *aisthēsis*] **:** SENSATION; *esp* **:** rudimentary sensation

esthetic *var of* AESTHETIC

es·thi·o·mene \esˈthīəˌmēn\ *n* -s [NL *esthiomenus*, fr. Gk *esthiomenos* decayed, infected, fr. pres. part. middle and passive of *esthiein* to eat; akin to Gk (Homeric) *edmenai* to eat — more at EAT] **:** the chronic ulcerated state of the vulva and clitoris characteristic of lymphogranuloma in the female

esthonian *usu cap, var of* ESTONIAN

es·ti·ma·ble \ˈestəməbəl\ *adj* [ME, fr. MF, fr. L *aestimabilis*, fr. *aestimare* to value, estimate + *-abilis* -able — more at ESTEEM] **1** *archaic* **:** of worth **:** VALUABLE **2 :** worthy of esteem or respect **:** deserving good opinion ⟨disappointing her father and jilting an ~ young man —Mary Austin⟩ ⟨a cultivated and eminently ~ dramatic critic —G.J.Nathan⟩ ⟨he is in many ways an admirable and even ~ figure —Irving Howe⟩ ⟨sober ~ paintings —*Time*⟩ — **es·ti·ma·ble·ness** *n* -ES

¹es·ti·mate \ˈestəˌmā|t *sometimes* -mə|; *usu* |d·+V\ *vb* -ED/-ING/-S [L *aestimatus*, past part. of *aestimare* to value, estimate] *vt* **1** *archaic* **a :** to consider or judge to be of a particular character or nature **b :** to consider or judge to be of value **:** hold in regard ⟨a man to ~ and welcome nobleness —George Meredith⟩ **2 :** to make an estimate of: as **a :** to judge the value, worth, or significance of; *esp* **:** to arrive at (a value judgment that is often valid but incomplete, approximate, or tentative) ⟨the egregious error of supposing that the dramatic merit of a dramatic work could be *estimated* without reference to its poetic merit —T.S. Eliot⟩ **b :** to fix sometimes accurately the size, extent, magnitude, or nature of ⟨a method of *estimating* deuterium⟩ ⟨small and manageable numbers of birds must be counted precisely; huge flocks can only be *estimated* —*Time*⟩ ⟨a prehistoric skeleton that is *estimated* by some anthropologists to be at least 20,000 years old —*Amer. Guide Series: Minn.*⟩ ⟨*estimating* the social importance of this movement —C.D.Lewis⟩ **c** (1) **:** to arrive at an often accurate but usu. only approximate statement of the cost of (a job to be done) (2) **:** to arrive at a sometimes only tentative price for which one is willing to undertake (a job to be done) **3 :** JUDGE, CONCLUDE ⟨he checked the chimneys off one by one and *estimated* that the fire was in the kitchen —Hugh MacLennan⟩ ~ *vi* **:** to make an estimate

syn VALUE, EVALUATE, RATE, ASSAY, ASSESS, APPRAISE: ESTIMATE is often used with judgments, either considered or casual, which are not entirely definitive ⟨we have first to *estimate* their effects upon complicated social conditions (largely a matter of guesswork) —John Dewey⟩ ⟨let us dispassionately consider the Codex Sinaiticus and try to *estimate* its position —Aldous Huxley⟩ VALUE may suggest definite but quick and temporary judgments ⟨one may pronounce a play fine or 'rotten'. If one term such direct characterization *valuing*, then criticism is *not valuing* —John Dewey⟩ It may on the other hand suggest more careful judgment ⟨you cannot *value* him alone; you must set him, for contrast and comparison, among the dead. I mean this as a principle of aesthetic . . . criticism —T.S.Eliot⟩ VALUE is used more often than the accompanying words in quick or rash hyperboles ⟨who *values* his own honor not a straw —Robert Browning⟩ EVALUATE has less connotational effect than others in this group. It is often used in situations in which criteria or principles of judgment are specified as new or important ⟨the current debate should be *evaluated*, not in terms of the excess profits tax we had during the last war, but in terms rather of an improved excess profits tax —L.G.Walinsky⟩ ⟨conventional ethical codes are assumed to be invalid or at least impractical for *evaluating* life as it is —C.C.Walcutt⟩ RATE indicates placing in a certain class, status, or bracket, perhaps without much serious reflection ⟨it is a curious thing this friend of yours you *rate* so monstrous high has not come nigh you in your sore affliction —Edna S. V. Millay⟩ ⟨as copper is *rated* very much above its real value, so silver is *rated* somewhat below it —Adam Smith⟩ ASSAY stresses careful analysis before judgment, as with the completeness of scientific methods ⟨alienation in the modern world is a major theme. In his later novels Greene has *assayed* it with acute analysis and philosophical breadth —J.M.Brinnin⟩ ASSESS likewise stresses careful analysis, as though according to better economic principles ⟨long before he arrived in the capital he had cast up his accounts with himself and made his decision. Soberly he *assessed* the elements of his power —John Buchan⟩ More than others in this group, APPRAISE may suggest expert and definitive judgment on difficult or subtle matters ⟨the cool, judicial regard, the scholarly eye of this trained historian resting on and *appraising* the turmoil and hysteria that marked the downfall of Adolf Hitler —Rosemary Benét⟩ ⟨this difficulty of *appraising* literature absolutely —A.T.Quiller-Couch⟩ **syn** see in addition CALCULATE

²**es·ti·mate** \'estəmə̇t *sometimes* -,māt; *usu* |d·+V\ *n* -s [L *aestimatus*, fr. *aestimatus*, past part. of *aestimare* to value] **1 a :** the act of appraising or valuing **:** VALUATION, CALCULATION ⟨the influence of their work upon the health and well-being of millions of Canadians is beyond ~ —F.C.James⟩ **b** *obs* **:** appraised value **c** *obs* **:** ESTEEM, REPUTE **2 :** an evaluation or judgment (as to the nature, character, or quality of a thing) ⟨an ~ of a man⟩ ⟨by general ~ at the period, the flour ground at the Brandywine Mills possessed an uncommon softness and whiteness —*Amer. Guide Series: Del.*⟩ ⟨in any ~ of human life there are two factors, both of which are extremely difficult to weigh —David Fairchild⟩ ⟨whether it is a benefit at all is a matter of forecast and ~ —O.W.Holmes †1935⟩ ⟨a generous ~ of one of the most intriguing and stimulating characters in modern fiction —Harrison Smith⟩ **:** ESTIMATION ⟨found that he had dropped somewhat in the ~ of the firm⟩ ⟨powerfully influenced an innocent public's ~ of an unfortunate woman —Ruth P. Randall⟩ ⟨in the last eight lines of the first stanza Keats makes one ~ of how this song could have thus affected him —C.S.Kilby⟩ **3 a :** a judgment made from usu. mathematical calculation esp. from incomplete data **:** a rough or approximate calculation (as of the number, amount, or size of anything) ⟨famous for a map of the inhabited earth and for reasonable ~*s* of the heights of mountains —Benjamin Farrington⟩ ⟨production figures for planes, tanks, and shipping actually exceeded the ~*s* projected by the program —*Current Biog.*⟩ ⟨some sort of ~ of the possible future developments —A.G.N.Flew⟩ ⟨impossible to give a precise ~ of the duration of these various Pleistocene ages —W.H. Dowdeswell⟩ **b :** a statement of the often approximate amount for which certain work will be done by one who undertakes it

estimated cost *n* **:** cost in cost accounting estimated in advance of production or construction

estimated weight *n* **:** the weight specified in tariffs and agreed upon by shippers and carriers to be that of certain commodities shipped in specified packages in order to avoid the weighing of each package

es·ti·mat·ing·ly *adv* **:** in an estimating or appraising manner

es·ti·ma·tion \,estə'māshən\ *n* -s [ME *estimacioun*, fr. MF *estimation* act of estimating, valuation, fr. L *aestimation-*, *aestimatio*, fr. *aestimatus* (past part. of *aestimare* to value, estimate) + *-ion-*, *-io* -ion — more at ESTEEM] **1 :** JUDGMENT, OPINION, POINT OF VIEW ⟨but apart from his own ~ of certain modern composers it is a conductor's duty to give all well-written works a trial —Warwick Braithwaite⟩ **2 a :** the act of estimating **:** the act of making an estimate (as of significance, size, or extent) ⟨the thermometer for the measurement of temperature and the barometer for the ~ of atmosphere pressure —S.F.Mason⟩ **b :** the value, number, amount, size, or price arrived at in an estimate **:** EVALUATION, ESTIMATE ⟨felt his ~ of the man was unfair⟩ ⟨staggering ~*s* of the future Canadian population —Aileen D. Ross⟩ **3 a** *archaic* **:** REPUTATION **b :** good reputation **:** ESTEEM, HONOR ⟨after the victory, the victor gained notably in general ~⟩ **c** *archaic* **:** IMPORTANCE, SIGNIFICANCE

es·ti·ma·tive \'estə,mād·iv, -,məd-\ *adj* [ME, fr. MF or ML; MF *estimatif*, fr. ML *estimativus*, fr. L *aestimatus* + *-ivus* -ive] **1 :** adapted for and capable of estimating and judging ⟨the ~ power⟩ **2 :** ESTIMATED ⟨send along only an ~ figure rather than an exact calculation of the cost⟩

es·ti·ma·tor \-,mād·ə(r), -ātə-\ *n* -s [ML, fr. L *aestimator*, fr. *aestimatus* + *-or*] **:** one that estimates: **a :** one who estimates the amount of material or labor needed to do a given job or the cost of a job or of an item of manufacture **b :** CRUISER 4a

estival *var of* AESTIVAL

estivate *var of* AESTIVATE

es·ti·vo–autumnal *also* **aes·ti·vo–autumnal** \¦estə(,)vō, e¦stī(-+\ *adj* [*estivo-* or *aestivo-* (fr. L *aestivus* of summer) + *autumnal* — more at AESTIVAL] **:** relating to or occurring in the summer and autumn — used chiefly of a form of malaria

es·toc \(')e¦stäk\ *n* -s [F (also, tree trunk), fr. OF, tree trunk, sword point, of Gmc origin; akin to OHG *stoc* stump, tree trunk — more at STOCK] **:** a thrusting sword chiefly of the Renaissance

es·to·ca·da \,estə'kädə\ *n* -s [Sp, fr. OSp *estoque* estoc (fr. MF *estoc*) + *-ada* -ade] **:** the thrust of the matador's sword used in the final stage of a bullfight and aimed to pass through the neck and kill by striking the aorta

es·to·fa·do \,estə'fä(,)dō\ *n* -s [Sp, fr. past part. of *estofar* to quilt, make estofado work, fr. *estofa* quilted material, fr. OSp, fr. MF *estoffe* stuff, material — more at STUFF] **:** the technique of finishing sculpture of wood and gesso with gilding, punched patterns, and paint

es·toile \(')e¦stöil, -twäl\ *n* -s [MF, star, fr. L *stella* — more at STAR] **:** a star conventionally represented in heraldry usu. with six wavy points

estoile

es·to·lide \'estə,līd, -lə̇d\ *n* -s [*ester* + *-ol* + *-ide*] **:** any of a class of long-chain esters formed usu. by hydroxy acids by reaction of two molecules either of the same or of different acids

es·to·nia \(')e¦stōnyə, -nēə\ *adj*, *usu cap* [fr. *Estonia*, country in northern Europe] **:** of or from Estonia **:** of the kind or style prevalent in Estonia **:** ESTONIAN

¹**es·to·nian** \(')e¦stōnyən, -ōnēən\ *also* **es·tho·nian** \(')es¦thō-, (')e¦stō-\ *adj*, *usu cap* [*Estonia*, *Esthonia* + E *-an*] **:** of or relating to Estonia, the Estonians, or their language

²**estonian** \"\ *also* **esthonian** \"\ *n* -s *cap* **1 :** a member of a Finno-Ugric-speaking people living chiefly in the former republic of Estonia on the Baltic sea **2 :** the Finno-Ugric language of the Estonian people — see URALIC LANGUAGES table

es·top \ə̇'stäp, e'-\ *vt* [ME *estoppen*, fr. MF *estoper*, *estouper*, fr. (assumed) VL *stuppare*, fr. L *stuppa* tow — more at STUPE] **1** *archaic* **:** to fill up **:** plug up **:** stop up **2 :** PRECLUDE, BAR, PROHIBIT ⟨sought to . . . ~ fighting on Sundays —K.S. Latourette⟩ ⟨if a person is pitch-deaf, he is *estopped* from the skillful use of inflectional change in his voice —A.T.Weaver⟩; *esp* **:** to impede or bar by estoppel

es·top·pel \-pəl\ *n* -s [prob. fr. MF *estoupail* bung, stopper, fr. *estouper*, v.] **:** a legal preclusion or bar by which one is prevented from alleging something he has previously denied in actuality or by implication in his action or from denying something he has similarly alleged

es·to·que \e'stō,kā\ *n* -s [Sp, fr. MF *estoc* — more at ESTOC] **:** a matador's sword with a flat blade curved at the tip

es·to·vers \ə̇'stōvə(r)z, e'-\ *n pl* [ME, fr. AF, fr. OF *estoveir*, *estovoir* to be necessary, fr. L *est opus* there is need, it is necessary] **:** necessary supplies; *esp* **:** wood that a tenant is allowed to take from the landlord's premises for the necessary fuel or implements used by himself and his resident servants or for necessary repairs

es·trade \e'sträd\ *n* -s [F, fr. Sp *estrado*, fr. L *stratum* bed, covering — more at STRATUM] **:** PLATFORM, DAIS

es·tra·di·ol *also* **oes·tra·di·ol** \,estrə'dī,ōl, -ī,ōl\ *n* -s [ISV *estra-*, *oestra-* (fr. *estrin*, *oestrin*) + *-diol*] **:** a white crystalline highly estrogenic hormone that is a phenolic steroid alcohol $C_{18}H_{24}O_2$ found esp. in the follicular fluid of the ovary and in the urine of pregnant mares but is usu. made synthetically (as from estrone by reduction or indirectly from cholesterol) and that is often used in the form of esters esp. in treating menopausal symptoms

es·tra·gole \'estrə,gōl\ *also* **es·dra·gol** \'ezdrə,gōl, -gōl\ *n* -s [*estragole* ISV *estragon* + *-ole*; *esdragol* fr. G, fr. *esdragon*, *estragon* (fr. F *estragon*) + *-ol* -ole] **:** a liquid ether $C_3H_5C_6H_4OCH_3$ that has an odor like aniseed, occurs in tarragon oil, turpentine, and other essential oils, and is used in perfumes and flavoring materials; *para*-allyl-anisole — called also *methyl chavicol*

es·tra·gon \'estrə,gän\ *n* -s [F, fr. MF, alter. of earlier *targon*, fr. Ar *ṭarkhun* — more at TARRAGON] **:** TARRAGON

estragon oil *n* **:** TARRAGON OIL

estral *var of* ESTROUS

es·trange \ə̇'strānj, e'-\ *vt* -ED/-ING/-S [MF *estranger*, fr. OF *estrangier*, fr. ML *extraneare*, fr. L *extraneus* foreign, strange — more at STRANGE] **1 :** to remove or keep at a distance esp. from customary environment or associations ⟨his constant need to travel served to ~ him from most family activities⟩ **2 :** to divert in affection or personal attachment **:** destroy one's confidence in **:** arouse enmity or indifference in where there had been originally love, affection, or friendliness ⟨the difference in religion brought on clashes between the two and ultimately *estranged* them⟩ ⟨the father's need to dominate quickly *estranged* all but one of the children⟩ ⟨poverty and misery had *estranged* him from his background —E.H.Erikson⟩ **3 :** to make alien or a stranger in condition, character, or appearance — now used with *from* ⟨writers who somehow felt *estranged* from their native life when the thread had once been broken —Van Wyck Brooks⟩ ⟨if a young man is not as anxious to work as he might be, let us remember that laws like that have helped ~ him from habits of industry —Elijah Adlow⟩

syn ALIENATE, DISAFFECT, WEAN: ESTRANGE may suggest development of hostility, separation, or divorcement ⟨the *estranging* film of defensive reticence which separates nearly all of us from our friends —C.E.Montague⟩ ALIENATE may not suggest separation but does indicate a changing of affection, sympathy, and interest to coldness, aloofness, or antipathy ⟨the governor and judges, who had *alienated* the people by arrogating to themselves the judicial, legislative, and executive powers of government —*Amer. Guide Series: Mich.*⟩ ⟨the colossal impudence of his comment on his former and now *alienated* associate —E.V.Lucas⟩ DISAFFECT indicates causing loss of warm and ready loyalty and inducing unrest and discontent ⟨the disloyalists tried to *disaffect* the militia, preaching treason —C.G.Bowers⟩ WEAN indicates separating commendably from someone or something that another is weakly dependent on or immaturely preoccupied with ⟨*wean* your minds from hankering after false Germanic standards —A.T.Quiller-Couch⟩ ⟨definitely *weaned* from close emotional dependency on his parents —John Dollard⟩

estranged *adj* **:** marked by or giving evidence of estrangement ⟨suggested a marriage counselor who might help out the ~ couple⟩ ⟨gave him an ~ look⟩

es·tranged·ness \-jə̇dnə̇s, -j(d)n-\ *n* -ES **:** the quality or state of being estranged

es·tran·ge·la \e'straŋgələ\ *or* **es·tran·ge·lo** *or* **es·tran·ghe·lo** \-,lō\ *n* -s *usu cap* [Syr *esṭrangĕlāyē* rounded (letters), fr. Gk *strongylos* rounded; akin to Gk *strangos* twisted — more at STRAIN (draw tight)] **:** the earlier form of the Syriac alphabet — compare SERTA

es·trange·ment \ə̇'strānjmənt, e'-\ *n* -s **:** the act of estranging or the condition of being estranged **:** alienation esp. in friendship ⟨the small difference of opinion snowballed into mutual resentment and resulted in final and total ~⟩ ⟨the hero, a middle-aged intellectual and student, has passed through successive ~*s* from bourgeois life —*Time*⟩ ⟨resulted in the almost complete ~ of arts and letters from the sciences —*Scientific American Reader*⟩

estranger *n* -s [ME, fr. MF *estrangier*, fr. OF *estrange* foreign, strange + *-ier* -er — more at STRANGE] *obs* **:** one from another family, district, or country **:** ALIEN, FOREIGNER, STRANGER

es·tra·pe·nia \,estrə'pēnēə, -nyə\ *n* -s [NL, fr. *estra-* (fr. ISV *cholinesterase*) + *-penia*] **:** deficiency of cholinesterase — **es·tra·pe·nic** \,estrə'pēnik\ *adj*

¹**es·tray** \ə̇'strā, e'-\ *vi* [MF *estraier* to roam about without a master — more at STRAY] *archaic* **:** STRAY

²**estray** \"\ *n* -s [AF, fr. OF *estraié* wandering, masterless, fr. *estraier*, v.] **1 :** a valuable domestic animal found wandering away from its home or enclosure **:** STRAY **2 :** something that has wandered or gone out of its usual or normal place — compare FREE ASTRAY

³**estray** \"\ *adj* [²*estray*] **:** being or having gone astray

¹**es·treat** \ə̇'strēt, e'-\ *n* -s [ME *estrete*, fr. AF, fr. OF *estraite*, fem. of *estrait*, past part. of *estraire* to extract, fr. L *extrahere* — more at EXTRACT] **:** a true copy, duplicate, or extract of an original writing or record (as of an amercement)

²**estreat** \"\ *vt* -ED/-ING/-S **1 :** to extract from the records of a court so as to enforce or prosecute **2 :** to exact or take by means of a levy or fine

es·trepe \ə̇'strēp, e'-\ *vt* -ED/-ING/-S [MF *estreper*, fr. L *exstirpare* to root out — more at EXTIRPATE] **:** to wreak needless destruction or waste upon — compare ESTREPEMENT

es·trepe·ment \-mənt\ *n* -s [AF *estrepement*, fr. OF *estreper*, v. + *-ment*] **:** waste or needless destruction of lands; *esp* **:** such waste in lands, woods, or houses wrought by a tenant for life to the damage of the reversioner

estriate \(')ē+\ *adj* [NL *estriatus*, fr. L *e-* + *striatus* striated — more at STRIATED] **:** not striated

estrich *or* **estridge** *obs var of* OSTRICH

es·trin *also* **oes·trin** \'estrə̇n\ *n* -s [NL *estrus*, *oestrus* + E *-in*] **:** an estrogenic hormone; *esp* **:** ESTRONE

es·trin·iza·tion \,estrə̇nə̇'zāshən, -,nī'z-\ *n* -s [*estrin* + *-ization*] **1 :** the uterine and vaginal mucosal alteration characteristic of estrus **2 :** treatment with estrogenic substances

es·tri·ol *also* **oes·tri·ol** \'e,strī,ōl, e's-, -ī,ōl\ *n* -s [blend of *estrin*, *oestrin* and *-triol*] **:** a white crystalline estrogenic hormone that is a phenolic steroid glycol $C_{18}H_{24}O_3$ and is usu. obtained from the urine of pregnant women — called also *theelol*

es·tro·gen *also* **oes·tro·gen** \'estrəjən, -,jen\ *n* -s [ISV *estro-*, *oestro-* (fr. NL *estrus*, *oestrus*) + *-gen*] **:** a sex hormone (as estradiol, estriol, estrone) produced esp. in the ovaries and usu. characterized by its ability to promote estrus and stimulate the development of secondary sex characteristics in the female; *also* **:** a substance occurring naturally in plants or made synthetically (as benzestrol or diethylstilbestrol) that has similar biological activity — compare ANDROGEN

es·tro·gen·ic *also* **oes·tro·gen·ic** \¦estrə¦jenik\ *adj* [ISV *estro-*, *oestro-* + *-genic*] **1 :** promoting estrus **2** [*estrogen*, *oestrogen* + *-ic*] **:** of, relating to, or caused by an estrogen — **es·tro·gen·i·cal·ly** \-nə̇k(ə)lē\ *adv*

Es·tron \'e,strän\ *trademark* **1** — used for a fiber made from partly hydrolyzed cellulose acetate **2 :** a yarn or fabric made of Estron fiber

es·trone *also* **oes·trone** \'e,strōn\ *n* -s [ISV *estrin*, *oestrin* + *-one*] **:** a white crystalline estrogenic hormone that is a phenolic steroid ketone $C_{18}H_{22}O_2$ usu. obtained from the urine of pregnant females (as mares or women) and that is used similarly to estradiol — called also *theelin*

es·trous *or* **oes·trous** \'estrəs, *chiefly Brit* 'ēs-\ *also* **es·tral** *or* **oes·tral** \-rəl\ *or* **es·tru·al** *or* **oes·tru·al** \-rəwəl\ *adj* [NL *estrus*, *oestrus* + E *-ous* or *-al*] **1 :** of, relating to, or characteristic of estrus ⟨the ~ state⟩ ⟨~ keratinization of the vaginal mucosa⟩ **2 :** exhibiting estrus **:** being in heat ⟨the ~ bitch⟩

estrous cycle *n* **:** the correlated phenomena of the endocrine and generative systems of a female mammal from the beginning of one period of estrus to the beginning of the next

es·tru·ate *or* **oes·tru·ate** \'estrə,wāt\ *vi* -ED/-ING/-S [back-formation fr. *estruation*, *oestruation*] **:** to undergo estrus

es·tru·a·tion *or* **oes·tru·a·tion** \,estrə'wāshən\ *n* -s [NL *estrum*, *oestrum* + E *-ation*] **1 :** the condition of being in estrus **2 :** ESTRUS

es·trus *or* **oes·trus** \'estrəs, *chiefly Brit* 'ēs-\ *also* **es·trum** *or* **oes·trum** \-rəm\ *n*, *pl* **estruses** *or* **oestruses** *also* **estrums** *or* **oestrums** *often attrib* [NL, fr. L *oestrus* gadfly, frenzy, fr. Gk *oistros* — more at IRE] **1 a :** a regularly recurrent state of sexual excitability during which the female of most mammals will accept the male and is capable of conceiving **:** HEAT **b :** a single occurrence of this state ⟨the next ~ was delayed⟩ **2 :** ESTROUS CYCLE

ests *pl of* EST

es·tu·a·rine \'es(h)chəwə,rīn\ *also* **es·tu·ar·i·al** \¦==¦wa(a)rēəl\ *adj* [*estuary* + *-ine*, *-ial*] **:** of, relating to, or formed in an estuary ⟨~ clays⟩ ⟨~ currents⟩ ⟨~ fisheries⟩ **:** suited to operate in estuaries ⟨*estuarial* craft⟩

estuarine crocodile *n* **:** SALTWATER CROCODILE

es·tu·ary \'es(h)chə,werē, -ri\ *n* -ES *often attrib* [L *aestuarium*, fr. *aestus* heaving of the sea, tide, boiling, heat + *-arium*; akin to L *aestas* summer — more at AESTIVAL] **1 a :** a water passage (as the mouth of a river) where the tide meets the current of a stream **:** TIDAL RIVER **b :** an arm of the sea at the lower end of a river **2 :** a drowned river mouth caused by the sinking of the land near the coast

estuate *vi* -ED/-ING/-S [L *aestuatus*, past part. of *aestuare* to be in commotion, boil, fr. *aestus*] *obs* **:** HEAVE, SURGE, BOIL — **estuation** *n* -s

es·tu·fa \e'stüfə\ *n* -s [Sp, lit., stove, warm room, fr. *estufar* to heat an apartment, fr. (assumed) VL *extufare* to heat by steam — more at STOVE] **:** an assembly room or council chamber of a Pueblo Indian dwelling in which a sacred fire is kept burning

ESU *abbr*, *usu not cap* electrostatic unit

esu·ri·ence \ə̇'su̇rēən(t)s, ē's-\ *also* **esu·ri·en·cy** \-nsē\ *n*, *pl* **esuriences** *also* **esuriencies :** the quality or state of being esurient

esu·ri·ent \-nt\ *adj* [L *esurient-*, *esuriens*, pres. part. of *esurire* to be hungry, desiderative of *edere* to eat — more at EAT] **:** VORACIOUS, GREEDY ⟨fell into the ~ embrace of a predatory enemy⟩ ⟨regarded the fellow with ~ eyes, the eyes of an avid curiosity —Carl Van Vechten⟩ — **esu·ri·ent·ly** *adv*

esurine *adj* [NL *esurinus*, fr. LL *esuries* hunger (fr. L *esurire* to be hungry) + L *-inus* -ine] **1** *obs* **:** consisting of a mineral acid **:** CORROSIVE **2** *obs* **:** VORACIOUS

et *dial past of* EAT

-et \¦et, ə̇t, *usu* ¦ed· *or* ə̇d+V\ *n suffix* -s [ME, fr. OF *-et* (masc.) & *-ete* (fem.), fr. LL *-itus* & *-ita*] **1 :** small one **:** lesser one **:** -LET ⟨baron*et*⟩⟨cellar*et*⟩⟨single*t*⟩ **2 :** group ⟨oct*et*⟩

-et- *comb form* [ISV, fr. *ethyl*] **:** ethyl radical C_2H_5 ⟨phen*et*idine⟩

ET *abbr* **1** eastern time **2** Easter term **3** electric telegraph **4** electrical transcription

Et *symbol* ethyl

¹**eta** \'ād·ə, |tə *also* 'ē|\ *n* -s [LL, fr. Gk *ēta*, fr. a Phoenician word akin to Heb *ḥēth*] **:** the seventh letter of the Greek alphabet — symbol H or η; see ALPHABET table

²**eta** \'ā,tä\ *n*, *pl* **eta** *also* **etas** *often cap* [Jap] **1 :** an outcast class formerly segregated in Japan (in pre-Meiji Japan the ~, or pariah class, ranked below the . . . warrior, farmer, artisan, and merchant —J.F.Embree⟩ **2 :** a member of the eta class

-eta *pl of* -ETUM

ETA *abbr or n* -s **:** estimated time of arrival

etaac \ā'täts\ *n* -s [origin unknown] **:** BLAUBOK

éta·gère *or* **eta·gere** \,ā,tä'zhe(ə)r\ *n* -s [F *étagère*, fr. MF *estagiere*, fr. *estage* floor of a building, sojourn, situation + *-iere* -er — more at STAGE] **:** a cabinet consisting of a tier of open shelves **:** WHATNOT

étain blue \'ā,taⁿ-\ *n* [F *étain* tin, pewter, fr. MF *estain*, fr. LL *stagnum*, *stannum* — more at STANNIC] **:** a very pale green to very pale blue

et al \(')ed·¦al, (')e¦tl, -|ōl, -|äl\ *abbr* **1** [L *et alibi*] and elsewhere **2** [L *et alii* (masc. pl.), *et aliae* (fem. pl.), or *et alia* (neut. pl.)] and others

eta·lon \'ād·ᵊl,än, 'ed-\ *n* -s [F *étalon* standard of weights and measures, fr. MF *estalon*, *estelon*, prob. of Gmc origin; akin to Fris *stal* shape, form] **:** an interferometer in which two parallel partially silvered glass plates at a fixed distance apart produce by multiple reflection interference spectra of high dispersion and resolution adapted to the fine-structure analysis of spectrum lines

eta·mine \'ād·ə,mēn, 'ed-\ *n* -s [F *étamine* — more at ESTAMIN] **:** a light cotton or worsted fabric with an open mesh

etanim *usu cap*, *var of* ETHANIM

eta·oin shrd·lu \'ed·|ē,ōin'shərd,lü, 'ēd·|, 'äd·|, |ə,ōi-, -n-(,)shərd'lü\ *n* -s **:** a combination of letters set by running a finger down the first and then the second left-hand vertical banks of six keys of a Linotype machine to produce a temporary marking slug not intended to appear in the final printing

eta palm *var of* ITA PALM

etap·ter·is \ə̇'taptərə̇s, ā'-,ē'-\ *n*, *cap* [NL, fr. Gk *ēta* eta + NL *-pteris*] **:** a form genus of Paleozoic ferns represented only by fossil leaves which are pinnate and with primary pinnal alternate on the rachis

etat·ism \ā'täd·,izəm\ *or* **éta·tisme** \ātätēsm(ᵊ), -s(mə)\ *also* **état·ism** \ā'tad·,izəm\ *n*, *pl* **etatisms** \-izəmz\ *or* **étatismes** \-sm(ᵊ), -s(mə)\ *or* **étatisms** \-izəmz\ [F *étatisme*, fr. *état* state (fr. MF *estat*) + *-isme* -ism — more at STATE] **:** STATE SOCIALISM

etat·ist *or* **état·ist** \ā'täd·ə̇st\ *adj* [F *étatiste*, fr. *étatiste*, n., one that favors etatism, fr. *état* state + *-iste* -ist] **:** based on or favoring state socialism

etc \ən'sō,f|ōrth |ōrth, |ōəth, |ō(ə)th *sometimes* =¦=¦=; et'sed·ərə, -setərə, -se·trə *also* ə̇t's-\ *abbr* [L *et cetera*] et cetera — sometimes used esp. formerly to| sbefore a letter-closing formula ⟨I am, Yours, ~⟩

et cet·era *also* **et cae·tera** \et'sed·ərə, -setərə, -se·trə *also* ə̇t's-\ [L] **:** and others esp. of the same kind **:** and so on **:** and so forth ⟨lovely scarves, handbags, *et cetera* —*Mademoiselle*⟩ ⟨children are always catching things from one another, bad manners, germs, *et cetera* —Evelyn Barkins⟩ ⟨amid the new movements, foreign influences, themes, *et cetera* —Stark Young⟩ ⟨other institutional components of a society, such as school, church, *et cetera* —L.S.Cottrell⟩ ⟨climb mountains, cross rivers, swim oceans, *et cetera* —Everett Carter⟩ — abbr. *etc.*; used to imply that other items are to be understood; used also as a reminder that semantic abstractions lack allness

et·cet·era \"\ *n* -s [*et cetera*] **1 :** a number of various unspecified persons or things ⟨a long ~ of illustrious names —Susan E. Ferrier⟩ **2 etceteras** *pl* **:** additional items **:** ODDS AND ENDS, SUNDRIES ⟨she began to pack back her compact, comb and other ~*s* into her handbag —Elizabeth Bowen⟩ ⟨it's roomy enough to hold small parcels, plus your important ~*s* —*Christian Science Monitor*⟩

¹**etch** \'ech\ *vb* -ED/-ING/-ES [D *etsen*, fr. G *ätzen* to feed, bite, cause to bite, etch, fr. OHG *azzen* to feed; akin to MD *etten* to put out to graze, ON *etja* to cause to fight, goad on, Goth *fraatjan* to distribute as food; causative fr. the root of E *eat* — more at EAT] *vt* **1 a :** to produce (as a design) usu. on a metal or glass surface by covering it with an acid-resistant ground through which a design is scratched with a

pointed instrument and submitting the surface to an acid bath or other mordant ⟨panels of glass ~*ed* to simulate clouds —*Amer. Guide Series: Minn.*⟩ **b :** to treat (as a copper or zinc plate) in a similar manner to produce a relief printing image by photoengraving — compare HALFTONE **c :** to treat (a lithographic printing surface) with dilute nitric or other acid in order to fix the design and make the exposed parts more repellent to grease **2 :** to corrode the surface of (as a metal) usu. with acid for the purpose of microscopic examination of structural details **3 a :** to draw the main features of (as a face) **:** OUTLINE ⟨a little leaned by the years, and the features a little more sharply ~*ed* —C.I.Lewis⟩ ⟨nor has the relationship between crime and politics been more clearly ~*ed* than in Chicago —Seth Agnew⟩ **b :** to set forth in a clear-cut manner **:** DELINEATE ⟨the most sharply ~*ed* character in the book —*Times Lit. Supp.*⟩ **4 :** to produce (a feature of the landscape) by erosion **:** ERODE, CHISEL ⟨barrier of towering peaks and deeply ~*ed* canyons —R.A.Billington⟩ ⟨streams ~*ed* out new valleys —*Amer. Guide Series: N.J.*⟩ **5 :** to impress usu. on the mind or in the memory **:** IMPRINT ⟨the place, the people, are ~*ed* in our minds to stay —*N.Y. Herald Tribune Bk. Rev.*⟩ ⟨lasting impressions on the American mind, ~*ed* deeply into a national consciousness —J.D.Hart⟩ ~ *vi* **1 :** to practice the art of etching **:** make etchings ⟨has been ~*ing* busily the past month⟩ **2 :** to be susceptible of etching with acid ⟨magnesium is said to ~ faster than copper or zinc⟩

²**etch** \" \ *n* -ES **1 :** the action or effect of an etching acid on metal or glass **:** BITE **2 :** a chemical agent used in etching; *specif* **:** a solution of acid and gum arabic used in lithography to desensitize the parts of the stone or metal surface that are not intended to print **3 :** TOBACCO ETCH

etch·ant \ˈechənt\ *n* -S [¹*etch* + *-ant*] **:** a reagent (as a dilute solution of an acid) used in etching

etched-out \ˈ=ˌ=\ *adj* **:** BURNT-OUT 2

etch·e·min \ˈechəmən\ *n, pl* **etchemin** *or* **etchemins** *usu cap* [F, of AmerInd origin] **:** MALECITE

etch·er \ˈechə(r)\ *n* -S **:** one that etches: as **a :** an artist who hand-etches on metal or glass **b** (1) **:** one that hand-etches copper or steel plates for use in printing (2) **:** a worker who immerses such plates in the acid-etching solution **c :** one that dips a copper roller for use in printing textiles into an acid bath to etch the design previously scratched on its surface **d :** one that etches designs, trademarks, figures, or numbers on cutlery or firearms by hand or machine **e :** a worker who cleans metal airplane parts with an acid to prepare them for welding

etch figure *or* **etching figure** *n* **:** a marking consisting usu. of a minute pit produced by a solvent on the crystal face of a mineral and revealing its molecular structure — usu. used in pl.

etching *n* -S **1 :** the act or process of etching (as a design); *specif* **:** the art of producing pictures or designs by printing from a metal plate prepared by covering with a ground on which the picture is scratched with a needlelike instrument and then etched — compare AQUATINT, CRAYON MANNER, PHOTOENGRAVING, RELIEF, SOFT GROUND **2 :** the result or product of etching: as **a :** an etched plate **b :** a design produced by etching **c :** an impression on paper or a similar substance taken in ink from an etched plate **3 :** a written sketch or impression ⟨a series of ~*s* he wrote —A.W.Long⟩ **4 :** a cracked state of the enamel of a tooth

etching ball *n* **:** a ball of the ground used in etching

etching needle *n* **:** a steel point or stylus used in etching to draw through the ground and expose the metal plate to the acid

etching press *n* **:** COPPERPLATE PRESS

¹**et·eo·cretan** \ˌēd·ē(ˌ)ō, ¦ed-·+\ *adj, usu cap* [Gk *Eteokrēt-, Eteokrēs* pre-Greek inhabitant of Crete (fr. *eteos* true + *Krēt-, Krēs* Cretan) + E *-an* — more at SOOTH] **:** of or relating to the pre-Greek inhabitants of Crete — compare MINOAN

²**eteocretan** \" \ *n* -S *cap* **1 :** a pre-Greek inhabitant of Crete **2 :** a pre-Greek language of Crete preserved in a small amount of inscriptional material partly in hieroglyphic characters

¹**eter·nal** \əˈtərnᵊl, ēˈ-, -tə̄n-, -təin-\ *adj* [ME, fr. MF *eternal, eternel*, fr. LL *aeternalis*, fr. L *aeternus* (alter. of *aeviternus*, prob. fr. *aevitas* age, lifetime of something, fr. the stem of *aevum* age, eternity + *-itas* -ity) + *-alis* -al — more at AYE] **1 a :** having infinite duration: (1) **:** infinite in past and future duration **:** having no beginning or end ⟨the ~ God is your dwelling place —Deut 33:27 (RSV)⟩ (2) **:** infinite in past duration **:** having no beginning (3) **:** infinite in future duration **:** having no end ⟨the soldiers were convinced that whatever happened, the end of the war would mark the opening of an era of ~ peace —R. de R. de Sales⟩ **b :** having infinite duration and characterized by abiding fellowship with God ⟨good teacher, what must I do to inherit ~ life? —Mk 10:17 (RSV)⟩ **c :** of or relating to eternity ⟨this ~ blazon must not be to ears of flesh and blood —Shak.⟩ **2 a :** continued without intermission **:** CEASELESS, UNCHANGING ⟨and fires ~ in thy temple shine —John Dryden⟩ **b :** seemingly endless often to the point of weariness or disgust **:** constantly recurring **:** INTERMINABLE ⟨there was also the ~ waiting in hotels for appointments with officials —Herbert Hoover⟩ **3** *archaic* **:** INFERNAL, DAMNED — used as an intensive ⟨some ~ villain . . . devised this slander —Shak.⟩ **4 :** valid or existing at all times **:** IMMUTABLE, UNCHANGEABLE ⟨right and wrong were ~ verities . . . which could not be changed and must not be tampered with —O.E.Rölvaag⟩ **5 :** outside or beyond temporal relationships **:** discrete from all times **:** TIMELESS ⟨a color is ~ —A.N.Whitehead⟩

²**eternal** \" \ *n* -S **1** *cap* **:** ²GOD — used with preceding *the* ⟨the great issue remains man's relationship to the *Eternal* —Ruth Suckow⟩ **2** *obs* **:** ETERNITY **3 :** something that is eternal ⟨the superiority of the spiritual and ~ over the carnal and temporal —H.O.Taylor⟩ — often used in pl. ⟨men so truly spiritual in the ~*s* of their creed —Thomas De Quincey⟩

³**eternal** *adv, obs* **:** FOREVER

eternal generation *n* **:** the theological doctrine that the Son was begotten of the Father from all eternity and is therefore coeternal with the Father

eter·nal·ism \-ᵊlˌizəm\ *n* -S **:** the doctrine of the eternalists

eter·nal·ist \-ᵊləst\ *n* -S **:** a believer in the eternity of the world, in a transcendent world, or in a transcendental domain — **eter·nal·is·tic** \ə¦==¦istik, ē¦=-, ¦ē,=-\ *adj*

eter·nal·i·ty \(ˌ)ēˌtərˈnaləd·ē, əˌt-, -tə̄ˈn-, -təiˈn-, -lətē, -i\ *n* -ES [ME *eternalite*, fr. MF *eternalité*, fr. ML *eternalitas*, fr. LL *aeternalis* eternal + L *-itas* -ity] **:** the quality or state of being eternal ⟨but to realize again the ~, the deathlessness and changelessness of youth —William Faulkner⟩

eter·nal·ize \əˈtərnᵊlˌīz, ēˈ-, -tə̄n-, -təin-\ *vt* -ED/-ING/-S **:** ETERNIZE

eter·nal·ly \-ᵊlē, -ᵊli\ *adv* [ME, fr. *eternal* + *-ly*] **1 :** throughout eternity **:** FOREVER ⟨whosoever liveth and believeth in Him shall not die ~ —*Bk. of Com. Prayer*⟩ **2 :** with continual recurrence **:** CONSTANTLY ⟨he was ~ in need of money —Rudyard Kipling⟩ **3 :** IMMUTABLY, UNALTERABLY ⟨there is such a thing as the ~ right and the unchangeably good —J.P.Hopps⟩

eter·nal·ness \-ᵊlnəs\ *n* -ES **:** ETERNALITY

eternal object *n* **1** *in Whiteheadian philosophy* **:** an enduring potential for becoming **2 :** a subsistent form or idea

eternal recurrence *n* **:** the infinitely cyclical repetition of all things and situations with respect to a finite universe — used in Nietzschean philosophy

eterne \əˈtərn, ēˈ-\ *adj* [ME, fr. MF, fr. L *aeternus* — more at ETERNAL] *archaic* **:** ETERNAL

eter·ni·ty \əˈtərnəd·ē, ēˈt-, -nətē, -i\ *n* -ES [ME *eternite*, fr. MF *eternité*, fr. L *aeternitas*, fr. *aeternus* eternal + *-itas* -ity] **1 :** the quality or state of being eternal **:** eternal existence ⟨God enjoys himself only by contemplation of his goodness, ~, infiniteness and power —Izaak Walton⟩ **2 :** a totality of infinite time: **a :** a totality of infinite past and future time **b :** a totality of infinite past time **c :** a totality of infinite future time **3 eternities** *pl* **:** AGES ⟨to unfold through the ages, yea, through the *eternities* —E.H.Sears⟩ **4 :** the condition that begins at death **:** IMMORTALITY ⟨all that lives must die, passing through nature to ~ —Shak.⟩ **5 a :** something that transcends time or involves or includes timeless reality **b :** absolute timelessness **6 :** an indefinite, immeasurable, or seemingly endless period of time ⟨it seemed an ~, not a few hours ago, when her mother had sat there reading —Ellen Glasgow⟩ **7 eternities** *pl* **:** the eternal truths or realities ⟨if a man cannot get some glimpse into the *eternities* —Thomas Carlyle⟩

eternity ring *n* **:** a narrow ring to be worn by a woman and usu. set with a continuous line of gems

eter·nize \əˈtərˌnīz, ēˈ-, -tə̄ˌn-, -təiˌn-; ˈēd·ə(r)ˌnīz, ˈētə-\ *vt* -ED/-ING/-S [MF *eterniser*, fr. *eterne* + *-iser* -ize] **1 a :** to make eternal in duration or character ⟨the mortal soul shall be . . . *eternized* —P.J.Bailey⟩ **b :** to prolong indefinitely **:** PERPETUATE ⟨my perpetual quarrels which they take care to ~ —Mary W. Montagu⟩ **2 :** to make forever famous **:** IMMORTALIZE ⟨my verse your virtues rare shall ~ —Edmund Spenser⟩

¹**ete·sian** \əˈtēzhən, ēˈt-\ *adj, often cap* [L *etesius* (fr. Gk *etēsios*, fr. *etos* year) + E *-an* — more at WETHER] **:** recurring annually — used of northerly winds that blow during the summer over the eastern Mediterranean

²**etesian** \" \ *n* -S *often cap* **:** an etesian wind — usu. used in pl.

eth *var of* EDH

eth- *or* **etho-** *comb form* [ISV, fr. *ethyl*] **:** ethyl ⟨*eth*aldehyde⟩ ⟨*etho*chloride⟩

¹**-eth** \əth\ *or* **-th** \th\ *vb suffix* [ME, fr. OE *-eth, -ath, -th*, 3d sing. pres. indic. endings of various classes of verbs; akin to OHG *-it, -ōt, -ēt*, 3d sing. pres. indic. endings, early ON (runic) *-ith, -īth, -ōth, -ēth*, Goth *-ith, -eith, -oth, -aith*, L *-t* (preceded by various thematic vowels), Gk *-ti*, 3d sing. pres. indic. ending of unthematic verbs, Skt *-ti* (preceded by various thematic vowels or by a consonant), 3d sing. pres. indic. ending] — used to form the archaic third person singular present indicative of verbs ⟨go*eth*⟩ ⟨do*th*⟩ ⟨think*eth*⟩ ⟨ha*th*⟩ ⟨sai*th*⟩ ⟨mak*eth*⟩ ⟨lead*eth*⟩

²**-eth** — see -TH

eth *abbr* **1** ether **2** ethical; ethics

eth·a·nal \ˈethəˌnal\ *n* -S [ISV *ethane* + *-al*] **:** ACETALDEHYDE

eth·ane \ˈeˌthān\ *n* -S [ISV *eth-* + *-ane*] **:** a colorless odorless water-insoluble gaseous paraffin hydrocarbon CH_3CH_3 occurring in natural gas, produced as a by-product in the cracking of petroleum, and used chiefly as a fuel or as a source of ethylene by dehydrogenation

eth·a·nim \ˈethəˌnim\ *also* **et·a·nim** \ˈed·ə-\ *n* -S *usu cap* [Heb *Ēthānīm*] **:** the 7th month of the ancient Hebrew calendar corresponding to Tishri

eth·a·nol \ˈethəˌnōl, -ˌnȯl\ *n* -S [ISV *ethane* + *-ol*] **:** ALCOHOL 3 — used in the system of nomenclature adopted by the International Union of Pure and Applied Chemistry

eth·a·nol·amine \ˌethəˈnōləˌmēn, -nȯl-\ *n* [ISV *ethanol* + *amine*] **1 :** a colorless liquid basic amino alcohol $HOCH_2CH_2NH_2$ made usu. from ammonia and ethylene oxide and used chiefly as a solvent, in scrubbing acidic gases from gas streams, in making detergents, and in synthesis (as of pharmaceuticals); 2-amino-ethanol; 2-hydroxyethyl-amine — called also *monoethanolamine* **2 :** an amino alcohol containing hydroxyethyl attached to amino nitrogen — see DIETHANOLAMINE, TRIETHANOLAMINE

eth·a·no·lic \ˌethəˈnōlik, -nȯl-\ *adj* [*ethanol* + *-ic*] **:** of, relating to, containing, or derived from ethyl alcohol **:** ALCOHOLIC 1

eth·a·nol·y·sis \ˌethəˈnäləsəs, -nȯl-\ *n, pl* **ethanoly·ses** \-ləˌsēz\ [NL, blend of ISV *ethanol* + NL *-lysis*] **:** alcoholysis with ethyl alcohol

eth·el \ˈethəl\ *n* -S [ME, fr. OE *ēthel, ōthel* — more at ATHELING] **:** ancestral land

etheling *often cap, var of* ATHELING

eth·ene \ˈeˌthēn\ *n* -S [ISV *eth-* + *-ene*] **:** ETHYLENE — used in the system of nomenclature adopted by the International Union of Pure and Applied Chemistry

eth·e·noid \ˈethəˌnȯid\ *adj* [*ethene* + *-oid*] **:** resembling ethylene in chemical properties **:** like ethylene or its double bond in unsaturation **:** characterized by or produced by virtue of a double bond **:** ETHYLENIC ⟨~ fatty acids⟩ ⟨~ resins⟩

etheo·genesis \ˌē¦thēō, ˌe¦+\ *n* [NL *etheo-* (fr. Gk *ētheos* unmarried youth) + NL *-genesis* — more at WIDOW] **:** male parthenogenesis **:** development of an unfertilized male gamete into an organism

¹**ethe·os·to·moid** \ˌēthē¦ästəˌmȯid, ¦eth-\ *adj* [NL *Etheostoma*, genus of fishes (fr. *etheo-* — fr. Gk *ēthein* to sift, strain — + *-stoma*) + E *-oid* — more at ETHMOID] **:** of or relating to the darters

²**etheostomoid** \" \ *n* -S **:** DARTER 2

ether *also* **ae·ther** \ˈēthə(r)\ *n* -S [ME *ether*, fr. L *aether*, fr. Gk *aithēr*, fr. *aithein* to kindle, blaze — more at EDIFY] **1 a :** the clear sky **:** HEAVEN, AIR ⟨all the unmeasured ~ flames with light —Alexander Pope⟩ **b :** the element formerly held to form the material of the heavenly spheres and bodies from the moon to the fixed stars **c :** the upper regions of space or the rarefied element formerly held to fill these regions **:** EMPYREAN **2 a :** a medium of unusual qualities (as extreme tenuity, absolute continuity, and high rigidity and elasticity) postulated in the undulatory theory of light as permeating all space and as transmitting transverse waves **b :** the medium of transmission of radio waves ⟨jamming of BBC output became a regular feature of the war in the ~ —J.B.Clark⟩ **3 a :** a light volatile flammable water-insoluble fat-soluble liquid $(C_2H_5)_2O$ that has a characteristic aromatic odor, is obtained by the distillation of alcohol with sulfuric acid, and is used chiefly as a solvent and anesthetic — called also *diethyl ether, ethyl ether, ethyl oxide* **b :** any of a class of relatively inert organic compounds typified by ethyl ether and characterized by an oxygen atom attached to two carbon atoms that are usu. contained in hydrocarbon radicals — see EPOXIDE **c :** ESTER: *esp* **:** ETHYL ESTER — now little used **4 :** something that resembles the medium of ether **:** ATMOSPHERE ⟨the narrator's autoanalysis . . . is the ~ in which the great work exists —Bernard DeVoto⟩

ether alcohol *n* **:** a compound that is both an ether and an alcohol

ether·ate \ˈēthəˌrāt, -rət\ *n* -S [*ether* + *-ate*] **:** a compound with an ether (as ethyl ether) ⟨boron trifluoride ~ $BF_3\text{-}(C_2H_5)_2O$⟩

ether drift *n* **:** a relative motion held to exist between a body and the medium of ether

ethe·re·al *also* **ethe·ri·al** *or* **aethe·re·al** *or* **aethe·ri·al** \əˈthirēəl, ēˈ-,eˈ-, -thēr-\ *adj* [L *aetherius, aethereus* (fr. Gk *aitherios*, fr. *aithēr* ether) + E *-al*] **1 a :** of or relating to the regions beyond the earth ⟨liberty, far from being an ~ thing, is always . . . related to specific and present situations —Max Ascoli⟩ **b :** CELESTIAL, HEAVENLY ⟨go, heavenly guest, ~ messenger —John Milton⟩ **2 a :** resembling or having the characteristics of the element of ether **:** AIRY, IMMATERIAL ⟨have been obliged to work with physical rather than ~ forms —L.A.White⟩ **b :** characterized by unusual delicacy and refinement **:** DAINTY, EXQUISITE ⟨this smallest, most ~, and daintiest of birds —William Beebe⟩ ⟨a chocolate cake of quite ~ lightness —*New Yorker*⟩ **3 :** of, relating to, or having the characteristics of the medium of ether ⟨~ waves⟩ **4 :** relating to, containing, or resembling the liquid ether or an ether ⟨~ oxygen⟩ ⟨an ~ solution⟩ — **ethe·re·al·ly** \-ēəlē, -li\ *adv* — **ethe·re·al·ness** \-ēəlnəs\ *n* -ES

ethereal blue *n* **:** SKY BLUE

ethe·re·al·i·ty \əˌthirēˈaləd·ē, (ˌ)ēˌth-, eˌth-, -thēr-, -lətē, -i\ *n* -ES **:** the quality or state of being ethereal

ethe·re·al·i·za·tion *or* **ethe·ri·al·iza·tion** \=ˌ=rēələˈzāshən, -ˌlīˈz-\ *n* -S **:** the act or process of etherealizing

ethe·re·al·ize *or* **ethe·ri·al·ize** \=ˈ=rēəˌlīz\ *vt* -ED/-ING/-S **:** to make ethereal: **a :** to refine, exalt, or spiritualize ⟨our tastes have been *etherealized*, our perceptions exalted —W.S. Gilbert⟩ **b :** to give an ethereal appearance to ⟨the moonlight cast a kind of dreamy beauty and quite *etherealized* the low brick wall —Olive Schreiner⟩

ethereal oil *n* **1 :** ESSENTIAL OIL **2 :** a mixture of heavy oil of wine with an equal volume of ether

ethereal salt *n* **:** ESTER

ethereal sulfate *n* **:** any of various esters of sulfuric acid that are formed as products of metabolism and excreted in the urine

ethereal tincture *n* **:** a tincture prepared by using a menstruum composed of one volume of ether and two volumes of alcohol

ethe·re·ous \=ˈ=rēəs\ *adj* [L *aethereus* ethereal] *archaic* **:** ETHEREAL

ether extract *n* **:** the part of a complex organic material that is soluble in ether and consists chiefly of fats and fatty acids — used esp. in analyses of animal feeds

ethe·ria \əˈthirēə, ēˈ-,eˈ-, -thēr-\ *n, cap* [NL, fr. L *aetheria*, fem. of *aetherius* ethereal — more at ETHEREAL] **:** a genus (the type of the family Etheriidae) of freshwater lamellibranch mollusks of Africa and Madagascar that attach themselves by one valve to rocks in deep water

ether·ic *also* **ae·ther·ic** \əˈtherik, ēˈ-,eˈ-; ˈēthərik\ *adj* [*ether, aether* + *-ic*] **:** ETHEREAL ⟨poetry is to some degree the ~ body of the poet —Edith Sitwell⟩

ether·i·fi·ca·tion \əˌtherəfəˈkāshən, ēˌ-; ˌēthər-\ *n* -S [*ether* + *-i-* + *-fication*] **:** the process of etherifying

ether·i·fy \əˈtherəˌfī, ēˈ-; ˈēthər-\ *vt* -ED/-ING/-ES [*ether* + *-ify*] **:** to convert (an alcohol or phenol) into an ether

ether·in *also* **ae·ther·in** \ˈēthərən\ *n* -S [ISV *ether, aether* + *-in*] **1** *archaic* **:** ethylene believed to be a basic radical and a constituent of alcohol, ether, and various other compounds **2** *archaic* **:** a white crystalline hydrocarbon found in heavy oil of wine

ether·iza·tion \ˌēthərəˈzāshən, -ˌrīˈz-\ *n* -S **1 :** the administration of ether to produce anesthesia **2 :** the exposure of a dormant plant to the fumes of an ether under controlled conditions in order to stimulate growth

ether·ize \ˈēthəˌrīz\ *vt* -ED/-ING/-S **1 :** to treat or anesthetize with ether ⟨couldn't bear to ~ cats and eviscerate frogs —*New Yorker*⟩ **2 :** to make numb as if by anesthetizing **:** TORPIFY ⟨stillness *etherized* the whole train —Truman Capote⟩

ether·iz·er \-zə(r)\ *n* -S **:** one that etherizes

ether·o·phone *also* **ae·ther·o·phone** \ˈēthərəˌfōn; əˈther-, ēˈ-\ *n* -S [*ether, aether* + *-o-* + *-phone*] **:** THEREMIN

eth·ic \ˈethik, -thēk\ *n* -S [ME *etik, ethik*, fr. MF *ethique*, fr. LL *ethica* & L *ethice*, fr. Gk *ēthikē*, fr. *ēthikē*, adj., fem. of *ēthikos* moral, ethic] **1 ethics** *pl but usu sing in constr* **:** the discipline dealing with what is good and bad or right and wrong or with moral duty and obligation ⟨the sphere of ~*s* for the Greeks was not distinguished from the sphere of aesthetics —Havelock Ellis⟩ **2 a :** a group of moral principles or set of values ⟨the Christian ~⟩ ⟨even the code of the gangster . . . has its own ~ —R.P.Warren⟩ ⟨Puritan ~⟩ ⟨Lincoln had been pondering the ~*s* of slavery —A.C.Cole⟩ **b :** a particular theory or system of moral values ⟨a materialistic ~⟩ ⟨naturalistic ~*s*⟩ **c ethics** *pl but sing or pl in constr* **:** the principles of conduct governing an individual or a profession **:** standards of behavior ⟨social ~*s*⟩ ⟨professional ~*s*⟩ ⟨a certain ~*s* makes it impossible for me to review the production . . . which I directed —*New Republic*⟩ **3 :** character or the ideals of character manifested by a race or people ⟨while the rituals . . . are complex and stylized, the meaning behind them and their significance shows how far advanced was Indian religious culture and ~ —Seth Agnew⟩ — compare ETHOS

¹**eth·i·cal** \ˈethəkəl, -thēk-\ *or* **eth·ic** \-thik, -thēk\ *adj* [ME *etik*, fr. L *ethicus*, fr. Gk *ēthikos*, fr. *ēthos* custom, usage, character, dwelling + *-ikos* -ic, -ical; akin to L *sodalis* comrade, Gk *ethos* custom, habit, Skt *svadhā* self-position, own condition or place, custom, L *sui* of oneself — more at SUICIDE] **1 a :** of or relating to the field of ethics or morality **:** relating to or involving questions of right and wrong ⟨~ principles⟩ ⟨~ theories⟩ **b :** dealing with or concerned with ethics ⟨~ tracts⟩ ⟨modern ~ analysts⟩ ⟨~ literature⟩ **2 :** involving or expressing moral approval or disapproval ⟨~ judgments⟩ **3 a :** being in accord with approved standards of behavior or a socially or professionally accepted code **:** MORAL ⟨~ conduct⟩ ⟨~ practices⟩ **b :** conforming to professionally endorsed principles and practices ⟨an ~ lawyer⟩ ⟨~ medical practice⟩ **4** *of a drug* **:** restricted to sale only on a doctor's prescription ⟨digitalis is an ~ drug but aspirin is not⟩ ⟨the ~ drug business⟩ — compare OVER-THE-COUNTER, PROPRIETARY

syn see MORAL

²**ethical** \" \ *n* -S **:** an ethical drug

ethical dative *n* **:** a colloquial use of the dative of a pronoun for a person to whom it imputes a vague concern with the matter in question (as German *mir*, literally "for me", in *bleibe mir nur gesund* "I just hope you stay well")

ethical genitive *n* **:** the use of the possessive *your* to impute only a vague concern (as in *she is not at all one of your bluestockings*)

eth·i·cal·i·ty \ˌethəˈkaləd·ē, -lətē, -i\ *n* -ES **:** ethical quality, character, or aspect **:** ethical principle

eth·i·cal·ly \ˈethək(ə)lē, -thēk-, -li\ *adv* **:** in an ethical manner **:** according to ethical principles **:** from an ethical point of view ⟨little can be said ~ . . . for foolish things written —*Saturday Rev.*⟩

eth·i·cal·ness \-kəlnəs\ *n* -ES **:** the quality or state of being ethical

ethical truth *n* **:** NORMATIVE TRUTH

ethi·cian \eˈthishən\ *or* **eth·i·cist** \ˈethəsəst\ *n* -S [*ethics* + *-ian* or *-ist*] **:** a specialist in ethics

eth·i·cize \ˈethəˌsīz\ *vt* -ED/-ING/-S **:** to make ethical or endow with ethical qualities ⟨~ nature⟩

ethico- *comb form* [NL, fr. L *ethicus* moral, ethical — more at ETHICAL] **:** ethical and ⟨*ethico*religious⟩ **:** ethics ⟨*ethico*-centered⟩

eth·ide \ˈeˌthīd, -ˌthəd\ *n* -S [*eth-* + *-ide*] **:** a binary compound of ethyl ⟨sodium ~ C_2H_5Na⟩

ethine *var of* ETHYNE

ethinyl *var of* ETHYNYL

ethinyl estradiol *or* **ethynylestradiol** *n* **:** a white crystalline potent orally effective estrogen $C_{20}H_{24}O_2$ prepared from estrone

eth·iodide \(ˈ)eˈth+ˌ-\ *n* [*eth-* + *iodide*] **:** a compound with ethyl iodide

ethi·on·ic acid \ˌē¦thē¦änik-, ¦ē¦, ˌthī¦\ *n* [*ethionic* ISV *e-* (fr. *ether*) + *-thion-* (fr. Gk *theion* brimstone) + *-ic* — more at THI-] **:** an unstable diacid $HO_3SCH_2CH_2OSO_3H$ known only in solution and obtainable by adding water to ethionic anhydride

ethionic anhydride *n* **:** a crystalline cyclic compound $C_2H_4O_6S_2$ formed by the action of sulfur trioxide on ethylene or alcohol — called also *carbyl sulfate*

ethi·o·nine \eˈthīəˌnēn, -nən\ *n* -S [*eth-* + *-ionine* (as in *methionine*)] **:** a crystalline amino acid $C_2H_5SCH_2CH_2CH(NH_2)COOH$ that is the ethyl homologue of methionine and is biologically antagonistic to methionine

¹**ethi·op** \ˈēthēˌäp\ *or* **ethi·ope** \-ēˌōp\ *also* **ae·thi·op** \ˈēth-\ *n* -S *cap* [ME *Ethiope*, fr. L *Aethiops*, fr. Gk *Aithiops*] **:** ETHIOPIAN ⟨*Ethiops* were selling picture postcards —Osbert Sitwell⟩

²**ethiop** \" \ *adj, usu cap, archaic* **:** black in complexion

ethi·o·pia \ˌēthēˈōpēə\ *adj, usu cap* [fr. *Ethiopia*, country of northeast Africa] **:** of or from Ethiopia **:** of the kind or style prevalent in Ethiopia **:** ETHIOPIAN

¹**ethi·o·pi·an** \ˌēthēˈōpēən\ *n* -S *cap* [ME *Ethiopien*, fr. *Ethiopia* + ME *-en* -an] **1** *also* **aethiopian :** a member of any of the mythical or actual peoples that the ancient Greeks designated by the name *Aithiopes* usu. described as being dark-skinned and living far to the south; *esp* **:** a native or inhabitant of a country south of Egypt and extending east to the Red sea **2 :** NEGRO **3 :** a native or inhabitant of the modern nation of Ethiopia

²**ethiopian** \" ¦==¦===\ *adj, usu cap* **1** *also* **aethiopian a :** of, relating to, or characteristic of the ancient Ethiopians **b :** of, relating to, or characteristic of any of the regions or countries anciently or formerly known as Aethiopia or Ethiopia **2 a :** of, relating to, characteristic of, or being a Negro **b** (1) **:** representing or purporting to represent the Negro esp. of the cultural type found on plantations in the southern U.S. in the 19th cent. — used esp. of entertainers (usu. white men wearing blackface) in Negro minstrel shows and of the entertainment that they offered ⟨*Ethiopian* serenaders⟩ (2) **:** characteristic of, suitable for, or done in the style of the entertainment offered in Negro minstrelsy ⟨*Ethiopian* dialogue⟩ ⟨*Ethiopian* song⟩ **3 :** of, relating to, or being the biogeographic region that includes Africa south of the Sahara, southern Arabia, and sometimes Madagascar and the adjacent islands **4 a :** of, relating to, or characteristic of the modern nation of Ethiopia **b :** of, relating to, or characteristic of the people of the modern nation of Ethiopia **5 :** of or relating to the ancient Monophysite church of Ethiopia that was founded in the 4th century A.D., is governed by an abuna appointed by

the Coptic patriarch, and follows Coptic doctrine, discipline, and worship but uses Ethiopic as its liturgical language

[1]**ethi·opic** \ˌēthēˈäpik, -ˈōp-\ *adj, usu cap* [L *Aethiopicus*, fr. Gk *Aithiopikos*, fr. *Aithiopia* Ethiopia + Gk *-ikos* -ic] **1 :** ETHIOPIAN 1, 4 **2 a :** of, relating to, characteristic of, or constituting the language Ethiopic **b :** of, relating to, characteristic of, or constituting a group of related Semitic languages spoken in Ethiopia including the classical Ethiopic, Tigre, Tigrinya, Amharic, Argobba, Harari, and Gurage

[2]**ethiopic** \"\ *n, cap* **1 :** a Semitic language formerly spoken in Ethiopia and still in use as the liturgical language of the Christian church in Ethiopia — called also *Geez* **2 :** the Ethiopic group of the Semitic branch of the Afro-Asiatic family of languages

ethiopic alphabet *n, usu cap E* **:** an alphabet of South Semitic origin in which the vocalization is indicated by modification of the basic character (as by the addition of small appendages or by shortening or lengthening of one of the main strokes) and in use since the 4th century A.D. in writing Ethiopic and since about 1600 in adapted form also for Amharic, Tigre, and Tigrinya

ethiops *n* [NL, fr. L *Aethiops* Ethiopian] *obs* **:** any of various chemical preparations (as metallic salts) of a black or very dark color

ethiops mineral *n* **:** impure black mercuric sulfide prepared by rubbing together mercury and sulfur

ethis·ter·one \əˈthistəˌrōn\ *n* -s [*ethinyl* + testo*sterone*] **:** a synthetic crystalline orally effective female sex hormone $C_{21}H_{28}O_2$ administered in cases of deficiency of progesterone; 17-ethynyl-testosterone — called also *anhydrohydroxyprogesterone*

ethmo- *comb form* [Gk *ēthmo-* strainer (influenced in meaning by E *ethmoid*), fr. *ēthmos*] **:** ethmoidal and ⟨*ethmo*frontal⟩ **:** ethmoid and ⟨*ethmo*sphenoid⟩

[1]**eth·moid** \ˈethˌmȯid\ *or* **eth·moi·dal** \(ˈ)ethˈmȯidᵊl\ *adj* [*ethmoid* fr. F *ethmoïde*, fr. MF, fr. Gk *ēthmoeidēs* like a strainer, perforated, ethmoid, fr. *ēthmos* strainer, colander (fr. *ēthein* to sift, strain) + *-oeidēs* -oid; *ethmoidal* fr. F *ethmoïde* + E *-al;* akin to ON *sáld* sieve, MIr *síthlad* act of sifting, W *hidl* strainer, OSlav *sito*, and perh. to L *serere* to sow — more at SOW] **:** of, relating to, or adjoining one or more bones forming part of the walls and septum of the nasal cavity; *also* **:** of or relating to the whole region of the nasal capsule

[2]**ethmoid** \"\ *n* -s **:** ETHMOID BONE

ethmoid bone *n* **:** a delicate essentially cubical cartilage bone of the skull that is made up of thin plates enclosing irregular vacuities, forms much of the walls of the nasal cavity and part of that of the orbits, and is subject to considerable variation in different vertebrate groups

eth·moid·itis \ˌethˌmȯiˈdīdəs\ *n* -ES [NL, fr. E *ethmoid* + NL *-itis*] **:** inflammation of the ethmoid or its sinuses

eth·mo·lith \ˈethməˌlith\ *n* -s [ISV *ethmo-* + *-lith*] **:** a body of igneous rock intruded into stratified rocks and narrowing downward like a funnel

[1]**eth·mo·turbinal** \ˌeth(ˌ)mō+\ *n* [*ethmo-* + *turbinal*] **:** an ethmoturbinal bone

[2]**eth·mo·turbinal** *also* **eth·mo·turbinate** \"+\ *adj* [*ethmo-* + *turbinal, turbinate*] **:** of, relating to, or consisting of the lateral masses of the ethmoid bone that bear or consist largely of the turbinated bones in mammals

eth·narch \ˈethˌnärk\ *n* -s [Gk *ethnarchēs* ruler of a tribe or nation, fr. *ethnos* nation + *-archēs*, fr. *archos* ruler — more at ARCHI-] **:** the governor of a province or people (as of the Byzantine Empire) ⟨the ~ of Cyprus⟩

eth·nar·chy \-kē\ *n* -ES [Gk *ethnarchia* office of ethnarch, fr. *ethnarchēs* ethnarch + *-ia* -y] **:** the dominion of an ethnarch or his office or rank

[1]**ethnic** *n* -s [ME, fr. LL *ethnicus*, fr. Gk *ethnikos*, adj.] *obs* **:** HEATHEN, PAGAN ⟨impure ~s —John Milton⟩

[2]**eth·nic** \ˈethnik, -nēk\ *adj* [ME, fr. LL *ethnicus*, fr. Gk *ethnikos* foreign, gentile, national, fr. *ethnos* nation + *-ikos* -ic — more at ETHNOS] **1 :** of or relating to the Gentiles or to nations not converted to Christianity **:** HEATHEN, PAGAN ⟨ancient ~ revels of a faith long since forsaken —H.W. Longfellow⟩ **2 a :** relating to community of physical and mental traits possessed by the members of a group as a product of their common heredity and cultural tradition ⟨influenced by ~ and cultural ties —J.F.Kennedy⟩ ⟨the boundaries along the West African coast were not plotted with regard to the ancient ~ frontiers —A.H.Young-O'Brien⟩ **b :** having or originating from racial, linguistic, and cultural ties with a specific group ⟨Negroes, Irish, Italians, Germans, Poles, and other ~ groups —F.J.Brown & J.S.Roucek⟩ ⟨displaced persons, 653 of them ~ Germans —*N.Y. Herald Tribune*⟩ **3 :** originating in an exotic primitive culture ⟨~ music⟩

[3]**ethnic** \"\ *n* -s [Gk *ethnikon*, neut. of *ethnikos* national] **:** ETHNICON

eth·ni·cal \-nəkəl, -nēk-\ *adj* [*ethnic* + *-al*] **:** ETHNIC 2, ETHNOLOGIC

eth·ni·cal·ly \-k(ə)lē, -li\ *adv* **:** from an ethnic or ethnologic point of view **:** RACIALLY

eth·ni·cism \ˈethnəˌsizəm\ *n* -s *archaic* **:** PAGANISM, HEATHENISM

eth·nic·i·ty \ethˈnisədē\ *n* -ES **:** ethnic quality or affiliation ⟨the influence of ~ upon the character of community status arrangements —G.P.Stone & W.H.Form⟩ ⟨~, occupation, and language spoken are the crucial factors in . . . intermarriage —*Soc. Abstracts*⟩

eth·ni·con *also* **eth·ni·kon** \ˈethnəˌkän\ *n, pl* **ethni·ca** *also* **ethni·ka** \-ˌkə\ [Gk *ethnikon*, neut. of *ethnikos* national — more at ETHNIC] **:** the name of a tribe, ethnic group, race, or people (as *Hopi, Ethiopian, Phoenician*) ⟨the ~ *Veneti* is not limited to Italy —Joshua Whatmough⟩

ethno- *comb form* [F, fr. LGk, fr. Gk *ethnos* nation — more at ETHNOS] **1 :** race, people, cultural group ⟨*ethno*graphy⟩ ⟨*ethno*genic⟩ **2 :** characteristic of or believed by a people, race, or group ⟨*ethno*meteorology⟩ **:** used by or related to a people or race ⟨*ethno*biology⟩ ⟨*ethno*flora⟩

eth·no·biological \ˌeth(ˌ)nō+\ *adj* **:** of or relating to ethnobiology

eth·no·biology \"+\ *n* [*ethno-* + *biology*] **:** the branch of biology that deals with the relation between usu. primitive human societies and the plants and animals of their environment

eth·no·botanic *or* **eth·no·botanical** \"+\ *adj* **:** of or relating to ethnobotany

eth·no·botanist \"+\ *n* **:** a specialist in ethnobotany

eth·no·botany \"+\ *n* [*ethno-* + *botany*] **:** the plant lore of a race or people; *also* **:** the systematic study of such lore

eth·no·centric \ˌethnō, -nə+\ *adj* [*ethno-* + *-centric*] **1 :** centering upon race as a chief interest or end ⟨the religion of the future must more and more deal with the salvation of society; it must be ~ —Gamaliel Bradford⟩ **2 a :** inclined to regard one's own race or social group as the center of culture ⟨any profession . . . is somewhat ~ regarding outsiders —L.W. Doob⟩ **b :** exhibiting an incapacity for viewing foreign cultures dispassionately ⟨the ~ view that the rest of the world must become worthy of us by . . . imitating our way of life —G.E.Taylor⟩ ⟨a Greek ~ legend about Persian morals —W.H.Goodenough⟩ — **ethnocentrically** \"+\ *adv* — **ethnocentricity** \"+\ *n* -ES

eth·no·cen·trism \ˌethnōˈsenˌtrizəm, -thnōˈ-\ *n* -s [*ethno-* + *centr-* + *-ism*] **1 :** a habitual disposition to judge foreign peoples or groups by the standards and practices of one's own culture or ethnic group ⟨this is the more usual form that ~ takes . . . — a gentle insistence on the good qualities of one's own group —M.J.Herskovits⟩ **2 :** a tendency toward viewing alien cultures with disfavor and a resulting sense of inherent superiority ⟨the ~ of national groups . . . causes them to regard their culture as superior to that of all other nations —Mabel Elliott & Francis Merrill⟩ ⟨with perhaps pardonable ~, the Americans have acted on the assumption that the best preparation for freedom is Americanization —Raymond Kennedy⟩ ⟨intolerant ~ and super nationalism can only result in the narrowest sort of isolationism —*Amer. Scholar*⟩

eth·no·flora \ˌethnə+\ *n* [NL, fr. *ethno-* + *flora*] **:** the part of the flora of a region used by its human aborigines

eth·no·gen·ic \ˌethnəˈjenik\ *adj* **:** of or relating to ethnogeny

eth·nog·e·nist \ethˈnäjənəst\ *n* -s **:** an ethnologist who specializes in the study of the origin and evolution of races

eth·nog·e·ny \-jənē\ *n* -ES [F *ethnogénie*, fr. *ethno-* + *-génie* -geny] **:** a branch of ethnology that deals primarily with the evolution of races

eth·no·geographer \ˌeth(ˌ)nō+\ *n* **:** an ethnologist who specializes in ethnogeography

eth·no·geographic \"+\ *adj* **:** of or relating to ethnogeography

eth·no·geography \"+\ *n* [*ethno-* + *geography*] **:** the study of the geographical distribution of races or peoples and their relation to the environments in which they live — compare ANTHROPOGEOGRAPHY

eth·nog·ra·pher \ethˈnägrəfə(r)\ *also* **eth·nog·ra·phist** \-fəst\ *n* -s **:** a specialist in ethnography

eth·no·graph·ic \ˌethnəˈgrafik, -fēk\ *or* **eth·no·graph·i·cal** \-fəkəl, -fēk-\ *adj* **:** of or relating to ethnography — **eth·no·graph·i·cal·ly** \-fək(ə)lē, -fēk-, -li\ *adv*

eth·nog·ra·phy \ethˈnägrəfē, -fi\ *n* -ES [F *ethnographie*, fr. *ethno-* + *-graphie* -graphy] **:** a branch of anthropology that deals historically with the origin and filiation of races and cultures **:** ETHNOLOGY; *specif* **:** a branch of ethnology dealing with description of cultures rather than comparison and analysis **:** descriptive anthropology — compare ANTHROPOGRAPHY

eth·no·historian \ˌeth(ˌ)nō+\ *n* [*ethno-* + *historian*] **:** a specialist in ethnohistory

eth·no·historical *also* **eth·no·historic** \"+\ *adj* [*ethno-* + *historical, historic*] **:** of or relating to ethnohistory

eth·no·history \ˌethnō+\ *n* [*ethno-* + *history*] **:** a study of the development of cultures; *specif* **:** the interpretation of the significance of archaeological findings by means of documentary material

eth·no·linguistic \ˌeth(ˌ)nō+\ *adj* [*ethno-* + *linguistic*] **:** of or relating to ethnolinguistics

eth·no·linguistics \"+\ *n pl but sing in constr* [*ethno-* + *linguistics*] **:** a study of the relations between linguistic and nonlinguistic cultural behavior

eth·no·log·ic \ˌethnəˈläjik\ *or* **eth·no·log·i·cal** \-jəkəl, -jēk-\ *adj* **:** of or relating to ethnology — **eth·no·log·i·cal·ly** \-jək(ə)lē, -jēk-, -li\ *adv*

eth·nol·o·gist \ethˈnäləjəst\ *also* **eth·nol·o·ger** \-jə(r)\ *n* -s **:** a specialist in ethnology

eth·nol·o·gy \-jē, -ji\ *n* -ES [*ethno-* + *-logy*] **1 :** a science that deals with the division of mankind into races, with their origin, distribution, and relations, and with the peculiarities that characterize them — see ETHNOGENY, ETHNOGRAPHY **2 :** cultural or social anthropology including the comparative and analytical study of cultures and excluding the subject matter of archaeology and physical anthropology **3 :** the materials of ethnology ⟨the ~ of the American Indian⟩

eth·no·psychological \ˌeth(ˌ)nō+\ *adj* [*ethno-* + *psychological*] **:** of or relating to ethnopsychology — **ethnopsychologically** \"+\ *adv*

eth·no·psychology \"+\ *n* [*ethno-* + *psychology;* trans. of G *völkerpsychologie*] **:** the psychology of races and peoples **:** folk psychology

eth·nos \ˈethˌnäs\ *n* -ES [Gk, nation, people, caste, tribe; prob. akin to Gk *ēthos* custom — more at ETHICAL] **:** an ethnic group — compare DEMOS

eth·no·zoological \ˌeth(ˌ)nō+\ *adj* **:** of or relating to ethnozoology

eth·no·zoology \"+\ *n* [*ethno-* + *zoology*] **:** the animal lore of a race or people; *also* **:** the systematic study of such lore

etho- — see ETH-

etho·hexa·di·ol \ˌe(ˌ)thōˌheksəˈdīˌȯl, -īˌōl\ *n* [*etho-* + *hexane* + *-diol*] **:** an odorless oily glycol $C_8H_{16}(OH)_2$ applied to the skin as an insect repellent; 2-ethyl-hexane-1,3-diol

etho·log·i·cal \ˌēthəˈläjəkəl, ˌeth-\ *adj* **:** of or relating to ethology — **etho·log·i·cal·ly** \-jək(ə)lē\ *adv*

ethol·o·gy \ēˈthäləjē, ēˈ-\ *n* -ES [L *ethologia* art of depicting character, fr. Gk *ēthologia*, fr. *ēthos* + *-logia* -logy] **1 :** a systematic study of the formation of human character **2 :** a scientific study of animal behavior

ethos \ˈēˌthäs *sometimes* ˈe,- *or* -thōs\ *n* -ES [NL, fr. Gk *ēthos* character, delineation of character, custom, accustomed place — more at ETHICAL] **1 :** character, sentiment, or moral nature: **a :** the guiding beliefs, standards, or ideals that characterize or pervade a group, a community, a people, or an ideology **:** the spirit that motivates the ideas, customs, or practices of a people, an epoch, or a region ⟨the general ~ of the people they have to govern . . . determines the behavior of politicians —T.S.Eliot⟩ ⟨every age or epoch is inspired by what may be called its inevitable idea — the ~ of the century —*Life*⟩ ⟨our democratic ~⟩ ⟨the quasi-moral American ~ of production at any cost —William Troy⟩ ⟨the commercial ~ . . . of the 19th century —C.W.Hendel⟩ **b :** the complex of fundamental values that underlies, permeates, or actuates major patterns of thought and behavior in any particular culture, society, or institution ⟨the value system, the ~ of a group —Kurt Lewin⟩; *also* **:** such a complex permeating a literary or scientific work or an intellectual discipline ⟨the ~ of science⟩ **2 a** *in Aristotelian philosophy* (1) **:** the character or personality of a man esp. with respect to a balance between the passions and caution (2) **:** an element (as moral purpose) in dramatic character which determines what a man does in contrast to what he thinks — compare DIANOIA **b :** the disposition, fundamental outlook, moral attitude, or system of values of an individual ⟨that fateful summer of 1940 when Churchill alone, endowed with prophetic ~ and a keen sense of the realities of war and peace, turned the tide —*Atlantic*⟩ ⟨there was a distinctly athletic ~ about her, as if . . . she might have majored in physical education —J.D.Salinger⟩

eth·oxide \eˈth+ˌ-\ *n* -s [*ethoxyl* + *-ide*] **:** a binary compound of ethoxyl; *esp* **:** a base formed from ethyl alcohol by replacement of the hydroxyl hydrogen with a metal ⟨aluminum ~ $Al(OC_2H_5)_3$⟩

eth·oxy \(ˈ)eˈthäksē\ *adj* [*ethoxy-*] **:** relating to or containing ethoxyl

ethoxy- *comb form* [ISV, fr. *ethoxyl*] **:** containing ethoxyl — in names of chemical compounds ⟨*ethoxy*caffeine⟩

ethoxy·carbonyl \(ˌ)eˌthäksē+\ *n* [*ethoxy-* + *carbonyl*] **:** CARBETHOXYL

eth·oxyl \(ˈ)eˈthäksəl\ *n* -s [*eth-* + *oxygen* + *-yl*] **:** a univalent radical C_2H_5O— composed of ethyl united with oxygen

eth·ox·y·line resin \eˈthäksəˌlēn-, -ˌlən-\ *n* [*ethoxyl* + *-ine*] **:** EPOXY RESIN

eth·rog *or* **et·rog** \eˈthrōg, et-ˈrōg, ˈ=,=\ *or* **es·rog** \ˈesˌrōg\ *n, pl* **eth·ro·gim** *or* **et·ro·gim** \ˌethrōˈgim, ˌet·r-\ *or* **es·ro·gim** \esˈrōgim\ *or* **ethrogs** *or* **etrogs** *or* **esrogs** [Heb *ethrōgh*] **:** the fruit of the citron (*Citrus medica*) anciently used with the palm branch in the celebration of Sukkoth and still used by Jews as a symbol of that occasion — compare LULAB

eth·yl \ˈethəl, *chiefly by Brit chemists* ˈēˌthīl\ *n* -s [ISV *ether* + *-yl*] **:** a univalent hydrocarbon radical C_2H_5 or CH_3CH_2 derived from ethane by removal of one hydrogen atom — compare TETRAETHYL LEAD

ethyl acetate *n* **:** a colorless fragrant volatile flammable liquid ester $CH_3COOC_2H_5$ made from ethyl alcohol and acetic acid and used chiefly as a solvent and in organic synthesis

ethyl acetoacetate *n* **:** a colorless liquid ester with pleasant odor important for its tautomerism [keto form $CH_3COCH_2COOC_2H_5$, enol form $CH_3C(OH){=}CHCOOC_2H_5$] and for the numerous condensations it can undergo — called also *acetoacetic ester*

eth·yl·acetylene \ˈethəl+\ *n* [ISV *ethyl* + *acetylene*] **:** BUTYNE a

ethyl alcohol *n* **:** ordinary alcohol **:** ALCOHOL 3

eth·yl·amine \ˌethələˈmēn\ *n* [ISV *ethyl* + *amine*] **1 :** a colorless flammable volatile liquid base $C_2H_5NH_2$ that has an ammoniacal odor, is usu. made from ammonia and ether or alcohol, and is used chiefly in organic synthesis — called also *monoethylamine* **2 :** an amine containing ethyl attached to amino nitrogen — see DIETHYLAMINE, TRIETHYLAMINE

ethyl aminobenzoate *n* **:** BENZOCAINE

[1]**eth·yl·ate** \ˈethəˌlāt, -ˌlət\ *n* -s [*ethyl* + *-ate*] **:** ETHOXIDE

[2]**eth·yl·ate** \-ˌlāt\ *vt* -ED/-ING/-s [*ethyl* + *-ate*, v. suffix] **:** to introduce the ethyl group into (a compound) — **eth·yl·a·tion** \ˌethəˈlāshən\ *n* -s

eth·yl·ben·zene \ˈ==ˌ=,=, ˈ==ˌ=ˈ=\ *n* [ISV *ethyl* + *benzene*] **:** a liquid hydrocarbon $C_6H_5C_2H_5$ that is made usu. from benzene and ethylene and is used chiefly in the manufacture of styrene

ethyl bromide *n* **:** a volatile liquid compound C_2H_5Br of aromatic odor; bromo-ethane

ethyl butyrate *n* **:** a colorless liquid ester $C_3H_7COOC_2H_5$ with a pineapple odor found in fruits and also synthesized and used in artificial rum, pineapple oil, and perfumes

ethyl carbamate *n* **:** URETHANE

ethyl cellulose *n* **:** any of various white granular tough thermoplastic substances made by ethylating alkali cellulose and used chiefly in making plastics and lacquers

ethyl chaulmoograte *n* **:** a pale-yellow liquid containing a mixture of the ethyl esters of the acids of chaulmoogra oil and formerly used in the treatment of leprosy

ethyl chloride *n* **:** a colorless pungent flammable gaseous or volatile liquid compound C_2H_5Cl that is usu. made from chlorine and ethane or from hydrogen chloride and ethylene or ethyl alcohol and that is used chiefly in synthesis (as of tetraethyl lead and ethyl cellulose) and as a local surface anesthetic — called also *chloroethane*

ethyl cyanide *n* **:** PROPIONITRILE

eth·yl·ene \ˈethəˌlēn\ *n* -s [ISV *ethyl* + *-ene*] **1 :** a colorless flammable gaseous olefin hydrocarbon $CH_2{=}CH_2$ found in coal gas, now usu. obtained by pyrolysis of petroleum hydrocarbons, and used chiefly in organic synthesis (as of ethyl alcohol, polyethylene, and styrene), in promoting growth of plants and ripening of fruits, and as an anesthetic **2 :** a bivalent hydrocarbon radical $-CH_2CH_2-$ derived from ethane by removal of one hydrogen atom attached to each carbon atom or from ethylene by breaking of the double bond

ethylene chlorohydrin *n* **:** a colorless toxic liquid alcohol $ClCH_2CH_2OH$ made usu. by reaction of ethylene with chlorine and water esp. in the presence of alkali and used chiefly in organic synthesis (as of ethylene oxide and ethylene glycol) and as a solvent

ethylene cyanohydrin *n* **:** a straw-colored toxic liquid alcohol $CNCH_2CH_2OH$ made usu. from ethylene oxide and hydrogen cyanide and used chiefly in making acrylonitrile and esters of acrylic acid

eth·yl·ene·diamine \ˌethəˌlēn+\ *n* [ISV *ethylene* + *diamine*] **:** a colorless volatile liquid base $NH_2CH_2CH_2NH_2$ that has an ammoniacal odor, is made from ethylene dichloride and ammonia, and is used chiefly as a solvent and in organic synthesis — symbol *en*

ethylenediaminetetraacetate \+ˌteˌtrə+\ *n* [*ethylenediamine* + *tetra-* + *acetate*] **:** a salt of ethylenediaminetetraacetic acid

ethylenediaminetetraacetic acid \+ˌteˌtrə+. . .-\ *n* [*ethylenediamine* + *tetra-* + *acetic*] **:** a colorless crystalline acid $(HOOCCH_2)_2NCH_2CH_2N(CH_2COOH)_2$ used esp. in the form of its salts (as the tetrasodium salt or the calcium disodium salt) as a chelating and sequestering agent in industry, in chemical analysis, and in pharmacy and medicine (as in the treatment of lead poisoning) — abbr. *EDTA*

ethylene dibromide *or* **ethylene bromide** *n* **:** a colorless heavy toxic liquid compound $BrCH_2CH_2Br$ made by direct union of ethylene and bromine and used chiefly with tetraethyl lead in antiknock compositions and as a solvent; 1, 2-dibromo-ethane

ethylene dichloride *or* **ethylene chloride** *n* **:** a colorless heavy toxic liquid compound $ClCH_2CH_2Cl$ that has an odor like chloroform, is made usu. by direct union of ethylene and chlorine, and is used chiefly as a solvent (as for fats and oils) and insecticidal fumigant; 1,2-dichloro-ethane

ethylene glycol *n* **:** a thick sweet colorless liquid dihydroxy alcohol $HOCH_2CH_2OH$ made usu. by the hydration of ethylene oxide and used chiefly as an antifreeze, as a coolant (as in airplane engines), in hydraulic fluids, and in the manufacture of dynamites, plasticizers, and resins; 1,2-ethane-diol — called also *glycol*

ethylene linkage *or* **ethylenic linkage** *n* **:** a carbon-to-carbon double bond

ethylene oxide *n* **:** a colorless flammable toxic gaseous or liquid compound C_2H_4O made by reaction of ethylene chlorohydrin and alkali or by catalytic oxidation of ethylene and used chiefly in organic synthesis (as of ethylene glycol and ethanolamines) and in sterilization and fumigation — compare STRUCTURAL FORMULA

$$H_2C{-}CH_2 \text{ (bridged by O)}$$

ethylene oxide

ethylene series *n* **:** the homologous series of unsaturated hydrocarbons C_nH_{2n} of which ethylene is the lowest member — compare OLEFIN

eth·yl·e·nic \ˌethəˈlēnik\ *adj* [ISV *ethylene* + *-ic*] **:** relating to or derived from ethylene **:** resembling ethylene esp. in having a double bond **:** ETHENOID — **eth·yl·e·ni·cal·ly** \-nək(ə)lē\ *adv*

ethylenic isomerism *n* **:** CIS-TRANS ISOMERISM a

eth·yl·en·imine *or* **eth·yl·ene·imine** \ˌethəˈlēnəˌmēn\ *n* [ISV *ethylene* + *imine*] **:** a colorless liquid toxic base C_2H_4NH made by dehydration of ethanolamine and used esp. in making finishing agents for textiles

ethyl ester *n* **:** an ester that yields ethyl alcohol on hydrolysis ⟨*ethyl esters* of fatty acids⟩

ethyl ether *n* **1 :** ETHER 3a **2 :** an ether in which one of the radicals united to oxygen is ethyl ⟨an *ethyl ether* of a phenol⟩

eth·yl·hex·o·ate \ˌethəlˈheksəˌwāt\ *n* -s [*ethylhexoic* + *-ate*] **:** a salt or ester of ethylhexoic acid — called also OCTOATE

eth·yl·hex·o·ic acid \ˌethəlˌhekˈsōik-\ *n* [*ethyl* + *hexoic*] **:** a colorless liquid acid $CH_3(CH_2)_3CH(C_2H_5)COOH$ made synthetically and used in the form of its salts (as the cobalt or lead salt) chiefly as varnish driers; 2-ethyl-hexanoic acid

ethyl·ic \(ˈ)eˈthilik\ *adj* [ISV *ethyl* + *-ic*] **:** relating to, derived from, or containing ethyl ⟨an ~ ester⟩

ethyl·i·dene \eˈthiləˌdēn, ˈethəl-\ *n* [ISV *ethyl* + *-idene*] **:** a bivalent hydrocarbon radical $CH_3CH<$ isomeric with ethylene ⟨~ chloride CH_3CHCl_2⟩

ethyl iodide *n* **:** a colorless liquid compound C_2H_5I made by the interaction of ethyl alcohol, red phosphorus, and iodine and used chiefly in organic synthesis; iodo-ethane

ethyl lactate *n* **:** a colorless water-soluble liquid ester $CH_3CH(OH)COOC_2H_5$ of low volatility used chiefly as a solvent (as for cellulose derivatives in lacquers)

ethyl mercaptan *n* **:** a colorless flammable volatile liquid compound C_2H_5SH of disagreeable odor used as a warning agent in fuel-gas systems; ethane-thiol

ethylmorphine \ˈ==ˌ=,=, ˈ==ˌ=ˈ=\ *n* [ISV *ethyl* + *morphine*] **:** a synthetic toxic alkaloid $C_{19}H_{23}NO_3$ that is an ethyl ether of morphine and is used esp. in the form of its white crystalline hydrochloride similarly to morphine and codeine

ethyl nitrite *n* **:** a pale-yellow flammable volatile liquid ester C_2H_5ONO of ethereal odor

ethyl nitrite spirit *n* **:** a solution of ethyl nitrite in alcohol formerly used as a diuretic and diaphoretic — called also *spirit of nitrous ether, sweet spirit of nitre*

ethyl oxide *n* **:** ETHER 3a — used esp. of ether not intended for use in anesthesia

ethyl phthalate *n* **:** an ethyl ester of phthalic acid; *esp* **:** DIETHYL PHTHALATE

ethyls *pl of* ETHYL

ethyl silicate *n* **:** a colorless flammable liquid ester $(C_2H_5)_4SiO_4$ that hydrolyzes to silica and ethyl alcohol and is used esp. in paints and coatings (as for weatherproofing stone and cement) and as a bonding agent (as for molds for casting metals) — called also *tetraethoxysilane, tetraethyl orthosilicate*

ethyl sulfate *n* **:** an ethyl ester of sulfuric acid; *esp* **:** the fragrant oily diethyl ester $(C_2H_5)_2SO_4$ made usu. by reaction of ethyl alcohol and oleum and used as an ethylating agent

ethyl vanillin *n* **:** a white crystalline aldehyde $C_2H_5O(OH)C_6H_3CHO$ that is the ethyl analogue of vanillin, has a more intense odor and flavor than vanillin, and is used as a flavoring agent — called also *bourbonal*

ethyl violet *n, usu cap E&V* **:** a basic dye — see DYE table I (under *Basic Violet 4; Pigment Blues 5 & 14*)

eth·yne *also* **eth·ine** \ˈeˌthīn, eˈth-\ *n* -s [ISV *eth-* + *-yne, -ine*] **:** ACETYLENE

ethy·nyl *or* **ethi·nyl** \eˈthīnᵊl\ *n* -s [*ethyne, ethine* + *-yl*] **:** a univalent unsaturated radical $HC{\equiv}C-$ derived from acetylene by removal of one hydrogen atom

ethy·nyl·a·tion \(ˌ)eˌthīnᵊlˈāshən\ *n* -s **:** the introduction of the ethynyl radical into a compound usu. by reaction with acetylene ⟨~ of aldehydes yields acetylenic alcohols⟩

ethynylestradiol *var of* ETHINYL ESTRADIOL

-et·ic \ˈed·|ik, |et|, |ēk\ *adj suffix* [L & Gk; L *-eticus*, fr. Gk

-etikos, ētikos, fr. *-etos, -ētos*, ending of certain verbals + *-ikos* -ic] **:** -IC ⟨alg*etic*⟩ — usu. used to form adjectives corresponding to nouns ending in *-esis* (as *genetic* : *genesis*)

etio- *or* **aetio-** *comb form* [ML *aetio-*, fr. Gk *aitio-*, fr. *aitia* — more at ETIOLOGY] **1 :** cause ⟨*etio*logic⟩ ⟨*etio*genic⟩ **2 :** formed by chemical degradation of a (specified) compound ⟨*etio*phyllin⟩

¹eti·o·late \ˈēd-ēə,lāt\ *vt* -ED/-ING/-S [F *étioler* + E *-ate* (v. suffix)] **1 :** to bleach and alter or weaken the natural development of (a green plant) by excluding sunlight **2 :** to make pale and sickly ⟨remembering how drink hardens the skin and how drugs ~ it —Jean Stafford⟩ **3 :** to rob of natural vigor **:** prevent or inhibit the full physical, emotional, or mental growth of (as by sheltering or pampering) ⟨the shade of Poets' walk, a green tunnel that has *etiolated* so many . . . poets —Cyril Connolly⟩

²etiolate \"\ *adj* [F *étiolé* + E *-ate* (adj. suffix)] **:** COLORLESS, PALE, ETIOLATED

etiolated *adj* **1 :** grown in absence of sunlight **:** BLANCHED ⟨~ celery⟩ **2 :** lacking in vigor or natural exuberance **:** lacking in strength of feeling or appetites **:** EFFETE ⟨~ poetry⟩

eti·o·la·tion \,ēd-ēəˈlāshən\ *n* -S **1 :** the act, process, or result of growing a plant in darkness **:** the yellowing or whitening of a green plant through lack of sunlight **2 :** the loss or lessening of natural vigor **:** overrefinement of thought or emotional sensibilities **:** DECADENCE

eti·o·log·ic *or* **ae·ti·o·log·ic** \ˌē|d-ēə¦läjik, |tē- *also* ¦e|\ *or* **eti·o·log·i·cal** *or* **ae·ti·o·log·i·cal** \-jəkəl, -jēk-\ *adj* [Gk *aitiologikos* inquiring into causes, fr. *aitiologia* + *-ikos* -ic, -ical] **:** relating to etiology **:** assigning or seeking to assign a cause ⟨~ myth⟩ — **eti·o·log·i·cal·ly** *or* **ae·ti·o·log·i·cal·ly** \-jək(ə)lē, -jēk-, -li\ *adv*

eti·ol·o·gy *or* **ae·ti·ol·o·gy** \,⁼⁼ˈäləjē, -ji\ *also* **ai·ti·ol·o·gy** \,ī|, ,ā|\ *n* -ES [ML *aetiologia* allegation of a cause or reason, fr. Gk *aitiologia*, fr. *aitia* cause + *-logia* -logy; akin to L *aemulus* rivaling, envious, rival, OIr *ães* age, Gk *ainumai* I take, seize, *aisa* destiny, share, Av *aēta-* punishment] **1 :** CAUSE, ORIGIN ⟨~ of an old custom⟩; *specif* **:** all of the causes of a disease or an abnormality ⟨~ of malaria⟩ ⟨~ of crown rot⟩ **2 a :** a science or doctrine of causation or of the demonstration of causes **b :** a branch of knowledge concerned with the causes of particular phenomena; *specif* **:** a branch of medical science concerned with the causes and origins of diseases

etio·porphyrin *or* **ae·tio·porphyrin** \¦ē|d-ē(,)ō *also* ¦e|+\ *n* [*etio-, aetio-* + *porphyrin*] **:** any of four isomeric porphyrins $C_{20}H_6N_4(CH_3)_4(C_2H_5)_4$; *esp* **:** a violet crystalline pigment occurring in nature (as in petroleum and coal) and formed by degradation of chlorophyll and of heme

et·i·quette \ˈed-|əkət, -et|, |ēk-, -,ket, *usu* -kəd· *or* -ked· +V\ *n* -S [F *étiquette* — more at TICKET] **1 :** the forms required by good breeding or prescribed by authority to be observed in social or official life **:** observance of the proprieties of rank and occasion **:** conventional decorum ⟨the strict ~ of court functions⟩ **2 :** an item of behavior prescribed by rule or custom **3 :** the rules of conduct, action, or practice binding on members of a profession (as medicine or law) esp. in their relations with one another

et·na \ˈetnə\ *n* -S [fr. Mt. *Etna*, Sicily; fr. its cone shape] **:** a device formerly used for heating liquids and consisting of a cup fixed in a saucer in which alcohol is burned

et·ne·an \(ˈ)etˈnēən\ *adj, usu cap* [L *Aetnaeus*, fr. Gk *Aitnaios* (fr. *Aitnē* Etna, volcano in Sicily) + E *-an*] **:** of or relating to Mt. Etna in Sicily

étoile \ā·ˈtwäl\ *n* -S [F, fr. MF *estoile* star — more at ESTOILE] **1 :** a star or a pattern in the shape of a star **2 :** a principal dancer in a ballet company

eton \ˈētᵊn\ *adj, usu cap* [fr. *Eton* College, public school in Eton, Bucks, England] **:** resembling the clothes or appearance of boys at Eton College ⟨a short *Eton* crop for women⟩

eton blue *n, often cap E* [so called fr. its being the school color] **:** a light bluish green that is bluer and duller than average aqua green (sense 1) or average turquoise green and bluer and deeper than robin's-egg blue (sense 2) — called also *Cambridge blue*

eton cap *n, usu cap E* **:** a boy's cap with a short visor

eton collar *n, usu cap E* **:** a wide turnover collar for wear with an Eton jacket

eton game *or* **eton fives** *n, usu cap E* **:** the game of fives played on a court with front and side walls — compare RUGBY GAME

¹eto·ni·an \ēˈtōnēən\ *n* -S *cap* [*Eton* College + E *-ian*] **:** a student or former student of Eton College

²etonian \(ˈ)⁼¦⁼⁼⁼\ *adj, usu cap* **:** of or relating to Eton College

eton jacket *n, usu cap E* [so called from its being worn by boys at Eton College] **1 :** a black jacket having long sleeves, wide lapels, and an open front and reaching just below the waistline in length **2** *also* **eton** -S **:** a woman's jacket that is usu. waist-length, often short-sleeved, and without lapels

eton wall game *n, cap E* [so called from being originated there] **:** an early form of English school football played by two teams on a strip of ground bounded on one side by a high wall

Eton jacket 1

étouf·fé \¦ā,tü¦fā\ *adj* [F, fr. past part. of *étouffer* to stifle, smother, mute, fr. MF *estouffer* to smother, suffocate] **:** STIFLED, SMOTHERED — used esp. of a damping or muting of the tone on a stringed instrument (as the harp)

etrog *var of* ETHROG

etru·me·us \əˈtrümēəs\ *n, cap* [NL] **:** a genus of rather small chiefly tropical marine fishes (family Dussumieriidae) that includes round herrings of economic importance esp. in parts of the Pacific — see JAPANESE HERRING

¹etru·ri·an \əˈtrurēən, ēˈt-\ *n* -S *cap* [L *Etruria*, ancient country of central Italy + E *-an*] **:** ETRUSCAN

²etrurian \"\ *adj, usu cap* **:** ETRUSCAN

etru·ria ware \-rēə-\ *n, usu cap E* [fr. *Etruria*, factory in Staffordshire, England, where it was made] **:** Wedgwood wares made at the Etruria factory

¹etrus·can \əˈtrəskən, ēˈ-\ *adj, usu cap* [L *Etruscus* of Etruria, Etruscan + E *-an*] **:** of, relating to, or characteristic of Etruria or its inhabitants, art, language, or civilization

²etruscan \"\ *n* -S **1** *cap* **:** a native or inhabitant of ancient Etruria **:** TYRRHENIAN **2** *cap* **:** the language of the Etruscans which is of unknown affiliation and whose surviving records have been imperfectly interpreted **3** *often cap* **:** TUSCAN BROWN

etruscan alphabet *n, usu cap E* **:** an alphabet derived from the Greek alphabet, used for writing Etruscan, and having 26 letters in its earliest known form of the 7th or 8th century B.C. and subsequently 23 and then 20

etruscan red *n, often cap E* **:** a grayish reddish orange that is slightly darker than hyacinth red, yellower and darker than Persian melon, and duller than light persimmon

etruscan ware *n, usu cap E* **:** a black ware ornamented with encaustic colors chiefly in red and white and invented by Josiah Wedgwood and patented by him in 1770

etrusco- *comb form, cap* [L *Etruscus*] **:** Etruscan and ⟨*Etrusco*-Roman⟩

etrus·col·o·gist \(,)ē,trəˈskäləjəst, ə,-\ *n* -S *usu cap* **:** a specialist in Etruscan language and antiquities

etrus·col·o·gy \-jē\ *n* -ES *usu cap* [*Etrusco-* + *-logy*] **:** a study of Etruscan and Etruscan antiquities

-ets *pl of* -ET

ETS *abbr* expiration of term of service

et se·quens \etˈse,kwān(t)s, -sē,kwenz, -sēkwənz\ [L] **:** and the following one — abbr. *et seq.*

et se·quen·tes \,etse'kwen-,tās, -səˈkwen(·,)tēz\ *or* **et sequentia** \-səˈkwentē,ä, -səˈkwench(ē)ə\ [L *et sequentes* (masc. & fem. pl.), *et sequentia* (neut. pl.)] **:** and those that follow — abbr. *et seq., et seqq., et sq., et sqq.*

-ette \ˈet *sometimes* ət; *usu* ¦ed· *or* ,əd· +V\ *n suffix* -S [ME, fr. MF, fem. dim. suffix, fr. OF *-ete* — more at -ET] **1 :** little one (of the thing or class specified) **:** -LET ⟨wagon*ette*⟩ ⟨kitchen*ette*⟩ ⟨din*ette*⟩ **2 :** group (of so many) ⟨oct*ette*⟩ **3 :** female ⟨major*ette*⟩ ⟨farmer*ette*⟩ ⟨suffrag*ette*⟩ **4 :** imitation **:** substitute ⟨ermin*ette*⟩ ⟨beaver*ette*⟩ — used chiefly in commercial names

et·ter·cap \ˈed·ər,kap\ *n* -S [ME *attercop, attercoppe*, fr. OE *ātorcoppe*, fr. *ātor* poison, venom + *-coppe* spider, fr. *copp* top, summit — more at ATTER, COP] **1** *Scot* **:** SPIDER **2** *Scot* **:** an ill-tempered or spiteful person

et·tings·hau·sen effect \ˈed·iŋz,hauzᵊn-\ *n, usu cap E* [fr. the name *Ettingshausen*] **:** a transverse temperature gradient produced when a metal in which an electric current is flowing is placed in a magnetic field whose direction is perpendicular to that of the current

¹et·tle \ˈed·ᵊl\ *vb* [ME *ettlen, atlen*, fr. ON *ætla;* akin to OE *eahtian* to consider, estimate, watch over, *eaht* consideration, estimation, OHG *ahtōn* to consider, believe, estimate, *ahta* consideration, attention, esteem, Goth *ahjan* to believe, think, *aha* understanding, mind, Gk *oknos* hesitation, fear, and perh. to OE *ēage* eye — more at EYE] *vt* **1** *chiefly Scot* **:** INTEND, PLAN, DESIGN **2** *chiefly Scot* **:** ATTEMPT, VENTURE **3** *chiefly Scot* **:** GUESS, SUPPOSE ~ *vi, chiefly Scot* **:** AIM, ASPIRE, PLAN

²ettle \"\ *n* -S *Scot* **:** INTENT, PURPOSE

³ettle \"\ *n* -S [by alter. (resulting from incorrect division of *a nettle*)] *dial Eng* **:** NETTLE

et·tring·ite \ˈe·triŋ,īt\ *n* -S [G *ettringit*, fr. *Ettringen*, Rhine Province, Germany, its locality + G *-it* -ite] **:** a mineral $Ca_6Al_2(SO_4)_3(OH)_{12}.26H_2O$ consisting of hydrous basic sulfate of calcium and aluminum

et·ua tree \ˈed·əwə-, ˈet·wə-\ *n* [of African origin; akin to Twi *etwa*, a prickly plant] **:** a tropical African tree (*Kigelia pinnata*) of the family Bignoniaceae with sausage-shaped pods borne on the old wood

étude \ˈā,tüd, ˈā-,työd, ⁼ˈ⁼\ *n* -S [F, lit., study, fr. MF *estude, estudie* — more at STUDY] **:** a piece of music for the practice of some special point of technical execution **:** STUDY, EXERCISE; *also* **:** a composition built upon a technical motive but played for its artistic value ⟨concert ~⟩

etui *also* **etwee** \āˈtwē, etˈwē, ˈ⁼,⁼\ *n* -S [F *étui* — more at TWEEZE] **:** an ornamental case for an article or small articles (as toilet articles, glasses, scissors, needles) in daily use

-e·tum \ˈēd·əm, ˈēt|əm\ *n suffix, pl* **-e·ta** \|ə\ *or* **-etums** [L *-etum*] **1 :** garden or group of a (specified) kind of plant ⟨ros*etum*⟩ ⟨pin*etum*⟩ **2 :** consocies (of a specified plant genus or family) ⟨characetum⟩

et ux *abbr* [L *et uxor*] and wife

et·y·mol·o·ger \,ed·əˈmäləj(ə)r, ,etə-\ *n* -S [prob. fr. obs. *etymologe*, v., to derive etymologically (fr. Gk *etymologein*, fr. *etymon* + *-logein* to discourse, fr. *logos* speech) + ¹*-er* — more at ¹LEGEND] *archaic* **:** ETYMOLOGIST

et·y·mo·log·i·cal \¦⁼⁼,məˈläjəkəl, -jēk-\ *also* **et·y·mo·log·ic** \-jik, -jēk\ *adj* [*etymological* fr. L *etymologicus* etymological (fr. Gk *etymologikos*, fr. *etymologia* + *-ikos* -ic) + E *-al; etymologic* fr. L *etymologicus*] **:** belonging to, based on, or in accord with etymology — **et·y·mo·log·i·cal·ly** \-jək(ə)lē, -jēk-, -li\ *adv*

et·y·mo·log·i·con \,⁼⁼⁼ˈ⁼jə,kän, -jē-, -,kən\ *n* -S [Gk *etymologikon*, fr. neut. of *etymologikos*] **:** an etymological dictionary or manual

et·y·mol·o·gist \,ed·əˈmäləjəst, ,etə-\ *n* -S [fr. *etymologize*, after such pairs as E *catechize: catechist*] **:** one that etymologizes **:** a specialist in etymology

et·y·mol·o·giz·able \-,jīzəbəl\ *adj* **:** capable of being etymologized

et·y·mol·o·gize \-z\ *vb* -ED/-ING/-S [ML *etymologizare*, fr. L *etymologia* etymology + LL *-izare* -ize] *vt* **:** to discover, formulate, or state an etymology for ~ *vi* **1 :** to study etymology **:** formulate etymologies **2 :** to define etymologically

et·y·mol·o·gy \,ed·əˈmäləjē, ,etə-, -ji\ *n* -ES [alter. (influenced by L *etymologia*) of ME *ethimologie*, prob. fr. ML *ethimologia*, alter. of L *etymologia*, fr. Gk, fr. *etymon* + *-logia* -logy] **1 a :** the history often including the prehistory of a linguistic form (as a word or morpheme) as shown by tracing its phonetic, graphic, and semantic development since its earliest recorded occurrence in the language where it is found, by tracing the course of its transmission from one language to another, by analyzing it into the component parts from which it was put together, by identifying its cognates in other languages, or by tracing it and its cognates back to a common ancestral form in a recorded or assumed ancestral language **b :** a branch of linguistics concerned with etymologies **2 :** ACCIDENCE **3 :** the etymological meaning of a word

et·y·mon \ˈ⁼⁼,män\ *n, pl* **ety·ma** \-,mä, -,mə\ *also* **etymons** [L, origin of a word, fr. Gk, literal meaning of a word according to its origin, fr. neut. of *etymos* true; akin to Gk *eteos* true — more at SOOTH] **1 a :** the original form of a word either in the same language or in an ancestral language **b :** the word in a foreign language that is the source of a particular loanword ⟨the ~ of English *cantata* is Italian *cantata*⟩ **2 :** the literal meaning of a word according to its origin **3 :** a word or morpheme from which words are formed by composition or derivation

eu- *comb form* [ME, fr. L, fr. Gk, fr. *ey, eu*, fr. neut. of *eys* good; akin to Hitt *asus* good and perh. to Skt *asti* he is — more at IS] **1 a :** well **:** easily ⟨*eu*plastic⟩ — opposed to *dys-* **b :** good ⟨*eu*daemon⟩ — opposed to *dys-* **2 a :** most typical **:** true ⟨*Eu*ascomycetes⟩ ⟨*eu*chromosome⟩ **b :** truly ⟨*eu*coelomate⟩ **c :** having a complete life cycle ⟨*eu*-form⟩ **3 :** improved derivative of a (specified) substance ⟨*eu*codeine⟩

EU *abbr* entropy unit

Eu *symbol* europium

eu·arc·tos \yüˈ(w)ärktəs, -,täs\ *n, cap* [NL, fr. *eu-* + Gk *arktos* bear — more at ARCTIC] *in some classifications* **:** a genus of bears comprising the American and sometimes the Asiatic black bears — compare SELENARCTOS, URSUS

eu·as·ca·les \,yü,aˈskā(,)lēz\ *n pl, cap* [NL, fr. *eu-* + *asc-* + *-ales*] *in some classifications* **:** an order equivalent to the class Euascomycetes

eu·ascomycetes \(¦)yü,(w)+-,\ *n pl, cap* [NL, fr. *eu-* + *Ascomycetes*] **:** a subclass of the Ascomycetes having the asci borne in or on an ascocarp and usu. from ascogenous hyphae — compare HEMIASCOMYCETES, PROTOASCOMYCETES

eu·as·co·my·cet·i·dae \(,)yü,(w)askō,mīˈsed·ə,dē\ [NL, fr. *eu-* + *Ascomycetes* + *-idae*] *syn of* EUASCOMYCETES

eu·ascomycetous \(¦)⁼+\ *adj* [NL *Euascomycetes* + E *-ous*] **:** of or relating to the Euascomycetes

eu·aster \(ˈ)yü¦(w)+-,\ *n* [NL, fr. *eu-* + *aster*] **:** a sponge spicule in the shape of a modified aster in which the rays meet at a common center — compare STREPTASTER

eu·bacteria \¦yü+\ [NL, fr. *eu-* + *bacteria*] *syn of* EUBACTERIALES

eu·bac·te·ri·a·les \,yü(,)bak,tirēˈā(,)lēz\ *n pl, cap* [NL, fr. *eu-* + *bacteri-* + *-ales*] **:** an order of Schizomycetes comprising relatively simple nonfilamentous unbranched bacteria showing no visible sulfur or iron particles and including spherical and rod-shaped forms

eu·bacterium \¦yü+\ *n* [NL, fr. *eu-* + *bacterium*] **:** one of the Eubacteriales **:** a typical bacterium

eu·ba·sid·i·ae \,yübəˈsidē,ē\ *n pl, cap* [NL, fr. *eu-* + *-basidiae* (fr. *basidium*)] *in some classifications* **:** a subclass of fungi (class Basidiomycetes) including the orders Polyporales and Agaricales and characterized by one-celled basidia which produce spores on terminal sterigmata — compare HETEROBASIDIAE, TELIOSPOREAE

eu·ba·sid·ii \-dē,ī\ *n pl, cap* [NL, fr. *eu-* + *-basidii* (fr. *basidium*)] *in some classifications* **:** a subclass of fungi including all those basidiomycetes in which the basidium arises directly from vegetative cells of the dicaryotic mycelium (as the puffballs, jelly fungi, pore fungi, and related forms) — compare HEMIBASIDII, HETEROBASIDIOMYCETES

¹eu·boe·an \(ˈ)yüˈbēən\ *adj, usu cap* [*Euboea*, island of Greece northeast of Attica and Boeotia + E *-an*] **:** EUBOIC

²euboean \"\ *n* -S *cap* [*Euboea* + E *-an*] **:** a native or inhabitant of Euboea

eu·bo·ic \(ˈ)yüˈbōik\ *adj, usu cap* [L *euboicus*, fr. Gk *euboikos*, fr. *Euboia* Euboea + Gk *-ikos* -ic] **:** of or relating to the island of Euboea or the sea which separates it from the Greek coast — compare CHALCIDIAN

eu·branchipus \(ˈ)yü+\ *n, cap* [NL, fr. *eu-* + *Branchipus*] **:** a genus of freshwater branchiopod crustaceans comprising fairy shrimps formerly classed in the genus *Branchipus*

eu·bryales \¦yü+\ *n pl, cap* [NL, fr. *eu-* + *Bryales*] **:** an order of Musci comprising mosses that have perennial erect gametophores, stems with many rows of leaves, and drooping capsules with a double peristome of well-developed teeth

eu·caine \yüˈkān, ˈ⁼,⁼\ *n* -S [ISV *eu-* + *-caine;* orig. formed as G *eucain* (now *eukain*)] **:** a local anesthetic $C_{15}N_{21}NO_2$ derived from piperidine and usu. administered as the white crystalline hydrochloride — called also *beta-eucaine*

eu·cai·rite *also* **eu·kai·rite** \yüˈkī,rīt, -kā-\ *n* -S [Sw *eukairit*, fr. Gk *eukairos* seasonable, opportune (fr. *eu-* + *kairos* time, season) + Sw *-it* -ite; fr. its being found soon after the discovery of selenium] **:** a mineral CuAgSe consisting of a grayish metallic-looking copper silver selenide (sp. gr. 7.50)

eu·ca·lypt \ˈyükə,lipt\ *n* -S [NL *Eucalyptus*] **:** a tree of the genus *Eucalyptus* — **eu·ca·lyp·tic** \¦⁼⁼ˈliptik\ *adj*

eu·ca·lyp·tog·ra·phy \,yükə,lipˈtägrəfē\ *n* -ES **:** a treatise upon or study of the genus *Eucalyptus*

eu·ca·lyp·tol \,yükəˈlip,tōl\ *also* **eu·ca·lyp·tole** \-,tōl, -,tōl\ *n* -S [ISV *eucalypt-* (fr. NL *Eucalyptus*) + *-ol, -ole*] **:** CINEOLE

¹eu·ca·lyp·tus \,yükəˈliptəs\ *n* [NL, fr. *eu-* + Gk *kalyptos* covered, fr. *kalyptein* to cover, conceal; fr. the hemispherical or conical covering of the buds — more at HELL] **1** *cap* **:** a genus of evergreen timber trees or rarely shrubs (family Myrtaceae) mostly native to western Australia, having rigid entire leaves, umbellate flowers, and rather woody fruits, and yielding gums, resins, oils, and tars as well as useful woods — compare BLOODWOOD, BLUE GUM, CIDER GUM, EUCALYPTUS GUM, PEPPERMINT TREE, STRINGYBARK **2** *pl* **eucalyp·ti** \-,tī\ *or* **eucalyptuses :** any tree or shrub of the genus *Eucalyptus* **:** EUCALYPT **3** *or* **eucalyptus green** -ES **:** a grayish yellow to yellow green

²eucalyptus \¦⁼⁼¦⁼⁼\ *adj* **:** of or relating to the eucalyptus **:** made of eucalyptus wood

eucalyptus gum *or* **eucalyptus kino** *n* **:** a reddish brown dried gummy exudation from a red gum tree (*Eucalyptus rostrata*) of Australia and several other eucalypts used as a base for lozenges and troches — called also *Botany Bay kino, red gum*

eucalyptus oil *n* **:** any of various essential oils obtained from the leaves of various eucalypts (as *Eucalyptus globulus*) and used in pharmaceutical preparations (as antiseptics, cough drops), in perfumes, and in the flotation process for concentrating ores

eu·carida \(¦)yü+\ *n pl, cap* [NL, fr. *eu-* + *-carida* (fr. L *carid-, caris*, a kind of sea crab) — more at -CARIS] **:** an extensive group of crustaceans having the thoracic segments covered by and fused with a carapace and the eyes on movable stalks and constituting the orders Euphausiacea and Decapoda of the subclass Malacostraca

eu·car·pic \(ˈ)yüˈkärpik\ *adj* [*eu-* + *-carpic*] **1 :** having only part of the thallus transformed into a fruiting body or sporangium ⟨~ algae⟩ ⟨~ fungi⟩ **2 :** gaining nourishment by means of haustoria or rhizoids — compare HOLOCARPIC

eucaryote *var of* EUKARYOTE

euc·atropine \(ˈ)yü¦k+-\ *n* [*eucaine* + *atropine*] **:** a synthetic alkaloid related in structure to eucaine and atropine, obtained in the form of its white crystalline hydrochloride $C_{17}H_{25}NO_3.HCl$, and used as a mydriatic

eu·ceph·a·lous \(ˈ)yüˈsefələs\ *also* **eu·ce·phal·ic** \¦yüsəˈfalik\ *adj* [ISV *eu-* + *-cephalous* or *-cephalic*] **:** having a well-developed head — used of the larvae of certain flies; compare HEMICEPHALOUS

eu·cestoda \¦yü+\ *n pl, cap* [NL, fr. *eu-* + *Cestoda*] *in some classifications* **:** a subclass of Platyhelminthes comprising the tapeworms and including all the cestodes except the cestodarians

eu·cha·ris \ˈyük(ə)rəs\ *n* [NL, fr. LL, gracious, charming, fr. Gk, fr. *eu-* + *charis* grace; akin to Gk *chairein* to rejoice — more at YEARN] **1** *cap* **:** a small genus of So. American scapose herbs (family Amaryllidaceae) having white umbellate flowers — see AMAZON LILY **2** *or* **eucharis lily** -ES **:** any plant of the genus *Eucharis*

eu·cha·rist \ˈyük(ə)rəst\ *n* -S *usu cap* [ME *eukarist*, fr. MF *eucariste*, fr. LL *eucharistia*, fr. Gk, Eucharist, giving of thanks, gratitude, fr. *eucharistos* grateful (fr. *eu-* + — assumed — *charistos*, verbal of Gk *charizesthai* to show favor, fr. *charis* favor, grace) + *-ia* -y] **1 a :** the sacrament of the Lord's Supper; *specif* **:** a central rite in many Christian churches in which bread and wine are consecrated by the officiating clergyman, shared with the people, and consumed as memorials of Christ's death or as symbols for the realization of a spiritual union between Christ and communicant or as the body and blood of Christ — called also *Communion, Holy Communion* **b :** the consecrated elements of bread and wine **2 a :** an act of giving thanks **b :** an act of worship in which thanksgiving is central **3** *Christian Science* **:** spiritual communion with God

eu·cha·ris·tial \,yükəˈris(h)chəl\ *n* -S [ML *eucharistiale*, fr. neut. of *eucharistialis* of the Eucharist, fr. LL *eucharistia* + L *-alis* -al] **:** a vessel for consecrated bread **:** PYX

eu·cha·ris·tic \¦yükə¦ristik, -tēk\ *adj* [*eucharist* + *-ic*] **1** *often cap* **:** of, relating to, or resembling the Eucharist **2 :** manifesting or expressing praise and thanksgiving ⟨the poem's ~ intent⟩ — **eu·cha·ris·ti·cal·ly** \-tək(ə)lē, -tēk-, -li\ *adv* **:** in a eucharistic manner

eu·cha·ris·ti·cal \-təkəl, -tēk-\ *archaic var of* EUCHARISTIC

eu·cha·rist·ize \ˈyükərə,stīz, ,⁼⁼ˈri,stīz\ *vt* -ED/-ING/-S [*eucharist* + *-ize*] *archaic* **:** to consecrate as elements of the Lord's Supper

eu·cheu·ma \yüˈk(y)ümə\ *n, cap* [NL, fr. *eu-* + Gk *cheuma* stream, fr. *chein* to pour — more at FOUND] **:** a genus of red algae (family Solieriaceae) having terete or flattened thalli often with abundant spiny branchlets

eu·chite \ˈyü,kīt\ *n* -S *usu cap* [LGk *euchitēs*, fr. Gk *euchē* prayer, vow (fr. *euchesthai* to pray, vow) + *-itēs* -ite — more at VOW] **1 :** one of an ecstatic mendicant vagrant Christian sect of the 4th to the 8th centuries in Mesopotamia, Syria, and Asia Minor that believed man's congenital devil could be expelled only by unremitting prayer **2 :** one of an 11th century Thracian sect similar to the Euchite and probably descended from it through 8th and 10th century migrations

eu·chlae·na \yüˈklēnə\ *n, cap* [NL, fr. *eu-* + Gk *chlaina* cloak; fr. the bracts around the ear] **:** a small genus of Mexican grasses that are closely related to and readily hybridize with Indian corn and have the pistillate spike reduced to a row of hard joints resembling seeds — see TEOSINTE

eu·chlo·rin \yüˈklōrən, ˈyüklər-\ *n* -S [It *euclorina*, fr. Gk *euchlōros* greenish (fr. *eu-* + *chlōros* greenish yellow) + It *-ina* -ine; fr. the color — more at YELLOW] **:** a mineral $(K,Na)_8Cu_9(SO_4)_{10}(OH)_6$ composed of a basic sulfate of copper, sodium, and potassium found in lava at Vesuvius

eu·cho·lo·gion \,efkōˈlōyōn\ *n, pl* **eucholo·gia** \-yä\ [MGk, fr. *eucho-* (fr. Gk *euchē* prayer) + *-logion* (fr. Gk *legein* to collect) — more at LEGEND] **:** a principal service book of liturgies, prayers, and occasional rites used in the Eastern Orthodox Church

eu·chol·o·gy \yüˈkäləjē\ *n* -ES [MGk *euchologion*] **:** EUCHOLOGION

eu·chor·da \yüˈkȯrdə\ *n pl, cap* [NL, fr. *eu-* + *-chorda* (fr. *chorda*)] *in some classifications* **:** a subphylum or other division of Chordata comprising the lancelets and true vertebrates

eu·chordata \¦yü+\ [NL, fr. *eu-* + *Chordata*] *syn of* EUCHORDA

¹eu·chre *also* **eu·cher** \ˈyükə(r)\ *n* -S [origin unknown] **1 :** a card game in which each player is dealt five cards and the player or side that makes the trump must take three tricks to win a hand — see BOWER **2 :** the action of euchring an opponent

²euchre *also* **eucher** \"\ *vt* **euchred** *also* **euchered; euchred** *also* **euchered; euchring** *also* **euchering** \ˈyük(ə)riŋ\ **euchres** *also* **euchers 1 :** to prevent (the maker of trump in the game of euchre) from winning three tricks **2 :** CHEAT, DECEIVE, TRICK, OUTWIT ⟨*euchred* me out of a fortune —Richard Stanton⟩

eu·chred \ˈyükə(r)d\ *adj* [origin unknown] *dial* **:** made slightly tart by an acid or spice ⟨~ figs⟩

eu·chro·ite \ˈyükrō,īt\ *n* -S [G *euchroit*, fr. Gk *euchroos* well-colored (fr. *eu-* + *-chroos* -chroous) + G *-it* -ite] **:** a mineral $Cu_2(AsO_4)(OH).3H_2O$ consisting of a basic copper arsenate in emerald-green orthorhombic crystals (hardness 3.5–4, sp. gr. 3.39)

eu·chromatic \¦yü+\ *adj* [*euchromatin* + *-ic*] **:** of or relating to euchromatin

eu·chromatin \(ˈ)yü+\ *n* [G, fr. *eu-* + *chromatin*] **:** the portion of chromatin that is genetically active and is held to be largely made up of genes and that stains less intensely than heterochromatin

eu·chro·ma·ti·za·tion \yü,krōməd·ə'zāshən\ *n* -s [*euchromat-* (fr. *euchromatin*) + *-ization*] **:** the transformation of a portion of chromatin into euchromatin — compare HETEROCHROMATIZATION

eu·chromocenter \(ˈ)yü+\ *n* [ISV *eu-* + *chromocenter;* prob. orig. formed as F *euchromocentre*] **:** PROCHROMOSOME, CHROMOCENTER

eu·chromocentric \(ˌ)yü+\ *adj* **:** of, relating to, or characterized by the presence of euchromocenters — used esp. of plant-cell nuclei that appear homogeneous during metabolic phases

eu·chromosome \(ˈ)yü+\ *n* [*eu-* + *chromosome*] **:** AUTOSOME

euchrysine GG *n, usu cap E* [*euchrysine* ISV *eu-* + *chrys-* + *-ine*] **:** a basic dye — see DYE table I (under *Basic Yellow 9*)

eu·ciliata \(ˌ)yü+\ *n pl, cap* [NL, fr. *eu-* + *Ciliata*] **:** the subclass of Ciliata comprising protozoans having a trophic macronucleus and a reproductive micronucleus and reproducing sexually by conjugation and including the four orders Holotricha, Spirotricha, Chonotricha, and Peritricha — compare PROTOCILIATA — **eu·ciliate** \(ˈ)yü+\ *adj or n*

eu·cirripedia \(ˌ)yü+\ *n pl, cap* [NL, fr. *eu-* + *Cirripedia*] *in some classifications* **:** a group of barnacles consisting of the more typical forms as distinguished from the Rhizocephala

eu·clase \'yü,klās, -āz\ *n* -s [F, fr. *eu-* + Gk *klasis* breaking, fr. *klan* to break — more at HALT] **:** a rare brittle silicate of beryllium and aluminum $BeAlSiO_4(OH)$ occurring in pale-yellow, green, or blue prismatic crystals and sometimes used as a gem

eu·clea \yü'klēə\ *n, cap* [NL, fr. Gk *eukleia* glory, fr. *euklees* famous (fr. *eu-* + *-klees,* fr. *kleos* report, fame) + *-ia* -y; akin to Gk *klytos* famous— more at LOUD] **:** a genus of African trees and shrubs (family Ebenaceae) having evergreen leaves, dioecious racemose flowers, and hard wood — see CAPE EBONY

¹**eu·cle·id** \'yüklēəd\ *adj* [NL *Eucleidae*] **:** of or relating to the Eucleidae

²**eucleid** \"\ *n* -s **:** a moth of the family Eucleidae

eu·cle·i·dae \yü'klēə,dē\ *n pl, cap* [NL, fr. *Euclea,* type genus (fr. Gk *eukleia* glory) + *-idae*] **:** a family of hairy robust yellow to brown moths often strikingly marked with color and including some with severely urticating hairs — see CUP MOTH

eu·clid \'yükləd\ *n* -s *often cap* [after *Euclid fl ab* 300 B.C. Greek geometer] **:** EUCLIDEAN GEOMETRY

eu·clid·e·an *also* **eu·clid·i·an** \(ˈ)yü¦klidēən\ *adj, often cap* **:** adopting Euclid's assumptions with respect to space **:** relating to geometry as developed in Euclid's *Elements*

euclidean construction *n, often cap E* **:** a geometric construction by the use of ruler and compasses

euclidean geometry *n, often cap E* **1 :** the geometry based on Euclid's axioms **2 :** the geometry of a Euclidean space

euclidean space *n, often cap E* **:** the space to which Euclid's axioms and definitions (as of straight and parallel lines, angles of plane triangles) apply

eu·clid's algorithm \'yükləd̮z-\ *n, often cap E* **:** a rule for finding the greatest common divisor of two positive integers

eu·coelomate \(ˈ)yü+\ *adj* [*eu-* + *coelomate,* adj.] **:** having a body cavity that is a coelom — distinguished from *acoelomate* and *pseudocoelomate*

eu·co·lite *also* **eu·ko·lite** *or* **eu·ko·lyte** \'yükə,līt\ *n* -s [G *eukolit,* fr. Gk *eukolos* easily satisfied + G *-it* -ite; fr. a conception that its difference in composition from woehlerite is a disadvantage that it has to endure] **:** a mineral similar to eudialyte but optically negative

eu·com·mia \yü'kämēə\ *n, cap* [NL, fr. *eu-* + *-commia* (fr. Gk *kommi* gum) — more at GUM] **:** a monotypic genus (coextensive with the family Eucommiaceae of the order Rosales) containing a hardy Chinese tree that yields rubber and has alternate leaves and solitary unisexual flowers in the leaf axils

eu·cone \'yü,kōn\ *also* **eu·con·ic** \(ˈ)yü¦känik\ *adj* [*eucone* ISV *eu-* + *cone; euconic* fr. *eucone* + *-ic*] **:** having fully developed crystalline cones in the ommatidia — used of the eyes of insects and crustaceans; compare ACONE, EXOCONE, PSEUDOCONE

eu·copepoda \¦yü+\ *n pl, cap* [NL, fr. *eu-* + *Copepoda*] **:** an order of copepods consisting of the typical free-swimming forms and the lernaeans as distinguished from the Branchiura

eu·cos·mi·dae \yü'käzmə,dē\ [NL, fr. *Eucosma,* included genus (irreg. fr. Gk *eukosmos* well adorned, fr. *eu-* + *kosmos* order, ornament) + *-idae*] *syn of* OLETHREUTIDAE

eu·cot·y·lid \yü'kād·ᵊləd\ *n* -s [NL *Eucotylidae*] **:** a worm of the family Eucotylidae

eu·co·tyl·i·dae \,yükə'tilə,dē\ *n pl, cap* [NL, fr. *Eucotyle,* type genus (fr. *eu-* + Gk *kotylē* cup, anything hollow) + *-idae* — more at KETTLE] **:** a family of digenetic trematode worms including numerous parasites of the kidneys and ureters of gallinaceous birds

eu·cra·sia \yü'krāzh(ē)ə\ *n* -s [NL, fr. ML, mixture of the humors in good proportions, fr. Gk *eukrasia,* fr. *eu-* + *-krasia* (fr. *krasis* mixing, combination) — more at CRASIS] **:** a normal state of health **:** physical well-being — opposed to *dyscrasia*

eu·cra·site \'yükrə,sīt, -,zīt\ *n* -s [Sw *eukrasit,* fr. Gk *eukrasia* mixture of the humors in good proportions, good temperature + Sw *-it* -ite] **:** a variety of thorite

eu·crite \'yü,krīt\ *n* -s [G *eukrit,* fr. Gk *eukritos* easily discerned, fr. *eu-* + *kritos* separated, chosen, fr. *krinein* to separate — more at CERTAIN] **1 :** a meteorite composed essentially of anorthite and augite **2 :** a very basic gabbro whose feldspar contains at least as much lime as does bytownite

eu·crustacea \¦yü+\ *n pl, cap* [NL, fr. *eu-* + *Crustacea*] *in some classifications* **:** a primary division of Crustacea comprising all recent and extinct forms which do not have the body divided into median and lateral lobes — used when trilobites are considered crustaceans

eu·cryph·ia \yü'krifēə\ *n, cap* [NL, fr. *eu-* + Gk *kryphia,* fem. of *kryphios* concealed, fr. *kryptein* to conceal, hide — more at CRYPT] **:** a genus (coextensive with the family Eucryphiaceae of the order Parietales) of tall evergreen trees native to Australia and Chile that have dark shining opposite leaves, large flowers, and a woody or leathery capsular fruit — **eu·cryph·i·a·ceous** \(ˌ)yü¦krifē¦āshəs\ *adj*

eu·cryp·tite \yü'krip,tīt\ *n* -s [G *eukryptos* easily hidden (fr. *eu-* + *kryptos* hidden) + E *-ite* — more at CRYPT] **:** a mineral $LiAlSiO_4$ consisting of a colorless or white lithium aluminum silicate occurring in hexagonal crystals (sp. gr. 2.67)

euctical *adj* [Gk *euktikos* constituting a prayer or vow (fr. *euktos* wished for, vowed — fr. *euchesthai* to pray, vow — + *-ikos* -ic) + E *-al* — more at VOW] *obs* **:** SUPPLICATORY

eu·cyclic \(ˈ)yü+\ *adj* [ISV *eu-* + *cyclic*] *of a flower* **:** cyclic with alternate isomerous whorls

eu·daemon *also* **eu·demon** \(ˈ)yü+\ *n* [*eu-* + *demon*] **:** a good spirit **:** ANGEL — opposed to *cacodemon*

eu·dae·mo·nia \,yüdē'mōnēə\ *also* **eu·dai·mo·nia** \-,dī'-, -(,)dā'-\ *n* -s [Gk *eudaimonia,* fr. *eudaimon-, eudaimōn* having a good attendant or indwelling spirit, lucky, happy (fr. *eu-* + *daimon-, daimōn* spirit) + *-ia* -y— more at DEMON] **1 :** WELL-BEING, HAPPINESS **2** *Aristotelianism* **:** a life of activity governed by reason

eu·dae·mon·ic \¦yüdē¦mänik, -nēk\ *also* **eu·dae·mon·i·cal** \-nəkəl, -nēk-\ *adj* [*eudaemonic* fr. Gk *eudaimonikos,* fr. *eudaimon-, eudaimōn* + *-ikos* -ic; *eudaemonical* fr. Gk *eudaimonikos* + E *-al*] **:** producing happiness **:** based on the idea of happiness as the proper end of conduct

eu·dae·mon·ics \,══'mäniks, -nēks\ *n pl but sing or pl in constr* [Gk *eudaimon-, eudaimōn* + E *-ics*] **1 :** the practice of eudaemonism **:** an art or means of attaining happiness **2 :** the science of happiness — contrasted with *aretaics*

eu·dae·mon·ism \yü'dēmə,nizəm\ *also* **eu·dai·mo·nism** \-dīm-, -dām-\ *or* **eu·de·mon·ism** \-dēm-\ *n* -s [prob. fr. G *eudämonismus,* fr. Gk *eudaimon-, eudaimōn* + G *-ismus* -ism] **:** an ethical theory that defines moral obligation by reference to happiness or personal well-being esp. through a life governed by reason as distinguished from pursuit of pleasure— compare HEDONISM

eu·dae·mon·ist \-,nəst\ *n* -s [prob. fr. G *eudämonist,* fr. Gk *eudaimon-, eudaimōn* + G *-ist*] **:** an adherent of eudaemonism

eu·dae·mon·is·tic \(ˌ)yü¦dēmə¦nistik, -tēk\ *adj* **:** of or relating to eudaemonism **:** based on a conception of eudaemonia — **eu·dae·mon·is·ti·cal·ly** \-tək(ə)lē, -tēk-, -li\ *adv*

eu·dae·mo·ny \yü'dēmənē, -ni\ *n* -ES [Gk *eudaimonia*] **:** EUDAEMONIA

eu·da·lene \'yüdᵊl,ēn\ *n* -s [*eudesmol* + *naphthalene*] **:** a liquid hydrocarbon $C_{14}H_{16}$ formed by dehydrogenation of various sesquiterpenoids; 7-isopropyl-1-methyl-naphthalene

eu·de·mis moth \'yüdəməs-\ *n* [NL *Eudemis,* former genus name, fr. *eu-* + *-demis* (fr. Gk *demas* body, fr. *demein* to build) — more at TIMBER] **:** a small European tortricid moth (*Polychrosis botrana*) that is destructive to the grape

eu·den·dri·um \yü'dendrēəm\ *n, cap* [NL, fr. *eu-* + *-dendrium* (fr. Gk *dendrion,* dim. of *dendron* tree) — more at DENDR-] **:** a genus of hydrozoans (order Anthomedusae) forming a branching colony of pink hydranths with a chitinous perisarc

eu·der·ma \yü'dərmə\ *n, cap* [NL, fr. *eu-* + *-derma*] **:** a genus of bats containing the jackass bat

eu·des·mol \yü'dez,mōl, -mōl\ *n* -s [*eudesm-* (fr. NL *Eudesmia* — syn. of *Eucalyptus* —, fr. *eu-* + *desm-* + *-ia*) + *-ol*] **:** a crystalline sesquiterpenoid alcohol $C_{15}H_{25}OH$ found in eucalyptus oils and used in perfumery as a fixative

eu·de·ve \eü'dā,vā\ *n, pl* **eudeve** *or* **eudeves** *usu cap* [Sp, of AmerInd origin] **1 a :** a division of the Opata people of Mexico **b :** a member of this division **2 :** the language of the Eudeve people

eu·di·a·lyte \yü'dīə,līt\ *n* -s [G *eudialyt,* fr. Gk *eudialytos* easy to dissolve, fr. *eu-* + *dialytos* capable of being dissolved, fr. *dialyein* to dissolve — more at DIALYSIS] **:** a mineral $Na_4(Ca,Fe)_2ZrSi_6O_{17}(OH,Cl)_2$ consisting of a brownish red silicate chiefly of sodium, iron, zirconium, and calcium that occurs in crystals or masses and is optically positive (H.5–5.5, sp. gr. 2.9–3.0)

eu·did·y·mite \yü'didə,mīt\ *n* -s [Norw *eudidymit,* fr. *eu-* + Gk *didymos* twin + Norw *-it* -ite; fr. its occurrence in twin crystals — more at DIDYM-] **:** a mineral $NaBeSi_3O_7(OH)$ consisting of a white glassy sodium beryllium silicate

eu·di·om·e·ter \,yüdē'äməd·ə(r)\ *n* [It *eudiometro,* fr. *eudio-* (fr. Gk *eudia* fair weather, fr. *eu-* + *-dia* weather — akin to L *dies* day) + *-metro* -meter; fr. a former belief that the proportion of oxygen in the air is higher in fair than in bad weather — more at DEITY] **:** an instrument (as a graduated glass tube) for the volumetric measurement and analysis of gases that involves the explosion of one of the components of a mixture by the passage of an electric spark — compare BURETTE 1 — **eu·di·o·met·ric** \¦yüdēə¦me·trik\ *adj*

eu·dist \'yüdəst\ *n* -s *cap* [F *eudiste,* fr. Jean *Eudes* †1680 Fr. priest and founder + F *-iste* -ist] **:** a member of the Roman Catholic Congregation of Jesus and Mary established in 1643 for diocesan priests and lay brothers and now devoted chiefly to teaching and missionary work

eu·doc·i·mus \yü'däsəməs\ *n, cap* [NL, fr. Gk *eudokimos* glorious, famous, fr. *eu-* + *dokimos* esteemed, fr. *dokein* to seem good — more at DECENT] **:** a genus of ibises containing the New World white and scarlet ibises

eu·do·ri·na \,yüdə'rīnə, -rēnə\ *n, cap* [NL, fr. NL Gk *eudōros* generous (fr. *eu-* + *-dōros,* fr. *dōron* gift) + NL *-ina;* akin to Gk *didonai* to give — more at DATE] **:** a genus related to *Volvox* and comprising flagellates that produce markedly anisogamous gametes and form spherical or ellipsoidal colonies

eu·dox·ian \yü'däksēən, -kshən\ *n* -s *usu cap* [*Eudoxius* †A.D.370, bishop of Constantinople and a leader of the Anomoeans + E *-an*] **:** a follower of Bishop Eudoxius

eu·dro·mi·as \yü'drōmēəs\ *n, cap* [NL, fr. Gk, rapid swimmer, fr. *eudromos* swift, running well, fr. *eu-* + *dromos* course, racecourse; akin to Gk *dramein* to run — more at DROMEDARY] **:** a genus of plovers that includes the common dotterel of Europe

eu·echinoidea \(ˌ)yü+\ *n pl, cap* [NL, fr. *eu-* + *Echinoidea*] *in some classifications* **:** a division of Echinoidea including all living sea urchins and comprising the orders Cidaroida, Centrechinoida, and Exocycloida — compare PALAEECHINOIDEA

eu-form \'yü,fȯrm\ *n* **:** a rust having a complete life cycle of pycnial, aecial, uredinial, and telial stages — compare OPSIS-FORM

eu·ge \'eü,gā, 'yü,jē\ *n* -s [L, well done!, fr. Gk, fr. *eu* well — more at EU-] **:** an act or expression of approval **:** BRAVO

eu·gene poplar \'yü,jēn-, ═'═-\ *n, usu cap E* [prob. fr. the name *Eugene*] **:** a hybrid poplar (*Populus canadensis eugenei*) of pyramidal habit originated near Metz in 1832 and used for ornament esp. as a street tree

eu·genesis \¦yü+\ *n* [NL, fr. *eu-* + L *genesis*] **:** fertility between hybrids

eu·ge·nia \yü'jēnyə, -nēə\ *n* [NL, fr. *Eugene,* prince of Savoy †1736 Austrian general + NL *-ia*] **1** *cap* **:** a large genus of tropical trees and shrubs (family Myrtaceae) having aromatic leaves, tetramerous flowers, baccate fruit, and wood that is often hard and valuable — see SURINAM CHERRY **2** -s **:** any tree of the genus *Eugenia*

eugenia red *n, often cap E* **:** a moderate red that is yellower and paler than cerise, claret (sense 3a), or average strawberry (sense 2a) and bluer and paler than Turkey red

eu·gen·ic \(ˈ)yü¦jenik, -nēk\ *also* **eu·gen·i·cal** \-nəkəl, -nēk-\ *adj* [Gk *eugenēs* wellborn (fr. *eu-* + *-genēs* born) + E *-ic, -ical* — more at -GEN] **:** relating to or fitted for the production of good offspring **:** relating to or aiming at the improvement of race or breed — contrasted with *dysgenic* — **eu·gen·i·cal·ly** \-nək(ə)lē, -nēk-, -li\ *adv*

eu·gen·i·cist \yü'jenəsəst\ *n* -s **:** a student or advocate of eugenics

eu·gen·ics \yü'jeniks, -nēks\ *n pl but usu sing in constr* **1 :** a science that deals with the improvement of hereditary qualities in a series of generations of a race or breed esp. by social control of human mating and reproduction — compare EUTHENICS, GENETICS **2 :** the process or means of race improvement (as by restricting mating to superior types suited to each other)

eu·gen·ism \yü'je,nizəm, yü'jē,-, 'yüjə,-\ *n* -s [Gk *eugenēs* + E *-ism*] **:** the combination of influences best suited to improve the hereditary qualities of a race or breed, esp. the human race

eu·gen·ist \-,nəst\ *n* -s [Gk *eugenēs* + E *-ist*] **:** EUGENICIST

eu·ge·nol \'yüjə,nōl, -nōl\ *n* -s [ISV *eugen-* (fr. *Eugenia caryophyllata,* species of clove that is a source of clove oil) + *-ol;* orig. formed as F *eugénol*] **:** a colorless aromatic liquid phenol $CH_2CH{:}CH_2C_6H_3(OCH_3)OH$ found esp. in clove oil and cinnamon-leaf oil and used chiefly in flavors and perfumes, in dentistry as an anodyne and disinfectant, and in the synthesis of vanillin; 4-allyl-guaiacol

eu·geosynclinal \(ˌ)yü+\ *adj* **:** of the nature of or relating to a eugeosyncline

eu·geosyncline \"+\ *n* [*eu-* + *geosyncline*] **:** a narrow rapidly subsiding geosyncline usu. with volcanic materials mingled with clastic sediments — compare MIOGEOSYNCLINE

eu·glan·di·na \,yü,glan'dīnə, -dēnə\ *n, cap* [NL, fr. *eu-* + *Glandina* genus of snails, fr. L *gland-, glans* acorn + NL *-ina* — more at GLAND] **:** a genus of land snails (family Oleacinidae) found esp. in the southern U.S. and in Mexico that are largely carnivorous in habits

eu·gle·na \yü'glēnə\ *n, cap* [NL, fr. *eu-* + Gk *glēnē* eyeball, socket of a joint; prob. akin to Gk *glainoi* ornaments — more at CLEAN] **:** a genus (order Euglenoidina) of green flagellates that are often classed as algae, are cosmopolitan in stagnant fresh water, usu. have a distinct pellicle more or less sculptured and striated, and are capable of writhing plastic movement as well as flagellar motility — see EUGLENACEAE

eu·gle·na·ce·ae \yüglə'nāsē,ē\ *n pl, cap* [NL, fr. *Euglena,* type genus + *-aceae*] **:** a family of algae (class Euglenophyceae) that includes *Euglena* and numerous related genera when these are considered to be algae

eu·gle·na·les \-ā(,)lēz\ *n pl, cap* [NL, fr. *Euglena* + *-ales*] **:** an order of algae (class Euglenophyceae) comprising forms in which the motile flagellate is the dominant phase in the life cycle — compare COLACIALES

eu·gle·ni·da \yü'glēnədə, -len-\ *or* **eu·gle·noi·di·da** \,yüglə'nȯidədə\ [*Euglenida* fr. NL, fr. *Euglena* + *-ida; Euglenoidida* fr. NL, fr. *Euglena* + L *-oides* -oid + NL *-ida*] *syn of* EUGLENOIDINA

eu·gle·nin·e·ae \,yüglə'ninē,ē\ [NL, fr. *Euglena* + *-ineae*] *syn of* EUGLENOPHYCEAE

¹**eu·gle·noid** \yü'glē,nȯid, 'yüglə,n-\ *adj* [NL *Euglenoidina*] **:** of or relating to the order Euglenoidina

²**euglenoid** \"\ *n* -s [NL *Euglenoidina*] **:** a flagellate of the order Euglenoidina

eu·gle·noi·di·na \,yüglə,nȯi'dīnə, -dēnə\ *n pl, cap* [NL, fr. *Euglena* + L *-oides* -oid + NL *-ina*] **:** an order of Phytomastigina comprising extremely varied flagellates that are typically solitary green or colorless stigma-bearing organisms with one or two flagella emerging anteriorly from a well-defined gullet — see EUGLENA

euglenoid movement *n* **:** writhing usu. nonprogressive protoplasmic movement characteristic of plastic-bodied euglenoids but known to occur in other groups (as certain sporozoans) — called also *metabolic movement*

eu·gle·no·phy·ce·ae \yü,glēnə'fīsē,ē, -'fis-\ *n pl, cap* [NL, fr. *Euglena* + *-o-* + *-phyceae*] **:** a class (coextensive with a division Euglenophyta) of mostly green and free-swimming algae comprising the family Euglenaceae and related forms

eu·gle·noph·y·ta \,yüglə'näfəd·ə\ *n pl, cap* [NL, fr. *Euglena* + *-o-* + *-phyta*] **:** a division or other category of algae that is coextensive with the zoological order Euglenoidina

eu·globulin \(ˈ)yü+\ *n* [ISV *eu-* + *globulin*] **:** a simple protein insoluble in half-saturated ammonium sulfate or sodium sulfate and insoluble in pure water — distinguished from *pseudoglobulin*

eu·gly·pha \'yügləfə, yü'glifə\ *n, cap* [NL, fr. *eu-* + Gk *glyphē* carving, fr. *glyphein* to carve or hollow out — more at CLEAVE] **:** a genus (the type of a cosmopolitan family Euglyphidae) of freshwater amoeboid protozoans with a plated test, one or two nuclei, and dichotomously branched filopodia — **eu·gly·phid** \-fəd\ *adj or n*

eu·gon·ic \(ˈ)yü¦gänik\ *adj* [*eu-* + *gon-* + *-ic*] **:** growing readily on artificial media — used esp. of tubercle bacteria; opposed to *dysgonic*

eu·greg·a·rine \yü'gregə,rīn, -,rən\ *n* -s [NL *Eugregarinina*] **:** one of the Eugregarinina

eu·gregarinida \(ˌ)yü+\ [NL, fr. *eu-* + *Gregarinida*] *syn of* EUGREGARININA

eu·gregarinina \"+\ *n pl, cap* [NL, fr. *eu-* + *Gregarinina*] **:** a suborder of Gregarinida comprising sporozoans that do not exhibit asexual schizogonous reproduction — compare SCHIZOGREGARINARIA

eu·harmonic \(ˌ)yü+\ *adj* [*eu-* + *harmonic*] **:** not tempered **:** ENHARMONIC 3

eu·he·dral \(ˈ)yü¦hēdrəl\ *adj* [*eu-* + *-hedral*] **:** IDIOMORPHIC

eu·he·mer·ism \yü'hēmə,rizəm, -hem-\ *n* -s [*Euhemerus,* 4th cent. B.C. Greek mythographer + E *-ism*] **1** *often cap* **:** a theory held by Euhemerus that the gods of mythology were but deified mortals **2** *sometimes cap* **:** interpretation of myths as traditional accounts of historical persons and events

eu·he·mer·ist \-,rəst\ *n* -s *often attrib* **:** an advocate of euhemerism — **eu·he·mer·is·tic** \(ˌ)═¦═══¦ristik\ *adj* — **eu·he·mer·is·ti·cal·ly** \-tək(ə)lē\ *adv*

eu·he·mer·ize \═'══,rīz\ *vt* -ED/-ING/-S **:** to interpret (mythology) on the theory of euhemerism

eukairite *var of* EUCAIRITE

eu·kary·ote *also* **eu·cary·ote** \yü'kar(ə)rē,ōt\ *n* -s [*eu-* + *kary-* + *-ote* (as in *zygote*)] **:** an organism composed of one or more cells with visibly evident nuclei — **eu·kary·ot·ic** *also* **eu·car·yot·ic** \(ˌ)yü,ka(a)rē¦äd·ik\ *adj*

eu·kinetics \¦yü+\ *n pl but usu sing in constr* [prob. fr. Gk *eukinētos* easily moved, agile (fr. *eu-* + *kinētos* moving, movable, fr. *kinein* to move, set in motion) + E *-ics* — more at HIGHT] **:** a science of well-controlled body movement (as of dancers)

eukolite *or* **eukolyte** *var of* EUCOLITE

eu·la·chon *also* **eu·la·chan** \'yülə,kän, -ləkən\ *or* **oo·la·chan** \'ü-\ *n, pl* **eulachon** *or* **eulachons** *also* **eulachan** *or* **eulachans** *or* **oolachan** *or* **oolachans** [Chinook Jargon *ulâkân*] **:** CANDLEFISH 1

eu·la·lia \yü'lālēə, -lyə\ *n* -s [NL, prob. fr. the name *Eulalia*] **:** any of several ornamental grasses belonging to the genus *Miscanthus* (esp. *M. sinensis*)

eu·lamellibranch \¦yü+\ *n* [NL *Eulamellibranchia*] **:** a eulamellibranchiate mollusk

eu·lamellibranchia \"+\ *n pl, cap* [NL, fr. *eu-* + *Lamellibranchia*] **:** an order of Lamellibranchia comprising bivalve mollusks that have filamentous gills forming two continuous flattened layers on each side of the body, the foot usu. large, and a byssus reduced or absent and that include the oysters, freshwater mussels, clams, cockles, shipworms, and numerous related mollusks — **eu·lamellibranchiate** \"+\ *adj or n*

eu·lamellibranchiata \"+\ [NL, fr. *eu-* + *Lamellibranchiata*] *syn of* EULAMELLIBRANCHIA

eu·la·mia \yü'lāmēə\ [NL, fr. *eu-* + *Lamia,* former name of a genus of fishes, fr. L *lamia* — more at LAMIA] *syn of* CARCHARHINUS

eu·ler diagram \'ȯilə(r)-\ *or* **eu·ler's diagram** \-)z-\ *n, usu cap E* [after Leonhard *Euler* †1783 Swiss mathematician and physicist] **:** a graphic method employing circles to represent relations between and operations on classes and the terms of propositions by inclusion, exclusion, and intersection — compare VENN DIAGRAM

euler's equation *n, usu cap E* **1 :** an equation in alternating-current theory: $e^{ix} = \cos x + i \sin x$ **2 :** any of several differential equations of dynamics

euler's formula *n, usu cap E* **:** a general engineering formula relating to the strength of a long strut and obtained by mathematical analysis assuming the strut to be initially very slightly bent and neglecting the $\left(\frac{dy}{dx}\right)^2$ term in the curvature equation: $P = c\frac{\pi^2 EI}{l^2}$, where P = axial load, E = Young's modulus, I = moment of inertia of transverse section of strut, l = length of strut, c = a constant depending upon the manner of fixing the ends

eu·littoral \(ˈ)yü+\ *n* [*eu-* + *littoral*] **:** a landward subdivision of the littoral zone of a body of water; *esp* **:** the benthic zone that falls between the limits of fluctuation level

eu·lo·gia \yü'lōj(ē)ə\ *n, pl* **eulogi·ae** \-jē,ē\ [MGk, fr. Gk, praise, blessing, gift, fr. *eu-* + *-logia* -logy] **:** ANTIDORON

eu·log·ic \yü'läjik, -lōj-\ *or* **eu·lo·gi·cal** \-jəkəl\ *adj* [*eulogy* + *-ic* or *-ical*] **:** EULOGISTIC

eu·lo·gi·ous \yü'lōjēəs\ *adj* [*eulogy* + *-ous*] *archaic* **:** EULOGISTIC

eu·lo·gism \'yülə,jizəm\ *n* -s [*eulogy* + *-ism*] **:** an expression of eulogy

eu·lo·gist \-jəst\ *n* -s [*eulogy* + *-ist*] **:** one that eulogizes

eu·lo·gis·tic \¦yülə¦jistik, -tēk\ *adj* **:** of, relating to, or characterized by eulogy **:** bestowing praise **:** PANEGYRICAL, LAUDATORY — opposed to *dyslogistic* — **eu·lo·gis·ti·cal·ly** \-tək(ə)lē, -tēk-, -li\ *adv*

eu·lo·gi·um \yü'lōjēəm\ *n, pl* **eulo·gia** \-ēə\ *or* **eulogiums** [ML] **:** EULOGY

eu·lo·gi·za·tion \,yüləjə'zāshən, -,jī'z-\ *n* -s **:** the act of eulogizing **:** PRAISE

eu·lo·gize *also* **eu·lo·gise** \'yülə,jīz\ *vt* -ED/-ING/-S [*eulogy* + *-ize, -ise*] **:** to speak or write in strong commendation of **:** extol in speech or writing **:** PRAISE ⟨one of those rare days in June *eulogized* by poets —Evelyn Barkins⟩

eu·lo·giz·er \-zə(r)\ *n* -s **:** one that eulogizes **:** EULOGIST

eu·lo·gy \'yüləjē, -ji\ *n* -ES [ME *euloge,* fr. ML *eulogium,* alter. (influenced by L *elogium* maxim, saying, inscription on a tombstone) of *eulogia,* fr. Gk, praise, blessing — more at EULOGIA, ELOGE] **1 :** a composition (as a set oration) in commendation of someone or something (as of the character and services of a deceased person) **:** ENCOMIUM **2 :** an expression characteristic of eulogies **:** PRAISE, LAUDATION ⟨mingle ~ with admonition⟩ ⟨the inflated tone of ~ in which their insect authors are lauded —Frances Trollope⟩

¹**eu·loph·id** \yü'läfəd, 'yüləf-\ *adj* [NL *Eulophidae*] **:** of or relating to the Eulophidae

²**eulophid** \"\ *n* -s **:** a chalcid fly of the family Eulophidae

eu·loph·i·dae \yü'läfə,dē\ *n pl, cap* [NL, fr. *Eulophus,* type genus (fr. Gk *eulophos* well plumed, fr. *eu-* + *lophos* nape of the neck, crest) + *-idae*] **:** a large cosmopolitan family of narrow-winged chalcid flies usu. with 4-jointed tarsi that are parasitic as larvae in or on the larvae of various other insects

eu·ly·tite \'yülə,tīt\ *also* **eu·ly·tine** \-,tēn, -,tᵊn\ *n* -s [*eulytite* fr. *eulytine* + *-ite; eulytine* fr. G *eulytin,* fr. Gk *eulytos* easily dissolved (fr. *eu-* + *lytos* soluble, fr. *lyein* to dissolve, release) + G *-in* -ine — more at LOSE] **:** a mineral $Bi_4Si_3O_{12}$ consisting of a bismuth silicate occurring usu. in minute dark-brown or grayish tetrahedral crystals (sp. gr. 6.11)

eu·malacostraca \(ˌ)yü+\ *n pl, cap* [NL, fr. *eu-* + *Malacostraca*] **:** a group of malacostracan crustaceans comprising all Malacostraca except the Leptostraca — **eu·malacostracan** \"+\ *adj or n*

eu·me·ces \yüˈmē(ˌ)sēz\ *n, cap* [NL, fr. Gk *eumēkēs* tall, long, fr. *eu-* + *-mēkēs* (fr. *mēkos* length); akin to Gk *makros* long — more at MEAGER] **:** a large genus of cosmopolitan diurnal carnivorous lizards (family Scincidae) with opaque scaly eyelids and pterygoid teeth

eu·melanin \(ˈ)yü+\ *n* [ISV *eu-* + *melanin*] **:** a dark melanin pigment — compare PHAEOMELANIN

eu·me·nes \ˈyüməˌnēz\ *n, cap* [NL, fr. Gk *eumenēs* well-disposed, fr. *eu-* + *-menēs* (fr. *menos* spirit, intent) — more at MIND] **:** a widely distributed genus (family Vespidae) comprising chiefly black or black and yellow solitary wasps that build jug-shaped cells of mud singly or in rows and stock them with caterpillars as food for the larval wasps — see POTTER WASP — **eu·me·nid** \ˈyüməˌnid, yüˈmenəd\ *adj or n*

eu·men·i·dae \yüˈmenəˌdē\ *n pl, cap* [NL, fr. *Eumenes*, type genus + *-idae*] *in some classifications* **:** a family of wasps containing those solitary mason wasps and potter wasps that are now usu. included in Vespidae — compare EUMENES

eu·metazoa \(ˌ)yü+\ *n pl, cap* [NL, fr. *eu-* + *Metazoa*] *in some classifications* **:** a major division of the animal kingdom comprising all multicellular forms except the sponges — compare PARAZOA — **eu·metazoan** \"+\ *adj or n*

eu·me·to·pi·as \ˌyüməˈtōpēəs\ *n, cap* [NL, fr. *eu-* + Gk *metōpias* having a broad forehead, fr. *metōpon* forehead — more at METOPION] **:** a genus of sea lions including the Australian sea lion and the Steller's sea lion

eu·mitosis \ˌyü+\ *n* [ISV *eu-* + *mitosis*] **:** typical mitosis (as of unicellular organisms)

eu·mitotic \"+\ *adj* [ISV *eu-* + *mitotic*] **1 :** ANASCHISTIC **2 :** of or relating to eumitosis

eu·mol·pique \ēmōlpēk\ *n* -s [F, fr. Gk *eumolpein* to sing well (fr. *eu-* + *-molpein*, akin to Gk *melpein* to sing) + F *-ique* -ic] **:** a poetic measure consisting of two unrhymed Alexandrines with alternate masculine and feminine endings

eu·mor·phic \(ˈ)yüˈmȯrfik\ *adj* [*eu-* + *-morphic*] **:** MESOMORPHIC 2, ATHLETIC 3 — distinguished from *brachymorphic* and *dolichomorphic*

eu·my·ce·tae \ˌyüˌmīˈsēd·(ˌ)ē\ *also* **eu·my·ce·te·ae** \-d·ēˌē\ [NL, fr. *eu-* + *-mycetae*, *-myceteae* (irreg. fr. *-myces*)] *syn of* EUMYCETES

eu·my·cete \yüˈmīˌsēt, ¦==¦=\ *n* -s [NL *Eumycetes*] **:** a fungus of the subdivision Eumycetes

eu·my·ce·tes \ˌyüˌmīˈsēd·ēz\ *n pl, cap* [NL, fr. *eu-* + *-mycetes*] **:** a subdivision of thallophytes comprising all the true fungi as distinguished from myxomycetes and schizomycetes — compare THALLOPHYTA — **eu·my·ce·tic** \¦==¦sēd·ik\ *adj*

eu·nec·tes \yüˈnek(ˌ)tēz\ *n, cap* [NL, fr. *eu-* + Gk *nēktēs* swimmer, fr. *nēchein* to swim; akin to L *nare* to swim — more at NOURISH] **:** a genus of snakes (family Boidae) comprising the anaconda

eu·ni·ce \yüˈnī(ˌ)sē\ *n, cap* [NL, fr. the name *Eunice*] **:** a genus (the type of the family Eunicidae) of marine polychaete worms with complex chitinous jaws including the palolo worm and related forms — **eu·ni·ce·an** \yüˈnīsēən, -nis-\ *adj or n* — **eu·ni·cid** \-səd\ *adj or n*

eu·no·mi·an \yüˈnōmēən\ *n* -s *usu cap* [LGk *eunomianos*, fr. *Eunomios* Eunomius †ab A.D.393 Roman Catholic ecclesiastic who became bishop of Cyzicus in 360] **:** ANOMOEAN

eu·no·mi·an·ism \-ēəˌnizəm\ *n* -s *usu cap* **:** the doctrines of Eunomians **:** extreme Arianism

eu·no·my \ˈyünəmē\ *n* -ES [Gk *eunomia*, fr. *eunomos* having good laws (fr. *eu-* + *nomos* law) + *-ia* -y — more at NIMBLE] **:** civil order under good laws

eu·no·to·sau·rus \ˌyüˌnōd·əˈsȯrəs\ *n, cap* [NL, prob. fr. Gk *eunōtos* stout-backed (fr. *eu-* + *nōtos*, *nōton* back) + NL *-saurus* — more at NATES] **:** a genus of small generalized reptiles from the Middle Permian of southern Africa that have the vertebrae reduced in number and the ribs broad and somewhat leaf-shaped, are often considered ancestral to the turtles, and are commonly placed in a separate suborder of Chelonia

eu·nuch \ˈyünək, -nik, -nēk\ *n* -s [ME *eunuk*, fr. L *eunuchus*, fr. Gk *eunouchos*, fr. *eunē* bed + *-ochos* (fr. *echein* to have, have charge of) — more at SCHEME] **1 :** a castrated man in charge of a harem or employed as a chamberlain in a palace; *often* **:** any chamberlain **2 :** a man or boy whose testes or external genitals have been removed or who is deprived of testicular function by other cause (as inflammation or injury) **3 :** CASTRATO **4 :** one who is impotent, ineffective, or lacking in manhood in any respect ⟨intellectual ~⟩ ⟨political ~⟩

eunuch flute *n* **:** KAZOO

eu·nuch·ism \-ˌkizəm\ *n* -s [LL *eunuchismus*, fr. Gk *eunouchismos*, fr. *eunouchos* + *-ismos* -ism] **:** the condition of being a eunuch

eu·nuch·ize \-ˌkīz\ *vt* -ED/-ING/-s [LL *eunuchizare*, fr. Gk *eunouchizein*, fr. *eunouchos* eunuch + *-izein* -ize] **:** EMASCULATE

¹eu·nuch·oid \-ˌkȯid\ *also* **eu·nuch·oi·dal** \¦==¦kȯidᵊl\ *adj* [*eunuchoid* fr. Gk *eunouchoeidēs*, fr. *eunouchos* + *-oeides* -oid; *eunuchoidal* fr. *eunuchoid* + *-al*] **:** of, relating to, or characterized by eunuchoidism ⟨~ voice⟩ **:** resembling a eunuch

²eunuchoid \"\ *n* -s **:** a sexually deficient individual; *esp* **:** one lacking in sexual differentiation and tending toward the intersex state

eu·nuch·oid·ism \ˈ==ˌkȯiˌdizəm\ *n* -s [ISV *eunuchoid* + *-ism*] **:** a state suggestive of that of a eunuch in being marked by deficiency of sexual development, by persistence of prepuberal characteristics, and often by the presence of characteristics typical of the opposite sex

eu·nuch·ry \ˈ==ˌkrē, -ri\ *n* -ES **:** the state of being a eunuch

eu·o·nym \ˈyüəˌnim\ *n* -s [*eu-* + *-onym*] **:** a name well suited to the person, place, or thing named

eu·on·y·min \yüˈänəmən\ *n* -s [ISV *euonym-* (fr. NL *Euonymus*, genus name of *Euonymus atropurpureus*) + *-in* — more at EUONYMUS] **:** a mixture of impure active principles derived from a wahoo (*Euonymus atropurpureus*); *also* **:** the dry powdered extract of this plant

eu·on·y·mous \(ˈ)=¦==məs\ *adj* [Gk *euōnymos* having an auspicious name] **:** suitably named

eu·on·y·mus \=ˈ==məs\ *n* [NL, fr. L *euonymos* spindle tree, fr. Gk *euōnymos*, fr. *euōnymos* having an auspicious name, fr. *eu-* + *-ōnymos* (fr. *onyma*, *onoma* name) — more at NAME] **1** *cap* **:** a genus of often evergreen shrubs, small trees, or vines (family Celastraceae) of north temperate regions having usu. 4-angled branches, opposite leaves, flowers solitary or in axillary cymes, fruit a lobed capsule, and seed enclosed in a scarlet or orange aril — see SPINDLE TREE, STRAWBERRY BUSH, WAHOO **2** -ES **:** any plant of the genus *Euonymus* **3** -ES **:** the dried bark of the root of a shrub (*Euonymus atropurpureus*) used as a cathartic

euonymus scale *n* **:** a rectangular grayish brown to black scale (*Unaspis euonymi*) that infests euonymus and is common in greenhouses

eu·or·ni·thes \yüˈȯrnəˌthēz, ˌyüˌȯrˈnī(ˌ)thēz\ [NL, fr. *eu-* + *-ornithes*] *syn of* NEOGNATHAE

eu·pa·to·ri·a·ceous \ˌyüpəˌtōrēˈāshəs\ *adj* [NL *Eupatorium* + E *-aceous*] **:** of or belonging to *Eupatorium* or related genera

eu·pa·to·rin \ˌyüpəˈtōrən\ *n* -s [It *eupatorina*, fr. NL *Eupatorium* + It *-ina* -in] **1 :** a bitter glucoside $C_{35}H_{58}NO_{10}$ occurring in boneset **2 :** an eclectic resinoid prepared from boneset and formerly used as a tonic and expectorant

eu·pa·to·ri·um \ˌyüpəˈtōrēəm\ *n* [NL, fr. Gk *eupatorion* hemp agrimony, fr. Mithridates VI *Eupator* †63B.C. king of Pontus] **1** *cap* **:** an immense genus of chiefly tropical herbs (family Compositae) having heads of white or purplish flowers arranged in cymose clusters, a capillary pappus, and 5-angled achenes — see BONESET, HEMP AGRIMONY, JOE-PYE WEED, MISTFLOWER **2** -s **:** any plant of the genus *Eupatorium*

eupatorium purple *n* **:** a moderate reddish purple that is redder, lighter, and stronger than bishop's violet and bluer, lighter, and stronger than heliotrope (sense 4b)

eu·pa·to·ry \ˈyüpəˌtōrē\ *n* -ES [ME *eupatorie* wild sage, fr. LL *eupatorion* horehound, fr. Gk, hemp agrimony] **:** a plant of the genus *Eupatorium*

eu·pat·rid \yüˈpa·trəd, ˈyüpə·t-\ *n, pl* **eupatri·dae** \yüˈpa·trəˌdē\ *often cap* [Gk *eupatridēs*, fr. *eu-* + *patr-*, *patēr* father + *-idēs*, patronymic suffix — more at FATHER] **:** one of the hereditary aristocrats of ancient Athens who in early times exclusively made and administered the law

eu·pav·er·ine \yüˈpavəˌrēn, -rən\ *n* -s [*eu-* + *papaverine*] **:** a synthetic alkaloid $C_{19}H_{15}NO_4$ related to papaverine and used as a relaxant to nonstriated muscle

eu·pep·sia \yüˈpepshə, -epsēə\ *also* **eu·pep·sy** \ˈyüˌpepsē, =ˈ==\ *n, pl* **eupepsias** *also* **eupepsies** [NL *eupepsia*, fr. *eu-* + *-pepsia*] **:** good digestion — opposed to *dyspepsia*

eu·pep·tic \(ˈ)yü¦peptik, -tēk\ *adj* [prob. fr. *eupepsia*, after such pairs as E *dyspepsia: dyspeptic*] **1 :** of, relating to, produced by, or having good digestion — opposed to *dyspeptic* **2 :** CHEERFUL, OPTIMISTIC

eu·phau·si·a·cea \(ˌ)yüˌfȯzēˈāshēə\ *n pl, cap* [NL, fr. *Euphausia*, included genus (perh. fr. *eu-* + Gk *pha-* — fr. *phainein* to show — + *ousia* substance) + *-acea* — more at FANCY, OUSIA] **:** an order of small commonly luminescent malacostracan crustaceans (division Eucarida) related to the Decapoda, resembling shrimps, and in some areas forming an important element of marine plankton — **eu·phau·sid** \(ˈ)yü¦fȯzəd\ *adj or n* — **eu·phau·si·id** \-zēəd\ *adj or n*

eu·phe·mi·ous \(ˈ)yü¦fēmēəs\ *adj* [Gk *euphēmos* auspicious, sounding good + E *-ious*] **:** EUPHEMISTIC — **eu·phe·mi·ous·ly** *adv*

eu·phe·mism \ˈyüfəˌmizəm, -fᵊm,i-\ *n* -s [Gk *euphēmismos*, fr. *euphēmos* auspicious, sounding good (fr. *eu-* + *-phēmos*, fr. *phēmē* speech, fr. *phanai* to say) + *-ismos* -ism — more at -PHEMIA] **1 :** the substitution of an agreeable or inoffensive word or expression for one that is harsh, indelicate, or otherwise unpleasant or taboo **:** allusion to an offensive thing by an inoffensive expression — contrasted with *dysphemism* **2 :** a polite, tactful, or less explicit term used to avoid the direct naming of an unpleasant, painful, or frightening reality (as *pass away* for *die; underprivileged* for *poor*)

eu·phe·mis·tic \ˌyüfə¦mistik, -fᵊm¦i-, -tēk\ *also* **eu·phe·mis·ti·cal** \-təkəl, -tēk-\ *adj* [fr. *euphemism*, after such pairs as E *optimism: optimistic, optimistical*] **:** relating to or of the nature of euphemism **:** containing a euphemism — **eu·phe·mis·ti·cal·ly** \-tək(ə)lē, -tēk-, -li\ *adv*

eu·phe·mize \ˈyüfəˌmīz, -fᵊmˌīz\ *vb* -ED/-ING/-s [fr. *euphemism*, after such pairs as E *criticism: criticize*] *vt* **:** to express by a euphemism ⟨the uneasy effort in America to ~ death —W.J.Fisher⟩ ~ *vi* **:** to make use of euphemistic expressions

eu·phe·miz·er \-zə(r)\ *n* -s **:** one that euphemizes

eu·phone \ˈyüˌfōn\ *n* -s [Gk *euphōnos* sweet-voiced, musical] **:** an 8-foot or 16-foot free-reed organ stop giving a soft expressive tone

¹euphonia *n* -s [LL] *obs* **:** EUPHONY

²eu·pho·nia \yüˈfōnēə, -nyə\ [NL, fr. LL, euphony] *syn of* TANAGRA

³euphonia \"\ *n* -s [NL *Euphonia*] **:** a tanager of the genus *Tanagra*

eu·phon·ic \yüˈfänik, -nēk\ *adj* [*euphony* + *-ic*] **1 :** of or relating to euphony **:** in accordance with the principles of euphony **2** *of an intervocalic consonant* **:** serving to avoid a hiatus (as \t\ in French \ate(l)\ *a-t-il*) — **eu·phon·i·cal·ly** \-nək(ə)lē, -nēk-, -li\ *adv*

eu·phon·i·cal \-nəkəl, -nēk-\ *archaic var of* EUPHONIC

eu·pho·nious \yüˈfōnēəs, -nyəs\ *adj* [*euphony* + *-ous*] **:** pleasing in sound **:** having euphony — **eu·pho·nious·ly** *adv* — **eu·pho·nious·ness** *n* -ES

eu·pho·ni·um \-nēəm\ *n* -s [Gk *euphōnos* sweet-voiced, musical + E *-ium* (as in *harmonium*)] **1 :** a tenor tuba similar in shape, pitch, and range to the baritone but with a larger bore, a mellower tone quality, and often a double bell **2 :** EUPHONE

euphonium

eu·pho·nize \ˈyüfəˌnīz\ *vt* -ED/-ING/-s [*euphony* + *-ize*] **:** to make euphonious

eu·pho·nous \ˈyüfənəs\ *adj* [Gk *euphōnos*] **:** EUPHONIOUS

eu·pho·ny \ˈyüfənē, -ni\ *n* -ES [F *euphonie*, fr. LL *euphonia*, fr. Gk *euphōnia*, fr. *euphōnos* sweet-voiced, musical (fr. *eu-* + *-phōnos*, fr. *phōnē* voice) + *-ia* -y — more at BAN] **1 :** pleasing or sweet sound **:** the acoustic effect produced by words so formed and combined as to please the ear; *esp* **:** a harmonious succession of words having a pleasing sound or striking the ear as being appropriate to the meaning — opposed to *cacophony* **2 :** tendency to greater ease of pronunciation resulting in regularly observed combinative changes that seem to be caused by increased speed of utterance and economy of effort

eu·phor·bia \yüˈfȯ(r)bēə\ *n* [NL, alter. (influenced by NL *-ia*) of L *euphorbea* euphorbia, fr. *Euphorbus* 1st cent A.D. physician to Juba, king of Mauretania] **1** *cap* **:** a large genus of plants (family Euphorbiaceae) of greatly diverse appearance some being fleshy and like cactus, others leafy and herbaceous or shrubby, but all having milky juice and flowers without a calyx and included in an involucre which surrounds a group of several staminate flowers and a central pistillate flower with 3-lobed pistils **2** -s **:** any plant of the genus *Euphorbia* **:** SPURGE

eu·phor·bi·a·ce·ae \=ˌ=ˈāsēˌē\ *n pl, cap* [NL, fr. *Euphorbia*, type genus + *-aceae*] **:** a widely distributed family of herbs, shrubs, or trees (order Geraniales) with usu. milky often poisonous juice, unisexual flowers, and a superior usu. trilocular ovary and including several medicinal plants (as those yielding castor oil and croton oil), several trees yielding caoutchouc, and the cassava — see HEVEA, MANIHOT — **eu·phor·bi·a·ceous** \=¦==¦āshəs\ *adj*

eu·phor·bi·um \=ˈ=bēəm\ *n* -s [ME *euforbium*, fr. ML, fr. Gk *euphorbion* euphorbium, euphorbia, fr. *Euphorbus*] **:** a yellow or brownish very acrid gum resin derived from a Moroccan spurge (*Euphorbia resinifera*) and other African spurges and formerly employed medicinally as an emetic and cathartic but now used chiefly in veterinary medicine as a vesicant

eu·pho·ria \yüˈfōrēə, -fȯr-\ *n* -s [NL, fr. Gk, fr. *eu-* + *-phoria*] **:** a feeling of well-being or elation; *esp* **:** one that is groundless, disproportionate to its cause, or inappropriate to one's life situation

¹eu·pho·ri·ant \-ēənt\ *n* -s [*euphoria* + ¹*-ant*] **:** a drug that tends to induce euphoria

²euphoriant \"\ *adj* [*euphoria* + ²*-ant*] **:** tending to induce euphoria ⟨a ~ drug⟩

eu·phor·ic \yüˈfȯrik, -fär-,-fōr-\ *adj* [*euphoria* + *-ic*] **:** characterized by or based on euphoria ⟨a ~ mood⟩

eu·pho·ry \ˈyüfərē\ *n* -ES [NL *euphoria*] **:** EUPHORIA

eu·pho·tic \(ˈ)yü¦fōd·ik\ *adj* [ISV *eu-* + *photic*] **:** of, relating to, or constituting the upper layers of a body of water into which sufficient light penetrates to permit growth of green plants

eu·phra·sia \yüˈfrāzh(ē)ə\ *n, cap* [NL, fr. ML *eufrasia* euphrasy] **:** a large genus of hemiparasitic herbs (family Scrophulariaceae) widely distributed outside the tropics and having flowers with the upper lip of the corolla 2-cleft and its margin recurved

eu·phra·sy \ˈyüfrəsē\ *n* -ES [ME *eufrasie*, fr. ML *eufrasia*, fr. Gk *euphrasia* good cheer, fr. *euphrainein* to gladden, fr. *eu-* + *-phrainein* (fr. *phrēn* mind) — more at FRENETIC] **:** an eyebright (*Euphrasia officinalis*)

eu·phra·te·an \yüˈfrād·ēən\ *adj, cap* [*Euphrates*, river in southwest Asia + E *-an*] **:** of or belonging to the Euphrates river or its valley

eu·phroe \ˈyüˌfrō\ *n* -s [D *juffrouw*, *juffer* miss, madam, lady, euphroe, fr. MD *joncfrouwe, juffrouwe* miss, madam, young lady; akin to OFris *jungfrouwe* young lady, girl, OHG *jungfrouwa*; all fr. a prehistoric WGmc compound whose first constituent is represented by OE *geong* young and whose second constituent is represented by OHG *frouwa* mistress, lady — more at YOUNG, FRAU] **1 :** a block or slat of wood perforated for the passage of the parts of a crowfoot **2 :** TENT SLIDE

eu·phu·ism \ˈyüfyəˌwizəm\ *n* -s [*Euphues*, character in the prose romances *Euphues, the Anatomy of Wit* (1579) and *Euphues and his England* (1580) by John Lyly †1606 Eng. author + E *-ism*] **1 :** an affected style of conversation and writing fashionable in the time of Elizabeth I and characterized by antithesis, alliteration, similes, and a pervading effort after elegance; *also* **:** an example of such style **2 :** artificial and excessive elegance of language **:** high-flown diction — **eu·phu·ist** \-ˌwəst\ *n* -s — **eu·phu·is·tic** \¦==¦wistik\ *or* **eu·phu·is·ti·cal** \-təkəl\ *adj* — **eu·phu·is·ti·cal·ly** \-k(ə)lē\ *adv*

eu·phu·ize \ˈ==ˌwīz\ *vi* -ED/-ING/-s [*Euphues* + E *-ize*] **:** to use euphuistic language

eu·phyllopoda \ˌyü+\ [NL, fr. *eu-* + *Phyllopoda*] *syn of* BRANCHIOPODA

eu·plastic \(ˈ)yü+\ *adj* [*eu-* + *plastic*] **:** adapted to the formation of tissue **:** BLASTEMATIC

eu·plec·tel·la \ˌyüˌplekˈtelə\ *n, cap* [NL, fr. Gk *euplektos* well plaited (fr. *eu-* + *plektos* plaited, fr. *plekein* to plait) + NL *-ella* — more at PLY] **:** a genus of hyalosponges comprising the Venus's-flower-basket, having a skeleton of interwoven siliceous spicules, and growing in the form of a cornucopia

eu·plex·op·te·ra \ˌyüˌplekˈsäptərə\ [NL, fr. *eu-* + *plexo-* (fr. L *plexus*, past part. of *plectere* to plait, weave) + *-ptera* — more at PLY] *syn of* DERMAPTERA

¹eu·ploid \ˈyüˌplȯid\ *adj* [ISV *eu-* + *-ploid*] **:** having a chromosome number that is an exact multiple of the monoploid number

²euploid \"\ *n* -s **:** a euploid individual, strain, or cell; *esp* **:** one having three or more identical genomes

eu·ploidy \-dē\ *n* -ES **:** euploid quality or state

eu·plo·tes \yüˈplōd·(ˌ)ēz\ *n, cap* [NL, fr. *eu-* + *-plotes* (prob. irreg. fr. Gk *plōt-*, *plōs* swimmer, fr. *plein* to sail, swim) — more at FLOW] **:** a genus (the type of the family Euplotidae) of large rigid ovoid hypotrichous ciliates extremely common in fresh and salt water — **eu·plo·tid** \-ōd·əd\ *adj or n*

eup·nea *also* **eup·noea** \ˈyüpnēə, =ˈ==\ *n* -s [NL, fr. Gk *eupnoia*, fr. *eupnoos*, *eupnous* breathing freely (fr. *eu-* + *-pnoos*, *-pnous*, fr. *pnoē* breathing, fr. *pnein* to breathe) + *-ia* — more at SNEEZE] **:** normal respiration — distinguished from *dyspnea* — **eup·ne·ic** \(ˈ)yüp¦nēik\ *adj*

eu·po·li·de·an \ˌyüˌpälə¦dēən, ˌyüpəl-; ˌyüpə¦lidē-\ *n* -s *usu cap* [Gk *eupolideion* Eupolidean (fr. neut. of *eupolideios* in the style of Eupolis, fr. *Eupolid-*, *Eupolis* Eupolis, 5th cent. B.C. Greek writer of comedies) + E *-an*] **:** the characteristic meter used by Eupolis composed of two polyschematist choriambic dimeters the second of which is catalectic (as oooo-◡◡- oooo-◡-)

eu·po·ma·tia \ˌyüpəˈmāsh(ē)ə\ *n, cap* [NL, fr. *eu-* + Gk *pōmat-*, *pōma* lid + NL *-ia* — more at POMACENTRIDAE] **:** a small Australasian genus (the type of the family Eupomatiaceae of the order Ranales) comprising trees and shrubs with large staminodia that resemble petals between the anther-bearing stamens and the stigma so that pollination can only be effected by insects

eu·potamic \ˌyü+\ *adj* [*eu-* + *potamic*] *of aquatic organisms* **:** thriving in both flowing and still fresh waters — compare AUTOPOTAMIC, TYCHOPOTAMIC

eu·prac·tic \(ˈ)yü¦praktik\ *adj* [fr. *eupraxia*, after E *apraxia: apractic*] **:** relating to or having normally coordinated muscular performance

eu·prax·ia \yüˈpraksēə, -kshə\ *n* -s [NL, fr. *eu-* + *-praxia*] **:** normally coordinated muscular performance — contrasted with *apraxia*

eup·tel·ea \yüpˈtelēə, -tēl-\ *n, cap* [NL, fr. *eu-* + Gk *ptelea* elm — more at PTELEA] **:** a small genus of Asiatic shrubs and trees (family Trochodendraceae) with apetalous showy red flowers

eup·te·ro·ti·dae \ˌyüptəˈrōd·əˌdē, -räd-\ *n pl, cap* [NL, fr. *Eupterote*, type genus (fr. *eu-* + Gk *pterōtē*, fem. of *pterōtos* feathered, fr. *pteron* feather) + *-idae* — more at FEATHER] **:** a family of large moths having strongly pectinate antennae and lacking proboscis and tympanum

eu·pyr·chro·ite \ˌyüpə(r)ˈkrōˌīt\ *n* -s [*eu-* + Gk *pyr* fire + *chroia*, *chroa* color + E *-ite*; akin to Gk *chrōs* skin, color — more at CHROMATIC] **:** a mineral composed of a concretionary variety of apatite

eu·pyrene \(ˈ)yü+\ *adj* [ISV *eu-* + *-pyrene* (fr. Gk *pyrēn* stone of a fruit); prob. orig. formed as G *eupyren* — more at FURZE] **:** having a normal nucleus ⟨a ~ sperm⟩ — compare APYRENE, OLIGOPYRENE

eu·pyr·i·on \yüˈpirēən\ *n* -s [*eu-* + Gk *pyreion* fire stick, fr. *pyr* fire — more at FIRE] **:** an early-19th-century match having a tip coated with sugar and potassium chlorate to be ignited by being dipped in sulfuric acid

eur- *or* **euro-** *comb form, cap* [*Europe*] **:** European and ⟨*Eurafrican*⟩

¹eur·african \(ˈ)yůr+\ *adj, usu cap* [ISV *Eur-* + *African*] **1 :** of or belonging to the continents of Europe and Africa combined **2 :** of or relating to the biogeographic region that includes most of Europe and northern Africa south to the Sahara **3 :** of mixed European and African descent

²eurafrican \"\ *n, cap* **1 :** an assumed prehistoric subrace or type from which originated Mediterraneans of Europe and certain No. African peoples (as in Algeria, Egypt, and Ethiopia); *also* **:** a person of such a subrace or type **2 :** a person of European and African descent

eur·american \ˌyůr+\ *or* **euro-american** \ˌyů(ˌ)rō+\ *adj, cap E & usu cap A after hyphen* [*Eur-* + *American*] **:** common to Europe and America **:** OCCIDENTAL ⟨*Euramerican* flora⟩ ⟨culture patterns that are variants of our common *Euramerican* culture —W.H.Wickwar⟩

euraquilo *usu cap, var of* EUROAQUILO

eur·asian \yər, (ˈ)yůr+\ *adj, usu cap* [*Eur-* + *Asian*] **:** relating to Europe and Asia as a whole **:** common to adjacent parts of Europe and Asia or to the whole **:** of a mixed European and Asiatic origin ⟨*Eurasian* race⟩ ⟨*Eurasian* fauna⟩

²eurasian \"\ *n, cap* **:** a person of mixed European and Asian descent — often taken to be offensive esp. in India; compare ANGLO-INDIAN

eur·asiatic \(ˌ)yůr, yər+\ *adj, usu cap* [fr. *Eurasia*, Europe and Asia as one continent, after *Asia:* E *Asiatic*] **1 :** of or relating to Europe and Asia taken as a unit **:** EURASIAN **2 :** PALAEARCTIC

eu·re·ka \yəˈrēkə\ *interj* [Gk *heurēka* I have found, 1st pers. sing. perf. indic. act. of *heuriskein* to find; fr. the exclamation attributed to Archimedes †212B.C., Greek mathematician and inventor, on discovering a method for determining the purity of gold — more at HEURISTIC] — used to express triumph concerning a discovery

eureka red *n* **:** PUCE

eu·rhodine \yəˈrōˌdēn, -ˌdᵊn\ *n* -s [ISV *eu-* + *rhod-* (fr. Gk *rhodon* rose) + *-ine*; orig. formed as G *eurhodin* — more at ROSE] **:** any of a class of amino-substituted phenazine dyes (as neutral red)

eu·rho·dol \-ˌdȯl, -ˌdōl\ *n* -s [ISV *eurhod-* (fr. *eurhodine*) + *-ol*] **:** any of a class of dyes differing from the eurhodines only in containing hydroxyl in place of an amino group or groups

eurhythmic *var of* EURYTHMIC

eu·rip·i·de·an \yə¦ripə¦dēən\ *adj, usu cap* [L *euripideus* Euripidean (fr. Gk *euripideios*, fr. *Euripidēs* Euripides, 5th cent. B.C. Greek playwright) + E *-an*] **:** of, relating to, or characteristic of Euripides or his tragedies

eu·ri·pus \yəˈrīpəs\ *n, pl* **euri·pi** \-ˌpī\ [L, fr. Gk *euripos*] **1 :** a narrow tract of water where the tide or a current flows and reflows with violence **:** STRAIT, CHANNEL **2 :** a condition of rapid or dangerous fluctuation

eu·ro \ˈyů(ˌ)rō\ *n, pl* **euro** *or* **euros** [native name in Australia] **:** a large reddish gray kangaroo (*Macropus robustus*) — called also *wallaroo*

euro- — see EUR-

euro-american *usu cap E&A, var of* EURAMERICAN

eu·ro·aq·ui·lo \ˌyůrəˈakwəˌlō\ *also* **eur·aq·ui·lo** \yəˈrak-\ *n* -s *usu cap* [LL *euroaquilo*, fr. *euro-* (fr. L *eurus* east wind, fr. Gk *euros*) + L *aquilo* north wind] **:** GREGALE

eu·ro·bin \yəˈrōbən\ *n* [ISV *eu-* + *-robin* (as in *chrysarobin*); orig. formed in G] **:** the triacetate of chrysarobin formerly used as a substitute therefor in ointments

eu·roc·ly·don \yəˈräkləˌdän\ *n* -s *usu cap* [Gk *euroklydōn*, MS var. (in Acts 27:14) of *eurakylōn*, fr. *eur-* (fr. *euros* east wind) + (assumed) Gk *akylōn* north wind, fr. L *aquilon-*, *aquilo*] **:** GREGALE

eu·rope \ˈyůrəp, ˈyür-\ *adj, usu cap* [fr. *Europe*, continent extending west from Asia] **:** of or from the continent of Europe **:** of the kind or style prevalent in Europe **:** EUROPEAN

[1]**eu·ro·pe·an** \¦yu̇rə¦pēən, ¦yür-\ *adj, usu cap* [L *europaeus* European (fr. Gk *eurōpaios*, fr. *Eurōpē* Europe) + E *-an*] **1** : of, relating to, or belonging to Europe or its inhabitants **2** *of a plant or animal* : native to Europe : originating in Europe — used esp. (1) to distinguish Old World forms from New World forms known by the same name ⟨*European* robin⟩ and (2) to distinguish an introduced form from a native New World form ⟨*European* corn borer⟩

[2]**european** \"\ *n* -s *cap* **1 a** : a native or inhabitant of Europe **b** : a person of European descent **2 a** : a member of a race inhabiting Europe **b** *in southern and eastern Africa and Asia* : a white person : CAUCASIAN

european alder *n, usu cap E* **1** : a tree (*Alnus vulgaris*) with woody fruiting aments and leaves hairy beneath **2** : GRAY ALDER

european apple sawfly *n, usu cap E* : an Old World sawfly (*Hoplocampa testudinea*) now established on both coasts of No. America and becoming a serious pest esp. of early apples

european ash *n, usu cap E* : a tall Eurasian tree (*Fraxinus excelsior*) having leaves that are dark green and glabrous above and paler and often pubescent on the veins beneath with 7 to 11 oval leaflets

european aspen *n, usu cap E* : a small open-headed tree (*Populus tremula*) of Europe, northern Africa, and Siberia having leaves with rounded irregular notches

european barberry *n, usu cap E* : COMMON BARBERRY

european beachgrass *n, usu cap E* : a beach grass (*Ammophila arenaria*)

european beech *n, usu cap E* : a European tree (*Fagus sylvatica*) with smooth gray bark and minutely toothed often purple leaves widely planted in No. America as an ornamental

european bindweed *n, usu cap E* : FIELD BINDWEED

european bird cherry *n, usu cap E* **1** : a small to medium-sized cherry (*Prunus padus*) closely resembling the chokecherry (*Prunus virginiana*) but having larger flowers and a strongly ridged stone **2** : the small black fruit of the European bird cherry

european bittersweet *n, usu cap E* : BITTERSWEET 2a

european blastomycosis *n, usu cap E* : CRYPTOCOCCOSIS

european brooklime *n, usu cap E* : WALL INK

european canker *n, usu cap E* **1** : a disease of the apple, pear, and other fruit and shade trees caused by a fungus (*Nectria galligena*) producing cankers on the trunks and branches characterized by concentric rings of callus **2** : a disease of poplars caused by a fungus (*Dothichiza populea*)

european chafer *n, usu cap E* : an Old World May beetle (*Amphimallon majalis*) now established in parts of eastern No. America where the larvae are a destructive pest feeding on the roots of turf grasses

european chestnut *n, usu cap E* : SPANISH CHESTNUT

european chicken flea *n, usu cap E* : a flea (*Ceratophyllus gallinae*) native to northern Europe that has become a serious pest of domestic fowls in parts of northern and western No. America

european columbine *n, usu cap E* : a common garden columbine (*Aquilegia vulgaris*) with spurred blue flowers

european cranberry *n, usu cap E* : a small red-fruited trailing cranberry (*Vaccinium oxycoccus*) found in arctic and cool regions of the northern hemisphere with leaves ovate, acute, and conspicuously whitened beneath, flowers terminal, and fruit ¼ to ⅓ inch in diameter — called also *small cranberry*; compare AMERICAN CRANBERRY

european earwig *n, usu cap 1st E* : a large earwig (*Forficula auricularia*) native to Europe but now a pest in various parts of the world

european elder *n, usu cap 1st E* : an elder tree or bush native to Europe; *esp* : BOURTREE

european elm *n, usu cap 1st E* : ENGLISH ELM

european elm scale *n, usu cap 1st E* : a reddish brown unarmored scale (*Gossyparia spuria*) introduced into No. America from Europe, feeding esp. on the underside of the limbs of various elms, secreting great quantities of honeydew, and sometimes killing the trees

european fly honeysuckle *n, usu cap E* : a cultivated Eurasian shrub (*Lonicera xylosteum*) with twin yellowish white flowers and scarlet fruit

european foulbrood *n, usu cap E* : a foulbrood that is caused by a bacillus (*Bacillus alvei*) and that differs from American foulbrood chiefly in the absence of ropiness of affected larvae

european fruit scale *n, usu cap E* : an armored scale (*Aspidiotus ostreaeformis*) common on ornamental and deciduous fruit trees in Europe and No. America

european gooseberry *n, usu cap E* : ENGLISH GOOSEBERRY

european grape *n, usu cap E* : VINIFERA

european honeysuckle *n, usu cap E* **1** : EUROPEAN FLY HONEYSUCKLE **2** : a woodbine (*Lonicera periclymenum*)

european house borer *n, usu cap E* : a wood-boring beetle (*Hylotrupes bajulus*) native to northern Europe but widely distributed by commerce that feeds as larva and adult in dry timbers and is esp. destructive in soft woods

eu·ro·pe·an·ism \,==ˈ=ə,nizəm\ *n* -s *usu cap* **1** : traditions, customs, ideals, or traits distinctive of Europeans **2** : the ideal or advocacy of the political and economic unification of Europe ⟨believes that Germany and France are pursuing, under the guise of *Europeanism* or internationalism, a purely national policy —Hans Kohn⟩

eu·ro·pe·an·iza·tion \-ənəˈzāshən, -ə,nīˈz-\ *n* -s *usu cap* : the act, process, or result of Europeanizing

eu·ro·pe·an·ize \-ˈpēə,nīz\ *vt* -ED/-ING/-s *often cap* **1** : to modify to accord with a continental European pattern in characteristics, customs, or ideas **2** : to denationalize and subject (a territory) to the supervision of an agency of a European community of nations

european larch *n, usu cap E* : a larch (*Larix decidua*) having pubescent cone scales — compare TAMARACK 1a

eu·ro·pe·an·ly \¦==¦===\ *adv, usu cap* : in a European manner

european mountain ash *n, usu cap E* : ROWAN TREE 1

european oyster *n, usu cap E* : the common edible oyster (*Ostrea edulis*) of northern and western Europe

european partridge *n, usu cap E* : HUNGARIAN PARTRIDGE

european pasqueflower *n, usu cap E* : a highly variable European perennial herb (*Anemone pulsatilla*) typically having violet or white campanulate flowers in spring

european pine shoot moth *n, usu cap E* : an olethreutid moth (*Rhyacionia buoliana*) native to Europe but introduced in eastern No. America and having a larva that feeds on the tips of pines (as the red pine)

european plan *n, usu cap E* : a hotel rate whereby guests are charged a fixed sum for lodging and service only and meals are not included — contrasted with *American plan*

european plum *n, usu cap E* : any of several cultivated plums derived chiefly from a plum (*Prunus domestica*) of southwestern Asia — compare AMERICAN PLUM

european pond tortoise *or* **european pond turtle** *n, usu cap E* : a small European freshwater turtle (*Emys orbicularis*)

european raspberry *n, usu cap E* : an upright diffuse red-fruited shrub (*Rubus idaeus*) of Europe extensively cultivated and sometimes an escape in America

european red elder *n, usu cap 1st E* : a glabrous European ornamental shrub (*Sambucus racemosa*) with paniculate cymes of yellow or white flowers followed by red fruits

european red mite *n, usu cap E* : a very small bright or brownish red oval mite (*Panonychus ulmi*) that is now nearly cosmopolitan in distribution and is a destructive orchard pest that sucks juices and chlorophyll from the leaves of fruit and other trees

european spruce *n, usu cap E* : NORWAY SPRUCE

european spruce sawfly *n, usu cap E* : a sawfly (*Diprion hercyniae*) native to Europe but introduced into Canada and the northern U.S. the larva of which seriously defoliates spruce

european tortoise *n, usu cap E* : a small land tortoise (*Testudo graeca*) of southern Europe with olive carapacial shields bordered in black

european vervain *n, usu cap E* : a perennial European herb (*Verbena officinalis*) with small spicate bluish purple flowers — called also *herb-of-the-cross*

european walnut *n, usu cap E* : ENGLISH WALNUT

european wheat stem sawfly *n, usu cap E* : a sawfly (*Cephus pygmaeus*) native to Europe but now widespread in grain-growing areas that has larvae which bore in the stalks of growing wheat and other small grains

european white birch *n, usu cap E* : a birch (*Betula pendula*) with slender pendulous branches and white peeling bark that is often confused with a white birch (*B. alba*)

european wildcat *n, usu cap E* : a brown or grayish black-striped wildcat (*Felis sylvestris*) native to most of Europe but now extinct over most of its range and regarded as one of the ancestors of the domestic cat

european winter moth *n, usu cap E* : a European geometrid moth (*Operophtera brumata*) introduced in parts of Nova Scotia and having a looper larva very destructive as a defoliator of fruit and other deciduous trees

eu·ro·peo- \¦yu̇rə¦pē(,)ō, ¦yür-\ *comb form, cap* [L *europaeus* European — more at EUROPEAN] : European and ⟨*Europeo-*Asiatic⟩

eu·ro·pic \yəˈrōpik\ *adj* [NL *europium* + E *-ic*] : relating to compounds of europium in which it is trivalent

eu·ro·pi·um \yəˈrōpēəm\ *n* -s [NL, fr. *Europe* + NL *-ium*] : a bivalent and trivalent metallic element of the rare-earth group found in very small amounts in monazite sand — symbol *Eu*; see ELEMENT table

eu·ro·poid \ˈyu̇rə,pȯid, ˈyür-; yəˈrō,p-\ *or* **eu·ro·pid** \ˈyu̇rə,pid, ˈyür-, -,pəd; yəˈrōpəd\ *n* -s *usu cap* [ISV *europ-* (fr. *Europe*) + *-oid* or *-id*] : CAUCASOID

eu·ro·pous \yəˈrōpəs\ *adj* [NL *europium* + E *-ous*] : relating to compounds of europium in which it is bivalent

euros *pl of* EURO

eu·ro·ti·a·les \yə,rōd·ēˈā(,)lēz, -ōshē-\ *n pl, cap* [NL, fr. *Eurotium*, included genus (fr. Gk *eurōt-*, *eurōs* mold + NL *-ium*) + *-ales*] : an order (subclass Euascomycetes) of fungi (as the blue molds) having a closed ascocarp with the asci scattered rather than collected into a hymenial layer

eury- *comb form* [NL, fr. Gk, fr. *eurys*; akin to Skt *uru* broad, wide] : broad ⟨*eury*gnathic⟩ : wide ⟨*eury*benthic⟩ ⟨*eury*haline⟩ — opposed to *sten-*

eu·rya \ˈyu̇rēə\ *n, cap* [NL, irreg. fr. Gk *eurys*] : a genus of Asiatic evergreen trees and shrubs (family Theaceae) having foliage resembling that of holly, small white flowers, and globose black fruit and being cultivated in mild regions as ornamentals

eu·ry·a·lae \yəˈrīə(,)lē\ [irreg. fr. NL *Euryale*] *syn of* EURYALIDA

eu·ry·a·le \-(,)lē\ *n, cap* [NL, fr. Gk *Euryalē*, one of the Gorgons] : a widely distributed genus of basket stars

eu·ry·al·i·da \,yu̇rēˈaləda\ *n pl, cap* [NL, fr. *Euryale* + *-ida*] : an order or other division of Ophiuroidea comprising the basket stars and related forms with the arms dichotomously branched and capable of acting as tentacles — **eu·ry·al·i·dan** \¦==¦=əd°n\ *adj or n*

eu·ry·apteryx \¦yu̇rē+\ *n, cap* [NL, fr. *eury-* + *Apteryx*] : a genus of moas closely related to *Anomalopteryx*

eu·ry·bath·ic \¦yu̇rə¦bathik, -rē¦-\ *adj* [*eury-* + Gk *bathos* depth + E *-ic* — more at BATHOS] : living on the bottom of a body of water at varying depths — opposed to *stenobathic*

eu·ry·ben·thic \-¦ben(t)thik\ *adj* [*eury-* + Gk *benthos* depth + E *-ic* — more at BENTHOS] : EURYBATHIC

eu·ry·cea \yəˈrish(ē)ə, -isēə\ *n, cap* [NL] : a common genus of No. American neotenic salamanders (family Plethodontidae)

eu·ry·ce·phal·ic \¦yu̇rə|sə¦falik, -rē|\ *also* **eu·ry·ceph·a·lous** \¦ˈsefələs\ *adj* [NL *eurycephalus* eurycephalic person (fr. *eury-* + *-cephalus*) + E *-ic* or *-ous*] : having a cephalic index of 80 to 84 : BRACHYCEPHALIC

eu·ry·cne·mic \¦yu̇rə(k)¦nēmik, -rē(-\ *adj* [*eury-* + *-cnemic* (as in *platycnemic*)] *of a shinbone* : dorsoventrally flattened with a platycnemic index of 70 or more

eu·ry·ene \ˈyu̇rē,ēn, -rē,ēn\ *adj* [G *euryen*, fr. *eury-* + *-en* (fr. Gk *-ēnēs* in *prosēnēs* gentle and *apēnēs* cruel, taken as having the etymological meanings "with face turned toward one" and "with averted face" respectively); perh. akin to Skt *ānana* mouth, face] : having a short or broad forehead or both with an upper facial index of 45 to 50 — **eu·ry·eny** \-nē\ *n* -ES

eu·ry·gae·an \¦yu̇rə¦jēən\ *adj, usu cap* [NL *Eurygaea* Palaearctic region (fr. *eury-* + *-gaea*) + E *-an*] : PALAEARCTIC

eu·ryg·a·mous \yəˈrigəməs\ *also* **eu·ry·gam·ic** \¦yu̇rə¦gamik\ *adj* [*eury-* + *-gamous* or *-gamic*] *of insects* : mating on the wing : engaging in a nuptial flight — opposed to *stenogamous*

eu·ry·gnath·ic \¦yu̇rə(g)¦nathik, -rē(-\ *also* **eu·ryg·na·thous** \yəˈrignəthəs\ *adj* [F *eurygnathe* eurygnathic (fr. *eury-* + *-gnathe* -gnathous) + E *-ic* or *-ous*] : having a wide jaw — **eu·ryg·na·thism** \yəˈrignə,thizəm\ *n* -s

eu·ry·ha·line \¦yu̇rə¦hā,līn, -ha,-, -,lən\ *also* **eu·ry·ha·lin** \-,lən\ *adj* [ISV *eury-* + *-haline*, *-halin* (fr. Gk *halinos* of salt, fr. *hals* salt) — more at SALT] : able to live in waters of a wide range of salinity — opposed to *stenohaline*

eu·ry·lai·mi \,yu̇rəˈlī,mī, -lā,-\ *n pl, cap* [NL, fr. *Eurylaimus*, included genus, fr. *eury-* + Gk *laimos* throat; perh. akin to OE *lathian* to invite — more at LURE] : a suborder (coextensive with the family Eurylaimidae) of Passeriformes consisting of the broadbills

eu·ry·mer·ic \¦yu̇rə¦merik, -rē¦-\ *adj* [*eury-* + *-meric* (as in *platymeric*)] : having a broad femur with a platymeric index of 85 to 100

eu·ry·on \ˈyu̇rē,än\ *n* -s [NL, irreg. fr. Gk *eurys* broad] : either of the lateral points marking the ends of the greatest transverse diameter of the skull

eu·ry·pel·ma \,yu̇rəˈpelmə\ *n, cap* [NL, fr. *eury-* + Gk *pelma* sole of the foot; akin to L *pellis* skin, hide — more at FELL] : a genus of large hairy burrowing spiders (family Theraphosidae) of the western U.S. popularly held to be venomous that includes the typical New World tarantulas

eu·ry·phage \ˈyu̇rə,fāj\ *n* -s [ISV *eury-* + *-phage*] : a euryphagous animal

eu·ryph·a·gous \yəˈrifəgəs\ *adj* [ISV *eury-* + *-phagous*] : eating various kinds of foods : POLYPHAGOUS — opposed to *stenophagous*

eu·ry·plas·tic \¦yu̇rə¦plastik, -rē¦-\ *adj* [*eury-* + *plastic*] : exhibiting great capacity for modification and adaptability to a wide range of environmental conditions : capable of great evolutionary differentiation — opposed to *stenoplastic*; compare PSEUDOPLASTIC — **eu·ry·plas·ty** \ˈ==,plastē\ *n* -ES

eu·ry·prognathous \¦yu̇rə, -rē+\ *adj* [*eury-* + *prognathous*] : having broad prognathous jaws

eu·ry·prosopic \¦yu̇rə, -rē+\ *adj* [G *euryprosop* euryprosopic (fr. *eury-* + Gk *prosōpon* face) + E *-ic* — more at PROSOP-] : having a short or broad face or both with a facial index of 80 to 85 — **eu·ry·pros·o·py** \,==+ˈpräsəpē, -prəˈsōpē\ *n* -ES

[1]**eu·ryp·te·rid** \yəˈriptərəd\ *adj* [NL *Eurypterida*] : of or relating to the Eurypterida

[2]**eurypterid** \"\ *n* -s : one of the Eurypterida

eu·ryp·ter·i·da \,yu̇rə(p)ˈterəda, -ürə(-\ *n pl, cap* [NL, fr. *Eurypterus*, included genus (fr. *eury-* + *-pterus*) + *-ida*] : an order of aquatic Paleozoic arthropods commonly forming with the related king crabs the class Merostomata, having a cephalothorax with six pairs of limbs of which the last pair were usu. shaped like paddles and a tapering abdomen of 13 segments, and including the largest known arthropods, some exceeding 6 feet in length

[1]**eu·ryp·te·roid** \yəˈriptə,rȯid\ *adj* [NL *Eurypteroidea*] : resembling or relating to the Eurypterida

[2]**eurypteroid** \"\ *n* -s : one of the Eurypterida

eu·ryp·te·roi·dea \yə,riptəˈrȯidēə\ [NL, fr. *Eurypterus* + *-oidea*] *syn of* EURYPTERIDA

eu·ry·py·ga \,yu̇rəˈpīgə\ *n, cap* [NL, fr. *eury-* + *-pyga*] : a genus (coextensive with the family Eurypygidae) that includes solely the sun-grebes — compare GRUIFORMES

eu·ry·py·lous \¦yu̇rə¦pīləs\ *or* **eu·ry·pyl·lous** \-¦piləs\ *adj* [*eurypylus* fr. *eury-* + *pyl-* + *-ous*; *eurypyllous* alter. of *eurypylous*] : having a wide opening; *specif, of a sponge* : having a direct connection between the flagellated chambers and their apopyles and prosopyles

eu·ry·some \ˈyu̇rə,sōm\ *also* **eu·ry·so·mat·ic** \¦yu̇rəsō¦mad·ik\ *or* **eu·ry·so·mic** \-¦sōmik\ *adj* [*eurysome* ISV *eury-* + *-some*; *eurysomatic* prob. alter. (influenced by *somatic*) of *eurysome*; *eurysomic* prob. fr. *eurysome* + *-ic*] *anthrop* : having a broad thickset body build — opposed to *leptosome*

eu·ry·stom·a·tous \¦yu̇rə¦stäməd·əs, -rē¦-, -tōm-\ *adj* [prob. fr. NL *eurystomatus*, fr. *eury-* + *-stomatus* -stomatous] *zool* : having a broad mouth : having the mouth dilatable

eu·ry·therm \ˈyu̇rə,thərm\ *n* -s [prob. fr. G *eurytherm* eurythermal, fr. *eury-* + *-therm* (fr. Gk *thermē* heat) — more at THERM] : an organism that tolerates a wide range of temperature

eu·ry·ther·mal \¦yu̇rə¦thərməl, -rē¦-\ *or* **eu·ry·ther·mic** \-mik\ *or* **eu·ry·ther·mous** \-məs\ *adj* [prob. fr. G *eurytherm* + E *-al* or *-ic* or *-ous*] : able to live in a wide range of temperatures — opposed to *stenothermal*

eu·ryth·mic *or* **eu·rhyth·mic** \(ˈ)yü¦rithmik *sometimes* -th-\ *also* **eu·ryth·mi·cal** *or* **eu·rhyth·mi·cal** \-məkəl\ *adj* [*eurythmy* + *-ic* or *-ical*] **1** : HARMONIOUS ⟨~ proportions in architecture⟩ **2** : of or relating to eurythmy or eurythmics

eu·ryth·mics *also* **eu·rhyth·mics** \=ˈ=miks\ *n pl but usu sing in constr* **1** : the art of harmonious and expressive bodily movement; *specif* : this art as applied in music education through expressive timed movements in response to improvised musical effects chiefly according to a system devised by Émile Jaques-Dalcroze **2** : eurythmy applied to dancing; *specif* : a kind of dancing based on musical patterns and used in the study of musical rhythm and phrasing

eu·ryth·my *also* **eu·rhyth·my** \=ˈ=mē, ˈ=,=mē\ *n* -ES [L *eurythmia*, fr. Gk, fr. *eurythmos* rhythmical, well proportioned (fr. *eu-* + *rhythmos* rhythm, proportion) + *-ia* -y — more at RHYTHM] **1** : harmonious proportion or movement **2** [G *eurhythmie*, fr. L *eurythmia*] : a system of harmonious body movement to the rhythm of spoken words devised for dance training by Rudolph Steiner

eu·ry·tom·i·dae \,yu̇rəˈtämə,dē\ *n pl, cap* [NL, fr. *Eurytoma*, type genus (fr. *eury-* + *-toma*) + *-idae*] : a family of black or black and yellowish chalcid flies which have the abdomen rounded and compressed and some of which are parasitic on other insects while others are plant feeders and important pests esp. of grains — see JOINTWORM

eu·ry·top·ic \¦yu̇rə¦täpik\ *adj* [prob. fr. G *eurytop* eurytopic (fr. *eury-* + *-top*, fr. Gk *topos* place) + E *-ic* — more at TOPIC] : having a wide range of tolerance to variation of one or more environmental factors — compare STENOTOPIC — **eu·ry·to·pic·i·ty** \,==,tōˈpisəd·ē\ *n* -ES

eu·ry·tre·ma \,yu̇rəˈtrēmə\ *n, cap* [NL, fr. *eury-* + *-trema*] : a genus of digenetic trematode worms (family Dicrocoeliidae) infesting the pancreatic and bile ducts of various ruminants, rodents, and primates chiefly in tropical areas

eu·ry·zy·gous \¦yu̇rə¦zīgəs, yəˈrizəgəs\ *adj* [*eury-* + *-zygous*] : having wide zygomatic arches

-e·us \,ēəs\ *n comb form, pl* **-ei** \,ē,ī\ *also* **-euses** [NL, fr. L, adj. suffix, composed of, of the nature of, or resembling (a specified substance) — more at -EOUS] : muscle that constitutes, has the form of, or joins a (specified) part, thing, or structures ⟨*gluteus*⟩ ⟨*rhomboideus*⟩ ⟨*iliococcygeus*⟩

eu·schis·tus \yüˈskistəs\ *n, cap* [NL, fr. Gk *euschistos* easy to split, fr. *eu-* + *schistos* split, divided, fr. *schizein* to split — more at SHED] : a genus of pentatomid bugs some of which cause catfacing of peaches

[1]**eu·se·bi·an** \yüˈsēbēən\ *n* -s *usu cap* [*Eusebius* of Nicomedia †*ab* A.D.342 Arian leader and bishop + E *-an*, n. suffix] : a follower of Eusebius, bishop of Nicomedia : ARIAN

[2]**eusebian** \"\ *adj, usu cap* **1** [*Eusebius* of Caesarea †*ab* A.D.340 theologian and church historian + E *-an*, adj. suffix] : of or belonging to Eusebius, bishop of Caesarea and church historian **2** [*Eusebius* of Nicomedia + E *-an*, adj. suffix] : of or belonging to Eusebius, bishop of Nicomedia, who was a friend and protector of Arius

eusebian canons *n pl, usu cap E* [[2]*eusebian* (Eusebius of Caesarea)] : a set of tables presenting a harmony of the Gospels in outline form by use of section numbers

[1]**eu·selachii** \¦yü+\ *n pl, cap* [NL, fr. *eu-* + *Selachii*] : a subclass or other division of Chondrichthyes comprising the recent sharks and rays and certain extinct related forms

[2]**euselachii** \"\ [NL, fr. *eu-* + *Selachii*] *syn of* PLEUROTREMATA

eus·ka·ra *or* **eus·ke·ra** \ˈeuskə,rä\ *n* -s *cap* [Basque] : the Basque language

eus·kar·i·an \yüˈska(a)rēən\ *n* -s *usu cap* [Basque *euskara* Basque (the language) + E *-ian*, n. suffix] **1** : the Basque language **2** : the language family of which Basque is the only member

eu·smi·lus \yüˈsmīləs\ *n, cap* [NL, fr. *eu-* + *-smilus* (fr. Gk *smilē* carving knife) — more at SMITH] : a genus of early saber-toothed tigers with extremely large canines known from the Oligocene of Europe and No. America

eu·spongia \(ˈ)yü+\ [NL, fr. *eu-* + *Spongia*] *syn of* SPONGIA

eu·spo·ran·gi·a·tae \,yüspə,ranjēˈäd·,ē, -ˈād-\ *n pl, cap* [NL, fr. fem. pl. of (assumed) NL *eusporangiatus*] *in some classifications* : a group comprising all the ferns in which sporangium formation is eusporangiate — compare LEPTOSPORANGIATAE

eu·spo·ran·gi·ate \¦yüspə¦ranjēət, -ē,āt\ *adj* [fr. (assumed) NL *eusporangiatus*, fr. NL *eu-* + *sporangium* + L *-atus* -ate] : having sporangia which rise from a group of epidermal cells ⟨~ ferns of the families Ophioglossaceae and Marattiaceae⟩ — opposed to *leptosporangiate*

eu·sta·chian \yüˈstāshən *also* -āshēən *or* -ākēən\ *adj, often cap* [Bartolommeo *Eustachio* †1574 Ital. anatomist + E *-an*] : of or relating to Eustachio or to the eustachian tube : located in or adjoining the eustachian tube

eustachian tonsil *n, often cap E* : a mass of lymphoid tissue at the pharyngeal opening of the eustachian tube

eustachian tube *n, often cap E* : a bony and cartilaginous tube connecting the cavity of the middle ear with the nasopharynx and serving to equalize air pressure on both sides of the tympanic membrane — see EAR illustration

eustachian valve *n, often cap E* : a crescent-shaped fold of the lining membrane of the heart at the entrance of the vena cava inferior that directs the blood through the foramen ovale to the left auricle in the fetus but is rudimentary and functionless in the adult

eu·sta·cy \ˈyüstəsē\ *n* -ES [ISV *eu-* + *-stacy* (irreg. fr. Gk *stasis* condition of standing still) — more at STASIS] : worldwide change of sea level as contrasted with local diastrophic uplift or subsidence of the land

eu·sta·sism \ˈyüstə,sizəm\ *or* **eu·sta·tism** \-tə,tiz-\ *n* -s [*eustasism* prob. irreg. fr. *eustacy* + *-ism*; *eustatism* ISV *eustat-* (fr. *eustatic*) + *-ism*] : EUSTACY

[1]**eu·sta·thi·an** \yüˈstāthēən\ *n* -s *cap* **1** [*Eustathius* of Sebaste †*ab* A.D.380 Semi-Arian bishop of Sebaste in Armenia + E *-an*, n. suffix] : a follower of the Semi-Arian bishop Eustathius who established a monastic institute which was condemned by the Synod of Gangra in A.D.340 **2** [*Eustathius* of Antioch †*ab* A.D.360 bishop of Antioch in Syria + E *-an*, n. suffix] : one of an orthodox party whose protest against the deposition by an Arian synod of Eustathius, bishop of Antioch, led to a schism that lasted till A.D.413

[2]**eustathian** \"\ *adj, cap* [*Eustathius* + E *-an*, adj. suffix] : of or relating to Eustathius or to a Eustathian

eu·stat·ic \(ˈ)yü¦stad·ik\ *adj* [ISV *eu-* + *static*] : relating to or characterized by eustacy — **eu·stat·i·cal·ly** *adv*

eu·stele \(ˈ)yü+\ *n* [*eu-* + *stele*] : a stele (as in most higher vascular plants) in which the vascular cylinder is broken up by both leaf gaps and interfascicular areas

eu·sternum \"\ *n, pl* **eusterna** [NL, fr. *eu-* + *sternum*] : the anterior plate of a sternum of an insect : BASISTERNUM; *also* : any of certain other sclerites of the ventral part of the insect thorax

eus·the·nop·te·ron \,yüsthəˈnäptə,rän\ *n, cap* [NL, fr. *eustheno-* (fr. Gk *eusthenēs* strong, fr. *eu-* + *-sthenēs*, fr. *sthenos* strength) + Gk *pteron* wing; fr. the strongly developed fins — more at ASTHEN-, FEATHER] : a genus of Upper Devonian lobe-finned fishes (order Rhipidistia)

eu·stom·a·tous \(ˈ)yü¦stäməd·əs, -tōm-\ *adj* [prob. fr. (assumed) NL *eustomatus*, fr. NL *eu-* + *-stomatus* -stomatous] : having a distinct and well-developed mouth — used esp. of ciliates and larval nematodes

eu·style \ˈyü,stīl\ *n* [L *eustylos* having columns at the best distances, fr. Gk, fr. *eu-* + *stylos* pillar — more at STOW] : an intercolumniation of 2¼ diameters

eu·su·chia \yüˈsükēə\ *n pl, cap* [NL, fr. *eu-* + Gk *souchos* crocodile + NL *-ia*] : a suborder or other division of Loricata including the typical members of that group (as the existing gavials, alligators, and crocodiles and post-Cretaceous fossil forms) having the internal nasal opening situated far back and surrounded by the pterygoid bone — **eu·su·chi·an** \-ēən\ *adj*

eu·syn·chite \yü'sin,kīt, -iŋ,k-, 'yüs°n,k-\ *n* -s [G *eusynchit*, fr. *eu-* + Gk *syncheïn*to commingle, confuse (fr. *syn-* + *chein* to pour) + G *-it* -ite — more at FOUND] **:** DESCLOIZITE

eu·tae·nia \yü'tēnēə\ [NL, fr. *eu-* + Gk *tainia* band, fillet — more at TAENIA] *syn of* THAMNOPHIS

eu·tamias \(')yü+\ *n, cap* [NL, fr. *eu-* + *Tamias*] **:** a genus of rodents comprising the chipmunks of western No. America

eu·tax·ic \yü¦taksik\ *adj* [*eutaxy* + *-ic*] **:** of or relating to stratified ore deposits — opposed to *ataxic*

eu·taxy \'yü,taksē\ *n* -ES [Gk *eutaxia*, fr. *eutaktos* orderly (fr. *eu-* + *taktos* ordered, fr. *tattein, tassein* to put in order) + *-ia* -y — more at TACTICS] **:** good order or management ⟨whose keeping of Christmas . . . was an annual example of that competent ~ in which her life was ordered —Rose Macaulay⟩

¹eu·tec·tic \(')yü¦tektik\ *adj* [ISV *eutect-* (fr. Gk *eutēktos* easily melted, fr. *eu-* + *tēktos* melted, fr. *tēkein* to melt) + *-ic* — more at THAW] **:** relating to a eutectic or its composition ⟨~ mixture⟩ or the temperature at which it melts or freezes ⟨~ point⟩

²eutectic \"\ *n* -s **1 :** an alloy or solution having its components in such proportions that the melting point is the lowest possible with those components **2 :** the characteristic microstructure resulting from solidification of metal of eutectic composition — compare EUTECTOID

¹eu·tec·toid \yü'tek,tȯid\ *n* -s [ISV *eutect-* (fr. *eutectic*) + *-oid*, n. suffix] **:** a eutectoid alloy (as pearlite) formed when a solid solution transforms during cooling into new solid phases, the change taking place entirely in the solid state

²eutectoid \(')=¦=,=\ *adj* **:** like a eutectic — used esp. of steel in the form of pearlite

eu·tele·genesis \(,)yü,telə+\ *n* [NL, fr. *eu-* + *tel-* + L *genesis*] **:** ARTIFICIAL INSEMINATION

eu·tely \'yüd·°lē; 'yü,telē, =¦==\ *n* -ES [prob. fr. G *eutelie*, fr. Gk *euteleia* thrift, economy, fr. *eutelēs* cheap, frugal, fr. *eu-* + *-telēs* (fr. *telos* end, toll, expenditure) — more at WHEEL] **:** the condition of having a body made up of a constant number of cells (as in certain rotifers and some lower worms)

eu·ter·pe \yü'tər(,)pē\ *n, cap* [NL, fr. L *Euterpe*, one of the Muses (in late Roman times characterized as the Muse of the flute), fr. Gk *Euterpē*, one of the Muses] **:** a genus of graceful tropical American pinnate-leaved palms having a small globose fruit about the size of a pea — see ASSAI

eu·ter·pe·an \(')yü¦tərpēən\ *adj, usu cap* [L *Euterpe* + E *-an*] **:** relating to the muse Euterpe or to music

eu·tex·ia \yü'teksēə, -kshə\ *n* -s [Gk *eutēxia*, fr. *eutēktos* easily melted + *-ia* -y] **1 :** the quality of melting at a minimum temperature **2 :** the principle or process of forming from given components the eutectic alloy

eu·tha·mia \yü'thāmēə\ *n, cap* [NL, fr. *eu-* + *tham-* (prob. fr. Gk *thamees* crowded) + *-ia*; akin to Gk *tithenai* to place — more at DO] *in some classifications* **:** a genus of composite herbs including those members of the genus *Solidago* in which the flower heads are flat topped

eu·tha·na·sia \,yüthə'nāzh(ē)ə\ *n* -s [Gk, easy death, fr. *eu-* + *-thanasia* (fr. *thanatos* death) — more at THANAT-] **1 :** an easy death or means of inducing one **2 :** the act or practice of painlessly putting to death persons suffering from incurable conditions or diseases — **eu·tha·na·sic** \¦yüthə¦nāzik\ *adj*

eu·then·ics \yü'theniks\ *n pl but sing or pl in constr* [Gk *euthenein* to thrive (fr. *eu-* + *-thenein* to swell) + E *-ics*; akin to Lith *gana* enough, Skt *ghana* compact, dense] **:** a science that deals with developing human well-being and efficient functioning through the improvement of environmental conditions — compare EUGENICS

eu·then·ist \yü'thenəst, 'yüthən-\ *n* -s [*euthenics* + *-ist*] **:** a student or advocate of euthenics

eu·theria \(')yü+\ *n pl, cap* [NL, fr. *eu-* + *Theria*] **:** a major division of Mammalia originally coextensive with the subclass Theria but in modern usage an infraclass or other division of Theria comprising the placental mammals as opposed to the Metatheria — **eu·the·ri·an** \(')yü¦thirēən\ *adj or n*

eu·thermic \(')yü+\ *adj* [*eu-* + *thermic*] **:** inducing or promoting warmth

eu·tho·scop·ic \¦yüthə¦skäpik\ *adj* [*eutho-* (irreg. fr. Gk *euthys* straight) + *-scopic*] *of a photoreceptor* **:** capable of perceiving the presence, direction, and relative intensity of light but unable to form a visual image

eu·thy·neu·ra \,yüthə'n(y)u̇rə\ *n pl, cap* [NL, fr. *euthy-* (fr. Gk, fr. *euthys* straight) + *-neura*] **:** a large subclass of Gastropoda comprising the Opisthobranchia and Pulmonata — **eu·thy·neu·ral** \¦=¦=rəl\ *or* **eu·thy·neu·ran** \-rən\ *or* **eu·thy·neu·rous** \-rəs\ *adj*

eu·thyn·nus \yü'thinəs\ *n, cap* [NL, fr. *eu-* + Gk *thynnos* tunny — more at TUNNY] **:** a genus of comparatively small tunas with teeth on the palatine bones that includes the little tuna cosmopolitan in tropical seas

eu·thyroid \(')yü+\ *adj* [*eu-* + *thyroid*] **:** characterized by normal thyroid function **:** having a thyroid that functions normally — **eu·thyroidism** \¦yü+\ *n*

eu·to·cia \yü'tōsh(ē)ə\ *n* -s [NL, fr. Gk *eutokia*, fr. *eutokos* giving birth easily (fr. *eu-* + *tokos* childbirth, parturition) + *-ia*; akin to Gk *teknon* child — more at THANE] **:** normal parturition — opposed to *dystocia*

eutomous *adj* [*eu-* + *-tomous*] *obs, of a mineral* **:** cleaving readily or distinctly

eu·to·pia \yü'tōpēə, eu̇'t-\ *n* -s *usu cap* [NL, fr. *eu-* + *-topia* (fr. Gk *topos* place + *-ia*) — more at TOPIC] **:** a country of ideal felicity and perfection; *sometimes* **:** UTOPIA — **eu·to·pi·an** \(')=¦=pēən\ *adj, usu cap*

eu·tracheata \(¦)yü+\ *n pl, cap* [NL, fr. *eu-* + *Tracheata*] **:** a group of Arthropoda comprising all arthropods (as insects, chilopods, diplopods, and a few related forms) that have a tracheal respiratory system and a single pair of antennae — **eu·tracheate** \(')yü+\ *adj or n*

eu·trombicula \¦yü+\ *n, cap* [NL, fr. *eu-* + *Trombicula*] **:** a genus of rather large mites (family Trombidiidae) that have the body clearly demarked into cephalothorax and abdomen, are free-living as adults, and have larvae which are typical chiggers

eu·troph·ic \(')yü¦träfik, -rōf-\ *adj* [prob. fr. *eutrophy* + *-ic*] **1 :** relating to or being in a well-nourished condition **2** [prob. fr. G *eutroph* eutrophic (fr. Gk *eutrophos* well nourished, nourishing) + E *-ic*] *of a lake* **:** rich in dissolved nutrients but frequently shallow and with seasonal oxygen deficiency in the hypolimnion — compare DYSTROPHIC, OLIGOTROPHIC

eu·troph·i·ca·tion \(,)yü,träfə'kāshən, -rōf-\ *n* -s [*eutrophic* + *-ation*] **:** the process of becoming more eutrophic either as a natural phase in the maturation of a body of water or artificially (as by fertilization)

eu·tro·phy \'yü·trəfē\ *n* -ES [Gk *eutrophia*, fr. *eutrophos* well nourished, nourishing (fr. *eu-* + *trophos* feeder, fr. *trephein* to nourish) + *-ia* -y — more at ATROPHY] **1 :** healthy nutrition **:** healthy action of the nutritive functions **2** [prob. fr. G *eutrophie*, fr. Gk *eutrophia*] *of a lake* **:** the quality or state of being eutrophic

eu·tych·i·an \(')yü¦tikēən\ *n* -s *usu cap* [*Eutyches* †A.D.454? heresiarch, presbyter, and archimandrite of the Eastern Church in Constantinople + E *-ian*] **:** a follower of Eutyches in the belief that the divine and the human in the person of Christ so blend as to constitute but one nature so that Christ is *of* two natures but not *in* two **:** MONOPHYSITE — compare NESTORIAN — **eu·tych·i·an·ism** \-,nizəm\ *n* -s *usu cap*

eux·e·nite \'yüksə,nīt\ *n* -s [G *euxenit*, fr. Gk *euxenos* hospitable (fr. *eu-* + *xenos* guest, stranger) + G *-it* -ite; fr. the rare elements it contains] **:** a brownish black mineral (Y, Ca, Ce, U, Th) (Cb, Ta, Ti)$_2$O$_6$ that consists of oxide of calcium, cerium, columbium, tantalum, titanium, and uranium, that has a metallic luster, and that is isomorphous with polycrase (hardness 6.5, sp. gr. 4.7–5.0)

eux·ine \'yüksən, -,sīn\ *adj, usu cap* [L *euxinus*, fr. Gk *euxeinos* (esp. in *Pontos Euxeinos* Black sea), fr. *euxenos, euxeinos* hospitable] **:** of, relating to, or having to do with the Black sea

eux·in·ic \(')yük¦sinik\ *adj* [*euxine* + *-ic*] **:** relating to a rock facies that includes black shales and graphitic sediments of various kinds

eu·xoa \yük'sōə\ *n, cap* [NL] **:** a genus of brownish noctuid moths having larvae that are voracious cutworms — see RED-BACKED CUTWORM

ev *abbr* evangelical

EV *abbr, often not cap* electron volt

Evac·tor \ə'vaktə(r), ē'-\ *trademark* — used for a jet pump

¹evac·u·ant \ə'vakyəwənt, ē'-\ *n* -s [L *evacuant-, evacuans*, pres. part. of *evacuare*] **:** an evacuant agent

²evacuant \"\ *adj* [L *evacuant-, evacuans*, pres. part. of *evacuare*] **:** EMPTYING, EMETIC, DIURETIC, PURGATIVE, CATHARTIC

evac·u·ate \ə'vakyə,wāt, ē'-, *usu* -ād·+V\ *vb* -ED/-ING/-S [L *evacuatus*, past part. of *evacuare*, fr. *e-* + *vacuus* empty — more at WANE] *vt* **1 a :** to make empty **:** empty out ⟨~ an abscess⟩ **b :** DEPRIVE ⟨a naturalistic logic which *evacuated* Christianity of all religious values —*Times Lit. Supp.*⟩ **2** *archaic* **:** to make void **:** NULLIFY, VACATE **3 :** to discharge through the excretory passages **:** VOID **4 :** to remove something (as a gas or water) from esp. by pumping **:** EXHAUST ⟨a highly *evacuated* glass tube⟩ **5 a :** to remove (troops equipment, civilians) esp. from a military position or zone **:** remove (sick and wounded) from a combat area **b :** to withdraw from military occupation of (a fort or region) **c :** to remove (a person or thing) from some place in an organized way esp. as a protective measure ⟨*evacuated* the people of the towns threatened by the forest fire⟩ ⟨~ American citizens from the war-torn land⟩ ⟨during the war their school had been *evacuated* to the country —Margaret Kennedy⟩ ⟨the irreplaceable treasures had been *evacuated* to safety —*Amer. Library Assoc. Bull.*⟩ ⟨the pigs had been *evacuated* and were not brought back —*Time*⟩ **d :** to remove the inhabitants of (a place or area) esp. as a protective measure ⟨~ a city under attack⟩ **e :** to give up the occupancy of (premises) ~ *vi* **1 :** to withdraw in an organized way from a place or territory esp. as a protective measure or as a military operation ⟨the decision to ~ was made as flood waters reached a new height⟩ ⟨enemy troops were to ~ in 10 days⟩ **2 :** DEFECATE, URINATE

evac·u·a·tion \=,=='wāshən\ *n* -s [ME *evacuacioun*, fr. MF & LL; MF *evacuation*, fr. LL *evacuation-, evacuatio*, fr. L *evacuatus* + *-ion-, -io* -ion] **1 :** the act of emptying, clearing of the contents, or discharging ⟨easy and resounding ~ of words —Philip Wylie⟩ ⟨it is very wrong . . . to hold back a natural ~ of joy —Robertson Davies⟩: as **a :** the withdrawal of troops from a town or fortress, of a population from a city or territory, or of sick and wounded from a combat area ⟨demanded the immediate ~ of foreign troops⟩ ⟨~ of the threatened city had begun⟩ **b :** any organized withdrawal or removal (as of persons or things) from a place or area esp. as a protective measure ⟨as flood waters rose ~ of families and farm animals was begun⟩ ⟨advised ~ of the precious art collection to a neutral country⟩ **c :** discharge of any matter by the natural passages of the body or by an artificial opening **:** DEFECATION **2 :** something that is evacuated or discharged by natural or artificial means

evacuation hospital *n* **:** a mobile or partly mobile hospital where casualties are received usu. from collecting stations and where major medical and surgical treatment can be given before evacuation to rear installations

evac·u·a·tive \=¦==,wād·iv\ *adj* **:** of or relating to evacuation

evac·u·ee \=¦==¦wē\ *also* **evac·ué** *or* **evac·u·ée** \-wā\ *n* -s [F *évacué* (masc.) & *évacuée* (fem.), fr. past part. of *évacuer* to evacuate, fr. L *evacuare* — more at EVACUATE] **:** a person who is removed from his home or community in time of war or pressing danger as a protective measure ⟨the villagers fed and housed the ~s from the blitzed city⟩

evad·able \ə'vādəbəl, ē'-\ *adj* **:** capable of being evaded ⟨these obligations are not easily ~⟩

evade \ə'vād, ē'-\ *vb* -ED/-ING/-S [MF & L; MF *evader*, fr. L *evadere*, fr. *e-* + *vadere* to go, walk — more at WADE] *vi* **1 :** to slip away **:** give someone the slip ⟨submariners have always despised the need to ~ in order to escape —S.D.Cutter⟩ **2 :** to take refuge in evasion **:** use craft or stratagem in avoidance **:** avoid facing up to something ⟨wisdom consists . . . in learning when to ~, when to stave off, and when to oppose head on —Irving Howe⟩ ⟨the adult who regresses to the infantile . . . ~s —H.A.Overstreet⟩ ~ *vt* **1 a** (1) **:** to get away from (a pursuer or enemy) by dexterity or stratagem **:** avoid capture by **:** shun or avoid contact or confrontation with **:** ELUDE, ESCAPE, AVOID ⟨*evaded* the police and crossed the border into safety⟩ ⟨he . . . tried to ~ her kisses —Winifred Bambrick⟩ ⟨guiltily *evaded* her accusing look⟩ (2) **:** to avoid facing up to (a fact or condition) ⟨though she knew . . . her father would never be up again, she united with her mother in *evading* the fact —Ellen Glasgow⟩ ⟨prefers to ~ home truths . . . by saying what he does not really mean —*Va. Quarterly Rev.*⟩ **b** (1) **:** to manage to avoid the performance of (an obligation) **:** escape from doing or experiencing (something disagreeable) **:** CIRCUMVENT, DODGE ⟨I have a horror of the men who *evaded* service during the war —Rose Macaulay⟩ ⟨the French had been limited to a hundred thousand troops . . . but they had managed . . . to ~ this limit —Upton Sinclair⟩ ⟨several very safe and easy methods of *evading* the law —Adam Smith⟩; *specif* **:** to fail to pay or to minimize (taxes) in violation of law ⟨served a term . . . for *evading* his income tax —H.H.Martin⟩ (2) **:** to get around (an intellectual obstacle) ⟨the traditional way of *evading* the difficulty . . . is to have recourse to . . . "vitalism" —A.N.Whitehead⟩ **c :** to avoid answering directly (as a question or a questioner) **:** turn aside **:** PARRY ⟨tried to ~ his query but he was not to be put off⟩ ⟨tried to ~ this nonsensical demand —Alfred Burmeister⟩ **2 :** BAFFLE, ELUDE **:** be baffling or elusive to ⟨the simple, personal meaning *evaded* them —C.D. Lewis⟩ **syn** see ESCAPE

evad·er \-də(r)\ *n* -s **:** one that evades ⟨prosecuting tax ~s⟩

eva·ga·tion \,ēvə'gāshən, ,ē(,)vā'-, ,evə'-\ *n* -s [ME *evagacioun*, fr. MF or ML; MF *evagation*, fr. ML *evagation-, evagatio*, fr. L, wandering, fr. *evagatus* (past part. of *evagari* to wander, fr. *e-* + *vagari* to stroll, wander) + *-ion-, -io* ion — more at VAGARY] **1** *obs* **:** a wandering of the mind **2** [L *evagation-, evagatio*] *archaic* **:** the act or an instance of wandering

evag·i·na·ble \ə'vajənəbəl, ē'-\ *adj* **:** capable of being evaginated

¹evag·i·nate \-,nāt\ *vb* -ED/-ING/-S [L *evaginatus*, past part. of *evaginare* to unsheathe, fr. *e-* + *vagina* sheath — more at VAGINA] *vt* **:** to turn (as a body part) inside out **:** cause (a part) to protrude by eversion of an inner surface ~ *vi, of a part or structure* **:** to protrude by eversion of an inner surface **:** turn inside out

²evag·i·nate \-,nət, -,nāt\ *adj* [L *evaginatus*, past part.] **:** EVAGINATED

evag·i·na·tion \ə,vajə'nāshən, (,)ē,v-\ *n* -s [LL *evagination-, evaginatio* act of unsheathing, fr. L *evaginatus* + *-ion-, -io* -ion] **1 :** the act or an instance of evaginating **2 :** a product of evaginating **:** OUTGROWTH

eval·u·ate \ə'valyə,wāt, ē'v-, *usu* -ād·+V\ *vb* -ED/-ING/-S [back-formation fr. *evaluation*] *vt* **1 a :** to set down or express the mathematical value of **:** express numerically **b :** to estimate or ascertain the monetary worth of **:** VALUE ⟨the inspector *evaluated* the horses at thirty-five dollars a head —F.B.Gipson⟩ **2 :** to examine and judge concerning the worth, quality, significance, amount, degree, or condition of **:** APPRAISE, RATE ⟨using trained observers to visit and ~ teachers in their classrooms —*Educational Research Bull.*⟩ ⟨X-ray and radium therapy must be further explored before their efficacy can be *evaluated* —W.S.Middleton⟩ ⟨*evaluated* a new novel⟩ ⟨~ a student's ability⟩ ⟨at the first visit, an attempt should be made to ~ the patient as a whole —*Therapeutic Notes*⟩ ⟨~ a new political trend⟩ ~ *vi* **:** to make an evaluation ⟨it is not enough to count, we must ~ —Havelock Ellis⟩ ⟨we . . . come . . . as critics, to scrutinize and ~ —R.W. Stallman⟩ **syn** see ESTIMATE

eval·u·a·tion \ə,valyə'wāshən, (,)ē,v-\ *n* -s [F *évaluation*, fr. MF *evaluation*, fr. *evaluer* to evaluate (fr. *e-* + *value*) + *-ation* — more at VALUE] **:** the act or result of evaluating **:** JUDGMENT APPRAISAL, RATING, INTERPRETATION ⟨a man can be labeled a security risk for presenting his ~ of a political situation —*Civil Liberties*⟩ ⟨if we examine the great writers, we find that their moral ~s are often either below, or above, the level of their material —William Barrett⟩ ⟨every woman should have a thorough examination, including ~ of the pelvic organs —*Therapeutic Notes*⟩

eval·u·a·tive \ə'==,wād·|iv, -,wəl, |t|, |ēv *also* |əv\ *adj* **:** serving or tending to evaluate ⟨the literary judge uses ~ terms freely —C.W.Shumaker⟩

eval·u·a·tor \-,wād·ə(r), -ātə-\ *n* -s **:** one that evaluates ⟨an intelligence officer is supposed to be a professional ~ —Perry Miller⟩

ev·a·nesce \¦evə¦nes, *chiefly Brit* ¦ēv-\ *vi* -ED/-ING/-S [L *evanescere* — more at VANISH] **:** to dissipate and disappear like vapor **:** disappear gradually ⟨I touch a scarf and it falls into air and light and seems to ~ —William Goyen⟩ **syn** see VANISH

ev·a·nes·cence \,=='nes°n(t)s\ *n* -s **1 :** the process or fact of evanescing **:** a vanishing away ⟨the possible ~ of her passion for him —Thomas Hardy⟩ **2 :** evanescent quality ⟨the fleeting ~ of all things that are —J.L.Lowes⟩

ev·a·nes·cent \¦==¦nes°nt\ *adj* [L *evanescent-, evanescens*, pres. part. of *evanescere*] **1 :** tending to vanish or pass away like vapor **:** of short life or duration **:** VANISHING, FLEETING, IMPERMANENT ⟨slight and ~ as an April storm —Elinor Wylie⟩ ⟨~ isotopes⟩ ⟨an ~ eruption⟩ ⟨~ flowers⟩ **2** *archaic* **:** becoming imperceptible by diminution **:** INFINITESIMAL **3 :** characterized by extreme delicacy or fineness of form, structure, or texture **:** light and airy **:** FRAGILE, DIAPHANOUS, UNSUBSTANTIAL ⟨with the . . . ~ brushwork and psychological clarity since lost in English painting —*New Republic*⟩ ⟨many beautiful creatures, . . . so ~ that they are only discoverable by the faint shadows which they cast on the bottom —William Beebe⟩ **syn** see TRANSIENT

ev·a·nes·cent·ly *adv* **:** in an evanescent manner

¹evan·gel \ə'vanjəl, ē'-, -vaan-\ *n* -s [ME *evangile, evangell*, fr. MF *evangile*, fr. LL *evangelium*, fr. Gk. *euangelion* good news, glad tidings, gospel, fr. *euangelos* bringing good news, fr. *eu-* + *-angelos*, fr. *angelos* messenger — more at ANGEL] **1 a :** the Christian gospel **b** *usu cap* **:** one of the four Gospels of the New Testament **2 :** good news **:** announcement of good news **3 :** a doctrine regarded as having special grace, sanction, or efficacy ⟨a contemporary situation invested atomism . . . with the attributes of an ~ —Benjamin Farrington⟩

²evangel \"\ *n* -s [LL *evangelus*, fr. Gk *euangelos*, adj.] **:** one who proclaims a gospel message **:** EVANGELIST ⟨never joined in the public confessions of his fellow ~s —*Time*⟩

evan·ge·lary \-,lerē\ *n* -ES [modif. of ML *evangeliarium*, fr. LL *evangelium* + L *-arium* -ary] **:** EVANGELISTARY

¹evan·gel·ic \¦ē,van¦jelik, ¦evən-, ¦ē,vaan-, ¸ē,va(a)n-, ə-,va(a)n-\ *adj* [ME, fr. LL *evangelicus*] **:** EVANGELICAL

²evangelic \"\ *n* -s *archaic* **:** EVANGELICAL

¹evan·gel·i·cal \-ləkəl, -lēk-\ *adj* [LL *evangelicus* (fr. Gk *euangelikos*, fr. *euangelion* + *-ikos* -ic) + E *-al*] **1 :** of, relating to, contained in, or in agreement with the Christian gospel esp. as it is presented in the four Gospels of the New Testament **2** *sometimes cap* **:** PROTESTANT ⟨mobs attacked ~ property⟩ **3 :** of, relating to, or being a religious group emphasizing salvation by faith in the atoning death of Jesus Christ through personal conversion, the authority of Scripture, and the importance of preaching as contrasted with ritual **4 a** *usu cap* **:** of or relating to the Evangelical Church in Germany **b** *sometimes cap* **:** of or relating to Fundamentalism or Fundamentalists ⟨an ultraconservative ~ message⟩ **c** *usu cap* **:** of or relating to Low Church adherents in the Church of England and the Protestant Episcopal Church as distinguished from High Church Anglo-Catholics; *also* **:** of or relating to Wesleyans or Methodists who stand in the tradition of the 18th century evangelical revival in England **5 :** characteristic or suggestive of an evangelist **:** characterized by or reflecting a missionary, reforming, or redeeming impulse or purpose **:** EVANGELISTIC, ZEALOUS, ARDENT, MILITANT, CRUSADING ⟨did not feel the passion for writing or preaching that more ~ authors have felt —F.A.Swinnerton⟩ ⟨the rise and fall of ~ fervor within the Socialist movement —*Times Lit. Supp.*⟩ ⟨propaganda . . . reinforced the mood of ~ patriotism —J.D. Hart⟩ ⟨the Marxist impulse in American literary criticism was chiefly hortatory and ~ —C.I.Glicksberg⟩ — **evan·gel·i·cal·ness** *n* -ES

²evangelical \"\ *n* -s *usu cap* **:** one holding evangelical principles or belonging to an evangelical party or church

evan·gel·i·cal·ism \,=,=¦==kə,lizəm, ,==¦=-, =,=¦=-\ *n* -s *usu cap* **:** evangelical principles or beliefs; *also* **:** adherence to the party or churches holding them

evan·gel·i·cal·i·ty \,ē,va(a)n,jelə'kaləd·ē, ,evən-\ *n* -ES **:** the state of being evangelical

evan·gel·i·cal·ly \¦ē,va(a)n¦jelək(ə)lē, ¦evən-, ¸ē,va(a)n-, ə-,va(a)n-, -lēk-, -li\ *adv* **:** in an evangelical manner **:** in the manner of an evangelist ⟨~ pleaded for individual regeneration —*Time*⟩

evan·gel·i·cism \,=,=¦=lə,sizəm, ,==¦=-, =,=¦=-\ *n* -s *sometimes cap* **:** EVANGELICALISM

evan·ge·lion \,e,văn'gyelyȯn\ *n* -s [LGk *euangelion*, fr. Gk, good news, gospel — more at EVANGEL] **1** *Eastern Church* **:** EVANGELISTARY **2** *Eastern Church* **:** a pericope of a gospel as read in the liturgy

evan·ge·lism \ə'va(a)njə,lizəm, ē'-\ *n* -s [LGk *euangelismos*, fr. Gk *euangelizesthai, euangelizein* to evangelize] **1 :** the proclamation of the gospel; *esp* **:** the presentation of the gospel to individuals and groups by such methods as preaching, teaching, and personal or family visitation programs **2 :** missionary, militant, or crusading zeal for or earnest advocacy of any cause ⟨stumped the state, denouncing the Fugitive Slave law and . . . electrifying his audiences with his Free-Soil ~ —W.E.Smith⟩

evan·ge·list \-ləst\ *n* -s [ME, fr. OF & LL; OF *evangeliste*, fr. LL *evangelista*, fr. Gk *euangelistēs*, fr. *euangelizesthai, euangelizein*] **1** *usu cap* **:** a writer of any of the four Gospels **2 a :** a member of the primitive church who brought the first news of the gospel message, paving the way for the more systematic work of settled church officers **:** a traveling missionary or wandering teacher **b :** one who converts (as a nation) to Christianity **:** EVANGELIZER, APOSTLE **c :** an occasional preacher having no fixed charge **:** a traveling missionary: as (1) **:** a minister of the Disciples of Christ who organizes church societies and sets churches and their officers in order (2) **:** a minister or layman among various Protestant denominations who goes about from place to place preaching at special services to awaken religious interest **:** REVIVALIST **3 :** PATRIARCH 4 **4 :** a person characterized by evangelical zeal for and earnest advocacy of any cause ⟨a fervent ~ for the mutual interests of labor and management —*Time*⟩

evan·ge·lis·ta·ry \=,==¦listərē, -ri\ *n* -ES [ML *evangelistarium*, fr. LL *evangelista* + L *-arium* -ary] **:** a book consisting of the four Gospels that is used as a lectionary

evan·ge·lis·tic \=¦==¦listik, -tēk\ *adj* **1 :** of or relating to evangelism **:** designed or used for the purpose of evangelization ⟨the ~ concerns of the early church⟩ ⟨an ~ tent⟩ **2 :** EVANGELICAL ⟨an ~ interpretation of the Bible⟩ **3 :** of, relating to, or led by an evangelist ⟨an ~ service⟩ ⟨~ writings⟩ **4 a :** having a missionary or revivalist character or purpose ⟨the ~ movement on the American frontier⟩ **b :** marked by evangelism — **evan·ge·lis·ti·cal·ly** \-tək(ə)lē, -tēk-, -li\ *adv*

evan·ge·lis·tics \=,==¦=stiks, -tēks\ *n pl but sing in constr* **:** the science of the propagation of Christianity

evan·ge·li·za·tion \-,lə'zāshən, -,lī'z-\ *n* -s [LL *evangelization-, evangelizatio*, fr. *evangelizatus* (past part. of *evangelizare*) + L *-ion-, -io* -ion] **:** the act or process of evangelizing **:** the state of being evangelized

evan·ge·lize \ə'==,līz\ *vb* -ED/-ING/-S [ME *evangelisen*, fr. LL *evangelizare*, fr. Gk *euangelizesthai, euangelizein*, fr. *euangelion* + *-izesthai, -izein* -ize] *vt* **:** to instruct in the gospel **:** to preach the gospel to **:** convert to Christianity ⟨~ the world⟩ ~ *vi* **:** to preach the gospel; *esp* **:** to preach in the manner of an evangelist

evan·ge·liz·er \-zə(r)\ *n* -s [ME *evangeliser*, fr. *evangelisen* + *-er*] **:** one that evangelizes

evangely *n* [ME *evangelie*, fr. LL *evangelium* — more at EVANGEL] *obs* **:** ¹EVANGEL

evan·id \ə'vanəd, ē'-\ *adj* [L *evanidus*; akin to L *evanescere* to vanish — more at VANISH] *archaic* **:** EVANESCENT, FAINT, ILLUSORY

ev·a·ni·idae \,evə'nīə,dē\ *n pl, cap* [NL, fr. *Evania*, type genus (fr. Gk *euanios* taking trouble easily, fr. *eu-* + *ania* trouble) + *-idae*] **:** a family of hymenopterous insects comprising the ensign flies

evan·ish \ə̇, ē+\ *vi* [ME *evanisshen*, fr. MF *esvaniss-*, stem of *esvanir* — more at VANISH] **1 :** VANISH, DISAPPEAR **2 :** to cease to be

evanishment \"+\ *n* **:** the act or process of vanishing **:** DISAPPEARANCE

ev·a·ni·tion \ˌevəˈnishən\ *n* -s [fr. *evanish*, after such pairs as E *abolish: abolition*] **:** EVANISHMENT

ev·ans blue \ˈevənz-\ *n, usu cap E* [after Herbert M. *Evans* †1971 Am. anatomist] **:** a disazo dye $C_{34}H_{24}N_6Na_4O_{14}S_4$ that is obtained as a green, bluish green, or brown powder and that on injection into the blood stream combines with serum albumin and serves as a means of determining blood volume colorimetrically

ev·ans·ite \ˈevənˌzīt\ *n* -s [Brooke *Evans* †1862 Eng. nickel refiner + E *-ite*] **:** a massive basic aluminum phosphate $Al_3(PO_4)(OH)_6.6H_2O$

ev·ans'–root \ˈevənzˌ≠\ *n* [by folk etymology fr. *avens*] **:** WATER AVENS

ev·ans·ville \ˈevənzˌvil, -ˌvəl\ *adj, usu cap* [fr. *Evansville*, Ind.] **:** of or from the city of Evansville, Ind. **:** of the kind or style prevalent in Evansville

evap·o·ra·ble \ə̇ˈvap(ə)rəbəl, ēˈ-\ *adj* **:** capable of being evaporated

evap·o·rate \ə̇ˈvapəˌrāt, ēˈ-, *usu* -ād·+V\ *vb* -ED/-ING/-S [ME *evaporaten*, fr. L *evaporatus*, past part. of *evaporare*, fr. *e-* + *vapor* steam, vapor — more at VAPOR] *vi* **1 a :** to pass off in vapor **:** escape and be dissipated either as a visible cloud or in particles that are too minute to be visible **b** (1) **:** to pass away or disappear without leaving a trace **:** pass off harmlessly ⟨the principal secret . . . *evaporated* with the advent of the Russian bomb —*Atlantic*⟩ ⟨a book so beguiling that the faintest impulse to criticize ~*s* —Dan Wickenden⟩ ⟨suddenly the anger left him and his pugnaciousness *evaporated* —Erle Stanley Gardner⟩ (2) **:** to shrink or diminish sharply or quickly ⟨the industry's stocks of scrap *evaporated*, leaving only a few days' supply in some areas —*New Internat'l Yr. Bk.*⟩ (3) **:** to grow weak **:** lose in substance, force, or value **:** DECLINE ⟨a thing of infinite beauty in the hands of a master . . . ~*s* into meaningless overrefinement in his imitators —R.A.Hall b.1911⟩ (4) **:** to take sudden leave **:** depart without leaving a trace **:** VANISH ⟨after his first wife *evaporated*, he married the girl —Hugh McGovern⟩ ⟨a foreigner, for the purpose of *evaporating*, paid in advance for the hire of a boat —Norman Douglas⟩ **2** *obs* **:** to issue forth as vapor **:** become exhaled **3 :** to give forth vapor **:** undergo evaporation — compare SUBLIME ~ *vt* **1 a :** to convert from a liquid state into vapor **:** dissipate or draw off in vapor or fumes **b :** to deposit in the form of a film (as a metal or metallic salt) by sublimation of the material from a nearby solid source **c :** EXPEL ⟨~ neutrons from a nucleus⟩ ⟨~ electrons from a thermionic filament⟩ **2 :** to cause to disappear **:** do away with **:** DISSOLVE, WEAKEN, DISSIPATE ⟨the contradiction between ends and means . . . is what Marxism and like ideologies pretend to ~ —David Riesman⟩ **3 :** to expel moisture from (as by heat) leaving the solid portions **:** subject to evaporation ⟨~ apples⟩ **4** *obs* **:** to send out as if vapor **:** give vent to **:** give off (as smoke or an odor) **:** EMIT **syn** see VANISH

evaporated milk *n* **:** milk without added sugar concentrated through evaporation by heat under partial vacuum to one half or less of its bulk and usu. containing a specified amount of milk fat and milk solids — compare CONCENTRATED MILK; see CONDENSED MILK, PLAIN CONDENSED MILK

evaporating dish *n* **:** a shallow usu. lipped vessel often of porcelain used esp. for concentrating solutions on a small scale by evaporation of the solvent

evaporating dish

evap·o·ra·tion \≠ˌ≠≠ˈrāshən\ *n* -s [ME *evaporacioun*, fr. MF or L; MF *evaporation*, fr. L *evaporation-, evaporatio*, fr. *evaporatus* + *-ion-, -io* -ion] **1 a :** the change by which any substance is converted from a liquid state into and carried off in vapor; *specif* **:** the conversion of a liquid into vapor in order to remove it wholly or partly from a liquid of higher boiling point or from solids dissolved in or mixed with it — compare DISTILLATION 1, SUBLIMATION **b :** the process by which molecules of a heated metal or metallic compound are released to be subsequently deposited as a film on neighboring cooler surfaces **:** SUBLIMATION **c :** the expulsion of particles (as of neutrons from a nucleus or electrons from a thermionic filament) **2 :** the process of evaporating or concentrating by conversion of a part into vapor ⟨~ of syrup⟩ **3** *archaic* **:** the product or result of evaporating **:** vapor formed or a reaction effected by evaporating **4 a :** the process of passing away or off without leaving a trace **:** DISAPPEARANCE, DISSIPATION ⟨~ of the fortune took less time . . . and in the early thirties he was on his uppers —R.H.Rovere⟩ ⟨the gradual ~ of humanitarian and democratic spirit —Carl Landauer⟩ **b :** the process of passing into a weaker, less substantial, or inferior state or form **:** WEAKENING, DECLINE ⟨a danger of ~ into a vague . . . mysticism —P.E.More⟩

evaporation tank *n* **:** an experimental tank used to determine the amount of evaporation from the surface of water under measured or observed climatic and cultural conditions

evap·o·ra·tive \ə̇ˈvapəˌrād·|iv, ēˈ-, -p(ə)rə|, |t|, |ēv *also* |əv\ *adj* [ME, fr. LL *evaporativus*, fr. L *evaporatus* + *-ivus* -ive] **:** relating to, producing, or produced by evaporation ⟨~ coating⟩ — **evap·o·ra·tive·ly** \|əvlē, -li\ *adv*

evap·o·ra·tiv·i·ty \əˌvap(ə)rəˈtivəd·ē, ēˌv-, -vətē, -i\ *n* -ES **:** tendency to evaporate **:** rate of evaporation

evap·o·ra·tor \ə̇ˈvapəˌrād·ə(r), ēˈ-, -ātə-\ *n* -s **:** one that evaporates: as **a :** a workman in charge of an evaporation process **b :** a usu. closed apparatus for driving off superfluous liquid (as in a concentration plant for sugar and syrup) or for evaporating liquid for subsequent condensation to purify it (as from salts held in solution) **c :** the part of a refrigeration system in which cooling is produced by evaporation of the liquid refrigerant **d :** a kiln for evaporating

evap·o·rim·e·ter \ə̇ˌvapəˈrimәd·ə(r), ēˌ-\ *also* **evap·o·rom·e·ter** \-ˈräm-\ *n* [*evaporate* + *-i-* or *-o-* + *-meter*] **:** ATMOMETER

evap·o·rite \ə̇ˈvapəˌrīt, ēˈ-\ *n* -s [*evaporation* + *-ite*] **:** a sedimentary rock (as gypsum or salt) that originates by evaporation of sea water in enclosed basins

evap·o·rize \ə̇ˈvapəˌrīz, ēˈ-, -văp-\ *vt* [*e-* + *vaporize*] **:** VAPORIZE

evapo·transpiration \ə̇|va(ˌ)pō, ē|-+\ *n* [*evaporation* + *transpiration*] **:** loss of water from the soil both by evaporation from the surface and by transpiration from the plants growing thereon; *also* **:** the volume of water lost in this way

eva·sé \ˌāˌväˈzā\ *adj* [F *évasé*, fr. past part. of *évaser* to widen the mouth of, flare out, fr. MF *evaser*, fr. *e-* + *vase* — more at VASE] **:** enlarging gradually — used esp. of chimneys or outlet ducts

eva·sion \ə̇ˈvāzhən, ēˈ-\ *n* -s [ME *evasioun*, fr. MF or LL; MF *evasion*, fr. LL *evasion-, evasio*, fr. L *evasus*, (past part. of *evadere* to evade) + *-ion-, -io* -ion — more at EVADE] **1 a :** physical escape or flight ⟨every abolitionist took part in a conspiracy of ~ —S.E.Morison & H.S.Commager⟩ ⟨rented a house . . . for midweek ~*s* of Paris —Janet Flanner⟩ **b :** mental escape ⟨on this basis the springs of action are cleansed without ~ into a false spirituality —A.N.Wilder⟩ **c :** means of escape ⟨war and travel have been the accredited ~ by which a member . . . may relax the pursuit of decorum without derogation of dignity —F.J.Mather⟩ **2 a :** the act or an instance of evading, dodging, or equivocating **:** failure to answer or state one's position directly or candidly ⟨it was not a case of ~, quibbling, or concealment . . . it was sheer, blank, bottomless ignorance —S.H.Adams⟩ ⟨you always come back to my point, in spite of your wrigglings and ~*s* and sophistries —G.B.Shaw⟩ **b :** the act of evading, dodging, or circumventing a law, responsibility, or obligation; *specif* **:** the act of failing to pay taxes or of minimizing taxes in violation of law ⟨opportunities for tax ~ . . . favor self-employment —R.B.Goode⟩

eva·sion·al \-zhənᵊl,-zhnəl\ *adj* **:** constituting an evasion **:** EVASIVE ⟨faces away from his obstacles and seeks his triumph through various ~ procedures —H.A.Overstreet⟩

eva·sive \-ās|iv, |ēv *also* -āz| *or* |əv\ *adj* [*evasion* + *-ive*] **1 a :** tending to evade **:** not direct, candid, or forthright **:** EQUIVOCAL ⟨his answers were brief, constrained, and ~ —T.L.Peacock⟩ ⟨if one persists in merely asking for the truth, they suspect hidden motives and become ~ —Norman Douglas⟩ **b :** avoiding confrontation **:** SHIFTY ⟨the monotonous voice, ~ eyes, and grim, tired face —Peggy Durdin⟩ **2 a :** not easily caught **:** ELUSIVE ⟨dug vigorously for the ~ prey, half fish, half eel —Anne D.Sedgwick⟩ ⟨inspiration is not forever ~ —Warren Beck⟩ **b :** directed toward avoidance of or escape from enemy fire ⟨mentioned . . . for skillful ~ tactics when . . . under attack by German night fighters —*McGill News*⟩ — used esp. in the phrase *evasive action* ⟨all pilots are taught to take ~ action should their ammunition be exhausted —Keith Ayling⟩ **c :** escaping perception or definition **:** VAGUE, NEBULOUS, ELUSIVE ⟨this menace from the north was intangible and ~ —John Buchan⟩ ⟨since she had been brought so close to reality she had had less patience with ~ idealism —Ellen Glasgow⟩

eva·sive·ly \|əvlē, -li\ *adv* **:** in an evasive manner **:** with the use of evasion ⟨answered his questions grudgingly and ~⟩

eva·sive·ness \|ivnə̇s, |ēv- *also* |əv-\ *n* -ES **:** the quality or condition of being evasive ⟨the most crushing blow of all has been the ~ of peace —T.H.Fielding⟩

¹**eve** \ˈēv\ *n* -s [ME, var. of *even*] **1 :** EVENING ⟨from morn to noon he fell, from noon to dewy ~ —John Milton⟩ **2 :** the evening or the day before a holiday, a saint's day, or any important day **3 :** the period immediately preceding some particular event ⟨believed that America was on the ~ of a tremendous theoretical and cultural development—J.T.Farrell⟩

²**eve** \"\ *n* -s *usu cap* [ME, after *Eve*, the first woman in the Bible] **:** a woman having qualities typically associated with womankind **:** WOMAN ⟨an effortlessly feminine creature whose personal career never interferes with her role as a charming, eternal *Eve* —*Newsweek*⟩

³**evé** *usu cap, var of* EWE

evec·tion \ə̇ˈvekshən, ēˈ-\ *n* -s [L *evection-, evectio* act of going up, fr. *evectus* (past part. of *evehere* to carry out, raise up, fr. *e-* + *vehere* to carry) + *-ion-, -io* -ion — more at WAY] **1 :** perturbation of the moon's motion in its orbit due to the attraction of the sun **2** *in certain filamentous algae* **:** displacement of the base of a new branch with respect to its parent cell so as to result in apparent dichotomy — **evec·tion·al** \-shənᵊl,-shnəl\ *adj*

eve green *n, often cap E* [²*eve*] **:** a strong to brilliant yellowish green

evejar \ˈ≠ˌ≠\ *n* [¹*eve* + *jar*] **:** NIGHTJAR

eve method \ˈēv-\ *n, usu cap E* [after Frank C. *Eve*, 20th cent. Brit. physician] **:** artificial respiration by seesawing the victim head up and head down on a stretcher so that the alternating pressure and release of pressure of the abdominal organs against the diaphragm promotes expiration and inspiration

¹**even** \ˈēvən\ *n* -s [ME *even, eve*, fr. OE *ǣfen;* akin to OFris *ēvend* evening, OS *āband*, OHG *āband*, ON *aptann* evening, and perh. to Gk *epi* on — more at EPI-] **1** *archaic* **:** EVENING **2** *archaic* **:** ¹EVE 2

²**even** \"\ *adj, sometimes* -ER/-EST [ME, fr. OE *efen;* akin to OFris *even* even, equal, OS *eban*, OHG *eban*, ON *jafn*, Goth *ibns*] **1 a** (1) **:** having a horizontal surface **:** not sloping **:** FLAT, LEVEL ⟨toiling up the mountain they at last came to ~ ground⟩ (2) **:** being without gross deviation from a geometrical plane ⟨pneumatic hammers . . . work across the . . . block, producing a rough but ~ surface —*Amer. Guide Series: Vt.*⟩ **b :** being without break, indentation, roughness, or other irregularity **:** SMOOTH, CONTINUOUS ⟨the coastline was always ~ and unbroken —Valter Schytt⟩ **c :** being in the same plane or line **:** LEVEL, PARALLEL — used chiefly with *with* ⟨the man came ~ with the corner —Robert Murphy⟩ ⟨houses ~ with each other⟩ ⟨that great wind had laid the tree ~ with the ground⟩ **2 a** (1) **:** being without variation or fluctuation **:** REGULAR, SMOOTH, EQUAL, STEADY, UNIFORM ⟨~ distances apart⟩ ⟨the ~ motion of the airplane⟩ ⟨the ~ beat of raindrops on the roof⟩ ⟨his straight nose and clear ~ features went well with his blondness —Louis Auchincloss⟩ (2) **:** uniform or consistent in character or quality ⟨the darkling sky was all of an ~ slate color⟩ ⟨the texture of his writing is ~ and finished —*Times Lit. Supp.*⟩ (3) **:** LEVEL 5 **b :** not easily disturbed **:** SERENE, UNRUFFLED, CALM, PLACID ⟨the child . . . was naturally of an ~ temper —Samuel Butler †1902⟩ ⟨the ~ tenor of his life⟩ ⟨speaks in a thoughtful, ~ voice —Stuart Keate⟩ **3 a** *obs* **:** STRAIGHTFORWARD, PLAIN, DIRECT **b :** equal in quality, opportunity, or station ⟨they started out ~, since neither had had any playing experience⟩ **c :** giving no advantage to either side ⟨an ~ exchange⟩ ⟨the ~ balance of its interests —F.L.Paxson⟩ **:** FAIR, IMPARTIAL, JUST **d** (1) **:** leaving nothing due on either side **:** SQUARE, QUITS ⟨we shall not be ~ till you repay my visit⟩ (2) **:** fully revenged — often used in the phrase *get even with* ⟨get ~ with his tormentor⟩ **e :** being in equilibrium **:** BALANCED ⟨the scales hang ~⟩; *specif* **:** being neither loser nor gainer **:** showing neither profit nor loss ⟨the firm has had to do an enormous business in order to stay ~ —Harold Koontz & Cyril O'Donnell⟩ **4 :** equal in size, number, or quantity ⟨~ shares⟩ **5 a :** being any member of a sequence of positive integers beginning with two and counting by twos **:** being always exactly divisible by 2 — opposed to *odd* **b :** having an even number as one of a series ⟨an ~ page in a book⟩ ⟨an *even*-pinnate leaf⟩ **c :** containing an even number of individuals ⟨analyzing a committee chairman's tie-breaking function . . . we see that . . . in an ~ committee he is never pivotal —L.S.Shapley & Martin Shubik⟩ **6 :** having neither more nor less than the named or understood amount, extent, or number **:** EXACT ⟨an ~ mile⟩ ⟨an ~ dollar⟩ **7 :** as likely as not **:** nicely balanced **:** FIFTY-FIFTY ⟨it is at least an ~ chance that he will prosper⟩ ⟨he stands an ~ chance of winning⟩ ⟨the chances of success or failure are ~⟩ **syn** see LEVEL, STEADY — **at even hand** *or* **at even hands** *obs* **:** on equal terms — **of even date :** of the same date — used esp. of letters and documents ⟨*of even date* with the treaty was the protocol —J.S.Reeves⟩ — **on even keel** *or* **on an even keel** **1** *of a ship* **a :** having approximately the same draft forward and aft; *sometimes* **:** having the load water line of the ship parallel to the surface of the water (as in a ship whose natural draft is much greater aft than forward) **b :** without list **2** *of an aircraft* **:** in proper fore-and-aft trim **3** *usu on an even keel* **:** in a sound or stable condition **:** STABLE, STEADY, UNSHAKEN ⟨struggling to keep the firm *on an even keel* during the dismal depression years⟩ ⟨a man of character, he stayed *on an even keel* while the others panicked⟩

³**even** \ˈēvən *or except in sense 1b* ˈēᵊm *or* ˈēbᵊm\ *adv* [ME *evene, even*, fr. OE *efne*, fr. *efen*, adj.] **1 a** *obs* **:** without disagreement **:** in accord **b** *knitting* **:** without change by increasing or decreasing — used chiefly in the phrase *work even* ⟨work ~ until armhole measures same as back armhole —*Nat'l Needlecraft Bureau*⟩ **2 a :** as well **:** PRECISELY, JUST, EXACTLY ⟨~ as you and I, children need warmth and affection⟩ ⟨some can appreciate character ~ as other men —Nora Waln⟩ **b :** to a degree that extends **:** FULLY, QUITE ⟨~ to the shedding of some natural tears —William Wordsworth⟩ ⟨to be faithful ~ unto death⟩ **c :** at the very time **:** ALREADY ⟨~ as the fish's head fell from the crocodile's munching mouth there was a swoop of white wings —Francis Birtles⟩ ⟨perhaps ~ now the time has arrived —Walt Whitman⟩ **d** *archaic* **:** to be sure **3 a :** TRULY, INDEED, NAY — used as an intensive that serves to emphasize the identity or character of something ⟨we, ~ we, henceforth flaunt out masterful —Walt Whitman⟩ ⟨a huge, ~ monstrous animal⟩ **b** — used as an intensive serving to indicate an extreme, hypothetical, or unlikely case or instance of something ⟨corruption is so diffused that no one ~ protests —Gilbert Seldes⟩ ⟨refused ~ to look at her⟩ ⟨~ if help comes, it will be too late⟩ ⟨ravaged it ~ to the precious library and family Bible —*Amer. Guide Series: N.C.*⟩ **c** — used as an intensive serving to stress the comparative degree ⟨did ~ better under the new coach⟩ ⟨emeralds are ~ scarcer than rubies⟩ **4 :** in an even manner

⁴**even** \ˈēvən\ *vb* **evened; evened; evening** \ˈēv(ə)niŋ\ **evens** [ME *evenen*, fr. OE *efnan*, fr. *efen*, adj.] *vt* **1 a :** to make (a surface) smooth or even ⟨~ out the soil with a spade⟩ **b :** to make regular or uniform **:** free of fluctuations **:** STABILIZE — often used with *out* ⟨giant reservoirs . . . ~ out the flow of the river by controlling floods in winter and releasing water in dry periods —G.R.Clapp⟩ ⟨~ out the activities of the construction industry . . . providing a reasonable level of construction throughout the year —Beardsley Ruml⟩ **2** *archaic* **a :** to regard as being on the same level **:** treat as equal **:** COMPARE **b :** to come up to **:** MATCH, RIVAL **c :** to bring down to a certain level **3** *dial Brit* **:** ASCRIBE, IMPUTE **4 :** to make even in advantage **:** make (accounts or some other reckoning) balanced **:** make quits ⟨things are ~*ed* up in this world —*Irish Digest*⟩ ⟨his mind . . . is suggestible to suspicious jealousy, and he cannot cease until he is ~*ed* with the Moor wife for wife —*College English*⟩ ~ *vi* **:** to be or become even ⟨odds have probably ~*ed* somewhat between us and the Russians in the air-atomic field —R.W.Frase⟩

even-aged \ˈ≠≠ˌ|ājd\ *adj, of a forest* **:** consisting of trees of a single age

even break *n* **:** an equal chance esp. for success **:** fair chance ⟨a nation that doesn't spy today is not giving its people an *even break* —E.B.White⟩

even court *n,* **:** the right half court in a singles racket game — compare ODD COURT

evendown \ˌ≠≠ˈ≠\ *adj* **1** *dial* **:** straight up and down **:** PERPENDICULAR **2** *dial* **:** OUT-AND-OUT, DOWNRIGHT, SHEER **3** *dial* **:** STRAIGHTFORWARD, CANDID

even·er \ˈēv(ə)nə(r)\ *n* -s **:** one that makes even: as **a :** a pivoting bar of wood which is often reinforced with metal and at each end of which a pivoting singletree is attached **b :** any of various devices on textile machines that regulate the flow or size of material

evenfall \ˈ≠≠ˌ≠\ *n* [¹*even* + *fall*] **:** the beginning of evening ⟨all through the quiet ~ —P.G.Wodehouse⟩

even function *n* **:** a function such that $f(x)=f(-x)$ where the value remains unchanged if the sign of the independent variable is reversed

evenglow \ˈ≠≠ˌ≠\ *n* [¹*even* + *glow*] **:** a reddish gray that is yellower and deeper than mist and lighter, stronger, and slightly bluer than opal gray

evenhanded \ˌ≠≠ˈ≠≠\ *adj* **:** FAIR, IMPARTIAL, UNBIASED ⟨~ justice⟩ ⟨~ rulings⟩ — **even·hand·ed·ly** *adv* — **even·hand·ed·ness** *n* -ES

eve·ning \ˈēvniŋ, -nēŋ *sometimes* ÷ -vən-\ *n* -s *often attrib* [ME, fr. OE *ǣfnung*, fr. *ǣfnian* to grow towards evening (fr. *ǣfen* evening) + *-ung* -ing — more at EVEN] **1 a :** the latter part and close of the day and early part of darkness or night **b** *chiefly South & Midland* **:** the time extending roughly from noon to twilight **:** AFTERNOON ⟨it was about 3 o'clock in the ~⟩ **c :** the part of the day from noon to midnight — used in the Bible **d :** the period from sunset or from the evening meal to bedtime **2 :** the latter portion **:** the period of decline ⟨in the ~ of life⟩ ⟨the ~ of his country's glory⟩ **3 a :** the period of an evening's entertainment ⟨an ~ at the theater⟩ ⟨an ~ of bridge⟩ **b :** an evening party **:** SOIREE ⟨their ~ became widely known for the distinction and wit of the people assembled —C.A.Dinsmore⟩

evening campion *or* **evening lychnis** *n* **:** WHITE CAMPION a

evening dress *n* **:** conventional dress for formal or semiformal evening social occasions: as **a :** a woman's gown with skirt usu. of floor or ankle length **b** (1) **:** men's clothing consisting of a tailcoat and matching trousers usu. in black or midnight blue, a white stiff-bosomed shirt, and white bow tie (2) **:** men's clothing consisting of a tuxedo jacket usu. in black, midnight blue, or white, a black bow tie, a stiff-bosomed or soft pleated shirt, and usu. a cummerbund — compare MORNING DRESS

evening dress b(1)

evening emerald *n* **:** PERIDOT

evening grosbeak *n* **:** a grosbeak (*Hesperiphona vespertina*) which is related to the European hawfinch, which is found in western No. America but occas. strays to eastern Canada and New England, and the male of which is chiefly olivaceous and yellow with some black and white

evening prayer *n, often cap E&P* **:** EVENSONG

evening primrose *n* **:** any of several plants of the family Onagraceae and esp. of the genus *Oenothera; usu* **:** a coarse biennial herb (*O. biennis*) with yellow flowers that open in the evening

evening-primrose family *n* **:** ONAGRACEAE

evening rose *n* **:** any of several nocturnal flowering plants of the family Onagraceae

eve·nings \-ŋz\ *adv* **:** in the evening repeatedly **:** on any evening ⟨he had seen and listened to them playing their guitars ~ around the quad —James Jones⟩ ⟨teenagers and adults use the building ~ for recreation —W.A.Kinney⟩

evening school *n* **:** NIGHT SCHOOL

evening-snow \ˌ≠≠ˈ≠\ *n* **:** a small California annual herb (*Linanthus dichotomus*) with white flowers

evening star *n* **1 a :** a bright planet (as Venus) seen in the western sky after sunset **b :** any planet that rises before midnight **c :** any of the five planets that may be seen with the naked eye at sunset **2 :** a small bulbous plant (*Cooperia drummondii*) of Texas with grasslike leaves and star-shaped white flowers

evening stock *n* **:** a low-growing annual stock (*Mathiola bicornis*) with small purplish flowers

evening student *n* **:** a student at evening school

eveningtide \ˈ≠≠ˌ≠\ *n* **:** EVENTIDE

evening trumpet flower *n* **:** YELLOW JESSAMINE 2

evenk \ə̇ˈveŋk\ *n, pl* **evenk** \"\ *or* **evenks** \-ks\ *or* **even·ki** \-kē\ *usu cap* [Russ] **:** TUNGUS

even·ly \ˈēvənlē, -li\ *adv* [ME *evenliche, evenly*, fr. OE *efenlīce*, fr. *efen* even + *-līce* -ly — more at EVEN] **1 a :** in an even manner or degree **:** in equal parts ⟨a career ~ divided between stage and screen⟩ **b :** IMPARTIALLY, FAIRLY, JUSTLY ⟨she never talked about politics, but was ~ courteous to everyone —H.E.Scudder⟩ **c :** on an equal basis ⟨hoped to found a Latin-American economic bloc strong enough to bargain ~ with U.S. commercial power —*Time*⟩ **2 :** without variation or fluctuation **:** in the same manner or proportion throughout **:** SMOOTHLY, UNIFORMLY ⟨spread plaster ~⟩ ⟨run ~⟩ ⟨there is no climactic choice in the story; it moves ~ on a chain of circumstances —C.C.Walcutt⟩ **3 :** without raising the voice **:** in a flat expressionless voice **:** QUIETLY, UNEMOTIONALLY ⟨"this is a lie," she said ~ —Guy Fowler⟩ ⟨"I'll raise the bloody roof," he said ~ —Nevil Shute⟩

even money *n* **:** equal stakes in betting **:** the same amount on each side in a wager ⟨he bet him *even money*⟩ ⟨an *even money* proposition⟩ ⟨an *even money* bet⟩

even·ness \ˈēvən(n)ə̇s\ *n* -ES [ME *evennesse*, fr. OE *efennes*, fr. *efen* even + *-nes* -ness] **:** the quality or condition of being even: as **a** *archaic* **:** FAIRNESS, IMPARTIALITY **b :** balanced condition ⟨ensure the ~ of the scales of justice⟩ **c :** freedom from variation or fluctuation **:** UNIFORMITY, CONSISTENCY, REGULARITY ⟨her tone regained . . . its ~ of texture from the bottom register to the top —*Current Biog.*⟩ ⟨pronounced each syllable with great ~⟩ **d :** PLACIDITY, EQUANIMITY ⟨kindness and ~ of temper were two of his salient characteristics⟩ **e :** absence of expression esp. in speech **:** FLATNESS ⟨although deeply moved, he spoke with a strange ~⟩

even on *adv, Scot* **:** all the time **:** CONTINUOUSLY

eve·noo \ˌēv(ə)ˈnü, ˌäv-\ *adv, Scot* [³*even* + Sc *noo* now] **:** just now **:** in this moment

even pitch *n* **:** the pitch of a screw to be cut having the number of threads per inch a multiple or a submultiple of the number of threads per inch of the lead screw of the lathe used to cut it

¹**evens** *pres 3d sing of* EVEN, *pl of* EVEN

²**evens** \ˈēvənz\ *n pl but usu sing in constr* [²*even* + *-s*] **1** *Brit* **:** EVEN TIME ⟨a schoolboy who was repeatedly breaking ~ for 100 yards —*Sydney (Australia) Sunday Telegraph*⟩ **2** *Brit* **:** EVEN MONEY ⟨his prospects became dimmer to round thirty-two when ~ was freely offered about him —*Irish Digest*⟩

evensong \ˈ≠≠ˌ≠\ *n, often cap* [ME, fr. OE *ǣfensang*, fr. *ǣfen* evening + *sang* song — more at EVEN, SONG] **1 :** the sixth in a system of seven canonical hours **:** VESPERS **2 :** an evening worship service in the Anglican communion related in origin to vespers and compline — called also *evening prayer*

even–span greenhouse *n* : a greenhouse in which the pitch of the roof is the same on both sides

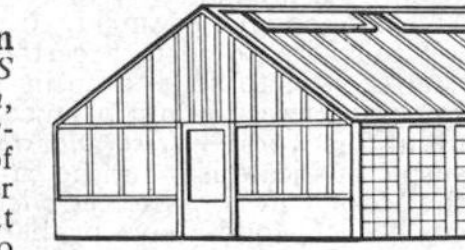
even-span greenhouse

even ste·phen *or* **even ste·ven** \ˌ==ˈstēvən\ *adj, often cap S* [fr. the name *Stephen, Steven,* used as rhyming slang] : having the same score : capable of going one way or the other : TIED, EVEN, FIFTY-FIFTY ⟨at the end of the seventh the two teams were *even Stephen,* no hits, no runs, no errors⟩ ⟨dividing up on an *even Stephen* basis —J.D.Ratcliff⟩ ⟨a few more undecided, and the race will be *even Stephen* —R.L.Neuberger⟩

event \ə'vent, ē'- *chiefly South sometimes* 'ē,v-\ *n* -s [MF or L; MF, fr. L *eventus,* fr. *eventus,* past part. of *evenire* to happen, fr. *e-* + *venire* to come — more at COME] **1 a** (1) : something that happens : OCCURRENCE ⟨this day's ~ has laid on me the duty of opening out my heart —William Wordsworth⟩ ⟨such an ~ would shock the conscience of the world⟩ (2) : course of events : ACTIVITY, EXPERIENCE ⟨ending my brief account of long ~ —D.C.Peattie⟩ ⟨from his dark berth he could see without moving this whole immense and immediate theater of human ~ —Thomas Wolfe⟩ — often used in pl. ⟨~*s* proved the folly of such calculations⟩ **b** : a noteworthy occurrence or happening : something worthy of remark : an unusual or significant development ⟨her new book was the intellectual ~ of the year⟩ ⟨the great ~ of his childhood was a voyage to America⟩ ⟨the flat monotonous plains stretch away . . . a single tree becomes an ~ —Alan Moorehead⟩ **2 a** *obs* : the end to which a person or thing comes : FATE **b** (1) *archaic* : the outcome or consequence of anything : ISSUE, CONCLUSION, RESULT ⟨then very doubtful was the war's ~ —Edmund Spenser⟩ ⟨curiosity as to the ~ of an evening which had raised such splendid expectations —Jane Austen⟩ (2) : the issue or outcome of a legal action or proceeding as finally determined **c** : an outcome, condition, or contingency that is assumed or postulated : CASE, EVENTUALITY — used chiefly in the phrase *in the event* ⟨in the ~ of the king's death, the prince succeeds⟩ ⟨in the ~ he has not been told, I will tell him⟩ ⟨in the ~ you are right, I have been tricked and cheated⟩ **3 a** : any one of the contests in a program of sports ⟨track and field ~*s*⟩ **b** : a competitive contest of a specified kind or class ⟨a bow shot in the same manner as in a regulation target ~⟩ **c** : FIXTURE 3a(1) **4** : an occurrence, phenomenon, or complex of processes occupying a restricted portion of four-dimensional space-time : a happening represented by a point designated by *x, y,* and *z* as coordinates of place and *t* as time in the space-time continuum, it being a fundamental assumption of the theory of relativity that all physical measurements reduce to observations of relations between happenings **syn** see EFFECT, OCCURRENCE — **at all events** *adv* : no matter what else may be : in any case ⟨*at all events,* we shall be free of his company⟩ — **in any event** *adv* : at all events : in any case : at any rate : at least : ANYHOW ⟨*in any event,* you will find him in comfortable circumstances⟩ — **in the event** *adv* : as it turns out : in the sequel : in the result ⟨vaguely he expects "something" to happen, but *in the event* hardly anything ever does —*Times Lit. Supp.*⟩ ⟨*in the event* nearly twice as many French prisoners were sent back as English —Olive Anderson⟩

event·ful \-fəl\ *adj* **1** : full of or rich in events ⟨an ~ period of history⟩ **2** : MOMENTOUS : deeply important ⟨an ~ affair that brought two countries to the verge of war⟩ — **event·ful·ly** \-fəlē, -li\ *adv* — **event·ful·ness** \-fəlnəs\ *n* -ES

eventide \'==,=\ *n* [ME, fr. OE *ǣfentīd,* fr. *ǣfen* evening + *tīd* time — more at EVEN, TIDE] : the time of evening : EVENING

eventide home *n, Brit* : a Salvation Army home for old people

eventilate *vt* [L *eventilatus,* past part. of *eventilare* to fan, winnow, fr. *e-* + *ventilare* to fan, winnow — more at VENTILATE] *obs* : VENTILATE — **eventilation** *n* -s *obs*

even time *n* : the running time of exactly 10 seconds for the 100-yard dash

event·less \ə'ventləs, ē'-\ *adj* : being without event : being without incident ⟨two ~ weeks passed by⟩

ev·en·tog·na·thi \ˌē,venˈtägnə,thī\ *n pl, cap* [NL, irreg. fr. *eu-* + *ent-* + *-gnathi*] *in some classifications* : an order or other group of soft-finned freshwater fishes comprising the carps, suckers, and loaches — **ev·en·tog·na·thous** \ˌ=ˌ=ˈ=nəthəs\ *adj*

even·tra·tion \ˌē,venˈtrāshən\ *n* -s [F *éventration,* fr. *é-* e- + *ventre* belly (fr. L *ventr-, venter*) + *-ation* — more at VENTER] : protrusion of abdominal organs through the abdominal wall — compare EVISCERATION

even·tual \ə'vench(ə)wəl, ē'-, -chəl\ *adj* [L *eventus* event + E *-al* — more at EVENT] **1 a** *obs* : relating to, consisting in, or being an event **b** *obs* : happening to exist : CHANCE, FORTUITOUS **c** *archaic* : dependent or contingent upon certain conditions : CONDITIONAL **2** : taking place, arising, or becoming something at an unspecified later time : ultimately resulting : ULTIMATE, FINAL ⟨hoped for the ~ replacement of the old buildings by others⟩ ⟨predicted the ~ decay and extinction of the monarchical system⟩ ⟨the ~ successor to the presidency⟩ **syn** see LAST

even·tu·al·i·ty \ə,=chəˈwaləd·ē, -lətē, -i\ *n* -ES **1** : something that may possibly happen : CONTINGENCY, POSSIBILITY ⟨preparation for the ~ of war⟩ ⟨positions which, in certain *eventualities,* might early become the scene of military operations —*Current History*⟩ **2** : ultimate result or consequence ⟨some *eventualities* we can predict, but not the circumstances of their realization —L.J.Halle⟩

even·tu·al·ly \-ch(ə)lē, -li, -ch(ə)wəl-\ *adv* : at an unspecified later time : in the end : at last : FINALLY, ULTIMATELY ⟨that plan . . . was ~ abandoned as impracticable —Havelock Ellis⟩ ⟨~ achieved success⟩

even·tu·ate \-chə,wāt, *usu* -ād· +V\ *vi* -ED/-ING/-S [L *eventus* + E *-ate*] : to come out finally or in conclusion : come to pass : turn out : RESULT ⟨as things *eventuated* orthodoxy and revolution were not left to fight it out —F.L.Allen⟩ ⟨his illness *eventuated* in death⟩ — **even·tu·a·tion** \ə,=chəˈwāshən\ *n* -s

¹even-up \ˌ==ˈ=\ *adj* [²*even* + *up*] : EVEN 7

²even-up \"\ *adv* : without odds or a handicap being granted by either side in a bet or competition

eveque \āˈvek\ *n* -s [F *évêque* bishop, fr. LL *episcopus* — more at BISHOP] : MADDER VIOLET

¹ev·er \'evə(r)\ *adv* [ME, fr. OE *ǣfre;* prob. akin to OE *ā* always — more at AYE] **1 a** : at all times : ALWAYS, CONSTANTLY, CONTINUOUSLY ⟨he is ~ making the same mistake⟩ ⟨interference in their affairs became ~ less as they became more capable of managing them —B.K.Sandwell⟩ **b** : through all time : through an indefinite time ⟨he will ~ be regarded with gratitude by his countrymen⟩ ⟨I have not seen him ~ since⟩ **c** : in each and every case : INVARIABLY ⟨war and suffering have ~ gone hand in hand⟩ **2** : at any time : on any occasion : at any period or point of time ⟨he is seldom if ~ a visitor⟩ : in any way : by any chance ⟨how could I ~ have lost it⟩ ⟨how can I ~ thank you⟩ : at all ⟨what can I ~ do to repay you⟩ **3 a** : KNOWN — used as an intensive with a superlative ⟨it was New York City and State's worst wreck ~ —*Springfield (Mass.) Union*⟩ **b** (1) — used as an intensive esp. with *so* ⟨the primary data are ~ so often not even cataloged —L.D. Reddick⟩ ⟨does an *ever*-so-cute little dance —*Time*⟩ ⟨thank you ~ so much⟩ ⟨it did him ~ so much good⟩ (2) : EXTREMELY, IMMENSELY — used as an intensive preceding and modifying an adjective after an inverted verb-subject construction ⟨boy . . . was I ~ green —Richard Bissell⟩ ⟨is he ~ proud of it⟩

²ever \"\ *adj* [by shortening] *dial* : EVERY ⟨that's what I say ~ time —Helen Eustis⟩

ever and again *or* **ever and anon** *adv* : from time to time : now and then

everbearer \ˌ==ˈ==, ˈ==,==\ *n* : a plant that is everbearing

everbearing \ˌ==ˈ==\ *adj* : bearing more or less continuously ⟨an ~ strawberry⟩ — compare EVERBLOOMING

everbearing grape *n* : a slender low-growing grape (*Vitis munsoniana*) of the West Indies and the extreme southeastern U.S. that is closely related to the muscadine and ripens its fruit over a long period

everbloomer \ˌ==ˈ==, ˈ==,==\ *n* : an everblooming plant

everblooming \ˌ==ˈ==\ *adj* : blooming more or less continuously throughout the growing season — opposed to *seasonal*

everblooming cherry *n* : ALL SAINTS' CHERRY

everduring \ˌ==ˈ==\ *adj, archaic* : EVERLASTING

ev·er·est \'ev(ə)rəst, -vərst, -və,rest\ *n* -s *usu cap* [fr. Mount *Everest* in the Himalayas between Nepal and Tibet, the highest mountain in the world] : the highest point : CLIMAX, APEX ⟨has reached an *Everest* of vulgarity that may well stand as a mark —*Time*⟩ ⟨the everlasting *Everest* of all classic puns —*Holiday*⟩

ev·er·ett *also* **ev·er·ette** \ˌevəˈret\ *n* -s [origin unknown] : a man's lounging slipper having a low back and a front reaching to the instep

everett

ev·er·glades kite \'evə(r),glādz-\ *or* **everglade kite** \-d-\ *n, often cap E* [fr. the *Everglades,* a large tract of marshland in southern Florida] : a small bluish gray kite (*Rostrhamus sociabilis plumbeus*) ranging from So. America to Florida

¹evergreen \'==,=\ *adj* [¹*ever* + *green*] **1** : remaining verdant ⟨an ~ coniferous tree⟩ ⟨~ tropical plants⟩ — compare DECIDUOUS **2** : ever retaining its freshness, interest, or popularity : ever enduring : PERENNIAL, UNCEASING, PERPETUAL ⟨the plot is the ~ one —Henry Hellssen⟩ ⟨keep us in ~ remembrance of the days of old —Daniel O'Connell⟩ ⟨the . . . author of ~ romances —*Brit. Book News*⟩

²evergreen \"\ *n* **1** : an evergreen plant (as the pine, holly, ivy, laurel, rhododendron, and most tropical plants); *also* : CONIFER **2 evergreens** *pl* : twigs and branches of evergreen plants used for decoration **3 a** : ORPINE **b** : either of two club mosses (*Lycopodium clavatum* and *L. complanatum*) **c** : PIPSISSEWA **d** : CHERRY LAUREL 2 **4** : a dark green that is bluer and less strong than forest green (sense 1) and bluer than average bottle green **5** : something that ever retains its freshness, interest, or popularity ⟨a trio of jazz ~*s* —Wilder Hobson⟩

evergreen beech *n* : a tree of the genus *Nothofagus*

evergreen bittersweet *n* : an Asiatic woody vine (*Euonymus radicans vegetus*) with pinkish fruits

evergreen blueberry *n* : a shrub (*Vaccinium myrsinites*) of the southeastern U.S. with shining evergreen leaves and bluish black fruit

evergreen cherry *n* **1** : CHERRY LAUREL 2 **2** : ISLAY

evergreen grass *n* : TALL OAT GRASS

evergreen magnolia *n* **1** : a magnolia (*Magnolia grandiflora*) of the southern U.S. having evergreen foliage and large white flowers **2** : the wood of the evergreen magnolia

evergreen millet *n* : JOHNSON GRASS

evergreen oak *n* : any of various oaks with foliage that persists for two years so that the plant is more or less continuously green: as **a** : HOLM OAK **b** : COAST LIVE OAK — see LIVE OAK

evergreen thorn *n* **1** : FIRE THORN **2** : an evergreen hawthorn (*Crataegus oxyacantha*) of southeastern Europe

evergreen winterberry *n* : INKBERRY 1

evergreen wood fern *n* **1** : a No. American fern (*Dryopteris marginalis*) with evergreen fronds **2** : CHRISTMAS FERN

¹everlasting \ˌ==ˈ==\ *adj* [ME, fr. ¹*ever* + *lasting,* pres. part. of *lasten* to last — more at LAST] **1** : lasting or enduring through all time : ETERNAL ⟨what a peace is mine, leaning on the ~ arms —E.A.Hoffman⟩ ⟨belief in unchanging and ~ laws governing the physical universe⟩ **2 a** (1) : continuing indefinitely or during a long period : PERPETUAL ⟨reached the zone of ~ snow⟩ ⟨the one thing that seemed to her immutable and ~ was the poverty of the soil —Ellen Glasgow⟩ (2) *of a plant* : retaining its form or color for a long time when dried ⟨~ flowers⟩ **b** : wearisome or tedious from repetition : CONTINUAL ⟨she had grown tired of his ~ whimpering —O.E. Rölvaag⟩ **3** : wearing indefinitely : DURABLE ⟨~ cotton homespun⟩

²everlasting \"\ *n* [ME (*the*) *Everlastinge,* fr. *everlasting,* adj.] **1** *cap* : GOD — used with *the* ⟨the *Everlasting*⟩ **2** : eternal duration : ETERNITY — used chiefly in the phrase *from everlasting* ⟨from ~ thou! —S.T.Coleridge⟩ **3** *or* **everlasting flower a** : any of several plants chiefly of the family Compositae that have flowers which can be dried without loss of form or color: as (1) : LADIES' TOBACCO (2) : STRAWFLOWER 1 (3) : CUDWEED a (4) : a plant of the genus *Anaphalis* (5) : STATICE (6) *usu everlasting flower* : a plant of the Australian genus *Waitzia* **b** : the flower or bloom of any everlasting **4** : a strong durable woolen material of twill or satin weave similar to lasting

ev·er·last·ing·ly *adv* [ME, fr. *everlasting* + *-ly*] **1** : in an everlasting manner ⟨his name will be ~ remembered⟩ ⟨a bird whose plumage remains ~ green —*Publ's Mod. Lang. Assoc. of Amer.*⟩ ⟨this shoe wears ~⟩ ⟨he was ~ whining⟩ **2** : most certainly or completely : IMMEASURABLY ⟨splendidly and ~ right in his determination not to be pressured into war —*New Republic*⟩

ev·er·last·ing·ness *n* [ME *everlastingnesse,* fr. *everlasting* + *-nesse* -ness] : the quality or condition of being everlasting : ETERNITY, IMMORTALITY ⟨a belief in the ~ of our spiritual nature —W.R.Inge⟩

everlasting pea *n* : any of several perennial plants of the genus *Lathyrus* (esp. *L. latifolius*) having usu. purple flowers

everlasting thorn *n* : a fire thorn (*Pyracantha coccinea*)

ev·er·ly \'evə(r)lē\ *adv* [ME, fr. ¹*ever* + *-ly*] *dial* : CONTINUALLY

evermore \ˌ==ˈ=\ *adv* [ME *evermo, evermore,* fr. OE *ǣfre mā,* fr. *ǣfre* ever + *mā* more — more at EVER, MORE] **1** : during eternity : at all times : ALWAYS, FOREVER ⟨brightly beams our Father's mercy from his lighthouse ~ —P.P.Bliss⟩ **2** : at any future time : in the future : ever again ⟨means to lead a blameless life ~ —W.S.Gilbert⟩ ⟨I may not ~ acknowledge thee —Shak.⟩ **3** *dial* : CERTAINLY, DEFINITELY ⟨he can ~ ride a horse —R.P.Warren⟩

ever·nia \ə'vərnēə, ē'-\ *n, cap* [NL, irreg. fr. Gk *euernēs* sprouting well (fr. *eu-* + *ernos* sprout) + NL *-ia*] : a genus of lichens (family Usneaceae) having a fruticose or pendulous thallus with a cottony medulla

ever-normal granary *n* : stocks of farm products established under a governmental policy of buying and storing surpluses in order to stabilize prices and as a safeguard against crop failures

ever·si·ble \ē'vərsəbəl, ə'-, -rzə-\ *adj* [*eversion* + *-ible*] : capable of being everted

ever·sion \-rzhən, -rsh-\ *n* -s [ME *eversioun,* fr. MF, fr. L *eversion-, eversio,* fr. *eversus* (past part. of *evertere*) + *-ion-, -io* -ion] **1** *obs* : the act of everting : DESTRUCTION **2** : the act of turning inside out : the state of being turned inside out ⟨~ of the eyelid⟩ ⟨~ of the bladder⟩ **3** : the condition of being turned outward ⟨~ of the foot⟩

eversporting \ˌ==ˈ==\ *adj, biol* : producing sports repeatedly

evert \ē'vərt, ə'-\ *vt* -ED/-ING/-S [L *evertere* to turn out, overturn, overthrow, destroy, fr. *e-* + *vertere* to turn — more at WORTH] **1** : OVERTHROW, UPSET ⟨dash it all! It ~*s* my pet theory —W.H.Wright⟩ **2** : to turn outward (as the foot) or inside out

evertebrate \(ˈ)ē+\ *adj or n* [*e-* + *vertebrate*] : INVERTEBRATE

ever·tor \ē'vərd·ə(r), ə'-\ *n* -s [NL, irreg. fr. L *evertere* + *-or*] : a muscle that rotates a part outward

everwhich \ˌ==ˈ=\ *pron* [by alter.] *dial* : WHICHEVER

everwho \ˌ==ˈ=\ *pron* [by alter.] *dial* : WHOEVER

¹ev·ery \'evrē, |i *sometimes* 'evər|\ *adj* [ME *everich, every,* fr. OE *ǣfre ǣlc,* fr. *ǣfre* ever + *ǣlc* each — more at EVER, EACH] **1 a** : being each individual or part of a class or group whether definite or indefinite in number without exception ⟨listened carefully to his ~ word⟩ ⟨~ citizen of the town was there⟩ ⟨has ~ quality needed for success⟩ **b** : being each in a series or succession of similar things ⟨out of ~ five men only two were fit⟩ **c** : being each in a succession of intervals ⟨~ few days⟩ ⟨~ little while⟩ **2** *obs* : being all taken severally **3** *archaic* : EVEN — used with *the* and a superlative ⟨~ the least iota⟩ **4** : being each and all within the range of contemplated possibilities ⟨given ~ chance⟩ ⟨~ prospect of success⟩ **5** : COMPLETE, ENTIRE ⟨have ~ confidence in him⟩ — **every now and then** *or* **every now and again** *or* **every so often** : at intervals : OCCASIONALLY, REPEATEDLY ⟨*every now and then* the public gives a great heave of boredom —Cyril Connolly⟩ ⟨dogs sailed out *every so often,* yelping and howling —Marion Hargrove⟩

²every *like* ¹EVERY\ *pron* [ME *everich, every,* fr. *everich, every,* adj.] *archaic* : EVERYONE ⟨occasions given to ~ of us —Richard Hooker⟩

every bit *adv* : in every way : QUITE ⟨the end was *every bit* as good as the beginning —Rumer Godden⟩

ev·ery·body \'evrē,bädē, 'evri,bädi, 'evrə,b- *sometimes* -(,)bəd-, *chiefly in substand or rapid speech* 'evə(r)(,)b-\ *pron* [ME, fr. ¹*every* + *body*] **1** : every person : EVERYONE ⟨~ must do what his conscience dictates⟩ ⟨a theory arguing that ~ is motivated by self-interest⟩ **2 a** : every person forming part of a particular group ⟨there is a seat for ~ in the room⟩ — usu. referred to by the third person singular ⟨~ is bringing his own lunch⟩ but sometimes by a plural personal pronoun ⟨~ had made up their minds⟩ **b** : every person considered worthwhile (as in a particular group or in society) ⟨~ will be there⟩

¹everyday \'==,= *sometimes* ˌ==ˈ=\ *adj* [*every day*] **1 a** : used or occurring routinely or typically ⟨the community . . . was once entirely Gaelic speaking and still retains the lilt of it in ~ speech —*Current Biog.*⟩ ⟨the class provides training for meeting and solving ~ problems⟩ ⟨the needs of the ~ movie audience —H.G.Weinberg⟩ **b** *of clothes* : suitable or designed for wear on ordinary days as contrasted with those worn on holidays or special occasions **2** : lacking in unusual or distinctive quality or incident : PLAIN, UNVARNISHED, HOMELY, ORDINARY, COMMONPLACE, DRAB ⟨his characters speak a plain ~ speech, free of literary bombast or rhetoric⟩ ⟨wrote of ~ people who grew out of the soil, not about exceptional individuals —Willa Cather⟩ ⟨feels deeply for such ~ characters as scrubwomen —Wolcott Gibbs⟩ ⟨their life is ordinary and their story is ~ —Katharine Scherman⟩

²everyday \ˌ==ˈ=\ *n* : the typical, routine, or ordinary day : ordinary existence or routine ⟨I wore this dress — I wear it for ~ —Eudora Welty⟩ ⟨the trite and feeble language of ~ —C.S.Kilby⟩

ev·ery·day·ness \ˌ==ˈdānəs\ *n* -ES : everyday quality : COMMONPLACENESS, TYPICALITY ⟨paints the objects themselves in all their vulgar ~ —Roger Fry⟩

everyhow \ˌ==ˈ=\ *adv* [¹*every* + *how*] : in every way

¹ev·ery·man \'==,man, -maa(ə)n\ *pron* [ME *every man*] : EVERYBODY

²everyman \"\ *n, pl* **everymen** *often cap* [after *Everyman,* allegorical character in *The Summoning of Everyman,* 15th cent. English morality play] : the typical or ordinary man ⟨an *Everyman,* salt of the earth, graduate of the school of hard knocks —E.B.Garside⟩

ev·ery·one \'==,wən *sometimes* -,wən\ *pron* : EVERYBODY

everyplace \'==,=\ *adv* : in every place : EVERYWHERE

everything \'==,=\ *pron* [ME *every thing*] **1 a** : all that exists or is conceived as existing : ALL ⟨a theory that ~ can be apprehended by the human mind⟩ **b** : every thing forming part of an aggregate ⟨~ in this room belongs to me⟩ **c** : all that relates to the subject under consideration ⟨the substitute housekeeper . . . turned out to be ~ that was wrong —Helen Daringer⟩ ⟨tell the fine gentlemen at court that I know ~, and have marvelous disclosures to make —Max Peacock⟩ **2 a** : something that is most important or excellent : the sum total of all desirable or needed qualities : all that counts ⟨he said that in the theater he thought that the author was ~ —Arnold Bennett⟩ ⟨the Bible was ~ to him —L.C.Powys⟩ ⟨to the Puritan the inward relation of the soul to God is ~ —G.L. Dickinson⟩ ⟨this means ~ to me⟩ ⟨that third baseman has ~⟩ **b** : all of one's capacity or ability : the sum total of one's efforts — often used with following *have* ⟨allowed himself to be persuaded to give a solo item and put ~ he had into a piece —*Irish Digest*⟩ ⟨giving his keynote address ~ he had⟩ **3** : all sorts of other things — used with *and* to indicate the existence of related but unspecified facts or conditions ⟨there's a ticklish situation in the world, with international politics all mixed up and ~ —Sinclair Lewis⟩ ⟨people . . . are not going to shell out any more than about 35 cents for a book, especially if they are hungry and ~ —Mac Hyman⟩ — **like everything** *adv* : with maximum energy, effort, or effect ⟨he ran *like everything*⟩ ⟨it shook him up *like everything*⟩

every-way \ˌ==ˈ=\ *adv* : in every way or respect ⟨his brother is *every-way* superior in talent⟩

everywhen \ˌ==ˈ=\ *adv* : at any or all times ⟨the universal operation of Spirit manifested everywhere and ~ —J.H. Muirhead⟩

¹everywhere \'==,=\ *adv* [ME, fr. *every* + *where*] **1** : in every place : in all places ⟨poverty anywhere is a danger to prosperity and peace ~ —*Current History*⟩ **2** : in every part : THOROUGHLY, ALTOGETHER ⟨his own prose is ~ a vivid demonstration of disdain for brevity —S.E.Fitzgerald⟩ **3** : WHEREVER ⟨~ you go, people are much the same⟩

²everywhere \"\ *n* **1** : every place : all places ⟨~ seemed silent, but for the rattle of trains —D.H.Lawrence⟩ ⟨people came from ~ for the auction⟩ **2** : boundless space ⟨where did you come from, baby dear? out of the ~ into the here —George Macdonald †1905⟩

ev·ery·wheres \-z\ *adv* [*everywhere* + *-s*] *chiefly dial* : EVERYWHERE

every which way *adv* [prob. by folk etymology fr. ME *everich wey,* fr. *everich* every + *wey* way — more at EVERY, WAY] **1** : in every direction ⟨blasting his tanks *every which way* with direct fire —Walter Karig⟩ **2** : in a disorderly manner : IRREGULARLY ⟨big jagged boulders piled up *every which way* —*Jewelers' Circular-Keystone*⟩

¹eves *pl of* EVE

²evés *pl of* EVÉ

eve's constant \'ēvz-\ *n, usu cap E* [after Arthur S. *Eve* †1948 Brit. physicist] : a measure of the intensity of radioactivity of a given substance consisting of the number of ions produced per second per cubic centimeter of ordinary air at a distance of one centimeter from one gram of the substance when in radioactive equilibrium

eve's needle *or* **eve's–darning–needle** \'ēvz-\ *n, usu cap E* [after *Eve,* the first woman in the Bible] : ADAM'S NEEDLE 1

eveweed \'==,=\ *n* [¹*eve* + *weed;* fr. its high fragrance in the evening] : DAME'S VIOLET

evg *abbr* evening

evian water \(')āvˈyäⁿ-\ *n, usu cap E* [after *Évian*-les-Bains, town in southeastern France where it is found] : a noneffervescent alkaline mineral water

evict \ə'vikt, ē'-\ *vt* -ED/-ING/-S [ME *evicten,* fr. LL *evictus,* past part. of *evincere,* fr. L, to vanquish, win a point in an argument, demonstrate — more at EVINCE] **1 a** : to recover (property) of or from a person by legal process or by virtue of a superior title **b** : to put out (a person) from property by legal process or by virtue of a paramount right or claim of such right : EJECT, OUST **2** : to force out : EXPEL ⟨a heavy counterattack ~*ed* the enemy from the town⟩ **3** [L *evictus*] *obs* **a** : to conquer in disputation : CONFUTE, CONVINCE **b** : to establish by reason or evidence : PROVE **syn** see EJECT

evict·ee \ə,vikˈtē\ *n* -s [*evict* + *-ee*] : one that is evicted ⟨the ~*s* rolled up in a truck with all their furniture —*Time*⟩

evic·tion \ə'vikshən\ *n* -s [ME, fr. LL *eviction-, evictio,* fr. *evictus* + L *-ion-, -io* -ion] **1** : the act or process of evicting or the state of being evicted **2 a** : the recovery of lands or tenements from another's possession by due course of law — compare EJECTMENT, OUSTER **b** : dispossession in virtue of a paramount title **c** : dispossession of a tenant by his landlord **3** *obs* : conclusive evidence : PROOF

evic·tor \-ktə(r)\ *n* -s [ML, fr. LL *evictus* + L *-or*] : one that evicts

¹ev·i·dence \'evədən(t)s *also* -d'n- *or* -,den-\ *n* -s [ME, fr. MF, fr. LL *evidentia,* fr. L *evident-, evidens* evident + *-ia* -y — more at EVIDENT] **1 a** : an outward sign : INDICATION, TOKEN ⟨~*s* of prosperity⟩ ⟨let's have an ~ of good faith⟩ **b** : something that furnishes or tends to furnish proof : means of making proof : medium of proof : PROOF, TESTIMONY ⟨on every ~ we now have —*N.Y.Times*⟩ ⟨on the ~ of many people who have seen such paintings, . . . their imagery has a very haunting quality —Herbert Read⟩; *specif* : something legally submitted to a competent tribunal as a means of ascertaining the truth of any alleged matter of fact under investigation before it — see CIRCUMSTANTIAL EVIDENCE **2** : one who bears witness; *esp* : one who voluntarily confesses a crime and testifies for the prosecution against his accomplices usu. in the expectation of lenient treatment — see KING'S EVIDENCE, STATE'S EVIDENCE **3** *archaic* : the state of being evident : CLEARNESS — **in evidence 1** : to be seen : PROMINENT, CONSPICUOUS ⟨two members of the committee were not *in evidence*⟩ ⟨he was much *in evidence* during the bitterest fighting of the war⟩ ⟨trim lawns and gardens are everywhere *in evidence* —*Amer. Guide Series: N.C.*⟩ **2** : as evidence ⟨papers submitted *in evidence*⟩

[2]**evidence** \"\ *vb* -ED/-ING/-S *vt* : to offer or constitute evidence of : PROVE, DISPLAY, EVINCE ⟨initiative is *evidenced* by willingness to accept responsibility —A.W.McCain⟩ ⟨certificates *evidencing* stock ownership —*U.S. Code*⟩ ⟨the friendliness she had formerly *evidenced* to the U.S. —V.G.Heiser⟩ ~ *vi, archaic* : to give evidence **syn** see SHOW

ev·i·den·cy \-nsē\ *n* -ES [LL *evidentia*] *archaic* : EVIDENCE

[1]**ev·i·dent** \-nt\ *adj* [ME, fr. MF, fr. L *evident-, evidens,* fr. *e-* + *vident-, videns,* pres. part. of *vidēre* to see — more at WIT] **1 a** : capable of being perceived esp. by sight : distinctly visible : being in evidence : DISCERNIBLE ⟨nature in England, slow and ~ in its process, mild in its changes —Francis Hackett⟩ ⟨quaint ways are still ~ in these moneymaking times —F.H.Eliot⟩ ⟨there is no ~ impairment of the organs⟩ ⟨an ~ erasure in the manuscript⟩ ⟨a considerable amount of placer mining is still ~ —*Amer. Guide Series: Oregon*⟩ **b** : clear to the understanding : OBVIOUS, MANIFEST, APPARENT ⟨his leadership qualities soon became ~⟩ ⟨rose with the ~ intention of leaving the room⟩ — often used with impersonal *it* ⟨it is ~ that we do not understand each other⟩ **2** *obs* : CONVINCING, CONCLUSIVE

syn APPARENT, PATENT, MANIFEST, PLAIN, CLEAR, DISTINCT, OBVIOUS, PALPABLE, along with EVIDENT, are often interchangeable without much variation in meaning, implication, or suggestion; any of these words could be substituted for EVIDENT in the sentence "at this point my opponent's disregard for truth becomes *evident*". Since EVIDENT rather naturally suggests *evidence*, it may imply the existence of signs and indications that must lead to an identification or inference ⟨it is abundantly *evident* that American citizens everywhere are demanding and supporting speedy and complete action —F.D. Roosevelt⟩ APPARENT may occas. suggest a longer period of observation or reasoning ⟨as experience accumulated it gradually became *apparent* that the oils of any of the trees . . . were equally efficacious —V.G.Heiser⟩ ⟨a few years ago this inconsistency became *apparent* to some —C.H.Grandgent⟩ PATENT may stress ease of sight and lack of any obscuring or concealing factor ⟨to compress and define a character or story and make it *patent* at a glance, within the narrow scope attainable by sculpture —Nathaniel Hawthorne⟩ ⟨in Roosevelt's case the imposture is less *patent;* he died before it was fully unmasked —H.L.Mencken⟩ MANIFEST may add to PATENT suggestions or very open showing or exhibiting and may suggest a shade of purposefulness while PATENT stresses only the fact of openness ⟨the *manifest* will of the king to free himself from parliamentary control estranged the Lower House —J.R.Green⟩ ⟨his May devotions were so largely attended, esp. by the young people of the parish, in whom a notable increase of piety was *manifest* —Willa Cather⟩ PLAIN may connote an ease in perception through absence of confusing adventitious matter ⟨in the unlikely event of any European at all being familiar with the "full inside story" . . . it would be his *plain* duty to make his facts known to the police —*Times Lit. Supp.*⟩ CLEAR may suggest easy and assured perception with sharp definiteness and evident certainty ⟨a principle of science based on proof as sharp and *clear* as anything which is known —K.K.Darrow⟩ ⟨until our flow of supplies gives us *clear* superiority we must keep on striking our enemies —F.D.Roosevelt⟩ DISTINCT stresses sharpness of outline, delineation, or definition, and hence unmistakable impression ⟨those shapes *distinct* that yet survive insculptured on the walls of palaces —William Wordsworth⟩ OBVIOUS, often contrasted with *subtle*, stresses ease of perception or interpretation or, more strongly, inevitability of notice ⟨axioms so familiar to us that they seem *obvious* truths —Havelock Ellis⟩ ⟨new mechanical and electrical devices . . . automobiles, electric refrigerators, and radios, to mention the most *obvious* examples —J.B.Conant⟩ PALPABLE, in other uses a synonym for *tangible*, may suggest the ease and inevitability of perception associated with solid masses ⟨the least provident of barbaric despots may raise a massive pile of buildings because it is the most *palpable* proof of his present wealth and power —Alfred Marshall⟩ With these words general similarity of meaning is more noteworthy than occasional differences in connotation.

[2]**evident** \"\ *n* -S [ME (Sc dial.), fr. *evident*, adj.] *archaic* : a thing that serves as evidence

ev·i·den·tial \ˌevəˈdenchəl\ *adj* [ML *evidentialis*, fr. LL *evidentia* evidence + *-alis* -al — more at EVIDENCE] : being, relating to, or affording evidence ⟨conducted an exhaustive examination of the scene for ~ signs of a forced entrance —W.H.Wright⟩ — **ev·i·den·tial·ly** \-ch(ə)lē, -li\ *adv*

ev·i·den·tia·ry \-ch(ə)rē, -ri\ *adj* [LL *evidentia* + E *-ary*] **1** : EVIDENTIAL **2** : determined by, concerning, or deriving its validity from the law of evidence ⟨~ fact⟩ ⟨~ technique⟩ ⟨~ value⟩

ev·i·dent·ly \ˈevədəntlē, ˈevəˌden-, ˌevəˈden-, ˈevədᵊn-, -li\ *adv* [ME, fr. *evident* + *-ly*] : in an evident manner : PERCEPTIBLY, CLEARLY, OBVIOUSLY, PLAINLY ⟨~ the most strenuous exertions must be made by all —Sir Winston Churchill⟩

ev·i·dent·ness \ˈevədəntnəs, -ˌden-\ *n* -ES : evident quality : CLEARNESS ⟨youth's fire surpasses in ~ the settled glow of the forties —Reginald Farrer⟩

[1]**evil** \ˈēvəl *sometimes* -(ˌ)vil\ *adj, sometimes* **eviler** *or* **eviller**; **evilest** *or* **evillest** [ME *ivel, evel, evil,* fr. OE *yfel;* akin to OFris *evel* evil, OS *ubil*, OHG *ubil*, Goth *ubils* evil, and perh. to OE *ūp* up; fr. the concept that evil is beyond the limits of accepted conduct — more at UP] **1 a** : not good morally : marked by bad moral qualities : violating the rules of morality : WICKED, SINFUL ⟨fell into ~ courses⟩ ⟨never was a more ~ attitude toward life transmitted to the young —Stephen Duggan⟩ ⟨an ~ piece of work⟩ **b** : arising from actual or imputed bad character or conduct ⟨this tribe has acquired an ~ name among its neighbors⟩ ⟨a man of ~ fame⟩ **2 a** *archaic* : unsound or inferior in quality : WORTHLESS, POOR ⟨it is hard to believe this ~ tree could produce so beneficent a wine —Andrew Young⟩ **b** : causing discomfort or repulsion : UNCOMFORTABLE, OFFENSIVE, PAINFUL, FOUL ⟨a liquid with an ~ smell⟩ ⟨awoke with a start from a most realistic and ~ dream⟩ ⟨the strange fruit had an ~ taste⟩ ⟨it was an ~ trip through fever-ridden jungles —S.H.Adams⟩ ⟨forward progress halted because of ice and ~ weather —*All Hands*⟩ **c** : ANGRY, DISAGREEABLE, UNPLEASANT, WRATHFUL, MALIGNANT ⟨found him ailing and in an ~ temper⟩ ⟨cast an ~ glance at his opponent⟩ ⟨he was ever an ~ companion the morning after a drinking bout⟩ **3 a** : causing or tending to cause harm : BANEFUL, HARMFUL, PERNICIOUS ⟨the reaction of the slave system upon the southern people . . . was wholly ~ —V.L.Parrington⟩ ⟨people . . . remember sins committed secretly and wonder whether they have caused the ~ sequence —John Steinbeck⟩ ⟨other spots . . . without the ~ concomitants of lagoon and fever-breeding vapors —Helen T. Lowe⟩ **b** : portending harm or misfortune ⟨messengers . . . coming in from all sides with ~ rumors of an immediate attack —T.E.Lawrence⟩ ⟨they spit on the ground to avert the ~ omen —J.G.Frazer⟩ **c** : WRETCHED, MISERABLE, UNFORTUNATE ⟨~ weather caused a postponement⟩ ⟨~ luck was presaged by the flight of a bird past the window —*Amer. Guide Series: Ind.*⟩ ⟨the fish of ~ hap which . . . had been caught and frozen fast in the transparent ice —Llewelyn Powys⟩ ⟨found himself in a most ~ plight⟩ **d** : marked or signalized by misfortune or calamity : UNLUCKY, INAUSPICIOUS ⟨the school fell upon ~ days⟩ ⟨made his friendship in an ~ hour⟩ ⟨my days have been few and ~ —Ann E. Bleecker⟩ **syn** see BAD

[2]**evil** \"\ *adv* [ME *ivel, evel, evil,* fr. OE *yfele, yfle,* fr. *yfel,* adj.] *archaic* : in an evil manner : BADLY

[3]**evil** \"\ *n* -S [ME *ivel, evel, evil,* fr. *ivel, evel, evil,* adj.] **1 a** : the fact of suffering and wickedness : the totality of undesirable, harmful, wicked acts, experiences, and things ⟨attempts to explain the origin of ~ in the world⟩ ⟨regarding ~ . . . as a necessary means of realizing the good —Frank Thilly⟩ **b** : a cosmic force producing evil actions or states **c** (1) : WICKEDNESS, SIN ⟨don't make the mistake of thinking that you are dealing with a woman, . . . you happen to be dealing with ~ in its most absolute form —Hamilton Basso⟩ (2) : the wicked or undesirable element or portion of anything ⟨the ~ in that man outweighs the good⟩ **d** (1) : evil actions or deeds — used chiefly with *do* ⟨lived a blameless life, doing no ~ to others, showing charity to all⟩ (2) : slanderous or malicious speech ⟨hearing and speaking no ~⟩ (3) : an evil person : one that embodies or personifies wickedness ⟨it seemed impossible that the ancient ~ was alive after all these years —Archie Binns⟩ **2 a** : something that is injurious to moral or physical happiness or welfare : MISFORTUNE, CALAMITY, DISASTER ⟨if it is an ~ to lose our liberty in a war, it is much worse to sacrifice it ourselves on the altar of fear —M.R.Cohen⟩; *esp* : something (as a condition or practice) that has harmful effects ⟨the narcotics ~⟩ ⟨the drink ~⟩ ⟨erosion of the soil on the slopes . . . is one of the great ~*s* in this region —Samuel Van Valkenburg & Ellsworth Huntington⟩ ⟨struggling with the alternate ~*s* of bad seasons and bad markets —G.E.Fussell⟩ **b** : a harmful consequence : ill effect ⟨it is only necessary to remember that the deserts of No. Africa once grew wheat to realize what ~*s* can follow the maltreatment . . . of the land —Henry Beresford-Peirse⟩ **3** : MALADY, DISEASE; *esp* : SCROFULA

syn ILL: EVIL is the antithesis of *good*, esp. in moral or moralistic considerations; it may indicate a quality, trait, condition, practice, cause, or desire ⟨obvious *evils:* the beggars, the terrible poverty, the prevalence of disease, the anarchy and corruption in politics —Bertrand Russell⟩ ⟨war is perhaps the greatest of all human *evils* and follies —W.R.Inge⟩ ILL now applies mainly to anything distressing, painful, fretting, or injurious that one suffers ⟨a pathetic lack of medical services, poor housing, poor schooling, and a hundred other *ills* flowing from the same source of poverty —A.E.Stevenson b. 1900⟩ ⟨the diversification of crops long advocated by agricultural economists as a cure for the *ills* of the cotton belt —*Amer. Guide Series: Ark.*⟩

[4]**evil** \"\ *n* -S [prob. fr. OE *geafol, gafol* fork — more at GAFFLE] *dial Eng* : PITCHFORK

evildoer \ˈ=(ˌ)=ˈ==\ *n* [ME *evyl doer*] : one who does evil

evildoing \ˈ=(ˌ)=ˈ==\ *n* : the act or action of doing evil ⟨the recurrent cycle of ~ —O.J.Baab⟩

evil eye *n* : the glance of a person that is believed to be capable of inflicting injury ⟨many people are reputed to . . . cause harm by staring at someone with an *evil eye* —Pamela Gulliver & P.H.Gulliver⟩ ⟨contamination by *evil eye* is usually unwitting on the part of . . . the causal agent —O.G.Simmons⟩; *also* : a person believed to have such power ⟨what's that *evil eye* up to —Nelson Algren⟩

evilhearted \ˈ==ˈ==\ *adj* : having an evil heart

evil·ly \ˈēvəl(l)ē, -)i *sometimes* -(ˌ)vil-\ *adv* : in an evil manner : WICKEDLY, BADLY ⟨grinning ~ down upon him —Farley Mowat⟩ ⟨the world was an evil place, . . . and it had treated him ~ —Max Peacock⟩

evil-minded \ˈ==ˈ==\ *adj* : having an evil disposition or evil intentions : disposed to mischief or sin : MALICIOUS; *also* : tending to interpret words or sayings in a dirty sense — **evil-mind·ed·ly** *adv* — **evil-mind·ed·ness** *n* -ES

evil·ness *n* -ES [ME *ivelnes, evelnes, evilnes,* fr. OE *yfelnes,* fr. *yfel* evil + *-nes* -ness — more at EVIL] : the quality of being evil : BADNESS

evince \əˈvin(t)s, ēˈ-\ *vt* -ED/-ING/-S [L *evincere* to vanquish, win a point in an argument, demonstrate, fr. *e-* + *vincere* to conquer — more at VICTOR] **1** *obs* : CONQUER, SUBDUE **2** *obs* : CONVINCE, CONFUTE **3 a** : to constitute evidence of : PROVE, CONFIRM ⟨the congestion, poverty, and lack of ambition *evinced* by these poor houses on the part of the working people —Samuel Van Valkenburg & Ellsworth Huntington⟩ **b** : to display clearly : EXHIBIT, MANIFEST, REVEAL, EXPRESS ⟨his musical talent *evinced* itself at an early age⟩ ⟨*evinced* the greatest disregard for the feelings of others⟩ **4** : to call forth : OCCASION, PROVOKE ⟨he could ~ no response from his stolid taciturn companion⟩ **syn** see SHOW

evinc·ible \-səbəl\ *adj* : capable of being proved or evinced : DEMONSTRABLE

evin·cive \-siv\ *adj* : tending to prove : DEMONSTRATIVE

Ev·i·pal \ˈevəˌpal, -pȯl\ *trademark* — used for hexobarbital

ev·i·rate \ˈevəˌrāt, ēˈvīˌ-\ *vt* -ED/-ING/-S *archaic* [L *eviratus*, past part. of *evirare*, fr. *e-* + *vir* man — more at VIRILE] : CASTRATE, EMASCULATE

evis·cer·ate \əˈvisəˌrāt, ēˈ-, *usu* -ād·+V\ *vb* -ED/-ING/-S [L *evisceratus*, past part. of *eviscerare*, fr. *e-* + *viscera* — more at VISCERA] *vt* **1 a** : to take out the entrails of : DISEMBOWEL, GUT ⟨~ a turkey⟩ **b** : to deprive of essential or vital content or force : weaken decisively : DEVITALIZE ⟨recklessly ~*s* the ground forces in favor of . . . long-range bombers —Walter Millis⟩ ⟨the book is *eviscerated* and left a mere story for boys —Montgomery Belgion⟩ **2** : to remove an organ from (a patient) or the contents of (an organ) ~ *vi* **1** *of a part* : to protrude through a surgical incision **2** *of a patient* : to suffer protrusion of a part through an incision

evis·cer·a·tion \=ˌ=='rāshən\ *n* -S [ML *evisceration-, evisceratio*, fr. L *evisceratus* + *-ion-, -io* -ion] **1** : the act or process of eviscerating **2 a** : protrusion of viscera through the body wall esp. through a surgical incision **b** : removal of an organ or of the contents of an organ

evis·cer·a·tor \='==ˌrād·ə(r), -ātə-\ *n* -S : one that eviscerates; *specif* : a worker who eviscerates animal carcasses (as poultry or fish)

ev·i·ta·ble \ˈevəd·əbəl, ˈev(ə)təb-\ *adj* [L *evitabilis*, fr. *evitare* to avoid + *-abilis* -able] : AVOIDABLE ⟨even nonhistorical events are ~ —Sidney Hook⟩

evite \əˈvīt, ēˈ-, -vēt\ *vt* -ED/-ING/-S [MF or L; MF *eviter*, fr. L *evitare*, fr. *e-* + *vitare* to shun] *archaic* : SHUN, AVOID ⟨I have *evited* striking you . . . under muckle provocation —Sir Walter Scott⟩

eviternal *adj* [L *aeviternus* eternal + E *-al* — more at ETERNAL] *obs* : ETERNAL, EVERLASTING

ev·i·ter·ni·ty \ˌevəˈtərnəd·ē\ *n* -ES : EVERLASTINGNESS

evittate \(ˈ)ē+\ *adj* [*e-* + *vittate*] : destitute of oil tubes — used of the fruit of certain plants; compare VITTA

evng *abbr* evening

ev·o·ca·ble \ˈevəkəbəl, əˈvōk-, ēˈvōk-\ *adj* [F *évocable*, fr. *évoquer* to evoke + *-able* — more at EVOKE] : capable of being evoked

evo·cate \ˈē(ˌ)vōˌkāt, ˈevəˌ-, ˈevōˌ-\ *vt* -ED/-ING/-S [L *evocatus*, past part. of *evocare* — more at EVOKE] *archaic* : EVOKE

evo·ca·tion \ˌē(ˌ)vōˈkāshən, ˌevəˈ-, ˌevōˈ-\ *n* -S [L *evocation-, evocatio*, fr. *evocatus* + *-ion-, -io* -ion] **1** : the act or fact of evoking or calling forth, out, or up : SUMMONING, CITATION ⟨the most conspicuous result of these four laws was the ~ of protests from many states —W.C.Ford⟩ ⟨both amazed and amused by this ~ of the old Hebrew principle —C.G.Bowers⟩: as **a** : the summoning of a spirit by incantation; *also* : the ritual used in such incantation : SPELL ⟨emotion is an ~ and in ways beyond the senses alters events—creating good and evil luck —W.B.Yeats⟩ **b** : the calling upon a deity for assistance : INVOCATION ⟨there are no prayers, only continuous ~*s* —Negley Farson⟩ **c** *obs* : the summoning of a case from an inferior by a superior court (as on appeal) **2** : the act or an instance of artistic imaginative re-creation or portrayal (as of a mood, time, place, or personality) esp. in such a manner as to produce a compelling impression of reality or authenticity ⟨a garrulous, gossipy, and engaging ~ of a vanished age —W.H.Hale⟩ ⟨an ~ of the locomotive in musical terms —*Newsweek*⟩ ⟨not so in his most deeply felt portraits, as in that heroic and pathetic ~ of himself in old age —F.J.Mather⟩ ⟨terse and vivid, precise and realistic in its ~ of disagreeable detail —*Amer. Guide Series: Ind.*⟩ ⟨excellent powers of description and ~ —Alexander Klein⟩ **3** *embryol* : INDUCTION 4f; *specif* : initiation of development of a primary embryonic axis — contrasted with *individuation*

evoc·a·tive \əˈväkəd·iv, ēˈ-, -kətiv\ *adj* [LL *evocativus*, fr. L *evocatus* + *-ivus* -ive] **1** : serving or tending to evoke or call forth something ⟨a preface ~ . . . of interest —*Times Lit. Supp.*⟩ ⟨the function of alcoholic overindulgence on some individuals . . . is not . . . ~ of socially or personally disapproved behavior —R.M.Lindner⟩ **2 a** : tending to evoke an emotional response : charged with emotion as well as meaning ⟨the ideas of Thomas Jefferson will always be ~ . . . read or heard they inspire and arouse any audience —W.S.Lynch⟩ ⟨spheres of discourse . . . rich in ~ or emotive overtones —F.W.Leakey⟩ **b** (1) : tending by artistic imaginative means to re-create (as a mood, time, place, or personality) esp. in such a manner as to produce a compelling impression of reality ⟨superbly ~ account, rooted in fact but crowned with imagination —E.M.Lustgarten⟩ ⟨one of his book's most ~ passages . . . describes the effect of this lotus land on the American soldiers —*Time*⟩ ⟨a war novel . . . powerful and terse, with ~, minute details of war —Richard Plant⟩ (2) : tending to inspire or evoke vivid memories, recollections, or associations ⟨the old photographs are charmingly ~ —Lee Rogow⟩ ⟨described and illustrated the apples of England: their ~ names, subtle flavors, and the season of highest quality for each —Herbert & Mary Miles⟩

evoc·a·tive·ly *adv* : in an evocative manner

evoc·a·tive·ness *n* -ES : evocative quality ⟨the enormous ~ of the picture and its curious feeling of timelessness —R.M. Coates⟩

evo·ca·tor \ˈē(ˌ)vōˌkād·ə(r), ˈevə-, ˈevō-\ *n* -S [L, fr. *evocatus* + *-or*] : one that evokes; *esp* : the specific chemical constituent responsible for the physiological effects of an inductor or organizer

evoc·a·to·ry \əˈväkəˌtōrē\ *adj* [LL *evocatorius*, fr. L *evocatus* + *-orius* -ory] : EVOCATIVE

evo·dia \əˈvōdēə, ēˈ-\ *n, cap* [NL, irreg. fr. Gk *euōdia* fragrance, fr. *euōdēs* fragrant (fr. *eu-* + *-ōdēs*, fr. *ozein* to smell) + *-ia* -y — more at ODOR] : a genus of Asiatic and Australasian shrubs and trees (family Rutaceae) having opposite aromatic leaves, unisexual flowers, and dry fruits

evoke \əˈvōk, ēˈ-\ *vt* -ED/-ING/-S [F *évoquer*, fr. L *evocare*, fr. *e-* + *vocare* to call — more at VOCATION] **1 a** : to call forth or up (a spirit or other supernatural being) : SUMMON ⟨the people avoid mentioning the names of the gods, because . . . to name them is to ~ them —J.G.Frazer⟩ ⟨controls his demons largely through ritual which can both ~ and propitiate them —Francis Huxley⟩ **b** : to cite esp. with approval or for support : INVOKE ⟨a list of qualities which men in more religious days *evoked* with familiar approval, but some of which have grown pale —C.W.deKiewiet⟩ ⟨the name of Socrates is not one that would ordinarily be *evoked* by a defender of artists —*Times Lit. Supp.*⟩ **2 a** : to call forth (a response) : ELICIT ⟨his action *evoked* official displeasure⟩ ⟨that remark *evoked* nothing, not even curiosity —Clarissa F. Cushman⟩ **b** : to call into being : cause to arise ⟨these exigencies *evoked* a university in Bologna, Paris, and Oxford —H.O.Taylor⟩ ⟨advertising created modern American radio . . . , *evoked* the modern slick periodical —D.M.Potter⟩ **c** : to call up (memories, recollections, associations) ⟨the place ~*s* memories of happier years⟩ ⟨all of them *evoking* historical and literary associations of worldwide fame —Sam Pollock⟩ **3** : to re-create, depict, or suggest by artistic imaginative means esp. in such a manner as to produce a compelling impression of reality : bring to life ⟨the opening chapters of the book, although they contain very few descriptive passages, ~ the place marvelously —Basil Taylor⟩ ⟨the sights, the sounds, the smells of Spain are *evoked* with a vividness that has a physical impact —Harriet de Onís⟩ ⟨to ~ Lincoln the man in marble and bronze was not an easy task for any sculptor —R.P. Basler⟩ **syn** see EDUCE

[1]**evo·lute** \ˈevəˌlüt *also* ˈēv- *or* -vəlˌyüt\ *n* -S [L *evolutus*, past part. of *evolvere* to unroll, unfold — more at EVOLVE] **1** *math* : the locus of the center of curvature or the envelope of the normals of another curve — compare INVOLUTE **2** : a curving wavelike scroll used decoratively on friezes and moldings

[2]**evolute** \"\ *adj* [L *evolutus*, past part.] *bot* : turned back : UNFOLDED

[3]**evolute** \"\ *vb* -ED/-ING/-S [back-formation fr. *evolution*] : EVOLVE, DEVELOP ⟨if we ever ~ into a really satisfactory political and economic life, we won't like it —*Scribner's*⟩

evo·lu·tion \ˌevəˈlüshən *also* ˌēv- *or* -vəlˈyü-\ *n* -S [L *evolution-, evolutio* act of unrolling, fr. *evolutus* + *-ion-, -io* -ion] **1 a** : a series of related changes in a certain direction : process of change : organic development : UNFOLDING, MOVEMENT, TRANSFORMATION ⟨the ~ of his hair has been from brown to gray, to bald —*Current Biog.*⟩ ⟨the ~ of a complicated plot⟩ ⟨it should be remembered that even in the biological world, ~ is not always in the direction of progress —A.B.Novikoff⟩ ⟨the ~ of the seasons⟩ ⟨there has been much discussion as to . . . the possible ~ of benign adenomas into invasive carcinoma —*Jour. Amer. Med. Assoc.*⟩ **b** (1) : a process of continuous change from a lower, simpler, or worse condition to a higher, more complex, or better state : progressive development : GROWTH, PROGRESS ⟨the ~ of the capitalist forms of business organization, from primitive units to the modern corporation —W.C.Scoville⟩ ⟨the ~ from childhood to manhood⟩ ⟨the ~ of physics from Galileo to Einstein⟩ ⟨the ~ of the rifle⟩ (2) : a process of gradual and relatively peaceful social, political, and economic advance or amelioration — often contrasted with *revolution* ⟨a British pattern of change by ~ . . . which contrasts with less attractive changes by revolution in other countries —*Current History*⟩ **c** : the end product of an evolutionary process : something that is evolved ⟨economically it is an ~ of the ancient system of barter —*Encyc. Americana*⟩ ⟨the style of the King James version . . . is . . . an ~ . . . , the resultant of a long selective process —J.L.Lowes⟩ **2** : one of a set of prescribed movements or motions (as those of a skater, dancer, a body of troops, a fleet, or other formation) : any movement designed to effect a new arrangement by passing from one position to another : MANEUVER ⟨~*s* of the eight pink bridesmaids and the eight black ushers —Edith Wharton⟩ **3** : the process of working out or developing (as an idea, design, or theme) ⟨the greatest task facing agricultural scientists in this region is the ~ of an adaptable farming system —*Farmer's Weekly (So. Africa)*⟩ **4** *math* : the extraction of roots — opposed to *involution* **5 a** (1) *archaic* : the development of an organism by gradual unfolding of parts (as in the growth of a plant from a seed) (2) : the presumed process of development in which a germ containing the adult parts in miniature was stimulated to differentiate by the action of fertilization — opposed to *epigenesis;* compare ENCASEMENT **b** : the development of a race, species, or other group : PHYLOGENY : the process by which through a series of changes or steps any living organism or group of organisms has acquired the morphological and physiological characters which distinguish it : the theory that the various types of animals and plants have their origin in other preexisting types, the distinguishable differences being due to modifications in successive generations — compare DARWINISM, HEREDITY, MUTATION, NATURAL SELECTION, VARIATION, WEISMANNISM **6 a** : the progressive development of civilization and social institutions in a fixed sequence of stages — called also *unilinear evolution;* see EVOLUTIONISM **b** : a process of cultural change determined esp. by technological factors and marked by a movement from simplicity to complexity and the gradual increase of man's control over his environment **7 a** : the process of the whole universe conceived as a progression of interrelated phenomena **b** : the theory of such progression — compare EMERGENT EVOLUTION, SPENCERIANISM

evo·lu·tion·al \ˈ=vəˈlüshənᵊl, -shnəl *also* -vəlˈyü-\ *adj* : EVOLUTIONARY — **evo·lu·tion·al·ly** \-ᵊl|ē, -əl|, |i\ *adv*

evo·lu·tion·ar·i·ly \ˌ==ˈ=shəˈnerəlē, -li\ *adv* : in an evolutionary way : from the evolutionary point of view ⟨moved ~ some way apart —*Biol. Symposia*⟩

[1]**evo·lu·tion·ary** \ˈ==ˈ=shəˌnerē, -ri\ *adj* [*evolution* + *-ary*] : of, relating to, or produced by evolution

[2]**evolutionary** \"\ *n* -ES : EVOLUTIONIST

evo·lu·tion·ism \ˌ=='=shəˌnizəm\ *n* -S **1** : a theory of evolution (as in philosophy, biology, or sociology) — see DARWINISM **2** : adherence to or belief in evolution esp. of living beings

[1]**evo·lu·tion·ist** \ˌ=vəˈlüsh(ə)nəst, -vəlˈyü-\ *n* -S [*evolution* + *-ist*] : a student of or adherent to a theory of evolution

[2]**evo·lu·tion·ist** \ˈ==ˈ=(=)=\ *or* **evo·lu·tion·is·tic** \ˌ=vəˈlüshəˈnistik, -tēk *also* -vəlˈyü-\ *adj* : of or relating to evolution or evolutionists — **evo·lu·tion·is·ti·cal·ly** \-tək(ə)lē, -tēk-, -li\ *adv*

evo·lu·tive \ˈ=vəˈlüd·iv, -vəlˈyü-\ *adj* [*evolution* + *-ive*] : of, relating to, or promoting evolution or development ⟨~ conditions⟩

evolv·able \pronunc at EVOLVE +əbəl\ *adj* : capable of being evolved

evolve \ə'välv, ē'-, -'vȯlv *also* -'vä(ü)v *or* -'vōv\ *vb* -ED/-ING/-S [L *evolvere* to unroll, unfold, fr. *e-* + *volvere* to roll — more at VOLUBLE] *vt* **1** *archaic* **a** : UNFOLD, UNROLL **b** : to disclose by degrees to view : DISENTANGLE **2** : to give off : EMIT ⟨natural cheese, during the course of its aging, ~s carbon dioxide —*Modern Packaging*⟩ **3 a** : DERIVE, EDUCE ⟨from these premises he *evolved* a startling new set of philosophic axioms⟩ ⟨out of their writings . . . Hitler and his disciples *evolved* the racial myth —Raoul de R. de Sales⟩ **b** : to work out or develop esp. by experience, experimentation, or intensive care or effort ⟨*evolved* . . . a fresh and personal approach to residential design —*Amer. Guide Series: N.Y.*⟩ ⟨I lay awake for an hour or so *evolving* a plan —Irving Stone⟩ ⟨~ a solution for the problem⟩ ⟨independently *evolved* a lamp based upon this principle —S.F.Mason⟩ ⟨*evolved* a new and improved variety of this plant⟩ **c** : to develop or produce by natural evolutionary processes ⟨the Protozoa . . . *evolved* the types that were transitional to higher animals —R.W. Miner⟩ ~ *vi* : to develop by or as if by evolution : undergo evolutionary change ⟨hygiene . . . has *evolved* into preventive medicine —Victor Robinson⟩ ⟨show . . . that life has *evolved* according to a Creator's plan—J.P.Marquand⟩ **syn** see UNFOLD

evolve·ment \-mənt\ *n* -S : the act or process of evolving : the state of being evolved

[1]**evon·y·mus** \ə'vänəməs, e'-,ē'-\ [NL, fr. L *euonymos* spindle tree — more at EUONYMUS] *syn of* EUONYMUS

[2]**evonymus** \"\ *n* -ES : EUONYMUS 2

evot·o·mys \ə'vädəməs, e'-,ē-, -vōd-\ [NL, irreg. fr. *eu-* + *ot-* + *-mys*] *syn of* CLETHRIONOMYS

evul·gate \ə'vəl,gāt, ē'-\ *vt* -ED/-ING/-S [L *evulgatus*, past part. of *evulgare*, fr. *e-* + *vulgare* to spread abroad, publish, divulge, fr. *vulgus* multitude — more at VULGAR] *archaic* : PUBLISH, DIVULGE — **evul·ga·tion** \,ē,vəl'gāshən\ *n* -S

evulse \ə'vəls, ē'- *also* -lts\ *vt* -ED/-ING/-S [L *evulsus*, past part. of *evellere*, fr. *e-* + *vellere* to pluck — more at VULNERABLE] : to extract forcibly ⟨~ a tooth⟩

evul·sion \-lshən\ *n* -S [L *evulsion-*, *evulsio*, fr. *evulsus* + *-ion-*, *-io* -ion] : the act of plucking out : a rooting or casting out

ev·zone \'ev,zōn\ *n* -S [NGk *euzōnos*, fr. Gk *euzōnos* active, lit., well girt, fr. *eu-* + *zōnē* girdle — more at ZONE] : a member of a select infantry corps in the Greek army

EW *abbr* enlisted woman

[1]**ewe** \'yü, *esp among farm dwellers* 'yō\ *n* -S [ME, fr. OE *ēowu*; akin to OHG *ou*, *ouwi* ewe, ON *ær* ewe, Goth *awethi* flock of sheep, L *ovis* sheep, Gk *ois*, Skt *avi*] : the female of the sheep esp. when mature; *also* : the female of various related animals (as goats or the smaller antelopes)

[2]**ewe** *also* **evé** \'ā,wā, 'ā,vā\ *n, pl* **ewe** *or* **ewes** *also* **evé** *or* **evés** *usu cap* **1 a** : a Negro people of Ghana and Togo and border regions of Dahomey **b** : a member of such people **2** : a Kwa language of the Ewe people

ewe hogg *or* **ewe hogget** *also* **ewe hog** *n, chiefly Brit* : a young female sheep usu. between weaning and first shearing

ewe lamb *n* : a young usu. unweaned female sheep

ewelease \'=,=\ *n, dial Eng* : a sheep pasture

ewe-neck \'=,=\ *n* : a thin sheeplike neck having an insufficient, faulty, or concave arch and occurring as a defect in certain dogs and horses — **ewe-necked** \'=,=\ *adj*

[1]**ew·er** \'yüə(r), -ü(ə)r,-üə\ *n* -S [ME, fr. AF, fr. OF *evier*, fr. (assumed) VL *aquarium*, fr. neut. of L *aquarius* of water, fr. *aqua* water + *-arius* -ary — more at ISLAND] : a usu. vase-shaped pitcher or jug with a handle and often a spout for ease of pouring

ewer

[2]**ewer** \"\ *n* -S [prob. of Scand origin; akin to OSw *iūwer*, *iūger* udder, ON *jūgr* — more at UDDER] *dial Eng* : UDDER

ew·ery \-ərē\ *n* -ES [ME *ewerie*, fr. AF, fr. *ewer* + *-ie* -y] : a room for ewers, table linen, and towels (as in a royal palace)

ew·est \'yüəst\ *adj* [ME (Sc dial.), alter. (resulting from incorrect division) of *anewest*, fr. OE *on nēawiste* in the neighborhood] *Scot* : NEAREST, NEXT

ew·ing's sarcoma *also* **ewing's tumor** \'yüiŋz-, -iēŋz-\ *n*, *usu cap E* [after James Ewing †1943 Am. pathologist] : a tumor of bone that invades the shaft of a long bone, tends to recur, but rarely metastasizes

[1]**ex** \'eks\ *n* -ES [*ex-*] : one that formerly held a specified position or place; *esp* : a former spouse ⟨took my ~ and the children to dinner⟩

[2]**ex** \(')eks\ *prep* [L] **1** : out of : FROM ⟨sturdy plants ~ 3-inch pots⟩: as **a** : from a specified place or source — used chiefly in commerce ⟨the goods will be supplied ~ stock or ~ factory at the option of the buyer⟩ **b** — a function word used by breeders to identify the dam of an animal ⟨a promising calf by Eric XVI ~ Heatherbell⟩ **2** : free from : WITHOUT: as **a** : without an indicated value or right (as a dividend declared, interest accrued, or a preferential right to purchase shares) — used esp. of securities ⟨was willing to buy the shares ~ rights⟩ **b** : free of charges precedent to removal from the specified place, purchaser to provide means of subsequent transportation ⟨~ dock⟩ ⟨~ warehouse⟩ — used also attributively with a hyphen between *ex* and the noun

[3]**ex** \'eks\ *n* -ES : the letter *x*

[4]**ex** \"\ *n* -ES [alter. of E dial. *ax*, fr. OE *eax* axis, axle — more at AXIS] *dial* : AXLE

[5]**ex** \"\ *n* -ES [by shortening] **1** : EXPENSE **2** : EXAMINATION

[1]**ex-** *variants not shown in the pronunciations of "ex-" words below are* ə *or* ē *for the "e" when the prefix is unstressed and esp when a stressed syllable immediately precedes without pause, and* ks *for the "x" in words in which only* gz *is shown, as "exact"*\ *or* **ef-** *prefix* [ME, fr. OF & L; OF, fr. L (also, perfective and intensive prefix), fr. *ex* out of, from; akin to Gk *ex* out of, from, OIr *ess-*, OSlav *iz*, *izŭ*, *is*] **1** : out of : away from : outside of ⟨*excircle*⟩ ⟨*exclave*⟩ **2** : without : lacking ⟨*exalate*⟩ ⟨*exalbuminous*⟩ **3** \(')eks\ [ME *ex-*, fr. LL, fr. L] : out of (the office or condition named by the main word) : former : sometime — usu. joined to second element by a hyphen ⟨*ex-president*⟩ ⟨*ex-convict*⟩; often with phrases ⟨*ex-child actor*⟩ ⟨*ex-man-about-town*⟩; usu. *ef-* in senses 1 & 2 before *f* ⟨*efform*⟩ ⟨*effuse*⟩; always *ex-* in sense 3

[2]**ex-** — see EXO-

ex *abbr* **1** examined **2** example **3** exception **4** exchange **5** excluding **6** excursion **7** executed; executive **8** exempt **9** exercise **10** exhibit **11** export **12** express **13** extra **14** extract **15** extremely

ex·ac·er·bate \ig'z|asə(r),bāt, eg'z|, ek's|, |aas-, *usu* -ād·+V\ *vb* -ED/-ING/-S [L *exacerbatus*, past part. of *exacerbare*, fr. *ex-* [1]ex- + *acerbus* harsh, bitter, unpleasant, fr. *acer* sharp — more at EDGE] *vt* **1** : to make more violent or bitter : intensify the bad qualities of ⟨foolish words *exacerbating* a quarrel⟩ ⟨all the frictions that *exacerbated* the long-drawn-out negotiations —Howard Taubman⟩ **2** : to cause (a disease or its symptoms) to become more severe ⟨her condition was *exacerbated* by lack of care⟩ ~ *vi* : to cause exacerbation ⟨what charms and consoles in the private house may distract and ~ in the public office —Virginia Woolf⟩ — used chiefly as a participial adjective ⟨*exacerbating* factors in modern life⟩

syn EXACERBATE, EMBITTER, and SOUR can mean in common to cause to become, or become increasingly, severe or bitter. EXACERBATE stresses intensification in harshness or grievousness or an increase in virulence or violence, as of pain, disease, or hatred ⟨the injuries to his pride, *exacerbated* by her desertion of him —Edith Sitwell⟩ ⟨their prejudices have not been unduly *exacerbated* —Cabell Phillips⟩ ⟨the reduction of diseases may merely *exacerbate* the world's poverty and hunger by increasing the number of people —Eric Larrabee⟩ ⟨they may *exacerbate* rather than cure that unnatural craving for excess and novel thrills —J.D.Adams⟩ EMBITTER implies the making of an experience (esp. a normally pleasant experience) unpleasant or of an unpleasant experience increasingly hard to endure or of a person bitter or resentful ⟨the remoter outcome of the case was that competition was *embittered* rather than allayed —*Times Lit. Supp.*⟩ ⟨his last years were *embittered* by disputes among his sons —*Encyc. Americana*⟩ ⟨violence . . . *embittered* the fight between capitalism and socialism —Stringfellow Barr⟩ ⟨the irresponsibility of privilege that *embitters* even men of goodwill —*Time*⟩ SOUR implies a making or a becoming acidulous, hostile, resentful, peevish, or cynical ⟨his heart was *soured* in his weary old hide, and his hopes had curdled in his breast —Amy Lowell⟩ ⟨they were almost truculent, as if they had been *soured* by heavy and unwelcome duties —John Buchan⟩ ⟨the anxiousness of some might *sour* to enmity under the acerbity of his attack —H.O.Taylor⟩ ⟨the condition of the city government *soured* most of the thinking citizens⟩

ex·ac·er·bat·ing·ly *adv* : in an exacerbating manner : so as to cause exacerbation

ex·ac·er·ba·tion \ig,==ˈbāshən, (,)eg-, (,)ek-\ *n* -S [ME *exacerbacioun*, fr. LL *exacerbation-*, *exacerbatio*, fr. L *exacerbatus* + *-ion-*, *-io* -ion] : the act of exacerbating or state of being exacerbated

[1]**ex·act** \ig'zakt, eg-\ *vb* -ED/-ING/-S [ME *exacten*, fr. L *exactus*, past part. of *exigere* to drive out, demand, exact (payment), weigh, measure, fr. *ex-* [1]ex- + *-igere* (fr. *agere* to drive, lead, act, do) — more at AGENT] *vt* **1** : to demand and force or compel (payment, surrender, concession, performance, compliance) : WRING, EXTORT, WREST ⟨from them has been ~*ed* the ultimate sacrifice —D.D.Eisenhower⟩ ⟨qualms which ~*ed* rites of expiation —John Dewey⟩ **2** : to require despite difficulty or reluctance : call for as necessary, appropriate, or desirable ⟨a task so delicate ~s the scholar and philosopher —B.N.Cardozo⟩ **3** *archaic* : to draw (as a meaning) out : EXTRACT ~ *vi, obs* : to practice exaction **syn** see DEMAND

[2]**exact** \"\ *adj, often* -ER/-EST [L *exactus*, fr. past part. of *exigere*] **1** : exhibiting or characterized by strict, particular, and complete accordance with fact, truth, or an established standard or original : devoid of any addition, subtraction, or other variation from fact or a standard ⟨the ~ time⟩ ⟨not only is ~ description difficult —Aldous Huxley⟩ ⟨an ~ account of the quarrel⟩ ⟨extremely ~ in conduct⟩ **2** : characterized or marked by thorough consideration or minute measurement of small factual details usu. leading to incontestably true conclusions : not incomplete or approximate ⟨a power of intuition greater than that of an ~ investigator —Havelock Ellis⟩ ⟨the ~ measurements of physical science⟩ **syn** see CORRECT

ex·act·able \-təbəl\ *adj* : that may be exacted ⟨there is a limit to the interest lawfully ~⟩

exact differential *n* : a differential expression of the form $X_1dx_1 + \ldots + X_ndx_n$, where the *X*'s are the partial derivatives of a function $f(x_1 \ldots x_n)$, with respect to $x_1 \ldots x_n$ respectively

exacting *adj* **1 a** : tryingly or unremittingly severe in making demands or requiring the fulfillment of obligations ⟨an ~ employer⟩ **b** : requiring careful attention and precise accuracy ⟨an ~ task⟩ **2** : unable to thrive except under special conditions (as of nutrition, temperature, or moisture) : FASTIDIOUS ⟨an ~ microbe⟩ ⟨certain highly specialized xerophytes are extremely ~ in their requirements⟩ **syn** see ONEROUS

ex·act·ing·ly *adv* : in an exacting manner

ex·act·ing·ness *n* -ES : the quality or state of being exacting

ex·ac·tion \-kshən\ *n* -S [ME *exaccioun*, fr. L *exaction-*, *exactio*, fr. *exactus* + *-ion-*, *-io* -ion] **1 a** : the act or process of exacting : compulsion to furnish : a levying esp. by force ⟨the ~ of tribute⟩ ⟨~ of various dues and fees⟩ **b** : the levying or demanding of some benefit (as a fee or gratuity) that is not lawfully or properly due : EXTORTION ⟨the ~s of dishonest officials who demand fees to perform their sworn duty⟩ **2** : something exacted; *usu* : a fee, reward, or contribution demanded or levied with severity or injustice

ex·ac·ti·tude \-ktə,tüd, -ə,tyüd\ *n* -S [F, fr. *exact* (fr. L *exactus*) + *-i-* + *-tude*] : the quality or an instance of being exact ⟨the ~s of careful expression⟩ ⟨a man of great ~⟩

ex·act·ly \ig'zak(t)lē, eg-, -li\ *adv* **1 a** : in an exact manner : precisely according to a rule, standard, or fact : ACCURATELY **b** : ENTIRELY, ALTOGETHER ⟨do ~ as you wish this afternoon⟩ ⟨our pleas got us ~ nothing⟩ **2** : quite so : as you say or state — used to express agreement or concurrence

ex·act·ness \-k(t)nəs\ *n* -ES : EXACTITUDE, PRECISION ⟨a neat ~ of caricaturing⟩

ex·ac·tor *also* **ex·act·er** \-ktə(r)\ *n* -S [ME *exactour*, fr. L *exactor*, fr. *exactus* + *-or*] : one that exacts esp. by authority

exact science *n* : a science whose laws are capable of accurate quantitative expression (as physics, chemistry, astronomy)

ex·a·cum \'eksəkəm\ *n* [NL, fr. L, a kind of centaury, fr. Gaulish] **1** *cap* : a genus of tropical Asiatic and African plants (family Gentianaceae) including one species (*E. affine*) of herbaceous biennials with bluish to dark lavender flowers that are often cultivated in the greenhouse **2** -S : any plant of the genus *Exacum*

ex ae·quo et bo·no \ek¦sīkwōet'bō(,)nō, -ōət-\ [L] : according to what is equitable and good : on the merits of the case — used esp. in international law when a case by agreement of the principals is to be decided on grounds of equity and reason rather than specific points of law

ex·ag·ger·ate \ig'zajə,rāt, eg-, *usu* -ād·+V\ *vb* -ED/-ING/-S [L *exaggeratus*, past part. of *exaggerare*, fr. *ex-* [1]ex- + *aggerare* to pile up, fr. *agger* heap, mound, breastwork, fr. *aggerere* to carry toward, fr. *ad-* + *gerere* to carry — more at JEST] *vt* **1** *obs* : to heap up : ACCUMULATE **2** : to enlarge beyond bounds or the truth : delineate extravagantly : overstate the truth concerning ⟨a friend ~s a man's virtues —Joseph Addison⟩ ⟨*exaggerated* their difficulties in order to enhance their accomplishments⟩ **3** : to enlarge or increase esp. beyond the normal ⟨the brightly flowered dress ~s her corpulence⟩ ⟨the *exaggerated* crests of certain fowls⟩ ~ *vi* : to misrepresent on the side of largeness (as of size, extent, or value) : overstate the truth

ex·ag·ger·at·ed·ly *adv* : in an exaggerated manner : with exaggeration

ex·ag·ger·at·ing·ly *adv* : so as to exaggerate ⟨an ~ described incident⟩

ex·ag·ger·a·tion \=,==ˈrāshən\ *n* -S [L *exaggeration-*, *exaggeratio*, fr. *exaggeratus* + *-ion-*, *-io* -ion] **1** : the act of exaggerating : a going beyond the bounds of truth, reason, or justice : OVERSTATEMENT ⟨their ~ of their wealth caused much later confusion⟩ **2** : the state or an instance of being exaggerated ⟨this ridiculous ~ was instantly seen through⟩ ⟨the ~ of his height by built-up heels⟩

ex·ag·ger·a·tive \='==,rā|d·|iv, -,rə|, |t|, |ēv *also* |əv\ *adj* **1** : tending to exaggerate **2** : given to or involving exaggeration — **ex·ag·ger·a·tive·ly** \|əvlē, -li\ *adv*

ex·ag·ger·a·tor \-,rād·ə(r), -ātə-\ *n* -S : one that exaggerates

exagitate *vt* -ED/-ING/-S [L *exagitatus*, past part. of *exagitare*, fr. *ex-* [1]ex- + *agitare* to drive, agitate — more at AGITATE] **1** *obs* : to stir up : AGITATE **2** *obs* : DISCUSS, DEBATE **3** *obs* : HARASS, CENSURE — **ex·ag·i·ta·tion** *n* -S *obs*

ex·alate \(')eks+\ *adj* [[1]*ex-* + *alate*] *bot* : lacking winglike appendages

ex·albuminous \¦ek,s+\ *adj* [[1]*ex-* + *albuminous*] : EXENDOSPERMOUS

ex-all \(')=¦=\ *adv* [[2]*ex* + *all* (pron.)] : without any accrued supplementary values, rights, or privileges — used chiefly in respect to transactions in securities ⟨sold his shares *ex-all*⟩

ex·alt \ig'zȯlt, eg-\ *vb* -ED/-ING/-S [ME *exalten*, fr. MF & L; MF *exalter*, fr. L *exaltare*, fr. *ex-* [1]ex- + *altus* high — more at OLD] *vt* **1** : to raise high : put in an eminent position : ELEVATE ⟨I will ~ my throne above the stars of God —Isa 14:13(AV)⟩ ⟨sold at ~*ed* prices⟩ **2** : to raise esp. in rank, dignity, wealth, power, or character ⟨the king ~*ed* his victorious admiral to a place on the privy council⟩ : DIGNIFY ⟨a nation ~*ed* by fair dealings⟩ **3** : to elevate by praise or in estimation ⟨my father ~*ed* dramatic poetry above all other kinds —W.B.Yeats⟩ : MAGNIFY, EXTOL, GLORIFY ⟨~ ye the Lord —Ps 99:5(AV)⟩ **4** *obs* : to lift up (as with joy, pride, or success) : inspire with delight or satisfaction : ELATE **5 a** : to enhance the activity of : stimulate to greater or higher activity : HEIGHTEN, INTENSIFY ⟨~*ing* the imagination to new flights of fancy⟩ **b** : REFINE, CONCENTRATE — used esp. in alchemy **c** *archaic* : to make more complete or perfect **d** : to cause (virulence) to increase ⟨virulence ~*ed* by addition of mucin to a bacterial culture⟩; *also* : to increase the virulence of ⟨~ a virus by repeated rapid passage through susceptible hosts⟩ ~ *vi* : to induce exaltation : ELEVATE ⟨the power of brilliant conversation to excite and ~⟩ ⟨the ~*ing* beauty of the forest⟩

syn MAGNIFY, AGGRANDIZE: EXALT may indicate a raising up in prestige or significance, often with concomitant depreciation of something else ⟨crisis government, of course, inevitably *exalts* any agency best situated for supplying vigorous and effective direction of affairs —F.A.Ogg & Harold Zink⟩ MAGNIFY means to increase markedly in actual or apparent size or significance ⟨kind, quiet, nearsighted eyes, which his round spectacles *magnified* into lambent moons —Margaret Deland⟩ ⟨public opinion which thus *magnifies* patriotism into a religion —W.C.Brownell⟩ ⟨to minimize the power of the judiciary and the executive, and *magnify* the power of the legislature —V.L.Parrington⟩ AGGRANDIZE indicates making great in power, authority, sway, or eminence ⟨if we *aggrandize* ourselves at the expense of the Mahrattas —Duke of Wellington †1852⟩

ex·al·ta·tion \,eg,zȯl'tāshən, ,ek,sȯ-\ *n* -S [ME *exaltacioun*, fr. MF or L; MF *exaltation*, fr. LL *exaltation-*, *exaltatio*, fr. L *exaltatus* (past part. of *exaltare*) + *-ion-*, *-io* -ion] **1** : the part of the zodiac in which in astrology a planet is thought to exert its strongest influence — opposed to *descension* **2 a** : an act of exalting or the state of being exalted : ELEVATION **3** : refinement, concentration, or intensification esp. by distilling — used chiefly in old chemistry or alchemy **4** *of larks* : FLOCK **5 a** : marked or excessive intensification of a mental state or of the activity of a bodily part or function **b** : an abnormal sense of personal well-being, power, or importance : a delusive euphoria **c** : a state of extreme spiritual elevation usu. marked by a more or less transitory sense of unity with the Deity or with all things natural or divine

exaltation of the cross *usu cap E and C* : a feast observed in the Roman Catholic and Eastern Orthodox churches on September 14 in commemoration of what is held to be the historical recovery of the true cross from the Persians and its return to Jerusalem in the 7th century — called also *Holy Cross Day*

exalted *adj* : exhibiting or characterized by exaltation ⟨~ raptures⟩: as **a** : raised to or having high rank ⟨an ~ personage⟩ **b** : exceedingly or excessively high or favorable ⟨an ~ opinion of his own worth⟩ — often used in negative expressions ⟨took no ~ view of the situation⟩ **c** : marked by nobility of thought or elegance of utterance ⟨an ~ literary style⟩ ⟨we allowed it to be a highly ~ way of telling how so-and-so climbed a hill for a better view —A.T.Quiller-Couch⟩ ⟨the ~ outpourings of a great mind⟩ **d** : CONCENTRATED, STRONG — now used chiefly of seasonings ⟨an ~ essence⟩ ⟨the insipid flesh . . . has need of an ~ seasoning —*Punch*⟩ **e** : partially intoxicated : TIPSY — **ex·alt·ed·ly** *adv* — **ex·alt·ed·ness** *n* -ES

ex·alt·er \ig'zȯltə(r), eg-\ *n* -S [ME, fr. *exalten* + *-er*] : one that exalts

Ex·al·to·lide \ig'zȯltə,līd, eg-\ *trademark* — used for a crystalline macrocyclic lactone used in perfumes

Ex·al·tone \-,tōn\ *trademark* — used for a crystalline macrocyclic synthetic ketone used in perfumes

ex·am \ig'zam, eg-, -zaa(ə)m\ *n* -S [by shortening] : EXAMINATION

ex·a·men \ig'zāmən, eg-\ *n* -S [L, tongue of a balance, consideration, examination, fr. *exigere* to drive out, weigh, measure — more at EXACT] **1** : examination, inquiry, or investigation esp. when conducted to study or weigh the worth or state of something ⟨a regular ~ of conscience⟩ ⟨show a periodic structure under electron microscope ~ —*Biol. Abstracts*⟩ **2** : a critical study (as of a writer or a phenomenon) ⟨a sound, often brilliant ~ of the most powerful English poet of this century —Robert Halsband⟩

ex·am·in·able \ig'zam(ə)nəbəl, eg-\ *adj* [LL *examinabilis*, fr. L *examinare* + *-abilis* -able] : suitable or fit for examination ⟨an ~ subject⟩

ex·am·i·nant \-mənənt\ *n* -S [L *examinant-*, *examinans*, pres. part. of *examinare*] **1** : EXAMINER **2** *or* **ex·am·i·nate** \-,nāt, -,nət\ : one that is examined or is subject to examination (as a witness or deponent)

ex·am·i·na·tion \ig,zamə'nāshən, eg-\ *n* -S [ME *examinacioun*, fr. MF *examination*, fr. LL *examination-*, *examinatio*, fr. L *examinatus* (past part. of *examinare*) + *-ion-*, *-io* -ion] **1** : the act or process of examining or state of being examined : SEARCH, INVESTIGATION, SCRUTINY ⟨a careful ~ of the terrain showed no signs of human habitation⟩ **2** : an exercise or a series of exercises designed to examine progress or test qualification: **a** : a test given to a candidate for a certificate or a position and concerned typically with problems to be solved, skills to be demonstrated, or tasks to be performed ⟨a civil service ~⟩ ⟨a driver's ~⟩ **b** : an oral or written test given by a teacher to a class or an individual student to determine the amount and quality of learning over a period of time ⟨the final ~ will decide your grade for the course⟩ ⟨college entrance ~s may be taken in April or June⟩ **3** : a formal interrogation (as of a witness in a legal action); *also* : the deposition or statements made in such an examination

ex·am·i·na·tion·al \=¦==¦nāshən°l, -shnəl\ *adj* : of or relating to examination ⟨~ methods⟩

examination in chief : DIRECT EXAMINATION

ex·am·i·na·tor \='==,nād·ə(r)\ *n* -S [LL, fr. L *examinatus* + *-or*] *chiefly Scot* : a person in charge of an examination (sense 2)

ex·am·i·na·to·ri·al \ig¦zamənə¦tōrēəl, eg-\ *also* **ex·am·i·na·to·ry** \='====,rē\ *adj* [*examinatorial* fr. LL *examinatorius* (fr. L *examinatus* + *-orius* -ory) + E *al*; *examinatory* fr. LL *examinatorius*] : of or relating to an examiner or examination

[1]**ex·am·ine** \ig'zamən, eg-\ *vb* **examined**; **examined**; **examining** \-ni(ə)niŋ\ **examines** [ME *examinen*, fr. MF *examiner*, fr. L *examinare*, fr. *examin-*, *examen* tongue of a balance, consideration, examination — more at EXAMEN] *vt* **1** : to test by an appropriate method : INVESTIGATE: as **a** : to look over : inspect visually or by use of other senses (as for the determination of accuracy, propriety, or quality) ⟨*examining* title deeds⟩ ⟨carefully *examined* his steward's accounts⟩ ⟨*examining* the cloth and its embroidery⟩ **b** : to inspect or test for evidence of disease or abnormality ⟨the doctor *examined* the young men and found them in perfect health⟩ **c** : to inquire into the state of esp. by introspective processes ⟨first ~ your own conscience⟩ ⟨he *examined* his inmost thoughts⟩ **d** : to search (as baggage) esp. for contraband or dutiable items **2** : to seek to ascertain : attempt to determine ⟨attempt to ~ whether and to what extent the enormous growth in the economic welfare of this nation has been . . . aided by our knowledge of economics —Fritz Machlup⟩ ⟨sat brooding and *examining* how he was at fault⟩ **3** : to interrogate closely (as in a judicial proceeding) : try or test by question ⟨*examining* witnesses in court⟩ ⟨*examined* the students in French⟩ ⟨~ a bankrupt regarding the state of his property⟩ ~ *vi* : to make or give an examination ⟨the doctor will ~ at the infirmary⟩ — usu. used with *into* ⟨let us ~ into the basic mechanism involved⟩ ⟨spent some time *examining* into the rumor that an underground passage led from the castle to the marsh⟩ **syn** see ASK, SCRUTINIZE

[2]**examine** \"\ *n* -S *archaic* : EXAMINATION, SCRUTINY

examined copy *n* : a copy (as of a legal document) that has been compared with the original

ex·am·in·ee \ig¦zamə¦nē, eg-\ *n* -S : a person who is examined

ex·am·in·er \='zam(ə)nə(r)\ *n* -S : one that examines: as **a** : a court officer empowered to administer the oath and take testimony **b** : a person charged with the conducting of examinations into the attainments or qualifications (as of students or applicants) **c** : a person whose work is to inspect usu. a specified thing or situation ⟨the government ~ checked the scene of the crash⟩ ⟨hosiery ~s⟩ ⟨a qualified cable ~⟩ ⟨bank ~⟩

ex·am·in·ing·ly *adv* : in an examining manner : with careful scrutiny : SEARCHINGLY

examplar *archaic var of* [1]EXEMPLAR

[1]**ex·am·ple** \ig'zampəl, eg-, -zaam-,-zaim-,-zām-\ *n* -S [ME *exaumple*, fr. MF *example*, *exemple*, alter. (influenced by L *exemplum*) of *essample*, *essemple*, fr. L *exemplum*, fr. *eximere* to take out, remove, fr. *ex-* [1]ex- + *-imere* to take (fr. *emere*

to buy, obtain) — more at REDEEM] **1 :** a particular single item, fact, incident, or aspect that may be taken fairly as typical or representative of all of a group or type ⟨a most outstanding ~ of a war fought with a purpose was our own American Revolution —Wendell Willkie⟩ **2 a :** a pattern or representative action or series of actions tending or intended to induce one to imitate or emulate ⟨we make the mistake of thinking that all can be done by precept, when . . . ~ is no less potent a force —A.C.Benson⟩ **b :** a pattern of action that by its ill result should discourage emulation ⟨learn from me, if not by my precepts, at least by my ~, how dangerous is the acquirement of knowledge —Mary W. Shelley⟩ — often used with a qualifying adjective (as *bad*) **3 :** a parallel or closely similar case, incident, or item esp. when serving as a precedent or model ⟨such temperate order in so fierce a cause doth want ~ —Shak.⟩ **4 a :** an incident or situation in which one individual's punishment or plight may serve to admonish others **b :** an individual so punished ⟨to make an ~ of a malingering soldier⟩ **5 :** an instance (as a problem to be solved) serving to illustrate a rule or precept or to act as an exercise in the application of the rules of any study or branch of science ⟨in mathematics problems assigned are ~s designed to test and apply rules previously learned⟩ ⟨we have 10 ~s in our homework⟩ **syn** see INSTANCE, MODEL — **for example** \f(ə)r-\ *adv* **:** as an example

²**example** \"\ *vt* **exampled; exampled; exampling** \-p(ə)liŋ\ **examples** [ME *exemplen, exaumplen,* fr. MF *exempler,* fr. LL *exemplare,* fr. L *exemplum*] **1 a :** to serve or use as an example of, for, or to — used in the passive ⟨his novel writing, best *exampled* in the somewhat cruel satire —Fanny Butcher⟩ ⟨their spirit may be *exampled* by the way they help one another⟩ **b** *archaic* **:** to be or set an example to **:** teach through example **2** *obs* **:** to constitute a precedent for **:** PARALLEL, MATCH ⟨I may ~ my digression by some mighty precedent —Shak.⟩

exams *pl of* EXAM

¹**ex·animate** \(ˈ)egˈz, (ˈ)ekˈs+ .-\ *adj* [L *exanimatus,* past part. of *exanimare* to deprive of life or courage, terrify, fr. *ex-* ¹ex- + *anima* breath, soul — more at ANIMATE] **1 :** lacking in animation **:** SPIRITLESS **2 :** LIFELESS, DEAD; *also* **:** appearing lifeless

²**exanimate** *vt* -ED/-ING/-S [L *exanimatus,* past part.] *obs* **:** to deprive of life or of animation — **exanimation** *n* -S *obs*

ex ante \(ˈ)ˌ=ˈ==\ *adj* [²*ex* + *ante* (adv.)] **:** based on assumption and prediction and being essentially subjective and estimative ⟨an *ex ante* plan for the budget⟩ ⟨consistency of market behavior, and therefore reasonable conformity of *ex ante* expectations with ex post reality, is basically determined by the social stability of the community —Werner Hochwald⟩ — opposed to *ex post*

ex·an·them \egˈzan(t)thəm, ˈek,san,them\ *also* **ex·an·the·ma** \,eg,zanˈthēmə, ,ek,s-\ *n, pl* **exanthems** \-əmz, -,themz\ *also* **exan·them·a·ta** \-ˈthemәd·ə, -ˈthēm-\ *or* **exanthemas** [NL *exanthema,* fr. LL, skin rash, fr. Gk *exanthēma,* fr. *exanthein* to bloom, to break out (as with a rash), fr. *ex-* (fr. *ex* out of) + *anthein* to bloom, fr. *anthos* flower — more at EX-, ANTHOLOGY] **1 :** an eruptive disease or its symptomatic eruption — used esp. of eruptions attended with fever (as in measles, smallpox, and scarlatina); distinguished from *enanthem* **2** *usu exanthema* **:** a copper-deficiency disease of plants that is esp. prevalent in citrus and olive and is characterized by gummosis often accompanied by dieback and by glossy brownish blotches on leaves and fruit — **ex·an·the·mat·ic** \(ˈ)eg¦zan(t)thə¦mad·ik, (ˈ)ek¦s-\ *or* **ex·an·them·a·tous** \¦=ˌ=ˈthemәd·əs\ *adj*

ex·ant·la·tion \,eg,zantˈlāshən, ,ek,sa-\ *n* -S [L *exantlatus, exanclatus* (past part. of *exantlare, exanclare* to draw out, fr. Gk *exantlein,* fr. *ex-* + *antlein* to bail out, draw out, fr. *antlos* bilge) + E *-ion*] *archaic* **:** the act of drawing out

ex·a·rate \ˈeksə,rāt\ *adj* [L *exaratus,* past part. of L *exarare* to plow up, write on a tablet, fr. *ex-* ¹ex- + *arare* to plow — more at EAR] **1 :** grooved or furrowed **2** *of a pupa* **:** having the appendages not cemented to the body — compare OBTECT

ex·a·ra·tion \,eksəˈrāshən\ *n* -S [LL *exaration-, exaratio,* fr. L *exaratus* + *-ion-, -io* -ion] **:** an act of writing or a product of writing (as a composition or inscription)

¹**ex·arch** \ˈek,särk\ *n* -S [LL *exarchus,* fr. LGk *exarchos,* fr. Gk, leader, chief, fr. *exarchein* to begin, take the lead in, rule, fr. *ex-* (fr. *ex* out) + *archein* to begin, rule — more at EX-, ARCHI-] **1 :** a viceroy of a province under the Byzantine emperors — used as a title or mode of address **2** *Eastern Church* **a :** the head of a chief see or province during the early periods of church history **b :** a bishop inferior to a patriarch and superior to a metropolitan **c :** a deputy of a patriarch usu. holding the rank of bishop **d :** the head of an independent church — **ex·arch·al** \(ˈ)ek¦särkəl\ *adj*

²**exarch** \"\ *adj* [*exo-* + *-arch*] **:** formed or taking place from the periphery toward the center — used of the primary xylem (as of a root) or its development; compare ENDARCH, MESARCH

ex·arch·ate \ˈek,sär,kāt, -rkət\ *n* -S [ML *exarchatus,* fr. LL *exarchus* + L *-atus* -ate] **:** the office or the province of an exarch

ex·arch·ist \ˈek,särkəst\ *n* -S *usu cap* **:** a member of a politico-religious party in Macedonia (1872-1915)

¹**ex·as·per·ate** \igˈzaspə,rāt, eg-, -zaas-,-zás-, *usu* -ād·+V\ *vb* -ED/-ING/-S [L *exasperatus,* past part. of *exasperare,* fr. *ex-* ¹ex- + *asperare* to roughen, irritate, fr. *asper* rough] *vt* **1 :** to excite or inflame the anger of **:** ENRAGE ⟨~ them against the king of France —Joseph Addison⟩; *often* **:** to cause irritation or annoyance to ⟨the general reader will . . . be *exasperated* at a certain cavalier curtness of narrative —C.H.Driver⟩ ⟨she's a good child but her slowness often ~s me⟩ **2** *obs* **:** to make grievous or more grievous or malignant **3** *obs* **:** to make harsh or harsher ~ *vi, obs* **:** to become irritated **syn** see IRRITATE

²**ex·as·per·ate** \-ˌrət, -ˌrāt\ *adj* [L *exasperatus,* past part.] **1 :** EXASPERATED **2** *biol* **:** roughened with irregular prickles or elevations ⟨an ~ carapace⟩ ⟨~ seed coats⟩

exasperated *adj* **:** irritated or annoyed esp. to the point of injudicious action — **ex·as·per·at·ed·ly** *adv*

exasperating *adj* **:** causing or tending to cause exasperation — **ex·as·per·at·ing·ly** *adv*

ex·as·per·a·tion \=ˌ==ˈrāshən\ *n* -S [LL *exasperation-, exasperatio,* fr. L *exasperatus* + *-ion-, -io* -ion] **1 :** the state of being exasperated **:** marked irritation or annoyance ⟨threw the book down in ~⟩ ⟨it should be real anger, and not merely the ~ that comes of fretted nerves or facile emotion —F.A. Swinnerton⟩; *sometimes* **:** violent or bitter anger **:** RAGE **2 :** an act or source of exasperating **:** a cause of irritation ⟨the petty ~s of daily life⟩

ex·auc·to·rate \egˈzóktə,rāt, ekˈsó-\ *vt* -ED/-ING/-S [L *exauctoratus,* past part. of *exauctorare,* fr. *ex-* ¹ex- + (*se*) *auctorare* to hire oneself out, fr. *auctor* author, bail, security — more at AUTHOR] *archaic* **:** to deprive of authority **:** DISMISS — **ex·auc·to·ra·tion** \(,)=ˌ==ˈrāshən\ *n* -S *archaic*

ex·au·gu·ral \(ˈ)ek¦sógyərəl, ÷ -gər-\ *adj* [¹*ex-* + *-augural* (as in *inaugural*)] **:** occurring at the close of a term of office — opposed to *inaugural* ⟨an ~ message⟩

exc *abbr* **1** excellency; excellent **2** except; excepted; exception **3** exchange **4** exciter **5** [L *excudit*] (he) engraved (it) **6** excuse

ex·calcarate \(ˈ)eks+\ *adj* [¹*ex-* + *calcarate*] **:** ECALCARATE

ex·camb \ekˈskam(b)\ *vb* -ED/-ING/-S [ME (Sc dial.) *excamben,* fr. ML *excambiare,* prob. modif. of OF *eschangier* to exchange — more at EXCHANGE] *Scots law* **:** EXCHANGE

ex·cam·bi·on \-mbēən\ *n* -S [ME (Sc dial.), fr. ML *excambium,* prob. modif. of OF *eschange* — more at EXCHANGE] *Scots law* **:** exchange of land

ex·can·des·cence \,ekskənˈdesᵊn(t)s, -,kan-\ *also* **ex·can·des·cen·cy** \-desᵊnsē\ *n, pl* **excandescences** *also* **excandescencies** [L *excandescentia,* fr. *excandescent-, excandescens* (pres. part. of *excandescere* to grow hot, glow, burn, fr. *ex-* ¹ex- + *candescere* to glow, grow red hot, incho. of *candēre* to shine) + *-ia* -y — more at CANDID] *archaic* **:** a feverish condition brought on by anger or passion

ex·can·ta·tion \,ek,skanˈtāshən\ *n* -S [L *excantatus* (past part. of *excantare* to bring out by charms, fr. *ex-* ¹ex- + *cantare* to sing) + E *-ion* — more at CHANT] *archaic* **:** an act of freeing by enchantment

ex·car·di·na·tion \(,)ek,skärdᵊnˈāshən\ *n* -S [¹*ex-* + *-cardination* (as in *incardination*)] **:** the transference of a cleric from one diocese to another

excarnate *vt* -ED/-ING/-S [LL *excarnatus,* past part. of *excarnare,* fr. L *ex-* ¹ex- + *carn-, caro* flesh — more at CARNAL] *obs* **:** to deprive or strip of flesh

ex·car·na·tion \,ek,skärˈnāshən\ *n* -S **1 :** removal of flesh (as by putrefaction) **2 :** separation of soul from body (as at death)

ex cathedra \(ˈ)eks+\ *adv* (*or adj*) [L, from the chair] **:** by virtue of or in the exercise of one's office **:** with authority ⟨speaking *ex cathedra*⟩ ⟨an *ex cathedra* pronouncement⟩

ex·ca·vate \ˈekskə,vāt, *usu* -ād·+V\ *vb* -ED/-ING/-S [L *excavatus,* past part. of *excavare,* fr. *ex-* ¹ex- + *cavare* to make hollow, fr. *cavus* hollow — more at CAVE] *vt* **1 :** to hollow out **:** form a cavity or hole in ⟨*excavating* the side of a hill⟩ ⟨an *excavated* wisdom tooth⟩ **2 :** to form by hollowing **:** shape by removing material so as to leave a space ⟨will ~ the cellar as soon as the frost goes⟩ ⟨*excavated* a tunnel under the river⟩ **3 :** to dig out and remove (as earth or mineral matter) ⟨over a million tons of rich ore were *excavated* from that one pocket⟩ **4 :** to expose to view by or as if by digging away a covering ⟨*excavated* the remains of 10 separate cultures⟩ ⟨*excavated* several forgotten accounts of the brawl⟩ ~ *vi* **1 :** to make excavations or become hollowed out ⟨the mollusk uses its pointed foot to ~ in the mud⟩ ⟨an area of infarction in soft tissue often tends to ~⟩ **syn** see DIG

ex·ca·va·tion \,=ˈvāshən\ *n* -S [L *excavation-, excavatio,* fr. *excavatus* + *-ion-, -io* -ion] **1 a :** the action or process of excavating **b :** the removal of superposed material (as earth, stone, or buildings) from the remains or structures of an age or civilization earlier than the present **2 :** a cavity formed by cutting, digging, or scooping **3 a :** an uncovered cutting in the earth — distinguished from *tunnel* **b :** the material dug out in making a channel or cavity

ex·ca·va·tor \ˈ==,vād·ə(r), -ātə-\ *n* -S **:** one that excavates: as **a :** a worker who digs out material or digs cavities (as in quarrying or for building construction) **b :** any of various machines (as a steam shovel) for excavating earth **c :** an instrument used to open bodily cavities (as in the teeth) or remove material from them

ex·ca·va·to·ry \ˈekskəvə,tōrē, ekˈskavə-; ¦ekskə¦vād·ərē\ *adj* **:** concerned with excavation or its results ⟨~ archaeology⟩

excecate *vt* -ED/-ING/-S [L *excaecatus,* past part. of *excaecare,* fr. *ex-* ¹ex- + *caecare* to blind, fr. *caecus* blind — more at CECUM] *obs* **:** to blind physically or mentally — **excecation** *n* -S *archaic*

ex·ceed \ikˈsēd, ek-\ *vb* -ED/-ING/-S [ME *exceden,* fr. MF *exceder,* fr. L *excedere,* fr. *ex-* ¹ex- + *cedere* to go, proceed — more at CEDE] *vt* **1 :** to extend outside of or enlarge beyond — used chiefly in strictly physical relations ⟨if this rain keeps up, the river will ~ its banks by morning⟩ **2 a :** to be greater than or superior to **:** SURPASS ⟨his brother ~s him in height⟩ ⟨their accomplishment ~*ed* our expectation⟩ ⟨the cost must not ~ one year's income⟩ **b :** to be too much for **:** be beyond the comprehension of ⟨the mercy of God ~s our finite minds⟩ **3 :** to go beyond a limit set by (as an authority or privilege) **:** do more than is justified by or allowable under (as a commission or order) ⟨he ~*ed* his authority when he paid his brother's gambling debts with money from the trust⟩ ⟨the captain ~*ed* his orders when he quartered men in private houses⟩ ~ *vi* **1** *obs* **a :** to go too far **:** pass the proper or usual bounds (as of conduct) **b :** to eat or drink to excess **2 :** to stand out among or be more or greater than others **:** PREDOMINATE

syn SURPASS, TRANSCEND, EXCEL, OUTDO, OUTSTRIP: EXCEED indicates a going over or topping what is under consideration in a companion or what is set as a standard or limit ⟨far *exceeding* the production figures from last year⟩ ⟨an Inferno which *exceeds* anything that Dante imagined —Henry Miller⟩ ⟨the number of representatives shall not *exceed* one for every thirty thousand —*U.S. Constitution*⟩ ⟨he seemed to think I'd *exceeded* my authority in disposing of the rebels as I saw fit —Kenneth Roberts⟩ SURPASS is a close synonym of EXCEED; it is likely to be used in reference to superiority in quality, merit, virtue, or skill, although it may be used to describe what is more evil or reprehensible ⟨he wanted himself to *surpass* Caesar in deeds and his legions to *surpass* the achievements of the legions of Caesar —J.T.Farrell⟩ ⟨in the moral essence of tragedy it is safe to say that in this play Middleton is *surpassed* by one Elizabethan alone, and that is Shakespeare —T.S.Eliot⟩ ⟨in the imputation of things evil and in putting the worst construction on things innocent, a certain type of good people may be trusted to *surpass* all others —Rudyard Kipling⟩ ⟨his tyrannies *surpassed* those of his predecessor⟩ TRANSCEND may suggest a rising notably or remarkably above an accustomed standard or level ⟨sorrow transcending all sorrows, darker than death, immitigable, eternal —W.H.Hudson †1922⟩ ⟨in Virgil we find that divine afflatus which *transcends* the most balanced wisdom and the deftest technical skill —John Buchan⟩ ⟨certain problems are raised, if an ideal, embodied into law, *transcends* the "realities" too far —Reinhold Niebuhr⟩ In intransitive uses EXCEL implies reaching a preeminence in accomplishment or achievement; in transitive ones it is a close synonym of SURPASS ⟨*excelling* in terse narrative⟩ ⟨*excelling* in athletics⟩ ⟨during their seminary years he had easily *surpassed* his friend in scholarship, but he always realized that Joseph *excelled* him in the fervor of his faith —Willa Cather⟩ ⟨if some *excelled* him in learning and scholarly productivity, not many *surpassed* him in personal attractiveness —H.E.Starr⟩ OUTDO, a more colloquial word, may apply to topping, bettering, or exceeding what has been done before ⟨the military engines he devised for the defense of Syracuse seem never to have been *outdone* in the ancient world —Benjamin Farrington⟩ ⟨a competition in deceit in which, I admit, he *outdid* them —Owen Wister⟩ OUTSTRIP suggests surpassing in a race or competition or similar endeavor ⟨swimming was his chief delight, and so it came about that one day when he was far from land, having *outstripped* all his fellows in a race, he was hardly surprised to see a dolphin plunging alongside of him —Norman Douglas⟩ ⟨bituminous coal had far *outstripped* anthracite in the industrial markets —S.A.Hale⟩ ⟨instead of allowing his reader the easy victory, he takes pride in *outstripping* him completely —Edmund Wilson⟩

ex·ceed·able \-dəbəl\ *adj* **:** suitable for or capable of being exceeded ⟨a safely ~ speed limit⟩

ex·ceed·er \-də(r)\ *n* -S **:** one that exceeds

exceeding *adj* [fr. pres. part. of *exceed*] **:** exceptional in amount, quality, or degree **:** greater than is customary or desirable or predictable ⟨the ~ disorder of the room⟩ ⟨the ~ pallor of her skin⟩

ex·ceed·ing·ly *also* **exceeding** *adv* **:** to a marked degree or extent **:** EXTREMELY, NOTABLY, VERY ⟨ground to an ~ fine powder⟩ ⟨an *exceeding* high hill —Isak Dinesen⟩

ex·cel \ikˈsel, ek-\ *vb* **excelled; excelled; excelling; excels** [ME *excellen,* fr. L *excellere,* fr. *ex-* ¹ex- + *-cellere* to rise, project (akin to L *collis* hill) — more at HILL] *vt* **1 :** to surpass or outshine (as in some quality possessed or activity engaged in) ⟨a charming child who instinctively ~s other children in all the social graces⟩ ⟨he *excelled* his brother at sports but not in school⟩ ⟨his journeys *excelled* most . . . of theirs in miles, speed, and comfort —Vilhjalmur Stefansson⟩ **2** *obs* **:** to go beyond ~ *vi* **:** to surpass others esp. in good qualities, laudable actions, or acquirements **:** be distinguishable by superiority — usu. used with *in* ⟨he ~s in mathematics⟩ ⟨some painters ~ in precise delineation of detail⟩ ⟨a new melon that ~s in flavor⟩ **syn** see EXCEED

ex·cel·lence \ˈeks(ə)lən(t)s\ *n* -S [ME, fr. MF, fr. L *excellentia,* fr. *excellent-, excellens* + *-ia* -y] **1 :** the quality of being excellent **:** the state of possessing good qualities in an eminent degree **2 :** an excellent or valuable quality **:** VIRTUE **3 :** EXCELLENCY 2

syn MERIT, VIRTUE, PERFECTION: EXCELLENCE indicates a high degree or the highest degree of good qualities, of qualities that make for especial worth or merit; it may be limited explicitly by some such word as *particular* or *distinctive* or by its context ⟨spoke of the rude health of their children as if it were a result of moral *excellence;* in a peculiar tone which seemed to imply some contempt for people whose children were liable to be unwell at times —Joseph Conrad⟩ ⟨*excellences* achieved with the sure touch of craftsmanship —*Saturday Rev.*⟩ MERIT, often contrasted with *demerit* in critical estimates, may refer broadly to any good, commendable, worthy, or valuable quality or feature ⟨the result might have been a permanent aristocracy, possessing the *merits* and defects of the Spartans —Bertrand Russell⟩ ⟨the *merits* and defects of Cowper's version —Matthew Arnold⟩ ⟨the subject of my choice has the *merit* of universal appeal —R.W.Chapman⟩ VIRTUE may apply to a peculiar or distinctive power, strength, or efficacy, to a characteristic indicating moral goodness, or to some conspicuous character merit ⟨flexibility and adaptation are the cardinal *virtues* of successful aging —George Lawton⟩ ⟨the fine balance with which Johnson weighed and sustained his judgments of human flaws and virtues —H.V.Gregory⟩ ⟨define as *virtues* those mental and physical habits which tend to produce a good community, and as vices those that tend to produce a bad one —Bertrand Russell⟩ PERFECTION suggests attainment to faultlessness, to the highest excellence ⟨the effort to make such windows was never repeated. Their jeweled *perfection* did not suit the scale of the vast churches of the thirteenth century —Henry Adams⟩ ⟨defective as they are in every branch of knowledge, and in every other species of refinement, it seems wonderful that they should arrive at such *perfection* in the dance —William Cowper⟩

ex·cel·len·cy \-nsē, -si\ *n* -ES [ME *excellencie,* fr. L *excellentia*] **1 :** EXCELLENCE; *usu* **:** outstanding or valuable quality — used chiefly in pl. ⟨noting one another's *excellencies* and defects⟩ **2 :** a person of notable position, dignity, or worth — used in a title or in a mode of address to certain high dignitaries (as a Roman Catholic bishop, a governor of a state, an ambassador, a viceroy) and then usu. cap. ⟨His *Excellency* the Bishop⟩

¹**ex·cel·lent** \-nt\ *adj, sometimes* -ER/-EST [ME, fr. MF, fr. L *excellent-, excellens,* fr. pres. part. of *excellere* to excel — more at EXCEL] **1** *archaic* **:** excelling or exceeding in kind or degree **2 :** of high station, rank, or office — used as a title or in a mode of address and often cap. ⟨the most ~ chief of the lodge will preside at the meeting⟩ **3 :** meritoriously near the standard or model **:** very good of its kind **:** FIRST-CLASS ⟨this vase is an ~ imitation of the antique⟩; *broadly* **:** of great worth **:** eminently good ⟨an ~ man⟩ ⟨~ breeding⟩ ⟨crossbred wool was in ~ demand⟩ ⟨many ~ Americans are fighting this hysteria —Hugh Gaitskell⟩

²**excellent** \"\ *adv* [ME, fr. ¹*excellent*] *archaic* **:** EXCELLENTLY, EXCEEDINGLY

ex·cel·lent·ly *adv* [ME, fr. ¹*excellent* + *-ly*] **1 :** in an excellent manner **:** to marked advantage **:** very well **:** EFFECTIVELY, FINELY ⟨~ reasoned arguments⟩ ⟨getting along ~⟩ **2 :** to or in a marked or unusual degree **:** EXCEEDINGLY, NOTABLY, VERY ⟨lunched ~ well⟩

ex·cel·lent·ness *n* -ES **:** EXCELLENCE

excelse *adj* [L *excelsus,* fr. past part. of *excellere* to raise, rise, excel — more at EXCEL] *obs* **:** EMINENT, LOFTY

ex·cel·sin \ikˈselsən, ek-\ *n* -S [NL *excelsa* (specific epithet of *Bertholettia excelsa,* fr. fem. of *excelsus* high) + E *-in*] **:** a crystalline globulin obtained from the meat of the Brazil nut

ex·cel·si·or \ikˈselsēə(r), ek- *also* -lts- *sometimes* -lshə- *or* ÷ -l(t)sə- *or* -l(t)sē,ȯ(ə)r *or* -l(t)sē,ȯ(ə)r\ *n* -S [L, higher, comparative of *excelsus*] **:** fine curled shavings of wood forming a resilient mass and used esp. for packing fragile items

ex·center \ˈek(s)+,-\ *n* [¹*ex-* + *center*] **:** the center of an escribed circle

¹**ex·centric** \ik, (ˈ)ek(s)+\ *var of* ECCENTRIC

²**excentric** \"\ *or* **ex·central** \ik-, (ˈ)ek(s)+\ *adj* [¹*ex-* + *centric* or *central*] **:** not centrally located **:** ONE-SIDED — used esp. of the relation of stipe to pileus in certain fungi

excentrical *archaic var of* ECCENTRIC

¹**ex·cept** \ikˈsept, ek-\ *vb* -ED/-ING/-S [ME *excepten,* fr. MF *excepter,* fr. L *exceptare,* fr. *exceptus,* past part. of *excipere,* to take out, make an exception of, take, receive, fr. *ex-* ¹ex- + *-cipere* (fr. *capere* to take) — more at HEAVE] *vt* **1 :** to take or leave out (something) from a number or a whole **:** exclude or omit (as from consideration) ⟨it is desirable to ~ all first-calf heifers in determining butterfat production averages⟩ **2** *obs* **:** to offer as objection; *also* **:** to protest against ~ *vi* **1 :** to take exception **:** OBJECT — usu. used with *to,* sometimes with *against* ⟨~ to a witness⟩ ⟨except thou wilt ~ against my love —Shak.⟩ **2 :** to enter an exception in law

²**except** \=ˈ=, *rapid* (,)sep(t)\ *also* **excepting** *prep* [*except* fr. ME, fr. L *exceptus,* past part.; *excepting* fr. ME, fr. pres. part. of *excepten*] **1 :** with the exclusion or exception of ⟨the stores will remain open daily ~ Sundays⟩ ⟨*excepting* Christmas we did not have one really pleasant holiday⟩ **:** SAVE ⟨he could do little ~ write⟩ **2 :** otherwise, elsewhere, or for other reason than **:** other than **:** BUT ⟨you cannot hope to keep them ~ in sealed containers⟩ ⟨you could never have lost your way ~ by your own carelessness⟩ ⟨I take no orders ~ from the king —G.B.Shaw⟩

³**except** \"\ *also* **excepting** *conj* [*except* fr. ME, fr. L *exceptus,* past part.; *excepting* fr. *excepting,* prep.] **1 :** on any other condition than that **:** UNLESS ⟨I will not let thee go, ~ thou bless me —Gen 32:26 (AV)⟩ ⟨horses had been man's only means of land travel, ~ he walked —Hugh McCausland⟩ ⟨I wouldn't go near the old gossip ~ I had to⟩ ⟨never does he sit down at table ~ it is crowded with guests —Upton Sinclair⟩ **2 :** ONLY — used with or without *that* ⟨I would buy a new suit ~ I have no money⟩ ⟨a furious energy drove me to all kinds of bodily and mental exercise, without any particular direction ~ that I felt sure I was going to be a great poet —John Reed⟩

⁴**except** *vt* -ED/-ING/-S [ME *excepten,* fr. L *exceptus,* past part.] *obs* **:** ACCEPT

ex·cept·able \ikˈseptəbəl, (ˈ)ek¦s-\ *adj* [¹*except* + *-able*] **:** fit for excepting or suitable for being excepted

except for *prep* **:** ²EXCEPT 1 ⟨*except for* your presence I would be bored⟩

ex·cep·tio \ikˈsepshē,ō, ek-, -ptē,ō; ekˈskeptē,ō\ *n, pl* **ex·cep·ti·o·nes** \ik,sepshēˈō,nēz, (,)ek,-, -septēˈō,nēz, -skeptēˈō,nās\ [L] **:** an exception in pleading at law

ex·cep·tion \ikˈsepshən, ek-\ *n* -S [ME *excepcioun,* fr. MF & L; MF *exception,* fr. L *exception-, exceptio,* fr. *exceptus* (past part. of *excipere* to take out, make an exception) + *-ion-, -io* -ion — more at EXCEPT] **1 :** the act of excepting or excluding **:** exclusion or restriction (as of a class, statement, or rule) by taking out something that would otherwise be included **2 :** one that is excepted or taken out from others ⟨almost every general rule has its ~s⟩ ⟨eight of the pups were beauties; the only ~ was a potbellied little male⟩ **3 a :** something offered or offerable as objection or as a ground of objection or taken as objectionable ⟨witnesses whose authority is beyond ~ —T.B.Macaulay⟩ — now usu. used with *take* ⟨taking ~ to the majority vote —Bennett Cerf⟩ ⟨to whose musical ideas one would seldom take ~ —A.T.Davison⟩ **b** *archaic* **:** OFFENSE ⟨she takes ~s at your person —Shak.⟩ **4 a :** an oral or written objection (as to a ruling of a judge or something in his charge to a jury) taken in the course of an action or proceeding at law **b :** a clause by which a grantor (as of a deed) excepts something out of what he before granted **5 a :** a special plea in defense in Roman law setting up allegations which if they are true will bar the claim even when the facts on which the claim is based are true, the plea being set up in a formula directing that it be tried first; *also* **:** any plea in defense whether peremptory in complete bar or dilatory in delay of the plaintiff's claim **b :** SPECIAL PLEA IN BAR **c** *Scots law* **:** DEFENSE 1b **d :** an objection alleging insufficiency of some pleading or proceeding in equity

ex·cep·tion·able \-sh(ə)nəbəl\ *adj* **1 :** such as may cause objection **:** OBJECTIONABLE ⟨a thoroughly unpleasant highly ~ piece of writing⟩ **2 :** EXCEPTIONAL — **ex·cep·tion·ably** \-blē, -li\ *adv*

ex·cep·tion·al \-shənᵊl, -shnəl\ *adj* **1 :** forming an exception; *usu* **:** being out of the ordinary **:** UNCOMMON, RARE ⟨they made an ~ group⟩ ⟨there have been an ~ number of rainy days this year⟩ **2 :** better than the average **:** SUPERIOR ⟨his ~ skill⟩ ⟨this is an ~ opportunity⟩ **3** *of a child* **:** requiring special educational or psychological aid in social adjustment whether because of superior ability or because of physical or mental defect — **ex·cep·tion·al·i·ty** \=,=shə'naləd-ē\ *n* -ES — **ex·cep·tion·al·ly** \=ˈ=shən°l|ē, -shnəl|ē, |i\ *adv* — **ex·cep·tion·al·ness** \-°lnəs, -əl-\ *n* -ES

ex·cep·tion·al·ism \=ˈsepshən°l,izəm, -shnə,li-\ *n* -S **:** a theory or doctrine (as of social or political action) based on the assumption that exceptional circumstances will result in distortion of a generally predictable course in certain instances

ex·cep·tion·al·ist \-°ləst, -ələ-\ *n* -S **:** one that accepts or advocates exceptionalism

ex·cep·tion·less \-shənləs\ *adj* **:** admitting of no exception

exception principle *n* **:** a method or plan of supervision (as of a business) under which only significant deviations from normally expected results or conditions are brought to the attention of a supervisor for consideration and decision

ex·cep·tious \-shəs\ *adj* [exception + -ous] *archaic* **:** disposed to take exception — **ex·cep·tious·ness** *n* -ES *archaic*

ex·cep·tive \-ptiv, -tēv *also* -təv\ *adj* [ML *exceptivus*, fr. L *exceptus* + *-ivus* -ive] **1 :** relating to, containing, or constituting exception: as **a** *of a word* **:** serving to introduce a verbal exception ⟨an ~ preposition⟩ **b** *of a proposition in logic* **:** having the subject limited by exception **2** *archaic* **:** EXCEPTIOUS — **ex·cep·tive·ly** \-tə̇vlē, -li\ *adv*

excepts *pres 3d sing of* EXCEPT

excern *vt* [L *excernere* to sift out, separate, discharge (as feces) — more at EXCRETE] *obs* **:** EXCRETE, DISCHARGE

[1]**ex·cerpt** \(ˈ)ek¦s|ərpt, ik's|, |əpt, |əipt *sometimes* (ˈ)eg¦z| *or* ig'z|\ *vb* -ED/-ING/-S [L *excerptus*, past part. of *excerpere*, fr. *ex-* [1]ex- + *-cerpere* (fr. *carpere* to gather, pluck, divide) — more at HARVEST] *vt* **1 :** to select (passages or details) as typical of a larger store **:** select for quoting **:** EXTRACT ⟨a compendium of quotable sayings ~*ed* from the writings of a variety of modern writers —*Book-of-the-Month Club News*⟩ **2** *obs* **:** to take out **:** REMOVE **3 :** to shorten by selecting parts of ⟨a new biography that is to be ~*ed* for serial publication in three installments⟩ ~ *vi* **:** to make excerpts

[2]**ex·cerpt** \ˈek,s| *sometimes* ˈeg,z|\ *n* -S [L *excerptum*, fr. neut. of *excerptus*, past part.] **:** a selection or fragment (as from a writing or a work of music) ⟨played ~*s* from the opera⟩ **:** a chosen portion or sample ⟨cabled daily ~*s* of life in the Orient⟩

ex·cerp·ta \ek's|, ik's| *sometimes* eg'z| *or* ig'z|\ *n pl* [L, pl. of *excerptum*] **:** brief bits of writing; *often* **:** clippings or résumés

ex·cerpt·er *also* **ex·cerp·tor** *pronunc at* [1]EXCERPT+ə(r)\ *n* -S **:** a maker of excerpts

ex·cerpt·ible *pronunc at* [1]EXCERPT+əbəl\ *adj* **:** fit or suitable for use as a source of excerpts

ex·cerp·tion \ek's|ərpshən, ik's|, |əp-, |əip- *sometimes* eg'z- *or* ig'z-\ *n* -S [L *excerption-, excerptio*, fr. *excerptus* + *-ion-, -io* -ion] **1** *archaic* **:** EXTRACT **2 :** an act or process of excerpting esp. in the selection of material for an abridgment

[1]**ex·cess** \ik'ses, ˈek,ses, ek'ses\ *n* -ES [ME, fr. MF or LL; MF *excès*, fr. LL *excessus*, fr. L, departure, fr. *excessus*, past part. of *excedere* to go forth, exceed — more at EXCEED] **1 a :** a state of surpassing or going beyond limits **:** the fact of being in a measure beyond sufficiency, necessity, or duty **:** SUPERFLUITY, SUPERABUNDANCE ⟨~ of grief⟩ ⟨an ~ of provisions⟩ **b :** something that exceeds what is usual, proper, proportionate, or specified ⟨she was serious almost to ~ —Aldous Huxley⟩ **c :** the amount or degree by which one thing or number exceeds another ⟨there was an ~ of 10 bushels over what was needed to fill the bin⟩ ⟨the ~ of 12 plus 2 over 12 minus 2 is 4⟩ **2 :** undue or immoderate indulgence **:** intemperance esp. in eating and drinking ⟨~ at table is seldom healthful⟩ — often used in pl. ⟨their ~*es* led to their expulsion from the congregation⟩

syn SUPERFLUITY, SURPLUS, SURPLUSAGE, OVERPLUS: EXCESS may be used of any exceeding or going beyond measure, limits, or accustomed bounds ⟨an *excess* of carbon dioxide in the air⟩ ⟨an *excess* of supply over demand⟩ It is often used in connection with culpable lack of moderation, temperance, and restraint ⟨I have a considerable affection for the Empire style, of which I bought a houseful when it could be bought for half nothing. But the *excesses* of the style are terrible —Arnold Bennett⟩ ⟨Washington began with the prestige of a unanimous election and ended, as his farewell address plainly reveals, with a deep abhorrence of the *excesses* of intense party spirit —A.N.Holcombe⟩ SUPERFLUITY may refer to a vain, wasteful, or embarrassing excess, over actual needs ⟨as I have a certain amount of money to spare and am possessed by the strange desire to collect unnecessary objects, I succumb easily to anyone who asks me to buy *superfluities* and luxuries —Aldous Huxley⟩ ⟨not the lack of expressive power, but the *superfluity*. He was profusely and indiscriminately loquacious —Virginia Woolf⟩ SURPLUS applies to whatever is left after all needed has been used or expended; it is often used in reference to money or to valuable commodities ⟨the company books showing a *surplus*⟩ ⟨the Patent Office has become one of the relatively few government establishments that not only pay their way, but normally yield a *surplus* —F.A.Ogg & P.O. Ray⟩ ⟨nearly every farmer had an apple press with which he prepared adequate quantities of cider and vinegar for family consumption, and frequently there were *surpluses* to market —W.M.Kollmorgen⟩ SURPLUSAGE may refer to an unjustified or useless excess ⟨the Senate conferees took the position that the usage of the word "prior" was unnecessary and was mere *surplusage* —*U.S.Code*⟩ OVERPLUS may designate an unnecessary addition or adventitious augmentation ⟨we entered the Rectory drive, the car poked at by the wild *overplus* of vegetation which was certainly not that of a normal garden —Wyndham Lewis⟩

— **in excess of** *prep* **:** to an amount or degree beyond **:** OVER ⟨gifts *in excess of* $1,000,000 —T.M.Gordon⟩ ⟨is regarded as *in excess of* that which the law should permit —W.L.Sperry⟩ ⟨made demands on the climbers *in excess of* what was required —E.F.Norton⟩ — **to excess** *adv* **:** IMMODERATELY ⟨started drinking *to excess* and eventually became an alcoholic —Polly Adler⟩

[2]**ex·cess** \ˈek,ses, ik'ses, ek's-\ *adj* [ME, fr. *excess*, n.] **1 :** more than or above the usual or specified amount **:** that constitutes an excess ⟨~ property on hand after a contract ends⟩ ⟨the body tends to rid itself of its ~ nitrogen —H.G.Armstrong⟩ ⟨~ sleep may be a sign of a disturbance —Morris Fishbein⟩ **2 :** exceeding in weight or size an allowance transportable without charge ⟨~ baggage⟩

excess condemnation *n* **:** condemnation under eminent domain of an area of land greater than needed for the immediate purposes for which the land is being condemned

excess insurance *n* **1 :** insurance in which the underwriter's liability does not arise until the loss exceeds a stated amount and then only on the excess above that amount **2 :** insurance over and above that necessary to meet the requirements of a coinsurance clause

ex·ces·sive \ik'sesiv, (ˈ)ek¦s-, -esēv *also* -esəv\ *adj* [ME, fr. MF *excessif*, fr. ML *excessivus*, fr. L *excessus* (past part.) + *-ivus* -ive] **:** characterized by or present in excess: as **a :** exceeding the usual, proper, or normal ⟨~ rainfall⟩ ⟨an ~ penchant for intellectual and verbal hairsplitting —J.W. Beach⟩ ⟨gross and ~ language⟩ **b :** very large, great, or numerous **:** greater than usual ⟨the early rains induced an ~ vegetative growth⟩ **c :** given to excess **:** INTEMPERATE

syn IMMODERATE, INORDINATE, EXTRAVAGANT, EXORBITANT, EXTREME: EXCESSIVE describes whatever notably exceeds the reasonable, usual, proper, necessary, just, or endurable ⟨outraged farmers had clamored against the railroad monopoly, charging that it gouged them with *excessive* freight charges —Allan Nevins & H.S.Commager⟩ ⟨*excessive* bail shall not be required, nor *excessive* fines imposed, nor cruel and unusual punishments inflicted —*U.S. Constitution*⟩ IMMODERATE may suggest blameworthy lack of restraint and moderation ⟨I can testify that the Mass gave him extreme, I may even say *immoderate*, satisfaction. It was almost orgiastic —T.S.Eliot⟩ ⟨Mr. Hilary saw, at one view, all the circumstances of the adventure, and burst into an *immoderate* fit of laughter —T.L.Peacock⟩ INORDINATE connotes an excess transcending reason or judgment ⟨his pride was *inordinate*. Rather than humble himself, rather than bend, he flings himself to the dogs —Henry Miller⟩ ⟨his insensate wrath seemed to pass all ordinary bounds . . . Even Heath was startled by Rex's *inordinate* malignity —W.H.Wright⟩ EXTRAVAGANT connotes a similar excess; the word may imply a wild, prodigal, or foolish wandering from fit restraints and accustomed bounds ⟨she tore her hair and beat her breast, and abandoned herself to all the violences of *extravagant* emotion —Bram Stoker⟩ ⟨the absence of a customary norm of consumption was most conspicuous in the *extravagant* life of the courts. To externalize the desire for power, wealth, and privilege, the princes of the Renascence lavished upon private luxury and display enormous amounts of money —Lewis Mumford⟩ ⟨altogether too *extravagant* and impossible to be regarded in any other light than as a monstrous joke —Charles Dickens⟩ EXORBITANT likewise suggests a notable excessive departure from the customary; frequently applied to prices asked, demands, or exactions ⟨a continuation of the law for the renegotiation of war contracts — which will prevent *exorbitant* profits and assure fair prices to the government —F.D.Roosevelt⟩ ⟨blinded by so *exorbitant* a lust of gold, the youngster straightway tasked his wits, casting about to kill the lady —Robert Browning⟩ EXTREME may suggest an attaining to, approaching to, and tending toward the greatest excess possible, although it frequently means only to a notably high degree ⟨the fascination of crime is perpetual, especially in its *extreme* form as murder —A.C.Ward⟩ ⟨there are wings *extreme* to the point of anarchy —J.L.Lowes⟩

ex·ces·sive·ly \-sə̇vlē, -li\ *adv* [ME, fr. *excessive* + *-ly*] **:** to an exceptional or even improper degree **:** to excess **:** EXTREMELY ⟨~ fond of fine dress and luxury⟩

ex·ces·sive·ness \-sivnəs, -sēv- *also* -səv-\ *n* -ES **:** the quality or state of being excessive ⟨the townspeople chafed under the ~ of the tax imposed on them⟩

excessive verdict *n* **:** a verdict considered by the court as awarding shockingly and unreasonably high damages to the plaintiff even assuming that all the evidence most favorable to the plaintiff is true

excess-loss reinsurance *n* **:** reinsurance by a company agreeing to bear any loss in excess of a stipulated amount often with some maximum limitation — compare EXCESS INSURANCE, EXCESS REINSURANCE

excess-profits tax *n* **:** a tax imposed esp. during war on business profits that are in excess of the average profits over a specified base period, of a specified rate of return on invested capital, or of a specified rate of return on certain military contracts

excess reinsurance *n* **:** reinsurance by a company assuming liability on the risk only for that amount of insurance which is over and above a stated sum with the principle of contribution applying in payment of losses

exch *abbr* **1** exchange **2** exchequer

[1]**ex·change** \iks'chānj, eks'ch *also* ˈeks,ch-\ *n, often attrib* [ME *eschaunge, exchaunge*, fr. MF *eschange*, fr. *eschangier*] **1 :** the act of giving or taking one thing in return for another as if equivalent: as **a :** the restoration to their fellows of persons captured during military action usu. by each contesting side in equivalent numbers **b :** the process of reciprocal transfer of ownership (as between persons) **:** TRADE, BARTER; *broadly* **:** a complex of transactions that results in the actual interchange of goods and services (as among primitive peoples) even though any one transfer may be widely separated in space and time from another and may take place under the guise of presenting gifts or in consequence of traditional ceremonies — compare KULA **c :** a mutual grant under the law of equal interests one being in consideration of the other **d :** reciprocal transfer (as of military or naval commissions) between individuals usu. with some added gratuity to the individual accepting the less desirable **2 a :** the act of substituting one thing in the place of another ⟨the gradual ~ of her grief for quiet peace⟩ ⟨the startling transformation wrought by the ~ of his rags for royal raiment⟩ **b :** reciprocal giving and receiving (as of courtesies, blows, or words) **c :** a mutual capture of men in chess or checkers **d :** reciprocal interchange of sisters or daughters whereby two men in certain primitive societies obtain wives for themselves or for their brothers or sons ⟨the custom of marriage by ~⟩ **e :** a chemical reaction or process in which one atom, ion, or group changes places with another ⟨isotopic ~⟩ — see ION EXCHANGE; compare DOUBLE DECOMPOSITION, SUBSTITUTION 1d **3 :** something offered, given, or received in an exchange (as goods, blows, or words): as **a :** a usu. brief and often heated, acrid, or witty dialogue **b :** a publication (as a periodical) given (as by a publisher or author) in return for another publication; *also* **:** an item or article reprinted from a newspaper **4 a :** funds (as drafts, checks, or bills of exchange) payable currently at a distant point either in (1) a foreign currency or (2) in domestic currency — called also respectively (1) *foreign exchange*, (2) *domestic exchange* **b :** the amount paid for the collection (as of a draft, bill of exchange, or check drawn in one place upon another) **c** (1) **:** interchange or conversion of the money of two countries or of current and uncurrent money with allowance for difference in value (2) **:** RATE OF EXCHANGE (3) **:** the amount of the difference in value between two currencies or between values at two places — compare ARBITRAGE **d exchanges** *pl* **:** the items (as drafts, checks) that are presented in a clearinghouse for settlement by mutual interchange of credits and debits and payment of balances **5 :** a place where things or services are exchanged: as **a** *obs* **:** a money changer's place of business **b :** a place devoted to the transaction (as between merchants, bankers, and brokers) of business usu. at the professional level — often used in combination ⟨the grain ~⟩ ⟨a southern stock ~⟩ **c :** an organized market or center for trading in certain commodities at wholesale or on contracts calling for future delivery ⟨a produce ~⟩ **d :** a store or shop where merchandise usu. of a particular type is bought, resold, or repaired ⟨a typewriter ~⟩ **e :** a cooperative store or society ⟨a farmers' ~⟩ **f** *archaic* **:** BARROOM, SALOON **g :** TELEPHONE EXCHANGE **h :** POST EXCHANGE — **in exchange** *adv* **:** as a substitute ⟨what will you give me *in exchange*⟩; *sometimes* **:** as payment ⟨he received $10 *in exchange* for a couple of hours of work⟩

[2]**exchange** \"\ *vb* [ME *eschaungen*, fr. MF *eschangier*, fr. (assumed) VL *excambiare*, fr. L *ex-* [1]ex- + *cambiare* to exchange — more at CHANGE] *vt* **1 a :** to part with, give, or transfer in consideration of something received as an equivalent ⟨the boy *exchanged* his mother's cow for a handful of beans⟩ **b :** to supply (something else) in place of goods returned ⟨do you think the store will ~ something more up-to-date for the high shoes my aunt bought?⟩; *also* **:** to have (goods returned to the seller) replaced by other merchandise ⟨I'm sure you can ~ the blouse but probably not return it for a refund⟩ **2 :** to part with for a substitute ⟨*exchanging* future security for immediate enjoyment⟩ **:** to lay aside, quit, or resign (something presently possessed) in return for some alternate ⟨*exchanged* his youth and health for the burdens of wealth⟩ ⟨who would not ~ loneliness for happy companionship?⟩ **3 :** to give and receive reciprocally (as things of the same kind) **:** BARTER, SWAP ⟨let's ~ hats⟩ ⟨I would ~ horses if you had a better horse⟩ ⟨if she could ~ natures with her brother⟩ ⟨*exchanging* heated words and finally blows⟩ **4** *obs* **:** ALTER, CHANGE ~ *vi* **1 :** to pass or be received in exchange — used with *for* ⟨when the pound ~*s* for less than $3⟩ **2 :** to engage in an exchange esp. of a commission or appointment ⟨anxious to ~ out of that provincial regiment⟩

ex·change·able \-jəbəl\ *adj* **1 :** capable of being exchanged **:** fit or proper to be exchanged **2 :** available for making exchanges **:** RATABLE — **ex·change·ably** \-blē, -li\ *adv*

exchange charge *n* **:** a small deduction from the face value of a check or draft on a distant point made by the bank that cashes such a document

exchange control *n* **:** governmental regulation of the conversion of currencies, the purchase of foreign coin or gold, and the transfer of funds between countries

exchange depreciation *n* **:** reduction of the foreign exchange value of a currency below its true relative value (as for the purpose of stimulating exports)

ex·chang·ee \¦eks,chān¦jē, iks¦ch-, eks¦ch-\ *n* -S [[2]*exchange* + *-ee*] **:** a participant or former participant in an exchange program (as of students or teachers)

exchange note *n* **:** CHANGE NOTE

exchange office *also* **exchange post office** *n* **:** a post office assigned to and having special facilities for the interchange of mail with foreign countries

ex·chang·er *pronunc at* [1]EXCHANGE +ə(r)\ *n* [ME *eschaungeour*, fr. AF *eschaungeor*, fr. OF *eschangier* to exchange + *-eor* -or] **1 :** one that exchanges **2 :** MONEY CHANGER, BANKER; *esp* **:** one formerly appointed in England to exchange plate and bullion for coin under royal authority **3 :** an agent or apparatus for carrying out exchange reactions or processes: as **a :** ION EXCHANGER **b :** HEAT EXCHANGER

exchange rate *n* **:** the ratio at which the principal unit of two currencies may be traded whether arbitrarily established by government action or based on the relative capacity of each currency to buy (as gold) on a free market ⟨an *exchange rate* of nearly 800 to 1⟩ — compare PEG

exchanges *pl of* EXCHANGE, *pres 3d sing of* EXCHANGE

exchange student *n* **:** a student usu. from a foreign country received free into an institution in exchange for one sent to that country on the same terms

exchange teacher *n* **:** a teacher teaching at an institution other than his own in exchange with a teacher from that institution

exchange ticket *n* **:** a slip exchanged between stockbrokers to check accuracy of a transaction — called also *comparison slip*

exchange transfusion *n* **:** simultaneous withdrawal of the recipient's blood and transfusion with the donor's blood esp. in the treatment of erythroblastosis

exchanging *pres part of* EXCHANGE

excheat *obs var of* ESCHEAT

[1]**ex·che·quer** \ˈeks,chekə(r) *also* iks'ch- *or* eks'ch-\ *n* -S [ME *escheker, eschequer*, fr. AF *escheker, eschekier*, fr. OF *eschequier* chessboard, counting table — more at CHECKER] **1** *usu cap* **:** a department or office of state in medieval England charged with the collection and management of the royal revenue and the judicial determination of all revenue causes **2** *usu cap* **:** a former superior court having jurisdiction in England and Wales primarily over revenue matters but also over causes in equity and a concurrent jurisdiction with the courts of common law and now forming a division of the Court of King's Bench **3** *often cap* **a :** the department or office of state in Great Britain and Northern Ireland charged with the receipt and care of the national revenue and headed by a chancellor **b :** the national banking account or purse of this realm **4 :** TREASURY; *esp* **:** a national or royal treasury **5 :** pecuniary possessions or resources **:** PURSE, FINANCES ⟨the ~ is low just now⟩

[2]**exchequer** \"\ *vt* -ED/-ING/-S **:** to proceed against in the Court of Exchequer

exchequer bill *n* **:** a former British short-time bill of credit or promissory note issued by governmental authority and bearing interest — compare TREASURY BILL

exchequer bond *n* **:** a British government interest-bearing bond constituting part of the unfunded debt

exchequer of the jews *usu cap E&J* **:** a department of the English royal exchequer charged in the 13th century with the supervision of all business with the Jews

ex·cide \ek'sīd, ik-\ *vt* -ED/-ING/-S [L *excidere* — more at EXCISE] **:** to cut out **:** EXCISE

[1]**ex·cip·i·ent** \ik'sipēənt, (ˈ)ek¦s-\ *adj* [L *excipient-, excipiens*, pres. part. of *excipere* to take out, make an exception of, take, receive — more at EXCEPT] **:** taking exception

[2]**excipient** \"\ *n* -S [L *excipient-, excipiens*, pres. part.] **:** an inert substance (as gum arabic, syrup, lanolin, or starch) that forms a vehicle (as for a drug or antigen); *esp* **:** one that in the presence of sufficient liquid imparts to a medicated mixture the adhesive quality needed for the preparation of pills or tablets

ex·ci·ple \ˈeksəpəl\ *also* **ex·ci·pule** \-,pyül\ *n* -S [NL *excipulum*, fr. L, a kind of vessel, fr. *excipere*] **:** a saucer-shaped rim around the hymenium of various lichens formed (1) from the hypothecium or (2) from the upper layer of the thallus — called also respectively (1) *proper exciple*, (2) *thalloid exciple*

ex·cip·u·la·ce·ae \(,)ek,sipyə'lāsē,ē\ *n pl, cap* [NL, fr. *Excipula*, type genus (fr. L *excipulum* receptacle, fr. *excipere* to catch, take out, receive) + *-aceae* — more at EXCEPT] **:** a family of imperfect fungi (order Sphaeropsidales) characterized by cup-shaped pycnidia

ex·cip·u·li·form \ek'sipyələ,fȯrm\ *adj* [NL *excipulum* + E *-iform*] **:** resembling or having the shape of an exciple

ex·cip·u·lum \-ləm\ *n, pl* **excipula** [NL] **:** EXCIPLE

excircle \ˈek(s)+,-\ *n* [[1]*ex-* + *circle*] **:** an escribed circle

ex·cis·able *pronunc at* [1]EXCISE +əbəl\ *adj* [[2]*excise* + *-able*] **:** subject to excise

[1]**ex·cise** \ˈek,sīz *also* -īs *sometimes* ek's- *or* ik's-\ *n* -S *often attrib* [obs. D *accijs, excijs* (now *accijns*), fr. MD *excijs*, prob. modif. of OF *assise* session, settlement, assessment, tax — more at ASSIZE] **1** *or* **excise tax a** *obs* **:** DUTY, TOLL, TAX **b :** an internal tax, duty, or impost levied upon the manufacture, sale, or consumption of a commodity within a country and usu. forming an indirect tax that falls on the ultimate consumer **c :** any of various duties or fees levied on producers of excisable commodities **d :** any of various taxes upon privileges (as of engaging in a particular trade or sport, transferring property, or engaging in business in a corporate capacity) that are often assessed in the form of a license or other fee **2 :** a former department or bureau of the British public service charged with collection of the excise taxes and now merged in the Bureau of Customs and Excise

[2]**excise** \"\ *vt* -ED/-ING/-S **1 :** to lay or impose an excise upon **2** *now dial Brit* **:** to impose upon **:** OVERCHARGE

[3]**ex·cise** \(ˈ)ek¦sīz, ik's-\ *vt* -ED/-ING/-S [L *excisus*, past part. of *excidere*, fr. *ex-* [1]ex- + *-cidere* (fr. *caedere* to cut) — more at CONCISE] **1 :** to cut out ⟨~ a tumor⟩ **:** remove by or as if by cutting out **:** RESECT, EXTIRPATE — compare AMPUTATE **2 :** to make an excision in **:** hollow out — used chiefly as a participial adjective ⟨antenna bases *excised*⟩

ex·cise·man *pronunc at* [1]EXCISE +mən\ *n, pl* **excisemen** [[1]*excise* + *man*] **:** an officer who inspects and rates articles liable to excise under British law and often collects or enforces payment of excise due

ex·ci·sion \ek'sizhən, ik-\ *n* -S [MF, fr. L *excision-, excisio*, fr. *excisus* + *-ion-, -io* -ion] **:** the act or procedure of excising: as **a :** EXTIRPATION, DESTRUCTION, ERASURE **b :** excommunication from a church **c :** surgical removal (as of a diseased part) **:** RESECTION

ex·ci·sion·al \-zhən°l,-zhnəl\ *adj* **:** pertaining to or involving excision ⟨~ surgery⟩

ex·cit·abil·i·ty \ik,sīd-ə'biləd-ē, ek-, -ītə-, -lətē, -i\ *n* -ES **:** the quality of being excitable

ex·cit·able \ik'sīd-əbəl, ek-, -ītə-\ *adj* [LL *excitabilis*, fr. L *excitare* to call forth, arouse, excite + *-abilis* -able] **1 :** capable of being readily roused into action or a state of excitement or irritability **2** *of living tissue or an organism* **:** capable of being activated by and reacting to stimuli **:** exhibiting irritability — **ex·cit·able·ness** *n* -ES

[1]**ex·cit·ant** \ik'sīt°nt, ek'-; ˈeksəd-ənt, -sətənt *also* -sət°nt\ *adj* [L *excitant-, excitans*, pres. part. of *excitare*] **:** tending to excite **:** EXCITING ⟨an ~ drug⟩

[2]**excitant** \"\ *n* -S **:** something that excites; *usu* **:** an agent that arouses or augments physiologic (as nervous) activity

ex·ci·ta·tion \,ek,sī'tāshən, ,eksə'-\ *n* -S [ME *excitacioun*, fr. MF *excitation*, fr. LL *excitation-, excitatio*, fr. L *excitatus* (past part. of *excitare*) + *-ion-, -io* -ion] **1 :** the act of exciting or state of being excited **:** EXCITEMENT ⟨astir with delicious ~ —Agnes Repplier⟩ **2 :** electric energizing: as **a :** production of a magnetic field (as in a dynamo, motor, or loudspeaker); *also* **:** the magnetizing force producing a particular magnetic field **b :** the application of signal voltage to a control electrode of an electron tube; *also* **:** the voltage so applied **3 :** the arousing of activity (as by neural or electrical stimulation) in an individual, organ, or tissue; *broadly* **:** the disturbed or altered condition resulting from such arousal **4 :** the process of exciting an electron, atomic nucleus, atom, molecule, or other particle

ex·cit·ative \ik'sīd-əd-iv, (ˈ)ek¦s-\ *adj* [MF *excitatif*, fr. *exciter* + *-atif* -ative] **:** having power to excite **:** tending or serving to induce excitation

ex·cit·ato·ry \ik'sīd-ə,tōrē, ek-\ *adj* [*excitation* + *-ory*] **1 :** EXCITATIVE **2 :** exhibiting or marked by excitement or excitation

ex·cite \ik'sīt, ek-, *usu* -īd-+V\ *vt* -ED/-ING/-S [ME *exciten*, fr. MF *exciter*, fr. L *excitare* to call forth, arouse, excite, fr.

ex- ¹ex- + *citare* to put in movement, summon, rouse — more at CITE] **1 a :** to call to activity in any way **:** stir up (as a person or a hive of bees) to combined or general activity **b :** to rouse to feeling **:** kindle to passionate emotion **2 :** to energize (as an electromagnet) **:** produce a magnetic field in ⟨~ a dynamo⟩ **3 :** to arouse or increase the activity of (a living organism or any of its parts) **:** STIMULATE **4 :** to raise (an atomic nucleus, an atom, a molecule, an electron, or other particle) to a higher energy level (as by heating, irradiation, or bombardment) ⟨radiation ~*s* and ionizes the atoms of material through which it passes —R.S.Rochlin⟩ **syn** see PROVOKE

ex·cit·ed·ly *adv* **:** in an excited manner **:** with excitement

ex·cit·ed·ness *n* -ES **:** the quality or state of being excited ⟨experienced a certain ~ at the prospect of a trip⟩

excited state *n* **:** any of the states of a physical system (as of atoms, molecules, atomic nuclei) that is higher in energy than the ground state

ex·cite·ment \-ītmənt\ *n* -S **1 :** the act of exciting or state of being excited **:** AGITATION, STIR **2 a :** something that excites or rouses ⟨the ~*s* of the journey⟩ **b** *archaic* **:** something (as a motive or incitement) that induces action **3 a :** aroused, augmented, or abnormal activity of an organism or functioning of an organ or part **b :** extreme motor hyperactivity (as in catatonic schizophrenia or manic-depressive psychosis)

ex·cit·er \-īd·ə(r), -ītə-\ *n* -S [ME, fr. *exciten* + *-er*] **1 :** one that excites **2 a :** a dynamo or battery that supplies the electric current used to produce the magnetic field in another dynamo or motor **b :** an electrical oscillator that generates the carrier frequency (as for a radar or frequency-modulation transmitter)

exciter lamp *n* **:** a lamp whose light passes through the sound track of a motion-picture film and enters a photoelectric cell causing the current fluctuations that actuate the loudspeaker

exciting *adj, sometimes* -ER/-EST **1 :** being a source of or marked by excitement **:** absorbingly interesting ⟨an ~ adventure⟩ ⟨an ~ period in the history of our nation⟩ **2 :** inducing a state of excitement or excited interest **:** INTRIGUING, STIMULATING ⟨an ~ person to know⟩ ⟨the ~ mystery of Christmas packages⟩ **3 :** having an immediate effect **:** PRECIPITATING — used of various agents or causes (as of disease); contrasted with *remote* ⟨they had long been on bad terms but the ~ cause of the quarrel was her comments on his drinking⟩ ⟨the ~ agent of brucellosis is a specific bacterium⟩ — **ex·cit·ing·ly** *adv*

exciting current *n* **1 :** a current that excites or energizes an electrical apparatus (as the field magnets of a dynamo) **2 :** the current taken by the primary of a transformer on no load

excito- *comb form* [excitor & L *excitare* to excite] **1 :** excitor and ⟨*excito*motory⟩ ⟨*excito*secretory⟩ **2 :** exciting **:** stimulating **:** causing activity (of a specified kind) ⟨*excito*catabolism⟩

ex·ci·ton \'eksə,tän\ *n* -S [ISV *excitation* + *-on*] **:** a concentration of energy assumed to exist in crystalline semiconductors under the influence of radiation, to be resident in the electric field between a displaced electron and the hole left by it, to be a mobile unit behaving like a neutral particle with mass and momentum, and to have wave-mechanical characteristics

ex·ci·tor \ik'sīd·ə(r), ek-, -ītə-\ *n* -S **1** *archaic* **:** EXCITER **2 :** an afferent nerve arousing increased action of the part that it supplies

ex·ci·tron \'eksə·,trän\ *n* -S [*excitation* + *-tron*] **:** a single-anode mercury-arc rectifier having its output controlled by a grid and an arc that is started by means of a mercury spray

excl *abbr* **1** exclamation **2** excluded; excluding; exclusive

¹**ex·claim** \ik'sklām, ek-\ *vb* -ED/-ING/-S [MF *exclamer*, fr. L *exclamare*, fr. *ex-* ¹ex- + *clamare* to cry out, call — more at CLAIM] *vi* **1 :** to cry out or speak in strong or sudden emotion **:** give a cry or utter a word indicative of surprise, pain, anger, delight, or other emotion ⟨~*ed* with wonder as the view unfolded⟩ ⟨~*ing* over the compactness of the trailer⟩ ⟨~*ed* in delight⟩ **2 :** to speak loudly or vehemently (as in blame, mockery, or protest) — used with *against, at, on,* or *upon* ⟨~ against oppression⟩ ⟨~*ed* furiously upon the wickedness of the plot⟩ ~ *vt* **:** to utter sharply, passionately, or vehemently **:** PROCLAIM ⟨powers of air whose tongues ~ dominion —R.P.Warren⟩

syn EXCLAIM, CRY (*out*), EJACULATE, BLURT (*out*), SNORT can mean, in common, to express oneself in sudden, usu. vehement and unpremeditated, utterance. EXCLAIM usu. implies the force of strong emotion, as anger, joy, or surprise, or the sudden force of protest, criticism, praise, or reproach ⟨"Oh, the troubles of the young!" her mother *exclaimed* —Irving Bacheller⟩ ⟨"Well done!" the instructor *exclaimed*⟩ CRY and CRY (*out*) stress loud, exclamatory tones ⟨"I forbid you!" *cried* my master —W.J.Locke⟩ ⟨as we drove past, a man *cried out* that the road ahead was washed out⟩ EJACULATE usu. stresses sudden, forceful, and abrupt utterance as from astonishment, sudden delight, or great disgust ⟨striding up and down in front of her and *ejaculating* horrible oaths —W.J. Locke⟩ ⟨shook his head, and *ejaculated*, "Whew! Whew! Whew!" as though he were overcome with disgust —V.G. Heiser⟩ ⟨"Fifty thousand! My goodness gracious me!" *ejaculated* Mrs. Berry in flattering accents —George Meredith⟩ BLURT (*out*) is similar to EJACULATE but puts more stress upon the impulsiveness of the remark, suggesting an irresistible, often naive, compulsion to speak ⟨security officers reported overhearing him *blurt out* secret information —*Time*⟩ ⟨stung by his reproaches, I *blurted out* that he had no right to talk to me, even in fun, in such a way —W.H.Hudson †1922⟩ ⟨wished to *blurt out* his indignation —Joseph Conrad⟩ SNORT implies explosive utterance resembling a snort, motivated by contempt, scorn, or indignation ⟨"Running away, and leaving Johnnie to take the blame!" he *snorted* in disgust at himself —Rex Ingamells⟩ ⟨"Talk of his successful son", *snorted* my father, whom I had fairly roused. "He is not fit to black his father's boots" —Samuel Butler †1902⟩ ⟨*snorted* with disdain at such vulgarity —C.S.Forester⟩

²**exclaim** \"\ *n* -S *archaic* **:** OUTCRY, CLAMOR

ex·claim·er \-mə(r)\ *n* -S **:** one that exclaims

ex·cla·ma·tion \,eksklə'māshən\ *n* -S [ME *exclamacioun*, fr. L *exclamation-, exclamatio*, fr. *exclamatus* (past part. of *exclamare*) + *-ion-, -io* -ion] **1 :** the act of exclaiming **:** a sharp or sudden utterance expressive of strong feeling ⟨he uttered an ~ of pain⟩ ⟨amid ~*s* of delight the cake was brought in⟩ **2 :** vehement expression (as of protest, reproach, or complaint) ⟨~*s* of social prejudice —Bernard Smith⟩ **3 :** a word, phrase, clause, or sentence used as an outcry or interjection **4 :** EXCLAMATION POINT — **ex·cla·ma·tion·al** \¦==¦māshənᵊl, -shnəl\ *adj*

exclamation point *or* **exclamation mark** *n* **:** the mark ! used in writing and printing after an interjection, after a sentence or phrase of assertion, wish, or command, and after a direct or indirect question to indicate forceful utterance or strong feeling — called also *mark of exclamation, note of exclamation*

ex·clam·a·tive \ik'sklamәd·iv, ek-\ *adj* [*exclamation* + *-ive*] *archaic* **:** EXCLAMATORY

ex·clam·a·to·ri·ly \ik¦sklamə¦tōrəlē, (,)ek-, -tȯr-, -li\ *adv* **:** in an exclamatory manner

ex·clam·a·to·ry \=ˈ=mə,tōrē, -tȯr-, -ri\ *adj* [*exclamation* + *-ory*] **1 :** containing, expressing, using, or relating to exclamation ⟨an ~ phrase⟩ ⟨~ speakers⟩ **2 :** showing emotion on the part of speaker or writer by its elliptical form (as in *Oh, for a camera! You an author!*) or by an intensifying expression (as an interrogative pronoun or adverb or other part of speech in an emphatic position like an interjection) ⟨an ~ noun⟩ **3 :** like or having the effect of an exclamation esp. in lending emphasis or focusing attention ⟨set off by a bright ~ scarf⟩

ex·clave \'ek,sklāv\ *n* -S [¹*ex-* + *-clave* (as in *enclave*)] **:** a portion of a country that is separated from the main part and surrounded by politically alien territory and that is an enclave in respect to the surrounding country ⟨after World War I East Prussia became an ~ of Germany⟩

ex·clo·sure \ek'sklōzhə(r), ik-\ *n* -S *often attrib* [¹*ex-* + *-closure* (as in *enclosure*)] **:** an area from which intruders (as browsing animals) are excluded by fencing or other means ⟨the ~ plot is used to keep an area in a natural condition, free from grazing by deer or domestic livestock —*Wildlife Management Handbook for Forest Officers*⟩ — compare ENCLOSURE

ex·clud·abil·i·ty \ik,sklüdə'biləd·ē, (,)ek-, -ətē, -i\ *n* -ES **:** the condition of being excludable **:** suitability for exclusion ⟨the ~ of certain income for purposes of tax computation⟩

ex·clud·able *or* **ex·clud·ible** \ik'sklüdəbəl, (')ek¦s-\ *adj* **:** subject to exclusion ⟨~ classes of aliens include those with certain specified mental or physical defects⟩ ⟨~ income⟩

ex·clude \ik'sklüd, ek-\ *vt* -ED/-ING/-S [ME *excluden*, fr. L *excludere*, fr. *ex-* ¹ex- + *-cludere* (fr. *claudere* to close) — more at CLOSE] **1 a :** to shut out **:** restrain or hinder the entrance of ⟨immigrants must be screened to ~ the small fraction of undesirables⟩ ⟨if you draw the blind it will ~ the glare⟩ ⟨that high ridge tends to ~ the breezes⟩ **b :** to bar from participation, enjoyment, consideration, or inclusion ⟨there was no need to ~ your brother from our talks⟩ ⟨that request must be *excluded* from further consideration⟩ **c :** to prevent or refuse to tolerate the occurrence, use, or existence of ⟨such words are *excluded* from polite conversation⟩ ⟨true faith ~*s* all doubt⟩ ⟨would ~ any oppressive measures no matter how expedient⟩ **2 a :** to put out **:** expel esp. from a place or position previously occupied ⟨the executed queen's child was specifically *excluded* from the succession⟩ **b :** to eject esp. in giving birth or hatching ⟨as soon as the larva was *excluded* from the egg⟩

syn DEBAR, BLACKBALL, ELIMINATE, RULE (*out*), SHUT (*out*), DISBAR, SUSPEND: EXCLUDE is a general term for shutting out or preventing entrance or admission ⟨*exclude* light from the rooms⟩ ⟨*exclude* hospital visitors⟩ ⟨minority groups who are *excluded* from some activities simply because their ancestors belonged to the less privileged classes in a time when social status was a matter of birth rather than ability —J.R. Everett⟩ ⟨*exclude* these subjects from consideration⟩ DEBAR may suggest the effect of a bar, sometimes literal but usu. figurative, in keeping from belonging or enjoying ⟨the Blue mountains . . . presented a cruel, awful barrier to the earlier settlers, and for a long time *debarred* them from the land beyond —Anthony Trollope⟩ ⟨that movement was condemned as heretical and its adherents were expelled from the Church and *debarred* from the communion —K.S.Latourette⟩ ⟨dangerous and foolish talk — of a sort that should *debar* its author from further serious consideration by intelligent Americans —*New Republic*⟩ BLACKBALL suggests exclusion from membership by adverse vote of those belonging ⟨he was very nearly *blackballed* at a West End club of which his birth and social position fully entitled him to become a member —Oscar Wilde⟩ ELIMINATE indicates a discharging, casting out, or getting rid of something figuring as a constituent member or part or an included element ⟨if children are *eliminated* from the statistics and only persons above the age of fifteen are taken into consideration —Morris Fishbein⟩ ⟨it is always wise to *eliminate* the personal equation from our judgments of literature —J.R.Lowell⟩ RULE (*out*) indicates formal or authoritative exclusion or elimination ⟨a play *ruled out* by the referee⟩ ⟨candidacies *ruled out* by the election laws⟩ ⟨the dean *ruled out* any special celebration⟩ SHUT (*out*) may indicate an effective, forceful, or definitive exclusion ⟨always *shut out* from public office⟩ ⟨the purpose of cartels is to *shut out* newcomers to an industry unless the newcomers are willing to join in and be subjected to cartel arrangements —*Wall Street Jour.*⟩ DISBAR refers to the formal processes whereby a lawyer is prevented from further practice or to similar exclusions ⟨the first proceeding in American history seeking to *disbar* an attorney for having invoked an historic constitutional privilege —*New Republic*⟩ ⟨*disbarred* from further teaching⟩ SUSPEND applies to a temporary elimination or exclusion pending investigation of fitness, occurrence of new developments, or full consideration of the matter ⟨*suspended* from the university for bad conduct⟩

ex·clud·er \-də(r)\ *n* -S **:** one that excludes: as **a :** a person who tries to keep another out of office **b :** a screen with divisions large enough to permit passage of workers but not a queen bee that is placed between chambers or supers of a beehive esp. to control the distribution of brood **c** *Brit* **:** a heavy rubber overshoe **:** GALOSH

ex·clu·si·ble \ik'sklüzəbəl, ek-\ *adj* [L *exclusus* + E *-ible*] **:** subject to or deserving of exclusion ⟨emergencies, miscellanea, entertainment, such items are not ~ from the well-planned budget⟩

ex·clu·sion \ik'sklüzhən, ek-\ *n* -S [L *exclusion-, exclusio*, fr. *exclusus* (past part. of *excludere* to exclude) + *-ion-, -io* -ion] **1 :** the act or an instance of excluding **:** the state of being excluded **:** DEBARRING, REJECTION; *specif* **:** refusal of entry into a country by immigration authorities **2 :** an exclusive disjunction

ex·clu·sion·ary \-zhə,nerē, -ri\ *adj* **:** tending to or so as to exclude ⟨~ policy⟩ ⟨~ separation of powers⟩ **:** EXCLUSIVE

exclusion clause *n* **:** a clause in an insurance policy barring certain losses or risks from coverage

¹**ex·clu·sion·ist** \-zh(ə)nəst\ *also* **ex·clu·sion·er** \-nə(r)\ *n* -S [*exclusion* + *-ist* or *-er*] **:** one who would exclude another from some right or privilege

²**exclusionist** \"\ *adj* **1 :** of, relating to, or involving exclusion (as from a right or privilege) ⟨~ policies⟩ **2** *of a tariff* **:** designed to reduce competition of foreign goods

exclusion principle *n* **:** PAULI EXCLUSION PRINCIPLE

¹**ex·clu·sive** \ik'sklüs|iv, (')ek¦s-, -üz|, |ēv *also* |əv\ *adj* [MF *exclusif*, fr. ML *exclusivus*, fr. L *exclusus* + *-ivus* -ive] **1 a :** excluding or having power to exclude (as by preventing entrance or debarring from possession, participation, or use) ⟨~ regulations⟩ **b :** limiting or limited to possession, control, or use (as by a single individual or organization or by a special group or class) ⟨~ privileges of the citizens of a country⟩ ⟨the Puritan's God was a somewhat ~ possession —Agnes Repplier⟩ **2 :** excluding or inclined to exclude others (as outsiders) from participation (as in an association or privilege) or from cordial relations ⟨an ~ nation⟩; *sometimes* **:** snobbishly aloof ⟨an ~ clique⟩ ⟨an ~ attitude⟩ ⟨~ standards⟩ **3 a :** admitting of or soliciting only a socially restricted patronage (as of the upper classes) ⟨~ hotels or haberdashers⟩ **b :** STYLISH, FASHIONABLE ⟨~ styles⟩ **c :** EXPENSIVE; *often* **:** restricted in distribution, use, or appeal because of expense ⟨~ suburban neighborhoods⟩ **4 a :** SINGLE, SOLE ⟨an ~ agent⟩ ⟨~ jurisdiction⟩ **b :** UNDIVIDED, WHOLE ⟨giving the question his ~ attention⟩ **c** *of a news item* **:** being an exclusive **5** *in grammar* **:** referring to the speaker and another or some others but excluding the hearer

²**exclusive** \"\ *n* -S **1 a :** a person who fastidiously limits his acquaintance to a few **b :** an organism restricted in distribution to a single ecological community **2 :** something exclusive: as **a :** a newspaper story at first released to or printed by only one newspaper **b :** an exclusive right (as to sell a particular product in a certain area)

exclusive listing *n* **:** a formal agreement giving a broker the sole right to sell or to rent a property during a specified period of time

ex·clu·sive·ly \|əvlē, -li\ *adv* **:** in an exclusive manner

ex·clu·sive·ness \|ivnəs, |ēv- *also* |əv-\ *n* -ES **:** the quality or state of being exclusive

exclusive of *prep* **:** not taking into account **:** excluding from consideration ⟨there were four of us *exclusive of* the guide⟩ ⟨*exclusive of* artillery⟩

exclusive proposition *n* **:** a proposition in logic whose predicate is asserted to apply to its subject and no other ⟨"none but the brave deserve the fair" is a simple *exclusive proposition*⟩

ex·clu·siv·ism \ik'sklüs|ə,vizəm, ek-, -üz|, |ē,-\ *n* -S **:** the practice of excluding or of being exclusive

ex·clu·siv·ist \-,vəst\ *n* -S *often attrib* **:** a practitioner of exclusivism — **ex·clu·siv·is·tic** \=¦==¦vistik, -tēk\ *adj*

ex·clu·siv·i·ty \,ek,sklü'sivəd·ē, -'zi-, -vətē, -i\ *n* -ES **1 :** EXCLUSIVENESS **2 :** exclusive rights or services

ex·clu·so·ry \ik'sklüs(ə)rē, -üz(-, -ri\ *adj* [LL *exclusorius*, fr. L *exclusus* + *-orius* -ory] **:** able to exclude **:** excluding or tending to exclude

excoct *vt* -ED/-ING/-S [L *excoctus*, past part. of *excoquere*, fr. *ex-* ¹ex- + *coquere* to cook, boil, melt — more at COOK] *obs* **:** to obtain, refine, or drive off by heat — **excoction** *n* -S *obs*

ex·coe·car·ia \,eksē'ka(a)rēə\ *n, cap* [NL, irreg. fr. L *excaecare* to blind + NL *-aria* — more at EXCECATE] **:** a genus of timber trees or shrubs (family Euphorbiaceae) of Asia, Africa, and Australia that have a poisonous acrid milky juice and in some species a bark used for dyeing

ex·cog·i·tate \(')ek¦skäjə,tāt, *usu* -ād·+V\ *vb* [L *excogitatus*, past part. of *excogitare*, fr. *ex-* ¹ex- + *cogitare* to cogitate — more at COGITATE] *vt* **1 :** to examine mentally with thoroughness and care so as to attain thorough grasp and comprehension of ⟨a much-*excogitated* topic⟩ ⟨to consider what ought to be written . . . he must first think and ~ his matter —Samuel Johnson⟩ **2 :** to evolve, invent, or contrive in the mind **:** think out or up ⟨*excogitating* arguments against hard work⟩ ⟨there may have been a time when the scientific inquirer sat still in his chair to ~ science —John Dewey⟩ ⟨socialism was not an ideal . . . *excogitated* by wise men — *Times Lit. Supp.*⟩ ~ *vi* **:** COGITATE **syn** see CONSIDER

ex·cog·i·ta·tion \(,)=,==ˈtāshən\ *n* [L *excogitation-, excogitatio*, fr. *excogitatus* (past part. of *excogitare*) + *-ion-, -io* -ion] **1 :** the act of excogitating **2 :** a product of mental analysis and invention **:** something thought out or up **:** CONTRIVANCE

ex·cog·i·ta·tive \=ˈ==,tād·iv\ *adj* **:** of, relating to, or involving excogitation

ex co·mi·ta·te \,ek,skämə'täd·ē\ [L] **:** from courtesy

ex·com·mu·ni·ca·ble \¦ekskə¦myünəkəbəl, -nēk-\ *adj* [*excommunicate* + *-able*] **:** liable to or deserving excommunication

¹**ex·com·mu·ni·cate** \,ekskə'myünə,kāt, *usu* -ād·+V\ *vt* [ME *excommunicaten*, fr. LL *excommunicatus*, past part. of *excommunicare*, fr. L *ex-* ¹ex- + LL *communicare* to communicate — more at COMMUNICATE] **:** to put out of communion or fellowship; *esp* **:** to cut off or shut out by an ecclesiastical sentence from communion with the church

²**excommunicate** \¦==¦=nəkət, -nēk-; -nə,kāt\ *adj* [LL *excommunicatus*, past part.] **:** interdicted from the rites of the church **:** EXCOMMUNICATED

³**excommunicate** \"\ *also* **ex·com·mu·ni·cant** \,=ˈ==kənt\ *n* -S [³*excommunicate* fr. ²*excommunicate; excommunicant* alter. (influenced by *communicant*) of ³*excommunicate*] **:** an excommunicated person

ex·com·mu·ni·ca·tion \,==,=nə'kāshən\ *n* [ME *excommunicacioun*, fr. LL *excommunication-, excommunicatio*, fr. *excommunicatus* + L *-ion-, -io* -ion] **:** the act of excommunicating **:** exclusion from fellowship; *esp* **:** an ecclesiastical censure whereby the person against whom it is pronounced is for the time cast out of the communion of the church — see MAJOR EXCOMMUNICATION, MINOR EXCOMMUNICATION

ex·com·mu·ni·ca·tive \,ekskə'myünə,kād|iv, -nәk|əl, -nēk|əl, |t|, |ēv *also* |əv\ *adj* **:** tending toward, decreeing, or favoring excommunication

ex·com·mu·ni·ca·tor \-nə,kād·ə(r), -ātə-\ *n* [LL, fr. *excommunicatus* + L *-or*] **:** one that excommunicates

ex·com·mu·ni·ca·to·ry \-nəkə,tōrē, -nēk-, -tȯr-, -ri\ *adj* [ML *excommunicatorius*, fr. LL *excommunicatus* + L *-orius* -ory] **:** relating to, causing, or declaring excommunication

excommunion *n* [*ex-* + *communion*] *obs* **:** EXCOMMUNICATION

ex·con·ju·gant \(')eks+\ *n* [¹*ex-* + *conjugant*] **:** a protozoan just after the separation following conjugation

ex con·trac·tu \,ekskən'trak(,)t(y)ü\ [L] **:** upon or from a contract — used of legal actions or obligations

¹**ex·co·ri·ate** \ek'skōrē,āt, ik-, -kȯr-, *usu* -ād·+V\ *vt* -ED/-ING/-S [ME *excoriaten*, fr. LL *excoriatus*, past part. of *excoriare*, fr. L *ex-* ¹ex- + *corium* skin, hide — more at CUIRASS] **1 :** to strip or wear off the skin of **:** FLAY, ABRADE, GALL; *also* **:** to break and remove the cuticle of **2 :** to censure scathingly

²**ex·co·ri·ate** \-ēət, -ē,āt\ *adj* [LL *excoriatus*, past part.] *archaic* **:** GALLED, ABRADED — used esp. of skin or other covering

ex·co·ri·a·tion \(,)ek,=ˈāshən, ik-\ *n* -S [ME *excoriacioun*, fr. MF & ML; MF *excoriation*, fr. ML *excoriation-, excoriatio*, fr. LL *excoriatus* + L *-ion-, -io* -ion] **1 :** the act of excoriating or state of being excoriated either physically or verbally ⟨marked chafing and ~ of the skin⟩ ⟨his violent ~ of his adversaries⟩ **2 :** an instance or product of excoriation: as **a :** a raw irritated lesion (as of the skin or a mucosal surface) **b :** a scathingly censorious utterance

ex·cor·ti·cate \(')ek¦skȯ(r)d·ə,kāt\ *vt* -ED/-ING/-S [LL *excorticatus*, past part. of *excorticare*, fr. L *ex-* ¹ex- + *cortic-, cortex* bark — more at CORTEX] **:** DECORTICATE

excpt *abbr* exception

¹**ex·cre·ment** \'ekskrəmənt\ *n* -S [L *excrementum*, fr. *excre-* (stem of *excernere* to sift out, separate, discharge — as feces —) + *-mentum* -ment — more at EXCRETE] **1 a :** waste matter discharged from the body; *usu* **:** waste discharged from the alimentary canal **:** fecal matter **:** DUNG — compare EXCRETION **b excrements** *pl* **:** DROPPINGS, STOOLS **:** fecal pellets **2** *obs* **:** DREGS, LEES, REFUSE

²**excrement** *n* -S [LL *excrementum*, fr. L *excre-* (stem of *excrescere* to grow out) + *-mentum* -ment] **1** *obs* **:** an excrescence or appendage esp. of hair or feathers **:** OUTGROWTH **2** *obs* **:** GROWTH, INCREASE

ex·cre·men·ti·tious \¦ekskrə,men¦tishəs, -,mən-\ *also* **ex·cre·men·tal** \¦==¦mentᵊl\ *adj* [¹*excrement* + *-itious* or *-al*] **:** of or relating to excrement **:** concerned with or caused by dung ⟨~ odors⟩ — **ex·cre·men·ti·tious·ly** \-shəslē\ *also* **ex·cre·men·tal·ly** \-tᵊlē\ *adv*

ex·cre·men·tous \¦==¦mentəs\ *adj* [¹*excrement* + *-ous*] **:** like or constituting excrement

ex·cres·cence \ek'skres³n(t)s, ik-\ *n* -S [ME, fr. MF *excressance*, fr. L *excrescentia*, pl., fr. neut. pl. of *excrescent-, excrescens*, pres. part. of *excrescere* to grow out, fr. *ex-* ¹ex- + *crescere* to grow, increase — more at CRESCENT] **1 a :** a growing out esp. to an abnormal extent **:** abnormal or excessive increase **b** *archaic* **:** EXCESS, SUPERFLUITY **2 :** an outgrowth or enlargement: as **a :** a natural and normal appendage or development ⟨hair is an ~ from the scalp⟩ ⟨several small glandular ~*s*⟩ **b :** an abnormal outgrowth ⟨warty ~*s*⟩ **3 :** EXCRESCENCY 3

ex·cres·cen·cy \-nsē, -si\ *n* -ES [L *excrescentia*] **1 :** EXCRESCENCE 2 ⟨it would be a well-proportioned house if you stripped off the Victorian *excrescencies*⟩ **2 :** the state of being excrescent; *esp* **:** abnormal protrusion or growth **3 :** occurrence of an excrescent sound or letter

ex·cres·cent \(')ek¦skres³nt, ik's-\ *adj* [L *excrescent-, excrescens*, pres. part. of *excrescere*] **1** *archaic* **:** constituting an excess **:** SUPERNUMERARY **2 :** growing out or forming an outgrowth; *usu* **:** forming an abnormal, excessive, or useless outgrowth **:** SUPERFLUOUS ⟨pruning ~ witches'-broom from blueberry bushes⟩ **3** *phonet* **a :** EPENTHETIC, INTRUSIVE **b :** present but substandard ⟨the ~ second \t\ sound in \'wəntst\ for *once*⟩ **c :** epenthetic as a result of folk etymology ⟨the ~ second \r\ sound in *bridegroom*⟩ — **ex·cres·cent·ly** *adv*

ex·cres·cen·tial \¦ekskrə¦senchəl, ¦ek(,)skre¦-\ *adj* [L *excrescentia* + E *-al*] **:** relating to or being an excrescence

excression *n* -S [modif. of LL *excretion-, excretio* — more at EXCRETION (excrescence)] *obs* **:** EXCRESCENCE

ex·cre·ta \ek'skrēd·ə, ik-, -ētə\ *n pl* [NL, fr. L, neut. pl. of *excretus*, past part. of *excernere*] **:** waste matter eliminated or separated from an organism; *usu* **:** EXCRETIONS — **ex·cre·tal** \(')ek¦skrēd·ᵊl, ik's-, -ētᵊl\ *adj*

ex·crete \(')ek¦skrēt, ik's-, *usu* -ēd·+V\ *vt* -ED/-ING/-S [L *excretus*, past part. of *excernere* to sift out, separate, discharge (as feces), fr. *ex-* ¹ex- + *cernere* to sift — more at CERTAIN] **1 :** to separate and eliminate or discharge (waste, superfluous, or harmful material) from the blood or tissues in animals or from the active protoplasm in plants and animals **2 :** to give off (as something expendable or in some way inferior) ⟨the shell-like covering which our souls have *excreted* to house themselves —Virginia Woolf⟩ ⟨a foundation ~*s* an extraordinary quantity of typed and mimeographed words —*New Yorker*⟩

ex·cret·er \-ēd·ə(r), -ētə-\ *n* -S **:** one that excretes; *esp* **:** one that gives forth from his body an atypical product (as a pathogenic microorganism)

¹**ex·cre·tion** \ek'skrēshən, ik-\ *n* -S [*excrete* + *-ion*] **1 :** the process of eliminating useless, superfluous, or harmful matter (as the waste products of metabolism) from the body of an organism or from its protoplasm, usu. through the action of special cells or tissues — compare SECRETION **2 a :** something eliminated by the process of excretion comprising chiefly the

urine and sweat in man and other mammals and comparable materials in other animals, characteristically including products of protein degradation (as urea or uric acid), usu. differing from ordinary bodily secretions by lacking any further utility to the organism that produces it, and being distinguished from waste materials (as feces) that have merely passed into or through the alimentary canal without being incorporated into the body proper **b :** a waste product (as urine, feces, vomitus) eliminated from the confines of an animal body **:** EXCREMENT — not used technically **c :** any of various materials stored in or secreted by plants (as certain intracellular crystals, nectar, or the water and carbon dioxide produced in respiration) that are believed to have a basically excretory function

²excretion *n* -s [LL *excretion-, excretio*, fr. L *excretus* (past part. of *excrescere* to grow out) + *-ion-, -io* -ion — more at EXCRESCENT] *obs* **:** EXCRESCENCE

ex·cre·to·ry \'ekskrə,tōrē, -tȯr-, -ri, *chiefly Brit* ek'skrētəri *or* ik-\ *adj* [*excrete* + *-ory*] **:** of, relating to, concerned with, or serving for excretion

¹ex·cru·ci·ate \ik'skrüshē,āt, ek- *sometimes* -üsē-, *usu* -ād.+V\ *vt* -ED/-ING/-S [L *excruciatus*, past part. of *excruciare*, fr. *ex-* ¹ex- + *cruciare* to torment, crucify, fr. *cruc-, crux* cross — more at CROSS] **1 a** *obs* **:** to torture esp. by the rack **b :** to inflict intense pain upon **:** subject to the utmost physical suffering ⟨a man *excruciated* by facial neuralgia⟩ **2 :** to subject to intense mental distress **:** irritate or annoy exceedingly ⟨the very sound of his voice ~*s* me⟩ ⟨what panic and gnashing of teeth would ~ the propagandists —Peter Viereck⟩

²excruciate *adj* [L *excruciatus*, past part.] **1** *obs* **:** suffering intensely **2** *obs* **:** causing intense suffering

excruciating *adj* **1 :** TORTURING, RACKING, AGONIZING **2 :** so intense as to cause great pain or anguish ⟨the ~ spasms of angina⟩ ⟨an ~ fear⟩; *often* **:** very intense **:** EXTREME ⟨~ pain⟩ ⟨the characters are paired off with an ~ regard for balance —Douglas Watt⟩ ⟨~ delight⟩ — **ex·cru·ci·at·ing·ly** *adv*

ex·cru·ci·a·tion \ik,skrüshē'āshən, (,)ek- *also* -üsē-\ *n* -s [LL *excruciation-, excruciatio*, fr. L *excruciatus* + *-ion-, -io* -ion] **:** the act of excruciating or the state or an instance of being excruciated

ex·cul·pate \'ek(,)skəl,pāt, ek's-, ik's-, *usu* -ād.+V\ *vt* -ED/-ING/-S [ML *exculpatus*, past part. of *exculpare*, fr. L *ex-* ¹ex- + *culpare* to blame — more at CULPABLE] **:** to clear from alleged fault or guilt **:** prove to be guiltless ⟨the court *exculpated* him after a thorough investigation⟩ ⟨specifically ~*s* all countries from any special responsibility for bringing on the catastrophe —*Saturday Rev.*⟩

syn ABSOLVE, EXONERATE, ACQUIT, VINDICATE: EXCULPATE indicates a freeing from blame, fault, or guilt, esp. fault or guilt with blameworthy intent ⟨directly Harding was blameless for what was going on. Indirectly he cannot be wholly *exculpated* —S.H.Adams⟩ ABSOLVE indicates a releasing either from charges or suspicions of guilt or from consequences or responsibilities of guilt, often unconfessed guilt ⟨society was at least good-natured and was inclined to take the view that if a fellow had faced his punishment and taken it he was pretty well *absolved* —F.M.Ford⟩ ⟨since the emperor was willing to make the necessary promises, however, he as a priest was bound to *absolve* the contrite sinner —M.W.Baldwin⟩ EXONERATE may imply complete clearance not only from an immediate charge or accusation but from suspicious or attendant denigration ⟨he was subsequently tried for murder, but was completely *exonerated* by the testimony of his crew and passengers, who testified that the ship was in deadly peril of seizure by mutineers —C.C.Cutler⟩ ACQUIT may apply to a formal decision freeing one from a charge ⟨at his trial the next year he was *acquitted* of dishonesty, although his reputation for intelligence suffered —Louise P. Kellogg⟩ VINDICATE may apply to the eventual demonstration by subsequent developments of freedom from guilt, dishonor, wrong, folly, or weakness ⟨both his knowledge and his honesty were *vindicated* when the river was discovered —G.R.Stewart⟩ ⟨then came the fatal letter, the desolating letter, which *vindicated* Constance's dark apprehensions —Arnold Bennett⟩ ⟨*vindicating* the old adage about great minds —Ring Lardner⟩

ex·cul·pa·tion \,ek(,)skəl'pāshən\ *n* -s [ML *exculpation-, exculpatio*, fr. *exculpatus* + L *-ion-, -io* -ion] **:** the act or fact of exculpating from alleged fault or crime ⟨his ~ was complete when his partner confessed to the theft⟩ **2 :** an excuse or explanation by way of vindication ⟨this is not said by way of ~ of Aristotle —C.J.O'Neil⟩ ⟨blaming Americans is a familiar ~ —*Time*⟩

ex·cul·pa·to·ry \ek'skəlpə,tōrē, ik-, -tȯr-, -ri\ *adj* **:** tending to exculpate **:** serving as an exculpation ⟨~ testimony⟩ ⟨an ~ statement⟩

ex·current \(')eks+\ *adj* [L *excurrent-, excurrens*, pres. part. of *excurrere* to run out, make an excursion, project, extend, fr. *ex-* ¹ex- + *currere* to run — more at CURRENT] **:** running or flowing out: as **a** *of a plant or plant part* (1) **:** having the axis prolonged to form an undivided main stem or trunk (as in the spruce and other conifers) — opposed to *deliquescent* (2) **:** projecting beyond the apex — used esp. of the midrib of a mucronate leaf **b :** characterized by a current that flows outward — used esp. of those channels in sponges through which water flows toward the osculum ⟨~ canals⟩

¹ex·curse \ek'skərs, ',=\ *n* -s [L *excursus*, fr. *excursus*, past part. of *excurrere*] **:** a sally or digression

²excurse \"\ *vi* [L *excursus*, past part.] **1 :** DIGRESS, RAMBLE **2 :** to journey or pass through **:** make an excursion

¹ex·cur·sion \ik'skərzhən, ek-, -kō|, -kəi|, *chiefly Brit* |shən\ *n* -s [L *excursion-, excursio*, fr. *excursus* (past part.) + *-ion-, -io* -ion] **1 :** a going out or forth as from a place of confinement: as **a :** a military expedition **:** RAID, SORTIE — obs. except in the phrase *alarums and excursions* **b** *in Elizabethan stage directions* **:** a movement of soldiers across the stage **c :** a journey chiefly for recreation **:** a usu. brief pleasure trip; *often* **:** a trip (as by rail or steamship) at special reduced rates ⟨the railway ran Sunday ~*s* to the city⟩ **d :** a trip made with the positive intention of returning to the starting point **:** ROUND TRIP **:** a trip that is not planned to involve prolonged or definite separation from one's usu. or normal place or way of life ⟨his summer ~*s* to the Colorado Rockies⟩ ⟨made several ~*s* into the Amazon valley⟩ **2 :** the persons participating in or going together on an excursion **3 :** departure from a direct or proper course **:** deviation from a definite path; *usu* **:** a wandering from a subject **:** DIGRESSION ⟨his ~*s* into abstruse theory⟩ **4** *obs* **:** a projection or extension (as of a building) **5** *archaic* **:** a sally or outburst (as of wit or feeling) esp. when overstepping accepted or customary bounds **6 :** a movement outward and back or from a mean position or axis **7 a :** a single vibratory motion (as of a diaphragm or membrane); *sometimes* **:** the distance traversed in such a movement **:** AMPLITUDE **b :** one complete movement of inspiratory expansion and expiratory contraction of the lungs and their membranes

²excursion \"\ *vi* **excursioned; excursioned; excursioning** \-zh(ə)niŋ, -sh(-\ **excursions :** to go on an excursion

³excursion \"\ *adj* **:** relating to or used for excursions ⟨an ~ rate⟩ ⟨~ trains⟩ ⟨a packed ~ steamer⟩

ex·cur·sion·al \-zhən°l, -zhnəl, -sh-\ *or* **ex·cur·sion·ary** \-zhə,nerē, -sh-, -ri\ *adj* **:** of or relating to an excursion ⟨~ fare⟩

ex·cur·sion·ist \-zh(ə)nəst, -sh-\ *n* -s **:** a person who goes on an excursion; *esp* **:** one of a party on a pleasure trip

excursion ticket *n* **:** a special-rate ticket for making a round-trip journey on an excursion

ex·cur·sive \ik'skər|siv, (')ek|s-, -kō|, -kəi|, |z|, |ēv *also* |əv\ *also* **ex·cur·so·ry** \|(ə)rē, -ri\ *adj* [L *excursus* (past part.) + E *-ive* or *-ory*] **1 :** constituting a digression ⟨his ~ remarks⟩ **2 :** characterized by or prone to digression ⟨an amusingly ~ style⟩ — **ex·cur·sive·ly** \|əvlē, -li\ *adv*

ex·cur·sus \ik'skərsəs, ek-\ *n, pl* **excursuses** *also* **excursus** [L, digression — more at EXCURSE] **1 :** a dissertation that is appended to a work and that contains a more extended exposition of some point or topic **2 :** an incidental discussion **:** DIGRESSION

ex·curvature \(')eks+\ *also* **ex·curvation** \¦eks+\ *n* [¹*ex-* + *curvature* or *curvation*] **:** excurved state or an excurved part

ex·curved \'eks+,-\ *or* **ex·cur·vate** \'ek,skər,vāt, (')ek¦skərvət\ *adj* [¹*ex-* + *curved* or *curvate* (fr. ³*curve* + *-ate*)] **:** curved outward or away from a central part

ex·cus·able \ik'skyüzəbəl, (')ek¦s-\ *adj* [ME, fr. MF, fr. L *excusabilis*, fr. *excusare* + *-abilis* -able] **:** capable of or fit for being excused, forgiven, justified, or acquitted of blame **:** PARDONABLE ⟨an ~ oversight⟩ — **ex·cus·able·ness** \-nəs\ *n* -ES

excusable homicide *n* **:** homicide done by accident or misadventure or in self-defense and without criminal intent

excusable neglect *n, law* **:** neglect for which there is a reasonable excuse

ex·cus·ably \-blē, -li\ *adv* **:** in an excusable manner

ex·cus·al \ik'skyüzəl, ek-\ *n* -s **:** the act or fact of excusing esp. from the payment of an assessment or tax due

excusation *n* -s [ME *excusacioun*, fr. MF & L; MF *excusation*, fr. L *excusation-, excusatio*, fr. *excusatus* (past part. of *excusare*) + *-ion-, -io* -ion] *obs* **:** EXCUSE

ex·cu·sa·tor \'ekskyü,zād·ə(r), ,==¦==\ *n* -s [LL, fr. L *excusatus* + *-or*] **:** APOLOGIST

ex·cus·ato·ry \ik'skyüzə,tōrē, (')ek¦s-, -tȯr-, -ri\ *adj* [ML *excusatorius*, fr. L *excusatus* + *-orius* -ory] **:** making or containing excuse or apology **:** APOLOGETIC

¹ex·cuse \ik'skyüz, ek-, in "*excuse me*" *often* 'sky-\ *vb* -ED/-ING/-S [ME *excusen*, fr. OF *escuser, excuser*, fr. L *excusare*, fr. *ex-* ¹ex- + *-cusare* (fr. *causa* cause, apology) — more at CAUSE] *vt* **1 a :** to offer excuse for **:** make apology for ⟨he *excused* his delay as due to the weather⟩ **b :** to try to remove blame from **:** seek indulgence for **:** seek to extenuate ⟨*excusing* himself for his delay⟩ **2 a :** to seek or obtain exemption or release for ⟨asked the school principal to ~ the boys from religious services⟩ **b** *obs* **:** to serve as a means of exemption from **:** serve as a substitute for **3 :** to accept an excuse for **:** regard as excusable **:** forgive entirely or admit to be little censurable and to overlook **:** PARDON ⟨we ~ irregular conduct when circumstances justify it⟩ **4 :** to regard with indulgence **:** OVERLOOK ⟨it is easy to ~ one's own faults⟩ — often used as an introductory apology (as when interrupting or expressing disagreement) ⟨~ me, but do you mind if I shut the window?⟩ **5 a :** to grant exemption or release to or from **:** free from an obligation or duty ⟨the judge *excused* the young man's fine because of the unusual circumstances⟩ **b :** to permit to leave a place or stop an activity or task ⟨class is *excused*⟩ ⟨you are *excused* the rest of the translation⟩ **6 a :** to serve as excuse for **:** free from imputation of fault **:** clear from guilt **:** EXCULPATE, JUSTIFY ⟨one's own assurance of propriety cannot ~ jeopardizing another's happiness⟩ ⟨perhaps, knowing what you do, you can ~ him⟩ **b** *obs* **:** to release from a charge ~ *vi* **:** to ask or grant excuse ⟨while some accuse, others ~⟩ **:** serve as an excuse ⟨such loving self-sacrifice goes far toward *excusing*⟩

syn CONDONE, PARDON, FORGIVE: EXCUSE indicates a passing over of some fault, omission, neglect, or failure without further consideration, censure, or punishment, redress, or retaliation in view of extenuating conditions ⟨the plea of 'frontier conditions' could no longer *excuse* the lack of an adequate public-school system —*Amer. Guide Series: Mich.*⟩ ⟨guilty of contributory negligence, in default, at least, of special circumstances *excusing* the omission —B.N.Cardozo⟩ ⟨the injustice with which he had been treated would have *excused* him if he had resorted to violent methods of redress —T.B.Macaulay⟩ CONDONE may indicate accepting without protest, censure, or punishment some reprehensible action or condition because of circumstances ⟨those Anglo-Saxon critics of the brutality of the bullfight who *condone* the hunting of the fox or the killing of deer —W.D.Patterson⟩ ⟨often he got into scrapes, but they were the manly scrapes that are easily *condoned* —D.H.Lawrence⟩ ⟨institutionalized suicide, *condoned*, approved, or even exacted by a code and therefore by the culture —A.L.Kroeber⟩ PARDON may indicate waiving of punishment or censure and reinstatement to grace esp. by a superior and in legal, formal, or social situations ⟨*pardoned* by the state governor⟩ ⟨it became necessary for us both to fly for our lives. In the circumstances we could not look to be *pardoned*, even on the score of youth —W.H.Hudson †1922⟩ ⟨the most good-natured of women *pardoned* the error —W.M. Thackeray⟩ FORGIVE may apply to genuine, sincere change of feeling whereby resentment and desire for retaliation on or punishment of an offender are no longer felt ⟨the Mayor invariably gazed stormfully past him, like one who had endured and lost on his account, and could in no sense *forgive* the wrong —Thomas Hardy⟩ ⟨he *forgave* injuries so readily that he might be said to invite them —T.B.Macaulay⟩

²ex·cuse \ik'skyüs, ek-\ *n* -s [ME, fr. MF, fr. *excuser*] **1 :** the act of excusing (as by apologizing, exculpating, pardoning, or releasing) **:** ACQUITTAL, RELEASE, ABSOLUTION, JUSTIFICATION ⟨pleading so wisely in ~ of it —Shak.⟩ **2 a :** something offered as grounds for being excused **:** a justifying explanation of a fault or defect ⟨what's your ~ for being late this morning?⟩ ⟨he made his ill health an ~ for everything⟩ **b excuses** *pl* **:** an expression of regret for failure to do or participate in something often conveyed through a third party ⟨make my ~*s* to your cousin, I'm sorry to miss her tea⟩ **c :** a note of explanation (as from a parent or teacher) concerning the absence of an individual (as from class or work) **3 a :** something that serves to excuse **:** anything that justifies or extenuates a fault or defect ⟨I suppose his youth is an ~ for his flighty ways⟩ ⟨forgetfulness is no ~ for bad manners⟩ **b :** a purpose or use that justifies **:** JUSTIFICATION, REASON ⟨such loveliness is enough ~ for being⟩ **4 :** an inferior example or instance of a kind specified ⟨finally turned in a bluffed ~ for a composition⟩ ⟨this rattletrap is a poor ~ for a car⟩ **syn** see APOLOGY

ex·cuse·less *adj* **1** *obs* **:** having or offering no excuse **2** \-üzləs, -üsl-\ **:** impossible to excuse **:** INEXCUSABLE

ex·cus·er \-üzə(r)\ *n* -s **:** one that excuses

excuses *pres 3d sing of* EXCUSE, *pl of* EXCUSE

ex·cus·ing \(ik)'skyüz°n\ *prep* [fr. pres. part. of ¹*excuse*] *chiefly South & Midland* **:** EXCEPT ⟨ain't done much ~ fret and worry —Marjorie K. Rawlings⟩

ex·cus·ing·ly *adv* **:** in an excusing manner

ex·cu·sive \ik'skyüs|iv, ek-, -üz|\ *adj* **:** tending to excuse — **ex·cu·sive·ly** \|əvlē\ *adv*

ex·cuss \ik'skəs, ek-\ *vt* -ED/-ING/-ES [L *excussus*, past part. of *excutere*, fr. *ex-* ¹ex- + *-cutere* (fr. *quatere* to shake) — more at QUASH] **1** *obs* **:** to shake off or out **:** DISCARD **2** *obs* **:** to investigate as if by shaking out **:** DISCUSS **3 :** to proceed against (a principal debtor) before falling back on a surety

excussion *n* -s [LL *excussion-, excussio*, fr. L *excussus* + *-ion-, -io* -ion] *obs* **:** the act of excussing

ex·cyst \(')ek(s)¦sist\ *vi* -ED/-ING/-S [¹*ex-* + *cyst* (n.)] **:** to emerge from a cyst (as of a protozoan) — **ex·cys·ta·tion** \,ek(s),si'stāshən\ *n* -s — **ex·cyst·ment** \ek(s)'sis(t)mənt\ *n* -s

exd *abbr* examined

ex de·bi·to jus·ti·ti·ae *adj* (*or adv*) \eks'debə,tō,yü'stid·ē,ī\ [NL] **:** of or by reason of an obligation of justice **:** as a matter of right

ex de·lic·to \,eksdə'lik(,)tō\ *adj* (*or adv*) [LL] **:** of or by reason of a wrong **:** arising from a wrongful act

ex dividend *adv* (*or adj*) [²*ex*] **:** with the value of a pending dividend excluded from the sale price of a security, the buyer not being entitled to the dividend when paid — opposed to *cum dividend;* abbr. *ex div.*

ex·e·at \'eksē,at\ *n* -s [L, let him or her go out, 3d pers. sing. pres. subj. of *exire* to go out, fr. *ex-* ¹ex- + *ire* to go —more at ISSUE] **1** *Brit* **:** a permit for temporary absence (as from a college or monastery) **2 :** a letter of permission allowing a cleric to transfer from one diocese to another **:** a letter of excardination

ex·ec \ig'zek, eg-\ *n* -s [by shortening] **:** EXECUTIVE OFFICER

exec *abbr* executed; execution; executive; executor

ex·e·cra·ble \'eksəkrəbəl, -sēk-\ *adj* [ME, expressing a curse, deserving to be execrated, fr. L *execrabilis, exsecrabilis*, fr. *execrare, exsecrare* + *-abilis* -able] **1** *obs* **:** expressing a curse **2 :** deserving to be execrated **:** DAMNABLE, DETESTABLE, ABOMINABLE, HORRIFYING ⟨~ crimes⟩ **3 :** very bad **:** WRETCHED ⟨~ verses⟩ ⟨~ taste⟩ — **ex·e·cra·ble·ness** \-lnəs\ *n* -ES — **ex·e·cra·bly** \-blē, -li\ *adv*

ex·e·crate \'eksə,krāt, *usu* -ād.+V\ *vb* -ED/-ING/-S [L *execratus, exsecratus*, past part. of *execrari, exsecrari*, fr. *ex-* ¹ex- + *-secrari* (fr. *sacr-, sacer* sacred) — more at SACRED] *vt* **1** *archaic* **:** to call down curses upon **:** put under a curse **:** pronounce accursed **2 :** to declare to be evil or detestable **:** DENOUNCE, DAMN, REVILE ⟨he was *execrated* as a murderer and adulterer⟩ **3 :** to detest utterly **:** ABHOR ⟨finally came to ~ the Victorian values —*New Yorker*⟩ ~ *vi* **:** CURSE, SWEAR ⟨he longed to ~ aloud —James Joyce⟩

syn CURSE, DAMN, ANATHEMATIZE, OBJURGATE: EXECRATE indicates a violent denouncing with intense loathing and, usu., furious passion ⟨for a little while he was *execrated* in Rome; his statues were overthrown, and his name was blotted from the records —John Buchan⟩ ⟨the murder will be added to the many crimes of Egidio Gambara, that posterity may *execrate* his name —Rafael Sabatini⟩ CURSE and DAMN both signify fervent angry denunciation by oaths; the former may seem somewhat more literary than the latter ⟨in literature, with his usual charming violence, he *cursed* Conrad's style —F.A. Swinnerton⟩ ⟨he told me great tales of their cruelty, and he *cursed* them most bitterly —Hugh Walpole⟩ ⟨he mentally *damned* the cook as the real cause of his distress —F.M. Crofts⟩ ⟨*damn* the torpedoes, full speed ahead —David Farragut⟩ ANATHEMATIZE indicates solemn, although perhaps impassioned, formal denunciation or condemnation, as a churchman's denunciation of evil ⟨in the course of the proceedings of the Council, the earlier deposition of Arius by an Alexandrian synod was confirmed and his teachings were *anathematized* —Frank Thilly⟩ OBJURGATE may apply to the chiding of extremists ⟨*objurgating* the present incumbent of the White House⟩

ex·e·cra·tion \,eksə'krāshən\ *n* -s [L *execration-, exsecration-, execratio, exsecratio*, fr. *execratus, exsecratus* + *-ion-, -io* -ion] **1 :** the act of cursing or denouncing ⟨~, if followed by submission, is devoid of motive power —B.N.Cardozo⟩; *also* **:** the curse so uttered ⟨excommunicated with all the somber maledictions, ~*s*, and anathemas —L.K.Anspacher⟩ ⟨the ~*s* of the mob⟩ **2 :** an object of curses **:** a detested thing

ex·e·cra·tive \'eksə,krād·iv, -,krəd-\ *adj* **:** EXECRATORY — **ex·e·cra·tive·ly** \-d·əvlē\ *adv*

ex·e·cra·tor \-,krād·ə(r)\ *n* -s [LL *execrator, exsecrator*, fr. L *execratus, exsecratus* + *-or*] **:** one that execrates

ex·e·cra·to·ry \'eksəkrə,tōrē\ *adj* **:** of or relating to execration **:** IMPRECATORY

ex·e·cut·able \'eksə,kyüd·əbəl, -ütə-, ,==¦===\ *adj* **:** capable of execution **:** FEASIBLE

¹ex·ec·u·tant \ig'zekyəd·ənt, eg-, ÷ -kə-, -ətənt *also* -ət°nt\ *n* -s [F *exécutant*, fr. pres. part. of *exécuter* to execute] **:** one who executes or performs; *esp* **:** one skilled in the technique of an art **:** PERFORMER

²executant \"\ *adj* [F *exécutant*, pres. part. of *exécuter* to execute, fr. MF *executer*] **1 :** performing esp. for an audience ⟨~ musicians⟩ **2 :** of, related to, or connected with an executant ⟨~ music⟩

ex·e·cute \'eksə,kyüt, *usu* -üd.+V\ *vt* -ED/-ING/-S [ME *executen*, fr. MF *executer*, back-formation fr. *executeur* executor (fr. L *executor, exsecutor*), *execution*, and *executoire* executory (fr. LL *executorius, exsecutorius* executory, putting into effect)] **1 :** to put into effect **:** carry out fully and completely **:** PERFORM, EFFECT ⟨~ a purpose⟩ ⟨~ the king's will⟩ ⟨~ a dance step⟩ ⟨~ a military maneuver⟩ **2** *obs* **a :** to give practical expression to (as a sentiment, a passion) **b :** to make use of (a weapon) **c :** to carry out (as a ceremony) **:** CONDUCT **3 :** to give effect to **:** do what is provided or required by ⟨~ the provisions of a will⟩ **:** perform the requirements of **:** perform the acts necessary to the effectiveness of ⟨~ a decree⟩ **4 :** to inflict capital punishment on **:** put to death in conformity to a legal sentence ⟨*executed* him as a traitor⟩ **5 :** to make or produce (as a work of art) esp. by carrying out a design ⟨a statue *executed* in bronze⟩ ⟨~ a facade in red sandstone⟩ **6 :** COMPLETE ⟨~ legal instrument⟩ **:** perform what is required to give validity to (as by signing and perhaps sealing and delivering) ⟨~ a deed⟩ **7 :** PLAY ⟨~ a piece of music⟩ **syn** see KILL, PERFORM

executed *adj* [fr. past part. of *execute*] **:** carried out **:** carried out legally according to its terms **:** PERFORMED— see EXECUTORY

ex·e·cu·tion \,eksə'kyüshən\ *n* -s [ME *execucioun*, fr. MF *execution*, fr. L *execution-, exsecution-, executio, exsecutio*, fr. *executus, exsecutus* (past part. of *exequi, exsequi* to execute, fr. *ex-* ¹ex- + *sequi* to follow) + *-ion-, -io* -ion — more at SUE] **1 :** the act or process of executing **:** PERFORMANCE, ACCOMPLISHMENT ⟨there was nothing to prevent the ~ of his purpose⟩ ⟨put a new plan into ~⟩ **2 a** *archaic* **:** a punishment ordered legally **b :** a putting to death as a legal penalty **:** CAPITAL PUNISHMENT **3 a :** the process for carrying into effect the judgment or decree of a court; *esp* **:** the enforcement of such judgment or decree by arrest of the person or seizure of the property of a debtor **b :** a judicial writ by which an officer is empowered to carry a judgment into effect — called also *final process* **c :** the act of signing, sealing, and delivering a legal instrument or giving it the forms required to make it valid ⟨the ~ of a deed⟩ ⟨the ~ of a will⟩ **4 :** the act or mode or result of performance in any of the arts or in anything that requires a special skill or technique ⟨~ of a carving⟩ ⟨~ of a violin solo⟩ ⟨the fineness of ~ of the iron balcony and of the railing —*Amer. Guide Series: N.Y. City*⟩ **5 :** effective or destructive action — used usu. with *do* ⟨as soon as day came, we went out to see what we had done —Daniel Defoe⟩ **6** *archaic* **:** the military act of plundering

ex·e·cu·tion·al \¦==¦kyüshən°l, -shnəl\ *adj* **:** relating to execution

ex·e·cu·tion·er \,==¦kyüsh(ə)nə(r)\ *n* -s **1 a :** one that executes or performs **b :** one that executes a judgment; *esp* **:** one that inflicts an authorized punishment **2 :** one that puts to death **:** HANGMAN

¹ex·ec·u·tive \ig'zekyəd·iv, eg-, ÷ -kə-, -ətiv *sometimes* ÷ -ktiv *or* ÷ -ktēv\ *adj* **1 :** designed or fitted for or relating to execution or carrying into effect ⟨~ board⟩ ⟨~ skill⟩ ⟨~ plan⟩ ⟨~ committee⟩ **2 :** qualified for, concerned with, or relating to the execution of the laws or the conduct of public and national affairs ⟨~ duties⟩ ⟨~ authority⟩ **:** belonging to the branch of the government that is charged with such powers as diplomatic representation, supreme command of the armed forces, superintendence of the execution of the laws, and appointment of officials and that usu. has some power over legislation (as through the veto, the initiation of legislation, and dissolution of the legislature) ⟨~ department⟩ — distinguished from *judicial* and *legislative* **3 :** active, effectual, or skillful in managing, directing, or accomplishing ⟨the ~ aspects of the ego —Abram Kardiner⟩ ⟨under the supervision of his very strong-minded, ~ wife —Margaret Mead⟩ **4 :** relating or belonging to an executive ⟨~ rewards⟩ ⟨~ suite of offices⟩ — **ex·ec·u·tive·ly** \-əvlē, -li\ *adv* — **ex·ec·u·tive·ness** \-ivnəs, -ēv- *also* -əv-\ *n* -ES

²executive \"\ *n* -s **1 :** the executive branch of a government; *also* **:** the person or persons who constitute the executive magistracy of a state **2 :** a directing or controlling body of an organization (as a political party, a labor union) **:** an executive council or committee **3 :** one who holds a position of administrative or managerial responsibility in a business or other organization **:** ADMINISTRATOR, OFFICER ⟨chief sales ~⟩

executive agreement *n* **:** an agreement between the U.S. and a foreign government made by the executive branch of the government alone without approval by the Senate and dealing usu. with routine matters not thought to require the formality of a treaty

executive council *n* **1 :** a council constituted to advise or share in the functions of a political executive: as **a :** a council composed of the principal government officials and sometimes unofficial appointees that is constituted to advise the governor of a British colony ⟨the Governor shall . . . preside at all meetings of the *Executive Council* —*Royal Instructions (Nigeria)*⟩ **b :** a council in several member nations of the British Commonwealth that resembles the Privy Council in power and function ⟨in New Zealand . . . the Cabinet and the *Executive Council* have the same membership —Walter Nash⟩ **2 :** a council that exercises supreme executive power **:** a plural executive ⟨in Switzerland . . . the *Executive Council* is not based upon a party majority in the representative bodies —C.J.Friedrich⟩ ⟨replacing the Uruguayan president with an *executive council*⟩

executive officer *n* **1 :** the principal staff officer in a command below division level **2 :** the military officer second in command of a company or similar organization **3 :** the second in command of a ship, station, or air squadron in the navy

executive order *n* **:** REGULATION 2b (2)

executive secretary *n* **:** a secretary having administrative duties; *specif* **:** a paid full-time official who is responsible for organizing and administering the activities and business affairs of an organization or association

executive session *n* **:** a usu. closed session of a legislative or other body acting in the function of an executive council (as of the U.S. Senate when considering appointments or the ratification of treaties)

ex·ec·u·tor \ig'zekyəd·ə(r), eg-, ÷ -kə-, -ətə(r), *in sense 1a* " *or* 'eksə,kyüd·ə(r) *or* -,kyütə-\ *n* -s [ME *executour*, fr. OF *executor*, fr. L *executor*, *exsecutor*, fr. *executus*, *exsecutus* (past part. of *exequi*, *exsequi* to execute) + *-or* — more at EXECUTION] **1 a :** one who executes something (as a purpose, duty, function, work of art) **:** DOER, PERFORMER, AGENT **b** *obs* **:** EXECUTIONER **2 :** the person appointed by a testator to execute his will or to see its provisions carried into effect after his decease

executor-dative \=¦=≡=¦==\ *n* [*executor* + *dative*, adj.] *civil, Scots, & canon law* **:** an executor or administrator appointed by a bishop or magistrate or ecclesiastical or civil court — distinguished from *executor-nominate*

executor de son tort \-də,sōⁿ'tȯ(ə)r\ *n* [AF, executor of his own wrong] **:** a person who without legal authority assumes control of a decedent's property as if he were executor

ex·ec·u·to·ri·al \ig¦zekyə¦tōrēəl, (¦)eg-, ÷kə¦-, -tȯr-\ *adj* [ME (Sc), fr. ML *executorialis*, fr. LL *executorius*, *exsecutorius* executory, putting into effect + L *-alis* -al] **1** *chiefly Scots law* **:** of or relating to the execution of a mandate or of legal process **2 :** of or relating to an executor

executor-nominate \=¦=≡=¦==(,)=\ *n, civil, Scots, & canon law* **:** an executor or administrator nominated in the will — distinguished from *executor-dative*

ex·ec·u·tor·ship \='≡=,ship\ *n* **:** the office of executor

ex·ec·u·to·ry \ig'zekyə,tōrē, eg-, ÷-kə,-, -tȯr-, -ri\ *adj* [ME *executorie* operative, being in effect, putting into effect, fr. LL *executorius*, *exsecutorius* putting into effect, fr. L *executus*, *exsecutus* (past part. of *exequi*, *exsequi* to execute) + *-orius* -ory] **1 :** relating to administration or to putting the laws in force **:** EXECUTIVE **2 :** designed or of such a nature as to be executed in time to come or to take effect on a future contingency ⟨an agreement to sell is an ~ contract⟩

executory devise *n* **:** a devise of land which takes effect by terminating a preceding interest

executory interest *n* **:** an interest that takes effect through an executory limitation

executory limitation *n* **:** a dispositive provision that becomes effective by divesting a prior interest

ex·ec·u·trix \ig'zekyə,triks, eg-, ÷-kə-,-\ *n, pl* **executri·ces** \=,=='trī,sēz\ *or* **executrixes** [ME, executrix of a will, fr. ML, fr. LL, *executrix*, *exsecutrix* woman that executes something, fem. of L *executor*, *exsecutor* executor — more at -TRIX] **:** a woman exercising the functions of an executor

ex·ec·u·try \-(y)ə·tri\ *n* -ES [prob. irreg. fr. *executor* + *-y*] *Scots law* **:** the movable estate passing to the executor for distribution

exede *vt* -ED/-ING/-S [L *exedere* to eat up, fr. *ex-* ¹ex- + *edere* to eat — more at EAT] *obs* **:** CORRODE

ex·e·dent \'eksədənt\ *adj* [L *exedent-*, *exedens*, pres. part. of *exedere*] **:** WASTING, ULCERATING

ex·e·dra \'eksədrə, ek'sēd-, eks'hed-\ *also* **ex·he·dra** \ek'sēd-, eks'hēd-\ *n, pl* **exe·drae** \-,drē\ [L *exedra*, fr. Gk, fr. *ex* out of, out + *hedra* seat, fr. *hezesthai* to sit — more at EX-, SIT] **1** *in ancient Greece and Rome* **:** a room for conversation usu. open like a portico and furnished with seats **2 :** a large out-of-door nearly semicircular seat or bench with a solid back — **ex·e·dral** \-rəl\ *adj*

exeem *vt* -ED/-ING/-S [fr. *exemption*, after E *redemption*: *redeem*] *obs* **:** EXEMPT

ex·e·ge·sis \,eksə'jēsəs\ *n, pl* **exege·ses** \-ē,sēz\ [NL, fr. Gk *exēgēsis*, fr. *exēgeisthai* to explain, interpret, fr. *ex* out of, out + *hēgeisthai* to lead — more at SEEK] **:** EXPOSITION, EXPLANATION; *esp* **:** critical interpretation of a text or portion of Scripture

ex·e·ge·sist \-ēsəst\ *n* -S [*exegesis* + *-ist*] **:** EXEGETE

ex·e·gete \'eksə,jēt\ *n* -S [Gk *exēgētēs*, fr. *exēgeisthai*] **:** one who practices exegesis

ex·e·get·ic \¦eksə¦jed·ik\ *or* **ex·e·get·i·cal** \-d·əkəl\ *adj* [*exegetic* fr. Gk *exēgētikos*, fr. *exēgētēs* + *-ikos* -ic; *exegetical* fr. Gk *exēgētikos* + E *-al*] **:** relating to exegesis **:** EXPLANATORY, EXPOSITORY — **ex·e·get·i·cal·ly** \əkə(ə)lē\ *adv*

ex·e·get·ics \,eksə'jed·iks\ *n pl but sing or pl in constr* **:** the science of interpretation esp. of the Scriptures

ex·e·get·ist \,eksə'jed·əst, '≡=,=\ *n* -S [*exegetic* + *-ist*] **:** EXEGETE

exempla *pl of* EXEMPLUM

¹ex·em·plar \ig'zemplə(r), eg-, -,plär, -,plȧ(r\ *n* -S [ME *exaumplere*, *exemplar*, fr. MF & L; ME *exaumplere* fr. MF *exemplaire*, *examplaire*, fr. LL *exemplarium*, alter. of L *exemplar*; ME *exemplar* fr. L, fr. *exemplum* model, example, copy — more at EXAMPLE] **:** one that serves as a model or example: as **a :** an ideal model ⟨Plato, the classic ~ of the moral theory —Hunter Mead⟩ **b :** a typical or standard specimen **c :** a copy of a book **d :** a manuscript or copy of a text from which other copies were made **e :** a philosophical archetype; *specif* **:** UNIVERSAL **syn** see MODEL

²exemplar *adj* [L *exemplaris*] *obs* **:** EXEMPLARY

ex·em·plar·i·ly \ig¦zemplərəlē, -,zem-, -li, *chiefly Brit* ig'zemplərəli *or* eg'z-\ *adv* **:** in an exemplary manner **:** by way of example

ex·em·pla·ri·ness *pronunc at* ¹EXEMPLARY + nəs\ *n* -ES **:** the quality or state of being exemplary

ex·em·plar·ism \ig'zemplə,rizəm, eg-\ *n* -S [¹*exemplar* + *-ism*] **:** a theological doctrine that the divine ideas are the ontological basis of finite realities and of their knowability

ex·em·plar·i·ty \,eg,zem'plarəd·ē, -,zəm-\ *n* -ES [trans. of It *esemplarità*] **:** exemplary quality **:** EXEMPLARINESS

¹ex·em·pla·ry \ig'zemplərē, eg-, -ri *sometimes* 'egzəm,pler- *or* 'eg,zem,pler-\ *n* -ES [ME *exemplarie*, *exaumplarie*, fr. LL *exemplarium*] **:** EXEMPLAR

²exemplary \"\ *adj* [L *exemplaris*, fr. *exemplum* + *-aris* -ar] **1 a :** serving as or in the nature of an exemplar, form, or pattern ⟨the realm of ~ ideas⟩ **b :** deserving imitation **:** COMMENDABLE ⟨the ~ lives of saints⟩ **2 :** serving as a warning **:** MONITORY ⟨~ justice⟩ **3 :** serving as an example, instance, or illustration ⟨~ passages⟩ **4 :** consisting of or relating to exempla ⟨medieval ~ literature⟩

³exemplary *adv*, *obs* **:** EXEMPLARILY

exemplary damages *n pl* **:** PUNITIVE DAMAGES

ex·em·pli·fi·able \ig'zemplə,fīəbəl, eg-, =,=='≡=\ *adj* **:** capable of being exemplified

ex·em·pli·fi·ca·tion \=,=pləfə'kāshən\ *n* -S [ME *exemplificacion*, fr. AF & ML; AF *exemplification*, fr. ML *exemplification-*, *exemplificatio*, fr. *exemplificatus* (past part. of *exemplificare* to copy, show by example) + L *-ion-*, *-io* -ion] **1** *law* **:** an exemplified copy **2 a :** the act or process of exemplifying **:** a showing or illustrating by example ⟨the formation of a general idea . . . and the observation of its ~ in a variety of occasions —A.N.Whitehead⟩ **b :** a case in point **:** INSTANCE, EXAMPLE **3 :** the presentation or working of degrees (as by the various Masonic bodies) **:** a setting forth of the work of a lodge or fraternal order for purposes of instruction or conferral of a degree and under the supervision of a qualified officer

ex·em·pli·fi·ca·tive \='≡=,kād·iv\ *adj* [ML *exemplificatus* + E *-ive*] **:** EXEMPLIFYING

ex·em·pli·fi·ca·to·ry \-,kə,tōrē, *chiefly Brit* =¦≡=¦kātəri\ *adj* [ML *exemplificatus* + E *-ory*] **:** EXEMPLIFYING **:** designed to exemplify

ex·em·pli·fy \ig'zemplə,fī, eg-\ *vt* -ED/-ING/-S [ME *exemplifien*, fr. MF *exemplifier*, fr. ML *exemplificare* to copy, show by example, fr. *exempli-* (fr. L *exemplum* model, example, copy) + L *-ficare* -fy — more at EXAMPLE] **1** *obs* **:** to set an example to **2 :** to show or illustrate by example **:** furnish with examples ⟨the chief value . . . lies not so much in any novelty of thesis as in the instances and insights which ~ and enrich his elaboration —Lucius Garvin⟩ **3** *obs* **a :** to put forward or point to as an example **b :** to make an example of by public punishment **4 a :** COPY, TRANSCRIBE **b :** to make an attested copy or transcript of (a document) under seal **5 a :** to be an instance of or serve as an example of **:** EMBODY ⟨an organism can manifest and ~ mechanical principles in itself —Weston La Barre⟩ **b :** to be typical of **:** ILLUSTRATE ⟨his works ~ the taste of the period⟩ **6 :** to go through the ceremonies and rituals of (as a degree of a fraternal order)

ex·em·pli gra·tia \ig¦zem,plē'grād·ē,ä, eg-\ *adv* [L] **:** for the sake of example **:** for example or instance — abbr. *e.g.*

ex·em·plum \-'zempləm\ *n, pl* **exem·pla** \-lə\ [LL, fr. L, model, example, copy] **1 :** an anecdote or short narrative used (as in a medieval sermon) to point a moral or sustain an argument **2** [L] **:** EXAMPLE, MODEL

¹ex·empt \ig'zem(p)t, eg-\ *adj* [ME, fr. L *exemptus*, past part. of *eximere* to remove, free, fr. *ex-* ¹ex- + *-imere* (fr. *emere* to buy, acquire) — more at REDEEM] **1** *obs* **:** set apart **:** cut off **:** EXCLUDED **2 :** not subject to an authority or jurisdiction (as of a bishop) ⟨~ monastery⟩ **3 :** free or released from some liability to which others are subject **:** excepted from the operation of some law or obligation **:** not subject to **:** not liable to — used with *from* ⟨goods ~ from execution⟩ ⟨~ from jury service⟩ ⟨tax-*exempt*⟩

²exempt \"\ *vt* -ED/-ING/-S [ME *exempten*, fr. L *exemptus*, past part. of *eximere*] **1** *obs* **:** to set apart **:** REMOVE, EXCLUDE **2 :** to release or deliver from some liability or requirement to which others are subject **:** except or excuse from the operation of a law or obligation ⟨~ a man from military service⟩ ⟨~ a student from a generally required course⟩

³exempt \"\ *n* -S [L & F; F *exempt* subordinate in the cavalry commanding in the absence of the higher company officers, fr. *exempt*, adj., fr. L *exemptus*, past part. of *eximere*] **1 :** one exempted or freed from duty **:** one not subject **2 a :** a subordinate in the French cavalry who is in command when the higher company officers are absent and is exempt from common duty; *also* **:** a similar French police officer **b :** EXON **c :** an honorably discharged fire fighter who enjoys certain exemptions (as from jury duty)

exempt carrier *n* **:** a transport agency specializing in services (as taxi service) or commodities (as farm products or bulk cargo) exempt from regulation by the Interstate Commerce Act

ex·emp·tion \-m(p)shən\ *n* -S [ME *exempcioun*, fr. MF or ML; MF *exemption*, fr. ML *exemption-*, *exemptio*, fr. L, removal, fr. *exemptus* (past part. of *eximere*) + *-ion-*, *-io* -ion] **1 :** the act of exempting or state of being exempt **:** freedom from any charge or obligation to which others are subject **:** IMMUNITY ⟨~ from an entrance examination⟩ ⟨~ from customs duty⟩ **2 :** a cause for exempting (as a portion of taxable income) ⟨claim ~ for a dependent⟩ **3** *Roman Catholicism* **:** release from the jurisdiction of the ordinary and subjection only to that of the Holy See

ex·emp·tive \-m(p)tiv\ *adj* [²*exempt* + *-ive*] **:** relating to, securing, or providing exemption

exempt job *n* **:** a job that is removed from seniority provisions in that while the holder may be laid off he may not be replaced by someone of senior service

ex·endospermous *also* **ex·endospermic** \(¦)eks+\ *adj* [¹*ex-* + *endosperm* + *-ous* or *-ic*] **:** lacking endosperm — used of seeds ⟨~ beans⟩

¹ex·en·ter·ate \ek'sentə,rāt\ *vt* -ED/-ING/-S [L *exenteratus*, past part. of *exenterare*, modif. of Gk *exenterizein*, fr. *ex* out of, out + *enteron* intestine + *-izein* -ize — more at EX-, INTER-] **1 :** DISEMBOWEL, EVISCERATE **2 :** to remove the contents of (as the orbit, pelvis, or a sinus) — **ex·en·ter·a·tion** \(,)ek,sentə'rāshən\ *n* -S

²ex·en·ter·ate \(')=¦=≡rət\ *adj* [L *exenteratus*, past part. of *exenterare*] **:** EVISCERATED

ex·e·qua·tur \,eksə'kwād·ə(r), -wäd-\ *n* -S [L *exequatur*, *exsequatur* let him perform, 3d pers. sing. pres. subj. of *exequi*, *exsequi* to perform, execute — more at EXECUTION] **1 :** a written official recognition and authorization of a consular officer issued by the government to which he is accredited **2 :** permission granted by a sovereign for the exercise of a bishop's functions under papal authority or for the publication of papal bulls

ex·e·qui·al \(')ek¦sēkwēəl\ *adj* [L *exequialis*, *exsequialis*, fr. *exequiae*, *exsequiae* + *-alis* -al] **:** of or relating to funerals **:** FUNEREAL

ex·e·quy \'eksəkwē\ *n, pl* **exequies** [ME *exequies*, *exequise*, sing. & pl., fr. MF & L; MF *exequies*, pl., fr. L *exequiae*, *exsequiae*, pl., fr. *exequi*, *exsequi* to follow, perform, execute] **:** a funeral rite or ceremony; *sometimes* **:** a funeral procession — now chiefly used in pl.

exerce *vb* -ED/-ING/-S [ME *exercen*, fr. L *exercēre*] *obs* **:** EXERCISE

ex·er·cent \ig'zərsᵊnt, eg-\ *adj* [L *exercent-*, *exercens*, pres. part. of *exercēre*] *archaic* **:** EXERCISING, PRACTICING

ex·er·cis·able \'eksə(r),sīzəbəl, ,=='≡=\ *adj* **:** capable of being exercised ⟨~ right⟩

¹ex·er·cise \'eksə(r),sīz\ *n* -S [ME, fr. MF *exercice*, fr. L *exercitium*, fr. *exercitus*, past part. of *exercēre* to drive on, keep busy, fr. *ex-* ¹ex- + *-ercēre* (fr. *arcēre* to hold off, enclose) — more at ARK] **1 a :** the act of bringing into play or realizing in action **:** EXERTION, USE ⟨avoid accidents by the ~ of foresight⟩ ⟨the violent . . . ~ of royal authority —T.B. Macaulay⟩ **b :** the discharge of an official function or professional occupation ⟨~ of his judicial duties⟩ **2 a :** regular or repeated appropriate use of a faculty, power, or bodily organ ⟨willpower is strengthened by ~⟩ ⟨muscles atrophy from lack of ~⟩ **b :** bodily exertion for the sake of developing and maintaining physical fitness ⟨he plays golf chiefly for the ~⟩ **3 :** something that is performed or practiced in order to develop or improve a specific power or skill: as **a :** a set task (as a piece of writing) designed to improve a pupil's ability or to test his comprehension of a subject ⟨do the ~ at the end of each chapter⟩ ⟨spelling ~⟩ **b :** an artificially devised bodily action or set of actions prescribed for regular or repeated practice as a means of gaining strength, dexterity, suppleness, or all-around competence in some field of performance ⟨finger ~⟩ ⟨bowing ~⟩ ⟨vocal ~s⟩ ⟨breathing ~s⟩ **4 a :** a composition or work of art performed chiefly in order to practice or display a specific technical point or aspect **:** STUDY ⟨~ in double-stops⟩ ⟨~ in light and shadow effects⟩ **b :** an artistic or intellectual performance whose value is greater in the doing than in the final result or greater for the performer than for the beholder ⟨a mere literary ~⟩ ⟨to balance forms, calculate proportions, and harmonize colors can be an intellectual ~ rather than an act of creative imagination —Herbert Read⟩ **c :** any performance having a strongly marked or identifiable secondary or ulterior aspect ⟨a biography that . . . is a truly formidable ~ in unrelieved contempt —*New Yorker*⟩ **d :** habitual act **:** PRACTICE ⟨the casting of metal forms in molds was an ~ older than recorded history⟩ **5 :** an act of religious practice esp. in worship (as of preaching, expounding, or praying) ⟨~s of devotion⟩ **6 :** a public exhibition or ceremony: as **a :** a maneuver, operation, or drill carried out for training and discipline ⟨a field ~⟩ **b :** an academic disputation, oral examination, or discourse required of a candidate for a degree and often carried on in public **c exercises** *pl* **:** a program including speeches, announcements of awards and honors, and various traditional practices of secular or religious character ⟨commencement ~s⟩ **d :** an activity forming part of a regular academic routine ⟨salute the national flag as part of a daily school ~ —Felix Frankfurter⟩

²exercise \"\ *vb* -ED/-ING/-S [ME *exercisen*, fr. *exercise*, n.] *vt* **1 a :** to bring into play **:** make effective in action ⟨privileges if not *exercised* are often lost⟩ ⟨he failed to ~ good judgment in buying the car⟩ **:** bring to bear **:** EXERT ⟨will can only be *exercised* in the presence of something which retards or resists it —W.R.Inge⟩ ⟨~ her influence among all the nations of the world —Norman Angell⟩ **b** *obs* **:** to carry on (an occupation) or carry out the functions of (an office) **2 a :** to use repeatedly in order to strengthen or develop (a muscle or a bodily faculty) ⟨*exercising* his fingers daily to restore them⟩ **b :** to train (as troops) by drills and maneuvers ⟨Tom was being *exercised* like a raw recruit —George Meredith⟩ **c :** to give exercise to **:** put through exercises **3 a :** to engage the attention and effort of ⟨a problem which is much *exercising* the minds of the city fathers —Sam Pollock⟩ **b :** to cause anxiety, alarm, or indignation in **:** VEX, HARASS ⟨was ever a human generation so *exercised* about its education as ours? —C.G.Osgood⟩ ~ *vi* **1** *obs* **:** to perform one's office **2 :** to exert oneself **:** take exercise **:** DRILL, TRAIN **3 :** to take part in religious observances **syn** see PRACTICE

ex·er·cis·er \-zə(r)\ *n* -S **:** one that exercises: as **a :** an apparatus for use in physical exercise **b :** a groom who exercises horses

ex·er·ci·tant \ig'zərsəd·ənt, eg-\ *n* -S [F, prob. fr. LL *exercitant-*, *exercitans*, pres. part. of *exercitare* to meditate, fr. L, to exercise diligently, fr. *exercitus*, past part. of *exercēre* to drive on, keep busy — more at ¹EXERCISE] **:** one engaged in spiritual exercises

ex·er·ci·ta·tion \ig,zərsə'tāshən, (,)eg-\ *n* -S [ME *exercitacioun*, fr. L *exercitation-*, *exercitatio*, fr. *exercitatus* (past part. of *exercitare* to exercise diligently) + *-ion-*, *-io* -ion] *archaic* **:** EXERCISE

ex·er·ci·tor \='=səd·ə(r)\ *or* **exercitor ma·ris** \-'ma(a)rəs\ *n* -S [*exercitor* fr. L, exerciser, fr. *exercitus* (past part. of *exercēre* to drive on, keep busy) + *-or*; *exercitor maris* fr. NL, lit., exerciser of the sea] *civil & Scots law* **:** the one (as owner, charterer, or mortgagee in possession) to whom the profits of a ship belong at a particular time

ex·er·ci·to·ri·al \ig¦zərsə¦tōrēəl, (¦)eg¦-\ *adj* **:** of or relating to an exercitor

ex·er·e·sis \ek'serəsəs, eg'ze-\ *n, pl* **exere·ses** \-ə,sēz\ [NL, fr. Gk *exairesis* removal, taking out, fr. *exairein* to remove, take out (fr. *ex* out of, out + *hairein* to take) + *-sis* — more at EX-, HERESY] **:** surgical removal of a part or organ (as a nerve)

ex·er·gon·ic \¦ek(,)sər¦gänik\ *adj* [*exo-* + Gk *ergon* work + E *-ic* — more at WORK] **:** producing work or energy — opposed to *endergonic*; used esp. of a chemical reaction occurring in a biological process

ex·ergu·al \(')ek¦sərgəl, (')eg¦zər-\ *adj* **:** relating to the exergue of a coin or medal

ex·ergue \'ek,sərg, 'eg,zərg, ='=\ *n* -S [F *exergue*, fr. NL *exergum*, fr. Gk *ex* out of, out + *ergon* work] **:** a space on a coin, token, or medal usu. on the reverse below the central part of the design, sometimes marked off from it by a line, and often containing the date

ex·ert \ig'zər\|t, eg-, -zə̄l, -zəi\|, *usu* \|d.+V\ *vt* -ED/-ING/-S [L *exertus*, *exsertus*, past part. of *exerere*, *exserere* to thrust out, fr. *ex-* ¹ex- + *serere* to join together — more at SERIES] **1** *obs* **:** to thrust forth **:** EMIT **2 a :** to put forth or put out (as strength, power, or effort) **:** bring (as a force) into play **:** set in operation **:** make effective ⟨he had to ~ all his strength to move the stone⟩ **b :** to put (oneself) into action or to tiring effort ⟨if people are to ~ themselves they must be convinced —A.J.P.Taylor⟩ **3** *obs* **:** SHOW, REVEAL **4 :** to bring (as a force, an influence) to bear esp. with sustained effort or lasting effect ⟨never would have entered the political arena at all if his father had not ~*ed* relentless pressure —Bennett Cerf⟩ ⟨forms which ~*ed* a profound influence on late buildings —*Amer. Guide Series: N.Y. City*⟩ ⟨his long poetic career . . . continues to ~ a special fascination —Delmore Schwartz⟩ **5 :** EXERCISE, WIELD ⟨a chance to ~ leadership in a constructive way —*Education Digest*⟩ ⟨disguised aristocracies, where courtiers or even courtesans frequently ~ the real power —M.R.Cohen⟩

ex·er·tion \|shən\ *n* -S **:** the act of exerting **:** active exercise of any power or faculty ⟨a diversion requiring little mental ~⟩ **:** EFFORT; *esp* **:** a laborious or perceptible effort ⟨panting from the ~ of climbing the stairs⟩ **syn** see EFFORT

ex·ert·ive \|d·iv\ *adj* **:** having power or a tendency to exert

exes *pl of* EX

ex·e·unt \'eksē(,)ənt, -se,ünt\ [L, they go out, 3d pers. pl. pres. indic. of *exire* to go out — more at EXEAT] **:** go out **:** go off the stage — used as a stage direction to specify that all or certain named characters leave the stage; compare MANENT

exeunt om·nes \-(,)ənt'äm,nēz, -,ünt·'ȯm,nās\ [NL, they all go out] **:** all go out **:** all go off the stage — a stage direction to specify that all the characters leave the stage

ex fa·cie \ek'sfākē,ā\ *adv* (*or adj*) [NL, lit., from the face] **:** in the light of what is apparent — used in ref. to a legal instrument ⟨the deed appears *ex facie* to be in order⟩

ex·filtration \¦eks+\ *n* [¹*ex-* + *filtration*] **:** a filtering out **:** a gradual escape (as through a membrane or a wall) **:** LEAK

¹ex·flagellant \(¦)eks+\ *adj* [*exflagell*ate + *-ant*, adj. suffix] **:** relating to or marked by exflagellation

²exflagellant \"\ *n* [*exflagell*ate + *-ant*, n. suffix] **:** one that exflagellates

ex·flagellate \(')eks+\ *vi* [back-formation fr. *exflagellation*] **1** *biol* **:** to cast off cilia or flagella **2** *of sporozoans* **:** to form microgametes by extrusion of nuclear material into peripheral processes of gametocyte cytoplasm that resemble flagella

ex·flagellation \(¦)eks+\ *n* [¹*ex-* + *flagellum* + *-ation*] **:** the action or process of exflagellating

ex·fo·li·ate \ek'sfōlē,āt\ *vb* [LL *exfoliatus*, past part. of *exfoliare* to strip of leaves, fr. L *ex-* ¹ex- + *-foliare* (fr. *folium* leaf) — more at BLADE] *vt* **1 :** to cast or throw off from the surface in scales, laminae, or splinters **2 :** to remove or take off the surface of in scales or laminae **3 :** to open, spread, or extend by or as if by opening out leaves ⟨in twenty-three chapters he ~*s* his program of moral transformation —O.L. Reiser⟩ ~ *vi* **1 :** to split into or give off scales, laminae, or body cells esp. from the surface **2 :** to come off in a thin piece **:** scale or flake off **3 :** to grow or develop by or as if by producing or unfolding leaves ⟨criticism has *exfoliated* until the work of art is sometimes smothered beneath it —Malcolm Cowley⟩

ex·fo·li·a·tion \(,)=,=='āshən\ *n* [prob. fr. (assumed) ML *exfoliation-*, *exfoliatio*, fr. LL *exfoliatus* (past part. of *exfoliare* to strip of leaves) + L *-ion-*, *-io* -ion] **:** the action or process of unfolding or exfoliating: as **a :** the peeling of the horny layer of the skin (as in some skin diseases) **b :** the shedding of surface components (as cells from internal body surfaces when diseased) **c :** the shedding of a superficial layer of bone (as a sequestrum) or of a tooth or part of a tooth **d :** the phase of weathering that involves the breaking loose of thin concentric shells, slabs, spalls, or flakes from rock surfaces

exfoliation dome *n* **:** a large dome-shaped rock mass (as of granite) produced by exfoliation

ex·fo·li·a·tive \(')ek¦sfōlē,ād·iv, -lēəd-\ *adj* [F *exfoliatif*, fr. MF, fr. LL *exfoliatus* (past part. of *exfoliare* to strip of leaves) + MF *-if* -ive] **:** causing or characterized by exfoliation

exfoliative cytology *n* **:** the study of cells shed from body surfaces esp. for determining the presence or absence of a cancerous condition

ex gr *abbr* [L *exempli gratia*] for example

ex gra·tia \eks'grād·ē,ä, -grāsh(ē)ə\ *adj* (*or adv*) [NL, by favor] **:** as a favor **:** not compelled by legal right ⟨*ex gratia* pension payments⟩

¹ex·hal·ant *or* **ex·hal·ent** \(')eks¦hālənt\ *adj* [L *exhalant-*, *exhalans*, pres. part. of *exhalare*] **:** having the function of exhaling or of being exhaled **:** EMISSIVE ⟨the ~ siphon of a clam⟩

²exhalant *or* **exhalent** \"\ *n* -S **:** an exhaling duct

exhalate *vt* -ED/-ING/-S [L *exhalatus*, past part. of *exhalare*] *obs* **:** EXHALE

ex·ha·la·tion \,eks(h)ə'lāshən\ *n* -S [ME *exalacioun*, fr. MF & L; MF *exalation*, fr. L *exhalation-*, *exhalatio*, fr. *exhalatus* (past part. of *exhalare* to exhale) + *-ion-*, *-io* -ion] **1 :** an exhaling or sending forth (as in steam or vapor) **:** EVAPORATION, EXPIRATION ⟨noisy ~*s* of a locomotive⟩; *specif* **:** the action of forcing air out of the lungs by means of a complex of essentially reflex actions that involve changes in the diaphragm and in muscles of the abdomen and thorax which cause contraction of the chest cavity and lungs resulting in production of relative positive pressure within the lung so that air flows out until the pressure is restored to equality with that of the atmosphere **2 :** something that is exhaled or given off or that rises in the form of gas, fumes, or steam **:** EFFLUVIUM, EMANATION ⟨a foul ~ from the marsh⟩

¹ex·hale \eks'hāl, *chiefly before pause or consonant* -ə̄l\ *vb* -ED/-ING/-S [ME *exalen*, fr. L *exhalare*, fr. *ex-* ¹ex- + *halare* to breathe; akin to L *anima* breath — more at ANIMATE] *vt* **1 :** to breathe out **:** let or force out of the lungs ⟨*exhaled* carbon dioxide) ⟨*exhaled* a sigh⟩ **2 :** to give off or give forth (gas or odor) **:** EMIT ⟨the turned earth *exhaled* in the warm sun a delicate fragrance —Mary Austin⟩ **3** *archaic* **:** to draw out (moisture) **:** EVAPORATE **4 :** to discharge through a membranous surface — used in old medical terminology ~ *vi* **1 :** to rise or be given off as vapor ⟨a bad smell *exhaling* from the kitchen —Glenway Wescott⟩ **:** EMANATE; *also* **:** to vanish by or as if by evaporation ⟨dried his hands . . . instead of suffering the moisture to ~ —Sir Walter Scott⟩ **2 :** to breathe out **:** let or force the breath out — opposed to *inhale* **3 :** to percolate through a membrane **:** OOZE — used in old medical terminology **syn** see EMIT

²exhale *vt* [¹*ex-* + *hale* (to draw)] *obs* **:** to draw or force out ⟨and what those sorrows could not thence ~, thy beauty hath, and made them blind with weeping —Shak.⟩

ex·hale·ment \eks'hā(ə)lmənt\ *n* -S [¹*exhale* + *-ment*] *archaic* **:** EXHALATION

¹ex·haust \ig'zȯst, eg-\ *vb* -ED/-ING/-S [L *exhaustus*, past part. of *exhaurire*, fr. *ex-* ¹ex- + *haurire* to draw; akin to MHG *æsen* to empty, ON *ausa* to besprinkle, Gk *exauein* to take out] *vt* **1** *obs* **:** to draw forth (as tears) **2** *obs* **:** to draw in **:** drink up **3 a :** to draw off or let out wholly **:** drain off completely ⟨~ the water of a well⟩ ⟨~ the air from a bell jar⟩ **b :** to empty by drawing off or draining ⟨~ a wine cask⟩ ⟨~ a bank account⟩; *specif* **:** to create a vacuum in (as the receiver of an air pump) **:** EVACUATE 4 **4 a :** to use up the whole supply or store of **:** expend or consume entirely ⟨~ a coal vein⟩ ⟨till her lover had ~*ed* his eloquence —T.L.Peacock⟩ **b :** to deprive wholly of strength, patience, or resources **:** tire out **:** wear out **:** WEARY ⟨~*ed* from a day's shopping⟩ ⟨~*ed* himself working in the heat⟩ **c :** to destroy the fertility of ⟨steady cropping ~*ed* the soil⟩ **5 a :** to develop (a subject) completely **:** discuss thoroughly **b :** to make use of or try out or otherwise account for the whole number of ⟨~*ed* the possibilities⟩ **c :** to take complete advantage of (legal remedies) ⟨all administrative remedies must be ~*ed* before application to the courts can be made⟩ **6 :** to deprive completely of removable ingredients **:** deprive of strength or virtue ⟨~ a photographic developer⟩: as **a :** to extract completely with a solvent ⟨~ a drug successively with water, alcohol, and ether⟩ **b :** to free as far as possible from sugar or other ingredient by crystallization ⟨~ molasses⟩ **c :** to transfer dye from (a dyebath); *also* **:** to transfer (a dye) completely from a dyebath onto a fabric ~ *vi* **1 :** DISCHARGE, EMPTY ⟨the engine ~*s* through a muffler⟩ **2 :** to flow or pass out ⟨the steam ~*s* into the condenser⟩ **3 :** to pass from a dyebath onto a fabric ⟨substantive dyes ~ reasonably well onto cellulose⟩ **syn** see DEPLETE, TIRE

²exhaust \"\ *n* -S **1 a :** the escape or removal of working substance (as gas or vapor) from an engine cylinder after it has done its work on the piston **b :** the gas or vapor thus escaping **c :** the conduit including muffler and stack through which the gases escape **d :** an arrangement (as of fans) for withdrawing undesirable fumes, dusts, or odors from an enclosure (as a factory room or a kitchen) **2 :** the production of a partial vacuum (as by an air pump) **:** EXHAUSTION

exhaust collector ring *n* **:** the exhaust manifold of a radial engine

exhaust cone *n* **:** the tapered exhaust pipe of a jet engine

exhaust draft *n* **:** a draft produced by suction on the outlet side (as of a ventilation system) rather than by pressure on the intake side

ex·haust·er \-tə(r)\ *n* -S **1 :** a fan, pump, or other device for exhausting gases **2 :** one who operates a retort for the final cooking of canned foods **3 :** an operator of an exhaust machine for removing air, gas, and impurities from radio tubes

exhaust-gas analyzer *n* **:** a device for indicating the fuel-air ratio of the fuel mixture of an engine (as of an airplane) that consists of an element sensitive to carbon dioxide placed in the exhaust manifold — called also *fuel-mixture indicator, smoke feeler*

exhaust head *n* **:** a conical casing containing baffle plates that is attached to the end of an exhaust pipe for separating out the entrained oil and water and reducing the noise

ex·haust·ibil·i·ty \ig,zȯstə'biləd·ē, (,)eg-, -lətē, -i\ *n* -ES **:** the quality or state of being exhaustible

ex·haust·ible \ˈ=ˈ=təbəl\ *adj* **:** capable of being exhausted

exhausting *adj* [fr. pres. part. of ¹*exhaust*] **:** producing exhaustion ⟨~ labors⟩ — **ex·haust·ing·ly** *adv*

ex·haus·tion \ig'zȯschən, eg-\ *n* -S [LL *exhaustion-, exhaustio*, fr. L *exhaustus* (past part. of *exhaurire* to exhaust) + *-ion-, -io* -ion — more at EXHAUST] **1 :** the act or process of exhausting or the state of being exhausted ⟨he felt ready to drop from ~⟩ **2 :** neurosis following overstrain or overexertion ⟨combat ~⟩

ex·haus·tive \-stiv, -tēv *also* -təv\ *adj* **:** serving or tending to exhaust **:** testing all possibilities or considering all the elements **:** THOROUGH ⟨an ~ investigation⟩ ⟨~ list⟩ **:** COMPLETE ⟨~ methylation⟩ — **ex·haus·tive·ly** \-təvlē, -li\ *adv* — **ex·haus·tive·ness** \-tivnəs, -tēv- *also* -təv-\ *n* -ES

ex·haust·less \-tləs\ *adj* **:** not to be exhausted **:** INEXHAUSTIBLE ⟨~ wealth⟩ — **ex·haust·less·ly** *adv* — **ex·haust·less·ness** *n* -ES

exhaust manifold *n* **:** the manifold that receives the exhaust gases from each of several engine cylinders

exhaust nozzle *n* **:** the terminal portion of the tail pipe of a jet engine

exhausts *pres 3d sing of* EXHAUST, *pl of* EXHAUST

exhaust stroke *n* **:** the movement of an engine piston (as of a 4-stroke-cycle engine) that forces the used gas or vapor out through the exhaust ports

exhaust-suction stroke *n* **:** a piston stroke (as of a 2-cycle engine) that simultaneously expels used gases and draws in fresh fuel mixture

exhbn *abbr* exhibition

exhedra *var of* EXEDRA

ex·her·e·da·tion \(,)eks,herə'dāshən\ *n* -S [ME *exheredacioun*, fr. L *exheredation-, exheredatio*, fr. *exheredatus* (past part. of *exheredare*) + *-ion-, -io* -ion] **:** DISINHERITANCE

ex·her·i·date *also* **ex·her·e·date** \ˈ=ˈ==,dāt\ *vt* -ED/-ING/-S [L *exheredatus*, past part. of *exheredare*, fr. *exhered-, exheres* disinherited person, fr. *ex-* ¹ex- + *hered-, heres* heir — more at HEIR] **:** DISINHERIT

¹ex·hib·it \ig'zibət, eg-, *usu* -bəd·+V\ *vb* -ED/-ING/-S [ME *exhibiten*, fr. L *exhibitus*, past part. of *exhibēre* to present, show, fr. *ex-* ¹ex- + *-hibēre* (fr. *habēre* to have, hold) — more at HABIT] *vt* **1 :** to present to view **:** SHOW, DISPLAY: as **a :** to show (as a feeling) or display (as a quality) outwardly esp. by visible signs or actions ⟨~*ed* no fear⟩ ⟨~*ed* a mastery of the keyboard⟩ **b :** to have as a readily discernible quality or feature ⟨buildings ~*ing* the stark functionalism of a toy village —J.P.Marquand⟩ ⟨in all cultures we know, men ~ an aesthetic sense —H.J.Muller⟩ **c :** to represent or make clear by a drawing, plan, or other visual method esp. so as to show detail or spatial relations **:** PICTURE ⟨orbit is to be diagrammatically ~*ed* by a series of dots —A.N.Whitehead⟩ **d :** to show publicly **:** put on display in order to attract notice to what is interesting or instructive or for purposes of competition or demonstration ⟨~ goods in a store⟩ ⟨~ a painting⟩ **:** show off ⟨proudly ~*ed* a fine buck he had shot⟩ **2 :** to submit (as a document) to a court or officer in course of proceedings; *also* **:** to present or offer officially or in legal form **:** BRING ⟨~ a charge⟩ **:** file of record **3 a** *obs* **:** to offer (as a sacrifice) or present (as a grant) **b :** to administer as a remedy **c** *obs* **:** ADMINISTER ⟨~ an oath⟩ **4 :** to make clear to the understanding **:** EXPLAIN ⟨article . . . in which he ~*s* this distrust as narrow-minded in its origin —B.N.Cardozo⟩ ~ *vi* **:** to display something for public inspection **:** put on an exhibition ⟨he first ~*ed* in the salon at the age of 14 —*Amer. Guide Series: Conn.*⟩ **syn** see SHOW

²exhibit \"\ *n* -S **1 :** an act or instance of exhibiting **:** DISPLAY, EXHIBITION ⟨a new ~ in the library⟩ ⟨a school ~⟩ **2 :** something exhibited; *specif* **:** an article or a collection of articles displayed in an exhibition **3 :** a document or material object produced and identified in court or before an examiner for use as evidence; *also* **:** a paper or document referred to by way of explanation or evidence (as in a pleading or petition) ⟨introduced the weapons into evidence as ~*s* A and B⟩ **4 exhibits** *pl, Brit* **:** the documents that a clergyman may be required to produce at the first visitation after his admission; *also* **:** the fees then payable

ex·hib·it·able \-bəd·əbəl, -bətə-\ *adj* **:** capable of being exhibited **:** suitable for exhibition

ex·hib·i·tant \-əd·ənt, -ətənt *also* -itᵊnt\ *n* -S **:** EXHIBITOR

ex·hi·bi·tion \,eksə'bishən *sometimes* ,egzə-\ *n* -S [ME *exhibicioun*, fr. MF *exibition, exhibition*, fr. L *exhibition-, exhibitio* presentation, fr. *exhibitus* (past part. of *exhibēre* to present, show) + *-ion-, -io* -ion — more at EXHIBIT] **1 :** an act or instance of showing, evincing, or showing off ⟨an ~ of bad manners⟩ ⟨a notable ~ of courage⟩ ⟨out of training as he was, he was afraid of making an ~ of himself⟩ **2 a** *obs* **:** allowance esp. for food and drink **:** SUSTENANCE, MAINTENANCE **b** *obs* **:** SALARY, PENSION **c** *obs* **:** PRESENT **d :** a grant formerly given by a private benefactor and now drawn from the funds of the institution to help maintain a student at a school, college, or university in the British Commonwealth **3 :** a public show or showing: as **a :** a display esp. of works of art or objects of manufacture — often used with *on* ⟨the coin collection will be on ~ next week⟩; *specif* **:** a display or show where the display itself is the chief object and from which the exhibitor derives or expects to derive a profit ⟨an industrial ~⟩ **b** (1) **:** a public examination of school or college students (2) **:** a public display of the attainments of the pupils of a school **:** EXERCISE **c :** a public display of athletic or other skill often in the form of a contest or game but usu. without importance with respect to winning or losing ⟨a fencing ~⟩ ⟨an ~ baseball game⟩ ⟨an ~ billiards match⟩ **4 :** the act of administering a remedy

ex·hi·bi·tion·er \-sh(ə)nə(r)\ *n* -S **1** *Brit* **:** one who holds an exhibition (sense 2d) **2 :** EXHIBITOR

exhibition game fowl *n* **:** a game fowl of the Modern Game class bred for show and selected esp. for perfection of form, carriage, and feathering — compare PIT GAME FOWL

ex·hi·bi·tion·ism \-shə,nizəm\ *n* -S [ISV *exhibition* + *-ism*] **1 a :** a perversion marked by a tendency to indecent exposure of the person so as to excite or gratify oneself sexually by such exposure **b :** such exposure or an act of such exposure **2 :** the act or practice of behaving so as to attract attention to oneself **:** extravagant and willfully conspicuous behavior

¹ex·hi·bi·tion·ist \-sh(ə)nəst\ *n* -S [ISV *exhibition* + *-ist*] **:** one who engages in or is addicted to exhibitionism

²exhibitionist \ˈ=ˈ=(ə)=\ *or* **ex·hi·bi·tion·is·tic** \ˈ== ˈbishəˈnistik\ *adj* **:** of, relating to, or given to exhibitionism

ex·hib·i·tive \ig'zibəd·iv, eg-, -ət\ *adj* [NL *exhibitivus*, fr. L *exhibitus* (past part. of *exhibēre*) + *-ivus* -ive] **:** having the function of exhibiting — **ex·hib·i·tiv·ely** \əvlē, -li\ *adv*

ex·hib·i·tor *also* **ex·hib·it·er** \ə(r)\ *n* -S **1 :** one that exhibits (as in an exhibition) **2 :** one who shows motion pictures to the public

ex·hib·i·to·ry \-bə,tōrē, -tȯr-, -ri\ *adj* **:** relating to or intended for exhibition

exhibits *pres 3d sing of* EXHIBIT, *pl of* EXHIBIT

ex·hil·a·rant \ig'zilərənt, eg-\ *adj* [L *exhilarant-, exhilarans*, pres. part. of *exhilarare*] **:** EXHILARATING

ex·hil·a·rate \-ə,rāt, *usu* -ād·+V\ *vt* -ED/-ING/-S [L *exhilaratus*, past part. of *exhilarare*, fr. *ex-* ¹ex- + *hilarare* to cheer, gladden, fr. *hilarus* cheerful — more at HILARITY] **1 :** to make cheerful **:** ENLIVEN, CHEER, GLADDEN ⟨the sun and wind . . . on his back . . . *exhilarated* him —Grace Campbell⟩ **2 :** REFRESH, INVIGORATE, STIMULATE ⟨watching the flood, awed yet somehow *exhilarated* by the terrible, incalculable power of rushing water —Louis Bromfield⟩ **syn** see PLEASE

exhilarating *adj* [fr. pres. part. of *exhilarate*] **:** that exhilarates **:** CHEERING, GLADDENING, INVIGORATING, INTOXICATING ⟨the ~ effect of mountain air⟩ ⟨found something ~ and oddly exciting in all this unusual bright costume —H.G.Wells⟩ — **ex·hil·a·rat·ing·ly** *adv*

ex·hil·a·ra·tion \ˈ=,==ˈrāshən\ *n* -S [LL *exhilaration-, exhilaratio*, fr. L *exhilaratus* (past part. of *exhilarare*) + *-ion-, -io* -ion] **1 :** the action of exhilarating **2 :** the feeling or the state of being exhilarated

ex·hil·a·ra·tive \ˈ=ˈ==,rād·|iv, -,rə|, |t|, |ēv *also* |əv\ *adj* **:** tending to exhilarate ⟨nature was ~ and restorative —R.L. Cook⟩

ex·hil·a·ra·tor \-ād·ə(r), -ātə-\ *n* -S **:** one that exhilarates

¹ex·hort \ig'z|ȯ(ə)r|t, eg'z|, |ȯ(ə)| *also* ik's| *or* iks'h| *or* ek's| *or* eks'h|, *usu* |d·+V\ *vb* -ED/-ING/-S [ME *exhorten*, fr. MF *exhorter*, fr. L *exhortari*, fr. *ex-* ¹ex- + *hortari* to incite, urge — more at YEARN] *vt* **:** to incite by argument or advice **:** urge strongly **:** ADVISE, WARN ⟨we have been ~*ed* to drive all negative fears out of our minds —W.J.Reilly⟩ ~ *vi* **:** to give warnings or advice **:** make urgent appeal **:** PREACH 2 ⟨ministers and converted Christians rushed about the camp praying and ~*ing* —J.C.Brauer⟩ **syn** see URGE

²exhort *n* -S *obs* **:** EXHORTATION

ex·hor·ta·tion \,ek,sȯ(r)'tāshən, ,eg,zȯ(r)-, ,eksə(r)-, ,eks|-,hȯ(r)-\ *n* -S [ME *exhortacioun*, fr. MF & L; MF *exhortation*, fr. L *exhortation-, exhortatio*, fr. *exhortatus* (past part. of *exhortari*) + *-ion-, -io* -ion] **:** an act or instance of exhorting **:** SERMON ⟨~*s* to young men to continue their education⟩ **2 :** language intended to incite and encourage **:** ADVICE, COUNSEL; *specif* **:** a liturgical formulary of this nature

ex·hor·tative *pronunc at* ¹EXHORT + əd·|iv *or* ət|\ *adj* [ME, fr. L *exhortativus*, fr. *exhortatus* (past part. of *exhortari*) + *-ivus* -ive] **:** serving to exhort **:** HORTATIVE — **ex·hort·ative·ly** \|əvlē, -li\ *adv*

ex·hor·ta·to·ry \|ə,tōrē, -tȯr-, -ri\ *adj* [ME, fr. LL *exhortatorius*, fr. L *exhortatus* + *-orius* -ory] **:** HORTATORY

ex·hort·er \|ə(r)\ *n* -S **:** one that exhorts **:** PREACHER; *specif* **:** a layman authorized to exhort under ministerial direction

ex·hort·ing·ly *adv* [*exhorting* (pres. part. of ¹*exhort*) + *-ly*] **:** in the manner of one exhorting ⟨a speech marked by ~ passionate appeals for action⟩

ex·hu·mate \eks'(h)yü,māt, eg'zü-, egz'yü-\ *vt* -ED/-ING/-S [ML *exhumatus*, past part. of *exhumare*] **:** EXHUME

ex·hu·ma·tion \,eks(,)(h)yü'māshən, ,eg(,)zü-, ,egz(,)yü-\ *n* -S [F, fr. *exhumer* + *-ation*] **:** the act or process of exhuming, disinterring, or digging up

ex·hume \ig'züm, igz'yüm, iks'(h)yüm, eg-,ek-\ *vt* -ED/-ING/-S [F or ML; F *exhumer*, fr. ML *exhumare*, fr. L *ex-* ¹ex- + *humus* earth — more at HUMBLE] **1 :** to dig out of the ground **:** to take out of a place of burial **:** DISINTER ⟨the body was *exhumed* and burned⟩ **2 :** to bring back from neglect or obscurity **:** REVIVE ⟨~ a minor poet⟩ ⟨~ an old play⟩ **3 :** to uncover or expose by erosion ⟨*exhumed* landscapes⟩ **syn** see DIG

ex·hum·er \-mə(r)\ *n* -S **:** one that exhumes

ex hy·po·the·si \,eks,hī'päthə,sī\ *adv* [NL, from the hypothesis] **:** by hypothesis **:** HYPOTHETICALLY, THEORETICALLY, SUPPOSEDLY

ex·i·gence \'eksəjən(t)s *also* 'egzə-\ *n* -S [MF *exigence*, fr. ML *exigentia*] **:** EXIGENCY

ex·i·gen·cy \-nsē, -si; ig'zij-,eg'zij-\ *n* -ES [ML *exigentia*, fr. LL, demand, fr. L *exigent-, exigens* + *-ia* -y] **1 :** the quality or state of being exigent **:** PRESSURE, URGENCY ⟨the president is the sole judge of the ~ demanding the use of federal troops —Herman Beukema⟩ **2 :** such need or necessity as belongs to the occasion **:** DEMANDS, REQUIREMENTS — usu. used in pl. ⟨the *exigencies* of French politeness are not necessarily at variance with truthfulness —Norman Douglas⟩ ⟨regret that the *exigencies* of party politics should deprive our government of so much talent —Frank Altschul⟩ **syn** see JUNCTURE

¹ex·i·gent \'eksəjənt *also* 'egzə-\ *n* -S [ME *exigent, exigend*, fr. AF *exigende*, fr. ML *exigenda*, fr. L, fem. sing. or neut. pl. of *exigendus*, gerundive of *exigere* to drive out, demand] *English law* **:** a writ formerly issued summoning a person on pain of outlawry

²exigent *n* -S [ME, prob. fr. L *exigent-, exigens*] *obs* **:** time of crisis or need **:** EXIGENCY, EXTREMITY

³ex·i·gent \'eksəjənt *also* 'egzə-\ *also* **ex·i·geant** \āgzēzhäⁿ\ *adj* [*exigent* fr. L *exigent-, exigens*, pres. part. of *exigere* to drive out, demand; *exigeant* fr. F, pres. part. of *exiger* to demand, fr. L *exigere* — more at EXACT] **1 :** exacting or requiring immediate aid or action **:** PRESSING, CRITICAL ⟨regarded literary questions as ~ and momentous —H.L. Mencken⟩ **2 :** requiring or calling for much **:** hard to satisfy **:** DEMANDING, EXACTING ⟨they have so much to guard in the way of social status that they have become very ~ in their ideas of what they are willing to do⟩ **syn** see PRESSING

ex·i·gent·ly *adv* **:** in an exigent manner

ex·i·gi·ble \'eksəjəbəl, 'egzə-\ *adj* [F, fr. *exiger* to demand + *-ible*] **:** liable to be exacted **:** REQUIRABLE, DEMANDABLE

ex·i·gi fa·ci·as \ˌeksəˌgē'fākē,äs\ *n* [ML, you should cause to be demanded] **:** ¹EXIGENT

ex·i·gu·i·ty \,eksə'gyüəd·ē, ,egzə-\ *n* -ES [L *exiguitat-, exiguitas*, fr. *exiguus* + *-itat-, -itas* -ity] **:** exiguous state or character **:** SCANTINESS, SMALLNESS ⟨an ~ of cloth that would only allow of miniature capes —George Eliot⟩

ex·ig·u·ous \(')eg'zigyəwəs, (')ek'si-\ *adj* [L *exiguus*, fr. *exigere* to drive out, demand, weigh, measure] **:** scanty in amount **:** MEAGER, NARROW ⟨~ budget⟩ **syn** see MEAGER

ex·ig·u·ous·ly *adv* **:** in an exiguous manner **:** MEAGERLY

ex·ig·u·ous·ness *n* -ES **:** EXIGUITY

ex·i·larch \'egzə,lärk, 'eksə-, -,zī-, -,sī-,\ *n* -S [¹*exile* + *-arch*; trans. of Aram *rēsh gālūtā*] **:** one of a line of Jewish civil and judicial rulers of the exiles in Babylon from about the third to the tenth centuries A.D. to whom Jews in all countries paid tribute

ex·i·larch·ate \ˈ=(,)=,lärkət, -,kāt, ,=(,)='=(,)=\ *n* -S **1 :** the office or term of office of an exilarch **2 :** the territory or people ruled by an exilarch

¹ex·ile \'eg,zīl, 'ek,sīl, *chiefly archaic* =ˈ= *or* ig'z- *or* ik's-\ *n* -S [ME *exil*, fr. MF *exil, essil*, fr. L *exilium*, fr. *ex-* ¹ex- + *-ilium* (prob. akin to Gk *alasthai* to wander) — more at AMBLE] **1 a :** forced removal from one's native country **:** expulsion from home **:** BANISHMENT **b :** voluntary absence from one's country **2 a :** a person expelled from his country by authority **b :** one who separates himself from his home **3** *obs* **:** DEVASTATION, RUIN, WASTE

²exile \"\ *vt* -ED/-ING/-S [ME *exilen*, fr. MF *exilier, essilier*, fr. LL *exiliare* to exile, fr. L *exilium*] **1 :** to banish or expel from one's own country or home **:** drive away ⟨calling home our *exiled* friends abroad —Shak.⟩ **2** *obs* **:** DEVASTATE, RUIN **syn** see BANISH

³exile \ˈ=,=, =ˈ=\ *adj* [ME, fr. L *exilis*, prob. fr. *exigere* to drive out, demand, weigh, measure] *archaic* **:** SLENDER, THIN; *also* **:** SCANTY, POOR

ex·il·er \'eg,zīlə(r), 'ek,sī-\ *n* -S [ME *exilere*, fr. *exilen* + *-er, -ere* -er] **:** one that exiles

ex·il·i·an \eg'zilēən *also* ek'si-\ *adj* **:** EXILIC

ex·il·ic \-lik\ *adj* **:** relating or belonging to exile (as that of the Jews in Babylon) ⟨~ books of the Old Testament⟩

exility *n* -ES [ME *exilite*, fr. L *exilitat-, exilitas*, fr. *exilis* + *-itat-, -itas* -ity] **1** *obs* **:** SMALLNESS, MEAGERNESS, SLENDERNESS, FINENESS, THINNESS **2** *obs* **:** TENUITY, SUBTLETY

eximious *adj* [L *eximius*, fr. *eximere* to take out, remove, free — more at EXEMPT] *obs* **:** SELECT, CHOICE, EXCELLENT — **eximiously** *adv, obs*

ex·in·a·ni·tion \(,)eg,zinə'nishən\ *n* -S [L *exinanition-, exinanitio*, fr. *exinanitus* (past part. of *exinanire* to empty, exhaust, fr. *ex-* ¹ex- + *inanire* to empty, fr. *inanis* empty) + *-ion-, -io* -ion] **1** *archaic* **:** an emptying or enfeebling **:** EXHAUSTION **2 :** HUMILIATION, ABASEMENT

ex·ine \'ek,sēn, |īn\ *also* **ex·tine** \'ek,st|\ *n* -S [*exine* prob. fr. G, fr. L *ex* out of, out; *extine* prob. modif. of G *exine* — more at EX-] **:** the outer of the two layers forming the wall of certain spores (as pollen grains) — called also *exosporium;* compare INTINE, PERINIUM

ex·i·nite \'eksə,nīt\ *n* -S [*exine* + *-ite*] **:** organic material that occurs in coal and that is composed essentially of spores, spore debris, and cuticular matter

ex·ist \ig'zist, eg-\ *vi* -ED/-ING/-S [L *existere, exsistere* to step forth, emerge, come into being, exist, fr. *ex-* ¹ex- + *sistere* to cause to stand; akin to L *stare* to stand — more at STAND] **1 :** to have actual or real being whether material or spiritual **:** have being in space and time ⟨by whom we ~ and cease to be —Shak.⟩ **2 :** to have being in any specified condition or place or with respect to any understood limitation ⟨salt ~*s* in solution in the sea⟩ ⟨queer notions ~ in his mind⟩ **3 :** to continue to be **:** maintain being ⟨some industrial activity does ~ in the urban fringe —N.R.Heiden **4 :** to have life or the functions of vitality **:** LIVE ⟨men cannot ~ without oxygen⟩ **5** [trans. of Dan *eksistere* & G *existieren*] *in existentialism* **:** to have contingent but free and responsible being; *also* **:** to live as one that has such being

ex·is·tence \-tən(t)s\ *n* -S [ME, fr. MF, fr. LL *existentia, exsistentia* state or fact of having being, fr. L *existent-, exsistent-, existens, exsistens* + *-ia* -y] **1** *obs* **:** reality or actuality as opposed to appearance **2 a :** the state or fact of having being esp. as considered independently of human consciousness and as contrasted with nonexistence ⟨the ~ of other worlds⟩ **b :** the manner of being that is common to every mode of being **:** the state common to physical objects, living beings, objects of thought, and anything else ⟨both of noumena and of phenomena we may affirm simple ~ —J.S. Mill⟩ **3 a :** being with reference to some limiting condition or under a particular aspect (as a mode of being, determined being, or a manner of existing) ⟨the ~ of a fictive world⟩ **b :** being as given in experience or in the act of experiencing: (1) *in scholasticism* **:** being in its actuality as contrasted with its essence (2) [trans. of Dan *eksistens* & G *existenz*] *in existentialism* **:** the condition of man in his factuality characterized by a passionate self-consciousness and sense of responsibility in the face of contingency and freedom **4 :** sentient or living being **:** LIFE ⟨God, Nature, Self, are the fundamental facts of ~ —Henry Sidgwick⟩ **5 :** continued or repeated manifestation **:** actual or present occurrence ⟨~ of a state of war⟩ **6 :** something that exists: as **a :** the totality of being **b :** a particular being, individual, or entity **:** EXISTENT ⟨concepts . . . are tyrants rather than servants when treated as real ~*s* —B.N.Cardozo⟩

existency *n* -ES [LL *existentia, exsistentia*] *obs* **:** EXISTENCE

¹ex·is·tent \-nt\ *adj* [L *existent-, exsistent-, existens, exsistens*, pres. part. of *existere, exsistere*] **1 :** having existence, being, or actuality **:** EXISTING ⟨chimeras are classified as subsistent but not ~ —R.J.Butler⟩ **2 :** existing now or at the present time **:** CONTEMPORARY, EXTANT ⟨keep abreast with things military as ~ in other nations of the world —H.H.Arnold & I.C.Eaker⟩

²existent \"\ *n* -S **1 :** a particular existing thing, event, person, or entity **2 :** something that exists ⟨to debate whether the ~ is merely appearance⟩ **3** *in existentialism* **:** one who has existence aware of oneself as an ~⟩

ex·is·ten·tial \ˌeg(,)zi'stenchəl, -gzə¦-, ¦ek(,)si¦-, -ksə¦-\ *adj* [LL *existentialis, exsistentialis*, fr. *existentia, exsistentia* + L *-alis* -al] **1 :** of, relating to, or dealing with existence ⟨the ~ 'is' which in our logic connects the two parts of a proposition —E.R.Hughes⟩ **2** *logic* **a :** assertive either explicitly or by implication of existence or actuality as opposed to mere possibility, conceivability, or ideality or to mere explication of a meaning ⟨definitions are not ~ propositions⟩ **b :** making an assertion about the extension as opposed to the intension of the subject term **3 a :** grounded in existence **:** having being in time and space ⟨formal logicians . . . are not concerned with ~ matters which are precisely what artists are concerned with —John Dewey⟩ **b :** based on the experience of existence **:** empirical as contrasted with theoretical or abstract ⟨the problem of aesthetic objectivity or, more precisely, the ~ status of aesthetic values —Hunter Mead⟩ **4** [trans. of Dan *eksistentiel* & G *existential*] **:** concerned with or involving human existence or its nature **:** EXISTENTIALIST — **ex·is·ten·tial·ly** \-əlē, -li\ *adv*

ex·is·ten·tial·ism \ˌ=(,)=ˈ=chə,lizəm\ *n* -S **:** an introspective humanism or theory of man that holds that human existence is not exhaustively describable or understandable in either scientific or idealistic terms and relies upon a phenomenological approach that emphasizes the analysis of critical borderline situations in man's life and esp. of such intensely subjective phenomena as anxiety, suffering, and feelings of guilt in order to show the need for making decisive choices through a utilization of man's freedom in an uncertain, contingent, and apparently purposeless world: **a :** a theory stating that man's individual existence precedes his essence and stressing his responsibility for fashioning his self **b :** CHRISTIAN EXISTENTIALISM

¹ex·is·ten·tial·ist \-,ləst\ *n* -S **1 :** a proponent or adherent of philosophical existentialism **2 :** a writer who develops or emphasizes in literary form the principles of existentialism

²existentialist \ˈ=(,)=ˈ===\ *adj* **1 :** dealing with, subscribing to, or based on existential philosophy ⟨~ thought⟩ ⟨~ terminology⟩ ⟨~ writers⟩ **2 :** of, relating to, or involving existentialism or existentialists **:** EXISTENTIAL ⟨an ~ question⟩

⟨the ~ character of his ideas⟩ ⟨an ~ group⟩ — **ex·is·ten·tial·is·tic** \¦=(,)=¦=chə¦listik\ *adj* — **ex·is·ten·tial·is·ti·cal·ly** \-tək(ə)lē\ *adv*

ex·is·ten·tial·ize \,=(,)=ˈ=chə,līz\ *vt* -ED/-ING/-S : to cause to become existential or transform into existential terms

existential operator *or* **existential quantifier** *n, logic* : a quantifier that asserts at least one value of a variable in a formula

existential philosophy *n* : EXISTENTIALISM

existential psychology *n* : a psychology that emphasizes sensory experience as its object of study — compare CONTENT PSYCHOLOGY, STRUCTURALISM

ex·is·tenz \eksiˈsten(t)s\ *n* -ES [G, fr. LL *existentia, exsistentia* state or fact of having being — more at EXISTENCE] : EXISTENCE 3b(2)

ex·ist·er \igˈzistə(r), eg-\ *n* -S : one that exists

existimation *n* -S [L *existimation-, existimatio,* fr. *existimatus* (past part. of *existimare* to estimate, esteem, fr. *ex-* ¹ex- + *-istimare,* fr. *aestimare* to value, estimate, esteem) + *-ion-, -io* -ion — more at ESTEEM] *obs* : ESTEEM, OPINION, ESTIMATION

existing *pres part of* EXIST

exists *pres 3d sing of* EXIST

¹**ex·it** \ˈegzət, ˈeksət, *usu* -əd·+V\ [L, he or she goes out, 3d pers. sing. pres. indic. of *exire* to go out — more at EXEAT] : goes out : goes off the stage — used as a stage direction ⟨~ Hamlet⟩ ⟨pick up tray and ~ left⟩ — compare MANET

²**exit** \"\ *n* -S [partly fr. ¹*exit,* partly fr. L *exitus* departure, way out, end, fr. *exitus,* past part. of *exire* to go out] **1** : the departure of a player from the stage — compare ENTRANCE **2 a** : the act of going out or going away : act of leaving the scene of action : DEPARTURE **b** : DEATH **3 a** : a way out : a passage out of an enclosed place or space : OUTLET **b** : a door or passage for escape in case of fire **c** (1) : a place of egress from a limited-access highway (2) : a roadway or ramp affording egress from such a highway **4** *card games* : the act or means of losing a trick so as to escape the obligation of leading : a card that when led cannot win the trick

³**exit** \"\ *vi* -ED/-ING/-S **1** : to go out : DEPART **2** : DIE **3** *card games* : to lead a losing card in order to avoid the obligation of leading again

exit cone *n* : the portion of a wind tunnel into which the air flows from the test section

ex·ite \ˈek,sīt\ *n* -S [*exo-* + *-ite*] : a movable appendage or lobe on the exterior side of the limb of a generalized arthropod (as a branchiopod)

exitial *adj* [L *exitialis,* fr. *exitium* destruction, departure (fr. *exitus,* past part. of *exire*) + *-alis* -al] *obs* : DESTRUCTIVE, FATAL

exit interview *n* : an interview held by a personnel officer with an employee who is leaving the company

exitious *adj* [L *exitiosus,* fr. *exitium* + *-osus* -ose] *obs* : DESTRUCTIVE, FATAL

exit pupil *n* : the image of the entrance pupil of an optical system viewed from the image space (as at the eyepiece)

ex·i·tus \ˈeksəd·əs\ *n, pl* **exitus** [L, departure, way out, end] **1** *obs* : EXIT, EXODUS **2** : ISSUE, OUTCOME, END **3** [ML, fr. L] : an export duty **4** : DEATH; *esp* : fatal termination of a disease **5** [NL, fr. L] : an excretory outlet

ex le·ge \ekˈslā,gā, -ge\ *adv* [LL, from law] : as a matter of law : by operation of law

¹**exlex** *n* -ES [ML, fr. L, bound by no law, lawless] *obs* : OUTLAW

²**ex·lex** \ˈek,sleks\ *adj* [G *exlex-,* fr. L *exlex* bound by no law, lawless, fr. *ex-* ¹ex- + *lex* law — more at LEGAL] : without legal authority ⟨~ government⟩

ex li·bris \ekˈslēbrəs, -lē(,)brēs *sometimes* -lī(,)brēs *or* -librəs *or* -lībrəs\ *n, pl* **ex libris** [NL, from the books; fr. the use of the Latin phrase before the owner's name on bookplates] : BOOKPLATE

ex–li·brism \-,brizəm\ *n* -S [*ex libris* + *-ism*] : the collecting of bookplates

ex–li·brist \-,brəst\ *n* -S [*ex libris* + *-ist*] : a collector of bookplates

ex ma·le·fi·cio \,ek,smälə'fikē,ō\ *adj* [LL, from wrongdoing] : guilty of malfeasance ⟨a trustee *ex maleficio*⟩

¹**ex-meridian** \¦eks+\ *adj* [¹*ex-* + *meridian*] : EXTRAMERIDIONAL

²**exmeridian** \"\ *n* : EXTRAMERIDIAN

ex·moor \ˈek,smu̇(ə)r, -mō(-\ *n, usu cap* [*Exmoor,* district in Somersetshire, England] **1** *or* **exmoor horn** : a breed of horned sheep of Devonshire, England, that are valuable for mutton **2** *or* **exmoor pony** : a breed of hardy heavy-maned ponies native to the Exmoor district

exmr *abbr* examiner

ex new \(ˈ)=¦=\ *adv (or adj)* [²*ex*] *Brit* : without the right to claim participation in an issue of new stock — used of a quoted price of a stock

ex ni·hi·lo \ekˈsnēhə,lō, -ēə,-, -ēhē,- *sometimes* -nihi,- *or* -nī(h)ə,-\ *adv (or adj)* [L] : from or out of nothing ⟨creation *ex nihilo*⟩

exo \ˈek(,)sō\ *adj* [*exo-*] *chem* : being, having, or characterized by valence bonds of a 6-membered ring in its boat-shaped conformation that are directed outward ⟨the ~ side of a ring⟩ — compare EXO- 2

exo- *or* **ex-** *comb form* [Gk *exō* out of, out, outside of, outside, fr. *ex* out of — more at ¹EX-] **1 a** : outside ⟨*exogamy*⟩ : outer ⟨*exocarp*⟩ ⟨*exoskeleton*⟩ — opposed to *end-*; compare ECT- **b** : producing ⟨*exergonic*⟩ — opposed to *end-* **2** *exo-, usu ital* : having a 6-membered ring in its boat-shaped conformation with one or more substituents directed outward ⟨2,5-methylene-*exo*-cyclohexyl-amine⟩ — compare END- 2

exo·adaptation \¦ek(,)sō+\ *n* [*exo-* + *adaptation*] *biol* : modification of an organism resulting in more effective interaction with its external environment — compare ENDOADAPTATION

exo·as·ca·ce·ae \,ek(,)sōaˈskāsē,ē\ [NL, fr. *Exoascus,* type genus + *-aceae*] *syn of* TAPHRINACEAE

exo·as·ca·les \-ā(,)lēz\ [NL, fr. *Exoascus* + *-ales*] *syn of* TAPHRINALES

exo·as·cus \-ōˈaskəs\ *n, cap* [NL, fr. *exo-* + *ascus*] *in some esp former classifications* : a genus of fungi (family Taphrinaceae) distinguished from *Taphrina* by the formation of not more than eight ascospores in each ascus but now usu. included in *Taphrina*

exo·ba·sid·i·a·ce·ae \,ek(,)sōbə,sidēˈāsē,ē\ *n pl, cap* [NL, fr. *Exobasidium,* type genus + *-aceae*] : a family comprising fungi parasitic on higher plants and producing their hymenium as a thin coating on the surface of the host plant and without differentiation of a fruiting body — see EXOBASIDIUM, EXOBASIDIALES

exo·ba·sid·i·a·les \-ā(,)lēz\ *n pl, cap* [NL, fr. *Exobasidium* + *-ales*] : an order of Homobasidiomycetes coextensive with the family Exobasidiaceae

exo·basidium \¦ek(,)sō+\ *n, cap* [NL, fr. *exo-* + *basidium*] : the type and chief genus of the family Exobasidiaceae comprising fungi parasitic esp. on various heath plants on which they cause swollen thickenings resembling galls — see FALSE BLOSSOM

exo·cannibalism \"+\ *n* [ISV *exo-* + *cannibalism;* orig. formed as G *exokannibalismus*] : cannibalism of persons from outside one's family or tribe— contrasted with *endocannibalism*

exo·carp \ˈeksō,kärp\ *n* -S [ISV *exo-* + *-carp*] : EPICARP

¹**ex·occipital** \¦eks+\ *adj* [ISV *exo-* + *occipital*] : of or relating to a bone or region on each side of the foramen magnum of the skull

²**exoccipital** \"\ *n* : either of a pair of bones lying one on each side of the foramen magnum and free in lower vertebrates but forming in man a part of the occipital bone

exo·centric \¦eksō+\ *adj* [*exo-* + *-centric*] : not having the same grammatical function as a nonmodifying immediate constituent — used of a compound (as *barefoot,* which is unlike *foot* in function) or construction (as *in the yard* in the sentence "they played in the yard," which is unlike *in* or *yard* in function); compare ENDOCENTRIC

exo·chor·da \,eksōˈkȯrdə\ *n, cap* [NL, fr. *exo-* + L *chorda* cord; fr. the free placentary cords supposed to be external to the carpels — more at CORD] : a genus of Asiatic shrubs (family Rosaceae) having spikes of white flowers succeeded by fruits each of which consists of five bony carpels in the form of a star — see PEARLBUSH

exo·chorion \¦ek(,)sō+\ *n, pl* **exochoria** [NL, fr. *exo-* + *chorion*] : the outer of the two layers that form the hardened covering of an insect egg

exo·cli·nal \¦eksō¦klīnᵊl\ *adj* : relating to or resembling an exocline

exo·cline \ˈ==,klīn\ *n* -S [*exo-* + *-cline*] *geol* : an inverted fan fold

exo·coele *or* **exo·coel** \-,sēl\ *n* -S [*exo-* + *-coele*] : the space between adjacent pairs of mesenteries in the anthozoan polyp — compare ENDOCOELE — **exo·coe·lic** \¦==¦sēlik\ *adj*

exo·coelom \¦eksō+\ *n* [ISV *exo-* + *coelom*] : the extra-embryonic part of the body cavity of the embryo of an amniotic vertebrate — **exo·coelomic** \"+\ *adj*

¹**exo·coe·tid** \¦eksō¦sēd·əd\ *adj* [NL *Exocoetidae*] : of or relating to the Exocoetidae

²**exocoetid** \"\ *n* -S : a flying fish of the family Exocoetidae

exo·coe·ti·dae \,==ˈsēd·ə,dē\ *n pl, cap* [NL, fr. *Exocoetus,* type genus (fr. L, fish that sleeps on the shore, fr. Gk *exōkoitos,* fr. *exō* outside + *koitos* resting place, bed, fr. *keist* to lie) + *-idae* — more at EXO-, CEMETERY] : a family (order Synentognathi) of marine fishes that are closely related to the half-beaks and include all the true flying fishes

exo·cone \ˈeksə,kōn\ *adj* [*exo-* + *cone*] : having the crystalline cone replaced by an ingrowth of transparent cuticular material from the cornea — used chiefly of insect eyes

exo·cor·tis \,eksəˈkȯrd·əs\ *n* -ES [ISV *exo-* + *-cortis* (irreg. fr. *cortex*)] : a disease of oranges that is esp. important in trees grafted on trifoliate stock, is characterized by peeling of the outer bark in narrow dry strips and by dwarfing of the tree, and is caused prob. by either a virus or a genetic factor

ex·o·crine \ˈeksəkrən; -,krin,-,īn,-ēn\ *adj* [ISV *exo-* + *-crine* (fr. Gk *krinein* to separate) — more at CERTAIN] : secreting externally — used of glands that discharge their secretion through a duct; opposed to *endocrine*

exocrine gland *n* : a gland that produces an exocrine secretion — called also *gland of external secretion*

exoculation *n* -S [ML *exoculation-, exoculatio,* fr. L *exoculatus* (past part. of *exoculare* to put out the eyes, fr. *ex-* ¹ex- + *-oculare,* fr. *oculus* eye) + *-ion-, -io* -ion — more at EYE] *obs* : the act of putting out the eyes (as in execution of a judicial sentence)

exo·cuticle \¦ek(,)sō+\ *n* [*exo-* + *cuticle*] : the intermediate layer of a typical cuticle being sometimes considered in insects the outer part of the endocuticle

ex·o·cy·cla \,eksōˈsīklə\ *or* **ex·o·cyc·li·ca** \-ˈsikləkə\ [NL, fr. *exo-* + *-cycla* (fr. Gk *kyklos* ring, circle, wheel) or *-cyclica* (fr. Gk *kyklika,* neut. pl. of *kyklikos* circular, cyclic, fr. *kyklos* + *-ikos* -ic) — more at WHEEL] *syn of* EXOCYCLOIDA

ex·o·cy·clic \¦eksō¦sīklik, -¦sik-\ *adj* [NL *Exocyclica*] : belonging to or characteristic of the Exocycloida

ex·o·cy·cloi·da \,ek(,)sō,sīˈklȯidə\ *n pl, cap* [NL, fr. *exo-* + *cycl-* + *-oida*] : an order of sea urchins comprising forms with the periproct posterior or oral in position and including the heart urchins and sand dollars

ex·ode \ˈek,sōd, ˈeg,zōd\ *n* -S [F or L; F *exode,* fr. L *exodium,* fr. Gk *exodion* part of a drama following the last song of the chorus, fr. neut. of *exodios* of a departure or exit, fr. *exodos* departure, going out] **1** : a comic afterpiece in the ancient Roman theater : FARCE, TRAVESTY **2** : EXODUS 2

ex·o·derm \ˈeksō,dərm\ *n* -S [ISV *exo-* + *-derm*] **1** : EXODERMIS **2 a** : ECTODERM **b** : an external integument — **ex·o·der·mal** \¦eksō¦dərməl\ *adj*

ex·o·der·mis \,eksōˈdərməs\ *n* -ES [NL, fr. *exo-* + *-dermis*] **1** : a layer of the outer living cortical cells that by becoming cutinized or suberized takes over the functions of the epidermis in roots such as those of the monocotyledons and some dicotyledons which lack secondary thickening **2** : the single layer of cells just below the corky epidermis of various orchid roots

ex·od·ic \(ˈ)ek¦sädik, (ˈ)eg¦zä-\ *adj* [Gk *exodos* departure, going out + E *-ic*] : EFFERENT

ex·o·dist \ˈeksədəst, ˈegzə-\ *n* -S [*exodus* + *-ist*] : EMIGRANT

ex·o·di·um \ekˈsōdēəm, egˈzō-\ *n, pl* **exo·dia** \-ēə\ [L] : EXODE 1

ex·o·don·tia \,eksəˈdänch(ē)ə\ *n* -S [NL, fr. ¹*ex-* + *-odontia*] : a branch of dentistry that deals with the extraction of teeth — **ex·o·don·tist** \-ntəst, ˈ==,==\ *n* -S [NL *exodontia* + E *-ist*] : a specialist in exodontia

ex·o·dus \ˈeksədəs *also* ˈegzə-\ *n* -ES [*Exodus,* Old Testament book that tells of the departure of the Israelites from Egypt, fr. ME, fr. LL, fr. Gk *Exodos,* fr. *exodos* departure, going out, fr. *ex* out of, out + *hodos* way, journey — more at EX-, CEDE] **1** : a mass departure : EMIGRATION ⟨the ~ of the cotton mills from New England to the South —J.A.Morris b. 1918⟩ **2** *also* **ex·o·dos** \-,däs\ [Gk *exodos,* lit., departure] : the part of a Greek drama following the last song of the chorus

ex·o·dy \-ədē\ *n* -ES [Gk *exodia* expedition, journey out, fr. *exodos* + *-ia* -y] : EXODUS

exo·enzyme \¦eksō,w+-\ *n* [ISV *exo-* + *enzyme*] : an enzyme that acts outside the cell (as in yeasts) : an extracellular enzyme — distinguished from *endoenzyme*

exo·ergic \¦eksō¦wərjik\ *adj* [*exo-* + *erg-* + *-ic*] : releasing energy : EXOTHERMIC ⟨~ nuclear disintegration⟩ — opposed to *endoergic*

exo·erythrocytic \¦eksəw, ¦ek,sō+\ *adj* [*exo-* + *erythrocytic*] : occurring outside of the red blood cells — used of stages of malaria parasites

ex of·fi·cio \¦eksə¦fishē,ō, -i(,)shō\ *also* **ex offici·is** \-ishē,ēs\ *adv (or adj)* [LL] : by virtue or because of an office or offices ⟨all heads of departments . . . are called upon to serve *ex officiis* as members of . . . boards —F.A.Ogg & P.O.Ray⟩ ⟨acting as *ex officio* chairman of the board⟩

ex·o·gam·ic \¦eksō¦gamik\ *adj* [*exogamy* + *-ic*] : EXOGAMOUS

ex·og·a·mous \(ˈ)ek¦sägəməs\ *adj* [*exo-* + *-gamous*] : of, relating to, or characterized by exogamy

ex·og·a·my \ekˈsägəmē\ *n* -ES [*exo-* + *-gamy*] **1** : marriage outside of a specific group esp. as required by custom or law : OUTBREEDING — contrasted with *endogamy* **2** : sexual reproduction between organisms not closely related

exo·gastrula \¦eksō+\ *n* [NL, fr. *exo-* + *gastrula*] : an abnormal gastrula that has the presumptive endoderm increased in quantity and incapable of invagination and is therefore unable to develop further — **exo·gastrulation** \"+\ *n*

ex·o·gen \ˈeksəjən, -,jen\ *n* -S [F *exogène,* fr. *exogène* exogenous, fr. *exo-* + *-gène* (fr. Gk *-genēs* born) — more at -GEN] : a plant that develops by exogenous growth — compare ENDOGEN

exo·gene \ˈeksə,jēn\ *or* **exo·ge·net·ic** \¦eksōjə¦ned·ik\ *or* **ex·o·gen·ic** \¦eksō¦jenik\ *adj* [*exogene* prob. fr. F *exogène; exogenetic* fr. *exo-* + *genetic; exogenic* prob. fr. F *exogène* + E *-ic*] : EXOGENOUS

ex·og·e·nism \ekˈsäjə,nizəm\ *n* -S [*exogenous* + *-ism*] : the state of being exogenous

ex·og·e·nous \(ˈ)ek¦säjənəs\ *adj* [F *exogène* exogenous + E *-ous*] : produced from without : originating from or due to external causes: as **a** : growing from or on the outside ⟨~ spores⟩ : growing by addition to the exterior ⟨~ stems⟩ **b** (1) : caused by a factor (as food) or an agent from outside the organism and not due primarily to structural or functional failure ⟨~ obesity⟩ ⟨~ heart disease associated with rheumatic fever⟩ — compare ENDOGENOUS (2) : introduced from or produced outside the organism ⟨~supply of a vitamin⟩ **c** : arising from other than hereditary factors ⟨~ mental deficiency⟩ **d** : of, relating to, or produced by the metabolism of nitrogenous substances obtained from food : DIETARY ⟨~ uric acid⟩ — compare ENDOGENOUS **e** *of rocks* : composed of materials derived from processes of erosion or produced by metamorphism through contact with adjacent igneous intrusion **f** : originating from outside an economic system (as from political, accidental, and technological forces) — compare ENDOGENOUS — **ex·og·e·nous·ly** *adv*

exo·geosyncline \¦ek(,)sō+\ *n* [*exo-* + *geosyncline*] : a transverse basin extending from an orthogeosyncline into a craton

ex·og·nath \¦eksəg,nath\ *n* -S [*exo-* + Gk *gnathos* jaw; akin to Gk *genys* jaw — more at CHIN] : EXOGNATHITE

exo·gnathion \¦eksō+\ *n* [NL, fr. *exo-* + *gnathion*] : the maxilla not including the premaxilla

exo·gnath·ite \¦eksō¦na,thīt, ekˈsägnə,th-\ *n* [*exo-* + *gnathite*] : the external branch of an oral appendage of a crustacean

ex·o·go·ni·um \,eksəˈgōnēəm\ *n, cap* [NL, fr. *exo-* + *-gonium* (fr. Gk *gōnia* corner, angle) — more at DIAGONAL] : a genus of tropical American nearly woody vines (family Convolvulaceae) having showy tubular flowers with exserted stamens and a capitate stigma — see JALAP

ex·o·graph \ˈeksə,graf, -raf\ *n* [*exo-* (irreg. fr. *X ray*) + *-graph*] : a radiograph made with X rays

ex·og·y·nous \(ˈ)ek¦säjənəs\ *adj* [prob. fr. (assumed) NL *exogynus,* fr. *exo-* + *-gynus* -gynous] *bot* : having the style longer than the corolla and exserted beyond it

ex·o·gy·ra \,eksəˈjīrə\ *n, cap* [NL, fr. *exo-* + *-gyra* (fr. Gk *gyros* ring, circle, fr. *gyros* round) — more at COWER] : a genus of Upper Jurassic and Cretaceous bivalve mollusks that have thick shells and spirally twisted beak and are related to the true oysters

exolete *adj* [L *exoletus,* past part. of *exolescere* to go out of use, become out of date, fr. *ex-* ¹ex- + *-olescere* (as in *adolescere* to grow up) — more at ADULT] **1** *obs* : DISUSED, OBSOLETE **2** *obs* : STALE, INSIPID, FADED

exolution *n* -S [L *exsolution-, exsolutio,* fr. *exsolutus* (past part. of *exsolvere* to release, fr. *ex-* ¹ex- + *solvere* to loosen, release) + *-ion-, -io* -ion — more at SOLVE] *obs* : a setting free : RELEASE, RELAXATION

ex·o·mol·o·ge·sis \,eksə,mäləˈjēsəs\ *n, pl* **exomologeses** \-ē,sēz\ [LL, fr. LGk *exomologēsis,* fr. Gk, confession, fr. *exomologeisthai* to confess (fr. *ex* out of, out + *homologeisthai,* pres. middle infin. of *homologein* to agree, grant, confess, fr. *homologos* assenting, agreeing) + *-sis* — more at EX-, HOMOLOGOUS] : a penitential rite with public confession of sins that was practiced in the early Christian church

ex·o·mor·phic \¦eksō¦mȯrfik\ *adj* [*exo-* + *-morphic*] : relating to or produced by exomorphism — opposed to *endomorphic*

ex·o·mor·phism \,==ˈmȯr,fizəm\ *n* -S [ISV *exo-* + *-morphism;* orig. formed as F *exomorphisme*] : a change (as hardening or the formation of new minerals) produced in a rock mass by igneous intrusion from without : metamorphism by external contact

ex·on \ˈek,sän\ *n* -S [modif. of F *exempt* subordinate in the cavalry commanding in the absence of the higher company officers — more at EXEMPT] : one of four officers of the yeomen of the British royal guard ranking below ensign who in turn act as resident commanders in the absence of superior officers — called also *exempt*

exo·narthex \¦eksō+\ *n* [*exo-* + *narthex*] : the outer narthex of a church having two narthexes; *sometimes* : the whole atrium — compare ESONARTHEX

exo·nephric \"+\ *adj* [*exo-* + *nephric*] : having the excretory organs discharge through the body wall (as in some annelid worms)

ex·on·er \igˈzänər, eg-\ *vt* -ED/-ING/-S [L *exonerare*] *Scots law* : EXONERATE

¹**ex·on·er·ate** \igˈzänə,rāt, eg-\ *vt* -ED/-ING/-S [ME *exoneraten,* fr. L *exoneratus,* past part. of *exonerare* to relieve, free, unload, fr. *ex-* ¹ex- + *onerare* to load, fr. *oner-, onus* load — more at ONEROUS] **1** : to relieve esp. of a charge, obligation, or hardship ⟨no reason for *exonerating* him from the ordinary duties of a citizen —O.W.Holmes †1935⟩ : clear from accusation or blame : EXCULPATE ⟨defendant was *exonerated* from any criminal offense⟩ **2** *obs* : UNLOAD, DISBURDEN, DISCHARGE **syn** see EXCULPATE

²**exonerate** *adj* [L *exoneratus,* past part. of *exonerare*] *obs* : EXONERATED

ex·on·er·a·tion \ig,zänəˈrāshən, eg-\ *n* -S [LL *exoneration-, exoneratio,* fr. L *exoneratus* + *-ion-, -io* -ion] **1** : the act of disburdening, discharging, or freeing morally or legally (as from a charge, imputation, duty, obligation, or responsibility); *also* : the state of being so freed **2 a** : a remedy in equity available to the surety who has discharged the obligation of his defaulting principal or of a prior surety **b** : the right of a surety to require a person or estate subject to a liability prior to his to discharge that liability thus relieving the surety

ex·on·er·e·tur \-ˈräd·ə(r), -ˈred-\ *n* -S [L, let him or her be relieved, 3d pers. sing. pres. subj. pass. of *exonerare*] : an entry on a bailpiece discharging a surety

exo·peptidase \¦eksō+\ *n* [*exo-* + *peptidase*] : one of a group of enzymes that hydrolyze peptide bonds formed by the terminal amino acids of peptide chains : PEPTIDASE — distinguished from *endopeptidase;* compare AMINOPEPTIDASE, CARBOXYPEPTIDASE, DIPEPTIDASE

ex ope·re oper·an·tis \ek¦sōpərē,ōpəˈrän təs\ [ML, lit., from the work of the worker] : in virtue of the agent — used of a sacrament considered in relation to the conditions required for its valid administration or for its worthy reception; compare EX OPERE OPERATO

ex ope·re oper·a·to \-ˈräd·(,)ō\ [ML, lit., from the work done] : in virtue of the action — used of a sacrament considered independently of the merits of the minister or the recipient; compare EX OPERE OPERANTIS

exo·peridium \¦ek(,)sō+\ *n* [NL, fr. *exo-* + *peridium*] : the outer peridium when the peridium has two layers (as in the puffballs) — compare ENDOPERIDIUM

ex·o·pha·sia \,eksōˈfāzh(ē)ə\ *n* -S [NL, fr. *exo-* + *-phasia*] : speech that is actually formed with the speech organs : uttered speech : vocalized speech — contrasted with *endophasia* — **ex·o·pha·sic** \¦eksō¦fāzik\ *adj*

ex·o·pho·ria \,eksəˈfōrēə\ *n* -S [NL, fr. *exo-* + *-phoria*] : latent strabismus in which the visual axes tend outward toward the temple — **ex·o·phor·ic** \¦eksə¦fȯrik\ *adj*

ex·oph·thal·mia \,ek,säfˈthalmēə, ÷-säp'th-\ *n* -S [NL, fr. Gk *exophthalmos* + NL *-ia*] : EXOPHTHALMOS

ex·oph·thal·mic \¦=,=¦=mik\ *adj* [ISV *exophthalm-* (fr. NL *exophthalmos*) + *-ic*] : relating to or characterized by exophthalmos

exophthalmic goiter *n* : hyperthyroidism with protrusion of the eyeballs

ex·oph·thal·mos \,=,=ˈ=məs, -,mäs\ *also* **exophthal·mus** \-məs\ *n* -ES [NL, fr. Gk *exophthalmos* having prominent eyes, fr. *ex* out of, out + *ophthalmos* eye — more at EX-, OPHTHALMIA] : abnormal protrusion of the eyeball

ex·o·phyt·ic \¦eksō¦fid·ik\ *adj* [*exo-* + *-phytic* (as in *endophytic*)] **1** : growing on or deposited on the outside of plant tissues **2** : tending to grow outward beyond the surface epithelium from which it originates — used of tumors; opposed to *endophytic*

exo·plasm \ˈeksō,plazəm\ *n* [ISV *exo-* + *-plasm*] : ECTOPLASM 1

ex·op·o·dite \ekˈsäpə,dīt\ *also* **ex·o·pod** \ˈeksə,päd\ *n* [ISV *exo-* + *-podite*] : the external branch on the protopodite of a typical limb of a crustacean — **ex·op·o·dit·ic** \(¦)eksäpə¦did·ik, ¦eksə,pä¦di-\ *adj*

ex·op·ter·y·go·ta \¦ek,säp,terə¦gōd·ə, ¦ek(,)sō,ter-\ [NL, fr. *exo-* + Gk *pterygōta,* neut. pl. of *pterygōtos* winged — more at PTERYGOTA] *syn of* HEMIMETABOLA

ex·op·ter·y·gote \¦=(,)=¦=,gōt\ *adj* [NL *Exopterygota*] : HEMIMETABOLOUS

exor *abbr* executor

ex·o·ra·ble \ˈeks(ə)rəbəl, ˈegz-\ *adj* [L *exorabilis* — more at INEXORABLE] : capable of being moved by entreaty

ex·or·bi·tance \igˈzȯ(r)bəd·ən(t)s, eg-, *also* -bətᵊn(t)s\ *n* -S [ME *exorbitaunce,* prob. fr. MF *exorbitance,* fr. *exorbitant,* after such pairs as MF *abundant: abundance*] **1** : an exorbitant action or procedure; *esp* : excessive deviation from rule, right, or propriety **2** *archaic* : the fact or action of being exorbitant : irregularity esp. in law or morals **3** : tendency or disposition to be exorbitant : EXTRAVAGANCE ⟨she had earned the right to folly and ~ —V.S.Pritchett⟩

ex·or·bi·tan·cy \-ənsē, -ᵊn-, -si\ *n* -ES [fr. *exorbitance,* after such pairs as E *elegance: elegancy*] *archaic* : EXORBITANCE

ex·or·bi·tant \-nt\ *adj* [ME, fr. MF, fr. LL *exorbitant-, exorbitans,* pres. part. of *exorbitare* to deviate, fr. L *ex-* ¹ex- + LL *-orbitare* (fr. L *orbita* track, rut) — more at ORB] **1** *archaic* : wandering or deviating from the normal or ordinary course : ABNORMAL, IRREGULAR **2** : not within the orbit or scope of the law **3 a** : exceeding in intensity, quality, force, power, scope, or size the customary, due, or appropriate limits ⟨required an ~ quantity of fuel⟩ : EXCESSIVE **b** *of a price, charge, or rate* : grossly exceeding normal, customary, fair, and just limits ⟨~ rent⟩ ⟨~ profits⟩ **syn** see EXCESSIVE — **ex·or·bi·tant·ly** *adv* : in an exorbitant manner : EXCESSIVELY

exorbitate *vi* -ED/-ING/-S [LL *exorbitatus,* past part. of *exorbitare*] *obs* : to go out of the track : deviate from an orbit

ex·or·ci·sa·tion *or* **ex·or·ci·za·tion** \,ek,sȯ(r)səˈzāshən,

ˌeksə(r)sə'z-, ˌeksə(r)ˌsī'z- *also* ˌegˌzȯ- *or* ˌegzə-\ *n* -s [ME *exorcisacioun*, fr. MF *exorcization*, fr. LL *exorcization-, exorcizatio*, fr. *exorcizatus* (past part. of *exorcizare*) + L *-ion-, -io* -ion] : EXORCISM

ex·or·cise *also* **ex·or·cize** \'ekˌsȯ(r)ˌsīz *also* 'eksə(- *or* 'egˌzȯ- *or* 'egzə-\ *vt* -ED/-ING/-S [ME *exorcisen*, fr. MF *exorciser*, fr. LL *exorcizare*, fr. Gk *exorkizein*, fr. *ex* out of, out + *horkizein* to cause to swear, bind by oath, adjure, fr. *horkos* oath; akin to Gk *herkos* fence, L *sarcire* to patch, mend — more at EX-] **1 a** : to drive out or drive away (an evil spirit) by adjuration esp. by use of a holy name or magic rites **b** : to get rid of (something that is troublesome or menacing or oppressive) ⟨trying to ~ her feeling of alarm —Rebecca West⟩ **2** : to relieve (a person or place) from the presence or influence of an evil spirit : PURIFY **3** *obs* : to address or summon by adjuration : conjure up

ex·or·cis·er *or* **ex·or·ciz·er** \-zə(r)\ *n* -s : EXORCIST

ex·or·cism \-ˌsizəm\ *n* -s [ME *exorcisme*, fr. MF or LL; MF *exorcisme*, fr. LL *exorcismus*, fr. Gk *exorkismos* administration of an oath, fr. *exorkizein* to administer an oath, conjure, exorcise] **1** : the act or practice of exorcising **2** *obs* : the conjuration of evil spirits **3** : a spell or formula used in exorcising

ex·or·cis·mal \¦=(ˌ)=¦sizməl\ *or* **ex·or·ci·so·ry** \¦=(ˌ)=¦sīzərē\ *adj* [*exorcismal* fr. *exorcism* + *-al*; *exorcisory* fr. *exorcise* + *-ory*] : of or relating to exorcism

ex·or·cist \'=(ˌ)=ˌsist, -sə̇st\ *n* -s [ME *exorciste*, fr. LL *exorcista*, fr. Gk *exorkistēs*, fr. *exorkizein*] **1** : one who exorcises or conjures evil spirits **2 a** : a member of a minor order in the early Christian church **b** : the second highest office of the minor orders in the Roman Catholic Church ranking immediately below that of acolyte

ex·or·cis·tate \ˌ=(ˌ)='siˌstāt\ *n* -s : the office or order of exorcist

ex·or·cis·ti·cal \¦=(ˌ)=¦sistə̇kəl\ *also* **ex·or·cis·tic** \-istik\ *adj* : of or relating to exorcism

ex·or·di·al \(')eg¦zȯ(r)dēəl, (')ek¦sȯ-\ *adj* [*exordium* + *-al*] : relating to an exordium : INTRODUCTORY

ex·or·di·um \=ˈ=dēəm\ *n, pl* **exordiums** \-ēəmz\ *or* **exor·dia** \-ēə\ [L, fr. *exordiri* to begin, begin a web, lay a warp, fr. *ex-* ¹ex- + *ordiri* to begin, begin a web — more at ORDER] : BEGINNING, INTRODUCTION; *esp* : the introductory part of a discourse or composition

ex·organic \¦eks+\ *adj* [¹*ex-* + *organic*] : having lost organic character

exo·rha·son \ek'sȯrə̇sȯn\ *n* [NGk, fr. Gk *exo-* + MGk *rhason*] : RHASON 2

ex·or·na·tion \ˌekˌsȯ(r)'nāshən\ *n* -s [L *exornation-, exornatio*, fr. *exornatus* (past part. of *exornare* to embellish, equip, fr. *ex-* ¹ex- + *ornare* to embellish, furnish) + *-ion-, -io* -ion — more at ORNATE] : EMBELLISHMENT, ORNAMENTATION

exo·scop·ic \¦eksō¦skäpik\ *adj* [*exo-* + *-scopic*] *bot* : having the apex of the embryo pointed toward the neck of the archegonium — compare ENDOSCOPIC 2

exo·skeletal \¦ek(ˌ)sō+\ *adj* [*exoskeleton* + *-al*] : of or relating to an exoskeleton

exo·skeleton \"+\ *n* [*exo-* + *skeleton*] **1** : an external skeleton or supportive covering of an animal (as the system of sclerites covering the body of an insect or of bony plates covering an armadillo) — compare ENDOSKELETON **2** : bony or horny parts (as nails, hoofs, or scales) of a vertebrate that are produced from epidermal tissues

ex·osmosis \¦eks+\ *n* [alter. (influenced by Gk *-sis*) of earlier *exosmose*, fr. F, fr. *ex-* ¹ex- + Gk *ōsmos* action of thrusting or pushing — more at ENDOSMOSIS] **1** : osmotic diffusion toward the outside of a cell or vessel **2** : passage of material through a membrane from a region of higher to a region of lower concentration — used chiefly in biology; compare ENDOSMOSIS 1

ex·osmotic \"+\ *adj* [ISV *exosm-* (fr. *exosmosis*) + *-otic*] : of or relating to exosmosis

exo·sphere \'eksō+ˌ-\ *n* [ISV *exo-* + *sphere*] : the outer fringe region of the atmosphere variously estimated to begin at an altitude of 200 to 600 miles

ex·o·spor·al \¦eksə¦spōrəl, (')ek¦säspər-\ *or* **ex·o·spor·ous** \-rəs\ *adj* : of or relating to an exospore

exo·spore \'eksə+ˌ-\ *n* [ISV *exo-* + *spore*] **1** : EPISPORE 1a **2** : one of the asexual spores formed by abstriction from a parent cell (as in phycomycetous fungi) — compare ENDOSPORE

ex·o·spo·re·ae \ˌeksə'spōrēˌē\ *n pl* [NL, fr. *exo-* + *spor-* + *-eae*] : a subclass of fungi (class Myxomycetes) distinguished by having the spores borne externally and germinating to produce a protoplasmic body which then develops a group of eight swarm spores — compare MYXOGASTRES

ex·o·spo·ri·um \-rēəm\ *n, pl* **exospo·ria** \-ēə\ [NL, fr. *exo-* + *-sporium*] : EXINE

exossate *vt* -ED/-ING/-S [L *exossatus*, past part. of *exossare* to deprive of bones, fr. *ex-* ¹ex- + *-ossare* (fr. *oss-, os* bone) — more at OSSEOUS] **1** *obs* : to deprive of bones **2** *obs* : to cause (fruits) to grow without stones

ex·o·ste·ma \ˌeksə'stēmə\ *n, cap* [NL, fr. *exo-* + LGk *stēma* stamen, fr. Gk, shaft, fr. *histanai* to cause to stand; fr. the exserted stamens — more at STAND] : a genus of tropical American trees or shrubs (family Rubiaceae) with small salverform white flowers and capsular fruits — see PRINCEWOOD

ex·o·stome \'eksəˌstōm\ *n* -s [ISV *exo-* + *-stome*; prob. orig. formed in F] **1** *bot* : the opening of the outer integument of an ovule that has two integuments **2** : the outer part of the peristome of a moss

ex·os·tosis \ˌekˌsä'stōsə̇s\ *n, pl* **exosto·ses** \-ōˌsēz\ [NL, fr. Gk *exostōsis*, fr. *ex* out of, out + *osteon* bone + *-ōsis* -osis — more at EX-, OSSEOUS] **1** : a spur or bony outgrowth from a bone or the root of a tooth **2** : the formation of knots upon the surface of wood in trees

ex·os·tot·ic \¦=,=¦täd·ik\ *adj* [*exostosis* + *-otic*] : of or relating to exostosis

ex·ostracize \eks+\ *vt* [Gk *exostrakizein*, fr. *ex* out of, out + *ostrakizein* to ostracize] : OSTRACIZE

¹**ex·o·ter·ic** \¦eksə¦terik, -rēk\ *adj* [L & Gk; L *exotericus*, fr. Gk *exōterikos*, lit., external, fr. *exōterō* more outside (compar. of *exō* outside) + *-ikos* -ic — more at EXO-] **1 a** : suitable to be imparted to the public : readily comprehensible ⟨the ~ doctrine⟩ — compare ESOTERIC **b** : belonging to the outer or less initiate circle ⟨~ rites⟩ **c** : publicly known : POPULAR **2** : relating to the outside : EXTERNAL, EXTERIOR — **ex·o·ter·i·cal·ly** \-rə̇k(ə)lē, -rēk-, -li\ *adv*

²**exoteric** \"\ *n* -s **1** : LAYMAN, OUTSIDER **2 exoterics** *pl* : doctrines or discourses for the uninstructed or the general public

ex·o·ter·i·ca \ˌeksə'terə̇kə\ *n pl* [NL, fr. L, neut. pl. of *exotericus*] : exoteric doctrines or works

ex·o·ter·i·cism \-rəˌsizəm\ *n* -s : exoteric doctrines or practices esp. in religion; *also* : the holding of such doctrines or engaging in such practices

exo·thermal \¦eksō+\ *adj* [*exo-* + *thermal*] : EXOTHERMIC — **exo·thermally** \"+\ *adv*

exo·thermic \"+\ *adj* [ISV *exo-* + *thermic*] : characterized by or formed with evolution of heat : EXOERGIC ⟨~ chemical reactions⟩ — opposed to *endothermic* — **exo·ther·mic·i·ty** \ˌek(ˌ)sō(ˌ)thər'misəd·ē\ *n* -ES

¹**ex·ot·ic** \ig'zäd·ik, eg'z-, -ät\, |ēk *sometimes* ik'sä- *or* ek'sä-\ *adj* [L *exoticus*, fr. Gk *exōtikos*, fr. *exō* outside] **1** : from another country : not native to the place where found : FOREIGN ⟨~ flower⟩ ⟨~ fish⟩ ⟨~ dishes⟩ **2** *archaic* : OUTLANDISH, ALIEN **3 a** : strikingly out of the ordinary : rarely met with : STRANGE **b** : excitingly strange : having the appeal of the unknown : MYSTERIOUS, ROMANTIC, PICTURESQUE, GLAMOROUS **c** : strikingly unusual in color or design : RICH, SHOWY, ELABORATE — **ex·ot·i·cal·ly** \ə̇k(ə)lē, |ēk-, -li\ *adv* — **ex·ot·ic·ness** \ikn*ə*s, |ēk-\ *n* -ES

²**exotic** \"\ *n, pl* **exotics** \-ks\ : one (as a plant or a word) that is exotic

¹**ex·ot·i·ca** \|əkə, |ēkə\ *n* -s [L, fem. of *exoticus*] : an acidanthera (*Acidanthera bicolor*) with creamy-white flowers that are blotched chocolate-brown within

²**exotica** \"\ *n pl* [L, neut. pl. of *exoticus*] : things excitingly different or unusual; *esp* : literary or artistic items having an exotic theme or nature

exotical *adj* [L *exoticus* + E *-al*] *obs* : EXOTIC

ex·ot·i·cism \|əˌsizəm\ *n* -s **1** : the quality or state of being exotic **2** : interest in or adoption of the exotic **3** : a foreign trait of expression or behavior

ex·ot·i·cist \|əsə̇st\ *n* -s : one who specializes (as in writing) in the exotic : one who exploits the appeal of the exotic

exotic stream *n* : a stream (as the Nile) that has its source in well-watered lands and crosses a desert on its way to the sea

ex·o·tism \'eksəˌtizəm, 'egzə-\ *n* -s [*exotic* + *-ism*] : EXOTICISM

exo·toxic \¦eksō+\ *adj* [*exotoxin* + *-ic*] : of, relating to, or acting as an exotoxin

exo·toxin \"+\ *n* [ISV *exo-* + *toxin*] : a soluble poisonous substance that passes into the medium during growth of certain bacilli or other microorganisms ⟨tetanus ~⟩ — compare ENDOTOXIN

ex·o·tro·pia \ˌeksə'trōpēə\ *n* -s [NL, fr. *exo-* + *-tropia*] : WALLEYE 2b

ex·ot·ro·pism \ek'sä-trəˌpizəm\ *n* [ISV *exo-* + *-tropism*] : curvature away from the main axis

exp *abbr* **1** expansion **2** ex parte **3** expense **4** experience **5** experiment; experimental **6** expiration **7** explosive **8** exponential **9** export **10** exposure **11** express

ex·pand \ik'spand, ek-, -paa(ə)nd\ *vb* -ED/-ING/-S [ME *expaunden*, fr. L *expandere*, fr. *ex-* ¹ex- + *pandere* to spread, unfold — more at FATHOM] *vt* **1** : to spread out : open wide : UNFOLD ⟨~*ed* his thick underlip and stared . . . with distended eyes —Liam O'Flaherty⟩ **2** : to increase the extent, size, number, volume, or scope of : ENLARGE ⟨~*ed* this regiment into a brigade —B.I.Wiley⟩ ⟨we need to ~ our factual information concerning the behavior of the economy —L.V.Chandler⟩ ⟨business is ~*ing* its interest in the liberal arts —C.C.Brown⟩ **3 a** : to express fully : develop in detail : AMPLIFY ⟨these views he announced and ~*ed* in three monographs —J.S.Bassett⟩ **b** : to write out in full ⟨contractions have been ~*ed* and spellings modernized —J.L.Clifford⟩ **c** *math* : to state in enlarged form : develop in a series ~ *vi* **1** : to spread itself out : open out ⟨each stalk ~*ing* at the top into a . . . flower head —C.S.Forester⟩ **2** : to increase in extent, size, number, volume, or scope : become larger : GROW ⟨measure how rapidly the water warmed up and ~*ed* while it was warming —K.K.Darrow⟩ ⟨this trend toward conformity will ~ and accelerate —P.H.Odegard⟩ ⟨his mind never ~*ed*; his emotions never deepened —Kenneth Clark⟩ **3** : to speak or write fully or in detail : EXPATIATE — usu. used with *on* or *upon* ⟨I propose . . . to ~ on three of these common problems —W.R.Bascom⟩ **4** : to experience a feeling of well-being : become expansive ⟨the subtle flattery . . . made the eminent Victorian ~ and glow —Osbert Sitwell⟩

syn AMPLIFY, SWELL, DISTEND, INFLATE, DILATE: EXPAND, often interchangeable with others in this list, may indicate any enlarging by opening out, spreading, unfolding, extending, or increasing ⟨the captain established a tavern here, *expanding* it after 10 years into an elaborate stone structure —*Amer. Guide Series: Pa.*⟩ ⟨gradually psalm singing *expanded* into oratorios and concerts of sacred music —*Amer. Guide Series: N.J.*⟩ ⟨she hungered for a full environment in which to *expand* her new powers —Havelock Ellis⟩ AMPLIFY often applies to extending by magnifying the volume or scope or adding details ⟨a pipe organ and an *amplifying* system over which programs can be sent to the entire town —*Amer. Guide Series: Mich.*⟩ ⟨it is on the main argument that the book is to be judged, and I must *amplify* a summary of it —Julian Huxley⟩ SWELL sometimes applies to an abnormal expanding, puffing up or out, or increasing in intensity or volume ⟨now the trickle continued throughout the war, and *swelled* to a flood soon after the war ended —William Clark⟩ ⟨Servia's ambitions had been *swollen* enormously by her successes —A. D.H.Smith⟩ ⟨when at anchor here I ride, my bosom *swells* with pride —W.S.Gilbert⟩ ⟨a great determination *swelled* in him —A.J.Cronin⟩ DISTEND applies to an extending out or a swelling out, often brought about by internal pressures, or to an appearance of swelling or protruding ⟨sails *distended* by the wind⟩ ⟨a stomach *distended* by gas⟩ ⟨her eyes were black with terror, and so *distended* that the white showed all the way round them —Edith Sitwell⟩ ⟨when a piece of oratory intended for a public occasion impresses us as *distended*, which is to say, filled up with repetition, periphrasis, long grammatical forms, and other impediments to directness —R.M. Weaver⟩ INFLATE usu. implies distention or puffing up by or as if by an air or gas or something else relatively insubstantial ⟨*inflate* a balloon⟩ ⟨*inflated* currency⟩ ⟨poems *inflated* with fine language⟩ ⟨the psychological problems of *inflated* national ego, heroic delusions of grandeur, and theories of historical inevitability —R.A.Newhall⟩ DILATE is likely to refer to a swelling or widening of something known or viewed as circular or spherical ⟨arteries *dilated* by the drug⟩ ⟨the pupils of his eyes were *dilated*⟩ ⟨some stirring experience, the drastic stimulus given by some masterpiece in an art or by some personal emotion, may swiftly *dilate* your field of consciousness —C.E.Montague⟩

ex·pand·abil·i·ty \ikˌspandə'biləd·ē, ek-, -paan-, -lətē, -i\ *n* -ES : EXPANSIBILITY

ex·pand·able *also* **ex·pand·ible** \=ˈ=dəbəl\ *adj* : capable of being expanded

expanded *adj* [fr. past part. of *expand*] **1 a** : spread out : OUTSTRETCHED, UNFOLDED ⟨then with ~ wings he steers his flight aloft —John Milton⟩ **b** *heraldry* : OPEN, DISPLAYED **c** *of a letter or typeface* : having a somewhat wider face than that of a typeface not so characterized — compare CONDENSED, EXTENDED **2 a** : increased in volume or scope : ENLARGED ⟨~ public-relations programs⟩ **b** : PERIPHRASTIC used of the progressive-tense forms in *-ing* (as *am writing, was writing, is being written*) — **ex·pand·ed·ness** *n* -ES

expanded metal *n* : sheet metal cut and stretched into a lattice

expanded plastic *n* : a lightweight cellular material usu. made by introducing gas into a plastic or resin and used esp. in insulation and lamination — called also *foamed plastic, plastic foam*

expanded metal

ex·pand·er \=ˈ=də(r)\ *n* -s **1** : one that expands: as **a** : an operator of a machine that expands metal tubes **b** : a tool designed to expand a boiler tube at its end so as to fit it snugly into the flue sheet **2** : any of several colloidal substances of high molecular weight (as special preparations of gelatin or dextran) used as a blood or plasma substitute in transfusion for increasing the volume of the circulating blood esp. in the treatment of shock — called also *extender*

expanding *adj* [fr. pres. part. of *expand*] : that expands or may be expanded; *esp* : GROWING ⟨an ~ economy⟩

expanding brake *n* : a brake in which a flexible band or a set of circular segments is sprung outward against the inside rim of a hub or wheel

expanding bullet *n* : a soft-nosed bullet — compare DUMDUM

expanding pulley *n* : a pulley whose diameter can be varied

expanding universe *n* : a relativistic concept of the material universe according to which all celestial bodies are becoming steadily farther apart with the result that those more remote recede from the earth at greater speeds

expands *pres 3d sing of* EXPAND

¹**expanse** *vt* -ED/-ING/-S [L *expansus*, past part. of *expandere* to spread out, expand — more at EXPAND] *obs* : EXPAND

²**ex·panse** \ik'span(t)s, ek-, -paa(ə)n-\ *n* -s [NL *expansum* firmament, fr. L, neut. of *expansus*, past part. of *expandere*] **1** : something that is spread out typically over a wide area: as **a** : FIRMAMENT ⟨moon and stars . . . silvering in the blue ~ —Christopher Smart⟩ **b** : an extensive and usu. unbroken stretch of land or sea ⟨great ~ of country spread around and below —D.H.Lawrence⟩ ⟨majestic ~ of calm water —Tom Marvel⟩

ex·pan·si·bil·i·ty \ikˌspan(t)sə'biləd·ē, (ˌ)ek-, -paan-, -lətē, -i\ *n* -ES : the quality or state of being expansible

ex·pan·si·ble \=ˈ==bəl\ *adj* [L *expansus* + E *-ible*] : EXPANDABLE

ex·pan·sile \-n(t)səl, -nˌsīl\ *adj* [L *expansus* + E *-ile*] **1** : capable of expansion ⟨gases are more ~ than liquids⟩ **2** : of, relating to, or characteristic of expansion ⟨~ movements⟩

ex·pan·sion \ik'spanchən, ek-, -paan-\ *n* -s [LL *expansion-, expansio*, fr. L *expansus* + *-ion-, -io* -ion] **1** : the act or process of expanding: as **a** (1) : the act or process of spreading out ⟨the easy ~ of the wing of a bird —Nehemiah Grew⟩ (2) : the mushrooming of a bullet upon striking the target **b** (1) : the act or process of increasing in extent, size, number, volume, or scope : ENLARGEMENT, GROWTH ⟨localized pain along nerve trunks may be due to the ~ of the dissolved nitrogen without actual bubble formation —H.G.Armstrong⟩ ⟨the bewildering ~ of science during the last century —C.H. Grandgent⟩ ⟨this desire for territorial ~ is deeply rooted in human history —C.J.Friedrich⟩ (2) *in an electronic sound amplifier* : the widening of the range of an audio-frequency signal by making the gain vary directly with the amplitude of the input signal so that weak sounds become weaker and loud sounds louder **c** (1) : the act of expressing fully or of developing in detail : AMPLIFICATION ⟨these lectures with some slight ~ . . . are here printed as delivered —A.N.Whitehead⟩ (2) *math* : the developed result of an indicated or possible operation : the expression of a function in the form of a series ⟨the ~ of $(a+b)^2$ is $a^2+2ab+b^2$⟩ (3) *logic* : the operation or result of making the terms in a formula more explicit or of introducing new terms without changing the logical significance of the expression **2** : the quality or state of being expanded ⟨the gilded clouds in fair ~ lie —Alexander Pope⟩ **3** : EXPANSE ⟨the sky's serene ~ —Thomas Hood †1845⟩ **4** *obs* : pure space ⟨lost in ~, void and infinite —Richard Blackmore⟩ **5 a** : the increase in volume of working fluid (as steam) in an engine cylinder after cutoff or in an internal-combustion engine after explosion by which it continues to propel the piston while expending part of its internal energy and losing in pressure and temperature **b** : the period during which such expansion occurs **c** : amount of increase of length, area, or volume **6 a** : an expanded part ⟨the great ~ of the St. Lawrence called the Lake of St. Peter —Francis Parkman⟩ **b** : something that results from an act of expanding ⟨this book was an ~ of a notable series of articles —A.C.Ames⟩ **7** : EXPANSIVENESS ⟨gradually tones of careless freedom, moments of reckless ~ come in, though never . . . any trace of sentimentality or of adoration —Havelock Ellis⟩

ex·pan·sion·al \-chənᵊl, -chnəl\ *adj* : of or relating to expansion

ex·pan·sion·ary \-chəˌnerē\ *adj* : tending toward expansion ⟨an ~ factor⟩ ⟨an ~ economy⟩

expansion attic *n* : an unfinished attic area usu. with dormers in an otherwise finished house that is suitable for conversion into habitable space

expansion bit *n* : EXPANSIVE BIT

expansion bolt *n* : a bolt operating in or by an expanding attachment fitted in wood, iron, or masonry

expansion chamber *n* : CLOUD CHAMBER

expansion coupling *n* : EXPANSION JOINT 1

ex·pan·sion·ism \-chəˌnizəm\ *n* -s : the policy, practice, or advocacy of expansion, esp. territorial expansion ⟨furnish specific guarantees to countries which lay in the path of Soviet ~ —P.E.Mosely⟩

¹**ex·pan·sion·ist** \-ch(ə)nə̇st\ *n* -s : one who favors expansionism: **a** : an advocate of an enlarged paper currency **b** : an advocate of territorial expansion

²**expansionist** \"\ *adj* : practicing, advocating, or tending toward expansion; *specif* : pressing for a policy of extending a nation's political and economic dominance ⟨we must make it perfectly clear that we are not ourselves ~ —H.L.Stimson⟩

ex·pan·sion·is·tic \=¦=chə¦nistik\ *adj* : EXPANSIONIST

expansion joint *n* **1** : a coupling (as of steam pipes) designed to permit an endwise movement that compensates for expansion or contraction resulting from temperature changes **2** : a joint or gap (as in concrete work) designed to permit expansion or contraction resulting from temperature changes

expansion shield *n* : a device for anchoring attachments to masonry or concrete surfaces consisting of a metal insert that is driven into a drilled hole and expanded tightly against the sides of the hole

expansion trunk *n* : a trunk that extends above a cargo tank in an oil tanker and that permits the change in volume resulting from temperature changes to be accommodated by a change in the level in the trunk

expansion valve *n* : a valve through which liquid or gas under pressure is allowed to expand to a lower pressure and greater volume

ex·pan·sive \ik'span(t)siv, ek-, -paan-, -sēv *also* -səv\ *adj* [L *expansus* (past part. of *expandere* to expand) + E *-ive* — more at EXPAND] **1** : having a capacity or a tendency to expand ⟨~ materials⟩ **2** : causing or tending to cause expansion ⟨the ~ force of fire⟩ **3 a** : characterized by high spirits or benevolent inclinations : freely communicative : GENIAL ⟨like all secretive persons she could be suddenly ~ at times —Arnold Bennett⟩ ⟨some kindly or helpful act, some ~ expression of fellowship —S.H.Adams⟩ **b** : marked by or indicative of exaggerated euphoria and delusions of self-importance **4** : applying, working by, or capable of expansion ⟨an ~ engine⟩ ⟨an ~ gear⟩ **5** : having considerable extent : BROAD, EXTENSIVE ⟨came abreast of the ~ glittering lake —William Bartram⟩ ⟨a course of lectures on the religions of the world . . . or on something equally ~ —Agnes Repplier⟩ **6** : characterized by largeness or magnificence of scale : AMPLE, SPACIOUS ⟨those glorious days of ~ living were soon curtailed —Frank Monaghan⟩ ⟨they were liberal with good timber in those ~ days —George Farwell⟩ **7** : EXPANSIONIST

syn see ELASTIC

expansive bit *n* : a bit with a cutting blade that can be adjusted to various sizes — called also *expansion bit*

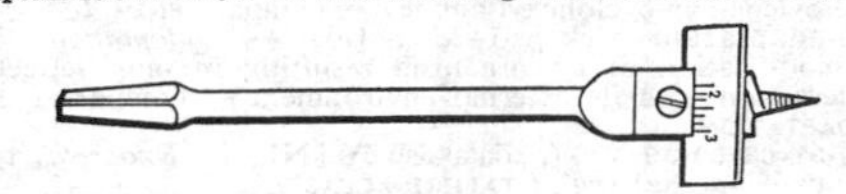

expansive bit

expansive classification *n* : a library classification using both numbers and letters in its notation and having seven complete schedules each one after the first being more minutely subdivided than the previous one — called also *Cutter classification*

ex·pan·sive·ly \-sə̇vlē, -li\ *adv* : in an expansive manner

ex·pan·sive·ness \-sivnə̇s, -sēv- *also* -səv-\ *n* -ES : the quality or state of being expansive

ex·pan·siv·i·ty \ˌekˌspan'sivəd·ē, ik-, -paan-, -vətē, -i\ *n* -ES **1** : EXPANSIVENESS; *esp* : the capacity to expand **2** : COEFFICIENT OF EXPANSION

ex·pan·sum \ik'span(t)səm\ *n* -s [NL — more at EXPANSE] *archaic* : EXPANSE a

ex·pan·sure \ik'spanchə(r)\ *n* -s [L *expansus* + E *-ure*] **1** *obs* : the process of expanding **2** : EXPANSE ⟨the lowland's dark ~ —T.C.Irwin⟩

ex par·te \(')eks¦pärd·ē\ *adj (or adv)* [ML, on behalf] **1** : on or from one side only — used of such legal matters as injunctions, commissions, hearings, and testimony and ordinarily implying a hearing or examination in the presence of or on papers filed by one party and in the absence of and often without notice to the other party **2** : from a one-sided or partisan point of view ⟨the bully proceeds at once by superior power to enforce his own *ex parte* notion of what is right —*Christian Century*⟩ ⟨was discussed *ex parte* by vehement propagandists on both sides —F.L.Allen⟩

ex·pa·ti·ate \ek'spāshēˌāt, ik-, *usu* -ād·+V\ *vb* -ED/-ING/-S [L *expatiatus, exspatiatus*, past part. of *expatiari, exspatiari* to wander from the course, digress, fr. *ex-* ¹ex- + *spatiari* to take a walk, fr. *spatium* space, walk, course — more at SPEED] *vi* **1** : to move about freely or at will : WANDER ⟨fetters to be snapped asunder in order that the human spirit might ~ at liberty —Irving Babbitt⟩ **2** : to speak or write at length or in considerable detail : ELABORATE, ENLARGE — usu. used with *on* or *upon* ⟨his knowledge of the country enabled him to ~ with fluency on the strategical situation —C.S.Forester⟩ ⟨the promoter of the raffle . . . was *expatiating* upon the value of the fabric —Thomas Hardy⟩ ~ *vt* **1** *obs* : EXPAND, SPREAD ⟨princes ~ their dominions —Thomas Adams⟩ **2** *obs* : to allow (oneself) to expatiate ⟨an oration wherein he *expatiated* himself in his praises for the nobility —William Cave⟩ **syn** see DISCOURSE

ex·pa·ti·a·tion \(ˌ)ekˌspās(h)ē'āshən, ik-\ *n* -s [*expatiate* + *-ion*] : the act or an instance of expatiating ⟨it is a very risky thing to ask a professional officer . . . to give a weekly ~ on the war —Sir Winston Churchill⟩

¹ex·pa·tri·ate \ek'spā·trē,āt, *usu* -ād·+V, *chiefly Brit* -pa·-\ *vb* -ED/-ING/-S [ML *expatriatus*, past part. of *expatriare* to leave one's native country, fr. L *ex-* ¹ex- + LL *-patriare* (fr. L *patria* native country, fr. fem. of *patrius* of a father, paternal, fr. *patr-, pater* father) — more at FATHER] *vt* **1 :** to drive into exile **:** BANISH ⟨this minister after having been *expatriated* outlived his great enemy —Isaac D'Israeli⟩ **2 a :** to withdraw (oneself) from residence in one's native country ⟨*expatriated* himself for years at the Cape of Good Hope —R.W.Emerson⟩ **b :** to withdraw (oneself) from allegiance to one's native country ⟨although the father had . . . *expatriated* himself, the son was appointed a cadet "at large" at West Point —T.M.Spaulding⟩ **~** *vi* **:** to leave one's native country ⟨the population again died out or *expatriated* —George Grote⟩; *specif* **:** to renounce allegiance to one's native country **syn** see BANISH

²ex·pa·tri·ate \(')=¦==,ā|t, -,ə|t, *usu* |d·+V\ *adj* [ML *expatriatus*, past part. of *expatriare*] **:** living or occurring in a foreign country **:** EXPATRIATED ⟨an indoctrination school for the training of . . . ~ U.S. employees —*Lamp*⟩ ⟨the equivalent in our day of his early ~ experiences in the Twenties —J.W. Aldridge⟩

³expatriate \"\ *n* -s **:** one who lives in a foreign country ⟨there are both disadvantages and attractions to the life of a foreign correspondent: he is an ~ —F.L.Mott⟩; *specif* **:** one who has renounced his native country ⟨becomes a downright ~ and a more or less active agent of anti-American feeling —H.L.Mencken⟩

ex·pa·tri·a·tion \(,)=,==ˈāshən\ *n* -s [F, fr. *expatrier* to expatriate (fr. ML *expatriare* to leave one's native country) + *-ation*] **:** the act or action of expatriating: as **a :** residence in a foreign country ⟨had recently come back from Paris after long years of ~ . . . for an operation —Louis Auchincloss⟩ **b :** renunciation of allegiance to one's native country ⟨the passage of his bill acknowledging the right of ~ —C. G.Bowers⟩

expdn *abbr* expedition

¹ex·pect \ik'spekt, ek-\ *vb* -ED/-ING/-S [L *expectare, exspectare* to await, look forward to, fr. *ex-* ¹ex- + *spectare* to look at, fr. *spectus*, past part. of *specere* to look — more at SPY] *vi* **1** *obs* **:** WAIT ⟨a dog ~s till his master has done picking of the bone —Henry More⟩ **2 :** to look forward **:** look with anticipation ⟨we love to ~, and when expectation is disappointed or gratified we want to be again ~*ing* —Samuel Johnson⟩ **3 :** to anticipate the birth of a child **:** be pregnant — used in progressive tenses ⟨his wife is ~*ing*⟩ **~** *vt* **1** *archaic* **a :** to wait for **:** AWAIT ⟨with what anxiety I ~ your news of her health —P.B.Shelley⟩ **b :** to wait in order to see and know ⟨~*ing* what should be the event thereof —Richard Knolles⟩ **c :** to be in store for ⟨if any other fate ~s me —Conyers Middleton⟩ **2 :** SUPPOSE, THINK, BELIEVE ⟨I ~ that those Indians are on their way to war —Meriwether Lewis⟩ **3 a :** to look for; *specif* **:** to anticipate the coming or receipt of ⟨she had not ~*ed* the others and there was a great scurrying about to make coffee . . . for them —Louis Bromfield⟩ **b :** to look forward to; *specif* **:** to anticipate the occurrence of ⟨she had spent the night ~*ing* death in the morning, but then was told . . . that she was not to die till noon —Edith Sitwell⟩ **4 a :** to consider probable or certain ⟨he can never ~ . . . that reason will ever hold in leash the emotions —Havelock Ellis⟩ ⟨scurvy was to be ~*ed* in ships that had been long at sea —C.S. Forester⟩ **b :** to consider reasonable, just, proper, due, or necessary ⟨he ~*ed* and demanded hard work of his students —M.H.Thomas⟩ ⟨rich men . . . sometimes ~ a deference which they refuse to claim —J.W.Krutch⟩ **c :** to consider (a person) obligated or in duty bound ⟨England ~s every man to do his duty —Horatio Nelson⟩ ⟨a scholar . . . is ~*ed* to know the latest work on his own speciality —T.H. Savory⟩ **5** *obs* **:** DEMAND, REQUIRE ⟨one assertion in it . . . ~*ed* greater evidence —Joseph Boyse⟩

syn EXPECT, HOPE, HOPE (*for*), LOOK (*to*), LOOK (*for*), and AWAIT can mean, in common, to anticipate in the mind a thing or an event more or less likely or certain to occur. EXPECT usu. implies a high degree of certainty to the point of making preparations or anticipating particular things, actions, or feelings ⟨an old three-story brick, nothing like what he had *expected* —Lenard Kaufman⟩ ⟨Bainbridge's men could *expect* to be starved and cold and verminous, as indeed they were —C.S.Forester⟩ ⟨we can *expect* to import only a fraction of the feeding stuffs formerly obtained from abroad —Laurence Easterbrook⟩ ⟨a person of authority, who is awaited, *expected*, and now comes —Virginia Woolf⟩ HOPE and HOPE (*for*) imply little certainty but suggest confidence and sometimes assurance that what one desires or longs for will happen ⟨makes the reading of it as rewarding as anything short of real, bona fide firsthand experience can ever *hope* to be —H.C.Adamson⟩ ⟨I could not remain a moment in the place, although he considerately *hoped* I would stay —Effie Gray⟩ ⟨what I *hope for* and work for today is for a mess more favorable to artists than is the present one —E.M.Forster⟩ ⟨a boy who showed intellectual promise was encouraged to *hope for* a college education —H.E.Scudder⟩ LOOK (*to*) implies a freedom from doubt that expectations will be fulfilled ⟨*look to* help from the family in times of uncertainty⟩ ⟨*look to* profit from an enterprise⟩ LOOK (*for*) implies less assurance and suggests an attitude of expectancy and watchfulness ⟨*look for* trouble when the enemy begins to move his forces⟩ ⟨*look for* snags that will almost inevitably occur in putting any theory into practice⟩ AWAIT suggests a being in readiness for something expected or watched for; unlike the preceding words it may have as its subject the thing awaited and as its object the person awaiting ⟨nothing for me to do but *await* their return —A.J.Broadwater⟩ ⟨the punishment which *awaits* unrepented sin —R.A.Hall b. 1911⟩ ⟨the fate that *awaits* a sovereign who would display talents and expert authority —A.M.Young⟩

²expect *n* -s *obs* **:** EXPECTATION

ex·pect·able \-təbəl\ *adj* [L *expectabilis, exspectabilis*, fr. *expectare, exspectare* + *-abilis* -able] **:** to be expected ⟨differences of opinion . . . are quite ~ in the present stage of knowledge —J.H.Steward⟩

ex·pect·ably \-blē, -li\ *adv* **:** as might be expected ⟨the passing years, ~, have made his sense of crisis ever more urgent —Lionel Trilling⟩

ex·pect·an·cy \-tənsē, -si\ *or* **ex·pect·ance** \-n(t)s\ *n, pl* **expectancies** *or* **expectances** [ML *expectantia, exspectantia*, fr. L *expectant-, exspectant-, expectans, exspectans* + *-ia* -y] **1** *archaic* **a :** the act of waiting **b :** the state of waiting **2 a :** the act or action of anticipating ⟨the thirst did feel abatement of its edge e'en from *expectance* —H.F.Cary⟩ **b :** the state of anticipating ⟨suspicion . . . gave way to a more submissive ~ —George Eliot⟩ **3 :** the state of being expected ⟨a large fortune in ~⟩ **4 a** (1) **:** something that is expected **:** the object of expectation or hope ⟨each of us had come . . . with his own purposes and *expectancies* —Esther Warner⟩ (2) **:** the expected amount (as of the number of years of life) based on statistical probability — compare LIFE EXPECTANCY **b** *archaic* **:** something that gives rise to expectations ⟨the ~ and rose of the fair state —Shak.⟩

¹ex·pect·ant \ik'spektənt, (')ek¦s-\ *adj* [ME *expectaunt*, fr. L *expectant-, exspectant-, expectans, exspectans*, pres. part. of *expectare, exspectare* to await, look forward to] **1 a :** characterized by expectation **:** EXPECTING, WAITING ⟨the ~ crowds all curious to catch a glimpse of some familiar face —*London Calling*⟩ ⟨spoke as one ~ of unquestioning obedience —S.H. Adams⟩ **b :** expecting the birth of a child ⟨an ~ father⟩; *specif* **:** PREGNANT ⟨~ mothers⟩ **2 :** having expectations **:** PROSPECTIVE ⟨scruples . . . raised in the mind of the ~ heir —Jonathan Swift⟩ **3 :** existing in expectation **:** in prospect **:** EXPECTED ⟨the fee ~ on his wife's life estate —Thomas Jarman⟩ **4** *of the treatment of disease* **:** involving alleviation of immediate distress without basic interference with the development of the pathologic process **:** CONSERVATIVE

²expectant \"\ *n* -s **:** one who is expectant; *specif* **:** a candidate for a position

ex·pect·ant·ly *adv* **:** in an expectant manner **:** with expectation

ex·pec·ta·tion \,ek,spek'tāshən *also* ik-\ *n* -s [L *expectation-, exspectation-, expectatio, exspectatio*, fr. *expectatus, exspectatus* (past part. of *expectare, exspectare*) + *-ion-, -io* -ion] **1** *archaic* **a :** the act of waiting ⟨a daily ~ at the gate is the readiest way to gain admittance into the house —Robert South⟩ **b :** the state of waiting ⟨sat the livelong day with patient ~ —Shak.⟩ **2 a :** the act or action of looking forward **:** ANTICIPATION ⟨had given rise to a general ~ of their marriage —Jane Austen⟩ **b :** the state of looking forward **:** the mental attitude of one who anticipates ⟨no fear of worse . . . would torment me with cruel ~ —John Milton⟩ **3 :** something that is expected **:** the object of expectancy ⟨the hope and ~ of thy time is ruined —Shak.⟩ **4 a :** the basis for expecting something ⟨my soul, wait thou only upon God; for my ~ is from him —Ps 62:5 (AV)⟩ **b :** prospects of inheritance — usu. used in pl. ⟨a rich old uncle . . . from whom I have the greatest ~s —R.B.Sheridan⟩ **5 :** the state of being expected — used esp. in the phrase *in expectation* ⟨benefits in ~⟩ **6 a :** EXPECTANCY 4a(2) **b :** the value of a chance measured by the product of the amount to be received if an event takes place and the probability of the event — called also *mathematical expectation* **7 :** ASSUMPTION, SUPPOSITION, SURMISE ⟨the ~ that you are always from home prevents my writing to you —Thomas Jefferson⟩

expectation of life : LIFE EXPECTANCY

expectation sunday *n, cap E & S* **:** the Sunday before Whitsunday

expectation week *n, cap E&W* [so called fr. its being the period commemorating the apostles' expectation of and prayer for the promised coming of the Holy Spirit] **:** the 10 days between Ascension Day and Whitsunday

¹ex·pect·ative \ik'spektəd·iv, (')ek¦s-, -tətiv\ *adj* [ME (Sc), conferring the right of succession to a benefice, fr. ML *expectativus, exspectativus*, fr. L *expectatus, exspectatus* + *-ivus* -ive] **:** relating to, characterized by, or constituting an object of expectation

²expectative \"\ *n* -s [ML *expectativa, exspectativa* grant of a benefice not yet vacant, fr. fem. of *expectativus, exspectativus*] **:** something that is expected ⟨though blessedness seems to be but an ~, a reversion reserved to the next life —John Donne⟩; *specif* **:** EXPECTATIVE GRACE

expectative grace *n* [alter. of ME (Sc) *grace expectative*, part trans. of ML *gratia expectativa*, fr. L *gratia* grace + ML *expectativa* (fem. of *expectativus*)] **:** a grant of a benefice not yet vacant

expected *past of* EXPECT

expected value *n* **:** the mean value of a random variable

ex·pect·er \ik'spektə(r), (')ek¦s-\ *n* -s **:** one that expects

expecting *pres part of* EXPECT

expectingly *adv* [*expecting* (pres. part. of ¹*expect*) + *-ly*] **:** in an expectant manner

¹ex·pec·to·rant \ik'spektərənt, ek's-\ *adj* [prob. fr. (assumed) NL *expectorant-, expectorans*, pres. part. of (assumed) NL *expectorare*] **:** tending to facilitate expectoration or to promote discharge of mucus from the respiratory tract

²expectorant \"\ *n* -s [prob. fr. (assumed) NL *expectorant-, expectorans*, fr. pres. part. of (assumed) NL *expectorare*] **:** an expectorant agent

ex·pec·to·rate \-,rāt, *usu* -ād·+V\ *vb* -ED/-ING/-S [prob. fr. (assumed) NL *expectoratus*, past part. of (assumed) NL *expectorare*, fr. L, to cast out of the mind, fr. *ex-* ¹ex- + *-pectorare* (fr. *pector-, pectus* breast, soul, mind) — more at PECTORAL] *vt* **1** *obs* **:** to bring about the ejection of (phlegm) **2 a** *obs* **:** to cast out of the mind **b** *archaic* **:** to relieve the mind of **3 a :** to eject (as phlegm) from the throat or lungs by coughing or hawking and spitting **b :** SPIT **~** *vi* **1 :** to discharge matter from the throat or lungs by coughing or hawking and spitting **2 :** SPIT

ex·pec·to·ra·tion \ik,spektə'rāshən, (,)ek,s-\ *n* -s [prob. fr. (assumed) NL *expectoration-, expectoratio*, fr. (assumed) NL *expectoratus* + L *-ion-, -io* -ion] **1 :** the act or an instance of expectorating **2 :** expectorated matter

ex·pec·to·ra·tor \ik'spektə,rād·ə(r), ek's-, -ātə-\ *n* -s **:** one that expectorates

expects *pres 3d sing of* EXPECT, *pl of* EXPECT

ex·pede \ek'spēd\ *vt* -ED/-ING/-S [L *expedire* to set free, make ready] *Scots law* **:** to obtain, issue, or take out officially ⟨the letter formerly *expeded* under the dictation of your right honorable mother —Sir Walter Scott⟩

ex·pe·di·ate \ik'spēdē,āt, ek-\ *vt* -ED/-ING/-S [by alter. (influence of *-ate*)] **:** EXPEDITE ⟨fires had been lighted in the grate beneath the climbing boy in order to ~ his efforts —*Ireland's Mag.*⟩

ex·pe·di·en·cy \ik'spēdēənsē, ek-, -si\ *or* **ex·pe·di·ence** \-n(t)s\ *n, pl* **expediencies** *or* **expediences** [*expediency* fr. LL *expedientia* advantage, fr. L *expedient-, expediens* + *-ia* -y; *expedience* fr. ME, advantage, fr. LL *expedientia*] **1** *obs* **:** HASTE, DISPATCH ⟨three thousand men of war are making hither with all due *expedience* —Shak.⟩ **2** *obs* **:** ENTERPRISE, EXPEDITION ⟨let me hear . . . what yesternight our council did decree in forwarding this dear *expedience* —Shak.⟩ **3 :** the quality or state of being suited to the end in view **:** FITNESS, SUITABILITY ⟨the whip of shame and pain could drive her . . . into an appreciation of the ~ of morality —Margaret Deland⟩ **4 :** cultivation of or adherence to means and methods that are opportune or temporarily advantageous as distinguished from those that are right or just; *specif* **:** SELF-INTEREST ⟨the struggle between ethics and politics, between right and ~, had begun —C.W.De Kiewiet⟩ **5 :** a means of achieving a particular end **:** EXPEDIENT ⟨had found a number of simple *expediencies* by which to dissolve what was once the most solemn contract of all —Hamilton Basso⟩

¹ex·pe·di·ent \-nt\ *adj* [ME, fr. MF or L; MF *expedient*, fr. L *expedient-, expediens*, pres. part. of *expedire* to be advantageous, set free, make ready, fr. *ex-* ¹ex- + *-pedire* (fr. *ped-, pes* foot) — more at FOOT] **1 :** characterized by suitability, practicality, and efficiency in achieving a particular end **:** fit, proper, or advantageous under the circumstances ⟨the harvest had been bad, and it was found ~, for their better provision, to disperse the troops over a broader area —J.A.Froude⟩ ⟨it is not necessary, and probably not even ~, to pilfer the secret files of the foreign office —H.J.Morgenthau⟩ **2** *obs* **:** EXPEDITIOUS ⟨I will with all ~ duty see you —Shak.⟩ **3 :** characterized by concern with the opportune or temporarily advantageous as distinguished from the just or right; *specif* **:** governed by self-interest ⟨morality, for the state, means doing what is ~ —H.S.Agar⟩

syn POLITIC, ADVISABLE: EXPEDIENT applies to what is advantageous and opportune under the immediate circumstances in question, often without much regard to ethics ⟨so long as the Stuarts were ruling at St. James's, speculative theocrats found it *expedient* to gloss their principles with nice distinctions between temporal and spiritual overlords —V.L.Parrington⟩ ⟨purely for *expedient* reasons he let the Iroquois alone —Hervey Allen⟩ POLITIC may apply to what is judicious and wise according to the practicalities of the situation ⟨before he faced the head of the Osborne house with the news which it was his duty to tell, Dobbin bethought him that it would be *politic* to make friends of the rest of the family, and, if possible, have the ladies on his side —W.M.Thackeray⟩ ⟨the alacrity with which the German intellectual world submitted to Hitler is proof that, if it knew nothing of politics, it at least knew how to be *politic* —Martin Greenberg⟩ ADVISABLE describes what is practical, prudent, and advantageous and lacks the occas. derogatory implications of EXPEDIENT and POLITIC ⟨in the circumstances, Superintendent, it seems to me *advisable* to adjourn the inquest until you have completed your investigations —Dorothy Sayers⟩ ⟨I do not say that either psychology or medicine or penology has yet arrived at such a stage as to make a revolution in our system of punishment *advisable* —B.N. Cardozo⟩

²expedient \"\ *n* -s [F *expédient*, fr. MF *expedient*, fr. *expedient*, adj.] **1 :** something that is expedient **:** a means to an end ⟨rules of thumb generally . . . are a lazy man's ~ for ridding himself of the trouble of thinking and deciding —B.N. Cardozo⟩ **2 :** a means devised or used in an exigency **:** MAKESHIFT ⟨through so much traveling I had had to learn all sorts of ~s and prepare for all sorts of emergencies —V.G.Heiser⟩ **syn** see RESOURCE

ex·pe·di·en·tial \ik,spēdē¦enchəl, (,)ek¦-\ *adj* [fr. *expediency*, after such pairs as E *potency: potential*] **:** of, characterized by, or governed by expediency ⟨doubtful if government by congressional committees can be justified on either democratic or ~ grounds —E.E.Schattschneider⟩

ex·pe·di·ent·ist \=ˈ==,əntəst\ *n* -s **:** one who uses or advocates expedients

ex·pe·di·ent·ly *adv* [ME, fr. *expedient* + *-ly*] **:** in an expedient manner

ex·ped·i·tate \ek'spedə,tāt, ik-\ *vt* -ED/-ING/-S [ML *expeditatus*, past part. of *expeditare*, fr. L *ex-* ¹ex- + ML *-peditare* (fr. L *ped-, pes* foot)] **:** to cut off three claws or the ball of each forefoot of (a dog) so as to prevent the chasing of deer ⟨the mastiffs which were *expeditated* . . . were allowed to be kept in the forest without a special license —Nicholas Biddle⟩

ex·ped·i·ta·tion \(,)ek,spedə'tāshən, ik-\ *n* -s [ML *expeditation-, expeditatio*, fr. *expeditatus* + L *-ion-, -io* -ion] **:** the act of expeditating a dog

¹ex·pe·dite \'ekspə,dīt, *usu* -īd· +V\ *adj* [ME *expedit* accomplished, fr. L *expeditus*, past part. of *expedire*] **1** *obs* **:** QUICK, SPEEDY, PROMPT **2** *obs* **:** free from obstacles, impediments, or difficulties **:** UNHAMPERED, UNIMPEDED **3 a** *obs* **:** ready for action **:** ALERT **b** *archaic* **:** ready for use **:** HANDY **4** *archaic* **:** lightly equipped **:** UNENCUMBERED

²expedite \"\ *vt* -ED/-ING/-S [L *expeditus*, past part. of *expedire* to set free, make ready — more at EXPEDIENT] **1 :** to carry through with dispatch **:** execute promptly ⟨such is my wish: dare thou to ~ it —Bayard Taylor⟩ **2** *obs* **a :** to remove the difficulties from **:** FACILITATE ⟨a broad way now is paved to ~ your glorious march —John Milton⟩ **b :** to set free **:** EXTRICATE ⟨this active gentleman had much ado to ~ himself and save his life —Thomas Fuller⟩ **3 :** to accelerate the process or progress of **:** speed up **:** HASTEN ⟨an administration measure intended to ~ the shipbuilding program —T.W. Arnold⟩ **4 :** to send out **:** ISSUE, DISPATCH ⟨*expedited* a letter under cover to the duke —Fanny Burney⟩

expedite freight *or* **expedited freight** *n* **:** a special railroad freight service giving preference in transportation to specified commodities (as fruit, vegetables, livestock)

ex·pe·dit·er *or* **ex·pe·di·tor** \-īd·ə(r), -ītə-\ *n* -s **:** one that expedites: as **a :** one employed to ensure adequate supplies of raw materials and equipment for filling production contracts **b :** one employed to coordinate the flow of materials, tools, parts, and processed goods within a plant in order to facilitate continuous production **c :** one employed to attend to the shipping of products on schedule

ex·pe·di·tion \,ekspə'dishən\ *n* -s [ME *expedicioun*, fr. MF & L; MF *expedition*, fr. L *expedition-, expeditio*, fr. *expeditus* (past part. of *expedire* to set free, make ready) + *-ion-, -io* -ion] **1 a :** a journey, voyage, or excursion undertaken for a specific purpose ⟨had charge of the ~ to observe the transit of Venus in China —W.C.Rufus⟩ ⟨military ~s⟩ ⟨an archaeological ~⟩ ⟨a whaling ~⟩ **b :** the group of persons making such an expedition ⟨the gun belongs to the ~ —C.B.Hitchcock⟩ **2 :** efficient promptness **:** SPEED, HASTE ⟨put her things on with remarkable ~ —Arnold Bennett⟩ **3** *obs* **:** the quality or state of being expedited ⟨let us deliver our puissance into the hand of God, putting it straight in ~ —Shak.⟩ **syn** see HASTE

¹ex·pe·di·tion·ary \-shə,nerē, -ri\ *adj* **:** of, relating to, or constituting an expedition; *specif* **:** sent on military service abroad ⟨a British ~ force bound for China was diverted to Calcutta —A.N.Whitehead⟩

²expeditionary \"\ *n* -ES **:** one who goes on an expedition ⟨the *expeditionaries* founded a town . . . and set up the first European colony on the American mainland —*Time*⟩

ex·pe·di·tion·er \-sh(ə)nə(r)\ *n* -s **:** EXPEDITIONARY ⟨the ~s left Reykjavik on June 22 —Thomas Foster⟩

ex·pe·di·tion·ist \-sh(ə)nəst\ *n* -s **:** EXPEDITIONARY ⟨a lookout from which Indians as well as returning ~s could be watched —*Amer. Guide Series: Minn.*⟩

ex·pe·di·tious \¦ekspə¦dishəs\ *adj* [fr. *expedition*, after such pairs as E *sedition: seditious*] **:** characterized by expedition: **a :** acting or performed with promptness and efficiency **:** SPEEDY ⟨where wages are high . . . we shall always find the workmen more active, diligent, and ~ —Adam Smith⟩ ⟨~ service⟩ **b :** conducive to prompt efficient performance **:** QUICK ⟨stamped out the rebellion by the most ~ means —Virginia W. Valentine⟩ ⟨an ~ system⟩ **syn** see FAST

ex·pe·di·tious·ly *adv* **:** in an expeditious manner **:** with expedition ⟨they traveled as ~ as possible —Jane Austen⟩

ex·pe·di·tious·ness *n* -ES **:** the quality or state of being expeditious ⟨the boss was pleased with the ~ with which the enterprise was completed⟩

ex·ped·i·tive \ek'spedəd·iv\ *adj* **:** EXPEDITIOUS

ex·pel \ik'spel, ek-\ *vt* **expelled; expelled; expelling; expels** [ME *expellen*, fr. L *expellere*, fr. *ex-* ¹ex- + *pellere* to drive — more at FELT] **1 :** to force out from or as if from a receptacle **:** drive out **:** cast out **:** EJECT, DISLODGE ⟨the gigantic explosion . . . *expelled* some four and a half cubic miles of pumice —Howel Williams⟩ ⟨filled her lungs with a long inhalation and *expelled* the smoke —B.A.Williams⟩ ⟨superstitions become lodged in our mental constitutions and sometimes are modified or *expelled* only with the greatest difficulty —F.A.Geldard⟩ **2 :** to drive away from a place or country **:** compel to leave ⟨citizens organized vigilante committees and *expelled* or subdued the undesirables —*Amer. Guide Series: Tenn.*⟩; *specif* **:** DEPORT ⟨an alien within a deportable class had to be *expelled* —*Harvard Law Rev.*⟩ **3 :** to cut off from membership in or the privileges of an institution or society ⟨the boy attended school but was *expelled* for fighting with his teacher —A.F.Harlow⟩ **4** *obs* **:** to dismiss from attention or consideration **:** REFUSE ⟨would you not poor fellowship ~, myself would offer you to accompany —Edmund Spenser⟩ **5** *obs* **:** to keep out **:** EXCLUDE ⟨O, that that earth . . . should patch a wall to ~ the winter's flaw —Shak.⟩ **6** *obs* **:** DISCHARGE, SHOOT ⟨was not slow to ~ the shaft from her contracted bow —John Dryden⟩ **syn** see EJECT

ex·pel·la·ble \-ləbəl\ *adj* **:** capable of being expelled **:** liable to expulsion

¹ex·pel·lant *or* **ex·pel·lent** \-lənt\ *n* -s [*expellant* fr. *expel* + *-ant*, n. suffix; *expellent* fr. L *expellent-, expellens*, pres. part. of *expellere*] **:** an expellant medicine

²expellant *or* **expellent** \"\ *adj* [*expellant* fr. *expel* + *-ant*, adj. suffix; *expellent* fr. L *expellent-, expellens*, pres. part. of *expellere*] **:** tending or serving to expel **:** EXPULSIVE

ex·pel·lee \,ek,spe¦lē, -,spə¦-; ik¦spe¦lē, ek¦-\ *n* -s **:** a person expelled esp. from his native or adopted country; *specif* **:** one transferred from the country of residence for resettlement in the country with which he is ethnically associated

ex·pel·ler \ik'spelə(r), ek-\ *n* -s **:** one that expels: as **a :** a screw press for expressing vegetable oil from soybeans or other seeds **b :** an operator of a machine for pressing liquid and tallow from tankage

expeller man *n, pl* **expeller men 1 :** EXPELLER b **2 :** an operator of a machine for expressing oil from soybeans

ex·pend \ik'spend, ek-\ *vb* -ED/-ING/-S [ME *expenden*, fr. L *expendere* to weigh out, expend, fr. *ex-* ¹ex- + *pendere* to weigh, pay — more at SPAN] *vt* **1 :** to pay out or distribute **:** SPEND ⟨the social services upon which public revenue is ~*ed* —J.A.Hobson⟩ **2 :** to consume by use **:** use up ⟨little guys — the ones who are ~*ed* — never get to see the broad picture of the war —W.L.White⟩ ⟨still mourns the apparent eclipse of books on which he ~*ed* great energies —Harry Hansen⟩ **~** *vi* **:** to spend money ⟨he rode a horse, lived high, ~*ed* largely —George Meredith⟩ **syn** see SPEND

ex·pend·abil·i·ty \ik,spendə'bilәd·ē, (,)ek-, -lətē, -i\ *n* -ES **:** the quality or state of being expendable

¹ex·pend·able \ik'spendəbəl, (')ek¦s-\ *adj* **:** that may be expended: as **a :** normally used up or consumed in service ⟨such ~ supplies as pencils, ink, and paper⟩ **b :** more economically replaced than rescued, salvaged, or protected; *specif* **:** sacrificed according to plan in order to accomplish a military mission ⟨in a war anything can be ~ — money or gasoline or equipment or most usually men —W.L.White⟩

²expendable \"\ *n* -s **:** one that is expendable — usu. used in pl. ⟨when an army is retreating, a small force is left behind to cover the retreat and be sacrificed to the enemy: they are ~s —Drew Pearson⟩

ex·pend·er \=ˈ=də(r)\ *n* -s **:** one that expends

ex·pen·di·tor \=ˈ=dəd·ər, -də,tȯ(ə)r\ *n* -s [ML, fr. L *expendere* to expend, prob. after L *vendere* to sell: *venditor* seller] **:** PAYMASTER; *specif* **:** an officer formerly appointed in England to expend the money collected by tax for the repair of sewers

ex·pend·i·ture \ik'spendəchə(r), ek-, -dēchə(r); -də,chu̇(ə)r, -u̇ə, -də,tu̇-, -də-,tyu̇-\ *n* -s [*expendit-* (as in *expenditor*) + *-ure*] **1** : the act or process of expending ⟨with the ~ of five or six thousand dollars for refurbishing, lighting, advertising, she could have held her own —Mary J. Rolfs⟩ ⟨individual stars which maintain their luminosity by the ~ of nuclear energy —George Gamow⟩ **2** : something that is expended : DISBURSEMENT, EXPENSE ⟨only after ten years of practice did his income equal his ~*s* —R.H.Shryock⟩ **3** *in accrual-basis accounting* : an outlay or the creation of a liability for an asset or expense item

¹ex·pense \ik'spen(t)s, ek- *sometimes* 'ek,s-\ *n* -s [ME, fr. AF or LL; AF *expense*, fr. LL *expensa*, fr. L, fem. of *expensus*, past part. of *expendere*] **1 a** (1) *archaic* : the act or practice of expending money : SPENDING ⟨this exuberance of money displayed itself in wantonness of ~ —Samuel Johnson⟩ (2) *obs* : EXTRAVAGANCE ⟨all of them . . . dread a woman of ~ —James Fordyce⟩ **b** (1) *archaic* : the act or process of using up : CONSUMPTION ⟨the sun is not wasted by ~ of light —Benjamin Franklin⟩ (2) *obs* : LOSS ⟨and moan the ~ of many a vanished sight —Shak.⟩ **2 a** : something that is expended in order to secure a benefit or bring about a result ⟨those who have no experience of teaching are incapable of imagining the ~ of spirit entailed by any really living instruction —Bertrand Russell⟩ **b** : the financial burden involved typically in a course of action or manner of living : COST ⟨at his own ~ he built a fort and persuaded others to join him there —*Amer. Guide Series: Maine*⟩ ⟨was obliged to spend most of each year earning his tuition and living ~*s* —R.F.Seybolt⟩ **c** (1) : the charges that are incurred by an employee in connection with the performance of his duties and that typically include transportation, meals, and lodging while traveling — usu. used in pl. (2) : money given to an employee as reimbursement for such charges — usu. used in pl. **d** : an item of outlay incurred in the operation of a business enterprise allocable to and chargeable against revenue for a specific period **3** : a cause or occasion of expenditure ⟨a country estate is a great ~⟩ **4** : loss, injury, or detriment as the necessary price of something gained or as the inevitable result or penalty of an action : SACRIFICE — usu. used in the phrase *at the expense of* ⟨the spread of the city civilization at the ~ of the villages —Benjamin Farrington⟩ ⟨develop a boy's physique at the ~ of his intelligence —Bertrand Russell⟩

²expense \"\ *vt* -ED/-ING/-S **1** : to charge with expenses **2** : to charge to an expense account : write off as an expense expenditure

expense account *n* : an account of expenses reimbursable to an employee

expense constant *n* : a flat amount included in workmen's compensation insurance rates for small risks in order to cover the costs of issuing and servicing the policy

expenseful *adj* **1** *obs* : EXPENSIVE **2** *obs* : EXTRAVAGANT

ex·pense·less \s'ˌslə̇s\ *adj*, *archaic* : INEXPENSIVE

ex·pen·sive \ik'spen(t)siv, ek-, -sēv *also* -səv\ *adj* **1** *archaic* : given to lavish expenditure : EXTRAVAGANT ⟨young men of this age are . . . so ~ both of their health and fortune —Richard Steele⟩ **2** : attended with or involving losses, sacrifices, or continued drains on one's resources : COSTLY, DEAR ⟨they . . . tightened credit, raising discount rates and otherwise making it more ~ to borrow —L.H.Haney⟩ ⟨an aggressive foreign policy meant ~ alliances —J.H.Plumb⟩ **3** : characterized by high price or cost that sometimes exceeds a thing's intrinsic worth or a prospective buyer's financial resources ⟨wind and water power were free; but coal was ~ —Lewis Mumford⟩ ⟨three ~ but flourishing weeklies devoted to absolutely nothing but the life of the rich and titled —Aldous Huxley⟩ **syn** see COSTLY

ex·pen·sive·ly \-səvlē, -li\ *adv* : in an expensive manner

ex·pen·sive·ness \-sivnə̇s, -sēv- *also* -səv-\ *n* -ES : the quality or state of being expensive

exper *abbr* **1** experience; experienced **2** experiment; experimental

ex·per·ge·fac·tion \ek¦spərjə¦fakshən\ *n* [LL *expergefaction-, expergefactio*, fr. L *expergefactus* (past part. of *expergefacere* to awaken, fr. *expergisci* to become awake — fr. *ex-* ¹ex- + *-pergisci*, fr. *pergere* to proceed, go on, fr. *per* through + *regere* to lead straight, guide, rule — + *facere* to make, do) + *-ion-, -io* -ion — more at FARE, RIGHT, DO] *archaic* : AWAKENING

¹ex·pe·ri·ence \ik'spirēən(t)s, ek-, -pēr-\ *n* -s [ME, fr. MF, fr. L *experientia*, fr. *experient-, experiens* (pres. part. of *experiri* to try, fr. *ex-* ¹ex- + *-periri* — akin to *periculum* attempt, peril) + *-ia* -y — more at FEAR] **1** *obs* **a** : a trial or test ⟨make ~ of my loyalty by some service —James Shirley⟩ **b** : a tentative trial : EXPERIMENT ⟨a story of I know not what ~*s* they have made —Walter Blithe⟩ **c** : a conclusive proof : DEMONSTRATION ⟨the ~ that Pyrrhus hath given of the Roman power —Walter Raleigh †1618⟩ **2** : direct observation of or participation in events : an encountering, undergoing, or living through things in general as they take place in the course of time ⟨what we call education and culture is . . . the substitution of reading for ~, of literature for life, of the obsolete fictitious for the contemporary real —G.B.Shaw⟩ ⟨she knew by prevision what most women learn only by ~ —Thomas Hardy⟩ **3 a** : the state, extent, duration, or result of being engaged in a particular activity (as a profession) or in affairs generally ⟨ten years' ~ had made my eye learned in the valuing of motion —Thomas De Quincey⟩ ⟨gaining . . . business ~ and developing a character recognized for its industry and ambition —C.W.Mitman⟩ **b** *obs* : something approved by or made on the basis of such experience ⟨saw the schools . . . full of pretty curiosities and ~*s*, mechanical, mathematical, and hydraulic —Richard Lassels⟩ **4** : knowledge, skill, or practice derived from direct observation of or participation in events : practical wisdom resulting from what one has encountered, undergone, or lived through ⟨tell him that he ought to get ~, see the world, join a political party, and . . . make sure that he participates in the habitual activities of his society —Delmore Schwartz⟩ **5 a** : the sum total of the conscious events that make up an individual life ⟨all that we know and feel and do, all our facts and theories, all our emotions and ideals and ends may be included in . . . ~ —James Ward⟩ **b** : the sum total of events that make up the past of a community or nation or that have occurred within the knowledge of mankind generally ⟨the organized groups whose life has been the ~ of the peoples of the West —*Official Register of Harvard Univ.*⟩ **6** : something personally encountered, undergone, or lived through: as **a** : an event observed or participated in ⟨a series of the author's reprinted papers which augment the stories of his personal ~*s* —John Cushing⟩ **b** (1) : a state of mind that forms a significant and often crucial part of one's inner religious life and that is sometimes accompanied by intense emotion ⟨in the writings of the earlier Friends, in the diaries and journals that record their intimate and inward ~*s* —Kate W. Tibbals⟩ (2) : an account of such an experience — see EXPERIENCE MEETING **c** : illicit sexual relations ⟨a mere nineteen, a kid, when he had his ~ with her —James Jones⟩ **7** : something by which one is stimulated or moved ⟨the only one of our new playwrights who has given me . . . an ~ in the theater —Louis Kronenberger⟩ ⟨New Mexico was the greatest ~ from the outside world that I have ever had —D.H.Lawrence⟩ **8** *philos* **a** : the act or process of perceiving or apprehending ⟨~ is a matter of the interaction of organism with its environment, and environment that is human as well as physical, that includes the materials of tradition and institutions as well as local surroundings —John Dewey⟩ **b** : the content or the particular result of such experience **c** : the discriminative reaction or the nonconscious response of an organism to events or happenings within its environment **9** : insurance loss record ⟨the favorable mortality ~ of the past several years —P.M.Fraser⟩

²experience \"\ *vt* -ED/-ING/-S **1 a** *archaic* : to put to the test : TRY ⟨persuade their governess to ~ their zeal —Thomas Pennant⟩ **b** *obs* : to ascertain, prove, or reveal by observation or participation ⟨this trial has . . . *experienced* to me my sad weakness —Rachel Russell⟩ **2** *obs* : to teach by experience : EXERCISE, TRAIN ⟨~ thy soul in the comforts of Christ's dying —Richard Whitlock⟩ **3 a** : to have experience of : meet with : FEEL, SUFFER, UNDERGO ⟨the first need for the reader of poetry is to ~ its impact —Mary M. Colum⟩ ⟨the reason death was feared was because no man could twice ~ it —Stuart Cloete⟩ ⟨the cane planters often ~ a lack of workers —P.E.James⟩ **b** : to learn by experience : find out : DISCOVER ⟨I have *experienced* that a landscape and the sky unfold the deepest beauty —Nathaniel Hawthorne⟩ **4** : to respond or react discriminatively to (a set of events within the environment) — used of an organism

syn UNDERGO, SUSTAIN, SUFFER: EXPERIENCE indicates an actual living through something and coming to know it firsthand rather than through hearsay or report ⟨a weak and transient feeling to what I now *experienced* —W.H.Hudson⟩ ⟨real people, not labor units, figures in reports, but persons? It is persons who *experience* life —J.B.Priestley⟩ UNDERGO may apply esp. to that which one bears or endures or is subjected to ⟨*undergoing* a major operation⟩ ⟨the air was charged with tension. She saw that he was *undergoing* a difficult struggle —Irving Stone⟩ ⟨part of the ceremony of purification which he must *undergo* before partaking of the new fruits of the season —J.G.Frazer⟩ SUSTAIN in this sense suggests undergoing affliction or infliction without necessarily bearing up with resolution ⟨the two dropped supine into chairs at opposite corners of the ring as if they had *sustained* excessive fatigue —G.B.Shaw⟩ ⟨a few years later he *sustained* something like a heatstroke, which weakened his resistance to climatic conditions —A.D.H.Smith⟩ ⟨the company *sustained* large-scale losses in the venture⟩ SUFFER, often interchangeable in this sense with SUSTAIN, may more strongly implicate wrong or injury ⟨here is a ruthless anatomy of that loneliness which continues life in the Arctic and is a continuing mystery because the men who *suffer* it gladly have thick enough skins to find an easy shelter —*Times Lit. Supp.*⟩ ⟨women in government are democratic and will not *suffer* the servility of subordination —H.J.Laski⟩ ⟨with frightful atrocities *suffered* mostly by the McCoys —A.F.Harlow⟩

—**experience religion** : to undergo religious conversion

ex·pe·ri·ence·able \-səbəl\ *adj* : capable of being experienced

experienced *adj* [fr. past part. of ²*experience*] **1** *archaic* : approved by test : TRIED ⟨counteract by ~ remedies every new tendency —Samuel Johnson⟩ **2** : having experience : made skillful or wise through observation of or participation in a particular activity or in affairs generally : PRACTICED ⟨advocated so widely by thoughtful and ~ people in all classes —G.B.Shaw⟩ **3** : encountered or undergone in the course of experience ⟨a cautious and guiltless reformation of ~ grievances —Archibald Alison⟩

ex·pe·ri·ence·less \-slə̇s\ *adj* : being without experience

experience meeting *n* : a meeting at which persons relate their religious experiences

ex·pe·ri·enc·er \-sə(r)\ *n* -s : one that experiences ⟨signs or symbols calling for one response or another on the part of the ~ —E.M.Bartlett⟩

experience rating *n* : merit rating (as in a state unemployment compensation system) that consists of the manual rate modified by the loss experience of the particular risk

experiences *pl of* EXPERIENCE, *pres 3d sing of* EXPERIENCE

experiencing *pres part of* EXPERIENCE

¹ex·pe·ri·ent \-nt\ *adj* [ME, fr. L *experient-, experiens*, pres. part. of *experiri* to try — more at ¹EXPERIENCE] : having experience

²experient \"\ *n* -s : a person undergoing an experience or having experience

ex·pe·ri·en·tial \ik¦ˌˌ¦enchəl, (ˌ)ek¦-\ *adj* [ML *experientialis* experimental, fr. L *experientia* experience, test + *-alis* -al] : derived from, based on, or relating to experience : EMPIRICAL ⟨the rich ~ content of the teachings of the older philosophers —Benjamin Farrington⟩ — **ex·pe·ri·en·tial·ly** \-chəlē, -li\ *adv*

ex·pe·ri·en·tial·ism \ik,ˌˌ¦echə,lizəm, (ˌ)ek-\ *n* -s : a philosophical theory that experience is the source of all knowledge not purely deductive, formal, or tautological — compare EMPIRICISM

¹ex·pe·ri·en·tial·ist \-chələ̇st\ *n* -s : one who believes in experientialism

²experientialist \"\ *or* **ex·pe·ri·en·tial·is·tic** \ik,ˌˌ¦ˌˌ¦listik, (ˌ)ek-\ *adj* : of or relating to experientialism

experiential time *n* : SUBJECTIVE TIME

¹ex·per·i·ment \ik'sperəmənt, ek- *also* ˌ-pir-\ *n* -s [ME, fr. MF *experiment*, fr. L *experimentum*, fr. *experiri* to try + *-mentum* -ment] **1 a** : a test or trial ⟨make another ~ of his suspicion —Shak.⟩ **b** (1) : a tentative procedure or policy; *esp* : one adopted in uncertainty as to whether it will answer the desired purpose or bring about the desired result ⟨is going to put this hope to the test by trying a political ~ of bold proportions —Harold Callender⟩ (2) : the tangible result of such a procedure or policy ⟨Benavente's earliest literary ~*s* were four little romantic fantasies published . . . in 1892 —*Current Biog.*⟩ **c** : an act or operation carried out under conditions determined by the experimenter (as in a laboratory) in order to discover some unknown principle or effect or to test, establish, or illustrate some suggested or known truth ⟨the ~*s* of the defendant's experts lead . . . to the opinion that a typhoid bacillus could not survive the journey —O.W.Holmes †1935⟩ **2** *obs* : EXPERIENCE ⟨by sad ~ I know how little weight my words with thee can find —John Milton⟩ **3** *obs* : EXPEDIENT, REMEDY ⟨you will find it a sure ~ for the quinsy —William Coles⟩ **4** : the process or practice of trying or testing : EXPERIMENTATION ⟨the result of some centuries of ~ tended to raise rather than silence doubt —Henry Adams⟩

²ex·per·i·ment \-,ment, -mənt —*see* ²-MENT\ *vb* -ED/-ING/-S [ME *experimenten*, fr. *experiment*, n.] *vt* **1** *obs* : to have experience of : EXPERIENCE, FEEL ⟨thy fatherly mercy . . . so often ~*ed* by me —Henry Hammond⟩ **2** *archaic* : to discover by experiment ⟨that may be easily ~*ed* in a small bird —Benjamin Martin⟩ **3** *archaic* : to make a trial or test of ⟨several articles were proposed to be ~*ed*, and if found good . . . to be confirmed —John Entick⟩ ~ *vi* : to engage in experimentation : make experiments ⟨the world has become a laboratory where immature and feverish minds ~ with unknown forces —John Buchan⟩ ⟨studied drawing and painting in an art school . . . and ~*ed* in painting at home —W.H.Downes⟩

¹ex·per·i·men·tal \ik¦sperə¦mentᵊl, ˌ-pir-, ek¦-, ,ek,ˌˌ¦ˌˌ\ *adj* [ME, fr. ML *experimentalis*, fr. L *experimentum* + *-alis* -al] **1** : of, relating to, or based on experience : EMPIRICAL ⟨misgivings, intensified . . . by ~ knowledge of the difficulties to be overcome, seem to hem me in —Arnold Bennett⟩ **2 a** : founded on, derived from, or discovered by experiment ⟨the heart of the ~ method is the direct control of the thing studied —B.F. Skinner⟩ **b** : given to or skilled in experiment ⟨~ philosophers could only indicate how gravity operated —S.F.Mason⟩ **3 a** : serving the ends of or used as a means of experimentation ⟨~ animals⟩ ⟨the ~ theater⟩ ⟨an ~ school⟩ **b** *of a disease* : intentionally produced esp. in laboratory animals for the purpose of study ⟨~ tuberculosis⟩ **4** : relating to or having the characteristics of experiment : TENTATIVE ⟨~ flights will start this autumn — in fact, almost as soon as the two machines can be fitted with floats —*London Calling*⟩ ⟨free verse is not yet out of the ~ stage —J.L.Lowes⟩

²experimental \"\ *n* -s **1** *obs* : something learned by experience ⟨as to ~*s* . . . a mere novice —Samuel Richardson⟩ **2 a** : something experimental ⟨don't try ~*s* until you've had plenty of experience with the straight radio play —Josephina Niggli⟩ **b** : a plant or animal used in an experiment — compare CONTROL

experimental design *n* : a method of research in the social sciences (as sociology or psychology) in which a controlled experimental factor is subjected to special treatment for purposes of comparison with a factor kept constant

experimental engineer *n* : an engineer whose training or specialization is in experimental engineering

experimental engineering *n* : research and development work in some branch of engineering

ex·per·i·men·tal·ism \ik,ˌˌ'mentᵊl,izəm, (ˌ)ek-\ *n* -s **1 a** : a theory advocating experimental or empirical principles and procedures **b** : pragmatist or instrumentalist theories, principles, and practices; *specif* : those of John Dewey and his followers — compare INSTRUMENTALISM, PRAGMATISM **2** : the practice of relying on experiment

ex·per·i·men·tal·ist \-ˌə̇st\ *n* -s **1** : a person conducting scientific experiments **2** : one who likes to experiment as an innovator, artist, or explorer ⟨a bold ~ with paragraph and punctuation —H.G.Wells⟩

ex·per·i·men·tal·ize \-,īz\ *vi* -ED/-ING/-S : to make experiments : engage in experimentation

ex·per·i·men·tal·ly *pronunc at* ¹EXPERIMENTAL +ē *or* i\ *adv* : in an experimental manner: **a** : by experience : as a result of experience ⟨a king . . . ~ acquainted with the ways . . . of flatterers —Robert South⟩ **b** : by experiment : as an experiment ⟨the curvature of the runners was determined ~ —E.K. Kane⟩

experimental psychology *n* : PSYCHOLOGY 1b

ex·per·i·men·ta·tion \ik,ˌˌmən·tāshən, (ˌ)ek-, -,men-\ *n* -s **1** : the act, process, or practice of making experiments ⟨a tendency among lay critics to confine ~ to scientists in the laboratory —John Dewey⟩ **2** : an instance of experimentation : EXPERIMENT ⟨an outgrowth and culmination of numerous ~*s* and inventions —William Chomsky⟩

ex·per·i·men·ta·tive \ik,ˌˌ'mentəd·iv, (ˌ)ek-, -tətiv\ *adj* : inclined to experimentation : having the characteristics of an experiment

ex·per·i·men·ta·tor \ik'ˌˌmən,tād·ə(r), ek-, -,men-, -ātə-, ik,ˌˌ(ˌ)ˌ'ˌˌ, (ˌ)ek,ˌˌ(ˌ)ˌ'ˌˌ\ *n* -s [ML, fr. LL *experimentatus* (past part. of *experimentare* to test by experience, fr. L *experimentum* test) + L *-or*] : EXPERIMENTER

ex·per·i·men·tee \ik¦ˌˌ(ˌ)ˌ¦tē, ek-\ *n* -s : one subjected to an experiment

ex·per·i·ment·er \ˌ'ˌˌ,mentə(r)\ *or* **ex·per·i·men·tor** \",(ˌ)ˌ,ˌ'men·,tȯ(ə)r, -ō(ə)r\ *n* -s : one that experiments or conducts an experiment; *specif* : one that conducts an experiment in introspective psychology by arranging and determining the physical conditions of the observer's experience

ex·per·i·men·tize \ˌ'ˌˌmən·,tīz\ *vi* -ED/-ING/-S : EXPERIMENT

experiments *pl of* EXPERIMENT, *pres 3d sing of* EXPERIMENT

experiment station *n* : an establishment for scientific research in such fields as agriculture, biology, or meteorology where experiments are carried out, studies of practical application are made, and information is disseminated — called also *field station*

¹ex·pert \'ek,spər|t, -pə̄|, -pəi|, ik's-,ek's-; 'ek,spə(r)|; *usu* |d·+V\ *adj* [ME, fr. MF & L; MF *expert*, fr. L *expertus*, past part. of *experiri* to try — more at ¹EXPERIENCE] **1** *obs* : proved or approved by test : EXPERIENCED ⟨his bark is stoutly timbered and his pilot of very ~ and approved allowance —Shak.⟩ **2** : having special skill or knowledge derived from training or experience : knowing and ready as a result of wide experience or extensive practice : CLEVER, SKILLFUL ⟨an ~ bridge player⟩ ⟨an artist ~ in shaping his material into one comprehensive design —S.C.Chew⟩ ⟨had become ~ at learning scientific formulas and principles by heart —Upton Sinclair⟩ **3 a** : involving or displaying special skill or knowledge, extensive practice, or wide experience ⟨the acting was fresh, warm, self-assured . . . , and ~ —John Mason Brown⟩ ⟨the shoemaker whose . . . hands had never been so nimble and ~ —Charles Dickens⟩ **b** : of or relating to an expert ⟨his presence was frequently required in an ~ capacity at the League's general conferences —*Current Biog.*⟩ **syn** see PROFICIENT

²expert *like* ³EXPERT\ *vb* -ED/-ING/-S [in sense *vt* 1, fr. ME *experten*, fr. *expert*, adj.; in other senses, fr. ³*expert*] *vt* **1** *obs* : EXPERIENCE **2** : to serve as an expert for ⟨wanted to know whatever happened to the man who had been sent to ~ their business —*Woman*⟩ ~ *vi* : to serve as or set oneself up as an expert ⟨read the newspapers and books of the countries on which they are ~*ing* —*Hispania*⟩

³ex·pert \'ek,spər|t, -spə̄|t,-pəi| *also* -spə(r)-\, *usu* |d·+V\ *n* -s [F, fr. *expert*, adj.] **1** : one who has acquired special skill in or knowledge of a particular subject through professional training or practical experience : AUTHORITY, SPECIALIST ⟨being an amateur . . . in philosophy he naturally looks for guidance to the ~*s* and professionals —William James⟩ ⟨this problem . . . was extremely difficult, and an ~ in geodesy was brought from the U.S. —V.G.Heiser⟩; *broadly* : one having skill or knowledge not possessed by mankind in general ⟨every man arranged his knapsack and blanket bag . . . with the practiced discretion of an ~ —E.K.Kane⟩ **2 a** : the highest classification given to a member of the military for skill in the use of arms **b** : a soldier having such a classification

syn ADEPT, ARTIST, ARTISTE, VIRTUOSO, WIZARD: each of these six nouns designates a person who shows mastery in a subject, an art, or a profession, or who shows unusual skill in execution, performance, or technique. EXPERT implies experience, knowledge, and achievement, and usu. recognition as an authority in the subject, art, or profession ⟨an *expert* in foreign policy⟩ ⟨an *expert* in mathematics⟩ ⟨an *expert* at skiing⟩ ⟨an *expert* in the art of evasion⟩ ADEPT, usu. connoting understanding of the mysteries of an art or craft or penetration into secrets beyond the reach of exact science, implies, in the most modern use, subtlety or ingenuity ⟨an *adept* in religions of the East⟩ ⟨an *adept* in the Platonic philosophy —Benjamin Farrington⟩ ⟨an *adept* at understatement —John Buchan⟩ ARTIST stresses extraordinary skill in execution usu. involving a high degree of imagination or taste ⟨an *artist* at flower arrangement⟩ ⟨an *artist* in manipulating public opinion —Samuel Lubell⟩ ⟨an *artist* at invective —W.A.Swanberg⟩ ARTISTE, orig. applied to actors, singers, and dancers, is now also often humorously applied to workers in crafts where adeptness and taste are indispensable ⟨a cook, a tragedian, or a music-hall *artiste* —Osbert Sitwell⟩ ⟨a Hollywood musical about life among the radio *artistes* —John McCarten⟩ ⟨a tightrope *artiste* quickly crossing the wire —George Bellairs⟩ VIRTUOSO, usu. applied to musicians, esp. pianists or violinists, stresses the display of great technical skill or brilliance in execution ⟨one of the piano *virtuosos* of international reputation —*Current Biog.*⟩ ⟨a frightfully wonderful *virtuoso* in the old art of love —G.B.Shaw⟩ WIZARD implies a knowledge or skill so great that it seems to border on the magical ⟨a mathematical *wizard*⟩ ⟨a *wizard* with cards —Malcolm Cowley⟩ ⟨a *wizard* in calculating distance —*Current Biog.*⟩

ex·per·tise \,ek,spər'tēz, -per-\ *n* -s [F, fr. MF, expertness, fr. *expert*, adj.] **1** : expert opinion or commentary ⟨is there an ~ on the question of the relative importance of preserving competition which should induce judges to defer to commissioners? —L.B.Schwartz⟩ **2** : specialized skill or technical knowledge : expertness in a particular field : KNOW-HOW ⟨the mental commodity most in demand will be practical wisdom rather than specialized ~ —Walter Moberly⟩ ⟨his bravery, his sure judgment in the most difficult situations, his ~ in the science of war —H.L.Merillat⟩

ex·pert·ism \'ek,spər|d·,izəm, -,spə̄|, -,spəi|, -,spə(r)|, |,tiz-\ *n* -s : EXPERTISE 2 ⟨looks like a doctor . . . who in his ~ has discovered . . . how to prolong his years —Janet Flanner⟩

ex·pert·ize \-d·,īz, -,tīz\ *vb* -ED/-ING/-S *vi* : to give a professional opinion usu. after careful study or examination ⟨would . . . be pointless for me to ~ on the specific subject —R.F. Cassidy⟩ ~ *vt* : to examine and give expert judgment on ⟨a philatelic society which ~*s* the stamps of its members for a moderate fee —R.B.Yardley⟩

ex·pert·ly *pronunc at* ¹EXPERT + lē *or* li\ *adv* : in an expert manner : ADROITLY

ex·pert·ness *pronunc at* ¹EXPERT +nə̇s\ *n* -ES : the quality or state of being expert : SKILL

ex·pi·a·ble \'ekspēəbəl\ *adj* [LL *expiabilis*, fr. L *expiare* to expiate + *-abilis* -able] : capable of being expiated : ATONABLE

¹ex·pi·ate \'ekspē,āt\ *vb* -ED/-ING/-S [L *expiatus*, past part. of *expiare* to atone for, purify, fr. *ex-* ¹ex- + *piare* to appease, atone for — more at PIOUS] *vt* **1** *obs* : to put an end to : cause to die out ⟨somewhat to ~ their savage fury —Thomas Adams⟩ **2** *obs* : to purify with sacred rites : CLEANSE ⟨he lustrated and *expiated* the city —Thomas Stanley⟩ **3 a** : to extinguish the guilt incurred by : make propitiation for ⟨trying to ~ by justice and mercy the dark deeds of his bloodstained youth —Charles Kingsley⟩ **b** : to pay the penalty for ⟨the casual offender ~*s* his offense in the company of defectives —B.N.Cardozo⟩ **c** : to make amends for ⟨sought to ~ their failures by adding a few sprigs or posies —Lewis Mumford⟩ **4** : to ward off by sacred rites : AVERT ⟨disaster shall fall upon you, which you will not be able to ~ —Isa 47:11 (RSV)⟩ ~ *vi* : to make expiation ⟨we are willing enough to repent, but the Higher Law requires that we ~ —W.L.Sullivan⟩

²expiate *adj* [L *expiatus*, past part. of *expiare*] *obs* : fully come ⟨make haste; the hour of death is ~ —Shak.⟩

ex·pi·a·tion \ˌekspēˈāshən\ *n* -s [ME *expiacioun*, fr. L *expiation-, expiatio*, fr. *expiatus* + *-ion-, -io* -ion] **1 :** the act of making atonement **:** the extinguishing of guilt by suffering or penalty ⟨the tree remains a symbol of agony and ~ —P.B. Sears⟩ **2 :** the means by which atonement is made **:** something done as an act of atonement ⟨the payment of money was ever welcomed as the ready ~ of crime —J.A.Froude⟩ — **ex·pi·a·tion·al** \ˌ;ekspē;āshənᵊl, -shnəl\ *adj*

ex·pi·a·tive \ˈekspē,ād·iv\ *adj* **:** EXPIATORY

ex·pi·a·tor \-ād·ə(r)\ *n* -s [LL, fr. L *expiatus* + *-or*] *n* -s **:** one that expiates

ex·pi·a·to·ry \ˈekspēə,tōrē, -,tȯr-\ *adj* [LL *expiatorius*, fr. L *expiatus* + *-orius* -ory] **:** having power to make expiation **:** serving to expiate **:** ATONING ⟨the sacrifice ~ for our offenses was to be a lamb without blemish —Isaac Barrow⟩

ex·pi·la·tion \ˌekspəˈlāshən, -,spī-\ *n* -s [L *expilation-, expilatio*, fr. *expilatus* (past part. of *expilare* to plunder, fr. *ex-* ¹ex- + *-pilare*, perh. akin to L *pila* pillar, pier) + *-ion-, -io* -ion — more at PILE] *archaic* **:** the act of plundering **:** SPOLIATION ⟨whence . . . proceeds this ravenous ~ of the state —Samuel Daniel⟩

ex·pi·ra·tion \ˌekspəˈrāshən *sometimes* -(,)spī- *or* -,spē-, *chiefly Brit* ˌek,spīˈ-\ *n* -s [ME *expiracioun*, fr. L *expiration-, exspiration-, expiratio, exspiratio*, fr. *expiratus, exspiratus* (past part. of *expirare, exspirare*) + *-ion-, -io* -ion] **1 :** the act, action, or process of expiring: **a** (1) **:** the action or process of releasing air from the lungs through the nose or mouth (2) **:** the escape of carbon dioxide from the body protoplasm (as through the blood and lungs or by diffusion) **b** *obs* **:** the emission of volatile matter **:** EXHALATION ⟨the true cause of cold is an ~ from the globe of the earth —Francis Bacon⟩ **c** *archaic* **:** the last emission of breath **:** DEATH ⟨the attendants did not discern the exact time of his ~ —Samuel Johnson⟩ **2 :** the fact of coming to an end **:** TERMINATION, CLOSE, EXTINCTION ⟨what effect the ~ of the excess-profits tax will have on corporate giving —J.A.Morris b. 1904⟩ **3 :** something that is expired or produced by breathing out ⟨the aspirate "he" which is . . . a gentle ~ —Granville Sharp⟩

ex·pi·ra·tor \ˈ=(,)=,rād·ə(r)\ *n* -s [*expire* + *-ator*] **:** one that expires; *specif* **:** an instrument for sending out a stream of air, gas, or vapor

ex·pi·ra·to·ry \ikˈspīrə,tōrē, ek-, -tȯr-; ˈeksp(ə)rə-, -ri\ *adj* [prob. fr. *expiration*, after such pairs as E *exploration: exploratory*] **1 :** of, relating to, or employed in the expiration of air from the lungs ⟨the ~ muscles⟩ **2** *of accent* **:** characterized by variations dependent on variation in force of expiration — compare DYNAMIC, STRESS ACCENT

ex·pire \ikˈspīr, ek-\ *vb* -ED/-ING/-S [ME *expiren*, fr. MF or L; MF *expirer*, fr. L *expirare, exspirare*, fr. *ex-* ¹ex- + *spirare* to breathe — more at SPIRIT] *vi* **1 :** to breathe one's last breath **:** DIE ⟨was carried home by his two old counselors and soon *expired* —D.G.Hoffman⟩ **2 :** to come to an end **:** CEASE: **a :** to reach a close (as of a period of time) **:** TERMINATE ⟨the period of ten years for which the court was established *expired* in 1918 —B.H.Williams⟩ **b :** to become void through the passage of time ⟨now all his powerful patents have *expired* —C.B.Fisher⟩ **c :** to become extinct **:** die out ⟨the title of the daughters *expired* on the birth of the son —William Cruise⟩ **3 :** to emit the breath ⟨the whales . . . *expired* with a rushing sound the instant the blowhole was exposed —P.H.Gosse⟩ **4** *obs* **:** to burst forth **:** fly out with or as if with a blast ⟨furious winds . . . pent in blind caverns, struggling to ~ —George Sandys⟩ ~ *vt* **1** *obs* **:** to breathe out in the act of dying ⟨as soon as their apostle had *expired* his last breath —Jeremy Taylor⟩ **2** *obs* **:** to bring to an end **:** CONCLUDE ⟨would ~ the misery of his unspeakable tormenting uncertainty —Thomas Nash⟩ **3 :** to breathe out from or as if from the lungs **:** release from the nose or mouth in the process of respiration ⟨the basal metabolism test . . . measures the amount of carbon dioxide *expired* by the lungs —J.D. Ratcliff⟩ — distinguished from *inspire* **4** *archaic* **:** to give off **:** EXHALE, EMIT ⟨every shrub ~*s* perfume —Charles Churchill⟩

ex·pir·ee \ˌek,spīˈrē; ik;spīˈrē, ek;-\ *n* -s **:** an Australian convict whose time of penal servitude has expired

ex·pir·er \ikˈspīrə(r), ek-\ *n* -s **:** one that expires

ex·pir·ing·ly *adv* [*expiring* (pres. part. of *expire*) + *-ly*] **:** in the manner of one expiring ⟨spoke in an ~ weak voice⟩

ex·pi·ry \ikˈspīrē, ekˈs-, ˈek,s-; ˈekspərē\ *n* -ES [*expire* + *-y*] **:** EXPIRATION: **a :** exhalation of breath ⟨that deep intake of breath, that brief and passionate ~ were not the components of a sigh —Aldous Huxley⟩ **b :** DEATH ⟨on ~, the rebellious soul shall other bodies enter —P.J.Bailey⟩ **c :** DESTRUCTION, EXTINCTION ⟨ancient history ought . . . not to cease with the ~ of the Roman Empire —William Taylor †1836⟩ **d :** TERMINATION, CLOSE, END ⟨at the ~ of these eight years he dismissed the subject and sold the books —A.N.Whitehead⟩; *esp* **:** the termination of a time or period fixed by law, contract, or agreement ⟨on the ~ of the State Governor's term of office —Noreen Routledge⟩

ex·pis·cate \ˈekspə,skāt, ekˈspi,s-\ *vt* -ED/-ING/-S [L *expiscatus*, past part. of *expiscari*, fr. *ex-* ¹ex- + *piscari* to fish, fr. *piscis* fish — more at FISH] *chiefly Scot* **:** to discover by careful examination or investigation **:** search out ⟨has with much ingenuity endeavored to ~ the truth —W.L.Alexander⟩ — **ex·pis·ca·tion** \ˌekspəˈskāshən, -(,)spiˈs-\ *n* -s *chiefly Scot*

ex·pis·ca·to·ry \ekˈspiskə,tōri\ *adj, chiefly Scot* **:** tending to expiscate **:** SEARCHING

ex·plain \ikˈsplān, ek-\ *vb* -ED/-ING/-S [ME *explanen*, fr. L *explanare* to level, make plain or clear, fr. *ex-* ¹ex- + *-planare*, fr. *planus* level, flat — more at FLOOR] *vt* **1 a :** to make manifest **:** present in detail **:** EXPOUND, DISCLOSE ⟨promised to ~ the secret of his success⟩ **b :** to make plain or understandable **:** clear of complexities or obscurity **:** INTERPRET, CLARIFY ⟨a commentary that ~*s* the more difficult passages of the poem⟩ **c :** to give the meaning or significance of **:** provide an understanding of ⟨~*ed* the concept in straightforward language⟩ **d :** to give the reason for or cause of **:** account for ⟨was unable to ~ his strange conduct⟩ **2** *obs* **:** to spread or open out **:** UNFOLD, EXPAND ⟨the horse chestnut is . . . ready to ~ its leaf —John Evelyn⟩ **3 a :** to show the logical development of **:** EXPLICATE ⟨~ an intellectual argument⟩ **b :** to subsume under a scientific theory or exhibit as an instance of a scientific law ⟨~ natural events⟩ **c :** to deduce from stated premises **:** PROVE ⟨~ a mathematical result⟩ **4 :** to state by way of explanation — used in direct or indirect discourse ~ *vi* **1 :** to give an explanation ⟨a poet whose words intimate rather than define, suggest rather than . . . ~ —Irwin Edman⟩ **2** *obs* **:** to speak one's mind ⟨the public . . . begins to ~ upon him —Earl of Chesterfield⟩

syn ACCOUNT (*for*), JUSTIFY, RATIONALIZE: to EXPLAIN is to clarify or make acceptable to the understanding something that it finds mysterious, causeless, or inconsistent ⟨*explain* an inconsistency in a financial report⟩ ⟨there is no comprehensive theory that *explains* these phenomena⟩ ⟨the mountainous character of Greece *explains* its division into a crowd of petty states —Edward Clodd⟩ To ACCOUNT (*for*) suggests a making acceptable by the fitting of the thing to be accounted for into some acceptable scheme (as logical or mathematical consistency, or an order of nature) ⟨their presence could not be *accounted for* by some temporary catastrophe, such as the Mosaic Flood —S.F.Mason⟩ ⟨the presence of buffalo *accounted for* the character of the Indian civilizations frontiersmen encountered when they entered the Great Plains —R.A. Billington⟩ ⟨*account for* the loss of a company's money⟩ To JUSTIFY is to account for or explain, or attempt to account for or explain, to one's or someone's satisfaction, esp. by explaining away guilt or blame ⟨the playhouse was forced to *justify* itself as a serious cultural endeavor —*Amer. Guide Series: Pc.*⟩ ⟨decided after the second day of the hearings that not enough people were watching to *justify* the expense —Gilbert Seldes⟩ ⟨an opinion *justified* by the facts⟩ To RATIONALIZE in an older sense stresses the idea of something acceptable to reason but in modern use signifies frequently to justify by false, esp. self-deceptive, reasoning ⟨cooperation with those from whom we differ is possible only if we *rationalize* our beliefs and thus make them intelligible to those having different backgrounds —M.R.Cohen⟩ ⟨we *rationalize* our cumbersome habit, taking for granted or explaining that this custom is intrinsically and logically best —A.L.Kroeber⟩ — **explain oneself :** to make clear the meaning of one's statements or the reasons for one's conduct

ex·plain·able \-nəbəl\ *adj* **:** capable of being explained

explain away *vt* **1 :** to get rid of by or as if by explanation ⟨was trying to speak some words that . . . would *explain away* all the mistakes and misunderstandings of life —Ellen Glasgow⟩ **2 :** to minimize the significance of by or as if by explanation ⟨evidence which it was hard to *explain away* —A.G.N.Flew⟩

ex·plain·er \-nə(r)\ *n* -s **:** one that explains

ex·pla·nan·dum \ˌekspləˈnandəm\ *n, pl* **explanan·da** \-də\ [NL, fr. L, neut. of *explanandus*, gerundive of *explanare* to explain, make plain or clear] **:** a word or an expression whose meaning is to be explained — used chiefly in philosophy; contrasted with *explanans*

ex·pla·nans \ˈekˈsplā,nanz\ *n, pl* **ex·pla·nan·tia** \ˌeksplə-ˈnanchēə\ [NL, fr. L, pres. part. of *explanare*] **:** the meaning of a word or an expression — used chiefly in philosophy; contrasted with *explanandum*

ex·pla·nate \ˈeksplə,nāt, ekˈsplā,n-\ *adj* [L *explanatus*, past part. of *explanare* to level] *biol* **:** extending outward in a flat form

ex·pla·na·tion \ˌeksplәˈnāshən\ *n* -s [ME *explanacioun*, fr. L *explanation-, explanatio*, fr. *explanatus* (past part. of *explanare* to level, make plain or clear) + *-ion-, -io* -ion] **1 :** the act or process of explaining **:** EXPOSITION, INTERPRETATION, CLARIFICATION ⟨~ consists in successfully comparing new phenomena with older and more familiar ones —J.H. Woodger⟩ **2 :** something that explains or that results from the act or process of explaining; *specif* **:** a statement incorporating an explanation ⟨the ~*s* offered for mistakes followed a set pattern —V.G.Heiser⟩ **3 :** a mutual discussion designed to correct a misunderstanding or reconcile differences **:** RECONCILIATION ⟨another person I should like an ~ with —Elizabeth Bowen⟩

ex·plan·a·tive \ikˈsplanəd·iv, ek-\ *adj* [LL *explanativus*, fr. L *explanatus* + *-ivus* -ive] **:** EXPLANATORY — **ex·plan·a·tive·ly** \-d·əvlē\ *adv*

ex·pla·na·tor \ˈeksplə,nād·ə(r)\ *n* -s [L, fr. *explanatus* + *-or*] **:** EXPLAINER

ex·plan·a·to·ri·ly \ik;splanə;tōrəlē, ek;-, ,ek,==ˈ===, -tȯr-, -li\ *adv* **:** in an explanatory manner **:** by way of explanation

ex·plan·a·to·ry \ikˈsplanə,tōrē, ek-, -tȯr-, -ri\ *adj* [LL *explanatorius*, fr. L *explanatus* + *-orius* -ory] **:** serving or disposed to explain **:** offering explanation ⟨textual and ~ . . . notes appear at the bottom of the page —I.M.Price⟩ ⟨was surprised to find herself cool, ~, and reasonable —Elizabeth Bowen⟩

¹ex·plant \(ˈ)eks+\ *vt* [*ex-* + *plant*, v.] **:** to remove (living tissue) to a place or medium outside the natural habitat esp. in tissue culture — **ex·plan·ta·tion** \ˌeks+\ *n* -s

²ex·plant \ˈeks+,\ *n* -s **:** living tissue removed from its place in the body and placed in an artificial medium for tissue culture

ex·ple·ment \ˈeksplәmənt\ *n* -s [L *explementum* something that fills, fr. *explēre* + *-mentum* -ment] **:** the difference between an angle and 360 degrees — **ex·ple·men·tal** \ˌ;ekspləˈmentᵊl\ *adj*

ex·ple·men·ta·ry angle \ˌ;ekspləˈmentərē-, -n·trē-\ *n* [*explement* + *-ary*] **:** either of two angles whose sum is 360 degrees

explete *vt* -ED/-ING/-S [ME *expleiten, expleten*, partly fr. MF *expleiter, espleiter, exploiter, esploiter* to achieve, perform & partly fr. L *expletus*, past part. of *explēre* — more at EXPLOIT] *obs* **:** SATISFY, COMPLETE — **expletion** *n* -s *obs*

¹ex·ple·tive \ˈeksplə|d·iv, |tiv, *chiefly Brit* ekˈsplē| *or* ikˈs-\ *adj* [LL *expletivus*, fr. L *expletus* (past part. of *explēre* to fill, fr. *ex-* ¹ex- + *plēre* to fill) + *-ivus* -ive; akin to L *plenus* full — more at FULL] **1 a :** serving to fill up or added to fill out ⟨~ phrases . . . to plump his speech —Isaac Barrow⟩ **b** *of a word* **:** used as a grammatical subject or grammatical object **2 :** marked by the use of expletives ⟨resigned his post in a letter of great ~ violence —F.M.Ford⟩

²expletive \"\ *n* -s **1 a :** a syllable, word, or phrase inserted to fill a vacancy (as in a sentence or a metrical line) without adding to the sense ⟨while ~*s* their feeble aid do join and ten low words oft creep in one dull line —Alexander Pope⟩; *esp* **:** an expletive word (as *it* in "it is easy to say so" or *it* in "make it clear which you prefer") **b :** an exclamatory word or phrase; *esp* **:** one that is obscene or profane ⟨wrote with chalk on the steps and doors the old four-letter Anglo-Saxon ~*s* —Shelby Foote⟩ **2 :** one that serves as a filler or is added as a filling ⟨a gooseberry tart with other ornamental ~*s* of the same kind —Richard Graves⟩ ⟨he is a sort of ~ at the table serving to stop gaps —O.W.Holmes †1935⟩

ex·ple·to·ry \ˈeksplə,tōrē; ekˈsplēd·ərē, ikˈs-\ *adj* [L *expletus* + E *-ory*] **:** EXPLETIVE

ex·plica·ble \ekˈsplikəbəl, ikˈs-, ˈek(,)s-, ˈeksplək-\ *adj* [L *explicabilis*, fr. *explicare* + *-abilis* -able] **:** capable of being explicated **:** EXPLAINABLE

ex·pli·can·dum \ˌeksplәˈkandəm\ *n, pl* **explican·da** \-də\ [NL, fr. L, neut. of *explicandus*, gerundive of *explicare* to explicate] **:** a word or an expression whose meaning is to be explicated — used chiefly in philosophy; contrasted with *explicans*

ex·pli·cans \ˈeksplə,kanz\ *n, pl* **explican·tia** \ˌeksplə-ˈkanchēə\ [NL, fr. L, pres. part. of *explicare*] **:** the meaning of a word or an expression — used chiefly in philosophy; contrasted with *explicandum*

¹ex·pli·cate \ˈeksplə,kāt\ *vt* -ED/-ING/-S [L *explicatus*, past part. of *explicare*, lit., to unfold, fr. *ex-* ¹ex- + *plicare* to fold — more at PLY] **1 a :** to give a detailed account of **:** EXPOUND, DISCLOSE ⟨an unfairness . . . which this would not be quite the proper place for *explicating* —Charles Lamb⟩ **b :** to unfold the meaning or sense of **:** INTERPRET, CLARIFY ⟨trying to ~ not vocabulary or techniques but the experience out of which these works were written —Perry Miller⟩ **2** *obs* **:** to lay open **:** UNFOLD, EXPAND ⟨the rose of Jericho will . . . ~ its flowers —Sir Thomas Browne⟩ **3** *obs* **:** DISENTANGLE, EXTRICATE ⟨no way to ~ the Kingdom out of those intricacies —Edward Hyde⟩ **4 :** to develop what is involved or implied in (as a statement or notion) **:** analyze logically ⟨this principle has been *explicated* into three general axioms —Francis Bowen⟩

²explicate *adj* [L *explicatus*, past part. of *explicare*] *obs* **:** EXPLICATED

ex·pli·ca·tion \ˌeksplәˈkāshən\ *n* -s [L *explication-, explicatio*, fr. *explicatus* + *-ion-, -io* -ion] **1 :** the act or process of explicating **:** EXPLANATION ⟨he quite naturally brought to the ~ of those principles tastes and predilections which were very much of his time —C.S.Singleton⟩ **2 :** something that explicates or that results from the act or process of explicating: as **a :** a detailed description, exposition, or interpretation ⟨a precise ~ of how to drive an automobile —C.A.Fenton⟩ **b :** a statement containing a logical analysis

ex·pli·ca·tion de texte \eksplēkäsyōⁿd(ə)tekst\ *n, pl* **explications de texte** \"\ [F, lit., text explanation] **1 :** a method of literary criticism involving a detailed examination of each part of a work and an exposition of the relationship of these parts to each other and to the whole work **2 :** a critical analysis employing explication de texte

¹ex·plic·a·tive \(ˈ)ekˈsplikəd·iv, ikˈs-, ˈeksplə,kād·-\ *adj* **:** serving to explicate **:** EXPLANATORY; *specif* **:** serving to explain logically what is contained in the subject ⟨an ~ proposition⟩ — **ex·plic·a·tive·ly** \-d·əvlē\ *adv*

²explicative \"\ *n* -s **:** an explicative expression

ex·pli·ca·tor \ˈeksplə,kād·ə(r)\ *n* -s [L, fr. *explicatus* + *-or*] **:** one that explicates **:** EXPOSITOR

ex·plic·a·to·ry \ekˈsplikə,tōrē, ikˈs-, ˈek(,)splik-, ˈek,splək-; ;eksplə;kād·ərē\ *adj* **:** EXPLICATIVE

ex·pli·ca·tum \ˌeksplәˈkād·əm, -kād·-\ *n, pl* **explica·ta** \-d·ə\ [NL, fr. L, neut. of *explicatus*, past part. of *explicare*] **:** EXPLICANS

¹ex·pli·cit \ˈeksplə,kit *sometimes* ekˈsplisət\ *n* -s [LL, prob. short for L *explicitus* unrolled, past part. of *explicare* to unroll, unfold; fr. the gradual unrolling of a scroll during the course of writing on it and its completely unrolled state when the writing is finished] **:** a statement formerly used at the end of a book or manuscript or section of a book or manuscript (as to indicate authorship or place and date of copying)

²ex·plic·it \ikˈsplisət, ek-, *usu* -sәd·+V\ *adj* [F or ML; F *explicite*, fr. ML *explicitus*, fr. L, free from obstacles, fr. *explicitus*, past part. of *explicare* to unfold — more at EXPLICATE] **1 :** characterized by full clear expression **:** being without vagueness or ambiguity **:** leaving nothing implied **:** UNEQUIVOCAL ⟨that there might be no mistake as to the meaning of his satire Brackenridge set down . . . an ~ statement of his purpose —V.L.Parrington⟩ — compare IMPLICIT **2 :** clearly and fully developed or formulated **:** DEFINITE ⟨how impossible it is . . . to have a clear and ~ notion of that which is infinite —Robert South⟩ **3** *obs* **:** having no complexities **:** SIMPLE ⟨and that commonly called the plot, whether intricate or ~ —John Milton⟩ **4 :** unreserved and unambiguous in expression **:** speaking fully and clearly **:** OUTSPOKEN ⟨he would not be more ~ about it; the wells of his loquacity were dried up —C.S.Forester⟩ **5 :** externally visible **:** clearly observable ⟨~ movements⟩ ⟨an ~ pattern of culture⟩ **6 :** involving direct payment **:** MONETARY ⟨~ costs⟩ ⟨~ rent⟩

syn DEFINITE, SPECIFIC, EXPRESS, CATEGORICAL: the chief emphasis of the word EXPLICIT is on the notion of plain distinct expression that leaves no need for the reader or hearer to infer; the antonym of this word is *implicit*. It may also connote plainness, frankness, force, or fullness ⟨these things are implicit in Augustine and existed before him: with Gregory they have become *explicit*, elaborated, and insisted on with recurrent emphasis —H.O.Taylor⟩ ⟨he [Hamilton] pointed out that all the powers of the national government could not be set down in *explicit* words, for that would mean intolerable detail —Allan Nevins & H.S.Commager⟩ DEFINITE, which has for its antonym *indefinite*, stresses the clear certainty of wording that leaves nothing unclear or doubtful, certainty sometimes attained by unadorned, flat statement, sometimes by careful limitation or definition ⟨do the quinine derivatives act by attaching themselves to the bacteria or by changing the body fluids? It was a simple, clear, *definite* question —Sinclair Lewis⟩ SPECIFIC indicates on the one hand being specified, particular, or individual or on the other marked by particulars and details sufficiently or amply treated ⟨religion refers to the fundamental issues of human existence, while magic always turns round *specific*, concrete, and detailed problems —B.K.Malinowski⟩ ⟨captions and legends in these pages are often mere generalized comments, devoid of *specific* information — e.g., identification of the illustration as to date, place, photographer —*Saturday Rev.*⟩ EXPRESS stresses the idea that whatever is under consideration has been expressed and not left to tacit understanding; it may suggest stress, cogency, directness, pointedness, or special emphasis in expression ⟨if no *express* acknowledgment of these rights had been made . . . they were practically observed —J.R.Green⟩ ⟨an *express* provision of the act required that the codes should not promote monopolies —F.D.Roosevelt⟩ CATEGORICAL stresses a positive or absolute absence of reserving qualification, demurrer, tentative condition ⟨the question is always *categorical*: is this man guilty or not —W.G.Sumner⟩ ⟨when documentary testimony was not the appropriate answer, Secretary Chapman gave specific *categorical* replies under oath —*Saturday Rev.*⟩

explicit definition *n* **:** a definition giving an exact equivalent for the term defined — contrasted with *contextual definition*

explicit function *n* **:** a mathematical function containing only the independent variable or variables — opposed to *implicit function*

ex·plic·it·ly *adv* **:** in an explicit manner **:** EXPRESSLY

ex·plic·it·ness *n* -ES **:** the quality or state of being explicit **:** CLEARNESS, DIRECTNESS

explicit relation *n* **:** a functional relation in mathematics in which the dependent variable is stated directly in terms of the independent variable

ex·plode \ikˈsplōd, ek-\ *vb* -ED/-ING/-S [L *explodere, explaudere*, fr. *ex-* ¹ex- + *plodere, plaudere* to clap, applaud] *vt* **1** *archaic* **:** to drive from the stage by noisy disapproval **:** hoot off **2 :** to expose decisively the hollowness or invalidity of **:** bring into disrepute or discredit ⟨*exploding* conventional theories of courtship and marriage —H.L.Myers⟩ ⟨~ a rumor⟩ **3 a :** to cause to explode or burst noisily **:** DETONATE ⟨~ powder⟩ ⟨~ a bomb⟩ **b :** to cause the fibers of (wood chips) to separate into pulp under high steam pressure which is suddenly released **c :** to hit (a golf ball) out of a sand trap with an explosion shot **d :** to separate the covers and panes or leaves of (a stamp booklet) by removing the staples **e :** to utter with explosion (sense 2d) ~ *vi* **1 a** (1) **:** to undergo rapid combustion with sudden release of energy in the form of heat that causes violent expansion of the gases formed and consequent production of great disruptive pressure and a loud noise ⟨dynamite ~*s*⟩ (2) **:** to undergo an atomic nuclear reaction with similar but more violent results ⟨an atom bomb ~*s*⟩ (3) **:** to burst violently as a result of pressure from within ⟨a steam boiler may ~⟩ **b :** to hit a golf ball out of a sand trap with an explosion shot **2 :** to give a sudden, strong, and usu. noisy release to an emotion **:** burst forth ⟨*exploded* with wrath⟩ ⟨race tension was *exploding* all around us —H.W.Young⟩ ⟨he is apt to ~ into picturesque profanity —Carl Markwith⟩ **3 :** to resound with a sudden loud noise **4 :** to shatter esp. with a loud report ⟨threw a glass on the stone floor and it *exploded* like a shot —Jean Stafford⟩ **5 :** to suggest an explosion (as in appearance or effect) ⟨clay jars *exploded* with bouquets —Jack Kerouac⟩ ⟨a clever aphorism . . . ~*s* with a brilliant shower of sparks —V.L.Parrington⟩ ⟨the road inches deep in rough ice and the blizzard *exploding* in the middle of the windshield —Joyce Cary⟩ ⟨when your fist *explodes* against the target —Jack Dempsey⟩ **6 a :** to change state or appearance expansively and suddenly or rapidly ⟨touched by a flicker of flame, the parched woods ~ —W.B.Greeley⟩ **:** break or burst forth ⟨maples have *exploded* into clouds of rosy buds —Walter O'Meara⟩ ⟨~ into a grin⟩ ⟨suburbs are *exploding* outward —*New Republic*⟩ **b :** to come to a sudden violent breaking point or point of release ⟨this situation at last ~*s* in an overt action —Howard Nemerov⟩ — **explode a bombshell :** to introduce a proposal, theory, statement, or item of information unexpectedly and forcefully so as to compel attention or stimulate action ⟨*exploded a bombshell* that was followed, for the most part, by a stunned silence —Oliver La Farge⟩

exploded *adj* [fr. past part. of EXPLODE] **:** showing the parts (as of an apparatus or machine) separated but in positions that indicate their correct relationship to each other ⟨an ~ view of a carburetor⟩ — compare PHANTOM

ex·plod·ent \-dᵊnt\ *n* -s [*explode* + *-ent*] **:** EXPLOSIVE

ex·plod·er \-də(r)\ *n* -s **1 :** one that explodes **2 :** a device for firing or detonating an explosive charge: as **a :** BLASTING CAP **b :** BLASTING MACHINE **c :** SQUIB

¹ex·ploit \ˈek,splȯit *also* ikˈs- *or* ekˈs-, *usu* -ȯid·+V\ *n* -s [ME *exploit, expleit, esploit, espleit* outcome, success, enterprise, fr. OF, accomplishment, success, revenue, fr. L *explicitum*, neut. of *explicitus*, past part. of *explicare* to unfold, set in order — more at EXPLICATE] **:** DEED, ACT; *esp* **:** a notable or heroic act **:** FEAT ⟨the ~*s* of Columbus⟩ ⟨a gallant ~⟩

²ex·ploit \ikˈsplȯit, (ˈ)ek;s-, *usu* -ȯid·+V\ *vt* -ED/-ING/-S [ME *expleiten, esploiten, espleiten*, fr. MF *exploiter, expleiter, esploiter, espleiter*, fr. OF *exploitier, expleitier, esploitier, espleitier*, fr. *exploit, expleit, esploit, espleit*, n.] **1** *obs* **:** ACHIEVE, PERFORM **2 a** (1) **:** to turn (a natural resource) to economic account **:** WORK, CULTIVATE ⟨~ a mine⟩ ⟨~ the virgin lands of the West⟩ (2) **:** to take advantage of **:** UTILIZE ⟨~*ed* his distinctive talent for book illustration —Herbert Read⟩ ⟨~*ing* the materials . . . and the techniques of our time —*N.Y. Times*⟩ **b :** to make use of meanly or unjustly for one's own advantage or profit **:** take undue advantage of ⟨~*s* his friends⟩; *specif* **:** to utilize the labor power of (a person) without giving a just or equivalent return ⟨struck by the degree in which the peasant was ~*ed* by the noble —M.H. Dodwell⟩

ex·ploit·able \-ȯid·əbəl, -ȯitə-\ *adj* **:** capable of being exploited

ex·ploi·ta·tion \ˌek,splȯiˈtāshən *sometimes* ,ik-\ *n* -s [F, fr. *exploiter* to exploit (fr. OF *exploitier, expleitier, esploitier, espleitier* to achieve, perform) + *-ation*] **1 :** an act of exploiting ⟨here we get incessant ~ of the author's social and political observations —F.B.Millett⟩ ⟨widespread ~ of antibiotics for nonmedical use —*Americana Annual*⟩: as **a :** utilization or working of a natural resource ⟨the sheep . . . finds its living by ~ of pastures —Allan Fraser⟩ ⟨~ of water power⟩;

sometimes : a wasteful or destructive utilization of a natural resource ⟨the spectacular results of uncontrolled ~ of the soil . . . awakened the American people to their danger —K.D. White⟩ **b** : an unjust or improper use of another person for one's own profit or advantage ⟨~ of the tourist destroys trade —*Americas*⟩; *specif* : utilization of the labor power of another person without giving a just or equivalent return ⟨that magic word "colonies", which means "trusteeship" to an Englishman and ~ in Karachi or Delhi —*Economist*⟩ ⟨capitalist ~⟩ **c** : coaction between organisms in which one is benefited at the expense of the other — used esp. of relationships (as that between an epiphyte and the plant on which it grows) in which the effect is less extreme than in parasitism or predation **2** : PUBLICITY, ADVERTISING ⟨allotted . . . $250,000 for the film's new ~ campaign —*Newsweek*⟩ ⟨the ~ that a dozen American composers are getting today — Deems Taylor⟩ — **ex·ploi·ta·tion·ist** \-sh(ə)nəst\ *adj*

ex·ploit·ative \ik'splȯid·ə·|iv, (ˈ)ek¦s-, -ȯitət|\ *adj* [²*exploit* + *-ative*] : relating to exploitation: as **a** : relating to the utilization or working of a natural resource ⟨the ~ activities of this region include lumbering and mining⟩ **b** : relating to the wasteful or destructive utilization of a natural resource ⟨reaping the fruits of an ~ type of agriculture —Bernard Frank & Anthony Netboy⟩ **c** : relating to the utilization of the labor power of a person without giving a just or equivalent return ⟨a stage in the decay of ~ capitalism —*New Republic*⟩ — **ex·ploit·ative·ly** \|əvlē, -li\ *adv*

ex·ploit·ato·ry \ik'splȯid·ə,tōrē, ek-, -tȯr-, -ri\ *adj* [fr. *exploitation*, after such pairs as E *explanation: explanatory*] : EXPLOITATIVE

ex·ploi·tee \ˌek,splȯi¦tē; ik¦s-, ek¦s-\ *n* -s : one that is exploited

ex·ploit·er \ik'splȯid·|ə(r), (ˈ)ek¦s-, -ȯit|\ *n* -s : one that exploits

ex·ploit·ive \|iv, |ēv *also* |əv\ *adj* : EXPLOITATIVE

ex·plo·ra·tion \ˌeksplə'rāshən, -lō'r-, -lȯ'r-\ *n* -s [L *exploration-, exploratio*, fr. *exploratus* + *-ion-, -io* -ion] : an act or an instance of exploring : EXAMINATION, INVESTIGATION, SEARCH ⟨a voyage of ~⟩ ⟨extensive ~s of the psychoneurotic aspects of literature —C.I.Glicksberg⟩ ⟨we encourage ~ and development of additional mineral reserves —*Americana Annual*⟩ ⟨surgical ~ of a visceral organ⟩

ex·plo·ra·tion·al \¦==¦rāshənᵊl, -shnəl\ *adj* : of or relating to exploration

ex·plor·ative \ik'splōrəd·|iv, (ˈ)ek¦s-, -lȯr-, -rət|\ *adj* [fr. *exploration*, after such pairs as E *deliberative: deliberation*] : EXPLORATORY — **ex·plor·ative·ly** \|əvlē, -li\ *adv*

ex·plor·ato·ry \ik'splōrə,tōrē, ek-, -lȯr-, -tȯr-, -ri\ *adj* [ME, fr. L *exploratorius*, fr. *exploratus* (past part. of *explorare* to explore, spy out) + *-orius* -ory] : of, relating to, or connected with exploration : serving in or intended for exploration : SEARCHING ⟨an ~ reconnaissance of . . . the least-known inhabited part of the world —R.C.Andrews⟩ ⟨drilling an ~ well in the Gulf of Mexico —*Wall Street Jour.*⟩ ⟨an ~ surgical operation⟩ : designed to orient in or acquaint with the outlines or first elements of a subject : PRELIMINARY ⟨an ~ course in art⟩ ⟨~ talks between diplomats⟩

ex·plore \ik'splō(ə)r, ek-, -ō(ə)r,-ōə,-ō(ə)\ *vb* -ED/-ING/-S [L *explorare* to explore, spy out, fr. *ex-* ¹ex- + *plorare* to cry out, wail, prob. of imit. origin; prob. fr. the outcry of hunters on sighting game] *vt* **1** *obs* : to seek for or after : strive to attain by search **2** : to search through or into : make a first or preliminary study of : INVESTIGATE, EXAMINE ⟨~ archives never before utilized by scholars⟩ ⟨~ the possibilities of reaching an agreement⟩ ⟨~ the economic and social conditions of the period⟩: as **a** : to examine minutely (as by surgery) esp. for diagnostic purposes ⟨operation seemed indicated and the patient was *explored* —J.G.Scannell & L.L.Robbins⟩ **b** : to penetrate into or range over for purposes of geographical discovery ⟨~ a trackless wilderness⟩ ~ *vi* : to make or conduct a systematic search ⟨~ for oil⟩

ex·plor·er \-ōrə(r), -ȯrə-\ *n* -s : one that explores: as **a** : a person who travels or is sent in search of geographical or scientific information ⟨an arctic ~⟩ **b** : a youth of 14 years or over, who participates in an exploring program of the Boy Scouts of America — compare BOY SCOUT, CUB SCOUT **c** : an instrument for exploring cavities esp. in teeth : PROBE 1a

explorer tent *n* : a variously shaped tent having a ridgepole, a maximum amount of floor space, and a minimum of standing room

exploring coil *n* [*exploring* fr. gerund of *explore*] : FLIP COIL

ex·plor·ing·ly *adv* [*exploring* (pres. part. of *explore*) + *-ly*] : in the manner of one that explores

ex·plo·si·bil·i·ty \ik,splōzə'biləd·ē, (ˌ)ek,s-, -ōsə-, -lətē, -i\ *n* -ES : the quality of being explosible

ex·plo·si·ble \=¦=zəbəl\ *adj* [*explos-* (as in *explosive*) + *-ible*] : capable of being exploded

ex·plo·sim·e·ter \ˌeksplō'zimәd·ə(r), -ō'si-\ *n* [*explosibility* + *-meter*] : an instrument for testing explosibility by measuring the concentration of combustible gases and vapors in air

ex·plo·sion \ik'splōzhən, ek-\ *n* -s [L *explosion-, explosio* action of driving from the stage by noisy disapproval, fr. *explosus* (past part. of *explodere, explaudere* to drive from the stage by noisy disapproval) + *-ion-, -io* -ion — more at EXPLODE] **1** : an act of exposing something as invalid or baseless : REJECTION, COLLAPSE, FIASCO ⟨the ~ of that pseudo philosophy of science —P.E.More⟩ **2 a** : an act of exploding : a violent expansion or bursting that is accompanied by noise and is caused by a sudden release of energy from a very rapid chemical reaction, from a nuclear reaction, or from an escape of gases or vapors under pressure (as in a steam boiler) — compare DEFLAGRATION, DETONATION **b** : the noise made by such bursting **c** (1) : a large-scale, rapid, and spectacular expansion, outbreak, or other upheaval ⟨increasing the world food supply to offset the ~ of population —Bruce Bliven b. 1889⟩ ⟨ideal material for a revolutionary ~⟩ (2) : an outburst of temper manifested by excited language or action ⟨an ~ of national rage shattered the plan forever —*Holiday*⟩ **d** : the release of stoppage-impounded breath that occurs in one kind of articulation of stop consonants (as when a vowel or syllabic consonant immediately follows the stop, as in *mica, sodden*)

explosion gun *n* : an impact tool deriving its thrust from the detonation of a cartridge in its cylinder

explosion shot *n* : a golf shot made by driving the club head into sand just behind the ball

¹**ex·plo·sive** \-ōs|iv, |ēv *also* -ōz| *or* |əv\ *adj* [L *explosus* (past part. of *explodere, explaudere*) + E *-ive*] **1 a** : relating to, characterized or operated by, or suited to cause explosion ⟨~ force⟩ ⟨an ~ engine⟩ ⟨the ~ increase of population⟩ ⟨an ~ epidemic of rheumatic fever⟩ **b** : tending to explode ⟨a blustering ~ person⟩ **2** : characterized by explosion — **ex·plo·sive·ly** \|əvlē, -li\ *adv* — **ex·plo·sive·ness** \|ivnəs, |ēv- *also* |əv-\ *n* -ES

²**explosive** \"\ *n* -s **1** : an explosive substance : a substance that on ignition by heat, impact, friction, or detonation undergoes very rapid decomposition (as combustion) with the production of heat and the formation of more stable products (as gases) which exert tremendous pressure as they expand at the high temperature produced; *esp* : a solid chemical compound or mixture of compounds that is used to release energy for performing work (as in blasting or propelling projectiles) — see HIGH EXPLOSIVE, LOW EXPLOSIVE **2** : a consonant characterized by explosion in its articulation when it occurs in certain environments : STOP

explosive evolution *n* : the appearance esp. early in the biological history of a group of a great variety of forms few of which become permanently established as lines within the group

explosive oil *n* : nitroglycerin esp. when mixed with a substance (as a nitrated glycol) that lowers the freezing point for use in dynamite

explosive rivet *n* : a rivet containing an explosive charge that is exploded either by touching the head with a heated iron or placing it in a high frequency electromagnetic field

explosive train *n* : a series of explosive elements of a land mine, bomb, or projectile that serve to set off the detonating charge

expn *abbr* **1** exposition **2** expiration

¹**ex·po·nent** \ik'spōnənt, ek's-, 'ek,s-\ *adj* [L *exponent-, exponens*, pres. part. of *exponere* to explain, expound, set forth — more at EXPOUND] : giving exemplification : EXPLAINING ⟨in his characters we find not so much people who are ~ types of a region as personifications of various human qualities —J.W.Wilson⟩

²**exponent** \"\ *n* -s **1** : a symbol written above and to the right of a symbol, expression, or quantity to indicate a mathematical operation to be performed (as in involution where 2 in a^2 indicates how many times the operand is to be taken as a factor: $a \times a$; or in extraction of a root where ⅓ in $a^{⅓}$ indicates a cube root of a: $\sqrt[3]{a}$) **2 a** : an expounder or explainer esp. of a doctrine ⟨an ~ of profound economic truths —*Current Biog.*⟩ : an interpreter esp. of an art ⟨an important ~ of the living Bach as opposed to the dry and pedantic Bach —A.E.Wier⟩ ⟨the most controversial figure in the modern dance and . . . its most successful ~ —Walter Terry⟩ : a representative or practitioner esp. of a profession or other activity ⟨a well-known ~ of the science of anthropology —*Current Biog.*⟩ **b** : one that champions, advocates, or exemplifies ⟨the best known ~ of this use of free association in verse —C.D.Lewis⟩ ⟨a leading ~ of arbitration in labor-management disputes —*Current Biog.*⟩

ex·po·nen·tial \ˌekspə¦nenchəl, -pō¦-\ *adj* [²*exponent* + *-i-* + *-al*] **1** : of or relating to an exponent : involving a variable exponent ⟨an ~ expression⟩ **2** : approximately expressible by an exponential equation ⟨~ distribution⟩ — used esp. in indicating variation in which one variable factor depends upon another variable factor ⟨culture is said to grow in an ~ manner; and the number of inventions is a function of the size of the cultural base —F.H.Hankins⟩ — **ex·po·nen·tial·ly** \-chəlē\ *adv*

exponential curve *n* : a graph of an exponential function

exponential equation *n* : an equation involving exponential functions of a variable

exponential function *also* **exponential** *n* : a mathematical function in which an independent variable appears in one of the exponents

exponential horn *n* : a loudspeaker horn whose sectional area varies exponentially along its length

exponential series *n* : a series derived from the development of exponential expressions; *specif* : the fundamental expansion $e^x = 1 + \frac{x}{1} + \frac{x^2}{1\cdot2} + \frac{x^3}{1\cdot2\cdot3} + \frac{x^4}{1\cdot2\cdot3\cdot4} + \ldots$, absolutely convergent for all finite values of x

¹**ex·po·ni·ble** \ik'spōnəbəl, ek's-\ *n* -s [ML *exponibilis*, adj.] : an exponible proposition

²**exponible** \ik's, (ˈ)ek¦s-\ *adj* [ML *exponibilis*, fr. L *exponere* + *-ibilis* -ible] **1** : capable of being explained **2** : needing restatement — used of a proposition in logic

¹**ex·port** \(ˈ)ek¦spō(ə)r|t, ik's-, -ȯ(ə)r|, -ōə|, -ō(ə)|, *usu* |d·+V\ *vb* -ED/-ING/-S [L *exportare*, fr. *ex-* ¹ex- + *portare* to carry — more at PORT] *vt* **1** : to carry away : REMOVE ⟨only the finer debris is ~*ed* by wind —Arthur Holmes⟩ ⟨the blood . . . ~*s* waste products from the tissues —W.E.Swinton⟩ **2 a** : to carry or send (a commodity) to some other country or place — opposed to *import* **b** : to transmit or cause the spread of (as an idea or institution) to another part of the world ⟨unable to ~ its democratic faith to . . . other nations —A.M. Schlesinger b. 1917⟩ ⟨we cannot even ~ freedom —F.L.Schuman⟩ ~ *vi* : to export something abroad ⟨the U.S. ~*s* to many foreign countries⟩

²**ex·port** \'ek,s-\ *n* -s **1** : something that is exported; *specif* : a commodity conveyed from one country or region to another for purposes of trade **2** : an act of exporting : EXPORTATION ⟨the ~ of wheat or tobacco⟩

³**export** \"\ *adj* [²*export*] : of, relating to, or concerned with exportation or exports ⟨an ~ duty⟩ ⟨the ~ trade⟩ : suitable or designed for exportation ⟨an ~ crop⟩

ex·port·able \(ˈ)ek¦spōr|d·əbəl, ik's-, -ȯr|, -ōə|, -ō(ə)|, |tə-\ *adj* : capable of being exported

ex·por·ta·tion \ˌek,spōr'tāshən, -ō(r)'-,-ōə'- *also* -ˌpə(r)'-\ *n* -s [L *exportation-, exportatio*, fr. *exportatus* (past part. of *exportare*) + *-ion-, -io* -ion] **1** : an act of exporting; *also* : a commodity exported : EXPORT **2** : a direct inference from a statement of the form *pq*⊃*r* to one of the form *p*⊃(*q*⊃*r*) — used in formal logic

export bar *n* : a bar or ingot of pure gold used in making gold shipments to settle international exchange balances

export credit *n* : a credit opened by an importer with a bank in the country of an exporter to finance an export transaction — compare IMPORT CREDIT

ex·port·er *pronunc at* ¹EXPORT + ə(r)\ *n* -s : one that exports; *specif* : a wholesaler who sells to merchants or industrial consumers in foreign countries

export point *n* : the quotation for a foreign currency on the gold standard at which it pays to export gold in place of buying a bill of exchange — compare GOLD EXPORT POINT, GOLD IMPORT POINT

export tax *or* **export duty** *n* : a tax or duty on articles exported from a country

¹**ex·pose** \ik'spōz, ek-\ *vt* -ED/-ING/-S [ME *exposen*, fr. MF *exposer*, modif. (influenced by *poser* to put, place) of L *exponere* to expose, explain, set forth (perfect stem *expos-*), fr. *ex-* ¹ex- + *ponere* to put, place — more at POSITION, POSE] **1 a** : to lay open (as to attack, danger, trial, or test) : make accessible to something that may prove detrimental : deprive of shelter, protection, or care ⟨~ him to the weather⟩ ⟨~ troops needlessly⟩ ⟨a coast *exposed* to severe gales⟩ **b** : to submit or subject to an action or influence ⟨~ children to good books⟩ ⟨think . . . they can arrest the fall of rain by *exposing* to it a boulder —J.G.Frazer⟩ ⟨~ a man to new impressions⟩; *specif* : to subject (a sensitive photographic film, plate, or paper) to the action of radiant energy **c** : to abandon (an infant) esp. by leaving in the open : DESERT ⟨the foundation of lying-in hospitals and orphanages . . . kept the children alive, . . . prevented them being *exposed* —J.H. Plumb⟩ **2** : to lay open to view : lay bare : make known : set forth : EXHIBIT, DISPLAY ⟨*exposing* a sun-tanned back⟩ ⟨each had started *exposing* his views —F.M.Ford⟩ ⟨the new display object is to ~ the package —*Printers' Ink*⟩: as **a** : to offer publicly for sale ⟨all of which I shall ~ for sale at public auction —*Detroit Law Jour.*⟩ — sometimes used with *to* ⟨the markets at which the corn, the cattle, the wool . . . of the surrounding country were *exposed* to sale —T.B.Macaulay⟩ **b** : to exhibit (a religious relic or the Host) for public veneration **c** : to reveal the face of (a playing card) — used chiefly in games in which such exposure is contrary to the rules **d** : to conduct (oneself) as an exhibitionist **3 a** : to disclose or reveal the faults, frailties, or unsoundness of : bring to light (as something criminal or shameful) : UNMASK ⟨took a leading part in *exposing* the pretensions of this quack⟩ ⟨has behaved like a cad and ought to be *exposed* —Kingsley Martin⟩ ⟨~ a voting fraud⟩ ⟨~ the abuses of the day —John Mason Brown⟩ **b** *obs* : RIDICULE, SATIRIZE **syn** see SHOW

²**ex·po·sé** *or* **ex·po·se** \ˌek(ˌ)spō¦zā, -ˌspə¦- *sometimes* ek'spō,zā *or* ik's-\ *n* -s [F *exposé*, fr. past part. of *exposer*] **1** : a formal recital or exposition of facts : STATEMENT ⟨the best ~ of the full Platonic metaphysical synthesis that we know —W.N.Clarke⟩ **2** : an exposure or revelation of something discreditable ⟨novelists were making fictional ~*s* of plutocratic iniquity —W.A.White⟩ ⟨has written a startling ~ of missionary mentality —Lucy Crockett⟩ ⟨a newspaper ~ of crime conditions⟩

ex·posed \ik'spōzd, ek-\ *adj* [fr. past part. of ¹*expose*] **1** : open to view ⟨left acres of large flat stones ~ —*Amer. Guide Series: Tenn.*⟩; *specif, of a playing card* : dealt or placed so that its face shows whether legally or illegally **2** : not shielded or protected : so situated as to invite or make likely an attack, injury, or other adverse development ⟨must do something to protect her ~ northeast frontier —Geoffrey Godsell⟩; *specif* : not adequately insulated, guarded, or isolated — used of equipment ⟨an ~ electric wire⟩ **syn** see LIABLE

ex·posed·ness \-z(ə)dnəs\ *n* -ES : the quality or state of being exposed ⟨the very ~ of the position on the stage conduced to mild stage fright⟩

ex·pos·er \-zə(r)\ *n* -s : one that exposes

ex·pos·it \ik'späzət, ek-\ *vt* -ED/-ING/-S [L *expositus*, past part. of *exponere*] : EXPOUND ⟨~*s* a pluralism of interests and corresponding types of criticism —René Wellek & Austin Warren⟩

ex·po·si·tion \ˌekspə'zishən, -pō'-\ *n* -s [ME *exposicioun*, fr. MF *exposition*, fr. L *exposition-, expositio*, fr. *expositus* (past part. of *exponere* to explain, expound, set forth) + *-ion-, -io* -ion — more at EXPOUND] **1** : a setting forth of the meaning or purpose (as of a writing or discourse) : an expounding of the sense or intent (as of a law) : an interpretation esp. of a parable : EXEGESIS **2 a** (1) : the art or procedure of expository discourse : the art of presenting a subject matter in detail apart from criticism, argument, or development : ELUCIDATION (2) : a verbal statement or presentation of some subject matter or point of view whether expository, critical, or argumentative ⟨overawed by such a splendid piece of advocacy and ~ —Stewart Cockburn⟩ (3) : presentation or interpretation of any kind ⟨demands a clarity of ~ somewhat foreign to the modern piano —P.H.Lang⟩ **b** : discourse or an example of it designed to convey information or explain what is difficult to understand; *esp* : a statement embodying an analysis of the subject matter and the use of familiar illustrations or analogies **c** : a part of a composition (as of music or drama) in which the theme or subject is presented or opened out: as (1) : the first part of a musical composition in sonata form in which the thematic material of the movement is presented (2) : the opening section of a fugue **3** : an act or an instance of exposing: as **a** : abandonment of an infant **b** : an open display of a religious relic or the Host for public veneration **c** : a public exhibition or show (as of industrial and artistic productions)

ex·po·si·tion·al \¦==¦zishənᵊl, -shnəl\ *adj* : EXPLANATORY

ex·pos·i·tive \ik'späzəd·iv, (ˈ)ek¦s-\ *adj* [L *expositus* (past part. of *exponere* to explain, expound, set forth) + E *-ive* — more at EXPOUND] : DESCRIPTIVE, EXPOSITORY — **ex·pos·i·tive·ly** \-d·əvlē\ *adv*

ex·pos·i·tor \=¦=zəd·ə(r)\ *n* -s [ME *expositour*, fr. MF *expositeur*, fr. LL *expositor*, fr. L *expositus* + *-or*] : one that expounds or explains : EXPOUNDER, COMMENTATOR — **ex·pos·i·to·ri·al** \ik¦späzə¦tōrēəl, (ˌ)ek¦-\ *adj* — **ex·pos·i·to·ri·al·ly** \-ēəlē\ *adv*

ex·pos·i·to·ri·ly \ik¦späzə¦tōrəlē, (ˌ)ek¦-, -tȯr-, -li\ *adv* : in an expository manner ⟨in his book the events were presented ~ rather than with any imaginative or creative alteration⟩

ex·pos·i·to·ry \ik'späzə,tōrē, ek-, -tȯr-, -ri\ *adj* [LL *expositorius*, fr. L *expositus* + *-orius* -ory] : of, relating to, or containing exposition : serving to elucidate or interpret : EXEGETIC ⟨the failure of composition teachers to solve the problem of clean ~ writing —H.L.Creek⟩ ⟨occasional textual and explanatory but not ~ notes —I.M.Price⟩

ex post \(ˈ)ek¦spōst\ *adj* [¹*ex post (facto)*] : based on knowledge and retrospection and being essentially objective and factual ⟨consistency of market behavior, and therefore reasonable conformity of ex ante expectations with *ex post* reality, is basically determined by the social stability of the community —Werner Hochwald⟩ — opposed to *ex ante*

¹**ex post fac·to** \ˌek,spōst¦fak(ˌ)tō\ *adj* [LL, from a thing done afterward] : done, made, or formulated after the fact and on the basis of current premises, conditions, or knowledge : disregarding the previous status or setting of the event or thing concerning which a conclusion is reached or at which action is directed : RETROSPECTIVE, RETROACTIVE ⟨*ex post facto* punishment⟩ ⟨the general gave his *ex post facto* approval —W.H.Upson⟩ ⟨*ex post facto* rationalizations of behavior —Edward Sapir⟩ ⟨the results of scientific inquiry are always subject to *ex post facto* interpretation —H.M.Magid⟩

²**ex post facto** \"\ *adv* : after the fact : in a retrospective or retroactive manner ⟨no lawmaker can alter the fact, *ex post facto* —C.A.Beard⟩

ex post facto law *n* : a criminal or penal statute that imposes a punishment for an act not punishable when committed, or alters to the defendant's disadvantage the punishment prescribed at the time of the act, or takes away from the substantial protection afforded the defendant by the then existing law; *also* : a civil or criminal law enacted with a retroactive effect

ex·pos·tu·late \ik'späschə,lāt, ek-, *usu* -ād·+V\ *vb* -ED/-ING/-S [L *expostulatus*, past part. of *expostulare*, fr. *ex-* ¹ex- + *postulare* to ask for, demand — more at POSTULATE] *vt* **1** *obs* : to call for : DEMAND **2** *obs* **a** : DISCUSS, EXAMINE **b** : to complain of ~ *vi* **1** *obs* : to talk earnestly : COMPLAIN **2** : to reason earnestly with a person for purposes of dissuasion or remonstrance : REMONSTRATE ⟨it is useless to ~ with a stubborn man⟩ ⟨send for the maître d'hôtel; you have a right to ~ —Margaret Lane⟩ ⟨reporters at his press conference *expostulated* against playing favorites —*New Republic*⟩ **syn** see OBJECT

ex·pos·tu·lat·ing·ly \ik¦späschə¦lād·iŋlē, ek¦-, ˌek,==¦===\ *adv* [*expostulating* (pres. part. of *expostulate*) + *-ly*] : in the manner of one that expostulates ⟨raised a hand ~ to try to stop the flow of abuse⟩

ex·pos·tu·la·tion \ik,späschə'lāshən, (ˌ)ek,-\ *n* -s [L *expostulation-, expostulatio*, fr. *expostulatus* + *-ion-, -io* -ion] **1** : an act or an instance of expostulating with a person : REMONSTRANCE ⟨all his ~*s* proved futile⟩ **2** : a speech or writing of remonstrance or dissuasion ⟨wrote an ~ to the minister of education defending their right to function —*Collier's Yr. Bk.*⟩

ex·pos·tu·la·to·ry \=¦==lə,tōrē, -tȯr-, -ri\ *adj* : relating to or containing expostulation

ex·po·sure \ik'spōzhə(r), ek-\ *n* -s [*expose* + *-ure*] **1** : an act of exposing, laying open, or setting forth: as **a** : disclosure to view : DISPLAY ⟨skillful ~ of goods in a store window⟩ ⟨her ~ of a shapely leg⟩ **b** (1) : a disclosure esp. of a weakness or something shameful or criminal : UNMASKING ⟨continued his ~ of electoral frauds⟩ ⟨the battle was finally won with the ~ of the Tory commissioner as a grafter —*Current Biog.*⟩; *also* : the condition of being unmasked or shown up ⟨he feared ~ above all else⟩ (2) : PRESENTATION, EXPOSITION ⟨a dispassionate ~ of fundamental passions of any time and any place —T.S.Eliot⟩ ⟨how terrifying an ~ he was making of the emptiness of life without belief —F.O.Matthiessen⟩ ⟨suites were considered too heavy for ~ in the concert hall —Roland Gelatt⟩ **c** : an act of abandoning (as an infant) esp. in the open ⟨reject all regulation of the birth rate by infanticide, ~, . . . or any other means —H.E.Barnes & Howard Becker⟩ **d** (1) : the act of exposing a sensitized photographic material (2) : a section of a film for an individual picture ⟨a roll containing eight ~*s*⟩ (3) : the total amount of light or other radiant energy received per unit area on the sensitized material — usu. expressed for cameras in terms of the time and the lens *f*-number ⟨an ~ of 1/50 second at *f*/8⟩ **e** : an act of subjecting to an experience or influence ⟨denounced ~ of children to such corrupting literature⟩ **2 a** : a condition or an instance of being laid bare or exposed to view ⟨particularly striking . . . are the picturesque ~*s* of the somber banded clays —*Earth Science Digest*⟩ **b** : a condition of being exposed to danger or loss : liability or accessibility to something that may affect detrimentally ⟨~ to infection⟩ : RISK, VULNERABILITY ⟨insurable under a policy having less ~ —Charles Ray⟩ ⟨~ to sudden attack by the enemy⟩; *specif* : the condition of being exposed to the elements ⟨she died as a result of ~ suffered after a shipwreck —*Amer. Guide Series: Maine*⟩ ⟨the work is hard . . . and ~ is part of the routine —E.P.Hohman⟩ **c** : a condition or an instance of being subjected to an experience or influence ⟨long ~ to the temperature of boiling water —J.B.Conant⟩ ⟨the permanent effects of his early ~ to Catholicism —William Troy⟩ ⟨wearily cynical from years of ~ to human misery —*N.Y. Times*⟩ **d** : a position with respect to the points of compass or to climatic or weather influences ⟨a kitchen with a western ~⟩ **3** : something (as a bed of mineral material) exposed to view ⟨thousands of ~*s* of many different kinds of rock have been examined —W.E.Swinton⟩ **4** : the product of the flux density of radiation falling upon a surface by the time during which the surface is exposed to the radiation

exposure hazard *n* : the chance that a particular building and its contents may sustain loss or damage from fire in a neighboring property

exposure index *n* : a number that is assigned to a photographic film or plate for use with an exposure meter to aid a photographer in obtaining the correct camera exposure

exposure meter *n* : a device for indicating correct photographic exposure under varying conditions of illumination (as by measuring the light falling on or reflected from the subject by means of a photoelectric photometer)

exposure suit *n* : a suit (as of rubber) designed for a flier forced down at sea and for a person exposed to extreme cold or drenching

ex·pound \ik'spau̇nd, ek-\ *vb* -ED/-ING/-S [ME *expounden, expounen*, fr. MF *expondre, espondre*, fr. L *exponere* to explain, expound, set forth, fr. *ex-* ¹ex- + *ponere* to put, place — more at POSITION] *vt* **1 a :** to set forth **:** STATE, PRESENT, TEACH ⟨~s his conviction that the economic outlook is brightening⟩ ⟨~ing a philosophy from which she shrank —William McFee⟩ ⟨~ing to the literate but uninformed some of the mysteries of economics —Quincy Howe⟩ ⟨it's the personality of the teacher that counts, far more than the topic he ~s —R.B.Merriman⟩ ⟨~ed with distinguished precision the difference between an extinct and an extirpated bird —Edmund Wilson⟩ **b :** to defend with argument **:** ADVOCATE ⟨welcomed . . . the suggestions of a union with the Church of England, which some . . . clergymen in the two churches ~ed because of an alleged similarity in spirit and ritual —R.C.Wood⟩ **2 :** to make clear the meaning of **:** comment on **:** INTERPRET, EXPLAIN, CONSTRUE, GLOSS ⟨~ed to his monks . . . the religious significance of . . . the Song of Songs —G.C.Sellery⟩ ⟨spent much of his time ~ing the conflict between Christianity and Communism —*Current Biog.*⟩ ⟨used to take me riding before breakfast and ~ my shortcomings —John Buchan⟩ ⟨~ a law⟩ ~ *vi* **1 :** to make a statement **:** present a view **:** DISCOURSE, COMMENT — often used with *on* ⟨when executives ~ on the subject their views coincide remarkably —W.H.Whyte⟩ ⟨~ on the many good reasons for getting to know Great Britain —Richard Joseph⟩ ⟨sportsmen will ~ for hours on their observations —G.J.Knudsen⟩ **2 :** to make explanatory comments **:** EXPLAIN ⟨you speak of the time assigned . . . I . . . would like you to ~ —O.W.Holmes †1935⟩

ex·pound·er \-də(r)\ *n* -S [ME *expoundere, expounere*, fr. *expounden, expounen* + *-er, -ere* -er] **:** one that expounds

¹**ex·press** \ik'spres, ek- *sometimes* 'ek,s-\ *adj* [ME, fr. MF *expres, express*, fr. L *expressus*, past part. of *exprimere* to express, press out, fr. *ex-* ¹ex- + *-primere* (fr. *premere* to press) — more at PRESS] **1 a :** directly and distinctly stated or expressed rather than implied or left to inference **:** not dubious or ambiguous **:** DEFINITE, CLEAR, EXPLICIT, UNMISTAKABLE ⟨with the ~ injunction that I was to show them to no one —Anita Pollitzer⟩ ⟨with the ~ provision that they remain away from the coast settlement —Mabel R. Gillis⟩ **b :** exactly represented **:** EXACT, PRECISE ⟨he was the ~ image of his father⟩ **c** *obs* (1) **:** OUTSPOKEN (2) **:** STEADFAST, UNWAVERING **2 a :** specially designed or chosen for its purpose **:** adapted to its purpose ⟨what a piece of work is man! . . . in form and moving how ~ and admirable! —Shak.⟩ **b :** of a particular or special sort **:** SPECIFIC ⟨he came for that ~ purpose⟩ **3 a :** dispatched with or traveling at special or high speed; *specif* **:** traveling between terminal or specified points without stop or with a limited number of stops ⟨an ~ train⟩ ⟨an ~ bus⟩ ⟨an ~ elevator⟩ — compare LOCAL **b :** adapted or suitable for or characterized by travel at special or high speed ⟨an ~ highway⟩; *also* **:** specially fast ⟨traveling at ~ speed⟩ **c** *Brit* **:** delivered or to be delivered without delay by special messenger ⟨~ letter⟩ ⟨~ mail⟩; *also* **:** performing or paying for such service ⟨~ messenger⟩ ⟨~ charges⟩ **4 :** designed for an express rifle — used of a cartridge, load, or bullet **syn** see EXPLICIT

²**express** \"\ *adv* [ME *expres*, fr. *expres, express* adj.] **1** *obs* **:** EXPRESSLY **2** [⁴*express*] **:** by express ⟨send a package ~⟩

³**express** \"\ *vb* -ED/-ING/-ES [ME *expressen*, fr. MF & L; MF *expresser, espresser*, fr. OF, fr. *expres, espres*, adj., fr. L *expressus*, past part. of *exprimere* to express] *vt* **1 a :** to make or offer a representation of **:** show by a copy or likeness **:** DELINEATE, DEPICT ⟨among the striking patterns in modern printed textiles were seen many geometrical and abstract designs gracefully ~ed —*Americana Annual*⟩ **b** (1) **:** to represent in words **:** STATE, UTTER ⟨~ an opinion⟩ ⟨~ his views⟩ (2) **:** to give expression to ⟨an emotion or feeling⟩ ⟨when I ~ed disgust he and others laughed —David Livingstone⟩ ⟨her countenance ~ed both shame and defiance⟩ **c :** to give or convey a true impression of **:** display fully or exactly **:** SHOW, SIGNIFY, EXHIBIT, REFLECT, EMBODY ⟨all these thrusting, driving words became the slogans which ~ed the folk ideals —W.P.Webb⟩ ⟨its proud edifices ~ material riches so overwhelming as to transcend materialism —Gerald Sykes⟩ ⟨no words can ~ the grandeur of that scene⟩ ⟨in Constantinople was ~ed all the life and culture of the Byzantine Empire —W.G.East⟩ **d** *obs* **:** to give a full and explicit statement of **:** RECOUNT, DESCRIBE, DESIGNATE, SIGNIFY **e** (1) **:** to make known the opinions or feeling of (oneself) **:** declare what is in the mind of (oneself) ⟨~ himself very strongly on that subject⟩ ⟨asked the members of the panel to ~ themselves freely⟩ (2) **:** to give expression to the artistic or creative impulses or abilities of (oneself) ⟨in one of our modern schools, where the little darlings are supposed to ~ themselves —H.W. Van Loon⟩ **f :** to represent by a sign or symbol **:** SYMBOLIZE ⟨the sign = ~es equality⟩ **2 a :** to force out by pressure **:** press or squeeze out (as the juice of a fruit) ⟨estimated that the daily water requirements of one person could be ~ed from six to seven pounds of fish —N.B.Marshall⟩ **b :** to empty by pressure or squeezing **:** subject to pressure so as to extract something ⟨the seeds . . . are ~ed to yield the neutral liquid fat —C.H.Thienes⟩ **3** [⁴*express*] **:** to send by express messenger **:** transport by express service ⟨~ a package⟩ ~ *vi* [⁴*express*] **:** to travel by express train

syn VENT, UTTER, VOICE, BROACH, AIR, VENTILATE: these can mean, in common, to give some form to in letting out (usu. what one feels or thinks). EXPRESS, the most general and comprehensive, can mean merely to say or put into words, but more generally implies any degree of more comprehensive revelation involving thoughts, feelings, moods, attributes, or qualities and a putting into any form that reveals, as words, gestures, bodily positions or facial aspects, arrangements of line, mass, or color (in painting), variations of tone, tempo, rhythm in the playing of notes, phrases, or harmonic progressions (in music), or the like ⟨*express* one's views⟩ ⟨*express* agreement⟩ ⟨to be an artist means . . . to *express* emotion —C.W.H.Johnson⟩ ⟨*express* surprise and anger⟩ ⟨music *expressing* repose and serenity⟩ ⟨a novel *expressing* character⟩ VENT implies some inner compulsion to express or let out as with a pent-up emotion or powerful passion that demands an outlet or cannot be controlled ⟨*vent* a grievance⟩ ⟨*vent* one's spleen against an enemy⟩ ⟨compensate for a lifetime of frustration by *venting* their aggressive drives against an acceptable villain —Walter Goodman⟩ UTTER stresses the use of the voice though not necessarily speech, generally implying a short, usu. significant, often carefully formulated expression ⟨*utter* a grunt⟩ ⟨the ruler who *uttered* the divine command —B.N.Cardozo⟩ ⟨he *uttered* a spell —J.G.Frazer⟩ ⟨*utter* platitudes⟩ ⟨*utter* a dictum⟩ ⟨his impetuosity and eagerness to *utter* what was in him —H.O.Taylor⟩ VOICE suggests expression or formulation in words though not necessarily in vocal utterance ⟨*voice* an opinion⟩ ⟨*voice* resentment⟩ ⟨poetry *voicing* one's yearnings and frustrations⟩ BROACH stresses mention for the first time, esp. of something long thought over and usu. awaiting an opportune moment for disclosure ⟨the idea of religious radio broadcasts was first *broached* in 1923 —*Current Biog.*⟩ ⟨I *broached*, as a practical measure, in my plan of organization, the system which I had discussed tentatively —A.D.White⟩ ⟨*broach* a touchy subject with care⟩ AIR implies exposure, often a parading of one's views, sometimes a much needed expressing of them as a form of relief or in the hope of gaining attention or, occas., to gain sympathy ⟨*air* one's views⟩ ⟨*air* grievances⟩ VENTILATE implies a thorough scrutiny by bringing to light or exposing all phases or aspects of a matter, usu. suggesting a desire to get at the truth by discovering the real issues or by a careful weighing of pros and cons ⟨persuading their legislative representatives to *ventilate* the question in Parliament —S.O.Eklund⟩ ⟨discussion programs of this kind, whose aim is to *ventilate* economic problems —William Salter⟩

⁴**express** \"\ *n* -ES [¹*express*] **1 a** *Brit* **:** a messenger sent on a special errand **b** *Brit* **:** a dispatch conveyed by a special messenger **c** (1) **:** an intercity and international system for the prompt and safe transportation of parcels, money, or goods with pickup and delivery service and at rates higher than standard freight charges — compare FREIGHT (2) **:** a company operating a merchandise freight service (3) **:** the goods or shipments transported by express **d** *or* **express delivery** *Brit* **:** delivery of express mail **:** SPECIAL DELIVERY **2** [³*express*] *obs* **:** EXPRESSION, MANIFESTATION; *esp* **:** a verbal manifestation **:** UTTERANCE, DECLARATION, INJUNCTION **3 :** EXPRESS TRAIN

ex·press·age \-sij\ *n* -S **:** a carrying of parcels by express; *also* **:** a charge for such carrying

express assumpsit *n* **:** an action on contract brought to recover damages on a bilateral contract express or implied in fact — called also *special assumpsit*

express car *n* **:** a railroad car built for carrying express

expressed *past of* EXPRESS

expressed almond oil *n* **:** ALMOND OIL 1a

ex·press·er *or* **ex·pres·sor** \-sə(r)\ *n* -S **:** one that expresses ⟨the ~ of a minority opinion⟩

expresses *pres 3d sing of* EXPRESS, *pl of* EXPRESS

ex·press·ible *also* **ex·press·able** \-səbəl\ *adj* **:** capable of being expressed ⟨an ~ emotion⟩ ⟨the presence of natural ~ liquids in the meat —*Meat & Meat Cookery*⟩

expressing *pres part of* EXPRESS

ex·pres·sion \ik'spreshən, ek-\ *n* -S [ME *expressioun*, fr. ML *expression-, expressio*, fr. L, action of pressing out, fr. *expressus* (past part. of *exprimere* to express, press out) + *-ion-, -io* -ion — more at EXPRESS] **1 a :** an act, process, or instance of representing, manifesting, or conveying in words or some other medium **:** MANIFESTATION, UTTERANCE, ISSUE ⟨the sacred principle of freedom of ~ of ideas⟩ ⟨his anger found ~ in a string of oaths⟩ ⟨his talent found ~ in the plastic arts⟩ **b** (1) **:** something that manifests, represents, reflects, embodies, or symbolizes something else **:** SIGN, TOKEN ⟨a country in which socialism found its practical ~⟩ ⟨an assortment of gifts as ~s of his fans' admiration —*Current Biog.*⟩ ⟨the first clinical ~ of the disease⟩ (2) **:** a significant word or phrase ⟨he uses some very odd ~s⟩ (3) **:** a sign or character or a finite sequence of signs or characters (as logical or mathematical symbols) representing a quantity or operation (4) **:** the detectable effect of a gene; *also* **:** EXPRESSIVITY **2 a** (1) **:** a mode, means, or use of significant representation or symbolism ⟨dignified ~ in writing⟩; *esp* **:** felicitous or vivid indication or depiction of mood or sentiment ⟨read a poem with ~⟩ (2) **:** a manipulation of formal artistic means or an interpretation of subject matter to reveal forcefully the artist's conception, mood, or attitude (3) **:** features of musical performance other than mechanical reproduction of the notes commonly including gradations of tempo and dynamics, phrasing and articulation, and nuance whether indicated by expression marks or left to the performer's discretion (4) **:** use of artistic means or the artistic interpretation of subject matter for the imaginative recreation of objects from nature or life ⟨delightful and illuminating journey through 150 years of graphic ~ —Una E. Johnson⟩ ⟨the aestheticians of romanticism invented the term ~ to describe the artistic purpose to which apparent imitation was subservient —J.W.Krutch⟩ **b** (1) **:** the quality or fact of being expressive ⟨eyes full of fire and ~⟩ (2) **:** facial aspect or vocal intonation as indicative of feeling ⟨she tried to read something in his face . . . but was not yet capable of understanding its ~ —Joseph Conrad⟩ **3 :** an act or product of pressing out ⟨~ is a process of forcibly separating liquids from solids —E.F.Cook & E.W.Martin⟩

ex·pres·sion·al \-shən°l, -shnəl\ *adj* **:** of or relating to expression

ex·pres·sion·ism \-shə,nizəm\ *n* -S [G *expressionismus*, fr. F *expression* (fr. ML *expression-, expressio*) + G *-ismus* -ism] **1 :** a theory or practice in art esp. of the late 19th and 20th centuries of seeking to depict not objective reality but the subjective emotions and responses that objects and events arouse in the artist with wide use of distortion, exaggeration, and symbolism — often contrasted with *impressionism* **2 :** a theory or practice in the literature and theater of the 20th century of presenting the subjective or subconscious thoughts and emotions of characters, the struggle of abstract forces, or the inner realities of life by a wide variety of nonnaturalistic techniques that include abstraction, distortion, and symbolism **3 :** a theory or practice in music esp. of the 20th century of avoiding the traditional tonalities and techniques and seeking to express the composer's inner experience — often contrasted with *impressionism*

¹**ex·pres·sion·ist** \-sh(ə)nəst\ *adj* **:** of or relating to expressionism ⟨how ~ line and color can give a strong feeling of emotion —A.H.Barr⟩

²**expressionist** \"\ *n* -S **:** a practitioner or adherent of expressionism

ex·pres·sion·is·tic \ik¦spreshə¦nistik, ek¦-, ,ek,==¦==\ *adj* **:** EXPRESSIONIST ⟨her art has always been highly ~, which is to say that it is basically motivated by psychological forces and not solely by the autonomous demands of plastic form —Rhys Gwyn⟩ — **ex·pres·sion·is·ti·cal·ly** \-tək(ə)lē, -tēk-, -li\ *adv*

ex·pres·sion·less \=¦=shənləs\ *adj* **:** lacking expression ⟨eyes . . . as numb and ~ as a brace of gray oysters on the half shell —R.P.Warren⟩ — **ex·pres·sion·less·ly** *adv*

expression mark *n* **:** a sign or mark used in music to denote a specific expressive quality

ex·pres·sio uni·us est ex·clu·sio al·te·ri·us \ek'spresē,ō-'ünē,ü,se,stek'sklüsē,ō,äl'terē,ùs\ [NL, expression of the one is exclusion of the other] **:** a principle in law: when one or more things of a class are expressly mentioned others of the same class are excluded

ex·pres·sive \ik'spresiv, ek-, -sēv *also* -səv-\ *adj* **1 :** of or relating to expression ⟨the ~ function of language⟩ ⟨architecture . . . has its limitations as an ~ medium —Robin Boyd⟩ **2 :** serving to express, utter, or represent **:** INDICATIVE ⟨spent much time in Arizona . . . and left many canvases ~ of its vitality and color —*Amer. Guide Series: Ariz.*⟩ ⟨poems and prayers . . . ~ of the deepest religious experiences —*Saturday Rev.*⟩ **3 :** forcefully representing the meaning or feeling meant to be conveyed **:** full of expression **:** SIGNIFICANT, EMPHATIC ⟨richly ~ gestures⟩ ⟨an ~ silence⟩ ⟨a homely whistling sound which . . . was terribly ~ — William Zukerman⟩ ⟨still cling to their "'tain't so" and "'twan't nothin'" because their fathers found these so ~ —*Amer. Guide Series: N.C.*⟩

syn ELOQUENT, SIGNIFICANT, MEANINGFUL, PREGNANT, SENTENTIOUS: EXPRESSIVE describes that which clearly shows or communicates an idea, mood, or emotion forcefully or vividly ⟨her forehead had been strikingly *expressive* of an engrossing terror and compassion that saw nothing but the peril of the accused —Charles Dickens⟩ ⟨he used foul and novel terms *expressive* of rage —H.G.Wells⟩ ⟨described by such epithets as vital, characteristic, picturesque, individual — in short, on the element that may be summed up by the epithet *expressive* —Irving Babbitt⟩ ELOQUENT may intensify the notions of EXPRESSIVE, esp. in evoking emotional ideas or arousing deep feeling ⟨no man is *eloquent* save when someone is moved as he listens —John Dewey⟩ ⟨there was a burst of applause, and a deep silence which was even more *eloquent* than the applause —Thomas Hardy⟩ ⟨I could scarcely remove my eyes from her *eloquent* countenance: I seemed to read in it relief and gladness mingled with surprise and something like vexation —W.H.Hudson †1922⟩ SIGNIFICANT is applicable to whatever expresses a meaning, sometimes a covert or hidden meaning, sometimes a clearly ascertainable idea, sometimes an important meaning ⟨those who lay down that every sentence must end on a *significant* word, never on a preposition —Havelock Ellis⟩ ⟨every sentence is doubly *significant*, and the sense of our author is as broad as the world —S.P.Sherman⟩ MEANINGFUL may have the suggestion of SIGNIFICANT; it may be used simply to indicate presence of meaning ⟨some brilliant minds to whom the carefully turned phrase and the *meaningful* metaphor are very important —D.W.Maurer & V. H. Vogel⟩ PREGNANT may describe that which conveys a rich or weighty meaning, often with force or conciseness ⟨who has not had the experience of resolving a difficulty with the help of a sentence *pregnant* with life's meaning, some well-phrased words of wisdom, or a poem that came to mind at a critical moment? —Vivian T. Thayer⟩ ⟨no talent for revealing a character or resuming the significance of an episode in a single *pregnant* phrase —W.S.Maugham⟩ SENTENTIOUS may apply to what is full of significance and expressed tersely ⟨clarity is gained by a brief and almost *sententious* statement at the outset of the problem to be attacked —B.N.Cardozo⟩ ⟨the peculiarly sardonic and *sententious* style in which Don Luis composed his epigrams —Hervey Allen⟩

ex·pres·sive·ly \-səvlē, -li\ *adv* **:** in an expressive manner ⟨sentiments ~ fashioned into verse⟩

ex·pres·sive·ness \-sivnəs, -sēv- *also* -səv-\ *n* -ES **:** the quality of being expressive

ex·pres·siv·i·ty \,ek,spre'sivəd·ē, -vətē, -i\ *n* -ES [ISV *expressive* + *-ity*; orig. formed as G *expressivität*] **1 :** the relative capacity of a gene to modify the organism of which it is a part — compare PENETRANCE **2** [*expressive* + *-ity*] **:** the quality of being expressive ⟨works in which intellectual interest . . . is held in perfect balance with ~ —Edward Cushing⟩

ex·press·less \ik'spresləs, (')ek¦s-\ *adj, archaic* **:** INEXPRESSIBLE

express liner *n* **:** a fast liner equipped chiefly for carriage of passengers, mails, and high-class cargo

ex·press·ly \ik'spreslē, ek's- *sometimes* 'ek,s-\ *adv* [ME *expresli*, fr. ¹*express* + *-li* -ly] **1 :** in direct or unmistakable terms **:** in an express manner **:** EXPLICITLY, DEFINITELY, DIRECTLY ⟨he had ~ rejected at one time or another dialectical materialism —J.G.Colton⟩ **2 :** for the express purpose **:** PARTICULARLY ⟨the need for a city hospital ~ for the cure of addicts —*Current Biog.*⟩

ex·press·man \ik'spre,sman, ek-, -,smən\ *n, pl* **expressmen** **:** a person employed in the express business

expressor *var of* EXPRESSER

express rifle *n* [prob. fr. ⁴*express* (train)] **:** a sporting rifle for use at short ranges employing a large charge of powder and a light bullet

express train *n* **1 :** a train formerly run expressly for the occasion **2 a :** a train of express freight **b :** a passenger train operated at high speed with few stops

express truck *n* **:** a light motor truck for quick delivery (as of express packages)

express trust *n* [¹*express*] **:** a trust created directly and explicitly by deed, will, or declaration of trust — compare CONSTRUCTIVE TRUST, RESULTING TRUST

ex·pres·sure \ik'spreshə(r), ek-\ *n* -S [³*express* + *-ure*] *archaic* **:** EXPRESSION

express wagon *n* **1 :** a wagon used for moving and delivering goods sent by express **2 :** a low 4-wheeled wagon with an open rectangular body like a flat box and a retroflex tongue made for the play or use (as for carrying newspapers) of a child

express wagon 2

expressway \=¦=,=\ *n* **:** a high-speed divided highway for through traffic with access partially or fully controlled and grade separations at important intersections with other roads — compare FREEWAY, PARKWAY, TURNPIKE

ex·pro·brate \'ekspro͞,brāt\ *vt* -ED/-ING/-S [L *exprobratus*, past part. of *exprobrare*, fr. *ex-* ¹ex- + *-probrare* (fr. *probrum* disgraceful act, infamy) — more at OPPROBRIUM] *archaic* **:** CENSURE, UPBRAID

ex·pro·bra·tion \,==¦brāshən\ *n* -S [ME *exprobracioun*, fr. L *exprobration-, exprobratio*, fr. *exprobratus* + *-ion-, -io* -ion] *archaic* **:** an act or an instance of exprobrating **:** REPROACH

ex·pro·mis·sion \,ekspro͞'mishən\ *n* -S [NL *expromission-, expromissio*, fr. L *expromissus* (past part. of *expromittere* to promise to pay, fr. *ex-* ¹ex- + *promittere* to promise) + *-ion-, -io* -ion — more at PROMISE] **:** an act of binding oneself for another's debt and thereby releasing him from obligation — compare INTERCESSION 2

ex·pro·mis·sor \,ekspro͞'misə(r)\ *n* -S [LL, fr. L *expromissus* + *-or*] **:** one that performs an act of expromission

ex·pro·pri·ate \ek'sprōprē,āt, ik-, *usu* -ād·+V\ *vt* -ED/-ING/-S [ML *expropriatus*, past part. of *expropriare*, fr. L *ex-* ¹ex- + *propriare* to appropriate, fr. *proprius* own — more at PROPER] **1 :** to deprive of possession or proprietary rights — used esp. of the action of a state; see EXPROPRIATION **2 :** to take (something) out of the possession of another **:** transfer (the property of another) to one's own possession ⟨the landowners *expropriated* the countryside, but they developed it —Roy Lewis & Angus Maude⟩ ⟨they have also *expropriated* another cherished word from the lexicon of western European peoples —R.G.Cowherd⟩ — used esp. of the action of a state ⟨promulgate laws which tended to ~ Jewish possessions —*Collier's Yr. Bk.*⟩ ⟨the government had *expropriated* nearly 68,000 hectares of privately owned property —*Americana Annual*⟩

ex·pro·pri·a·tion \(,)ek,sprōprē'āshən, ik,-\ *n* -S [ML *expropriation-, expropriatio*, fr. *expropriatus* + L *-ion-, -io* -ion] **:** an act of expropriating or a state of being expropriated; *specif* **:** the action of the state in taking or modifying the property rights of an individual in the exercise of its sovereignty (as where property is sold under eminent domain)

ex·pro·pri·a·tor \=¦==,ād·ə(r), -ātə-\ *n* -S **:** one that expropriates

ex pro·prio vi·go·re \ek'sprōprē,ōvə'gōrē\ [NL] **:** of its own force

expt *abbr* **1** experiment **2** expert **3** export

exptl *abbr* experimental

exptr *abbr* exporter

expugn *vt* -ED/-ING/-S [ME *expugnen*, fr. L *expugnare*, fr. *ex-* + *pugnare* to fight; akin to L *pugnus* fist — more at PUNGENT] **1** *obs* **:** to take by storm **2** *obs* **:** VANQUISH

ex·pug·na·ble \ek'spəgnəbəl, -'spyünə-\ *adj* [L *expugnabilis*, fr. *expugnare* + *-abilis* -able] **:** capable of being conquered or taken by storm

ex·pug·na·to·ry \ek'spəgnə,tōrē\ *adj* [LL *expugnatorius* overpowering, fr. L *expugnatus* + *-orius* -ory] **:** adapted for attack

ex·pulse \ik'spəl(t)s, ek-\ *vt* -ED/-ING/-S [ME *expulsen*, fr. L *expulsare*, fr. *ex-* ¹ex- + *pulsare* to push — more at PUSH] **:** EXPEL ⟨the country had just *expulsed* the detested . . . invaders —Galbraith Welch⟩

ex·pul·sion \ik'spəlshən, ek-\ *n* -S [ME *expulsioun*, fr. L *expulsion-, expulsio*, fr. *expulsus* (past part. of *expellere* to expel) + *-ion-, -io* -ion — more at EXPEL] **:** an act of expelling or a state of being expelled **:** a driving or forcing out **:** summary removal (as from membership or association) ⟨on the occasion of my ~ from college —A.J.Liebling⟩ ⟨~ from Germany had cost them their homes —Oscar Handlin⟩

expulsion fuse *n* **:** an electrical fuse that is blown out of its cartridge by a short circuit

ex·pul·sive \-lsiv, -sēv *also* -lts- *or* -səv\ *adj* [ME *expulsif*, fr. MF & ML; MF *expulsif*, fr. ML *expulsivus*, fr. L *expulsus* + *-ivus* -ive] **:** having the power of expelling **:** serving to expel ⟨the ~ power of an exhausting emotional experience —Hunter Mead⟩

ex·punc·tion \ik'spəŋ(k)shən, ek-\ *n* -S [L *expunctus* (past part. of *expungere*) + E *-ion*] **:** an act of expunging or a state of being expunged **:** ERASURE ⟨making some ~ —J.M.Conly⟩

ex·punge \ik'spənj, ek-\ *vt* -ED/-ING/-S [L *expungere* to mark for deletion by dots placed above or below, fr. *ex-* ¹ex- + *pungere* to prick — more at PUNGENT] **1 a :** to strike out, obliterate, or mark for deletion (as a word, line, or sentence) **b :** to obliterate (a material record or trace) by any means ⟨~ the sound of a voice from a tape recording⟩ ⟨~ a man's fingerprints⟩ **c :** DROP, EXCLUDE, DISCARD, OMIT ⟨that condemnation stood for priests to read . . . until the seventeenth century, when it was silently *expunged* —G.G.Coulton⟩ **d :** to cause (something intangible) to be effaced ⟨could not ~ those bitter memories from his mind⟩ ⟨the most primitive ways of thinking may not yet be wholly *expunged* —William James⟩ **2 a :** to cause the physical destruction of **:** ANNIHILATE ⟨the nuclear explosives that can ~ in a fraction of a second . . . the units of . . . civilization —*Saturday Rev.*⟩ ⟨the race of man *expunging* itself by its own hand —Sara H. Hay⟩ **b :** to treat or cause to be regarded as nonexistent **:** consign to oblivion **:** destroy in any manner **:** ERADICATE ⟨released her with a warning and . . . considered the episode *expunged* —Josephine Johnson⟩ ⟨~ the power of labor in politics —Bruce Bliven b. 1889⟩ ⟨official efforts to ~ the popular hero from history⟩ **syn** see ERASE

ex·pur·gate \'ekspə(r),gāt, *usu* -ād·+V\ *vt* -ED/-ING/-S [L *expurgatus*, past part. of *expurgare* to purge, purify, vindicate, fr. *ex-* ¹ex- + *purgare* to purge, purify — more at PURGE] **:** to cleanse of something morally harmful, offensive, or erroneous : PURGE; *esp* : to expunge before publication or presentation obscene or otherwise objectionable parts from ⟨~ a book⟩ ⟨~ a play⟩

ex·pur·ga·tion \ˌ==ˈgāshən\ *n* -s [ME *expurgacion*, fr. L *expurgation-, expurgatio* vindication, fr. *expurgatus* + *-ion-, -io* -ion] : an act of expurgating, purging, or cleansing : purification from something morally harmful, offensive, sinful, or erroneous

ex·pur·ga·tor \ˈ==ˌgād·ə(r), -ātə-\ *n* -s : one that expurgates

ex·pur·ga·to·ri·al \ikˌspərgəˈtōrēəl, ekˌ-, ˌek,==ˈ===\ *adj* [NL *expurgatorius* + E *-al*] : relating to expurgation or an expurgator : EXPURGATORY

ex·pur·ga·to·ry \=ˈ=gəˌtōrē\ *adj* [NL *expurgatorius*, fr. L *expurgatus* + *-orius* -ory] : serving to purify from something morally harmful, offensive, or erroneous : CLEANSING, PURIFYING

[1]**ex·quis·ite** \ekˈskwizət, ˈek,skwiz-, ˈekskwəz-, ikˈskwiz-, *usu* -zəd.+V\ *adj* [ME *exquisit*, fr. L *exquisitus*, fr. past part. of *exquirere* to search out, seek, fr. *ex-* [1]ex- + *-quirere* (fr. *quaerere* to seek, gain, obtain, ask)] **1 a** : carefully selected or sought out : ingeniously devised : CHOICE, RECHERCHÉ ⟨I have given her the best advice, . . . making the most ~ moral reflections — but to no purpose —Iris Origo⟩ **b** *obs* : FARFETCHED, AFFECTED **2** *archaic* : careful or exact in working or operation : ACCURATE, NICE, EXACT **3 a** : marked by flawless craftsmanship or by beautiful, ingenious, delicate, or elaborate execution ⟨Sung vases and ~ lacquers —James Hilton⟩ ⟨an ~ cameo⟩ ⟨an ~ portrait⟩ **b** : marked by nicest discrimination, keenest appreciation, deepest sensitivity, or most subtle understanding ⟨a far more keen and ~ observer than her brother —J.L.Lowes⟩ ⟨an ~ choice⟩ ⟨an ~ critic⟩ : marked or perceptible by or calling for keenest sensitivity ⟨an ~ sense of hearing⟩ ⟨~ variations in color⟩ **c** : transcending and superlative : marked by acute discrimination and selection, faultless execution, and maximum effectiveness ⟨paints with ~ art the charm of the deep country —John Buchan⟩ ⟨the ~ transparency and delicate finish of her work —P.E.More⟩ **d** : ACCOMPLISHED, FINISHED, PERFECTED ⟨an ~ gentleman⟩ **4 a** : affording or accompanied by keen delight, rapture, or pleasure esp. through beauty, fitness, delicacy, or perfection : DELIGHTFUL, DELECTABLE ⟨the night-blooming cereus . . . an ~ white blossom with a spicy fragrance —*Amer. Guide Series:Ariz.*⟩ ⟨~ brushwork⟩ **b** : perfect and unrelieved : TRANSCENDING, ACUTE, EXTREME, CONSUMMATE ⟨the most ~ pitch of joy and happiness to which life could thrill —Jack London⟩ ⟨an ~ pain shot through his arm⟩ ⟨wondered at the ~ stupidity of the hearers —S.M.Crothers⟩ **c** : marked by uncommon, esoteric, or precious appeal ⟨the ~, the finely drawn, the rich trappings of legend —Sara H. Hay⟩ **syn** see CHOICE

[2]**exquisite** \"\ *n* -s : one who is overnice in dress or ornament ⟨young ~s, perfumed and foppish⟩

ex·quis·ite·ly *adv* : in an exquisite manner

ex·quis·ite·ness *n* -ES : the quality of being exquisite

ex·quis·i·tive·ly \ekˈskwizəd·ivlē\ *adv, archaic* : EXQUISITELY

exr *abbr* executor

ex·radius \(ˈ)eks+\ *n* [[1]ex- + *radius*] : a radius of an escribed circle or sphere — opposed to *inradius*

ex re·la·ti·o·ne \ˌeksrə,lād·ēˈōnē\ *prep* [L] : by or on the relation or information of — used in the title of informations and special proceedings to designate the person at whose instance the state or a public officer is acting; abbr. *ex rel.*

ex rights *adv (or adj)* [[2]ex] : without carrying or conferring the right to subscribe to a pending new issue of stock ⟨stock that sells *ex rights*⟩

exrx *abbr* executrix

ex·san·gui·nate \ek(s)ˈsaŋgwə,nāt\ *vt* -ED/-ING/-S [L *exsanguinatus* bloodless, fr. *ex-* [1]ex- + *sanguin-, sanguis* blood + *-atus* -ate] : to make bloodless : drain of blood — **ex·san·gui·na·tion** \(ˌ)=,==ˈnāshən\ *n* -s

ex·san·guine \(ˈ)ek(s)ˈsaŋgwən\ *adj* [irreg. (influence of *sanguine*) fr. L *exsanguis*, fr. *ex-* [1]ex- + *sanguis* blood] : BLOODLESS, ANEMIC — **ex·san·guin·i·ty** \ˌek(s)ˌsaŋˈgwinəd·ē, -saŋˈg-\ *n* -ES

ex·san·guin·e·ous \ˌek(s)ˌsaŋˈgwinēəs, -saŋˈg-\ *adj* [[1]ex- + *sanguineous*] : EXSANGUINE

ex·san·gui·no·transfusion \ek(s)ˌsaŋgwə,nō+\ *n* [[1]*exchange* + *sanguino-* + *transfusion*] : EXCHANGE TRANSFUSION

ex·san·gui·nous \(ˈ)ek(s)ˈsaŋgwənəs\ *adj* [[1]ex- + *sanguinous*] : EXSANGUINE

ex·san·gui·ous \(ˈ)ek(s)ˈsaŋgwēəs\ *adj* [irreg. fr. L *exsanguis*] : EXSANGUINE

ex·scind \ekˈsind\ *vt* -ED/-ING/-S [L *exscindere* to cut or tear out, fr. *ex-* [1]ex- + *scindere* to cut, tear — more at SHED (to throw off)] : to cut off or out : EXCISE ⟨these words were ~*ed* from the text⟩

exscribe *vt* [L *exscribere*, fr. *ex-* [1]ex- + *scribere* to write — more at SCRIBE] *obs* : COPY, TRANSCRIBE

ex·sculp·tate \ekˈskəlp,tāt\ *adj* [L *exsculptus* (past part. of *exsculpere* to carve out, fr. *ex-* [1]ex- + *sculpere* to carve) + E *-ate* — more at SCULPTOR] : having variable and irregular depressed lines that resemble sculptured work

ex·scutellate \(ˈ)ek(s)+\ *adj* [[1]ex- + NL *scutellum* + E *-ate*] : ESCUTELLATE

ex·sect \(ˈ)ekˈsekt\ *vt* -ED/-ING/-S [L *exsectus*, past part. of *exsecare*, fr. *ex-* [1]ex- + *secare* to cut — more at SAW] : to cut out : EXCISE ⟨an ~*ed* uterus⟩

ex·sec·tile \(ˈ)ekˈsektᵊl, -,tīl, -(ˌ)til\ *adj* : capable of being exsected

ex·sec·tion \(ˈ)ekˈsekshən\ *n* [L *exsection-, exsectio*, fr. *exsectus* + *-ion-, -io* -ion] : EXCISION

[1]**ex·sert** \(ˈ)ekˈsərt\ *vt* -ED/-ING/-S [L *exsertus, exertus*, past part. of *exserere, exerere* — more at EXERT] : to thrust forth or out : cause to protrude : cause to project : stick out ⟨a bee ~*ing* its sting⟩

[2]**exsert** \"\ *adj* [L *exsertus, exertus*, past part.] : EXSERTED

exserted *adj* : projecting beyond an enclosing organ or part ⟨~ stamens⟩

ex·ser·tile \(ˈ)ekˈsərd·ᵊl, -r,tīl, -r(ˌ)til\ *adj* : capable of being exserted ⟨the highly ~ tongue of this snake⟩

ex·ser·tion \(ˈ)ekˈsərshən\ *n* -s : the action of exserting or state of being exserted

ex·sheath \(ˈ)ek(s)ˈshēth, -th\ *vb* [[1]ex- + *sheath* (n.)] *vi* : to escape from the residual membrane remaining from a previous stage of development — used of certain larval nematodes (as filaria) ~ *vt* : to cause (nematode larvae) to exsheath — **ex·sheath·ment** \-mənt\ *n* -s

ex ship *adv (or adj)* [[2]ex] : without shipment costs to the consignee until receipt overside of the shipment at destination, the consignee being required to accept delivery at the ship's side and assume all subsequent liability ⟨the firm agreed to receive the lumber *ex ship*⟩ — compare FREE ON BOARD

ex·sic·ca·tae \ˌeksəˈkä,tē, -kā,-, -ä,tī\ *also* **ex·sic·ca·ti** \-ä,tī, -ā,-, -ä,tē\ *n pl* [NL, fr. L, fem. & masc. pl. respectively of *exsiccatus*] : a collection or series of dried herbarium specimens

ex·sic·cate \ˈeksə,kāt, ekˈsi,-\ *vt* -ED/-ING/-S [L *exsiccatus*, past part. of *exsiccare*, fr. *ex-* [1]ex- + *siccare* to dry, fr. *siccus* dry — more at SACK] : to drive moisture from (as by the action of heat) : make dry : DEHYDRATE ⟨*exsiccated* salt⟩ : drain of moisture : dry up ⟨an *exsiccated* swamp⟩ : DESICCATE — now used chiefly in passive — **ex·sic·ca·tion** \ˌeksəˈkāshən\ *n* -s

ex·sic·co·sis \ˌeksəˈkōsəs\ *n* -ES [NL, fr. L *exsiccare* + NL *-osis*] : insufficient intake of fluids or the state of bodily dehydration produced thereby

ex si·len·tio \ˌek(s)səˈlenchē,ō, -)ˌsī-\ *or* **e silentio** \ˌēsə-, ˌē,sī-\ *adv (or adj)* [L *ex silentio* from silence] : from the fact of lack of specific evidence (as of written or oral attestation) ⟨an argument that was built up wholly *ex silentio*⟩

ex·solution \ˌek(s)+\ *n* [L *exsolution-, exsolutio* release, fr. *exsolutus* (past part. of *exsolvere*) + *-ion-, -io* -ion] : the action or process of exsolving

ex·solve \(ˈ)ek(s)+\ *vb* [L *exsolvere* to loosen, untie, release, fr. *ex-* [1]ex- + *solvere* to loosen, release — more at SOLVE] : to separate or precipitate from a solid crystalline phase : UNMIX

ex·stipulate \(ˈ)ek(s)+\ *adj* [[1]ex- + *stipule* + *-ate*] : having no stipules ⟨~ leaves⟩

ex store *adv (or adj)* [[2]ex] : with shipment costs to be paid by the consignee after the shipment leaves the stock — opposed to *free on board*; compare IN STORE

ex·stro·phy \ˈekstrəfē\ *n* -ES [[1]ex- + *-strophy* (fr. Gk *strophein* to turn + E -y) — more at STROPHE] : eversion of a part or organ; *specif* : a congenital malformation of the bladder in which the normally internal mucosa of the organ lies exposed on the abdominal wall because of failure of union between the halves of the pubic symphysis and between the adjacent halves of the abdominal wall

ex·suc·cous \(ˈ)ek(s)ˈsəkəs\ *adj* [L *exsuccus*, fr. *ex-* [1]ex- + *succus* juice — more at SUCCULENT] : devoid of all juices or sap : having no moisture whatsoever : dried up ⟨a withered ~ piece of fruit⟩

exsudation *obs var of* EXUDATION

ex·suf·fla·tion \ˌeksəˈflāshən\ *n* [LL *exsufflation-, exsufflatio*, fr. *exsufflatus* (past part. of *exsufflare* to blow away, fr. L *ex-* [1]ex- + *sufflare* to inflate, blow upon) + L *-ion-, -io* -ion — more at SUFFLATE] **1** : the action of breathing forth or blowing; *esp* : this action used as an exorcism in some rites of baptism **2** : forcible breathing or blowing out (as in clearing the respiratory tract) : forcible expiration

ext *abbr* **1** extended; extension **2** exterior **3** external **4** extinct **5** extinguisher **6** extra **7** extract **8** extreme; extremely

ex·tant \ˈekstənt, ekˈstant, ˈek,stant, ikˈstant, -taa(ə)nt\ *adj* [L *exstant-, exstans, extant-, extans*, pres. part. of *exstare, extare* to stand out, project, be in existence, fr. *ex-* [1]ex- + *stare* to stand — more at STAND] **1 a** *archaic* : standing, projecting, or protruding out or above ⟨its naked body half ~ from the coarse blanket —George Borrow⟩ **b** *archaic* : standing out in a way that is adapted to physical or mental perception : easily seen or understood : clearly evident ⟨the truth should be visibly ~ —A.W.Kinglake⟩ **2 a** : currently or actually existing : that is in existence ⟨the most charming writer ~ —G.W. Johnson⟩ **b** : still existing : continuing to exist : maintaining existence : not exterminated, destroyed, or lost ⟨in the specimens of graphic art found among ~ barbaric folk —Edward Clodd⟩ ⟨one of the oldest works ~ on that subject⟩

ex·ta·sy *archaic var of* ECSTASY

ext d&c color \ˈeks(t),dēənˌsē-\ *n, usu cap E&D & 1st C* [abbr. of *external drug and cosmetic color*] : any of the synthetic dyes that in certified batches are permitted for use only in drugs and cosmetics to be applied externally — compare D&C COLOR, FD&C COLOR; see DYE table II

ex·tem·po·ral \(ˈ)ekˈstemp(ə)rəl, ikˈs-\ *adj* [L *extemporalis*, fr. *ex tempore* + *-alis* -al] *archaic* : EXTEMPORANEOUS, EXTEMPORE — **ex·tem·po·ral·ly** \-rəlē\ *adv, obs*

ex·tem·po·ra·ne·i·ty \(ˌ)ek,stempərəˈnēəd·ē, ik,-, -ēətē, -i\ *n* -ES : the quality or state of being extemporaneous

ex·tem·po·ra·ne·ous \(ˌ)ekˌstempəˈrānēəs, ikˌ-\ *adj* [LL *extemporaneus*, fr. L *ex tempore* + *-aneus* (as in *subterraneus* subterranean)] **1 a** : composed, performed, or uttered on or as if on the spur of the moment ⟨an ~ musical composition⟩ ⟨an ~ piece of verse⟩ : impromptu ⟨~ comment⟩ or apparently impromptu (as by avoiding use of rigid memorization, reading, or notes) ⟨a brilliant ~ speech⟩ : marked by or as if by no previous thought, study, or other preparation : IMPROVISED, UNPREMEDITATED **b** : skilled at, given to, or marked by extemporaneous composing, performance, or utterance ⟨one of the funniest ~ wits of our time —E.J.Kahn⟩ **c** : happening suddenly, often unexpectedly, and usu. without clearly known causes or relationships ⟨a great deal of criminal and delinquent behavior is . . . ~ —W.C.Reckless⟩ **2** : provided, made, or put to use as a temporary expedient : suggested by or hurriedly adapted to the occasion : MAKESHIFT ⟨preparing an ~ meal⟩ ⟨using an ~ shelter⟩ **3** *of a pharmaceutical preparation* : compounded according to a physician's prescription as needed : prepared when ordered : not ready-made — **ex·tem·po·ra·ne·ous·ly** *adv* — **ex·tem·po·ra·ne·ous·ness** *n* -ES

ex·tem·po·rar·i·ly \ikˌstempəˌrerəlē, -li, (ˌ)ekˌ==ˈ===, ekˌ==-, ˌ===\ *adv* : in an extemporary manner

ex·tem·po·rary \ikˈstempə,rerē, ek-, -eri\ *adj* [L *ex tempore* + E *-ary*] : EXTEMPORANEOUS

[1]**ex·tem·po·re** \ikˈstempərē, ek-, -ri, -,rē *also* -,rā\ *adv* [L *ex tempore* instantaneously, on the spur of the moment, fr. *ex* out of + *tempore*, abl. of *tempus* time — more at EX-, TEMPORAL] : in an extempore manner : EXTEMPORANEOUSLY

[2]**extempore** \"\ *n, pl* **extempores** *also* **extempore** *archaic* : something that is extemporaneous : IMPROVISATION

[3]**extempore** \"\ *adj* : EXTEMPORANEOUS ⟨his effusions were genuinely ~ —W.G.Lane⟩

ex·tem·po·ri·za·tion \ikˌstempərəˈzāshən, (ˌ)ekˌ-, -ˌrīˈz-\ *n* -s **1** : the act of extemporizing : IMPROVISATION **2** : something produced or marked by extemporization ⟨ingenious ~s were employed to provide substitutes for customary foods, clothing, and household articles —A.D.Kirwan⟩

ex·tem·po·rize \=ˈ==,rīz\ *vb, see -ize in Explan Notes* [[1]*extempore* + *-ize*] *vi* **1** : to do something extemporaneously : IMPROVISE; *esp* : to speak extemporaneously ⟨the rarely *extemporized* and never on grave occasions —John Buchan⟩ **2** : to get along in a makeshift manner adapted to the occasion : regularly meet necessity with temporary expedients : live with little or no advance planning ⟨the world, facing the need to organize itself internationally, drifted and *extemporized* —Charles McKinley⟩ ⟨*extemporizing* without a plan has long been regarded by many as a necessary and inherent part of movie making —Hortense Powdermaker⟩ ~ *vt* **1** : to compose, perform, or utter extemporaneously : IMPROVISE ⟨a cleverly *extemporized* organ accompaniment⟩ ⟨*extemporizing* an after-dinner speech⟩ **2** : to provide, make, or put to use as a temporary expedient ⟨the ungainly but useful vessels which Caesar had *extemporized* —J.A.Froude⟩ ⟨beyond the *extemporized* bandstand —Graham Greene⟩ : produce, put together, devise, or contrive hurriedly or in a makeshift manner to meet an immediate need or emergency ⟨trying to ~ a competent personnel⟩ ⟨*extemporizing* a plan to overwhelm the opposition⟩

ex·tem·po·riz·er \-zə(r)\ *n* -s : one that extemporizes

ex·tend \ikˈstend, ek-\ *vb* -ED/-ING/-S [ME *extenden*, fr. MF or L; MF *estendre, extendre*, fr. L *extendere*, fr. *ex-* [1]ex- + *tendere* to stretch — more at THIN] *vt* **1** [ME *extenden*, fr. ML *extendere* (fr. L) or AF *estendre*, fr. OF *estendre, extendre*] **a** *Brit* : to assess the value of (as lands or buildings) **b** *Brit* : to take possession of by a writ of extent **c** *obs* : to take by force : SEIZE **2** : to lay out at full length ⟨with his body ~*ed* on the ground⟩ : put into a horizontal and usu. straight position ⟨~*ing* their arms in front of them⟩ : straighten out (as a limb or other bodily part) : UNBEND ⟨alternately flexing his arm and ~*ing* it⟩ **3 a** : to stretch out esp. forcibly : stretch out to fullest length ⟨with the sails ~*ed* by yards⟩ **b** *obs* : to stretch, fill, or inflate beyond normal limits : STRAIN, DISTEND **c** : to cause (as a horse) to move at full stride ⟨a promising racehorse that had so far never been really ~*ed*⟩ : push to full stride **d** : to apply or exert (oneself) energetically or to full capacity ⟨people who would rather accept federal bounties than ~ themselves —F.L.Allen⟩ ⟨his capacity for handling an immense amount of work without appearing to ~ himself —*Lamp*⟩ **e** : to increase the quantity or bulk of (a product) by the addition of a relatively inexpensive or otherwise readily available substance so as to reduce cost, improve efficiency, or attain other desired effects ⟨~*ing* ground meat with cereal⟩; *sometimes* : ADULTERATE **4 a** : to stretch forth : hold out ⟨she ~*ed* both her hands to him —W.F.deMorgan⟩ ⟨a bald eagle with its wings ~*ed*⟩ **b** : to present for acceptance or rejection : make the offer of : PROFFER ⟨~*ing* their greetings⟩ ⟨~*ed* hospitality to them⟩ **c** : to make available (as a fund or privilege) often in response to an explicit or implied request : GRANT ⟨financial aid will be ~*ed* where needed —Paul Wooton⟩ **5 a** : to cause to stretch out or reach (as from one point to another) ⟨~*ing* the railroad to the next city⟩ : cause to span an interval (as of distance, space, or time) ⟨a rope bridge was ~*ed* over the chasm⟩ : push to a farther point ⟨~*ing* the frontiers of knowledge⟩ ⟨city boundaries were ~*ed* to take in the entire county —*Amer. Guide Series: Pa.*⟩ : open out (a compass) **b** : to cause to be longer : LENGTHEN, PROLONG, PROTRACT ⟨~*ing* their visit⟩; *specif* : to prolong the time of payment of (as a debt) beyond the time orig. stipulated **c** : to cause to project in one or more directions : stick out ⟨when disturbed, the creature ~*s* its spines⟩ **d** : to bring to a further degree of development ⟨the Anglo-Saxons ~*ed* the use of the plow —L.D.Stamp⟩ : cause to be more nearly complete or perfect : ADVANCE, FURTHER ⟨~*ing* man's knowledge of the universe⟩ ⟨the rest of the decade consolidated and ~*ed* those gains —Oscar Handlin⟩ **e** : to transfer (figures) from one column to another (as in bookkeeping) : carry forward **f** : to compute the amount of (as in accounting) : indicate the amount of ⟨the credit balance will be ~*ed* on the accounts⟩ **6 a** : to cause to be of greater area or volume ⟨~*ing* the surface of metal plates by hammering⟩ : increase the size of : ENLARGE : make greater in extent ⟨trying to ~ its staff of trained personnel⟩ **b** : to increase the scope, meaning, or application of ⟨~*ing* the sense of a word⟩ ⟨the name . . . was easily ~*ed* to the new land —P.E.James⟩ ⟨~ the force of the laws⟩ : increase the action or capacity of ⟨beauty, I suppose, opens the heart, ~*s* the consciousness —Algernon Blackwood⟩ : make more comprehensive, inclusive, or intensive : BROADEN, AMPLIFY ⟨~*ing* the range of their duties⟩ **c** *archaic* : to enlarge upon in imagination : EXAGGERATE **d** : to write out (as shorthand notes) in expanded form : write out or set forth in detail ~ *vi* **1** : to stretch out (as in distance, space, or time) : RANGE ⟨rugged hills and ravines ~ in all directions —*Amer. Guide Series: Minn.*⟩ ⟨occupation of the fortress ~*ed* from the second century B.C. to the first century A.D. —J.E.M.White⟩ : REACH, SPREAD **2** : to span an interval (as of distance, space, or time) ⟨an ancient bridge ~*s* over the river⟩ **3** : to jut out : stick out : PROTRUDE, PROJECT ⟨through a cupola . . . ~*s* a thin square chimney —*Amer. Guide Series: Minn.*⟩ ⟨fruit trees that ~*ed* out over the farm fences —Sherwood Anderson⟩ **4** *of a serviceman* : to agree to remain on active duty for another term

syn LENGTHEN, ELONGATE, PROLONG, PROTRACT: EXTEND, like others in this group, applies to a drawing out in length; it may suggest also similar or comparable drawing out in breadth, size, or range ⟨*extend* a road⟩ ⟨an *extended* trip⟩ ⟨*extending* his vacation⟩ ⟨federal grants to the states to *extend* and improve their health and welfare services for mothers and children —*Americana Annual*⟩ LENGTHEN is likely to refer to what constitutes or may be thought of as similar in some way to a line ⟨*lengthen* a road⟩ ⟨a *lengthened* period⟩ ⟨the *lengthening* of the average life span by more than twenty years since the last century —*Collier's Yr. Bk.*⟩ ELONGATE suggests a stretching out resulting in a long narrow frame or shape or to unusual length ⟨*elongated* fibers⟩ ⟨an *elongated* segment⟩ ⟨the old man's gaunt and *elongated* frame⟩ PROLONG is likely to indicate a drawing out or stretching out in duration ⟨a *prolonged* discussion⟩ ⟨withstanding a *prolonged* siege⟩ ⟨a strange, secret life, *prolonged* for half a century in Paris —Van Wyck Brooks⟩ PROTRACT, often close to EXTEND or PROLONG, may suggest needlessness, boredom, vexation, indefiniteness ⟨litigation *protracted* through a decade⟩ ⟨the *protracted* interruption of steel production by labor difficulties —*Americana Annual*⟩ ⟨his temptation will be to *protract* negotiations on the minor points still outstanding —*New Statesman & Nation*⟩

extended *adj* [ME, fr. past part. of *extenden*] **1 a** : drawn out in length ⟨an ~ meandering river⟩ esp. in length of time ⟨their ~ residence in England⟩ ⟨an ~ visit⟩ : LENGTHY ⟨an ~ tale⟩ : PROLONGED, PROTRACTED **b** *of a letter or typeface* : having a face considerably wider than that of a typeface not so characterized — compare CONDENSED, EXPANDED **2 a** : fully stretched out ⟨his ~ limbs raised in an attitude of prayer⟩ : widely spread out ⟨an ~ battle line⟩ **b** : stretched forth : held out ⟨refusing to accept her ~ hand⟩ **c** *of a horse's stride* : FULL ⟨an ~ gallop⟩ — compare COLLECTED 3 **d** : INTENSIVE ⟨the groundwork is laid for more ~ efforts —Dorothy Barclay⟩ ⟨an ~ course in college mathematics⟩ **3** : having the property of extension : having spatial magnitude ⟨~ substances⟩ **4** : EXTENSIVE: as **a** : having great area ⟨~ farm lands⟩ : WIDESPREAD, FAR-FLUNG ⟨an ~ empire⟩ **b** : having a wide range : greatly diversified : of great scope ⟨an ~ vocabulary⟩ ⟨a word with ~ meanings⟩ : notable in extent ⟨surgeons who have had ~ experience —Morris Fishbein⟩ **c** : ENLARGED, AMPLIFIED : more complete, comprehensive, or detailed ⟨lectures that were later brought out in ~ book form⟩ — **ex·tend·ed·ly** *adv* — **ex·tend·ed·ness** *n* -ES

extended coverage *n* : coverage extending a fire insurance policy so that additional hazards (as those arising from storms or explosions) are included

extended family *n* : a larger family group which includes near relatives (as patrilineal descendants) and in which collateral lines are kept fairly distinct — distinguished from *clan*; opposed to *nuclear family*

extended harmony *n* : OPEN HARMONY

extended insurance *or* **extended term insurance** *n* : life insurance that after cessation of premium payments is continued in its original amount for the period allowed by the cash value

extended order *n* : an arrangement of troops for skirmishing not in exact formation or at fixed intervals but usu. as widely separated as the tactical situation and the terrain permit — distinguished from *close order*

extended play *n* : a 45-rpm phonograph record that has a playing time of about 6 to 8 minutes obtained by the use of closer groove spacing and utilization of a greater part of the surface area than in the standard 45-rpm record — abbr. *EP*

extended river *or* **extended consequent** *n* : a stream lengthened by the extension of its course downstream across newly emerged land (as on a coastal plain)

ex·tend·er \-də(r)\ *n* -s **1 a** : a substance added to a product esp. in the capacity of a diluent, adulterant, or modifier: as (1) *or* **extender pigment** : a colorless or white mineral pigment (as whiting) used with one or more other pigments usu. to achieve certain physical properties (as improved surface characteristics or working properties in paint or printing ink) — called also *filler, inert* (2) : a substance usu. having some adhesive action (as flour) that is added to an adhesive for reducing the cost or sometimes for improving the viscosity (3) : a substance (as a petroleum oil) used for increasing the bulk or improving the processing characteristics of a rubber compound, a plastic, or a resin **b** : EXPANDER 2 **2** *Brit* : a teacher of university extension classes

ex·tend·ibil·i·ty \ikˌstendəˈbiləd·ē, (ˌ)ekˌ-, -lətē, -i\ *n* -ES : capability of being extended

ex·tend·ible *or* **ex·tend·able** \ikˈstendəbəl, (ˈ)ekˈs-\ *adj* : capable of being extended

extending *pres part of* EXTEND

extends *pres 3d sing of* EXTEND

ex·tense \ikˈsten(t)s, (ˈ)ekˈs-\ *adj* [L *extensus*, past part. of *extendere* to extend — more at EXTEND] *archaic* : widely extended

ex·ten·si·bil·i·ty \ikˌsten(t)səˈbiləd·ē, (ˌ)ekˌ-, -lətē, -i\ *n* -ES : capability of being extended; *specif* : the extent to which something can be stretched without breaking

ex·ten·si·ble \ikˈsten(t)səbəl, (ˈ)ekˈs-\ *adj* [L *extensus* + E *-ible*] : capable of being extended ⟨~ school building⟩; *esp* : capable of being protruded ⟨an ~ tongue⟩ or opened out ⟨an ~ measuring rule⟩

ex·ten·sile \ikˈsten(t)səl, (ˈ)ekˈs-, -n,sīl, -n(t)(ˌ)sil\ *adj* [L *extensus* + E *-ile*] : EXTENSIBLE

extensimeter *var of* EXTENSOMETER

ex·ten·sion \ikˈstenchən, ek-, *in sense 3c* " *or* estänsyōⁿ\ *n, pl* **extensions** \-ənz,-ōⁿ(z)\ *often attrib* [ME *extensioun*, fr. MF or LL; MF *extension*, fr. LL *extension-, extensio*, fr. L *extensus* + *-ion-, -io* -ion] **1 a** : the action of extending or state of being extended : a stretching out or stretching forth : a carrying forward : LENGTHENING, FURTHERING, DEVELOPING **b** : the action of spreading out (as in area) or state of being spread out : EXPANSION, ENLARGEMENT, AUGMENTATION, INCREASE **c** : something extended **2 a** : the total range over which something extends or can be extended : COMPASS ⟨the ~ of the human mind⟩ **b** : DENOTATION 4 ⟨*plant* is a word with wider ~ than *orchid*⟩ — contrasted with *intension* **3 a** : the stretching of a fractured or luxated limb so as to restore it to its natural position **b** : the straightening out of a flexed limb **c** : a dance movement in which the leg is extended at an angle to the body; *also* : an exercise (as for a ballet dancer) in which this movement is used **4 a** : a property whereby something occupies or apparently occupies a greater or lesser part of space : spatial magnitude **b** : something marked or delimited by the property of extension **5** : an increase in length of time : increased or continued duration; *specif* : an agreement on or concession of additional time (as for meeting an overdue debt or fulfilling a legal formality) **6 :** the making available of the educational opportunities or other resources of an institution by special programs or methods (as evening classes in a university, off-campus instruction centers, correspondence courses, library branches, or bookmobiles) to persons otherwise unable to take advantage of such opportunities and resources; *also* **:** a service or system by which such opportunities or resources are made available **7 a :** a part that is extended from or attached to a main body or section as an addition, supplement, or enlargement ⟨a house with two ~*s*⟩ or that is capable of being so extended or attached ⟨a table with side ~*s*⟩ **:** a section that forms an additional length ⟨an ~ for an electric-light cord⟩ ⟨the ~ of a railway⟩ **:** PROLONGATION; *also* **:** something having extensions (as a table) **b :** an extra telephone connected to the principal line ⟨they have a downstairs phone and an ~ in each of the bedrooms⟩ **8 :** an indicated figure or amount: as **a :** a figure transferred or carried forward (as in bookkeeping) **b :** an amount computed (as by multiplying a number of units by the cost of each unit) ⟨~*s* on an invoice⟩

extension agent *n* **:** COUNTY AGENT

ex·ten·sion·al \ik'stenchən°l, (')ek¦s-, -chnəl\ *adj* **1 :** of, relating to, or marked by extension; *specif* **:** DENOTATIVE ⟨the ~ meaning of *cow* is the group comprising all existing cows —P.D.Wienpahl⟩ **2 :** of, relating to, or marked by practical values, relationships, and applications **:** PRAGMATIC ⟨an ~ nonsubjective approach to social problems⟩ **:** concerned with objective reality **:** CONCRETE, FACTUAL — **ex·ten·sion·al·ly** \-°lē, -əlē, -li\ *adv*

ex·ten·sion·al·ism \ik'stenchən°l,izəm, ek-, -chnə,li-\ *n* -s **:** EXTENSIONALITY

ex·ten·sion·al·i·ty \ik,stenchə'naləd·ē, (,)ek,-\ *n* -ES **:** the quality or state of being extensional

ex·ten·sion·al·iza·tion \ik,stenchən°lə'zāshən, (,)ek,-, -chnələ-, -°l,ī'z-, -ə,lī'z-\ *n* -s **:** the act of extensionalizing or condition of being extensionalized

ex·ten·sion·al·ize \ik'stenchən°l,īz, ek-, -chnə,līz\ *vt* -ED/-ING/-S **:** to make extensional

extension bolt *n* **:** a bolt set flush and vertically (as at the top or bottom of a door) having a long extended rod by which it may be conveniently slid into place

extension-gap lathe *also* **extension lathe** *n* **:** a gap lathe with an upper extendible bed

ex·ten·sion·ist \ik'stench(ə)nəst, ek-\ *n* -s **:** one that advocates extension

extension jamb *n* **:** a jamb extending beyond the head of a door or window usu. to the ceiling

extension ladder *n* **:** a ladder consisting of usu. two sections arranged so that they fit together or extend on a sliding mechanism almost to the full length of the two sections

ex·ten·sion·less \-chənləs\ *adj, philos* **:** having no extension ⟨~ time⟩

extension rule *n* **:** a sliding attachment to a folding rule for the measuring of inside distances between objects

extension spring *n* **:** a closely coiled spring made to resist a

extension spring

force pulling in the direction of its length

extension table *n* **:** a table that can be extended in length by the insertion of a leaf

ex·ten·si·ty \ik'sten(t)səd·ē, ek-\ *n* -ES [L *extensus* + E *-ity*] **1 :** the quality of having extension ⟨two characteristic facts about an emotional experience . . . are its intensity and its ~ —H.H.Britan⟩ **:** degree of extension **:** RANGE ⟨changes in the severity and ~ of punishment for crimes —P.A.Sorokin⟩ **2** *psychol* **:** an attribute of sensation whereby space or size are perceived

ex·ten·sive \ik'sten(t)siv, (')ek¦s-, -sēv *also* -səv\ *adj* [LL *extensivus*, fr. L *extensus* (past part. of *extendere* to extend) + *-ivus* -ive — more at EXTEND] **1** *obs* **:** capable of being extended **:** APPLICABLE ⟨inability . . . may be more general and ~ to all acts —Jonathan Edwards⟩ **2 :** of, relating to, or marked by logical extension ⟨an ~ proposition⟩ or spatial extension ⟨the ~ nature of the physical world⟩ **:** EXTENSIONAL **3 a :** widely extended in scope or application **:** broad in range **:** WIDE, COMPREHENSIVE ⟨~ reading in literature⟩ ⟨~ repairs⟩ ⟨~ privileges⟩ **:** very complete **:** THOROUGH, FAR-REACHING ⟨an ~ knowledge of languages⟩ ⟨taking ~ precautions⟩ **b :** widely extended in area ⟨~ farms and prairies⟩ **:** extending over a large surface or space ⟨~ stretches of ocean —S.F.Mason⟩ **:** ranging over a wide area ⟨~ travels in Europe⟩ **c :** marked by considerable length ⟨a book with an ~ introduction⟩ ⟨an ~ trip⟩ or detail ⟨an ~ report on the trial⟩ **d :** large in amount ⟨~ funds will be needed⟩ or extent ⟨an ~ business⟩ ⟨~ railroad development⟩ ⟨~ efforts⟩ **e :** considerable in number **:** NUMEROUS ⟨~ examples of picture writing⟩ **4 :** of, relating to, or involving farming in which large areas of land are utilized with minimum outlay and labor ⟨producing wheat under ~ conditions⟩ ⟨agriculture of the ~ type⟩ — opposed to *intensive* — **ex·ten·sive·ly** \-sə̇vlē, -li\ *adv* — **ex·ten·sive·ness** \-sivnəs, -sēv- *also* -səv-\ *n* -ES

ex·ten·siv·i·ty \(,)ek,sten'sivəd·ē, ik,-\ *n* -ES **:** the quality or state of being extensive

ex·ten·som·e·ter \(,)ek,sten'sämәd·ə(r), ik,-\ *also* **ex·ten·sim·e·ter** \-sim-\ *n* [*extension* + *-o-* or *-i-* + *-meter*] **:** an instrument for measuring minute deformations of test specimens under stress (as of tension, compression, bending, or twisting)

ex·ten·sor \ik'sten(t)sər, ek-, -n,sȯ(ə)r\ *n* -s [NL, fr. L *extensus* + *-or*] **:** a muscle that serves to extend a limb or other bodily part — opposed to *flexor*

extensor thrust *n* **:** a sudden reflex extension of a leg in response to upward pressure applied to the sole

ex·tent \ik'stent, ek-\ *n* -s [ME *extente*, fr. AF & MF; AF *estente, extente* valuation, fr. MF, extension, area, land survey, fr. fem. of *estent, extent*, past part. of *estendre, extendre* to extend — more at EXTEND] **1 a** *archaic* **:** valuation or assessment (as of land) in Great Britain esp. when made for the purpose of taxation ⟨an ~ of the realm made on the king's behalf —R.H.I.Palgrave⟩; *also* **:** an instance or record of such valuation or assessment **b** *archaic* **:** the value assigned by such an extent **:** assessed value **2** *obs* **:** the act of exercising (as justice) or showing (as courtesy) ⟨the ~ of equal justice —Shak.⟩ **3 a :** seizure (as of land) in execution of a writ of extent in Great Britain or the condition of being so seized; *also* **:** the right of making such an extent **b :** WRIT OF EXTENT **c :** a writ giving to a creditor temporary possession of his debtor's property (as lands) **4** *obs* **:** ASSAULT ⟨this uncivil and unjust ~ against thy peace —Shak.⟩ **5 a** (1) **:** the range (as of inclusiveness or application) over which something extends **:** SCOPE, COMPASS, COMPREHENSIVENESS ⟨within the ~ of human knowledge⟩ ⟨the ~ of his authority⟩ ⟨the ~ of the law⟩ (2) **:** the point or degree to which something extends ⟨they spent money to the ~ of $1500⟩ **:** the limit to which something extends ⟨exerting the full ~ of his power⟩ ⟨to a certain ~ she was fond of him⟩ **b :** the amount of space which something occupies or the distance over which it extends **:** the length, width, height, thickness, diameter, circumference, or area of something **:** DIMENSIONS, PROPORTIONS, SIZE, MAGNITUDE, SPREAD ⟨a farm of considerable ~⟩ ⟨the ~ of a bird's wings⟩ ⟨20 square miles in ~⟩ **c** (1) **:** something that is extended esp. in area **:** a usu. level stretch or expanse ⟨sailing over the vast ~ of the sea⟩ **:** an extended tract or region ⟨the sloping ~ of the forest⟩ ⟨in the whole ~ of France⟩ (2) **:** DENOTATION 4

syn see SIZE

¹extenuate *adj* [ME *extenuat*, fr. L *extenuatus*, past part.] *obs* **:** EXTENUATED

²ex·ten·u·ate \ik'stenyə,wāt, ek-, *usu* -ād·+V\ *vt* -ED/-ING/-S [L *extenuatus*, past part. of *extenuare*, fr. *ex-* ¹ex- + *tenuare* to make thin or small, fr. *tenuis* thin, small — more at THIN] **1 a** *archaic* **:** to treat as of small importance **:** make light of ⟨not by *extenuating* or by exaggerating the damage —Isaac Taylor⟩ **:** UNDERRATE, UNDERESTIMATE **b** (1) **:** to lessen or to try to lessen the real or apparent seriousness of (as a crime, offense, or fault) or extent of (guilt) by making partial excuses ⟨they neither concealed nor *extenuated* their crime⟩ or by affording a basis for excuses ⟨the fact of his extreme youth certainly *extenuated* the act⟩ **:** MITIGATE (2) **:** to make partial excuses for **:** try to justify (as by making partial excuses) ⟨he thought it necessary to ~ the length of time he kept the dinner on the table —Charles Lamb⟩ **c** *obs* **:** to lessen the worth of **:** DISPARAGE, BELITTLE ⟨every man seemed wholly bent to ~ the sum which fell to his share —Henry Fielding⟩ **2** *archaic* **a :** to make (as a person) thin or emaciated ⟨peasants were . . . *extenuated* by hunger —W.E.H.Lecky⟩ **b :** to lessen the strength or extent of **:** WEAKEN, DIMINISH ⟨in friendship the individual element is intensified, in fraternity it is *extenuated* —W.C.Brownell⟩ **3 a** *obs* **:** to diminish esp. in size, number, or amount **b** *archaic* **:** to lessen the force or effect of (as a law) **4** *archaic* **:** to make (as a liquid or gas) less concentrated **:** lessen the density of ⟨*extenuating* the air —Samuel Vince⟩ **:** thin out **:** ATTENUATE, RAREFY **syn** see PALLIATE, THIN

extenuating *adj* **:** that extenuates ⟨an ~ circumstance⟩ — **ex·ten·u·at·ing·ly** *adv*

ex·ten·u·a·tion \ik,stenyə'wāshən, (,)ek,-\ *n* -s [MF or L; MF, fr. L *extenuation-, extenuatio*, fr. *extenuatus* + *-ion-, -io* -ion] **1 :** the act of extenuating or state of being extenuated; *esp* **:** partial justification ⟨there is surely much to be said in ~ of it —Stewart Cockburn⟩ **2 :** something that extenuates; *esp* **:** a partial excuse ⟨it was a comfort to him, this ~ —Audrey Barker⟩

ex·ten·u·a·tive \ik'stenyə,wād·iv, ek-, -,wəd-\ *adj* **:** EXTENUATING

ex·ten·u·a·tor \-,wād·ə(r)\ *n* -s **:** one that extenuates

ex·ten·u·a·to·ry \-,wə,tōrē\ *adj* [LL *extenuatorius*, fr. L *extenuatus* + *-orius* -ory] **:** tending to extenuate

¹ex·te·ri·or \(')ek¦stirēə(r), -tēr-, ik's-\ *adj* [L, comp. of *exter*, *exterus* outward, on the outside, foreign, strange, fr. *ex* out of, from — more at EX-] **1 :** EXTERNAL; *esp* **:** situated at and forming the outer surface or limit ⟨the ~ surface of a tennis ball⟩ or a part of the outer surface or limit ⟨the ~ slope of a mountain⟩ — opposed to *interior* **2 a :** of or relating to an exterior ⟨an ~ appearance of happiness⟩ **b :** suitable for use on outside surfaces (as of a house) **:** capable of withstanding normal wear and tear of weather conditions for a considerable period of time ⟨an ~ paint⟩ ⟨an ~ finish for the clapboarding⟩ **syn** see OUTER

²exterior \"\ *n* -s **1 :** something that is exterior: as **a** *archaic* **:** exterior features **:** EXTERNALS — usu. used in pl. **b :** exterior part (as of a building) ⟨the house has an old ~⟩ or surface ⟨the ~ of a tennis ball⟩ or appearance ⟨under a cheerful ~ I have got a spirit that is angry —Mark Twain⟩ **2 a :** a representation of an outdoor scene (as a stage or motion-picture set) ⟨remarkably realistic ~*s*⟩ **b :** a background or acting sequence photographed or played outdoors (as for motion pictures or television) ⟨~*s* for the movie will be filmed in Arizona⟩

exterior angle *n* **1 :** the angle between any side of a polygon and an adjacent side prolonged **2 :** an angle between a line crossing two parallel lines and either of the latter on the outside

e g a b c h d f

ega, egb, fhc, fhd
exterior angles

exterior ballistics *n pl but usu sing in constr* **:** a science that deals with the factors affecting the behavior of a projectile after the projectile leaves the muzzle of the firing weapon (as the initial velocity of the projectile, the force of gravity, and atmospheric conditions) — compare INTERIOR BALLISTICS

exterior caste *n* **:** UNTOUCHABLES

exterior crest *n* **:** the line of intersection of the superior and the exterior slopes of a fortification

ex·te·ri·or·i·ty \(,)ek,=='ȯrəd·ē, ik,-, -'är-, -rətē, -i\ *n* -ES **:** the quality or state of being exterior or exteriorized **:** EXTERNALITY — contrasted with *interiority*

ex·te·ri·or·iza·tion \-rēərə'zāshən, -rēə,rī'z-\ *n* -s **:** the act of exteriorizing or the state of being exteriorized

ex·te·ri·or·ize \=ˈ==rēə,rīz\ *vt* -ED/-ING/-S *see -ize in Explan Notes* **1 :** to make exterior **:** EXTERNALIZE **2 :** to bring (an organ) out of the abdomen (as for surgery) ⟨*exteriorizing* the colon⟩

exterior lines *n pl* **:** lines of operations of one or more armed forces converging upon a centrally situated opponent

ex·te·ri·or·ly *adv* **:** on or with regard to the exterior **:** EXTERNALLY ⟨situated ~⟩ ⟨quite unobjectionable ~⟩

exterior planet *n* **:** SUPERIOR PLANET

exterior slope *n* **:** the slope connecting the exterior crest of a fortification with the berm

ex·ter·mi·nate \ik'stərmə,nāt, ek-, -stəm-, -stəim-, *usu* -ād·+V\ *vt* -ED/-ING/-S [L *exterminatus*, past part. of *exterminare*, fr. *ex-* ¹ex- + *terminus* boundary, limit, end — more at TERM] **1** *obs* **:** to drive out or away (as from the boundaries of a country) **:** BANISH, EXPEL **2 :** to get rid of (as by killing) ⟨*exterminating* rats⟩ **:** put an end to **:** root out **:** ERADICATE, EXTIRPATE ⟨*exterminating* every error⟩ **:** put out of existence **:** utterly destroy **:** ANNIHILATE ⟨the cataclysm *exterminated* all life⟩

syn EXTERMINATE, EXTIRPATE, ERADICATE, UPROOT, DERACINATE, and WIPE (*out*) can mean to bring about the destruction or abolition of something. EXTERMINATE implies utter extinction usu. by killing off ⟨using every feeble attempt at retaliation as an excuse to *exterminate* whole tribes —R.A.Billington⟩ ⟨following the attempt of the people to *exterminate* feudalism —*Amer. Guide Series: N.J.*⟩ EXTIRPATE usu. applies to the extinction of a race, family, species, or growth, often by the destruction or removal of the means by which a thing is propagated ⟨the gray wolf and the black bear have been *extirpated* —*Amer. Guide Series: Mass.*⟩ ⟨the trailing arbutus . . . has been almost *extirpated* —*Amer. Guide Series: Del.*⟩ ⟨the ancient Athenians had been *extirpated* by repeated wars and massacres —Robert Graves⟩ ⟨another set of measures are intended to get closer to the roots of the evil and to *extirpate* them —Frank Gorrell⟩ ERADICATE implies the driving out or elimination of something that has taken root or has established itself ⟨federal and municipal housing groups are cooperating to *eradicate* slums —*Amer. Guide Series: N.Y. City*⟩ ⟨if you *eradicate* a fault, you leave room for a worse one to take root and flourish —L.P.Smith⟩ UPROOT suggests a forcible removal as by tearing up by the roots, not often suggesting elimination ⟨a tribe *uprooted* by war and famine and forced to settle in new territory⟩ ⟨nor was it going to be easy to *uproot* deep-seated tendencies toward corruption —*Collier's Yr. Bk.*⟩ DERACINATE implies an uprooting or, more commonly, a separation from a rootstock ⟨he is not the *deracinated* and rootless author he has sometimes been thought to be —R.B.West⟩ ⟨although the author is himself a Negro, his book is so *deracinated*, without any of the lively qualities of the imagination peculiar to his people —*Commentary*⟩ WIPE (*out*) is often interchangeable with EXTERMINATE but often applies to a canceling or obliteration as by payment or retaliation or by exhaustion of supplies ⟨discover which species still survive and which have been *wiped out* —*Manchester Guardian Weekly*⟩ ⟨a nerve gas that could *wipe out* the populations of enemy cities —*N.Y. Times*⟩ ⟨*wipe out* corruption⟩ ⟨*wipe out* a debt⟩ ⟨the depression *wiped out* his savings⟩

ex·ter·mi·na·tion \ik,=='nāshən, (,)ek,-\ *n* -s [LL *extermination-, exterminatio*, fr. L *exterminatus* + *-ion-, -io* -ion] **1** [ME *exterminacioun* (influenced in meaning by L *exterminare* to banish), fr. LL *extermination-, exterminatio* annihilation, destruction] *obs* **:** BANISHMENT, EXPULSION **2 :** the act of exterminating or the condition of being exterminated **:** total destruction **:** ERADICATION, ANNIHILATION

ex·ter·mi·na·tive \=ˈ==,nād·iv, -,nəd-\ *adj* **:** EXTERMINATORY

ex·ter·mi·na·tor \-,nād·ə(r), -ātə-\ *n* -s [LL, fr. L *exterminatus* + *-or*] **:** one that exterminates: as **a :** one that rids a place of vermin by fumigating — called also *fumigator* **b :** something (as a chemical preparation) used for exterminating

ex·ter·mi·na·to·ry \-,nə,tōrē, -tȯr-, -ri\ *adj* **:** of, relating to, or marked by extermination ⟨an ~ war⟩ **:** tending to exterminate ⟨harsh ~ political moves⟩

extermine *vt* -ED/-ING/-S [ME *exterminen*, fr. MF or L; MF *exterminer*, fr. L *exterminare* — more at EXTERMINATE] *obs* **:** EXTERMINATE

¹ex·tern \(')ek¦stərn\ *adj* [MF or L; MF *externe*, fr. L *externus*] *archaic* **:** of, relating to, or situated on or at the outside **:** EXTERNAL, OUTER

²ex·tern *also* **ex·terne** \'ek,stərn\ *n* -s [F *externe*, fr. *externe*, adj.] **1 :** a person connected with an institution but not living or boarding in it: as **a :** a day student of a school **b :** a nonresident doctor or medical student at a hospital **2 :** a nun of a strictly enclosed order (as the Carmelites) that lives within the convent but outside the enclosure and attends to the convent's outside affairs

ex·ter·na \ek'stərnə\ *n, pl* **exter·nae** \-,nē, -,nī\ *or* **externas** [NL, fr. L, fem. of *externus*] **:** the outer layer of a blood vessel made up chiefly of connective tissue — compare INTIMA, MEDIA

¹ex·ter·nal \(')ek¦stərn°l, ik's-, -tən-, -təin-\ *adj* [ME, fr. L *externus* (fr. *exter, exterus* outward, on the outside) + ME *-al* — more at EXTERIOR] **1 a** (1) **:** of, relating to, or consisting in outward form, appearance, or action ⟨the ~ aspect of religion⟩ (2) **:** capable of being perceived outwardly **:** BODILY, PHYSICAL, VISIBLE ⟨~ signs of a disease⟩ **b** (1) **:** merely outward and lacking in or totally devoid of inner nature, spirit, or motivation **:** having the appearance of something with little or none of the reality **:** SUPERFICIAL ⟨her gaiety was of a conventional ~ kind —J.C.Powys⟩ (2) **:** not intrinsic or essential **:** ACCIDENTAL ⟨~ circumstances⟩ ⟨~ factors affecting their decision⟩ **2 a** (1) **:** of, relating to, or connected with the outside or an outer part ⟨the ~ features of the building are very attractive⟩ (2) **:** situated at, on, or near the outside ⟨an ~ protective covering⟩ ⟨an ~ muscle⟩ **b** (1) **:** acting on or exerted upon the outside ⟨sunbaths and other ~ treatments⟩ ⟨the box collapsed after prolonged ~ pressure⟩ (2) **:** directed toward the outside ⟨~ perception⟩ **:** having an outside object ⟨eyesight and the other ~ senses⟩ **c :** used by applying to the outside ⟨an ~ lotion⟩ **3 a** (1) **:** of, relating to, or connected with something outside, apart, or beyond ⟨~ evidence⟩ ⟨the club's ~ activities⟩ (2) **:** situated outside, apart, or beyond ⟨people almost always want something ~ to themselves —Samuel Butler †1902⟩; *specif* **:** situated away from the mesial plane ⟨the ~ condyle of the humerus⟩ (3) **:** arising or acting from outside **:** having an outside origin ⟨~ force⟩ ⟨~ causes⟩ ⟨~ stimuli⟩ **b :** of or relating to dealings or relationships with foreign countries **:** FOREIGN ⟨~ policies⟩ ⟨~ commerce⟩ ⟨the ~ exchange position of the dollar⟩ ⟨~ affairs⟩ **c :** of, relating to, or consisting of something outside the mind **:** having existence independent of the mind **:** belonging to the spatio-temporal world ⟨sensations aroused by ~ phenomena⟩ ⟨~ reality⟩ ⟨man's efforts to understand the workings of the ~ world —James Jeans⟩ **syn** see OUTER

²external \"\ *n* -s **1 :** something that is external: as **a** *archaic* **:** an outer part **:** OUTSIDE, EXTERIOR **b :** an external feature or aspect — usu. used in pl. ⟨the ~*s* of religion⟩ **2 :** a house organ designed for circulation among outsiders (as dealers, customers, stockholders)

external account *n* **:** an account of a firm or corporation with any outside party

external acoustic meatus *n* **:** EXTERNAL AUDITORY MEATUS

external angle *n* **:** EXTERIOR ANGLE

external audit *n* **:** INDEPENDENT AUDIT

external auditory meatus *n* **:** the passage leading from the external-ear opening to the eardrum

external ballistics *n pl but usu sing in constr* **:** EXTERIOR BALLISTICS

external brake *n* **:** a brake in which the lining operates on the outside of the brake drum

external capsule *n* **:** CAPSULE 1b(2)

external carotid *n* **:** the branch of the carotid artery that supplies the face, tongue, and external parts of the head

external-combustion engine *n* **:** a heat engine that derives its heat from fuel consumed outside the engine cylinder (as a steam engine or hot-air engine) — compare INTERNAL-COMBUSTION ENGINE

external degree *n* **:** a degree granted by a university to a student who has studied at another institution affiliated with or approved by it — compare INTERNAL DEGREE

external ear *n* **:** the parts of the ear that are external to the eardrum; *also* **:** PINNA 2b

external examination *n* **:** an examination prepared by someone outside the faculty of the school where the examination is given (as by a testing bureau)

external gill *n* **:** a gill that projects from the surface of the body and is not enclosed by the body wall and that is characteristic of certain larval fishes and amphibians

ex·ter·nal·ism \ek'st==,izəm, ik-\ *n* -s **1 a :** EXTERNALITY 1a **b :** attention to externals; *esp* **:** excessive preoccupation with externals ⟨the ~ of some religions⟩ **2 :** a doctrine dealing only with immediate experience and with objects of sense perception and discounting the validity of other knowledge **:** PHENOMENALISM

ex·ter·nal·ist \-°ləst\ *n* -s **:** one that practices or adheres to externalism

ex·ter·nal·i·ty \,ek,stər'naləd·ē\ *n* -ES **1 a :** the quality or state of being external or externalized; *esp* **:** OBJECTIVITY ⟨the ~ of some writers⟩ **b :** EXTERNALISM 1b **2 :** something that is external (as an external object, event, or feature) ⟨the *externalities* of wealth, of friends, of fame —Irwin Edman⟩

ex·ter·nal·iza·tion \(,)ek,stərn°lə'zāshən, ik,-, -°l,ī'z-\ *n* -s **1 a :** the action or process of externalizing **b :** the quality or state of being externalized **2 :** something that has been externalized

ex·ter·nal·ize \=ˈ==,īz\ *vt* -ED/-ING/-S *see -ize in Explan Notes* **1 a :** to make external **:** embody in an outward form ⟨spoken language ~*s* thought⟩ **b :** to consider or treat as if consisting only of externals ⟨a tendency to ~ all religions⟩ **2 a :** to transform from a mental image into an apparently real object (as in hallucinations) **:** attribute (a mental image) to external causation ⟨*externalizing* an obsession⟩ **b :** to invent an explanation for (an inner conflict, emotion, or problem whose actual basis is known only subconsciously) by attributing to causes outside the self **:** RATIONALIZE, PROJECT ⟨*externalized* his inability to succeed⟩ **3 :** to direct outward socially **:** EXTROVERT ⟨attempts to ~ the individual and to divert his energies into social and recreational channels —L.R. Wolberg⟩

external loan *n* **:** a loan that a government obtains by selling its securities in a foreign country

external lobe *n* **:** the median lobe of the suture on the venter of an ammonoid

ex·ter·nal·ly \(')ek¦stərn°lē, ik's-, -tən-, -təin-, -°li\ *adv* **:** in an external manner

externally fired boiler *n* **:** a boiler whose furnace is neither wholly nor partly surrounded by water — compare INTERNALLY FIRED BOILER

external oblique *n* **:** a chiefly subcutaneous sheet of diagonally arranged abdominal muscle on each side of the trunk

external phase *n* **:** DISPERSION MEDIUM

external relation *n* **:** a relation that is external to the terms or things it relates; *specif* **:** one that does not affect its relata or is not a part of its relata — contrasted with *internal relation*

external respiration *n* **:** exchange of gases (as oxygen and carbon dioxide) between the external environment and some distributing system (as the lungs of higher vertebrates or the tracheal tubes of insects) of the animal body; *also* **:** the exchange of such gases in higher vertebrates between the blood and the alveolae of the lungs — compare INTERNAL RESPIRATION

externals *pl of* EXTERNAL

external student *n* **:** a student studying outside the university at which he has matriculated and from which he expects to receive a degree — compare INTERNAL STUDENT

external thread *n* **:** a screw thread on the outside of a cone or cylinder (as the thread on a plug gage)

external work *n* **:** work done (as by expanding) against a contrary external force

externas *pl of* EXTERNA

ex·ter·na·tion \,ek,stər'nāshən\ *n* -s [¹*extern* + *-ation*] *archaic* **:** EXTERNALIZATION

externe *var of* EXTERN

ex·ter·ni·ty \ek'stərnəd·ē\ *n* -ES [¹*extern* + *-ity*] *archaic* **:** EXTERNALITY

ex·ter·ni·za·tion \(,)ek,stərnə'zāshən\ *n* -s *archaic* : EXTERNALIZATION

ex·ter·nize \ek'stər,nīz\ *vt* -ED/-ING/-S [¹*extern* + *-ize*] *archaic* : EXTERNALIZE

ex·ter·no·median \ek'stər(,)nō, ,ek,stərnō+\ *adj* [L *externus* external + E *-o-* + *median* — more at EXTERNAL] : extending to a median line or plane

externs *pl of* EXTERN

ex·ter·o·cep·tive \'ekstərō'septiv\ *adj* [L *exter* outward, on the outside + E *-o-* + *-ceptive* (as in *receptive*) — more at EXTERIOR] : activated by, relating to, or constituting stimuli impinging on the organism from outside (as in touch, smell, or sight) — distinguished from *interoceptive* and *proprioceptive*

ex·ter·o·cep·tor \-ptə(r)\ *n* -s [NL, fr. L *exter* + NL *-o-* + *-ceptor* (as in *receptor*)] : a sense organ excited by stimuli arising outside the body (as those of touch, temperature, smell, vision, or hearing) — compare INTEROCEPTOR, PROPRIOCEPTOR

ex·ter·o·fec·tive \-'fektiv\ *adj* [L *exter* + E *-o-* + *-fective* (as in *effective*)] : of, relating to, dependent on, or constituting the cerebrospinal nervous system — distinguished from *interofective*

ex·terrestrial \'eks+\ *adj* [¹*ex-* + *terrestrial*] : EXTRATERRESTRIAL

ex·territorial \(')eks+\ *adj* [¹*ex-* + *territorial*] : EXTRATERRITORIAL — **ex·territorially** \"+\ *adv*

ex·territoriality \(')eks+\ *n* : EXTRATERRITORIALITY

ex·territorialize \'eks+\ *vt, see -ize in Explan Notes* : EXTRATERRITORIALIZE

ex·till \ek'stil\ *vb* -ED/-ING/-S [L *exstillare, extillare*, fr. *ex-* ¹ex- + *stillare* to drip, trickle — more at DISTILL] *archaic* : EXUDE, DISTILL

ex·ti·ma \'ekstəmə\ *n, pl* **exti·mae** \-,mē, -,mī\ *or* **extimas** [NL, fr. L, fem. of *extimus*, superl. of *exter, exterus* outward, on the outside — more at EXTERIOR] : EXTERNA

extimulate *vt* -ED/-ING/-S [L *exstimulatus, extimulatus*, past part. of *exstimulare, extimulare*, fr. *ex-* ¹ex- + *stimulare* to goad, stimulate — more at STIMULATE] *obs* : to stir up : spur on : INCITE — **extimulation** *n* -s *obs*

¹**ex·tinct** \ik'stiŋ(k)t, (')ek¦s-\ *adj* [ME, fr. L *exstinctus, extinctus*, past part. of *exstinguere, extinguere* to extinguish — more at EXTINGUISH] **1 a** : no longer burning : put out : EXTINGUISHED, QUENCHED ⟨he threw his ~ cigarette into the rapid brown water —C.S.Forester⟩ ⟨all hope was ~⟩ **b** *of a volcano* : marked by total cessation of eruptions : no longer active **2 a** : no longer living : DECEASED, DEAD ⟨~ relatives and friends⟩ **b** : that has died out altogether ⟨an ~ nation⟩ : lacking living representatives : lacking survivors ⟨an ~ royal family⟩ ⟨~ prehistoric animals⟩ : no longer to be found : no longer in existence : VANISHED ⟨a truly kind person of a type almost ~⟩ **c** : that no longer exists in its original form ⟨members of an ~ Indian people now living on a reservation⟩ **3 a** : gone out of use : SUPERSEDED ⟨like a woman dressed in a fashion long ~ —William Beebe⟩ ⟨an ~ language⟩ ⟨~ laws and customs⟩ : OBSOLETE ⟨~ verb suffixes⟩ **b** *of a title of nobility* : being without a qualified claimant ⟨an ~ dukedom⟩

²**extinct** \"\ *vt* **extincted; extincted** *or* **extinct; extincting; extincts** [ME *extincten*, fr. L *exstinctus, extinctus*, past part.] *archaic* : EXTINGUISH ⟨give renewed fire to our ~*ed* spirits —Shak.⟩

ex·tinc·teur \,ek,staŋk'tər(·)\ *n* -s [F, fr. L *exstinctor, extinctor* one that extinguishes, fr. *exstinctus, extinctus* + *-or*] : a chemical fire extinguisher

ex·tinc·tion \ik'stiŋ(k)shən, ek-\ *n* -s [ME *extinccioun*, fr. L *exstinction-, exstinctio, extinction-, extinctio*, fr. *exstinctus, extinctus* + *-ion-, -io* -ion] **1 a** : the act of making extinct or causing to be extinguished : QUENCHING, SUPPRESSION, EXTERMINATION, DESTRUCTION, ANNIHILATION ⟨the ~ of all life in the region⟩ : CANCELLATION, ABOLITION ⟨~ of a debt⟩ **b** : the condition or fact of being extinct or extinguished : the process of becoming extinct or extinguished ⟨~ of a species⟩ **2 a** : progressive decrease in the intensity of radiation (as of the light of the sun) by absorption and scattering in the medium (as the atmosphere) traversed **b** : the condition of a crystal of appearing dark when viewed in polarized light with crossed nicols **3** : elimination of a conditioned response by not reinforcing the response

extinction angle *n* : the angle through which a crystal is revolved from a definite line (as that of the crystallographic axis) to the plane of maximum extinction

extinction coefficient *n* : the sum of the absorption coefficient and the scattering coefficient for a medium that both absorbs and scatters radiation

extinction meter *n* : an exposure meter that indicates the intensity of light usu. by gradually attenuating the light until a selected design (as a number superimposed on a ground-glass screen) is barely visible or disappears completely

ex·tinc·tive \ik'stiŋ(k)tiv, (')ek¦s-, -tēv *also* -təv\ *adj* [²*extinct* + *-ive*] : capable of making extinct or of extinguishing : tending to make extinct or to extinguish ⟨an ~ factor⟩

extine *var of* EXINE

ex·tin·guish \ik'stiŋgwish, -wēsh, *chiefly in pres part* -wəsh; ÷-ŋw-\ *vb* -ED/-ING/-ES [L *exstinguere, extinguere* (fr. *ex-* ¹ex- + *stinguere* to extinguish) + E *-ish* (as in *abolish*); akin to L *instigare* to urge on, incite — more at STICK] *vt* **1 a** : to cause (as a fire or light) to cease burning : put out : QUENCH ⟨~*ing* the flames⟩ ⟨threw water on the glowing coals to ~ them⟩ ⟨the lamps were all ~*ed*⟩ **b** (1) : to bring (as life or hope) to an end : make an end of : cause to die out : do away with entirely : blot out of existence : wipe out : make extinct : DESTROY, ANNIHILATE ⟨a way of life which one might expect to have been ~*ed* almost two generations ago —E.H.Spicer⟩ ⟨death will not ~ us —W.L.Sullivan⟩ ⟨~*ing* the last glimmer of hope⟩ : suppress (an institution or an official position) ⟨~*ing* monasteries by an act of the king⟩ ⟨whose office of paymaster of works was ~*ed* by these efforts —John Craig⟩ (2) : to reduce to silence or ineffectiveness : choke off : STIFLE, SMOTHER ⟨a very nearly ~*ed* voice —Elizabeth Bowen⟩ ⟨~*ing* his opponents with a single word⟩ : make powerless or inoperative : CRUSH, CHECK ⟨a point at which the popular will is ~*ed* —T.E.Utley⟩ (3) : to cause extinction of (a conditioned response) ⟨the more specific a response the easier it is to ~ it —Ralph Linton⟩ **c** : to cause the brightness of to appear relatively dim or to disappear altogether (as by setting next to a superior brilliancy) : cause to seem lackluster or tawdry : ECLIPSE ⟨a glittering costume that ~*ed* all the others⟩ ⟨her face looked pale and ~*ed*, as if dimmed by the rich red of her dress —Edith Wharton⟩ **2 a** : to cause (as a claim or right) to be void : make legally nonexistent : NULLIFY, ABOLISH ⟨titles to the land had not been ~*ed* —C.G.Bowers⟩ **b** : to get rid of (a debt or other liability) by payment or other compensatory adjustment — compare SUSPEND, TRANSFER ~ *vi, archaic* : to become extinguished : die out **syn** see ABOLISH, CRUSH

ex·tin·guish·able \-shəbəl\ *adj* : capable of or subject to being extinguished

ex·tin·guish·ant \-shənt\ *n* -s : an agent (as water) that extinguishes fire

ex·tin·guish·er \-shə(r)\ *n* -s **1** : one that extinguishes; *specif* : EXTINGUISHANT **2 a** : a hollow conical cap typically of metal that is used for extinguishing the flame of a candle, lamp, or torch **b** : a mechanical device that throws out fire-extinguishing chemicals : FIRE EXTINGUISHER

ex·tin·guish·ment \-shmənt\ *n* -s : the act of extinguishing or the state of being extinguished : EXTINCTION ⟨the ~ of the Indians' rights to lands —D.E.Clark⟩

extirp *vt* -ED/-ING/-S [ME *extirpen*, fr. L *exstirpare, extirpare*] *obs* : EXTIRPATE

ex·tir·pate \'ekstə(r),pāt *also* ek'stər,p- *or* ik's- *or* -'stə,p- *or* -'stəi,p- *or* '=,=,=; *usu* -ād·+V\ *vt* -ED/-ING/-S [L *exstirpatus, extirpatus*, past part. of *exstirpare, extirpare*, fr. *ex-* ¹ex- + *stirp-, stirps* trunk, root — more at TORPID] **1 a** : to pull up or out by or as if by the roots or stem : pluck out : root out : ERADICATE ⟨serpent worship which the Mosaic curse and Christianity alike have not succeeded in *extirpating* —Norman Douglas⟩ **b** : to destroy totally : wipe out : kill off : make extinct : EXTERMINATE ⟨many species have been *extirpated* from large areas —William Vogt⟩ **c** : to cut out by surgery **2** *obs* : to drive away : EXPEL **syn** see EXTERMINATE

ex·tir·pa·tion \,ekstə(r)'pāshən *also* -,stə'p- *or* -,stəi'p-\ *n* -s [ME *extirpacioun*, fr. L *exstirpation-, exstirpatio, extirpation-, extirpatio*, fr. *exstirpatus, extirpatus* + *-ion-, -io* -ion] : the act of extirpating or state of being extirpated ⟨~ of weeds⟩ ⟨~ of evil⟩

ex·tir·pa·tor *pronunc at* EXTIRPATE +ə(r)\ *n* -s [L *exstirpator, extirpator*, fr. *exstirpatus, extirpatus* + *-or*] : one that extirpates

extl *abbr* external

ex·tol *also* **ex·toll** \ik'stōl, ek- *sometimes* -täl *or* -tòl\ *vt* **extolled; extolled; extolling; extols** *also* **extolls** [ME *extollen*, fr. L *extollere*, fr. *ex-* ¹ex- + *tollere* to lift up — more at TOLERATE] **1** : to praise highly : GLORIFY, LAUD, EULOGIZE ⟨they ~ the largely nonexistent virtues of bygone eras —Adam Abruzzi⟩ **2** *obs* : to lift up : raise up : ELEVATE

ex·tol·ler \-lə(r)\ *n* -s : one that extols

ex·tol·ling·ly *adv* : in an extolling manner

ex·tol·ment \-lmənt\ *n* -s *archaic* : the act of extolling

ex·torsion \(')eks+\ *n* [¹*ex-* + *torsion*] : outward rotation (as of a body part) about an axis or fixed point — compare INTORSION

ex·tor·sive \ik'stȯrsiv, (')ek¦s-\ *adj* [L *extors-* (stem of *extorquēre*) + E *-ive*] : serving for or obtained by extortion — **ex·tor·sive·ly** \-səvlē\ *adv*

ex·tort \ik'stȯ(ə)r|t, ek-, -ȯ(ə)|, *usu* |d·+V\ *vb* **extorted; extorted** *or obs* **extort; extorting; extorts** [L *extortus*, past part. of *extorquēre* to wrench out, obtain by force, extort, fr. *ex-* ¹ex- + *torquēre* to twist — more at TORTURE] *vt* **1 a** (1) : to obtain from an unwilling or reluctant person by physical force, intimidation, or the abuse of legal or official authority : get by compelling : FORCE, EXACT ⟨till the injurious Romans did ~ this tribute from us we were free —Shak.⟩ ⟨~ bribes⟩ (2) : to obtain from an unwilling or reluctant person by importunity, argument, or ingenuity ⟨~ a confession⟩ ⟨she did at last ~ from her father an acknowledgment that the horses were engaged —Jane Austen⟩ ⟨~*ed* his resignation in exchange —Seymour Freidin⟩ **b** : to elicit from someone unwilling by the obvious or apparent existence of an intrinsic compelling force ⟨his intelligence ~*ed* the admiration even of his worst enemies⟩ **2** : to derive (as a meaning or conclusion) by strained or perverse reasoning ⟨they ~*ed* a bizarre sense from the few words that had been spoken⟩ ~ *vi, archaic* : to obtain something forcibly from someone unwilling **syn** see EDUCE

ex·tor·tion \|shən\ *n* -s [ME *extorsioun, extorcioun*, fr. MF *or* ML; MF *extorsion, extortion*, fr. ML *extorsion-, extorsio, extortion-, extortio*, fr. LL *extortion-, extortio* torture, fr. L *extortus* (past part. of *extorquēre*) + *-ion-, -io* -ion] **1** : the act or practice of extorting esp. money or other property; *specif* : the offense committed by an official who practices extortion **2** : something that is extorted; *esp* : a gross overcharge

ex·tor·tion·ary \-shə,nerē\ *adj, archaic* : EXTORTIONATE, EXORBITANT

ex·tor·tion·ate \-sh(ə)nət, *usu* -əd·+V\ *adj* : characterized by extortion : EXCESSIVE, EXORBITANT ⟨~ prices⟩ ⟨~ fees⟩ — **ex·tor·tion·ate·ly** *adv*

ex·tor·tion·er \-sh(ə)nə(r)\ *n* -s [ME *extorsiouner, extorcioner*, fr. *extorsioun, extorcioun* + *-er*] : one that practices or is given to extortion

ex·tor·tion·ist \-sh(ə)nəst\ *n* -s : EXTORTIONER

extortious *adj, obs* : EXTORTIONATE

ex·tort·ive \ik'stȯrd·iv, (')ek¦s-\ *adj* : of, relating to, or using extortion : EXTORTIONATE

extr *abbr* extruded; extrusion

¹**ex·tra** \'ekstrə, *chiefly in substand speech* -rē *or* -ri\ *adj* [prob. short for *extraordinary*] **1 a** : beyond or greater than what is due, usual, expected, necessary, or essential : SPECIAL, ADDITIONAL ⟨doing ~ work⟩ ⟨using ~ effort⟩ **b** : subject to or marked by an additional charge ⟨room service is ~⟩ **2** : better than ordinary : SUPERIOR ⟨~ quality⟩; *specif* : marked by superiority of hand workmanship and material ⟨an *extra*-bound leather book⟩

²**extra** \"\ *n* -s **1** : something extra or additional: as **a** : an added charge or fee ⟨television is available in each of the hotel rooms as an ~⟩ ⟨the basic cost and the ~*s*⟩ **b** : a special edition of a newspaper issued in addition to the regular editions or at a time different from that of the regular editions ⟨the city was flooded with ~*s* that screamed the news⟩ **c** : an additional point : an additional score; *specif* : a run in the game of cricket that is scored but is not made from a hit (as a run made from a bye) **d** : an additional worker; *specif* : one hired for a motion picture or stage production to augment the number of people in a crowd or group scene **2** : something of superior quality or grade ⟨a hi-fi set that is a real ~⟩

³**extra** \"\ *adv* **1** : to a degree or extent beyond the usual : UNUSUALLY, UNCOMMONLY, EXTREMELY ⟨those who may be ~ gullible about witches and demons —W.W.Howells⟩ : very particularly : ESPECIALLY ⟨he was ~ glad to see them⟩ **2** : in excess of a usual, regular, or specified size or amount ⟨these trousers are ~ long⟩

extra- \¦=+\ *prefix* [ME, fr. L, fr. *extra*, adv. & prep., outside, except, beyond, fr. *exter* outward, on the outside — more at EXTERIOR] : outside : beyond — esp. in adjectives formed from adjectives ⟨*extra*cranial⟩ ⟨*extra*legal⟩ ⟨*extra*vascular⟩ ⟨*extra*-urban⟩ ⟨*extra*historic⟩

extra-base hit *n* : a hit in baseball or softball good for more than one base

extra binder *n* : one that produces extra bindings — compare ¹EXTRA 2

ex·tra·branchial \¦==+\ *adj* [*extra-* + *branchial*] : situated outside the branchial arches

ex·tra·bronchial \¦==+\ *adj* [*extra-* + *bronchial*] : situated outside the bronchial tubes

ex·tra·bulbar \¦==+\ *adj* [*extra-* + *bulbar*] : situated or originating outside the medulla oblongata

ex·tra·canonical \¦==+\ *adj* [*extra-* + *canonical*] : being outside the body of officially accepted writings : not included in a list of authorized books; *specif* : being outside a canon of books held to be sacred ⟨an ~ writing⟩

ex·tra·capsular \¦==+\ *adj* [*extra-* + *capsular*] : situated outside a capsule; *esp* : situated outside a capsular ligament

ex·tra·cellular \¦==+\ *adj* [*extra-* + *cellular*] : situated or occurring outside a cell or the cells of the body — **ex·tra·cellularly** \¦==+\ *adv*

ex·tra·chance \¦==+\ *adj* [*extra-* + *chance* (n.)] : greater than could be anticipated on a basis of chance : showing a level of frequency or uniformity beyond what can reasonably be attributed to coincidence ⟨wherever parapsychology can yield ~ results —G.R.Price⟩

ex·tra com·mer·cium \¦==kə'mərsh(ē)əm\ *adj* [L, lit., outside of commerce] *Roman & civil law* : not subject to private ownership or acquisition (as of the air, navigable waters, property owned by the government) — opposed to *in commercio*

extra cover *or* **extra cover point** *n* : a position in the game of cricket between cover point and mid off; *also* : a fieldsman playing this position — see CRICKET illustration

¹**ex·tract** \ik'strakt, ek's-, *in sense 3a usu & in other senses sometimes* 'ek,s-\ *vt* **extracted; extracted** *or obs* **extract; extracting; extracts** [ME *extracten*, fr. L *extractus*, past part. of *extrahere*, fr. *ex-* ¹ex- + *trahere* to draw, pull — more at DRAW] **1 a** : to draw forth ⟨~*ing* a letter from his pocket⟩; *esp* : to pull out (as something embedded or otherwise firmly fixed) forcibly or with great effort ⟨~*ing* a tooth⟩ ⟨~*ing* the bullet from the wound⟩ ⟨~*ing* the stump of a tree⟩ **b** : to obtain (as money or knowledge of a secret) by much maneuvering and effort from or as if from someone unwilling ⟨before you try to ~ money from anyone —Edith Sitwell⟩ ⟨~*ing* a promise⟩ ⟨~*ing* information⟩ ⟨~*ing* the truth⟩ **c** : to derive (as pleasure) or deduce (as the meaning of a word) from a specified source as if by drawing forth ⟨~*ing* happiness from what many would consider a humdrum existence⟩ ⟨~*ing* a strange meaning from what she had said⟩ **d** : to separate or otherwise obtain (as constituent elements or juices) from a substance by treating with a solvent (as alcohol), distilling, evaporating, subjecting to pressure or centrifugal force, or by some other chemical or mechanical process ⟨~*ing* an essence⟩ ⟨~*ing* the juice of apples⟩ ⟨~*ed* honey⟩ — compare LEACH 1b **e** : to treat with a solvent so as to remove soluble substances ⟨adrenal cortex is ~*ed* with acetone⟩ — compare LEACH 1a **f** : to separate (an ore or mineral) from a deposit; *also* : to separate (a metal) from an ore **g** : to separate (flour) from broken grain kernels in the process of grinding grain **h** : to separate (a particular genetic character) in the form of a homozygote from a heterozygous strain ⟨~*ed* albinos⟩ ⟨~*ed* dominants and recessives⟩ **2** : to determine (the root of a number or quantity) by mathematical calculation ⟨~*ing* the square root of 64⟩ **3 a** : to make out an extract (sense 1b) of **b** : to select (excerpts) and copy out or cite ⟨I have ~*ed* out of that pamphlet a few notorious falsehoods —Jonathan Swift⟩ **4** : to subject to any action or process of extracting **syn** see EDUCE

²**ex·tract** \'ek,strakt\ *n* -s [ME, fr. ML *extractus, extracta, & extractum*, fr. L, masc., fem., & neut. respectively of the past part. of *extrahere*] **1 a** *obs* : SUMMARY, OUTLINE **b** : a certified copy of a document that forms part of or is preserved in a public record **c** : a selection from a writing or discourse : EXCERPT, QUOTATION **2** : something extracted: as **a** : a preparation obtained by evaporation (as of a solution of a drug or the juice of a plant) **b** : the portion of a mixture that is dissolved by a solvent and later separated from part or from all of the solvent (as by distillation) **c** : a solution in alcohol of flavor and odor constituents (as from an aromatic plant) ⟨the use of vanilla ~ and lemon ~ in cooking⟩ **d** : a preparation containing the essence of the substance from which it is derived : ESSENCE, CONCENTRATE ⟨beef ~⟩ **e** : the total soluble constituents of beer with the exception of alcohol and carbon dioxide **3** *obs* : EXTRACTION 2

³**extract** *or* **extracted** *adj* [fr. past part. of ¹*extract*] *obs* : derived or descended

ex·tract·abil·i·ty \ik,straktə'biləd·ē, (,)ek,-\ *n* -ES : capability of being extracted

¹**ex·tract·able** *also* **ex·tract·ible** \ik'straktəbəl, (')ek¦s-\ *adj* [¹*extract* + *-able* or *-ible*] : capable of being extracted

²**extractable** *also* **extractible** \"\ *n* -s : EXTRACTIVE

ex·tract·ant \=ˈ=tənt\ *n* -s [¹*extract* + *-ant*] : a solvent (as alcohol or sulfuric acid) used in extracting

ex·trac·tion \ik'strakshən, ek-\ *n* -s [ME *extraccioun*, fr. LL *extraction-, extractio*, fr. L *extractus* + *-ion-, -io* -ion] **1 a** : the act or process of extracting ⟨~ of a tooth⟩ **b** *obs* : EXTRACT 2 **2** [MF (also, act of extracting), fr. LL *extraction-, extractio*] : ORIGIN, LINEAGE, DESCENT, BIRTH ⟨a workman of German ~⟩ **3 a** (1) : the proportion of ore that can be separated from the total mined mass of an ore occurrence (2) : the proportion of valuable metal or mineral recovered from an ore **b** : the proportion of flour obtained from each 100 pounds of milled grain ⟨an ~ of 74 percent⟩

extraction turbine *n* : a steam turbine provided with taps through which steam may be drawn off at various stages for purposes (as heating) other than driving the turbine

¹**ex·trac·tive** \ik'straktiv, (')ek¦s-, -tēv *also* -təv\ *adj* [¹*extract* + *-ive*] **1 a** : of, relating to, involving, or making use of extraction : marked by extraction ⟨~ processes⟩ ⟨~ industries⟩ **b** : tending to or resulting in withdrawal of natural resources by extraction with no provision for and often no possibility of replenishment of the resources ⟨mining, quarrying, and other ~ occupations⟩ ⟨~ agriculture⟩ **2 a** : capable of being extracted ⟨the ~ constituents of aromatic plants⟩ **b** (1) : of, relating to, or having the nature of an extract ⟨an ~ substance⟩ (2) : containing extractive matter ⟨a full-bodied and highly ~ beer⟩

²**extractive** \"\ *n* -s **1 a** : something extracted or capable of being extracted; *specif* : an extractable substance that gives a characteristic flavor to meat **b** : a substance that can be separated from an extract ⟨these ~*s* are recovered by removal of the solvent⟩ **2** : a dark-colored insoluble substance produced in the preparation of extracts by evaporation

extractive distillation *n* : a combined continuous fractional distillation and extraction in which a relatively high-boiling solvent (as furfural) flowing down the distillation column selectively scrubs one or more of the components from a mixture of compounds of similar vapor pressures (as butanes and butylenes)

ex·trac·tor \ik'straktə(r), (')ek¦s-\ *n* -s **1** : one that extracts: as **a** : a forceps or other instrument used in extraction (as of a tooth) **b** : a device for withdrawing a cartridge or spent cartridge case from the chamber of a firearm **c** : a machine that exerts centrifugal force in extraction (as of honey from honeycombs or moisture from wet materials) **d** : a device to pull ferrules from tube plates **e** : an apparatus for extracting substances by means of solvents **f** : a device used for extracting fruit juice (as by squeezing) **2** : a worker who operates an extractor

extract printing *n* : DISCHARGE PRINTING

extracts *pres 3d sing of* EXTRACT, *pl of* EXTRACT

extract wool \'ek,strakt-\ *n* : wool fiber extracted from material containing both wool and cotton or rayon by carbonizing the cotton or rayon

ex·tra·curricular *also* **extracurriculum** \'ekstrə+\ *adj* [*extra-* + *curricular* or *curriculum*] **1** : outside a regular curriculum : not falling within the scope of a regular curriculum; *specif* : of or relating to officially or semiofficially approved and usu. organized student activities (as athletics, dramatics, or publication of a school newspaper) connected with the students' school and usu. carrying no academic credit **2 a** : outside the regular duties of one's job or profession; *esp* : outside and in pleasant contrast to such duties ⟨reading detective stories as an ~ pastime⟩ **b** : outside and in direct opposition to or violation of the conventionally established limits or rights of one's position ⟨the ~ activities of a philandering husband⟩

ex·tra·cystic \¦==+\ *adj* [*extra-* + *cystic*] : situated or originating outside a cyst or bladder

ex·tra·dit·able \'ekstrə,dīd·əbəl, -īta-, ,=='===\ *adj* **1** : subject or liable to extradition ⟨an ~ criminal⟩ **2** : making liable to extradition ⟨an ~ offense⟩

ex·tra·dite \'ekstrə,dīt, *usu* -īd·+V\ *vt* -ED/-ING/-S [back-formation fr. *extradition*] **1** : to deliver up to extradition : subject to extradition **2** : to obtain the extradition of **syn** see BANISH

ex·tra·di·tion \,ekstrə'dishən\ *n* -s [F, fr. *ex-* ¹ex- + L *tradition-, traditio* act of handing over, surrendering — more at TRADITION] **1** : the surrender or delivery of an alleged criminal usu. under the provisions of a treaty or statute by one country, state, or other power to another having jurisdiction to try the charge **2** : localization of a sensation at a point removed from the center of the sensation

ex·tra·dos \'ekstrə,däs, -,dōs, -,dō; ek'strā|,däs, -rä|, |,dəs\ *n, pl* **extrados** \-,dōz\ *or* **extradoses** \-äsəz,-ōsəz,-əsəz\ [F, fr. L *extra* outside + F *dos* back — more at EXTRA-, DOSSIER] **1** : the exterior curve of an arch; *specif* : the upper curved face of the body of voussoirs which forms the arch **2** : the outer surface of a vault — compare INTRADOS

1 extrados

ex·tra·dotal \'ekstrə+\ *adj* [*extra-* + *dotal*] : PARAPHERNAL

extra dry *adj* [³*extra*] *of a beverage* : having little or no sweetness; *specif* : EXTRA SEC

ex tra·du·ce \ek'strādü,kā\ *adj* [LL *ex traduce*, lit., from a vine layer] *archaic, of the soul* : having direct origin from the souls of the parents

ex·tra·dural \'ekstrə +\ *adj* [*extra-* + *dural*] : situated or occurring outside the dura mater but within the skull ⟨an ~ hemorrhage⟩

ex·tra·embryonic *also* **ex·tra·embryonal** \¦==+\ *adj* [*extra-* + *embryonic, embryonal*] : situated outside the embryo proper; *esp* : developed from the zygote but not part of the embryo ⟨~ membranes⟩

extraembryonic coelom *n* : the space between the chorion and amnion which in early stages is continuous with the coelom of the embryo proper

ex·tra·enteric \'ekstrə +\ *adj* [*extra-* + *enteric*] : situated outside the enteron : PERIVISCERAL

ex·tra·familial \¦==+\ *adj* [*extra-* + *familial*] : lying outside the family or its control ⟨~ interests⟩

extra-fare \¦=¦=\ *adj* [*extra fare*] **1** : requiring or involving an extra fare **2** : providing better than regular accommodation or service

ex·tra·fascicular cambium \ˌekstrə +...-\ *n* [*extra-* + *fascicular*] **:** SECONDARY CAMBIUM

ex·tra·floral \ˌekstrə +\ *adj* [*extra-* + *floral*] *of a plant part* **:** not forming part of a flower **:** located elsewhere than in the flower ⟨~ nectaries⟩

ex·tra·foraneous \ˌ⸗⸗+\ *adj* [*extra-* + ML *foraneous* external, fr. L *foris, fores* door — more at DOOR] **:** OUTDOOR

ex·tra·galactic \ˌ⸗⸗+\ *adj* [ISV *extra-* + *galactic*] **:** lying or coming from outside the Milky Way

extragalactic nebula *n* **:** GALAXY 1b

ex·tra·genic \ˌ⸗⸗+\ *adj* [*extra-* + *genic*] **:** not involving or not entering into the composition of the genes ⟨mutations due to ~ causes⟩

ex·tra·genital \ˌ⸗⸗+\ *adj* [ISV *extra-* + *genital*] **:** situated or originating outside the genital region or organs ⟨~ sexual responses⟩

ex·tra·hazardous \ˌ⸗⸗+\ *adj* [*extra-* + *hazardous*] **:** extremely hazardous

ex·tra·hepatic \ˌ⸗⸗+\ *adj* [*extra-* + *hepatic*] **:** situated or originating outside the liver ⟨~ jaundice⟩ — compare INTRAHEPATIC

ex·tra-illustrate \ˌ⸗⸗+\ *vt* [[3]*extra* + *illustrate*] **:** to illustrate (as a book) by inserting material (as photographs or engravings) collected from other sources (as books) — compare GRANGERIZE — **ex·tra-illustration** \"+\ *n*

ex·tra·judicial \ˌ⸗⸗+\ *adj* [*extra-* + *judicial*] **1 a :** lying outside or beyond court proceedings **:** forming no valid part of a case before a court ⟨an ~ investigation⟩ **b** (1) **:** not made before a judge or court in due course of legal proceedings ⟨an ~ confession⟩ ⟨an ~ oath⟩ (2) **:** not made or delivered officially **:** INFORMAL, PRIVATE ⟨the judge made it clear that the opinion he voiced was ~⟩ **2 :** lying outside, beyond, or contrary to the ordinary course of law or justice **:** not legally authorized ⟨~ infliction of the death penalty⟩ — **ex·tra·judicially** \"+\ *adv*

ex·tra·lateral \ˌ⸗⸗+\ *adj* [*extra-* + *lateral*] **:** of or relating to the right of a lode locator on the public domain to certain portions of all veins apexing within his claim though these portions lie in adjoining land

ex·tra·lecithal \ˌ⸗⸗+\ *adj* [*extra-* + *lecithal*] *of an egg* **:** having the yolk arranged in a layer superficial to the protoplasm

ex·tra·legal \ˌ⸗⸗+\ *adj* [*extra-* + *legal*] **:** being beyond the province of law **:** not regulated by law ⟨~ law of the mining camps —P.S.Fritz⟩ ⟨voluntary ~ associations of educational institutions which exist for the purpose of improving education —Norman Burns⟩ — **ex·tra·legally** \"+\ *adv*

ex·tra·limital \ˌ⸗⸗+\ *adj* [*extra-* + [1]*limit* + *-al*] **:** not present in a given area — used esp. of organisms or kinds of organisms (as species)

ex·tra·literary \ˌ⸗⸗+\ *adj* [*extra-* + *literary*] **:** lying outside what is literary **:** lying outside the province of literature

ex·tral·i·ty \ekˈstralədˌē\ *n* -ES [by alter.] **:** EXTRATERRITORIALITY

ex·tra·marginal \ˌekstrə+\ *adj* [*extra-* + *marginal*] **:** lying outside or beyond a margin; *specif* **:** lying outside or beyond the margin of awareness ⟨~ perception⟩

ex·tra·marital \ˌ⸗⸗+\ *adj* [*extra-* + *marital*] **:** relating to sexual relationship with another than one's spouse **:** ADULTEROUS ⟨involved in ~ experiences⟩

ex·tra·mastoid \ˌ⸗⸗+\ *adj* [*extra-* + *mastoid*] **:** situated on or affecting the outer surface of the mastoid bone ⟨~ infection⟩

ex·tra·matrical \ˌ⸗⸗+\ *adj* [*extra-* + *matrical*] **:** lying or growing outside a substratum ⟨~ branches from the body of the host plant⟩ — used chiefly of aerial parts of parasitic fungi

ex·tra·matrimonial \ˌ⸗⸗+\ *adj* [*extra-* + *matrimonial*] **:** EXTRAMARITAL

ex·tra·medullary \ˌ⸗⸗+\ *adj* [ISV *extra-* + *medullary*] **:** lying outside a medulla; *esp* **:** EXTRABULBAR

ex·tra·mental \ˌ⸗⸗+\ *adj* [*extra-* + *mental*] **:** existing outside the mind ⟨the ~ world⟩

ex·tra·meridian \ˌ⸗⸗+\ *n* [back-formation fr. *extrameridional*] **:** an observation of a celestial body when it is near the meridian

ex·tra·meridional \ˌ⸗⸗+\ *adj* [*extra-* + *meridional*] **:** of or relating to deviation from the meridian **:** taken near the meridian

ex·tra·metrical \ˌ⸗⸗+\ *adj* [*extra-* + *metrical*] **:** exceeding the usual or prescribed number of syllables in a given meter **:** not counted in metrical analysis

ex·tra·morainic *also* **ex·tra·morainal** \ˌ⸗⸗+\ *adj* [*extra-* + *morainic, morainal*] **:** situated outside the area occupied by a glacier and its lateral and terminal moraines ⟨~ deposits⟩

ex·tra·mundane \ˌ⸗⸗+\ *adj* [LL *extramundanus*, fr. L *extra*, adv. & prep., outside, beyond (as in *extra mundum* beyond the world) + *mundanus* of the world — more at MUNDANE] **:** EXTRATERRESTRIAL

[1]**ex·tra·mural** \ˌ⸗⸗+\ *adj* [*extra-* + *mural*] **1 :** existing outside or beyond the walls, boundaries, or precincts of an organized unit ⟨an ~ basilica⟩ ⟨~ hospital care and treatment⟩ **2 a :** of, relating to, or taking part in extension courses or facilities ⟨~ classes⟩ ⟨the ~ department of a university⟩ **b :** relating to or taking part in informal interschool contests arranged for competition between special groups or classes rather than varsities ⟨~ athletics⟩ — opposed to *intramural;* distinguished from *intercollegiate* and *interscholastic* **3 :** EXTRACURRICULAR 2b ⟨a husband's ~ affair —J.W.Krutch⟩ — **ex·tra·murally** \"+\ *adv*

[2]**extramural** \"\ *n* **:** an extramural contest

ex·tra·ne·i·ty \ˌekstrəˈnēəd-ē, -(ˌ)strāˈ-\ *n* -ES **:** the quality or state of being extraneous

ex·tra·ne·ous \(ˈ)ekˈstrānēəs, ikˈs-\ *adj* [L *extraneus* — more at STRANGE] **1 a :** existing or originating outside or beyond **:** external in origin **:** coming from the outside ⟨~ light in a camera⟩ ⟨protecting the contents of the container from ~ moisture⟩ ⟨no premiums or other ~ inducements⟩ **b :** brought in, introduced, or added from an external source or point of origin ⟨a valley bottom covered with ~ soil⟩ ⟨relying upon an ~ income⟩ **2 a :** not forming an essential or vital part **:** not belonging to something as a proper or natural part **:** not intrinsic **:** ACCIDENTAL, FOREIGN ⟨~ sounds⟩ ⟨they considered art to be ~ to reality⟩ ⟨a ballet that struck me as ~ and somewhat out of keeping with the rest of the play —Wolcott Gibbs⟩ ⟨~ incidents in a novel⟩ ⟨a building with ~ ornamentation⟩ **b :** having little or no relevance **:** IRRELEVANT **:** not pertinent ⟨an unexpected and altogether ~ remark⟩ ⟨an ~ digression⟩ **c :** having little or no interdependence or connection **:** UNRELATED ⟨a series of ~ books⟩ ⟨~ events⟩ **syn** see EXTRINSIC

ex·tra·ne·ous·ly *adv* **:** in an extraneous manner

ex·tra·ne·ous·ness *n* -ES **:** the quality or state of being extraneous

ex·tra·ne·us he·res \ekˈstrānēəsˈhi(ˌ)rēz\ *n, pl* **extra·nei here·des** \-nēˌīhəˈrē(ˌ)dēz\ [L, lit., outside heir] **:** an heir other than a suus heres either of an intestate or under a will in whom the inheritance can be vested only upon his definite acceptance

ex·tra·nuclear \ˌekstrə+\ *adj* [*extra-* + *nuclear*] **:** situated in, involving elements situated in, or affecting the parts of a cell external to the nucleus **:** CYTOPLASMIC ⟨~ viruses⟩

ex·tra·ocular muscle \ˌekstrə+...-\ *n* [*extra-* + *ocular*] **:** any of the six small voluntary muscles that pass between the eyeball and the orbit and control the movements of the eyeball in relation to the orbit

ex·traor·di·nar·i·ly \ikˌstrȯ(r)dᵊnˌerəlē, (ˌ)ekˌ-, -li *also* ˌekstrəˈȯ- *sometimes* -dᵊnˌe-\ *adv* **:** in an extraordinary manner **:** to an extraordinary degree

ex·traor·di·nar·i·ness \ikˈstrȯ(r)dᵊnˌerēnəs, ekˈs-, -rin-, *also* ˌekstrəˈȯ- *sometimes* -dᵊˌne-\ *n* **:** the quality, state, or fact of being extraordinary

[1]**ex·traor·di·nary** \-ˌerē,-eri *sometimes* -dˌner-\ *adj* [ME *extraordinarie*, fr. L *extraordinarius*, fr. *extra*, adv. & prep., outside, beyond (as in *extra ordinem* out of course, in an extraordinary manner) + *ordinarius* ordinary — more at EXTRA-, ORDINARY] **1 a :** more than ordinary **:** not of the ordinary order or pattern ⟨ordinary and ~ expenses⟩ **:** going beyond what is usual, regular, common, or customary **:** not following the general pattern or norm ⟨held the office for an ~ period of time⟩ ⟨giving ~ powers to the president⟩ **b** (1) **:** exceptional to a very marked extent **:** most unusual **:** far from common ⟨enjoying ~ popularity⟩ ⟨an ~ capacity for work⟩ **:** very outstanding ⟨an ~ leader⟩ **:** very remarkable ⟨~ technical progress⟩ **:** rarely equaled **:** SINGULAR, PHENOMENAL ⟨a woman of ~ beauty⟩ **:** strikingly impressive **:** ARRESTING ⟨an ~ family resemblance⟩ (2) **:** having little or no precedent and usu. totally unexpected ⟨an ~ combination of circumstances⟩ (3) **:** very curious, strange, or surprising **:** AMAZING ⟨how ~ that she should not understand⟩ **2 a :** of, relating to, or having the degree of care, caution, or diligence typical of that exercised by an extremely prudent person ⟨revealing an ~ foresight⟩ **b :** of, relating to, or having the nature of a proceeding or action not normally required by law or not prescribed for the regular administration of the law ⟨an ~ session of a legislature⟩ ⟨an ~ court⟩ ⟨~ jurisdiction⟩ **c :** of, relating to, or having the nature of an occurrence (as an accident or casualty) or risk of a kind other than what ordinary experience or prudence would foresee **3 a :** serving in addition to the regular officials or employees **:** having a special and usu. occasional rather than regular function **:** entrusted with a special responsibility **:** employed for or sent upon an unusual service ⟨an ambassador ~⟩ **b** *obs* **:** EXTRA

[2]**extraordinary** \"\ *n, archaic* **:** something extraordinary

[3]**extraordinary** \"\ *adv, archaic* **:** EXTRAORDINARILY ⟨the quite ~ large quantity of furniture —Osbert Lancaster⟩

extraordinary ray *n* **:** the part of a ray divided in two by double refraction that does not follow the ordinary laws of refraction because its speed varies with its direction in the doubly refracting medium

extraordinary writ *n* **:** PREROGATIVE WRIT

ex·tra·organismal \ˌekstrə+\ *adj* [*extra-* + *organismal*] **:** situated or originating outside an organism ⟨~ conflicts⟩ ⟨~ infective agents⟩

extra pat·ri·mo·ni·um \-ˌpa·trəˈmōnēəm\ *adj* [L, lit., outside of inheritance] **:** EXTRA COMMERCIUM

ex·tra·physical \"+\ *adj* [*extra-* + *physical*] **:** not subject to physical laws or methods

ex·tra·planetary \"+\ *adj* [*extra-* + *planetary*] **:** situated or originating outside the region of the planetary orbits; *also* **:** relating to space outside this region

extra point *n* **1 :** a point scored in football after a touchdown esp. by drop-kicking or place-kicking from scrimmage over the bar between the goalposts **2 extra points** *pl* **:** a score of two points gained after a touchdown in football by advancing the ball across the goal line in one play from scrimmage

ex·trap·o·late \ikˈstrapəˌlāt, ek-, *usu* -ād·+V\ *vb* -ED/-ING/-S [L *extra* outside, beyond + E *-polate* (as in *interpolate*) — more at EXTRA-] *vt* **1 :** to infer from a trend within an already observed interval (the usu. probable values of a mathematical variable in an unobserved interval) **:** calculate from the terms of a known series (the terms not included in the series) **2 a** (1) **:** to project, extend, or expand (known data or experience) into an area not known or experienced so as to arrive at a usu. conjectural knowledge of the unknown area by inferences based on an assumed continuity, correspondence, or other parallelism between it and what is known ⟨events ... can be traced in the past and *extrapolated* into the future —D.J.Bogue⟩ ⟨*extrapolating* the present geological state of the earth to its state billions of years ago⟩ (2) **:** to extend to a greater length or into a new area ⟨~ a straight line⟩ (3) **:** to cause to move further, develop, or expand on the basis of often unwarranted assumptions or speculations **:** draw out or amplify ⟨*extrapolating* some unpleasant personal experience into a generalized slur on his hosts —L.G.Crocker⟩ ⟨metaphysicians that ~ themselves to the point of absurdity⟩ **b :** to gain knowledge of (an area not known or experienced) by extrapolating **:** estimate or predict by or as if by extrapolating ⟨*extrapolating* public opinion from the public's known reactions to other issues⟩ ~ *vi* **:** to perform the act or process of extrapolating — compare INTERPOLATE

ex·trap·o·la·tion \ikˌstrapəˈlāshən, (ˌ)ekˌ-\ *n* -S **:** the act or process of extrapolating **:** PROJECTION, EXTENSION

extrapolation chamber *n* **:** an ionization chamber used as a dosimeter and having adjustments that permit the accurate determination of dosage over a surface by means of extrapolation from measurements on finite layers

ex·trap·o·la·tive \ikˈstrapəˌlād·iv, ek-\ *adj* **:** of, relating to, or obtained by extrapolation

ex·trap·o·la·tor \-ād·ə(r)\ *n* -S **:** one that extrapolates

ex·trap·o·la·to·ry \-pələˌtōrē\ *adj* **:** EXTRAPOLATIVE

ex·tra·psychic *or* **ex·tra·psychical** \ˌekstrə+\ *adj* [*extra-* + *psychic, psychical*] **:** being or occurring outside the psyche, the mind, or the personality — **extrapsychically** *adv*

ex·tra·punitive \ˌekstrə+\ *adj* [*extra-* + *punitive*] **:** tending to direct blame or punishment toward persons other than the self — opposed to *intropunitive* — **extrapunitiveness** *n* -ES

ex·tra·pyramidal \ˌ⸗⸗+\ *adj* [ISV *extra-* + *pyramidal*] **:** situated outside or independent of the pyramidal tracts ⟨~ brain lesions⟩

ex·tra-regarding \ˌ⸗⸗+\ *adj* [[1]*extra*] **:** ALTRUISTIC

extra river *n* **:** a diamond of the very highest grade

extras *pl of* EXTRA

ex·tra·scientific \ˌ⸗⸗+\ *adj* [*extra-* + *scientific*] **:** lying outside what is scientific **:** lying outside the province of science ⟨an ~ area of experience⟩

extra sec *adj* [[3]*extra*] *of champagne* **:** containing from 1.5 to 3 percent sugar by volume **:** somewhat dry **:** drier than sec and sweeter than brut

ex·tra·sensorial \ˌ⸗⸗+\ *adj* [*extra-* + *sensorial*] **:** EXTRASENSORY — **ex·tra·sensorially** \"+\ *adv*

ex·tra·sensory \ˌ⸗⸗+\ *adj* [*extra-* + *sensory*] **:** residing beyond or outside the ordinary senses **:** not limited to the senses ⟨mental telepathy and other instances of ~ perception⟩

ex·tra·systole \ˌ⸗⸗+\ *n* [NL, fr. L *extra* outside, beyond + NL *systole* — more at EXTRA-, SYSTOLE] **:** a premature beat of one of the chambers of the heart that leads to momentary arrhythmia, the fundamental rhythm being maintained — **ex·tra·systolic** \"+\ *adj*

ex·tra·tension \ˌ⸗⸗+\ *n* [*extratensive* + *-ion*] **:** the state or fact of having extratensive qualities or responses

ex·tra·tensive \ˌ⸗⸗+\ *adj* [*extra-* + *tensive*] **:** showing a predominance of color responses on the Rorschach test and characterized by the urge to live in the world outside oneself, by restless motility, and by unstable affective reactions — contrasted with *introversive*

ex·tra·terrestrial \ˌ⸗⸗+\ *adj* [*extra* + *terrestrial*] **:** originating, occurring, or existing outside the earth or its atmosphere ⟨the possibility of ~ life⟩

ex·tra·territorial \ˌ⸗⸗+\ *adj* [*extra-* + *territorial*] **:** situated outside the territorial limits of a jurisdiction — **ex·tra·territorially** \"+\ *adv*

ex·tra·territoriality \ˌ⸗⸗+\ *n* **:** a quality, state, or privilege of general or partial exemption from the application of local law or jurisdiction of local tribunals ⟨the ~ of diplomats⟩

ex·tra·territorialize \ˌ⸗⸗+\ *vt, see -ize in Explan Notes* **:** to cause to be extraterritorial

ex·tra·tropical cyclone \ˌ⸗⸗+...-\ *n* [*extra-* + *tropical*] **:** a cyclone in the middle latitudes being often 1500 miles in diameter and usu. containing a cold front that extends toward the equator for hundreds of miles from the center of low pressure and that divides the warmer humid winds of the forward portion from the cooler dry winds of the rear portion

ex·tra·tubal \ˌ⸗⸗+\ *adj* [*extra-* + *tubal*] **:** situated outside a body duct or esp. outside the fallopian tube ⟨~ pregnancy⟩

ex·tra·tympanic \ˌ⸗⸗+\ *adj* [*extra-* + *tympanic*] **:** situated outside the middle ear

ex·tra·uterine pregnancy \ˌ⸗⸗+...-\ *n* [ISV *extra-* + *uterine*] **:** pregnancy in which the fetus develops outside the uterus (as in a fallopian tube)

ex·trav·a·gance \ikˈstravəgən(t)s, ek-, -vēg-\ *n* -S [F, fr. MF, fr. *extravagant*] **1** *obs* **:** a wandering away from a set course **:** DEVIATION **2 a :** an instance of excess or prodigality ⟨have never observed any of the ~s of a lover in your conduct —G.B.Shaw⟩; *esp* **:** a very great or excessive outlay of money or other resources ⟨living simply and avoiding ~s⟩ **b :** something that is extravagant ⟨that coat is an ~ you can't afford⟩ **3 :** the quality, condition, or fact of being extravagant **:** excess or prodigality ⟨living in idle ~⟩ ⟨words that to some might seem wild, even insane, in their ~ —W.H.Hudson †1922⟩

ex·trav·a·gan·cy \-nsē, -si\ *n* -ES [*extravagant* + *-cy*] **:** EXTRAVAGANCE

[1]**ex·trav·a·gant** \-nt\ *adj* [ME *extravagaunt*, fr. MF *extravagant*, fr. ML *extravagant-, extravagans*, fr. L *extra-* + *vagant-, vagans*, pres. part. of *vagari* to wander about — more at VAGARY] **1 a** *archaic* **:** wandering away **:** VAGRANT ⟨rare ~ spirits —R.W.Emerson⟩ **b** *obs* **:** spreading or projecting beyond usual limits **c** *obs* **:** differing greatly **:** widely divergent **d** *obs* **:** STRANGE, CURIOUS **2 a :** exceeding the limits of reason or necessity **:** exceeding proper bounds **:** going beyond what is justifiable ⟨an ~ theory⟩ ⟨demanding ~ privileges⟩ ⟨usurping ~ power⟩ ⟨making ~ claims⟩ **b** (1) **:** almost totally lacking in moderation, balance, and restraint **:** wildly excessive **:** going much too far ⟨~ generalizations⟩ **:** INTEMPERATE ⟨~ praise⟩ ⟨~ enthusiasm⟩ (2) **:** extremely and often excessively impetuous and vehement and marked by sudden and abrupt changes ⟨the ~ language of a lover⟩ (3) **:** extremely or excessively elaborate, vivid, and showy and colored by startling and often apparently capricious contrasts ⟨a play filled with ~ dialogue⟩ ⟨gazing at the ~ display of the setting sun⟩ **c :** wildly exaggerated often to the point of absurdity **:** pushed beyond credibility **:** utterly fantastic ⟨~ accusations⟩ ⟨~ reports of what they had seen⟩ **3 a :** spending or tending to spend much more than necessary **:** spending lavishly, recklessly, or wastefully **:** spending improvidently like a spendthrift **:** PRODIGAL ⟨~ in everything she bought⟩ ⟨to keep up appearances they became ~⟩ **b :** pouring forth liberally **:** very bountiful **:** exceedingly or excessively generous in giving or spending **:** PROFUSE ⟨he can be counted on to be ~ toward the poor⟩; *often* **:** excessively effusive or exuberant ⟨without wishing to be ~ in expressing their admiration⟩ **c :** marked by great abundance often to an extreme or excessive degree **:** most plentiful ⟨a tropical island with ~ vegetation⟩ **4 :** extremely and often unreasonably high in price **:** costing an excessive amount ⟨interested only in ~ clothes⟩ **:** EXORBITANT ⟨~ prices⟩ **:** LAVISH ⟨an ~ new musical⟩ **syn** see EXCESSIVE

[2]**extravagant** \"\ *n* -S *archaic* **:** one that is extravagant

ex·trav·a·gant·ly *adv* **:** in an extravagant manner

ex·trav·a·gan·za \ikˌstravəˈganzə, (ˌ)ekˌ- *sometimes* -gän- *or* -gán-\ *n* -S [It *estravaganza, stravaganza*, lit., extravagance, fr. *estravagante, stravagante* extravagant, fr. ML *extravagant-, extravagans*] **1 :** a literary fantasy that is freely imaginative in subject, structure, and development and that often includes elements of burlesque or parody **2 a :** a musical composition marked by freedom of form and by elements of burlesque or parody **b :** a lavish or spectacular show or event ⟨a winter sports ~⟩; *esp* **:** a lavish musical production (as a stage show or motion picture) typically marked by spectacular and elaborate settings, unusual scenic effects, costly costuming, a large cast of singers and dancers, extensive choral numbers and choreography, and a loosely unifying theme or plot that is usu. light and comic **3 a :** a decorative article of clothing or a clothing accessory designed or used for a striking ornamental effect ⟨such ~s as hats of velvet and dresses sprinkled with sequins⟩ **b :** an object that is strikingly unusual and often bizarre; *esp* **:** a usu. large and opulent architectural structure of freely imaginative design and striking ornamental effects **4 :** an effusion or burst of activity that captures or holds one's attention like an extravaganza ⟨another ~ of fun —Ernest Beaglehole⟩

ex·trav·a·gate \ˈ⸗ˈ⸗⸗ˌgāt\ *vi* -ED/-ING/-S [*extravagant* + *-ate*] **1** *archaic* **a :** to wander off **:** STRAY **b :** to wander about without control **:** ROAM **2** *archaic* **:** to go beyond the limits of what is reasonable, necessary, or proper — **ex·trav·a·ga·tion** \ˌ⸗ˌ⸗⸗ˈgāshən\ *n* -S

ex·tra·vaginal \ˌekstrə+\ *adj* [*extra-* + *vaginal*] **:** bursting through an enclosing sheath ⟨the ~ shoots of many grasses⟩

[1]**ex·trav·a·sate** \ikˈstravəˌsāt, ek-, -ˌzāt\ *vb* -ED/-ING/-S [L *extra* outside + *vas* vessel + E *-ate* (v. suffix) — more at EXTRA-, VASE] *vt* **1 :** to force out (as blood) or cause to escape from a proper vessel or channel (as a blood vessel) **2 :** to cause (as molten lava) to pour out or erupt (as from a vent in the earth) ~ *vi* **1 :** to pass by infiltration or effusion from a proper vessel or channel into surrounding tissue (as of blood from a blood vessel) **2 :** to pour out or erupt (as of lava from a vent in the earth)

[2]**extravasate** \"\ *adj* [L *extra* + *vas* + E *-ate* (adj. suffix)] *archaic* **:** EXTRAVASATED

[3]**extravasate** \"\ *n* -S **:** an extravasated fluid (as blood) or a deposit (as of solidified lava) formed from extravasation

ex·trav·a·sa·tion \ikˌstravəˈsāshən, (ˌ)ekˌ-\ *n* -S [[1]*extravasate* + *-ion*] **1 :** the action of extravasating **:** the condition of being extravasated ⟨the ~ of lava from a volcano⟩ **:** EFFUSION, ERUPTION **2 :** an extravasated fluid or a deposit formed from extravasation **:** EXTRAVASATE

ex·tra·vascular \ˌekstrə+\ *adj* [*extra-* + *vascular*] **1** *anat* **:** not contained in vessels **2** *anat* **:** destitute of vessels **:** NONVASCULAR

ex·trav·ased \ikˈstravəst\ *adj* [F *extravaser* to extravasate (fr. L *extra* + *vas*) + E *-ed*] *archaic* **:** EXTRAVASATED

extraversion *var of* EXTROVERSION

extravert *var of* EXTROVERT

ex·tra·visceral \ˌekstrə+\ *adj* [*extra-* + *visceral*] **:** situated or originating outside the viscera ⟨~ abdominal pain⟩

ex·tra·visible \ˌ⸗⸗+\ *adj* [*extra-* + *visible*] **:** lying outside the range of visible wavelengths ⟨the ~ regions of the spectrum⟩

ex·tra·zonal \ˌ⸗⸗+\ *adj* [*extra-* + *zonal*] **:** lying outside a zone ⟨in the American sector of the region and in the ~ part⟩

extrema *pl of* EXTREMUM

[1]**ex·treme** \ikˈstrēm, ekˈ-, *in "extreme unction" often* ⸗ˌek-(ˌ)strēm\ *adj, often* -ER/-EST [ME, fr. MF, fr. L *extremus*, superl. of *exter, exterus* on the outside, outward — more at EXTERIOR] **1 a :** existing in the highest or the greatest possible degree **:** very great **:** very intense ⟨living in ~ poverty⟩ ⟨the ~ cold of the polar regions⟩ **b :** marked by great severity or violence **:** most severe **:** most stringent **:** DRASTIC, DESPERATE ⟨resorting to ~ measures to combat crime⟩ ⟨an ~ action that crushed their spirits⟩ **c** (1) **:** going to great or exaggerated lengths **:** UNCOMPROMISING, RADICAL, FANATICAL ⟨he was quite ~ in his views on the matter⟩ (2) **:** going beyond the limits of reason, necessity, or propriety **:** IMMODERATE ⟨avidly following the most ~ fashion in clothes⟩ ⟨a religion whose tenets were austere and ~⟩ **:** exceeding the ordinary, usual, or expected **:** EXCESSIVE ⟨an ~ descent⟩ **d :** having an implied or specified characteristic to the fullest possible extent ⟨the nature of real need can be studied best in ~ cases⟩ ⟨in politics he sits at the ~ right⟩ **2** *archaic* **:** LAST, FINAL ⟨thy ~ hope, the loveliest and the last —P.B.Shelley⟩ **3 a :** situated at the farthest possible point from a center **:** most remote **:** FARTHEST, OUTERMOST ⟨the ~ edge of the city⟩ ⟨traveling to the ~ borders of the country⟩ ⟨an ~ outpost⟩ **b :** situated at the very tip of either of two ends (as of a line) ⟨the ~ end of the road⟩ **4 a :** farthest advanced in any direction **:** most advanced **:** UTMOST ⟨standing at the ~ edge of the river⟩ **b :** MAXIMUM ⟨a folding table with an ~ length of 6 feet⟩ **syn** see EXCESSIVE

[2]**extreme** \"\ *n* -S **1 a :** an extreme state or condition ⟨an ~ of poverty⟩ **b extremes** *pl, obs* **:** critical circumstances **:** STRAITS, HARDSHIPS ⟨resolute in most ~s —Shak.⟩ **2 a** (1) **:** an extreme variation ⟨~s of behavior weaving into one another as if to spite all moralists —Irving Howe⟩ **:** something situated at, serving to mark, or terminating one end or the other of a total range or extent ⟨the temperature in the desert ranges astonishingly between ~s of heat and cold⟩ (2) **:** one of two things related in some way (as by nature, condition, or position) and at the same time removed from, contrasting with, or opposed to each other to a very great extent or as far as possible ⟨the ~s of passion that are called love and hatred⟩ **b** (1) **:** the first term or the last term of a mathematical proportion (2) **:** the greatest or the least of several magnitudes **c** *logic* **:** a term appearing in an extreme position: as (1) **:** the subject or predicate of a proposition — contrasted with *copula* (2) **:** the major term or minor term of a syllogism — compare MIDDLE TERM **3** *archaic* **:** a terminal part of a body **:** EXTREMITY **4 a** (1) **:** a very pronounced or excessive degree ⟨there is no need to grieve to such an ~⟩ ⟨a more stable and democratic regime with less ~s of wealth and poverty —William Clark⟩ ⟨he aroused ~s of admiration and hostility —Robert Lawrence⟩ **:** EXCESS ⟨this world of violent ~s —Huntington Hartford⟩ (2) **:** the utmost conceivable or tolerable degree **:** the utter limit ⟨enthusiasm that was carried to an ~⟩ **:** MAXIMUM ⟨prejudice is found at its ~ in that century⟩ **b :** an extreme measure or expedient **:** an extreme step ⟨forced to an unpleasant ~⟩ **:** utmost length ⟨he went to ~s to satisfy their curiosity —P.J.O'Brien⟩; *also* **:** an extreme instance or case ⟨an ~ they could not visualize⟩

—**in the extreme :** to the greatest possible extent or degree ⟨would find the task wearisome *in the extreme* —Lionel McColvin⟩
³**extreme** \"\ *adv, archaic* **:** EXTREMELY
extreme and mean ratio *n* **:** GOLDEN SECTION
extreme breadth *n* **:** BREADTH EXTREME
extreme fiber *n* **:** one of the longitudinal elements of a structural member (as a beam) that are at the greatest distance from the neutral axis
extreme fiber stress *n* **:** the stress per unit of area in an extreme fiber of a structural member subjected to bending
ex·treme·ly *adv* **:** in an extreme manner **:** to an extreme extent
extremely high frequency *n* **:** a radio frequency in the highest range of the radio spectrum — see RADIO FREQUENCY table
ex·treme·ness *n* -ES **:** the quality or state of being extreme ⟨the ~ of the measures to combat crime was almost as bad as the crime itself⟩
extremer *comparative of* EXTREME
extremest *superlative of* EXTREME
extreme unction *n, often cap E&U* **:** a sacrament (as in the Roman Catholic Church) that consists of praying over and anointing a person who is in danger of death
ex·tre·mism \ik'strē,mizəm, ek-\ *n* -S **:** the quality or state of being extreme; *specif* **:** RADICALISM
¹**ex·trem·ist** \-ēməst *sometimes* -em-\ *n* -S [²*extreme* + *-ist*] **:** an adherent or advocate of extremism; *esp* **:** RADICAL
²**extremist** \"\ *also* **ex·trem·is·tic** \;=(,)=¦mistik\ *adj* **:** of, relating to, or favoring extremism or extremists
ex·trem·i·ty \ik'stremәd·ē, ek-, -mәtē, -i\ *n* -ES [ME *extremite*, fr. MF *extremité*, fr. L *extremitat-, extremitas*, fr. *extremus* extreme + *-itat-, -itas* -ity — more at EXTREME] **1 :** something that is extreme: as **a** (1) **:** an outlying or terminal part, section, or point ⟨one ~ of the mountain range is located to the east⟩ **:** the farthest or most remote part, section, or point **:** the most advanced part **:** the farthest extent **:** the farthest projection ⟨the region's wooded northern ~⟩ ⟨the inhabitants of the southern ~ of the continent⟩ **:** the very end ⟨at the ~ of a small path —William Black⟩ ⟨the sting at the ~ of a scorpion's tail⟩ (2) **:** a limb (as of the body) or other appendage **:** an arm or leg ⟨circulation of blood in the *extremities*⟩; *usu* **:** a hand or foot ⟨coldness in the *extremities*⟩ **b** (1) **:** a condition of extreme urgency or necessity **:** a highly crucial state of affairs **:** a time of extreme danger or critical need **:** extreme adversity ⟨in this ~ she took refuge in grief —G.B.Shaw⟩ ⟨to whom in the depths of his ~ he turned for sympathy —F.W.Crofts⟩ (2) **:** a moment marked by imminent destruction or dissolution ⟨anchors thrown out by a vessel in its last ~ —A.C.Clarke⟩ (3) *archaic* **:** the point of death ⟨the king was at ~ —G.P.R. James⟩ **c** (1) **:** an extremely intense degree (as of emotion or pain) **:** extreme intensity ⟨in his first ~ of grief —H.G.Wells⟩ ⟨enduring *extremities* of torture —Edith Sitwell⟩ (2) **:** a culminating point (as of emotion or pain) **:** HEIGHT, APEX, CLIMAX ⟨some went so far as to kneel on the sharp stones in the very ~ of terror —Elinor Wylie⟩ ⟨an ~ of passion⟩ (3) *archaic* **:** extreme severity or rigor **:** ASPERITY **d** *obs* **:** an instance or act of extravagant behavior **:** EXTRAVAGANCE **e :** the fullest possible extent **:** utmost limit **:** utmost degree ⟨the thought worried her to the ~ of her endurance⟩ ⟨they were definitely provoked to ~ before they did this deed —Rex Ingamells⟩ **f** (1) **:** a very severe, violent, drastic, or desperate act or measure ⟨reduced to the ~ of telling everything they knew⟩ ⟨forced to *extremities*⟩ (2) **:** a single remaining source of help or plan of action **:** sole recourse **:** final resort ⟨as a last ~ there's only one thing that can be done⟩ **2 :** the quality or state of being extreme ⟨avoiding *extremities*⟩ ⟨they vied with one another in the ~ of their opinions —H.G.Wells⟩ ⟨the ~, violence, and anguish which have characterized much of the literature —K.I. Lansner⟩ — **in extremities :** at the end of one's resources **:** in a most crucial or dangerous condition or position **:** at the point of death — **to the last extremity :** to the point of death **:** to the death
ex·tre·mum \ik'strēməm\ *n, pl* **extre·ma** \-ēmə\ [NL, fr. L, end, fr. neut. of *extremus*] **:** a stationary value of a mathematical function that is either a maximum or a minimum
ex·trica·ble \ek'strikəbəl, ik'strik-, 'ekstrәk-, 'ek(,)strik-\ *adj* [L *extricare* + E *-able*] **:** capable of being extricated
ex·tri·cate \'ekstrə,kāt, *usu* -ād·+V\ *vt* -ED/-ING/-S [L *extricatus*, past part. of *extricare*, fr. *ex-* ¹ex- + *tricae* trifles, impediments, perplexities; perh. akin to L *torquēre* to twist — more at TORTURE] **1 a** *archaic* **:** to separate the tangled threads of **:** UNRAVEL, DISENTANGLE **b :** to distinguish (one thing) from a related thing by recognition of common and variant elements **:** DISCRIMINATE, DIFFERENTIATE ⟨a plant that cannot easily be *extricated* from similar ones⟩ ⟨*extricating* the typical culture of a people from its behavior patterns⟩ **c** *archaic* **:** to clear up the involved condition of **:** clear of complication or confusion **2 a :** to draw out from or forth from and set free of a tangled, jumbled, confused, or otherwise involved heap, mass, or situation **:** separate and set aside ⟨*extricating* the one unbroken dish from the pile of fragments⟩ **b** (1) **:** to draw out from or as if from a fixed position **:** remove with effort ⟨he *extricated* the two heavy gas cylinders from the bottom of the boat —C.S.Forester⟩ **:** pull out **:** get out ⟨many who were trapped perished before they could be *extricated* —O.S.Nock⟩ **:** EXTRACT ⟨the horse could not ~ its foot from the mudhole⟩ ⟨the kind of dust that, once it infiltrates one's lungs, seems never to be altogether *extricated* —E.J.Kahn⟩ (2) **:** to release from or as if from a confining, restraining, difficult, embarrassing, dangerous, or otherwise undesirable condition or situation **:** get free **:** DISENGAGE, LIBERATE ⟨*extricating* himself from the straitjacket⟩ ⟨golf players *extricating* themselves from a sand trap⟩ ⟨what he expected of me was to ~ him from a difficult situation —Joseph Conrad⟩ ⟨my success in having *extricated* myself from an awkward predicament —Victor Heiser⟩ ⟨trying to ~ themselves from debt⟩ **3** *archaic* **:** to set (as a gas) free from a state of combination

syn EXTRICATE, DISENTANGLE, UNTANGLE, DISENCUMBER, and DISEMBARRASS can mean in common to free or release from what binds or holds one back. EXTRICATE implies an entanglement, as in difficulties or perplexities, a restraining from free action so great that only force, ingenuity, or persistence will bring release ⟨on the point of *extricating* itself from the snarls of conflicting claims —*Amer. Guide Series: N.J.*⟩ ⟨give us what aid you can in *extricating* a generous young man from such a pair of schemers as this father and daughter seem to be —W.M. Thackeray⟩ ⟨personality is to be *extricated* from the loyalties which disintegrate it —Donald Meyer⟩ DISENTANGLE is similar to EXTRICATE but often stresses more the things, esp. intricately complex, which entangle other things ⟨*disentangle* one's foot from a fish net⟩ ⟨so picturesque a figure that biography is unable to *disentangle* him from legend —*Amer. Guide Series: N. C.*⟩ ⟨a moralization which must be slowly *disentangled* from the driftings and confusions of everyday life —V.S.Pritchett⟩ ⟨he can *disentangle* facts from impressions —J.G.Cozzens⟩ UNTANGLE is often popularly used in the sense of DISENTANGLE, with the same implications ⟨*untangle* one's foot from a fish net⟩ DISENCUMBER implies a freeing from what weighs down, clogs, or imposes a heavy burden ⟨they *disencumber* themselves of many garments —George Meredith⟩ ⟨he cannot *disencumber* himself of his lifelong methods of composition —H.O.Taylor⟩ ⟨*disencumber* oneself of a weight of debts⟩ DISEMBARRASS implies a release from what impedes, hampers, or hinders ⟨I was glad to *disembarrass* myself of the bag and give it to a duty officer —Basil Black⟩ ⟨decide to *disembarrass* themselves of him by killing or banishing him —Merriam McCulloch⟩ ⟨*disembarrass* ourselves of the curse of ignorance and learn to work together —Alvin Johnson⟩
ex·tri·ca·tion \,==¦kāshən\ *n* -S [LL *extrication-, extricatio*, fr. L *extricatus* + *-ion-, -io* -ion] **1 :** the action of extricating **2 :** the process of being extricated
ex·trin·sic \(')ek¦strinz|ik, ik's-, -n(t)s|, |ēk\ *adj* [F & LL; F *extrinsèque*, fr. LL *extrinsecus*, fr. L, adv., from without, on the outside, fr. (assumed) L *extrim* (fr. L *exter, exterus* outward, on the outside) + L *-secus* (fr. *sequi* to follow) — more at EXTERIOR, SUE] **1 a :** lying outside **:** not forming part of or belonging properly to **:** not contained in or occurring in **:** EXTRANEOUS ⟨~ to native capacities⟩ **b** (1) **:** arising outside **:** originating or operating from or on the outside ⟨looking for aid⟩ ⟨disdaining ~ pressure groups⟩; *specif* **:** originating outside a part and acting upon the part as a whole ⟨the ~ muscles of the tongue⟩ (2) **:** derived from an external source **:** not inherent **:** not essential **:** ACCESSORY, ADVENTITIOUS ⟨~ evidence⟩ **:** ACCIDENTAL, CONTINGENT **2 :** of or relating to the outside of **:** OUTER, OUTWARD, EXTERNAL ⟨an ~ feature of the new building⟩

syn EXTRANEOUS, FOREIGN, ALIEN: EXTRINSIC applies to what is definitely not contained in something else, esp. not contained in or derived from its essential nature ⟨that style is something *extrinsic* to the subject, a kind of ornamentation laid on to tickle the taste —A.T.Quiller-Couch⟩ ⟨the special quality of such presuppositions is that they are inherent and not *extrinsic* —Walter Moberly⟩ EXTRANEOUS applies to what is exterior or unrelated but may be interjected with or interpreted as part of an intrinsic essence ⟨simony was no *extraneous* stain to be washed off from the body ecclesiastic, but rather an element of its actual constitution —H.O.Taylor⟩ ⟨it is simply a close rendering of the Latin text, and it contains little, if any, *extraneous* matter of the kind which in other works illustrates the character of Alfred's thought —F.M.Stenton⟩ ⟨no *extraneous* beauty or vigor was ingrafted on the decaying stock —T.B. Macaulay⟩ FOREIGN applies to what is exterior, notably different, or unlikely to be assimilated with or to become part of ⟨the mysticism so *foreign* to the French mind and temper —W.C.Brownell⟩ ⟨executive inaction in such a situation, courting national disaster, is *foreign* to the concept of energy and initiative in the executive as created by the founding fathers —*Current History*⟩ ALIEN may be stronger than FOREIGN in suggesting opposition, incompatibility, repugnance, or irreconcilability ⟨an emotional quality totally *alien* to the austerity of the rest of the sermon⟩ ⟨though such frankness would, in the past, have been wholly *alien* to her nature, she now began to tell him of her experience —Francis King⟩
ex·trin·si·cal \|əkəl, |ēk-\ *adj* [F *extrinsèque* or L *extrinsecus* + E *-al*] *archaic* **:** EXTRINSIC
ex·trin·si·cal·ly \|ək(ə)lē, |ēk-, -li\ *adv* **:** in an extrinsic manner **:** with regard to what is extrinsic **:** from the outside **:** EXTERNALLY
extrinsic factor *n* **:** a dietary substance that was thought to interact with the intrinsic factor of the gastric secretion to produce the antianemic factor and that is now known to be vitamin B_{12}
extrinsic fraud *n* **:** fraud (as that involved in making a false offer of compromise) that induces one not to present a case or deprives one of the opportunity of being heard; *also* **:** fraud that is not involved in the actual issues presented to a court or jury and that prevents a full and fair hearing
extro- *prefix* [modif. (influenced by *intro-*) of L *extra* — more at EXTRA-] **:** outside **:** outward ⟨*extro*vert⟩ — opposed to *intro-*
ex·trorse \'ek,strórs, ek'stró(ə)rs\ *adj* [prob. fr. (assumed) NL *extrorsus*, fr. LL *extrorsus*, adv., outward, fr. L *extra* + *-orsus* (as in *introrsus* inward) — more at INTRORSE] **:** turned away from the axis of growth ⟨an ~ anther⟩ — compare INTRORSE — **ex·trorse·ly** *adv*
ex·tro·spec·tion \¦ekstrə¦spekshən, -rō¦-\ *n* -S [*extro-* + *-spection* (as in *introspection*)] **:** examination or observation of what is outside oneself — opposed to *introspection*
ex·tro·spec·tive \-ktiv\ *adj* [*extro-* + *-spective* (as in *introspective*)] **:** of, relating to, or marked by extrospection — opposed to *introspective*
ex·tro·ver·sion \¦ekstrə'vər|zhən, -trō'-, -vā|, -vəi| *also* |shən\ *n* -S [*extro-* + L *versus* (past part. of *vertere* to turn) + E *-ion* — more at WORTH] **1 :** EXTROPHY **2** *also* **ex·tra·ver·sion** \-trə'-\ [G, fr. *extra-* (fr. L) or *extro-* (alter. of *extra-*) + L *versus* + G *-ion*] **a** (1) **:** the act of directing attention toward and obtaining gratification from what is outside the self (2) **:** the state of being wholly or predominantly concerned with and interested in what is outside the self **b :** an habitual tendency toward such extroversion — opposed to *introversion*
ex·tro·ver·sive *also* **ex·tra·ver·sive** \¦==¦=|siv *also* |ziv\ *adj* **:** of, relating to, or tending to extroversion — opposed to *introversive* — **ex·tro·ver·sive·ly** \|səvlē, |zə-\ *adv*
¹**ex·tro·vert** *also* **ex·tra·vert** \'==,vər|t, -vә|, -vəi|, ,=='=, *usu* |d·+V\ *vb* -ED/-ING/-S [in sense 1, fr. *extro-* or *extra-* + L *vertere*; in other senses fr. ²·³*extrovert*] *vt* **1** *archaic* **:** to turn or push outward **2 :** to cause to be extroversive **:** make an extrovert of **:** cause to be an extrovert **:** produce extroversion in — opposed to *introvert* **~** *vi* **:** to become extroversive **:** become an extrovert **:** act in an extroversive manner
²**extrovert** *also* **extravert** \'==,=\ *adj* [modif. of G *extrovertiert, extravertiert*, fr. *extra-* or *extro-* + *-vertiert* (fr. L *vertere*)] **:** EXTROVERTED
³**extrovert** *also* **extravert** \"\ *n* -S **1 :** one whose attention and interests are directed wholly or predominantly toward what is outside the self **:** one characterized by extroversion — opposed to *introvert* **2** [*extro-* or *extra-* + L *vertere*] **:** an extrusile proboscis (as that of certain marine and parasitic worms)
extroverted *also* **extraverted** \'==,==, ,=='==\ *adj* [modif. of G *extrovertiert, extravertiert*] **:** having the characteristics of an extrovert **:** marked by extroversion — opposed to *introverted*
ex·tro·vert·ish \'==,=ish\ *adj* **:** somewhat extroverted
ex·tro·ver·tive *also* **ex·tra·ver·tive** \¦=¦=¦vərd·iv\ *adj* **:** EXTROVERSIVE
ex·trude \ik'strüd, ek-\ *vb* -ED/-ING/-S [L *extrudere*, fr. *ex-* ¹ex- + *trudere* to thrust, push — more at THREAT] *vt* **1 a** (1) **:** to thrust out **:** cause to protrude **:** stick out ⟨an insect *extruding* its proboscis⟩ (2) **:** to cause to emerge by or as if by squeezing out **:** press out ⟨mollusks *extruding* fecal pellets⟩ **:** cause to move to or appear at the surface or the outside ⟨a land upheaval that *extruded* molten rock⟩ **b :** to cast out or get rid of forcibly or violently by or as if by pushing or shoving **:** throw out **:** EJECT, EXPEL ⟨the offender . . . is *extruded* as unworthy of an honorable calling —R.M.MacIver⟩ **2 :** to shape (as metal, plastic, rubber) by forcing through a specially designed opening often after a previous heating of the material or of the opening or of both — compare DRAW *vt* 4e **~** *vi* **1 a :** to jut out as or as if a result of being extruded **:** PROTRUDE, PROJECT ⟨land masses *extruding* into the sea⟩ **b :** to move to or appear at the surface or the outside **:** EMERGE ⟨lava *extruding* from early fissures⟩ **2 :** to undergo shaping done by the process of extruding ⟨a material that does not ~ well⟩
ex·trud·er \-də(r)\ *n* -S **:** one that extrudes; *specif* **:** a machine that shapes materials by the process of extruding
ex·tru·si·ble \-üsəbəl, -üzə-\ *adj* [L *extrusus* + E *-ible*] **:** EXTRUSILE
ex·tru·sile \ik'strü,|sīl, ek-, -|səl, -(,)|sil, |z|\ *adj* [L *extrusus* + E *-ile*] **:** capable of being extruded
ex·tru·sion \ik'strüzhən, ek-\ *n* -S [ML *extrusion-, extrusio*, fr. L *extrusus* (past part. of *extrudere*) + *-ion-, -io* -ion] **1 a :** the act or process of extruding **b :** the fact of being extruded **:** subjection to the act or process of extruding **2 a :** an article or product (as of metal, plastic, rubber) made by the process of extruding **b :** something (as lava or mud) forced out (as through a fissure) upon the earth's surface
¹**ex·tru·sive** \ik'strüsiv, (')ek¦s-, -üziv\ *adj* [*extrusion* + *-ive*] **:** of, relating to, or produced by geological extrusion ⟨volcanic eruptions and other ~ phenomena⟩ ⟨~ rocks formed after lava reached the earth's surface⟩ — contrasted with *intrusive*
²**extrusive** \"\ *n* -S **:** a mass (as an igneous rock) produced by geological extrusion
ex·tu·bate \ek'st(y)ü,bāt, '=,=,=\ *vt* -ED/-ING/-S [¹*ex-* + *tube* + *-ate*] **:** to take a tube out of (as the larynx) — **ex·tu·ba·tion** \,=,=¦bāshən\ *n* -S
ex·tu·ber·ance \ik'st(y)übərən(t)s, ek-\ *n* -S [L *extuberare* to swell out (fr. *ex-* ¹ex- + *tuber* hump, swelling) + E *-ance* — more at TUBER] *archaic* **:** PROTUBERANCE
ex·tu·ber·ant \-nt\ *adj* [L *extuberant-, extuberans*, pres. part. of *extuberare*] *archaic* **:** swelled out
ex·u·ber·ance \ig'züb(ə)rən(t)s, eg-\ *n* -S [F *exubérance*, fr. L *exuberantia*, fr. *exuberant-, exuberans* + *-ia* -y] **1 :** the quality or state of being exuberant **2 :** an act or expression that is marked by exuberance **:** an individual instance of exuberance
ex·u·ber·an·cy \-nsē, -si\ *n* -ES [L *exuberantia*] **:** EXUBERANCE
ex·u·ber·ant \-nt\ *adj* [ME *exuberaunt*, fr. MF *exuberant*, fr. L *exuberant-, exuberans*, pres. part. of *exuberare* to be fruitful, abundant, fr. *ex-* ¹ex- + *uberare* to be fruitful, fr. *uber* fruitful, fertile, fr. *uber* udder — more at UDDER] **1 a** (1) **:** joyously unrestrained and enthusiastic **:** extremely or excessively high-spirited and uninhibited ⟨there were plays which he wrote with an ~ gaiety —Van Wyck Brooks⟩ ⟨her ~ capacity for pleasure —Paul Roche⟩ **:** full of life **:** VIVACIOUS ⟨his warm ~ personality —Douglas Cleverdon⟩ (2) **:** diffuse and undisciplined ⟨~ remarks⟩ **:** effusively inflated **:** excessively ornate or otherwise overdone **:** TURGID, PROFUSE, FLAMBOYANT ⟨a reporter who overwrote his story with ~ images and exaggerated figures —F.L.Mott⟩ ⟨heaping ~ praise on them⟩ **b :** extreme or excessive in degree, size, or extent **:** surpassing fixed, usual, or expected limits ⟨a person of ~ talent⟩ ⟨the nation enjoyed ~ prosperity⟩ ⟨mountains of ~ bulk⟩ ⟨~ zeal⟩ **c :** LAVISH, EXTRAVAGANT, PRODIGAL ⟨that ~ vista of gilding and crimson velvet —Max Beerbohm⟩ **2 a** (1) **:** extremely luxuriant **:** produced in extreme or excessive abundance **:** PLENTIFUL ⟨~ foliage and vegetation⟩ ⟨~ crops⟩ ⟨an ~ growth of hair⟩ (2) *med* **:** characterized by excessive proliferation ⟨~ warts⟩ **b :** extremely fertile or creative **:** richly productive **:** FECUND, FRUITFUL, PROLIFIC ⟨gifted with an ~ imagination⟩ **syn** see PROFUSE
ex·u·ber·ant·ly *adv* **:** in an exuberant manner
ex·u·ber·ant·ness *n* -ES **:** EXUBERANCE
ex·u·ber·ate \-bə,rāt, *usu* -ād·+V\ *vi* -ED/-ING/-S [L *exuberatus*, past part. of *exuberare*] **1** *archaic* **:** OVERFLOW ⟨one whose . . . breast *exuberated* with human kindness —W.M. Thackeray⟩ **2 :** to be exuberant **:** feel exhilarated ⟨*exuberating* in the knowledge of having contributed to victory⟩ **:** show exuberance ⟨an actor who knows how to ~ —James Agate⟩
¹**ex·u·date** \'eksə,dāt, -k(,)sü-, *sometimes* -ksyə- *or* -ks(,)yü-; 'egzə,-, -g(,)zü-, *sometimes* -gzyə- *or* -gz(,)yü-\ *vb* -ED/-ING/-S [L *exsudatus, exudatus*, past part. of *exsudare, exudare* — more at EXUDE] *archaic* **:** EXUDE
²**exudate** \"\ *n* -S [*exude* + *-ate* (n. suffix)] **:** exuded matter; *specif* **:** the material composed of serum, fibrin, and white blood cells in variable amounts that escapes from blood vessels into a superficial lesion or an area of inflammation
ex·u·da·tion \,=(,)=¦dāshən\ *n* -S [LL *exsudation-, exsudatio, exudation-, exudatio*, fr. L *exsudatus, exudatus* + *-ion-, -io* -ion] **1 :** the process of exuding **2 :** EXUDATE
exudation pressure *n* **:** ROOT PRESSURE
ex·ud·a·tive *pronunc at* EXUDE +əd·iv\ *adj* **:** of, relating to, or marked by exudation
ex·u·da·to·ri·um \ig,züdə'tōrēəm, eg- *sometimes* ik,sü- *or* ek,sü- *or* -gz,yü- *or* -ks,yü-\ *n, pl* **exudato·ria** \-ēə\ [NL, fr. L *exsudatus, exudatus* + NL *-orium*] **:** one of the papillae present on certain ant and termite larvae that secrete substances attractive to adults of the same species
ex·ude \ig'züd, eg- *sometimes* ik'süd *or* ek'süd *or* -gz'yüd *or* -ks'yüd\ *vb* -ED/-ING/-S [L *exsudare, exudare*, fr. *ex-* ¹ex- + *sudare* to sweat — more at SWEAT] *vi* **1 a :** to ooze out slowly in small drops through openings (as pores) **:** emerge like drops of sweat ⟨beads of moisture *exuding* from the clammy walls⟩ **b :** to flow slowly out **:** issue slowly forth ⟨a sticky substance *exuded* from the end of the cut branch⟩ **2 :** to undergo diffusion (as of an odor) **:** EMANATE ⟨an air of respectability *exuded* from them⟩ **~** *vt* **1 a :** to discharge slowly in small drops through openings **:** cause to ooze out or to emerge like drops of sweat ⟨pine trees *exuding* resin⟩ **b :** to cause to flow slowly out ⟨tar was *exuded* through the cracks⟩ **2 :** to cause (as a vapor or odor) to spread out in all directions ⟨the bubbling stew *exuded* a delicious aroma⟩ **:** DIFFUSE **:** breathe forth **:** give off ⟨*exuding* the charm which is held to be Irish —John Mason Brown⟩ ⟨a voice that ~*s* confidence —Vance Packard⟩ **:** EXHALE ⟨shawls . . . *exude* the odor of moth balls —John Steinbeck⟩ **syn** see EMIT
¹**ex·ulcerate** \egz+\ *vt* -ED/-ING/-S [L *exulceratus*, past part. of *exulcerare*, fr. *ex-* ¹ex- + *ulcerare* to ulcerate — more at ULCERATE] *archaic* **:** ULCERATE
²**exulcerate** *adj* [L *exulceratus*, past part.] *obs* **:** ULCERATED
ex·ult \ig'zəlt, eg-\ *vb* -ED/-ING/-S [MF *exulter*, fr. L *exsultare, exultare*, lit., to leap up, fr. *ex-* ¹ex- + *-sultare* (fr. *saltare* to leap) — more at SALTANT] *vi* **1** *obs* **:** to leap for joy **2 :** to be extremely joyful **:** be very glad or elated **:** feel great delight **:** experience great happiness ⟨~*ing* over their good luck⟩ **:** feel jubilant **:** rejoice very much esp. with feelings and often an outward display of triumph or exuberant self-satisfaction **:** GLORY ⟨~*ing* in their victory⟩ ⟨who had once ~*ed* in abundant strength —Arnold Bennett⟩ ⟨Indian warriors ~*ing* over their slain enemies⟩ **~** *vt* **:** to cause to exult **:** GLADDEN, DELIGHT ⟨it did not exactly ~ him —W.A.White⟩
ex·ult·ance \-tᵊn(t)s, -tən-\ *or* **ex·ult·an·cy** \-nsē, -si\ *n, pl* **exultances** *or* **exultancies** [LL *exultantia, exultantia*, fr. L *exsultant-, exsultans, exultant-, exultans* + *-ia* -y] **:** EXULTATION
ex·ult·ant \-nt\ *adj* [L *exsultant-, exsultans, exultant-, exultans*, pres. part. of *exsultare, exultare*] **:** filled with extreme joy **:** manifesting triumphant elation **:** JUBILANT ⟨he was ~ and could not conceal his delight —Sherwood Anderson⟩ ⟨the ~ laugh of youth —Ellen Glasgow⟩ — **ex·ult·ant·ly** *adv*
ex·ul·ta·tion \,eksəl'tāshən, ,egzəl- *also* -k,s- *or* -g,z-\ *n* -S [ME *exultacioun*, fr. MF *exultation*, fr. L *exsultation-, exsultatio, exultation-, exultatio*, fr. *exsultatus, exultatus* (past part. of *exsultare, exultare*) + *-ion-, -io* -ion] **1 a :** the act of exulting **b :** the state of being exultant **2 :** very great or triumphant joy **:** joyous transport ⟨the ~ of victory and the thrill of power —John Buchan⟩
ex·ul·tet \ig'zül,tet, eg-\ *n* -S *usu cap* [L *exsultet, exultet* let (it) rejoice, 3d pers. sing. pres. subj. of *exsultare, exultare*] **:** a hymn of praise sung in the Roman Catholic Church at the blessing of the paschal candle on Easter eve
ex·ult·ing·ly *adv* **:** in an exultant manner
ex·um·brel·la \¦ek(,)səm¦brelə\ *n* [NL, fr. *exo-* + *umbrella*] **:** the top of the umbrella of a jellyfish — **ex·um·brel·lar** \-lə(r)\ *adj*
ex·un·da·tion \,ek(,)sən'dāshən\ *n* -S [L *exundation-, exundatio*, fr. *exundatus* (past part. of *exundare* to overflow, fr. *ex-* ¹ex- + *undare* to surge, overflow, fr. *unda* wave, billow) + *-ion-, -io* -ion — more at WATER] *archaic* **:** OVERFLOW, FLOODING
exuperance *n* -S [L *exsuperantia, exuperantia*, fr. *exsuperant-, exsuperans, exuperant-, exuperans* (pres. part. of *exsuperare, exuperare* to excel, surpass, fr. *ex-* ¹ex- + *superare* to rise above, surmount exceed, excel, surpass) + *-ia* -y — more at SUPERABLE] *obs* **:** the amount by which one thing exceeds another; *also* **:** SUPERABUNDANCE
ex·urb \'ek,sərb, 'eg,zərb\ *n* -S [¹*ex-* (out of) + *-urb* (as in *suburb*)] **:** a region or district outside a city and usu. beyond its suburbs that is inhabited chiefly by well-to-do families ⟨the ~ is generally further from New York than the suburb on the same railway line —A.C.Spectorsky⟩ ⟨the city, the suburbs, and the ~*s* —H.S.Commager⟩
ex·ur·ban·ite \ek'sərbə,nīt, eg'zər-, ig'z-\ *n, often attrib* [¹*ex-* + *-urbanite* (as in *suburbanite*)] **:** one that chooses to live in an exurb after residence in the city, that cherishes and preserves an urban manner of living, and that derives income chiefly from urban businesses (as publishing)
ex·ur·bia \-bēə\ *n* -S [¹*ex-* + *-urbia* (as in *suburbia*)] **:** the generalized region of exurbs ⟨commuting to New York from ~⟩
ex·ute \ig'züt\ *vt* -ED/-ING/-S [L *exutus*, past part. of *exuere*] *archaic* **:** STRIP ⟨*exuted* of all his preferments —Robert Southey⟩
ex·u·vi·ae \ig'züvē,ē, eg-\ *n pl* [L, fr. *exuere* to take off, fr. *ex-* ¹ex- + *-uere* to put on; akin to ORuss *izuti* to take off shoes and stockings, Arm *aganim* I put on, Av *aothra-* shoe, and perh. to OIr *fuan* coat] **:** the natural covering of an animal (as the skin of a snake) after it has been sloughed off — **ex·u·vi·al** \-vēəl\ *adj*
ex·u·vi·ate \-vē,āt\ *vb* -ED/-ING/-S [*exuvial* + *-ate*] **:** MOLT — **ex·u·vi·a·tion** \ig,==¦āshən, (,)eg,-\ *n* -S
¹**ex-vo·to** \eks'vōd·(,)ō, -vō(,)tō\ *n* -S [L *ex voto* according to a vow] **:** a votive offering
²**ex-voto** \(')=¦=(,)=\ *adj* **:** VOTIVE
exx *abbr* **1** examples **2** executrix
-ey — see -Y, -IE
ey·ak \'ī,ak, 'ē,-\ *n, pl* **eyak** *or* **eyaks** *usu cap* [fr. *Eyak*, lake, village, & river in Alaska] **1 a :** an Indian people of the Copper river delta in Alaska **b :** a member of such people **2 a :** the language of the Eyak people **b :** a language stock of the Na-dene phylum comprising only Eyak
ey·as *or* **ey·ess** \'īəs\ *n* -ES [ME, alter. (resulting fr. incorrect division of *a neias*) of *neias, nyesse*, fr. MF *niais* fresh from the nest, fr. (assumed) VL *nidax* nestling, fr. L *nidus* nest — more at NEST] **1 :** an unfledged bird; *specif* **:** a nestling hawk

2 : a hawk or falcon taken young from the nest for training — compare HAGGARD

¹eye \ˈī\ *n* -s [ME *eie, eye, eighe*, fr. OE *ēage*; akin to OHG *ouga* eye, ON *auga*, Goth *augo*, L *oculus* eye, Gk *osse* (two) eyes, *ōps* eye, face, Skt *akṣi* eye] **1 a** (1) : an organ of sight consisting typically of a light-recipient mechanism that by variation of state of pigmentation or refractive index or by muscular or other adjustment regulates the light that reaches a light-sensitive region which projects sensory stimuli due to impinging light to the central nervous system : PHOTORECEPTOR : the human eyeball protected by movable upper and lower eyelids, movable in its bony orbit by means of four rectus and two oblique muscles, and having externally a tough fibrous sclerotic coat of which the anterior one sixth forms the transparent cornea, a middle highly vascular coat modified anteriorly into the iris, ciliary body, and related structures separated from the cornea by the anterior chamber of the eye and posteriorly into the choroid that underlies the retina, and the retina which is an inner receptive layer, lining the posterior and lateral walls of the large posterior chamber of the eye and on which light passing through the cornea and pupil of the iris is focused by a crystalline lens to form an inverted image of objects in the visual field that is transmitted along sensory paths of the optic nerves to the brain — see ACCOMMODATION 6, VISION 3b; compare FOCUS 2, IMAGE 2a (2) : the eye and any closely associated supporting or protective structures (as an eyelid, eyelash, or eyebrow) : the whole region within and surrounding the orbit of the eye (3) : the iris of the eye; *specif* : the distinctively colored anterior surface of the iris ⟨a girl with blue ~*s*⟩ **b** (1) : the faculty of seeing with or as if with the eyes ⟨a keen ~ for significant detail —C.A.Lejeune⟩ : SIGHT, VISION : power of perceiving physically or mentally ⟨a good ~ for what is essential⟩ (2) : the ability to see very keenly or with special clarity : keen discernment : keen discrimination and appreciation ⟨an ~ for beauty⟩ ⟨he has an artist's ~⟩ (3) : range of vision : VISUAL FIELD **c** (1) : LOOK, GLANCE, GAZE, VIEW ⟨peering through the window with an eager ~⟩ ⟨universities have cast a critical ~ on both the methods and the materials —R. de Kieffer⟩ ⟨they were often in the public ~⟩ (2) : a very attentive look : close watch : close observation or supervision : SCRUTINY ⟨the workmen were at almost all times immediately under the ~ of their employers —Ben Riker⟩ ⟨I've got to keep an ~ on the road —Ellen Glasgow⟩ **d** : POINT OF VIEW : way of looking at something : JUDGMENT ⟨in the ~ of the law⟩ ⟨in his ~*s* she was beautiful —Edith Sitwell⟩ **2** : something having an appearance suggestive of an eye: as **a** (1) : the hole through the head of a needle (2) : a hole designed to receive a rope, shaft hook, or other object; *specif* : a hole in an implement (as an ax or hammer) designed for the insertion of a handle (3) : the hole in an upper millstone (4) : the central opening in a centrifugal impeller **b** : one of the holes formed in some cheeses (as Swiss cheese) during ripening **c** (1) : a usu. circular marking (as on a peacock's tail or on the wings of a butterfly); *also* : a small dark spot (as on an egg) (2) : a bright spot, band, or circular area (as of light) ⟨the trolley car rumbled toward them, a clanking ~ of light in the distance —Irwin Shaw⟩ (3) : an aggregate of minerals exposed in the surface of a rock and having an appearance contrasting with the surface so as to form a more or less conspicuous area **d** (1) : a loop (as at the end of a rope) (2) : a loop (as of thread) or other catch (as a transverse piece of metal) designed to receive a hook (as for fastening together the opposite edges of a garment) ⟨hooks and ~*s* on a dress⟩ (3) : a bound or stitched slit or a loop through which a button is passed : BUTTONHOLE (4) : a ring through which a rod (as for a curtain) is passed (5) : a loop at either end of the bowstring of an archer's bow used for attaching the string to the bow (6) : a loop bent in the end of the shank of a fishhook or a hole drilled through the shank for attaching a line or leader **e** (1) : an undeveloped bud (as on a potato) (2) : the depression at the calyx end of some fruits (as apples or pears) (3) : the hilum (as of a bean) **f eyes** *pl* : CRAB'S-EYE **g** (1) : the opening from which the water of a spring wells out of the earth (2) : an opening that leads into a mine shaft (3) : an opening at the top of a cupola — compare OCULUS (4) : a peephole in the walls of a furnace (5) : an aperture through which light enters; *specif* : the lens of a camera **h** : an area like a hole or column in the center of a tropical cyclone marked by only light winds or complete calm with no precipitation and sometimes by a sunlit clear sky ⟨the ~ of a hurricane⟩ **i** : the center of a flower esp. when differently colored or marked : the disk in composites **j** (1) : the indentation on the inside of a bivalve shell (as the oyster) where the adductor muscle is inserted : CICATRIX (2) : the adductor muscle of a bivalve mollusk esp. when used as food ⟨the ~*s* of scallops⟩ (3) : the osculum of a fibrous sponge **k** (1) : a triangular piece of beef cut from between the top and bottom of the round (2) : the chief muscle of a chop (3) : a compact mass of muscular tissue usu. embedded in fat in a rib or loin cut of meat **l** : a very small nugget of gold or platinum **m** : a device (as a photoelectric cell) that functions in a manner analogous to human vision : ELECTRIC EYE **3** : something that is central or is felt to be central (as in location or importance) : focal point : CENTER **4** *obs* : a light touch of color : TINGE **5 a** : the direction from which the wind is blowing ⟨sailing into the wind's ~⟩ **b eyes** *pl* : the forward part in the bows of a ship near the hawseholes **6** *slang* : DETECTIVE ⟨a private ~⟩ **7** : MELATOPE — **all eyes** : marked by rapt attention to something seen or about to be seen ⟨she was *all eyes* as I unwrapped the package⟩ — **all one's eye** *or* **all the eye** *or* **all in the eye** *chiefly Brit* : utter nonsense ⟨their opinions are *all my eye*⟩ — **at eye** : at a glance : without effort — **cut an eye 1** *archaic* : to cast a look : GLANCE **2** *archaic* : to make eyes — **do in the eye** : to take complete and unfair advantage of (as by trickery) ⟨born to *do* the other fellow *in the eye* and enjoy life —Alva Johnston⟩ — **give an eye to** : to look after : give attention to ⟨go into the garden and *give an eye to* your children —Katherine Mansfield⟩ — **give the big eye** : to make eyes — usu. used with *to* — **give the eye to** : to look at ⟨people walk past here just to *give me the eye* —Joseph Mitchell⟩ esp. in admiration or with a more or less open display of sexual interest ⟨sailors *giving the eye to* every girl in the port⟩ — **have an eye to 1** : to look after : give attention to **2** : to have as an objective ⟨*having an eye to* the furnishing of a new flat —Sam Pollock⟩ — **have eyes only for 1** : to look at nothing else but **2** : to desire nothing else but — **have in one's eye** : to have in mind : have a mental picture of ⟨I *have* one particular friend *in my eye* at this moment —A.C.Benson⟩ — **have one's eye on 1** : to look at **2** : to watch constantly and attentively : keep one's eyes on **3** : to have as an objective — **in a pig's eye** *slang* : by no means : under no circumstances : NEVER — **keep an eye out** : to be on the lookout : keep watch attentively and expectantly ⟨*keep an eye out* for modern trends in school designs —Cecile Starr⟩ — **keep one's eyes open** *or* **keep one's eyes peeled** *also* **keep one's eyes skinned** : to be on the alert : be watchful : be careful — **make eyes** : to look with a more or less open display of sexual interest : gaze amorously : FLIRT, OGLE ⟨a waitress *making eyes* at every customer⟩ — **my eye** — used to express mild disagreement or sometimes surprise ⟨you can do it as well as he can, *my eye!*⟩ — **see eye to eye** : to be in entire agreement : agree without exception ⟨we *see eye to eye* in everything we do⟩ — **set one's eyes by** : to have a great affection for : esteem highly — **throw eyes at** *or* **throw the eye at** *chiefly Austral* : to make eyes at ⟨jealous because her young man began to *throw eyes at* me —Rex Ingamells⟩ — **to the eye** : in appearance : on the surface : APPARENTLY ⟨prejudices that *to the eye* are rather complex —W.S.White⟩ — **up to one's eyes** *or* **up to the eyes** : extremely busy : very much occupied : deeply immersed ⟨*up to their eyes* in paper work⟩ — **with an eye to** : with a view to ⟨*with an eye to* the future⟩ : with the object of ⟨*with an eye to* robbing him —S.M.Fitzgerald⟩ — **with half an eye** : with only a hurried glance : without paying full attention ⟨*with half an eye* he could see what their plan was⟩

eye, 1 a (1): *1* optic nerve, *2* blind spot, *3* sclera, *4* anterior chamber, *5* cornea, *6* lens, *7* pupil, *8* iris, *9* posterior chamber, *10* suspensory ligament, *11* conjunctiva, *12* choroid, *13* macula and fovea, *14* ciliary muscle

²eye \"\ *vb* **eyed; eyed; eyeing** *or* **eying; eyes** [ME *eyen*, fr. *eie, eye*, n.] *vt* **1 a** : to fix the eyes on : turn the eyes toward ⟨after speaking with her he *eyed* the letter she was carrying⟩ : look at : look upon : VIEW : gaze upon ⟨the child *eyed* the wonder from a safe distance —Edison Marshall⟩ : stare at ⟨the detective *eyed* the bald man searchingly —T. M.Johnson⟩ **b** *archaic* : to have a visual perception of : get a look at : catch sight of : SEE **2 a** : to keep a close watch on : watch carefully : study closely : keep an eye on ⟨*eyeing* every change in the stock market⟩ **b** : to have or keep (as an objective or point of reference) in view : look to ⟨the cold calculations of statesmen *eyeing* the national advantage —Oscar Handlin⟩ : aim at **3** : to furnish with an eye : make an eye in **4** : to remove the undeveloped buds of (a potato) ~ *vi* **1** *obs* : to appear to the eye : SEEM, LOOK ⟨they do not ~ well to you —Shak.⟩ **2** : to become eyed ⟨in 30 to 45 days the eggs begin to ~ up —*Scientific American*⟩

eye·able \ˈīəbəl\ *adj* : **1** *archaic* : that may be seen **2** *archaic* : visually attractive

eye agate *n* : ALEPPO STONE

eye appeal *n* : visual attractiveness — **eye-appealing** \ˈ⸗,⸗ˈ⸗⸗\ *adj*

eye backer *or* **eye bender** *n* : an operator of a machine for forming the eyes of leaf springs

¹eyeball \ˈ⸗,⸗\ *n* [¹*eye* + *ball*] : the more or less globular capsule of the eye of vertebrates that is formed by the sclera and cornea together with its contained structures : the ball of the eye : the eye proper

²eyeball \"\ *vt, slang* : to look at intently or fixedly : stare at : EYE ⟨his triggermen huddled over a table in the corner, ~*ing* me —Milton Mezzrow & Bernard Wolfe⟩

eyebalm \ˈ⸗,⸗\ *n* : GOLDENSEAL

eye bank *n* : a storage place for a reserve supply of human corneas removed from the newly dead for transplanting to the eyes of those blinded because of defects of the cornea

eyebar \ˈ⸗,⸗\ *n* : a metal bar that is usu. rectangular in cross section and that is enlarged at each end for holes forming eyes; *sometimes* : I BAR

eye-beam \ˈ⸗,⸗\ *n, archaic* : a radiant glance of the eye

eyeberry \ˈī-— *see* BERRY\ *n* **1** : PARTRIDGEBERRY 1 **2** : WINTERGREEN 2a

eyebolt \ˈ⸗,⸗\ *n* : a bolt with a looped head or an opening in the head

eye bone *n* : one of the ossified plates in the sclera of the eye that are esp. well developed in birds and many reptiles

eyebright \ˈ⸗,⸗\ *n, pl* **eyebrights** *or* **eyebright 1** : any of several herbs of the genus *Euphrasia* (esp. *E. officinalis* of Europe) formerly regarded as a remedy for eye ailments **2 a** : SCARLET PIMPERNEL **b** : INDIAN TOBACCO **c** : INDIAN PIPE **d** : GERMANDER SPEEDWELL **e** : a sundew (*Drosera rotundifolia*) **f** : BLUET 1c(1)

eyebolt

¹eyebrow \ˈ⸗,⸗\ *n* [ME, fr. *eie, eye* eye + *brow*] **1 a** : the arch or ridge over the eye; *also* : the covering of hair growing on this ridge **b** : the narrow surface between the upper border of the orbit and the orbital cavity of fiddler crabs **2 a** : a molding over a window **b** : FILLET 4 **c** : a low dormer over which the roofing is carried in wave line **3** : a projection above an air port to divert water trickling down the side of a ship — called also *wriggle* **4** : fibrous waste that accumulates on machines during the spinning of yarn and that often forms defects in the yarn

²eyebrow \"\ *vi* : to form eyebrow (sense 4)

eyebrow pencil *n* : a cosmetic pencil for the eyebrows

eye-catcher \ˈ⸗,⸗⸗\ *n* : something that strongly attracts the eye ⟨ads that were real *eye-catchers*⟩

eye-catching \ˈ⸗,⸗⸗\ *adj* : strongly attracting the eye : STRIKING ⟨*eye-catching* posters⟩

eye color *n* : pigmentation of the iris in man

eyecup \ˈ⸗,⸗\ *n* **1 a** : a small oval cup that has a rim curved to fit the orbit of the eye and that is used for bathing the eyes or for applying liquid remedies to them **b** : an oval part shaped like a cup that extends backward from each of the rims of a pair of goggles and that is designed to fit snugly about the orbit of the eye so as to give the eye added protection from sparks or other hazards **2** : a round hollowed piece with a peephole in it on the rear sight of a firearm

eyecup 1a

eyed \ˈīd\ *adj* [ME *eied, eyed*, fr. *eie, eye* + *-ed*] **1 a** : having eyes ⟨now they were swimming, making a long ~ line —A.B.Guthrie⟩ or an eye ⟨an ~ fishhook⟩ **b** : having markings suggestive of eyes ⟨~ like a peacock —John Keats⟩ **2** *of a fish egg* : developed to the point that the eyes are clearly visible

eye dialect *n* : the use of misspellings that are based on standard pronunciations (as *sez* for *says* or *kow* for *cow*) but are usu. intended to suggest a speaker's illiteracy or his use of generally nonstandard pronunciations

eyed·ness \ˈī(ə)dnəs\ *n* -ES : preference for the use of one or the other eye (as in sighting a gun) — compare HANDEDNESS

eye doctor *n* : a specialist (as an optometrist or ophthalmologist) in the examination, treatment, or care of the eyes

eye draft *n* : a drawing made from sight

eyedropper \ˈ⸗,⸗⸗\ *n* : DROPPER 4a

eye·drop·per·ful \ˈ⸗,⸗⸗,fu̇l\ *n* -s : the amount held by an eyedropper

eyed skate *n* : WINTER SKATE

eyed skink *n* : a bronzy insectivorous skink (*Chalcides ocellatus*) marked with black spots that is native to Asia Minor but sometimes kept in terraria

eye-ear plane *n* : a conventional position in which a human skull is placed for craniometric study marked so that the lower margin of the orbits is on the same horizontal plane as the upper margin of the auditory meatus — called also *Frankfurt horizontal*

eye-filling \ˈ⸗,⸗⸗\ *adj* : visually attractive : EYE-APPEALING

eye fold *n* : EPICANTHIC FOLD

eye·ful \ˈī,fu̇l\ *n* -s **1 a** : a full or completely satisfying view : a good look : all that one could want to see ⟨they wanted to see life in the raw and they got a real ~⟩ **b** : something or someone visually attractive; *esp* : a strikingly beautiful woman **2** : a quantity of something thrown into the eye

eyeglass \ˈ⸗,⸗\ *n* **1 a** *obs* : the lens of the eye **b** : the eyepiece of an optical instrument (as a microscope or a telescope) **c** : a lens for personal wear that is used to aid vision or correct defects of vision; *specif* : MONOCLE **d eyeglasses** *pl* : GLASSES, SPECTACLES **2** : EYECUP 1a

eye·glassed \ˈī,glast, -laa(ə)st,-laist,-lȧst\ *adj* [*eyeglasses* + *-ed*] : wearing eyeglasses

eye·glassy \-sē\ *adj* [*eyeglass* (monocle) + *-y*] : SNOBBISH

eye gnat *or* **eye fly** *n* : a small fly attracted (as by lachrymal secretions) to the eyes of man or other animals — compare CHLOROPIDAE

eyeground \ˈ⸗,⸗\ *n* : the fundus of the eye; *esp* : the retina as viewed through an ophthalmoscope

eyehole \ˈ⸗,⸗\ *n* **1** : one of the orbits of the skull **2** : a hole (as in a mask) through which one looks : PEEPHOLE

eye indexing *n* : the indexing of potatoes that is done by preplanting an eye of each potato — called also *tuber indexing*

eyeing *pres part of* EYE

eye·ish \ˈīish, ˈēsh\ *n, pl* **eyeish** *usu cap* [Sp *ayas*, of AmerInd origin] **1** : a Caddo people of northeastern Texas **2** : a member of the Eyeish people

eyelash \ˈ⸗,⸗\ *n* : the fringe of hair that edges the eyelid; *usu* : a single hair of this fringe

eye lens *n* : the lens nearest the eye in an eyepiece

eye·less \ˈīləs\ *adj* **1 a** (1) : having no natural eyes : lacking eyes ⟨~ fishes in caves⟩ (2) : being without an eye or eyes ⟨an ~ needle⟩ **b** : no longer having one's natural eyes : having had the eyes removed : deprived of one's eyes : made sightless : BLINDED ⟨blind as an ~ beggar —Dorothy Sayers⟩ **2 a** : lacking sight : BLIND ⟨the dread of being ~⟩ **b** : not using the eyes : failing to use the eyes : moving or acting blindly ⟨an ~ leader⟩ — **eye·less·ness** *n* -ES

¹eye·let \ˈīlət, *usu* -əd·+V\ *n* -s [ME *oilet*, fr. MF *oillet*, dim. of *oil* eye, fr. L *oculus* — more at EYE] **1 a** : a small hole usu. round and buttonholed and designed to receive a cord, lace, pin, or button shank or used only for decoration (as in embroidery) **b** (1) : a small ring of durable material typically metal that is inserted into an eyelet to reinforce it : GROMMET; *also* : a small barrel-shaped piece of such material (2) : an eyelet (as of a shoe or a mailbag or at the edge of a sail) that is reinforced with such a ring or piece or that is lined with such material **2** : a small hole (as in a wall) usu. for observation : PEEPHOLE, EYEHOLE, LOOPHOLE **3** : a small eye; *specif* : OCELLUS

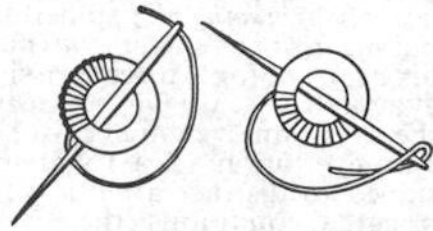
eyelets 1a

²eyelet \"\ *vt* **eyeleted** *also* **eyeletted; eyeleted** *also* **eyeletted; eyeleting** *also* **eyeletting; eyelets** : to make an eyelet in : equip with eyelets — **eye·let·er** *also* **eye·let·ter** \-lə̇d·ə(r), -lətə-\ *n* -s

eye·le·teer \ˌīləˈti(ə)r\ *n* -s : a small instrument with a sharp point used in making eyelet holes

eyelid \ˈ⸗,⸗\ *n* [ME *eielid, eyelid*, fr. *eie, eye* + *lid*] : one of the movable lids of skin with which an animal covers or uncovers the eyeball, most vertebrates above fishes having both an upper lid and a lower lid and many of them having also a nictitating membrane

eyelike \ˈ⸗,⸗\ *adj* : resembling or suggestive of an eye ⟨~ markings on a butterfly's wings⟩

eyeline \ˈ⸗,⸗\ *n* **1** : the level of the eyes : eye level ⟨above his ~ he saw her frown —Richard Llewellyn⟩ **2** : a linear ridge connecting each eye with the glabella in most early trilobites

eye-minded \ˈ⸗,⸗⸗\ *adj* : marked by a predominance of visual imagery in one's thought processes or mental productions : given to extensive or excessive visualization in one's mental operations — compare EAR-MINDED, MOTOR-MINDED — **eye-mind·ed·ness** *n* -ES

eye muscle *n* : either of two long large muscles one of which runs along the right side of the backbone and the other along the left side of the backbone — called also *longissimus dorsi*

eye·n \ˈīən\ *archaic pl of* EYE

eye-opener \ˈ⸗,⸗(⸗)⸗\ *n* **1** : a drink intended to wake one up fully or clear one's head esp. when taken early in the day or shortly after awakening **2 a** : something that opens one's eyes with astonishment or that causes one to stare or gape **b** : something (as a sudden or unexpected disclosure, experience, or occurrence) that causes great surprise and that makes inescapably clear or certain what had not been realized ⟨news of the industry's collapse was an *eye-opener*⟩ : something very enlightening or revealing ⟨the book was an *eye-opener* to complacent party members⟩ **c** : something or someone of remarkable and often startling visual attractiveness ⟨she was a real *eye-opener*⟩

eye-opening \ˈ⸗,⸗(⸗)⸗\ *adj* : that opens the eyes (as with astonishment) : most surprising or enlightening

eyepiece \ˈ⸗,⸗\ *n* **1** : the lens or combination of lenses at the eye end of an optical instrument (as a telescope) through which the image is viewed — see PRISM BINOCULAR illustration **2 a** : a piece of transparent material (as mica) that resists intense heat and that is mounted and fitted in the side of a furnace to permit a view of the interior **b** : a piece of transparent material (as glass) that is mounted and fitted in the facepiece of a gas mask or other respirator to permit vision

eyepiece micrometer *n* : a scale in the field of vision of an eyepiece used as a measuring device — called also *ocular micrometer*

eyepit \ˈ⸗,⸗\ *n* : EYEHOLE

eyepoint \ˈ⸗,⸗\ *n* : the point at which the eye is placed in using an optical instrument (as a microscope) and which is coincident with the exit pupil of the instrument

eye-popper \ˈ⸗,⸗⸗\ *n* **1** : something that astonishes : EYE-OPENER **2** : something thrilling or exciting ⟨a Western novel that's a surefire *eye-popper*⟩

eye-popping \ˈ⸗,⸗⸗\ *adj* **1** : EYE-OPENING **2** : thrilling or exciting ⟨the climber has an *eye-popping* view the full length of Zion Canyon —L.F.Clark⟩

ey·er \ˈī(ə)r, ˈīə\ *n* -s : one that eyes

eye relief *n* : the distance of the eye from the eye lens of an optical instrument that is best suited to the use of the instrument

eye rhyme *n* : an imperfect rhyme that appears to have identical vowel sounds from similarity of spelling (as *move* and *love* or *bough* and *though*) or that arises from a former similarity of vowel sound (as *far* and *war*)

eye-ring \ˈ⸗,⸗\ *n* : the inner margin of the eyelids of a fowl

eyeroot \ˈ⸗,⸗\ *n* : GOLDENSEAL

eyes *pl of* EYE, *pres 3d sing of* EYE

eye screw *n* : a screw (as a wood screw) that has a head in the form of an eye; *often* : such a screw with a head that is not closed

eye-servant \ˈ⸗,⸗⸗\ *n, archaic* : one that attends to duty only when watched

eye-server \ˈ⸗,⸗⸗\ *n, archaic* : EYE-SERVANT

eye-service \ˈ⸗,⸗⸗\ *n, archaic* : attendance to duty only when being watched

eyeshade \ˈ⸗,⸗\ *n* : a visor for shielding the eyes from strong light that is held on the head by a band

eye shadow *n* : a cosmetic cream in various colors that is applied to the eyelids to accent the eyes

eyeshine \ˈ⸗,⸗\ *n* : reflection of light from the inner surface of an eye through the pupil so that the eye has a luminous appearance (as in a cat)

eyeshade

eyeshot \ˈ⸗,⸗\ *n* **1** : the range of the eye : the distance that the eye can see : SIGHT ⟨there wasn't a living soul walking or standing or sitting anywhere within ~ —Dorothy Sayers⟩ **2** *archaic* : a look of the eye : GLANCE

eyesight \ˈ⸗,⸗\ *n* [ME *eiesight, eyesight*, fr. *eie, eye* + *sight*] **1 a** : the faculty of seeing : ability to see : SIGHT, VISION ⟨a young man with good ~⟩ **b** *archaic* : the act of seeing or looking : OBSERVATION **2** *archaic* : EYESHOT

eye socket *n* : ORBIT 1a

eye·some \ˈīsəm\ *adj* [¹*eye* + *-some*] *archaic* : visually attractive

eyesore \ˈ⸗,⸗\ *n* [ME *eiesor, eyesor* soreness or disease of the eye, fr. *eie, eye* + *sor* sore] : something offensive to the sight ⟨the old church and historic burying ground had fallen into decay and had become an ~ —L.H.Beck⟩

eye splice *n* : a splice formed by bending a rope's end back and splicing it into the rope so that a loop is formed

eyespot \ˈ⸗,⸗\ *n* **1 a** : a simple visual organ in many invertebrates that consists of pigment or pigmented cells covering a sensory termination : OCELLUS **b** : a small pigment body in various unicellular algae that is supposedly sensitive to light **2 a** : a usu. small spot of color (as on the wings of certain butterflies) **b** : a darkish area around the hilum of a seed (as some beans and cowpeas) **3** : any of several fungous diseases of plants characterized by yellowish oval lesions on the leaves and stems; *esp* : a disease of sugarcane and various other grasses caused by a fungus (*Helminthosporium sacchari*)

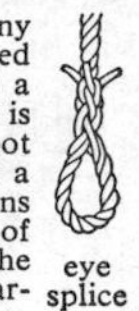
eye splice

eye-spotted \ˈ⸗,⸗⸗\ *adj* : marked by spots of color : having eyespots

eye-spotted bud moth *n* : a dark brown tortricid moth (*Spilonota ocellana*) with a light band on each wing and a dark brown black-headed larva that feeds in a web on fruit buds, leaves, and fruit (as apples or plums)

eyess *var of* EYAS

eyestalk \ˈ=,=\ *n* **:** one of the movable peduncles bearing the eyes at the tip in a decapod crustacean
eyestrain \ˈ=,=\ *n* **:** weariness or strained condition of the eye (as from overuse or uncorrected defects of vision)
eyestrings *n pl, obs* **:** organic eye attachments (as muscles of the eye) once popularly viewed as causing blindness by breaking or as breaking at death
eye·tie *also* **ey·tie** \ˈīd·ē, ˈī,tī\ *adj or n, usu cap* [by shortening & alter.] **:** ITALIAN — usu. used disparagingly
eyetooth \ˈ=ˌ=\ *n, pl* **eyeteeth** **1 :** a canine tooth of the upper jaw **2** *eyeteeth, pl* **:** something of great value — used in the phrase *give one's eyeteeth* ⟨many a young reporter would give his *eyeteeth* for a foreign assignment —F.L.Mott⟩
¹**eyewash** \ˈ=,=\ *n* [¹*eye* + *wash*] **1 a :** a liquid used in bathing the eyes **:** an eye douche **b :** a medicinal solution for the eyes **:** an eye lotion **2 a :** statements, actions, or procedures designed to distract attention from or conceal ulterior motives or actual conditions ⟨the ~ handed out by dictators⟩ **b :** statements, actions, or procedures undertaken merely to make a good impression **:** empty display ⟨disgusted with all the ~ of political campaigns⟩ **c :** pretentious nonsense **:** DRIVEL, CLAPTRAP ⟨preposterous claims that were the purest ~⟩
²**eyewash** \"\ *vt* **:** to give a misleading appearance to **:** doctor up **:** PRETTIFY ⟨he'll line up his peg tents and ~ his base camps with the old parade-ground touch —J.W.Bellah⟩
eyewater \ˈ=,==\ *n* **1** *archaic* **a :** TEARS **b :** AQUEOUS HUMOR **2** *archaic* **:** EYEWASH 1
eyewhite \ˈ=,=\ *n* **:** WHITE 2a(2)
eyewink \ˈ=,=\ *n* **1 :** a wink of the eye **2** *obs* **:** LOOK, GLANCE
eyewinker \ˈ=,==\ *n* **1 :** EYELASH; *also* **:** EYELID **2 :** something (as a foreign particle lodged in the eye) that irritates the eye and causes winking
¹**eyewitness** \ˈ=ˈ==\ *n, often attrib* [¹*eye* + *witness*] **1 :** one that sees or has seen an occurrence or an object with his own eyes and so is able to give a firsthand report on it **:** one that gives a report on or testifies to what he has actually seen ⟨an ~ of the crime⟩ **2** *obs* **:** a report by an eyewitness
²**eyewitness** \"\ *vt* **:** to see with one's own eyes ⟨correspondents who ~*ed* the recent riots —*Time*⟩
eye worm *n* **:** a parasitic worm found in the eye: as **a :** either of two slender nematode worms (*Oxyspirura mansoni* and *O. petrowi*) living beneath the nictitating membrane of the eyes of chickens or other birds **b :** a member of a genus (*Thelazia*) of spiruroid nematodes living in the tear duct and beneath the eyelid of dog, cat, sheep, man, and other mammals and sometimes causing blindness **c :** an African filarial worm (*Loa loa*) that migrates through the subdermal tissues and eyeball of man — compare CALABAR SWELLING
eyewort \ˈ=,=\ *n* [so called fr. its use as a remedy for eye ailments] **:** EYEBRIGHT 1
eying *pres part of* EYE
eyne \ˈīn\ *archaic pl of* EYE
eyot \ˈā(ə)t\ [ME *ait, eit* — more at AIT] *var of* ¹AIT
ey·ra \ˈārə\ *n* -s [AmerSp & Pg, fr. Tupi *eirara, irara*] **:** a solid-colored reddish wildcat usu. regarded as a color phase of the jaguarundi but sometimes considered to constitute a separate species (*Felis eyra* or *Herpailurus eyra*)
eyre \ˈa(a)|(ə)r, ˈe|, |a\ *n* -s [ME *eire*, fr. AF, fr. OF *erre* trip, journey, round, fr. *errer* to travel — more at ERR] **1 :** the circuit court held by justices in eyre **2 :** the record of an eyre
eyrie *var of* AERIE
ey·rir \ˈā,rir\ *n, pl* **au·rar** \ˈœu,rär\ [Icel, fr. ON, ounce (usu. of silver), money (in pl.), prob. fr. L *aureus*, a gold coin — more at AUREUS] **1 :** a unit of monetary value in Iceland worth 1/100 of a krona — see MONEY table **2 :** a small coin representing one eyrir unit
ey·ry *like* EYRIE — *see* AERIE\ *archaic var of* AERIE
-eys *pl of* -EY
ey·sell \ˈā|səl, ˈē|, |zəl\ *var of* ESILL
eytie *var of* EYETIE

1f \ˈef\ *n, pl* **f's** *or* **fs** \ˈefs\ *often cap, often attrib* **1 a :** the sixth letter of the English alphabet **b :** an instance of this letter printed, written, or otherwise represented **c :** a speech counterpart of orthographic *f* (as *f* in *fife, wafer,* or Spanish *fuero*) **2 a :** the keynote of F major or F minor **b :** the tone F **3 :** a printer's type, a stamp, or some other instrument for reproducing the letter *f* **4 :** someone or something arbitrarily or conveniently designated *f* esp. as the sixth in order or class **5 a :** a grade assigned by a teacher or examiner rating a student's work as so inferior as to be failing ⟨no student with more than one *F* in a major subject may be advanced to a higher grade without a special examination⟩ **b :** one graded or rated with an F ⟨an *F* student in history⟩ **6 :** something having the shape of the letter F

2f *abbr, often cap* **1** [L *fac*] make **2** Fahrenheit **3** failure **4** fair **5** family **6** farad **7** farthing **8** father **9** fathom **10** fawn **11** feast **12** [L *fecit*] he made **13** fellow **14** female **15** feminine **16** [L *fiat*] let it be done; let it be made **17** fiction **18** field **19** fighter **20** [L *filius*] son **21** filly **22** finance; financial **23** fine **24** finish **25** fire **26** firm **27** fixed **28** flat **29** fleet **30** florin **31** flower **32** fluid **33** fluid ounce **34** fog **35** folio **36** following **37** foot **38** for **39** force **40** forma **41** formed **42** formula **43** forte **44** forward **45** foul **46** fragile **47** fragmentation **48** franc **49** [L *frater*] brother **50** French **51** frequency **52** friar **53** from **54** fuel **55** full **56** function **57** furlong

3f *symbol* **1** *cap* Faraday **2** *cap* luminous flux **3** *cap* filial; filial generation **4** *cap* fluorine **5** focal length **6** *cap* folio **7** the relative aperture of a photographic lens — often written *f/* or *f:*

fa \ˈfä\ *n, pl* **fas** *or* **fa's** [ME, fr. ML, fr. L *famuli* servants, a word sung to this note in a medieval hymn to St. John the Baptist] **1 :** the fourth tone of the diatonic scale in solmization **2 :** the tone *F* in the fixed-do system

fa' \ˈfä, ˈfȯ\ *chiefly Scot var of* FALL

FA *abbr* **1** field artillery **2** financial adviser **3** football association **4** forage acre **5** free alongside **6** free astray **7** free of all average **8** freight agent

FAA *abbr* free of all average

faags \ˈfägz, ˈfagz\ *var of* FEGS

fab *abbr* fabricated

1fa·ba \ˈfäbə\ *n, cap* [NL, fr. L, bean — more at BEAN] *in some classifications* **:** a genus of leguminous plants comprising the broad bean and now usu. included in *Vicia*

2faba *var of* FAVA

fa·ba·ce·ae \fəˈbāsēˌē\ *n pl, cap* [NL, fr. *Faba,* type genus + *-aceae*] *in some classifications* **:** a large nearly cosmopolitan family that comprises the peas, beans, and related herbaceous or woody plants with pealike flowers and a legume as fruit and that is now usu. included in the family Leguminosae

fa·ba·ceous \-āshəs\ *adj* [LL *fabaceus,* fr. L *faba* bean + *-aceus* -aceous] **1 :** of or relating to the Leguminosae **:** LEGUMINOUS **2 :** relating to, like, or being a bean

fabe \ˈfāb\ *n* -s [prob. alter. of ME *theve* bramble, gooseberry — more at FEABERRY] *dial Brit* **:** GOOSEBERRY 1a

fa·bel·la \fəˈbelə\ *n, pl* **fabel·lae** \-eˌlē\ [NL, dim. of L *faba*] **:** a small fibrocartilage ossified in many animals and sometimes in man in the tendon of the gastrocnemius muscle, behind one or both of the femoral condyles

1fa·bi·an \ˈfābēən\ *adj, usu cap* [L *fabianus,* fr. Quintus *Fabius* Maximus Cunctator †203 B.C. Roman dictator and general + L *-anus* -an] **1 a :** of, relating to, or in the manner of the Roman general Quintus Fabius Maximus who defeated Hannibal in the Second Punic War by avoiding decisive contests and harassing him by marches and countermarches **b :** notably conservative and cautious in making advances or changes **2** [*Fabian* (*Society*); fr. the members' belief in slow orderly rather than revolutionary change in government] **:** being or belonging or relating to a society of socialists organized in England in 1884 to spread socialistic principles gradually

2fabian \"\ *n* -s *usu cap* **:** a member of or sympathizer with the Fabian Society of socialists

fa·bi·ana \ˌfābēˈanə, -ˈä- *also* -ˈā-\ *n, cap* [NL, after Francisco *Fabián* y Fuero †1801 Span. archbishop and naturalist] **:** a genus of heathlike evergreen shrubs (family Solanaceae) of Central and So. America that have numerous small white or lavender tubular flowers and are sometimes cultivated in the cool greenhouse or in the open in frost-free areas

fa·bi·an·ism \ˈfābēəˌnizəm\ *n* -s *usu cap* **:** the doctrines or principles of the Fabian socialists

fa·bi·form \ˈfäbəˌfȯrm\ *adj* [L *faba* bean + E *-iform*] **:** shaped like a bean

1fa·ble \ˈfābəl\ *n* -s [ME, fr. MF, fr. L *fabula* conversation, narrative, tale, play, fable, fr. *fari* to speak, say — more at FAME] **1 :** a fictitious narrative or statement **:** an invented tale **:** FICTION: as **a :** UNTRUTH, FALSEHOOD ⟨the ~*s* and misrepresentations of this pamphlet⟩ **b :** a story of supernatural or highly marvelous happenings (as in legend, myth, or folklore) **c :** a narration intended to enforce some useful truth or precept; *esp* **:** one in which animals and even inanimate objects speak and act like human beings ⟨the ~ of the fox in the barnyard⟩ — see BEAST FABLE **d :** casual, idle, or foolish report or talk ⟨old wives' ~*s*⟩; *broadly* **:** common talk **2 a :** a subject of fable **:** something (as a mysterious event) productive of fabulous accounts or explanations; *broadly* **:** a theme of popular talk and speculation ⟨he became the chief ~ of the village⟩ **b :** a product of fable **:** something having reality only in fabulous accounts ⟨if personal immortality is not a ~⟩ **3 :** the plot, story, or connected series of events forming the theme of a literary work (as an epic poem or play) **syn** see ALLEGORY, FICTION

2fable \"\ *vb* **fabled; fabled; fabling** \-b(ə)liŋ\ **fables** [ME *fablen,* fr. MF *fabler,* fr. L *fabulari* to talk, fr. *fabula*] *vi* **1 a :** to compose or tell fictitious tales **b** *obs* **:** to talk idly **2** *archaic* **:** to write or speak what is not true **:** utter falsehoods **:** LIE ~ *vt* **:** to devise and recount as if real **:** report as if literally true ⟨it is *fabled* that Norsemen built the tower⟩ ⟨the bird of paradise was *fabled* to have no feet⟩ ⟨how he fell from Heaven they *fabled* —John Milton⟩

fabled *adj* **1 :** told or mentioned in fable **:** MYTHICAL, LEGENDARY **2 :** having no real existence **:** FICTITIOUS ⟨~ sorrows⟩

fa·ble·ist \-b(ə)ləst\ *n* -s **:** a teller or writer of fables **:** FABULIST

fa·bler \-b(ə)lə(r)\ *n* -s [ME, fr. MF *ableur,* fr. *fabler* + *-eur* -or] **:** FABULIST

fab·li·au \ˈfablēˌō\ *also* **fa·bleau** \faˈblō\ *n, pl* **fabli·aux** *also* **fa·bleaux** \-ō(z)\ [F, fr. OF *fablel, fableau, fabliau,* dim. of *fable*] **:** a short metrical tale of a type composed chiefly by jongleurs for and about the lower classes; *also* **:** the genre of such metrical tales being usu. comic, frankly coarse, and often cynical esp. in their treatment of women

fabling *n* -s [ME, fr. gerund of *fablen* to fable] **:** an act of one who fables **:** ROMANCING, PREVARICATION

fa·braea \fəˈbrēə\ *n, cap* [NL, prob. after Jean H. *Fabre* †1915 Fr. entomologist] **:** a genus of ascomycetous fungi (family Mollisiaceae) that includes several leaf parasites with multicellular ascospores

1fab·ric \ˈfabrik, -rēk\ *n* -s [MF *fabrique,* fr. *fabriquer* to fabricate, fr. L *fabricari,* fr. *fabrica* artisan's workshop, skillfully wrought object, building — more at FORGE] **1 a :** a product of building (as a house or ship) ⟨four high houses . . . of the sort lane-dwellers call ~*s* —Daniel Corkery⟩ **b :** underlying structure **:** FRAMEWORK ⟨the work of restoring the ~ of Westminster Abbey —Conrad Voss Bark⟩ ⟨the very ~ of daily life⟩ ⟨whether the political ~ had the strength to withstand war —S.E.Morrison & H.S.Commager⟩ **2** *obs* **:** CONTRIVANCE, DEVICE; *esp* **:** a military engine **3 :** an act of constructing **:** CONSTRUCTION, ERECTION; *specif* **:** the construction and maintenance of a church building **4 a :** structural plan or style of construction ⟨the whole complex ~ of flowers and floral organs that makes up the head of a composite plant⟩ ⟨soil ~ (arrangement of the constituents of the soil in relation to each other) —L.D.Baver⟩ **b :** TEXTURE, QUALITY — used chiefly of textiles ⟨a linen cloth of fine silky ~⟩ **c :** the form of the planchet of a medal or coin ⟨a coin with thick ~⟩ **5 a** *archaic* **:** something made by man **:** ARTIFACT, PRODUCT ⟨the earliest ~ of the Venetian glassblowers⟩ **b :** CLOTH 1a **c :** cloth of a particular kind ⟨satin is a ~ with a smooth shining surface⟩ or for a particular use ⟨a sheer curtain ~⟩ **d :** a material (as leather or woven wire) that in some respect resembles cloth **6 :** a place devoted to manufacture **:** FACTORY ⟨the chief shapes manufactured in this ~ were bowls —V.G.Childe⟩ **7:** structural material ⟨the more usual ~ was timber or coursed masonry⟩ ⟨using a ~ of silken threads the spider builds her web⟩ **8 :** the appearance or pattern that is produced by the shapes and arrangement of the crystal grains or of these with glass in a rock and that includes those orientation features which are not evident from grain shape alone

2fabric *vt* **fabricked; fabricked; fabricking; fabrics** [F *fabriquer*] *obs* **:** FRAME, BUILD, CONSTRUCT

fab·ri·cant \ˈfabrəkənt\ *n* -s [F, fr. L *fabricant-, fabricans,* pres. part. of *fabricari*] **:** a maker or producer esp. of a commercial product **:** MANUFACTURER

fab·ri·cate \-əˌkāt, *usu* -d·+V\ *vt* -ED/-ING/-S [ME *fabricaten,* fr. L *fabricatus,* past part. of *fabricari* — more at FABRIC] **1 a :** to form by art and labor **:** MANUFACTURE, PRODUCE ⟨*fabricated* some of the finest English pottery⟩ ⟨an organization devoted to *fabricating* deluxe editions of the classics⟩ **b :** to form into a whole by uniting parts **:** CONSTRUCT, BUILD ⟨*fabricated* a bridge of steel beams⟩ ⟨planning to ~ a house of wholly synthetic materials⟩; *often* **:** to build up into a whole by uniting interchangeable standardized parts ⟨*fabricating* automobiles on the assembly line⟩ **2 a :** to make, shape, or prepare (parts) according to standardized specification so as to be interchangeable ⟨*fabricating* brake assemblies for one of the new cars⟩ **b :** to cause (raw material or stock) to be manufactured **:** SHAPE ⟨*fabricating* sheet steel into plates⟩ ⟨what steel to use or how to ~ it —*Dun's Rev.*⟩ **3 a :** INVENT, FORMULATE ⟨philosophers *fabricating* new theories of the universe⟩ **:** CREATE ⟨his brave attempts to ~ something permanent and holy out of his personal animal feelings —T.S. Eliot⟩ **b** (1) **:** to make up with intent to deceive ⟨*fabricated* an involved explanation of his absence⟩ (2) **:** FORGE **syn** see MAKE

fab·ri·ca·tion \ˌ==ˈkāshən\ *n* -s [ME *fabricacioun,* fr. L *fabrication-, fabricatio,* fr. *fabricatus* + *-ion-, -io* -ion] **1 :** the act or process of fabricating: as **a :** the assembly of materials into a structure ⟨~ of a bridge⟩ **b :** the invention or utterance of something calculated to deceive ⟨the unconscious ~ of an honest man trying to put his best foot forward⟩ **c :** the process of converting one form of metal into another (as ingots into rolled shapes, rolled shapes into structural members, castings into weldments, wire into springs, forgings into gears) **2 :** a product of fabrication: as **a :** FALSEHOOD, DECEIT, FORGERY ⟨all the petty ~*s* with which he hoped to fool his fellows⟩ **b :** a fabricated structure or structural element ⟨the whole ~ of the house⟩ **syn** see FICTION

fabrication-in-transit \ˌ===ˈ===ˈ=\ *n* **:** an arrangement by which a continuous through rate is charged by a transporting agent (as a railway) for articles that are made up into a new form at some point on the way — compare MILLING-IN-TRANSIT

fab·ri·ca·tive \ˈfabrəˌkād·iv\ *adj* **:** tending or able to fabricate **:** concerned with manufacture

fab·ri·ca·tor \-ād·ə(r), -ātə-\ *n* -s [L, fr. *fabricatus* + *-or*] **:** one that fabricates: as **a :** one that invents a false statement or commits forgery **:** LIAR, FORGER **b :** an implement for fabricating; *specif* **:** a neolithic flint used as a tool for fashioning other implements **c :** a workman who shapes, finishes, or assembles objects **d :** a firm or establishment that converts metal from one form into another — compare FABRICATION 1c

fabricature *n* -s *obs* **:** CONSTRUCTION, STRUCTURE

fabric tire *n* **:** a pneumatic tire having a carcass with a woven fabric — compare CORD TIRE

Fab·ri·koid \ˈfabrəˌkȯid\ *trademark* — used for an imitation leather

fa·bro·ni·a·ce·ae \fəˌbrōnēˈāsēˌē\ *n pl, cap* [NL, fr. *Fabronia,* type genus (after G.V.M. *Fabroni* †1822 Ital. naturalist) + *-aceae*] **:** a family of chiefly tropical mosses (order Hypnobryales) that grow on tree trunks and have erect branches and exserted capsules with the operculum beaked

fab·u·la \ˈfabyələ\ *n, pl* **fabu·lae** \-yəˌlē\ [L — more at FABLE] **:** STORY; *usu* **:** a traditional tale **:** FOLKTALE

fabula pal·li·a·ta \-ˌpalēˈäd·ə, -ˈād·ə\ *n, pl* **fabulae pallia·tae** \-ˈäd·ˌē, -ˈād·ˌē\ [L, lit., drama in himations; fr. the Greek himations worn by the actors] **:** an ancient Roman comedy based on a Greek model and treating a Greek subject — compare FABULA TOGATA

fabula prae·tex·ta \-prēˈtekstə\ *also* **fabula prae·tex·ta·ta** \-(ˌ)prēˌtekˈstäd·ə, -ād·ə\ *n, pl* **fabulae praetex·tae** \-ˌstē\ [L, lit., drama in praetextae; fr. the praetextae worn by the actors] **:** an ancient Roman drama with a theme from Roman history or legend

fab·u·lar \ˈfabyələ(r)\ *adj* [L *fabularis,* fr. *fabula* + *-aris* -ar] **:** like or relating to fable

fab·u·la·tion \ˌ==ˈlāshən\ *n* -s [*fabulous* + *-ation*] **:** the act of inventing or retailing false or fantastic tales ⟨unrestrained ~*s* and several otherworldly visions —Susan A. Taubes⟩

fabula to·ga·ta \-tōˈgäd·ə, -ād·ə\ *n, pl* **fabulae toga·tae** \-ˈäd·ˌē, -ād·ˌē\ [L, lit., drama in togas; fr. the togas worn by the actors] **:** ancient Roman comedy based on a Greek model but treating native Roman subjects — compare FABULA PALLIATA

fab·u·la·tor \ˈfabyəˌlād·ə(r)\ *n* -s [L, fr. *fabulatus* + *-or*] *archaic* **:** FABULIST

fab·u·list \-ləst\ *n* -s [MF *fabuliste,* fr. L *fabula* tale, fable + MF *-iste* -ist — more at FABLE] **1 :** a creator or writer of fables esp. that carry a moral lesson **2** *obs* **:** a professional teller of tales **3 :** an inventor of falsehoods **:** LIAR, PREVARICATOR

fab·u·lize \-ˌlīz\ *vt* -ED/-ING/-S [L *fabula* + E *-ize*] **:** FABLE; *esp* **:** to give a false account of

fab·u·los·i·ty \ˌ==ˈläsəd·ē\ *n* -ES [L *fabulositas,* fr. *fabulosus* fabulous + *-itas* -ity] **1 :** fabulous quality or character **2** *archaic* **:** a fabulous statement or tale **:** FABLE

fab·u·lous \ˈfabyələs\ *adj* [ME, fr. L *fabulosus,* fr. *fabula* + *-osus* -ous] **1 :** given to telling fables **2 :** celebrated or known from fables only **:** belonging to fables alone **:** not real, actual, or historical ⟨the ~ mill which ground old people young —Charles Dickens⟩ ⟨the ~ German smith, who made feather clothes for flight —Lewis Mumford⟩ **3 a :** characteristic of fables **:** like the contents of fables in being marvelous, incredible, absurd, extreme, exaggerated, or approaching the impossible ⟨a hero who, after many ~ exploits . . . , bolted to the Spanish Main —G.B.Shaw⟩ ⟨[Lincoln] grows vaguer and more ~ as year follows year —H.L.Mencken⟩ **b :** outstanding or remarkable esp. in some acceptable or pleasing quality ⟨a ~ year for the Republicans —*New Republic*⟩ ⟨the ~ view of the mountains from her porch⟩ ⟨~ jewelry⟩ ⟨a career . . . recognized as the most famous and ~ in U.S. diplomacy —Claude Pepper⟩ **syn** see FICTITIOUS

fab·u·lous·ly *adv* **:** in a fabulous manner **:** to a fabulous degree or extent **:** VERY, EXTREMELY, EXCESSIVELY ⟨~ expensive clothes⟩

fab·u·lous·ness *n* -ES **:** the quality or state of being fabulous

fa·bur·den \ˈfabə(r)dᵊn\ *n* -s [ME *faburdoun,* fr. MF *faux-bourdon* — more at FAUXBOURDON] **:** FAUXBOURDON

fac *abbr* **1** facsimile **2** factor **3** factory **4** faculty

1fa·cade *also* **fa·çade** \fəˈsäd, -sad *also* faˈ-\ *n* -s [F *façade,* fr. It *facciata,* fr. *faccia* face (fr. — assumed — VL *facia*) + *-ata* -ade] **1 a :** the front of a building **b :** a face (as a flank or rear facing on a street or court) of a building that is given emphasis by special architectural treatment **2 :** a false, superficial, or artificial appearance or effect ⟨maintaining a ~ of contentment⟩ ⟨in the winter of 1929 the brilliant ~ of American prosperity fell into ruin almost overnight —*Times Lit. Supp.*⟩ **:** FACE, FRONT; *often* **:** FALSE FRONT 1

facade 1a

2facade *also* **façade** \"\ *vt* -ED/-ING/-S **:** to impose a facade on ⟨*facading* civilization with formalities⟩ ⟨a building *facaded* with white tile⟩

1face \ˈfās\ *n* -s *often attrib* [ME, fr. OF, fr. (assumed) VL *facia,* fr. L *facies* form, shape, face, fr. *facere* to make, do — more at DO] **1 a :** the front part of the human head including the chin, mouth, nose, cheeks, eyes, and usu. forehead **:** VISAGE, COUNTENANCE **b :** the corresponding part of the head of a lower animal **c :** the part of the vertebrate skull in front of and below the cranium and including the nasal region, jaws, and associated structures **d :** the part of the insect head lying anterior to the vertex, above the mouth, and between the compound eyes **2** *archaic* **:** PRESENCE, SIGHT, VIEW ⟨thou fleddest from the ~ of Esau —Gen 35:1 (AV)⟩ **3 a :** cast of features as expressing emotion or character **:** expression of countenance ⟨a grave stern ~⟩ ⟨turned an angry ~ on his erring son⟩ **b :** beauty or glory of countenance ⟨in ~ far exceeding her sisters⟩ ⟨the Lord make his ~ shine upon thee —Num 6:25 (AV)⟩ **4 a :** outward appearance or aspect **:** SEMBLANCE ⟨the whole village presented a ~ of placid contentment⟩ **:** visible or apparent state or condition ⟨his report put a new ~ on the matter⟩; *also* **:** a cursory or superficial examination or its result ⟨this testimony is false on the ~ of it⟩ ⟨on the ~ of your report I have no valid objection to raise⟩ **b :** an outward appearance of dignity or prestige or of freedom from abashment, confusion, anger, or distress ⟨though he was obviously distressed he put the best ~ he could on the matter⟩; *broadly* **:** DISGUISE, PRETENSE **c :** ASSURANCE, CONFIDENCE ⟨maintaining a firm ~ in spite of adversity⟩; *often* **:** brash or bold conduct or outlook **:** EFFRONTERY ⟨how anyone could have the ~ to ask such a question⟩ — compare CHEEK, NERVE **d :** DIGNITY, PRESTIGE ⟨a man of considerable ~ in the local community⟩ ⟨trying to save ~⟩; *also* **:** concern for or preservation of one's prestige ⟨~ is sometimes a major consideration in diplomatic negotiations⟩ **5 a :** GRIMACE, MOUE; *esp* **:** an expression of distaste ⟨made a ~ at the taste of the medicine⟩ **b :** MASK ⟨the children bought some funny ~*s* for the party⟩ **c :** facial makeup ⟨she'll be here as soon as she gets her ~ on⟩ **6 a :** the surface of something esp. where only one surface is commonly considered ⟨mist moving over the ~ of the water⟩ ⟨driven from the ~ of the earth⟩ **b** (1) **:** the physical features (as of a country) (2) *obs* **:** a description of a country in its physical features **7 :** a front, upper, or outer surface or a surface presented to view or regarded as principal: as **a :** the front of anything having two or four sides — opposed to *back;* usu. distinguished from *side* **b :** the facade esp. of a building **c :** an exposed surface of rock (as in a wall or a cliff) **d :** one of the broad surfaces of a coin **:** an obverse or reverse ⟨lettering on the edge as well as on the ~ of a coin⟩; *also* **:** the obverse of a currency note **e :** the dial of a watch or clock ⟨a watch with a black enamel ~ and raised gold figures⟩ **f :** any of the plane surfaces that bound a polyhedron (as a crystal) or other geometrical solid **g :** the grille of a hot-air or cold-air register **8 :** a side or surface dressed, finished, or specially prepared: **a :** the principal dressed surface (as of a plate, disk, or pulley) **b :** the dressed side of a board finished only on one surface; *sometimes* **:** the side having the better appearance or quality when both are dressed **c :** the right side (as of cloth or leather); *esp* **:** the front side of a fabric in which that side is distinguished from the back by differences of finish, weave, or appearance **d :** the inscribed or printed side of something (as a document or a leaf bearing a map or illustration) that has one blank surface; *broadly* **:** the side of something inscribed or printed on both sides that can be considered the front (as by reason of containing major matter) ⟨the ~ of a stock certificate⟩ **e :** the variously colored scoring surface of a target **f :** the front side of a book or book cover **g :** the side of a playing card that is marked to designate its rank and suit **h :** the top or bottom layer of fruit or vegetables in a container esp. as arranged for purposes of display **i :** the flat surface of a propeller blade that corresponds to the undersurface of a wing **9 :** an acting surface (as of a tool or implement): as **a :** the edge of a cutting implement (as a knife) **b :** the striking surface of the head (as of a hammer or golf club) **c :** the grinding surface of a molar tooth **d** (1) **:** the uppermost part of a relief printing surface (as type or a plate) that receives the ink and transfers it to the paper — see TYPE (2) **:** TYPEFACE — often used in combination ⟨bold*face*⟩ ⟨light*face*⟩ **10 a :** the end or wall of a mine tunnel, drift, or excavation at which work is progressing or was last done **:** BREAST — called also *working face* **b :** the working surface of a pit or quarry **11 a :** the part of the acting surface of a gear tooth that projects beyond the pitch line **b :** the width of a pulley or the length of a gear tooth from end to end **c :** the sole of a carpenter's plane **12** *astrology* **:** one third of a zodiacal sign or 10 degrees of longitude **13 :** FACE CARD — used chiefly in the expression *neither ace nor face* **14 :** FACE VALUE **15 :** a cut made in a pine or other tree from which resin exudes **16 :** FACE-OFF

syn COUNTENANCE, VISAGE, PHYSIOGNOMY, MUG, PUSS: these six nouns can all designate the front part of the head including the mouth, nose, eyes, cheeks, and, usu., the forehead. FACE is the most general, having the common meaning of the group ⟨a person with a pale *face*⟩ ⟨a dog with white markings about the *face*⟩ COUNTENANCE, applied only to the human face, stresses appearance, esp. as revealing or seeming to reveal an inner condition, as thoughts, character, mood, or frame of mind ⟨their hideous *countenances* were all bloody and sweaty —Charles Dickens⟩ ⟨an expressive *countenance*⟩ ⟨something of dignity in his *countenance* —Jane Austen⟩ ⟨a benign *countenance*⟩ ⟨serious illness and suffering stared from his dark *countenance* —A.C.Cole⟩ In an older use it can mean a normal, composed expression and suggest a composed state ⟨far beyond them all in person, *countenance,* air, and walk —Jane Austen⟩ VISAGE, a bookish term very close to COUNTENANCE in meaning, stresses appearance and often suggests attention to the shape and proportion of the face or to the general impression of character or frame of mind it gives, often distinctive or esp. significant ⟨the very *visage* of a man in love —Edna S. V. Millay⟩ ⟨more horrible and cruel than the *visages* of the wildest savages —Charles Dickens⟩ ⟨withered, wrinkled, and loathsome of *visage* —Oscar Wilde⟩ PHYSIOGNOMY is chiefly used when the interest is the contours of face, shape of features, or characteristic expression as indicating race, temperament, or general character; it is applied today, however, more frequently to the distinguishing aspect or features of things other than the face ⟨a man of saturnine *physiognomy*⟩ ⟨a few of many features from two to three thousand years old which have given Chinese civilization a *physiognomy* all its own —A.L.Kroeber⟩ MUG has a humorous intent in suggesting an ugly, though usu. not displeasing, physiognomy ⟨getting your *mug* in the papers is one of the shameful ways of making a living —Norman Mailer⟩ PUSS, Irish in origin, is as symptomatic as any of a wealth of slang words (*map, kisser, pan, mush*) applying to the face or the central area of it, the nose and mouth, and signifying pretty much what the tenor of the remark containing it would suggest, from a mere synonym for FACE to a humorous or grim implication of ugliness or offensiveness ⟨he put on a very sour *puss* when he saw the priest along with me —Frank O'Connor⟩

— in the face of *or* **in face of :** in opposition to **:** in defiance of **:** DESPITE ⟨succeed *in the face of* great difficulties⟩ ⟨the aggression was seen *in face of* all evidence as a defensive war⟩ **— to one's face :** in one's presence or so that one is fully aware of what is going on **:** OPENLY, FRANKLY, BOLDLY

2face \"\ *vb* -ED/-ING/-S [ME *facen,* fr. *face,* n.] *vt* **1 :** to confront, controvert, or maintain impudently, brashly, or with excessive assurance **:** BROWBEAT, BULLY — now usu. used with *down* or *out* ⟨the look with which she *faced* down all opposition in the club⟩ ⟨determined to ~ out the situation he answered all questions curtly⟩ **2 a :** to stand or sit opposite to **:** occupy a position with the face toward ⟨the audience *faced* the speaker⟩ ⟨he stood *facing* the window⟩ ⟨a large mirror *faced* the door⟩ **b :** to be face-to-face with ⟨they *faced* one another for the last time⟩; *often* **:** to be on the page opposite to ⟨the color plate *facing* page 857⟩ **c :** to front on or toward ⟨the house *faced* the river⟩ ⟨a sheltered valley that ~*s* the morning sun⟩ **3 :** to meet face-to-face without shrinking, cringing, or withdrawing ⟨I can't bear to ~ your sister after what has happened⟩ ⟨gone with a clear conscience to ~ his Lord⟩: as **a :** to meet or oppose firmly and without evasion ⟨we must ~ the facts⟩ **b :** to meet for the purpose of stopping or opposing ⟨such untrained militia can never hope to ~ veterans successfully⟩ **c :** to master, check, or bring to heel by confronting with firm assurance and steady determination to resist or control — used with *down* ⟨*facing* down the forces of reaction⟩ ⟨we must ~ down every aggressor⟩ ⟨she *faced* down the rebellious students and sent them back to their books⟩ **4 a :** to recognize or contemplate as an often unpleasant or difficult eventuality confronting one ⟨*facing* the risk of the operation and weighing it against the certainty of continued suffering⟩ ⟨*facing* the need to retrench he decided to give up luxuries⟩ **b :** to be likely or possible and often imminent to or for ⟨extermination ~*s* many of the larger mammals as urbanization destroys their habitats⟩ ⟨the king was *faced* with the loss of his throne unless immediate reforms were instituted⟩ **c :** to be an immediate prospect for **:** THREATEN ⟨death ~*s* everyone sooner or later⟩ ⟨our gambling losses left us *faced* with ruin⟩ **5 :** to cover the front or surface of with something (as a protective or ornamental coating) ⟨a building *faced* with marble⟩ ⟨several water-resistant fabrics are *faced* with plastics⟩ **6 :** to bring directly to the attention of **:** CONFRONT — usu. used with *with* ⟨*faced* him with evidence of treachery⟩ ⟨*faced* by two tragic alternatives⟩ **7 :** to finish an edge of (a textile article) by applying a lining **:** reinforce (as a section of a garment) by applying a piece of cloth on the inside **8 :** to improve the appearance of (cheaper grades of green tea) by use of additives (as coloring matter and soapstone) **9 :** to position (a full-page illustration) at right angles to the text — see ²DOWN 10b, ¹UP 13c **10 :** to turn face up: as **a :** to turn (a playing card) so that the face is exposed usu. deliberately — compare EXPOSE *vt* **b :** to arrange (mail) so that addresses on all pieces in a batch face the same way **11 :** to arrange (fruits or vegetables) in a container so as to display a face ⟨berries are much more salable when neatly *faced*⟩ **12 a :** to make the surface of flat or smooth **:** dress the face of (as a stone or a casting) — often used with *off* **b :** to shape or smooth the flat as distinguished from the cylindrical surface of (an object being made on a lathe) — often used with *up* **13 :** to cause (troops) to face in a particular direction on command ⟨the captain *faced* his company to the left⟩ **14 :** to put (a lacrosse ball) in play by dropping between the crosses of two opposing forwards each of whom stands with his left toward the goal he is attacking; *also* **:** to put (a hockey puck) in play by a similar method **~** *vi* **1** *obs* **:** to present a false appearance **:** play the hypocrite **2 a :** to turn the face ⟨quickly *faced* to her right⟩ **b :** to have or lie so as to have a face or front in a specified direction ⟨the house *faced* south⟩ **3 :** to face the puck or ball in certain sports

syn BRAVE, CHALLENGE, DARE, BEARD, DEFY: FACE means to confront face-to-face or as if face-to-face. It may imply either resolution and fortitude or realistic appraisal of one's situation ⟨I shuddered, but unflinchingly *faced* an awful possibility —Rose Macaulay⟩ ⟨here we are together *facing* a group of mighty foes —Sir Winston Churchill⟩ BRAVE stresses the fact of underlying courage, fortitude, or bravado inciting one to dare or endure ⟨though Archbishop Warham mournfully assured the Queen that "the anger of the King is death", not a few Englishmen were increasingly ready to *brave* his anger —Francis Hackett⟩ ⟨if you find yourself in trouble before them, call on your courage and resolution: *brave* out every difficulty —Kenneth Roberts⟩ CHALLENGE expresses the notion of confronting to invite into competition or contest or to oppose by imputing weakness or fault ⟨Henry IV . . . had in a manner curbed Bouillon's power, but he tolerated it, and he hesitated to *challenge* it —Hilaire Belloc⟩ ⟨the best medical practitioner turned out by the school, who once dared to *challenge* the power of the chief of the witch doctors —V.G.Heiser⟩ DARE may imply venturesomeness, daring, boldness, love of danger, or even vainglory in risking or tempting fate or retribution ⟨those who *dare* an enemy greatly should be prepared for the fullest consequences —S.L.A.Marshall⟩ BEARD suggests a bold confronting, resolute daring, or mocking of someone or something dangerous or powerful ⟨a bold heart yours to *beard* that raging mob —Alfred Tennyson⟩ ⟨for years she led the life of a religious tramp, *bearding* bishops and allowing herself many eccentricities which . . . brought her more than once into serious suspicion of Lollardy —G.G. Coulton⟩ DEFY suggests confronting an opponent with resolution, boldness, and confident assertiveness, sometimes with mocking, arising from the feeling that the strongest efforts thus provoked will fail ⟨fiend, I *defy* thee . . . Foul tyrant both of Gods and Humankind, one only being shalt thou not subdue —P.B.Shelley⟩ ⟨*defy* the enemies of our constitution to show the contrary —Edmund Burke⟩ **syn** see in addition MEET

— face the music : to meet resolutely an unpleasant situation, a danger, or the consequences of one's actions ⟨had made a mistake and now had to *face the music*⟩

face·able \ˈfāsəbəl\ *adj* **:** capable of or fit for being faced

face-about \ˈ≈ˌ≈\ *n* -S [fr. *face about!*] **:** ABOUT-FACE

face and fill *n* **:** a method of packing fresh fruit or vegetables in containers with only the surface layer regularly arranged

face angle *n* **:** an angle formed by two edges of a polyhedral angle

face-bedded \ˈ≈ˌ≈≈\ *adj* **:** bedded in masonry so that the naturally horizontal surface forms the face of the work — used of a quarried stone; compare JOINT-BEDDED

face bone *n* **:** CHEEKBONE

face·bow \ˈfās,bō\ *n* **:** a device used in dentistry to determine the positional relationships of the maxillary arch of a patient

facebread \ˈ≈ˌ≈\ *n* [trans. of Heb *leḥem happānīm*] **:** SHEWBREAD

face brick *n* **:** brick used in the face of a wall; *usu* **:** brick made esp. for facing purposes by selecting clays to produce desired color or by special surface treatment

face card *n* **:** a playing card bearing a stylized picture of a king, queen, or knave

face-centered \ˈ≈ˌ≈≈\ *adj* **:** relating to a crystal space lattice in which each cubic unit cell has an atom at the center and at the corners of each face

facecloth \ˈ≈ˌ≈\ *n* **1 a :** a cloth laid over the face of a corpse **b :** a small cloth used for washing one's face or person **:** WASHCLOTH **2 a :** a cloth with warp threads predominating on the surface **b :** a cloth with a distinctly better appearance on one side often produced by napping or finishing

face cord *n* **:** a cubic measure for wood equivalent to a pile whose length is 8 feet, whose height is 4 feet, and whose width varying with the length of the pieces is usu. from 12 to 36 inches

faced \ˈfāst\ *adj* [¹*face* + *-ed*] **:** provided with a face or a facing ⟨a neatly ~ terrace⟩ ⟨a well-*faced* lapel⟩ — used chiefly in combination with an attributive noun or adjective indicating a particular kind of face or facing ⟨a marble-*faced* brick building⟩ ⟨satin-*faced* lapels⟩ ⟨a dog-*faced* boy⟩ ⟨rosy-*faced* dawn⟩

facedown \ˈ≈ˌ≈\ *adv* **:** with the face downward ⟨coasting ~⟩

faced wall *n* **:** a wall in which the masonry facing and backing are so bonded as to exert common action under load

face flannel *n, Brit* **:** WASHCLOTH

face gear *n* **:** a gear having teeth on its face

face guard *n* **:** a guard for the face; *usu* **:** a complete or partial mask (as one worn by workmen exposed to heat or flying particles of metal or by football players or fencers)

face-harden \ˈ≈ˌ≈≈\ *vt* **:** to harden the face or surface of

face joint *n* **:** a joint in the face of a wall usu. more carefully struck or pointed than one less visible

face·less \ˈfāsləs\ *adj* **:** lacking a face: as **a** *obs* **:** COWARDLY **b :** regarded as a member of a category and as such lacking individuality ⟨he might have been any barber in town — ~, pleasant, trusted —Luke Short⟩ ⟨the ~ men who make up statistics⟩ **c :** unidentified or unidentifiable esp. by deliberate intent ⟨the ~ accusers of the police state⟩

face·less·ness *n* -ES **:** faceless state or quality; *esp* **:** lack of individuality

face-lift \ˈ≈ˌ≈\ *vt* **:** to engage in or perform a face-lifting of ⟨some manufacturers usually just *face-lift* their cars when bringing out new models⟩

face-lifting \ˈ≈ˌ≈≈\ *also* **face-lift** \ˈ≈ˌ≈\ *n* -S **1 :** a plastic operation for removal of facial wrinkles, sagging skin, and certain other defects usu. associated with aging **2 :** an alteration (as of a building) or restyling (as of an automobile design) intended to modernize or to increase comfort or salability

fa·cel·lite \fəˈse,līt\ *n* -S [It, fr. Gk *phakelos* bundle, faggot + It *-lite*] **:** KALIOPHILITE

facemaking \ˈ≈ˌ≈≈\ *n* -S **:** GRIMACING

face·man \ˈfāsmən, -ˌman\ *n, pl* **facemen :** a worker (as in a quarry or coal mine) who actually works the face as distinguished from one who serves in various supplementary capacities (as in mucking, loading, or hauling)

face mill *n* **:** a cutter for face milling

face milling *n* **:** the process of milling flat surfaces that are at right angles to the axis of rotation of the cutter

face mite *n* **:** FOLLICLE MITE, DEMODEX

face mold *n* **:** the template used to outline forms to be cut out of wood, metal, or other sheet material (as by carpenters or sheet-metal workers); *esp* **:** a pattern for the practical projection of a wreath in stair building

face-nail \ˈ≈ˌ≈\ *vt* **:** to fasten by means of face nailing ⟨the boards should be *face-nailed* solidly at each bearing point —*Amer. Builder*⟩

face nailing *n* **:** nailing in which the nailheads are exposed to view and which is used in the fastening of facing wood to a base

face-off \ˈ≈ˌ≈\ *n* -S [fr. *face off*, v.] **:** the act of facing the playing piece (as a puck or ball) in certain games (as hockey)

facepiece \ˈ≈ˌ≈\ *n* **1 a :** the part of an overcheck that connects the bit with the cavesson and overcheck rein **b :** an ornamental harness brass placed pendant from the cavesson **2 :** the part of a gas mask or other respirator that fits over the face and is provided with eyepieces and a breathing device

face pit *n* **:** FACIAL PIT

faceplate \ˈ≈ˌ≈\ *n* **1 :** a disk fixed with its face at right angles to the live spindle of a lathe and provided with holes, slots, and other devices for the attachment of the work which thus rotates with the spindle **2 a :** a protective plate for a machine or device (as a door lock) **b :** a protective covering for the human face (as of a diver)

faceplate jaw *n* **:** a dog attachment for a faceplate to convert it into a chuck

face play *or* **face playing** *n* **:** display or simulation of emotion by use of the muscles of the face (as in certain styles of acting)

face presentation *n* **:** presentation of the fetus face first at the mouth of the uterus during parturition

fac·er \ˈfāsə(r)\ *n* -S **1** *obs* **:** one that puts on a false show **:** BRAGGART, SWAGGERER **2** *obs* **:** a tankard esp. when filled **:** BUMPER **3 a :** a blow in the face (as in boxing) **b :** a severe or stunning check or defeat ⟨his refusal to participate was a ~ for me⟩ **4 :** one (as a machine or worker) that faces: as **a :** a cutter for facing or surfacing or a machine-tool attachment for holding such a cutter **b :** a garment worker who sews facings and reinforcements **c :** a worker who polishes the faces of jewel bearings **5 :** something that forms or acts as a face: as **a :** FACE TITLE **b :** a selected specimen for use in facing (as of a pack of fruit or vegetables) **c :** any of certain broad low-growing plants used in border plantings to hide unattractive basal parts of larger background items

faces *pl of* FACE, *pres 3d sing of* FACE

face-saver \ˈ≈ˌ≈≈\ *n* **:** something that saves face; *usu* **:** something that constitutes such grounds or justification as to permit compromise or compliance without jeopardizing the dignity or prestige of the compromising or complying parties

face-saving \ˈ≈ˌ≈≈\ *n* **:** the act or an instance of preserving one's prestige or dignity ⟨he often effected compromises which, in permitting a certain *face-saving*, did not yield the right —Merle Curti⟩

face spanner *n* **:** a spanner with pins at the ends for fitting into holes in the face of the part to be adjusted

face stone *n* **:** a stone used or usable as part of a facing

face string *n* **:** the outermost string of a stair often of superior material and separate from the roughstrings which in a wooden stair it conceals

¹fac·et \ˈfasət, ˈfaas-, *usu* -əd·+V\ *also* **fa·cette** \faˈset\ *n* -S [F *facette*, dim. of *face* — more at FACE] **1 a :** one of the small plane surfaces produced on a diamond or other precious stone in cutting esp. to enhance its brilliance and beauty — see BRILLIANT illustration **b :** a similar surface on other material (as one cut on a pebble by natural forces) **2 :** any of the sharply defined or definable aspects that make up a subject or object of consideration **:** PHASE ⟨no other ~ of his leadership could be more revealing⟩ **3** *anat* **:** a smooth flat or nearly flat circumscribed surface ⟨the articular ~ of a bone⟩ **4 :** the fillet between the flutes of a column **5 a :** the external corneal surface of an ommatidium of a compound eye **b :** OMMATIDIUM **syn** see PHASE

²facet \"\ *vt* **faceted** *or* **facetted** \-səd·əd,-sətəd\ **faceted** *or* **facetted**; **faceting** *or* **facetting**; **facets :** to cut facets upon ⟨the skill with which he ~*ed* the great diamond⟩

facet *abbr* **1** facetiae **2** facetious

fa·cete \fəˈsēt\ *adj* [L *facetus* courteous, elegant, witty, facetious] *archaic* **:** FACETIOUS, WITTY — **fa·cete·ly** *adv, archaic*

fac·et·ed *also* **fac·et·ted** \ˈfasəd·əd, ˈfaas-, -sətəd\ *adj* **:** having or made with facets

facet head *n* **:** a device to aid in orienting the facets being cut on a gemstone

fa·ce·ti·ae \fəˈsēshē,ē\ *n pl* [L, pl., of *facetia* jest, witticism, fr. *facetus* + *-ia* -y] **1 :** witty or humorous writings or sayings **2 a :** short humorous frequently obscene tales **b :** EROTICA

face tile *n* **:** tile with one surface designed for use on a face and usu. specially finished or treated (as to enhance appearance, ease of cleaning, or resistance to weathering)

fa·ce·ti·os·i·ty \fə,sēshēˈäsəd·ē, -ətē, -i\ *n* -ES [fr. *facetious*, after such pairs as E *ponderous: ponderosity*] **:** a facetious quality or item ⟨the ponderous ~ of his pronouncements⟩

fa·ce·tious \fəˈsēshəs\ *adj* [MF *facetieux*, fr. *facetie* jest (fr. L *facetia*) + *-eux* -ous] **1 a :** given to jesting that is sometimes crude ⟨a ~ companion⟩ **b** *obs* **:** gay and witty **2 :** characterized by pleasantry or levity **:** exciting laughter **:** JOCOSE ⟨a ~ story⟩ ⟨his impudently ~ reply⟩ **syn** see WITTY

fa·ce·tious·ly *adv* **:** in a facetious manner

fa·ce·tious·ness *n* -ES **:** the quality or state of being facetious

face title *n* **:** a left-hand page facing the title page of a book; *esp* **:** such a page bearing advertising matter (as a list of titles by the same author or publisher)

face-to-face \ˌ≈≈ˈ≈\ *adv (or adj)* [ME] **1 :** within each other's sight or presence **:** involving close contacts **:** in person ⟨a *face-to-face* meeting of the two leaders⟩ ⟨we met *face-to-face* for the first time⟩ **2 :** under the necessity of having to make a decision or to take action ⟨surgeon *face-to-face* with an emergency case⟩ **3 :** OPPOSITE ⟨printed *face-to-face*⟩

face towel *n* **:** a towel that is smaller than a bath towel, is often of smooth-surfaced material (as linen), and is used esp. for drying the face

face up *vi* **:** to confront or meet something or someone esp. boldly ⟨he *faced up* and considered his situation⟩ — usu. used with *to* ⟨finally *faces up* to the young hoods terrorizing these subway riders —A.H. Weiler⟩

faceup \ˈ≈ˌ≈\ *adv* **:** with the face upward ⟨floating ~⟩

face validity *n* **:** apparent but untested statistical validity

face value *n* **1 :** the value indicated on the face of an instrument: as **a :** the principal amount of a bond or note **b :** the maturity value of a life-insurance policy **c :** the par value of a municipal bond **2 :** the apparent value ⟨if their results may be taken at *face value*⟩

face wall *n* **:** BREAST WALL

facework \ˈ≈ˌ≈\ *n* **:** the often ornamental or superior material of the outside or front side (as of a wall) **:** FACING

face worker *n* **:** a miner who works at the face of a mine

facia *var of* FASCIA

¹fa·cial \ˈfāshəl\ *adj* [ML *facialis*, fr. L *facies* form, shape, face + *-alis* -al] **1 :** of, relating to, situated in, or affecting the face ⟨~ neuralgia⟩ **2 :** of or relating to an outer surface **:** SUPERFICIAL ⟨a ~ layer of grime⟩ **3 :** concerned with or used in improving the appearance or freshness of the human face esp. by the use of massage or cosmetics ⟨~ pack⟩ — **fa·cial·ly** \-shəlē, -li\ *adv*

²facial \"\ *n* -S **1 :** a treatment or massage for the face **2 :** a facial part (as a nerve or artery)

facial angle *n* **:** a measure of relative prognathism made by determining the angle at which a line connecting the nasion and prosthion intersects the eye-ear plane

facial artery *n* **:** an artery that arises from the external carotid artery just superior to the lingual artery and gives off a number of branches supplying the neck and face

facial bone *n* **:** any of the bones of the facial region of the skull that do not take part in forming the braincase and that in man include 14 bones: two nasals, two maxillaries, two lacrimals, two zygomatics, two palatines, two inferior conchae, one vomer, and one mandible

facial canal *n* **:** a passage in the petrous part of the temporal bone that extends from the internal auditory meatus to the stylomastoid foramen and transmits various branches of the facial nerve

facial colliculus *n* **:** a medial eminence on the floor of the fourth ventricle of the brain produced by the nucleus of the abducent nerve and the flexure of the facial nerve around it

facial disk *n* **:** the disk of an owl

facial index *n* **:** the ratio of the breadth of the face to its length multiplied by 100, the breadth used being usu. the bizygomatic and the length either that from ophryon to gnathion or that from nasion to gnathion

facial nerve *n* **:** either of the seventh pair of cranial nerves leaving the cranium on either side by the internal auditory meatus, passing through the facial canal, emerging at the stylomastoid foramen to supply motor fibers to the facial muscles and to the stylohyoid and posterior belly of the digastric, and sending a separate mixed branch to the tongue that carries the gustatory fibers from the anterior two thirds of the tongue and parasympathetic fibers to the sphenopalatine and submaxillary ganglia

facial pit *n* **1 :** a gland-containing depression of the skull surface in front of the orbit in certain ruminants **2 :** one of the paired sensory pits of a pit viper — compare JACOBSON'S ORGAN

facial vein *n* **:** any of several veins draining the face and neighboring parts

facial vision *n* **:** an awareness of obstacles independent of vision that is often considerably developed in blind persons and probably dependent on tactile perception of reflected sound waves

fa·ci·a·tion \ˌfāshēˈāshən\ *n* -S [L *facies* + E *-ation*] **:** a subdivision of an ecological association that is characterized by the codominance of two or more but not all the dominant forms of the association and that constitutes a community of considerable extent, its area usu. being related to a climatic variation within the area of the association — compare LOCIATION

fa·cient \ˈfāshənt\ *n* -S [L *facient-*, *faciens*, pres. part.] **:** one that does something **:** DOER, AGENT

-fa·cient \ˈfāshənt\ *adj comb form* [L *facient-*, *faciens*, pres. part. of *facere* to do, make (as in *calefacere* to warm) — more at DO, CHAFE] **:** making **:** causing ⟨somni*facient*⟩

facier *comparative of* FACY

fa·ci·es \ˈfāshē,ēz, ˈfāshēz\ *n, pl* **facies** [NL, fr. L, form, shape, face — more at FACE] **1 a :** the general appearance or makeup esp. of a natural group (as a fauna) **b :** a particular local aspect or modification of an ecological community **c :** a specialized and commonly localized segment of a cultural community **2 :** an appearance and expression of the face characteristic or indicative of a disease or abnormal condition ⟨peptic ulcer ~⟩ ⟨adenoid ~⟩ **3 a** *geol* **:** a group of stratified beds differing in lithologic character or fossil contents from other beds of the same age **b :** a rock or group of rocks that differs from comparable rocks (as in composition, fabric, or age)

facies-suite \ˈ≈≈ˌ≈ˌ≈, ˈ≈≈ˌ≈\ *n* **:** a collection or group of rocks that exhibits variations in a single rock mass

faciest *superlative of* FACY

fac·ile \ˈfasəl *also* -(ˌ)sil, *chiefly Brit* -ˌsīl\ *adj* [MF, fr. L *facilis*, fr. *facere* to make, do + *-ilis* -ile — more at DO] **1 a :** easily accomplished or attained **:** involving no special difficulty or expenditure of skill or effort **:** EASY ⟨a ~ victory⟩; *sometimes* **:** SPECIOUS, SUPERFICIAL ⟨the work is well-organized but the conclusions and interpretations are often unduly ~⟩ ⟨I am not concerned . . . with offering any ~ solution for so complex a problem —T.S.Eliot⟩ **b :** used or comprehended with ease ⟨the techniques of paper chromatography have provided ~ means of separating complex organic mixtures⟩ ⟨the report proved to be surprisingly ~ reading⟩ **c** *of feelings, emotions, attitudes* **:** readily experienced or manifest and often lacking sincerity, depth, or real basis ⟨sick of words and phrases and ~ emotions and situations and insincerities —Rose Macaulay⟩ ⟨we must possess a peculiarly ~ turn of mind when we can virtuously condemn the cruelties perpetrated in other countries, while . . . we avert our eyes from the cruelties we ourselves continue to condone —Farley Mowat⟩ **2 a** *archaic* **:** easily led or prevailed upon **:** COMPLIANT, DOCILE, YIELDING **b** *Scots law* **:** so easily influenced as to require curatorship or guardianship — used of the mentally weak; compare FACILITY 3b **3 :** mild or pleasing in manner or disposition: **a** *archaic* **:** lenient and gentle **:** not stern, severe, or harsh **b** *obs* **:** kind and affable **c :** exhibiting ease of bearing or manner **:** ASSURED, POISED **4 :** free and unrestrained in performing or expressing **:** READY, RESOURCEFUL, QUICK, FLUENT, EXPERT **:** not hesitant, barren, slow, or awkward ⟨a man ~ in expedients⟩ ⟨the most ~ and prolific of humorists —Alfred Kreymborg⟩ **syn** see EASY

fac·ile·ly \-əl(l)ē, -il(l)ē, -īll\, \|i\ *adv* **:** in a facile manner **:** with ease or assurance

fac·ile·ness \-əlnəs, -iln-, -īln-\ *n* -ES **:** the quality or state of being facile ⟨impressed by the ~ of the man's mind⟩

fa·cil·i·tate \fəˈsilə,tāt, *usu* -ād·+V\ *vt* -ED/-ING/-S [F *faciliter* (fr. MF, fr. OIt *facilitare*, fr. *facilità* facility, fr. L *facilitat-*, *facilitas*) + E *-ate*) — more at FACILITY] **1 :** to make easier or less difficult **:** free from difficulty or impediment ⟨~ the execution of a task⟩ ⟨*facilitating* free cultural interchange⟩ ⟨measures intended to ~ economic recovery⟩ **2 :** to lessen the labor of (as a person) **:** ASSIST, AID

fa·cil·i·ta·tion \fə,siləˈtāshən\ *n* -S **1 :** the act of facilitating **:** the state of being facilitated ⟨the ~ of trade that results from free intercourse of peoples⟩ ⟨social ~ is essentially an adaptive condition⟩ **2 :** something that facilitates **:** AID, HELP ⟨such notes provide a real ~ to the memory⟩ **3 a :** the lowering of the threshold for reflex conduction by the passage of another preceding or simultaneous stimulation esp. from a reflex of different origin **b :** the lowering of the threshold for reflex conduction along a particular neural pathway that results from repeated use of that pathway **c :** SUMMATION 3

fa·cil·i·ta·tive \ˈ≈ˌ≈≈ˌtād·iv\ *adj* **:** tending to facilitate

fa·cil·i·ta·tor \fəˈsilə,tād·ə(r)\ *n* -S **:** one that facilitates

fa·cil·i·ta·to·ry \fəˈsilətə,tōrē, fə¦siləˈtād·ərē\ *adj* **:** tending to induce or involved in facilitation esp. of reflex action

facilities contract *n* **:** a lease, rental agreement, or other contractual agreement governing the acquisition, use, or disposition of government-owned machinery, tools, building installations, or other property furnished to or acquired by a war contractor for war production purposes other than incorporation in a finished product

fa·cil·i·ty \fəˈsiləd·ē, -ətē, -i\ *n* -ES [ME *facilite*, fr. MF & L; MF *facilité*, fr. L *facilitat-*, *facilitas*, fr. *facilis* easy + *-itat-*, *-itas* -ity — more at FACILE] **1 :** the quality of being easily performed **:** freedom from difficulty **:** EASE **2 :** ease in performance **:** readiness proceeding from skill or use **:** DEXTERITY ⟨practice gives a wonderful ~⟩ **3 a :** easiness to be persuaded **:** READINESS, COMPLIANCE, PLIANCY **b** *Scots law* **:** mental weakness, compliancy, or responsiveness to undue influence sufficient to justify curatorship or guardianship **4** *archaic* **:** easiness in manner **:** AFFABILITY, GRACIOUSNESS **5 a :** something that promotes the ease of any action, operation, transaction, or course of conduct — usu. used in pl. ⟨excellent *facilities* for graduate study⟩ **b :** something (as a hospital, machinery, plumbing) that is built, constructed, installed, or established to perform some particular function or to serve or facilitate some particular end

facility of payment clause : a provision in an industrial life-insurance policy permitting the company to pay the death benefit to a relative of the insured or any other person entitled thereto by reason of his having paid expenses in the insured's behalf

[1]**fac·ing** \ˈfāsiŋ\ *n* -s [fr. gerund of [2]*face*] **1** : the act of one that faces ⟨his brave ~ of the enemy⟩; *also* : an instance of such act **2 a** : a plain or decorative lining applied to an edge of a textile article (as a garment or drapery) and turned either to the inside (as for hems or slashes) or to the outside (as for revers or cuffs) **b facings** *pl* : the collar, cuffs, and trimmings of some military or other uniform coats commonly of a color different from that of the coat and often prescribed for a particular group (as an arm of the service, a regiment, or a hotel staff) **3 a** : a covering in front usu. for ornament or protective purposes : an exterior covering or sheathing ⟨a ~ of stone blocks on an earthen dam⟩ ⟨had to replace the clutch ~ on his car⟩ **b** : a front of porcelain or plastic used in dental crowns and bridgework to face the metal replacement and simulate the natural tooth **4** : material used or suitable for facing ⟨you will need 12 yards of ribbon ~ for the ruffles⟩ **5** : a powdered substance (as graphite) applied to the face of a mold or mixed with the sand that forms the mold to give a smooth surface to the casting **6** : a turning of men in formation to face in a given direction usu. at command

[2]**facing** *adj* [fr. pres. part. of [2]*face*] **1** : used for or suitable for use in facing ⟨a strong ~ sateen⟩ **2** : arranged or placed opposite one another ⟨the ~ ornaments on the mantel⟩

facing brick *n* : FACE BRICK

facing distance *n* : the minimum distance (as 14 inches) between men necessary to make the facings in military drill

facing-point lock *n* : a mechanical lock for a railroad switch, derail, or movable-point frog comprising a plunger stand and a plunger which engages a lock rod attached to the switch point to lock the operated unit

facing-point switch *n* : a railroad switch so set that a train faces the points as it passes them — distinguished from *trailing-point switch*

facing sand *n* : sand in contact with a foundry pattern

facing slip *n* : a printed or written direction slip or label to be attached to a package of mail

facing tile *n* : FACE TILE

fa·cin·o·rous \fəˈsinərəs\ *also* **fac·i·ne·ri·ous** \ˌfasəˈnirēəs\ *adj* [L *facinorosus, facinerosus*, fr. *facinor-, facinus* deed, evil deed, crime (fr. *facere* to do) + *-osus* -ous — more at DO] *archaic* : atrociously wicked : INFAMOUS — **fa·cin·o·rous·ness** *n* -ES *archaic*

facio- *comb form* [ISV, fr. L *facies* form, shape, face — more at FACE] **1** : facial and ⟨*faciolingual*⟩ **2** : facial ⟨*facioplegia*⟩

fa·cio ut des \ˈfäkē,ōˌu̇tˈdās\ *n* [L, I do that you may give] : a commutative contract in which one party performs something in order that another may give something in return

facio ut fa·ci·as \-ˈfäkē,äs\ *n* [L, I do that you may do] : a commutative contract in which one party performs something in order that another may perform something in exchange

fack \ˈfak\ *dial var of* FACT

fack·el·tanz \ˈfäkəl,tänts\ *n, pl* **fackeltän·ze** \-,tentsə\ [G, fr. *fackel* torch (fr. OHG *faccala, facchela*, fr. L *facula* small torch) + *tanz* dance, fr. MHG, fr. OF *dance* — more at FACULA, DANCE] **1** : a pavane for a ceremonial torchlight procession formerly celebrating a royal marriage in certain German courts **2** : POLONAISE

fa·con \fäˈkōn\ *n* -ES [AmerSp *facón*, aug. of Sp *faca* large knife, prob. fr. Pg, knife] : a large heavy belt knife carried by So. American gauchos

[1]**fa·con·ne** \ˌfasəˈnā\ *adj* [F *façonné*, fr. past part. of *façonner* to work, fashion, fr. *façon* make, fashioning, manner, fr. L *faction-, factio* action of making, company, faction — more at FASHION] *of textiles* : having a pattern that consists of small scattered figures or a fancy weave

[2]**faconne** \ˈ"\ *n* -s [F *façonné*, fr. *façonné*, adj.] **1** : a faconne fabric (as a jacquard) **2** : the pattern or a figure of the pattern on a faconne fabric

[1]**fac·sim·i·le** \fakˈsiməlē, -li\ *n* -s *often attrib* [L *fac simile!* make something similar!, fr. *fac* (imp. of *facere* to make, do) + *simile*, neut. of *similis* like, similar — more at DO, SAME] **1** : an exact and detailed copy of something (as of a book, document, painting, or statue) **2** : the process of transmitting and reproducing (as printed matter or still pictures) orig. by facsimile telegraph but now chiefly by a system of radio communication in which the subject matter is scanned by a pinprick of light and differences between light and dark are noted by a photoelectric cell, transmitted by radio broadcast, and intercepted by a radio receiver equipped with a stylus or other device that produces a printed record on paper ⟨a ~ recorder⟩

[2]**facsimile** \ˈ"\ *vt* -ED/-ING/-S **1** : to be an exact copy of **2** : to make a facsimile of or reproduce by the process of facsimile

facsimile signature *n* : a signature produced by mechanical means but recognized as valid by law for many banking, financial, and business transactions

facsimile telegraph *n* : a telegraphic apparatus that reproduces matter (as messages, drawings, or pictures) in facsimile

fac·sim·i·list \-ləst\ *n* -s : a maker of facsimiles (as in the preparation of lithographs)

fac·sim·i·lize \-ə,līz\ *vt* -ED/-ING/-S : FACSIMILE

fact \ˈfakt\ *n* -s [L *factum*, fr. neut. of *factus*, past part. of *facere* to do, make — more at DO] **1** : a thing done : DEED: as **a** *obs* : an action in general : ACTION, CONDUCT **b** *obs* : a meritorious or valorous deed **c** : a wrong or unlawful deed : CRIME — used in the phrase *after the fact* ⟨an accessory after the ~⟩ **2** *obs* : DOING, MAKING, PREPARING, PERFORMING, ACT **3 a** : something that has actual existence : EVENT **b** : an occurrence, quality, or relation the reality of which is manifest in experience or may be inferred with certainty; *specif* : an actual happening in time or space ⟨~ in its primary meaning, as an object of direct experience, is distinguished from truth⟩ ⟨stubborn ~s⟩ ⟨given ~s⟩ **c** : a verified statement or proposition; *also* : something that makes a statement or a proposition true or false **4 a** : the quality or character of being actual or of being made up of facts : ACTUALITY ⟨a question of ~ hinges on the actual evidence⟩ **b** : physical actuality or practical experience as distinguished from imagination, speculation, or theory ⟨the realm of ~ is distinct from fancy⟩ **5** : an assertion, statement, or information containing or purporting to contain something having objective reality ⟨you must marshal your ~s to combat his assertions⟩; *broadly* : something presented rightly or wrongly as having objective reality ⟨his ~s are open to question⟩ **6** *usu pl* **a** : any of the circumstances of a case at law as it exists or is alleged to exist in reality : something proved by the evidence to be or alleged to be of actual occurrence **b** : the reality of events or things the actual occurrence or existence of which is to be determined by evidence — **in fact** *adv* : in truth : ACTUALLY, REALLY ⟨painters who are *in fact* anything but unsophisticated —Cyril Ray⟩ ⟨these tests *in fact* marked an important stage in the development of atomic weapons —J.G.Palfrey⟩

facta *pl of* FACTUM

fac·ta·ble \ˈfak,tābəl\ *n* -s [alter. of earlier *fractable, fract table*, fr. L *fractus* (past part. of *frangere* to break) + E *table* — more at BREAK] : [1]COPING

fact finder *n* : one occupied in determining the realities of a particular case, situation, or relationship; *often* : an impartial examiner appointed by a government agency to investigate and appraise the facts underlying a dispute between labor and management

fact-finding \ˈ=,==\ *n* : the action of a fact finder or a group or committee of fact finders

Fac·tice \ˈfaktəs\ *trademark* — used for a vulcanized oil

fac·ti·cide \ˈfaktə,sīd\ *n* -s [*fact* + *-i-* + *-cide*] : perversion of fact; *also* : a perverter of fact

fac·tic·i·ty \fakˈtisəd·ē\ *n* -ES [F or G; F *facticité*, fr. G *faktizität*, fr. *faktum* fact (fr. L *factum*) + *-izität* (fr. L *-icitat-, -icitas* -icity)] : the quality or state of being a fact (as an inescapable and unalterable fact) : FACTUALITY

fact in controversy : a fact other than a fact in issue that is collateral to the issue and controverted between the parties (as evidential facts merely of aid in reaching a verdict) — distinguished from *fact in issue*

fact in issue : a fact that is raised by the pleadings directly and is necessary to be determined by the decision so that it will become res judicata — distinguished from *fact in controversy*; compare ISSUE OF LAW

[1]**fac·tion** \ˈfakshən\ *n* -s [MF & L; MF *faction*, fr. L *faction-, factio* action of making, company, faction — more at FASHION] **1** : a party, combination, or clique (as within a state, government, or other association) often contentious, self-seeking, or reckless of the common good **2** : party spirit or tumult esp. as manifested in discord, dissension, or intrigue ⟨~, or the irreconcilable conflict of parties —Ernest Barker⟩ **3** *obs* **a** : ACTION, DEED, BEHAVIOR **b** : a set or class of persons **c** : DISPUTE, QUARREL, INTRIGUE **4** : one of the divisions of charioteers contesting in the ancient Roman circus and distinguished by the color of their costumes; *often* : the part of the populace favoring and supporting one of these factions

[2]**faction** *also* **factionate** *vb* -ED/-ING/-S *vi, obs* : to act factiously : INTRIGUE ~ *vt, obs* : to gather into factions

-fac·tion \ˌfakshən\ *n comb form* -s [ME *-faccioun*, fr. MF & L; MF *-faction*, fr. L *-faction-, -factio* (as in *satisfaction-, satisfactio* satisfaction) — more at SATISFACTION] : making : -FICATION ⟨rare*faction*⟩ — in nouns derived from verbs ending in *-fy*

fac·tion·al \ˈfakshənᵊl, -shnəl\ *adj* **1** : of or relating to a faction ⟨a ~ leader⟩ **2 a** : characterized by faction **b** : occurring between factions ⟨~ disputes within the party⟩ — **fac·tion·al·ism** \-ᵊl,izəm, -ə,li-\ *n* -s — **fac·tion·al·ly** \-ᵊlē, -əlē, \i\ *adv*

fac·tion·al·ist \-ᵊləst, -əl-\ *n* -s : an advocate of or adherent to factionalism

[1]**fac·tion·ary** \ˈfakshə,nerē, -ri\ *n* -ES [[1]*faction* + *-ary* (n. suffix)] : PARTISAN

[2]**factionary** \ˈ"\ *adj* [[1]*faction* + *-ary* (adj. suffix)] : of or relating to a faction : PARTISAN

fac·tion·eer \ˌfakshəˈni(ə)r\ *n* -s [[1]*faction* + *-eer*] : PARTISAN

fac·tion·ist \ˈfaksh(ə)nəst\ *n* -s : a person who promotes factions or engages in faction

fac·tious \ˈfakshəs\ *adj* [MF or L; MF *factieux*, fr. L *factiosus*, fr. *factio* faction + *-osus* -ous — more at FASHION] **1** : given to faction : addicted to form parties or factions and raise dissensions; *sometimes* : SEDITIOUS **2** : relating to faction : proceeding from or characterized by faction ⟨~ and detailed political or moral analyses —Frances Keene⟩ **syn** see INSUBORDINATE

fac·tious·ly *adv* : in a factious manner

fac·tious·ness *n* -ES : the quality or state of being factious

fac·ti·tial \(ˈ)fakˈtishəl\ *adj* [by alter.] : FACTITIOUS; *usu* : induced by deliberate human action with or without intention to produce a lesion or disease ⟨~ rectal lesions following irradiation⟩ ⟨a ~ hyperthyroidism resulting from surreptitious ingestion of thyroid products⟩

fac·ti·tious \-shəs\ *adj* [L *facticius, factitius*, fr. *factus* (past part. of *facere* to make, do) + *-icius, -itius* -itious — more at DO] **1** : produced by human art, skill, or effort : not occurring or arising through unaided nature ⟨it seems probable that several of the mounds are ~⟩ — compare FACTITIAL **2 a** : formed by or adapted to an artificial or conventional standard ⟨~ tastes and values⟩ ⟨a ~ report on a situation⟩ **b** : produced artificially or by special effort (as for a particular situation) : not natural or spontaneous ⟨~ popular enthusiasm in the totalitarian state⟩ ⟨a ~ British accent⟩ **syn** see ARTIFICIAL

fac·ti·tious·ly *adv* : in a factitious manner ⟨prepared to be ~ gay⟩ : with factitious quality : ARTIFICIALLY

fac·ti·tious·ness *n* -ES : the quality of being factitious; *often* : studied quality : ARTIFICIALITY

[1]**fac·ti·tive** \ˈfaktəd·|iv, -tət|\ *adj* [NL *factitivus*, irreg. fr. L *factus* (past part. of *facere* to make, do) + *-ivus* -ive — more at DO] **1 a** : being or relating to a transitive verb that in certain constructions requires besides its object an objective complement (as in "he made the water wine", "they called him Teddy", "boil the eggs hard") **b** : serving as objective predicate ⟨a ~ adjective⟩ ⟨the ~ object in this sentence⟩ **2** : indicating that the subject of a verb causes an action to be performed or a condition to come into being — compare CAUSATIVE — **fac·ti·tive·ly** \|əvlē, -li\ *adv*

[2]**factitive** \ˈ"\ *n* -s : a factitive verb

[1]**fac·tive** \ˈfaktiv, -tēv, -təv\ *adj* [ML *factivus*, fr. L *factus* + *-ivus* -ive] **1** *obs* : having power to make : CONSTRUCTIVE **2 a** *of a grammatical case* : denoting a process of becoming or transmutation **b** : FACTITIVE

[2]**factive** \ˈ"\ *n* -s : the factive case of a language; *also* : a form in the factive case

-fac·tive \ˌfaktiv, -tēv, -təv\ *adj comb form* [MF *-factif*, fr. *-faction* + *-if* -ive] : making : causing : -POIETIC ⟨putre*factive*⟩

fac·to \ˈfak(ˌ)tō\ *adv* [L, abl. of *factum* deed, act — more at FACT] : in or by the fact

fact of life 1 facts of life *pl* : the fundamental physiological processes and reactions involved in sex and reproduction ⟨the mistake of bringing up children in ignorance of the *facts of life*⟩ **2** : something that exists and must be taken into consideration (as in developing a plan of action or comprehending a situation) ⟨that communism has a real appeal to the Asian is a *fact of life* we cannot ignore⟩

[1]**fac·tor** \ˈfaktə(r) *also* -ˌtȯ(ə)r *or* -ˌō(ə)\ *n* -s [ME *factour*, fr. MF *facteur*, fr. L *factor* maker, doer, fr. *factus* + *-or*] **1 a** : person that acts or transacts business for another : AGENT, DEPUTY: as **a** : a commercial agent who sells or buys goods for others on commission : CONSIGNEE; *esp* : one permitted to buy and sell in his own name and entrusted with the possession and control of goods — compare BROKER **b** *now chiefly Scot* : a steward or bailiff of an estate; *also* : one appointed by law to have charge of forfeited or sequestered property **c** : an employee of the former East India Company of Britain that ranked above a writer and below a merchant **d** : the agent in charge of a trading post of the Hudson's Bay Company who adds to the usual duties of a factor the care of the company's territory and often exercises a quasi police control of the surrounding region **e** : a commercial banker or finance company specializing in financial services to producers and dealers (as the discounting of accounts receivable) **2** *obs* **a** : PARTISAN, ADHERENT **b** : a maker, author, or doer of anything **3 a** : something (as an element, circumstance, or influence) that contributes to the production of a result : CONSTITUENT, INGREDIENT ⟨people and people's doings are the essential ~ —I.J.C.Brown⟩ ⟨such ~s as availability of adequate power, transportation, and a labor source must be considered in appraising an industrial site⟩ ⟨hereditary predisposition, malnutrition, and overexertion are common ~s in the development of many diseases⟩ **b** *or* **factor of production** : a good or service (as land, labor, or capital) used in the process of production **c** : one of the elements determined in job evaluation to be essential to a job (as skill and training required, effort demanded, responsibility and working conditions involved) — called also *job factor* **4 a** : GENE **b** : a presumed equivalent of a gene (as a plasmagene) ⟨some authorities recognize more than one kind of cytoplasmic ~⟩ **5 a** : any of the numbers, quantities, or symbols in mathematics that when multiplied together form a product **b** : a quantity by which a given quantity is multiplied or divided in order to express it in other terms; *also* : a quantity by which a given quantity is multiplied or divided in order to indicate a difference in measurement **c** : the number by which a given time is multiplied in photography to give the complete time for exposure or development **d** : a number that converts by multiplication the weight of one substance into the chemically equivalent weight of another substance — called also *gravimetric factor* **6** : a substance (as a hormone or vitamin) promoting or functioning in a particular physiological process; *esp* : such a substance of which the exact nature or mode of action is unknown ⟨the role of extrinsic ~s in blood formation⟩ **syn** see ELEMENT

[2]**fac·tor** \-tə(r)\ *vb* **factored; factored; factoring** \-t(ə)riŋ\ **factors** *vi* **1** : to resolve into factors : FACTORIZE **2** : to act as factor for ⟨~ed his cousin's estate after he got out of the army⟩ ~ *vi* : to act as a factor esp. in discounting accounts receivable

fac·tor·able \-t(ə)rəbəl\ *adj* : capable of representation as the product of numbers of a given field — opposed to *prime*

fac·tor·age \-tərij\ *n* -s [[1]*factor* + *-age*] **1 a** : the charges made by a factor for his services : commission or allowance of a factor **b** : the functions or business of a factor **2** : factors esp. of a situation

factor analysis *n* : a statistical method for the identification of each of several statistical variables that fluctuate together and for the determination of their relative contribution to a mingled influence

factoress *n* -ES *obs* : a female factor

[1]**fac·to·ri·al** \fakˈtōrēəl, -tȯr-\ *adj* [[1]*factor* + *-ial*] **1 a** : of, relating to, or involving the use of factorials ⟨~ mathematics⟩ **b** : involving or based on replication with a variable introduced in each replicate ⟨a ~ experiment⟩ ⟨~ study of mental processes⟩ **2** : of, relating to, or involving a factor ⟨advantages of ~ supervision of an estate⟩ — **fac·to·ri·al·ly** \-ēəlē, -li\ *adv*

[2]**factorial** \ˈ"\ *n* -s [[1]*factor* + *-ial*] : a function of a positive integer n denoted by $n!$ and defined by the relation $n! = 1 \cdot 2 \cdot 3 \cdots n$ with the convention that $0!$ is usu. assigned the value one

fac·to·ried \ˈfakt(ə)rēd, -rid\ *adj* : having or characterized by factories ⟨~ towns along the rivers⟩

factoring *n* -s **1** : the act or process of resolving something (as a mathematical expression) into its constituent factors **2** : the purchase of accounts receivable from a business by a factor who thereby assumes the risk of loss in return for some agreed discount

fac·tor·ist \ˈfaktərəst\ *n* -s [[1]*factor* + *-ist*] : an adherent to the theory that mental abilities depend on several factors, some specific and affecting success with one kind of task only, others general and affecting all undertakings

fac·tor·i·za·tion \ˌfaktərəˈzāshən, -ˌrīˈz-\ *n* -s : the act or process or an instance of factorizing

fac·tor·ize \ˈfaktəˌrīz\ *vt* -ED/-ING/-S **1** : GARNISHEE 1 **2** : [2]FACTOR 1

factor of production : FACTOR 3b

factor of safety : the ratio of the ultimate strength of a member or piece of material (as in an airplane) to the actual working stress or the maximum permissible stress when in use

factors *pl of* FACTOR, *pres 3d sing of* FACTOR

fac·tor·ship \ˈfaktə(r),ship\ *n* : the office or status of a factor

fac·to·ry \ˈfakt(ə)rē, -ri\ *n* -ES *often attrib* [MF *factorie*, fr. *facteur* factor + *-erie* -ery — more at FACTOR] **1** : an establishment (as a trading station) where factors or agents reside and transact business for their employers **2 a** : a building or collection of buildings with facilities (as power-driven machinery) for the manufacture of goods often from raw materials : a place where work is done in the fabricating of goods, wares, or utensils **b** *or* **factory ship** : a ship equipped to process at sea whales or fishes brought to it by other ships **c** : a place that is a seat of some kind of production ⟨the leaf is a ~ for carbohydrate production⟩ ⟨the vice *factories* of the slums⟩ **3** *chiefly Scot* : the office or function of a factor : FACTORSHIP **4** *now dial* : unbleached muslin

factory committee *n* : a group in each Soviet Russian factory elected by the workmen that at first managed the factory but later acted as the local organ of the trade union — compare SHOP COMMITTEE

factory farm *n* : a farm managed and operated like a factory

factory lumber *n* : lumber for or of a grade suitable for further processing (as in making sashes and doors)

factory mutual *n* : a mutual insurance company organized for the purpose of insuring factories and factory properties exclusively

factory system *n* : the system of manufacturing that began in the 18th century with the development of the power loom and the steam engine and is based on concentration of industry into large establishments — contrasted with *domestic system*

fac·to·tum \fakˈtōd·əm, -ōtəm\ *n* -s [NL, fr. L *fac totum!* do everything!, fr. *fac* (imp. of *facere* to do, make) + *totum*, neut. of *totus* all — more at DO] **1** : a person having many diverse activities or responsibilities : a general servant **2** : an ornamental oversize capital letter used in printing

fac·trix \ˈfaktriks\ *n* -ES *Scots law* : a female factor

facts *pl of* FACT

fac·tu·al \ˈfakch(əw)əl, -ksh-; -kshwəl\ *adj* [*fact* + *-ual* (as in *actual*)] **1** : of, relating to, or concerned with facts ⟨~ considerations⟩ ⟨the ~ aspects of the case⟩ **2** : restricted to, involving, or based on fact esp. as opposed to the imaginative or theoretical ⟨a carefully ~ presentation of the evidence⟩ ⟨~ studies⟩ ⟨a ~ account⟩ — **fac·tu·al·ly** \-əlē, -li\ *adv*

fac·tu·al·ism \-ə,lizəm\ *n* -s **1** : adherence or dedication to facts ⟨the ~ of the scientist⟩ **2** : a theory based on or emphasizing the importance of facts

fac·tu·al·ist \-ələst\ *n* -s : an adherent of factualism — **fac·tu·al·is·tic** \ˌ=(=)=ˈ=s=\ *adj*

fac·tu·al·i·ty \ˌfakchəˈwaləd·ē, -ətē, -i\ *also* **fac·tu·al·ness** *n* -ES : the quality or state of being fact or factual ⟨the ~ of his report⟩

fac·tum \ˈfaktəm\ *n, pl* **fac·ta** \-tə\ *also* **factums** [NL, fr. L, act, deed — more at FACT] **1** *law* : a man's own act and deed: as **a** : an instrument under seal **b** : the due execution of a will **2** [LL, fr. L] **a** : FACT, EVENT **b** : a statement of facts (as of a case in court) : MEMORIAL

fac·ture \ˈfakchə(r), -ksh-\ *n* -s [ME, fr. MF, fr. L *factura* act of making, formation — more at FEATURE] **1** : the manner in which something is made or finished : EXECUTION; *often* : the quality or handling of a surface (as in painting) ⟨Dali's neat, tight Vermeerish ~ has its aesthetic as well as Picasso's bold, plangent viscous brushwork —Herbert Read⟩ **2** *archaic* : the act or process of making something **3** : INVOICE

fact verdict *n* : SPECIAL VERDICT

facty \ˈfaktē, -ti\ *adj* -ER/-EST : filled with facts

fac·u·la \ˈfakyələ\ *n, pl* **facu·lae** \-yə,lē\ [NL, fr. L, small torch, dim. of *fac-, fax* torch] : any of the bright regions of the sun's photosphere seen most easily near the sun's edge and occurring most frequently in proximity to sunspots — **fac·u·lar** \-lə(r)\ *adj* — **fac·u·lous** \-ləs\ *adj*

fac·ul·ta·tive \ˈfakəl,tād·iv\ *adj* [F *facultatif*, fr. *faculté* faculty + *-atif* -ative] **1 a** : having relation to or concerned with the grant of a privilege ⟨~ legislation or enactments⟩ : involving permission rather than compulsion ⟨the licensing provision is purely ~⟩ **b** *of money* : used for convenience and having no status as legal tender ⟨at one time local subdivisions of France issued ~ coins of small value⟩ **c** : OPTIONAL ⟨~ courses in the sciences⟩ **2 a** : having characteristics that permit alternate responses (as of doing or not doing or of happening or not happening) under different conditions ⟨there is no ~ plurality in the mind; it is a single organ of true judgment —James Martineau⟩ ⟨~ homosexuals⟩ **b** : able to live or thrive under more than one set of conditions ⟨certain ~ parasites that are capable of a free-living saprophytic existence⟩ ⟨many bacteria are ~ anaerobes⟩ **3** : of or relating to the faculties **4** : NONDISTINCTIVE

fac·ul·ta·tive·ly *adv* : in a facultative manner : not obligatorily ⟨~ parasitic fungi⟩

facultative referendum *n* : OPTIONAL REFERENDUM

facultative reinsurance *n* : a separate reinsurance agreement drawn up for a single risk

fac·ul·ty \ˈfakəltē, -ti\ *n* -ES *often attrib* [ME *faculte*, fr. MF *faculté*, fr. ML & L; ML *facultat-, facultas* branch of learning, academic faculty, fr. L, ability, power, abundance, supply, property, fr. OL *facul* (neut. of L *facilis* easily done, easy) + L *-tat-, -tas* -ty — more at FACILE] **1 a** *obs* : a branch of learning **b** : a branch of teaching or learning in an institution usu. involving the interaction of several academic departments and providing education leading to a particular degree ⟨in medieval universities the *faculties* usually recognized were theology, law, medicine, and arts⟩ **c** *archaic* : something in which one is trained or qualified (as an art, craft, trade, or profession) **2 a** : the holders of graduate degrees and often the student candidates for degrees in theology, law, medicine, or arts **b** : the members of a profession or calling ⟨the medical ~⟩ **c** : the teaching staff and those members of the administrative staff having academic rank in a college, university, or other educational institution or one of its divisions ⟨an excellent mathematics ~⟩ **3** : pecuniary state as evidenced by ability to pay; *often* : MEANS, PROPERTY, RESOURCES ⟨the levying of ~ taxes〉 **4 a :** ability to act or do whether inborn or cultivated 〈man . . . how infinite in ~ —*Shak.*〉 **b :** an inherent capability, power, or function — now used chiefly of the living body or its parts 〈the ~ of hearing〉 〈the digestive ~〉 **c :** one of the powers or agencies into which psychologists formerly divided the mind (as will, reason, instinct) and through the interaction of which they endeavored to explain all mental phenomena **d** *obs* **:** personal characteristics or capacity **:** DISPOSITION **e :** natural aptitude 〈he has a ~ for saying the right thing〉 **f :** executive ability **:** COMPETENCE 〈a natural ~ for managing a household〉 **g :** a special mental endowment 〈Coleridge employed his analytical ~ frequently and brilliantly upon the works of Shakespeare —James Benziger〉 **5 a :** power, authority, or prerogative given or conferred (as by a superior) 〈by its constituting authority the state has the ~ to define treason〉 **b :** a permit from the consistory in the Church of England without which no considerable alterations can be made in a church's fabric, ornaments, or monuments **c :** a right, authority, license, or dispensation granted or delegated by ecclesiastical authority — often pl. in constr. even when sing. in meaning **d** *Scots law* **:** a power or ability created by one to be exercised at any time by another in accordance with the terms of the instrument creating it; *specif* **:** a power to make provision for the support of someone or to apportion or appoint property in which the holder of the power need not necessarily have any ownership **syn** see GIFT

faculty psychology *n* **:** an outmoded school of psychology that attempted to account for human behavior by positing various mental powers or agencies on an a priori basis — compare FACULTY 4c

faculty theory *n* **:** a theory of taxation: every individual should contribute to the support of the public burdens according to his ability

fa·cund \'fakənd, fə'kənd\ *adj* [ME *facound,* fr. L *facundus,* fr. *fari* to speak — more at FAME] **:** ELOQUENT

fa·cun·di·ty \fə'kəndəd·ē, fə'-\ *n* -ES [L *facunditas,* fr. *facundus* + *-itas* -ity] **:** ELOQUENCE

facy \'fāsi\ *adj* -ER/-EST [¹*face* + *-y*] *now dial Brit* **:** BRASH, IMPUDENT, INSOLENT

fad \'fad, 'faa(ə)d\ *n* -S [origin unknown] **1 :** a pursuit or interest followed usu. widely but briefly and capriciously with exaggerated zeal and devotion 〈the fancy, fashionable cleverness and egocentric brilliance of each passing modern ~ —Peter Viereck〉 **2 :** the object of a fad **:** RAGE 〈crossword puzzles were the ~ of the year〉 **syn** see FASHION

FAD \,ef,ā'dē\ *abbr or n* -S **:** flavin adenine dinucleotide

FAD *abbr* free air delivered

fad·ding *var of* ¹FADING

fad·dish \'fadish, 'faad-,-ēsh\ *adj* **1 :** inclined to take up fads 〈~ wealthy widows〉 **2 :** constituting or resembling a fad 〈~ collecting of special stamps〉 — **fad·dish·ly** *adv*

fad·dism \-,dizəm\ *n* -S **:** inclination to take up fads **:** fondness or enthusiasm for fads 〈aping another's scale out of snobbery or ~ —Hayward Keniston〉

fad·dist \-,dəst\ *n* -S **:** one that is inclined to take up fads 〈the literary ~*s* — those people who affect newness of manner —Lodwick Hartley〉; *often* **:** one that enthusiastically accepts and practices quack notions 〈food ~*s* who like to live on strangely restricted diets —Morris Fishbein〉 — **fad·dis·tic** \(')fa¦distik,(')faa¦-\ *adj*

fad·dle \'fadᵊl\ *n* -S [origin unknown] *chiefly dial* **:** NONSENSE, FOOLISHNESS

fad·dy \'fadē, 'faad-, -di\ *adj* -ER/-EST **:** FADDISH

¹**fade** \'fād,'fȧd\ *adj* [ME, fr. OF, fr. (assumed) VL *fatidus,* alter. (influenced by L *sapidus* wise, tasty & *vapidus* flat-tasting) of L *fatuus* foolish, silly, tasteless — more at SAGE, VAPID, BAT (club)] **:** INSIPID, VAPID, TRITE, COMMONPLACE 〈a sauce . . . which . . . struck me as rather more ~ than delicate —*New Yorker*〉

²**fade** \'fād\ *vb* -ED/-ING/-S [ME *faden,* fr. MF *fader,* fr. *fade*] *vi* **1 a :** to lose freshness, vigor, vitality, or health **:** LANGUISH, WITHER, DROOP 〈the old flowers in the vase were *fading*〉 **b :** to undergo loss of the appeal or attractiveness of the young or new 〈Mexican wives are expected to do all the domestic work, and ~ early —*Amer. Guide Series: Texas*〉 〈a *fading* child star in Hollywood〉 〈the metaphors contained in countless words *faded* so long, long ago —E.S.McCartney〉 **c :** to decline with or as if with approaching death or invalidism 〈a fell disease from which . . . she was now *fading* —F.M.Ford〉 **d :** to lose force and drive and cease to be a contender 〈the horse *faded* in the stretch〉 **e :** to lose strength **:** suffer loss of significance, consequence, or effectiveness **:** become enervated, unsubstantial, immaterial, or unreal 〈as optimism and security *faded* in the Thirties —Anthony Boucher〉 〈as the dream of building a society of Saints *faded* —Carl Bridenbaugh〉 〈countless small towns had boomed for a few years and then *faded* into ghosts —*Amer. Guide Series: Ark.*〉 **f** *of an automobile brake* **:** to lose braking power gradually (as because of wear or temperature change of parts) — often used with *out* **2 a** (1) **:** to lose freshness of color **:** become dingy 〈there were vivid paintings on the entrance walls . . . they have not entirely *faded* —Green Peyton〉 〈a little mill village with *faded* wooden houses —*Amer. Guide Series: Vt.*〉 (2) **:** to lose brilliance **:** change color by decreasing in saturation or increasing in lightness or both **:** DIM 〈the fabrics *faded* in the strong sunshine〉 〈at about half-past seven, when the light was beginning to ~ —Nevil Shute〉 〈the long Roman twilight *faded* into darkness —Herbert Agar〉 **b** *of a sound* **:** to dwindle or die away gradually 〈heard at night, when daytime sounds have *faded* —Tom Marvel〉 **3 a :** to recede into indistinctness and lack of clarity of outline and detail **:** BLUR 〈now ~*s* the glimmering landscape on the sight —Thomas Gray〉 〈we stood out to sea till the coastline itself began to ~ —Kenneth Roberts〉 **b :** to disappear slowly and die out in effect **:** lapse gradually into desuetude **:** pass gradually from clear consideration or memory 〈memories of transatlantic antecedents *faded* —Oscar Handlin〉 〈this story seems to have *faded* out of the popular mind —Norman Douglas〉 **c :** to undergo gradual disappearance or gradual change or transition **:** become gradually submerged or absorbed **:** BLEND 〈the mountains ~ into lowlands —L.D.Stamp〉 〈that nationalism might gradually ~ into a universal humanism —Bertrand Russell〉 **4 a :** to pass gradually from a certain stage, condition, or situation 〈murmuring to herself and visibly *fading* back into the mist in which she lived —Marcia Davenport〉 **b :** to dwindle away gradually **:** vanish slowly **:** melt away 〈his audience . . . had *faded* away like snow before the sun —Ernest Beaglehole〉 〈the smile *faded* from his face〉 **c :** to draw back **:** go away or backward typically quietly, unobtrusively, or furtively **:** RETREAT, LEAVE 〈the protective plumage that enabled him to ~ effortlessly into the background —Hamilton Basso〉 〈you can ~ away and the sergeant and I will take over —F.W.Crofts〉 **d** *of a football back* **:** to move back from the line of scrimmage 〈the quarterback *faded* back and threw a pass〉 **e** *of a ball* **:** to swerve from a true course **:** CURVE **f** *of a coin* **:** to wear away so that the design becomes indistinct or vanishes **5 :** to switch focus of attention 〈you can immediately ~ to the detective questioning members of the household —Richard Harrison〉 **6 a :** to change gradually in loudness or visibility — used of a motion-picture image or of an electronics signal or image and usu. with *out* to specify change from loud to soft or bright to dark and with *in* to specify change from soft to loud or dark to bright **b :** to begin to operate or to cease to operate — used esp. of a camera or piece of sound equipment and usu. with *out* to specify decreasing operation and with *in* to specify increasing operation ~ *vt* **1 :** to cause to lose freshness or vitality **:** WITHER 〈time has not completely *faded* the humor of these verses —G.H.Genzmer〉 **2 :** to cause to alter and esp. decrease in brightness, loudness, intensity, or distinctness: as **a :** to cause to change color by decreasing in saturation or increasing in lightness or both **b** (1) **:** to cause (as a motion-picture, radio, or television sound or image) to change gradually in loudness or visibility — usu. used with *in* or *out* (2) **:** to cause (as a camera or piece of sound equipment) to begin gradually to operate or to cease to operate — usu. used with *in* or *out* **3 :** to accept a bet offered by (one gambling) **:** COVER 19; *esp* **:** to cover all or a specified part of the center bet of (a crapshooter) **4 :** to curve (a ball) to the player's off side (as in golf or bowling) — opposed to *hook* **syn** see VANISH

³**fade** \"\ *n* -S **1 a :** FADE-IN **b :** FADE-OUT **2 :** a gradual changing of one picture to another in a motion-picture or television sequence **3 :** a fading of an automobile brake

fadeaway \'ˌ=ˌ=\ *n* -S [fr. *fade away,* v.] **1 :** an act or instance of fading away **2 a :** a baseball pitch that breaks downward and toward a right-handed batter **b :** a slide in which a base runner throws his body sideways to avoid the tag

fad·ed·ly *adv* **:** in the manner of one that has faded 〈a ~ handsome woman〉

fad·ed·ness *n* -ES **:** the quality or state of being faded

faded rose *n* **:** OCHER RED

fade–in \'ˌ=ˌ\ *n* -S [fr. *fade in,* v.] **:** an act or instance of fading in **:** gradual emergence of a picture from darkness to full visibility or of a sound from silence to full volume

fade·less \'fādləs\ *adj* **:** exempt from fading **:** not susceptible to fading 〈the ~ blooms of youth —Thomas Moore〉 — **fade·less·ly** *adv*

Fade–Om·e·ter \fā'dämәd·ə(r)\ *trademark* — used for an apparatus containing a carbon-arc lamp that emits radiation approximating sunlight for use in accelerated tests of light-fastness under controlled conditions

fade–out \'ˌ=ˌ\ *n* -S [fr. *fade out,* v.] **1 a :** gradual decrease in visibility or distinctness of a motion-picture or television image esp. for signaling transition or conclusion **b :** diminution or disappearance of sound impulse sent by radio either purposive for dramatic effect or natural as caused by ionospheric disturbances **2 a :** the concluding scene of or as if of a motion picture 〈the standard *fade-out* kiss —*Current Biog.*〉 **b :** gradual disappearance from prominence 〈the slow *fade-out* of auction bridge〉 **c :** VANISHING, DISAPPEARING

fad·er \'fādə(r)\ *n* -S **1 :** one that fades **2 a :** a device for varying the volume of reproduced sound of a motion picture **b :** an electronic device by which fade-in or fade-out can be controlled

fades *pres 3d sing of* FADE, *pl of* FADE

¹**fadge** \'faj\ *n* -S [ME (Sc dial.) *faige*] **1 a** *chiefly Scot* **:** a round thick loaf of bread **b** *chiefly Irish* **:** potato cake or bread **2 :** BUNDLE **3** *Austral* **:** an irregular package of wool weighing from 60 to 150 pounds

²**fadge** \"\ *vi* -ED/-ING/-S [origin unknown] **1 a** *archaic* **:** to fit surroundings and consequently to thrive or avail **b** *obs* **:** SUIT, AGREE **2 a** *obs* **:** to be compatible **b** *archaic* **:** SUCCEED

¹**fad·ing** \'fadiŋ\ *n* -S [origin unknown] *archaic* **:** an Irish dance

²**fad·ing** \'fādiŋ\ *n* -S [fr. gerund of ²*fade*] **:** fluctuation in intensity of received radio waves while the adjustments of sending and receiving apparatus remain unchanged

fad·ing·ly *adv* **:** in the manner of one that is fading 〈a ~ attractive beauty of yesterday〉

fa·do \'fä(,)thü\ *n* -S [Pg, lit., fate, fr. L *fatum* — more at FATE] **:** a Portuguese folk song typically plaintive or mournful

fads *pl of* FAD

fady \'fād·ē, -i\ *adj* -ER/-EST **:** tending to fade

¹**fae** \'fā\ *prep* [alter. of *frae*] *Scot* **:** FROM

²**fae** \"\ *archaic Scot var of* FOE

faecal *var of* FECAL

faem \'fām\ *Scot var of* FOAM

fa·e·na \fä'ānə\ *n* -S [Sp, lit., task, fr. obs. Catal (now *feina*), fr. L *facienda* things to be done, fr. neut. pl. of *faciendus,* fut. passive participle of *facere* to make, do, make — more at DO] **:** the series of final passes by the matador with sword and muleta leading to the kill

fae·nus *or* **fe·nus** *or* **foe·nus** \'fēnəs\ *n* [L; prob. akin to L *femina* woman — more at FEMININE] *Roman law* **:** INTEREST 3a

faenus nau·ti·cum \-'nȯd· əkəm\ *n* [LL, lit., maritime interest] *Roman law* **:** interest paid on maritime loans to be repaid only when a ship and its cargo safely reach port

fa·en·za ware \fä'enzə-, -ntsə-\ *n, usu cap F* [fr. *Faenza,* commune in northern Italy] **:** pottery of majolica technique made at Faenza, Italy, in the 16th century

fa·er·ie *also* **fa·ery** \'fā(ə)rē, 'fa(a)r-,'fer-, -ri\ *n, pl* **faeries** [MF *faerie* fairyland, enchantment — more at FAIRY] **1 :** the imagined realm of fairies **:** an imaginary land of enchantment **2 :** FAIRY

¹**faero·ese** *or* **faro·ese** \¦fa(a)rə¦wēz, ¦fer-, -ēs\ *adj, usu cap* [*Faeroes,* islands in the north Atlantic comprising a county of Denmark + E *-ese*] **:** of or relating to the Faeroese people or their language

²**faeroese** *or* **faroese** \"\ *n, pl* **faeroese** *or* **faroese** *cap* **1 a :** the Germanic people inhabiting the Faeroes **b :** a member of such people **2 :** the North Germanic language of the Faeroese people

fa·ery *also* **fa·er·ie** \'fā(ə)rē, 'fa(a)r-,'fer-, -ri\ *adj* **:** of, relating to, or suggesting faerie 〈pines and crags ~ with September mists —Hervey Allen〉

faex com·pres·sa \¦fekskəm'presə\ *n* [L] **:** COMPRESSED YEAST

FAF *abbr* flyaway factory

faff \'faf\ *vi* -ED/-ING/-S [imit.] *dial Brit* **:** to make a fuss over nothing

¹**fag** \'fag, -aa(ə)g,-aig\ *n* -S [ME *fagge* flap, knot in cloth] **1 :** FAG END **2 :** CIGARETTE; *sometimes* **:** a cheap cigarette

²**fag** \"\ *vb* **fagged; fagged; fagging; fags** [obs. E *fag* to droop, perh. fr. ¹*fag*] *vi* **1 :** to become weary **:** TIRE, FLAG **2 :** to work to exhaustion **:** DRUDGE, TOIL 〈*fagging* away at all the extra work〉 **3 a :** to be a fag **:** serve as a fag 〈*fagging* for older boys during his first year〉 **b :** to serve as a fag in the field in British school games (as cricket) ~ *vt* **1 :** to compel to serve as a fag 〈what right have the fifth-form boys to ~ us —Thomas Hughes〉 **2 :** to exhaust by toil, drudgery, or sustained heavy activity — often used with *out* 〈the long march *fagged* them out〉 **3 :** to make (the end of a rope) frayed or untwisted **syn** see TIRE

³**fag** \"\ *n* -S **1** *chiefly Brit* **:** a fatiguing task **:** DRUDGERY 〈it is such a ~; I came back tired to death —Jane Austen〉 **2 a :** an English public-school boy who acts as servant to another boy in a higher form **b :** MENIAL, DRUDGE, SERVITOR

⁴**fag** \"\ *or* **fag·got** \'fagət\ *n* -S [origin unknown] *slang* **:** HOMOSEXUAL

fa·ga·ce·ae \fə'gāsē,ē\ *n pl, cap* [NL, fr. *Fagus,* type genus + *-aceae*] **:** a family of trees and shrubs (order Fagales) having the staminate flowers in cymose heads or drooping aments and pistillate flowers with an urn-shaped to oblong perianth that occur singly or in clusters and are succeeded by one-seeded nuts — see CASTANEA, FAGUS, QUERCUS — **fa·ga·ceous** \-āshəs\ *adj*

fa·ga·les \fə'gā(,)lēz\ *n pl, cap* [NL, fr. *Fagus* + *-ales*] **:** an order of dicotyledonous trees and shrubs distinguished chiefly by the inferior unilocular ovary containing two or more ovules

fa·ga·ra \fə'garə\ [NL, fr. Ar] *syn of* ZANTHOXYLUM

fa·ge·lia \fə'jēlēə, -lyə\ [NL, fr. Kaspar *Fagel* †1688 Dutch statesman + NL *-ia*] *syn of* CALCEOLARIA

fag end *n* [¹*fag*] **1 a :** the last part or coarser end of a web of cloth **b :** the untwisted end of a rope **c :** an end or other part showing poor quality or spoiled condition **2 :** a worn, poor, or useless ending or remnant unlikely to afford either pleasure or profit

fag·gery \'fagərē, -ri\ *n* -ES [³*fag* + *-ery*] **:** the fagging system formerly common in English public schools

fa·gin \'fāgən\ *n* -S *often cap* [after *Fagin,* a fence and trainer of children as pickpockets in the novel *Oliver Twist* (1837-39) by Charles Dickens †1870 Eng. novelist] **:** an adult who instructs others in crime; *esp* **:** one who teaches children to steal 〈a kindly ~ who harbors a nest of adolescent thieves as runners for his goods —*Time*〉

fa·gine \'fā,jēn,-jən\ *n* -S [NL *Fagus* + E *-ine*] **:** a volatile narcotic principle present in the husks of beechnuts

fagmaster \'ˌ=ˌ=\ *n* [³*fag* + *master*] **:** a schoolboy who has a fag

fag·o·py·rism \,fagō'pī,rizəm\ *also* **fag·o·py·ris·mus** \-,pī'rizməs\ *n, pl* **fagopyrisms** *also* **fagopyris·muses** [G *fagopyrismus,* fr. NL *Fagopyrum* + G *-ismus* -ism] **:** a photosensitization esp. of swine and sheep that is due to eating large quantities of buckwheat and that appears principally on the nonpigmented parts of the skin as an intense redness and swelling with severe itching and the formation of vesicles and later sores and scabs — compare BIGHEAD 1b, HYPERICISM

fag·o·py·rum \-'pīrəm\ *n, cap* [NL, fr. L *fagus* beech + NL *-o-* + *-pyrum* (fr. Gk *pyros* wheat) — more at BEECH, FURZE] **:** a genus of European and Asiatic annual plants (family Polygonaceae) having the achene much exceeding the perianth but otherwise resembling members of the genus *Polygonum* — see BUCKWHEAT

¹**fag·ot** *or* **fag·got** \'fagət,'faig-, *usu* -əd·+V\ *n* -S [ME *fagot,* fr. MF *fagot,* prob. fr. OProv, perh. fr. (assumed) VL *facus,* modif. of Gk *phakelos*] **1 :** a bundle of sticks or twigs esp. as used for fuel, as a fascine, or as a means of burning heretics alive **2 :** BUNDLE, BUNCH **3 :** a bundle of pieces of wrought iron to be worked over into bars or other shapes by rolling or hammering at high temperature **4 :** an unpleasant or objectionable woman **5** *obs* **:** a person paid for use of his name to complete a roster **6** *Brit* **:** FAGOT VOTE **7 a :** BOUQUET GARNI **b :** a portion of the viscera of the hog, chopped, seasoned with herbs, shaped into a ball or stick, and fried or baked

fagot 1

²**fagot** \"\ *or* **faggot** *vb* **fagoted** *or* **faggoted; fagoted** *or* **faggoted; fagoting** *or* **faggoting; fagots** *or* **faggots** *vt* **1 :** to set fagots around (as a heretic) preparatory to execution by burning **2 :** to make a fagot of **:** bind together into a bundle 〈~*ed* sticks〉 〈he ~*ed* all the pamphlets together〉 **3 :** to embroider or work in fagoting **:** seam with fagoting ~ *vi* **:** to make fagots

fagot cinnamon *n* **:** a cinnamon bark from an Asiatic tree (*Cinnamomum burmanni*) — called also *Batavia cassia*

fag·ot·er \'fagəd·ə(r)\ *n* -S **:** one that makes fagots or works with fagoting: as **a :** one who sews together or decorates with fagoting by hand or by machine **b :** a sewing machine attachment for making fagoting

fag·ot·ing *or* **fag·got·ing** \-əd·iŋ\ *n* -S **1 a :** an embroidery produced by pulling threads in one direction and tying the exposed threads into groups of an hourglass shape **b :** a decorative openwork stitching forming a ladderlike or zigzag line that is used esp. in seams of garments and table linens **2 :** the act or operation of cutting up puddled iron into lengths and piling in a reheating furnace for subsequent heating and rolling or hammering into bars

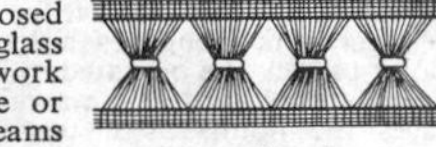

fagoting 1a

fagot iron *n* **:** iron in bars or masses made from fagots

fa·gott \fä'gȯt\ *n, pl* **fa·got·te** \-ōtə\ [G, fr. It *fagotto*] **:** BASSOON — **fa·got·tist** \fə'gäd·əst\ *n* -S

fa·got·ti·no \,fägə'tē(,)nō\ *n* -S [It, dim. of *fagotto*] **:** TENOROON

fa·got·to \fə'gäd·(,)ō *It* fä'gȯt(,)tō\ *n, pl* **fagot·ti** \-äd·(,)ē, -ȯt(,)tē\ [It, lit., fagot, fr. Prov *fagot* — more at FAGOT] **1 :** BASSOON **2 :** an 8-foot pipe-organ stop of the same general quality as the bassoon

fagot vote *n, Brit* **:** the vote of one made a property holder for party purposes to qualify him as a voter

fags *pl of* FAG, *pres 3d sing of* FAG

fa·gus \'fāgəs\ *n, cap* [NL, fr. L, beech — more at BEECH] **:** a genus of trees (family Fagaceae) having the staminate flowers in small pendulous heads and the fruit sharply 3-angled — compare CASTANEA, QUERCUS; see BEECH, COPPER BEECH

fah *abbr, usu cap* Fahrenheit

fa·ham \'fä,häm\ *n* -S [F, fr. a native name in the Mascarene islands] **1 :** the leaves of an orchid (*Angrecum fragrans*) of Réunion and Mauritius used in France as a substitute for Chinese tea **2 :** the plant that produces faham leaves

fahl·band \'fäl,bänt, -band\ *n* [G, fr. *fahl* pale, faded, dun-colored (fr. OHG *falo*) + *band,* fr. OHG *bant;* fr. its pale color at decomposition — more at FALLOW, BAND] **:** a band or stratum in crystalline rock containing metallic sulfides

fahl·erz \'fä,lerts\ *also* **fahl·ore** \-lō(ə)r\ *n, pl* **fahler·ze** \-tsə\ *also* **fahlores** [*fahlerz* fr. G, fr. *fahl* + *erz* ore, fr. OHG *aruz, aruzzi;* akin to OS *arut* ore, ON *örtog,* a small coin; all prob. of non-IE origin; akin to Sumerian *urud* copper; *fahlore* part trans. of G *fahlerz*] **:** TETRAHEDRITE

fah·lun·ite \'fälə,nīt\ *n* -S [Sw *fahlunit,* fr. *Fahlun* (Falun), Sweden + Sw *-it* -ite] **:** an altered form of cordierite

fahr *abbr, usu cap* Fahrenheit

¹**fahr·en·heit** \'farən,hīt *also* 'fer-, *usu* -īd·+V\ *adj, usu cap* [after Gabriel D. *Fahrenheit* †1736 Ger. physicist] **:** relating or conforming to a thermometric scale on which under standard atmospheric pressure the boiling point of water is at 212 degrees and the freezing point at 32 degrees above the zero of the scale, the zero point approximating the temperature produced by mixing equal quantities by weight of snow and common salt 〈10° *Fahrenheit*〉 — abbr. *F, Fah, Fahr*

²**fahrenheit** \"\ *n* -S *usu cap* **:** a Fahrenheit thermometer or scale

fai·blesse \fābles\ *n, pl* **fai·blesses** \"\ [F, fr. OF *flebesse, feblesse, foiblesse,* fr. *flebe, feble, foible* weak — more at FEEBLE] **:** WEAKNESS, FOIBLE

fa·ience *or* **fa·ïence** *also* **fa·yence** \fā'än(t)s, -äⁿs, 'ˌ=ˌ=\ *n* -S [F, fr. *Faenza,* city in northern Italy] **:** earthenware decorated with opaque colored glazes

faïence d'oi·ron \fāyäⁿsdwärōⁿ\ *n, usu cap O* [F, lit., faïence from Oiron (commune in western France)] **:** SAINT-PORCHAIRE FAÏENCE

faik \'fāk\ *vt* -ED/-ING/-S [short for Sc *defaik,* alter. of E *defalk*] *Scot* **:** SPARE, EXCUSE

¹**fail** \'fāl, *esp before pause or consonant* -āəl\ *vb* -ED/-ING/-S [ME *faillen, failen,* fr. OF *faillir,* fr. (assumed) VL *fallire,* alter. of L *fallere* to deceive, be concealed from, escape observation, be ignorant of; prob. akin to Gk *phēlos* deceitful, Skt *hrunāti* he gets lost, OSlav *zŭlŭ* bad, evil] *vi* **1 a :** to undergo loss of vigor or activity **:** lose strength, power, vitality, or intensity **:** become enfeebled 〈his health ~*ed* and he retired young〉 〈the breeze ~*ed* and we were becalmed〉 〈the warm sun is ~*ing* . . . the pale flowers are dying —P.B.Shelley〉 〈the never ~*ing* river of student life —J.B.Conant〉 **b :** to diminish in amount or quantity to a point of inadequacy **:** dwindle away **:** run short 〈the supplies of the defenders ~*ed*〉 **c :** to cease to be encountered **:** be or become nonexistent 〈should the rains ~ . . . the numbers of the game depreciate —James Stevenson-Hamilton〉 **d :** to become extinct **:** die away 〈until our family line ~*s*〉 **e :** to be inadequate 〈time ~*s* for recounting all his exploits〉 **f :** to lose strength and control rapidly as a prelude to dying 〈the old man was ~*ing* and they decided to spare him the shock of the news〉 **g :** to grow dim and difficult or impossible to perceive 〈the radio signals ~*ed*〉 〈the landward marks have ~*ed* —Rudyard Kipling〉 **h :** to weaken and come to function very imperfectly 〈his eyesight was ~*ing*〉 〈the senile old woman's mind was ~*ing*〉 **i :** to stop functioning 〈the patient's heart ~*ed*〉 〈one of the plane's engines ~*ed*〉 **j :** to fall away from an expected or hoped-for yield 〈the peach crop ~*ed*〉 **2 a :** to miss attainment **:** fall short of achievement or realization — usu. used with *of* 〈this chronicle . . . may ~ of effect —Clifton Fadiman〉 〈the senator ~*ed* of reelection〉 〈music that ~*s* of beauty〉 **b :** to miss success in some effort **:** become forced to leave incomplete an attempt or enterprise — used with infinitive 〈he ~*ed* to finish the race〉 〈when a rainmaker ~*s* to produce rain —J.G.Frazer〉 **c :** to neglect to do something **:** leave something undone **:** be found wanting in not doing something — used with infinitive 〈the janitor had ~*ed* to call the fire department〉 〈had criminally ~*ed* to latch the street door —Arnold Bennett〉 〈if our civilization has ~*ed* to enable us to look further than our own egoistic ends —Havelock Ellis〉 **d :** to miss success **:** be unavailing **:** MISCARRY — used of things, devices, and arrangements 〈the commission ~*ed* to settle the refugee question〉 〈the jack ~*ed* to raise the truck〉 **e :** to end without success **:** miss successful achievement of a result 〈I ~*ed,* yet still I clung to the hope —Mary W. Shelley〉 〈the neurotic personality wishes to ~〉 **f :** to leave some possible or expected action unperformed or leave some condition unachieved 〈he usually ~*s* to remember his dreams〉 〈they could hardly ~ to meet〉 〈explosive statements that rarely ~*ed* to startle his hearers —D.D.Eisenhower〉 〈meals that ~ to satisfy〉 〈a . . . section that the continental glacier ~*ed* to cover —*Amer. Guide Series: Minn.*〉 〈a rise in prices that ~*ed* to develop〉 **3 a :** to be deficient or inadequate **:** LACK 〈Aristophanes could ridicule all the literary Homeric

gods but must never ~ in respect to Athena —Gilbert Murray⟩ **b** : to prove inadequate, deficient, or unavailing on trial : give way or break down ⟨the attack ~*ed*⟩ ⟨the supporting brace ~*ed*⟩ **c** : to become unable to meet financial engagements; *esp* : to become bankrupt or insolvent ⟨banks were ~*ing*, unemployment was soaring —N.M.Clark⟩ **d** : to be deficient or unable to meet a test or standard of attainment ⟨he ~*ed* in arithmetic⟩ ⟨a ~*ing* term paper⟩ **4** *obs* : to err in judgment : be in error ~ *vt* **1** : to disappoint the expectations or trust of : be found wanting at the time of need of (a person) : miss performing expected or hoped-for service, assistance, or function for ⟨his allies ~*ed* him when the battle started⟩ ⟨if a man's English subordinates ~ him in India, he comes to a hard time indeed —Rudyard Kipling⟩ ⟨she reached for a chair and sat down suddenly, as if her legs had ~*ed* her —Ellen Glasgow⟩ ⟨for once his ready wit ~*ed* him⟩ **2** : to be deficient in : LACK ⟨our youth . . . never ~*ed* an invincible courage —Douglas MacArthur⟩ **3** *obs* : to leave undone or unperformed ⟨his morning prayer, which he never ~*ed*⟩ **4** *archaic* : to disappoint or leave unfulfilled (a trust, hope, or expectation) ⟨the book ~*s* the reader's hopes⟩ **5 a** : to prove so deficient in knowledge or skill as not to pass (as a test or course) ⟨she ~*ed* her driving test⟩ ⟨he ~*ed* chemistry⟩ **b** : to rate (as a pupil) as deficient in achievement for not meeting the standard required for passing ⟨the teacher ~*ed* only his two worst students⟩

²**fail** *n* [ME *faille, faile,* fr. OF *faille,* fr. (assumed) VL *fallia,* fr. LL *fallire*] **1 a** *obs* : failure to occur **b** : omission of doing or performing something — usu. used in the phrase *without fail* **2** *obs* : want of success

failance *n* -S *obs* : FAILURE

failed *adj* : having failed : having been unsuccessful ⟨a ~ candidate⟩ ⟨a ~ novelist⟩

¹**failing** *n* -S [ME *failling, failing,* fr. gerund of *faillen, failen* to fail] : an often slight or venial disadvantageous foible, personality defect, or character weakness ⟨has all the ~*s* of our common lot —Ronald Rubinstein⟩ **syn** see FAULT

²**failing** *prep* [fr. pres. part. of ¹*fail*] : in absence, default, or lack of : in case of nonoccurrence of : WITHOUT ⟨~ specific instructions, use your own judgment⟩ ⟨~ brothers and sisters, cousins may inherit⟩

fail·ing·ly *adv* : in the manner of one that is failing ⟨a ~ dim beam of light⟩ ⟨a ~ faint cry⟩

faille \ˈfīl, *esp before pause or consonant* -īəl\ *n* -S [F] : a semilustrous closely woven fabric with good draping qualities for use in clothing and interior decoration that is made in plain weave of silk, rayon, or cotton and is characterized by slight flat ribs in the weft

fails *pres 3d sing of* FAIL

fail spot *or* **fail place** *n* : a place where forest reproduction has failed

fail·ure \ˈfālyə(r)\ *n* -S [alter. (influenced by *-ure*) of earlier *failer,* fr. AF *failer,* fr. OF *faillir* to fail — more at FAIL] **1 a** : omission of performance of an action or task; *esp* : neglect of an assigned, expected, or appropriate action ⟨the mechanic's ~ to adjust the brake⟩ ⟨the ~ of students to write complete sentences⟩ ⟨the scout's ~ to rejoin the party⟩ **b** : the fact of a certain action or process not having occurred : the fact of nonoccurrence ⟨~ of the water to pass through the pipe⟩ ⟨the ~ of the drug to have a harmful effect⟩ **2** : want of success : lack of satisfactory performance or effect ⟨the ~ of the attack on the fort⟩ ⟨the ~ of the candidate in the election⟩ **3** *obs* : FAILING, LAPSE **4 a** : DEFICIENCY, LACK : the fact of being cumulatively inadequate or not matching hopes or expectations ⟨the crop ~*s* brought on near famine⟩ **b** : ABSENCE, NONEXISTENCE ⟨through ~ of heirs, most of the state societies had disintegrated —A.F.Harlow⟩ **c** : marked weakening : the fact of becoming exhausted or enfeebled : DETERIORATION ⟨any impairment or ~ of his bodily vigor through sickness or age —J.G.Frazer⟩ **d** *med* : inability to perform a vital function ⟨heart ~⟩ **e** : a collapsing, fracturing, or giving way under stress : inability of a material or structure to fulfill an intended purpose **5 a** : BANKRUPTCY ⟨the ~ of the company⟩ ⟨the ~ of a friend whose note he had endorsed⟩ **b** : a venture financially unsuccessful ⟨although a contribution to literature, the play was a box-office ~⟩ **6** : a person or thing that has failed ⟨people who were either ~*s* or had had no ambitions —Louis Bromfield⟩ ⟨the war against the confederation was a ~⟩ **7 a** : the fact of failing in a test or course **b** : a failing grade **c** : a student who has failed

syn NEGLECT, DEFAULT, MISCARRIAGE, DERELICTION: FAILURE implies a lack or absence of something expected esp. in performance or achievement ⟨the *failure* of the courts in the past to formulate any principle for drawing a boundary line around the right of free speech —Zechariah Chafee⟩ ⟨the ailing civilization pays the penalty for its *failure* of vitality by becoming disintegrated —A.J.Toynbee⟩ ⟨nutritional *failure* due to inadequate intake of proteins and vitamins —*Jour. Amer. Med. Assoc.*⟩ NEGLECT implies carelessness or inattentiveness resulting in incompleteness or inadequacy of performance or achievement ⟨any *neglect* to take into consideration the relations of the social framework can only lead to a defective understanding —M.F.A.Montagu⟩ ⟨so intent on taking care of the physical mechanics of getting things done, their creative and imaginative faculties suffer from *neglect* —*Phoenix Flame*⟩ ⟨driven to extreme bitterness by public *neglect* of his work —*Amer. Guide Series: N.Y.*⟩ DEFAULT, now chiefly in legal context, implies a failure to perform something required, usu. by total omission of any action at all ⟨some of our decisions . . . are arrived at by *default* — that is, by "letting things go" —W.J.Reilly⟩ ⟨betraying by *default* the privileges of citizenship in a democratic society —Vera M. Dean⟩ ⟨in some *default* of faith too base for words —William Alfred⟩ MISCARRIAGE is often used when one cannot assign or wishes to avoid assigning specific blame for a failure ⟨it seems to me a *miscarriage* of the artist's job if his reputation does his work for him —William Arrowsmith⟩ ⟨we fear . . . some *miscarriage* in the details of our plan —J.W.Krutch⟩ ⟨a *miscarriage* of justice⟩ DERELICTION is extremely strong in signifying or implying a neglect or nonobservance amounting to a reprehensible abandonment of a morally compelling duty, law, or principle ⟨there is a moral *dereliction* in failure by any member of a profession to apply in professional practice the standards which, by consensus of opinion in the profession, are necessary —*Jour. Amer. Med. Assoc.*⟩ ⟨every good reporter knows that his friendship for a news source must never extend so far as disregard of official *dereliction* or incompetence —F.L.Mott⟩ ⟨a manager who fails to throw out hour-old coffee and replace it with fresh coffee is warned not to repeat his *dereliction* —Jack Alexander⟩

failure of issue : a lack of living descendants (as of a designated person) resulting from death or from complete lack of issue — see DEFINITE FAILURE OF ISSUE, INDEFINITE FAILURE OF ISSUE

faim·ly \ˈfāmli\ *Scot var of* FAMILY

¹**fain** \ˈfān\ *adj* -ER/-EST [ME *fagen, fayn,* fr. OE *fægen;* akin to OS *fagin, fagan* glad, happy, OHG *faginōn* to rejoice, ON *fegiun* happy, Goth *faginon* to rejoice, OE *fæger* beautiful — more at FAIR] **1** *archaic* : PLEASED, HAPPY ⟨if thou wouldst grant his asking and make his heart full ~ —William Morris⟩ **2 a** : GLAD, WILLING : INCLINED, DESIROUS ⟨men and birds are ~ of climbing high —Shak.⟩ ⟨something which the scientists approached with reluctance and which they were ~ to leave to the linguists —C.B.Tinker⟩ **b** *archaic* : OBLIGED, CONSTRAINED, COMPELLED ⟨such a clamor that we were ~ to comply —Tobias Smollett⟩ **3** *Scot* : FOND — **fain·ly** *adv*

²**fain** \"\ *adv* [ME *fagen, fayn,* fr. *fagen, fayn,* adj.] **1** : HAPPILY, JOYFULLY : with glad preference ⟨~ would I woo her —Shak.⟩ **2** : by preference or acquiescence in view of the circumstances ⟨Macbeth, who, though he would ~ repent —H.S.Wilson⟩

³**fain** \"\ *interj* [by alter.] *chiefly Brit* : ³FEN

fai·naigue \fəˈnāg\ *vi* -ED/-ING/-S [origin unknown] **1** *dial Brit* : RENEGE **2** *dial Brit* : to shirk work

fai·ne·an·cy \ˈfānēənsē\ *also* **fai·ne·ance** \-ēən(t)s\ *n, pl* **faineancies** *also* **faineanc·es** : remiss indolence : INACTIVITY ⟨~ and neglect of civic affairs⟩

¹**fai·ne·ant** \-nt\ *n* -S [F *fainéant,* fr. MF *fait-nient,* lit., (he) does nothing, by folk etymology fr. *faignant,* fr. pres. part. of *feindre, faindre* to feign, shirk, be inactive (as in *se feindre* to be lazy) — more at FEIGN] : an irresponsible or weak idler

²**faineant** \"\ *adj* : showing a faineant's character : idle and ineffectual : INDOLENT ⟨~ kings under whose rule the country languished⟩ **syn** see LAZY

fainéant deity *n* : a deity not acting in human affairs

fai·né·an·tise \fānāäⁿtēz\ *n, pl* **fainéan·tises** \"\ [F, fr. *fainéant*] : FAINEANCY

fain·ness \ˈfānnəs\ *n* -ES [ME *faynnesse,* fr. *fayn* fain + *-nesse* -ness] : WILLINGNESS, EAGERNESS

fains \ˈfānz\ *or* **fain it** *or* **fains I** *interj* [alter. of ³*fen*] *chiefly Brit* : ³FEN

¹**faint** \ˈfānt\ *adj* -ER/-EST [ME *faint, feint* (also, deceitful, feigned), fr. OF, fr. past part. of *faindre, feindre* to feign, shirk — more at FEIGN] **1** : lacking courage and spirit : COWARDLY, SPIRITLESS — now usu. used in the phrase *faint heart* **2** : feeble, dizzy, and likely to faint through or as if through hunger, illness, pain, shock, or emotion ⟨he felt suddenly ~ . . . he had eaten nothing —Pearl Buck⟩ ⟨sick and ~ from the pain —Jack London⟩ ⟨~ with her happiness —Ethel Wilson⟩ **3 a** : having an appearance of underlying weakness : lacking vigor or strength ⟨fair young man, with a long, pale nose, a ~ chin —Booth Tarkington⟩ **b** : performed, acted, or accomplished in a weak, feeble, or hesitant manner : marked by halfhearted forcelessness ⟨believed the assertion at once, but he made a ~ effort to resist conviction —G.B.Shaw⟩ ⟨damning with ~ praise⟩ **4** : likely to make one faint : OPPRESSIVE ⟨the ~ atmosphere of a tropical port⟩ **5 a** : making only a feeble impression on the senses : hardly perceptible : INDISTINCT, BLURRED, DIM ⟨he tied his shoelaces in hard knots because he couldn't see in the ~ light —Erskine Caldwell⟩ ⟨a ~ hissing sound became audible —H.G.Wells⟩ **b** : not making or accompanied by a clear mental impression : OBSCURE ⟨these ~ lights of intuition —G.W.Russell⟩ ⟨a ~ clue to the origin of these mystery people —R.W.Murray⟩ ⟨had not the ~*est* idea what was meant⟩

²**faint** \"\ *n* -S [ME *faint, feint,* fr. *faint, feint,* adj.] : the act or condition of fainting : SWOON ⟨the classic signs of the ordinary ~ — marked facial pallor and moist cold skin —*Today's Health*⟩

³**faint** \"\ *vb* -ED/-ING/-S [ME *fainten, feinten,* fr. *faint, feint,* adj.] *vi* **1** *archaic* : to lose heart : become discouraged or afraid : give way : FLAG **2** *archaic* : to grow weak or feeble : DECLINE ⟨but his strength dwindled and ~*ed*⟩ **3** : to suffer syncope : SWOON **4 a** : to lose brilliance, color, or intensity ⟨the aroma soon ~*s*⟩ **b** : to lose distinctness and clarity ~ *vt, archaic* : to make faint : DEPRESS, ENFEEBLE ⟨it ~*s* me to think what follows —Shak.⟩

⁴**faint** \"\ *adv* [¹*faint*] : FAINTLY

⁵**faint** *var of* FEINT

¹**faintheart** \ˈ=,=\ *adj* [alter. of *fainthearted*] : COWARDLY, TIMID, IRRESOLUTE

²**faintheart** \"\ *n* : a timorous or irresolute person : COWARD ⟨the ~*s* who broke and ran —Bruce Catton⟩

fainthearted \ˈ=ˈ==\ *adj* [ME *feint herted*] : lacking courage or resolution : FAINTHEART ⟨the ~ wished to surrender —J.A. Froude⟩ — **faint·heart·ed·ly** *adv* — **faint·heart·ed·ness** *n*

fainting *n* -S [ME *fainting, feinting,* fr. gerund of *fainten, feinten* to faint] : the act of one who faints: **a** : a growing faint : DEPRESSION **b** : loss of consciousness resulting from arrest of the blood supply to the brain : SYNCOPE

fainting fit *or* **fainting spell** *n* : FAINTING, SWOON, SYNCOPE

faint·ing·ly *adv* : in the manner of one that faints ⟨a ~ weak voice⟩

faint·ly *adv* **1** : in a faint manner ⟨for a few seconds he ~ struggled with the man —Charles Dickens⟩ ⟨his senses alive so ~ as to be useless —Nigel Dennis⟩ **2** : to a faint degree : SLIGHTLY, INDISTINCTLY ⟨showing ~ at the right of the picture —G.R.Stewart⟩ ⟨~ blue hills —Hugh Walpole⟩ ⟨rumors . . . which weren't even ~ true —Scott Fitzgerald⟩

faint·ness *n* -ES [ME *faintnesse, feintnesse,* fr. *faint, feint* + *-nesse* -ness] : the quality or state of being faint: as **a** : loss of strength : partial or near loss of consciousness **b** : lack of courage or spirit ⟨~ of heart⟩ **c** : feebleness of impression or of intensity of color or contrast : lack of distinctness ⟨~ of an old photograph⟩ ⟨~ of his recollection of the event⟩

faints *var of* FEINTS

fainty \ˈfāntē\ *adj* [ME *ffaynty,* fr. *faint, feint* + *-y*] *chiefly dial* : liable to faint : FEEBLE

fa·i·pu·le \fīˈpü,lā\ *n* -S [Samoan, fr. *fai* to do, make + *pule* rule] : a Samoan native councillor heading a political district and belonging to a fono

¹**fair** \ˈfa(a)(ə)r, ˈfe|, |ə\ *adj* -ER/-EST [ME *fager, fair,* fr. OE *fæger;* akin to OS & OHG *fagar* beautiful, ON *fagr* beautiful, Goth *fagrs* suitable, and perh. to MHG *vegen* to clean, sweep, ON *fāga* to clean, decorate, Lith *puošti* to decorate] **1 a** : attractive in appearance : pleasant to view : BEAUTIFUL, HANDSOME, COMELY ⟨the innkeeper had two ~ daughters⟩ ⟨forever wilt thou love and she be ~ —John Keats⟩ ⟨bedecked with garlands and flowers ~⟩ ⟨our ~ city⟩ ⟨settle down in such a ~ fat land and call good acres his own —Charles Kingsley⟩ **b** *archaic* : DEAR, KIND — used in formal salutation chiefly in the phrase *fair sir* ⟨your servant, ~ sir —Max Peacock⟩ **c** : FEMININE ⟨the ~ sex⟩ ⟨his ~ companions⟩ **2** : pleasing to hear : inspiring hope or confidence often delusively : GRACIOUS, AFFABLE, CIVIL, SPECIOUS ⟨in an evil hour she trusted his ~ promises⟩ ⟨trusted the enemy's ~ words, and were immediately murdered —J.A.Froude⟩ **3 a** : having attraction or admirable qualities : pleasant to contemplate : AGREEABLE, RICH, CONSIDERABLE, WORTHY ⟨the ~ life of ancient Athens⟩ ⟨a ~ estate⟩ ⟨cheapening a ~ cause with shabby tactics⟩ **b** : somewhat above average : moderately numerous or large : pretty good : being without marked lack or defect : SATISFACTORY, PASSABLE, SUFFICIENT, ADEQUATE ⟨a ~ proportion of the people . . . could read and write —G.M. Trevelyan⟩ ⟨a ~ knowledge of English and a smattering of Latin —W.E.Smith⟩ ⟨made some ~ guesses about the shape . . . of the universe —B.J.Bok⟩ ⟨a crop of scrub pine, grown already to a ~ height —Ellen Glasgow⟩ ⟨received a grade of ~ in English⟩ ⟨his work is only ~, certainly not distinguished⟩ **c** *of livestock* (1) : of middling quality; *specif* : third grade (2) : reasonably plentiful in supply : not scarce **4 a** : free from spots or dirt : not sullied ⟨a sheet of ~ white paper⟩ **b** *of water, archaic* : not dirtied, soiled, or contaminated : PURE **c** : free from moral stain : UNSULLIED, UNBLEMISHED ⟨her ~ name⟩ **d** (1) : DISTINCT, LEGIBLE ⟨easily deciphering the old manuscript written in a ~ hand⟩ (2) : free from corrections : being the final draft ⟨no private bill is permitted to be sent up . . . until a certificate is endorsed on the ~ printed bill —T.E.May⟩ **e** : straight or smoothly curving : having no sudden angular deviation **f** : properly aligned : fitting together ⟨~ rivet holes⟩ **5 a** : not stormy or foul : FINE, CLOUDLESS ⟨a ~ sky⟩ ⟨a ~ day⟩ **b** : free or nearly free from rain, hail, or snow — used in the predictions issued by the U.S. Weather Bureau even if the weather is cloudy and threatening if less than one hundredth of an inch of precipitation occurs **6** : not dark or brunet : LIGHT, CLEAR, BLOND ⟨~ . . . with great wavy masses of golden hair —Bram Stoker⟩ **7 a** : characterized by honesty and justice : free from fraud, injustice, prejudice, or favoritism ⟨you will find him a very ~ man⟩ ⟨determined to win by ~ means or foul⟩ **b** (1) : conforming to an established commonly accepted code or rules of a game or other competitive activity ⟨observers disagreed as to whether the blow was ~⟩ ⟨believes in ~ play in sports and business⟩ (2) *of a baseball field* : lying between the foul lines (3) : equitable as basis for exchange : REASONABLE ⟨a ~ valuation⟩ ⟨a ~ wage⟩ (4) : conforming to its merits or importance : DUE ⟨the subject has received its ~ share of attention⟩ (5) : having a certain basis in evidence or of reason : JUSTIFIED, VALID ⟨a ~ assumption that regularities occur in history⟩ ⟨he has a ~ complaint⟩ (6) : being a sufficient, equitable, or adequate basis for judgment or evaluation : TYPICAL, REPRESENTATIVE ⟨a ~ sample of his work⟩ ⟨that is not a ~ example⟩ **c** : legitimately open to attack or pursuit ⟨the hypocrite is ~ game to the satirist⟩ **8 a** (1) : PROMISING, AUSPICIOUS, LIKELY ⟨his prospects of future wealth were exceedingly ~ —Jane Austen⟩ ⟨in a ~ way to realize a profit —Arnold Bennett⟩ ⟨its cultures and institutions seem ~ to become stabilized —Clark Wissler⟩ (2) *of the wind* : favorable to a ship's course ⟨sailed for France with a ~ wind⟩ (3) *of the tide* : running in the general direction of a ship's course **b** : neither favorable and promising nor unfavorable and discouraging : EVEN ⟨a ~ bet that his team would win⟩ **9** *archaic* : free from obstacles : UNOBSTRUCTED, OPEN **10** *archaic* : plainly visible : DISTINCT **11** : UTTER, REAL, COMPLETE, FULL, STARK, ABSOLUTE ⟨a ~ miracle⟩ ⟨a ~ treat to watch him outsnob the snobs —*New Republic*⟩ ⟨when a ~ month had elapsed I did meet him again —James Stephens⟩

syn FAIR, JUST, EQUITABLE, IMPARTIAL, UNBIASED, DISPASSIONATE, UNCOLORED, and OBJECTIVE can apply, in common, to judgments, judges, or acts resulting from judgments, and signify freedom from improper influence. FAIR, the most general of the terms, implies a disposition in a person or group to achieve a fitting and right balance of claims or considerations that is free from undue favoritism even to oneself, or implies a quality or result in an action befitting such a disposition ⟨a *fair* trial for all offenders⟩ ⟨a *fair* distribution of profits⟩ ⟨a *fair* judge in a criminal trial⟩ ⟨a *fair* estimate of his achievements⟩ JUST stresses, more than FAIR, a disposition to conform with or conformity with the standard of what is right, true, or lawful, despite strong, esp. personal, influences tending to subvert that conformity ⟨a severe but *just* decision of the court⟩ ⟨a *just* estimate of her personal qualities⟩ ⟨a *just* statement of the facts⟩ ⟨he was *just* — but not charitable; he was magnanimous — but not tolerant —H.S.Commager⟩ EQUITABLE implies fair and equal treatment of all concerned, suggesting often a less rigid standard than JUST, as one that provides relief where rigid adherence to law would make for unfairness ⟨the *equitable* distribution of essential commodities —*U.S. Dept. of State Bull.*⟩ ⟨develop an *equitable* and adequate tax structure throughout the country —*Collier's Yr. Bk.*⟩ ⟨techniques that will make for more *equitable* access to higher education and vocational opportunity —W.H.Hale⟩ IMPARTIAL stresses an absence of favor or prejudice in judgment ⟨judges as a rule sincerely and ardently desire to be *impartial* and just —M.R.Cohen⟩ ⟨the law provides for the examination by neutral, *impartial* psychiatric experts of all persons indicted for a capital offense —*Current Biog.*⟩ UNBIASED emphasizes even more strongly than IMPARTIAL the absence of prejudice, favoritism, or prepossession ⟨to furnish the cabinet with *unbiased* and helpful advice on matters of state —R.M. Dawson⟩ ⟨it is difficult to convince the average spectator or juror that the law enforcement officer is an *unbiased* objective witness —Paul Wilson⟩ DISPASSIONATE usu. implies freedom from all unduly influencing feeling or preconception, often implying temperateness or coolness, even coldness, in judgment ⟨the *dispassionate* study of history —John Baillie⟩ ⟨a *dispassionate* and objective description of the region —G.M. Foster⟩ ⟨an economic report studiously *dispassionate* in temper and analytic in mode —Robert Leckachman⟩ UNCOLORED stresses a freedom from influences as prejudices or impulses to dramatize or embellish that detract from truthfulness or accuracy, as of news report ⟨it is often difficult to find a newspaper with *uncolored* accounts of the news⟩ ⟨to strive to give an *uncolored* report of one's experiences⟩ OBJECTIVE implies a looking at something as apart, as disentangled from all personal feeling, prejudice, or opinion ⟨he is not *objective* . . . but the slightest insight into historical processes to discover that objectivity, in the usual sense of that term, is unattainable in a serious political struggle —Philip Rahv⟩ ⟨it has no direct interest in the construction industry and could be expected to approach the problem from a purely *objective* standpoint —*Housing & Home Finance Agency Technical Bull.*⟩ ⟨we shall be like ice when relating passions and adventures . . . we shall be . . . *objective* and impersonal —William Troy⟩ **syn** see in addition BEAUTIFUL

— **fair to middling** : just average : pretty good : TOLERABLE ⟨the food is *fair to middling*⟩

²**fair** \"\ *adv* -ER/-EST [ME *faire, fair,* fr. OE *fægre,* fr. *fæger,* adj.] **1 a** : in a fair manner : in an attractive or agreeable manner : PLEASANTLY ⟨the sun shone ~⟩ **b** : GRACIOUSLY, COURTEOUSLY — used chiefly in the phrase *speak (one) fair* ⟨the sheriff felt that he must speak the prisoner ~ —C.W. Chesnutt⟩ **c** : in an equitable manner ⟨play ~⟩ **d** : AUSPICIOUSLY, PROMISINGLY ⟨events promise ~⟩ **e** : CLEARLY, PLAINLY ⟨write ~⟩ **2** *obs* : QUIETLY, MODERATELY **3** : EVENLY, SQUARELY, FULL, PLUMP, STRAIGHT ⟨the torpedo had struck ~ on the starboard side —*Time*⟩ ⟨the gabled houses leaned out over the streets, planted ~ upon sturdy timbers —Lord Dunsany⟩ ⟨you could have thrashed a battleship ~ down midstream —C.E.W.Bean⟩ **4** : QUITE, COMPLETELY, ABSOLUTELY ⟨he ~ spurned the earth with arrogance —J.H.Wheelright⟩ ⟨~ take one's breath away —David Hardman⟩ ⟨~ blinding you with his headlights —Richard Llewellyn⟩

³**fair** \"\ *vb* -ED/-ING/-S [ME *fairen,* fr. *fair,* adj.] *vt* **1** *obs* : to make beautiful : BEAUTIFY **2** : to make smooth without hollows or bumps : even out (a curve or line) : SHAPE ⟨~ a ship's lines⟩ — often used with *up* or *off* ⟨it'll take a lot of . . . cookery to ~ out the hollows in your outline —Llewellyn Howland⟩ **3 a** : to join one part of a structure with (another part) in such a way that there is a smooth blending of external surfaces — often used with *into* ⟨an engine *faired* into a wing⟩ ⟨a radiator from another make car with the original hood ~*ed* into it —B.H.Scott⟩ **b** : to provide (an airplane part) with a fairing ~ *vi, of the weather* : CLEAR ⟨it ~*ed* as the night went on —R.L.Stevenson⟩ — often used with *up* or *off* ⟨stopped on this porch till it ~*ed* up —*Reader's Digest*⟩ ⟨it's ~*ed* off . . . we'll have a clear day tomorrow —Jessamyn West⟩

⁴**fair** \"\ *n* -S [ME, fr. OE *fæger,* fr. *fæger,* adj.] **1** *obs* : FAIRNESS, BEAUTY **2** *archaic* : a lovely woman : SWEETHEART **3** *archaic* : something that is fair or fortunate : good fortune ⟨~ befall thee —Shak.⟩ — **for fair** *adv* : to the greatest extent or degree : CERTAINLY, DEFINITELY, FULLY ⟨opened up with everything they had . . . and caught the bomber *for fair* —Alfred Friendly⟩ ⟨the rush was on *for fair* —R.L.Neuberger⟩ — **no fair** : something that is not according to the rules : something that is not right or proper ⟨that's *no fair*⟩ — often used interjectionally ⟨you mustn't peek! *no fair!*⟩

⁵**fair** \"\ *n* -S [ME *feire, faire,* fr. OF *feire, foire,* fr. ML *feria* (also, weekday), fr. LL, festal day (also, day of the week), back-formation fr. L *feriae* days of rest, holidays, festivals — more at FEAST] **1 a** : a gathering of buyers and sellers at a particular place at a fixed time for purposes of trade ⟨the village has a ~ once a month —J.M.Mogey⟩ **b** : a competitive exhibition (as of wares, farm products, livestock) with prizes for excellence ⟨an agricultural ~⟩ — see COUNTY FAIR **c** : an exhibition designed to acquaint prospective buyers or the public at large with the range and quality of currently available or planned products ⟨a book ~⟩ ⟨a shoe ~⟩ **2** : a bazaar or sale of a collection of articles usu. for some charitable purpose ⟨a church ~⟩

fair and square *adj (or adv)* : marked by honesty and fairness ⟨be so much easier too if he weren't so damn *fair and square* —Sinclair Lewis⟩ : in an honest and fair manner ⟨see that everything was done *fair and square* —S.E.Fletcher⟩

fair ball *n* : a batted baseball that settles within the foul lines in the infield, that first touches fair territory in the outfield, or that is on or over fair territory when bounding to the outfield past first or third base

fair catch *n* **1** : a catch of a kicked football by a player who having given a prescribed signal forfeits his right to advance the ball and may not be tackled **2** *rugby* : a catch made direct from a kick or knock-on by a player of the opposing side who at the same time marks with his heel the spot where the catch is made — called also *mark*

fair·child·ite \ˈfa(a)r,chīl,dīt, ˈfer,-\ *n* -S [John G. *Fairchild* b1882 Am. chemist + E *-ite*] : a mineral $K_2Ca(CO_3)_2$ consisting of carbonate of potassium and calcium that is found in fused wood ash in partly burned trees

fair comment *or* **fair criticism** *n* : the legal privilege everyone has to criticize and comment on matters of public interest provided he states facts truly and without malice and expresses his opinion honestly and provided any criticism he makes imputes no corrupt or dishonorable motive not reasonably warranted by the facts notwithstanding that such criticism may be voiced in a style calculated to attract attention and to entertain and may involve some exaggeration, humor, or irony

fair competition *n* **:** competition reasonable in view of the interests of those competing and the public and not involving practices condemned by law as inimical to the public interest — compare UNFAIR COMPETITION

fair copy *n* **:** a neat and exact copy esp. of a corrected or revised draft of a document; *also* **:** the form of such a copy

fair cow *n, slang Austral* **:** something exceedingly troublesome or unpleasant

fair dinkum *adj* [²*fair*] *slang Austral* **:** unquestionably good or genuine **:** EXCELLENT — often used as a general expression of approval ⟨these cigars are good — *fair dinkum*⟩

fair employment *n* **:** employment of workers on a basis of equality without discrimination or segregation esp. because of race, color, or creed

fairer *comparative of* FAIR

fairest *superlative of* FAIR

fair–faced \ˈ=ˌ=\ *adj* **1 :** having a light complexion **:** beautiful of countenance **2** *Brit, of a brick wall* **:** not plastered

fair·field·ite \ˈfa(a)rˌfēlˌdīt, ˈfer-\ *n* -S [*Fairfield* co., Conn. + E *-ite*] **:** a mineral $Ca_2Mn(PO_4)_2.2H_2O$ consisting of a white or pale yellow hydrous calcium manganese phosphate and usu. occurring foliated or fibrous (sp. gr. 3.07–3.15)

fairgoer \ˈ=ˌ=(=)\ *n* **:** one that attends a fair

fairground \ˈ=ˌ=\ *n* **:** an enclosure where outdoor fairs, circuses, or exhibitions are held — sometimes used in pl. with sing. constr. ⟨what a spot for a ~*s* —W.L.Gresham⟩

fair–haired \ˈ=ˈ=\ *adj* **1 :** having fair or light-colored hair **2 :** specially favored **:** DARLING — used chiefly in the phrase *fair-haired boy* ⟨I was something of a *fair-haired* boy with my employer —P.B.Williamson⟩

fair hearing *or* **fair trial** *n* **:** a hearing conducted impartially in accordance with due process of law of which a party has had reasonable notice as to the time, place, and issues or charges, for which he has had a reasonable opportunity to prepare, at which he is permitted to have the assistance of a lawyer, and during which he has a right to present his witnesses and proof, to cross-examine his adversary's witnesses, to argue that a decision be made in accordance with the law and the evidence, and often to have a trial before a jury

fairies *pl of* FAIRY

fairies'–butter \ˈ==ˈ==\ *n* **:** a blue-green alga (*Nostoc commune*) forming gelatinous sheets or pellets

fairies'–table \ˈ==ˈ==\ *n* **1 :** the meadow mushroom or any of several similar fungi **2 a :** a European marsh pennywort (*Hydrocotyle vulgaris*) **b :** the flat peltate leaf of the European marsh pennywort

fair·i·ly \ˈfa(a)rəlē, ˈfer-,ˈfār-, -li\ *adv* **:** in the manner of a fairy **:** lightly and delicately

¹**fair·ing** \ˈfa(a)riŋ, ˈfer-\ *n* -S [⁵*fair* + *-ing*] *Brit* **:** a present, cake or sweet, or souvenir purchased at a fair ⟨a ~ to be bought for those at home —Flora Thompson⟩

²**fairing** *n* -S [fr. gerund of ³*fair*] **:** a member or structure the primary function of which is to produce a smooth outline and to reduce drag or head resistance (as on an airplane)

fair·ish \ˈfa(a)rish, ˈfer-, -rēsh\ *adj* [¹*fair* + *-ish*] **:** tolerably good or large ⟨serves ~ food at controlled prices —Bruce Bliven b. 1889⟩ ⟨a ~ demand for . . . rarer items —Clifton Fadiman⟩ — **fair·ish·ly** *adv*

fair isle *n, often cap F&I* [fr. *Fair Isle*, one of the Shetland islands, where it originated] **:** a style of knitting consisting of simple geometric patterns in two or more colors forming horizontal bands

fair·lead \ˈ=ˌlēd\ *n* **1 a** *also* **fair·lead·er** \-ēdə(r)\ **:** a block, ring, or strip of plank with holes that serves as a guide for the running rigging or any ship's rope and keeps it from chafing **b :** a course of running ship's rope that avoids all chafing **2 :** an insulating tube through which the antenna passes from outside to the inside of an airplane; *also* **:** a guide or support for an airplane control cable that prevents chafing or fouling **3 :** a device that consists of pulleys or rollers arranged to permit reeling in of a cable from any direction and that is used in conjunction with winches and similar apparatus esp. in logging

fair leather *n* **:** leather not artificially colored

fair·ly *adv* [ME, fr. ¹*fair* + *-ly*] **1 a** (1) **:** HANDSOMELY, BEAUTIFULLY ⟨she likes to be overlooking the table with its ~ set dishes and silver —Eve Langley⟩ (2) *of writing* **:** in the manner of a final draft **:** NEATLY, ELEGANTLY ⟨one little essay . . . written out ~ for the press but never published —Richard Garnett †1906⟩ ⟨you excelled in writing ~ —George Lillo⟩ **b** *obs* **:** SOFTLY, QUIETLY, GENTLY **c** *obs* **:** COURTEOUSLY **2 a :** to the full degree or extent **:** CLEARLY, DEFINITELY, ACTUALLY, PLAINLY, DISTINCTLY, FULLY ⟨when the captain is on board and we are ~ off —Rachel Henning⟩ ⟨amongst the boys scurrying to their ten-o'clocks I ~ caught sight of him —*Atlantic*⟩ ⟨when I had him ~ seated in a hackney coach with me —James Boswell⟩ ⟨the chestnut, finding himself ~ in for it, struck out gamely —Henry Lapham⟩ ⟨badly wounded before the battle had ~ begun⟩ **b :** as it were **:** so to speak **:** ABSOLUTELY, POSITIVELY, DOWNRIGHT ⟨the pages ~ quiver with indignation —Alban Baer⟩ ⟨its waters . . . are ~ alive with crocodiles —Tom Marvel⟩ ⟨~ boiling over with pride —Dorothy C. Fisher⟩ ⟨~ lifted the waters of the gulf and hurled them through the city —A.F.Harlow⟩ **c :** SQUARELY, CLEANLY ⟨one of her 8-inch salvos smashed ~ into a large warship —*Time*⟩ **3 a :** in conformity with the evidence, with reason, or with one's merits **:** JUSTIFIABLY, PROPERLY, LEGITIMATELY, RIGHTFULLY ⟨our business is to show that the doctrine is false and this we may ~ claim to have done —A.J.Ayer⟩ ⟨his services have ~ earned him promotion⟩ **b** (1) **:** in a just or lawful manner **:** without fraud, injury, or unfair advantage **:** EQUITABLY ⟨fought and beat him ~⟩ ⟨come by something ~⟩ (2) **:** without bias or distortion **:** IMPARTIALLY, CANDIDLY, ACCURATELY, OBJECTIVELY ⟨the merits of the plea were ~ considered⟩ ⟨~ described as all very decayed and horrible⟩ **4 :** TOLERABLY, MODERATELY, RATHER ⟨a ~ difficult scientific text⟩ ⟨a ~ steady diet of lamb and beef⟩ **:** moderately well ⟨how are you getting along? Only ~⟩ **:** PLEASANTLY ⟨the evening passed away very ~ —Henry Lapham⟩

fairm \ˈfārm, ˈferm\ *Scot var of* FARM

fair maid *n* [by folk etymology fr. *fumado*] **:** a scup (*Stenotomus aculeatus*)

fair–maids–of–france \ˈ=ˌ=ˌ=ˈ=\ *n pl but sing or pl in constr, cap 2d F* **:** the double garden form of any of several European plants (as garden buttercup, sneezewort, meadow saxifrage, or ragged robin)

fair–minded \ˈ=ˈ==\ *adj* **:** UNPREJUDICED, JUST, JUDICIAL, HONEST ⟨a *fair-minded* man⟩ ⟨his *fair-minded* and dispassionate analysis —*Times Lit. Supp.*⟩ ⟨attempt to be as *fair-minded* as possible —W.L.Sperry⟩

fair–mindedness *n* -ES **:** the quality or state of being fair-minded ⟨his resolute refusal to retaliate, his restraint and *fair-mindedness* won out —S.H.Adams⟩

fair·ness *n* -ES [ME *fairnesse*, fr. OE *fægernes*, fr. *fæger* fair + *-nes* -ness — more at FAIR] **1 :** the quality or state of being fair; *esp* **:** fair or impartial treatment **:** REASONABLENESS ⟨the guarantees of ~ contained in the judicial process —*Harvard Law Rev.*⟩ **2 :** the degree of streamlining (as of an airplane)

fairn·tick·le \ˈfernˌtikəl\ *var of* FERNTICKLE

fair play *n* **:** equitable or impartial treatment **:** JUSTICE ⟨passage of the *fair-play* amendment abolishing the practice of contested delegates voting in their own and other delegate contests —Roscoe Drummond⟩

fairs *pres 3d sing of* FAIR, *pl of* FAIR

fair shake *n* **:** fair chance ⟨give the negative side a *fair shake* —S.L.Payne⟩

fair–spoken \ˈ=ˈ==\ *adj* [ME *faire-spoken*] **:** using fair speech or uttered with fairness **:** BLAND, CIVIL, COURTEOUS, PLAUSIBLE

fairstitcher \ˈ=ˌ==\ *n* **:** an operator of a fair-stitching machine

fair stitching *n* **:** stitching that appears on the extension of a welt shoe to ornament and to bind the outsole to the welt

fair trade *n* **:** trade in conformity with a fair-trade agreement ⟨a *fair-trade* product⟩ ⟨abandonment of price fixing in small home appliances was a staggering blow to *fair trade* —A.R. Zipser⟩

fair–trade \ˈ=ˈ=\ *vt* [*fair trade*] **:** to market (a commodity) in compliance with the provisions of a fair-trade agreement — **fair trader** *n*

fair–trade agreement *n* **:** an agreement between a producer and a vendor (as a manufacturer and a retailer) that commodities bearing a trademark, label, or brand name of that producer be sold at or above a certain price, the agreement often being binding on all vendors in a state after one vendor has signed

fair–traded *adj* **:** protected or covered by a fair-trade agreement ⟨working for a law designed to end price cutting of *fair-traded* books⟩

fair–trade law *n* **:** a law authorizing fair-trade agreements

fair use *n* **:** a legal doctrine that portions of copyrighted materials may be used (as by publishing) without permission of the copyright owner provided the use is fair and reasonable, does not substantially impair the value of the materials, and does not curtail the profits reasonably expected by the owner, such use often being accompanied by fair comment

fair value *n* **:** a reasonable value (as set by courts and regulatory commissions) for property — used esp. in application to public-utility property for rate-making purposes

fairwater \ˈ=ˌ==\ *n* [³*fair* + *water*] **1 :** a device (as a sleeve about a propeller shaft) that is used to fair the lines of an underwater fitting **2 :** a streamlined bridge and conning tower of a submarine

fairway \ˈ=ˌ=\ *n* **1 a :** a navigable part of a river or bay through which boats enter or depart **:** a part of a harbor or channel that is kept open and unobstructed **b :** a stretch of clear or open water adjacent to an airport and used by seaplanes in landing and taking off **2 :** a clear or open path or space ⟨situated . . . in the very ~ of migrating bird hosts —Douglas Carruthers⟩ ⟨the ~ for cars is often choked by stream-lined hummocks of clay —G.W.Murray⟩ **3 :** a part of a golf course exclusive of tees, putting greens, and hazards that is prepared for play by cutting the grass to provide a fair lie for the ball — compare ROUGH

fair–weather \ˈ=ˈ==\ *adj* [*fair weather*] **1 :** suitable for, done during, or made in fair weather ⟨a *fair-weather* sail⟩ **2 :** active, effective, suitable or loyal only during a time of prosperity or when no danger or hardship is involved ⟨a *fair-weather* friend⟩ ⟨our banking system was often spoken of as a *fair-weather* system —E.W.Kemmerer⟩

fair white *n* **:** a light-complexioned or blond white person

¹**fairy** \ˈfa(a)rē, ˈfer-,ˈfār-, -ri\ *n* -ES [ME *faierie, fairie* fairyland, fairy people, enchantment, fr. OF *faerie, faierie*, fr. *fee, feie, fayee* fairy (fr. L *Fata* goddess of fate, fr. *fatum* fate) + *-erie* -ery — more at FATE] **1 :** a mythical being of folklore and romance usu. having diminutive human form and magic powers and dwelling on earth in close relationship with man: **a :** a dwarf creature typically having green clothes and hair, living underground or in stone heaps, and usu. exercising his magic powers to benevolent ends **b :** a diminutive sprite usu. in the shape of a delicate beautiful ageless winged woman dressed in diaphanous white clothing, inhabiting fairyland, but making usu. benevolent intervention in personal human affairs **c :** a tiny mischievous and protective creature in a household usu. associated with the hearth — compare BROWNIE, ELF, GOBLIN, LEPRECHAUN, PUCK **2 :** FAIRY GREEN **3 a :** HOMOSEXUAL **b :** a markedly effeminate man suspected of homosexual tendencies

²**fairy** \"\ *adj* **1 :** of or relating to a fairy **:** being a fairy ⟨the sprite made his ~ home in the cleft of an ancient tree⟩ ⟨the nuptials of the ~ queen⟩ **2 :** resembling or suggestive of a fairy in its delicacy or grace ⟨their porcelains . . . showed a subtle ~ fragility —*Time*⟩ ⟨the viaduct comes into view, so slender, so exquisitely graceful, that . . . it seems a mere ~ thing —O.S.Nock⟩

fairy arrow *n* **:** a flint arrowhead — compare THUNDERSTONE

fairy bell *n* **1** *also* **fairy cap** *or* **fairy finger** *or* **fairy glove :** FOXGLOVE 1 **2 :** a woodland herb (*Disporum lanuginosum*) of eastern No. America with terminal greenish flowers and red pulpy berries

fairy bluebird *n* **:** any of several largely brilliant blue Indian or East Indian passerine birds related to the leafbirds and constituting the genus *Irena*

fairy bouquet *n* **:** TOADFLAX 1

fairy butter *n* **1 :** any of various fungi (order Tremellales) having a gelatinous fruiting body (as *Exidia glandulosa* or *E. albida*) **2 :** FAIRIES'-BUTTER

fairy candle *n* **:** a bugbane (*Cimicifuga racemosa*)

fairy circle *n* **1 :** FAIRY RING **2 :** a shrubby form of the common juniper that often grows in ring-shaped masses

fairy club *n* **:** CLUB FUNGUS

fairy creeper *n* **:** CLIMBING FUMITORY

fairy cup *n* **1 :** COWSLIP 1a **2 :** BLOOD CUP **3 :** a miterwort (*Mitella diphylla*) of northeastern No. America usu. with two opposite leaves on the erect flowering stem that terminates in an upright raceme of white flowers

fairy fans *n pl but sing or pl in constr* **:** an annual Californian herb (*Clarkia breweri*) with showy pink fan-shaped petals

fairy flax *n* **:** PURGING FLAX

fairy–fringe \ˈ=ˌ=ˈ=\ *n* **:** PURPLE-FRINGED ORCHID a

fairy godmother *n* **:** a generous friend or benefactor; *esp* **:** one that appears unexpectedly or at a time of urgent need ⟨our needy unemployed would be cared for when, as, and if some *fairy godmother* should happen on the scene —F.D.Roosevelt⟩

fairy gold *or* **fairy money** *n* **1 :** money held to be given by fairies but turned into rubbish when put to use **2 :** wealth or prosperity that may vanish as swiftly as it is acquired **:** precarious or illusory wealth ⟨was to have been, according to those who profited most from its *fairy gold*, an era that would transcend the business cycle —Stringfellow Barr⟩

fairy green *also* **fairy** *n* -ES **:** a moderate yellowish green that is greener and paler than tarragon, paler than malachite green, and less strong and slightly yellower than verdigris

fairy·ism \-ˌizəm\ *n* -S **:** the state of being or of being like a fairy

fairy lamp *n* **:** a candle-burning night-light usu. of colored glass with separate base and shade

fairy·land \ˈ==ˌland, -aa(ə)nd\ *n* **1 :** the land or habitat of fairies **2 :** a place of delicate beauty or magical charm ⟨a winter ~ of iced boughs and sparkling snow⟩

fairy lantern *n* **:** any of various plants of the genus *Calochortus* (esp. *C. alkus*)

fairylike \ˈ==ˌ=\ *adj* **:** resembling a fairy or what is made or done by fairies ⟨the ~ beauty of the moonlit glade⟩ ⟨a delicate ~ butterfly⟩

fairy lily *n* **1 :** ATAMASCO LILY **2 :** a rain lily (*Cooperia pedunculata*); *also* **:** its white flower resembling a lily

fairy lint *n* **:** PURGING FLAX

fairy martin *n* **:** an Australian swallow (*Hylochelidon ariel*) that builds flask-shaped nests of mud on cliffs

fairy palm *n* **:** a common shallow-water solitary hydroid (*Corynomorpha palma*) of the Pacific coast of No. America

fairy primrose *n* **1 :** a Chinese primrose (*Primula malacoides*) with long-stalked leaves and lilac or rose flowers **2 :** a European alpine primrose (*Primula minima*)

fairy prion *n* **:** a small Australian prion (*Pachyptila turtur*)

fairy ring *n* **1 :** a ring of mushrooms (*Marasmius oreades* or other basidiomycetes) that is produced at the periphery of mycelium which has grown centrifugally from an initial growth point and that increases in diameter from year to year; *also* **:** a ring of luxuriant vegetation associated with these mushrooms that also increases in diameter from year to year **2** *or* **fairy–ring mushroom :** a mushroom (esp. *Marasmius oreades*) that commonly grows in fairy rings

fairy ring spot *n* **:** a disease of carnations found esp. in the greenhouse and caused by a fungus (*Heterosporium echinulatum*) that produces on the leaves bleached spots with concentric dark zones

fairy rose *n* **:** any of various dwarf roses constituting a variety (*Rosa chinensis minima*) of the China rose and having small single or double flowers

fairy shrimp *n* **:** any of several freshwater branchiopod crustaceans (order Anostraca) so called from their delicate colors, transparency, and graceful motions (as the European *Eubranchipus diaphanus* or the No. American *E. vernalis*)

fairy slipper *n* **:** a bog orchid (*Calypso bulbosa*) native to Eurasia and established widely in No. America

fairy stone *n* **1 :** a stone arrowhead **2 :** any of various concretions and fossils of odd or fantastic shape: as **a :** a staurolite crystal **b :** a fossil sea urchin

fairy tale *or* **fairy story** *n* **1 a :** a simple narrative dealing with supernatural beings (as fairies, magicians, ogres, dragons) that is typically of folk origin and written or told for the amusement of children ⟨these ten short *fairy tales* to read aloud to younger children are in an old-fashioned mood —Louise S. Bechtel⟩ **b :** a more sophisticated narrative containing supernatural or obviously improbable events, scenes, and personages and often having a whimsical, satirical, or moralistic character ⟨an unusual adult *fairy tale* well designed to while away an evening —*N.Y. Times Book Rev.*⟩ **2 :** an implausible, incredible, or lying story **:** a story designed to delude or mislead ⟨in spite of various *fairy tales* that have been spread . . . your power system is still paying taxes to the community —F.D.Roosevelt⟩

fairy–tale \ˈ==ˌ=\ *adj* [*fairy tale*] **:** characteristic of or suitable to a fairy tale **:** marked by exquisite or unreal beauty, grace, or perfection ⟨a thing of beauty, a *fairy-tale* body of water surrounded by little houses with red roofs —J.A.Michener⟩ ⟨the sort of *fairy-tale* dresses most women dream about —*Time*⟩ ⟨the *fairy-tale* America manufactured in Hollywood —J.W. Aldridge⟩

fairy tern *n* **:** any of various small terns: **a :** either of two pure white terns constituting a genus (*Gygis*) and living in tropical seas **b :** a small white black-capped tern (*Sterna nereis*) of the Australian region

fairy thimbles *n pl* **:** the blossoms of the foxglove

fairy wand *n* **:** a blazing star (*Chamaelirium luteum*) with a spike of white to greenish or yellow flowers

fairy wren *n* **:** any of numerous small Australian warblers (genus *Malurus*) having the male usu. brilliantly colored and the female drably brown

fais–do·do \ˌfāˌdōˈdō\ *n* -S [LaF, fr. F (baby-talk) *fais dodo!* go to sleep!; prob. fr. the fact that small children who attend the dances are expected to go to sleep during the festivities] **:** a country-dance or dancing party held usu. on a Saturday night in southern Louisiana

fait \ˈfāt\ *n* -S [ME, fr. MF, fr. L *factum* — more at FACT] **:** a legal deed, writing, or fact

fait ac·com·pli \ˌfād·əˌkämˈplē, ˌfed-, -d·(ˌ)a,k-, ˌfe(ˌ)tä,k-, -ˌkōm-, -ˌkō(ⁿ)m-, *Brit also* ˌfātəˈkäm(ˌ)plē, *F* fetäkōⁿplē\ *n, pl* **faits accomplis** \-ē(z)\ [F, accomplished fact] **:** a thing accomplished and presumably irreversible **:** an accomplished fact ⟨intended to present the people with a *fait accompli* —Tor Myklebost⟩ ⟨was only asking formal approval of a *fait accompli* —*Current History*⟩

¹**faith** \ˈfāth\ *n, pl* **faiths** \-āths *also* -āthz\ [ME *feith, fey*, fr. OF *feid* (*d* prob. pronounced \th\), *fei, foi*, fr. L *fides*; akin to L *fidere* to trust — more at BIDE] **1 a :** the act or state of wholeheartedly and steadfastly believing in the existence, power, and benevolence of a supreme being, of having confidence in his providential care, and of being loyal to his will as revealed or believed in **:** belief and trust in and loyalty to God ⟨people earnestly prayed in the ages of ~ . . . to be delivered from sudden death —J.A.Pike⟩ ⟨lost his ~ at an early age⟩ **b** (1) **:** an act or attitude of intellectual assent to the traditional doctrines of one's religion **:** orthodox religious belief (2) **:** a decision of an individual entrusting his life to God's transforming care in response to an experience of God's mercy **c** *among Roman Catholic theologians* **:** a supernatural virtue by which one believes on the authority of God himself all that God has revealed or proposes through the Church for belief **2 a** (1) **:** firm or unquestioning belief in something for which there is no proof ⟨for the scientist ~ can be no virtue, because it is inconsistent with the resolution to accept the fact as supreme —P.W.Bridgman⟩ ⟨clinging to the ~ that her missing son would one day return⟩ (2) **:** uncritical grounds for belief — used chiefly in the phrase *on faith* ⟨you will have to accept my statements on *faith*⟩ **b :** CONFIDENCE; *esp* **:** firm or unquestioning trust or confidence in the value, power, or efficacy of something ⟨have ~ in prayer⟩ ⟨~ in his medical skill⟩ ⟨the ~ on which science rests, the ~ in the value of truth seeking —H.T.Muller⟩ **3 a :** an assurance, promise, or pledge of fidelity, loyalty, or performance ⟨gave his ~ that he would come on the appointed day⟩ — often used in the phrases *to keep faith* or *to break faith* ⟨to have hitchhiked would have been breaking ~, for all who use the country's youth hostels are honor bound to reach them under their own power —H.V.Morton⟩ **b :** fidelity to one's promises **:** allegiance to a duty or a person **:** sincerity or honesty of intentions **:** LOYALTY — often used with the qualifiers *good* or *bad* to specify a state of mind of one trying to be honest and faithful ⟨observed perfect good ~ and strictly fulfilled their engagements —Marjory S. Douglas⟩ or of one trying to deceive, mislead, or defraud ⟨accused him of bad ~⟩ **4** *obs* **:** AUTHORITY, CREDIT, CREDIBILITY **5 :** something that is believed or adhered to esp. with strong conviction: as **a** (1) **:** a system of religious beliefs **:** RELIGION ⟨an individual of the Jewish ~⟩ (2) **:** the body of believers **:** an organized church or denomination ⟨a movement supported by all the great ~*s*⟩ **b :** the cherished values, ideals, or beliefs of an individual or people **:** WELTANSCHAUUNG, CREED, CREDO ⟨a free world which is strong in its ~ and in its material progress —Dean Acheson⟩ **c :** the fundamental tenets, views, or beliefs of an individual or group on a particular subject or in a particular field ⟨a profession of literary ~⟩ ⟨I state my own ~ at once . . . organic union under the Crown is vital —R.G.Menzies⟩ ⟨she visits the prisoners of her own political ~ —Katharine A. Porter⟩ **6** *often cap* **:** the true religion from the point of view of the speaker — usu. used with *the* ⟨the king, temporal head of the ~⟩ **syn** see BELIEF, RELIGION, TRUST — **in faith :** by my faith **:** VERILY

²**faith** \"\ *vt* -ED/-ING/-S [ME *feithen*, fr. *feith*, n.] *archaic* **:** BELIEVE, TRUST

faith cure *n* **:** a method or practice of treating diseases by prayer and exercise of faith in God **:** a cure held to have been achieved by this method

fai·ther \ˈfāthər, ˈfeth-\ *dial var of* FATHER

¹**faith·ful** \ˈfāthfəl\ *adj* [ME *feithful*, fr. *feith* faith + *-ful*] **1** *archaic* **:** full of faith **:** ready to believe esp. in the declarations and promises of God **2 :** true and constant in affection or allegiance **:** LOYAL ⟨a ~ friend⟩ ⟨a ~ dog⟩ **3 :** firm in adherence to promises, oaths, or undertakings **:** firm and thorough in the observance of duty **:** CONSCIENTIOUS ⟨a ~ public official⟩ ⟨~ to his plan of economy —W.M.Thackeray⟩ **4 :** given with strong or solemn assurances **:** BINDING ⟨a ~ promise⟩ **5 :** conforming to the facts or to an original **:** worthy of credence **:** ACCURATE, RELIABLE, EXACT, CREDIBLE ⟨the book presents a ~ picture of life in that century⟩ ⟨the painter . . . concerned . . . with the ~ rendering of the observed facts —*Encounter*⟩ ⟨a very ~ source⟩

syn LOYAL, LEAL, TRUE, CONSTANT, STAUNCH, STEADFAST, RESOLUTE: FAITHFUL implies firm and unhesitating adherence to whatever one is bound to by ties of honor, friendship, allegiance, or love ⟨the story of Lilla, *faithful* thane, who flung himself between his Northumbrian king, Edwin, and the sword of the assassin —H.O.Taylor⟩ ⟨she proved a good and *faithful* helpmate, assisted me much by attending the shop; we throve together, and have ever mutually endeavored to make each other happy —Benjamin Franklin⟩ LOYAL may indicate a continuing, reliable faithfulness and allegiance secure against wavering and temptation ⟨a trained and *loyal* army willing to sacrifice for the good of a common discipline —F.D.Roosevelt⟩ ⟨there was no man more *loyal* to his commander. On the morning of the mutiny there had not been a moment's hesitation in deciding where his duty lay —C.B.Nordhoff & J.N. Hall⟩ LEAL is a Scots or archaic form of *loyal* ⟨thou, Scotland's son, that would'st be *leal* and true —J.S.Blackie⟩ TRUE may add implications of deep inner fidelity and devotion ⟨goodhearted and *true*, full of sturdy, homely sense, willing to take care of a man's money, and make him a straightforward wife —George Moore⟩ ⟨in my judgment the Quakers are the *truest* Christians in the modern world —W.R.Inge⟩ CONSTANT indicates the fact of firm attachment or adherence but implies less than other words in this set about resolution or deep feeling ⟨if he will be *constant* and kind, and not forsake her —W.M.Thackeray⟩ ⟨his last and most *constant* love was for a Roman girl named Morosina —R.A.Hall b. 1911⟩ STAUNCH suggests resolution, fortitude, and conviction in adherence and imperviousness to influences which would weaken it ⟨*staunch* adherence to majority decisions and determination at all costs to preserve the unity of the party in the face of the political enemy are their forte —Woodrow Wyatt⟩ ⟨ever a *staunch*

Federalist, he viewed the policies of Jefferson and his followers with repugnance —E.E.Curtis⟩ STEADFAST indicates unwavering adherence unchanged over a period; like STAUNCH it may imply resolution ⟨hundreds of obscure martyrs now followed in the same path to another world, where surely they deserved to find their recompense if *steadfast* adherence to their faith, and a tranquil trust in God amid tortures and death too horrible to be related, had ever found favor above —J.L. Motley⟩ ⟨if President Lowell had not stood *steadfast* against alumni pressure, we would have today a giant stadium built in the gay twenties on borrowed money —J.B.Conant⟩ RESOLUTE implies steady firm determination to adhere ⟨an earthquake in the midst of the proceedings terrified every prelate but the *resolute* primate —J.R.Green⟩ ⟨your clients, sir, are happy in having so *resolute* a guardian of their confidence —Bram Stoker⟩

2**faithful** \"\ *n, pl* **faithful** *or* **faithfuls** : one that is faithful: as **a** : one of the adherents of a system of religious belief ⟨an Eastern Orthodox ~ is expected to attend church regularly⟩ ⟨sectarian schools supported by the fees and contributions of the ~ —C.A. & Mary Beard⟩ **b** : baptized Christians as opposed to catechumens — used with *the* ⟨the division between the liturgy of the catechumens and the liturgy of the ~ is still preserved in the Eastern Orthodox Church⟩ **c** : church members in full communion and good standing — used with *the* **d** : the body of adherents of the Muslim religion — used with *the* ⟨the Muslim congregation of all the ~ is a democratic one —Percival Spear⟩ **e** : a devoted or loyal follower of a cause or member of an organization ⟨only the party ~*s* and ignorant, duped immigrants . . . favored his cause —M.D. Hirsch⟩ ⟨Dixieland jazz itself was losing popularity, except with the ~ who gathered in small, smoky cellar clubs to listen to it —Grady Johnson⟩ ⟨party ~*s* will prepare tea and meals for the crowd —Ernie Hill⟩

faith·ful·ly \-fəlē, -li\ *adv* [ME *feithfully*, fr. *feithful* + *-ly*] : in a faithful manner: **a** : DUTIFULLY, LOYALLY **b** : ACCURATELY

faith·ful·ness \-fəlnəs\ *n* -ES [ME *feithfulnesse*, fr. *feithful* + *-nesse* -ness] : the quality or state of being faithful

faith healer *n* : one that practices faith healing

faith healing *n* : a method or practice of treating diseases by prayer and exercise of faith in God

faith·less \'fāthləs\ *adj* [ME *feithles*, fr. *feith* faith + *-les* -less] **1** *archaic* : not believing : not giving credence **2 a** *archaic* : not believing in God or religion **b** : being without a faith : lacking strong convictions ⟨we live in a skeptical and ~ time⟩ **3** : false to promises or agreements : not true to allegiance or duty : PERFIDIOUS, TREACHEROUS, DISLOYAL ⟨few of its teachers . . . have been ~ to their society —C.W. de Kiewiet⟩ ⟨the abandoned one wife and was ~ to another —J.R.Green⟩ : INCONSTANT, FICKLE ⟨she had been too successful, and a ~ public was tired of her —Carl Van Vechten⟩ **4 a** : not to be relied on : UNSTABLE, ERRATIC ⟨they are at the mercy of an unseen instructor who can simulate violent weather and ~ machinery —*Time*⟩ **b** : not conforming to a standard or to an original : not true or accurate ⟨the disc has a heavy surface and the tone is ~ —Edward Sackville-West & Desmond Shawe-Taylor⟩

syn FALSE, DISLOYAL, TRAITOROUS, TREACHEROUS, PERFIDIOUS: FAITHLESS applies to any lack of adherence or devotion to a vow, pledge, allegiance, or loyalty ⟨the *faithless* conduct of the allies toward this dethroned monarch, who, after giving himself generously up to their mercy, was consigned to an ignoble and cruel banishment —W.M.Thackeray⟩ ⟨a woman who has been deserted by her lover will make a straw effigy of the *faithless* gallant —J.G.Frazer⟩ FALSE may center attention on the fact of failing to be true, reasons ranging from fickle negligence to cold treachery ⟨from the first hour of Edward's rule the threads of his diplomacy ran over Europe in almost inextricable confusion. And to all who dealt with him he was equally *false* and tricky —J.R.Green⟩ ⟨men, when they're *false*, and try to deceive young girls, and are playing their own wicked game with them, do not like to be bothered about such things —Anthony Trollope⟩ DISLOYAL indicates lack of complete faith, loyalty, and adherence to a person, cause, or country ⟨they had already assumed a tone in their correspondence which must have seemed often *disloyal*, and sometimes positively insulting, to the governor —J.L.Motley⟩ ⟨the *disloyal* subject who had fought against his rightful sovereign —T.B.Macaulay⟩ TRAITOROUS applies to committing, countenancing, or contemplating actual treason or similar serious betrayal ⟨*traitorous* generals collaborating with the enemy⟩ ⟨charged with *traitorous* contempt of the emperor —S.T. Coleridge⟩ TREACHEROUS is wider and less specific than TRAITOROUS; it may refer to any serious betrayal or inclination to betray or to anything likely to bring sudden peril or disaster unless one is quite wary ⟨thy kin of the days of old were an evil and *treacherous* folk, and they lied and murdered for gold —William Morris⟩ ⟨lighthouses were placed on *treacherous* parts of the coast —Lewis Mumford⟩ PERFIDIOUS may add to FAITHLESS implications of a base incapacity for fidelity; the word now seems rather declamatory or oratorical ⟨betrayed by his *perfidious* allies⟩ ⟨a *perfidious* violation of a treaty⟩ ⟨*perfidious* Mrs. Albion who had her spouse, Albion I, murdered by a lover acquired for the purpose —Claudia Cassidy⟩

faith·less·ly *adv* : in a faithless manner

faith·less·ness *n* -ES : the quality or condition of being faithless

faiths *pl of* FAITH, *pres 3d sing of* FAITH

fai·tour \'fād·ə(r)\ *n* -S [ME, fr. AF, fr. OF *faitor* founder, perpetrator, fr. L *factor* maker, doer — more at FACTOR] *archaic* : CHEAT, IMPOSTOR

fai·tours grass \'fād·ərz-\ *n* [ME *faytowrys gresse*] : LEAFY SPURGE

faits *pl of* FAIT

faize \'fāz\ *Scot var of* 2FEAZE

faja \'fä(,)hä\ *n* -S [Sp, sash, band, prob. fr. Catal *faixa*, fr. L *fascia* band, bandage — more at FASCIA] : a wide bright sash worn around the waist by Spaniards and Latin Americans

1**fake** \'fāk\ *or* **flake** \'flāk\ *vt* -ED/-ING/-S [ME *faken*] : to coil (as a ship's rope, line, or hawser or a fire hose) in fakes esp. by winding in layers usu. of zigzag or figure-eight form, to prevent twisting and fouling when running out — often used with *down* ⟨~ down line⟩ or *out* ⟨there's an old twelve-inch hawser *faked* out down there —Chesley Wilson⟩

2**fake** \"\ *or* **flake** \"\ *n* -S : one loop of a coil (as of ship's rope) that is coiled free for running

3**fake** \"\ *vb* -ED/-ING/-S [origin unknown] *vt* **1** : to alter, manipulate, or treat so as to impart a false character to for legitimate or illegitimate reasons : cause to appear something other than it is : tamper with : DOCTOR, COLOR ⟨the well-known biologist who did ~ his results was driven to suicide by the disgrace of exposure —H.J.Muller⟩ ⟨~ the fight until the twelfth round, for the sake of the money —Donn Byrne⟩ ⟨~ the perspective in such a way that the stage appears grander the farther one is from it —*Atlantic*⟩ — often used with *up* ⟨in consequence of the *faked*-up narrative the world of Columbus's discovery would be named America —S.E. Morison⟩ ⟨two small beds *faked* up to look like an enormous bed —Daniel Curley⟩ **2 a** : to counterfeit or make a counterfeit of with fraudulent intent ⟨~ a painting⟩ **b** : to devise an acceptable substitute for ⟨a printer may ~ a foreign accent not carried in stock⟩ **3 a** : to create the illusion of the reality or existence of : cause (something inexistent) to appear as real or existing : CONCOCT, FABRICATE, SIMULATE, PRETEND ⟨*faked* 38 claims . . . for damages incurred in mythical automobile accidents —Henry La Cositt⟩ ⟨*faked* his own kidnapping in order to avoid extradition to England —M.S.Mayer⟩ ⟨had *faked* an interview with the prime minister that caused a sensation⟩ ⟨*faked* a surprise that was transparently bogus⟩ **b** : to deceive (an opponent) in a sports contest by a simulated movement ⟨busily *faking* two other men out of position —Roy McHugh⟩ **4** *slang* : IMPROVISE, AD-LIB ⟨whistle a few bars . . . and I'll ~ the rest —Robert Sylvester⟩ ⟨~ a bass accompaniment⟩ ~ *vi* : to engage in faking something : PRETEND ⟨he's not sick, he's just *faking*⟩

4**fake** \"\ *n* -S **1 a** : an article or object simulating one that is genuine; *often* : a worthless or spurious imitation passed off as genuine to deceive esp. for gain ⟨experts called the priceless antique a ~⟩ **b** : a report, story, or account spurious in its details, conclusions, or presentation; *esp* : one intended to delude for gain or advantage ⟨the adventures of the spy turned out to be a series of ~*s*⟩ **c** : a device, plan, stratagem, or act designed to fool, trick, or defraud : FEINT, TRICK, HOAX ⟨the new wonder gasoline was a complete ~⟩: as (1) : a simulated movement in a sports contest (as a pretended kick or pass) designed to deceive an opponent (2) *or* **feke** \"\ : a device or apparatus used by a magician to achieve the illusion of magic in a trick **d** : a person passing himself off for what he is not : PRETENDER, IMPOSTOR, CHARLATAN ⟨medical ~ —Agnes N. Keith⟩ **2** : a genuine postage stamp fraudulently treated in an attempt to convert it into a more valuable philatelic variety **3** : a mixture of waxes and dressing for finishing edges and bottoms of shoe soles **syn** see IMPOSTURE

5**fake** \"\ *adj* [4*fake*] : simulating the genuine person, thing, or article : being a fake : FALSE, SHAM, SPURIOUS, COUNTERFEIT, PRETENDED ⟨skirt is supplied with flap pockets that are completely ~ —*New Yorker*⟩ ⟨a phony physicist and one ~ air force colonel —Greer Williams⟩ ⟨~ patriotism⟩ ⟨~ amnesia victims⟩ ⟨hand-screened prints and crusts of ~ diamonds and pearls —*advt*⟩ **syn** see COUNTERFEIT

fake·ment \-mənt\ *n* -S [3*fake* + *-ment*] : something faked : a contrivance or device used to deceive

fak·er \'fākə(r)\ *n* -S [3*fake* + *-er*] : one that fakes: as **a** : a person who makes fakes ⟨sought by the genealogical scholar and the pedigree ~ alike —A.R.Wagner⟩ **b** : a street or fair vendor who seeks to deceive by ascribing great value or efficacy to cheap or worthless products : FRAUD, SWINDLER ⟨the business objective of the old medicine-show ~*s* was to . . . defraud the public —C.M.Babcock⟩ **c** : one that passes himself off as something other than he is or pretends to qualities or abilities that he does not possess : PRETENDER, IMPOSTOR, PHONY ⟨more honest than the majority of art lovers and concertgoers, most of whom he regards as . . . cultural ~*s* —Hunter Mead⟩

fak·ery \-k(ə)rē, -ri\ *n* -ES [3*fake* + *-ery*] : the practice or a product of faking ⟨this, according to insurance men, was something unique in ~ —Henry La Cossitt⟩ ⟨were persuaded that the bells were not cast-iron *fakeries* only after sledgehammers failed to crack them —*Time*⟩

fakey \'fākē, -ki\ *adj* [4*fake* + *-y*] : FAKE

fa·kir \fə'ki(ə)r *or* fä'- *or* fa'- *or* -iə, *in sense 2* 'fākə(r)\ *n* -S [Ar *faqīr* poor] **1** *or* **fa·qir** *or* **fa·quir** \"\ : a Muslim mendicant or ascetic; *also* : an itinerant wonder-worker of other religions **2** [by folk etymology fr. *faker*] : FAKER; *esp* : SWINDLER ⟨the ~*s* who accompany a circus came up in full force to ply their games —D.D.Martin⟩ **3** : PEACHBLOW 1

fa la *also* **fal la** \(')fä(l)'lä\ *n* -S [fr. *fa-la*, frequent meaningless syllables in the refrains of such songs] : a 16th and 17th century part-song that is like a dance in character : BALLAD ⟨another kind of ballets commonly called *fa las* —Thomas Morley⟩

fa·la·na·ka \,falə'näkə\ *also* **fal·a·nouc** \,falə'nük\ *n* -S [Malagasy] : a viverrine mammal (*Eupleres goudotii*) of Madagascar closely related to the Asiatic palm civet

fa·lan·gist \fə'lanjəst *also* 'fā,l- *or* fā'l-\ *n* -S *often cap* [Sp *Falangista*, fr. *Falange* (*Española*) Spanish Phalanx, a Spanish fascist organization; Sp *falange*, fr. L *phalang-*, *phalanx* — more at PHALANX] : a member of the Spanish fascist organization Falange

fa·la·sha \fə'läshə\ *n, pl* **falasha** *or* **falashas** *usu cap* [Amharic *fālasha*, fr. *fālasi* sojourner, stranger] **1** : a people in Ethiopia that are Jewish in religion but similar in biological type to the Galla **2** : a member of the Falasha people

fal·ba·la \'falbələ\ *n* -S [F, fr. F dial. *ferbelà*, *farbélla*] : a flounce or trimming for a woman's garment (as a petticoat, apron, or scarf)

fal·ca·ta \fal'kād·ə, fȯl-, -kād·ə\ [NL, fr. L, *falcatus* falcate] *syn of* AMPHICARPA

fal·cate \'fal,kāt, 'fȯl-\ *adj* [L *falcatus*, fr. *falc-*, *falx* sickle, scythe + *-atus* -ate] : hooked or curved like a sickle ⟨a ~ leaf⟩ ⟨a ~ claw⟩ — used also of the moon or an inferior planet when less than half its disk is illuminated

fal·cat·ed \-ād·əd\ *adj* [L *falcatus* + E *-ed*] : FALCATE

falcated teal *also* **falcated duck** *n* : a teal (*Anas falcata*) of Asia, the male having an iridescent bronze head with slightly shaggy crest and drooping scapulars

falces *pl of* FALX

fal·chion \'fȯlchən, -lsh-\ *n* -S [ME *fauchoun*, fr. OF *fauchon*, fr. *fauchier* to mow, fr. (assumed) VL *falcare*, fr. L *falc-*, *falx* sickle, scythe] **1** *archaic* : a broad-bladed slightly curved sword used in the middle ages **2** *archaic* : a sword of any kind

fal·cial \'falshəl, 'fȯl-, -lch-\ *adj* [NL *falc-*, *falx* + E *-ial*] : of or belonging to a falx

fal·ci·form \'falsə,fȯrm, 'fȯl-\ *adj* [L *falc-*, *falx* sickle + E *-iform*] : having the shape of a scythe or sickle

falciform ligament *n* : an anteroposterior fold of peritoneum attached to the under surface of the diaphragm and sheath of the rectus muscle and along a line on the anterior and upper surfaces of the liver extending back from the notch on the anterior margin

fal·cip·a·rum malaria \fal'sipərəm-, fȯl\ *n* [*falciparum*, NL (specific epithet of *Plasmodium falciparum*), fr. L *falci-* (fr. *falc-*, *falx* sickle) + L *-parum* (neut. of *-parus* -parous)] : severe malaria caused by a malaria parasite (*Plasmodium falciparum*) and marked by recurrence of paroxysms usu. in less than 48 hours — called also *malignant malaria, subtertian malaria*; compare VIVAX MALARIA

fal·co \'fal(,)kō, 'fȯl-\ *n, cap* [NL, fr. LL, falcon] : the type genus of Falconidae comprising the typical falcons

1**fal·con** \'falkən *also* 'fȯlk- *sometimes* 'fōk-\ *n* -S [ME *faucoun*, *falcon*, fr. OF *faucon*, *falcon*, fr. LL *falcon-*, *falco*, prob. of Gmc origin; akin to OHG *falcho* falcon, MLG *valke*, and to the masculine name *Falco* attested among Lombards, Visigoths, and Franks; prob. fr. a prehistoric Gmc compound whose constituents are akin respectively to OHG *falo* pale, faded, dun-colored and OHG *-h*, *-ch* (suffix designating a bird) — more at FALLOW] **1 a** : any of various hawks trained or adapted for use in the sport of hawking; *esp* : PEREGRINE FALCON — used technically only of a female; see TIERCEL; compare IGNOBLE HAWK, NOBLE HAWK **b** : any of various hawks of the family Falconidae distinguished by their long wings, by having a distinct notch and tooth or sometimes two teeth on the edge of the upper mandible where it begins to bend down, and by their usu. plunging down on their prey from above in hunting — compare ACCIPITER **c** : HAWK 1a **2** : a light piece of ordnance used from the 15th to the 17th centuries

2**falcon** \"\ *vi* **falconed**; **falconed**; **falconing** \-k(ə)niŋ\ **falcons** : to hunt with falcons

falcon-beaked \',=='=\ *adj* : having a curved beak

fal·con·er \-k(ə)nə(r)\ *n* -S [ME *fauconer*, fr. OF *fauconier*, fr. *faucon* + *-ier* -er — more at FALCON] : a person who breeds or trains hawks for taking birds or game : one who follows the sport of fowling with hawks

fal·co·nes \fal'kō(,)nēz, fȯl-\ *n pl, cap* [NL, fr. pl. of *Falcon-*, *Falco*] : a suborder of Falconiformes comprising the hawks, falcons, eagles, Old World vultures, ospreys, caracaras, and secretary birds — compare CATHARTAE

fal·con·et \,falkə'net, ,fȯlk-, ,fōk-\ *n* -S [1*falcon* + *-et*] **1** : a smaller type of falcon (sense 2) **2** : any of several very small Asiatic falcons constituting a genus (*Microhierax*) **3** : any of several Australian insectivorous passerine birds (genus *Falcunculus*) — called also *shrike tit*

falcon-gentle \',=='=\ *n* [ME *faucoun gentil* peregrine falcon, fr. MF *faucon gentil*, lit., noble falcon] : the female peregrine falcon — used in the technical language of falconry

fal·con·i·dae \fal'känə,dē, fȯl-, -kōn-\ *n pl, cap* [NL, fr. *Falcon-*, *Falco*, type genus + *-idae*] : a family of diurnal birds of prey now usu. restricted to the long-winged swift-flying falcons and the caracaras but formerly including most hawks, eagles, buzzards, Old World vultures, and related forms — compare ACCIPITRIDAE

fal·co·ni·for·mes \(,)fal,kōnə'fȯr(,)mēz, (,)fȯl-\ *n pl, cap* [NL, fr. *Falcon-*, *Falco* + *-iformes*] : an order of chiefly diurnal flesh-eating birds having short stout hooped bills and strong feet with four toes, the young being helpless at hatching and fed in the nest, and including the hawks, eagles, vultures, and related birds — see CATHARTAE, FALCONES

fal·co·nine \'falkə,nīn, 'fȯlk-, 'fōk-\ *adj* [1*falcon* + *-ine*] : belonging to or resembling a falcon

fal·con·ry \-kənrē, -ri\ *n* -ES [F *fauconnerie*, fr. *faucon* falcon + *-erie* -ery — more at FALCON] **1** : the art of training falcons to pursue and to attack wild fowl or game **2** : the sport of taking wild fowl or game by the use of falcons — called also *hawking*

fal·cu·la \'falkyələ, 'fȯl-\ *n* -S [L, lit., small sickle, dim. of *falc-*, *falx* sickle] : a curved and sharp-pointed claw or process (as of a cat); *specif* : the cerebral falx

fal·cu·lar \-lə(r)\ *adj* [L *falcula* + E *-ar*] **1** : shaped like a sickle **2** : belonging to or indicating a falcula or falx ⟨~ cilia⟩

fal·cu·late \-,lāt\ *adj* [L *falcula* + E *-ate*] *zool* : curved and sharp-pointed

faldage *var of* FOLDAGE

falderal *var of* FOLDEROL

faldistory *n* -ES [ML *faldistorium*] *obs* : FALDSTOOL 1

fald·stool \'fȯl(d),stül\ *n* [part trans. of ML *faldistolium*, *faldistorium*, of Gmc origin; akin to OS *faldistōl* folding chair — more at FAUTEUIL] **1** : a folding stool or chair; *specif* : such a chair used by a bishop when not occupying his throne or when officiating outside his own cathedral church **2** : a similar stool or small desk at which one kneels during devotions; *esp* : one used by the king of England at his coronation **3** : the desk from which the litany is read in churches of the Anglican Communion

faldstool 1

1**fa·le·ri·an** \fə'lirēən\ *adj, usu cap* [*Falerii*, ancient city of central Italy (now Civita Castellana) + E *-an*] : of or relating to ancient Falerii

2**falerian** \"\ *n* -S *cap* **1** : an inhabitant of Falerii **2** : FALISCAN

fa·ler·ni·an \fə'lərnēən\ *adj, usu cap* [L *falernus* Falernian + E *-ian*] : of or coming from a district of Campania called Falernus ager by the Romans — used esp. of a wine celebrated by Horace

Fa·ler·num \fə'lərnəm\ *trademark* — used for a sweet white flavoring syrup of low alcoholic content often used as a cocktail ingredient

1**fa·lis·can** \fə'liskən\ *adj, usu cap* [L *Faliscus* + E *-an*] : of or relating to the Falisci who inhabited the city of Falerii and its region in ancient Etruria; *also* : relating to or constituting their dialect : FALERIAN

2**faliscan** \"\ *n* -S *cap* **1** : one of the Falisci **2** : the dialect of Latin of the Faliscans that is known from a small body of inscriptions written in an alphabet of Etruscan origin and is sometimes regarded as a language

fa·lis·ci \fə'li,sī, -li,skē\ *n pl, cap* [L] : an ancient people of Italic origin who were located in southern Etruria in the 5th century B.C. and whose chief town was Falerii

1**fall** \'fȯl\ *vb* **fell** \'fel\ **fall·en** \'fȯlən *also in poetry & sometimes* + V *in prose* -ln\ *also dial* **fell**; **falling**; **falls** [ME *fallen*, fr. OE *feallan*; akin to OFris & ON *falla* to fall, OS & OHG *fallan*, and perh. to Lith *pulti* to fall, OPruss *aupallai* he finds, Arm *p'ul* fall, plunge] *vi* **1 a** (1) : to descend by the force of gravity when freed from suspension or support : DROP ⟨the rain ~*s*⟩ ⟨ripe fruit ~*ing* off a tree⟩ (2) : to pass downward in a certain direction : drop in a guided descent ⟨the water ~*s* over the ledge⟩ ⟨the mercury ~*s* in the thermometer⟩ ⟨the lash *fell* on his shoulders⟩ (3) : to hang freely : extend downward ⟨her hair ~*s* loosely⟩ ⟨his cloak ~*s* from his shoulders⟩ (4) : to let oneself down usu. swiftly and suddenly to a sitting, reclining, or kneeling position ⟨she *fell* on the window seat by the coat closet and began to sob —Louis Auchincloss⟩ ⟨I was her slave; I *fell* at her feet —A.W.Long⟩; *sometimes* : to leap from a great height ⟨the column was popular with suicides, some of whom *fell* to their death before the top was enclosed in a cage —*Sydney* (*Australia*) *Bull.*⟩ **b** (1) : to become born — now usu. used of lambs (2) : to drop to a lower degree ⟨the temperature *fell*⟩ or level ⟨blood pressure *fell* to 140 systolic⟩ (3) : to decrease in volume of sound : drop in pitch ⟨his voice *fell*⟩ ⟨the music rose and *fell*⟩ (4) : ISSUE — used of speech ⟨the excellent advice that *fell* from his lips⟩ (5) : to come or come to pass as if by falling ⟨an ominous stillness *fell* upon the room⟩ ⟨night *fell* upon the village⟩ ⟨a heavy vengeance *fell* upon the rebels⟩ (6) : to become lowered — used of a glance or the eyes **2 a** : to drop suddenly and involuntarily ⟨~ down on the ice⟩ ⟨slipped and *fell* heavily to the ground⟩ **b** (1) : to enter as if blindly or unawares into a dangerous or undesirable state or situation : STUMBLE, STRAY — used with *in* or *into* ⟨*fell* into the enemy ambush⟩ ⟨~*ing* into the moral snares of a great city⟩ ⟨*fell* into grave doctrinal errors⟩ ⟨the novel ~*s* into a cloying sentimentality⟩ (2) *of a structure* : to collapse esp. in fragments ⟨many houses *fell* as a result of the earthquake⟩ ⟨the building *fell* of its own weight⟩ (3) : to drop to the ground wounded or dead ⟨men were ~*ing* all about him under the enemy fire⟩; *esp* : to die in battle ⟨the *fallen* included numerous officers⟩ ⟨*fell* in the first skirmish of the war⟩ (4) : to suffer destruction, capture, or total military defeat : COLLAPSE ⟨scholars still argue about why the Roman Empire *fell*⟩ ⟨the city *fell* after a siege of many months⟩ (5) : to lose office esp. as a result of an adverse parliamentary vote — used of a government or ministry ⟨the coalition government fell after only 6 months in office⟩ (6) : to suffer ruin, defeat, or failure : fail utterly ⟨we will stand or ~ together⟩ — used chiefly of projects or undertakings and in the phrase *fall through* ⟨your paper's ~*ing* through for no money and you want me to give you some? —Josephine Johnson⟩ ⟨I do not remember why the deal *fell* through —A.L.Guérard⟩ (7) : LAPSE, EXPIRE : PERISH, DISAPPEAR ⟨the conversation *fell* for a few minutes —Arnold Bennett⟩ ⟨his anger suddenly *fell*⟩ — often used with *away* ⟨if you have some other witness . . . this difficulty will ~ away —*Farmer's Weekly* (*So. Africa*)⟩ (8) *card games* : to become played — used of a card whose holder must legally though unwillingly play it (9) *cricket, of a wicket* : to become lost by the dismissal of a batsman ⟨the first wicket *fell* with 50 runs on the board⟩ **c** : to yield to temptation : commit an immoral act ⟨if ~*ing* were all that ever happened to a good man, all his days would be a simple matter of striving and repentance —Owen Wister⟩; *esp* : to lose one's chastity **3 a** (1) *of a river* : to flow down : DEBOUCH, EMPTY — used with *into* ⟨the rivers that ~ into the sea⟩ (2) : to move or extend in a generally downward direction ⟨the land ~*s* to a river⟩ — often used with *away* ⟨the ridge ~*s* away quickly where it approaches the sea —Norman Cousins⟩ ⟨the ground ~*ing* away from the highest point —Osbert Lancaster⟩ **b** (1) : to cease to be violent : SUBSIDE, ABATE ⟨the flames rose and *fell*⟩ ⟨the wind *fell*⟩ : EBB ⟨the ~*ing* tide⟩ (2) : to decline in quality, character, activity, or quantity ⟨the party's representation in the legislature *fell* from seven seats to six⟩ ⟨after his book on the circulation of the blood came out . . . he *fell* mightily in his practice —John Aubrey⟩ ⟨greater increases would merely influence traffic to ~ more sharply —*Collier's Yr. Bk.*⟩ ⟨how low can a man ~ ?⟩ — often used with *off* or *away* ⟨the tourist trade *fell* off markedly in January —R.F.Warner⟩ ⟨the play ~*s* off toward the end⟩ ⟨his work *fell* off badly⟩ ⟨subscriptions *fell* away —C.L.R.James⟩ ⟨the poem does not ~ away from its opening line —Oscar Cargill⟩ (3) : to lose physical tone, condition, or weight : become wasted — usu. used with *off* or *away* ⟨the cattle have *fallen* off badly in the drought⟩ ⟨you'd scarcely believe anybody could ~ off so rapidly —Ellen Glasgow⟩ ⟨she's *fallen* away terribly⟩ (4) : to assume a look of shame, disappointment, or dejection — used of the face ⟨his face *fell*⟩ (5) : to decline in financial value or price : suffer a decline in prices ⟨stocks *fell* several points⟩ ⟨the market is ~*ing*⟩ **c** : to make a hostile move or attack physically or verbally — now used with *on* or *upon* ⟨*fell* upon the enemy and routed him⟩ ⟨the opposition speakers *fell* clamorously on the tottering government⟩ **4 a** (1) : to come or occur at a certain time : ARRIVE ⟨prevent the harvest seasons from coming in time to ~ outside of their proper agricultural seasons —T.H.Gaster⟩ ⟨the beginnings of his career *fell* at the period . . . when the vogue of field games . . . was beginning —E.P.Tanner⟩ (2) : to come by chance

: happen to come ⟨it *fell* into my mind to write you a letter⟩ ⟨hurried me frequently into intrigues with low women that *fell* in my way —Benjamin Franklin⟩ **b** (1) : to come or pass by lot, assignment, inheritance, or as a burden or duty : DEVOLVE ⟨the estate *fell* to his brother⟩ ⟨the lot *fell* on him⟩ ⟨it *fell* to him to break the news⟩ (2) *dial Brit* : to have need or occasion : become obliged or due — used with *to* **c** *archaic* : to come or be due in the course of events — followed by *to be* and usu. a participle **d** (1) : to lie in a certain position ⟨the point ~*s* to the right of a given line⟩ : have the proper place or station ⟨the accent ~*s* on the second syllable⟩ (2) : to come within the limits, scope, or jurisdiction of something : have a definite position in a classificatory system or arrangement — often used with *into, within,* or *under* ⟨this word ~*s* into the class of verbs⟩ ⟨obviously *fell* within the Soviet sphere of influence —Max Ascoli⟩ ⟨~*s* within the jurisdiction of this city⟩ ⟨species ~ under genera⟩ (3) : to divide naturally — usu. used with *into* ⟨his creative output ~*s* into three distinct classes⟩ ⟨the area ~*s* into a number of physiographic regions⟩ (4) : to break up : SEPARATE ⟨they *fell* into two factions —R.A.Billington⟩ ⟨under the enemy thrust, the division *fell* to pieces⟩ **5 a** : to pass usu. somewhat suddenly and passively into a certain state of body or mind or a new condition or relation : BECOME ⟨*fell* at musing —Hugh McCrae⟩ ⟨I *fell* silent⟩ ⟨*fell* prey to dangerous diseases⟩ ⟨the brittle dish *fell* apart⟩ ⟨the tax ~*s* due this month⟩ ⟨*fell* heir to the estate⟩ ⟨*fell* in love⟩ — often used with *into* ⟨*fell* into a heavy slumber⟩ ⟨ran a street or two . . . and then *fell* into a walk —Arthur Morrison⟩ ⟨the word *fell* into disuse⟩ **b** : to come by chance into close or friendly dealings with a particular individual or group : have a chance encounter ⟨at college he *fell* into a congenial crowd of artistic and literary young men⟩ — often used in the phrases *fall among* or *fall in with* ⟨a bluff and simple country gentleman who had inadvertently *fallen* among politicians —C.H.Driver⟩ ⟨*fell* in with a Russian gentleman and his daughter —Norman Douglas⟩ ⟨he thought he was close to land when he *fell* in with a ship —Walter Hayward⟩ **c** : to set about usu. heartily or actively : BEGIN — often used with an infinitive of action ⟨*fell* to work⟩ or a verbal noun after the prefix *a-* ⟨*fell* a-laughing⟩ **6** *archaic* **a** : to revert to a feudal superior — used of a benefice **b** : to become vacant — used of an office **7** : to have a certain direction or point of incidence : STRIKE, IMPINGE ⟨a ray of light *fell* on the table⟩ ⟨music ~*ing* on the ear⟩ ⟨the shot *fell* a great distance from its target⟩ **8 a** : to form an ardent and usu. sudden attachment : become passionately or blindly fond or enamored ⟨one look at the girl and he *fell* — but hard⟩ — usu. used with *for* ⟨have you *fallen* for that young female grasshopper . . . at your age —Sinclair Lewis⟩ ⟨he has *fallen* for the ravishing widow —C.J.Rolo⟩ **b** : to become victim of a hoax or deception : become gulled or deceived ⟨they just don't ~ any more —Reed Whittemore⟩ — usu. used with *for* ⟨a reform movement that has *fallen* for a panacea —F.L. Allen⟩ **9** *slang* : to undergo arrest ⟨he *fell* twice, for theft and burglary —Wallace Beene⟩ **~** *vt* **1** *archaic* : to let drop or bring down (as tears or a weapon) **2** *dial Eng* : to receive as one's share : GET **3** : FELL *vt* 1

syn FALL, DROP, SINK, SLUMP, and SUBSIDE can mean in common to go or to let go downward freely. FALL, intransitive, suggests a descent by the force of gravity, always implying a loss of support opposing gravity in extension applying to anything extending downward or going figuratively in a downward direction ⟨let a glass *fall* to the ground and shatter⟩ ⟨the supports gone, the structure *fell* in a heap⟩ ⟨the roof had *fallen* in on another speaker —Bennett Cerf⟩ ⟨hair *falling* over a woman's shoulders⟩ ⟨the birthrate *fell* over a 6-month period, then rose⟩ ⟨let *fall* a remark about the weather⟩ DROP usu. stresses a speed, directness, unexpectedness, or casualness in falling or allowing to fall ⟨*dropped* a coin into a pond⟩ ⟨*dropped* seeds into holes⟩ ⟨*dropping* to the ground at the sound of an air-raid warning⟩ ⟨*dropping* a hint of coming trouble⟩ ⟨income figures *dropped* during the slow winter season⟩ SINK implies a gradual descending motion, esp. into something, often to the point of total submersion ⟨the ship *sank* gradually into the placid sea⟩ ⟨the float on the fish line *sank* a moment, then bobbed furiously⟩ ⟨the thermometer *sank* to far below zero —Douglas Carruthers⟩ ⟨*sinking* to her knees from exhaustion⟩ SLUMP now implies a falling or collapsing as of someone suddenly powerless or suddenly totally enervated ⟨*slumping* to the ground, unconscious⟩ ⟨*slumped* in his seat⟩ ⟨prices *slumped* badly in the winter⟩ ⟨when a bird falls asleep, it relaxes and *slumps* down until its body rests against the perch —J.H.Baker⟩ SUBSIDE suggests a gradual descent or return to a normal or usual position, action, or condition after an undue rising, expanding, boiling up; often it can suggest a sinking below a normal or usual level ⟨a wind rising then *subsiding*⟩ ⟨he lost a quarter of an hour waiting for the flood to *subside* —Mary Austin⟩ ⟨the bustle *subsides* and relative calm is resumed —*Amer. Guide Series: N.C.*⟩ ⟨the child's quick temper *subsided* into listlessness —Agnes Repplier⟩ ⟨after the boom prices *subsided* to a level far below normal⟩

—**fall a cropper** : to come a cropper — **fall by the wayside** **1** : to fall from grace **2** : to suffer defeat esp. in a contest ⟨many party stalwarts *fell by the wayside* on election day⟩ ⟨some *fell by the wayside* in encounters with unconquered squads —*N.Y. Times*⟩ — **fall down** : to sail or drift down (as a river or harbor) — **fall flat** : to produce no response or result : fail of the intended effect ⟨his homespun jokes . . . *fell flat* on those grim-faced men —R.W.Thorp⟩ — **fall foul** **1** : to have a collision : become entangled — used chiefly of ships **2** : to have a quarrel : CLASH — often used with *of* ⟨*fell foul* of one another⟩ **3** *archaic* : to make an attack — **fall from** *obs* : fail in duty to : DESERT — **fall from grace** **1** : to forfeit one's state of acceptance with God ⟨some believe that it is not possible for a saved person to *fall from grace* —J.C. Swaim⟩ **2** : BACKSLIDE — **fall home** : to curve inward — used of the timbers or upper parts of a ship's side that are much within a perpendicular; compare TUMBLE HOME — **fall into line** **1** : to fall in **2** : to comply or concur with a certain course of action or policy — **fall off the roof** : MENSTRUATE — **fall on** *or* **fall upon** : to meet with (a particular and usu. unfortunate kind of experience) : come upon ⟨an aristocratic girl . . . *fallen on* hard times —*Newsweek*⟩ ⟨*fell on* evil days⟩ — **fall on one's face** : to fail completely or resoundingly : fail so completely as to appear ridiculous ⟨efforts to increase production have up to now *fallen on their face*⟩ — **fall over oneself** *or* **fall over backward** : to display great or excessive eagerness ⟨*fell over themselves* in their efforts to accommodate the new administration —*Atlantic*⟩ ⟨juries *fell over backward* in favor of progressive art —Aline B. Saarinen⟩ — **fall short** **1** : to become or be deficient ⟨the expedition's supplies began to *fall short*⟩ **2** : to fail to attain, reach, arrive at, or perform something ⟨the shot *fell short*⟩ ⟨our efforts have *fallen short*⟩

²**fall** \"\ *n* -s [ME, fr. OE *feall;* akin to OFris, OS, & OHG *fal* fall, ON *fall*, deverbatives fr. the root of E ¹*fall*] **1 a** (1) : the act of dropping or descending by the force of gravity ⟨the ~ of a stone⟩ ⟨a ~ from a horse⟩ ⟨the leading cause of home deaths continued to be ~*s* —*Americana Annual*⟩ ⟨a ~ on the ice⟩ (2) : a guided descent or drop through the air ⟨the ~ of an ax⟩ ⟨the ~ of a man's foot⟩; *specif* : a descent to the floor in modern-dance technique that can be effected in a variety of ways and that resolves into a recovery or rise (3) : a position in which a wrestler's scapular area is held in contact with the mat for a given period of time; *also* : the act of putting an opponent in this position for the prescribed time **b** (1) : a falling out, off, or away : DROPPING, SHEDDING ⟨the ~ of leaves⟩ ⟨a ~ of snow⟩ (2) : the season when leaves fall from trees : AUTUMN (3) : the approach or onset esp. of night or darkness ⟨he came along the road in the chill ~ of the evening —Padraic Colum⟩ **c** (1) : a thing or quantity that falls or has fallen ⟨examined the ~ of earth at the mouth of the tunnel —G.A.Wagner⟩ ⟨a freak 20-inch ~ of rain⟩; *specif* : one or more meteorites or their fragments that have fallen together at one place and time (2) : birth or production by birth; *also* : something which is so produced ⟨a good ~ of lambs⟩ **d** : something that hangs down ⟨pushed back the ~ of hair from her forehead —Berton Roueché⟩: as (1) : a costume decoration of lace or thin fabric arranged to hang loosely and gracefully esp. from the back edge of a bonnet (2) : a very wide collar of fine fabric and lace worn in the 17th century esp. by Cavaliers (3) : the part of a turned-over collar from the crease to the outer edge — compare STAND (4) : a wide front flap on trousers (as those worn by sailors) (5) : the freely hanging lower edge of the skirt of a coat — often used in pl. ⟨would have done it . . . had I not taken him by the ~*s* of his skirt —Hugh McCrae⟩ (6) : one of the three outer and often drooping segments of the flower of an iris — usu. used in pl. (7) : long hair overhanging the face of certain terriers (8) : a hoisting-tackle rope or chain; *esp* : the part of it to which the power is applied (9) : BOAT FALL **e** : the manner in which something hangs down ⟨the ~ of a woman's hair⟩ **2 a** : loss of greatness, power, status, influence, or dominion : COLLAPSE, DOWNFALL ⟨the ~ of the Roman Empire⟩ ⟨the rise and ~ of business firms —*Economic Jour.*⟩; *specif* : loss of office by a government or ministry esp. as a result of an adverse parliamentary vote ⟨the ~ of a government on a vote of confidence⟩ **b** : the surrender or capture of a besieged fortress or town ⟨the ~ of Troy⟩ **c** (1) : lapse or departure from innocence or goodness : spiritual ruin ⟨~ from virtue⟩ — used with *the* and often cap. in reference to the fall of man reported in Gen 3 (2) : loss of a woman's chastity (3) : the cause of falling from virtue, grace, or power ⟨his stubbornness was his ~⟩ **3 a** : the descent of land or a hill : downward direction : SLOPE, DECLIVITY ⟨the well-remembered ~ of the land, dropping away to the old rice fields —Hamilton Basso⟩ **b** : precipitous descent of water : CASCADE, CATARACT, WATERFALL ⟨the first ~ is about 60 feet high —*Amer. Guide Series: Tenn.*⟩ — usu. pl. but often sing. in constr. ⟨the ~*s* of Niagara⟩ ⟨the upper ~*s* has a sheer plunge of 20 feet —*Jour. of Geol.*⟩ **c** (1) : a musical cadence (2) : DOUBLE APPOGGIATURA **d** : a falling-pitch intonation in speech **4** : diminution or decrease in size, quantity, or degree : DECLINE ⟨the persistently steep ~ in immigration —Peter Scott⟩ ⟨it was a compensation for a ~ in excitement and satisfaction in their . . . lives —W.D. Howells⟩ ⟨the main ~ in the average family size . . . had already taken place —Roy Lewis & Angus Maude⟩ ⟨the steady ~ in purchasing power⟩; *specif* : diminution or decrease in price or value ⟨recent heavy ~*s* in the stock market⟩ ⟨a ~ of rents⟩ **5 a** : the distance or extent to which something falls or slopes : the difference between levels ⟨a cultivated field . . . with a ~ of five feet in a hundred feet —J.B.Robson⟩ ⟨a ~ of five points in the price of a stock⟩ ⟨the Mississippi has a ~ of 620 feet between Minnesota and the Gulf —*Amer. Guide Series: Minn.*⟩ **b** : INCLINATION, PITCH ⟨a flat roof with a barely perceptible ~⟩ ⟨adjust the ~ of the gutter so the water would run along it faster⟩ **6 a** : the act of felling **b** : the quantity of trees cut down **7** *Scot* : something that befalls one : FORTUNE, LOT ⟨may good fortune be your ~⟩ **8** *slang* : ARREST ⟨served time on narcotics and prostitution ~*s* —Jack Lait & Lee Mortimer⟩ — **take a fall out of** *or* **get a fall out of** : to cause the discomfiture of : get the best of ⟨some of his sharper-tongued confreres occasionally *took a fall out of* him —S.H.Adams⟩

³**fall** \"\ *adj* : of fall or autumn : being such as occurs, matures, is done, or is suited for use or wear in the fall ⟨bought a ~ coat⟩ ⟨brisk ~ weather⟩

fall- *or* **fallo-** *comb form* [*Fallopian*] : fallopian tube ⟨*fallectomy*⟩ ⟨*fallotomy*⟩

fal la *var of* FA LA

fal·la·cious \fə'lāshəs\ *adj* [MF *fallacieux,* fr. L *fallaciosus,* fr. *fallacia* + *-osus* -ous] **1** : embodying or presenting a fallacy ⟨the demand was plausible, but the more I thought upon it the more . . . ~ . . . it seemed —A.D.White⟩ ⟨some ~ conclusions regarding drugs and crime —D.W.Maurer & V.H.Vogel⟩ ⟨read him a second time in order that I might state . . . articulately the points at which I thought he became ~ —O.W.Holmes †1935⟩ **2** : DECEPTIVE, MISLEADING, DELUSIVE, DISAPPOINTING ⟨the ~ hope that the propriety of going to bed may at any moment dawn upon the paternal mind —W.L.Alden⟩ ⟨a region . . . where . . . the ~ colocynth, the wild melon, scatters its globes of bitter gold —Norman Douglas⟩ — **fal·la·cious·ly** *adv*

fal·la·cious·ness *n* -ES : the quality of being fallacious

fal·la·cy \'faləsē, -si\ *n* -ES [L *fallacia,* fr. *fallac-, fallax* deceitful (fr. *fallere* to deceive) + *-ia* -y — more at FAIL] **1 a** *obs* : GUILE, TRICKERY **b** : deceptive or false appearance : something that misleads the eye or the mind : DECEPTION ⟨it appears that . . . the descent is perpendicular but this . . . is a ~ of the eye caused by the distance —Anthony Trollope⟩ **2 a** : a false or erroneous idea ⟨parents console themselves by the American ~ that one can only be young once —Elizabeth Bowen⟩ **b** : erroneous or fallacious character : ERRONEOUSNESS ⟨the ~ of such a suit for military use should at once be apparent —H.G.Armstrong⟩ **3** : a plausible reasoning that fails to satisfy the conditions of valid argument or correct inference — see FORMAL FALLACY, MATERIAL FALLACY, VERBAL FALLACY

fallacy of accident : the fallacy that consists in arguing from some accidental character as if it were essential or necessary (as in *the food you buy you eat; you buy raw meat; therefore you eat raw meat*)

fallacy of composition : the fallacy of arguing from premises in which a term is used distributively to a conclusion in which it is used collectively or of assuming that what is true of each member of a class or part of a whole will be true of all together (as in *if my money bought more goods I should be better off; therefore we should all benefit if prices were lower*)

fallacy of division : a fallacy in which a term taken collectively is used as if taken distributively

fallacy of the antecedent : the logical fallacy of denying the antecedent : DENIAL OF THE ANTECEDENT

fallacy of the consequent : the logical fallacy of affirming the consequent : AFFIRMATION OF THE CONSEQUENT

fal-lal \(')fa(l)¦lal, -¦läl, fə'l-\ *n* -s [perh. alter. of *falbala*] : an ornament or trimming esp. in dress

fall armyworm *n* : the larva of an American noctuid moth (*Spodoptera frugiperda*) that migrates northward as far as New England and is destructive esp. to grasses and small grains

fall away *vi* **1 a** : to withdraw friendship or support ⟨they had only been the companions of his pleasures and would be the surest to *fall away* in affliction —Marcia Davenport⟩ — often used with *from* ⟨the party leaders *fell away* from him, and his popularity seemed on the wane⟩ **b** : to renounce one's faith : APOSTATIZE ⟨those who had *fallen away* during the recent persecutions —K.S.Latourette⟩ **2 a** : to diminish in size or height : grow gradually smaller ⟨although the limbs are long and powerful . . . the animal *falls away* behind —James Stevenson Hamilton⟩ **b** : to swerve or drift off a line of direction ⟨the boat kept *falling away* to starboard⟩ ⟨*falling away* from the second baseman's tag and hooking the base with his toe as he slid past⟩

fallaway \'⸗⸗,⸗\ *n* -s [*fall away*] : a ballroom position in which both partners face in the same direction

fall back *vi* : to give way : RETREAT, RECEDE ⟨the infantry *fell back* before the determined enemy attack⟩ ⟨rivers . . . were *falling back* from their flood peaks —E.L.Dale⟩ — **fall back on** *or* **fall back upon** **1** : to retreat to (a stronger position) **2** : to have recourse to (a reserved fund or some available expedient or support) ⟨it's always good to have at least two things you can do because . . . if one folds, you can always *fall back on* the other —Eamonn Andrews⟩

fallback \'⸗,⸗\ *n* [*fall back*] **1** : a falling back : RETREAT ⟨there would be a rapid and orderly ~ to break contact —*N.Y. Times*⟩ **2** : something on which one can fall back : RESERVE ⟨there is a certain ~ against the risk of failure . . . on the part of the Allies —H.V.Hodson⟩

fall block *n* : a pulley block used with a fall (sense 1d(8))

fall board *n* : the cover of a piano keyboard

fall cankerworm *n* : a green or brown white-striped looper that is the larva of a small widespread No. American geometrid moth (*Alsophila pometaria*) with gray-winged males and wingless females and that is a destructive defoliator of fruit trees and deciduous shade trees

fall chronometer *n* : an instrument used in experimental psychology having a body which may fall practically without friction and which makes or breaks electrical contacts as it drops so that time intervals can be determined

fall dandelion *n* : a European scapose herb (*Leontodon autumnalis*) naturalized in the U.S.

fall down *vi* **1** : to prostrate oneself in worship **2** : to fail or disappoint expectation — often used with *on* ⟨he *fell down* on the job⟩

fall duck *n* : any of various migratory ducks (as the pintail, the teal, the redhead)

fallen *past part of* FALL

fallen star *n* : any of various blue-green algae of the family Nostocaceae growing on moist ground

fallen wool *n* **1** : wool rubbed off the backs of sheep and collected from the ground or elsewhere **2** : wool taken from dead sheep

fall·er \'fòlə(r)\ *n* -s [ME, one that falls, fr. *fallen* to fall + *-er* — more at FALL] **1** : a logger who fells trees — called also *feller* **2** : a machine part that acts by falling: as **a** : the activating part of some stop motions **b** : a falling or controlling device (as the hammer in a fulling machine, a tensioning device on a mule-spinning machine, or one of a series of pins in a gill box)

fallfish \'⸗,⸗\ *n* : any of several common No. American cyprinoid fishes; *esp* : a fish (*Semotilus corporalis*) of the streams of northeastern No. America — compare CHUB

fall front \'⸗,⸗\ *n* : DROP FRONT

fall grain *n* : grain sown in the autumn and harvested the following spring or summer

fall guy *n* **1** : one who assumes or on whom is placed the blame or responsibility : one who takes the rap : SCAPEGOAT ⟨public officials use the correctional institution as a *fall guy* for their own apathy, inertia, and ignorance —C.W.Leonard⟩ ⟨becoming the *fall guy* for the ring which operated the houses of prostitution in that district —R.M.Lindner⟩ **2** : one that is made the victim of a swindle or deception : one that is easily gulled or victimized ⟨his friends were laughing at him . . . had he been marked early for a *fall guy* —Irving Stone⟩

fall herring *n* : a herring (*Pomolobus mediocris*) of the Atlantic coast from Cape Cod south

fal·li·bi·lism \'faləbə,lizəm\ *n* -s [ML *fallibilis* + E *-ism*] : a theory that it is impossible to attain absolutely certain empirical knowledge because the statements constituting it cannot be ultimately and completely verified — opposed to *infallibilism* — **fal·li·bi·list** \-,ləst\ *n* -s — **fal·li·bi·lis·tic** \¦⸗⸗⸗¦listik\ *adj*

fal·li·bil·i·ty \,falə'biləd·ē, -lətē, -i\ *n* -ES : liability or proneness to err ⟨the critics of the romantic period were pioneers, and exhibit the ~ of discoverers —T.S.Eliot⟩ ⟨the ~ of human perceptions —A.S.Eddington⟩

fal·li·ble \'faləbəl\ *adj* [ME, fr. ML *fallibilis,* fr. L *fallere* to deceive + *-ibilis* -ible — more at FAIL] **1** : liable to err ⟨all men are ~⟩ **2** : liable to be erroneous or inaccurate ⟨a ~ rule⟩ — **fal·li·ble·ness** \-bəlnəs\ *n* -ES — **fal·li·bly** \-blē, -li\ *adv*

fall in *vi* **1** : to sink inward ⟨the roof *fell in*⟩ **2 a** : to come to an end : TERMINATE, LAPSE — used of a lease or annuity **b** : to come into the owner's possession after a lease **c** : to become operative or available (as of a reversion) **3** *obs* : to rush in or come in **4** *archaic* : OCCUR, HAPPEN **5** : to take one's proper place in a military formation and come to the position of attention **~** *vt* : to cause (troops) to take proper positions in ranks : cause (a military unit) to form ranks — **fall in for** : to come in for : INCUR ⟨*fell in for* the major share of the blame⟩ — **fall in with** **1** : to agree or concur with : yield to : conform to ⟨I had to *fall in with* her wishes as much as possible —Frank Sargeson⟩ ⟨requested me to *fall in with* the custom of the day —Tyrone Power †1841⟩ **2** : to harmonize with : join with ⟨it *falls in* exactly *with* my views⟩

falling *adj* [fr. pres. part. of ¹*fall*] : passing from a more vigorous to a less vigorous physical condition : DECLINING — used esp. of domestic livestock; compare RISING

falling asleep *n, usu cap F&A* [trans. of MGk *koimēsis*] : an Eastern Church feast celebrating the corporeal assumption of the Virgin Mary that is observed on August 15 and that corresponds to the Western feast of the Assumption

falling band *n* : FALL 1d(2)

falling diphthong *n* : a diphthong with less stress on the second element than on the first (as \ȯi\ in \'nȯiz\ *noise*) — compare RISING DIPHTHONG

falling disease *n* : the typical terminal manifestation of severe copper deficiency in which an animal collapses and dies apparently from heart failure consequent to myocardial damage

falling evil *n* [ME *falling evil*] : EPILEPSY

falling fit *n* : an epileptic seizure of a domestic animal — compare EPILEPSY

falling hinge *n* : a horizontal hinge (as for a trapdoor)

falling leaf *n* : an aerobatic flight maneuver in which an airplane is allowed to stall and is then slipped successively to the right and left, the nose being held to point in the same direction throughout

falling mold *n* : a pattern for templating the side of a wreath after using the face mold in stairbuilding

falling of the womb : prolapse of the uterus into the vagina

falling-out \¦⸗⸗¦⸗\ *n, pl* **fallings-out** *or* **falling-outs** [fr. gerund of *fall out*] : an instance of falling out : QUARREL ⟨Papa had *falling-outs* with a lot of people —Alan Le May⟩

falling rhythm *n, prosody* : rhythm with stress occurring regularly on the first syllable of each foot — opposed to *rising rhythm;* compare CADENCE 5

falling sickness *n* **1** : FALLING FITS **2** : EPILEPSY

falling star *n* : METEOR 2a

falling weather *n, chiefly Midland* : weather characterized by heavy rain, snow, or hail : bad weather

falling wedge *n* : a wedge to drive into the kerf of a tree in order to direct its fall — called also *felling wedge*

fall leaf *n* : the drop leaf of a table

fall line *n* **1** : a line joining the waterfalls on a number of rivers that marks the point where each river descends from the upland to the lowland and the limit of its navigability **2** : the natural downward course (as for skiing) between two points on a slope

fall meadow rue *n* : TALL MEADOW RUE

fall money *n, slang* : money set aside or deposited with some other person by a professional criminal or group of criminals for use in an emergency (as for legal fees)

fallo- — see FALL-

fall off *vi* **1** : to step aside : WITHDRAW **2** : TREND — used of a coastline **3** *of a ship* : to deviate or trend to leeward of the point to which her head was directed

falloff \'⸗,⸗\ *n* -s [*fall off*] : a decline esp. in quantity ⟨a ~ in exports which helped to pay for Europe's vital imports —*Newsweek*⟩

fall of the hammer : the customary stroke of the hammer or gavel made by an auctioneer to denote that the sale is closed and the highest previous bid is accepted — compare *by inch of candle* at ¹INCH

fal·lo·pi·an \fə'lōpēən\ *adj, often cap* [Gabriel *Fallopius* (Gabriello *Fallopio*) †1562 Ital. anatomist + E *-an*] : relating to or discovered by Fallopius

fallopian aqueduct *or* **fallopian canal** *n, often cap F* : FACIAL CANAL

fallopian tube *n, often cap F* : the oviduct in mammals : either of the pair of tubes that conduct the egg from the ovary to the uterus, have at the upper end a funnel-shaped expansion receiving the egg as it escapes from the ovary, and are continuous with the uterus at the lower end

fall out *vi* **1** : to turn out : RESULT, OCCUR, HAPPEN ⟨as it *fell out,* the building was deserted at the time of the explosion⟩ ⟨all *fell out* very well indeed⟩ ⟨this strangeness of life, this unexpected and even perverse element of things as they *fall out* —G.K.Chesterton⟩ **2** : to have a quarrel : DISAGREE **3 a** : to leave one's place in the ranks **b** : to leave a building to meet a formation ⟨you will *fall out* of the barracks in 10 minutes for retreat⟩

fallout \'⸗,⸗\ *n* -s [*fall out*] **1** : the descent through the atmosphere of often radioactive particles stirred up by or resulting from a nuclear explosion **2** : the particles that descend through the atmosphere following a nuclear explosion

fall over *vi, Scot* : to go to sleep

¹**fal·low** \'fa(,)lō, -lə, *often* -ləw+V\ *adj* [ME *falow,* fr. OE *fealo, fealu;* akin to OHG *falo* pale, faded, dun-colored,

fallow, OS *falu*, ON *fölr* pale, fallow, L *pallēre* to be pale, Gk *polios* gray, Skt *palita* gray, hoary, OSlav *plavŭ* white] **:** of the color fallow ⟨a ~ greyhound⟩; *also* **:** of any pale color or warm hue

2**fallow** \"\ *n* -s **:** a light yellowish brown that is lighter and slightly redder and stronger than khaki, less strong and slightly yellower and darker than walnut brown, yellower and paler than cinnamon, and less strong than manila

3**fallow** \"\ *n* -s [ME *falwe, falow,* fr. OE *fealg, fealh* — more at FELLY] **1** *obs* **:** plowed land or a piece of it **2 :** land ordinarily used for crop production when allowed to lie idle either in a tilled or untilled condition during the whole or the greater portion of the growing season **3 :** the plowing or tilling of land without sowing it for a season; *also* **:** the state or period of being fallow ⟨summer ~ is a method of destroying weeds⟩

4**fallow** \"\ *vt* -ED/-ING/-S [ME *falwen, falowen,* fr. OE *fealgian,* fr. *fealg,* n.] **1** *obs* **:** to plow (land) for sowing **2 :** to plow, harrow, and break up (land) without seeding for the purpose of destroying weeds and conserving soil moisture

5**fallow** \"\ *adj* [ME *falwe, falow,* fr. *falwe, falow,* n.] **1 :** left untilled or unsown after plowing **:** UNCULTIVATED ⟨~ ground⟩ **2** *obs* **:** fit for cultivation **:** plowed ready for sowing **3 a :** not pregnant ⟨a ~ sow⟩ **b :** marked by the absence of pregnancy ⟨a long ~ period followed by the birth of two sons in rapid succession⟩ **4 a :** having large potential value or utility but being unused — used esp. in the phrase *to lie fallow* ⟨at this very moment there are probably important inventions lying ~ —*Harper's*⟩ ⟨the skills of the men displaced by . . . up-to-date machinery will not lie ~ for long —Sam Pollack⟩ **b :** characterized by a state of creative or recuperative rest or dormancy **:** gathering strength while lying idle — used esp. in the phrase *to lie fallow* ⟨and now the period of lying ~, of incorporating a new approach, came to an end —Dorothy Lee⟩ ⟨the spirit that actuated the grandfather having lain ~ in the son and being refreshed by repose so as to be ready for fresh exertion in the grandson —Samuel Butler †1902⟩

6**fallow** \"\ *Scot var of* FELLOW

fallowchat \ˈ=,=\ *n* [3*fallow* + *chat*] **:** WHEATEAR

fallow deer *n* [1*fallow*] **:** a European deer (*Dama dama*) much smaller than the red deer that has the antlers palmate near the ends and the coat spotted with white in summer and that is commonly domesticated in England where it is often kept in private parks — see DEER illustration

fal·low·ness *n* -ES [5*fallow* + *-ness*] *archaic* **:** the state of being unused or unworked

fall phonometer *n* **:** an instrument used in experimental psychology designed to furnish sounds whose intensities are in known ratios by permitting balls to drop from different heights upon plates of metal or slate

fall-pipe \ˈ=,=\ *n* **:** DOWNSPOUT

fall-plow \ˈ=;=\ *vt* **:** to plow (land) in autumn

fall riv·er \(ˈ)fȯl¦rivə(r)\ *adj, usu cap F&R* [fr. *Fall River,* Mass.] **:** of or from the city of Fall River, Mass. ⟨a *Fall River* resident⟩ **:** of the kind or style prevalent in Fall River

fall rope *n* **:** a rope used for hoisting (as in a derrick)

fall rose *n* **:** CHINA ASTER

falls *pres 3d sing of* FALL, *pl of* FALL

fall snipe *n* **:** RED-BACKED SANDPIPER

fall-sow \ˈ=;=\ *vt* **:** to sow (seed or land) in autumn

falltime \ˈ=,=\ *n* **:** AUTUMN

fall to *vi* **:** to set about doing something esp. actively: as **a :** to begin to fight **b :** to begin to eat ⟨*fell to* as soon as dinner was served⟩

fall together *vi* **:** to become identical **:** become leveled — used of speech sounds or forms

fall-trap \ˈ=,=\ *n* **:** a trap with a door or a weight that falls upon the victim

fall webworm *n* **:** a pale yellow dusky-striped hairy caterpillar that is the larva of either of two common white arctiid moths (*Hyphantria cunea* and *H. textor*) and that lives gregariously in nests of webbing at the ends of branches of many deciduous trees — compare TENT CATERPILLAR

fall wheat *n* **:** WINTER WHEAT

fall wind *n* **:** a katabatic wind

fall witchgrass *n* **:** a tufted No. American perennial grass (*Leptoloma cognatum*) with flat leaves, brittle culms, and very diffuse terminal panicles that break away at maturity and become tumbleweeds

fall zone *n* **:** FALL LINE

fals *var of* FELS

fal·sa·ry \ˈfȯl(t)sərē\ *n* -ES [ME *falsarie,* fr. L *falsarius,* fr. *falsus* + *-arius* -ary] *archaic* **:** FALSIFIER, DECEIVER; *specif* **:** FORGER

1**false** \ˈfȯls *also* -lts\ *adj* -ER/-EST [ME fals, *faus,* fr. OF & L; OF *fals, faus,* fr. L *falsus,* past part. of *fallere* to deceive — more at FAIL] **1 a :** not corresponding to truth or reality **:** not true **:** ERRONEOUS, INCORRECT ⟨his assumption that this is the only possible interpretation is demonstrably ~ —M.R.Cohen⟩ **b :** intentionally untrue **:** LYING ⟨~ claims are frequently made of automobile ownership —S.L.Payne⟩ ⟨the ~ testimony of suborned witnesses⟩ **2 a :** speaking falsehood **:** not truthful **:** DISHONEST, DECEITFUL ⟨slanders of her ~ accusers —Shak.⟩ ⟨especially heavy consequences for people . . . attracted to unworthy, ~, and callous persons —H.E.Salisbury⟩ **b** (1) **:** made or tampered with to deceive ⟨~ scales⟩ ⟨~ dice⟩ ⟨~ bottom of a glass⟩ (2) *archaic* **:** tending to distort **:** DEFECTIVE ⟨tears are ~ spectacles —John Donne⟩ (3) **:** inaccurate in pitch **:** out of tune **c :** tending to mislead **:** DECEPTIVE, ILLUSORY ⟨the ~ warmth of the January thaw —Louis Bromfield⟩ **3 :** not faithful or loyal (as to obligations, allegiance, or vows) **:** TREACHEROUS, PERFIDIOUS ⟨a ~ friend⟩ ⟨a ~ lover⟩ **4 a** (1) **:** being other than what is purported or apparent **:** assumed or designed to deceive **:** not genuine or real **:** COUNTERFEIT, ARTIFICIAL, SHAM, FORGED, SPECIOUS ⟨~ tears⟩ ⟨~ modesty⟩ ⟨privateersmen sailing under ~ colors⟩ ⟨~ deeds of ownership⟩ ⟨the ~ glamor of war⟩ ⟨listening to ~ prophets⟩ (2) **:** artificially made or assumed ⟨a set of ~ teeth⟩ ⟨buying ~ hair from impoverished country girls —Lois Long⟩ **b :** BLANK 5b ⟨a ~ door⟩ ⟨a ~ window⟩ **c :** of a kind related to, resembling, or having properties similar to another species that commonly bears the unqualified vernacular — used in plant names ⟨~ oats⟩ ⟨a ~ pea⟩ **d** (1) **:** not essential or permanent — used of parts of a structure that are temporary or supplemental ⟨~ siding⟩ ⟨~ pillar⟩ ⟨~ roof⟩ (2) **:** fastened to or fitting over a main part to strengthen it, to protect it or anything that comes in contact with it, or to disguise its appearance ⟨~ deck⟩ ⟨~ jaw of a chuck or vise⟩ ⟨~ post⟩ **e :** formed through unawareness or misunderstanding of the etymology ⟨pea is a ~ singular formed from the real singular *pease*⟩ **f :** VOIDED 2 **g :** lacking realism, naturalness, or authenticity **:** failing to produce an effect of artistic rightness or inevitability **:** appearing forced, strained, or incongruous **:** ARTIFICIAL, UNCONVINCING ⟨there are only two seriously ~ scenes . . . and they occur toward the end —V.S. Pritchett⟩ ⟨a vocabulary affected and often . . . ludicrously ~ —Gilbert Highet⟩ **5 a :** not based on facts or correct premises **:** not well founded **:** IMPRUDENT, UNWISE, INCORRECT ⟨our time is for the most part spent in hesitation, ~ starts, and painful retracing of our steps —M.R.Cohen⟩ ⟨make a ~ turn in his canoe —*Amer. Guide Series: La.*⟩ ⟨practice ~ economy⟩ ⟨this marriage is ~ —George Meredith⟩ ⟨a sense of ~ security⟩ **b :** appearing inconsistent with one's true character or intentions **:** COMPROMISING, AWKWARD ⟨by accepting the support of such dubious elements he put himself in an extremely ~ position⟩ **6** *dial Eng* **:** SHARP, CLEVER ⟨it's a ~ child that knows its own father⟩ **syn** see FAITHLESS

2**false** \"\ *vt* -ED/-ING/-S [ME *falsen, fausen,* fr. OF *falser, fausser,* fr. LL *falsare,* fr. L *falsus*] *obs* **:** FEIGN

3**false** \"\ *adv* [ME *false, fals,* fr. *fals, faus,* adj.] **1** *archaic* **:** ERRINGLY, INCORRECTLY, WRONGLY **2 :** FAITHLESSLY, TREACHEROUSLY — usu. used with *play* ⟨his wife played him ~⟩

false acacia *n* **:** LOCUST 3a (2)

false alarm *n* **:** one who raises but fails to meet expectations ⟨rising to attention on waves of their discoverers' ardor, most of them soon . . . sink back to the sea of *false alarms* —*Yale Rev.*⟩

false albacore *n* **:** LITTLE TUNA

false aloe *n* **1 :** any of various plants of the genus *Agave; esp* **:** a bulbous herb (*Agave virginica*) of the southeastern U. S. **2 :** a colicroot (*Aletris farinosa*)

false alumroot *n* **:** a hairy perennial herb (*Tellima grandiflora*) of the western U. S. with racemes of greenish flowers that have fringed petals and that gradually turn pink or reddish as they fade — compare ALUMROOT

false angostura bark *n* **:** the bark of the nux vomica tree

false annual ring *n* **:** FALSE RING

false arborvitae *n* **:** a tree or shrub of the genus *Thujopsis*

false arch *n* **:** a member having the appearance of an arch though not of arch construction; *specif* **:** CORBEL ARCH

false arrest *n* **:** an arrest not justifiable under law

false asphodel *n* **:** a plant of the genus *Tofieldia*

false attic *n* **:** a compartment that is situated like an attic immediately under a roof but does not have windows and does not enclose rooms

false azalea *n* **:** a shrub (*Menziesia ferruginea*) of the Rocky mountains having foliage with a bluish tinge and bell-shaped inconspicuous flowers

false baby's breath *n* **:** any of various plants of the genus *Galium; esp* **:** WILD MADDER 2a

false banana *n* **:** PAPAW 2a

false bark *n* **:** a bark used commercially as a substitute for cinchona

false bearing *n* **:** a bearing (as of a lintel or beam) not directly on a vertical support

false-bedded \ˈ=¦==\ *adj* **:** CROSS-BEDDED — **false bedding** *n*

false beechdrops *n* **:** a pinesap (*Monotropa hypopiths*)

false bittersweet *n* **:** BITTERSWEET 2b

false blossom *n* **1 :** a disease of the cranberry caused by a fungus (*Exobasidium oxycocci*) producing erect flower buds which produce malformed flowers that set no fruit or are sometimes replaced by a whorl of leaves or a branch — called also *rosebloom* **2 :** a similar disease of cranberries caused by a virus and transmitted by a leafhopper (*Scleroracus vaccinii*) — called also *Wisconsin false blossom*

false body *n* **:** a higher apparent consistency exhibited on standing than that resulting from stirring or brushing; *also* **:** the property or phenomenon of exhibiting such a change in consistency **:** THIXOTROPY — used esp. of paints and varnishes

false boneset *n* **:** a plant of the genus *Kuhnia; esp* **:** a perennial resinous No. American herb (*K. eupatorioides*) with purplish white flowers

false box *or* **false boxwood** *n* **:** a small tree or shrub (*Gyminda grisebechii*) of the southeastern U.S., Mexico, northern So. America, and parts of the West Indies having small leathery leaves resembling those of the box (*Buxus sempervirens*)

false branching *n* **:** a branched arrangement of the cells of certain filamentous bacteria and algae resulting from a slipping of the end of one cell past that of another following cell division, from continued growth of the free end of a trichome through the sheath in various blue-green algae, or esp. from continued growth of parts of a filament separated by one or more intervening dead cells or by heterocysts — compare TRUE BRANCHING

false branching in an alga

false bromegrass *n* **:** either of the two European fodder grasses (*Brachypodium pinnatum* and *B. sylvaticum*)

false buckthorn *n* **:** a spiny tree (*Bumelia lanuginosa*) of the southern U.S. having oblong to obovate leaves with the undersurface dull and woolly, small greenish white flowers followed by dark globular fruits, and very hard tough wood

false buckwheat *n* **:** an American herbaceous vine (*Polygonum scandens*) with seeds resembling buckwheat

false buffalo grass *n* **:** a low tufted grass (*Munroa squarrosa*) of the western U.S. with stiff leaves and wiry branches

false bugbane *n* **:** a tall herb (*Trautvetteria carolinensis*) of the family Ranunculaceae of the eastern U.S. with large basal leaves and white apetalous flowers

false cadence *n* **:** DECEPTIVE CADENCE

false-card \ˈ=¦=\ *n* **:** a card played with the intention of deceiving an opponent as to the content of one's hand

falsecard \"\ *vi* [*false card*] **:** to play a false-card

false cast *n* **:** a cast made when fly-fishing in which neither fly nor line touches the water

false cedar *n* **:** any of several trees resembling cedars of the genus *Thuja* esp. in odor; *specif* **:** SPANISH CEDAR

false ceiling *n* **:** a ceiling that is hung some distance below the ceiling joists

false chamomile *n* **:** a plant of the genus *Boltonia*

false chinaroot *n* **:** AMERICAN CHINAROOT

false chinch bug *n* **:** a small dark bug (*Nysius ericae*) resembling the related chinch bug in appearance and habits though commonly feeding on weeds and not often seriously destructive to cultivated crops

false cirrus *n* **:** a cirrus cloud of appreciable thickness originating from a cumulonimbus cloud — called also *thunderstorm cirrus*

false claims statute *n* **:** a statute penalizing the maker of knowingly false claims against the government or any department or agency thereof

false cockle *n* **:** CARDITA 2

false coltsfoot *n* **:** WILD GINGER 2a

false cypress *n* **:** any of several coniferous shrubs or trees (as members of the genus *Chamaecyparis*) with foliage resembling that of a cypress

falsed *past of* FALSE

false dandelion *n* **:** any of various American herbs (family Compositae) having flower heads resembling those of a dandelion

false dawn *n* **:** a faint light on the eastern horizon sometime before dawn; *often* **:** ZODIACAL LIGHT

false death cap *n* **:** an agaric (*Amanita mappa*) often confused with the death cup (*A. phalloides*) but having the cap usu. lemon yellow or white with no trace of green and a very bulbous stem base with the volva separated from the stem by a distinct groove

false dichotomy *n* **:** a branching in which the main axis appears to divide dichotomously at the apex but is in reality suppressed, the growth being continued by lateral branches (as in the dichasium)

false dragonhead *n* **1 :** a plant of the genus *Physostegia* **2 :** DRAGONHEAD

false face \ˈ=,=\ *n* **:** a caricature of human or animal features that is made of cloth, plaster, or similar material and worn over the face **:** MASK

false-face \"\ *adj* **:** disguised by a false face

false flax *n* **:** a plant of the genus *Camelina* — see GOLD OF PLEASURE, SMALL-SEEDED FALSE FLAX

false floor *n* **:** a floor usu. with open cracks placed about 18 inches above the main floor of a farm fruit or vegetable storage to facilitate free circulation of air

false foot *n* **:** PSEUDOPODIUM

false foxglove *n* **:** any of several gerardias having yellow flowers that resemble those of a foxglove

false front *n* **1 :** a facade extending beyond and esp. above the true dimensions of a building to give it a more imposing appearance **2 :** false hair usu. used for bangs or curls at the front hairline **3 :** appearance or manner intended to deceive

false fruit *n* **:** ACCESSORY FRUIT

false galena *n* **:** SPHALERITE

false garlic *n* **:** a bulbous herb (*Nothoscordum bivalve*) of the southern U.S. and the West Indies

false gid *n* **:** a disease of sheep that resembles gid and is caused by larvae of a botfly (*Oestrus ovis*) in the nasal chambers

false goatsbeard *n* **:** a plant of the genus *Astilbe*

false goldenrod *n* **:** a No. American herb (*Solidago sphacelata*) having sessile or subsessile heads in glomerules along the branches

false gromwell *n* **:** a plant of the genus *Onosmodium*

false guinea grass *n* **:** JOHNSON GRASS

false header *n* **:** SNAP HEADER

falsehearted \ˈ=¦==\ *adj* **:** having a disloyal heart ⟨a ~ traitor —Shak.⟩

false heather *n* **1 :** any of several ericaceous plants that resemble true heather; *esp* **:** BEACH HEATHER **2 :** a small heath-like So. American solanaceous shrub (*Fabiana imbricata*) that is sometimes cultivated as an ornamental usu. in the coolhouse

false hedge hyssop *n* **:** a plant of the genus *Ilysanthes*

false heliotrope *n* **:** GARDEN HELIOTROPE 1

false hellebore *n* **1 :** WHITE HELLEBORE **2 :** PHEASANT'S-EYE 1

false hemp *n* **1 :** HEMP NETTLE **2 :** SUNN

false·hood \ˈfȯl(t)s,hu̇d\ *n* [ME *falshede, falshod,* fr. *fals* false + *-hede, -hod* -hood — more at FALSE] **1 a :** absence of truth or accuracy **:** FALSITY ⟨the ~ of this doctrine must be patent to any careful student⟩ **b :** an untrue assertion esp. when intentional **:** LIE ⟨told two flat ~s about what had happened in secret session —Elmer Davis⟩ **c :** the practice of lying **:** MENDACITY ⟨it is a trite . . . observation that courts are the seat of ~ and dissimulation —Earl of Chesterfield⟩ **2** *Scots law* **:** the fraudulent imitation or suppression of truth by words, writing, or conduct to the damage of another

false hoof *n* **:** a hoof terminating a vestigial digit in many ungulates (as deer and pigs)

false hybrid *n* **:** an individual produced by an essentially parthenogenetic process from an egg of one species activated by a sperm of another without the entry of sperm chromosomes to form a synkaryon

false imprisonment *n* **:** the imprisonment of a person contrary to law; *also* **:** any unlawful interference with another's right of free location

false indigo *n* **1 :** a shrub of the genus *Amorpha:* as **a :** a shrub (*A. fruticosa*) of the eastern U.S. **b :** a shrub (*A. californica*) of the Pacific coast **2 :** INDIGO BROOM

false indusium *n* **:** the revolute margin of some fern pinnae (as in the bracken and maidenhair ferns)

false ipecac *n* **1 :** an herb of the genus *Gillenia* that has properties similar to those of ipecac **2 :** BLOODFLOWER 1

false keel *n* **:** a thin keel or strip below the main keel used to serve as a protection and to increase a ship's lateral resistance — see SHIP illustration

false key *n* **:** PICKLOCK

false killer whale *n* **:** a small cosmopolitan toothed whale (*Pseudorca crassidens*) resembling and closely related to the killer whale

false labor *n* **:** pains resembling those of normal labor but without effacement or dilation of the cervix

false larch *n* **:** a tree of the genus *Pseudolarix; esp* **:** GOLDEN LARCH

false leaf *n* **:** CLADOPHYLL

false leg *n* **:** PROLEG

false ligaments *n pl* **:** folds of peritoneum assisting to retain the bladder in position

false lily of the valley *n* **:** a small 2-leaved herb (*Maianthemum canadense*) of the northern U. S. and parts of Canada

false logwood *n* **:** a West Indian timber tree (*Haemocharis haematoxylon*) of the family Theaceae with red wood

false loosestrife *n* **:** an American plant of the genus *Ludwigia*

false lupine *n* **:** an American plant of the genus *Thermopsis* with yellow pealike flowers — called also *golden pea, yellow pea*

false·ly *adv* [ME *falsly,* fr. *fals* false + *-ly*] **:** in a false manner: as **a :** WRONGLY, INCORRECTLY ⟨~ assumed that he was familiar with the subject⟩ **b :** not truthfully **:** DISHONESTLY ⟨recently cleared of a murder charge to which he had ~ confessed as a result of police brutality —Curtis Bok⟩ ⟨swore ~ that he had seen me that morning⟩ **c :** without cause **:** UNJUSTLY ⟨led to the exoneration of a man ~ convicted of forgery —*Current Biog.*⟩ **d :** DECEITFULLY, INSINCERELY ⟨smiled ~ at her unwelcome visitor⟩ **e :** not genuinely **:** SPECIOUSLY ⟨the difficulty in presenting Elizabethan plays is that they are liable to be made too modern or ~ archaic —T.S.Eliot⟩

false mallow *n* **1 :** an American plant of the genus *Malvastrum* **2 :** GLOBE MALLOW **3 a :** INDIAN MALLOW 2 **b :** any of several other plants of the genus *Sida*

false mange *n* **:** severe seborrhea of domestic animals

false manna *n* **:** a product similar to the manna from ash trees but obtained from other plants

false membrane *n* **:** a fibrinous deposit with enmeshed necrotic cells formed esp. in croup and diphtheria

false mermaid *n* **:** a plant of the genus *Floerkea; esp* **:** a slender annual aquatic herb (*F. proserpinacoides*) of eastern No. America with small white flowers

false-mermaid family *n* **:** LIMNANTHACEAE

false mesquite *n* **:** a dwarf somewhat prostrate shrub (*Calliandra eriophylla*) sometimes used for forage in the western U. S.

false mildew *n* **:** DOWNY MILDEW

false mistletoe *n* **:** MISTLETOE 2a

false miterwort *n* **:** an American white-flowered woodland spring-blooming herb (*Tiarella cordifolia*) — called also *coolwort, foamflower*

false music *n* **:** MUSICA FICTA

false·ness *n* -ES [ME *falsnesse,* fr. *fals* false + *-nesse* -ness] **:** the quality or state of being false: as **a :** contrariety to the fact **:** INACCURACY ⟨the ~ of a wicked rumor⟩ **b** (1) **:** UNFAITHFULNESS, TREACHERY, PERFIDY ⟨upbraided him for his ~ to his wife⟩ (2) **:** lack of integrity or uprightness **:** INSINCERITY ⟨there is a certain ~ about the man that I dislike⟩

false nettle *n* **:** any of several plants of the genera *Boehmeria* and *Laportea*

false nostril *n* **:** a blind pouch two or three inches long of unknown function lying between the nasal and premaxillary bones of the horse and related animals

false nutmeg *n* [so called fr. the shape of the fruit] **:** a tree of the genus *Torreya*

false oat grass *n* **1 :** TALL OAT GRASS **2 :** YELLOW OAT GRASS

false paca *n* **:** any of several So. American rodents constituting a genus *Dinomys* closely related to the pacas and chiefly distinguished by their long tails — called also *long-tailed paca*

false-packed \ˈ=¦=\ *adj* **:** containing other than the specified grade or amount — used of a bale of cotton

false papers *n pl* **:** documents carried by a ship giving false representations respecting her cargo, destination, or other matters for the purpose of deceiving

false pareira *n* **:** the root of a tropical vine (*Cissampelos pareira*) that is sometimes used like So. American pareira

false parenchyma *n* **:** PSEUDOPARENCHYMA

false pelvis *n* **:** the upper broader portion of the pelvic cavity

false pennyroyal *n* **:** an American annual mint (*Isanthus brachiatus*) with sticky entire leaves and blue flowers

false pimpernel *n* **1 :** CHAFFWEED **2 :** a plant of the genus *Ilysanthes* **3 :** a plant of the genus *Lindernia* (family Scrophulariaceae) with usu. purplish flowers having only two fertile stamens

false position *n* **:** a method of solution of a problem that uses the result obtained by replacing the unknown by trial values

false-positive \ˈ=¦=(=)=\ *n* **:** an individual under test whose laboratory data or scores classify him esp. because of imperfection or hypersensitivity of the method in a reference group or diagnostic category he does not belong in

false pregnancy *n* **:** PSEUDOCYESIS, PSEUDOPREGNANCY

false pretenses *n pl* **:** false representations concerning past or present facts or events for the purpose of defrauding another

false proscenium *n* **:** a frame within the fixed proscenium used to make smaller the exposed area of the inner stage

false quantity *n* **:** faulty pronunciation or metrical use of a vowel with respect to its quantity (as in reading Latin verse)

false quarter *n* **:** a cleft in the quarter of a horse's foot

falser *comparative of* FALSE

false ragweed *n* **1 :** a plant of the genus *Franseria* having spiny seeds and resembling a ragweed **2 :** BURWEED MARSH ELDER

false relation *n* **:** the discrepancy in traditional harmony caused by using in different musical voice parts either simultaneously or in successive chords any given tone and one of its chromatic derivatives — called also *cross relation*

false representation *n* **1 :** an untrue representation willfully made to deceive another to his damage **2 :** a representation in fact untrue but recklessly made when the maker has no knowledge as to its truth or falsity **3 :** a promise made with no intention of carrying it out — see DECEIT, FRAUD

false return *n* **1 :** an incorrect report ⟨*false returns* on an income-tax blank⟩ **2 :** an untrue return made to a legal process by the officer to whom it was delivered for execution

false rib *n* **:** any of the ribs with cartilages which unite indirectly or not at all with the sternum

false ring *also* **false annual ring** *n, forestry* **:** a layer of wood less than a full season's growth and sometimes not all around the trunk — compare ANNUAL RING

false rue anemone *also* **false rue** *n* **:** a slender white-flowered herb (*Isopyrum biternatum*) of the family Ranunculaceae of eastern No. America closely resembling meadow rue

falses *pres 3d sing of* FALSE

false saffron *n* **:** SAFFLOWER

false sandalwood *n* **1 :** a small spiny often shrubby tropical tree (*Ximenia americana*) that has an astringent bark rich in tannins, leathery opposite leaves, whitish flowers, and a yellow to orange edible fruit which resembles a plum and contains a very oily seed and that yields a very dense heavy aromatic wood **2 :** the wood of the false sandalwood sometimes substituted for sandalwood

false sanicle *n* **:** FAIRY CUP 3

false sarsaparilla *n* **:** any of several American plants of the genus *Aralia:* as **a :** WILD SARSAPARILLA 1 **b :** FALSE SOLOMON'S SEAL

false scab *n* **:** severe seborrhea of domestic animals

false scorpion *n* **:** BOOK SCORPION

false sisal *n* **:** a fiber derived from a plant (*Agave decipiens*) closely related to sisal

false smut *n* **1 :** GREEN SMUT **2 :** a disease of palms (as those of the genus *Phoenix*) that is caused by a fungus (*Graphiola phoenicis*) and characterized by small cylindrical protruding pustules surrounded often by yellowish leaf tissue

false solomon's seal *n, usu cap 1st S* **:** a plant of the genus *Smilacina* differing from Solomon's seal in having the flowers in a terminal raceme or panicle

false spider mite *n* **:** any of several phytophagous mites that do not web the plants on which they feed

false spikenard *n* **:** a false Solomon's seal (*Smilacina racemosa*)

false spirea *n* **:** a plant of the genus *Sorbaria*

falsest *superlative of* FALSE

false sting *n* **:** a virus disease of apples causing malformation of the fruit which resembles injury from insect feeding

false stripe *n* **:** a seed-borne virus disease of barley that causes light brown linear mottling of the leaves

false sunflower *n* **:** BURWEED MARSH ELDER

false syringa *n* **:** MOCK ORANGE 1

false tack *n* **:** a coming up into the wind and filling away again on the same tack

false tamarisk *n* **:** GERMAN TAMARISK

false title *n* **:** HALF TITLE 1

false topaz *n* **:** a yellow transparent variety of quartz **:** CITRINE

false truffle *n* **:** the subterranean basidial fruit of various fungi (families Sclerodermataceae and Hymenogastraceae) somewhat like the ascus fruit of the truffle

¹fal·set·to \fȯl'sed·(,)ō, -e(,)tō\ *n* -s [It, fr. *falso* false, (fr. L *falsus*) + *-etto* (dim. suffix) — more at FALSE] **1 :** an artificially high voice; *esp* **:** an artificially produced singing voice that overlaps and extends above the range of the full voice esp. of a tenor and is noticeably less rich, expressive, and powerful than the full voice **2 :** a singer (as a male alto) who uses falsetto — contrasted with *castrato*

²falsetto \"\ *adj* **:** relating to falsetto

³falsetto \"\ *adv* **:** in falsetto ⟨to sing ~⟩

false umbel *n* **:** a cyme in which the main axis is of the same length as the secondary axes (as in various pelargoniums)

false unicorn root *also* **false unicorn** *or* **false unicorn plant** *n* **1 :** BLAZING STAR b **2 :** a colicroot (*Aletris farinosa*)

false vampire bat *n* **:** any of various carnivorous bats of the families Megadermatidae and Phyllostomatidae

false violet *n* **:** DEWDROP

false vocal cord *n* **:** either of the upper pair of vocal cords that are not directly concerned with speech production

false wall cress *n* **:** a purple-flowered or violet-flowered perennial herb (*Aubrietia deltoidea*) of southern Europe used as an ornamental

false water lily *n* **:** WATER SOLDIER 1

false wild oats *n* **:** FATUOID

false willow *n* **:** a shrub (*Baccharis glutinosa*) with viscid lanceolate leaves

false wing *n* **:** BASTARD WING

false wintergreen *n* **:** a widely distributed shinleaf (*Pyrola rotundifolia americana*) — called also *wild lily of the valley*

false winter's bark *n, usu cap W* **:** CANELLA BARK

false wireworm *n* **:** a slender hard-coated brownish or yellowish grub that is the larva of any of various tenebrionid beetles (genus *Eleodes*) and that is often destructive to germinating wheat in western No. America

falsework \'=,=\ *n* **1 :** temporary construction work on which a main work is wholly or partly built and supported until it is made strong enough to support itself ⟨~ of a bridge⟩ **2 :** a temporary framework used to support a part of a structure during demolition

fal·si cri·men \,fȯl,sē'krēmən, -sī'krīm-, -,men\ *n* [LL, crime of falsifying] **:** the infamous crime of falsifying including in Roman law every crime committed by fraud and deceit, in modern civil law mainly forgery but also perjury and similar offenses, and in English and U. S. law also counterfeiting — called also *crimen falsi*

fal·sie \'fȯl(t)sē, -si\ *n* -s ['*false* + *-ie*] **:** a breast-shaped usu. fabric or rubber cup that is used to pad a brassiere — usu. used in pl.

fal·si·fi·abil·i·ty \,fȯl(t)sə,fīə'bilәd·ē, -bilәtē, -i\ *n* -ES **:** the quality or state of being falsifiable

fal·si·fi·able \'==,=əbəl, ,==='===\ *adj* **:** capable of being proved false **:** DEFEASIBLE

fal·si·fi·ca·tion \,fȯl(t)səfə'kāshən\ *n* -s [MF, fr. ML *falsification-, falsificatio*, fr. *falsificatus* (past part. of *falsificare*) + L *-ion-, -io* -ion] **1 :** the act or an instance of falsifying: as **a :** a counterfeiting (as of a work of art) **b :** a usu. willful misstatement or misrepresentation **:** DISTORTION ⟨a far-reaching and fateful ~ of German cultural history —W.A.Kaufmann⟩ ⟨of *Othello* . . . one can say bluntly . . . that it suffers in current appreciation an essential ~ —F.R.Leavis⟩ **2 :** the act or an instance of showing something to be false or erroneous **3 :** a fraudulent alteration of or tampering with (as an account or judgment)

fal·si·fi·er \'==,fī(ə)r, -īə\ *n* -s **:** one that falsifies

fal·si·fy \-,fī\ *vb* -ED/-ING/-ES [ME *falsifien*, fr. MF *falsifier*, fr. ML *falsificare*, fr. L *falsus* false + *-ificare* -ify — more at FALSE] *vt* **1 :** to prove to be false **:** CONFUTE ⟨other records or traces which seemed to ~ the hypothesis based on the records that I found —H.N.Lee⟩; *specif* **:** to prove false so as legally to avoid, defeat, or rectify ⟨~ a judgment⟩ **2 a :** to make false by mutilation or addition **:** tamper with ⟨~ a passport⟩ ⟨~ a will⟩ **b :** COUNTERFEIT, FORGE, ADULTERATE ⟨producing *falsified* champagne for sale to hotels⟩ **3** *obs* **:** to cause (as one's word) to be violated or betrayed **4 :** to prove unsound or untrue by experience **:** DISAPPOINT, FRUSTRATE ⟨its spacious promises of a new era have almost every one of them been *falsified* —W.M.Citrine⟩ **5 :** to represent falsely **:** MISREPRESENT, DISTORT ⟨contended that the history of early Virginia had been *falsified* by the Court party in England —T.J.Wertenbaker⟩ ⟨a low-priced sunglass lens said to be completely effective without ~*ing* the colors seen through it —*Newsweek*⟩ ⟨the novelist has distorted the characters and *falsified* their motives —Bernard De Voto⟩ ~ *vi* **1 :** to violate the truth **:** tell lies ⟨impressed with the fact that he has *falsified* in his answer —H.G.Armstrong⟩ **2 :** to engage in misrepresentation or distortion ⟨his account *falsifies* from beginning to end⟩

falsing *pres part of* FALSE

fal·si·ty \'fȯl(t)səd·ē, -sətē, -i\ *n* -ES [ME *falsete, falste*, fr. OF *falseté, falsité*, fr. LL *falsitat-, falsitas*, fr. L *falsus* + *-itat-, -itas* -ity] **1 a :** the character or quality of not conforming to the truth or facts **:** UNTRUTH ⟨truth (or ~) is a property of declarative statements —Philip Hallie⟩ **b :** DECEITFULNESS, UNTRUSTWORTHINESS, FAITHLESSNESS ⟨the ~ of an ally⟩ **c :** specious, artificial, insincere, or unreal character ⟨the ~ of her smile⟩ ⟨the contrast between the reality of history and the ~ of the most commercialized and popular art of the times —J.T. Farrell⟩ **2 :** something that is false or unreal **:** FALSEHOOD, LIE, SHAM ⟨here we do not escape easily into a pleasant ~ —M.S.Dworkin⟩

fal·staff·ian \(')fȯl'stafēən, -l;st-, -taaf-,-taif-,-täf-\ *adj, usu cap* [Sir John *Falstaff*, character in Shakespeare's *Merry Wives of Windsor* and *Henry IV* + E *-ian*] **1 :** resembling the fat, jovial, humorous, dissolute Shakespearean character Sir John Falstaff ⟨a *Falstaffian* figure, fantastically overfed and fat —C.G.Bowers⟩ **:** like that of Sir John Falstaff ⟨the romanticism of Brahmin culture with all its *Falstaffian* vulgarity deleted —V.L.Parrington⟩ **2 :** resembling the ragged regiment raised by Sir John Falstaff

fal·sum \'fȯl(t)səm\ *n* -s [L, fr. neut. of *falsus*, past part. of *fallere* to deceive — more at FAIL] **:** FALSI CRIMEN

falt·boat \'fält,=, 'fōl-\ *n* [part trans. of G *faltboot* folding boat, fr. *falten* to fold (fr. OHG *faldan*) + *boot* boat — more at FOLD] **:** a small collapsible canoe made of rubberized sailcloth stretched over a knockdown framework — called also *foldboat*

¹fal·ter \'fȯltə(r)\ *vb* **faltered; faltered; faltering** \-ltəriŋ, -l·tr-\ **falters** [ME *falteren*, perh. of Scand origin; akin to Icel *faltrask* to be burdened, be unsure, Faeroese *fjaltra* to tremble] *vi* **1 a :** to walk in an unsteady or wavering manner **:** STUMBLE, STAGGER ⟨the naked stranger ~*s* out of the thicket and drops to his knees —Dudley Fitts⟩ **b :** to be unsteady on one's feet **:** give way **:** TOTTER ⟨being eighty-nine, he had a chair . . . but . . . he stood without complaint or ~*ing* —Joseph Bryan⟩ ⟨he could feel his legs ~⟩ **c :** to move waveringly or unsteadily as if uncertain ⟨her eyes ~*ed* away from his —Erle Stanley Gardner⟩ ⟨forced to bail out of ~*ing* airplanes over the Alps —*Nat'l Geographic*⟩ **2 :** to speak brokenly or weakly **:** HESITATE, STAMMER ⟨his voice ~*ed* just the least bit —Joseph Conrad⟩ **3 a :** to hesitate in purpose or action **:** WAVER, FLINCH ⟨never ~*ed* in his determination to make good⟩ ⟨warned the Western democracies to suffer no division or ~*ing* in their duty —*Current Biog.*⟩ **b :** to lose drive, effectiveness, or momentum in some way **:** WEAKEN, DECLINE, FAIL ⟨his powers of musical invention never ~ or flag⟩ ⟨when a symbolist poem ~*s* for a moment it is irretrievably lost —Burns Singer⟩ ⟨Britain's vaunted prosperity was ~*ing* —*Time*⟩ ~ *vt* **:** to utter with hesitation or in a broken, trembling, or weak manner ⟨~ an excuse⟩

syn see HESITATE

²falter \"\ *n* -s **:** the act or an instance of faltering ⟨I managed to do what was required of me without ~ —Lonnie Coleman⟩; *esp* **:** QUAVER ⟨a ~ in her voice⟩

fal·ter·er \-tərə(r\ *n* -s **:** one that falters

fal·ter·ing·ly *adv* **:** in a faltering manner **:** HESITANTLY, UNCERTAINLY ⟨she gave her answer ~⟩

falus *pl of* FELS

falx \'falks, 'fōl-\ *n, pl* **fal·ces** \-l,sēz\ [NL, fr. L, lit., sickle] **:** a sickle-shaped part or structure; *esp* **:** either of two folds of the dura mater separating the hemispheres of the brain, the larger being between the cerebral hemispheres and containing the sagittal sinuses, the smaller between the lateral lobes of the cerebellum — called respectively *falx ce·re·bri* \-k(s)'serə,brī\, *falx ce·re·bel·li* \-,serə'be,lī\

fam *abbr* **1** familiar **2** family **3** famous

FAM *abbr* foreign airmail

fa·ma·ti·nite \,famə'tē,nīt, ,fäm-\ *n* -s [G *famatinit*, fr. Sierra de *Famatina*, mountain range in northwest Argentina + G *-it* -ite] **:** a mineral Cu_3SbS_4 consisting of a reddish gray copper antimony sulfide (sp. gr. 4.57)

¹fame \'fām\ *n* -s [ME, fr. OF, fr. L *fama*; akin to Gk *phēmē* utterance, report; derivative fr. the root of L *fari* to speak, Gk *phanai* to say, *phōnē* sound — more at BAN] **1 a :** public estimation of a person or thing **:** REPUTATION ⟨ought to . . . inquire into her former and present ~ —John Chamberlayne⟩ **b :** general recognition for outstanding achievement **:** popular acclaim **:** GLORY, RENOWN ⟨~ is the thirst of youth —Lord Byron⟩ **c :** recognition of an unfavorable kind **:** NOTORIETY ⟨achieved ~ . . . when its school board became the first in the state to require a loyalty oath from the officers of all organizations seeking to use the school facilities —David Clinton⟩ **2** *archaic* **:** common talk **:** RUMOR ⟨and the ~ thereof was heard in Pharaoh's house —Gen 45:16 (AV)⟩

syn NOTORIETY, REPUTATION, REPUTE, CELEBRITY, ÉCLAT, HONOR, RENOWN, GLORY: in this set FAME is a general term used to indicate a state of being quite widely known. It is likely to be favorable in its connotations but, perhaps more than any of the accompanying words, may be qualified widely ⟨he still shines when the light of his successors is fading away; they had celebrity, Spinoza has *fame* —Matthew Arnold⟩ ⟨*fame* is proof that people are gullible —R.W. Emerson⟩ NOTORIETY, sometimes still neutral in its suggestions and indicating the fact of being widely known, is likely to suggest being widely known for evil, shameful, reprehensible, or eccentric behavior ⟨if the occupation of steamboats be a matter of such general *notoriety* that the court may be presumed to know it —John Marshall⟩ ⟨that brilliant, extravagant, careless Reverend Doctor Dodd who acquired some fame and much *notoriety* as an eloquent preacher —Havelock Ellis⟩ REPUTATION usu. suggests the commonly circulated and accepted judgment of one's character; unmodified, it may suggest a quite good reputation, a measure of fame on some particular account ⟨the downfall of his first political *reputation* following the disaster of the Dardanelles expedition —*New Republic*⟩ ⟨he went on writing war poetry and gained a good deal of *reputation* as one of our soldier poets —Rose Macaulay⟩ REPUTE may suggest high esteem ⟨the *repute* which a classical Latin style and the ancient classics had acquired in Renaissance Italy —G.C.Sellery⟩ CELEBRITY in this sense may suggest sudden fame and widespread popularity which may turn out to be ephemeral ⟨there was a time in London when no one could afford to say he had not read the *Poems Descriptive of Rural Life and Scenery*, but that was in the spring of 1820, and the season of *celebrity* was often quite as short then as it is today —H.V.Gregory⟩ ÉCLAT in this sense may suggest a certain suddenness whereby something becomes well known or a certain brilliancy or flashiness in its reputation ⟨this letter was sprung, with great *éclat*, in public hearing —*New Republic*⟩ ⟨consider what luster and *éclat* it will give you . . . to be the best scholar, of a gentleman, in England —Earl of Chesterfield⟩ HONOR in this sense indicates widespread fame and esteem through achievement or position ⟨wherever the bright sun of heaven shall shine, his *honor* and the greatness of his name, shall be, and make new nations —Shak.⟩ ⟨admirals all, for England's sake, *honor* be yours and fame —H.J. Newbolt⟩ RENOWN means much the same as HONOR; it may imply additional acclaim ⟨filled with a nation's praise, filled with *renown* —Alfred Tennyson⟩ GLORY is the strongest and most complimentary word in this group; it suggests lasting, extreme, and deserved fame ⟨there he [Washington] lived in noble simplicity, there he shall be in *glory* —Edward Everett⟩

²fame \"\ *vt* -ED/-ING/-s [ME *famen*, fr. *fame*, n.] **1 :** to report, consider, or repute — usu. used in passive ⟨the fancy cannot cheat so well as she is *famed* to do —John Keats⟩ **2 a :** to make famous or renowned — usu. used in passive ⟨an inn . . . that was *famed* for its corn bread —*Amer. Guide Series: Md.*⟩ **b** *obs* **:** to make notorious or infamous ⟨foes enough would ~ thee in their hate —Ben Jonson⟩

³fame \"\ *Scot var of* FOAM

famed *adj* [fr. past part. of *²fame*] **:** FAMOUS ⟨development of the world's most ~ garden spot —*Monsanto Mag.*⟩

fameflower \'=,=\ *n* ['*fame* + *flower;* prob. fr. the transitoriness of its petals] **:** a linear-leaved herb (*Talinum teretifolium*) of the eastern U. S. with scapes of ephemeral pink flowers

fame·less \'fāmləs\ *adj* **:** little known **:** OBSCURE, UNDISTINGUISHED

fames *pl of* FAME, *pres 3d sing of* FAME

fa·meuse \fə'myüz\ *n* -s *usu cap* [F, fem. of *fameux* famous] **:** any of various apples having deep red stripes and crisp white flesh

fa·mil·ia \fə'milēə, -lyə\ *n, pl* **famili·ae** \-lē,ē, -lē,ī\ [L — more at FAMILY] **1** *Roman law* **:** the paterfamilias, his legitimate descendants and their wives, and all persons adopted into his family and their wives — compare POTESTAS **2** *Old English law* **a :** the servants of one master **b :** a quantity of land adequate for the maintenance of one family

fa·mil·ial \fə'milyəl, -lēəl\ *adj* [F, fr. L *familia* family + F *-al*] **1 :** of, relating to, or having the characteristics of a family ⟨children of the same ~ background —E.L.Volpe⟩ **2 :** having a tendency to occur in different members of a family to a degree greater than chance would allow ⟨a ~ disease⟩ — compare CONGENITAL, HEREDITARY

¹fa·mil·iar \fə'milyə(r), *chiefly in substand speech* fər'milyər\ *n* -s [ME *familier* member of one's household, intimate associate, fr. OF, member of one's household, fr. *familier*, adj.] **1 :** an intimate associate **:** COMPANION ⟨with ~*s* he has the unvarnished candor of old people and children —Janet Flanner⟩ **2 :** a member of the household of a high official **:** one who belongs to an official family ⟨a mile away 269 . . . ~*s* or courtiers were buried —V.G.Childe⟩; *specif* **:** a layman employed as a resident servant in a Roman Catholic institution or in the household of a high dignitary of the Roman Catholic church **3 :** a confidential officer of the Inquisition whose task was to apprehend and imprison the accused **4 :** a supernatural spirit often embodied in an animal and at the service of a person ⟨the loathsome toad, the witches' ~ —Harvey Graham⟩ **5 a :** one who is well acquainted with something ⟨~*s* of the measure —C.G.Poore⟩ **b :** one who frequents a place ⟨~*s* of the embassy —Rebecca West⟩

²familiar \"\ *adj* [ME *familier, familiar*, fr. OF *familier*, fr. L *familiaris*, fr. *familia* + *-aris* -ar — more at FAMILY] **1 :** closely associated **:** INTIMATE: as **a :** on a family footing ⟨his ~ friend —Marjory S. Douglas⟩ **b :** having a supernatural relationship with people ⟨a prayer to the ~ sharks . . . which have exchanged souls with living men —C.E.Fox⟩ **c :** sexually intimate ⟨the girl with whom he has been ~ having to leave school —Evelyn M. Duvall⟩ **2** *obs* **:** affable and courteous **:** SOCIABLE ⟨bland and ~ to the throne he came —Alexander Pope⟩ **3 a :** of or relating to a family ⟨~ domestic happenings —G.F. Whicher⟩ ⟨it is convenient to refer to many of the natural acids by their ~ names —T.P.Hilditch⟩ **b :** designed for family use **:** frequented by families ⟨a ~ resort . . . favored by couples with children —Betty de Sherbinin⟩ **4 :** of an informal nature **:** UNCEREMONIOUS: as **a :** free and easy ⟨a child's ~ access to his eminent . . . circle —W.V.O'Connor⟩ **b :** marked by informality and nonadherence to rigid structure ⟨he learned to write a passable ~ essay —J.W.Krutch⟩ ⟨functional varieties may roughly be grouped together in the two classes ~ and formal writing and speaking —J.S.Kenyon⟩ **c :** overly free and unrestrained **:** PRESUMPTUOUS ⟨he was rather noisily ~ with them —Robertson Davies⟩ **5** *of a wild animal* **:** used to human company **:** not alarmed by proximity to people **:** moderately tame ⟨he is tame and ~ and sings on the tree over your head or on the rock a few paces in advance —John Burroughs⟩ **6 a :** frequently seen or experienced **:** easily recognized ⟨he was a ~ figure at the opera —Edna Yost⟩ ⟨some ~ scent can carry one back to early childhood —Stuart Chase⟩ **b :** of everyday occurrence **:** COMMON, ORDINARY ⟨emotions which he has never experienced will serve his turn as well as those ~ to him —T.S.Eliot⟩ **c :** currently accepted or previously tested **:** WELL-KNOWN ⟨America's most ~ poet —Lewis Leary b. 1906⟩ ⟨the new can be learned successfully only in terms of the ~ —W.M.Mason⟩ **7 :** well acquainted through personal knowledge or study **:** CONVERSANT ⟨~ with what is being taught to our children in schools —Vera M. Dean⟩

syn INTIMATE, CONFIDENTIAL, CLOSE, THICK, CHUMMY: FAMILIAR may suggest natural ease, informality, lack of reserve, constraint, or stiffness, ensuing from long acquaintanceship, as among members of a family ⟨she was constantly referring to dear friends by their Christian names, in a casual and *familiar* way —Havelock Ellis⟩ ⟨the *familiar*, if not rude tone, in which people addressed her —Nathaniel Hawthorne⟩ INTIMATE always indicates closeness of relationship and it usu. suggests a closeness, warmth, personal nearness, or emotionalism which transcends and intensifies the more factual suggestion of FAMILIAR ⟨*intimate* as man is with his habitat —L.A.White⟩ ⟨the *intimate* political relation subsisting between the President of the U. S. and the heads of departments —John Marshall⟩ ⟨*intimate* letters . . . love letters which were never written to be published —Havelock Ellis⟩ ⟨man never derives any *intimate* help, any heart sustenance, from his brother man, but from woman —Nathaniel Hawthorne⟩ CONFIDENTIAL stresses a reposing of confidence, a willingness to confide innermost thoughts and feelings ⟨the growing harmony and *confidential* friendship which daily manifest themselves between their majesties —William Pitt †1778⟩ ⟨a tone as sad and *confidential* as if he were . . . preluding a declaration of love —W.M.Thackeray⟩ CLOSE in this sense suggests strong liking and accustomed agreement and compatibility leading to steady association ⟨I would be with Adam a lot . . . she'd tag along, for she and Adam were very *close* —R.P.Warren⟩ ⟨being *close* to Peggy, [he] was aware that she . . . acted by her own secret intuitions —Morley Callaghan⟩ THICK indicates an accustomed close association or cooperation, often in devious ways or for dishonest purposes ⟨he . . . does a lot of bail bond business . . . and is pretty *thick* with . . . the chief of police —Dashiell Hammett⟩ ⟨he'd told me that you and Pamela Dean were as *thick* as thieves —Dorothy Sayers⟩ CHUMMY takes its color from the word *chum* and describes easy, steady, confidential association with compatibility of interests ⟨an unprecedented thing . . . for a captain to be *chummy* with the cook —Jack London⟩ **syn** see in addition COMMON

fa·mil·iar·ism \-yə,rizəm\ *n* -s *archaic* **:** COLLOQUIALISM

fa·mil·iar·i·ty \fə,mil'yarəd·ē, -lē'(y)ar-, -l'yar-, -rətē-, -i *also* -(y)er-\ *n* -ES [ME *familiarite*, fr. OF *familiarité*, fr. L *familiaritat-, familiaritas*, fr. *familiaris* + *-itat-, -itas* -ity] **1 a :** a state of close personal relationship **:** INTIMACY ⟨they never exposed their idolatry to the test of domestic ~ —G.B.Shaw⟩ **b** *obs* **:** a circle of intimate friends or relatives ⟨leaving of parents or other ~ —John Milton⟩ **2 a :** absence of ceremony **:** INFORMALITY ⟨began to treat him first with ~ and then with contumely —Robert Graves⟩ **b :** an overly informal act or expression **:** IMPROPRIETY ⟨employs insulting *familiarities* —*New Republic*⟩ **c :** sexual intimacy ⟨she is unwise enough to permit affectionate *familiarities* when she is with boys —Valeria H. Parker⟩ **3 :** close acquaintance with or knowledge of something ⟨~ with the forces in the world which tend to define our policies —W.A.Parker⟩

fa·mil·iar·iza·tion \fə,milyərə'zāshən, -,rī'z-\ *n* -s **:** the act or process or an instance of familiarizing

fa·mil·iar·ize \fə'milyə,rīz\ *vb* -ED/-ING/-s *see -ize in Explan Notes, vt* **1 :** to make known through experience or repetition **:** remove strangeness from ⟨Shakespeare . . . ~*s* the wonderful —Samuel Johnson⟩ **2** *archaic* **:** to accustom to something **:** HABITUATE ⟨intending to ~ my parishioners to it little by little —J.H.Newman⟩ **3 a** *archaic* **:** to make more affable **:** cause to unbend ⟨for the cure of this particular sort of madness it will be necessary to . . . ~ his carriage by the use of a good cudgel —Richard Steele⟩ **b** *archaic* **:** to introduce as a friend ⟨I should be glad . . . to be *familiarized* to the ladies of your family —Samuel Richardson⟩ **4 :** to make well acquainted **:** make conversant ⟨~ students with the use of periodicals —Frances Eldredge⟩ **5** *archaic* **:** to bring into common use **:** POPULARIZE ⟨I have *familiarized* the terms of philosophy —Samuel Johnson⟩ ~ *vi, archaic* **:** to act in an informal way **:** make oneself agreeable ⟨he . . . *familiarized* with his equals —Roger North⟩

fa·mil·iar·ly *adv* [ME *familierly*, fr. *familier*, adj. + *-ly* — more at ²FAMILIAR] **1 :** in a familiar manner: as **a :** INTIMATELY ⟨he was widely known to many but ~ acquainted with few⟩ **b :** COMMONLY ⟨the frankfurter is ~ called a hot dog⟩ **c :** INFORMALLY ⟨hailed him ~ by his nickname⟩ **d :** PRESUMPTUOUSLY ⟨pinched her cheek ~ when they were introduced⟩ **2 :** without shyness or fear **:** BOLDLY ⟨the phoebe bird . . . comes ~ about the house —John Burroughs⟩

fa·mil·iar·ness *n* -ES **:** the quality or state of being familiar

familiar spirit *n* **1 :** a supernatural often malignant spirit in the service of an individual ⟨medicine men . . . can summon to their aid at any time their *familiar spirits* —G.P.Murdock⟩ — compare DEMON **2 :** the spirit of a dead person invoked by a medium to advise or prophesy ⟨a consultor with *familiar spirits* —Deut 18:11 (AV)⟩ — compare ²CONTROL 3d

familiar verse *n* **:** LIGHT VERSE

fam·i·lism \'famə,lizəm\ *n* -s [*family* + *-ism*] **1** *sometimes cap* **:** the tenets and practices of the familists ⟨men who follow Anabaptism, ~, antinomianism, and other fanatic dreams —John Milton⟩ **2 :** a social pattern in which the family and familial solidarity, tradition, and social status tend to assume a position of ascendance over individual rights and interests within society ⟨the reduced emphasis on ~ of the middle-class family —M.B.Sussman⟩

fam·i·list \-ləst\ *n* -s *often cap* [*family* + *-ist*] **:** a member of a mystical and somewhat antinomian sect of 16th and 17th century Europe

fam·i·lis·tic \ˌfaməˈlistik\ *adj* [*familist* + *-ic*] **:** of, relating to, or based on a family or familism; *specif* **:** based on the family as a primary unit ⟨such stories as those of . . . Joseph and his brethren, and the prodigal son had a direct bearing upon life in a ~ society —A.D.Rees⟩

fa·mille jaune \fəˌmēˈzhōn\ *n* [F, lit., yellow family] **:** Chinese porcelain the decoration of which has a rich yellow background

famille noire \-mēnˌwär, -mēnəˈwär\ *n* [F, lit., black family] **:** Chinese porcelain the decoration of which has a black background

famille rose \-mēˈrōz\ *n* [F, lit., pink family] **:** Chinese porcelain in the decoration of which a rose color predominates

famille verte \-mēˈve(ə)rt\ *n* [F, lit., green family] **:** Chinese porcelain in the decoration of which green predominates

1fam·i·ly \ˈfam(ə)lē, ˈfaamlē, -li\ *n* -ES [ME *familie*, fr. L *familia* servants of a household, household including not only the servants but also the head of the household and all persons in it related to him by blood or marriage, fr. *famulus* servant; perh. akin to Skt *dhāman* dwelling place, *dadhāti* he puts, places — more at 1DO] **1 a** *archaic* **:** a group of persons in the service of an individual ⟨he had a great ~, that is to say . . . many slaves who worked in his bronze foundry —Maurice Samuel⟩ **b :** the retinue or staff of a nobleman or high official ⟨invited . . . to join his military ~ as aide-de-camp —H.E. Scudder⟩ **c :** a group of people bound together by philosophical, religious, or other convictions **:** FELLOWSHIP ⟨belongs to the Kantian ~ —W.E.Schlaretzki⟩ **d :** a body of employees or volunteer workers united in a common enterprise ⟨reference is made not just to the administrators, but to every single member of the community hospital ~ —G.W.Gilbert⟩ **2 a :** a group of persons of common ancestry **:** CLAN ⟨let us assail the ~ of York —Shak.⟩; *specif* **:** a group of persons of distinguished lineage ⟨the office has always been held by men of ~ —Oswald Banon⟩ **b :** a people or group of peoples regarded as deriving from a common stock **:** RACE ⟨the worldwide ~ of human beings —K.F.Mather⟩ **3 a :** a group of individuals living under one roof **:** HOUSEHOLD ⟨the ~ includes a poodle —*TV Guide*⟩ **b :** the body of persons who live in one house and under one head including parents, children, servants, and lodgers or boarders; *specif* **:** a group of persons sharing a common dwelling and table considered for census purposes to include at one extreme a single person living alone and at the other the residents of a hotel or the inmates of a prison **4 a :** a group of things having common features or properties: as **a** (1) *in the classification of languages of the eastern hemisphere* **:** a number of related languages comprising all those held to be demonstrably descended from a single ancestral language that itself is not demonstrably related to any other language by descent from a common ancestral language ⟨the Afro-Asiatic language ~⟩ (2) *in the classification of languages of the western hemisphere* **:** a number of related languages comprising all those held to be demonstrably descended from a single ancestral language believed to have existed approximately 5 to 25 centuries ago **b :** musical instruments having the same basic method of tone production ⟨the double-reed ~⟩ ⟨the viol ~⟩ **c :** a set of typefaces of the same name and basic design that are cast in various sizes, weights, and widths ⟨the Cheltenham ~⟩ — compare FONT, SERIES **d :** a closely related series of elements or chemical compounds: (1) **:** a subgroup in the periodic table ⟨the chromium ~⟩ (2) **:** RADIOACTIVE SERIES ⟨the radium ~⟩ (3) **:** a homologous series of organic compounds ⟨the paraffin ~⟩ **e :** a group of rocks of the same general mineralogical and chemical composition **f** (1) **:** a group of asteroids whose orbits have similar characteristics which remain little changed over long periods of time prob. because of their common origin (2) **:** a group of comets whose aphelion points are near that of one of the major planets prob. as a result of successive gravitational encounters with the planet **g :** a group of soils that have similar profiles and include one or more series — called also *soil family* **5 a :** the basic biosocial unit in society having as its nucleus two or more adults living together and cooperating in the care and rearing of their own or adopted children ⟨the association of adults . . . is the necessary nucleus of any ~ —Ralph Linton⟩ **b :** one's children ⟨a young mother scouring her numerous ~ with flat pancakes of . . . river clay —Marguerite Steen⟩ **c :** a male and female animal with their young ⟨the typical gorilla band has as many as five associated *families* —Weston La Barre⟩ **6 a :** a group of related plants or animals forming a category ranking above a genus and below an order, usu. comprising several to many genera, but sometimes including a single genus of notably distinctive characters **b** *in livestock breeding* (1) **:** the descendants or line of a particular individual esp. of some outstanding female (2) **:** an identifiable strain within a breed **c :** an ecological community consisting of a single kind of organism and usu. being of limited extent and representing an early stage of a succession **7** *math* **:** an infinite set — used of curves and surfaces

2family \"\ *adj* **1 :** of or relating to a family ⟨a strong ~ resemblance⟩ **2 :** adapted to family use or participation ⟨a ~ room⟩ ⟨~ dances⟩

family allowance *n* **:** a grant to an employee made typically by a government or an employer in addition to regular salary and graded according to occupation and the number of dependent children

family altar *n* **1 :** a place of family devotions **2 :** the custom of family devotions

family bible *n, usu cap B* **:** a large Bible usu. having special pages for recording births, marriages, and deaths

family car doctrine *or* **family purpose doctrine** *n* **:** the legal doctrine whereby the owner of an automobile is liable for the negligence or misconduct of a member of his family who while using the automobile with the owner's permission though not as his agent or servant causes injury to another

family circle *n* **:** a gallery in a theater or opera house usu. located above or behind a gallery containing more expensive seats

family contract *or* **family settlement** *n* **:** a contract between the members of a family settling the distribution or descent of its estates

family court *n* **:** COURT OF DOMESTIC RELATIONS

family doctor *or* **family physician** *n* **:** a general practitioner regularly called by a family in time of illness

family expense *n* **:** an expense incurred for whatever is used or kept for use in the family whether necessaries or luxuries — used in statutes making both husband and wife legally liable for such an expense

family fare *n* **:** a special transportation rate offered by public carriers on certain light-traffic days whereby a wife or children each pay half fare when accompanying a full-fare passenger — called also *family fare plan, family travel plan*

family farm *n* **:** a farm on which the farmer and members of his family do a substantial part of the work

family flour *n* **:** ALL-PURPOSE FLOUR

family income policy *n* **:** a term insurance policy on the life of a breadwinner providing special income benefits beyond the face amount that continue for the remainder of the child-rearing period after the death of the insured

family maintenance policy *n* **:** a term insurance policy on the life of a breadwinner providing special income benefits in addition to the face amount that continue for a specified number of years after the death of the insured

family man *n* **1 :** a man who has a family, esp. a wife and children living with him and dependent upon him **2 :** a responsible man of domestic habits

family meeting *n* **:** a formal meeting of not less than five relatives or next friends of a minor or other person held by official appointment under civil law to consider and give advice in his interest

family name *n* **1 :** SURNAME 2a **2 :** the name of an individual that identifies him with his family **3 :** a male forename that is the surname of another family (as of the mother or grandmother)

family of nations **1 :** the group of nations recognized as having equal status under international law ⟨oceans are regarded as the common property of the *family of nations*⟩ **2 :** a group of nations united by common historical, political, or ideological ties ⟨members of the British *family of nations* —Herbert Dorn⟩

family of orientation **:** the family of one's parents and relatives

family of procreation **:** the family created by marriage

family romance *n* **:** a childhood fantasy in which the individual believes that his actual parents are not his own and that he is really of higher birth

family skeleton *n* **:** a secret or hidden source of embarrassment or disgrace to a family — compare SKELETON IN THE CLOSET

family style *adv* (*or adj*) **:** with the food placed on the table in serving dishes from which those eating may help themselves as often as they like ⟨meals are served *family style*⟩ ⟨a *family style* dinner⟩

family tree *n* **1 :** GENEALOGY ⟨my services were enlisted by a wealthy snob . . . who was anxious to pursue his *family tree* —Wallace Clare⟩; *specif* **:** the relationships of languages of common parent stock **2 :** a schematic description of genealogical relationships ⟨the totem pole was their *family tree* —L.H.Appleton⟩; *specif* **:** a diagram showing the relationships of languages of common parent stock

family-tree theory *n* [trans. of G *stammbaumtheorie*] **:** a theory in linguistics: at various periods branches (as Germanic) sprang from a parent language (as Indo-European) and subsequently forked into subbranches (as West Germanic, North Germanic) that later split up into the various modern languages (as English, German, Swedish) — called also *pedigree theory;* compare WAVE THEORY

family wage *n* **1 :** the total income of a family **2 :** the income needed for the subsistence of a family

family way *n* **:** condition of being pregnant — used with *in* and *the* or *a* ⟨she is in the *family way* again —Mary W. Shelley⟩ ⟨she gets herself in a *family way* and is then, as a matter of course, married off —G.H.Shuster⟩

fam·ine \ˈfamən\ *n* -S [ME, fr. MF, fr. (assumed) VL *famina*, fr. L *fames* hunger — more at DAZE] **1 :** a severe food shortage **:** a period of extreme scarcity of food ⟨six seasons of dearth approaching ~ —Samuel Van Valkenburg & Ellsworth Huntington⟩ **2** *archaic* **:** lack of food **:** extreme hunger **:** STARVATION ⟨horses . . . recovered from past ~ and fatigue —Washington Irving⟩ **3** *archaic* **:** a ravenous appetite ⟨death grinned . . . to hear his ~ should be filled —John Milton⟩ **4 :** a great scarcity or shortage of something ⟨a ~ of television sets —Irwin Edman⟩

famine bread *n* **:** a lichen (*Umbilicaria arctica*) found in arctic regions and sometimes used as food

famine fever *n* **:** RELAPSING FEVER

faming *pres part of* FAME

fam·ish \ˈfamish, -mēsh, *esp in pres part* -məsh\ *vb* -ED/-ING/-ES [ME *famishen*, prob. alter. (influenced by such verbs as *finishen* to finish) of *famen* to famish, starve, modif. of MF *afamer*, fr. (assumed) VL *affamare*, fr. L *ad-* + (assumed) VL *-famare* (fr. L *fames* hunger)] *vt* **1 :** to reduce to extremities for lack of food or other necessities — usu. used in passive ⟨both were dirty, travel-weary, ~*ed* for food and slumber —David Walden⟩ **2** *archaic* **:** to kill by withholding food or water **:** cause to starve ⟨did he marry me to ~ me? —Shak.⟩ ~ *vi* **1** *archaic* **:** to die for lack of food **:** STARVE ⟨they suffer us to ~ and their storehouses crammed with grain —Shak.⟩ **2** *archaic* **:** to suffer for lack of something necessary ⟨you are all resolved rather to die than to ~ —Shak.⟩ ⟨you ~ for promotion —Benjamin Disraeli⟩

fam·ish·ment \-shmənt\ *n* -S [ME *famishement*, fr. *famishe-* (fr. *famishen*) + *-ment*] **1 :** the quality or state of being famished **2 :** the act or process of famishing

fam·men·i·an \fəˈmēnēən, faˈm-, -men-\ *adj, usu cap* [irreg. fr. *Famenne*, district in Belgium + E *-ian*] **:** of, relating to, or constituting a subdivision of the European Devonian — see GEOLOGIC TIME table

fa·mose \fəˈmōs\ *vt* -ED/-ING/-S [ME *famosen*, fr. *famose*, adj., famous, fr. L *famosus*] *archaic* **:** FAMOUS

1fa·mous \ˈfāməs\ *adj* [ME, fr. MF *fameux*, fr. L *famosus*, fr. *fama* fame + *-osus* -ose — more at FAME] **1 a :** much talked about **:** WELL-KNOWN ⟨puffer fish . . . are ~ for their ability to inflate themselves when annoyed —S.W.Tinker⟩ **b :** honored for achievement **:** CELEBRATED ⟨he knows innumerable ~ people from the theatrical world⟩ **c :** discreditably renowned **:** NOTORIOUS ⟨~ for her shrewish tongue —Peggy Durdin⟩ **2** *obs* **:** COMMON, USUAL ⟨taking the word . . . in its most ~ signification —John Lewis⟩ **3 :** EXCELLENT, FIRST-RATE ⟨a ~ dinner⟩

2famous \"\ *vt* -ED/-ING/-ES *archaic* **:** to make famous ⟨the painful warrior ~*ed* for fight —Shak.⟩

fa·mous·ly *adv* **1 :** in a celebrated manner **:** NOTABLY ⟨he was a novelist and dramatist but most ~ a poet⟩ **2 :** in a superlative fashion **:** EXCELLENTLY ⟨asked how he was bearing up under the strain of his relentless schedule . . . he replied that he was doing ~ —Robert Shaplen⟩ **3 :** to an unusual degree **:** VERY ⟨the cost of good TV time is ~ high —Walter Goodman⟩

fa·mous·ness *n* -ES **:** the quality or state of being famous

fam·u·lus \ˈfamyələs\ *n, pl* **famu·li** \-ˌlī\ [G, academic assistant to a university professor, fr. L, servant — more at FAMILY] **:** a private secretary or attendant esp. upon a scholar or magician

1fan \ˈfan, ˈfaa(ə)n\ *n* -S *often attrib* [ME, fr. OE *fann*, fr. L *vannus* — more at WINNOW] **1 a :** a basket or wooden shovel formerly used for tossing grain into the air to let the chaff be blown away **b :** any of various devices for winnowing grain **2 :** an instrument or device for producing an artificial current of air (as by a wafting or revolving motion of a broad surface): as **a :** a device for cooling the person usu. having the form of a segment of a circle and consisting of material (as feathers, paper, or silk) mounted on thin rods or slats moving about a pivot so that the device may be closed compactly when not in use **b :** any revolving vane used for producing a current of air (as in blowing a fire or ventilating a room or for governing rapid rotary motion by the resistance of the air) **c :** a fan wheel revolved to cool the radiator of an automobile engine **d :** a fly that controls the striking mechanism of a clock **e :** one of the small vanes on a smock windmill that receive the impulse of the wind and are so located as to keep the large sails in the direction of the wind **f** *slang* **:** an aircraft propeller **3 :** something felt to resemble an open fan: as **a :** a fan-shaped leaf (as of certain palms) **b :** the wing of a bird **c :** the tail of a bird **d :** any of several fan-shaped architectural members; *esp* **:** FANLIGHT **e :** a gently sloping fan-shaped body of detritus commonly at a place where there is a notable decrease in gradient; *usu* **:** one deposited by a stream **:** ALLUVIAL FAN

fan 2a

2fan \"\ *vb* **fanned; fanned; fanning; fans** [ME *fannen*, fr. OE *fannian*, fr. *fann*, n.] *vt* **1 a :** to separate and drive away the chaff of (grain) by means of a current of air **b :** to eliminate (as chaff) by winnowing **2 :** to move or impel (air) with or as if with a fan **3 :** to blow or breathe upon ⟨the breeze *fanned* her hair⟩ **4 :** to direct a current of air upon with or as if with a fan: as **a :** to cool and refresh by moving the air with a fan ⟨*fanned* her perspiring face⟩ **b :** to drive or scare with or as if with a fan ⟨~ away the smoke with a newspaper⟩ **c :** to force or seek to force to glow or flame up by a draft of air ⟨*fanning* the coals into a brisk blaze⟩ **d :** to stir up to activity as if by fanning **:** STIMULATE ⟨this conduct *fanned* his rage⟩ ⟨they tried to ~ our interest with coy hints⟩ **5** *archaic* **:** to move to and fro like a fan **:** WAVE **6** *slang* **:** BEAT, TAN, WHIP **7 a :** to spread like a fan — often used with *out* ⟨*fanning* out the cards in his hand⟩ **b :** to spread (as the leaves of an unbound book) with one edge of each element extending slightly beyond the next — often used with *out*, sometimes with *over* or *up* **8** *slang* **:** to feel (a person's clothing) in order to locate prospective loot; *broadly* **:** to search or examine (as a person or place) ⟨the guards found a gun when they *fanned* the cell block⟩ ⟨routinely *fanning* him for weapons⟩ **9 :** to strike (a batter) out in baseball or softball **10 :** to fire (a revolver) by squeezing the trigger and striking the hammer to the rear with the free hand thereby rotating the cylinder so that a new cartridge is detonated when it lines up with the firing pin ~ *vi* **1 :** to move like a fan **:** FLAP, FLUTTER ⟨muslin curtains *fanning* in the breeze⟩ ⟨white butterflies were *fanning* on the goldenrod⟩ **2 :** to spread like a fan — often used with *out* ⟨the glacial debris *fanned* out over the slope⟩ ⟨picnickers ~ out along each highway⟩ **3 a :** to drift gently as if in a current of air produced by a fan **b** *dial* **:** to move briskly **:** HUSTLE **4** *of a batter* **:** to strike out in a baseball or softball game

3fan \(ˈ)fan, ˌfən\ *Scot var of* WHEN

4fan \ˈfan, ˈfaa(ə)n\ *var of* FEN

5fan *usu cap, var of* FANG

6fan \ˈfan, ˈfaa(ə)n\ *n* -S *often attrib* [prob. short for *fanatic*] **1 :** an enthusiastic devotee of a sport (as baseball) or diversion (as ballet) usu. as a spectator rather than a participant **2 :** an ardent admirer or champion (as of a person, technique, or pursuit) **:** ENTHUSIAST ⟨the president's thousands of ardent ~*s*⟩ ⟨camera ~*s*⟩ ⟨science-fiction ~*s*⟩ ⟨~ clubs⟩

fa·na \fəˈnä\ *n* -S [Ar *fanā'* annihilation, dissolution] *Islam* **:** the annihilation (as in Sufism) of the individual human will before the will of God

fa·na·ga·lo \ˌfänəgəˈlō\ *or* **fa·na·ka·lo** \-nəkə-\ *n* -S *cap* **:** a pidgin language based on Xhosa, Zulu, English, and Afrikaans and spoken in the mines in So. Africa

fa·nal \fəˈnal, -ˈnäl, ˈfanᵊl, ˈfänᵊl\ *n* -S [It *fanale*, fr. MGk *phanarion*, fr. Gk *phanos* torch, fr. *phanos* bright; akin to Gk *phainein* to show — more at FANCY] *archaic* **:** a beacon on a ship or lighthouse

fan·a·lo·ka \ˌfanᵊlˈōkə\ *n* -S [prob. native name in Madagascar] **:** a civet (*Fossa fossa*) of Madagascar

fa·nam \fəˈnäm\ *n* -S [prob. modif. of Tamil *panam*, prob. fr. Skt *pana* bet, reward, wealth] **1 a :** an old gold or silver coin of southern India **b :** a silver coin of Travancore worth ⅛ of a rupee issued up until Indian independence in 1947 **2 :** a unit of value corresponding to a fanam

fanariot *usu cap, var of* PHANARIOT

1fa·nat·ic \fəˈnad·ik, -at|, |ēk\ *or* **fa·nat·i·cal** \|əkəl, |ēk-\ *adj* [*fanatic* fr. L *fanaticus* frantic, inspired by a deity, fr. *fanum* sanctuary, temple — more at FEAST] **1** *obs* **:** possessed by or as if by a demon; *broadly* **:** CRAZED, FRANTIC, MAD **2 :** governed, produced, or characterized by too great zeal ⟨~ enthusiasms⟩ **:** EXTRAVAGANT, UNREASONABLE **:** excessively enthusiastic esp. on religious subjects ⟨certain ~ sects⟩ — **fa·nat·i·cal·ly** \|ək(ə)lē, |ēk-, -li\ *adv* — **fa·nat·i·cal·ness** \|əkəlnəs, |ēk-\ *n* -ES

2fanatic \"\ *n* -S **1** *obs* **a :** LUNATIC **b :** a religious maniac **c :** an English nonconformist — used derogatorily esp. in the 17th century **2 :** a person exhibiting excessive enthusiasm and intense uncritical devotion usu. toward some controversial matter (as in religion, politics, or philosophy) and commonly urging his beliefs zealously and with unreasonable and uncompromising insistence; *broadly* **:** ENTHUSIAST ⟨the duchess became a boating ~⟩ **syn** see ENTHUSIAST

fa·nat·i·cism \-əˌsizəm\ *n* -S **:** fanatic outlook or behavior esp. as exhibited by excessive enthusiasm, unreasoning zeal, or wild and extravagant notions on some subject

fa·nat·i·cize \-ˌsīz\ *vb* -ED/-ING/-S *vt* **:** to cause to become a fanatic **:** imbue with fanaticism — used chiefly as a participial adjective ⟨a *fanaticized* mob⟩ ~ *vi* **:** to act or feel like a fanatic

fan·a·tism \ˈfanəˌtizəm\ *archaic var of* FANATICISM

1fanback \ˈ=,=\ *adj, of a chair* **:** having a fan-shaped back; *esp, of a Windsor chair* **:** having the spindles of the back spread fanwise from the seat to the top rail

2fanback \"\ *n* **:** a fanback chair

fan blower *n* **:** a wheel with vanes on a rotating shaft in a case or chamber used to create a blast of air for a forge or a current for draft and ventilation — called also *fanner*

fan brake *n* **:** a fan or propeller used to provide resistance for its driving mechanism (as an engine or a dynamometer for measuring power)

fanback

fan·chon·ette \ˌfanchəˈnet\ *n* -S [F, fr. *Franchonette*, dim. of *Franchon*, nickname of *Françoise* Frances] *n* -S **:** an open tart covered with meringue or sometimes whipped cream

fan·ci·able \ˈfan(t)sēəbəl, ˈfaan-, ˈfain-, -sīə-\ *adj* **1 :** IMAGINABLE **2 :** ATTRACTIVE

fan·ci·cal \-səkəl\ *adj* [*fancy* + *-ic* + *-al*] *adj, now dial Eng* **:** FANCIFUL

fancied *adj* [fr. past part. of 2*fancy*] **1 :** formed or conceived by the fancy **:** IMAGINED, UNREAL ⟨a ~ wrong⟩ **2 :** FAVORITE, CHOSEN ⟨mounted on a ~ horse⟩ **3** *archaic* **:** artistically devised **:** FANCIFUL, ORNAMENTAL

1fan·ci·er \ˈfan(t)sē(ə)r, ˈfaan-,ˈfain-, -sīə-\ *n* -S [2*fancy* + *-er*] **1 a :** one that has a special liking for or interest in a particular object, subject, or field **:** ENTHUSIAST ⟨a ~*s* of liturgical music⟩ **b :** a person who breeds or grows some kind of animal or plant with the intent of approaching some standard of excellence ⟨a pigeon ~⟩ ⟨the multitude of African violet ~*s*⟩ **2 :** one that employs or depends upon imagination (as in artistic designing or reaching decisions) **:** IMAGINER ⟨a ~ of foolish schemes⟩

2fancier *comparative of* FANCY

fancies *pl of* FANCY; *pres 3d sing of* FANCY

fanciest *superlative of* FANCY

fan·ci·fi·ca·tion \ˌfan(t)səfəˈkāshən, ˌfaan-, ˌfain-\ *n* -S [fr. *fancify*, after such pairs as E *gratify: gratification*] **:** the art or an instance of making fanciful esp. by ornate elaboration ⟨a stilted ~ of language⟩

fan·ci·ful \ˈfan(t)səfəl, -aan-,-ain-, -sēf-\ *adj* **1 :** given to fancy, unrestrained imagination, or whim **:** guided by fancy, imagination, or illusion rather than by reason, experience, or fact ⟨I am not a ~ person, but . . . I seemed to hear Moriarty's voice screaming at me —A. Conan Doyle⟩ **2 a :** marked by fancy and unrestrained imagination in conception, thought, or consideration **:** not governed or ascertained by facts, realities, and reason ⟨~ image of primitive man, uncontaminated by science or art, undepraved by thought —C.H. Grandgent⟩ **b :** existing in fancy only **:** having no existence in fact ⟨the falsehood about some ~ secret treaties —F.D. Roosevelt⟩ **3 :** marked by or as if by fancy, whim, or imagination in design, construction, or execution ⟨the thin blue wreaths of smoke that curled up in such ~ whorls —Oscar Wilde⟩ **syn** see IMAGINARY

fan·ci·ful·ly \-f(ə)lē, -li\ *adv* **:** in a fanciful manner

fan·ci·ful·ness \-fəlnəs\ *n* -ES **:** fanciful quality **:** WHIMSICALITY

fan·ci·fy \-səˌfī\ *vb* -ED/-ING/-ES [1*fancy* + *-fy*] *vt* **:** to make ornate, elaborate, or fancy ⟨a substantial dish and one easily *fancified* for a buffet supper⟩ ~ *vi* **:** to indulge in fancies ⟨resisting an impulse to ~ she turned back to work⟩

fan·ci·less \-sēləs, -sil-\ *adj* **:** being without ideas or imagination **:** purely factual and lacking fancy or fanciful quality

fan·ci·ly \-səlē, -li\ *adv* **1 :** with fancy or imagination esp. when studied or affected ⟨a play with a sound plot but much too ~ developed⟩ **2 :** ELABORATELY, ORNATELY ⟨a ~ embroidered smock⟩ ⟨~ carved ornaments⟩

fan·ci·ness \-sēnəs, -sin-\ *n* -ES **:** fancy quality or form; *often* **:** overly elaborate or studied quality (as of literary style)

fan coral *n* **:** any of several gorgonians (as of the genus *Rhipidogorgia*) that form flat colonies resembling fans

fan-crested \ˈ=ˌ==\ *adj, of a bird* **:** having a median erectile crest of feathers resembling a fan

1fan·cy \ˈfan(t)sē, -aan-,-ain-, -si\ *n* -ES [ME *fantsy*, contr. of *fantasie* fantasy, fancy, fr. MF, fantasy, fr. LL *phantasia* imagination, fr. L, mental image, fr. Gk, appearance, image, faculty of imagination, fr. *phantazein* to make visible, present to the mind, fr. *phainein* to show; akin to OE *gebōned* polished, MD *boenen* to scour, scrub, Gk *phaos, phōs* light, Skt *bhāti* it shines] **1 a :** a liking formed by caprice rather than reason **:** INCLINATION ⟨a ~ for a stroll by the river this evening⟩ ⟨how does this strike your ~?⟩ ⟨had a ~ for rich delicacies⟩ **b :** amorous fondness **:** love or desire ⟨sometimes the queen took a ~ to handsome lads about the court⟩ **2 a :** an opinion or notion formed without much reflection **:** CAPRICE, WHIM ⟨the prediction of his return is based on a mere ~⟩ **b :** an image or representation of something formed in the mind ⟨what sorry *fancies* trouble you so?⟩ **c :** a product of mental conception (as an invention, device, or design) ⟨what a pretty ~ her drawing is⟩ ⟨an excellent trout fly, my father's own ~⟩ **3 :** a short instrumental composition of impromptu character — compare FANTASIA **4** *archaic* **:** fantastic quality or state **5 a** *obs* **:** something that pleases or entertains the taste or caprice **:** CONCEIT **b :** a fabric or an article of clothing manufactured to meet the demand of temporary styles and characterized by novelty in weave, color, design **c :** a diamond of gemstone quality and a color other than white or blue-white **6 a :** imagination esp. of a capricious sort; *often* **:** ILLUSION **:** delusive imagination **b :** the power of conception and representation used in artistic expression (as by a poet or painter) **:** IMAGINATION; *esp* **:** the power of conceiving and giving artistic form to that which is not existent, known, or experienced **c :** the invention of the novel and the unreal by recombining the elements found in reality so that life is represented in alien surroundings or essentially changed in natural physical and mental constitution (as in centaurs or giants) — distinguished from *imagination* **d :** the conceiving power which concerns itself with imagery (as figures of speech and details of a decorative design) **:** CONCEIT **7 :** judgment or taste (as in matters of art or dress) ⟨a person of delicate ~⟩ **8 :** a plant having variegated or parti-colored flowers; *also* **:** a variegated or parti-colored flower **9 a :** persons who pursue or are enthusiastic over some particular art, practice, or amusement: as (1) **:** sporting characters (2) **:** the followers of pugilism (3) **:** fanciers of animals ⟨the bulldog ~⟩ **b :** the object of interest of such a fancy; *esp* **:** PUGILISM **10** *also* **fancy roller :** a carding roller with long teeth used to raise fiber to the top of the main cylinder

syn FANCY, FANTASY, PHANTASY, PHANTASM, VISION, DREAM, DAYDREAM, and NIGHTMARE can signify, in common, a vivid idea or image present in the mind but having no concrete or objective reality. FANCY applies to anything conceived purely in the imagination whether it combines the elements of reality or is pure invention, usu. however, carrying the implication of something consequently more or less trifling ⟨was this only the *fancy* of a visionary, or . . . would it come true in the end? —Ellen Glasgow⟩ ⟨the status of archeological fact and *fancy* in the world today —W.W.Taylor⟩ FANTASY is an imaginative product (often extended and often in literary or artistic form) the greater part or the significant part of which has no correspondence with an objective reality, usu. implying an unrestrained inventiveness ⟨lost himself in a pictured *fantasy* of a London working-class shopping district on a Saturday night —C.S.Forester⟩ ⟨understood Bloom's mind as a river of nonsequiturs and *fantasies* of fear, guilt and desire —*Time*⟩ ⟨intoxicated by *fantasies* of world conquest —Nathaniel Peffer⟩ ⟨to cleanse our minds of all *fantasy* and daydream —*Economic Council Letter*⟩ PHANTASY, generally interchangeable with FANTASY, sometimes applies more to the psychological image-making power in general or its product, often also standing as a clearer antonym of *truth* or *reality* ⟨the distinctions between dream and reality, imagination and fact are blurred, and the speeches and activities of his characters are a further acting out of the schizophrenic's lonely *phantasy*-life, a charade in which the fixed meaning is contactlessness —Isaac Rosenfeld⟩ ⟨on the stage *phantasy*, a strange persuasive illusion, reigns —Leonide Zarine⟩ ⟨probably in his life, certainly in his poetry, there is no sharp boundary between *phantasy* and reality —H.S.Canby⟩ PHANTASM may apply to a phantasy, a mental image, or to a fantasy, esp. a hallucination ⟨held that only the Supreme Being exists and all that we call the natural world is illusion, a *phantasm* of the human mind having no real existence of its own —Radhagovinda Basak⟩ ⟨the figures in the rooming house, in the bars and cabarets slid out of his thoughts like *phantasms* that had no real existence —Donn Byrne⟩ VISION generally applies to what the mind sees so clearly or concretely as to suggest concrete reality, as if revealed by a supernatural power or by vivid intuition, sometimes applying to an image of something one wishes strongly to realize, often suggesting something spiritual in essence and therefore beyond the general grasp of the senses ⟨what *visions* and revelations God may have granted —Willa Cather⟩ ⟨*visions* of suddenly acquired wealth began to float in their minds —Sherwood Anderson⟩ ⟨our *vision* of world law and some sort of worldwide law enforcement agency —*Saturday Rev.*⟩ DREAM applies to the ideas and esp. the images present to the mind in sleep. Figuratively, like DAYDREAM, it suggests vague or idle, commonly happy, imaginings of future events or imaginative projections of the ideal self or life; unlike DAYDREAM, however, DREAM can apply to a serious, though usu. idealized, envisioning of a realizable, often planned, future event or state of affairs ⟨to wake from a bad *dream*⟩ ⟨were it not for the oppressions and monotonies of daily experience, the realm of *dream* and reverie would not be attractive —John Dewey⟩ ⟨a *dream* of a better society in which to live⟩ ⟨the shock that will bring them out of their *daydreams* into today's realities —*Science News Letter*⟩ ⟨a *daydream*, which is wishful thinking and an attempt to escape the experience of oneself —*Life*⟩ ⟨*daydreams* of a better world —*Fortune*⟩ NIGHTMARE applies to any frightful and oppressive dream which occurs in sleep or by extension to any vision or experience which inspires terror or cannot easily be shaken off ⟨to wake in a cold sweat from a *nightmare*⟩ ⟨how many of our daydreams would darken into *nightmares*, were there a danger of their coming true —L.P.Smith⟩ ⟨a marriage might be a *nightmare* to both partners —F.L.Allen⟩ **syn** see in addition IMAGINATION

²**fancy** \"\ *vb* -ED/-ING/-ES *vt* **1 a :** to be pleased with esp. on account of external appearance or manners **:** LIKE, ENJOY **:** have a taste for ⟨it's natural to ~ people who agree with us⟩ ⟨could ~ a bowl of chowder right now⟩ **b** *obs* **:** to love or desire (a person) **2** *obs* **a :** to suit the fancy of **:** PLEASE **b :** to arrange according to a conception of fancy **:** DESIGN, DEVISE **3 :** to form a conception of **:** IMAGINE — used imperatively to imply surprise ⟨~ that⟩ or to attract attention (as to a point of view) ⟨~ our embarrassment⟩ ⟨just ~ how we felt⟩ **4 :** to believe without any evidence or on the basis of false evidence or misconception **5 :** to believe without being certain **:** be inclined to think ⟨I ~ he will act quickly⟩ **6 :** to transform in fancy **:** visualize or interpret as ⟨I had such a scare; I *fancied* that rock was a crouching wolf⟩ — often used with *to be* ⟨I *fancied* myself to be a child once more⟩ ~ *vi* **1 :** to believe or imagine something without proof or proper grounds **:** build up fancies ⟨idly ~*ing* about all sorts of things as we drowsed in the shade⟩ ⟨let me ~ while I may⟩ **2** *obs* **:** to experience love or desire **syn** see LIKE, THINK

³**fancy** \"\ *adj* -ER/-EST **1 :** dependent or based on fancy **:** WHIMSICAL, IRREGULAR ⟨a ~ display of bad manners⟩ **2 a :** adapted to please the fancy or senses; *usu* **:** ornamental or elegant rather than utilitarian — often opposed to *plain* ⟨skilled in plain sewing and ~ needlework⟩ ⟨~ shoes with satin bows and 3-inch heels⟩ **b :** of particular excellence **:** of a quality distinctly above the average **:** specially selected — used esp. of foodstuffs and in some schemes of grading designating the highest of a series of grades of quality ⟨~ peaches packed in heavy syrup⟩ ⟨~ fresh fruits and vegetables⟩ **c** *of a gem* **:** of a color other than that usu. considered standard ⟨~ diamonds occur in red, green, blue, and golden to brownish yellow and include the most costly gemstones⟩ **d** *of an animal or plant* **:** bred for special qualities esp. such as lack practical utility ⟨~ goldfish with bulging eyes and immense fins⟩ **3 :** based on conceptions of the fancy rather than reality ⟨~ sketches of nature⟩ **4 a :** dealing in fancy goods ⟨a ~ department stocking notions, bric-a-brac, and other fripperies⟩ or in goods of fancy quality ⟨in the long run it often pays to patronize a ~ butcher who properly grades and trims his meats⟩ ⟨a ~ delicatessen⟩ **b :** above real value or the usual market price ⟨they ask ~ prices at that stand but everything is fresh and good⟩ **:** PREMIUM, TOP; *often* **:** EXCESSIVE, EXTRAVAGANT ⟨during the war ~ rents were paid for mere hovels⟩ **5 :** executed with manner or method requiring technical skill and with superior grace, ease, and harmony ⟨~ diving⟩ ⟨~ techniques in schooling horses⟩ **6** *of a plant or plant part* **:** PARTI-COLORED ⟨~ carnations⟩

fancy bread *n* **:** bread in other form than the conventional yeast-raised loaf; *esp* **:** any of various raised breads enriched (as with eggs, sweetenings, or nuts and fruit) and often baked in some other shape than an elongated loaf (as a braid or twist or an individual portion)

fancy-bred \ˈ══ˌ═\ *adj* **1 :** evoked by fancy **2** *of an animal* **:** having a highly desirable pedigree ⟨*fancy-bred* bulls should produce good progeny⟩

fancy dan \ˈ══ˌdan, -daa(ə)n\ *n, often cap D* [³*fancy* + *Dan*, nickname of *Daniel*] **:** a showy fellow more impressive than effective; *esp* **:** a boxer who depends on technical skill and lacks hitting power

fancy dive *n* **:** DIVE 1a(1)

fancy dress *n* **:** a costume (as for a masquerade or party) departing from currently conventional style and usu. representing a fictional or historical character, an animal, the fancy of the wearer, or a particular occupation; *sometimes* **:** formal evening dress

fancy dress ball *also* **fancy ball** *n* **:** a ball at which persons appear in fancy dress

fancy-free \ˈ══ˈ═\ *adj* [¹*fancy*] **:** free to imagine or fancy ⟨stage designers, in exercising their *fancy-free* talents —Donald Oenslager⟩ **:** not centering thoughts or attentions on one object; *usu* **:** free from amorous attachment or engagement

fancy geranium *n* **:** MARTHA WASHINGTON GERANIUM

fancy goods *n pl* **1 :** ¹FANCY 5b **2 :** items (as novelties, accessories, or notions) that are primarily ornamental or designed to appeal to taste or fancy rather than essential

fancy house *n* **:** BROTHEL

fancy line *n* **1 :** a line rove through a block at the jaws of a gaff to haul it down **2 :** any of several short lines used chiefly on shipboard for various purposes (as the control of sash windows)

fancy man *n* **1 a** *archaic* **:** a male sweetheart **b :** a woman's paramour **c :** a man who lives on the earnings of a prostitute **:** PIMP **2** *archaic* **:** a man who is a member of a fancy **3 :** DECORATOR d

fancy meat *n* **:** VARIETY MEAT

fancy pants *n pl but sing in constr* **:** an overly elegant, affected, and often somewhat epicene man

fancy roller *n* **:** FANCY 10

fancysick \ˈ══ˌ═\ *adj* **:** LOVE-SICK

fancy up *vt* [³*fancy*] **:** to add superficial adornment esp. in order to refurbish ⟨that dress will do if you *fancy* it *up* with a bright scarf⟩

fancy woman *or* **fancy girl** *or* **fancy lady** *n* **:** a woman of questionable morals or reputation; *specif* **:** PROSTITUTE

fancywork \ˈ══ˌ═\ *n* **:** decorative needlework (as embroidery and crocheting)

fand \ˈfand\ *chiefly Scot past of* FIND

fan dance *n* **:** a solo dance act performed in or as if in the nude, the dancer using one or more large fans for covering — compare BUBBLE DANCE

fan·dan·gle \fanˈdaŋgəl, ˈ═ˌ══\ *n* -S [perh. alter. of *fandango*] **1 :** an ornate or fantastic ornament ⟨stitched all over . . . with ~*s* in fruit-colored threads —Audrey Barker⟩ **2 :** NONSENSE, TOMFOOLERY

¹**fan·dan·go** \fanˈdaŋ(ˌ)gō, faan-, -daiŋ-\ *n* -S [Sp, perh. fr. (assumed) Pg *fadango*, fr. Pg *fado* — more at FADO] **1 a :** a lively Spanish or Spanish-American dance usu. performed by a man and a woman with castanets and in triple time **b :** music for such a dance **2** *chiefly Southwest* **:** a ball or other party featuring dancing **3 :** tomfoolery esp. in public affairs or other matters of serious import **:** ridiculous or childishly improper behavior or speech ⟨the continued ~*s* of this committee are subjecting the whole senate to public contempt⟩

²**fandango** \"\ *vi* -ED/-ING/-ES **:** to dance a fandango or to move or comport oneself as if dancing a fandango ⟨fighter planes ~*ing* in the sky⟩

F and D *abbr* freight and demurrage

fan delta *n* **:** an alluvial fan merging with a delta — called also *delta fan*

F and F *abbr* furniture and fixtures

fan·dom \ˈfandəm, ˈfaan-\ *n* -S **:** all the fans (as of a particular sport) ⟨~ impatiently awaits publication of the new football rules⟩

¹**fane** \ˈfān\ *n* -S [ME, fr. OE *fana* banner, flag — more at VANE] *archaic* **:** FLAG, PENNANT, BANNER; *also* **:** WEATHERCOCK

²**fane** \"\ *n* -S [ME, temple, fr. L *fanum* — more at FEAST] **1 :** TEMPLE **2** *archaic* **:** CHURCH

fa·ne·ga \fəˈnāgə\ *n* -S [Sp, fr. Ar *faniqah* large sack] **1 :** any of various units of capacity used in Spain and Spanish-American countries; *esp* **:** one of about 1.6 bushels **2 a :** any of various Spanish units of land area (as of 1.59 acres) **b :** a Mexican land area of 8.81 acres

fan·fa·rade \ˌfanfəˈrād\ *n* -S [*fanfare* + *-ade*] **:** FANFARE

¹**fan·fare** \ˈfan,fa(a)(ə)r, ˈfaan-, -fe(, |ə\ *n* [F, prob. of imit. origin] **1 :** a sounding of trumpets (as in coming into the lists); *specif* **:** a short and lively air performed on hunting horns during the chase **2 :** a showy outward display or motion **:** FLOURISH ⟨such devout phrases could easily be classed as introductory ~ —Paul Blanshard⟩ ⟨great political ~⟩ **3 :** an orchestral passage in which the brass instruments are prominent

²**fanfare** \"\ *vt* **:** to make public or call attention to with much clamor ⟨the crash of trees *fanfared* the spread of material civilization —R.G.Lillard⟩

fan·fa·ron \ˈfanfəˌrän\ *n* -S [Sp *fanfarrón*, prob. of imit. origin] **1 :** an empty boaster **:** BRAGGART, SWAGGERER **2 :** FANFARE

fan·far·o·nade \ˌfanˌfarəˈnād, -nȧd\ *n* -S [F *fanfaronnade*, fr. Sp *fanfaronada*, fr. *fanfarrón* + *-ada* -ade (fr. LL *-ata*)] **1 :** SWAGGERING **:** empty boasting **:** BLUSTER; *often* **:** ostentatious or gaudy display **2 :** FANFARE

fanflower \ˈ═ˌ══\ *n* **:** a tropical shrub (*Scaevola koenigii*) of the family Goodeniaceae having white flowers

fan fold *n* [¹*fan* + *fold*, n.] **:** a fold of geologic strata in which both limbs are overturned forming an anticline if the limbs dip toward each other or a syncline if they dip away from each other

fanfold \ˈ═ˌ═\ *n, often attrib* [¹*fan* + *fold*, n.] **:** a collection of sheets or forms (as for billing) interleafed with carbon paper so as to permit a multiple record (as of a transaction) to be made with a single written or typed impression

fanfoot \ˈ═ˌ═\ *also* **fanfooted gecko** \ˈ═ˌ══-\ *n* -S **:** a gecko with toes expanded into lobes for adhesion; *esp* **:** a harmless Egyptian gecko (*Ptyodactylus hasselquistii*) that is thought by natives to have venomous toes

¹**fang** \ˈfaŋ\ *vb* -ED/-ING/-S [ME *fangen, fongen*, alter. of *fon* (past *feng*, past part. *fangen, fongen*), fr. OE *fōn* (past *fēng*, past part. *fangen, fongen*) — more at PACT] *vt* **1** *now dial Brit* **:** to lay hold of **:** SEIZE **2** *obs* **a :** to get into one's power or possession **:** SNARE, CAPTURE, OBTAIN, PROCURE **b :** to receive as a guest **c :** to set about **:** COMMENCE, UNDERTAKE, BEGIN **d :** TAKE, CONSUME **3** *now dial Eng* **:** to receive as due **:** EARN ~ *vi, dial Eng* **:** to act as sponsor at baptism — usu. followed by *to*

²**fang** \ˈfaŋ, ˈfaiŋ\ *n* -S [ME, fr. OE; akin to OHG *fang* seizure, ON *fang* grip; derivative fr. the root of OE *fōn* to seize] **1** *chiefly Scot* **:** BOOTY, PLUNDER **2** *obs* **:** a seizing or capture **:** CATCH; *also* **:** GRIP, GRASP **3 a :** a long sharp tooth by which the prey of an animal is seized and held or torn **:** a long pointed tooth; *esp* **:** one of the long, hollow or grooved, and often erectile, teeth of venomous serpents **b :** one of the chelicerae of a spider at the tip of which a poison gland opens **4 :** the root of a tooth or one of the processes or prongs into which a root divides **5 :** any of various sharp or elongated processes: as **a** *dial Eng* **:** TALON, CLAW **b :** a projecting tooth or prong (as on a lock, the plate of a belt clamp, or the end of a tool) **c :** a branch on a normally unbranched thickened tap root (as of a sugar beet or carrot) **6** *obs* **:** VANG

1 fangs 3a

³**fang** \"\ *vt* -ED/-ING/-S **1 :** to strike with or as if with fangs ⟨he jumped aside but the snake ~*ed* him⟩ ⟨the wind . . . ~*ed* his ears —Countee Cullen⟩ **2 :** to supply (a pump) with water so as to make it work **:** PRIME **3 :** to fit with or as if with fangs ⟨the gray rocks were ~*ed* with long icicles —Victor Canning⟩

⁴**fang** \ˈfaŋ, ˈfäŋ\ *also* **fan** \ˈn\ *n, pl* **fang** *or* **fangs** *or* **fan** *or* **fans** *usu cap* [F *Fan*, perh. modif. of Fang *Mpangwe*] **1 a :** an African people occupying the Ogowe basin, French Equatorial Africa and noted for their carved and painted religious masks **b :** a member of such people — called also *Pahouin, Pangwe* **2 :** a Bantu language of the Fang people

fang bolt *n* **:** a bolt having for a nut a triangular plate with sharp fangs projecting from its corners and used for attaching iron to wood — compare JAG BOLT

fanged \ˈfaŋd, ˈfaiŋd\ *adj* [²*fang* + *-ed*] **:** having fangs or processes resembling fangs ⟨the ice-*fanged* eaves⟩

¹**fan·gle** \ˈfaŋgəl, ˈfaiŋ-\ *n* -S [prob. fr. *newfangle*, adj.] **1 :** a fashion esp. when foppish or silly — used with *new* and usu. derogatorily **2** *obs* **:** a silly or fantastic contrivance **:** GEWGAW, GAUD

²**fangle** \"\ *vt* -ED/-ING/-S *now dial* **:** FASHION, DRESS **:** deck out

fan·gle·ment \-mənt\ *n* -S **1 :** CONTRIVANCE, DEVICE **2 :** FRIPPERY, GEWGAW

fang·less \ˈfaŋlės, ˈfaiŋ-\ *adj* **:** having no fangs; *also* **:** having lost the power to do harm

fan·glom·er·ate \(ˈ)fanˈgläm(ə)rət\ *n* -S [¹*fan* + *-glomerate* (as in *conglomerate*)] **:** the material of an alluvial fan in which the rock fragments are only slightly waterworn — **fan·glom·er·at·ic** \ˌ═ˌ══məˈrad·ik\ *adj*

fan·go \ˈfaŋ(ˌ)gō, ˈfäŋ-\ *n* -S [It, mud, of Gmc origin; akin to Goth *fani* clay — more at FEN] **:** MUD, MIRE; *esp* **:** a clay mud from hot springs at Battaglio, Italy, that is used in the form of hot external applications in certain medical treatments

fang shih \ˈfäŋˈshē\ *n, pl* **fang shih** [Chin *fang*¹ *shih*⁴, fr. *fang*¹ prescription, formula + *shih*⁴ scholar, teacher] **:** a priest-magician flourishing in China 249 B.C.–A.D. 220 whose office was to provide divinational and magical formulas to those seeking immortality and supernatural powers

fangy \ˈfaŋē, ˈfaiŋ-, -ŋi\ *adj* -ER/-EST [²*fang* + *-y*] **:** having fangs; *specif, of certain root crops* **:** producing roots with fangs ⟨sugar beets are often ~ on acid soil⟩

fan·ion \ˈfanyən\ *n* -S [F, fr. *fanon* maniple, pennon — more at FANON] **:** a small flag used orig. by horse brigades and now by soldiers and surveyors to mark positions

fank \ˈfaŋk\ *n* -S [ScGael *fang*, prob. fr. E ²*fang*] *Scot* **:** SHEEPFOLD

fanleaf palm \ˈ═ˌ═-\ *n* **:** FAN PALM; *esp* **:** WASHINGTON PALM

fan letter *n* **:** a letter sent to a public figure (as in sports or the theater) by an admirer

fanlight \ˈ═ˌ═\ *n* **:** a semicircular window made with radiating sash bars like the ribs of a fan and placed over a door or window; *broadly* **:** a window over a door or window

fanlighted \ˈ═ˌ══\ *adj* **:** surmounted by a fanlight

fanlike \ˈ═ˌ═\ *adj* **1 :** resembling a fan or the action of a fan ⟨a ~ motion⟩ **2 :** folded up like a closed fan **:** PLICATE — used esp. of leaves

fan magazine *n* **:** a magazine devoted to the exploitation of popular interest in the personalities of the sports or entertainment world (as movie, radio, TV)

fanlight

fan mail *n* **:** FAN LETTERS

fan·man \ˈ═ˌman, maa(ə)n\ *n, pl* **fanmen :** a worker who operates a ventilation system (as by fans for cooling kilns or for forcing hot air through furnaces)

fan marker *n* **:** a radio beacon located near an airport and on a radio range that transmits a vertical fan-shaped beam with distinctive code signal usu. crossing one leg of the range station as an aid to landing — compare RADIO MARKER

fan mussel *n* [so called fr. the shape of the shell] **:** PEN SHELL

fanned *past of* FAN

fan·ner \ˈfanə(r), ˈfaan-\ *n* -S **:** one that fans: as **a** (1) **:** FAN WHEEL (2) **:** FAN BLOWER (3) **:** FANNING MILL **b :** KESTREL **c** [so called fr. its early use as a winnowing basket] *dial* **:** a broad flat basket esp. for carrying or displaying fresh produce **d :** a stationary engineer who tends the ventilation system of a mine

fan-nerved \ˈ═ˌnərvd\ *adj* **:** having the nerves or veins radially disposed ⟨a *fan-nerved* leaf⟩

fan·nia \ˈfanēə\ *n, cap* [NL, perh. irreg. fr. Gk *phanos* bright, conspicuous + NL *-ia*; akin to Gk *phainein* to show — more at FANCY] **:** a genus of two-winged flies (family Anthomyiidae) resembling but smaller than the common housefly and including the lesser housefly and the latrine fly

fanning *n* -S [ME, winnowing of grain, fr. gerund of *fannen* to fan, winnow] **1 :** the act of one that fans **2 :** an instance or product of fanning: as **a fannings** *pl* **:** coarse tea siftings **b :** a whipping or beating

fanning mill *n* **:** a machine for winnowing

fan·ny \ˈfanē, -aan-\ *n* -ES [fr. *Fanny*, nickname of *Frances*] **1** *slang Brit* **:** ³BILLY **2** *also* **fany** \"\ *usu cap* [*fanny* irreg. (influence of the nickname *Fanny*) fr. First Aid Nursing Yeomanry; *fany* fr. First Aid Nursing Yeomanry] **:** a member of a British women's ambulance unit **3 :** BUTTOCKS

fan·on \ˈfanən, fəˈnōn\ *n* -S [ME *fanoun* maniple, fr. MF *fanon*, of Gmc origin; akin to OHG *fano* cloth — more at VANE] **:** any of several articles used in religious ceremonials: as **a :** MANIPLE **b :** an oblation cloth for carrying vessels and bread for the Eucharist **c :** ¹CORPORAL **d :** a vestment that resembles a short cape and is worn by a Roman pontiff at solemn pontifical mass — called also *orale* **e :** INFULA 2a

fan palm *n* **:** a palm having simple fan-shaped leaves (as the cabbage palmetto of the southern U.S., the hemp palm of Europe, the talipot of Asia, the Chinese fan palm, and the Washington palm of California) — called also *fanleaf palm*; see DWARF FAN PALM

fan roof *n* **:** a vaulted roof with fan tracery

fans *pl of* FAN, *pres 3d sing of* FAN

fan-shaped \ˈ═ˌ═\ *adj* **:** shaped like a fan and often having or made up of radiating parts (as wings, ribs, or individuals) that are felt to resemble the supporting sticks of a fan

fan shell *n* **1 :** a scallop or its shell **2 :** PEN SHELL

fantad *var of* FANTOD

fantail \ˈ═ˌ═\ *n, often attrib* **1 :** a tail or end with the shape of a fan **2 a** *often cap* **:** a domestic pigeon of a variety characterized by a broad rounded tail often having 30 or 40 feathers instead of the usual 12 **b :** any of numerous flycatchers constituting a genus *Rhipidura* of the family Muscicapidae of Asia, Australia, and the southwest Pacific and having a fanlike tail that is often widely spread during flight **c** *often cap* **:** a goldfish of a fancy breed having double anal and tail fins **d :** a wild or low grade range horse **3 :** an architectural part resembling or likened to a fan; *specif* **:** a centering (as of an arch) of radiating struts **4 :** a counter or after overhang of a ship that is shaped like a duck's bill

fantail deer *also* **fantail** *n* **:** a small white-tailed deer (*Odocoileus virginianus couesi*) of the southwestern U.S. and western Mexico

fan-tailed \ˈ═ˌtāld\ *adj* **:** having a tail broadly expanded and suggesting a fan — used esp. of certain breeds of birds and fishes

fan-tailed darter *n* **:** a small darter (*Catonotus flabellaris*) of the central U.S.

fan-tailed pigeon *n* **:** FANTAIL 2a

fan-tailed warbler *n* **:** any of various small Old World warblers (genus *Cisticola*) that build delicate nests woven of cobwebs and down

fantail joint *n* **:** DOVETAIL JOINT

fantail mullet *or* **fan-tailed mullet** *n* **:** a mullet (*Querimana trichodon*) found from Brazil to Key West where it is used as food

fan-tan \ˈfanˌtan\ *n* -S [Chin *fan*¹*-t'an*¹] **1 :** a Chinese gambling game in which a banker counts off a large handful of small objects (as beans) in fours and the players bet on what number from one to four will be left at the end of the count **2 :** a card game in which the object is to play sevens and other cards that form sequences in the same suits as the sevens and to be first to have played all one's cards — called also *sevens*

fan·ta·sia \fanˈtā|zhə, faan- *also* |z(h)ēə *sometimes* fän- *or* fən- *or* -tä| *or* -tä| *or* -ta(i); ˌfantəˈzēə, ˌfaan-, ˌfän-, ˌfən-, -teˈsēə\ *also* **fan·ta·sie** \ˌfäntəˈzē, ˌfan-, ˌfaan-, ˌfän- *or like* FANTASY\ *n* -S [It *fantasia*, lit., fancy, fr. LL *phantasia* imagination, fr. L, mental image — more at FANCY] **1 a :** an instrumental composition of the 16th and 17th centuries written in contrapuntal style and akin to the motet **b :** a free instrumental composition not in strict form (as the development section of sonata form) **c :** FREE FANTASIA **d :** a composition based generally on one theme ⟨~ on spring⟩ **e :** a potpourri of operatic arias or familiar airs ⟨~ on Christmas carols —Ralph Vaughan Williams⟩ **2 :** a work (as a poem or play) in which the author's fancy roves unrestricted by set form or verisimilitude **3 :** something strange or foreign by reason of grotesque, bizarre, or seemingly unreal qualities ⟨psychologists like to dismiss myths as mere ~ —Robert Graves⟩ ⟨the jungle's boggy ~ —*Time*⟩ **4 :** an Arab performance featuring dancing and often evolutions on horseback, gun firing, and shouting all in a rapid rhythm

fan·ta·sied *or* **phan·ta·sied** \ˈfantəs|ēd, ˈfaan-, -təz|, |id\ *adj* [fr. past part. of *fantasy*, v.] **1 :** existing only in the imagination : FANCIED — now used esp. in psychiatry **2** *obs* **:** full of fancies or strange whims

fantasies *pl of* FANTASY, *pres 3d sing of* FANTASY

fan·ta·sie·stück \ˌfäntäˈzē,shtu̇k\ *n, pl* **fantasie·stücke** \-kə\ [G *fantasiestück, phantasiestück*, fr. *phantasie* fantasia (fr. It *fantasia*) + *stück* piece, fr. OHG *stucki* — more at STOCK] **:** FANTASIA 1b **:** CHARACTER PIECE

fan·ta·sist \fan·ˈtäzhəst; ˈfantəsəst, -təzə-\ *n* -s [*fantasy*, n. + *-ist*] **:** a composer of fantasias or fantasies

fan·ta·size \ˈfantə,sīz\ *vb* -ED/-ING/-S [*fantasy*, n. + *-ize*] *vt* **1 :** FANTASY 1 ⟨likes to ~ that he has inherited a fortune⟩ **2 :** to view as fantastic ⟨nothing will be gained by *fantasizing* our position⟩ ~ *vi* **:** to create or develop imaginative and often fantastic views, ideas, or explanations — often used with *about* ⟨*fantasizing* about her neighbors⟩

fantasm *var of* PHANTASM

¹fan·tasque \(ˈ)fan·ˈtask\ *n* -s [F, fr. *fantasque*, adj.] **:** FANCY, FANTASY, WHIM

²fantasque \"\ *adj* [F, fr. MF, prob. contr. of *fantastique*] **:** FANTASTIC, FANCIFUL

fan·tast *or* **phan·tast** \ˈfan·,tast\ *n* -s [G *phantast, fantast*, prob. fr. (assumed) ML *fantasta*, prob. back-formation fr. ML *fantasticus*] **1 :** VISIONARY, DREAMER **2 a :** a fantastic or eccentric person **b :** FANTASIST

¹fan·tas·tic \(ˈ)fan·ˈtastik, -aan-, fən·ˈt-, -taas-, -stēk\ *also* **fan·tas·ti·cal** \-stəkəl, -stēk-\ *or* **phan·tas·tic** *or* **phan·tas·ti·cal** *adj* [*fantastic* fr. ME *fantastic, fantastik*, fr. MF & ML; MF *fantastique*, fr. ML *fantasticus*, fr. LL *phantasticus* imaginary, fr. Gk *phantastikos* able to produce a mental image, fr. *phantazein* to make visible; *fantastical* fr. ME, fr. *fantastic, fantastik* + *-al* — more at FANCY] **1** *obs* **:** of, belonging to, or constituting fantasy; *esp* **:** PHANTASMAL **2** *usu fantastic* **a :** based on fantasy rather than reason **:** IMAGINARY, IRRATIONAL, UNREAL ⟨this ~ assumption of neutralism is not unknown among some ritualistic liberals —Sidney Hook⟩ *broadly* **:** FOOLISH, UNREALISTIC ⟨a ~ idea of his own importance⟩ **b :** conceived or giving the impression of having been conceived by unrestrained fancy ⟨~ new space and nuclear weapons —Jack Raymond⟩ **:** exhibiting strange, grotesque, inappropriate, or startlingly novel characteristics ⟨~ as the situation was — a landlubber second in command —Jack London⟩; *often* **:** UNSUITABLE, QUAINT, ECCENTRIC ⟨a ~ costume for street wear⟩ **c :** so extreme as to challenge belief esp. by reason of magnitude or extent **:** UNBELIEVABLE ⟨the bomb did ~ damage⟩ ⟨a ~ industrial complex of steel, coal, machine tools, and other heavy industries —M.S.Handler⟩; *broadly* **:** exceedingly or excessively large or great ⟨spent ~ sums on his library⟩ ⟨the housing shortage reached ~ proportions —Gerda Luft⟩ **3 a** *sometimes fantastical* **:** given to or marked by extravagant fantasy, unrestrained imagination, or extreme individuality and deviation from some accepted norm **:** ODD, ECCENTRIC ⟨one need not have a very ~ imagination to see spirits there —Thomas Gray⟩ ⟨a strange ~ mind⟩ ⟨a man *fantastical* in dress⟩ **b :** following no set pattern **:** CAPRICIOUS ⟨~ acts of kindness⟩ ⟨the ~ irregularity of the dunes⟩

syn BIZARRE, GROTESQUE, ANTIC: FANTASTIC suggests unrestrained imagination and unbridled fancy, extravagant conception, or wild or highly imaginative remoteness from reality ⟨explosions, *fantastic*, far off, bright green or violet or golden —C.P.Aiken⟩ ⟨*fantastic* figures, with bulbous heads, the circumference of a bushel, grinned enormously in his face —Nathaniel Hawthorne⟩ ⟨helped their panic as best he could by sending Congo natives over to the Tanganyika side to spread the most *fantastic* rumors he could dream up —Joseph Millard⟩ BIZARRE applies to the sensationally, colorfully queer or strange, often through violent contrasts and incongruities ⟨temple sculpture became *bizarre* — rearing monsters, fiery horses, great pillared halls teeming with sculptures —*Atlantic*⟩ ⟨the restaurants of *bizarre* design — one like a hat, another like a rabbit, a third like an old shoe, another a fish —*Amer. Guide Series: Calif.*⟩ ⟨it was *bizarre* in the extreme. It was as if a judge, wearing the black cap, had suddenly put out his tongue at the condemned —J.C.Powys⟩ GROTESQUE applies to the incongruously distorted, to ridiculous ugliness or incompatibility ⟨there was a *grotesque* look in his face, as if it had been pulled out of shape by some sudden twist —Ellen Glasgow⟩ ⟨the crescendo and diminuendo of the planes, the agitated noise of patrol vessels and the vicious challenge of the guns were all *grotesque* against the still serenity of the moonlight —Eleanor Dark⟩ ⟨*grotesque* serpents eight fathoms long that churned the seas, huge reptiles that beat the air with wings of nightmare breadth —P.E.More⟩ ANTIC, now less common than others in this set, may suggest ludicrous clownish exuberance of action ⟨the Friday-night Mad Arts Balls, Mad Hatters Balls, Pagan Routs, and similar *antic* gatherings —Lillian Ross⟩ ⟨in the course of Kaye's *antic* fun with this plot, he makes an entrance with his head on platter, gorges himself in fast motion at a feast, keeps a roomful of conspirators hidden from one another, tugs frantically at a sword that refuses to come out of its scabbard —*Time*⟩ **syn** see in addition IMAGINARY

²fantastic \"\ *n* -s **1** *archaic* **:** a person with fantastic ideas **2** *obs* **:** a person given to fantastic behavior (as in choice of dress or in manners)

fan·tas·ti·cal·i·ty \(,)=,=stəˈkaləd·ē\ *n* -ES **1 :** fantastic quality ⟨consider the ~ of enforcing loyalty by oath —W.T. Hastings⟩ **2 :** a fantastic incident, event, or account ⟨an amusing volume of natural *fantasticalities*⟩

fan·tas·ti·cal·ly \(ˈ)fan·ˈtastək(ə)lē, -aan-, fən·ˈt-, -taas-, -stēk-, -li\ *adv* **1 :** in a fantastic manner **:** GROTESQUELY, ODDLY ⟨a ~ plotted novel⟩ **2 :** to a fantastic degree **:** UNBELIEVABLY, EXTREMELY ⟨~ expensive clothes⟩ **3** *archaic* **:** CAPRICIOUSLY

fan·tas·ti·cal·ness *n* -ES **:** the quality or state of being fantastic **:** ECCENTRICITY, WHIMSICALITY ⟨the charm and ~ of these little sketches⟩ ⟨the sheer ~ of their behavior⟩

fan·tas·ti·cate \=ˈ=stə,kāt\ *vb* -ED/-ING/-S *vi* **:** to indulge in fantastic notions ~ *vt* **:** to render fantastic ⟨time and climate *fantasticated* the cliffs⟩ ⟨*fantasticating* life far beyond the limits of pure drama —W.B.Adams⟩ — **fan·tas·ti·ca·tion** \(,)=,=ˈkāshən\ *n* -s

fan·tas·ti·cism \=ˈ=stə,sizəm\ *n* -s **:** adherence to or employment of fantasy (as in literature or art)

fantasticly *obs var of* FANTASTICALLY

fan·tas·tic·ness *archaic var of* FANTASTICALNESS

fan·tas·ti·co \fan·ˈtastə,kō, fən-\ *n* -ES [It, fantastic (adj.), fr. ML *fantasticus*] **:** a pretentiously fantastic person

¹fan·ta·sy *or* **phan·ta·sy** \ˈfantəs|ē, -aan-, -təz|, |i\ *n* -ES [ME *fantasie* — more at FANCY] **1** *obs* **a :** the act or function of forming images or representations whether in direct perception or in memory; *also* **:** an image or impression derived through sensation **b :** HALLUCINATION; *sometimes* **:** PHANTOM, APPARITION **c :** DESIRE, INCLINATION **2 :** imagination or fancy; *esp* **:** the free play of creative imagination as it affects perception and productivity usu. as expressed in an art form or as elicited by projective techniques of formal psychology **3 :** a creation of the imaginative faculty whether expressed or merely conceived: as **a :** a fanciful design or invention ⟨a ~ of delicate tracery⟩ **b :** a chimerical or fantastic notion **c :** FANTASIA 1 **d** *also* **fantasy fiction :** imaginative fiction dependent for effect on strangeness of setting (as other worlds or times) and of characters (as supernatural or unnatural beings); *sometimes* **:** SCIENCE FICTION **4 :** mood or mental prepossession; *often* **:** a whimsical or capricious mood **5 :** the power or process of creating mental images (as of unrealistic or improbable happenings or distortions of previously perceived persons, objects, or events) esp. with erotic content or implication in response to psychological need or through the action of drugs or illness ⟨an object of ~⟩; *also* **:** a mental image so created **:** DAYDREAM ⟨sexual *fantasies* of adolescence and middle age⟩ **syn** see FANCY, IMAGINATION

²fantasy *or* **phantasy** \"\ *vb* -ED/-ING/-ES [ME *fantasien*, fr. *fantasie*, n.] *vt* **1 :** to portray in the mind **:** FANCY, IMAGINE **2** *obs* **:** to have a fancy for ~ *vi* **1 :** to indulge in fantasy or reverie **:** DAYDREAM **2 :** to improvise in playing a musical instrument **:** play fantasias

fan·tee *also* **fan·ti** \ˈfantē\ *adj* [*Fanti*] *chiefly Brit* **:** wild, unrestrained, or primitive — used chiefly as a predicate adjective and usu. in the phrase *go fantee*

fan·ti *or* **fan·te** *also* **fan·tee** \", ˈfän-\ *n, pl* **fanti** *or* **fante** *or* **fantis** *or* **fantes** *cap* **1 a :** an African Negro nation of Ghana **b :** a member of such nation **2 :** a dialect of Akan spoken by the Fanti people **3 :** a literary language based on the Fanti dialect and used by the Fanti and related peoples

fan·tigue *or* **fan·teeg** \fan·ˈtēg\ *n* -s [perh. blend of *fantastic* and *fatigue*] *dial chiefly Eng* **:** a state of excitement or great tension ⟨his nerves were in a proper ~ —John Galsworthy⟩

fan·toc·ci·ni \ˌfäntəˈchēnē, ˌfan-\ *n pl* [It, pl. of *fantoccino*, dim. of *fantoccio* doll, lay figure, aug. of *fante* servant, boy, child, fr. L *infant-, infans* infant — more at INFANT] **1 :** puppets moved by strings or mechanical devices **2 :** puppet shows in which fantoccini are used

fan·tod \ˈfan·,täd\ *also* **fan·tad** \-tad\ *n* -s [perh. alter. of *fantigue*] **1** *usu* **fantods** *pl* **a :** a state of irritability, fidget, and tension; *sometimes* **:** a state of acute worry and distress **b :** a state of bodily or mental disorder esp. when ill-defined and more or less chronic **2** *sometimes* **fantods** *pl* **a :** an instance or occurrence of the fantods **b :** a violent or irrational outburst **3 :** a fidgety fussy officer of a ship

fantom *var of* PHANTOM

fan tracery *n* **:** decorative tracery on fan vaulting

fan–trained \ˈ=ˌ=\ *adj, of a tree or vine* **:** trained in growing so that the main branches radiate in one plane like the sticks of a fan

fan tree *n* **1 :** FAN PALM **2 :** a fan-trained tree

fan truss *n* **:** a truss (as of a roof) characterized by the radiating lines of the king post and appended struts or of the queen posts and appended struts

fan vault *n* **:** a vault produced by fan vaulting

fan vaulting *n* **:** an elaborate system of vaulting in which the ribs diverge somewhat like the rays of a fan and that was used esp. in the latest English Gothic architecture

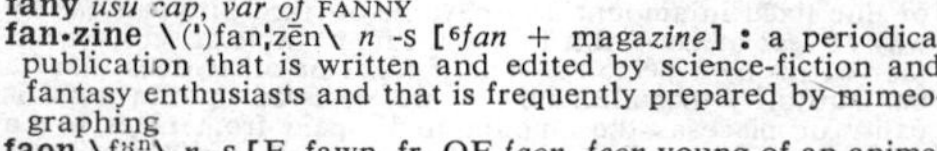

fan vaulting

fanweed \ˈ=ˌ=\ *n* **:** PENNYCRESS

fan wheel *n* **:** the wheel of a fan blower

fan window *n* **:** a window (as a fanlight) with radiating sash bars like the sticks of a fan

fan–wing fly *n* **:** an artificial dry fly with fan-shaped wings

fanwise \ˈ=ˌ=\ *adv* (*or adj*) **:** over a segment of a circle **:** in the manner or position of the sticks of an open fan ⟨highways arranged ~ to the north of the city⟩ ⟨the ~ spread of the turkey gobbler's tail⟩

fanwork \ˈ=ˌ=\ *n* **:** FAN TRACERY

fanwort \ˈ=ˌ=\ *n* **:** a plant of the genus *Cabomba*; *esp* **:** WATER SHIELD

fany *usu cap, var of* FANNY

fan·zine \(ˈ)fanˌzēn\ *n* -s [⁶*fan* + *magazine*] **:** a periodical publication that is written and edited by science-fiction and fantasy enthusiasts and that is frequently prepared by mimeographing

faon \ˈfäⁿ\ *n* -s [F, fawn, fr. OF *faon, feon* young of an animal — more at FAWN] **:** FAWN 3

fap \ˈfap\ *adj* [origin unknown] *archaic* **:** INTOXICATED

FAP *abbr* first-aid post

fape \ˈfāp\ *n* -s [prob. by shortening & alter. fr. *feaberry*] *dial Brit* **:** GOOSEBERRY 1a

FAQ *abbr* **1** fair average quality **2** free at quay

fa·qih \fäˈkē\ *n, pl* **faqihs** \-ēz\ *or* **fu·qa·ha** \füˈkä,hä\ [Ar *faqīh* (pl. *fuqahā'*)] **:** a Muslim theologian versed in the religious law of Islam

faqir *or* **faquir** *var of* FAKIR

¹far \ˈfär, ˈfä(r\ *adv* **far·ther** \ˈfärt͟hər, ˈfät͟hə(r\ *or* **fur·ther** \ˈfərt͟hər, ˈfət͟hə(r, ˈfəithə(r, *in southern US often* ˈfət͟hə(r *or* ˈfət͟hər\ **far·thest** \-t͟həst\ *or* **fur·thest** \-t͟həst\ [ME *fer*, fr. OE *feorr*; akin to OHG *ferro* far, ON *fjarri*, Goth *fairra* far, OE *faran* to go — more at FARE] **1 a :** to a considerable distance in space **:** to a remote place ⟨wandered ~ from home⟩ ⟨the force of the gale was felt ~ inland⟩ **b :** at a considerable distance in space **:** at a remote place ⟨lived ~ up the mountain⟩ **2 :** at a considerable distance in time ⟨this was not ~ from the year 1115 —H.O.Taylor⟩ **3 a :** to a great extent **:** MUCH — often used with comparatives and superlatives ⟨the book is ~ richer than any of the others I have recommended —M.R.Ridley⟩ **b :** by a broad space **:** WIDELY ⟨the new site is never ~ distant from the old —C.D. Forde⟩ **c :** of a distinctly different quality or attitude — usu. used with *from* ⟨it is ~ from easy to say what makes a nominee . . . emerge as the successful candidate —H.J.Laski⟩ ⟨news reporters are ~ from blind —F.L.Mott⟩ **4 a :** to an advanced point or extent **:** a long way ⟨if the right peace officer is assigned to this contact work he can go ~ —Spencer Parratt⟩ ⟨went ~ toward determining the schedule and character of all his subsequent service —J.C.Archer⟩ ⟨drove the stake ~ into the ground⟩ **b :** to a late hour ⟨works or reads ~ into the night —Gertrude Samuels⟩ — **by far** *adv* **:** far and away — **how far :** to what extent, degree, or distance ⟨didn't know *how far* to trust him⟩ — **so far** *adv* **1 :** to a certain extent, degree, or distance ⟨when the water has risen *so far* the pumps will be brought into action⟩ **2 :** up to the present ⟨he has written only one novel *so far*⟩ — **thus far** *adv* **:** so far ⟨good luck *thus far* in fixing plumbing⟩

²far \"\ *adj* **farther** *or* **further; farthest** *or* **furthest** [ME *fer*, fr. OE *feorr*; akin to OFris *fir* far, OS *ferr*; derivative fr. the root of OE *feorr*, adv.] **1 a :** remote in space **:** DISTANT ⟨snow is shining on the ~ volcanoes —Muriel Rukeyser⟩ **b :** distinctly different in quality or relationship **c :** remote in time ⟨go back in the ~ past to a common origin —A.L. Kroeber⟩ **2 a :** of a considerable distance **:** LONG ⟨a ~ journey⟩ **b :** of notable extent **:** COMPREHENSIVE ⟨a man of ~ vision and deep convictions —*Catalog of Hollins Coll.*⟩ **3 :** the more distant of two ⟨on the near side was a tobacconist's and on the ~ a public house —F.W.Crofts⟩

³far \"\ *dial Brit var of* WHERE

far *abbr* **1** farad **2** farthing

far·ad \ˈfa,rad, -rəd\ *n* -s [after Michael *Faraday* †1867 Eng. physicist] **1 :** the practical mks unit of capacitance equal to the capacitance of a capacitor between whose plates there appears a potential of one volt when it is charged by one coulomb of electricity, the unit being taken as the standard in the U.S. **2 :** a unit of capacitance that is equal to .999505 farad and that was formerly taken as the standard in the U.S. — called also *international farad*

far·a·day \ˈfarə,dā *also* -ˌdē *or* -ˌdi\ *also* **faraday constant** *n* -s *sometimes cap F* [after Michael *Faraday*] **:** the quantity of electricity transferred in electrolysis per equivalent weight of any element or ion, being equal to about 96,500 coulombs per gram equivalent

faraday cage *n, usu cap F* **:** a grounded metallic screen completely surrounding a space to protect it from external electrostatic influence

faraday dark space *n, usu cap F* **:** a dark space of low light intensity between the positive column and the negative glow from the cathode in a vacuum tube

faraday disk *n, usu cap F* **:** a metal disk through which a current of electricity is passed and in which an induced current occurs as the disk rotates on a metal axis between the poles of a magnet

faraday effect *n, usu cap F* **:** the optical rotation produced in a beam of polarized light traversing certain isotropic media along the lines of force of a magnetic field

faraday shield *n, usu cap F* **:** a number of parallel wires arranged in one plane, connected at one end, and usu. grounded to provide electrostatic shielding

faraday's law *n, cap F* **:** either of two laws in physics: **a :** the mass of any substance deposited or dissolved by electrolysis is proportional to the product of the equivalent weight of the substance multiplied by the quantity of electricity passed during the reaction **b :** the electromotive force induced in a circuit by variation of the magnetic flux through the circuit is proportional to the negative of the time rate of change of the magnetic linkage

fa·rad·ic \fəˈradik, (ˈ)fa|ra-\ *also* **far·a·da·ic** \ˌfarəˈdāik\ *adj* [*faradic* fr. F *faradique*, fr. Michael *Faraday* + F *-ique* -ic; *faradaic* fr. Michael *Faraday* + E *-ic*] **:** of or relating to an asymmetric alternating current of electricity produced by an induction coil; *also* **:** produced by or using such a current — distinguished from *galvanic*

far·a·dism \ˈfarə,dizəm\ *also* **far·a·di·za·tion** \ˌfarədəˈzāshən, -,dīˈz-\ *n* -s [*faradism* fr. F *faradisme*, fr. Michael *Faraday* + F *-isme* -ism; *faradization* fr. F *faradisation*, fr. *faradiser* to faradize + *-ation*] **:** the application of a faradic current of electricity (as for therapeutic purposes)

far·a·dize \ˈfarə,dīz\ *vt* -ED/-ING/-S [F *faradiser*, fr. Michael *Faraday* + F *-iser* -ize] **:** to treat by faradism — **far·a·diz·er** \-zə(r)\ *n* -s

faradmeter \ˈ=(,)=,==\ *n* **:** an electrical instrument for measuring capacitances and usu. having a scale graduated in farads

farado- *comb form* [*faradic* + *-o-*] **:** resulting from or involving faradic stimulus ⟨*farado*contractility⟩ ⟨*farado*therapy⟩

fa·ran·cia \fəˈranch(ē)ə, -n(t)sēə\ *n, cap* [NL] **:** a genus of snakes (family Colubridae) including only the No. American hoop snake

far and away *adv* **:** by a considerable margin **:** DECIDEDLY ⟨*far and away* the best player on the team⟩

farandine *n* -s [F *ferrandine*, fr. *Ferrand*, 17th cent. Fr. inventor] *obs* **:** a fabric of silk mixed with wool or hair

far·and·man \ˈfarən(d)ˌman\ *n, pl* **farandmen** [ME (Sc), fr. ME (northern dial.) *farand* (pres. part. of ME *faren* to go, travel) + ME *man* — more at FARE] *Scot* **:** WAYFARER; *usu* **:** a traveling peddler or merchant

far and near *or* **far and wide** *adv* **:** on all sides **:** in every direction **:** EVERYWHERE ⟨searched for the child *far and near*⟩ ⟨the story spread *far and wide* —F.D.Ommanney⟩

far·an·dole \ˈfarən,dōl, ˌ==ˈ=\ *also* **fa·ran·do·la** \fəˈrandələ\ *n* -s [F *farandole*, fr. Prov *farandoulo*] **1 :** a lively Provençal chain dance in sextuple measure and serpentine path **2 :** the music for a farandole

fa·ra·on \ˌfä,räˈōn\ *n, pl* **faraon** \"\ *or* **fara·o·nes** \-ō,nās\ *usu cap* [AmerSp *faraón*, prob. fr. Sp, pharaoh, fr. LL *Pharaon-, Pharao* — more at PHARAOH] **:** MESCALERO

¹faraway \ˌ==ˈ=\ *adj* [*far away* (adverbial phrase), fr. ME *fer away*, fr. *fer* far (adv.) + *away* (adv.)] **1 a :** distant in space ⟨~ places⟩ **b :** remote in time ⟨the ~ future⟩ **c :** coming or seeming to come from a distance — used esp. of sounds ⟨the ~ tinkle of a cowbell⟩ **2 :** DREAMY, ABSTRACTED — used esp. of a look or the eyes ⟨a ~ expression⟩

²faraway \"\ *n* -s **1 :** something remote (as from physical or mental vision) **2 :** the unknown

far·away·ness *n* -ES **:** remoteness esp. from experience or comprehension ⟨~ from life —Dan Levin⟩

far back *adv* (*or adj*) **1 :** at a considerable distance to the rear ⟨from our *far-back* position⟩ ⟨we stood *far back*⟩ **2 :** in or into the remote past ⟨a *far-back* ancestor⟩ ⟨venturing *far back* we can perhaps explore the beginnings of reason⟩

far between *adj* **:** separated by considerable intervals ⟨good workhorses are few and *far between* these days⟩

¹farce \ˈfärs, ˈfäs\ *vt* -ED/-ING/-S [ME *farsen*, fr. MF *farcir*, fr. L *farcire* to stuff; akin to MIr *barc* attack, Gk *phrassein, phrattein* to enclose, fence in] **1** *obs* **a :** to stuff (as poultry) with forcemeat or other stuffing **b :** to stuff (as oneself) with food **:** GORGE **c :** to make full **:** CRAM, STUFF **2 a** *obs* **:** to fatten or enlarge by or as if by cramming **b :** to enlarge, amplify, or expand (as a literary work) by interpolation or addition often of witty material or quotations; *esp* **:** FARSE

²farce \"\ *n* -s [ME *farse*, fr. MF *farce*, fr. (assumed) VL *farsa*, fr. L, fem. of *farsus*, past part. of *farcire*] **1 :** FORCEMEAT; *broadly* **:** any savory stuffing (as for poultry or roasts) **2 a :** a light dramatic composition of satirical or humorous cast in which great latitude is allowed as to probability of happenings and naturalness of characters ⟨an amusing ~ based on confused relationships⟩ **b :** the class or form of drama made up of such compositions ⟨the place of ~ in the modern theater⟩ **3 a :** the element of broad humor that goes to make up theatrical farce **:** comic trait, feature, or characteristic **b :** a passage containing such comic element ⟨the father's speech is sheer ~⟩ **4 :** ridiculous or empty show ⟨the authorities have indulged in a ~ of stubborn resistance —Bosley Crowther⟩; *often* **:** something so much less than it could or should be as to constitute a mockery ⟨a procedure . . . that would have revived the ~ of the veto —A.P.Ryan⟩ ⟨observance and upholding of the law became a ~⟩

farce–comedy \ˈ=,===\ *n* **:** comedy of a marked farcical character

farc·er \ˈfärsər\ *n* -s [²*farce* + *-er*] **:** FARCEUR

far·ceur \(ˈ)fär|sər(·)\ *n* -s [F, fr. MF *farseur*, fr. *farser, farcer* to joke, fr. OF, fr. (assumed) OF *farce* theatrical farce (whence MF *farce*), fr. OF *farce* forcemeat — more at FARCE] **1 :** JOKER, WAG **2 :** a person skilled in farce, esp. in the writing or acting of a farce

far·ceuse \ˈfär|sərz, -|səz, -|süz, -|səz\ *n* -s [F, fem. of *farceur*] **:** a woman who is a farceur; *esp* **:** an actress skilled in playing farce

¹far·ci *or* **far·cie** \(ˈ)fär|sē\ *adj* [F *farci* (masc.), *farcie* (fem.), fr. *farci*, past part. of *farcir*] *of food* **:** stuffed esp. with forcemeat — usu. used postpositively ⟨oysters ~⟩

²farci \"\ *n* -ES **:** a stuffed dish (as a roast or fowl)

¹far·ci·cal \ˈfärsəkəl, ˈfäs-, -sēk-\ *adj* [²*farce* + *-ical*] **1 :** constituting or resembling farce in boisterous or nonsensical disregard of the serious or through extravagance or unnaturalness ⟨a wild ~ exuberance of the clownish and swinish side of man —W.L.Sullivan⟩ **2 :** receiving or meriting laughter or amused scorn as utterly without claim to serious consideration or as laughably inept ⟨am I such a ~ bungler . . . that I should erect an obvious dummy and expect that some of the sharpest men in Europe would be deceived? —A. Conan Doyle⟩ **syn** see LAUGHABLE

²farcical \"\ *adj* [*farcy* + *-ical*] **:** of, relating to, or affected with farcy

far·ci·cal·i·ty \ˌfärsəˈkaləd·ē, ˌfäs-, -lətē, -i\ *n* -ES **:** farcical quality

far·ci·cal·ly \ˈ=sək(ə)lē, -sēk-, -li\ *adv* **:** in a farcical manner

far·ci·cal·ness \-kəlnəs\ *n* -ES **:** the quality or state of being farcical

far·cied \ˈfärsēd\ *adj* **:** suffering from or affected with farcy ⟨a badly ~ horse⟩

farcin *obs var of* FARCY

far·cist \ˈfärsəst\ *n* -s **:** a maker of farces

far–come \ˈ=ˌ=\ *adj* **:** come from a distance

far corner *n* **:** a distant and usu. obscure place — used esp. in the phrase *far corners of the world*

farc·tate \ˈfärk,tāt\ *adj* [L *farctus* (past part. of *farcire* to stuff) + E *-ate*] *of the stipe of certain fungi* **:** having the center solid but softer in consistency than the peripheral layers

far·cy \ˈfärsē\ *n* -ES [ME *farsi, farsin*, fr. MF *farcin*, fr. LL *farcimen*, fr. L, sausage, fr. *farcire* to stuff — more at FARCE] **1 :** GLANDERS; *esp* **:** cutaneous glanders **2 :** a chronic ultimately fatal disease of cattle that is caused by an actinomycete (*Nocardia farcinica* or *Actinomyces farcinicus*), that is marked by indurative lymphadenitis and lymphangitis of the subcutaneous tissues leading to cold abscess formation, and that usu. terminates in pulmonary involvement — called also *bovine farcy, cattle farcy*

farcy bud *also* **farcy button** *n* **:** a swollen subcutaneous lymph gland characteristic of cutaneous glanders

farcy pipe *n* **:** a hard corded sometimes ulcerating subcutaneous lymphatic vessel characteristic of cutaneous glanders

¹fard \ˈfärd\ *vt* -ED/-ING/-S [ME *farden*, fr. MF *farder*, of Gmc origin; akin to OHG *faro* colored — more at PERCH (fish)] **1 :** to paint (the face) with cosmetics — now used only as a participial adjective ⟨thickly ~*ed* cheeks⟩ **2** *archaic* **:** to gloss over (as a fault)

²fard \"\ *n* -s [MF, fr. OF, fr. *farder*, v.] *archaic* **:** paint used on the face

³fard \" *or* **fardh** \"\ *n* -s [Ar *fard*] **:** a shiny dark brown date grown in eastern Arabia and in California

¹far·del \ˈfärdᵊl\ *n* -s [ME, fr. MF, fr. OF, fr. *farde* bundle, load, prob. fr. Ar *fardah* bundle, bale of goods] **1 a :** a bundle or parcel (as of raw silk) **b** *archaic* **:** BURDEN **2 :** a miscellaneous lot or collection **3** *dial* **:** OMASUM

²fardel *vt* **1** *obs* **:** to make up into a bundle **2** *obs* **:** FURL

³far·del \'färd°l\ *n* -s [ME (Sc), contr. of ME (northern dial.) *ferde del* fourth part, fr. ME (northern dial.) *ferde* fourth (fr. OE *fēartha, fēortha*) + ME *deel, del* part — more at FOURTH, DEAL] **1** *now dial* **:** a fourth part of something **:** QUARTER **2** *now dial* **:** a piece or fragment ⟨a ~ of bread⟩

fardel–bound \'=,=\ *adj* [¹*fardel* + *bound*] *dial, of cattle* **:** COSTIVE

far·den \'färd°n\ *dial Brit var of* FARTHING

farder *obs var of* FARTHER

fardest *obs var of* FARTHEST

far·din·gale \'färd°n,gāl, -diŋ,g-\ *archaic var of* FARTHINGALE

far·dle \'färd°l\ *archaic or dial var of* FARDEL

far–down \'=;=\ *or* **far–downer** \"+ə(r)\ *n* -s **:** a native of the north of Ireland — often used disparagingly

¹fare \'fa(a)|(ə)r, 'fe|, |ə\ *vi* -ED/-ING/-S [ME *faren*, fr. OE *faran;* akin to OHG *faran* to go, travel, ON *fara*, Goth *faran* to go, travel, L *per* through, *portare* to carry, Gk *peran* to pass through, *poros* ford, passage, path, *poreuein* to convey, Skt *piparti* he brings over] **1 :** to go or travel ⟨~ into the marshes . . . and shoot partridges —Kenneth Roberts⟩ ⟨*faring* on through the fading dusk⟩; *often* **:** to commence on a course or journey — usu. used with *forth* ⟨*fared* forth daily into the streets —C.G.Bowers⟩ ⟨*fared* forth regretfully from his childhood home⟩ **2 :** to get along **:** make out or turn out **:** SUCCEED, PROGRESS ⟨went to see how the lambs were *faring* on the upper pastures⟩ ⟨it is hard to guess how minorities will ~ at the hands of the new government⟩ ⟨a concise characterization usually ~*s* well at the hands of the critics⟩ ⟨the admiral *fared* no better than his predecessors⟩ **3 :** to consume food **:** EAT, DINE ⟨they *fared* very plainly, eating on a few cents a day to stretch their funds⟩ ⟨we all *fared* alike⟩ **4** *dial Eng* **:** APPEAR, SEEM ⟨how does he ~ to feel about it?⟩ ⟨they don't ~ to remember⟩

²fare \"\ *n* -s [ME, fr. OE *faru* & OE *fær;* OE *faru* akin to OFris *fere* journey, MHG *var* (fem.), ON *fōr;* OE *fær* akin to MHG *var* (neut.) shore, ferry, ON *far* ship, passage, track; derivatives fr. the root of OE *faran*] **1** *obs* **a :** a journey or expedition **:** GOING, PASSAGE **b :** PATH, TRACK, WAY **2 a :** the price charged to transport a person or persons usu. together with a limited amount of baggage or goods **b** *obs* **:** the price charged to transport goods from one place to another **c :** the passenger or passengers hiring a public vehicle ⟨he drove his ~ home⟩ **3** *archaic* **:** state of things **:** FORTUNE ⟨what ~? what news abroad —Shak.⟩ **4 a :** range or stock of food **:** DIET ⟨the ~ in this restaurant⟩ ⟨a rich and delicate ~⟩ **b :** material provided for use, consumption, or enjoyment — used esp. of entertainment media ⟨the current literary ~⟩ ⟨much of our everyday ~ is Bach —Marcia Davenport⟩ ⟨the reviewing of theater ~ —*Theatre Arts*⟩ **5 :** the catch taken by a fishing boat

³fare \"\ *n* -s [obs. *fare*, v., to farrow, alter. of *farrow*, v.] *dial Eng* **:** a litter of pigs

far eastern *adj, usu cap F&E* **:** of, relating to, or concerned with the countries of the Far East — used of (1) China, Japan, Korea, Manchuria, Mongolia, and eastern Siberia or (2) the Asian countries bordering on the Pacific ocean and including the Philippines and Indonesia or (3) the countries of eastern and southern Asia including those of the Indian subcontinent, Tibet, the Malay peninsula and archipelago, China, Japan, Korea, Manchuria, Mongolia, and eastern Siberia; compare MIDDLE EASTERN, NEAR EASTERN

far·er \'fa(a)rə(r), 'fer-\ *n* -s [ME *-farere* (in *weyfarere* wayfarer), fr. *faren* to go + *-er, -ere* -er] **:** TRAVELER — used esp. in combination ⟨*seafarer*⟩ ⟨*wayfarer*⟩

fare–thee–well *or* **fare–you–well** *also* **fare–ye–well** \¦=(,)=¦=\ *n* -s **1 :** a state of perfection and completion ⟨the cake was done to a *fare-thee-well*⟩ ⟨he took off his uncle's brusque mannerisms to a *fare-thee-well*⟩ **2 :** the utmost degree ⟨worked to a *fare-you-well*⟩ ⟨he drubbed the little pest to a *fare-ye-well*⟩

fareway *dial var of* FAIRWAY

¹farewell \(')=¦=\ *v imper* [ME *farewel, fare wel*, fr. *fare* (imper. of *faren* to go, get along, succeed) + *wel* well — more at FARE] **:** get along well — used interjectionally to or by one departing (as from a place, a group, or a way of life) and often separated by a pronoun ⟨*fare you well*⟩ ⟨~ old year, welcome new⟩

²farewell \"\ *n* -s [ME *farewel*, fr. *farewel*, v. imper.] **1 a :** a wish of happiness or welfare at parting **:** GOOD-BYE, ADIEU ⟨as soon as the visitors had made their ~*s* and left⟩ **2 a :** act of departure **:** LEAVE-TAKING ⟨his ~ to life⟩ ⟨before I take my ~ of the subject —Joseph Addison⟩ **b :** a formal event or ceremonial occasion for honoring a person about to withdraw from the public eye ⟨held a great ~ for the retiring senator⟩; *often* **:** a gala performance honoring a theatrical personality about to retire **3** *dial* **:** AFTERTASTE ⟨the coffee left a good ~ in his mouth⟩

³farewell \"\ *vb* -ED/-ING/-S [¹*farewell*] *vt* **:** to bid farewell ⟨~*ing* the parting guests⟩ ~ *vi* **:** to take one's leave **:** say farewell

⁴farewell \"\ *adj* [¹*farewell*] **:** PARTING, VALEDICTORY, FINAL ⟨a ~ concert⟩ ⟨one ~ gift⟩ ⟨made his ~ bow⟩

farewell–summer \,=,=¦=\ *n* **1 :** SOAPWORT **2 :** any of certain late-flowering asters; *esp* **:** HEATH ASTER

farewell–to–spring \(,)=,==¦=\ *n* **:** a summer-flowering annual herb (*Godetia amoena*) cultivated for its showy flowers

far–famed \'=¦=\ *adj* **:** widely and favorably known ⟨this *far-famed* hostelry —John Galsworthy⟩

far·fa·ra \'färfərə\ *n* -s [NL (specific epithet of the coltsfoot *Tussilago farfara*), fr. ML, coltsfoot, alter. of L *farferum, farfarum*] **:** the dried leaves of coltsfoot (sense a) used in folk medicine for coughs and as a tonic

far·fel \'färfəl\ *or* **fer·fel** \'fer-\ *n, pl* **farfel** *or* **ferfel** [Yiddish (pl.), fr. MHG *varveln* (pl.) noodles, noodle soup] **:** noodle dough in the form of small pellets or granules

farfet *adj* [ME *fer-fet*, fr. *fer* far + *fet*, past part. of *fetten* to fetch — more at FAR, FET] *obs* **:** FARFETCHED

¹farfetch *n* [back-formation fr. *farfetched*] *obs* **:** a deep or complicated and obscure stratagem

²farfetch \'=¦=\ *vb* [back-formation fr. *farfetched*] *vt* **:** to derive (as a word) in a farfetched manner ~ *vi* **:** to make farfetched derivations

farfetched \'=¦=\ *adj* [¹*far* + *fetched*, past part. of *fetch*] **1 a :** brought from a distance ⟨oranges and other ~ delicacies were rarities in those days⟩ **b** *obs* **:** from a remote time or place **2 :** not easily or naturally deduced or introduced **:** not based on probable or reasonable grounds or relationships **:** FORCED, STRAINED ⟨a ~ theme for a play⟩ ⟨such ~ ideas⟩ ⟨his stand seemed ~ and unreasonable⟩ — **far·fetched·ness** \-ch(t)nəs, -chədn-\ *n* -ES

far–flung \'=¦=\ *adj* **1 :** widely spread or distributed **:** having a wide range (as in space, time, or variation) **:** covering a large area ⟨the *far-flung* mountain ranges of the West⟩ ⟨*far-flung* trading operations⟩ ⟨the *far-flung* research fields of this foundation⟩ **2 :** distant from a point of reference ⟨this *far-flung* corner of the continent⟩ **:** REMOTE ⟨a *far-flung* tributary of the Nile⟩

far–forth \'=¦=\ *adv* [ME *ferforth*, fr. *fer* far + *forth*, adv. — more at FAR, FORTH] **:** to a great or definite distance, degree, or extent **:** FAR

fargoing \'=¦==\ *adj* **:** having extended influence **:** FAR-REACHING ⟨the ~ effects of this legislation⟩

¹far–gone \'=¦=\ *adj* **:** remote in some respect (as from a standard or a beginning) ⟨*far-gone* places⟩ **:** nearing an end ⟨sitting in the *far-gone* night over their rum⟩: as **a :** nearing complete exhaustion or death ⟨too *far-gone* to raise his head⟩ **b :** nearly worn out ⟨my shoes were *far-gone* but I patched the soles with cardboard each night⟩

²far–gone \"\ *adv, dial* **:** by far **:** UNQUESTIONABLY ⟨known to be *far-gone* the best hound —Vereen Bell⟩

fa·ri·na \fə'rēnə *also chiefly Brit* -rīnə\ *n* -s [L, meal, flour, fr. *far* spelt — more at BARLEY] **1 a :** a fine meal of vegetable matter (as cereal grains, nuts, or sea moss) used chiefly for puddings or as a breakfast cereal **b :** the coarsely ground bolted endosperm of wheats other than durum, free from fine flour and from bran **c** *chiefly Brit* **:** starch esp. from the potato **2 :** any of various powdery substances that suggest flour or meal: as **a :** the pollen of a plant — not now used technically **b** *archaic* **:** a pruinous coating on various plants and insects

far·i·na·ceous \¦farə¦nāshəs\ *adj* [L *farinaceus*, fr. *farina* + *-aceus* -aceous] **1 a** *archaic* **:** containing or made of meal or flour **b :** containing or rich in starch **:** STARCHY ⟨~ foods⟩ ⟨a ~ diet lacking in animal protein⟩ **2 :** having a powdery surface that appears to be covered with meal — used esp. of plant and insect parts ⟨elytra ~⟩ **3 :** like meal in texture or quality ⟨a ~ surface⟩; *also* **:** having an odor like that of freshly ground wheat — **far·i·na·ceous·ly** *adv*

farinaceous ipecacuanha *n* **:** the emetic root of the Mexican clover (*Richardia scabra*)

fa·rine \fə'rēn\ *n* -s [modif. of Pg *farinha*] **:** FARINA 1a; *esp* **:** edible meal made from cassava root

faring *n* -s [fr. gerund of ¹*fare*] *dial Eng* **:** ²FARE 4a

fa·ri·nha \fə'rēnyə\ *n* -s [Pg, cassava meal, meal, flour, fr. L *farina* meal, flour] **:** cassava meal

fa·ri·no·gram \fə'rēnə,gram\ *n* [ISV *farino-* (fr. L *farina*) + *-gram*] **:** a graphic record of the quality of a dough by means of a farinograph

fa·ri·no·graph \-af,-àf\ *n* [ISV *farino-* (fr. L *farina*) + *-graph*] **:** a recording dough mixer designed to measure qualitatively and record automatically the dough-forming properties of different wheats under controlled conditions of temperature — **fa·ri·no·graph·ic** \¦=¦==¦grafik\ *adj* — **far·i·nog·ra·phy** \,farə'nägrəfē\ *n* -ES

far·i·no·sae \,farə'nō(,)sē\ [NL, fr. LL, fem. pl. of *farinosus* mealy] *syn of* XYRIDALES

far·i·nose \'farə,nōs\ *adj* [LL *farinosus* mealy, fr. L *farina* + *-osus* -ose] **1 a :** yielding farina ⟨~ roots⟩ **b :** like farina esp. in texture **2 :** covered with a whitish mealy powder ⟨~ leaves⟩ ⟨the ~ bodies of certain insects⟩ **:** MEALY, FARINACEOUS — **far·i·nose·ly** *adv*

far·ish \'färish\ *adj* [²*far* + *-ish*] *dial* **:** somewhat far (as in age or drunkenness) — used with *on* ⟨he's ~ on for so early in the evening⟩

far·kle·ber·ry \'färkəl- — *see* BERRY\ *n* [prob. alter. of *whortleberry*] **:** a shrub or small tree (*Vaccinium arboreum*) of the southeastern U.S. having coriaceous often evergreen leaves and a black dry berry with hard stony seeds — called also *sparkleberry*

farl *or* **farle** \'färl\ *n* -s [contr. of ³*fardel*] **1** *Scot* **a :** a wedge of oatcake **b :** the fourth part of a bannock **2** *Scot* **:** a small scone

far·leu \'fär(,)lü\ *or* **far·ley** \-rlē\ *n* -s [origin unknown] **:** money or chattels given by a feudal tenant to his lord in lieu of a heriot

far·ley maidenhair \'färlē-\ *n, usu cap F* [*Farley* Hill, country house in Barbados where it was discovered] **:** a brittle maidenhair of a widely cultivated variety (*Adiantum tenerum farleyense*)

¹farm \'färm, 'fàm\ *vt* -ED/-ING/-S [ME *fermen*, fr. OE *feormian* to cleanse; akin to OHG *āfermī* filth] *dial Eng* **:** CLEANSE, EMPTY

²farm \"\ *n* -s *often attrib* [ME *ferme* rent, lease, fr. OF, lease, fr. *fermer* to make a contract, fix, fasten, fr. L *firmare* to make firm, fr. *firmus* firm — more at FIRM] **1** *obs* **:** a sum or due fixed in amount and payable at fixed intervals (as by way of rent or tax) **2 a :** a fixed sum payable at set intervals (as yearly) by a person in lieu of taxes or other dues that he has authority to collect **b :** a sum assessed upon a municipality or place as the amount to be paid from taxes to be collected within its limits **c :** a letting out of revenues or taxes for a fixed sum to one authorized to collect and retain them **d :** the farmers of public revenues **3 a :** the condition of being let out at a fixed rent **b** *obs* **:** LEASE **4 :** a district or division of a country leased out for the collection of the revenues of government **5 a :** a piece of land held under lease for cultivation **b :** any tract of land whether consisting of one or more parcels devoted to agricultural purposes generally under the management of a tenant or the owner **:** any parcel or group of parcels of land cultivated as a unit **6 a :** a plot of land devoted to the raising of domestic or other animals ⟨a chicken ~⟩ ⟨a fox ~⟩ **b :** a tract of water reserved for the artificial cultivation of some aquatic life-form ⟨an oyster ~⟩ **c :** TREE FARM **7 :** FARMHOUSE — obs. except in proper names **8 a :** FARMER 5 — used with *the* **b :** the pool in the game of farmer **9 :** a minor-league baseball club associated with a major-league club as a subsidiary to which recruits are assigned until needed or for further training **10 :** a rurally located rest home for alcoholics or other psychiatric patients

³farm \"\ *vb* -ED/-ING/-S [ME *fermen*, fr. *ferme*, n.] *vt* **1** *obs* **:** RENT **2 :** to collect and take the fees or profits of (an occupation or business) on payment of a fixed sum **3 :** to give up (as an estate, a business, or the revenue) to another on condition of receiving in return a fixed sum **4 :** to contract for the maintenance and care of (a person or thing) at a fixed price ⟨the town ~*s* its paupers⟩ — see FARM OUT **5 a :** to devote (land) to agriculture ⟨they decided to clear and ~ the north forty⟩ **b :** to manage and cultivate (land) as a farm ⟨he ~*ed* a small holding beside the river⟩ ~ *vi* **:** to engage in the business of raising crops or livestock ⟨he ~*ed* for nearly 50 years⟩ **:** manage or conduct a farm **:** work as a farmer

farm belt *n, sometimes cap F&B* **:** an area (as of the north central U.S.) devoted to large-scale commercial farming

farm bloc *n* **:** a combination of members of the U. S. Congress that transcends party lines in order to support the special interests of agriculture

farm·er \-mə(r)\ *n* -s [ME *fermour, fermer*, fr. MF *fermer, fermier* lessee, renter, fr. OF, fr. *ferme* lease + *-ier* -er — more at FARM] **1 :** a person who pays a fixed sum for some privilege or source of income: as **a :** one that obtains the right to collect taxes, customs, excises, or other duties, paying a fixed sum and retaining the moneys collected **b** *obs* **:** a lessee or renter **c :** the lessee of a government monopoly **2 :** a person who cultivates land or crops or raises livestock: as **a :** one that as steward, bailiff, or agent cultivates or supervises the cultivation of the lands of another **b :** one that rents or leases land for cultivation **:** TENANT FARMER **c :** a person whose primary occupation is the raising of crops or livestock — see GENTLEMAN FARMER; compare RANCHER **d :** a person engaged in a particular kind of farming ⟨fruit ~*s*⟩ ⟨a leading dairy ~⟩ **3 :** a person that agrees to perform certain duties for a fixed sum; *specif* **:** one that agrees to keep babies or paupers for a fixed sum per head **4 a :** an ignorant rustic **:** YOKEL, BUMPKIN **b :** a clumsy stupid fellow **:** DOLT **c** *slang* **:** a green hand inexperienced or incompetent in the trade at which he is working **5 :** a variation of twenty-one in which the object is to draw cards totaling sixteen in value; *also* **:** the dealer in this game

farmer cheese *n* **:** a pressed cheese of whole milk or partly skimmed milk made on farms

farm·er·ess \-mərəs\ *n* -ES **1** *archaic* **:** a female farmer **2** *archaic* **:** a farmer's wife

farm·er·ette \¦=mə¦ret\ *n* -s **:** a woman or girl who farms or works on a farm; *esp* **:** one that does farm labor as a civic duty during emergencies

farmer–general \¦==¦=(=)=\ *n, pl* **farmers–general** [trans. of F *fermier général*] **:** one of the men who farmed certain taxes in France from 1697 to 1789

farmer in the dell : a ring game in which one player chosen as the farmer occupies the center of the ring, others being called to join him as wife, child, nurse, cat, rat, and cheese and then sent away in reverse order while the players remaining in the ring circle about the farmer singing appropriate verses

farmer–laborite \,==¦==,=\ *n* -s *usu cap F&L* **:** a member of the Farmer-Labor party which is a minor political party in the U.S.

farm·er·ly \'färmərlē, 'fàməlē, -li\ *adj* **:** befitting or suggesting a farmer ⟨a tall ~ fellow —Lewis Nordyke⟩

farmer's lung *n, chiefly Brit* **:** an acute pulmonary disorder that is characterized by sudden onset, fever, cough, expectoration, and breathlessness and that results from the inhalation of dust from moldy hay or straw

farmers' mutual *n* **:** a mutual insurance company organized for the purpose of insuring farmers and farm property exclusively

far·mer's reducer \'färmərz-, 'fàməz-\ *n, usu cap F* [after E. Howard *Farmer* †1944 Eng. photographic technician who originated it] **:** a 20 to 25 percent solution of hypo to which a few drops of a 10 percent solution of potassium ferricyanide are added and which is used for reducing the image density and fog density of photographic negatives and prints

farmer's satin *n* **:** a lustrous durable fabric in satin weave with a cotton warp and a worsted or cotton filling used esp. for linings and dresses

farm·ery \'färmərē\ *n* -ES [²*farm* + *-ery*] *chiefly Brit* **:** the buildings and yards of a farm **:** FARMSTEAD

farmhand \'=,=\ *n* **1 :** a farm laborer; *esp* **:** a hired laborer on a farm **2 :** a baseball player assigned to a farm team

farmhold \'=,=\ *or* **farmholding** \'=,==\ *n* -s [*farmhold* fr. ME *fermehold*, fr. *ferme* rent, lease + *hold* land that is held; *farmholding* fr. ²*farm* + *holding*, n. — more at FARMS, HOLD] *archaic* **:** a tract of land cultivated as a farm

farmhouse \'=,=\ *n* **1 :** the dwelling on a farm as distinguished from utility buildings (as a barn, corncrib, milk house) ⟨took the milk from the cow shed up to the ~⟩ **2 :** the dwelling and adjacent buildings (as a barn) on a farm

farming *n* -s [fr. gerund of ³*farm*] **:** the practice of agriculture

farm labor camp *n* **:** any of certain residential facilities provided chiefly by government agencies for migratory or seasonal farm labor

farmland \'=,land\ *n* **:** land used or suitable for farming ⟨the decreasing supply of good ~⟩

farm loan bond *n* **:** a bond issued by a U.S. Federal Land bank and secured by a first mortgage on farmland

farm management *n* **:** the phase of agricultural economics dealing with the management of a farm

farmost \'=,=\ *adj* **:** FARTHEST

farm out *vt* **1 :** to turn over for performance (as a job or part of an operation) or for use (as a property or privilege) usu. on contract or for some agreed payment to one not usu. responsible for such performance or entitled to such use ⟨it is often desirable to *farm out* highly specialized operations⟩ ⟨the candidate was willing to *farm out* a few votes to check the rise of the new party⟩ **2 a :** to put (as children or prisoners) into the hands of a private individual for care in return for a fee ⟨*farmed out* the baby with her grandmother and went to work in town⟩ ⟨state wards are often *farmed out* to private families⟩ **b :** to send (a professional athlete) to a farm team **3 a :** to exhaust (land) by farming, esp. by continued cropping under a monoculture system ⟨much of the foothills has been *farmed out* with tobacco⟩ **b :** to drill (oil wells) on a piece of ground to the extent permitted by law, the terms of a lease, or circumstances

farmout \'=,=\ *n* -s [*farm out*] **:** a sublease granted by an oil company to another for drilling on partially proven ground

farmplace \'=,=\ *n* **:** a farmhouse or farmstead

farms *pres 3d sing of* FARM, *pl of* FARM

farmstead \'=,=\ *also* **farmsteading** \'=,==\ *n* -s **1 :** the buildings and adjacent service areas of a farm; *broadly* **:** a farm with its buildings **2 :** a farmhouse or a rural or suburban residence designed to suggest a farmhouse

farm system *n* **:** the several minor-league baseball clubs subsidiary to a single major-league club; *also* **:** the practice of having such subsidiary clubs

farmwife \'=,=\ *n, pl* **farmwives :** the mistress of a farm; *esp* **:** a farmer's wife

farmyard \'=,=\ *n* **:** space immediately adjoining and often more or less enclosed by the buildings making up a farmstead; *esp* **:** BARNYARD

far·ne·sol \'färnə,sōl, -,zl, |ōl\ *n* -s [ISV *farnes-* (fr. NL *farnesiana* — specific epithet of the huisache *Acacia farnesiana* —, after Odoardo *Farnese fl* 1600 Ital. cardinal) + *-ol;* orig. formed in G] **:** a liquid alcohol $C_{15}H_{25}OH$ that has a floral odor, occurs in various essential oils (as neroli oil, citronella oil, and oil of amber seed), and is used in perfumes

far·ness *n* -ES [ME *fernesse*, fr. *fer* far + *-nesse* -ness — more at FAR] **1 :** the quality or state of being far off **:** remote state or situation ⟨the ~ of her house from the station⟩ **2** *archaic* **:** distant parts or regions ⟨from the ~ of the stars⟩

faro \'fa(a)|(,)rō, 'fe|\ *n* -s [prob. alter. of *pharaoh*] **:** a banking game in which players place bets on a special layout as to which cards will be winners or losers as they are drawn one at a time from a dealing box, each two cards drawn constituting a turn after which bets are settled

faro bank *n* **1 :** an establishment where faro is played **2 :** FARO

faro banker *n* **:** the proprietor or conductor of a faro bank

faroese *cap, var of* FAEROESE

far·oe step \'fa(a)|(,)rō, 'fe|\ *n, usu cap F* [*Faroe* islands (Faeroes), islands in the north Atlantic comprising a county of Denmark] **:** a dance step similar to the branle used in sung rounds of the Faroe islands

far–off \'=¦=\ *adj* [*far off* (adverbial phrase), fr. ME *fer of*, fr. *fer* far (adv.) + *of* off (adv.) — more at FAR, OFF] **1 :** remote in time or space **:** DISTANT ⟨*far-off* happier times⟩ ⟨rumblings of *far-off* thunder⟩ **2 :** directed toward the distance **:** ABSTRACTED ⟨*far-off* wandering thoughts⟩

fa·rol \fə'rōl, -rōl\ *n, pl* **farols** \-lz\ *or* **fa·ro·les** \-,lās\ [Sp, lit., lantern, prob. modif. of Catal *faró*, fr. Gk *pharos* lighthouse — more at PHAROS] **:** a pase in bullfighting in which the matador swirls the cape back over his head, drawing the bull closely around

fa·rouche \fə'rüsh\ *adj* [F, shy, unwilling to make friends, wild, fr. OF *farouche, forasche*, fr. LL *forasticus* having come from elsewhere, fr. L *foras* out of doors, out; akin to L *foris, fores* door — more at DOOR] **:** lacking social graces and experience **:** marked by shyness and lack of polish ⟨their manners . . . were ~ beyond reason —Rose Macaulay⟩; *sometimes* **:** wild or disorderly ⟨an extremely ~ bohemian household⟩ — **fa·rouche·ness** *n* -ES

far point *n* **:** the point farthest from the eye at which an object is accurately focused on the retina when the accommodation is completely relaxed, being theoretically equatable with infinity or, for practical purposes in respect to the normal eye, with any distance greater than 6 meters or 20 feet — compare NEAR POINT; see RANGE OF ACCOMMODATION

far·rag·i·nous \fə'rajənəs\ *adj* [L *farragin-, farrago* + E *-ous*] **:** formed of various materials in no fixed order or arrangement ⟨the report is a ~ mass of disordered detail⟩ **:** forming a disordered whole ⟨a ~ body of complex ceremonial⟩

far·ra·go \fə'rä(,)gō, -rā(-, -ra(-\ *n* -ES [L *farragin-, farrago* mixed fodder for cattle, mash, mixture, fr. *far* spelt — more at BARLEY] **1 :** MIXTURE, MEDLEY ⟨a ~ of protein, fiber, and mineral salts —*New Yorker*⟩ **2 a :** a confused, disordered, or irrational assemblage (as of words or ideas) ⟨his ~ of facts would need sifting —O.W.Holmes †1935⟩ ⟨arranged as 'South is London of Brighton' they make a ~ which is neither true nor false, but nonsense —Gilbert Ryle⟩ **b :** a presentation (as of mingled fact and fancy) designed to deceive ⟨a ~ of half-truths intended to put the party line in the best light⟩ ⟨tricked many shrewd men with her wistful ~*es* of the helpless orphan girl⟩

far·rand \'farənd\ *or* **far·rant** \-nt\ *adj* [ME *farand, farende*, pres. part. of *faren* to go, get along, turn out — more at FARE] *chiefly Scot* **:** having a specified appearance or disposition ⟨he was ill, ~, and revengeful⟩ — **far·rand·ly** *or* **far·rant·ly** *adv*

farrash *var of* FERASH

farre *archaic var of* FAR

far–reaching \'=¦==\ *adj* **:** having a wide range or scope **:** having an influence or effect that reaches far in space, time, or relationships ⟨a *far-reaching* reform⟩ ⟨*far-reaching* forests⟩ ⟨*far-reaching* influence⟩ — **far–reach·ing·ly** *adv*

far·ri·er \'farēə(r)\ *n* -s [prob. alter. (influenced by *-er, -ier, -yer*, n. suffix) of obs. *ferrer*, fr. ME *ferrour* blacksmith who shoes horses, veterinarian, fr. MF, blacksmith who shoes horses, fr. OF *ferreor*, fr. *ferrer* to fit with iron, fr. (assumed) VL *ferrare*, fr. L *ferrum* iron, prob. of southwest Asiatic origin; akin to the source of Heb & Phoenician *barzel* iron, Syr *parzlā*, Akkadian *parzillu*] **1** *chiefly Brit* **:** one that attends a sick horse; *broadly* **:** a veterinarian esp. when practicing without full qualification **2** *chiefly Brit* **:** BLACKSMITH 1b **3 :** a noncommissioned officer in a cavalry regiment who has charge of the horses or their shoeing

farrier's hammer *n* **:** a hammer with a curved head having a flat poll at one end and a plain claw at the other

far·ri·er's knife *n* **:** a knife with curved blade and handle that has a square-cut hook on the end of the blade and is used for trimming hooves during shoeing (as of horses)

far·ri·ery \-ēərē\ *n* -ES [*farrier* + *-y*] **:** the art or practice of a farrier

¹far·row \ˈfa(ˌ)rō, -rə *also* ˈfe(-, *often* -rəw+V\ *vb* -ED/-ING/-S [ME *farwen*, fr. (assumed) OE *feargian*, fr. OE *fearh* young pig; akin to OHG *farah* young pig, L *porcus* domestic pig, Lith *paršas* barrow] *vt* **:** to give birth to (a farrow) ~ *vi, of swine* **:** to bring forth young — often used with *down* ⟨planned to have the gilts ~ down about the end of March⟩

²farrow \ˈ"\ *n* -S **1 :** a litter of pigs **2 :** an act of farrowing

³farrow \ˈ"\ *adj* [ME (Sc) *ferow, ferrow*, prob. fr. (assumed) MD (Flemish dial.) *verwe-, varwe-* (whence Flem *verwe-, varwe-* in *verwekoe, varwekoe* cow that has ceased bearing); prob. akin to OE *fearr* bull, ox — more at PARE] *of a cow* **:** not in calf **:** not settled

far·ru·ca \fəˈrükə\ *n* -S [Sp, fr. fem. of *farruco* Galician or Asturian outside of his native region, fr. *Farruco*, nickname of *Francisco* Francis] **:** a Spanish gypsy dance having sudden changes of mood and tempo

far·sakh \ˈfärˌsak\ *or* **far·sagh** \-ag\ *also* **far·sang** \-aŋ\ *n, pl* **farsakh** [Ar & Per; Ar *farsakh*, fr. Per *farsang*] **:** a Persian unit of distance equal to about 4 miles; *also* **:** a Persian metric unit equal to 10 kilometers or 6.21 miles

¹farse *obs var of* FARCE

²farse \ˈfärs\ *n* -S [ML *farsa*, fr. (assumed) VL *farsa* forcemeat — more at FARCE] **:** an interpolation (as an explanatory phrase) inserted in a liturgical formula; *usu* **:** an addition or paraphrase, often in the vulgar language, formerly permitted in the sung portions of the Mass

³farse \ˈ"\ *vt* -ED/-ING/-S **:** to amplify (a liturgical formula) by interpolation **:** insert a farse in; *also* **:** to interpolate (a farse)

farseeing \ˈ=ˈ==\ *adj* **1 :** able to see to a great distance **:** FARSIGHTED **2 :** having foresight

far·si \ˈfär(ˌ)sē\ *n, pl* **farsi** *or* **farsis** *cap* [Per *fārsī*, fr. *Fārs* Persia] **:** a native or inhabitant of Fars, Iran

far side *n* **:** the farther side — **on the far side of :** BEYOND ⟨just *on the far side of* middle age⟩

far–sight \ˈ=ˌ=\ *n* **:** ability to see far

farsighted \ˈ=ˈ==\ *adj* **1 a :** seeing or able to see to a great distance **b :** having foresight **:** able to anticipate and plan for the future; *broadly* **:** having good judgment **:** SAGACIOUS ⟨a state under the leadership of ~ men⟩ **2 :** HYPEROPIC — **far·sight·ed·ly** *adv*

far·sight·ed·ness *n* -ES **1 :** the quality or state of being farsighted **2 :** HYPEROPIA

¹fart \ˈfär|t, ˈfȧ|, *usu* |d·+V\ *vi* -ED/-ING/-S [ME *ferten, farten;* akin to OHG *ferzan* to break wind, ON *freta*, Gk *perdesthai*, Skt *pardate* he breaks wind] **:** to expel intestinal gas from the anus **:** break wind — usu. considered vulgar

²fart \ˈ"\ *n* -S [ME *fert, fart*, fr. *ferten, farten*; v.] **:** an expulsion of intestinal gas — sometimes used of a person as a generalized term of abuse; usu. considered vulgar

¹far·ther \ˈfärthər, ˈfȧthə(r\ *adv* [ME *ferther*, alter. (influenced by *ferre* — compar. of *fer*, adv., far —, fr. OE *fierr, fyrr*, compar. of *feorr*, adv., far) of *further* — more at FURTHER (adv.), FAR] **1 a :** to a greater distance in space **:** to a more remote place ⟨drive ~ north⟩ ⟨swallows . . . are gathering to fly ~ away —Padraic Colum⟩ **b :** at a greater distance in space **:** at a more remote place ⟨~ down the corridor —Willa Cather⟩ **c :** at a greater distance in time ⟨it may go back still ~ to racial Druid memories —Marjorie K. Rawlings⟩ **d :** more divergent ⟨nothing had been ~ from his thoughts —C.S. Forester⟩ **2 :** to or at a more advanced point **:** beyond a given limit ⟨if he could go a little ~ . . . he might become a very fine poet —C.P.Aiken⟩ **3 :** ¹FURTHER 3 **4 :** to a greater degree or extent ⟨we do not extend the one-man idea any ~ than we have to —G.F.Eliot⟩

²farther \ˈ"\ *adj* [ME *ferther*, fr. *ferther*, adv.] **1 a :** more distant in space **:** REMOTER ⟨the ~ side of town⟩ ⟨flood the ~ parts of your fields —Oliver La Farge⟩ **b :** more divergent in character or relationship ⟨the ~ the machines get from immediate and practical application —Robert Bendiner⟩ **c :** more remote in time ⟨a memory of a ~ childhood —*Yale Rev.*⟩ **2 :** ²FURTHER 2 **3 :** the more distant of two ⟨the ~ side —C.E.Craddock⟩ ⟨her glance fixed itself . . . upon the ~ room —Virginia Woolf⟩

³farther \ˈ"\ *vt* -ED/-ING/-S [ME *fertheren*, fr. *ferther*, adv. & adj.] **:** FURTHER

far·ther·most \ˈ==ˌmōst *also chiefly Brit* -ˌməst\ *adj* **:** most remote **:** FARTHEST

¹far·thest \ˈfärthəst, ˈfȧth-\ *adj* [ME *ferthest*, fr. *ferther*, after comparatives and superlatives in ME *-er*: *-est* — more at -ER, -EST] **1 a :** most distant in space **:** REMOTEST ⟨the rage for these authors had traveled to the ~ frontier —Van Wyck Brooks⟩ ⟨to their ~ caverns sent —Matthew Arnold⟩ **b :** most remote in time **:** LATEST ⟨a few months or a year at ~ —Mary S. Watts⟩ **2 :** most advanced **:** ULTIMATE ⟨girls in beach pajamas already making the ~ use of their smiles —Hortense Calisher⟩

²farthest \ˈ"\ *adv* [ME *ferthest*, fr. *ferthest*, adj.] **1 a :** to or at the greatest distance in space **:** REMOTEST ⟨see who could jump the ~⟩ ⟨chose the seat ~ from the door⟩ **b :** at the greatest distance in time ⟨~ reach of memory⟩ **c :** of the most divergent quality ⟨~ thing from the ordinary —*New Republic*⟩ **2 :** to the most advanced point ⟨goes ~ toward giving us sculpture —G.L.K.Morris⟩ **3 :** by the greatest degree or extent **:** MOST ⟨the essay ~ removed from this reviewer's comprehension —*Saturday Rev.*⟩

far·thing \ˈfärthiŋ, ˈfȧth, -theŋ\ *n* -S [ME *ferthing*, fr. OE *fēorthung*; akin to OFris *fiardunge, fiardeng* one fourth of a mark, MHG *vierdunc, vierdinc* fourth part, ON *fjōrthungr*; derivative fr. the root of OE *fēortha* fourth — more at FOURTH (adj.)] **1 a :** a British unit of value equal to ¼ of a penny **b :** a coin orig. of silver, later of copper, and after 1860 of bronze representing this unit **2 a :** an ancient English gold coin worth ¼ noble **b :** a somewhat later coin worth ¼ of a ryal **3 :** any very small Roman bronze coin (as a quadrans) **4 a** *obs* **:** a very small quantity **b :** something of small value **:** MITE ⟨I don't care a ~⟩ **5** *obs* **:** any of various measures or quantities of land (as a quarter of an acre or of a virgate)

far·thin·gale \ˈfärthənˌgāl, -thiŋ,g-\ *n* -S [modif. of MF *verdugale*, modif. of OSp *verdugado*, fr. *verdugo* young shoot of a tree, fr. *verde* green, fr. L *viridis* — more at VERDANT] **:** a support (as of hoops or a padded roll) worn esp. in the 16th century beneath a skirt to swell out and extend it at the hip line

farthingale

farthingale chair *n, often cap F* **:** a broad-seated chair without arms, current in England during the reigns of Elizabeth I and James I

far·thing·deal \ˈfärthinˌdēl\ *n* [by folk etymology (influence of *farthing*) fr. earlier *farthendele*, fr. ME *ferthendel*, fr. OE *fēorthandǣl* fourth part, fr. *fēorthan* (accus. of *fēortha* fourth) + *dǣl* part — more at FOURTH, DEAL] *archaic* **:** one fourth acre **:** ROOD

far·thing·land \-ˌland\ *n, archaic* **:** a farthingdeal or other measure of land

farting *pres part of* FART

far to seek : hard to find **:** RARE ⟨a really conscientious man is *far to seek*⟩ — usu. used negatively ⟨the causes of this oversight were not *far to seek*⟩

far–traveled \ˈ=ˈ==\ *adj* **:** having traveled far esp. to varied and widely separated places

farts *pres 3d sing of* FART, *pl of* FART

far–western \(ˈ)=ˈ==\ *adj* **:** of, relating to, or situated in the part of the U.S. west of the Mississippi river or esp. west of the Great Plains

fas *or* **fa's** *pl of* FA

FAS *abbr* **1** firsts and seconds **2** free alongside ship

fasc *abbr* fascicle

fas·ces \ˈfaˌsēz\ *n pl but often sing in constr* [L, fr. pl. of *fascis* bundle; akin to L *fascia* band] **1 :** a bundle of rods having among them an ax with the blade projecting, borne before Roman magistrates as a badge of authority in ancient Rome **2 :** the authority symbolized by the fasces

fas·cet \ˈfasət\ *n* -S [origin unknown] **:** a tool (as a rod or wire basket) used in glass manufacturing to carry bottles to the annealing furnace

fasces

fasci *pl of* FASCIO

fas·cia *or* **fa·cia** \ˈfash(ē)ə, ˈfāsh-, *in sense 1c usu* ˈfāsh-\ *n, pl* **fasci·ae** \-shēˌē\ *or* **fascias** *or* **facias** \-sh(ē)əz\ [It *fascia* band, bandage, architectural fascia, fr. L, band, bandage; akin to MIr *basc* necklace] **1 a :** a flat horizontal member of an order or building having the form of a flat band or broad fillet; *esp, in the Ionic order* **:** one of the three bands which make up the architrave — see MOLDING illustration **b** *usu facia* **:** a plate or tablet over the front of a shop (as one bearing the name or business of the owner) **c** *usu facia, also* **facia board** *or* **fascia board** *Brit* **:** the dashboard of an automobile **2** *usu facia* [L] **:** a band, sash, or fillet (as on a garment) **3** *usu fascia* [NL, fr. L] **:** a broad and well-defined band of color (as on the wing of an insect) **4** *usu fascia* [NL, fr. L] **:** a sheet or layer of more or less condensed connective tissue covering, ensheathing, supporting, or binding together internal parts or structures of the body and being continuous with the other connective-tissue structures (as the ligaments, periosteum, or tendons); *also* **:** tissue of this character — see APONEUROSIS, DEEP FASCIA, SUPERFICIAL FASCIA

fascia board *n* **:** a horizontal board fascia covering the joint between the top of a wall and the projecting eaves

fas·cial \ˈfash(ē)əl\ *adj* [NL *fascialis*, fr. *fascia* + L *-alis* -al] **:** of or relating to a fascia ⟨~ planes of the neck⟩ **:** taking place through a fascia ⟨a ~ hernia⟩

fascia la·ta \ˌ=(=)=ˈläd·ə, -ād·ə\ *n, pl* **fasciae la·tae** \ˌ==,=-ˈläd·ˌē, -ˈlād·ˌē\ [NL, wide fascia] **:** the deep fascia that forms a complete sheath for the thigh and presents in front, just below Poupart's ligament, the saphenous opening

fas·ci·ate \ˈfashēˌāt, -ēət\ , *or* **fas·ci·at·ed** \-ˌād·əd\ *adj* [*fasciate* prob. fr. (assumed) NL *fasciatus*, fr. NL *fascia* + L *-atus* -ate; *fasciated* prob. fr. (assumed) NL *fasciatus* + E *-ed*] **1 :** banded or striped; *esp* **:** broadly banded with color **2 a :** FASCICLED **b :** exhibiting fasciation

fas·ci·a·tion \ˌ==ˈāshən\ *n* -S [prob. fr. (assumed) NL *fasciation-, fasciatio*, fr. (assumed) NL *fasciatus* + L *-ion-, -io* -ion] **:** malformation (as in stems of plants) resulting from more or less disorganized tissue growth commonly manifested as enlargement and flattening and sometimes spiral curving as if several stems were fused and often accompanied by an abnormal number and arrangement of floral organs

fas·ci·cle \ˈfasəkəl\ *n* -S [L *fasciculus* small bundle, dim of *fascis* bundle — more at FASCES] **1 :** a small bundle or collection **:** a compact cluster: as **a :** an inflorescence consisting of a compacted cyme that is less capitate than a glomerule; *broadly* **:** any compact cluster of similar plant parts ⟨a ~ of larch needles⟩ **b :** BUNDLE 1d **c :** FASCICULUS 1 **2 :** one of the divisions of a book published in parts — called also *fascicule*

fas·ci·cled \-kəld\ *adj* **:** arranged in fascicles ⟨~ leaves of the larch⟩

fas·cic·u·lar \fəˈsikyələ(r), faˈ-\ *adj* [fr. *fascicle*, after such pairs as E *auricle*: *auricular*] **:** of or belonging to a fascicle **:** made up of fasciculi ⟨~ plant tissues⟩ **:** FASCICLED; *specif* **:** relating to or consisting of bundles of acicular crystals in a rock — **fas·cic·u·lar·ly** *adv*

fascicular cambium *n* **:** cambium within the vascular bundle — compare INTERFASCICULAR CAMBIUM

fascicular tissue *n* **:** VASCULAR TISSUE

fas·cic·u·late \fəˈsikyələt, -ˌlāt, faˈ-\ *or* **fas·cic·u·lat·ed** \-ˌlād·əd\ *adj* [*fasciculate* fr. LL *fasciculatus*, past part. of *fasciculare* to bundle, fr. L *fasciculus* small bundle; *fasciculated* fr. LL *fasciculatus* + E *-ed*] *biol* **:** FASCICLED — **fas·cic·u·late·ly** *adv*

fas·cic·u·la·tion \=ˌ==ˈlāshən\ *n* -S [prob. fr. (assumed) NL *fasciculation-, fasciculatio*, fr. LL *fasciculatus* + L *-ion-, -io* -ion] **1** *zool* **:** the condition of being fascicled **2** [*fasciculus* + *-ation* (as in *fibrillation*)] **:** muscular twitching involving contiguous groups of muscle fibers — compare FIBRILLATION

fas·ci·cule \ˈfasəˌkyül\ *n* -S [F, fr. L *fasciculus*] **:** FASCICLE 2

fas·cic·u·lus \fəˈsikyələs,faˈ-\ *n, pl* **fascicu·li** \-ˌlī\ [NL, fr. L] **1** *anat* **:** a slender bundle of fibers: **a :** a bundle of skeletal muscle cells bound together by fasciae and forming one of the constituent elements of a muscle **b :** a bundle of nerve fibers coursing together but not necessarily having like functional connections (as in certain subdivisions of the funiculi of the spinal cord) **c :** TRACT 2b(2) **2** [L] **:** FASCICLE 2

fas·ci·nate \ˈfasᵊnˌāt, ˈfaas-, *usu* -ād·+V\ *vb* **fascinated; fascinated; fascinating** \-sᵊnˌād·iŋ, -ātiŋ *also* -ˌsnā-\ **fascinates** [L *fascinatus*, past part. of *fascinare*, prob. modif. (influenced by L *fari* to speak) of Gk *baskainein* to bewitch, speak evil of, fr. *baskanos* sorcerer, slanderer, prob. fr. a Thracian or Illyrian word akin to Gk *phaskein* to say, *phanai* to say — more at BAN] *vt* **1** *obs* **:** to cast a spell over **:** BEWITCH, ENCHANT **2 a :** to transfix and hold spellbound by or as if by an irresistible power ⟨believed that the serpent was capable of *fascinating* its prey before striking⟩ ⟨the changing vivid colors of the sunset *fascinated* the eye⟩ ⟨the younger and weaker man was *fascinated* and helpless before the creeping approach of so monstrous a wrath —G.D.Brown⟩ ⟨the bright light of a hooded lantern or a flashlight ~s the fleet-footed animal, making him a target for the huntsman's bullet —*Amer. Guide Series: Maine*⟩ **b :** to command the attention or interest of strongly or irresistibly often by the artful, subtle, challenging, strange, or piquant ⟨was *fascinated* by the personality of the tall, dark-haired young actress —J.K.Newnham⟩ ⟨men . . . who were not either *fascinating* women or obeying them —G.K.Chesterton⟩ ~ *vi* **:** to have or exercise the power of charming, alluring, or enthralling **:** be irresistibly attractive or interesting **:** engage and powerfully hold the attention or interest ⟨the very style of the book ~s, never mind the content⟩ ⟨since she had proved that she could farm as well as a man there was less need for her to endeavour to ~ as a woman —Ellen Glasgow⟩ **syn** see ATTRACT

fascinated *adj* [fr. past part. of *fascinate*] **:** FASCINATING, ENTHRALLING ⟨the ~ interest of her new novel⟩ ⟨an atmosphere of ~ suspense —W.H.Bucher⟩

fas·ci·nat·ed·ly *adv* [*fascinated* (past part. of *fascinate*) + *-ly*] **:** in the manner of one that is fascinated ⟨watched the man ~ as he juggled seven plates at a time⟩

fascinating *adj* [fr. pres. part. of *fascinate*] **:** holding the interest as if by a spell **:** ENTHRALLING **:** extremely interesting or charming ⟨~ old shops and alleys with the dust of another century upon them —*Amer. Guide Series: Maine*⟩ ⟨a ~ man of varied talents —Green Peyton⟩ ⟨the fickle yet ~ moods of British weather —L.D.Stamp⟩ ⟨India is an astounding and ~ country —Gerald Priestland⟩

fas·ci·nat·ing·ly *adv* **:** in a manner that fascinates

fas·ci·na·tion \ˌfasᵊnˈāshən,ˌfaas-\ *n* -S [L *fascination-, fascinatio*, fr. *fascinatus* + *-ion-, -io* -ion] **1** *obs* **:** the act of placing under a spell or the state of being under a spell; *also* **:** SPELL, ENCHANTMENT **2 a:** the quality of fascinating **:** the quality of holding the interest strongly esp. as if by a spell **:** the ability to enthrall **:** irresistible attraction or charm ⟨attracted by the ~ of discovery and the prospect of spiritual conquest —*Amer. Guide Series: Minn.*⟩ ⟨the Rio Grande . . . offers ~s for geologists and bird lovers —Stanley Walker⟩ ⟨it is so dreadful, in fact, that it begins to have its own morbid ~ and it is almost impossible . . . to put it down —B.R.Redman⟩ ⟨they found a certain ~ in combat —Mack Morriss⟩ **b :** a characteristic or peculiarity that gives this quality or ability ⟨tired of her ~s . . . he began to blame her for all his misfortunes —Edith Sitwell⟩ **3 :** the state of being fascinated **:** the state of feeling an intense interest in ⟨his lifelong ~ for clowns and their art —*Current Biog.*⟩ ⟨James's ~ by brutality and violence —John Farrelly⟩ ⟨Hunt's ~ with the mechanics and engineering of public opinion —T.H.White b. 1915⟩ **4 :** one form of the game of solitaire

fas·ci·na·tor \ˈ==ˌād·ə(r)\ *n* -S **1 :** one that fascinates **2 :** a woman's light head scarf usu. of crochet or lace

¹fas·cine \faˈsēn,fəˈ-\ *n* -S [F, fr. L *fascina* bundle of sticks, fr. *fascis* bundle — more at FASCES] **:** a long cylindrical bundle of wooden sticks bound together at intervals by a choker or withy and used for filling ditches, strengthening ramparts, or making parapets, revetments or mats for river banks, dams or jetties

²fascine \ˈ"\ *vt* -ED/-ING/-S **:** to cover, protect, or strengthen with fascines

fa·scio \ˈfä(ˌ)shō\ *n, pl* **fa·sci** \-(ˌ)shē\ *sometimes cap* [It, bundle, political group, local branch of the Fascisti, fr. L *fascis* bundle] **:** a local branch of the Fascisti

fas·ci·o·la \fəˈsēələ, -sīə-\ *n* [NL, fr. L, small bandage, dim. of *fascia* bandage — more at FASCIA] **1** *pl* **fascio·lae** \-ˌlē\ *or* **fasciolas :** a narrow fascia or band of color **2** *cap* **:** a genus (the type of the family Fasciolidae) of digenetic trematode worms including common liver flukes of ruminants and various other mammals including man

fas·ci·o·lar \-lə(r)\ *adj* **:** of or relating to a fasciola

fas·ci·o·lar·ia \ˌfasēōˈla(a)rēə\ *n, cap* [NL, fr. L *fasciola* small bandage + NL *-aria*] **:** a genus (the type of the family Fasciolariidae) of large stenoglossate marine snails comprising the typical band shells

fas·ci·ole \ˈfas(h)ēˌōl\ *n* -S [NL *fasciola*, fr. L, small bandage] **:** a band of minute tubercles bearing modified commonly ciliated spines on the test of certain sea urchins

fas·ci·o·li·a·sis \fəˌsēəˈlīəsəs,fəˌsī-\ *also* **fas·ci·o·lo·sis** \-ˈlōsəs\ *n, pl* **fasciolia·ses** \-əˌsēz\ *also* **fasciolo·ses** \-ōˌsēz\ [NL, fr. *Fasciola* + *-iasis*] **:** infestation with or disease caused by liver flukes (genus *Fasciola*) **:** LIVER ROT, DISTOMATOSIS

fas·ci·o·li·ci·dal \fəˌsēələˈsīdᵊl,fəˌsīə-\ *adj* **:** of or belonging to a fasciolicide ⟨~ effect⟩ ⟨~ efficacy⟩

fas·ci·ol·i·cide \fəˈsēələˌsīd,fəˈsī-\ *n* -S [NL *Fasciola* + E *-i-* + *-cide*] **:** an agent that destroys liver flukes of the genus *Fasciola*

fas·ci·ol·i·dae \ˌfasēˈäləˌdē\ *n pl, cap* [NL, fr. *Fasciola*, type genus + *-idae*] **:** a cosmopolitan family of digenetic trematodes chiefly infesting the livers of mammals and typically having a flattened leaf-shaped body with the ventral sucker near the anterior end — see FASCIOLA, FASCIOLOIDES, FASCIOLOPSIS

fas·ci·o·loid \fəˈsēəˌlȯid, fəˈsī-\ *adj* [NL *Fasciola* + E *-oid*] **:** of, relating to, or resembling worms of the genus *Fasciola* or the family Fasciolidae

fas·ci·o·loi·des \fəˌsēəˈlȯi(ˌ)dēz,fəˌsī-\ *n, cap* [NL, fr. *Fasciola*, genus name + L *-oides* -oid] **:** a genus of trematode worms (family Fasciolidae) including the giant liver flukes of ruminant mammals that are serious pests of livestock and game in parts of western No. America

fas·ci·o·lop·si·a·sis \-ˌläpˈsīəsəs\ *n* -ES [NL, fr. *Fasciolopsis* + *-iasis*] **:** infestation with or disease caused by the large intestinal fluke (*Fasciolopsis buski*) of man

fas·ci·o·lop·sis \-ˈläpsəs\ *n, cap* [NL, fr. *Fasciola* + *-opsis*] **:** a genus of trematode worms (family Fasciolidae) that includes an important intestinal parasite of man and swine that is prevalent in much of eastern Asia

fas·cism \ˈfa|ˌshizəm, ˈfaa|, ˈfai| *also* |ˌsi- *sometimes* ˈfä| *or* ˈfȧ|\ *n* -S [It *fascismo*, fr. *fascio* bundle, political group + *-ismo* -ism] **1** *often cap* **:** the principles of the Fascisti; *also* **:** the movement or governmental regime embodying their principles **2 a :** any program for setting up a centralized autocratic national regime with severely nationalistic policies, exercising regimentation of industry, commerce, and finance, rigid censorship, and forcible suppression of opposition **b :** any tendency toward or actual exercise of severe autocratic or dictatorial control (as over others within an organization) ⟨the nascent ~ of a detective who is not content merely to do his duty —George Nobbe⟩ ⟨early instances of army ~ and brutality —J.W.Aldridge⟩ ⟨a kind of personal ~, a dictatorship of the ego over the more generous elements of the soul —Edmond Taylor⟩

fa·scis·mo \fäˈshez(ˌ)mō\ *n* -S *often cap* [It] **:** FASCISM

¹fas·cist \ˈfa|shəst, ˈfaa|, ˈfai| *also* |səst *sometimes* ˈfä| *or* ˈfȧ|\ *n* -S *often cap* [It *fascista*, fr. *fascio* + *-ista* -ist] **:** one who adheres to, advocates, or practices fascism

²fascist \ˈ"\ *or* **fas·cis·tic** \(ˈ)=ˈ|shistik, fəˈ| *also* |si-\ *adj* **1** *usu cap* **:** of or belonging to the Fascisti, their organization, or their program **2** *sometimes cap* **a :** of, belonging to, sponsored by, or embodying fascism **:** according with or favoring fascism **b :** of or belonging or relating to fascists — **fas·cis·ti·cal·ly** \(ˈ)=ˈ|shistək(ə)lē, fəˈ|, |si-, -tēk-, -lī\ *adv*

fa·scis·ta \fäˈshēs(ˌ)tä\ *n, pl* **fascis·ti** \-(ˌ)tē\ [It] **1** *usu cap* **:** a member of an Italian political organization that was founded in 1919 and was dedicated to violently nationalistic and totalitarian principles and that under Benito Mussolini gained control of Italy and reorganized its political and social structure to accord with fascism — compare BLACKSHIRT **2 :** a member of an organization similar to that of the Italian Fascisti **:** FASCIST

fa·scis·ti·za·tion \ˌfa|s(h)əstəˈzāshən, ˌfaa|, ˌfai| -ˌstīˈz| *sometimes* ˌfä| *or* ˌfȧ|\ *n* -S **:** the act or process of fascistizing or the state of being fascistized

fa·scis·tize \ˈ==ˌstīz\ *vt* -ED/-ING/-S **:** to make over or transform into a fascista **:** convert to the principles of fascism

fasels *n pl* [ME *fasele* (sing.) kidney bean, fr. L *phaselus* — more at FRIJOL] **1** *obs* **:** KIDNEY BEANS **2** *obs* **:** CHICK-PEAS

¹fash \ˈfash\ *vb* -ED/-ING/-ES [MF *fascher*, fr. (assumed) VL *fastidiare* to disgust, fr. L *fastidium* loathing, disgust — more at FASTIDIOUS] *vt, chiefly Scot* **:** INCONVENIENCE, TROUBLE, BOTHER ⟨don't ~ yourself about me⟩ ~ *vi, chiefly Scot* **:** to take trouble or pains ⟨no need to ~⟩ — **fash one's beard** *or* **fash one's head** *or* **fash one's thumb** *dial Brit* **:** to trouble oneself

²fash \ˈ"\ *n* -ES *chiefly Scot* **:** fuss and bother **:** ANNOYANCE ⟨if you don't want to hear it, I am saved the ~ of telling it⟩

³fash \ˈ"\ *n* -ES [prob. alter. of obs. *fas* tassel, fr. ME, tassel, rootlets of a leek, fr. OE *fæs* fringe; akin to MD *vese* fringe, frayed edge, OHG *faso, fasa* fiber, fringe, Russ *pasmo* part of a skein of yarn] **:** an irregular seam on a boat

fash·er·ie *or* **fash·ery** \ˈfash(ə)ri\ *n, pl* **fasheries** [MF *fascherie*, fr. *fascher* + *-erie* -ery] **1** *dial Brit* **:** ANNOYANCE, BOTHER **2** *dial Brit* **:** unnecessary ornament or ceremony

¹fash·ion \ˈfashən, ˈfaash-, ˈfaish-\ *n* -S [ME *facioun, fasoun* shape, manner, fr. OF *façon*, fr. L *faction-, factio* action of making, company, faction, fr. *factus* (past part. of *facere* to make) + *-ion-, -io* -ion — more at DO] **1 a :** the form of something or the way it is constructed **:** appearance or mode of structure **:** STYLE, SHAPE ⟨do not like the ~ of your garments —Shak.⟩; *also* **:** a distinctive or peculiar form, shape, or cut (as of attire) ⟨the cut of the coat was a ~ of his own⟩ **b** *archaic* **:** KIND, SORT **2 a :** MANNER, WAY ⟨expressed himself in a striking ~⟩ ⟨turn out munitions in wholesale ~ following the outbreak of war —R.L.Buell⟩ ⟨the phonetics of Chinese are introduced in summary ~ in the first weeks —*Georgetown Univ. Bull.*⟩ **b :** mode of action or operation **:** ⟨threshing grain after the old ~⟩; *also, archaic* **:** DEMEANOR, BEARING, BEHAVIOR **c :** a distinctive or peculiar and often habitual manner, way, gesture, or action ⟨defending demagogy after his ~ —E.R. Bentley⟩ ⟨Carlyle's bad ~ of ignoring the best forces of his own age —Bliss Perry⟩ **d** *archaic* **:** SHOW, PRETENSE **3** *obs* **:** the act or process of making something (as an ornamentation on silver) **:** CRAFTSMANSHIP **4 a :** a prevailing usu. short-lived custom, usage, or style **:** FAD ⟨there are ~s in kinds of novels and ~s in ways of writing them —Bernard DeVoto⟩ ⟨not even changing ~s in warfare have diminished the island's strategic importance —Franc Shor⟩ ⟨Classicism, the Enlightenment, Romanticism, Realism, were not mere literary ~s —A.L.Guérard⟩ ⟨in six weeks she was the ~ of the town —Willa Cather⟩ ⟨there was a ~ for it some forty years ago as a depressant in cases of mania —Margery Allingham⟩ **b :** the prevailing or accepted style or group of styles in dress or personal decoration established or adopted during a particular time or season **:** VOGUE ⟨the ~ in hairdressing of the preceding century⟩ ⟨jewelry and clothing ~s vary with the season⟩ ⟨a high forehead from which swept back thick bronze hair scrupulously trimmed according to the day's ~ —W.J.Locke⟩ ⟨followed the line and general ~ of female court clothes of the day —Anatole Chujoy⟩; *also* **:** a garment in such a style ⟨we tried on the latest ~s today⟩ **c** *often cap* **:** such prevailing customs or styles considered as an abstract force ⟨a woman who lets *Fashion* dictate most of her actions⟩ ⟨as for the peculiar stamp of the scientific thought of an age, we must make due allowance for ~ and the example of leaders —*Times Lit. Supp.*⟩ **d :** social standing or prominence esp. as signalized by dress or conduct that meticulously accords with the most approved prevalent style or mode ⟨the captain, who was speaking a few parting words to some passengers of ~ —Winston Churchill⟩

syn FASHION, STYLE, MODE, VOGUE, FAD, RAGE, CRAZE, DERNIER CRI, CRY can mean, in common, a way of dressing, behaving, dancing, decorating, or an interest (as in a recreation) that is considered esp. up-to-date or noticeably following the contemporary trend in such activities. FASHION, in this context, is the prevailing conventional usage or custom ⟨dressed in the height of *fashion*⟩ ⟨the gloom of modern writing is no more than a *fashion*, which will pass as all fashions pass —Douglas Stewart⟩ ⟨one of a group of elegant, narrative biographies which may be setting a modern *fashion* —*Saturday Rev.*⟩ STYLE, often interchangeable with FASHION, can suggest the elegant or distinguished way of dressing, behaving, and so on, characteristic of those of taste in a given period ⟨dressed in the current *style*⟩ ⟨a house in the *style* of the late 19th century architecture⟩ ⟨the . . . house . . . has space, simplicity, *style* —Lillian Hellman⟩ ⟨a woman of both beauty and *style*⟩ MODE stresses, more than the others, the peak of contemporary fashion especially in dress and behavior, often suggesting a certain transiency ⟨its three bedrooms . . . all done in the modern *mode* —*Monsanto Mag.*⟩ ⟨the romantic landscape of England became a *mode* accepted without question in Sydney —Bernard Smith⟩ ⟨the rule of taste results in the tyranny of the *mode* —W.C.Brownell⟩ VOGUE, when it is not interchangeable with FASHION, often puts stress upon obvious popularity and wide acceptance, esp. of dress or decoration ⟨when fanciful scrollwork trim, cupolas, and brackets were in *vogue* —*Amer. Guide Series: Ariz.*⟩ ⟨the fashionable *vogue* for ultramodern art —*Encyc. Americana*⟩ ⟨a *vogue* at the moment of the red ties and red skirts —Frank Gorrell⟩ FAD designates a fashion that is usu. short lived, and connotes capriciousness in the interest and quick decline of interest shown in it ⟨unconcerned with *fads*, with whims of the moment —Clifton Fadiman⟩ ⟨a *fad* is a small fashion in some secondary matter or detail —N.A.Brisco⟩ ⟨whether the long skirts, high necks, pinched waists, padded hips, and bulky hats are here to stay for a while, or are merely a passing *fad* —*Modern Beauty Shop*⟩ RAGE and CRAZE designate a fad adopted with short lived but intense enthusiasm, often implying a certain senselessness ⟨one of the very latest *rages* — sterling silver charm bracelets that spell out your name —*N.Y. Times Mag.*⟩ ⟨for part of the Grimaldi period, performing dogs were the *rage* —Robert Turley⟩ ⟨the current *craze* for cyclecars —*Current Biog.*⟩ ⟨to satisfy the *craze* for wild-bird feathers on women's hats —J.H.Baker⟩ DERNIER CRI, sometimes with the French article *le*, and the equivalent English CRY (as in the phrase *all the cry*) designate the very latest style, fashion, or fad, esp. in art or clothes ⟨women garbed in the *dernier cri* from Paris —S.J.Perelman⟩ ⟨purporting to be the quintessence of scholarly research, the *dernier cri* in intelligent social theory and practice —*Current History*⟩ ⟨the last *cry* today may be a far cry from that of yesterday⟩ **syn** see in addition METHOD

— **after a fashion** *adv* : in an approximate or rough way ⟨became an artist *after a fashion* but never achieved distinction⟩

²fashion \"\ *vb* **fashioned; fashioned; fashioning** \-sh(ə)niŋ\ **fashions** [ME *faciounen*, fr. *facioun*, n.] *vt* **1 a** : to give shape or form to : FORM, MOLD ⟨~ the clay in the figure of a donkey⟩ ⟨sit once more at the feet of the ancient wisdom and ~ their lives upon the principle that the soul is more than the meat and the body than raiment —V.L.Parrington⟩ ⟨human nature is ~*ed* to a large extent by surrounding cultural configurations —Bernard Rosenberg⟩ ⟨as intelligent creatures, ~*ed* by the hand and in the image of an all-wise God —W.F. Hambly⟩ **b** : ALTER, MODIFY, TRANSFORM ⟨new frontiers were established which ~*ed* the political and social institutions of the old —W.P.Webb⟩ **c** : to mold into a particular character by influencing, instructing, training, or conditioning ⟨the teacher ~*ed* the student into a fine pianist⟩ ⟨the painful metaphysical struggle or religious revolt that ~*ed* Joyce's soul in youth and first manhood —Sean O'Faolain⟩ ⟨choose a dog specifically designed by nature, and ~*ed* by man, to hunt —*Holiday*⟩ **d** : MAKE, CONSTRUCT ⟨~*ed* a canoe from a huge pine —R.S.Monahan⟩ ⟨~ out of paper a representation of the person whom the magician wishes to injure —J.G.Frazer⟩ ⟨well-kept houses of brick ~*ed* from the red clay —*Amer. Guide Series: Pa.*⟩ ⟨each writer had to find or ~ for himself an artistic credo —Max Lerner & Edwin Mims⟩ ⟨his ability to ~ personal triumphs from the most unlikely materials —R.H. Rovere⟩ **2** : FIT, ADAPT, ACCOMMODATE ⟨she was always ~*ed* to the subtle, disguising whalebone of common sense —V.S. Pritchett⟩ **3 a** *obs* : to bring about by devising : CONTRIVE **b** : REPRESENT, PICTURE ⟨the subordinate characters are expertly ~*ed* too —T.C.Chubb⟩ **c** *obs* : to make pretense of : COUNTERFEIT **4** : to make up : CONSTITUTE ⟨from these yards was recruited Noah Brown's heroic band who ~*ed* Commodore Perry's fleet for the Battle of Lake Erie —*Amer. Guide Series: N. Y. City*⟩ **5** : to increase or decrease stitches in ~ *vi, dial Eng* : to have the nerve : DARE **syn** see MAKE

³fashion *n* [by folk etymology fr. obs. *farcin* farcy, fr. ME *farsin* — more at FARCY] *obs* : FARCY

fash·ion·a·bil·i·ty \ˌfash(ə)nəˈbiləd·ē, ˌfaash-, ˌfaish-, -lətē, -i\ *n* -ES : FASHIONABLENESS

¹fash·ion·a·ble \ˈfash(ə)nəbəl, ˈfaash-, ˈfaish-\ *adj* [¹*fashion*, ²*fashion* + -*able*] **1 a** : conforming to the custom, fashion, or established mode esp. in dress or behavior : observant of the fashion : dressing or behaving according to the prevailing fashion ⟨a ~ lady⟩ ⟨a ~ society⟩ : in accordance with prevailing form or fashion : STYLISH, MODISH ⟨a ~ dress⟩ ⟨a ~ hairdo⟩ **b** : of or belonging to the world of fashion : frequented or patronized by persons of fashion or by those who conform to fashion ⟨the ~ stores⟩ ⟨a ~ vacation spot⟩ : popular among those who conform to fashion ⟨during the height of St. Martinville's ~ period, steamboats landed passengers regularly at its door —*Amer. Guide Series: La.*⟩ ⟨eventually became a ~ surgeon —*Time*⟩ ⟨there are some ~ books that one must read, because they are ingredients of the talk of the day —T.L.Peacock⟩ ⟨went to Europe because it was the ~ thing to do⟩ ⟨asking the ~ questions of the moment —Max Beloff⟩ **c** : merely echoing or imitating thoughtlessly or irresponsibly a contemporary fashion rather than acting responsibly or with a full awareness of essential issues ⟨the martyr-toned, bogus moralizing now ~ among scientists and their hero worshipers —*Time*⟩ ⟨it is ~ — and easy — to define tolerance in such a way as to evade all responsibility —Paul Blanshard⟩ ⟨an Age of Anxiety in which "escape" itself is becoming increasingly frequent and even ~ —*College English*⟩ ⟨a ~ neurosis —Miriam Allott⟩ **2** *obs* : capable of being shaped or molded **3** *obs* : of or belonging to mere outward show or form **4** *obs* : of good appearance — **fash·ion·a·ble·ness** \-bəlnəs\ *n* -ES — **fash·ion·a·bly** \-blē, -li\ *adv*

²fashionable \"\ *n* -S : a fashionable person ⟨trying to keep up with the young ~*s* of Rome —Grace Frick⟩ ⟨the ~*s* were now arriving, including a number of chic Muslims wearing tasseled chechias above their handsomely tailored European clothes —A.J.Liebling⟩

fash·ion·er \-nə(r)\ *n* -S : one that fashions, forms, or gives shape to something ⟨the ~*s* of the screens, choir stalls, corbels, and hammer posts of the great cathedrals —L.F.Herreshoff⟩ ⟨for the mind (the "spiritual") is a maker and a ~ of quite formidable proportions —Weston La Barre⟩ ⟨America's most expert ~ of the wholesome love story —*Time*⟩; *esp* : one that makes clothing

fashion gray *n* : a dark gray that is darker than Oxford gray, Dover gray, or pelican — called also *cruiser, pilgrim, Plymouth*

fash·ion·ist \-sh(ə)nəst\ *n* -S : a maker, leader, specialist in, or follower of fashions

fash·ion·less \-shənləs\ *adj, archaic* : without a definite shape : SHAPELESS

fashion mark *n* : the stitch distortion resulting from an increase or decrease in full-fashioned knitting

fashionmonger \ˈ≈≈ˌ≈≈\ *n* : one that studies, imitates, or sets the fashion ⟨~*s* say they must adapt their production and advertising to irrational consumer behavior —P.M.Gregory⟩

fashion piece *n* : one of the timbers at the ends of the transom that define the shape of a ship's stern

fashion plate *n* **1** : an illustration of a clothing style **2** : a person who dresses in the newest fashion ⟨the wealthy woman who . . . is little more than an animated *fashion plate* —H.A. Overstreet⟩

fashions *pl of* FASHION, *pres 3d sing of* FASHION

fash·ious \ˈfashəs\ *adj* [MF *fascheux*, fr. *fascher* to trouble, bother + -*eux* -ous — more at ¹FASH] *dial Brit* : TROUBLESOME, ANNOYING

fasnacht *var of* FASTNACHT

fa·so·la \ˌfäˌsōˈlä\ *n* -S [*fa* + *so* + *la*] : a system of solmization used in England and America in the 17th and 18th centuries using of the original six Guidonian syllables only the four fa, sol, la, and mi and often used in conjunction with the shape-note system of musical notation

fas·sa·ite \ˈfasəˌīt\ *n* -S [G *fassait*, fr. Val di *Fassa*, Venezia Tridentina, northeast Italy + G -*it* -ite] : a mineral consisting of a pale green to dark green variety of augite

fas·set \ˈfasət, *also* -ɔd·+V\ *dial var of* FAUCET

¹fast \ˈfast, -aa(ə)-, -ai-, -á-\ *adj* -ER/-EST [ME, fr. OE *fæst*; akin to OHG *festi* firm, ON *fastr*, Arm *hast* firm, Skt *pastya* homestead] **1 a** : firmly fixed : immovable or moved only with the greatest difficulty ⟨the roots of the tree were so ~ in the ground we left them there⟩ ⟨a flagpole set ~ in its concrete socket⟩ ⟨a gun ~ in its carriage⟩ ⟨a ~ and impassable barrier between them⟩ **b** : tightly shut : unable to be opened or very difficult to open ⟨after the damp weather all the drawers became ~⟩ ⟨the trunk lid was ~ so that even after the key was turned it would not budge⟩ : FASTENED, LOCKED ⟨the windows and doors were all ~ so that thieves could not enter⟩ **c** : unable to be separated after being fastened together ⟨the boards were ~ a few hours after being glued together⟩ ⟨made the ropes ~ with a solid square knot⟩ **d** : not easily extricated or freed : STUCK ⟨when his foot went through the rotten floor it became ~ between two of the floor timbers⟩ ⟨a shell ~ in the chamber of a gun⟩ **e** : not able to leave something — usu. used in combination ⟨bed*fast*⟩ **f** : BUSY, ENGAGED **g** : somewhat permanently settled : STABLE **h** : UNCHANGEABLE ⟨hard and ~ rules⟩ **2** *obs* **a** *of a fortification* : UNYIELDING, IMPREGNABLE **b** *of a place* : secure against attack **3** : turned from one's purpose only with great difficulty: as **a** : firmly loyal : STAUNCH, STEADFAST — used in the phrase *fast friend* **b** *archaic* : UNREMITTING — used in the phrase *fast foe* **4 a** *obs* : COMPACT, DENSE, SOLID **b** *archaic* : frozen over solid **5 a** : characterized by quick motion: (1) : moving or able to move rapidly : FLEET, SWIFT ⟨a ~ car⟩ ⟨a ~ horse⟩ (2) *of a baseball* : thrown at the pitcher's highest speed ⟨threw more ~ balls than curves⟩ (3) : moving ahead swiftly ⟨a society that was ~ as far as improvement is concerned⟩ (4) : taking a comparatively short time ⟨a ~ race⟩ (5) : following in rapid succession ⟨took two ~ shots⟩ (6) : imparting quickness of motion ⟨a ~ bowler⟩ ⟨a ~ mechanism on the gun trigger⟩ (7) : accomplished or capable of being accomplished quickly ⟨~ work⟩ (8) : marked by abrupt decision or action esp. as impelled by a quick temper or irascible nature ⟨a bit too ~ with his fists in an argument⟩ (9) *of a dramatic or literary work* : holding the interest by reason of the sustained conflict, vivid writing, or the rapid advancement of a story ⟨a taut and ~ play⟩ ⟨a ~ rollicking tale⟩ (10) : agile of mind ⟨an excellent witness — eloquent, confident, ~ beyond belief —Michael Straight⟩ (11) : having a rapid effect ⟨the medicine was a ~ one⟩ ⟨the acid was chosen because it was ~⟩ **b** : having qualities which are conducive to rapidity of play or action ⟨a ~ track⟩ ⟨a ~ tennis court⟩ ⟨a ~ gun holster⟩ ⟨the roads were ~ between the towns⟩: as (1) *of a wicket* : in such condition as to cause a bowled cricket ball to leave the ground swiftly after landing — contrasted with *slow*; compare FIERY (2) : allowing the rapid passage of a gas or fluid ⟨a ~ nipple on the baby bottle⟩ **c** (1) *of timepieces or time reports* : indicating time in advance of what is correct (2) *of weighing instruments* : registering more than the correct weight of the thing weighed (3) : according to daylight saving time **d** : contributing to a shortening of exposure time — used of a photographic lens or photographic emulsion **e** *slang* (1) *of money or profits* : acquired with unusually little effort and usu. in a rapid transaction ⟨made a ~ fortune in real estate⟩ ⟨made some ~ money on horseracing⟩ and often by shady or dishonest methods ⟨made a ~ dollar in a con scheme⟩ (2) : involving unusually little effort in proportion to the money gained thereby ⟨tried to think of a show he could do for a ~ thirteen weeks that would pay for the baby —Pete Martin⟩ (3) : unusually quick and ingenious or cunning in finding or recognizing and profiting by easy and often shady ways of making or acquiring money ⟨a particularly ~ man with a buck —*Time*⟩ (4) : marked by trickery and unfairness ⟨worked a ~ deal on a friend⟩ **6 a** : securely attached or fixed to someone or something ⟨a rope ~ to the wharf⟩ ⟨when the handcuffs were snapped on, the culprit was ~ to the police officer⟩ **b** : TENACIOUS ⟨a ~ hold on the purse⟩ **c** (1) *of a knot* : firmly tied (2) *of an alliance or agreement* : not easily broken or betrayed : CERTAIN, SECURE **d** (1) *of a harpoon* : stuck securely in a whale (2) *of a whale* : secured by a harpoon; *esp* : harpooned securely by a certain crew and consequently the rightful possession of that crew regardless of subsequent claims (3) *of a whaleboat* : secured to a whale by harpoon **7 a** *archaic* : sound asleep **b** *of sleep* : not easily disturbed : SOUND ⟨fell into a ~ sleep⟩ **8 a** : not fading or changing color readily : permanently dyed : COLORFAST ⟨~ colors⟩ ⟨~ dyeings⟩ **b** : yielding colors of this kind — used esp. of the diazo components of azoic dyes ⟨~ color bases⟩; see DYE table I (under *Acid, Azoic, Diazo, Disperse, Mordant*) **c** : proof against fading under exposure to a particular agency or action ⟨the dye is made ~ to perspiration —*Know Your Merchandise*⟩ ⟨a color that is ~ to sunlight⟩ — often used in combinations ⟨sun*fast*⟩ ⟨boil*fast*⟩ ⟨wash*fast*⟩ **9 a** : marked by or given to living that is unusually active ⟨his health would not allow so ~ a life and he was forced to slow down⟩ esp. in pursuit of excitement or pleasure ⟨~ living⟩ **b** (1) : DISSIPATED, WILD ⟨associating with a pretty ~ bunch⟩ (2) : markedly or promiscuously given to a flouting of the proprieties in the matter of personal behavior esp. in sexual relations — usu. used of a woman ⟨he thought how in 1910 a painted woman was said to be ~ —T.H.Raddall⟩ (3) : of or characteristic of a person of this kind ⟨a lot of ~ talk and promiscuous behavior⟩ **10** : resistant to change, esp. to destructive action — used chiefly of organisms and in combination with the name of the agent resisted ⟨acid-*fast* bacteria⟩ ⟨arsenic-*fast* insects⟩ ⟨a streptomycin-*fast* patient⟩

syn RAPID, SWIFT, FLEET, QUICK, SPEEDY, HASTY, EXPEDITIOUS: FAST and RAPID are often interchangeable; FAST often describes moving objects or creatures and may suggest constant speedy course, flight, or procedure; RAPID may refer to actions and their rate of speed and suggest successful course ⟨a *fast* runner⟩ ⟨a *fast* horse⟩ ⟨a *fast* train⟩ ⟨a *fast* worker⟩ ⟨a *rapid* approach⟩ ⟨a *rapid* gait⟩ ⟨*rapid* progress⟩ ⟨*rapid* operations⟩ SWIFT may suggest speed or rapidity accompanied by easy facility, sure flight, brisk activity, or lack of interference and delay ⟨flawless and chaste and *swift* in their machined perfection which even the airplane has never been able to rival —Robert Payne⟩ ⟨so *swift* was Caesar that his greatest exploits were measured by days —J.A.Froude⟩ ⟨the flight of his imagination is very *swift*; the following of it often a breathless business —C.D. Lewis⟩ FLEET, sometimes rather poetic or literary, may suggest nimble or graceful lightness and swiftness ⟨the Indian bands swept over the hills on their *fleet* little ponies and wiped out emigrant wagon trains —*Amer. Guide Series: Ariz.*⟩ ⟨how the *fleet* creature would fly before the wind —Herman Melville⟩ QUICK applies to lively action with alacrity or to prompt occurrence with short duration ⟨am a *quick* man with my hands, and in a minute and a half I had done what I wanted to do —G.K.Chesterton⟩ ⟨a *quick* brain for intrigue —John Buchan⟩ ⟨in passing *quick* rather than deliberate judgment on the literature of the day —M.R.Cohen⟩ SPEEDY may suggest velocity or quickness along with promptness, dispatch, or haste ⟨orders for the fastest plane, the swiftest motorboat, the *speediest* racing car that money and American ingenuity could produce —Gerald Beaumont⟩ ⟨industries where there is a need for exceptionally *speedy* reinforcement —Sir Winston Churchill⟩ ⟨in all criminal prosecutions the accused shall enjoy the right to *speedy* and public trial —*U.S. Constitution*⟩ HASTY suggests precipitate hurried rapidity, sometimes ineffective or nervous ⟨it had a hurried evacuated look. Many houses had that. The look of the *hasty* choice made of what to take along —R.H.Newman⟩ ⟨we must, this time, have plans ready — instead of waiting to do a *hasty*, inefficient, and ill-considered job at the last moment —F.D.Roosevelt⟩ EXPEDITIOUS suggests efficient rapidity ⟨to assist me in every way in making the journey as *expeditious* as may be —Elinor Wylie⟩ ⟨if you suggested *expeditious* English methods of settling accounts he would laugh at you; he does not want his accounts settled —Norman Douglas⟩

²fast \"\ *adv* -ER/-EST [ME *faste*, fr. OE *fæste*; akin to OHG *fasto* firmly; derivative fr. the root of E ¹*fast*] **1** : in a fast manner: as **a** : FIRMLY, FIXEDLY, SECURELY, SOUNDLY ⟨frozen ~⟩ ⟨fixed ~ in the hardened cement⟩ ⟨~ welded⟩ ⟨~ asleep⟩ **b** : LOYALLY, STAUNCHLY, UNWAVERINGLY ⟨held ~ to his belief in justice⟩ ⟨labor held ~ to its right to strike —F.L.Paxson⟩ **c** : leaving no room for play : in the manner of one caught and immovable : TIGHTLY ⟨a foot stuck ~ between the boards of the floor⟩ ⟨holding his mother's hand ~⟩; *also* : leaving no access or outlet ⟨a door shut ~⟩ ⟨the blinder over his eyes as ~ as ever —Mary Deasy⟩ **d** : in a rapid manner : QUICKLY, SWIFTLY ⟨run ~⟩ ⟨perils had thickened about him ~ —Charles Dickens⟩ ⟨a building ~ going to ruin⟩; *also* : READILY, EAGERLY ⟨complete the task ~ if paid enough⟩ **e** : in quick succession ⟨bullets coming thick and ~⟩ **f** : with speed and accuracy of mental process : with intellectual agility ⟨a man who could think ~ in a crisis⟩; *also* : continuously and facilely with the intent of influencing or deceiving someone or evading trouble or confusing an issue ⟨when the police caught him in the act he talked ~ to try to prove his innocence⟩ ⟨what he lacks in knowledge he can make up for by talking ~ —Stuart Chase⟩ **g** : in a wild or dissipated way ⟨living too ~ for his health⟩ : so as to flout the conventions, esp. sexual convention in one's behavior ⟨living ~ and free⟩ ⟨playing ~ with the ladies⟩ **h** : ahead or in advance of a correct time or posted schedule ⟨a clock that runs ~⟩ ⟨a train running two minutes ~⟩ **2** *obs* : with a fixity of attention : ZEALOUSLY, STEADILY **3** *archaic* : CLOSE, NEAR ⟨sat ~ by hell's gate —John Milton⟩ **4** *obs* : AT ONCE; IMMEDIATELY

³fast *vt* -ED/-ING/-S [ME *fasten*, *festen* fr. OE *fæstan*; akin to OHG *festen* to make fast, ON *festa* to settle, fix; derivative fr. the root of E ¹*fast*] *obs* : to make fast : BIND

⁴fast \"\ *interj* [²*fast*] — used as an exclamation in archery expressing a warning to one about to pass in the line of an arrow's flight

⁵fast \"\ *vb* -ED/-ING/-S [ME *fasten*, fr. OE *fæstan*; akin to OHG *fastēn* to fast, ON *fasta*, Goth *fastan*; derivative fr. the root of E ¹*fast*] *vi* **1** : to abstain from food : omit to take nourishment in whole or in part : go hungry **2** : to practice abstinence from food voluntarily for a time as a religious exercise or duty ⟨to counsel men to ~ and pray⟩ **3** : to restrict one's diet by eating sparingly or by abstaining from certain foods ⟨~ in Lent⟩ ~ *vt* : to cause to go without food : deny food to ⟨the patient is ~*ed* and given a mild hypnotic —*Lancet*⟩ — **fast on** *or* **fast upon** *or* **fast against** *Irish law* : to sit fasting at the door of a defendant or debtor until the demand or debt is met or a pledge is given as is often required before the judicial seizure of property

⁶fast \"\ *n* -S [ME *faste*, fr. ON *fasta*; akin to OHG *fasta* fast; derivative fr. the root of OHG *fastēn* to fast, ON *fasta*] **1 a** : voluntary abstinence from food or from certain kinds of food for a space of time as a spiritual discipline or as a religious exercise ⟨a day for a general ~⟩ **b** : abstinence from food : the omission of or failure to take food for an unusual length of time **2** : a time of fasting ⟨observe the ~*s* and feasts of the church⟩ ⟨went on a ~ of a month as a protest⟩

⁷fast \"\ *n* -S [alter. (influenced by ¹*fast*) of ME *fest*, fr. ON *festr* rope, mooring cable, fr. *fastr* firm — more at ¹FAST] : something that fastens or holds a fastening ⟨a door ~⟩ ⟨a window ~⟩: as **a** : a mooring rope or cable ⟨a stern ~⟩ ⟨a quarter ~⟩ — compare BREAST FAST **b** : a post on a pier or on shore around which hawsers are passed in mooring

fast and loose *adv* : RECKLESSLY, IRRESPONSIBLY : in a craftily deceitful way — formerly used in the phrase *to play at fast and loose*; now usu. used in the phrase *to play fast and loose* ⟨playing *fast and loose* with concepts of right and wrong to justify our own actions⟩ ⟨some dressmakers have played *fast and loose* with the original Black Watch design —*Newsweek*⟩ ⟨playing *fast and loose* with someone else's money⟩

fa station \ˈeˈfā-\ *n, usu cap F&A* : an aeronautical radio station

fast back *n, chiefly Brit* : TIGHT BACKBONE

fastball *n, Canad* : SOFTBALL

fast baller \ˈ≈ˌbȯlə(r)\ *n* : a baseball pitcher who relies chiefly on a fast ball

fast break *n* : a basketball maneuver calculated to move the ball toward the opponents' basket for a shot as quickly as possible after gaining possession of the ball

fast-breaking \ˈ≈ˌ≈≈\ *adj, of a news story* : becoming news suddenly in rapidly revealed successive details

fast color salt *n, often cap F&C, sometimes cap S* : an azoic diazo component — see DYE table I (under *Azoic Diazo*)

fast day *n* [ME *faste day*, fr. *faste* fast + *day* — more at ⁶FAST] : a day appointed for fasting and prayer often as a means of invoking the favor of God: as **a** *cap* : a day usu. in the spring appointed by the magistrates and governors of some of the New England colonies and states as a holiday for the purpose of fasting and prayer **b** : such a legal holiday often in the summer observed in Scotland

fasted *adj* [fr. past part. of ⁵*fast*] : having been subjected to fasting ⟨a ~ animal⟩ : resulting from having been fasted ⟨the animal's ~ weight⟩

¹fas·ten \ˈfasᵊn, -aas-, -ais-, -ás-\ *vb* **fastened; fastened; fastening** \-s(ᵊ)niŋ\ **fastens** [ME *fastnen*, fr. OE *fæstnian* to make fast; akin to OHG *festinōn* to make fast, ON *fastna* to pledge; derivative fr. the root of E ¹*fast*] *vt* **1** *obs* **a** : to make firm or strong : RATIFY, CONFIRM **b** : to make stable or unwavering : place solidly : ESTABLISH **c** : to make fast (as a color) ⟨we ~ the dyes into the cloth first —H.I.Poleman⟩ **2 a** : to cause to hold to something else : attach esp. by pinning, tying, or nailing **b** : to cause (parts which are separate) to hold together : make fast and secure ⟨~ the ends of the rope⟩ ⟨~ my hair⟩ ⟨~ her dress⟩ **c** : to fix firmly or securely in position ⟨~ the flagpole so that it does not waver⟩ : secure against opening ⟨~ a door shut⟩ ⟨~ a window⟩; *also* : fix firmly by implanting (as in the memory) ⟨~*ed* firmly in my mind the main facts and principles —A.D.White⟩ **d** : to secure within limits (as within a fenced area) by fastening or enclosing — usu. used with *in* or *up* ⟨~ up the dog in the yard⟩ ⟨~ in the prisoners at nightfall⟩ **e** : to pin, nail, tie, or otherwise make immovable — usu. used with *down* ⟨~ down a flapping shutter⟩ ⟨~ down the lifeboats on deck⟩ **3 a** : to focus or direct (as the attention) intently or steadily ⟨~ his attention upon a fire in the distance⟩ : place (as one's hopes) strongly ⟨~*ed* his hopes on a quick recovery⟩ **b** : to focus or direct the attention or interest markedly upon ⟨~*ed* him with her clear blue eyes —Hamilton Basso⟩ **4** *obs* : to deliver (as a blow) forcefully; *also* : to imprint or implant (as a kiss) on the cheek **5** : to take a firm grip with ⟨the dog ~*ed* his teeth in the man's leg⟩ **6 a** : to attach, affix, or associate (oneself) persistently and usu. objectionably or with or as if with intent to annoy or exploit or with the result of limiting the freedom of another ⟨~*ed* himself upon anyone who would listen to his sad story⟩ ⟨the con man ~*s* himself on any likely looking sucker⟩ **b** : to place forcefully : bring about the imposition of : IMPOSE ⟨too often ~*ed* the blame on the wrong man⟩ ⟨~*ed* on the community a merciless totalitarian system —J.E.Neole⟩ ⟨sought to ~ upon him the stigma of atheism —V.L.Parrington⟩ **c** : GIVE, AFFIX ⟨to which . . . later the name of "Llewellen" was ~*ed* by American breeders —W.F.Brown b.1903⟩ ~ *vi* **1 a** : to become fast or fixed ⟨where the phrase has ~*ed*, let it stick —Robert Browning⟩ **b** : to become firmly attached to a whale by means of a well placed harpoon — used of one harpooning or the boat from which the harpoon is launched **c** : to close and lock (as with catches) ⟨the lock of the bag was so damaged it would not ~⟩ **2 a** : take a firm grip or hold ⟨the stranger ~*ed* on my arm⟩ ⟨the flames ~*ed* upon the roof⟩ **b** : to focus or markedly fix attention ⟨his blue eyes ~*ed* sharply and eagerly upon the general —Kenneth Roberts⟩ ⟨the interest of the prosecution ~*ed* on one small inconsistency in the story⟩ ⟨they ~*ed* exclusively and resentfully on everything I said about power and progress —Norman Smith⟩

syn FIX, ATTACH, AFFIX: these four verbs signify in common to make to stay firmly in place. FASTEN commonly implies tying, binding, nailing, or some such process, or using a lock, catch, hook and eye, or other device, to keep a thing from moving, or it may apply to any action that suggests the use of one of these processes or devices ⟨*fasten* a sign to a post with a nail⟩ ⟨*fasten* a door by throwing a lock⟩ ⟨we will put aside the theology and *fasten* attention on the politics and the economics of the struggle —V.L.Parrington⟩ FIX is often interchangeable with FASTEN ⟨had to *fix* my collar onto my shirt with a paper clip —J.B.S.Haldane⟩ It usu. implies an attempt to keep something from falling down or losing its place and generally suggests a driving in or implanting ⟨*fix* a post in the ground⟩ ⟨he glanced about the washroom for what hooks might be *fixed* in the walls —Kay Boyle⟩ In figurative use FIX may sometimes be distinguished from FASTEN in suggesting a forthright, normal, or reasonable attitude as opposed to a devious, underhanded, or predatory one ⟨*fix* their affection upon a good person⟩ ⟨*fasten* your affection upon a mere child⟩ ⟨did not *fix* the blame on the right person⟩ ⟨*fasten* the blame upon an innocent man⟩ ATTACH suggests strongly a connection or union, a bond or link to prevent motion or keep one thing with another ⟨*attach* a cover by means of a brass hinge⟩ ⟨*attach* a card to the package⟩ ⟨guinea fowl *attach* themselves firmly to the place where they were born —F.D. Smith & Barbara Wilcox⟩ AFFIX is sometimes interchangeable with FASTEN or ATTACH ⟨*affix* a card to the package⟩ but usu. implies attachment by the imposition of one thing upon another, esp. with glue or mucilage ⟨*affix* a stamp to a letter⟩ ⟨*affix* a seal and signature to a document⟩

²**fasten** *n* -s [ME, fast, fr. OE *fæsten*, fr. *fæstan* to fast — more at ⁵FAST] **1** *obs* **:** a fast day **2** *obs* **:** the act of fasting

fastened *past of* FASTEN

fas·ten·er \-s(ᵊ)nə(r)\ *n* -s **:** one that fastens: as **a :** a device (as a button, hook and eye, zipper, or snap) that joins together separate parts or closes an opening (as on a garment) **b :** a device for holding shut or preventing opening ⟨attached a chain ~ to the door⟩ ⟨a catch ~ on a traveling bag⟩ **c :** a worker who fastens together the timbers, subassemblies, steel plates, and other parts in the construction of ships

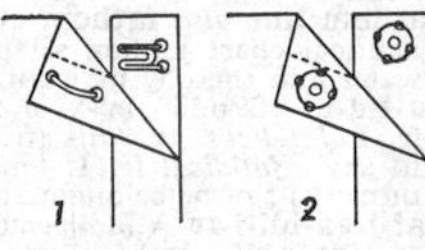

fasteners a: *1* hook and eye, *2* snap

fastening *n* -s [ME *fastninge*, fr. *fastnen* to make firm, make fast + *-inge*, *-ing* -ing — more at ¹FASTEN] **:** something that binds, holds one thing to another, or makes something fast **:** FASTENER; *specif* **:** the spikes, joint bars, bolts, and nuts used to connect rails in railroad track and affix them to ties

fastens *pres 3d sing of* FASTEN

fast·en's e'en \ˌfasᵊnˈzēn\ *or* **fast·en's** \ˈfasᵊnz\ *n* [ME (Sc) *fastinnys evin*, fr. *fastinnys* (gen. of ME — Sc — *fastin* fast, var. of ME *fasten*) + *evin* (var. of ME *even* evening, eve) — more at ²FASTEN, ¹EVEN] *dial Brit* **:** SHROVE TUESDAY

faster *comparative of* FAST

fast·ern's e'en \ˌfasərnˈzēn\ *or* **fast·ern's** \ˈfasərnz\ *n* [ME (Sc) *fasternis evin*, fr. *fasternis* (gen. of *fastern* fast, fr. OE — Northumbrian dial. — *fæstern*, fr. OE *fæstan* to fast) + *evin* — more at ⁵FAST] *chiefly Scot* **:** SHROVE TUESDAY

fastest *superlative of* FAST

fast green *n, often cap F&G* **:** any of several relatively fast green dyes belonging for the most part to the class of triphenylmethane dyes — see DYE table I (under *Acid Green 11*)

fast ice *n* **:** sea ice fastened to the shore

fas·tid·i·ous \faˈstidēəs *sometimes* fəˈ-\ *adj* [ME, haughty, disgusting, fr. MF & L; MF *fastidieux* disgusting, fr. L *fastidiosus* squeamish, haughty, disgusting, fr. *fastidium* aversion, disgust (prob. irreg. fr. *fastus* pride, arrogance + *taedium* irksomeness, disgust) + *-osus* -ose; akin to L *fastigium* top, extremity — more at ¹BRISTLE, TEDIUM] **1** *archaic* **:** SCORNFUL, HAUGHTY **2** *obs* **:** DISGUSTING, DISAGREEABLE **3 a :** overly difficult to please **:** overly nice or delicate in matters of taste ⟨grew ~ with easy living⟩ ⟨highbrow critics who are so esoteric and so ~ that they can talk only to a small circle of initiates —Granville Hicks⟩ ⟨a man falsely ~, finical, effeminate —Matthew Arnold⟩ **b :** marked by a meticulous, sensitive, or demanding attitude (as in matters of taste) ⟨an extremely stylish and ~ person⟩ ⟨~ about cleanness of the person⟩ ⟨~ attention to detail —Robert Evett⟩ ⟨a ~ aristocrat by birth and habit, he was a fine critic both of art and music —F.J.Mather⟩ **:** sensitive and particular ⟨the ~ puritanism of Virgil —John Buchan⟩ ⟨~ and well-bred and incurably polite —Elinor Wylie⟩ ⟨amahs and houseboys ~ in white jackets and black trousers —*New Yorker*⟩ **c :** reflecting a meticulous, sensitive, or demanding attitude ⟨an oar took shape with marvelous rapidity — trimmed and smoothed with a neatness almost ~ —John Burroughs⟩ ⟨Europe's intellectuals, editorial writers, and theologically ~ churchmen —*Newsweek*⟩ ⟨his ~ regard for the court's dignity —John Mason Brown⟩ **4 :** having complex nutritional requirements — used of bacteria that grow only in specially fortified artificial culture media **syn** see NICE

fas·tid·i·ous·ly *adv* **:** in a fastidious manner ⟨dressed ~ for the occasion⟩ ⟨exchanging . . . pungent plantation retorts for ~ phrased compliments of the nineties —Edmund Wilson⟩

fas·tid·i·ous·ness *n* -ES **:** the quality or state of being fastidious ⟨neatness and ~ in housekeeping⟩ ⟨a ~ of dress⟩

fas·tid·i·um \-dēəm\ *n* -s [L — more at FASTIDIOUS] **:** a mood of scornful distaste; *also* **:** SQUEAMISHNESS

fas·tig·ial \faˈstij(ē)əl\ *adj* [*fastigium* + *-al*] **:** of or associated with the fastigium

fas·tig·i·ate \-jēət\ *or* **fas·tig·i·at·ed** \-ēˌādəd\ *adj* [prob. fr. (assumed) NL *fastigiatus*, fr. ML *fastigiatus* lofty, fr. L *fastigium* top, extremity + *-atus* -ate] **:** narrowing toward the top: **a :** having or consisting of more or less upright clustered branches ⟨the lombardy poplar is ~⟩ ⟨the ~ cortex of the thallus of certain lichens⟩ **b** *zool* **:** united into a conical bundle — **fas·tig·i·ate·ly** \-ēətlē\ *adv*

fas·tig·i·um \-jēəm\ *n* -s [L, summit, top, extremity] **:** APEX, SUMMIT, PEAK: **a :** the ridge of a house **b :** GABLE END, PEDIMENT **c** [NL, fr. L] **:** the period at which the symptoms of a disease (as a febrile disease) are most pronounced **d** [NL, fr. L] **:** the angle in the roof of the fourth ventricle

¹**fasting** *n* -s [ME *fastinge*, *fasting*, fr. *fasten* to fast + *-inge*, *-ing* -ing — more at ⁵FAST] **:** the act of abstaining from food esp. for an unusual time and often as a form of religious observance or for therapeutic purposes

²**fasting** *adj* [fr. pres. part. of ⁵*fast*] **:** of or from a fasting subject ⟨~ urine⟩ ⟨~ blood-sugar level⟩

fast·ish \ˈfastish, -aas-,-ais-,-ás-\ *adj* **:** rather fast

fast-joint \ˈ≈ˌ≈\ *adj, of a hinge* **:** having its pin permanently secured in position ⟨a *fast-joint* butt⟩ ⟨a *fast-joint* hinge⟩

fast·land \ˈfastˌland, ˈfaast-, ˈfaist-, ˈfást-, -ˌlaa(ə)nd\ *n* -s [trans. of G *festland* mainland] **:** MAINLAND; *esp* **:** land that is high and dry near water **:** UPLAND

fast·ly *adv* [ME, fr. OE *fæstlīce*, fr. *fæstlīc* firm, solid, fr. *fæst* fast + *-līc* -ly (adj. suffix) — more at ¹FAST] *archaic* **:** FAST

fast-mass \ˈ≈ˌ≈\ *n* **:** SHROVETIDE

fast-moving \ˈ≈ˌ≈≈\ *adj* **1 :** moving or capable of moving rapidly usu. with sustained speed ⟨a *fast-moving* vehicle for freight transport⟩ **2** *of a dramatic or literary work* **:** full of sustained action or conflict usu. with the result of sustaining the interest

fast·nacht *also* **fas·nacht** \ˈfäsh(t)ˌnäkt, ˈfäs(-\ *n* -s [modif. of PaG *fasnachtkuche*, fr. *fasnacht* Shrove Tuesday, festival held on Shrove Tuesday (fr. MHG *vastnaht*, *vasnaht* Shrove Tuesday, fr. *vaste* fast — fr. OHG *fasta* — + *naht* night, fr. OHG) + *kuche* cake, fr. OHG *kuocho* — more at ⁶FAST, NIGHT, CAKE] **1 :** a doughnut made of yeast-leavened dough and traditionally eaten on Shrove Tuesday **2** *usu cap* [PaG *fasnacht* & G *fastnacht* Shrove Tuesday, festival held on Shrove Tuesday, fr. MHG *vastnaht*, *vasnaht* Shrove Tuesday] **:** a festival of Christians of Germanic origin held on the last day before Lent and observed as a time of merrymaking preceding Lenten fasting

fast·ness \ˈfas(t)nəs, -aas-,-ais-,-ás-\ *n* -ES [ME *fastnesse*, fr. OE *fæstnes*, fr. *fæst* fast + *-nes* -ness — more at ¹FAST, -NESS] **1 :** the quality or state of being fast: as **a :** firmness or fixedness **:** fixed attachment **:** FIXITY **b** *obs* **:** SECURITY, INACCESSIBILITY **c :** SWIFTNESS, SPEED **d :** resistance to color change **:** the quality of being colorfast — used of dyes or dyed materials **e :** resistance to the action of certain esp. toxic substances (as that developed by some organisms) **2** *obs* **:** DENSITY, SOLIDITY **3 a :** a fortified or secure place **:** STRONGHOLD, FORT, FORTRESS, CASTLE **b :** a place of retreat or privacy ⟨visited them in their desert ~ —Simon Bourgin⟩ ⟨the poet can retire into the ~ of himself —Clifton Fadiman⟩ — often used in pl. ⟨into the ~*es* of the pine- and oak-covered hills —*Amer. Guide Series: Tenn.*⟩ ⟨down in the remote ~*es* of Staten Island —Richard Burke⟩

fast of es·ther \-ˈestə(r)\ *cap F&E* [after *Esther*, Jewish heroine in the Old Testament who became the queen of King Ahasuerus of Persia and successfully interceded with him for her people after three days of fasting] **:** a Jewish fast day commonly observed on the 13th of Adar, the day before Purim, in honor of Queen Esther

fast of ge·da·liah \-gəˈdälyə, -ˌgedəˈlīə\ *cap F&G* **:** a Jewish fast day observed on the 3d day of Tishri and commemorating the assassination of Gedaliah, Nebuchadnezzar's governor in Judah

fast of tammuz *cap F&T* **:** a Jewish fast day observed on the 17th of Tammuz and commemorating the breach of the walls of Jerusalem by the Romans

fast of tebet *cap F&T* **:** a Jewish fast day observed on the 10th day of Tebet in commemoration of the beginning of the siege of Jerusalem by the Babylonians

fast-paced \ˈ≈ˌ≈\ *adj, of a narrative* **:** FAST-MOVING ⟨an extraordinary story as *fast-paced* with as much sheer narrative power as any novel of recent years —*N.Y.Times*⟩

fast pin *n* **:** a pin, screw, or nail or something resembling one of these that fastens securely or immovably; *specif* **:** the nonremovable rod that holds together the flaps on a fast-joint hinge

fast pulley *n* **:** a pulley fastened rigidly to a shaft

fast red *n, often cap F&R* **:** any of several fast red azo dyes: as **a :** a monoazo acid dye that dyes wool and silk red — called also *Fast Red A*; see DYE table I (under *Acid Red 88*) **b :** a monoazo acid dye that dyes wool and silk claret and is used chiefly as a biological stain — called also *Bordeaux B, Bordeaux red, Fast Red B*; see DYE table I (under *Acid Red 17*)

fast red base *n, often cap F&R, sometimes cap B* **:** any of several bases used as such or in the form of fast color salts in producing azoic dyes — see DYE table I (under *Azoic Diazo*)

fasts *pres 3d sing of* FAST, *pl of* FAST

fast salt *n, often cap F & sometimes cap S* **:** FAST COLOR SALT

fast scarlet R base *n, often cap F&S* **:** an orange-red crystalline amine $CH_3OC_6H_3(NO_2)NH_2$ that is often sold in the form of its stabilized diazonium complex salt with zinc chloride and is used in producing azoic dyes; 4-nitro-*ortho*-anisidine — see DYE table I (under *Azoic Diazo 13*)

fast spine *n, chiefly Brit* **:** TIGHT BACKBONE

fast-stepping \ˈ≈ˌ≈≈\ *adj* **1** *of a horse* **:** FAST, SWIFT **2 :** notable for purposeful and usu. tireless activity or drive ⟨a *fast-stepping* businessman⟩ **3 :** characterized by a fast, active, and often wild social life

fast-talk \ˈ≈ˌ≈\ *vt* [¹*fast* + *talk*, n.] *slang* **:** to influence or persuade by fluent and facile and usu. deceptive or tricky talk ⟨*fast-talked* tribal chieftains . . . out of a parcel of rain-drenched, tropical real estate —*Newsweek*⟩ ⟨he's *fast-talked* you into trying to be something you're not —Martin Dibner⟩

fas·tu·ous \ˈfaschəwəs\ *adj* [F or L; F *fastueux*, fr. L *fastuosus*, fr. *fastus* pride, arrogance + *-osus* -ose; akin to L *fastigium* top, extremity — more at BRISTLE] **1 :** HAUGHTY, ARROGANT, PRIDEFUL ⟨a ~ air of finality —Carl Van Vechten⟩ **2 :** OSTENTATIOUS, SHOWY ⟨the most ~ spectacle ever offered in the present opera house —Janet Flanner⟩ ⟨the ~ pomps and magnificence of ancient Carthage —*Times Lit. Supp.*⟩ — **fas·tu·ous·ly** *adv*

fast worker *n* **:** one who is fast and usu. smooth and shifty in his manner of gaining his personal ends (as profit, advantage, or sexual conquest)

¹**fat** \ˈfat, *usu* -ad·+V\ *n* -s [ME, fr. OE *fæt* — more at VAT] **1** *obs* **:** a large tub, cistern, or vessel **:** VAT **:** a wine cask **2** *archaic* **:** a barrel or receptacle for dry articles **3 :** a measure of quantity varying with the commodity

²**fat** \"\ *adj* **fatter; fattest** [ME, fr. OE *fǣtt*, past part. of *fǣtan* to cram; akin to OHG *feizit* fat (past part. of *feizen* to fatten, cram), *feiz* fat, ON *feita* to fatten, *feitr* fat, L *opimus* fat, fertile, copious, Gk *pidyein* to gush forth, *pidax* spring, *pimelē* lard, Skt *pīvan* fat, robust, *payate* he swells, grows] **1 :** notable for having an unusual amount of fat: **a :** well fed **:** PLUMP ⟨a cute ~ little baby⟩ ⟨ate a ~ capon for supper⟩ **b :** fleshy with superfluous nonmuscular flabby tissue **:** CORPULENT, OBESE ⟨a woman of medium height, a little plump but not ~ —Mary McCarthy⟩ **c** *of an animal* **:** fatted and likely to yield much red meat **d** *of food* **:** OILY, GREASY ⟨a ~, rich cheese⟩ **2 a :** well filled out **:** of sizable proportions **:** THICK ⟨a ~ letter⟩ ⟨a ~ volume of verse⟩ **:** BIG ⟨a resistor spark plug . . . permits a wider gap, thus a *fatter* hotter spark —*Newsweek*⟩ **:** unusually large ⟨he had to pay a ~ price to move his factory —Martin Turnell⟩ **:** substantial and impressive ⟨point to some ~ facts and figures to justify his claim —*Time*⟩ ⟨a ~ bank account⟩ ⟨make a mule of myself for a ~ fee on the stage —Harry Bailey⟩; *also* **:** FULL, RICH ⟨a gorgeous ~ bass voice —*Irish Digest*⟩ ⟨the ~ aroma of chocolate and coffee —Marcia Davenport⟩ **b :** well furnished, filled, or stocked ⟨a ~ refrigerator⟩ ⟨a ~ shelf⟩ ⟨this book is ~ with first-hand information —Frank Rounds⟩ **:** ABUNDANT ⟨a ~ feast⟩; *also* **:** PROSPEROUS, WEALTHY ⟨grew ~ on the war —*Time*⟩ **c** *of a type face* **:** characterized by wide letters; *also* **:** characterized by wide letters with heavy downstrokes and light upstrokes **d** *of a line of copy or type* **:** too wide to fit the measure ⟨a ~ heading⟩ **e** *of a slug* **:** cast larger than its normal body size ⟨trimming knives set to cast slugs .0015 inch ~⟩ **3 a :** richly rewarding ⟨a ~ part in a new play⟩ **:** markedly profitable or lucrative or presenting a marked opportunity of profit or advantage ⟨a nice ~ job⟩ ⟨a ~ opening in a business firm⟩ ⟨landed in the ~ post of governor of Buenos Aires —*Time*⟩ **b** *slang* **:** practically nonexistent **:** NEGLIGIBLE ⟨the depression left us with a ~ chance of making our first million⟩ ⟨a ~ lot of good it did him —Arthur Koestler⟩ **c** *archaic, of matter printed on a handpress* **:** easy and profitable **d :** making few if any demands **:** SLOTHFUL ⟨the dull, soft, ~ routine of peace —F.E.Robin⟩ **4 :** PRODUCTIVE, FERTILE, FRUITFUL ⟨growing soft on the ~ land and the easy living⟩ ⟨a ~ year for crops⟩ **5 a** *of clay or soil* **:** containing a high proportion of minerals that make clay or soil greasy to the touch, highly plastic, cohesive and compressible, difficult to work when wet, and strong when dry **b** *of beer or wine* **:** fullbodied and smooth **c** *of air or mist* **:** filled with moisture or odors **d** *of wood* **:** having a high resin content ⟨pine splinters ~ with pitch —Rebecca Caudill⟩ **e** *of coal* **:** having a high content of volatile matter **f** *of a pavement* **:** having too high a content of bitumen **g** *of mortar* **:** containing a high cement or lime content **h** *of lime* **:** pure or nearly so and slaking rapidly **6 a :** heavy, coarse, gross, or slow-witted in a way suggesting an overfed animal ⟨a foolish smile on his ~ face⟩ ⟨~ stupidity⟩ **b :** FOOLISH, EMPTY ⟨got myself in trouble because I did not use my ~ head⟩

syn FLESHY, STOUT, CORPULENT, OBESE, CHUBBY, ROTUND, PORTLY, PLUMP: FAT suggests an abundance of flesh, esp. adipose, nonmuscular flesh; it may be uncomplimentary ⟨the unreasonably *fat* woman with legs like tree trunks —Katherine A. Porter⟩ ⟨he remained *fat*, and his round, red cheeks shone like ripe apples —W.S.Maugham⟩ FLESHY is a close synonym for FAT but may suggest an abundance of muscular flesh as well as adipose ⟨my appetite is plenty good enough, and I am about as *fleshy* as I was in Brooklyn —Walt Whitman⟩ STOUT suggests a thickset figure with abundant flesh, but is a less uncomplimentary word than FAT ⟨one very *stout* gentleman, whose body and legs looked like half a gigantic roll of flannel —Charles Dickens⟩ CORPULENT suggests a bulky excess of flesh, either graceless or burly ⟨a large burly man, gradually growing *corpulent*, with a soft oily face —Anthony Trollope⟩ OBESE suggests a graceless excess of flesh; it is often used in medical or pathological discussion and is always quite uncomplimentary ⟨a woman of robust frame . . . though stout, not *obese* —Charlotte Brontë⟩ ⟨a retarded, *obese* child who died young⟩ CHUBBY may suggest rounded ample flesh; it is often used in reference to children and suggests well-nurtured health and appeal ⟨[children] looked so fresh and pink and *chubby* —Bruce Marshall⟩ ROTUND stresses the notion of roundness and is applicable without being uncomplimentary to more-or-less short men and women of ample girth ⟨a *rotund* governor, five feet six inches in height, six feet five inches in circumference⟩ PORTLY suggests a thickset body with quite ample girth sustained with presence and carried with dignity ⟨large, imposing, *portly* people . . . with the air of grave responsibility which sometimes marks the man of large and imperious physical organism —Havelock Ellis⟩ PLUMP suggests a soft, pleasing, ample, buxom fullness with well-rounded curves and lack of sharp angularity ⟨his wife was . . . *plump* where he was spare —Dorothy Sayers⟩

³**fat** \"\ *vb* **fatted; fatted; fatting; fats** [ME *fatten*, fr. OE *fǣttian*, fr. *fǣtt* fat — more at ²FAT] *vi* **:** to grow fat, plump, or fleshy ⟨large *fatting* pigs —*Brit. Ministry of Agric. Advisory Leaflet*⟩ ~ *vt* **1 :** to make fat **:** FATTEN; *specif* **:** to feed (animals) with the intention of making fat for use as food — often used with *up* or *out* ⟨*fatted* out as porkers —E.W. Lloyd⟩ ⟨~ her up and kill her —Aldous Huxley⟩ **2** *archaic* **:** FERTILIZE, ENRICH **3 a :** to dress or impregnate (leather) with fat or fatty material **b :** to incorporate a fat, grease, or oil in ⟨a well-*fatted* soap⟩

⁴**fat** \"\ *n* -s [ME, fr. *fat*, adj. — more at ²FAT] **1 :** a part of the tissues of an animal that consists chiefly of cells distended with greasy or oily matter ⟨the ~ of meat⟩ **2 a :** the oily or greasy substance that makes up the bulk of the cell contents of adipose tissue and occurs in smaller quantities in many other parts of animals and in plants (as in seeds) **b :** any of a class of neutral solid, semisolid, or liquid chemical compounds that are insoluble in water but soluble in ether and other organic solvents, that are glycerides $C_3H_5(OOCR)_3$ of one or more fatty acids, that are obtained industrially from adipose tissues of animals, from oilseeds, and from the pulp of some fruits, and that are used chiefly in making soap, in protective coatings (as paints and varnishes), as lubricants and softening agents (as in dressing leather), and as cooking fats and a source of energy in foods by furnishing about 9.3 large calories per gram — see LIPID; compare OIL 1a, WAX **c :** a solid or semisolid fat (as lard, beef or mutton tallow, butterfat) obtained chiefly from land animals — distinguished from *fatty oil;* compare BUTTER 2b **3 a :** the best or richest productions **:** the best part ⟨living on the ~ of the land⟩ **b :** an effective part or effective lines or business given to an actor in a dramatic work **4 :** the condition of fatness **:** CORPULENCE, OBESITY ⟨a person somewhat inclined to ~⟩ **5 :** a meat animal that is fat and ready for market — usu. used in pl. ⟨commercial producers, all of whose pigs are being sold as ~*s* —*New Zealand Jour. of Agric.*⟩ **6 a :** something in excess or expendable **:** SUPERFLUITY ⟨slicing a little ~ off the city budget —Anthony West⟩ ⟨the new reserves would have to come from the remaining ~ of the U.S. not yet stripped for total war —*Time*⟩ **b :** resources in excess of those needed immediately **:** SAVINGS, RESERVES ⟨while the country is in a relative depression, it can still live for a time off its ~ —*Newsweek*⟩

⁵**fat** \(ˌ)fat, ˌfət\ *Scot var of* WHAT

⁶**fat** *var of* PHAT

fat acid *n* **:** FATTY ACID 2

fa·tal \ˈfādᵊl, -ātᵊl\ *adj* [ME, fr. L & MF; MF *fatal*, fr. L *fatalis*, fr. *fatum* fate + *-alis* -al — more at FATE] **1** *obs* **a :** decreed or appointed by destiny **:** FATED **b :** DOOMED, CONDEMNED **2 :** attended by or fraught with acts or a potential act of fate **:** FATEFUL ⟨a ~ hour⟩ ⟨a ~ spot⟩ **3 a :** of or belonging to fate ⟨this science sets a ~ necessity on things —H.O.Taylor⟩ **:** concerned with or dealing in fate ⟨the ~ thread of his life had nearly run out⟩ **:** resembling fate in foretelling destiny **:** PROPHETIC ⟨felt he could console himself by arguing that death was written in the ~ books⟩ **b :** like fate in proceeding according to an inevitable or fixed sequence ⟨there was always physical exercise, but that had a ~ way of coming after a time to raise more problems than it solved —Rebecca West⟩ **c** *obs* **:** OMINOUS, FOREBODING **d :** determining one's fate ⟨this ~ gift of enthusiasm, an inherited trait which determined her later life —E.S.Bates⟩ ⟨the ~ flaw in this dazzling woman: a total lack of taste —Marya Mannes⟩ **4 a :** causing death ⟨a ~ blow⟩ ⟨the ~ weapon was found by the police⟩ ⟨a ~ diabetic coma —Havelock Ellis⟩ **b :** causing or resulting in destruction or ruin **:** CALAMITOUS, DISASTROUS ⟨the ~ weekend on which he lost his total fortune in a fire⟩ ⟨the ~ eruption of the volcano that destroyed people and towns and ruined the countryside⟩ **c :** difficult to avoid and causing a harm or evil less grievous than death or ruin ⟨the ~ moment in which she accepted his proposal and began a life of boredom and frustration⟩ ⟨a ~ invitation to triviality —Mark Schorer⟩; *specif, of a woman* **:** ruinously attractive **:** being a femme fatale **syn** see DEADLY

fa·tal·ism \-ˌizəm\ *n* -s [prob. fr. *fatalist*, after such pairs as E *atheist: atheism*] **1 :** the doctrine that all things are subject to fate; *specif* **:** the doctrine that the occurrence of events is necessitated or is fixed in advance for all time in such a manner that human beings are powerless to change them — compare DETERMINISM **2 a :** the mental attitude of a fatalist; *specif* **:** a belief in fatalism **b :** compliance with what are believed to be the dictates of fate ⟨~ can take the form of abject submissiveness but also of heroism⟩

fa·tal·ist \-ˌəst\ *n* -s [prob. fr. F *fataliste*, fr. MF, fr. *fatal* + *-iste* -ist] **:** an adherent of fatalism; *specif* **:** one whose conduct is regulated by belief in fatalism

fa·tal·is·tic \ˈ≈≈ˌistik, -tēk\ *adj* [*fatalist* + *-ic*] **1 :** relating to, implying, or consisting of fatalism ⟨a ~ philosophy⟩ ⟨sorrowful but ~ acceptance —A.D.Coleman⟩ **2 :** believing in or inclined to fatalism ⟨a ~ people⟩ — **fa·tal·is·ti·cal·ly** \-tək(ə)lē, -tēk-, -li\ *adv*

fa·tal·i·ty \fāˈtalədˌē, fəˈ-, -lətē, -i\ *n* -ES [MF *fatalité*, fr. LL *fatalitat-*, *fatalitas*, fr. L *fatalis* decreed by destiny + *-itat-*, *-itas* -ity] **1 :** something brought about or established by fate or necessity ⟨this necessary fact and even duty of nationality is accidental; like age or sex it is a physical ~ —George Santayana⟩ **2 a :** the quality or state of causing or being likely to cause death or destruction ⟨the degree of ~ of certain diseases is higher than one imagines⟩ **b :** the quality or condition of being fated **:** subjection to fate **:** predetermination by necessity; *specif* **:** the quality or condition of being destined for disaster ⟨afraid of the ~ that seemed to mark his family's history⟩ **3 a :** invincible necessity as a principle or fact in nature **:** FATE 1 ⟨to believe in ~⟩ **b :** FATALISM **4 :** the agent or agency of fate ⟨their destiny established by an overruling ~⟩ **5 a :** a fatal outcome; *esp* **:** death resulting from a disaster ⟨a car crash that was the cause of several *fatalities*⟩ **b :** something experiencing or subject to a fatal outcome ⟨one of the *fatalities* in the drownings was a small child⟩

fa·tal·ize \ˈfādᵊlˌīz\ *vt* -ED/-ING/-S *archaic* **:** to ordain or establish by or subject to fate

fa·tal·ly \ˈfādᵊlē, ˈfātᵊl-, -ᵊli\ *adv* [ME, fr. *fatal* + *-ly*] **1 :** in a way established or determined by fate ⟨who would not say, with Huxley, let me be wound up every day like a watch, to go right ~, and I ask no better freedom —William James⟩ ⟨the temptation becomes more and more insidious and she is more ~ bound to yield —H.M.Parshley⟩ **2 :** in a manner suggesting fate or an act of fate **:** inevitably or implacably ⟨a man ~ stern⟩ ⟨a kind of action that brings one ~ to perdition⟩: as **a :** in a manner resulting in death **:** MORTALLY ⟨~ wounded by the accidental discharge of a gun⟩ **b :** beyond repair **:** IRREVOCABLY ⟨find himself ~ humiliated before a hard cadre of French officers because he had not pulled his chauffeur out of a burning jeep —J.W.Chase⟩ ⟨a conflict of ideas that will ~ divide the victors if they are not reconciled —F.S.Kinney⟩ **c :** in a manner resulting in ruin or evil **:** DISASTROUSLY ⟨this ~ ingenious explanation proved an obstacle for some time to a true view of the function of the arterial system —Benjamin Farrington⟩ ⟨it is ~ easy to pass off our prejudices as our opinions —W.F.Hambly⟩ **d :** IRRESISTIBLY ⟨~ attracted by vigorous, strong-willed women —*Time*⟩ ⟨thinks she is ~ attractive —J.W.Krutch⟩

fa·tal·ness \-ᵊlnəs\ *n* -ES **:** the quality or state of being fatal ⟨a poison of such ~ as to result in death⟩

fa·ta mor·ga·na \ˌfädə,mȯ(r)ˈgänə\ *n, pl* **fata morganas** *sometimes cap F&M* [It, mirage, Morgan le Fay (sorceress of Arthurian legend)] **1 :** MIRAGE ⟨suddenly — like a *fata morgana* rising out of the desert clouds — houses, trees, and people materialized —Joseph Wechsberg⟩; *esp* **:** one with marked displacement and distortion **2 :** something insubstantial or illusory ⟨the *fata morgana* of romantic love —Anthony West⟩

fatback \ˈ≈ˌ≈\ *n* [²*fat* + *back*, n.] **1 :** MENHADEN **2 :** BLUE-

FISH 1 **3 :** the strip of fat from the back of a hog carcass usu. cured by dry-salting — see PORK illustration

fatbird \ˈ=,=\ *n* **1 :** OILBIRD **2 :** PECTORAL SANDPIPER

fat body \ˈ=,==\ *n* **1 :** a lobulated mass of fatty tissue attached to each genital gland in amphibians **2 :** a fatty tissue enveloping the viscera or forming a layer under the integument and serving as a reserve of nutrition in many insects esp. in nearly mature larval stages — compare ADIPOSE TISSUE

fatcake \ˈ=,=\ *n* **:** DOUGHNUT, FRIEDCAKE

fat cat *n* **1** *slang* **a :** a wealthy contributor to a political campaign fund; *esp* **:** one who is also a political candidate **b :** a wealthy and consequently privileged person **c :** BIG SHOT **2 :** a lethargic complacent person

fat cell *n* **:** one of the constituent fat-laden cells characteristic of adipose tissue

fat-chewing \ˈ=,==\ *n* -S **:** CHATTING ⟨endless shoptalk and *fat-chewing* with many authors —Laura Z. Hobson⟩

fat-choy \ˈfatˈchȯi, ˈfätˈ-\ *n* -S [Chin (Cant) *faat ts'oi,* fr. *faat* hair + *ts'oi* vegetable] **:** an edible blue-green alga (*Nostoc commune* var. *flagelliforme*)

fat crab *n* **:** a crab that soon will shed its shell

fat dormouse *n* **:** a common dormouse (*Glis glis*) of Central Europe and Asia Minor introduced into parts of England

¹fate \ˈfāt, *usu* -ād·+V\ *n* -S [ME, fr. L or MF; MF *fate,* fr. L *fatum* prophetic declaration, oracle, what is ordained by the gods, destiny, fate, fr. neut. of *fatus,* past part. of *fari* to speak — more at BAN] **1 a :** the principle or determining cause or will by which things in general are supposed to come to be as they are or events to happen as they do **b :** foreordination by which either the universe as a whole or particular happenings are predetermined; *specif* **:** necessity as inherent in the nature of things to which the gods as well as men are subject ⟨~ in Greek tragedy becomes the order of nature in modern thought —A.N.Whitehead⟩ — compare DETERMINISM **2 a :** whatever is destined or inevitably decreed esp. for a person **:** an appointed lot ⟨her ~ was to remain a spinster⟩ **b :** RUIN, DISASTER; *esp* **:** DEATH ⟨the villain met his ~ at the hands of the hero⟩ **c :** ultimate lot or disposition **:** final outcome **:** END ⟨the congress decided the bill's ~ by a single vote⟩ ⟨the explorer's party left no trace of the ~ that overcame them⟩ ⟨the importance of an individual thinker . . . depends upon the ~ of his ideas in the mind of his successors —A.N.Whitehead⟩ **d :** the circumstances that befall something ⟨all human beings live as members of organized groups and have their ~ inextricably bound up with that of the group to which they belong —Ralph Linton⟩ **3 :** one of the goddesses of fate or destiny esp. of classical times supposed to determine the course of human life — usu. used in pl. and then sometimes cap. ⟨waiting there, standing like a ~ in the center of the carpet, a gaunt, gray, somber woman —G.W.Brace⟩ ⟨my great-aunts, formidable ~*s* who sat in judgment on all the events of their time —Hugh Dickinson⟩ ⟨the ~*s* . . . have smiled with an astonishing kindness on his wanderings in the jungle —*Geog. Jour.*⟩

syn FATE, DESTINY, LOT, PORTION, and DOOM agree in signifying the condition or end decreed by a higher power. FATE presupposes a determining supernatural or divine agency, as the gods, God, or the law of necessity, and usu. implies inevitability, but can extend to include a human agency whose decision is finally determinative, in both applications usu. implying a more or less adverse condition or end ⟨no matter how absurd or meaningless our *fate* may be, we still must accept it and play our role —J.M.O'Brien⟩ ⟨through knowledge man can control his own *fate* —Abram Kardiner⟩ ⟨it is the *fate* of all these lakes to disappear —*Amer. Guide Series: Minn.*⟩ ⟨preparing for the end, for the final grim defense, when his men would retreat upon the one last strong fort, and there await their *fate* —Gilbert Parker⟩ ⟨the *fate* of the congressional bill was uncertain⟩ DESTINY implies an irrevocable determination, course, or appointment, as by the will of the gods, but out of context specifies neither a good nor bad course or end, more often, possibly, implying a course conceived of as good by the one destined because it is conceived of as a natural fulfillment ⟨not to impose their view of life upon any people but to inspire in all peoples an understanding of their common *destiny* —Stephen Duggan⟩ ⟨for good or ill, that clubfoot, like the mark of Jason in her life, had been his *destiny* —Ellen Glasgow⟩ ⟨always had with him, too, the special conviction of *destiny* — that his was a great age of history, and that he was born to act in and dominate these times —Henry Wallace⟩ ⟨the conception of a lordly splendid *destiny* for the human race, to which we are false when we revert to wars and other atavistic follies —Bertrand Russell⟩ LOT and PORTION imply a distribution by fate or destiny, LOT suggesting more a blind chance, PORTION implying a more or less fair apportioning of good and evil ⟨shunned extremes of passion or suffering, declaring that these were seldom the common *lot* —*Encyc. Americana*⟩ ⟨it fell to the *lot* of the U.S. to scrap thirty-two ships —C.E.Black & E.C. Helmreich⟩ ⟨poverty was his *portion* all his days —Kemp Malone⟩ ⟨a feeling of guilty remorse was her daily *portion* —Susan Ertz⟩ ⟨she is not the saint he deems it the *portion* of every creature wearing petticoats to be —George Meredith⟩ DOOM implies a final, usu. grim and calamitous, award or fate ⟨thirty-two brave men of Gonzales, who marched in even after the *doom* of the fort seemed certain —*Amer. Guide Series: Texas*⟩ ⟨lured unsuspecting ships to their *doom* on the rocks on dark and stormy nights —Richard Joseph⟩ ⟨the poor beast's ribs stood out under a coating of snow as it stood there, awaiting its *doom* —F.V.W.Mason⟩

²fate \"\ *vt* -ED/-ING/-S **:** DESTINE ⟨the two seemed *fated* for each other⟩; *also* **:** DOOM ⟨the deep antipathy . . . seeming to ~ them to antagonism —Les Savage⟩ ⟨novel about a *fated* beauty —*Newsweek*⟩

³fate \"\ *dial Brit var of* FEAT

fated *adj* [fr. past part. of ²*fate*] **1 a :** determined or controlled by fate ⟨all life is lived in a ~ field —*N.Y. Times*⟩ ⟨an ill-*fated* expedition⟩ **b :** marked by fate **:** chosen to be the locale of disastrous events ⟨the spot was ~ and narrowly escaped being the scene of a second catastrophe as frightful as the first —J.A.Froude⟩ **2 :** FATEFUL ⟨from the first there had been a ~ air about the Gallipoli expedition —Alan Moorehead⟩ ⟨the story unfolds with a tragic, ~ quietness —*Times Lit. Supp.*⟩

fate drama *n* **:** a play esp. popular in early 19th century Germany in which a malignant destiny drives the protagonist to commit a horrible crime often unsuspectingly

fate·ful \ˈfātfəl\ *adj* **1** *of an utterance* **:** OMINOUS, PROPHETIC ⟨ready at the nurse's ~ whisper to fetch whatever was needed or telephone for the physician —Ellen Glasgow⟩ **2 :** having the power of serving or accomplishing fate **:** fraught with fate **:** involving momentous consequences ⟨that ~ meeting of the U.N. when . . . it declared war on North Korea —*Saturday Rev.*⟩; *esp* **:** bringing on adverse fate **:** DEADLY, CATASTROPHIC ⟨during the ~ time the slayings occurred —*Fortnight*⟩ **3 :** controlled by fate **:** determined by irresistible and foreordained forces **syn** see OMINOUS

fate·ful·ly \-fəlē, -li\ *adv* **:** in a fateful manner

fate·ful·ness \-fəlnəs\ *n* -ES **:** the quality or state of being fateful ⟨unaware of the ~ of their meeting until it resulted in both their deaths⟩

fate line *n, sometimes cap F* **:** LINE OF FATE ⟨a double *Fate line* denotes an eventful life —Alice D. Jennings⟩

fate map *n* **:** a plan of an early embryo indicating the potentialities for development and differentiation of the various embryonic areas

fates *pl of* FATE, *pres 3d sing of* FATE

fath *abbr* fathom

fathead \ˈ=,=\ *n* **1 :** a slow-witted or stupid person **:** FOOL **2 a :** FATHEAD MINNOW **b :** SHEEPSHEAD 2c

fatheaded \ˈ=ˈ==\ *adj* **:** dull-witted **:** markedly foolish **:** STUPID, IDIOTIC

fat·head·ed·ness *n* -ES **:** the quality or state of being fatheaded

fathead minnow *also* **fatheaded minnow** *n* **:** a widely distributed No. American cyprinid fish (*Pimephales promelas*) occurring from southern Canada and New York westward down the Mississippi valley and into Mexico and in some areas esteemed as a panfish

fat hen *n* **1 :** any of several succulent or fleshy-leaved plants esp. of the genus *Chenopodium* (as lamb's-quarters) **2 :** any of certain plants of the genus *Atriplex* (esp. *A. lastata* and *A. patula*) **3 :** GROUND IVY **4 :** BUCKWHEAT 1 **5 :** SHEPHERD'S PURSE **6 :** MUGWORT 1

¹fa·ther \ˈfät͟hə(r), ˈfȧt͟hə(r\ *n* -S [ME *fader,* fr. OE *fæder;* akin to OHG *fater* father, ON *fathir,* Goth *fadar,* L *pater,* Gk *patēr,* Skt *pitṛ*] **1 a :** a man who has begotten a child **:** a male parent **:** SIRE **b** *cap* (1) **:** ²GOD, DEITY 1b ⟨our Father who art in heaven —Mt 6:9 (RSV)⟩ (2) **:** the first person of the Trinity ⟨Father, Son, and Holy Ghost⟩ **2 : a** male ancestor more remote than a parent **:** FOREFATHER, ANCESTOR **3 :** one related to another in a way paralleling or suggesting the relationship of father to child: as **a :** one to whom a filial affection and respect are usu. due **:** adoptive father **:** FATHER-IN-LAW, STEPFATHER **:** a male relative who assumes the rights and obligations as well as the title of a father **b :** CONFESSOR 3 **c :** one who is the marked and usu. revered guide or most notable influence in another's spiritual, intellectual, or artistic development; *also* **:** one who is in a position of authority as guide and benefactor ⟨he had become a ~ to the village —Keith Ellis⟩ **d :** an old man — used as a respectful form of address **4** *often cap* **:** an early Christian writer accepted widely or generally as a trustworthy witness to or expositor of the early history or teachings of the church **5 a :** one that originates or institutes **:** one that first constructs, designs, or frames ⟨the ~ of modern radio⟩ ⟨~ of science fiction —D.H.Menzel⟩ ⟨the influence of Babylonian and Egyptian mathematics upon the ~*s* of Greek science, esp. Pythagoras —*Times Lit. Supp.*⟩ **b :** one of the first American colonists **:** PILGRIM FATHER **c :** an early American statesman; *esp* **:** one of the creators of the Constitution ⟨the founding ~*s*⟩ **d :** SOURCE, ORIGIN ⟨the wish is ~ to the thought⟩ ⟨such an attitude of mind may easily become the ~ of criticism —V.L.Parrington⟩ ⟨the doctrine that strife is the ~ of all things —M.R.Cohen⟩ **e :** PROTOTYPE ⟨a totem board at least fifteen feet high . . . the ~ of all totem boards —Daisy Bates⟩ **6 :** any of various ecclesiastics — used in direct address and as a title prefixed to the name (as of a priest in the Roman Catholic, Anglican, or Eastern Orthodox churches, and sometimes a deacon or a superior of a monastic house) **7 :** one of the leading men of a country, city, or council — usu. used in pl. ⟨four proposals were before the city ~*s* —Wayne Robinson⟩ ⟨surrounded by a council of the town ~*s* —Frank Yerby⟩ **8 :** the oldest or the presiding member of an associated group (as a society, a profession, or a legislative assembly) ⟨the ~ of the chapel in a printing plant⟩ ⟨the ~ of the bar⟩

²father \"\ *vt* **fathered; fathered; fathering** \-t͟h(ə)riŋ\ **fathers** [ME *faderen,* fr. *fader* father — more at ¹FATHER] **1 a :** to make oneself the father of **:** BEGET ⟨~ three strapping sons⟩ ⟨cowards ~ cowards —Shak.⟩ **b :** to make oneself the father or author of by adoption or acknowledgment ⟨professed himself willing to have ~*ed* it —Richard Garnett †1906⟩ **c :** to be the founder, creator, or author of **:** ORIGINATE ⟨though he was no great poet he ~*ed* a school of notable poets⟩ ⟨~*ed* a plan for improving the city's schools⟩ **d :** to be at the center, base, or source of ⟨this moral fault which ~*s* democratic politics —T.V.Smith⟩ **e :** to produce by educating or training ⟨one of the most promising doctors the school had ever ~*ed*⟩ **2 a :** to fix the paternity or origin of ⟨investigation ~*ed* the child upon the lover⟩ ⟨like caterpillars . . . not to be tracked or ~*ed* —William Wordsworth⟩ **b :** to place responsibility for the origin or cause of ⟨~ a crime upon the first likely suspect⟩ **3** *archaic* **:** to care for or look after as a father might **4 :** IMPOSE, FASTEN, FOIST ⟨bent upon ~*ing* a scurrilous significance upon a perfectly innocent remark⟩ **5** *now dial Eng* **:** to bear a strong resemblance to the father of (oneself)

father christmas *n, cap F&C, chiefly Brit* **:** the Christmas spirit personified **:** SANTA CLAUS

father confessor *n* **1 :** a priest who hears confessions; *specif* **:** a priest who is one's regular spiritual guide **2 :** a person who is one's intimate spiritual guide and counselor

fa·thered \ˈ=t͟hə(r)d\ *adj* [¹*father* + *-ed*] **:** provided with a father ⟨worse off in being fatherless than I was, ~ —Elizabeth B. Browning⟩

father family *n* **:** patrilineal family **:** patrilineal sib or gens

father figure *n* **:** one who serves as an emotional substitute for a father

fa·ther·hood \ˈ==,hu̇d\ *n* -S [ME *faderhod,* fr. *fader* + *-hod* -hood] **1 :** the quality or state of being a father **:** the character or authority of a father **:** PATERNITY **2** *usu cap* **:** Godhood in its paternal aspect

father hu·go's rose \,==ˈ(h)yü(,)gōz-\ *n, usu cap F&H* [after *Father Hugo* (Hugh Scallan) *fl* 1889 Catholic missionary who introduced it into England from China] **:** a very early blooming shrub rose (*Rosa hugonis*) with mahogany-red drooping canes, delicate leaves, and solitary but very numerous clear yellow single flowers

father image *n* **1 :** an idealization of one's father constitutive of the ego ideal and often projected onto someone to whom one then looks for guidance and protection **2 :** FATHER FIGURE

fa·ther-in-law \ˈfät͟hə(r)ən,lȯ, ˈfȧth-, -thrən-, -t͟hə(r)n-\ *n, pl* **fathers-in-law** \-ə(r)zən-\ [ME *fader in lawe*] **1 :** the father of one's spouse **2 :** STEPFATHER

fa·ther·land \ˈ==,land, -laa(ə)nd\ *n* **1 :** one's native land or country **:** the country to which one claims native allegiance **2 :** the native land or country of one's father or ancestors

father-lasher \ˈ==,==\ *n* [so called fr. the fact that the male guards the eggs and that it defends itself by lashing out with its tail and spines] **:** either of two small darkly mottled sculpins (*Cottus bubalis* and *C. scorpius*) found chiefly along the coasts of northwestern Europe and the British Isles

fa·ther·less \-ləs\ *adj* [ME *faderles,* fr. OE *fæderlēas,* fr. *fæder* father + *-lēas* -less — more at FATHER, -LESS] **1 a :** having no father; *esp* **:** having no father living ⟨a quiet, thoughtful little lad with the man-of-the-house air of responsibility sometimes worn by ~ only sons —Flora Thompson⟩ **b :** ILLEGITIMATE **2 :** having no known author — **fa·ther·less·ness** *n* -ES

fa·ther·li·ness \-lēnəs, -lin-\ *n* -ES **:** paternal quality **:** the kindness or benignity of or befitting a father ⟨the gentleness and ~ of the strange old man eased the young girl's fears⟩

¹fa·ther·ly \-lē, -li\ *adj* [ME *faderly,* fr. OE *fæderlic,* fr. *fæder* + *-lic* -ly] **1 :** of, belonging to, befitting, or proper to a father ⟨unwilling to take on ~ responsibilities⟩ ⟨gave ~ counsel to the boy in the absence of a parent⟩ **2 :** like a father in affection, care, feeling, or conduct **:** paternally kind, solicitous, or benign **:** PATERNAL ⟨placed a ~ hand on his head and wished him well in his new venture⟩ ⟨noted for his ~ concern for the welfare of his company's employees —*Current Biog.*⟩

²fatherly *adv* [ME *faderly,* fr. OE *fæderlīce,* fr. *fæderlīc,* adj.] *obs* **:** in a fatherly manner

father right *n* **:** descent and inheritance in the male line

father's day *n, usu cap F&D* **:** a day (as the third Sunday in June) appointed for the special honoring of fathers by their children

fa·ther·ship \ˈfät͟hə(r),ship, fȧt͟hə,sh-\ *n* -S [ME *fadership,* fr. *fader* + *-ship*] **:** the quality or state of being a father; *esp* **:** the state of being the oldest member of a society or associated group (as the British House of Commons)

father-sib \ˈ==,=\ *n* **:** sib based on patrilineal descent **:** GENS

father time *n, usu cap F&T* **:** time personified esp. as an old man who is bald, bearded, and holding a scythe and water jar or sometimes an hourglass

fath·o·gram \ˈfat͟hə,gram\ *n* -S [*fatho-* (as in *fathometer*) + *-gram*] **:** a record made by means of a sonic depth finder

¹fath·om \ˈfat͟həm\ *n* -S [ME *fadme,* fr. OE *fæthm* embracing or outstretched arms, fathom (unit of length); akin to OHG *fadum* thread, ON *fathmr* embracing arms, fathom (unit of length), L *patēre* to be open, *pandere* to spread, unfold, Gk *petannynai* to spread out] **1 a** *obs* **:** a full stretch of the arms in a straight line; *also* **:** GRASP, REACH **b :** intellectual grasp, penetration, or profundity **:** COMPREHENSION ⟨the themes display a newer ~ than the technical modernism of the composer's earlier works —*Newsweek*⟩ **2 a :** a unit of length equal to 6 feet based on the distance between fingertips of a man's outstretched arms and used esp. for measuring the depth of water — sometimes used in the singular when qualified by a number ⟨five ~ deep⟩ **b** *archaic* **:** any of several units of length varying around 5 and 5½ feet **c** *Brit* **:** the quantity of wood in a pile of any length measuring 6 feet square in cross section **d :** a unit of area equal to 6 square feet used by miners for measuring areas in the plane of a vein

²fathom \"\ *vb* -ED/-ING/-S [ME *fadmen,* fr. OE *fæthmian;* akin to ON *fathma* to embrace; derivative fr. the root of E ¹*fathom*] *vt* **1** *archaic* **:** to encircle (as for measuring) with outstretched arms **2 a :** to measure by a sounding line **b :** to penetrate (as a mystery) and come to understand **:** comprehend where one had not understood previously **:** get to the bottom of ⟨found the man's motives very difficult to ~⟩ ⟨trying to ~ the universe —C.S.Kilby⟩ ~ *vi* **:** to take soundings; *also* **:** PROBE, INVESTIGATE

fath·om·able \-məbəl\ *adj* **1 :** that can be sounded **2 :** capable of being comprehended

Fa·thom·e·ter \faˈt͟häməd·ə(r), ˈfat͟hə(m),mēd·ə(r)\ *trademark* — used for a sonic depth finder

fath·om·less \ˈfat͟həmləs\ *adj* [²*fathom* + *-less*] **:** incapable of being fathomed **:** IMMEASURABLE ⟨the ~ depths of the ocean⟩ ⟨a man of wealth and ~ energy —Bruce Catton⟩ **:** INCOMPREHENSIBLE ⟨a philosophy complex and, to the ordinary thinker, quite ~⟩ — **fath·om·less·ly** *adv* — **fath·om·less·ness** *n* -ES

fathom line *also* **fathom curve** *n* **:** a usu. sinuous line on a nautical chart joining all points having the same depth of water and thereby indicating the contour of the ocean floor

fa·tid·ic \fāˈtidik, fəˈ-\ *or* **fa·tid·i·cal** \-dəkəl\ *adj* [*fatidic* fr. L *fatidicus,* fr. *fati-* (fr. *fatum* fate) + *-dicus* (fr. *dicere* to say); *fatidical* fr. L *fatidicus* + E *-al* — more at FATE, DICTION] **:** of or belonging to prophecy **:** PROPHETIC

fat·i·ga·bil·i·ty \,fad·ə̇gəˈbilədē, ,fat|, |ēg-, -lətē, -i\ *also* **fa·tigu·abil·i·ty** \fəˌtēgəˈb-\ *n* -ES **:** susceptibility to fatigue

fat·i·ga·ble \ˈfad·ə̇gəbəl, ˈfat|, |ēg-\ *also* **fa·tigu·able** \fəˈtēgəbəl\ *adj* [*fatigable* fr. LL *fatigabilis,* fr. L *fatigare* + *-abilis* -able; *fatiguable* fr. ²*fatigue* + *-able*] **:** easily tired **:** susceptible to fatigue

¹fatigate *adj* [ME *fatigat,* fr. L *fatigatus,* past part. of *fatigare*] *obs* **:** TIRED, WEARY, FATIGUED

²fatigate *vt* -ED/-ING/-S [L *fatigatus,* past part. of *fatigare*] *obs* **:** FATIGUE, TIRE

¹fa·tigue \fəˈtēg, *chiefly dial* -tig\ *n* -S [F, fr. MF, fr. *fatiguer,* v.] **1 a :** weariness from labor or exertion **:** exhaustion of strength; *also* **:** tiredness or physical or nervous exhaustion from causes other than physical or intellectual exertion (as from anoxia, motion sickness, or emotional tension) **b :** loss of power resulting from continued work but removable by rest **c :** exhaustion in productive power (as of soil) **d :** the transitory refractory state induced in a sensory receptor or motor end organ by continued or repeated stimulation — compare ADAPTATION **2 a :** a tiring duty **:** LABOR, TOIL **b** (1) **:** manual or menial work often assigned as a punishment; *esp* **:** such work (as the cleaning up of a camp area or the building of a road) performed in the course of service by a member of one of the military services other than the navy (2) **:** one such task ⟨punishments include loss of rewards or privileges, temporary loss of recreation (usu. associated with a ~ such as floor scrubbing or potato peeling) —*Lancet*⟩ **c fatigues** *pl* **:** the uniform or work clothing worn on fatigue and in the field **3 a :** the tendency of a material (as a metal) to break under repeated cyclic loading at a stress considerably less than the tensile strength in a static test **b :** the decrease of efficiency (as of a luminescent or light-sensitive material) with use

²fatigue \"\ *vb* -ED/-ING/-S [F *fatiguer,* fr. MF, fr. L *fatigare;* akin to L *affatim* sufficiently, *fatisci* to fall apart, become exhausted, and prob. to L *fames* hunger — more at DAZE] *vt* **1 :** to weary with labor or exertion **:** TIRE **2 :** to induce a condition of fatigue in (as a material or an effector organ) ~ *vi* **1 :** to undergo or suffer fatigue (as of a metal) **2 :** to perform fatigue (as in the army) **syn** see TIRE

³fatigue \"\ *adj* [¹*fatigue*] **:** consisting of, done, or used in fatigue ⟨~ detail⟩ ⟨a ~ uniform⟩ **:** belonging to fatigues ⟨a ~ cap⟩ ⟨grabbed his ~ collar and pulled him out of line⟩

fatigue call *n* **:** a bugle call warning those detailed for fatigue duty to report to a designated place

fatigue curve *n* **:** a graph showing the rate of decline of strength or speed in long-continued work

fa·tigue·less \-ləs\ *adj* **:** incapable of tiring **:** UNTIRING

fatigue limit *n* **:** the highest stress that a material can withstand for an infinite number of cycles without breaking — called also *endurance limit;* compare FATIGUE STRENGTH

fatigue ratio *n* **:** the ratio of the fatigue limit or fatigue strength to the static tensile strength of a material — called also *endurance ratio*

fa·tigue·some \fəˈtēgsəm\ *adj* **:** FATIGUING, WEARISOME

fatigue strength *n* **:** the highest stress that a material can withstand for a given number of cycles without breaking — called also *endurance strength;* compare FATIGUE LIMIT

fatigue syndrome *n* **:** COMBAT FATIGUE

fa·tigu·ing·ly *adv* [*fatiguing* (pres. part. of ²*fatigue*) + *-ly*] **:** in a manner that tires or wearies

fa·ti·ha *or* **fa·ti·hah** \ˈfätē,hä\ *n* -S *often cap* [Ar *fātihah* that which opens or begins] **:** the short opening sura of the Koran used by Muslims as a prayer

fa·til·o·quent \fāˈtiləkwənt, fəˈ-\ *adj* [modif. (influenced by E *eloquent*) of L *fatiloquus,* fr. *fati-* (fr. *fatum* fate) + *-loquus* (fr. *loqui* to speak) — more at FATE, LOQUACIOUS] *archaic* **:** PROPHETIC

fat·i·mid \ˈfad·əməd, -(,)mid\ *also* **fat·i·mite** \-,mīt\ *n* -S *cap, often attrib* [*Fatima* †A.D.632 daughter of Muhammad by his first wife + E *-id* or *-ite*] **:** a descendant of Fatima, a daughter of Muhammad, and Ali, the cousin of Muhammad and fourth caliph of Islam, regarded by the Shi'ites as a true heir to the caliphate; *esp* **:** a member of the Fatimid dynasty ruling portions of No. Africa during the period A.D. 909–1171

fating *pres part of* FATE

fat-kidneyed *adj, obs* **:** GROSS, CLUMSY

fat·less \ˈfatləs\ *adj, of meat* **:** LEAN

fatlike \ˈ=,=\ *adj* **:** resembling fat **:** FATTY

fat·ling \ˈfatliŋ\ *n* -S **:** a young animal (as a calf, lamb, or kid) fattened for slaughter

fat liquor *n* [¹*fat* + *liquor*] **:** a liquor made of an emulsion of soap and fat (as castor oil or degras) or of sulfonated oil and used in tanning leather

fat-liquor \ˈ=,==\ *vt* [*fat liquor*] **:** to fill the fiber of (a leather) with oil or fat **:** treat (leather) with fat liquor

fat·ly *adv* [ME, fr. ²*fat* + *-ly*] **1 :** RICHLY, LUXURIANTLY ⟨a ~ prosperous landscape⟩ **2 :** in the manner of one that is fat ⟨walking ~ down the road —Claud Cockburn⟩ ⟨turned ~ and looked at him —William Faulkner⟩ **3 :** SMUGLY, COMPLACENTLY ⟨any of the reasons usu. given so patly and ~ —Sinclair Lewis⟩

fat mouse *n* [so called from its accumulation of oily fat before hibernation] **:** any of several silky furred tropical and southern African short-tailed mice (genus *Steatomys*) regarded as a great delicacy by the natives

fat·ness *n* -ES [ME *fatnesse,* fr. OE *fǣtnes,* fr. *fǣtt* fat + *-nes* -ness — more at FAT] **1 a :** the quality or state of being fat or rich in fats **:** fullness of flesh **:** CORPULENCE, OBESITY **b :** FERTILITY, FRUITFULNESS ⟨the ~ of the orchards⟩ ⟨a land of all but incredible ~ and beauty —Russell Lord⟩ **2** *obs* **:** greasy or oily substance found in animal or vegetable matter **:** FAT **3 :** something that makes rich or fertile ⟨let it come like the abundant ~ of the clouds upon the thirsting earth —Benjamin Fine⟩

fat paint *n* **:** FATTY PAINT

fat pine *n* **1** *chiefly Midland* **:** KINDLING WOOD **2 :** any of several trees (as the longleaf pine) abounding in pitchy heartwood

fat pork *n* **1 :** the fruit of a wild fig (*Clusia flava*) **2 :** the fruit of the coco plum

fat-rumped sheep \ˈ=,=-\ *n* **:** a coarse-wooled sheep widespread in western and central Asia that develops large accumulations of fat on the rump during periods of abundant feed

fats *pl of* FAT, *pres 3d sing of* FAT

fat scab *n* : RAIN ROT
fats·hed·era \fat'sed(ə)rə, -ts'he-\ *n* -s *sometimes cap* [*fatsia* + NL *Hedera*] : a vigorous upright ornamental foliage plant with glossy deeply lobed palmate leaves that is a hybrid between the common ivy (*Hedera helix*) and a fatsia (*Aralia elata*)
¹**fat·sia** \'fatsēə\ [NL] *syn of* ECHINOPANAX
²**fatsia** \"\ *n* -s **1** : DEVIL'S CLUB **2** : a prickly tree (*Aralia elata*) with immense leaves and large flower clusters
fat·so \'fat(,)sō\ *n* -ES [prob. fr. *Fats,* nickname of a fat person (fr. ²*fat* + -*s,* noun plural suffix used in casual nicknames such as *Whiskers* or *Cuddles* identifying a person by a characteristic feature or activity) + -*o*] *slang* : a fat person — often used as a disparaging form of address
fat-soluble \'⸗'⸗⸗⸗\ *adj* : soluble in fats or fat solvents (as ether) : OIL-SOLUBLE — used esp. of certain vitamins ⟨*fat-soluble* vitamin A⟩
fatstock \'⸗,⸗\ *n* : livestock that is fat and ready for market
fat-tailed lemur \'⸗,⸗-\ *n* : any of several Malagasy mouse lemurs (genus *Cheirogaleus*) with much-thickened tails sometimes regarded as constituting a separate genus (*Atililemur* or *Opolemur*)
fat-tailed sheep *n* : a coarse-wooled mutton sheep that has great quantities of fat on each side of the tail bones, that is widely distributed in southeastern Europe, No. Africa, and Asia, and that occurs in many local breeds or races
fatted *adj* [fr. past part. of ³*fat*] : FATTENED, FAT ⟨killed for him the ~ calf —Lk 15:30 (RSV)⟩
fat·ten \'fatᵊn\ *vb* **fattened; fattened; fattening** \-t(ᵊ)niŋ\ **fattens** [²*fat* + -*en*] *vt* **1 a** : to make fat, fleshy, or plump — often used with *up* ⟨attempting to ~ her children up with potatoes, spaghetti, and creamed dishes⟩ : make bigger or more substantial ⟨~ the record by making false entries⟩ ⟨~ the young author's self-esteem —E.J.Simmons⟩; *esp* : to feed (as a stock animal) for slaughter **b** (1) : to add to (a pot) in a card game esp. by an additional ante (2) : to play a high-scoring card to (a trick one's partner or a favored opponent is expected to win, as in pinochle) **2** : to make fertile and fruitful : ENRICH ~ *vi* : to grow fat, corpulent, or plump ⟨herds ~*ing* on the early clover⟩ : grow rich and prosperous ⟨early kings ~*ing* on the labor of slaves and enemy captives⟩ ⟨boulevard papers with large circulations ~*ing* on sex, crime, and scandal —*Newsweek*⟩ — often used with *out* ⟨a skinny cow ~*ing out* into a good carcass⟩
fat·ten·er \-t(ᵊ)nə(r)\ *n* -s **1** : one that fattens ⟨selling young goslings to ~*s*⟩ **2** : stock to be fattened for slaughter ⟨some of the pigs were singled out as breeders and the rest left as ~*s*⟩
fattening *adj* [fr. gerund & pres. part. of *fatten*] : used in or subject to the process of fattening up for slaughter ⟨a ~ pen⟩ ⟨a ~ hog⟩
¹**fatter** *comparative of* FAT
²**fat·ter** \'fad·ə(r), 'fatə(r)\ *n* -s [³*fat* + -*er*] **1** : FATTENER **2** [⁴*fat* + -*er*] : a worker who trims excess fat from meat or who cuts fat from intestines for rendering into lard
fattest *superlative of* FAT
fat·ti·ly \'fad·ᵊlē, -at|, |ᵊli\ *adv* : in a fatty manner
fat·ti·ness \|ēnəs, |in-\ *n* -ES : the quality or state of being fatty ⟨made ill by the excessive ~ of the meal⟩ ⟨made greasy by the ~ of the wool⟩
fatting *pres part of* FAT
fat·tish \'fad·|ish, -at|, |ēsh\ *adj* [ME, fr. ²*fat* + -*ish*] : somewhat fat ⟨a ~ girl⟩ ⟨an almost white . . . tenacious ~ clay —William Bartram⟩
fat·trels \'fa·trəlz\ *n pl* [origin unknown] *Scot* : ends of ribbons ⟨the ~ on a lady's bonnet⟩
¹**fat·ty** \'fad·|ē, -at|, |i\ *adj* -ER/-EST [ME, fr. ⁴*fat* + -*y,* adj. suffix] **1 a** : containing fat esp. in unusual amounts ⟨a rather ~ steak⟩ : ADIPOSE ⟨getting ~ around the hips⟩ : CORPULENT ⟨a short ~ woman in black —John Updike⟩ ⟨the curious ~ grace of the butcher —Josephine Johnson⟩ **b** : having the qualities of fat : GREASY ⟨a rather ~ wool⟩ ⟨the constant frying left a ~ deposit on the kitchen woodwork⟩ **c** : having or marked by too great a deposit of fat ⟨a ~ liver⟩ ⟨~ cirrhosis⟩ **d** : STICKY, COHESIVE — used of cement pastes, mortars, concretes, or clays **2** : derived from or chemically related to the fats : ALIPHATIC ⟨~ alcohols⟩
²**fatty** \"\ *n* -ES [²*fat* + -*y,* n. suffix] : one that is fat ⟨the pill would weigh almost two ounces, for a 150-pound person . . . would be . . . still bigger for a ~ —*Springfield* (*Mass.*) *Daily News*⟩
fatty acid *n* **1** : any of the series of saturated aliphatic monocarboxylic acids $C_nH_{2n+1}COOH$ (as acetic acid or lauric acid) many of which occur naturally usu. in the form of esters in fats, waxes, and essential oils **2** : any of the saturated or unsaturated monocarboxylic acids that occur naturally in the form of glycerides in fats and fatty oils, that in almost all cases contain an even number of carbon atoms most commonly 12 to 24 in the higher acids (as palmitic acid or oleic acid), that in a few cases contain a substituting group (as hydroxyl in ricinoleic acid), that are obtained by hydrolysis of fats or by synthesis, and that are used chiefly in making soap, detergents, metallic soaps, and other derivatives
fatty degeneration *n* **1** : a process of tissue degeneration marked by the deposition of fat globules in the cells **2** : moral or artistic degeneration esp. as a result of sloth or complacency, overindulgence, or luxury
fatty infiltration *n* : infiltration of the tissue of an organ with excess amounts of fat
fatty oil *n* : a fat that is liquid at ordinary temperatures and that is obtained from plants or marine animals — called also *fixed oil;* distinguished from *essential oil* and *volatile oil;* compare OIL 1a
fatty paint *n* : a liquid paint in which the oil has become unduly polymerized, oxidized, or thickened to a pasty buttery abnormal consistency
fa·tu·i·tous \fə'tüəd·əs, fə'tyü-, -ᵊlətəs\ *adj* [*fatuity* + -*ous*] : characterized by fatuity : FATUOUS
fa·tu·i·ty \-üəd·ē, -üətē, -i\ *n* -ES [MF *fatuité* foolishness, fr. L *fatuitat-, fatuitas,* fr. *fatuus* foolish + -*itat-,* -*itas* -ity] **1 a** : something foolish, silly, absurd, or stupid (as an action) ⟨the exaggerated patience of all children dealing with the *fatuities* of all adults —*New Yorker*⟩ **b** : FOOLISHNESS, INANITY, ABSURDITY ⟨in the light of what has happened, this remark has a poisonous ~ —Anthony West⟩ ⟨refined her good manners into docility, her gentleness almost to ~ —Louis Auchincloss⟩; *also* : STUPIDITY ⟨the vessels . . . had just arrived at the landing place — and here, with incredible ~, were allowed to remain, with most of their indispensable contents still on board —Francis Parkman⟩ **2** *archaic* : IMBECILITY, IDIOCY, DEMENTIA
fat·u·oid \'fachə,wȯid\ *n* -s [NL *fatua* (specific epithet of *Avena fatua,* fr. L, fem. of *fatuus*) + E -*oid*] : an aberrant form arising in cultivated oats that is believed to be a mutation and that resembles both the parent variety and the wild oat (*Avena fatua*) — called also *false wild oats*
fat·u·ous \'fachəwəs\ *adj* [L *fatuus* foolish, silly — more at BAT] **1 a** : marked by want of intelligence and rational consideration; *esp* : marked by futile ill-founded hope or desire, by witless complacent disregard of reality, or by inane lack of consideration ⟨the ~ adorer of that dilapidated, horrible woman —Arnold Bennett⟩ ⟨men do argue about religion, and it is ~ for those who argue on one side to try also to discredit all rational arguments —M.R.Cohen⟩ : inanely foolish ⟨aware that a ~ expression was spreading like melted wax over his features —Ellen Glasgow⟩ : ABSURD ⟨one of the most ~ plans for city improvement ever devised⟩ : STUPID, SILLY ⟨a foolish woman given to ~ remarks⟩ **b** *chiefly Scots law* : DEMENTED, IMBECILE **2** *archaic* : resembling an ignis fatuus : without reality : ILLUSORY **syn** see SIMPLE
fat·u·ous·ly *adv* : in a fatuous manner : FOOLISHLY, INANELY
fat-witted \'⸗'⸗⸗\ *adj* : STUPID, IDIOTIC, FATHEADED
fatwood \'⸗,⸗\ *n, South & Midland* : LIGHTWOOD 1
fau·bourg \(')fō¦bu̇(ə)r, 'fō,bu̇rg, -,bərg, F fōbüːr\ *n* -s [alter. (influenced by F *faubourg* suburb, fr. MF *fauxbourg*) of ME *faubour, fabor,* fr. MF *fauxbourg,* by folk etymology (influence of MF *faux* false, fr. L *falsus*) fr. *forsbourg,* fr. OF *forsborc,* fr. *fors* outside of, outside (fr. L *foris* out of doors, out) + *borc* town; akin to L *foris, fores* door — more at FALSE, DOOR, BOURG] **1** : a suburban area : SUBURB; *esp* : a suburb of a French city **2 a** : a district formerly outside a city's wall but now within the city **b** : a city quarter

¹**fau·cal** \'fȯkəl\ *adj* [L *fauces* + E -*al*] **1** : FAUCIAL **2** : formed or occurring in or near the fauces : PHARYNGEAL
²**faucal** \"\ *n* -s : a faucal sound
fau·cal·ize \-ə,līz\ *vb* -ED/-ING/-S : to modify by faucal articulation
faucal plosive *n* : a stop consonant released through the nasal cavity by sudden lowering of the velum (as the \t\ in \'kätᵊn\ *cotton*)
fau·ces \'fȯ,sēz\ *n pl* [L, pl., fauces, throat] **1** *usu sing in constr* : the narrow passage from the mouth to the pharynx situated between the soft palate and the base of the tongue and bounded laterally by two curved folds enclosing the tonsil on each side — called also *isthmus of the fauces* **2** : the throat of a gamopetalous corolla **3** : the portion of the interior of a spiral shell that can be seen by looking into the aperture
fauces ter·rae \¦fau̇,kā'ste,rī, ¦fȯ,sēz'te,rē\ *n pl* [L, gulf] : headlands or promontories enclosing an arm of the sea that under international law is territorial water and not part of the high seas
fau·cet \'fȯsət,'fä-, *archaic* 'fa-; *usu* -əd·+V\ *n* -s [ME, fr. MF *fausset,* fr. *fausser,* to damage, be false to, fr. LL *falsare* to falsify, fr. L *falsus* false — more at FALSE] **1** *now dial* : a peg used to stop a vent hole in a cask or other vessel **2** : a fixture for drawing a liquid from a pipe, cask, or other vessel : TAP, COCK **3** : HUB 5a (1)

faucet 2

fau·chard \(')fō¦shär\ *n* -s [F, fr. OF *fausart, fauchart,* fr. *faus, faux* sickle, scythe (fr. L *falx*) + -*ard,* -*art* -ard] : a long-handled medieval weapon with a long convex edge
faucht \'fäkt\ *Scot var of* FOUGHT
fau·cial \'fȯshəl\ *adj* [L *fauces* + E -*ial*] : of or involving the fauces ⟨a ~ tonsil⟩ ⟨~ diphtheria⟩
faud \'fȯd,'fäd\ *dial Brit var of* FOLD
faugh *a forcefully articulated p-sound or a forceful trilling of the lips; often read as* 'fȯ\ *interj* — used to express contempt, disgust, or abhorrence
faught \'fȯkt\ *Scot var of* FIGHT
fau·ja·site \'fōzhə,sīt,-,zīt\ *n* -s [F, fr. Barthélemy *Faujas* de Saint-Fond †1819 Fr. geologist + F -*ite*] : a mineral $(Na_2,Ca)Al_2Si_4O_{12}.6H_2O$ consisting of a colorless or white hydrous aluminosilicate of sodium and calcium (hardness 5, sp. gr. 1.92)
fauj·dar *or* **fouj·dar** \'fau̇j,där\ *n* -s [Hindi *fawjdār,* fr. Per, fr. Ar *fawj* host, troop + Per -*dār* holder — more at BHUMIDAR] **1** *India* : a petty officer (as one in charge of police) **2** *India* : a criminal judge
fauj·da·ri *or* **fouj·da·ry** \-rē\ *n, pl* **faujdaris** *or* **foujdaries** [Hindi *fawjdārī,* fr. Per, fr. *fawjdār*] **1** *India* : a faujdar's jurisdiction **2** *India* : a criminal court
faul·chion *var of* FALCHION
fauld \'fȯld\ *chiefly Scot var of* FOLD
¹**fault** \'fȯlt, *archaic* 'fȯt\ *n* -s [ME *faute, faulte,* fr. OF *faute,* fr. (assumed) VL *fallita,* fr. fem. of (assumed) VL *fallitus,* past part. of L *fallere* to deceive — more at FAIL] **1** *obs* **a** : LACK, SCARCITY ⟨one it pleases me, for ~ of a better, to call my friend —Shak.⟩ **b** : NEGLECT, DEFAULT **2** : a defect in quality or constitution : an imperfection in character or disposition : FAILING, WEAKNESS; *esp* : a blameworthy moral weakness less serious than a vice **b** : a physical or intellectual imperfection or impairment ⟨a theory with some serious ~*s*⟩ : FLAW, BLEMISH : a damaged part ⟨a ~ in a bolt of cloth⟩ **c** (1) : a violation of a rule in a racket game which results in loss of service or a point for the opponent or both (as a failure to serve the ball legitimately into the proper court) (2) : a service in a racket game that strikes outside the proper service court **d** : a defective point in an electric circuit due to a crossing of wires, a ground, a break in the circuit, a failure of insulation **3** : a failure to do what is right : **a** : a moral transgression : SIN ⟨fell down at the pope's feet confessing his ~ —R.W. Southern⟩ **b** : a wrongdoing of an excusable kind : MISDEMEANOR ⟨a small boy's ~*s*⟩ **c** : MISTAKE, ERROR ⟨a subtle ~, committed most . . . when we are least aware of it —S.L. Payne⟩ **d** : a failure to do something required by law or the doing of something forbidden by law — compare NEGLIGENCE **4 a** : responsibility for wrongdoing or failure ⟨it was not the driver's ~ that the car went out of control⟩ **b** : the wrongdoing or failure attributable to a particular inadequacy, flaw, or failure ⟨the accident was the ~ of a broken steering rod⟩ **5** : a fracture in the earth's crust accompanied by a displacement of one side of the fracture with respect to the other and in a direction parallel to the fracture **6** : a lost scent in hunting; *also* : the act of losing the scent : CHECK
syn FAILING, FRAILTY, FOIBLE, VICE: FAULT implies some falling short, though usu. not far, of a standard of moral perfection in disposition or action ⟨his lack of interest in theology is a weakness but not a major *fault* —C.H.Hopkins⟩ ⟨there are *faults* which are not *faults* of will, but *faults* of mere inadequacy to some unforeseen position —J.A.Froude⟩ ⟨a victim of many small *faults* of envy and spitefulness⟩ FAILING implies a shortcoming, usu. a weakness of character of which one may be unaware ⟨the one *failing* — common to all elderly observers since Adam's hair turned gray — of imagining that the entire youth of the world is going to the dogs —Douglas Stewart⟩ ⟨we should keep in mind the *failings* of resting on what seem to be our laurels and being content with an optimism grown on sheer apathy —H.A.Sosland⟩ FRAILTY stresses a general weakness of character or an instance of usu. chronic weakness deriving from such a character ⟨that shuddering relish for the horrors of conventions at their worst I grant to be a purely human *frailty,* like a fondness for detective stories —J.L. Lowes⟩ FOIBLE usu. implies a harmless weakness of character, often no more than an idiosyncrasy ⟨to indulge on occasion in a kind of willful coquettishness hardly appropriate to her age or appearance . . . was the result rather of a *foible* than of any fundamental folly —J.W.Krutch⟩ ⟨his dear father's one intellectual *foible* — that willful blindness of his to the march of time —Robert Graves⟩ ⟨it is a *foible* in most decent human beings to hope that whatever our failings, at least we are not disfigured by vulgarity of spirit —Kate O'Brien⟩ VICE usu. stresses violation of moral law but in this comparison can apply to any large or small imperfection or weakness of character ⟨the great *vices* such as mendacity, vanity —Norbert Guterman⟩ ⟨she was criminally proud. That was her *vice* —Arnold Bennett⟩ ⟨his only *vice* was . . . an insatiable lust for power —*Time*⟩ ⟨reading was his *vice.* How could he solace his inactive hours? —Sydney Greenbie⟩ ⟨the great *vice* of English drama from Kyd to Galsworthy has been that its aim of realism was unlimited —T.S.Eliot⟩
— **at fault 1 a** : unable to find the scent and continue chase **b** : in trouble or embarrassment and unable to proceed **2** *also* **in fault** : responsible or to blame for a mistake or blemish : CULPABLE ⟨looking for the person *at fault* for an inadequately constructed house⟩ ⟨if war should break out it would be difficult to determine who is really *at fault*⟩ — **for fault of** *or* **for the fault of** *obs* : in default of : through want of — **to a fault** *adv* : almost to the point of absurdity : EXCESSIVELY ⟨gentle *to a fault*⟩ ⟨meticulous *to a fault* in all matters of dress⟩ — **with all faults** *adv* : with no guarantee against defects ⟨merchandise sold *with all faults*⟩
²**fault** \"\ *vb* -ED/-ING/-S [ME *fauten,* fr. *faute,* n. — more at ¹FAULT] *vi* **1** : to commit a fault : go wrong : ERR, BLUNDER ⟨not one singer forgot a word; not a pianist ~*ed* —Hartzell Spence⟩ ⟨his tongue stammering and ~*ing* with rage —Earl of Chesterfield⟩ : fall short : FAIL **2** : to fracture so as to produce a geologic fault ~ *vt* **1 a** : to find a fault or flaw in ⟨conducted himself with such calm dignity that few could ~ him —*Newsweek*⟩ ⟨he had been ~*ed* by professional critics for the lack of music in his speaking of verse —Tyrone Guthrie⟩ ⟨his arguments were logical and hard to ~ —Anthony West⟩ ⟨I ~ this speech in three ways —J.E.Agate⟩; *specif* : to grade (a person or animal) down for imperfect performance or feature in a contest ⟨the dog was ~*ed* in stance⟩ **b** *now dial* : BLAME, SCOLD, CENSURE ⟨don't ~ him for that⟩ **2** : to produce a geologic fault in; *also* : to place in a particular position or shape by reason of such a fault ⟨sediments ~*ed* down against older rocks —Frank Dixey⟩ — used chiefly in the passive **3** : to commit an error in : BUNGLE ⟨the acrobat deliberately ~*ed* the performance once to make it look difficult⟩

fault·age \'fȯltij\ *n* -s : geologic faulting : geologic faults
fault block *n* : a body of rock bounded by faults
fault breccia *or* **fault rubble** *n* : a rock composed of angular fragments that have resulted from movement along a fault : CRUSH BRECCIA
fault cliff *n* : a cliff formed by faulting
fault conglomerate *n* : CRUSH CONGLOMERATE
fault·ed \'fȯltəd\ *adj* [¹*fault* + -*ed*] : marked by faults : FAULTY ⟨a book that is good although ~⟩
fault·er \-tər\ *n* -s [alter. (influenced by -*er,* n. suffix) of ME (Sc) *fautor, fautour* wrongdoer, fr. ME *fauten* to commit a fault + -*or,* -*our* -ə(r)] *dial Brit* : a wrongdoer esp. against the church
faultfinder \'⸗,⸗⸗\ *n* : one esp. given to faultfinding
¹**faultfinding** \'⸗,⸗⸗\ *n* -s [¹*fault* + *finding,* fr. gerund of *find*] : the tendency to unremitting petty esp. unjustified criticisms or the act of persistently finding petty flaws and inadequacies in another ⟨reviews of appreciation and not of contemptuous ~ —A.C.Benson⟩
²**faultfinding** \"\ *adj* [¹*fault* + *finding,* fr. pres. part. of *find*] : disposed to or given to faultfinding : unreasonably or perversely noticing and stressing faults ⟨his *faultfinding* critic —J.T.Field⟩ **syn** see CRITICAL
fault·ful \-fəl\ *adj* : full of faults — **fault·ful·ly** \-fəlē\ *adv*
fault gouge *n* : finely comminuted uncemented rock characteristic of fault zones
fault·i·ly \'fȯltəlē,-li\ *adv* : in a faulty or blamable manner ⟨denial of statements ~ attributed to the secretary of state —*Current Biog.*⟩
fault·i·ness \-tēnəs, -tin-\ *n* -ES : the quality or state of being faulty ⟨the notable ~ of a man's reasoning⟩
faulting *n* -s [fr. gerund of *fault*] : the act or process of fracturing so as to produce a fault; *also* : FAULT
fault·less \'fȯltləs\ *adj* [ME *fautles,* fr. *faute* fault + -*les* -less — more at FAULT] : having no fault : free from defect, imperfection, failing, blemish, or error : IRREPROACHABLE ⟨gave a ~ performance on his first appearance as a concert pianist⟩ ⟨a ~ complexion⟩ ⟨~ workmanship⟩ — **fault·less·ly** *adv* — **fault·less·ness** *n* -ES
fault line *n* : the geologic line determined by the intersection of a fault with the earth's surface or with some other plane of reference
fault-line scarp *n* : a cliff or escarpment resulting from the erosion of soft rock that has been brought against hard rock by faulting
fault-line valley *also* **fault valley** *n* : a valley that follows a fault line
fault plane *n* : a fault surface that is not notably curved
fault rock *n* : a rock that consists of fragments produced by the crushing and grinding which accompany a dislocation and is often found along the fault plane — compare CRUSH BRECCIA, CRUSH CONGLOMERATE
faults *pl of* FAULT, *pres 3d sing of* FAULT
fault scarp *n* : a cliff or escarpment directly resulting from an uplift along one side of a fault
fault slip *n* : a geologic fault
fault surface *n* : the surface along which the dislocated masses have moved in a geologic fault — see FAULT PLANE
fault terrace *n* : a topographic bench or step on a hill slope formed by displacement by two approximately parallel faults along each of which the downhill side has moved down relatively to the uphill side
fault trace *n* : a line of intersection of a fault plane with the earth's surface
fault trough *n* : a usu. long and narrow depression bounded on either side by faults — compare GRABEN
fault vent *n* : a volcanic vent situated on a fault
faulty \'fȯltē, -ti\ *adj* -ER/-EST [ME *fauty,* fr. *faute* fault + -*y*] **1 a** : marked by a fault : having a fault, blemish, or defect : IMPERFECT, UNSOUND ⟨a ~ mechanism⟩ ⟨a ~ argument⟩ ⟨~ digestion⟩ ⟨his technique was ~ and his taste was worse —J.B.Priestley⟩ **b** : prone to faults ⟨memory is often ~ among the mentally ill —Hartzell Spence⟩ : apt to do wrong ⟨this pleasant ~ world —C.E.Montague⟩ **c** : not fit for the use or result intended or desired ⟨the first mate's ~ stowage plan causes a cargo shift —E.B.Garside⟩ **2** *archaic* **a** : guilty of a fault **b** : consisting of a fault : BLAMABLE
fault zone *n* : an area in which there are several closely spaced faults
faun \'fȯn, 'fän\ *n* -s [ME, fr. L *faunus;* akin to Goth *afdauiths* maltreated, Russ *davit'* to press, crush, strangle] : an Italic deity of fields and herds represented as having human shape, with pointed ears, small horns, and sometimes a goat's tail, or as half goat and half man

faun

fau·na \'fȯnə,'fänə\ *n, pl* **fau·nas** \-nəz\ *also* **fau·nae** \-,nē\ [NL, fr. LL *Fauna,* Roman goddess connected with the fauns, fr. L *faunus*] **1** : animals in general or animal life esp. as distinguished from flora; *esp* : the animals or animal life characteristic of or peculiar to a region or locality, period, or geological stratum **2** : the animals or animal life occurring, developed, or adapted for living in a specified environment ⟨cave ~⟩ ⟨protozoal ~ of the human intestine⟩ **3** : a systematic treatise upon the animals of an area or period — compare FLORA 1
fau·nal \'fȯnᵊl, 'fän-\ *adj* [*fauna* + -*al*] : of or relating to fauna — **fau·nal·ly** \-nᵊlē\ *adv*
faunal area *n* : a region characterized by a particular kind of animal community
fau·nat·ed \'fȯ,nād·əd, 'fä,-\ *adj* [*fauna* + -*ate* + -*ed*] : possessing an extensive intestinal fauna of commensal microorganisms — used of certain animals (as termites)
faunch \'fȯnch,'fä-\ *vi* -ED/-ING/-ES [origin unknown] *dial* : to display angry excitement : rant and rave ⟨it was enough to make anybody ~⟩
fau·nist \'fȯnəst, 'fän-\ *n* -s [*fauna* + -*ist*] : a specialist on faunas
fau·nis·tic \(')fȯ¦nistik,(')fä¦-\ *or* **fau·nis·ti·cal** \-tə̇kəl\ *adj* : of or relating to zoogeography : FAUNAL — **fau·nis·ti·cal·ly** \-tə̇k(ə)lē\ *adv*
fau·ni·zone \'fȯnə,zōn, 'fän-\ *n* -s [*fauni-* (fr. *fauna*) + *zone*] : a group of geologic beds deposited during the life span of a particular assemblage of organisms and thus characterized by the fossils of a particular fauna
fau·nol·o·gy \fȯ'näləjē, fä'-, -ji\ *n* -s [*fauno-* (fr. *fauna*) + -*logy*] : ZOOGEOGRAPHY
faunt·le·roy \'fȯntlə,rȯi, 'fän-\ *adj, usu cap* [after Lord *Fauntleroy,* boy hero of Frances Hodgson Burnett's novel *Little Lord Fauntleroy* (1886)] : characterized by a short tailored jacket, knee-length trousers, rather frilly shirt, wide collar with rounded corners, or large loose bow ⟨dressed the boy in *Fauntleroy* clothes and kept his hair in curls —R.L.Taylor⟩ ⟨a ~ suit⟩ ⟨a ~ collar⟩
fau·nule \'fȯ,nyül, 'fä,-\ *also* **fau·nu·la** \-nyələ\ *n, pl* **faunules** \-lz\ *also* **faunu·lae** \-yə,lē\ [NL *faunula,* fr. *fauna* + -*ula*] : a diminutive fauna; *esp* : an association of animal fossils found in a single stratum or a succession of strata of limited thickness
faur \(')fȯr\ *Scot var of* WHERE
faured \'fȯrd\ *Scot var of* FAVORED
fause \'fȯs\ *adj* [by alter.] *chiefly Scot* : FALSE
fau·sen \'fȯsᵊn\ *n* -s [origin unknown] *archaic* : EEL — used chiefly of catadromous eels and sometimes specif. of developmental forms (as the elver or the yellow eel) in their life cycle

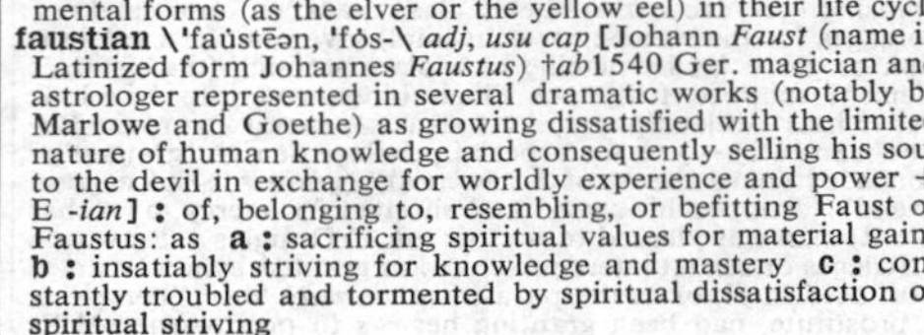

faustian \'fau̇stēən, 'fȯs-\ *adj, usu cap* [Johann *Faust* (name in Latinized form Johannes *Faustus*) †*ab*1540 Ger. magician and astrologer represented in several dramatic works (notably by Marlowe and Goethe) as growing dissatisfied with the limited nature of human knowledge and consequently selling his soul to the devil in exchange for worldly experience and power + E -*ian*] : of, belonging to, resembling, or befitting Faust or Faustus: as **a** : sacrificing spiritual values for material gains **b** : insatiably striving for knowledge and mastery **c** : constantly troubled and tormented by spiritual dissatisfaction or spiritual striving

faust slipper \'faůst-\ *n, usu cap F* : a high-cut house shoe having in the sides V-shaped cuts without goring — compare ROMEO

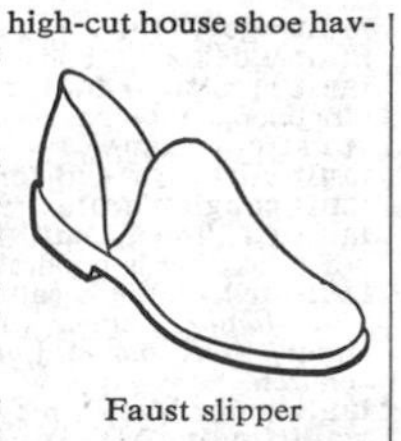

Faust slipper

faut \'fȯt\ *chiefly Scot var of* FAULT

[1]**faute de mieux** \fōtdəmyœ̄\ *adv* [F, for lack of something better] : for lack of something better or more desirable ⟨sherry made him dopey but he drank it *faute de mieux* —F.T. Marsh⟩ ⟨we would welcome it — *faute de mieux* — even if it were only mediocre —F.B.Agard & W.G. Moulton⟩

[2]**faute de mieux** \"\ *adj* : adopted or undertaken for lack of something better ⟨only the result of a *faute de mieux* formula, and not of a desired stylization —R.J.Goldwater⟩ ⟨such marriages . . . were *faute de mieux* and usually accepted because there was no other alternative —L.S.B.Leaky⟩

fau·teuil \(')fō¦tər(·), (')fō¦tə̄ē, *F* fōtœœy\ *n, pl* **fau·teuils** \-ərz,-ə̄ēz,-œœy\ [F, fr. OF *faudestuel* folding chair, of Gmc origin; akin to OE *fyldestōl* folding chair, OS *faldistōl*, OHG *faltistuol;* all these fr. a prehistoric WGmc compound whose first constituent is akin to OHG *faldan* to fold and whose second constituent is represented by OHG *stuol* chair — more at FOLD, STOOL] **1** : ARMCHAIR; *esp* : an upholstered chair with open arms **2** *Brit* : a theater stall

[1]**fau·tor** \'fȯd·ə(r)\ *n* -s [ME *fautour*, fr. L or MF; MF *fauteur*, fr. L *fautor*, fr. *fautus* (past part. of *favēre* to be favorable) + *-or* — more at FAVOR] *archaic* : one that gives support : PATRON, PROTECTOR, PARTISAN, ABETTOR

[2]**fau·tor** \'fȯtər\ *Scot var of* FAULTER

fautress *or* **fautrix** *n* [*fautress* fr. *fautor* + *-ess; fautrix* fr. L, fem. of *fautor* — more at -TRIX] *obs* : a female fautor

[1]**fauve** \'fōv\ *n* -s [F, lit., wild animal, fr. *fauve*, adj., wild, tawny, fr. OF, tawny, of Gmc origin; akin to OHG *falo* fallow — more at FALLOW] **1** : a painter whose work is marked by fauvism : FAUVIST **2** : a rebel or nonconformist in art

[2]**fauve** \"\ *adj* : of or relating to the fauvists or to fauves

fau·vette \fō'vet\ *n* -s [F, fr. OF *fauvete*, fr. *fauve* + *-ete* -ette] *archaic* : any of several small singing birds (as the garden warbler of Europe)

fau·vism \'fō,vizəm\ *n* -s *often cap* [F *fauvisme*, fr. *fauve*, n. + *-isme* -ism] : a movement or a practice in painting typified by the work of the French painter Henri Matisse and characterized by markedly vivid colors and the free treatment of form resulting in a marked vibrant and decorative effect

fau·vist \-_vəst\ *n* -s *often cap* [[1]*fauve* + *-ist*] : one who practices or advocates fauvism; *specif* : a member of a group of French artists who about 1906 revolted from the restrictiveness of academic and neo-impressionist art

faux·bour·don \'fōbə(r),dän, ¦==¦dōⁿ\ *n* -s [F *faux-bourdon*, fr. MF, fr. *faux* false (fr. L *falsus*) + *bourdon* bass horn — more at FALSE, BOURDON] **1** : harmonic progressions of the 15th century characterized by parallel fourths in the two upper voices and based chiefly on parallel sixth chords **2** : a sacred homophonic choral composition

faux·bourg *like* FAUBOURG\ *archaic var of* FAUBOURG

faux jour \(')fō¦zhů(ə)r\ *n, pl* **faux jours** \-r(z)\ [F, lit., false light] : a window in a partition opposite one in an outer wall that allows daylight to pass

faux pas \(')fō¦pä\ *n, pl* **faux pas** \-ä(z)\ [F, lit., false step] : BLUNDER; *esp* : a social blunder **syn** see ERROR

faux sa·ti·ne \¦fō,satᵊn'ā\ *n* [perh. fr. F *faux* false + *satiné* — more at SATINÉ] : a light-tan oily wood that is obtained from cypress knees and is valued chiefly for its crotch figure which is used in ornamental veneers

fav *abbr* favorite

fa·va \'fävə\ *or* **fava bean** *also* **fa·ba** \'fäbə\ *n* -s [*fava* fr. It, fr. L *faba* bean; *faba* fr. NL (specific epithet of the broad bean *Vicia faba*), fr. L, bean — more at BEAN] : BROAD BEAN

fa·vel·la \fə'velə\ *n, pl* **favel·lae** \-e,lē\ [NL, fr. L *favus* honeycomb + NL *-ella*] : an agglomeration of spores in various red algae (family Ceramiaceae) resembling cystocarps but naked or with only a thin membrane or gelatinous envelope

fav·el·lid·i·um \,favə'lidēəm\ *n, pl* **favellid·ia** \-ēə\ [NL, fr. *favella* + *-idium*] : a favella immersed in an algal frond

fa·vel·loid \fə've,lȯid\ *adj* [*favella* + *-oid*] : relating to or resembling a favella

fav·en·tine \'favən·,tēn, -tīn\ *adj, usu cap* [L *faventinus*, fr. *Faventia* (now *Faenza*, city in northern Italy) + L *-inus* -ine] : of or belonging to Faenza, Italy ⟨*Faventine* majolica⟩

fa·ve·o·late \fə'vēələt, -ə,lāt\ *adj* [prob. fr. (assumed) NL *faveolatus*, fr. NL *faveolus* + L *-atus* -ate] : HONEYCOMBED, ALVEOLATE

fa·ve·o·lus \-ələs\ *n, pl* **faveo·li** \-ə,lī\ [NL, dim. of L *favus* honeycomb] : ALVEOLA 1

fav·e·rolle \'favə,rōl, ,=='=\ *n* [prob. fr. *Faverolles*, northern France] **1** *usu cap* : a breed of general purpose fowls developed in France by intercrossing Houdan, Dorking, and Asiatic fowls and comprising moderate-sized deep-bodied birds with five toes, partially feathered shanks, a single comb, and very distinctive feather beard and muffs below the bill and on the cheeks **2** -s *often cap* : a bird of the Faverolle breed

favi *pl of* FAVUS

fa·vi·form \'fāvə,fȯrm, 'fav-\ *adj* [prob. fr. (assumed) NL *faviformis*, fr. (assumed) NL *favi-* (fr. L *favus* honeycomb) + L *-formis* -form] : resembling a honeycomb in structure

fa·vil·la \fə'vilə\ *n, pl* **favil·lae** \-i,lē\ [L, glowing ashes; akin to L *fovēre* to warm — more at DAY] : a small incandescent fragment of lava from a volcano

fa·vism \'fä,vizəm\ *n* -s [It *favismo*, fr. *fava* broad bean + *-ismo* -ism — more at FAVA] : a severe allergic reaction caused by eating the broad bean or by inhaling its pollen that is marked by hemolytic anemia, eosinophilia, jaundice, fever, and often diarrhea and is observed chiefly in southern Italy

fa·vo·ni·an \fə'vōnēən\ *adj* [L *favonianus*, fr. *favonius* west wind + *-anus* -an; akin to L *fovēre* to warm] : of or belonging to the west wind : MILD, BLAND

[1]**fa·vor** \'fāvə(r)\ *n* -s *see -or in Explan Notes* [ME *favour*, *favor* friendly regard, attractiveness, fr. OF *favor* friendly regard, fr. L, fr. *favēre* to be favorable; akin to OHG *gouma* attention, ON *gā* to heed, OSlav *gověti* to revere] **1** *archaic* **a** : a quality that arouses approbation : CHARM **b** : APPEARANCE **c** : COUNTENANCE, FACE; *also* : a feature of the face **2 a** (1) : friendly regard, goodwill, or esteem shown toward another esp. by a superior ⟨a politician attempting to keep the ~ of the voters⟩ (2) : the act of approving or the state of being approved of : APPROBATION ⟨look with ~ upon an enterprise⟩ ⟨enjoy ~ in an enterprise⟩ (3) *obs* : the object of approval ⟨his chief delight and ~ —John Milton⟩ **b** : bias in favor : PARTIALITY ⟨the judge showed ~ toward the plaintiff⟩ ⟨the students naturally showed ~ toward their own team⟩ **c** *archaic* : LENIENCY; *also* : a lenient action **d** *archaic* : INDULGENCE, PERMISSION, LEAVE **e** : POPULARITY ⟨it was a fad, something that would lose ~ quickly⟩ **3 a** : kindness esp. when marked by benevolence in the agent or great gratification in the one benefiting ⟨enjoying the ~ of a rich and generous patron⟩; *also* : an act or instance of such kindness ⟨showering ~*s* on the needy and deserving⟩ **b** *archaic* : HELP, ASSISTANCE **c favors** *pl* : effort in one's behalf or interest : ATTENTION ⟨vying for the king's ~*s*⟩; *also* : the product of such effort or interest ⟨magazines paid well for the young writer's ~*s*⟩ **4 a** : an object or token of favor (as a glove or ribbon) given esp. formerly by a lady to a favored one (as a lover or a favored knight in a tournament) to be worn conspicuously **b** : appropriate knickknacks, small gifts, or amusing or decorative items (as crackers, noisemakers, corsages for the women, or souvenirs) given out at a celebration or party (as by placing at a place setting) ⟨the younger element snapped frilly ~*s* which blossomed into frivolous paper hats —Silas Spitzer⟩ **c** : EMBLEM, BADGE ⟨wore the Republican party ~⟩ **5 a** : a special privilege or right granted or conceded ⟨have the ~ of a new trial⟩ ⟨grant a ~ to a good friend⟩ ⟨dropped his sword and shouted for mercy, a ~ that the Roman was pleased to bestow —L.C.Douglas⟩ **b** : sexual privileges or sexual intercourse usu. as granted by a woman — usu. used in pl. or in the phrase *the ultimate favor* ⟨her niece, a prostitute, had been granting her ~*s* to policemen —M.R. Werner⟩ ⟨a young woman . . . worked for a publishing firm and was generally supposed to have granted the ultimate ~ to every male author on the list who sold over 20,000 copies —Clifton Fadiman⟩ **6** *archaic* : LETTER, COMMUNICATION **7 a** : BEHALF, INTEREST ⟨a man who acts only in his own ~⟩ **b** : a difference that favors ⟨of the speed of the two swimmers there is a slight ~ for the first⟩ — **in favor of** *prep* **1** : to the special advantage or benefit of ⟨there shall be no discrimination *in favor of*, or to the prejudice of, either race —*Amer. Guide Series: N.C.*⟩: as **a** : in accord or sympathy with : on the side of ⟨*in favor of* the group working for greater sanitation⟩ **b** : for the acquittal of ⟨the jury returned *in favor of* the man accused of robbery⟩ : in support of ⟨the court's decision was *in favor of* the corporation that brought the suit⟩ **2** : to the order of — used of a check or other draft — **in one's favor 1** : in one's good graces ⟨doing extra works to get back *in the teacher's favor*⟩ **2** : to one's advantage according to the laws of probability ⟨the odds in the gambling game were *in the bettor's favor*⟩ — **out of favor** *adv* : under displeasure : DISLIKED; *also* : not popular : NEGLECTED ⟨certain ideas . . . however much obscured and *out of favor* for a time, live on —C.I. Glicksberg⟩ — **under favor** *adv, archaic* : with permission (of one addressed or implied) : subject to being overruled

[2]**favor** \"\ *vt* **favored; favored; favoring** \-v(ə)riŋ\ **favors** *see -or in Explan Notes* [ME *favouren*, *favoren*, fr. *favour*, *favor*, n. — more at [1]FAVOR] **1 a** : to regard or treat with favor, goodwill, or approval : show favor to : treat with consideration ⟨~ any bill that cuts my taxes⟩ ⟨as a father he ~*ed* little girls⟩; *also* : to act in a way that encourages ⟨the board ~*ed* the protection of labor without freezing it —*Current Biog.*⟩ **b** : to do a kindness for or oblige esp. with a gift ⟨the author ~*ed* us with a copy of his latest book⟩; *also* : to provide with a special quality, characteristic, or possession ⟨he was ~*ed* with great intelligence and phenomenal good looks⟩ **c** : to treat gently or carefully : avoid overworking : SPARE ⟨like a hound ~*ing* a sore foot —Nelson Algren⟩ ⟨sorry to hear you had a return of your rheumatism — I do hope you will ~ yourself more —Walt Whitman⟩ **d** : to give (oneself) free course ⟨typically tends to ~ himself with special foods and laborsaving devices⟩ **2 a** : to show partiality toward ⟨the jurors clearly ~*ed* the defendant⟩ ⟨a ~*ed* class of citizens⟩ : side with ⟨the neutral nations seemed to ~ neither side⟩ : to regard above others : PREFER ⟨the patient said he would ~ a harder bed⟩; *esp* : to prefer as a matter of passing favor or temporary enthusiasm or popularity ⟨certain ~*ed* movie stars⟩ ⟨the most ~*ed* gun on the skeet field today . . . seems to be the very heavy 12-gauge autoloader —Bob Nichols⟩ **b** : to choose as a favorite in or as if in betting ⟨the Russians are ~*ed* to win —Samuel Reshevsky⟩ **c** : to tend to have as if by preference ⟨in the spring, suits ~*ed* moderately full to very wide skirt hemlines —*Collier's Yr. Bk.*⟩ **3 a** : to give support or confirmation to : SUSTAIN ⟨adducing facts which ~*ed* his contention⟩ : AID ⟨he felt that God was ~*ing* him in his efforts⟩ **b** : to afford advantages for success to : FACILITATE ⟨the continued good weather distinctly ~*ed* the vacation trade⟩ : be propitious for ⟨a wind ~*ing* their speedy return⟩ ⟨high humidity ~*ed* the incidence of disease —G.G.Weigend⟩ **4** : to bear a resemblance to ⟨the daughter rather ~*ed* the father's side of the family⟩

syn COUNTENANCE, ENCOURAGE: FAVOR may be used in reference to a well-disposed inclination, an expressed preference, active support, or, more broadly, a circumstance or agency conducive to a result ⟨a number of wealthy and influential Newport folk *favored* dramatic performances, although a majority of their fellow citizens continued to condemn them —*Amer. Guide Series: R.I.*⟩ ⟨in general the marshmen *favor* a broad, roomy canoe —Wilfred Thesiger⟩ ⟨we had been *favored* by tail winds and would put down at Idlewild —Bennett Cerf⟩ ⟨the summer weather at Maudheim *favored* the formation of this type of snow —Valter Schytt⟩ COUNTENANCE may indicate mere toleration; it may imply more positive favoring ⟨really fail to see why you should *countenance* immorality just to please your father —Sheila Kaye-Smith⟩ ⟨her popularity had been retrieved, grievances against her silenced, her past *countenanced*, and her present irradiated by the family approval —Edith Wharton⟩ ⟨several of them appeared at the bar to *countenance* him when he was tried at the Horsham assizes —T.B.Macaulay⟩ ENCOURAGE indicates heartening stimulation, inciting or inducing esp. by expressions of approval, confidence, liking, or comfort ⟨openly *encouraged* from Germany and Italy, fascist organizations, although from time to time banned, carried on insidious and demoralizing propaganda —F.A.Ogg and Harold Zink⟩ ⟨*encouraged* her in her ambition to be an actress —*Current Biog.*⟩ **syn** see in addition OBLIGE

fa·vor·able \'fāvər(ə)bəl, -vrəb-\ *adj* [ME *favourable*, *favorable*, fr. MF *favorable*, fr. L *favorabilis* popular, pleasing, fr. *favor* + *-abilis* -able — more at FAVOR] **1 a** : disposed to favor : FAVORING, APPROVING, PARTIAL ⟨taking a ~ attitude toward our request⟩ : expressing approval : COMMENDATORY ⟨a ~ recommendation⟩ ⟨a ~ grade on an exam⟩; *also* : giving a result that is in one's favor ⟨a ~ comparison⟩ **b** *obs* : GRACIOUS, OBLIGING **c** : granting or obliging in what is desired : AFFIRMATIVE ⟨gave a ~ answer to our request⟩ **2** : winning approval : PLEASING, AGREEABLE ⟨made a ~ impression on his future colleagues⟩ **3 a** : tending to promote or facilitate : ADVANTAGEOUS ⟨a ~ wind blew us into port without a mishap⟩ ⟨a business climate ~ to almost any enterprise⟩ **b** : having the value of exports exceed that of imports ⟨a ~ balance of trade⟩ **4 a** : indicative of a successful outcome : affording cheer or reason for optimism : boding well ⟨~ weather for our yacht trip⟩ ⟨~ conditions for opening a new business⟩ **b** : marked by success : turning out in the way desired or hoped ⟨a ~ demonstration of a new invention⟩ ⟨made a ~ adjustment to the new conditions of her life⟩

syn BENIGN, AUSPICIOUS, PROPITIOUS: FAVORABLE describes persons, events, or conditions whose disposition or effect is kindly, helpful, advantageous, or encouraging and likely to presage or facilitate a happy outcome ⟨a hot dry summer, *favorable* to contemplative life out of doors —Joseph Conrad⟩ ⟨they won't take a chance of battle unless they can feel sure of most *favorable* conditions —Alexander Forbes⟩ ⟨my position in reference to them, being paternal and protective, was *favorable* to the growth of friendly sentiments —Nathaniel Hawthorne⟩ BENIGN may apply to persons or agencies that have power or position to harm, hinder, or check but whose disposition appears kindly and encouraging ⟨that *benign* friend who had previously comforted him in his misery —Anthony Trollope⟩ ⟨always *benign*, there was not a grain of ill will anywhere in him —A.N.Whitehead⟩ ⟨the *benign* and fatherly old man put his arm round her waist —Arnold Bennett⟩ AUSPICIOUS describes events or conditions pointing toward good or favorable outcomes or developments ⟨court astrologers pronounced March 2, 1949, an *auspicious* date for the coronation —*Current Biog.*⟩ ⟨at least pay the boy then; I have no pice with me, and he brought *auspicious* news —Rudyard Kipling⟩ PROPITIOUS describes, perhaps more mildly so than AUSPICIOUS, events or conditions that are favorable. PROPITIOUS may describe that which lacks any discouraging indication without having the optimistic ring of AUSPICIOUS ⟨although it was already late in the autumn, the weather was *propitious* —J.L.Motley⟩ ⟨after so *propitious* an opening it seemed that acerbities might be quelled, rivalries mitigated —S.H.Adams⟩

fa·vor·able·ness *n* -ES : the quality or state of being favorable ⟨pleased by the ~ of the court's decision⟩

fa·vor·ably \-blē, -li\ *adv* [ME *favourably*, *favourablely*, fr. *favourable* + *-ly*] : in a favorable manner

fa·vored \¦fāvə(r)d\ *adj* [fr. past part. of [2]*favor*] **1** : endowed with special advantages, good qualities, or gifts ⟨a ~ position in the firm⟩ ⟨a place ~ by nature⟩ ⟨a student clearly ~⟩ **2** [[1]*favor* + *-ed*] : having an appearance or features of a particular kind — usu. used in combination ⟨a well-*favored* community⟩ ⟨an ill-*favored* child⟩ ⟨hard-*favored*⟩ **3** : providing preferential treatment ⟨better management of the existing collective farms with ~ rates of credit —Jack Raymond⟩

fa·vor·er \-vərə(r)\ *n* -s : one that favors, furthers, or promotes

favoring *pres part of* FAVOR

[1]**fa·vor·ite** \'fāv(ə)rə̇|t, -vər|, *usu* |d·+V\ *n* -s [It *favorito*, past part. of *favorire* to favor, fr. *favore* favor, fr. L *favor*] **1 a** : something treated or regarded with special favor : something esp. liked or loved ⟨like other fertile districts, this territory was once a ~ with the Indians —*Amer. Guide Series: Mich.*⟩ ⟨of all books, the Bible was his ~⟩; *specif* : one unusually loved, trusted, or provided with favors by a person of high rank or authority ⟨the Duke of York . . . granted the area between the Hudson and Delaware rivers to two of his ~*s* —*Amer. Guide Series: N.J.*⟩ ⟨the political rule, by palace intrigue, of ~*s*, women, and eunuchs —W.G.Sumner⟩ ⟨committing to a wicked ~ all public cares —John Milton⟩ **b** : something having marked esp. lasting popularity ⟨approximately thirty active winter playland areas in Vermont . . . include old ~*s* of all sizes —*N.Y. Times*⟩ **2** *obs* : SUPPORTER, FOLLOWER, PARTISAN **3** : a short curl at the temple fashionable in the 17th and 18th centuries — usu. used in pl. **4** : a competitor (as a horse in a race) judged most likely to win : the competitor against whom the shortest odds are laid in the betting **syn** see PARASITE

[2]**favorite** \"\ *adj* : constituting a favorite ⟨a ~ picnic place⟩ : accorded special treatment or attention usu. loving or affectionate ⟨a ~ daughter⟩; *specif* : markedly popular esp. over an extended period of time ⟨~ melodies from light opera⟩ ⟨small dogs are ~ pets⟩

favorite sentence *n* : the most common sentence type in a language (as in English the actor-action type, as *he won*)

favorite son *n* : a person favored as their candidate by the delegates of his state at the presidential nominating convention of a party

fa·vor·it·ism \'fāv(ə)rə̇|d·,izəm, -vər|, |,di-\ *n* -s **1** : the treating of one person, family, or class of men with special favor or partiality to the correlative neglect of others ⟨~ in federal tax legislation —C.S.Shoup⟩ ⟨the workers think that most raises are based on ~ —S.L.Payne⟩ **2** : the state or fact of being a favorite

favorless *adj, obs* : showing no favor : UNPROPITIOUS

favors *pl of* FAVOR, *pres 3d sing of* FAVOR

fa·vose \'fā,vōs\ *adj* [prob. fr. (assumed) NL *favosus*, fr. L *favus* honeycomb + *-osus* -ose] : ALVEOLATE — **fa·vose·ly** *adv*

fav·o·site \'favə,sīt\ *n* -s [NL *Favosites*] : a fossil coral of the genus *Favosites* or a related genus

fav·o·si·tes \,=='sīd·(,)ēz\ *n, cap* [NL, prob. fr. (assumed) NL *favosus* + NL *-ites* -ite] : a genus (the type of a large exclusively Paleozoic family Favositidae) of extinct corals having polygonal cells with perforated walls esp. abundant in the Silurian and Devonian rocks — **fav·o·sit·oid** \¦==¦sīd·,ȯid\ *adj*

fa·vour \'fāvə(r)\ *Brit var of* FAVOR

fa·vous \'fāvəs\ *adj* [L *favus* honeycomb + E *-ous*] : FAVOSE

Fa·vrile \fəv'rē(ə)l\ *trademark* — used for glassware of delicate design and with an iridescent surface

fa·vus \'fāvəs\ *n* [NL, fr. L, honeycomb] **1** -ES : a contagious skin disease caused by a fungus (as *Achorion schoenleinii*) occurring in man on hairy surfaces that become covered with yellowish crusts and often depilated and also attacking many domestic animals and fowls **2** *pl* **fa·vi** \-,vī\ : a tile or flagstone cut into a hexagonal shape to produce a honeycomb pattern (as in a pavement)

faw \'fȯ, 'fä\ *dial var of* FALL

[1]**fawn** \'fȯn, 'fän\ *vi* -ED/-ING/-S [ME *faunen*, fr. OE *fagnian*, *fægnian* to rejoice, fr. *fagen*, *fægen* glad — more at FAIN] **1** : to show delight or affection in such behavior as wagging the tail or licking — used esp. of dogs ⟨the puppy was ~*ing* on its master as if it understood what he suffered⟩ **2** : to act in a sycophantic way : court favor by a cringing or overly flattering manner : GROVEL ⟨they ~ and slaver over us —Robinson Jeffers⟩ ⟨died, still ~*ing* like the coward that he had always been —Bernard Pares⟩ ⟨your knights here, who ~ on a damsel with soft words in the hall, and will kiss the dust off their queen's feet —Charles Kingsley⟩ ⟨courtiers who ~ on a master while they betray him —T.B.Macaulay⟩

[2]**fawn** *n* -s *obs* : the act of fawning

[3]**fawn** \'fȯn, 'fän\ *n* -s [ME *foun*, fr. MF *faon*, *feon* young of an animal, fr. OF, fr. (assumed) VL *feton-*, *feto*, fr. L *fetus* offspring — more at FETUS] **1** : a young deer; *esp* : one still unweaned or retaining a distinctive baby coat **2** : [1]KID 1 **3** *or* **fawn brown** : a variable color averaging a light grayish brown that is yellower, darker, and slightly stronger than Deauville sand — called also *autumn blond*, *faon* **4** : one that is fawn colored

[4]**fawn** \"\ *vi* -ED/-ING/-S [ME *faunen*, fr. MF *faonner* to give birth to young (said of an animal), fr. OF, fr. *faon*, *feon* young of an animal] : to give birth to a fawn

fawning *adj* [fr. pres. part. of [1]*fawn*] : characteristic of one that fawns : servilely abject : SYCOPHANTIC ⟨sent the most objectionable ~ greetings⟩ — **fawn·ing·ness** *n* -ES

fawn·ing·ly *adv* : in a fawning manner : in an overly flattering, cringing, servile, or groveling manner

fawn lily *n* : any of several plants of the genus *Erythronium; esp* : a Californian dogtooth violet (*E. californicum*) with creamy white flowers sometimes yellow tinged

fawny \'fȯnē, 'fänē\ *adj* -ER/-EST [[3]*fawn* + *-y*] : of a color approximating fawn

[1]**fay** \'fā\ *vb* -ED/-ING/-S [ME *feien*, fr. OE *fēgan;* akin to OS *fōgian* to fit, join, OHG *fuogen* to fit, join, L *pangere* to fasten — more at PACT] *vt, in shipbuilding* : to fit, fasten, or join closely or tightly ~ *vi* **1 a** : to fit closely together or nicely esp. against something else (as a surface) ⟨paint a ~*ing* surface before making an overlapping metal joint⟩ — often used with *in*, *into*, *with*, or *together* **b** *archaic* : AGREE, JIBE **2** *dial Eng* : SUCCEED, PROSPER

[2]**fay** \"\ *vt* -ED/-ING/-S [ME *feien*, fr. ON *fægja* to clean, polish; akin to ON *fāga* to clean, decorate — more at FAIR] *dial Brit* : CLEAN : clear away — often used with *up* or *out*

[3]**fay** \"\ *n* [ME *fai*, *fei*, fr. OF *fei* — more at [1]FAITH] *obs* : FAITH

[4]**fay** \"\ *n* -s [ME *faie*, *fei* someone or something enchanted, fr. MF *fee*, *feie* fairy — more at FAIRY] : FAIRY, ELF

[5]**fay** \"\ *adj* -ER/-EST [ME *faie* having magical powers, enchanted, fr. *faie*, *fei*, n.] : like an elf ⟨a ~ and delicate daughter⟩

[6]**fay** \"\ *n* -s [perh. by shortening] *slang* : OFAY

fa·yal·ite \fə'yä,līt, fī'ä-\ *n* -s [G *fayalit*, fr. *Fayal*, island in the Azores + G *-it* -ite] : a mineral Fe_2SiO_4 consisting of an iron silicate isomeric with olivine and occurring in crystals or massive (sp. gr. 4.1)

fayence *var of* FAIENCE

fay in *vb, NewEng* : [1]FAY

[1]**fa·yum·ic** *or* **fay·yum·ic** \(')fā¦yümik, (')fī¦-\ *adj, usu cap* **1** : of, belonging to, or situated in the Fayum, a fertile depression in Egypt south of Cairo and connected with the Nile valley by a narrow pass **2** : of, belonging to, being, or composed in Fayumic

[2]**fayumic** *or* **fayyumic** \"\ *n* -s *usu cap* : a dialect of Coptic spoken in the early Christian period in Middle Egypt of which fragments of a New Testament translation survive

faze *also* **phase** \'fāz\ *vt* -ED/-ING/-S [alter. of *feeze*] : to disturb the composure of : DISCONCERT, WORRY, BOTHER, DAUNT ⟨he had never navigated a ship up the St. Lawrence before, but that didn't ~ him —James Dugan⟩ ⟨calamitous personal defeat did not seem to ~ him⟩ **syn** see EMBARRASS

fa·zen·da \fə'zendə\ *n* -s [Pg, fr. L *facienda* things to be done — more at HACIENDA] **1** : a Brazilian plantation; *esp* : a coffee plantation **2** : the house on a fazenda

fa·zen·dei·ro \,fazᵊn'dā(,)rō\ *n* -s [Pg, fr. *fazenda*] : a Brazilian planter or cattleman

FB *abbr* **1** fire brigade **2** flying boat **3** freight bill **4** fullback

FBI \¦ef,bē'ī\ *n* -s [*F*ederal *B*ureau of *I*nvestigation, a bureau of the U.S. Department of Justice that investigates violations of certain federal statutes] : a governmental investigating agency ⟨toying with the idea of dissolving the discredited German *FBI* —*Springfield (Mass.) Daily News*⟩

FBM *abbr* foot board measure

fc *abbr* franc

FC *abbr* **1** fideicommissum **2** fire control **3** flood control **4** follow copy **5** food control **6** football club **7** foot-candle **8** free church

FC&S *abbr* free of capture and seizure

fc&s warranty *n, usu cap F&C&S* : a clause in a marine insurance policy excluding coverage if loss is caused by capture or seizure of the insured ship or by atomic fission or radioactive force

fcap *abbr* foolscap

FCC *abbr* first-class certificate

f center *n, usu cap F* **:** a point in a crystalline compound (as a silver halide) at which a negative ion missing from the crystal lattice has been replaced by an electron

fcg *abbr* facing

f clef *n, usu cap F* **:** a clef placing the F below middle C on the fourth line of the staff — called also *bass clef;* see CLEF illustration; compare C CLEF, G CLEF

fco *abbr* [It *franco*] postage free; delivered free

fcp *abbr* foolscap

FCS *abbr, often not cap* free of capture and seizure

fcst *abbr* forecast

fc station *n, usu cap F&C* **:** a coast radio station

fcty *abbr* factory

fcy *abbr* fancy

fd *abbr* **1** field **2** forced **3** ford **4** found **5** fund

FD *abbr* **1** [L *Fidei Defensor*] Defender of the Faith **2** fire department **3** first day **4** focal distance **5** forced draft **6** free delivery **7** free discharge **8** free dispatch **9** free dock

fd&c color *n, usu cap F&D & 1st C* [Food, Drug, *and* Cosmetic Act + *color*] **:** any of the synthetic dyes that in certified batches are permitted for use in foods, drugs, and cosmetics by the Federal Food, Drug, and Cosmetic Act of 1938 and subsequent legislation — compare D&C COLOR, EXT D&C COLOR; *see* DYE table II

FDC *abbr* **1** fire direction center **2** first-day cover

FDD *abbr* [F *franc de droits*] free of charge

fdg *abbr* funding

fdn *abbr* foundation

fdry *abbr* foundry

Fe *symbol* **1** [L *ferrum*] iron **2** quadragesimo-octavo

fea·ber·ry \ˈfē-, ˈfā- — *see* BERRY\ *n* [*fea-* (perh. alter. of ME *theve-* as in *thevethorn* bramble, fr. OE *thefanthorn*) + *berry;* akin to OHG *depandorn* bramble] *dial Eng* **:** GOOSEBERRY 1a

feak *n* -S [origin unknown] *obs* **:** a lock or curl of hair

¹feal \ˈfē(ə)l\ *vt* [ME *felen,* fr. ON *fela;* akin to OE *fēolan* to undergo, enter, OHG *felahan* to conceal, Goth *filhan* to conceal, OE *fell* skin, hide — more at FELL] *dial Eng* **:** CONCEAL

²feal \"\ *adj* [MF, fr. OF, alter. (influenced by OF *-al,* fr. L *-alis*) of *feil,* fr. L *fidelis* faithful, fr. *fides* faith — more at FAITH] *archaic* **:** FAITHFUL, LOYAL

feal and divot *n* [*feal* fr. ME (Sc) *faile* turf] *Scots law* **:** the right of taking turf for making fences or thatching houses

fe·al·ty \ˈfē(ə)ltē, -ti\ *n* -ES [alter. (influenced by MF *fealté*) of ME *feute, feaute,* fr. OF *feauté, fealté,* alter. (influenced by *feal* faithful) of *feelté,* fr. L *fidelitat-, fidelitas* fidelity, fr. *fidelis* faithful + *-itat-, -itas* -ity] **1 a :** the fidelity of a vassal or feudal tenant to his lord **b :** the obligation of such fidelity ⟨received him as king and lord of Ireland, vowing loyal obedience to him and his successors, and acknowledging ~ to them forever —Owen Wister⟩ **c :** an oath committing one to such fidelity ⟨swore ~ to his overlord⟩ **2 a :** FAITHFULNESS, ALLEGIANCE ⟨the board . . . to be appointed by the President, presumably from names submitted by the Academy or those holding strong ~ to it —M.L.Cooke⟩ ⟨~ to facts⟩; *specif* **:** faithfulness or allegiance conceived as an obligation or duty ⟨the ~ owed by a citizen to the best interest of his country⟩ **b :** an oath committing one to such fidelity or allegiance ⟨swore ~ to the Constitution with his hand resting upon a Bible —*Time*⟩ **syn** see FIDELITY

¹fear \ˈfi(ə)r, -iə\ *n* -S [ME *fer, fere,* fr. OE *fǣr* sudden danger, disaster; akin to OHG *fāra* ambush, danger, ON *fār* harm, misfortune, Goth *ferja* spy, L *periculum* attempt, peril, Gk *peiran* to attempt, OE *faran* to go — more at FARE] **1 a :** an unpleasant emotional state characterized by anticipation of pain or great distress and accompanied by heightened autonomic activity esp. involving the nervous system **:** agitated foreboding often of some real or specific peril — compare ANXIETY **b :** an instance or manifestation of this feeling ⟨they have created ~ of the free mind —John Mason Brown⟩ **c :** calm recognition or consideration of whatever may injure or damage **:** reasoned caution **:** intelligent foresight **2 a :** the state or habit of feeling agitation or dismay **:** a condition between anxiety and terror either natural and well-grounded or unreasoned and blind ⟨anesthetics have removed the ~ of physical pain —H.W.VanLoon⟩ ⟨the only thing we have to fear is ~ itself —F.D.Roosevelt⟩ ⟨living in ~⟩ **b :** anxious concern **:** SOLICITUDE ⟨a ~ that the boy will not make out well in his examination⟩ **3 :** profound reverence and awe ⟨the ~ of the Lord is the beginning of wisdom —Ps 111:10 (RSV)⟩ ⟨godliness and holy ~⟩ **4 :** something that is the object of apprehension or alarm **:** a ground for fear **:** DANGER ⟨starvation is still a real ~ in the minds of many peoples of the world⟩

syn DREAD, FRIGHT, ALARM, DISMAY, CONSTERNATION, PANIC, TERROR, HORROR, TREPIDATION: with the possible modified exception of DISMAY and CONSTERNATION, these nouns in one sense which they have in common signify the agitation aroused by anticipation of danger or the actual awareness of a present danger. FEAR, the most general of the terms, implies apprehension and anxiety and sometimes a loss of courage amounting to cowardice ⟨the human *fear* of death —Douglas Stewart⟩ ⟨a *fear* of failure⟩ ⟨the *fear* of the unknown⟩ ⟨tremble and grovel with *fear*⟩ DREAD is similar to FEAR but usu. adds the idea of extreme fear-inspired reluctance to face or meet a particular dreaded person or situation ⟨we face the threat —not with *dread* and confusion—but with confidence and conviction —D.D.Eisenhower⟩ ⟨though she was without definite fear, an obscure *dread* was beating against the wall of her consciousness —Ellen Glasgow⟩ FRIGHT implies the shock of sudden, startling, and short-lived fear ⟨a face to inspire *fright*⟩ ⟨the sound produces a kind of horror that is something more than mere *fright* —Ernie Pyle⟩ ⟨disquietude had developed into *fright; fright* quickly developed into terror —Emile Gaboriau⟩ ALARM suggests intense, usu. sudden, apprehension ⟨instantly the *alarm* began in her nerves; she felt the warning quiver dart through them like the vibration in a wire —Ellen Glasgow⟩ ⟨with an astonishment bordering on *alarm* —Jane Austen⟩ DISMAY, of these words the least generally associated with the idea of fear, usu. implies a sudden discouragement or loss of courage or initiative, generally accompanied by a certain mental confusion usu. induced by an unexpected turn of events ⟨view a difficult task with *dismay*⟩ ⟨when the child told her first lie her foster-mother was nearly sick with *dismay* and anxiety —Margaret Deland⟩ ⟨he is flung neck and crop into a world which he does not comprehend, and his *dismay* is hysterical —John Buchan⟩ CONSTERNATION implies fear only incidentally, stressing rather the idea of a temporary confusion or paralysis of faculties induced by something startlingly contrary to expectation or hope or something shocking ⟨he looked down on her with stirrings of tender pride which altered to *consternation* as slow tears came stealing down the nearest cheek —Mary Austin⟩ ⟨the more adventurous drivers enjoyed timing the trip down to the last second so that they could race the tide to safety, much to the *consternation* of their passengers —*Amer. Guide Series: Calif.*⟩ PANIC is overmastering and unreasoning fear or fright usu. as manifesting itself in hysterical activity ⟨thrown into a *panic* by the threat of raids by pirates —*Amer. Guide Series: Mich.*⟩ ⟨all the possible phases of that sort of anguish, beginning with instinctive *panic,* through the bewildered stage, the frozen stage, and the stage of blanched apprehension, down to the instinctive prudence of extreme terror —Joseph Conrad⟩ TERROR is extreme violent fear or dread, such as might conduce to panic ⟨his appeal was to fear, and he so impressed his hearers that frequently they fell to the floor or shrieked in *terror* —H.E. Starr⟩ ⟨in *terror,* the wild horse seems to lose possession of his senses and plunges ahead regardless of obstacles —*Amer. Guide Series: Ariz.*⟩ HORROR throws emphasis upon the idea of strong abhorrence or shuddering revulsion induced or accompanied by fear ⟨such a *horror* of his cruelty, duplicity, and power, that I could scarce conceal a shudder —R.L. Stevenson⟩ ⟨he saw, to his *horror,* that the three pairs of legs continued to parade but there seemed to be no bodies above them —*Amer. Guide Series: R.I.*⟩ TREPIDATION carries the idea of a trembling fear, born of timidity ⟨they went in *trepidation,* almost afraid that the delight of exploring this ruin might be denied them —D.H.Lawrence⟩ ⟨I should very shortly perish of *trepidation* and suspense in so sinister an environment —Elinor Wylie⟩

— **for fear :** by reason of an apprehension lest ⟨worried *for fear* the child will hurt himself⟩ — **without fear or favor :** in a manner uninfluenced by fear, prejudice, or partiality

²fear \"\ *vb* -ED/-ING/-S [ME *feren,* fr. OE *fǣran,* fr. *fǣr* sudden danger— more at ¹FEAR] *vt* **1** *now dial* **a :** FRIGHTEN, TERRIFY ⟨be careful not to ~ the horse by shouting⟩ **b :** to scare away ⟨~ the crows out of the corn⟩ **2** *obs* **:** DETER **3** *archaic* **:** to feel fear in (oneself) ⟨I ~ me he is slain —Christopher Marlowe⟩ **4 a :** to have a reverential awe of ⟨~ God⟩ **b :** to stand in awe of ⟨~ anyone in authority⟩ **5 a :** to be afraid of **:** consider, expect, or anticipate with feelings of alarm, foreboding, or solicitude ⟨most men ~ death⟩ ⟨~ the unexpected and unknown⟩ ⟨~ evil and misfortune⟩ **b :** to hesitate (to do something) for fear of doing wrong or causing unhappiness ⟨~ to disturb someone's thoughts⟩ **c :** to suspect or conclude regretfully ⟨I ~ I have made too many mistakes⟩ **~** *vi* **:** to be apprehensive **:** be afraid ⟨I ~ lest we commit an inexcusable blunder⟩ ⟨if the night seems cold, you need not ~ if the house is well heated⟩ — **fear·er** *n*

feared \ˈfi(ə)rd, -iəd\ *adj* [ME *fered,* past part. of *feren* to frighten] *chiefly dial* **:** AFRAID ⟨he was ~ to go⟩

fear·ful \ˈfi(ə)rfəl, -iəf-\ *adj, sometimes* -ER/-EST [ME *ferful,* fr. *fer, fere* fear + *-ful* — more at ¹FEAR] **1 a :** inspiring or likely to inspire fear, fright, or alarm **:** dangerous and alarming ⟨spent a ~ night alone in the woods⟩ ⟨won the war but at a ~ cost⟩ **b :** caused by, indicative of, or attended by fear ⟨casting ~ glances at the large dog as he passed it⟩ **2 :** full of fear, alarm, awe, concern, or apprehension: **a :** AFRAID, APPREHENSIVE ⟨Henry, ~ lest his prize should escape him at the last, was driven to offer terms —J.R.Green⟩ ⟨~ for his safety⟩ **b :** inclined to fear **:** TIMOROUS ⟨heaped scorn on all ~ people who strove only for comfort and security⟩ **c** *archaic* **:** CAUTIOUS **d :** marked by awe or reverence ⟨riveted his eyes in ~ ecstasy —Thomas Gray⟩ **3 a :** extremely bad, shocking, or revolting ⟨~ slum conditions⟩ **b :** EXTREME, LARGE, NUMEROUS — usu. used as a generalized intensifier with the force of a superlative ⟨a patron who had taken a ~ shellacking wagered every last chip —Bennett Cerf⟩ ⟨she exercises a ~ attraction —C.W.Cunnington⟩ ⟨a ~ litter of paper —Arnold Bennett⟩

syn AWFUL, DREADFUL, FRIGHTFUL, TERRIBLE, TERRIFIC, HORRIBLE, HORRIFIC, SHOCKING, APPALLING, DIRE: in loose use most of these words may be used to mean little more than *extreme.* More precisely, FEARFUL applies to what makes one feel fear, fright, alarm, agitation, or loss of courage ⟨our *fearful* trip is done, the ship has weathered every rack —Walt Whitman⟩ ⟨a *fearful* battlefield, the earth of it gaped open by shells and bombs —Ira Wolfert⟩ ⟨monsters, ghosts, spirit voices, and other *fearful* sights and sounds —*Time*⟩ AWFUL describes that which strikes one profoundly with overpowering awareness of might, power, or significance transcending the individual ⟨he looked at war and he saw through all the sham glory to the *awful* evil beneath —Edith Hamilton⟩ ⟨the *awful* impersonality of those great rock-creatures, the terrible impartiality of that cold, clinging wind which swept by, never an inch lifted above ground —John Galsworthy⟩ ⟨the *awful* arithmetic of the atomic bomb —D.D.Eisenhower⟩ DREADFUL applies to what fills one with a haunting shuddering fear or yearning to escape, often unanalyzable and persistent ⟨he perished, he and his house, struck by a thunderbolt in the midst of a *dreadful* storm —J.G.Frazer⟩ ⟨in his delirium his ravings have been *dreadful;* of wolves and poison and blood; of ghosts and demons —Bram Stoker⟩ FRIGHTFUL is applicable either to what causes consternated fright at the moment or to what is generally awful, outrageous, or enormous ⟨the Ghost of a Lady, dressed in deep mourning, a scar on her forehead, and a bloody handkerchief at her breast, *frightful* to behold —George Meredith⟩ ⟨look at what the British did in Greece — the most *frightful* military blunder, for which they are paying now —Upton Sinclair⟩ ⟨a *frightful* spectacle of poverty, barbarity, and ignorance —T.B.Macaulay⟩ TERRIBLE describes whatever inspires terror or extreme desperate dominating fear; it may describe something unendurable or excruciating to feelings or sensibilities ⟨so *terrible* was his wrath at their resistance that the Dean of St. Paul's, who stood forth to remonstrate, dropped dead of sheer terror at his feet —J.R.Green⟩ ⟨three *terrible* days in the hospital, tortured by a monster headache, a frightful thirst —Xavier Herbert⟩ ⟨one of those *terrible* women produced now and then by the Roman stock, unsexed, implacable, filled with an insane lust of power —John Buchan⟩ TERRIFIC applies to what compels terror, often by force, stunning effect, release of energy, explosive manifestation ⟨eyes starting with frantic terror at the *terrific* scene that met them —C.G.D.Roberts⟩ ⟨a *terrific* barrage of shell and bomb fragments, smoke, flame and debris from the stricken vessel —F.D.Roosevelt⟩ ⟨in 1848 a $75,000 dam was completed, and on the same day it was swept away by the *terrific* pressure, incorrectly calculated, of the water behind it —*Amer. Guide Series: Mass.*⟩ HORRIBLE describes that which instills a combination of terror and loathing or one of pure loathing at hideousness or hatefulness ⟨there came a most *horrible* yell — the most dreadful sound, Mr. Holmes, that ever I heard. It will ring in my ears as long as I live. I sat frozen with horror for a minute or two —A. Conan Doyle⟩ ⟨every *horrible* detail of Nazi atrocity —*Encounter*⟩ ⟨the most *horrible* monsters and tortures, and the most loathsome and noisome abominations, that his fervid imagination could concoct —C.W.Eliot⟩ HORRIFIC is close to HORRIBLE but may stress actual effect rather than the potential effect of the latter ⟨that *horrific* yarn "The Body-Snatcher" —C.E.Montague⟩ ⟨there was a *horrific,* splitting, tearing roar, and then I knew no more —A.C.Whitehead⟩ SHOCKING is a milder term applying to what startles, esp. as contrary to expectations, taste, sensibilities, or morality ⟨his face has been terribly mutilated, and — what seems even more *shocking* — the poor fellow's hands have been cut right off at the wrists —Dorothy Sayers⟩ ⟨the *shocking* realities of a world in which the principles of common humanity and common decency are being mowed down by the firing squads of the Gestapo —F.D.Roosevelt⟩ APPALLING describes what terrifies and also dismays or dumbfounds ⟨a huge bomb had . . . gone off with such *appalling* violence that it killed thirty people outright and injured hundreds —F.L.Allen⟩ ⟨an *appalling* exhaustion rendered her helpless —Arnold Bennett⟩ DIRE applies to the extremely fearful and dread or ominous ⟨prophets of the downfall of American democracy have seen their *dire* predictions come to naught —F.D.Roosevelt⟩ ⟨the *dire* possibilities of a head-on collision —O.S.Nock⟩ ⟨wolves ran in ferocious packs, *dire* wolves, larger than any wolf man has seen —Marjory S. Douglas⟩ **syn** see in addition AFRAID

fear·ful·ly \-f(ə)lē, -li\ *adv* [ME *ferfulli,* fr. *ferful* fearful + *-li* -ly] **:** in a fearful manner — usu. used as a generalized intensifier with the force of a superlative ⟨~ talented people —Harvey Breit⟩ ⟨a ~ difficult role —Winthrop Sargeant⟩ ⟨a ~ hot day⟩

fear·ful·ness \-fəlnəs\ *n* -ES **1 :** the quality or state of being afraid **:** TIMIDITY **2 :** the quality of causing fear or awe **:** DREADFULNESS

fear·less \ˈfi(ə)rləs, -iəl-\ *adj* **1 :** marked by freedom from fear and by resolution in braving dangers **:** not timid **:** BOLD ⟨a ~ soldier⟩ ⟨a less courageous man would have hesitated, but Parker was utterly ~ —V.L.Parrington⟩ **2** *obs* **:** looked upon without fear **:** not arousing fear **:** HARMLESS **syn** see BRAVE

fear·less·ly *adv* **:** in a fearless manner ⟨advanced ~ upon the enemy⟩

fear·less·ness *n* -ES **:** the quality or state of being without fear **:** BRAVERY

fearnought *also* **fearnaught** \ˈ⸗,⸗\ *n* -S [²*fear* + *nought, naught*] **1 :** a thick heavy overcoating that is made of wool often mixed with shoddy and that has a rough shaggy face; *also* **:** a garment made of this material — called also *dreadnought* **2 a :** a machine for disentangling woolen fiber prior to carding that consists usu. of one large cylinder with hooked teeth and several worker and stripper rollers **b :** a picker preceding the card

fears *pl of* FEAR, *pres 3d sing of* FEAR

fear·some \ˈfi(ə)rsəm, -iəs-\ *adj* **1 a :** arousing or likely to arouse fear, fright, or terror ⟨a ~ monster⟩ ⟨a ~ place it is, with a straight drop to the sea, hundreds of feet below —C.B. Nordhoff & J.N.Hall⟩ ⟨a shadowy garret; sordid, dark, and ~ —John Mason Brown⟩ **b :** AWE-INSPIRING — often used as a generalized intensifier with the force of a superlative ⟨the moment had a magical and ~ quality⟩ ⟨he had a ~ sincerity that made good manners seem false —Mary McCarthy⟩ ⟨she had acquired a perfectly ~ artificial tact —Mary M. Colum⟩ **2 :** TIMID, TIMOROUS ⟨a little ~ beast⟩ ⟨the ~ cook did not like dogs —Virginia D. Dawson & Betty D. Wilson⟩ — **fear·some·ly** *adv* — **fear·some·ness** *n*

fea·si·bil·i·ty \ˌfēzəˈbilədē, -lətē, -i\ *n* -ES **:** the quality of being feasible **:** PRACTICABILITY ⟨a plan so complex its ~ was doubtful⟩ ⟨established the ~ of polar flying —*Current Biog.*⟩

fea·si·ble \ˈfēzəbəl\ *adj* [ME *faisible,* fr. MF, fr. *fais-* (stem of *faire* to make, do, fr. L *facere*) + *-ible* — more at DO] **1 :** capable of being done, executed, or effected **:** possible of realization ⟨irradiation of pork is simple, rapid, commercially ~ and sanitary —*Biol. Abstracts*⟩ ⟨a ~ method⟩ ⟨a ~ plan⟩ **2 :** capable of being managed, utilized, or dealt with successfully **:** SUITABLE ⟨all odd moments were spent upon the links, in any garment ~ to the opportunity —Clive Arden⟩ ⟨coal, oil, and waterfalls are the most ~ sources of power in sight at present —C.C.Furnas⟩ **3 :** REASONABLE, LIKELY ⟨gave an explanation that seemed ~ enough⟩ **syn** see POSSIBLE

fea·si·ble·ness *n* -ES **:** the quality or state of being feasible ⟨spent an hour discussing the ~ of the plan for city improvement⟩

fea·si·bly \-blē, -li\ *adv* **:** in a feasible manner

¹feast \ˈfēst\ *n* -S [ME *feste* festival, holiday, feast, fr. OF, festival, fr. L *festa* (neut. pl.), fr. neut. pl. of *festus* solemn, festal; akin to L *fanum* temple, *feriae* holidays, Arm *dikʻ* gods] **1 a :** an elaborate meal often accompanied by a ceremony or entertainment **:** BANQUET **b :** something partaken of or shared in with delight **:** something highly agreeable and usu. sumptuous ⟨the ~ of reason —Alexander Pope⟩ ⟨a ~ for the eyes⟩ **2 :** a religious festival of rejoicing as opposed to a fast **a :** a holy day set apart annually for solemn commemoration (as of an event in the life of Christ) ⟨the ~ of the Nativity⟩ **b :** an anniversary marked out in the church calendar for special services or devotions ⟨the ~ of Corpus Christi⟩ **3** *archaic* **:** FEASTING, FESTIVITY

²feast \"\ *vb* -ED/-ING/-S [ME *festen,* fr. *feste,* n.] *vi* **1 :** to have or take part in a feast **:** dine on rich provisions **2 :** to enjoy some unusual pleasure or delight **~** *vt* **1 :** to present a feast to **:** entertain lavishly esp. by a banquet ⟨we were ~*ed* on filet mignon and strawberry shortcake⟩ **2 :** DELIGHT, GRATIFY ⟨~*ing* our eyes on the colors and contours of the landscape in autumn⟩ **3 :** to commemorate annually and with religious ceremonies — **feast·er** *n*

feast day *n* [ME *feste day,* fr. *feste* festival + *day*] **:** a day set as a commemorative festival; *esp* **:** a periodic religious festival

feast·ful \ˈfēstfəl\ *adj* [ME *festful,* fr. *feste* festival + *-ful*] *archaic* **:** devoted to feasting **:** FESTIVE, FESTAL ⟨~ days —John Milton⟩

feast of booths *usu cap F&B* **:** SUKKOTH

feast of dedication *usu cap F&D* **:** HANUKKAH

feast of fools *usu cap both Fs* [trans. of ML *festum stultorum*] **:** a medieval burlesque festival held esp. in France usu. on the feast of the Circumcision (January 1), a prominent feature being mummeries such as a burlesque of the high mass conducted by the lower clergy under a leader elected for the occasion with a burlesque title

feast of ingathering *usu cap F&I* **:** SUKKOTH

feast of lanterns *usu cap F&L* **1 :** a Chinese annual festival on the 15th day of the 1st month according to the old Chinese calendar that is the concluding part of the new-year celebration **2 :** ²BON

feast of lights *usu cap F&L* **:** HANUKKAH

feast of lots *usu cap F&L* **:** PURIM

feast of orthodoxy *usu cap F&O* **:** a solemn feast of the Eastern Orthodox Church celebrated on the first Sunday of Lent and commemorating the victory over iconoclasm, the restoration of images to churches, and the victory over all heresies

feast of tabernacles *usu cap F&T* **:** SUKKOTH

feast of unleavened bread *usu cap F&U&B* **:** an ancient 7-day agricultural feast marked by the offering of new grain to the Lord which began on the 15th day of the 1st month, the day after the 1st day of the Passover, and finally became one continuous festival with the Passover

feast of weeks *usu cap F&W* **:** SHABUOTH

feast-or-famine \ˌ⸗⸗ˈ⸗⸗\ *adj* **:** marked by extremes (as of success and failure or prosperity and depression) ⟨ski-area operators agree that theirs is uniquely a *feast-or-famine* business —William Gilman⟩ ⟨it follows . . . that mineral exploitation is a *feast-or-famine* industry —H.A.Meyerhoff⟩

¹feat \ˈfēt, *usu* -ēd.+V\ *n* -S [ME *fait, fet* action, act, deed, fr. MF, deed, fr. L *factum,* fr. neut. of *factus,* past part. of *facere* to make, do — more at DO] **1** *obs* **a :** TECHNIQUE, KNACK, SKILL **b :** a deed or act of a specialized kind **c :** skilled or specialized activity **:** PROFESSION **2 a :** ACT, DEED **b :** a deed notable esp. for courage **:** a heroic achievement **:** EXPLOIT ⟨a story of knights and ~*s* in arms⟩ ⟨the amazing ~*s* of ordinary foot soldiers⟩ **c :** an act or product of skill, endurance, dexterity, or ingenuity **:** ACCOMPLISHMENT ⟨~*s* of an acrobat⟩ ⟨~*s* of scholarship⟩ ⟨a difficult engineering ~⟩

²feat \"\ *adj* -ER/-EST [ME *fete, fayt,* fr. MF *fait* made (past part. of *faire* to make, do), fr. L *factus,* past part. of *facere*] **1** *now dial Eng* **:** SUITABLE, FITTING, APPROPRIATE **2** *now dial Brit* **a :** clever and graceful **b :** DEXTEROUS, ADROIT **3** *now dial Brit* **a :** attractively neat **:** TRIM **b** *of dress* **:** BECOMING **4** *obs* **:** AFFECTED, OVERNICE **syn** see DEXTEROUS

¹feath·er \ˈfeth̲ə(r)\ *n* -S [ME *fether,* fr. OE; akin to OHG *federa* wing, ON *fjǫthr* feather, L *petere* to go to or toward, seek, Gk *petesthai* to fly, *piptein* to fall, *pteron* wing, feather, Skt *patati* he flies, falls] **1 a :** one of the light horny epidermal outgrowths that form the external covering of the body of birds and the greater part of the surface of their wings, that arise from the surface epidermis of vascular dermal papillae lying in depressed follicles, and that consist of a shaft divided into a hollow proximal quill and a distal rachis furrowed on one side, filled with a pithy substance, and bearing on each side a series of somewhat obliquely directed barbs which bear barbules which in turn bear barbicels commonly ending in hooked hamuli and interlocking with the barbules of an adjacent barb to link the barbs into a continuous vane — see AFTERSHAFT, DOWN, FILOPLUME, PINFEATHER, PTERYLA **b feathers** *pl, obs* **:** WINGS ⟨set ~*s* to thy heels —Shak.⟩ **c** (1) *obs* **:** PLUMAGE (2) **:** ATTIRE, DRESS, CLOTHES — usu. used in pl. **d** (1) *archaic* **:** a decorative crest or badge consisting of a feather or group of feathers **:** PLUME — often used in pl. (2) **:** a foaming crest of a wave **e** (1) *obs* **:** BIRD (2) *archaic* **:** feathered game **f :** the vane of an arrow — see ARROW illustration **2 :** a feathery tuft or fringe of hair; *specif* **:** a fringe of long hair (as that on the legs of certain dogs or horses) — see DOG illustration **3 a :** something extremely light or insignificant ⟨so frightened that he shied at ~*s*⟩ ⟨you could have knocked me over with a ~⟩ **b** [by shortening] **:** FEATHERWEIGHT **4 :** KIND, NATURE, SPECIES ⟨the typical tavern-keeper was a panderer, a thief, and an all-around rascal and . . . his clients were of the same ~ —L.C. Douglas⟩ **5 a :** CONDITION, TRIM, FETTLE ⟨feeling in fine ~ on the day of the race⟩ **b :** MOOD, SPIRITS ⟨woke up in good ~⟩ **6 :** a projecting strip, rib, fin, or flange: as **a :** a strength-

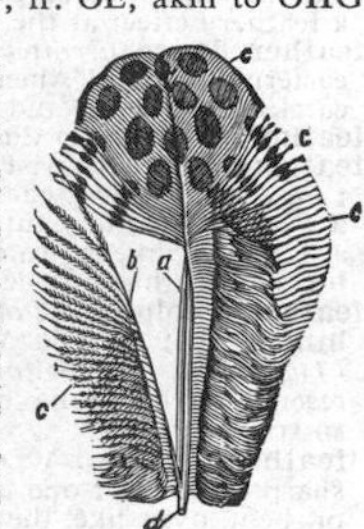

feather 1a: *a* shaft with some of the barbs cut away from the left, *b* aftershaft with barbs cut away on the right, *c* barbs, *d* quill

ening rib, web, or bracket **b :** a tongue fixed or cut (as in the edge of a board) to fit into a corresponding groove (as in another board) to make a flush joint without nails, screws, or pegs **:** FEATHER KEY **7 :** a feathery flaw in the eye or in a precious stone **8 a :** the act of feathering an oar **b :** the angular adjustment of an oar blade as it leaves the water **9 :** one of two wedge-shaped short metal rods curved at the upper end and driven into a hole drilled in rock and forced apart by another rod driven in between them in order to split the rock **10 :** the wake made by the periscope of a submarine running submerged — **a feather in one's cap :** an honor, a trophy, or a mark of distinction **:** a notable accomplishment ‹it was *a feather in the governor's cap* that he had stayed above corruption throughout his term›

²**feather** \"\ *vb* **feathered; feathered; feathering** \-th(ə)riŋ\ **feathers** [ME *fetheren*, fr. OE *gefetheran*, *gefitherian*, fr. *fether*, n. — more at ¹FEATHER] *vt* **1** *obs* **:** to give wings to; *also* **:** to help to speed **2 a :** to furnish with a feather (as an arrow or a cap) **b :** to cover, clothe, or adorn with or as if with feathers ‹birches and oaks still ~*ed* the narrow ravines —Sir Walter Scott› ‹red-*feathered* skies —Virginia Woolf› **3 a :** to reduce the edge of to the fineness of a featheredge esp. by cutting, shaving, or wearing away **b :** to thin and cut (the hair) in short tapered lengths **c :** to spread out (as paint) esp. around the edges of a particular area in order to blend in with adjoining matter **4 a** (1) *of a bird* **:** to cut (the air) with a wing (2) *of a fish* **:** to cut (the water) with a fin **b :** to turn (an oar or paddle blade) parallel to the surface of the water during recovery to eliminate air resistance **c** *aeronautics* (1) **:** to rotate (propeller blades) so that the chords become approximately parallel to the thrust axis thus reducing drag and preventing windmilling in case of engine failure; *also* **:** to rotate the propeller blades of (an engine) in such a manner (2) *in a rotary-wing aircraft* **:** to increase and decrease periodically the angle of incidence of (a rotor blade) by rotation about the axis to equalize the lift produced by advancing and retreating blades in forward flight **5 a :** to dye (fur) by applying dye to the top hairs with a feather **b :** to apply a slip decoration to in ceramics by light brushing **6 :** to join by a tongue and groove **7 :** to adjust (the main light) in photographic portraiture so that the subject is illuminated by the outer part of the light beam ~ *vi* **1 :** to grow or form feathers **:** become fledged — often used with *out* ‹birds ~*ing* out› **2 :** to have or take on the appearance of a feather or something feathered **:** grow or spread to give the effect of something feathered **3** *of a hound* **:** to move the stern nervously from side to side (as in searching for a trail) **4 :** to soak in and spread **:** BLUR — used of writing in ink or a printed impression on soft or unsized paper **5 :** to feather an oar or an airplane propeller blade **6 :** to produce branches or laterals **7 :** to spread and thin out esp. at the edges — often used with *away* or *out* ‹bits of smoke began to ~ away from the top of the hill —Walt Sheldon› **8 :** to form a shape resembling a feather in emerging ‹the soaring white streams that ~*ed* from the nozzles of the swarming fireboats —Robert O'Brien› — **feather one's nest :** to provide for oneself esp. reprehensibly while in a position of trust (as from property confided to one's care) ‹this genius at fund raising was also able to *feather his nest* most adequately by an adroit manipulation of the nation's funds with his own —Sidney Warren›

³**feather** \"\ *adj* [¹*feather*] **:** consisting of or resembling a feather **:** having a feather **:** composed of or containing feathers ‹a ~ edge to the board› ‹a ~ pillow›

feather alum *n* **1 :** HALOTRICHITE **2 :** ALUNOGEN

feather ball *n* **:** a low tuberculate Mexican cactus (*Neomammillaria plumosa*) with white feathery spines

feather bed *n* [ME *fetherbed*, fr. *fether* feather + ¹*bed* — more at FEATHER] **1 a :** a feather mattress **b :** a bed having a feather mattress **2 :** a markedly easy and comfortable state or position **:** SINECURE **3 :** a bed often formed in pools and shallow lakes by the crowded growth of stoneworts; *also* **:** a stonewort of the genus *Chara*

¹**featherbed** \ˈ==ˌ=\ *adj* **:** calling for, requiring, or sanctioning featherbedding ‹a ~ rule› **:** created by or resulting from featherbedding ‹a ~ job›

²**featherbed** \"\ *vi* **1 :** to require more workmen than are strictly needed or a placing of workmen in nonproductive or unnecessary jobs or a limiting of productive output under a featherbed rule **2 :** to do featherbed work or to put in time in a featherbed job or under a featherbed rule ~ *vt* **1 :** to bring under a featherbed rule ‹many tasks are *featherbedded* to employ two craftsmen . . . where one would do —*Time*› **2 :** to assist or stimulate (as an industry or an economy) by government aid

featherbedding \ˈ==ˌ==\ *n* [fr. gerund of ²*featherbed*] **:** the requiring of an employer usu. under a union rule or by safety statute to pay more employees than are needed for a particular job or to pay full wages for nonproductive labor or unnecessary or duplicating jobs or made-work or for output artificially restricted below normal working capacity

feather bell *n* **:** FEATHER-FLEECE

feather boarding *n* **:** featheredged boarding

featherbone \ˈ==ˌ=\ *or* **featherboning** \ˈ==ˌ==\ *n* **:** a corset bone made from the quills of domestic fowl or of plastic

featherbrain \ˈ==ˌ=\ *n* **:** a foolish scatterbrained person

featherbrained \ˈ==ˌ=\ *adj* [¹*feather* + *brained*] **:** not very bright **:** FOOLISH, FRIVOLOUS ‹too ridiculous and ~ a man for any position of responsibility›

feather bunchgrass *n* **:** a sparingly branched feather grass (*Stipa viridula*) with a narrow erect panicle that is densely flowered from near the base

feather coral *n* [so called fr. the appearance of the septa] **:** TETRACORAL

feather crotch *n* **:** a feathery pattern in the grain of veneer cut from the crotch

feathercut \ˈ==ˌ=\ *n* **:** a style of cutting women's and girls' hair in short tapered lengths that shape into small curls with a feathery effect at the tips

feather dance *n, often cap F&D* **:** a ceremonial dance of eastern woodland Amerinds in which male participants orig. carried feathered wands

feather duster *n* **:** a dusting brush made of feathers

feathered *adj* [fr. past part. of ²*feather*] **:** resembling or suggesting a feather: as **a :** having feathery tufts or markings that are shaped like a feather ‹~ asparagus› **b :** shaved thin on the edge ‹a ~ board›

feather duster

feathered columbine *also* **feather columbine** *n* **1 :** an Old World meadow rue (*Thalictrum aquilegifolium*) with foliage resembling that of the columbine **2 :** EARLY MEADOW RUE

¹**featheredge** \ˈ==ˌ=\ *n* **1 a :** a very thin sharp edge; *esp* **:** one that is easily broken or bent over like the edge of a feather **b :** such an edge that is bent or curled over on a cutting tool **2 a :** a thin edge of a board of triangular or trapezoidal section **b :** a board with one edge thinner than the other **3 :** DECKLE EDGE **4 :** the thin edge of a gravel road built on a flat subgrade, the thickness of the gravel surface being gradually increased from the edges to the center line **5 :** a blurred edge (as of a written or printed character) caused by feathering **6 :** a fringe of hair; *esp* **:** a thin narrow fringe at the nape of the neck

²**featheredge** \"\ *vt* **1 a :** to produce a featheredge upon **b :** to make into a featheredge ‹the thin boards were *featheredged* for clapboards› **2 :** to smooth out one edge of as thin as possible ‹~ the new paint along the edge of the painted area› **3 :** to make the edge of (a photograph) thin (as by cutting, tearing, or sandpapering) so as to match smoothly with other photographs in a mosaic

³**featheredge** \"\ *adj* **1 :** FEATHEREDGED **2 :** consisting of or being a featheredge

featheredge file *n* [*featheredge* fr. ³*feather* + *edge*] **:** a file of narrow rhomboidal or double half-round section

featheredger \ˈ==ˌ==\ *n* [*feather edge* (fr. ³*feather* + *edge*) + *-er*] **:** FEATHERER

feathered serpent *n* **:** the symbolic representation of Quetzalcoatl, one of the chief Aztec gods

feathered shot *n* **:** FEATHER SHOT

feath·er·er \ˈfeth̲ərə(r)\ *n* -s **:** a worker who feathers the edges of shoe welts to leave the edge of the outsole more accessible for trimming — called also *featheredger*

feather fern *n* **:** a Japanese herb (*Astilbe japonica*) with feathery compound leaves and paniculate white flowers

feath·er·few \ˈfeth̲ə(r),fyü\ *n* -s [ME *fetherfewe* feverfew, centaury, modif. (influenced by *fether* feather) of (assumed) AF *fevrefue*, fr. LL *febrifugia* centaury — more at FEBRIFUGE, FEATHER] *chiefly dial* **:** FEVERFEW

feather-fleece \ˈ==ˌ=\ *n* **:** a bulbous often branched leafy plant (*Stenanthium robustum*) of the family Liliaceae with linear leaves, linear lanceolate perianth segments, and winged seeds

featherfoil \ˈ==ˌ=\ *n* [¹*feather* + *foil* (leaf)] **:** a plant of the genus *Hottonia*

feather-footed \ˈ==ˌ==\ *adj* **:** moving very lightly and silently ‹*feather-footed* dancers›

feather geranium *n* **:** JERUSALEM OAK 1

feather germ *n* **:** the undifferentiated feather forming a dermal papilla in the skin of a bird

feather grass *n* **1 :** a grass of the genus *Stipa* (esp. the European *S. pennata*) **2 :** a grass (*Leptochloa filiformis*) of the southern U.S. and tropical America

featherhead \ˈ==ˌ=\ *n* **:** a foolish or scatterbrained person ‹that ultraprofound look of the pretty ~ who suddenly turns serious —J.B.Priestley›

featherheaded \ˈ==ˌ==\ *adj* [¹*feather* + *headed*] **:** being a featherhead **:** markedly not bright **:** FOOLISH, SCATTERBRAINED ‹grown into one of the most ~ of her sex —*New Statesman & Nation*›

featherier *comparative of* FEATHERY

featheriest *superlative of* FEATHERY

feath·er·i·ness \ˈfeth̲(ə)rēnəs, -rin-\ *n* -ES **:** the quality or state of being feathery or extremely light

feathering *n* -s [partly fr. ¹*feather* + *-ing*, partly fr. gerund of ²*feather*] **1 a :** a covering of feathers **:** PLUMAGE; *collectively* **:** FEATHERS **b :** a style in which feathers are attached to the shafts of arrows; *also* **:** the feathers of an arrow **2 :** a fringe of hair (as on the legs of a dog) **3 :** FOLIATION 5 **4 :** a shaving or small bit of cinnamon bark **5 :** a process in which the fat in homogenized milk precipitates or flocculates at the surface of hot coffee or tea; *also* **:** the precipitate so formed **6 :** photographic illumination by means of feathering

feathering screw *n* [*feathering* fr. gerund of ²*feather*] **:** a screw propeller on a ship the blades of which may be moved while revolving to alter the pitch, to reverse the ship, or to move edgeways through the water

feather joint *n* **1 :** a joint formed by making a mating groove in each of the contiguous pieces and inserting a feather in the opening formed when the pieces are butted together **2 :** one of a set of joints that are developed by shear and tension in a zone of deformation of the earth's crust (as along a fault) and that resemble in pattern the barbs and shaft of a feather

feather key *n, in machinery* **:** a sunk key without taper that is permanently fixed in one of the connected pieces and that is a sliding fit in a keyway in the other so as to permit relative longitudinal motion — called also *spline*

featherleaf cedar \ˈ==ˌ=-\ *n* **:** AMERICAN ARBORVITAE

feather-legged *US usu* ˈ==ˌlegəd, *Brit usu* -gd\ *adj* **1** *of a domestic fowl* **:** having feathers on the outer surface of the shank and usu. extending onto the outer or outer and middle toe **2** *South & Midland* **:** unwilling to fight **:** COWARDLY

feath·er·less \ˈfeth̲ə(r)ləs\ *adj* [ME *fetherles*, fr. *fether* feather + *-les* -less] **:** having no feathers — **feath·er·less·ness** *n* -ES

featherlight \ˈ==ˌ=\ *adj* **:** extremely light ‹he hung on tenaciously, his body ~ —I.L.Idriess› ‹operated by a ~ touch —*advt.*›

feath·er·man \ˈ==mən, -ˌman\ *n, pl* **feathermen** [ME *fetherman*, fr. *fether* feather + *man* — more at FEATHER] **:** a tradesman or hawker of former times who dealt in feathers or plumes

feather merchant *n, slang* **:** one in a position that involves little effort or responsibility or that calculatedly evades effort or responsibility **:** LOAFER

feather mite *n* **:** any of several small mites living on the feathers and feeding on the blood of domestic and wild birds

feather mosaic *n* **:** FEATHERWORK

feather moss *n* [so called fr. the feathery branches] **:** a moss of *Hypnum* or related genera

feather ore *n* **:** a capillary or fibrous form of jamesonite

feather out *vi* **:** to end irregularly (as of a lenticular rock formation)

feather palm *n* **:** a palm with pinnate leaves

featherpate \ˈ==ˌ=\ *n* **:** FEATHERHEAD

featherpated \ˈ==ˌ==\ *adj* **:** FEATHERHEADED

feather picking *n* **:** a common vice of young chickens and turkeys involving pecking at or pulling the developing feathers of other members of the flock, a practice that is related to and may lead to cannibalism

feather poke *n* [¹*feather* + *poke* (bag)] *dial Eng* **:** any of several birds that line their pocket-shaped nests with feathers (as the long-tailed titmouse)

feather rot *n* **:** a common rot of both dead and living tree trunks caused by a fungus (*Poria subacida*) and characterized by the white stringy or spongy nature of the rotted tissue

feathers *pl of* FEATHER, *pres 3d sing of* FEATHER

feather shot *n* **:** copper granulated by being poured molten into cold water

feather star *n* [so called fr. the superficial resemblance of the arms to feathers] **:** COMATULID

¹**featherstitch** \ˈ==ˌ=\ *n* **:** an embroidery stitch consisting of a line of diagonal blanket stitches worked alternately to the left and right

²**featherstitch** \"\ *vb* **:** to embroider in featherstitch

feather tip *n* **:** a very thin end in lumber (as in certain grades of shingles)

feather-tongue \ˈ==ˌ=\ *vt* **:** to make with a tongue fitting a groove

feathertop \ˈ==ˌ=\ *or* **feathertop grass** *n* **:** any of several grasses having feathery panicles (as members of the genera *Pennisetum* and *Calamagrostis*)

featherstitch

feather tract *n* **:** PTERYLA

feather tree *n* **1 :** SMOKE TREE 1a **2 :** a mountain mahogany (*Cercocarpus montanus*) that is usu. a low spreading evergreen shrub, is widely distributed in interior uplands of western No. America, and is a major browse plant over much of its range

feather tye \ˈ==ˌtī\ *n* [¹*feather* + E dial. *tye* tick (of a mattress or pillow), perh. fr. ME, small box, case, fr. OE *tēag*] *dial* **:** FEATHER BED 1

featherweed \ˈ==ˌ=\ *n* **1 :** CATFOOT **2 :** a red alga of the genus *Ptilota*

¹**featherweight** \ˈ==ˌ=\ *n* **1 :** a very light weight; *specif* **:** the lightest weight a racehorse may carry in a handicap **2 :** one that is very light in weight: as **a :** a boxer or wrestler of a weight falling within a fixed class of very light body weights: (1) **:** a professional boxer weighing between 118 and 120 lbs — compare BANTAMWEIGHT, FLYWEIGHT, HEAVYWEIGHT, MIDDLEWEIGHT, WELTERWEIGHT (2) **:** an intercollegiate boxer weighing between 125 and 134 lbs (3) **:** a wrestler weighing between 123 and 134 lbs **b** (1) **:** a paper that is bulky but light in weight (as some book papers) (2) **:** a paper that is light in weight (as some thin writing papers) **3 :** a person that is not very bright **:** FEATHERBRAIN ‹a giant on the football field but a ~ in the classroom›

²**featherweight** \"\ *adj* **1 :** constituting or being a featherweight **:** extremely light in weight ‹a ~ boxer› ‹a bicycle of ~ construction› **2 :** very light or careful in touch or handling ‹the book is ~ in its treatment of the incendiary theme› **3 :** of small significance ‹a ~ comedy› ‹a ~ but charming novel —*New Yorker*›

featherwood \ˈ==ˌ=\ *n* **1 :** an Australian timber tree (*Polyosma cunninghamii*) of the family Escalloniaceae **2 :** the wood of the featherwood resembling hickory — called also *hickory*

featherwork \ˈ==ˌ=\ *n* **1 :** a net or fabric completely covered with overlapping feathers usu. having a design — called also *feather mosaic* **2 :** the art or method of making featherwork

feath·ery \ˈfeth̲(ə)rē, -ri\ *adj, often* -ER/-EST **1 :** resembling or suggesting a feather, a bunch of feathers, or the barbs of a feather in shape, texture, quality, or weight: as **a :** light and delicate ‹a ~ touch on the piano keys› **:** almost weightless and delicately unsubstantial ‹~ snow› ‹~ ash› **b :** delicately marked or flecked as if with a feather or in a way resembling feather markings ‹a ~ sky› **:** marked by delicate tracery or extremely lightly applied decoration or decorative elements ‹an orchestra playing with a ~ elegance› **c :** light and fluffy ‹~ pastry› **d :** fanning out gracefully and delicately like feathers in a plume ‹~ palm trees› **2 :** covered with or as if with feathers ‹joined the ~ congregation of jays› ‹a ~ landscape›

¹**feat·ly** \ˈfētlē, -li\ *adv* [ME *fetly*, fr. *fete*, *fayt* suitable + *-ly* — more at FEAT] **1 a :** FITLY, PROPERLY **b :** neatly and beautifully ‹a chick ~ feathered in royal scarlet —Llewelyn Powys› **2 :** gracefully and nimbly or dexterously ‹foot it ~ here and there —Shak.› ‹convinced that a conductor should handle himself as ~ as his orchestra —*Time*› **3 :** SKILLFULLY

²**featly** \"\ *adj, often* -ER/-EST **1 :** GRACEFUL ‹one of the lead horses . . . lifting his forefeet in ~ fashion —Howard Taubman› **2** *obs* **:** neat and comely; *also* **:** APPROPRIATE, JUST, FITTING

feat·ness *n* -ES *now dial Brit* **:** the quality or state of being feat

feats *pl of* FEAT

¹**fea·ture** \ˈfēchə(r)\ *n* -s [ME *feture*, fr. MF *faiture*, *feture*, fr. L *factura* act of making, formation, fr. *factus* (past part. of *facere* to make, do) + *-ura* -ure — more at DO] **1 a :** the makeup, structure, form, or outward appearance of a person or thing ‹a man of large ~› **b** *obs* **:** a part of the body **:** LIMB **c :** something that goes to make up something else **:** ELEMENT, PART, CONSTITUENT ‹a ~ of English grammar is the number of periphrastic forms› ‹it is also possible to hear ~*s* of pitch and intonation —Stanley Newman› ‹this course teaches the student the ~*s*, operation, and care of darkroom equipment —*Bull. of Meharry Med. Coll.*› ‹it was a bad evening from then on, its only good ~ being its shortness —Lloyd Alexander› **2 a :** the makeup or cast of the face or its parts **:** facial aspect or appearance ‹stern of ~ even when he smiled› **b** (1) **:** a part of the face **:** LINEAMENT ‹a man with oriental ~*s*› ‹her head . . . seems too small for her generous ~*s* —*Time*› (2) **features** *pl* **:** FACE, COUNTENANCE ‹an embarrassed blush on his ~*s*› **c** *obs* **:** physical beauty ‹cheated of ~ by dissembling nature —Shak.› **d :** distinctive outline, form, or quality ‹could not well describe the ~*s* of the painting› ‹an experience with no special or distinctive ~› **3** *archaic* **:** a shape or a thing with form **:** a visible form **:** APPARITION **4 a :** a marked element of something **:** something that is esp. prominent **:** PECULIARITY, CHARACTERISTIC ‹sparse pine growth was a ~ of the landscape› **b :** something offered to the public or to a clientele that is exhibited or advertised as particularly attractive **:** a special inducement: as (1) **:** a distinctive, prominent, or unusual article, story, or picture (as one with strong emotional or human-interest appeal) in a newspaper or periodical ‹an account of the fire was a ~ of the Sunday supplement›; *esp* **:** a newspaper story that consists of background or analysis or that depends on unusual treatment as contrasted with a straight news story (2) **:** a special department in a newspaper or periodical ‹detailed weather reports are a ~ of the morning paper› (3) **:** the main presentation in a program at a motion-picture theater **:** a film of considerable length presented as the main attraction at a theater **5 :** an evidence of human occupation (as a house floor, fire pit, or storage pit) encountered in archaeological excavation

²**feature** \"\ *vb* **featured; featured; featuring** \-ch(ə)riŋ\ **features** *vt* **1** *now dial* **:** to resemble in features **:** FAVOR **2 :** to be a feature of ‹another performance of the Haydn Mass . . . *featured* our stop in Atlanta —R.K.Leopold› ‹agricultural radicalism *featured* the period from 1880 to 1896 —C.A.M. Ewing› **3 :** to picture or portray in the mind **:** IMAGINE ‹can you ~ wearing a necktie out here —K.M.Dodson› **4 a :** to make a feature of **:** give special prominence to ‹the newspaper *featured* the story of the murder› ‹the theater was *featuring* a murder-mystery film› **b :** to be marked by **:** have as a characteristic or feature ‹the string quartets ~ a style more characteristic of the last century than this one› **c :** to provide with a special feature ‹their annual Blossom Festival, *featured* by parades, balls, concerts —*Amer. Guide Series: Mich.*› ~ *vi* **:** to play a significant part **:** comprise a feature ‹other lesser-known figures who ~ in the book —*Times Lit. Supp.*› ‹a Ten-Year Plan in which . . . urgently needed rehousing, hydroelectric, and other development schemes were intended to ~ largely —*New Statesman & Nation*›

³**feature** \"\ *adj* **:** being a special or main attraction **:** constituting a feature ‹a ~ story on candidates' wives› ‹a ~ performer› ‹a ~ picture›

fea·tured \-chə(r)d\ *adj* [ME *fetured*, fr. *feture* feature + *-ed* — more at ¹FEATURE] **1** *obs* **a :** SHAPED, FASHIONED **b :** well shaped **:** attractive of appearance **2 a :** provided with form or lineaments (as by carving) **b :** having facial features of a particular kind — usu. used in combination ‹a grim-*featured* man› ‹a heavy-*featured* face› ‹a sharp-*featured* woman› **3** [fr. past part. of ²*feature*] **a :** displayed, advertised, or presented as a feature ‹a ~ attraction› ‹a ~ story›; **b :** given special prominence **:** STARRING ‹a ~ actor›

fea·ture·less \ˈfēchə(r)ləs\ *adj* **1 :** having no distinct or distinctive features ‹the top is largely ~ plateau —*London Calling*› ‹the long ~ months with no special credit or romance —Mary Webb› ‹vast tracts of ~ ocean —W.H.Dowdeswell› **2 :** inactive and without any material price change — used of business or market activity

fea·ture·ly \-lē,-li\ *adj* **:** HANDSOME ‹~ warriors of Christian chivalry —S.T.Coleridge›

fea·tur·ette \ˌfēchəˈret\ *n* -s **1 :** a short feature film **2 :** SHORT 8e

fea·tur·ish \ˈfēch(ə)rish\ *adj* **:** having the quality or some of the qualities usu. marking a feature article in a newspaper **:** tending to use eye-catching or sensational matter or devices in the presentation of news

¹**feaze** *var of* FEEZE

²**feaze** \ˈfāz, ˈfēz\ *vi* -ED/-ING/-S [prob. fr. obs. D *vase*, *vese* fringe, frayed edge, fr. MD — more at FASH] **1** *dial Brit* **:** to become frayed — usu. used with *out* ‹his coat was all *feazed* out at the edges› **2** *dial Brit* **:** to become rough or jagged at the edges

feazings *n pl* [fr. pl. of *feazing*, gerund of ²*feaze*] **:** the unlaid end of a rope

febri- *comb form* [LL, fr. L *febris* — more at FEVER] **:** fever ‹*febri*cide›

fe·bric·i·ty \fəˈbrisəd·ē, fē'-\ *n* -ES [ML *febricitat-*, *febricitas*, irreg. fr. L *febris* fever + *-itat-*, *-itas* -ity] **:** the quality or state of being feverish

fe·bric·u·la \-ˈbrikyələ\ *n* -s [L, dim. of *febris*] **:** a slight and transient fever

fe·brif·ic \-ifik\ *adj* [prob. fr. (assumed) NL *febrificus*, fr. LL *febri-* + L *-ficus* -fic] *archaic* **:** producing fever

fe·brif·u·gal \fəˈbrif(y)əgəl, fē'-, ˌfebrəˈfyügəl\ *adj* [prob. fr. (assumed) NL *febrifuga*, n., febrifuge + E *-al*] **:** mitigating or removing fever

feb·ri·fuge \ˈfebrəˌfyüj\ *n or adj* [F *fébrifuge*, prob. fr. (assumed) NL *febrifuga*, fr. LL *febrifuga*, *febrifugia* centaury, fr. *febri-* + *-fuga*, *-fugia* (fr. L *fugare* to put to flight) — more at -FUGE] **:** ANTIPYRETIC

fe·brif·u·gine \fəˈbrifyəˌjēn, fē'-, -jən\ *n* -s [NL *febrifuga* (specific epithet of the ch'ang shan *Dichroa febrifuga*) (fr. fem. of — assumed — NL *febrifugus*, adj., antipyretic, fr. — assumed — NL *febrifuga*, n., antipyretic) + E *-ine* — more at FEBRIFUGE] **:** a toxic emetic crystalline alkaloid $C_{16}H_{19}N_3O_3$ that is obtained from ch'ang shan and is a potent antimalarial

feb·rile \ˈfebrəl, ˈfēb-, -ˌbrīl\ *adj* [ML *febrilis*, fr. L *febris* fever] **:** of or relating to fever **:** marked by fever **:** FEVERISH ‹a ~ reaction caused by an allergen› ‹the ~ tempo of the city's social life in winter› ‹a book obviously written by a talented, if ~ intellect —Janet Flanner›

fe·bril·i·ty \fəˈbriləd·ē, fē'-, fe'-, -ətē, -i\ *n* -ES **:** FEVERISHNESS

fe·bris \ˈfebrəs, ˈfēb-\ *n* -ES [L] **:** FEVER

¹**fe·bro·ni·an** \fəˈbrōnēən\ *adj, cap* [Justinus *Febronius* (pseudonym of Johann N. von Hontheim †1790 German

Roman Catholic prelate) + E *-an*] **:** of, relating to, or advocating Febronianism

²febronian \"\ *n* -s *cap* **:** an advocate of Febronianism

fe·bro·ni·an·ism \-ə,nizəm\ *n* -s *usu cap* **:** the principle applied in 1763 to the Roman Catholic Church by Johann N. von Hontheim, suffragan bishop of Treves, that final ecclesiastical authority belongs to the whole church and not merely to the papacy, that papal power is inferior to that of the whole body of the episcopate, and that papal power is limited in matters of doctrine by general church councils and in matters of discipline by national churches

feb·ru·ary \÷ˈfeb(y)ə,werē, |i, ˈfebrə,wer| *also* ÷-b,wer| *or* ÷-b,rer| *sometimes* ÷-bə,rer| *or* ÷-bwər| *or* ÷-b(ə)r| *or* ÷-brər| *or* ÷-b,yer|\ *n, pl* **februaries** *or* **februarys** *usu cap* [ME *februarie*, fr. L *februarius*, fr. *februa*, pl., feast of purification held on the 15th of February + *-arius* -ary; perh. akin to L *fumus* smoke, vapor — more at FUME] **:** the second month in the Gregorian calendar — abbr. *Feb.*; see MONTH table

february daphne *n, usu cap F* **:** MEZEREON 1

february fill-dike \-ˈ=,=\ *n, usu cap 1st F* **:** FEBRUARY; *also* **:** the period of the sun's occupation of Aquarius according to astrology

feb·ru·a·tion \,febrəˈwāshən\ *n* -s [L *februation-, februatio*, fr. *februatus* (past part. of *februare* to purify, fr. *februa*) + *-ion-, -io* -ion] *archaic* **:** purification by a religious ceremony

fec *abbr* [L *fecit*] he made

fe·cal *also* **fae·cal** \ˈfēkəl\ *adj* [MF *fecal*, fr. L *faec-, faex* dregs, sediment + MF *-al*] **:** of, relating to, being, or involving feces ⟨a ~ mass⟩ ⟨~ egg counts⟩

fe·ca·lith *also* **fae·ca·lith** \-kə,lith\ *n* -s [*fecal* + *-lith*] **:** a concretion of dry compact feces occas. formed in the intestine or vermiform appendix

fe·cal·oid \-kə,lȯid\ *adj* [ISV *fecal* + *-oid*] **:** resembling dung

fe·ces *also* **fae·ces** \ˈfē(,)sēz\ *n pl* [ME *feces* (pl.), *fece* (sing.), *fex* (sing.), fr. L *faec-, faex* dregs, sediment] **1 :** the sediment formed after infusion or distillation **:** DREGS, REFUSE **2 :** bodily waste discharged through the anus **:** DUNG, MANURE

fech·ne·ri·an \(ˈ)fek¦nirēən, -ek¦-\ *adj, usu cap* [Gustav Theodor *Fechner* †1887 Ger. physicist, philosopher, & experimental psychologist + E *-ian*] **:** of, relating to, or discovered by G. T. Fechner, German physicist considered to be a founder of psychophysics and experimental psychology

fech·ner's law \ˈfek|nə(r)z-, -k|\ *n, usu cap F* **:** WEBER-FECHNER LAW

fecht \ˈfekt\ *Scot var of* FIGHT

fecial *var of* FETIAL

fe·cit \ˈfākət\ [L, 3d pers. sing. perf. indic. of *facere* to make, do — more at DO] **:** (he) created or executed (it) — used with the name of the executing artist or craftsman on a painting, piece of sculpture, or other art object or piece of craftsmanship

feck \ˈfek\ *n* [ME (Sc) *fek*, by shortening & alter. fr. ME *¹effect*] **1** *Scot* **a :** the greater share **:** MAJORITY — usu. used with *the* ⟨the ~ of the town council didn't fancy his backers —John Buchan⟩ **b :** PART, PORTION ⟨took the best ~ of a year⟩ ⟨sold the best ~ of the litter⟩ **2** *Scot* **:** VALUE, WORTH ⟨no ~ would come from it⟩ **3** *Scot* **:** a number or quantity esp. when large ⟨a whole ~ of them came⟩

feck·et \ˈfekət\ *n* -s [origin unknown] *Scot* **:** VEST 2a

feck·ful \ˈfekfəl\ *adj* [*feck* + *-ful*] **1** *chiefly Scot* **:** EFFICIENT, EFFECTIVE **2** *chiefly Scot* **a :** STURDY, TRUSTY **b :** POWERFUL, VIGOROUS — **feck·ful·ly** \-əlē\ *adv, chiefly Scot*

feck·less \-kləs\ *adj* [*feck* + *-less*] **1 a :** weak in mind or body **:** HELPLESS, INCOMPETENT ⟨a pretty, ~ little widow who is not very good at "managing" —*New Statesman & Nation*⟩ **b :** INEFFICIENT ⟨a day of ~ house heating⟩ **2 :** having no real worth or purpose **:** MEANINGLESS, PURPOSELESS ⟨a ~ figurehead⟩ ⟨what strikes most at first, frequently turns out to be ~ —Amy Lowell⟩ ⟨three years of ~ negotiations —*Time*⟩ **3 a :** lazy and worthless ⟨here were failure and defeat visiting the energetic along with the ~, the able along with the unable —F.L.Allen⟩ **b :** indifferent to responsibility **:** UNRELIABLE **4 :** awkward and unskilled **5 :** UNTHINKING, IRRESPONSIBLE ⟨a certain childish, ~ gaiety⟩ **6 :** impractical and shiftless ⟨he was ~, a gambler, a lover of what is called low company, but he was generous —Robert Lynd⟩ — **feck·less·ly** *adv* — **feck·less·ness** *n* -ES

feck·ly \-lī\ *adv* [*feck* + *-ly*] **1** *chiefly Scot* **:** for the most part **2** *chiefly Scot* **:** ALMOST, NEARLY

fec·u·la \ˈfekyələ\ *n, pl* **fecu·lae** \-,lē\ [NL, fr. L *feces* dung (fr. L *faeces*, pl. of *faec-, faex* dregs, sediment) + *-ula*] **:** a fecal pellet of an insect

fec·u·lence \-lən(t)s\ *n* -s [F *féculence*, fr. LL *faeculentia*, fr. *faeculentus* + *-ia* -y] **1 :** something that is feculent **:** SEDIMENT, DREGS, FECES **2 :** the quality or state of being feculent **:** MUDDINESS, FOULNESS

fec·u·len·cy \-nsē, -si\ *n* -ES [LL *faeculentia*] *archaic* **:** FECULENCE

fec·u·lent \-nt\ *adj* [ME, fr. L *faeculentus*, fr. *faec-, faex* dregs, sediment] **:** foul with impurities or excrement **:** covered with filth **:** abounding in sediment or noxious matter **:** FECAL

fe·cund \ˈfēkənd, ˈfek-\ *adj* [ME *fecund, fecound*, fr. MF *fecond*, fr. L *fecundus* — more at FEMININE] **1 a :** characterized by having produced many offspring or by having yielded vegetation, fruit, or crops to a marked or satisfying degree ⟨~ pastures⟩ ⟨~ herds⟩ **b :** capable of producing **:** not sterile or barren **:** markedly fertile ⟨born into a notably ~ family⟩ **2 :** marked by noteworthy intellectual productivity and inventiveness ⟨ideas are, in Paris, so far more numerous and ~ . . . that Paris has on an average some eighty odd daily papers —W.C.Brownell⟩ ⟨a good part of these inventions came to birth — or were further nourished — in the ~ mind of Leonardo da Vinci —Lewis Mumford⟩ **syn** see FERTILE

fec·un·date \ˈfekən,dāt, ˈfēk-\ *vt* -ED/-ING/-S [L *fecundatus*, past part. of *fecundare* to fertilize, fr. *fecundus* fecund] **1 :** to make fruitful or prolific ⟨a flow of ideas *fecundating* the very atmosphere of the college⟩ **2 :** to make fertile **:** IMPREGNATE ⟨males are needed to ~ the young virgin females —W.C.Allee⟩ ⟨the sterile eggs of reason never *fecundated* by sense —P.E. More⟩ — **fec·un·da·tion** \,==ˈdāshən\ *n* -s

fe·cun·da·tive \fēˈkəndəd·iv, ˈfekən,dād-, ˈfēk-\ *adj* **:** serving to fecundate **:** making fertile

fec·un·da·tor \ˈfekən,dād·ə(r), ˈfēk-\ *n* -s [LL, fr. L *fecundatus* + *-or*] **:** one that fecundates

fe·cun·da·to·ry \fēˈkəndə,tōrē\ *adj* **:** of or relating to fecundation

fe·cun·di·ty \fēˈkəndəd·ē, -ədē, -i\ *n* -ES [ME *fecundite*, fr. L *fecunditat-, fecunditas*, fr. *fecundus* fecund + *-itat-, -itas* -ity] **1 a :** the quality or the power of producing fruit esp. in abundance **:** FRUITFULNESS ⟨the ~ of the earth⟩ **b :** productive quality or power ⟨the ~ of the pocket-book publishers —James Rorty⟩ **c :** richness of imagination or invention ⟨the ~ of Shakespeare's genius⟩ **2 a :** the power of producing offspring esp. in large numbers or the quality that conduces to this **:** the potential reproductive capacity (as of a hen) as measured by the individual production of mature eggs and sperm **b :** the power of germinating (as in seeds) **c :** the power or quality of increasing rapidly in number or quantity or of being so increased in number or quantity **3** *archaic* **:** the power of making fruitful or fertile

¹fed \ˈfed\ *adj* [fr. past part. of *feed*] **1** *of poultry or stock* **:** specially nourished or fattened for market ⟨a deck of ~ lambs averaging about 95 lbs. —*Chicago Daily Drovers Jour.*⟩ **2** *slang* **:** FED UP ⟨~ with people scrounging our liquor before four o'clock —J.H.Burns⟩ — **fed to the gills** *or* **fed to the teeth :** FED UP ⟨*fed to the teeth* with this little pension that you euphemistically call a high-grade resort hotel —R.E. Sherwood⟩

²fed \"\ *n* -s *often cap* [by shortening] **1 :** FEDERAL 1 **2** *slang* **:** FEDERAL 2 ⟨so one night I stole a car and took it over the state line to sell it and the *Feds* got me —H. W. Van Couenhoven⟩

fed *abbr* federal; federated; federation

fedai *sometimes cap, var of* FIDA'I

fedarie *n* -s [alter. (influenced in meaning by L *foeder-, foedus* league) of *feodary*] *obs* **:** CONFEDERATE, ACCOMPLICE

fe·da·yee \fəˈda'(y)ē, -dä'-, ==ˈ=\ *n, pl* **feda·yeen** \-ēn\ [Ar *fidā'ī* one who offers himself for his native land, fr. *fidā'* redemption] **:** a member of an Arab commando group esp. operating against Israel

fed·dan \fəˈdän, -dan\ *n, pl* **feddan** *or* **feddans** [Ar *faddān* yoke of oxen, feddan] **:** an Egyptian unit of area equal to 1.038 acres

fed·der \ˈfedə(r)\ *dial Brit var of* FEATHER

fed·e·li·ni \,fedᵊlˈēnē\ *n* -s [It (pl.), alter. of *fidellini*, dim. of It dial. (Genoese) *fidelli* (pl.) vermicelli, prob. fr. Sp *fideos* (pl.), fr. Judeo-Spanish *fidear* to grow, fr. Ar *fāda* to abound, overflow] **:** alimentary paste smaller than vermicelli

fed·er·a·cy \ˈfed(ə)rəsē\ *n* -ES [prob. back-formation fr. *confederacy*] *archaic* **:** ALLIANCE, CONFEDERACY, FEDERATION

¹fed·er·al \ˈfed(ə)rəl\ *adj* [L *foeder-, foedus* league, compact + E *-al*; akin to L *fides* faith — more at FAITH] **1 a :** of or relating to a compact, league, or treaty; *esp* **:** of, relating to, or derived from a compact between states which by the terms of the compact surrender their general sovereignty and consolidate into a new state ⟨a ~ union⟩ **b :** of, relating to, or expressing a covenant between God and the human race or its members, esp. the covenant of works and the covenant of grace — compare FEDERAL THEOLOGY **2 a :** of or relating to a state formed by the consolidation of several states which retain limited residuary powers of government under the common sovereignty of the new state **:** being or befitting such a state ⟨some ~ states have political parties peculiar to one area⟩ **b :** of, characterized by, or constituting a form of government in which power is distributed among a number of constituent territorial units ⟨~ governments often evolved out of leagues or confederations —C.J.Friedrich⟩ ⟨a ~ system⟩ **c** *often cap* **:** of or relating to the central government of a nation having the character of a federation as distinguished from the governments of the constituent units (as states or provinces) **3** *usu cap* **:** advocating or friendly to the principle of a federal government with strong centralized powers; *esp* **:** of or relating to the American Federalists **4** *often cap* **:** of, relating to, or loyal to the federal government or the Union armies of the U.S. in the American Civil War **5** *usu cap* **:** being or belonging to a style of architecture and decoration current in the U.S. following the Revolution and before the period of Classic Revival **6** *of a British university* **:** consisting of an association of colleges that function to a very large degree as independent units — **fed·er·al·ly** \-rəlē, -lī\ *adv*

²federal \"\ *n* -s *usu cap* **1 :** a supporter of the government of the U.S. in the Civil War; *specif* **:** a soldier in the federal armies ⟨*Federals* and Confederates lie buried together⟩ **2 :** a federal agent or officer

federal assembly *n, often cap F&A* **:** the two parliamentary houses constituting the legislative division of certain governments (as that of Switzerland)

federal case *n* **:** an act or activity that is or is likely to be subject to investigation by one of the criminal-investigation agencies (as the FBI) of the U.S. government

federal chancellor *n* **:** CHANCELLOR 4

federal council *n, often cap F&C* **1 :** a central legislative group or assembly in certain governments **2 :** a central executive council in certain governments (as that of Switzerland)

federal court *n* **:** a court established by authority of a federal government; *esp* **:** one established under the constitution and laws of the U.S.

federal deposit insurance *n* **:** federal insurance of bank deposits in the U.S. up to a stated limit per depositor created under the Banking Act of 1933

federal district *n* **:** a district set apart by a country as the seat of the national government (as the District of Columbia in the U.S.)

federal district court *n* **:** a district trial court of law and equity that hears cases under federal jurisdiction

fed·er·al·ese \¦fed(ə)rə¦lēz, -ēs\ *n* -s *often cap, slang* **:** prose that is marked by a needlessly involved and awkwardly pretentious sentence structure and use of a jargon of polysyllabic words and that is sometimes said to characterize the documents of federal bureaus in the U.S. ⟨an enigma wrapped in ~ and tied with red tape —*Time*⟩

fed·er·al·ism \ˈfed(ə)rə,lizəm\ *n* -s **1 a** *often cap* **:** the federal principle of national, European, or world organization or its support **b :** the principle of federal organization of any group of more or less autonomous units or the support of such a principle **2** *usu cap* **:** the principles of the Federalists **3** *usu cap* **:** the principles of federal theology **4** *sometimes cap* **:** federal control ⟨in the lower schools the trend toward ~ is . . . apparent in the proposal for Federal aid to education —Raymond Moley⟩

¹fed·er·al·ist \-ləst\ *n* -s **1 :** an advocate of federalism: as **a** *often cap* **:** an advocate of a federal union between the American colonies after the Revolution and of the formation and adoption of a constitution **b** *often cap* **:** WORLD FEDERALIST **2** *usu cap* **:** a member or adherent of the American Federalist party that in the early years of the U.S. was in favor of a strong centralized federal power as opposed to a central government of limited sovereignty and few powers and that went out of existence between 1821 and 1825

²federalist \"\ *or* **fed·er·al·is·tic** \¦fed(ə)rə¦listik, -tēk\ *adj* **:** of, relating to, or favoring federalism or federalists

fed·er·al·iza·tion \,fed(ə)rələˈzāshən, -,līˈz-\ *n* -s **:** the state or process of federalizing or being federalized ⟨the ~ of higher education⟩ ⟨the ~ of post-office employees⟩

fed·er·al·ize \ˈfed(ə)rə,līz\ *vt* -ED/-ING/-S [F *fédéraliser*, fr. *fédéral* federal (prob. fr. E *¹federal*) + *-iser* -ize] **1 :** to unite in or under a federal compact or a federal government ⟨attempting to ~ the independent states of Europe⟩ **2 :** to bring under the usu. sole jurisdiction of the federal government ⟨it does not ~ the unemployment-compensation system —H.S. Truman⟩

federal labor union *n* **:** a local labor union affiliated directly with the American Federation of Labor

federal land bank *n, usu cap F&L* **:** one of 12 regional banks established under the Federal Farm Loan Act of 1916 to facilitate the furnishing of capital to farms by making long-term loans available through subsidiary cooperative farm-loan associations or through agents on first mortgages up to one half the value of the farm plus 20 percent of the value of permanent improvements on it

federal public law *n* **:** the federal law as embodied in the rules, regulations, and decisions of public federal administrative agencies entrusted with the enforcement of various federal statutes as distinguished from the decisions of the federal courts interpreting and applying these statutes in individual cases

federal reserve agent *n, usu cap F&R* **:** the director who is designated by the board of governors of the Federal Reserve system as chairman of the board of directors of a Federal Reserve bank and who acts as official representative of the board of governors to the bank

federal reserve bank *n, usu cap F&R* **:** one of 12 banks set up under the Federal Reserve system by the Federal Reserve Act of Dec. 23, 1913, one in each of 12 districts, and serving as banks of reserve and discount for affiliated banks including all national banks and many state banks and trust companies

federal reserve district *n, usu cap F&R* **:** one of the 12 districts set up under the Federal Reserve system each of which contains a Federal Reserve bank

federal reserve note *n, usu cap F&R* **:** a currency note issued by the Federal Reserve banks and secured by a gold-certificate reserve of 25 percent and the balance of 75 percent in gold certificates, commercial paper, or U.S. government obligations

federal theology *n* **:** the theological system which rests upon the beliefs (1) that before the Fall man was under a covenant of works by which God through Adam promised man eternal blessedness if he kept his commandments and (2) that since the Fall man has been under a covenant of grace by which God by his grace promises the same blessings to all who believe in Christ — called also COVENANT THEOLOGY

federary *n* -ES [alter. (influenced in form and meaning by L *foeder-, foedus* league) of *feodary*] *obs* **:** FEDARIE

¹fed·er·ate \ˈfed(ə)rət\ *adj* [L *foederatus*, fr. *foeder-, foedus* league, compact + *-atus* -ate — more at ¹FEDERAL] **:** united by compact **:** forming an alliance **:** FEDERATED

²fed·er·ate \ˈfedə,rāt, *usu* -ād·+V\ *vb* -ED/-ING/-S *vi* **:** to unite in a league or association ⟨several nations willing to ~⟩ ~ *vt* **1 :** to organize into a federal organization ⟨~ the world⟩ ⟨a *federated* state⟩ ⟨the British provinces, then separate but now *federated* as Canada —T.H.LeDuc⟩ **2 :** to unite in a league or alliance or federation ⟨officially *federated* with Ethiopia —*Americana Annual*⟩

federated church *n* **:** a local church formed by the coming together of two or more congregations of different denominational backgrounds that unite in a common program while maintaining their separate denominational ties

fed·er·a·tion \,fedəˈrāshən\ *n* -s [F *fédération* league, alliance, fr. LL *foederation-, foederatio*, fr. L *foederatus* + *-ion-, -io* -ion] **1 :** the act of uniting in a league; *esp* **:** the formation of a single sovereign power by the uniting of separate states, provinces, or colonies so that each retains the management of its own local affairs **2 :** something formed by federation: as **a :** a sovereign state formed by the union of several states that have given up certain powers to the central government while retaining for themselves control over local matters — compare CONFEDERATION 2 **b :** a union of societies or organizations ⟨a ~ of labor unions⟩ ⟨a ~ of women's clubs⟩ — **fed·er·a·tion·al** \¦==¦rāshənᵊl, -shnəl\ *adj*

fed·er·a·tive \ˈfedə,rād·iv, ˈfed(ə)rəl, |t|, |ēv *also* |əv\ *adj* [L *foederatus* + E *-ive*] **:** of or relating to a federation or covenant or its formation **:** based on or inclined to federation — **fed·er·a·tive·ly** \|əvlē, -lī\ *adv*

fed·er·a·tor \ˈfedə,rād·ə(r), -ātə-\ *n* -s [*²federate* + *-or*] **:** one that forms a federation **:** one that takes part in a federation

fe·de ring \ˈfā(,)dā-, *It* ˈfāādā\ *n* [It *fede* faith, fr. L *fides* — more at FAITH] **:** a finger ring typically bearing a device in the shape of two clasped hands and used esp. among Europeans as a token of loyalty or faith between two persons; *sometimes* **:** WEDDING RING

federita *var of* FETERITA

fedifragous *adj* [L *foedifragus*, fr. *foedi-* (fr. *foedus* league, compact) + *-fragus* (fr. *frangere* to break) — more at ¹FEDERAL, BREAK] *obs* **:** FAITHLESS, PERFIDIOUS

fedity *n* -ES [L *foeditat-, foeditas*, fr. *foedus* foul, ugly + *-itat-, -itas* -ity — more at BEBUNG] *obs* **:** FOULNESS, VILENESS, IMPURITY

fedn *abbr* federation

fe·do·ra \fəˈdōrə, -dȯrə\ *n* -s *sometimes cap* [*Fédora* (1882), drama by V. Sardou †1908 Fr. playwright] **:** a soft felt hat with a low crown creased lengthwise and with or without a high roll on the side brim

fedora

fed up *adj* **:** sated to the point of disgust **:** bored beyond endurance **:** disgusted and totally out of patience ⟨a generation that is rapidly becoming *fed up* with novels about sensitive young men⟩ ⟨a great many who are *fed up* and disgusted with their jobs —*Encore*⟩ — **fed-upness** \(ˈ)=ˈ==\ *n* -ES

¹fee *n* -s [ME, fr. OE *feoh* cattle, property, money; akin to OHG *fihu* cattle, ON *fē* cattle, sheep, money, Goth *faihu* money, wealth, L *pecus* cattle, *pecunia* money, *pectere* to comb, Gk *pekein* to comb, *pokos* fleece, Skt *paśu* cattle; basic meaning: to fleece, pluck (wool)] *obs* **:** personal property **:** GOODS, LIVESTOCK, MONEY

²fee \ˈfē\ *n* -s [ME, fr. OF *fé, fié, fief*, of Gmc origin; akin to OHG *fihu* cattle] **1 a :** a heritable estate in land held in English feudal law of a superior lord by whom the estate was granted and who retains rights in the land or tenement and acquires rights against the tenant **b :** a feudal benefice or estate in land held of a feudal lord in feudal law; *also* **:** the interest or right of the lord in the land so held **c :** territory held in this way **d :** an estate of inheritance — see FEE SIMPLE, FEE TAIL **2 a** *obs* **:** PERQUISITE; *esp* **:** an allowance esp. of food to a cook or of game to a forester **b** *obs* **:** REWARD, PRIZE **c** *dial Brit* **:** WAGES; *esp* **:** those of a servant **d** *obs* **:** BRIBE **e** *archaic* **:** GRATUITY, TIP **3 a :** a fixed charge for admission (as to a museum) **b :** a charge fixed by law or by an institution (as a university) for certain privileges or services ⟨a license ~⟩ ⟨a toll-road ~⟩ ⟨a college-admission ~⟩ ⟨research ~*s*⟩ ⟨laboratory ~*s*⟩ ⟨tuition ~*s*⟩ **4 a :** a charge fixed by law for the services of a public officer ⟨a sheriff's ~⟩ **b :** compensation often in the form of a fixed charge for professional service or for special and requested exercise of talent or of skill (as by an artist) ⟨a doctor's ~⟩ ⟨a lawyer's retainer ~⟩ ⟨teach them this art if they shall wish to learn it, without ~ or stipulation —*Hippocratic Oath*⟩ **5** *dial Brit* **:** employment as a servant ⟨I come here to seek a ~⟩ **syn** see WAGE — **in fee 1** *also* **of fee :** as a feudal fee **2** *also* **at a fee** *or* **with fee** *obs* **:** in service **:** under obligation **3 :** in fee simple **4** *archaic* **:** as an absolute and legal possession

³fee \"\ *vt* **feed; feed; feeing; fees** [ME *feen* to enfeoff, hire, fr. *²fee*] **1** *obs* **:** BRIBE **2 a** *chiefly Scot* **:** HIRE ⟨~ a servant⟩ **b** *now dial Brit* **:** to make use of **:** EMPLOY ⟨~ every occasion —Shak.⟩ **3 :** to reward or pay for usu. personal services rendered or to be rendered **:** give a gratuity to **:** TIP ⟨~ a waiter⟩

feeb \ˈfēb\ *n* -s [short for *feebleminded*] *slang* **:** a feebleminded person ⟨considered purely as playgoers, what ~*s* and addlepates they are —Russell Maloney⟩

fee bill *n* **:** a schedule of the minimum or customary fees charged by lawyers, sheriffs, or other officers of a court for specified services; *also* **:** a list of the fees taxable as costs in a particular law case

¹fee·ble \ˈfēbəl\ *adj, usu* **feebler** \-b(ə)lə(r)\ **feeblest** \-b(ə)ləst\ [ME *feble*, fr. OF *flebe, feble, foible*, fr. L *flebilis* lamentable, wretched, fr. *flēre* to weep — more at BLEAT] **1 a :** markedly lacking in normal strength or endurance **:** WEAK, DEBILITATED, INFIRM ⟨a ~ old man⟩ ⟨~ in mind and body⟩ **b :** unequal to strain **:** YIELDING, FRAGILE ⟨a shaky buttress providing only ~ support⟩ ⟨a flower with a ~ stem⟩ **c :** indicating weakness or infirmity ⟨taking only ~ steps⟩ ⟨gave a ~ moan⟩ **2 a :** deficient in qualities or resources that indicate or give vigor, authority, force, or efficiency **:** not strong or effective (as in character, mental ability, tone, or color) ⟨a ~ personality⟩ ⟨a ~ intelligence⟩ ⟨~ imagery⟩ ⟨a ~ attempt at a novel⟩ **b :** INADEQUATE, INFERIOR ⟨forced to deal with ~ human nature⟩ ⟨could muster only the *feeblest* of thoughts on the occasion⟩ ⟨making ~ excuses⟩ **syn** see WEAK

²feeble \"\ *vt* -ED/-ING/-S [ME *feblen*, partly fr. ME *feble*, adj., partly fr. OF *feblir, flebir* to make or become feeble, fr. *flebe, feble, foible*, adj.] *archaic* **:** to make feeble **:** ENFEEBLE

³feeble \"\ *n* -s [ME *feble*, fr. *feble*, adj.] **1** *obs* **:** a feeble person **2 a** *archaic* **:** FOIBLE 1 **b :** FOIBLE 2

feebleminded \¦==¦==\ *adj* **1** *obs* **:** irresolute and fainthearted **2 :** mentally deficient **3 :** FOOLISH, STUPID — **fee·ble·mind·ed·ly** *adv* — **fee·ble·mind·ed·ness** *n* -ES

fee·ble·ness *n* -ES [ME *feblenesse*, fr. *feble* + *-nesse* -ness] **:** the quality or state of being feeble ⟨the old man's halting steps revealed the ~ of his constitution⟩ ⟨the writing was marked by ~ of style and inanity of content⟩

feeble-wit \ˈ==,=\ *n* **:** one that is deficient in intelligence or common sense

fee·bling \ˈfēb(ə)liŋ\ *n* -s [blend of *¹feeble* and *-ling*] **:** one that is feeble in mind or body

fee·blish \-lish\ *adj* **:** somewhat feeble

fee·bly \ˈfēb(ə)lē, -lī\ *adv* [ME *febly*, fr. *feble* feeble + *-ly* — more at ¹FEEBLE] **1 :** POORLY, SCANTILY, INSUFFICIENTLY ⟨a ~ handled newsreel talk —Gilbert Seldes⟩ **2 :** in a feeble manner **:** INEFFECTIVELY, WEAKLY ⟨a criminal only ~ prosecuted⟩ ⟨nations have ~ tried to humanize and regulate war —Vera M. Dean⟩ **:** MILDLY ⟨a ~ alcoholic wine⟩ **:** DIMLY ⟨a light shining ~ through the mist⟩

¹feed \ˈfēd\ *vb* **fed** \ˈfed\ **fed; feeding; feeds** [ME *feden*, fr. OE *fēdan*; akin to OHG *fuoten* to feed, ON *fœtha*, Goth *fodjan*; denominative fr. the root of E *food*] *vt* **1 a :** to give food to **:** supply with nourishment **:** satisfy the hunger of ⟨~ several guests⟩ ⟨~ the chickens⟩; *also* **:** SUCKLE ⟨~ a baby at the breast⟩ **b :** to convey food to the mouth of ⟨a patient so weak he had to be *fed*⟩ ⟨~*ing* a small child in a high chair⟩ **c :** to supply emotional, intellectual, or spiritual sustenance to ⟨looking for what would ~ the soul⟩ ⟨a capacity for love that found nothing to ~ it⟩ **d :** to convey to or into the mind of as if feeding a child ⟨the governed can be unknowingly *fed* with untruths —Harrison Brown⟩ ⟨thought the man was ~*ing* him all kinds of nonsense⟩ **2 a :** to furnish esp. with something that is essential or that improves or enhances ⟨~*ing* plants with fertilizer⟩ ⟨the intelligence *fed* by reading⟩ ⟨most adults do stop ~*ing* their minds —R.H.Wittcoff⟩ **b :** to supply or keep supplied esp. with something consumed ⟨lakes and rivers which ~ the Congo —Tom Marvel⟩ ⟨~*ing* a furnace with coal⟩ ⟨checks the items that are *fed* to him by the usual run of press agents —*Saturday Rev.*⟩ **c :** to pass or throw a ball or puck to (a teammate) esp. for a shot at the goal ⟨kept ~*ing* the tall center⟩ **d :** to supply (a fellow actor) with the cue lines and situations that give greater effectiveness or significance to a role; *also* **:** to supply (as cue lines) to an actor **e :** to provide a supply of (electrical energy) ⟨power is usually *fed* to the antenna —*Radio Amateur's Handbook*⟩; *also* **:** to supply electrical energy to **f** (1) **:** to supply esp. to an electronic circuit **:** send esp. through an electronic circuit — used of a signal (as in radar, radio, or telegraphy) (2) **:** to send (a radio or television program) by wire to a transmitting station for broadcast **3 a :** to produce food for ⟨the pasture *fed* the cows poorly⟩ **b :** to provide food for ⟨enough wheat to ~ the troops for a week⟩ **c :** to provide material for **:** supply (as a talent) with substance or occasion for exercise ⟨immense learning . . . drawn upon to ~ a fine sense of humor —R.M.Lovett⟩ **4 a :** SATISFY, GRATIFY ⟨*fed* his desire for revenge⟩ ⟨I will ~ fat the ancient grudge I bear him —Shak.⟩ **b :** to give support or encouragement to ⟨~*ing* false hopes⟩ **c :** AGGRAVATE, AUGMENT ⟨~ his feelings of indignation⟩ ⟨*fed* his resentment by mulling over the circumstances that aroused it⟩ ⟨vanity *fed* by flattery⟩ ⟨sensational . . . papers *fed* the public outcry with near-hysterical headlines —*Time*⟩ ⟨the public acclaim *fed* the dictator's ego⟩ **5 a :** to supply (the material to be operated upon) to a machine ⟨to ~ paper to a printing press⟩ **b :** to produce progressive operation upon or with (as in woodworking and metalworking machines) so that the work moves to the cutting tool or the tool to the work **6 a :** to give as food ⟨~ grain to chickens⟩ **b :** to furnish for use or consumption ⟨~*ing* coal to a furnace⟩ often in appropriate or convenient amounts ⟨hurried to another hospital to borrow a machine which he hoped would ~ the oxygen mechanically —Grace Reiten⟩ — often used with *out* ⟨the flatbed press *fed* out papers each afternoon about as fast as I could deal cards —C.C. Wertenbaker⟩ **7 a :** to put (cattle) to graze **b :** to cause (land or crops) to be grazed **~** *vi* **1 a** (1) **:** to consume food **:** EAT — often used with a derogatory implication when applied to a person ⟨cattle ~*ing* in a barn⟩ ⟨we determined to ~ only once a day at a restaurant —M.C.A.Henniker⟩ (2) **:** to take a meal esp. in restaurants ⟨you can ~ better here than in most other cities⟩ **b :** to satisfy the appetite **:** feed oneself **:** PREY — used with *on* or *upon* or *off* ⟨a vulture ~*ing* on carrion⟩ ⟨an animal ~*ing* off smaller animals⟩ **c :** to become nourished, strengthened, satisfied, sustained, or augmented as if by food ⟨convictions ~ . . . on many things, including items of knowledge and considerations of logic —Lucius Garvin⟩ **d :** to consume or utilize feed — used of an engine or other mechanical device ⟨a gas turbine ~*ing* on the fuel it pumps⟩ **2 :** to supply a fellow actor with the cue lines and situations that give greater effectiveness or significance to his role **3 a :** to move in or as if in supplying something with what it uses or consumes ⟨the river ~*s* into the Atlantic ocean⟩ **b :** to move into a machine or opening in order to be used or processed ⟨bullets ~ into a machine gun⟩ ⟨oil ~*s* into an engine⟩ ⟨wire ~*s* into a conduit⟩ **4 :** to load a cartridge into the chamber of a firearm esp. by the operation of the action in magazine or clip-fed arms

syn NOURISH, PASTURE, GRAZE: FEED is a general term applicable to persons, animals, and plants and anything else given material to consume or enjoy for purposes of sustaining or continuing operation ⟨to *feed* the refugees⟩ ⟨to *feed* the chickens⟩ ⟨to *feed* a furnace⟩ ⟨Hugh's growing vanity was *fed* by the thought that Clara was interested in him —Sherwood Anderson⟩ ⟨the dissatisfactions that *feed* the cause of the rebels⟩ NOURISH is applicable to supplying what furnishes elements essential to growth, well-being, and building up ⟨the humid prairie heat, so *nourishing* to wheat and corn, so exhausting to human beings —Willa Cather⟩ ⟨our press has helped to *nourish* this legend by stretching and distorting certain of the more horrendous and eccentric features —S.L.A. Marshall⟩ ⟨all writers are *nourished* by the sense of having an audience —Malcolm Cowley⟩ PASTURE suggests leading cows or sheep to grassy areas or permitting them to go to such areas ⟨*pasturing* cows in the meadow⟩ GRAZE is often synonymous with PASTURE ⟨sheep *grazing* in a field⟩ but may suggest free ranging over a less circumscribed area ⟨*grazing* cattle on the range⟩

²**feed** \"\ *n* -s **1 a** *obs* **:** the act of eating **b :** MEAL; *esp* **:** a sumptuous meal ⟨a bath and a shave and clean clothes and a good ~ —I.L.Idriess⟩ **2 a** *obs* **:** the right of pasture on a piece of land **b** *obs* **:** GRAZING **c** *obs* **:** pasture land **d** *dial Eng* **:** CROPS **3 a :** food esp. for livestock **:** FODDER ⟨he needed food for his family and ~ for his livestock —A.F.Gustafson⟩ **b :** a food of this kind **:** a mixture or preparation used for feeding livestock **c :** the amount given at each feeding **4 :** the fermenting wort drawn off from yeast troughs in brewing and added to the fermenting unions to keep them full and so enable the yeast to work out **5 a :** the motion or process of carrying forward the material to be operated upon (as cloth to the needle in a sewing machine) or of producing progressive operation upon any material or object in a machine (as in a lathe by moving the cutting tool along or in the work) **b** (1) **:** the degree of feeding material to a machine ⟨a fine or coarse ~⟩ (2) **:** the advance of a cutting tool at each revolution of the tool or of the work ⟨a ~ of ⅛ inch⟩; *specif* **:** the thickness of the chip cut per tooth of a milling cutter **c :** material supplied to a machine or apparatus (as lubricant to an engine, water to a steam boiler, coal to a furnace, or petroleum to a distilling column) **d :** a mechanism by which the action of feeding is produced **:** FEED MOTION **6 :** the system or surfaces of the action of a firearm that serve to move a cartridge from its magazine or clip to the chamber or act as a surface for such motion — **off one's feed 1 :** having little appetite for food **:** unwilling to eat a normal amount of food ⟨the child was *off his feed* and cried a good deal⟩ **2 :** not feeling well **:** UPSET

³**feed** *past of* FEE

feedback \'≈,≈\ *n* -s *often attrib* **1 :** the return to the input of a part of the output of a machine, system, or process: as **a :** the return to the input of a part of the output of an electronic amplifying system leading to increased amplification or decreased amplification or control of the quality of the signal — see NEGATIVE FEEDBACK, POSITIVE FEEDBACK **b :** the return to the input of a part of the output of a mechanism, this part of the input constituting information that reports discrepancies between intended and actual operation and leads to a self-correcting action that can be utilized (as in the automatic operation of machinery) ⟨~ control system⟩ **2 :** the partial reversion of the effects of a given process to its source or to a preceding stage so as to reinforce or modify it — used esp. of biological, psychological, and social systems

feed bag *n* **:** NOSE BAG — **put on the feed bag** *slang* **:** to begin eating

feedboard \'≈,≈\ *n* **:** a board (as on a printing press or folding machine) to hold material fed to the machine

feedbox \'≈,≈\ *n* **1 :** a container for feed or fodder **2 :** a casing on a machine enclosing the feed motion and the shifting mechanism

feed bunk *n* **:** ²BUNK 3

feed case *n* **:** a detachable metal case that contains cartridges and is used in feeding certain machine guns

feed cutter *n* **:** a machine that cuts up feed or fodder (as cornstalks or alfalfa)

feed dog *n* **:** a sewing-machine device consisting of a notched piece of metal that automatically moves the material under the needle

feed efficiency *n* **:** EFFICIENCY 3d

¹**feeder** \'fēdə(r)\ *n* -s [ME *feder, federe*, fr. *feden* to feed + *-er, -ere* -er — more at ¹FEED] **1 :** one that gives or provides food or nourishment: as **a :** one that fattens cattle for slaughter **b :** a device or apparatus for supplying food (as to an animal) ⟨an automatic poultry ~⟩ ⟨a calf ~⟩ **c :** a normal pigeon used as a foster parent for the young of short-beaked pigeons **2 :** one that eats or is notable for eating ⟨the man was a prodigious ~⟩: as **a** *obs* **:** one dependent on another for food (as a servant) **b :** an animal being fattened or one suitable for fattening — compare STOCKER **3 :** one that ministers (as to another's welfare, mind, or passions): as **a :** one that incites ⟨the ~ of . . . riots —Shak.⟩ **b** *archaic* **:** an academic tutor or crammer **4 a :** one that feeds material into or through a machine or device that operates upon it or consumes it: as (1) **:** a device that supplies crushed stone to a conveyor (2) **:** a device for supplying coal automatically to a furnace (3) **:** a worker who charges lead ore and other substances into a blast furnace (4) **:** a worker who feeds aluminum sheets into a rolling mill **b :** a strong discharge of gas from a fissure in a mine **c :** FEEDHEAD **5 :** a small lateral lode connecting with the main lode of a mine **6 a :** one that replenishes or connects with and supplies something **:** a source of supply for the maintenance or effectiveness of something else of the same general kind ⟨farm baseball teams that act as ~*s* for the major-league teams⟩ ⟨it was thought that Broadway had become a ~ for Hollywood⟩ **b :** TRIBUTARY **c** *or* **feeder line :** a branch transportation line: as (1) *also* **feeder airline :** a local-service airline connecting smaller communities with larger terminal cities and trunk lines (2) **:** a local bus line that runs into a terminal used by a trunk line **d** (1) **:** a heavy wire conductor supplying electricity at some point of any system of electric distribution (as from a substation to a distribution point) (2) **:** a conductor connecting a major unit of a radio transmitting or receiving apparatus with another; *esp* **:** the line from the aerial to the receiver or transmitter **e :** FEEDER ROAD **7 a :** a part in a play designed as a foil for one more important **b :** an actor playing such a part **:** one who feeds a fellow actor **8 :** an assorter in a garment factory **9** *chiefly Brit* **:** a baby's bib

²**feeder** \"\ *adj* **1 :** being, acting, or serving as a feeder ⟨a ~ root⟩ ⟨a ~ device⟩ ⟨~ air service⟩ ⟨a ~ belt⟩ ⟨a ~ cable⟩ ⟨a ~ farmer⟩ **2 :** suitable for fattening ⟨~ cattle⟩

feeder head *n* **:** FEEDHEAD

feeder man *n* **:** a workman who climbs a pole to high-tension lines and with a long insulated rod switches off the flow of current so that the lines may be repaired with safety

feeder road *n* **:** a road that serves as a traffic feeder to a more important road (as a turnpike) — compare SECONDARY ROAD

feed guide *or* **feed gauge** *n* **:** a device in a printing press for holding and releasing a sheet

feedhead \'≈,≈\ *n* **:** an excess of metal left above a foundry mold to supply molten metal to a solidifying casting and thus compensate for shrinkage that cannot be fed from the gate — called also *riser*

feed-in \'≈,≈\ *adj* **:** being or belonging to something that feeds material (as into a machine) or to the process of feeding in this way ⟨a *feed-in* device connecting the main source of power to the subsidiary outlets⟩ ⟨used the main switch box as a *feed-in* point for too many electrical outlets⟩

feeding *n* -s [ME *feding*, fr. OE *fēding*, fr. *fēdan* to feed + *-ing*] **1 a :** the act or process of one that feeds or the act or process of being fed ⟨all fruit purchased will be used to assist in relief ~ in foreign countries —*Collier's Yr. Bk.*⟩ ⟨the jamming of the mechanism stopped the ~ of the coke into the furnace⟩ **b :** an instance of feeding esp. something more or less incapable of providing its own food or of feeding itself ⟨give your lawn a late fall ~ of fertilizer⟩ ⟨gave the baby eight ounces of milk at each ~⟩ **2 :** land used for grazing

feeding board *n* **:** FEEDBOARD

feeding bottle *n* **:** NURSING BOTTLE

feeding cup *n* **:** a vessel with a spout rising near its base for use in feeding the bedfast

feeding ground *n* **:** the area in which an animal or group of animals customarily feed (as by grazing) ⟨a lion skulking about the *feeding ground* of a herd of antelope⟩ ⟨a *feeding ground* for small game⟩

feeding head *n* **:** FEEDHEAD

feeding rod *n* **:** an iron rod to keep clear the passage between riser and casting in founding

feeding station *n* **:** a central or convenient place at which food is provided (as for soldiers during a military operation); *specif* **:** a device (as a hanging platform) on which food is placed to attract birds for observation or study or for feeding birds during winter months

feedlot \'≈,≈\ *n* **:** a lot or plot of land on or in which livestock are fed or fattened for market — compare DRYLOT

feed mill *n* **:** a mill in which stock feeds are prepared

feed off *vt* **:** to dispose of (a crop) by turning in livestock to pasture

feed out *vt* **:** to feed or fatten (animals) to a marketable condition

feed pump *n* **:** a force pump for supplying water to a steam boiler

feed ratio *n* **:** the ratio expressing feed efficiency

feed roll *n* **1** *or* **feed roller :** a roll or one of two or more rolls by which material is drawn or fed into a machine **2 :** one of a set of small rubber rolls under the platen of a typewriter that help to roll the paper and hold it in place during typing

feeds *pres 3d sing of* FEED, *pl of* FEED

feed screw *n* **:** a screw that imparts feed motion (as in a lathe or other machine tool) — compare LEAD SCREW

feedstock \'≈,≈\ *n* **:** raw material supplied to a machine or processing plant (as pulpwood to a paper mill)

feedstore \'≈,≈\ *n* **:** a store selling livestock feeds

feedstuff \'≈,≈\ *or* **feedingstuff** \'≈≈,≈\ *n* **:** a feed for domestic animals; *usu* **:** any of the constituent nutrients of an animal ration ⟨cotton-seed meal has proved a useful ~ in fattening rations⟩ ⟨the basic ~*s*, carbohydrate, fat, and protein⟩

feedwater \'≈,≈≈\ *n* **:** water sometimes preheated or purified and supplied to a boiler (as for steam) or still

feedway \'≈,≈\ *n* **:** an aisle between rows of stalls in a barn along which feed is distributed to the mangers

feed wheat *n* **:** low-grade wheat used as stock feed

fee farm *n* [ME *fee ferme*, fr. AF *fé ferme*, fr. OF *fé* fee, fief + *ferme* lease — more at ²FEE, ²FARM] **:** land held of another in fee simple subject to a perpetual fixed rent without homage, fealty, or any other service than that mentioned in the feoffment; *also* **:** the estate or land so held or the rent paid

fee-faw-fum \,fē,fȯ'fəm\ *or* **fee-fo-fum** \-fō'-\ *n* -s **1 :** a bloodthirsty person **:** OGRE ⟨were all *fee-faw-fums* . . . and the sooner that was admitted, the sooner some sort of solution could be reached —William Manchester⟩ **2 :** something designed to impose upon the timid and ignorant ⟨black magic or whatever is the technical name for this sort of *fee-fo-fum* —J.C.Snaith⟩

fee gouging *n* **:** the charging of excessive fees esp. for professional services — compare FEE SPLITTING

feeing *pres part of* FEE

feeing market *also* **feeing fair** *n* [*feeing* fr. gerund of ³*fee*] *Scot* **:** a market where servants gather to be hired for the coming season or year

¹**feel** \'fēl, *esp before pause or consonant* -ēəl\ *vb* **felt** \'felt\ **felt; feeling; feels** [ME *felen*, fr. OE *fēlan;* akin to OHG *fuolen* to feel, ON *fālma* to fumble, grope, L *palpare* to caress, and perh. to Gk *pallein* to shake, brandish — more at POLEMIC] *vt* **1 a** (1) **:** to perceive by tactile, muscular, integumental, or other sensation excited by some physical stimulus **:** be aware of esp. on contact in the body or limbs ⟨~ a sharp blow⟩ ⟨~ a cold draft⟩ ⟨*felt* a sudden pain⟩ ⟨after an hour of climbing we began to ~ fatigue⟩ (2) *archaic* **:** to perceive by smell or taste **b** (1) **:** TOUCH, HANDLE ⟨*felt* the coat to see if it was wet⟩ (2) *slang* **:** to feel up **c :** to examine or explore by such methods as touching, lifting, or sounding **:** make a trial of **:** test by touching, lifting, or sounding ⟨*felt* the rock to see how heavy it was⟩ **2 a :** to experience or undergo passively **:** endure without taking any positive action against ⟨~ inconvenience at having to stay overnight⟩ ⟨continually *felt* the resentment of his competitors⟩ ⟨though I was tired I *felt* the music with more pleasure now —Chandler Brossard⟩ **b :** to be conscious of (a subjective state) ⟨~ pleasure in her company⟩ ⟨~ a strong sense of our own importance⟩ ⟨*felt* a mild inclination to cry —T.B.Costain⟩ **c :** to suffer from **:** have one's sensibilities markedly affected by ⟨~ the insult deeply⟩ ⟨~ his son's ingratitude as if it were a wound⟩ **d :** to experience the special or typical effect of (as a subjective experience) ⟨~ the judge's wrath⟩ ⟨experience the intoxicating effect of (as an alcoholic drink) ⟨drank for a long time before they began to ~ the liquor⟩ ⟨experience the emotional force of ⟨young conductors don't bother much anymore to ~ music —Virgil Thomson⟩ **3 a :** to find out by or as if by the tactile sense — used with a clause as object ⟨~ if any bones had been broken⟩ ⟨~ how the tiller worked⟩ **b :** to ascertain (as a man's attitude) by cautious trial **:** sound out ⟨by diplomatic query tried to ~ the sentiments of the neighborhood⟩ **:** discover by careful and tentative investigatory methods ⟨when the architects designed their first building they were clearly ~*ing* their way⟩ — often used with *out* ⟨~*ing* out the sentiments of their neighbors on the subject of school improvement⟩ **4 a :** to be aware of (something objective) by instinct or inference rather than through actual experience or sensation ⟨~ the presence of an intruder in the room⟩ ⟨~ trouble brewing⟩ **b :** to be persuaded or convinced of emotionally rather than intellectually **:** believe esp. on indefinite grounds ⟨*felt* that the move would be unwise although she could give no positive reason⟩ ⟨*felt* that what he said was probably true⟩ **c :** BELIEVE, THINK, HOLD — now used with a clause as object ⟨they *felt* that their own argument was as sound as that of their opponents⟩ ⟨I am a reader, so I ~ I have a right to criticize authors —Alice Hamilton⟩ ⟨we feel that he should retire⟩ **~** *vi* **1 :** to receive or be able to receive a tactile sensation **:** perceive by touching or making contact ⟨lost all ability to ~ in his fingertips⟩ **2 a :** to search for something or guide oneself using the sense of touch esp. in the fingers **:** GROPE ⟨she *felt* in her purse for her keys⟩ ⟨*felt* along the wall in the dark for an opening⟩ ⟨*felt* under the table with his foot for the spoon he had dropped⟩ **b :** to seek or search out with caution or uncertainty ⟨went quietly through the woods ~*ing* for the enemy⟩ ⟨began to explain at random while ~*ing* for an excuse⟩ **c :** to find by trial and error ⟨in the absence of a book of instructions we had to ~ for the best way to rig the mechanism⟩ **3 :** to manifest itself to the tactile sense or to physical sensation — usu. used with a specifying adjective ⟨it ~*s* cold outside⟩ ⟨how it ~*s* to be hungry⟩ **4 a :** to have sympathy or pity ⟨capable of ~*ing* for the poverty stricken and underfed⟩ **b :** to achieve or experience aesthetic identification ⟨we ~ for the hero who is in danger . . . and we unconsciously desire to realize the escape —John Erskine †1951⟩ **5 a :** to be conscious of an inward particular impression, state of mind or feeling, or physical condition **:** perceive oneself to be ⟨~ assured⟩ ⟨~ friendly⟩ ⟨~ sick⟩ ⟨~ in a happy frame of mind⟩ ⟨~ bad⟩ ⟨~ good⟩ **b :** to have a marked sentiment or opinion pro or con ⟨~ strongly about the disposition of school funds⟩ **6 :** to react emotionally or instinctively rather than as a result of rational or meditative analysis ⟨a man who ~*s* but seldom thinks⟩ — **feel in one's bones :** to feel strongly and instinctively (as that something is true or false) **:** hold a strong opinion based on no concrete evidence — **feel like :** to have an inclination for ⟨*feel like* taking a walk⟩ ⟨*feel like* being alone⟩ — **feel no pain :** to be drunk — **feel of :** to examine by touching **:** FEEL ⟨*feel of* a fabric to discover its texture⟩ ⟨*feel of* a pear to see if it is ripe⟩ — **feel one's oats : 1** *of a horse* **:** to act spirited or frisky **2 a :** to be actively exuberant ⟨the children were *feeling their oats* and running madly around the house⟩ **b :** to act in a newly self-confident and often self-important manner — **feel the helm** *of a ship* **:** to obey the helm

²**feel** \"\ *n* -s [ME *fele*, fr. *felen* to feel — more at ¹FEEL] **1 a :** the sense of touch ⟨a blanket soft to the ~⟩ **b** (1) **:** an instance of or opportunity of feeling by touching ⟨took a ~ of the bump on his head⟩ (2) *slang* **:** an instance or opportunity of feeling up **2 :** EXPERIENCE, SENSATION, FEELING ⟨the ~ of an insect's bite⟩ ⟨the ~ of joy⟩ ⟨learned to relish the ~ of power —A.W.Long⟩ ⟨there was a ~ of the train's being about to leave —Eudora Welty⟩ **3 a :** the quality or properties of a thing as imparted or its typical quality or properties as recognized or determined through or as if through touch or handling ⟨a greasy ~⟩ ⟨testing the ~ of the cloth⟩ ⟨the warm ~ of her flesh —Stuart Cloete⟩ **b :** typical or peculiar quality, air, or atmosphere ⟨the house had the ~ of a home⟩ ⟨the place has the ~ of an old English pub —James Cerruti⟩ **4 a :** knack, facility, or skill often deriving from an innate ability — used with *for* ⟨a good ~ for the handling of planes⟩ ⟨he will develop a ~ for words which will help to make him articulate —*Nat'l Catholic Educational Assoc. Bull.*⟩ ⟨these provincial companies have a ~ for opera that you'll find nowhere else in the world —T.H.Fielding⟩ **b :** a quality (as in an art work) resulting from such knack, facility, or skill — used with *for* ⟨a strong ~ in the artist's work for balance and proportion⟩ **5 :** an awareness of the spirit or temper of something or of its distinguishing or special qualities ⟨the ~ of the country⟩ — often used with *for* ⟨he has a sensitive ~ for the vast reaches in which his particular war took place —James Michener⟩

³**feel** \"\ *Scot var of* FOOL

⁴**feel** \"\ *var of* FEIL

feel·er \'fēlə(r)\ *n* -s [ME *feler* one that feels, fr. *felen* to feel + *-er, -ere* -er] **1 :** a tactile process of an animal: as **a :** a sensory tentacle **b :** ANTENNA 1 **c :** VIBRISSA **2 :** something ventured (as a proposal, remark, or tentative action) to ascertain the views or reactions of others ⟨ready to explore any peace ~*s* no matter what their origin —*Current Biog.*⟩ ⟨~*s* being put out by certain manufacturers in an effort to determine whether or not stripings and patterns are due for reacceptance in popularity —*Apparel Arts*⟩ ⟨the letter was a ~ to see how Washington would look upon such a movement —H.E.Scudder⟩ **3** *or* **feeler gage :** a thin metal strip of known thickness used as a gage or one of a set of metal strips of graduated thicknesses so used **4 :** a loom device in textile manufacturing that replaces nearly empty bobbins in shuttles

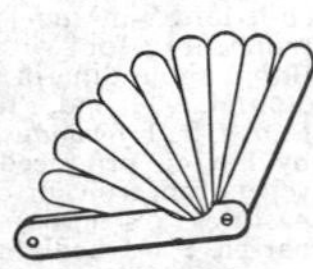
feeler 3

feeler pin *n* **:** a pin controlling a tripping mechanism on various duplicating machines that allows the printing roll or rolls to come into position for printing only while there is paper in the machine

fee-less \'fēləs\ *adj* **:** being without a fee **:** yielding no fee **:** requiring no fee

¹**feeling** *n* -s [ME *felinge, feling*, fr. *felen* to feel + *-inge, -ing* -ing — more at ¹FEEL] **1 a :** the one of the five senses of which the skin is the chief end organ and of which the sensations of touch, contact, temperature, and pressure are characteristic **b :** a sensation experienced through this sense; *esp* **:** a sensation of touch **2 :** a sensation, a complex of sensations, or a perception belonging to the more general forms of sensibility: **a :** bodily consciousness **:** organic sensation **b :** a generalized sensation involving touch, contact, temperature, pressure, or physical pain or pleasure **c :** appreciative or responsive awareness or recognition ⟨experience a ~ of safety⟩ ⟨a ~ of injury followed the unfair decision of the court⟩ **d :** sympathetic aesthetic response **3 a :** the undifferentiated background of one's awareness considered apart from any identifiable sensation, perception, or thought **b :** the overall quality of one's awareness esp. as measured along a pleasantness-unpleasantness continuum — compare ¹AFFECT 2, EMOTION **4 a :** the condition of one that feels **:** an emotional state **:** EMOTION ⟨a kindly ~ inside him whenever he was treated decently⟩ ⟨experienced a ~ of pride at the accomplishment⟩ ⟨a ~ of reverential awe for these immemorial shelters —Norman Douglas⟩; *also* **:** a particular emotion ⟨human ~*s* — human hopes, aspirations, fears, and sorrows —H.R.Collins⟩ **b feelings** *pl* **:** SENSIBILITIES ⟨a biting remark that hurt the ~*s* of a good friend⟩ **c :** emotional reaction ⟨so unable to control her ~*s* that she broke down and wept⟩; *specif* **:** the emotional reaction of one person or group to another or the emotional relationship of one person or group to another or of two persons or groups ⟨wished to improve the ~ between the two countries⟩ ⟨bad ~ existed wherever he went and he expected an outburst of hostilities at any moment⟩ ⟨the act promoted the best ~ possible between the families⟩ **d :** a reaction consisting of or combining hostility, distrust, dislike, opposition, resentment, or hatred and usu. marked by belligerence ⟨there was ~ between the groups so we hesitated to intervene⟩ ⟨~ ran high at the proposal⟩ **e :** tender emotion **:** FONDNESS, AFFECTION, LOVE ⟨don't have any ~ anymore about you —Louis Auchincloss⟩ **5 a :** OPINION, BELIEF ⟨asked the professor what his ~*s* were on the international

crisis〉 **b :** unreasoned opinion **:** frame of mind **:** emotional attitude **:** SENTIMENT 〈expressing the ~s of an essentially irrational child〉 〈impossible to imagine the ~ about so controversial a person〉 **6 :** capacity to feel emotion **:** emotional responsiveness 〈found out how much ~ his mother really had〉; *esp* **:** delicate and sympathetic emotional responsiveness 〈a man of fine ~〉 **7 a :** a character or quality ascribed to or associated with something as a result of one's impression or emotional state **:** FEEL, ATMOSPHERE 〈the place had the ~ of a haunted house〉; *esp* **:** the emotional quality (as of a work of art or literature) that calls to mind a particular era, period, place, culture, or civilization 〈a collection of scenic wallpapers that . . . have a slight Japanese ~ —*New Yorker*〉 〈a Baroque ~ in the architecture〉 〈the ~ of the outdoors has been realized with sky-blue ceiling and natural colors —*Playthings*〉 **b :** the impression something gives to one observing or experiencing 〈thoroughfares and railways alive with busy traffic . . . give the ~ of energy and power —Samuel Valkenburg & Ellsworth Huntington〉 **c** *or* **feeling tone :** the quality of a work of art which embodies, conveys, or is calculated to convey emotion **8 :** the ability to deal with or handle something with sensitivity and facility — used with *for* 〈he has no true ~ for words —*Geog. Jour.*〉 〈a young painter with a good ~ for color〉 **9 :** PRESENTIMENT 〈recent attempts to combine quantum mechanics and electrodynamics have produced . . . relatively little ~ of a final result —W.V.Houston〉 〈these may all be short and scattered straws on which to base my ~ of a trend —W.I.Nichols〉

syn AFFECTION, EMOTION, SENTIMENT, PASSION: FEELING, the most general of the terms in this connection, denotes any partly mental, partly physical (but not entirely sensory) response, or the resulting state, marked by pleasure, pain, attraction, or repulsion 〈hostile *feelings* toward strangers〉 〈the sentimental song aroused no *feeling* in him at all〉 〈expressions of patriotic *feeling* —D.W.Brogan〉 〈she had a *feeling* that all would be well —Gilbert Parker〉 AFFECTION is usu. applied to feelings marked by inclination toward, liking, or fondness 〈his personality aroused the lasting *affection* of the generations of students he instructed —W.S.Rusk〉 〈the authors' *affection* for the buildings they have seen in China —Jane G. Mahler〉 〈without fear or favor, *affection* or ill-will —F.T.Giles〉 EMOTION usu. suggests a condition that involves more of the total mental and physical response than does FEELING, or implies feelings marked by a certain excitement or agitation 〈rousing the patriotic *emotions* of the citizenry —Oscar Handlin〉 〈every other *emotion* — affection, tenderness, sympathy, sentiment —Ellen Glasgow〉 〈the *emotions* which we ordinarily distinguish — ambition, lust, pity, pride, anger, and many others —Stuart Hampshire〉 SENTIMENT suggests a larger intellectual element than do the other terms, applying commonly to an emotion inspired by an idea, often suggesting a refined or an affected feeling 〈one of the centers of antislavery *sentiment* —*Amer. Guide Series: Tenn.*〉 〈a considerable *sentiment* in favor of the proposition —J.H.Easterby〉 〈man of liberal *sentiments* and cultivated understandings —T.B. Macaulay〉 PASSION suggests a strong, esp. a controlling, emotion, implying urgency of desire (as for possession or revenge) 〈the love of dancing amounts almost to a *passion* —*Amer. Guide Series: La.*〉 〈this consuming *passion* for law —H.E.Scudder〉 **syn** see in addition SENSATION

²**feeling** *adj* [ME *feling*, fr. *felen* to feel + *-inge*, *-ing* (alter. of *-inde*, *-ende*)] **1 a :** SENTIENT, SENSITIVE 〈not a mere lump of clay but a ~ creature〉; having the capacity to feel or respond emotionally **b :** easily affected or moved emotionally 〈a ~ heart〉 **2 :** expressing or evincing great sensitivity or emotional susceptibility 〈wrote in passionate ~ language〉 **3** *obs* **:** deeply or keenly felt 〈a ~ grief〉 — **feel·ing·ness** *n* -ES

feel·ing·ful \ˈfēliŋfəl, -lēŋ-\ *adj* **:** marked by strong feeling 〈a ~ expression of his hope for peace〉

feel·ing·less \-ŋləs\ *adj* **:** having no feeling **:** devoid of a normal capacity to feel 〈their arms got tired, then heavy and achy, then dead and ~ —H.L.Davis〉 〈an unsympathetic and positively ~ man〉 — **feel·ing·less·ly** *adv*

feel·ing·ly *adv* [ME *felingly*, fr. *feling*, adj. + *-ly*] **:** with great feeling 〈spoke ~ of his early childhood when he had been extremely happy〉

feeling tone *n* **1 a :** FEELING 7c **b :** a particular quality of one's awareness measured in terms of pleasantness and unpleasantness **2 a :** the overall quality of an experience esp. as attributed to the thing experienced 〈a second translation which I think reproduces the *feeling tone* of the original —Ernest Beaglehole〉 **b :** one of the emotional shades of an experience esp. as attributed to the thing experienced

feel out *vt* **1 :** to sound out the sentiments of 〈*felt out* the neighbors on the subject of local political reform〉 — compare FEEL *vt* 3b **2 :** to test the validity or practicability of by cautious investigation, trial, or application 〈*feel out* a new idea by submitting it to a group of colleagues〉

feels *pres 3d sing of* FEEL, *pl of* FEEL

feel up *vt*, *slang* **:** to caress the upper thighs and genital area of

fee patent *n* **:** a patent for an estate in fee simple

feer \ˈfēr\ *vi* -ED/-ING/-S [prob. fr. ME (northern dial.) *feren* to plow, fr. OE *fȳrian* to make a furrow, fr. *furh* furrow — more at FURROW] *chiefly Scot* **:** to mark off land for plowing

feerie *var of* FEIRIE

feering *n* -S [fr. gerund of *feer*] *chiefly Scot* **:** feered or furrowed land

fee·ry-fa·ry \ˈfēri¦fāri\ *n* [redupl. of obs. Sc *fary* state of confusion or excitement, fr. ME (Sc), fairyland, state of confusion or excitement, fr. ME *faierie*, *fairie* fairyland — more at FAIRY] *chiefly Scot* **:** BUSTLE, TUMULT

fees *pl of* FEE, *pres 3d sing of* FEE

fee simple *n*, *pl* **fees simple** [ME, fr. AF *fé simple*, fr. *fé* fee, fief (fr. OF) + MF *simple* — more at ²FEE, SIMPLE] **:** a freehold estate of inheritance in land or hereditaments that may last forever and may be inherited by all classes of both lineal and collateral heirs of an individual owner or grantee — distinguished from *fee tail*; see FEE SIMPLE ABSOLUTE, FEE SIMPLE DEFEASIBLE

fee simple absolute *n*, *pl* **fees simple absolute :** a fee simple that has no limitation, qualification, or condition affecting it and is the maximum possible ownership in real estate under system of property founded on the English common law

fee simple conditional *n*, *pl* **fees simple conditional :** an estate in fee granted to a person and his issue or to a designated class of his issue that is subject to the possibility of reversion in case there is no such issue or no alternative gift to a designated person in case there is no such issue and that exists in states where the English Statute De Donis of 1285 or a similar statute converting such an estate into a fee-tail estate has not been adopted — compare FEE TAIL, REVERSION

fee simple defeasible *n*, *pl* **fees simple defeasible :** a fee-simple estate that may come to an end under a stipulated provision; *sometimes* **:** FEE SIMPLE DETERMINABLE

fee simple determinable *n*, *pl* **fees simple determinable :** a fee-simple estate subject by the provisions of the instrument creating it to come to an end automatically upon the occurrence of an event stated therein

fee splitter *n* **:** a physician who engages in fee splitting

fee splitting *n* **:** a dividing of a professional fee for specialist's medical services with the recommending physician

fee system *n* **:** a system by which a sheriff or warden is compensated through county, municipal, or state funds for boarding prisoners

¹**feet** [ME *fet*, *feet*, fr. OE *fēt*] *pl of* FOOT

²**feet** \ˈfēt\ *n pl*, *Scot* **:** FOOTWEAR; *specif* **:** shoes and stockings 〈you're soaking wet; sit by the stove and change your ~〉

feet·age \ˈfēd·ij\ *n* -S [¹*feet* + *-age*] **:** FOOTAGE — sometimes used of lumber and leather

fee tail *n*, *pl* **fees tail** [ME *fee taille*, fr. AF *fé taillé*, fr. OF *fé* fee, fief + *taillé*, *taillié*, past part. of *taillier* to cut, decide, determine — more at ²FEE, TAIL (entailed)] **:** an estate in fee granted to a person and his issue or a designated class of his issue that is subject to the possibility of reversion if there is no such issue or no alternative gift to a designated person in case there is no such issue, that is subject under modern statutes to being converted into a fee simple absolute by the owner's barring the entail by executing a deed in his lifetime or to being converted to other types of estates more in harmony with present social conditions, and that is the estate created by the English Statute De Donis of 1285 or a similar statute operating upon a grant that would otherwise create a fee simple conditional — compare REVERSION

feetfirst \ˈ=ˈ=\ *adv* **1 :** with both feet or all four feet foremost 〈jumped into the water ~〉 **2** *slang* **:** in a coffin **:** DEAD 〈carried out ~〉

feet foremost *adv* **:** FEETFIRST 2

feet of clay [so called fr. the feet (partly of iron and partly of clay) of the image in Nebuchadnezzar's dream in Dan 2:33] **1 :** a generally concealed or unobserved but marked weakness or frailty in one hitherto idolized for qualities seemingly superior to those of common humanity or feared because of formidable and seemingly unassailable command or strength **2 :** a focal weakness (as cowardice or fear) in a seemingly commanding person

¹**feeze** *or* **feaze** \ˈfēz, ˈfāz\ *vt* -ED/-ING/-S [ME *fesen*, fr. OE *fēsian*; perh. akin to Norw *fuse* to gush, rush, ON *fjūka* to be driven by the wind — more at FOG] **1** *obs* **:** to drive away **:** put to flight **2 :** FAZE

²**feeze** \"\ *n* -S [ME *veze*, fr. *fesen*, *vesen* to drive away — more at ¹FEEZE] **1** *now dial* **:** a violent impact **:** RUSH **2** *dial* **:** a state of alarm or excitement

³**feeze** \"\ *vt* -ED/-ING/-S [obs. Sc *fize*, n., screw, fr. Flem *vize*, fr. MD *vise*, fr. MF *vis* — more at VISE] *dial Brit* **:** to tighten by turning **:** TWIST 〈~ a fiddle string〉

feg \ˈfeg\ *chiefly Scot var of* FIG

fe·ga·ry \fəˈgāri\ *n* -ES [alter. of *vagary*] **1** *now dial Brit* **a :** WHIM **b :** an eccentric prank **2** *now dial Brit* **:** GEWGAW — usu. used in pl.

feg·a·tel·la \ˌfegəˈtelə\ [NL, fr. It, liverwort, dim. of *fegato* liver, fr. LL *ficatum* liver of an animal fattened with figs (trans. of Gk *sykōton*), fr. L *ficus* fig + *-atum* (neut. of *-atus* -ate) — more at FIG] *syn of* CONOCEPHALUM

fegs \ˈfegz, ˈfāgz\ *n* [alter. of ¹*faith*] *chiefly Scot* **:** FAITH — used interjectionally to express surprise or as a mild invocation

feh·ling solution \ˈfāliŋ-\ *or* **fehling's solution** \-ŋz-\ *n*, *usu cap F* [after Hermann *Fehling* †1885 Ger. chemist] **:** a blue solution that is made by mixing an alkaline solution of Rochelle salt with a solution of copper sulfate and that is used as a mild oxidizing agent esp. in testing for glucose and other reducing sugars and for aldehydes, being itself reduced to red cuprous oxide which precipitates

feh·me \ˈfāmə\ *n*, *pl* **fehmen** *or* **fehmes** *often cap* [G *feme*, fr. MHG (Westphalian dial.) *vēme*; akin to OFris *fēma* to outlaw, MD *veme* secret tribunal] **1 :** a late medieval German secret tribunal **2 :** a unit of a secret Nazi organization intent upon seeking out and executing those considered enemies of National Socialism

feh·mic \-mik\ *adj* **:** of or relating to the Fehme

fei \ˈfā,ē\ *n*, *pl* **feis** *or* **fei** [Tahitian] **:** a wild banana (*Musa fehi*) widely cultivated in Polynesia and distinguished by an upright fruiting stalk bearing large thick fruits that have reddish orange or yellow skin and are edible only when cooked

feif·teen \(ˈ)fefˈtēn\ *Scot var of* FIFTEEN

feign \ˈfān\ *vb* -ED/-ING/-S [ME *feinen*, *feignen*, fr. OF *feign-*, stem of *feindre*, fr. L *fingere* to shape, form, devise, feign — more at DOUGH] *vt* **1 a :** to cause (oneself) to appear 〈~ himself to be sick〉 〈~*ed* herself above such paltry activities〉 **b :** to give a sham appearance of **:** simulate falsely 〈~ sickness〉 〈a limp merely to arouse sympathy〉 〈one of the birds which ~s death when taken in the hand — lying limply with closed eyes —E.A.Armstrong〉 **:** PRETEND 〈~*ed* to be asleep〉 **:** give a false impression 〈everybody had ~*ed* . . . that his wife was as other wives —Arnold Bennett〉 **c** *obs* **:** conceal esp. by disguising **:** DISSEMBLE **2 a :** to fashion by inventing (as a story or accusation) or by forging (as a document) **b :** to assert or relate as if true **:** ALLEGE 〈~ that he was not feeling well so that he could leave the party early〉 **c** *archaic* **:** to give fictional or fabled representation to **:** relate in fiction or fable **d** *archaic* **:** to give an imitation of (as a voice or manner) **:** COUNTERFEIT **3 a** *archaic* **:** to give a mental existence to or conjure up (something unreal) **:** IMAGINE **b** *obs* **:** to believe erroneously ~ *vi* **1** *obs* **:** to give false information **:** LIE **2 :** DISSEMBLE, PRETEND 〈he told the truth because he was no good at ~*ing*〉 **3 :** to create or invent fictional representations 〈the ~*ing* novelist —W.V.O'Connor〉 **syn** see ASSUME

feigned \ˈfānd\ *adj* [ME *feined*, *feigned*, past part. of *feinen*, *feignen* to feign] **1 :** FICTITIOUS, IMAGINARY 〈an actual or ~ account of what happened〉 **2 a :** not real or genuine **:** INSINCERE, FALSE 〈showered him with ~ compliments〉 **b :** PRETENDED, COUNTERFEIT 〈he slipped into the part of the tranquil, fearless matador, and the ~ calm brought him genuine calm —Barnaby Conrad〉 〈presented him with a ~ copy, not with the original〉; *also* **:** altered to deceive **:** DISGUISED 〈spoke in a ~ voice and a foreign accent〉 — **feigned·ly** \ˈfān(ə)dlē, -li\ *adv*

feigned issue *n* **:** an issue framed often by an equity court or by arrangement of the parties in order to try before a jury a question of fact which the court either has not the power to try or is unwilling to try **:** an issue of fact that does not actually exist between the parties to litigation since it is based upon an obvious fiction

feign·er \ˈfānə(r\ *n* -S **:** one that feigns

fei·joa \fāˈyōə, fāˈhōə\ *n* [NL, fr. Juan de Silva *Feijó*, 19th cent. Span. naturalist] **1** *cap* **:** a small genus of So. American shrubs or trees (family Myrtaceae) having opposite leaves, fragrant white or purplish white flowers, and edible greenish red fruit **2** -S **:** any plant of the genus *Feijoa* **3** -S **:** the fruit of a feijoa

fei·jo·a·da \ˌfāzhəˈwäthə\ *n* -S [Pg, fr. *feijão* bean, fr. L *phaseolus* kidney bean — more at FRIJOL] **:** a thick stew that is made of black beans and preferably fatty meat (as sausage) with vegetables and that is popular in Brazil and some other So. American countries

feil \ˈfēl\ *adj* [perh. fr. ¹*feel*] *chiefly Scot* **:** neat and cosy **:** COMFORTABLE

feinne *also* **fein** \ˈfēn\ *n pl*, *usu cap* [IrGael *fianna*, *fēinne*, pl. of *fiann* band of Fenians] **:** FENIANS 1

¹**feint** *adj* [ME — more at ¹FAINT] *archaic* **:** FEIGNED

²**feint** \ˈfānt\ *n* -S [F *feinte*, fr. OF *fainte* fabrication, feigning, fr. *faint*, *feint*, past part. of *faindre*, *feindre* to feign — more at FEIGN] **:** something feigned or intended to deceive esp. for an advantage **:** a false or deceptive act **:** TRICK; *specif* **:** a mock blow or attack on or toward one part in order to distract opposition while one attacks another part (as in fencing, boxing, or military strategy) **syn** see TRICK

³**feint** \"\ *vb* -ED/-ING/-S *vi* **:** to make a feint 〈moved about with the grace of a ballet dancer, could counter and ~ —Nat Fleischer〉 ~ *vt* **1 :** to lure or deceive with a feint 〈the guard was ~*ed* out of position〉 **2 :** to make a pretense of 〈the assailant ~*ed* a rush, then stopped abruptly〉

⁴**feint** \"\ *or* **faint** \"\ *adj* [*feint* alter. of ¹*faint*; *faint* fr. ¹*faint*] **:** being or belonging to fine pale horizontal lines produced by pen ruling (as in account books) 〈~ lines〉 〈~ ruling〉

⁵**feint** *or* **faint** \"\ *n* -S **:** a feint line

feints *or* **faints** \ˈfān(t)s\ *n pl* [¹*faint* + *-s*] **:** the weak and impure spirit containing fusel oil that is produced in the very first and the last part of the distillation of liquor (as whiskey) and that requires rectification

fei·rie \ˈfērē\ *adj* [ME (Sc) *fery*, fr. ME *fere* sound, strong + *-y* — more at FERE] **1** *Scot* **:** sturdy and strong **2** *Scot* **:** active and agile; *specif* **:** able to walk

¹**feis** \ˈfesh\ *n*, *pl* **fei·sean·na** \-shənə\ *often cap* [IrGael, fr. MIr, feast; akin to OE *wist* food, feast, existence, OHG *wist* food, ON *vist* food, dwelling, Goth *wists* nature, essence, OE *wesan* to be — more at WAS] **1 :** an assembly in ancient Ireland for the promulgation of laws and for competition in artistic, intellectual, and physical prowess — compare AENACH **2 :** an Irish folk festival or convention patterned on the ancient feis and featuring games and competitions and usu. traditional Irish music and dancing — compare EISTEDDFOD

²**feis** *pl of* FEI

feist *or* **fice** *or* **fist** \ˈfīs(t)\ *n* -S [by shortening & alter. fr. obs. *fisting* \ˈfīstiŋ\, adj., breaking wind (in such expressions as *fisting dog*, *fisting hound*), fr. pres. part. of obs. *fist* \ˈfist\, v., to break wind, fr. ME *fisten*, fr. *fist* flatus; akin to MHG *vist*, *vīst* flatus, emission of gas from the colon, ON *físa* to break wind — more at SPIRIT] **1** *chiefly dial* **:** a small dog of uncertain ancestry **:** MONGREL, CUR **2** *chiefly dial* **a :** a person of little worth **b :** someone with a bad temper

feisty \-tē\ *adj* -ER/-EST [*feist* + *-y*] **1** *chiefly South & Midland* **:** like a feist in behavior or appearance **2** *chiefly South & Midland* **:** being in a state of excitement or agitation: as **a :** full of nervous energy **:** FIDGETY **b :** touchy and quarrelsome **:** looking for trouble **c :** frisky and exuberant **3** *chiefly South & Midland* **a :** inclined to put on airs **:** AFFECTED, HAUGHTY **b :** WILFUL, PETULANT

fei ts'ui \ˈfāˈtswē, ˈfāchˈwē\ *n* -S [Chin (Pek) *fei*³ *ts'ui*⁴ *yü*⁴, fr. *fei*³ *ts'ui*⁴ kingfisher + *yü*⁴ jade] **:** emerald-green jadeite from Burma

feke *var of* FAKE

feld·sher \ˈfel(d)shə(r)\ *n* -S [Russ *fel'dsher*, fr. G *feldscher*, *feldscherer* field surgeon, fr. *feld* field (fr. OHG) + *scherer* barber, surgeon, fr. OHG *skerāri* shearer, fr. *skeran* to shear + *-āri* -er — more at FIELD, SHEAR, -ER] **:** a practitioner of medicine in certain east European countries and esp. Russia without the full training or the status of a qualified doctor; *esp* **:** an assistant to a physician esp. on the battlefield

feld·spar \ˈfelz,pär, -l(d),sp-, -pä(r\ *also* **feld·spath** \-path\ *n* -S [*feldspar* part trans. of obs. G *feldspath* (now *feldspat*); *feldspath* fr. obs. G *feldspath* (now *feldspat*), fr. G *feld* field (fr. OHG) + obs. G *spath* spar (now *spat*), fr. MHG *spat*, *spāt*; akin to OHG *spān* chip of wood — more at SPOON] **:** any of a group of usu. white or nearly white, flesh-red, bluish, or greenish minerals that are closely related in crystalline form, that are all aluminum silicates with potassium, sodium, calcium, or barium, that occur in crystals and crystalline masses which are vitreous in luster and break rather easily in two directions at approximately right angles to each other, that are essential constituents of nearly all crystalline rocks (as granite, gneiss, most kinds of basalt, and trachyte), that on decomposition yield a large part of the clay of the soil and also the mineral kaolinite, and that include the monoclinic species orthoclase and celsian and the triclinic species microcline, anorthoclase, anorthite, albite, and other plagioclases (hardness 6–6.5, sp. gr. 2.5–2.9)

feld·spath·ic \(ˈ)felz¦pathik, -l(d)¦sp-\ *also* **feld·spath·ose** \ˈ=ˌ=ˌthōs\ *adj* [*feldspathic* fr. ISV *feldspath* + *-ic*; *feldspathose* fr. *feldspath* + *-ose*] **:** being, belonging to, or containing feldspar — used esp. of a porcelain glaze containing feldspar

feld·spath·iza·tion \ˌ=ˌ=ˌthəˈzāshən\ *n* -S [ISV *feldspath* + *-ize* + *-ation*] **:** the process of feldspathizing or of being feldspathized

feld·spath·ize \ˈ=ˌ=ˌtīz\ *vb* -ED/-ING/-S [*feldspath* + *-ize*] **:** to develop into feldspar by metamorphism

feld·spath·oid \-ˌthȯid\ *n* -S [ISV *feldspath* + *-oid*] **:** a mineral consisting of an aluminous silicate (as leucite nepheline) that has too little silica to form feldspar — **feld·spath·oi·dal** \ˌ=ˌ=ˈthȯidᵊl\ *adj*

felf \ˈfelf\ *dial Eng var of* ¹FELLY

fe·li·bre \fāˈlēbrə, -rᵊ\ *n*, *pl* **felibres** \-rəz,-rᵊ\ *often cap* [F *félibre*, fr. Prov *felibre* felibre, any one of the learned men with whom Jesus at the age of twelve disputed in the Temple (Lk 2:46), perh. fr. LL *fellebris* being not yet weaned, fr. L *fellare*, *felare* to suck — more at FEMININE] **:** a member or supporter of the Felibrige, a literary association of Provençal writers founded near Avignon in 1854 esp. for the maintenance and purification of Provençal as a literary language

fe·li·bre·an \-rēən\ *adj*, *often cap* [F *félibréen*, fr. *félibre*] **:** of or relating to the felibres

fe·li·cia \fəˈlish(ē)ə, -lēshə\ *n*, *cap* [NL, fr. L *felic-*, *felix* happy + NL *-ia*] **:** a large genus of So. African herbs or subshrubs (family Compositae) with solitary flower heads and bright blue rays — see BLUE DAISY

fe·li·cide \ˈfēləˌsīd\ *n* -S [*feli-* (fr. L *feles*, *felis* cat) + *-cide*] **:** the killing of a cat

fe·li·cif·ic \ˌfēlə¦sifik\ *adj* [L *felic-*, *felix* happy + E *-i-* + *-fic*] **1 :** bringing about or designed to bring about or produce happiness 〈conclude that the validity of ethical judgments is not determined by the ~ tendencies of actions —A.J.Ayer〉 **2 :** measured or measuring value in terms of happiness 〈an ethics that is ~ in character〉

¹**felicitate** *adj* [LL *felicitatus*, past part. of *felicitare* to make happy, fr. L *felicitas* felicity] *obs* **:** made happy

²**fe·lic·i·tate** \fəˈlisəˌtāt, usu -ād·+V\ *vt* -ED/-ING/-S [LL *felicitatus*, past part. of *felicitare*] **1** *archaic* **:** to make happy or prosperous **2 a :** to reckon or consider as happy or fortunate 〈*felicitating* himself on having so good a wife〉 **b :** CONGRATULATE 〈make a point of *felicitating* those you know whenever there is an occasion in their lives for rejoicing —Agnes M. Miall〉 — **fe·lic·i·ta·tor** \-ād·ə(r), -ātə-\ *n* -S

fe·lic·i·ta·tion \=ˌ==ˈtāshən\ *n* -S [F *félicitation*, fr. *féliciter* to make happy, congratulate (fr. LL *felicitare* to make happy) + *-ation*] **:** the act or an instance of felicitating **:** CONGRATULATION

fe·lic·i·tous \fəˈlisəd·əs, -isətəs\ *adj* [*felicity* + *-ous*] **1 a :** happily suited to an occasion or purpose **:** expressed or applied with a fastidious appropriateness or telling effectiveness 〈a ~ expression of affection〉 〈handled the delicate matter in a most ~ manner〉 **b :** marked by happy or fastidious appropriateness of expression or manner 〈a ~ writer〉 **2 a :** marked by general happiness or good fortune 〈a ~ life〉 〈a ~ country〉 〈she had everything . . . life was indeed ~ —Rose Macaulay〉 **b :** PLEASANT, CHARMING, DELIGHTFUL 〈the ride through the countryside is a ~ journey for city people〉 **syn** see FIT

fe·lic·i·tous·ly *adv* **:** in a felicitous manner 〈~ translated into English〉

fe·lic·i·tous·ness *n* -ES **:** the quality or state of being felicitous 〈pleased by the ~ of the phrasing〉

fe·lic·i·ty \fəˈlisəd·ē, -sətē, -i\ *n* -ES [ME *felicite*, fr. MF *felicité*, fr. L *felicitat-*, *felicitas*, fr. *felic-*, *felix* happy, fruitful + *-itat-*, *-itas* -ity — more at FEMININE] **1 a :** the quality or state of being happy 〈everlasting joy and ~ —*Bk. of Com. Prayer*〉 〈no one more entitled by unpretending merit, or better prepared by habitual suffering, to receive and enjoy ~ —Jane Austen〉 **b :** something that promotes or is the source of happiness **2** *archaic* **a :** good fortune **:** SUCCESS **b :** a fortunate achievement **:** a stroke of fortune **3 a :** a felicitous manner, faculty, or quality esp. in art or language **:** telling or elegant neatness or appropriateness **:** APTNESS, GRACE 〈~ in the painting of children〉 〈pleased by the ~ of the expression〉 〈a writer of fluency and ~, of graciousness and gentleness —Saxe Commins〉 〈the special *felicities* of water color as opposed to oil〉 **b :** a felicitous turn of phrase or artistic expression **:** a happy achievement **:** an apt expression 〈a style marked by *felicities*〉 〈a poem is more than the sum of its *felicities* —*Times Lit. Supp.*〉 **syn** see HAPPINESS

¹**fe·lid** \ˈfēləd\ *n* -S [NL *Felidae*] **:** one of the Felidae **:** CAT

²**felid** \"\ *adj* **:** of or relating to the Felidae

fe·li·dae \ˈfēləˌdē\ *n pl*, *cap* [NL, fr. *Felis*, type genus + *-idae*] **:** a cosmopolitan family comprising lithe-bodied digitigrade carnivorous mammals having soft and often strikingly patterned fur, comparatively short limbs with soft pads on the feet, usu. sharp curved retractile claws, a broad and somewhat rounded head with short but powerful jaws equipped with teeth suited to grasping, tearing, and shearing through flesh, erect ears, and typically eyes with narrow or elliptical pupils and esp. adapted for seeing in dim light and including the true cats (as the lion, tiger, jaguar, leopard, or cougar), the cheetah, and extinct related forms

fe·li·form \ˈfēləˌfȯrm\ *adj* [*feli-* (fr. L *feles*, *felis* cat) + *-form*] **:** resembling a cat

¹**fe·line** \ˈfēˌlīn\ *adj* [L *felinus*, fr. *feles*, *felis* cat + *-inus* -ine] **1 :** of or relating to the genus *Felis* or the family Felidae 〈the ~ tribe〉 **2 :** resembling or suggesting a cat in manner or quality: **a :** sleekly graceful 〈the women . . . were fair to look upon, ~ in movement —Douglas Carruthers〉 **b :** SLY, TREACHEROUS 〈a ~ old gossip〉 **c :** STEALTHY — **fe·line·ly** *adv* — **fe·line·ness** \-līnnəs\ *n* -ES

²**feline** \"\ *n* -S **:** a feline animal **:** CAT

feline distemper *n* **1** *or* **feline enteritis :** PANLEUCOPENIA **2 :** a disease of cats closely related or identical to panleucopenia in which gastrointestinal symptoms predominate

fe·lin·i·ty \fēˈlinəd·ē\ *n* -ES **:** the quality of being feline; *also* **:** a feline characteristic 〈those elusive *felinities* — beauty, sleekness, grace, and movement —*All-Pets Mag.*〉

fe·lis \ˈfēləs\ *n*, *cap* [NL, fr. L *feles*, *felis* cat] **:** the type genus of Felidae comprising the true or typical cats

1**fell** \'fel\ *n* -s [ME *fel* skin, fr. OE *fell;* akin to OHG *fel* skin, ON *berfjall* skin of a bear, Goth *thrūtsfill* leprosy, L *pellis* skin, Gk *pelma* sole, Russ *pelena* swaddling clothes, covering] **1 a :** an animal skin with or without the original hair or wool **:** PELT, HIDE **b :** the skin of a human being **2 :** the flesh immediately under the skin **:** a thin tough membrane covering a carcass immediately under the hide and consisting of superficial fascia more or less intermingled with fatty tissue **3 :** a body covering of esp. thick hair or wool **:** FLEECE

2**fell** \"\ *vt* -ED/-ING/-S [ME *fellen,* fr. OE *fellan, fyllan;* akin to OHG *fellen* to fell, ON *fella;* causative fr. the root of E *fall* (v.)] **1 :** to cut, beat, or knock down or bring down (as with a missile) ⟨~ a tree⟩ ⟨~ an opponent⟩ ⟨strong enough to ~ an ox⟩ ⟨~*ed* the deer with a single shot⟩ ⟨got as far as the top of the prison wall where a live electric wire ~*ed* him —*N.Y. Times*⟩; *also* **:** KILL ⟨a final attack of pneumonia ~*ed* him —*Time*⟩ **2** *chiefly Scot* **a :** SLAUGHTER ⟨~ a fat swine⟩ **b :** to bring to a state of exhaustion or prostration esp. by beating ⟨~*ed* the old mare⟩ **3 :** to sew with a flat-fell seam **:** HEM, BLINDSTITCH

3**fell** \"\ *n* -s **1 a :** the act of felling something (as a tree) **b :** the timber cut down in one season **2 a :** the junction of the last filling thread with unwoven warp threads when a cloth is being woven **b :** the final yard or so in weaving out a warp

4**fell** \"\ *past tense and dial past part of* FALL

5**fell** \"\ *adj* -ER/-EST [ME *fel,* fr. OF *fel* (nom. case form) cruel, fierce, fr. ML *fellon-, fello* villain, rogue — more at FELON] **1 a :** FIERCE, CRUEL, SAVAGE ⟨a ~ and barbarous enemy⟩ ⟨swoop down and massacre his relatives, carrying off two young girls for their own ~ purpose —*Time*⟩ **b :** AWESOME, SINISTER, MALEVOLENT ⟨turned on him a ~ countenance⟩ **c :** killing or markedly sickening or destroying **:** DEADLY, MURDEROUS, DIRE ⟨a ~ poison⟩ ⟨a ~ disease⟩ ⟨a murderer bent on his ~ purpose⟩ **2** *chiefly Scot* **a :** EAGER, INTENT ⟨~ on seeing him⟩ **b :** SHREWD, CLEVER ⟨~ at poetry⟩ **c :** SHARP, PUNGENT ⟨~ cheese⟩ **d :** SPIRITED, ENERGETIC **3** *chiefly Scot* **:** strange and inexplicable ⟨a ~ part of her died with him⟩ **syn** see FIERCE

6**fell** \"\ *adv* [ME *fel,* fr. *fel,* adj.] **1** *chiefly Scot* **:** in a fell manner: as **a :** FIERCELY, CRUELLY **b :** VIGOROUSLY, EAGERLY **2** *chiefly Scot* **:** VERY, GREATLY

7**fell** \"\ *n* -s [ME, fr. ON *fell, fjall;* akin to OHG *felis* rock, MIr *all* cliff, LGk *pella* stone, Skt *pāṣāṇa*] **1** *chiefly Scot* **:** MOUNTAIN, HEIGHT — now used chiefly in place names ⟨Capel Fells⟩ **2** *dial Brit* **:** an elevated wild field **:** a hill moor

fell·age \'felij\ *n* -s **:** the act or process of felling (as a tree)

fel·la·gha \fə'lägə, -lagə\ *n, pl* **fellaghas** *also* **fellagha** [Ar *fallāq* (pl. *fallāqah*) bandit, robber] **:** a member of an Algerian or Tunisian Muslim and nationalist guerrilla band

fel·lah \'felə, fə'lä\ *n, pl* **fella·hin** *or* **fella·heen** \ˌfeləˈhēn, fəˌläˈhēn\ [Ar *fallāḥ*] **1 :** a peasant or agricultural laborer in Egypt, Syria, and other Arabic-speaking countries **2 :** one of a race type in modern Egypt descended from ancient Egyptians

fel·la·ta \fə'läd·ə\ *n, pl* **fellata** *or* **fellatas** *usu cap* **:** FULA 1

fel·la·tio \fə'lāshē,ō, fe'-, -lād·ē-\ *also* **fel·la·tion** \-lāshən\ *n* -s [NL *fellation-, fellatio,* fr. L *fellatus, felatus* (past part. of *fellare, felare* to suck) + *-ion-, -io* -ion — more at FEMININE] **:** the practice of obtaining sexual satisfaction by oral stimulation of the penis

felled *past of* FELL

fel·len \'felən\ *n* -s [prob. by shortening & alter. fr. *felonwood* & *felonwort*] **:** BITTERSWEET 2a

fell·er \'felə(r)\ *n* -s [ME *fellere,* fr. *fellen* to fell + *-er, -ere* -er] **:** one that fells: as **a :** FALLER 1 **b :** a worker who fells seams or binds the seams of knitted garments; *also* **:** a sewing machine attachment for flat-fell seams

fellfare *var of* FIELDFARE

fell–field \'⸗,⸗\ *n* **:** a treeless rock-strewn area that is above the timberline or in the frigid zones and that is dominated by low plants or by grasses and sedges

fellies *pl of* FELLY

felling *n* -s [ME, fr. *fellen* to fell + *-inge, -ing* -ing] **1 :** FELLAGE **2 :** an area on which trees have been or are to be felled

felling ax *n* **:** an ax designed esp. for cutting down trees

felling wedge *n* **:** FALLING WEDGE

fellmonger \'⸗,⸗⸗\ *n* -s *Brit* **:** one whose vocation is the removal of hair or esp. wool from hides in preparation for leather making

fellmongered \'⸗,⸗(⸗)⸗\ *adj* [fr. *fellmongering,* after such pairs as E *covering: covered*] *Brit, of wool* **:** removed in fellmongering

fellmongering \'⸗,⸗(⸗)⸗\ *n* -s *Brit* **:** the trade or occupation of a fellmonger

fellmongery \'⸗,⸗(⸗)⸗\ *n* -ES [*fellmonger* + *-y*] **1** *Brit* **:** the place of business of a fellmonger **2** *Brit* **:** fellmongering as a business

fell·ness *n* -ES [ME *felnes,* fr. *fel* fell + *-nes* -ness] **:** the quality or state of being fell **:** extreme cruelty, harshness, or destructiveness of character or effect ⟨a ~ of aspect⟩ ⟨the ~ of the blow staggered him⟩

felloe *var of* FELLY

1**fel·low** \'fe(,)lō, -lə, *often* -ˌləw+V\ *n* -s [ME *felawe,* fr. OE *fēolaga,* fr. ON *fēlagi,* fr. *fē* cattle, sheep, money + *-lagi* (akin to ON *leggja* to lay) — more at FEE, LAY] **1 a** *obs* **:** one associated with another as a sharer **:** PARTNER **b :** COMPANION, COMRADE, ASSOCIATE — used chiefly of men **c** *archaic* **:** ACCOMPLICE, HENCHMAN **2 a :** an equal in rank, power, or character **:** PEER ⟨more like a ~ than a subject⟩ ⟨the final line of seventeen syllables has no ~ —H.O.Taylor⟩ **b :** one of a pair: as (1) *obs* **:** SPOUSE (2) **:** something that matches or resembles another ⟨the vase is the exact ~ to one on the shelf⟩ **3 :** a member of a company or group having common characteristics or common interests: as **a :** a creature of the same kind **:** one of a usu. relatively homogeneous group ⟨all men are ~*s* in their need of food, clothing, and companionship⟩ **b :** CONTEMPORARY ⟨didn't like the company of his ~*s* but preferred to associate by way of reading and study with ancient Romans⟩ **c** *sometimes cap* **:** a member of an incorporated literary, scientific, and often professional society ⟨a ~ of several scholarly associations⟩ ⟨a ~ of the American College of Surgeons⟩ ⟨a ~ of the Royal Geographical Society⟩; *often* **:** such a member given a rank usu. of distinction with the title *Fellow* **d fellows** *pl* **:** a social group of usu. youngsters or teen-agers or the male members of such group **4 a** *obs* **:** a person of one of the lower social orders — used as a customary form of address to servants or those of lower social rank **b** *archaic* **:** a worthless or contemptible person **c :** MAN ⟨saw three strange ~*s* standing in a doorway⟩ — often used in phrases of familiar address ⟨no trouble at all, my dear ~⟩ ⟨I say, old ~, could you give me a lift home⟩ **d :** THING, CREATURE — used of children or animals ⟨the poor little ~ had fallen off his tricycle⟩ ⟨I fired twice but the big ~ got away and we lost his trail⟩ **e :** ONE ⟨the queer way you look at a ~ you'd think I'd committed a crime⟩ **5 a :** an incorporated member of a college or collegiate foundation esp. in a British university **b :** a member of the corporation or governing body in one of certain colleges or universities **c :** a scholar of some note who is appointed by a British university to reside and work in one of its colleges **6 :** a person appointed to one of a number of positions granting a stipend and allowing for advanced study: as **a :** a graduate student in an American university who is granted money to continue research usu. in preparation for an advanced degree and often with certain teaching duties **b :** a young physician who has completed training as intern and resident and has been granted a stipend and position allowing him to do further study and research in a specialty **c :** one who has been granted money to do research by a foundation

2**fellow** \"\ *vt* -ED/-ING/-S [ME *felawen* to join in partnership, fr. *felawe,* n. — more at 1FELLOW] *archaic* **:** to produce or find an equal to **:** MATCH

3**fellow** \"\ *adj* [1*fellow*] **1 a :** belonging to the same group or class as oneself or as another — used only in attributive position ⟨a ~ creature⟩ ⟨a ~ lodge member⟩ ⟨a ~ trainee⟩ ⟨a ~ disciple⟩ ⟨a ~ pupil⟩ ⟨a ~ employee⟩ **b :** having or sharing the same occupation or avocation ⟨a ~ musician⟩ ⟨a ~ plumber⟩ ⟨a ~ golfer⟩ **c :** experiencing or suffering the same fate (as misfortune) ⟨a ~ paraplegic⟩ ⟨a ~ prisoner⟩ ⟨a ~ exile⟩ **d :** having the same weaknesses or strengths ⟨a ~ mortal⟩ ⟨a ~ sinner⟩ ⟨a ~ saint⟩ **e :** subject to the same government or political or civil obligations or having the same allegiance ⟨a ~ citizen⟩ ⟨a ~ American⟩ **2 :** accompanying one **:** accompanying another ⟨a ~ voyager⟩ **3 :** sympathetic as if one were of the same group as another or in the same circumstance ⟨the Indian's ~ feeling for wild things —*Amer. Guide Series: Tenn.*⟩

fellow commoner *n* **:** an undergraduate at Oxford, Cambridge, or Trinity College, Dublin, formerly permitted to dine at the same table as the fellows of his college

fellowcraft *n* **1 :** the second degree of Freemasonry **2 :** one who has taken the degree of fellowcraft — compare BLUE LODGE

fellow feeling *n* **1 :** SYMPATHY **2 :** a feeling of community of interest or of mutual understanding ⟨that sympathy must be more than the mere *fellow feeling* of other craftsmen —H.L.Mencken⟩

1**fel·low·ly** \-ˌlōl|ē, -ləl|, |i\ *adj* [ME *felawely,* fr. *felawe* fellow + *-ly* — more at FELLOW] **:** SOCIABLE, COMPANIONABLE

2**fellowly** \"\ *adv* [ME *felawely,* fr. *felawely,* adj.] **:** in a fellowly manner

fel·low·man \ˌ⸗⸗'man, -maa(ə)n\ *n, pl* **fellowmen 1 :** a kindred human being ⟨the question of the meaning of existence is answered neither by a god nor a ~ —Karl Lowith⟩ **2 :** fellow human beings ⟨a shrewd judge of his ~⟩ ⟨trying to be of service to his ~⟩

fellow servant *n* **:** an employee working with another employee on a common enterprise of their employer under such circumstances that each employee if negligent may expose the other to harm which the employer cannot reasonably be expected to guard against or be held legally liable for

1**fel·low·ship** \'⸗⸗,ship\ *n* -s [ME *felaweshipe,* fr. *felawe* fellow + *-shipe* -ship] **1 a :** the companionship of persons on equal and friendly terms **:** COMPANY, SOCIETY ⟨looking for the ~ of companionable people⟩ ⟨the inability of the individual to find satisfactory ~ in the group —N.A.Ford⟩ **b :** the state of being together or sharing (as in an activity or experience) **:** mutual participation, interest, or experience **:** common interest or experience ⟨their ~ in crime —A.J.Ayer⟩ **c :** intimate mutual personal intercourse ⟨a ~ with great men⟩ ⟨a ~ with the glorious firmament —E.J.Banfield⟩ **2 :** a company or group of equals or associates **:** UNION, ASSOCIATION ⟨he belongs to an organized ~ that circulates a devotional literary criticism —Bernard DeVoto⟩: as **a** *archaic* **:** the fellows of a college or university **b** *archaic* **:** a guild or corporation **c :** BROTHERHOOD, FRATERNITY; *also* **:** a group with the intimate relationship or common purposefulness of a brotherhood or fraternity ⟨a ~ of women and girls devoted to the task of realizing in our common life those ideals . . . to which we are committed as Christians —*Current Biog.*⟩ **d :** a local group of 10 or more Unitarians or Universalists ineligible for church status and usu. without a minister but recognized and regulated by the denomination **3 :** the quality or state of being comradely **:** FRIENDLINESS, COMRADESHIP **4 a :** the state or relationship of being an equal or an associate **b** *obs* **:** membership in a society **:** PARTNERSHIP, ALLIANCE **c :** mutual relation between members or branches of the same church **:** COMMUNION 3a **5 a :** the position or rank of a fellow (as of a university, college, or hospital) **b** (1) **:** the stipend or endowments of a fellow (as of a college or university) (2) **:** a sum of money offered or granted by an educational institution, a public or private agency, organization, or foundation for advanced study or research or for creative writing **c :** a foundation for the providing of such a stipend or sum

2**fellowship** \"\ *vt* **fellowshiped** *or* **fellowshipped; fellowshiped** *or* **fellowshipped; fellowshiping** *or* **fellowshipping; fellowships** [ME *felaweshipen* to join in fellowship, fr. *felaweshipe,* n.] **:** to join in fellowship or be in communion with (a church or church member)

fellow–travel \ˌ⸗⸗'⸗⸗\ *vi* [back-formation fr. *fellow traveler*] **:** to be or act as a fellow traveler ⟨continued to *fellow-travel* with the Communists in various front organizations —H.L. Varney⟩

fellow traveler *n* [trans. of Russ *poputchik*] **:** one that sympathizes with and often furthers the ideals and program of an organized group (as the Communist party) without membership in the group or participation in its activities

fell pony *n* [prob. fr. 7*fell*] **1** *usu cap F* **:** a breed of small hardy English ponies native to the regions west of the Pennine range **2** *often cap F* **:** an animal of the Fell pony breed formerly much used for pack purposes

fells *pl of* FELL, *pres 3d sing of* FELL

fell seam *n* **:** FLAT-FELL SEAM

fellside \'⸗,⸗\ *n* -s **:** HILLSIDE, MOUNTAINSIDE

fell system \'fel-\ *n, usu cap F* [after *Fell,* 19th cent. engineer who used it in a mountain railway across Mont Cenis that was opened in 1868] **:** a system of tracking for mountain railroads that uses a central elevated double-headed rail laid sideways and gripped tightly on each side by horizontal wheels attached to the locomotive

fellup *usu cap, var of* FELUP

fellwort *var of* FELWORT

1**fel·ly** \'felē, -li\ *also* **fel·loe** \-(,)lō\ *n, pl* **fellies** *also* **felloes** [ME *fely, felive,* fr. OE *felg;* akin to OS & OHG *felga* felly, OE *fealg, fealh* piece of plowed land, Russ *polosa* strip, plot of ground, region] **:** the exterior rim or a segment of the rim of a wheel supported by the spokes

f felly

2**fel·ly** \'fel(l)ē, -)i\ *adv* [ME *felly,* fr. *fel* fell + *-ly* — more at FELL (fierce)] **:** in a fell manner: as **a :** FIERCELY, CRUELLY, BARBAROUSLY, SAVAGELY, DESTRUCTIVELY **b** *obs* **:** KEENLY, BITTERLY, TERRIBLY

felo–de–se \ˌfe(,)lōdə'sā, -'sē, ˌfā-(,)lōdə'sā, ˌfē(,)lōdə'sē\ *n, pl* **fe·lo·nes–de–se** \fə'lō(,)nēzd-, fe'-\ *or* **felos–de–se** [ML *felo de se,* fr. *felo, fello* rogue, evildoer, felon + L *de* of, from + *se* (abl.) oneself — more at FELON, DE-, SUICIDE] **1 :** one that deliberately kills himself or dies from the effects of his commission of an unlawful malicious act **2 :** the act of deliberate self-destruction — compare SUICIDE

fe·loid \'fē,lȯid\ *adj* [NL *Feloidea*] **:** of or relating to the Aeluroidea

fe·loi·dea \fē'lȯidēə, fə'-\ [NL, fr. *Felis* + *-oidea*] *syn of* AELUROIDEA

1**fel·on** \'felən\ *adj* [ME *feloun,* fr. OF *felon* (oblique case form), fr. ML *fellon-, fello* villain, rogue, prob. fr. (assumed) OFrk *fillo* one who skins, one who whips; akin to OHG *fillen* to skin, whip, *fel* skin — more at FELL] **1** *archaic* **a :** CRUEL, FIERCE; *also* **:** MURDEROUS **b :** SAVAGE, WILD **2** *archaic* **:** WICKED, EVIL

2**felon** \"\ *n* -s [ME *feloun,* fr. OF *felon* (oblique case form) villain, rogue, fr. ML *fellon-, fello*] **1 :** a person who has committed a felony **2** *archaic* **:** one that is wicked **:** VILLAIN **syn** see CRIMINAL

3**felon** \"\ *n* -s [ME *feloun* suppurative sore, fr. OF *felon,* lit., villain] **1 :** a usu. suppurative infection involving the deep tissues on the palmar surface of a fingertip — called also *whitlow;* compare PARONYCHIA **2 :** a severe inflammation on a finger or toe esp. if involving the bone

felon de se *or* **felon of oneself** *n, pl* **felones de se** *or* **felons of oneself** [*felon de se* part trans. of ML *felo de se; felon of oneself* trans. of ML *felo de se*] *obs* **:** FELO-DE-SE

felon herb *n* **1 :** MUGWORT 1 **2 :** MOUSE-EAR 1a

fe·lo·ni·ous \fə'lōnēəs, fe'-\ *adj* [ME, fr. *felonie* felony + -ous] **:** of, relating to, or having the quality of a felony **:** being against the law **:** VILLAINOUS, CRIMINAL — **fe·lo·ni·ous·ly** *adv* — **fe·lo·ni·ous·ness** *n* -ES

felonious homicide *n* **:** the killing of a human being without legal justification

fel·on·ry \'felənrē\ *n* -ES **:** FELONS; *specif* **:** the convict population of a penal colony

felonweed \'⸗⸗,⸗\ *n* [*felon* (infection) + *weed;* fr. its use as a remedy for felons] **:** TANSY RAGWORT

felonwood \'⸗⸗,⸗\ *n* **:** BITTERSWEET 2a

felonwort \'⸗⸗,⸗\ *n* **1 :** BITTERSWEET 2a **2 :** CELANDINE 1 **3 :** MASTERWORT a **4 :** HERB ROBERT

fel·o·ny \'felənē, -ni\ *n* -ES [ME *felonie,* fr. OF, treachery, ill will, misdeed, fr. *felon* villain, rogue] **1 :** an act on the part of a vassal involving the forfeiture of his fee or an act of a lord involving the forfeiture of his lordship in feudal law **2 :** a grave crime (as murder, manslaughter, rape, robbery, larceny, burglary, mayhem, arson, rescue of a felon, some types of prison breach, some offenses for which benefit of clergy was abolished, and sometimes treason) declared expressly as distinguished from a misdemeanor in English common law and resulting in outlawry if the offender fled and until the Forfeiture Act of 1870 resulting upon conviction in the offender's loss of his goods or lands or both and sometimes in punishment by loss of a member, whipping, death, or long imprisonment **3 a :** one of several grave crimes that are distinguished from treason or minor misdemeanors, that are expressly declared to be such by the common law or judicial decisions or statutes of a state that follows the English common law, and that sometimes include sodomy and offenses deemed serious in more modern times (as kidnapping or wilful evasion of income taxes) **b :** a crime declared a felony by statute because it may be punished by death or by imprisonment in a penitentiary or state prison regardless of the punishment actually imposed **c :** a crime declared to be a felony by statute because of the punishment actually imposed (as death or imprisonment for the length of time prescribed by the statute) **d :** any crime for which the punishment in federal law may be death or imprisonment for more than one year

felos–de–se *pl of* FELO-DE-SE

fels \'fels\ *also* **fals** \'fals\ *n, pl* **fa·lus** \fə'lüs\ [Ar *fals* (pl. *fulūs*), fr. LGk *phollis,* a small coin, fr. LL *follis,* fr. L, bellows, leather moneybag — more at BLOW] **:** an Arabic copper coin

fel·sen·meer \'felzən,me(ə)r\ *n* -s [G, fr. *felsen, fels* rock (fr. OHG *felis*) + *meer* sea (fr. OHG *meri*) — more at FELL (mountain), MARINE] **:** an assemblage of angular and subangular rock fragments completely mantling the surface and commonly present in mountainous regions above timberline where slopes are not too steep to retain the loose debris

fel·sic \'felsik\ *adj* [*feldspar* + *silica* + *-ic*] **:** consisting of or chiefly consisting of feldspar or feldspathoid quartz

fel·site \'fel,sīt\ *n* -s [*felspar* + *-ite*] **:** a dense macrocrystalline igneous rock that is like flint in fracture and that consists almost entirely of feldspar and quartz — **fel·sit·ic** \(')fel'sid·ik\ *adj*

fel·so·phyre \'felsə,fī(ə)r\ *n* -s [G *felsophyr,* fr. *felso-* (fr. *felsit* felsite, fr. E *felsite*) + *-phyr* -phyre] **:** a porphyritic rock having a felsitic groundmass — **fel·so·phyr·ic** \ˌ⸗⸗'firik, -fīr-\ *adj*

fel·spar *n* -s [by alter. (influenced by G *fels* rock)] *chiefly Brit* **:** FELDSPAR

fel·spath·ic *adj* [irreg. (influenced by *felspar*) fr. ISV *feldspathic*] *chiefly Brit* **:** FELDSPATHIC

1**felt** \'felt\ *n* -s [ME, fr. OE; akin to OS *filt* felt, OHG *filz* felt, Sw dial. *filta* to beat, L *pellere* to drive, beat, push, Gk *pelas* near] **1 a :** a cloth constructed usu. of wool and fur fibers often mixed with natural or synthetic fibers by the interlocking of the loose fibers through the action of heat, moisture, chemicals, and pressure without spinning, weaving, or knitting **b :** a firm woven cloth of wool or cotton heavily napped and shrunk to form a smooth resilient texture and used widely by manufacturers esp. of printing presses, pianos, and textiles **2 a :** an article of felt cloth; *esp* **:** a soft hat made of felt **b :** a length of felt used as protective or absorbent padding esp. in industry — see SILENCE CLOTH **3 :** any of several materials resembling felt in composition: as **a :** a heavy paper of organic or asbestos fibers impregnated with asphalt and used in building construction (as under shingling) **b :** pressed boards of rags or old paper used as insulation (as in a refrigerator) **c :** sheets of semirigid pressed fiber insulation used under the sheathing of a building or between rough and finish flooring **4 a :** a blanket of absorbent material (as wool) between pairs of which wet sheets of handmade paper are pressed in papermaking **b :** an endless belt commonly of textile material on which a web is carried (as after leaving the wire) in a papermaking machine

2**felt** \"\ *vb* -ED/-ING/-S [ME *felten,* fr. *felt,* n.] *vt* **1 :** to make into felt or a substance like felt **2 :** to cause to adhere and mat together (as the fibers in paper) **3 :** to cover with felt ⟨~ a cylinder⟩ ⟨a ~*ed* roof⟩ **~** *vi* **:** to become felted — sometimes used with *up* ⟨mustn't ~ up after repeated washing —*Punch*⟩

3**felt** *past of* FEEL

felted *adj* [fr. past part. of *felt*] **1 a :** made of or into felt ⟨~ cloth⟩ **b :** covered with felt **2 a :** MATTED — used esp. of woolen cloth that has shrunk **b :** having hairs, filaments, or hyphae closely woven or matted together

1**felt·er** \'feltə(r)\ *vt* -ED/-ING/-S [ME *filteren, felteren,* fr. (assumed) AF *feltrer* to cover with felt, fr. (assumed) OF *feltrer* (whence OF *feutrer*), fr. OF *feltre, feutre* felt, of Gmc origin; akin to OS *filt* felt] *now dial Brit* **:** to mat together like felt **:** INTERTWINE

2**felter** \"\ *n* -s **:** one that makes felt or works with felt: as **a :** an operator of a machine that produces felting **b :** a worker who attaches felt weather stripping

felt fern *n* **:** TONGUE FERN

felt finish *n* **:** the finish applied at the wet press in papermaking by a felt of special weave

felt fungus *n* **:** a fungus (*Septobasidium pseudopedicellatum*) that frequently encircles the twigs and branches of various trees (as citrus in the southern U.S.)

felting *n* -s [fr. gerund of *felt*] **1 a :** the process by which fibers are made to mat together esp. in the manufacture of felt **b :** the material made by this process; *esp* **:** FELT **c :** the quality of fibers that causes them to felt **2 :** a felted mass (as of hair) **3 :** the action of shrinking into a matted state — used esp. of such shrinking in woolen cloth

feltlike \'⸗,⸗\ *adj* **:** resembling felt in appearance or texture **:** soft and matted **:** having a napped somewhat fuzzy appearance or quality

felt·man \'⸗mən, -,man\ *n, pl* **feltmen :** a maintenance mechanic who replaces the clothing used on papermaking machines

felt paper *n* **:** a highly porous absorbent paper used in the manufacture of some building and roofing papers

felt rust *n* **:** the telia of a rust (*Cronartium ribicola*) on currants and gooseberries — compare WHITE PINE BLISTER RUST

felt side *n* **:** the side of a sheet of machine-made paper that was not in contact with the wire of the papermaking machine during manufacture — called also *right side, top side*

feltwork \'⸗,⸗\ *n* [*felt* (cloth)] **:** a fibrous network ⟨in the meshes of a loose ~ of silk, the young spiders are destined to live for some time —*Nature Mag.*⟩

feltwort \'⸗,⸗\ *n* [ME, fr. OE *feltwyrt,* fr. *felt* + *wyrt* herb — more at FELT (cloth), WORT] **:** a mullein (*Verbascum thapsus*) with thick woolly leaves

felty \'feltē\ *adj* -ER/-EST [*felt* + *-y*] **1 :** resembling or suggesting felt or a felted mass; *specif* **:** belonging to or having a texture that is like felt and that is produced by unoriented microlites of various minerals **2 :** FELTED

fe·lu·ca *also* **fe·lu·ca** \fə'lükə, -'ləkə\ *n* -s [It *feluca,* prob. fr. Sp *falúa, faluca,* perh. fr. Ar *fulūk,* pl. of *fulk* ship, fr. Gk *epholkion* small boat towed behind a ship, fr. *ephelkein* to drag along, tow, fr. *epi-* + *helkein* to drag, pull — more at SULCUS] **:** a narrow fast lateen-rigged commonly two or three-masted sailing ship chiefly of the Mediterranean area that is usu. low and decked at the ends or from stem to foremast and often has an awning and provision for the use of oars

fe·lup *or* **fel·lup** *or* **fu·lup** \fə'lüp\ *n, pl* **felup** *or* **felups** *or* **fellup** *or* **fellups** *or* **fulup** *or* **fulups** *usu cap* **:** a member of a Negro people on the Atlantic coast of the western Sudan

fel·wort *or* **fell·wort** \'fel,⸗\ *n* [ME *feldwurt,* fr. OE *feldwyrt,* fr. *feld* field + *wyrt* herb — more at FIELD] **:** any of several plants of the family Gentianaceae

fem *var of* FEMME

fem *abbr* **1** female **2** feminine

1**fe·male** \'fē,māl\ *n* -s [ME, alter. (influenced by *male*) of *femel, femelle,* fr. MF & ML; MF *femelle,* fr. ML *femella,* fr. L, young woman, girl, dim. of *femina* woman — more at FEMININE] **1 :** an individual that bears young or produces eggs as distinguished from one that begets young ⟨the ~ has to carry an embryo inside her body⟩: as **a :** a female animal **b :** a woman or girl as distinguished from a man or boy

⟨74 percent of the employees were ~s⟩ ⟨when she was a few days old she became . . . the richest ~ in France —William Maxwell⟩ **2 :** WOMAN ⟨the guide perceived that the ~s could command their steeds —J.F.Cooper⟩ — now usu. used disparagingly ⟨ladies of culture and refinement or coarse common ~s⟩ ⟨the backbiting of catty ~s⟩ **3 :** a pistillate plant

²**female** \"\ *adj* [ME, alter. (influenced by *male*) of *femel, femelle*, fr. MF & ML; MF *femel, femelle*, fr. ML *femellus*, fr. L *femella*, n.] **1 a :** of, by, for, or being the sex that bears young or a member of that sex: as (1) **:** being a woman or girl or composed of members of the female sex ⟨a ~ heir⟩ ⟨the ~ population⟩ **:** WOMAN ⟨a ~ pilot⟩ (2) **:** belonging to, peculiar to, or characteristic of a woman ⟨a ~ name on the doorplate⟩ ⟨composed for ~ voices⟩ ⟨~ sensitiveness⟩ (3) **:** engaged in or exercised by women ⟨~ tillage of the fields⟩ ⟨~ suffrage⟩ **b :** exhibiting femaleness ⟨exceptional ~ behavior by the male bird⟩; *specif* **:** producing or capable of producing eggs ⟨the uterus is a ~ organ⟩ — symbol ♀ **2 a :** having some quality (as passiveness, gentleness, delicacy of color or sound, highness of pitch) associated with the female sex ⟨the ~ castanet . . . gives a delicate sound while the male . . . with its deeper tone plays the role of accompaniment —F.C.Schang⟩ **b** (1) **:** designed with a hollow into which a corresponding male part fits ⟨the ~ coupling of a hose⟩ ⟨the ~ molding of a table hinge⟩ (2) **:** faced with a character in intaglio ⟨a ~ stamping die⟩ ⟨a ~ typefounding matrix⟩ **3 :** FEMININE 4 **4** *of a dialect or speech form* **:** normally used only by women or by men speaking to women **5 :** of, associated with, or being the material, receptive, or productive principle of the cosmos — compare YIN

syn FEMININE, WOMANLY, WOMANLIKE, WOMANISH, EFFEMINATE, LADYLIKE: FEMALE, opposed to *male*, stresses the fact of sex and usu. lacks the rich connotation of various of the others in this set ⟨a *female* voice⟩ ⟨use of *female* labor in the mills⟩ ⟨*female* fashions⟩ ⟨the tender ministries of *female* hands —Alfred Tennyson⟩ FEMININE, opposed to *masculine*, has practically supplanted FEMALE in references to what is characteristic of or appropriate to women, esp. women's attitudes, qualities, and attributes ⟨the sweet, rich, almost *feminine* curves of his sensitive mouth —J.C.Powys⟩ ⟨the *feminine* task of mending a pair of gloves —Nathaniel Hawthorne⟩ ⟨the strangely *feminine* jealousies and religiousness —John Steinbeck⟩ ⟨the *feminine* touch of embroidery and lace —*N.Y. Times*⟩ WOMANLY, opposed to *manly* and also, from another point of view, to *girlish*, often describes qualities that befit a woman or make her particularly attractive ⟨yet more *womanly* was the purity with which she passed through the brutal warriors of a medieval camp —J.R.Green⟩ ⟨a *womanly* tenderness such as any man might prize at a sanctified hearthside —R.P.Warren⟩ WOMANLIKE may be used in reference to faults or foibles ascribed to women ⟨*womanlike*, taking revenge too deep for a transient wrong —Alfred Tennyson⟩ WOMANISH is often derogatorily used in situations in which manliness might be wanted or expected ⟨*womanish* entreaties and lamentations —T.B.Macaulay⟩ ⟨the lank and gray-haired, long-nosed, elderly poet whose head leaned with a weak, *womanish* tilt —H.V.Gregory⟩ EFFEMINATE often describes or suggests unmanly softness, delicacy, enervation, or lack of strength ⟨his manner, in spite of his rugged appearance, was oddly *effeminate* —John Buchan⟩ ⟨he saw in delicate, laborious, discriminating taste, an *effeminate* pedantry, and would, when the mood was on him, delight in all that seemed healthy, popular, and bustling —W.B.Yeats⟩ In reference to girls and young women LADYLIKE suggests decorous propriety; in references to boys and men it sarcastically suggests daintiness, delicacy, softness, primness, and lack of masculine force and strength ⟨your daughter may be better paid, better dressed, more gently spoken, more *ladylike* than you were in the old mill —G.B.Shaw⟩ ⟨that *ladylike* quality which is the curse of southern literature —Margaret Leech⟩

female complaint *n* **:** any of various ill-defined or imaginary disorders of the human female usu. associated with or attributed to the generative function

female dragon *also* **female water dragon** *n* **:** WATER ARUM

female fern *n* **1 :** LADY FERN **2 :** the common brake (*Pteridium aquilinum*)

female fluellin *n* **:** a cancerwort (*Kickxia spuria*)

female hormone *n* **:** a sex hormone (as an estrogen) primarily produced and functioning in the female

female impersonator *n* **:** a male entertainer who plays the role of a woman (as in vaudeville)

female nervine *n* **:** SHOWY LADY'S SLIPPER

fe·male·ness *n* -ES **:** the qualities (as of form, physiology, or behavior) that distinguish an individual that produces large usu. immobile gametes from one that produces spermatozoa or spermatozoids **:** FEMININITY — opposed to *maleness; see* SEX

female pronucleus *n* **:** the nucleus that remains in a female gamete after reduction and extrusion of polar bodies and that contains only one half of the number of chromosomes characteristic of its species — compare MALE PRONUCLEUS

female rhyme *n* **:** FEMININE RHYME

females *pl of* FEMALE

fem·cee \ˈfemˌsē\ *n* -S [blend of *female* and *emcee*] **:** a mistress of ceremonies esp. on a radio or television program

feme \ˈfem, ˈfēm\ *n* -S [AF, fr. OF, woman, wife, female, fr. L *femina* woman, female] **1** *also* **femme** \ˈfem\ **:** WIFE — used in heraldry correlatively with *baron* **2** *law* **:** WOMAN ⟨the ~ plaintiff⟩

feme cov·ert \ˌfemˈkəvərt, fēm-, -kōv-\ *also* **femme cou·verte** \ˌfemkü've(ə)rt\ *n, pl* **femes covert** *also* **femmes couvertes** \-mz(ˈ)k-\ [AF] *law* **:** a married woman — distinguished from *feme sole*

fem·er·ell \ˈfem(ə)rəl, -məˌrel\ *n* -S [ME *femerell, fumerel*, fr. MF *fumeraille* & *fumeril*, modif. of LL *fumariolum* vent, smoke hole — more at FUMAROLE] **:** a small open structure on a roof (as of a medieval kitchen) for ventilation **:** LOUVER

feme sole \ˈfemˈsōl, ˈfēm-\ *n, pl* **femes sole** \-m(z)ˈs-\ [AF] **1** *law* **:** a woman not in the married state — distinguished from *feme covert* **2** *law* **:** a married woman acting or contracting with respect to her separate estate

fem·ic \ˈfemik, fē-\ *adj* [*fe*rro*m*agnesian + *-ic*] **1 :** belonging to or being a group of mostly ferromagnesian minerals including amphibole and pyroxene **2 :** MAFIC

fem·i·nal \ˈfemənᵊl\ *adj* [L *femina* woman + E *-al*] **:** FEMININE — **fem·i·nal·i·ty** \ˌ==ˈnaləd·ē\ *n* -ES

fem·i·ne·i·ty \ˌ==ˈnēəd·ē\ *n* -ES [L *feminеus* womanly (fr. *femina* woman) + E *-ity*] **:** FEMININITY

fem·i·nie \ˈfemənē\ *n pl* [ME *femenie, feminie*, fr. MF, fr. OF, fr. L *femina* + OF *-ie* -y] **1 :** the world of women **:** WOMANKIND **2 :** a class of women **:** WOMEN ⟨when a man . . . wishes to go on a great duty . . . this selfishness on the part of the ~ is rather too much —Iris Origo⟩

¹**fem·i·nine** \ˈfemənən\ *adj* [ME *feminin, feminine*, fr. MF *feminin*, fr. L *femininus*, fr. *femina* woman, female + *-inus* -ine; akin to OE *delu* nipple, OHG *tila* female breast, ON *dilkr* sucking lamb, Goth *daddjan* to suckle, L *felare* to suck, suckle, *filius* son, *felix, fetus*, & *fecundus* fruitful, Gk *thēlys* female, *thēlē* nipple, Skt *dhayati* he sucks; basic meaning: to suck, suckle] **1 :** FEMALE 1a ⟨the ~ members of society⟩ ⟨the ~ lead in the play⟩ **2 :** characteristic of or appropriate or peculiar to women ⟨the gentler virtues which are especially ~⟩ **:** marked by or having features, attitudes, or qualities associated with women ⟨frilly ~ fashions⟩; *specif* **:** receiving or enduring action **:** PASSIVE ⟨each individual showing a mixture of masculine aggression and ~ tendencies⟩ **3 :** belonging to, connected with, or constituting the gender that ordinarily includes most words or grammatical forms referring to females ⟨the ~ gender⟩ ⟨a ~ noun⟩ ⟨a ~ form of an adjective⟩ ⟨a ~ ending⟩ — compare MASCULINE, NEUTER **4** *of a sign of the zodiac* **:** having a feminine influence ⟨beginning with Taurus alternate signs are ~⟩ **5 a :** having an unstressed and usu. hypermetric final syllable ⟨a line of iambic verse with a ~ ending⟩ **b :** having the final chord occurring on a weak beat ⟨music typified by ~ cadences⟩ **syn** see FEMALE

²**feminine** \"\ *n* -S [ME *feminin, feminine*, fr. *feminin, feminine*, adj.] **1 :** WOMAN ⟨sat serene, the eternal ~ of all the ages —Winston Churchill⟩ ⟨an anthology of fiction, articles, and cartoons all dealing with the ~ —Ward Moore⟩; *specif* **:** a markedly feminine woman or girl ⟨charming ~s and sloppy females⟩ **2 a :** a noun, pronoun, adjective, or inflectional form or class of the feminine gender **b :** the feminine gender

feminine caesura *n* **:** a caesura that follows an unstressed or short syllable — see EPIC CAESURA, LYRIC CAESURA

fem·i·nine·ly *adv* **:** in a feminine manner ⟨a ~ fair complexion⟩

fem·i·nine·ness \-nən(n)əs\ *n* -ES **:** the quality or state of being feminine

feminine rhyme *n* **:** double rhyme in verses with feminine endings (as *motion, ocean*)

fem·i·nin·i·ty \ˌfeməˈninəd·ē, -ətē, -i\ *n* -ES [ME *femininite*, fr. *feminin, feminine*, adj. + *-ite* -ity] **1 :** the quality or nature of the female sex **:** WOMANLINESS ⟨disarmed by her delicate ~⟩ ⟨accused of catty ~⟩ **2 :** WOMANISHNESS, EFFEMINACY ⟨the ~ of his manner⟩ **3 :** WOMEN, WOMANKIND ⟨neither in Oriental women nor in the confident ~ of his own country⟩

fem·i·nism \ˈ==ˌnizəm\ *n* -S [¹*feminine* + *-ism*] **1 :** the presence of female characteristics in males **2** [prob. fr. F *féminisme*, fr. *féminin* feminine + *-isme* -ism] **a :** the theory of the political, economic, and social equality of the sexes **b :** organized activity on behalf of women's rights and interests; *specif* **:** the 19th and 20th century movement seeking to remove restrictions that discriminate against women

¹**fem·i·nist** \-ˌnəst\ *n* -S [F *féministe*, fr. *féminin* feminine + *-iste* -ist] **:** one that advocates or practices feminism

²**feminist** \"\ *also* **fem·i·nis·tic** \ˌ==ˈnistik\ *adj* **:** of or relating to feminism

fe·min·i·ty \feˈminəd·ē\ *n* -ES [ME *feminite*, fr. MF *feminité*, fr. OF, fr. *feminin* feminine + *-ité* -ity] **:** FEMININITY

fem·i·ni·za·tion \ˌfemənəˈzāshən, -ˌnīˈz-\ *n* -S **:** the process or condition of being feminized; *specif* **:** development of female characteristics in a male or castrate

fem·i·nize \ˈfeməˌnīz\ *vt* -ED/-ING/-S [F *féminiser*, fr. MF, fr. *feminin* feminine + *-iser* -ize] **1 :** to give a feminine quality to ⟨changes that ~ the hat⟩ ⟨influences that will ~ their robust morality⟩ **2 :** to cause (a male or castrate) to take on feminine characters (as by implantation of ovaries or administration of estrogenic substances) **3 :** to cause (as a population) to be made up more of females than of males **:** render preponderantly feminine in composition ⟨low salaries have *feminized* the teaching profession⟩

femino- *comb form* [L *femina* — more at FEMININE] **:** woman ⟨*feminology*⟩

¹**femme** *var of* FEME

²**femme** *or* **fem** \ˈfem\ *n* -S [F *femme*, fr. L *femina*] *slang* **:** WOMAN 1

femme couverte *var of* FEME COVERT

femme du monde \ˌfemdüˈmänd, *F* fȧmdümōⁿd\ *n, pl* **femmes du monde** \"\ [F, lit., woman of the world] **:** a sophisticated or worldly woman

femme fa·tale \ˌfemfəˈtal, ˌfam-, fǟm-, -fəˈtäl,fäˈtäl, *F* fȧmfȧtȧl\ *n, pl* **femmes fatales** \-mf . . . al(z), -äl(z), *F* -mf . . . ȧl\ [F, lit., disastrous woman] **1 :** a seductive woman who lures men into dangerous or compromising situations **:** SIREN ⟨the glittering eye of a *femme fatale* in any Hollywood film —Katherine Anne Porter⟩ **2 :** a woman who attracts men by an aura of charm and mystery ⟨vying for the attention of a young *femme fatale* —E.D.Radin⟩

femora *pl of* FEMUR

¹**fem·o·ral** \ˈfemərəl\ *adj* [LL *femoralis*, fr. L *femor, femur* thigh, femur + *-alis* -al] **:** of, relating to, or located near the femur or thigh

²**femoral** \"\ *n* -S **:** either of two femoral shields of the plastron of a turtle

femoral artery *n* **:** the chief artery of the thigh lying in the anterior inner part of the thigh and being undivided as far as a point about two inches below Poupart's ligament where it divides into (1) a large deep branch and (2) a smaller superficial branch — called also respectively (1) *deep femoral artery*, (2) *superficial femoral artery*

femoral canal *n* **:** the space between the femoral vein and the inner wall of the femoral sheath, being from a quarter to half an inch long and extending from the femoral ring to the saphenous opening

femoral nerve *n* **:** the largest branch of the lumbar plexus that in man comes from the 2d, 3d, and 4th lumbar nerves and supplies extensor muscles of the thigh and skin areas on the front of the thigh and medial surface of the leg and foot and that sends articular branches to the hip and knee joints — called also *anterior crural nerve*

femoral ring *n* **:** the oval upper opening of the femoral canal often the seat of a hernia — see CRURAL SEPTUM

femoral sheath *n* **:** the fascial sheath investing the femoral vessels

femoral triangle *or* **femoral trigone** *n* **:** SCARPA'S TRIANGLE

femoral vein *n* **:** the chief vein of the thigh constituting a continuation of the popliteal vein that accompanies the femoral artery in the upper part of its course and continues above Poupart's ligament as the external iliac vein

femoro- *comb form* [NL, fr. L *femor-, femur* thigh] **:** femoral ⟨*femorocele*⟩ **:** femoral and ⟨*femorofibular*⟩

fem·o·ro·tibial index \ˌfemə(ˌ)rō+ . . . -\ *n* [*femoro-* + *tibial*] **:** the ratio of the length of the femur to the length of the tibia multiplied by 100 ⟨compared the *femorotibial indexes* of fossil men and modern anthropoids⟩

fe·mur \ˈfēmə(r)\ *n, pl* **femurs** \-ə(r)z\ *or* **fem·o·ra** \ˈfemərə\ [L] **1 :** one of the three flat narrow spaces separating the grooves of a triglyph **:** SHANK **2 a :** the proximal bone of the hind or lower limb that is in man the longest and largest bone, extending from the hip to the knee, articulating above with the acetabulum by a rounded head connected with the shaft of the bone by an oblique neck that bears a pair of trochanters for the attachment of muscles, and articulating with the tibia below by a pair of condyles — called also *thighbone* **b :** THIGH **3** [NL, fr. L] **a :** the segment of an insect's leg that is third from the body, is often enlarged, and constitutes the principle horizontal element **b :** MEROPODITE

¹**fen** \ˈfen\ *n* -S [ME, fr. OE *fenn* marsh, mud, dirt; akin to OHG *fenna* marsh, ON *fen*, Goth *fani* clay, Skt *paṅka* mud, mire] **:** low peaty land covered wholly or partly with water unless artificially drained

²**fen** \"\ *dial var of* FEND

³**fen** \"\ *also* **fan** \ˈfan\ *or* **fin** \ˈfin\ *or* **vents** \ˈven(t)s\ *interj* [prob. alter. of ¹*fend*] — used as a ritual call by children esp. in certain games (as marbles) to prevent certain actions by an opponent or teammate or to exempt the first caller from a task or action

⁴**fen** \ˈfən\ *or* **fan** \ˈfän\ *n* -S [Chin (Pek) *fên¹*] **:** CANDAREEN 1

fenagle *var of* FINAGLE

¹**fence** \ˈfen(t)s\ *n* -S *often attrib* [ME *fens*, short for *defens* — more at DEFENSE] **1** *archaic* **:** a means of protection or security **:** DEFENSE ⟨my whole body wanted a ~ against heat and cold —Jonathan Swift⟩ **2 a :** a barrier intended to prevent escape or intrusion or to mark a boundary ⟨large areas of range were put under ~⟩: as (1) **:** a structure of posts and boards, wire, pickets, or rails commonly used as an enclosure for a field or yard ⟨erected a ~ that was horse high, hog tight, and bull strong⟩ (2) **:** something legally constituting an enclosure around land (as a bank of earth high enough to confine livestock) **b :** something resembling a fence in appearance or function ⟨a teapot rimmed with a silver ~⟩ ⟨a ~ of mountains around the valley⟩ ⟨built a radar ~ across the continent⟩ **:** an immaterial barrier or boundary line ⟨erected legislative ~s to control the development of industrial and residential areas⟩ ⟨on the other side of the ~ in the argument⟩ **c** (1) **:** an obstacle met in fox hunting that can be jumped (as a fence, hedge, brook, or chicken coop) (2) **:** an artificial obstacle on the course of a steeplechase or horse show **:** JUMP **d :** FENCING 3 **3 :** FENCING 4 ⟨books of ~⟩ **4 a :** a receiver of stolen property **:** a dealer in stolen goods **b :** a place where stolen goods are bought and sold **5 a :** an attachment to a plane, saw bench, or woodworking machine that controls the location or extent of the cut — see BEADING PLANE illustration **b :** an attachment to a marking gauge that serves to guide the marking **6 :** a projection on a lock forming an obstruction to throwing the bolt except when the gatings of the tumblers are properly arranged (as by the key) to allow the fence to pass **7 :** a means of political support for an officeholder, candidate, or institution **:** a political interest — usu. used in pl. ⟨building his ~s for election as governor —*Springfield* (*Mass.*) *Daily News*⟩ ⟨the tedious, tricky, and often tense art of diplomatic *fence*-mending —*Newsweek*⟩ **8 :** a fixed plate that projects from the upper surface of an airplane wing and sometimes continues around the leading edge, that is substantially parallel to the airstream, and that is used to prevent spanwise flow — called also *stall fence* — **on the fence :** in a position of neutrality or indecision ⟨some who had been *on the fence* came out in favor of the plan⟩

²**fence** \"\ *vb* -ED/-ING/-S [ME *fensen*, fr. *fens*, n.] *vt* **1 a :** to surround, separate, or delineate with or as if with a fence **:** erect a fence around or along (as a field or boundary) ⟨he *fenced* his yard with white pickets⟩ ⟨mountains ~ in the valley⟩ ⟨~ off a corner of the sea with dikes⟩ ⟨the canonical books are those the church has *fenced* off from other writings⟩ **b :** to keep in or out with or as if with a fence: as (1) **:** to secure in an enclosure **:** CONFINE ⟨~ sheep⟩ (2) **:** to restrict the activity of ⟨minds that were *fenced* round with dogma⟩ (3) **:** to ward off **:** REPEL, EXCLUDE ⟨laws that ~ out undesirable immigrants⟩ **2 :** to provide a defense or screen for **:** give security to **:** PROTECT ⟨a motorcycle escort on each side *fenced* the celebrity's limousine⟩ **:** SHIELD ⟨she had *fenced* his tatters even from her own eyes —Mary King⟩ **:** HEDGE ⟨~s his doctrines with the specious plea that statesmen must live as the world lives —*Times Lit. Supp.*⟩ **3** *Scots law* **a :** to open the proceedings of (the parliament or a court of law) with a form of words forbidding persons to interrupt or obstruct the proceedings unnecessarily **b :** to secure or strengthen (a provision in a contract) by a condition (as by a clause imposing forfeiture) **4 :** to sell (stolen property) with criminal intent **:** dispose of (stolen goods) gainfully esp. to a fence ⟨the gang stole cars and *fenced* them themselves⟩ — compare RECEIVE **5 :** to turn aside **:** EVADE, PARRY ⟨the chairman ~s awkward questions⟩ **~** *vi* **1 a :** to practice the art of fencing ⟨he ~s daily with a skilled foilsman⟩ **b :** to use tactics of attack and defense resembling those of fencing (as thrusting, guarding, parrying) ⟨the tennis players *fenced* for an opening⟩ **c :** to baffle inquiry by equivocation or evasion **:** parry arguments by shifting ground ⟨he ~s skillfully on the witness stand⟩ **2** *obs* **:** to provide protection or security **:** guard or defend oneself — used with *against* ⟨a constant endeavor to ~ against the infirmities of ill health —Laurence Sterne⟩ **3 :** to leap a fence — used of a horse and rider or a greyhound ⟨the hunter ~s leaving a safe but not wasteful space above the jump⟩ **4 :** to build or repair a fence ⟨when farmers *fenced* with rails⟩ **syn** see DODGE, ENCLOSE — **fence the tables** *in Scottish Presbyterian churches* **:** to make a solemn address to those who present themselves to commune at the Lord's Supper on the conditions prerequisite to the service in order to hinder those who are unworthy from approaching the table

fence arbor *n* **:** an arbor connecting the spindle and tumblers of a combination lock

fence law *n* **:** one of the laws enacted by most states regulating the erection and maintenance of a fence sufficient to prevent trespass by livestock on cultivated ground ⟨two angry factions: the crop people who wanted *fence laws*, and the stock people who wanted free range —Carl Withers⟩

fence·less \-ləs\ *adj* **1 :** being without enclosure ⟨the ~ prairies of the old West⟩ **2** *archaic* **:** being without defense ⟨marked his ~ dwelling for their wrath —C.G.D.Roberts⟩ — **fence·less·ness** *n* -ES

fence lizard *n* **1 :** PINE LIZARD **2 :** AMERICAN CHAMELEON

fence month *n* **:** the closed season for deer in England lasting from June 9 to July 9

fence nail *n* **:** a heavy cut nail of tapered cross section used in building fences

fence-off \ˈ=ˌ=\ *n* -S [²*fence* + *off* (as in *play-off*)] **:** a fencing bout for deciding a tie between individuals or teams

fenc·er \ˈfen(t)sə(r)\ *n* -S **1 :** one that fences as: **a :** one who practices the art of fencing **:** SWORDSMAN **b :** one who builds or repairs fences **c :** a horse trained to jump fences **2 :** an electric-fence controller

fence rider *n* **:** a ranch hand who inspects and repairs fences

fence·row \ˈ=ˌrō\ *n* [¹*fence* + *row*] **:** the land occupied by a fence including the uncultivated area on each side

fences *pl of* FENCE, *pres 3d sing of* FENCE

fence-sitter \ˈ=ˌ==\ *n* [¹*fence* + *sitter*] **:** an undecided or neutral person ⟨whether he is a *fence-sitter* by conviction or is waiting to see which side wins⟩

fence-sitting \ˈ=ˌ==\ *n* [¹*fence* + *sitting* (n.)] **:** a state of indecision or neutrality with respect to conflicting positions ⟨his reluctance to commit himself publicly has the appearance of *fence-sitting*⟩

fence viewer *n* **:** a local official who administers the fence laws (as by inspection of new fence and settlement of disputes arising from trespass by livestock that have escaped enclosure)

fen·chene \ˈfenˌchēn\ *n* -S [G *fenchen*, fr. *fenchel* fennel (fr. OHG *fenihhal*, fr. L *feniculum*) + G *-en* -ene — more at FENNEL] **:** any of several isomeric liquid terpenes $C_{10}H_{16}$ obtained esp. by dehydration of fenchyl alcohol

fen·chol \-ˌchōl, -ōl\ *n* -S [ISV *fench*ene + *-ol*] **:** FENCHYL ALCOHOL

fen·chone \-ˌchōn\ *n* -S [G *fenchon*, fr. *fenchel* fennel + *-on* -one] **:** an oily terpenoid ketone $C_{10}H_{16}O$ that is isomeric with camphor and has a camphoraceous odor, that exists in three optically different forms, occurring as the dextrorotatory form esp. in fennel oil and as the levorotatory form in thuja oil, and that is used chiefly as a pine scent; 1,3,3-trimethyl-2-keto-norbornane

fen·chyl alcohol \-ˌchil-, -ˌchəl-\ *n* [ISV *fench*ene + *-yl*] **:** either of two stereoisomeric alcohols $C_{10}H_{17}OH$ made by hydrogenation of fenchone; *esp* **:** the solid racemic alpha-fenchyl alcohol obtained from pine oil from the stumps of southern pine

¹**fen·ci·ble** \ˈfen(t)səbəl\ *adj* [ME *fensable, fensible*, short for *defensable, defensible* — more at DEFENSIBLE] **1** *chiefly Scot, of a man* **a :** capable of defending or bearing arms for his country **b :** eligible for military service **2** *archaic* **:** capable of being defended ⟨this old tower . . . is ~ —Sir Walter Scott⟩ **3 :** being of the corps of fencibles ⟨~ and militia regiments⟩

²**fencible** \"\ *n* -S **:** a soldier in a corps enlisted only for home service and for the duration of a war esp. in Britain and the U.S. during the second half of the 18th and first half of the 19th centuries

fencing *n* -S [ME *fensing*, fr. gerund of *fensen* to protect — more at FENCE] **1 :** FENCE 2a(1) ⟨makeshift ~ blocked the gaps between the buildings⟩ **2 :** the fences of a property or region ⟨the ~ of the farm was in poor repair⟩ **3 :** material used in building a fence **4 :** the art or practice of attack and defense with foil, epee, or saber which has as its object the scoring of a touch and for which blunted weapons and usu. protective clothing and masks are used — compare PARRY

fencing patent *n* **:** a patent broader in scope than the product or process actually intended to be manufactured thereunder that is procured to hinder competitors — called also *blocking patent*

¹**fend** \ˈfend\ *vb* -ED/-ING/-S [ME *fenden*, short for *defenden* — more at DEFEND] *vt* **1 :** DEFEND, PROTECT ⟨~*ing* himself from her clamor —Elizabeth M. Roberts⟩ **2 a :** to keep off **:** prevent from entering or hitting **:** ward off **:** REPEL ⟨raised his arm up to ~ branches from his eyes⟩ — often used with *off* ⟨her policy of ~*ing* off her suitor was no good; she would have to rebuff him —Rex Ingamells⟩ **b :** to push or keep (a boat) from a shore, dock, or ship **:** SHOVE — often used with *off* **3** *dial Brit* **:** to provide for **:** SUPPORT **~** *vi* **1** *dial Brit* **a :** to make an effort **:** STRUGGLE **b :** to get along **:** FARE **2 a :** to look out (for oneself) **:** MANAGE ⟨parents who go out and leave their young children to ~ for themselves⟩ **b :** to supply a livelihood (as for oneself) **:** PROVIDE ⟨told at the age of 18 to ~ for himself⟩ ⟨three children to ~ for⟩

²**fend** \"\ *n* -S *chiefly Scot* **:** an effort or attempt esp. at self-support ⟨he makes a good ~⟩

fend·er \ˈfendə(r)\ *n* -S *often attrib* [ME *fendour*, fr. *fenden*, v. + *-our* -or] **1 :** a device attached or set up to prevent something from sustaining or inflicting damage: as **a** (1) **:** a buffer (as a camel or pudding) between a ship and wharf or between two ships that absorbs and distributes shock and prevents

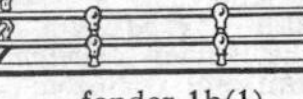
fender 1b(1)

chafing (2) **:** a pile or a row or cluster of piles placed to protect a dock or bridge pier from damage by docking ships or floating objects (3) **:** a timber or other obstruction set up to protect a scaffold base from impact or interference **b** (1) **:** a low often ornamental fence of iron or brass set before a hearth to confine coals and ashes — see CURB 5g (2) **:** FIRE SCREEN **c :** a device in front of a locomotive or streetcar that is designed to catch or throw aside an object struck **d** (1) **:** a guard or protective covering over a wheel of an automobile or other vehicle (2) *Brit* **:** [4]BUMPER 2a **e :** a rail in a farrowing pen that prevents the sow from crushing the little pigs against the wall when she lies down **f :** a sheet temporarily inserted between the pastedown and flyleaf of a book in the course of binding to protect the pages (as from paste and pressure on the covers) **g :** an oblong or triangular shield of leather attached to the stirrup leather of a saddle to protect a rider's legs — see STOCK SADDLE illustration **2 :** a strip of stiff paper glued to the tympan of a platen press to prevent the sheets from sliding over the feed guides

fender bar *n* **:** a long fore-and-aft fender for a ship

fender beam *n* **1 :** the inclined advance piece of an icebreaker **2 :** the horizontal top beam into which the posts of a saw gate are framed

fender bolt *n* **1 :** a bolt with a projecting head designed to protect the adjacent parts **2 :** a bolt securing a fender

fender boom *n* **:** a boom used to keep floating logs in a course

fend·ered \'fendə(r)d\ *adj* [*fender* + *-ed*] **:** protected with a fender ‹the ship should be well ~ amidships›

fend·er·ing \-d(ə)riŋ\ *n* -s [*fender* + *-ing*] **:** material used for fenders (as on a ship)

fen·der·less \-dələs, -dᵊl-\ *adj* **:** having no fenders

fender post *n* **:** one of the guiding stanchions of a saw gate

fender skid *n* **:** a log placed on the lower side of a skidding trail to keep the logs on the trail

fender skirt *n* **:** a panel that fits flush with the side of an automobile fender and conceals the upper part of a wheel

fender stool *n* **:** a long stool placed near or extending from a fireplace fender

fendy \'fendi\ *adj* [[1]*fend* + *-y*] **1** *chiefly Scot* **:** capable and resourceful (as at managing and providing) **2** *dial Brit* **:** ECONOMICAL, THRIFTY

feneration *n* -s [L *faeneration-, faeneratio*, fr. *faeneratus, feneratus* (past part. of *faenerari, fenerari* to lend on interest, irreg. fr. *faenor-, faenus, fenor-, fenus* interest) + *-ion-, -io* -ion — more at FAENUS] *obs* **:** the act or practice of lending money on interest **:** USURY

fen·es·tel·la \,fenə'stelə\ *n* [L, small opening or window, dim. of *fenestra* window] **1** -s **a :** a niche like a window in the south wall of the sanctuary near the altar (as of a Roman Catholic church) containing the piscina and often also the credence **b :** a small window or opening like a window (as in an altar front for allowing relics within to be seen) **2** *cap* [NL, fr. L, small window] **:** a genus (the type of the family Fenestellidae) of Paleozoic bryozoans whose colonies form lacy fronds — compare LACE BRYOZOAN

fen·es·tel·lid \-eləd\ *n* -s [NL *Fenestellidae*, family of bryozoans, fr. *Fenestella*, type genus + *-idae*] **:** a bryozoan of the genus *Fenestella* or the family Fenestellidae

fen·es·tel·loid \¦==¦=,lȯid\ *adj* [NL *Fenestella* + E *-oid*] **:** resembling or related to the genus *Fenestella*

fe·nes·tra \fə'nestrə\ *n, pl* **fenes·trae** \-,strē, -,strī\ [NL, fr. L, opening in a wall for air and light, window] **1** *anat* **:** a small opening; *esp* **:** either of two membrane-covered apertures in the bone between the middle and inner ear: (1) an oval opening between the middle ear and the vestibule having the base of the stapes or columella attached to its membrane and (2) a round opening between the middle ear and the cochlea — called also respectively (1) *fenestra ova·lis* \-ō'vāləs, -väl-, -val-\ or *fenestra ves·ti·bu·li* \-ve'stibyə,lī\ and (2) *fenestra ro·tun·da* \-rō'təndə\ or *fenestra coch·le·ae* \-'käklē,ē, -lē,ī\ **2 a :** an opening like a window cut in bone (as in the inner ear in the fenestration operation) **b :** a window cut in a surgical instrument (as an endoscope) **3 a :** a transparent spot (as in the wings of certain moths) **b :** one of two pits covered with membrane on the head of certain cockroaches **c :** the fontanel of a termite

[1]**fe·nes·tral** \-,strəl\ *n* -s [ME, fr. MF, fr. OF, window, opening, fr. *fenestre*, fr. L *fenestra*] **:** a casement or window sash closed with cloth or translucent paper instead of glass

[2]**fenestral** \"\ *adj* [L *fenestra* + E *-al*] **1 :** of or relating to a window **2** [NL *fenestra* + E *-al*] **:** of or relating to, or having a fenestra

fe·nes·trate \fə'ne,strāt, 'fenə,s-\ *adj* [L *fenestratus*] **:** FENESTRATED 2

fen·es·trat·ed \'fenə,strād·əd, fə'ne,s-\ *adj* [L *fenestratus* (past part. of *fenestrare* to provide with openings or windows, fr. *fenestra* opening, window) + E *-ed*] **1 :** provided with or characterized by windows ‹symmetrically ~ buildings› **2 :** having one or more openings or transparent spots **:** PERFORATED ‹~ forceps with loops at the grasping end› **:** RETICULATED ‹part of the dress may be flimsy, ~, or transparent —P.M.Gregory› ‹the ~ leaves of some plants›

fenestrated membrane *n* **:** an elastic membrane of the inner coat of large arteries composed of broad elastic fibers that become fused to form a perforated sheet

fen·es·tra·tion \,fenə'strāshən\ *n* -s [L *fenestratus* + E *-ion*] **1 a :** the arrangement, proportioning, and design of windows and doors in a building **b** (1) **:** openings admitting daylight to a building ‹classroom ~ consists of glass block panels over continuous windows› (2) **:** the furnishing of a building with fenestration ‹~ with louvered wall and continuous windows to control the amount and distribution of daylight› **2 a :** an opening or break in a surface (as in a wall or membrane) ‹the level of brightness at the ~s› **b :** the presence of such openings **3** *or* **fenestration operation :** the operation of cutting an opening in the bony labyrinth between the inner ear and tympanum to replace natural fenestrae that are not functional because of sclerotic or other changes and to improve hearing impaired by such fenestrae

fen·es·tra·to \,fenə'sträd·(,)ō\ *n* -s [It *finestrato*, adj., provided with windows, fr. L *fenestratus*, past part. of *fenestrare*] **:** a group of windows considered as a single window divided by mullions or colonnettes (as in Venetian palaces)

fe·nes·trule \fə'ne,strül\ *n* -s [L *fenestrula* small window, dim. of *fenestra* opening, window] **:** one of the small openings between intersecting branches of a lacy bryozoan colony

fen fire *n* [[1]*fen*] **:** IGNIS FATUUS

fêng huang *or* **fung-hwang** \'fəŋ'(h)wäŋ\ *n* [Chin (Pek) *fêng*[4] *huang*[2], fr. *fêng*[4] male phoenix + *huang*[2] female phoenix] **1 :** the bird that in Chinese myth watches with the dragon, tortoise, and kylin over the empire and appears in times of prosperity and that is often represented in art as composite in appearance sometimes as a symbol of the empress **2 :** a bird with rich plumage and graceful form and movement domestic in the former imperial court of China, associated with the mythical fêng huang as an emblem of good fortune, and identified by some with the ocellated argus

feng·ki·eh \'fəŋjē¦ä\ *adj, usu cap* [fr. *Fengkieh* (Kweichow), city in Szechwan, central China] **:** of or from the city of Fengkieh, China **:** of the kind or style prevalent in Fengkieh

fen groundsel *n* [[1]*fen*] **:** either of two European groundsels (*Senecio paludosus* and *S. palustris*) found in wet places

fêng shui \'fəŋ'shwā\ *n* [Chin (Pek) *fêng*[1] *shui*[3], lit., wind and water, fr. *fêng*[1] wind + *shui*[3] water] **:** a system of geomancy employed in China to bring practice into harmony with natural forces (as in determining the site of a grave or house)

[1]**fe·nian** \'fēnēən, -nyən\ *n* -s *usu cap* [modif. (influenced by *Feni* ancient inhabitants of Ireland) of IrGael *fēinne* (pl. of *fiann* band of Fenians) + E *-ian*] **1 :** one of a legendary band of warriors who defended Ireland in the 2d and 3d centuries A.D. ‹the cycle of romance describing the battles, hunts, and rivalries of the *Fenians*› **2 :** a member of a secret organization consisting mainly of Irishmen and men of Irish birth or ancestry and having for its aim the overthrow of British rule in Ireland

[2]**fenian** \"\ *adj, usu cap* **:** of, relating to, or characteristic of the Fenians ‹*Fenian* conspirators›

fe·nian·ism \-ə,nizəm\ *n* -s *usu cap* **:** the principles and practices of the Fenians ‹embers of the old *Fenianism* were quickened into flame —*Manchester Guardian Weekly*›

fen·land \'fen,land, -lənd\ *n* [[1]*fen* + *land*] **:** an area of low often marshy ground ‹towns of the ~› — often used in pl. ‹undrained marsh and ~s of considerable extent —*Ecology*›

fen·man \-mən\ *n, pl* **fenmen** [[1]*fen* + *man*] **:** an inhabitant of a fen esp. of the lowlands of southeastern Lincolnshire and adjacent English counties known as the Fens

fen·nec \'fenik\ *n* -s [Ar *fanak*] **:** a small African fox (*Fennecus zerda*) of a pale fawn color that is remarkable for the large size of its ears; *sometimes* **:** any of various related foxes

fen·nel \'fenᵊl\ *n* -s [ME *fenel*, fr. OE *finugl, finul, finol*, fr. (assumed) VL *fenuculum*, fr. L *feniculum, faeniculum*, dim. of *fenum, faenum* hay; perh. akin to L *fetus* fruitful — more at FEMININE] **1 :** a perennial European herb (*Foeniculum vulgare*) adventive in No. America and cultivated for the aromatic flavor of its seeds **2 :** the seed of the fennel **3 :** a staminate plant of the hemp (*Cannabis sativa*)

fennel-flower \'==,=\ *n* **:** NIGELLA 2

fennel oil *n* **:** a colorless or pale yellow essential oil obtained from fennel seed and used chiefly as a flavoring material

fennel seed *n* [ME *fenel-seed*, fr. OE *finolsǣd*, fr. *finol* fennel + *sǣd* seed — more at SEED] **1 :** the seed of fennel **2 :** the seed of a fennel-flower (*Nigella sativa*) sometimes used as a condiment

fennel water *n* **:** a saturated solution of fennel oil in distilled water used as a stimulant and carminative

fen nightingale *n* **:** a croaking frog

fenno- *comb form, usu cap* [Sw, fr. L *Fenni* Finns] **1 :** Finnish and ‹*Fenno*-German› **2 :** including Finland ‹*Fenno*-Scandinavia›

fen·no·man \¦fenō¦män\ *n* -s *usu cap* [Sw, fr. *fenno-* + *-man* maniac, fr. F *-mane*, back-formation fr. *manie* mania) — more at BIBLIOMANIA] **:** a partisan of the nationalist movement in Finland that began in the middle of the 19th century by advocating the use and cultivation of the Finnish language — compare SWEKOMAN

fen·no·scan·di·an \¦fe(,)nō¦skandēən\ *adj, usu cap* [*Fennoscandia*, the part of northern Europe comprising Finland, Sweden, Norway, and Denmark + E *-an*] **:** of or relating to the region of Fennoscandia ‹the *Fennoscandian* ice cap . . . had central thickness not far from three miles —R.A.Daly›

fen·ny \'fenē, -ni\ *adj* [ME, fr. OE *fennig*, fr. *fenn* marsh + *-ig* -y — more at FEN] **1 :** having the characteristics of a fen **:** BOGGY ‹the ~ ground along the lake shore› **2 :** peculiar to or found in a fen ‹long ~ grass› ‹fillet of a ~ snake, in the caldron boil and bake —Shak.›

fen orchid *or* **fen orchis** *n* **:** a small terrestrial orchid (*Liparis loeselii*) of eastern No. America and Europe with two nearly basal leaves and racemose irregular flowers

fen·ouil·let *or* **fen·ouil·lette** \¦fenᵊl¦et\ *n* -s [F *fenouillette*, lit., small fennel, dim. of *fenouil* fennel, fr. MF *fenoil*, fr. (assumed) VL *fenuculum* — more at FENNEL] **:** a liqueur flavored with fennel seed

fens *pl of* FEN

fen·ster \'fenztə(r), -n(t)st-\ *n* -s [G, lit., window, fr. OHG; akin to OE *fenester* window, MLG & MD *venster, venstere*; all fr. a prehistoric WGmc word borrowed fr. L *fenestra*] **:** an erosional opening down through overthrust rock exposing the underlying rock — called also *window*

fent \'fent\ *n* -s [ME *fente, fent*, fr. MF *fente* — more at VENT (hole)] **1** *dial Eng* **:** a slit or opening in a garment; *esp* **:** a neck opening or placket **2 :** a remnant of cloth; *specif* **:** a short and often imperfect end or length of finished fabric

fen·u·greek \'fen(y)ə,grēk, -nē,g-\ *also* **foenn·greek** \-n,g-\ *or* **foen·u·greek** \-n(y)ə,g-, -nē,g-\ *n* [ME *fenigrek*, fr. MF & L; MF *fenegrec, fenugrec*, fr. L *fenum Graecum, faenumgraecum*, lit., Greek hay, fr. *fenum, faenum* hay + *Graecum*, neut. of *Graecus* Greek — more at FENNEL, GREEK] **:** a leguminous annual Asiatic herb (*Trigonella foenumgraecum*) with aromatic seeds used in making curry, imitation vanilla flavoring, and some veterinary medicines

fenus *var of* FAENUS

feod \'fyüd\ *n* -s [ML *feodum*] *obs* **:** [3]FEUD — **feod·al** \-dᵊl\ *adj, obs* — **feo·dal·i·ty** \fyü'daləd·ē\ *n* -ES *obs*

feo·da·ry \'fyüdərē\ *n* -ES [ME, fr. ML *feodarius*, fr. *feodum* + L *-arius* -ary] **1 a :** a feudal tenant **:** VASSAL **b :** SUBJECT, DEPENDENT, SERVANT **2 :** an officer of the ancient English Court of Wards appointed to receive rents **3** [influenced in meaning by L *foeder-, foedus* league — more at FEDERAL] *obs* **:** CONFEDERATE, ACCOMPLICE **4** [ME, fr. ML *feodarium*, fr. *feodum* + L *-arium* -ary] **:** a book compiling the details of feudal duties and services

feo·dum \'fyüdəm, 'feüd-\ *n, pl* **feo·da** \-də\ [ML *feodum, feudum* — more at FEUD (estate)] **:** [3]FEUD — opposed to *alodium*

feoff \'fef, 'fēf\ *vt* -ED/-ING/-S [ME *feffen, feoffen*, fr. AF *feoffer* & OF *fieffer*, fr. *fiu, fief* fief — more at FEE (estate)] **:** to invest with a fee or feud **:** put in possession of a freehold interest in corporeal hereditament or of a leasehold **:** ENFEOFF

feoff·ee \(')fe¦fē, (')fē¦fē\ *n* -s [ME *feffe, feoffe*, fr. AF *feoffé*, past part. of *feoffer*, v.] **:** the person to whom a feoffment is made **:** the person enfeoffed; *specif* **:** a trustee in England invested with a freehold estate (as a member of certain boards holding land for public uses)

feoff·ment \'fefmənt, 'fēf-\ *n* -s [ME *feffement, feoffement*, fr. AF, fr. *feffer, feoffer*, v. + *-ment*] **1 :** the granting of a feudal fee **2 :** the act of granting a freehold estate in land by actual delivery of possession orig. by livery of seizin **3 :** a deed of enfeoffment

feof·for \'fefər, 'fēf-, (')=¦fō(ə)r\ *or* **feoff·er** \'=fər\ *n* -s [ME *feoffor, feffour*, fr. AF *feoffour*, fr. *feoffer*, v. + *-our* -or] **:** one that makes a feoffment to another **:** one that enfeoffs

FEP *abbr* fore edges painted

fer \'fər(·), 'fə(r)\ *dial var of* FAR

-fer \,fə(r)\ *n comb form* -s [F & L; F *-fère*, fr. L *-fer* (n. & adj. comb. form), fr. *ferre* to bear, carry — more at BEAR] **:** one that bears ‹aquifer› ‹conifer›

fe·ra·cious \fə'rāshəs\ *adj* [L *ferac-, ferax* (fr. *ferre* to bear) + E *-ious*] **:** producing abundantly **:** PROLIFIC, FRUITFUL ‹a world so ~, teeming with endless results —Thomas Carlyle›

fe·rae \'fe,rī; 'fe,rē, 'fi,-\ *n pl, cap* [NL, fr. L, wild animals, fr. fem. pl. of *ferus*, adj., wild — more at FIERCE] **1** *in some classifications* **:** a subdivision of Mammalia coextensive with Carnivora **2** *in some former classifications* **:** a subdivision of Mammalia comprising Carnivora together with a varied assemblage of chiefly carnivorous marsupials, bats, insectivores, rodents, and primates

ferae na·tu·rae \'fe,rīnə'tü,rē; 'fe,rēnə'tü,rē, 'fi,-\ *adj* [L, of a wild nature] *of an animal* **:** wild by nature **:** not usu. tamed — used of such animals as foxes and wild ducks in which at the common law no one can claim absolute property although a qualified property may be obtained by capturing them, by owning the land on which they are found, or by having a special privilege of hunting them

fer·a·ghan *or* **fer·e·ghan** \¦ferə¦gän\ *n* -s *usu cap* [fr. *Fergana, Ferghana*, region in west central Asia (fr. Per *Farghāna*)] **:** a usu. small heavy Persian rug chiefly of cotton having usu. a web and a fringed end, a deep blue or rose field with an allover herati sometimes guli hinnai design and a main border with a turtle design, and being highly prized if antique

[1]**fe·ral** \'firəl, 'fer-\ *adj* [ML *feralis*, fr. L *fera* wild animal (fr. fem. of *ferus* wild) + *-alis* -al] **1 a :** suggestive of a beast of prey ‹~ teeth›; *specif* **:** characterized by inhuman ferocity ‹the ~ hostility of his fellow officers as they denounced and judged him —Albert Hubbell› **b :** being, characteristic of, or suggesting an animal in the state of nature ‹the human and ~ inhabitants of the forest› ‹as ~ in her wariness as the fierce . . . dogs that stalked the countryside —Ann F. Wolfe› **c :** lacking a human personality due to being reared in isolation from all or nearly all human contacts **:** not socialized ‹~ children who had been adopted by wolves› **2 a :** existing in a state of nature **:** not domesticated or cultivated ‹~ and semidomestic animals› **b :** having escaped from domestication and become wild ‹several species introduced by settlers soon became ~› **syn** see BRUTAL

[2]**feral** \"\ *adj* [L *feralis*] **1** *archaic* **:** causing death **:** DEADLY, FATAL ‹thence come . . . ~ diseases —Robert Burton› **2 :** of or relating to the dead **:** FUNEREAL, GLOOMY ‹in ~ order slow the slaughter barges go —F.T.Palgrave›

fe·ra·lia \fə'rālēə\ *n pl, cap* [L, fr. neut. pl. of *feralis* of the dead] **:** public religious ceremonies of ancient Rome held in honor of the dead upon the last day of the Parentalia — compare MANES

fe·rash *also* **far·rash** *or* **fer·rash** \fə'räsh\ *n* -ES [Hindi *farrāsh*, fr. Ar, spreader of carpets] **:** an Oriental servant (as in the Indian subcontinent) usu. employed in menial work

fer·bam \'fər,bam, 'fe(ə)r,-\ *n* -s [*ferric dimethyl-dithiocarbamate*] **:** a fungicide $[(CH_3)_2NCSS]_3Fe$ obtained as a black powder; ferric dimethyl-dithiocarbamate

fer·ber·ite \'fərbə,rīt, 'fer-\ *n* -s [G *ferberit*, fr. Rudolph *Ferber*, 19th cent. German + G *-it* -ite] **:** a mineral $FeWO_4$ consisting of a valuable ferrous tungstate occurring in black granular masses

fer-de-lance \¦ferdə¦lan(t)s, ¦fər-, -lȧn-\ *n, pl* **fer-de-lance** [F, lit., lance iron, spearhead] **:** a large extremely venomous pit viper (*Bothrops atrox*) that has a horny spine terminating the tail and that is widely distributed in Central and So. America and in some of the West Indies where it infests the sugar plantations and is greatly dreaded — called also *bonetail*

fer-de-mo·line \,ferdəmō'lēn\ *or* **fer-de-mou·lin** \-mü'laⁿ\ *n, pl* **fers-de-moline** *or* **fers-de-moulin** \-rdə-\ [F *fer de moulin* mill-iron] **:** MILLRIND 2

[1]**fere** \'fi(ə)r\ *n* [ME, fr. OE *gefēra*, derivative fr. the root of *faran* to travel — more at FARE] **1** *archaic* **a :** MATE, COMPANION ‹the lamb . . . raceth freely with his ~ —Alfred Tennyson› **b :** a wife or husband ‹own her ~ and plighted lord —E.G.Bulwer-Lytton› **2** *now dial Brit* **:** a person of the same rank or competence **:** EQUAL, PEER, MATCH

[2]**fere** \'fēr\ *adj* [ME, fr. OE *fēre* able to go, fit for military service; akin to OHG *gifuori* fit, suitable, ON *fœrr* able, strong, fit for use, OE *faran* to travel] *now chiefly Scot* **:** in good health **:** SOUND, STRONG — often used in the phrase *hale and fere*

fer·e·to·ry \'ferə,tōrē\ *n* -ES [ME *fertre, feretory, firetree*, fr. AF *fertre* & MF *fiertre*, fr. ML *feretrum*, fr. L, litter, bier, fr. Gk *pheretron*, fr. *pherein* to carry — more at BEAR] **1 :** an ornate often portable bier for the relics of a saint **2 :** a place for keeping a feretory; *esp* **:** a narrow space behind the high altar of a medieval cathedral or large church

ferfel *var of* FARFEL

fer·gha·nite *also* **fer·ga·nite** \fər'gä,nīt, 'fərgə,n-\ *n* -s [Russ *ferganit*, fr. *Fergana*, region in west central Asia + Russ *-it* -ite] **:** a mineral $U_3(VO_4)_2.6H_2O$ consisting of a hydrated uranium vanadate occurring in sulfur-yellow scales

fer·gu·son·ite \'fərgəsə,nīt\ *n* -s [Robert *Ferguson* †1865 Scot. physician + E *-ite*] **:** a brownish black mineral (Y,Er,-Ce,Fe)(Nb,Ta,Ti)O_4 consisting essentially of an oxide of yttrium, erbium, niobium, and tantalum with other metals often including uranium and isomorphous with formanite (hardness 5.5–6)

[1]**fe·ria** \'firēə, 'fer-\ *n, pl* **feri·as** \-ēəz\ *also* **feri·ae** \'firē,ē, 'ferē,ī\ [ML, fr. LL, festal day, day of the week (as in *prima feria* Sunday, *secunda feria* Monday, etc., orig. designations for the days of Easter week) — more at FAIR] **:** a day of the Roman Catholic or Anglican church calendar other than Sunday on which no feast regularly falls often having a special commemorative office ‹the Sundays and ~s of Lent› — see GREATER FERIA

[2]**fe·ria** \'ferēə, -r(,)yä\ *n* -s [Sp, fair, market, fr. ML — more at FAIR] **:** a market festival in Spain and places affected by Spanish culture often celebrating a local religious holiday (as the day of a town's patron saint) **:** FAIR ‹the annual bullfight at the start of a 3-day ~›

[1]**fe·ri·al** \'firēəl, 'fer-\ *adj* [ME, fr. MF & ML; MF *ferial*, fr. ML *ferialis*, fr. LL *feria* + L *-alis* -al] **1 :** of, relating to, or being a feria; *esp* **:** belonging to any day of an ecclesiastical calendar that is marked by no special observance ‹a cloth of gold vestment can be worn for festal as well as for dominical and ~ offices› **2** *archaic* **:** of or being a legal holiday when labor is suspended and judicial proceedings may not be held or process served

[2]**ferial** \"\ *n* -s **:** [1]FERIA

fe·ri·a·tion \,firē'āshən, ,fer-\ *n* -s [ML *feriation-, feriatio*, fr. L *feriatus* (past part. of *feriari* to rest from work, keep holiday, fr. *feriae* days of rest, holidays) + *-ion-, -io* -ion — more at FEAST] *archaic* **:** the keeping of a holiday esp. by refraining from work

fe·rine \'fe,rīn, 'fi,-, 'fe,-\ *adj* [L *ferinus*, fr. *fera* wild animal (fr. fem. of *ferus* wild) + *-inus* -ine — more at FIERCE] **:** [1]FERAL 1a,1b

fe·rin·ghee *or* **fe·rin·ghi** *or* **fe·rin·gi** \fə'riŋgē\ *n* -s *usu cap* [Per *Firinghī, Farangī*, fr. Ar *Faranjī, Ifranjī*, modif. of MF *Franc* Frank — more at FRANK] **1** *India* **:** EUROPEAN 1a **2** *India* **:** a Eurasian esp. of Portuguese-Indian blood — usu. used disparagingly

fer·i·ty \'ferəd·ē\ *n* -ES [L *feritas*, fr. *ferus* wild + *-itas* -ity] **:** the state of being feral **:** WILDNESS, BARBARITY ‹the ~ of the animals of the deep forests›

ferk \'fərk, 'fe(ə)rk\ *var of* FIRK

[1]**fer·lie** \'ferlē\ *adj* [ME *ferly, ferlich*, fr. OE *fǣrlic* sudden, unexpected, fr. *fǣr* sudden danger or attack, calamity + *-lic* -ly — more at FEAR] *now dial* **:** STRANGE, SURPRISING ‹a ~ sight outside the door›

[2]**fer·lie** *also* **fer·ly** \"\ *n, pl* **ferlies** [ME, fr. *ferly*, adj.] **1** *Scot* **:** a strange or unusual sight **:** WONDER **2** *Scot* **:** a freakish person or animal sometimes seen in hallucinations ‹when he was real drunk and the ~s came sniftering out of the whiskey bottles at him —L.G.Gibbon› **3** *Scot* **:** NEWS, GOSSIP — usu. used in pl. **4** *Scot* **:** SURPRISE, AMAZEMENT

[3]**ferlie** *also* **ferly** \"\ *vb* **ferlied; ferlied; ferlying; ferlies** [ME *ferlien*, fr. *ferly*, adj.] *Scot* **:** WONDER

ferling *n* -s [ME, fr. OE *fēorthling*, fr. *fēortha* fourth + *-ling* — more at FOURTH] *obs* **:** a fourth part; *specific* **:** FARTHING

ferm \'fə(ə)rm\ *n* -s [ME *ferme* rent, lease — more at FARM] **:** [2]FARM ‹~s paid in kind or money by landowners in Anglo-Saxon and Norman times›

fer·mail \'fər,māl\ *n* [MF *fermail, fermaille*, fr. ML *firmaculum*, fr. L *firmare* to make fast + *-culum* -cle — more at FIRM (v.)] **:** a medieval clasp for clothing; *esp* **:** a late medieval English or French closed-ring brooch worn by both sexes (as to close a robe at the throat)

fer·man·agh \fə(r)'manə\ *adj, usu cap* [fr. *Fermanagh*, county in Northern Ireland] **:** of or from County Fermanagh, Northern Ireland **:** of the kind or style prevalent in Fermanagh

fer·ma·ta \fer'mäd·ə\ *n* -s [It, stop, pause, fr. *fermata* (fem. of *fermato*, past part. of *fermare* to stop, fr. L *firmare* to make fast), fr. L *firmata*, fem. of *firmatus*, past part. of *firmare*] **1 :** a prolongation at the discretion of the performer of a musical note, chord, or rest beyond its given time value **2 :** a sign consisting of a dot under or over a half circle placed over or under a note, chord, or rest indicating a fermata — called also *hold, pause*

fer·mat's principle \(')fer¦mäz—\ *n, usu cap F* [after Pierre de *Fermat* †1665 Fr. mathematician, its formulator] **:** a statement in optics: the path actually followed by a ray of light undergoing reflection or refraction is one of either minimum or maximum time as compared with adjacent arbitrary paths except for reflection or refraction at an aplanatic surface or passage through an aplanatic lens for which the time is constant

[1]**fer·ment** \fə(r)'ment, ¦fər¦m-, ¦fə¦m-, ¦fəi¦m-\ *vb* -ED/-ING/-S [ME *fermenten*, fr. MF & L; MF *fermenter*, fr. L *fermentare* to cause to rise or ferment, fr. *fermentum*, n.] *vi* **1 :** to undergo fermentation **:** WORK ‹spores survive and the fruit ~s› **2 a :** to be in a state of individual or social ferment **:** be inwardly active ‹everything ~s in him — his thoughts, sensations, and memories; nothing stays quiet —Janet Flanner› **:** become mentally or emotionally agitated ‹the squire continued ~*ing* to the highest degree of exasperation —T.L.Peacock› **:** SEETHE; *also* **:** to undergo a process of ferment **:** develop by agitated inner activity ‹but underneath things will be ~*ing*, basic decisions shaping up that will have far-reaching effects —*Kiplinger Washington Letter*› ‹still have a novel ~*ing* in my system —Virginia D. Dawson & Betty D. Wilson› **b :** to act as a ferment in an individual or society **:** arouse agitation or promote change ‹the idea of the self-rule of the people took hold and ~*ed* vigorously› **~** *vt* **1 :** to cause to undergo fermentation ‹enzymes that ~ tobacco› **2 a :** to produce or bring to maturity as if by fermentation ‹oppressive poverty ~*ed* violent discontent› ‹travel and reflection ~*ed* his already full mind› **b :** to cause ferment (as of emotion) in **:** work into

a state of ferment **:** AGITATE, EXCITE, FOMENT ⟨quick-spreading rumors ~*ed* the city and violence soon broke out⟩

²**fer·ment** \ˈfər,ment, ˈfə̄,m-, ˈfəi,m- *sometimes* ,=ˈ= *or* ,fə(r)ˈm- *or chiefly Brit* ˈ=,mənt\ *n* -s [ME, fr. L *fermentum* leaven, yeast — more at BARM] **1 a :** an agent capable of bringing about fermentation and other metabolic processes: (1) **:** a living organism (as a yeast or bacterium) that acts by virtue of its enzymes — called also *organized ferment;* used chiefly commercially; compare STARTER 3d (2) **:** ENZYME — called also *unorganized ferment* **b :** a person or thing that stimulates agitation or the active working out of change in an individual or society ⟨the possessive instinct, the most violent of ~*s* —Havelock Ellis⟩ ⟨the active ~ at work in China . . . was that of nationalism —*Times Lit. Supp.*⟩ **2 a :** FERMENTATION 1 **b :** a state of unrest **:** AGITATION, EXCITEMENT, TUMULT ⟨that ~ in the air which accompanies an election —John Buchan⟩ ⟨she was thrown into a ~ by his unexpected arrival⟩; *also* **:** a process of active often disorderly development in an individual life or in a society **:** the painful or disturbing transition from old to new ⟨a continent in ~, awakening to a new era after centuries of stagnation —Tad Szulc⟩ ⟨the great period of creative ~ in literature —William Barrett⟩

fer·ment·abil·i·ty \(,)=,mentəˈbiləd-ē, -lətē, -i\ *n* -ES **:** the quality or state of being fermentable

fer·ment·able \(,)=ˈmentəbəl\ *adj* **:** capable of undergoing esp. alcoholic fermentation

fer·men·tal \(ˈ)=¦mentᵊl\ *adj* [²*ferment* + -*al*] **:** FERMENTATIVE

fermentate *vt* -ED/-ING/-S [L *fermentatus*, past part.] *obs* **:** to cause to ferment

fer·men·ta·tion \,fərmən'tāshən, ,fə̄m-, ,fəim-, -,men-\ *n* -s [ME *fermentacioun*, fr. LL *fermentation-, fermentatio*, fr. L *fermentatus* (past part. of *fermentare* to cause to rise or ferment) + -*ion-*, -*io* -ion — more at FERMENT] **1 a :** a chemical change accompanied by effervescence and suggestive of changes produced in organic materials by yeasts **b :** any of various enzymatic transformations of organic substrates (as the formation of alcohol from sugars or of vinegar from cider or the souring of milk); *esp* **:** a transformation of a carbohydrate material that yields such products as alcohols, acids, and carbon dioxide and that typically involves decomposition without the participation of oxygen — see ALCOHOLIC FERMENTATION; compare GLYCOLYSIS **c** (1) **:** any of various controlled aerobic or anaerobic processes used for the manufacture of certain products (as alcohols, acids, vitamins of the B complex, or antibiotics) by the action usu. of yeasts, molds, or bacteria (2) **:** any of various industrial processes for improving esp. flavor, aroma, or quality (as of tea, tobacco, or cheese) by means of fermentation **2 :** FERMENT 2b

fermentation tube *n* **:** a modified culture tube with an upright closed arm for collecting gas formed in broth cultures by microorganisms

fermentation tube

fer·ment·ative \fə(r)ˈmentəd·iv\ *also* **fer·men·tive** \-entiv\ *adj* **1 :** causing or having power to cause fermentation ⟨the ~ substance in yeast⟩ **2 :** of or produced by fermentation ⟨the ~ process⟩ ⟨~ gases⟩ **3 :** FERMENTABLE

fer·ment·er *pronunc at* ¹FERMENT+ə(r)\ *n* -s **1 :** one that ferments: as **a :** a worker who attends a fermentation process (as of moistened tobacco or of mash for beer) **b :** an organism that causes fermentation **2** *or* **fer·men·tor** \"\ **a :** a vessel in which mash is fermented during the brewing process **:** a fermenting tank **b :** a laboratory apparatus for carrying out fermentation

fer·men·tes·ci·ble \¦fərmən¦tesəbəl\ *or* **fer·men·tis·ci·ble** \-tis-\ *adj* [*fermentescible* fr. L *fermentescere* to swell, rise, ferment (fr. L *fermentum* leaven, yeast + -*escere*, incho. verb ending) + -*ible; fermentiscible* irreg. fr. L *fermentescere* + E -*ible* — more at BARM] **:** FERMENTABLE

fer·men·tol·o·gist \,==·ˈtäləjəst\ *n* -s **:** a specialist in fermentology; *specif* **:** a chemist who experiments with ingredients and production processes of alcoholic beverages in order to control and improve taste, color, odor, and other characteristics — called also *oenologist*

fer·men·tol·o·gy \-əjē\ *n* -ES [²*ferment* + -*alogy*] **:** a science that deals with ferments and fermentation — compare ENZYMOLOGY

ferments *pres 3d sing of* FERMENT, *pl of* FERMENT

fer·me·ture \ˈfərmə,chů(ə)r\ *n* -s [F, lit., act of closing, apparatus for closing, fr. MF, fr. ML *firmatura* lock, clasp, fr. L *firmatus* (past part. of *firmare* to make fast) + -*ura* -ure — more at FIRM (v.)] **:** the mechanism closing the breech of a breech-loading firearm

fer·mi-di·rac distribution \¦fer(,)mēdə¦rak—\ *n, usu cap F&D* [after Enrico *Fermi* †1954 Ital. physicist and Paul A. M. *Dirac* b1902 Eng. physicist] **:** an assumed statistical distribution of speeds among the electrons responsible for thermal conduction in metals

fermi-dirac statistics *also* **fermi statistics** *n, usu cap F&D* **:** quantum-mechanical statistics according to which subatomic particles of a given class (as electrons, protons, and neutrons) have a quantum-mechanical symmetry that makes it impossible for more than one particle to occupy any particular quantum-mechanical state — compare BOSE-EINSTEIN STATISTICS

fer·miere \fermyeer\ *adj* [F (*à la*) *fermière* in the manner of the farmer's wife] *of a food* **:** prepared in plain country style

fer·mi·on \ˈfermē,än, ˈfər-\ *n* -s [Enrico *Fermi* + E -*on*] **:** a particle (as an electron, proton, or neutron) having a half-odd-integer number of quantum units of spin and conforming to the Fermi-Dirac statistics

fer·mi·um \-ēəm\ *n* -s [NL, fr. Enrico *Fermi* + NL -*ium*] **:** a radioactive metallic element artificially produced (as by bombardment of plutonium with neutrons) — symbol *Fm;* see ELEMENT table

fer·mor·ite \ˈfərmə,rīt\ *n* -s [Lewis L. *Fermor* †1954 Eng. geologist + E -*ite*] **:** a mineral $(Ca,Sr)_5[(As,P)O_4]_3$ that consists of an arsenate, phosphate, and fluoride of calcium and strontium and that is related to apatite and found in white crystalline masses

fern \ˈfərn, ˈfə̄n, ˈfəin\ *n* -s *often attrib* [ME *fern, ferne*, fr. OE *fearn;* akin to OHG *farn* fern, MIr *raith* fern, Skt *parṇa* wing, feather, leaf, and perh. to OE *faran* to travel — more at FARE] **1 a :** any of numerous nonflowering vascular plants constituting a class (Filicineae) of the division Tracheophyta; *esp* **:** a plant of the order Filicales resembling seed plants in being differentiated into root, stem, and leaflike fronds and in having vascular tissue but differing in reproducing by spores that are borne usu. in sori on fertile fronds or fertile portions of vegetative fronds and that upon germination commonly produce a flat typical thallus which produces antheridia and archegonia upon its surface, the egg of the archegonium giving rise to the sporophyte which is the conspicuous generation in the life cycle — see FROND illustration **b :** a frond of a fern **c :** a growth or quantity of ferns ⟨admiring the ~ of the park⟩ ⟨decorated with white roses banked with ~⟩ **2 :** any of various plants with fernlike foliage — usu. used in combination ⟨asparagus ~⟩ ⟨sweet ~⟩

fern ally *n* **1 a :** a pteridophyte other than a member of the order Filicales **b :** any of various pteridophytes (as horsetails or club mosses) that are not leafy in habit as distinguished from the leafy true ferns **2 :** WATER FERN 1

fer·nam·bu·co wood \¦fərnəm¦b(y)ü(,)kō-, ¦fernəm¦bü(,)kō-\ *n, usu cap F* [fr. *Fernambuco* (now *Pernambuco*), state of Brazil, fr. Pg] **:** PERNAMBUCO WOOD

fer·nan·de·ño \,fərnən'dān(,)yō, ,fer-\ *n, pl* **fernandeño** *or* **fernandeños** *usu cap* [Sp *fernandeño*, fr. San *Fernando*, Franciscan mission in Los Angeles county, Calif. + Sp -*eño* (suffix added to place names to form names of inhabitants)] **1 :** a Shoshonean people of the valley of the Los Angeles river, California **2 :** a member of the Fernandeño people

fer·nan·di·nite \,fərnən'dē,nīt\ *n* -s [Eulagio E. *Fernandini*, 20th cent. Peruvian mine owner + E -*ite*] **:** a mineral consisting of a massive dull green hydrous calcium vanadyl vanadate

fern asparagus *n* **:** ASPARAGUS FERN

fern ball *n* **:** a ball composed of the compacted rhizomes of several small drooping ferns that is usu. imported in a dry dormant condition from Japan for use in house decoration — see BALL FERN

fernbird \ˈ=,=\ *n* [*fern* + *bird*] **:** a small passerine bird (*Bowdleria punctata*) of New Zealand that frequents marshy ground and is becoming rare

fernbrake \ˈ=,=\ *n* [*fern* + *brake* (thicket)] **:** a dense growth of ferns

fern-bush \ˈ=,=\ *n* **:** a low densely branched very leafy white-flowered shrub (*Chamaebatiaria milbefolium*) of the family Rosaceae that is widely distributed in dry uplands of the western U.S. — called also *desert sweet*

fern clubmoss *n* **:** an epiphytic Australasian fern ally (*Tmesipteris tannensis*) with large lanceolate green leaves that grows on trunks of tree ferns

fern cycad *n* **:** CYCAD FERN

ferned \ˈfərnd, ˈfə̄nd, ˈfəind\ *adj* **:** abounding in or covered with ferns

fer·nent \fə(r)ˈnent\ *or* **fer·ninst** \-ˈnin(t)st, -ˈninzt\ *var of* FORNENT

fern·ery \ˈfərn(ə)rē, ˈfə̄n-, ˈfəin-, -ri\ *n* -ES **1 a :** a place where ferns are growing **b :** a planter for ferns **2 :** a collection of growing ferns

fernery

fern·flö·te \ˈfern,flœtə\ *n* -s [G, fr. *fern* far (fr. OHG *ferrana* from far, fr. *ferro* far) + *flöte* flute — more at FAR, BLOCKFLÖTE] **:** a very soft organ pipe of flute tone and 8-foot or 4-foot pitch

fern fruit *n* **:** SORUS a

ferngale \ˈ=,=\ *n* [*fern* + *gale* sweet gale, fr. ME *gale, gayl*, fr. OE *gagel;* akin to MLG & MD *gagel* sweet gale] **:** SWEET FERN 1a

fern green *n* **:** a moderate yellow green that is greener and paler than average moss green, duller than average pea green, and duller and very slightly greener than apple green (sense 1)

fernleaf \ˈ=,=\ *n, pl* **fernleaf 1 :** a delicate red alga (*Callithamnion gracillimum*) with finely divided thallus **2 :** a disease of tomatoes caused by the cucumber mosaic virus and characterized by mottling and fernlike narrowing of the leaves

fernlike \ˈ=,=\ *adj* **:** resembling a fern esp. in leaf shape

fern moss *n* **:** any of various fernlike mosses esp. of the genus *Thuidium*

fern owl *n* **:** a nightjar (*Caprimulgus europaeus*)

fern palm *n* **:** any of several cycads with palmlike foliage

fern poisoning *or* **fern staggers** *n* **:** BRACKEN POISONING

ferns *pl of* FERN

fern scale *n* **:** a tropical armored scale (*Pinnaspis aspidistrae*) common on potted ferns and in greenhouses

fern seed *n* **:** the dustlike asexual spores of ferns that were formerly taken for seeds and reputed to render one invisible

fern·tick·le \ˈfern,tikəl\ *n* -s [ME *ferntikel, ferntikill*, fr. *fern* + -*tikel*, -*tikill*, prob. fr. L -*ticula* (as in *lenticula* lentil, group of freckles) — more at LENTIL] *n, chiefly Scot* **:** FRECKLE — **fern·tick·led** \-kəld\ *adj*

fern tree *n* **:** TREE FERN

fern weevil *n* **:** a weevil (*Syagrius fulvitarsis*) of Australia and the Pacific islands that feeds on ferns

fernwort \ˈ=,=\ *n* **:** a plant belonging to the Pteridophyta **:** FERN ALLY **:** FERN

ferny \ˈfərnē, ˈfə̄nē, ˈfəinē, -ni\ *adj, usu* -ER/-EST [ME, fr. *fern* + -*y*] **1 :** of or abounding in ferns **2 :** FERNLIKE ⟨the ~ shadows of locust leaves —W.V.T.Clark⟩

fer·o·cac·tus \,ferəˈkaktəs, ,fir-\ *n, cap* [NL, fr. *fero-* (fr. L *ferus* wild, fierce) + *cactus*] **:** a genus of nearly globular deeply ribbed cacti of Mexico and the adjacent U. S. having numerous spines, large funnel-shaped flowers, and dry fruits

fe·ro·ce \fāˈrō(,)chā\ *adj* [It, fr. L *feroc-, ferox*] **:** FIERCE, FEROCIOUS — used as a direction in music

fe·ro·cious \fəˈrōshəs\ *adj* [L *feroc-, ferox* fierce (fr. *ferus* wild, fierce + -*oc-*, -*ox* looking, appearing — akin to L *oculus* eye) + E -*ious* — more at FIERCE, EYE] **1 a :** characterized by wild or extreme rapacity, cruelty, acrimony, or destructiveness **:** violently aggressive **:** BLOODTHIRSTY ⟨a ~ tiger⟩ ⟨the raiders' ~ butchery of women and children⟩ **:** BITTER ⟨the ~ word battles he has had with other editors⟩ **:** DEVASTATING ⟨the ~ torrents of the flood⟩ **b :** suggesting a ferocious character or mood **:** FORMIDABLE ⟨a ~ beard⟩ ⟨a ~ smile⟩ **2 :** very great **:** EXTREME, EXCESSIVE ⟨he was a ~ bore⟩ **:** FURIOUS ⟨sought to forget his troubles through ~ activity⟩ ⟨a ~ wind swept the sea⟩ **syn** see FIERCE

fe·ro·cious·ly *adv* **:** in a ferocious manner ⟨pounces ~ on a trivial error of fact —C.W.Shumaker⟩ ⟨a ~ logical system⟩

fe·ro·cious·ness *n* -ES **:** FEROCITY

fe·roc·i·ty \fəˈräsəd-ē, -sətē, -i\ *n* -ES [F & L; F *férocité*, fr. L *ferocitas*, fr. *feroc-, ferox* fierce + -*itas* -ity] **1 :** the quality or state of being ferocious **:** savage wildness **:** FURY ⟨turned on them with a ~ which made a savage of him on the spot —Virginia Woolf⟩ **:** extreme or furious intensity **:** ARDOR ⟨a wild ~ of joy overcame him —Liam O'Flaherty⟩ **2 :** an instance of ferocity ⟨has his great sentimentalities to compensate for his chronic *ferocities* —Edmund Wilson⟩

-**fer·ous** \f(ə)rəs\ *adj comb form* [ME, fr. L -*fer* & MF -*fere* (fr. L -*fer*) + E -*ous* — more at -FER] **:** bearing **:** producing **:** yielding ⟨auri*ferous*⟩ ⟨ovuli*ferous*⟩ — almost always preceded by *i* — -**fer·ous·ly** *adv comb form* — -**fer·ous·ness** *n comb form* -ES

fer·rai·o·lo·ne \fə,rīəˈlōnē\ *n* -s [It, aug. of *ferraiolo* large mantle, cloak, prob. fr. Ar *feryūl* wool cape, fr. L *palliolum* small Greek mantle, dim. of *pallium* Greek mantle — more at PALL] **:** a large full length cloak having a large flat collar, varying in color according to the wearer's rank, and forming the necessary complement of full ecclesiastical dress among Roman Catholic clergy on nonliturgical occasions (as an academic ceremony or papal audience)

fer·ra·ra \fəˈrärə\ *adj, usu cap* [fr. *Ferrara*, Italy] **:** of or from the city of Ferrara, Italy **:** of the kind or style prevalent in Ferrara

¹**fer·ra·rese** \fəˈrä,rēz, -ēs, ¦ferə¦r-\ *adj, usu cap* [It, adj. & n., fr. *Ferrara* Italy + It -*ese*] **1 :** of, relating to, or characteristic of Ferrara, a city in Italy **2 :** of, relating to, or characteristic of the people of Ferrara

²**ferrarese** \"\ *n, pl* **ferrarese** *cap* **:** a native or resident of Ferrara, Italy

ferrash *var of* FERASH

fer·rate \ˈfe,rāt\ *n* -s [ISV *ferr-* (fr. L *ferrum* iron) + -*ate*] **:** any of various classes of compounds containing iron and oxygen in the anion or regarded as so constituted: as **a :** a strongly oxidizing dark red salt analogous to the chromates and sulfates and formed in various ways (as by heating iron filings with a nitrate) ⟨potassium ~ K_2FeO_4⟩ — called also *ferrate(VI)* **b :** FERRITE

fer·rei·ro \fəˈrā(,)rō\ *n* -s [Pg, lit., blacksmith, fr. L *ferrarius*, fr. *ferrum* iron + -*arius* -ary — more at FARRIER] **:** a Brazilian tree frog (*Hyla faber*) that produces notes resembling measured beating on a copper plate

fer·rel \ˈferəl\ *archaic var of* FERRULE

fer·rel's law \ˈferəlz-\ *n, usu cap F* [after William *Ferrel* †1891 Am. meteorologist, its formulator] **:** a statement in meteorology: a wind in any direction tends to deflect to the right in the northern hemisphere and to the left in the southern with a force that is directly proportional to the mass of wind in question, its velocity, the sine of the latitude, and the angular velocity of the earth's rotation

fer·re·ous \ˈferēəs\ *adj* [L *ferreus*, fr. *ferrum* iron] **:** of, like, or containing iron

ferrer *n* -s [ME *ferrour* blacksmith who shoes horses, veterinarian — more at FARRIER] **1** *obs* **:** IRONSMITH **2** *obs* **:** FARRIER

¹**fer·ret** \ˈferət, *usu* -əd·+V\ *n* -s [ME *feret, ferret, furet*, fr. MF *furet, fuiret*, fr. (assumed) VL *furittus*, lit., small thief, dim. of L *fur* thief — more at FURTIVE] **1 a :** a semidomesticated variety of the European polecat sometimes treated as a separate species (*Mustela furo*) that is usu. albino with red eyes and is much used for hunting rodents and sometimes rabbits in Europe and occas. in the U. S. **b :** BLACK-FOOTED FERRET **2 :** a person who searches actively and persistently (as for incriminating information) ⟨German ~s who constantly spied on the Allied prisoners of war⟩ **3 :** an airplane equipped to detect a radar installation and analyze its signals

²**ferret** \"\ *vb* -ED/-ING/-S [ME *fereten, fureten*, fr. *feret, furet*, n.] *vt* **1 :** to hunt with a ferret: **a :** to hunt over ⟨they have *ferreted* the duke's fields⟩ **b :** to hunt for **:** TAKE *esp* **:** to drive esp. from covert ⟨they *ferreted* a number of rabbits⟩ **2 :** to worry or harry as with a ferret ⟨the king kept *ferreting* the rebellious baron⟩ ~ *vi* **1 :** to hunt game or drive out vermin with a ferret ⟨some U. S. states have laws against *ferreting*⟩ **2 :** to search carefully or diligently and sometimes presumptuously **:** search about **:** PRY ⟨old-fashioned . . . to go *ferreting* into people's pasts —Virginia Woolf⟩

³**ferret** \"\ *also* **fer·ret·ing** \-əd·iŋ\ *n* -s [*ferret* fr. earlier *ferret silk*, prob. modif. of It *fioretti* floss silk, fr. pl. of *fioretto* small flower, dim. of *fiore* flower, fr. L *flor-, flos; ferreting* fr. *ferret* + -*ing* — more at BLOW (blossom)] **1 :** a narrow silk tape or ribbon for trimming or decorative lacing **2 :** a strong tape of cotton or wool for binding or shoelaces

ferret-badger \ˈ==,==\ *n* **:** any of several heavy-bodied mammals (as *Helictis moschata*) of southeastern Asia that resemble the weasel — called also *pahmi*

fer·ret·er \ˈferəd·ə(r)\ *n* -s [ME *fereter, fureter*, fr. *feret, furet* ferret + -*er*] **:** one that ferrets ⟨paid a ~ to drive out the rats⟩

ferret out *vt* **:** to find or uncover with keen, diligent, crafty, or shrewd search ⟨*ferret out* the enemies of the country⟩ ⟨*ferret* the facts *out* after hours of painstaking examination of records⟩ **syn** see SEEK

ferret-polecat \¦==ˈ=,=\ *n* **:** an unusually vicious ferret valuable as a rodent destroyer, closely resembling the wild European polecat, and said to result from interbreeding the domestic ferret with the wild polecat

fer·rety \ˈferəd-ē\ *adj* [¹*ferret* + -*y*] **:** suggestive of a ferret ⟨into his ~ eyes there came a gentler look —Norman Douglas⟩

ferri- *comb form* [L *ferri-*, fr. *ferrum* iron] **1 :** iron ⟨*ferri*ferous⟩ **2** [*ferric*] **:** containing ferric iron ⟨ferrihemoglobin⟩

fer·ri·age *or* **fer·ry·age** \ˈferēij, -riij\ *n* -s [ME *feriage*, fr. *ferien* to ferry + -*age* — more at FERRY] **1 :** the act or business of transporting by ferry ⟨cross the larger streams by ~⟩ **2 :** the fare to be paid for a ferry passage ⟨no money to pay the ~⟩

fer·ri·an \ˈferēən\ *adj* [*ferri-* + -*an*] **:** containing ferric iron

fer·ric \-rik\ *adj* [L *ferrum* iron + E -*ic* — more at FARRIER] **:** of, relating to, or containing iron — used esp. of compounds in which this element has a higher valence, usu. three, than in the ferrous compounds or of iron with such a valence

ferric acetate *n* **:** either of two acetates of iron used chiefly in the textile industry as mordants and formerly in medicine as tonics: **a :** the normal acetate $Fe(C_2H_3O_2)_3$ known best in solution **b :** a basic acetate $Fe(OH)(C_2H_3O_2)_2$ obtained as brownish red scales or powder

ferric ammonium citrate *n* **:** a complex salt containing varying amounts of iron, one type being obtained as red crystals or a brownish yellow powder and another type as green crystals or powder and both being used in medicine for treating iron-deficiency anemia and in photography for making blueprints

ferric chloride *n* **:** a deliquescent salt $FeCl_3$ that is obtained in anhydrous form (as by heating iron in chlorine) as dark crystals appearing red by transmitted light and green by reflected light, that forms several crystalline hydrates (as the yellow hexahydrate $FeCl_3.6H_2O$), and that is used chiefly as an oxidizing agent, as a catalyst, as an etching agent in photoengraving, as a coagulant in treating industrial wastes, and in medicine in a water solution or tincture usu. as an astringent or styptic; iron trichloride

ferric hydroxide *n* **:** any of several hydrates $Fe_2O_3.nH_2O$ of ferric oxide that are capable of acting both as bases and weak acids **:** hydrated ferric oxide: as **a :** a reddish brown gelatinous precipitate obtained by adding an alkali to a ferric salt solution and often regarded as the trihydrate $Fe(OH)_3$ **b :** a red to reddish brown crystalline oxide and hydroxide FeO-(OH) occurring in nature as lepidocrocite

ferric oxide *n* **:** the red or black crystalline sesquioxide of iron Fe_2O_3 that is found in nature both as hematite and as hydrated forms (as rust and limonite) and is also obtained synthetically (as by calcining ferrous sulfate or hydrated ferric oxide) and that is used chiefly as a pigment and polishing material and in the removal of hydrogen sulfide from gases — called also *iron(III) oxide;* compare IRON OXIDE a, IRON RED, ROUGE 2

ferric sulfate *n* **:** a salt $Fe_2(SO_4)_3$ that is found in nature as the hydrated minerals coquimbite and quenstedtite and is also obtained synthetically (as by oxidation of ferrous sulfate) in the white anhydrous form and that is used chiefly in making iron alums, in pickling metals, as a mordant in dyeing, and as a coagulant in treating industrial wastes

fer·ri·cyanic acid \¦fe,rī, ¦ferē+. . .-\ *n* [*ferri-* + *cyanic*] **:** a brown crystalline unstable acid $H_3Fe(CN)_6$ obtained by treating ferricyanides with strong acids

fer·ri·cyanide \"+\ *n* -s [ISV *ferri-* + *cyanide*] **:** a salt of ferricyanic acid obtained usu. by oxidation of a ferrocyanide — see IRON BLUE ⟨cupric ~ $Cu_3[Fe(CN)_6]_2$⟩

fer·ri·did·dle \¦ferē¦didᵊl\ *n* -s [origin unknown] *dial* **:** CHIPMUNK

ferried *past of* FERRY

¹**fer·ri·er** \ˈferēə(r), -eriə-\ *n* -s [ME *ferier*, fr. *ferien* to ferry + -*er* — more at FERRY] **:** FERRYMAN

²**ferrier** \"\ *var of* FARRIER

ferries *pres 3d sing of* FERRY, *pl of* FERRY

fer·rif·er·ous \fəˈrif(ə)rəs, (ˈ)fe¦r-\ *adj* [*ferri-* + -*ferous*] **:** containing iron **:** iron-bearing ⟨highly ~ carbonates⟩

fer·ri·hemoglobin \¦fe,rī, ¦ferē+\ *n* [*ferri-* + *hemoglobin*] **:** METHEMOGLOBIN

fer·ri·magnetic \"+\ *adj* [ISV *ferri-* + *magnetic*] **:** of or relating to a class of substances (as ferrite) characterized by magnetization in which the polarization in one group of magnetic ions is antiparallel to the polarization in another group — **fer·ri·magnetism** \"+\ *n*

fer·ri·molybdite \"+\ *n* [ISV *ferri-* + *molybdite*] **:** a mineral $Fe_2(MoO_4)_3.8H_2O(?)$ consisting of hydrated iron molybdate

fer·ri·natrite \¦fe,rī'nā-,trīt, ,ferē'-\ *n* -s [alter. (influenced by *ferri*) of *ferronatrite*, fr. *ferro-* + *natron* + -*ite*] **:** a mineral $Na_3Fe(SO_4)_3.3H_2O$ consisting of a greenish or white sodium ferric iron double sulfate usu. occurring in spherical forms

fer·ri·porphyrin \¦fe,rī, ¦ferē+\ *n* [*ferri-* + *porphyrin*] **:** a red-brown to black ferric derivative of a porphyrin that differs from a ferroporphyrin by the additional combination of a univalent anion (as chloride) with the iron atom

fer·ri·protoporphyrin \"+\ *n* [*ferri-* + *protoporphyrin*] **:** a ferriporphyrin in which the porphyrin is protoporphyrin — see HEMATIN, HEMIN

fer·ri·sicklerite \"+\ *n* [ISV *ferri-* + *sicklerite*] **:** a mineral $(Li,Fe,Mn)(PO_4)$ consisting of phosphate of lithium, ferric iron, and manganese with more iron than manganese and isomorphous with sicklerite

fer·ris wheel \ˈferəs-\ *n, usu cap F* [after George Washington Gale *Ferris* †1896 Am. engineer who designed such a wheel for the World's Columbian Exposition in Chicago in 1893] **:** an amusement device consisting of a large power-driven wheel made in two parallel sections having seats suspended between the sections, the seats maintaining a horizontal position while the wheel rotates in a vertical plane

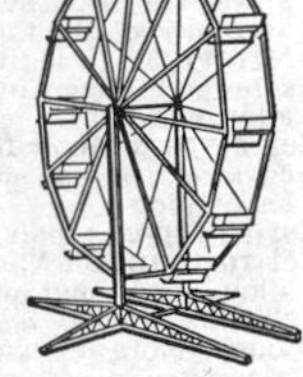

Ferris wheel

fer·rite \ˈfe,rīt\ *n* -s [L *ferrum* iron + E -*ite*] **1 :** any of several compounds formed usu. by treating hydrated ferric oxide with an alkali or by heating ferric oxide with a metallic oxide and regarded in some cases as salts of a ferric hydroxide acting in its capacity of an acid and in other cases as spinels ⟨sodium ~ $NaFeO_2$⟩ ⟨zinc ~ $ZnFe_2O_4$ has a spinel structure⟩ — called also *ferrate, ferrate(III)* **2 :** a solid solution in which alpha iron is the solvent

fer·rit·ic \fəˈrid·ik, (ˈ)fe¦r-\ *adj* **:** composed chiefly of ferrite ⟨~ stainless steel⟩

fer·ri·tin \ˈferətᵊn\ *n* -s [ISV *ferr-* (fr. L *ferrum* iron) + -*ite* + -*in*] **:** an amber-colored crystalline protein that contains more than 20 percent of iron in the form of a ferric hydroxide-phosphate complex with apoferritin, that is abundant esp. in the liver and spleen, and that constitutes a body mechanism for the storage of reserves of iron

fer·ri·tize \-rə,tīz\ *vt* -ED/-ING/-S **:** to convert (as steel) into ferrite

fer·ri·tungstite \ˌfe,rī, ˌferē+\ *n* [*ferri-* + *tungstite*] **:** a mineral $Fe_2(WO_4)(OH)_4.4H_2O$ consisting of a hydrous ferric tungstate and occurring as yellow ocherous powder

fer·riv·o·rous \fəˈrivərəs, (ˈ)feˈr-\ *adj* [*ferri-* + *-vorous*] **:** feeding on iron

ferro- *comb form* [ML *ferro-*, fr. L *ferrum* iron — more at FARRIER] **1 :** iron **:** containing iron ⟨*ferro*concrete⟩ **2 :** iron and ⟨*ferro*nickel⟩ — chiefly in names of alloys **3** [*ferrous*] **:** containing ferrous iron ⟨*ferro*ferricyanide⟩

fer·ro·alloy \ˌfe(ˌ)rō+\ *n* [*ferro-* + *alloy*] **:** a crude alloy of iron with one or more other elements, (as metals) used for deoxidizing molten steel and making alloy steels

fer·ro·aluminum \"+\ *n* [*ferro-* + *aluminum*] **:** an alloy of iron and aluminum that is sometimes added to molten steel to deoxidize the metal or to provide aluminum (as in steel for nitriding)

fer·ro·an \ˈferəwən, ˈfe,rōən\ *adj* [*ferro-* + *-an*] **:** containing ferrous iron

fer·ro·bacteria \ˌfe(ˌ)rō+\ *n pl* [*ferro-* + *bacteria*] **:** IRON BACTERIA

fer·ro·boron \"+\ *n* [*ferro-* + *boron*] **:** an alloy of iron and boron sometimes added to molten steel

fer·ro·car·bon titanium \ˌferōˌkärbən-\ *n* **:** a crude alloy of iron, carbon, and titanium containing 15 to 20 percent titanium and 3 to 8 percent carbon and sometimes added to molten steel

fer·ro·cene \ˈferə,sēn\ *n* -S [*ferro-* + cyclopenta*diene*] **:** a crystalline very stable organometallic compound $(C_5H_5)_2Fe$ of cyclopentadiene and iron; *also* **:** any analogous compound with other heavy metals (as chromium)

fer·ro·cerium \ˌfe(ˌ)rō+\ *n* [NL, fr. *ferro-* + *cerium*] **:** a crude iron alloy containing a high percentage of cerium and used for flints in cigarette lighters

fer·ro·chromium \"+\ *or* **fer·ro·chrome** \ˈferə,krōm\ *n* [NL, fr. *ferro-* + *chromium*] **:** a crude alloy of iron and chromium used chiefly to incorporate chromium in iron or steel

fer·ro·columbium \ˌfe(ˌ)rō+\ *n* [NL, fr. *ferro-* + *columbium*] **:** a crude alloy of iron and niobium used chiefly to add niobium to steel

fer·ro·concrete \"+\ *n* [*ferro-* + *concrete*] **:** REINFORCED CONCRETE

fer·ro·cyanic acid \"+...-\ *n* [*ferrocyanic* ISV *ferro-* + *cyanic*] **:** a white crystalline acid $H_4Fe(CN)_6$ obtained by treating ferrocyanides with acids

fer·ro·cyanide \"+\ *n* [ISV *ferrocyanic* + *-ide*] **:** a salt of ferrocyanic acid obtained usu. by reaction of a cyanide (as calcium cyanide) with ferrous sulfate or by recovery from spent oxide ⟨calcium ~ $Ca_2Fe(CN)_6$⟩ — see IRON BLUE, PRUSSIAN BLUE

fer·ro·dolomite \"+\ *n* [*ferro-* + *dolomite*] **:** a mineral component $CaFe(CO_3)_2$ consisting of calcium iron carbonate in ankerite

¹fer·ro·electric \"+\ *adj* [*ferro-* + *electric*] **:** having dielectric properties (as electric hysteresis or a saturation limit for electric polarization) ⟨~ crystals⟩ — **fer·ro·electricity** \"+\ *n*

²ferroelectric \"\ *n* **:** a ferroelectric substance

fer·ro·equi·nol·o·gist \ˌfe(ˌ)rō,ēkwəˈnäləjəst, -ē,kwīˈn-\ *n* -S [*ferroequino-* "iron horse" (fr. *ferro-* + *equino-*, fr. L *equinus* equine + *-logy* + *-ist* — more at EQUINE] **:** RAILFAN

fer·ro·gabbro \ˌfe(ˌ)rō+\ *n* [*ferro-* + *gabbro*] **:** a gabbro having pyroxene and olivine that are abnormally high in iron

fer·ro·hemoglobin \"+\ *n* [*ferro-* + *hemoglobin*] **:** HEMOGLOBIN 1b

¹fer·ro·magnesian \"+\ *adj* [*ferro-* + *magnesian*] **:** containing iron and magnesium

²ferromagnesian \"\ *n* -S **:** a ferromagnesian mineral

fer·ro·magnet \"+\ *n* [*ferro-* + *magnet*] **:** a magnet composed of ferromagnetic material

¹fer·ro·magnetic \"+\ *adj* [*ferro-* + *magnetic*] **:** of or relating to a class of substances characterized by abnormally high magnetic permeability, definite saturation point, and appreciable residual magnetism and hysteresis — **fer·ro·mag·netism** \"+\ *n*

²ferromagnetic \"\ *n* **:** a ferromagnetic substance (as iron, nickel, cobalt, and numerous alloys)

fer·ro·manganese \"+\ *n* [*ferro-* + *manganese*] **:** an alloy of iron and manganese containing usu. about 80 percent manganese and used in steelmaking — compare SPIEGELEISEN

fer·ro·molybdenum \"+\ *n* [*ferro-* + *molybdenum*] **:** a crude alloy of iron and molybdenum used to add molybdenum to iron or steel

fer·ro·nickel \"+\ *n* [*ferro-* + *nickel*] **:** a crude alloy of iron and nickel sometimes used in making nickel steel

fer·ron·nière *also* **fer·ro·nière** \ˌferənˌye(ə)r\ *n* -S [F *ferronnière*, after *La Belle Ferronnière*, portrait of a woman wearing such a jewel painted by Leonardo da Vinci †1519 Ital. artist] **:** a pendant jewel worn (as by women in 15th century Italy and early 19th century England) in the middle of the forehead

fer·ro·phosphorus \ˌfe(ˌ)rō+\ *n* [*ferro-* + *phosphorus*] **:** a crude alloy of iron and phosphorus

fer·ro·porphyrin \"+\ *n* [*ferro-* + *porphyrin*] **:** a red ferrous derivative of a porphyrin in which the iron atom is held by nitrogen atoms of the porphyrin

fer·ro·protoporphyrin \"+\ *n* [*ferro-* + *protoporphyrin*] **:** HEME

fer·ro·prussiate process \"+ . . . -\ *n* [*ferro-* + *prussiate*] **:** the process of making a blueprint

fer·ro·silicon \"+\ *n* [*ferro-* + *silicon*] **:** a crude alloy of iron and silicon containing 15 to 95 percent silicon and used for deoxidizing molten steel and making silicon steel and high-silicon cast iron

fer·ro·sil·ite \ˌferōˈsi,līt\ *n* -S [*ferro-* + *silicate*] **:** a mineral component consisting of an iron silicate $FeSiO_3$ in hypersthene — compare CLINOFERROSILITE, ORTHOFERROSILITE

ferroso- *comb form* [NL *ferrosus* ferrous — more at FERROUS] **:** ferrous and ⟨*ferroso*ferric⟩

fer·ro·so·ferric oxide \fəˌrōsə, feˌ+ . . . -\ *n* [ISV *ferroso-* + *ferric*] **:** a black magnetic iron oxide Fe_3O_4 found in nature as magnetite, also obtained synthetically (as from iron by heating in steam or from a ferrous salt and an alkali by precipitation and oxidation), and used chiefly as a pigment and polishing material — called also *iron(II,III) oxide*

fer·ro·spinel \ˌfe(ˌ)rō+\ *n* [*ferro-* (fr. *ferromagnetic*) + *spinel*] **:** any of several synthetic crystalline magnetic substances of spinel structure that contain iron and are poor electrical conductors

fer·ro·titanium \"+\ *n* [*ferro-* + *titanium*] **:** an alloy of iron and titanium containing 15 to 45 percent titanium and used in steelmaking

fer·ro·tungsten \"+\ *n* [*ferro-* + *tungsten*] **:** a crude alloy of iron and tungsten used in making alloy steels

¹fer·ro·type \ˈferə,tīp\ *n* [*ferro-* + *type*] **1 :** a positive photograph made by a collodion process on a thin iron plate and having a darkened surface (as of black enamel) — called also *tintype* **2 :** the process by which a ferrotype is made

²ferrotype \"\ *vt* **:** to give a gloss to (a photographic print) by squeegeeing facedown while wet upon a ferrotype plate and allowing to dry

ferrotype plate *or* **ferrotype tin** *n* **:** a highly polished black-enameled or chromium-plated metal sheet that is used in ferrotyping

fer·ro·typ·er \-pə(r)\ *n* **:** one that ferrotypes

fer·ro–uranium \ˌfe(ˌ)rō+\ *n* [*ferro-* + *uranium*] **:** a crude alloy of iron and uranium

fer·rous \ˈferəs\ *adj* [NL *ferrosus*, fr. L *ferrum* iron + *-osus* -ous — more at FARRIER] **1 :** of, relating to, or containing iron — used specif. of compounds in which this element is bivalent or of bivalent iron; compare FERRIC **2** *of an alloy* **:** containing more iron than any other metal

ferrous carbonate *n* **:** a salt $FeCO_3$ occurring in nature as the mineral siderite, obtained synthetically as a white easily oxidizable precipitate, and used in medicine in treating iron-deficiency anemia

ferrous chloride *n* **:** a deliquescent salt $FeCl_2$ obtained in anhydrous form as colorless crystals (as by heating iron in hydrogen chloride) and used chiefly in the textile industry as a mordant and in metallurgy; iron dichloride

ferrous hydroxide *n* **:** a basic compound $Fe(OH)_2$ that is usu. obtained as a nearly white gelatinous precipitate by adding an alkali to a ferrous salt solution and that turns green and finally reddish brown in air on oxidation to ferric hydroxide

ferrous oxalate *n* **:** a yellow crystalline salt $FeC_2O_4.2H_2O$ found in nature as humboldtine and formerly used in potassium oxalate solution as a photographic developer

ferrous oxide *n* **:** the monoxide of iron FeO obtained as a readily oxidizable black powder (as by heating ferrous oxalate) — called also *iron(II) oxide*

ferrous sulfate *n* **:** an astringent salt $FeSO_4$ obtained usu. in the form of the pale green efflorescent crystalline heptahydrate $FeSO_4.7H_2O$ as a by-product (as in pickling iron or steel) and used chiefly in making other iron salts, pigments, and ink, in treating industrial wastes, and in medicine esp. for treating iron-deficiency anemia

ferrous sulfide *n* **:** the monosulfide of iron FeS found in nature as pyrrhotite and as troilite, obtained as brown or black metallic masses by fusing iron and sulfur or as a black precipitate by adding an alkaline sulfide to the solution of a ferrous compound, and used chiefly in making hydrogen sulfide

fer·ro·vanadium \ˌfe(ˌ)rō+\ *n* [*ferro-* + *vanadium*] **:** a crude alloy of iron and vanadium used in making steel or cast iron

fer·ro·zirconium \"+\ *n* [*ferro-* + *zirconium*] **:** a crude alloy of iron and zirconium usu. containing 12 to 40 percent zirconium

fer·ruc·cite \fəˈrü,chīt\ *n* -S [It, fr. *Ferruccio* Zambonini †1932 Ital. mineralogist + It *-ite*] **:** a mineral $NaBF_4$ consisting of sodium fluoborate occurring in minute orthorhombic crystals at Vesuvius

fer·ru·gi·nate \fəˈrüjə,nāt, fe'-\ *vt* -ED/-ING/-S [*ferruginous* + *-ate*] **:** to charge or stain (as rock) with a compound of iron — **fer·ru·gi·na·tion** \-ˌ==ˈnāshən\ *n* -S

¹fer·ru·gi·nous \fəˈrüjənəs, fe'-\ *also* **fer·ru·gin·e·ous** \ˌfer(y)əˈjinēəs\ *adj* [L *ferruginus, ferrugineus*, fr. *ferrugin-, ferrugo* iron rust, fr. *ferrum* iron — more at FARRIER] **1 :** of or containing iron **2 :** resembling iron rust in color

²ferruginous \"\ *n* -ES **:** a dark reddish orange to strong brown that is less strong than English red (sense 2a)

ferruginous roughleg *or* **ferruginous rough-legged hawk** *n* **:** a rather large light-colored rough-legged hawk (*Buteo regalis*) that feeds chiefly on rodents and is widely distributed in western No. America

¹fer·rule \ˈferəl\ *n* -S [alter. (influenced by L *ferrum* iron) of ME *virell, verelle, virole*, fr. MF *virelle, virole*, fr. OF *virol*, fr. L *viriola* small bracelet, dim. of *viria* armlet, bracelet, of Celt origin; akin to OIr *fiar* oblique — more at VEER] **1 a :** a band or cap usu. of metal enclosing the end of a cane, tool handle, table leg, or similar object to strengthen it or prevent splitting and wearing **b :** the protective point or knob on the far end of an umbrella **c :** the edge or corner covering of a book **2 :** a tube or bushing making a tight joint between a tube and tube plate or between two tubes or pipes (as of different metals) **3 a :** the metal band around a paint brush that binds the bristles to the head **b :** a metal or plastic band holding an eraser to a pencil **4 :** one of the complementary parts of a joint of a demountable fishing rod consisting of a sleeve and a shaft fitting into it to join the sections — called also respectively *female ferrule, male ferrule* **5 :** a metal band or socket in which the terminal of a wire or wiring system is secured for firm grip **6 :** a plug for a cleanout in a plumbing trap or soil pipe

²ferrule \"\ *vt* -ED/-ING/-S [alter. (influenced by L *ferrum* iron) of ME *virellen*, fr. MF *vireler*, fr. OF *viroler*, fr. *virol*, n.] **:** to supply with a ferrule

fer·rum \ˈferəm\ *n* -S [L] **:** IRON — symbol *Fe*

fer·ru·mi·nate \fəˈrümə,nāt\ *vt* -ED/-ING/-S [L *ferruminatus, feruminatus*, past part. of *ferruminare, feruminare*, fr. *ferrumin-, ferrumen, ferumin-, ferumen* solder, glue; perh. akin to L *firmus* firm — more at FIRM] **:** to join together (as metals) **:** SOLDER — **fer·ru·mi·na·tion** \-ˌ==ˈnāshən\ *n* -S

¹fer·ry \ˈferē, -ri\ *vb* -ED/-ING/-ES [ME *ferien*, fr. OE *ferian* to carry, bring, convey; akin to OHG *ferien, ferren* to transport, convey, ON *ferja* to transport, ferry, Goth *farjan* to travel in a boat; frequentatives fr. the root of OE *faran* to go, travel — more at FARE] *vt* **1 a :** to convey over a river or other body of water by boat ⟨*ferried* himself across the river⟩ ⟨~ troops from ship to shore⟩ ⟨~ supplies out to the island⟩ **b :** to cross (as a river) by a ferry ⟨whether they swim, ford, or ~ the river⟩ **2 a :** to convey from one place to another **:** TRANSPORT ⟨official cars could ~ the delegates over to the . . . reception —A.J.Liebling⟩ ⟨had to ~ a rare book across the Atlantic —Bernard Kalb⟩ **b :** to fly (an airplane) from the factory or other shipping point to the designated delivery point or from one base to another ⟨~ large planes to overseas bases⟩ **c :** to transport (as across an ocean) in an airplane ⟨our domestic airlines . . . ~ high-ranking military personnel between the United Nations —*Congressional Record*⟩ **~** *vi* **:** to pass over water in a boat or by a ferry ⟨reached Hoboken late . . . and *ferried* across to New York —G.A.Hamid⟩ ⟨~ across the river⟩

²ferry \"\ *n* -ES *often attrib* [ME *ferie, fery*, prob. fr. ON *ferja*, fr. *ferja*, v.] **1 :** a place where persons or things are carried across a river or other body of water in a boat ⟨rowed the traveler over the ~⟩ **2 a :** a service for carrying usu. on schedule persons, animals, vehicles, or goods across a ferry on a boat ⟨the opening of the new bridge and the termination of the ~⟩ **b :** an organized service and route for flying airplanes esp. across a sea or continent for delivery to the user ⟨the Atlantic ~ to British bases⟩ **c :** air transportation of persons or things that operates regularly between two points ⟨via the air ~ that carries tourists and their cars to the island⟩ ⟨a ~ plane⟩ **3 :** FERRYBOAT ⟨take the passenger and automobile ~ across the lake⟩ ⟨the railway ~ operating on the cross-channel route⟩ **4 :** a franchise or right to operate as a common carrier a ferry service across a body of water

ferryage *var of* FERRIAGE

ferryboat \ˈ==,=\ *n* [ME *feryboot*, fr. *fery* ferry + *boot* boat — more at BOAT] **:** a boat used in ferry service

ferry bridge *n* **:** a floating or hanging structure hinged or movably fastened to a wharf to facilitate passing on or off a ferryboat

ferry car *n* **:** a railroad car used generally within terminal limits to distribute or collect shipments of less than a carload to or from industries on private sidings — called also *trap car*

ferry–flat \ˈ==,=\ *n* **:** a flatboat used chiefly for ferrying (as on the Mississippi river)

ferry–house \ˈ==,=\ *n* **1 :** the house of the keeper of a ferry **2 :** the structure on a ferry wharf usu. containing a ticket office, waiting room, and other facilities

fer·ry·man \-mən, -,man\ *n, pl* **ferrymen** [ME *feryman*, fr. *fery* + *man*] **:** a person who operates a ferry

ferry–place \ˈ==,=\ *n* [ME *fery place*, fr. *fery* ferry + *place*] **:** a place used or usable for a ferry landing

ferry push car *n* **:** a long flatcar used as a bridge between a locomotive and the cars it is moving on or off a car ferry where the land-to-ferry incline is too steep for the locomotive to operate

fers *n* -ES [ME, fr. MF *fierce*, fr. Ar *farzan*, fr. Per *farzīn*] *obs* **:** a chess queen

-fers *pl of* -FER

fers·man·ite *also* **fers·man·nite** \ˈfərzmə,nīt, -rsm-\ *n* -S [Russ *fersmanit*, fr. Aleksandr E. *Fersman* †1945 Russ. mineralogist + Russ *-it* -ite] **:** a mineral $(Na,Ca)_2(Ti,Cb)Si(O,F)_6$ consisting of a silicate fluoride of sodium, calcium, titanium, and columbium

fers·mite \-,mīt\ *n* -S [Russ *fersmit*, fr. A. E. *Fersman* + Russ *-it* -ite] **:** a mineral $(Ca,Ce)(Cb,Ti)_2(O,F)_6$ consisting of an oxide and fluoride of calcium and columbium with cerium and titanium

fer·tile \ˈfərdᵊl, fəl, fəil, ˌtᵊl *sometimes* ˌ(ˌ)til, *chiefly Brit* ˌtīl\ *adj* [ME, fr. MF & L; MF *fertile*, fr. L *fertilis*, fr. *ferre* to bear, produce — more at BEAR] **1 a :** characterized by production of great quantities **:** abundant in yield **:** PRODUCTIVE ⟨prodigally ~ fields of ripening corn and oats⟩ ⟨peopled chiefly by three ~ families⟩ ⟨a ~ author with 50 books already published⟩ ⟨a philosophic tradition ~ in lucid writers⟩; *specif* **:** characterized by abundant resourcefulness of thought or imagination **:** CREATIVE, INVENTIVE ⟨his mind ~ in projects for the advancement of his fellows —H.W.H.Knott⟩ ⟨the ~ handling of folk themes in his new composition⟩ **b :** produced abundantly **:** NUMEROUS, TEEMING ⟨GI's . . . wading into the shore in numbers . . . prodigally ~ —John Mason Brown⟩ **2 a** (1) **:** capable of sustaining abundant and vigorous vegetation **:** favorable to plant growth ⟨~ fields of loam⟩ ⟨made the soil ~ again by adding the needed chemicals⟩ ⟨a ~ region awaiting the plow⟩ (2) **:** making the soil fertile **:** FERTILIZING (3) **:** affording favorable conditions or abundant possibilities for development ⟨countries where such misery exists are ~ soil for Communist infiltration —*N. Y. Times Mag.*⟩ ⟨what happens to responses during this period . . . would seem to offer a ~ field for research —Ralph Linton⟩ **b** *of a seed or egg* **:** capable of growing or developing **c** (1) **:** capable of producing fruit **:** fruit-bearing ⟨~ flowers⟩ ⟨~ trees⟩ (2) *of an anther* **:** containing pollen (3) **:** developing spores or spore-bearing organs **d** (1) **:** capable of breeding or reproducing esp. as indicated by the prior production of viable offspring ⟨a bull warranted ~⟩ (2) **:** likely to conceive or beget offspring ⟨few men over 60 are highly ~⟩ (3) **:** potentially reproductive ⟨few men of ~ age⟩ (4) *of an estrous cycle* **:** marked by the production of one or more viable eggs **e** *of a bee* **:** producing eggs **3 :** capable of being converted into fissionable material ⟨~ uranium 238⟩

syn FECUND, FRUITFUL, PROLIFIC: FERTILE may apply to a soil facilitating ready growth or to something likened to a productive seed bed; it may also apply to persons or animals able to produce young ⟨past fields where the wheat was high. Peaches grew in the orchards; it was a *fertile* country —S.V. Benét⟩ ⟨planted so deeply in *fertile* minds that even now they are sending up fresh crops —H.S.Canby⟩ ⟨India, where the people are more *fertile* than the land —*Time*⟩ FECUND may apply to whatever yields in abundance or with rapidity ⟨giving lessons to a few of the *fecund* king's offspring —E.J.Kahn⟩ ⟨a good part of these inventions came to birth — or were further nourished — in the *fecund* mind of Leonardo da Vinci —Lewis Mumford⟩ FRUITFUL may apply to anything bearing or borne in abundance or in gratifying numbers or to conditions that facilitate such bearing ⟨prefer that a coconut palm should be planted by an old woman who has many children, because they believe that a tree planted by so *fruitful* a woman will bear a plentiful crop of coconuts —J.G.Frazer⟩ ⟨rewarding land, too, much of it; rich, wide, and in years when the rains came, wonderfully *fruitful* —Russell Lord⟩ ⟨the enormously *fruitful* discovery that pitch of sound depends upon the length of the vibrating chord —Havelock Ellis⟩ PROLIFIC stresses rapidity in production or reproduction and may or may not be derogatory ⟨the defectives are appallingly *prolific*: the others have fewer children —G.B.Shaw⟩ ⟨the starling is so *prolific* that the flocks become immense —Richard Jefferies⟩ ⟨an extremely *prolific* writer whose literary output, if collected, might easily fill half-a-hundred volumes —*Encyc. Americana*⟩

fertile frond *n* **:** a frond bearing spores and often differing markedly in color, form, and size from the sterile fronds (as in sensitive fern)

fer·tile·ly \-ᵊl(l)ē, -il(l)ē, -īll, ˌli\ *adv* **:** in a fertile or fruitful manner

fer·tile·ness *n* -ES **:** FERTILITY

¹fer·til·i·ty \ˌfərˈtiləd·ē, fə'-, fəi'-, ˌfə(r)'-, -lətē, -i\ *n* -ES [ME *fertilite*, fr. MF *fertilité*, fr. L *fertilitas*, fr. *fertilis* fertile + *-itas* -ity] **1 :** the quality or state of being fertile: **a :** an actual state of productive abundance ⟨insure the ~ of the rice crop⟩ ⟨a theme he develops with ~ and power⟩ **b :** a capacity for producing or reproducing ⟨the ~ of the theory should provoke new developments in research⟩ ⟨a high degree of ~ in one member of a childless couple and relative infertility in the other **c :** a capacity to provide the necessary nutriments or conditions for plant growth ⟨used manure to keep up the ~ of their land⟩ **d :** actual reproductive capacity as measured by production of offspring ⟨a ram of proven ~⟩ ⟨a breed noted for its high ~⟩ — compare FECUNDITY **2 :** the birthrate of a population (as of a national, religious, or ethnic group) **:** reproductive performance — opposed to *mortality*

²fertility \"\ *adj* **1 :** of or relating to fertility ⟨the serpent was a ~ symbol —A.P.Davies⟩ ⟨~ statistics⟩ **2 :** of or associated with a fertility cult ⟨~ rites practiced by the Canaanites⟩ ⟨~ gods⟩ ⟨~ myths⟩; *also* **:** believed to promote the fertility of the land and its animals and people ⟨~ dances surviving in medieval Europe⟩

fertility cult *n* **1 :** a system of nature worship involving rites and ceremonies believed to ensure productiveness of plants, animals, and people and often directed toward the propitiation of a special deity **2 :** the body of followers and practitioners of such a system

fer·til·iz·abil·i·ty \ˌfər|d·ᵊl,īzəˈbiləd·ē, ˌfəl, ˌfəil, ˌtᵊl-, -bilətē, -i\ *n* -ES **:** capability of being fertilized; *specif* **:** the period in the life of an egg during which it is able to participate effectively in fertilization ⟨the length of life of an egg and the length of its ~ —George Barth⟩

fer·til·iz·able \ˈ==,=zəbəl, ,=='===\ *adj* **:** capable of being fertilized

fer·til·iza·tion \ˌ==əˈzāshən, -ˌīˈz-\ *n* -S **1 :** the act or process of making or becoming fertile: **a** (1) **:** the application of fertilizer (2) **:** the bringing about or promoting of an intellectual or economic development **:** ENRICHMENT **b** (1) **:** the act or process of fecundation, insemination, impregnation, or pollination — not often used technically (2) **:** the process of union of two germ cells whereby the somatic chromosome number is restored and the development of a new individual is initiated in animals typically involving penetration of a large passive female cell by a smaller active male cell followed by completion of the maturation of the female cell and by fusion of the haploid gamete pronuclei to form a diploid synkaryon within a new initially unicellular zygote and in most seed plants depending upon penetration of the ovule and embryo sac containing the egg by a pollen tube that discharges the nonmotile male nucleus — compare CONJUGATION, DOUBLE FERTILIZATION, PARTHENOGENESIS, POLYSPERMY **2 :** an instance of fertilization — **fer·til·iza·tion·al** \ˌ==(ˌ)=ˈzāshənᵊl, -shnəl\ *adj*

fertilization cone *n* **:** ENTRANCE CONE

fertilization membrane *n* **:** a resistant membranous layer that separates from the surface of many eggs immediately after entry of a sperm and thus prevents multiple fertilization

fertilization tube *n* **:** a branch that projects from the antheridium and pierces the oogonium to provide for passage of the male nucleus in certain phycomycetous fungi

fer·til·ize \ˈfər|d·ᵊl,īz, ˈfəl, ˈfəil, |tᵊl-\ *vb* -ED/-ING/-S *see -ize in Explan Notes* [prob. fr. F *fertilizer*, fr. MF, fr. *fertile*, adj. + *-iser* -ize] *vt* **:** to make fertile: as **a** (1) **:** to apply compost, manure, or commercial fertilizer to (a growing medium) in order to supply nutriments or make available nutriments already present ⟨~ the fishpond with commercial fertilizer to promote plankton growth⟩ (2) **:** to stimulate, supply, or enrich the development of ⟨the struggles of the war had . . . *fertilized* and quickened the thinking and feeling of the region —Van Wyck Brooks⟩ ⟨~ the country's economy with foreign capital⟩ ⟨reading that will ~ his vocabulary⟩ **b** (1) **:** to cause or tend to cause fertilization in (as by pollinating or inseminating) ⟨the wind ~*s* many plants⟩ — not used technically (2) **:** to participate with (a germ cell of the opposite sex) in fertilization ⟨under certain circumstances spermatozoa from one species may ~ ova from another⟩ **~** *vi* **:** to make something fertile; *specif* **:** to apply fertilizer to soil ⟨who raise grain but do not ~⟩

fer·til·iz·er \-zə(r)\ *n* -S **1 :** one that fertilizes ⟨he was not only a very distinguished writer but . . . a ~ of other talents —Lloyd Morris⟩ **2 :** a substance (as manure, lime, or commercial fertilizer) used to fertilize soil; *esp* **:** one chemically prepared that supplies nutrients (as a mixture containing varying percentages of nitrogen, available phosphate, and water-soluble potash)

fertilizer analysis *or* **fertilizer grade** *n* **:** ANALYSIS 4c

fer·til·i·zin \(ˌ)fərˈtiləzən, ˈfərd·ᵊl,īz-\ *n* -S [*fertilize* + *-in*] **:** a sperm-agglutinating agent produced by an egg (as of an ascidian) that plays a part in the preliminaries of fertilization

fe·ru \fəˈrü\ *n* -S [Yoruba] **:** a bast fiber derived from an African tree (*Cochlospermum tinctorium*) and used in making rope

fer·u·la \ˈfer(y)ələ\ *n* [NL, fr. L, giant fennel — more at FESTUCA] **1** *cap* **:** a large genus of Old World plants (family Umbelliferae) with deeply divided leaves, compound umbels of yellow flowers, and membranous-winged fruit with three threadlike ridges — see ASAFETIDA, GALBANUM **2** -S **:** any plant of the genus *Ferula*

¹fer·ule \ˈferəl\ *also* **fer·u·la** \ˈfer(y)ələ\ *n* -S [L *ferula* giant fennel, whip, rod for punishment] **1 :** any of several instruments (as a rod, switch, or ruler) used to punish school children; *specif* **:** a flat piece of wood like a ruler used esp. on the hands **2 :** punishment with a ferule ⟨as boys that slink from ~ —Alfred Tennyson⟩ **3 :** school discipline ⟨this tutelage under Miss Newcomb's ~ —Dixon Wecter⟩

²ferule \"\ *vt* -ED/-ING/-S **:** to punish with a ferule

fe·ru·lic acid \fəˈrülik-\ *n* [*ferula* + *-ic*] **:** a white crystalline acid $HO(CH_3O)C_6H_3CH{:}CHCOOH$ that is structurally related to vanillin and is obtained esp. from various resins (as asafetida or opopanax)

fer·un·gu·la·ta \ˌfer+\ *n pl, cap* [NL *Ferae* + *Ungulata*] *in some classifications* **:** a major division of eutherian mammals comprising the Ungulata and the Carnivora

fer·va·nite \ˈfərvəˌnīt\ *n* -S [*fer*rum + *va*nadium + *-ite*] **:** a mineral $Fe_4V_4O_{16}.5H_2O$ consisting of a rare hydrated iron vanadate occurring with radioactive minerals but not itself radioactive

fer·ven·cy \ˈfərvənsē, ˈfə̄v-, ˈfəiv-, -si\ *n* -ES [ME *fervence, fervency,* fr. MF *fervence,* fr. LL *ferventia,* fr. L *fervent-, fervens* (pres. part.) + *-ia* -y] **:** FERVOR ⟨calmness as opposed to ~ in writing —Fanny Butcher⟩

fer·vent \-vənt\ *adj* [ME, fr. MF & L; MF *fervent,* fr. L *fervent-, fervens,* pres. part. of *fervēre* to boil, glow — more at BURN] **1 :** intensely hot ⟨the tessellated plain . . . seemed on this ~ day to be half-molten —Mary Webb⟩ **2 :** of great intensity ⟨the ~ heat . . . merely communicated a genial warmth to their half-torpid systems —Nathaniel Hawthorne⟩; *specif* **:** characterized by often deep fervor of feeling or expression ⟨~ patriotism⟩ ⟨expressed a ~ hope⟩ ⟨the religious center . . . was the austere yet ~ meetinghouse —Ruth Suckow⟩ ⟨setting ~ kisses upon his hands —Paul Bowles⟩ ⟨~ diction —H.O.Taylor⟩ **:** ENTHUSIASTIC ⟨had no longer any cause to grow ~ or furious about —Edmund Wilson⟩ **:** EARNEST ⟨a ~ moral sense⟩ **:** ZEALOUS ⟨he is known as a ~ champion of the trivial detail —R.L.Taylor⟩ ⟨a moment ends the ~ din —William Wordsworth⟩ **syn** see IMPASSIONED

fer·vent·ly *adv* [ME, fr. *fervent* + *-ly*] **:** in a fervent manner ⟨discussed the issue ~⟩ ⟨wished ~ that he might⟩

fer·vent·ness *n* -ES [ME *ferventnes,* fr. *fervent* + *-nes* -ness] **:** FERVOR

fer·vid \ˈfərvəd, ˈfə̄v-, ˈfəiv-\ *adj* [L *fervidus,* fr. *fervēre* to boil] **1 :** giving off intense heat **:** very hot **:** BURNING ⟨set out on an expedition when the ~ heat subsides —Frances Trollope⟩ **2 :** characterized by often extreme fervor of feeling or expression **:** IMPASSIONED ⟨overcome by ~ enthusiasm⟩ **:** ZEALOUS ⟨the voters . . . have always taken ~ partisans somewhat humorously —G.W.Johnson⟩ **:** VEHEMENT ⟨~ eloquence with which he urged his proposal⟩ **:** EBULLIENT ⟨the most loathsome and noisome abominations that his ~ imagination could concoct —C.W.Eliot⟩ **syn** see IMPASSIONED

fer·vid·i·ty \ˌfərˈvidəd·ē, fə̄'-, fəi'- -dətē, -i\ *n* -ES **:** FERVOR ⟨writes with ~, faith, and feeling —*New Yorker*⟩

fer·vid·ly *adv* **:** in a fervid manner **:** PASSIONATELY, INTENSELY ⟨to believe not perfunctorily but ~ that the power that orders nature and history is on one's side —Brand Blanshard⟩

fer·vid·ness *n* -ES **:** FERVOR

fer·vor \ˈfərvər, ˈfə̄və(r, ˈfəivə(r\ *n* -S *see -or in Explan Notes* [ME *fervour,* fr. MF & L; MF *ferveur,* fr. L *fervor,* fr. *fervēre* to boil, glow + *-or*] **1 :** intense heat ⟨those deserts . . . whose . . . ~s scarce allowed a bird to live —P.B.Shelley⟩ **2 a :** intensity of feeling or expression **:** PASSION ⟨rejected communism with as much ~ as they had accepted it —Margaret Marshall⟩ ⟨she cried quietly but with ~ —Robert Murphy⟩; *specif* **:** deep or excited interest in or enthusiasm for something ⟨the book has been greeted by Frenchmen with a ~ that no previous book on art ever aroused —George Duthuit⟩ **:** EARNESTNESS ⟨the moral ~ of a reformer⟩ ⟨ages of spiritual ~ . . . in which . . . men have been unusually excited about their souls —Clive Bell⟩ **:** ZEAL ⟨the tackling on both sides attains the ~ of a holy war —*New Yorker*⟩ **b :** an instance of emotional fervor ⟨the almost hysterical ~s of wartime⟩ **syn** see PASSION

fer·vor·ous \-v(ə)rəs\ *adj* **:** full of fervor

fès *or* **fes** *usu cap, var of* FEZ

fes·cen·nine \ˈfesᵊnˌīn, -ˌēn\ *adj, usu cap* [L *fescenninus,* prob. fr. *Fescenninus* of Fescennium, fr. *Fescennium,* ancient town in Etruria, Italy, famous for such songs and verses + L *-inus* -ine] **1 :** sung or read at a rural festival or a wedding in ancient Italy and marked by often obscene mockery ⟨~ songs⟩ ⟨lively ~ verses on the emperor's marriage⟩ **2 :** SCURRILOUS, OBSCENE ⟨street corner idlers making ~ comments on passing girls⟩

¹fes·cue \ˈfe(ˌ)skyü\ *n* -S [ME *festu,* fr. MF, fr. VL *festucum,* fr. L *festuca* — more at FESTUCA] **1** *obs* **:** STRAW, RUSH, TWIG **2 :** a small pointer (as a straw, stick, or quill) used to point out letters to or by children learning to read **3** *also* **fescue grass :** a grass of the genus *Festuca* — see MEADOW FESCUE, SHEEP FESCUE

²fescue *vt* -ED/-ING/-S *obs* **:** to assist (a reader) with a fescue

fescue foot *n* **:** a disease of the feet of cattle resembling ergotism but considered due to feeding on certain grasses of the genus *Festuca* which contain a toxic principle similar to ergot

fesh \ˈfesh\ *Scot var of* FETCH

¹fess *also* **fesse** \ˈfes\ *n, pl* **fesses** [ME *fes, fesse,* fr. MF *faisse, fesse,* fr. L *fascia* band — more at FASCIA] **:** a broad bar drawn horizontally across the middle of a heraldic field — **in fess** *adv* **1 :** in a line in the direction of a fess — used of two or more charges; usu. used only of charges in a line across the middle of the field; compare BARWISE 2, ¹BASE 5a, *in chief* at ¹CHIEF **2 :** FESSWISE 1, BARWISE 1 — **per fess :** divided in two by a horizontal line across the middle

fess

²fess \"\ *vb* -ED/-ING/-ES [short for *confess*] *slang* **:** CONFESS, OWN — usu. used with *up* ⟨~ up to having put something over on me⟩ ⟨~ up you're still carrying the torch for her —W.G.Smith⟩

³fess \"\ *adj* [perh. alter. of *fierce*] **1** *dial Eng* **:** LIVELY, SMART ⟨what a ~ little bonfire —Thomas Hardy⟩ **2** *dial Eng* **:** CONCEITED, IMPUDENT

fess point *n* **:** the center of a heraldic field

fesswise *also* **fesseways** *or* **fessewise** *or* **fessways** \ˈ=,=\ *adv* **1 :** in the direction of a fess **:** HORIZONTALLY, BARWISE 1 ⟨three keys ~ in pale⟩ **2 :** in fess ⟨three escarbuncles ~⟩

-fest \ˌfest\ *n comb form* -S [G *fest* festival, holiday, fr. MHG *vest,* fr. L *festum,* fr. neut. of *festus* solemn, festal — more at FEAST] **1 :** festive gathering esp. for competition ⟨shooting*fest*⟩ ⟨turner*fest*⟩ ⟨song*fest*⟩ **2 :** session often informal or spontaneous ⟨gab*fest*⟩ **:** outburst of activity ⟨slug*fest*⟩

fes·ta \ˈfestə\ *n* -S [It, fr. L, festival — more at FEAST] **:** CELEBRATION; *specif* **:** an annual local celebration in Italy of the day of the patron saint

fes·tal \ˈfestᵊl\ *adj* [L *festa* or *festum* festival + E *-al*] **1 :** of or belonging to a religious feast ⟨the ~ day of that saint⟩ ⟨~ celebration of the Holy Communion⟩ **2 :** of, given over to, or suited to festivity ⟨~ occasions⟩ ⟨~ crowds⟩ ⟨~ garments⟩ — **fes·tal·ly** \-təlē, -li\ *adv*

festal letter *n* **:** PASCHAL LETTER

¹fes·ter \ˈfestə(r)\ *n* -S [ME *fester, festre,* fr. MF *festre,* fr. L *fistula* pipe, tube, a kind of ulcer] **1 :** a suppurating sore **:** PUSTULE, ABSCESS **2 :** pus from an abscess

²fester \"\ *vb* **festered; festered; festering** \ˈfest(ə)riŋ\ **festers** [ME *festren,* fr. *festre,* n.] *vi* **1 :** to generate pus ⟨the wound becomes inflamed and ~s⟩ **2 :** to become putrid **:** PUTREFY, ROT ⟨a heritage of blackened ruins and ~*ing* cemeteries —G.B.Shaw⟩ **3 a :** to produce continual or progressive irritation or malignancy (as in a mind or population) **:** RANKLE ⟨an injustice that will ~ in their minds until the situation is corrected⟩ ⟨resentment that ~*ed* until it broke out in violence⟩ **b :** to develop by becoming increasingly virulent or malignant ⟨the quarrel . . . burst out again and quickly ~*ed* into the definitive schism of 1054 —A.J.Toynbee⟩ **c :** to undergo or exist in a state of often progressive deterioration ⟨comradeship can ~ into hatred —Merle Miller⟩ **:** reek with corruption ⟨the city's ~*ing* slums⟩ ~ *vt* **:** to exert a malignant influence on **:** INFLAME, CORRUPT ⟨the Argentina situation stood out as the sorest thumb of Pan-America, continuing to ~ and fever the whole system —*Annals of Amer. Acad. of Polit. & Soc. Sci.*⟩

¹fes·ti·nate \ˈfestəˌnāt, -ˌnət\ *adj* [L *festinatus,* past part.] **:** HASTY ⟨not likely to survive the wrecker's ~ crowbar —J.C. Adams⟩ — **fes·ti·nate·ly** *adv*

²fes·ti·nate \-ˌnāt\ *vi* -ED/-ING/-S [L *festinatus,* past part. of *festinare* to hasten, make haste — more at BORZOI] **:** HASTEN; *specif* **:** to accelerate the gait involuntarily in walking (as in certain nervous diseases) ⟨a *festinating* gait⟩

fes·ti·na·tion \ˌ==ˈnāshən\ *n* -S [L *festination-, festinatio,* fr. *festinatus* (past part.) + *-ion-, -io* -ion] **:** an act or instance of festinating

fes·ti·no \feˈstē(ˌ)nō\ *also* **fes·tine** \feˈstēn\ *n* -S [It *festino,* dim. of *festa* feast, holiday, festival, fr. L *festa* festival — more at FEAST] *archaic* **:** FEAST, ENTERTAINMENT

¹fes·ti·val \ˈfestəvəl\ *adj* [ME, fr. MF, fr. OF, fr. L *festivus* festive, gay + OF *-al* — more at FESTIVE] **:** of, belonging to, appropriate to, or set apart as a festival ⟨the ~ celebration of the Holy Communion⟩ ⟨playing ~ concerts⟩ ⟨their mood was ~⟩ ⟨on a ~ day⟩ — **fes·ti·val·ly** \-vəlē, -li\ *adv*

²festival \"\ *n* -S **1 :** a time of celebration marked by special observances: **a :** an occasion observed with religious ceremonies ⟨the planting and harvest ~s of primitive peoples⟩ **:** FEAST ⟨the great ~s of Whitsuntide, Trinity Sunday, and Corpus Christi —S.E.Morison⟩ **b :** an occasion devoted to festive community observances often held annually to celebrate the anniversary of a notable person or event or the harvest of an important product **:** a program of public festivity ⟨the best known ~ at the college is Founder's Day⟩ **2 a :** a program of cultural events consisting typically of a series of performances of works in the arts sometimes devoted to a single artist or a particular genre and often held annually for a period of several days or weeks ⟨a Bach ~⟩ ⟨a Shakespeare ~⟩ ⟨a crama ~⟩ ⟨a dance ~⟩ **b :** something resembling such a festival ⟨the radio station held a ~ of books with readings, talks, and discussions⟩ ⟨a cartoon ~ for children advertised by the local theater⟩ ⟨the occasional ~s at which the square-dance clubs of the area gather⟩ **3 :** CONVIVIALITY, GAIETY, CHEERFULNESS ⟨alcohol had always loosened . . . his sense of ~ but now it only dragged him down into despondency —Budd Schulberg⟩ **4 a :** ⁵FAIR 2 **b :** STRAWBERRY FESTIVAL

festival of freedom *usu cap both Fs* **:** PASSOVER 1

festival of lanterns *usu cap F&L* **:** FEAST OF LANTERNS

festival of lights *usu cap F&L* **:** HANUKKAH

festival of weeks *usu cap F&W* **:** SHABUOTH

fes·tive \ˈfestiv, -tēv *also* -təv\ *adj* [L *festivus,* fr. *festum* festival, feast + *-ivus* -ive — more at -FEST] **1 :** of, belonging to, or befitting a feast, festival, or other celebration ⟨banqueting merrily round the ~ board⟩ ⟨raise the flag on public holidays and other ~ occasions⟩ ⟨a set of diamond . . . cuff buttons for ~ wear —Ring Lardner⟩ **2 :** of or marked by gaiety, conviviality, or revelry **:** JOYOUS, MERRY, SPORTIVE ⟨came across the floor with a ~ stride —Theodore Dreiser⟩ ⟨a ~ party of sailors and girls at the next table⟩ — **fes·tive·ly** \-təvlē, -li\ *adv* — **fes·tive·ness** \-tivnəs, -tēv- *also* -təv-\ *n* -ES

fes·tiv·i·ty \feˈstivəd·ē, fəˈs-, -vətē, -i\ *n* -ES [ME *festivite,* fr. MF *festivité,* fr. L *festivitas,* fr. *festivus,* adj. + *-itas* -ity] **1 :** FESTIVAL ⟨the Pickwickian Christmas . . . was mainly a gratuitous ~ —Aldous Huxley⟩ **2 :** the quality or state of being festive **:** joyfulness in company (as at a social gathering) **:** GAIETY ⟨hung with banners which give it an air of restrained ~ —Kay Fuller⟩ **3 :** festive activity **:** REJOICING, MERRY-MAKING ⟨general ~ is to follow the parade⟩ — often used in pl. ⟨the *festivities* end with a fireworks display⟩

fes·ti·vous \ˈfestəvəs\ *adj* [L *festivus* + E *-ous*] **:** FESTIVE

¹fes·toon \(ˈ)feˈstün\ *n* -S [F *feston,* fr. It *festone,* fr. *festa* celebration, feast — more at FESTA] **1 a :** a decorative chain (as of flowers or leaves) hanging typically in a curve between two points ⟨decorated with ~s of flowers and ivy intertwined⟩ **b :** a carved, molded, or painted ornament representing a festoon **:** SWAG ⟨around the mirror were carved ~s of flowers wound with ribbon⟩ **c :** a piece of fabric suspended or bound at intervals to form graceful rounded folds ⟨a fringed damask ~ for the archway⟩ **2 :** a usu. hanging open loop or curve ⟨the paper is looped over these spars in long ~s —F.H.Norris⟩; *esp* **:** something suspended in a curve between two points ⟨between the mulberry trees swing long ~s of grapevines⟩ **3 :** something resembling a pendent garland ⟨live oaks with long . . . ~s of Spanish moss —F.B. Gipson⟩ **4 :** one of the somewhat quadrangular segments bordering the body of certain ticks — see TICK illustration

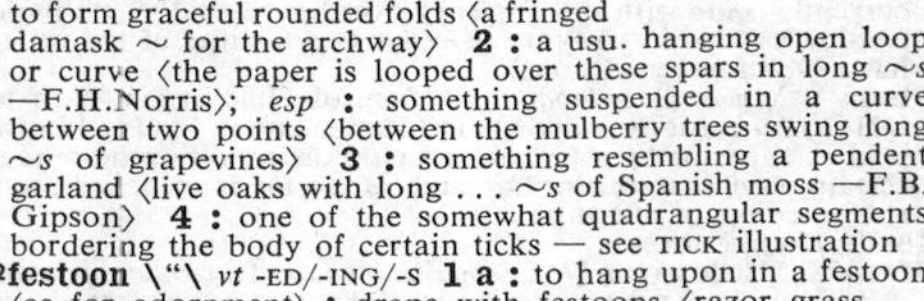

festoon 1a

²festoon \"\ *vt* -ED/-ING/-S **1 a :** to hang upon in a festoon (as for adornment) **:** drape with festoons ⟨razor grass . . . hung in emerald loops from branch to branch, ~*ing* living foliage and dead stump alike —William Beebe⟩ **b :** hang down from like a pendent garland ⟨blossoms ~ the vine⟩ ⟨bearded moss ~s the branches⟩ ⟨icicles ~ the eaves⟩ **c :** to hang upon or adorn as if comprising a festoon ⟨the old wooden carriages . . . have passengers . . . hanging from the sides; the more hardy commuters even ~ tender and locomotive —H.T. De Sa⟩ ⟨the margins of the manuscript were ~*ed* with additions and corrections⟩ **2 :** to form into a festoon **:** suspend in festoons ⟨the telegraph wires whipped back and ~*ed* themselves round our machine —Francis Yeats-Brown⟩; *specif* **:** to hang (material) in festoons for drying **3** *dentistry* **a :** to shape (a crown or band) to conform to the contour of tissues with which there is to be association **b :** to mold (the plate of a denture) about the base of the teeth or facings to resemble the natural gum line

festoon cloud *n* **:** MAMMATOCUMULUS

festoon drier *n* **:** a mechanism for supporting material in loops while it is being dried by circulating air

festoon drying *n* **:** the drying of material (as rubber, plastic, impregnated fabric, or a web of paper) by supporting it in long loops and moving it through a drying chamber

fes·toon·er \-nə(r)\ *n* -S **:** a sewing-machine operator who finishes the edges of knit goods

fes·toon·ery \feˈstünərē, -ri\ *n* -ES **:** festoons (as of a room) considered as a group ⟨the elegant ~ of the ballroom⟩

festoon lighting *n* **:** lighting by festoons of electric lamps wired to a flexible cable

festoon pine *n* **:** a creeping evergreen plant (*Selaginella rupestris*) of eastern No. America with tufted stems

-fests *pl of* -FEST

fest·schrift \ˈfestˌshrift\ *n, pl* **fest·schrif·ten** \-ftən\ *or* **festschrifts** *often cap* [G, fr. *fest* festival + *schrift* writings, fr. OHG *scrift,* fr. *scrīban* to write — more at -FEST, SCRIBE] **:** a usu. miscellaneous volume of writings from several hands for a celebration; *esp* **:** one of learned essays contributed by students, colleagues, and admirers to honor a scholar on a special anniversary

fes·tu·ca \feˈst(y)ükə, fəˈ-\ *n, cap* [NL, fr. L, stalk, straw, rod for touching slaves in manumission; prob. akin to L *ferula* giant fennel] **:** a large genus of mostly tufted perennial grasses comprising the fescues and having flat leaves and panicled spikelets with acute pointed or awned flowering scales — see BUFFALO BUNCHGRASS, SHEEP'S FESCUE, TALL FESCUE

fes·tu·cine \ˈfest(y)əˌsīn, -sən\ *adj* [L *festuca* stalk, straw + E *-ine*] **:** of the color straw yellow

fet \ˈfet\ *vt* **fet; fet; fetting; fets** [ME *fetten, feten,* fr. OE *fetian* — more at FETCH] *dial Eng* **:** FETCH

fe·ta \ˈfed·ə\ *n* -S [NGk (*tyri*) *pheta,* fr. *tyri* cheese + *pheta* slice, fr. It *fetta*] **:** a white cheese made of the milk of sheep or goats and cured in brine

fe·tal *also* **foe·tal** \ˈfēd·ᵊl, -ētᵊl\ *adj* [*fetus, foetus* + *-al*] **:** of, relating to, characteristic of, or in the stage or condition of a fetus

fetal circulation *n* **:** the course of the blood in the vessels of the fetus, impure blood passing in man and the higher mammals to the placenta by the umbilical arteries, returning purified and charged with nutriment by the umbilical vein, and entering the inferior vena cava either directly by the ductus venosus or after passing through the liver

fe·tal·iza·tion *also* **foe·tal·iza·tion** \ˌ===ˈzāshən, -ˌīˈz-\ *n* -S **:** a retention in the postnatal life of higher forms of conditions occurring during development of related lower forms ⟨the human skull shows ~ in comparison to the gorilla's since it resembles the simple infant gorilla skull rather than the massive specialized adult skull⟩

fetal membrane *n* **:** an embryonic membrane

fetal rickets *n* **:** human achondroplasia

fe·ta·tion *also* **foe·ta·tion** \fēˈtāshən\ *n* -S [*fetus, foetus* + *-ation*] **:** the formation of a fetus **:** PREGNANCY

¹fetch \ˈfech\ *vb* -ED/-ING/-ES [ME *fecchen,* fr. OE *feccan, fetian;* akin to OE *fatian* to fetch, OHG (*sih*) *vazzōn* to climb, ascend, ON *feta* to step, find one's way, OE *fōt* foot — more at FOOT] *vt* **1 a :** to go after and bring back **:** go and get ⟨escaped while the guard was out to ~ their supper⟩ ⟨~ me a drink⟩ ⟨had to leave her alone while he ~*ed* the doctor from town⟩; *broadly* **:** to convey or conduct from one place to another **:** come and get ⟨inside the station as I waited for my friends to ~ me —D.L.Cohn⟩ **:** BRING ⟨the souvenirs he ~*ed* back from Europe⟩ ⟨come and ~ along your family⟩ **:** TAKE ⟨had enough money to ~ him from New York to Philadelphia⟩ **b** *now dial* **:** to carry off **:** FILCH **c :** to draw from an often remote source **:** DERIVE, DEDUCE ⟨~*ed* his arguments from afar⟩ ⟨~ analogies from nature⟩ **2 a :** to cause to come ⟨~ the discussion to a close⟩ ⟨one shot ~*ed* it down⟩ **:** draw forth **:** ELICIT ⟨the sound of the sob ~*ed* tears to the eyes —Arnold Bennett⟩ ⟨~ a laugh from the audience⟩ ⟨a scamper of feet ~*ed* me out of my berth and up on deck —A.T.Quiller-Couch⟩ **b :** to bring as a price or similar return **:** sell for ⟨the pigs ~*ed* a good price at the market⟩ **:** bring in **:** REALIZE ⟨risk capital ~*es* a higher interest rate⟩ ⟨professional skill . . . ~*es* very much smaller pay in Germany —J.A.Hobson⟩ **c :** to win the interest or admiration of **:** ATTRACT ⟨two of the men . . . were ~*ed* by the notion of striking it rich —*Newsweek*⟩ ⟨he doesn't ~ the girls like William —D.H.Lawrence⟩ **d** *chiefly dial* **:** to revive from unconsciousness **:** bring around — often used with *to* or *around* **e :** to bring to agreement **:** CONVINCE — often used with *round* ⟨his argument ~*ed* her round⟩ **3 a :** to give (a blow) by striking **:** DEAL ⟨~ him a clip on the chin⟩ — not often in formal use **b** *now chiefly dial* **:** to bring about (a movement or action) **:** PERFORM, ACCOMPLISH ⟨I meant to go . . . but time was short and I didn't ~ it —O.W.Holmes †1935⟩; *specif* **:** to take into the lungs **:** DRAW ⟨sat ~*ing* her breath in dry sobs —Ngaio Marsh⟩ **c :** to bring forth (a sound or speech) ⟨~ a sneeze⟩ **:** UTTER ⟨~ a loud whoop⟩ **:** HEAVE ⟨~ a sigh⟩ **d :** to make an end of (as a person) **:** do for **:** KILL ⟨got in another shot and ~*ed* him —Bret Harte⟩ — not often in formal use **4 a :** to make (a point) by sailing esp. despite adverse wind or tide ⟨~ the harbor before the storm breaks⟩ **b :** to arrive at **:** REACH ⟨~*ed* home after his long ride⟩ **5 :** DAMN — used in an oath ⟨dad ~ it⟩ ~ *vi* **1 :** to get and bring something ⟨the German housewife has to spend a lot of time ~*ing* and carrying —Marieluise Capitaine⟩; *specif* **:** to retrieve killed game **:** SEEK — often used in the imperative as a command to a dog **2 :** to take a roundabout way **:** CIRCLE — usu. used with *about, around,* or *round* ⟨working through the parts beyond Jago Row, he ~*ed* round into Honey Lane —Arthur Morrison⟩ **3** *of a boat* **:** GO, COME ⟨~ about⟩ **:** hold a course ⟨~ to windward⟩ **4** *chiefly Scot* **:** to breathe with difficulty ⟨she ~*es* and fights for breath —Robert Burns⟩ **5** *dial* **:** to recover consciousness, health, or weight **:** REVIVE — often used with *up* ⟨give him another glass — then he'll ~ up —Thomas Hardy⟩ — **fetch about** *obs* **:** to effect a change in ⟨*fetch about* this form of speech —2 Sam 14:20 (AV)⟩ — **fetch a compass :** to circle around ⟨from thence we *fetched a compass* —Acts 28:13 (AV)⟩ — **fetch a pump :** to prime a pump — **fetch off** *obs* **:** to get the better of ⟨as I return I will *fetch off* these justices —Shak.⟩

²fetch \"\ *n* -ES [¹*fetch*] **1 :** an act or instance of fetching ⟨in the trial for two sheep dogs each must keep its own side till the ~ is finished⟩ **2 :** a stratagem contrived in a far-fetched, ingenious, or devious way **:** ARTIFICE, SOPHISM ⟨the mere ~ of a debater at a loss for arguments⟩ **:** TRICK ⟨one of the cunningest ~*es* of Satan that he . . . dodging behind this neighbor or that acquaintance compels us to wound him through them —J.R.Lowell⟩ **3** *dial Eng* **:** a catch in the throat or voice; *specif* **:** a dying gasp **4 :** the distance along open water or land over which the wind blows **:** SWEEP ⟨wind coming from the . . . deserts with a clear ~ of a thousand miles —Joseph Furphy⟩; *specif* **:** the distance traversed by waves without obstruction (as when caused by steady winds)

³fetch \"\ *n* -ES [origin unknown] **1 a :** the phantom double of a living person appearing as an omen of the death of the person **:** WRAITH **b :** something that looks or acts exactly like another **:** COUNTERPART ⟨the muddy field before them which was the exact ~ of the muddy field behind —*Strand Mag.*⟩ **2 :** GHOST, APPARITION ⟨a harrowing graveyard with . . . a ~ —*Saturday Rev.*⟩

⁴fetch *var of* FITCH

fetch away *or* **fetch way** *vi* **:** to move from place as a result of a ship's rolling or pitching **:** SHIFT, SLIDE ⟨some of the cargo had been loosely stowed and *fetched away* a little when the storm hit⟩

fetch candle *n* [perh. fr. ³*fetch*] **:** a corpse candle supposed to pass between the home and the grave of the beholder

fetching *adj* [fr. pres. part. of ¹*fetch*] **:** tending to win interest or admiration **:** ATTRACTIVE ⟨a memoir that must be one of the most ~ tourist baits in all the state —S.H.Holbrook⟩ ⟨a ~ gown⟩ — **fetch·ing·ly** *adv*

fetch up *vt* **1 :** to bring up or out **:** PRODUCE ⟨a tyrant *fetched up* by frightened capitalists —H.J.Muller⟩ **:** RECALL ⟨can *fetch up* anecdotes on almost any phase of straits historic lore —R.M.Dorson⟩ **2 :** to make up (as leeway or lost time) **3** *chiefly dial* **:** to bring up **:** RAISE, REAR ⟨she *fetched up* three boys⟩ **4 :** to bring to a stop ⟨he was *fetched up* short by a stop light⟩ ~ *vi* **:** to come to a standstill, stopping place, or result **:** end up **:** STOP ⟨*fetched up* suddenly against the wall⟩ **:** ARRIVE ⟨it was enough to make the voyage at all, and indeed he should have *fetched up* in Virginia —Alan Villiers⟩ **:** CONCLUDE ⟨counted the wooden boxes . . . and *fetched up* with fourteen —Frederick Way⟩

fetch-up \ˈ=,=\ *n* -S [*fetch up*] **:** an abrupt stop (as at the end of a fall) ⟨injured in the *fetch-up* of the toboggan against the tree⟩

¹fete *or* **fête** \ˈfāt, *usu* -ād·+V\ *n* -S [F *fête,* fr. MF *feste,* fr. OF — more at FEAST] **:** a festive celebration or entertainment **:** FESTIVAL ⟨the ~ of the Assumption of the Virgin in Paris⟩ ⟨the village ~s go on, as English as a cowslip —C.G.Glover⟩ ⟨Class Day, the great ~ of the year —Catherine D. Bowen⟩; *specif* **:** an often outdoor entertainment on a lavish scale ⟨~s in the park of the Château of Versailles with sky, water, and sylvan illuminations and empyrical music and discourses —Janet Flanner⟩

²fete *or* **fête** \"\ *vt* -ED/-ING/-S [F *fêter,* fr. MF *fester,* fr. OF, fr. *feste,* n.] **:** to honor (a person) or commemorate (an event) with a fete ⟨*feted* the royal visitors with banquets and parades⟩ **:** ENTERTAIN ⟨when the circus came to town . . . he would welcome the train in the railway yards, ~ the performers —Green Peyton⟩ **:** CELEBRATE ⟨*feted* his recovery with ice cream and cake⟩ ⟨literary weeklies here all *feted* her with photographs of herself and with the compliments of others —*New Yorker*⟩ **:** EXTOL ⟨Sade has been *feted* as a great thinker —François Bondy⟩

fête cham·pê·tre \ˌfāt,shäⁿˈpetr(ᵊ), -shäⁿp-, -pät-, -t(rə)\ *n, pl* **fêtes champêtres** \-t,sh. . .tr(ᵊ), . . .trə(z), . . .t(s)\ [F, lit., rural festival] **1 :** a gathering for amusements in a rural setting of members of an 18th century French court costumed as shepherds and shepherdesses **2 :** an outdoor entertainment **:** a large garden party

fête ga·lante \-gəˈläⁿt\ *n, pl* **fêtes galantes** \-tg. . .nt(s)\ [F, lit., gay festival] **:** FÊTE CHAMPÊTRE 1

fet·er·i·ta *also* **fed·er·i·ta** \ˌfed(·)əˈrēd·ə\ *n* -S [Sudanese Ar; akin to Ar *faṭīrah* unleavened bread] **:** any of various grain sorghums that are derived from a Sudanese sorghum (*Sorghum vulgare* var. *caudatum*) and are characterized by compact oval heads of exceptionally large soft white seeds

feth \ˈfeth\ *Scot var of* FAITH

feth·er *dial var of* FEATHER

feti- — see FETO-

¹fe·tial *or* **fe·cial** \ˈfēshəl\ *n, pl* **fetials** \-lz\ *or* **fe·ti·a·les** \ˌfād·ēˈäˌlās\ *or* **fecials** [L *fetialis,* prob. fr. (assumed)

OL *fetis* statute, treaty (akin to Goth *gadeths* deed) + L *-alis* -al — more at DEED] : a member of a priestly board in ancient Rome responsible for overseeing diplomatic negotiations

²**fetial** *or* **fecial** \"\ *adj* [L *fetialis* of a fetial, fr. *fetialis*, n.] : dealing with matters (as a treaty or declaration and rules of war) affecting relations between nations ⟨the ~ law of Rome⟩ : DIPLOMATIC ⟨a member of the ~ profession⟩

fe·ti·ci·dal *also* **foe·ti·ci·dal** \ˌfēd-əˌsīdᵊl\ *adj* : of or relating to feticide : tending to cause intrauterine death of a fetus ⟨a ~ infection⟩

fe·ti·cide *also* **foe·ti·cide** \ˈfēd-əˌsīd\ *n* -s [*feti-, foeti-* + *-cide*] : the act of killing a fetus : ILLEGAL ABORTION

fet·id *also* **foet·id** \ˈfe|d-əd, |təd *sometimes* ˈfē|\ *adj* [ME *fetid*, fr. L *fetidus, foetidus*, fr. *fetēre, foetēre* to have an offensive smell, stink; akin to L *fumus* smoke — more at FUME] **1** : having an offensive smell : STINKING, RANK ⟨store fronts ~ with the smell of old vegetables —A.J.Liebling⟩ ⟨the air of the room was ~ with stale tobacco smoke —A. Conan Doyle⟩ **2** : containing the volatile constituents of asafetida — **fet·id·ly** *adv* — **fet·id·ness** *n* -ES

fetid aloe *n* **1** : GIANT CABUYA **2** **fetid aloes** *pl* : CABALLINE ALOES

fetid buckeye *n* : OHIO BUCKEYE

fetid cassia *n* : SICKLEPOD 2

fetid chamomile *n* : MAYWEED 1

fetid cress *n* : a European peppergrass (*Lepidium ruderale*) adventive in No. America

fetid currant *n* : SKUNK CURRANT

fetid hellebore *n* **1** : BEAR'S-FOOT **2** : SKUNK CABBAGE 1a

fetid horehound *n* : BLACK HOREHOUND

fe·tid·i·ty \feˈtidəd-ē, fēˈ-, -idətē, -i\ *n* -ES : FETIDNESS

fetid marigold *n* : a prairie weed (*Dyssodia papposa*) of the western U. S. with ill-smelling herbage

fetid marsh fleabane *n* : a marsh fleabane (*Pluchea foetida*) with fetid foliage

fetid nightshade *n* : HENBANE

fetids *n pl, obs* : fetid drugs

fetid shrub *n* : a papaw (*Asimina triloba*)

fetid wood witch *n* : STINKHORN

fetid yew *n* : STINKING CEDAR 1

fe·tii \fəˈtēˌē\ *n, pl* **fetii** [Tahitian *feti'i*] *in French Oceania* : a member of one's extended family : RELATION

feting *pres part of* FETE

fe·tip·a·rous *or* **foe·tip·a·rous** \fēˈtipərəs\ *adj* [*feti-, foeti-* + *-parous*] : that bear young very incompletely developed ⟨~ marsupials⟩

fet·ish *also* **fet·ich** \ˈfed|-|ish, |t|, |ēsh *also* ˈfē| *or* ˈfā|\ *n* -ES *often attrib* [F & Pg; F *fétiche*, fr. Pg *feitiço*, fr. *feitiço*, adj., artificial, false, fr. L *facticius* factitious — more at FACTITIOUS] **1 a** : a natural or artificial object (as an animal tooth or a wood carving) believed among a primitive people to have a preternatural power to protect or aid its owner often because of ritual consecration or animation by a spirit; *broadly* : any material object regarded with superstitious or extravagant trust or reverence ⟨all our ~*es* . . . Sunday school cards, a silver cross that I had for my baptism, a Bible —*Amer. Mercury*⟩ **b** : an object of extreme or irrational reverence or devotion : PREPOSSESSION ⟨security . . . may be sought excessively and become a ~ —Bertrand Russell⟩ ⟨a goose-stepping army which makes a ~ of discipline —*Scribner's*⟩ ⟨accept the ~ that birth and station presuppose any innate superiority —Theodore Dreiser⟩ **c** : an object (as a shoe or glove) or a part of the body that arouses libidinal interest often to the exclusion of genital impulses **2** : a rite or incantation or cult of fetish worshipers ⟨their tribal custom and ~⟩ **3** : irrational reverence or attachment : FIXATION ⟨had a ~ for red hair and so married a redhead⟩

fet·ish·ism *also* **fet·ich·ism** \-ˌshizəm\ *n* -s **1** : belief in and use of magical fetishes ⟨tribes that still practice ~⟩ : a religion marked by the use of fetishes **2** : extravagant irrational devotion to some object, idea, or practice : WORSHIP ⟨~ of the Bible as a material object⟩ ⟨a ~ of luxury goods⟩ ⟨suffers from ~ of weekly housecleaning⟩ **3** : the often pathological displacement of erotic or libidinal interest and satisfaction to a fetish (as an inanimate object) — compare PARTIALISM

fet·ish·ist *also* **fet·ich·ist** \-ˌshəst\ *n* -s **1** : a believer in magical fetishes **2** : one addicted to fetishism ⟨a ~ about gadgets⟩ ⟨a shoe ~ and other sex deviants⟩

fet·ish·is·tic *also* **fet·ich·is·tic** \ˌfe|d-|iˈshistik, |t|, |ēsh-, -istēk *also* ˌfē| *or* ˌfā| *also* **fe·tish·ic** \feˈtishik, fēˈ-,fāˈ-, -shēk\ *adj* **1** : of, belonging to, or characterized by fetishism **2 a** : invested with extraphysical or symbolic significance ⟨~ objects gathered in shrines⟩ ⟨the injection had become a ~ symbol —Wenzell Brown⟩ **b** : marked by fixed irrational regard ⟨its ~ veneration for education —D.S.Savage⟩ ⟨a ~ response to women's shoes⟩ — **fet·ish·is·ti·cal·ly** \ˌ==ˈstək(ə)lē, -stēk-, -li\ *adv*

fet·ish·ize \ˈfe|d-|iˌshīz, |t|, |ēˌsh- *also* ˈfē| *or* ˈfā|\ *vt* -ED/-ING/-S : to make a fetish of : treat or regard as a fetish ⟨an Australian *fetishizes* a piece of wood; a devout believer, an ikon or the name of a saint . . .; a Communist, the portrait of Lenin or Stalin —P.A.Sorokin⟩

¹**fet·lock** \ˈfetˌläk\ *n* -s [ME *fitlok, fetlak*; akin to MHG *vizzelach, vizlach, vizloch* fetlock, *vezzel, vizzel* pastern, OE *fōt* foot — more at FOOT] **1** : a projection like a cushion bearing a tuft of long hair on the back side of the leg above the hoof of the horse and similar animals **2** : the tuft of hair itself **3** *or* **fetlock joint** : the joint of the limb at the fetlock between the great pastern bone and the metatarsal or metacarpal

1 fetlock 1

²**fetlock** \"\ *n* -s [by alter. (influence of ¹*fetlock*)] : ¹FETTERLOCK

fet·low \ˈfetˌlō\ *n* -s [perh. alter. (influenced by ³*felon*) of *whitlow*] : a felon in cattle

feto- *or* **feti-** *also* **foeto-** *or* **foeti-** *comb form* [*feto-, foeto-* fr. L *fetus, foetus; feti-, foeti-* fr. L, fr. *fetus, foetus*] : fetus ⟨*fetocide*⟩ : fetal and ⟨*fetoplacental*⟩

fe·tor *also* **foe·tor** \ˈfēd-ə(r)\ *n* -s [ME *fetour*, fr. L *fetor, foetor*, fr. *fetēre, foetēre* to have an offensive smell, stink + *-or* — more at FETID] : a usu. strong offensive smell : STENCH, FETIDNESS ⟨burned sugar to dispel the ~ of the sickroom —Jean Stafford⟩ ⟨~ of breath⟩

fets *pres 3d sing of* FET

¹**fet·ter** \ˈfed-ə(r), -etə-\ *n* -s [ME *feter*, fr. OE *feter, fetor, feotur*; akin to OHG *fezzera* fetter, MD *veter*, ON *fjöturr* fetter, OE *fōt* foot — more at FOOT] **1** : a chain or shackle for the feet : BOND ⟨a cow dragging her ~ chain and picket⟩ — used chiefly in the pl. ⟨the ~*s* of the galley slave⟩ **2** : something that confines or restrains : RESTRAINT ⟨would like to have world trade free of political ~*s*⟩ **3** : a long link in an ornamental chain

²**fetter** \"\ *vt* **fettered; fettered; fettering; fetters** [ME *feteren*, fr. OE *gefeterian*, fr. *feter, fetor*, n.] **1** : to put fetters upon : shackle the feet of with a chain **2** : to bind (one thing or person) to another as if with a chain ⟨God who has ~*ed* our everyday senses to an understanding of nothing but the things immediately around us —T.B.Costain⟩ **3 a** : to restrain from free action : deprive of freedom ⟨we reverence tradition but we will not be ~*ed* by it —W.R. Inge⟩ **b** : to render helpless or impotent ⟨deafness, by ~*ing* the powers of utterance, cheats many of their birthright of knowledge —Malachy Hynes⟩ **syn** see HAMPER

fetterbush \ˈ==ˌ=\ *n* **1** : a showy shrub (*Lyonia lucida*) of the southern U.S. with persistent leaves and angled branchlets **2** : MOUNTAIN FETTERBUSH **3** : a plant of the genus *Leucothoe*

fettered cat *n* : KAFFIR CAT

fet·ter·less \-ərləs, *-R* -əl- *or* -ᵊl-\ *adj* : having no fetters : FREE, UNBOUND

¹**fetterlock** \ˈ==ˌ=\ *n* [ME *feterlok*, fr. *feter* fetter + *lok* lock — more at LOCK (fastening)] **1** : a device formerly attached to a horse's leg to hamper running away : CLOG — called also *fetlock* **2** : an armorial representation of a fetterlock

²**fetterlock** \"\ *n* [by alter. (influence of ¹*fetterlock*)] : ¹FETLOCK

fet·ti·cus \ˈfed-əkəs\ *n* -ES [modif. of D *vettekous*, fr. *vet* fat (fr. MD) + *kous* stocking, fr. MD *couse*, fr. OF (Picardy dial.) *cauce*, fr. ML *calcea*; akin to OE *fǣtt* fat — more at FAT, CHAUSSES] : CORN SALAD

fetting *pres part of* FET

¹**fet·tle** \ˈfed-ᵊl, -etᵊl\ *n* -s [fr. (assumed) ME *fetel*, fr. OE, belt; akin to OHG *fezzil* sword belt, ON *fetill*, and prob. to OE *fæt* vessel — more at VAT] *dial Brit* : straw or hay esp. when used as a basket handle

²**fettle** \"\ *vb* **fettled; fettled; fettling** \ˈfed-ᵊliŋ, -t(ᵊ)l-\ **fettles** [ME *fetlen* to shape, prepare; prob. akin to OE *fæt* vessel — more at VAT] *vt* **1** *chiefly Brit* : to set in working order : MEND, REPAIR ⟨~ a gun⟩ **2** *dial Brit* : to make neat or orderly : ARRANGE ⟨~ up the house⟩ **3** *dial Brit* **a** : to feed and care for (a domestic animal) **b** : to groom and harness (a horse) **c** : to dress up : ARRAY **4** *dial Eng* : MULL ⟨~ a beverage⟩ **5** : to cover or line the hearth of (a reverberatory furnace) with fettling **6 a** : to clean and smooth (as a metal or plastic) after casting or molding : DRESS **b** : to trim off excess clay at the seams of (cast and partly dried pottery ware) **c** : to remove excess dried glaze from (tile) before firing **7** : to clean accumulated fibers from the card clothing of (a woolen or worsted carding machine) ~ *vi* **1** *dial Eng* : to make preparations : get ready **2** *dial Eng* : to fuss esp. over trifles **3** *dial Eng* : to get along : FARE

³**fettle** \"\ *n* -s **1 a** : a state of fitness or order : CONDITION, TRIM ⟨in pretty good ~ for a man of his years —R.L.Duffus⟩ **b** : state of mind : SPIRITS ⟨the good news put him in fine ~⟩ **2** : FETTLING

fet·tler \ˈfed-ᵊlə(r), -et(ᵊ)l-\ *n* -s [²*fettle* + *-er*] : one that fettles: as **a** *chiefly Brit* : a repairman or maintenance man (as on a railway) **b** : a pottery worker who smooths greenware with a knife, felt, emery, and a wet sponge **c** : a worker who sands or cuts excess glaze from tile

fettling *n* -s [fr. gerund of ²*fettle*] : loose material (as ore or sand) that is thrown on the hearth of a furnace esp. to protect it

fet·tuc·cel·le \ˌfed-əˈchelē\ *n* -s [It *fettuccelle*, pl. of *fettuccella*, dim. of *fettuccia* small slice, ribbon, dim. of *fetta* slice] : pasta in ribbon shape

fet·tuc·ci·ne *or* **fet·tu·ci·ni** *also* **fet·tu·ci·ne** *or* **fet·tuc·ci·ni** \-ˈchēnē\ *n pl but sing or pl in constr* [It *fettuccine*, pl of *fettuccina*, dim. of *fettuccia*] : pasta in the form of narrow ribbons; *also* : a dish of which fettuccine is the base

fe·tus *also* **foe·tus** \ˈfēd-əs, -ētəs\ *n, pl* **fetuses** *also* **foetuses** *or* **foe·ti** \ˈfēˌtī\ [L, action of bearing young, offspring, fetus, fr. *fetus, foetus*, adj., pregnant, fruitful, newly delivered — more at FEMININE] : an unborn or unhatched young vertebrate esp. after passing through the earliest developmental stages and attaining the basic structural plan of its kind; *specif* : a developing human from usu. three months after conception to birth — compare EMBRYO

¹**feu** *or* **few** \ˈfyü\ *n* -s [ME (Sc dial.) *feu*, fr. MF *fé, fié, fief, fieu* — more at FEE] **1** *Scots law* : a feudal benefice : FEE **2** *Scots law* **a** : a tenure where the vassal in place of military services makes a return in grain or in money — compare BLANCH, WARDHOLDING **b** : a grant of land to be so held **c** : a perpetual lease for a fixed rent — compare EMPHYTEUSIS **3** *Scots law* : a piece of land held under one of these tenures

²**feu** \"\ *vt* **feued; feued; feuing; feus** *Scots law* : to grant (land) upon feu

feu·ar \ˈfyüər\ *n* -s [¹*feu* + *-ar* (Sc var. of *-er*) *Scots law* : one who holds a feu

feu charter *n, Scots law* : the charter securing a feu

feucht \ˈfyükt\ *Scot past of* FIGHT

¹**feud** \ˈfyüd\ *n* -s [alter. of ME *fede, feide*, fr. MF *faide, feide, fede*, of Gmc origin; akin to OE *fǣhth* enmity, hostility, feud, OHG *fēhida*, OFris *feithe, faithe*; derivatives fr. the root of OE *fāh* hostile — more at FOE] : a prolonged or inveterate mutual enmity marked by bitter and often violent conflicts : a war of revenge or rivalry between individuals or factions : a relationship of aggressive hostility : STRIFE, QUARREL ⟨a political ~ of long standing⟩ ⟨a new outbreak of the virulent ~ between labor and management⟩ ⟨had they been united, they might have prevailed; but they were always at ~ with each other —Goldwin Smith⟩; *specif* : BLOOD FEUD

²**feud** \"\ *vi* -ED/-ING/-S : to carry on a feud : BATTLE ⟨is currently ~*ing* with the Treasury over her refusal to withhold employees' taxes —*Newsweek*⟩ ⟨the two families of the valley have ~*ed* for generations⟩

³**feud** \"\ *n* -s [ML *feodum, feudum*, of Gmc origin; akin to OHG *fihu* cattle — more at FEE] : an estate in land held of a lord or superior by a tenant or vassal on condition he render certain services to the lord or superior : a feudal benefice : FEE, FIEF — compare ALODIUM

feuda *pl of* FEUDUM

¹**feu·dal** \ˈfyüdᵊl\ *adj* [ML *feodalis, feudalis*, fr. *feodum, feudum* + L *-alis* -al] **1 a** : of, relating to, or having the characteristics of a feud or fief : founded upon or involving the relation of lord and vassal with tenure of land in feud ⟨~ rights and services⟩ ⟨~ tenure⟩ ⟨~ polity⟩ — distinguished from *domanial* **b** : of, existing in, characterized by, or relating to the feudal system ⟨the ~ era⟩ ⟨his ~ lord⟩ ⟨the ~ states of medieval Europe⟩ ⟨a volume of ~ studies⟩ **c** : of feudal times ⟨ruins of a ~ castle⟩ ⟨a map of ~ England⟩ **2** : resembling that of a medieval lord in imperiousness or impressiveness : characterized by a grand style or manner ⟨lived in almost ~ ease among devoted retainers and entertained with a lavish hand —A.C.Cole⟩ : IMPOSING ⟨owner of the . . . railroad had built his ~ castle —Harrison Smith⟩ **3 a** : marked by or upholding the domination of a privileged class : OLIGARCHIC ⟨replace the ~ bureaucracy with an equitable civil service⟩ ⟨strongly ~ by instinct, he led the opposition to . . . demands for equal electoral privileges —Andrew Boyle⟩; *specif* : controlled absolutely by and for the benefit of an individual or small group (as of landowners) ⟨the Arab governments, representing largely ~ societies in which the masses are incredibly poor —Peter Allen⟩ ⟨textile-mill towns are ~ empires with their own stores . . . courts . . . police, and jails —Lawrence Lader⟩ **b** : of, belonging to, or constituting a ruling class ⟨the ~ bourgeois type . . . represented a coalition of the army, the bureaucracy, and the owners of the large estates and factories for the joint exploitation of the state —Franz Neumann⟩; *specif* : ruling absolutely within a limited domain ⟨the last survivor of the ~ tribal chieftains —Robert Payne⟩ **4** : of or marked by division into independent often absolutely ruled domains ⟨where no central government has replaced the ~ structure of tribal society⟩ **5** : characterized by reciprocal and contractual relations between members (as of a society) ⟨monarchical and democratic societies, ~ or caste-divided ones, priest-ridden and relatively irreligious ones . . . evolve —A.L.Kroeber⟩

²**feudal** \"\ *adj* [¹*feud* + *-al*] : of, associated with, or engaged in a retaliatory or competitive feud ⟨~ hatred⟩ ⟨the man who rescued a ~ enemy —*Emporia (Kans.) Gazette*⟩

feu·dal·ism \-dᵊlˌizəm\ *n* -s [¹*feudal* + *-ism*] **1 a** : the system of polity flourishing in Europe from the 9th to about the 15th centuries, based upon the relation of lord to vassal with the holding of all land in fee (as of the king), and having as its principal incidents homage, service of tenants under arms and in court, wardship, and forfeiture **b** : the principles or relations and usages on which the feudal system was based — compare COMMENDATION, FEUD, LIEGE, LORD, PRECARIUM, VASSAL **2** : any social system in which great landowners or hereditary overlords exact revenue from the land and also exercise the functions of government in their domains **3** : control by an entrenched minority esp. for its own benefit : social, political, or economic oligarchy ⟨he was a pioneer of industrial ~, a benevolent despot —F.W.Coburn⟩

feu·dal·ist \-dᵊləst\ *n* -s **1** : a representative or upholder of feudalism **2** : a specialist in medieval feudalism

feu·dal·is·tic \ˌ==ˈistik, -tēk\ *adj* : of or having the character of feudalism or feudalists ⟨~ institutions⟩; *esp* : characterized by control by and for an entrenched minority ⟨~ and vested economic interests⟩ ⟨a reactionary and ~ regime⟩

feu·dal·i·ty \fyüˈdaləd-ē, -lətē, -i\ *n* -ES [modif. of F *féodalité*, fr. *féodal* feudal (fr. ML *feodalis*) + *-ité* -ity] **1** : the quality or state of being feudal : feudal principles or practice ⟨the trend to ~ dissolved the empire into many independent domains⟩ **2** : a feudal holding, domain, or concentration of power ⟨a league of Greek *feudalities* led by Agamemnon —*Time*⟩ ⟨the eviction of the great economic . . . *feudalities* and the return to the nation of . . . the sources of mineral wealth —C.J.Friedrich⟩ **3** : the feudal aristocracy or ruling group ⟨the ~, scornful and fearful of the new men . . . were ready to rally to her banner —Basil Henning⟩

feu·dal·iza·tion \ˌfyüdᵊləˈzāshən, -dᵊlˌīˈz-\ *n* -s : the act or process of feudalizing ⟨the Norman Conquest brought only partial ~ to England⟩

feu·dal·ize \ˈfyüdᵊlˌīz\ *vt* -ED/-ING/-S : to make feudal : reduce to feudal tenure or dependence ⟨~ alodial lands⟩ ⟨*feudalized* the bourgeoisie⟩

feu·dal·ly \-dᵊlē, -dᵊli\ *adv* : in a feudal manner

feudal system *n* : a feudal system of polity : FEUDALISM

¹**feu·da·tary** \ˈfyüdəˌterē\ *n* -ES [ML *feudatarius*, fr. *feudatarius*, adj.] *archaic* : ²FEUDATORY 1

²**feudatary** *adj* [ML *feudatarius*, fr. *feudatus* (past part. of *feudare* to enfeoff, fr. *feudum* fief, feud) + L *-arius* -ary — more at FEUD] *obs* : ¹FEUDATORY

feu·da·to·ri·al \ˌ==ˈtōrēəl, -tȯr-\ *adj* : FEUDAL

¹**feu·da·to·ry** \ˈfyüdəˌtōrē, -tȯrē, -ri\ *adj* [ML *feudatorius*, fr. *feudatus* + L *-orius* -ory] **1** : standing in or belonging to the relation of a feudal vassal to his lord **2** *of a kingdom or state* : under the overlordship of a foreign state

²**feudatory** \"\ *n* -ES [ML *feudatorius*, fr. *feudatorius*, adj.] **1 a** : one holding lands by feudal tenure : the tenant of a feud; *esp* : a feudal lord **b** : a prince or ruler subject to the overlordship of a foreign ruler **2 a** : a dependent lordship : FEUD **b** : a feudatory state

feu de joie \fœdəzhwȧ\ *n, pl* **feux de joie** \"\ [F, lit., fire of joy] **1** : BONFIRE 2 **2** : a salute fired by rifles in rapid succession along a line of troops (as to celebrate a victory)

feuding *pres part of* FEUD

¹**feud·ist** \ˈfyüdəst\ *n* -s [³*feud* + *-ist*] : a specialist in feudal law

²**feudist** \"\ *n* -s [¹*feud* + *-ist*] : one who is party to a hostile feud

feuds *pl of* FEUD, *pres 3d sing of* FEUD

feu·dum \ˈfyüdəm\ *n, pl* **feu·da** \-də\ *or* **feudums** [ML — more at FEUD] : ³FEUD

feu–duty \ˈ=ˌ==\ *n, Scots law* : the annual rent paid by the tenant of a feu

feued *past of* FEU

feu·er·bach·i·an \ˌfȯiə(r)ˈbäkēən, -äkē-\ *adj, usu cap* [Ludwig A. *Feuerbach* †1872 Ger. philosopher + E *-ian*] : of or relating to the sensationalistic and materialistic theories of Ludwig Feuerbach

feuil·lage \fœyȧäzh\ *n* -s [F, fr. MF *fuellage* — more at FOLIAGE] : FOLIAGE

feuille \fœœy\ *n, pl* **feuilles** \"\ [F, lit., leaf, fr. OF *fuelle, fueille, foille* — more at FOIL] : TERRAPIN 2

feuille morte \-mȯrt\ *n* [F, lit., dead leaf] : a brownish orange that is deeper and slightly redder than leather, yellower and deeper than spice, and yellower and deeper than gold pheasant — called also *autumn leaf, dead leaf, foliage brown, leather lake, oakleaf brown, philamot, withered leaf*

feuil·le·ton \ˌfəryəˈtōⁿ, ˌfəyə-, ˌfœyə-, F fœytōⁿ\ *n* -s [F, fr. *feuillet* sheet of paper, folio, fr. OF *fuellet, foillet* small leaf, sheet of paper, dim. of *fuel, fueil, foil* leaf — more at FOIL] **1** : a part of a European newspaper or magazine devoted to material designed to entertain the general reader : a feature section **2** : a writing printed in a feuilleton (as an installment of a serialized novel) **3 a** : a novel printed in installments : SERIAL **b** : a work of fiction catering to popular taste **4** : a short literary composition often having a familiar tone and reminiscent content : SKETCH ⟨these ~*s* are self-analytical studies and personal confessions, memories, scenes of animal life, symbolic stories dealing with personal and national problems —Izidor Cankar⟩ — **feuil·le·ton·ism** \-ˈtōⁿˌnizəm\ *n* -s

feuil·le·ton·ist \-nəst, -ˌnist\ *n* -s [F *feuilletoniste*, fr. *feuilleton* + *-iste* -ist] : a writer of feuilletons; *esp* : a writer of regularly appearing critical or familiar essays or of a column

feuing *pres part of* FEU

feul·gen reaction \ˈfȯilgən-\ *n, usu cap F* [after Robert *Feulgen* *b*1884 Ger. physiologist] : the development of a purplish color in a microscopic preparation hydrolyzed and stained with a modified Schiff reagent that is considered to indicate the presence of chromatin and used to identify chromatinic structures in cells or as an aid in distinguishing nuclei in various microorganisms

feus *pl of* FEU, *pres 3d sing of* FEU

¹**fe·ver** \ˈfēvə(r)\ *n* -s *often attrib* [ME, fr. OE *fēfer, fēfor*, fr. L *febris*; akin to L *fovēre* to warm — more at DAY] **1 a** : a rise of body temperature above the normal whether a natural response (as to infection) or artificially induced for therapeutic reasons **b** : an abnormal bodily state characterized by increased production of heat, accelerated heart action and pulse, and systemic debility with weakness, loss of appetite, and thirst **c** : any of various diseases of which fever is a prominent symptom ⟨typhoid ~⟩ ⟨yellow ~⟩ ⟨quartan ~⟩ **2 a** : a state of heightened or intense emotion (as of excitement, anxiety, or desire) : abnormal intensity ⟨in a fervor and ~ of resentment colonists all over the land voluntarily carried their tea to public bonfires —C.G.Bowers⟩ ⟨terror hung over the West, the frontier was in a ~, forts and blockhouses were hastily constructed —*Amer. Guide Series: Ind.*⟩ ⟨a ~ of passionate love —T.L.Peacock⟩ **b** : a widely contagious usu. transient enthusiasm (as for gold prospecting, migration to the West, or stock speculation) : CRAZE ⟨caught uranium ~⟩ ⟨football ~ raged in the university⟩ ⟨gripped by a ~ for emigration⟩ **3** : a state of agitated or intense activity : urgent haste ⟨what a ~ of preparation seized the fort on the afternoon before that great day —Walter O'Meara⟩ ⟨worked at a ~ pitch⟩ **4** : an abnormal often unstable condition of mind or society ⟨the ~ is over; already unemployment . . . has started to drop —*Economist*⟩

²**fever** \"\ *vb* **fevered; fevered; fevering** \-v(ə)riŋ\ **fevers** *vt* : to throw into a fever : affect with fever : HEAT, AGITATE ⟨the gold coin, clutched deep in his trouser pocket, ~*ed* him —A.J. Cronin⟩ ~ *vi* **1** : to contract or be in a fever : be or become feverish ⟨the malaria victim ~*s* intermittently⟩ ⟨he ~*ed* for his far-off home⟩ **2** : to move or live feverishly ⟨Germany has not experienced a revolution; she has only ~*ed* through a convulsion caused by overexertion and fright —Maximillian Harden⟩

fever and ague *n* : MALARIA 2

fever bark *n* : any bark used in the treatment of fevers: as **a** : CINCHONA BARK **b** : bark of the bitterbark (*Alstonia constricta*)

fever blister *also* **fever sore** *n* : COLD SORE

feverbush \ˈ==ˌ=\ *n* **1** : SPICEBUSH 1 **2** : BLACK ALDER 1

fever cabinet *also* **fever box** *n* : an electric apparatus used in fever therapy to raise the body temperature of a patient above the normal level

fever chart *n* **1** : a chart indicating the course of a patient's fever **2** : the rising and falling course of conditions (as in politics or business)

fevercup \ˈ==ˌ=\ *n* : PITCHER PLANT a

fe·ver·few \ˈfēvə(r)ˌfyü\ *n* -s [ME *feverfew, feverfu*, fr. (assumed) AF *fevrefue*, feverfew, centaury, fr. LL *febrifugia* centaury — more at FEBRIFUGE] : a perennial European herb (*Chrysanthemum parthenium*)

fevergum \ˈ==ˌ=\ *n* : a blue gum (*Eucalyptus globulus*)

fever heat *n* **1** : the state of a human body when the oral temperature exceeds 98.6° Fahrenheit **2** : FEVER PITCH

fe·ver·ish \ˈfēv(ə)rish, -rēsh\ *adj* [ME, fr. *fever* + *-ish*] **1 a** : showing symptoms indicating fever (as increased heat and thirst, delirium) : having a fever ⟨the patient is ~⟩; *specif* : abnormally hot ⟨the child's forehead felt ~⟩ **b** : of or indicating fever ⟨a ~ condition⟩ ⟨a ~ spot burned on each cheek⟩ **c** : infected with or tending to cause fever ⟨a damp, ~, unhealthy spot —R.L.Stevenson⟩ **2 a** : marked by aroused or intense feeling or activity or by irregular variations : characterized by fever : AGITATED ⟨lay sleepless while his ~ mind went over the catastrophes of the day⟩ : ARDENT ⟨novels . . . in which every young man is sleek and ~ for an unattainable success —Marjory S. Douglas⟩ : HECTIC ⟨a burst of ~ activity just before sailing time⟩ : UNSTABLE ⟨a ~ condition of the stock market with extreme fluctuations between gains and losses⟩ **b :** suggesting in appearance the delirium of a fever ⟨a wallpaper with a ~ contemporary design⟩ **3 :** uncomfortably hot **:** SULTRY ⟨the afternoon was ~ for so temperate a seacoast —Robinson Jeffers⟩ — **fe·ver·ish·ly** *adv* — **fe·ver·ish·ness** *n* -ES

fe·ver·less \ˈfēvə(r)ləs\ *adj* **:** having no fever

fe·ver·ous \ˈfēv(ə)rəs\ *adj* [ME, fr. *fever* + *-ous*] **:** FEVERISH

fever pitch *n* **:** a degree of abnormal excitement that usu. develops rapidly among a number of people and sometimes leads to impulsive violence ⟨worked themselves to *fever pitch* while watching their team lose —*N.Y.Times*⟩ ⟨when at last the hour of the full-dress trial drew near, popular excitement rose to *fever pitch* —E.M.Lustgarten⟩ ⟨fanned his wrath to *fever pitch* —Jack London⟩

fever plant *n* **1 :** an evening primrose (*Oenothera biennis*) **2 :** an African shrub (*Ocimum viride*)

feverroot \ˈ≈,≈\ *n* [¹*fever* + *root*] **:** a coarse American herb (*Triosteum perfoliatum*) — called also *horse gentian, tinker's root*

fevers *pl of* FEVER, *pres 3d sing of* FEVER

fever therapy *n* **:** a treatment of disease by fever induced by various artificial means

fever thermometer *n* **:** CLINICAL THERMOMETER

fever tick *n* **:** a tick that transmits the causative agent of a fever; *specif* **:** a cattle tick of the genus *Boophilus* that transmits piroplasmosis or anaplasmosis

fever tree *n* **:** any of several usu. tropical or subtropical shrubs or trees thought to indicate regions free from fever or planted because they yield remedies for fever: as **a :** a blue gum (*Eucalyptus globulus*) **b :** an ornamental tree (*Pinckneya pubens*) of the southeastern U.S. that yields Georgia bark **c :** an African tree (*Acacia xanthophloea*) supposed to mark healthful regions **d :** FEVER PLANT 2

fevertwig \ˈ≈,≈\ *also* **fevertwitch** \ˈ≈,≈\ *n* **:** BITTERSWEET 2b

feverweed \ˈ≈,≈\ *n* **1 :** any of several plants of the genus *Eryngium* (as *E. aquaticum* of the southern U.S. or *E. campestre* of Europe) **2 :** an American false foxglove (*Gerardia pedicularia*) **3 :** a verbena (*Verbena stricta*) of the southwestern U.S.

feverwort \ˈ≈,≈\ *n* **1 :** FEVERROOT **2 :** BONESET

¹**few** \ˈfyü\ *pron, pl in constr* [ME *fewe*, pron. & adj., fr. OE *fēawa, fēa;* akin to OHG *fao, fō, fōh* little, ON *fār* little, taciturn, Goth *fawai* few, L *paucus* little, *pauper* poor, Gk *pauros* small, slight, *paid-, pais* child, Skt *putra* son, child] **:** not many persons or things ⟨many are called but ~ are chosen —Mt 22:14 (RSV)⟩ ⟨~ of the statements are true⟩

²**few** \"\ *adj* **fewer** \ˈfyüə(r); -ü(ə)r, -üə\ **fewest** \-üəst\ [ME *fewe*] **1 :** consisting of or amounting to a small number **:** not many ⟨one of his ~ pleasures⟩ ⟨has relatively ~ friends⟩ ⟨less construction means ~*er* jobs⟩ ⟨holidays were ~ and far between⟩ ⟨was applauded by the ~ people present⟩ **2 :** some at least **:** not many but some — used with a preceding *a* to designate being some rather than none ⟨caught a ~ fish⟩ ⟨leave a ~ flowers for the next person⟩; see ²A 1 **3** *dial* **:** LITTLE ⟨a piece of salt jowl meat and a ~ syrup —G.S. Perry⟩

³**few** \"\ *n, pl in constr* [ME *fewe*, fr. *fewe*, pron. & adj.] **1 :** a small number of units or individuals — used with preceding *a* ⟨sold a ~ of the old books⟩ ⟨a ~ of the soldiers were wounded⟩ **2 :** a special limited number **:** MINORITY — used with preceding *the* ⟨a society based on privileges for the ~⟩ ⟨a car built for the discriminating ~⟩ **3 :** an indefinite but not very large number of drinks — used with preceding *a* ⟨went into a crummy-looking beer joint and had a ~ —Len Zinberg⟩ — **a few** *chiefly dial* **:** to some degree or extent **:** a little ⟨we'd already made out that he could ride *a few* —*Smart Set*⟩ — **a good few** *dial chiefly Eng* **:** quite a few — **in few** *archaic* **:** in short **:** BRIEFLY ⟨the firm resolve I here *in few* disclose —Alexander Pope⟩ — **not a few :** quite a few ⟨*not a few* of the members were absent⟩ ⟨a custom followed in *not a few* countries⟩ — **quite a few :** a considerable number **:** a good many ⟨*quite a few* of the merchants cut prices⟩ ⟨owns *quite a few* horses⟩ ⟨maybe not a hundred but *quite a few*⟩

⁴**few** \"\ *var of* FEU

fewer *pron, pl in constr* [ME *fewere*, fr. OE *fēawran*, fr. compar. of *fēawa*, adj, few — more at FEW] **:** a smaller number of persons or things ⟨few know and ~ care⟩ ⟨~ are here than had been expected⟩ ⟨to the ~ ye shall give the less inheritance —Num 33:54 (AV)⟩

fewmet *var of* ¹FUMET

few·ness *n* -ES [ME *fewenesse*, fr. OE *fēawnes, fēanes*, fr. *fēawa, fēa* few + *-nes* -ness] **1 :** the state of being few **:** PAUCITY **2 :** smallness in amount or quantity ⟨according to the ~ of years —Lev 25:16 (AV)⟩

fewterer *n* -S [ME *vewter, feutrere, fewterer*, fr. MF *veltrier, veautrier*, fr. *veltre, veautre* greyhound, fr. LL *vertragus*, fr. Gaulish] *obs* **:** a keeper of dogs (as greyhounds) **:** SLIPPER

few·trils \ˈfyü·trəlz\ *n pl* [origin unknown] *dial Eng* **:** odds and ends **:** TRIFLES

¹**fey** \ˈfā\ *adj* -ER/-EST [ME *feie, feye, fay*, fr. OE *fǣge;* akin to OS *fēgi, fēg* doomed to die, OHG *feigi*, ON *feigr*, and perh. to OE *fāh* hostile, outlawed — more at FOE] **1 a** *now chiefly Scot* **:** fated to die **:** DOOMED ⟨they dashed and hewed and smashed till ~ men died away —Robert Burns⟩ **b :** marked or disturbed by an apprehension of death or calamity ⟨another and lesser man . . . gave a ~ lonely warning —Hodding Carter⟩ **2 a :** being in a wild or elated state of mind formerly believed to portend death **:** behaving in an excited irresponsible manner **:** beside oneself ⟨she must be ~ and in that case has not long to live —Sir Walter Scott⟩ ⟨was ~ that night, with a kind of febrile gaiety, because the favored lover of the moment was home —Frances Towers⟩ **b :** out of one's mind **:** MAD ⟨he went ~⟩ **:** TOUCHED ⟨the apparently ~ but sharply pointed eccentricities —Louis Untermeyer⟩ **3** [prob. influenced in meaning by ⁴*fay*] **a :** able to see fairies or to have intuitions about the future **:** possessing a sixth sense **:** CLAIRVOYANT ⟨what qualifications have I to discuss fairies; am I ~ —O.S.J. Gogarty⟩ ⟨not being ~ he never suspected what it would lead to⟩ **b :** characterized by an unworldly air or attitude **:** ELFIN ⟨she has that half shy, half ~ smile and that birdlike perkiness —A.G.Ogden⟩ ⟨the ~ quality was there, the ability to see the moon at midday —John Mason Brown⟩ **:** VISIONARY ⟨a Celtic penchant for ~ fancies that contrasted with the other's stolid matter-of-factness⟩

²**fey** \"\ *var of* ²FAY

fey·ther \ˈfāthə(r)\ *dial Brit var of* FATHER

¹**fez** *or* **fès** *or* **fes** \ˈfez\ *adj, usu cap* [fr. *Fez* (*Fès*), Morocco] **:** of or from the city of Fez, Morocco **:** of the kind or style prevalent in Fez

²**fez** \ˈfez\ *n, pl* **fezzes** *also* **fezes** [F, fr. *Fez* (*Fès*), Morocco] **:** a brimless cone-shaped hat that has a flat crown usu. with a long tassel attached, is usu. made of red felt, is worn by men in eastern Mediterranean countries (as Turkey), and has been adapted for women's hats in Europe and America

fez

fez·zani \fəˈzanē, fəˈz-, -zänē\ *n, pl* **fezzani** *or* **fezzanis** *cap* [fr. *Fezzan*, region in southwestern Libya] **1 :** a people in Fezzan, Libya, of mixed Negroid and Arab ancestry **2 :** a member of the Fezzani people

fez·zi \ˈfezē\ *n* -S *cap* [fr. *Fez*, Morocco] **:** a native or resident of Fez, Morocco

ff *abbr* **1** [L *fecerunt*] they made **2** folios **3** following **4** fortissimo

FF \(ˈ)efˈef\ *n* -S **1 :** FIRST FAMILY **2 :** a member of a first family ⟨a snobbish *FF*⟩

FF *abbr* **1** first family **2** fixed focus **3** thick fog **4** folded flat **5** [L *fratres*] brothers **6** freight forwarder **7** French fried **8** full-fashioned

FFA *abbr* **1** foreign freight agent **2** for further assignment **3** free foreign agency **4** free from alongside **5** free from average

fff *abbr* [It *fortississimo*] as loud as possible

FFI *abbr* free from infection

f flat *n, usu cap 1st F* **:** the tone a half step below F and sounding enharmonically the same as E in the tempered scale

FFT *abbr* for further transfer

FFV *abbr* first families of Virginia

ffy *abbr* faithfully

FG *abbr* **1** fine grain **2** flat grain **3** friction glaze **4** fuel gas **5** fully good

FGA *abbr* **1** foreign general agent **2** foreign general average **3** free of general average

fgn *abbr* foreign

fgt *abbr* freight

f-head \ˈ≈,≈\ *adj, cap F* **:** having one valve in the head and the other on the side of the engine cylinder ⟨an *F-head* engine⟩

f-hole \ˈ≈,≈\ *n* **:** one of the two *f*-shaped sound holes in the top of a violin or other bowed stringed instrument

f horn *n, usu cap F* **:** a French horn in F

f i *abbr* for instance

FIA *abbr* full interest admitted

fi·a·cre \fēˈäkr(ᵊ), |kr(ə), *F* fyȧ|\ *n, pl* **fiacres** \|kr(ᵊ), |krə(z), |k(s)\ [F, fr. the Hotel St. *Fiacre*, Paris, where such vehicles were first hired out] **:** a small hackney coach

fi·a·dor \ˌfēəˈdō(ə)r\ *n* -S [Sp, lit., guarantor, fr. *fiado* (past part. of *fiar* to trust, guarantee, fr. — assumed — VL *fidare*, alter. of L *fidere* to trust) + *-or* — more at BIDE] **:** a cord fastened to a hackamore and acting as a throatlatch

fi·an·cé \ˌfēˌänˈsā, fēˈ|, |äⁿ|;-, |än|;-\ *n* -S [F, fr. MF, fr. past part. of *fiancer* to vow, promise, betroth, fr. OF *fiancier*, fr. *fiance* vow, promise, trust, fr. *fier* to trust (fr. — assumed — VL *fidare*) + *-ance*] **:** a man engaged to be married — usu. used with preceding possessive

fi·an·cée \"\ *n* -S [F, fem. of *fiancé*] **:** a woman engaged to be married — usu. used with preceding possessive

¹**fi·an·chet·to** \÷,fēənˈched·(,)ō, -nˈke-\ *n, pl* **fianchet·ti** \-d·(,)ē\ [It, dim. of *fianco* flank, side, fr. OIt, fr. OF *flanc* — more at FLANK] **:** a position or opening in chess with one or both pawns at Kt3 to make room for the bishop on Kt2

²**fianchetto** \"\ *vb* -ED/-ING/-ES **:** to develop (a bishop) in a chess game to Kt2

fi·an·na \ˈfēənə\ *n pl, usu cap* [IrGael *fianna, fēinne*, pl. of *fiann* band of Fenians] **:** FENIANS

fiants *n pl but sing or pl in constr* [MF *fientes*, pl. of *fiente* dung, fr. (assumed) VL *femita*, fr. LL *femus*, alter. of L *fimus;* prob. akin to L *fumus* smoke — more at FUME] *obs* **:** the dung of the fox, wolf, boar, or badger

¹**fi·ar** \ˈfēər\ *n* -S [ME (Sc dial.) *fiar, fear*, fr. *fe* fee + *-ar* -er — more at FEE] *Scots law* **:** one in whom the fee simple of an estate is vested subject to a liferent

²**fiar** \"\ *n* -S [ME *feor*, fr. OF *fuer, feor* market price, price, fr. L *forum* market — more at FORUM] **1** *Scot* **:** PRICE, STANDARD **2 fiars** *also* **fiars prices** *pl* **:** prices of grain in Scotland fixed for the year by law

fiard \ˈfēˌärd, ˈfyä-\ *n* -S [Sw *fjärd, fjord*, fr. OSw *fiordher, fiærdher;* akin to ON *fjörthr* fjord — more at FORD] **:** FJORD

fi·as·co \fēˈas(ˌ)kō, -ˈaa-,-ˈai-, *in sense 1 & sometimes in sense 2* -ˈä- *or* -ˈȧ-\ *n, pl* **fiascoes** *also* **fiascos** \-kōz\ *see sense 1* [It, in sense 1, fr. ML *flasco*, of Gmc origin; akin to OHG *flaska* bottle — more at FLASK] **1** *pl* **fias·chi** \-kē\ **:** BOTTLE, FLASK; *specif* **:** a bottle of wine **2 :** an utter and often ridiculous failure esp. of an ambitious or pretentious undertaking ⟨the campaign to abolish the sales tax ended in a ~⟩

¹**fi·at** \ˈfī,a\|t, -ə|; ˈfē,a|, ˈfēə|, ˈfē,ä|, ˈfē,ȧ|; *usu* |d·+V\ *n* -S [L, let it be done, 3d sing. pres. subj. of *fieri* to become (used as passive of *facere* to do) — more at BE, DO] **1 :** official endorsement or sanction **:** PERMISSION ⟨a colonial governor acting under the ~ of the king⟩ **2 :** a command or act of will that creates something without or as if without further effort **3 :** an authoritative decision of consciousness **:** mental determination of one of two or more alternatives ⟨the ~ of will⟩ ⟨a ~ of conscience⟩ **4 :** an arbitrary edict **:** a summary judicial or executive pronouncement ⟨the question of what conduct shall be made criminal . . . should never be determined by police ~ —*Harvard Law Rev.*⟩

²**fiat** \"\ *adj* **:** established, sanctioned, or created by or as if by fiat ⟨~ value⟩

fiat money *n* **:** money (as paper currency) that is not convertible into coin or specie of equivalent value and thus is dependent for its value on the decree of government

¹**fib** \ˈfib\ *n* -S [perh. by shortening & alter. fr. *fable*] **:** a trivial falsehood **:** an innocuous lie ⟨a child who tells ~*s*⟩

²**fib** \"\ *vi* **fibbed; fibbed; fibbing; fibs :** to tell a fib **syn** see LIE

³**fib** \"\ *vb* **fibbed; fibbed; fibbing; fibs** [origin unknown] *Brit* **:** BEAT, PUMMEL ⟨*fibbing* him on the ear —David Garnett⟩

FIB *abbr* **1** free into barge **2** free into bunker

fib·ber \ˈfibə(r)\ *n* -S **:** one that tells fibs

fib·bery \-b(ə)rē\ *n* -ES **:** the practice of fibbing **:** FALSEHOOD

¹**fi·ber** *or* **fi·bre** \ˈfībə(r)\ *n* -S [F *fibre*, fr. L *fibra*] **1 :** a thread or a structure or object resembling a thread: as **a** (1) **:** a slender root (as of a grass) (2) **:** an elongate tapering cell that has at maturity a small lumen and no protoplasm content, that is found in many plant organs and is esp. well developed in the xylem and phloem of the vascular system, and that imparts elasticity, flexibility, and tensile strength to the plant or organ — compare SCLEREID **b** (1) **:** the axis cylinder of a nerve cell with its sheath (2) **:** one of the structures composing most of the intercellular matrix of ordinary and elastic connective tissues (3) **:** one of the elongated contractile cells constituting muscular tissue **c :** a natural or man-made object that has a length usu. many hundred or thousand times greater than its width, that possesses considerable tensile strength, pliability, and resistance esp. against heat, light, some chemicals, and mechanical abrasion, that is obtained from animals (as wool, hair, silk, fur), vegetable matter (as cotton, flax, hemp, straw), or minerals or metals (as asbestos, aluminum, gold) or that is synthesized industrially (as rayon, nylon, glass fiber), and that may be wholly crystalline like asbestos and metal wires, wholly amorphous like glass, or in the case of the most widely used fibers, which are high polymers, partly crystalline and partly amorphous with elongated crystalline domains embedded in an amorphous matrix consisting of the same chemical substance; *specif* **:** a fiber sufficiently long, pliable, cohesive, and strong to be spun into a yarn made into a fabric or cordage or used in loose masses for stuffing (as in pillows or mattresses) — see FIBRIL c, MICELLE; compare FILAMENT a(3) **2 :** a material made of or from fibers: as **a :** a durable material resembling straw that is woven of prepared paper and used esp. for suitcases, furniture, mats, and caps **b :** the vegetable tissues constituting the major raw material of most papers **c :** VULCANIZED FIBER **3 a :** an element that imparts strength, body, or substance ⟨his objectivity gave ~ to his point of view⟩ **b :** basic toughness **:** DURABILITY, FORTITUDE, STRENGTH ⟨hurdles that might have seemed insurmountable to persons of lesser ~ —R.L.Taylor⟩ **c :** essential structure or makeup **:** ESSENCE ⟨the very ~ of a person's thought⟩ **4 :** CRUDE FIBER **5 :** the pattern of directional structure in a wrought metal (as wire)

²**fi·ber** \ˈfē,b|e(ə)r, |beə, ˈfībə(r)\ *n* [NL, fr. L, beaver — more at BEAVER] *syn of* ONDATRA

fiberboard \ˈ≈,≈\ *n* **:** a material made by compressing fibers (as of wood) into thick stiff sheets; *also* **:** a board or a sheet of this material

fiber box *also* **fiberboard box** *n* **:** a shipping container made from corrugated or solid paperboard by slotting, scoring, joining, folding, and sealing

fiber can *n* **:** a rigid multi-ply paperboard container generally cylindrical but sometimes oval or rectangular with rounded corners having inserted or formed paper ends

fi·bered \ˈfībə(r)d\ *adj* **1 :** having or made up of fibers **2 :** possessing fiber ⟨the tough-*fibered* spirit of our times —Dana Burnet⟩

fiber glass *n* **:** glass in fibrous form used in making various products (as glass wool, yarns, textiles) ⟨*fiber glass* insulation⟩ ⟨a *fiber glass* boat⟩ — called also *fibrous glass, spun glass*

fiber grease *n* **:** a lubricating grease having a fibrous consistency

fi·ber·iza·tion \,fībərəˈzāshən, -,rīˈz-\ *n* -S **:** the process of fiberizing

fi·ber·ize \ˈfībə,rīz\ *vt* -ED/-ING/-S **:** to reduce to fibers **:** separate into fibers by crushing or beating **:** DEFIBRATE; *also* **:** to treat or mix with fibers (as in the manufacture of rubber fabric)

fi·ber·iz·er \-zə(r)\ *n* -S **:** one that fiberizes

fi·ber·less \ˈfībə(r)ləs\ *adj* **:** lacking fiber **:** devoid of fibers

fiber of corti *usu cap C* **:** ROD OF CORTI

fiber of mül·ler \-ˈmyülə(r), -ˈmil-,-ˈmul-,-ˈməl-, *G* ˈmʊel-\ *usu cap M* [after Heinrich M. *Müller* †1864 Ger. anatomist] **:** any of certain neuroglia fibers that extend through the entire thickness of the retina and act as support for the other structures

fiber of re·mak \-ˈrā,mäk\ *usu cap R* [after Robert *Remak* †1865 Ger. physiologist] **:** an unmedullated nerve fiber

fiber of shar·pey \-ˈshärpē\ *usu cap S* [after William *Sharpey* †1880 Scot. anatomist] **:** any of the thready processes of the periosteum that penetrate the tissue of the superficial lamellae of bones

fiber plant *n* **:** a plant yielding a useful fiber (as hemp, flax)

fiber plaster *n* **:** a gypsum plaster used in building to which hair fiber or wood fiber has been added as a binder

fiber-reactive dye *n* **:** a dye that combines chemically with fibers, esp. cellulose — see DYE table I

fiber saturation point *n* **:** the point in drying wood at which all free moisture has been removed from the cell itself while the cell wall remains saturated with absorbed moisture

fiber tracheid *n* **:** a tracheid having pointed ends, a relatively thick wall, and a narrow lumen as in a fiber but with small bordered pits and prob. functioning in support rather than conduction

fiber tract *n* **:** TRACT

fibr- *or* **fibro-** *comb form* [L *fibra*] **1 a :** fiber **:** fibrous and **:** fibrous tissue ⟨*fibrogenic*⟩ ⟨*fibrocaseous*⟩ ⟨*fibrosis*⟩ **b :** of or containing fibrous tissue ⟨*fibrocartilage*⟩ ⟨*fibroangioma*⟩ ⟨*fibrocarcinoma*⟩ **2 :** fibrotic ⟨*fibrobronchitis*⟩ **3 a :** fibroma and **:** fibromatous ⟨*fibromyxoma*⟩ ⟨*fibrochondroma*⟩ **b :** a fibroma containing ⟨*fibrocyst*⟩ **4 :** fibrin and ⟨*fibrohemorrhagic*⟩ ⟨*fibropurulent*⟩

fi·brat·ed \ˈfī,brād·əd\ *adj* [L *fibratus* (fr. *fibra* fiber + *-atus* -ate) + E *-ed*] **:** containing fibers or fibrous material

fi·bra·tion \fīˈbrāshən\ *n* -S [prob. fr. F, fr. *fibr-* + *-ation*] **:** the arrangement or formation of fibers or fibrous structure

fibre *var of* FIBER

fi·bril \ˈfībrəl, ˈfib-, -(,)bril\ *n* -S [NL *fibrilla*, dim. of L *fibra* fiber] **:** a small thread or small fiber: as **a** (1) **:** a filamentous outgrowth of the thallus in lichens (2) **:** ROOT HAIR **b** (1) **:** one of the fine threads into which a striated muscle fiber may be longitudinally split after treatment with alcohol — compare MYOFIBRIL (2) **:** NEUROFIBRIL **c :** one of the minute elongated elements that make up the structure of fibers of certain natural and synthetic materials (as textile fibers, wood, or fibrous proteins) and that are held to be made up ultimately of long-chain molecules oriented in a bundle in one direction — compare CRYSTALLITE 2

fi·bril·la \fīˈbrilə, fəˈ-\ *n, pl* **fibril·lae** \-,lē\ [NL] **:** FIBRIL c

fi·bril·lar \ˈfībrələ(r), ˈfib-; fīˈbril-,fəˈbril-\ *adj* [NL *fibrilla* + E *-ar*] **1 :** of or like fibrils or fibers ⟨a ~ network⟩ **2 :** of or exhibiting fibrillation ⟨~ twitchings⟩

fibrillar theory *n* **:** a theory of protoplasmic structure: protoplasm is essentially composed of fine sometimes branched fibrils that interlace but do not form a continuous network and are bathed in a fluid matrix

fi·bril·lary \ˈfībrə,lerē, ˈfib-; fīˈbrilərē, fəˈb-\ *adj* [NL *fibrilla* + E *-ary*] **1 :** of or relating to fibrils or fibers ⟨~ overgrowth⟩ **2 :** of, relating to, or marked by fibrillation ⟨~ chorea⟩

¹**fi·bril·late** \ˈfībrə,lāt, ˈfib-\ *vb* -ED/-ING/-S [NL *fibrilla* + E *-ate* (v. suffix)] *vi* **:** to undergo or exhibit fibrillation ~ *vt* **:** to cause to undergo or exhibit fibrillation; *specif* **:** to cause (the heart) to fibrillate

²**fi·bril·late** \ˈfībrə,lāt, ˈfib-; fīˈbrilət, fəˈb-\ *or* **fi·bril·lat·ed** \ˈfībrə,lād·əd, ˈfib-\ *adj* [*fibrillate* fr. NL *fibrilla* + E *-ate*, adj suffix; *fibrillated* fr. past. part. of ¹*fibrillate*] **:** having a fibrous structure **:** furnished with fibrils **:** FRINGED

fi·bril·la·tion \,fībrəˈlāshən, ,fib-\ *n* -S **1 :** the act or process of forming fibrils or the state of being fibrillate **2 a :** muscular twitching involving individual muscle fibers acting without coordination — compare FASCICULATION **b :** very rapid irregular contractions of the muscle fibers of the heart resulting in a lack of synchronism between heartbeat and pulse beat — see AURICULAR FIBRILLATION, VENTRICULAR FIBRILLATION **3 :** the breaking down of fibers such as occurs in beating paper pulp

fi·brilled \ˈfībrəld, ˈfib-, -(,)brild\ *adj* [*fibril* + *-ed*] **:** FIBRILLATE

fi·bril·li·form \fīˈbrilə,fȯrm, fəˈb-\ *adj* [NL *fibrilla* + E *-iform*] **:** resembling a fibril

fi·bril·lo·gen·ic \ˌfībrəlōˈjenik, ˈfib-; fīˌbril|-, fəˌb-\ *adj* [NL *fibrilla* + E *-o-* + *-genic*] **:** inducing fibrillation esp. of the heart — **fi·bril·lo·gen·i·cal·ly** \-nək(ə)lē\ *adv*

fi·bril·lose \ˈfībrə,lōs, ˈfib-\ *adj* [NL *fibrilla* + E *-ose*] **:** furnished with or consisting of fibril

fi·bril·lous \-ləs\ *adj* [NL *fibrilla* + E *-ous*] **:** belonging to or composed of fibrils

fi·brin \ˈfībrən\ *n* -S [ISV *fibr-* + *-in*] **:** a white insoluble fibrous protein formed from fibrinogen by the action of thrombin esp. in the clotting of blood but capable of being solubilized by certain enzymes (as plasmin, pepsin, or trypsin)

fibrin film *n* **:** a pliable translucent film prepared from fibrinogen and thrombin from human blood plasma and used in the surgical repair of defects

fibrin foam *n* **:** a spongy substance prepared from fibrinogen and thrombin from human blood plasma and used esp. after saturation with thrombin as an absorbable clotting agent in surgical wounds

fi·brin·o·gen \fīˈbrinəjən, -,jen\ *n* -S [ISV *fibrin* + *-o-* + *-gen;* orig. formed in G] **:** a globulin that is produced in the liver, is present esp. in blood plasma, and is converted into fibrin normally by the action of thrombin during clotting of blood

fi·brin·o·gen·o·pe·nia \(,)fī,brinə,jenəˈpēnēə, -nyə\ *n* -S [NL, fr. ISV *fibrinogen* + NL *-o-* + *-penia*] **:** a deficiency of fibrin or fibrinogen or both in the blood

fi·brin·oid \ˈfībrə,nȯid\ *n* -S *often attrib* **:** a material that somewhat resembles fibrin and is derived from connective tissue which occurs in the normal placenta and in certain pathological processes (as caseous necrosis) postnatally

fi·bri·nol·y·sin \,fībrəˈnäləsən\ *n* -S [ISV *fibrin* + *-o-* + *lysin*] **1 :** PLASMIN **2 :** STREPTOKINASE

fi·bri·nol·y·sis \-səs\ *n* -ES [NL, fr. ISV *fibrin* + NL *-o-* + *-lysis*] **:** the breakdown of fibrin to soluble products usu. through enzymatic action — **fi·bri·no·lyt·ic** \,fībrənōˈlid·ik, fī,brinə|-\ *adj*

fi·bri·no·pe·nia \,fībrənōˈpēnēə, -nyə\ *n* -S [NL, fr. ISV *fibrin* + NL *-o-* + *-penia*] **:** FIBRINOGENOPENIA

fi·bri·no·purulent \,fībrə(,)nō, fī,brinə+\ *adj* [*fibrin-* + *-o-* + *purulent*] **:** containing, characterized by, or exuding fibrin and pus (as in certain inflammations)

fi·brin·ous \ˈfībrənəs\ *adj* [ISV *fibrin* + *-ous*] **:** marked by the presence of fibrin ⟨~ pericarditis⟩ ⟨~ exudate⟩

fibro- — see FIBR-

fi·bro·adenoma \,fī(,)brō+\ *n* [NL, fr. *fibr-* + *adenoma*] **:** adenoma with a large amount of fibrous tissue

fi·bro·blast \ˈfībrə,blast\ *n* [ISV *fibr-* + *-blast*] **:** an undifferentiated mesenchyme cell giving rise to connective tissue — **fi·bro·blas·tic** \ˌ≈ˈblastik\ *adj*

fi·bro·cartilage \,fī(,)brō+\ *n* [ISV *fibr-* + *cartilage*] **:** cartilage in which the matrix except immediately about the cells is largely composed of fibers like those of ordinary connective tissue; *also* **:** a structure or part composed of such cartilage — **fi·bro·cartilaginous** \"+\ *adj*

fi·bro-cement \"+\ *n* [*fibr-* + *cement*] *Brit* **:** ASBESTOS CEMENT

fi·bro·crystalline \"+\ *adj* [*fibr-* + *crystalline*] **:** composed of or characterized by fibrous crystals

fi·bro·cyte \ˈfībrə,sīt\ *n* -S [ISV *fibr-* + *-cyte*] **:** FIBROBLAST; *specif* **:** a spindle-shaped connective-tissue cell characteristic of fibrous tissue — **fi·bro·cyt·ic** \ˌ≈ˈsid·ik\ *adj*

fi·bro·elastic \,fī(,)brō+\ *adj* [*fibr-* + *elastic*] **:** consisting of both fibrous and elastic elements

fi·bro·fer·rite \,fībrōˈfe,rīt\ *n* [G *fibroferrit*, fr. *fibr-* + L *ferrum* iron + G *-it* -ite — more at FARRIER] **:** a mineral $Fe(SO_4)(OH).5H_2O$ consisting of a fibrous hydrated basic ferric sulfate

¹**fi·broid** \ˈfī,brȯid\ *adj* [*fibr-* + *-oid*] **:** like, forming, or composed of fibrous tissue

²**fibroid** \"\ *n* -S **:** a benign fibromyoma of the uterine wall

fi·bro·in \ˈfībrəwən\ *n* -S [F *fibroïne*, fr. *fibr-* + *-ine*] **:** the insoluble protein of silk comprising the filaments of the raw fiber held together by sericin

fi·bro·lite \'fībrə,līt\ *n* -s [*fibr-* + *-lite*] : SILLIMANITE — **fi·bro·lit·ic** \¦==¦lid·ik\ *adj*

fi·bro·ma \fī'brōmə\ *n, pl* **fibromas** \-məz\ *also* **fibroma·ta** \-məd·ə\ [NL, fr. *fibr-* + *-oma*] : a benign tumor consisting mainly of fibrous tissue — **fi·brom·a·tous** \(')fī¦brämәd·əs, -rōm-\ *adj*

fi·bro·ma·to·gen·ic \fī¦brōməd·ō¦jenik\ *adj* [NL *fibromat-*, *fibroma* + E *-genic*] : inducing or tending to induce the development of fibromas

fi·bro·ma·toid \fī'brōmə,tȯid\ *adj* [NL *fibromat-*, *fibroma* + E *-oid*] : resembling a fibroma

fi·bro·ma·to·sis \(,)fī,brōmə'tōsəs\ *n, pl* **fibromato·ses** \-ō,sēz\ [NL, fr. *fibromat-*, *fibroma* + *-osis*] : a condition marked by the presence of or a tendency to develop multiple fibromas

fi·bro·myoma \¦fī(,)brō+\ *n, pl* **fibromyomas** *also* **fibro·myomata** [NL, fr. *fibr-* + *myoma*] : a mixed tumor containing both fibrous and muscle tissue — **fi·bro·myomatous** \"+\ *adj*

fibromyositis \"+\ *n* [NL, fr. *fibr-* + *myositis*] : inflammation of fibrous and muscle tissue

fi·bro·pla·sia \,fībrə'plāzh(ē)ə\ *n* -s [NL, fr. *fibr-* + *-plasia*] : the process of forming fibrous tissue (as in wound healing) — **fi·bro·plas·tic** \¦==¦plastik\ *adj*

fi·bro·plaster \'fībrō+,-\ *n* [*fibr-* + *plaster*] : FIBROUS PLASTER

fi·bro·sarcoma \¦fī(,)brō+\ *n* [NL, fr. *fibr-* + *sarcoma*] : a sarcoma of relatively low malignancy made up chiefly of spindle-shaped cells that tend to form collagenous fibrils — called also *spindle-cell sarcoma*

¹fi·brose \'fī,brōs\ *adj* [L *fibra* fiber + E *-ose*] : FIBROUS

²fibrose \"\ *vi* -ED/-ING/-S : to form fibrous tissue ‹a *fibrosed* wound›

fi·bro·sis \fī'brōsəs\ *n, pl* **fibro·ses** \-ō,sēz\ [NL, fr. *fibr-* + *-osis*] : a condition marked by a relative increase in the formation of interstitial fibrous tissue in any organ or region of the body : fibrous degeneration — **fi·brot·ic** \(')fī¦bräd·ik\ *adj*

fi·bro·sit·ic \¦fībrə¦sid·ik\ *adj* [NL *fibrositis* + E *-ic*] : of, relating to, or characteristic of fibrositis

fi·bro·si·tis \,==ˈsīd·əs\ *n* -ES [NL, fr. *fibrosus* fibrous (fr. ISV *fibrous*) + *-itis*] : a painful muscular condition that is believed to originate in the connective tissue associated with muscles and joints and in some instances to involve a psychosomatic factor and that is commonly accompanied by the formation of painful subcutaneous nodules

fi·bro·spon·gi·ae \,fībrə'spənjē,ē, -pän-\ *n pl, cap* [NL, fr. *fibr-* + *-spongiae*] *in former classifications* : an order of Porifera comprising sponges with fibrous skeletons and including all forms not placed in Calcispongiae

fi·brous \'fībrəs\ *adj* [F *fibreux*, fr. *fibre* fiber (fr. L *fibra*) + *-eux* -ous] **1 a** : containing, consisting of, or like fibers ‹~ roots› ‹the ~ husk of a coconut› ‹~ proteins› **b** : characterized by fibrosis **c** : capable of being separated into fibers ‹a ~ mineral›; *also* : breaking in a manner that exposes needlelike grains **2** : possessing body, strength, or toughness : SINEWY, HARDENED — **fi·brous·ly** *adv* — **fi·brous·ness** *n* -ES

fibrous glass *n* : FIBER GLASS

fibrous plaster *n* : plastering reinforced with fiber (as Manila hemp or sisal) or provided with a cloth backing and used chiefly as sheeting, cornice molding, and cover strips

fibrous ring *n* : a strong laminated ring of fibrous tissue that forms the outer part of an intervertebral disk — see PULPY NUCLEUS

fibrous root *n* : a root (as in most grasses) that has no prominent central axis and that branches in all directions — distinguished from *taproot and tuberous root* — see ROOT illustration

fibrous-rooted begonia \¦==¦==-\ *n* : a begonia with fibrous rather than rhizomatous or tuberous roots; *esp* : any of numerous rather small bushy free-flowering begonias with white, pink, or red single or double flowers that have been developed in cultivation from a Brazilian wild plant (*Begonia semperflorens*) — compare RHIZOMATOUS BEGONIA, TUBEROUS BEGONIA

fi·bro·vascular \¦fī(,)brō+\ *adj* [*fibr-* + *vascular*] : having or consisting of fibers and conducting cells (as vessels) — compare VASCULAR

fibrovascular bundle *n* : VASCULAR BUNDLE

fibs *pl of* FIB, *pres 3d sing of* FIB

fib·ster \'fibztə(r), -bst-\ *n* -s [¹*fib* + *-ster*] : FIBBER

fib·u·la \'fibyələ\ *n, pl* **fibu·lae** \-,lē\ *or* **fibulas** [L, prob. fr. *figere, fivere* to fasten, pierce — more at DIKE] **1** : a clasp somewhat resembling a safety pin used by the ancient Greeks and Romans **2** [NL, fr. L] **a** : the outer or postaxial and usu. the smaller of the two bones of the hind limb below the knee that is rudimentary and often ankylosed with the tibia in most birds and many mammals (as the horse and the ruminants) and in man the slenderest bone of the body in proportion to its length and that articulates above with the external tuberosity of the tibia and below with the talus, its lower end forming the external malleolus of the ankle **b** : JUGUM 2

fibulae 1

fib·u·lar \-lə(r)\ *adj* [NL *fibula* + E *-ar*] : of, relating to, or lying in the direction of the fibula

fib·u·la·re \,fibyə'lärē, -la(a)rē\ *n, pl* **fibula·ria** \-rēə\ [NL, fr. *fibula* + L *-are* (neut. of *-aris* -ar)] : the outer or postaxial element or bone of the proximal row of the tarsus; *specif, in higher vertebrates* : CALCANEUM

fib·u·lo·calcaneal \¦fibyə(,)lō+\ *adj* [NL *fibula* + E *-o-* + *calcaneal*] : belonging to the fibula and the calcaneum

-fic \fik, fēk\ *adj suffix* [MF & L; MF *-fique*, fr. L *-ficus*, fr. *facere* make, do — more at DO] : making : causing : bringing about ‹acidi*fic*› ‹proli*fic*›

fi·car·ia \fī'ka(a)rēə\ *n, cap* [NL, fr. L *ficus* fig + NL *-aria*; fr. the appearance of the roots — more at FIG] : a small genus of European herbs (family Ranunculaceae) closely related to the buttercups but having three sepals and swollen smooth achenes

fic·a·ry \'fikərē\ *n* -ES [NL *Ficaria*] : LESSER CELANDINE

-fi·ca·tion \fə'kāshən\ *n comb form* -s [ME *-ficacioun*, fr. MF & L; MF *-fication*, fr. L *-fication-*, *-ficatio*, fr. *-ficatus* (past part. ending of verbs ending in *-ficare* to make, fr. *-ficus* -fic) + *-ion-*, *-io* -ion] : making : production ‹paci*fication*› ‹vini*fication*› ‹russi*fication*› — compare -FACTION; -FY

fice *var of* FEIST

fice dog *n* : FEIST 1

¹fich·te·an \'fiktēən, -ikt-\ *adj, usu cap* [Johann Gottlieb *Fichte* †1814 Ger. philosopher + E *-an*] : of or having to do with Johann Gottlieb Fichte or his idealist philosophy

²fichtean \"\ *n* -s *usu cap* : an adherent of Fichteanism

fich·te·an·ism \-,nizəm\ *n* -s *usu cap* : a post-Kantian idealist philosophy in which an attempt is made to perfect the Kantian system by connecting practical reason with pure reason through deducing a priori from the ego not only the categories of our knowledge of nature but also the doctrines of ethical and legal obligations and thereby uniting these two critiques in one system — compare ABSOLUTE EGO

fichu \'fi(,)shü *sometimes* (')fē¦shü\ *n* -s [F, neckerchief, small shawl, fr. past part. of *ficher* to drive in, pin, fasten, fr. (assumed) VL *figicare*, fr. L *figere* to fasten, pierce — more at DIKE] : a woman's scarf often of sheer white fabric in a triangular shape that is draped over the shoulders and fastened in front or worn to fill in a low neckline

fic·i·dae \'fisə,dē\ *n pl, cap* [NL, fr. *Ficus*, type genus + *-idae*] : a family of chiefly tropical marine gastropod mollusks (suborder Taenioglossa) — see FICUS 2, FIGSHELL

fi·cin \'fīsᵊn\ *n* -s [NL *Ficus* (genus name of *Ficus doliaria*, species that produces it) + E *-in*] : a proteinase obtained usu. as a pale tan powder from the latex of fig trees and used as an anthelmintic and protein digestant (as for curdling milk)

fichu

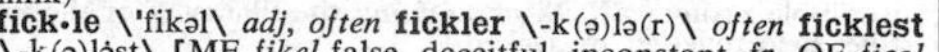

¹fick·le \'fikəl\ *adj, often* **fickler** \-k(ə)lə(r)\ *often* **ficklest** \-k(ə)ləst\ [ME *fikel* false, deceitful, inconstant, fr. OE *ficol* guileful, deceitful; akin to OE *befician* to deceive, *fācen* deceit, fraud, OHG *feihhan* deceit, guile, ON *feikn* terror, misfortune, L *piget* it irks, disgusts, and prob. to OE *fāh* hostile — more at FOE] : marked by lack of steadfastness, constancy, stability : given to ready change, inconstancy, whimsical choice, or unpredictable variability ‹the conventionally ~ woman —J.L. Lowes› ‹because the people are so easily misled, and so ~ in their views —Will Durant› **syn** see INCONSTANT

²fickle \"\ *vt* -ED/-ING/-S [perh. fr. ME *fikelen* to deceive, beguile, fr. *fikel*, adj.] **1** *chiefly Scot* : PERPLEX, BAFFLE **2** *chiefly Scot* : OUTWIT

fick·le·ness *n* -ES : the quality or state of being fickle

fick's law \'fiks-\ *n, usu cap F* [after Adolf *Fick* †1901 Ger. physiologist] : a law of chemistry and physics: the rate of diffusion of one material in another is proportional to the negative of the gradient of the concentration of the first material

fi·co \'fē(,)kō\ *n* -ES [modif. of It *fica*, fr. (assumed) VL — more at FIG] : FIG 6b

¹fi·coid \'fī,kȯid\ *adj* [NL *Ficus* + E *-oid*] **1** : resembling a fig or a plant of the genus *Ficus* **2** [NL *Ficoideae*] : of or relating to the Aizoaceae

²ficoid \"\ *also* **fi·coi·dal** \(,)fī¦kȯidᵊl\ *n* -s : a plant of the family Aizoaceae

fi·coi·de·ae \fī'kȯidē,ē\ [NL, fr. *Ficoides* (syn. of *Mesembryanthemum*) (fr. *Ficus* + L *-oides* -oid) + *-eae*] *syn of* AIZOACEAE

fict *abbr* **1** [L *fictilis*] earthen **2** fiction **3** fictitious

¹fic·tile \'fiktᵊl, -(,)til, -,tīl\ *adj* [L *fictilis*, fr. *fictus* (past part. of *fingere* to shape, form, devise, feign) + *-ilis* -ile — more at DOUGH] **1** : molded or capable of being molded into the form of an art work or artifact **2 a** *of an art work or artifact* : molded of earth, clay, or other soft material **b** : of or belonging to pottery or earthenware **3** : capable of being led or directed : PLIABLE ‹~ masses of people ripe for propaganda›

²fictile \"\ *n* -s [L, fr. neut. of *fictilis*] : a piece of fictile ware

fic·tion \'fikshən\ *n* -s [ME *ficcioun*, fr. MF *fiction*, fr. L *fiction-*, *fictio*, fr. *fictus* + *-ion-*, *-io* -ion] **1** : the act of creating something imaginary : a fabrication of the mind **2 a** : an intentional fabrication : a convenient assumption that overlooks known facts in order to achieve an immediate goal **b** : an unfounded, invented, or deceitful statement ‹the ~s on a bottle of patent medicine› **3 a** : fictitious literature (as novels, tales, romances) **b** : a work of fiction; *esp* : NOVEL **4 a** : an assumption of a possible thing as a fact irrespective of the question of its truth; *specif* : an allegation or supposition in law of a state of facts assumed to exist which the practice of the courts allows to be made in pleading and refuses to allow the adverse party to disprove — distinguished from *presumption* **b** : an assumption concealing or affecting to conceal that a law has undergone an alteration by which in its operation it is modified while in its letter it remains unchanged **5** *archaic* : the act of fashioning or inventing **6 a** : unfounded belief : ASSUMPTION ‹all the ~s that go to make up a man's public reputation› **b** : a practical or useful illusion or pretense ‹it was only a ~ of independence his mother gave him; he was almost totally under her power —G.A.Wagner› **c** : an imaginary, ideal, logical, or hypothetical construct without a known counterpart in reality or a conception of assumed validity or actuality that serves heuristic purposes esp. in the guidance of practical affairs ‹the average man is a ~›

syn FIGMENT, FABRICATION, FABLE: FICTION may refer to any composition wholly an invention of the imagination or noticeably more the product of the imagination than of factual reporting ‹when we call a piece of literature a work of *fiction* we mean no more than that the characters could not be identified with any persons who have lived in the flesh, nor the incidents with any particular events that have actually taken place —A.J.Toynbee› ‹at a loss what to invent to detain him, beyond the stale *fiction* that his father was coming tomorrow —George Meredith› FIGMENT may suggest a product of unrestrained fancy or quite free imagination ‹a gigantic fancy of his own! And all these figures were *figments* of his brain —John Galsworthy› ‹the metaphysical *figments* of our own creation —Havelock Ellis› FABRICATION may apply to an account made up with artifice, deft or clumsy, and with specific intent to deceive ‹the doctor was a great liar, but a valuable liar. His *fabrications* seemed to be the framework of a forgotten but imposing plan —Djuna Barnes› ‹the government story was not a complete *fabrication* but a careful distortion—Christopher Devlin› FABLE may apply to an obviously fictitious narrative in which the impossible, marvelous, and incredible are employed, often to suggest some moral ‹the *fables* of Aesop› ‹whispered suspicions, old wives' tales, *fables* invented by men who had nothing to do but loaf in the drugstore and make up stories —Sherwood Anderson› ‹witchcraft and diabolical possession and diabolical disease have long since passed into the region of *fables* —W.E.H.Lecky›

fic·tion·al \-shənᵊl,-shnəl\ *adj* : of, relating to, characterized by, or suggestive of fiction — **fic·tion·al·ly** \-ᵊlē,-əlē, -i\ *adv*

fic·tion·al·ism \-shənᵊl,izəm, -shnə,li-\ *also* **fic·tion·ism** \-shə,nizəm\ *n* -s : a theory describing or advocating the use of fictions (sense 6c)

fic·tion·al·is·tic \¦fikshənᵊl¦istik, -shnə¦li-\ *adj* : FICTIONAL

fic·tion·al·iza·tion \,fikshənᵊlə'zāshən, -shnələ'-, -ᵊl,ī'z-, -ə,lī'z-\ *or* **fic·tion·iza·tion** \,fiksh(ə)nə'z-, -shə,nī'z-\ *n* -s : an act, process, or product of fictionalizing; *esp* : a fictionalized version (as of a summer vacation)

fic·tion·al·ize \'fikshənᵊl,īz, -shnə,līz\ *or* **fic·tion·ize** \'fikshə,nīz\ *vt* -ED/-ING/-S : to make into, treat in the manner of, or regard as fiction ‹~ the diary he kept in prison›

fic·tion·eer \,fikshə¦ni(ə)r\ *n* -s : one who writes fiction esp. in quantity ‹the strident din of the popular ~s — E.A.Boyd›

fictioneering *n* -s : the production of or practice of writing fiction in quantity or of commonplace quality ‹she never quite goes over the limit into blatant ~ —G.W.Johnson›

fic·tion·er \,fiksh(ə)nə(r)\ *n* -s : FICTIONIST

fic·tion·ist \-nəst\ *n* -s : a writer of fiction; *esp* : NOVELIST

fic·tious \'fikshəs\ *adj* [*fiction* + *-ous*] *archaic* : given to fiction : FICTITIOUS

fic·ti·tious \(')fik¦tishəs\ *adj* [L *fictitius*, *ficticius*, fr. *fictus* (past part. of *fingere* to shape, form, devise, feign) + *-itius*, *-icius* -itious — more at DOUGH] **1** : of, relating to, or suggestive of fiction or a fiction ‹~ value› : IMAGINARY **2 a** (1) : conventionally or hypothetically assumed ‹a ~ entity› ‹a ~ concept› (2) : accepted although known to be untrue, unnatural, or unreal : arbitrarily accepted as genuine ‹like a jealous stepmother . . . wary of the favors she bestows on her ~ offspring —J.F.Cooper› **b** *of a name* : ASSUMED **c** *of a celestial object* : assumed at a given time to be in the position that would be occupied if the apparent motion were perfectly uniform ‹the ~ sun› **3** : FEIGNED, SIMULATED : not genuinely felt ‹sure that his equanimity was ~ —George Meredith›

syn FABULOUS, LEGENDARY, MYTHICAL, APOCRYPHAL: FICTITIOUS applies to fabrication or contrivance, often artful, without necessary intent to deceive, or to false evaluation ‹a *fictitious* reconstruction of primitive life before the coming of the white man —*Amer. Guide Series: Oregon*› ‹he was a novelist: his amours, and his characters, were *fictitious* —O.S. J.Gogarty› ‹a *fictitious* expansion of expenditure creating a morbid speculation —Norman Angell› FABULOUS applies to the marvelous or incredible; it describes that which, existent or not, transcends accustomed sober reality ‹*fabulous* atomic weapons› ‹the *fabulous* pirate treasures of Captain Kidd› ‹out in Montana in the 1860s *fabulous* mining strikes made boom towns overnight —*Saturday Rev.*› ‹the mouth of the converter belched fire like some *fabulous* dragon, its flames leaping forty or fifty feet into the air —Allan Nevins & H.S.Commager› LEGENDARY may apply to that which undergoes distortion, elaboration, or exaggeration by popular tradition ‹*legendary* wonders, such as the Seven Cities which, situated on great heights, had jewel-studded doorways and whole streets of busy goldsmiths —Allan Nevins & H.S.Commager› ‹*legendary* history reported in the next generation that the elements had been pregnant with auguries: images had sweated; the sky had blazed with meteors —J.A.Froude› MYTHICAL suggests quite fanciful or imaginative creation, embellishment, or exaggeration and implies nonexistence ‹these ancestors are not creations of the *mythical* fancy but were once men of flesh and blood —J.G.Frazer› ‹the *mythical* islands, Antilia, St. Brendan, and the rest, with which map makers had for centuries decorated their maps —G.C.Sellery› APOCRYPHAL suggests lack of known authentic source and implies spuriousness or dubiousness about what is described ‹it is not possible to attach much weight to the Sanson memoirs — they are so plainly *apocryphal* —Agnes Repplier› ‹tales, possibly *apocryphal* and certainly embroidered, of his feats of intelligence work in the eastern Mediterranean —R.W.Firth›

fic·ti·tious·ly *adv* : in a fictitious manner

fic·ti·tious·ness *n* -ES : the quality or state of being fictitious

fictitious person *n* **1** : a supposed but in fact nonexistent person referred to in some legal documents or proceedings (as the "Richard Roe" in English ejectment cases or the payee "Cash" in a check) **2** : JURISTIC PERSON

fic·tive \'fiktiv\ *adj* [*fiction* + *-ive*] **1** : of, relating to, or capable of imaginative creation ‹~ art› ‹~ talent› **2** : not genuine : IMAGINARY, FEIGNED ‹~ sympathy› — **fic·tive·ly** \-tәvlē\ *adv*

fi·cus \'fīkəs\ *n, cap* [NL, fr. L, fig — more at FIG] **1** : a large genus of tropical trees or shrubs (family Moraceae) distinguished usu. by their leaves and by their fruit which consists of a pear-shaped or globose receptacle enclosing numerous minute diclinous flowers — see BANYAN, FIG 2a, PIPAL, RUBBER PLANT **2** : the type genus of Ficidae comprising gastropods with light thin spirally ribbed and sculptured shells that are more or less pear-shaped or fig-shaped — compare FIGSHELL

¹fid \'fid\ *n* -s [origin unknown] **1** : a wooden or metal bar or pin: as **a** : a square bar of wood or iron used to support the topmast or a topgallant mast and passed through a hole or mortise at its heel and resting on the trestletrees **b** : a pin usu. of hard wood that tapers to a point and is used in opening the strands of a rope (as in splicing) or in stretching eyes — compare MARLINESPIKE **2 a** *obs* : a plug of oakum to stop the vent of a cannon **b** *dial Eng* : CHUNK, LUMP ‹a ~ of tobacco›

fid 1b

²fid \"\ *vt* **fidded; fidded; fidding; fids** : to secure (as a topmast) and support in place with a fid

fid *abbr* **1** fidelity **2** fiduciary

-fid \fəd, ,fid\ *adj comb form* [L *-fidus*, fr. the root of *findere* to split — more at BITE] : divided into (so many) parts ‹sexi*fid*› or (such) parts ‹pinnati*fid*›

fi·da'i *or* **fi·da'i** *or* **fi·dai** \fi'dä,ē\ *also* **fi·da·wi** \-ä̈wē\ *or* **fe·dai** \-ä,ē\ *n, pl* **fida'is** *or* **fida'is** *or* **fidai** *or* **fidais** *also* **fidawi** *or* **fidawis** *or* **fedai** *or* **fedais** *sometimes cap* [Per *fidā'ī*] : a member of an Ismaili order of assassins known for their willingness to offer up their lives in order to carry out delegated assignments of murdering appointed victims

fidate *vt* -ED/-ING/-S [prob. fr. L *fidus* trusty, safe + E *-ate*; akin to L *fidere* to trust — more at BIDE] : to exempt in chess from capture (as in problems) — **fi·da·tion** \fī'dāshən, fə'-\ *n* -s

-fi·date \fədə¦t, fə,dāt, fə,dā\, *usu* |d·+V\ *adj comb form* [L *-fidatus*, fr. *-fidus* -fid + *-atus* -ate] : -FID

¹fid·dle \'fidᵊl\ *n* -s [ME *fithele*, *fidel*, fr. OE *fithele*, prob. fr. ML *vitula*, perh. fr. L *vitulari* to celebrate, be joyful] **1** : a bowed stringed instrument: **a** : a folk instrument used esp. to accompany dancing ‹the sound of the ~ on the village green› **b** : VIOLIN **c** : an instrument that resembles the violin ‹a gourd ~› **2** : FIDDLER **3** : a flat restraining surface (as a slat, rack, or light railing of cords on shipboard to keep dishes from sliding off a cabin table during rough weather) **4** : FIDDLESTICKS

²fiddle \"\ *vb* **fiddled; fiddled; fiddling** \-d(ᵊ)liŋ\ **fiddles** [ME *fithelen*, *fidelen*, fr. *fithele*, *fidel*, n.] *vi* **1** : to play on a fiddle **2 a** : to keep the hands or fingers moving nervously — usu. used with *with* ‹~ about with his tie› **b** : to work aimlessly, fruitlessly, or pointlessly : TINKER — usu. used with *with* ‹*fiddled* around with the engine for hours› **c** : MEDDLE, TAMPER — usu. used with *with* ‹a back window broken out or a door lock *fiddled* with —MacKinlay Kantor› ~ *vt* **1** : to play (as a tune) on a fiddle **2** : CHEAT, SWINDLE

fiddle away *vt* : to waste or fritter away ‹he *fiddled away* his time and strength›

fiddleback \'==,=\ *n, often attrib* : something resembling a fiddle: as **a** *or* **fiddleback chasuble** : a chasuble with a broad backpiece — see CHASUBLE illustration **b** : a wavy grain in wood due to an irregular arrangement of the fibers that gives an undulating appearance to a smooth surface **c** : an Australian beetle (*Eupoecila australasiae*) related to the goliath beetles

fiddleback chair *n* : a chair usu. in Queen Anne style having a splat resembling the outline of a violin

fiddle beetle *n* : any of several large flattened long-legged Oriental ground beetles of the genus *Mormolyce* having an elongated head and thorax and expanded wing cases and resembling a violin in outline

fiddle block *n* : a tackle block having two sheaves of different diameters one above the other instead of side by side as in a common double block

fiddle bow *n* : FIDDLESTICK

fiddle case *n* : the fruit of the rattle (sense 3a)

fiddleback chair

fid·dle·dee·dee \,fidᵊldē'dē\ *interj* — used to express impatience, disbelief, or scorn

fiddle dock *n* : a dock (*Rumex pulcher*) with fiddle-shaped leaves

fiddle drill *n* : BOW DRILL

¹fid·dle-fad·dle \'fidᵊl¦fadᵊl\ *n* [redupl. of ¹*fiddle*] : trifling or foolish talk, comment, or action : NONSENSE — often used interjectionally

²fiddle-faddle \"\ *vb* **fiddle-faddled; fiddle-faddled; fiddle-faddling** \-ad(ᵊ)liŋ\ **fiddle-faddles** : TRIFLE, MEDDLE, FIDDLE — **fid·dle-fad·dler** \-d(ᵊ)lə(r)\ *n* -s

fiddle flower *n* : a bleeding heart (*Dicentra spectabilis*)

fiddle-footed \¦==¦==\ *adj* **1** : SKITTISH, JUMPY ‹a *fiddle-footed* horse› **2** : prone to wander or drift ‹*fiddle-footed* cowboys›

fiddlehead \'==,=\ *n* **1** : an ornament on a ship's bow curved like the scroll at the head of a violin **2** : one of the young unfurling fronds of certain ferns (as the cinnamon fern and ostrich fern) that are often eaten as greens

fiddleheaded \¦==¦==\ *adj* : having a head shaped like a violin ‹a ~ spoon›

fiddle-leaf fig *n* : an African fig tree (*Ficus lyrata*) that has very large violin-shaped or guitar-shaped leaves and that is often cultivated as a pot or tub plant

fiddle-neck \'==,=\ *n* [so called fr. the shape of the flower racemes] **1** : a hairy annual Californian herb (*Phacelia tanacetifolia*) with large pinnately divided leaves and bluish flowers **2** : a plant of the genus *Amsinckia*

fid·dler \'fid(ᵊ)lə(r)\ *n* -s [ME *fitheler*, *fideler*, fr. OE *fithelere*, fr. *fithele* fiddle + *-ere* -er — more at FIDDLE] **1 a** : one that fiddles **b** : VIOLINIST **2 a** *also* **fiddlerfish** \'=(=)=,=\ : any of several rays of the family Rhinobatidae that resemble a violin in outline — called also *fiddlefish, fiddle shark* **b** *also* **fiddler cat** *or* **fiddler catfish** : SPOTTED CAT

fiddler beetle *n* : any of certain beetles: as **a** : FIDDLEBACK **b** : a root-girdling beetle (*Prepodes vittatus* or a related species) destructive to citrus in Jamaica

fiddler crab *also* **fiddler** *n* **1** : any of numerous burrowing crabs of the genus *Uca* widely distributed in salt marshes and along sandy or muddy shores of No. and So. America, the Indian ocean, and other areas and having in the male one claw much enlarged and often held in a position suggesting that in which a fiddle is held — called also *beckoning crab, fighting crab* **2** : any of several crabs structurally similar to the fiddler crab

fiddler crab 1

fiddler's green *n, usu cap F&G* : a heaven reserved for sailors or soldiers, esp. cavalrymen

fiddles *pl of* FIDDLE, *pres 3d sing of* FIDDLE

fiddlestick \'==,=\ *n* [ME *fidel stik*] **1 a :** the bow usu. strung with horsehair that is used in playing the fiddle **b :** a stick on a seeding machine that is worked back and forth to broadcast seed **2 a :** TRIFLE ⟨she didn't care a ~ for that⟩ **b :** NONSENSE — usu. used in the pl. ⟨nothing but utter ~*s*⟩ **c** — used in the pl. interjectionally to express disapproval, disbelief, or derision

fiddle waist *n* **:** an extremely narrow shank on a shoe

fiddlewood \'==,=\ *n* **1 :** any of several trees of the family Verbenaceae esp. of the genus *Citharexylum* **2 :** the hard wood of a fiddlewood

fid·dley *or* **fid·ley** \'fid(ᵊ)lē\ *n* -s [origin unknown] **:** the uppermost part of the stokehole of a steamship or an alleyway across this on a level with the between decks and roofed usu. with a grating for ventilation

fiddley hatch *n* **:** a hatch around the smokestack and uptake on the weather deck of a ship for ventilation of the boiler room

¹fiddling *adj* [fr. pres. part. of ²*fiddle*] **:** TRIFLING, PETTY

²fiddling *n* [fr. gerund of ²*fiddle*] **:** the process of sewing book sections together by hand with cross-stitch or overcast stitch from one section or group of leaves to the next in alternation often for use in books having a number of single leaves and having cords or bands in sawed-in grooves

¹fi·dei·com·mis·sary \ˌfīdēˌīˈkämə,serē, -dē,īkəˈmisərē\ *n* -ES [LL *fideicommissarius*, fr. *fideicommissum* + L *-arius* -ary (n. suffix)] **:** a person who is the beneficiary under civil law of a fideicommissum and who is nearly equivalent to a cestui que trust of common law

²fideicommissary \ˌ==,=ˈ==,==, ˌ==,==ˈ===\ *adj* [LL *fideicommissarius*, fr. *fideicommissum* + L *-arius* -ary (adj. suffix)] **:** of, having to do with, or of the nature of a fideicommissum

fideicommissary heir *n* **:** one that receives property from a fiduciary heir

fideicommissary substitution *n* **1 :** the substitution under Roman and civil law of another heir or donee by a fideicommissum or direction that the original heir or donee at his death or upon some stated event or condition transfer the inheritance or gift or a part thereof to the substituted heir or donee **2 :** a gift of property under Roman and civil law by will or gift inter vivos wherein the donee (as an heir of the testator or an heir of such person) is directed and under a duty to transfer the property to another or other persons designated as donees

fi·dei·com·mis·sion \ˌfīdēˌīkəˈmishən\ *n* [*fideicommissum* + *-ion*] **:** the making of a fideicommissum

fi·dei·com·mis·sion·er \-sh(ə)nə(r)\ *n* **:** the fiduciary of a fideicommissum

fi·dei·com·mis·sor \-kəˈmisər, -ˈkämə,sȯ(ə)r\ *n* -S [*fideicommissum* + *-or*] **:** the grantor of a fideicommissum

fi·dei·com·mis·sum \-kəˈmisəm\ *n, pl* **fideicommis·sa** \-sə\ [LL, fr. neut. of *fideicommissus*, past part. of *fideicommittere* to bequeath in trust, fr. *fidei* (gen. of *fides* faith, trust) + *committere* to connect, entrust — more at FAITH, COMMIT] **1 :** a gift under Roman law of property stipulated by the donor to be transferred by the donee at a given time or upon a stated condition to a third person for his benefit and made between living persons in contemplation of death or by will **2 :** the substantial equivalent of a gift to a donee under civil law upon a trust created to transfer the property to another — compare SUBSTITUTION

fi·de·ism \ˈfē(ˌ)dā,izəm, ˈfīdē,-\ *n* -s [prob. fr. F *fidéisme*, fr. L *fides* faith + F *-isme* -ism — more at FAITH] **:** exclusive or basic reliance upon faith alone accompanied by a consequent disparagement of reason and utilized esp. in the pursuit of philosophical or religious truth — **fi·de·ist** \-ēəst\ *n* -s — **fi·de·is·tic** \ˌfīdēˈistik\ *adj*

fi·de·jus·sio \ˌfīdēˈjəsē,ō\ *n, pl* **fidejussi·o·nes** \ˌ===,==ˈō(ˌ)nēz\ [LL] **:** FIDEJUSSION

fi·de·jus·sion \ˌfīdēˈjəshən\ *n* -s [LL *fidejussion-, fidejussio*, fr. *fidejussus* (past part. of *fidejubēre* to give surety, fr. L *fide* — abl. of *fides* — + *jubēre* to order) + L *-ion-, -io* -ion — more at JUSSIVE] **1 :** the contract of guaranty or suretyship under Roman and civil law made by stipulation accessory to an existing contract — compare INTERCESSION **2 :** the contract or obligation (as under Scots law) of guaranty or suretyship — **fi·de·jus·sion·ary** \-shə,nerē\ *adj*

fi·de·jus·sor \-ˈjəsə(r)\ *n* -s [LL, fr. *fidejussus* + L *-or*] **:** one under Roman and civil law who enters into or authorizes a fidejussion, a guarantor, or surety

fi·del·i·ty \fəˈdeləd·ē, fīˈ-, -lətē, -i\ *n* -ES [ME *fidelite*, fr. MF *fidelité*, fr. L *fidelitat-, fidelitas* — more at FEALTY] **1 a :** the quality or state of being faithful or loyal (as to a person, cause, party, or nation) **:** LOYALTY; *specif* **:** adherence to the marriage contract **:** conjugal loyalty **b :** accuracy in details (as in the reproduction of a manuscript, the reporting of an event, the performance of a duty) **:** EXACTNESS **2** *obs* **:** WORD OF HONOR **3 a :** the degree to which an electronic device (as a radio receiving set, phonograph, or recording device) accurately reproduces at its output end the signal or wave form received at its input end **b :** the relative tendency of a kind of organism (as a species) to be restricted to the ecological community to which it is most perfectly adapted — often used with a percentage expressing the degree to which such a tendency has developed ⟨a substory plant of the beech-maple community with a 90 percent ~⟩ — compare EXCLUSIVE 1b

syn ALLEGIANCE, FEALTY, LOYALTY, DEVOTION, PIETY: FIDELITY implies strict and continuing faithfulness as to an obligation, trust, or duty ⟨a profound reverence for and *fidelity* to the truth, sometimes almost amounting to fanaticism —H.L.Mencken⟩ ⟨the oath which might be exacted — that of *fidelity* to the constitution — is prescribed —John Marshall⟩ ⟨it is equally certain, without any groundless aspersion of Harriet's conjugal *fidelity*, that the fault was not Shelley's —Richard Garnett †1906⟩ ALLEGIANCE suggests adherence as that of medieval vassal to his lord or of a modern free citizen to his country ⟨I pledge *allegiance* to the Flag of the United States of America and to the Republic for which it stands —Francis Bellamy⟩ ⟨to exclude unnaturalized foreigners; the latter forming no part of the sovereignty, owing it no *allegiance*, and therefore under no obligation to defend it —R.B.Taney⟩ ⟨he claims no political *allegiance*, is a member of the bipartisan National Committee on Strengthening Congress —*Current Biog.*⟩ FEALTY implies a strict fidelity acknowledged and cherished by the individual ⟨abolitionism, to which I swore *fealty* —J.R.Lowell⟩ ⟨constant in *fealty* to his faith, extracting fresh allegiance —W.O. Clough⟩ ⟨profoundly grateful and emboldened by their comradeship and their *fealty* —A.E.Stevenson †1965⟩ LOYALTY may imply steadfast and reliable personal attachment; in today's English it is taken to indicate absence of anything treasonable or subversive ⟨the *loyalties* which lead men to go to war —Virginia Woolf⟩ ⟨western man subordinated religious *loyalties* to national ones —Isaac Deutscher⟩ ⟨*loyalty* in these terms is allegiance to the democratic way of life, to the process or system that welcomes into free competition even the most loathsome ideas —*New Republic*⟩ DEVOTION may indicate zealous self-dedication and ardent attachment ⟨in the Declaration of the Rights of Man adopted amid swirling revolution in 1789, France rose to a height of *devotion* to human liberties from which she has never receded —F.A. Ogg & Harold Zink⟩ ⟨he loved with a passionate intensity of *devotion* the greatness of Roman traditions, and the memory of the mighty dead —Agnes Repplier⟩ ⟨a *devotion* to the welfare of children, a complete absorption in the business of parenthood, and a willingness not only to subordinate all other interests to those of the offspring, but, if necessary, to lay down life itself upon the altar of family duty —J.W. Krutch⟩ PIETY applies to fidelity to spiritual or natural obligations ⟨*piety* is the knowledge and worship of the gods: it consists in forming an adequate conception of them and imitating their perfection —Frank Thilly⟩ ⟨the principle of filial *piety*, which has existed throughout the world and is embodied in the Fifth Commandment —Bertrand Russell⟩

fidelity bond *n* **:** a bond or other form of contract for indemnifying an employer against financial loss due to the dishonesty of an employee — see INSURANCE

fidelity insurance *n* **:** insurance against loss by reason of the dishonesty or nonperformance of an employee or fiduciary

fi·de·pro·mis·sion \ˌfīdēprōˈmishən\ *n* -s [LL *fidepromission-, fidepromissio*, fr. *fidepromissus* (past part. of *fidepromittere* to give surety, fr. L *fide* — abl. of *fides* faith, trust — + *promittere* to promise) + L *-ion-, -io* -ion] **:** contract of guaranty or suretyship under Roman law by stipulation — **fi·de·pro·mis·sor** \-prōˈmisər, -ˈprämə,sȯ(ə)r\ *n* -s

fi·des fac·ta \ˌfē,dāˈsfäktə\ *n* [ML, lit., assurance given] **:** a ceremony in Teutonic law required for the making of a binding contract except in cases of bailment and consisting of making faith with a gage and pledge

fidge \ˈfij\ *n or vb* [prob. alter. of ³*fitch*] *dial* **:** FIDGET

¹fid·get \ˈfijət, *usu* -əd.+V\ *n* -s [irreg. fr. *fidge*] **1 :** the quality or state of being restless **:** a condition marked by incessant changes of position or nervous movement **:** DYSPHORIA ⟨in a terrible ~ over unpaid bills⟩ — often used in pl. ⟨a person suffering from the ~*s*⟩ **2** [²*fidget*] **:** one that exhibits or suffers from the fidgets ⟨his aunt being a regular old ~⟩

²fidget \ˈ"\ *vb* -ED/-ING/-S *vi* **1 :** to move uneasily one way and the other **:** act nervously or impatiently ⟨the speaker kept ~*ing* and clearing his throat⟩ **2 :** to be nervously uneasy **:** WORRY ⟨always ~*ing* about her health⟩ **3 :** to tinker or play nervously or absently — used with *with* ⟨~*s* with his tie⟩ ~ *vt* **1 :** to cause physical uneasiness in **:** make nervous ⟨a pitcher ~*ed* by the constant movement of a batter⟩ **2 :** to move or play with restlessly ⟨a policeman eyeing traffic and ~*ing* his whistle⟩

fid·get·er \-əd·ə(r), -ətə-\ *n* -s **:** one that fidgets

fid·get·i·ness \-d·ēnəs, -t|, |in-\ *n* -ES **:** the quality or state of being fidgety

fid·get·ing·ly *adv* **:** in a fidgety manner

fid·gety \ˈfijəd·ē, -ətē, -i\ *adj* **1 a :** inclined to fidget ⟨a ~ person⟩ **b :** exhibiting nervous jumpy movements ⟨~ hands⟩ **2 a :** making unnecessary ado **:** FUSSY ⟨a ~ old man⟩ **b :** showing overmuch care or attention to detail ⟨~ ornamentation⟩

fidg·in fain \ˈfijən,fān\ *adj* [*fidgin* fr. pres. part. of *fidge*] *chiefly Scot* **:** restless with curiosity or excitement

fid hole *n* **:** a hole in the heel of a topmast or topgallant mast through which the fid or other spar passes

fid hook *n* **:** a stout steel hook with a slot in the flattened end for connecting chains (as in lumbering)

fid·ia \ˈfidēə\ *n* [NL] **1** *cap* **:** a genus of small beetles (family Chrysomelidae) including the grape rootworm (*F. viticida*) and being very injurious to vines in America **2** -s **:** any beetle of the genus *Fidia*

fid·i·bus \ˈfidəbəs\ *n, pl* **fidibuses** *or* **fidibus** [G (orig. student slang), fr. L. dat. pl. of *fides* lyre (a jocular allusion to a line of Horace); akin to Gk *sphides* sausage] **:** a paper spill for lighting pipes

fidley *var of* FIDDLEY

FIDO \ˈfī(ˌ)dō\ *abbr or n* -s [*F*og *I*nvestigation *D*ispersal *O*perations] **:** a system in which fog above runways is evaporated by the heat from liquid-fuel burners at their sides to permit aircraft to operate

fids *pl of* FID, *pres 3d sing of* FID

fi·du·cia \fəˈd(y)üsh(ē)ə, fīˈ-\ *n, pl* **fiduci·ae** \-shē,ē\ [L, lit., trust, confidence, fr. *fidere* to trust — more at BIDE] **:** a contract used under Roman and civil law (as in the emancipation of children, in connection with testamentary gifts, and in pledges) and constituting essentially a contract of sale to a person usu. by mancipation coupled with an agreement that the purchaser should sell the property back upon the fulfillment of certain conditions — called also *contractus fiduciae*

fi·du·cial \fəˈd(y)üshəl, fīˈ-\ *adj* [LL *fiducialis*, fr. L *fiducia* + *-alis* -al] **1 :** founded on faith or trust ⟨his ~ reliance on certain religious beliefs⟩ **2 :** having the nature of a trust **:** FIDUCIARY ⟨a ~ power⟩ **3 :** taken as an origin or zero of reference ⟨a ~ point on a scale⟩ — **fi·du·cial·ly** \-əlē\ *adv*

fi·du·ci·ar·i·ly \fəˈd(y)üshēˌerəlē, fīˌ-, ˌfīˌ==ˈ===\ *adv* **:** in a fiduciary manner

¹fi·du·ci·ary \fəˈd(y)üshē,erē, fīˈ-, -ri\ *adj* [L *fiduciarius*, fr. *fiducia* trust + *-arius* -ary] **1 :** holding, held, or founded in trust or confidence **2 :** of, having to do with, or involving a confidence or trust **:** of the nature of a trust ⟨a ~ capacity⟩ ⟨a ~ relation⟩ **3 :** resting upon public confidence for value or currency ⟨~ fiat money⟩

²fiduciary \ˈ"\ *n* -ES **:** one (as a corporate trust company or the trust department of a bank) that holds a fiduciary relation or acts in a fiduciary capacity to another (as one whose funds are entrusted to it for investment)

fiduciary bond *n* **:** a surety bond filed by a fiduciary (as the administrator of an estate) to guarantee faithful performance of his duties

fiduciary coemption *n* **:** a fictitious sale under Roman law by which a woman can change her guardian or gain legal capacity to make a will — compare COEMPTIO

fiduciary contract *n* **:** FIDUCIA

fiduciary heir *n* **:** an heir in Roman Dutch law who takes the property subject to its passing to another (as the fideicommissary heir) on fulfillment of certain conditions

fiduciary relation *n* **1 :** the relation that is declared by a court to exist between parties to a transaction when the court desires to hold the offending party responsible to prevent unjust enrichment as though he were in fact a trustee for the other **2 :** the relation existing when one person justifiably reposes confidence, faith, and reliance in another whose aid, advice, or protection is sought in some matter **:** the relation existing when good conscience requires one to act at all times for the sole benefit and interests of another with loyalty to those interests **:** the relation by law existing between certain classes of persons (as confidential advisor and the one advised; executors or administrators and legatees or heirs; conservators and wards, trustees, or beneficiaries; partners, joint adventurers, corporate directors or officers and stockholders; majority and minority stockholders; factors, agents, or brokers and principals; attorneys and clients; promoters and stock subscribers; mutual savings banks or investment corporations and their depositors or investors; receivers, trustees in bankruptcy, or assignees in insolvency and creditors)

fie \ˈfī\ *interj* [ME *fi, fy*, fr. OF] — used to express disgust, dislike, or the affectation of being shocked

-fied *past of* -FY

fied·ler·ite \ˈfēdlə,rīt\ *n* -s [G *fiedlerit*, fr. Karl G. *Fiedler* †1853 Ger. mine commissioner + G *-it* -ite] **:** a lead mineral $Pb_3(OH)_2Cl_4$ that is prob. a hydroxychloride and occurs in colorless monoclinic crystals

fief \ˈfēf\ *n* -s [F, fr. OF *fief, fié*] **1 :** a feudal estate **:** FEE **2 :** something over which one has rights or exercises control

fief·dom \-dəm\ *n* -s [*fief* + *-dom*] **:** an area over which one exercises control

¹field \ˈfēld, *chiefly before pause or consonant* -ēəld\ *n* -s [ME *feld, fild, field*, fr. OE *feld*; akin to OFris, OS, & OHG *feld* field, OE *fold* earth, OS *folda*, ON *fold*; akin to OE *flōr* floor — more at FLOOR] **1 a** (1) **:** a land area free of woodland, cities, and towns **:** open country (2) **:** the open country near or belonging to a city — usu. used in pl. **b** (1) **:** an area of cleared enclosed land used for cultivation or pasture ⟨a ~ of wheat⟩ ⟨a ~ of cattle⟩ (2) **:** an area of land containing, yielding, or worked for a natural resource ⟨a coal*field*⟩ ⟨oil ~*s*⟩ ⟨diamond ~*s*⟩ **c :** the place where a battle is fought **:** BATTLEGROUND **d :** a large unbroken expanse of sea ice **2 a :** an area, category, or division wherein a particular activity or pursuit is carried out ⟨a lawyer eminent in his ~⟩ ⟨a wide ~ of speculation⟩ ⟨the ~ of analytical chemistry⟩ **b** (1) **:** the sphere of practical operation of an organization or enterprise; *specif* **:** the place or territory where direct contacts (as with customers) may be made or firsthand knowledge obtained ⟨salesmen in the ~⟩ (2) **:** the scene of observation (as of actual phenomena) outside of a laboratory ⟨geologists working in the ~⟩ **c :** an area outside of a military post where exercises or maneuvers are carried out ⟨new equipment being tested in the ~⟩ **d** (1) **:** an athletic or sports area or space (as an outdoor enclosure for baseball, cricket, football) (2) **:** the portion enclosed by the racing track of an indoor or outdoor sports area on which are contested events of a track-and-field meet **3 :** a space or ground on which something is drawn or projected: as **a :** the space on either surface of a coin, token, or medal that does not contain the central figure of the design, the inscription, or the exergue **b :** the ground of each division in a flag **c** *heraldry* (1) **:** the whole surface of an escutcheon (2) **:** so much of an escutcheon as is shown unconcealed by the different bearings upon it **d :** the area of a seal inside the inscription or other device about the circumference **4 :** BATTLE ⟨an extremely costly ~⟩ **5 :** the persons, participants, or elements that make up all or part of a sports activity: **a :** all the participants with the exception usu. of the favorite in an athletic contest or sporting event where more than two are entered; *esp* **:** the horses or dogs that are for purposes of pari-mutuel betting grouped together usu. as the 12th betting unit when the number of entries exceeds 12 **b :** all the players that are in action esp. in football ⟨ran through a broken ~⟩ **c :** the side of a team not at bat **d :** a fielder in cricket; *collectively* **:** the members of the fielding side **e :** the group of numbers 2, 3, 5, 9, 10, 11, and 12 or 2, 3, 4, 9, 10, 11, and 12 on which a bet in craps pays even money **6 a :** a continuously distributed entity in space that accounts for actions at a distance ⟨electric ~⟩ ⟨gravitational ~⟩ **b :** FIELD INTENSITY **c :** a complex of coexistent forces (as biological, psychological, and social or interpersonal) which serve as causative agents or as a frame of reference in human experience and behavior **7 a** *math* **:** a domain or aggregate of elements or magnitudes that when combined by addition, subtraction, multiplication, and division, the divisor 0 being excluded, always produce an element of the aggregate **b :** a region of embryonic tissue potentially capable of a particular type of differentiation ⟨a neural ~⟩ ⟨an ear ~⟩ **c :** a region of space in which a given effect (as gravity, magnetism, or electricity) exists and has a definite value at each point **8 a** (1) **:** the usu. circular area visible through the lens system of an optical instrument (as a microscope or telescope) (2) **:** the whole area of a television image **b :** the site of a surgical operation **c :** the total range of meanings associated with a set of words which are related but not identical in meaning (as *mind, thought, intellect, spirit, intelligence, insight*) — called also *semantic field, word field* **d :** CARD FIELD **9 a :** the field magnet of a generator — see DYNAMO illustration **b :** a series of open-joint drain tiles that leads off septic-tank overflow to its absorption area

syn DOMAIN, PROVINCE, SPHERE, TERRITORY, BAILIWICK: FIELD denotes a limited and demarcated area of knowledge or endeavor to which pursuits, activities, and interests are confined, often one determinedly chosen at a certain time or by the necessities of a situation ⟨the provincial governments and the federal government in Ottawa share some *fields* of government business —*Canadian Citizenship Series*⟩ ⟨organizations functioning in the *field* of cartography —*Americana Annual*⟩ ⟨a writer whose reputation . . . has been pretty much confined to the whodunit *field* —James Kelly⟩ DOMAIN may apply to a clearly defined area of activity marked by a degree of exclusive mastery and control discouraging outside interference or unwarranted intrusion ⟨advances in the *domain* of the history of ideas —Benjamin Farrington⟩ ⟨the *domain* of artifact typology or cultural taxonomy —Philip Phillips & G.R.Willey⟩ ⟨great work in the *domain* of physiological chemistry of the cornea —*Americana Annual*⟩ PROVINCE indicates an area of special jurisdiction, responsibility, competence, power, or influence ⟨economic theory is not the *province* of the lawyer or courts of law —C.A.Cooke⟩ ⟨the almost impertinently realistic explorations into behavior which are the *province* of the psychiatrist —Edward Sapir⟩ ⟨a decision that, in any case, was not within the *province* of the F.B.I. —*New Statesman & Nation*⟩ SPHERE may more strongly imply circumscribed limits setting apart activities and interests ⟨a long and profound process of social change . . . but this time in the economic *sphere* —John Strachey⟩ ⟨the congress and the president, acting in their proper *spheres*, must perform their duties to the American people in support of our highest traditions —D.D.Eisenhower⟩ ⟨composing, in which *sphere* he is a prolific worker —*London Calling*⟩ TERRITORY is close to DOMAIN but lacks its suggestions of inviolability ⟨prose has preempted a lion's share of the *territory* once held, either in sovereignty or on equal terms, by poetry —J.B.Lowes⟩ BAILIWICK may suggest a petty area of individual power and authority ⟨love the Romantics, and feel that lyric poetry and impassioned prose are their proper *bailiwick* —Katharine F. Gerould⟩ ⟨to achieve an authoritative position within your own little *bailiwick* —W.J.Reilly⟩

²field \ˈ"\ *vb* -ED/-ING/-S *vt* **1 :** to expose (as grain, malt, or fiber) to the action of the air and sun in the field **2 :** to handle (as a batted ball) while playing in the field **3 a :** to put (a team or designated players) into the field for actual play ⟨~ a weak team⟩ **b :** to put into the field ⟨the greatest army any nation ever ~*ed*⟩ ~ *vi* **1** *obs* **:** to take to the battlefield **:** engage in battle **2 :** to play as a fielder

³field \ˈ"\ *adj* **1 :** of or having to do with a field: as **a :** growing in or inhabiting the fields or open country or cleared land **b :** made, conducted, or used in the field ⟨~ operations⟩ ⟨~ equipment⟩ **c :** operating or active in or assigned to the field ⟨a ~ agent⟩ ⟨a ~ worker for a benevolent society⟩ **2 :** of, relating to, or contested on the field and not on the track — see FIELD EVENT

field ambulance *n* **:** AMBULANCE 1

field archery *n* **:** competitive archery in which shooting is done at a simulated hunting ground

field army *n* **:** a military unit organized to be capable of independent action and consisting conventionally of a headquarters, two or more corps, and auxiliary troops

field arrow *n* **:** a hunting arrow

field artillery *n* **:** artillery other than antiaircraft artillery used with armies in the field and classified according to the weight and caliber of its cannon as light, medium, or heavy

fieldball \ˈ=,=\ *n* **:** a game played on a soccer field with a soccer ball or basketball by two teams of 11 members each and combining many of the techniques of basketball and soccer with the object being to score by throwing the ball under the crossbar between the uprights of the opponents' goal

field balm *n* **1 :** a European perennial savory (*Satureia nepeta*) naturalized in the U. S. and having stiff branches and axillary clusters of lilac or violet flowers **2 :** GROUND IVY

field basil *n* **:** WILD BASIL

field bean *n* **1 :** BROAD BEAN **2 :** a bean grown primarily for its ripe edible seeds ⟨always put in a plot of *field beans* for our own winter baked beans⟩

field bed *n* **1 :** a bed used in the field **2 :** a four-poster of moderate height with a canopy supported on a frame that is strongly arched so as to give greater height at the center than at the ends

field bed 2

field bee *n* **:** a honey-gathering worker bee

field beet *n* **:** MANGEL-WURZEL

field betony *n* **:** a bristly annual European hedge nettle (*Stachys arvensis*) with purplish flowers

field bindweed *n* **:** a prostrate or weakly climbing European perennial plant (*Convolvulus arvensis*) established in No. America where it often becomes a serious weed — called also *wild morning glory*

fieldbird \ˈ=,=\ *n* **:** PLOVER: as **a :** GOLDEN PLOVER **b :** UPLAND PLOVER

field book *n* **:** a notebook used for keeping field notes in surveying

field brome *n* **:** an annual or biennial weed grass (*Bromus arvensis*) with soft pubescent leaf sheaths and an open panicle — called also *bromegrass*

field capacity *n* **:** the water-retaining capacity of a soil usu. including both the hygroscopic and capillary water of the soil and being expressed as a percentage of the dry weight of the soil ⟨a silty loam with a *field capacity* of 35 percent⟩ — called also *field moisture capacity*

field captain *n* **1 a :** the official in charge of the men's division of an archery tournament **b :** the chief official in an all-men's archery tournament **2 :** a player on the field esp. in football who acts as representative of the team (as in accepting or refusing penalties of the opposing team)

field chamomile *n* **:** a European white-flowered weed (*Anthemis arvensis*) naturalized in No. America — called also *corn chamomile*

field chickweed *n* **:** a densely tufted perennial chickweed (*Cerastium arvense*) of the north temperate zone
field chopper *n* **:** an implement that while moving across a field mows the standing crop and chops and loads it as silage
field code *n* **:** a code book for use in combat areas
field coil *n* **:** a current-bearing coil used to excite a field (as of a generator, motor, or loudspeaker)
field conventicle *n* **:** a religious meeting held out of doors
field corn *n* **:** an Indian corn (as dent corn, flint corn, or soft corn) grown for feeding stock or for market grain and having kernels that are usu. white or yellow and not sweet
field-cor·net \ˈ;=,kȯrˈnet, =ˈkȯrnət\ *n* -s [trans. of Afrik *veldkornet*] **1 :** a commander of the burghers in Cape Province during the former native risings **2 :** a minor magistrate similar to a justice of the peace who represents the government in a rural district in Cape Province — **field-cor·net·cy** \-sē\ *n* -ES
field crane's-bill *n* **:** ALFILARIA
field cress *n* **:** a wild European peppergrass (*Lepidium campestre*) naturalized in America — called also *cow cress, crowdweed, field peppergrass*
field cricket *n* **:** any of several crickets of *Gryllus* and related genera; *esp* **:** a common American cricket (*Acheta assimilis*) sometimes destructive to crops
field crop *n* **:** a crop (as hay, grain, or cotton) grown for agricultural purposes covering a large area but excluding fruits, vegetables, and ornamental plants
field crowfoot *n* **:** CORN CROWFOOT
field current *n* **:** the current supplied to the field windings of a generator or motor to establish the magnetic field for its operation
field cypress *n* **:** GROUND PINE 1
field daisy *n* **:** DAISY 1b
field day *n* **1 a :** a day when troops are given exercises or maneuvers in the field **b :** an outdoor get-together held for entertainment and relaxation ⟨the annual *field day* of a company union⟩ **c :** a day of open-air sports and athletic competition (as in schools) **2 :** a thorough general cleaning in the navy **3 a :** an occasion marked usu. by extreme fun or hilarity ⟨the children had a *field day* when the teacher left the room⟩ **b :** an occasion or opportunity for unrestrained ridicule ⟨the newspapers had a *field day* with the scandal⟩ **c :** a period when full opportunity suddenly, unexpectedly, or finally appears to unleash and satisfy natural powers, thwarted ability, or restrained desire ⟨the artillery had a *field day* with the retreating infantry⟩
field dodder *n* **:** a very widespread annual (*Cuscuta pentagona*) parasitic on various herbaceous plants
field dog *n* **:** a dog (as a pointer) used for hunting in the field
field driver *n* **:** a town officer esp. in early New England authorized to round up and impound domestic farm animals roaming at large
fielded *adj* [fr. pres. part. of ²*field*] *obs* **:** fighting in the battlefield and not in a fort
fielded panel *n* **:** a raised or recessed panel with a wide flat surface surrounded by moldings; *also* **:** such a panel divided into smaller panels
field emission *n* **:** the emission of electrons from a metallic conductor due solely to the action of an electric field — compare PHOTOEMISSION, THERMIONIC EMISSION
fielden *adj, obs* **:** of or having to do with fields **:** RUSTIC
field·er \ˈfēldə(r)\ *n* -s **:** one that fields: as **a :** a player stationed in the field (as in baseball or cricket) **b :** a player considered as to his ability at fielding
fielder's choice *n* **:** an attempt by a fielder handling a batted baseball to retire a base runner other than the batter when a play to first base would probably retire the batter
field event *n* **:** an athletic contest involving the broad jump, high jump, pole vault, shot put, and the discus, javelin, and hammer throws — compare TRACK
field exercise *n* **:** a military training exercise simulating war conditions in the field with one side fully or partly equipped and manned and the other represented only on paper or by token forces — compare MANEUVER, WAR GAME
field·fare \ˈ=,fa(a)(ə)r, -,fe|\ *also* **fell·fare** \ˈfel,-\ *n* -s [ME *fildefare, feldefare*, fr. OE *feldeware*, fr. *feld* field + *-ware* dweller — more at FIELD] **1 :** a medium-sized thrush (*Turdus pilaris*) that breeds in northern Europe and western Asia and winters in Britain, central and southern Europe, and parts of Africa and Asia and that has the head, nape, and lower part of the back ash-colored and the upper part of the back and wing coverts chestnut **2 :** ROBIN 1c
field fever *n* **:** a European leptospirosis of man
field fortification *n* **:** fortification for more or less temporary use constructed in the field
field frame *n* **:** the principal magnetic structure of a motor or generator including the poles if they are an integral part — called also *yoke*
field garlic *n* **:** CROW GARLIC
field glass *n* **:** a hand-held optical instrument for use outdoors usu. consisting of two telescopes on a single frame with a focusing device — usu. used in pl.

field glasses

field goal *n* **1 :** a score in football made by drop-kicking or place-kicking the ball over the crossbar from ordinary play — compare EXTRA POINT **2 :** a basket in the game of basketball made while the ball is in play
field grade *n* **:** the grade of a field officer
field gray *n* **:** a dark gray (as of some military field uniforms)
field gromwell *n* **:** CORN GROMWELL
field guide *n* **:** a manual that identifies objects in a class and esp. natural objects and that is suitable for carrying into the field ⟨a *field guide* to birds⟩
field hand *n* **:** an outdoor farm laborer; *specif* **:** a Negro slave in America before 1865 who worked in the fields in distinction from one employed about the house of the master
field-handball \(ˈ)=ˈ;=,=\ *n* **:** FIELDBALL
field hockey *n* **:** a game played on a turfed field between teams of 11 players each whose object is to hit a hard leather or plastic ball into the goal cage by the use of curved sticks that have a blade flattened on the left side and rounded on the right

diagram of hockey field: *A*, point for initial bully; *C,C*, striking circles; *EF, EF*, sidelines; *EE, FF*, goal lines; *G,G*, goals

field horsetail *n* **:** a horsetail (*Equisetum arvense*) of the U.S. and Canada that produces from the same rhizomes brownish reproductive shoots in early summer and greenish chlorophyll-bearing vegetative shoots usu. after the former have shed their spores
field hospital *n* **:** a military organization of surgeons, nurses, and orderlies with equipment for establishing a temporary hospital in the field
field house *n* **1 :** a building on or near an athletic field for housing equipment and providing dressing facilities **2 :** a building enclosing a stadium or arena suitable for track events, basketball, and gymnastics
field ice *n* **:** floating ice in large comparatively flat tracts
fielding *pres part of* FIELD
fielding average *n* **:** a ratio in baseball obtained by dividing the number of total chances into the number of total putouts and assists
field intensity *n* **1 :** the attribute of a magnetic, electric, gravitational, or other field of force that at any point is measured by the force which the field exerts upon a unit pole, unit charge, or unit mass placed at that point — called also *field strength* **2 :** the intensity of radiation at any point in a radiation field
field jacket *n* **:** a military jacket issued for wear in the field
field kale *n* **:** CHARLOCK
field kitchen *n* **:** the place where food for a military unit in the field is prepared; *also* **:** the portable cooking apparatus used in such a place
field lark *n, South & Midland* **:** MEADOWLARK
field larkspur *n* **:** an annual European larkspur (*Delphinium consolida*) naturalized in No. America having flowers with two petals succeeded by smooth follicles
field lens *n* **1 :** a lens located at or near the plane of a real image whose function is to collect and redirect the rays into some other element of the optical system **2 :** the one of two lenses forming the eyepiece of a telescope or compound microscope that is nearer the object glass and that directs the rays into the eye lens
field line *n* **:** any one of a system of nonintersecting lines so drawn in mapping a vector field that the direction of the tangent to it at any point is that of the vector at that point
field madder *n* **:** an annual European weed (*Sherardia arvensis*) of the family Rubiaceae with square stems, whorled leaves, and heads of blue or pink flowers — called also *blue field madder*
field magnet *n* **:** a magnet for producing and maintaining a magnetic field esp. in a generator or electric motor
field·man \ˈfē(ə)l(d)mən, -,man, -,maa(ə)n\ *n, pl* **fieldmen** **:** one that works in the field: as **a :** a traveling representative of a business organization (as a man who negotiates with farmers for the raising of crops under contract for a food-processing company) **b :** an investigator or advisor who works outdoors or away from the center of administration or activity (as a man who conducts educational programs for milk producers in an assigned territory)
field maneuver *n* **:** a maneuver in which troops in training oppose each other in given military situations
field marigold *n* **:** CORN MARIGOLD
field mark *n* **:** a marking (as of a bird) useful for identification from a distance
field marshal *n* **:** an officer (as in the British and several other armies) of the highest rank who corresponds in rank to a general of the army in the U.S. Army
field martin *n* **:** KINGBIRD
field milkwort *n* **:** PURPLE MILKWORT
field mint *n* **1 :** CATNIP **2 :** CORN MINT
field moisture *n* **:** the water in the ground above the water table
field moisture capacity *n* **:** FIELD CAPACITY
field mouse *n* **:** any of various mice that inhabit open fields: as **a :** any mouse of the New World genus *Microtus* **b :** any mouse of the Old World genus *Apodemus*
field mushroom *n* **1 :** MEADOW MUSHROOM **2 :** HORSE MUSHROOM
field music *n* **:** the drummers, fifers, buglers, and pipers attached to military companies who sound the various calls for the troops and play for marching in the absence of the band; *also* **:** the music produced by drummers, fifers, pipers, or buglers
field mustard *n* **:** CHARLOCK
field name *n* **:** a name that can be applied to a rock without critical microscopic or chemical analysis in a laboratory
field negro *n, cap N* **:** a Negro field hand
field note *n* **:** an item in a systematic record of the measurements made by a surveyor or the observations of a researcher in the field
field of consciousness **:** the totality of consciousness at any one time
field officer *n* **1 :** a military officer of the rank of colonel, lieutenant colonel, or major — compare GENERAL OFFICER **2 :** a member of the Salvation Army responsible for administration of a corps center
field of fire **:** the area that can be covered by the fire from a weapon or a group of weapons from a given position
field of force **:** a vector field in which the vector associated with each point is measurable by a force
field of honor **1 :** a place where a duel is fought **2 :** BATTLEFIELD
field of vision **:** VISUAL FIELD
field order *n* **:** a combat order of prescribed form giving instructions for a specific operation
field pea *n* **:** a pea (*Pisum sativum* var. *arvense*) native to the Mediterranean region and northern Africa that is widely grown esp. in the U. S. and Canada for forage and food and has short flower stalks a little longer than the stipules, colored flowers, and small pods and seeds — called also *Austrian winter pea*
field pennycress *n* **:** PENNYCRESS
field peppergrass *n* **:** FIELD CRESS
fieldpiece \ˈ=,=\ *n* **:** a gun or howitzer for use in the field **:** a piece of field artillery
field pine *n* **:** BEACH HEATHER
field plover *n* **:** any of certain plovers: as **a :** GOLDEN PLOVER **b :** UPLAND PLOVER
field poppy *n* **:** CORN POPPY
field pumpkin *n* **:** PUMPKIN 1a(1)
field ration *n* **:** any of the various types of rations provided when troops are actually issued food in distinction from a money allowance
field rheostat *n* **:** a rheostat for regulating the current supplied to the field winding of a generator or motor
field rivet *n* **:** a rivet driven in place on work in the field — opposed to *shop rivet*
field run *n* **:** a crop product that has not been graded or sorted
field rush *n* **:** the common wood rush
fields *pl of* FIELD, *pres 3d sing of* FIELD
field scabious *n* **:** a perennial European scabious (*Scabiosa arvensis*) introduced in eastern U.S. and having bluish lilac flowers
field scorpion grass *n* **:** a common forget-me-not (*Myosotis arvensis*) of Europe and No. America with small blue or white flowers in one-sided racemes
field service *n* **1 :** service (as of troops, company agents, social-service workers) in the field **2 :** labor in the fields performed by Negro slaves in America before 1865
field slave *n* **:** a slave field hand
fields·man \ˈfēl(d)zmən\ *n, pl* **fieldsmen** **:** FIELDER
field sorrel *n* **:** SHEEP SORREL 1
field sow thistle *n* **:** PERENNIAL EUROPEAN SOW THISTLE
field spaniel *n* **:** a large usu. black hunting and retrieving spaniel that has a dense flat or slightly waved coat and that is now nearly extinct as a separate breed
field sparrow *n* **:** a sparrow that frequents fields: **a :** a small American sparrow (*Spizella pusilla*) closely related to the chipping sparrow but paler colored **b :** HEDGE SPARROW
field speedwell *n* **:** an annual speedwell (*Veronica agrestis*) of Europe widely naturalized in No. America having oval stalked leaves and minute blue axillary flowers on long stalks
field spider *n* **:** SPIDER 5e
field spool *n* **:** SPOOL 1a(3)
field station *n* **:** EXPERIMENT STATION
fieldstone \ˈ=,=\ *n* **:** stone used as taken from the field (as in building) ⟨the clay-daubed ~ chimney —William Faulkner⟩
field stop *n* **:** a diaphragm that determines the size of the field of an optical instrument
field strength *n* **:** FIELD INTENSITY
field-strip \ˈ=,=\ *vt* **:** to take apart (a weapon) to the extent authorized for routine cleaning, lubrication, and minor repairs
field system *n* **:** the prevailing system of husbandry in medieval times in England and parts of western Europe whereby the arable land of a village unit was composed of unenclosed strips held by the different owners or cultivators subject to use as a common for pasture during a certain period of each year
field theory *n* **1 a :** a theory in physics: the interaction of two separated physical systems is attributed to the intermediary of a field that propagates or extends from one to the other **b :** a theory in physics: particles are assumed to be the manifestation of quantum fields **2 :** a method of analysis in behavioral science that describes actions or events as the resultant of dynamic interplay among sociocultural, biomechanical, and motivational forces
field thistle *n* **:** a prickly stout No. American thistle (*Cirsium discolor*) with heads of purplish pink flowers
field thyme *n* **:** FIELD BALM 1
field tile *n* **:** unglazed clay drain tile without bell ends
field train *n* **:** the portion of the transportation including personnel of military units lower than a division that carries reserve stocks of supplies of all kinds not immediately required during combat
field trial *n* **:** a trial of sporting dogs in actual performance — compare BENCH SHOW
field trip *n* **:** a visit made by students and usu. a teacher for purposes of firsthand observation (as to a factory, farm, clinic, museum)
field vole *n* **:** a small European vole (*Microtus agrestis*) often troublesome in grainfields
field winding *n* **:** the winding of the field magnet of a dynamo or motor
fieldwork \ˈ=,=\ *n* **1 :** a temporary fortification thrown up by an army in the field **2 a :** work done in the field (as by students) to gain practical experience through firsthand observation **b :** the gathering of anthropological or sociological data through the interviewing of subjects in the field
field wormwood *n* **:** a European wormwood (*Artemisia campestris*) that is similar to common wormwood in its properties
fieldwort \ˈ=,=\ *n* **:** a bastard gentian (*Gentiana acuta*) or its European relative (*G. amarella*)
field woundwort *n* **:** FIELD BETONY
field-wren \ˈ=,=\ *n* **:** any of several more or less streaked brown Australian warblers (genus *Calamanthus*) chiefly of open fields and scrubby areas
field yam-root \ˌ=ˈ=,=, ˈ=,=,=\ *n* **:** the root of a carrion flower (*Smilax herbacea*)
fiend \ˈfēnd\ *n* -s [ME *feend, fiend* enemy, devil, demon, fr. OE *fēond, fiond*; akin to OHG *fīant* enemy, ON *fjāndi*, Goth *fijands*, all fr. the pres. part. of a Gmc verb represented by OE *fēon, fēogan* to hate, OHG *fiēn, fijēn*, ON *fjā*, Goth *fijan*; akin to Goth *faian* to scorn, Skt *pīyati* he scorns] **1 a :** the arch enemy of man **:** DEVIL, SATAN **b :** an infernal being **:** DEMON **c :** a person of great wickedness or maliciousness **2 :** a person excessively devoted to or captivated by a pursuit, practice, or object of study **:** FANATIC, BUG ⟨a golf ~⟩ ⟨a target-shooting ~⟩ **3 :** a person who uses or consumes immoderate or excessive quantities ⟨an aspirin ~⟩ ⟨a cigar ~⟩ ⟨a ~ for ice cream⟩ **4 :** a person remarkably clever at some skill or study ⟨a ~ at mathematics⟩
fiend·ish \-dish,-dēsh\ *adj* **1 :** perversely diabolical **:** HIDEOUS ⟨a ~ pleasure in hurting people⟩ **2 :** extremely cruel or wicked ⟨a ~ old man⟩ **3 :** excessively bad, unpleasant, or difficult ⟨~ weather⟩ ⟨a ~ punishment⟩ — **fiend·ish·ly** *adv* — **fiend·ish·ness** *n* -ES
fiend·ly \-dlē,-dli\ *adj* -ER/-EST [ME *feendly, fiendly*, fr. OE *fēondlic, fiendlic*, fr. *fēond, fiend* fiend + *-lic* -ly] *archaic* **:** of, relating to, or befitting a fiend **:** FIENDISH
fient \ˈfēnt, ˈfint\ *n* -s [alter. of *fiend*] *Scot* **:** FIEND, DEVIL — often used in imprecations
fier \ˈfēr\ *Scot var of* FERE
¹fi·e·ras·fer \,fīəˈrasfə(r) ,fēə-\ [NL, fr. Prov *fielat-fèr, fierasfèr*, fr. *fielat, fieras* net, moray (fr. OProv *filat*, fr. *fil* thread, fr. L *filum*) + *fèr* fierce, wild, fr. L *ferus* — more at FILE] *syn of* CARAPUS
²fierasfer \ˈ"\ *n* -s **:** any of the small inquiline fishes of the genus *Carapus* — **fi·e·ras·fer·oid** \ˌ;==ˈ;=fə,rȯid\ *n or adj*
fi·e·ras·fer·id \,==ˈ=fərəd\ *n* -s [NL *Fierasferidae*] **:** FIERASFER, PEARL FISH
fi·e·ras·fer·i·dae \,==,raˈsferə,dē\ [NL, fr. *Fierasfer* + *-idae*] *syn of* CARAPIDAE
¹fierce \ˈfi(ə)rs, ˈfiəs\ *adj* -ER/-EST [ME *fers, fiers*, fr. OF, fr. L *ferus* wild, savage, cruel; akin to Gk *thēr* wild animal, OSlav *zvěrĭ*] **1 a :** marked by grim, pugnacious, or wild hostility **:** MERCILESS ⟨~ fighting⟩ **b :** given to fighting or killing **:** savagely intractable and likely to attack ⟨~ native tribes⟩ **2 a :** marked by furious unrestrained zeal or vehemence ⟨a ~ argument⟩ **:** heated or violent in nature **:** without moderation, restraint, or control ⟨a ~ temper⟩ **b** (1) **:** extremely vexatious, disappointing, or hard to bear **:** CRUSHING ⟨~ pain⟩ (2) **:** unpleasantly or uncomfortably intense or extreme ⟨a ~ light⟩ ⟨a ~ silence⟩ **3 a** *obs* **:** PROUD, ARROGANT **b :** wild, unfriendly, or menacing in aspect or appearance ⟨a ~ old hermit⟩ ⟨~ and barren moors⟩ **4 a :** furiously active **:** extremely eager ⟨a ~ effort⟩ **:** VIOLENT ⟨a ~ dash up the mountainside⟩ **b** *dial Eng* **:** in vigorous health or spirits **:** CHIPPER

syn FEROCIOUS, FELL, SAVAGE, CRUEL, INHUMAN, BARBAROUS are applied to persons and their actions. FIERCE may connote wild menacing demonstration, grim, invincible determination, or feral combativeness ⟨the treaty was received with a *fierce* outburst of indignation. Jay was burned in effigy by wild mobs; angry orators and editors heaped execration upon Washington —Allan Nevins & H.S.Commager⟩ ⟨the *fiercest* and most treacherous of foes, whose way is to dash upon their prey amid the tempest —H.O.Taylor⟩ ⟨a *fierce* tiger of crime, which could only be taken fighting hard with flashing fang and claw —A. Conan Doyle⟩ FEROCIOUS may indicate a complete insensible lack of mercy, a wild bloodthirstiness ⟨the *ferocious* slaughters instituted . . . by barbarian conquerers —Lewis Mumford⟩ ⟨*ferocious* countenances which had been glaring at the prisoner a moment before, as if with impatience to pluck him out into the streets and kill him —Charles Dickens⟩ FELL may combine notions of direness, malignancy, murderousness, or wasting enervation ⟨murdered by his cruel uncle's mandate *fell* —S.T.Coleridge⟩ ⟨like a famine or plague or aught more *fell* —P.B.Shelley⟩ ⟨we cannot tell what the course of this *fell* war will be as it spreads, remorseless —Sir Winston Churchill⟩ SAVAGE may indicate the wild mercilessness of uncivilized tribal society or an utter, nearly animal lack of compunction or inhibition ⟨the son . . . had been trained in *savage* Sicilian loyalty and lived only to avenge his father —G.K.Chesterton⟩ CRUEL indicates pleasure in or callous indifference to pain inflicted on or anticipated or wished for another ⟨he became haughty, tyrannical, and *cruel*. You must have heard tales in Tahiti of how he punished his men by whipping them till the blood ran down their backs —C.B.Nordhoff & J.N.Hall⟩ ⟨*cruel*, and full of hate and malice and a petty rage —G.D. Brown⟩ INHUMAN indicates a nonhuman insensateness to pain or suffering or, occas., to concern, vexation, or chagrin ⟨there an *inhuman* and uncultured race . . . rushed to war, tore from the mother's womb the unborn child —P.B.Shelley⟩ ⟨there were few *inhuman* barbarities aside from the custom of scalping —*Amer. Guide Series: Maine*⟩ BARBAROUS suggests the cruelty or indifference to suffering and pain of the uncivilized ⟨you have been wantonly attacked by a ruthless and *barbarous* aggressor. Your capital has been bombed, your women and children brutally murdered —Sir Winston Churchill⟩ ⟨he required as a condition of peace that they should sacrifice their children to Baal no longer. But the *barbarous* custom was too inveterate and too agreeable to Semitic modes of thought to be so easily eradicated —J.G.Frazer⟩

²fierce \ˈ"\ *adv* [ME *fers, fiers*, fr. *fers, fiers*, adj.] **:** FIERCELY, TERRIBLY, AWFULLY
fierce·ly *adv* [ME *fersly, fiersly*, fr. *fers, fiers* + *-ly*] **:** in a fierce manner
fierc·en \ˈfirsᵊn, -iəs-\ *vi* -ED/-ING/-S **:** to become fierce or fiercer ⟨the storm ~*ed* hour by hour⟩
fierce·ness \-snəs\ *n* -ES [ME *fersnesse, fiersnesse*, fr. *fers, fiers* + *-nesse* -ness] **:** the quality or state of being fierce **:** FEROCITY
fi·eri fa·ci·as \ˌfīərēˈfākē,as\ *n* [ME, fr. L, cause (it) to be done!] **:** a common-law writ lying for one who has recovered judgment in debt or damages commanding the sheriff that he cause satisfaction to be made of the goods and chattels of the defendant in the sum claimed — compare CAPIAS, ELEGIT, EXECUTION, LEVARI FACIAS
fi·er·i·ly \ˈfī(ə)rəlē, -li\ *adv* **:** in a fiery manner ⟨a book that is ~ opinionated⟩
fi·eri·ness \-rēnəs, -rin-\ *n* -ES **:** the quality or state of being fiery ⟨impressed by the ~ of the man's speech⟩ ⟨there was ~ in her glance⟩
¹fi·ery \ˈfī(ə)rē, -ri\ *adj, often* -ER/-EST [ME *firy, fiery*, fr. *fir, fire, fier* fire + *-y* — more at FIRE] **1 a :** made up of fire ⟨~ tongues playing about the roof of a burning building⟩ **b** (1) **:** BURNING, BLAZING ⟨the ~ interior of a furnace⟩ (2)

heraldry : vomiting flames ⟨a ~ lynx⟩ **c** : using fire ⟨the ~ experiments of the ancient alchemists⟩ **d** : liable to catch fire or explode ⟨a ~ vapor⟩ **e** : containing flammable substances ⟨a ~ mine⟩ **2 a** : hot like a fire ⟨savoring the ~ taste of red pepper⟩ **b** (1) : INFLAMED ⟨a raw, ~ throat⟩ ⟨a ~ boil⟩ (2) : hot and dry and often reddened : feverish and flushed ⟨his forehead was ~ to the touch⟩ **c** *of a sign of the zodiac* : having a hot and dry complexion **3 a** : of the color of fire : RED ⟨a ~ sunset⟩ **b** : intensely or unnaturally red ⟨~ lips and fingernails⟩ **4 a** : full of, charged with, or exuding emotion, spirit, or passion ⟨a ~ speech⟩ ⟨a ~ love affair⟩ ⟨a ~ horse⟩ **b** : easily provoked : IRRITABLE ⟨a ~ personality⟩ **5** *of a wicket* : in such a condition as to cause a bowled ball in cricket to rise high and fast after landing — compare FAST

2fiery \"\ *adv* : in a fiery manner : FIERILY

fiery azalea *n* : FLAME AZALEA

fiery cross *n* **1** : a cross of wood partly charred and sometimes stained with blood formerly carried from clan to clan as a rallying signal in the Highlands of Scotland — called also *crostarie* **2** : a burning cross; *esp* : a burning cross used as a symbol of the Ku Klux Klan

fiery red *n* : a strong reddish orange that is paler and slightly yellower than poppy, redder and paler than paprika, and redder and darker than fire red — called also *firecracker, minium, red lead;* compare FLAME, FLAME RED

-fies *pres 3d sing of* -FY

fi·es·ta \fē'estə\ *n* -s [Sp, fr. L *festa* — more at FEAST] **1** : FESTIVAL; *specif* : a religious celebration (as in Spain and Latin America) featuring processions and dances of pagan heritage addressed to Christian saints **2** : a deep pink that is bluer, lighter, and stronger than average coral (sense 3b), yellower than begonia, and yellower and stronger than sweet william

fiesta flower *n* : a straggling annual Californian herb (*Nemophila aurita*) with deep purple or violet flowers

fi·este·ro \ˌfēə'ste(ˌ)rō\ *n* -s [MexSp, fr. Sp *fiesta* + *-ero* -er (fr. L *-arius*)] : one of a group of persons among the Cahita, Mayo, and Yaqui responsible for the conduct of a fiesta

fi fa *abbr* fieri facias

1fife \'fīf\ *n* -s [G *pfeife* fife, whistle, pipe, fr. OHG *pfīfa* — more at PIPE] **1** : a small transverse flute with shrill tone used chiefly to accompany the drum **2** : a shrill flute stop in a pipe organ of 1-foot or 2-foot pitch

fife 1, with raised finger holes and gutta-percha embouchure

2fife \"\ *vb* -ED/-ING/-S *vi* : to play a fife ~ *vt* : to play (a tune) on a fife

fif·er \'fīfə(r)\ *n* -s : one that plays a fife

fife rail *n* **1** : a railing around the bulwarks of a quarterdeck **2** : a rail about the mast near the deck to which running rigging is belayed

fife·shire \'fīfˌshi(ə)r, -iə, -ˌshə(r)\ *or* **fife** *adj, usu cap* [fr. *Fifeshire* or *Fife* county, Scotland] : of or from the county of Fife, Scotland : of the kind or style prevalent in Fife

fif·ie \'fīfē\ *n* -s [*Fife* county, Scotland + E *-ie*] : a Scottish fishing lugger with straight stem and sternposts

FIFO \'fī(ˌ)fō\ *abbr* first in, first out

1fif·teen \(')fif¦tēn\ *adj* [ME *fiftene*, fr. OE *fīftīene, fīftȳne, fīftēne* (akin to OHG *finfzehan*, ON *fimmtān*, Goth *fimftaihunim*, dat.), fr. *fīf* five + *-tīene, -tȳne, -tēne* (fr. *tien, tȳn, tēn* ten) — more at FIVE, TEN] : being one more than 14 in number ⟨~ years⟩ — see NUMBER table; used prepositively to designate various years of the 16th century ⟨the *fifteen-eighties*⟩ ⟨the early *fifteen*-hundreds⟩

2fifteen \"\ *pron, pl in constr* [ME *fiftene*, fr. OE *fīftīene, fīftȳne, fīftēne*, fr. *fīftīene, fīftȳne, fīftēne*, adj.] : 15 countable persons or things not specified but under consideration and being enumerated ⟨~ are here⟩ ⟨~ were found⟩

3fifteen \"\ *n* -s **1** : 10 and five : three times five **2 a** : 15 units or objects ⟨a total of ~⟩ **b** : a group or set of 15 ⟨arranged by ~*s*⟩ **3** : the numerable quantity symbolized by the arabic numerals 15 **4** : the 15th in a set or series; *esp* : an article of clothing of the 15th size ⟨wears a ~⟩ **5** : a combination of cards in cribbage whose total value is 15, each such combination counting two points **6** : the first score in a game of tennis — called also *five*

fifteen ball *n* : a pool game using a cue ball and 15 numbered balls racked in order with the highest at the apex of the triangle and in which players are credited with points corresponding to the number on the pocketed ball, the first to score 61 points being the winner

fif·teen·er \-nə(r)\ *n* -s : a line of verse of 15 syllables

fifteen-pounder \¦=¦=¦==\ *n* : a gun whose missile weighs 15 pounds

fifteen-spined stickleback \¦=¦=¦=\ *n* : a large European marine stickleback (*Spinachia spinachia*) with 15 spines

1fif·teenth \(')fif¦tēn(t)th\ *adj* [ME *fiftenthe*, adj. & n., alter. (influenced by *fiftene*) of *fiftethe*, fr. OE *fīftēotha* (akin to ON *fimmtāndi* fifteenth, Goth *fimftataihundin*, dat. sing. neut.), fr. *fīftīene, fīftȳne, fīftēne* + *-otha, -tha* -th] **1** : being number 15 in a countable series ⟨the ~ day⟩ — see NUMBER table **2** : being one of 15 equal parts into which something is divisible ⟨a ~ share of the money⟩

2fifteenth \"\ *n, pl* **fifteenths** \-n(t)s, -n(t)ths\ [ME *fiftenthe*] **1** : number 15 in a countable series ⟨the ~ of the month⟩ **2** : the quotient of a unit divided by 15 : one of 15 equal parts of something ⟨one ~ of the total⟩ **3** : a tax of one fifteenth on personal property that formed a part of a grant to the English king from 1272 to 1624 **4 a** : a 2-foot stop in a pipe organ **b** : an interval or compass of a double octave

1fifth \'fif(t)th, 'fift, *rapid or substand* 'fith\ *adj* [ME *fifte, fifthe*, adj. & n., fr. OE *fīfta* (akin to OHG *fimfto, finfto*, ON *fimmti*), fr. *fīf* five + *-ta* (fr. *-otha, -tha* -th) — more at FIVE] **1** : being number five in a countable series ⟨the ~ day⟩ — see NUMBER table **2** : being one of five equal parts into which something is divisible ⟨a ~ share of the money⟩

2fifth \"\ *n, pl* **fifths** \'fif(t)ths, 'fif(t)s, *rapid or substand* 'fiths\ [ME *fifte, fifthe*] **1** : number five in a countable series ⟨the ~ of the month⟩ **2** : the quotient of a unit divided by five : one of five equal parts of something ⟨one ~ of the total⟩ **3 a** : the musical interval embracing five diatonic degrees **b** : the tone at this interval; *specif* : DOMINANT 2b **c** : the harmonic combination of two tones at this interval **4** : a unit of capacity for liquor equal to one fifth of a U. S. gallon; *also* : a bottle holding this quantity of liquor **5** : QUINTE

3fifth \"\ *adv* ['fifth] **1** : in the fifth place **2** : with four exceptions ⟨the nation's ~ largest city⟩

fifth column *n* [trans. of Sp *quinta columna;* fr. the fact that during the Spanish Civil War rebel sympathizers in Madrid were so called when in 1936 four rebel columns advanced against this city] : a group of secret sympathizers or supporters of an enemy that engage in espionage, sabotage, and other subversive activities within the defense lines or borders of a nation — **fifth columnism** *n* — **fifth columnist** *n*

fifth cranial nerve *or* **fifth nerve** *n* : TRIGEMINAL NERVE

fifth day *n, usu cap F* : THURSDAY — used chiefly by the Friends

fifth estate *n* : a class or group existing in addition to the traditional four ⟨scientists who today make up a *fifth estate*⟩

fifth freedom *n* : the right of an international airline to pick up and deliver at intermediate points along a route

fifth·ly \'fif(t)thlē, 'fiftlē, -li\ *adv* : in the fifth place

fifth monarchy *n* : a universal monarchy supposed to be prophesied in Daniel 2 and to follow the monarchies of the Assyrians, Persians, Greco-Macedonians, and Romans

fifth monarchy man *n, usu cap F & both Ms* : a member of a fanatical sect in England at the time of the Commonwealth who believed that the fifth monarchy during which Christ would reign on earth a thousand years was near at hand and that they must assist to establish it by force

fifth quarter *n* : the parts of a slaughtered animal other than offal that supplement the four quarters (as the giblets in poultry and the head, tail, hide, horns, hoofs, fat, tallow, tongue, heart, and liver in cattle and sheep)

fifth wheel *n* **1 a** : a horizontal wheel or segment of a wheel that consists of two parts rotating on each other about the kingbolt above the fore axle of a carriage or wagon and beneath the body and that forms an extended support to prevent tipping **b** : a coupling in the form of two disks rotating on each other for attaching a vehicle body to the front axle so as to support it in turning **c** : a similar coupling between tractor and trailer of a semitrailer **2 a** : a spare wheel **b** : a light wheel trailed behind an automobile for measuring speed or distance **3** : one that is superfluous or burdensome ⟨committees without authority to act are *fifth wheels* —F.L.Allen⟩

1fif·ti·eth \'fiftēəth, -tiəth\ *adj* [ME *fiftithe*, adj. & n., fr. OE *fīftigotha* (akin to ON *fimmtugandi*), fr. *fīftig* fifty + *-otha, -tha*, -th] **1** : being number 50 in a countable series ⟨the ~ day⟩ — see NUMBER table **2** : being one of 50 equal parts into which something is divisible ⟨a ~ share⟩

2fiftieth \"\ *n* -s [ME *fiftithe*] **1** : number 50 in a countable series **2** : the quotient of a unit divided by 50 : one of 50 equal parts of something ⟨one ~ of the total⟩

1fif·ty \'fiftē, -ti\ *adj* [ME, fr. OE *fīftig*, fr. *fīftig*, n., group of 50, fr. *fīf* five + *-tig* group of ten — more at FIVE, EIGHTY] : being one more than 49 in number ⟨~ years⟩ — see NUMBER table

2fifty \"\ *pron, pl in constr* [ME, fr. *fifty*, adj.] : 50 countable persons or things not specified but under consideration and being enumerated ⟨~ are here⟩ ⟨~ were found⟩

3fifty \"\ *n* -ES [ME] **1** : five tens : twice 25 : 10 fives **2 a** : 50 units or objects ⟨a total of ~⟩ **b** : a group or set of 50 ⟨arranged by *fifties*⟩ **3 a** : the numerable quantity symbolized by the arabic numerals 50 **b** : the letter L **4** : the 50th in a set or series; *esp* : an article of clothing of the 50th size ⟨a ~ is too big⟩ **5** : something having as an essential feature 50 units or members **6 fifties** *pl* **a** : the numbers 50 to 59 inclusive ⟨a score in the *fifties*⟩ ⟨low grades in the *fifties*⟩ **b** : the members of a series or set of successive numbers that end in 50 to 59 inclusive ⟨the *fifties* of the preceding century⟩ ⟨lives in the *fifties* in the next block⟩ **c** : the portion of a continuum lying between 50 and 60 on a scale of measurement or segmentation ⟨temperatures in the *fifties* tomorrow⟩ ⟨a man in his *fifties*⟩ ⟨dresses selling in the *fifties*⟩ ⟨in the latitude of the *fifties*⟩ **7 a** : a fifty-pound note **b** : a fifty-dollar bill **8** : a 50 caliber gun — usu. written .50

1fifty-eight \¦==¦=\ *adj* : being one more than 57 in number ⟨*fifty-eight* years⟩ — see NUMBER table

2fifty-eight \"\ *pron, pl in constr* : 58 countable persons or things not specified but under consideration and being enumerated ⟨*fifty-eight* are here⟩ ⟨*fifty-eight* were found⟩

3fifty-eight \"\ *n* **1** : eight and 50 : 29 times two **2 a** : 58 units or objects ⟨a total of *fifty-eight*⟩ **b** : a group or set of 58 **3** : the numerable quantity symbolized by the arabic numerals 58 **4** : the 58th in a set or series

1fifty-eighth \¦==¦=\ *adj* **1** : being number 58 in a countable series ⟨the *fifty-eighth* day⟩ — see NUMBER table **2** : being one of 58 equal parts into which something is divisible ⟨a *fifty-eighth* share of the money⟩

2fifty-eighth \"\ *n* **1** : number 58 in a countable series **2** : the quotient of a unit divided by 58 : one of 58 equal parts of something ⟨one *fifty-eighth* of the total⟩

1fifty-fifth \¦==¦=\ *adj* **1** : being number 55 in a countable series ⟨the *fifty-fifth* day⟩ — see NUMBER table **2** : being one of 55 equal parts into which something is divisible ⟨a *fifty-fifth* share of the money⟩

2fifty-fifth \"\ *n* **1** : number 55 in a countable series **2** : the quotient of a unit divided by 55 : one of 55 equal parts of something ⟨one *fifty-fifth* of the total⟩

1fifty-fifty \¦==¦==\ *adv* : EQUALLY ⟨profits shared *fifty-fifty*⟩

2fifty-fifty \"\ *adj* **1** : shared, assumed, or borne equally (as by two people) ⟨a *fifty-fifty* proposition⟩ **2** : half favorable and half unfavorable ⟨a *fifty-fifty* chance to live⟩ : half pro and half con ⟨a *fifty-fifty* decision⟩

1fifty-first \¦==¦=\ *adj* **1** : being number 51 in a countable series ⟨the *fifty-first* day⟩ — see NUMBER table **2** : being one of 51 equal parts into which something is divisible ⟨a *fifty-first* share of the money⟩

2fifty-first \"\ *n* **1** : number 51 in a countable series **2** : the quotient of a unit divided by 51 : one of 51 equal parts of something ⟨one *fifty-first* of the total⟩

1fifty-five \¦==¦=\ *adj* : being one more than 54 in number ⟨*fifty-five* years⟩ — see NUMBER table

2fifty-five \"\ *pron, pl in constr* : 55 countable persons or things not specified but under consideration and being enumerated ⟨*fifty-five* are here⟩ ⟨*fifty-five* were found⟩

3fifty-five \"\ *n* **1** : five and 50 : five times 11 : 11 fives **2 a** : 55 units or objects ⟨a total of *fifty-five*⟩ **b** : a group or set of 55 **3** : the numerable quantity symbolized by the arabic numerals 55 **4** : the 55th in a set or series

1fifty-four \¦==¦=\ *adj* : being one more than 53 in number ⟨*fifty-four* years⟩ — see NUMBER table

2fifty-four \"\ *pron, pl in constr* : 54 countable persons or things not specified but under consideration and being enumerated ⟨*fifty-four* are here⟩ ⟨*fifty-four* were found⟩

3fifty-four \"\ *n* **1** : four and 50 : three times 18 : six times nine **2 a** : 54 units or objects ⟨a total of *fifty-four*⟩ **b** : a group or set of 54 **3** : the numerable quantity symbolized by the arabic numerals 54 **4** : the 54th in a set or series

1fifty-fourth \¦==¦=\ *adj* **1** : being number 54 in a countable series ⟨the *fifty-fourth* day⟩ — see NUMBER table **2** : being one of 54 equal parts into which something is divisible ⟨a *fifty-fourth* share of the money⟩

2fifty-fourth \"\ *n* **1** : number 54 in a countable series **2** : the quotient of a unit divided by 54 : one of 54 equal parts of something ⟨one *fifty-fourth* of the total⟩

1fifty-nine \¦==¦=\ *adj* : being one more than 58 in number ⟨*fifty-nine* years⟩ — see NUMBER table

2fifty-nine \"\ *pron, pl in constr* : 59 countable persons or things not specified but under consideration and being enumerated ⟨*fifty-nine* are here⟩ ⟨*fifty-nine* were found⟩

3fifty-nine \"\ *n* **1** : nine and 50 **2 a** : 59 units or objects ⟨a total of *fifty-nine*⟩ **b** : a group or set of 59 **3** : the numerable quantity symbolized by the arabic numerals 59 **4** : the 59th of a set or series

1fifty-ninth \¦==¦=\ *adj* **1** : being number 59 in a countable series ⟨the *fifty-ninth* day⟩ — see NUMBER table **2** : being one of 59 equal parts into which something is divisible ⟨a *fifty-ninth* share of the money⟩

2fifty-ninth \"\ *n* **1** : number 59 in a countable series **2** : the quotient of a unit divided by 59 : one of 59 equal parts of something ⟨one *fifty-ninth* of the total⟩

1fifty-one \¦==¦=\ *adj* : being one more than 50 in number ⟨*fifty-one* years⟩ — see NUMBER table

2fifty-one \"\ *pron, pl in constr* : 51 countable persons or things not specified but under consideration and being enumerated ⟨*fifty-one* are here⟩ ⟨*fifty-one* were found⟩

3fifty-one \"\ *n* **1** : one and 50 : three times 17 **2 a** : 51 units or objects ⟨a total of *fifty-one*⟩ **b** : a group or set of 51 **3** : the numerable quantity symbolized by the arabic numerals 51 **4** : the 51st in a set or series

1fifty-second \¦==¦==\ *adj* **1** : being number 52 in a countable series ⟨the *fifty-second* day⟩ — see NUMBER table **2** : being one of 52 equal parts into which something is divisible ⟨a *fifty-second* share of the money⟩

2fifty-second \"\ *n* **1** : number 52 in a countable series **2** : the quotient of a unit divided by 52 : one of 52 equal parts of something ⟨one *fifty-second* of the total⟩

1fifty-seven \¦==¦==\ *adj* : being one more than 56 in number ⟨*fifty-seven* years⟩ — see NUMBER table

2fifty-seven \"\ *pron, pl in constr* : 57 countable persons or things not specified but under consideration and being enumerated ⟨*fifty-seven* are here⟩ ⟨*fifty-seven* were found⟩

3fifty-seven \"\ *n* **1** : seven and 50 : three times 19 **2 a** : 57 units or objects ⟨a total of *fifty-seven*⟩ **b** : a group or set of 57 **3** : the numerable quantity symbolized by the arabic numerals 57 **4** : the 57th in a set or series

1fifty-seventh \¦==¦==\ *adj* **1** : being number 57 in a countable series ⟨the *fifty-seventh* day⟩ — see NUMBER table **2** : being one of 57 equal parts into which something is divisible ⟨a *fifty-seventh* share of the money⟩

2fifty-seventh \"\ *n* **1** : number 57 in a countable series **2** : the quotient of a unit divided by 57 : one of 57 equal parts of something ⟨one *fifty-seventh* of the total⟩

1fifty-six \¦==¦=\ *adj* : being one more than 55 in number ⟨*fifty-six* years⟩ — see NUMBER table

2fifty-six \"\ *pron, pl in constr* : 56 countable persons or things not specified but under consideration and being enumerated ⟨*fifty-six* are here⟩ ⟨*fifty-six* were found⟩

3fifty-six \"\ *n* **1** : six and 50 : four times 14 : seven times eight **2 a** : 56 units or objects ⟨a total of *fifty-six*⟩ **b** : a group or set of 56 **3** : the numerable quantity symbolized by the arabic numerals 56 **4** : the 56th in a set or series

1fifty-sixth \¦==¦=\ *adj* **1** : being number 56 in a countable series ⟨the *fifty-sixth* day⟩ — see NUMBER table **2** : being one of 56 equal parts into which something is divisible ⟨a *fifty-sixth* share of the money⟩

2fifty-sixth \"\ *n* **1** : number 56 in a countable series **2** : the quotient of a unit divided by 56 : one of 56 equal parts of something ⟨one *fifty-sixth* of the total⟩

1fifty-third \¦==¦=\ *adj* **1** : being number 53 in a countable series ⟨the *fifty-third* day⟩ — see NUMBER table **2** : being one of 53 equal parts into which something is divisible ⟨a *fifty-third* share of the money⟩

2fifty-third \"\ *n* **1** : number 53 in a countable series **2** : the quotient of a unit divided by 53 : one of 53 equal parts of something ⟨one *fifty-third* of the total⟩

1fifty-three \¦==¦=\ *adj* : being one more than 52 in number ⟨*fifty-three* years⟩ — see NUMBER table

2fifty-three \"\ *pron, pl in constr* : 53 countable persons or things not specified but under consideration and being enumerated ⟨*fifty-three* are here⟩ ⟨*fifty-three* were found⟩

3fifty-three \"\ *n* **1** : three and 50 **2 a** : 53 units or objects ⟨a total of *fifty-three*⟩ **b** : a group or set of 53 **3** : the numerable quantity symbolized by the arabic numerals 53 **4** : the 53d in a set or series

1fifty-two \¦==¦=\ *adj* : being one more than 51 in number ⟨*fifty-two* years⟩ — see NUMBER table

2fifty-two \"\ *pron, pl in constr* : 52 countable persons or things not specified but under consideration and being enumerated ⟨*fifty-two* are here⟩ ⟨*fifty-two* were found⟩

3fifty-two \"\ *n* **1** : two and fifty : four times 13 **2 a** : 52 units or objects ⟨a total of *fifty-two*⟩ **b** : a group or set of 52 **3** : the numerable quantity symbolized by the arabic numerals 52 **4** : the 52d in a set or series

1fig \'fig\ *n* -s [ME *fige, figue*, fr. OF *fige, figue*, fr. OProv *figa*, fr. (assumed) VL *fica*, fr. L *ficus* fig tree, fig, of non-IE origin; akin to the source of Gk *sykon* fig, Arm *t'uz*] **1 a** : an oblong to pear-shaped or nearly globose edible fruit of warm regions that is greenish, yellowish to orange, or purple when ripe, that has a thick soft skin enclosing a sweet pulp full of tiny seeds, and that is available commercially chiefly dried — see COMMON FIG, SMYRNA FIG, SYCONIUM **b** *obs* : poison given in a fig **2** *or* **fig tree** : a tree of the genus *Ficus; usu* : any of the cultivated or escaped trees derived from a tree (*F. carica*) native to southwestern Asia but extensively grown in several varieties in warm regions of the New and Old Worlds for the edible figs that are their fruit — see CAPRIFIG **3 a** *Austral* : any of several woody plants that resemble fig trees or produce fruits resembling figs: as (1) : BLUEBERRY ASH (2) : a slender twining xerophytic vine (*Marsdenia australis*) that produces pear-shaped fruits sometimes eaten by the aborigines **b** : FIG BANANA **c** : COCHINEAL FIG **d** *dial chiefly Eng* : RAISIN **4** : something resembling the fruit of the fig tree (as piles or a warty excrescence on the frog of a horse's hoof) **5** : a small piece of tobacco **6 a** [MF *figue* (in *faire la figue* make a fig), fr. It *fica* (in *far la fica*), fr. *fica* fig, vulva, fr. (assumed) VL *fica* fig] : a gesture or sign of contempt (as thrusting a thumb between two fingers) **b** : the least bit : the merest trifle : PARTICLE ⟨he doesn't give a ~ for his appearance⟩ ⟨who cares a ~ for widows swindled in the . . . real-estate boom —Lee Rogow⟩ — often used interjectionally to express scorn or contempt ⟨a ~ for housework! she said to herself —Glenway Wescott⟩

2fig \"\ *vt* **figged; figged; figging; figs** *obs* : to insult by giving the sign of the fig to

3fig \"\ *vi* [perh. alter. of ME *fiken* — more at FIKE] *now dial Eng* : to move about restlessly : pace back and forth

4fig \"\ *vt* **figged; figged; figging; figs** [origin unknown] **1** : to dress or adorn — used with *out* or *up* ⟨a richly *figged* out dowager⟩ **2** : to put ginger or pepper in the anus or vagina of (a horse) to stimulate action or improve carriage

5fig \"\ *n* -s **1** : DRESS, ARRAY ⟨the appealing figure of a young woman in dazzling royal full ~ —Mollie Panter-Downes⟩ **2** : CONDITION, FORM ⟨in fine ~ for a race⟩

fig *abbr* **1** figurative **2** figure

figa·ro sauce \'figəˌrō-, 'fēg|\ *n* [prob. after *Figaro*, the hero of *Le Barbier de Séville* (1775) and *Le Mariage de Figaro* (1784), comedies by P. A. Caron de Beaumarchais †1799 Fr. playwright] : hollandaise sauce with tomato puree added

figary *var of* FEGARY

fig banana *n* : a small plump tropical American banana having a flavor somewhat like a fig

fig bar *n* **1** : a bar-shaped form of pressed figs **2** : a bar-shaped cookie with a fig filling

fig-bird \'=ˌ=\ *n* : any of several largely greenish yellow Australian orioles (genus *Sphecotheres*) that feed chiefly on figs and other fruits

figeater \'=ˌ==\ *n* **1** : GREEN JUNE BEETLE **2** : BECCAFICO

figent *adj* [alter. of *fidge* + *-ent*] *obs* : FIDGETY, VOLATILE

fig family *n* : MORACEAE

fig faun *n* : one of a class of rural deities or monsters supposed to live on figs and referred to in Jer 50 : 39 (DV)

figged \'figd\ *adj* **1** *dial chiefly Eng* : made with figs or raisins ⟨a ~ pudding⟩ **2** *dial chiefly Eng* : SPECKLED, SPOTTED

fig·ging \'figiŋ\ *n* -s : a granular appearance in soft soap that resembles the seeds of a fig, that is held to be due to the crystallization of a harder soap, and that is sometimes considered an indication of superior quality

fig·gy \'figē\ *adj* -ER/-EST : containing or resembling figs

1fight \'fīt, *usu* -īd.+V\ *vb* **fought** \'fȯt, *usu* -ȯd.+V\ *or dia* **fit** \'fit, *usu* -id.+V\ *or* **fout** \'fōt, 'faůt, *usu* |d.+V\ **fought** *or dial* **fit** *or* **fought·en** \'fȯtᵊn\ *or* **fout; fighting; fights** [ME *fighten*, fr. OE *feohtan*; akin to OFris *fiuchta* to fight, OS & OHG *fehtan* to fight, L *pectere* to comb — more at FEE] *vi* **1 a** : to contend physically for victory with vigor, fierceness, and determination ⟨*fought* on the ridge until nightfall⟩ : strive to overcome or destroy a person, animal, or thing esp. by blows or weapons — often used with *against* or *with* ⟨brother ~*ing* against brother⟩ **b** : to engage in prize-fighting esp. as a profession or career : BOX **2 a** : to put forth a grim, determined, or dogged effort (as for the achievement of a goal or purpose) — often used with *for* ⟨~ for freedom⟩ or *to* ⟨~ to bring about some needed changes⟩ **b** *of a Salvationist* : to war aggressively against evil and for the cause of God ~ *vt* **1 a** (1) : to contend against in or as if in battle or physical combat esp. with determination to cease only upon achieving victory or sustaining defeat ⟨~ the invaders of his homeland⟩ (2) : to box against in the prize ring ⟨*fought* several strong challengers⟩ **b** (1) : to attempt to prevent the success, fruition, or effectiveness of ⟨the company *fought* the strike for months⟩ (2) : to oppose the passage, development, or appearance of ⟨the northern senators *fought* the bill bitterly⟩ ⟨~ a bad habit⟩ **2 a** : to carry on : WAGE ⟨~ a war⟩ ⟨~ a battle⟩ **b** : to take part in (as a boxing match) ⟨*fought* a dozen professional matches before he was 20 years old⟩ **3 a** : to struggle with the inconvenience, discomfort, or hardship of ⟨~ a leaky roof all year⟩ **b** : to struggle to endure or surmount — used with *out* ⟨a ship ~*ing* out a storm at sea⟩ **4 a** : to win or gain by struggle ⟨*fought* his way through the underbrush⟩ **b** : to resolve or surmount by struggle — used with *out* ⟨the two men *fought* out their differences in court⟩ or *down* ⟨*fought* down his fear⟩ **5 a** (1) : to manage (a ship) in a battle or storm (2) : to cause to struggle or contend ⟨~ cocks⟩ **b** : to handle, treat, or manage in an unnecessarily rough or overly deliberate manner ⟨she always *fought* the shift and could wear a transmission out in six months⟩ **6** : to become unnecessarily or unnaturally difficult for ⟨the minute your work starts ~*ing* you, give up —Marian Corey⟩ **syn** see CONTEND, CONTEST — **fight shy of** : to avoid meeting : refuse to face up to

2fight \"\ *n* -s [ME, fr. OE *feoht*; akin to OFris *fiucht* fight, OHG *gifeht*; derivative fr. the root of OE *feohtan* to fight] **1** *archaic* : the act of fighting **2 a** : a hostile encounter between opposing forces or individuals : BATTLE, COMBAT **b** : a boxing match **c** : a verbal disagreement **3** : a struggle to achieve a goal or an objective ⟨an uphill ~ for reelection⟩ **4** *obs* : a screen put up to protect combatants on a naval vessel **5** : strength or disposition for fighting : PUGNACITY ⟨he still has a lot of ~ in him⟩ **syn** see CONTEST

fight·able \ˈfīd·əbəl, -ītə-\ *adj* **1 :** fit for fighting ⟨a ~ ship⟩ **2 :** eager to fight ⟨an opponent still excited and ~⟩

fight·er \ˈfīd·ə(r), -ītə-\ *n* -s [ME, fr. OE *feohtere*, fr. *feohtan* + *-ere* -er] **:** one that fights: as **a** (1) **:** WARRIOR, SOLDIER (2) **:** a pugnacious or game individual (3) **:** PRIZEFIGHTER, BOXER **b** *or* **fighter plane :** a military or naval airplane of high speed, high rate of climb, excellent maneuverability, and armament designed to destroy enemy aircraft in the air

fighter-bomber \ˈ≈≈ˌ≈≈\ *n* **:** a fighter aircraft fitted to carry bombs, rockets, or napalm tanks in addition to its normal armament and used to support friendly ground troops and to cut enemy supply lines so as to isolate the battlefield and also to engage enemy aircraft

fighter-interceptor \ˈ≈≈,≈≈ˈ≈≈\ *n* **:** a fighter aircraft designed to intercept and destroy enemy aircraft in the air

fighting *adj* [ME, fr. pres. part. of *fighten* to fight] **1 :** designed or intended to fight ⟨a ~ ship⟩ **2 a :** fit to fight ⟨a boxer in ~ condition⟩ **b :** that qualifies to fight ⟨a boxer at ~ weight⟩ **3 a** (1) **:** prone to fight **:** WARLIKE ⟨a ~ tribe⟩ (2) **:** liable to provoke a fight ⟨those are ~ words⟩ **b :** showing a readiness to fight **:** GAME, PLUCKY ⟨a ~ spirit⟩ — **fight·ing·ly** *adv*

fighting chair *n* **:** a chair from which a salt-water angler plays a hooked fish

fighting chance *n* **:** a chance that may be realized by a struggle **:** a possible but not easy chance ⟨the patient had a *fighting chance* to live⟩

fighting cock *n* **:** GAMECOCK

fighting crab *n* **:** FIDDLER CRAB

fighting fish *n* **:** BETTA

fighting top *n* **:** the top (sense 4b) on a warship

fight-off \ˈ≈,≈\ *n* -s [²*fight* + *-off* (as in *play-off*)] **:** a prizefight to decide a tie or to determine a single winner in a class — compare PLAY-OFF

fights *pres 3d sing of* FIGHT, *pl of* FIGHT

fight talk *n* **:** a pregame or intermission talk made (as by a football coach) to inspire the players and spur them to their best possible efforts **:** PEP TALK

fig leaf *n* **1 :** the leaf of a fig tree **2 :** something that conceals, masks, or camouflages usu. inadequately, prudishly, or dishonestly ⟨the rhetorical *fig leaves* by which the pursuit of wealth and power hid itself from the public gaze —H.J.Laski⟩

fig marigold *n* **:** any of several plants of the genus *Mesembryanthemum* cultivated for their showy white or pink flowers — see AIZOACEAE

fig·ment \ˈfigmənt\ *n* -s [ME, fr. L *figmentum*, fr. *fig-* (stem of *fingere* to shape, form, devise, feign) + *-mentum* -ment — more at DOUGH] **:** something made up, fabricated, or contrived ⟨uses this dim ~ of the chronicles as an excuse to present the doubts and indecisions of a humanistic age —Herbert Read⟩ ⟨a ~ of an author's imagination⟩ **syn** see FICTION

fig mite *n* **:** a minute blister mite (*Aceria ficus*) that feeds on the leaves of figs causing rusting

fig moth *n* **:** ALMOND MOTH

Fig New·tons \ˈfigˈn(y)üt³nz\ *trademark* — used for bar-shaped cookies having fig filling

figo *n* -s [modif. of OSp or Pg *figa* fig, vulva, fr. (assumed) VL *fica* fig — more at FIG] *obs* **:** FICO

fig parrot *n* **:** LORILET

figpecker \ˈ≈,≈≈\ *n* **:** BECCAFICO

fig rust *n* **:** a rust disease of figs that is troublesome in the southeastern U.S. and is caused by a fungus (*Physopella fici*)

figs *pl of* FIG, *pres 3d sing of* FIG

fig scale *n* **:** an elongate armored scale (*Lepidosaphes ficus*) that is related to the typical oystershell scale and that feeds on fig trees

figshell \ˈ≈,≈\ *n* **1 :** a gastropod mollusk of the family Ficidae that has a fig-shaped shell; *also* **:** the shell of one of these mollusks **2 :** any of several mollusks of the family Tonnidae

fig soap *n* **:** a soft soap showing figging

fig sunday *n, usu cap F&S* [so called fr. the custom of eating figs on this day] **:** PALM SUNDAY

fig tree *n* **:** ¹FIG 2

fig·ur·able \ˈfig(y)ərəbəl\ *adj* **1 :** capable of being figured **2 :** capable of being brought to a fixed form or shape

fig·ur·al \-rəl\ *adj* [ME, fr. LL *figuralis*, fr. L *figura* figure + *-alis* -al — more at FIGURE] **1** *obs* **:** FIGURATIVE 1 **2 :** FIGURATIVE 2 **3 :** FIGURATE 2 **4 :** relating to or consisting wholly or for the most part of human or animal figures ⟨a ~ composition⟩ ⟨finely etched with bands of floral and ~ subjects⟩ — **fig·ur·al·ly** \-rəlē\ *adv*

fig·u·rant \ˌfigyəˌränt, -rä^n,-rant, ˌ≈≈ˈ≈; ˈfigyərənt\ *n* -s [F *figurant*, fr. pres. part. of *figurer* to figure, represent, appear — more at FIGURE] **1 :** a member of a dance troupe who dances only in groups or figures **2 :** one that figures in a scene without speaking or without taking a prominent part

fig·u·rante \ˈfigyəˌränt, -rant, ˌ≈≈ˈ≈; ˈfigyərənt\ *n* -s [F, fem. of *figurant*] **:** a female figurant; *esp* **:** a member of a ballet troupe

fig·u·rate \ˈfigyərət, -ˌrāt\ *adj* [L *figuratus*, past part. of *figurare* to form — more at FIGURE] **1 :** relating to, composed of, or suggestive of a figure **2 :** involving passing discords by the freer melodic movement of one or more voice parts **:** FLORID ⟨~ counterpoint⟩ — contrasted with *simple* — **fig·u·rate·ly** *adv*

figurate number *n* **:** any of a progression of numbers formed from an arithmetical progression in which the first term is 1 and the difference an integer by taking the first term, and the sums of the first two, first three, first four, and so on as the successive terms of a new progression and by operating on this in the same way, and so on, the numbers in each sequence being such that points representing them are capable of arrangement in geometrical figures

fig·u·ra·tion \ˌfigyəˈrāshən\ *n* -s [ME *figuracioun*, fr. MF or L; MF *figuration*, fr. L *figuration-, figuratio*, fr. *figuratus* (past part. of *figurare* to figure) + *-ion-, -io* -ion — more at FIGURE] **1 :** the act or action of creating or providing a figure ⟨Dante's unique ~ of the underworld⟩ **2 :** FORM, SHAPE, OUTLINE ⟨he studied words and ~s on pieces of money —Carl Sandburg⟩ **3 :** the act or action of representation in figures and shapes **:** emblematic or typical representation; *also* **:** the result of such an act or action ⟨the new cubism was explained as a synthesis of colored ~s of objects —Janet Flanner⟩ **4 :** the ornamental treatment of a musical passage by the use of decorative and usu. repetitive figures specif. in variations of a theme ⟨brilliant string ~s first for violins and then for cellos and basses —Cecil Gray⟩

fig·u·ra·tive \ˈfig(y)ərəd·iv, -grəl, |tiv\ *adj* [ME, fr. MF or LL; MF *figuratif*, fr. LL *figurativus*, fr. L *figuratus* + *-ivus* -ive] **1 :** representing or represented by a figure or resemblance ⟨the ~ art of the humanistic tradition —Herbert Read⟩ **2 :** transferred in sense from literal or plain to abstract or hypothetical (as by the expression of one thing in terms of another with which it can be regarded as analogous) **:** METAPHORICAL ⟨~ language⟩ ⟨in a ~ sense, civilization marches up and down —Lewis Mumford⟩ **3 :** characterized by figures of speech or elaborate expression ⟨a ~ description⟩ ⟨a ~ author⟩ — **fig·u·ra·tive·ly** \|d·əvlē, |təv-, -li; ˈfigər|\ *adv* — **fig·u·ra·tive·ness** \-ivnəs\ *n* -ES

¹fig·ure \ˈfigyə(r), *usual in Brit speech & frequent in US speech but regarded by many in the US as substand* -gə(r); *"figur-" followed by a vowel other than "e" is usually or often pronounced with* y *in Brit speech*\ *n* -s [ME, fr. OF, fr. L *figura*, fr. *fig-* (stem of *fingere* to shape, form, devise, feign) + *-ura* -ure — more at DOUGH] **1 a :** a number symbol (as one of the arabic numerals) **:** NUMERAL, DIGIT **b figures** *pl* **:** figures used in arithmetical calculating ⟨~s can be made to prove anything⟩ **:** arithmetical calculations ⟨he is good at ~s⟩ **c :** a written or printed character (as a letter, mathematical symbol, or cipher) **d :** value esp. as expressed in numbers **:** PRICE, AMOUNT, SUM ⟨the house sold at a low ~⟩ **e :** a numeral of a continuo in music **2 a :** a body apparent chiefly in outline **:** an object significant or noticeable only in its form ⟨a ~ moving slowly in the dusk⟩ **b :** a surface shape in a work of art visually appreciable and separable from its surroundings ⟨*figure*-ground relationship⟩ **c :** the part of a total stimulus situation which is most clearly perceived by an observer and to which he responds **3 a :** the representation of a form (as by drawing, painting, modeling, carving, embroidering); *specif* **:** a representation of the human form esp. in the nude **b :** a diagram or pictorial illustration (as a linecut or photoreproduction) augmenting text matter (as of a book) — abbr. *fig.* **4 :** a person, thing, or action conceived of as analogous to another person, thing, or action of which it is a type or representative ⟨Adam . . . who is the ~ of him that was to come —Rom 5:14 (AV)⟩ **5 :** a diagram made to represent any definite combination of geometric elements **6 :** an imagined form **:** PHANTASM ⟨a ~ of idle dreaming⟩ **7 a :** a figure of speech: as (1) **:** METAPHOR (2) **:** SIMILE **b :** an intentional deviation from the ordinary form or syntactical relation of words (as in syncope) **8 a :** the two-dimensional proportions of a body or object ⟨the ~ of a ship on the horizon⟩ **b :** the shape of the human body ⟨a woman with a good ~⟩ **9 :** a diagram or scheme representing the heavens at a given moment (as at the moment of birth) **:** HOROSCOPE **10 :** the form of a syllogism with respect to the relative position of the middle term — compare MOOD **11 a :** a pattern or design (as in nature or in a cloth, paper, or other manufactured article) wrought out often repetitively in systematic arrangement ⟨the beautiful ~s of crystals⟩ ⟨a polka-dot ~⟩ **b :** the pattern produced on a wood surface by irregular coloration and by sawing through growth rings, knots, burls, and other deviations from regular grain; *esp* **:** any such wood surface of decorative value **12 a :** consequence in station or mode of living **:** RANK, GRANDEUR ⟨a person of ~⟩ **b :** conspicuous part or appearance **:** impressive effect — often used with *cut* or *make* ⟨the couple cut quite a ~⟩ **c :** appearance made or impression produced ⟨a person who always presented a sorry ~⟩ **13 a :** a series of movements that form one unit of a dance (as bowing to partners in a square dance) **b :** an outline representation of a form traced by means of a series of evolutions (as with skates on an ice surface or by an airplane in the air) **14 :** a prominent personality **:** PERSONAGE ⟨whether people are impressed with you as a ~ or a person —Anthony Perkins⟩ **15 :** a short coherent group of notes or tones or chords constituting a germ which by varied repetition and association with other figures may grow into a phrase, theme, or accompaniment or entire musical composition — compare MOTIVE **syn** see FORM, NUMBER

THE FOUR SYLLOGISTIC FIGURES*

S=SUBJECT M=MIDDLE TERM P=PREDICATE

(1)	(2)	(3)	(4)
M is P	P is M	M is P	P is M
S is M	S is M	M is S	M is S
∴ S is P	∴ S is P	∴ S is P	∴ S is P

*The first three figures were formulated by Aristotle, the fourth reputedly by Galen

²figure \ˈ"\ *vb* **figured; figured; figuring** \-gyəriŋ,-g(ə)riŋ\ **figures** [ME *figuren*, fr. MF *figurer*, fr. L *figurare*, fr. *figura*] *vt* **1 a :** to represent by or as if by a figure **:** PORTRAY ⟨an emblem wherein the apostles were *figured*⟩ **b** *archaic* **:** to represent or express by a metaphor **:** SYMBOLIZE **c** *obs* **:** FORESHADOW **2 a :** to adorn or embellish with a pattern or design ⟨*figured* cloth⟩ **b** (1) **:** to write figures over or under (the bass) in order to indicate the accompanying chords of a musical composition (2) **:** to embellish in music with passing notes or figures **3 a :** to indicate or represent by numerals ⟨water depth *figured* along a wharf piling⟩ **b :** to provide with numerals ⟨a watch dial *figured* in luminescent green⟩ **4 :** to give the requisite shape to (as a mirror, lens, or prism) **5 a** (1) **:** COMPUTE, RECKON ⟨~ expenses⟩; *specif* **:** ADD — usu. used with *up* ⟨~ up an account⟩ (2) **:** to determine or ascertain — usu. used with *out* ⟨~ a way out of a difficulty⟩ **b** (1) **:** SOLVE — usu. used with *out* ⟨~ a problem out⟩ (2) **:** CONCLUDE, DECIDE ⟨he *figured* there was no use in further effort⟩ (3) *slang* **:** to perceive the true makeup of **:** UNDERSTAND ⟨he *figured* the whole scheme right away⟩ **6 a :** REGARD, CONSIDER ⟨~ himself a good candidate⟩ **b :** THINK, ASSUME ~ *vi* **1 :** to make a figure **:** be or appear important ⟨the vice-president really *figured* in the company⟩ **2 :** to perform a figure in dancing **3 :** COMPUTE, CALCULATE ⟨a carpenter *figuring* on a board with a stub of pencil⟩ **4** *slang* **:** to seem rational, normal, or expected **:** be understandable ⟨sure, that ~s⟩ — **figure on 1 :** to take into consideration (as in planning or reckoning) ⟨*figuring on* $50 a month extra income⟩ **2 :** to rely on ⟨a person you can always *figure on* to pay his bills⟩ **3 :** PLAN ⟨I *figure on* going over to town to buy some stores —Helen Eustis⟩

figure caster *n, obs* **:** ASTROLOGER

figured *adj* [ME, fr. past part. of *figuren*] **1 :** REPRESENTED, PORTRAYED ⟨a lion ~ on a coin⟩ **2 :** adorned with, formed into, or marked with a figure ⟨~ muslin⟩ **3 :** FIGURATIVE ⟨~ language⟩ **4 a :** FIGURATE 2 **b :** indicated in music by figures **5 :** expressed in logic in the form of a figure ⟨a ~ syllogism⟩

figured bass *n* **:** CONTINUO; *esp* **:** the system or practice of indicating harmonic progression by numerals placed under the bass notes

figured glass *n* **:** sheet glass that is rolled with an intaglio figure or pattern on one side and that has powerful light-diffusing properties but is not transparent

figure eight *also* **figure of eight** *n* **:** something felt to resemble the arabic numeral eight in form or shape: as **a :** a small stopper knot **b :** a stitch used in embroidery **c :** a weave used in basketry **d :** a dance pattern; *esp* **:** a square-dance figure in which a couple passes between the partners of an adjacent couple and around each **e :** a figure executed by a skater in any of several prescribed ways

figure eight a

figure-four scissors *n* **:** a wrestling hold secured from a rear position by wrapping one leg around the opponent's waist and hooking the foot of this leg beneath the knee of the holder's other leg

figure-four trap *n* **:** a trap in which the trigger and support are fixed in the shape of the figure four and which when sprung causes a box or heavy lid to fall upon the game

figurehead \ˈ≈≈,≈\ *n* **1 :** the figure, statue, or bust on the bow of a ship at the stemhead **2 :** a nominal but not real head or chief; *esp* **:** one who allows his name to be used to give standing to enterprises in which he has no responsible interest or duties

figure in *vt* **1 :** to include esp. in a reckoning ⟨forgetting to *figure in* occasional expenses in a budget⟩ **2 :** to be a part of **:** be implicated in ⟨persons who *figured in* a robbery⟩

fig·ure·less \ˈfig(y)ə(r)ləs\ *adj* **:** lacking or devoid of a figure **:** SHAPELESS

figure-of-eight bandage *n* **:** a bandage in which the successive turns cross each other as in the figure eight — see BANDAGE illustration

figurehead 1

figure of merit : a numerical quantity based on one or more characteristics (as of a device or solution) under specified conditions and used for indicating comparative efficiency or effectiveness; *specif* **:** the current in amperes that must flow through a galvanometer to produce a deflection of one scale division

figure of speech : an expression (as a metaphor or euphemism) that substitutes a variation in point of view by which one thing or notion is referred to as if it were different in some way (as in identity, degree, shape) from what it actually is or seems to be but so related that the expression successfully implies an intended meaning or effect either slightly or greatly different from what is literally said (as "the apple of my eye", "forever chasing rainbows", "she didn't go to the party because she had nothing to wear", "a pretty pickle")

figure of the earth : the precise geometric shape of the planet — compare GEOID

fig·ur·er \ˈfig(y)ərə(r)\ *n* -s **:** one that figures; *specif* **:** a molder of figures for pottery

figures *pl of* FIGURE, *pres 3d sing of* FIGURE

figure skate *n* **:** a skate used for figure skating and having a hollow-ground blade slightly curved from heel to toe with a row of jagged points on the forepart of the blade

figure skate

figure skating *n* **:** skating in which the skater describes or outlines prescribed figures or performs various jumps, spins, and dance movements

figure stone *n* **:** AGALMATOLITE

fig·u·rine \ˌfig(y)əˈrēn\ *n* -s [F, fr. It *figurina*, dim. of *figura* figure, fr. L — more at FIGURE] **:** a small carved or molded figure; *esp* **:** a statuette in terracotta or similar material that is often adorned with painting or gilding and that is found in ancient tombs and ruins — compare TANAGRA

figuring *pres part of* FIGURE

figurist *n* -s *obs* **:** one that believes in the figurative presence of Christ in the Eucharist

fig wasp *n* **:** a minute insect (*Blastophaga psenes*) of the family Agaontidae that breeds in the caprifig and is important as the agent in the process of caprification; *broadly* **:** an insect of the family Agaontidae

fig wax *n* **:** GONDANG WAX

figwort \ˈ≈,≈\ *n* **:** a plant of the family Scrophulariaceae esp. of the genus *Scrophularia* **:** PILEWORT 2

figwort family *n* **:** SCROPHULARIACEAE

¹fi·ji \ˈfē(ˌ)jē, -ji, *chiefly Brit* (ˈ)fēˈjē\ *n, pl* **fiji** *or* **fijis** *usu cap* [Fiji *Viti*] **1 a :** a Melanesian people of the Fiji islands **b :** a member of this people **2 :** the Austronesian language of the Fiji people

²fiji \ˈ"\ *adj, usu cap* **:** FIJIAN

¹fi·ji·an \ˈfē(ˌ)jēən, -jiən, *chiefly Brit* (ˈ)fēˈjēən\ *adj, usu cap* [*Fiji* islands, southwest Pacific + E *-an*] **1 :** of or relating to the Fiji islands **2 :** of or relating to the Fijian people **3 :** of or relating to the Fijian language

²fijian \ˈ"\ *n* -s *cap* **:** FIJI

fiji disease *n, usu cap F* **:** a virus disease of sugarcane first reported from the Fiji islands and characterized by elongated white to brown swellings on the underside of the leaves followed by stunting and death

¹fike \ˈfīk\ *vb* -ED/-ING/-s [ME *fiken*, prob. of Scand origin; akin to ON *fikjask* to desire eagerly, *fikenn* eager, Norw *fika* to strive, hurry, Dan *fige*; akin to OE *fācian* to try to obtain, to get] *vi* **1** *dial Brit* **:** to move restlessly **:** FIDGET **2** *dial Brit* **:** WORRY, FUSS ⟨don't ~ about it⟩ **3** *dial Brit* **:** to bustle about **:** create a fuss over nothing ~ *vt, chiefly Scot* **:** to bring pain to **:** HURT

²fike \ˈ"\ *n* -s **1** *dial Brit* **:** FIDGET, WORRY **2** *dial Brit* **:** a passing fancy **:** FAD, WHIM

³fike *var of* FYKE

fik·ery \ˈfīk(ə)ri\ *n* -ES *chiefly Scot* **:** FUSSINESS

fik·ie \ˈfīkē\ *adj* **1** *chiefly Scot* **:** FIDGETY, RESTLESS **2** *chiefly Scot* **:** tricky and troublesome ⟨a ~ task⟩ **3** *chiefly Scot* **:** elaborate and decorative ⟨a ~ gown⟩

fil \ˈfil\ *var of* FILS

fil *abbr* **1** filament **2** fillet **3** fillister **4** filter

fila *pl of* FILUM

filabeg *var of* FILLEBEG

fi·la·go \fəˈlā(ˌ)gō, -lä(-\ *n* [NL, fr. ML, a plant, prob. cudweed, fr. L *filum* thread + *-ago* (as in *plantago* plantain) — more at FILE, PLANTAIN] **1** *cap* **:** a genus of small woolly herbs (family Compositae) with entire leaves and small flower heads in capitate clusters **2** -s **:** any plant of the genus *Filago* — see COTTON ROSE

filagree *var of* FILIGREE

fil·a·ment \ˈfiləmənt\ *n* -s [MF, fr. ML *filamentum*, fr. LL *filare* to spin + L *-mentum* -ment — more at FILE] **:** a long thin flexible object that has a small cross section **:** a fiber of great or indefinite length: as **a** (1) **:** the fine tenuous material of a spider web (2) **:** one of the two continuous cores of the fiber of silk; *also* **:** the whole fiber (3) **:** a single continuous man-made fiber produced from a liquid bath (as by extrusion through a small orifice) and used either in the form of a monofilament or in groups for textile yarns with little or no twist or for cordage — often distinguished from *staple* (4) **:** a slender barb of a down feather **b** (1) **:** a metal wire drawn very fine ⟨tungsten ~s⟩ (2) **:** a fine conductor (as of carbon or metal) that is rendered incandescent by the passage of an electric current; *specif* **:** a cathode in the form of a metal wire in an electron tube heated by current passing through — see INCANDESCENT LAMP illustration **c** (1) **:** a thin and fine elongated constituent part of a gill (2) **:** an elongated thin series of cells attached one to another or a very long cylindrical single cell (as of certain algae, fungi, and bacteria) **d :** the anther-bearing stalk of a stamen — see FLOWER illustration **e :** a body in mathematics whose transverse dimensions are negligible compared with its length

fil·a·men·ta·ry \ˌfiləˈmentərē, -n·trē, -ri\ *adj* **:** having the characteristics of a filament **:** formed by or consisting of filaments ⟨~ crystals⟩ ⟨a ~ structure⟩

filament battery *n* **:** A BATTERY

fil·a·ment·ed \ˈfiləˌmentəd\ *adj* **:** having or provided with one or more filaments

filament lamp *n* **:** a lamp containing a filament heated to incandescence

fil·a·men·tous \ˌfiləˈmentəs\ *also* **fil·a·men·tose** \ˌ≈≈ˈmen,tōs, ˈ≈≈mən-\ *adj* [*filamentous* fr. F *filamenteux*, fr. MF, fr. *filament* + *-eux* -ous; *filamentose* fr. *filament* + *-ose*] **:** resembling a filament **:** composed of filaments **:** THREADY ⟨~ algae⟩ ⟨~ fibers⟩

¹fil·amer·ican \ˌfil+\ *adj, usu cap* [*Filipino* + *American*] **:** being Filamerican ⟨a *Filamerican* soldier⟩ **:** consisting of Filamericans ⟨the *Filamerican* troops⟩

²filamerican \ˈ"\ *n, cap* **:** a Filipino with sympathetic or loyal feelings toward America

fi·lan·der \fəˈlandə(r)\ *n* -s [D, after Kornelis *Philander* de Bruyn †1726? Dutch traveler] **:** a kangaroo (*Macropus brunii*) native to the Aru islands

fi·la·ni \fəˈlänē\ *or* **fi·la·nin** \-nən\ *n, pl* **filani** *or* **filanis** *or* **fillanin** *or* **fillanins** *usu cap* **:** FULA

fi·lao \fəˈlau̇, -lä(ˌ)ō\ *n* -s [Sp, fr. Malagasy] **:** a beefwood (*Casuarina equisetifolia*) with very pendulous branches

fi·lar \ˈfīlə(r)\ *adj* [L *filum* thread + E *-ar* — more at FILE] **:** of or relating to a thread or line; *esp* **:** possessing threads across the field of view ⟨a ~ eyepiece⟩ ⟨a ~ microscope⟩

fil·a·ree \ˌfiləˈrē, ˌ≈≈ˈ≈\ *or* **fil·a·ria** \ˌ≈≈ˈrēə\ *n* -s [modif. of AmerSp *alfilerillo* — more at ALFILARIA] **:** ALFILARIA

fi·lar·ia \fəˈla(a)rēə\ *n* [NL, fr. L *filum* + NL *-aria*] **1** *pl* **filar·i·ae** \-ēˌē, -ēˌī\ **:** any of an important group of slender filamentous nematodes that as adults are parasites in the blood or tissues of mammals and as larvae usu. develop in biting insects, that belong to the Filariidae and related families, and that for the most part were once included in the genus *Filaria* and are now divided among various genera (as *Wuchereria* and *Onchocerca*) **2** *cap* **:** the type genus of Filariidae

fi·lar·i·al \fəˈla(a)rēəl\ *adj* [NL *filaria* + E *-al*] **:** of, relating to, infested with, transmitting, or caused by filariae or related parasitic worms

fil·a·ri·a·sis \ˌfiləˈrīəsəs\ *also* **fi·lar·i·o·sis** \fəˌla(a)rēˈōsəs\ *n, pl* **filaria·ses** \-īəˌsēz\ *also* **filario·ses** \-ōˌsēz\ [NL, fr. *filaria* + *-iasis* or *-osis*] **:** infestation with or disease caused by filariae — compare BANCROFTIAN FILARIASIS, ELEPHANTIASIS

fi·lar·i·at·ed \fəˈla(a)rēˌād·əd\ *adj* [NL *filaria* + E *-ate* + *-ed*] **:** marked by the presence of filariae ⟨a ~ person⟩

fi·lar·i·ci·dal \fəˌla(a)rəˈsīd³l\ *adj* [NL *filaria* + E *-cidal*] **:** destructive to filariae

fi·lar·i·cide \-ˈ≈≈,sīd\ *n* -s [NL *filaria* + E *-cide*] **:** a filaricidal agent

fi·lar·i·form \-ˌfȯrm\ *adj* [NL *filaria* + E *-form*] *of a larval nematode* **:** resembling a filaria esp. in having a slender elongated form and in possessing a delicate capillary esophagus

¹fi·lar·i·id \fəˈla(a)rēəd\ *or* **fi·lar·id** \-rəd, ˈfilərəd\ *adj* [NL *Filariidae*] **:** of or relating to Filarioidea, Filariidae, or filariae

²filariid \ˈ"\ *or* **filarid** \ˈ"\ *n* -s **:** FILARIA 1

fil·a·ri·idae \ˌfiləˈrīəˌdē\ *n pl, cap* [NL, fr. *Filaria*, type genus + *-idae*] **:** a family of nematode worms formerly

coextensive with Filarioidea and now usu. restricted to a few forms not of medical importance
fi·lar·i·oid \fə'la(a)rē,ȯid\ *adj* [NL *Filarioidea*] **:** of or relating to the Filarioidea
fi·lar·i·oi·dea \fə,la(a)rē'ȯidēə\ *n pl, cap* [NL, fr. *Filaria* + *-oidea*] **:** a large superfamily of the nematode order Spirurida that comprises the medically important filarial worms and related forms having a slender thready body, a simple anterior end with the oral lips inconspicuous, a cylindrical esophagus lacking a bulbus, and often unequal and dissimilar copulatory spicules in the male
filar micrometer *n* **:** an instrument for accurately measuring small distances or angles usu. consisting of two parallel fine platinum wires mounted in the focal plane of a microscope or telescope, one wire being fixed and the other movable by means of a finely threaded screw
fi·lasse \fə'las\ *n* -s [F, fr. OF *filace*, fr. (assumed) VL *filacea*, fr. L *filum* thread + *-acea* (fr. fem. of *-aceus* -aceous) — more at FILE] **:** vegetable fiber (as jute or ramie) prepared for manufacture
fi·late \'fī,lāt\ *adj* [L *filum* + E *-ate*] **:** slender and without appendages **:** THREADY
fil·a·ture \'filə,chu̇(ə)r, -,chər\ *n* -s [F, fr. LL *filatus* (past part. of *filare* to spin) + F *-ure* — more at FILE] **1 :** the reeling of silk from cocoons **2 :** a reel for drawing off silk from cocoons **3 :** a factory where silk is reeled
fil·beard \'fil,bird\ *dial Eng var of* FILBERT
fil·bert \'filbə(r)t, *usu* -d.+V\ *n* -s [ME *filberd, filbert*, fr. AF *philber*, after St. *Philibert* †684 Frankish abbot whose feast day (Aug. 20) falls in the nutting season] **1 a :** either of two European hazels (*Corylus avellana pontica* and *C. maxima*) **b :** the thick-shelled and sweet-flavored nut produced by the filberts and for which they are frequently cultivated **c :** HAZELNUT **2** *or* **filbert brown :** HAZEL 4 **3** *slang* **:** a person who presumes to be an expert analyst ⟨a football ~⟩
filbert blight *n* **:** a blight of the filbert caused by a bacterium (*Xanthomonas corylina*) and characterized esp. by the formation on the trunk of cankers which often girdle and kill the tree
filbert worm *n* **:** the pink or whitish larva of an olethreutid moth (*Melissopus latiferreanus*) that is a destructive borer in acorns, filberts, chestnuts, and various other nuts and fruits throughout the U.S.
1**filch** \'filch\ *vt* -ED/-ING/-ES [ME *filchen* to attack, steal, perh. fr. OE *gefylce* band of men, troop, army; akin to ON *fylki* band of men, shire, OE *folc* folk — more at FOLK] **:** to steal furtively **:** PILFER ⟨~*ed* some cigarettes⟩ **syn** see STEAL
2**filch** \"\ *n* -ES *obs* **:** a hooked staff used by thieves to snatch articles (as from windows)
1**file** \'fīl, *esp before pause or consonant* -īəl\ *n* -s [ME, fr. OE *fēol, fīl*; akin to OHG & OS *fīla* file, ON *thēl*, and prob. to Skt *piṁśati* he cuts or hacks out — more at PAINT] **1 a :** a hardened steel tool in the form of a bar or rod that has cutting ridges on its surface made by chisel cuts and that is used for forming or smoothing surfaces esp. of metal by means of the cutting or abrading action of the ridges — see BLUNT FILE, DOUBLE-CUT FILE, FLOAT-CUT FILE, MACHINE FILE, RASP, ROTARY FILE, SINGLE-CUT FILE, TAPER FILE **b :** a narrow instrument for shaping fingernails with a fine rough metal or emery surface **2 :** the corrugated part of the stridulating organ of an insect that produces sound when rubbed **3 :** a shrewd or crafty person ⟨an old ~ of a storekeeper⟩

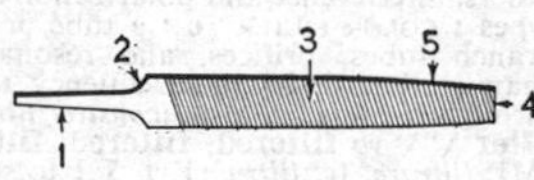

file 1a: *1* tang, *2* heel, *3* face, *4* tip, *5* edge

2**file** \"\ *vb* -ED/-ING/-S [ME *filen*, fr. OE *fēolian, fīlian*; akin to OHG *fīlōn* to file, ON *thēla*; derivative fr. the root of OE *fēol, fīl*] *vt* **1 a :** to rub, smooth, or cut with a file ⟨~ a piece of stock⟩ ⟨*filed* away the rough edges⟩ **b :** to sharpen with a file ⟨~ a saw⟩ **2 :** to refine esp. by careful revision ⟨a prose style with all ineptitudes *filed* away⟩ ~ *vi* **:** to use or work with or as if with a file
3**file** \"\ *vt* -ED/-ING/-S [ME *filen*, fr. OE *fȳlan*, fr. *fūl* foul — more at FOUL] **1** *chiefly dial* **:** DEFILE, BEFOUL **2** *chiefly dial* **:** DEBAUCH, DISHONOR
4**file** \"\ *vb* -ED/-ING/-S [ME *filen*, fr. MF *filer* to string documents on a string or wire, fr. *fil* thread, string, fr. L *filum*; akin to W *gewyn* sinew, Lith *gija* thread, *gysla* vein, sinew, Arm *jil* sinew, cord] *vt* **1 :** to arrange (as papers, cards, or letters) in a particular order for preservation and reference **2** *obs* **:** THREAD, STRING **3 a** (1) **:** to deliver (as a legal paper or instrument) after complying with any condition precedent (as the payment of a fee) to the proper officer for keeping on file or among the records of his office (2) **:** to send (newspaper copy) to a newspaper or news agency by telephone, telegraph, or cable ⟨*filed* a good story⟩ **b :** to place (as a paper or instrument) on file among the legal or official records of an office esp. by formally receiving, endorsing, and entering **c :** to return (a law case) to the office of the clerk of a court without action on the merits **d :** to fill out and submit (an income tax return) to the appropriate office **4 :** to perform the first act of (as a lawsuit) **:** COMMENCE ~ *vi* **:** to register as a candidate esp. in a primary election ⟨~ for county attorney⟩
5**file** \"\ *n* -s [MF *fil*] **1 a :** a wire or cord that documents are strung from esp. in an order devised to facilitate reference **b :** a container (as a folder or a metal cabinet) in which papers are kept usu. in chronological or alphabetical order for ready reference **2** *obs* **:** THREAD **3 a** *obs* **:** ROLL, LIST **b :** a collection of cards or papers usu. arranged or classified ⟨a ~ of newspapers⟩ ⟨a letter ~⟩ **4 :** LABEL 3
6**file** \"\ *n* -s [MF *file* row, fr. *filer* to spin, fr. LL *filare*, fr. L *filum* thread] **1 a :** a row of persons, animals, or things arranged one behind the other ⟨a ~ of infantrymen⟩ ⟨to pass in ~⟩ — compare RANK **b :** a row of squares extending vertically across a chessboard ⟨a knight's pawn may capture on the rook's or the bishop's ~⟩ **2 a :** a man in a military formation who occupies a position in a single rank **b :** a number or numerical position on the lineal list for promotion ⟨a navy ~⟩
7**file** \"\ *vi* -ED/-ING/-S [MF *filer*, fr. *file*, n.] **:** to march in a line not abreast but one after another
8**fi·lé** \fə'lā, (')fē¦lā, (')fē¦lā\ *n* -s [AmerF (Louisiana) fr. F, past part. of *filer* to twist, spin] **:** powdered young leaves of sassafras used to thicken soups or stews
9**file** \'fī(ə)l\ *n* -s [ME, perh. of Celt origin; akin to OIr *fīla* dirty fellow] *dial Eng* **:** RASCAL
10**file** \(')fī(ə)l\ *Scot var of* WHILE
11**file** \"\ *n* -s [D *feil*] *dial* **:** a cloth esp. for wiping a floor or table
1**file card** *n* [1*file*] **:** a wire brush for cleaning files
2**file card** *n* [5*file*] **:** a card of a size and shape suitable to be used in a file
file case *n* [5*file*] **:** an attaché case with a file for papers in the lid
file clerk *n* [5*file*] **:** a clerk who works on files; *esp* **:** a clerk who arranges materials or records in accordance with a particular filing system
file closer *n* [6*file*] **:** a commissioned or noncommissioned officer in the rear of a line or on the flank of a column who rectifies mistakes and ensures steadiness in the ranks
filefish \'=,=\ *n* [1*file* + *fish*] **:** any of certain fishes with rough granulated leathery skins: as **a :** TRIGGERFISH **b :** any of numerous closely related oddly shaped fishes (family Monocanthidae) differing from the triggerfishes in having the scales reduced to prickles like those of shagreen and the first dorsal fin to a single long spine
file-hard \'=¦=\ *adj* [1*file*] **:** so hard as not to be cut by a file
file holder *n* [1*file*] **:** a handle sometimes used in benchwork with clamps for attaching to the heel and point of a file and provision for springing the center of the file downward
file meristem *n* [6*file*] **:** RIB MERISTEM
file off *vi* [7*file*] **:** to march in a single file from some other formation
1**fil·er** \'fīlə(r)\ *n* -s [2*file* + *-er*] **:** one that files; *specif* **:** a worker who smooths, shapes, or sharpens with a file
2**filer** \"\ *n* -s [4*file* + *-er*] **:** one that files; *specif* **:** FILE CLERK
files *pl of* FILE, *pres 3d sing of* FILE
file shell *n* [1*file*] **:** any of a family (Limidae) of small equivalve bivalve mollusks with the yellowish or white valves closely ribbed and covered with spiny scales suggesting a rasp or file
file signal *n* [5*file*] **:** a small movable colored tab attached to a filed card or folder as a temporary indicator
file snake *n* [1*file*] **:** any of several large harmless African colubrid snakes of the genus *Mehelya* that have a steeply ridged back making them resemble a 3-cornered file
file-soft \'=¦=\ *adj* [1*file*] **:** soft enough to be readily cut by a file
1**filet** *var of* FILLET
2**fi·let** \fə'lā, 'fi(,)lā\ *also* **filet lace** *n* -s [F *filet*, lit., net, fr. OF *filé*, fr. OProv *filat* — more at FIERASFER] **:** a lace with geometric designs made by darning patterns on a square-mesh ground or by crocheting ⟨a tablecloth of fine damask and the frilly cloth of ~ —*Amer. Cookery*⟩
file-tailed rat \'=,=-\ *n* [1*file*] **:** ROUND-TAILED MUSKRAT
file-tail shark *n* [1*file*] **:** a small dark brown shark (*Parmaturus xaniurus*) of the coast of southern and Lower California having a broad crowded band of enlarged scales on the upper edge of the tail
file 13 *n* **:** WASTEBASKET
fi·let mi·gnon \,fi(,)lā(,)mēn'yōⁿ, fə,lā-, -'mēn,-\ *n, pl* **filets mignons** [F, lit., dainty fillet] **:** a fillet of beef cut from the thick end of a beef tenderloin — compare TOURNEDOS
file wrapper *n* [5*file*] **:** the written record in the patent office of negotiations between an applicant and that office preceding the issuance or rejection of a patent
file wrapper estoppel *n* **:** a doctrine in patent law that one who has acquiesced in the rejection of a broad claim in his application for a patent may not later assert that a claim deliberately more restricted is equivalent to the original claim
fi·li \'fil(y)ə\ *n, pl* **fi·li** \fi'lē\ [OIr, lit., seer; akin to W *gweled* to see — more at BULTO] **:** a poet in ancient Ireland of higher rank than a bard and belonging to a class who were also lawyers, historians, genealogists, and storytellers
fili- *comb form* [L *filum* — more at FILE] **:** thread or threads **:** something resembling thread or threads ⟨*filicauline*⟩ ⟨*filiferous*⟩
fil·ial \'filēəl *also* -lyəl\ *adj* [ME, fr. LL *filialis*, fr. L *filius* son + *-alis* -al — more at FEMININE] **1 :** of or relating to a son or daughter; *esp* **:** becoming to a child in relation to his parents ⟨~ obedience⟩ **2 :** bearing or assuming the relation of a child or offspring — **fil·ial·ly** \-ēəlē, -yəlē, -li\ *adv* — **fil·ial·ness** \-əlnəs\ *n* -ES
filial generation *n* **:** a generation in a cross successive to a parental generation — symbol F_1 for the first, F_2 for the second, etc.
fil·ial·i·ty \,filē'aləd·ē, fil'ya-\ *n* -ES [LL *filialitas*, fr. *filialis* + L *-itas* -ity] **:** the relation or attitude of a child to a parent
filial piety *n* [trans. of Chin (Pek) *hsiao*4] **:** reverence for parents considered in Chinese ethics the prime virtue and the basis of all right human relations
fil·i·ate \'filē,āt, *usu* -ād.+V\ *vt* -ED/-ING/-S [ML *fillatus*, past part. of *filiare*, fr. L *filius* son] **:** to declare (an illegitimate child) the offspring of a particular father **:** AFFILIATE
fil·i·a·tion \,filē'āshən\ *n* -s [ME *filiacioun*, fr. LL *filiation-, filiatio*, fr. L *filius* + *-ation-, -atio* -ation] **1 a :** relationship esp. of a son to his father **b :** the relationship between a parent and a child whether legitimate or illegitimate **2 :** one that is derived from a parent or source **:** OFFSHOOT ⟨~*s* from a common stock⟩ **3 a :** the act or action of determining relationship ⟨a scholar's careful ~ of manuscripts⟩ **b :** adjudication of paternity **:** AFFILIATION **4 :** descent from or as if from a parent ⟨to determine the ~ of a language⟩ **5 :** the formation of branches or offshoots
filibeg *var of* FILLEBEG
fil·i·bran·chia \,filə'braŋkēə\ *n pl, cap* [NL, fr. *fili-* + *-branchia*] **:** an order of Lamellibranchia that comprises marine bivalve mollusks having two pairs of laminated gills formed of distinct V-shaped filaments with interfilamentary junctions either absent or formed by groups of interlocking cilia and nonvascular and that includes mussels, ark shells, and scallops — **fil·i·bran·chi·ate** \¦=¦=¦=kēət, -ē,āt\ *adj*
fil·i·branchiata \¦filə+\ [NL *fili-* + *Branchiata*] *syn of* FILIBRANCHIA
1**fil·i·bus·ter** \'filəbəstə(r)\ *n* -s [Sp *filibustero*, lit., freebooter, prob. fr. F *flibustier, fribustier*, fr. E *fleebooter, freebooter* — more at FREEBOOTER] **1 a :** an American who in the mid-19th century took part in fomenting revolutions and insurrections in a Latin-American country **b :** an irregular military adventurer; *specif* **:** an organizer or member of a hostile expedition to a country with which his own is at peace **2** [2*filibuster*] **a :** the use of extreme dilatory tactics (as speaking merely to consume time) by an individual or group in an attempt to delay or prevent action by the majority in a legislative or deliberative assembly; *also* **:** an instance of this ⟨~*s* are most often associated . . . with proceedings in the U.S. Senate —H.D.Scott⟩ ⟨a Communist ~ designed to prevent passage of a new Italian electoral law —*Springfield (Mass.) Union*⟩ **b :** FILIBUSTERER
2**filibuster** \", ,=¦=¦=\ *vb* **filibustered; filibustered; filibustering** \-t(ə)riŋ\ **filibusters** *vi* **1 :** to carry out insurrectionist or revolutionary activities esp. in a foreign country **2 :** to engage in a filibuster ⟨he had ~*ed* for 22 hours and 26 minutes without leaving the Senate floor —*Time*⟩ ~ *vt* **:** to subject to filibustering ⟨any . . . proposal to alter the rules could be ~*ed* —P.H.Douglas⟩
fil·i·bus·ter·er \-tərə(r)\ *n* -s **:** one that filibusters
fil·i·bus·ter·ism \-tə,rizəm, ,=¦=¦=,=\ *n* -s **:** the practice of filibustering
fil·i·cal \'filəkəl\ *adj* [NL *Filicales*] **:** of or relating to the order Filicales
fil·i·ca·les \,filə'kā(,)lēz\ *n pl, cap* [NL, fr. *Filic-, Filix* + *-ales*] **:** an order of herbaceous, arborescent, or occas. climbing plants (class Filicineae) that comprise the true ferns, that are characterized by exstipulate fronds, leptosporangiate sporangial development, and small thin-walled sporangia which are usu. borne in sori on the undersides of the fronds, and that have a characteristic ring of thick-walled cells which assists in dehiscence of the spores — compare FERN ALLY, PTERIDOPHYTA
fili·cauline \¦filə, ¦fīlə+\ *adj* [*fili-* + *cauline*] **:** having a filamentous stem
fil·i·ces \'filə,sēz\ [NL, fr. *Filic-, Filix*] *syn of* FILICALES
fi·lic·ic acid \fə'lisik-\ *n* [ISV *filic-* (fr. NL *Filic-, Filix*) + *-ic*] **:** a phenolic anthelmintic substance that is obtained as a colorless powder from the rhizome of the common male fern
fil·i·ci·dal \¦filə¦sīdᵊl\ *adj* **:** of or relating to filicide
fil·i·cide \'filə,sīd\ *n* -s [L *filius* son & *filia* daughter + E *-cide* — more at FEMININE] **:** the murdering of a son or daughter; *also* **:** the parent who commits such a murder
fi·lic·i·form \fə'lisə,fȯrm\ *adj* [L *filic-, filix* fern + E *-iform*] **:** shaped like a fern or fern frond
fil·i·cin \'filəsən\ *n* -s [ISV *filic-* (fr. NL *Filic-, Filix*) + *-in*] **:** FILICIC ACID; *also* **:** the mixture of active principles obtained in the chemical assay of the male fern
fil·i·ci·nae \,filə'sī,nē\ *syn of* FILICINEAE
fil·i·cin·e·ae \,filə'sinē,ē\ *n pl, cap* [NL, fr. *Filic-, Filix* + *-ineae*] **1 :** a class of Pteropsida comprising plants (as the typical ferns) that produce no seeds and have large often complex leaves, sperms which must be transported by water, and well-developed alternation of generation usu. with independent gametophytes and sporophytes which often differ radically in size and form and including the orders Marattiales, Ophioglossales, and Filicales with living representatives and the extinct order Coenopteridales — compare ANGIOSPERMAE, GYMNOSPERMAE **2** *in some classifications* **:** a class or other group coextensive with Filicales — **fil·i·cin·e·an** \¦filə¦sinēən\ *adj*
fil·i·cite \'filə,sīt\ *n* -s [ISV *filic-* (fr. L *filic-, filix* fern) + *-ite*] **:** a fossil fern
fil·i·ci·tes \,=¦=¦sīd·(,)ēz\ *n pl, cap* [NL, fr. ISV *filicite*] *in former classifications* **:** a group including all fossil ferns
fil·i·col·o·gy \,filə'käləjē\ *n* -ES [L *filic-, filix* fern + E *-o-* + *-logy*] **:** PTERIDOLOGY
fil·i·cor·nia \-'kȯ(r)nēə\ [NL, fr. *fili-* + L *cornu* horn + NL *-ia* — more at HORN] *syn of* ADEPHAGA
fi·lif·er·ous \(')fī¦lif(ə)rəs, fə'l-\ *adj* [*fili-* + *-ferous*] **:** bearing threads
1**fil·i·form** \'filə,fȯrm, 'fīl-\ *adj* [*fili-* + *-form*] **:** having the shape of a thread or filament ⟨a ~ peduncle⟩ — see ANTENNA illustration
2**filiform** \"\ *n* -s **:** an extremely slender bougie
filiform apparatus *n* **:** a prolongation of the synergids beyond the summit of the embryo sac
fili·formed \'=,=-md\ *adj* [*fili-* + *formed*] **:** FILIFORM
filiform papilla *n* **:** any of numerous minute pointed papillae on the tongue
fi·lig·er·ous \(')fī¦lijərəs, fə'l-\ *adj* [*fili-* + *-gerous*] **:** FLAGELLATE
fil·i·grain *also* **fil·i·grane** \'filə,grān\ *n* -s [F *filigrane*] **:** FILIGREE — **fil·i·grained** \-nd\ *adj*
1**fil·i·gree** *also* **fil·a·gree** \'filə,grē\ *n* -s *often attrib* [short for earlier *filigreen, filagreen*, modif. of F *filigrane*, fr. It *filigrana*, fr. *fili-* (fr. L *filum* thread) + *grana* grain, fr. L, pl. of *granum* grain — more at FILE, CORN] **1 :** ornamental work formerly with grains or beads but now esp. of fine wire of gold, silver, or copper that is used chiefly to decorate gold and silver surfaces **2 a :** ornamental openwork of delicate or intricate design **b :** a pattern or design resembling such openwork

filigree 2a

2**filigree** \"\ *vt* **filigreed; filigreed; filigreeing; filigrees** **:** to adorn with or as if with filigree
1**filing** *n* -s [ME, fr. gerund of *filen* to file — more at FILE] **1 :** an act or instance of using a file (as for abrading or smoothing) **2 :** a fragment or particle rubbed off in filing ⟨iron ~*s*⟩
2**filing** *n* -s [fr. gerund of 4*file*] **:** preservation and methodical arrangement (as of documents, papers, letters) ⟨a ~ system⟩ ⟨a ~ card⟩ ⟨have some ~ to do⟩
fil·io·pietistic \¦filē(,)ō+\ *adj* [L *filius* son + E *-o-* + *pietistic* — more at FEMININE] **:** of or relating to an often excessive veneration of ancestors or tradition
filip *var of* FILLIP
fil·i·pen·du·la \,filə'penjələ, -nd(y)ələ\ *n* [NL, fr. *fili-* + L *pendula*, fem. of *pendulus* hanging — more at PENDULOUS] **1** *cap* **:** a small genus of perennial herbs (family Rosaceae) of north temperate regions with pinnately divided leaves and small white or pink flowers in cymose panicles **2** -s **:** any plant of the genus *Filipendula*
fil·i·pen·du·lous \¦=¦=¦=ləs\ *adj* [*fili-* + *pendulous*] **:** suspended by or strung upon a thread
fil·i·pi·na \,filə'pēnə\ *n* -s *cap* [Sp, fem. of *filipino*] **:** a female Filipino
fil·i·pi·ni·za·tion \,filə,pēnə'zāshən\ *n* -s *usu cap* **:** the act of Filipinizing **:** the condition of being Filipinized
fil·i·pi·nize \,=¦=¦pē,nīz, '=,=,=\ *vt* -ED/-ING/-S *usu cap* **:** to provide with personnel preponderantly or totally Filipino ⟨*Filipinized* the police force⟩
1**fil·i·pi·no** \,filə'pē(,)nō\ *n* -s *cap* [Sp, adj. & n., fr. (*Islas*) *Filipinas* Philippine islands] **1 :** a native of the Philippine islands; *specif* **:** a member of a Christianized Philippine people as distinguished from a member of a people predominantly pagan or Muslim **2 :** a citizen of the Republic of the Philippines
2**filipino** \¦=¦=(,)=\ *adj, usu cap* [Sp] **1 :** of, relating to, or characteristic of the Filipinos **2 :** of, relating to, or characteristic of the Philippines **:** PHILIPPINE
fi·li·us nul·li·us \¦fēlēəsnə'lēəs, -'snülēəs\ *n, pl* **fi·lii nullius** \¦fēlē,ēnə'l-, -ē,ē'nül-\ [L, nobody's son] **:** an illegitimate child **:** BASTARD
filius po·pu·li \¦fēlēə'spȯpə,lē\ *n, pl* **fi·lii populi** \¦fēlē,ē'pȯ-\ [L, son of the people] **:** FILIUS NULLIUS
fi·lix \'fīliks, 'fil-\ [NL, fr. L, fern] *syn of* CYSTOPTERIS
fi·lix-mas \¦fīlik'smas, ¦filik'smäs\ *n* -ES [NL *filix mas* male fern] **:** ASPIDIUM 2
1**fill** \'fil\ *vb* -ED/-ING/-S [ME *fillen*, fr. OE *fyllan*; akin to OHG *fullen* to fill, ON *fylla*, Goth *fulljan*; causative fr. the root of E 1*full*] *vt* **1 a** (1) **:** to supply with as much as can be held or contained ⟨*filling* the holes in the road⟩ (2) **:** to place or put as much material in as can be often conveniently contained ⟨~ a box⟩ **:** pour as much of a substance into as can be often conveniently held ⟨~ a cup⟩ ⟨~ a barrel with apples⟩ (3) **:** to furnish (as a container) esp. in proportion **:** PROVIDE ⟨~ a glass with water⟩ ⟨~ a page with print⟩ (4) **:** to provide (as a container) with a specified amount ⟨~ it half full⟩ (5) **:** POUR ⟨~ wine into bottles⟩ **:** LOAD, PUT ⟨~ coal into bins⟩ (6) **:** to make full or complete (as a partly empty line or an incomplete column in printed matter) by respacing the existing printed matter or by adding matter (7) **:** to give a pleasingly full form to (as a dress) in wearing — often used with *out* ⟨she ~*ed* the dress nicely⟩ ⟨he began to ~ his suits out well as he grew older⟩ **b** (1) **:** to stop up **:** OBSTRUCT ⟨wreckage ~*ed* the channel⟩ — often used with *up* ⟨the traffic jam *filled* the street up completely⟩ (2) **:** to make an embankment in or raise the level of (a low place) with earth, gravel, or rock **c** (1) **:** PLUG ⟨~ a chink⟩ **:** CAULK ⟨~ the seams with oakum⟩ (2) **:** to stop up the interstices, crevices, or pores of (as cloth, wood, leather) with some foreign substance for the sake of hardening, dressing, or adulterating (3) **:** LOAD 3c(1) (4) **:** to close up (a cavity in a tooth) with gold, silver, or other comparatively inert material **d** *obs* **:** IMPREGNATE **e** (1) **:** to feed and water (livestock) immediately before sale to increase the apparent weight (2) **:** to stuff (a food) with a filling ⟨~*ed* rolls⟩ **2 a :** to occupy the whole of ⟨his huge bulk ~*ed* the chair⟩ **b :** to swarm in **:** PERVADE ⟨shoppers ~*ed* the city⟩ **c** (1) **:** PACK, LOAD, SURFEIT ⟨her presence ~*ed* his heart with joy⟩ ⟨~*ed* his head with foolish ideas⟩ (2) **:** SATISFY, SATIATE ⟨~ their guest with good food⟩ (3) **:** to belly out **:** DISTEND — often used with *out* ⟨the wind ~*ed* the sails out⟩ **d** (1) **:** to supply fully or completely ⟨~ a long-felt want⟩ (2) **:** STOCK ⟨~ a stream with trout⟩ **3 a :** to execute or fulfill the requirements of (a business order) **b :** to complete or make out — often used with *out* ⟨~ out a check⟩ or *up* ⟨~ up the blanks in a questionnaire⟩ or *in* ⟨~ in the tax form⟩ **c :** to make up (a prescription) **4 a :** OCCUPY, HOLD ⟨~ a throne⟩ **b :** to provide with incumbents ⟨~ vacancies left by retirements⟩ — often used with *up* **c :** to possess and perform the duties of ⟨~ an office⟩ **5 :** to trim (a sail) so that the wind will blow on the after side **6 :** to cover the surface of with a layer of precious metal — used chiefly as a past participle ⟨a gold-*filled* watch⟩ **7 :** to draw the cards in poker necessary to complete (a full house, a flush, or a straight) ~ *vi* **1 a** (1) **:** to become full ⟨the rivers ~*ed*⟩ (2) *of the eyes* **:** to become full with tears (3) **:** to become so suffused with ink (as of the bowl of a letter or the space between the dots of a halftone) as to print improperly — often used with *in* or *up* **b :** to have the whole capacity occupied ⟨the stadium ~*ed* and overflowed⟩ **c :** to fill a cup or glass for drinking **2 a :** to become blocked, burdened, or obstructed by or as if by accumulations — often used with *in* ⟨the harbor gradually ~*ed* in⟩ or *up* ⟨the channel ~*ed* up⟩ **b** (1) **:** to become heavy, choked, or fraught ⟨his heart ~*ed* at the words⟩ ⟨their expressions ~*ed* with grief⟩ (2) **:** to swell out in or as if in fullness ⟨the sails ~*ed* with wind⟩ ⟨her body began to ~ out⟩ ⟨the balloon ~*ed* up⟩ **3 :** to complete a full house, flush, or straight in poker — **fill one's shoes :** to take one's place **:** take over one's job or position and usu. handle its duties or responsibilities satisfactorily — **fill the bill :** to answer a need **:** serve the purpose usu. satisfactorily
2**fill** \"\ *n* -s [ME *fille*, fr. OE *fyllo*; akin to OHG *fulli* fill, abundance, ON *fyllr*, Goth *ufarfullei* great abundance; derivative fr. the root of E 1*full*] **1 :** a full supply; *esp* **:** a quantity that satisfies or satiates — usu. used with a possessive ⟨eat your ~⟩ ⟨she wept her ~⟩ **2 a** (1) **:** material used to fill a receptacle, cavity, or passage ⟨~ for a trench⟩ — see BACKFILL; compare GOB (2) **:** an embankment (as in railroad construction) to fill a hollow or ravine or the place filled by such an embankment; *also* **:** the depth of the filling material when in place (3) **:** material that is used to take up unused or unoccupied periods (as in a radio or television schedule) **b :** the

contents of the digestive tract of an animal **3 :** the maximum width of the paper producible by a particular papermaking machine

³fill \"\ *n* -s [by alter.] *chiefly dial* **:** THILL

fillanin *usu cap, var of* FILANI

fill away *vi* **1 :** to trim a sail so that it will catch the wind full **2 :** to proceed on the course esp. after being brought up in the wind ⟨the fleet had . . . begun to *fill away* on a northerly course —S.E.Morison⟩

fill cap *n* **:** a metal cap screwed on the top of the pipe through which a fuel-oil tank is filled

fill-dike \ˈ=,=\ *n* **:** FEBRUARY FILL-DIKE

fil·le·beg *or* **fil·i·beg** *or* **fil·a·beg** *or* **phil·a·beg** *or* **phil·i·beg** \ˈfilə,beg, ˈfēl-\ *n* -s [ScGael *fēile-beag*, fr. *fēileadh* kilt + *beag* little; akin to OIr *becc, bec* small, W *bach*] **:** KILT

filled *past of* FILL

filled board *n* **:** a board or paper made on a cylinder machine in which the inner layers differ in material from the outer layers

filled cheese *n* **:** a product made from whole or skim milk enriched by the addition of foreign fatty material

fille de joie \ˌfēdəˈzhwä\ *n, pl* **filles de joie** \"\ [F, lit., pleasure girl] **:** PROSTITUTE

filled milk *n* **:** skim milk enriched in fat content by the addition of vegetable oils

filled soap *n* **:** a soap from which the water and glycerol have not been removed by salting out or to which an adulterant that is not necessarily an inactive one has been added

¹fill·er \ˈfilə(r)\ *n* -s [¹*fill* + *-er*] **1 a :** something that fills: as (1) **:** a substance added to a product to increase the bulk or weight of the product (as in the case of wood flour added to a plastic) or to dilute expensive materials and often also to improve the product (as in its mechanical or electrical properties) **:** EXTENDER — compare DILUENT (2) **:** any inert material or one containing little plant food that is added to commercial fertilizers or pest-control chemicals to secure the weight or bulk needed to give the desired composition or physical condition (3) **:** a composition (as of powdered silica and oil) used to fill the pores and grain of a wood or other surface before paint or varnish is applied (4) **:** mineral matter (as clay, talc, or titanium dioxide) that is added to paper in papermaking (as in the beater) to increase opacity and improve printing quality (5) **:** asphalt, cement, or coal-tar pitch used to fill the joints of brick and stone-block pavements (6) **:** dry limestone dust, dust from another appropriate stone, or portland cement used in the surface mixture of sheet-asphalt pavement (7) **:** a plate or other piece used to cover or fill in a space between two parts of a structure **b** (1) **:** a standing tree or standard higher than the surrounding coppice — usu. used in pl. (2) **:** any rapidly growing plant used to occupy idle space in a permanent planting; *esp* **:** an early maturing variety in orcharding planted between the regular units (3) **:** a stream that fills a lake **c** (1) **:** tobacco used to add bulk to cigarettes without modifying their flavor or to form the bulk of plugs and twists; *esp* **:** tobacco used to form the core of a cigar — compare BINDER, WRAPPER (2) **:** filling for a pie or a layer cake **d** (1) **:** copy used primarily to fill extra space in a column or page of a newspaper or periodical; *esp* **:** a brief item of fact (as from a reference book) appearing in a newspaper ⟨a ~ from an encyclopedia⟩ (2) **:** paper used in a loose-leaf notebook (3) **:** the inner layer or layers of a filled board **e** (1) **:** a worker who fills pillows, comforters, cushions (2) **:** a worker who puts rags and chemicals into a boiler that will clean and bleach the rags for use in papermaking (3) **:** BACKFILLER (4) **:** a worker who fills and tests aircraft inclinometers **f** (1) **:** a light form made often of wood and placed in a shoe to maintain its shape while on display **:** material used to fill the space between the outsole and the insole of a shoe (2) **:** a device or implement (as a funnel, pipe, or syringe) that supplies or conducts the filling material to its receptacle ⟨a fountain pen ~⟩ **g :** a card (as a ten or nine) that adds to the strength of a hand in bridge but is not recognized by a given method of evaluating the hand's strength **:** INTERMEDIATE **2 :** a worker who measures marble blocks, marks them for cutting, and verifies their measurements after cutting

²fill·er \"\ *n* -s [³*fill* + *-er*] *now dial* **:** THILL HORSE

³fil·ler \ˈfi,le(ə)r, -eə\ *n, pl* **fillers** *or* **filler** [Hung *fillér*] **1 :** a Hungarian unit of value worth before 1925 $^1/_{100}$ korona, from 1925 to 1946 $^1/_{100}$ pengő, after 1946 $^1/_{100}$ forint — see MONEY table **2 :** a coin representing one filler

filler-in \ˌ=ˈ=\ *n, pl* **fillers-in** [*fill in* + *-er*] **1 :** one that fills in (as colors, designs, materials); *specif* **:** one that paints designs on pottery or porcelain by hand **2 :** one that substitutes

filler man *n* **:** a tobacco worker who places filler leaves on trays so that air can circulate among them and dry them to the proper moisture content for use in cigars

filler vase *n* **:** a funnel-shaped vase with a small handle near the top esp. characteristic of Minoan potters

¹fil·let \ˈfilət, *usu* -əd·+V; *in sense 2e* " *or like* FILET\ *also* **fi·let** \fəˈlā, ˈfi(,)lā\ *n* -s [ME *filet*, fr. MF *filet*, dim. of *fil* thread — more at FILE] **1 :** a narrow strip of ornamental material (as a ribbon for a woman's hair or a border or edging of a painting) **2 :** a thin narrow strip of any material: as **a :** a narrow strip of card clothing **b :** a strip of metal from which coin blanks are punched **c :** a scantling smaller than a batten **d :** a band of fibers; *specif* **:** LEMNISCUS **e** [F *filet*, fr. MF] **:** a piece or slice of boneless meat or fish; *specif* **:** the tenderloin of beef — compare FILET MIGNON **3 a :** a concavely curved section at the angle formed by the junction of two surfaces **:** a rounded inside corner; *also* **:** a strip fitted into the angle of such a junction or corner to form a concave section **b :** a fairing member of metal, wood, or fabric employed to promote smooth airflow at an internal angle produced by the juncture of two surfaces on an aircraft **c :** a bead of cementing material placed along a joint formed by two parts or pieces to strengthen the joint or make it watertight **4 :** a narrow flat member: **a :** a flat molding separating other moldings **:** REGLET — see BASE illustration **b :** the space between two flutings in a shaft **5 a :** a metal wheel for impressing designs on book covers — called also *roulette* **b :** the plain line or repetitive design in blind or gold rolled on a book by a fillet

fillet 1

²fillet \"\ *vt* -ED/-ING/-S **1 :** to bind, furnish, or adorn with or as if with a fillet **2 :** to round off (a corner, hollow, or reentrant angle) with a fillet **3 a :** to cut into fillets **b :** to treat as a fillet

fil·let·er \ˈfilәd·ә(r), fәˈlāә(r)\ *n* -s **:** one that fillets; *specif* **:** one that slices fillets from the sides of fish

fillet gauge *n* **:** a gauge for gauging convex or concave surfaces

filleting *n* -s **1 :** the protecting of a joint (as between roof and parapet wall) with mortar or cement where flashing is sometimes used **2 :** FILLETS; *also* **:** the material used for fillets

fillet weld *n* **:** a weld of approximately triangular section external to the pieces being welded

fill in *vt* **1 :** INSERT ⟨*fill in* figures⟩ **2 :** to enrich (as a design) with detail **3 :** to give (a person) lacking, necessary, or recently acquired information — often used with *on* ⟨his friend *filled* him *in* on the details⟩ **~** *vi* **:** to fill a vacancy usu. temporarily **:** SUBSTITUTE ⟨when I am called on to *fill in* in an emergency —Milton Cross⟩

fill-in \ˈ=,=\ *n* -s [*fill in*] **1 :** something that fills in: as **a** (1) **:** an insert esp. in the low neckline of a woman's dress or blouse (2) **:** an insertion made of a name, address, date, or salutation in a form or letter already printed **b** (1) **:** goods purchased to replenish stock **:** REPLACEMENTS (2) **:** mechandise purchased to supplement a line or assortment of goods in stock or substituted for an advertised article that is out of stock (3) **:** an order to replenish or complete stock or an assortment on hand **c :** written or typewritten matter inserted in blank spaces left for the purpose (as in printed or mimeographed forms or form letters) **2 :** a person who fills another's place

filling *n* -s [ME, fr. gerund of *fillen* to fill — more at FILL] **1 :** an act or instance of filling ⟨the ~ of bottles⟩ ⟨the ~ of an order⟩ **2 :** something used to fill a cavity, container, or depression **:** FILLER, FILL **3 :** something that completes or rounds off: as **a** (1) **:** the yarn interlacing the warp at right angles in the weaving of fabrics; *also* **:** yarn for the shuttle (2) **:** a pattern of fancy stitches used to cover or complete the open spaces in embroidery and lace designs **b :** a sweet or savory food mixture used to fill pastry, cake, or sandwiches **c :** ¹FILLER 1a(4) **4 :** simple sporadic lymphangitis of the leg of a horse commonly due to overfeeding and underexercising

filling fork *n* **:** a loom feeler that actuates a stop motion when filling yarn breaks or is not properly laid

filling knitting *n* **:** WEFT KNITTING

filling notch *or* **filling slot** *n* **:** an opening cut into the shoulders of a ball bearing to permit introduction of the balls

filling point *n* **:** the level in a liquid container (as a bottle) up to which it is usu. filled or at which it has its nominal capacity

filling station *n* **:** a retail station for servicing automobiles and other motor vehicles esp. with gasoline and oil

fill-in light *also* **fill light** *n* **:** a light used in photography to illuminate the deep shadows caused by the main light

fill-in test *n* **:** COMPLETION TEST

¹fil·lip *also* **fil·ip** \ˈfiləp\ *n* -s [prob. of imit. origin] **1 a :** a blow or gesture made by the sudden forcible straightening of a finger curled up against the thumb **b :** a short smart blow **:** BUFFET ⟨giving her a . . . ~ on the shoulder with his heavy gloves —Glenway Wescott⟩ **2 a :** something added that tends to arouse or excite ⟨the Declaration of Independence gave a brief ~ to patriotism but only for a short period —S.E.Morison & H.S.Commager⟩ **b :** a stimulating or rousing agent ⟨businessmen . . . cannot see where the next big ~ for business will come from —*Newsweek*⟩ **3 :** a trivial addition **:** a minor embellishment ⟨quite necessary adjuncts instead of merely extra ~s —Lois Long⟩

²fillip \"\ *vt* -ED/-ING/-S **1 a :** to strike by holding the nail of a finger against the ball of the thumb and then suddenly releasing it from that position **b :** to make a filliping motion with ⟨the man ~*ed* his fingers toward his accuser —S.H. Adams⟩ **2 :** to project quickly by or as if by a fillip **:** SNAP ⟨~*ed* crumbs off the table⟩ **3 :** to urge on **:** STIMULATE ⟨with this to ~ his spirits —Robert Westerby⟩

fil·li·peen \ˈfilə,pēn, ,==ˈ=\ *or* **fil·li·peen·er** \-nə(r)\ *n* -s [by alter.] **:** PHILOPENA

fil·lis·ter \ˈfiləstə(r)\ *n* -s [origin unknown] **:** an adjustable rabbet plane; *also* **:** a rabbet esp. on the outer edge of a window-sash bar)

fillister head *or* **fillister screwhead** *n* **:** a slotted cylindrical screwhead with a convex or flat top

fillmass \ˈ=,=\ *n* [¹*fill* + *mass*; trans. of G *füllmasse*] **:** massecuite used esp. in beet-sugar making

fill out *vt* **:** to make (as an account or report) more complete or more substantial by amplifying or expanding matter already touched on or by giving additional pertinent details ⟨*filled* his story of the battle *out* by reporting the reactions of both officers and men⟩

fil·low·ite \ˈfilə,wīt\ *n* -s [A. N. *Fillow*, 19th cent. Am. mine owner + E *-ite*] **:** a mineral $H_2Na_6(Mn,Fe,Ca)_{14}(PO_4)_{12}.H_2O(?)$ consisting of a brown, yellow, or colorless hydrous phosphate of manganese, iron, sodium, and other metals

fills *pres 3d sing of* FILL, *pl of* FILL

fill-up \ˈ=,=\ *n* -s [fr. *fill up*, v.] **:** something that fills up **:** FILLER, FILL

fil·ly \ˈfilē, -li\ *n* -ES [ME *fyly*, fr. ON *fylja*; akin to OHG *fuli* foal, ON *foli* — more at FOAL] **1 :** a young female horse usu. of less than four years **2 :** a young woman **:** GIRL ⟨the attempts of a middle-aged gentleman to keep up with a ~ half his age —John McCarten⟩

¹film \ˈfilm, ˈfiụm, *dial or substand* ˈfiləm\ *n* -s *often attrib* [ME *filme*, fr. OE *filmen, fylmen*; akin to OFris *filmene* skin, Gk *pelma* sole of the foot, OE *fell* skin — more at FELL] **1 a :** a thin skin **:** a membranous covering **:** PELLICLE **b :** a pathological growth on or in the eye **2 a :** HAZE, MIST **b :** a thin covering or coating or veil **3 a** (1) **:** an exceedingly thin layer **:** LAMINA ⟨a ~ of soil⟩ ⟨a coal ~⟩ (2) **:** a split sheet of mica 0.001 to 0.009 inch thick — usu. used in pl. **b** (1) **:** a thin often flexible transparent sheet (as of cellophane, polyethylene, rubber, or an adhesive) used esp. as a wrapping or packaging material (2) **:** a thin flexible transparent sheet of cellulose acetate, cellulose nitrate, or other plastic material that is used for taking photographs and that is coated with a light-sensitive emulsion which when exposed and developed contains negative or positive images in black silver or in color **4 :** MOTION PICTURE ⟨a ~ of the life of our first president⟩ ⟨~ coverage of a sporting event⟩ **5 :** FILM COLOR

²film \"\ *vb* -ED/-ING/-S *vt* **1 :** to cover with or as if with a film **2 a :** to make a motion picture of ⟨~ a scene⟩ **b :** to make a motion picture from a scenario based upon ⟨~ a novel⟩ **~** *vi* **1 :** to become covered or obscured with or as if with a film **2 a :** to be suitable for photographing ⟨she ~*s* well⟩ **b :** to make a motion picture

film·able \-məbəl\ *adj* **:** suitable for being filmed or adapted to motion pictures ⟨~ novels and plays —Andrew Buchanan⟩ ⟨of all the novelists of his day . . . the most ~ —Stanley Kauffmann⟩

film badge *n* **:** a dosimeter of photographic film

film base *n* **:** BASE 2d(1)

film clip *n* **:** a strip of motion-picture film; *specif* **:** one inserted in a live telecast

film color *n* **:** a vague soft smooth expanse of color (as seen when the eyes are closed or when looking at certain kinds of sky) that appears as nontransparent, not on the surface of an object, and at no definite distance; *broadly* **:** a colored expanse of soft texture

film cutout *n* **:** a thin insulating film that breaks down when a series filament street lamp fails and that short-circuits the lamp so as not to interrupt the service elsewhere

film·dom \ˈfilmdəm, ˈfiụmd-\ *n* -s **1 :** the motion-picture industry **2 :** the personnel of the motion-picture industry

film·er \-mə(r)\ *n* -s **:** one that films

film gate *n* **:** a portion of a motion-picture mechanism which positions the film while it remains stationary or passes before the aperture

filmgoer \ˈ=,==\ *n* **:** one that goes to see motion pictures ⟨weekly ~*s* —*Irish Digest*⟩ ⟨inveterate ~*s* —George Woodcock⟩

film holder *n* **:** a lighttight container for photographic film

film·ic \-mik\ *adj* **:** of, relating to, resembling, or having the characteristics of motion pictures — **film·i·cal·ly** *adv*

film·i·ly \-məlē, -li\ *adv* **:** in a filmy manner

film·i·ness \-mēnəs, -min-\ *n* -ES **:** the quality or state of being filmy ⟨pleased by the ~ of the dress material⟩

film·iza·tion \,filməˈzāshən, ,fiụm-\ *n* -s **:** an adaptation (as of a novel or play) for motion pictures

film·ize \ˈfil,mīz, ˈfiụ,-\ *vt* -ED/-ING/-S **:** CINEMATIZE

filmland \ˈ=,=\ *n* **:** FILMDOM

filmlike \ˈ=,=\ *adj* **:** FILMY

film pack *n* **:** a flat package of sheet films for daylight loading with each film being attached to a paper tab by which after exposure it is withdrawn from the front and moved to the back of the package

film phonograph *n* **:** a phonograph for playing only the sound recording on a photographic or magnetic film

film pickup *n* **:** the transmission by television of events outside the studio or of motion pictures

film play *n* **:** MOTION PICTURE

film recorder *n* **:** a recorder of sound on a photographic or magnetic film

filmslide \ˈ=,=\ *n* **:** a photographic transparency for projection consisting of a small piece of film mounted between two clear glass plates or cardboard masks

filmstrip \ˈ=,=\ *n* **:** a strip of film usu. 35 millimeters wide bearing photographs, diagrams, or printed or other graphic matter intended for still projection ⟨~*s*, recordings, maps . . . were used —Joeseph Alessandro⟩ — called also *slidefilm, stripfilm*

filmwright \ˈ=,=\ *n* **:** one who writes the script for a motion picture

filmy \ˈfilmē, ˈfiụmē, -mi\ *adj* -ER/-EST **1 a :** light, transparent, and fluffy ⟨the ~ seeds of dandelions⟩ **:** GAUZY ⟨~ curtains⟩ **b :** TENUOUS, SLIGHT ⟨a ~ vesture of rhythm —*Sewanee Rev.*⟩ **2 a :** covered with haze **:** slightly misty ⟨a ~ sky⟩ **b :** GLAZED, GLASSY ⟨~ eyes⟩

film yeast *n* **:** FLOR

filmy fern *or* **film fern** *n* **1 :** a fern of the family Hymenophyllaceae **2 :** BRISTLE FERN

filo·plume \ˈfilə,plüm, ˈfī-\ *n* [L *filum* thread + E *-o-* + *plume* — more at FILE] **:** a hairlike feather; *specif* **:** a feather with a slender scape and with but few barbs

fil·o·po·di·um \,=ˈpōdēəm\ *also* **fil·o·pod** \ˈ==,päd\ *n, pl* **filopo·dia** \-ōdēə\ *also* **filopods** [NL, fr. *filo-* (fr. L *filum*) + *-podium*] *zool* **:** a filamentous chiefly ectoplasmic pseudopodium typical of testaceous rhizopods

fi·lose \ˈfī,lōs\ *adj* [L *filum* + E *-ose*] **1 :** FILAMENTOUS **2 :** terminating in a threadlike process

fil·o·selle \ˌfiləˌsel, -ˌzel\ *n* -s [F, silk floss, filoselle, fr. MF, fr. OIt (dial.) *filosello* silkworm cocoon, silk floss, modif. (influenced by *filo* thread, fr. L *filum*) of (assumed) VL *follicellus*, alter. of L *folliculus* small bag, husk, pod — more at FILE, FOLLICLE] **:** soft silk thread for embroidery

filo silk \ˈfī(,)lō-, ˈfē\ *n* [*filoselle* + *silk*] **:** FILOSELLE

fils \ˈfils, ˈfēls\ *also* **fil** \ˈfil\ *n, pl* **fils** [Ar *fils, fals*] **1 :** a unit of value equal to $^1/_{1000}$ dinar (as in Bahrain, Iraq, Jordan, Kuwait, Southern Yemen) or $^1/_{1000}$ dirham (United Arab Emirates) — see MONEY table **2 :** a coin representing one fils

¹fil·ter \ˈfiltə(r)\ *n* -s *often attrib* [ME *filtre*, fr. ML *filtrum* felt, piece of felt used for straining liquids, of Gmc origin; akin to OS *filt* felt — more at FELT] **1 :** a porous article or mass (as of cloth, paper, or sand) that serves as a medium for separating from a liquid or gas passed through it matter held in suspension or dissolved impurities or coloring matter: as **a :** a circular piece of filter paper folded twice or fluted to fit a conical funnel or used flat (as in a Büchner funnel) esp. for laboratory filtrations **b** *also* **filter candle :** a candle-shaped hollow cylinder closed at one end and made of diatomite or unglazed porcelain with minute pores that prevent the passage of cells or bacteria and other microscopic organisms but not of ultramicroscopic bodies (as the filterable viruses) **2 a :** an apparatus (as a tube or tank) containing a filter medium and operating by gravity, pressure, or vacuum **b :** TRICKLING FILTER **3 :** a device or material for suppressing or minimizing waves or oscillations of certain frequencies passing through it without greatly altering the intensity of others: **a :** a combination of capacitors and inductors in an electric circuit that transmits only frequencies within a selected band — called also *band-pass filter;* see HIGH-PASS FILTER, LOW-PASS FILTER **b :** a transparent material (as glass or gelatin) that usu. transmits radiant energy of some wavelengths more freely than others, interference and polarization effects being used in some types **:** COLOR FILTER **c :** a tube or a combination of tubes, branch tubes, orifices, and resonant cavities in a sound channel that limits the frequency range of sounds passing through it — called also *acoustic filter*

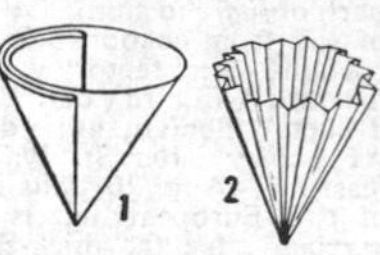

filters 1a **:** *1* plain, *2* fluted

²filter \"\ *vb* **filtered; filtered; filtering** \-t(ə)riŋ\ **filters** [ML *filtrare*, fr. *filtrum*] *vt* **1 :** to subject to the action of a filter **:** pass (a liquid or gas) through a filter for the purpose of purifying or separating or both **:** STRAIN; *also* **:** to act as a filter toward **2 :** to remove from a fluid by means of a filter — usu. used with *off* or *out* ⟨~ off impurities⟩ **~** *vi* **1 a :** to pass through or as if through a filter **:** PERCOLATE **b** *of light* **:** to pass through something that partially obstructs ⟨daylight ~*ing* through thick clouds —Francis Stuart⟩ ⟨sunlight ~*ing* through the shutters —T.B.Costain⟩ **2 a :** INFILTRATE 2 ⟨~ through the front lines⟩ **b :** to enter or cross over in small units over a period of time ⟨races which ~*ed* into Europe toward the end of the old stone age —Emma Hawkridge⟩

fil·ter·abil·i·ty \,filt(ə)rəˈbiləd·ē, -lətē, -i\ *n* -ES **:** the quality or state of being filterable

fil·ter·able *or* **fil·tra·ble** \ˈfilt(ə)rəbəl\ *adj* **:** capable of being filtered or of passing through a filter

filterable virus *or* **filtrable virus** *n* **:** any of the infectious agents that remain virulent after a fluid containing them passes through a filter of diatomite or unglazed porcelain and that include the viruses as presently understood and various other groups (as the mycoplasmas and rickettsias) which were orig. considered viruses before their cellular nature was established — see VIRUS 2b

filter aid *n* **:** an agent consisting of solid particles (as of diatomite) that improves filtering efficiency (as by increasing the permeability of the filter cake) and that is either added to the suspension to be filtered or placed on the filter as a layer through which the liquid must pass

filter alum *n* **:** ALUMINUM SULFATE

filter bed *n* **:** a bed of sand, gravel, or similar matter used for filtering large quantities of water or sewage

filter-bottom block *n* **:** a hollow vitrified salt-glazed clay block used in the floors of trickling filters in sewage-treatment plants

filter cake *n* **:** the solid mass remaining on a filter after the liquid that contained it has passed through; *specif* **:** the residue of impurities filtered from clarified juice of sugarcane that is used as a fertilizer

filter center *n* **:** a station in a military aircraft warning net that receives information on aircraft sighted at observation posts and relays it to stations where it is evaluated for action

fil·ter·er \ˈfiltərə(r)\ *n* -s **:** a worker who tends a filtration process in any of various capacities (as by operating a filter press) — called also *filterman*

filter factor *n* **:** a number by which the normal exposure time must be multiplied to compensate for the use of a color filter with a given photographic material and source of illumination

filter feeder *n* **:** an animal that obtains its food by filtering organic matter or minute organisms from a current of water that passes through some part of its system

filter flask *or* **filtering flask** *n* **:** a flask that is used for receiving a filtering liquid and that is usu. of heavy-walled glass and is often provided with a side tube to connect with a suction pump

filter flask with side tube

filter fly *n* **:** any of a number of long-legged hairy-bodied two-winged flies (family Psychodidae) common about sewage filters

fil·ter·man \ˈfiltə(r)mən\ *n, pl* **filtermen** **1 :** FILTERER **2 :** DECKER MAN

filter paper *n* **:** porous unsized paper used esp. for filtering; *specif* **:** such a paper chemically treated for use in quantitative analysis

filter press *n* **:** a filter consisting usu. of a series of rigid corrugated plates with intervening filter medium (as cloth) assembled in a framework so that the suspension to be filtered can be forced under pressure into the assembled press and the solids can collect as cake between the plates — see PLATE-AND-FRAME FILTER

filter-press \ˌ==ˌ=\ *vt* [*filter press*] **:** to pass through a filter press

filter stick *n* **:** a short tube (as of glass or porcelain) provided with a filter plate or filter medium at one end and used esp. in microanalysis for siphoning off liquid above a precipitate

filter tip *n* **:** a cigar or cigarette tip of cotton, crepe paper, asbestos fiber, alpha cellulose, or cellulose acetate designed to filter the smoke before it enters the smoker's mouth; *also* **:** a cigar or cigarette provided with such a tip — **filter-tipped** \ˌ==ˌ=\ *adj*

filth \ˈfilth *also* -ltth\ *n* -s [ME, fr. OE *fȳlth* (akin to OHG *fūlida* foulness, OS *fūlitha*) fr. OE *fūl* foul + *-th* — more at FOUL] **1 :** the quality or state of being dirty ⟨moral ~⟩ ⟨the faded aristocrat who lives in drunkenness and ~ —William Peden⟩ **2 :** something that tends to corrupt or disgust ⟨literature full of ~ and perversion⟩ **3** *now dial Eng* **a :** RASCAL, SCOUNDREL **b :** WHORE, SLUT **4 a :** rotten, foul, or unhealthy matter ⟨the ~ of a slaughterhouse⟩ **b** *chiefly Midland* (1) **:** underbrush and unwanted vegetation ⟨to cut ~⟩ (2) **:** WEEDS, TARES ⟨the hay bales were full of ~⟩

filth disease *n* **:** a disease due to pollution of the soil or water or to insanitary and filthy surroundings and habits

filth·i·ly \-thəlē, -li\ *adv* **:** in a filthy manner

filth·i·ness \-thēnəs, -thi-\ *n* -ES **:** the quality or state of being filthy ⟨saw only the disorder of his hair and the ~ of his clothes and person⟩

filthy \-thē,-thi\ *adj* -ER/-EST [ME, fr. *filth* + *-y*] **1 :** covered with, having the appearance of, or containing filth **:** very dirty ⟨~ clothes⟩ ⟨~ streets⟩ **2 a :** UNDERHANDED, VILE ⟨~ politics⟩ **b :** OBSCENE ⟨a ~ joke⟩ **syn** see DIRTY

filthy lucre *n* **1** *obs* **:** shameful gain **2 :** MONEY

filtrable *var of* FILTERABLE

¹fil·trate \ˈfil·trāt, *usu* -ād·+V\ *vb* -ED/-ING/-S [ML *filtratus*, past part. of *filtrare* to filter — more at FILTER] **:** FILTER

²filtrate \"\ *n* -S **:** something that has been filtered (as the fluid that has passed through a filter)

fil·tra·tion \fil·ˈtrāshən\ *n* -S **1 :** the process of filtering **2 :** the process of passing through or as if through a filter **:** PERCOLATION; *also* **:** DIFFUSION

fi·lum \ˈfīləm\ *n, pl* **fi·la** \-lə\ [NL, fr. L, thread — more at FILE] **:** a filament or threadlike structure

fi·lum aquae \ˌfīləˈmāˌkwē, ˌfēləˈmäˌkwī\ *n, pl* **fi·la aqua·rum** \ˌfīlə·əˈkwa(a)rəm, ˌfēlə·əˈkwärəm\ [ML, lit., thread of water] **:** the thread of a stream

fi·lum ter·mi·na·le \ˌfīləmˌtermə'nā(ˌ)lē, ¦fēləmˌtermə'nä¦lā\ *n, pl* **fila termina·lia** \¦fīləˌtərmə'nālēə, ¦fēləˌtermə'nälēə\ [NL, lit., terminal thread] **:** the slender threadlike prolongation of the spinal cord below the origin of the lumbar nerves **:** the last portion of the pia mater

fim·ble \ˈfimbəl\ *or* **fimble hemp** *n* -S [MD *femeel, fimele*, fr. OF (*chanvre*) *femelle*, fr. *chanvre* hemp + *femelle* female — more at FEMALE] **:** a male hemp plant; *also* **:** the fiber of this plant

fim·bria \ˈfimbrēə\ *n, pl* **fimbri·ae** \-rēˌē, -ēˌī\ [NL, fr. L, fringe] **1 a** *fimbriae, pl* **:** a bordering fringe; *esp* **:** such a fringe at the entrance of the fallopian tubes **b :** a band of nerve fibers bordering the hippocampus and joining the fornix **2 :** a border that resembles a fringe (as the peristome of a moss)

fim·bri·al \-rēəl\ *adj* [NL *fimbria* + E *-al*] **:** of, relating to, or marked by fimbriae

¹fim·bri·ate \-rēˌāt\ *vt* -ED/-ING/-S [L *fimbria* + E *-ate* (v. suffix)] **:** to furnish with a fimbriation

²fim·bri·ate \-rēət, -rēˌāt\ *adj* [L *fimbriatus* fringed, fr. *fimbria* + *-atus* -ate (adj. suffix)] **1 :** having the edge or extremity bordered by slender processes **:** FRINGED ⟨~ petals⟩ **2 :** FIMBRIATED

fim·bri·at·ed \-ēˌād·əd\ *adj* [L *fimbriatus* + E *-ed*] **1 :** FIMBRIATE **2 :** having a narrow border of specified tincture

fim·bri·a·tion \ˌ==ˈāshən\ *n* -S [ML *fimbriation-, fimbriatio*, fr. L *fimbriatus* + *-ion-, -io* -ion] **1 :** FRINGE, BORDER **2** *heraldry* **:** a narrow border to an ordinary

fim·bril·late \ˈfimbrəˌlāt, (ˈ)fim¦brilət\ *also* **fim·bril·lose** \ˈfimbrəˌlōs\ *adj* [NL *fimbrilla* minute fringe (dim. of L *fimbria* fringe) + E *-ate or -ose*] **:** bordered with a minute fringe

fim·bri·sty·lis \ˌfimbrəˈstīləs\ *n, cap* [NL, fr. *fimbria* + *-stylis* (fr. *stylus*)] **:** a genus of sedges (family Cyperaceae) having small usu. brownish flowers in loose umbels

fi·mic·o·lous \(ˈ)fī¦mikələs, fəˈm-\ *adj* [ISV *fimi-* (fr. L *fimus* dung) + *-colous* — more at FIANTS] **:** inhabiting or growing on dung

¹fin \ˈfin\ *n* -S [ME *finne, finn*, fr. OE *finn*; akin to MLG & MD *vinne* fin, MHG *vinne* nail, OSw *fina* fin, L *spina* thorn, spine — more at SPINE] **1 :** a membranous process resembling a wing or a paddle in fishes and certain other aquatic animals that is used in propelling, balancing, or guiding the body **2 :** something resembling a fin esp. in appearance or function: **a :** a sharp plate or projection used as the colter of a plow **b :** HAND, ARM **c** (1) **:** an appendage of a boat (as a submarine); *also* **:** FIN KEEL (2) **:** a fixed or adjustable airfoil attached to an airplane approximately parallel to the vertical plane of symmetry to afford directional stability (3) **:** one of a pair of usu. slender projections at the rear of an automobile or other vehicle usu. consisting of an extension of the fender line or an upsweep above the fender line and intended to ornament or to provide added stability in motion — called also *tail fin* **d :** FLIPPER 1b — usu. used in pl. **e :** a ridge or piece of excess metal left along the edge of a casting where metal overflows the mold, at the edges of the groove when rolling with grooved rolls, around the parting line of a drop forging, or on a welded joint; *also* **:** a piece of excess material (as plastic or glass) left along the edge of a casting where the material overflows the mold **f** (1) **:** a thin sheet of metal squeezed out between the collars of the rolls in rolling or through the joints of a mold (2) **:** any of the projecting ribs on a radiator or internal-combustion engine cylinder **g :** FEATHER KEY, SPLINE **h :** a thin wall or panel used for screening of light or interruption of a view

²fin \"\ *vb* **finned; finned; finning; fins** *vi* **1 :** to show the fins above the water **:** break water — used of fish ⟨the fish is often sighted *finning* near the surface —I.N.Gabrielson⟩ **2 :** to propel oneself through the water on the back using the hands alone in a finning motion while the arms remain at the sides ~ *vt* **:** to construct or equip with fins — usu. used as past participle ⟨the cylinder head and barrel are heavily *finned* for strength —*Principles of Automotive Vehicles*⟩ ⟨short-*finned*⟩ ⟨steam is condensed in a *finned* coil —*Mech. Engineering*⟩

³fin \"\ *adj* **:** relating to a plow colter shaped like a fin

⁴fin *var of* FEN

⁵fin \ˈfin\ *n* -S [Yiddish *finf* five, fr. MHG *vumf, vimf*, fr. OHG *funf, finf* — more at FIVE] *slang* **:** a five-dollar bill ⟨you owe me a ~ already —Chandler Brossard⟩

fin *abbr* **1** finance; financial **2** finis **3** finish; finished

fin·able *or* **fine·able** \ˈfīnəbəl\ *adj* [ME *finable*, fr. *finen* to pay, pay a fine (fr. MF *finer*) + *-able* — more at FINE] **:** subject to the payment of a fine or liable to a fine

fi·na·gle *also* **fe·na·gle** \fəˈnāgəl\ *vb* **finagled** *also* **fenagled; finagled** *also* **fenagled; finagling** *also* **fenagling** \-g(ə)liŋ\ **finagles** *also* **fenagles** [perh. alter. of *fainaigue*] *vt* **1 :** to arrange for **:** WANGLE, MANAGE ⟨~ a 10-day leave⟩ **2 :** to obtain by chicanery or trickery **:** SWINDLE ⟨he bluffed and *finagled* his way into a fortune⟩ ~ *vi* **:** to use devious or questionable methods to achieve one's ends **:** MANEUVER

fi·na·gler \-g(ə)lə(r)\ *n* -S **:** one that finagles **:** CHEATER, SWINDLER

finagling *n* -S **:** maneuvering or manipulation esp. of a political or financial nature and sometimes of a dishonest character ⟨trying to cover up his financial ~*s*⟩ ⟨a master of backstairs ~⟩

¹fi·nal \ˈfīnᵊl\ *adj* [ME, fr. MF *final, finel*, fr. L *finalis*, fr. *finis* boundary, limit, end + *-alis* -al; perh. akin to L *figere* to pierce, fasten — more at DIKE] **1 a** (1) **:** not to be altered or undone **:** CONCLUSIVE, DECISIVE ⟨a genuinely popular ballad can have no fixed and ~ form, no sole authentic version —F.J.Child⟩ ⟨all sales are ~⟩ ⟨the industry was heading toward its ~ decline —R.H.Brown⟩ ⟨in all free states the Constitution is ~ —John Adams⟩ (2) **:** constituting the ultimate in degree, achievement, or utilization **:** approaching perfection **:** PERFECT **:** not to be done again **:** DEFINITIVE ⟨a concept of art as disinterested, digested, measured, disciplined, and ~ —S.E.Hyman⟩ ⟨line, color, and tonal relations coalesce with ~ surety —Bernard Smith⟩ ⟨they have succumbed to the ~ sin, despair —*The Reporter*⟩ ⟨a meticulously detailed, authentic, and one would imagine ~ biography —Evelyn Eaton⟩ **b** (1) **:** ending a court action or proceeding leaving nothing further to be determined by the court or to be done except the administrative execution of the court's finding but not precluding an appeal — used of a court order, decision, judgment, decree, or sentence; compare INTERLOCUTORY (2) **:** being a court finding that is conclusive as to jurisdiction and precluding the right to appeal to or continue the case in any other court upon the merits ⟨in some minor matters the decisions of the lower courts are usu. made ~⟩ — often used in the phrase *final and conclusive* (3) **:** being a judgment or decree of the Supreme Court of the U.S. given under the provisions of the statutes giving it jurisdiction over appeals and writs of error that eliminates the litigation between the parties on the merits and leaves nothing for the inferior court to do in case of an affirmance except to execute the judgment or decree (4) *of a court hearing* **:** being the last at which evidence may be presented or the last at which argument may be made **2 a :** relating to or occurring at the end or conclusion **:** LAST, TERMINATING ⟨~ illness⟩ ⟨the ~ day of a school term⟩ ⟨one ~ comment is necessary⟩ ⟨in the ~ analysis, this is a second-rate work⟩ **b** (1) **:** last in a series of economic increments — compare MARGINAL (2) **:** not to be processed further but consumed or utilized as is **:** ULTIMATE — used of a commodity **c :** of that form regularly employed only at the end of a word — used of a letter in any of a number of alphabets (as the Hebrew and Arabic) that has two or more positional forms ⟨writing a ~ letter in medial position⟩ **3 a :** relating to an end or object to be gained **:** related to the purpose or ultimate end in view **b :** expressive of purpose — used of a subordinate clause, sometimes also of a conjunction (*that, in order that, lest*) introducing it **syn** see LAST

²final \"\ *n* -S **:** something that is final: as **a :** a deciding match, game, heat, or trial — usu. used in pl. ⟨qualified to play in the ~*s*⟩ **b :** the last examination in a course — usu. used in the pl. with *the* ⟨busily preparing for the ~*s*⟩; *also* **:** the last examination or set of examinations taken by a candidate for an advanced degree ⟨after his thesis was accepted, he'd come down . . . and take his ~ —G.R.Stewart⟩ **c** [ML *finalis*, fr. L, adj.] **:** the keynote of an ecclesiastical mode ⟨the ~ is d in Dorian mode⟩ **d :** the final sound or letter of a syllable, morpheme, or word **e :** a form of an alphabetical letter (as in the Hebrew and Arabic alphabets) that regularly is used only at the end of a word **f :** FINAL EDITION

final cause *n* [ME] **:** something that is the end or purpose of a process — used in Aristotelianism and some other teleological doctrines

final common path *also* **final common pathway** *n* **:** a motoneuron that forms the terminal step of one or more reflex circuits transmitting their stimuli to an effector end organ

final drive *n* **:** the means for transmitting power from the propeller shaft to the rear axle in an automotive vehicle

fi·nale \fəˈnalē, fēˈ-, -näl-, -nal-, -li\ *n* -S [It, fr. *finale*, adj., final, fr. L *finalis* — more at FINAL] **:** the close or termination of something: as **a** (1) **:** the last section or movement of an instrumental musical composition (2) **:** the last section or piece in any act of an opera usu. arranged for a large ensemble **b :** the closing part, piece, scene, or number in any public performance ⟨the ~ of a ballet⟩ **c :** the close or conclusion of any sequence, series, or action **:** the last and often climactic event or item in a series ⟨this was the sad ~ of every reflection —Jane Austen⟩ ⟨the novel has its ~ at a cocktail bar⟩ ⟨drop over a high cliff as a ~ to a succession of cascades —*Amer. Guide Series: Oregon*⟩ ⟨the ~ is cut-up fresh fruit —Jane Nickerson⟩

final edition *n* **:** the last edition of a morning, afternoon, or evening newspaper issued on any one day

fi·na·lis \fēˈnäləs\ *n, pl* **fina·les** \-ˌlās\ [ML, fr. L, adj., final] **:** ²FINAL c

fi·nal·ism \ˈfīnᵊlˌizəm\ *n* -S **:** a belief in final causes **:** teleological doctrine — compare TELEOLOGY

¹fi·nal·ist \-ᵊləst\ *n* -S [F *finaliste*, fr. *final* + *-iste* -ist] **1 :** a believer in or advocate of finalism **2 :** any of the contestants who meet in the final round of a competition

²finalist \"\ *or* **fi·nal·is·tic** \¦==¦istik\ *adj* **:** TELEOLOGICAL

fi·nal·i·ty \fīˈnaləd·ē, fəˈ-, -lətē, -i\ *n* -ES **1 a :** the character or condition of being final, finished, conclusive, irrevocable, or complete **:** CONCLUSION ⟨there is a ~ to a diplomatic defeat that cannot be overcome —*New Republic*⟩ ⟨has not been able to bring to ~ many of the interesting ideas . . . generated by his fertile mind —W.E.L.Clark⟩ ⟨there appears to be a disposition not to accept the ~ of the revolution in China —Aneurin Bevan⟩ **b :** the quality, manner, or air of being final or decisive ⟨walked across the court with a kind of ~ in his stride —R.P.Warren⟩ ⟨spoke with curt ~⟩ ⟨certitude and ~ mark their assertions —Paul Radin⟩ **2 :** the condition of being so perfect or finished as to be incapable of improvement **:** the condition of being the ultimate authority or the last word **:** PERFECTION, INEVITABILITY ⟨in the work of the great classical writers a ~ of effect which places certain of their scenes beyond the reach of change —Virginia Woolf⟩ ⟨we cannot claim ~ of judgment —Herbert Reade⟩ ⟨the authentic ~ of his autobiography —W.T.Scott⟩ **3 :** the categorial or causal relation of end or purpose to its means **:** TELEOLOGY 1 **4 :** something that is final **:** a final, ultimate, or fundamental fact, action, detail, condition, or belief ⟨a code of *finalities* is a necessary condition of profitable talk between two persons —O.W. Holmes †1935⟩ **5 :** ¹CLOSURE 11

fi·nal·iza·tion \ˌfīnᵊləˈzāshən, -ᵊlˌīˈz-\ *n* -S **:** the act, process, or an instance of finalizing ⟨the ~ of a sound doctrine set forth in service manuals for use and guidance in future maneuvers —Kalman Siegel⟩

fi·nal·ize \ˈfīnᵊlˌīz\ *vb* -ED/-ING/-S *vt* **:** to put in final or finished form **:** FINISH, COMPLETE, CLOSE ⟨soon my conclusions will be *finalized* —D.D.Eisenhower⟩ ⟨the couple ~ plans to marry at once —S.J.Perelman⟩ ⟨empowered to . . . ~ the deal —James Joseph⟩ **:** give final approval to ⟨the list has not been *finalized* by the deputy, but it won't be changed now —Robertson Davies⟩ ⟨ties up the day's loose ends, *finalizing* the papers prepared and presented by his staff —*Newsweek*⟩ ~ *vi* **:** to bring something to completion ⟨if we don't ~ tonight, those two . . . will get suspicious and sell to someone else —I.L. Idriess⟩

fi·nal·ly \ˈfīn(ᵊ)lē, -li\ *adv* [ME, fr. ¹*final* + *-ly*] **1 a :** after a certain space of time **:** as the last act or occurrence in a series **:** in the end **:** at last **:** EVENTUALLY ⟨he carefully adjusted his tie, took one last look about the room, and ~ walked out the door⟩ ⟨the theologians . . . ~ adjusted theology to the new conceptions —G.C.Sellery⟩ ⟨pressure falls steadily and may ~ reach a point at which shock occurs —Morris Fishbein⟩ **b :** in the last analysis **:** ULTIMATELY ⟨the creation of the work of art is what ~ concerns us —Michael Kitson⟩ ⟨the generality and heartiness of assent on which laws ~ depend for effectiveness —*Modern Churchman*⟩ ⟨can positively and ~ depend upon him —Walter de la Mare⟩ **c :** by way of conclusion **:** as the last point ⟨~, I wish to thank all who cooperated in this important project⟩ ⟨~, the essayist considers the vexing problem of free will⟩ **2 :** for all time **:** beyond change **:** IRREVOCABLY, CONCLUSIVELY, DECISIVELY ⟨this question which you have answered so ~ —Willa Cather⟩ ⟨reluctance to commit himself ~ to one extreme or the other —E.D.H.Johnson⟩

final process *n* **:** EXECUTION 3b

final record *n* **1 :** the court record corresponding to the common-law judgment record **2 :** the record of a case in its final form as shown by the permanent docket entries made by the recording officer of the court

final recovery *n* **:** the ultimate judgment or decree of a court on the merits; *sometimes* **:** the verdict rendered by a jury

final utility *n* **:** MARGINAL UTILITY

¹fi·nance \fəˈnan(t)s, ˈfīˌn-, -naa(ə)n- *also* fīˈn-\ *n* -S [ME *finaunce* ending, settlement, payment, ransom, fr. MF *finance*, fr. *finer* to end, pay + *-ance* — more at FINE] **1 finances** *pl* **:** the pecuniary affairs or resources of a state, company, or individual ⟨school had to close for lack of ~*s*⟩ ⟨his ~*s* were in bad shape⟩ ⟨company with ample ~*s*⟩ **2 :** the obtaining of funds or capital **:** FINANCING ⟨productive business expansion for which ~ would otherwise be unavailable —F.D.Roosevelt⟩ **3 :** the system that includes the circulation of money, the granting of credit, the making of investments, and the provision of banking facilities ⟨people employed in . . . trade, ~, personal services, and government —P.H. Landis⟩

²finance \"\ *vb* -ED/-ING/-S [ME *finauncen*, fr. *finaunce*, n.] *vt* **1 :** to raise or provide funds or capital for ⟨~ a war⟩ ⟨~ a new home⟩ ⟨encouraged and *financed* a career⟩ ⟨~ a new venture⟩ **2 :** to provide with necessary funds in order to achieve a desired end ⟨~ a son through school⟩ ⟨~*ed* the government through this emergency⟩ **3 :** to sell on credit **:** to supply on credit ⟨the early motor-vehicle producers were not in a position to ~ . . . the automobile distributors and dealers who wished to obtain cars for resale to consumers —C.W. Phelps⟩ ⟨your store bill is too high, we just can't ~ you any longer⟩ ~ *vi* **:** to secure needed funds or capital ⟨governments and individuals ~ through borrowing⟩ — **fin·ance·able** *adj*

finance bill *n* **1 :** a bill of exchange drawn usu. by one bank on another bank for the purpose of transferring funds as a result of loans or for temporarily procuring money by discounting the bill **2 :** a legislative act to provide the necessary funds for the public treasury **:** a revenue bill — compare MONEY BILL

finance capitalism *n* **:** a stage of capitalism in which economic and political domination is exercised by financial institutions or financiers rather than by industrial capitalists

finance company *n* **:** a company that buys accounts receivable from business usu. in the form of installment notes covering the purchase of durable goods (as automobiles)

fi·nan·cial \fəˈnanchəl, (ˈ)fī¦n-, -naan-\ *adj* [¹*finance* + *-ial*] **1 :** relating to finance or financiers ⟨rumors heard in high ~ circles⟩ ⟨found himself in severe ~ difficulties⟩ ⟨the ~ aspect of a college education⟩ **2 :** in good standing as to payment of dues **:** paying dues **:** not honorary — used of a member of a society, trade union, or other association

financial institution *n* **:** an enterprise specializing in the handling and investment of funds (as a bank, trust company, insurance company, savings and loan association, or investment company)

fi·nan·cial·ly \-ch(ə)lē, -li\ *adv* **:** in respect to finance **:** from a financial point of view ⟨~ Constantinople was the center of an area much more extensive than the Empire —R.W. Southern⟩ ⟨the project is ~ unsound⟩

financial year *n* **:** FISCAL YEAR

¹fin·an·cier \ˌfinənˈsi(ə)r, fəˌnanˈ-, fəˌnaanˈ-, -ˈsiə *also* ˈfīˌna(a)n¦- *or* ¦fīˌna(a)n¦- *or* ¦fīnən¦- *chiefly Brit* fīˈnansiə(r) *or* fiˈnansiə(r)\ *n* -S [F, fr. MF, fr. *finance* + *-ier* -er] **1 a** *obs* **:** an officer who administers the public revenues **b :** a large-scale investor **:** CAPITALIST **c :** a person who undertakes to secure large funds for a government or business **:** INVESTMENT BANKER **2** *obs* **:** a receiver, farmer, or administrator of public taxes in France before the Revolution

²financier \"\ *vi* -ED/-ING/-S **:** to conduct financial operations often by sharp, fraudulent, or reprehensible practices ⟨put an end to such ~*ing* and unhallowed practices —Hartley Withers⟩ ⟨cold-eyed ~*ing* —Carlos Baker⟩

fi·nan·cière \fēnäⁿsyeer\ *adj* [F (*à la*) *financière*, lit., in the manner of a financier] **:** having or being a garnish or a sauce the principal ingredients of which are truffles, mushrooms, olives, Madeira wine, and sometimes balls of forcemeat ⟨sweetbreads ~⟩

financing *n* -S **:** the act, process, or an instance of raising or providing funds ⟨announcement of new ~ has almost invariably been followed by a drop in the stock of the company concerned —*Time*⟩; *also* **:** the funds thus raised or provided ⟨new ~ will consist of $34,000,000 additional first mortgage bonds —*Barron's*⟩

finback \ˈ=,=\ *n* [so called fr. the prominent dorsal fin] **:** a whalebone whale of the genus *Balaenoptera* **:** RORQUAL; *esp* **:** a common whale of the Atlantic coast of the U. S. (*B. physalus*) attaining a length of over 60 feet and now the commonest large whale of the region

fin boom *n* **:** an adjustable boom used in logging on navigable streams where permanent booms are not allowed

fin·ca \ˈfēŋkə, ˈfiŋ-\ *n* -S [Sp, fr. *fincar* to remain, fr. (assumed) VL *figicare*, fr. L *figere* to pierce, fasten — more at DIKE] **:** a rural property, ranch, or estate in Spain or Spanish America; *esp* **:** a landed estate in Spanish America devoted to the cultivation of tropical crops

finch \ˈfinch\ *n* -ES [ME, fr. OE *finc*; akin to OHG *fincho* finch, MD *vinke* finch, Sw *spink* small bird, sparrow, Gk *spingos, spiza, spinos* chaffinch, *spizein* to chirp, Skt *phingaka* drongo] **1 :** a bird of the family Fringillidae including the sparrows, grosbeaks, crossbills, goldfinches, linnets, buntings, and related birds, being of small or moderate size and rather stout build, having generally a short stout conical bill adapted for crushing seeds, being often very beneficial to agriculture by destroying the seeds of weeds, and being sometimes fine singers (as the canary) — used often in combination ⟨bull*finch*⟩ ⟨chaf*finch*⟩ ⟨gold*finch*⟩; see BILL illustration **2 :** any of various African and Australian weaverbirds (family Ploceidae) — see FIRE FINCH, GOULDIAN FINCH

finch falcon *n* **:** FALCONET 2

fin colter *n* **:** a colter having a fin-shaped hanging knife

¹find \ˈfīnd\ *vb* **found** \ˈfau̇nd\ **found; finding; finds** [ME *finden*, fr. OE *findan*; akin to OE *fētha* foot soldier, troop of foot soldiers, OS *findan, fīthan* to find, *fāthi* act of going, OHG *findan* to find, *fendo, fendeo* one that walks, ON *finna* to find, Goth *finthan* to find, find out, L *pont-, pons* bridge, Gk *pontos* sea, *patos* path, Skt *patha* way, path, course; basic meaning: going, stepping] *vt* **1 a** (1) **:** to come upon accidentally **:** gain the first sight of (as something new or unknown) ⟨*found* the tracks of some unknown animal⟩ ⟨*found* a large stone blocking the way⟩ ⟨the child *found* a coin in the street⟩ ⟨the well diggers *found* a number of Indian artifacts⟩ (2) **:** to fall in with (a person) **:** ENCOUNTER ⟨~*s* interesting people wherever he goes⟩ **b** (1) **:** to meet with (a particular kind of reception or treatment) ⟨he hoped to ~ favor in her sight⟩ ⟨his doctrines *found* no acceptance among scholars⟩ (2) **:** to obtain or come to have (something desirable) as if without effort ⟨the book *found* a host of readers⟩ ⟨the new product *found* few buyers⟩ **2 a :** to come upon (a material object) by searching or effort ⟨they *found* water at a depth of 10 feet⟩ ⟨the committee must ~ a suitable man for the job⟩ ⟨*found* his missing brother at last⟩ **b :** to discover by study or experience directed to an object or end ⟨~ the answer to a complex mathematical problem⟩ ⟨scientific research is ~*ing* important new principles nearly every day —C.E.Kellogg⟩ ⟨~*s* that . . . the volumes of the other gas . . . are in the ratio 1:2 —L.K.Nash⟩ **c :** to hit upon **:** DEVISE, INVENT, CONTRIVE ⟨*found* a more modern method of treating the processed material⟩ **d :** to secure or obtain (something needed or desirable) by effort or management **:** summon up **:** PROCURE ⟨*found* the time to continue his studies⟩ ⟨~ bail for a prisoner⟩ ⟨~ the courage to address a large audience⟩ **e :** to attain to **:** arrive at **:** REACH ⟨the bullet *found* its mark⟩ **f :** to discover by sounding ⟨preliminary surveys failed to ~ any solid bottom —O.S.Nock⟩ **g :** to obtain as if by effort ⟨the spirit of adventure . . . *found* vent in the life of the explorer —B.K.Sandwell⟩ ⟨authors whose textbooks ~ publication —James Britton⟩ ⟨the new system has *found* its first codification —*Reporter*⟩ **3** *dial* **:** to perceive or detect by or as if by the senses; *specif* **:** FEEL, SUFFER ⟨~ pain⟩ ⟨~ punishment⟩ ⟨grandpa *found* his rheumatism again this morning⟩ **4 a :** to learn by experience or trial **:** discover by the intellect or the feelings **:** PERCEIVE, EXPERIENCE, DETECT, REGARD, FEEL ⟨*found* him a very sensible and tactful man⟩ ⟨~ much pleasure in his company⟩ ⟨*found* something repellent about the man⟩ ⟨~ no logic in his argument⟩ ⟨*found* a strange odor in the room⟩ **b** (1) **:** to perceive (oneself) to be in a certain place or condition ⟨when he awoke, he *found* himself in a luxuriously furnished apartment⟩ ⟨~ herself in a dilemma⟩ ⟨*found* themselves in the presence of the sovereigns⟩ (2) **:** to perceive (oneself) with respect to a certain condition with respect to health — usu. used in a question ⟨how do you ~ yourself to-day? —Winston Churchill⟩ **c** (1) **:** to gain or regain the use or power of ⟨after a second's pause, he *found* broken speech —Arthur Morrison⟩ ⟨a baby just beginning to ~ her feet⟩ (2) **:** to attain to (the exercise of one's inherent powers) **:** establish (a place or footing) in a profession or career **:** recover from (a financial, moral, or other downfall) — often used in such phrases as *find one's wings, find one's feet* ⟨the youthful poet had just begun to ~ his wings⟩ ⟨continue a small unearned allowance while his son *found* his feet at the bar —Geoffrey Gorer⟩ ⟨when he *found* his feet the army . . . decided to overlook the prison record and accept his reform —Gordon Harrison⟩ **d :** to bring (oneself) to a consciousness of one's powers, capacities, or of one's proper sphere of activity **:** raise (oneself) to that point of efficiency, effectiveness, achievement or to that mode of life of which one is inherently capable ⟨it was an army that had *found* itself —F.V.W. Mason⟩ ⟨must help the student to ~ himself as an individual —N.M.Pusey⟩ ⟨she suddenly ~*s* herself, and becomes the acknowledged leader of all the women of the neighborhood —Vernon Jarratt⟩ **5 a** (1) **:** to provide for the use of **:** provide with **:** SUPPLY ⟨for selected children the church ~*s* half of this sum, leaving the parent to ~ the rest —Ernest & Pearl Beaglehole⟩ — often used with *in* ⟨there'd be all the neighbors to ~ in victuals and drink —Mary Webb⟩ ⟨we are *found* in everything—house, servants, food —Rachel Henning⟩ (2) **:** to provide (room and board) esp. as a condition of employment **:** MAINTAIN ⟨he was chopping by day's work—75 cents a day—and *found* himself —Herman Melville⟩ — often used in the phrases *everything found, all found* ⟨combining business and pleasure in a new kind of holiday camp with all *found* —Fred Majdalany⟩ ⟨no worries, everything *found*, and lots of Saturday-night spirits —Lionel Shapiro⟩ ⟨why should you go to the workhouse? I offer you 14 pounds and everything *found* —George Moore⟩ **b :** to equip with what is needful or necessary ⟨the boat comes fully *found*, ready to go —*Holiday*⟩ **6 :** to arrive at (a conclusion) **:** come to (a finding) **:** determine and declare (as a verdict in a judicial proceeding) **:** agree or settle upon and deliver ⟨he was *found* guilty⟩ ⟨~ a verdict⟩ ⟨~ a true bill of indictment against an accused person⟩ **7** *chiefly Midland* **:** to give birth to — used of animals ⟨about February . . . the mother bears ~ their cubs —Mary Sloop⟩ ~ *vi* **1 :** to discover the game or scent — used chiefly of hunting dogs ⟨when the hounds *found*, they went off at a very fast clip —*Scientific Monthly*⟩ ⟨harked back to the famous runs of his youth, telling me where they had *found*, where killed, and hazards in between —Adrian Bell⟩ **2 :** to determine a case judicially or quasi-judicially by a verdict or decision — used of a court, jury, or a quasi-judicial administrative body — **find fault :** to discover and proclaim some defect or censurable action or quality **:** criticize unfavorably ⟨he is chronically *finding fault*⟩ — often used with *with* ⟨at times *found fault* with interpretation, balance, tone quality —*Current Biog.*⟩ — **find in one's heart** *archaic* **:** to be willing or disposed ⟨I could *find in my heart* to ask your pardon —Philip Sidney⟩ — **find one's way 1 a :** to make one's way by searching, inquiry, or trial and error **:** manage to reach some destination ⟨could not *find his way* to my house⟩ ⟨*found his way* to the pantry in total darkness⟩ **b :** to go to or reach some place by or as if by chance or after an interval of wandering ⟨maybe fur traders *found their way* to California —R.A.Billington⟩ ⟨when the white men first *found their way* to this continent⟩ **:** move along a certain route or path ⟨the waters *find their way* . . . through the lake's outlet —Tom Marvel⟩ **2 :** to be carried or brought to some place ⟨the tapestry was cut into three sections . . . and the various parts *found their* separate *ways* to the U.S. —*Time*⟩ **:** obtain entrance **:** ENTER ⟨dozens of curious little crackpot movements *found their way* into the curriculum —Martin Gardner⟩ **3 :** to end up ⟨a considerable portion of . . . the land grants . . . *found its way* into the hands of private speculators —*Amer. Guide Series: Oregon*⟩

[2]**find** \"\ *n* -s **1 :** the act or an instance of finding esp. something valuable **:** DISCOVERY ⟨announced the ~ of an important manuscript⟩ ⟨a ~ of high-quality ore deposits⟩; *specif* **:** discovery of game or a scent by a hunting dog ⟨his first ~ was at the far end of one of the stubble fields —*Popular Dogs*⟩ **2 a :** something that is found ⟨any small archaeological ~ may provide valuable historical evidence⟩; *esp* **:** a valuable discovery ⟨these letters constitute a real ~⟩ ⟨an important uranium ~⟩ **b :** a person whose ability or value proves to be surprisingly or unexpectedly great ⟨the boy . . ., not yet 24 years old, was a ~ —Will Irwin⟩ ⟨the young actress was the theatrical ~ of the year⟩

find·er \ˈfīndə(r)\ *n* -s [ME, fr. *finden* + *-er*] **1 :** one that finds **2 :** one that deals in findings (as of a shoemaker) **3 :** a small astronomical telescope of low power and wide field attached to a larger telescope parallel to its axis for the purpose of finding an object more readily **4 :** a device sometimes used by artists to aid in the selection or arrangement of a subject and usu. made of a card with a rectangular opening through which the object may be viewed as if within a picture frame **5 :** a device attached to or forming a part of a camera for showing the area of the subject that will be included in the picture (as by reflecting upon a viewing lens an image formed by a lens of short focus or by viewing directly with a sight held at eye level) **6 :** one that discovers a financial opportunity, passes it on to another, and often acts as a go-between in subsequent negotiations

finders' leather *n* **:** sole leather specially processed for use by shoe repairers

finder switch *n* **:** an electric switch that automatically finds a circuit out of a large number of circuits from which a signal comes — used esp. in telephone circuits

fin-de-siè·cle \ˌfandəsˈyekl(ə), -sēˈek-, -k(lə)\ *adj* [F *fin de siècle* end of the century] **1 a :** of or relating to the close of the 19th century ⟨recreated in its *fin-de-siècle* splendor on a sound stage in London —T.F.Brady⟩ **b :** of, relating to, characterized by, or resembling in one or another respect the late 19th century literary and artistic climate of sophistication, escapism, extreme aestheticism, world-weariness, and fashionable despair **:** DECADENT **2 a** ⟨this attitude grew into a *fin-de-siècle* one of cultivated fatigue and bored aestheticism —Peter De Vries⟩ ⟨queer that in 1917 a man of 29 should be writing in so adolescent and *fin-de-siècle* a manner —Jacob Isaacs⟩ ⟨early dabblings in the mood of the *fin-de-siècle* aesthetes —R.D.Jacobs⟩ **2 :** of or relating to the end of an era

findfault \ˈ=,=\ *n* [*find* + *fault*] *dial Eng* **:** FAULTFINDER

finding *n* -s [ME, fr. gerund of *finden* to find — more at FIND] **1 :** FIND 2a ⟨archaeological ~s along the route . . . led some authorities to conclude that the district was once the home of the mound builders —*Amer. Guide Series: Mich.*⟩ **2 findings** *pl* **a :** the small parts and the materials other than leather that enter into the making of a shoe (as nails, eyelets, laces, buckles) **b :** small articles used in various trades (as buttons, thread, zippers for dressmakers, or catches, swivels, clasps, wire for jewelers) **3 a :** the result of a judicial or quasi-judicial examination or inquiry esp. into matters of fact as embodied in the verdict of a jury or decision of a court, referee, or administrative body **b :** the result or conclusion of any inquiry or investigation — usu. used in pl. ⟨the ~s of natural science⟩ ⟨published his ~s in scholarly journals⟩

finding list *n* **:** an index, catalog, or list (as of books or rare coins) usu. without being full in description and annotation **:** CHECKLIST

fin·don haddock \ˌfin(d)ən-\ *n, usu cap F* [*Findon* (or *Finnan*), village near Aberdeen, Scotland, noted for its smoked fish] **:** FINNAN HADDIE

find out *vt* **1 a :** to catch in a theft or offense of any kind ⟨the Indian ate one of the loaves, and was . . . *found out* —Edward Clodd⟩ **b :** DETECT, DISCOVER ⟨*found out* that he was divorced⟩ **:** LEARN ⟨the press *found out* and proclaimed his youthful sins⟩ ⟨vainly tried to *find out* his name and occupation⟩ **2 a :** to penetrate to the true character or identity of **:** penetrate the disguise of **:** UNMASK ⟨if I tried to wear a halo and faked it, I'd be *found out* for sure —Jackie Gleason⟩ ⟨afraid the truth would *find* them *out* —H.S.Reuss⟩ **b :** to bring retribution upon **:** visit with retribution ⟨his sins have *found* him *out*⟩ ⟨the fallacies in their doctrine and their own imperfect abilities have *found* them *out* —*Time & Tide*⟩ ~ *vi* **:** to discover, learn, or verify something secret, unknown, or uncertain ⟨you don't know for sure, and how are you going to *find out*⟩

finds *pres 3d sing of* FIND, *pl of* FIND

findspot \ˈ=,=\ *n* [[2]*find* + *spot*] **:** the place where an archaeological object has been found

[1]**fine** \ˈfīn\ *n* -s [ME *fin, fine,* fr. OF *fin,* fr. L *finis* boundary, limit, end — more at FINAL] **1** *obs* **:** END, CONCLUSION, CLOSE **2 a :** a sum formerly paid as compensation or for exemption from punishment but now imposed as punishment for a crime — distinguished from *forfeiture* and *penalty* **b :** a forfeiture or penalty paid to an injured party in a civil action **c :** a sum of money ordered paid by one in contempt of court to vindicate the court's authority **d** (1) **:** a sum paid to a library as a penalty for keeping a book beyond the date due (2) **:** the monetary penalty imposed for infraction of a rule or obligation ⟨club members who were late had to pay a 25-cent ~⟩ **3 a** *feudal law* (1) **:** a money payment made by a tenant to his lord on a particular occasion (as a transfer of the tenant right) (2) **:** an endowment whereby a tenant's widow was permitted to claim her dower **b** (1) **:** a final amicable agreement or compromise of an actual or fictitious controversy or suit formerly made in England by leave of the king or his justices (2) **:** a settlement giving exemption or release; *esp* **:** one obtained by a payment of money **c** *or* **fine of lands :** a compromise of a fictitious suit used as a form of conveyance of lands where ordinary conveyances were less efficacious (as in cases involving married women or entailed estates) **d** *English & early American law* **:** an agreement effecting a conveyance of estates in land by entering into a friendly lawsuit whereby one party's claim of title was formally recognized by the other, putting an end to all litigation between them **e** *English law* **:** a sum of money charged for any benefit, favor, or privilege (as obtaining or renewing a lease) — **in fine :** in conclusion **:** in short ⟨it is shorn of all pathos, sympathy, understanding, and romance—of everything human, *in fine* —O.S.J.Gogarty⟩

[2]**fine** \"\ *vb* -ED/-ING/-S [ME *finen,* fr. MF *finer* to end, pay (as a fine), fr. *fin,* n., end] *vt* **1 :** to pay by way of fine or composition **2** [[1]*fine*] **:** to set a fine on by judgment of a court esp. as a punishment **:** punish by fine ~ *vi, archaic* **:** to pay a fine, penalty, composition, ransom, or consideration for any special privilege or exemption; *esp* **:** to pay for release from accepting the duties of an office — often used with *for, off,* or *down*

[3]**fine** \"\ *adj* -ER/-EST [ME *fin, fine,* fr. OF *fin,* fr. L *finis,* n., boundary, limit, end (as in such phrases as *finis honorum* the height of honor, the highest honor); trans. of Gk *telos,* lit., end) — more at FINAL, WHEEL] **1 a :** free from impurity **:** brought to perfection **:** highly purified **:** REFINED, SUPERIOR, PURE ⟨~ gold and silver⟩ **b** *of a metal* **:** having a stated proportion of pure metal in the composition ⟨gold 23 karats ~⟩ — compare FINENESS 2b **c** *of glass* **:** freed from bubbles **2 a** (1) **:** very small **:** MINUTE ⟨~ print⟩ (2) **:** marked by subtlety, refinement, or intricacy of thought or expression **:** HAIRSPLITTING ⟨very ~ legal points were involved⟩ ⟨I cannot follow these ~ distinctions⟩ (3) **:** performed with extreme care and accuracy ⟨~ measurement⟩ ⟨~ adjustment⟩ (4) *of bodily tremors* **:** of slight excursion **b :** not coarse **:** constituting small particles ⟨~ sand⟩ ⟨~ flour⟩ **c** (1) **:** not thick or clumsy **:** SLENDER, FILMY ⟨~ thread⟩ ⟨~ chiffon⟩ ⟨a fine-boned hand⟩ (2) *of wool* **:** having a diameter similar to that of merino wool (3) *of paper* **:** of a grade suitable for writing, printing, or drawing **d :** THIN, KEEN, ATTENUATED ⟨a sword with a ~ edge⟩ **e** (1) **:** made of delicate materials **:** delicately fashioned or proportioned **:** exquisite in texture **:** LIGHT, CLEAR, FAIR, FRAGILE ⟨he was ~ in profile, in the texture of his fair skin —Osbert Sitwell⟩ ⟨many of the present inhabitants have ~ skins, fair hair, and florid complexions —Tobias Smollett⟩ ⟨~ linen⟩ ⟨~ china⟩ (2) **:** sharp forward or aft — used of a ship **f** (1) **:** trained to a point of weight and muscular activity close to the limit of efficiency — used of an athlete or animal (2) *cricket* **:** being to the rear of the defending batsman and nearer than usual to the line of flight of a bowled ball ⟨caught at ~ leg⟩ — compare SQUARE **g :** having a delicate or subtle quality ⟨the ~ scent of burning wax —Vicki Baum⟩ ⟨the ~ bouquet of a vintage wine⟩ ⟨the ~ irony of it all⟩ ⟨~, rapier-edged humor⟩ **3 a** *obs* **:** CLEVER, INGENIOUS, CUNNING, CRAFTY **b :** subtle, sensitive, or acute in perception or feeling ⟨he has a ~ ear for the . . . idiomatic English that passes for conversation among the youths of the day —Max Wilk⟩ **4 a :** superior in character, nature, ability, or prospects **:** NOBLE, SKILLFUL, EXCELLENT ⟨a ~ man⟩ ⟨a ~ ship⟩ ⟨a ~ musician⟩ ⟨you have a ~ future before you⟩ **b :** superior in construction, execution, design, or expression ⟨a ~ work of art⟩ ⟨a ~ orchestra was playing⟩ **c :** of noble or attractive appearance **:** BEAUTIFUL, HANDSOME, PLEASANT, BRIGHT ⟨a ~ view⟩ ⟨a ~ morning⟩ ⟨a very ~ garden⟩ **d** (1) **:** ORNATE, SHOWY **:** ELEGANT ⟨~ feathers make ~ birds⟩ ⟨wore a ~ new dress⟩ (2) *of writing* **:** excessively ornate **:** affectedly elegant **:** FLORID, RHETORICAL ⟨this last sentence is so ~ I am quite ashamed —Thomas Gray⟩ (3) **:** marked by or displaying elegance or refinement often affected or excessive **:** FASTIDIOUS, DAINTY ⟨our ~ neighbors wouldn't speak to the likes of us⟩ ⟨sneered at the stranger's ~ ways⟩ **5 a :** SPLENDID, NOTABLE, ADMIRABLE ⟨spoke with ~ enthusiasm⟩ ⟨his terrible slashing wit, his ~ scorn of stupidity and cowardice —John Reed⟩ ⟨what a ~ darling baby⟩ **b :** GREAT, TERRIFIC, AWFUL — used as an intensive ⟨had come running in a ~ embarrassment —Glenway Wescott⟩ ⟨you make a ~ mistake if you think I'm out for quarreling —Mrs. Patrick Campbell⟩ **c :** very well **:** EXCELLENT ⟨I feel ~⟩

[4]**fine** \"\ *adv* [ME *fin, fine,* fr. *fin, fine,* adj.] **1 :** FINELY: as **a :** ELEGANTLY, MINCINGLY ⟨talks and walks so ~, just like a great lady⟩ **b :** SPLENDIDLY, WELL ⟨you did ~⟩ ⟨he made out ~⟩ ⟨I liked it ~⟩ **c :** SUBTLY, DELICATELY, MINUTELY ⟨the line between victory and defeat . . . will be ~ drawn⟩ **2** *Scot* **:** SURELY **:** for certain ⟨~ I know him though I haven't seen him for years —John Buchan⟩ **3 :** with a very narrow margin of time or space — often used with *cut* or *run* ⟨close thing . . . mustn't run it so ~ another time —P.G.Wodehouse⟩

[5]**fine** \"\ *vb* -ED/-ING/-S [ME *finen,* fr. *fin, fine,* adj.] *vt* **1 :** REFINE, PURIFY, CLARIFY ⟨~ and filter wine⟩ ⟨beer is sometimes *fined* before bottling —B.M.Brown⟩ ⟨~ gold⟩ ⟨the glass will be fully *fined* before being admitted to the working chamber —*Glass Industry*⟩ **2 :** to make finer or less coarse or dull in quality, size, bulk, texture, or appearance ⟨~ his wits⟩ **:** SHARPEN, PULVERIZE — often used with *down* ⟨the one-way disc plow . . . ~s the soil to the extent of increasing losses from blowing —*Soils & Men*⟩ ⟨the women, except . . . where Italian influence has *fined* down the bone structure, are . . . well built —Don Smith⟩ ⟨material *fined* and refined until every . . . word . . . has its place in an artistic whole —*Times Lit. Supp.*⟩ ⟨*fined* his tuning, eliminating the interference —Rayne Kruger⟩ ⟨in this story . . . human beings are *fined* down to bee size —*N.Y. Herald Tribune*⟩ **3 :** to make less or finer by graduations — used with *away* or *down* ⟨~ down a ship's lines⟩ ~ *vi* **1 :** to become fine, pure, or clear ⟨the weather gradually *fined*⟩ ⟨the ale will ~⟩ — often used with *off* **2 :** to become fine in lines or proportions **:** DIMINISH, DWINDLE — often used with *away* or *down* ⟨even her fatness seemed puppy fat . . . that must ~ down before very long —Mollie Panter-Downes⟩

[6]**fi·ne** \ˈfē(ˌ)nā\ *n* [It, fr. L *finis* boundary, limit, end — more at FINAL] **:** END — used as a direction in music to mark the closing point after a repeat

[7]**fine** \fēn\ *n* -s [F, short for *fine champagne*] **:** ordinary French brandy; *esp* **:** one of undisclosed origin sold in French restaurants

fineable *var of* FINABLE

fine aggregate *n* **:** that portion of the aggregate used in concrete that is smaller than about 3/16 inch

fine art \ˈ=ˈ=\ *n* [back-formation fr. *fine arts,* pl., trans. of F *beaux-arts*] **1 a :** art that is concerned primarily with the creation of beautiful objects **:** art for which aesthetic purposes are primary or uppermost **b :** the objects themselves ⟨the fetishes of the Negro sculptor . . . are *fine art* —John Dewey⟩ **2 :** any art (as painting, drawing, architecture, sculpture, music, ceramics, or landscape architecture) for which aesthetic purposes are primary or uppermost — usu. used in pl.

finebent \ˈ=,=\ *n* **:** any of several grasses of the genus *Agrostis; esp* **:** RHODE ISLAND BENT

fine-bore \ˈ=ˈ=\ *vt* **:** to bore accurately (a gun or gun barrel) so as to give a fine finish

fine cham·pagne \fēnshänpäny\ *n* [F] **:** a French brandy designated by French law as one distilled from wine made from grapes grown in the vineyards Grande Champagne and Petite Champagne in Charente department, France — called also *grande champagne*

fine chemical *n* **:** a chemical (as a photographic chemical, a perfume, or a pharmaceutical) produced and handled in relatively small amounts and usu. in a more or less pure state — compare HEAVY CHEMICAL

finecomb \ˈ=ˈ=\ *vt* **:** to search thoroughly ⟨technicians ~ed the liquor stores for clues —Al Spiers⟩

fine cut *n* **:** tobacco cut into small shreds for chewing or smoking

fined *past of* FINE

fine-draw \ˈ=ˈ=\ *vt* **:** to make a concealed joining of; *esp* **:** to mend (torn edges) by drawing together with invisible stitches

fine-drawn \ˈ=ˈ=\ *adj* **:** drawn out to extreme subtlety ⟨I don't follow his *fine-drawn* speculations⟩

fine frame *n* **:** SPEEDER 1b

fine-grain \ˈ=ˈ=\ *adj* **1 :** producing images of low graininess so that considerable enlargement without undue coarseness is permitted — used of a photographic developer **2** *also* **fine-grained** \ˈ=ˈ=\ **:** characterized by comparatively fine graininess — used of a photographic image or photographic emulsion

fine gravel *n* **:** gravel having particles ranging between 1 and 2 mm in diameter

fine harness *n* **:** a show class of light harness horses; *also* **:** a horse trained to participate in such a class

fine herbs \ˈfīˈnərbz, ˈfīnˈhər- — *see* HERB\ *n pl* [trans. of F *fines herbes*] **:** FINES HERBES

fine-leaved heath \ˈ=ˌ=-\ *n* **:** a common European heath (*Erica cinerea*) with very slender leaves in whorls of three

fine·less \ˈfīnləs\ *adj* [[1]*fine* (end) + *-less*] *archaic* **:** ENDLESS

fine·ly *adv* [ME, fr. *fin, fine* + *-ly*] **:** in a fine manner: as **a :** EXCELLENTLY, SPLENDIDLY, ADMIRABLY ⟨the house has been ~ restored⟩ ⟨a large modern plant ~ housed and staffed —*Amer. Guide Series: N.H.*⟩ **b :** with nice or close discrimination **:** to a fine point **:** DISCRIMINATINGLY, PRECISELY ⟨with color lines so ~ drawn that a contemporary record recognized 250 different blood combinations —*Time*⟩ ⟨~ detailed maps and guide books —E.W.Smith⟩ **c :** with delicacy or subtlety (as in action, expression, or feeling) **:** SENSITIVELY ⟨you play a little too ~ . . . I want some roughness here —*Time*⟩ ⟨~ modulated thought —Cecil Sprigge⟩ ⟨he was a deeply and ~ feeling man —T.W.Beach⟩ **d :** in small particles **:** MINUTELY ⟨~ divided nickel⟩ **e :** in an impressive or elegant manner **:** BRAVELY ⟨she moves ~, with a slow steady elegance —Kenneth Tynan⟩ **f :** GREATLY, REALLY — used as an intensive ⟨had his temper ~ up now—Mary Deasy⟩

fine·ness \ˈfīnnəs\ *n* -ES [ME *finenesse,* fr. *fin, fine* + *-nesse* -ness] **1 :** exquisite perfection or elaborateness of form, texture, or construction **:** superior quality ⟨this material surpasses all others in ~⟩ **2 a :** freedom from foreign matter or alloy **:** CLEARNESS, PURITY ⟨the ~ of the gold⟩ **b :** the proportion of pure silver or gold in jewelry, bullion, or coins often expressed in parts per thousand and being in U.S. silver coin 9/10 or .900 fine and in English gold coin 11/12 or .9166 fine — compare KARAT **3 a** (1) **:** brave or striking appearance **:** ELEGANCE, DELICACY ⟨he was struck by the ease, the poise, the ~ of every motion —S.H.Adams⟩ ⟨the ~, the perfection, the chiseled quality of her features⟩ (2) **:** sensitivity or delicacy of touch or manipulation ⟨the pianist's notable ~ of rendition⟩ ⟨the ~ of the surgeon's technique⟩ **b :** SUBTLETY, SENSITIVITY, ACUITY ⟨not in the name of some high-flown ~ of feeling but in the name of simple social practicality —Lionel Trilling⟩ ⟨this does not mean that there is no ~ of discrimination in his handling of its themes —T.W.Beach⟩ **4 :** the condition or degree of slenderness, thinness, or sharpness ⟨the ~ of wire⟩ ⟨the ~ of a knife's edge determines its cutting power⟩ **5 a :** the condition of being finely divided **:** the condition of being finely composed (as of particles, threads, or fibers) ⟨marveled at the ~ of the sand⟩ **b :** the extent of subdivision of a substance as indicated under prescribed conditions (as of cement, sand, gravel, or pigments) **c :** the relative width, diameter, linear density, or weight per unit length (as of fibers or yarns) expressed in a number of units

fineness ratio *n* **:** the ratio of the length of a streamlined body (as a fuselage) to its maximum diameter

fine of lands : [1]FINE 3c

fine print *n* **:** a part of a contract (as an insurance policy) or a certificate of ownership (as of stock) printed in type of small size or in footnotes that contains qualifications, limitations, or exceptions which make a contractual agreement less favorable ⟨be sure to read the *fine print*⟩ — called also *small print*

[1]**finer** *comparative of* FINE

[2]**fin·er** \ˈfīnə(r)\ *n* -s [ME *finour, finer,* fr. *finen* to refine + *-our* -or or *-er* — more at FINE] **1 :** a workman who refines **:** ROLLER, TRIMMER **2 :** one who puts the mainspring assembly into clocks

[1]**fin·ery** \ˈfīn(ə)rē, -ri\ *n* -ES [[5]*fine* + *-ery*] **:** REFINERY

[2]**finery** \"\ *n* -ES [[3]*fine* + *-ery*] **1** *obs* **:** FINENESS, BEAUTY, ELEGANCE; *esp* **:** ostentatious luxury or lavishness **2 a :** ornament or decoration esp. in excessive amounts **b :** showy clothing and jewels; *also* **:** an individual's best or dressy clothing ⟨a modest woman, dressed out in all her ~ —Oliver Goldsmith⟩

fines \ˈfīnz\ *n pl* [[3]*fine* + *-s*] **1 :** finely crushed or powdered material (as ore); *esp* **:** material finer than the minimum for any specified grade or passing through a screen on which the coarser material is retained **2 :** very small particles; *esp* **:** those smaller than average in a mixture of particles of various sizes ⟨the ~ in glacial drift⟩ **3 :** very small fragments of fiber

fine sand *n* **:** sand composed of grains ranging from 0.10 to 0.25 mm in diameter

fines herbes \fēnzerb\ *n pl* [F, lit., fine herbs] **:** a mixture of culinary herbs (as parsley, chervil, chives, tarragon, thyme) in various combinations used as a seasoning when chopped or as a garnish when whole

fine sight *n* **:** disposition of the gunsight in firing so that only the tip of the front sight is seen through the notch of the rear sight

finespun \ˈ=ˈ=\ *adj* **1 :** developed or elaborated with extreme care, skill, delicacy, ingenuity ⟨the satire touches also, with ~ ridicule, every kind of human pretense or affectation —Carl van Doren⟩ ⟨a ~ novel⟩ **2 :** too subtle, tenuous, or refined **:** engrossed or concerned with narrow or minute detail **:** developed in excessively fine or hairsplitting detail ⟨the emergency . . . does not permit of ~ distinctions and long arguments —*Newsweek*⟩ ⟨~ theories⟩ ⟨economics has long enjoyed the reputation of being the most ~ . . . of the social sciences —R.A.Lester⟩

[1]**fi·nesse** \fəˈnes\ *n* -s [ME, fr. MF, fr. *fin* fine — more at FINE] **1 :** fineness or delicacy esp. of workmanship, structure, texture, or flavor ⟨trinkets of an extreme ~ —Arnold Rosin⟩ ⟨the wines . . . make up in richness and bigness what they lack in ~ —H.T.Grossman⟩ **2 :** delicate skill **:** exquisite grace **:** SUBTLETY, REFINEMENT ⟨it is no surprise to find him playing with persuasion and ~ —Howard Barnes⟩ **3 a :** adroit maneuvering **:** CUNNING, STRATEGY ⟨Danish ~, which consists of a fine balance of imagination and horse sense —*Atlantic*⟩ **b :** TRICK, STRATAGEM ⟨it is a frequently available ~, in such positions, not to capture hostile pawns, but to pass them by —C.T.S.Purdy⟩ **4 :** deliberate omission to play one's highest card in a suit in bridge or deliberate omission to trump in the hope or assurance that a lower card played from one's own or one's partner's hand will take the trick because the only higher opposing card is in the hand of an opponent who has already played to the trick

[2]**finesse** \"\ *vb* -ED/-ING/-S *vi* **:** to make a finesse in playing cards — sometimes used with *for* ⟨~ for the jack⟩ or *against* ⟨~ against opponent on the right⟩ ~ *vt* **1 a :** to play (a card) as a finesse ⟨can ~ the jack if the queen lies on the right⟩ **b :** to play a card one lower than (the middle card of a three-card sequence) ⟨hoped by playing the jack to ~ the queen⟩ **c :** to refrain from topping the lead of (one's partner) with a card two points higher in hope that the intervening card is not in the fourth hand and therefore cannot win the trick **2 :** to bring about or manage by adroit maneuvering **:** MANEUVER ⟨the man who *finessed* the entry of American troops into New Caledonia without firing a shot —Joseph Driscoll⟩ ⟨~ his way through tight places where the flick of an eyelash might mean death —Marquis James⟩ **:** get the better of by adroit maneuvering **:** get around **:** EVADE, TRICK ⟨trying to ~ an eagle-eyed editor who's on to all the tricks —J.C.G.Conniff⟩ ⟨*finessed* rather than faced the hottest critical barrage of his prime-ministership —*Time*⟩ ⟨felt that in some way he had been *finessed*, and was trying to figure out where —Robertson Davies⟩ **3 :** to play (a croquet ball) into a position where it will be of the least use to an opponent

[1]**finest** *superlative of* FINE

[2]**fin·est** \ˈfīnəst\ *n, pl in constr* [[1]*finest*] **:** POLICEMEN — usu. qualified and localized explicitly or implicitly by the possessive form of a city ⟨a dozen of the city's ~⟩

fine stuff *n* **:** the material (as plasterer's putty or a mixture of fine sand with plasterer's putty) used for the final coat of a plastered wall

fine-tooth comb *n* **1 :** a comb with teeth set close together used esp. for cleaning lice, nits, and other matter from the hair **2 :** an attitude or system of thoroughly searching or scrutinizing ⟨went through that house with a *fine-tooth comb* —Merle Miller⟩

fine-tooth-comb \ˈ=ˌ=ˈ=\ *vt* [*fine-tooth comb*] **:** to search or scrutinize intensively or minutely ⟨I *fine-tooth-combed* that patch of roadside, inch by inch —*True Crime Cases*⟩ ⟨scientists have gone to *fine-tooth-comb* the Urals and mid-Asia for new raw materials and power resources —Joseph Prescott⟩

finetop \ˈ=,=\ *n* **:** RHODE ISLAND BENT

fine–top salt grass *n* **:** a perennial dropseed grass (*Sporobolus airoides*) that forms dense clumps and has open panicles

fine–wool \'=;=\ *adj* **:** having or producing wool similar to that of the merino in fineness ⟨a *fine-wool* sheep⟩ ⟨*fine-wool* breeding⟩

finfish \'=,=\ *n pl* **:** true fish — distinguished from *shellfish*

fin fold *n* **:** a median fold of integument which extends along the body of an embryo fish and from which the dorsal, caudal, and anal fins are developed

finfoot \'=,=\ *n, pl* **finfoots :** SUN-GREBE

fin·gent \'finjənt\ *adj* [L *fingent-, fingens,* pres. part. of *fingere* to shape, form — more at DOUGH] **:** PLIABLE, FLEXIBLE, YIELDING ⟨showing a somewhat more ~ mood —C.L.Sulzberger⟩

[1]**fin·ger** \'fiŋgə(r)\ *n* -s [ME, fr. OE; akin to OHG *fingar* finger, ON *fingr,* Goth *figgrs,* and perh. to OE *fīf* five — more at FIVE] **1 :** one of the five terminating members of the hand **:** a digit of the forelimb; *specif* **:** one of the four extremities of the hand other than the thumb **2 a :** something that resembles or does the work of a finger ⟨a ~ of toast⟩ ⟨a ~ of land extending into the sea⟩ ⟨the ~ of a clock⟩ **b :** a part of a glove into which a finger is inserted **c :** one of the bananas or plantains in a hand **d :** a vegetable drug cut or compressed into the size and shape of a finger ⟨a ~ of rhubarb⟩ **e :** a projecting rod, wire, or piece (as a pawl for a ratchet) that is brought into contact with an object to effect, direct, or restrain a motion **3 a :** FINGERBREADTH **b :** an amount of liquor equal to the quantity in a glass filled up to one fingerbreadth **4 a :** CONCERN, INTEREST, PART, SHARE ⟨he seems always to have a ~ in some magisterial affair —V.L.Parrington⟩ — often used in the phrase *to have a finger in the pie* ⟨has a ~ in every political pie⟩ **b fingers** *pl* **:** POSSESSION ⟨marries the boss's daughter, and gets his ~s on the armament industry —Sherwood Anderson⟩ **5** *slang* **:** one who keeps tabs on or reports on a person **:** FINGER MAN, INFORMER ⟨first they get a ~ on him —J.M.Cain⟩ — **lift a finger :** to make an effort **:** WORK

[2]**finger** \"\ *vb* **fingered; fingered; fingering** \-ŋg(ə)riŋ\ **fingers** [ME *fingeren,* fr. *finger,* n.] *vt* **1 :** to touch or feel with the fingers **:** toy with **:** HANDLE ⟨eyeing her . . . as a broker buys a diamond . . . as a country woman ~s a bolt of tweed —Francis Hackett⟩ ⟨~ed his scraggy chin before he answered —C.G.D.Roberts⟩ ⟨~ed his heavy underlip as if probing it for a cold sore —Kenneth Roberts⟩ **2** *obs* **:** STEAL, PILFER, PURLOIN **3 a :** to play (a musical instrument) with the fingers **b :** to play with a specific fingering **c :** to mark the notes of (a music score) as a guide in playing **4 :** to extend into or penetrate in the shape of a finger ⟨the long beams of the searchlights ~*ing* the sky —R.H.Newman⟩ ⟨new roads ~*ing* once trackless plains⟩ **5 :** to point out **:** IDENTIFY, INDICATE, DESIGNATE ⟨far be it from me to ~ any individual to be blasted by the presidential wrath —G.W.Johnson⟩ ⟨the man he ~*ed* for the mayor's job was an old-time politician⟩ ⟨practically all of them had been ~*ed* by the more reliable ex-Communists —Elmer Davis⟩: as **a :** to point out, name, or identify to the police esp. in a police lineup ⟨she ~*ed* a boy friend . . . as one of the killers —Lew Arthur⟩ **b :** to indicate to a criminal (as the intended victims or the place or object to be robbed) ⟨in those days you merely ~*ed* the victim . . . and in a few days your enemy's body was discovered in the gutter —Danny Ahearn⟩ ⟨sometimes the dock boss . . . ~s the load to be stolen —Malcolm Johnson⟩ **c** *slang* **:** to keep tabs on **:** report on **:** SHADOW ⟨we've been ~*ing* him for months —L.A.Norris⟩ ~ *vi* **1 :** to touch or handle something ⟨the rosaries, the strings of round bells . . . brought them toward him . . . snatching and ~*ing* —Marjory S. Douglas⟩ **2 a :** to use the fingers in playing a musical instrument **b :** to have a certain fingering (as of a musical instrument) ⟨it ~s like a cornet⟩ **3 :** to extend in the shape or manner of a finger ⟨the docks ~*ed* out into the water —R.P.Warren⟩ ⟨forests, farms, industries . . . ~*ing* through great river valleys —Betty F. Martin⟩ ⟨searchlights ~*ed* across the black water —*Time*⟩

finger alphabet *n* **:** MANUAL ALPHABET

finger and toe *also* **finger–and–toe disease** *n* **:** CLUBROOT

finger bar *n* **:** CUTTER BAR

fingerboard \'=,=\ *n* **1 a :** the part of a stringed instrument against which the fingers press the strings to vary the pitch — see VIOLIN illustration **b :** the keyboard of a piano or organ **:** MANUAL **2 a :** FINGERPOST **b :** a pointed guideboard often bearing a symbol representing a hand with extended index finger ⟨weather-beaten ~s —F.V.W.Mason⟩

finger bowl *n* **1 :** a bowl or basin to hold water for rinsing the fingers at table **2** *biol* **:** a round shallow bowl of heavy glass used esp. for culturing aquatic organisms

fingerbreadth \'=,=\ *n* **:** a unit of length based on the breadth of a finger **:** DIGIT 2

finger brush *n* **:** a brush for applying size to book covers

finger clamp *n* **:** a flat clamp of which the end that holds the work is shaped to fit into a hole in the work

finger–cone pine *n* **:** WESTERN WHITE PINE 1

finger coral *n* **:** SEA GINGER

finger cymbal *n* **:** CASTANET

fin·gered \'fiŋgə(r)d\ *adj* **1 :** having fingers ⟨the ~ roots of giant trees⟩ **2 :** DIGITATE 2

fingered citron *also* **fingered lemon** *n* **:** BUDDHA'S-HAND

fingered kelp *n* **:** DEADMAN'S HAND 1c

fin·ger·er \'fiŋgərə(r)\ *n* -s [[1]*finger* + *-er*] **:** one that makes the fingers of gloves

finger fern *n* **1 :** SCALE FERN **2 :** any fern of the genus *Asplenium* **3 :** HART'S-TONGUE 1

fingerfish \'=,=\ *n* **:** STARFISH

fingerflower \'=,=\ *n* **:** FOXGLOVE 1

finger–foxed \'=;=\ *adj* **:** having a quarter or foxing so designed that the upper portion extends forward to the throat of a shoe in a narrow strip below the upper part of the quarter

finger fracture *n, med* **:** a breaking of the fibers of the mitral commissure to relieve stenosis of the mitral valve that is performed by a finger thrust through the valve — compare COMMISSUROTOMY

finger grass *n* **1 :** CRABGRASS 1a **2 :** any grass of the genus *Chloris* **3 :** YARD GRASS

finger guard *n* **:** a metal piece attached to the shaft of a carving fork for protecting the fingers from the carving knife

fingerhold \'=,=\ *n* **1 :** a hold or grasp by the fingers **2 :** any weak hold or support ⟨it gave a ~ to her theories and suspicions —Victor Canning⟩

finger hole *n* **1 :** a hole in a wind instrument for changing the pitch of the tone according as it is left open or closed by the finger **2 :** either of two holes bored in a large bowling ball to provide a grip **3 :** any of the small holes in the disk of a dial telephone by which the number desired is dialed

[1]**fingering** *n* -s [ME, fr. gerund of *fingeren* to finger] **1 a :** the act or method of using the fingers (as in playing a musical instrument or typing) **b :** the marking of the method of fingering (as by figures on a music score) **2 :** the controlling of the position of a fencing foil by the action of the fingers only

[2]**fin·ger·ing** \'fiŋg(ə)riŋ\ *or* **fingering yarn** *n* -s [fr. earlier *fingram,* prob. fr. F *fin grain* fine grain] **:** a plied worsted yarn for hand knitting

finger joint *n* **:** a joint in cabinetmaking formed by cutting two board ends into matching fingerlike projections that fit together

finger lake *n* **:** any of several long relatively narrow lakes in central New York state; *also* **:** a lake of similar shape elsewhere

fin·ger·less \'fiŋgə(r)ləs\ *adj* **:** having no fingers **:** having lost the fingers

fingerlike \'=,=\ *adj* **:** resembling a finger esp. in slender elongated form and flexibility **:** DIGITATE 2 ⟨~ projections of the margin of the ostium of a fallopian tube⟩ ⟨~ tendrils by which the vine clings⟩

finger lime *n* **:** a spiny Australian citrus shrub or tree (*Microcitrus australasica*) with smooth slender elongated fruits

fin·ger·ling \'fiŋgə(r)liŋ\ *n* -s [[1]*finger* + *-ling*] **:** a small fish no longer than a finger; *esp* **:** a young fish from two weeks after complete absorption of the yolk sac up to one year of age

finger man *n* **:** one who fingers (as for a gangster) ⟨Chicago gangster methods, with *finger men* pointing out unreliables for the triggermen to kill —*Newsweek*⟩ ⟨the miraculous finder of lost boys and girls, the brilliant *finger man* of thousands of sheriff's posses and private trailers —James Thurber⟩

finger millet *n* **:** RAGGEE

fingernail \'=,=, ,==;=\ *n* [ME *finger neil*] **:** the nail of a finger

fingernail clam *also* **fingernail shell** *n* **:** a small freshwater bivalve mollusk of a cosmopolitan genus (*Sphaerium*)

finger nut *n* **:** WING NUT

finger of apollo *usu cap A* [after *Apollo,* Greco-Roman god of the sun] **:** the third finger that when long and prominent is usu. held by palmists to indicate predominance of qualities characterizing an Apollonian

finger of jupiter *usu cap J* [after *Jupiter,* Roman god of the sky, fr. L *Juppiter* — more at DEITY] **:** the first finger that when long and prominent is usu. held by palmists to indicate predominance of qualities characterizing a Jupiterian

finger of mercury *usu cap M* [fr. *Mercury* (planet)] **:** the little finger that when long and straight is often held by palmists to indicate mental capacity for making use of talents and opportunities and power of expression esp. in speaking

finger of saturn *usu cap S* [after *Saturn,* Roman god connected with the sowing of seeds, fr. L *Saturnus*] **:** the second finger that when long and prominent is usu. held by palmists to indicate predominance of qualities characterizing a Saturnian

finger paint *n* **:** a pigment of the consistency of jelly

finger–paint \'=,=\ *vi* **:** to apply finger paint in splotches to wet paper and spread it mainly with the fingers ~ *vt* **:** to form (a design) with finger paint

finger painting *n* **1 :** the technique of using finger paint **2 :** a picture or design made with finger paint

fingerparted \'=;=;=\ *adj* **:** DIGITATE

finger plate *n* **:** a protective plate (as of metal, glass, or plastic) used to prevent soiling of a surface (as of a door) by finger marks

fingerpost \'=,=\ *n* **1 :** a guidepost bearing one or more index fingers **2 :** something that serves as a clue, indication, or aid to understanding or knowledge ⟨many admirable ~s to the study of old London have been written —Elizabeth Montizambert⟩ ⟨despite these significant ~s to her intention, the book has been somewhat inexplicably assigned a literal exactness —John McKellar⟩

fingerpost 1

[1]**fingerprint** \'=,=\ *n* [[1]*finger* + *print*] **:** the impression of a fingertip on any surface (as upon glass or polished metal); *esp* **:** an impression of the lines upon the finger taken in ink for purpose of identification

[2]**fingerprint** \"\ *vt* **:** to take fingerprints of ⟨hustled him into the sheriff's office, where he was ~*ed* . . . and locked in the bullpen to await bond —H.H.Martin⟩

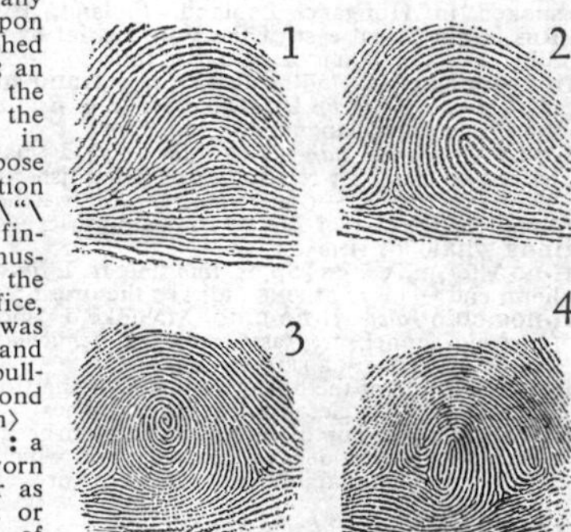

fingerprints: *1* arch, *2* loop, *3* whorl, *4* composite

finger ring *n* **:** a metal ring worn on the finger as an ornament or as a token of marriage or betrothal

finger roll *n* **1 :** bread shaped in long slender rolls **2 :** an Italian breadstick

fingerroot \'=,=\ *n* **:** FOXGLOVE 1

fingers *pl of* FINGER, *pres 3d sing of* FINGER

finger spelling *n* **:** communication by means of one of the manual alphabets **:** DACTYLOLOGY

finger sponge *n* **:** a sponge having finger-shaped lobes; *esp* **:** a common red or orange sponge (*Chalina oculata*) related to the important commercial sponges and widely distributed in shallow waters on both coasts of the Atlantic ocean

fingerstall \'=,=\ *n* [ME, fr. [1]*finger* + *stall*] **:** [1]COT 3b

finger–tame \'=;=\ *adj, of a pet bird* **:** trained to perch on a finger

[1]**fingertip** \'=,=\ *n* [[1]*finger* + *tip*] **1 :** the tip of a finger **2 :** a protective covering for the end joint of a finger **3 :** a southern California succulent herb (*Stylophyllum edule*) of the family Crassulaceae with pencil-shaped leaves — **at one's fingertips 1 :** within easy reach ⟨thanks to an excellent filing system, he has all the figures *at his fingertips*⟩ **2 :** instantly or readily produced or available as a result of thorough familiarity with the subject ⟨he had the whole answer *at his fingertips*⟩ — **to one's fingertips :** COMPLETELY, THOROUGHLY ⟨a gentleman *to his fingertips*⟩

fingertip 2

[2]**fingertip** \"\ *adj* **:** extending from the shoulder to mid-thigh — used of coats, veils, and similar clothing

finger wave *n* **:** a method or style of setting hair by dampening with water or wave solution and forming waves with fingers and a comb and shaping curls by winding strands of hair around the operator's finger

finger weaving *n* **:** the intertwisting or weaving of threads without a shuttle; *esp* **:** BRAIDING

fin·gery \'fiŋg(ə)rē, -ri\ *adj* **:** branching like or resembling fingers ⟨the chestnuts . . . with their interknit ~ leaves —Elizabeth Bowen⟩

fin·go \'fiŋ(,)gō\ *n, pl* **fingo** *or* **fingos** *or* **fingoes** *usu cap* **1 a :** a So. African people descended from a group of Negro refugees who were driven southward in native wars and later settled east of Great Fish river, Union of So. Africa **b :** a member of this people **2 :** the Bantu language of the Fingo people

fin·i·al \'finēəl, *chiefly Brit* 'fīn-\ *n* -s [ME, fr. *finial,* adj., final, alter. of *final* — more at FINAL] **1 :** a usu. foliated ornament forming the upper extremity (as of a pinnacle, canopy, or gable) esp. in Gothic architecture; *sometimes* **:** the pinnacle itself **2 :** any terminating or capping ornament or detail (as a vase in a broken pediment or an ornament on an automobile instrument panel or topping a lampshade)

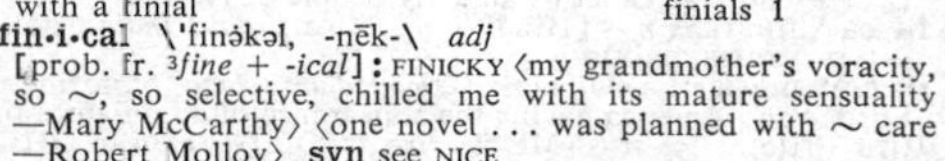
finials 1

fin·i·aled \-ld\ *adj* **:** provided with a finial

fin·i·cal \'finəkəl, -nēk-\ *adj* [prob. fr. [3]*fine* + *-ical*] **:** FINICKY ⟨my grandmother's voracity, so ~, so selective, chilled me with its mature sensuality —Mary McCarthy⟩ ⟨one novel . . . was planned with ~ care —Robert Molloy⟩ **syn** see NICE

fin·i·cal·i·ty \,finə'kaləd·ē\ *n* -ES **:** FINICALNESS

fin·i·cal·ly \-k(ə)lē, -li\ *adv* **:** in a finical manner ⟨~ tasting the unaccustomed dishes⟩

fin·i·cal·ness \-kəlnəs\ *n* -ES **:** the quality or state of being finical

fin·ick *also* **fin·nick** \'finik, -nēk\ *vi* -ED/-ING/-S [back-formation fr. *finicking*] **1 :** to become excessively or affectedly dainty or refined in speech or manner **:** put on airs **2 :** to dawdle about ⟨~*ed* with her food —Elizabeth Taylor⟩ ⟨she was not one who had time to ~ about snipping at blossoms —Adrian Bell⟩

fin·ick·i·ness \-nəkēnəs, -nēk-, -kin-\ *n* -ES **:** the quality or state of being finicky ⟨instability, irritability, ~ about food, a tendency to sudden whims and . . . fancies —Margaret Mead⟩ ⟨the gourmet's ~ with his appetite —William Becker⟩

fin·ick·ing \-kiŋ,-kin\ *or* **fin·i·kin** \-kən\ *adj* [alter. of *finical*] **:** FINICKY ⟨they seem to have approached the usually ~ processes involved . . . in a singularly carefree manner —R.M.Coates⟩

fin·ick·ing·ly *adv* **:** in a finicking manner

fin·ick·ing·ness \-kiŋnəs,kən(n)əs\ *n* -ES **:** the quality or state of being finicking

fin·icky *also* **fin·nicky** \'finəkē, -ki\ *adj, sometimes* -ER/-EST [alter. of *finicking*] **:** excessively nice, dainty, or exacting in taste or standards **:** marked by or displaying too much concern with trifles or details **:** hard to please **:** overly scrupulous **:** OVERNICE, METICULOUS, FUSSY, PARTICULAR ⟨his ~ concern for the detailed order of his existence —Jack Richmond⟩ ⟨very ~ about his food⟩ ⟨of all fruits, strawberries are most ~ about soil and climate —*House Beautiful*⟩

fin·i·fy \'finə,fī, 'fīn-\ *vt* -ED/-ING/-ES [[3]*fine* + *-ify*] *now dial* **:** to deck out **:** make fine in appearance **:** ADORN ⟨ladies minced about, *finified* in their gala best —S.H.Adams⟩

fining *n* -s [fr. gerund of [5]*fine*] **1 :** the act or process of fining: as **a :** the conversion of pig iron into wrought iron in a hearth or charcoal fire, a process now superseded by puddling **b :** the process of freeing molten glass of bubbles usu. by the addition of certain chemical agents **c :** the operation or process by which a beverage (as wine or beer) is clarified (as by bringing suspended matter to the bottom) **2 :** material (as isinglass, gelatin, egg white) used for clarifying a liquid (as a beverage) — often used in pl. ⟨when ~s are poured into a cask . . . they should reach every part of the wine —A.L. Simon⟩

fin·is \'finəs, 'fīn- *also* 'fēn-\ *n* -ES [ME, fr. L — more at FINAL] **:** END, CONCLUSION ⟨white settlers poured onto the prairies . . . and wrote ~ to their carefree existence —D.F.Symington⟩ ⟨the story . . . is far from complete because ~ is not yet written —R.G.Whalen⟩

[1]**fin·ish** \'finish, *chiefly in pres part* -nəsh\ *vb* -ED/-ING/-ES [ME *finisshen,* fr. MF *feniss-, finiss-,* stem of *fenir, finir,* fr. L *finire* to limit, finish, end, fr. *finis* boundary, limit, end — more at FINAL] *vt* **1 a :** to bring to an end **:** arrive at the end of **:** TERMINATE, COMPLETE ⟨he ~*ed* speaking, and a long silence fell⟩ ⟨he ~*ed* his days in poverty and loneliness⟩ ⟨a rapid reader, he can ~ a chapter in a few minutes⟩ **b :** to use, consume, or dispose of entirely ⟨he ~*ed* the meal to the last crumb —Louis Bromfield⟩ — often used with *off* ⟨the sailors lounging in the bar began to ~ off their drinks —Allen Upward⟩ **c :** to serve as the close or last item of ⟨a pleasant wine ~*es* the meal, nicely accenting the dessert⟩ ⟨a thrilling 100-yard dash ~*ed* the meet⟩ **2 a :** to expend the final labors on **:** bring to completion or issue ⟨tried to ~ the work his illustrious predecessor had started⟩ **b :** to perform completely **:** perfect with all possible labor and attention **:** give the ultimate touches to ⟨he always spoke in completed sentences . . . he ~*ed* his thought —W.A.White⟩ — often used with *up* ⟨advised him to ~ up the painting a little before exhibiting⟩ **c :** to complete the education of; *esp* **:** to prepare (a young woman) for entrance into society ⟨she received her ~*ing* in Paris⟩ **d :** to fatten (an animal) esp. for the market **e :** to put on as a finish ⟨all interior walls are ~*ed* with lime plaster —*Amer. Guide Series: Minn.*⟩ **f :** to cut, sort, trim, count, and pack (paper after it leaves the paper machine) **g :** to tool the title and decoration on (a hand-bound book) **h** (1) **:** to give (as cloth) special characteristics that improve appearance and usefulness by processing (as mercerizing, fulling, calendering, embossing) (2) **:** to complete work on (a garment); *esp* **:** to finish (a raw edge) by hemming, pinking, overcasting, facing **i :** to subject (newly formed soap or a kettle of soap) to the processes of fitting and settling **3 a :** to bring to an end the significance, usefulness, or effectiveness of **:** exhaust the power, worth, or vitality of **:** deal a mortal blow to ⟨the combination of . . . unfamiliar car, narrow streets, and strange town will just about ~ you —Richard Joseph⟩ ⟨his stunning defeat ~*ed* the young congressman as a political force⟩ — often used with *off* ⟨the romance of chivalry was already moribund and the new economic and social trends ~*ed* it off⟩ **b** (1) **:** to bring about the death of **:** KILL ⟨after wounding me with his spear he was about to ~ me with his knife —W.H.Hudson †1922⟩ — often used with *off* ⟨his woman ~*ed* him off . . . with a skinning knife —Walter O'Meara⟩ (2) **:** to bring about the decisive or final defeat of ⟨the cavalry charge ~*ed* the enemy; they broke and ran⟩ ~ *vi* **1 a :** to come to an end **:** TERMINATE, END ⟨the Civil War ~*ed* in 1865⟩ ⟨until British rule ~*ed* one had to obtain a visa from the British Foreign Office —W.B.Fisher⟩ **b** (1) **:** to come to the end of a course, task, or undertaking **:** complete a task or assignment ⟨it was noon, and he still had not ~*ed*⟩ ⟨he ~*ed* by reciting a cycle of sonnets⟩ ⟨I shall ~ with a Chopin nocturne —Lillian Hellman⟩ — often used with *up* ⟨you can ~ up now⟩ (2) **:** to finish a race or other competition in a certain manner or position ⟨the gelding ~*ed* strong and lost only by a nose⟩ ⟨he ~*ed* third in the oratorical contest⟩ **c :** to have a certain issue or outcome **:** RESULT ⟨any illness must ~ fatally for him —Osbert Sitwell⟩ **2 :** to become smooth (as of lumber) **3 :** to attend a finishing school **4** *of an animal* **:** to become suitably fat for marketing **syn** see CLOSE — **finish with 1 :** to have done with **:** cease to have relations with ⟨she decided to *finish with* him for good⟩ **2 :** to complete work upon ⟨as soon as he had *finished with* the statue he went on to a more ambitious project⟩

[2]**fin·ish** \"\ *n* -ES **1 a :** the final stage **:** CONCLUSION, END ⟨a fight to the ~⟩ ⟨flaunted the riskiest of their stunts and then . . . broke into their whirlwind ~ —Winifred Bambrick⟩ ⟨turned a slow start into a fast ~⟩ **b :** the cause of one's ruin **:** DOWNFALL ⟨his taste for gambling was his ~⟩ **2 :** something that finishes, completes, or perfects: as **a** (1) **:** the joiner work and other fine work required for the completion of a building esp. of the interior — see INSIDE FINISH, OUTSIDE FINISH (2) **:** the higher grade of lumber used for this work — called also *uppers* (3) **:** decorative surface treatment (as on paper, wood, stone, brick, plaster, or stucco) (4) **:** a finishing material used in painting ⟨oil ~⟩ — see FINISHING COAT **b :** the labor required for the last stage (as of a work of art) ⟨the sculptor is now doing the ~ on this splendid head⟩ **c :** a plain or decorative method of completing a part or an edge of a garment by use of a hem, binding, arrowhead, edging **d :** FAT; *esp* **:** the layer of fat lying beneath the skin of an animal well fattened for market or show **e :** the top or closure part of a glass container including the pouring lip and the threads or other means of attaching or inserting a closure **f :** the final treatment or coating of a surface **3 a :** the result or product of a finishing process esp. with regard to its quality, appearance, or characteristics ⟨a fabric with a water-resistant ~⟩ ⟨a cloth with a glazed ~⟩ ⟨paper with a glossy ~⟩; *specif* **:** the state of a surface (as of furniture or pottery) after the tool marks have been obliterated **b :** [6]FIT 3 **c :** the quality or state of being perfected or minutely elaborated **:** impeccable, finished, or flawless quality **:** PERFECTION ⟨the exquisite ~ of this artist's work⟩ ⟨the machine . . . worked with neither the accuracy nor the ~ of these girls —Sam Pollock⟩ ⟨his novels have a ~, a flavor, that the cultivated recognize and relish⟩ ⟨at the age of 60 he danced . . . and still displayed great ~ and fine style —Anatole Chujoy⟩ **d :** cultivation in manners and speech **:** social polish

finished *adj* **1 :** brought to conclusion **:** ENDED, COMPLETED ⟨typing the ~ letters on company letterheads —J.R.Gregg⟩ ⟨gave me the ~ manuscript to read⟩: as **a :** ready for packing, shipment, or sale — used of materials or goods **b :** PROCESSED ⟨storage facilities for both raw and ~ water —*U. S. Geol. Survey List*⟩ **c** *of an animal* **:** fattened esp. for the market **d :** in a hopeless condition **:** defeated, wounded, or ailing beyond hope of recovery **:** done for **:** DOOMED ⟨about that time I was feeling very feeble and ~ —O.W.Holmes †1935⟩ ⟨so the press telegrapher was ~, or practically so —C.B. Davis⟩ ⟨a lot of wishful thinkers assume that the enemy is ~⟩ ⟨their class, the upper middle, was ~ politically and economically —Mary McCarthy⟩ **2 :** possessed of, brought to, or displaying the highest degree of skill, polish, or excellence **:** marked by the highest quality **:** CONSUMMATE, PERFECTED ⟨written with the ~ workmanship which always delights us —Edward Sackville-West⟩ ⟨the texture of his writing is even and ~ —*Times Lit. Supp.*⟩ ⟨a group of gentle, highly ~, memorable stories —Paul Pickrel⟩ ⟨a glitteringly ~ troupe from the start —Wilder Hobson⟩ ⟨he's the most ~ blackmailer in America —Donn Byrne⟩

fin·ish·er \-shə(r)\ *n* -s **1 :** one that finishes: as **a :** a worker who performs the finishing steps of shaping, assembling, adjusting, smoothing, painting, polishing, cleaning, or decorating an item of manufacture **b :** a machine that performs the finishing steps in a processing, manufacturing, or similar operation **2 :** something that finishes or settles a matter decisively ⟨I looked to have a knife through me forthwith as a ~ —J.H.Wheelwright⟩

finisher card *n* **:** the last and finest of three cards used in producing wool sliver — compare BREAKER CARD, INTERMEDIATE 5a

finish hardware *n* **:** visible or exposed hardware fittings (as locks, hinges, fasteners, handles, plates) used in building construction

finishing *n* -s [ME *finisshing*, fr. gerund of *finisshen* to finish — more at FINISH] **:** the act or process of completing **:** the final work upon or ornamentation of a thing; *specif* **:** the processing applied to cloth after it is taken from the loom

finishing coat *also* **finish coat** *n* **1 :** the final usu. white coat of plastering applied to walls and ceilings **2 :** the final coat of paint

finishing hydrate *n* **:** hydrated lime used in the finishing coat for plastered walls

finishing machine *n* **:** a mechanical device running on forms that is used to strike off and shape concrete surfaces (as highway and airfield pavements)

finishing nail *n* **:** a wire nail used for finishing whose small cylindrical head is easily countersunk and the resulting hole concealed by a filler

finishing powder *n* **:** a dry sizing for making gold adhere to book covers while finishing

finishing room *n* **:** a room or department where the last steps of a manufacturing, processing, or assembling operation are performed; *specif* **:** a part of the plant in a paper mill where the paper is cut, sorted, trimmed, counted, and packed for shipment

finishing school *n* **:** a private school that prepares young women for social life (as by emphasizing cultural accomplishments and social graces) rather than for a vocational or professional career

finishing stove *n* **:** a small rack-topped stove for heating a bookbinder's finishing tools

finish line *n* **:** a line marking the end of a racecourse

fi·ni·tary \ˈfīnəˌterē, ˈfin-\ *adj* [*finite* + *-ary*] **:** having a finite character; *specif* **:** capable of being completed in a finite number of steps — used of a proof or other logical procedure

¹**fi·nite** \ˈfīˌnīt, *usu* -nīd.+V\ *adj* [ME *finit*, fr. L *finitus*, past part. of *finire* to limit, finish, end — more at FINISH] **1 a :** having definite or definable limits or boundaries **:** not illimitable **:** LIMITED, BOUNDED ⟨a ~, although not very definite, thickness will reduce the intensity to a point where it is relatively insignificant —Samuel Glasstone⟩ ⟨the power of credence, of imaginatively realizing a supreme event . . . is ridiculously ~ —Arnold Bennett⟩ ⟨the absorption of all peoples into a ~, small community —C.E.Odegaard⟩ ⟨a universal theory cannot be induced from a ~ number of facts —Maurice Cranston & J.W.N.Watkins⟩ **b :** having a nature, character, or existence subject to limitations or marked by imperfections **:** limited in power **:** not absolute **:** HUMAN, MORTAL ⟨a ~ God who struggles in his great and comprehensive way as we struggle in our weak and silly way —H.G.Wells⟩ ⟨the impossible gulf between the ~ Easterner and the infinite, pure virtue of the cowboy —D.B.Davis⟩ ⟨incurable ills such as death, destruction . . . and ignorance . . . will always be characteristic of ~ beings —M.R.Cohen⟩ ⟨fate was inhuman, it was cruel, it excited and crushed every ~ wish —F.R.Leavis⟩ ⟨have pity on ~ us —Don May⟩ **2 a :** having a character or being completely determinable in theory or in fact either as an object of thought or as susceptible of complete enumeration or of physical measurement **b :** subject to experience **c :** neither infinite nor infinitesimal **3 a :** less than an arbitrary positive integer and greater than the negative of that integer — used of a quantity, magnitude, or number **b :** having a finite number of elements ⟨the set of integers is ~⟩ **4 :** of, relating to, or being a verb or verb form that can function as a predicate or as the main element of one and that is limited (as in tense, person, and number) — **fi·nite·ly** *adv*

²**finite** \ˈ"\ *n* -s **:** a finite thing or being **:** something that is finite

³**finite** *vt* -ED/-ING/-s **:** to make finite **:** LIMIT

finite canon *n* **:** a musical canon that comes to a definite end with its theme — contrasted with *circular canon*

fi·nite·ness *n* -ES **:** the quality or state of being finite ⟨recoiled at the thought that the quality of ~ was not foreign to Eden —Thomas Hardy⟩

finite proposition *n* **:** a logical proposition with a limited or definite predicate (as *is white* or *is human*) as contrasted with one whose predicate is an indefinite negative (as *not white* or *not man*)

finite set *n, math* **:** a set consisting of a finite number of elements

fi·nit·ism \ˈfīˌnīdˌizəm\ *n* -s **:** a theory or belief holding that a particular entity or domain (as the world, God, or knowledge) is finite ⟨cosmological ~⟩ ⟨a theistic ~⟩

fi·nit·ist \-d.əst\ *or* **fi·nit·is·tic** \ˌ=,=ˈistik\ *adj* **:** relating to or being finitism ⟨a ~ system⟩

fin·i·tive \ˈfinəd.iv, -ətiv\ *adj* [L *finitus* (past part. of *finire* to limit, finish, end) + E *-ive* — more at FINITE] **:** TERMINATIVE

fin·i·tude \ˈfīnəˌtüd, ˈfin-, -nəˌtyüd\ *n* -s [blend of ¹*finite* and *-tude*] **:** the quality or state of being finite ⟨human ~⟩

fin·i·ty \ˈfinəd.ē, -nətē, -i\ *n* -ES [¹*finite* + *-y*] **:** FINITUDE

¹**fink** \ˈfiŋk\ *n* -s [origin unknown] **1** *slang* **:** INFORMER, SQUEALER **2** *slang* **:** STRIKEBREAKER ⟨couple of minutes ago I saw a guy I recognized for a company ~ —Alexander Saxton⟩

²**fink** \ˈ"\ *vi* -ED/-ING/-s **1** *slang* **:** SQUEAL, INFORM ⟨you have to ~ on somebody . . . to get a parole —*Police Dragnet*⟩ **2** *slang* **:** to act as a strikebreaker ⟨he ~*ed* back in the 1934 and 1936 strikes —R.F.Mirvish⟩

³**fink** \ˈ"\ *n* -s [Afrik *vink*, fr. MD *vinke* — more at FINCH] *Africa* **:** FINCH

fin keel *n* **1 :** a plate of metal fixed to the keel of a shallow boat to provide lateral resistance usu. supplemented by a cigar-shaped bulb of lead to provide stability **2 :** a long narrow and shallow ship (as a yacht) fitted with a fin keel and lead bulb **3 :** a yacht with shallow body carried down in an extension of wood or metal which in turn carries a metal keel

fin·land \ˈfinlənd\ *adj, usu cap* [fr. *Finland*, country in northern Europe, fr. Sw, fr. *finne* Finn (fr. OSw) + *land* country, fr. OSw; akin to ON *land* — more at LAND] **:** of or from Finland **:** of the kind or style prevalent in Finland **:** FINNISH

fin·land·er \-ˌlandə(r), -lən-\ *n* -s *cap* **:** FINN 2

fin·lay process \ˈfinlē-, -(ˌ)lā-\ *n, usu cap F* [after Clare L. *Finlay* †1936 Brit. photography expert] **:** an additive process of color photography in which exposure is made on a panchromatic plate behind a regular mosaic three-color screen — called also *Paget process*

fin·less \ˈfinləs\ *adj* **:** having no fin **:** devoid of fins ⟨a ~ animal⟩

fin·let \ˈfinlət\ *n* -s [*fin* + *-let*] **:** a little fin **:** one of the parts of a divided fin

¹**finn** \ˈfin\ *n* -s *cap* [Sw *finne*, fr. OSw; akin to ON *finnr* Finn, OE *Finnas*, pl.] **1 a :** a member of a people speaking Finnish **b :** a member of a people speaking a language akin to Finnish **c :** a member of a people speaking or formerly speaking a Uralic language **2 a :** a native or inhabitant of Finland **b :** one that is of Finnish descent

²**finn** \ˈ"\ *adj, usu cap* **:** FINNISH

fin·nage \ˈfinij\ *n* -s [*fin* + *-age*] **:** the whole set of fins of a fish

fin·nan had·die \ˌfinənˈhadē, -di\ *or* **finnan haddock** *n* [alter. of *findon haddock*] **:** smoked haddock

finned *past of* FIN

fin·ne·man·ite \ˈfinəməˌnīt\ *n* -s [K. J. *Finneman*, 20th cent. Swede who discovered it + E *-ite*] **:** a mineral $Pb_5(AsO_3)_3Cl$ consisting of arsenite and chloride of lead

fin·ner \ˈfinə(r)\ *n* -s [¹*fin* + *-er*] **:** FINBACK

finnes·ko *also* **finnes·koe** \ˈfinzˌkō, -n(ə),skō, -kü\ *n, pl* **finnesko** *also* **finneskoe** [Norw *finnsko*, fr. *finn* Finn, Lapp (fr. ON *finnr*) + *sko* shoe, fr. ON *skōr* — more at FINN, SHOE] **:** a boot made of tanned reindeer skin with the fur outside

¹**fin·nic** \ˈfinik\ *adj, usu cap* [¹*Finn* + *-ic*] **1 :** of or relating to the Finns (sense 1) **2 :** of, relating to, or constituting the branch of the Finno-Ugric subfamily of the Uralic family of languages that includes Finnish, Estonian, Lapp, Cheremis, Mordvin, Votyak, Permian, and various other languages — see URALIC LANGUAGES table

²**finnic** \ˈ"\ *n* -s *cap* **:** the Finnic languages

finnick *var of* FINICK

finnicky *var of* FINICKY

finning *pres part of* FIN

¹**finn·ish** \ˈfinish, -nēsh\ *adj, usu cap* [¹*Finn* + *-ish*] **1 :** of or relating to the Finns (sense 1) **2 :** of, relating to, characteristic of, or composed in the Finnish language **3 :** of or relating to Finland or its inhabitants

²**finnish** \ˈ"\ *n* -ES *cap* **1 :** a Finno-Ugric language spoken in Finland, Karelia, and small areas of Sweden and Norway — see URALIC LANGUAGES table **2 :** the form of the Finnish language spoken in Finland and adopted as the official language of that nation

finn·mark *or* **fin·mark** \ˈfinˌmärk\ *n* [Sw *finmark*, fr. *finne* Finn + *mark* (coin), fr. OSw; akin to ON *mörk* mark (coin and weight) — more at FINN, MARK] **:** a Finnish mark — compare MARKKA

fin·nock *also* **fin·noc** \ˈfinək\ *n* -s [ScGael *fionnag* whiting, fr. *fionn* white; akin to OIr *find* white, W *gwyn*, Corn *guyn*, Bret *gwenn* white, L *vidēre* to see — more at WIT] **:** a European sea trout: as **a :** a pale or whitish Scottish sea trout **b :** a young or grilse sea trout

¹**finno-ugrian** \ˈfi(ˌ)nō +\ *adj, usu cap F&U* [*Finno-* (fr. ¹*Finn* + *-o-*) + *Ugrian*] **1 :** of or relating to the Finno-Ugrians **2 :** FINNO-UGRIC 2

²**finno-ugrian** \ˈ"\ *n, cap F&U* **1 :** a member of any of various peoples of north and east Europe and western Siberia speaking related languages and historically antecedent to the Slavic expansion in those regions, including the ancestors and present members of the Finnish, Hungarian, Bulgarian, Ostyak and Vogul peoples, the Lapps, Estonians, and others **2 :** FINNO-UGRIC

¹**finno-ugric** \ˈ"+\ *adj, usu cap F&U* [*Finno-* + *Ugric*] **1 :** FINNO-UGRIAN 1 **2 :** of, relating to, characteristic of, or constituting the Finno-Ugric languages

²**finno-ugric** \ˈ"\ *n, cap F&U* **1 :** the Finno-Ugric languages **2 :** the extinct language from which the Finno-Ugric languages are descended

finno-ugric languages *n pl, cap F&U* **:** a subfamily of the Uralic family of languages comprising various languages spoken in Hungary, Lapland, Finland, Estonia, and in Russia north and east of the Volga as far as the Ob river in Siberia — see URALIC LANGUAGES table

finno-ugrist \ˌfi(ˌ)nō'(y)ügrəst\ *also* **finno-ugri·cist** \-grəsəst\ *n* -s *usu cap F&U* [²*Finno-Ugric* + *-ist*] **:** a specialist in the Finno-Ugric languages

fin·ny \ˈfinē, -ni\ *adj* -ER/-EST [*fin* + *-y*] **1 :** having or characterized by fins **2 :** relating to or being fish ⟨toothsome food of the ~ tribe —*Quartermaster Rev.*⟩ ⟨these would . . . complete the list of our ~ contemporaries —H.D.Thoreau⟩

finny whale *n* **:** FINBACK

fi·no \ˈfē(ˌ)nō\ *n* -ES [Sp, fr. *fino* fine, fr. L *finis*, n., boundary, limit, end — more at FINE (adj.)] **:** the driest Spanish sherry

fi·noc·chio *also* **fi·no·chio** \fəˈnōkēˌō, -nōk-\ *n* -s [It *finocchio* fennel, fr. (assumed) VL *fenuculum* — more at FENNEL] **:** FLORENCE FENNEL

fin ray *n* **:** one of the horny dermal rods that form the projecting part of the skeleton of the fins of fishes

fin rot *n* **:** a common disease of hatchery fishes in which the fin tissues become eroded and necrotic and which is believed to result from bacterial infection esp. in the presence of an inadequate diet

fins *pl of* FIN, *pres 3d sing of* FIN

fin·sen light \ˈfin(t)sən-, -nzən-\ *n, usu cap F* [after Niels R. *Finsen* †1904 Danish physician] **:** a mixture of blue, violet, and near ultraviolet light that is produced by a lamp using a high-temperature carbon arc or a mercury arc and that is used in the treatment of lupus and certain other skin conditions and in testing paints and other protective coatings

fin whale *n* **:** FINBACK

FIO *abbr* free in and out

fiord *var of* FJORD

fior dell'al·pi \ˌfē(ˌ)ōrdeˈlal(ˌ)pē\ *also* **fior di alpi** \-dēˈal(-\ *n* [It, lit., flower of the alps] **:** a yellow colored Italian liqueur containing a twig encrusted with crystallized sugar inside its bottle

fi·o·rin \ˈfīərən, ˈfēə-\ *n* -s [IrGael *fiorthann* wheat grass] **:** REDTOP 1

fi·o·rite \fēˈōrˌīt\ *n* -s [Santa *Fiora*, Tuscany, Italy, its locality + E *-ite*] **:** an opal occurring near hot springs in grayish or whitish incrustations that sometimes are fibrous and pearly

fio·ri·tu·ra \fēˌōrəˈtürə\ *n, pl* **fioritu·re** \-ˌrā\ [It, lit., bloom, flowering, fr. *fiorito* (past part. of *fiorire* to bloom, fr. LL *florire*) (fr. LL *floritus*, past part. of *florire* to bloom, alter. of L *florēre*) + *-ura* -ure — more at BLOW (to cause to blossom)] **:** ORNAMENT 5 — usu. used in pl.

fip \ˈfip\ *n* -s [by shortening] **:** FIPPENNY BIT ⟨wouldn't give a ~ for any other way of travel —S.H.Adams⟩

fip·pence \ˈfipən(t)s\ *n* [by alter.] *Brit* **:** FIVEPENCE

fip·pen·ny \ˈfip(ə)nē\ *n* [by alter.] *dial* **:** FIVEPENCE

fippenny bit *n* **:** a Spanish half real piece **:** a silver coin worth 1/16 of a Spanish dollar that circulated in the eastern U.S. before 1857 and passed current for about six cents — called also *fip*, *fourpence ha'penny*, *sixpence*

fip·ple \ˈfipəl\ *n* -s [origin unknown] **:** a grooved plug in the end of a whistle, flute, or organ pipe

fipple flute *n* **:** a wind instrument (as the recorder and flageolet) in which the air blown into the mouthpiece strikes a flat sharp lip, producing the sound waves within the body of the instrument

fi·que \ˈfē(ˌ)kā\ *n* -s [AmerSp, prob. fr. Quechua *ppiqui*, *phiqui* thread, fiber, vein] **:** MAURITIUS HEMP

fir *R* ˈfər, +V ˈfər-; *-R* ˈfə, + *suffixal vowel* ˈfər- *also* ˈfər, + *vowel in a following word* ˈfər- *or* ˈfə *also* ˈfər\ *n* -s [ME *firre*, *fir*, fr. OE *fyrh*, *furh*; akin to OHG *forha*, *foraha* fir, ON *fȳri* fir forest, *fura* fir, Goth *fairguni* mountain, L *quercus* oak] **1 :** any of several evergreen trees: as **a :** a tree of the genus *Abies* typically large and attractive in appearance and valued for its wood or resin — see BALSAM FIR **b :** any of various related coniferous trees — usu. used in combination ⟨Douglas ~⟩ ⟨Scotch ~⟩ **2 a :** the wood of any tree of the genus *Abies* distinguished from that of pine, spruce, or larch by the absence of resin ducts **b :** the wood from any of various other conifers: as (1) **:** SPRUCE 1b (2) *Brit* **:** PINE 2a **3** *or* **fir green :** a dark grayish green that is yellower and stronger than average ivy, yellower and deeper than Persian green, and yellower, lighter, and stronger than hemlock green

fir *abbr* firkin

fir balsam *n* **:** BALSAM FIR 1

fir·bolg \ˈfi(ə)rˌbələg\ *or* **fir·bolgs** \-gz\ *n pl, usu cap* [OIr *fir Bolg* men of the Builg (a Celtic people), fr. *fir* (pl. of *fer* man) + *Bolg*, gen. pl. of *Builg*; akin to W *gwr* man, Bret *gour*, L *vir* — more at VIRILE] **:** an early people of Ireland

fir·ca \ˈfi(ə)rkə\ *n* -s [Hindi *firqa*, fr. Ar *firqah*] *India* **:** COMMUNITY, TRIBE, GROUP

fir club moss *n* **:** a club moss (*Lycopodium selago*) of northern Europe and America having the appearance of a miniature fir

¹**fire** \ˈfī(ə)r, -īə\ *n* -s [ME *fir*, *fire*, fr. OE *fȳr*; akin to OHG *fiur* fire, ON *fȳrr*, *fūrr*, *funi*, Goth *fon*, Umbrian *pir*, Gk *pyr*, Arm *hur* fire, torch] **1 a :** the phenomenon of combustion as manifested in light, flame, and heat and in heating, destroying, and altering effects **:** IGNITION **b :** one of the four elements of the alchemists **c fires** *pl* **:** the heat, flame, or burning material of a specified place or thing ⟨the deep internal ~*s* of this volcanic region⟩ ⟨the ~*s* of hell⟩ **d** (1) **:** intense love or hate **:** PASSION ⟨the younger men, the warriors, the new leaders who had ~ in their hearts —Marjory S. Douglas⟩ (2) **:** ardor of spirit or temperament **:** DRIVE, COURAGE, ZEAL, ENTHUSIASM, FERVOR ⟨the glow and ~ of a faith that was content to bide its hour —B.N.Cardozo⟩ (3) **:** liveliness of imagination or fancy **:** GENIUS, INSPIRATION, VIVACITY ⟨color and ~ were imparted to the works of the classic master —A.E.Wier⟩ ⟨the force and ~ of his oratory⟩ **2 a :** fuel in a state of combustion (as on a hearth or in a stove or furnace) ⟨warmed his hands at the crackling ~⟩ ⟨stirred up the ~ with a poker⟩ — compare OPEN FIRE **b** *Brit* **:** a small gas or electric space heater ⟨electric ~*s* designed for efficiency —*Punch*⟩ **3 a :** a destructive burning (as of a house, town, or forest) ⟨engines clanging their way to the ~⟩ **b :** purposive destruction by burning — often used in the phrase *by fire and sword* ⟨he was going back . . . to carry the city by ~ and sword —Frank Yerby⟩ **c** (1) **:** death or torture by fire; *specif* **:** burning at the stake — used with *the* ⟨forced the shocked prelate, under threat of the ~, to confess heresies he was not guilty of —G.C.Sellery⟩ (2) **:** an experience that tests or tempers quality or character **:** a severe trial or ordeal ⟨he had proved himself in the ~ of battle⟩ — often used in pl. ⟨workers whose ideas have been tested in the ~*s* of performance —G.T.Trewartha⟩ **4 a** *dial Brit* **:** FUEL, FIREWOOD; *specif* **:** KINDLING **b** *archaic* **:** an inflammable composition or a device for producing a fiery display **:** FIREWORKS **5 a :** fever or inflammation esp. from a disease **b :** a plant disease producing a burnt appearance — see TULIP FIRE **6 :** BRILLIANCY, LUMINOSITY; *specif* **:** the play of prismatic colors in light flashes from a gemstone **7 a :** the discharge of firearms **:** FIRING ⟨troops rent by a heavy ~⟩ **b :** intense and usu. continuing criticism **:** verbal attack ⟨atomism had come under the ~ of the Socratic schools —Benjamin Farrington⟩ ⟨the ~ of his article is concentrated on the two hapless institutions —Nicolas Slonimsky⟩ **c :** a series (as of remarks) usu. following closely one upon the other ⟨they fell to, a running ~ of comments going on all the time —Robert Keable⟩ **8 :** the heating powers of a substance (as liquor) ⟨with the ~ of the drink melting the cold that was in the marrow of our bones —Mary Deasy⟩ — **on fire :** BURNING, EAGER

²**fire** \ˈ"\ *vb* -ED/-ING/-s [ME *firen*, fr. *fir*, *fire*, n.] *vt* **1 a :** to set on fire **:** set fire to ⟨*fired* the house⟩ **b** (1) **:** KINDLE, LIGHT, IGNITE ⟨the oven holds sufficient heat to ~ a fresh charge of coal —*Amer. Guide Series: Pa.*⟩ — often used with *up* ⟨he *fired* up a cigar —Gilbert Millstein⟩ (2) **:** to cause to explode by lighting or igniting ⟨*fired* the train of powder⟩ ⟨~ a mine⟩ (3) **:** to cause (an internal-combustion engine) to start operation (4) **:** to cause (an electron tube) to begin conducting a gas discharge **c** (1) **:** to give life or spirit to **:** ANIMATE, INSPIRE ⟨his description *fired* my imagination⟩ ⟨*fired* his ambition for a college education⟩ (2) **:** to fill with passion **:** INFLAME, AROUSE ⟨he was *fired* by her fresh young beauty⟩ **d :** to light up as if by fire **:** ILLUMINATE ⟨his eye had caught the flash of larkspur and snapdragons that *fired* the lawn —G.M. Smith⟩ **2 a :** to expel, purge, drive out, or drive away by or as if by fire ⟨such surrender is above all things delightful . . . it ~*s* the cold skepticism out of us —Virginia Woolf⟩ **b :** to discharge from employ or service usu. peremptorily or summarily ⟨*fired* him with one week's notice⟩; *also* **:** to throw out or eject forcibly **3 a** (1) **:** DETONATE ⟨~ a charge of dynamite⟩ (2) **:** to propel from or as if from a gun ⟨~ cannonballs⟩ ⟨~ an arrow⟩ ⟨~ a rocket⟩ **:** DISCHARGE ⟨~ a musket⟩ (3) **:** to score (a certain number) in a game or contest (as golf or target shooting) ⟨*fired* a 68⟩ **b :** to throw with speed or force **:** HURL ⟨stripped to his shorts and *fired* the wet clothes into the corner of the closet —Charles Jackson⟩ ⟨throwing clods at me by way of contempt and derision, and I *fired* back rocks —W.A. White⟩ ⟨*fired* a long pass to the left end⟩ **c :** to utter with force and rapidity ⟨*fired* questions at the prisoner⟩ **4 :** to apply fire, heat, or fuel to: as **a :** to prepare (as ceramics) by applying heat **:** burn in a kiln ⟨~ pottery⟩ **b :** to sear (the leg of a horse) with a hot iron in order to convert a crippling chronic inflammation into an acute inflammation that will stimulate the natural healing responses of the body **c :** to feed or serve the fire of ⟨~ a boiler⟩ **:** build a fire under in order to heat ⟨unless you have lived by lamplight or *fired* a washpot in the back yard, you'll never know what electricity means —James Street⟩ **d :** to heat gently in order to dry ⟨~ tea leaves⟩ **e :** to subject (a barnful of tobacco) to the drying and heating and combustion products of a charcoal fire for curing purposes **f :** to protect against freezing by the use of smudge pots ⟨a freeze comes in and I must ~ my young orange grove —Marjorie K. Rawlings⟩ ~ *vi* **1 a :** to take fire **:** KINDLE, IGNITE ⟨damp gunpowder will not ~⟩ **b :** to have the explosive charge ignite at the proper time — used of an internal-combustion engine **c :** GLOW, REDDEN ⟨her features *fired* at the thought; she clenched her hands in anger⟩ **d** (1) *of flax* **:** to become covered with dark blotches (2) **:** to turn yellow prematurely (as from drought) — used of corn or grain **2 :** to become irritated **:** become angry or inflamed with passion ⟨*fired* inwardly at these sarcasms —Tobias Smollett⟩ — often used with *up* ⟨*fired* up with a superb indignation —H.J. Laski⟩ **3 a :** to discharge artillery or firearms ⟨~ at point-blank range⟩ **b :** to emit forcefully or let fly an object ⟨as long as the tail is lowered, the skunk will not ~ —*Animal Trap Co. of Amer.*⟩ ⟨the archers raised their bows but did not ~⟩ **4 :** to undergo a change by the action of fire (as in the making of pottery) ⟨iron-bearing clays ~ to a red color⟩ **5 :** to light or tend a fire (as in a furnace) ⟨the ship's firemen went on strike, and there was no one to ~⟩ **6 :** to ring all the bells in a chime at once **syn** see DISMISS

³**fire** \ˈ"\ *adj* **1 :** involved in burning or the use of fire ⟨~ building⟩ ⟨~ floor⟩ **2 :** relating to, used in, or concerned with fire fighting ⟨~ bucket⟩ ⟨~ district⟩ ⟨~ hydrant⟩ **3 :** FIERY

fire agriculture *n* **:** the growing of crops by burning a forest and planting among the charred stumps

fire alarm *n* **:** a signal given on the breaking out of a fire; *also* **:** an apparatus for giving such a signal

fire and brimstone *n* [fr. *fire and brimstone*, a phrase used often in the Bible (esp. Rev 20 : 10) to designate God's means of destroying sinners] **:** eternal damnation and the torments of hell for sinners ⟨sermons full of *fire and brimstone*⟩

fire-and-brimstone \ˌ==ˈ=(ˌ)=\ *adj* [*fire and brimstone*] **:** of or relating to an ultimate day of violent reckoning and retribution **:** APOCALYPTIC ⟨a hive of revivalism, hymn singing, and *fire-and-brimstone* auguries from self-appointed minor prophets —Peter Ustinov⟩

fire ant *n* **:** a stinging ant; *specif* **:** any of numerous small fiercely stinging omnivorous ants constituting a genus (*Solenopsis*) now nearly cosmopolitan in warm regions

fire apparatus *n* **:** apparatus for fighting or extinguishing fire (as automobile fire engines or ladder trucks)

fire area *n* **:** one of various sections of a building that are separated from each other by fire-resistant walls

firearm \ˈ=ˌ=\ *n* **:** a weapon from which a shot is discharged by gunpowder — usu. used only of small arms

fire arrow *n* **:** an arrow bearing a flaming substance to set its mark afire

fire assay *n* **:** an assay in which the material is subjected to high heat (as in fusion, scorifying, and cupellation)

fire away *vi* **:** to begin speech and proceed with it rapidly ⟨useless to *fire away* with a lot of details —F.L.Mott⟩

fireback \ˈ=ˌ=\ *n* **1** *or* **fire-backed pheasant** \ˈ=ˌ=-\ **:** any of several pheasants (genus *Lophura*) of southern Asia and the East Indies having the lower back of the male a bright coppery or fiery maroon **2 :** the back wall or back lining of a fireplace or furnace; *also* **:** a decorated cast-iron plate to fit into the back of an open fireplace

fireball \ˈ=ˌ=\ *n* **1 :** a ball of fire or something resembling such a ball: as **a :** a brilliant meteor that may trail bright sparks — compare BOLIDE **b :** BALL LIGHTNING **c :** a ball filled with powder or other combustibles formerly used as a projectile to be thrown among the enemy **d** *heraldry* **:** a grenade or bomb fired proper **e :** the highly luminous cloud of vapor and dust created by a nuclear explosion **f** (1) **:** MALTESE CROSS 2 (2) **:** SUMMER CYPRESS **g :** a fast ball in baseball **2 :** a highly energetic indefatigable person **:** HUSTLER ⟨the British production ~ had one simple mission: get more of everything for the British —*Time*⟩

fire balloon *n* **1 :** a balloon raised by the buoyancy of air heated by a fire placed in the lower part **2 :** a balloon sent up at night with fireworks that ignite at a regulated height

fire-baptized \ˈ=ˌ=ˌ=, =ˈ=ˌ=\ *adj* **:** of or having experienced a baptism of fire

fire bar *n* **:** a bar of a grate or boiler furnace

fire bean *n* **:** SCARLET RUNNER

firebed \ˈ=ˌ=\ *n* **:** a layer of burning fuel (as that in the furnace under a boiler)

fire beetle *n* **1 :** a tropical American beetle of the genus *Pyrophorus*; *esp* **:** a common large beetle (*P. noctilucus*) having powerful luminous organs on the sides of the thorax and base

of the abdomen — compare FIREFLY **2** *Austral* **:** any of several beetles attracted to firelight
fire–bellied toad \'=,==-\ *n* **:** a toad (*Bombina bombina*) of central and eastern Europe with red or orange patches marbled with black on its underparts
firebird \'=,=\ *n* **:** any of several small birds having brilliant orange or red plumage (as the Baltimore oriole, the scarlet tanager, or the vermilion flycatcher)
fire blanket *n* **:** a blanket of fireproof or flameproof material for use in smothering small fires
fire blast *n* **:** a disease of plants (as hops) causing them to appear scorched
fire·blende \'fī(ə)r,blend, -īə,b-\ *n* [trans. of G *feuerblende*, fr. *feuer* fire + *blende*] **:** PYROSTILPNITE
fire blight *n* **1 :** a destructive highly infectious disease of apples, pears, and related fruits that is caused by a bacterium (*Erwinia amylovora*) and that produces a scorched or blackened appearance of the leaves and twigs, cankers on the trunk, or discoloration of flowers and fruit **2 :** the organism causing fire blight
fire blocks *n pl* **:** pieces of wood nailed horizontally between studs or joists to prevent the spread of fire and hot gases
fireboard \'=,=\ *n* **1 :** a screen or panel often painted or otherwise decorated to close a fireplace when not in use **2** *Midland* **:** MANTELPIECE
fireboat \'=,=\ *n* **:** a boat equipped with pumps and other apparatus for fighting fire on or from the water
firebolt \'=,=\ *n* **:** THUNDERBOLT, LIGHTNING
fire bomb *n* **:** INCENDIARY BOMB
fire boss *n* **:** one who examines a coal mine to determine whether firedamp is present, to search for fires caused by blasting, and to check on the general safety of the mine — called also *fireman, gasman*
fire·bote \'=,bōt\ *or* **fire·boot** \'=,büt\ *n* -s [ME *firbote*, fr. *fir*, *fire* + *bote* boot (profit) — more at BOOT] **:** the right of a tenant to take from the land occupied by him a reasonable amount of wood for maintaining fires in his house and in the houses of his servants; *also* **:** the wood or fuel used for this purpose
firebox \'=,=\ *n* **1 :** a chamber (as of a furnace or steam boiler) that contains a fire; *specif* **:** the compartment of a steam locomotive in which the fuel is burned **2 :** FIRE ALARM
firebrand \'=,=\ *n* [ME *firbrond, firbrand*, fr. *fir, fire* + *brond, brand* — more at FIRE, BRAND] **1 :** a piece of burning wood **2 :** a person who creates unrest, disaffection, or strife by noisy or violent agitation **:** TROUBLEMAKER, HOTHEAD, AGITATOR, INCENDIARY ⟨far from being considered ~*s*, young people of today are accused of being too quiet —*Harper's*⟩ ⟨a political ~⟩
firebrat \'=,=\ *n* **:** an insect (*Thermobia domestica*) of the family Lepismatidae of Europe and America that lives in warm moist places (as in buildings)
firebreak \'=,=\ *n* **:** a barrier of cleared or plowed land intended to check a forest fire or prairie fire
firebrick \'=,=\ *n* **:** a refractory brick (as of fireclay) capable of sustaining high temperature without fusion and used esp. for lining furnaces, fireplaces, and tall chimneys
fire bridge *n* **:** a low separating wall usu. of firebrick between the hearth and the grate in a reverberatory furnace
fire brigade *n* **:** a body of fire fighters: as **a :** a private, institutional, or temporary fire-fighting organization **b** *Brit* **:** FIRE DEPARTMENT
firebug \'=,=\ *n* **1 :** INCENDIARY, PYROMANIAC **2 :** one who patrols a metal mine looking for fire hazards and other dangers **3** *dial* **:** FIREFLY **4 :** an insect of the family Pyrrhocoridae
fireburn bush \'=,=-\ *n* **:** a West Indian woody vine (*Triopteris jamaicensis*) of the family Malpighiaceae with violet flowers and linear leaves
fire bush *n* **1 :** FIRE THORN **2 :** a low West Indian shrub (*Croton lucidus*) having small flowers in terminal racemes **3 :** SPINDLE TREE **4 :** SUMMER CYPRESS
fire chaser *n* **:** SMOKECHASER
fire check *n* **:** a fine shallow crack in an unglazed ceramic body or a glass article caused by sudden heating
fire cherry *n* **:** PIN CHERRY
fire chief *n* **1 :** the head of a fire department **2 :** FIRE MARSHAL
fireclay \'=,=\ *n* **:** clay that will withstand high temperatures without deforming, that is used for firebrick, crucibles, and many refractory shapes, and that approaches kaolin in composition, the better grades containing at least 35 percent alumina when fired
fire cock *n* **:** a cock to furnish water for extinguishing fires
fire company *n* **:** a body of men organized and equipped to extinguish fires
fire control *n* **1 :** all operations connected with the planning, preparation, and delivery of fire on targets **2 :** fire protection or extinction
firecracker \'=,==\ *n* **1 :** a cylinder that is usu. of thick paper, contains an explosive and a fuse, and is usu. discharged for amusement to make a noise **2** *California* **:** a young sardine **3 :** FIERY RED **4** *also* **firecracker flower :** a Californian herb (*Brodiaea coccinea*) with scarlet tubular flowers
firecrest \'=,=\ *n* *also* **fire-crested wren** \'=,==-\ *n* **:** a small European kinglet (*Regulus ignicapillus*) with a bright red crest
fire–cure \'=,=\ *vt* **:** to cure (tobacco) over open fires in direct contact with the smoke — compare FLUE-CURE
fire curtain *n* **:** CURTAIN BOARD
fire cut *n* **:** a slanted cut in the end of a wood beam or joist resting in a masonry wall that in case of fire allows the wood to fall out without wrecking the wall
fired \'fī(ə)rd, -īəd\ *adj, heraldry* **:** represented as on fire — used of a fireball
firedamp \'=,=\ *n* **:** a combustible gas that is formed in mines by decomposition of coal or other carbonaceous matter and that consists chiefly of methane; *also* **:** the explosive mixture formed by this gas with air
fire department *n* **1 a :** a permanent organization for preventing or putting out fires; *esp* **:** a government division (as in a municipality) having these duties **b :** FIRE COMPANY **2 :** the members of a fire department ⟨the . . . *fire department* . . . dashed up in three splendid long scarlet wagons —Nathaniel Burt⟩
fire direction *n* **:** tactical employment of firepower including the selection of targets and the massing of fires
fire direction center *n* **:** an element of an artillery command post consisting of gunnery and communication personnel and equipment by which the commander exercises fire direction and fire control
fire division wall *n* **:** a wall that subdivides a fire-resistive building to restrict the spread of fire
firedog \'=,=\ *n* **:** ANDIRON
fired–on \'=,=\ *adj, ceramics* **:** made a part of the ware by firing or fusing ⟨a *fired-on* enamel⟩
fire door *n* **1 :** the door or opening through which fuel is supplied to a furnace or stove **2 :** a fire-resistive door; *specif* **:** an automatic door secured in the open position by a fusible link or thermostatically operated device designed to release the door under the influence of heat and permit its closing by gravity or by weights or other contrivances
firedrake \'=,=\ *also* **firedragon** \'=,==\ *n* [ME *firdrake*, fr. OE *fȳrdraca*, fr. *fȳr* fire + *draca* dragon — more at FIRE, DRAKE] **:** a dragon breathing fire esp. in Teutonic mythology as the guardian of a treasure and in folk tales as the abductor or guardian of maidens
fire drill *n* **1 :** a primitive device for kindling fire consisting of a stick that is revolved rapidly between the hands or by means of a bow or thong with the stick's lower end being pressed into a hole made in a piece of wood **2 :** a practice drill with fire-extinguishing apparatus or in the conduct and manner of exit to be followed in case of fire
fire–eater \'=,==\ *n* **1 :** a performer who pretends to eat fire **2 a :** a person of violent, pugnacious, or swaggering disposition **:** BULLY ⟨another *fire-eater* . . . , mighty fighter and hunter whose deeds were already epic along the moving frontier —*Amer. Guide Series: Texas*⟩ **b :** a person who displays very militant or aggressive partisanship (as in political questions) ⟨inside all parties there are moderates and extremists . . . ; the pacific and the *fire-eaters* —Barbara & Robert North⟩; *specif* **:** a violent Southern proslavery partisan before the Civil War ⟨Southern *fire-eaters* . . . held the government had no power to ban slavery in the West —R.A.Billington⟩ — used chiefly by northern opponents
fire–eating \'=,==\ *adj* **:** violent, aggressive, belligerent, or highly militant in disposition, bearing, or policy ⟨a *fire-eating* radical⟩ ⟨the *fire-eating* partisans of immediate war⟩ ⟨a *fire-eating*, hectoring, swashbuckling bully⟩
fire engine *n* **:** an apparatus for throwing an extinguishing agent (as a jet of water) upon a fire: as **a :** a force pump with an air chamber to ensure a steady flow or an arrangement of two pumps working alternately or a direct-coupled steam engine and pump on wheels **b :** an automotive truck equipped with a motor-driven pump and hose and sometimes with a chemical fire-extinguishing unit **c :** any usu. mobile apparatus (as a ladder truck) used in connection with the extinguishing of fires
fire escape *n* **:** a device for facilitating escape from a burning building: as **a :** a stairway usu. of steel attached to the outside of a building **b** *Brit* **:** a wheeled extension ladder
fire–exit bolt *n* **:** a locking device for the exit doors of public buildings so designed that it is released by pressure applied from the inside of the building
fire extinguisher *n* **:** a portable or wheeled apparatus for putting out small fires by ejecting fire-extinguishing agents that may consist of water alone, water and chemicals (as soda-acid solutions or foam), or chemicals alone (as carbon tetrachloride, carbon dioxide, or dry chemicals)

portable fire extinguishers

fire–eyed \'=,=\ *adj, archaic* **:** having glowing eyes
firefall \'=,=\ *n* **:** a tree whose fall is caused by the partial destruction of its roots in a ground fire
firefang \'=,=\ *vi* [fr. obs. E *firefang*, v.t., to singe, scorch, fr. [1]*fire* + [1]*fang*] **:** to become overheated, excessively dry, and damaged as a result of slow oxidative decomposition of organic matter — used esp. of manure or grain
fire fight *n* **:** an exchange of fire between opposing military units as distinct from the fighting when the two forces close with each other (as during an assault)
fire fighter *n* **:** one who fights fires: as **a :** a member of a municipal fire department **b :** one of a crew that combats forest fires **c :** one who fights mine fires
fire fighting *n* **:** the activity of a fire fighter; *specif* **:** the effort to extinguish or to check the spread of a fire
fire finch *n* **:** any of several small African weaverbirds often kept as cage birds or in aviaries and noted for the brilliant largely red plumage of the male
firefinder \'=,==\ *n* **:** a device consisting of a map and a sighting instrument for determining (as from a fire tower) the location of a forest fire
fire–fish \'=,=\ *n* **:** a small scarlet and orange banded coral fish (*Pterois volitans*) of the Indo-Pacific region having the pectoral fin rays greatly prolonged into slender projections and the sharp dorsal spines equipped with venom and capable of causing painful injury
fireflaught \'=,=\ *n* **1** *chiefly Scot* **a :** SHEET LIGHTNING **b :** SHOOTING STAR **c :** WILL-O'-THE-WISP **d :** AURORA BOREALIS **2** *chiefly Scot* **:** a quick-tempered person
fire–float \'=,=\ *n* **:** a boat used to aid ships afire
fire flow *n* **:** the quantity of water available (as in a city) for fire-protection purposes in excess of that required for other purposes
fireflower \'=,=\ *n* **:** MEXICAN FIRE PLANT 1
firefly \'=,=\ *n* **1 :** a winged nocturnal light-producing insect usu. producing a bright soft intermittent light without sensible heat by oxidation of luciferin: as **a :** the male of various elongated flattened beetles of the family Lampyridae — compare GLOWWORM **b :** any of several tropical click beetles **2 :** a moderate to strong red that is bluer and lighter than blood red and yellower and very slightly darker than camellia
firefly squid *n* **:** a brilliantly luminescent squid (*Watseonia scintillans*) caught in great quantities off the western coast of Japan where it is used for fertilizer
fire–form \'=,=\ *vt* **:** to reshape a rifle cartridge case by loading and firing it until it conforms to the chamber of the rifle for which the case is being prepared ⟨using the new ammunition to *fire-form* to fit the large chamber —P.B.Sharpe⟩
fire frame *n* **:** a cast-iron frame made to be permanently set into a large fireplace to reduce its size
fire fungus *n* **1 :** any of various fungi (as those of the order Sphaeriales) that form dark or nearly black stromata or perithecia — called also *black fungus* **2 :** any fungus (as of the genus *Pyronema*) appearing esp. on burned areas or soil
fire gilding *n* **:** a mode of gilding with an amalgam of gold and quicksilver, the latter metal being driven off by heat
fire grass *n* [so called fr. its growing on burned land] **:** PARSLEY PIERT 1
fireground \'=,=\ *n* **:** an area in which fire-fighting operations are carried on
fireguard \'=,=\ *n* **1 :** FIRE SCREEN **2 :** FIREBREAK **3 :** one who watches for the outbreak of fire (as in a forest region); *also* **:** one whose duty is to extinguish small fires
fire gun *n* **1 :** a fire-hose nozzle having a handle shaped somewhat like a pistol grip **2 :** BLOWTORCH
firehall \'=,=\ *n, North & Canad* **:** FIRE STATION
fire hangbird *n* **:** BALTIMORE ORIOLE
fire hat *n* **:** a fireman's protective hat having a high domed crown and a brim extended at the rear as a neck guard
fire hook *n* [ME, fr. *fire* + *hook*] **1 :** a stout pole having a hooked metal head and used esp. in fire fighting for tearing down walls or ceilings **2 :** a hook for raking a furnace fire
firehorse \'=,=\ *n* **:** a horse specially trained for hauling a fire engine
firehouse \'=,=\ *n* [ME *firhous*, fr. OE *fȳrhūs*, fr. *fȳr* fire + *hūs* house — more at FIRE, HOUSE] **1** *dial Brit* **:** a dwelling house or unit having a fireplace — often contrasted with *outhouse* **2 :** FIRE STATION
firehouse pinochle *n* **:** pinochle played by four players in two partnerships
fire hunt *n* **1 :** a night hunt in which torches or other lights are used **2 :** a hunt in which fire is set to the woods in an area and the animals are killed as they attempt to escape
fire–hunt \'=,=\ *vt* **1 :** to hunt (animals) at night with the aid of a torch or light **2 :** to hunt by driving (animals) from the woods with a fire
fire insurance *n* **:** insurance against loss from damage or destruction of specified property by fire
fire iron *n* [ME *firiren*, fr. *fir, fire* + *iren* iron — more at IRON] **1 fire irons** *pl* **:** utensils for a fireplace or grate (as tongs, poker, and shovel) — compare SLICE BAR **2 :** ANDIRON — usu. used in pl.
fire laddie *n* **:** FIREMAN
fire lane *n* **:** FIREBREAK
fire·less \'fī(ə)rləs, -īəl-\ *adj* **:** having no fire
fireless cooker *n* **:** an insulated chamber that when heated to a cooking temperature by any of several means can maintain that temperature without the addition of further heat
fireless locomotive *n* **:** a steam locomotive of conventional design except that it has no firebox, its steam being obtained from an outside source, stored, and admitted to the cylinders at reduced pressure as required — called also *steam storage locomotive*
firelight \'=,=\ *n* **:** the light of a domestic fire or campfire
fire limits *n pl* **:** the limits fixed by a town or city government within which only structures meeting certain specifications with respect to fire resistance are permitted, there being sometimes two or three such zones with varying requirements
fire line *n* **1 a :** a police barrier or line about a burning building — usu. used in pl. **b :** a line of fire hose **2 a :** FIREBREAK **b :** a line of hardwood seedlings planted along abandoned railway grades for the protection of young conifers **c :** the gutter or strip dug or scraped in a forest-fire control line **d :** the front line of an advancing prairie or forest fire
firelit \'=,=\ *adj* **:** illuminated by an open flame
fire load *or* **fire loading** *n* **:** the weight of combustible material per square foot of floor space
firelock \'=,=\ *n* **1 :** a gunlock employing a slow match to ignite the powder charge; *also* **:** a gun having such a lock **2 a :** FLINTLOCK **b :** WHEEL LOCK
fire lookout *n* **:** a lookout stationed in a fire tower who keeps watch over a large area of forest and on sighting a fire notifies a dispatcher of its location — called also *towerman*
fire main *n* **:** a pipe for water to be used in putting out fire
fire maker *n* **1 :** a device formerly used for making fire that consists of a piece of flint which is held immovably in place by metal prongs and which is struck by a hammer like that of a musket by cocking the hammer and pulling a trigger, the spark thus produced falling into a metal box filled with wood shavings or other flammable material **2** *usu cap F&M* **:** the third of four ranks attained by camp fire girls — compare TORCH BEARER, TRAIL SEEKER, WOOD GATHERER
fire·man \'=mən\ *n, pl* **firemen** **1** *obs* **:** GUNNER **2 :** one who fights fires; *esp* **:** a member of a fire department below the rank of lieutenant **3 :** one who tends or feeds fires **:** STOKER; *specif* **:** the crew member of a locomotive whose principal duties include firing and operating the boiler if the locomotive is steam operated or servicing the motors if it is other than steam and assisting the locomotive engineer by watching for signals or track obstructions **4 :** an enlisted man in the U.S. Navy who performs general duties concerned with the operation of engineering machinery **5 :** FIRE BOSS **6 :** a relief pitcher in baseball
fire·man·ic \(')fī(ə)r¦manik\ *adj* **:** of or relating to fire fighters or to fire fighting
fire·man·ship \'fī(ə)rmən,ship\ *n* -s **:** the practice, skill, or occupation of fire fighting
fireman's red *n* **:** a vivid red commonly used for fire apparatus
fire mark *n* **:** a metal plate attached to a building to mark it as insured used by 18th century fire-insurance companies
fire marshal *n* **1 :** the head of a city, county, state, or provincial fire-prevention or fire-investigation bureau **2 :** one who is in charge of the fire-fighting personnel and equipment of an industrial establishment — called also *fire chief*
fire medusa *n* **:** a scyphozoan jellyfish (genus *Chiropsalmus*) of the tropical Pacific ocean having a severe sting that may cause serious injury or even death
fire mission *n* **:** the assignment of a specific target usu. including orders as to when to fire the amount of ammunition to be used
firemouth \'=,=\ *n* **:** a small cichlid fish (*Cichlasoma meeki*) that is fiery red along the belly and mouth with a metallic green blotch on the gill cover and that is often kept in tropical aquariums
fire–new \'=¦=\ *adj* **:** BRAND-NEW ⟨it may be considered a *fire-new* cross section of these lexicons —Paul Rosenfeld⟩
fir engraver *n* **:** an engraver beetle (*Scolytus ventralis*) very destructive to fir trees in western No. America
fire off *vt* **:** to complete the firing of (a kiln)
fire–on–the–mountain \¦=,=¦=\ *n, pl* **fires–on–the–mountain** **:** MEXICAN FIRE PLANT 1
fire opal *n* **:** GIRASOL 2
fire partition *n* **:** a fire-resistant interior wall intended to retard the spread of fire or to provide protection to occupants during the evacuation of a burning building
fire patrol *n* **:** SALVAGE CORPS
fire patrolman *n* **1 :** a member of a salvage corps who accompanies municipal fire trucks to protect property at the scene of the fire from unnecessary damage **2 :** one who patrols a certain area (as a mine, factory, or national forest) watching for fires or fire hazards
fire pink *n* **:** a scarlet-flowered sticky catchfly (*Silene virginica*) of the eastern U.S.
fire pit *n* **:** a pit whose floor is wholly or partly incandescent lava ⟨the *fire pit* of a crater⟩
fireplace \'=,=\ *n* **1 :** a square or rectangular opening made at the base of a chimney in or against the wall of a room and surrounded with brick, stone, or metal to hold an open fire for heating and formerly for cooking **:** HEARTH **2 :** an outdoor place made for cooking over an open fire contained within a low structure of stone, brick, or metal

fireplace 2

fire plant *n* **:** SUMMER CYPRESS
fire–plow *also* **fire–plough** \'=,=\ *n* **:** a stick which is rubbed in a groove of a board to produce fire
fireplug \'=,=\ *n* **:** a hydrant for drawing water from the mains (as in a street or building) for extinguishing fires
fire point *n* **:** the lowest temperature at which a volatile combustible substance continues to burn in air after its vapors have been ignited (as when heating is continued after the flash point has been determined) — compare IGNITION TEMPERATURE
fire–polish \'=¦==\ *vt* **:** to make (glassware) smooth, gloss, or brilliant in appearance by reheating in the process of manufacture
fire polish \"\ *n* **:** the smoothness or brilliancy of surface imparted to glassware by fire polishing
fire polishing *n* **:** the process of reheating glassware in order to impart a smooth or brilliant surface
firepot \'=,=\ *n* **:** a pot that holds fire: as **a :** a small earthen pot filled with combustibles formerly used as a missile in war **b :** the vessel that holds the fuel or fire in a furnace **c :** a solderer's furnace
firepower \'=,==\ *n* **:** the capacity (as of a military unit, a tank, a ship) to deliver prompt and effective fire on a specific target; *specif* **:** the aggregate of effective shells and missiles that can be placed upon a target
fire prevention *n* **:** measures and practices directed toward the prevention and suppression of destructive fires — **fire preventionist** *n*
[1]**fireproof** \'=¦=\ *adj* [[1]*fire* + *proof*] **:** proof against fire **:** relatively noncombustible: as **a** *of a building* **:** having all parts that carry weights or resist stresses and also all exterior and interior walls and stairways made of noncombustible materials and having all structural members that are made of steel and iron, which are injuriously affected by heat, protected effectively by other materials not so affected — compare FIRE-RESISTIVE, FIRE-RETARDANT, FLAMEPROOF **b** *of paper* **:** so treated that it will char but not burn on exposure to a flame — **fire·proof·ness** *n* -ES
[2]**fireproof** \"\ *vt* **:** to make fireproof
fireproofing *n* **1 :** the act or process of making a thing fireproof **2 :** the materials used in the process of fireproofing
fireproofing tile *n* **:** tile for use as a protection against fire for structural members
fire protection *n* **1 :** measures and practices for preventing or reducing injury and loss of life or property by fire **2 :** activities relating to the extinguishment of fire
fir·er \'fīrə(r)\ *n* -s **1 :** one that fires **:** one that lights, replenishes, and attends to a fire (as for a brickkiln) **2 :** a worker who bakes enameled jewelry settings to cause fusion of the enamel to the setting — called also *baker*
fire raft *n* **:** a raft loaded with combustibles for setting fire to an enemy's ships or waterfront
fire–raising \'=,==\ *n, Brit* **:** the crime of willfully or recklessly burning buildings or such property as stored cereals or growing woods
fire red *n* **1 :** a strong reddish orange that is yellower and paler than poppy or paprika, yellower and lighter than fiery red, and yellower and paler than average coral red — called also *mineral orange, Paris red;* compare FLAME, FLAME RED **2** *also* **fire red toner :** a brilliant orange-red azo dye that has good resistance to light and heat, is made from diazotized 2-chloro-4-nitroaniline, and is used as a pigment for paint and for lithographic and offset inks; chlorinated para red — called also *Permanent Red R;* see DYE table I (under *Pigment Red 4*)
fire resistance *n* **:** degree of resistance of material to fire often measured in terms of time of withstanding a standard test fire
fire–resistant *adj, of a structural element* **:** so resistant to fire that for a specified time and under conditions of a standard heat intensity it will not fail structurally or allow transit of heat and will not permit the side away from the fire to become hotter than a specified temperature
fire–resistive *or* **fire–resisting** \¦=¦==\ *adj* **:** immune to the

effects of exposure to fire of a certain specified severity and duration — compare FIREPROOF
fire-retardant \ˌ=ˌ=ˈ==\ *adj* **:** having the ability or tendency to slow up or halt the spread of fire (as by providing insulation) ⟨*fire-retardant* preservatives⟩ ⟨*fire-retardant* construction⟩
fire retardant *n* **:** a substance that is fire-retardant
fire-retarded \ˌ=ˌ=ˈ==\ *adj* **:** protected with a fire-retardant material
fireroom \ˈ=ˌ=\ *n* **1 :** STOKEHOLD **2** *obs* **:** a room heated by a fireplace
fire runner *n* **:** one who goes into a mine after the blasting to search for fires and to replace damaged brattices
fires *pl of* FIRE, *pres 3d sing of* FIRE
firesafe \ˈ=ˈ=\ *adj* **:** offering protection or protected against fire — **firesafety** \ˈ=ˌ==\ *n*
fire salamander *n* **:** SPOTTED SALAMANDER a
fire sale *n* **:** a sale of merchandise damaged or believed to be damaged as the result of a fire
fire sand *n* **1 :** a highly refractory sand that consists mainly of coarse quartz grains with alumina or clayey sand and that is used esp. for foundry purposes **2 :** a grayish green powder or granular refractory material obtained as a by-product in the manufacture of silicon carbide
fire saw *n* **:** an implement for producing fire by friction consisting of a piece of wood (as bamboo or rattan) that is sawed or rubbed against the grain of another
fire scarlet *n* **:** CASTILIAN RED
fire screen *n* **:** a protecting wire screen or grating placed before or fitting over the front of an open fireplace — compare FENDER 1b(1)
fire service *n* **:** an organized fire-fighting and fire-preventing service (as of a city); *also* **:** the occupation of fire fighting
fireset \ˈ=ˌ=\ *n* **:** a set of fire irons (as tongs, shovel, brush, and poker)
fire setting *n* **:** the process of softening or cracking the working face of a lode by the action of fire
fire ship *n* **:** a ship carrying combustibles or explosives sent among the enemy's ships or works to set them on fire
fire shutter *n* **:** a metal shutter constructed to resist fire for a period often specified as one hour
¹fireside \ˈ=ˌ=\ *n* [¹*fire* + *side*] **1 :** a place near the fire or hearth; *esp* **:** the sides of the fireplace where seats were formerly placed **2 a :** HOME ⟨shiploads of excellent gentlemen . . . were driven from their ~*s* —V.L.Parrington⟩ ⟨a virtuous people, fighting in defense of their altars and ~*s* —W.E.Channing⟩ **b** *archaic* **:** one's household **:** FAMILY ⟨by so doing she would bring comfort and relief to an anxious ~ —S.H.Adams⟩

fireset

²fireside \"\ *adj* **:** having an informal or intimate quality ⟨a report . . . written in ~ language —H.M.Baus⟩ ⟨a ~ chat⟩ ⟨~ commentator to musical America —R.D.Welch⟩
fire station *n* **:** a building housing fire apparatus and usu. firemen
fire step *n* **:** FIRING STEP
fire stick *n* [ME *fir sticke*, fr. *fir, fire* + *sticke* stick — more at STICK] **1 :** a hardwood stick that is rubbed or twirled to make fire by friction — compare FIRE DRILL 1 **2 :** FIREBRAND **3 a fire sticks** *pl* **:** primitive fire tongs made of two sticks **b :** POKER 1
firestone \ˈ=ˌ=\ *n* [ME *firston*, fr. OE *fȳrstān*, fr. *fȳr* fire + *stān* stone — more at FIRE, STONE] **1 :** pyrite formerly used for striking fire; *also* **:** FLINT **2 :** a stone that will endure high heat and is used esp. for lining furnaces and kilns — used esp. of a sandstone occurring in the south of England **3 :** a plate of iron covering the front of the furnace in a slag hearth except for a few inches of space between it and the bedplate
fire stop *n* **:** a member or material used to fill or close open parts of a structure for preventing the spread of fire and smoke — compare FIRE BLOCKS
fire-stop \ˈ=ˌ=\ *vt* [*fire stop*] **:** to provide with a fire stop
firestopping \ˈ=ˌ==\ *n* **:** a system of fire stops
fire storm *n* **:** an atmospheric disturbance caused by a large fire (as after the bombing of a city) in which the central column of rising heated air induces a strong wind often accompanied by rain
fire superiority *n* **:** fire superior in effect to that of the enemy; *also* **:** the degree of such superiority
fire support *n* **:** assistance to infantry and armored units by artillery fire, naval gunfire, and airplane strafing and bombing
firetail \ˈ=ˌ=\ *n* **:** any of several birds with red or reddish tails: as **a** *dial Eng* **:** REDSTART 1 **b :** DIAMOND SPARROW 1
fire test *n* **:** a test by fire (as one to determine the burning point of an oil or one to determine the resistance of porcelain or concrete to heat) — see TIME-TEMPERATURE CURVE
firetest \ˈ=ˌ=\ *vt* **:** to subject to a fire test
fire thorn *n* **:** a plant of the genus *Pyracantha; specif* **:** a European partly evergreen tree (*P. coccinea*) with white flowers and orange-red fruits
firetop \ˈ=ˌ=\ *n* **:** FIREWEED b
fire tower *n* **1 :** a tower from which a watch for fires is maintained **2 :** a fireproof and smokeproof compartment running vertically through or attached to a building and containing a fireproof stairway **3 :** WATER TOWER 2 **4 :** DRILL TOWER
firetrap \ˈ=ˌ=\ *n* **:** a building or other place so constructed as to make egress hazardous in case of fire; *also* **:** combustible rubbish creating a fire hazard
fire tree *n* **1 :** a New Zealand tree (*Metrosideros tomentosa*) with hard wood **2 :** SUN TREE
fire trench *n* **:** a trench constructed to facilitate the delivery of small-arms fire
fire truck *n* **:** an automotive vehicle equipped with fire-fighting apparatus
fire tube *n* **:** ³FLUE d
fire-tube boiler *n* **:** a boiler in which water surrounds the tubes through which hot gases pass from the furnace to the stack
fire wagon *n* **:** FIRE ENGINE
fire walking *n* **:** the ceremony or ordeal of walking barefooted through fire, over a bed of embers, or over hot stones
fire wall *n* **1 :** a wall to prevent the spread of fire usu. made of noncombustible materials; *esp* **:** a wall completely separating two parts of a building from the basement to three feet above the roof and consisting of fire-resistive material and having all openings protected by automatically closing fire doors **2 :** a wall to retain oil in case of its escape from a tank or to prevent the spread of burning oil
fire ward *n, archaic* **:** FIRE WARDEN
fire warden *n* **:** an officer who has responsibility for fire control in a particular area: as **a :** one who directs a crew in the suppression of forest fires **b :** a fire patrolman in a logging area
firewater \ˈ=ˌ==\ *n* [prob trans. of an AmerInd expression like Algonquian *scoutiouabou* firewater] **:** strong alcoholic beverage
fireweed \ˈ=ˌ=\ *n* **:** any of several weeds troublesome in clearings or burned districts: as **a :** a plant of the genus *Erechtites; esp* **:** an American weed (*E. hieracifolia*) **b :** a tall perennial (*Epilobium angustifolium*) with creeping rootstocks, lanceolate leaves, and long spikes of pinkish purple flowers that tends to occur in great abundance in burned over areas or recent clearings and is an important honey plant in parts of No. America **c :** JIMSONWEED **d :** HORSEWEED 1 **e :** HOARY PLANTAIN 1 **f :** a wild lettuce (*Lactuca canadensis*) **g :** ORANGE HAWKWEED
fire wheel *n* **1 :** INDIAN BLANKET **2 :** a wheel of fireworks
fire willow *n* **:** an erect willow (*Salix scouleriana*) of western No. America appearing soon on burned over areas
fire wind *n* **:** a wind caused by a fire storm
fire window *n* **:** a window constructed to resist a fire of known standard intensity for a specified time (as 20 minutes or one hour)
firewoman \ˈ=ˌ==\ *n, pl* **firewomen :** a female fire fighter
firewood \ˈ=ˌ=\ *n* [ME *firwode*, fr. *fir, fire* + *wode* wood — more at WOOD] **1 :** wood for fuel **2 :** LEATHERWOOD 1b

firework \ˈ=ˌ=\ *n, often attrib* **1 :** a device for producing a striking display (as of light, noise, or smoke) by the combustion of explosive or flammable compositions esp. for exhibition, signaling, or illumination and typically consisting of a paper case containing combustible material (as charcoal, sulfur, or a metal powder), an oxidizing agent (as a nitrate or chlorate), and a metal salt as coloring agent if color is desired **:** PYROTECHNIC ⟨the sodium rocket was not merely a beautiful . . . ~ —*Time*⟩ **2 fireworks** *pl* **:** a display of fireworks ⟨the celebration was marked by ~*s* and much oratory⟩ **3 a fireworks** *pl but sometimes sing in constr* **:** a display of fiery temper, great excitement, or intense activity ⟨whenever those two get together there were sure to be ~*s*⟩ ⟨political ~*s*⟩ ⟨a ~*s* of rage —W.A.White⟩ **b :** a spectacular display (as of musical or verbal brilliance ⟨a natural ~ of . . . wit too good to print —Winthrop Sargeant⟩ — usu. used in pl. ⟨many Spanish dancers tend to overdo the ~*s* —*Dance Observer*⟩
fireworm \ˈ=ˌ=\ *n* **1 :** the larva of various small tortricid moths that eats the leaves of the cranberry giving the vines a scorched look **2 :** GLOWWORM
fire worship *n* **:** religious homage to fire or to a deity symbolized by fire
fir green *n* **:** FIR 3
¹firing *n* -S [ME, fr. gerund of *firen* to fire — more at FIRE] **1 :** the act or an instance of treating, preparing, or curing by heat; *specif* **:** the process of maturing ceramic products by the application of heat **2 :** FIREWOOD, COAL, FUEL **3 :** the burning or scorching of plants esp. by unfavorable soil conditions or other environmental conditions
²firing *adj* [fr. pres. part. of ²*fire*] **:** of or relating to the operation or operating parts of a firearm ⟨~ cycle⟩ ⟨~ mechanism⟩
firing data *n pl* **:** the commands necessary for the settings (as of instruments or fuzes) in the firing of a weapon esp. in the artillery
firing iron *n* **:** an iron used by veterinarians in cauterizing or firing a horse
firing line *n* **1 a :** a line from which fire is delivered against the enemy **:** FRONT LINE **b :** a line from which target practice is conducted **2 :** the forefront of any activity — used esp. in the phrase *on the firing line* ⟨the man or woman engaged in advertising production must know what he must do when he is on the *firing line* —Ben Dalgin⟩
firing order *n* **:** the order in which the several cylinders of an internal-combustion engine are sparked and fired
firing pin *n* **:** the pin that strikes the primer of the cartridge in the breech mechanism of a firearm
firing point *n* **:** a position (as on a firing line) from which a weapon is fired
firing ring *n* **:** one of various flat clay rings so placed in a pottery kiln that they may be withdrawn successively as the firing proceeds, the amount of shrinkage of the ring indicating the intensity of the fire
firing squad *also* **firing party** *n* **1 :** a detachment detailed to fire volleys over the grave of one buried with military honors **2 :** a detachment detailed to carry out a sentence of death by shooting
firing step *n* **:** a ledge or board along the front wall of a trench used to stand on when firing
firing table *n* **:** a table giving the elements of standard trajectories for a particular gun and type of ammunition and for effects produced by conditions (as of temperature or wind) that are not standard
firing tread *n* **:** BANQUETTE TREAD
firk \ˈfərk, ˈfi(ə)rk\ *vb* -ED/-ING/-S [ME *ferken*, fr. OE *fercian* to convey, bring, proceed; akin to OE *faran* to go, travel — more at FARE] *vi* **1** *dial Brit* **:** to move quickly **:** HASTEN; *also* **:** to be lively or frisky **2** *dial Brit* **a :** JERK, TWITCH **b :** FIDGET, FUSS ~ *vt* **1** *archaic* **:** BEAT, STRIKE, CHASTISE, CONQUER ⟨I'll ~ you, I'll rattle you —Thomas Gray⟩ **2** *obs* **:** to get dishonestly **:** CONTRIVE, CHEAT
fir·kin \ˈfərkən, -ə̇k-,-ᵊik-\ *n* -S [ME *ferdkyn, firdekyn, fyrkyn*, fr. (assumed) MD *veerdelkijn, vierdelkijn*, dim. of MD *veerdel, vierdel* fourth, fr. *veerde, vierde* fourth (adj.) + *-del* (fr. *deel* part); akin to OE *fēortha* fourth and *dǣl* part — more at FOURTH, DEAL] **1 :** a small wooden vessel or cask of indeterminate size **2 :** any of various British units of capacity usu. equal to ¼ barrel: as **a :** a unit equal to 9 imperial gallons **b :** an old unit for ale equal to 8 ale gallons **3 :** any of various British units of weight; *specif* **:** a unit for butter equal to 56 pounds

firkin 1

fir·lot \ˈfi(ə)rlət, ˈfər-\ *n* -S [ME *ferlot*, fr. ON *fjōrthi hlotr* fourth part, fr. *fjōrthi* fourth + *hlotr* part; akin to OE *fēortha* fourth and OE *hlot* lot — more at FOURTH, LOT] **1 :** any of various old Scottish units of dry capacity equal to ¼ boll or from ½ to 1½ Winchester bushels **2 :** a container of one firlot capacity
¹firm \ˈfərm, -ə̇m,-ᵊim\ *adj* -ER/-EST [alter. (influenced by L *firmus*) of ME *ferm, ferme*, fr. MF *ferm*, fr. L *firmus*; akin to L *fretus* trusting, daring, Gk *thrēsasthai* to sit down, *thronos* chair, throne, Skt *dhārayati* he holds, carries, keeps; basic meaning: holding, supporting] **1 a :** securely or solidly fixed in place **:** not loose **:** IMMOVABLE ⟨his teeth were ~ —D.B. Chidsey⟩ ⟨~ in the saddle⟩ ⟨the gate and its pillars were ~, but at one side the fence had fallen —John Glassco⟩ **b** (1) **:** not weak, wavering, or uncertain **:** SOLID, ROBUST ⟨walked with a ~ tread⟩ ⟨a ~ handshake⟩ ⟨a ~ steady touch on the piano⟩ (2) **:** SOUND, HEALTHY ⟨her mind was still ~; but her limbs trembled . . . violently —Ellen Glasgow⟩ **c :** having a solid or compact structure or texture **:** withstanding stress or pressure **:** not flabby or soft ⟨~ flesh⟩ ⟨~ muscles⟩ ⟨the snow was ~, not powdery⟩ ⟨the creek has a ~ bottom⟩ **2 a** (1) **:** not subject to change, revision, or withdrawal **:** FIXED, SETTLED, DEFINITE, ESTABLISHED ⟨at this meeting . . . two ~ decisions were taken —*N.Y. Times*⟩ ⟨I cannot quote you a ~ price⟩ ⟨is this a ~ offer⟩ ⟨like a mother with no baby-sitter and a ~ date at the theater —E.B.White⟩ (2) **:** not subject to price weakness on an increase in offerings **:** STEADY — used esp. of commodities, securities, and interest rates (3) *of electric power* **:** dependable or flowing steadily because supplemented by a reserve source **b** (1) **:** not easily moved, shaken, excited, or disturbed **:** UNSHAKEN, CONVINCED, DETERMINED ⟨~ nerves⟩ ⟨a ~ believer in democracy⟩ ⟨~ confidence in his own ability⟩ (2) **:** not fickle or vacillating **:** STEADFAST, LOYAL, CONSTANT ⟨a ~ friend⟩ ⟨~ in his devotion⟩ (3) **:** making no concessions **:** showing no weakness **:** UNYIELDING, RIGOROUS, INFLEXIBLE, SEVERE, HARD ⟨a ~ and even tough diplomacy —Hugh Gaitskell⟩ ⟨when a strong hand must be used, be impersonal but ~ —Dorothy Barclay⟩ ⟨~ discipline —L.C.Douglas⟩ **c** (1) **:** not easily challenged or undone **:** ASSURED, SECURE, STRONG ⟨took ~ possession of the enemy's trenches⟩ ⟨holds a ~ position as the country's leading poet⟩ ⟨this horse is a ~ favorite for the big race⟩ (2) **:** WELL-FOUNDED, CERTAIN ⟨the fuller and ~*er* account would have set several facts in clearer . . . perspective —A.S.P.Woodhouse⟩ **:** THOROUGH ⟨he has a ~ knowledge of the subject⟩ (3) **:** marked by solidity, precision, or clarity **:** convincingly, realistically, or solidly drawn ⟨the plot is thin, but the atmosphere is ~ —Nicola Chiaromonte⟩ ⟨the deep richness of the book . . . and its ~ design —W.T. Scott⟩ **3 :** indicating firmness or resolution ⟨the ~ almost arrogant voice of a vigorous young man —E.K.Genn⟩ ⟨a ~ mouth⟩
syn HARD, SOLID: FIRM may apply to a resistant tight compactness or resilient consistency of substance withstanding strain, stress, or pressure; it may imply stability or resolution ⟨a *firm* weave⟩ ⟨a *firm* foundation⟩ ⟨the snow, far from being soft and powdery, was *firm* and hard —John Hunt & Edmund Hillary⟩ ⟨only the pier actually hit was demolished; the adjoining piers stood *firm* —O.S.Nock⟩ ⟨he stood *firm* on recommendations he believed were to the city's benefit, often in the face of popular opposition —*Current Biog.*⟩ ⟨she was *firm* and determined with a firmness that was impervious to assault⟩ HARD may apply to a strong and rigid resistance to pressure or a sound unyielding stability; it may imply unyielding or harsh obduracy ⟨*hard* coal⟩ ⟨*hard* wood⟩ ⟨*hard* cash⟩ ⟨a *hard* man to deal with⟩ ⟨the oppressive conflict between esthetic values and a *hard* materialistic view of nature and human nature —Victor Lowe⟩ SOLID, as opposed to *fluid*, indicates a density and coherence giving fixed form; as opposed to *flimsy* or *unsubstantial*, it indicates strong sound stability; in reference to persons, it may imply complete reliability or sobriety ⟨a *solid* substance⟩ ⟨the bungalow was a very *solid* one —Rudyard Kipling⟩ ⟨courses that are *solid* in purpose and preparation and that are backed up with a maximum of good scholarship —Elizabeth Jacobs⟩ ⟨all we knew was that there was something of force and majesty and authority, *solid*, consistent, and beautiful —R.A.Cram⟩
²firm \"\ *adv* -ER/-EST [ME *ferm, ferme*, fr. *ferm, ferme*, adj.] **:** FIXEDLY, STEADFASTLY, SOLIDLY, FIRMLY — used chiefly in the phrases *stand firm* and *hold firm* ⟨if England had not stood ~ . . . our way of life would have gone up the flue —Richard Joseph⟩ ⟨begged his men to hold ~ till relief came⟩
³firm \"\ *vb* -ED/-ING/-S [ME *fermen, firmen*, fr. MF & L; MF *fermer*, fr. L *firmare*, fr. *firmus*] *vt* **1 a** (1) **:** to cause to become firm in texture or consistency **:** make solid or compact ⟨~ cheese⟩ ⟨~*ing* a light soil by rolling or harrowing —F.D. Smith & Barbara Wilcox⟩ ⟨a new face cream that ~*s* your skin⟩ (2) **:** to make fast or secure **:** set firmly **:** TIGHTEN ⟨~ a post in the ground⟩ ⟨~*ing* the grip on the sword —Tom Lea⟩ **b :** to bolster the courage or resources of **:** strengthen in some way **:** ENCOURAGE ⟨~*ed* herself with great care for the day —R.O. Bowen⟩ — often used with *up* ⟨voted a state of siege to ~ up his government —*Time*⟩ ⟨unless other factors ~ up the . . . price index substantially, it goes down —*Wall Street Jour.*⟩ ⟨his failure to ~ up his materialism . . . with data from the natural and social sciences —P.B.Rice⟩ **c :** SETTLE ⟨~ a contract⟩ **:** CONFIRM, ESTABLISH **2** *obs* **:** SIGN, VALIDATE ~ *vi* **1 :** to become firm in some way **:** take clear, definite, or fixed shape **:** HARDEN, CRYSTALLIZE, JELL ⟨his face ~*ed* and he spoke with restrained anger⟩ ⟨confidence is ~*ing* that the slump will be of short duration⟩ — often used with *up* ⟨opinion on this is ~*ing* up, and it's more optimistic than it was —*Kiplinger Washington Letter*⟩ ⟨the cheese is ~*ing*⟩ ⟨diplomats said more informal soundings must take place before things ~ up —*N.Y. Herald Tribune*⟩ **2 :** to recover from a decline **:** expand or rise after a contraction or fall ⟨after a long decline prices are ~*ing* again⟩ — often used with *up* ⟨cattle prices are ~*ing* up⟩ ⟨the market ~*ed* up a bit⟩
⁴firm \"\ *n* -S [Sp *firma*, fr. *firmar* to affirm, confirm, sign, fr. L *firmare*] **1** *obs* **:** SIGNATURE; *esp* **:** official signature of state papers **2** [G *firma*, fr. obs. G, signature, fr. It, fr. *firmare* to sign, fr. L *firmare* to make firm, confirm] **a :** the name, title, or style under which a company transacts business **:** the firm name **b :** a partnership of two or more persons not recognized as a legal person distinct from the members composing it — compare COMPANY 3 **c :** a business unit or enterprise ⟨the organizational framework within which the Soviet ~ operates —Holland Hunter⟩
fir·ma·ment \ˈfərməmənt, ˈfə̄m-,ˈfəim-\ *n* -S [ME, fr. LL & L; LL *firmamentum* vault of the sky (trans. of Gk *stereōma*, lit., solid body, foundation, trans. of Heb *rāqīaʽ*), fr. L, strengthening, support, fr. *firmare* to make firm + *-mentum* -ment — more at FIRM] **1 :** the vault or arch of the sky **:** HEAVENS **2** *in ancient astronomy* **:** the orb of the fixed stars **:** the 8th and outermost celestial sphere; *sometimes* **:** any of the crystalline heavens ⟨the first ~ or primum mobile⟩ **3** *obs* **:** fixed foundation **:** established basis
fir·ma·men·tal \ˌ==ˈmentᵊl\ *adj* **:** relating to the firmament **:** being of the upper regions **:** CELESTIAL
firmament blue *n* **:** a pale blue to light greenish blue that is bluer than aquamarine
fir·man \fərˈmän, ˌfərˈmän, ˈfərmən\ *n* -S [Turk *ferman*, fr. Per *fermān*, fr. OPer *framānā*] **:** a decree or mandate, order, license, or grant issued by the ruler of an Oriental country
firmer *comparative of* FIRM
fir·mer chisel \ˈfərmər-\ *n* [modif. of F *fermoir*, alter. of MF *formoir* chisel, fr. *former* to form — more at FORM] **:** a woodworker's hand chisel having a thin flat blade usu. at least 6 inches long and ⅛ to 2 inches wide — see CHISEL illustration
fir·mer gouge \"-\ *n* [*firmer* (*chisel*)] **:** a woodworking gouge similar in length and thickness to the firmer chisel
firmest *superlative of* FIRM
fir·mi·ster·nal \ˌfərməˈstərnᵊl\ *adj* [NL *Firmisternia* + E *-al*] **1 :** having the epicoracoids meet in the median neutral line **2 :** of or relating to the Firmisternia
fir·mi·ster·nia \ˌ==ˈ=nēə\ *n pl, cap* [NL, fr. L *firmus* strong, firm + NL *sternum* + -ia — more at FIRM, STERNUM] *in some classifications* **:** a division of the amphibian suborder Linguata in which in the adult state the epicoracoids of the two sides meet in the median ventral line — compare ARCIFERA
firmland *n* [¹*firm* + *land*] *obs* **:** TERRA FIRMA
firm·ly *adv* [ME *fermely, firmely*, fr. *ferm, ferme* firm + *-ly* — more at FIRM] **:** in a firm manner **:** STEADFASTLY, RESOLUTELY, SOUNDLY, SOLIDLY, STRONGLY ⟨~ entrenched in the mountainous parts along the northern border —*Collier's Yr. Bk.*⟩ ⟨a group of staid brownstone and brick dwellings stands ~ against time —*Amer. Guide Series: N.Y. City*⟩
firm·ness *n* -ES **:** the quality or state of being firm
fir moss *n* **:** FIR CLUB MOSS
firm red heart *n* **:** an incipient decay of heartwood characterized by a reddish color
firm up *vt* **:** to assure a steady flow of (as hydroelectric power) by means of a reserve supplementary source of electric power
firn *or* **firn snow** \ˈfi(ə)rn\ *n* -S [G, fr. G dial. (Switzerland) *firn* of or relating to the previous year, fr. OHG *firni* old; akin to OE *fyrn, firn* former, ancient, Goth *fairneis* old, ON *fyrnd* age, antiquity, *forn* old, OE *faran* to go — more at FARE] **:** NÉVÉ
firn·ifi·ca·tion \ˌfirnəfəˈkāshən\ *n* -S [*firn* + *-i-* + *-fication*] **:** the process whereby snow is changed to névé
firn line *n* **:** NÉVÉ LINE
fir pine *n* **:** BALSAM FIR 1
fir·ring *n* -S [by alter.] **:** FURRING 3b(1)
fir·ry \ˈfər-ē, -ri *also* ˈfərē *or* -ri\ *adj* [*fir* + *-y*] **:** made of fir **:** abounding in firs
¹first \ˈfərst, ˈfə̄st, ˈfəist\ *adj* [ME, fr. OE *fyrst*; akin to OHG & OS *furist* first, ON *fyrstr*; superlative fr. the root of OHG & OS *furi* before, for, ON *fyr*; akin to OE *faran* to go — more at FARE] **1 a** (1) **:** being number one in a countable series ⟨the ~ day⟩ **:** beginning a series — see NUMBER table ⟨the ~ volume⟩ ⟨my ~ voyage⟩ (2) **:** being a type of grammatical declension or conjugation conventionally placed first in a standard arrangement of the types (3) **:** being the lowest forward gear or speed in an automotive vehicle **b :** preceding all others **:** earliest in time ⟨the ~ to come⟩ ⟨the ~ train leaves at noon⟩ **c :** foremost in position **:** being in front of all others ⟨~ in the race⟩ **d** (1) **:** foremost in rank, importance, or worth **:** CHIEF ⟨of ~ importance⟩ ⟨~ in the hearts of his countrymen —Henry Lee⟩ ⟨your ~ concern is to get well⟩ ⟨the ~ American actor of our day —Lee Rogow⟩ (2) **:** highest or most prominent in carrying the melody among several voices or instruments of the same class ⟨~ soprano⟩ ⟨~ violin⟩ (3) **:** having primary jurisdiction in the Mormon Church; *esp* **:** having jurisdiction throughout the church ⟨the ~ presidency⟩ **e :** having precedence over colleagues of the same general grade or duties — used in titles ⟨~ mate⟩ ⟨~ ballerina⟩ **2 :** smallest, slightest, or most rudimentary ⟨I haven't the ~ idea of what you mean⟩ **3 a** *North* **:** EAGER, ANXIOUS ⟨he was so ~ to hear about it⟩ **b** *dial Brit* **:** NEXT, FOLLOWING — often used postpositively with expressions of time ⟨I'll come to see him Sunday ~⟩ **4 a :** being between 0.51 and 1.50 on the magnitude scale — used of the magnitude of a star **b :** being 1.50 or brighter on the magnitude scale — used of the apparent visual magnitude of any of the 22 brightest stars in the sky
²first \"\ *adv* [ME, fr. OE *fyrst*, fr. *fyrst*, adj.] **1 :** before any or some other person or thing (as in time, space, rank, or importance) **:** as the first thing to be mentioned **:** to begin with ⟨I will pay you ~, and then the others⟩ ⟨~, I wish to consider the economic problem⟩ ⟨~ of all, let me say that I regard my opponent with great respect⟩ — often used with *off* ⟨~ off, he was likely to get a shave and a haircut —S.E.Fletcher⟩ ⟨~ off, we heard a splendid performance of Haydn's Symphony —Philip Hamburger⟩ **2 :** for the first time ⟨we ~ met at a formal party⟩ **3 :** in preference to anything else **:** rather than do, be, or bear something **:** SOONER ⟨surrender? we will die ~⟩ **4** *North* **:** JUST, ONLY ⟨are you back already or are you ~ leaving⟩

³**first** \"\ *n* -s [ME, fr. *first*, adj.] **1 a :** number one in a countable series ⟨the ~ of the month⟩ **b :** the first part : BEGINNING, OUTSET ⟨the last of life for which the ~ was made —Robert Browning⟩ ⟨from the ~ I disliked the man⟩ ⟨at ~ I didn't know what to make of it⟩ **c :** the first thing ⟨the ~ I knew, the fire had spread to the bedroom⟩ **2 :** the first occurrence or item of its kind ⟨out of doors marked "restricted" today flow the aviation ~*s* of tomorrow —*First in Flight*⟩ ⟨Vermont has several educational ~*s* —*Amer. Guide Series: Vt.*⟩; *specif* : a first edition (as of a book) **3 a :** the first gear or speed in an automotive vehicle **b :** FIRST BASE **c :** UNISON : PRIME 8c **d :** PRIME 7 **4 a :** an article of commerce of the finest grade — usu. used in pl. ⟨clear unspotted skins graded as ~*s*⟩ **b :** FIRST CLASS ⟨he took a ~ in classics⟩ **c :** the winning place in a race or other sports contest

first aid *n* **:** emergency and sometimes makeshift treatment given to someone (as a victim of an accident) requiring immediate attention where regular medical or surgical care is not available

first-aid·er \,fər'stādər; fə̄'stādə(r, fəi's-\ *n* **:** one trained in giving first aid

first and last *adv* **:** taking everything together : all in all : in the last analysis : ALTOGETHER ⟨she holds that he was *first and last* a poet —*Times Lit. Supp.*⟩

first angle *n* **:** an angle of the Great Triangle formed on the palm by the intersection of the lines of Head and Life and when clear, well pointed, and even usu. held by palmists to indicate diplomacy and refinement of thought and conduct — called also *upper angle;* compare SECOND ANGLE, THIRD ANGLE

first approximation *n* **:** a roughly approximate value of a quantity often preliminary to more precise determination ⟨the value of pi to a *first approximation* is 22⁄7⟩

first attack *n* **:** a member of the offense on a men's lacrosse team

first base *n* **1 a :** the base that must be touched first by a base runner in baseball **b :** the player position for defending the area around first base **2 :** the first step or stage in a course usu. involving several steps or stages ⟨the widely advertised romance never got to *first base* —Bennett Cerf⟩

first baseman *n, pl* **first basemen :** the baseball player stationed at the first-base position — see BASEBALL illustration

first bass *n* **:** the principal contrabass player of an orchestra

first bite *n, in line engraving* **:** the first etch or action of the acid upon the plate before the application of dragon's blood

first border *n* **:** a row of lights over the front of the stage parallel to the proscenium — called also *concert border*

¹**firstborn** \'⸗,⸗\ *adj* [ME, fr. *first* + *born* born] **:** first brought forth : first in the order of nativity : ELDEST

²**firstborn** \"\ *n, pl* **firstborn** *also* **firstborns** [ME, fr. ¹*firstborn*] **:** one that is firstborn; *esp* : a firstborn son

first bottom *n* **:** the floodplain of a river : low-lying flatland along a stream that may be inundated at flood stage

first call *n* **:** a warning bugle call usu. played 15 minutes before assembly (as for reveille or retreat)

first captain *n* **:** the highest ranking cadet officer of a cadet corps or a military school

first cause *n* **1** *in some philosophies* **:** the self-created being to which every chain of causes must ultimately go back **2** *usu cap F&C* **:** GOD — compare PRIME MOVER

first-chop \'⸗,⸗\ *adj* [¹*first* + *chop* (quality, class)] **:** FIRST-CLASS ⟨I believe London is simply teeming with *first-chop* unwritten plays —Katherine Mansfield⟩

first class *n* **1 a :** the first and usu. highest group in a classification; *specif* : the group of persons who have obtained highest distinction in an honors course at a British university **b :** a place in or a member of such a group **2 :** the highest of usu. three classes of accommodations (as on a passenger ship) — compare CABIN CLASS **3 :** a class of mail that comprises letters, postcards, any matter wholly or partly in handwriting or typewriting, and any matter sealed against inspection, that requires the highest rate of postage, and that is accorded privileged treatment such as free forwarding or return to sender in case of nondelivery to addressee **4 :** the third rank in the rising scale of ranks in the Boy Scouts of America or the Girl Scouts of America — compare SECOND CLASS, TENDERFOOT

¹**first-class** \'⸗¦⸗\ *adj* [*first class*] **1 :** of or relating to the highest grade in a series ⟨a *first-class* railway carriage⟩ ⟨a *first-class* honors degree⟩ **2 :** of the best quality : of the highest excellence ⟨a *first-class* telescope⟩ ⟨*first-class* work⟩

²**first-class** \"\ *adv* **:** by a first-class conveyance : with first-class accommodations ⟨they travel *first-class*⟩

first class·man \'⸗'⸗mən\ *n, pl* **first classmen :** a fourth-year student in a military school (as Annapolis or West Point)

first-class saloon *n, Brit* **:** a railroad car whose facilities are adaptable for day or night occupancy

first coat *n* **1 :** SCRATCH COAT **2 :** the first layer of paint

firstcomer \'⸗¦⸗\ *n* **:** one that comes first ⟨the ~*s* to the New World did not possess boats —W.T.Corlett⟩

first cousin *n* **:** COUSIN 1b

first cranial nerve *n* **:** OLFACTORY NERVE

first cross *n* **:** an animal produced by interbreeding members of two pure breeds — contrasted with *mongrel* and *purebred*

first day *n* **1** *usu cap F* **:** SUNDAY — used chiefly by the Friends **2 a :** a day when the postage stamps of a new issue are first placed on sale; *esp* : one on which recognition of the event is made by special cancellations and often by cachets on mail bearing the stamps **b :** FIRST-DAY COVER

first-day city *n* **:** a city officially chosen for the first-day sale of a new postage stamp

first-day cover *n* **:** a philatelic cover bearing postal markings showing that it was mailed on a first day at a first-day city and that its stamp belongs to the new issue of that first day

first defense *n* **:** a lacrosse player whose defensive position is in front of the goal

first-degree \'⸗⸗¦⸗\ *adj* [fr. *first degree* (as in such phrases as *of the first degree, to the first degree*)] **1 :** of the lowest or mildest in a series ⟨*first-degree* initiation⟩ ⟨*first-degree* laceration⟩ **2 :** of the highest or most serious in a series ⟨*first-degree* murder⟩

first-degree burn *n* **:** a mild burn characterized by heat, pain, and reddening of the burned surface but not exhibiting blistering or charring of tissues

first derivative *n, math* **:** the derivative of a function

first-desk \'⸗¦⸗\ *adj* **:** first in rank among players of the same instrument in an orchestra ⟨the *first-desk* players of the string section⟩

first division *n* **:** the highest ranking half of a sports league; *specif* : the five leading baseball teams in each of the major leagues

first down *n* **:** the first in a series of four downs in which a football team must net a 10-yard gain to retain possession of the ball; *also* : the right to start such a series

first edition *n* **1 a :** the copies of a literary work first printed from the same type and issued at the same time **b :** the first pressrun of a newspaper for a given date **2 :** a single copy from a first edition

first family *n, sometimes cap both Fs* **1 :** a family of high social rank or pretensions esp. due to descent from the first settlers of a place ⟨those few inhabitants of Boston who regard themselves as the . . . end-all of American civilization — the thirty or forty *first families* —Katharine Rosin⟩ — abbr. *FF* **2 :** the family enjoying preeminent status in some place ⟨the closest relatives of the young god-king automatically became the nation's *first family* —Heinrich Harrer⟩

first filial generation *n* **:** the first generation produced by a cross with all members heterozygous for characters in which the parents differ

first flight *n* **1 :** a first flight in which airmail is carried over a newly established route **2 :** FIRST-FLIGHT COVER

first-flight cover *n* **:** a philatelic airmail cover bearing postal markings such as special cancellation and often a cachet showing that it was carried on a first flight

first floor *n* **1 :** GROUND FLOOR **2** *Brit* **:** the floor next above the ground floor

¹**firstfoot** \'⸗¦⸗\ *n* -s [¹*first* + *foot*] **1** *Brit* **:** the first person entering a house on New Year's day, such a person being popularly believed to bring good luck to the household if brunet and bad luck if blond **2** *Brit* **:** the first person met on the way to a special event (as a christening or wedding)

²**firstfoot** \"\ *vt, Brit* **:** to enter (a household) as a firstfoot ~ *vi* **1** *Brit* **:** to be a firstfoot — usu. used with *it* **2** *Brit* **:** to go about to various houses intending to be firstfoot

first·foot·er \-ə(r)\ *n* **:** FIRSTFOOT 1

firstfruits \'⸗¦⸗\ *n pl* [ME *first fruites*] **1 :** the earliest gathered fruits of the season; *specif* : those offered by the ancient Hebrews and other ancient nations to the Deity in acknowledgment of the gift of fruitfulness **2 :** the income for the first year formerly payable to a superior by every holder of a feudal or ecclesiastical benefice or an office of profit **3 :** the earliest products, effects, or results of any work, endeavor, or process

first-generation \¦⸗,⸗⸗¦⸗⸗\ *adj* **1 :** born in the U. S. — used of an American of immigrant parentage **2 :** FOREIGN-BORN — used of a naturalized American

¹**firsthand** \'⸗¦⸗\ *adv* [fr. *(at) first hand*] **:** directly from the original source : by direct observation or experience ⟨they will learn them ~ — and they will not like them —H.S.Truman⟩ ⟨individual citizens should know ~ what goes on in the courts —Dorothy Barclay⟩

²**firsthand** \"\ *adj* **:** obtained or coming directly from the original source : obtained by or based on direct observation or experience : DIRECT, IMMEDIATE ⟨authentic ~ facts about business properties and market conditions —*advt*⟩ ⟨keep in ~ touch with the changing . . . situation —*Current Biog.*⟩ ⟨~ information⟩ ⟨a ~ account, written by the doctor of a small merchant ship —H.R.Viets⟩

first in, first out *adj* **:** being or relating to a method of valuing inventories by which items in the lot first received are assumed to be issued or sold first and requisitions are priced at the cost per item of the oldest lot on hand — compare LAST IN, FIRST OUT

first intention *n* **1 :** the healing of an incised wound by the direct union of skin edges without granulations — compare SECOND INTENTION **2 :** a conception of a thing (as man, stone) formed by the direct or primary application of the mind to an individual object — compare SECOND INTENTION

first inversion *n* **:** a triad in music with its third in the bass — see TRIAD illustration

first lady *n, often cap F&L* **1 a :** the wife of the president of the U. S. or if he has no wife the woman whom he chooses to act as hostess at the White House **b :** the wife or hostess of the chief executive of any other country or jurisdiction ⟨one of the daughters will serve as father's hostess and thus be the new *first lady* of California —*Time*⟩ ⟨cabinet ministers had gathered . . . as the . . . bulletins indicated that the *First Lady* lay dying —*N.Y.Times*⟩ **2 :** the leading woman representative or practitioner of any art or profession ⟨the *first lady* of French letters⟩ ⟨the *first lady* of the dance⟩

first law of thermodynamics : LAW OF THERMODYNAMICS 1

first lien *n* **:** a lien taking precedence over all other claims, charges, or encumbrances of the same general category but not necessarily over those imposed by the sanction of government (as taxes or costs of administration or other preferred claims given priority by law)

first lieutenant *n* **1 a :** a commissioned officer in the army, air force, or marine corps ranking below a captain and above a second lieutenant **b :** the naval officer responsible for the upkeep and cleanliness of a ship or station **2 :** a Salvation Army officer ranking above a second lieutenant and below a captain

first-line \'⸗¦⸗\ *adj* **1 :** available for immediate effective combat service ⟨*first-line* troops⟩ ⟨*first-line* ships⟩ **2 :** of the first quality or importance ⟨there are in the area no potential *first-line* industrial centers —S.G.Hanson⟩ ⟨a *first-line* tire⟩ ⟨attended by 50 *first-line* business executives —*Amer. Standards Assoc.*⟩

first·ling \'⸗liŋ, -lēŋ\ *n* -s **1 :** the first of a class or kind ⟨the ~*s* of my tiny library —C.E.Montague⟩ **2 :** the first produce, offspring, or result of something ⟨an offering of lambs, all ~*s*, laid on his altar —W.B.Smith & Walter Miller⟩

first lord of the treasury : the principal lord commissioner of the treasury whose office has only nominal official duties but is usu. held by the British prime minister

first·ly *adv* [¹*first* + *-ly*] **:** in the first place (as in a series of topics) : before anything else : FIRST

first man *n* **:** FIRST SLIP

first mean line *n* **:** ACUTE BISECTRIX

first meridian *n* **:** PRIME MERIDIAN

first mortgage *n* **:** a mortgage that has priority as a lien over all mortgages and liens except those imposed by paramount authority of law (as taxes, betterments, and public water charges); *sometimes* : a mortgage that has priority over other mortgages only

first-movement form *n, chiefly Brit* **:** SONATA FORM

first mover *n* **:** FIRST CAUSE

first name *n* **:** the name that stands first in one's full name : CHRISTIAN NAME, FORENAME ⟨called him by one of his *first names* —Thomas Wolfe⟩ — contrasted with *last name*

¹**first-name** \'⸗¦⸗\ *vt* [*first name*] **:** to address by the first name ⟨the doctor's son from Edinburgh and the boy from Abilene were soon *first-naming* each other —T.C.Mendenhall †1924⟩

²**first-name** \'⸗,⸗\ *adj* [*first name*] **:** familiar enough to speak and be spoken to by a first name or nickname ⟨on *first-name* terms with almost everyone —Keith Ellis⟩ ⟨on a *first-name* basis with scores of the neighborhood children —*Lamp*⟩

first nerve *n* **:** OLFACTORY NERVE

first·ness *n* -ES **:** a fundamental category in Peircean philosophy comprising qualities like redness, hardness, bitterness, and nobility and expressive of possibility, spontaneity, and chance — compare SECONDNESS, THIRDNESS

first night *n* **1 :** the night on which a theatrical production is first performed at a given place **2 :** the performance given on a first night

first-night·er \'⸗'⸗ə(r)\ *n* -s [*first night* + *-er*] **:** a spectator habitually present at first-night performances

first of aries *usu cap A, astron* **:** the first point of Aries

first off *adv* [²*first*] **:** right away ⟨won't want to have to see people *first off* —B.A.Williams⟩

first offender *n* **:** one legally convicted of an offense for the first time

first officer *n* **1 :** a first mate in the merchant service **2 :** COPILOT

first-order reaction *n* **:** a chemical reaction in which the rate of reaction is directly proportional to the concentration of the reacting substance — compare ORDER OF A REACTION

first or last *adv* **:** at one time or another : at the beginning or end ⟨and all are fools and lovers *first or last* —John Dryden⟩

first-page \'⸗,⸗\ *adj* **:** FRONT-PAGE

first papers *n pl* **:** papers declaring intention that are filed by an applicant for citizenship as the first step in the process of naturalization — compare SECOND PAPERS

first person *n* **1 a :** a set of linguistic forms (as verb forms, pronouns, and inflectional affixes) referring to the speaker or writer of the utterance in which they occur (Latin *vidimus* "we see" is in the *first person* plural) ⟨English *me* is an objective singular pronoun of the *first person*⟩ ⟨in Sanskrit verbs *-mi* is a much-used ending of the *first person* singular⟩ **b :** a linguistic form belonging to such a set ⟨Latin *video* "I see" and *eo* "I go" are *first persons*⟩ **c :** reference of a linguistic form to the speaker or writer of the utterance in which it occurs ⟨the Latin verb ending *-o* that marks the *first person*⟩ **2 :** a style of discourse characterized by the use of verbs and pronouns of the first person in the most essential statements ⟨fictitious narratives are sometimes put into the *first person* for greater vividness⟩

first personal *adj* **:** of or relating to the first person ⟨a *first personal* pronoun⟩

first philosophy *n, usu cap F&P* **1** *Aristotelianism* **:** a study of being as being dealing with the fundamental type of being or substance upon which all others depend and with the most fundamental causes — distinguished from *second philosophy;* compare METAPHYSICS **2** *Aristotelianism* **:** a study of supersensible immutable being — compare THEOLOGY

first point *n* **:** the westernmost point of a zodiacal sign

first presidency *n, usu cap F&P* **:** the presiding body in the Mormon Church comprising the president and two counselors

first principles *n pl* **:** principles that are basic or self-evident

first public examination *n* **:** an examination taken after a certain period of residence by every candidate for the B.A. degree (as at Oxford University) — see MODERATION 3

¹**first-rate** \'⸗¦⸗\ *adj* [¹*first* + *rate*] **1 :** of the first order of size or importance ⟨a *first-rate* blunder⟩ ⟨the temptation to rush into print . . . resulted in a *first-rate* headache —*Newsweek*⟩ ⟨a *first-rate* power⟩ ⟨a book of *first-rate* significance⟩ **2 :** of the first order of quality : extremely good : EXCELLENT, ADMIRABLE ⟨none of those ancestors of his was ever *first-rate*, not one —Hamilton Basso⟩ ⟨*first-rate* entertainment⟩ ⟨a *first-rate* book⟩ — **first-rate·ly** *adv* — **first-rate·ness** *n* -ES

²**first-rate** \"\ *adv* **:** very well : quite well ⟨have not felt *first-rate* myself —Walt Whitman⟩ ⟨the fan worked *first-rate* —Marquis James⟩

first-rat·er \(,)⸗'rād·ər, -ātə-\ *n* **:** one that is first-rate ⟨in all reports a *first-rater* —Charles Dickens⟩

first reader *n, usu cap F&R* **:** a member of a Christian Science church or society chosen to conduct services and meetings for a specified time and specif. to read aloud from the writings of Mary Baker Eddy — see SECOND READER

first reading *n* **:** the first reading of a measure before a quorum of a legislative assembly typically of the title or number only and usu. either upon its introduction or before its reference to a committee

first run *n* **1 :** the earliest and richest sap flow in the sugar maple **2** [*first-run*] **:** the first showing of a new motion picture ⟨a house that had specialized in *first runs* of distinguished British productions —Arthur Knight⟩ ⟨a *first run* . . . cost the exhibitor twenty times as much as a twentieth run —Lewis Jacobs⟩

first-run \'⸗¦⸗\ *adj* **:** relating to or specializing in the first showings of new motion pictures ⟨a *first-run* movie⟩ ⟨a deluxe *first-run* theater⟩

firsts *pl of* FIRST

first sergeant *n* **1 :** the chief enlisted assistant to the commander of a company or equivalent unit esp. in the army or marine corps **2 :** MASTER SERGEANT

first slip *n* **:** the slip positioned nearest to the wicketkeeper — see CRICKET illustration

first sound shift *n* **:** CONSONANT SHIFT 1

first speed *n* **:** the forward transmission gear ratio in an automotive vehicle giving the lowest ratio of propeller-shaft to engine-shaft speed and the highest multiplication of torque

first story *n* **:** FIRST FLOOR

first-string \'⸗¦⸗\ *adj* **1 :** being a regular as distinguished from a substitute (as on a football team) ⟨*first-string* quarterback⟩ **2 :** being of the first order of quality or importance ⟨drew highly favorable notices from nearly all the *first-string* critics —*Current Biog.*⟩ ⟨almost the only *first-string* American statesman who managed to combine high office with humor —A.J.Liebling⟩

first watch *n* **:** the watch on a ship from 8 p.m. to midnight

first water *n* **1 :** the highest quality or purest luster — used of gems (as diamonds and pearls) **2 :** the highest grade or excellence : the highest degree : the first quality ⟨this is choral music of the *first water* —P.H.Lang⟩ ⟨a fool of the *first water* —Thomas Wolfe⟩ ⟨an alarmist of the *first water* —Katherine Mansfield⟩

firth \'fərth\ *n* -s [ME, fr. ON *firth-, fjörthr* — more at FORD] **:** a narrow arm of the sea : the opening of a river into the sea

fisc \'fisk\ *n* -s [MF & L; MF, fr. L *fiscus*] **1 :** FISCUS **2 :** a state or royal treasury **3** *or* **fisk** \"\ *Scots law* **a :** the public or crown treasury to which estates escheat — used chiefly in the phrase *as to the fisk* **b :** the estate of a rebel or the crown's right to it

¹**fis·cal** \'fiskəl\ *n* -s [Sp, fr. *fiscal*, adj., fr. L *fiscalis*] **1 a :** a public officer (as a prosecutor or policeman) or colonial magistrate usu. concerned with law enforcement or revenue **2 :** a prosecuting attorney in the Philippines **3** [²*fiscal*] **:** REVENUE STAMP **4** *also* **fiscal shrike** [Afrik *fiskaal*, a government official, fiscal shrike, fr. *fiskaal*, adj., fiscal, fr. L *fiscalis*] **:** a common black-and-white African shrike (*Lanius collaris*)

²**fiscal** \"\ *adj* [L *fiscalis*, fr. *fiscus* rush basket, money basket, treasury + *-alis* -al; akin to L *fidelia* earthen vessel, Gk *pithos* wine jar, and perh. to Icel *bitha* milk jug, Norw *bide* butter tub] **1 :** of or relating to taxation, public revenues, or public debt management and policies **2 :** of or relating to financial matters generally — **fis·cal·ly** \-əlē, -əli\ *adv*

fiscal agent *n* **:** a bank or trust company acting as the financial representative of a corporation or service organization

fiscal cancellation *n* **:** a cancellation of a revenue stamp or a cancellation on a postage stamp showing that it was used as a revenue stamp

fis·cal·i·ty \fi'skaləd·ē\ *n* -ES **:** excessive regard for financial considerations : spirit of gain; *also* : fiscal policy or question

fiscal period *n* **:** a uniform period by or for which accounts are reckoned (as one year)

fiscal policy *n* **:** the financial policy of a government particularly as regards the budget and the method and timing of borrowings and esp. in relation to central-bank credit policy

fiscal shrike *n* **:** FISCAL 4

fiscal stamp *n* **:** REVENUE STAMP

fiscal year *n* **:** the year by or for which accounts are reckoned : the year between one annual time of settlement or balancing of accounts and another, ending regularly on December 31 for private individuals and institutions and on June 30 for the U.S. government

fisch·er·ite \'fishə,rīt\ *n* -s [G *fischerit*, fr. Gotthelf *Fischer* von Waldheim †1853 Ger. naturalist + G *-it* -ite] **:** a mineral $AlPO_4.Al(OH)_3+2\frac{1}{2}H_2O$ consisting of a green basic aluminum phosphate perhaps identical with wavellite

fischer-tropsch process *also* **fischer-tropsch synthesis** \¦fishə(r)¦trōp¦sh-, -rŏp¦, -räp¦\ *n, usu cap F&T* [after Franz *Fischer* †1948 Ger. chemist and Hans *Tropsch* †1935 Ger. chemist born in Czechoslovakia] **:** a process originated in Germany esp. for producing liquid and gaseous hydrocarbon fuels (as gasoline or gas oil) by passing a mixture of carbon monoxide and hydrogen over metal or other catalysts at elevated temperatures and at normal or higher pressures — see OXYL PROCESS, SYNTHESIS GAS

fis·cus \'fiskəs\ *n, pl* **fis·ci** \-,s(k)ī, -,skē\ [L, rush basket, money basket, treasury — more at FISCAL] **:** one of the three branches of the public treasury under the Roman Empire that was most under imperial control

fi·set·in \fə'zetᵊn\ *n* -s [G, fr. *fiset-* (in *fisetholz*, wood from a species of fustic) + *-in*] **:** a yellow crystalline flavone pigment $C_{15}H_{10}O_6$ obtained from the wood of various trees or shrubs (as fustet or sumac)

¹**fish** \'fish\ *n, pl* **fish** *or* **fishes** [ME, fr. OE *fisc;* akin to OHG

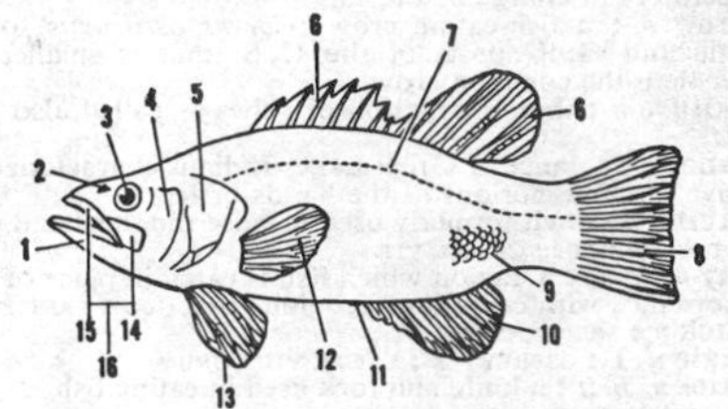

diagram of a fish: *1* mandible, *2* external naris, *3* eye, *4* cheek, *5* operculum, *6, 6* dorsal fins, *7* lateral line, *8* caudal fin, *9* scales, *10* anal fin, *11* anus, *12* pectoral fin, *13* pelvic fin, *14* maxilla, *15* premaxilla, *16* upper jaw

fisc fish, ON *fiskr*, Goth *fisks*, L *piscis*, OIr *īasc*] **1 :** an exclusively aquatic vertebrate or invertebrate animal — usu. used in combination ⟨star*fish*⟩ ⟨cuttle*fish*⟩ ⟨jelly*fish*⟩ **2 a :** any of numerous cold-blooded strictly aquatic water-breathing craniate vertebrates that include the cyclostomes, elasmobranchs, and higher gilled aquatic vertebrates with cartilaginous or bony skeletons or sometimes only the last of these groups, being on the one hand nearly coextensive with Pisces in its broadest use, on the other coextensive with Teleostomi, usu. with the addition of Choanichthyes, that have typically an elongated somewhat spindle-shaped body terminating in a broad caudal fin, limbs in the form of fins when present at all, and a 2-chambered heart by which blood is sent through the thoracic gills to be oxygenated before passing to the organs and tissues of the body and returning in venous condition to the heart, that are usu. oviparous, often producing great numbers of eggs which are fertilized in the water after they are laid, and that are important to man esp. as a source of food, fertilizers, and oils and for sport **b** : a particular kind of fish: as (1) *Brit* : SALMON (2) : COD (3) *Africa* : a dogfish served as food **3** : the flesh of fish used as food **4 a** : PERSON — often used with a disparaging qualifier ⟨regarded him as . . . a queer ~ —Nevil Shute⟩ ⟨as cold a ~ as you'd care to meet —*Saturday Rev.*⟩ ⟨a handful of poets, philosophers and other odd ~ —G.W. Johnson⟩ **b** : a person who is easily taken in : SUCKER ⟨I feel sorry for the poor ~⟩ **5** : something that resembles a fish: as **a** (1) : a purchase used to fish the anchor (2) : a piece of timber that is shaped like a fish and that is used to strengthen a mast or yard **b** : FISHPLATE **c** : FISH JOINT 1 **d** *slang* : TORPEDO 3 **e** : tools or other equipment lost down a drilled well and recoverable only by fishing **6 a** : a simplified form of the game of authors usu. played by children **b** : a counter (as in a game of chance) sometimes shaped like a fish **7** *slang* **a** *pl fish* : DOLLAR ⟨got over a thousand ~ apiece in back pay —Frederic Wakeman⟩ **b** : a new prison inmate ⟨three days after my arrival in Sing Sing prison as a new ~ in the teen-age bracket —Frank O'Leary⟩ **8** : a ballroom dance in which the partners move in close embrace — **fish out of water** : a person that is out of his proper sphere or element — **neither fish nor fowl** : one that does not belong to a definite class, party, or category : a nondescript person or thing; *also* : a person without convictions : TRIMMER — often used in the phrase *neither fish nor fowl nor good red herring* — **other fish to fry** : other affairs of interest or concern ⟨was asked to the party but had *other fish to fry*⟩

²fish \"\ *vb* -ED/-ING/-ES [ME *fisshen*, fr. OE *fiscian*; akin to OHG *fiscōn* to fish, ON *fiska*, Goth *fiskon*; denominative fr. the root of E ¹*fish*] *vi* **1 a** (1) : to attempt to catch fish by any means or for any purpose ⟨~ from a boat⟩ ⟨~ for cod⟩ (2) : to catch fish ⟨leaders a few inches long or too short . . . — there were always a hundred little things which could cause a boat not to ~ —E.K.Gann⟩ **b** (1) : to search for anything that is under water (as with a hook or dredge) ⟨~ for pearls⟩ (2) : to recover or attempt to recover tools or other equipment lost down a drilled well **c** : to engage in a search of any kind by or as if by groping or feeling ⟨~*ing* in the subconscious . . . brings to light . . . wayward associations —D.L.Bolinger⟩ ⟨for ten minutes or so this trio was busily engaged ~*ing* in the grass, for a lost token is a serious matter —O.S.Nock⟩ ⟨~*ing* in an inside pocket he handed me a square white envelope —Hartley Howard⟩ — often used with *for* ⟨he started to ~ around for a match —L.C.Stevens⟩ ⟨~*ing* for other applications the industry has produced a novel parade of articles —*Monsanto Mag.*⟩ **d** : to seek to elicit or draw forth by hinting or other roundabout means — often used with *for* ⟨~*ing* for praise of his ability —Arnold Bennett⟩ ⟨~*ing* for compliments⟩ **2** : to be in adjustment for catching fish — used of a net or other fishing device **3** : to be fishable ⟨this stream ~*es* well⟩ **4** *of a Salvationist* : to speak with individuals to help them make the decision to follow Christ : engage in personal evangelism ~ *vt* **1 a** : to catch or try to catch (as salmon); *also* : to collect (as coral) from the sea bottom **b** : to draw as if fishing ⟨he ~*ed* his one crutch from under the bed —Earle Birney⟩ ⟨~*ed* some cigarettes out of his shirt pocket —R.O.Bowen⟩ ⟨the ammunition also sank but was ~*ed* up —Frank Sebenham⟩ **2 a** : to fish in ⟨~*ed* the stream all morning⟩ **b** : to fish with : use in fishing (as a boat, net, or lure) **3** : to draw or pull (electric wires) through a conduit or between floors or walls with a hook and line or wire **4** : to hoist the flukes of (an anchor) — **fish or cut bait** : to make a choice between alternatives : cease temporizing or procrastinating; *specif* : to choose either to engage wholeheartedly or actively in some work or scheme or to withdraw from it completely

fish·abil·i·ty \ˌfishə'biləd·ē\ *n* -ES : the quality or state of being fishable

fish·able \'fishəbəl\ *adj* : suitable, promising, or legally open for fishing ⟨a ~ brook⟩

fish-and-chips \ˌ⸗⸗ˌ⸗\ *n pl* : fried fish and French fried potatoes

fish ball *n* : a globular cake made of fish (as salted codfish) shredded, mixed with mashed potato, and fried

fish basket *n* : a fishing device made of wooden slats usu. set in a running stream to trap fish moving downstream

fish beam *n* : a beam one of whose sides swells out like the belly of a fish

fishbed \'⸗,⸗\ *n* : a sedimentary stratum rich in fossil remains of fish

fish begonia *n* : an ornamental Brazilian herb (*Begonia maculata*) that is often cultivated and has showy spotted fishtail-shaped leaves

fish-bellied \'⸗,⸗⸗\ *adj* : bellying out on the underside; *specif* : bent downward in the middle and usu. also bent upward correspondingly — used of joists, beams, and similar structural members

fish belly rail *n, Brit* : a short-span rail supported on chairs and curved on the underside so as to be deeper at the middle than at the ends of the span

fish belly sill *n* : a side or center sill shaped like a fish and used in railroad car construction

fish·ber·ry \'fish- — *see* BERRY\ *n* : FISH POISON; *specif* : ²COCCULUS

fish blanket *n* : HORNWORT

fish-blooded \'⸗ˌ⸗⸗\ *adj* : COLD-BLOODED ⟨one of those brittle *fish-blooded* aristocrats who stand firm for kindness to animals and discipline for the lower classes —Leslie Charteris⟩

fish boat *n* [ME *fishboot*, fr. *fish* + *boot* boat — more at BOAT] : a boat from which fish are caught

fishbolt \'⸗,⸗\ *n, Brit* : a bolt for securing a fishplate; *specif* : a bolt joining two opposite fishplates

fishbowl \'⸗,⸗\ *n* **1** : a bowl for the keeping of live fish **2** : something that is open to inspection from all sides ⟨in the ~ of so small a town . . . it would have been impossible for . . . a secret to be kept —Robert Benton⟩

fish cake *n* : a flattened fish ball

fish car *n* : a railroad car equipped with water tanks for the transportation of live fish and also provided with quarters for the operators in charge of the car

fish crow *n* : a fish-eating crow (*Corvus ossifragus*) of the Atlantic and Gulf coasts of the U. S. that is smaller and quieter than the common crow

fish culture *n* : the propagation of fishes — called also *pisciculture*

fish dance *n* : a dance of Great Lakes Indians characterized by imitative flipping motions of the hands or feet

fish davit *n* : a davit formerly used to raise the fluke end of an anchor — compare CAT DAVIT

fish day *n* [ME] : a day on which fish is eaten in place of flesh in accordance with custom or religious practice : FAST DAY

fish duck *n* : MERGANSER

fish eagle *n* **1** : OSPREY **2** : EAGLE VULTURE

fish eater *n, Brit* : a knife and fork used in eating fish

fished *past of* FISH

fish·er \'fishə(r)\ *n* -S *see sense 2* [ME *fissher*, fr. OE *fiscere*, fr. *fisc* fish + *-ere* -er — more at FISH] **1** : one that fishes; *esp* : a person, animal, or boat that is engaged or is employed in fishing **2** *pl also* **fisher a** : a large dark brown somewhat vulpine arboreal carnivorous mammal (*Martes pennanti*) that is related to the marten and the weasels and that is native to much of the forested northern half of No. America but is now extinct over much of its former range due to excessive hunting because of its valuable pelt **b** : the fur or pelt of this animal

fisher-cat \'⸗⸗,⸗\ *n* : FISHER 2a

fisherfolk \'⸗⸗,⸗\ *n, pl in constr* : people whose occupation is fishing, esp. deep-sea fishing

fish·er·man \'fishə(r)mən\ *n, pl* **fishermen** [ME, fr. *fisher* + *man* man] **1** : one who engages in fishing as an occupation or for pleasure **2** : a ship used in commercial fishing

fisherman's bend *n* : a knot for tying a line to a spar or ring that is made by passing the end twice round the spar or through the ring and then back under both turns — called also *anchor bend*

fisherman's knot *n* : a knot for tying the ends of two lines together that is made by tying overhand knots in the ends around the opposite standing parts — called also *Englishman's knot, true lover's knot, waterman's knot*

fisherman's staysail *n* : a triangular or quadrilateral sail between the foremast and mainmast of a fishing schooner

fisherman's bend

fish·ery \'fish(ə)rē, -ri\ *n* -ES [²*fish* + *-ery*] **1** : the act, process, occupation, or season of taking fish or other sea products : FISHING ⟨the golden age of the whale ~⟩; *also* : the catch of a specified fish or sea product ⟨the menhaden ~ for the year⟩ **2** : a place for catching fish or taking other sea products ⟨an oyster ~⟩ ⟨a salmon ~⟩ **3** : a fishing establishment; *also* : its group of fishermen **4** : the legal right to take fish at a certain place or in particular waters esp. by drawing a seine or net — see COMMON FISHERY, FREE FISHERY, SEVERAL FISHERY **5** : the technology of fishery : a branch of knowledge concerned with the methods and economics of fishery and the utilization and preservation of fish resources — usu. used in pl. ⟨a number of schools of *fisheries* have been established⟩

fishery salt *n* : a coarse grade of common salt used in curing fish

fishes *pl of* FISH, *pres 3d sing of* FISH

fisheye \'⸗,⸗\ *n* **1** : a diamond or other gemstone cut too thin for proper brilliancy **2** : a large translucent globule of cooked tapioca — usu. used in pl. **3** : a small blemish in finished paper caused by the crushing and glazing of an adventitious particle by the calender **4** : ocular lymphomatosis of the fowl — compare LEUKOSIS **5** : a cold or suspicious stare ⟨I saw you guys giving me the ~ . . . so I ran —Eddie Krell⟩

fishfall \'⸗,⸗\ *n* : the tackle on a fish davit

fish-farming \'⸗,⸗⸗\ *n* : the rearing of fishes esp. in ponds for food

fish-finder \'⸗,⸗⸗\ *n* : a sonic depth finder used to determine the position of schools of fish in the sea

fish flake *n* : a frame on which fish are dried

fish flop *n* **1** : a semiaerial tumbling stunt consisting of a backward roll into a headstand followed immediately by the easing of the body down onto the chest, belly, and thighs and finishing in a stand **2** : a somersault with flipping of the feet in the air

fish flour *n* : flour made of pulverized dried fish

fish fly *n* : any of various insects (family Corydalidae) resembling but smaller than the dobsonfly

fish fork *n* **1** : a large short-handled fork used in loading and unloading fish **2 a** : an individual 4-tined fork larger than a salad fork that is used with an individual fish knife in eating fish **b** : a large broad 4-tined fork that is used with a broad serving knife in serving fish

fish fry *n* **1** : a picnic at which fish are caught, fried, and eaten; *also* : an indoor supper at which fish are fried and eaten **2** : fried fish

fish fungus *n* **1** : a water mold (*Saprolegnia ferax*) that attacks living fish esp. when crowded in hatcheries or aquariums **2** : a reddish fungus (*Clathrocystis roseopersicina*) sometimes appearing on salted codfish

fishgarth \'⸗,⸗\ *n* [ME, fr ¹*fish* + *garth*] : a dam or weir in a river or on the seashore for keeping fish or taking them

fish gelatin *n* : ISINGLASS

fish geranium *n* : an upright herb (*Pelargonium hortorum*) often cultivated for its scalloped crenate-toothed leaves with a broad color zone inside the margin

fish·gig \'fish,gig\ *n* [by folk etymology fr. *fizgig*] : a fish spear having two or more barbed prongs

fish glue *n* : either of two gelatinous substances obtained from fish waste products: **a** : ISINGLASS **b** : a strong adhesive obtained by heating with water esp. the skins, fins, and bones of fish (as cod, haddock, or hake) and used chiefly in liquid form in the cold

fish grass *n* : WATER SHIELD 2

fish guano *n* : a fertilizer prepared from fish : FISH MEAL

fish-handler's disease *n* : ERYSIPELOID

fish hatchery *n* : an establishment in which young fish are produced and reared esp. for later release in natural waters

fish hawk *n* : OSPREY

fish hoek skull \'fish,hu̇k-, 'fi,shu̇k-\ *n, usu cap F&H* [fr. *Fish Hoek* (Vishoek), town in Cape Province, Union of So. Africa, where it was discovered] : a southern African fossil skull that resembles that of a Bushman and that is found in association with artifacts suggesting an advanced type of the European Mousterian

fishhold \'⸗,⸗\ *n* : the hold in a fish boat for keeping fish

fish·hook \'fish,hu̇k, 'fi,shu̇k\ *n* [ME *fishhok*, fr. *fish* + *hok* hook — more at HOOK] **1** : a hook for catching fish **2** : a large hook with a pendant to the end of which the fish tackle is hooked in fishing an anchor

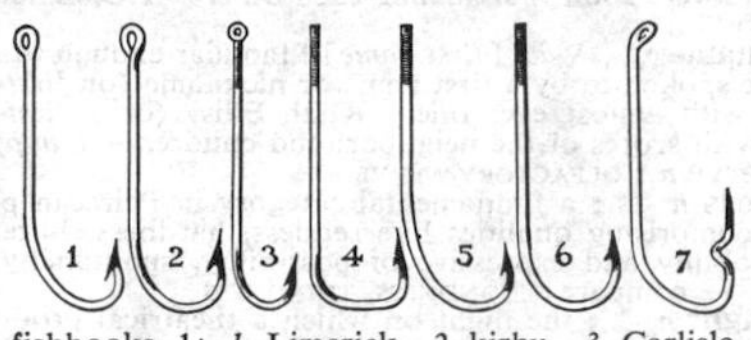

fishhooks 1: *1* Limerick, *2* kirby, *3* Carlisle, *4* Kendal sneck bent, *5* sproat, *6* Aberdeen, *7* barbless

fishhook cactus *n* **1** : CHOLLA **2** : a low cactus (*Ferocactus wislizenii*) of southwestern U. S. and adjacent Mexico

fishhook money *n* : Persian larin money

fish house *n* : BOB-HOUSE

fish house punch *n* : a punch usu. consisting of lemon juice, rum, peach liqueur, brandy, sugar, bitters, and carbonated or plain water

fishier *comparative of* FISHY

fishiest *superlative of* FISHY

fish·ify \'fishə,fī\ *vt* -ED/-ING/-ES : to change to fish

fish·i·ly \'fishəlē, -li\ *adv* : in a fishy manner ⟨looked at me ~⟩

fishing *n* -S [ME *fisshing*, fr. gerund of *fisshen* to fish — more at FISH] **1 a** : the act of one that fishes **b** : the occupation or pastime of catching fish **2 a** : a place for catching fish ⟨a descriptive list of the free and open mainland Scottish ~*s* —*Times Lit. Supp.*⟩ **b** : the right of taking fish

fishing banks *n pl* : a plateau under the sea at a comparatively small depth where fish frequently gather in schools

fishing bear *n* : a bear of northeastern Asia that constitutes a race (*Ursus arctos beringianus*) of the Eurasian brown bear and that lives largely on fish

fishing cat *n* : a spotted swamp-dwelling wildcat (*Felis viverrina*) of southeastern Asia that feeds mainly on fish and mollusks

fishing duck *n* : MERGANSER

fishing eagle *n* : any of several rather large birds of prey that commonly feed on fishes: as **a** : OSPREY **b** : a large eagle (*Ichthyophaga ichthyaetus*) of tropical Asia that resembles the osprey in habits **c** : a large eagle (*Haliaeetus leucoryphus*) of southeast Europe and central Asia that ranges southward to northern India and Burma **d** : EAGLE VULTURE

fishing expedition *n* **1** : a legal proceeding carried on for the primary purpose of interrogating an adversary or examining his property or books, papers, and records in order to discover information essential to and to be used as a basis for a later proceeding or defense **2** : an investigation that has no clearly defined objective or that does not stick to its stated or authorized objective and that engages in expedients of doubtful propriety or legality (as the irrelevant questioning of witnesses) in the hope of turning up incriminating or newsworthy evidence ⟨promised at the outset of the investigation that it would not . . . degenerate into a witch-hunt or a *fishing expedition* —Tom Fitzsimmons⟩

fishing float *n* : a scow used in seine fishing and designed to be moved from one fishing ground to another

fishing frog *n* : ANGLER 2

fishing ground *n* : an area in a body of water where fishes congregate and fishing is usu. good

fishing pole *n* : a slender tapering pole with a line attached to the tip used in fishing — compare FISHING ROD

fishing rod *n* : a springy tapering often jointed rod (as of wood, split bamboo, or steel) equipped with hand grip and line guides and used with fishing line and reel for catching fish

fishing space *n* : the space between the head and base of a railroad rail for seating the fishplate

fishing tool *n* : a tool for recovering objects from inaccessible places

fishing wand *n, Scot* : FISHING ROD

fishing worm *n* : FISHWORM 1

fish joint *n* **1** : a joint for forming separate limbs into a bow or bowstave by fitting a wedge end into a V slot or a double wedge into a W slot **2** : a butt joint in which the two abutting members are held in alignment by one or more fishplates

fish-joint \'⸗ˌ⸗\ *vt* : to fasten with a fish joint

fish kettle *n* : a long kettle for boiling fish whole that is usu. provided with a rack and handle

fish killer *n* : GIANT WATER BUG

fish knife *n* [ME *fishknif*, fr. ¹*fish* + *knif* knife — more at KNIFE] **1** : a small knife with an ornamental upper edge that is used with a fork in eating fish **2** : a large knife with broad blade and decorative upper edge that is used with a large 4-tined fork in serving fish

fish ladder *n* : a series of pools arranged like steps by which fishes can pass over a dam in going upstream

fish leaves *n pl* : the floating leaves of the common pondweed (*Potamogeton natans*)

fishline \'⸗,⸗\ *n* : a line used in fishing

fish-liver oil *n* : a fatty oil from the livers of various fishes (as cod, halibut, or sharks) used chiefly as a source of vitamin A and formerly also of vitamin D

fish louse *n* : any of various small crustaceans (as the carp louse) parasitic on fishes; *esp* : any of various true copepods that are found on the skin or gills or in the mouth of fishes and that exhibit varying degrees of degeneration in the adult state due to their parasitic habits — see LERNAEA

fish·man \'fishmən\ *n, pl* **fishmen** [ME, fr. ¹*fish* + *man*] **1** : one who cleans fish in preparation for cooking **2** : one who sells fish and other seafood

fish maw *n* : the air bladder of a fish

fish meal *n* : ground dried fish and fish waste used as fertilizer and in animal feeds

fish mint *n* : either of the two mints (*Mentha aquatica* and *M. longifolia*) that usu. grow in moist places

fish mold *n* : a water mold growing on fish — compare SAPROLEGNIALES

fishmonger \'⸗,⸗⸗\ *n* [ME, fr. ¹*fish* + *monger*] *chiefly Brit* : a fish dealer

fish moth *n* **1** : SILVERFISH **2** : FIREBRAT

fishmouth \'⸗,⸗\ *n* : TURTLEHEAD

fishnet \'⸗,⸗\ *n* [ME, fr. OE *fiscnett*, fr. *fisc* fish + *nett* net — more at FISH, NET] : netting fitted with floats and weights or with a supporting frame often oval for catching fish

fish oil *n* : a fatty oil from the bodies of fishes or marine mammals (as menhaden, sardines, or whales) used chiefly as a drying oil in paint and varnish and usu. after being hydrogenated for soapmaking

fish out *vt* : to exhaust the supply of fish in by fishing ⟨this lake has been *fished out*⟩

fish owl *or* **fishing owl** *n* : any of various fish-eating owls of the Old World genera *Scotopelia* and *Ketupa*

fish paper *n* : a tough flexible paper or board used for electrical insulation made largely from cotton fiber and vulcanized

fish pearl *n* : a glass bead lined or coated with essence d'orient to simulate a pearl

fish pier *n* : a pier for fish boats to tie up to

fish·plate \'⸗,⸗\ *n* : a steel plate lapping a joint of heavy timbers or railroad rails and secured to the sides so as to connect the members end to end

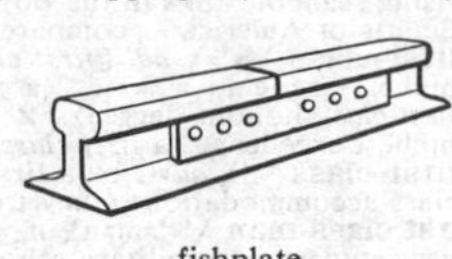
fishplate

fish poison *n* : any of numerous plants or drugs used to kill or stupefy fish by placing the drug or an extract of it in the water: as **a** : JAMAICA DOGWOOD **b** : RED BUCKEYE **c** : ²COCCULUS

fish poisoning *n* **1** : acute illness resulting from the consumption of fish: **a** : illness due to eating fish that normally contain neurotoxins in their flesh **b** : illness due to eating stale fish: (1) : a histamine intoxication (2) : a bacterial food poisoning **2** : ERYSIPELOID

fish pole *n* : FISHING POLE

fish pomace *or* **fish scrap** *n* : refuse of fish after the oil is expressed that is used for fertilizer

fishpond \'⸗,⸗\ *n* [ME, fr. ¹*fish* + *pond*] **1** : a pond stocked with edible fish **2** : a grab bag from which articles are extracted by means of a pole and line

fish pot *n* **1** : a structure built in a stream for catching fish ⟨in the construction of any such *fish pot* necessary portable slats, tilts, slides or escapes shall be installed —*Md. House Bill*⟩ — compare WEIR **2** : a receptacle for catching fish or shellfish — compare CRAB POT, LOBSTER POT

fishpound \'⸗,⸗\ *n* : a net attached to stakes that is used for catching fish : WEIR

fish scale *n* **1** : the scale of fish; *also* : something resembling it **2** : a defect in enamel on sheet iron characterized by blistering and the detachment of small flakes of enamel

fish screen *n* : a sometimes electrified screen designed to exclude fishes from an intake (as of a power plant or waterworks)

fish service *n* : a china service for fish consisting of a platter, sauce boat, and a specified number of plates

fishskin disease *or* **fish-scale disease** \'⸗,⸗-\ *n* : ICHTHYOSIS

fish stick *n* **1 a** *also* **fish water** : a by-product of fish processing containing considerable quantities of amino acids, animal protein factor, and other vitamins and minerals **b** : the product of its dehydration used chiefly in animal feeds **2** : a stick of fish ⟨*fish sticks* and French fried potatoes⟩

fish story *n* : an extravagant or incredible story

fish tackle *n* : a tackle or purchase used to raise the flukes of an anchor up to the gunwale

¹fishtail \'⸗,⸗\ *n* [ME *fish tail*] **1** : something suggesting the tail of a fish esp. in being somewhat triangular with a median notch: as **a** : an arrow that wobbles in flight **b** : a railroad semaphore the arm of which is notched at the end and which is used as an advance warning signal **2** : a turning ballroom step **3** : the aeronautical maneuver of fishtailing

²fishtail \"\ *also* **fishtailed** \'⸗,⸗\ *adj* : having a shape that imitates or resembles the shape of a fish's tail ⟨a gardener's knife with a sharp ~ blade —*New Yorker*⟩ ⟨the ~ gas jets in the square-sided station lamps —Anthony West⟩ ⟨some of the women were wound up in ~ skirts which defy description —G.H.Reed b.1887⟩

³fishtail \"\ *vi* **1** : to swing the tail of an airplane from side to side during a glide without altering the flight path in order to reduce speed in approaching the ground for a landing **2** *of a ship* : to move through the water with a side-to-side or whipping motion of the stern ⟨the short-ranged sleek destroyer ~*ing* alongside —K.M.Dodson⟩

fishtail bit *also* **fishtail** *n* : a drilling bit shaped like a fish's tail

fishtail burner *n* : a gas burner in which two jets of gas issuing from two holes inclined toward each other impinge and form a fan-shaped flame

fishtail cutter *n* : a flat milling cutter for milling (as slots, keyways)

fishtail palm *n* : a palm of the genus *Caryota*

fishtail wind *n* : a variable wind that blows toward the targets on a rifle range

fish tape *or* **fish wire** *n* : a flat tempered spring-steel tape or wire used in pulling electric wires and cables (as into conduit runs) — called also *snake wire*

fish tapeworm *n* : a large pseudophyllidean tapeworm (*Diphyl-*

lobothrium latum) as an adult infesting the human intestine and sometimes associated with a peculiar macrocytic anemia resembling pernicious anemia and having its early development in a copepod and intermediate stages in freshwater fishes, from which it is transmitted to man or other fish-eating mammals when raw fish is eaten

fish trap *n* **:** a device for catching fish that consists of a net or other structure which diverts the fish into an enclosure so arranged that egress is more difficult than ingress

fishway \ˈ=,=\ *n* **:** a contrivance for enabling fish to pass around a fall or dam in a stream; *specif* **:** FISH LADDER

fishweed \ˈ=,=\ *n* **1 :** MEXICAN TEA **2 :** PONDWEED

fishweir \ˈ=,=\ *n* [ME *fishwer,* fr. OE *fiscwer,* fr. *fisc* fish + *wer* weir — more at FISH, WEIR] **:** FISHGARTH

fish well *n* **:** a well for fish on a fish boat

fish wheel *n* **:** SALMON WHEEL

fishwife \ˈ=,=\ *n* [ME, fr. *fish* + *wife*] **1 :** a woman who sells fish at retail **2 :** a scurrilously abusive woman ⟨began to berate them in the coarse language of a ~ —Louis Bromfield⟩

fishwood \ˈ=,=\ *n* **1 :** STRAWBERRY BUSH 1a **2 :** JAMAICA DOGWOOD

fishworm \ˈ=,=\ *n* **1 :** an earthworm used as bait **2 :** a worm parasitic in or on fishes

fishy \ˈfishē, -shi\ *adj* -ER/-EST [ME, fr. ¹*fish* + *-y*] **1 :** of or relating to a fish **:** like a fish **:** abounding in fish ⟨the ~ deep⟩ ⟨a ~ odor⟩ ⟨a ~ taste⟩ **2 a :** inspiring doubt or suspicion **:** DUBIOUS, QUESTIONABLE, UNCONVINCING ⟨he could not help scenting something ~ about an Englishman who chose to live abroad —Margery Sharp⟩ ⟨that story sounds very very ~ to me —Erle Stanley Gardner⟩ ⟨there is something of a ~ nature going on in the office —Dorothy Sayers⟩ ⟨using his position to line his pocket through ~ and degrading commercial deals —*Time*⟩ **b :** lacking warmth or passion **:** FRIGID, COLD, SUSPICIOUS, LACKLUSTER, DULL ⟨they remembered his ~ handclasp and downcast eyes —H.S.Canby⟩ ⟨a fervent urge . . . to hit him between his damnable cold, ~, evasive eyes —Vicki Baum⟩ ⟨she looked with a ~ eye on the glamorous scenes that we loved —W.A.White⟩ ⟨drawled . . . in his usual cautious, ~ tone —Frank O'Connor⟩

fishyback \ˈ==,=\ *n* **:** the movement of truck trailers or freight containers by barge or ship — compare PIGGYBACK

fisk *var of* FISC

fissi- *comb form* [LL, fr. L *fissus,* past part. of *findere* to split — more at BITE] **1 :** divided **:** cleft ⟨*fissi*lingual⟩ **2 :** fission ⟨*fissi*parous⟩

fis·si·den·ta·ce·ae \,fisəden·ˈtāsē,ē\ *n pl, cap* [NL, fr. *Fissident-, Fissidens,* type genus (fr. *fissi-* + L *dent-, dens* tooth) + *-aceae* — more at TOOTH] **:** a family of chiefly tropical acrocarpous mosses (order Fissidentales) characterized by 2-ranked clasping vertically placed leaves — **fis·si·den·ta·ceous** \,===ˈtāshəs\ *adj*

fis·si·den·ta·les \,===ˈtā(,)lēs\ *n pl, cap* [NL, fr. *Fissident-, Fissidens* + *-ales*] **:** a small order of Musci coextensive with the family Fissidentaceae

fis·sile \ˈfisəl, -(,)sil, -,sīl\ *adj* [L *fissilis,* fr. *fissus* + *-ilis* -ile] **1 :** capable of being split, cleft, or divided in the direction of the grain ⟨~ wood⟩ or along natural planes of cleavage ⟨~ crystals⟩ **2 :** FISSIONABLE

fis·si·lin·gual \,fisə¦liŋgwəl\ *adj* [*fissi-* + *lingual*] **:** of or relating to the Fissilinguia

fis·si·lin·guia \,==ˈgwēə\ *n pl, cap* [NL, fr. *fissi-* + L *lingua* tongue + NL *-ia* — more at TONGUE] *in some classifications* **:** a group of lizards having the tongue forked (as members of the family Lacertilidae)

fis·sil·i·ty \fiˈsiləd·ē\ *n* **:** the quality of being fissile

¹**fis·sion** \ˈfishən *also* -izh-\ *n* -s [L *fission-, fissio,* fr. *fissus* (past part. of *findere* to split) + *-ion-, -io* -ion — more at BITE] **1 :** the process or an instance of cleaving, splitting, or breaking up into parts ⟨cites the ~ of many families during the civil strife —Boyd Keenan⟩ ⟨our diplomacy will have to be resourceful . . . to avert disastrous ~s in the free world during the next few weeks —E.K.Lindley⟩ **2 :** reproduction by spontaneous division of the body into two or more parts each of which grows into a complete organism, being the common mode of reproduction among the bacteria, fission algae, and protozoa — see BINARY FISSION, MULTIPLE FISSION **3 :** CLEAVAGE 5 **4 :** the splitting of an atomic nucleus (as by bombardment with neutrons) esp. into approximately equal parts resulting in the release of enormous quantities of energy when certain heavy elements (as uranium and plutonium) are split — called also *nuclear fission;* contrasted with *fusion;* distinguished from *spallation*

²**fission** \ˈ"\ *vb* **fissioned; fissioned; fissioning** \-sh(ə)niŋ, \-zh(-\ **fissions** *vt* **:** to cause to undergo fission ⟨an element ~*ed* by high energy particles⟩ ~ *vi* **:** to undergo fission ⟨the number of free atoms released when a U-235 atom ~*s* —*Scientific American*⟩

fis·sion·abil·i·ty \,fish(ə)nəˈbiləd·ē, -lətē, -i *also* ,fizh-\ *n* -ES **:** the property of being fissionable — used esp. of chemical elements and materials

¹**fis·sion·able** \ˈfish(ə)nəbəl *also* ˈfizh-\ *adj* [²*fission* + *-able*] **:** capable of undergoing fission ⟨~ nuclei⟩ ⟨~ material⟩

²**fissionable** \ˈ"\ *n* -s **:** fissionable material — usu. used in pl. ⟨large units capable of generating the volume required for production of ~s on a significant scale —*New Republic*⟩

fis·sion·al \-shənᵊl\ *adj* [¹*fission* + *-al*] **:** occurring in or by means of or involving division usu. of a cell ⟨~ reproduction⟩ ⟨~ irregularities⟩

fission alga *n* **:** BLUE-GREEN ALGA

fission bomb *n* **:** ATOM BOMB 1 — compare FUSION BOMB

fission fungus *n* **:** SCHIZOMYCETE, BACTERIUM

fission yeast *n* **:** a yeast that reproduces by division of each cell into two daughter cells of equal size (as members of the genus *Schizosaccharomyces*) — compare BUDDING YEAST

fis·sip·a·rous \(ˈ)fiˈsipərəs, fəˈs-\ *adj* [*fissi-* + *-parous*] **1 :** producing new biological units or individuals by fission **2 :** tending to break up into parts or to disintegrate **:** DIVISIVE, FACTIONAL, SEPARATIVE, DISINTEGRATIVE ⟨~ tenderness⟩ ⟨the problem of erecting a government on the shifting sands of the ~ center parties —*Newsweek*⟩ ⟨he knows how to reconcile ~ elements in his party —W.H.Stevenson⟩ — **fis·sip·a·rous·ly** *adv* — **fis·sip·a·rous·ness** *n* -ES

¹**fis·si·ped** \ˈfisə,ped\ *adj* [LL *fissiped-, fissipes,* fr. *fissi-* (fr. L *fissus,* past part. of *findere* to split) + *ped-, pes* foot — more at BITE, FOOT] **1 :** having the toes separated to the base **:** CLOVEN-FOOTED **2** [NL *Fissipeda*] **:** of or relating to the Fissipeda

²**fissiped** \ˈ"\ *n* -s **:** one of the Fissipeda

fis·sip·e·da \fəˈsipədə\ *n pl, cap* [NL, irreg. fr. LL *fissiped-, fissipes*] **:** a suborder of Carnivora that includes recent land carnivores (as cats, dogs, bears) and extinct related forms

fis·sip·e·dal \(ˈ)fiˈsipədᵊl, fəˈs-; ¦fisə¦pedᵊl, -¦pēd-\ *also* **fis·sip·e·date** \fəˈsipə,dāt, -,dət\ *adj* [LL *fissiped-, fissipes* + E *-al* or *-ate*] **:** FISSIPED

fis·si·pe·dia \,fisəˈpēdēə\ [NL, alter. of *Fissipeda*] *syn of* FISSIPEDA

fis·si·pe·di·al \¦==¦=dēəl\ *adj* [NL *Fissipedia* + E *-al*] **:** FISSIPED

fis·si·ros·tres \,fisəˈrä,strēz\ *n pl, cap* [NL, fr. *fissi-* + *-rostres* (fr. L *rostrum* beak) — more at ROSTRUM] *in former classifications* **:** a group of birds having the bill deeply cleft, including the swifts, goatsuckers, swallows, and others, and not representing natural relationships

fis·sive \ˈfisiv\ *adj* [L *fissus* (past part. of *findere* to split) + E *-ive* — more at BITE] **:** relating or tending to fission

¹**fis·sle** *or* **fis·tle** \ˈfisəl\ *vi* -ED/-ING/-S [prob. of imit. origin] **1** *chiefly Scot* **:** to make a rustling sound **2** *chiefly Scot* **a :** to bustle about **b :** FIDGET

²**fissle** *or* **fistle** \ˈ"\ *n* -s **1** *chiefly Scot* **:** a rustling sound **2** *chiefly Scot* **:** COMMOTION, FUSS

fis·su·ra \fəˈs(h)ürə\ *n, pl* **fissu·rae** \-,rē, -,rī\ [NL] **:** FISSURE 2

fis·sur·al \ˈfishərəl\ *adj* [*fissure* + *-al*] **:** of or relating to a fissure

fis·su·ra·tion \,fishəˈrāshən\ *n* -s [ISV *fissure* + *-ation*] **1 :** the act of fissuring **2 :** the state of being fissured

¹**fis·sure** \ˈfishə(r)\ *n* -s [ME, fr. MF, fr. L *fissura,* fr. *fissus* (past part. of *findere* to split) + *-ura* -ure — more at BITE] **1 a :** a narrow opening, chasm, or crack of some length and considerable depth usu. occurring from some breaking, rending, or parting **:** CLEAVAGE ⟨one of those abrupt ~*s* with which the earth in the Southwest is riddled —Willa Cather⟩ **b** (1) **:** a usu. profound disagreement or discord portending or making for total disruption or breakup **:** DIVISION ⟨the serious ~ in the Labor Party —Felix Morley⟩ (2) **:** a serious weakness or flaw ⟨the traders of the English colonies were eating their way into the French colonial system, exploring its ~*s* systematically —O.G.Creighton⟩ **2** [NL *fissura,* fr. L] **a :** one of the clefts separating the lobes of the liver and lodging peritoneal folds, ligaments, blood and lymph vessels, and other structures — called also *fossa* **b :** any of certain clefts between bones or parts of bones in the skull **c :** any of the deep clefts of the brain; *esp* **:** one of those collocated with elevations in the walls of the ventricles ⟨the dentate ~⟩ — compare SULCUS **d :** the cleft in the anterior or ventral part of the spinal cord; *also* **:** the posterior septum of the spinal cord **3 :** a slit in tissue usu. at the junction of skin and mucous membrane ⟨~ of the lip⟩ ⟨anal ~⟩ **syn** see CRACK

²**fissure** \ˈ"\ *vb* **fissured; fissured; fissuring** \-sh(ə)riŋ\ **fissures** *vt* **:** to break into fissures **:** CLEAVE ⟨sudden canyons deeply *fissured* the earth —Dan Wickenden⟩ ~ *vi* **:** CRACK, FRACTURE, DIVIDE ⟨the main castes *fissured* into scores, even hundreds, of subcastes —J.B.Noss⟩

fis·sure·less \-ləs\ *adj* **:** devoid of fissures ⟨a completely ~ large rock⟩

fis·su·rel·la \,fishəˈrelə\ *n, cap* [NL, dim. of L *fissura*] **:** a genus (the type of a cosmopolitan family Fissurellidae) of marine gastropods (suborder Rhipidoglossa) comprising the keyhole limpets and having a conical shell with an opening at the apex

fissure of ro·lan·do \-rōˈlan(,)dō, -län-\ *usu cap R* [after Luigi *Rolando* †1831 Ital. anatomist] **:** CENTRAL SULCUS

fissure of syl·vi·us \-ˈsilvēəs\ *usu cap S* [after Franciscus *Sylvius* (Franz de la Boë) †1672 Ger. anatomist] **:** LATERAL FISSURE

fissure vein *n* **:** a crack in the earth's crust filled with minerals deposited from aqueous solution including sometimes such adjacent rock as has been sufficiently mineralized to be mined as ore

fis·sur·iform \ˈfishərə,fȯrm, fiˈshür-\ *adj* [¹*fissure* + *-iform*] **:** resembling a fissure

fis·sury \ˈfishərē, -ri\ *adj* [¹*fissure* + *-y*] **:** abounding in fissures

¹**fist** \ˈfist\ *n* -s [ME, fr. OE *fȳst;* akin to OFris *fest* fist, OS & OHG *fūst,* OSlav *pęstĭ*] **1 :** a hand with fingers doubled into the palm **:** a clenched hand **2 a :** a hand when closed as if to grasp or grip **:** CLUTCH, GRASP ⟨once he gets his ~ on something he never lets go of it⟩ **b :** a hand whether closed or not ⟨let's make up; give me your ~⟩ **c :** HANDWRITING ⟨you wrote an exquisite ~ —J.E.Agate⟩ **d :** the manner of tapping out a message that is peculiar to a particular telegraph operator **3 a :** a piece of work performed in a specified manner or with a specified degree of success **:** ATTEMPT, EFFORT, JOB ⟨all make a fair ~ at criticizing what they call the capitalist system —A.J.Nock⟩ **b** *dial* **:** a poor job of work **:** MESS ⟨made a ~ of doing that painting⟩ **4 :** INDEX 9

²**fist** \ˈ"\ *vt* -ED/-ING/-S **1 :** to clench (one's hand) into a fist ⟨I'd ~*ed* my hands inside their mittens to keep the fingers warm —C.A.Lindbergh b. 1902⟩ **2 :** to grip with the fist **:** HANDLE ⟨he did his best at ~*ing* frozen canvas with the rest of us —Raymond McFarland⟩ ⟨the crack jehu ~*s* the ribbons above the capering leaders and snorting bays —*Saturday Rev.*⟩

³**fist** *var of* FEIST

fist cods *n pl but sing or pl in constr* [²*fist* + *cods* (testes)] **:** a slaughterhouse worker who removes the hide from the rear legs of lambs and calves and curries calf carcasses

fist·ed \ˈfistəd\ *adj* [¹*fist* + *-ed*] **1 :** having fists **2** *of the hand* **:** clenched into a fist ⟨turned and beat ~ hands upon the mantelpiece —*Chatelaine*⟩

fistfight \ˈ=,=\ *n* **:** a usu. spontaneous fight with bare fists ⟨anger provides that No. 1 difference between a ~ and a boxing bout —Jack Dempsey⟩

fist·ful \ˈfist,fu̇l\ *n* -s **1 :** HANDFUL ⟨a ~ of silver⟩ **2 :** a considerable number **:** COLLECTION ⟨a ~ of tired, outworn slogans —Bradford Smith⟩ ⟨last night a whole ~ of Chopin's greatest works were played —Virgil Thomson⟩

fist hatchet *also* **fist ax** *n* **:** HAND AX

fist·i·ana \,fistēˈanə, -ˈä-,-ˈā-\ *n* -s [¹*fist* + *-i-* + *-ana*] **:** the world of boxing ⟨one of ~'s most famous championship bouts⟩

fist·ic \ˈfistik, -tēk\ *adj* **:** relating to boxing or to fighting with the fists **:** PUGILISTIC ⟨she immediately became a ~ authority —Mickey Walker⟩

fist·i·cuff \ˈfistə,kəf, -tē,-\ *n* -s [alter. of earlier *fisty cuff,* fr. *fisty* + *cuff* (blow)] **1 :** a blow with the fist or hand **2 fisticuffs** *pl but sing or pl in constr* **:** a fight with the fists **:** BOXING ⟨intervillage or camp disputes were settled by ~*s* —R.P.Schaedel⟩

fist·i·cuff·er \-fə(r)\ *n* -s **:** BOXER

fistle *var of* FISSLE

fist·mele \ˈfist,mēl\ *n* -s [¹*fist* + *mele,* obs. var. of *meal* (measure)] **:** the breadth of a fist with thumb stuck out used esp. in archery to give the correct height of a string from a braced bow **:** about 7 inches

fistmele

fistnote \ˈ=,=\ *n* **:** a usu. important note (as in a book) preceded by a printing character in the shape of a fist with pointed index finger — symbol ☞

fis·tu·la \ˈfis(h)chələ\ *n, pl* **fistulas** \-ləz\ *or* **fistu·lae** -\,lē, -,lī\ [ME, fr. L] **1** *obs* **:** a reed instrument or pipe; *esp* **:** MUSETTE 1b **2 :** a congenital or acquired passage leading from an abscess or hollow organ to the body surface or from one hollow organ to another and permitting passage of fluids (as pus) or secretions ⟨a salivary ~⟩ ⟨prepared a ~ to obtain pure gastric juice from the dog⟩ — compare SINUS a **3 :** FISTULOUS WITHERS

fistula of the withers : FISTULOUS WITHERS

fis·tu·lar \-lə(r)\ *adj* [LL *fistularis,* fr. L *fistula* + *-aris* -ar] **:** FISTULOUS

fis·tu·la·ri·idae \,fis(h)chələˈrīə,dē\ *n pl, cap* [NL, fr. *Fistularia,* type genus (fr. L *fistula* + NL *-aria*) + *-idae*] **:** a family (type genus *Fistularia*) of hemibranchiate fishes of warm seas that have the head prolonged into a tube with the mouth terminal, that are otherwise structurally similar to the sticklebacks, and that comprise the cornetfishes

¹**fis·tu·lar·i·oid** \¦==¦la(a)rē,ȯid\ *adj* [NL *Fistularia* + E *-oid*] **:** related to or resembling the family Fistulariidae

²**fistularioid** \ˈ"\ *n* -s **:** a fistularioid fish

fis·tu·lat·ed \-,lād·əd\ *adj* [*fistula* + *-ate* + *-ed*] **:** having a fistula; *esp* **:** having an artificial fistula used for experiment (as on the digestive process)

fis·tu·li·na \,==ˈlīnə, -ˈlēnə\ *n, cap* [NL, fr. L *fistula* + NL *-ina*] **:** a genus of basidiomycetous fungi (family Polyporaceae) related to *Boletus* but having each of the pores separate although crowded

fis·tu·li·za·tion \-,ləˈzāshən, -,līˈz-\ *n* -s **:** the condition of being fistulized or having fistulas

fis·tu·lize \ˈ==,līz\ *vb* -ED/-ING/-S *see -ize in Explan Notes, vt* **:** to produce (an artificial channel) by surgical means (as for relieving pressure in glaucoma) ~ *vi* **:** to develop a fistula ⟨a *fistulizing* bone lesion⟩

fis·tu·lose \ˈfis(h)chə,lōs\ *adj* [L *fistulosus*] **:** FISTULOUS

fis·tu·lous \-ləs\ *adj* [ME, fr. L *fistulosus,* fr. *fistula* + *-osus* -ous] **1 :** having the form or nature of a fistula **:** relating to or having a fistula ⟨a ~ ulcer⟩ — compare FISTULOUS WITHERS **2 :** hollow like a pipe or reed

fistulous withers *n pl but usu sing in constr* **:** a deep-seated chronic inflammation of the withers of the horse usu. involving the cervical ligaments and the bursas of the vertebral spines and discharging seropurulent or bloody fluid through one or more openings which may be initiated by mechanical injury but of which the development depends on infection esp. with the bacterium (*Brucella abortus*) that causes bovine contagious abortion

fist wedge *n* **:** HAND AX

fisty \ˈfistē, -ti\ *adj* **:** FISTIC

¹**fit** \ˈfit, *usu* -id.+V\ *n* -s [ME, fr. OE *fitt;* akin to OS *fittea* division of a poem, text, OHG *fizza* skein, yarn, ON *fit* web (of an animal's foot), and perh. to OE *fōt* foot — more at FOOT] **1** *archaic* **:** a division of a poem or song **:** a canto or a similar division **2** *obs* **:** a strain of music

²**fit** \ˈ"\ *n* -s [ME, fr. OE *fitt* strife, conflict] **1** *obs* **:** a painful, dangerous, exciting, or mortal crisis or experience **2 a** *archaic* **:** a spell or bout of illness or of some specified disease **b :** a stroke of some disease (as epilepsy or apoplexy) that produces convulsions or unconsciousness **:** SEIZURE, PAROXYSM ⟨he was seized with a ~ which was repeated about every two hours until his death —D.D.Martin⟩ **c :** a sudden, severe, but transient attack of any physical disturbance ⟨~*s* of shivering that weaken knees and set teeth to chattering —Kenneth Roberts⟩ **3 :** a sudden often unaccountable burst or flurry (as of activity or emotion) **:** a brief period **:** SPELL, MOOD, IMPULSE ⟨a ~ of jealousy⟩ ⟨a ~ of idleness⟩ ⟨there is much praise or ridicule, as the ~ takes the onlookers —C.P.Conigrave⟩ ⟨something that grandpa threw together in a ~ of tinkering —*Car Life*⟩ ⟨he may have ~*s* of deep depression following ~*s* of anger —H.A.Overstreet⟩ ⟨went off into a quiet ~ of laughter —M.V.Reidy⟩ **4 :** an outburst of anger, chagrin, or intense excitement ⟨she simply had a ~ when she learned what had happened⟩ — **by fits** *or* **by fits and starts** *adv* **:** at intervals **:** impulsively and irregularly **:** FITFULLY, INTERMITTENTLY ⟨slow wandering footsteps that halted and came on *by fits* —Pearl Buck⟩ ⟨Japanese expansion proceeded not according to any coldly calculated master plan but rather *by fits and starts* —O.D.Tolischus⟩

³**fit** \ˈ"\ *adj* **fitter; fittest** [ME; akin to ME *fitten* to be suitable for] **1 a :** adapted to an end, object, or design **:** suitable by nature or by art **:** SUITED, QUALIFIED, APPROPRIATE ⟨found him a ~ officer and gentleman —*Time*⟩ ⟨soft water ~ for manufacturing is restricted to the central part of the district⟩; *specif* **:** so adapted to the environment as to be capable of surviving — often used in the phrase *the survival of the fittest* **b :** becoming from the viewpoint of propriety, convenience, or morality **:** SEEMLY, PROPER, MEET, PRUDENT, EXPEDIENT ⟨pictures . . . not ~ for young people to see —D.M.Davin⟩ ⟨it is not ~ for us to inquire into sacred things⟩ ⟨he gave credit where he thought ~ —Adrian Bell⟩ ⟨one can wish that the editors had seen ~ to include a few more illustrations —Stuart Preston⟩ **2 a** *obs* **:** made to fit **:** of the right dimensions **:** CLOSE-FITTING **b :** made or put in a suitable condition **:** READY, PREPARED ⟨corn . . . must be passed through a grain drier before it is ~ to store —F.D.Smith & Barbara Wilcox⟩ ⟨the work of getting the ship ~ for sea —Nevil Shute⟩ **c :** so affected as to be ready to do or suffer something **:** DISPOSED ⟨in ~ to cry I was —Bryan MacMahon⟩ ⟨shivering and shaking ~ to die with cold —*Time*⟩ **3 :** sound physically and mentally **:** qualified from the viewpoint of health **:** HEALTHY ⟨he keeps ~ by playing tennis and squash —*Current Biog.*⟩ ⟨you aren't ~ to get breakfast —Ellen Glasgow⟩ ⟨if you are young, ~, and keen you can be . . . an officer in the Royal Air Force —*Punch*⟩ ⟨the best prescription for a ~ old age is a bad illness in middle life —John Buchan⟩

syn SUITABLE, MEET, PROPER, APPROPRIATE, FITTING, APT, HAPPY, FELICITOUS: FIT suggests being adapted or adaptable to an end in view, situation, or occasion, sometimes an especial readiness for use ⟨a wooden image, movable and *fit* to be carried in procession —George Santayana⟩ ⟨the magnificent hall which seemed only a *fit* setting for her beauty —Nathaniel Hawthorne⟩ ⟨a ship *fit* for service⟩ SUITABLE applies to whatever answers demands or requirements smoothly, without difficulty, doubt, or objection ⟨the plain walls of the interior provide a *suitable* foil for the decorative color and woodwork —*Amer. Guide Series: Minn.*⟩ ⟨large tracts of land *suitable* for vineyards —Robert Hichens⟩ ⟨because of its proscribed theme, the play was not considered *suitable* movie material —*Current Biog.*⟩ ⟨after a *suitable* interval, not to seem importunate —Mary Austin⟩ MEET describes what is nicely adapted or rightly or justly applicable; it may be somewhat stronger and more complimentary than SUITABLE ⟨now that death has shut the door behind Kipling, leaving his completed work here with us, ready for the passionless estimate of posterity, it is *meet* for critics to weigh that work in their delicate scale —Katharine F. Gerould⟩ ⟨Sabbath was made a solemn day, *meet* only for preaching, praying, and Bible reading —C.A. & Mary Beard⟩ ⟨is it *meet* that an utter stranger should thus express himself? —W.S.Gilbert⟩ PROPER may suggest a fitness by nature or by right reason, good judgment, or social sanction ⟨water, the *proper* element for fish⟩ ⟨a few Yankees of the swindling kind who found their *proper* sphere in the peddling business —Van Wyck Brooks⟩ ⟨when a child has mastered a difficulty after persistent efforts, praise is a *proper* reward —Bertrand Russell⟩ ⟨the education *proper* to a hero —*Encyc. Americana*⟩ APPROPRIATE may suggest distinctive, peculiar, or distinguishing fitness ⟨the magician does not doubt that . . . the performance of the proper ceremony, accompanied by the *appropriate* spell, will inevitably be attended by the desired results —J.G. Frazer⟩ ⟨we have agreed that our writing should be *appropriate:* that it should fit the occasion —A.T.Quiller-Couch⟩ FITTING may suggest an especial harmony or congruousness ⟨the *fitting* expression for the deeds they do —G.W.Russell⟩ ⟨a *fitting* occasion to reassess the validity of the mechanical conception of the universe of which he was unwittingly the prime author —*Times Lit. Supp.*⟩ APT connotes a fitness marked by nicety and discrimination ⟨had shown that essential objectives could be gained by an *apt* combination of blackmail and negotiation —*Times Lit. Supp.*⟩ ⟨the *apt* and telling turns of expression, the phrases of homely vigor or happy pregnancy which have become a part of our linguistic stock in trade —J.L.Lowes⟩ ⟨what time so *apt* for inculcating obedience and other Christian virtues as this solemn hour —H.O.Taylor⟩ HAPPY applies to whatever is quite successfully, effectively, or pleasingly fit ⟨our ideal should be to make our battle a series of single combats, our ranks a *happy* alliance of agile commanders-in-chief —T.E. Lawrence⟩ ⟨of all writers he perhaps best combines in his style a felicitous elegance with a *happy* vernacular, the grace of philosophers and wits and the wit of the people —Carl Van Doren⟩ FELICITOUS suggests the opportunely or strikingly happy ⟨had a way of illuminating an array of factual data with *felicitous* theoretical insights —D.G.Mandelbaum⟩ ⟨some of the most *felicitous* turns of thought and phrase in poetry are the result of a flash of inspiration —J.L.Lowes⟩ — **fit to be tied :** angry or irritated to an extreme **:** ready to explode with wrath ⟨the hardheaded businessman looks *fit to be tied* —*New Republic*⟩ ⟨*fit to be tied* when she came home late⟩ — **fit to kill :** to an extreme ⟨dressed up *fit to kill*⟩ **:** at a great rate ⟨they were so happy that they blubbered *fit to kill* —S.J.Perelman⟩

⁴**fit** \ˈ"\ *adv* [ME, fr. *fit,* adj.] *archaic* **:** FITLY

⁵**fit** \ˈ"\ *vb* **fitted** *or* **fit; fitted** *or* **fit; fitting; fits** [ME *fitten,* fr. or akin to MD *vitten* to be suitable; akin to ON *fitja* to knit, OHG *fizzōn* to surround, *fizza* skein, yarn — more at ¹FIT] *vt* **1 a** (1) **:** to be suitable for or to **:** answer the requirements of **:** harmonize with **:** BEFIT, SUIT ⟨for all that it is a good constitution — a constitution that ~*s* us —Elmer Davis⟩ ⟨these fashions ~ the life of the sport car, the penthouse, modern furniture —*Women's Wear Daily*⟩ ⟨find . . . a gun that *fitted* you perfectly —Bob Nichols⟩ ⟨in appearance he *fitted* his job to perfection —S.H.Adams⟩ ⟨no program of work will ~ every community —Beatrice S. Rossell⟩ ⟨the name *fit* him to perfection —*Deerfield* (*Wis.*) *Republican*⟩ (2) *archaic* **:** to be seemly or proper for **:** become from the viewpoint of propriety, convenience, or morality — often used with impersonal *it* as subject ⟨it ~*s* us then to be as provident as fear may teach us —Shak.⟩ **b** (1) **:** to be correctly adjusted to or shaped for **:** conform to the contours of ⟨the coat ~*s* him beautifully⟩ ⟨the key ~*s* the lock⟩ ⟨I had grown tall enough to ~ my coffin —Sacheverell Sitwell⟩ (2) **:** to insert, apply, or adjust until snugly or correctly in place **:** cause to conform to the outlines or contours of a receptacle ⟨students are taught to ~ braces of different types⟩ ⟨~ a stopper into a bottle⟩ (3) **:** to make a place or room for (as by adjusting, maneuvering) **:** ACCOMMODATE ⟨he was *fitting* many concert appearances into a crowded schedule —*Current Biog.*⟩ ⟨always came in as though he . . . was *fitting* you in at great inconvenience —Fred Majdalany⟩ ⟨~ three or four men into a single

turret —Tom Wintringham⟩ ⟨most of his library had been *fitted* in here —Lucien Price⟩ **c :** to be in agreement with or accord with ⟨this theory ~*s* all the known facts⟩ ⟨does not quite ~ the assumption that the sole cause of the business slowdown is an attempt to cut inventories —George Shea⟩ **2 a :** to make fit or suitable **:** adapt to the purpose intended **:** put into a condition of readiness **:** PREPARE, QUALIFY ⟨a comfortable stall was *fitted* for the horse —*Irish Digest*⟩ ⟨each ant is *fitted* to his place in the community by a combination of structural specialization and instincts —Ralph Linton⟩ ⟨vigorous training ~*s* men for the ordeals of battle⟩ ⟨his temperament *fitted* him to understand an age of courageous exploits —Van Wyck Brooks⟩ **b :** to prepare for college ⟨he was *fitted* for college by his own father⟩ **c :** to till (land) in preparation for planting ⟨came up with the team and drag from the field . . . where he had been *fitting* the bean ground —Gordon Webber⟩ **d** (1) **:** to bring to a required form and size **:** shape rightly **:** adapt to a model **:** ADJUST ⟨*fitted* the garment to the client's specifications⟩ (2) **:** to cause to conform to or suit something else ⟨you must ~ the words to the music⟩ ⟨tried to ~ his spending to his income⟩ ⟨~ your conduct to your circumstances⟩ (3) **:** to determine the required specifications of something for **:** MEASURE ⟨came to the house and *fitted* you for handmade French lingerie —Margaret A. Barnes⟩ ⟨*fitted* me for glasses⟩ **:** determine the fit of a garment on ⟨*fitted* her with the dress and found that it needed alterations⟩ (4) **:** to supply with something that is shaped, adjusted, or designed for the use required **:** PROVIDE, EQUIP ⟨*fitted* the ship with new engines⟩ ⟨its many and diversified laboratories are *fitted* with the latest in equipment —*Investor's Reader*⟩ (5) **:** to finish (animals) for the show ring; *also* **:** to dress and prepare (animals) for showing (6) **:** to subject (newly formed soap) before settling to a process of boiling with steam or water and additional alkali as needed until the desired texture is attained (7) **:** to adjust (a smooth curve of specified type) to a given set of points in such a way as to minimize the sum of the squares of the distances measured parallel to the axis of ordinates from the given points to the curve (8) **:** to design (a character in a font) so that the apparent distance to any close-set adjacent character will be as nearly uniform as the shape of the individual characters allows (9) *of a hand or suit in bridge* **:** to contain cards that increase the trick-winning capacity of (a partner's hand) **~** *vi* **1** *archaic* **:** to be seemly, proper, or suitable **2 a :** to become adjusted to a particular shape or size **:** conform in contour when applied or assumed ⟨his coat ~*s* beautifully⟩ **b :** to be in harmony or accord **:** make the proper adjustment **:** meet the needs **:** become suited **:** COINCIDE, AGREE, CONFORM, BELONG, ADJUST ⟨a conservative in a semiliberal setting . . . doesn't seem to ~ —*Kiplinger Washington Letter*⟩ ⟨I'm glad that your new secretary seems likely to ~ —H.J.Laski⟩ ⟨none of the familiar labels . . . seems to ~ quite so well —J.W.Krutch⟩ — often used with *in, into,* or *with* ⟨where does the wife ~ into all this —W.H.Whyte⟩ ⟨his somber pessimism *fitted* in with her own mood⟩ ⟨many of them have been able to ~ into the white man's life without giving up the ancient ways —H.A.Overstreet⟩ ⟨we should have to determine where you would ~ in —C.B.Kelland⟩ ⟨employers were likely to select . . . those . . . who would ~ easily and docilely with the rest of the workers —Oscar Handlin⟩ **c** *of the hands of two partners* **:** to constitute a fit (sense 4) **3 :** to prepare for college esp. by attending a college-preparatory school **syn** see PREPARE

⁶fit \"\ *n* -s **1 a :** the quality or state of being fitted or adapted **:** the manner in which or the degree to which something fits or conforms to some standard **:** AGREEMENT, ACCORD, ADJUSTMENT ⟨yearning for the good old days and the job and the comfortable ~ of old ways —Dixon Wecter⟩ ⟨a qualitative verbal assessment of the degree of ~ between the interpretations —*Amer. Anthropologist*⟩ ⟨I believe the average American's notions about the average Briton are at least as bad a ~ —Richard Joseph⟩ **b :** the manner in which clothing fits a wearer ⟨advising me about the ~ of my corsets —Mary Austin⟩ ⟨the ~ of the dress is snug⟩ ⟨American man-produced fashions are the envy of all Europe because of their crisp styling and ~ —*Wall Street Jour.*⟩ **c :** the degree of closeness with which surfaces are brought together in an assembly of parts (as a shaft in a hole or a nut on a screw) **d :** the conformity of a set of statistical observations to a corresponding set of values or of a curve that represents observations to a corresponding curve that serves as a standard **2 :** a piece of clothing that fits ⟨the gown was an excellent ~⟩ **3 :** the texture attained in fitting soap — called also *finish* ⟨a close (soft) ~ is used on large kettles —G.W.Busby⟩ **4 :** such distribution of cards in the two hands of a bridge partnership that each can help the other to win tricks in every or nearly every suit

⁷fit \"\ *Scot var of* FOOT

⁸fit \"\ *dial past of* FIGHT

FIT *abbr* **1** free in truck **2** free of income tax

¹fitch \ˈfich\ *n* -ES [ME *ficche, fecche, vecche* — more at VETCH] **1** *dial* **:** VETCH **2 fitches** *pl* **:** SPELT ⟨lentiles, and millet, and ~*es* —Ezek 4:9 (AV)⟩ **3 fitches** *pl* **:** a forage herb (as tares) ⟨the ~*es* are beaten out with a staff —Isa 28:27 (AV)⟩

²fitch \"\ *or* **fitch·ew** \ˈfi(ˌ)chü\ *n, pl* **fitches** *or* **fitchews** [ME *fiche, ficheux, fitchewes,* fr. MF or MD; MF *fichau,* fr. MD *vitsau, fitsau, visse*] **1 a :** POLECAT 1a **b :** the fur or pelt of the fitch **2** *also* **fitch brush :** a small brush made of the hair of a fitch, skunk, or hog

³fitch \"\ *vi* -ED/-ING/-ES [ME *fichen,* prob. alter. of *fiken* — more at FIKE] *dial Brit* **:** FIDGET

⁴fitch \"\ *also* **fetch** \ˈfech\ *n* -ES [origin unknown] **:** a plait in which two canes or osiers are intertwined so as to bind the stakes and by-stakes in successive or alternate loops — see BASKET illustration

fitched \ˈficht\ *adj* [MF *fiché* + E *-ed*] **:** FITCHÉE

fitch·ée *or* **fitchy** *also* **fitché** \ˈfichē, (ˈ)fiˌchā\ *adj* [MF *fiché,* past part. of *ficher* to drive in, fasten — more at FICHU] *of a cross* **:** having the lower extremity pointed instead of ending in the form characteristic of the kind of cross in question ⟨a cross botonée ~⟩ ⟨a crosslet ~⟩ — **fitchée at the foot :** having a point descending from the lower extremity, the shape of which is not modified — used of a cross the outer aspects of whose arms are flat ⟨a cross formée ~⟩

fitch·et \ˈfichət\ *or* **fitchet weasel** *n* -S [²*fitch* + *-et*] **:** POLECAT 1a

fitching *n* -S [⁴*fitch* + *-ing*] **1 :** ⁴FITCH **2 :** the act of plaiting a fitch

fite \ˈfīt\ *Scot var of* WHITE

fit·ful \ˈfitfəl\ *adj* [²*fit* + *-ful*] **1** *obs* **:** characterized by fits or paroxysms ⟨life's ~ fever —Shak.⟩ **2 :** having a spasmodic, irregular, or intermittent character **:** changeable or uncertain in mood **:** occurring in fits or spurts **:** coming and going **:** VARIABLE, CAPRICIOUS, UNSTABLE, IMPULSIVE ⟨his education must have been ~, to say the most of it —Osbert Sitwell⟩ ⟨there was a ~ cannonade far away in the southwest —H.G. Wells⟩ ⟨one of the most constant complaints is of insomnia or . . . ~ sleep —H.G.Armstrong⟩ ⟨hitherto I've been gloomy, moody, ~ —W.S.Gilbert⟩ — **fit·ful·ly** \-fəlē, -li\ *adv* — **fit·ful·ness** *n* -ES

fit·i·fied \ˈfid·əˌfīd\ *adj* [²*fit* + *-ify* + *-ed*] **1** *Midland* **:** tending to have or be afflicted with fits; *specif* **:** EPILEPTIC **2** *Midland* **:** erratic and eccentric in behavior **:** TEMPERAMENTAL

fit·ly *adv* [³*fit* adj + *-ly*] **:** in a fit manner or at a fit time **:** SUITABLY, PROPERLY, DECOROUSLY ⟨his last book ~ presents his seasoned theological convictions⟩ ⟨the author may ~ regard it as the crown of an arduous . . . life's work —*Times Lit. Supp.*⟩

fit·ment \ˈfitmənt\ *n* -S [⁵*fit* + *-ment*] **1 a :** EQUIPMENT, FURNISHING, FURNITURE — used esp. of built-in furniture **b fitments** *pl* **:** FITTINGS **2 :** a dispensing or pouring device used with or as part of the closure of a bottle

fit·ness *n* -ES [³*fit* + *-ness*] **1 :** the quality or state of being fit or fitted ⟨the physical ~ . . . of large numbers of people had been impaired by poverty —F.A.Ogg & P.O.Ray⟩ **2 :** the condition of being qualified or suitable **:** ELIGIBILITY, SOUNDNESS, CAPACITY ⟨subjected to endurance tests to prove their ~ . . . for the status of manhood —Francis Birtles⟩ ⟨the law prescribed that the ordaining bishop should assure himself . . . of the candidate's ~ in education and morals —G.G. Coulton⟩ ⟨officials . . . should be chosen for their ~ to understand intellectual questions —Zechariah Chafee⟩ **3 :** essential rightness or reasonableness **:** PROPRIETY, CORRECTNESS, APPROPRIATENESS ⟨one observes a nice historical ~ in the fact —H.O.Taylor⟩ ⟨no one with a sense of ~ ever docked the tail of a Shetland pony —Ben Riker⟩ — often used in the phrase *fitness of things* ⟨the sheep . . . lay quiet enough, having an inborn sense of the ~ of things —John Galsworthy⟩ ⟨it does appear to be . . . inherent in the eternal ~ of things —T.L.Peacock⟩

fit out *vt* **:** to supply with necessaries or means **:** FURNISH, EQUIP, OUTFIT, PREPARE ⟨friends *fitted* him *out* with a new suit and new shoes⟩ ⟨*fit out* a privateer⟩ **~** *vi* **:** OUTFIT ⟨the ship, a former merchantman, was *fitting out* as a privateer⟩

fit plant *n* [²*fit*] **:** INDIAN PIPE

fitroot \ˈ=,=\ *also* **fits·root** \ˈfits,=\ *n* [²*fit* + *root*] **:** INDIAN PIPE

fits *pl of* FIT, *pres 3d sing of* FIT

fitted *adj* [fr. past part. of ⁵*fit*] **1 a :** shaped to conform to the lines of something else ⟨~ sheets⟩ ⟨~ closets⟩; *specif* **:** shaped to conform to the lines of the body ⟨a ~ coat⟩ ⟨a ~ sleeve⟩ **b :** equipped with accessories ⟨a genuine leather ~ case⟩ **2 :** ADAPTED, QUALIFIED ⟨for the accomplishments of the task . . . his energy and enthusiasm . . . make him peculiarly ~ —Arthur Fisher⟩

fit·ted·ness *n* -ES **:** FITNESS ⟨worried about his own ~ to carry on the work⟩

fit·ten \ˈfitᵊn\ *adj* [alter. of ¹*fitting*] *dial* **:** qualified or suited for **:** FIT ⟨a ~ place to live⟩

¹fitter *comparative of* FIT

²fit·ter \ˈfid·ə(r), -itə-\ *n* -S **:** one that fits or makes to fit: as **a :** a person who tries on, adjusts, or alters articles of clothing for a customer **b :** a worker who uses hand and machine tools to fit parts together and to assemble machinery and other equipment **c :** SHIPFITTER **d :** an upfitter of furniture or caskets **e :** one that sharpens and repairs saws **f :** one that selects trees to be felled for tanbark and after they have been felled cuts rings through the bark to prepare them for the peelers **g :** one that makes plaster casts of stumps, prepares them for use in making artificial limbs, and fits the assembled limbs to the wearers **h :** a finish carpenter who installs prefabricated window frames and sash

fit·ters \ˈfitə(r)z\ *n pl* [ME *fiteres;* akin to OHG *vetze* rag, ON *fat* vessel, dress — more at VAT] *now dial Eng* **:** RAGS, TATTERS, FRAGMENTS

fittest *superlative of* FIT

fittig reaction *or* **fittig synthesis** *n, usu cap F* [after Rudolf *Fittig* †1910 Ger. chemist] **:** the Wurtz-Fittig reaction applied to the synthesis of aromatic hydrocarbons

¹fitting *adj* [ME, fr. pres. part. of *fitten* to fit — more at FIT] **:** APPROPRIATE, SUITABLE, PROPER ⟨the ~ expression for the deeds they do —G.W.Russell⟩ ⟨a ~ rebuke for his rudeness⟩ **syn** see FIT

²fitting *n* -S [fr. gerund of ⁵*fit*] **1 a :** something used in fitting up **:** ACCESSORY, ADJUNCT, ATTACHMENT ⟨living quarters with splendid ~*s* — marble pavements, ivory doors, crystal chandeliers —Christopher Rand⟩ ⟨an unusual ~ in these days is a hand throttle, fitted to the instrument panel —*Country Life*⟩ ⟨the ~*s* of the violin have been considerably altered since the greatest period of violin making —Robert Donington⟩ **b :** a small often standardized part (as a coupling, valve, gauge) entering into the construction of a boiler, steam, water, or gas supply installation or other apparatus — usu. used in pl.; see GAS FITTING, PIPE FITTING **2 :** a trying-on of tailor-made clothes (as a suit or dress) in the process of completion **3** *Brit* **:** SIZE ⟨nylons are also being made in three ~*s* — for the slim, stocky, and oversize leg —*Irish Digest*⟩ ⟨~*s* for every foot —*Melbourne (Australia) Weekly Times*⟩

fit·ting·ly *adv* **:** in a fitting manner

fit·ting·ness *n* -ES **:** the quality or state of being fit

fit·tit \ˈfitət\ *Scot var of* FOOTED

fit·to·nia \fəˈtōnēə\ *n, cap* [NL, fr. Elizabeth and Sarah Margaret *Fitton,* 19th cent. Irish writers on botany + NL *-ia*] **:** a small genus of Peruvian trailing herbs (family Acanthaceae) that are cultivated as foliage plants and that have leaves with showy red or white venation and inconspicuous flowers in bracted terminal spikes

fit·ty \ˈfiti\ *adj* [³*fit* + *-y*] **1** *dial chiefly Eng* **:** suitable and becoming **:** APPROPRIATE **2** *dial chiefly Eng* **a :** being in good order **:** TRIM **b :** HANDSOME, STRIKING

fit up *vt* **:** to furnish with things suitable **:** make proper for use **:** EQUIP ⟨he *fitted up* one courtyard of the homestead and taught science to all . . . whom he could interest —Nora Waln⟩

¹fit-up \ˈ=,=\ *n* -S [*fit up*] **1** *Brit* **a :** a place (as an inn or hall) fitted up as a temporary theater or stage ⟨meager productions in village *fit-ups* —*Country Life*⟩; *also* **:** the makeshift or improvised scenery and properties used or carried by a traveling theatrical company **b** *or* **fit-up company :** a traveling theatrical group that carries its own scenery and properties ⟨I started my stage training . . . in a *fit-up company* —*Listener*⟩ **2 :** ⁶FIT 1c

²fit-up \"\ *adj* **:** of or relating to a fit-up ⟨having played much in inns and similar *fit-up* places —Arnold Bennett⟩

fit-up man *n* [*fit up*] **:** one who does the initial fitting together of parts of tanks, boilers, and other vessels in preparation for final assembly by the boilermaker

fitweed \ˈ=,=\ *n* [²*fit* + *weed*] **:** a tropical American herbaceous feverweed (*Eryngium foetidum*) with fetid prickly leaves

fitz·ger·ald contraction \(ˈ)fitsˈjerəld-\ *n, usu cap F&G* [after George F. *FitzGerald* †1901 Irish physicist] **:** a longitudinal contraction that according to relativity theory every moving body is believed to undergo in the dimension parallel to the direction of motion

fitz·hugh \ˈfits,(h)yü *sometimes* =ˈ=\ *n -s usu cap* [perh. alter. of *Foochow* (Minhow), city in southeastern China] **:** a pattern (as of pomegranates or butterflies) appearing on Chinese export porcelain of the 18th and earlier 19th centuries

fitz·roya \fitsˈrȯi(y)ə ˈ=,==\ *n, cap* [NL, after Robert *Fitzroy* †1865 Eng. naval commander & meteorologist] **:** a genus of commercially important evergreen timber trees (family Pinaceae) of Chile and Tasmania with irregular branching, ternate decurrent scalelike leaves, and small globose cones

¹five \ˈfīv\ *adj* [ME, adj. & pron., fr. OE *fīf;* akin to OHG *funf, finf* five, ON *fimm,* Goth *fimf,* L *quinque,* Gk *pente,* Skt *pañca*] **:** being one more than four in number ⟨~ years⟩ — see NUMBER table

²five \"\ *pron, pl in constr* [ME] **:** five countable persons or things not specified but under consideration and being enumerated ⟨~ are here⟩ ⟨~ were found⟩

³five \"\ *n* -S [ME, fr. *five,* pron. & adj.] **1 :** one more than four **2 a :** five units or objects ⟨a total of ~⟩ **b :** a group or set of five ⟨arranged by ~*s*⟩ **3 a :** the numerable quantity symbolized by the arabic numeral 5 **b :** the figure 5 **c :** the letter V **4 :** five o'clock — compare BELL table, TIME illustration **5 a :** a playing card marked to show that it is fifth in a suit **b :** a domino with five spots on one of its halves **c :** a die with five spots on the uppermost side **d :** an article of clothing of the fifth size ⟨wears a ~⟩ **6 a :** a five-pound note **b :** a five-dollar bill **7 :** a playing team of five members; *esp* **:** a basketball team **8 :** FIFTEEN 6

five-and-dime \ˌ=ˈ=\ *n* **:** FIVE-AND-TEN

five-and-ten \ˌ=ˈ=\ *n* **1 :** a store selling articles priced at 5 or 10 cents **2 :** a variety store selling inexpensive articles of merchandise

five back *n* **:** a bowling game in which four pins are spotted on the back line and one at the end of the line next in front and in which three balls not exceeding six inches in diameter are rolled in each inning — called also *fivepins*

five-centered arch \ˈ=ˌ==-\ *n* **:** an arch whose intrados curve is described from five centers

five-corners \ˈ=ˈ==\ *n pl but usu sing in constr* **:** the pentagonal fruit of any Australian shrub of the genus *Styphelia* (esp. *S. triflora*)

five-corns \ˈ=ˈ=\ *n pl* **:** the fruits of the cupseed

five-day week *n* **:** a week having five working days

five-eighth *or* **five-eighths** \(ˈ)=ˈ=\ *n* **:** a rugby player whose position is between the halfbacks and the three-quarter backs; *also* **:** the position of this player

five-em space *n* [contr. of *five-to-em space*] **:** a space in printing that is ⅕ of an em in thickness

five-figure \ˈ=ˈ==\ *adj* **:** containing five numerical figures **:** rated at an annual salary of $10,000 or more

five-finger \ˈ=ˌ==\ *n* **1 a :** CINQUEFOIL 1 **b :** OXLIP 2 **c :** BIRD'S-FOOT TREFOIL 1 **d :** VIRGINIA CREEPER **2 :** a 5-rayed starfish

five-fingered creeper \ˈ=ˌ==-\ *or* **five-fingered ivy** *n* **:** VIRGINIA CREEPER

five-fingered jack *n, usu cap J* **:** a common cinquefoil (*Potentilla canadensis*) of eastern No. America

five-fingered root *n* **:** the root of a water dropwort (*Oenanthe crocata*)

five-fingers \ˈ=ˌ==\ *n pl but sing in constr* **1 :** FIVE-FINGER 1 **2 :** GINSENG 2

five-flowered gentian \ˈ=ˌ=-\ *n* **:** an annual gentian (*Gentiana quinquefolia*) of eastern No. America

¹five·fold \ˈfīvˈfōld\ *adj* [ME *fiffold,* fr. OE *fīffeald,* fr. *fīf* five + *-feald* -fold] **1 :** having five parts or aspects **2 :** being five times as large, as great, or as many as some understood size, degree, or amount ⟨a ~ increase⟩

²fivefold \"\ *adv* **:** to five times as much or as many **:** by five times ⟨increased ~⟩

five hundred *n* **1 a :** the numerable quantity symbolized by the arabic numerals 500 — see NUMBER table **b :** the letter D **2 a :** a card game developed from euchre and played with a pack of cards varying from 24 to 62 cards and often including a joker in which 2 to 6 players bid for the right to name the trump suit or no trump and the first to score 500 points wins **b :** any of various games in which the objective is 500 points

five hundred rum *or* **five hundred rummy** *n* **:** a variety of rummy for from 2 to 4 players in which the object is to lay down 500 or more points in melds — called also *pinochle rummy*

five-leaf \ˈ=ˌ=\ *n* [ME *fivelef, fiflef,* fr. OE *fīflēaf,* fr. *fīf* + *lēaf* leaf — more at FIVE, LEAF] **:** CINQUEFOIL

five-leaved chaste tree \ˈ=ˌ=-\ *n* **:** an Asiatic shrub or small tree (*Vitex negundo*) with showy lilac panicled flowers

five-leaved ivy *n* **:** VIRGINIA CREEPER

five-leaved pine *n* **1 :** SWISS PINE **2 :** any of several pines with five needles; *esp* **:** WHITE PINE 1a

five-lined lizard \ˈ=ˌ=-\ *n* **:** BLUE-TAILED SKINK

five·ling \ˈfīvliŋ\ *n* -S **:** a twin crystal consisting of five individuals

five·pence *Brit* ˈfīvpən(t)s *or* ˈfī(f)pə- *or* ˈfipə-, *US* " *or* -īv-ˌpen-\ *n, pl* **fivepence** *or* **fivepences 1 :** the sum of five usu. British pennies **2 a :** five U.S. cents **b :** a five-cent piece

five·pen·ny morris \-nē-,-ni-, *or* ˈfipnē- *or* ˈfipni-\ *n* **:** morris played with five counters

five-per·cent·er \ˌfīvpə(r)ˈsentə(r)\ *n* -S **:** one that for a fee of five percent helps businessmen obtain government contracts or do other business with the government

fivepins \ˈ=ˌ=\ *n pl* **:** FIVE BACK

fiv·er \ˈfīvə(r)\ *n* -S **1** *slang* **:** a five-dollar bill **2** *slang* **:** a five-pound note

fives \ˈfīvz\ *n pl but sing in constr* [fr. pl. of ³*five*] **:** a game similar to handball for two or four players — see ETON GAME, RUGBY GAME

fivescore \ˈ=ˈ=\ *adj* **:** being 100 in number

five-shooter \ˈ=ˌ==\ *n* **:** a revolver with a five-round capacity

five-sisters \ˈ=ˈ==\ *n pl but sing in constr* **:** WHORLED LOOSESTRIFE

five·some \ˈfīvsəm\ *n* -S [²*five* + *-some*] **1 :** a group of five persons playing together **2 :** any group of five persons or things

five-spot \ˈ=ˌ=\ *n* **1 :** a California annual herb (*Nemophila maculata*) with showy flowers having a conspicuous purple blotch at the end of each corolla lobe **2 :** an oil well made to produce copiously by pumping water under pressure into four other holes surrounding it **3 a :** ³FIVE 5a **b** *slang* **:** a five-dollar bill

five-star \ˈ=ˈ=\ *adj* **1 :** being of five-star rank ⟨was made a *five-star* general⟩ **2** [so called fr. the use of multiple asterisks in the literary or dramatic reviews of some publications to symbolize degrees of merit] **:** being of the first class or quality ⟨there are not enough *five-star* works of art to go around —J.T.Soby⟩ ⟨a *five-star* book for those interested in the creation of our republic —J.R.Chamberlain⟩

five-star rank *n* [so called fr. the insignia on the uniform] **:** the rank of general of the army, general of the air force, or fleet admiral

fivestones \ˈ=ˌ=\ *n pl but sing in constr, Brit* **:** jacks played with five stones

five-ten limits \ˈ=ˈ=-\ *n pl* **:** limitations fixing the maximum liability of an insurer at $5000 for the bodily injury or death of any one person and subject to the same limit per person at $10,000 for any one accident irrespective of how many persons are killed or injured

five-toed jerboa \ˈ=ˌ=-\ *n* **:** any of several large active long-eared jerboas (genus *Allactaga*) of eastern Europe and Asia (as *A. sibirica*)

five-year cure \ˈ=ˌ=-\ *n* **:** survival without clinically evident recurrence for five years after treatment for certain diseases (as cancer)

five-year plan \ˈ=ˈ=-\ *n, often cap F&Y&P* [trans. of Russ *pyatiletka*] **1 :** one of a continuing series of Soviet governmental programs designed to achieve usu. specified goals in the planned, coordinated, and cumulative development of the Soviet economy and other sectors of Soviet life (as education and science) over a period of five years **2 :** a national governmental program of planned, coordinated, and cumulative economic and social development over a period of five years

FIW *abbr* free in wagon

¹fix \ˈfiks\ *vb* -ED/-ING/-ES [ME *fixen,* fr. L *fixus,* past part. of *figere* to fasten, pierce — more at DIKE] *vt* **1 a** (1) **:** to make (a material object) firm, stable, or stationary **:** make fast ⟨~ a post in the ground⟩ ⟨the internal passport system introduced . . . to ~ the population —Bernard Pares⟩ (2) **:** to implant firmly (as an idea or institution) **:** make permanent ⟨intent on ~*ing* a way of life outmoded in the home country —D.M. Friedenberg⟩ ⟨harsh words, threats . . . only ~ the habit deeper —H.R.Litchfield & L.H.Dembo⟩ (3) **:** to give a final or permanent form to **:** to make definite and settled **:** CRYSTALLIZE ⟨~*ed* the cultural pattern that dominates the contemporary scene —*Amer. Guide Series: Minn.*⟩ ⟨Greene and his fellows evolved the style of what was to become Shakespearean drama, and . . . Marlowe ~*ed* it —W.B.Adams⟩ (4) **:** to give definite, visible, or fixed form to (something that is intangible, fleeting, or elusive) **:** CAPTURE, EVOKE ⟨that other aspect of truth which the scientist tries to catch and ~ —J.L.Lowes⟩ ⟨~*ed* their fears . . . in ebony images —F.J.Mather⟩ ⟨a voyage of speculation that aimed rather to survey the world than to ~ a convincing vision —Edmund Wilson⟩ ⟨~ in words, before time blurs them, the clear lineaments of genius —*Dock Leaves*⟩ **b** (1) **:** to make nonvolatile or solid **:** cause to form a nonvolatile or solid compound ⟨~ ammonia⟩; *also* **:** COMBINE ⟨~ nitrogen to form ammonia⟩ ⟨leaves of many plants take up carbon dioxide and ~ it in organic acids⟩ (2) **:** to make (a fertilizer element or a trace element) insoluble by combination with soil minerals and thus often unavailable or only slowly available to plants (3) **:** to make (a perfume) more lasting by adding a substance that reduces the rate of evaporation (4) **:** to treat so as to make some condition permanent ⟨~ an oil in the vapor state by mixing it with a gas⟩ (5) **:** to make the image of (a photographic negative or positive) more permanent by changing the unused silver salts to a soluble form that can be removed by washing (6) **:** to kill, harden, and preserve (as organisms or fresh tissues) for microscopic study or other purposes usu. by immersion in dilute acids, alcohol, or solutions of substances that quickly coagulate living tissue (7) **:** to establish or make (as a trait, quality, peculiarity) permanent by selective breeding **c** (1) **:** FASTEN, ATTACH, AFFIX ⟨once the toxin has been combined with our tissues, it remains firmly ~*ed* to them —Justina Hill⟩ ⟨the old-fashioned scythe blade . . . usually works loose, unless skillfully ~*ed* —F.D.Smith & Barbara Wilcox⟩ ⟨will be able to ~ a silver and red badge to their vehicles —*N.Y. Times*⟩ (2) **:** to direct in an unwavering or concentrated manner **:** CONCENTRATE ⟨~*ed* his ambition upon orthopedic surgery as his lifework —J.M.Phalen⟩; *specif*

: to direct an unwavering gaze upon ⟨his mother ~*es* him icily —Samuel Taylor⟩ ⟨~*ed* her with his eye —Agnes S. Turnbull⟩ (3) : to hold fast : CAPTURE ⟨tried to ~ her eyes with his, but she was . . . looking away —Marcia Davenport⟩ ⟨seemed capable of being . . . attractive without wanting to ~ the attention of every man near her —Jane Austen⟩ **2 a** : to set or place definitely : STATION, SETTLE ⟨~*ed* his residence in the city⟩ ⟨~*ed* himself in New York⟩ **b** : to assign precisely : settle on : DETERMINE, DEFINE ⟨federal and state courts ~ not only wages but hours and working conditions as well —Nathaniel Peffer⟩ ⟨~ the limits of a debate⟩ ⟨wonder why such a lonely spot was ~*ed* in the first place —Sydney Moorhouse⟩ ⟨difficult to ~ the place of this remarkable statesman in history⟩ ⟨no time or place has yet been ~*ed* —Jess Whitworth⟩ **c** : ASSIGN, PLACE ⟨~ responsibility⟩ ⟨~ the guilt⟩ ⟨so many mistakes were made . . . that it was difficult to ~ the blame —Isaac Rosenfeld⟩ **3 a** : to set or place in order or in a certain pattern : adjust or settle properly or for a desired end ⟨~*ed* his face in an expression of mock disgust —C.B.Flood⟩ ⟨~*ed* his spectacles and read aloud —George Meredith⟩ ⟨~*ed* its door so that it couldn't be opened from the outside —Raymond Chandler⟩ **b** : to line the hearth of (a furnace) with fettling **4 a** (1) : to put in neat-appearing order : ARRANGE, PREPARE ⟨~*ed* the same room for you —Ellen Glasgow⟩ ⟨~*ed* their hair in the Hollywood manner—Norman Cousins⟩ ⟨asked me to ~ the table for the family dinner⟩; *specif* : to get (food) ready ⟨~*es* lunches for the children to take to school —*N.Y. Times*⟩ ⟨coffee ~*ed* with milk—Lorraine Calhoun⟩ ⟨~*ed* himself a drink⟩ (2) : REPAIR, MEND ⟨they know how to ~ their cars —Feliks Gross⟩ ⟨called in a plumber to ~ the drain⟩; *also* : to improve the physical condition of : RESTORE, CURE — often used with *up* ⟨that doctor ~*ed* up my son fine⟩ ⟨told her that food would ~ her up —E.D.Radin⟩ (3) : to take care of : see to : SOLVE ⟨getting your name in the society columns won't ~ anything —*Better Homes & Gardens*⟩ ⟨anything that's wrong with our life today, people expect the schools to ~ —Hannah Lees⟩ — often used with impersonal *it* as object ⟨the battalion surgeon ~*ed* it so I didn't have to go to the hospital —P.B.Kyne⟩ (4) : CASTRATE, SPAY (5) : to remove a principal means of defense from (as a pet skunk) **b** : to do for (someone) : get even with : PUNISH ⟨wish I could ~ them —P.G.Wodehouse⟩ ⟨God'll ~ you —Dan Browne⟩ ⟨the vigilante committee warned sheepmen away . . . on the threat of ~*ing* them up —*Amer. Guide Series: Oregon*⟩ **c** (1) : to determine the outcome of (a contest) by bribery or other improper methods ⟨all his fights have been ~*ed* —Budd Schulberg⟩ ⟨arrested for ~*ing* games —*Sports Illustrated*⟩ ⟨he can ~ an election so that one of his stooges becomes a key official —Malcolm Johnson⟩ : tamper with in advance ⟨a horse ~*ed* to lose a race⟩ ⟨a ~*ed* slot machine⟩ (2) : to induce by bribery or influence to give a favorable decision ⟨the jury had been ~*ed*⟩ : obtain the quashing or disposal of by tampering or other arrangement ⟨~*es* a traffic ticket or bribes a building inspector —Herman Kogan⟩ **5** *slang* : to give (someone) a narcotic ~ *vi* **1** : to become fixed; *esp* : to become firm or stable **2 a** : to settle or remain permanently : cease from wandering **b** : to direct the gaze or attention : FOCUS, FIXATE ⟨her eyes ~*ed* sideways for an instant⟩ — often used with *on* or *upon* ⟨the examinee is then directed to ~ on the examiner's right eye —H.G.Armstrong⟩ **c** : ARRANGE, DETERMINE, AGREE, DECIDE ⟨the general had ~*ed* to be out by that hour —Jane Austen⟩ — usu. used with *on* or *upon* ⟨~ with a contractor on a sum to be paid for the job —*Glasgow Sunday Post*⟩ ⟨had ~*ed* on the first week in November —Edna Ferber⟩ ⟨~*ed* on a cabin by the lake to spend vacation⟩ **3** : to get set : be about to : PREPARE, INTEND — used chiefly in the present participle ⟨are ~*ing* to ship some cattle —F.B.Gipson⟩ ⟨~*ing* to cop the first postwar contract in the shipbuilding industry —*Time*⟩ ⟨~*ing* to leave town for good —Erskine Caldwell⟩ ⟨~*ing* to rain⟩ **syn** see FASTEN, SET — **fix bayonets 1** : to attach a bayonet to a rifle — used as a command **2** : to raise the right hand in a mass swearing-in ceremony — used of Salvationists

²fix \"\ *n* -ES **1 a** : a position of difficulty or embarrassment : PREDICAMENT, DILEMMA ⟨found himself in an awful ~⟩ **b** : the position (as of a ship or airplane) obtained by bearings of fixed objects, by observations of heavenly bodies, or by radio means; *also* : a determination of one's position **2** : FETTLING **3 a** (1) : an arrangement whereby relative immunity from application of the law is obtained through the employment of economic, political, or social influence and esp. through the payment of money to law-enforcement officers or other authorities ⟨collusion between state party officials and the local collector of internal revenue led to tax ~*es* for gamblers, racketeers, and businessmen —*New Republic*⟩ (2) : the money paid (as by the owner of a gambling house) to a law-enforcement officer or other person wielding influence or authority for protection from the law : BRIBE **b** : an instance of collusion or private agreement that gives special or unfair advantage to one of the parties ⟨in the dream life of the little businessman the sure ~ is replacing the open market —C.W. Mills⟩; *specif* : a sports contest whose outcome is prearranged ⟨virtually impossible for a spectator to recognize a ~ even if he is told —O.R.Cohen⟩ **4** *slang* : a shot of a narcotic **5** : a tall drink made with alcoholic liquor, lemon juice, and sweetening, served in cracked ice, and decorated with fruit ⟨brandy ~⟩ ⟨gin ~⟩ **syn** see PREDICAMENT

fix·able \ˈfiksəbəl\ *adj* : capable of being fixed

fix·ate \ˈfik,sāt, *usu* -ād.+V\ *vb* -ED/-ING/-S [L *fixus* (past part. of *figere* to fasten, pierce) + E *-ate* — more at DIKE] *vt* **1** : to make fixed, stationary, or unchanging : FIX ⟨it is the groups that become *fixated* by orthodoxy that decline —D.F. Fleming⟩ ⟨Protestants have been *fixated* in defending the thought of the reforming sixteenth century —J.W.Nixon⟩ **2** : to focus one's eyes upon : concentrate one's gaze on ⟨~ a word on the moving sheet —R.S.Woodworth⟩ **3** : to direct (the libido) toward a pregenital form of gratification ~ *vi* **1** : to focus or concentrate one's gaze or attention — usu. used with *on* or *upon* ⟨an infant with normal vision . . . will ~ on a light held before him —*Jour. Amer. Med. Assoc.*⟩ **2** : to undergo arrestment at a certain stage of development ⟨men and women of a certain caliber ~ in any job —H.A.Overstreet⟩; *specif* : to undergo arrestment at a certain stage of psychosexual development

fixated *adj* [*fixate* + *-ed*] : arrested at a certain phase of adjustment or development; *esp* : arrested at a pregenital level of psychosexual development

fix·a·tif *like* FIXATIVE, *or* ˈfiksə¦tēf\ *n* -S [F, prob. fr. E *fixative*] : FIXATIVE

fix·a·tion \fikˈsāshən\ *n* -S [ME *fixacioun*, fr. ML *fixation-*, *fixatio*, fr. L *fixus* + *-ation-*, *-atio* -ation] **1** : the act of fixing or fixating : the state of being fixated ⟨~ of the kidney by operative means⟩ ⟨would entail the ~ of their present condition of inferiority —*New Republic*⟩ ⟨a marketing board should concentrate . . . on distribution and not on price ~ —*Farmer's Weekly (So. Africa)*⟩ **2** : the act or an instance of focusing the eyes upon an object **3** : a persistent concentration of libidinal energies upon pregenital zones, objects, persons, or substitute figures and consequent arrest of libidinal development at an immature level **4 a** : a habit formation : persistent, obsessive, or compulsive behavior **b** : an excessive, obsessive, or unhealthy preoccupation or attachment : OBSESSION ⟨public ~ on the rising tide of juvenile delinquency —*Nervous Child*⟩ ⟨~s about cleanliness⟩ ⟨isn't really love, it's just a ~ —Malcolm Cowley⟩ **5** : the immobilization of the parts of a fractured bone esp. by the use of various metal attachments **6** : NITROGEN FIXATION

fix·a·tive \ˈfiksəd·iv, -ativ\ *n* -S [fr. *fixative*, adj., "tending to fix", fr. ¹*fix* + *-ative*] : something that fixes or sets: as **a** : a substance (as musk or benzoin) added to a perfume esp. for preventing the more volatile ingredients from evaporating too rapidly **b** : a varnish usu. applied by spraying and used esp. for the protection of crayon drawings **c** : a substance or mixture of substances used to fix living tissue

fixed \ˈfikst\ *adj* [ME, fr. past part. of *fixen* to fix — more at FIX] **1 a** : securely placed or fastened ⟨a ~ piece of wood⟩ : not adjustable ⟨a ~ resistor⟩ : permanently and definitely located : STATIONARY, IMMOVABLE ⟨there were no ~ theaters in the provinces —G.M.Trevelyan⟩ **b** (1) : NONVOLATILE ⟨a ~ acid⟩ ⟨~ carbon⟩ (2) : COMBINED 1b, BOUND 6 ⟨~ nitrogen⟩ (3) : slowly soluble as a result of combination ⟨~ copper fungicides⟩ **c** (1) : not subject to change or fluctuation : ABSOLUTE, SETTLED, DEFINITE ⟨revolution . . . could never be a ~ right —S.W.Chapman⟩ ⟨urged the assembly to grant him a ~ salary⟩ ⟨a ~ rate pays for transportation . . . and food on tours —*Current Biog.*⟩ (2) : held to tenaciously and often blindly or obsessively : UNSWERVING, SET ⟨is very ~ in his ways and thought⟩ ⟨the man of ~ ideas . . . is today a public danger —*Nation*⟩ (3) : having a final or crystallized form or character : incapable of further development : FROZEN ⟨America is not yet a ~ and settled land —Barbara Ward⟩ ⟨the respect of the eighteenth century for ~ forms —R.B. West⟩ ⟨animal species are ~ and it is possible to define them in static terms —H.M.Parshley⟩ (4) : recurring on the same date from year to year ⟨~ feast⟩ **d** : RIGID, IMMOBILE, CONCENTRATED ⟨sat with a look of ~ attention on his face⟩ ⟨her thick glasses gave her eyes a ~ stare —Allen Tate⟩ **2** : supplied with a definite amount of something needed or desirable : PROVIDED ⟨how are we ~ for seamen —*Argosy*⟩; *esp* : supplied with money : WELL-FIXED

fixed accent *n* **1** : word accent occurring regularly on a specified syllable of a word or on a syllable which is specified in terms of vowel length or consonant combinations in the word **2** : word accent occurring on the same syllable in derivative and inflectional forms of a root or stem

fixed ammunition *n* : ammunition in which the projectile is permanently attached to a case that contains the primer and the propellant in distinction from separate-loading ammunition

fixed arch *n* : an arch without hinges

fixed armament *n* : guns or weapons that are permanently emplaced

fixed assets *n pl* : tangible assets (as land, buildings, machinery, equipment) of a permanent or long-term nature — compare CAPITAL ASSETS

fixed bayonet *n* : a bayonet when fitted in its place on the end of a rifle

fixed beam *n* : a restrained or built-in beam

fixed block *n* **1** : a tackle block that is immovable **2** : one of the sheaves in a ship's chesstree

fixed capital *n* : capital that is durable in character (as buildings and machinery) and can be used over an extended period of time without replacement

fixed cell *n* : a usu. large, irregular, and branching phagocytic cell existing in certain tissues (as connective tissue), lymph nodes, or spleen but sometimes becoming amoeboid and moving through the tissues — compare WANDERING CELL

fixed charge *n* : a recurring expense (as rent, insurance, depreciation, interest on funded debt, taxes on real estate) that is constant and does not fluctuate with business volume

fixed cost *n* : cost that remains constant and does not vary with short-term changes in production

fixed-do system \ˈfiks(t)ˈdō-\ *n* : the system of solmization in which a certain syllable (as *do* for C, C♯, C♭) is used for a given tone and its chromatic derivatives without regard to its key relation

fixed exchange *n* : a system of foreign exchange that quotes the value of a foreign unit of currency in terms of the money of the home country — called also *direct exchange*; compare INDIRECT EXCHANGE

fixed-focus \ˈ=¦=\ *adj* : not provided with a focusing adjustment — used of a camera having a lens of small aperture focused at about 8 to 15 feet

fixed gunnery *n* : the firing of a gun having no traverse so that the entire gun platform or aircraft must be maneuvered for aiming — compare FLEXIBLE GUNNERY

fixed idea *n* [prob. trans. of F *idée fixe*] **1** : a preconceived belief : PREPOSSESSION **2** : a usu. delusional idea that dominates the whole mental life during a prolonged period (as in certain mental disorders)

fixed-income \ˈ=¦=(,)=\ *adj* : having a uniform or relatively uniform annual income or yield ⟨bonds and preferred stocks are *fixed-income* securities⟩ ⟨inflation has its hardest impact on such *fixed-income* groups as people who have retired on social security⟩

fixed liability *n* : a liability (as a bond or mortgage) that does not mature for at least one year from the date incurred or from a given balance-sheet date — called also *funded debt*

fixed light *n* **1** : a light that emits constant beams — compare LIGHTHOUSE **2** : a circular port with a fixed glass and cover used on a ship (as in a deckhouse or skylight)

fixed·ly \-sədlē, -stl-, -li\ *adv* : in a fixed manner ⟨staring ~ into the empty fireplace —Aldous Huxley⟩ ⟨smiling ~ in a travesty of carefree good nature —Erle Stanley Gardner⟩

fixed·ness \-sədnəs, -s(t)n-\ *n* -ES : the quality or state of being fixed

fixed oil *n* : a nonvolatile oil; *esp* : FATTY OIL — distinguished from *essential oil*

fixed point *n* : any one of several definite temperatures determined by natural phenomena (as the freezing point of water) and used as reference points in the calibrating of thermometers

fixed price *n* **1** : a uniform price for all customers as opposed to a price obtained by bargaining **2** : a price fixed by international agreement or by a governmental price-fixing agency **3** : a price established by a contract and not subject to subsequent change

fixed service *n* : communication service carried on among fixed stations

fixed sign *n* : one of the four zodiacal signs Taurus, Leo, Scorpio, and Aquarius

fixed signal *n* : a signal of fixed location used to indicate a condition affecting the movement of a train or engine

fixed spool *n* : a fishing spool that remains stationary when line is wound onto it or cast off it

fixed-spool fishing *n* : SPINNING

fixed star *n* : a true star at such great distance that its motion can be measured only by very precise observations over long periods as distinguished from a planet or other obviously moving body

fixed station *n* : a permanently located radio transmitting station used for communicating with similar stations

fixed virus *n* : a virus made constant in its reactions by repeated passage through a host other than the usual host

fixed year *n* : a calendar year remaining constant in relation to the seasons

fix·er \ˈfiksə(r)\ *n* -S **1** : one that fixes: as **a** : a worker who sets up and adjusts knitting and sewing machines for specific operations **b** : LOOMFIXER **c** : one that is employed in industry to make parts for or to make repairs upon machinery **2 a** : one that intervenes with police officials or other authorities for a person in legal difficulty or with government officials for a person seeking a political favor often with use of corrupt methods and for a fee or other consideration : an influence peddler ⟨a big politico, a ~ you have to see if you want to open a gambling hall —Raymond Chandler⟩ **b** : a go-between (as a lawyer) employed by a circus to make arrangements with officials in advance of performance **c** : one that adjusts matters and esp. smooths over disputes (as between factions of a party) by negotiation : TROUBLESHOOTER ⟨party ~*s* hustled around to put the pressure on deviating Democrats —*Time*⟩ **d** : PLAY DOCTOR **3** : FIXATIVE; *specif* : a fixing bath in photographic work **4** *slang* : a peddler of dope

fixer mason *n* : a mason whose main occupation consists in placing the great blocks of stone accurately into position in a building

fixer-upper \¦fiksə(r)¦əpə(r)\ *n* -S : one that fixes up a person or thing ⟨storewide sale of *fixer-uppers* for walls and floors —Evelyn Kanter⟩

fixes *pres 3d sing of* FIX, *pl of* FIX

fixing *in sense 1 often* -ən *by persons who ordinarily pronounce the ending "-ing"* iŋ *or* ēŋ\ *n* -S [fr. gerund of ¹*fix*] **1 fixings** *pl* : TRIMMINGS, EMBELLISHMENTS, ACCESSORIES; *esp* : the accessories or supplements of a meal ⟨turkey with all the ~*s*, including mince pie⟩ **2** : FETTLING

fix·i·ty \ˈfiksəd·ē, -sətē, -i\ *n* -ES [ML *fixitas*, fr. L *fixus* (past part. of *figere* to fasten, pierce) + *-itas* -ity — more at DIKE] **1** : the quality or state of being fixed or stable ⟨the idea of the ~ of species —M.F.A.Montagu⟩ ⟨all grammars have the same degree of ~ —Edward Sapir⟩ **2** : something that is fixed ⟨the so-called *fixities* such as atoms or God —Frank Thilly⟩ ⟨now inventing rules, the unfixing of *fixities* —H.A.Overstreet⟩

fix·ture \ˈfikschə(r)\ *n* -S [modif. (influenced by *mixture*) of LL *fixura*, fr. L *fixus* + *-ura* -ure] **1** : the act of fixing : the state of being fixed ⟨its final definite ~ for the 25th was probably due to an attempt to harmonize it with the pre-Christian Roman calendar —G.G.Coulton⟩ **2 a** : something that is fixed or attached as a permanent appendage or a structural part ⟨hanging glass ~*s*⟩ ⟨a plumbing ~⟩; *specif* : an electric lighting device usu. ornamental and permanently mounted in place ⟨~*s* providing enough light to read by⟩ **b** (1) : a device for supporting work during machining without guiding the cutting tools (2) : a similar device for holding parts in the correct position during assembly or testing **c** (1) : a chattel that has been so wrought into or annexed to realty (as a house) that it may be regarded as legally a part of it usu. depending upon such considerations as whether it may be removed without irreparable damage, whether the parties (as landlord and tenant) regarded or are presumed by law to have regarded it as removable, whether its annexation was intended to be permanent and to further the purposes for which the structure is designed, or whether its annexation is really necessary to the contemplated use of the structure or only ornamental or convenient — called also *immovable fixture*; opposed to *fitting* (2) : such a chattel still legally the property of the annexer — called also *movable fixture* (3) : a chattel (as shelving or machinery) annexed to realty for purposes of trade or manufacture and legally still the property of the annexer — called also *trade fixture* **d** : an accessory or article that serves a special purpose ⟨an efficient cooking stove . . . alone represented the twentieth century in the ~*s* of the house —Arnold Bennett⟩ ⟨this new display ~ has been carefully designed to build you year-round sales —*Circle & Monogram*⟩ **3 a** (1) : one of a scheduled series of sporting events (as a game, contest, race) ⟨the winner will then meet the leader of the western section, where several ~*s* have still to be played —*Weekly Scotsman*⟩ (2) : a regularly scheduled event (as a festival or exhibition) ⟨a three-monthly classified calendar of ~*s* —*Britain: Information & Events*⟩ ⟨submitting a fairly large team of 2½-year-old rams at this ~ —*Westralian Farmers Co-op. Gazette*⟩ ⟨racegoers feel there should be more ~*s* there —*Sydney (Australia) Bull.*⟩ **b** : a familiar, invariably present, or permanent item, element, or feature in some particular setting ⟨a simile so vivid that it has become a ~ in anthologies —Bernard DeVoto⟩ ⟨resolved to make foreign economic aid a budget ~ as long as the cold war lasts —*Newsweek*⟩; *esp* : a person of long and continued association (as through residence or employment) with some place, activity, or other setting ⟨now a ~ in the stock department, being a member of the office force there —*Nightmare*⟩ ⟨the year in which he became a ~ at second base —*Current Biog.*⟩ ⟨a ~ in most rosters of the world's best-dressed women —*Time*⟩

fix up *vt* **1 a** : to arrange a settlement of : bring to a conclusion ⟨*fix up* a dispute⟩ ⟨today a contract was definitely *fixed up* —Arnold Bennett⟩ **b** : CONTRIVE, DEVISE ⟨*fixed up* an emergency mast⟩ **c** : FURNISH, EQUIP ⟨*fixed* the room *up* as a study⟩ **2** : to provide or accommodate with something needed or desirable : SUPPLY, FURNISH ⟨*fix up* a small loan⟩ — often used with *with* ⟨*fixed up* his relations with positions —*N.Y. Times*⟩ ⟨can sew up a client merely by *fixing* him *up* with a memorable game at his club —*Time*⟩ **3** : to dress up : spruce up ⟨*fixed* myself *up* as well as I could —J.B.Benefield⟩

fix·ure \ˈfikshə(r)\ *n* -S [LL *fixura* — more at FIXTURE] *archaic* : fixed position : FIRMNESS

fixy \ˈfiksē\ *adj* [¹*fix* + *-y*] *dial* : FUSSY, PARTICULAR, ELEGANT

fi·ze·ly·ite \fəˈzālē,īt\ *n* -S [Hung *fizélyite*, fr. Sandor *Fizély*, 20th cent. Hung. mining engineer, its discoverer + Hung *-it* -ite] : a mineral $Pb_5Ag_2Sb_8S_{18}$(?) consisting of a lead silver antimony sulfide occurring as a metallic lead-gray prism

fiz·gig \ˈfiz,gig\ *n* -S [alter. of earlier *fisgig*, perh. fr. *fise* flatus (fr. ME) + *gig* (girl); akin to ME *fist* flatus — more at FEIST] **1** *archaic* : a gadding flirting girl or woman **2** : a firework of damp powder that fizzes or hisses when it explodes **3** : WHIRLIGIG 1 **4** : FISHGIG

¹fizz \ˈfiz\ *vi* -ED/-ING/-ES [prob. of imit. origin] **1** : to make a hissing or sputtering sound (as of a freshly poured effervescent beverage or a burning fuse) : EFFERVESCE **2** : to exhibit strong excitement or exhilaration ⟨~*ing* with the desire to learn the latest hot news —P.G.Wodehouse⟩ ⟨letters home ~*ed* with high spirits —*Time*⟩

²fizz \"\ *n* -ES **1 a** : a hissing sound ⟨the ~ of champagne⟩ **b** : LIVELINESS, ACTIVITY **2** : an effervescent beverage (as ginger ale or champagne); *specif* : a tall drink variously made of spirituous liquor, carbonated water, and lemon juice often with the yolk or the white of an egg or both, sweetened, and chilled ⟨sloe-gin ~⟩ ⟨brandy ~⟩

fizz·er \-zə(r)\ *n* -S [¹*fizz* + *-er*] : a very fast ball in cricket

¹fiz·zle \ˈfizəl\ *vi* **fizzled; fizzled; fizzling** \-z(ə)liŋ\ **fizzles** [prob. alter. of *fist* to break wind (fr. ME *fisten*) + *-le* — more at FEIST] **1** *obs* : to break wind quietly **2** : to make a hissing or sputtering sound ⟨had to drink it hot while it *fizzled* —C.T.Jackson⟩ **3** : to fail or peter out esp. after a promising start : end feebly or lamely ⟨the attempt at surrender having *fizzled* —P.W.Thompson⟩ ⟨every coach knows the agony of watching a . . . rally ~ —W.L.Myers⟩ — often used with *out* ⟨all attempts at friendliness seemed to ~ out—Clive Arden⟩

²fizzle \"\ *n* -S **1** *archaic* : the act of breaking wind quietly **2** : HISS, SPUTTER, FIZZ **3** : an abortive effort : FAILURE, FIASCO ⟨the store was a ghastly ~ —E.J.Kahn⟩

fizzwater \ˈ=,==\ *n* : SODA WATER 2a

fizzy \ˈfizē, -zi\ *adj* -ER/-EST : EFFERVESCENT, FIZZING ⟨poured out the ~ liquid —G.A.Wagner⟩

fjäll \fēˈel, ˈfyel\ *n* -S *usu cap* [Sw, lit., mountain, fr. OSw *fiæll*; akin to ON *fjall* mountain, fell — more at FELL] : a Swedish breed of small white polled dairy cattle with red or black points and flecking on the sides

fjeld \fēˈel, ˈfyel\ *n* -S [Dan; akin to ON *fjall* mountain] : a barren plateau of the Scandinavian upland

fjord *or* **fiord** \fēˈȯ(ə)rd, ˈfyȯ|, |(ə)d\ *n* -S [Norw *fjord*, fr. ON *fjǫrthr* — more at FORD] : a narrow generally deep inlet of the sea between high cliffs or steep slopes (as on the coasts of Norway and Alaska); *also* : an embayment of the coast in a Scandinavian country regardless of the adjacent topography

fjord·ed \-ȯrdəd, -ō(ə)dəd\ *adj* : cleft by fjords

fjord shoreline *n* : a shoreline of submergence characterized by the presence of many fjords

fl *abbr* **1** flange **2** flash; flashing **3** flood **4** floor **5** [L *flores*] flowers **6** florin **7** [L *floruit*] he flourished **8** flour **9** fluid **10** flush **11** flute

FL *abbr* **1** [L *falsa lectio*] false reading **2** flag lieutenant **3** flight lieutenant **4** focal length **5** footlambert **6** foreign language

flab \ˈflab\ *n* -S [back-formation fr. *flabby*] : soft flabby body tissue

flab·ber·gast \ˈflabə(r),gast, -gaa(ə)st, -gaist,-gȧst\ *vt* -ED/-ING/-S [origin unknown] : to overwhelm with shock, surprise, or wonder (as by extraordinary statements or unexpected news) **syn** see SURPRISE

flab·ber·gast·ing·ly \ˈ==,===, ,==ˈ===\ *adv* [*flabbergasting* (pres. part. of *flabbergast*) + *-ly*] : to a flabbergasting degree ⟨a ~ precise young man⟩

flab·bi·ly \ˈflabəlē, -li\ *adv* : in a flabby manner

flab·bi·ness \-bēnəs, -bin-\ *n* -ES : the quality or state of being flabby ⟨the ~ of wasted unused muscles⟩ ⟨moral ~⟩

flab·by \ˈflabē, -bi\ *adj* -ER/-EST [alter. of *flappy*] **1** *of body tissues* **a** : slack and flaccid : yielding to the touch and easily moved or shaken : lacking tone and resilience or firmness ⟨a sagging ~ belly hanging over his belt⟩ **b** : weak and enfeebled ⟨muscles ~ from disuse⟩ **2** : weak and ineffective : FEEBLE ⟨~ liberals⟩ ⟨dull ~ writings⟩; *sometimes* : tending to cause a flabby state (as of the mind or will) ⟨roused from his ~ despondency⟩

flabel *n or vb* [*flabel*, n., fr. L *flabellum* fan; *flabel*, v., fr. *flabel*, n.] *obs* : FAN

flab·el·lar·i·um \,flabəˈla(a)rēəm\ *n, pl* **flabellar·ia** \-rēə\ [NL, fr. L *flabellum*] : VIBRACULUM

fla·bel·late \fləˈbelət, ˈflabə,lāt\ *also* **fla·bel·li·form** \fləˈbelə,fȯrm\ *adj* [*flabellate* prob. fr. (assumed) NL *flabellatus*, fr. L *flabellum* fan + *-atus* -ate; *flabelliform* prob. fr. (assumed)

NL *flabelliformis*, fr. L *flabelli-* + *-formis* -form] : resembling a fan in shape

flabelli- *comb form* [L, fan, fr. *flabellum*] : fan ⟨*flabelliform*⟩ ⟨*flabellinerved*⟩

fla·bel·li·nerved \flə'belə +,-\ *adj, of a leaf* : having the veins radiating like the spokes of a fan ⟨the ginkgo has ~ leaves⟩

fla·bel·lum \flə'beləm\ *n, pl* **flabel·la** \-elə\ [LL, fr. L, fan, dim. of *flabrum* breeze, fr. *flare* to blow — more at BLOW] **1** : a ceremonial fan: **a** : a fan used in religious ceremonies **b** : a fan displayed on state occasions among the appurtenances of certain dignitaries (as a pope or formerly a bishop or royal personage) **2** [NL, fr. L] : a body organ or part that resembles a fan: as **a** : the epipodite of certain limbs of crustaceans **b** : the proximal exite of the limb of a branchiopod

flabella 1b

flac·cid \'flaksəd, ÷'flasəd, ÷'flaasəd\ *adj* [L *flaccidus*, fr. *flaccus* flabby] **1 a** : yielding to pressure for want of firmness and stiffness : FLABBY ⟨a ~ muscle⟩ **b** *of a plant cell or tissue* : deficient in turgor **2** : weak and ineffective : lacking vigor or force ⟨~ leadership⟩ ⟨~ opinions drably expressed⟩ — **flac·cid·ly** *adv*

flac·cid·i·ty \flak'sidəd·ē, ÷fla(a)'si-, -idətē, -i\ *also* **flac·cid·ness** \'flaksədnəs, ÷'fla(a)səd-\ *n* -ES : the quality or state of being flaccid

flaccid paralysis *n* : paralysis in which muscle tone is lacking in the affected muscles and in which tendon reflexes are decreased or absent

fla·che·rie \,flashə'rē, fla'shrē, -lä-\ *also* **flach·ery** \'flashərē\ *n, pl* **flacheries** [F *flacherie*, fr. F dial. (Dauphiné) *flacharié*, fr. Prov *flacarié* flaccidity, flacherie, fr. *flac* flaccid, soft, fr. L *flaccus* flabby] : a disease of silkworms and other caterpillars marked by loss of appetite, sluggishness, dysentery, and flaccidity of the body, terminating fatally with rapid darkening and liquefaction of the body, and caused by an infective agent not certainly identified

¹fla·cian \'flāsh(ē)ən\ *n* -S *usu cap* [Matthias *Flacius* Illyricus †1575 Ger. Protestant theologian + E *-an*] : an adherent to Flacian doctrines or views

²flacian \"\ *adj, usu cap* : relating to or in accordance with the Lutheran teaching of Matthias Flacius Illyricus who accused Melanchthon and the adiaphorists of falsifying Luther's views

¹flack \'flak\ *vb* -ED/-ING/-S [ME *flacken*, perh. alter. of *flakeren* to flutter] *vi, now dial* : FLAP, FLUTTER ⟨clothes ~*ing* on the line⟩ ~ *vt, now dial* : FLICK ⟨~ the dust from your collar⟩

²flack \"\ *n* -S [imit.] **1** *dial Eng* : STROKE, BLOW, FLAP **2** : a recurrent sound of striking (as of a loose tire chain on a frozen road)

³flack \"\ *n* -S [origin unknown] : PRESS AGENT

⁴flack *var of* FLAK

flack·er \'flakə(r)\ *vi* -ED/-ING/-S [ME *flakeren*; akin to MD *flackeren* to flutter, MHG *vlackern* to flicker, ON *flökra* to roam around, and perh. to L *plangere* to beat — more at PLAINT] *dial Eng* : FLUTTER, PALPITATE

flac·on \'flakən\ *n* -S [F, fr. MF *flacon, flascon* — more at FLAGON] : a small usu. ornamental bottle with a tight cap

fla·cour·tia \flə'kůrd·ēə, fla'-, -kōr-\ *n, cap* [NL, fr. Étienne de *Flacourt* †1660 Fr. colonizer + NL *-ia*] : a small genus of often spiny trees or shrubs (family Flacourtiaceae) of tropical Asia and Africa with leaves pinnately veined, flowers in small axillary racemes or clusters, sepals imbricated, and seed enclosed in a stony covering which is surrounded by an edible pulp — see GOVERNOR'S PLUM

fla·cour·ti·a·ce·ae \=,==ˈāsē,ē\ *n pl, cap* [NL, fr. *Flacourtia*, type genus + *-aceae*] : a family of chiefly tropical trees and shrubs (order Parietales) having flowers with numerous stamens and often with enlarged receptacle and undifferentiated perianth and including the chaulmoogras — see FLACOURTIA — **fla·cour·ti·a·ceous** \=ˌ=ˈ=ˌāshəs\ *adj*

¹flae \'flā\ *chiefly Scot var of* FLAY

²flae \"\ *chiefly Scot var of* FLEA

¹flaff \'flaf\ *vb* -ED/-ING/-S [*flaff* fr. ME (Sc) *flaffen*, of imit. origin; *flaffer* freq. of *flaff*] *vi or* **flaf·fer** \-afər\ *chiefly Scot* : FLAP, FLUTTER ⟨~ in the wind⟩ ~ *vt, chiefly Scot* : to cause to flutter or flap ⟨the bird ~*s* his wings⟩

²flaff \"\ *n* -S **1** *chiefly Scot* : a movement made by flapping or fluttering **2** *chiefly Scot* : a burst or gust esp. of wind

¹flag \'flag, -aa(ə)-,-ai-\ *n* -S [ME *flagge* reed, rush] **1** : any of various monocotyledonous plants with long ensiform leaves: as **a** : a plant of the genus *Iris*: as (1) : the common yellow-flowered iris (*I. pseudacorus*) of Europe (2) : either of two blue-flowered No. American irises (*I. versicolor* and *I. prismatica*) **b** : SWEET FLAG **c** : CATTAIL 1 **2** : a leaf of a flag or of a cereal grass

²flag \"\ *vt* **flagged; flagged; flagging; flags** : to caulk (as the joints of a barrel) with cattails or other flags

³flag \"\ *n* -S [ME *flagge* piece of turf, flagstone, fr. ON *flaga* slab; akin to ON *flag* spot where the turf has been cut, OE *flēan* to skin — more at FLAY] **1** *dial Brit* : a piece of sod or turf **2** *dial Brit* : a slice of earth turned over in plowing **3 a** : a hard evenly stratified stone (as fine-grained sandstone or firm shale) that splits into flat pieces suitable for paving ⟨a valuable ~ quarry⟩ **b** : a piece of such stone; *esp* : a thin piece split from such stone ⟨looked down at the cracked ~*s* beneath which the roots spread —Virginia Woolf⟩ **c** : a surface of such stone ⟨scrubbed down the ~ of the terrace each morning⟩

walk paved with flags

⁴flag \"\ *vt* **flagged; flagged; flagging; flags** [ME *flaggen*, fr. *flagge*, n. — more at ³FLAG] : to lay (as a pavement) with flags : cover (as an earthen surface) with flat stones

⁵flag \"\ *n* -S [perh. fr. ¹*flag*] **1 a** : a usu. rectangular piece of fabric (as light flexible cloth) of distinctive design that is used as a symbol (as of a nation) or as a signaling device and is usu. displayed hanging free from a staff or halyard to which it is attached by one edge — see ²FLY 6c, HOIST; compare BANNER, ENSIGN, PENNANT, PENNON, STANDARD **b** : a flag that is the personal symbol of an admiral and is hoisted on a ship on which he is present and in command **c** : a representation of a flag ⟨embroidered a ~ on the cushion⟩ ⟨little ~*s* stenciled on the boxes⟩ ⟨a ~ of growing flowers⟩ **d** : something that is used like a flag to signal or attract attention **2 a flags** *pl, archaic* : the secondaries of a bird's wing **b** : the tail of certain dogs (as setters and hounds); *also* : the long hairs fringing a setter's tail **c** : the tail of a deer **3** : any of certain signaling devices: as **a** : one of the cross strokes on a musical note of less than a quarter-note time value ⟨the eighth note has one ~, the sixteenth two⟩ — called also *hook* **b** : a marker (as a piece of cardboard or a turned rule) inserted between lines of type to remind the compositor that an addition or correction must be made at that place — called also *watchman* **c** : RANGE POLE **d** : a thin oblong piece (as of metal or plastic) projecting from a movable rod by which it may be raised or lowered that is used for signaling (as of the availability of a taxi or the presence of mail in a rural delivery box) **e** : MASTHEAD 2a **f** : a usu. colored metal or plastic clip that may be attached to a card or sheet of paper as a reminder of some future attention required **g** : a marker (as a small strip of colored paper) placed to protrude from a roll of paper at a place where it has broken and been spliced **4** : the end of a bristle for use in brushes that is farthest from the root, is relatively soft and flexible and often somewhat frayed, and is usu. the free end in the finished brush **5** : something usu.

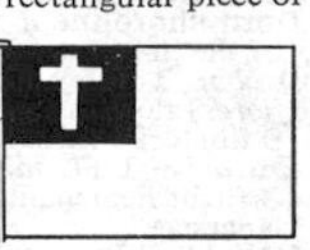
flag 1a

or properly symbolized by the display of a particular flag: as **a** : FLAGSHIP **b** : an admiral functioning in his office of command **c** : NATIONALITY; *esp* : the nationality of registration of a ship or airplane — called also *registry* **6** : FEATHER 7 **7** [⁷*flag*] : a wilted or dead leaf or a branch with such leaves on an otherwise healthy plant (as a tree) that is frequently indicative of an interference with the water supply to the leaves

syn ENSIGN, BANNER, STANDARD, COLORS, JACK, PENNANT, PENDANT, PENNON, STREAMER: FLAG is a very general term; in most situations it lends itself readily to substitutions for the more specific words following. ENSIGN, commonly used in naval or nautical affairs, often indicates a flag showing nationality or nation. BANNER, often a romantic and literary synonym for FLAG, is frequently used in situations involving emotional ties and appeals ⟨the star-spangled *banner*, oh! long may it wave —F.S.Key⟩ STANDARD is often used in reference to the flag, often an elongated one, of an individual, a cause or party, or a mounted or motorized unit, esp. when serving as a rallying point ⟨with the *standards* of the peoples plunging through the thunderstorm —Alfred Tennyson⟩ ⟨after the execution of Charles I, the royal *standard* was replaced by the Commonwealth *standard* —W.G.Perrin⟩ COLORS — the form more common than the singular COLOR — may refer to national flags, flags emblematic of affiliation or partisanship, flags of most military units ⟨the call to the *colors*⟩ ⟨to join the *colors*⟩ ⟨a ship carrying French *colors*⟩ ⟨afraid to show his *colors*⟩ ⟨the British *colors* were planted on the summit of the breach —Duke of Wellington †1852⟩ The following words are more specific and limited in use: JACK typically designates a small oblong flag indicating nationality and is used on the bowsprits of ships. PENNANT and PENDANT, the latter more English than American, typically refer to flags more or less triangular in shape used to identify individual units or to signal. PENNON may apply to a narrower flag, one suitable to hanging from a lance ⟨that squadron swung around . . . with a wicked whistling of wind in the *pennons* of its lances —Rudyard Kipling⟩ STREAMER is likely to refer to a long narrow flag capable of streaming in the wind.

⁶flag \"\ *vb* **flagged; flagged; flagging; flags** *vt* **1 a** : to put a flag on (as for decoration or identification) ⟨the course will be *flagged* at regular intervals⟩ ⟨he *flagged* the important pages with bright red tabs clipped to the margins⟩ **b** : to cause (a horse) to be docked **2 a** : to catch the attention of by or as if by signaling with a flag; *esp* : to signal to stop (as by waving the hand or a flag) ⟨hurry and ~ me a taxi or I'll miss my train⟩ — often used with *down* ⟨the watchman *flagged* down the truck⟩ **b** : to decoy (game) by waving a flag, handkerchief, or other object to arouse curiosity **c** : to convey (as a message) by means of flag signals ⟨*flagging* his orders to the other ships⟩ ~ *vi* **1** : to wave or signal with a flag **2** *of a pointing dog* : to wag the tail slightly when uncertain as to the exact position of birds

⁷flag \"\ *vb* **flagged; flagged; flagging; flags** [origin unknown] *vi* **1 a** *of flexible bodies* : to hang loose without stiffness : bend down : be loose, yielding, or limp **b** *of a plant* : to droop esp. from lack of water; *often* : to produce flags **2** *obs* : to move weakly — used chiefly of wings **3 a** : to become unsteady or feeble : slacken and decline : fall away ⟨his interest *flagged* as their lack of success continued⟩ ⟨the men get impatient and the morale ~*s* —Michael Gladych⟩ **b** : to grow spiritless and dull ⟨his wit *flagged* under such constant strain⟩ **c** : to decline in interest or attraction ⟨when everyone had had a say, the topic *flagged*⟩ ⟨such self-indulgent pleasures soon ~⟩ ~ *vt* **1** *archaic* **a** : to cease to use (as wings) vigorously : allow to move weakly **b** : to permit to droop or to fall into feebleness **2** : to exhaust the vigor or vitality of : ENERVATE ⟨such sorrow *flags* the strongest spirit⟩

syn see DROOP

⁸flag \"\ *adj, archaic* : PENDULOUS, DROOPING

⁹flag \"\ *n* -S [perh. modif. of (assumed) LG *vleger*, a Frisian coin, fr. MLG *vleger*] *Brit* : GROAT, FOURPENCE

¹⁰flag \"\ *n* -S [prob. alter. of *flake*] *chiefly Scot* : a large snowflake

flag alarm *n* [⁵*flag*] : a signal made by a small flag that appears on the indicator of an instrument which begins giving unreliable readings

flag badge *n* : a badge or cognizance used for distinction on a flag whose design except for the badge is used in common by two or more dominions, colonies, or territories within an empire

flag bag *n* : a metal or wooden locker or other container in which the signal flags of a ship are stored

flag blue *n* : a grayish to dark purplish blue that is bluer and less strong than independence

flag bottom *n* [¹*flag*] : a rush seat of a chair or settee — called also *flag seat*

flag bridge *n* [⁵*flag*] : the first bridge above the flight deck on an aircraft carrier : the admiral's bridge

flag captain *n* : the commanding officer of a flagship

flag carrier *n* : an air or sea transport line flying the flag of the country to which it belongs

flag country *n* : the part of a flagship set aside for the use of its flag officer

flag day *n* **1** *usu cap F&D* : an annual celebration or holiday (as June 14 in the U.S.) for commemorating the origin of or for honoring a national flag **2** *Brit* : a day on which contributions (as to a charity) are solicited and small flags are given to contributors — compare TAG DAY

flag discrimination *n* : preferential treatment of ships of a particular registry in the assignment of cargo

flagella *pl of* FLAGELLUM

¹flag·el·lant \'flajələnt, flə'jel-\ *n* -S [L *flagellant-, flagellans*, pres. part. of *flagellare* to whip] : one that whips: as **a** *usu cap* : a member of one of the organized groups that since the 12th century have practiced self-castigation as a religious rite **b** : a person who responds sexually to being beaten by or to beating another person — **flag·el·lant·ism** \-ən,tizəm\ *n* -S

²flagellant \"\ *adj* [L *flagellant-, flagellans*] **1** : FLAGELLATING, LASHING ⟨a vicious ~ speech⟩ **2** : believing in or practicing flagellation

fla·gel·lar \flə'jelə(r), 'flajəl-\ *adj* [*flagellum* + *-ar*] : of or relating to a flagellum

flagellar antigen *n* : any of various antigens associated with the flagella of motile bacteria and used in serological identification of various bacteria — distinguished from *somatic antigen*; called also *H antigen*

flag·el·lar·ia \,flajə'la(a)rēə\ *n, cap* [NL, fr. L *flagellum* whip, shoot of a plant + NL *-aria*] : a small genus (the type of the family Flagellariaceae) of tropical or subtropical monocotyledonous herbs with sheathing leaves terminating in a tendril and small persistent flowers in panicles — **flag·el·lar·i·a·ceous** \=ˌ==ˌ=ˈāshəs\ *adj*

¹flag·el·la·ta \,flajə'lād·ə, -lād·ə\ [NL, fr. *flagellum* + *-ata*] *syn of* MASTIGOPHORA

²flagellata \"\ [NL, fr. *flagellum* + *-ata*] *syn of* FLAGELLATAE

flag·el·la·tae \-lād·ē, -lā,tē, -lād·,ē\ *n, pl, cap* [NL, fr. *flagellum* + L *-atae* (fr. L, fem. pl. of *-atus* -ate)] *in some classifications* : a class of flagellated unicellular organisms comprising the Chrysomonadina, Cryptomonadina, Euglenoidina, and closely related flagellate and algal organisms and being nearly equivalent in scope to Phytomastigina of other classifications

¹flag·el·late \'flajə,lāt, *usu* -ād·+V\ *vt* -ED/-ING/-S [L *flagellatus*, past part. of *flagellare*, fr. *flagellum* whip, dim. of *flagrum* whip; akin to MD *blaken* to blow, wave, ON *blaka* to wave, flutter, Lith *blaškyti* to throw back and forth] **1** : WHIP, SCOURGE, FLOG **2** : to drive, punish, or stigmatize by or as if by whipping ⟨the papers *flagellated* the levity of his conduct⟩ ⟨*flagellating* herself to her daily task⟩

²flag·el·late \-lə̇t, -,lāt, flə'jelə̇t, *usu* |d·+V\ *adj* [NL *flagellatus*, fr. *flagellum* + L *-atus* -ate] **1 a** : having or bearing flagella **b** : shaped like a flagellum **2** [³*flagellate*] : of, relating to, or caused by flagellates ⟨~ dysentery⟩

³flagellate \"\ *n* -S [NL *Flagellata* & *Flagellatae*] : a flagellate protozoan or alga

⁴flag·el·late \'flajə,lāt, *usu* -ād·+V\ *vi* -ED/-ING/-S [back-formation fr. ²*flagellation*] : to develop a flagellum

flag·el·lat·ed \'flajə,lād·əd\ *adj* [²*flagellate* + *-ed*] : FLAGELLATE 1 ⟨~ organisms⟩

flagellated chamber *n* : one of the outpouchings of the wall of the central cavity of a sponge that is lined with choanocytes and connects with incurrent canals through prosopyles

¹flag·el·la·tion \,flajə'lāshən\ *n* -S [ME *flagellacion*, fr. L *flagellation-, flagellatio*, fr. *flagellatus* (past part. of *flagellare* to whip) + *-ion-, -io* -ion] : an act or instance of flagellating : BEATING, FLOGGING, SCOURGING; *esp* : the practice of a flagellant

²flagellation \"\ *n* -S [*flagellum* + *-ation*] : the formation of flagella; *also* : the flagella or the arrangement of flagella on an organism or surface

flag·el·la·tor \'==,lād·ə(r)\ *n* -S [ML, fr. L *flagellatus* + *-or*] : one that flagellates : SCOURGER, FLAGELLANT

flag·el·la·to·ry \'flajələ,tōrē, flə'jel-\ *adj* [¹*flagellate* + *-ory*] : relating to flagellation

flag·el·lif·er·ous \,flajə'lif(ə)rəs\ *adj* [prob. fr. F *flagellifère* flagelliferous (fr. *flagelli-* — fr. NL *flagellum* — + *-fère* -ferous — fr. L *-fer*) + E *-ous* — more at -FEROUS] : having flagella : FLAGELLATE

fla·gel·li·form \flə'jelə,fȯrm\ *adj* [ISV *flagelli-* (fr. NL *flagellum*) + *-form*] : elongated, slender, and tapering like a flagellum

flag·el·lo·sis \,flajə'lōsə̇s\ *n, pl* **flagello·ses** \-ō,sēz\ [NL, fr. *flagell-* (fr. *Flagellata*) + *-osis*] : infestation with or disease caused by flagellate protozoans

fla·gel·lum \flə'jeləm\ *n, pl* **flagel·la** \-elə\ *also* **flagellums** [L, whip, shoot of a plant] **1** : WHIP, SCOURGE **2** [NL, fr. L] : any of various elongated filiform appendages of animals: as **a** : the slender distal part of some antennae **b** : a sensory organ that suggests a comb on the chelicerae of most solpugids and pseudoscorpions **3** [NL, fr. L] : a long tapering process that projects singly or in groups from a cell or microorganism, is possibly equivalent to a much enlarged cilium, and is the primary organ of motion of flagellated protozoans and many algae, bacteria, and zoospores **4** : a long slender shoot (as a stolon or runner) of a plant

¹fla·geo·let \,flajə'let, -lā\ *n* -S [F, fr. OF *flajolet*, fr. *flajol* flute (fr. assumed VL *flabeolum*, fr. L *flare* to blow) + *-et* — more at BLOW] **1** : a small fipple flute resembling the treble recorder but having usu. four finger holes and two thumbholes and a cylindrical mouthpiece **2** : a labial 2-foot pipe-organ stop with a flute quality

flageolet

²fla·geo·let \'flazhōlā\ *n, pl* **flageolets** \"\ [F, modif. (influenced by *flageolet* flute) of Prov *faioulet*, fr. OProv *faiolet*, dim. of (assumed) OProv *faiol* kidney bean (whence Prov *faiou*), fr. (assumed) VL *fabeolus*, alter. (influenced by L *faba* bean) of L *phaseolus* kidney bean — more at FRIJOL, BEAN] : a green kidney bean of France

flageolet tone *n* : ²HARMONIC 1b

flagfish \'=,=\ *n* : any of several brilliantly colored fishes chiefly of tropical seas

flag flower *n* : an iris flower

flagged *past of* FLAG

flag·ger \'flagə(r), -laag-,-laig-\ *n* -S [¹*flag* + *-er*] *dial* : a wild iris

¹flag·ging \'flagiŋ, -laag-,-laig-, -gēŋ\ *adj* [fr. pres. part. of ⁷*flag*] **1** : LANGUID, WEAK **2** : DWINDLING, DIMINISHING, WEAKENING ⟨~ hopes⟩ ⟨~ demands for farm products⟩ — **flag·ging·ly** *adv*

²flagging \"\ *n* -S [³*flag* + *-ing*] **1** : flagstones for paving **2** : a pavement or walk of flagstones

flagging iron *n* [*flagging* fr. gerund of ²*flag*] : a prying tool with a double-hooked head used in caulking barrels with flags or for removing barrelheads

¹flag·gy \'flagē, -aag-,-aig-, -gi\ *adj* [ME *flaggi*, fr. *flagge* reed, rush + *-i, -y* -y] **1** : abounding with flags or other reedy plants ⟨a ~ marsh⟩ **2** *obs* : like an iris or other flag

²flaggy \"\ *adj* [⁷*flag* + *-y*] **1** *archaic* : soft and flabby **2** *archaic* : hanging limply : DROOPING

³flaggy \"\ *adj* [³*flag* + *-y*] **1** *of rock* : splitting or tending to split into layers of suitable thickness for use as flagstones : formed of laminated strata from 10 to 100 millimeters in thickness **2** *of soil* : full of pieces of flagstone

⁴flaggy \"\ *adj* [prob. fr. ⁵*flag* + *-y*] : split and frayed ⟨the ~ end of a bristle⟩ — compare ⁵FLAG 4

flag·i·tate \'flajə,tāt\ *vt* -ED/-ING/-S [L *flagitatus*, past part. of *flagitare*; akin to L *flagrum* whip] : IMPORTUNE — **flag·i·ta·tion** \,==ˈtāshən\ *n* -S

fla·gi·tious \flə'jishəs\ *adj* [ME *flagicious*, fr. L *flagitiosus*, fr. *flagitium* shameful or disgraceful thing + *-osus* -ose; akin to L *flagrum* whip — more at FLAGELLATE] **1** : disgracefully or shamefully criminal : grossly wicked : SCANDALOUS **2** : guilty of or characterized by enormous crimes or scandalous vices : VILLAINOUS, CORRUPT **syn** see VICIOUS

fla·gi·tious·ly *adv* : in a flagitious manner : VICIOUSLY, WICKEDLY

fla·gi·tious·ness *n* -ES : the quality or state of being flagitious : CORRUPTION, VICE, VILLAINY

flag law *n* : a law that prescribes rules concerning the use and display of the flag of a sovereign body (as a nation)

flag lieutenant *n* : an officer on an admiral's staff who acts as his personal aide

flag lily *n* : ¹FLAG 1a

flag line *n* : a sea or sometimes air transport line under a particular national registry ⟨American *flag lines* in the Pacific⟩; *often* : FLAG CARRIER

flag list *n* : a list of admirals of a particular navy

flag·man \'=mən\ *n, pl* **flagmen** **1** *obs* : ADMIRAL **2** : a person who signals with or as if with a flag esp. to warn of danger (as on a highway) or to direct some operation (as the use of hoisting equipment or the maneuvering of heavy machinery) **3** : a member of a surveying party who carries a range pole

flag of convenience : registry of a merchant ship under a foreign flag in order to compete with ships of foreign nations ⟨must operate under a *flag of convenience* or go out of business —Walter Hamshar⟩

flag officer *n* **1** : a naval officer entitled to display a flag with one or more stars that indicate his command rank ⟨in the U. S. Navy a *flag officer* with two stars is a rear admiral⟩ — compare GENERAL OFFICER **2** : a person (as the president of a yachting club) entitled to display a special identifying flag on his boat

flag of truce : a white flag carried or displayed to an enemy as an invitation to conference or parley or to signify a desire of making some communication not hostile; *sometimes* : the bearer of such a flag

flag·on \'flagən, -laig-\ *n* -S [ME *flakon, flakon*, fr. MF *flacon, flascon*, fr. LL *flascon-, flasco* bottle — more at FLASK] **1** : a vessel for liquid (as wine or liquor): as **a** : a large usu. metal or pottery vessel with handle and spout and often a lid **b** : a vessel used to hold eucharistic wine **c** : a large bulging short-necked bottle; *sometimes* : a glass flacon **2 a** : the contents of a flagon ⟨a ~ of wine⟩ **b** : a measure usu. of about two quarts

flagon 1b

flag plot *n* : the admiral's tactical and navigational control room aboard a flagship

flagpole \'=,=\ *n* **1** : a pole to raise a flag on **2** : RANGE POLE

fla·gran·cy \'flāgrənsē, -si *also* -la(i)g-\ *also* **fla·grance** \-n(t)s\ *n, pl* **flagrancies** *also* **flagrances** [L *flagrantia* glowing heat, fr. *flagrant-, flagrans* + *-ia* -y] **1** : the quality or state of being flagrant : ATROCITY ⟨the ~ of his vicious conduct⟩ **2** *obs* : a burning or heated state

flag rank *n* : any of the naval grades senior to that of captain — compare RANK table

¹fla·grant \'flāgrənt *also* -la(i)g-\ *adj* [ME, fr. ML *flagrant-, flagrans*, alter. of L *fragrant-, fragrans* — more at FRAGRANT] *dial* : FRAGRANT

²flagrant \"\ *adj* [L *flagrant-, flagrans*, pres. part. of *flagrare* to flame, burn — more at BLACK] **1** *archaic* : FLAMING, GLOWING, BURNING **2** *archaic, of a war or other contest* : carried on hotly : RAGING **3** : extremely, flauntingly, or purposefully

conspicuous usu. because of uncommon evil, unworthiness, unpleasantness, or truculence **:** glaringly evident **:** NOTORIOUS ⟨~ neglect of duty⟩ ⟨even in the most ~ crimes had denied the justice and righteousness of capital punishment —Jack London⟩
syn GLARING, GROSS, RANK: FLAGRANT may describe offenses or errors so conspicuously or outstandingly bad that it is impossible not to notice them ⟨ended their sinful career by open and *flagrant* mutiny and were shot for it —Rudyard Kipling⟩ ⟨the extremes of wealth and poverty were most *flagrant*, slums crowding the marble palaces of the rich —Allan Nevins & H.S.Commager⟩ GLARING applies to the obtrusively conspicuous; it may suggest the painfully and harshly vivid ⟨this evil is so *glaring*, so inexcusable by any sophistry that the cleverest landlord can devise —G.B.Shaw⟩ ⟨*glaring* imperfections which go far beyond a mere lack of verbal felicity —J.W.Krutch⟩ GROSS may refer to inexcusable faults or offenses displayed blatantly, callously, coarsely, and without mitigation or palliation ⟨my anger and disgust at his *gross* earthy egoism had vanished —W.H.Hudson †1922⟩ ⟨an ordinary Fascist type of state, *gross*, brutal, and violent —William Empson⟩ RANK may apply to what is openly objectionable in the extreme and utterly stigmatized ⟨*rank* heresy⟩ ⟨it was hatred, simple hatred, that *rank* poison fatal to Mr. Hazard's health, which now plagued his veins —Elinor Wylie⟩

fla·gran·te de·lic·to \flə¦grantēdə'lik(,)tō, flä¦-\ *adv* [ML, lit., while the crime is blazing] **:** in the very act of committing a misdeed ⟨caught the thief *flagrante delicto*⟩ — sometimes used substantively

fla·grant·ly *adv* [2*flagrant* + *-ly*] **:** in a flagrant manner **:** NOTORIOUSLY

fla·grant·ness *n* -ES **:** the quality or state of being flagrant ⟨punishment was according to the ~ of the crime⟩

flagration *n* -s [prob. back-formation fr. *conflagration*] *obs* **:** CONFLAGRATION, FIRE

flagroot \'=,=\ *n* **:** the root of the sweet flag

flags \'flagz, -aa(ə)gz,-aigz\ *n pl but sing or pl in constr, slang* **:** a naval signalman

flag seat \'=¦=\ *n* [1*flag*] **:** FLAG BOTTOM

flag secretary *n* **:** an admiral's aide who is usu. senior to the flag lieutenant and handles the correspondence

flagsetter \'=,==\ *n* **:** one that lays flagstones

flagship \'=,=\ *n* **1 :** the ship that carries the flag officer or the commander of a fleet or subdivision thereof and flies his flag **2 :** the finest or largest ship of a shipping line

flag-signal \'=¦==\ *vt* **:** to signal by flagging

flag smut *n* [1*flag*] **1 :** a smut of cereal and other grasses that chiefly affects the leaves and stems and is characterized by formation of linear chains of sori within the plant tissues which later rupture releasing black masses of spores and causing fraying of affected areas; *esp* **:** such a disease of wheat caused by a smut fungus (*Urocystis tritici*) **2 :** a smut fungus causing flag smut

flagstaff \'=,=\ *n* **:** a staff on which a flag is hoisted

flag station *n* **:** a flag stop on a railroad

flagstick \'=,=\ *n* **:** a stick with an attached flag that marks the location of the cup in golf

1flagstone \'=,=\ *n, often attrib* [3*flag* + *stone*] **:** 3FLAG 3 ⟨a large room with a ~ floor —Flora Thompson⟩

2flagstone \"\ *vt* **:** to lay flagstone upon

flag stop *n* **:** a point at which a vehicle engaged in public transportation stops only on prearrangement or signal (as by display of a flag)

flag-wagger \'=,==\ *n, chiefly Austral* **:** FLAG-WAVER

flag-waver \'=,==\ *n* **1 :** one that waves a flag (as in signaling) **2 a :** a chauvinistic patriot **b :** a vociferous partisan (as of a class or a political movement) **3 :** something (as a song) that tends to rouse patriotic sentiment

flag-waving \'=,==\ *n* -s **:** ardently or violently emotional appeal to or expression of patriotic or partisan sentiment

1flail \'flāl, *esp before pause or consonant* -āəl\ *n* -s [ME *fleil*, *flail* flail, whip, partly fr. (assumed) OE *flegel* flail (whence OE *fligel*) & partly fr. MF *flaiel*, *flael* flail, whip; (assumed) OE *flegel* akin to OHG *flegil* flail; both fr. a prehistoric WGmc word borrowed fr. LL *flagellum* flail, fr. L *flagellum* whip; MF *flaiel*, *flael* fr. LL *flagellum* flail & L *flagellum* whip — more at FLAGELLATE] **1 :** an instrument for threshing grain from the ear by hand consisting of a wooden handle at the end of which a stouter and shorter stick is so hung as to swing freely — see SWIPLE **2 a :** a primitive weapon (as a morning star) that resembles the agricultural flail in basic structure **b :** any of certain devices used to detonate mines; *sometimes* **:** a vehicle (as a tank) by which such a flail is propelled **3** *obs* **:** a swinging part (as a gate bar or a lever of a press)

2flail \"\ *vb* -ED/-ING/-s [ME *flailen*, fr. *fleil*, *flail*, n.] *vt* **1 :** SCOURGE, WHIP; *sometimes* **:** to drive by beating ⟨~*ed* the pig back to his sty⟩ **2 a :** to strike with or as if with a flail ⟨~*ing* his opponent about the head and shoulders⟩ ⟨startled wings ~*ed* the water⟩ **b :** to move, swing, or beat as though wielding a flail ⟨~*ed* his arms in front of his face to drive away the insects⟩ **3 :** to thresh (grain) with a flail ~ *vi* **1 :** to engage or participate in flailing ⟨propellers ~*ing* futilely⟩ ⟨they ~*ed* away at each other⟩ **2 :** to progress erratically as though along a path through which a flail moves in beating grain ⟨~*ed* up the slope with a rush⟩ ⟨~*ed* around for several months trying to decide to get a job⟩

3flail \"\ *adj* **:** exhibiting abnormal mobility and loss of response to normal controls — used of body parts (as joints) damaged by paralysis, accident, or surgery ⟨~ foot⟩ ⟨the arm remained ~ at the shoulder⟩

flail tank *n* **:** a tank equipped with chain flails to detonate mines

1flair *var of* FLARE

2flair \'fla(ə)(ə)r, 'fle|, |ə\ *n* -s [F, fr. OF, odor, fr. *flairier* to give off an odor, fr. LL *flagrare*, alter. of L *fragrare* to give off an odor, be fragrant — more at FRAGRANT] **1 :** discriminating sense **:** instinctive discernment ⟨an analysis with more ~ than penetration⟩ ⟨relying too much on taste and ~⟩ **2 :** natural ability or capacity ⟨a ~ for hospitality⟩ ⟨developed his ~ for cartooning⟩; *often* **:** an active liking commonly involving use or participation **:** BENT ⟨his ~ for the dramatic⟩ ⟨a developed ~ for the grotesque⟩ **syn** see LEANING

flaith \'flä\ *n* -s [IrGael] **:** an Irish chief or noble of one of several grades holding rent-free land

flaj·o·lo·tite \,flajə'lō,tīt\ *n* -s [F, fr. *Flajolot* fl1871 Fr. mineralogist who analyzed it + F *-ite*] **:** a mineral $4FeSbO_4 \cdot 3H_2O$ occurring as a hydrous iron antimonate in lemon-yellow nodular masses resembling clay

flak *also* **flack** \'flak\ *n, pl* **flak** [G *flak*, fr. *fliegerabwehrkanone* antiaircraft gun, fr. *fliegerabwehr* defense against air attack (fr. *flieger* aviator — fr. *fliegen* to fly, fr. OHG *fliogan* — + *abwehr* defense, fr. *abwehren* to ward off, fr. *ab* off, away — fr. OHG *aba* — + *wehren* to restrain, forbid, fr. OHG *werren* to defend) + *kanone* cannon, fr. It *cannone* — more at FLY, OF, WEIR, CANNON] **1 :** antiaircraft guns ⟨~ battery⟩ ⟨~ ship⟩ **2 :** the bursting shells fired from flak ⟨despite heavy ~ damage made a safe landing⟩

flak curtain *n* **:** flexible steel mesh or plates covered with canvas and used in military aircraft to protect vulnerable areas from enemy gunfire

1flake \'flāk\ *n* -s [ME *flake*, *fleke*, fr. ON *flaki*, *fleki* hurdle; akin to OE *flōc* flounder, MD *vlac* flat, smooth, OS *flaka* sole of the foot, OHG *flah* smooth, Norw *flak* disk, floe, L *plaga* region, Gk *pelagos* sea, L *placēre* to please — more at PLEASE] **1** *now dial* **:** a movable section of fence (as a paling or hurdle) **2 a :** a rack for storing provisions **b :** a stage, platform, or tray for drying fish or produce **3 :** a sheltering framework in a mine

2flake \"\ *n* -s [ME, of Scand origin; akin to Norw *flak* disk, floe] **1 a :** one of the small flocculent masses of ice crystals in which snow falls; *broadly* **:** any small loose mass or bit ⟨~*s* of froth on the horse's chest⟩ ⟨bright ~*s* of cloud⟩ **b :** a particle of incandescent or burning matter thrown off from a fire ⟨~*s* of flame⟩ **2 a :** a thin flattened piece or layer **:** CHIP, LAMINA, SCALE ⟨~*s* of flint detached by pressure were among early man's best tools⟩ ⟨slice the potatoes into ~*s*⟩; *often* **:** something flattened to resemble such a flake ⟨cereal ~*s*⟩ **b :** a lock of hair **c :** MYOCOMMA 1 **d :** MEDULLARY RAY; *also* **:** FLAKE FIGURE **3 :** a carnation with only two colors in the flower which has petals with large stripes **4 :** an internal fissure in ferrous metal

3flake \"\ *vb* -ED/-ING/-s [ME *flaken*, fr. *flake*, n.] *vi* **1 :** to fall as or like flakes of snow ⟨petals *flaking* down in the light breeze⟩ **2 a :** to separate into flakes ⟨sandstone ~*s* readily in heat⟩ **b :** to peel or scale off ⟨look how the paint has *flaked*⟩ ~ *vt* **1 :** to form or separate into flakes ⟨~ the fish for the salad⟩ **2 :** to cover with or as if with flakes (as of snow) ⟨her hair *flaked* with white⟩ ⟨shavings *flaked* the floor⟩ **3 a :** to remove flakes from (as a stone) **:** work (as flint) by pressing off flakes; *also* **:** to form (as an arrowhead) by flaking stone **b :** to remove (as worn paint) in flakes

4flake *var of* FAKE

5flake \'flāk\ *n* -s [perh. fr. 2*flake*] *Brit* **:** a dogfish esp. when used as food

flake figure *n* **:** a figure in lumber or veneer produced by sawing through the medullary rays

flake ice *n* **:** ice in the form of thin scales made usu. by freezing a thin film on a metal plate and scraping it off

flake·less \'flākləs\ *adj* **:** having no flakes **:** not tending to flake off ⟨a ~ paint⟩

flake·let \-lət\ *n* -s **:** a small flake (as of snow)

flake out *vi* [prob. fr. 4*flake*] *slang* **:** to fall asleep **:** collapse from exhaustion

flak·er \'flākə(r)\ *n* -s **:** one that flakes: as **a :** a person that produces flint flakes for striking fire or that manufactures flaked stone implements **b :** a worker who places cleaned fish on flakes for drying **c** *or* **flaking mill :** a machine for reducing material (as cereal grain, fish, soap, or ice) to flakes **d :** a prehistoric implement of bone or other material used to press off flakes of stone in making stone implements

flake stand *n* [2*flake*] **:** the vessel in which the worm of a still is cooled

flake tool *n* **:** a Stone-Age tool that is a flake of stone struck off from a larger piece and sometimes retouched — compare CORE TOOL

flake white *n* [2*flake*] **:** white lead selected for whiteness and fine texture esp. for artists' use

flak·i·ly \'flākəlē, -li\ *adv* **:** in a flaky manner

flak·i·ness \'flākēnəs, -kin-\ *n* -ES **:** the quality or state of being flaky

flak suit *or* **flak vest** *n* **:** body armor made of overlapping steel plates in a padded cover and worn by aircrewmen to protect them from shrapnel

flaky \'flākē, -ki\ *adj* -ER/-EST [2*flake* + *-y*] **1 :** consisting of flakes or full of small loose masses **:** not firmly united into a whole ⟨~ mica-filled sand⟩ **2 :** cleaving off in flakes or layers **:** FRIABLE ⟨a crisp ~ piecrust⟩

flaky fir *n* **:** a Chinese evergreen tree (*Abies squamata*) having shaggy purplish bark that comes off in thin papery layers and being sometimes cultivated as an ornamental

1flam \'flam, -aa(ə)m\ *n* -s [prob. short for *flimflam*] **1 a :** FALSEHOOD, TRICK, DECEPTION **b** *obs* **:** a fanciful bit of writing **2 :** HUMBUG, NONSENSE, RUBBISH

2flam \"\ *vb* **flammed; flammed; flamming; flams :** DECEIVE, TRICK, CHEAT

3flam \"\ *var of* 1FLAN

4flam \"\ *n* -s [prob. imit.] **:** a drumbeat of two strokes of which the first is a very quick grace note

flam·ant \'flamənt, -lām-\ *adj* [MF, pres. part. of *flamer* to flame, fr. OF — more at FLAME] *heraldry* **:** FLAMING; *esp* **:** having flames rising from the top

flamb \'flam\ *vt* -ED/-ING/-s [ME *flaumen*, *flamben* to flame, shine, baste — more at FLAME] *Scot* **:** 2BASTE

flam·bé \(')fläm¦bā\ *adj* [F, singed, passed through a flame, past part. of *flamber* to flame, singe, fr. OF, to flame, fr. *flambe* flame] **1 :** of, relating to, or being a Chinese ceramic glaze depending on partial reduction of copper oxides for its mingled red, purple, and greenish tones ⟨two Chinese ~ vases⟩ ⟨a fine ~ glaze⟩ **2** *also* **flam·béed** \-ād\ *of a food* **:** dressed or served covered with flaming brandy or other flaming liquor ⟨a perfectly browned ~ crepe suzette⟩

flam·beau \'flam,bō\ *n, pl* **flam·beaux** \-ōz\ *or* **flambeaus** [F, fr. MF, fr. *flambe* flame, fr. OF, alter. of *flamble* — more at FLAME] **1 :** a flaming torch usu. made by combining thick wicks saturated with a quick-burning substance (as pitch); *broadly* **:** TORCH **2 :** an ornamental candlestick **3 :** one of a group of kettles used in boiling sugar **4 :** ROYAL POINCIANA

flam·bor·ough \'flam,bərə\ *n* -s *usu cap* [prob. fr. *Flamborough* Head, promontory on east coast of Yorkshire, northern England] **:** an old English sword dance

flam·boy·ance \flam'bȯi(y)ən(t)s\ *also* **flam·boy·an·cy** \-vnsē, -si\ *n, pl* **flamboyances** *also* **flamboyancies** [*flamboyance* fr. *flamboyant*, after such pairs as E *compliant*: *compliance*; *flamboyancy* fr. *flamboyant* + *-cy*] **:** the quality or state of being flamboyant

1flam·boy·ant \(')=¦bȯi(y)ənt\ *adj* [F, lit., flaming, pres. part. of *flamboyer* to flame, blaze, fr. OF *flamboier*, fr. *flambe* flame] **1** *often cap, of architecture* **:** characterized by waving curves suggesting flames ⟨the ~ tracery of windows in the later French Gothic style⟩; *broadly* **:** belonging to the florid French Gothic school of architecture **2 a :** resembling a flame in form or color **b :** FLORID, ORNATE; *also* **:** RESPLENDENT **3 :** given to show or ostentation **:** SHOWY, UNRESTRAINED ⟨~ advertising⟩ **syn** see ORNATE

2flamboyant \"\ *n* -s **:** ROYAL POINCIANA

flam·boy·ant·ly *adv* **:** in a flamboyant manner **:** with flamboyance

flam·doo·dle \'flam¦düd^əl\ *n* [alter. (prob. influenced by 1*flam*) of *flapdoodle*] *dial* **:** NONSENSE; *esp* **:** pretentious nonsense

1flame \'flām\ *n* -s [ME *flaume*, *flambe*, fr. MF *flame*, *flamme* (fr. OF, fr. L *flamma*) & MF *flambe*, fr. OF, alter. of *flamble*, fr. L *flammula* small flame, dim. of L *flamma* flame; akin to L *flagrare* to burn — more at BLACK] **1 :** the glowing gaseous part of a fire **:** a body of gas or vapor that gives off energy usu. in the form of light and heat as a result of a rapid chemical reaction between a combustible material and air, oxygen or other oxidizing agent, that may be luminous, yellow, and smoky if it contains suspended incandescent particles (as of carbon in the case of a candle) or variously colored if certain elements or their compounds are present or predominantly nonluminous, bluish, and hotter as the proportion of air or oxygen in the burning mixture is increased, and that when nonluminous (as produced by a Bunsen burner) typically shows a bright inner cone constituting the flame front where the combustion starts and separating the incoming premixed fuel gas and air from a pale outer cone where the excess of fuel gas reacts with the oxygen of the surrounding air ⟨the ~ of a gas stove⟩ ⟨~*s* from the burning log⟩ ⟨the ~ in a rocket motor⟩ — see OXIDIZING FLAME, REDUCING FLAME **2 a :** a state of blazing combustion ⟨burst into ~⟩ **b :** a condition or appearance suggesting a flame (as a light ray) **c :** BRILLIANCE, BRIGHTNESS ⟨when the moon begins to show her silver ~ —H.W.Longfellow⟩ **3 :** burning zeal or passion **:** elevated and noble enthusiasm ⟨a ~ of righteous indignation filled him with zeal⟩ **4 :** a person beloved **:** SWEETHEART ⟨one of her old ~*s*⟩ **5 :** something (as an ornament, streak, or patch) resembling a flame in shape or color **6 :** a strong reddish orange that is yellower and paler than poppy or paprika and yellower and lighter than flame red — compare FIERY RED, FIRE RED

1 2 3

nonluminous flame produced by a Bunsen burner: *1* outer cone, *2* inner cone, *3* incoming premixed fuel gas and air

2flame \"\ *vb* -ED/-ING/-s [ME *flaumen*, *flamben* to flame, shine, baste, fr. MF *flamer*, *flammer* to flame (fr. OF, fr. L *flammare*, fr. *flamma* flame) & MF *flamber* to flame, fr. OF, fr. *flambe* flame — more at FLAME (n.)] *vi* **1 :** to burn with a flame or blaze **:** burn like gas emitted from bodies in combustion **:** burst into flame **:** BLAZE ⟨the overheated fat *flamed* up suddenly⟩ **2 :** to burst forth like flame **:** break out in violence of passion ⟨he *flamed* with indignation —T.B.Macaulay⟩ **3 a :** to seem or move like a flame **:** shine brightly ⟨the sun's rays *flamed* in the window⟩ **b :** to dart or flicker like a flame ⟨eyes *flaming* furiously⟩ ~ *vt* **1 :** to send or convey by means of flame ⟨the comet *flamed* a warning of dire portent⟩ ⟨a message could be *flamed* by signal fires from one village to the next⟩ **2** *obs* **a :** to consume by burning **:** BURN **b :** KINDLE, INFLAME, EXCITE **3 :** to treat or affect with flame: as **a :** to cleanse with or sterilize by fire ⟨~ the lip of each culture tube⟩ **b :** to dress food with flaming brandy or other liquor **c :** to sear and destroy (as weeds) with flame (as by use of a flamethrower) **4 :** to brighten with or as if with flame ⟨the fireplace *flamed* the opposite wall⟩ **:** give a burning appearance to ⟨the setting sun *flamed* the western sky⟩ **syn** see BLAZE

flame anneal *vt* **:** to soften (metal) by heating with a gas flame

flame azalea *n* **:** an azalea (*Rhododendron calendulaceum*) of the eastern U. S. with showy orange or yellow flowers — called also *fiery azalea*, *yellow azalea*

flame blue *n* **:** DARK WEDGWOOD

flame cell *n* **:** a large hollow cell containing a tuft of vibratile cilia and terminating the branches of the excretory vessels of many flatworms and rotifers and some other lower invertebrates

flame characin *or* **flame fish** *n* **:** a small orange-red So. American freshwater fish (*Hyphessobrycon flammeus*) with black-tipped fins that is frequently kept in the tropical aquarium

flame cultivator *n* **:** an agricultural device employing one or more flamethrowers to destroy small weeds between row crops by fire — called also *flame weeder*

flame-cut \'=,=\ *vt* **:** to cut (a metal) with a gas flame

flamed \'flāmd\ *adj* [1*flame* + *-ed*] **:** having markings suggesting flames ⟨a ~ maple veneer⟩; *esp, of a tulip* **:** having a broad irregular mark up the center of each petal

flameflower \'=,==\ *n* **:** KNIPHOFIA 2

flame-harden \'=,==\ *vt* **:** to harden (a ferrous alloy) by heating above the transformation temperature and then cooling as rapidly as necessary

flameholder \'=,==\ *n* **:** a device used to maintain continuous combustion in a flowing mixture in the combustion chamber of certain jet engines

flame·less \'flāmləs\ *adj* **:** having or producing no flame ⟨~ fuels⟩ — **flame·less·ly** *adv*

flame·let \'flāmlət\ *n* -s **:** a small or feeble flame

flame lily *n* **1 :** WOOD LILY 1b **2 :** ATAMASCO LILY

flame lousewort *n* **:** a lousewort (*Pedicularis flammea*) of arctic America and Europe with crimson-purple flowers

fla·men \'flāmən, -läm-\ *n, pl* **fla·mens** \-nz\ *or* **flam·i·nes** \'flamə,nēz, -läm-\ [ME *flamin*, fr. L *flamin-*, *flamen*; perh. akin to OE *blōtan* to sacrifice, OHG *bluozan*, ON *blōta* to sacrifice, Goth *blotan* to worship] **:** a priest devoted to the service of a particular god of the Roman pantheon

fla·men·co \flə'meŋ(,)kō\ *n* -s [Sp, Fleming, Flemish, buxom and ruddy, resembling a Gypsy, being in Gypsy style, gaudy, fr. MD *Vlaminc* Fleming] **1 a :** a vigorous rhythmic dance style of the Andalusian Gypsies; *also* **:** a dance in this style **b :** music or song accompanying or suitable to accompany such a dance which is often more or less impromptu and shows distinct Arab influence; *also* **:** a piece of such music **2 :** a Spanish Gypsy; *sometimes* **:** Spanish Gypsy custom or style **3 :** a brightly colored snapper (*Lutjanus guttatus*) of the Pacific coast from Mexico to Ecuador having the sides bright red, the back green, and the undersurface silvery and bearing red dorsal and caudal fins and yellowish anal and ventral fins

flame nettle *n* **:** a plant of the genus *Coleus*

flame-of-the-woods \¦=====¦=\ *n, pl* **flames-of-the-woods :** an East Indian shrub (*Ixora coccinea*) with showy scarlet flowers

flame orange *n* **:** a strong orange that is deeper and slightly redder than pumpkin and redder and deeper than cadmium orange

flameout \'=,=\ *n* -s [2*flame* + *out*] **:** the cessation of operation of a jet aircraft engine (as through improper combustion or exhaustion of the fuel supply) — called also *blowout*

flame peeling *n* **:** the exposure of fruit or vegetables to intense heat to char the peel and facilitate its rapid removal by a powerful stream of water

flame photometer *n* **:** a spectrophotometer in which a spray of metallic salts in solution is vaporized in a very hot flame and subjected to quantitative analysis by measuring the intensities of the spectrum lines of the metals present — **flame photometric** *adj* — **flame photometry** *n*

flame projector *n* **:** FLAMETHROWER

1flameproof \'=¦=\ *adj* **1 :** resistant to the action of flame **:** not burning on contact with flame; *esp* **:** not tending to propagate fire if ignited **2 :** safeguarded against causing destructive explosion (as by generating sparks) — used esp. of machinery in mines, oil refineries, cereal mills

2flameproof \"\ *vt* **:** to make flameproof

flam·er \'flāmə(r)\ *n* -s **:** one that flames

flame reaction *n* **:** the characteristic coloration that certain chemical elements or their compounds impart to a nonluminous flame (as yellow from sodium or green from copper)

flame red *n* **:** a strong reddish orange that is redder and slightly duller than poppy, redder and slightly paler than paprika, redder and deeper than flame, and redder and deeper than average coral red — compare FIERY RED, FIRE RED, FLAME

flames *pres 3d sing of* FLAME, *pl of* FLAME

flame scarlet *n* **:** a strong reddish orange that is yellower and lighter than fire red and yellower and paler than flame red, poppy, or flame — called also *Florentine*

flame spectrum *n* **:** the spectrum obtained by volatilizing substances in a nonluminous flame

flamethrower \'=,==\ *n* **:** a device that expels from a nozzle a burning stream of liquid or semiliquid fuel under pressure and is used in war esp. to penetrate enclosures (as tanks or pillboxes) or in agriculture to kill insects or weeds

flame trap *n* **:** a device (as a wire gauze across a nozzle inlet) for preventing the flame of burning gas from backing up into the supply pipe and causing an explosion

flame tree *n* **:** any of several trees or shrubs with showy scarlet or yellow flowers: as **a :** either of two Australian trees: (1) **:** a bottle tree (*Brachychiton acerifolium*) of southern Australia with panicles of brilliant scarlet flowers (2) **:** a small evergreen tree (*Nuytsia floribunda*) of the family Loranthaceae that is restricted to western Australia and is distinguished by axillary racemes of yellow-orange flowers **b :** ROYAL POINCIANA **c :** HUISACHE

flame tube *n* **:** a heat-resistant ceramic or metal tube inside the combustion chamber of a jet engine in which the actual combustion takes place

flame vine *n* **:** a Brazilian woody vine (*Pyrostegia ignea*) of the family Bignoniaceae that has tendril-bearing compound leaves and orange-red tubular flowers in clusters and that is widely cultivated in warm regions

flameware \'=,=\ *n* **:** cooking ware (as of glass) that can be used over an open flame without breaking

flame weeder *n* **:** FLAME CULTIVATOR

flamines *pl of* FLAMEN

1flaming *adj* [fr. pres. part. of 2*flame*] **1 :** emitting flames **:** BLAZING ⟨a ~ crackling fire⟩ **2 a :** of the color of flame; *usu* **:** of the color flame scarlet, flame red, flame, or fire red ⟨her ~ hat clashed madly with a purple coat and orange scarf⟩ **b :** highly chromatic **:** brilliantly colored ⟨the ~ sunset sky⟩ **3 :** suggesting a flame in having a wavy outline **4 a :** ARDENT, PASSIONATE ⟨a ~ devotion⟩ ⟨~ youth⟩ **b :** burning with zeal **:** irrepressibly earnest ⟨a ~ speaker kindling in his hearers a love of righteousness⟩ **c :** extravagant or monstrous ⟨repeated some of the most ~ tales⟩ **5** *slang Austral* — used as a generalized intensive; compare 1BLOODY 6 — **flam·ing·ly** *adv*

2flaming *n* -s [fr. gerund of 2*flame*] **:** the process of reheating glass in a reducing flame to bring out the color imparted by a metallic base

fla·min·gant \flämaⁿgäⁿ\ *n, pl* **flamingants** \-äⁿ(z)\ *usu cap* [F, Flemish-speaking, fr. pres. part. of F dial. (Walloon) *flaminguer* to speak Flemish, fr. Flem *Vlaming* Fleming, fr. MD *Vlaminc*] **:** one of the party among the Flemings of Belgium that seeks to revive Flemish to the exclusion of French

fla·min·go \flə'miŋ(,)gō\ *n, pl* **flamingos** *also* **flamingoes** [Pg, fr. Sp *flamenco*, prob. fr. OProv *flamenc*, fr. *flama* flame, blaze, fire (fr. L *flamma*) + *-enc* 2-ing, of Gmc origin — more at FLAME] **1 :** any of several aquatic birds that constitute the family Phoenicopteridae and with related extinct birds the suborder Phoenicopteri of the order Ciconiiformes, that have remarkably long legs and neck, webbed feet, a broad lamellated bill resembling that of a duck but abruptly bent downward, and usu. rosy-white plumage with scarlet wing coverts and black wing quills, and that are gregarious, breeding in colonies and building nests of mud in swamps and shallow lagoons and laying but one or two eggs **2 :** a moderate reddish orange that is duller and slightly redder than crab apple and redder and lighter than burnt ocher **3 :** a synchronized swimming stunt executed from a back layout position in which the legs are brought successively to the vertical and held in such position while the upper trunk drops backward to a head-down position after which the body is submerged

flamingo flower *or* **flamingo plant** *n* **:** either of two commonly cultivated anthuriums (*Anthurium scherzerianum* and *A. andraeanum*) with bright scarlet spathe and spadix

flaming pinkster *n* [*flaming* (pres. part. of 2*flame*) + *pinkster* (as in *pinkster flower*)] **:** FLAME AZALEA

flaming poppy *n* **:** WIND POPPY

fla·min·i·an \flə'minēən\ *adj, usu cap* [L *flaminianus*, fr. Gaius *Flaminius* †217B.C. Roman general and statesman + L *-anus* -an] **:** of or relating to the Roman censor Gaius Flaminius or the public works which he executed ⟨the *Flaminian* Way led northward from Rome⟩

fla·min·i·ca \flə'minəkə\ *n* -S [L, fr. *flamin-, flamen* flamen] **:** the wife of a flamen

flam·ma·bil·i·ty \,flamə'bilәd·ē, -lətē, -i\ *n* -ES **:** ability to support combustion **:** burning rate ⟨few materials completely lack ~⟩; *usu* **:** high capacity for combustion ⟨the dangerous ~ of certain otherwise valuable organic solvents⟩

1**flam·ma·ble** \'flaməbəl\ *adj* [L *flammare* to flame, set on fire + E *-able* — more at FLAME] **:** capable of being easily ignited and of burning with extreme rapidity — now used technically in preference to *inflammable;* compare COMBUSTIBLE, EXPLOSIVE ⟨cannot be used for safety reasons in coal mines in which ~ gases are present —A.C.Morrison⟩

2**flammable** \"\ *n* -S **:** a flammable substance

flam·ma·tion \fla'māshən, flə'-\ *n* -S [L *flammare* + E *-ation*] **:** an act of setting afire **:** IGNITING

flammed *past of* FLAM

flam·me·ous \'flamēəs\ *adj* [L *flammeus*, fr. *flamma* flame — more at FLAME] **:** consisting of or resembling the color of flame ⟨a ~ flycatcher⟩

flam·mif·er·ous \(')fla¦mif(ə)rəs, flə'm-\ *adj* [L *flammifer* flammiferous (*fr. flammi-* — fr. *flamma* flame — + *-fer*) + E *-ous*] **:** producing or bright with flame

flamming *pres part of* FLAM

flam·mu·lat·ed \'flamyə,lād·əd\ *adj* [L *flammula* small flame + E *-ate* + *-ed* — more at FLAME] **:** having flame-shaped markings — used of the plumage of certain birds — **flam·mu·la·tion** \,==='lāshən\ *n* -S

flam·mule \'fla,myül\ *n* -S [L *flammula*] **:** a small flame; *esp* **:** one shown in a picture of a Chinese or Japanese god

flams *pres 3d sing of* FLAM, *pl of* FLAM

flamy \'flāmē, -mi\ *adj* [ME *flaumy*, fr. *flaume* flame + *-y* — more at FLAME] **1 :** composed of flame **:** FLAMING, BLAZING **2 a :** resembling flame esp. in color **b :** of the color flame

1**flan** \'flan\ *n* -S [ME (Sc), fr. ON, rush, fr. *flana* to rush heedlessly; akin to Gk *planasthai* to wander — more at PLANET] *Scot* **:** a sudden gust of wind

2**flan** \"\ *vi* **flanned; flanned; flanning; flans** [perh. alter. (influenced by obs. *flan*, adj., spreading and shallow) of *flanch*, v.] *dial* **:** to expand or widen toward the top

3**flan** \'flan, 'flän, 'fläⁿ\ *n* -S [F, fr. OF *flaon*, fr. LL *fladon-, flado* flat cake, of Gmc origin; akin to OHG *flado* sacrificial cake; akin to Gk *platys* flat, broad — more at PLACE] **1 :** a large open pie usu. with straight sides filled with custard, cheese, jam, or fruit and often glazed with fruit syrup **2 :** the metal disk of a coin, token, or medal as distinguished from the design and lettering stamped on it

flan·card *or* **flan·chard** \'flaŋkə(r)d\ *n* -S [MF *flancard*, fr. *flanc* flank + *-ard*] *archaic* **:** a piece of armor for the thigh or flank

1**flanch** *also* **flanche** \'flanch, -á-\ *or* **flaunch** *or* **flaunche** \-ȯ-,-ä-\ *n* -ES [ME *flaunche*, prob. fr. MF *flanche* flank, fr. *flanc*] **:** either of two curved segments encroaching on a heraldic field one from each side

flanches

2**flanch** \'flánch\ *n* -ES [perh. fr. 1*flanch*] *Brit* **:** a flange esp. of a wheel

3**flanch** \"\ *vb* -ED/-ING/-ES *vi* **:** to slant outward **:** FLARE ~ *vt* **:** draw in toward the top — used with *up* and esp. of a chimney ⟨~ up the chimney so that it will shed rain⟩

flanched \-cht\ *adj* [1*flanch* + *-ed*] **:** having flanches

flan·con·nade *also* **flan·co·nade** \¦flaŋkə¦nād, -nȧd\ *n* -S [F, irreg. fr. *flanc* flank] **:** a bind in fencing that terminates in a thrust under the adversary's arm

flan·dan \'flan,dan\ *n* -S [origin unknown] **:** a woman's pinner of a style used in the 17th century

flan·der·kin \'flandə(r)kən\ *n* -S *usu cap* [*Flanders* + *-kin*] *archaic* **:** FLEMING

flan·ders baby \'flan|də(r)z-, 'flaan|, 'flân|\ *n, usu cap F* [*Flanders*, region in western Belgium and the adjacent part of northern France + E *baby*] **:** a wooden doll produced in the Netherlands and popular in England in the 18th and 19th centuries

flanders brick *n, usu cap F* **:** BATH BRICK

flanders poppy *n, usu cap F* **:** CORN POPPY

flane *n* -S [ME (Sc & dial. of northern England) *flan, flane*, fr. OE *flān;* akin to ON *fleinn* dart and perh. to OE *flint* — more at FLINT] *obs* **:** ARROW

flâ·ne·rie \(')flän¦rē\ *n* -S [F, fr. MF *flanerie*, fr. (assumed) MF dial. (Normandy) *flaner* to saunter aimlessly (whence F *flâner*) + MF *-erie* -ery] **:** aimless or idle quality or state

flâ·neur \(')flä¦nər(·)\ *n* -S [F *flâneur* idler, fr. MF *flaneur*, fr. (assumed) MF dial. (Normandy) *flaner* to saunter aimlessly (fr. ON *flana* to wander about) + MF *-eur* -or (fr. L *-or*) — more at FLAN] **:** an aimless and usu. self-centered and superficial person: as **a :** MAN-ABOUT-TOWN, BON VIVEUR **b :** an intellectual trifler

flâ·neuse \-¦nərz, -¦nōz\ *n* -S [F *flâneuse*, fem. of *flâneur*] **:** a woman who is or who behaves like a flaneur

1**flang** *dial past of* FLING

2**flang** \¦flaŋ, -aiŋ\ *n* -S [origin unknown] **:** a miner's pick with two points

1**flange** \'flanj, -aa(ə)nj\ *n* -S [perh. alter. of 1*flanch*] **1 :** a spreading out (as of a vein of ore) **2 a :** a rim or edge (as on a shaft or a pipe fitting) projecting at right angles to provide strength or means of attachment to another part **b :** a projecting edge around the inside rim of a car or locomotive wheel to guide and keep it on the track **c :** the wide portion at the top and bottom of an I beam, channel, or plate girder — compare WEB **d :** a projecting edge, tuck, or insert of cloth used for decoration on clothing **3 :** a foundry molder's tool for forming flanges

flange 2d

2**flange** \"\ *vb* -ED/-ING/-S *vt* **:** to make a flange on **:** furnish with a flange ⟨*flanging* the lead to make a joint⟩ ~ *vi* **1 :** to widen or spread — used with *out* ⟨the swollen stream *flanged* out over the lowlands⟩ **2 :** to shape flanges ⟨it is easier to ~ by machine than by hand⟩

flange·less \-ləs\ *adj* **:** lacking a flange

flangeless tire *n* **:** BALD TIRE

flange nut *n* **:** a nut with an enlarged base that obviates the need for a washer

flange plate *n* **:** COVER PLATE 2

flang·er \-jə(r)\ *n* -S **1 :** one that makes or repairs flanges: as **a :** a worker who flanges the tops of glass flasks **b :** a worker who prepares or adjusts flanges on metal plates (as in shipbuilding) **c :** a worker who forms the flanges of glass tubes used for hypodermic syringe cylinders **d :** a worker who shapes hat brims by pressing **e :** a tool or machine for forming flanges **2 :** a scraper for clearing ice and snow from the inside of railroad rails to provide clearance for the wheel flanges

flange rail *n* **1 :** a railroad rail with a flange on one side formerly used to keep wheels from running off the track and now replaced by the T rail **2 :** T RAIL — compare BULLHEADED 3b

flange steel *n* **:** steel ductile enough to be flanged esp. for the heads of steam boilers

flange turner *n* **:** a worker who performs any or all machine and hand operations necessary to form flanges on heavy steel plates used in boilermaking or automobile, locomotive, or ship building **:** FLANGER

flange union *n* **:** a pair of companion flanges for bolting or welding together

flangeway \'=,=\ *n* **:** the passageway for the flange of a wheel running on rails

1**flank** \'flaŋk, -aiŋk\ *n* -S *often attrib* [ME, fr. OF *flanc*, of Gmc origin; akin to OHG *hlanca* loin, flank — more at LANK] **1 a :** the fleshy part of the side between the ribs and the hip; *broadly* **:** the side of a quadruped ⟨the horse stood with quivering ~s⟩ — see COW illustration **b :** a cut of meat from this part of an animal — see BEEF illustration **c :** hide or leather from the flank or belly of an animal **2 a :** SIDE ⟨sheltering on the ~ of the hill⟩ **b :** the right or left of a formation (as a line of battle, a line of scrimmage, a marching column) ⟨attacked the enemy on both ~s⟩ **c :** the part of a bastion that reaches from the curtain to the face and defends the curtain and the flank and face of the opposite bastion **d :** either side of a fortification — see BASTION illustration **3 a :** the area along either side of an escutcheon — see POINT illustration **b :** the central part of this area **4 a :** the profile of the root of a gear tooth or the portion of a gear tooth between the root and the pitch circle **b :** the contacting face of a screw thread **c :** either side of a cutting tool (as a chisel) intersecting the cutting edge and adjacent to the face

2**flank** \"\ *vb* -ED/-ING/-S *vt* **1 :** to shelter or protect a side of ⟨used cavalry to stabilize and ~ the infantry during an attack⟩ ⟨a wall ~*ed* with tall towers⟩ **2 a :** to attack or threaten the flank of (as a body of troops) **b :** to turn the flank of ⟨the reserve forces were unexpectedly ~*ed* and immobilized by a detachment of tanks⟩ **3 a :** to stand or be situated at the side of **:** border esp. on each side ⟨a long avenue ~*ed* with lindens⟩ **b :** to place something on each side of ⟨by ~*ing* the mirror with tall candelabra⟩ **4** *archaic* **:** ESCAPE, EVADE ⟨successfully ~*ed* his pursuers⟩ ⟨the recruits ~*ed* drill whenever possible⟩ ~ *vi* **1 :** to be placed or move to, toward, or along a side ⟨at the wave of his handler's hand the dog ~*ed* off and turned the straggling sheep⟩ **2 :** to present the flank — used with *on* ⟨the fort ~*ed* on a swamp⟩

3**flank** \"\ *vt* -ED/-ING/-S [prob. imit.] **:** FLICK, FLIP

flank angle *n* **:** the angle between the flank of a screw thread and the perpendicular to the axis of the screw

1**flank·er** \-kə(r)\ *n* -S **:** one that flanks: as **a :** something that adjoins on the side (as a fort commanding the flank of an assailing force); *esp* **:** a lateral wing of a building ⟨the great kitchen took up most of the long west ~⟩ **b :** men so posted or marched as to protect the flank of a column on the march **c** *chiefly Brit* **:** a driver posted on the flank of the line of a grouse drive to turn birds that tend to break away **d** *West* **:** a cowhand who throws a roped calf on its side for branding **e :** an animal (as a sheep) that stays off to one side of a grazing herd **f :** a football player who takes a place on the line to the right of the right end or to the left of the left end

2**flank·er** \"\ *vt* -ED/-ING/-S *obs* **:** to defend or support by flankers

3**flan·ker** \"\ *n* -S [obs. *flanker*, v., to sparkle] **:** a large spark thrown off by a wood fire esp. up a chimney

flank guard *n* **:** a detachment charged with the protection of a flank of a marching force

flanking *n* -S [fr. gerund of 2*flank*] **:** the maneuvering of towed barges around a bend in a river by means of a towboat at the rear which is backed as a brake so that the barges are controlled but brought around the bend primarily by the current of the river

flanking fire *also* **flank fire** *n* **:** fire delivered on an enemy flank from a position to the side of that enemy

flank speed *n* **:** the full speed of which a ship is capable ⟨proceeding at *flank speed*⟩

flank steak *n* **:** the triangular internal oblique muscle of the beef flank — see BEEF illustration

flank vault *n* **:** a vault made with one supporting hand, both legs extended to one side, and the body facing ahead throughout

flankwise \'=,=\ *adv* (*or adj*) **:** on, along, about, or by way of the flank ⟨a ~ movement of cavalry⟩ ⟨charged the enemy ~⟩

flanky \'flaŋkē, -aiŋ-, -ki\ *adj* [1*flank* + *-y*] **1** *of leather* **:** having a loose coarse texture **2** *of a body* **:** well-developed in the flank region ⟨a soft ~ torso⟩

flanned *past of* FLAN

1**flan·nel** \'flan^əl\ *n* -S *often attrib* [ME *flaunneol*, a woolen cloth or garment, *flanyn*, a penitential garment, prob. fr. (assumed) MW *gwlanen* flannel (whence W *gwlanen*), fr. (assumed) MW *gwlân* wool (whence W *gwlân*); akin to L *lana* wool — more at WOOL] **1 a :** a soft twilled fabric with a loose texture and a slightly napped surface made in various weights of wool or worsted yarns and often in combination with cotton or synthetic yarns **b :** a napped cotton fabric of soft yarns simulating the texture of wool flannel: (1) **:** FLANNELETTE (2) **:** a stout cotton fabric usu. softly napped on one side and twilled on the other and used esp. for work gloves, filters, polishing cloths (as for shoes), and linings — called also *Canton flannel* (3) **:** OUTING FLANNEL **2 flannels** *pl* **a :** warm undergarments of flannel or sometimes of knit fabric; *esp* **:** men's long underdrawers **b :** outer garments of flannel; *esp* **:** men's trousers **c :** flannel garments forming a uniform (as of a club or team) **d** *Brit* **:** the place on a team represented by the wearing of such flannels or an individual holding such a place **3** *Brit* **:** WASHCLOTH

2**flannel** \"\ *vt* **flanneled** *or* **flannelled; flanneled** *or* **flannelled; flanneling** *or* **flannelling; flannels :** to clothe or enclose in or rub with flannel

flannel board *n* **:** a display board covered with flannel or felt to which suitably backed matter (as for the illustration of a lesson or lecture) adheres when pressed firmly in contact

flannelbush \'==,=\ *n* **:** a Californian and Mexican shrub (*Fremontia californica*) having a felty covering on the lower leaf surfaces

flannel cake *n, chiefly East & Midland* **:** a griddlecake esp. of wheat flour

flan·nel·ette \¦flan^əl¦et, *usu* -ed·+V\ *n* -S **:** a cotton flannel napped on one or both sides and used esp. for undergarments and nightwear

flannelflower \'==,=\ *n* **1 :** MULLEIN **2 :** a Brazilian vine (*Macrosiphonia longiflora*) of the family Apocynaceae having woolly leaves **3 :** an Australian plant (*Actinotus helianthi*) of the family Umbelliferae of which the umbels have a white velvety involucre — called also *satinflower*

flannelgraph \'==,=\ *n* **:** one of the figures used on a flannel board (as for illustrating a story or lecture) ⟨developed the idea with ~s against a pictorial background⟩

flannelleaf \'==,=\ *also* **flannel plant** *n* **:** a mullein (*Verbascum thapsus*)

flan·nel·ly \'flan^əlē, -^əli\ *adj* [1*flannel* + *-y*] **1** *of the voice* **:** blurred and muted as if heard through flannel **2 :** resembling flannel esp. in soft fluffy texture or appearance ⟨the sky full of ~ little clouds⟩

flannel moth *n* **:** a moth of the family Megalopygidae most of which have very hairy larvae

flannelmouth \'==,=\ *n* **:** a flannelmouthed person

flannelmouthed \¦==¦=\ *adj* **1 :** talking thickly with or as if with a brogue ⟨a ~ immigrant right off the boat⟩ **2 :** SMOOTH-SPOKEN **:** oily or tricky in speech

flannelmouthed sucker *n* **:** a large fish (*Catostomus latipinnis*) formerly used as food by Indians of the Colorado river region

flan·nen \'flanən\ *n* -S [ME *flanyn*, a penitential garment] *dial* **:** FLANNEL

flanning *pres part of* FLAN

flans *pres 3d sing of* FLAN, *pl of* FLAN

1**flap** \'flap\ *n* -S [ME *flappe*, prob. of imit. origin; in senses 5, 6, and 7, prob. fr. 2*flap*] **1** *obs* **:** STROKE, BLOW; *often* **:** a stroke with something broad (as the open hand) **:** SLAP **2** *obs* **:** something broad and flat (as a flyswatter) used for striking **3 :** something that is broad, limber, or flat and usu. thin and that hangs loose or projects freely: as **a :** a hinged leaf or fold (as of a table, door, or shutter) **b :** half of a hinge having two broad leaves through which screw holes are pierced esp. when one of them is to be screwed to the face of a door or shutter instead of to the edge — see STRAP HINGE **c** (1) **:** a piece on a garment that hangs free ⟨double ~s set off the pockets⟩ or can be adjusted to hang free ⟨a storm cap with a wool-lined ~ that can be pulled down to protect the ears⟩ (2) **:** a tongue of a shoe (3) **:** a brim of a hat **d** (1) **:** a projecting edge of a flexible book cover (as in a divinity circuit binding) (2) **:** a part of a book jacket that folds under the book's cover **e :** a piece of tissue partly severed from its place of origin for use in surgical grafting and repair of bodily defects **f :** an extended part that forms the closure of a bag, envelope, carton, or fiberboard case **g :** a cloth or rubber strip inserted between the tube and the beads of an automobile tire to protect the tube from contact with the rim **h :** a movable auxiliary airfoil usu. attached to the trailing edge of an airplane wing to increase wing resistance **4 :** a flat piece, slice, or layer ⟨a ~ of bread⟩ **5 a :** the motion of something broad and limber (as a sail or wing) ⟨the steady ~ of northbound wings⟩; *also* **:** a single stroke of such motion ⟨the sail gave a ~ as the breeze died⟩ **b :** the sound of such motion ⟨startled by the sudden ~ of a loose shutter⟩ **c :** a brush followed by a step on the same foot in tap dancing **6 :** an energetic single bouncing of the tip of the tongue against the hard palate (as in a frequent American articulation of the *tt* in *Betty* or a frequent southern British articulation of the *rr* in *berry*) **7 a :** a state of excitement or panicky confusion **:** HULLABALOO ⟨the president's statement had everybody in a ~⟩ **b :** CRISIS ⟨when there was a ~ abroad —Thomas Braden⟩

2**flap** \"\ *vb* **flapped; flapped; flapping; flaps** [ME *flappen*, fr. *flappe*, n.] *vt* **1 a** *obs* **:** STRIKE, CLAP **b :** to beat with or as if with a flap **:** strike with a surface (as of a bird's wing or of a flyswatter) ⟨the loose scarf *flapped* his face⟩ **2 a :** to toss sharply **:** FLING — usu. used with *down* ⟨*flapped* the paper down angrily⟩ **b :** to turn (as a pancake) by tossing **3 :** to move or cause to move in flaps ⟨a bird *flapping* its wings⟩ ⟨the uncertain breezes ~ the sails⟩ **4 :** to arouse the attention of by or as if by striking with a flap ⟨sent an emissary to ~ the local agents⟩ **5 :** to lower the flap of (as a hat or cap) **6 :** to break (the surface of the slag) in the fire-refining of copper by striking with a rabble, exposing the molten metal to the air, and hastening oxidation **7 :** to utter with a flap articulation ⟨a *flapped r*⟩ ~ *vi* **1 :** to give a quick blow (as with the hand) **:** CLAP **2 :** to sway loosely usu. with a noise of striking and esp. when moved by wind ⟨the tent *flapped* in the rising breeze⟩ **3 a :** to beat or pulsate wings or something suggesting wings ⟨the children *flapped* with their arms as they scurried down the hill⟩ **b :** to progress by flapping ⟨early ideas of airplanes that would ~ like birds⟩ **c** *of a rotor blade* **:** to move up and down while rotating at the center **4 a :** to flutter ineffectively (as by beating of wings) ⟨the bird *flapping* helplessly against the screen⟩ **b :** to act or move erratically or to little effect ⟨such childish *flapping* to and fro will get you nowhere⟩ **5 :** to talk foolishly or to no purpose — usu. used with *about* ⟨the thing's settled, there's no use *flapping* about it now⟩ ⟨all he does is ~ about his own importance⟩

flapdock \'=,=\ *n* **:** a foxglove (*Digitalis purpurea*)

flap·doo·dle \'flap,düd^əl\ *n* -S [origin unknown] **:** foolish, empty, and often specious talk, writing, ideas, or opinions **:** NONSENSE ⟨his book contains a number of good pieces and a quantity of ~ as well —John Lardner⟩

flapdragon \'=,==\ *n* **1 :** SNAPDRAGON 3 **2** *obs* **:** GERMAN, DUTCHMAN — usu. used disparagingly

flap-eared \'=¦=\ *adj* **1** *of a human* **:** having large ears standing well out from the head **2** *of a quadruped* **:** having large flexible or pendent ears

flap gate *n* **:** a gate hinged at the top and opening one way only and placed in a channel to close automatically on reversal of flow — compare FLAP VALVE

flap hinge *n* **:** STRAP HINGE

flapjack \'=,=\ *n* [2*flap* + *Jack* (the name)] **1 :** GRIDDLE CAKE **2** *chiefly dial* **:** a fruit turnover **3** *also* **flapjack terrapin** *or* **flapjack turtle :** a No. American soft-shelled turtle **4** *chiefly Brit* **:** a large flat circular compact for face powder

flap-jawed \'=¦=\ *adj* **:** inclined to talk excessively and often indiscreetly ⟨fed up at the *flap-jawed* way some . . . columnists were talking —*Time*⟩

flapmouthed \'=¦=\ *adj* **:** FLAP-JAWED

flapped \'flapt\ *adj* [1*flap* + *-ed*] **:** fitted or adorned with flaps ⟨a ~ pocket⟩

1**flap·per** \'flapə(r)\ *n* -S **1 :** one that flaps: as **a :** a person or thing that reminds or warns one of something likely to be overlooked ⟨a spring ~ can be built into the clutch to sound a warning —A.F.Cragne⟩ **:** one that jogs the memory ⟨till their memories were again roused by their ~s —Jonathan Swift⟩ **b :** something for use in flapping or striking (as a flyswatter) **c :** a part that hangs or droops (as the swingle of a flail) **d :** FLIPPER 1 **e** *Brit* **:** a young game bird; *esp* **:** a young wild duck not yet able to fly well **f** *slang* **:** HAND 1a(1) **g :** a worker who strikes the surface of molten metal with a rabble in copper refining **2 :** a young woman: **a** *archaic* **:** an immoral or dissolute young woman **b** *chiefly Brit* **:** a young girl not yet introduced to society — compare BUD **c :** a young woman who aggressively manifests freedom from constraint and conventions in conduct and dress — used esp. during the period of World War I and the following decade **d** *Brit* **:** a woman between 21 and 30 years of age — used disparagingly during the period that the vote was withheld from women below 30 years of age in Britain

2**flapper** \"\ *vi* **flappered; flappered; flappering** \-p(ə)riŋ\ **flappers :** to move in a flapping way

flapping *pres part of* FLAP

flapping meeting *also* **flapper meeting** *n, Brit* **:** an irregular horse race or series of horse races not under the supervision of any authoritative body

flap·py \'flapē, -pi\ *adj* -ER/-EST [2*flap* + *-y*] **1 :** SLACK, FLABBY ⟨~ skin⟩ **2 :** flapping or likely to flap ⟨long ~ hound ears⟩ ⟨loose ~ trousers⟩

flaps *pl of* FLAP, *pres 3d sing of* FLAP

flap table *n* **:** a drop-leaf table

flap tile *n* **:** a tile with a bent-up portion (as at a corner)

flap valve *also* **flapper valve** *n* **:** a valve (as in a pump) composed of a disk hinged on one edge and swinging one way only

1**flare** \'fla(a)|(ə)r, 'fle|, |ə\ *vb* -ED/-ING/-S [origin unknown] *vi* **1 a :** to stream or flutter in or as if in a current of air ⟨her coat *flared* behind her as she ran⟩ **b :** to burn with an unsteady or wavering flame ⟨the candle *flared* in the breeze as the door opened⟩ **2 a :** to shine with a sudden light **:** flame up brightly ⟨the fire *flared* brightly when the log crumbled into coals⟩; *often* **:** to emit a dazzling or painfully bright light ⟨the new snow *flaring* under the spring sun⟩ ⟨arc lights *flared*⟩ **b :** to become suddenly excited or angry **:** get in a passion (as of rage) — usu. used with *up* ⟨she ~s up at the slightest thing⟩ **c :** to express anger, passion, or vehement disapproval — usu. used with *out* ⟨she *flared* out at him furiously⟩ ⟨*flaring* out at such abuses⟩ **d :** to burst forth ⟨tempers *flared*⟩ **3 :** to open or spread outward **:** project beyond the perpendicular **:** have a flare usu. in a specified direction ⟨her skirt *flaring* about her legs⟩ ⟨a boat of shallow draft with the gunwales *flaring* out⟩ ~ *vt* **1 a :** to make to stream or flutter in or as if in a breeze ⟨the wind *flared* her skirts⟩ **b :** to display flaringly ⟨*flaring* a scarf from side to side to catch their eye⟩ **2 a :** to cause to flare ⟨the breeze *flared* the candle⟩ **b :** to give the appearance of a flaring flame ⟨sunset *flared* the western sky⟩ **c :** to signal with a flare or by flaring ⟨torches *flaring* the alarm⟩ **d :** to burn (a jet of waste gas) in the open air **3 :** to shape with a flare **:** spread gradually outward in shaping ⟨*flared* the coat with inset panels⟩ ⟨as the potter *flares* the neck of a jar⟩ ⟨gloved hands folded on a *flared* umbrella —Alan Brien⟩ **4 :** to level the flight path of (an airplane) just before making contact with the ground in landing so as to achieve a smooth transition from the steady glide to the ground run **syn** see BLAZE

2**flare** \"\ *n* -S **1 :** an unsteady glaring light **2 :** a strong or flaring fire or blaze of light: as **a** *or* **flare light :** such a flare used to illuminate or attract attention (as on an airfield or battleground at night or as a prearranged signal); *also* **:** a device or composition (as a torch, Very light, or magnesium ribbon) used to produce such a flare **b :** SOLAR FLARE **c :** the flame of a jet of waste gas (as from a sewage-disposal plant or coke oven) burned in open air for disposal **3 a :** a sudden outburst (as of sound, excitement, or anger) ⟨a harsh ~ of trumpets⟩ ⟨a ~ of temper⟩ **4** *sometimes* **flair :** a spreading outward or a place or part that spreads ⟨the ~ of a fireplace⟩ ⟨the ~ of an urn⟩: as **a :** the upward and outward curve of the bow of a ship that throws aside spray when in motion **b :** fullness produced by gradually increasing the width towards the edge of a garment (as a gored skirt) **c :** an area of skin flush resulting from and spreading out from a local center of vascular dilation and hyperemia ⟨urticaria ~⟩ **d** *usu* **flair :** a tapered widening of the flangeway at the end of the guard line of a railroad track structure (as at the end of a guardrail or at the end of a frog or crossing wing rail) **5 :** light resulting from interreflection (as between lens surfaces) or an effect of this light: **a :** non-image-forming light that reaches the sensitive film in a camera **b** *or* **flare spot :** the resulting fogged or dense area in a photographic negative

³flare \"\ *n* -s [perh. alter. of *⁴fleck*] *Brit* **:** LEAF FAT

flareback \ˈ=,=\ *n* -s [*¹flare* + *back*, adv.] **1 :** a burst of flame back or out from a furnace or similar space in opposition to the normal direction of the draft **2 :** an outburst (as of protest or angry rebuke) in response to a previous statement, criticism, or other cause **3 :** a burst of flame from the breech of a heavy gun that sometimes occurs on the opening of the breech when the gun has been fired and is due to gases left in the gun which ignite on admission of the air if a spark is present

flareboard \ˈ=,=\ *n* **:** a slanting extension of either side of an open box or frame (as on a wagon or motortruck) that increases the capacity

flare gun *or* **flare pistol** *n* **:** a handgun for firing signal rockets

flare kiln *n* **:** a kiln built of brick, shaped like the top and neck of a bottle, and formerly used to burn chalk and limestone into quicklime

flare·less \-ləs\ *adj* **:** free from flare: as **a** *of an explosive* **:** exploding without flame **b** *of a garment* **:** having straight lines without flared fullness

flare-out \ˈ=,=\ *n* -s [*¹flare* + *out*] **:** a leveling of the approach glide of an airplane made in such a way that the gliding angle is rapidly decreased by nosing up the airplane as it makes contact with the ground

flare path *n* **:** a path outlined by lights (as flares or electric lamps) on the ground to guide an airplane pilot in landing

flar·er \-a(a)rə(r), -erə-\ *n* -s **1 :** an operator of a machine that coils and flares strips of hoop steel for barrels — called also *coiler* **2 :** an operator of a machine that shapes riveted barrel hoops by alternate expansion and contraction

flare star *n* **:** a star (as a faint red dwarf) that undergoes sudden and unpredicted increases in brightness amounting often to several magnitudes in only a few minutes and fades as quickly

flare-up \ˈ=,=\ *n* -s [fr. *flare up* (verb phrase), fr. *¹flare* + *up*] **1 a :** a sudden bursting into flame or light **:** FLARING ⟨a sharp *flare-up* of the dying fire⟩ ⟨excessive head lamp *flare-up* when engine speed is increased —H.F.Blanchard & Ralph Ritchen⟩ **b** *or* **flare-up light :** a brilliantly flammable torch or flare used for signaling or emergency illumination (as on a fishing boat) **2 :** a sudden outburst: as **a :** an outburst of anger, discontent, or antagonism usu. leading to heated words or violent action ⟨struck his brother in a *flare-up* of fury⟩ **b :** a sudden intensification of something previously mild or quiescent ⟨a *flare-up* of labor disputes⟩ ⟨a new *flare-up* of border disorders⟩; *esp* **:** a sudden increase in the symptoms of a latent or subsiding disease ⟨a *flare-up* of malaria⟩

flaring *adj* [fr. pres. part. of *¹flare*] **1 a :** flaming or blazing brightly or unsteadily; *often* **:** DAZZLING **b :** gaudy and glaring ⟨a ~ resort hotel⟩ **2 a :** opening or spreading outward ⟨a ~ neckline⟩ **b :** having flare ⟨a graceful boat with a ~ bow⟩ — **flar·ing·ly** *adv*

flary \-a(a)rē, -erē, -ri\ *adj* [*²flare* + *-y*] **:** showy and bright **:** GAUDY

fla·ser \ˈfläzə(r)\ *n* -s [G, vein in wood or rock, prob. dial. modif. of *flader* vein in wood, veined wood, maple tree, fr. MHG *vlader* vein in wood, veined wood; perh. akin to Gk *platys* flat, broad — more at PLACE] **:** an irregular usu. streaked lens of granular texture found in a micaceous interstitial mass of rock and produced by shearing and pressure during metamorphism

¹flash \ˈflash, -aa(ə)-,-ai-\ *vb* -ED/-ING/-ES [ME *flaschen*, of imit. origin] *vi* **1 :** RUSH, DASH, SPLASH — used of flowing or tidal water ⟨flood waters ~*ing* over the rocky stream bed⟩ **2 a :** to break forth in or like a sudden flame **:** appear as a momentary flare ⟨the steel ~*ed*⟩ ⟨lightning ~*ing* in the sky⟩ ⟨the light ~*ed* on⟩ **b** *of a combustible* **:** to ignite with a flare ⟨the powder ~*ed*⟩ **c** *of a gun* **:** to give forth flame in the discharge **3 a :** to appear as suddenly as a flash ⟨an explanation ~*ed* into her mind⟩ **b :** to move with great speed **:** come, go, or pass like a flash ⟨the squirrel ~*ed* up a tree⟩ ⟨time ~*ed* by and we had to leave⟩ **4** *archaic* **:** to make a good showing **:** put one's best foot forward **:** show off **5 a :** to enter suddenly into another state (as of action or consciousness) ⟨he ~*ed* awake at the sound⟩ ⟨~*ing* into action as the starter's flag fell⟩ **b :** to break forth or out so as to make a sudden or unexpected display ⟨the sun ~*ed* from behind a cloud⟩ **c :** to act or speak vehemently and suddenly esp. in anger or disagreement — usu. used with *out* ⟨~*ing* out against such abuses⟩ ⟨sometimes she ~*es* out furiously before she thinks⟩ **6 a :** to light up or glow suddenly or intermittently ⟨fireflies ~*ing* in the meadow⟩ ⟨sunlight ~*ing* on the water⟩ **b :** to reflect light brilliantly or intermittently ⟨her diamonds ~*ed* and twinkled under the candles⟩ ⟨the windows ~*ed* with the setting sun⟩ **c** *of the eyes* **:** to glow or gleam esp. with animation or passion **:** SPARKLE ⟨eyes ~*ing* with delight⟩ **7** *in glass manuf* **:** to expand or open out into a sheet — used of a blown globe of glass **8** *of a liquid* **:** to change suddenly or violently into vapor ⟨as when released from pressure the oil ~*es* into vapor⟩ **~** *vt* **1 a** *archaic* **:** to cause (water) to splash **b :** to fill (as a channel) or pass (as a boat) over an obstacle by means of a sudden inflow of water **2 a :** to cause the sudden appearance of (light or a source of illumination) **:** EMIT ⟨the oars ~*ed* cold greenish light⟩ — often used with *on* ⟨he ~*ed* on the light⟩ **b :** to cause to burst violently into fire ⟨a lighted match probably ~*ed* the escaping gas⟩ **c :** to cause (light) to reflect or cause (as a mirror) to reflect light ⟨~*ing* spots of light on the ceiling with a mirror⟩ ⟨~*ing* a mirror in the sunlight⟩; *often* **:** to convey or communicate (information or a message) by means of flashes of light ⟨~*ed* his position with a torch⟩ ⟨the general's answer was ~*ed* by heliograph⟩ **d :** to cause to glow or gleam usu. suddenly or transiently ⟨~*ed* her bright eyes at the boy⟩ **e :** to burn (as a sample of explosive) under controlled conditions in order to determine the character and amount of residue **3 a :** to convey, make known, or cause to appear with great speed or instantaneously ⟨the news of the surrender was ~*ed* around the world by radio and telegraph⟩ ⟨the operator ~*ed* a message on the screen⟩ **b :** to show off **:** display obtrusively or ostentatiously ⟨only a fool would ~ a fat wallet in such company⟩ **c :** to expose to view suddenly and usu. briefly ⟨the detective ~*ed* his badge⟩ ⟨~*ing* a shy smile⟩; *esp* **:** to expose (the face of a playing card) momentarily whether by accident (as in dealing) or by design (as in certain card tricks) **d :** to type (a word or phrase) as a unit without thinking of the individual letters as they are struck **4 :** to cover with or form into a thin layer: as **a :** to protect (as the valley, hip, or edge of a roof) against rain by covering with sheet metal or a substitute laid over or under the edge of the roofing **b :** to coat (as plain glass) with a thin layer (as of colored glass or metal; *also* **:** to apply (as a layer of colored glass) to — often used with *on* **c :** to pass a blowtorch flame over the surface of a layer of melted wax (of an electrotype case) to remove air bubbles prior to use in an electrotype mold **5 a :** to cause (glass) to flash **b :** to reheat (glass) to intensify the color esp. when red or yellow **6 :** to subject (an exposed photographic negative or positive) to a supplementary uniform exposure to light before development in order to modify detail or tone **7 a :** to convert (a liquid) quickly into vapor (as in a flash boiler) **b :** to eliminate in the form of vapor esp. by exposure to intense or sudden heating — usu. used with off ⟨~*ing* off the turpentine in purifying gum⟩ **c :** to vaporize (a getter) by heating the vacuum-tube filament in order to clear the tube of residual gas **d :** to reduce the pressure of suddenly (as by releasing into a vaporizing chamber or tower under lower pressure) ⟨the hot tar is ~*ed* into a vacuum chamber⟩

²flash \"\ *n* -ES **1 a :** a sudden burst of light **:** a light instantaneously appearing and disappearing ⟨a ~ of lightning⟩ **b :** a transient light (as from a lantern or torch) displayed as a signal; *also* **:** a movement of a flag in signaling **2 :** a sudden and brilliant burst (as of wit or genius) **:** a momentary and sudden show ⟨occasional ~*es* of industry⟩ **3 :** the duration of a flash **:** a brief time ⟨answered in a ~⟩ ⟨for a ~ we thought we saw them⟩ **4 a :** SHOW, DISPLAY; *esp* **:** a vulgar ostentatious display **b** *archaic* **:** a showy ostentatious person **:** SWELL, FOP **c :** something or someone that attracts notice (as by gaudiness or excellence); *esp* **:** an outstanding athlete **d :** brightness of color in flue-cured tobacco **5** *obs* **a :** ostentatious or bombastic talk or phrasing **b** [perh. fr. *³flash*] **:** SLANG, CANT **6 a** *obs* **:** a splash or wave of water **b** *archaic* **:** a sudden stream of water released (as at a shoal or weir) to permit passage of a boat **7 :** something flashed: as **a :** GLIMPSE, LOOK ⟨caught a ~ of the scene as he hurried by⟩ **b :** SMILE **c :** a first brief news report; *usu* **:** one of an esp. newsworthy event sent to a newspaper or news broadcaster by wire — compare BULLETIN **d :** FLASHLIGHT c, d **e :** the quick-spreading flame or momentary intense outburst of radiant heat from the burst of a bomb, bazooka, or other explosive blast or from a flamethrower or welding arc **f** *Brit* **:** a bright tab worn as part of the insignia of a military uniform: (1) **:** a red shoulder patch — called also *shoulder flash* (2) **:** a red tab attached to a kilt garter as part of the uniform of certain Scottish units **g :** the body exposure at the end of a striptease **8 a :** FIN 2 e **b :** the recesses in a set of dies that receive the fin **9 :** a thin layer: as **a :** a layer of glass flashed on **b :** a very thin electroplated coating usu. less than 1/100,000 inch thick **c :** a surface coloration on brick or pottery produced in the kiln by metallic oxides, manipulation of flame, or accidentally **10 :** a strong red that is yellower, darker, and slightly less strong than geranium (sense 3a) and yellower and slightly lighter than Goya **11 :** the rapid conversion of a liquid into vapor **12 :** FLASHING 4

³flash \"\ *adj* [*²flash*] **1 a** *of a thing* **:** showy but counterfeit **:** cheap, pretentious, and vulgar ⟨~ finery⟩; *sometimes* **:** such as appeals to the uncritically fashionable **:** SMART ⟨a ~ hotel⟩ **b** *of a person* (1) **:** vulgarly pretentious **:** given to showy display (2) **:** belonging to a sporting set; *often* **:** SPORTY, FAST (3) **:** being a thief, tramp, or a member of some other class that is considered beyond the bounds of normal society **c :** of, relating to, or characteristic of flash things or people ⟨a ~ appearance⟩ ⟨~ behavior⟩ **2 a :** of sudden origin, swift advance, and usu. short duration ⟨a ~ fire⟩ ⟨a valley subject to ~ flooding⟩ **b** *of a food-processing method* **:** involving extremely brief exposure to some very intense altering agent (as heat or cold) ⟨~ drying of milk⟩ ⟨processed by ~ freezing⟩ **3 :** caused by or used to protect against flash ⟨~ injury⟩ ⟨~ gear⟩ — see FLASH BURN

⁴flash *adj* [ME *flasch* tepid, fr. MF *flache*, fem. of *flac* weak, feeble, slack, fr. L *flaccus* flabby] **1** *obs, of food* **:** lacking in savor **:** INSIPID, FLAT, TASTELESS **2** *obs* **:** lacking meaning or validity **:** TRASHY **:** weak and worthless — used esp. of essentially mental matters (as speech or reasoning)

⁵flash *n* [ME (Sc) *flasche*] *obs* **:** a sheaf of arrows

¹flashback \ˈ=,=\ *n* -s, *often attrib* [*¹flash* + *back*, adv.] **1 a :** a literary or theatrical technique used esp. in motion pictures and television that involves interruption of the chronological sequence of events by interjection of events or scenes of earlier occurrence often in the form of projected reminiscence **b :** a piece or instance of literary or theatrical flashback ⟨we got to the movie at the beginning of the ~ to the hero's school days⟩ — called also *backflash* **c :** a past incident recurring vividly in the mind ⟨he saw his whole life in a series of ~*s*⟩ **2 a :** a recession of flame to a position where it is not expected or not wanted (as into a blowpipe); *esp* **:** BACK DRAFT **b :** ARC-BACK

²flashback \"\ *vi* **1 :** to appear or become introduced as flashbacks ⟨his life ~*ed* before his eyes⟩ **2 :** to employ flashbacks ⟨the play ~*s* to the hero's childhood⟩ ⟨a writer who ~*s* in a masterly way to impart a feeling of vitality to his characters⟩

flashboard \ˈ=,=\ *n* [*¹flash* + *board*] **:** a board or one of a series of boards projecting above the top of a dam to increase the depth of the water — called also *flushboard*

flash boiler *n* **:** a steam boiler that has very strong tubes with little water space which are kept nearly red-hot so that the water coming to them in small amounts is flashed into steam and superheated

flash bomb *n* **:** an aerial bomb that explodes in the air to provide brilliant illumination for aerial photography of the ground at night

flashbulb \ˈ=,=\ *n* **:** an electric flash lamp in which metal foil or wire is burned

flash burn *n* **:** tissue injury caused by exposure to radiant heat of high intensity (as from electrical discharges or explosions)

flash card *n* **1 :** a card bearing words, numbers, or pictures briefly displayed by a teacher to a class during drills (as in reading, spelling, or arithmetic) **2 :** a card displayed by a judge to make known his scoring of a performance (as in diving or gymnastics)

flash color *n* **:** a patch of bright color that is apparent only during motion on an otherwise neutrally tinted animal and that is believed to distract the attention of pursuers who lose sight of the prey when it comes to rest and the bright patch is obscured — compare WARNING COLORATION

flash defilade *n* **:** a condition in which the flash of a gun when fired is concealed from enemy observation by an intervening obstacle (as a ridge)

flash-dry \ˈ=,=\ *vt* **:** to dry (as a granular material) quickly (as by placing in an up-current of hot air)

flashed *past of* FLASH

flash·er \-shə(r)\ *n* -s **:** one that flashes: as **a** *archaic* **:** a flashy or showy person **b :** TRIPLETAIL 1a **c :** a worker who flashes glass **d :** a device (as a traffic signal) that catches the attention by flashing **:** BLINKER **e :** a device for automatically lighting and extinguishing electric lamps by mechanical, thermal, or other means (as by regulating the flow of current through the lamps composing a display sign)

flashes *pres 3d sing of* FLASH, *pl of* FLASH

flash factor *n* **:** a number characteristic of a given photoflash lamp and a given film speed that when divided by the distance in feet between the lamp and the subject indicates the correct f-number for that distance

flash flood *n* **:** a local flood of relatively great volume and short duration that generally results from heavy rainfall in the immediate vicinity

flashflood \ˈ=,=\ *vt* [*flash flood*] **:** to flood suddenly **:** cause a flash flood in ⟨heavy rains ~*ed* the valley⟩

flashgun \ˈ=,=\ *n* **1 :** a device for holding and igniting flashlight powder **2 :** a device including a battery case, a lamp socket, and a reflector that is used for holding and operating a flashbulb

flashgun 2

flash hider *n* **:** a tubular device fitted to the muzzle of a firearm to conceal the flash of the burning powder gases

flash hole *n* **:** a hole in the bottom of the primer recess in the base of a cartridge case for admitting the flash of the ignited primer to the propelling charge

flashier *comparative of* FLASHY

flashiest *superlative of* FLASHY

flash·i·ly \-shəlē, -li\ *adv* **:** in a flashy manner or style ⟨a ~ dressed man⟩

flash in *vt* **:** to alter (details or tone) by flashing a photographic negative or positive

flash·i·ness \-shēnəs, -shin-\ *n* -ES **:** the quality or state of being flashy

flashing *n* -s [fr. gerund of *¹flash*] **1 :** the reheating of an article of glass at the furnace aperture to restore its plastic condition; *esp* **:** the reheating of a globe of crown glass to allow it to flash **2 :** strips of sheet metal (as copper or galvanized iron) bent to fit in the interior angle between a wall and a roof surface or in the valley between two intersecting roof surfaces in order to make a watertight joint — compare COUNTERFLASHING, FILLETING **3 :** a lap joint (as a bell-and-spigot joint) in plumber's leadwork **4 :** the small-stop exposure to white paper of the photographic emulsion as a preliminary step in making a halftone

flashing block *n* **:** a terracotta block built into a parapet wall and containing a groove to receive the upper end of roof flashing in order to avoid the use of counterflashing

flash·ing·ly *adv* [*flashing* (pres. part. of *¹flash*) + *-ly*] **:** in a flashing manner or style **:** SPARKLINGLY

flashing ring *n* **:** a ferrule around a pipe (as a drain) for holding it firm where it passes through a floor, wall, or ceiling

flashing tile *n* **:** a structural clay tile made with a recess to receive the flashing from a roof and used in a wall just above the junction of a flat roof with the wall — compare FLASHING BLOCK

flash in the pan 1 : the firing of the priming in the pan of a flintlock musket without discharging the piece **2 a :** a sudden spasmodic effort that accomplishes nothing **b :** a person of brilliant promise but little ultimate performance or worth

flash lamp *n* **:** a lamp for producing a brief but intense flash of light for taking photographs

flashlight \ˈ=,=\ *n, often attrib* **:** a flash of light or a light that flashes on and off: as **a** (1) **:** a scintillating light sometimes used in lighthouses (2) **:** a light shown by some lighthouses produced by revolution of reflectors or prismatic lenses so arranged as to show a bright light at regular intervals alternating with periods of dimness — called also *revolving light* **b :** a clear, sudden, or intermittent light used to signal (as on a ship) or illuminate (as an advertising sign) **c** (1) **:** a sudden bright artificial light used in taking photographic pictures (2) **:** metallic powder or other material to produce such a light (3) **:** a photograph taken by such a light **d :** a small battery-operated portable electric light

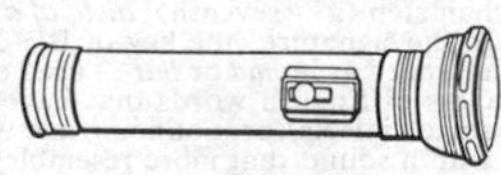

flashlight d

flashmeter \ˈ=,=\ *n* **:** TACHISTOSCOPE

flash·ness *n* -ES **:** the quality or state of being flash **:** FLASHINESS

flashold·er \ˈfla\|,shōldə(r), -laa\|, -lai\|, \|sh,hō-\ *n* [*²flash* (as in *flashbulb*) + *holder*] **:** FLASHGUN 2

flashover \ˈ=,=\ *n* -s *often attrib* [*¹flash* + *over*] **1 :** an electrical discharge or arc through the air to the ground from a high potential source or between two conducting portions of a machine or structure **2 :** the sudden spread of flame over an area when it becomes heated to the flash point

flashover voltage *n* **:** the voltage at which a current flashes from electrode to electrode or ground with the formation of a sustained arc

flashpan \ˈ=,=\ *n* **:** a pan for priming in a flintlock

flash paper *n* **:** thin paper (as tissue) treated with acid so that it will vanish in a flash when ignited

flash pasteurization *n* **:** pasteurization in which a fluid (as milk or fruit juice) is subjected very briefly to a relatively high temperature

flash photography *n* **:** photography by means of flashlight

flash plate *n* **:** a steel plate that protects the deck of a ship from the anchor chain

flash point *n* **1** *also* **flashing point :** the lowest temperature at which the vapors above a volatile combustible substance (as a petroleum product) ignite momentarily in air when tested usu. by applying a small flame under specified conditions ⟨the degree of flammability of a liquid is expressed mainly by means of its *flash point* —*Dict. of Fire Technology*⟩ **2 :** a point (as of interest or tension) at which someone or something bursts suddenly into action or being ⟨near the *flash point* of war⟩

flash ranging *n* **:** the locating of enemy weapons and the adjusting of friendly fire by observation of flashes from at least two observation posts — compare SOUND RANGING

flash spectrum *n* **:** a bright-line spectrum produced by the sun's reversing layer and observable for a few seconds at the beginning and end of a total solar eclipse

flashtube \ˈ=,=\ *n* **:** an electric flash lamp in which light can be obtained repeatedly by passing pulses of electric current through a gas **:** STROBE

flash-type \ˈ=,=\ *vt* **:** ¹FLASH 3d

flash weld *n* **:** a weld made by flash welding

flash welding *n* **:** butt welding in which a light initial pressure on the parts is quickly relieved and followed by a period of arcing and finally by heavy pressure

flashy \ˈflashē, -aash-,-aish-, -shi\ *adj* -ER/-EST [in sense 1, fr. *⁴flash* + *-y*; in other senses, fr. *¹flash* & *²flash* + *-y*] **1** *now chiefly dial* **:** flat and watery **:** INSIPID ⟨the heavy rains have brought on a crop of soft ~ grass that does not cure well⟩ **2 :** momentarily dazzling **:** transitorily or superficially bright or pleasing **3 :** FIERY, IMPETUOUS ⟨a ~ temper⟩ **4 a :** superficially attractive **:** BRIGHT; *often* **:** ostentatious or showy beyond the bounds of good taste ⟨~ manners⟩ **:** GAUDY ⟨~ dress⟩ **b** *of an animal* **:** noticeable by reason of excellent conformation and finish ⟨a ~ boxer bitch⟩ **syn** see GAUDY

¹flask \ˈflask, -aa(ə)-,-ai-,-à-\ *n* -s *often attrib* [MF *flasque* powder flask, prob. modif. of OSp *frasco* powder flask, flask for liquids, modif. of LL *flascon-, flasco* bottle, prob. of Gmc origin; akin to OE *flasce, flaxe* bottle, OHG & ON *flaska;* perh. derivative fr. the root of OHG *flehtan* to braid, plait — more at PLY] **1 :** a vessel (as of metal, glass, skin) somewhat narrowed or necked toward the outlet, often fitted with a stopper, cap, or other closure, and used as a container: as **a :** a container usu. of horn, metal, or leather used to carry powder for a muzzle-loading firearm **b :** a necked vessel for holding liquids; *esp* **:** a broad flattened vessel of metal or sometimes glass curved to fit a pocket and used esp. to carry alcoholic beverages on the person **c :** a standard iron container in which 76 pounds of mercury is sold; *also* **:** a unit of weight for mercury equal to 76 pounds **d :** any of various usu. blown-glass vessels used for technical purposes in a laboratory **2 :** a wooden or metal frame that holds the sand forming the mold used in a foundry

²flask \"\ *vt* -ED/-ING/-S **:** to enclose in a flask; *esp* **:** to place (a denture) in a flask for processing

flas·ker \-kə(r)\ *vb* -ED/-ING/-S [prob. imit.] *dial Eng* **:** FLUTTER

flask·et \-kət\ *n* -s [ME, a container, fr. (assumed) ONF *flasket* small bottle (OF *flaschet*), dim. of ONF *flaske* bottle (OF *flasche*), fr. (assumed) VL *flasca* bottle (whence ML *flasca*), prob. of Gmc origin; akin to OE *flasce, flaxe* bottle, OHG & ON *flaska* — more at FLASK] **1** *now dial Eng* **:** a long shallow basket **2 :** a small flask

flask-shaped \ˈ=ˈ=\ *adj* **:** resembling a typical flask in shape; *usu* **:** necked and either flattened in body

flasque \ˈflask, -aa(ə)-,-ai-,-à-\ *n* -s [perh. fr. F, cheek of a gun carriage] **:** a heraldic bearing similar to a flanch but narrower

¹flat \ˈflat, *usu* -ad.+V\ *adj* **flatter; flattest** [ME, fr. ON *flatr;* akin to OS *flat* shallow, OHG *flaz* flat, Latvian *plandīt* to make broad, Gk *platys* flat, broad — more at PLACE] **1 :** having or marked by a continuous surface that is horizontal or nearly so without significant curvature or inclination and without noteworthy elevations or depression ⟨a ~ top⟩ ⟨a ~ plateau⟩ ⟨a ~ deck⟩ **2 a :** lying at full length or spread out upon the ground **:** level with the ground or earth ⟨urged the pony ~ out and belly to the ground —Alan LeMay⟩ **:** PROSTRATE ⟨grass ~ after the storm⟩ **b :** utterly ruined, incapacitated, or destroyed **:** laid low ⟨buildings ~ from the blast⟩ ⟨was ~ with diphtheria⟩ ⟨my hopes all ~ —John Milton⟩ **c :** resting with a surface against or immediately adjoining something ⟨push the chairs ~ against the wall⟩ ⟨is ~ on his back in bed⟩ **3 a :** having a smooth or even surface whether horizontal or not ⟨use the *flatter* side for the face⟩ ⟨a ~ slab of rock⟩ **b :** smooth or even by comparison with something usu. implied ⟨a broad ~ face⟩ ⟨a design worked in ~ relief⟩ **c** *of a fur* **:** having a smooth sleek surface due to hairs lying strongly inclined to the surface; *sometimes* **:** having the hairs sparse and short **d** *of a knit fabric* **:** lacking ribs **:** FLAT-KNIT **4 :** arranged or laid out so as to be level, smooth, or even ⟨maps ~ on the desk⟩ **5 a :** having the major surfaces essentially parallel and distinctly greater than the minor surfaces ⟨a ~ piece of wood⟩ ⟨coins are usually round and ~⟩

b *of a shoe heel* **:** very low and broad; *also, of a shoe* **:** having a flat heel or no heel ⟨~ shoes for ballet⟩ **6 a :** clear and unmistakable **:** DOWNRIGHT, POSITIVE ⟨a ~ contradiction of his sister's statement⟩ ⟨a ~ failure⟩; *sometimes* **:** PEREMPTORY ⟨a ~ denial of responsibility⟩ **b :** not varied or varying (as from a fixed or normal amount or standard) **:** ABSOLUTE, FIXED ⟨a ~ service charge⟩ ⟨a ~ rate⟩; *also* **:** having no fraction either lacking or in excess **:** EXACT, PRECISE ⟨made the bus in a ~ 10 seconds⟩ ⟨ran the mile in four minutes ~⟩ **7 a :** weak or lacking in animation, spirit, zest, or vigor **:** lacking interest or qualities that please, interest, or stimulate **:** DULL, LIFELESS ⟨a ~ drab deadly round of work, eat, sleep⟩ ⟨~ puerile writing lacking both substance and style⟩ ⟨plays whose composition is neither lifelike nor unlifelike but just ~ —Marston Balch⟩ **b :** lacking mental alertness or vigor **:** dull and stupid ⟨~ cloddish minds⟩ **c :** lacking savor **:** INSIPID, TASTELESS ⟨the stew is too ~⟩ **d** *of an effervescent drink* **:** having given off the included gas and become still **:** lacking effervescence or sparkle ⟨beer goes ~ on standing⟩ **e :** commercially inactive **:** dull and depressed ⟨the market is very ~ for this time of year⟩ **f :** DEFLATED — used chiefly of pneumatic tires **g :** lacking funds **:** having no money **8 a :** characterized by lack of clearness, sharpness, accuracy of pitch, or sonority — used esp. of the tone quality of a musical instrument or voice ⟨the bell has a ~ sound as if cracked⟩ **b** *of a musical note or tone* **:** minor or lower by a half step ⟨a ~ seventh⟩; *also, of a key or tonality* **:** having a flat in the signature ⟨the key of B ~⟩ **c** *of the vowel a* (1) **:** pronounced as in *bad* or *bat* — used esp. when so pronounced in a class of English words that have the vowel of *palm* or *par* in some dialects ⟨pronouncing *ask* with a ~ *a*⟩ (2) **:** pronounced with a sound that more resembles in quality the *a* of *bat* than the *o* of *bother* without actually being the *a* of *bat* — used of the *a* of such words as *part, palm, father* as often pronounced in eastern New England **9 a :** having a low trajectory ⟨the bow shoots a ~ arrow⟩ ⟨made a ~ pass that was intercepted⟩ **b** *of a tennis ball* **:** hit squarely without being spun by the racket ⟨a ~ drive⟩ **10 :** not having an inflectional ending or sign — used esp. of an adherent noun, an infinitive without the sign *to*, or an adverb with no adverbial ending **11** *of a curve or angle* **:** GRADUAL, SHALLOW **:** not sharp or steep ⟨~ dive⟩ ⟨~ glide⟩ **12 a** *of a weather map* **:** showing little regional variation in barometric pressure **b** *of weather* **:** having not much wind or pressure variation **:** CALM **13** *of a sail* **:** made taut so as to prevent or reduce bellying ⟨eased before the wind with all sheets ~⟩ **14 a :** uniform in hue or shade ⟨figures standing out against a background of ~ wash⟩ **b** *of a painting* **:** having little or no illusion of depth, interest being concentrated on the surface treatment **c** *of a photograph or negative* **:** lacking contrast **d** *of a lighting arrangement* **:** not emphasizing shadows or contours — used esp. of an arrangement for photography in which light comes from a point that is in front of the subject and in line with the camera **e :** free from gloss ⟨a ~ paint⟩ **f** *of a proof* **:** made from an unfinished printing surface ⟨took a ~ proof from a form on the press but not yet made ready⟩ **15 :** having no bevel — used of ship timbers **16 :** being or relating to a transducer response or output that is in constant ratio to the input as the frequency varies so that there is distortionless reproduction over a specified frequency range **syn** see INSIPID, LEVEL

²flat \"\ *n* -S [ME, fr. *flat*, adj. — more at ¹FLAT] **1 a** (1) **:** a level surface of land with little or no relief **:** PLAIN (2) **:** a level tract lying at little depth below the surface of water or alternately covered and left bare by the tide **:** SHOAL, SHALLOW, STRAND (3) **:** a tract of wet low-lying level land **:** MARSH, SWAMP (4) *chiefly North & Midland* **:** BOTTOM 6 **b** (1) **:** one of the divisions of cropland used in common (2) *dial* **:** a field growing a crop **c :** a horizontal extension of a mineral vein; *also* **:** a flat horizontal deposit (as of ore) **d :** a running track or other course for a flat race ⟨a race for three-year-old trotters on the ~⟩ **e :** the part of a football field immediately adjacent to the flanks of either team **2 :** a flat part or surface: as **a :** one of the larger essentially parallel surfaces of something characterized by great disparity in the size of its surfaces — often opposed to *edge* ⟨struck the boy with the ~ of the ruler⟩ ⟨drive the stake with the ~ of your ax⟩ **b :** the palm of the hand sometimes together with the palmar surface of the fingers ⟨pat out the dough with the ~ of your hand⟩ **3 :** an improper die that because of imperfectly cubical form tends to present a particular face more frequently than a perfect die **4 a :** a musical note or tone one half step lower than a specified note or tone ⟨A flat is the ~ of A⟩ **b :** a character ♭ on a line or space of the musical staff indicating a pitch a half step lower than the line or space would otherwise indicate without it **5 :** something of broad shallow form: as **a :** a shallow basket, crate, or other container in which produce is shipped to market **b :** a broad-brimmed low-crowned straw hat **c :** a platform on wheels upon which displays (as of emblematic designs) are drawn in processions — compare FLOAT **d :** a shallow box in which seedlings are started **e :** a flat-bottomed boat with a shallow draft and without keel **f :** a flatcar or other draft vehicle (as a motortruck or handcart) without raised sides **g :** a pressed paper divider having shallow depressions in which eggs are placed to fill a single layer of an egg case **h :** a flat piece of theatrical scenery typically consisting of a wood frame covered with painted cloth and used to form a section of a set wall or ceiling or to mask a door or window **i :** one of the slats with teeth that are mounted on an endless chain above the cylinder of a carding machine and that assist in ordering the textile fiber being carded **6 :** something of broad and thin or flat form: as **a :** a plane mirror or reflector; *also* **:** a transparent disk with one or both surfaces accurately plane — called also *optical flat* **b :** a mature mushroom with a fully expanded cap — compare BUTTON 2d **c :** a picture-frame mat **d :** a level deck on a ship; *esp* **:** one onto which cabins open **e :** a shoe or slipper having a flat heel or no heel **f :** an architectural member having the form of a platform of generally horizontal character (as the deck of a roof with steep sides or any roof of which the slope does not much exceed one in twenty) **g :** a long flat square-edged artist's brush — compare BRIGHT, ROUND **h :** a collapsed or knocked down container as sent in bulk to the purchaser **i :** the straight part of the cutting edge of a machine tool **7 :** a punctured tire **:** a pneumatic tire with no air pressure **8 a :** a rolled metal bar of uniform rectangular cross section **b :** the cylindrical portion of the contour at either root or crest of certain screw threads **9 :** EUCLIDEAN SPACE **10 :** a surface (as of paint) that is not glossy **11 a :** an unfolded sheet of paper **b flats** *pl* **:** writing paper with a flat smooth surface **12 :** the thick glass on which negative films are laid close together for printing on sensitized metal in making a photoengraving; *also* **:** an assemblage of negative or positive films from which a photo-offset plate is made **13 :** an inferior grade of rough diamonds **14 a :** a dance step with the full surface of the foot **b :** the act of gliding upright on both edges of a skate blade during a curve where the single edge position is correct; *also* **:** the double track that shows on the ice when a flat occurs — called also *double edge*

³flat \"\ *adv* [¹*flat*] **1 :** in a flat manner **:** DIRECTLY, POSITIVELY ⟨came out ~ for less work and higher pay⟩ **2 a :** at full length ⟨fell ~ on his face⟩ **b :** on or against a flat surface ⟨lying ~ on his back⟩ ⟨spread out ~ on the ground⟩ **3 :** WHOLLY, COMPLETELY ⟨~ broke⟩ **4 :** without charging or without paying interest (as when giving or receiving credit); *esp* **:** without allowance or charge for accrued interest — used of the selling or quoting of bonds **5 :** below the proper musical pitch ⟨he sang slightly ~⟩ **6 :** with flat sail ⟨sailing ~ in a high wind⟩

⁴flat \"\ *vb* **flatted; flatted; flatting; flats** [¹*flat*] *vt* **1** *obs* **:** to lay flat **:** LEVEL, RAZE **2** *archaic* **:** to make flat or level **:** FLATTEN **3** *obs* **:** to make dull, insipid, or spiritless ⟨passions are allayed, appetites are *flatted* —Isaac Barrow⟩ **4 a :** to depress (a musical tone) in pitch **b :** to lower in pitch by a half step ⟨a *flatted* fifth⟩ **5 a :** to cover (a surface) with a flat coat (as of paint) **b :** to remove the gloss from (a painted or varnished surface) esp. by sanding **c :** to free (a paint) from the tendency to set with a glossy surface (as by the addition of turpentine) **6 :** to plant (as bulbs) in or transplant (as seedlings) into a flat ~ *vi* **1** *obs* **:** to become flat or flattened **:** sink or fall to an even surface **2** *of a musical tone* **:** to fall from the true or intended pitch ⟨could tell the approach of the milkman by the whistled notes that somehow always *flatted*⟩

⁵flat \"\ *n* -S [¹*flat*] **1 :** a floor, loft, or story in a building **2 a** *chiefly Brit* **:** an apartment or suite of rooms occupying or forming part of one floor of a building — compare MAISONETTE **b** *chiefly North* **:** an apartment on one floor usu. with separate outdoor entry and sometimes lacking amenities ⟨a cold-water ~⟩ — compare TENEMENT; see RAILROAD FLAT **3 :** a building divided into flats — often used in pl.

flat advertising rate *n* **:** a uniform rate of charge per unit of advertising space that is applicable irrespective of the amount of space contracted for

flat arch *n* **:** a spanning member constructed of mutually supporting voussoirs and having a straight or almost straight horizontal intrados and extrados

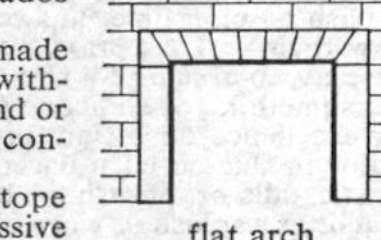

flat arch

flat back *n* **:** a book backbone made without rounding and sometimes without backing; *also* **:** a book so bound or the style of binding featuring this construction

flat–back stope *n* **:** an overhand stope in which the ore is mined in successive horizontal cuts

¹flatbed \'⸗,⸗\ *adj* [¹*flat* + *bed*] **:** having a horizontal bed on which a horizontal printing surface rests — usu. used of a cylinder press; compare ROTARY PRESS

²flatbed \"\ *n* [in sense 1, fr. ¹*flatbed;* in sense 2, fr. ¹*flat* + *bed*] **1 :** a flatbed printing press **2 :** a motortruck or trailer with a body in the form of a platform or shallow box

flat bet *n* **:** a bet at even money (as in craps)

¹flatboat \'⸗,⸗\ *n* **:** a boat with a flat bottom and square ends used for transportation of bulky freight esp. in shallow waters

²flatboat \"\ *vi* **:** to engage in the management of or labor or travel on a flatboat ~ *vt* **:** to transport (as supplies or passengers) by flatboat ⟨~*ed* his fruit to the city⟩

flat·boat·man \-mən\ *n, pl* **flatboatmen :** a member of the crew of a flatboat

flat–bodied \'⸗'⸗⸗\ *also* **flat–body** \'⸗,⸗⸗\ *adj* **:** having the body dorsoventrally flattened — used esp. of insects

flat bone *n* **:** any of various bones (as of the skull, the jaw, the pelvis, or the rib cage) not rounded in cross section

flat bow *n, archery* **:** a bow of uniform thickness that differs only in dimension from the longbow

flatbread \'⸗,⸗\ *or* **flat·brod** \'⸗,brōd\ *n* [*flatbread* trans. of Norw *flatbrød; flatbrod* modif. of Norw *flatbrød*, fr. *flat* (fr. ON *flatr*) + *brød* bread, fr. ON *brauth* — more at FLAT, BREAD] **:** a thin dry wafer made of rye flour dough and used esp. among Scandinavian peoples

flat bug *n* **:** an insect of the family Aradidae

flatcap \'⸗,⸗\ *n* **1 :** a round low-crowned cap worn in 16th and 17th century England esp. in London **2 :** a wearer of a flatcap; *esp* **:** LONDONER

flatcar \'⸗,⸗\ *n* **:** a railroad freight car without permanent raised sides, ends, or covering

flat carving *n* **:** carving (as on furniture) consisting of flat surfaces thrown into relief by cutting back the spaces around and between them

flatcatcher \'⸗,⸗⸗\ *n* [E slang *flat* dupe, fool (fr. E ¹*flat*) + E *catcher*] **1** *Brit* **:** SWINDLER **2** *Brit* **:** a horse that looks good but is not

flat chisel *n* **:** a chisel (as a cold chisel) of hardened and tempered steel used to obtain a flat and finished surface (as on wood or stone)

flat–coated retriever \'⸗,⸗⸗-\ *n* **:** an active medium-sized sporting dog of a breed of English origin characterized by a black or liver-colored dense close smooth coat and a rather long head

flat–compound \,⸗⸗'⸗, ⸗'⸗,⸗\ *vt* **:** to add to (the ordinary winding of a dynamo) a series field winding with the requisite number of turns to make the terminal voltage of a generator or the speed of a motor nearly independent of its load

flat cost *n* **:** the part of the cost (as of a building) representing direct outlay for labor and material

flat countersink *n* **:** a tool for countersinking in metal — see COUNTERSINK illustration

flat crab *n* **:** PORCELAIN CRAB

flat crepe *n* **:** a silk or rayon crepe similar to crepe de chine but with a flatter surface and a duller finish

flatcrown \'⸗,⸗\ *also* **flatcrown tree** *n* **:** a deciduous African tree (*Albizzia gummifera*) with hairy foliage, flowers in globular heads, and moderately heavy yellowish to grayish or brown wood used locally for carving

flat–earth·er \'⸗'ərthər\ *n* -S [*flat earth* + *-er*] **:** a person who maintains the earth to be a flat body

flat engine *n* **:** an internal-combustion engine having cylinders arranged by pairs on opposite sides of the crankshaft and in one horizontal plane

flat envelope *n* **:** a piece of paper cut ready to make into an envelope

flat etch *n* **:** FIRST BITE

flat–fell seam \'⸗,fel-\ *n* [obs. E *flat fell* (fr. E ¹*flat* + obs. E *fell*, n., action of felling a seam, felled seam, fr. E ²*fell*) + E *seam*] **:** a strong seam with two lines of stitching showing on the right side that is produced by folding one raw edge under the other and stitching it flat or slip-stitching it on the wrong side

flat-fell seam: *1* first stitching, joining pieces *A* and *B*; *2* second stitching

flat file *n* **:** a file of rectangular section about four times as wide as thick at the heel and tapering toward the point

flatfish \'⸗,⸗\ *n* **1 :** any of numerous marine teleost fishes that are usu. considered to constitute an order Heterosomata, that are distinguished as adults by swimming on one side of a laterally compressed body and by having both eyes on the upper side due to gradual twisting of the skull and the lower side blind and largely devoid of color, and that include important food fishes (as the halibuts, flounders, turbots, and soles) **2 :** any of various fishes with laterally compressed bodies that do not habitually swim on one side: as **a :** GIZZARD SHAD **b :** PUMPKINSEED **c :** INDIAN FISH 1a

¹flatfoot \'⸗'⸗, *in sense 3* '⸗,⸗\ *n, pl* **flatfeet** \'⸗'⸗\ **1 a :** a condition in which the arch of the instep is flattened so that the entire sole rests upon the ground **b :** a condition in horses in which the hoof is very large and sloping and the frog is excessively prominent **2 :** a foot affected with flatfoot **3 :** a person having or held likely to have flatfeet: as **a** *pl often* **flatfoots** *slang* **:** POLICEMAN; *esp* **:** a patrolman that walks a regular beat **b** *slang* **:** SAILOR

²flatfoot \'⸗'⸗\ *vi* **:** to walk in a flat-footed manner or style

¹flat–footed \'⸗'⸗⸗\ *adj* [¹*flat* + *footed*] **1 :** affected with flatfoot; *broadly* **:** walking with the somewhat dragging or shambling gait characteristic of a person with severe flatfeet **2 :** having a flat base ⟨a *flat-footed* rail⟩ **3 a :** firm and well balanced on the feet ⟨a *flat-footed* stance⟩ **b :** free from reservation **:** complete and determined **:** FORTHRIGHT ⟨*flat-footed* support for an idea⟩ **4 :** found in an unprepared state **:** UNREADY — used chiefly in the phrase *catch one flat-footed* — **flat–foot·ed·ly** *adv* — **flat–foot·ed·ness** *n* -ES

²flat–footed \"\ *adv* **:** openly and determinedly **:** FLATLY

flatfoot walk *also* **flat–footed walk** *n* **:** a slow 4-beat gait in which the horse's hooves touch the ground in the order right fore, left rear, left fore, right rear

flat glass *n* **:** a drawn sheet glass or rolled glass

flat grain *n* **:** a grain in lumber parallel or nearly parallel with the face of the piece (as of veneering stock) that is produced by sawing nearly at right angles to the annual rings

flat grain beetle *n* **:** a minute flattened oblong reddish brown cucujid beetle (*Cryptolestes pusillus*) common in stored grain where it feeds chiefly on damaged grains and debris

flat–hat \'⸗,⸗\ *vi* [¹*flat* + *hat*, n.; fr. an alleged incident in which a pedestrian's hat was crushed by the undercarriage of a low-flying plane] **1 :** to fly low in an airplane in an unnecessarily dangerous or reckless manner **:** HEDGEHOP **2 :** to show off — **flat–hatter** \'⸗,⸗⸗\ *n*

flat·head \'⸗,⸗\ *n, pl* **flatheads** *or* **flathead 1** *usu cap* **a :** any of several Indian peoples (as the Chinook, Catawba, Choctaw, and Waxhaw) of No. America that formerly practiced head-flattening **b :** a member of any of such peoples **2** *usu cap* **a :** a Salish people that formerly occupied most of western Montana **b :** a member of such people **3 a :** HOGNOSE SNAKE **b :** any of various fishes with more or less flat heads: as (1) **:** any of a family (Platycephalidae) of chiefly Indo-Pacific marine food fishes that resemble sculpins (2) **:** BARRAMUNDA a (3) **:** a large minnow (*Platygobio gracilis*) of rivers of the Rocky mountain area (4) **:** FLATHEAD CATFISH **4 a :** a flattened head of a rivet or bolt; *also* **:** a rivet or bolt with such a head **b :** a screw with a head flat on top and tapering to the shaft so that it can be countersunk **5 :** a stupid or gullible person **:** SIMPLETON **6** *South* **:** FALLER 1

flathead catfish *or* **flathead cat** *n* **:** a large yellowish brown-mottled catfish (*Pylodictis olivaris*) of the Mississippi drainage, the Gulf states, and westward to the Rio Grande

flat·head·ed \'⸗'⸗⸗\ *also* **flat·head** \'⸗'⸗\ *adj* **:** having a flat or flattened head ⟨a ~ nail⟩ ⟨~ snakes⟩

flatheaded adder *n* [so called fr. its habit of flattening its head when disturbed] **:** HOGNOSE SNAKE

flatheaded apple tree borer *n* **:** a flattened elongate-oval beetle (*Chrysobothris femorata*) bronze above and bright and brassy beneath that is widespread in hardwoods — called also *apple tree borer*

flatheaded borer *or* **flathead borer** *n* [so called fr. its much enlarged and flattened thorax] **:** any of numerous beetle larvae of the family Buprestidae that bore beneath the bark or in the sapwood of trees

flatheaded cat *n* **:** a wildcat (*Felis planiceps*) of southeastern Asia

flat hoop *n* **:** a wooden hoop dressed flat on both sides

flatiron \'⸗,⸗(⸗)\ *n* **1 :** an iron that has a flat smooth surface for ironing clothes and that typically has a base with the general contour of an isosceles triangle — compare BOX IRON, SADIRON **2** *geol* **:** a short triangular hogback that when viewed from the side resembles a huge flatiron standing on its heel **3** *also* **flatiron collier** *Brit* **:** a coal carrier with hinged funnels and masts used on the Thames river

flatiron 1

flat·ite \'flad,īt\ *n* -S *Austral* **:** a person who lives in a flat

flat joint *n* [prob. so called fr. the flat surface on which a shell game is played] **1** *slang* **:** a confidence game (as the shell game) carried out by an organized mob **2** *slang* **:** a gambling game or wheel usu. connected with a circus or carnival that can be manipulated at the will of the operator

flat–joint pointing *n* [*flat joint* (fr. ¹*flat* + *joint*) + *pointing*] **:** the making of a masonry joint that is flush with the wall surface

flat keel *n* **:** a ship's keel consisting of a heavy strake of plating stiffened by an upright vertical keel — called also *flat-plate keel*

flat key *n* **:** a rectangular key set upon a flat on a shaft and used for transmitting small torques

flat–knit \'⸗'⸗\ *adj* **:** knitted on a flat machine with needles arranged in a straight line — contrasted with *circular-knit*

flat knot *n* **:** REEF KNOT

flatland \'⸗,⸗\ *n* **1 a :** land that lacks significant variation in elevation ⟨the farm includes a valuable stretch of ~ along the river⟩ **b :** a region in which the land is predominantly flat — usu. used in pl. ⟨coastal ~*s*⟩ **2 :** a hypothetical two-dimensional world — **flat·land·er** \-də(r)\ *n* -S

flat·let \'flatlət\ *n* -S *Brit* **:** a small compact flat typically consisting of a single dwelling room with kitchenette and bath

¹flat·ling \-liŋ,-lən\ *or* **flat·lings** \-ŋz,-nz\ *or* **flat·lins** \-nz\ *adv* [ME *flatling, flatlinges*, fr. ¹*flat* + *-ling, -linges* -ling, -lings] **1** *now dial Brit* **:** in a flat or horizontal position ⟨had stumbled backwards and fallen *flatlings* into the ditch —J.H. McCarthy⟩ **2** *now dial Brit* **:** with a flat side or edge ⟨smote him ~ with his sheathed sword —William Morris⟩

²flat·ling \-liŋ\ *adj* **1** *obs, of a blow* **:** dealt with the flat side of a weapon **2 :** falling or pressing down on one ⟨we lift the weight of ~ years —Rudyard Kipling⟩

flatlock \'⸗,⸗\ *adj, of a seam* **:** made by bringing two raw edges together and covering them with machine stitching

flat·ly *adv* [ME (Sc), fr. ME ¹*flat* + *-ly*] **1** *obs* **:** into a flat position **:** PROSTRATE **2 a :** BLUNTLY, CATEGORICALLY, PLAINLY ⟨he ~ denied the charges⟩; *sometimes* **:** EMPHATICALLY, PEREMPTORILY ⟨presenting the case ~ and sternly⟩ ⟨~ challenged the truth of the statement⟩ **b :** ABSOLUTELY, WHOLLY ⟨acting ~ against his convictions⟩ **3 :** in a flat manner ⟨sagging ~ in his arms⟩: as **a :** without zest or spirit **:** in a dull and uninterested manner ⟨droned on ~ about her troubles⟩ **b :** without indication or development of a third dimension ⟨roses stenciled ~ on the chair backs⟩

flat machine *n* **:** a knitting machine with needles arranged on a horizontal flat bed

flat·ness *n* -ES [ME *flatnesse* flat surface, fr. ¹*flat* + *-nesse* -ness] **:** the quality or state of being flat

¹flat–out \'⸗'⸗\ *adj* **1** *chiefly dial* **:** frank and open **:** ALL-OUT, DOWNRIGHT **2 :** MAXIMUM, TOP ⟨no technical understanding of driving skill, and anything but *flat-out* speed is lost on them —Ken Purdy⟩

²flat–out \"\ *adv* **1** *chiefly dial* **:** bluntly and directly **:** OPENLY ⟨told him *flat-out* what I thought⟩ **2 :** at top speed

flat pass *n* **:** a forward pass in football thrown nearly level toward the sidelines

flat pea *n* **1 a :** a European perennial pea (*Lathyrus sylvestris*) sometimes cultivated for fodder or as a green-manure crop **b :** the seed of the flat pea **2 :** any of several Australian evergreen leguminous shrubs that constitute a small genus (*Platylobium*) and are sometimes cultivated in warm regions for their bright yellow pealike flowers

flat peach *n* [trans. of Chin (Pek) *pien³ t'ao²*] **:** PEEN-TO

flat–plate keel *n, Brit* **:** FLAT KEEL

flat point *or* **flat–point lace** *n* **1 :** needle-point lace with flat designs instead of raised or padded designs **2 :** bobbin-made lace in contrast to needlepoint lace

flat race *n* **:** a race on a level course without hurdles or other obstacles

flat racing *n* **:** the sport of riding in flat races

flat reinsurance *n* **:** a reinsurance agreement (as in marine insurance) that is not subject to cancellation or change

flat relief *n* **:** bas-relief in which projected parts have little or no modeling and the details are frequently marked by incised lines

flat–ring \'⸗'⸗\ *adj* **:** having or employing a flat ring **:** DISCOIDAL ⟨*flat-ring* winding of an induction coil⟩

flat–rolled \'⸗'⸗\ *adj* **:** formed by rolling between plain cylindrical rolls — used of metal sheet, strip, plate, and some bars

flat roof *n* **:** a nearly horizontal roof pitched for water drainage only

flat rope *n* **:** a rope of metal or fiber having a flat cross section and usu. formed by braiding or sewing rather than by twisting

flats *pl of* FLAT, *pres 3d sing of* FLAT

flat sage *n* **:** SPART GRASS

flat–sawn \'⸗'⸗\ *adj, of lumber* **:** sawed so as to produce a flat-grain surface

flat seizing *n* **:** a seizing in which the lines seized are parallel to each other and a single binding layer is used — compare ROUND SEIZING

flat silver *n* **:** knives, forks, spoons, and other eating or serving utensils made of or plated with silver

flat–slab construction *n* **:** reinforced-concrete floor construction not requiring beams and girders to transmit the floor load to supporting columns

flat sour *n* **:** fermentation of canned products (as peas or corn) that is caused by thermoduric microorganisms which survive the canning process and that is characterized by the formation of acid without gas; *sometimes* **:** the off-flavor produced by such fermentation

flat spin *n* **1 :** a spin in which the longitudinal axis of an airplane inclines downward at a smaller angle than 45 degrees **2** *slang* **:** a state of mental confusion

flat·tail mullet \'⸗,⸗-\ *also* **flat tail** \'⸗,⸗\ *n* **:** an Australian mullet (*Liza argentia*) that is an important food fish

flat·ted \'flatəd\ *adj* [⁵*flat* + *-ed*] *Brit, of a building* **:** divided into flats

flat·ten \'flat°n\ *vb* **flattened; flattened; flattening** \-t(°)niŋ\ **flattens** [¹*flat* + *-en*] *vt* **1 :** to reduce to an even or more nearly even surface **:** make flat **:** LEVEL, SMOOTH ⟨~ the seams with a steam iron⟩ ⟨time ~*s* the mountains⟩ **2 a :** to throw down **:** bring to the ground **:** PROSTRATE ⟨the hurricane ~*ed* the forest⟩ **b :** DEPRESS, DEJECT, DISPIRIT ⟨was ~*ed* by grief⟩ **c :** to completely overwhelm ⟨the senator ~*ed* his opposition⟩: as (1) **:** to ruin financially ⟨the depression ~*ed* many young or small businesses⟩ (2) *slang* **:** to knock out ⟨the boxer was ~*ed* in the seventh round⟩; *sometimes* **:** to defeat decisively in any contest (3) **:** to kill or destroy by or as if by crushing ⟨the car ~*ed* the farmer's hen⟩ (4) **:** to make (as oneself) helplessly drunk **3** *archaic* **:** to make vapid or insipid **4 a :** to make (as paint) lusterless **b :** to cover (a surface) with a priming coat or a coat of flat paint **5** *Brit* **:** FLAT 4 **6 :** to adjust (a sail) by hauling in the aftermost clew to help turn a sailboat — often used with *in* ~ *vi* **1 :** to become flat or flatter: as **a :** to become dull, savorless, or lacking in spirit **b :** to get, move, or extend in or into a flat position or form — often used with *out* ⟨hills ~*ing* into coastal plains⟩ ⟨the ruts ~*ed* out under the pressure of wheels⟩ **c :** to become uniform or stabilized often at a new higher or lower level — usu. used with *out* ⟨prices are expected to ~ out after the holiday buying⟩ ⟨performance tended to ~ out after an initial period of improvement⟩ **d** (1) **:** to manipulate an airplane so as to bring its longitudinal axis parallel with the ground (as after a climb or a dive) — used with *out* (2) *of an airplane* **:** to assume such a position — used with *out* **2 :** to extend oneself in making an effort ⟨the horses ~*ed* into their collars⟩ ⟨rose refreshed and ~*ed* to the task of grubbing roots⟩

flattened–strand rope *n* **:** a wire rope having the wires in each strand arranged so as to form flat surfaces on the strands

flat·ten·er \'flat(°)nə(r)\ *n* -s **:** one that flattens: as **a :** a worker who flattens materials (as metal, leather, paper, or glass) **b :** a machine for flattening or straightening plates or sheets

flattening oven *n* [*flattening* fr. gerund of *flatten*] **:** a heating chamber in which split glass cylinders are flattened and annealed

flattening stone *n* **:** a stone used in a flattening oven

¹flat·ter \'flad·ə(r), -atə-\ *vb* -ED/-ING/-S [ME *flateren*, irreg. fr. OF *flater* to lick, flatter, fr. (assumed) OFrk *flat*, adj., flat; akin to OHG *flaz* flat — more at FLAT] *vt* **1 :** to praise excessively or fulsomely esp. from motives of self-interest **:** gratify or appeal to the self-love or vanity of usu. by artful and interested commendation or attentions **2 a** *archaic* **:** to make more pleasant or less oppressive **:** BEGUILE, SOOTHE **b :** to encourage (as a person or his hopes) esp. by false or specious representations ⟨~*ed* the old man by asking him to climb the mountain⟩ **c :** to please or gratify (as oneself) usu. with the assurance that something (as a view or procedure) is right or acceptable ⟨~ myself that only the most caviling critics can take exception to my interpretation⟩ ⟨~*ed* himself that the young people wanted his company for its own sake, not the luxuries he provided⟩; *also* **:** to congratulate (oneself) in respect to something ⟨suppose I may ~ myself that I am not a fool⟩ **d :** GRATIFY ⟨balmy breezes ~*ed* his skin⟩ **3 a :** to portray too favorably ⟨that picture ~*s* him⟩ **b :** to display or set off to advantage **:** make the most of the good points of ⟨a draped neckline designed to ~ the stylish stout⟩ ⟨soft rosy light that ~*s* tired skins⟩ **4** *obs* **:** to touch caressingly **:** FONDLE ~ *vi* **1** *obs, of an animal* **:** to show fondness (as by fawning or cries) **2 :** to use flattery

²flatter *vi* -ED/-ING/-S [ME *flateren*, alter. of *floteren* to float, flutter — more at FLUTTER] *obs* **:** FLUTTER, FLOAT

³flatter *comparative of* ¹FLAT

⁴flat·ter \'flad·ə(r), -atə-\ *n* -s [⁴*flat* + *-er*] **:** one that flattens: as **a :** a drawplate with a narrow rectangular orifice for drawing flat strips (as watch springs) **b :** a flat-faced swage used in smithing

flatter b

flat·ter·er \-ad·ərə(r), -atə-\ *n* -s [ME *flaterer*, fr. *flateren* to flatter + *-er*] **:** one that flatters

flattering *adj* [fr. pres. part. of ¹*flatter*] **:** marked by flattery; *esp* **:** tending to display to advantage or to enhance the good points of something ⟨a ~ new shade of rose⟩ — **flat·ter·ing·ly** *adv*

flat·tery \'flad·ərē, -atə-, -ri\ *n* -ES [ME *flaterie*, fr. MF, fr. OF, fr. *flater* to flatter + *-erie* -ery] **1 a :** the act or practice of flattering **:** the act of pleasing by artful commendation **:** ADULATION **b :** something that flatters or is felt flatteringly; *often* **:** false, insincere, or excessive praise ⟨just praise is only a debt but ~ is a present —Samuel Johnson⟩ **2** *obs* **:** a pleasing self-deception

flattest *superlative of* FLAT

flat·tie *also* **flat·ty** \'flad·ē\ *n, pl* **flatties** [¹*flat* + *-ie, -y*] **:** something characterized by flatness: as **a :** a small working boat peculiar to Chesapeake Bay and more southern waters of the eastern U.S. that is sloop-rigged and that has a flat bottom, straight sides, and a centerboard **b :** FLAT 6e **c** *slang* **:** POLICEMAN

flatting *pres part of* FLAT

flatting agent *n* [*flatting* fr. gerund of ⁴*flat*] **:** a material added to a coating (as a paint or varnish) to cause it to set with a matte surface

flatting mill *n* **:** a rolling mill producing sheet metal (as ribbon for the planchets of a mint)

flatting oil *n* **:** a liquid that when added to pigment-oil paste produces a paint which dries with a flat appearance

flat·tish \'flad·|ish, -at|, |ēsh\ *adj* **:** somewhat flat

flattop \'⸗,⸗\ *n, often attrib* **:** something with a flat or flattened upper surface: as **a :** a plant of the genus *Eriogonum* **b :** a building with a flat roof **c :** AIRCRAFT CARRIER **d** *slang* **:** CREW CUT

flat–topped crab \'⸗,⸗-\ *n* **:** a porcelain crab (*Petrolisthes eriomerus*) of rocky shores along the Pacific coast of No. America

flat tuning *n* **:** tuning of a radio such that the current in the receiving apparatus is but slightly affected by a change in the frequency of the received waves — compare SHARP TUNING

flat turn *n* **:** a turn of an airplane made without banking

flat–turret lathe *n* **:** a turret lathe having a low flat turret and a cross-sliding headstock with power feed

flat·u·lence \'flachələn(t)s\ *also* **flat·u·len·cy** \-lənsē, -si\ *n, pl* **flatulences** *also* **flatulencies** [*flatulence* fr. *flatulency*, after such pairs as E *abstinency: abstinence*; *flatulency* fr. *flatulent* + *-cy*] **:** the quality or state of being flatulent

flat·u·lent \-nt\ *adj* [MF, irreg. fr. L *flatus* act of blowing, act of breaking wind, fr. *flatus*, past part. of *flare* to blow — more at BLOW] **1 :** full of air or other gas ⟨the burner content was very ~⟩ **2 :** marked by or affected with gases generated in the intestine or stomach ⟨~ dyspepsia⟩ ⟨feeling somewhat ~ after a heavy meal⟩ **3 :** causing or likely to cause flatulence of the intestine or stomach ⟨dried beans are popularly considered very ~ food⟩ **4 :** pretentious without real worth or substance ⟨the barren and ~ gods served by his countryman —V.L.Parrington⟩ **:** swollen and empty ⟨~ rhetoric⟩ **:** TURGID **syn** see INFLATED

flat·u·lent·ly *adv* **:** in a flatulent manner **:** with flatulence

flat·u·os·i·ty \,flachə'wäsəd·ē\ *n* -ES [*flatuous* + *-ity*] *archaic* **:** FLATULENCE

flat·u·ous \'flachəwəs\ *adj* [MF *flatueux*, fr. L *flatus* + MF *-eux* -ous] *archaic* **:** FLATULENT

fla·tus \'flād·əs, -ātəs\ *n* -ES [L, act of blowing, act of breaking wind] **1 :** a puff of wind **:** BREATH **2 :** gas generated in the stomach or bowels

fla·tus vo·cis \,flād·əs'vōkəs, -d·ə'swō-\ *n, pl* **flatus vocis** [ML, lit., breath of the voice] **:** a mere name, word, or sound without a corresponding objective reality — used by the nominalists of universals

flatware \'⸗,⸗\ *n* **:** tableware that is more or less flat and usu. formed or cast in a single piece: **a :** dishes (as plates, platters) that are flat or shallow as distinguished from deeper vessels (as tureens or pitchers) — compare HOLLOW WARE **b :** table knives, forks, spoons, and other eating or serving utensils — compare FLAT SILVER

flat warehouse *n* **:** a one-story building or room used for storing bagged grain

flat wash *n* **:** FLATWORK

flatweed \'⸗,⸗\ *n* **:** CAT'S-EAR 1

flat wheel *n* **:** a railroad wheel which has flat spots on the tread (as from skidding on the rail)

flatwise *or* **flatways** \'⸗,⸗\ *adv* **:** with the flat side presented in some expressed or implied position

flatwoods \'⸗,⸗\ *n pl* **:** low-lying dry timber land; *specif* **:** level pineland occupying most of the Florida peninsula and producing typically the longleaf pine

flatwork \'⸗,⸗\ *n* **:** articles (as sheets, towels, tablecloths) that in laundering can be finished mechanically as distinguished from those requiring hand ironing

flatwork ironer *n* **:** MANGLE

flatworm \'⸗,⸗\ *n* **:** a worm of the phylum Platyhelminthes; *esp* **:** TURBELLARIAN

flat wrack *n* **:** any of various seaweeds of the genus *Fucus* (esp. *F. spiralis*) with broad fronds

flat yard *n* **:** a railroad switchyard in which cars are moved by means of locomotives instead of by gravity

flau·ber·tian \flō'bərshən, flō'-, -'bərd·ēən; flō'bershən, -ō-'berd·ēən\ *adj, usu cap* [Gustave *Flaubert* †1880 Fr. novelist + E *-ian*] **:** relating to or characteristic of the writer Flaubert or his realistic novels ⟨*Flaubertian* realism⟩

flaucht *or* **flaught** \'flakt, -ó-\ *n* -s [ME *flaght, flawght*; prob. akin to OE *flēan* to skin — more at FLAY] **1** *chiefly Scot* **:** FLAKE; *esp* **:** SNOWFLAKE **2** *chiefly Scot* **:** a flash esp. of fire or lightning

flaucht·bred \-,bred\ *adv* [Sc *flocht* flutter, bustle, excitement (fr. ME — Sc — *flocht*) + *braid* (broad); ME (Sc) *flocht* prob. of Scand origin; akin to ON *flōtti* flight — more at FLIGHT (running away)] **1** *Scot* **:** with limbs outstretched **:** SPREAD-EAGLED **2** *Scot* **:** EAGERLY, ENTHUSIASTICALLY

¹flauch·ter *or* **flaugh·ter** \'flòkər, -läk-\ *vb* -ED/-ING/-S [Sc *flocht* flutter, bustle, excitement + E *-er* (freq. suffix)] *vi, chiefly Scot* **:** FLUTTER, FLICKER ⟨the candle ~*s* in the draft⟩ ~ *vt, chiefly Scot* **:** EXCITE, FLUSTER ⟨a little whiskey had ~*ed* him⟩

²flauchter *or* **flaughter** \"\ *n* -s *chiefly Scot* **:** FLICKERING

flaunch *or* **flaunche** *var of* FLANCH

¹flaunt \'flónt, -ä-, -á-\ *vb* -ED/-ING/-S [prob. of Scand origin; akin to Norw dial. *flanta* to gad about; akin to ON *flana* to rush heedlessly, Gk *planasthai* to wander — more at PLANET] *vi* **1 :** to wave or flutter showily ⟨their flag ~*s* in the breeze⟩ ⟨scarlet tulips ~*ing* in the spring sun⟩ **2 a :** to display or obtrude oneself to public notice esp. by reason of excessive or gaudy finery or impropriety of behavior **:** seek to attract attention esp. by appearing or acting brash and brazen ⟨a pair of pretty girls giggling and ~*ing* on the street corner⟩ **b :** to make a showy appearance **:** stand out brightly or distinctly ⟨warm short days ~*ing* with dahlia and marigold —C.G.Glover⟩ ~ *vt* **1 :** to display ostentatiously ⟨the winners ~*ing* their victory⟩ **:** make an impudent show of **:** PARADE **2 :** to treat contemptuously **:** FLOUT ⟨~ army regulations⟩ **syn** see SHOW

²flaunt \"\ *n* -s **1 :** act of flaunting **:** DISPLAY **2** *obs* **:** something displayed for vain show ⟨in these my borrowed ~*s* —Shak.⟩

flaunt·er \-tə(r)\ *n* -s **:** one that flaunts

flaunt·ing·ly *adv* **:** in a flaunting manner

flaunty \-tē, -ti\ *adj* -ER/-EST [¹*flaunt* + *-y*] **:** given to or characterized by flaunting **:** OSTENTATIOUS ⟨a ~ display of newly acquired possessions⟩

flau·tan·do \flau̇'tän(,)dō\ *also* **flau·ta·to** \-äd·(,)ō\ *adv* (*or adj*) [*flautando* fr. It, sounding like a flute, verbal of (assumed) It *flautare* to sound like a flute, fr. It *flauto* flute; *flautato* fr. It, sounded like a flute, past part. of (assumed) It *flautare*] **:** in the manner of a flute; *specif* **:** over the fingerboard — used as a direction in stringed-instrument playing

flau·ti·no \-'tē(,)nō\ *n* -s [It, dim. of *flauto* flute] **1 :** a small flute **:** PICCOLO **2 :** a small accordion **3 :** a labial pipe organ stop usu. of 4-foot pitch

flau·tist \'flód·əst, -laúd-\ *n* -s [It *flautista*, fr. *flauto* flute + *-ista* -ist] **:** FLUTIST

flau·to \'flau̇,tō\ *n, pl* **flau·ti** \-,tē\ [It, fr. OProv *flaut* — more at FLUTE] **1 :** FLUTE **2** *archaic* **:** RECORDER 3a

flauto ama·bi·le \-ä'mäbē,lā\ *n* [It, pleasing flute] **:** a sweet-toned labial pipe organ stop of 4-foot or 8-foot pitch

flauto dol·ce \-'dōl,chā\ *n* [It, sweet flute] **:** FLUTE-DOUCE

flauto piccolo *n* [It, small flute] **:** PICCOLO

flauto tra·ver·so \-trə'vər(,)sō, -ver-\ *n* [It, lit., transverse flute] **1 :** FLUTE 1b **2 :** a 4-foot or 8-foot organ stop of quality like that of the flute

flav- *or* **flavo-** *comb form* [L *flavus* — more at BLUE] **1 :** yellow ⟨*flav*in⟩ ⟨*flavo*-virescent⟩ **2 :** flavin ⟨*flavo*enzyme⟩

flav·a·none \'flavə,nōn, 'flāv-\ *n* -s [ISV *flav-* + *-ane* + *-one*] **:** a colorless crystalline ketone $C_{15}H_{12}O_2$; 2,3-dihydroflavone; *also* **:** any of the derivatives of this ketone many of which (as eriodictyol) occur in plants often in the form of glycosides (as hesperidin)

fla·van·throne \flā'van,thrōn, fla'-, ⸗¦⸗¦⸗\ *also* **fla·van·threne** \-rēn\ *n* -s [*flavanthrone* fr. *flavanthrene* + *-one*; *flavanthrene* ISV *flav-* + *-anthrene*] **:** a yellow vat dye $C_{28}H_{12}N_2O_2$ related to anthraquinone

fla·ve·do \flə'vē(,)dō, flā'-\ *n* -s [NL, fr. L *flavus* yellow] **:** the outer colored layer of the mesocarp of a citrus fruit — compare ALBEDO

fla·ve·ria \-'virēə\ *n, cap* [NL, perh. irreg. fr. L *flavus* yellow] **:** a genus of chiefly tropical American herbs (family Compositae) with opposite leaves and small yellow flowers in clustered heads

fla·ves·cence \-'vesən(t)s\ *n* -s [fr. *flavescent*, after such pairs as E *abstinent: abstinence*] **:** a yellowing or blanching of normally green plant parts that accompanies peach yellows, mosaic mottling, and certain other virus diseases and is due to diminution of chlorophyll

fla·ves·cent \-°nt\ *adj* [L *flavescent-, flavescens*, pres. part. of *flavescere* to turn yellow, fr. *flavus* yellow] **:** turning yellow **:** YELLOWISH

fla·vi·an \'flāvēən\ *adj, usu cap* [L *flavianus*, fr. *Flavius* (name borne by members of a particular Roman gens) + L *-anus* -an] **:** of or relating to the ancient Roman gens bearing the name Flavius and esp. to the three Roman emperors Vespasian, Titus, and Domitian who belonged to this gens

fla·vi·a·nate \'flāvēə,nāt, 'flav-\ *n* -s [ISV *flavian-* (as in *flavianic acid*) + *-ate*] **:** a salt of flavianic acid

fla·vi·an·ic acid \¦⸗⸗¦anik-\ *n* [*flavianic* prob. ISV *flav-* + *-ian* + *-ic*] **:** a yellow crystalline acid $C_{10}H_6N_2O_8S$ used chiefly in precipitating arginine, tyrosine, or organic bases as insoluble salts

fla·vid \'flāvəd, -lav-\ *adj* [L *flavidus*, fr. *flavus* yellow] **:** YELLOW ⟨a ~ gold coin⟩

fla·vin \'flāvən *also* -lav-\ *or* **fla·vine** \", -,vēn\ *n* -s [ISV *flav-* + *-in, -ine*] **1 :** a yellow dye obtained by extracting quercitron bark — see DYE table I (under *Natural Yellow 10*) **2 :** any of the yellow acridine dyes used in medicine for their antiseptic properties; *esp* **:** ACRIFLAVINE **3 :** any of a class of yellow water-soluble nitrogenous pigments derived from isoalloxazine and occurring in the form of nucleotides as coenzymes of flavoproteins; *esp* **:** RIBOFLAVIN

flavin adenine dinucleotide *n* **:** a coenzyme $C_{27}H_{33}N_9O_{15}P_2$ of certain flavoproteins (as xanthine oxidase); riboflavin 5'-adenosine-diphosphate — called also *FAD*

flavin enzyme *n* **:** FLAVOPROTEIN

flavin mononucleotide *n* **:** RIBOFLAVIN PHOSPHATE

flavo·bacterium \¦flā(,)vō, ¦fla(-+\ *n, cap* [NL, fr. *flav-* + *bacterium*] **:** a genus related to *Achromobacter* and comprising soil or water bacteria that produce yellow or orange pigments and often reduce nitrates to nitrites

fla·vone \'flā,vōn, 'fla,-, ⸗'⸗\ *n* -s [ISV *flav-* + *-one*; orig. formed as G *flavon*] **:** a colorless crystalline ketone $C_{15}H_{10}O_2$ found as a dust on the leaves, stems, and seed capsules of many primroses, and also prepared synthetically; 2-phenylchromone; *also* **:** any of the derivatives of this ketone many of which (as chrysin) occur as yellow plant pigments often in the form of glycosides (as apiin) — compare FLAVANONE, ISOFLAVONE

¹fla·vo·noid \'flāvə,nóid, 'flav-\ *adj* [*flavone* + *-oid*] **:** of, relating to, or like flavone or isoflavone in chemical structure

²flavonoid \"\ *n* -s **:** a flavonoid compound (as a plant pigment) — see BIOFLAVONOID; compare ANTHOCYANIDIN, ANTHOXANTHIN, CHALCONE

fla·vo·nol \-nól,-nōl\ *n* -s [ISV *flavone* + *-ol*; orig. formed in G] **:** any of various hydroxy derivatives of flavone; *esp* **:** the colorless crystalline 3-hydroxy compound $C_{15}H_9O_2(OH)$ many of whose derivatives occur as yellow plant pigments often in the form of glycosides (as quercetin, morin)

fla·vo·protein \¦flā(,)vō, ¦fla(-+\ *n* [ISV *flav-* + *protein*] **:** any of a class of dehydrogenases that contain a flavin and in some cases also a metal, that occur in animal and plant cells, and that play a major role in biological oxidations by oxidizing metabolites directly or through the agency of pyridine nucleotides and by being in turn oxidized usu. by cytochromes — called also *flavin enzyme*; compare YELLOW ENZYME

fla·vo·purpurin \"+\ *n* [ISV *flav-* + *purpurin*; orig. formed in G] **:** a yellow crystalline compound $C_{14}H_5O_2(OH)_3$ found in commercial synthetic alizarin and also made separately; 1,2,6-trihydroxy-anthraquinone

¹fla·vor \'flāvə(r)\ *n* -s *see -or in Explan Notes* [ME *flavour*, fr. (assumed) MF *flavour*, fr. OF *flavor*, alter. (influenced by OF *savor*) of *flaor, flaur*, fr. (assumed) VL *flator*, fr. L *flare* to blow — more at BLOW] **1 a** *archaic* **:** that quality of something which affects the sense of smell **:** ODOR, FRAGRANCE, AROMA **b :** that quality of something which affects the sense of taste or gratifies the palate **:** SAVOR ⟨condiments impart ~ to food⟩ **c :** the blend of taste and smell sensations evoked by a substance (as a portion of food or drink) in the mouth ⟨a pungent bitter ~⟩ **2 :** any agent (as a spice or extract) designed to impart flavor to or alter the flavor of something ⟨kept cinnamon, vanilla, and other ~*s* and extracts on a special shelf⟩ **3 :** characteristic or predominant quality ⟨the full ~ of English country life⟩; *often* **:** characteristic style (as of a school or individual) in literature or art ⟨the acrid ~ of his prose⟩ **syn** see TASTE

²flavor \"\ *vb* **flavored; flavored; flavoring** \-v(ə)riŋ\ **flavors** *see -or in Explan Notes* [ME *flavren* to give off an odor, fr. *flavour*, n.] *vt* **:** to give or add flavor to ⟨~*ed* the salad with herbs and vinegar⟩; *often* **:** to give character or zest to ⟨his witty ad libs ~ the whole performance⟩ ~ *vi* **:** to have a flavor **:** SMACK — used with *of* ⟨this ~*s* of treason⟩

flavored *adj* [fr. past part. of ²*flavor*] **:** having or indicating a particular flavor ⟨high-*flavored* cordials⟩ ⟨a hate-*flavored* and acrimonious discussion⟩

fla·vor·ful \-və(r)fəl\ *adj* **:** full of flavor **:** SAVORY, TASTEFUL — **fla·vor·ful·ly** \-əlē, -əli\ *adv*

flavoring *n* -s [fr. gerund of ²*flavor*] **:** FLAVOR 2 ⟨~ essences⟩

fla·vor·less \-və(r)ləs\ *adj* **:** lacking in flavor **:** FLAT, DRAB ⟨~ platitudes⟩ ⟨I cultivated her ~ friends with the object of getting asked to their parties —Edmund Wilson⟩

fla·vor·ous \-v(ə)rəs\ *adj* **:** FLAVORSOME ⟨a carefully wrought, ~ reminiscence —*N.Y. Herald Tribune*⟩

fla·vor·some \-və(r)səm\ *adj* **:** richly and usu. pleasingly flavored **:** FLAVORFUL, PALATABLE, TASTY; *often* **:** characterized by or tending to impart a particular flavor ⟨~ dialogue —John Gassner⟩ ⟨folksy, ~ yarns —Jay Walz⟩ **syn** see PALATABLE

fla·vory \-v(ə)rē, -ri\ *adj* [¹*flavor* + *-y*] **:** rich in flavor — used esp. of teas ⟨a ~ tea with a good bouquet⟩

fla·vous \'flāvəs, -lav-\ *adj* [L *flavus* yellow — more at BLUE] **:** YELLOW 1a; *esp* **:** of a clear pure yellow — used chiefly in technical descriptions in taxonomy and usu. postpositively ⟨elytra and antennae ~⟩; compare LUTEOUS

¹flaw \'flò\ *n* -s [ME *flaw, flawe*, prob. of Scand origin; akin to Sw *flaga* flaw, flake, ON *flaga* slab; akin to OE *flēan* to skin — more at FLAY] **1** *obs* **:** FLAKE, FRAGMENT, BIT ⟨this heart shall break into a hundred thousand ~*s* —Shak.⟩ **2 :** a faulty part **:** CRACK, BREACH, GAP, FISSURE ⟨a ~ in a gem or a vase⟩ ⟨a ~ in a bar of steel⟩ **3 :** a fault or defect esp. in a character or a piece of work ⟨the greatest ~ in his plan was failure to anticipate costs⟩ ⟨a complexion without a ~⟩; *esp* **:** a fault in a legal paper that may nullify it ⟨a ~ in a will⟩ ⟨found a ~ in the statute⟩ **4** *Scot* **:** LIE, FIB **5** *chiefly Scot* **:** a thin layer of turf or peat **6 :** a nearly vertical geological fault transverse to the strike of the rocks and characterized by horizontal displacement **syn** see BLEMISH

²flaw \"\ *vb* -ED/-ING/-S *vt* **1 :** to make flaws in **:** CRACK ⟨a ~*ed* diamond⟩ ⟨the brazen caldrons with the frosts are ~*ed* —John Dryden⟩ **2 :** to make a breach or defect in **:** VIOLATE, NULLIFY ⟨~ an agreement⟩ ⟨France hath ~*ed* the league —Shak.⟩ ~ *vi* **:** to become defective **:** CRACK, BREAK ⟨pavements warping and ~*ing* in the heat⟩ ⟨columns of smoke that . . . ~*ed* suddenly in the canyon wind —W.V.T.Clark⟩

³flaw \"\ *n* -s [of Scand origin; akin to Norw *flaga* gust, squall; akin to MHG & MLG *vlage* gust, attack, Lith *plakti* to beat, L *plangere* to beat — more at PLAINT] **1 :** a sudden burst of wind of short duration with or without rain or snow ⟨the wind changed with ~*s* from westward —Archibald MacLeish⟩; *also* **:** a spell of stormy weather **2** *obs* **:** an outburst esp. of passion or anger **:** a sudden tumult or disorder

flawed *adj* [fr. past part. of ²*flaw*] **:** having a flaw **:** DEFECTIVE, FAULTY

flaw·less \-ləs\ *adj* **1 :** lacking flaw or imperfection **:** PERFECT ⟨~ diction⟩ **2** *of a gemstone* **:** having no internal flaws — **flaw·less·ly** *adv* — **flaw·less·ness** *n* -ES

flawn \'flón, 'flän\ *n* -s [origin unknown] **:** MANILA GRASS

¹flawy \'flòi, -òē\ *adj, often* -ER/-EST [¹*flaw* + *-y*] **:** full of flaws (as cracks) **:** DEFECTIVE ⟨a ~ lot of pottery⟩

²flawy \"\ *adj, often* -ER/-EST [³*flaw* + *-y*] **:** subject to or characterized by sudden gusts of wind

flax \'flaks\ *n* -ES *often attrib* [ME *flax, flex*, fr. OE *fleax*, akin to OFris *flax*, OHG *flahs* flax, L *plectere* to plait, braid — more at PLY] **1 a :** a plant of the genus *Linum*; *esp* **:** a slender erect annual (*L. usitatissimum*) with linear leaves and blue flowers that is widely cultivated for (1) its long silky bast fibers which when freed from the stem by retting and mechanical processes are used in textile manufacture and are the source of linen and (2) its seeds which yield a valuable oil and a meal used esp. for cattle feed — see FLAXSEED **b :** the bast fiber of the flax plant esp. when cleaned and prepared for spinning **2 :** any of several plants resembling flax — usu. used with a qualifying term ⟨white ~⟩ ⟨several toad*flaxes*⟩ **3 :** a grayish yellow that is less strong and slightly greener than chamois, lighter and very slightly redder than old ivory, and redder and slightly lighter and stronger than crash — called also *peanut, pebble*

flax bellflower *n* **:** HAREBELL 1

flaxbird \'⸗,⸗\ *n* [so called fr. its habit of feeding on the seeds of flax] **:** GOLDFINCH 3

flax bollworm *n* **:** a grub that is the larva of a moth (*Heliothis ononis*) and is closely related to the cotton bollworm but feeds chiefly in the seedpods of flax

flax brake *also* **flaxbreak** *or* **flax breaker** *n* [*flax brake* fr. *flax* + *brake* (machine); *flax break & flax breaker* by folk etymology fr. *flax brake*] **:** a machine for separating the woody stem tissues from the fiber in flax

flax buncher *n* **:** a grain-binder attachment used to cut flax in unbound bunches

flax canker *n* **1 :** heat canker of flax **2** *or* **flax anthracnose :** a cankered condition of flax caused by a fungus (*Colletotrichum linicolum*)

flax comb *n* **:** HACKLE 1

flax dodder *n* **:** a dodder (*Cuscuta epilinum*) infesting cultivated flax — called also *flax vine*

flaxdrop \'⸗,⸗\ *n* **:** FLAX DODDER

Flax·e·dil \'flaksə,dil\ *trademark* — used for gallamine triethiodide

flax·en \'flaksən\ *adj* [ME *flaxen, flexen*, fr. *flax, flex* flax + *-en*] **1 a :** made of flax ⟨~ linens⟩ **b :** resembling flax esp. in being of pale soft strawy color — used chiefly of the hair ⟨~ curls⟩ **2** *archaic* **:** of or relating to flax

flax family *n* **:** LINACEAE

flaxflower blue \'⸗,⸗-\ *n* **:** a moderate blue to light purplish blue

flaxlike \'⸗,⸗\ *adj* **:** resembling flax ⟨a slender ~ herb⟩ ⟨soft but tough ~ fiber⟩

flax lily *n* **1 :** NEW ZEALAND FLAX **2 :** any of several plants constituting a genus (*Dianella*) of the family Liliaceae; *esp* **:** an Australian plant (*D. laevis*) that yields a long silky fiber formerly used by the aborigines for making baskets

flax–polled \'⸗,⸗\ *adj* **:** having flaxen hair

flax ripple *n* **:** a comb for removing bolls or seeds from flax

flax rust *n* **1 :** a disease of flax caused by a rust fungus (*Melampsora lini*) **2 :** the fungus causing flax rust

flax·seed \'flak,sēd *sometimes* -ks,sēd\ *n* **1 a :** a seed of the flax plant **b :** seeds of flax in bulk; *esp* **:** the commercial product consisting of these seeds that is used as a demulcent and emollient in inflammatory conditions of the respiratory, intestinal, and urinary passages and that yields linseed oil **2 :** a minute annual allseed (*Millegrana radiola*) that is closely related to true flax and is native to parts of Europe and Africa **3 :** the brown-shelled pupa of the Hessian fly resembling a flaxseed in size and appearance

flax–sick \'⸗,⸗\ *adj, of soil* **:** so infested with fungi (as *Fusarium lini*) that flax cannot be grown

flax star *n* **:** a low annual Mediterranean herb (*Asterolinon linumstellatum*) of the family Primulaceae bearing solitary greenish flowers

flax straw *n* **1 :** the whole flax plant after pulling and drying **2 :** the fiber flax retted and broken but not scutched

flax vine *n* **:** FLAX DODDER

flaxweed \'⸗,⸗\ *n* **:** TOADFLAX 1

flax wheel *n* **:** SAXON WHEEL

flax wilt *n* **:** a destructive disease of flax due to a fungus (*Fusarium lini*) which causes damping-off of young seedlings and wilting, yellowing, and death of older plants — compare FLAX-SICK

flaxy \'flaksē\ *adj* -ER/-EST [*flax* + *-y*] **:** resembling flax esp. in texture **:** FLAXEN

flay \'flā\ *vt* -ED/-ING/-S [ME *flen*, fr. OE *flēan*; akin to MD *vlaen* to skin, ON *flā* to skin, Lith *plēšti* to tear] **1 :** to strip off the skin or surface of **:** SKIN ⟨~ an ox⟩ ⟨~*ed* him with a lash⟩ ⟨with her nails she'll ~ thy wolfish visage —Shak.⟩ **2 :** to subject to treatment like or likened to skinning: as **a :** to strip of possessions ⟨the people ~*ed* by excessive taxes⟩ **b :** to reprove harshly **:** criticize severely **:** CENSURE, EXCORIATE ⟨his wife ~*ed* him when she heard where he had been⟩ **syn** see SKIN — **flay a flint :** to exact all possible gain

flay·er \'flāə(r), -le(ə)r, -leə\ *n* -S [ME *flear*, fr. *flen* to flay + *-ar, -er, -ere* -er] **:** one that flays

f layer *n, cap F* **1 :** the highest known and most densely ionized regular layer of the ionosphere occurring at night within the F region and resulting from the merger of the F_1 layer and F_2 layer **2 :** the zone in a forest soil characterized by abundant presence of plant remains actively undergoing decay

flayflint \'⸗,⸗\ *n, archaic* **:** SKINFLINT, MISER

fld *abbr* **1** field **2** fluid

¹flea \'flē\ *n* -S [ME *fle, flee*, fr. OE *flēah, flēa*; akin to OHG *flōh* flea, ON *flō*; prob. derivative fr. the root of E *flee*] **1 :** any of an order (Siphonaptera) of wingless bloodsucking insects that have a hard laterally compressed body, long legs adapted to leaping, and free-living larvae, feed on warm-blooded animals, and include important pests of man and domestic animals — see DOG FLEA, PULEX, STICKTIGHT FLEA **2 :** FLEA BEETLE **3 :** PUCE — **flea in one's ear :** an unwelcome and usu. unexpected hint or warning **:** an irritating rebuke ⟨I'll put a *flea in his ear* if he comes nosing around here⟩ ⟨sent the boy about his business with a *flea in his ear*⟩

²flea \"\ *vt* -ED/-ING/-S **:** to rid of fleas ⟨don't forget to ~ the dog⟩

fleabag \'⸗,⸗\ *n* **1 a :** BED; *often* **:** SLEEPING BAG ⟨he thrust one of his legs cumbrously out of the top of his ~ —F M. Ford⟩ **b :** an inferior hotel or rooming house ⟨three dollars for a room in a handy ~ —Jack Lait & Lee Mortimer⟩ **2 :** a flea-ridden animal **3 :** a slatternly old woman

fleabane \'⸗,⸗\ *n* **:** any of various plants of the family Compositae that are supposed to drive away fleas: as **a** *also* **fleabane mullet :** a hairy perennial herb (*Pulicaria dysenterica*) with yellow ray flowers that is native to Europe but widely naturalized **b :** any of several plants of the genera *Erigeron* and *Artemisia* — see DAISY FLEABANE

flea beetle *n* **:** any of various small chrysomelid beetles that have the thighs of the hind legs thickened and adapted for leaping, that constitute *Altica, Epitrix*, and numerous other genera, that feed on the leaves and tender new growth of plants, and that sometimes serve as vectors of virus diseases of plants — see POTATO FLEA BEETLE

fleabite \'⸗,⸗\ *n* **1 :** the bite of a flea; *also* **:** the red spot caused by such a bite **2 a :** a trifling wound or pain suggesting that of the bite of a flea **b :** a small irritation **:** a trifling annoyance **3 :** a minute amount

fleabiting *n* -S [*biting* fr. gerund of *bite*] *obs* **:** FLEABITE

flea–bitten \'⸗,⸗⸗\ *adj* **1 :** bitten by or infested with fleas ⟨a *flea-bitten* old hound⟩ ⟨*flea-bitten* lodgings⟩ **2** *of a horse* **:** having a white or gray coat flecked with minute dots of bay or sorrel ⟨a rangy *flea-bitten* gray⟩

flea bug *n* **1 :** FLEAHOPPER **2 :** TOBACCO FLEA BEETLE

flead \'flēd\ *n* -S [perh. alter. of ⁴*fleck*] *dial Brit* **:** unrendered leaf fat of the hog

fleadock \'⸗,⸗\ *n* -S **:** BUTTERBUR

fleahopper \'⸗,⸗⸗\ *n* **:** any of various small jumping bugs several of which feed on cultivated plants — see COTTON FLEAHOPPER, GARDEN FLEAHOPPER

fleam \'flēm\ *n* -S [ME *fleme*, fr. MF *flieme*, fr. LL *phlebotomus*, modif. of Gk *phlebotomon*, fr. *phleb-* + *-tomon* (fr. *temnein* to cut) — more at TOME] **1 :** a sharp lancet formerly much used for bloodletting **2 :** angle of bevel of the edge of a sawtooth with respect to the plane of the blade

flea market *also* **flea fair** *n* **:** an outdoor market at which antiques and secondhand articles (as furniture, pottery, or jewelry) are sold esp. from parked vehicles

flea mint *n* **:** PENNYROYAL 1

fleam tooth *n* **:** a sawtooth shaped like an isosceles triangle

fleaseed \'⸗,⸗\ *n* [so called fr. the resemblance of its seeds to fleas] **1 :** the seed of the fleawort **2 :** an oak-leaf gall of the southwestern U.S. that becomes detached and moves about independently due to the activity of the enclosed insect larva

flea soap *n* **:** soap to remove or kill fleas while cleansing

flea·some \'flēsəm\ *adj* **:** full of fleas

fleaweed \'⸗,⸗\ *n* [so called fr. the alleged power of its smell to drive off fleas] **1** *dial Eng* **:** YELLOW BEDSTRAW **2 :** BLUE CURLS 1

flea weevil *n* **:** any of various small broad weevils that have large eyes and hind legs adapted for leaping and that include some with larvae which are leaf miners on cultivated plants — see APPLE FLEA WEEVIL

fleawort \'⸗,⸗\ *n* [ME *flewort*, fr. OE *flēawyrt*, fr. *flēah, flēa* flea + *wyrt* herb, root — more at FLEA, WORT] **1 :** an Old World plantain (*Plantago psyllium*) having seeds that swell and become gelatinous when moist and that are used as a mild laxative — called also *psyllium* **2 :** any of various plants supposedly efficacious as destroyers of fleas

fleb·ile \'flebəl, 'flēb-\ *adj* [L *flebilis* lamentable, wretched — more at FEEBLE] **:** TEARFUL, DOLEFUL

flebotomus [NL, fr. LL *flebotomus, phlebotomus* lancet] *syn of* PHLEBOTOMUS — a prior name made unavailable by action of the International Commission on Zoological Nomenclature

flech \'flek\ *Scot var of* FLEA

flèche \'flāsh, -lesh\ *n* -S [F, lit., arrow, fr. OF *fleche*, of Gmc origin; akin to MD *vlieke* arrow, MLG *flieke* long arrow; akin to OHG *fliogan* to fly — more at FLY] **1 :** SPIRE; *esp* **:** a slender spire above the intersection of the nave and transepts of a church or cathedral and commonly carrying the Sanctus bell **2 :** a method of reaching the opponent that is used esp. in fencing with saber or épée and that consists of one or more rapid steps forward beginning with the rear foot

flèche 1

flé·chette \flā'shet, fle-\ *n* -S [F, fr. *flèche* arrow + *-ette*] **:** a small dart-shaped projectile clustered in an explosive warhead, dropped from an airplane, or fired from a hand-held gun

¹fleck \'flek\ *vt* -ED/-ING/-S [back-formation fr. *flecked*, adj., spotted, dappled (taken as a past part.), fr. ME, prob. modif. (influenced by ME ¹-*ed*) of ON *flekkōttr*, fr. *flekkr* spot; akin to MD *vlecke* spot, stain, OHG *flec, fleccho* spot, piece of land, and perh. to L *plaga* region — more at FLAKE] **:** STREAK, STRIPE **:** VARIEGATE, DAPPLE, SPOT ⟨blood ~*ed* the snow⟩

²fleck \"\ *n* -S **1 :** SPOT, MARK: as **a :** a blemish (as a freckle) on the skin **b :** a spot of color or brightness ⟨~*s* of fire rose from the embers⟩ ⟨a tweed brightened with ~*s* and nubs of bright wool⟩ **2 :** FLAKE, PARTICLE ⟨a ~ of soot on her nose⟩ ⟨scattered ~*s* of snow⟩ **3 :** any of various plant diseases of which the characteristic injury takes the form of small usu. elongated discolored lesions of the foliage ⟨~ in lilies appears to be a virus disease though similar conditions in other plants may be caused by fungi⟩

³fleck \"\ *vi* [perh. alter. of ¹*flack*] *now dial Brit* **:** FLIT, FLUTTER

⁴fleck \"\ *n* -S [alter. of ²*flick*] *dial Eng* **:** LEAF FAT

⁵fleck \"\ *n* -S [irreg. fr. *flea*] *Scot* **:** FLEA

fleck·er \-kə(r)\ *vt* -ED/-ING/-S [freq. of ¹*fleck*] **:** SPOT, STREAK — used chiefly as a participial adjective ⟨a quiet sun-*fleckered* spot beneath a tall elm⟩

fleck·less \-kləs\ *adj* **:** free from flecks; *esp* **:** FLAWLESS — **fleck·less·ly** *adv*

flec·tion *or* **flex·ion** \'flekshən\ *n* -S [*flection* alter. (influenced by such words as *correction*) of *flexion*, fr. L *flexion-, flexio* bend, turn, curve, fr. *flexus* (past part. of *flectere* to bend) + *-ion-, -io* -ion] **1 :** the act of flexing or bending **:** TURNING ⟨twisting and ~ of the vines by the wind⟩ **2 :** a part bent **:** BEND, FOLD, TURN ⟨an oxbow is a broad ~ of a stream⟩ **3 :** INFLECTION 4 **4** *usu flexion* **a :** a movement involving the bending of a joint esp. between the bones of a limb by which the angle between the bones is diminished **b :** a forward raising of the arm or leg by a movement at the shoulder or hip joint — opposed to *extension* **c :** the yielding of a horse to the pressure of the bit resulting in bending the head at the poll

flec·tion·al *or* **flex·ion·al** \-shənᵊl,-shnəl\ *adj* **:** capable of or relating to flection esp. of words

flec·tor \'flektə(r)\ *n* -S [obs. E *flect*, v., to bend (fr. L *flectere*) + E *-or*] **:** something used in bending; *esp* **:** FLEXOR

¹fledge \'flej\ *adj* [ME *flegge, flygge*, fr. OE *-flycge* (in *unflycge* not yet fledged); akin to MD *vlugge* able to fly, OHG *flucki*; derivative fr. the root of E *fly*] *archaic* **:** capable of or fitted for flying **:** FEATHERED, FLEDGED

²fledge \"\ *vb* -ED/-ING/-S *vi* **1 a** *of a bird* **:** to acquire the feathers necessary for flight **b** *of an insect* **:** to attain the winged adult stage (as by metamorphosis) **2 :** to attain the state of independence or competence characteristic of maturity ⟨the newly *fledged* dancer⟩ ~ *vt* **1 :** to rear or care for (a young bird) until plumage is developed enough for flying **2 a :** to cover with or as if with feathers or a feathery growth ⟨your master, whose chin is not yet *fledged* —Shak.⟩ **b :** to furnish (as a nest) with a feathery covering **3 :** to furnish (as an arrow) with feathers for flying

fledge·less \-ləs\ *adj* **:** UNFLEDGED

fledg·ling *also* **fledge·ling** \-jliŋ,-jlən\ *n* -S *often attrib* **1 a :** a young bird just fledged **b :** a young bird capable of leaving the nest and surviving **2 :** something or someone characterized by immaturity; *esp* **:** a person not fully experienced in some activity ⟨~ dramatists⟩

fledgy \'flejē, -ji-\ *adj, often* -ER/-EST [¹*fledge* + *-y*] **:** FEATHERED, DOWNY, FEATHERY ⟨a ~ sea-bird choir —John Keats⟩

¹flee \'flē\ *vb* **fled** \'fled\ **fled; fleeing; flees** [ME *flen*, fr. OE *flēon*; akin to OHG *fliohan* to flee, ON *flȳja*, Goth *thliuhan* to flee, and prob. to OE *flēogan* to fly — more at FLY] *vi* **1 a :** to run away from or as if from danger or evil **:** hasten off ⟨cowards ~*ing* before a revolution —R.W.Emerson⟩ ⟨a person . . . who shall ~ from justice —*U.S.Constitution*⟩ **b :** to hurry toward a source of security or protection — used with *to* or *into* ⟨he *fled* back to the shelter of his cab —Osbert Sitwell⟩ ⟨the survivors *fled* into the wilderness⟩ **2 :** to pass away swiftly **:** VANISH ⟨mists ~*ing* before the rising sun⟩ ⟨the truck was gathering speed . . . and the fields were ~*ing* past in the twilight —Kay Boyle⟩ **3** *archaic* **:** FLY, SPEED ⟨the arrow *fled* from the bow⟩ ~ *vt* **1 a :** to run away from **:** endeavor to avoid (as a threatened danger) or escape from (as an adversary) ⟨heard her ~*ing* his approach —T.B.Costain⟩ ⟨the lowlanders were ~*ing* the rising waters⟩ **b :** SHUN, AVOID, EVADE ⟨governments long in office are not inclined to ~ party and political considerations —S.L.A.Marshall⟩ **2 :** to leave abruptly **:** depart from suddenly or unexpectedly **:** ABANDON, FORSAKE ⟨when fortune *fled* her spoiled and favorite child —Lord Byron⟩ ⟨~*ing* the city for the hot months —Jerome Weidman⟩ **syn** see ESCAPE

²flee \"\ *chiefly Scot var of* FLY

³flee \"\ *dial Brit var of* FLAY

¹fleece \'flēs\ *n* -S [ME *flees*, fr. OE *flēos, flȳs*; akin to MD *vlies* fleece, MHG *vlius* fleece, L *pluma* down, small soft feather, Lith *pluskos* (pl.) tufts of hair] **1 a :** the coat of wool that covers a sheep or similar animal ⟨the ~ of the vicuna is very soft⟩ **b :** the wool obtained from a sheep at one shearing ⟨a ~ of over 16 pounds⟩ **c :** a heraldic representation of the fleece of a ram depicted complete with head and feet as if stuffed and suspended by a belt about its middle **2 :** any of various coverings resembling a fleece esp. in soft or woolly quality ⟨a heavy ~ of snow⟩ ⟨a cloud ~ half covered the sky⟩: as **a :** a covering of vegetation **b :** a head of hair **c :** a soft bulky knitted or woven fabric that has a deep pile or long nap and that is made usu. of wool or synthetic fibers and used chiefly for clothing **3 :** meat taken from either side of the hump of the buffalo **4** *obs* **a :** booty from the fleecing of a victim **b :** the act of fleecing a victim **5 :** a web of cotton or wool fiber during the carding process

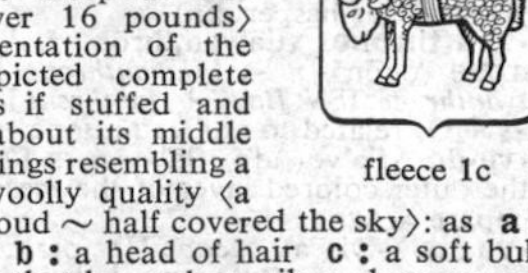

fleece 1c

²fleece \"\ *vt* -ED/-ING/-S **1 a :** to shear the fleece from (as a sheep) **b :** to remove (as wool) by shearing or plucking **2 a :** to strip (as a person) of property by fraud or extortion **:** DESPOIL, PLUNDER ⟨*fleeced* the church to build an estate for his sons⟩; *sometimes* **:** to charge excessively for service or goods ⟨garish roadhouses where the customer knew he would be *fleeced*⟩ **b :** to obtain by rapacious or improper means ⟨never hesitated to ~ a fee from a poor widow⟩ **3 :** to cover or fleck with (fleecy masses) ⟨a blue sky *fleeced* with little clouds⟩

fleece·able \-səbəl\ *adj* **:** capable of being or likely to be fleeced **:** GULLIBLE

fleeced \'flēst\ *adj* [¹*fleece* + *-ed*] **1 :** covered with or as if with a fleece ⟨*long-fleeced* sheep⟩ **2** *of textiles* **:** having a soft nap

fleeceflower *or* **fleecevine** \'⸗,⸗⸗\ *n* **:** SILVER-LACE VINE

fleece·less \'flēsləs\ *adj* **:** having no fleece

fleece–lined \'⸗;⸗\ *adj* **1 :** lined with fleece **2** *of knit goods* **:** having a heavily fleeced inner surface

fleec·er \'flēsə(r)\ *n* -S **:** one that fleeces

fleece wool *n* **:** wool sheared in a continuous fleece that is usu. dagged, folded, and tied individually

fleece worm *n* **:** any of various blowfly maggots developing in the wool of sheep; *esp* **:** the maggot of the black blowfly (*Phormia regina*)

fleech \'flēch\ *vb* -ED/-ING/-ES [ME (Sc) *flechen*] *dial* **:** to coax or wheedle esp. by flattery

fleec·i·ness \'flēsēnəs, -sin-\ *n* -ES **:** the quality or state of being fleecy

fleecy \-sē,-si\ *adj* -ER/-EST [¹*fleece* + *-y*] **:** covered with, made of, or resembling fleece or a fleece ⟨~ white clouds⟩ ⟨winter coats are getting *fleecier* —Lois Long⟩ ⟨stems ~ with soft hairs⟩

fleed \'flēd\ *var of* FLEAD

fleeing *pres part of* FLEE

fleem *chiefly dial var of* FLEAM

¹fle·er \'flēə(r), -lē(ə)r, -liə\ *n* -S [ME, fr. *flen* to flee + *-er, -ere* -er] **:** one that flees

²fleer \'fli(ə)r, -iə\ *vb* -ED/-ING/-S [ME *fleryen*, of Scand origin; akin to Norw *flire* to giggle, Sw (dial.) *flira* — more at FLIMFLAM] *vi* **1 a :** to laugh, grin, or grimace in a coarse manner **b :** to make a wry face in contempt or grin in scorn **:** SNEER, MOCK, GIBE **2** *obs* **:** to grin or smile with an often affected or artful air of civility ~ *vt* **:** to laugh at contemptuously **:** make a mock of **:** hold up to contempt **syn** see SCOFF

³fleer \"\ *n* -S **1 :** a word or look of derision or mockery ⟨and mark the ~*s*, the gibes, and notable scorns —Shak.⟩ **2 :** a grin simulating civility **:** LEER

fleer·er \'flirə(r)\ *n* -S **:** one that fleers

fleer·ing·ly *adv* **:** in a fleering manner **:** with a fleer

flee·rish \'flērish\ *n* -ES [alter. (influenced by *flint*) of earlier Sc *furisine*, prob. fr. (assumed) ME (Sc) *furisen*, prob. fr. MLG *vūrisern*, fr. *vūr* fire + *īsern* iron; akin to OHG *fiur* fire and to OHG *īsan, īsarn* iron — more at FIRE, IRON] *Scot* **:** STEEL 3c

flees *pres 3d sing of* FLEE

fleesh \'flēsh\ *chiefly Scot var of* FLEECE

¹fleet \'flēt, *usu* -ēd·+V\ *vb* -ED/-ING/-S [ME *fleten*, fr. OE *flēotan*; akin to OHG *fliozzan* to flow, float, ON *fljōta* to flow, float, Lith *plausti* to wash, OE *flōwan* to flow] *vi* **1** *now dial Brit* **:** FLOAT **2 a** *obs* **:** FLOAT, DRIFT ⟨clouds and mist ~*ing*⟩ **b :** to move waveringly **:** FLUCTUATE **3 a** *archaic* **:** to glide along or away **:** FLOW **b :** to fade away **:** DISSOLVE, VANISH **4** *obs* **:** to become filled **:** ABOUND **5 :** to fly swiftly **:** pass over quickly **:** HASTEN, FLIT ⟨clouds ~*ing* across the sky⟩ ~ *vt* **1 :** to cause (time) to pass **:** while away ⟨many young gentlemen . . . ~ the time carelessly —Shak.⟩ **2** *obs* **:** to pass over rapidly **:** skim the surface of **3** [alter. of ¹*flit*] **a :** to move or change in position — used only in certain nautical phrases ⟨~ aft the crew⟩ **b :** to draw apart the blocks of (a tackle) in order to shift the moving block **c :** to cause (as a cable or hawser) to slip down the barrel of a capstan or windlass

²fleet \"\ *n* -S [ME *flet, flete*, fr. OE *flēot* estuary, river; akin to MHG *vliez, vlieze* river, brook, ON *fljōt* river; derivative fr. the root of OE *flēotan* to float] **1** *now dial Eng* **:** a shallow inlet or estuary **:** a small creek **2** *now dial Eng* **:** SEWER, DRAIN

³fleet \"\ *n* -S [ME *flet, flete*, fr. OE *flēot* ship, fr. *flēotan* to float] **1 :** a number of warships under a single command **:** a naval force: **a :** an organization of ships and airplanes under a flag officer and suitable for undertaking major naval operations **b :** the whole naval forces afloat of a particular country **2 :** a group of boats in company or engaged in the same business ⟨the whaling ~⟩ ⟨the ~ of small craft now in the harbor⟩ **3** *now chiefly dial* **:** a group (as of birds) moving or acting together ⟨a ~ of crows pulling at the corn⟩ **4 a** *Brit* **:** a line of fishing nets joined together **b :** a fishing line having a hundred hooks **5 :** a group (as of airplanes or trucks) comparable to a fleet of ships ⟨a ~ of clouds overhead⟩; *esp* **:** such a group operated under unified control (as by a commercial or military organization) ⟨three separate taxi ~*s* operating in one area⟩ ⟨a ~ of 500 haulage units⟩ **6 :** a group of affiliated insurance companies esp. when handling fire insurance

⁴fleet \"\ *vt* -ED/-ING/-S [ME *fleten*, fr. OE *flēotan* to skim, fr. *flēotan* to float] *dial Eng* **:** to take the cream from (milk) **:** SKIM

⁵fleet \"\ *adj* -ER/-EST [prob. fr. ¹*fleet*] **1 :** swift in motion **:** moving or able to move with velocity ⟨the antelope is very ~⟩; *often* **:** light and quick in going from place to place **:** NIMBLE, AGILE ⟨the ~ scurryings of squirrels⟩ ⟨in mail their horses clad, yet ~ and strong —John Milton⟩ **2 :** lacking permanence or substance **:** EVANESCENT, FLEETING **syn** see FAST

⁶fleet \"\ *adv* (*or adj*) [prob. fr. ²*fleet*] **1** *now chiefly dial* **:** LIGHT, SHALLOW ⟨a ~ soil⟩ ⟨cream rising in ~ dishes⟩ **2** *now chiefly dial* **:** near the surface **:** SUPERFICIALLY ⟨potatoes with ~ eyes⟩ ⟨some soils should be plowed ~⟩

⁷fleet \"\ *n* -S [prob. fr. ¹*fleet*] **1 :** a long straight fake of a stowed rope **2 :** the act of fleeting **:** a change in position

fleet admiral *n* **:** a naval officer of the highest rank whose insignia is five stars

fleet–book evidence \'flēt-\ *n, usu cap F* [so called fr. the fact that books recording clandestine marriages in Fleet prison chapel, London, England, and in nearby houses were declared inadmissible as evidence in British courts] *Brit* **:** evidence usu. documentary that is inadmissible because inherently unreliable

fleet–foot \'⸗,⸗\ *also* **fleet–footed** \'⸗¦⸗⸗\ *adj* **:** swift of foot — **fleet–foot·ed·ness** *n*

fleet·ful \'flēt,fu̇l\ *n* -S **:** as many as would fill or make up a fleet ⟨whole ~*s* of students from distant lands⟩

fle·eth \'flēəth\ *archaic pres 3d sing of* FLEE

fleet in being : a fleet of naval vessels that because of its mere existence is a factor in the calculations of opposing strategists even though it is inactive or appears to be immobilized

fleeting *adj* [fr. pres. part. of ¹*fleet*] **:** passing swiftly **:** TRANSITORY, PASSING, BRIEF ⟨a ~ glimpse⟩ ⟨autumn's ~ beauty⟩ **syn** see TRANSIENT

fleet·ing·ly *adv* **:** for an instant **:** BRIEFLY

fleet·ing·ness *n* -ES **:** the quality or state of being fleeting

fleet·ings \'flētiŋz\ *n pl* [pl. of E dial. *fleeting* action of skimming, fr. ME *fletinge*, fr. *fleten* to skim + *-inge, -ing* -ing] *dial Eng* **:** milk curds (as for the making of cheese)

fleet insurance *n* **:** insurance by which a number of ships, automobiles, or airplanes are covered under one contract

fleet·ly *adv* **:** in a fleet manner **:** RAPIDLY

fleet marriage *n, usu cap F* **:** a marriage performed during the late 17th and early 18th centuries in or near the Fleet prison in London without public notice, witnesses, or consent of parents

fleet·ness *n* -ES **:** the quality or state of being fleet

fleet parson *n, usu cap F* **:** a disreputable clergyman who performed Fleet marriages

fleets *pres 3d sing of* FLEET, *pl of* FLEET

fleet street *n, usu cap F&S* [after *Fleet Street* (running from Ludgate Circus to the Strand), London, England, that has become the center of the London newspaper district] **:** the London press

¹fleg \'fleg\ *vt* [prob. alter. of *fley*] *Scot* **:** to scare out **:** FRIGHTEN

²fleg \"\ *n* -S *Scot* **:** FRIGHT, SCARE ⟨got a ~ and was ready to jump out of my skin —Sir Walter Scott⟩

³fleg \"\ *n* -S [origin unknown] *Scot* **:** BLOW; *esp* **:** KICK ⟨fortune gave him many a ~⟩

⁴fleg \"\ *vi* **flegged; flegged; flegging; flegs** [origin unknown] *Scot* **:** to rush around or away **:** FLEE

flegm *obs var of* PHLEGM

fleid \'flēid, -lād\ *var of* FLEYED

flei·shig *or* **flei·schig** \'flāshik, -lish-\ *adj* [Yiddish *fleyshig*, fr. MHG *vleischic* of meat, meaty, fat, fr. *vleisch* meat (fr. OHG *fleisk*) + *-ic* -y (fr. OHG *-ig*) — more at FLESH] *Jewish cookery* **:** made of, prepared with, or used for meat or meat products ⟨a ~ menu⟩ ⟨~ puddings made with chicken fat instead of butter⟩

flei·shigs *or* **flei·schigs** \-ks\ *n pl, Jewish cookery* **:** meat or meat products or dishes prepared with meat products rather than dairy products

fleiss·ner grille \'flīsnə(r)-\ *n, usu cap F* [after Eduard *Fleissner* von Wostrowitz, Austrian cryptographer] **:** a square grille designed to be reconstructed from a key word and used for cryptographic transposition without cover text and to be rotated 90 degrees on the paper whenever the spaces are exhausted so that a solid block of transposed ciphertext is produced after four successive turns or sometimes when reversal of the grille is provided for after eight turns

fleme \'flēm\ *vt* -ED/-ING/-S [ME *flemen*, fr. OE *flēman, flȳman*, fr. *flēam* flight; akin to OE *flēon* to flee — more at FLEE] *archaic, chiefly Scot* **:** to drive away **:** BANISH

flem·ing \'flemiŋ, -mēŋ\ *n* -S *cap* [ME, fr. MD *Vlaminc, Vleminc*, fr. *Vlam-* (akin to MD *Vlander* Flanders) + *-inc* -ing; akin to OHG *-ing* one belonging to — more at -ING] **:** a member of the Germanic people inhabiting northern Belgium (as Flanders, Antwerp, Brabant, and Limburg) and the Nord department of France — compare WALLOON

fleming valve \"-\ *n, usu cap F* [after Sir John Ambrose *Fleming* †1945 Eng. electrical engineer, its inventor] **:** DIODE

¹flem·ish \'flemish, -mēsh\ *adj, usu cap* [ME, fr. MD *vlamesch, vlemesch*, fr. *vlam-* (akin to MD *Vlander* Flanders) + *-esch* -ish; akin to OHG *-isk, -isc* -ish — more at -ISH] **1 :** relating to Flanders or to the Flemings **2 :** of, relating to, or in the Flemish language **3 :** of, relating to, or being a style of furniture developed in Flanders esp. in the 17th century that is similar to and greatly influenced the Jacobean style

²flemish \"\ *n* -ES *cap* [ME, fr. *flemish*, adj.] **1** *cap* **:** the West Germanic language used by the Flemings and made up of dialects of Dutch — see INDO-EUROPEAN LANGUAGES table **2 flemish** *pl, cap* **:** the Flemings **3** *usu cap* **:** FLEMISH GIANT

³flemish \"\ *vt* -ED/-ING/-ES *often cap* [¹*flemish*] **:** to lay (a ship's line) in a flemish coil — usu. used with *down*

flemish blue *n, often cap F* **:** a dark blue that is less strong and slightly redder than Peking blue, greener and paler than Japan

blue, and greener, lighter, and stronger than Majolica blue (sense 1)
flemish bond *n, often cap F* : a masonry bond in which each course consists of headers and stretchers alternately so laid as to always break joints

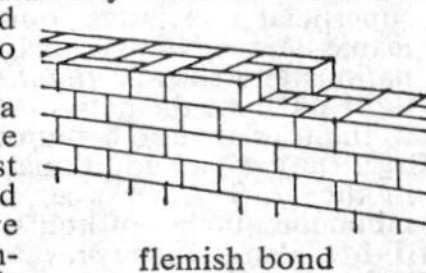
flemish bond

flemish coil *n, sometimes cap F* : a flat coil of rope with the end in the center and the turns lying against each other used esp. on shipboard
flemish eye *n, often cap F* : an eye formed at the end of a rope without splicing by dividing the strands and laying them over each other
flemish foot *n, often cap 1st F* : a furniture bun foot with a C-shaped or S-shaped scroll
flemish garden wall bond *n, often cap F* : a masonry bond in which all courses consist of one header to three or four stretchers, the courses breaking joints in a variety of patterns
flemish giant *n, usu cap F* : a rabbit of a breed prob. of Belgian origin that is characterized by large size, vigor, and solid coat color in black, white, or various grays
flemish horse *n, usu cap F* : a short footrope at the outer end of a yard on a ship — see SAIL illustration
flemish knot *n, usu cap F* : FIGURE EIGHT a
flemish scroll *n, often cap F* : a double scroll on furniture formed of two C-scrolls in opposite directions joined by an angle
flem·ming's fluid *or* **flemming's solution** \'flemiŋz-, -mēŋz-\ *n, usu cap F* [after Walther *Flemming* †1905 Ger. anatomist and cytologist] : a fixing fluid composed of osmium tetroxide, chromic anhydride, and acetic acid in aqueous solution and used in microscopy chiefly for preserving details of cells
flens·burg \'flenz,bərg, -n(t)s,bu̇(ə)rk\ *adj, usu cap* [fr. *Flensburg*, Germany] : of or from the city of Flensburg, Germany : of the kind or style prevalent in Flensburg
flense \'flen(t)s\ *also* **flench** \-nch\ *or* **flinch** \-linch\ *vt* **flensed** *also* **flenched** *or* **flinched**; **flensed** *also* **flenched** *or* **flinched**; **flensing** *also* **flenching** *or* **flinching**; **flenses** *also* **flenches** *or* **flinches** [D *flensen* or Dan & Norw *flense*; akin to MHG *vlans* large mouth, mouth of an animal, Norw *flans* horse's pizzle, Icel *flanni* penis] : to strip (as a whale or seal) of blubber or skin
flens·er \'flen(t)sə(r)\ *n* -s : one that flenses animals; *esp* : one that cuts free whale blubber as an occupation — compare LEMMER

flemish scroll

¹flesh \'flesh\ *n* -es *often attrib* [ME, fr. OE *flǣsc*; akin to OHG *fleisk* flesh, meat, ON *flesk* bacon, ham, *flīs* slice, splinter, and prob. to ON *flā* to flay — more at FLAY] **1 a** : the soft parts of the body of man or a lower animal (as a vertebrate) usu. excluding the integument **b** : the body parts composed chiefly of skeletal muscle with accompanying fat and connective tissues as distinguished from visceral structures and bone — called also *meat* **c** : sleek well-fatted condition of body : FAT ⟨the steer was in excellent ~ when shown⟩ ⟨lost ~ during his illness⟩ **d** : the surface or external appearance of the body — used esp. with reference to color ⟨sun-tanned ~⟩ **2 a** : food of animal origin comprising edible parts of any animal used as food ⟨*flesh*-eating mammals⟩ **b** : flesh of mammals or sometimes of mammals and birds as an article of diet ⟨abstain from ~ during religious fasts⟩ — distinguished from *fish* and often from edible organs (as liver or brains) or from foods of vegetable origin **3 a** : the physical being of man — distinguished from *soul* **b** : HUMAN NATURE: (1) : tender sensitivity (2) : carnal weakness : tendency to transient or physical pleasure : desire for sensual gratification ⟨indulgence of the ~⟩ **4 a** : human beings : MANKIND, HUMANITY **b** : living beings : animal life ⟨inconceivable that all ~ should be swept from the earth⟩ **c** : a stock, kindred, or race constituting a unified whole ⟨this English ~⟩ ⟨men of my own ~ and kin⟩ **5 a** : a fleshy mesocarp (as of an apple or stone fruit) : the sarcocarp of a fleshy fruit; *broadly* : the fleshy part of any fruit (as an aggregate or composite fruit) **b** : the part of an edible plant suitable for or actually consumed as food usu. excluding integuments and seeds even if these are also consumed ⟨a new tomato with splendid firm ~⟩ — used chiefly of parts (as fruits, fruiting bodies, or roots) that are more or less fleshy in structure **6** : a pale orange yellow to yellowish gray — called also *moonlight* **7** *or* **flesh side** : the inner side of a hide — compare GRAIN 4b(1) **8** *Christian Science* : an illusion that matter has sensation — **after the flesh** : in a natural, earthly, or gross manner or relationship — **in the flesh** : in person and alive ⟨saw him *in the flesh* not three days ago⟩ ⟨in movies . . . but never *in the flesh* —W.R.Inge⟩
²flesh \"\ *vb* -ED/-ING/-ES *vt* **1 a** : to feed (as a hawk or hound) with flesh from the kill to encourage interest in the chase — compare BLOOD *vt* 3a **b** : BLOOD *vt* 3b, 3c **c** *obs* : to arouse or habituate (as a person) to some emotion or response (as of lust, cupidity, or hate) esp. by experience **2** : to drive or thrust (as a weapon) into flesh ⟨the dog ~*ed* his fangs in the deer's leg⟩ **3** *archaic* : GRATIFY, SATIATE ⟨~ his cupidity⟩ **4 a** : to clothe or cover with or as if with flesh ⟨the modeler builds up his figure by ~*ing* a wire frame with clay⟩; *broadly* : to give substance or a feeling of reality to — usu. used with *out* ⟨they ~*ed* out the president's plan with statistics and procedural details⟩ ⟨the duchess was not as well ~*ed* out as the other characters in the play⟩ **b** : to cause to grow : FATTEN ⟨a garden ~*ed* by rain and sun⟩ — often used with *up* ⟨you'll have to ~ those steers up if you expect them to bring top prices⟩ **5** : to free from flesh; *esp* : to scrape (a skin) free of fat, membrane, or other adherent tissue ~ *vi* : to put on weight or substance : become fleshy — often used with *up* or *out* ⟨on a better diet the children soon began to ~ up⟩ ⟨that steer is ~*ing* out well⟩
flesh and blood *n* [ME *flesh and blod*] **1** : corporeal nature as composed of flesh and of blood with their infirmities and proclivities ⟨such neglect was more than *flesh and blood* could stand⟩ **2** : near kindred — used chiefly in the phrase *one's own flesh and blood* **3** : substance and reality ⟨attempting to give *flesh and blood* to nebulous ideas⟩
fleshburn \'=,=\ *n* : a brush with which to rub or cleanse the flesh of the body
flesh crow *n* : CARRION CROW
flesh·en \'fleshən\ *adj* [ME, fr. OE *flǣscen*, fr. *flǣsc* flesh + *-en*] : consisting of flesh
flesh·er \-shə(r)\ *n* -s [ME, fr. *flesh* + *-er*] **1** *Scot* : a meat seller : BUTCHER **2 a** : a primitive implement (as of bone or stone often with serrated edges) for fleshing hides **b** : a curved knife or other device used for fleshing skins or hides **3** : a worker who fleshes hides or pelts with a fleshing knife or a fleshing machine **4** : the inner layer of a split sheepskin generally tanned for chamois
flesh–fallen \'=,=(=)\ *adj* : become thin : EMACIATED
flesh fly *n* [ME *flesh-flie*, fr. *flesh* + *flie* fly] : any of numerous flies (superfamily Muscoidea) whose maggots feed on flesh (as a bluebottle or a blowfly); *esp* : any of various viviparous flies that deposit living larvae on fresh meat and that constitute the genus *Sarcophaga* — called also *meat fly*
flesh fork *n* : a large long-handled fork used to lift meat (as from the pot in which it was cooked)
fleshhook \'=,=\ *n* [ME, fr. *flesh* + *hook*] **1** : a hook for lifting pieces of flesh (as from a pot) **2** : a hook on which to hang meat (as in a butcher shop)
flesh hoop *n* : the hoop on which a drumhead is mounted — compare COUNTER HOOP
fleshier *comparative of* FLESHY
fleshiest *superlative of* FLESHY
flesh·i·ness \'fleshēnəs, -shin-\ *n* -ES [ME *fleshines*, fr. *fleshy* + *-nes* -ness] : the state of being fleshy : stout or plump habit of body : CORPULENCE
flesh·ing \'fleshiŋ, -shēŋ\ *n* -s [¹*flesh* + *-ing*] **1 fleshings** *pl* : close-fitting usu. flesh-colored tights **2 fleshings** *pl* : material removed in fleshing a hide or skin **3** [fr. pres. part. of ²*flesh*] **a** : the distribution of the lean and fat on an animal ⟨note the excellent ~ of the rump⟩ **b** : the capacity of an animal to put on flesh or finish ⟨easy ~ is important in the beef herd⟩
fleshing knife *or* **fleshing tool** *n* : a blunt concave knife or a flexible wire tool used to flesh a skin or hide
fleshing machine *n* : a machine used in tanneries for removing excess fat and flesh from hides and skins
flesh·less \-shləs\ *adj* [ME *fleshles*, fr. *flesh* + *-les* -less] **1** : lean and gaunt : EMACIATED ⟨a pale ~ face⟩ **2** : being without substance or body : DISEMBODIED ⟨~ ghosts⟩
fleshlike \'=,=\ *adj* : resembling flesh esp. in texture or appearance
flesh·li·ly \-shləlē, -əli\ *adv* [*fleshly* + *-ly*] : in a fleshly manner
flesh·li·ness \-shlēnəs, -lin-\ *n* -ES [ME, fr. OE *flǣsclicnes*, fr. *flǣsclic* fleshly + *-nes* -ness] : preoccupation with carnal matters
flesh·ly \-lē,-li\ *adj, often* -ER/-EST [ME, fr. OE *flǣsclic*, fr. *flǣsc* flesh + *-lic* -ly] **1 a** : of or relating to the flesh or body : CORPOREAL, BODILY ⟨~ strength⟩ ⟨the ~ eye⟩ **b** : of or relating to bodily appetites : CARNAL, SENSUAL; *esp* : LASCIVIOUS, LIBIDINOUS ⟨~ indulgences⟩ **c** : relating to or characteristic of the bodily life : not spiritual ⟨~ views of life⟩ : WORLDLY **2 a** : having or composed of flesh : FLESHY **b** *obs* : having much flesh : FAT **3** *of the heart* : easily moved (as to compassion) : kind and tender : SOFT ⟨can there be such deceit in Christians, or treason in the ~ heart of man? — Christopher Marlowe⟩ **4** : exhibiting or characterized by sensuous quality ⟨~ art⟩ ⟨a ~ poet⟩ **syn** see CARNAL
flesh–meat \'=,=\ *n* [ME *fleshmete*, fr. OE *flǣscmete*, fr. *flǣsc* flesh + *mete* food — more at FLESH, MEAT] : FLESH 2b — usu. distinguished from *fish*
fleshment *n* -s *obs* : excitement attending a successful beginning
fleshmonger \'=,==\ *n* [ME *fleshmonger*, *fleshmanger*, fr. OE *flǣscmangere*, fr. *flǣsc* flesh + *mangere* monger — more at MONGER] **1** *obs* : BUTCHER **2 a** *obs* : PANDER **b** : a dealer in slaves
flesh ocher *n* : a strong yellowish pink that is yellower and duller than salmon pink, yellower and darker than melon, and yellower and less strong than peach red
flesh–out \'=,=\ *adj, of shoe upper leather* : used with the grain side against the foot
flesh peddler *n, slang* : a theatrical agent
flesh pink *or* **flesh red** *n* **1** : a variable color that is pale and light yellowish pink **2** *of textiles* : a pale yellowish pink
fleshpot \'=,=\ *n* **1 fleshpots** *pl* : luxurious plenty : high living — used with *the* ⟨those who wallow heedlessly in the ~*s*⟩ **2** : an establishment catering to luxurious and usu. licentious tastes — usu. used in pl. ⟨elaborate urban ~*s* contain up to five distinct drinking areas —David Dodge⟩
flesh side *n* : FLESH 7
flesh wound *n* : an injury involving penetration of the body musculature without damage to skeletal or visceral structures
fleshy \'fleshē, -shi\ *adj* -ER/-EST [ME, fr. *flesh* + *-y*] **1 a** : marked by, characteristic of, or resembling flesh ⟨we lived ere yet this ~ robe we wore —S.T.Coleridge⟩ **b** : having or marked by ample or excess flesh whether merely adipose or muscular and sinewy ⟨bold ~ curves [of his face] had . . . far extended beyond the limits originally assigned them —Charles Dickens⟩; *usu* : PLUMP, CORPULENT, FAT ⟨a ~ woman⟩ **c** : composed of flesh only rather than bone or sinew ⟨he'd been shot through the ~ part of the leg and had lost a good deal of blood —C.B.Nordhoff & J.N.Hall⟩ **2** : FLESHLY; *esp* : sensual and libidinous ⟨enjoying a girly show and other ~ pleasures of life —Alan Levy⟩ **3 a** : SUCCULENT, PULPY ⟨soft ~ fruits⟩ **b** : having body or substance : not thin, dry, or membranaceous ⟨a ~ fungus⟩ **syn** see FAT
fleshy fruit *n* : a fruit consisting largely of soft succulent tissue (as a berry, drupe, or pome) — see FRUIT illustration
fleshy sponge *n* : a sponge (class Demospongiae) lacking a definite skeleton
¹flet \'flet\ *Scot var of* FLAT
²flet \"\ *adj* [fr. obs. past part. of ⁴*fleet*] *dial Eng* : made with skimmed milk : SKIMMED ⟨~ cheese⟩ ⟨~ milk⟩
fletch \'flech\ *vt* -ED/-ING/-ES [back-formation fr. *fletcher*] : FEATHER ⟨~ an arrow⟩ ⟨nursed a sharpened grudge . . . keeping it barbed and ~*ed* against the time when he might let fly with it —I.S.Cobb⟩
fletch·er \'flechə(r)\ *n* -s [ME *fleccher*, fr. OF *flechier*, fr. *fleche* arrow + *-ier* -er — more at FLÈCHE] : a maker of arrows
fletch·er·ism \-chə,rizəm\ *n* -s *usu cap* [Horace *Fletcher* †1919 Am. nutritionist + E *-ism*] : the practice of eating in small amounts and only when hungry and of chewing one's food thoroughly
fletch·er·ite \-,rīt\ *n* -s *usu cap* [Horace *Fletcher* + E *-ite*] : a believer in or practicer of Fletcherism
fletch·er·ize \-,rīz\ *vt* -ED/-ING/-S *often cap* [Horace *Fletcher* + E *-ize*] : to reduce (food) to tiny particles esp. by prolonged chewing
fletch·er radial burner \'flechə(r)-\ *n, usu cap F* [fr. the name *Fletcher*] : a low flat gas burner with a number of jets arranged in a radial pattern designed to heat a large container resting on it
fletcher scale *n, usu cap F* [James *Fletcher* †1908 Canadian entomologist] : an unarmored scale (*Lecanium fletcheri*) that is related to the brown soft scale and that is a widespread pest on ornamental evergreens
fletching *n* -s [fr. gerund of ¹*fletch*] : the feathers on an arrow; *also* : the particular arrangement in which such feathers are placed ⟨all arrows of a set should have similar ~⟩
¹fleth·er \'flethər\ *vi* -ED/-ING/-S [perh. blend of ¹*flatter* and ¹*blether*] *Scot* : to fawn and flatter
²flether \"\ *n* -s *Scot* : FLATTERY, FAWNING
flett·ner control \'fletnə(r)-\ *n, usu cap F* [after Anton *Flettner* b1885 Ger. engineer and inventor] : SERVO CONTROL
flet·ton \'fletᵊn\ *n* -s [fr. *Fletton*, urban district in Huntingdonshire, England, center of the brickmaking industry employing this process] : a yellowish red brick made by compressing moist ground clay in a steel mold
fleuk \'fl(y)ük, -lœk\ *chiefly Scot var of* FLUKE
fleur *n* -s [by shortening] : FLEUR-DE-LIS 2
fleur d'a·mour \,flərdə'mu̇(ə)r, ,flu̇r-\ *n, pl* **fleur d'amour** \"\ *or* **fleurs d'amour** \"\ [F, lit., flower of love] : TABERNAEMONTANA 2
fleur–de–lis *or* **fleur–de–lys** \,flərdᵊl'ē, ,fləd-, ,fləid- *also* ,flu̇rd- *or* -u̇əd- *sometimes* -'ēs\ *also* **fleur–de–luce** \-'üs\ *n, pl* **fleurs–de–lis** *or* **fleur–de–lis** *or* **fleurs–de–lys** *or* **fleur–de–lys** \-ərdᵊl'ē(z), -əd-, -əid- *also* -u̇rd- *or* -u̇əd- *sometimes* -'ēs\ *also* **fleurs–de–luce** \-'üs\ *or* **fleur–de–luc·es** \-'üsəz\ [alter. (influenced by F *fleur de lis*) of ME *flourdelis*, fr. MF *flor de lis*, *flour de lis*, lit., lily flower] **1** : ²IRIS 2; *esp* : the iris chosen for the royal emblem of France by Charles V which prob. belonged to a white-flowered variety (*Iris germanica florentina*) of the German iris **2** : a device common in artistic design and heraldry that is commonly supposed to be a conventionalized representation of an iris and that typically consists of oppositely posed C-scrolls on each side of an elongate lyrate figure, the three being closely juxtaposed or linked across the narrowest part of the scrolls by a horizontal ligature

fleur-de-lis 2

fleur·de·li·sé \,=(,)=(,)=ē;zā\ *adj* [F, fr. past part. of *fleurdeliser* to mark with fleurs-de-lis, fr. *fleur de lis*, fr. OF *flor de lis*, *flour de lis*] : marked or ornamented with one or more fleurs-de-lis
fleur–de–li·sée \"\ *adj* [F *fleurdelisée*, fem. of *fleurdelisé*] : FLEURETTÉE 1
fleur du mal \,flœrdᵊē'mal\ *n, pl* **fleurs du mal** \"\ [F, lit., flower of evil; fr. *Les fleurs du mal* (1857), volume of decadent poetry by Pierre-Charles Baudelaire †1867 Fr. poet] : a morbid or scandalous creation in literature or art
fleu·ret \,flər'et, (')flu̇'ret\ *n* -s [F, fr. MF *floret*, modif. of OIt *fioretto* lit., little flower, dim of *fiore* flower, fr. L *flor-*, *flos*; fr. the resemblance of the button at the end of its foil to a flower — more at BLOW (to bloom)] : a light fencing foil or small sword
fleu·rette \"\ *n* -s [F, lit., little flower, fr. OF *florete*, *flourete*, *flurete* — more at FLOWERET] : a decorative motif in the form of a small conventionalized flower
fleu·ret·tée *also* **fleu·ret·té** \,flər·ə'tā, ,flu̇rə'-\ *or* **flo·ret·tée** \,flōrə'-\ *or* **flo·ret·ty** \flō'red·ē\ *adj* [ME *florette*, *flourte*, *flortee*, fr. MF *flouretté* ornamented with flowery designs, fr. *flourette* small flower] **1** *also* **fleur·ty** \'flərd·ē, 'flu̇(ə)r-\ *of a cross* : having each arm terminated by the head of a fleur-de-lis which has the appearance of being attached to the end of the arm rather than constituting a part of it — see CROSS illustration **2** : FLEURY 2 **3** : SEMÉE-DE-LIS
fleu·ron \'flər,ün, 'flu̇,rün\ *n* -s [F, fr. MF *floron*, fr. *flor*, *flour*, *flur* flower — more at FLOWER] **1** : a flower-shaped ornament esp. when terminating an object or forming one of a series **2** : a printers' type ornament of floral motif often cast in units that may be combined to form borders
fleur vo·lante \,flərvō'länt, ,flu̇r-\ *n* [F, lit., flying flower] : a loop added in the body of the pattern of point lace
fleu·ry \'flər·ē, 'flu̇rē\ *adj* [alter. (influenced by F *fleur* flower) of ME *floury*, *flory*, fr. OF *floré*, fr. *flor*, *flour*, *flur* flower — more at FLOWER] **1** : semé with fleurs-de-lis — used of a heraldic field **2** *of a cross* : having the ends of the arms broadening out into the heads of fleurs-de-lis — compare FLEURETTÉE 1, PATONCE, PATY — see CROSS illustration **3** *of a heraldic ordinary* : having the heads of fleurs-de-lis projecting out from the edge
fleury counterfleury \'=='==,==\ *n* : FLORY COUNTERFLORY
flew *past of* FLY
flewed \,flüd\ *adj* : having flews usu. of an indicated kind ⟨a deep-*flewed* hound⟩
flew·it \'flüət\ *n* -s [origin unknown] *chiefly Scot* : a sharp blow : BUFFET
flews \'flüz\ *n pl* [origin unknown] : the pendulous lateral parts of the upper lip of a dog, esp. a hound — see DOG illustration
¹flex \'fleks\ *vb* -ED/-ING/-ES [L *flexus*, past part. of *flectere* to bend] *vt* **1** : to bend esp. repeatedly so as to form folds in ⟨sat ~*ing* the strap as he talked⟩ **2 a** : to move muscles so as to cause flexion of (a joint) ⟨stretching and ~*ing* his knees⟩ — compare EXTEND **b** : to move (a muscle or muscles) so as to flex a joint ⟨~*ed* their biceps and went to work⟩ ~ *vi* : to bend esp. so as to form a fold or to clasp ⟨the old man's hands ~*ed* on the head of his cane⟩ ⟨such a spring must ~ repeatedly without weakening or deforming permanently⟩
²flex \"\ *n* -ES **1** : an act or instance of flexing ⟨gave his muscles a ~ and heaved on the bar⟩ **2** [short for ²*flexible*] *chiefly Brit* : electric cord
flex–crack \'=,=\ *vi* : to develop cracks on the surface (as of rubber) as a result of repeated flexing
flexed *adj* : with knees drawn up to chin — used chiefly of the arrangement of the corpse for burial among certain primitive peoples ⟨buried in ~ position⟩ ⟨a ~ skeleton⟩
flex·i·bil·i·ty \,fleksə'biləd·ē, -lətē, -i\ *n* -ES [F *flexibilité*, fr. MF, fr. LL *flexibilitat-*, *flexibilitas*, fr. L *flexibilis* flexible + *-itat-*, *-itas* -ity] : the quality or state of being flexible ⟨balance and ~ in the armed forces —T.R.Phillips⟩ ⟨the ~ and spontaneity of performances —Brooks Atkinson⟩ ⟨the face of the mother, for all its amazing ~ —Thomas Wolfe⟩
flex·i·bi·lize \'fleksəbə,līz\ *vt* -ED/-ING/-S [L *flexibilis* + E *-ize*] : to render flexible : PLASTICIZE
¹flex·i·ble \'fleksəbəl\ *adj* [ME, fr. MF, fr. L *flexibilis*, fr. *flexus* + *-ibilis* -ible] **1** : capable of being flexed : capable of being turned, bowed, or twisted without breaking : PLIABLE ⟨using ointments to keep the healing surface ~⟩ ⟨slim ~ birches bowing in the wind⟩ **2** : willing or ready to yield to the influence of others : not invincibly rigid or obstinate : TRACTABLE, MANAGEABLE ⟨a ~ character, pleasant and cooperative but without strong convictions⟩ **3** : characterized by ready capability for modification or change, by plasticity, pliancy, variability, and often by consequent adaptability to new situations ⟨a highly ~ curriculum⟩ ⟨a living and ~ and growing morality —Havelock Ellis⟩ ⟨a ~ schedule of rates⟩ **4** : featuring flexible binding or flexible sewing ⟨a ~ edition⟩ — see SPINE illustration
syn ELASTIC, RESILIENT, SPRINGY, SUPPLE: FLEXIBLE is applicable to anything capable of being bent, turned, or twisted without being broken and with or without returning of itself to its former shape ⟨plumbing is easier with *flexible* copper tubing⟩ ⟨a *flexible* thin steel runner⟩ ELASTIC indicates ability to stretch, expand, or take on new shape under pressure, usu. with return to an original shape or position after pressure is withdrawn ⟨a body . . . is *elastic* when, and only when, it tends to recover its initial condition when the distorting force is removed. For example, lead, putty, and chewing gum are not elastic. Steel, rubber, air, most substances in fact, are more or less elastic —A.L.Foley⟩ RESILIENT stresses an ability to spring back and recover shape with the removal of pressure ⟨*resilient* natural rubber⟩ ⟨the *resilient* qualities of a tennis ball⟩ ⟨*resilient* mattresses and cushions⟩ SPRINGY is a nontechnical word with meanings and suggestions of both ELASTIC and RESILIENT ⟨a *springy* turf⟩ ⟨a bed of *springy* pine needles —S.E.White⟩ ⟨her bright brown hair rose in *springy* waves from her forehead, piled high on her head —Marcia Davenport⟩ SUPPLE applies to whatever bends, flexes, or folds with reasonable ease and shows resistance to cracking, breaking, or splitting ⟨*supplest* calfskin⟩ ⟨a pullover of *supple* chamois⟩
²flexible \"\ *n* -s : something that is flexible
flexible binding *n* **1** : bookbinding in which flexible sewing is used **2** : a book cover made of flexible rather than rigid boards
flexible collodion *n* : collodion to which small amounts of other ingredients (as camphor and castor oil) have been added to render the film left on evaporation pliable
flexible constitution *n* : a constitution that may be amended by the ordinary process of legislation and is therefore relatively easy to amend
flexible glue *n* : a mixture of glue, water, and a softening agent (as glycerol or sorbitol) used esp. in printers' rollers, bookbinding, and gasket binders
flexible gunnery *n* : the firing of swivel guns (as in an airplane) — compare FIXED GUNNERY
flex·i·ble·ness *n* -ES : FLEXIBILITY
flexible sandstone *n* : itacolumite in thin flexible layers
flexible sewing *n, bookbinding* : hand sewing in which the thread is passed through each section and over raised cords
flexible shaft *n* **1** : a shaft or shafting made of a flexible material (as wire wrapped around a core in alternately directed layers) or composed of a series of jointed links **2** : a high-speed rotating shaft so supported in its bearings (as by oil pressure or spring action) that a small lateral movement is possible
flexible tariff *n* : a tariff (as that established in the U. S. by the Fordney-McCumber Act of 1922) by which the executive under specified conditions may by proclamation modify any rate of duty by not more than a stipulated percent of the amount provided therefor
flexible wheelbase *n* : a wheelbase in a vehicle running on two or more pairs of wheels that is adjustable so that in rounding a curve the axles shift so as to be radial to the curve
flex·i·bly \'fleksəblē, -li\ *adv* : in a flexible manner : with flexibility
flex·ile \'fleksəl, -k,sīl, -k(,)sil\ *adj* [L *flexilis*, fr. *flexus* (past part. of *flectere* to bend) + *-ilis* -ile] : FLEXIBLE
flexing *pres part of* FLEX
flexion *var of* FLECTION
flex·ive \'fleksiv\ *adj* [L *flexus* (past part. of *flectere* to bend) + E *-ive*] *archaic* : FLEXIBLE
flex life *n* : the capability of a material (as nylon or rubber) to withstand repeated bending without fracture
flex·o·graph·ic printing \,fleksə,grafik-\ *n* [*flexo-* (fr. L *flexus*) + *-graphic*] : ANILINE PRINTING
flex·og·ra·phy \flek'sägrəfē\ *n* -ES [*flexo-* + *-graphy*] : ANILINE PRINTING
flex·om·e·ter \flek'säməd·ə(r)\ *n* [*flexo-* + *-meter*] : an instrument for testing the flexibility of materials (as textiles or rubber)
flex·or \'fleksər, -,sȯ(ə)r\ *n* -s [NL, fr. L *flexus* (past part. of *flectere* to bend) + *-or*] : a muscle that serves to bend a limb or part — opposed to *extensor*
flex·u·os·i·ty \,flekshə'wäsəd·ē\ *n* -ES [LL *flexuositas*, fr. L *flexuosus* + *-itas* -ity] **1** : the quality or state of being flexuous ⟨the ~ of the ureter⟩ **2** : a winding part ⟨a little ~ running along the base of the membrane⟩
flex·u·ous \'flekshəwəs\ *also* **flex·u·ose** \-,wōs\ *adj* [L *flexuosus*, fr. *flexus* + *-osus* -ous, -ose] **1 a** : having turns or

windings ⟨the ~ bed of the stream⟩ **b** *bot* **:** having alternate opposite curvatures **:** ZIGZAG, WAVY ⟨leaves with ~ margins⟩ **2 :** lacking rigidity in structure or action **:** FLEXIBLE: as **a :** ADAPTABLE **b :** FLICKERING, UNDULATING ⟨~ shadows⟩ — **flex·u·ous·ly** *adv*

flex·ur·al \'fleksh(ə)rəl\ *adj* **1 :** of, relating to, or resulting from flexure ⟨~ strength of wood⟩ **2 :** being or characterized by flexure ⟨~ elasticity⟩

flex·ure \'flekshə(r)\ *n* -s [L *flexura*, fr. *flexus* + *-ura* -ure] **1 :** the quality or state of being flexed **:** TURNING, FLECTION **2 :** TURN, BEND, FOLD ⟨a ~ in a rock stratum⟩ ⟨the ~ between thigh and abdomen⟩ **3** *obs* **:** ability or tendency to bend **:** PLIANCY **4 :** the last joint of a bird's wing **5 :** the slight bending of an astronomical observing instrument caused by the weight of its parts; *also* **:** the correction of the observed readings necessitated by this bending **6 :** a deformation of an elastic body wherein all points orig. in a straight line are displaced in the same plane to form a curve **7 :** one of three sharp bends of the anterior part of the primary axis of the vertebrate embryo that serve to establish the relationship of the parts of the developing brain — called also in order of occurrence *cephalic flexure, cranial flexure*, and *pontine flexure*

flexy \'fleksē\ *adj, often* -ER/-EST [1*flex* + *-y*] **:** tending to flex freely — used esp. of clothing ⟨soft ~ moccasins⟩

fley \'flāi, 'flā\ *vb* **fleyed; fleyed; fleying; fleys** [ME *flayen*, fr. OE *āflēgan, āflygan*, fr. *ā-, ar-*, perfective prefix + *-flēgan, -flygan*, causative fr. the root of E *flee* — more at ABEAR, FLEE] *vt* **1** *Scot* **:** to terrify or frighten esp. by startling **2** *Scot* **:** to frighten off — usu. used with *away* ~ *vi, Scot* **:** to become afraid

fley·some \-səm\ *adj, dial Brit* **:** TERRIFYING, FRIGHTENING

flg *abbr* **1** flange **2** flooring

flib·ber·ti·gib·bet \ˌflibə(r)d·ēˌjibət, -t|, |i|-, *usu* -jibəd.+V\ *n* -s [alter. of ME *flepergebet, flypyrgebet*] **1** *archaic* **:** GOSSIP, CHATTERER **2 :** a light-minded or silly restless person; *esp* **:** a pert young woman with such qualities — **flib·ber·ti·gib·bety** \-əd·|ē, -ət|, |i\ *adj*

fli·bus·tier \ˌflēbəˌsti(ə)r, ˌflib-\ *n* -s [F — more at FILIBUSTER] **1** *archaic* **:** FREEBOOTER **2** *archaic* **:** FILIBUSTER 1

flic \'flēk, 'flik\ *n* -s [F] **:** a Parisian policeman

flic-flac \'flik,flak\ *n* -s [F, of imit. origin] **:** a brushing movement of the foot used in ballet as a connecting step ⟨he teaches pirouettes and ~s —W.M.Thackeray⟩

flicht \'flikt\ *Scot var of* FLIGHT

1flich·ter \-tər\ *vi* -ED/-ING/-S [ME (northern dial.) *flichteren*, fr. *flicht, flight*, n. + *-eren* (freq. suffix) — more at FLIGHT] **1** *chiefly Scot* **:** to fly clumsily or ineptly **:** FLUTTER **2** *Scot* **:** QUIVER, THROB, PALPITATE **3** *Scot* **:** FLICKER

2flichter \"\ *n* -s *Scot* **:** FLICKER

flichtered *adj* [fr. past part. of 1*flichter*] **1** *Scot* **:** CONFUSED, FLUSTERED **2** *Scot* **:** FRIGHTENED

1flick \'flik\ *n* -s [ME *flik* pelt] *dial Eng* **:** fur esp. of a rabbit or hare

2flick \"\ *n* -s [ME *flicke*, fr. ON *flikki* — more at FLITCH] **1** *dial* **:** FLITCH **2** *dial Eng* **:** LEAF FAT

3flick \"\ *n* -s [imit.] **1 a :** a light sharp stroke, movement, or blow often with something flexible ⟨just a ~ or two with a light switch is enough to teach a puppy manners⟩ ⟨test the glass with the ~ of a finger⟩ **b :** a quick and usu. sudden movement (as of the wrist) made by angular or rotary flexion and used esp. in stroking a ball or shuttlecock **2 :** a light sound comparable to that produced by the flick of a whip ⟨the ~ of cards on polished wood⟩ ⟨the busy ~ and chatter of typewriter keys⟩ **3 a :** a splash or splotch esp. of mud or water **b :** FLICKER 1

4flick \"\ *vb* -ED/-ING/-S *vt* **1 a :** to strike lightly with a quick sharp motion ⟨~*ed* him in the face with his open hand⟩ ⟨~*ing* the old horse from time to time with his whip⟩ **b :** to remove with a light blow or a series of light blows ⟨~*ed* the dust from his boots with a handkerchief⟩ **2 a :** to move or cause to move with a jerk or a sharp light blow ⟨~*ing* the ashes from his cigar⟩ ⟨~*ed* a fly from the horse's rump⟩ **b :** to propel (as a ball) with a flick ~ *vi* **1 a :** to flutter or flit **b** *of an arrow in flight* **:** to suddenly deviate from the line of flight **2 :** to use flicks ⟨~*ing* away at his rival⟩; *esp* **:** to direct flicks at something ⟨he ~*ed* at the spot with a napkin⟩ ⟨~*ing* ineffectually at the mosquitoes⟩

5flick \"\ *vt* -ED/-ING/-S [origin unknown] *archaic* **:** CUT

6flick \"\ *n* -s [short for 2*flicker*] **:** MOVIE — usu. used in pl. ⟨take his girl to the ~s⟩

1flick·er \'flikə(r)\ *vb* **flickered; flickered; flickering** \-k(ə)riŋ\ **flickers** [ME *flikeren*, fr. OE *flicorian*; akin to OE *flacor* flying, MHG *vlackern* to flicker, ON *flökra* to flutter, *flakka* to flicker, flutter, L *plangere* to strike — more at PLAINT] *vi* **1 :** to flap the wings without flying **:** FLUTTER ⟨and ~*ing* on her nest made short essays to sing —John Dryden⟩ **2** *obs* **:** to make caressing motions or advances **3 a :** to waver unsteadily **:** wave or undulate like a flame in a current of air ⟨the embers ~*ed* into flame⟩; *sometimes* **:** to give a final flicker (as of light while expiring) ⟨shadows ~ on the wall⟩ — often used with *out* ⟨the light ~*ed* out⟩ **b** *of a fire or flame* **:** to burn fitfully **c :** to engage in brief and often surreptitious glances ⟨her glance ~*ed* at him⟩; *often* **:** to make an examination in brief glances ⟨the teacher's eyes ~*ed* doubtfully over the rapt pupils⟩ ~ *vt* **1 :** to cause to flicker **2 a :** to produce by flickering ⟨fitful flames ~*ing* dark horrors on the wall⟩ **b :** to make apparent or convey by some slight gesture ⟨~*ed* a warning with a lifted brow⟩

2flicker \"\ *n* -s **1 a :** an act of flickering ⟨the ~ of shadow on the wall⟩ **b :** a sudden brief movement or gesture ⟨a ~ of an eyelash⟩ **c :** a momentary quickening (as of interest or emotion) ⟨felt a ~ of renewed desire⟩ **d :** a tailspin of an ice-boat traveling at high speed **2 :** a product of flickering: as **a :** a brief interval of brightness ⟨the final ~ of a dying fire⟩ **b :** an uncertain wavering or intermittent light ⟨the uncertain ~ of a tallow dip⟩ **c :** the wavering or fluttering visual sensation produced by intermittent light when the rate of intermittence is not rapid enough to produce complete fusion of the individual impressions — contrasted with *fusion*; see CRITICAL FLICKER FREQUENCY **d** *slang* **:** MOTION PICTURE — usu. used in pl.

3flicker \"\ *n* -s [prob. fr. 4*flick* + *-er*] **:** YELLOW-SHAFTED FLICKER; *broadly* **:** any of various large No. American woodpeckers (genus *Colaptes*) widely distributed in the southern and western U.S. and often more or less brightly marked with red or reddish color esp. about the nape and usu. speckled underparts — usu. used in combination; see GILDED FLICKER, RED-SHAFTED FLICKER

flicker fusion *n* **:** FUSION 2d(2)

1flickering *adj* [ME *flikering*, fr. pres. part. of *flikeren*] **:** wavering and unsteady ⟨a ~ light⟩; *often* **:** uncertain and feeble **:** nearly extinguished ⟨held but a ~ hope of success⟩ — **flick·er·ing·ly** *adv*

2flickering *n* -s [ME *flikering*, fr. gerund of *flikeren*] **1 :** a wavering or uncertain movement or appearance (as of light) ⟨the ~ of gentle fingers over his face⟩ **2 :** a slight movement or trend **:** BEGINNING — often used in pl. ⟨there were ~*s* of unrest⟩ ⟨recurrent ~*s* of revolt⟩

flicker photometer *n* **:** a photometer for comparing the brightness of two lights based upon the principle that flicker between two alternating lights of different color is at a minimum when the brightness of the two is equal

flickertail \'==,=\ *n* **1 :** a ground squirrel (*Citellus richardsoni*) chiefly of the north-central U. S. and adjacent Canada **2** *usu cap* **:** NORTH DAKOTAN — used as a nickname

flick·ery \'flik(ə)rē, -ri\ *adj* **:** showing or moving with flickers **:** uncertain and wavering ⟨a ~ light⟩ ⟨flitted about like ~ black shadows —I.S.Cobb⟩

flick-flack \'flik,flak\ *n* -s [imit.] **:** the noise of repeated light blows ⟨the milk in the . . . churn . . . changed its squashing for a decided *flick-flack* —Thomas Hardy⟩

flicky \'flikē\ *adj, usu* -ER/-EST [fr. 4*flick* + *-y*] **:** jerky and brisk

flics *pl of* FLIC

flied *past of* FLY

fli·er *or* **fly·er** \'flī(ə)r, -īə\ *n* -s [ME, fr. *flien* to fly + *-er* — more at FLY] **1 :** one that flies with wings (as a bird or insect) or as if with wings: as **a :** FUGITIVE **b :** AERIALIST **c :** AIRCRAFT **d :** AIRMAN **2** *usu flyer* **:** one that moves with uncommon speed (as a fast coach or train) — often used in proper names ⟨the Western *Flyer*⟩ **3 :** a small dark-spotted greenish sunfish (*Centrarchus macropterus*) found in clear fresh waters near the coast from Virginia southward and in the lower Mississippi valley **4 :** a swift kangaroo; *specif* **:** BLUE DOE **5 :** any of various mechanical appliances of swift motion: as **a :** a vaned wheel that rotates the cap of a windmill as the wind veers **b :** a windmill sail **6 :** something entered into or undertaken without normal backing or reasonable grounds for assurance **:** a reckless or speculative venture ⟨took a ~ in politics soon after getting his degree⟩; *often* **:** a financial investment made with little knowledge of the facts or by one inexperienced in business in the expectation of realizing large profits **7** *usu flyer* **a :** a handbill or circular for mass distribution (as one bearing a political advertisement or the announcement of a coming sale) **b :** a supplementary catalog (as of a mail-order house) **8 :** a step in a straight flight made up of identically rectangular steps — compare WINDER **9** *usu* **flyers** *pl* **:** small floating particles; *esp* **:** hop particles in suspension in beer **10** *usu flyer, chiefly Brit* **:** DELIVERY 9 — often used in pl. but sing. in constr. **11** *usu flyer* **:** a device revolving above a spindle to guide and insert twist in slubbing, roving, or yarn and being usu. one of a series on a fly frame **12 :** a leaf or slip attached at one edge to another usu. larger leaf (as of printer's copy or a book) and typically containing an addition or correction **13 :** a shot that strikes a target well outside the area in which other shots of the same round have hit

flies *pres 3d sing of* FLY, *pl of* FLY

flif·fis *or* **flif·fus** \'flifəs\ *n* -ES [origin unknown] **:** a twisting double somersault performed on the trampoline

fligged \'fligd\ *dial Eng var of* FLEDGED

1flight \'flīt, *usu* -īd·+V\ *n* -s *often attrib* [ME, fr. OE *flyht*; akin to MD *vlucht* flight, OE *flēogan* to fly — more at FLY] **1 a :** the act or mode of passing through the air by the use of wings ⟨the ~ of a bee⟩ ⟨the ~ of bats⟩ **b :** ability to fly ⟨~ is natural to birds⟩ **c :** the extent of a flight ⟨a ~ of many hours⟩ ⟨a ~ of 100 miles⟩; *sometimes* **:** an instance of the flying of a hawk or falcon in pursuit of game **2 a :** a passing or mode of passing through the air analogous (as in duration or distance) to that of a winged creature **:** a journey or voyage through the air ⟨the ~ of a balloon⟩ ⟨an arrow's swift ~⟩; *also* **:** a passing through space beyond the earth's atmosphere ⟨~ of a rocket⟩ **b :** a swift passage (as of time) **3 a** *obs* **:** a bird's wing **b :** FLIGHT FEATHER — usu. used in pl. **4 :** a scheduled trip of an airplane ⟨on a 9 o'clock ~ to St. Louis⟩ **5 :** a number of similar beings or things passing through or capable of passing through the air together: as **a** (1) **:** a flock of birds esp. when flying or migrating together; *broadly* **:** the birds engaging in a particular migration ⟨the spring ~ of geese on the eastern flyway was unusually large⟩ (2) **:** the young birds produced by a nesting colony in one season esp. when about to fledge or newly fledged **b :** a swarm of insects **c :** a volley of arrows or other missiles ⟨loosed a swift ~ of arrows⟩ **d :** a group of angels **e :** a number of competitors (as in a sport) grouped together on the basis of demonstrated skill or ability or for purposes of elimination contests prior to a final test **f** (1) **:** a flight formation usu. made up of at least four airplanes; *also* **:** a larger formation made up of two or more such formations (2) **:** a parade formation made up of two or more squads **6 :** an act or instance of passing above or beyond ordinary bounds **:** a mounting or soaring esp. of mind or spirit ⟨~*s* of fancy⟩ ⟨soaring ~*s* of intellect⟩ **7 a** (1) **:** a continuous series of stairs from one landing to the next (2) **:** one or more of such series making the whole ascent from one floor to another (3) **:** FLOOR, STORY **b :** a series (as of canal locks, terraces, or hurdles) resembling a flight of stairs **8 :** the tail of the clapper of a bell **9 :** the range of an arrow **10 :** a vane or flat plate on an endless belt or chain in a conveyor or elevator **11 a :** FLYBOAT **b :** a sudden sharp rise in the lines of a vessel or any of its parts **12 :** a pen or cage large enough for birds to fly freely in **13** *cricket* **:** ability to flight

flights 7a(2)

2flight *adj, obs* **:** FLEET

3flight \'flīt, *usu* -īd·+V\ *vb* -ED/-ING/-S *vi* **1** *of birds, esp waterfowl* **:** to rise from or settle on resting or feeding grounds in a flock ⟨every evening the geese ~ on the marsh⟩ **2** *of birds* **:** to fly in flocks (as in migrating) ⟨hundreds of starlings ~*ed* toward the town⟩ ~ *vt* **1 :** to cause (waterfowl) to fly up from resting or feeding grounds or to shoot (waterfowl) while rising from such places **2 :** to put feathers on (an arrow) **:** FLETCH **3 :** to impart to (a cricket ball) a trajectory intended to make difficult a batsman's judgment of length

4flight \"\ *n* -s [ME, *fluht, fliht*; akin to OFris *flecht* flight (act of fleeing), OS & OHG *fluht*, ON *flōtti*, Goth *thlauhs*; derivatives fr. the root of OE *flēon* to flee — more at FLEE] **1 a :** an act or instance of running away (as to escape danger) ⟨fain by ~ to save themselves —Shak.⟩ ⟨his ~ was not discovered until the next day⟩ **b :** withdrawal or sudden transfer of capital (as from an enterprise or from one currency to another) to avoid risk or loss ⟨the ~ of capital that results from an unstable currency⟩ **2 :** means of escape

5flight \"\ *vt* -ED/-ING/-S **1** *obs* **:** to put to flight: ROUT **2** *archaic* **:** FRIGHTEN

flight arrow *n* **:** a light low-feathered arrow for long-distance shooting

flight bow *n* **:** a bow designed for distance shooting

flight check *n* **1 :** a test of the proficiency in flight of a member of an aircrew **2 :** a test in flight of an airplane or equipment on it

flight control *n* **1 :** the control from ground stations of airplanes in flight by means of information transmitted to the pilot by radio and other electronic devices; *also* **:** the office or system that provides this control **2 :** the system (as of levers, cables, and movable surfaces) that controls the movement of an airplane

flight cover *n* **:** FLOWN COVER

flight deck *n* **1 :** the uppermost complete deck of an aircraft carrier serving primarily as landing and takeoff area for airplanes **2 :** the forward compartment in some airplanes used by the pilot, copilot, and flight engineer

flight·ed \'flīd·əd\ *adj* [1*flight* + *-ed*] **1 :** FEATHERED — used chiefly of heraldic representations of arrows and usu. postpositively ⟨arrows ~ argent⟩ **2** *of steps* **:** arranged in flights often of a specified kind ⟨steep-*flighted* stairs⟩

flight engineer *n* **:** the member of the flight crew of an airplane responsible for its mechanical operation

flight·er \'flīd·ə(r)\ *n* -s *in brewing* **:** a horizontal vane revolving over the surface of wort in a cooler to hasten the cooling

flight feather *n* **:** one of the quills of a bird's wing or tail that support it in flight — compare CONTOUR FEATHER; see GOOSE illustration

flight formation *n* **:** two or more airplanes flying close to each other in a predetermined arrangement

flight·i·ly \'flīd·|əlē, -īt|, |əli, |əl-\ *adv* **:** in a flighty manner

flight·i·ness \|ēnəs, |in-\ *n* -ES **:** the quality or state of being flighty ⟨the ~ of her temper —Nathaniel Hawthorne⟩

flight·ing \'flīd·iŋ\ *n* -s [1*flight* + *-ing*] **:** a system of flights (as on a conveyor belt)

flight leader *n* **:** the pilot in command of a flight of military airplanes

flight·less \'flītləs\ *adj, of a bird* **:** lacking the ability to fly ⟨~ downy young⟩; *esp* **:** permanently unable to fly because of wing reduction accompanying evolutionary adaptation to certain specialized terrestrial habitats — used chiefly of ratite birds

flight lieutenant *n* **:** an aviation officer (as in the British Royal Air Force) equivalent in rank to a captain in the army

flight line *n* **:** the ground parking and servicing area for airplanes including hangars, operations building, and ramps but not runways or taxiways

flight nurse *n* **:** a registered nurse (as in the U. S. Air Force) who has had special training in aeromedicine and is assigned to care for patients being evacuated or transferred by air

flight officer *n* **:** an aviation officer (as in the U.S. Army Air Forces) having a rank equivalent to that of warrant officer junior grade

flight of ideas : a rambling from subject to subject with only superficial associative connections esp. in the manic phase of manic-depressive psychosis ⟨had visual and auditory hallucinations and showed *flight of ideas* —L.V.Der Horst⟩

flight path *n* **:** the path of the center of gravity of an airplane in flight relative to a stationary frame of reference

flight pay *n* **:** an additional pay allowance for hazard paid (as in the U. S. Air Force) to qualified aircrewmen who fly a minimum number of hours per month — called also *flying pay*

flights *pl of* FLIGHT, *pres 3d sing of* FLIGHT

flight shooting *n* **:** competitive shooting for distance with bow and arrow

flightshot \'=,=\ *n* **:** the distance to which an arrow may be shot **:** BOWSHOT

flight simulator *n* **:** an airplane pilot-training device in which the cockpit and instruments of an airplane are duplicated and the conditions of actual flight are simulated

flight song *n* **:** a song that is uttered by a bird while flying and that is often different in form from the song given while perched

flight strip *n* **1 :** an auxiliary or emergency landing field alongside a highway **2 :** a series of overlapping aerial photographs taken along a single course of flight

flight surgeon *n* **:** a medical officer (as in the U. S. Air Force) who has had additional training in the specialty of aeromedicine and who looks after the general health of the aircrewmen including the mental and physical problems associated with flying

flight-test \'=,=\ *vt* **:** to test (an airplane) in flight

flighty \'flīd·|ē, -īt|, |i\ *adj* -ER/-EST [1*flight* + *-y*] **1 :** FLEETING, SWIFT, TRANSIENT ⟨the ~ purpose never is o'ertook unless the deed go with it —Shak.⟩ **2 a :** indulging in or characterized by wild and unrestrained sallies (as of imagination, humor, caprice) **:** VOLATILE ⟨proofs of my ~ and paradoxical turn of mind —S.T.Coleridge⟩ ⟨~ young girls⟩ **b** *of a horse* **:** restless and mettlesome **:** SKITTISH **3** *archaic* **:** of disordered mind **:** mildly or transitorily insane

1flim·flam \'flim,flam, -aa(ə)m\ *n* -s [prob. of Scand origin; akin to ON *flim, flīm* mockery; akin to Norw *flire* to giggle, Sw (dial.) *flira*] **1 a :** FREAK, TRIFLE, CONCEIT **b :** DECEPTION, TRICK; *esp* **:** a trick (as in making change) by which one is swindled **2 :** TRIFLING, NONSENSE **:** deceptive humbug

2flimflam \"\ *vt* **flimflammed; flimflammed; flimflamming; flimflams :** to subject to a flimflam **:** TRICK; *sometimes* **:** SWINDLE

flim·flam·mer \-mə(r)\ *n* -s **:** one that gains his way by trickery and expedients **:** a user of flimflams esp. to get the better of another — **flim·flam·mery** \-m(ə)rē\ *n* -ES

1flim·mer \'flimə(r)\ *vi* -ED/-ING/-S [G *flimmern*] **:** GLIMMER, FLICKER

2flimmer \"\ *n* -s [G, lit., glitter, tinsel, fr. *flimmern*] **:** one of the delicate lateral filaments typical of some flagella — called also *mastigoneme*

flimp \'flimp\ *vt* -ED/-ING/-S [perh. fr. Flem *flimpen* to spirit away, make disappear] *slang Brit* **:** to rob (a person) esp. with the aid of a partner who provides a distraction; *also* **:** to steal (as a watch) from another's person

flim·si·ly \'flimzəlē, -li\ *adv* **:** in a flimsy manner

flim·si·ness \-zēnəs, -zin-\ *n* -ES **:** the quality or state of being flimsy

1flim·sy \'flimzē, -zi\ *adj* -ER/-EST [perh. alter. of 1*film* + *-sy* (as in *tipsy*)] **1 :** lacking in physical strength or substance ⟨a soft ~ silk⟩; *often* **:** of inferior materials and workmanship ⟨~ shacks⟩ **2 :** having little real worth ⟨could offer only very ~ security⟩; *often* **:** lacking real worth or plausibility ⟨making ~ pretenses at elegance⟩ **3** *of persons* **a :** frail and delicate **:** ENFEEBLED, WEAK **b :** frivolous and superficial **:** making a great show based on small attainments or accomplishments **:** TRIFLING ⟨faddish ~ rogues⟩

2flimsy \"\ *n* -ES **1 :** something thin, frail, or unsubstantial: as **a :** a sheet of manifold paper or other very thin paper **b flimsies** *pl* **:** women's sheer lightweight clothing; *esp* **:** sheer undergarments **2 :** manuscript or copy on flimsy: as **a :** a duplicate of a wire news story **b :** one of a number of manifolded copies of a news story supplied by a news agency **c :** a train order written on thin paper to permit making several carbon copies **d :** TELEGRAM, RADIOGRAM

1flinch \'flinch\ *vb* -ED/-ING/-S [MF *flenchir, flainchir*, prob. of Gmc origin; akin to MHG *lenken* to bend — more at LANK] *vi* **1 a :** to withdraw or shrink (as from an enterprise or responsibility) usu. because of danger, difficulties, or distress involved or foreseen ⟨~ at the thought of their own participation in partisan politics —John Lodge⟩ ⟨perilous to ~ from making the attempt —A.J.Toynbee⟩ **b :** to shrink from or as if from physical pain **:** WINCE, START ⟨~*ing* from the vile air —Marcia Davenport⟩ ⟨~*ing* from a dart of neuralgia —Ellen Glasgow⟩; *often* **:** to tense the muscles suddenly and involuntarily in anticipation of some startling unpleasant event ⟨many young shooters spoil their scores by ~*ing* just before they pull the trigger⟩ ⟨I cannot help ~*ing* when I hear the dentist's drill⟩ **2** *obs* **:** to slink off or away ~ *vt, archaic* **:** to draw back or hold back from (as some indulgence) **syn** see RECOIL

2flinch \"\ *n* -ES **:** an act or instance of flinching

3flinch *var of* FLENSE

1flinch·er \-chə(r)\ *n* -s [1*flinch* + *-er*] **1 :** one that flinches **2** *archaic* **:** a person who drinks sparingly

2flin·cher \"\ *n* -s [by alter.] **:** VELLINCH

flinch·ing·ly *adv* **:** in a flinching manner **:** as though shrinking from anticipated distress or discomfort

flin·ders \'flində(r)z\ *n pl* [ME *flenderis*, prob. of Scand origin; akin to Norw *flindra* thin piece or splinter of stone, *flinter* little piece; akin to D *flenter* piece of rag, tatter, thin piece, Fris *flanter* thin slice, dangling rag or rope, and prob. to OE *flint* flint, rock — more at FLINT] **:** pieces, splinters, or fragments ⟨broke the vase to ~⟩

flinders bar \'"-\ *n, usu cap F* [after Matthew *Flinders* †1814 Eng. mariner] **:** a soft-iron bar or bundle of soft-iron rods placed vertically near a ship's compass to counteract deviation due to magnetic induction from the earth in surrounding vertical ironwork

flinders grass *n, usu cap F* [after Matthew *Flinders*] **:** an Australian arid-land grass (*Iseilema membranacea*) valuable for pasture and forage

flin·der·sia \flin'dərzēə\ *n* [NL, fr. Matthew *Flinders* + NL *-ia*] **1** *cap* **:** a small genus of pinnate-leaved Australasian trees (family Meliaceae) having white flowers followed by woody capsular fruits and yielding strong hardwood lumber, often with an excellent figure, that is used in cabinetmaking and construction — see FLINDOSA **2** -s **:** any tree of the genus *Flindersia*

flin·do·sa \flin'dōzə\ *also* **flin·do·sy** \-zē\ *n, pl* **flindosas** *also* **flindosies** [modif. of NL *Flindersia*] **:** a tall Australian timber tree (*Flindersia australis*) with tough hard wood much used for hoops, staves, and similar items — called also *native beech*

1fling \'fliŋ\ *vb* **flung** \'fləŋ\ *also dial* **flang** \'flaŋ, -aiŋ\ **flung; flinging; flings** [ME *flingen, flengen* (also, to strike, lash out), of Scand origin; akin to ON *flengja* whip, throw, Norw, to tear loose, hurry; akin to ON *flā* to flay — more at FLAY] *vi* **1 :** to move hastily, brusquely, or violently often as an expression of mental or emotional turmoil ⟨she *flung* away from her brother's restraining hand⟩ ⟨~*ing* out of the room in a rage⟩ **2 a** *of an animal* **:** to kick or plunge wildly **:** aim a kick — now usu. used with *out* ⟨the mule *flung* out at him as he passed⟩ **b** *obs, of a person* **:** to struggle or fling oneself about (as in attempting to escape) **3** *Scot* **a :** to caper about **b :** to dance a fling ~ *vt* **1 a :** to throw esp. with force, violence, recklessness, or abandon **:** HURL ⟨as if a resistless flood had torn them loose from their foundations . . . ~*ing* them here and there —O.E.Rölvaag⟩ ⟨*flung* his books on the table⟩ — often used with an adverb of direction ⟨*flung* the report down in disgust⟩ ⟨*flung* up his hands in despair⟩ **b :** to cast aside by or as if by throwing forcibly **:** DISCARD, DISREGARD ⟨they *flung* off all restraint⟩ — often used with *away* ⟨~ away that dirty old cloth⟩ **2 a :** to bring, send, or put (a person) suddenly, violently, or unexpectedly into a different and usu. worse state or position — used with *into* ⟨the enemy was *flung* into confusion⟩ ⟨the new king *flung* his brothers into prison⟩ **b :** to throw off (as a rider) or down (as a wrestling opponent) **c** *archaic* **:** to get the better of **:** OVERTHROW **d** *archaic* **:** SWINDLE, CHEAT **3 :** to move (as a body part) suddenly or impetuously — usu. used with an adverb of direction ⟨*flung* her arms wide in greeting⟩ ⟨angrily ~*ing* up his head⟩ **4 a :** to give off or send forth **:** EMIT ⟨the sun ~*ing* its warm rays on the soil⟩ ⟨the massed roses *flung* their heady scent into the evening breeze⟩ **b :** to ejaculate or utter vigorously, curtly, or with strong emotion ⟨he *flung* a sharp reply as he left⟩ ⟨~*ing* a hasty word of consolation⟩ — see FLING OFF **5 :** to throw (as one's efforts) into something ⟨*flung* all their resources into the revolution⟩ **:** address (as oneself) to something usu. with vigor or strong emotional response ⟨she *flung* herself into her new tasks gratefully⟩ **syn** see THROW — **fling oneself at someone's head** *of a woman* **:** to make conspicuous efforts to win the attentions of as a possible suitor

²fling \"\ *n* -s [ME, fr. *flingen*, v.] **1 :** a sharp cast (as from the hand) **:** a hard throw ⟨give the thing a ~ and get rid of it for good⟩ **2 a :** a casual try **:** an effort not based on deep or sustained interest ⟨I'm willing to take a ~ at almost any job⟩ **b :** a usu. impulsive utterance indicative of contempt **:** GIBE, SARCASM ⟨not above taking an occasional sharp ~ at their folly⟩ **c** *archaic* **:** a hasty, impulsive, or impromptu act (as a journey) **3 :** lively and unconstrained action or activity: as **a :** a plunging or kicking esp. of a horse **b :** an affair or a period marked by uninhibited gaiety, self-indulgence, or dissipation ⟨determined to have one last ~ before he sailed⟩

fling·er \-ŋə(r)\ *n* -s **:** one that flings; *esp* **:** a baseball pitcher

fling·ing-tree \'≈,≈\ *n*, *chiefly Scot* **:** FLAIL

fling off *vt* **:** to give utterance or expression to usu. casually or carelessly ⟨*flung off* a hasty rhyme⟩ ⟨gracefully *flinging off* the proper compliments⟩ ~ *vi* **:** to depart hastily or brusquely ⟨*flung off* in a rage⟩ ⟨slammed the door and *flung off* to school⟩

flingy \'fliŋē\ *adj*, *often* -ER/-EST **:** given to or characterized by flinging **:** JERKY ⟨a loose ~ walk⟩

flink·ite \'fliŋ,kīt\ *n* -s [G or Sw *flinkit*, fr. Gustaf *Flink* †1931 Sw. mineralogist + G or Sw *-it* -ite] **:** a mineral $Mn_3(AsO_4)(OH)_4$ consisting of a greenish brown basic manganese arsenate in feathery forms (sp. gr. 3.87)

¹flint \'flint\ *n* -s *often attrib* [ME, fr. OE, flint, rock; akin to OHG *flins* pebble, hard stone, ON *flettugrjōt* slate, OSw *flinta* splinter of stone, and prob. to OHG *spaltan* to split — more at SPILL] **1 a :** a massive somewhat impure variety of quartz usu. gray to brown or nearly black in color, breaking with a conchoidal fracture and sharp edge, being very hard, and striking fire with steel **b :** a concretion or nodule of flint usu. embedded in other softer rock ⟨in certain areas the primitive nomads mined ~s from the soft chalk⟩ **c :** powdered quartz **:** POTTER'S FLINT **2 :** an implement of flint used by primitive man **3 a :** a piece of flint for striking fire formerly used for kindling fires or igniting material (as in a flintlock gun) **b :** a material used for striking fire; *esp* **:** an alloy of iron and cerium commonly used in cigarette lighters **4 :** something likened to flint in hardness or unyielding quality ⟨the ground was frozen to ~⟩ ⟨her heart became ~, she could only resist and deny⟩: as **a :** FLINT CORN **b :** FLINT GLASS

²flint \"\ *vt* -ED/-ING/-S *archaic* **:** to supply (as a gun) with flint

³flint \"\ *adj*, *usu cap* [fr. *Flint*, Michigan] **:** of or from the city of Flint, Mich. ⟨a *Flint* physician⟩ **:** of the kind or style prevalent in Flint

⁴flint *usu cap*, *var of* FLINTSHIRE

flint clay *n* **:** a hard flinty fireclay

flint corn *also* **flint maize** *n* **:** an Indian corn (*Zea mays indurata*) having hard, horny, rounded or short and flat kernels with the soft and starchy endosperm completely enclosed by a hard outer layer — called also *Yankee corn*; compare DENT CORN

flint-dried *also* **flint-dry** \'≈¦≈\ *adj* **:** dried to flinty hardness — used chiefly of unsalted hides

flint glass *n* **1 :** glass formerly made using calcined flints as a source of silica **2 :** heavy brilliant glass that contains lead oxide, that has a relatively high refractive index and dispersion value, and that now is used chiefly for optical structures (as lenses or prisms) — compare CROWN GLASS **3 :** a clear colorless glass

flint-glazed \'≈¦≈\ *adj*, *of paper* **:** given a hard glossy surface by rolling or rubbing esp. with a flint — compare FRICTION-GLAZED

flint gray *n* **:** a nearly neutral slightly yellowish medium gray that is darker than gull (sense 2a) or agate gray and very slightly greener than old silver

flint·head \'≈,≈\ *n* **:** WOOD IBIS 1

flinthearted \'≈¦≈≈\ *adj* **:** HARDHEARTED

flint hide *n* **:** a flint-dried hide

flint·ify \'flintə,fī\ *vt* -ED/-ING/-ES [¹*flint* + *-ify*] **:** to convert into or make like flint

flint·i·ly \-t°lē, -t°li, -təl-\ *adv* **:** in a flinty manner

flint·i·ness \-tēnəs, -tin-\ *n* -ES **:** the quality or state of being flinty; *often* **:** hardness esp. of heart

flintlike \'≈,≈\ *adj* **:** resembling flint **:** hard and resistant ⟨~ determination⟩

flintlock \'≈,≈\ *n* **1 :** a lock for an old-fashioned gun or pistol used chiefly in the 17th and 18th centuries having a flint fixed in the hammer that on striking the battery of the pan ignited the priming which communicated its fire to the charge through the touchhole — compare PERCUSSION LOCK, WHEEL LOCK **2 :** a firearm fitted with a flintlock; *esp* **:** an old-fashioned military musket so equipped

flintlock: *1* flint, *2* pan, *3* battery

flint mill *n* **1 :** TUBE MILL **2 :** a revolving cylinder containing flint pebbles used for grinding materials in the manufacture of portland cement

flint paper *n* **:** paper that has a surface of pulverized flint or quartz and that is used like sandpaper

flints *pl of* FLINT, *pres 3d sing of* FLINT

flint·shire \'flint,shi(ə)r, -,shiə, -,shə(r)\ *or* **flint** *adj*, *usu cap* [fr. *Flintshire* or *Flint* county, Wales] **:** of or from the county of Flint, Wales **:** of the kind or style prevalent in the county of Flint

flint wheat *n* **:** HARD WHEAT

flintwood \'≈,≈\ *n* **:** the very hard wood of an Australian tree (*Eucalyptus pilularis*)

flintwork \'≈,≈\ *n* **:** work in or with flint; *esp* **:** masonry in which flint forms a major structural or decorative element

flintworker \'≈,≈≈\ *n* **:** one that works with flint; *specif* **:** a maker of flint artifacts esp. by flaking

flinty \'flintē, -ti\ *adj* -ER/-EST **1 :** composed of, consisting of, or abounding in flint ⟨a ~ hillside⟩ ⟨poor ~ fields⟩ **2 :** resembling flint ⟨a ~ composition for driveways and walks⟩: as **a :** notably hard ⟨the bread was stale and ~⟩ ⟨~ coffee beans⟩ **b :** harsh and unyielding **:** rigorous and stern ⟨a ~ pride⟩ ⟨a strong ~ character yielding to no pressures⟩ **3 :** having a distinctive metallic taste — used of some European white wines

¹flip \'flip\ *vb* **flipped; flipped; flipping; flips** [prob. of imit. origin] *vt* **1 :** to put into motion with a small sharp impulse esp. so as to cause to turn over in the air ⟨*flipped* a coin to decide who should go⟩ ⟨boys *flipping* hazelnuts at one another⟩ **2 :** to touch or move with a flip **:** FLICK ⟨~ the dust from your feet⟩ ⟨*flipped* him on the ear with a peashooter⟩ **3 :** to propel (as oneself) with or as if with flippers ⟨various small creatures *flipping* themselves over the mud flats⟩ **4** *slang* **:** to get aboard (a vehicle in motion) ⟨beat his way west, *flipping* freights and hooking truck rides⟩ **5 :** FLAP 7 **6 :** to turn over (as a card in poker) ~ *vi* **1 :** to make a small sharp darting or twitching movement (as of the fingers) as though flipping something **:** strike at something with such a movement ⟨*flipping* at the daisy heads with a switch⟩ **2 :** to move jerkily or with or as if with flippers ⟨met a seal *flipping* over the rocks⟩ ⟨a small bird balancing and *flipping* on a twig⟩ — **flip one's lid** *also* **flip one's stack** *or* **flip one's top** *slang* **:** to lose self-control **:** become furiously angry

²flip \"\ *n* -s **1 :** an act, instance, or result of flipping: **a :** a smart quick blow or stroke ⟨give him a ~ on the ear and come on⟩ **b :** the motion used in flipping something ⟨anyone can make a stone skip; it's all in the ~ of the wrist⟩ **c :** a somersault esp. as performed in the air in certain gymnastic and diving exercises **d :** FLAP 6 **e :** a short quick football pass **f :** vibration of the barrel of a firearm that is caused by burning powder and movement of the projectile or shot load and that is distinct from motion of the barrel in the functioning of the action, recoil of the piece, or movement by the firer **g :** stud poker in which all cards are dealt face down **2 a :** a drink popular in 18th century England and colonial America consisting of rum and beer or ale sweetened and heated often with a hot poker or loggerhead **b :** an iced drink that consists of wine, brandy, rum, or a liqueur, sugar, and egg and that is shaken and dusted with nutmeg when served ⟨brandy ~⟩ ⟨sherry ~⟩ **c :** a hot drink of sweetened liquor usu. spiced and containing beaten egg

³flip \"\ *adj* **flipper; flippest 1** *dial* **:** SUPPLE, LIMBER; *esp* **:** NIMBLE **2 :** glib or pert in speech **:** FLIPPANT; *broadly* **:** violating good taste **:** fresh or smart in manner or conduct **:** SMART-ALECKY

⁴flip \"\ *n* -s [³*flip*] **:** a flip person **:** SMART ALECK

flip-book \'≈,≈\ *n* **:** a series of illustrations of an animated scene bound together in sequence so that an illusion of movement can be imparted by flipping them rapidly

flip coil *n* **:** a small coil of wire used to determine magnetic field intensity by suddenly rotating the coil through 180 degrees and measuring the resulting current surge with a ballistic galvanometer — called also *exploring coil*, *search coil*

flipe *var of* FLYPE

¹flip-flap \'flip,flap\ *adv* [¹*flip* + *flap* (v.)] **:** with repeated strokes and noise ⟨something going *flip-flap* in the dark⟩

²flip-flap \"\ *or* **flip-flop** \-,fläp\ *n* **1 :** the repeated sound and motion of something loose that is moved by recurrent impulses ⟨the *flip-flap* of the awning in the gusty wind⟩ **2 :** a backward somersault **3** *flip-flap* **:** a device used esp. in amusement parks that consists of a horizontal rotating arm pivoted at its center and supporting a passenger car at each end **4** *flip-flop* **:** FLIP-FLOP CIRCUIT

³flip-flap \"\ *vi* **:** to move flip-flap

flip-flop circuit *n* **:** an electronic circuit with two permanently stable conditions (as when one electron tube is conducting while the other is cut off) so that conduction is switched from one to the other by successive pulses

flip glass *n* **:** a large flaring often engraved glass vessel used esp. in the 18th and early 19th centuries for heating flip; *sometimes* **:** a smaller glass tumbler or goblet from which flip was drunk

flip jump *n* **:** a toe jump in figure skating executed at the finish of a three from an inside back edge landing on the outside back edge of the opposite foot after a full turn in the air

flip·ly *adv* **:** in a flip manner **:** PERTLY

flip·ness *n* -ES **:** FLIPPANCY

flip·pan·cy \'flipənsē, -si\ *n* -ES **:** the quality or state of being flippant

flip·pant \-nt\ *adj* [prob. fr. ¹*flip* + *-ant*] **1** *now dial* **:** NIMBLE, LIMBER **2** *archaic* **:** being of smooth, fluent, and easy speech **:** speaking with readiness and ease **:** having a voluble tongue **:** TALKATIVE ⟨it becometh good men, in such cases, to be ~ —Isaac Barrow⟩ **3 :** treating or tending to treat with unsuitable levity that which is serious or to which respect is due **:** PERT — **flip·pant·ly** *adv* — **flip·pant·ness** *n* -ES

¹flip·per \'flipə(r)\ *n* -s [¹*flip* + *-er*] **1 a :** a broad flat limb adapted for swimming (as those of seals, whales, or sea turtles) **b :** a broad flat usu. rubber shoe with the front expanded into a paddle used in skin diving and some other aquatic sports — called also *fin* **2 :** one that flips or is used in flipping: as **a** *slang* **:** ARM **b** (1) **:** GRIDDLE CAKE (2) **:** a utensil used to turn griddle cakes **c :** a device that is essentially a lever actuated by a small steam engine and that is used for moving lumber in a sawmill **d :** a sealed can (as of processed food) in which internal pressure causes the ends to bulge **3 :** a narrow flat hinged to a larger piece of theatrical scenery **4 :** a strip of rubberized fabric used to strengthen the union between the wire-cored bead and the sidewall of a pneumatic tire

flippers 1b

²flipper \"\ *vb* -ED/-ING/-S *vi* **:** to progress by means of flippers ~ *vt* **1 :** to equip with flippers **2 :** to move like a flipper ⟨languidly ~*ing* a washcloth to and fro —Christopher Morley⟩

flip·per·ling \-(r)liŋ\ *n* -s [¹*flipper* + *-ling*] **:** a small animal with flippers (as a baby seal)

flip·per·ty-flop·per·ty \¦flipə(r)d·ē¦fläpə(r)d·ē\ *adj* [irreg. fr. *flip-flop*] **:** loose and floppy ⟨a *flipperty-flopperty* hat⟩

¹flip·pery \'flip(ə)rē\ *n* -ES [by alter.] **:** FRIPPERY

²flippery \"\ *n* -ES [*flipp*ant + *-ery*] **:** FLIPPANCY

flippest *superlative of* FLIP

flipping *pres part of* FLIP

flip·pi·ty-flop \¦flipəd·ē¦fläp\ *adv* (*or adj*) [irreg. fr. *flip-flop*] **:** with a flip and a flop **:** FLIP-FLAP ⟨took a *flippity-flop* tumble on the stairs⟩

flips *pres 3d sing of* FLIP, *pl of* FLIP

flip-top table *n* **:** a table with a hinged leaf which lies on the top and folds outward to double the size

flip-up \'≈,≈\ *n* [fr. *flip up*, v.] **:** something designed to function by flipping up

¹flird \'flird\ *vi* -ED/-ING/-S [origin unknown] *Scot* **:** FLIRT *vi* 3a

²flird \"\ *n* -s **1** *Scot* **:** an object that is flimsy, gaudy, or unsubstantial **2** *Scot* **:** ²FLIRT 3

¹flirt \'flər|t, -lə|, -ləi|, *usu* |d·+V\ *vb* -ED/-ING/-S [origin unknown] *vt* **1 :** to throw with a jerk or quick effort **:** fling suddenly **:** FLIP, FLICK ⟨they ~ water in each other's faces⟩ ⟨~*ed* the ball from his left hand⟩ **2** *obs* **:** to tap smartly **3 :** to toss or throw about jerkily **:** open out or close briskly ⟨~ a fan⟩ ⟨a bird ~s its tail⟩ **4** *obs* **:** to jeer at **:** treat with contempt **:** MOCK ~ *vi* **1** *obs* **:** to turn up the nose (as in contempt) **2 a :** to move jerkily or by fits and starts **:** DART, FLIT ⟨butterflies ~*ing* among the flowers⟩ **b** *of an arrow* **:** to move suddenly out of the line of flight **3 a** *obs* **:** to turn inconstantly from one thing to another **b :** to play at courtship **:** act the lover without serious intent **:** COQUET; *often* **:** to trifle amorously esp. in discourse **c :** to evince superficial interest or liking **:** pay casual or spurious attention — used with *with* ⟨~*ing* with the idea⟩ ⟨a man who ~*ed* with all the arts but mastered none⟩ ⟨reactionary right-wing groups that ~*ed* with the fascists⟩

²flirt \"\ *n* -s **1 a** *now dial* **:** a quick blow **:** FLICK, TAP **b** *obs* **:** a turn or stroke of wit esp. when sharp or mocking **:** a witty jeer or gibe **2 :** a sudden sharp or darting movement ⟨dusted the table with a ~ of the cloth⟩; *sometimes* **:** a quick throw or throwing movement **:** TOSS ⟨released the ball with a ~ of his wrist⟩ **3 a** *archaic* **:** an inconstant, giddy, pert, or wanton person **b :** a person that flirts amorously **:** COQUETTE **4 :** a device (as a lever) for causing sudden or intermittent motion: as **a :** a lever used in some chime clocks to knock up the quarter-rack hook **b :** a lever that stops the balance in a chronograph

flirt·able \-əbəl\ *adj* **:** ready for flirtation

flir·ta·tion \,flər'tāshən, flə̄-,fləi'-\ *n* -s **:** an act or instance of flirting: as **a :** a playing at courtship **:** COQUETRY **b :** a transitory or coquettish love affair **c :** superficial or spurious indication of liking or approval esp. between parties normally or usu. opposed

flir·ta·tious \¦flər¦tāshəs, (')flə̄-, (')fləi¦-\ *adj* **:** inclined to flirt **:** COQUETTISH — **flir·ta·tious·ly** *adv*

flir·ta·tious·ness *n* -ES **:** flirtatious quality or manner ⟨the ~ of her walk⟩ ⟨her inherent ~ was always getting her in trouble⟩

flirt·er \'flər|d·ər, -lə|d·ə(r, -ləi|d·ə(r, |tə-\ *n* -s **:** one that flirts

flirt-gill *or* **flirt-gillian** *n* [²*flirt* + *gill* (girl)] *obs* **:** a pert or wanton woman

flirt·i·gig \'flirti,gig, 'flər-\ *n* -s [*flirty* + *gig* (girl)] *dial Eng* **:** a giddy girl

flirt·ing·ly *adv* **1 :** with a flirt ⟨the bird settled ~ on the swaying branch⟩ **2 :** COQUETTISHLY

flirt·ish \'flərd·ish\ *adj* **:** FLIRTATIOUS

flirty \-d·ē\ *adj* -ER/-EST **1 :** relating to or characterized by flirting ⟨a crisp ~ ruffle⟩ **2 :** FLIRTATIOUS

¹flisk \'flisk\ *vb* -ED/-ING/-S [prob. of imit. origin] *vt*, *chiefly Scot* **:** FLICK, WHISK ⟨a horse ~*ing* flies with his tail⟩ ~ *vi*, *chiefly Scot* **:** FRISK, CAPER

²flisk \"\ *n* -s *Scot* **:** a sudden action **:** WHIM

flisk·ma·hoy \¦fliskmə¦hȯi\ *n* -s [²*flisk* + *-mahoy* (perh. fr. *Dalmahoy*, town in Midlothian county, Scotland)] *Scot* **:** a flighty woman

¹flit \'flit, *usu* -id·+V\ *vb* **flitted; flitted; flitting; flits** [ME *flitten*, of Scand origin; akin to ON *flytja* to carry, convey, *flytjask* to move, migrate; akin to ON *fljōta* to flow — more at FLEET] *vi* **1 :** to pass usu. quickly or abruptly from one place to another **2** *now dial* **:** to change one's residence **:** move from one place to another ⟨we *flitted* last week to our new house⟩ **3 a :** to move swiftly or briskly **:** pass with a rapid motion **:** FLEET ⟨clouds *flitting* across the sky⟩ **b :** to move briskly, irregularly, or intermittently usu. from place to place ⟨butterflies *flitting* about the garden⟩ ⟨the hummingbird ~s from flower to flower⟩ **4 a** *archaic* **:** to shift esp. in direction, attention, or condition **:** be unstable or shifting **b** *of a flame* **:** to die down **:** flicker nearly out ⟨candles *flitting* and flaring in the light evening breeze⟩ **5** *of time* **:** PASS ~ *vt*, *now chiefly Scot* **:** to transfer from one residence to another **:** MOVE ⟨three wagons to ~ them and their furniture⟩

²flit \"\ *n* -s **:** an act or instance of the motion of flitting **:** FLUTTER ⟨the sleepy world that lies beneath the mind's restless ~ —Christopher Morley⟩

³flit \"\ *adj* [alter. (influenced by ¹*flit*) of ⁵*fleet*] *obs* **:** NIMBLE, QUICK, SWIFT

Flit \"\ *trademark* — used for an insecticide

¹flitch \'flich\ *n* -ES [ME *flicche*, fr. OE *flicce*; akin to MLG *vlicke* flitch, ON *flikki*, and prob. to ON *flā* to flay — more at FLAY] **1 a** *obs* **:** the side of any meat animal salted and cured **b :** a side of pork cured and smoked; *often* **:** the side meat of a hog after removal of shoulder, loin, ham, and bones cured and smoked as bacon **c :** a strip or steak of fish (as halibut) suitable for or prepared by smoking **2 a :** a longitudinal section of a log: as (1) **:** an outer slab cut off in shaping a timber (2) **:** a thick and often specially selected length of timber for further processing (as by cutting into veneer or turning) (3) **:** a thick cut of timber with bark on one or more edges (4) **:** a lengthwise half of a balk **b :** a complete package of thin sheets of veneer laid together in sequence as they are sawed or sliced **3 :** one of several elements (as planks or iron plates) that are secured together side by side to make a large girder or laminated beam

²flitch \"\ *vt* -ED/-ING/-ES **:** to cut into flitches (as fish) or cut flitches from (as logs)

flitch beam *or* **flitched beam** *n* **:** a beam built up of flitches between two of which a metal plate is sandwiched for reinforcement

flitch girder *n* **:** a girder that is built up in the manner of a flitch beam

flitch plate *n* **:** a metal plate sandwiched between planks in forming a flitch beam or girder

flite \'flīt\ *vi* -ED/-ING/-S [ME *fliten*, fr. OE *flītan* to contend, strive, wrangle; akin to OE, OFris & OS *flīt* strife, dispute, contention, OHG *flīz* strife, zeal, *flīzan* to contend, strive] **1** *now dial* **a :** CONTEND, QUARREL, WRANGLE **b :** to engage in sharp debate **2 :** to make or utter complaint

flit-gun \'≈,≈\ *n* [⁴*flit*] **:** a small hand insecticide sprayer chiefly for domestic use

flit·ing \'flīd·iŋ\ *n* -s [ME *fliting*, fr. gerund of *fliten* to quarrel] *archaic* **:** SCOLDING, BRAWLING, FLOUTING

¹flit·ter \'flid·ə(r), -itə-\ *vb* -ED/-ING/-S [freq. of ¹*flit*] *vi* **1 :** FLUTTER, FLICKER ⟨birds ~*ing* above the water⟩ ⟨boyish plans for the summer ~*ed* into his mind⟩ **2** *obs* **:** to burst into fragments, dust, or foam **3** *archaic* **:** WAVER, DROOP ~ *vt* **:** to cause to move rapidly to and fro ⟨the way a skilled shuffler ~s the cards⟩ ⟨a fledgling ~*ing* his wings preparatory to flight⟩

²flitter \"\ *n* -s [¹*flit* + *-er*] **:** one that flits; *esp*, *Brit* **:** a workman who moves a coal conveyor or cutting machine

³flitter \"\ *n* -s [G; akin to MHG *vlittern* to whisper, giggle, OHG *flitarezzen* to flatter, caress, OE *floterian* to flutter — more at FLUTTER] **1 :** a small bit or flake of metal **2 :** fine metal fragments usu. coarser than bronze powder that are used for ornamentation and often applied in a volatile vehicle or on an adhesive base (as of size)

⁴flitter \"\ *dial var of* ²FRITTER

flittermouse \'≈≈,≈\ *n*, *pl* **flittermice** [¹*flitter* + *mouse*; trans. of G *fledermaus*] **:** ³BAT 1

flit·tern \'flid·ə(r)n\ *n* -s [origin unknown] **:** a young oak ⟨~ bark is preferred by tanners⟩

flit·ters \'flid·ə(r)z\ *n pl* [alter. (influenced by ¹*flitter*) of *fitters*] **:** RAGS, TATTERS, FRAGMENTS ⟨fell all to ~ when he touched it⟩

¹flitting *n* -s [ME, fr. gerund of *flitten* to flit — more at FLIT] *dial* **:** the moving of an establishment from one place to another; *specif* **:** a household moving

²flitting *adj* [ME, fr. pres. part. of *flitten* to flit] **:** characterized by flitting; *broadly* **:** TRANSITORY, BRIEF, EVANESCENT ⟨a ~ touch of color⟩ ⟨~ moments⟩ — **flit·ting·ly** *adv*

¹fliv·ver \'flivə(r)\ *vi* -ED/-ING/-S [origin unknown] **1** *slang* **:** to be or become a failure **:** fall flat **:** FIZZLE **2** [²*flivver*] *slang* **:** to motor or tour in a flivver

²flivver \"\ *n* -s [perh. fr. ¹*flivver*] **1** *slang* **a :** a small and relatively inexpensive automobile **b :** a small airplane designed for private or personal use **c :** a small naval vessel; *esp* **:** a destroyer of minimal tonnage **2** *slang* **:** FAILURE, FRAUD, HOAX

¹flix \'fliks\ *n* -ES [perh. alter. of ¹*flick*] *archaic* **:** DOWN, FUR

²flix \"\ *n* -ES [ME *flex*, *flax* — more at FLAX] **:** FLAX 1a

flixweed \'≈,≈\ *n* [²*flix* + *weed*] **1 :** a branching annual tansy mustard (*Descurainia sophia*) that is native to Europe but widely naturalized in No. America **2 :** SAND ROCKET

¹float \'flōt, *usu* -ōd·+V\ *n* -s *often attrib* [partly fr. ME *flote* boat, fleet, float, act of floating, fr. OE *flota* ship & OE *flot* sea (as in *on flote* on the sea, afloat); partly fr. ²*float*; akin to OHG *flōz* raft, stream, MLG *vlote* raft, fleet, MD, stream, fleet, ON *flot* action of flowing, fat, *floti* raft, fleet; derivatives fr. the root of OE *flēotan* to flow — more at FLEET] **1 a :** the act or state of floating ⟨every ~ of her wide skirt—Christopher Morley⟩ **b :** a slight displacement of the axis of a rotating body (as of the armature of a generator) **c :** a floating movement ⟨the slow ~ of clouds across the sky⟩; *esp* **:** an easy loping stride used by distance runners in the intermediate part of a race **2 :** something broad and shallow and flat: as **a** *obs* **:** a brewing vat **b :** FLOATBOARD **c :** a floating tray for keeping shellfish (as crabs during shedding) in good condition until ready for marketing **3** *obs* **a :** a flowing or overflowing esp. of the tide or a river in flood **b :** something that flows (as the sea or a wave) **4 :** something that floats in or rests on the surface of a fluid (as to sustain a weight, mark the location of something submerged, or regulate a flow): as **a** (1) **:** a cork or bob used to buoy up the baited end of a fishline and keep it at a desired depth (2) **:** one of the cork, glass, or other floating devices attached to the edge of a fishnet to buoy it up (3) **:** a floating indicator marking the position of something (as a lobster pot) beneath the surface of a body of water **b :** a flat-bottomed boat **:** RAFT **c** (1) **:** a platform that floats and is anchored at or near the shore and used esp. for landing or the convenience of swimmers (2) **:** a support projected from each side of a small boat (as a canoe) **d :** a hollow metallic ball or similar object that floats usu. at the end of a lever in a cistern, tank, or boiler and regulates by its elevation or depression the level of the liquid; *also* **:** a similar often horseshoe-shaped device in a carburetor of a gasoline engine **e :** an inflated bag or pillow used to support on a water surface the head or other part of the body (as of a person learning to swim) **:** LIFE PRESERVER **f :** an air-filled glass

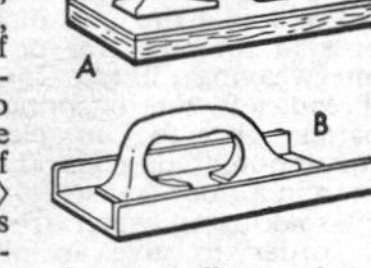

plasterer's floats: *A* regular; *B* angle

bulb used in a burette as an aid in measuring differences in the level of a liquid **g :** an air sac or other light structure containing air or gas serving to buoy up the body of a pelagic animal **:** PNEUMATOPHORE 1 **h :** a hollow vesicle found in certain algae (as of the genus *Fucus*) containing gases (as carbon dioxide) and serving to buoy up the plant **i :** a completely enclosed watertight structure fitted to an airplane to give it buoyancy and stability when in contact with a surface of water **5 :** any of several devices used in dressing, finishing, or smoothing surfaces: as **a :** a flat-faced tool for smoothing and finishing a plastic surface (as of unset concrete, plaster, or stucco) that is either rectangular with a handle on the back by which it is hand manipulated or disklike for mechanical rotation **b :** FLOAT-CUT FILE **c :** a usu. handled block used for polishing dressed stone **d** (1) **:** a platform of heavy overlapping planks cleated together that is drawn over soil to compact and smooth its surface, to improve its condition, or to crush clods — called also *clod smasher, drag, planker, slicker* (2) **:** a frame of heavy planks used for leveling land for irrigation **6 :** a trench for irrigation **7 a :** loose fragmentary rock, mineral, or ore detached from an outcrop or vein by natural forces (as weathering or the action of water) and deposited downslope often at a considerable distance from the source **b** *or* **floats** *pl but sing or pl in constr* **:** finely divided mineral material (as pulverized rock phosphate or flaky ores) that tends to remain in suspension in water ⟨~*s* is often used as a filler in mixed fertilizer⟩ ⟨~ gold⟩ ⟨asbestos ~*s*⟩ **8 :** a grant by the government of a fixed quantity of land that is not yet located by survey out of a larger specific tract of land and that will be later located with certainty in accordance with law **9 floats** *pl* **:** FOOTLIGHTS **10 a :** a portion of filling thread that passes over two or more warp threads or of warp thread that passes over two or more filling threads before interweaving; *also* **:** the passage of such thread **b :** a defective place in a fabric where warp and filling threads are not properly interlaced **c :** a portion of yarn that passes over several needles without interlacing and is usu. brought to the front at intervals to make colored patterns in knitting; *also* **:** the passage of such thread **11 a** *chiefly Brit* **:** a low underslung cart or platform on wheels used for drawing heavy loads **b :** a platform on wheels or a vehicle with a platform used as a base for a tableau or other exhibit in a procession; *broadly* **:** the entire unit of base and exhibit **12 :** a contrivance for supplying a copious stream of water to the heated surface of an object of large bulk (as an anvil or die) that is undergoing tempering **13 :** an amount of money represented at any one time by checks outstanding and in process of collection; *esp* **:** the amount of checks credited in a weekly statement to member banks of a system (as the Federal Reserve) but not yet collected by the crediting bank **14 :** a drink consisting of ice cream suspended in a liquid (as root beer)

[2]**float** \"\ *vb* -ED/-ING/-S [ME *floten,* fr. OE *flotian;* akin to ON *flota* to float; derivatives fr. the root of OE *flēotan* to flow — more at FLEET] *vi* **1 :** to become buoyed up by a fluid: as **a :** to rest on the surface of or partly submerged in a liquid ⟨a needle will ~ on water⟩ ⟨the boat ~*ed* away⟩; *esp* **:** to rest on one's back in water so that the face remains above the surface — often contrasted with *swim* ⟨he was a poor swimmer but could ~ for hours on quiet water⟩ **b :** to become waterborne by the action of rising water ⟨the logs will ~ when the river rises⟩ — often used with *off* ⟨their boat ~*ed* off as the tide came in⟩ **c :** to become suspended within the body of a fluid ⟨stars ~*ing* in the sky⟩ **2 a :** to move quietly and gently on, through, or as if on or through water or other fluid impelled by some external agent (as currents of the medium or gravity) ⟨the boat ~*ed* by⟩ ⟨yellow leaves ~*ing* down⟩ ⟨a flag ~*ing* in the breeze⟩ ⟨rumors ~*ed* about⟩ **b :** to move easily and smoothly as if floating in fluid ⟨she ~*ed* down the walk⟩ **c** *of a runner* **:** to run easily and at less than top speed ⟨a distance runner learns to spell himself by ~*ing* in the midstretch⟩ **d** *of a tool or mechanical part* **:** to remain virtually suspended in neutral position between contacts or limits set for motion **:** be free to move within limits **3 a** *obs* **:** to seem to waver **:** move uncertainly to and fro **:** WAVER — often used with *between* **b :** to be unstable (as in political affiliation or morals) **:** lack fixity of purpose or determination **c :** to make frequent changes (as of one's abode or occupation) **d :** to drift often aimlessly or heedlessly **4 a :** to fish with a float **b** *archaic* **:** to hunt deer at night from shallow boats **5 :** to become connected but adjusted so as not to share in output — used of a storage battery on the line or of an idle grid in an electron tube **6 :** to pass over or under two or more threads before interweaving **7** *of a defensive end in football* **:** to hang back to prevent the ball carrier from getting around the flank ~ *vt* **1 :** to cause to float: as **a :** to cause to rest on the surface of a fluid or to be suspended in and buoyed up by fluid ⟨the tide ~*ed* the ships⟩ **b :** to move or cause to move through the surface of water usu. by the action of an external agent (as a current) ⟨the stream ~*ed* the logs onto a sandbar⟩; *esp* **:** to convey to market by floating usu. down a river or stream ⟨the upriver farmers ~ their produce down on flatboats⟩ **c :** to cause to spread out on the surface of a liquid ⟨~ the liqueur on the surface of the coffee⟩ ⟨they ~ oil over the swamp to destroy mosquitoes⟩ **d :** to support (a building or structure) on a mat or raft foundation when the ground has low supporting value **e :** to arrange (a mechanical part) to operate smoothly by floating or as if by floating in a liquid **f :** to mount (a mechanical part) esp. in rubber so that vibration is not transmitted — see FLOATING POWER **2 :** to overflow with or as if with water **:** FLOOD — used both of natural flooding and that undertaken for military or agricultural purposes **3 :** to smooth or dress with a float: as **a :** to finish (as plaster or cement) with a float **b :** to work (land) with a float **c :** to smooth down (the teeth of an old horse) with a float **4 a :** to obtain popular support or acceptance of (as a scheme or idea) ⟨careful publicity is often required to ~ a really novel plan⟩ **b :** to offer (an issue of stocks or bonds) for sale in order to raise capital (as for beginning or expanding a business); *also* **:** to establish (as a company or enterprise) by floating securities ⟨hoped to raise enough money to ~ the company⟩ **c :** NEGOTIATE ⟨the company hoped to ~ a loan at lower interest rates⟩ **5 :** to grind (as a pigment in water) as a refining or levigating process **6 :** to solder the ends of (a tin can) — used with *up* **7 a :** to pass (a thread) over or under two or more threads before interweaving **b :** to form (a figure in textiles) by floating threads **8 a :** to connect (a storage battery) as a floating battery **b :** to join (electrical apparatus) at approximately equal potentials so that negligible current flows **9 a :** to keep in a float (sense 2c) **b :** to bloat (as oysters or scallops) by soaking in water fresher than that in the native habitat in order to give an abnormal appearance of plumpness **10** *slang* **:** to cause (a petty offender or vagrant who may become a financial burden) to move out of a community esp. by threats of legal action

float·abil·i·ty \ˌflōdəˈbiləd·ē\ *n* -ES **:** ability to float **:** floatable quality or state

float·able \ˈflōd·əbəl\ *adj* **1 a :** able to float **b** *of an ore or mineral* **:** suitable for treatment by a flotation process **2** *of a waterway* **:** suitable for the transport of floating objects (as logs)

floatage *var of* FLOTAGE

floatation *var of* FLOTATION

floatboard \ˈ⸗,⸗\ *n* **:** any of the radial rim boards of an undershot waterwheel or paddle wheel **:** VANE

float boat *n* **:** a shallow boat driven by an airplane engine and used on shallow waters and swamps esp. in Florida

float bowl *n* **:** FLOAT CHAMBER

float bridge *n* **:** a structure with tracks on an adjustable apron for transferring railroad cars to or from car floats at varying water levels

float chamber *n* **:** a chamber (as in a carburetor) having a float to regulate the level of the contained liquid

float coat *n* **:** a thin layer of mortar applied to a surface (as of concrete) and given a float finish

float-cut file \ˈ⸗,⸗-\ *n* **:** a coarse single-cut file usu. for filing soft materials

floated *past of* FLOAT

float·er \ˈflōd·ə(r), -ōtə-\ *n* -S **1 :** something that rests or drifts along on or in a fluid or is free or loose from its usual attachment: as **a :** a fired clay shape floating on molten glass in a tank to hold back scum **b floaters** *pl* **:** small particles in suspension in beer **c :** a plant (as a water hyacinth) that grows on the surface of water **d :** DRIFT BOTTLE **e :** a corpse found floating in the water **2 :** a person who floats something (as a company or a loan) or who works with a float ⟨a cement ~⟩ **3 a :** a person who votes illegally in various polling places either under false registration or under the name of a properly registered person who has not already voted **b :** a person (as a delegate to a convention or a member of a legislature) who represents an irregular constituency (as made up of the voters of two counties neither of which has sufficient population to entitle it to a separate representative) **4 :** a person who floats or drifts: as **a :** a person without fixed abode or regular employment **:** VAGRANT, TRAMP **b :** a person who tends to shift from job to job often within a particular industry for other than economic reasons ⟨~*s* increase the expense of handling a retirement system⟩ **:** BOOMER **c :** a person without fixed political or religious affiliations or convictions **d :** a worker without regular fixed duties who is available for assignment wherever extra help is needed ⟨larger hospitals usu. have a few nurses on the staff who act as ~*s* or substitutes⟩ **5** *slang Brit* **:** BLUNDER **6 a :** a slowly pitched baseball with little or no spin **b :** a soft pass in football that is long and high **7** *Brit* **:** a bearer security; *esp* **:** one unlisted but acceptable as collateral **8 :** a policy of insurance to protect against loss or damage of goods in transit or goods (as furs or jewels) naturally subject to use in various places — compare INLAND MARINE INSURANCE **9 :** an order (as by a court or police official) to a person considered an undesirable citizen to leave a town or locality; *usu* **:** a heavy sentence on a petty offender that is suspended on condition that he leave the jurisdiction of the court permanently

float finish *n* **:** a finish produced on plaster, mortar, or concrete surfaces by use of a float

float grass *n* **:** FLOATING GRASS

[1]**floating** *n* -S [fr. gerund of [2]*float*] **1 :** the act or action of one that floats **2 :** spotty or irregular flooding of paint; *sometimes* **:** separation of a pigment from a mixture whether in bulk or in a film **3 a :** the act or process of spreading or smoothing a surface (as of concrete, mortar, plaster, or stucco) with a float **b :** the second coat of three-coat plastering

[2]**floating** *adj* [fr. pres. part. of [2]*float*] **1 :** buoyed upon or in a fluid ⟨the ~ timbers of a wreck⟩ ⟨~ motes in the air⟩ ⟨~ aquatic vegetation made the canal unusable⟩ **2 a :** free from or lacking the usual attachment — used esp. of ribs that join the sternum by a cartilaginous rather than a bony union **b :** being out of the normal position; *esp* **:** abnormally movable and displaced downward or away from normal attachments — used esp. of the kidney **3 :** continually changing **:** characterized by shifting or drifting (as from one abode or occupation to another) ⟨the ~ population⟩: as **a :** shifting or variable in form, incidence, or subject matter ⟨~ rumors⟩ **b** *of funds or capital* **:** not presently committed or invested **c** *of a debt* **:** falling due within the year; *sometimes* **:** short-term and usu. not funded **d :** enforceable in equity as a lien against whatever assets a person may have from time to time leaving him meanwhile more or less free to dispose of or encumber his assets as if no lien existed ⟨a ~ charge⟩ ⟨~ security⟩ **e :** frequently shifted in location to evade detection and arrest of participants ⟨a ~ crap game⟩ **4 a :** connected or constructed so as to operate and adjust smoothly (as if floating) **b :** of, relating to, or having mechanical parts connected or constructed in this way ⟨a ~ transmission⟩ — **float·ing·ly** *adv*

floating accent *n* **:** PIECE ACCENT

floating anchor *n* **:** SEA ANCHOR

floating axle *n* **:** a live axle used in a self-propelled vehicle to turn the wheels, the dead weight of the vehicle being carried on the ends of a fixed axle housing or casing

floating bag *n* **:** a flexible tightly sealed protective barrier placed loosely around an object (as a metal part) in a shipping box

floating battery *n* **1 :** a storage battery connected across an electric line or feeder to equalize the load and maintain the voltage constant **2 :** a battery erected on a raft or the hull of a ship or a ship carrying heavy guns and designed as a gun platform rather than for navigation formerly used in coast defense and in attacking fortifications

floating bridge *n* **1 :** a temporary bridge supported by low flat-bottomed boats or pontoons **2 :** a double bridge that has the upper level projecting beyond the lower and capable of being moved forward by pulleys and was used formerly for carrying troops over narrow moats in attacking the outworks of a fort **3 :** a ferryboat drawn and guided by chains that are anchored on the sides of a stream and that mesh with wheels on the boat

floating dock *or* **floating dry dock** *n* **1 :** a dock that floats on the water and can be partly submerged to permit a ship to enter it and afterward floated to raise the ship high and dry as in a dry dock **2 :** a flatboat or barge used as a wharf adjustable to the stage of water

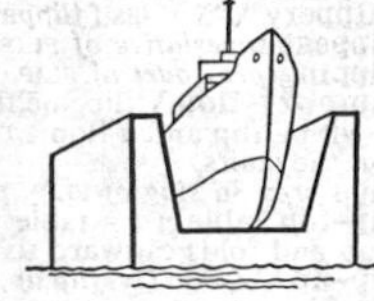

floating dock 1

floating fern *n* **1 :** any of several aquatic ferns of the genus *Ceratopteris* (esp. *C. thalictroides* and *C. pteridoides*) often used in aquariums — called also *water sprite* **2 :** FLOATING MOSS; *also* **:** a related plant (*Azolla caroliniana*)

floating floor *n* **:** a floor separated from its structural support by a layer of sand, building paper, or a sound-reducing blanket

floating foundation *n* **:** a building support on soft soil that consists of a stiff reinforced concrete slab which distributes the concentrated loads by columns to the soil so that the pressure intensity on the soil is nowhere more than the acceptable amount

floating gang *n* **:** a specially organized railroad track repair group that moves over various sections of the line

floating garden *n* **:** a planting on soil buoyed up (as on the surface of a lake) by rafts of interlaced branches or other floating support found chiefly in the Mexico City area and parts of Kashmir

floating grass *n* **:** any of several marsh or semiaquatic grasses: as **a :** FLOATING MANNA GRASS **b :** MARSH FOXTAIL

floating head *n* **:** a flesh hoop of a drum entirely free from the shell

floating heart *n* **:** a plant of the genus *Nymphoides; esp* **:** a small white-flowered aquatic (*N. cordata*) with heart-shaped floating leaves

floating holder *n* **:** a holder (as for a tap) that allows a certain amount of play or freedom to enable the tool to maintain the proper path relative to the work

floating inspector *n* **:** an inspector who inspects manufacturing operations as he chooses at various points in the process

floating island *n* **1 a :** FLOATING GARDEN **b :** a floating mass of vegetation with little or no soil (as in a lake or quiet tropical sea) usu. due to detachment of matted vegetation from a marshy shore **2 :** a dessert consisting of custard with floating masses of whipped whites of egg

floating lever *n* **:** a horizontal brake lever beneath a railroad car body having its fulcrum at the end of a rod that leads from another lever and thus is movable

floating liability *n* **:** CURRENT LIABILITY

floating light *n* **:** a light shown at the masthead of a ship moored over dangerous waters (as those above sunken rocks or shoals) to warn mariners **:** LIGHTSHIP; *also* **:** a light on a buoy

floating manna grass *n* **:** any of several aquatic grasses of the genus *Glyceria* (esp. *G. fluitans* and *G. septentrionalis*)

floating moss *n* **:** an aquatic plant (*Salvinia rotundifolia*) introduced from Mexico or So. America and locally established in the U.S.

floating policy *n* **1 :** a marine insurance policy designating the general nature of insured material but leaving the exact amount and kind, name of ship, and value to be fixed at a later date **2 :** FLOATER 8

floating power *n* **:** an arrangement of an automotive power plant such that a minimum of engine vibration is transmitted to the supporting chassis

floating primrose willow *n* **:** a widely distributed primrose willow (*Jussiaea repens glabrescens*) with creeping or floating stems

floating rib *n* **:** a rib not connected with the sternum or cartilages of other ribs ventrally, in man being the 11th and 12th on each side

floating screed *n* **:** a strip of plaster first laid on to serve as a guide for the thickness of the coat of plaster to be applied (as to a wall)

floating star *n* **:** FROST FLOWER 1a

floating supply *n* **:** the quantity of something (as a commodity, money, or securities) available immediately (as for purchase, loan, or delivery)

float·less \ˈflōtləs\ *adj* **:** not having a float **:** lacking in buoyancy

float master *n* **:** one that supervises the movement of freight by barge and lighter between a railroad yard and a ship — called also *boat dispatcher*

float·o·blast \ˈflōd·əˌblast\ *n* [[2]*float* + *-o-* + *-blast*] **:** a pelagic statoblast of certain bryozoans that lacks hooks or spines and has a specialized capsule containing air cells

float ore *n* **:** ore so finely divided as to be held in suspension by water for prolonged periods resulting in loss of mineral during refining or in movement of ore by water to considerable distances from its point of origin

floatplane \ˈ⸗,⸗\ *n* **:** a seaplane supported on the water by one or more floats — compare FLYING BOAT

float road *n* **:** a forest path (as in a swamp) cleared so that high water will take logs through

floats *pl of* FLOAT, *pres 3d sing of* FLOAT

float·sam \ˈflōtsəm\ *archaic var of* FLOTSAM

float seaplane *n* **:** FLOATPLANE

floats·man \ˈflōtsmən\ *n, pl* **floatsmen :** a worker who smooths stone (as marble or slate) usu. by holding it on a rotating sanding table

float-stone \ˈ⸗,⸗\ *n* **1 :** a light porous variety of opal occurring in concretionary masses **2 :** a bricklayer's rubstone for smoothing gauged brickwork

float switch *n* **:** an electric switch operated by a float on a liquid

float valve *n* **:** an automatic valve whose opening and closing are controlled by a float at the end of a lever

float-wing seaplane *n* **:** a seaplane that receives a substantial part of its support when on the water from buoyant forces acting on its wings

floaty \ˈflōd·ē\ *adj* -ER/-EST **:** tending to float **:** floating readily **:** BUOYANT, LIGHT

flob \ˈfläb\ *vi* **flobbed; flobbed; flobbing; flobs** [perh. alter. of [1]*flop*] **:** to be clumsy or aimless in moving

[1]**floc** \ˈfläk\ *n* -S [L *floccus* flock of wool — more at FLOCCUS] **1 :** a flocculent mass formed by the aggregation of a number of fine suspended particles (as in a precipitate or in smoke) **2 :** [3]FLOCK 1,2,3

[2]**floc** \"\ *vb* **flocced** \-kt\ **flocced** \"\ **floccing** \-kiŋ\ **flocs** *vi* **:** to aggregate into flocs **:** FLOCCULATE ~ *vt* **:** to cause (as a slime) to floc

flocci *pl of* FLOCCUS

floc·cil·la·tion \ˌfläksəˈlāshən\ *n* -S [L *floccus* + *-illus* dim. ending + E *-ation*] **:** CARPHOLOGY

floc·cose \ˈflä,kōs\ *adj* [LL *floccosus,* fr. L *floccus* + *-osus* -ose] **:** having or covered with tufts of soft woolly hairs that are often deciduous — used esp. of plants — **floc·cose·ly** \-lē\ *adv* — **floc·cos·i·ty** \fläˈkäsəd·ē\ *n* -ES

floc·cu·la·ble \ˈfläkyələbəl\ *adj* [*floccula*te + *-able*] **:** capable of being flocculated ⟨~ clays⟩

floc·cu·lant \-lənt\ *n* -S [*floccule* + *-ant*] **:** an agent that produces floccule or other aggregate formation esp. in soil ⟨lime alters soil pH and acts as a ~ in clay soils⟩; *esp* **:** a usu. acid reagent used in ceramic manufacture to increase the viscosity of a clay slip or the plasticity of tempered clay

floc·cu·lar \-lə(r)\ *adj* [NL *flocculus* + E *-ar*] **:** of or relating to a flocculus

[1]**floc·cu·late** \-lət, -ˌlāt\ *adj* [LL *flocculus* + E *-ate* (adj. suffix)] **:** bearing small tufts of hairs — often used postpositively ⟨a heavy-bodied bee with the dorsum of the thorax ~⟩

[2]**floc·cu·late** \-ˌlāt\ *vb* -ED/-ING/-S [NL *flocculus* + E *-ate* (v. suffix)] *vt* **:** to cause to aggregate or coalesce into small lumps or loose clusters or into a flocculent mass or deposit ⟨calcium ion tends to ~ clays⟩ ⟨essential to avoid *flocculating* the pulp fibers in early stages of paper manufacture⟩ — compare COAGULATE ~ *vi* **:** to aggregate or coalesce into small lumps or loose clusters or into a flocculent mass or deposit ⟨certain clays ~ readily⟩ ⟨the bacteria of a hay infusion tend to ~ with their products into a thick zooglea⟩

[3]**floc·cu·late** \-ˌlət, -ˌlāt\ *n* -S **:** something that has flocculated **:** a flocculent particle or mass **:** FLOC

floc·cu·la·tion \ˌfläkyəˈlāshən\ *n* -S **1 :** the act or process of flocculating **2 :** a product of flocculating; *broadly* **:** a cluster, conglomeration, or aggregate esp. of cultural traits

floc·cu·la·tor \ˈfläkyəˌlād·ə(r)\ *n* -S **:** something that induces flocculation; *esp* **:** an apparatus in which material (as water or sewage) flocculates certain suspended or dissolved constituents

floc·cule \ˈflä,kyül\ *n* -S [LL *flocculus* small flock of wool, dim. of L *floccus* flock of wool — more at FLOCCUS] **:** a small loosely aggregated mass of material suspended in or precipitated from a liquid **:** FLOC; *often* **:** one of the flakes of a flocculent precipitate

floc·cu·lence \ˈfläkyələn(t)s\ *also* **floc·cu·len·cy** \-nsē\ *n, pl* **flocculences** *also* **flocculencies 1 :** a flocculent state **2 :** something that gives a flocculent material or surface its character (as the waxy secretion of flocculent insects)

[1]**floc·cu·lent** \-nt\ *adj* [LL *flocculus* + E *-ent*] **1 :** of the appearance of wool; WOOLLY, FLOCKY ⟨~ cloud masses⟩ **2 :** containing, consisting of, or occurring in the form of loosely aggregated particles or soft flakes **:** made up of flocs ⟨a ~ white precipitate⟩ **3 :** covered with tufts of woolly material; *specif* **:** covered with a soft waxy substance often resembling wool — used chiefly of aphids and scales — **floc·cu·lent·ly** *adv*

[2]**flocculent** \"\ *n* -S **:** a flocculating agent **:** FLOCCULANT

floc·cu·lose \ˌlōs\ *also* **floc·cu·lous** \-ləs\ *adj* [LL *flocculus* + E *-ose* or *-ous*] **:** minutely floccose

floc·cu·lus \-ləs\ *n, pl* **floccu·li** \-ˌlī\ [LL *flocculus* — more at FLOCCULE] **1 :** a small loosely aggregated mass (as of wool) **:** FLAKE, FLOCCULE, FLOC **2** [NL, fr. LL] **:** a small irregular lobe on the under surface of each hemisphere of the cerebellum that is linked with the corresponding side of the nodulus by a peduncle **3** [NL, fr. LL] **:** a bright or dark patch on the sun seen in the light of calcium or hydrogen usu. in the vicinity of sunspots or other active regions — compare PLAGE

floc·cus \ˈfläkəs\ *n, pl* **floc·ci** \-äˌkī, -äˌkē, -äkˌsī, -äkˌsē\ [L, akin to OHG *blaha* coarse linen, OSw *blā, blār* oakum, ON *blæja* cloth, bed sheet] **1 :** a tuft of woolly hairs on a plant; *specif* **:** a mass of hyphal filaments or portion of mycelium of a fungus **2** [NL, fr. L] **:** one of the small masses or tufts making up certain cloud formations

[1]**flock** \ˈfläk\ *n* -S [ME, fr. OE *flocc;* akin to MLG *vlocke* crowd, herd of sheep, ON *flokkr* crowd, band, troop] **1 a** *archaic* **:** a band or company of people **b flocks** *pl* **:** great numbers **:** MULTITUDES ⟨the ~*s* of foreign students⟩ ⟨found ~*s* of witnesses willing to testify⟩ **2 a :** a natural assemblage of animals (as of gregarious birds or mammals) ⟨a ~ of wild geese⟩ **b :** a company of domestic mammals (as sheep or goats) herded together **c flocks** *pl* **:** holdings (as of a person) in sheep and goats — sometimes contrasted with *herds* ⟨immensely rich in ~*s* and herds⟩ **d :** a company of domestic poultry ⟨a small ~ of hens feeding on the lawn⟩ ⟨making the farm ~ pay⟩ **3 a :** all Christians in their relation to Christ **b :** a Christian church or congregation in their relation to the pastor or minister in charge **c :** a company in relation to one in charge; *esp* **:** the members of a family in relation to one member (as a father) who is responsible and in charge ⟨a father worrying over the future of his little ~⟩ **4 :** an aggregation, collection, or group of anything esp. when large ⟨returned with a ~ of new ideas⟩ ⟨the latest ~ of annual reports makes depressing reading⟩ ⟨drank a ~ of martinis⟩

²flock \"\ *vb* -ED/-ING/-S [ME *flocken*, fr. *flock*, n.] *vt* **1** *obs* **:** to assemble into a flock or company **2 a** *obs* **:** to crowd about (as a person) **b :** CROWD, THRONG ⟨vacationers ~*ed* the shore⟩ ~ *vi* **:** to gather into or move in bands or crowds ⟨~*ing* about the speaker⟩ ⟨people ~*ed* to the country for the weekend⟩

³flock \"\ *n* -S *often attrib* [ME; prob. akin to MHG *vlocke* snowflake, down, flock of wool (fr. OHG *floccho, flocko* down), MLG *vlocke* snowflake, flock of wool, Norw *flugsa, flygsa* snowflake, Latvian *plauki* snowflakes, *plaūkas* tufts of wool, fibers] **1 :** a lock or tuft of wool or other fiber (as cotton or hair) ⟨gleaning ~*s* from the bushes through which the sheep had passed⟩ **2 :** woolen or cotton refuse (as processing waste or old rags) reduced usu. by machinery and used esp. for stuffing furniture and mattresses ⟨cut into fragments to make ~*s* to stuff bedding —Flora Thompson⟩ **3 :** very short or pulverized fiber (as of wool, cotton, rayon, or silk) obtained often from the textile processes of shearing or napping, used esp. to form velvety patterns on cloth or paper or a soft protective covering on metal, and applied by blowing or shaking on a surface spread with adhesive **4 :** FLOC

⁴flock \"\ *vb* -ED/-ING/-S *vt* **1 :** to fill (as a mattress) with flock **2 a :** to coat (as an adhesive surface) or cover (as an evergreen bough) with flock **b :** to weight (woolen cloths) by blowing in short waste fibers and shrinking and pressing **c :** to decorate (as wallpaper) with raised patterns of flock ⟨finished with ~*ed* red wallpaper to look like velvet —Alice Griffin⟩ **3** [trans. of L *flocci facere*, lit., to make flocks] *obs* **:** to treat contemptuously ~ *vi* **:** FLOC

flock bed *n* [³*flock*] **:** a bed having or consisting of a mattress stuffed with flock

flock book *n* [¹*flock*] **:** a book containing the records and pedigrees of breeds of sheep or of a particular flock of sheep

flock duck *n* [¹*flock*] **:** SCAUP DUCK

flock·ing \ˈfläkiŋ\ *n* -S [³*flock* + *-ing*] **1 :** decorative work or a design in flock **2 :** ³FLOCK 3

flockmaster \ˈ=,==\ *n* **:** an owner or overseer of a flock (as of sheep)

flock–mate \ˈ=,=\ *vt* **:** to allow (poultry) to breed at random within a selected population — compare PEN-MATE

flockowner \ˈ=,==\ *n* **:** an owner of a flock of sheep

flock pigeon *n* **:** an Australian pigeon (*Histriophaps histrionica*) often seen in very large flocks

flock printing *n* [³*flock*] **:** a process in which material (as flock or metallic powder) is dusted or sprayed over matter (as Christmas cards or wallpaper) previously printed with an adhesive (as glue or varnish)

flockwise \ˈ=,=\ *adv* [¹*flock* + *-wise*] **:** in a flock

flocky \ˈfläkē\ *adj* -ER/-EST [ME, fr. ³*flock* + *-y*] **:** resembling or full of flock ⟨a ~ surface⟩ ⟨coarse ~ wool⟩

flocs *pl of* FLOC, *pres 3d sing of* FLOC

flodge \ˈfläj\ *n* -S [alter. of ME *floshe, flashe* swamp, pool, puddle, prob. fr. MF *flache*] *dial Eng* **:** POOL, PUDDLE

floe \ˈflō\ *also* **floe ice** *n* -S [prob. fr. Norw *flo* flat layer, fr. ON *flō* layer — more at PLEASE] **1 :** floating ice formed in a large sheet on the surface of the sea or other body of water **2 :** ICE FLOE

floeberg \ˈ=,=\ *n* **:** a mass of hummocky floe ice resembling an iceberg

floe rat *n* **:** RINGED SEAL

floer·kea \ˈflərkēə, ˈflōr-,ˈfler-\ *n, cap* [NL, after Heinrich G. *Floerke* †1835 Ger. botanist] **:** a small genus of aquatic or marsh herbs (family Limnanthaceae) having pinnately divided leaves and small solitary flowers with three sepals and three petals — see FALSE MERMAID

flog \ˈfläg *also* ˈflȯg\ *vb* **flogged; flogged; flogging; flogs** [perh. modif. of L *flagellare* — more at FLAGELLATE] *vt* **1 :** to beat or strike with a rod or whip **:** WHIP, LASH **2 :** to strike repeatedly as if beating ⟨wind-swept branches *flogging* the ground⟩; *often* **:** to cast a fishline repeatedly into ⟨*flogged* the stream for trout⟩ **3 a :** PUNISH 3 **b :** to criticize harshly or scathingly ⟨the opposition papers continue to ~ the government over the economic crisis⟩ **4** *chiefly Brit* **a :** DRIVE, PUSH **:** force into attention or action ⟨*flogging* his keen retentive memory —Nevil Shute⟩ ⟨*flogging* herself into a rage⟩ ⟨*flogged* his new car up to town⟩ **b :** to wear out **:** EXHAUST ⟨completely *flogged* when he got to the top⟩ ⟨pastures *flogged* by overgrazing⟩ **5** *slang* **:** to take (as government property) for purposes of resale ⟨*flogging* blankets from the army depot⟩ ~ *vi* **1 :** to flap or move violently or vigorously ⟨awnings *flogging* in the wind⟩ ⟨lambs racing to their mothers with their tails *flogging*⟩ **2 :** to progress or function by a repeated sequence of movements ⟨*flogging* down the road toward his home⟩ ⟨the idling motor *flogged* away quietly⟩ — **flog a dead horse :** to attempt to revive interest in a worn-out or forgotten subject

flog·ga·ble \-gəbəl\ *adj* **:** meriting a flogging ⟨a ~ offence⟩

flog·ger \-gə(r)\ *n* -S **:** one that flogs: as **a :** BUNG STARTER **b :** a foundry worker who knocks the loose sand from a casting just taken from the mold

flogging chisel *n* **:** a large cold chisel for chipping castings

flogging hammer *n* **:** a small sledgehammer used for driving a flogging chisel or for beating metal

flo·kite \ˈflō,kīt, -lä,-\ *n* -S [Dan *flokit*, fr. *Floki* Vilgerdarson, 9th cent. viking + Dan *-it* -ite] **:** a zeolitic mineral from Iceland occurring in slender colorless or yellowish green prismatic crystals

flong \ˈfläŋ, ˈflȯŋ\ *n* -S [F *flan* flan, flong — more at FLAN] **:** a sheet (as of several layers of tissue paper superposed on a sheet of heavier paper) used for making a stereotype matrix

flong paper *n* **:** MATRIX PAPER

¹flood \ˈfləd\ *n* -S *often attrib* [ME *flood, flod*, fr. OE *flōd*; akin to OHG *fluot* flood, ON *flōth*, Goth *flodus*; derivatives fr. the root of E *flow*] **1** *archaic* **:** a body of moving water (as a river or stream) esp. when large **2 a :** the flowing in of the tide **:** the semidiurnal swell or rise of water in the ocean ⟨there is a tide in the affairs of men which, taken at the ~, leads on to fortune —Shak.⟩ — opposed to *ebb* **b :** the highest point of a tide ⟨the tide is nearly at the ~⟩ **3 a :** a rising and overflowing of a body of water that covers land not usu. under water **:** DELUGE, FRESHET ⟨a covenant never to destroy the earth again by ~ —John Milton⟩ — used with *the* to identify a flood of esp. severity or local interest ⟨still date things around here from the ~, which was about the biggest excitement we ever had⟩ or, usu. cap., the worldwide deluge reported in Gen 7 ⟨the *Flood* in the days of Noah⟩ **b** (1) **:** an outpouring of considerable extent ⟨gave way in a ~ of tears⟩ (2) **:** a great downpour ⟨raining in ~*s*⟩ **4 :** the element water ⟨the rocky shore that forms a barrier between earth and ~⟩ ⟨willing to go through fire and ~ to gain his objective⟩ **5 a :** a great stream of something (as light or lava) that flows in a steady course **b :** a large quantity widely diffused **:** SUPERABUNDANCE ⟨a ~ of spurious bank notes⟩ ⟨soon had a ~ of invitations⟩ **6 :** FLOODLIGHT **syn** see FLOW

²flood \"\ *vb* -ED/-ING/-S *vt* **1 a :** to cover or overwhelm with a flood **:** INUNDATE, DELUGE ⟨the river ~*ed* the lowlands⟩ **b :** to cover or cause to be covered with water or other fluid ⟨in some places it is economical to irrigate by ~*ing* the fields at regular intervals⟩ ⟨~ the bearings with oil⟩ **2 :** to fill more or less completely with water or other fluid: **a :** to increase the elevation of the water in (a channel) esp. in splashing logs or in nullifying the effectiveness of a fall over a dam; *also* **:** SPLASH **b :** to supply to (the carburetor of an internal-combustion engine) an excess of fuel sufficient to raise the fuel level in the float chamber above the fuel nozzle **c :** to fill (as a compartment of a submarine) with water admitted from the sea **d :** to fill (an oil sand) with water to expel the oil **e :** to apply excessive ink to in printing ⟨the form was ~*ed* and the halftones are too heavy and dark⟩ **3 a :** to fill to full capacity or to excess ⟨shoppers ~*ed* the streets⟩ ⟨afferent impulses ~ the brain in certain hysteric states⟩ ⟨~*ing* the mails with circulars⟩ **b :** to distribute something in or provide with something in large quantities ⟨~*ing* the country with ads⟩ ⟨the room was ~*ed* with light⟩ ~ *vi* **1 a :** to pour or issue like a flood ⟨the milk ~*ed* over the table⟩ **:** OVERFLOW ⟨wine ~*ing* from the glass as her hand shook⟩ **b :** to become filled to excess with some fluid ⟨our cellar ~*s* after every heavy rain⟩ **c** *of a tide* **:** to run high ⟨could tell how the tide was ~*ing* —G.W.Brace⟩ **2 :** to have an excessive menstrual flow or a uterine hemorrhage after childbirth

flood·able \-dəbəl\ *adj* **:** capable of or subject to flooding

flood·age \-dij\ *n* -S **:** flooded state **:** INUNDATION

floodboard \ˈ=,=\ *n* **:** FLASHBOARD

flood bulb *n* **:** PHOTOFLOOD

floodcock \ˈ=,=\ *n* **:** a cock by which sea water can be admitted to flood part of a ship (as a powder magazine)

flood current *n* **:** a tidal current that moves toward a shore or up a tidal river

flood dam *also* **flooding dam** *n* **:** a dam to store floodwaters temporarily or to supply a surge of water (as for clearing a channel or splashing logs) — compare SPLASH DAM

flooded *adj* **:** covered or overfilled with water or other liquid ⟨~ fields⟩ ⟨a ~ carburetor⟩

flooded box *n* **:** an Australian tree (*Eucalyptus bicolor*) common on alluvial soils

flooded gum *n* **:** any one of several Australian gum trees (as *Eucalyptus tereticornis*, *E. grandis*, and *E. gunnii*) that grow on moist or alluvial soil

flood·er \-də(r)\ *n* -S **:** one that floods

flood fallowing *n* **:** a method of suppressing or eradicating soil-borne pathogens by flooding the land while it lies fallow

floodgate \ˈ=,=\ *n* [ME, fr. *flood* + *gate*] **1 a :** a gate for shutting out, admitting, or releasing a body of water **:** a sluice gate **:** SLUICE; *specif* **:** the lower gate of a lock **b :** something that acts to restrain an outburst ⟨tears do stop the ~*s* of her eyes —Shak.⟩ **2 :** the stream stopped or allowed to pass by a floodgate **:** FLOOD ⟨a whole ~ of facts —John Ward⟩

flood gull *n* **:** BLACK SKIMMER

flooding *n* -S [fr. gerund of ²*flood*] **1 :** a filling or becoming full with or as if with some fluid esp. to excess **2 :** something produced by flooding: as **a :** a concentration at the surface of a paint film of one of the ingredients of the pigment portion giving rise to a uniform change of color of the surface — compare FLOATING **b :** a coating (as of an adhesive) applied by flooding

flood insurance *n* **:** insurance against loss resulting from flood, tidal wave, and rising water

flood lamp *n* **:** FLOODLIGHT

floodland \ˈ=,=\ *n* **:** FLOODPLAIN 1

flood·less \ˈ=ləs\ *adj* **:** having no floods **:** devoid of floods ⟨a ~ year⟩ ⟨a ~ area⟩

¹floodlight \ˈ=,=\ *n* [¹*flood* + *light*] **1 :** artificial illumination in a broad beam; *also* **:** a source of such illumination **2** *also* **floodlight projector :** a lighting unit with a parabolic or other specially shaped reflector for projecting a beam of light for illumination (as of a show window, an athletic field, an airstrip)

²floodlight \"\ *vt* **:** to illuminate by means of one or more floodlights

floodlight 2

floodmark \ˈ=,=\ *n* [ME, fr. *flood* + *mark*] **:** the mark or line to which the tide or a flood rises **:** HIGH-WATER MARK

flood·om·e·ter \,flə'dämədə(r)\ *n* [¹*flood* + *-o-* + *-meter*] **:** an instrument for measuring the height of a flood

floodplain \ˈ=,=\ *n* **1 :** a flat or nearly flat surface that may be submerged by floodwaters **2 :** a plain built up or in the process of being built up by stream deposition

floods *pl of* FLOOD, *pres 3d sing of* FLOOD

flood stage *n* **:** the stage at which a stream will overflow its banks

flood tide *n* **1 a :** the rising tide — opposed to *ebb tide* **b :** a tide at its greatest height — compare SPRING TIDE **2 :** something felt to resemble a rising tide: as **a :** a moving mass of people ⟨a *flood tide* of laughing children burst from the school⟩ **b :** something overwhelming or overspreading ⟨the *flood tide* of recurrent barbarism⟩ **c :** a high point **:** PEAK, CLIMAX ⟨the army . . . which at its *flood tide* numbered 89 combat divisions —*Life*⟩ **d :** a great and usu. increasing quantity or number ⟨a *flood tide* of shoddy novels⟩ ⟨an effort to stem the *flood tide* of wheat that threatens to overrun the already jammed federal storehouses —*N.Y.Times*⟩

floodtime \ˈ=,=\ *n* **:** the season of floods

floodwall \ˈ=,=\ *n* **:** a wall (as a levee) built to prevent inundation by high water

floodwater \ˈ=,==\ *n* **:** the water of a flood

floodway \ˈ=,=\ *n* **:** an area or channel provided as an emergency course to divert floodwaters (as from more populous regions)

floodwood \ˈ=,=\ *n* **:** wood drifting on a stream or left stranded by a flood

floo·ey \ˈflüē, -üi\ *adv (or adj)* [origin unknown] **:** AWRY — usu. used in the phrase *go flooey* ⟨if I have to leave her it will all go ~ —Theodore Dreiser⟩ ⟨with my knees going ~ and an ache in my chest —Herbert Gold⟩ ⟨something went ~ with the time and all of a sudden it was a quarter of eight —Dorothy Baker⟩

¹floor \ˈflō(ə)r, -ō(ə)r,-ōə,-ȯ(ə)\ *n* -S *often attrib* [ME *flor*, fr. OE *flōr*; akin to OHG *fluor* cultivated field, meadow, ON *flōrr* floor of a cow stall, OIr *lār* floor, L *planus* level, flat, Gk *planan* to cause to wander, *planasthai* to wander, OSlav *polje* field; basic meaning: broad and flat] **1 :** the bottom or lower part of any room **:** the part of a room upon which one stands **2 a :** the lower inside surface of any hollow structure ⟨the ~ of a cave⟩ ⟨the ~ of the pelvis⟩ **b :** a lower ground surface (as the bottom of the sea or the invert of the chamber of a canal lock) ⟨the ~ of the valley⟩ **3 :** the structure of supporting beams, girders, and covering that divides a building horizontally; *broadly* **:** a story of a building **4 :** the surface or the platform of a structure on which to walk, work, or travel ⟨the ~ of a bridge⟩ ⟨the ~ of a prize ring⟩ **5 a :** the main level space in a room distinguished from a platform or gallery: as (1) **:** the part of a securities or commodity exchange on which trading takes place ⟨~ traders⟩ (2) **:** the part of a legislative chamber or meeting room occupied by the members (3) **:** an inside area (as in a restaurant or nightclub) used and usu. specially dressed and prepared for dancing — called also *dance floor* (4) **:** an area often specially prepared or marked on which an indoor sports event takes place ⟨the coach sent a substitute onto the ~⟩ **b :** the occupants of a floor ⟨the whole third ~ is furious over the situation⟩: as (1) **:** the members of an assembly **:** AUDIENCE ⟨the chairman appealed to the ~⟩ ⟨questions from the ~⟩ (2) **:** the dancers participating in a square dance **c :** the attention of an audience; *broadly* **:** the right esp. of a member to address an assembly **6 a :** the athwartship vertical plate connecting the frame and reverse frame of a steel ship — see SHIP illustration **b :** an athwartship member in a wood ship attached to a wood frame **7 :** the rock underlying an unconsolidated or stratified deposit **:** BASEMENT COMPLEX **8 a :** a nearly horizontal flat surface (as the top of a hard bed or stratum) that is utilized in mining operations **b :** the bottom of any nearly horizontal mine working (as a drift, level, flat stope, or slope); *sometimes* **:** a rock stratum **c :** one of the horizontal divisions of a stope that esp. in square-set stoping are generally spaced at regular intervals between levels **9 :** the layer of organic matter covering the soil of a forest **:** DUFF **10** *in malting* **:** a batch of grain spread out for germination **11 :** a lower limit or base: as **a :** one imposed by an authoritative ruling below which a given quantity or rate is not to be allowed to fall ⟨the right of the government to establish ~*s*⟩ ⟨a ~ under prices or wages⟩ **b :** a bottom level determined by economic factors ⟨increases in wages or freight rates raise the cost ~⟩

²floor \"\ *vt* -ED/-ING/-S [ME *floren*, fr. *flor*, n.] **1 a :** to cover with a floor **:** furnish with flooring ⟨will ~ the camp next weekend⟩ **b :** to form the floor of ⟨soft herbage ~*ed* the valley⟩ **2 :** to strike down or lay level with the floor **:** knock down; *broadly* **:** SILENCE, DEFEAT ⟨his answer ~*ed* me completely⟩ **3 :** to put, send, force, or display on or toward the floor ⟨the coach ~*ed* a whole new team⟩ ⟨he ~*ed* the accelerator and the car surged ahead⟩

³floor \ˈflü(ə)r\ *Scot var of* FLOWER

⁴floor \"\ *Scot var of* FLOUR

floor·age \ˈflōrij, -lȯr-\ *n* -S **:** floor space (as of a building) ⟨total ~ 21,000 square feet⟩

floor arch *n* **1 :** an arch having a flat extrados **:** a flat or segmental arch between floor beams **2 :** a flat concrete slab between beams

¹floorboard \ˈ=,=\ *n* [¹*floor* + *board*] **1** *also* **floorboarding** \ˈ=,==\ **:** board used for or suitable for floors **:** FLOORING ⟨seasoned oak ~⟩ **2 :** a board in a floor ⟨squeaky ~*s*⟩; *often* **:** one that can be removed to give access to something beneath it (as in a boat) ⟨raise the ~ to reach the battery⟩

²floorboard \"\ *vt, slang* **:** to press (the accelerator of a car) to the floor ~ *vi, slang* **:** to drive a car at full or excessive speed

floor box *n* **:** an electrical outlet set flush with a floor

floor boy *n* **:** a boy employed in a business concern to do errands and miscellaneous jobs

floor broker *n* **:** a broker who trades on the floor of an exchange for the account and risk of others — compare FLOOR TRADER

floor chisel *n* **1 :** a caulking iron for decks and floors **2 :** a chisel with a broad edge and long shank used for ripping out floorboards — see CHISEL illustration

floor clamp *or* **floor cramp** *or* **floor dog** *n* **:** a tool used to tighten seams of floorboards before nailing them in position

floorcloth \ˈ=,=\ *n* **:** cloth covering for a floor: **a** *obs* **:** a rug or carpet **b :** heavy cloth (as canvas) usu. oiled, painted with designs, and varnished that was formerly used for a floor covering — compare LINOLEUM **c :** canvas flooring (as for a tent or a theatrical stage)

floor·er \ˈflōrə(r), -lȯrə-\ *n* -S **:** one that floors: as **a :** a workman who lays floors **b :** something that discomfits or confuses one

floor furnace *n* **:** a small pipeless furnace located close below the floor and used esp. in houses having no basement

floor girl *n* **:** a girl or woman esp. in the needle trades to run errands and do odd jobs about a shop

floor hanger *n* **:** a stirrup iron to support a floor joist

floorhead \ˈ=,=\ *n* **:** an upper extremity of the floor timbers of a wooden ship

floor hinge *n* **:** a usu. double-acting hinge placed between the bottom of a door and the floor

floor·ing \ˈflōriŋ, -lȯr-, -rēŋ\ *n* -S [fr. ¹*floor* + *-ing*] **1 :** PLATFORM, FLOOR, PAVEMENT **2 :** material (as tongue-and-groove lumber) for floors ⟨the disadvantages of softwood ~*s*⟩

flooring saw *n* **:** a handsaw that has teeth on both edges, comes to a point, is used to cut out sections (as from a floor), and cuts its own entrance into the material

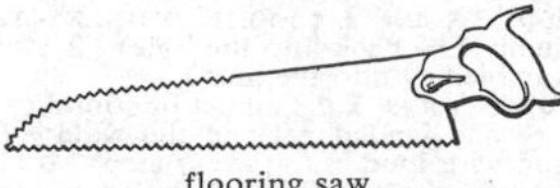

flooring saw

floor key *n* **:** a key that operates only a portion of the locks (as on one floor of a hotel) in a master-keyed system

floor knob *n* **:** a usu. rubber-ringed knob attached to a floor to prevent a door from striking the wall

floorlady \ˈ=,==\ *n* **:** FORELADY

floor lamp *n* **:** a tall usu. portable shaded lamp that stands on the floor

floor leader *n* **:** a member of a legislative body chosen by caucus of his party to have charge of its organization on the floor (as by making formal motions, opening debate, allotting time to other members of his party, and generally directing its strategy) — compare WHIP

floor–length \ˈ=,=\ *adj* **:** reaching to the floor ⟨*floor-length* draperies⟩

floor·less \-ləs\ *adj* **:** having no floor

floor light *n* **:** a window in the floor that is suitable for walking on and that admits light to space below

floor load *n* **:** the load that a floor (as of a building) may be expected to carry safely if uniformly distributed usu. calculated in pounds per square foot of area **:** the live load of a floor

floor machine *n* **:** a portable machine that removes the surface layer from rough or soiled wooden floors

floor·man \ˈ=mən\ *n, pl* **floormen 1 :** any of various laborers: as **a :** a horseshoer's helper who removes old shoes, trims hoofs, and makes himself useful about the shop **b :** a worker who stacks green bricks, tile, or ceramic pipe in a drying room — called also *set-off man* **c :** a worker performing labor (as hoisting, cleaning, polishing) concerned with the maintenance of a particular floor (as of an office building) **d :** one of a crew of men who assist in the drilling of oil wells (as in running drill pipe and casing in and out of wells) — called also *roustabout* **2 :** an employee who is to some degree a representative of his employer before the public: as **a :** FLOORWALKER **b :** an employee of a bowling establishment who assigns alleys, collects fees, and supervises pinsetters **c :** a supervisor who assigns taxicabs to drivers and approves reports of meter readings **d :** a supervisory employee in a gambling house not assigned to any one table and usu. superior to the head dealers of two or more tables **e :** CALLER d

floor lamp

floor manager *n* **1 :** FLOORWALKER **2 :** a person who directs something (as the maneuverings in favor of a candidate at a convention, the progress of a bill in a legislative assembly, or the handling of material in a warehouse) from the floor **3 :** the stage manager of a television show

floor panel *n* **:** a preassembled unit of floor joists, subflooring, finished flooring, and sometimes ceiling below supported by walls, columns, or beams

floor pattern *n* **:** the design described on the floor by the steps of a dancer

floor pit *n* **:** a pit or recess below a floor line provided to facilitate the reaching of parts beneath a machine

floor plan *n* **:** a diagrammatic representation of a floor and usu. its relation to other features (as openings in adjoining walls): as **a :** a scale diagram of a room or suite of rooms viewed from above and used esp. for planning effective use and arrangement of furnishings **b :** a similar diagram of a theatrical stage **:** a staging plan **c :** a diagram of positions to be taken or of patterns to be made by ballet dancers on a floor or stage

floor planning *n* **:** a system of financed wholesale purchasing of expensive items (as automobiles or major electrical appliances) whereby a retailer stocks his sales floor with a minimal outlay of cash

floor plate *n* **1 :** a plate (as of steel or iron) set in or forming part of a floor and sometimes provided with T slots to which heavy work and portable machine tools can be bolted to facilitate machining and erection **2 :** a wooden board lying flat on the floor and supporting the studs of a wall **3 :** a plate closing the bottom of the magazine recess in a bolt-action rifle having a clip-loaded magazine

floor plug *n* **:** an electrical receptacle with its face flush with or recessed in a floor

floor pocket *n* **:** a metal box containing one or more electrical outlets set into the floor of a theatrical stage

floors *pl of* FLOOR, *pres 3d sing of* FLOOR

floor sample *n* **:** an article (as a radio or kitchen cabinet) offered for sale at a reduced price because it has been used for display or demonstration

floor show *n* **:** an entertainment (as in a nightclub or cabaret) presented from the floor rather than an elevated stage and usu. consisting of singing and dancing and sometimes of comedy and burlesque without continuity

floor slab *n* **1 :** a paving slab **2 :** the slab forming the floor of a usu. reinforced-concrete structure

floor switch *n* **:** a switch in the shaft of an electric elevator at a height corresponding to a floor level and operated by a projection on the car

floor trader *n* **:** a trader who buys and sells on the floor of an exchange for his own account and risk — compare FLOOR BROKER

floor truck *n* **:** a hand-operated conveyance typically in the form of a box or basket on wheels or casters for indoor use (as in a factory or store)

floorwalker \ˈ=,==\ *n* **1 :** a retail-store employee who supervises the salespeople of a particular section of the store and is at hand to help with customers' problems and to handle returned goods — called also *floor manager, section manager* **2 :** FLOORMAN 2d

floor·ward \'ˌ=ˌwə(r)d\ *or* **floor·wards** \-dz\ *adv* **:** toward the floor ⟨pointing the stick ~⟩
floor wax *n* **:** a preparation made typically of a mixture of beeswax and vegetable waxes in a suitable vehicle and used for polishing and preserving the finish of floors
floorway \'=ˌ=\ *n* **:** the floor system of a bridge including the floor and supporting members
floorwoman \'=ˌ==\ *n, pl* **floorwomen :** FORELADY
floor work *n* **:** ritual circumambulation
floo·zy *or* **floo·zie** *or* **floo·sie** *also* **floo·sy** \'flüzē, -zi\ *n, pl* **floozies** *or* **floosies** [origin unknown] **1 :** an attractive young woman of loose morals ⟨fool enough to become entangled with a ~ —Richard Church⟩ ⟨frontier *floozies* —Lisle Bell⟩ ⟨a tight-gowned ~ smirking at a saloon bar —Walter Goodman⟩ **2** *slang* **:** a dissolute and sometimes slovenly woman
[1]**flop** \'fläp\ *vb* **flopped; flopped; flopping; flops** [alter. of [2]*flap*] *vi* **1 a :** to move irregularly to and fro or up and down **:** FLAP ⟨scarf *flopping* about her ears⟩ ⟨the fledgling's wings *flopped* again and again but it could not get off the ground⟩ **b :** to move or drop with heavy clumsiness as if inert ⟨*flopped* over on his other side for a last nap⟩ **c :** to strike about with something broad and flat ⟨the fish *flopped* helplessly on the bank⟩ **d :** to progress by flopping ⟨pelicans *flopping* across the sky⟩ **2 a :** to throw oneself down heavily, clumsily, or in a completely relaxed manner ⟨so tired that I *flopped* into the hammock without another word⟩ **b** *slang* **:** to dispose oneself for rest or sleep; *specif* **:** to go to bed ⟨it's time to ~⟩ **3 :** to change or turn suddenly (as from one course to another) **4 :** to fail abysmally ⟨anyone may ~ once without disgrace⟩ ⟨in spite of good reviews the show *flopped*⟩ ~ *vt* **1** *slang Brit* **:** to strike esp. heavily ⟨*flopped* his rival on the head⟩ **2 a :** to turn or drop suddenly and usu. heavily or noisily ⟨sat *flopping* the pages of the book⟩ ⟨*flopped* her bundles on the table⟩ **b :** to settle (oneself) with a heavy clumsy movement **:** PLUMP ⟨*flopped* himself into a chair⟩ ⟨*flopped* himself over without awaking⟩ **3 a :** to make (as a photoengraving) or print (as a picture) so that an image appears with right and left sides transposed **b :** to reverse (as a two-color form) so that the colors are transposed
[2]**flop** \"\ *adv* **1 :** RIGHT, JUST, EXACTLY ⟨fell ~ on his face⟩ ⟨jumped ~ back into the hole⟩ **2 :** with a sound of flopping ⟨tumbled ~ into the mud⟩
[3]**flop** \"\ *n* -s **1 a :** an act or sound of flopping ⟨the fish gave a ~ and landed back in the water⟩ ⟨squelched through the mud with loud ~*s* at every step⟩ **b :** ABOUT-FACE **:** a sudden change (as of policy) **2 a :** a sudden decline ⟨stocks took a ~ yesterday⟩ **:** FALL, COLLAPSE **b :** something that falls flat **:** FIZZLE, DUD ⟨everyone expected his new play to be a ~⟩ **c :** something or someone lacking success, effectiveness, or adequacy **:** FAILURE ⟨was a ~ as a reporter⟩ ⟨the new economic plan was a ~ from the very beginning⟩ **3** *slang* **:** a place to sleep; *usu* **:** a cheap rooming house or hotel catering to impoverished men or a bed in such a place — compare FLOPHOUSE
flop–eared \'=ˌ=\ *adj* **:** having long pendulous ears ⟨a *flop=eared* puppy⟩
flop·er·oo *also* **flop·per·oo** \ˌfläpə'rü\ *n* -s *slang* **:** a notable flop **:** complete failure
flophouse \'=ˌ=\ *n* **:** a cheap low-grade rooming house or hotel usu. catering chiefly to indigent men
flopover \'=ˌ==\ *n* -s [fr. *flop over*, v.] **:** a defect in television reception in which a succession of frames appear to traverse the screen vertically due to a temporary maladjustment of the relative horizontal and vertical sweep frequencies
flop·per \-pə(r)\ *n* -s **:** one that flops: as **a :** FLAPPER 1e **b** *slang* **:** a person who fakes an accident in order to collect money (as from insurance)
flop·pers \-(r)z\ *n pl but sing or pl in constr* **:** AIR PLANT 2
flop·pe·ty \'fläpəd·ē\ *adj* **:** tending to flop **:** FLOPPY ⟨a soft ~ straw hat⟩
flop·pi·ly \'fläpəlē, -əli\ *adv* **:** in a floppy manner
flop·pi·ness \-pēnəs, -pin-\ *n* -ES **:** the quality or state of being floppy
flop·py \-pē,-pi\ *adj* -ER/-EST **:** soft and flexible **:** tending to flop
flor \'flō(ə)r\ *n* -s [Sp, mold, flower, fr. L *flor-, flos* flower — more at BLOW] **:** a coating of microorganisms (as yeasts) including both yeasts and bacteria that is allowed to form on the surface of some sherry wines to which products of its fermentative activity impart a characteristic nutty flavor — called also *film yeast;* see MYCODERMA
flor *abbr* [L *floruit*] he flourished
flo·ra \'flōrə\ *n, pl* **floras** \-rəz\ *also* **flo·rae** \-r,ē\ [NL, after *Flora*, Roman goddess of flowers, fr. L, fr. *flor-, flos*] **1 :** a systematic treatise on or a list of the plants of an area, habitat, or period ⟨a ~ of No. America⟩ ⟨prepared a new ~ of the western mountains⟩ — compare FAUNA 3 **2 a :** plant life **:** PLANTS ⟨recent ~ exhibits many adaptations to habitat⟩ — often contrasted with *fauna* **b :** the plants or plant life characteristic of, peculiar to, or adapted for living in a particular situation (as a geological stratum, period, habitat, or region) ⟨the Devonian fossil ~⟩ ⟨postglacial ~*s*⟩ ⟨a lacustrine ~⟩ ⟨the intestinal ~⟩ **c :** plants or plant life of a particular kind or having some common characteristic ⟨the gram-negative ~ of the soil⟩ ⟨a large parasitic ~⟩ ⟨interesting moss ~*s*⟩ — see VEGETATION 3
flo·ra del·le al·pi \ˌflōrəˌdelə'al(ˌ)pē\ *n* [by alter.] **:** FIOR DELL'ALPI
flo·rai·son \flȯrāzōⁿ\ *n* -s [F, fr. *fleur* flower, fr. L *flor-, flos*] **:** FLOWERING, BLOSSOMING ⟨the ~ of the folk dance in the mid thirties⟩
[1]**flo·ral** \'flōrəl, -lȯr-\ *adj* [L *Floralis* of Flora, fr. *Flora* + L *-alis* -al] **1 a :** of, relating to, or associated with a flower ⟨~ organs⟩ **b :** resembling, made of, or based on flowers ⟨~ decorations⟩ ⟨an unusual ~ design⟩ **2 :** of, relating to, or concerned with a flora or floras ⟨characteristic alpine ~ elements⟩ ⟨isolated ~ relicts⟩ — **flo·ral·ly** \-rəlē, -li\ *adv*
[2]**floral** \"\ *n* -s **1 :** a design or pattern in which flowers predominate **2 :** something (as a fabric) with a floral design
floral element *n* **:** a group of plants forming one of the constituents of a flora and composed of plants geographically or habitally related
floral emblem *n* **:** a plant or flower recognized as symbolic of a group, organization, or sovereignty (as a club, school, or state) — see STATE FLOWER
floral envelope *n* **:** PERIANTH 1
flo·ra·lia \flō'rālēə\ *n pl, cap* [L, fr. neut. pl. of *Floralis*] **:** an ancient Roman festival celebrated on April 28 in honor of the goddess Flora and marked esp. by nude dancing of courtesans
floral leaf *n* **1 :** any of the modified leaves (as a sepal or petal) forming the perianth of a flower **2 :** BRACT
floral organ *n* **:** any of the modified leaves comprising the calyx, corolla, androecium, and gynoecium of a flower **:** FLORAL LEAF 1
floral water *n* **:** distilled water obtained by the steam distillation of flowers (as orange flowers, roses) and used as a perfume for lotions
flo·ra's–paintbrush \ˌflōrəz'=ˌ=, -ȯr-\ *n, pl* **flora's–paintbrushes** *usu cap F* [prob. after the goddess *Flora*] **1 :** ORANGE HAWKWEED **2 :** TASSEL FLOWER 1
-flo·rate \ˌflōr,āt, -ȯ,rāt, -rət, *usu* |d·+V\ *adj comb form* [L *flor-, flos* + E *-ate*] **:** flowered ⟨bi*florate*⟩
flo·re·at·ed *adj* [by alter.] **:** FLORIATED
floren *obs var of* FLORIN
[1]**florence** *n* -s *sometimes cap* [ME, fr. MF, fr. *Florence*, Italy] **1** *obs* **:** a gold florin **2** *obs* **:** CHIANTI
[2]**flor·ence** \'flȯrən(t)s, -lär-\ *adj, usu cap* [fr. *Florence*, Italy] **:** of or from the city of Florence, Italy **:** of the kind or style prevalent in Florence **:** FLORENTINE
florence brown *n, often cap F* **:** VANDYKE RED 1
flo·ren·cée \ˌflȯrən'sā, flə'ren(t)sē\ *adj* [F, fem. of *florencé*, fr. *Florence*, Italy + *-é* (fr. L *-atus* -ate); fr. the form of the lily in the arms of the city of Florence] *of a fleur-de-lis in art or heraldry* **:** having a figure in the form of a stem often seeded or flowered at the tip or leaflike or petallike in form arising between each C-scroll and the central lyrate figure ⟨the familiar fleur-de-lis ~ of the city of Florence⟩ — see FLORENTINE LILY
florence fennel *n, usu cap 1st F* **:** a fennel (*Foeniculum dulce*) with enlarged leaf bases used as a potherb and in salads — called also *finocchio*
florence flask *n, usu cap 1st F* **1 :** a round or pear-shaped glass flask with a long neck and often a covering of plaited raffia or straw in which olive oil or wine is shipped **2 :** a round usu. flat-bottomed glass laboratory vessel shaped like a Florence flask and usu. heat-resistant — called also *boiling flask*

Florence flask 2

florence leaf *n, usu cap F* **:** a yellow alloy or metal leaf or foil used for decorating
flor·enc·ite \-n,sīt\ *n* -s [Dr. W. *Florence*, 20th cent. scientist + E *-ite*] **:** a mineral $CeAl_3(PO_4)_2(OH)_6$ composed of basic phosphate of cerium and aluminum found in placer sands in Brazil
[1]**flor·en·tine** \'flȯrən,tēn, -lär- *sometimes* -tīn\ *n* -s [L *Florentinus*, of Florentia (Florence), fr. *Florentia* + *-inus* -ine] **1** *cap* **:** a native or resident of Florence **2** *often cap* **:** FLAME SCARLET
[2]**florentine** \"\ *adj, usu cap* [L *Florentinus*] **:** FLORENCE: as **a :** in or following a style of art originated in Florence during the Renaissance and noted for fine drawing, idealized portrayal, and humanist content — compare SIENESE **b :** served or dressed with spinach — usu. used postpositively ⟨eggs *Florentine*⟩
florentine flask *or* **florentine receiver** *n, usu cap 1st F* **:** a receiver of glass or metal having an outlet near the top and one near the bottom for separating the layers of two immiscible distillates (as oil and water in the steam distillation of essential oils)
florentine glass *n, usu cap F* **:** glass that is ornamented with embossed figures impressed (as by a roll) while the glass is still plastic
florentine iris *n, usu cap F* **:** a European iris (*Iris florentina*) having large white flowers with lavender-tinged falls and a rhizome that yields orris
florentine lake *n, usu cap F* **:** CRIMSON LAKE 1a
florentine lily *n, usu cap F* **:** a fleur-de-lis florencée
florentine marble *n, usu cap F* **:** a vase, statuette, or other ornament cut from a nearly white Italian alabaster
florentine mosaic *n, usu cap F* **:** a mosaic of hard or semiprecious stones chosen and arranged so that their natural colors represent figures (as of leaves or flowers) and inlaid in a background usu. of black or white marble
florentine orris *n, usu cap F* **:** [1]ORRIS
flo·res \'flōr(ˌ)ēz\ *n pl* [NL, fr. L, pl. of *flor-, flos* flower — more at BLOW (to bloom)] **:** a flaky or pulverulent form of an element or chemical compound obtained by sublimation
flo·res·cence \flō'resᵊn(t)s, flō'-,flə'-\ *n* -s [NL *florescentia*, fr. L *florescent-, florescens* (pres. part. of *florescere* to begin to bloom, incho. of *florēre* to bloom) + *-ia* -y — more at FLOURISH] **:** a state or period of being in bloom or of flourishing ⟨the highest ~ of a civilization⟩ **2 :** an act of unfolding into or as if into the open flower **:** ANTHESIS, BLOSSOMING
flo·res·cent \-nt\ *adj* [L *florescent-, florescens*, pres. part.] **1 :** being in the stage or at the point of florescence **2** *of a cultural level or period* **:** representing the attainment of the highest development of a particular society — used esp. of prehistoric Amerind groups
flo·ret \'flōrət, -lȯr-\ *n* -s [alter. (influenced by L *flor-, flos* flower) of ME *flourette* — more at FLOWERET, BLOW (to bloom)] **1 a :** a small flower ⟨dainty ~*s* of the bluet⟩ **b :** a single flower of a multiple-flowered inflorescence; *esp* **:** one of the small individual flowers that make up the head of a composite plant — compare DISK FLOWER, RAY FLOWER **2 :** FLEURON **3 :** yarn spun from floss silk
flo·ret·ed \-rəd·əd\ *adj* **:** decorated with small flowers
florettée *or* **floretty** *var of* FLEURETTÉE
flori- *comb form* [L, fr. *flor-, flos* — more at BLOW (to bloom)] **:** flower or flowers ⟨*flori*culture⟩ **:** something resembling a flower or flowers ⟨*flori*ated⟩
flo·ri·at·ed \'flōrē,ād·əd\ *also* **flo·ri·ate** \-rēət, -rē,āt\ *adj* [*flori-* + *-ated* (fr. *-ate* + *-ed*) or *-ate*] **:** having floral ornaments or a floral form ⟨~ lace⟩ ⟨a ~ pattern⟩
flo·ri·a·tion \ˌflōrē'āshən\ *n* -s [*flori-* + *-ation*] **:** floral ornamentation or a floral ornament
flo·ri·bun·da \ˌflōrə'bəndə\ *or* **floribunda rose** \ˌ==ˌ==-\ *n* -s [NL *floribunda*, fem. of *floribundus* flowering freely, fr. L *flori-* + *-bundus*, adj. suffix (as in *moribundus* moribund, but influenced in meaning by L *abundare* to abound)] **:** any of various bush roses derived from crosses of polyantha and tea roses and characterized by large seldom fragrant flowers in open clusters — called also *hybrid polyantha*
flo·ri·can \'flōrəkən\ *n* -s [origin unknown] **:** either of two bustards of India (*Houbaropsis bengalensis* and *Sypheotides indica*)
flo·ri·cul·tur·al \ˌflōrə'kəlch(ə)rəl\ *adj* **:** of, relating to, or concerned with floriculture — **flo·ri·cul·tur·al·ly** \-rəlē\ *adv*
flo·ri·cul·ture \'flōrə,kəlchə(r) *also* ˌ=='==\ *n* [*flori-* + *culture*] **:** the cultivation and management usu. on a commercial scale of ornamental and flowering plants — compare HORTICULTURE
flo·ri·cul·tur·ist \ˌflōrə'kəlch(ə)rəst\ *n* **:** a specialist in floriculture
flor·id \'flȯrəd, -lär-\ *adj* [L *floridus*, fr. *flor-, flos* flower — more at BLOW (to bloom)] **1 a** *obs* **:** covered with or abounding in flowers **:** FLOWERY **b :** embellished with flowers of rhetoric **:** excessively ornate **:** enriched to excess with or as if with figures ⟨a ~ literary style⟩ ⟨~ baroque architecture⟩ **c** *of music or counterpoint* **:** ornate and embellished **:** full of elaboration **:** FIGURATE **d :** showy and gaudy and usu. without solid worth or justification **2 :** flushed or tinged with red **:** RUDDY **:** of a lively reddish color ⟨a ~ complexion⟩ **3 :** marked by health and vigor ⟨a ~ old age⟩ **:** vigorous and flourishing ⟨she was a picture of ~ health⟩ **4** *of a disease* **:** fully developed **:** manifesting a complete and typical clinical syndrome ⟨~ rickets⟩ **syn** see ORNATE
[1]**flor·i·da** \'flȯrədə, -lär-\ *adj, usu cap* [*Florida*, state in the southeastern U. S., Sp, fr. (*Pascua*) *florida* Easter, fr. *Pascua* Easter, Pentecost, Twelfth Night, Christmas + *florida*, fem. of *florido* flowery, florid, fr. L *floridus*; fr. its having been discovered (on April 2, 1513) during the Easter season and fr. the blooming appearance of the land] **:** of or from the state of Florida ⟨*Florida* potatoes⟩ **:** of the kind or style prevalent in Florida **:** FLORIDIAN
[2]**florida** \"\ *n* -s *usu cap* **:** FLORIDA ORANGE
florida allspice *n, usu cap F* **:** a Carolina allspice (esp. *Calycanthus floridus*)
florida arrowroot *n, usu cap F* **1 :** an arrowroot obtained in Florida from the coontie **2 :** COONTIE
florida bayberry *n, usu cap F* **:** a white-barked evergreen shrub or small tree (*Myrica inodora*) of the Florida coast
florida bean *n, usu cap F* **:** the large seed of any of several West Indian leguminous plants (as that of cowage or the snuffbox bean) often polished and made into ornaments
florida beggarweed *n, usu cap F* **:** an annual upright tick trefoil (*Desmodium tortuosum*) of the southern U.S. and tropical America used for green manure
florida boxwood *or* **florida box** *n, usu cap F* **:** a small tree or shrub (*Schaefferia frutescens*) of southern Florida having very hard wood
florida caper *n, usu cap F* **:** a shrub or small tree (*Capparis cynophallophora*) of tropical America and Florida
florida cat's–claw *n, usu cap F* **:** CAT'S-CLAW 1b
florida cherry *n, usu cap F* **:** SURINAM CHERRY 2
florida clover *n, usu cap F* **:** MEXICAN CLOVER
florida cranberry *n, usu cap F* **:** ROSELLE
florida dogwood *or* **florida cornel** *n, usu cap F* **:** FLOWERING DOGWOOD
florida duck *n, usu cap F* **:** a duck (*Anas fulvigula fulvigula*) of Florida resembling the black duck
florida earth *n, usu cap F* **:** fuller's earth from or like that from Florida
florida gallinule *n, usu cap F* **:** a nearly cosmopolitan gallinule (*Gallinula chloropus*); *esp* **:** a dark bluish gray bird of the No. American subspecies (*G. c. cachinnans*) with white on the sides and beneath the tail, a whitish abdomen, and bright red on the bare forehead, bill, and tibias
florida gold *n, often cap F* **:** DUTCH ORANGE
florida grackle *n, usu cap F* **:** a small purple grackle (*Quiscalus quiscula quiscula*) of the southeastern U.S.
florida jay *n, usu cap F* **:** a gregarious crestless jay (*Aphelocoma coerulescens coerulescens*) of the Florida peninsula largely bluish gray in color
florida laurel *n, usu cap F* **:** SWEETLEAF
florida mahogany *n, usu cap F* **:** RED BAY
florida moss *n, usu cap F* **:** SPANISH MOSS 1
floridan *usu cap, var of* FLORIDIAN
florida orange *n, usu cap F* **:** an orange grown in Florida; *sometimes* **:** any orange other than a navel orange
florida pine *or* **florida yellow pine** *n, usu cap F* **:** LONGLEAF PINE
florida plum *n, usu cap F* **:** GUIANA PLUM
florida quinine *n, usu cap F* **:** GEORGIA BARK
florida red scale *n, usu cap F* **:** a rounded reddish armored scale (*Chrysomphalus aonidum*) that is a major pest of citrus in Florida and sometimes troublesome in greenhouses elsewhere
florida spruce pine *n, usu cap F* **:** SAND PINE 1
florida velvet bean *n, usu cap F* **:** VELVET BEAN
florida water *n, usu cap F* [fr. *Florida Water*, a trademark] **:** a light aromatic toilet water or perfume often containing orange-flower water and cinnamaldehyde or bergamot oil usu. in an alcoholic base
florida wax scale *n, usu cap F* **:** a wax scale (*Ceroplastes floridensis*) having a red body and a white waxy covering and sometimes becoming a destructive pest on cultivated plants in the southeastern U.S
florida yew *n, usu cap F* **1 :** STINKING CEDAR 1 **2 :** a rather rare bushy upright yew (*Taxus floridana*) of Florida with spreading branches and very narrow leaves
flo·rid·e·ae \flə'ridē,ē\ *n pl, cap* [NL, fr. L *floridus* flowery + NL *-eae* — more at FLORID] **1 :** a subclass of Rhodophyceae comprising red algae that have the cells connected by evident cytoplasmic strands, growth restricted to apical cells, and the carpogonium borne terminally on a special branch — compare BANGIOIDEAE **2** *in some classifications* **:** a group coextensive with Rhodophyceae — **flo·rid·e·an** \-dēən\ *adj*
[1]**flo·rid·i·an** \flə'ridēən, -lō'-,-lä'-,-lȯ'-\ *or* **flor·i·dan** \'flȯrədᵊn, -lär-, -dən\ *adj, usu cap* [*Florida* + E *-ian* or *-an*] **1 :** of, relating to, or characteristic of the state of Florida **2 :** of, relating to, or characteristic of the people of Florida
[2]**floridian** \"\ *or* **floridan** \"\ *n* -s *cap* **:** a native or resident of Florida
flo·ri·di·ana \flə,ridē'anə, -lō,-, -lä,-, -lȯ,-, -'ä-, -'ā- *also* -'ā-\ *n pl, usu cap* [*Florida* + E *-i-* + *-ana*] **:** material (as documents, anecdotes, or artifacts) distinctively bearing on or characteristic of Florida or its people or culture
floridian starch *n, often cap F* [NL *Florideae* + E *-an*] **:** a granular carbohydrate reserve in red algae that is not formed in plastids and that in several respects resembles glycogen rather than starch
flo·rid·i·ty \-'ridəd·ē\ *n* -ES **:** the quality or state of being florid ⟨the ~ of his prose⟩ ⟨a marked ~ of face⟩
flor·id·ly *adv* **:** in a florid manner **:** with floridity ⟨~ figurative prose —E.R.Bentley⟩
flor·id·ness *n* -ES **:** FLORIDITY
flo·rif·er·ous \flō'rif(ə)rəs\ *adj* [L *florifer* (fr. *flori-* + *-fer* -ferous) + E *-ous*] **1 :** bearing flowers; *esp* **:** blooming freely — used chiefly of ornamental plants **2 :** FLOWERY ⟨~ language⟩ — **flo·rif·er·ous·ly** *adv*
flo·rif·er·ous·ness *n* -ES **:** the quality or state of being floriferous; *esp* **:** a tendency or capacity to bear unusual quantities of flowers ⟨a new rose of outstanding ~⟩
flo·ri·form \'flōrə,fȯrm\ *adj* [*flori-* + *-form*] **:** having the form of a flower
flo·ri·gen \'flōrəjən, -,jen\ *n* -s [ISV *flori-* + *-gen*] **:** a hormone or hormonal agent that induces or promotes flowering — **flo·ri·gen·ic** \ˌflōrə'jenik\ *adj*
flo·ri·le·gi·um \ˌflōrə'lējēəm\ *n, pl* **florile·gia** \-jēə\ [NL, fr. L *florilegus* flower-culling (fr. *flori-* + *-legus*, fr. *legere* to gather) + *-ium* (as in *spicilegium* act of gleaning ears of grain) — more at LEGEND] **1** *archaic* **:** a usu. extravagantly illustrated book about flowers **2** [trans. of MGk *anthologia* — more at ANTHOLOGY] **:** a volume or collection of brief extracts or writings **:** ANTHOLOGY
flor·in \'flȯrən, -lär-,-lōr-\ *n* -s [ME, fr. MF, fr. OIt *fiorino*, fr. *fiore* flower (fr. L *flor-, flos*) + *-ino* -ine (fr. L *-inus*); fr. the Florentine lily on the reverse of the first florins — more at BLOW (to bloom)] **1 a :** an old gold coin first struck at Florence in 1252 weighing about 54 grains and noted for the purity of its gold **b :** any of certain gold coins of European countries patterned after the Florentine florin; *esp* **:** an English coin worth about 6 shillings issued by Edward III **2 :** a British silver coin worth two shillings first issued in 1849; *also* **:** any one of several similar coins issued in British Commonwealth countries (as Australia and the Union of So. Africa) **3 :** GULDEN **4 :** FORINT
flo·rip·a·rous \flō'ripərəs\ *adj* [LL *floriparus*, fr. L *flori-* + *-parus* -parous] *of a plant structure normally bearing fruits* **:** producing secondary or supplementary flowers rather than fruits
flor·i·pon·dio \ˌflȯrə'pändē,ō\ *n* -s [Sp, perh. modif. of NL *floribundus* flowering freely — more at FLORIBUNDA] **:** any of several tropical American shrubs or trees of the genus *Datura* (esp. *D. candida*) that have narcotic seeds from which an intoxicant is prepared and that are sometimes cultivated in warm regions esp. for their very large commonly white flowers
flo·ris·bad man \'flōrəs,bät-, -bad-\ *n, usu cap F* [fr. *Florisbad*, village near Bloemfontein, Union of So. Africa] **:** a primitive So. African man (*Homo helmei* or *Africanthropus helmei* syn. *Africanthropus florisbadensis*) that resembles Rhodesian man, is sometimes regarded as ancestral to certain living African races, and is based on a single skull of possibly mid-Pleistocene age, large and thick-boned, with prominent brow ridge, prognathous jaw, and flattened dorsal cranium which was found associated with artifacts suggesting those of the Eŭropean Acheulean
flo·rist \'flōrəst, -lȯr-,-lär-\ *n* -s [L *flor-, flos* flower + E *-ist* — more at BLOW (to bloom)] **:** one whose business is the raising of flowers and ornamental plants in a nursery or greenhouse or the selling of flowers and plants so raised
flo·ris·tic \flō'ristik\ *adj* **1 :** concerned with or relating to flowers, floral emblems, or a flora **2 :** of or relating to floristics — **flo·ris·ti·cal·ly** \-tək(ə)lē\ *adv*
flo·ris·tics \-ks\ *n pl but sing or pl in constr* **:** a branch of phytogeography that deals with plants and plant groups from the numerical standpoint
flo·rist·ry \'flōrəstrē, -lȯr-,-lär-, -tri\ *n* -ES **:** the florist's art or skill ⟨an expert at ~⟩ ⟨classes in ~⟩
florist's chrysanthemum *n* **:** any of certain large-flowered frost-susceptible chrysanthemums largely grown under glass for the cut-flower trade and derived chiefly by selection from and hybridizing of two perennial Chinese wild chrysanthemums (*Chrysanthemum morifolium* and *C. indicum*)
florists' flower *n* **:** a flower or plant commonly cultivated and sold by florists: **a** *Brit* **:** a cultigen grown primarily for its flowers **b :** a flower raised to be cut from the plant for sale (as the rose or carnation)
flo·ri·su·gent \ˌflōrə'süjənt\ *adj* [*flori-* + L *sugent-, sugens*, pres. part. of *sugere* to suck — more at SUCK] **:** sucking nectar from flowers — used of birds (as hummingbirds) that so feed
flo·riv·o·rous \flō'rivərəs\ *adj* [*flori-* + *-vorous*] **:** feeding on flowers **:** ANTHOPHAGOUS — used esp. of insects
-flo·rous \ˌflōrəs, -ȯr-\ *adj comb form* [LL *-florus*, fr. L *flor-, flos* flower — more at BLOW (to bloom)] **:** having or bearing (such or so many) flowers **:** -flowered **:** -ANTHOUS — in words whose first constituent ends in *i* ⟨nocti*florous*⟩ ⟨uni*florous*⟩
flo·ru·it \'flōr(y)əwət, -är-,-ōr-, *usu* -əd·+V\ *n* -s [L, (he) flourished, 3d sing. perf. indic. of *florēre* to flower, flourish — more at FLOURISH] **:** a period during which something (as a person, movement, or school) flourished most
flo·rule \'flōr,(y)ül, 'flȯr-\ *or* **florula** \-r(y)ələ\ *n, pl* **florules** \-r,(y)ülz\ *or* **floru·lae** \-r(y)ə,lē, -lī\ *also* **florulas** [NL *florula*, dim. of *flora*] **:** a small flora; *esp* **:** a fossil flora comparable to a faunule
flor·u·lent \'flȯr(y)ələnt, -rəl-\ *adj* [L *florulentus*, fr. *flor-, flos* flower] **:** FLOWERY, BLOSSOMING, FLORIATED
[1]**flo·ry** \'flōrē\ *adj* [ME *floury, flory* — more at FLEURY] **1 :** FLEURY **2 :** FLEURETTÉE 1
[2]**flory** \"\ *adj* [origin unknown] *Scot* **:** VAIN, CONCEITED
flory counterflory \'==ˌ==ˌ==\ *or* **flory and counterflory** *adj* [[1]*flory*] **:** COUNTERFLORY
flos·cu·lar \'fläskyələ(r)\ *adj* [L *flosculus* small flower (dim. of *flos* flower) + E *-ar* — more at BLOW (to bloom)] **:** FLOSCULOUS

flos·cu·lar·ia \ˌfläskyə'la(a)rēə\ *n, cap* [NL, fr. L *flosculus* + NL *-aria*] **:** the type genus of Flosculariidae comprising rotifers in which the female is attached and tubicolous with a lobed disk bearing long setae — **flos·cu·lar·i·an** \ˌ≈≈ˈ≈≈ən\ *adj or n*

flos·cu·la·ri·idae \ˌfläskyələ'rīəˌdē\ *n pl, cap* [NL, fr. *Floscularia*, type genus + *-idae*] **:** a family of rotifers (order Monogononta) with the male small in size and free-swimming and the adult female larger and tubicolous and usu. attached by a stalk derived from the modified foot

flos·cu·lous \'fläskyələs\ *also* **flos·cu·lose** \-ˌlōs\ *adj* [L *flosculus* + E *-ous* or *-ose*] **1 :** composed of florets **2** *of a floret* **:** tubular in form — used esp. of the disk flowers of a composite

flos fer·ri \flä'sfeˌrī\ *n* [NL, lit., flower of iron] **:** an aragonite that occurs in delicate white coralloid forms and is common in beds of iron ore

¹floss \'fläs, 'flȯs\ *n* -ES [fr. or akin to D *vlos;* akin to MLG *vlūs* fleece, flock of wool, MHG *vlus, vlius* fleece, Dan *flos* floss, Sw dial. *floss* long flock of wool — more at FLEECE] **1 :** waste or short silk fibers that cannot be reeled; *esp* **:** the short loose threads that form the outer part of the silkworm's cocoon **2 a :** soft loosely twisted thread of silk or mercerized cotton used chiefly for embroidery **b :** DENTAL FLOSS **c :** a lightweight loosely twisted wool knitting yarn **3 :** a fluffy fibrous mass of material ⟨~ candy⟩: as **a :** SILK COTTON; *esp* **:** KAPOK **b :** VEGETABLE SILK **c :** CORN SILK **d :** cotton staple **4 a :** something or someone showy or stylish **b :** people of fashion ⟨follow the ~ to the winter resorts⟩

²floss \"\ *n* -ES [G, lit., raft, fr. OHG *flōz* — more at FLOAT] **1 :** vitrified oxide or earth floating in a fluid state on the iron in the puddling furnace **2 :** FLOSS HOLE

³floss \"\ *n* -ES *Brit* **:** STREAM

flos·sa \'fläsə, 'flȯsə\ *n* -S *sometimes cap* [Sw, short for *flossamatta*, fr. Sw dial. *floss* long flock of wool + *matta* rug, carpet] **:** a Scandinavian handwoven carpet; *also* **:** the weave typical of such carpets

floss·er \-sə(r)\ *n* -S [¹*floss* + *-er*] **1 :** a worker who stitches boning into corsets and girdles **2 :** a machine for spraying out fertilizer, water, and grass seed in one operation used esp. for seeding roadsides

flossflower \'≈ˌ≈\ *n* **:** a plant or flower of the genus *Ageratum* **:** AGERATUM 2

flossflower blue *n* **:** a pale purple that is redder and paler than average lavender, redder and duller than mauvette or wistaria (sense 2a), and bluer and less strong than phlox pink — called also *ageratum blue*

floss hole *n* [²*floss*] **1 :** a hole at the back of a metallurgical furnace through which slag passes out **2 :** the taphole of a melting furnace

floss silk *n* **:** ¹FLOSS 1; *also* **:** floss (as for embroidery) of silk

floss–silk tree *n* **:** a thorny deciduous tree (*Chorisia speciosa*) of the family Bombacaceae that is native to Brazil and Argentina but often cultivated in warm regions for its large solitary pink flowers which appear while the tree is leafless and that is the chief source of vegetable silk — called also *samohu*

flossy \'fläsē, -lȯs-, -si\ *adj* -ER/-EST **1 :** relating to, made of, or resembling floss; *often* **:** light and soft **:** DOWNY ⟨~ baby hair⟩ **2 :** stylish or showy esp. in appearance **:** making a good superficial impression; *often* **:** ORNATE, FLASHY

flot \'flät\ *n* -S [by alter.] **:** FLAT 1c

flo·ta \'flōd·ə, -ō‚tä\ *n* -S [Sp — more at FLOTILLA] **:** FLEET; *esp* **:** a fleet of Spanish ships that formerly sailed every year from Cádiz to Vera Cruz in Mexico to obtain and transport to Spain the products of the Spanish colonies

flo·tage *also* **float·age** \'flōd·ij, -ōt|, |ēj\ *n* -S [*flotage* alter. of *floatage; floatage* fr. ²*float* + *-age*] **1 :** the act or state of floating **:** ability to float **2 :** material that floats on the sea or on bodies of fresh water **:** FLOTSAM **3** *usu floatage* **:** the charge for transferring railroad cars on a car float

flo·tant \'flōt³nt\ *adj* [F *flottant* floating, fr. pres. part. of *flotter* to float, fr. OF *floter*, of Gmc origin; akin to OE *flotian* to float — more at FLOAT] *heraldry* **:** flying in air ⟨a galley, sails furled, pennon ~⟩

flo·ta·tion *also* **floa·ta·tion** \flō'tāshən\ *n* -S [*flotation* alter. of *floatation; floatation* fr. ²*float* + *-ation*] **1 :** the act, process, or state of floating **2 :** an act or instance of financing (as a commercial venture, an issue of stock, or a loan) ⟨their last ~ of stock was successful⟩ ⟨the ~ of new securities is a specialized business⟩ **3 a :** the separation of the particles of a mass of finely pulverized ore according to their relative capacity for floating by virtue of the surface tension on a given liquid instead of according to their specific gravities **b :** any of various similar processes involving the relative capacity of materials for floating (as for separating oils from industrial wastes, pigments from impurities, or coal from slate) — see FROTH FLOTATION **4 :** the collection (as in sewage treatment) of substances immersed in a liquid by taking advantage of differences in specific gravities or of the buoyancy produced by the evolution of gas by chemicals or heat **5 :** the ability (as of a tire, crawler tread, platform, or vehicle) to stay on the surface of soft ground or snow

flotation gear *n* **:** emergency gear carried by a landplane to provide buoyancy in case of a forced landing on water

flo·ta·tive *also* **float·a·tive** \'flōd·əd·iv\ *adj* [*flotation, floatation* + *-ive*] **:** of, relating to, used in, or aiding flotation

flo·til·la \flō'tilə, flə'-\ *n* -S [Sp, dim. of *flota* fleet, fr. OSp, fr. OF *flote*, fr. ON *floti* raft, fleet — more at FLOAT] **1 :** a small fleet or a fleet of small watercraft: as **a :** a subdivision of a naval fleet consisting of two or more squadrons of destroyers or other small warships sometimes with supplementary ships and air support **b :** a group of ships (as canoes, rafts, or windjammers) with a common objective and sometimes a definite leader **c :** an organization of military landing craft consisting of two or more boat groups **2 :** a group (as of persons, planes, or tractors) resembling a fleet of ships

flo·to·ri·al \(')flō¦tōrēəl\ *or* **flo·te·ri·al** \-tir-\ *adj* [irreg. fr. *floater* + *-ial*] **1 :** running for or elected to office as a floater ⟨a ~ representative⟩ **2 :** represented by or entitled to be represented by a floater ⟨a ~ district⟩; *sometimes* **:** held by a floater ⟨a ~ post⟩

flot·sam \'flätsəm *sometimes* -lōt-\ *n* -S [alter. of earlier *flotsen*, fr. AF *floteson*, fr. *floter* to float, fr. OF — more at FLOTANT] **1 :** wreckage of a ship or its cargo found floating on the sea — distinguished esp. in legal usage from *jetsam* and *lagan* **2 :** something floating or drifting about on or as if on the surface of a body of water: as **a :** a floating population (as of useless, vagrant, or worthless people) ⟨the skid row ~⟩ **b :** an accumulation of unimportant, miscellaneous, and often disordered trifles

flot·ter \'flätər\ *vi* -ED/-ING/-S [ME *floteren* to be tossed by waves, float, flutter — more at FLUTTER] *Scot* **:** FLOAT

¹flounce \'flaůn(t)s\ *vb* -ED/-ING/-S [perh. of Scand origin; akin to Norw *flunsa* to hurry, Sw dial. *flunsa* to plunge] *vi* **1 a :** to move suddenly and usu. clumsily and jerkily in or as if in a state of emotional turmoil ⟨*flounced* away in a rage⟩ **b :** to move with a conscious awareness of self and usu. in a manner to draw attention to one's person ⟨*flouncing* across the hotel lobby⟩ **2 :** to spring, turn, or twist with sudden effort or violence **:** FLOUNDER, STRUGGLE ⟨the horse *flounced* wildly on the slippery paving⟩ **3 :** to enter or leave with an effect of flouncing ⟨*flounced* out of the room⟩ ⟨*flouncing* into the discussion⟩; *often* **:** to walk out **:** drop out — usu. used with *off* or *out* ⟨an actress who *flounces* out on her contract⟩ ⟨the seamstresses *flounced* off on strike⟩ ~ *vt, archaic* **:** to move or cause to move suddenly, violently, or jerkily (as in flinging, splashing, or slamming)

²flounce \"\ *n* -S **:** an act or instance of flouncing **:** a sudden or sharp jerk (as of the body) ⟨moved with a ~ to open the door⟩ ⟨giving the pillows a quick ~ to straighten and smooth them⟩

³flounce \"\ *adv* **:** with a flouncing motion

⁴flounce \"\ *n* -S [irreg. fr. *frounce*] **:** a strip of fabric that is straight, gathered, pleated, or circular-cut and is attached by one edge (as in finishing or trimming) so that the free edge will have maximum fullness ⟨a vanity with a chintz ~⟩; *often* **:** a wide ruffle

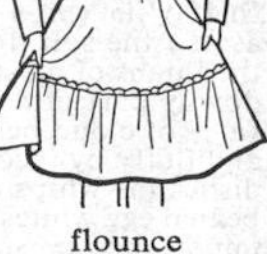

flounce

⁵flounce \"\ *vt* -ED/-ING/-S **:** to trim or finish with or as if with flounces

flounc·ing \'flaůn(t)siŋ\ *n* -S [⁴*flounce* + *-ing*] **:** material suitable for or made up into flounces; *esp* **:** yard goods of lace or embroidery with one plain straight edge and one fancy ornamented edge

¹flouncy *also* **flounc·ey** \-sē\ *adj* **flouncier; flounciest** [⁴*flounce* + *-y*] **:** ornamented or finished with flounces ⟨a ~ girlish evening dress⟩

²flouncy \"\ *adj* -ER/-EST [¹*flounce* + *-y*] **:** marked by flouncing; *often* **:** jerky and self-conscious

¹floun·der \'flaůndə(r)\ *n, pl* **flounder** *or* **flounders** *see sense 3* [ME *flundre, flounder*, of Scand origin; akin to Sw *flundra* flounder, Norw *flundra* flounder, flat stone, ON *flythra* flounder; akin to MHG *vluoder* flounder, ON *flatr* flat — more at FLAT] **1 :** any of numerous flattened fishes constituting the order Heterosomata **:** FLATFISH; *usu* **:** any of various fishes of the families Pleuronectidae and Bothidae which include a number of important marine food fishes — see SOUTHERN FLOUNDER, SUMMER FLOUNDER, WINTER FLOUNDER; compare SOLE **2 :** PUMPKINSEED **3** *pl flounders* **:** something (as a metal plate, a liver fluke, or a tool formerly used in crimping boot fronts) resembling a flounder in shape

²flounder \"\ *vi* **floundered; floundered; floundering** \-d(ə)riŋ\ **flounders** [prob. alter. (influenced by ¹*flounder*) of *founder*] **1** *obs* **:** STUMBLE **2 a :** to fling the limbs and body (as in making efforts to move) **:** struggle to move or obtain footing **b :** to proceed clumsily and often self-consciously **:** MUDDLE ⟨they ~*ed* on from blunder to blunder —William Hamilton †1856⟩ **syn** see WALLOW

³flounder \"\ *n* -S **:** an act or instance of floundering

floun·der·ing·ly *adv* **:** in a floundering manner

¹flour \'flaů(ə)r, -aůə, *esp in the South* -aůwə(r\ *n* -S *often attrib* [ME, flower, best of anything, flour — more at FLOWER] **1 a :** finely ground meal of wheat; *esp* **:** a commercial product that is obtained by milling and blending wheat more or less completely freed of bran and that consists essentially of starch and gluten of the endosperm — see WHOLE WHEAT FLOUR **b :** finely ground meal of other cereal grains or seeds (as rye, barley, buckwheat, rice, or bean) **c :** finely ground meal obtained from dried food products other than cereals (as potato, banana, or cassava) **2 :** a fine soft powder (as of mineral or plant matter) usu. obtained by grinding ⟨silica ~⟩ ⟨rock ~⟩ ⟨wood ~ production utilizes waste by-products and provides fuel for power⟩ **3 :** FINES

²flour \"\ *vb* -ED/-ING/-S *vt* **1 :** to convert (as wheat or wood) into flour **:** grind and bolt **:** MILL, PULVERIZE **2 :** to sprinkle or coat with or as if with flour ⟨his coat ~*ed* with snow⟩ **3 :** to break up (mercury) into fine particles — compare DEADEN 2e ~ *vi* **:** to break up into particles: as **a** *of mercury* **:** to break into particles and become coated with sulfides so as to become useless for amalgam formation **b** *of paint* **:** CHALK

flour beetle *n* **:** any of various beetles that breed in flour, meal, and similar substances and often render them unfit for food; *specif* **:** a rather elongated flattened brown beetle of the family Tenebrionidae and esp. of the genus *Tribolium* — see CONFUSED FLOUR BEETLE

flour copper *n* **:** fine copper occurring as float

flour corn *n* **:** SOFT CORN 1

flour gold *n* **:** fine gold occurring as float

flour gravy *n* **:** gravy of milk, water, or stock and fat and seasoning thickened with flour

¹flour·ish \'flər·ish, 'flə·r|, |ēsh, *chiefly in pres part* |əsh\ *vb* -ED/-ING/-ES [ME *florisshen*, fr. MF *floriss-*, stem of *florir*, fr. (assumed) VL *florire*, alter. of L *florēre*, fr. *flor-, flos* flower — more at BLOW (to bloom)] *vi* **1** *chiefly Scot* **:** to bear flowers **:** BLOSSOM **2 :** to grow luxuriantly **:** increase and enlarge **:** THRIVE — used chiefly of plants and animals ⟨blueberries ~ best on an acid soil⟩ **3 a :** to be prosperous **:** increase in wealth, honor, comfort, happiness, or whatever is desirable **:** PROSPER **b :** to be in a state of activity or production — used chiefly of creative workers (as painters or writers) **c :** to reach a height of development or influence — used chiefly of technical, artistic, or philosophic schools of thought **4 a :** to play a fanciful or improvised bit of music by way of ornament or prelude **b :** to play a fanfare on trumpets **c :** to play with a flourish **5 :** BOAST, BRAG ⟨spent the evening ~*ing* over a bottle or two⟩ **6 :** to use florid language **:** be flowery in speech or writing **7 :** to make bold and sweeping movements or gestures esp. by way of show or in bravado ⟨~*ing* about the streets⟩ ~ *vt* **1 :** to adorn or decorate esp. with flowers or figures **:** ORNAMENT ⟨the corners ~*ed* with little silver cherubs⟩ **2 :** to move about in bold and sweeping figures ⟨~*ed* his cane angrily at the children⟩ **3** *obs* **a :** to embellish with rhetorical figures or ostentatious eloquence **b :** to illuminate (a manuscript) with color or decorative figures **syn** see SUCCEED, SWING

²flourish \"\ *n* -ES **1** *chiefly Scot* **:** bloom or blossom esp. on a fruit tree ⟨the ~ of the apple trees⟩ **2** *obs* **:** blooming state or luxuriant growth usu. of plants or vegetation **3 a** *obs* **:** showy decoration or embellishment **b :** a florid bit of writing or speech (as a complicated figure or an ornate metaphor) **c :** a purely ornamental stroke usu. attached to or enveloping a letter or meaningful figure in a writing or engraving **4 a :** FANFARE **b :** a florid musical passage **5 :** the waving of a weapon or other thing ⟨with a last ~ of her handkerchief⟩ ⟨gave his cloak a ~ as he stepped from the coach⟩ **:** a brandishing esp. in salute or signal ⟨greeted him with a ~ of his cane⟩ ⟨caught the auctioneer's eye with a ~ of his catalog⟩ **6 :** a showiness or ostentation in the performance of something often intended to call forth or fix attention or admiration ⟨introduced his guest with a ~⟩ ⟨if I've got to give her a debut I'll do it with a ~⟩

flour·ish·er \-shə(r)\ *n* -S [ME *florissher*, fr. *florisshen* + *-er*] **:** one that flourishes

flourishing *adj* **:** increasing and growing **:** progressing well ⟨a ~ economy⟩ ⟨~ chicks⟩ — **flour·ish·ing·ly** *adv*

flour·ishy \-shē\ *adj* **:** characterized by flourishes **:** SHOWY

flour mite *n* **:** any of various mites that sometimes infest flour; *specif* **:** a small sarcoptoid mite (*Tyroglyphus farinae*) that is common in stored food products and may cause grocer's itch in persons handling infested materials

flour moth *n* **:** MEDITERRANEAN FLOUR MOTH

flour sulfur *n* **:** SULFUR FLOUR

flour worm *n* **:** the larva of any of various insects that breed in flour or meal; *esp* **:** the larva of the Mediterranean flour moth

floury \'flaů(ə)rē, -ri\ *adj* **1 :** of or resembling flour esp. in fine powdery texture ⟨a ~ clay⟩ **2 :** covered with flour ⟨wiped her ~ hands on her apron⟩

floury miller *n, Austral* **:** a large reddish brown cicada (*Abricta curvicosta*) having a whitish pubescence on the abdomen

¹flout \'flaůt, *usu* -aůd·+V\ *vb* -ED/-ING/-S [prob. fr. ME *flouten* to play the flute — more at FLUTE] *vt* **1 :** to treat with contempt **:** MOCK, INSULT **2** *obs* **:** to quote or say sarcastically or by way of mockery ~ *vi* **:** to engage in or practice mocking **:** SNEER, FLEER **syn** see SCOFF

²flout \"\ *n* -S **:** INSULT, JEER, MOCK, SCOFF; *sometimes* **:** MOCKERY, JEERING

flout·er \-ə(r)\ *n* -S **:** one that flouts

flout·ing·ly *adv* **:** in a mocking or contemptuous manner **:** with flouts

floutingstock *n, obs* **:** an object of mockery or contempt

¹flow \'flō\ *vb* **flowed** \-ōd\ **flowed** \"\ *also archaic* **flown** \-ōn\ **flowing; flows** [ME *flowen*, fr. OE *flōwan*; akin to OHG *flouwen* to rinse, wash, ON *flōa* to flow, L *pluere* to rain, Gk *plein* to sail, float, Skt *plavate* he swims] *vi* **1 a :** to issue in a stream **:** GUSH, SPRING, WELL **b :** to move with a continual change of place among the constituent particles or parts **:** RUN, STREAM — used of fluids and of plastic or particulate bodies that move like fluids ⟨the grain ~*ed* smoothly down the elevator chute⟩ ⟨water ~*ing* over a dam⟩ ⟨molasses ~*s* slowly in cold weather⟩ **c** *of paint or other coatings* **:** to spread out in a uniform layer without holding brush or other applicator marks ⟨this paint ~*s* very well with a roller⟩ **2 a** *obs* **:** to become liquid **:** FUSE, MELT **b :** to deform under stress without cracking, breaking, or rupturing — used of certain solids (as metals or rocks) **3** *of water* **:** to rise esp. in the influx of a tide — often opposed to *ebb* ⟨the tide ~*s* twice and ebbs twice in each 24 hours⟩ **4 a :** to issue forth **:** ARISE, PROCEED — usu. used with *from* ⟨his authority does not ~ from his office alone⟩ ⟨wealth continues to ~ from our commerce and industry⟩ **b :** to move in or as if in a stream — usu. used with adverbs of direction ⟨money continued to ~ in⟩ **5 a :** to be in abundance or excess **:** ABOUND ⟨a land ~*ing* with natural resources⟩ ⟨wine ~*ed* freely all evening⟩ ⟨rivers ~*ing* with fish⟩ **b :** to fill to overflowing ⟨her heart ~*ed* with gratitude⟩ **6 a :** to move or proceed smoothly and without harshness or asperities ⟨his speech ~*ed* on to a summation⟩ **:** issue easily or freely ⟨words ~*ed* from him as if from a faucet⟩ **b :** to have such a contour as to suggest a graceful unimpeded uninterrupted movement ⟨the *flowing* lines of the car⟩ ⟨the dress ~*ed* and shimmered⟩ **7 :** to hang loose and floatingly ⟨his cloak ~*ed* from his shoulders⟩ ⟨fair hair ~*ing* in the light air⟩ **8 :** to menstruate esp. profusely ~ *vt* **1 a :** to cause to flow ⟨~*ing* oil over the swamp to kill mosquito larvae⟩ **b :** to spread (as paint) in a thick layer without brushing out thinly in the usual manner **c :** to cause or permit (an oil or gas well) to produce **2 :** to cover (as land) with water or other liquid **:** FLOOD, INUNDATE ⟨~ land for irrigation⟩ **3 :** to discharge (something) in a flow ⟨brought in a new oil well that ~*ed* 100 barrels a day⟩ ⟨the cut ~*ed* blood for some time⟩ **4 :** to run (molten metal) through a foundry mold to carry off bubbles, slag, and dross **5 :** to slack the sheet of (a sail) to spill the wind **syn** see SPRING — **flow by heads :** to flow intermittently — used esp. of oil wells

²flow \"\ *n* -S [ME, fr. *flowen*, v.] **1 :** the act or manner of flowing (as of a liquid) ⟨a sudden ~ of tears⟩ ⟨the chuckling ~ of rills and brooklets⟩ **2 a :** the regular inflowing of tidal waters towards the shore **b :** OVERFLOWING, INUNDATION; *esp* **:** one regularly recurring (as along the course of the Nile) **3 a :** an easy smooth and uninterrupted progress or movement (as of thought, music, traffic) suggesting the steady flow of water in a river ⟨ideas arose in a steady ~ as he worked⟩ ⟨a pleasing ~ of distant melody⟩ ⟨there has been a satisfactory ~ of capital to new enterprises⟩ **b :** the progressive travel of material for manufacture or of semifinished or of finished product from place to place or from operation to operation **4 :** a stream of water or other fluid or a mass of matter (as lava) that has flowed when molten ⟨a rubble ~⟩; *broadly* **:** STREAM **5 a :** the quantity (as of water) that flows in a certain time under specified conditions ⟨a system able to handle a ~ of 100 gallons a second⟩ **b :** the percentage increase in diameter of a mass of concrete or mortar when subjected to a standardized flow-test procedure including a prescribed flow table **6 :** form or arrangement suggesting a gentle unbroken movement ⟨the ~ of her hair over her shoulders⟩ ⟨the draperies forming a continuous graceful ~ across the three windows⟩ **7 :** the ability of a paint, varnish, or other coating to flow out to a smooth film **8 a :** menstrual discharge **:** MENSTRUATION **b :** production of a fluid or an instance of such production ⟨a good ~ of milk⟩ ⟨the fall ~ of honey⟩ ⟨a good sap ~ last spring⟩ **9 a :** the motion characteristic of gases, liquids, and viscous solids in which there is freedom of motion among constituent particles and change of form under the action of forces — see LAMINAR FLOW, STREAMLINE FLOW, TURBULENT FLOW **b :** a continuous transfer of energy (as of electricity or heat)

syn STREAM, CURRENT, FLOOD, TIDE, FLUX: FLOW designates the characteristic movement of a fluid, gentle or rapid, copious or meager, showing unbroken continuity ⟨the *flow* of water from the pipe⟩ ⟨the *flow* of lava from the volcano⟩ ⟨the steady *flow* of casualties from the front⟩ ⟨she helped Ruth into her coat, keeping up a cheerful *flow* of conversation —B.A. Williams⟩ STREAM may focus attention on constant succession of individual units or on their volume or speed ⟨a *stream* of water through the cellar wall⟩ ⟨a continuous *stream* of messages came in by courier —Irving Stone⟩ ⟨the *stream* of immigration turned toward middle and west Tennessee, where soils were deep and rich —*Amer. Guide Series: Tenn.*⟩ ⟨Riverside Drive and the Henry Hudson Parkway with their constant *stream* of cars —*Amer. Guide Series: N.Y. City*⟩ CURRENT strongly suggests the fact of running or flowing in a set direction with noticeable force ⟨the main *current* of the stream⟩ ⟨the Labrador *current* in the Atlantic⟩ ⟨the *current* of air from the ventilator⟩ ⟨there are thus indications in the New Testament of several cross *currents* of thought, political and social, in the early Christian church —C.H.McIlwain⟩ FLOOD suggests abundant copiousness or torrential power ⟨the trickle became a stream and then a *flood* —*Amer. Guide Series: Oregon*⟩ ⟨the rising *flood* of students is very much like the barbarian invasions —Douglas Bush⟩ ⟨a *flood* of war orders that strained the capacity of factories long idle —Oscar Handlin⟩ TIDE may suggest either surging power or periodic alternation of direction ⟨the deadly glittering *tide* of Spanish conquest surged into Central and So. America —Marjory S. Douglas⟩ ⟨the *tide* of traffic flow recedes very rapidly and the movement of people out of doors after midnight is almost negligible —H.E.Agnew⟩ ⟨she was on the threshold of womanhood, borne this way and that by conflicting *tides* of feeling —Ruth Park⟩ FLUX stresses constant change, sometimes in components, sometimes in direction ⟨a brief illusion of stability in the eternal *flux* —P.E.More⟩ ⟨as far as nature is to us more than a *flux* lacking order in its mutable changes, as far as it is more than a whirlpool of confusions, it is marked by rhythms —John Dewey⟩

³flow \'flaů\ *n* -S [of Scand origin; akin to ON *flōi* wide mouth of a river, swampy place, Dan *flo* marsh; derivatives fr. the root of ON *flōa* to flow — more at ¹FLOW] **1** *chiefly Scot* **:** a wet swamp or bog **:** MORASS **2** *chiefly Scot* **:** an arm or basin of the sea — used chiefly in place names ⟨Scapa *Flow*⟩ **3** *Scot* **:** a small amount

flow·abil·i·ty \ˌflōə'biləd·ē\ *n* -ES **:** the capacity to move by flow that characterizes fluids and loose particulate solids

flow·able \'flōəbəl\ *adj* **:** capable of flowing or being flowed ⟨a good ~ paint⟩

flow·age \'flōij, -ōēj\ *n* -S **1 a :** an overflowing (as of a stream or impoundment) onto adjacent land **:** FLOODING **b :** a body of water formed by flowage or sometimes by damming **c :** floodwater esp. of a stream **2 :** gradual deformation of a body of plastic solid (as certain rocks) caused by intermolecular shear — sometimes distinguished from *fracture*

flowage line *n* **:** a contour line at the edge of a body of water (as a storage reservoir or lake) that corresponds to some particular water level

flowage texture *n* **:** FLUIDAL TEXTURE

flow bean *n* **:** FLOW NIPPLE

flow birefringence *n* **:** an anisotropic state of a liquid resulting from shear

flow–blue \'≈ˌ≈\ *n* **:** an underglaze blue that was popular esp. in the early 19th century on pottery ware, that is generally printed, and that is caused to spread in firing by the use of a powder placed in the sagger

flow box *n* **:** a mechanical reservoir that feeds beaten paper pulp onto the wire of a papermaking machine

flow chart *also* **flow diagram** *n* **:** a schematic diagram or expository outline showing the progress of material through the various steps of a manufacturing process or the succession of operations in a complicated activity

flow cleavage *n* **:** cleavage that results from flow in hard rock and that is characterized by more or less slaty structure and reorientation or recrystallization of certain included minerals into a platy form

flow counter *n* **:** a device for detecting low-level radiation involving essentially transport of emanations to a Geiger counter in a stream of inert gas

flowed *past of* FLOW

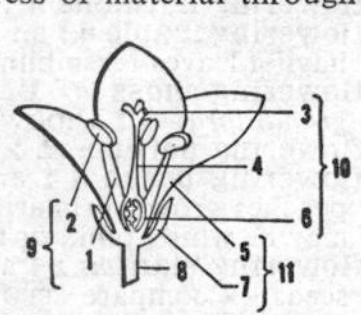

a flower in section: *1* filament, *2* anther, *3* stigma, *4* style, *5* petal, *6* ovary, *7* sepal, *8* pedicel, *9* stamen, *10* pistil, *11* perianth

¹flow·er \'flaů(ə)r, -aůə, *esp in the South* -aůwə(r\ *n* -S *often attrib* [ME *flour* flower, best of anything, flour, fr. OF *flor, flour, flur*, fr. L *flor-, flos* — more at BLOW (to bloom)] **1 a :** the part of a seed plant that normally bears reproductive organs esp. when some or all of its parts are conspicuous or brightly colored **:** BLOSSOM, INFLORESCENCE — not used technically **b :** a shoot of the sporophyte of a higher plant modified for reproductive purposes and consisting of a shortened axis bearing one or more series of floral leaves some or all of which are sporophylls; *esp* **:** such a shoot of a seed plant possessing an obvious external protective perianth often differentiated into calyx and corolla, an androecium of one or more stamens, and a gynoecium of one or more carpels **c :** BLOOM ⟨the tulips were in full ~⟩ **2 a :** the best, fairest, freshest, or choicest part, sample, or example of something ⟨she was the ~ of her family⟩ ⟨the ~ of chivalry⟩ **b :** the state or time of fresh vigor or bloom **:** PRIME ⟨in the ~ of youth and ardor⟩ **3 :** a very finely divided powder (as one that will pass through a screen of 400 meshes to the inch); *esp* **:** one produced by condensation or sublimation — usu. used in pl.; see FLOWERS OF SULFUR **4 flowers** *pl, archaic* **:** menstrual discharges **5 :** a plant cultivated or esteemed primarily for its blossoms ⟨we have separate ~ garden and kitchen garden⟩ **6 a :** an ornamental representation of a flower ⟨a skirt covered with little embroidered ~*s*⟩ **:** a floral design or artificial flower; *esp* **:** a printer's fleuron **b :** a flowery insertion or interpellation; *usu* **:** a figure of speech or other ornament of literary style **7 :** SEASON 6

²flower \"\ *vb* **flowered; flowered; flowering** \-aů(ə)riŋ, -aůwər-\ **flowers** [ME *flouren*, fr. *flour*, n.] *vi* **1 a :** to produce flowers **:** BLOOM, BLOSSOM ⟨some roses ~ throughout the growing season⟩ **b :** to arise and develop — often used with *out* ⟨quarrels that ~*ed* out as the community enlarged⟩ **2 :** to come into the finest or fairest condition ⟨girls tend to ~ early in the tropics⟩ **3** *obs, of an effervescent liquid* **:** to froth or foam — used esp. of beer ~ *vt* **1 :** to cause to bear flowers **:** grow until the bloom appears ⟨~*ing* azaleas under glass⟩ ⟨a rare tropical orchid that has never been ~*ed* in cultivation⟩ **2 :** to cover or decorate with floral designs or representations of flowers ⟨frost ~*ing* the window⟩ ⟨a gay vestee ~*ed* with silk⟩

flow·er·age \-aů(ə)rij, -aůwər-, -rēj\ *n* -s **:** flowers or flowering state

flower beetle *n* **:** a beetle that feeds upon flowers (as members of the family Cetoniidae)

flower box *n* **:** a usu. elongated box containing soil and used for growing ornamental plants

flower bud *n* **:** a plant bud that produces only a flower or flowers — compare LEAF BUD, MIXED BUD

flower cup *n* **1 :** CALYX **2 :** the cup-shaped interior of some flowers

flower-cup fern *n* **:** ALPINE WOODSIA

flower-de-luce \ˌ≈də¦lüs\ *n, pl* **flowers-de-luce** [ME *flour de luce*, fr. AF, alter. of MF *flor de lis, flour de lis*, lit., lily flower] **:** ²IRIS 2 — compare FLEUR-DE-LIS

flow·ered \ˈflaů(ə)rd, -aů(w)əd\ *adj* [ME *floured*, fr. *flour*, n. + *-ed*] **1 :** having or bearing flowers ⟨a ~ lawn⟩ **2 :** adorned or covered with flowers or floral figures or patterns ⟨a ~ carpet⟩ **3 :** made with or partly with petals or leaves of flowers ⟨~ tea⟩

flow·er·er \-aůrə(r), -aůwərə(r\ *n* -s **1 :** a plant that flowers esp. in some specified manner or season ⟨one of the best ~*s* among the miniatures⟩ ⟨tulips are among the showiest spring ~*s*⟩ **2 :** a person who makes representations of flowers (as on pottery or in embroidery) usu. as a trade

flow·er·et \-aů(ə)rət, -aůwər-, *usu* -əd+V\ *n* -s [ME *flourette*, fr. MF *florete, flourete, flurete*, dim. of *flor, flour, flur* flower — more at FLOWER] **:** FLORET; *sometimes* **:** one of the segments into which a head of cauliflower is divisible

flower fence *n* **:** PRIDE OF BARBADOS

flowerfly \ˈ≈,≈\ *n* **:** a syrphid fly

flower girl *n* **1 :** a girl peddling flowers in the street **2 :** a little girl generally carrying or strewing flowers before the bride at a formal wedding

flower head *n* **:** a compact shortened inflorescence; *esp* **:** the capitulum of a composite or other plant in which the individual flowers are sessile and so arranged that the whole inflorescence gives the effect of a single flower — see COMPOSITE illustration

flow·er·i·ly \ˈflaů(ə)rəlē, -aůwər-\ *adv* **:** in a flowery manner

flow·er·i·ness \-rēnəs, -rin-\ *n* -ES **:** the quality or state of being flowery esp. in the use of language

¹flowering *adj* [ME *flouring*, fr. pres. part. of *flouren* to flower, flourish — more at FLOWER] **1** *obs* **:** FLOURISHING **2 a :** bearing flowers esp. in the blooming stage ⟨a ~ branch⟩ **b :** covered with or full of flowers ⟨a ~ meadow⟩ **3 :** having conspicuous flowers **:** being of a kind grown primarily for its blossom — used chiefly in vernacular names of plants, the combination sometimes designating a plant that does not belong to the natural group indicated by the noun ⟨the fringe tree is sometimes called ~ ash⟩

²flowering *n* -s [ME *flouring*, fr. gerund of *flouren*] **1 a :** the act or state of producing flowers **:** ANTHESIS, FLORESCENCE ⟨have you ever watched the ~ of the cereus?⟩ **b :** the season when plants bloom ⟨~ will be late this year⟩ **2 :** something (as ornamentation) of floral form or suggesting a blooming **3 :** an unfolding or development ⟨the gradual ~ of his talent⟩ **4 :** the secondary fermentation with flor formation in the production of superior sherry wines; *sometimes* **:** FLOR

flowering almond *n* **:** any of three woody plants of the genus *Prunus* grown for their showy flowers: **a :** a Chinese shrub or small tree (*P. triloka*) with fruit furrowed and hairy but becoming smooth **b :** a low Chinese shrub (*P. glandulosa*) or a similar Japanese shrub (*P. japonica*) with smooth unfurrowed fruit

flowering ash *n* **1 :** any of three plants of the genus *Fraxinus*: **a :** MANNA ASH **b :** a large shrub or shrubby tree (*F. cuspidata*) of the southwestern U.S. that has fragrant white flowers **c :** a large shrub (*F. dipetala*) of the Pacific coast and coastal mountain ranges of the U.S. **2 :** FRINGE TREE

flowering box *or* **flowering boxberry** *n* **:** MOUNTAIN CRANBERRY

flowering cherry *n* **:** any of several shrubs or trees of the genus *Prunus* cultivated as ornamentals for their showy bloom — see JAPANESE FLOWERING CHERRY

flowering crab *or* **flowering crab apple** *or* **flowering apple** *n* **:** any of various crab apples mostly of Asiatic origin that are widely cultivated for their showy single or double white to rosy red flowers — see BECHTEL CRAB

flowering currant *n* **1 :** GOLDEN CURRANT **2 :** WILD BLACK CURRANT

flowering cypress *n* **:** TAMARIX 2

flowering dogwood *also* **flowering cornel** *n* **:** a common spring-flowering white-bracted dogwood (*Cornus florida*)

flowering fern *n* **:** a fern of the genus *Osmunda* in which the naked sporangia are on modified fronds that resemble flower clusters

flowering flag *n* **:** ²IRIS 2

flowering flax *n* **:** an erect leafy branching annual herb (*Linum grandiflorum*) of northern Africa cultivated for its red flowers

flowering glume *n* **:** LEMMA

flowering hazel *n* **:** WINTER HAZEL; *esp* **:** a widely cultivated Japanese shrub (*Corylopsis pauciflora*) with somewhat glaucous foliage

flowering hormone *n* **:** FLORIGEN

flowering maple *n* **:** an ornamental plant of the genus *Abutilon* having leaves resembling those of maples

flowering moss *n* **1 :** PYXIE **2 :** a portulaca (*Portulaca grandiflora*) **3 :** WIDOW'S CROSS

flowering nettle *n* **1 :** HEMP NETTLE **2 :** WHITE DEAD NETTLE

flowering peach *n* **:** any of various often dwarf or shrubby peaches grown primarily for their ornamental flowers which may be white, pink, or red and are often double

flowering plant *n* **1 :** a plant that produces flowers, fruit, and seeds — compare SEED PLANT **2 :** a plant notable or cultivated for its ornamental flowers

flowering plum *n* **:** any of several trees or shrubs of the genus *Prunus* cultivated chiefly for their blossom

flowering quince *n* **:** a shrub of the genus *Chaenomeles*; *esp* **:** JAPANESE QUINCE 2

flowering raspberry *n* **:** a shrubby bramble (*Rubus odoratus*) of eastern No. America having bristly stems, lobed leaves, showy rose to purplish flowers, and red edible fruit

flowering rush *n* **:** an aquatic or marsh plant (*Butomus umbellatus*) with sharp 3-cornered linear leaves and an umbel of rosy blossoms that is native to Europe but naturalized in waters adjacent to the St. Lawrence river

flowering shot *n* **:** INDIAN SHOT

flowering spurge *n* **:** a common spurge (*Euphorbia corollata*) of the eastern U.S. with showy white involucral appendages resembling petals

flowering straw *n* **1 :** any of several skeleton weeds of the southern U.S. **2 :** any of various branching leafy-stemmed composite herbs having small heads of pink or white flowers and constituting a genus *Stephanomeria* of western No. America

flowering thistle *n* **:** PRICKLY POPPY

flowering tobacco *n* **:** an ornamental plant of the genus *Nicotiana*

flowering willow *n* **:** DESERT WILLOW

flowering wintergreen *n* **:** GAYWINGS

flowering wood *n* **:** the portion of a woody plant that produces flower buds or mixed buds

flow·er·less \ˈflaů(ə)rl|əs-, -aů(w)əl|\ *adj* **:** having no flowers — **flow·er·less·ness** *n* -ES

flowerless plant *n* **1 :** a plant that produces no flowers **2 :** a plant that produces flowers that are not noticeable (as grasses or rushes) — not used technically

flow·er·let \|ət\ *n* -s **:** FLORET

flowerlike \ˈ≈,≈\ *adj* **:** like or having the characteristics of a flower ⟨a ~ simplicity —Max Beerbohm⟩ **:** resembling a flower esp. in beauty or grace ⟨~ hands —Oscar Wilde⟩

flower-of-an-hour *n, pl* **flowers-of-an-hour :** an annual weedy plant (*Hibiscus trionum*) with ephemeral yellow purple-eyed flowers

flower of jove \-¦jōv\ *usu cap J* [after *Jove* (Jupiter), chief god of the ancient Romans, fr. L *Jov-, Jupiter;* trans. of NL *flos jovis*, specific epithet of *Lychnis flos-jovis*] **:** a European campion (*Lychnis flos-jovis*) with white-tomentose foliage and pink flowers

flower of the winds : the figure of a compass printed on old charts that is represented with a rose in the center

flower-pecker \ˈ≈,≈\ *n* **:** any of numerous small short-tailed passerine birds of southeast Asia, the Pacific islands, and Australia that feed on the berries of tropical mistletoes and on insects and that constitute the family Dicaeidae

flower piece *n* **1 :** an ornamental arrangement of flowers **2 :** an ornament (as a painting) representing flowers

flowerpot \ˈ≈,≈\ *n* **1 a :** a container (as of earthenware or plastic) for earth in which plants are grown **b** *dial* **:** VASE; *also* **:** BOUQUET **2 :** a firework that sends up sparks in fountains or showers

flowerpots 1a

flowers *pl of* FLOWER, *pres 3d sing of* FLOWER

flowers of antimony : ANTIMONY TRIOXIDE

flowers of madder : the macerated ground root of madder

flowers of sulfur : sublimed sulfur in the form of a fine yellow powder used esp. in agriculture and in medicine

flowers of tan : a slime mold (*Fuligo septica*) forming yellowish brown crustose compound fructifications on dead wood, leaves, and bark (as on spent tanbark)

flowers of wine : a scum formed on wine in fermentation by certain yeasts; *sometimes* **:** a yeast producing such a scum

flowers of zinc : zinc oxide esp. as obtained as a light white powder by burning zinc for use in pharmaceutical and cosmetic preparations

flower spike *n* **:** SPIKE 2

flower stalk *n* **:** PEDUNCLE 1a

flower thrips *n* **:** a yellow and orange thrips (*Frankliniella tritici*) living and feeding chiefly on flowers and causing sterility in oats and other crop plants

flower way *n* **:** an elevated passage from the back of a traditional Japanese theater to the stage by which actors make their entrances and exits

flow·ery \ˈflaů(ə)rē, -ri, *esp in the South* -aůwər-\ *adj* [ME *floury*, fr. *flour* flower + *-y* — more at FLOWER] **1 a :** relating to or covered with flowers ⟨a ~ field⟩ **b :** suggesting or like that of a flower ⟨a ~ odor⟩ ⟨a light ~ wine⟩ **2 a** *of language* **:** ornate and florid **:** characterized by much use of figures ⟨a ~ farewell speech⟩ **b :** inclined to the use of flowery language ⟨a ~ speaker⟩

flowery pekoe *also* **flowery orange pekoe** *n* **:** high quality tea consisting essentially of the small unbroken terminal leaves and buds

flow gauge *n* **:** FLOWMETER 1

flow gun *n* **:** a nozzle with finger-controlled flow for applying liquids (as adhesives, lubricants, or caulking)

flowing *pres part of* FLOW

flowing furnace *n* **:** a furnace from which molten metal can be drawn (as through a taphole) **:** a foundry cupola

flow·ing·ly *adv* **:** so as to flow or seem to flow ⟨draperies arranged ~⟩

flow·ing·ness *n* -ES **:** the quality or state of being flowing

flowing sheet *n* **:** a sheet on a sailing ship when eased off (as when the wind is aft or abeam)

flowing tracery *n* **:** tracery characterized by waving or flame-shaped curves that is found in English architecture of the 14th century and in the French flamboyant

flowing well *n* **:** an oil or water well from which the product flows without pumping due to natural or artificially supplied subterranean pressure from air or other gas

flow line *n* **1 :** distinguishable differences (as of color, texture, or arrangement of crystals) indicative of flow having taken place in a plastic solid (as an igneous rock formation or wrought metal) **2 :** a pipe or gutter carrying a flow of liquid esp. at zero pressure head

flow·me·ter \ˈflō,mēd·ə(r)\ *n* **1 :** an instrument for measuring the velocity of flow of a liquid in a pipe **2 a :** an instrument for indicating pressure, velocity of flow, and rate of discharge of a gas or vapor flowing in a pipe ⟨a steam ~⟩ **b :** an apparatus for determining the flowing properties of materials (as paints or other coatings)

flow moss *n* [¹*flow*] *dial Brit* **:** a wet peat bog

¹flown *past part of* FLY

²flown *adj* [fr. archaic past part of ¹*flow*] **:** filled esp. to excess or repletion ⟨~ with anger —Francis Hackett⟩ ⟨well ~ with wine⟩

flown cover *n* **:** a cover (as an envelope) that has been carried by airmail

flow nipple *n* **:** a nipple placed in a pipe line to regulate the flow of oil from a well — called also *flow bean*

flow nozzle *n* **:** a tapered length of tube that causes a fall of pressure head in a liquid flowing through it from which the rate can be calculated

flowoff \ˈ≈,≈\ *n* -s [fr. *flow off*, v.] **:** RUNOFF 1a

flows *pres 3d sing of* FLOW, *pl of* FLOW

flow sheet *n* **:** FLOW CHART; *esp* **:** one used of metallurgical or chemical processing

flowstone \ˈ≈,≈\ *n* **:** a deposit of travertine found where water flowing in a very thin sheet over rocks has deposited mineral matter — used chiefly of such deposits in caves

flow structure *n* **:** oriented structure developed in rock during flow

flow table *n* **:** a device for measuring the consistency of freshly made concrete or mortar consisting of a table top that can be raised and dropped and a mold for shaping the test specimen — compare ²FLOW 5b

flow tank *n* **:** a settling tank in which crude oil direct from the wells is stored for a time to free it from sediment before passing it on to the refineries

flow test *n* **:** a test to determine the consistency of freshly mixed concrete by measuring its spread on a flat surface under jarring

flow texture *n* **:** FLUIDAL TEXTURE

flow valve *n* **:** a valve that closes when the velocity or the pressure gradient of the fluid passing through it reaches a certain value

flr *abbr* **1** floor **2** florin

flt *abbr* **1** fleet **2** flight **3** float

fltg *abbr* flotage; floating

flu \ˈflü\ *n* -s [short for *influenza*] **1 :** INFLUENZA **2 :** any of certain ill-defined transitory virus diseases marked by respiratory and usu. gastrointestinal symptoms — used often with a qualifying term ⟨intestinal ~⟩

flu·ate \ˈflü,āt\ *n* -s [by contr.] **:** FLUOSILICATE — used esp. of solutions for waterproofing building stone or concrete

flu·a·vil \ˈflüə,vil\ *n* -s [F *fluavile*] **:** an amorphous yellow resin extracted from gutta-percha and balata

¹flub \ˈfləb\ *vb* **flubbed; flubbed; flubbing; flubs** [origin unknown] *vt* **:** to perform or deal with in a blundering manner **:** make a botch of **:** fail at ⟨was always *flubbing* her lines⟩ ~ *vi* **:** to act in a blundering manner **:** do something poorly or inefficiently

²flub \"\ *n* -s **:** a clumsy or stupid failure **:** BLUNDER, BONER

flub·dub \ˈfləb,dəb\ *also* **flub·dub·bery** \-,dəb(ə)rē\ *n, pl* **flubdubs** *also* **flubdubberies** [origin unknown] *slang* **:** ornate show designed to deceive; *usu* **:** showy bombastic argument or language **:** BALDERDASH

fluc·tu·ant \ˈfləkchəwənt, -ksh-\ *adj* [L *fluctuant-, fluctuans*, pres. part. of *fluctuare*] **:** moving like a wave: **a :** wavering or fluctuating ⟨the ~ drift of mist —Arthur Foff⟩ **b :** varying and unstable **:** not fixed ⟨a ~ foreign exchange rate⟩ ⟨~ populations⟩ **c :** movable and compressible — used of abnormal body structures (as certain abscesses or tumors) ⟨a ~ mass⟩ ⟨the involved nodes became ~ and were removed surgically —*Biol. Abstracts*⟩

fluc·tu·ate \-,wāt, *usu* -ād+V\ *vb* -ED/-ING/-S [L *fluctuatus*, past part. of *fluctuare*, fr. *fluctus* action of flowing, flood, wave, fr. *fluctus*, past part. of *fluere* to flow — more at FLUID] *vi* **1 :** to become wavering, unsteady, irresolute, or undetermined **:** VACILLATE **2 a :** to move like a wave **:** roll hither and thither **:** WAVE **b :** to drift or float backward and forward as if on waves ⟨a *fluctuating* field of air⟩ ~ *vt* **:** to cause to move like a wave **:** put in motion **syn** see SWING

fluc·tu·at·ing·ly \ˈ≈≈,≈≈≈, ,≈≈ˈ≈≈≈\ *adv* **:** with fluctuation **:** in a fluctuating manner

fluc·tu·a·tion \,fləkchəˈwāshən, -ksh-\ *n* -s [ME *fluctuacioun*, fr. L *fluctuation-, fluctuatio*, fr. *fluctuatus* + *-ion-, -io* -ion] **1 :** a wavering or unsteadiness (as of opinion or prices) **2 :** a motion like that of waves **:** a moving in this and that direction ⟨the ~*s* of the sea⟩ **3 a :** a slight and nonheritable variation; *esp* **:** such a variation occurring in response to environmental factors **b :** recurrent and often more or less cyclic alteration (as of form, size, or color of a bodily part) **4 :** the wavelike motion of a fluid collected in a natural or artificial cavity of the body observed by palpation or percussion

fluc·tu·a·tion·al \¦≈≈¦wāshənᵊl, -shnəl\ *adj* **:** relating to or subject to fluctuation ⟨~ factors in the economy⟩

¹flue \ˈflü\ *n* -s [ME *flue, flowe, flew*, fr. MD *vlüwe, vlouwe;* akin to OE *flōwan* to flow — more at FLOW] **:** FISHNET; *esp* **:** DRAGNET

²flue \"\ *adj* [ME *flew*] *dial Eng* **:** SHALLOW, OPEN, FLARING

³flue \"\ *n* -s *often attrib* [origin unknown] **:** an enclosed passageway for establishing and directing a current of gas (as air): as **a** (1) *now dial* **:** CHIMNEY (2) **:** a channel in a chimney for conveying flame and smoke to the outer air ⟨a big 4-flue chimney⟩ **b :** a passageway for carrying a current of air from one place to another (as for heating, cooling, or ventilating) ⟨warmed air is forced through ~*s* between the studs⟩ **c** (1) **:** an air channel to the lip of a wind instrument (as a recorder) (2) **:** an organ flue pipe (3) **:** the opening in an organ flue pipe between the lower lip and the languet **d :** a passage for conveying flame and hot gases around or through water in a steam boiler

⁴flue \"\ *n* -s [Flem *vluwe*, fr. F *velu* shaggy — more at VELVET] **:** soft downy material: as **a :** soft fluffy lint or debris ⟨swept the ~ from under the beds⟩ **b :** feather vane freed from quill and shaft; *esp* **:** one of soft fluffy feathers (as of the ostrich) ⟨a dainty cap trimmed with curled ostrich ~⟩

⁵flue \"\ *adj* [origin unknown] *dial Eng* **:** thin and sickly **:** FEEBLE

flue-cure \ˈ≈¦≈\ *vt* [³*flue*] **:** to cure (tobacco) by means of heat transmitted through a flue without exposure to smoke or fumes — compare FIRE-CURE

flued \ˈflüd\ *adj* **:** having a flue

flue dust *n* **:** finely divided metal or metallic compounds escaping with the flue gases of a smelter or metallurgical furnace; *broadly* **:** such matter with accompanying fumes

flue gas *n* **:** the mixture of gases resulting from combustion and other reactions in a furnace, passing off through the smoke flue, composed largely of nitrogen, carbon dioxide, carbon monoxide, water vapor, and often sulfur dioxide, and sometimes serving as a source from which carbon dioxide or other compounds are recovered

fluegelhorn *var of* FLÜGELHORN

flue·less \ˈflüləs\ *adj, of a fire or combustion device* **:** having no flue **:** discharging by-products of combustion into the surrounding atmosphere ⟨a ~ oil heater⟩

flue lining *n* **:** a lining for chimney flues that consists of successive hollow sections of rectangular or circular hard burned clay and serves to protect the house against escape of gases or fire from the flue, the brick of the chimney usu. being built around the lining

flu·el·lin *also* **flu·el·len** \flüˈelən\ *n* -s [W *llysiau Llywelyn*, lit., Llewelyn's herbs, prob. after *Llywelyn* ab Iorwerth (Llewelyn the Great) †1240 or *Llywelyn* ab Gruffydd †1282 princes of Wales] **1 :** either of two speedwells (*Veronica officinalis* and *V. chamaedrys*) **2 :** TOADFLAX **3 :** CANCERWORT **4 :** MOUNTAIN PARSLEY

flu·el·lite \ˈflüə,līt, flüˈe,l-\ *n* -s [*fluorine* + *wavellite*] **:** a mineral $AlF_3.H_2O$ consisting of aluminum fluoride in colorless or white crystals

flue·man \ˈflümən, -,man\ *n, pl* **fluemen :** a worker who cleans boiler flues

flu·en·cy \ˈflüənsē, -si\ *n* -ES [LL *fluentia* action of flowing, fr. L *fluent-, fluens* + *-ia* -y] **1** *obs* **:** ABUNDANCE, PROFUSION **2 :** fluent quality **:** smoothness, ease, and readiness esp. of utterance ⟨spoke with great poise and ~⟩; *sometimes* **:** VOLUBILITY ⟨her ~ was like the insistent chatter of a stream⟩

¹flu·ent \ˈflüənt\ *adj* [L *fluent-, fluens*, pres. part. of *fluere* to flow — more at FLUID] **1 :** flowing or capable of flowing esp. with ease or freedom **:** LIQUID, FLUID ⟨a ~ stream⟩ ⟨~ metal in a crucible⟩ **2 :** FREE, EASY, SMOOTH ⟨a ~ technique⟩ ⟨the Moon upon her ~ route defiant of a road —Emily Dickinson⟩: as **a :** versed in the use of language **:** ready with words ⟨a speaker ~ in Japanese⟩; *sometimes* **:** noted for or addicted to the use of profanity ⟨George Washington, who was ~ himself . . . issued . . . orders against swearing in the ranks —Burges Johnson⟩ **b** *of language* **:** easy and flowing **:** pleasingly graceful ⟨~ speech⟩ **c** *of a performance* **:** smooth and finished **:** giving an effect of ease and accurate rendition ⟨a ~ reading of the part⟩ ⟨his versification is ~ —*Brit. Book News*⟩ **syn** see VOCAL

²fluent *n* -s [L *fluentum*, fr. *fluent-, fluens*] *obs* **:** a current of water **:** STREAM

flu·ent·ly *adv* **:** in a fluent manner **:** with fluency

flu·ent·ness *n* -ES **:** the quality or state of being fluent

flue pipe *n* **1 :** a pipe (as of an organ) whose tone is produced by the striking of a current of air upon an edge causing a wave motion in the air within — compare REED PIPE **2 :** a pipe connecting the smoke outlet of a furnace or stove with the flue of a chimney

flues *pl of* FLUE

flue stop *n* **1 :** a pipe-organ stop made up of flue pipes **2** *or* **flue stopper :** a stop for a flue opening

flue surface *n* **:** the aggregate surface area of boiler flues exposed to flame or hot gases

fluework \ˈ≈,≈\ *n* **:** pipe-organ stops in which the sound is caused by wind passing through a flue or fissure and striking an edge above — compare REEDWORK

¹fluff \ˈfləf\ *n* -s [prob. alter. of ⁴*flue*] **1 :** NAP, DOWN, FLUE: as **a :** the soft downy plumage on the abdomen and between the thighs of most birds — see GOOSE illustration **b :** the basal downy part of a feather **2 :** something fluffy **:** a fluffy mass ⟨a ~ of cloud near the horizon⟩: as **a :** a food rendered light and fluffy by incorporating air through beating — used esp. of dishes (as whips or soufflés) of which the texture depends on beaten egg whites **b :** something essentially trivial and lacking importance or solid worth; *esp* **:** a light amusing theatrical offering without real message or significance ⟨his latest is an amusing little ~ well suited to the summer theater⟩ **c** *slang* **:** a young woman — used chiefly in the phrase *bit of fluff* **3 :** an error, fault, or blunder ⟨the senator made a ~ when he called attention to his party's record on this issue⟩: as **a :** a forgetting or bungling of lines (as in a theatrical performance); *sometimes* **:** the missing of a cue **b :** a misplay in a sport or game

²fluff \"\ *vb* -ED/-ING/-S *vi* **1 a :** to become fluffy ⟨the omelet ~*ed* beautifully⟩ **b :** to move lightly like fluff ⟨streaks of cloud ~*ed* in from the water⟩ **2 :** to make a mistake **:** FAIL, BUNGLE: as **a :** to play a theatrical role blunderingly **:** forget one's lines or deliver them badly **b :** to misplay in a sport ⟨he was doing well until he ~*ed* at the seventh hole⟩ ~ *vt* **1 :** to make fluffy ⟨~ out your hair⟩ ⟨~*ing* up the pillows⟩ **2 :** to wheel (a skin) usu. to produce a smoothly napped or uniform surface **3 :** to make a mistake in **:** BUNGLE: as **a :** to play (a theatrical role) blunderingly **:** forget or deliver badly (one's lines) **b :** MISPLAY ⟨~*ed* his stroke and missed the green⟩ **:** BOTCH ⟨the quarterback ~*ed* the play and lost his side control of the ball⟩

³fluff \"\ *n* -S [prob. of imit. origin] *chiefly Scot* **:** a puff or whiff ⟨a ~ of smoke⟩

fluff·er \'fləfə(r)\ *n* -S **:** one that fluffs ⟨a constant pillow ~⟩

fluff-gib \'=,gib\ *n* [³*fluff* + *gib* (cat)] *Scot* **:** a gunpowder squib

fluff·i·ly \'fləfəlē, -li\ *adv* **:** in a fluffy manner

fluff·i·ness \-fēnəs, -fin-\ *n* -ES **:** the quality or state of being fluffy

fluff louse *n* **:** a small broad biting louse (*Goniocotes gallinae*) that lives and feeds on the fluff at the base of the feathers on domestic poultry and some other birds

fluff·ment \-fmənt\ *n* -S [¹*fluff* + *-ment*] **:** something light, loose, or showy ⟨a ~ of talk⟩ ⟨soft ~s of material flowing from the shoulder⟩

fluffy \-fē,-fi\ *adj* -ER/-EST [¹*fluff* + *-y*] **1 :** having, covered with, or resembling fluff or down ⟨a ~ young chick⟩ ⟨~ whiskers⟩: as **a :** light and soft or airy ⟨a ~ omelet⟩ ⟨big ~ cushions⟩ **b** *of soil* **:** loose and friable **c** *of snow* **:** consisting of large loose flakes with little tendency to cohere **d** *of clothing* **:** light and full ⟨a ~ summer dress⟩ **2 :** light in mind or intellectual content **:** lacking in brilliance or decisive quality ⟨a pleasant ~ little woman⟩ ⟨soft, vague, ~, uncertain policies —Geoffrey Crowther⟩ ⟨a ~ comedy⟩

fluffy-ruffle \'==,==\ *adj* **:** having a fluffy ruffled margin ⟨large *fluffy-ruffle* blossoms⟩

flü·gel *or* **flu·gel** \'flügəl\ *n* -S [G *flügel* lit., wing, fr. MHG *vlügel;* fr. the shape; akin to MLG *vlōgel* wing, MD *vlōgel, vleugel;* derivatives fr. the root of E *fly*] **:** the grand piano or its predecessor

flü·gel·horn *or* **flue·gel·horn** *also* **flu·gel·horn** \-,hȯrn\ *n* -S [G *flügelhorn,* fr. *flügel* wing, flank + *horn,* fr. OHG; fr. its use to signal the flanking drivers in a battue — more at HORN] **1 :** a bugle with valves that differs from the cornet only in having a larger bore **2 :** one of the bugle family of brass instruments similar to the saxhorn

flugelman *var of* FUGLEMAN

fluible *adj* [L *fluere* to flow + E *-ible*] *obs* **:** FLUID

¹flu·id \'flüəd\ *adj* [F or L; F *fluide,* fr. L *fluidus,* fr. *fluere* to flow; akin to Gk *phlyein, phlyzein* to boil over, chatter, L *flare* to blow — more at BLOW] **1 :** having particles that easily move and change their relative position without a separation of the mass and that easily yield to pressure **:** capable of flowing **2 a :** likely to change or move **:** not fixed or rigid ⟨a ~ military situation⟩ **b :** characterized by or employing a smooth easy style or producing such an effect esp. in literature or art ⟨a ~ style⟩ ⟨~ restful lines⟩ **c :** free or tending to alter in form or content ⟨~ consciousness⟩ **d :** available for a different use or application **:** not currently pledged or firmly engaged ⟨~ capital⟩; *esp* **:** such as may be rapidly or immediately converted into cash ⟨~ assets⟩ **e :** shifting from place to place **:** MOBILE ⟨the ~ population of large cities⟩ **3 a :** of, relating to, or like a fluid **b :** characteristic of a fluid ⟨the ~ state⟩ **c :** employing, based on, or acting through or like a fluid or the fluid state ⟨~ power⟩ ⟨~ catalytic cracking of oil⟩ — compare FLUIDIZE, FLUID CATALYST **syn** see LIQUID

²fluid \"\ *n* -S **1 :** a substance that alters its shape in response to any force however small, that tends to flow or to conform to the outline of its container, and that includes gases and liquids and in strictly technical use certain plastic solids and mixtures of solids and liquids capable of flow **2 :** a nonsolid substance in the body of an animal or a plant ⟨cerebrospinal ~⟩ ⟨body ~s⟩ **3 :** a hypothetical substance to which a particular phenomenon (as heat or electricity) was formerly attributed

flu·id·al \-dᵊl\ *adj* [²*fluid* + *-al*] **:** relating to or characteristic of a fluid or to flowing motion ⟨~ arrangement of components of metamorphic rock⟩ — **flu·id·al·ly** \-ᵊlē\ *adv*

fluidal texture *n* **:** texture of rock in which the arrangement of the minute crystals shows the lines of flow of the material while molten

fluid catalyst *n* **:** a solid catalyst in a finely divided state that is kept in constant motion in a stream of gas (as in the cracking of petroleum) **:** a fluidized catalyst

fluid coal *or* **fluidized coal** *n* **:** pulverized coal that is mixed with air and that is capable of being forced through pipes

fluid-compressed \'==;=,=\ *adj, of steel* **:** compressed while in a fluid state so as to eliminate all gases and increase structural homogeneity

fluid coupling *also* **fluid flywheel** *n* **:** a coupling (as a fluid drive) in which fluid (as oil) intervenes between moving members to transmit pressure and torque

fluid die *n* **:** one of a set of shaping dies in which a plunger descends upon a liquid previously placed in the shell to be shaped and causes the liquid to force the shell into the design in the dies

fluid dram *or* **fluid drachm** *n* **:** FLUIDRAM

fluid drive *or* **fluid clutch** *n* **:** an automotive power coupling that operates on a hydraulic turbine principle, the flywheel of the engine having a set of turbine blades connected directly to it and driving them in oil thereby turning another set of turbine blades attached to the transmission gears of the automobile

fluid dynamics *n pl but sing or pl in constr* **:** a branch of fluid mechanics that deals with fluid motion (as flow and wave motion)

fluidextract \'==;=,=\ *n* **:** a liquid preparation of a vegetable drug containing alcohol as a solvent or as a preservative or both with the therapeutic constituents of one gram of the standard drug in each milliliter — called also *liquid extract*

flu·id·glycerate \'==+\ *n* **:** a concentrated liquid preparation made by extracting a vegetable drug with a menstruum consisting of one volume of glycerol and three volumes of water to produce a drug strength equivalent to that of a fluidextract

flu·id·ible \'flüədəbəl, (')flü;id-\ *adj* **:** capable of flow under pressure ⟨the ~ state of metamorphic rock⟩

flu·id·ic \(')flü;idik\ *adj* **:** of, relating to, or having the characteristics of a fluid — used esp. by spiritualists

flu·id·i·form \-də,fȯrm\ *adj* [²*fluid* + *-iform*] **:** occurring in the form of or appearing to be a fluid **:** ethereal or intangible **:** FLUIDIC

flu·id·i·fy \flü'idə,fī\ *vb* -ED/-ING/-ES [¹*fluid* + *-ify*] *vt* **:** to make fluid or flowing ⟨rocks that have been *fluidified*⟩ ~ *vi* **:** to become fluid **:** accumulate fluid ⟨ore ~*ing* in the smelter⟩ ⟨the valley *fluidifies* each spring into a shallow lake as snow melts in the mountains⟩

flu·id·i·ty \-dəd·ē, -dətē, -i\ *n* -ES [prob. fr. F *fluidité,* fr. MF, fr. *fluide* fluid + *-ité* -ity — more at FLUID] **1 a :** the quality, state, or degree of being fluid **:** a liquid or gaseous state **b :** the physical property of a substance that enables it to flow and that is a measure of the rate at which it is deformed by a shearing stress as contrasted with viscosity **:** the reciprocal of viscosity **2 :** changeable or unstable quality: as **a :** easy adaptability **:** FLEXIBILITY ⟨showed the ~ of his mind by changing it frequently⟩ **b :** smooth flowing quality (as of language) ⟨the graceful ~ of the rhythm⟩ **c :** tendency to movement of population into or out of an area; *often* **:** the recurrent ebb and flow of population (as between an urban industrial and a suburban residential area)

flu·id·iza·tion \,flüədə'zāshən, -,dī'z-\ *n* -S **:** the process of fluidizing or the state of being fluidized ⟨~ of a catalyst⟩

flu·id·ize \'flüə,dīz\ *vt* -ED/-ING/-S **:** to cause to behave like a fluid; *specif* **:** to suspend (a finely divided solid) in a rapidly moving stream of gas or vapor so as to induce flowing movement of the whole (as in the transport of flour by air blast or in the catalytic cracking of petroleum) — **flu·id·iz·er** \-zə(r)\ *n* -S

flu·id·ly *adv* **:** in a fluid manner **:** with fluidity

fluid mechanics *n pl but sing or pl in constr* **:** a branch of mechanics that deals with the special properties of liquids and gases

fluid motor *n* **:** a motor commonly of the turbine type that is driven by water or compressed air

flu·id·ness *n* -ES **:** the quality or state of being fluid **:** FLUIDITY

fluidounce \'==;=\ *n* **:** either of two units of liquid capacity: **a :** a U.S. unit equivalent to 1/16 pint or 1.804 cubic inches **b :** a British unit equivalent to 1/20 pint or 1.7339 cubic inches — see MEASURE table

flu·idram *or* **flu·idrachm** \,flüə(d)'dram, -raa(ə)m\ *n* [¹*fluid* + *dram* or *drachm*] **:** either of two units of liquid capacity equal to ⅛ fluid ounce: **a :** a U. S. unit equivalent to 0.225 cubic inches **b :** a British unit equal to 0.2167 cubic inches — see MEASURE table

fluid stress *n* **:** stress associated with plastic flow in a solid

fluid transmission *n* **:** automotive transmission that incorporates a fluid drive

flu·i·gram *or* **flu·i·gramme** \'flüə,gram, -raa(ə)m\ *n* [¹*fluid* + *gram* or *gramme*] **:** a cubic centimeter of liquid

flu·ish \'flüish\ *adj* [*flu* + *-ish*] **:** mildly affected with influenza

¹fluke \'flük\ *n* -S [ME *fluke, floke,* fr. OE *flōc;* akin to ON *flōki* flounder, OHG *flah* smooth — more at FLAKE] **1 :** FLATFISH; *esp* **:** SUMMER FLOUNDER **2 :** a flattened, leaf-shaped or lanceolate digenetic trematode worm; *sometimes* **:** TREMATODE — see LIVER FLUKE

²fluke \"\ *n* -S [perh. fr. ¹*fluke;* fr. the flat shape, resembling a flounder] **1 :** the part of an anchor that fastens in the ground; *esp* **:** the broad end of each arm — see ANCHOR illustration **2 :** something shaped like the broad end of the arm of an anchor: as **a :** the barbed head or one of the barbs of a harpoon, whaling lance, arrow, or similar weapon **b :** one of the lobes of a whale's tail **c :** an instrument used to clean a hole in rock preparatory to blasting

³fluke \"\ *vt* -ED/-ING/-S **:** to make (a dead whale) fast by the tail (as for removing and processing blubber)

⁴fluke \"\ *n* -S [origin unknown] **1 :** an accidentally successful stroke at billiards or pool **2 :** an accidental advantage or result of an action **:** an extraordinary stroke of good or bad luck ⟨he won by a ~⟩ ⟨such a fall was a pure ~⟩

⁵fluke \"\ *vb* -ED/-ING/-S *vt* **:** to get, make, do, or succeed in by chance or accident ~ *vi* **:** to succeed or fail by chance

fluked \-kt\ *adj* [¹*fluke* + *-ed*] *of an animal* **:** infested with flukes

¹fluke·less \-kləs\ *adj* [¹*fluke* + *-less*] **:** free from flukes ⟨keep the flock as nearly ~ as possible⟩

²flukeless \"\ *adj* [²*fluke* + *-less*] **:** lacking a fluke

flukeworm \'=,=\ *n* [¹*fluke* + *worm*] **:** ¹FLUKE 2

¹fluky *also* **fluk·ey** \'flükē, -ki\ *adj* **flukier; flukiest** [¹*fluke* + *-y*] **:** infested with flukes ⟨~ meadows⟩ ⟨~ sheep⟩

²fluky \"\ *adj* -ER/-EST [⁴*fluke* + *-y*] **1 :** happening or depending on chance rather than skill **2 :** light and uncertain **:** UNSTEADY, CAPRICIOUS — used esp. of wind

flum \'fləm\ *Scot var of* FLAM

¹flume \'flüm\ *n* -S [prob. fr. obs. E, river, fr. ME *flum,* fr. OF *flum, flun,* fr. L *flumen,* fr. *fluere* to flow — more at FLUID] **1 :** a ravine or gorge with a stream running through **2 a :** an inclined channel for conveying water usu. from a distance for various uses (as power production, transportation, or irrigation) **b :** a channel (as of metal) placed in a stream of water to measure the volume or rate of flow **c :** a channel for admitting water to a water turbine

²flume \"\ *vb* -ED/-ING/-S *vt* **1 :** to divert the water of (a stream) by means of a flume; *also* **:** to divert (water) by means of a flume **2 :** to transport (as fish to a cannery or logs to a mill) by way of a flume ~ *vi* **:** to construct or use a flume ⟨*fluming* along the edge of the slope⟩

flu·mer·in \'flümərən, flü'mər·ən\ *n* -S [*fluorescein* + *mercury* + *-in*] **:** a dark red powder $C_{20}H_{10}O_6Na_2Hg$ with a greenish fluorescence that is the disodium salt of hydroxy-mercuri-fluorescein

flume runner *n* **:** a worker who prevents or releases log jams in a flume by moving logs with a cant hook or peavey — called also *herder*

flum·ma·did·dle *also* **flum·a·did·dle** \,fləmə'didᵊl\ *or* **flum·did·dle** \-m;-\ *or* **flum·mer·did·dle** \-mə(r);-\ *or* **flum·my·did·dle** \-mē;-\ *or* **fum·a·did·dle** \,fəmə;-\ *n* -S [perh. alter. of *flummery*] **1 :** something foolish or worthless **:** NONSENSE, TRASH **2 :** BAUBLE, FRILL

flum·mer \'fləmə(r)\ *vt* -ED/-ING/-S [back-formation fr. *flummery*] *archaic* **:** to get around (a person) esp. by coaxing or flattery **:** BEGUILE, HUMBUG

flum·mery \-m(ə)rē, -ri\ *n* -ES [W *llymru*] **1 a :** a soft jelly or porridge made of flour or meal — compare SOWENS **b :** any of several sweet dishes chiefly for dessert; *esp* **:** a molded cold sweet of cereal with fruit or nuts **2 a :** something poor, trashy, or not worth having **b :** empty compliment or foolish deceptive language **:** HUMBUG; *sometimes* **:** an instance or the use of this ⟨greatly addicted to ~⟩

¹flum·mox *also* **flum·mix** *or* **flum·mux** \'fləməks, -məks\ *vb* -ED/-ING/-ES [origin unknown] *vt* **:** to throw into perplexity **:** embarrass greatly **:** CONFOUND, DISCONCERT ~ *vi* **:** to fail or give up **:** COLLAPSE ⟨his scheme ~*ed* and left him high and dry⟩

²flummox *also* **flummix** *or* **flummux** \"\ *n* -ES **:** FAILURE; *also* **:** a state of confusion, perplexity, or embarrassment

¹flump \'fləmp\ *n* -S [imit.] **:** a dull heavy sound (as of a fall); *also* **:** a movement producing such a sound ⟨dropped into the chair with a ~⟩

²flump \"\ *vb* -ED/-ING/-S *vi* **:** to move or fall suddenly and heavily **:** PLUMP, PLOP ⟨~*ed* down into his chair with a sigh⟩ ~ *vt* **:** to place or drop with a flump ⟨~*ing* his books on the table⟩

flung *past of* FLING

¹flunk \'fləŋk\ *vb* -ED/-ING/-S [perh. blend of *flinch* and *funk*] *vi* **1 :** to fail esp. in a recitation or examination **2 :** to back out (as from an undertaking) through fear ~ *vt* **1 :** to fail or dismiss (a student) for deficiency or incompetence ⟨the professor ~*ed* him out after the midyear examination⟩ **2 :** FAIL ⟨~*ed* history⟩ ⟨expected to ~ his chemistry examination⟩ — **flunk·er** \-kə(r)\ *n* -S

²flunk \"\ *n* -S **:** an instance of a failure; *specif* **:** a failure in a recitation or examination

flun·ky *or* **flun·key** \'fləŋkē, -ki\ *n, pl* **flunkies** *or* **flunkeys** [fr. Sc dial., of unknown origin] **1 a :** a usu. liveried servant; *esp* **:** FOOTMAN — often used derogatorily **b :** any of various minor functionaries: as (1) **:** a ship's steward (2) **:** BULL COOK (3) **:** an engineer's helper in a logging camp (4) **:** an unskilled or general laborer **2 a :** an obsequious or cringing person **:** TOADY **b :** an unimportant or subordinate person

flun·ky·dom \-dəm\ *n* -S **:** FLUNKIES

flun·ky·hood \-,hu̇d\ *n* -S **:** the state of being a flunky

flun·ky·ish \-kēish, -kiish\ *adj* **:** resembling or suitable to a flunky

flun·ky·ism \-kē,izəm, -ki,-\ *n* -S **:** the quality or characteristics of a flunky

fluo- *comb form* [ISV, prob. by shortening] **:** FLUOR- 1 ⟨*fluo*beryllate⟩

fluo·aluminate \'flü(,)ō+\ *n* [*fluo-* + *aluminate*] **:** a complex salt (as cryolite) characterized by the anion AlF_6^{---} containing fluorine and aluminum

fluo·borate \'flüə+\ *n* [*fluo* + *-borate*] **:** a salt or ester of fluoboric acid — called also *borofluoride*

fluo·boric acid \"+...-\ *n* [*fluo-* + *boric*] **:** a poisonous strong acid HBF_4 made in solution by dissolving boron trifluoride in water or by adding boric acid to concentrated hydrofluoric acid and used in solution or in the form of salts chiefly in electroplating baths — called also *borofluoric acid*

fluo·bo·rite \,flüə'bȯr,īt, -bōr-\ *n* -S [*fluoborate* + *-ite*] **:** a mineral $Mg_3(BO_3)(F,OH)_3$ consisting of magnesium fluoborate occurring in hexagonal prisms

fluo·cerite *also* **fluo·cerine** \'flüə+\ *n* -S [*fluocerite* fr. G *fluozerit,* modif. (influenced by *-it* -ite) of F *fluocérine,* fr. *fluo-* + *cérine* cerine; *fluocerine* fr. F *fluocérine*] **:** a mineral (Ce,La,Nd)F_3 consisting of reddish yellow fluoride of cerium and related metals

flu·on·o·mist \flü'änəməst\ *n* -S [³*flue* + *-onomist* (as in *economist*)] *Brit* **:** CHIMNEY SWEEP 1

fluo·phosphate \'flüə+\ *n* [*fluo-* + *phosphate*] **:** FLUOROPHOSPHATE

flu·or \'flü,ȯ(ə)r, 'flü(ə)r\ *n* -S [in sense 1a, fr. L, fr. *fluere* to flow; in other senses, fr. NL, fr. L — more at FLUID] **1** *obs* **:** STREAM, FLOWING **b :** MENSTRUATION **2** *obs* **a :** the fluid state **b :** FLUID **:** a fluid mass **3 a** [trans. of G *fluss*] *obs* **:** a mineral belonging to a group including fluorite and characterized by the alchemists as resembling gems and usable as metallurgical fluxes **b** *chiefly Brit* **:** FLUORITE

fluor- *or* **fluoro-** *comb form* [F *fluor-,* fr. NL *fluor* (mineral belonging to a group including fluorite)] **1 a :** fluorine ⟨*fluor*hydric⟩ ⟨*fluoro*form⟩ **b** *now usu fluoro-* **:** containing fluorine in place of hydrogen — in names of organic compounds ⟨*fluoro*benzene⟩ **c** *now usu fluoro-* **:** containing fluorine regarded as replacing hydroxyl or oxygen or as coordinated to a central atom — in names of inorganic acids and salts ⟨*fluoro*molybdate⟩ **d :** containing fluorine as fluoride sometimes replacing another element or group — in names of minerals and salts ⟨*fluor*apatite⟩ ⟨*fluoro*chloride⟩ **2** *also* **fluori- :** fluorescence ⟨*fluor*ene⟩ ⟨*fluoro*scope⟩ ⟨*fluori*meter⟩

flu·o·ran·thene \,flü(ə)'ran,thēn, flō'-,flȯ'-\ *n* -S [ISV *fluor-* + *anthracene;* orig. formed as G *fluoranthen*] **:** a white crystalline hydrocarbon $C_{15}H_{10}$ obtained esp. from the coal-tar distillates having the highest boiling points and from petroleum; 1,8-*ortho*-phenylene-naphthalene

flu·or·apatite \flü(ə)'r, flō'r, flȯ'r + -\ *n* [G *fluorapatit,* fr. *fluor-* + *apatit* apatite] **:** an apatite containing fluorine: as **a :** apatite in which fluorine predominates over chlorine, hydroxyl, and carbonate **b :** calcium phosphate fluoride $Ca_5F(PO_4)_3$

fluor crown *n* [*fluor-*] **:** a crown glass that contains fluorine, that has a low refractive index, and that is used esp. for optical equipment

flu·o·rene \'flü(ə),rēn, 'flōr,ēn, 'flȯ,rēn\ *n* -S [ISV *fluor-* + *-ene;* orig. formed as F *fluorène*] **:** a colorless crystalline cyclic hydrocarbon $C_{13}H_{10}$ that has a violet fluorescence and that is obtained usu. from the coal-tar distillate which boils between naphthalene and anthracene; *ortho*-diphenylene-methane

flu·o·resce \(')flü(ə);res, (')flōr;es, (')flȯ;res\ *vb* -ED/-ING/-S [back-formation fr. *fluorescence* & *fluorescent*] *vi* **:** to produce, undergo, or exhibit fluorescence ~ *vt* **:** to produce (color) in fluorescing ⟨~s a dark red color under ultraviolet irradiation⟩

flu·o·res·ce·in \,flü(ə)'resēən, flō'-,flȯ'-\ *n* -S [*fluoresce* + *-in*] **:** a yellow granular or red crystalline phthalein dye $C_{20}H_{12}O_5$ giving a brilliant yellow-green fluorescence in alkaline solution and having a number of applications based chiefly on its visibility at high dilution or its ready conversion to eosin and related dyes — see DYE table I (under *Acid Yellow 73*)

fluorescein sodium *n* **:** URANIN

flu·o·res·cence \,flü(ə)'resᵊn(t)s, flō'-, flȯ'-\ *n* -S [*fluor* (fluorite) + *-escence*] **1 :** the emission by a substance of electromagnetic radiation esp. in the form of visible light as the immediate result of and only during the absorption of radiation from some other source; *also* **:** the property of emitting such radiation **2 :** the radiation emitted during fluorescence — compare LUMINESCENCE

fluorescence microscope *n* **:** a microscope equipped to irradiate material under examination with ultraviolet in order to detect or study fluorescent components — called also *ultraviolet microscope*

flu·o·res·cent \(')flü(ə);resᵊnt, (')flōr;e-, (')flȯ;re-\ *adj* [*fluor* (fluorite) + *-escent*] **:** having, characterized by, or showing fluorescence; *also* **:** caused by fluorescence

fluorescent brightener *n* **:** a chemical agent used for its fluorescent brightening effect — see DYE table I

fluorescent lamp *n* **:** a tubular electric lamp that is coated on its inner surface with a phosphor and that contains mercury vapor whose bombardment by electrons from the cathode provides ultraviolet light which causes the phosphor to emit visible light either of a selected color or closely approximating daylight

fluorescent screen *n* **:** a screen (as of cardboard or glass) one face of which is coated with a salt (as calcium tungstate) that emits light under the action of X rays or cathode rays

fluoresci- *comb form* [*fluorescence*] **:** fluorescence ⟨*fluoresci*genic⟩

fluori- — see FLUOR-

flu·o·ri·date \'flu̇rə,dāt, 'flōr-,'flȯr- *usu* -ād.+V\ *vt* -ED/-ING/-S [back-formation fr. *fluoridation*] **:** to add a fluoride to (as drinking water) — compare FLUORIDIZE, FLUORINATE

flu·o·ri·da·tion \,flu̇rə'dāshən, ,flōr-, ,flȯr-\ *n* -S [*fluoride* + *-ation*] **:** the addition of fluorine usu. as a fluoride to something: as **a :** the introduction of fluorine into rocks as indicated by the formation of such minerals as fluorite and topaz **b :** the adding of a fluoride to drinking water ⟨~ of public water supplies for prevention of tooth decay in children⟩

flu·o·ri·da·tion·ist \-sh(ə)nəst\ *n* -S **:** an advocate of the fluoridation of public water supplies

flu·o·ride \'flü(ə),rīd, 'flōr,īd, 'flȯ,rīd, -,rəd\ *n* -S [*fluor-* + *-ide*] **:** a binary compound of fluorine usu. with a more electropositive element or radical **:** a salt or ester of hydrofluoric acid

flu·o·ri·di·za·tion \,flu̇rədə'zāshən, ,flōr-, ,flȯr-, -,dī'z-\ *n* -S **:** the act or process of fluoridizing

flu·o·ri·dize \'==,dīz\ *vt* -ED/-ING/-S [*fluoride* + *-ize*] **:** to treat (as the teeth) with a fluoride — compare FLUORIDATE

fluorimeter *var of* FLUOROMETER

flu·o·ri·nate \'flu̇rə,nāt, 'flōr-,'flȯr-, *usu* -ād.+V\ *vt* -ED/-ING/-S [*fluorine* + *-ate*] **:** to treat or cause to combine with fluorine or any of certain compounds of fluorine **:** introduce fluorine into (as an organic compound) — compare FLUORIDATE

flu·o·ri·na·tion \,==;'nāshən\ *n* -S **:** the act or process of fluorinating

flu·o·rine \'flü(ə),rēn, 'flōr,ēn, 'flȯ,rēn, -rən\ *n* -S [F, fr. NL *fluor* (mineral belonging to a group including fluorite) + F *-ine*] **:** a nonmetallic univalent element belonging to the halogens that is normally a pale yellowish flammable irritating toxic gas, that is one of the most powerful oxidizing agents known, attacking water, most metals, and organic compounds, that occurs naturally only in combination in the form of minerals (as fluorite, cryolite, or fluorapatite) and in small amounts in several other minerals, in mineral waters, and in bones and teeth, that is best isolated by electrolysis of a molten mixture of hydrogen fluoride and potassium fluoride, and that is used chiefly in making fluorine compounds — symbol *F;* see ELEMENT table

fluorine test *n* **:** a determination of the relative age of fossil and subfossil bones that is based on the fact that the fluorine content of bones in contact with earth tends to increase through the ages and that is used chiefly in dating anthropological specimens

flu·o·rite \'flü(ə),rīt, 'flōr,īt, 'flȯ,rīt, *usu* -īd.+V\ *n* -S [It, fr. NL *fluor* + It *-ite*] **:** a transparent or translucent mineral of many different colors consisting of calcium fluoride, occurring commonly in crystalline cubes with perfect octahedral cleavage or in massive form, and being used as a flux, as a source of fluorine compounds, and in preparation of opalescent and opaque glasses and of vitreous enamels

fluorite green *n* **:** a moderate yellowish green that is greener, lighter, and stronger than tarragon, yellower, lighter, and slightly stronger than green, and yellower, stronger, and slightly lighter than verdigris

fluorite violet *n* **:** a dark to very dark purple

flu·o·ro \'flü(ə)(,)rō, 'flōr(,)ō, 'flȯ(ə)(,)rō\ *adj* [*fluor-*] **:** containing fluorine — used esp. of organic compounds; compare FLUOR- 1

fluoro- — see FLUOR-

flu·o·ro·acetate \'flü(ə)(,)rō, ;flōr(,)ō, ;flȯ(,)rō +\ *n* [*fluor-* + *acetate*] **:** a salt or ester of fluoroacetic acid; *esp* **:** SODIUM FLUORACETATE

flu·o·ro·acetic acid \"+...-\ *n* [*fluor-* + *acetic*] **:** a poisonous crystalline acid FCH_2COOH obtained from the gifblaar of southern Africa or made from chloroacetic acid

flu·o·ro·carbon \"+\ *n* [ISV *fluor-* + *carbon*] **:** any of a class of chemically inert compounds (as tetrafluoroethylene) composed entirely of carbon and fluorine and used chiefly as lubricants and in making resins and plastics **:** a perfluorinated hydrocarbon

flu·o·ro·chemical \"+\ *n* [*fluor-* + *chemical*] **:** any of various chemical compounds containing fluorine; *esp* **:** an organic compound (as a fluorocarbon) in which fluorine has replaced a large proportion of the hydrogen attached to carbon

flu·o·ro·chrome \'=(=)(,)=+,-\ *n* [ISV *fluor-* + *chrome*] **:** any of various fluorescent substances (as the alkaloid berberine or the dye auramine) used in biological staining to produce secondary fluorescence in the specimen

flu·o·ro·form \"+,-\ *n* [ISV *fluor-* + *-form* (as in *chloroform*)] **:** a colorless gas CHF_3 similar to chloroform; trifluoro-methane

flu·o·rog·ra·phy \flu̇(ə)'rägrəfē, flō'-,flȯ'-\ *n* -ES [*fluor-* + *-graphy*] **1 :** the art or process of etching on glass with hydrofluoric acid **2 a :** PHOTOFLUOROGRAPHY **b :** the photography of a fluorescing body

flu·o·roid \'flu̇(ə),rȯid, 'flōr,ȯid, 'flȯ,rȯid\ *n* -S [ISV *fluor-* + *-oid*] **:** TETRAHEXAHEDRON

Flu·o·rol \'flu̇(ə),rȯl, flōr,ȯl, 'flȯ,rȯl, -rōl\ *trademark* — used for a fluorescent brightener; see DYE table I (under *Fluorescent Brightener 74*)

flu·o·rom·e·ter \flu̇(ə)'rämәd·ə(r), flō'-,flȯ'-\ *or* **flu·o·rim·e·ter** \-rim-\ *n* [*fluor-* + *-meter*] **:** an instrument that measures fluorescence and is used esp. to determine intensities of radiations (as X rays) from the fluorescence they produce or concentrations of substances (as uranium or vitamins of the B complex) capable of forming fluorescent compounds — **flu·o·ro·met·ric** \¦flu̇(ə)rə¦me·trik, ¦flōr-, ¦flȯr-\ *adj* — **flu·o·ro·met·ri·cal·ly** \-trәk(ə)lē\ *adv* — **flu·o·rom·e·try** \flu̇(ə)'rämə·trē, flō'-,flȯ'-\ *n* -ES

flu·o·ro·phosphate \¦flu̇(ə)(,)rō, ¦flōr(,)ō, ¦flȯ(,)rō+\ *n* [ISV *fluor-* + *phosphate*] **:** a salt or ester of a fluorophosphoric acid (as mono-fluorophosphoric acid)

flu·o·ro·phosphoric acid \"+...-\ *n* [*fluor-* + *phosphoric*] **:** any of three acids made by reaction of phosphorus pentoxide with hydrogen fluoride; *esp* **:** the mono-fluoro acid H_2PO_3F obtained as a colorless viscous liquid and as salts and esters some of which are nerve gases

flu·o·ro·photometer \"+\ *n* [*fluor-* + *photometer*] **:** FLUOROMETER — **flu·o·ro·photometric** \"+\ *adj* — **flu·o·ro·photometry** \"+\ *n*

flu·o·ro·radiography \"+\ *n* [*fluor-* + *radiography*] **:** PHOTOFLUOROGRAPHY

flu·o·ro·roentgenography \"+\ *n* [*fluor-* + *roentgenography*] **:** PHOTOFLUOROGRAPHY

¹flu·o·ro·scope \'flu̇rə,skōp, 'flōr-,'flȯr-\ *n* [ISV *fluor-* + *-scope*] **:** an instrument used chiefly in industry and in medical diagnosis for observing the internal structure of opaque objects (as metals or the living body) by means of the shadow cast by the object examined upon a fluorescent screen when placed between the screen and a source of X rays — **flu·o·ro·scop·ic** \¦=+=¦skäpik, -pēk\ *adj* — **flu·o·ro·scop·i·cal·ly** \-pək(ə)lē, -pēk-, -li\ *adv*

²fluoroscope \"\ *vt* -ED/-ING/-S **:** to examine by fluoroscopy

flu·o·ros·co·pist \flu̇(ə)'räskəpə̇st, flō'-,flȯ'-\ *n* -S **:** one who specializes in the use of the fluoroscope

flu·o·ros·co·py \-pē,-pi\ *n* -ES [ISV *fluor-* + *-scopy*] **:** observation or examination by means of a fluoroscope

flu·o·ro·sis \flu̇(ə)'rōsə̇s, flō'-,flȯ'-\ *n* -ES [NL, fr. *fluor-* + *-osis*] **:** an abnormal or poisoned condition (as mottled enamel on human teeth or a condition resembling osteopetrosis in Indian cattle) caused by fluorine or its compounds — **flu·o·rot·ic** \(')flu̇(ə)¦räd·ik, (')flōr¦ä-, (')flȯ¦rä-\ *adj*

flu·o·ro·thene \'flu̇rə,thēn, 'flōr-,'flȯr-\ *n* -S [*fluor-* + *-thene* (fr. *ethylene*)] **:** any of various chemically inert insoluble plastics and resins made by polymerizing a derivative CF_2:CFCl of ethylene containing three atoms of fluorine and one of chlorine

fluor·spar \'flu̇(ə)r,=, 'flōr,-, 'flȯr,-, -u̇ə,-, -ōə,-, -ȯ(ə),-\ *n* [*fluor-* + *spar*] **:** FLUORITE

fluo·silicate \¦flüə+\ *n* [ISV *fluo-* + *silicate*] **:** a salt of fluosilicic acid — called also *silicofluoride*

fluo·silicic acid \"+ . . . -\ *n* [ISV *fluo-* + *silicic*] **:** an unstable corrosive poisonous acid H_2SiF_6 that is known chiefly in aqueous solution and in the form of its salts, that is made usu. by the reaction of silicon tetrafluoride with water (as in the manufacture of superphosphate), and that is used esp. as a hardening and waterproofing agent for building materials and ceramic products, as a disinfectant, and in some electrochemical processes — called also *hydrofluosilicic acid*

fluo·sulfonic acid \"+ . . . -\ *n* [ISV *fluo-* + *sulfonic*] **:** a fuming corrosive liquid acid FSO_3H that has an irritating odor, that is made by treating hydrogen fluoride with sulfur trioxide, and that is used chiefly as a catalyst in alkylation and polymerization reactions and as a reagent in organic synthesis

flure \'flu̇(ə)r, -u̇ə\ *dial var of* FLOOR

¹flurr \'flər(·)\ *vb* -ED/-ING/-S [prob. of imit. origin] *vt* **:** to throw scatteringly ~ *vi* **1 :** to fly or dash up **2** *of a bird* **:** to rise or pass with a whirring of wings

²flurr \"\ *n* -S **:** a splashing or whirring sound

flurried *adj* **:** disturbed by conflicting claims for attention **:** excited, confused, or embarrassed by a press of activities ⟨the ~ cook tried to hasten dinner⟩; *broadly* **:** agitated or disordered ⟨spoke in a ~ voice⟩ — **flur·ried·ly** \-ədlē, -ēd-, -li\ *adv*

flur·ri·ment \'flərēmənt\ *n* -S **:** a flurried state

¹flur·ry \'flər·ē, 'flə·rē, ¦i\ *n* -ES [prob. fr. ¹*flurr* + *-y*] **1 a :** a sudden and brief commotion of the air ⟨a ~ of wind⟩ **b :** a sudden shower or snowfall with a gust of wind **2 :** spasmodic agitation **:** nervous commotion **:** FLUTTER ⟨the racket and ~ of London life —*Blackwood's*⟩ **3 :** a sudden short-lived advance or decline in prices or outburst of trading activity on the stock exchange **4 :** the violent spasms of a whale dying after being harpooned **syn** see STIR

²flurry \"\ *vb* -ED/-ING/-ES *vt* **:** to cause to become agitated and confused **:** EXCITE ~ *vi* **:** to become flurried ⟨her heart *flurried* round within her breast—John Galsworthy⟩; *usu* **:** to move or function in a flurry ⟨*flurried* about her tasks⟩ **syn** see DISCOMPOSE

flus *pl of* FLU

¹flush \'fləsh\ *vb* -ED/-ING/-ES [ME *flusshen*, perh. of imit. origin] *vi* **1 a** *of a bird* **:** to take to wing suddenly **:** fly up (as from a place of concealment) **b** *obs, of persons* **:** to rush abroad or swarm together like a flock of birds **2 :** to cause a bird to flush ~ *vt* **1 :** to cause (a bird) to flush **:** put up (as a game bird)

²flush \"\ *n* -ES **1 :** a flight of flushed birds **2 :** the act of flushing birds

³flush \"\ *n* -ES [ME *floshe* — more at FLODGE] *dial Brit* **:** a low swampy place **:** a pool of standing water (as in a road)

⁴flush \"\ *n* -ES [perh. alter. (influenced by ¹*flush*) of ¹*flux*] **1 a :** a sudden flow (as of water) **:** a rush of liquid that fills or overflows whether naturally occurring or produced for a particular purpose ⟨the dam burst and sent a great ~ of water scouring down the valley⟩ ⟨a ~ of blood brightened her cheeks⟩ **b :** a cleansing or rinsing with or as if with water ⟨give the pot a ~ with boiling water before making the tea⟩ **2 :** a sudden increase or expansion: as **a :** a sudden and usu. abundant growth of vegetation ⟨the spring ~ of grass⟩ or of a particular plant part ⟨a second ~ of bloom⟩; *sometimes* **:** a tender young shoot (as of a tea plant) **b :** a sharp increase in milk production (as when cattle are first put out on good pasture) **c :** a sudden flood or rush of emotion ⟨a quick ~ of anger⟩ **:** THRILL **3 a :** a tinge of red or ruddy light or color (as produced on the cheeks by a sudden rush of blood) ⟨the healthy ~ of the child's face⟩ ⟨the ~ brightening a perfectly ripe peach⟩ **b :** a glowing, vigorous, or fresh state or quality ⟨a ~ of youthful ardor⟩ ⟨the first ~ of success⟩ **4 :** a transitory attack or sensation of extreme heat (as in response to certain drugs or in certain physiological states) ⟨harassed by the ~*es* natural to a woman of her age⟩ **5 :** a feed (as molasses or milk) used to stimulate the intestinal motility of domestic animals (as poultry)

⁵flush \"\ *vb* -ED/-ING/-ES *vi* **1 :** to flow and spread suddenly and freely **:** RUSH ⟨the tide ~*ed* through the narrow inlet⟩ ⟨as the blood ~*es* back to the extremities⟩ **2 a :** to glow suddenly, brightly, or with rich or ruddy color ⟨dawn was already ~*ing* beyond the line of hills⟩ ⟨the aurora ~*ed* far into the sky⟩ **b :** to become suddenly suffused (as with color); *esp* **:** BLUSH ⟨~*ed* hotly and denied everything⟩ **3** *of plants* **:** to start into growth **:** throw out shoots **4 :** to operate a placer mine where the continuous supply of water is insufficient by holding back water and releasing it periodically in a flood — compare BOOMING **5** *of sheep* **:** to come into breeding condition ~ *vt* **1 a :** to cause (as water) to flow ⟨~*ed* the water away⟩ **b :** to pour or cause water or other liquid to pour over or through (as a surface or a channel) ⟨~*ing* the meadow in the early fall⟩ ⟨~ the teapot with boiling water⟩; *usu* **:** to cleanse or wash out by means of a rush of liquid ⟨~ the stable floor with a hose⟩ ⟨~ the toilet⟩ **2 :** to fill with or inflame by **:** EXCITE, ANIMATE — now usu. used passively ⟨~*ed* with pride at his son's success⟩ ⟨~*ed* by a few minor successes⟩ **3 :** to make suddenly or temporarily red, rosy, or glowing as if suffused with blood or flooded with color **:** cause to blush ⟨the story ~*ed* her cheeks with shame⟩ **4 :** to prepare (sheep) for breeding by improving the ration for a time before turning the rams and ewes together **5 :** to transfer (pigment) directly from a water slurry to a dispersion in an oil or resinous base

⁶flush \"\ *adj* -ER/-EST **1 a :** filled to overflowing ⟨streams ~ with the spring runoff⟩ **b :** fully or generously supplied usu. with money **:** AFFLUENT ⟨particularly ~ this week⟩ **2 a** *archaic* **:** full of life and vigor **:** LUSTY, SPIRITED; *sometimes* **:** self-confident and assured **b :** of a ruddy or healthy color **:** FLUSHED **3 a** *of money or credit* **:** readily available **:** ABUNDANT ⟨money is so ~ just now that the poorest trash is bid up to ridiculous levels at the auctions⟩ **b :** prodigal or lavish esp. in expenditure ⟨so ~ you might buy your sister a trinket⟩ **4 a :** having or forming a continuous plane or unbroken surface ⟨~ paneling under the windows⟩ ⟨the river is ~ with its banks⟩; *also, of a boat* **:** having a flush deck **b :** directly abutting on or immediately adjacent to ⟨the windows of the overhang were ~ with the street⟩: as (1) *of printed matter* **:** set even with an edge or esp. with the left edge of a type page or column **:** having no indention (2) *of a cut* **:** trimmed to bleed the printing surface (3) *of a book cover* **:** trimmed even with the leaves (4) **:** arranged edge to edge so as to fit snugly ⟨be sure that the door is ~ with the casing⟩ ⟨~ wallpaper⟩ **5** *of a blow* **:** precisely delivered **:** ACCURATE, DIRECT ⟨floored his opponent with ~ shots to the chin⟩ **syn** see LEVEL

⁷flush \"\ *adv* [⁶*flush*] **:** without interruption: as **a :** STRAIGHT, SQUARELY ⟨caught his opponent ~ on the chin⟩ ⟨went ~ from school into politics⟩ ⟨the door came ~ with the threshold⟩ **b :** with a flush edge, cover, margin, or joining ⟨a line set ~⟩ ⟨books cut ~⟩ ⟨the timber butted ~ with the masonry⟩

⁸flush \"\ *vb* -ED/-ING/-ES [⁶*flush*] *vt* **:** to make, set, or trim flush ⟨~ all exposed joints in the wall⟩ ⟨often desirable to ~ a mounted stereotype⟩ ⟨~ all headings on the next three pages⟩ ~ *vi* **:** FLOAT 6

⁹flush \"\ *n* -ES [MF *flus*, *fluz*, fr. L *fluxus* flow — more at FLUX] **1 :** a hand of playing cards all of the same suit: as **a :** a poker hand with all five cards of the same suit but not in sequence — see STRAIGHT FLUSH; POKER illustration **b :** the five highest cards of the trump suit in pinochle scoring 150 points when melded **2** *or* **flush gate :** a series of three or more slalom gates set vertically on a slope

¹⁰flush \"\ *adj* [prob. alter. of ¹*fledge*] *archaic* **:** FLEDGED

¹¹flush \"\ *vi* -ED/-ING/-ES [perh. irreg. of ²*frush*] **1** *of a stone in a wall* **:** to break away at the edges through excess loading **2** *of mortar* **:** to become forced out to or from the joints through pressure

flushboard \'=,=\ *n* [⁴*flush* + *board*] **:** FLASHBOARD

flush box *n* [⁵*flush*] **:** FLUSH TANK

flush coat *n* [⁵*flush*] **:** a final coat of bituminous material spread, flushed, or sprayed on a surface to make a waterproof pavement

flush color *or* **flushed color** *n* [⁵*flush*] **:** a pigment dispersed in oil or varnish (as for use in printing ink) — compare DRY COLOR, PULP COLOR

flush deck *n* [⁶*flush*] **:** a deck on a boat continuous from bow to stern and usu. with no structure above

flush–decker \'=;=,=\ *n* -S **:** a boat with flush deck

flush door *n* [⁶*flush*] **:** a door with a flush surface that is not divided into panels and moldings — compare PANEL DOOR

flushed *past of* FLUSH

flush·er \'fləshə(r)\ *n* -S [⁵*flush* + *-er*] **:** one that flushes something; *usu* **:** a tank mounted on a vehicle and equipped with a battery of nozzles used for laying the dust on or flushing dirt from streets and roadways with a spray of water

flushes *pres 3d sing of* FLUSH, *pl of* FLUSH

flushgate \'=,=\ *n* [⁵*flush* + *gate*] **:** a gate or sluice used for flushing a channel below the gate in a dam or reservoir

flush gate *n* [⁹*flush*] **:** ⁹FLUSH 2

flush–head rivet *n* [⁶*flush*] **:** a rivet with a countersunk head

flush hydrant *n* [⁵*flush*] **:** CHUCK HYDRANT

¹flushing *adj* [fr. pres. part. of ⁵*flush*] **1 :** serving to flush ⟨a ~ mechanism⟩ **:** used in or concerned with flushing **2 :** of, relating to, or characterized by flushing; *often* **:** BLUSHING — **flush·ing·ly** *adv*

²flushing *n* -S [fr. gerund of ⁵*flush*] **:** transient reddening of the skin; *sometimes* **:** HOT FLASH

flushing bar *also* **flushing rod** *n* [fr. pres. part. of ¹*flush*] **:** a device attached in front of a mowing machine to flush ground-nesting game birds ahead of the cutter bar

flush joint *n* [⁶*flush*] **:** a joint in masonry in which the mortar is finished flush at the surface — see JOINT illustration

flush·ness *n* -ES [⁶*flush* + *-ness*] **:** the quality or state of being flush; *esp* **:** possession of abundant funds

flush·om·e·ter \,flə'shämәd·ə(r)\ *n* [fr. *Flushometer*, a trademark] **:** a valve for flushing toilets or urinals by operation of a handle that discharges a definite quantity of water under pressure directly into the fixture — called also *flush valve*

flush out *vt* [¹*flush*] **:** to bring to light **:** make public or available ⟨hoping to *flush out* some millions of hoarded dollars⟩ ⟨succeeded in *flushing out* many additional tax evaders⟩

flush plate *n* [⁶*flush*] **:** a small rectangular plate of metal or plastic that is used to cover a flush electrical switch or receptacle

flush plating *n* [⁶*flush*] **:** outside plating in steel ships joined edge to edge by edge strips and butt straps inside the plating or by welding

flush production *n* [⁴*flush*] **:** the yield of oil from a spontaneously flowing well

flush rim *or* **flushing rim** *n* [¹*flush*] **:** the rim of a water-closet bowl having a channel or perforated tube by which the bowl is flushed simultaneously from all sides

flush ring *n* [⁶*flush*] **:** a pull ring that when not in use drops flush into an opening in its supporting surface

flush switch *n* [⁶*flush*] **:** an electrical switch mounted with only its face exposed and with its sides surrounded by a box or case that is not a part of the switch

flush tank *n* [⁵*flush*] **1 :** a tank holding a supply of water or sewage for periodically flushing out a sewer **2 :** a small tank equipped with a float and ball valve for flushing a water closet

flush toilet *n* [⁵*flush*] **:** WATER CLOSET

flush valve *n* [⁵*flush*] **1 :** FLUSHOMETER **2 :** a ball valve in a water-closet flush tank

flushy \'fləshē\ *adj* -ER/-EST [⁴*flush* + *-y*] **:** somewhat flushed **:** REDDISH

¹flus·ker \'fləskə(r)\ *vi* -ED/-ING/-S [freq. of E dial. *flusk* to ruffle the feathers] **:** FLUTTER

²flusker \"\ *vt* -ED/-ING/-S [by alter.] *dial* **:** FLUSTER

¹flus·ter \'fləstə(r)\ *vb* **flustered**; **flustered**; **flustering** \-t(ə)riŋ\ **flusters** [ME *flostren*, prob. of Scand origin; akin to Icel *flaustur* hurry, *flaustra* to deal superficially (with); prob. akin to ON *flaustr* ship, *fljōta* to flow — more at FLEET] *vt* **1 :** to heat or inflame with or as if with drinking **:** make tipsy **:** BEFUDDLE **2 :** to put into a state of disorder or confusion **:** CONFUSE, MUDDLE **3 :** to utter in a confused or incoherent manner ~ *vi* **:** to move or behave in an agitated, confused, or excited manner ⟨~*ed* down the aisle to her seat⟩ **syn** see DISCOMPOSE

²fluster \"\ *n* -S **1** *obs* **:** a state of excitement or glow (as from intoxication) **2 :** agitation mingled with confusion **:** TO-DO ⟨took it all pretty coolly: no ~, no flood of tears or questions —C.D.Lewis⟩

flus·ter·er \-tərə(r)\ *n* -S **:** AMERICAN COOT

flus·tra \'fləstrə, 'flüs-\ *n, cap* [NL] **:** a genus (the type of a widely distributed family Flustridae) of marine bryozoans (class Gymnolaemata) that form broad flattened branching colonies — see SEA MAT

flus·trat·ed \'flə,strād·əd\ *or* **flus·ter·at·ed** \'fləstə,r-\ *adj* [¹*fluster* + *-ated* (as in *frustrated*)] **:** FLUSTERED

flus·tra·tion \,flə'strāshən\ *also* **flus·ter·a·tion** \,fləstə'r-\ *n* -S [¹*fluster* + *-ation* (as in *frustration*)] **:** the quality or state of being flustered

¹flute \'flüt, *usu* -üd.+V\ *n* -S [ME *floute*, fr. MF *flaute*, *flahute*, *fleute*, fr. OProv *flaut*, perh. alter. (influenced by *laut* lute) of *flaujol*, *flauja*, fr. (assumed) VL *flabeolum* — more at LUTE, FLAGEOLET] **1 :** a wind instrument stopped at one end with a vibrating air column used as a means of tone production: **a :** RECORDER **b :** an orchestral instrument consisting of a hollow cylinder with finger holes along its length, with a lateral hole for blowing into, and with a compass of three octaves up from middle C — called also *transverse flute* **2 :** FLUTIST; *usu* **:** a flute player in a band or orchestra **3 :** any of various flute-shaped things: as **a :** a long French breakfast roll **b** *or* **flute glass :** a tall slender wineglass **c :** a long shuttle used in weaving tapestry **d :** a grooved or ridged pleat used esp. in ruffles, edgings, or hat brims **e :** a groove (as in a reamer, twist drill, or tap) parallel or nearly parallel to the axis of a cylindrical piece **4 :** a groove of curved section: as **a :** any of a series of vertical grooves used to decorate columns and pilasters in classical architecture **b :** any of various similar ornamental grooves (as on furniture or silverware) **c :** one of the parallel grooves in corrugated board or glass (as in the lens of a headlight) **d** (1) **:** a natural groove or channel on a rock surface (as in a cave) (2) **: flutes** *pl* **:** scalloped or rippled rock surfaces — called also *fluting* **5 :** a molder's tool for forming grooves **6** *or* **flute stop :** a flue pipe-organ stop of flute quality and of 8-foot or 4-foot pitch

flute 1b

²flute \"\ *vb* -ED/-ING/-S [ME *flouten*, fr. MF *flauter*, fr. *flaute*] *vi* **:** to play on or as if on a flute **:** make a sound like that of a flute ~ *vt* **1 :** to play, whistle, or sing with a clear soft note like that of a flute **2 :** to form flutes in (as the shaft of a column or the crust of a pie)

³flute \"\ *n* -S [D *fluit*, lit., flute, fr. MD *flūte*, *fleute*, *floite*, fr. OF *flaute*, *flahute*, *fleute* — more at ¹FLUTE] **1 :** a flyboat usu. with a narrow cabin not projecting beyond the rudder-head **2 :** a former partially armed naval transport

flûte à bec \¦flüd·|ə¦bek, |(,)ä¦b-\ *n, pl* **flûtes à bec** \", -üts|\ [F, lit., flute with a beak] **:** FIPPLE FLUTE, RECORDER 3a

flute budding *n* **:** patch budding in which the stock is nearly girdled

flute co·nique \¦flütkō¦nēk, -kä¦-\ *n, pl* **flutes coniques** \-t(s)k-\ [F *flûte conique*, lit., conical flute] **:** a tapered pipe-organ flute stop yielding a tone similar to the Spitzflöte of 16-, 8-, 4-, and 2-foot pitches

fluted *adj* **1 :** formed or decorated with or as if with flutes **:** CHANNELED, GROOVED — see LEG illustration **2** *of a sound* **:** high, thin, and clear as if produced by a flute

flûte d'a·mour \¦flütdə¦mu̇(ə)r\ *n, pl* **flûtes d'amour** \-t(s)d-\ [F, lit., flute of love] **1 :** a flute ranging a minor third lower than the modern instrument **2 :** a labial pipe-organ stop usu. of 4-foot pitch and of delicate quality

flute–douce \(')flüt¦düs\ *n* -S [F *flûte douce*, lit., sweet flute] **1 :** RECORDER **2 :** a pipe-organ stop having a tone similar to that of a recorder

fluted scale *n* **:** COTTONY-CUSHION SCALE

flute glass *n* **:** ¹FLUTE 3b

flûte har·mo·nique \¦flüt,härmə¦nēk\ *n, pl* **flûtes harmoniques** \-t(s),h-\ [F, lit., harmonic flute] **:** an open flute organ pipe blown to yield the first harmonic instead of the fundamental

flutelike \'=,=\ *adj* **:** resembling a flute esp. in light clear sharp tone quality

flutemouth \'=,=\ *n* **:** CORNETFISH

flûte oc·ta·vi·ante \¦flüd·,äk,tavē¦änt, -tāv-\ *n, pl* **flûtes octaviantes** \", -üt,sä-\ [F, lit., octave flute] **:** FLÛTE HARMONIQUE

flûte ou·verte \-d·ü¦ve(ə)rt\ *n, pl* **flûtes ouvertes** \", -üts-\ [F, lit., open flute] **:** an open flute organ pipe of various pitches

flut·er \'flüd·ə(r), -ütə-\ *n* -S [ME *flauter*, *flautour*, fr. OF *flouteor*, fr. *flouter* to play the flute + *-eor* -or — more at FLUTE] **1** *archaic* **:** FLUTIST **2** [²*flute* + *-er*] **a :** a worker who flutes (as furniture parts or curtain ruffles) by hand or by machine **b :** a tool or implement for making flutings

flute stop *n* **:** ¹FLUTE 6

flûte tri·an·gu·laire \¦flüt,trī,angyə¦la(a)(ə)r\ *n, pl* **flûtes triangulaires** \-üt(s),t-\ [F, lit., triangular flute] **:** a 3-sided wooden flute organ pipe used to produce orchestral flute tone quality

flutey *var of* FLUTY

flutier *comparative of* FLUTY

flutiest *superlative of* FLUTY

fluting *n* -S [fr. gerund of ²*flute*] **1 a :** a flute or series of flutes esp. as ornamentation **:** a finish of flutes ⟨a narrow band of ~ sets off the margin of the table leaves⟩ ⟨decked with ~*s* and pipings⟩ **b :** fluted material ⟨need two yards of net ~ to finish the neck and cuffs⟩ **2 :** kinking or breaking of metal strip when bent on a small radius **3 :** ¹FLUTE 4d(2)

flut·ist \'flüd·ə̇st, -ütə̇-\ *n* -S [¹*flute* + *-ist*] **:** a flute player

flut·o·phone \'flüd·ə,fōn, -ütə-\ *n* [¹*flute* + *-o-* + *-phone*] **:** a simple wind instrument resembling a tonette but with the lower end flared like a clarinet

¹flut·ter \'fləd·ə(r), -ətə-\ *vb* -ED/-ING/-S [ME *floteren* to float, flutter, fr. OE *floterian* to be tossed by the waves, float to and fro, freq. of *flotian* to float — more at FLOAT] *vi* **1 :** to move or flap the wings rapidly without flying or with short flights ⟨butterflies ~*ing* among the flowers⟩ **2 :** to move with quick vibrations or undulations ⟨a sail ~*s* in the wind⟩ ⟨a ~*ing* fan⟩ ⟨his pulse ~*s*⟩ **3 a :** to move about agitatedly, irregularly, or with great bustle and show without much result **:** FLIT ⟨she ~*ed* through her chores, pausing often to chat⟩ **b :** to be in a state of trembling agitation (as from fear, hope, or anticipation) **:** QUAKE, QUIVER ⟨~*ed* at the sight of her escort⟩ ~ *vt* **1 :** to move or vibrate rapidly and often irregularly ⟨the young bird ~*ed* its wings but could not get off the ground⟩ **2 :** to throw into confusion or agitation ⟨a man to ~ girlish hearts⟩ **3 :** to utter with agitation or confusion ⟨~*ed* a few words of congratulation⟩

²flutter \"\ *n* -S **1 :** an act of fluttering **:** quick and irregular motion **:** FLICKERING, VIBRATION ⟨a ~ of flame⟩ ⟨the ~ of a fan⟩ **2 :** nervous or aimless activity or state **:** AGITATION, CONFUSION, DISORDER ⟨was in a ~ until he got home⟩: as **a :** a brief run or burst of speed **b :** a sudden but usu. slight stir (as of excitement or activity in the stock market) **:** FLURRY ⟨a ~ of buying of better-class bonds⟩ ⟨a ~ of indignation followed his remarks⟩ **c** *chiefly Brit* **:** a small speculative venture or gamble ⟨took a ~ on the ponies⟩ ⟨had a little ~ in grain futures that did well⟩ **d :** an abnormal state characterized by rapid spasmodic and usu. rhythmic motion of a body part ⟨diaphragmatic ~⟩ ⟨affected with a serious ventricular ~⟩ **3 a** *obs* **:** STIR, OSTENTATION, DISPLAY **b :** delicate fluffy daintiness (as of manner or dress) ⟨all femininity and ~⟩ **4 a :** a distortion in reproduced sound similar to wow in origin but of higher pitch **b :** fluctuation in the brightness of a television receiver image **5** *or* **flutter kick :** an alternating whipping motion of the legs used in swimming (as in the crawl and backstroke) **6 :** an oscillation of definite period but unstable character set up in a part (as an aileron) of an aircraft at a definite critical speed and maintained by a combination of aerodynamic, inertial, and elastic forces; *also* **:** such an oscillation occurring in other structures (as a bridge) **7 :** a group or collection of fluttering things ⟨a ~ of pretty girls⟩

flut·ter·a·tion \,fləd·ə'rāshən\ *n* -S [¹*flutter* + *-ation*] **:** a state of confusion or disorderly movement; *sometimes* **:** sound resulting from a flutteration ⟨heard the ~ of the mob⟩

flutterboard \'=,=,=\ *n* **:** a small rectangular board rounded at one end, made of cork, plastic, or wood, and used chiefly by swimmers to support the head and upper trunk when learning or practicing leg strokes

flutter echo *n* **:** a rapid series of echoes (as in broadcast and recording studios) originating in reflection between two parallel surfaces

flut·ter·er \'fləd·ərə(r), -lətə-\ *n* -S **:** one that flutters

flut·ter·ing·ly *adv* **:** with a flutter **:** in the manner of one that flutters

flutter kick *n* **:** [2]FLUTTER 5

flut·ter·ment \-d·ə(r)mənt\ *n* -S **:** fluttered or disturbed state ⟨gets into such a ~ when dinner is late⟩

fluttermill \ˈ⸗⸗,⸗\ *n, South & Midland* **:** a toy waterwheel

fluttermouse \ˈ⸗⸗,⸗\ *n* [alter. of *flittermouse*] **:** [3]BAT 1

flut·ter·some \-ə(r)səm\ *adj* [[1]*flutter* + *-some*] **:** FLUTTERY

flutter–tonguing \ˈ⸗⸗,⸗⸗\ *n* **:** a vibratory action of the tongue produced by rolling or trilling an *r* while playing on a wind instrument (as a trumpet)

flutter valve *n* **:** a valve (as in an engine carburetor) actuated by fluctuations of pressure in the fluid surrounding it rather than by any external control

flutter wheel *n* **:** a waterwheel of moderate diameter having radial floats and placed at the bottom of a chute so as to work by impact

flut·tery \ˈflədərē, -ətə-, -ri\ *adj* **:** given to or characterized by fluttering ⟨a light full ~ skirt⟩ ⟨~ mannerisms⟩

fluty *or* **flut·ey** \ˈflüdē\ *adj* **flutier**; **flutiest :** having a tone like that of a flute **:** resembling a flute esp. in sound

fluvi- *or* **fluvio-** *comb form* [L *fluvi-*, fr. *fluvius* — more at FLUVIAL] **1 :** river, stream ⟨*fluvi*coline⟩ ⟨*fluvio*logy⟩ **2 :** fluvial and ⟨*fluvio*volcanic⟩

flu·vi·al \ˈflüvēəl, -vyəl\ *adj* [L *fluvialis*, fr. *fluvius* river (fr. *fluere* to flow) + *-alis* -al — more at FLUID] **1 a :** of or relating to rivers ⟨~ law⟩ **b :** conforming to the changing course of a stream ⟨a ~ boundary⟩ **2 :** growing or living in streams ⟨~ vegetation⟩ **3 :** produced by river action ⟨a ~ plain⟩

flu·vi·a·les \ˌflüvēˈā(ˌ)lēz\ [NL, fr. L, masc. & fem. pl. of *fluvialis*] *syn of* NAIADALES

flu·vi·al·ist \-ləst\ *n* -S **:** one who emphasizes the action of streams in explanation of geological phenomena

flu·vi·at·ic \ˌflüvēˈad·ik\ *adj* [L *fluviaticus*, fr. *fluvius* river + *-aticus* (as in *aquaticus* aquatic)] **:** FLUVIATILE

flu·vi·a·tile \ˈflüvēəˌtil\ *adj* [MF, fr. L *fluviatilis*, fr. *fluvius* river + *-atilis* (as in *aquatilis* aquatile)] **:** belonging to, existing in or about, or produced by the action of streams or rivers

flu·vi·a·tion \ˌflüvēˈāshən\ *n* -S [L *fluvi-* + E *-ation*] **:** the action of streams

flu·vic·o·line \(ˈ)flüˈvikəˌlīn, -ˌlən\ *adj* [ISV *fluvi-* + *-coline*] **:** inhabiting or frequenting rivers or streams — used of animals

flu·vio–aeolian \ˌflüvē(ˌ)ō+\ *adj* [*fluvi-* + *aeolian*] **:** produced or caused by action of streams and wind ⟨*fluvio-aeolian* geologic formations⟩

flu·vio·glacial \"+\ *adj* [ISV *fluvi-* + *glacial*] **:** GLACIOFLUVIAL

fluvioglacial drift *n* **:** drift transported by waters emanating from a glacier

flu·vi·o·graph \ˈflüvēəˌgraf, -ˌrȧf\ *n* [ISV *fluvi-* + *-graph*] **:** an instrument for measuring and recording automatically the rise and fall of a river

fluv·io·lacustrine \ˌflüvē(ˌ)ō+\ *adj* [*fluvi-* + *lacustrine*] **:** of or relating to sedimentation partly in lake and partly in stream waters or to deposits laid down under alternating or overlapping lacustrine and fluviatile conditions

flu·vi·ol·o·gy \ˌflüvēˈäləjē\ *n* -ES [*fluvi-* + *-logy*] **:** a science dealing with watercourses

flu·vio·marine \ˌflüvē(ˌ)ō+\ *adj* [*fluvi-* + *marine*] **:** formed by the joint action of river and sea ⟨~ deposits at the mouths of rivers⟩ **:** ESTUARINE

flu·vi·om·e·ter \ˌflüvēˈäməd·ə(r)\ *n* [ISV *fluvi-* + *-meter*] **:** FLUVIOGRAPH

flu·vio·terrestrial \ˌflüvē(ˌ)ō+\ *adj* [*fluvi-* + *terrestrial*] **:** relating to the land and its streams ⟨~ shells⟩

flu·vio·volcanic \"+\ *adj* [*fluvi-* + *volcanic*] **:** of or relating to combined action of volcanoes and streams ⟨beds of ~ ash⟩

[1]**flux** \ˈfləks\ *n* -ES [ME, fr. MF & ML; MF, fr. ML *fluxus*, fr. L, flow, action of flowing, fr. *fluxus*, past part. of *fluere* to flow — more at FLUID] **1 a :** a flowing or discharge of fluid from the body; *usu* **:** an excessive and abnormal discharge from the bowels **:** DIARRHEA, DYSENTERY **b :** the matter discharged in a flux **2 :** an act of flowing: as **a :** a continuous moving on or passing by (as of a flowing stream) **b :** a continuing succession of changes ⟨language is subject to constant ~⟩ **3 :** a running stream (as of water) **:** a continued flow **:** FLOOD, OUTFLOW ⟨a ~ of words⟩ **4 a :** the setting in of the tide toward shore — compare REFLUX **b :** a state of uncertainty or absence of clearly directed action following or accompanying some event of moment and usu. preceding the establishment of a new course of action ⟨the ~ following the death of the emperor⟩ **5 a :** a substance used to promote fusion (as by removing impurities) esp. of metals or minerals **b :** a substance (as rosin or borax) applied to surfaces to be joined by soldering, brazing, or welding just prior to or during the operation to clean and free them from oxide and promote their union **c :** a substance (as borax) added in glassmaking for promoting vitrification **d** *or* **flux oil :** a viscous nonvolatile petroleum fraction used to soften asphalt **6 :** a fusible glass used as a base for enamels; *also* **:** an easily fusible enamel used as a ground for enamel painting **7 a :** the rate of transfer of fluid, particles, or energy (as radiant energy) across a given surface ⟨neutron ~⟩ ⟨light ~⟩ **b :** the surface integral of the normal component of field intensity over a given surface ⟨measurement of electric ~⟩ — see MAGNETIC FLUX **8 :** SLIME FLUX **syn** see FLOW

[2]**flux** \"\ *vb* -ED/-ING/-ES [ME *fluxen*, fr. *flux*, n.] *vt* **1 :** to cause to become fluid ⟨the intense heat ~*ed* the glass⟩ **2 :** to treat with a flux esp. in order to promote fusion or softening ⟨~ the edges to be joined with solder⟩ **3** *obs* **:** to treat (a patient or disease) so as to cause a discharge from an affected part; *often* **:** PURGE **~** *vi* **1 :** to flow freely **2 :** to become fluid **:** FUSE, MELT ⟨materials that soften and ~ under the influence of heat and pressure⟩ **3** *obs* **:** to undergo a flux; *specif* **:** to bleed copiously

[3]**flux** \"\ *adj* [L *fluxus*, fr. past part. of *fluere*] *archaic* **:** being in or characterized by a state of flux **:** VARIABLE, UNSTABLE

flux density *n* **:** magnetic, electric, or radiant flux per unit area normal to the direction of the flux

flux·er \-sə(r)\ *n* -S **:** a worker who fluxes seams of tin cans for soldering

flux gate *or* **flux valve** *n* **:** a device based on the earth-inductor principle and used to indicate the direction of the terrestrial magnetic field

flux·ible \-səbəl\ *adj* [ME, fr. MF, fr. LL *fluxibilis* fluid, fr. L *fluxus* (past part. of *fluere* to flow) + *-ibilis* -ible — more at FLUID] **1** *archaic* **:** capable of being fluxed **2** *obs* **:** flowing freely **:** FLUID **3** *archaic* **:** INCONSTANT, VARIABLE

flux·ile \-səl, -ˌsīl, -(ˌ)sil\ *adj* [LL *fluxilis*, fr. L *fluxus* (past part.) + *-ilis* -ile] **1** *obs* **:** FLUID **2** *archaic* **:** INCONSTANT, VARIABLE

flux·il·i·ty \ˌflәkˈsilәd·ē\ *n* -ES **:** the quality or state of being fluxile

flux·ion \ˈfləkshən\ *n* -S [MF, fr. L *fluxion-*, *fluxio*, fr. *fluxus* (past part.) + *-ion-*, *-io* -ion] **1 :** the action of flowing **2 :** something that flows; *sometimes* **:** continuing motion or change **3** *obs* **:** an unnatural or excessive flow of blood or fluid toward a body organ **4** *obs* **:** the derivative of a mathematical function

flux·ion·al \-shənᵊl, -shnəl\ *adj* **1 :** relating to or being a fluxion **2 :** subject to fluxion **:** VARIABLE, INCONSTANT — **flux·ion·al·ly** \-ᵊlē, -əlē\ *adv*

fluxional texture *n* **:** FLUIDAL TEXTURE

flux·ion·ary \-shəˌnerē\ *adj, archaic var of* FLUXIONAL

flux·ion·ist \-sh(ə)nəst\ *n* -S **:** one skilled in or using fluxions esp. in mathematics

flux·ive \ˈfləksiv\ *adj* [L *fluxus* (past part.) + E *-ive*] *archaic* **:** FLOWING, FLUID, FLUCTUATING

flux man *n* **:** a worker who mixes flux and supplies can-soldering machines with flux and solder

flux·me·ter \ˈfləkˌsmēd·ə(r)\ *n* [ISV *flux* + *-meter*] **:** an instrument for measuring magnetic-flux density usu. by electromagnetic induction

fluxweed \ˈ⸗,⸗\ *n* [[1]*flux* (dysentery) + *weed*] **1 :** a tansy mustard (*Descurainia sophia*) with spreading fruiting pedicels **2 :** SPOTTED CRANESBILL **3 :** SPOTTED SPURGE

flx *abbr* flexible

[1]**fly** \ˈflī\ *vb* **flew** \ˈflü\ **flown** \ˈflōn\ **flying**; **flies** [ME *flyen*, *flien*, *fleon*, fr. OE *flēogan*; akin to OHG *fliogan* to fly, ON *fljūga*, Lith *plaukti* to swim, OE *flōwan* to flow — more at FLOW] *vi* **1 a** *of a winged being* **:** to move in or pass through the air with wings ⟨insects ~*ing* over the water⟩ **b :** to move through the air or before the wind ⟨bullets *flew* in all directions⟩ ⟨the wind freshened and the schooner *flew* toward port⟩ ⟨clouds ~*ing* across the sky⟩ ⟨the plane *flew* south⟩ **c :** to float, wave, or soar in the air ⟨a flag *flies* from the tall staff⟩ ⟨the kite caught an updraft and *flew* up and up⟩ ⟨bright hair ~*ing* about her shoulders⟩ **2 a :** to take to flight **:** flee esp. from danger **:** run away ⟨forced to ~ for his life when his enemies came into power⟩ **b :** to fade and disappear **:** VANISH ⟨mists ~*ing* before the morning sun⟩ ⟨the hovering shadows had *flown* when the light went on⟩ **3 :** to move, pass, or act swiftly ⟨the horses *flew* down the stretch⟩ ⟨how such rumors do ~⟩ ⟨~*ing* to his sister's assistance⟩: as **a :** to spring or rush esp. suddenly or violently ⟨the rumor brought the citizens ~*ing* to arms⟩ — often used with *into* ⟨*flew* into a rage⟩ ⟨~ into tantrums —Gertrude Samuels⟩ **b :** to become suddenly or violently disordered, broken to bits, or forced apart or off **:** BURST ⟨the door *flew* open⟩ ⟨the glass *flew* to bits at the impact⟩ **c :** to become expended or dissipated rapidly — used esp. of money or property ⟨after he had become established in town his inheritance *flew*⟩ **d :** to seem to pass quickly ⟨our vacation had simply *flown*⟩ ⟨the hours *flew* as she busied herself about the house⟩ **4 a :** to hunt with a hawk — usu. used with *at* ⟨*flew* unsuccessfully at a low-flying duck⟩ **b :** to pursue or attack in or as if in flight ⟨hoped yet to ~ at higher game⟩ **5** *past or past part* **flied :** to hit a fly ball in baseball ⟨*flied* to left field⟩ **6 a :** to operate an airplane **b :** to travel in an airplane **~** *vt* **1 a :** to cause to fly or float in the air (as a bird, a flag) ⟨little boys ~*ing* their kites⟩ ⟨the club *flew* its pigeons every pleasant Saturday⟩ **b :** to operate (an airplane) in flight **2 a :** to flee or escape from ⟨the bird had *flown* its cage⟩ **b :** to avoid or shun ⟨sleep *flies* the wretch —John Dryden⟩ ⟨~ such a talkative woman⟩ **3 a :** to perform by flying ⟨the bat has *flown* his nightly flight⟩ **:** conform to in flying ⟨birds usually ~ the same flyway in both northward and southward migration⟩ **:** provide by flying ⟨fighters ~*ing* close escort for the transports⟩ **b :** to operate an airplane over ⟨~ the Atlantic⟩ **4 :** to fly (a hawk) at game **5 :** to transport by airplane **6** *past or past part usu* **flied :** to raise (as scenery not in use) to the flies of a theater stage **syn** see ESCAPE — **fly a kite** *or* **fly one's kite** *slang* **:** to cease importuning or troubling — usu. used with *go* in the imperative — **fly at one's throat 1 :** to attack by or as if by biting the throat ⟨the dog snapped the chain and *flew at his throat*⟩ **2 :** to assail suddenly and violently — **fly blind :** to fly an airplane solely by the aid of instruments — **fly by the seat of one's pants** *slang* **:** to fly an airplane by a sense of feeling without the aid of instruments — **fly contact :** to fly an airplane with the aid of visible landmarks or reference points — **fly high :** to be exuberantly ambitious **:** be elated — **fly in the face of** *or* **fly in the teeth of :** to act forthrightly or brazenly in a way that shows small respect and usu. contempt for ⟨*flying in the face of* convention⟩ ⟨*flying in the face of* other people's rights⟩ ⟨*flying in the teeth of* accepted opinion —F.L.Allen⟩ — **fly the coop** *slang* **:** to depart suddenly or surreptitiously **:** ESCAPE, FLEE

[2]**fly** \"\ *n* -ES [ME *flye*, fr. OE *flyge* — more at FLIGHT] **1 :** the action or process of flying **:** FLIGHT **2 :** the part of a compass on which the points are marked **:** COMPASS CARD **3 a :** a device consisting of two or more radial vanes capable of rotating on a spindle to act as a fan or to govern the speed of clockwork or very light machinery by the resistance of the air **b :** FLYWHEEL **c :** the arrangement consisting of a lever with end weights used to operate fly presses by its momentum when turned rapidly at the end of the screw; *also* **:** FLY PRESS **4 a :** a horse-drawn public coach or delivery wagon **b** *chiefly Brit* **:** a light covered vehicle (as a single-horse pleasure carriage or a hansom cab) **5 flies** *pl* **:** the space over the stage of a theater where scenery and equipment can be hung out of sight until needed **6 :** something attached by one edge: as **a :** a garment closing concealed by a fold of cloth extending over the fastener; *esp* **:** such a closing at the front of men's trousers — see FLY FRONT **b :** the outer canvas of a tent with double top usu. drawn over the ridgepole but so extended as to touch the roof of the tent at no other place; *often* **:** a piece of canvas suitable for such use **c** (1) **:** the length of an extended flag from its staff or support (2) **:** the outer or loose end of a flag **7** *textile manuf* **a :** FLIER 11 **b :** LATCH 3 **c :** FLY SHUTTLE **d :** airborne lint in a mill room; *specif* **:** short light waste fiber produced during carding, spinning, or napping **8 :** the course of something projected through the air ⟨the golf ball rose in a good straight ~ right down the fairway⟩; *often* **:** FLY BALL **9 :** FLYLEAF **10 a :** the fore flap of a bootee **b :** the overlapping part of a shoe upper **11** *or* **fly ladder :** the top section of an aerial ladder — **on the fly :** in motion: as **a :** continuously active **:** very busy ⟨*on the fly* all day long⟩ **b :** on the point of or in the course of departure ⟨answered *on the fly*⟩ **c :** while still in the air **:** before striking the ground ⟨caught the ball *on the fly*⟩

[3]**fly** \"\ *adj* [prob. fr. [1]*fly*] *slang chiefly Brit* **:** KEEN, ARTFUL

[4]**fly** \"\ *vb* **flied** *or* **flyed**; **flied** *or* **flyed**; **flying**; **flies** [[2]*fly* (carriage)] *vt, archaic* **:** to convey in a horse-drawn fly **~** *vi, archaic* **:** to travel in a fly

[5]**fly** \"\ *n* -ES [ME *flie*, fr. OE *flēoge*, *flȳge*; akin to OHG *flioga* fly, ON *fluga*, MD *vlieghe*; derivatives fr. the root of E [1]*fly*] **1 :** a winged insect — now used chiefly in combination ⟨emerging may*flies*⟩ ⟨an outbreak of turnip *flies*⟩ ⟨a large caddis ~⟩ ⟨beautiful butter*flies*⟩; *collectively* **:** winged insects of a particular kind or in a specified relationship ⟨~ is bad on turnip this season⟩ ⟨had a lot of trouble with ~ on the sheep in this wet weather⟩ **2 a :** an insect of the order Diptera **:** TWO-WINGED FLY — called also *true fly* **b :** any of various rather large and stout-bodied two-winged flies (as horseflies or houseflies) as distinguished from typically smaller and slenderer two-winged flies (as mosquitoes or midges) — not used technically **c :** TSETSE FLY ⟨~ is present in much of eastern Africa⟩ **3** *obs* **a :** a demon associate (as of a witch) **:** FAMILIAR **b :** SPY **c :** PARASITE **4 :** a fishhook dressed (as with feathers or tinsel) to suggest an insect for use as a lure in angling **5 a** *archaic* **:** FLYBOY **b :** DELIVERY 9 — **flies on :** lack of alertness about — used in negative expressions ⟨there's no *flies on* him⟩ ⟨he hasn't any *flies on* him⟩ — **fly in the ointment :** a detracting factor or element **:** an agent that spoils something that is otherwise pleasing

fly 4: *1* tag, *2* butt, *3* tail, *4* joint, *5* hackle, *6* body, *7* ribbing, *8* wing, *9* cheek, *10* topping, *11* horns, *12* head, *13* eye, *14* hook

[6]**fly** \"\ *adj* [*fly-fishing*] **:** used in or relating to fly-fishing ⟨improving his ~ technique⟩

fly·abil·i·ty \ˌflīəˈbiləd·ē\ *n* -ES **:** the quality or state of being flyable

fly·able \ˈflīəbəl\ *adj* **:** suitable for flying **:** fit to be flown ⟨~ weather⟩ ⟨a barely ~ airplane⟩

fly–about \ˈ⸗⸗,⸗\ *adj* [fr. *fly about*, v.] **1 :** given to or characterized by irregular, casual, or aimless activity or motion ⟨soft *fly-about* hair⟩ ⟨a *fly-about* boy⟩ **2** *of a horse* **:** SKITTISH

fly agaric *or* **fly amanita** *n* **:** a poisonous mushroom (*Amanita muscaria*) that has a variably colored but typically bright-red pileus with a warty white scurf on the surface and a prominent bulb at the base of the stipe, that with the related death cup is responsible for most cases of severe mushroom poisoning, that has been used as a source of poison for flypaper, and that is extensively used chiefly in northeastern Asia as an intoxicant esp. for the hallucinatory effects that it produces — called also *fly mushroom*

fly anchor *n* **:** SEA ANCHOR, DRAG

fly ash *n* **:** fine solid particles of noncombustible ash with or without accompanying combustible particles carried out of a bed of solid fuel by the draft and deposited in quiet spots within a furnace and flues or within a boiler setting or carried out of a chimney with the waste gases and often recovered for use as a constituent in commercial products (as phonograph records, cements, and bricks)

[1]**flyaway** \ˈ⸗⸗,⸗\ *adj* [fr. *fly away*, v.] **1** *of a person* **:** volatile and flighty **:** lacking in order and practical sense ⟨a pretty ~ sort of woman⟩ **2 a** *of clothing* **:** loose and floating **:** having unconfined fullness esp. at the back ⟨a trim ~ jacket⟩ **b :** having a pointed form suggestive of a wing ⟨~ eyebrows⟩ ⟨a ~ cuff⟩ **3 a :** ready to fly — used of aircraft esp. at the factory **b :** packaged or designed to be transported in an airplane — used of supplies to be carried by military aircraft of the units that will use them **c :** relating to or involving flyaway aircraft or supplies ⟨~ price⟩ ⟨~ delivery⟩ ⟨a ~ bin⟩

[2]**flyaway** \"\ *n* -S [partly fr. [1]*flyaway*; partly fr. *fly away*, v.] **1 :** a flyaway person or thing **2 :** a mirage of land seen at sea **3 :** a dismount from a horizontal bar consisting of a somersault executed at the front or back end of an arm swing **4 :** an airplane flown (as from the factory) instead of being shipped

[3]**flyaway** \"\ *adv* [[1]*flyaway*] **:** as ready to fly away — used of aircraft ⟨a light plane priced $8400 ~⟩

flyaway grass *n* **:** ROUGH BENT

[1]**flyback** \ˈ⸗,⸗\ *adj* [fr. *fly back*, v.] **:** tending to fly back or capable of flying back: as **a** *of a stopwatch or chronograph* **:** having a sweep second hand that may be made to fly back to zero **b** *of fur, hair, or feathers* **:** having a tendency to fall back into position when brushed the wrong way

[2]**flyback** \"\ *n* [fr. *fly back*, v.] **1 :** the return to zero of the second hand or the split-second hand of a stopwatch or chronograph **2 :** the return of a cathode-ray beam in a television picture tube after it has traced one picture before it traces the next

fly ball \ˈ⸗,⸗\ *n* **:** a ball hit in baseball into the air at least high enough to be caught by a fielder before touching the ground — compare GROUNDER

flyball \ˈ⸗,⸗\ *adj* **:** relating to or having ball weights that tend to fly outward when revolving and exert an effect through centrifugal force ⟨a ~ governor⟩

flybane \ˈ⸗,⸗\ *n* **:** any of several plants considered to be destructive to houseflies (as a catchfly or the fly agaric)

flybelt \ˈ⸗,⸗\ *n* **:** an area infested with tsetse fly

fly–bitten \ˈ⸗,⸗⸗\ *adj* **:** marked by or as if by the bite of flies

fly block *n* **:** a block whose position shifts to suit the working of the tackle with which it is connected; *esp* **:** the double upper block of the topsail halyards of a sailing ship

[1]**flyblow** \ˈ⸗,⸗\ *n* [[5]*fly* + *blow* (deposit of insect eggs)] **1 :** one of the eggs or young larvae deposited by a flesh fly or blowfly **2 :** FLY-STRIKE

[2]**flyblow** \"\ *vt* **1 :** to deposit flyblows in **2 :** to cause (as a reputation) to be contaminated **:** TAINT

flyblown \ˈ⸗,⸗\ *adj* [[5]*fly* + *blown*, past part. of *blow*] **1 a :** infested with flyblows ⟨a ~ sheep⟩ **b :** covered with flyspecks ⟨dirty ~ walls⟩ **2 :** TAINTED, IMPAIRED ⟨a ~ reputation⟩ **3** *often* **flyblowed** \ˈ⸗,⸗\ *slang Austral* **:** having no money

fly·boat \ˈflī,⸗\ *n* [part modif., part trans. of D *vlieboot*, fr. *Vlie*, channel between the North sea and the Wadden Zee, Netherlands + *boot* boat] **1 :** a large flat-bottomed coasting boat formerly widely used but now chiefly Dutch **2 :** any of various fast boats (as a fishing boat, a ship's boat)

fly bomb *var of* FLYING BOMB

fly book *n* **:** a case usu. in the form of a book for storing anglers' flies

flyboy \ˈ⸗,⸗\ *n* [[5]*fly* + *boy*] **1 :** a worker who removes printed sheets from a handpress **2 :** a printshop worker whose chief duty is to load and unload presses

fly–boy \"\ *n* [[1]*fly* + *boy*] *slang* **:** AIRCREWMAN; *esp* **:** a pilot in an air force

flybrush \ˈ⸗,⸗\ *n* **:** a device (as of feathers) formerly used to drive away houseflies

flyby \ˈ⸗,⸗\ *n* -S [fr. *fly by*, v.] **1 :** FLYOVER 1 **2 a :** a flight of a spacecraft past a celestial body (as Mars) close enough to obtain scientific data **b :** a spacecraft that makes a flyby

[1]**fly–by–night** \ˈflībəˌnīt, *usu* -nīd·+V\ *n* **1 :** one given to being abroad at night **2** *also* **fly–by–night·er** \ˌflībəˈnīd·ə(r), -nītə-\ **a :** one that escapes at night from his creditors **b :** one without established reputation or standing and therefore regarded as a poor risk (as for credit or future productivity) **3 :** a square sail sometimes spread on fore-and-aft-rigged ships when running before the wind

[2]**fly–by–night** \"\ *adj* **1** *of a business enterprise or promoter* **:** established or prepared to take advantage of an opportunity for immediate profit and often shady or irresponsible and inadequately financed for stability ⟨a *fly-by-night* salesman⟩ ⟨*fly-by-night* insurance plans⟩ ⟨a *fly-by-night* cut-rate drugstore⟩ **2 :** TRANSITORY, PASSING ⟨a *fly-by-night* political disorder⟩ **:** UNRELIABLE, UNSTABLE ⟨the symphony was no *fly-by-night* venture —Green Peyton⟩

fly camp *n* **:** a temporary advanced camp at a distance from a base camp

fly cap *n* **:** a woman's cap with sides resembling wings and worn in the 17th and 18th centuries

fly–cast \ˈ⸗,⸗\ *vb* **:** FLY-FISH

flycaster \ˈ⸗,⸗⸗\ *n* **:** an angler specializing in fly-fishing

fly casting *n* **:** the action of throwing the lure when fly-fishing

flycatcher \ˈ⸗,⸗⸗\ *n* **1 :** any of numerous birds (order Passeriformes) that feed upon insects taken on the wing: **a :** a member of the Old World passerine family Muscicapidae (as the spotted flycatcher) **b :** any of numerous New World birds of the family Tyrannidae (as the kingbird, peewee, and least flycatcher) — called also *tyrant flycatcher* **2 :** DROSOPHYLLUM 2

fly–catching \ˈ⸗,⸗⸗\ *adj, of a bird* **:** having the habit of catching insects on the wing

fly–catching warbler *n* **:** any of numerous American wood warblers having strong rictal bristles at the base of the bill and customarily feeding on insects caught on the wing

fly cop *n* [prob. fr. [3]*fly*] *slang* **:** PLAINCLOTHESMAN **:** DETECTIVE

fly cutter *n* [[2]*fly*] **:** a cutting tool set transversely to and revolving with the arbor of a lathe and acting upon work fed into its circular path

fly dope *n* **1 :** a dressing that makes angling flies water-resistant so that they will float **2 :** an insect repellent

fly dresser *n* **:** a maker of artificial flies for angling

flyed *past of* FLY

flyer *var of* FLIER

fly–fish \ˈ⸗,⸗\ *vi* **:** to angle with artificial flies **~** *vt* **:** to fly-fish in

fly–fisher \ˈ⸗,⸗⸗\ *also* **fly–fisherman** \ˈ⸗,⸗⸗⸗\ *n, pl* **fly-fishers** *also* **fly-fishermen :** an angler who uses or prefers the technique of fly-fishing

fly–fishing \ˈ⸗,⸗⸗\ *n* **:** the technique or act of angling by casting an artificial fly as lure

[1]**flyflap** \ˈ⸗,⸗\ *n* [ME *flieflappe*, fr. *flie* fly + *flappe* flap — more at FLY, FLAP] **:** a device (as a fan) for driving away or killing flies

[2]**flyflap** \"\ *vt, archaic* **:** to strike with or as if with a flyflap; *broadly* **:** BEAT, LASH **~** *vi* **:** to drive away flies with a flyflap — **flyflapper** \ˈ⸗,⸗⸗\ *n*

flyflower \ˈ⸗,⸗⸗\ *n* **:** DUTCHMAN'S-BREECHES

fly frame *n* **1** *in textile manuf* **:** any of various slubbing, roving, intermediate, and other frames on which flyers are used **2** *in glass manuf* **:** a grinding and polishing machine

fly front *n* **:** a concealed closing on the front of coats, skirts, shirts, dresses — compare [2]FLY 6a

fly fungus *n* **1 :** FLY AGARIC **2 :** a fungus (*Entomophthora muscae*) that is parasitic on flies — called also *fly mold*

fly gallery *or* **fly floor** *n* **:** a narrow raised platform at the side of a theatrical stage from which the lines for flying scenery are manipulated

fly governor *n* **:** [2]FLY 3a

fly half *n* **:** STANDOFF HALF

fly honeysuckle *n* **1 :** any of several shrubs of the genus *Lonicera:* as **a :** EUROPEAN FLY HONEYSUCKLE **b :** a straggling shrub (*L. canadensis*) with leaf margins and petioles ciliate — called also *American fly honeysuckle* **c :** TARTARIAN HONEYSUCKLE **2 :** an African shrub (*Halleria lucida*) of the family Scrophulariaceae

fly in *vt* **:** to switch (a railroad car) by a flying switch

fly–in \ˈ⸗,⸗\ *n* [fr. *fly in*, v.] **1 :** an act of flying to a destination ⟨planned the *fly-in* of the rescue planes⟩ **2 :** an outdoor theater planned for the patronage of persons remaining in their private planes — compare DRIVE-IN

[1]**flying** *adj* [ME, fr. pres. part. of *flien* to fly — more at FLY] **1 :** moving or capable of moving in the air with or as if with wings ⟨~ clouds⟩ **2 :** moving or made by moving lightly or

rapidly ⟨sped on ~ feet⟩ ⟨made a ~ start⟩ **:** intended for rapid movement or action ⟨a ~ coach⟩ **3 :** passing about freely and usu. without evident authority ⟨~ rumors⟩ **4 :** FLEETING, TRANSITORY, BRIEF ⟨a ~ impression⟩ ⟨a ~ visit⟩ **5 :** having stylized wings — see BRAND illustration **6** *of stairs* **:** ascending without a turn

²flying *n* -s [ME, fr. gerund of *flien*] **1 flyings** *pl* **:** ²FLY 7d **2 flyings** *pl, South & Midland* **:** the lower leaves of the tobacco plant **3 :** locomotion by air

flying bent *n* **:** MOOR GRASS 2

flying boat *n* **:** a seaplane whose hull is the means of support on water — compare FLOATPLANE

flying bomb *or* **fly bomb** *n* **:** ROBOT BOMB

flying bond *n* **:** a bond in masonry formed by inserting headers at considerable intervals only

flying boom *n* **:** a rigid fuel pipe flexibly joined to the tail of a tanker airplane and fitted at its after end with airfoils which are controllable from the tanker and which permit it to be guided into contact with an airplane being refueled in flight

flying bridge *n* **1 :** a suspended or floating usu. temporary bridge (as a pontoon bridge) **2 :** FLYING FERRY **3 :** the highest bridge on a ship having more than one

flying buttress *n* **:** a masonry structure typically consisting of a straight inclined bar carried on an arch and a solid pier or buttress against which it abuts that is used to take up the thrust of a roof or vault which cannot be supported by ordinary buttresses

flying buttress

flying camp *n* **1 :** a temporary military camp **2 :** a company, squadron, or other body of troops formed for rapid movement from place to place

flying cat *n* **1 :** FLYING MARMOT **2 :** FLYING LEMUR

flying circus *n* **1 :** a rotary echelon formation of airplanes in action **2 :** an organized group of pilots engaged in public exhibition flying

flying coachman *n* **:** a black-and-yellow honey eater (*Zanthomiza phrygia*) of Australia — called also *regent honey eater*

flying colors *n pl* **:** complete success ⟨passed his exams with *flying colors*⟩

flying column *n* **:** a strong military detachment that operates at a distance from the main force

flying deck *n* **:** a deck on a ship supported at the side by railings, stanchions, or other open framing

flying disk *n* **:** FLYING SAUCER

flying doe *n* **:** a female red kangaroo of Australia

flying dragon *n* **1 :** DRAGON 7a **2 :** DRAGONFLY

flying facade *n* **:** a front wall of a building when extended up above the roof **:** FALSE FRONT

flying fence *n* **:** a fence that in the hunting field can be cleared at a gallop

flying ferry *n* **:** a raft used as a ferry and held by an anchor cable fastened upstream from the ferry site

flying field *n* **:** a field with a graded portion for the taking off and landing of airplanes and sometimes with buildings for their shelter and maintenance

flying fish *n* **1 :** any of numerous fishes chiefly of tropical and warm seas that have long pectoral fins suggesting wings, that are capable of leaving the water and moving some distance through the air chiefly by the motion of the tail before they entirely leave the water, and that constitute the family Exocoetidae **2 :** BUTTERFLY FISH 1e; *broadly* **:** any of various related So. American fishes reputed to skim over the surface of the water **3 :** a sea robin of the genus *Prionotus* **4 :** FLYING GURNARD

flying fox *n* **1 :** FRUIT BAT **2** *Austral* **:** a carrier (as for mining material or produce) operating on cables over a gorge or other obstacle

flying frog *n* **:** any of several East Indian tree frogs of the genus *Polypedates* having very large and broadly webbed feet that serve as parachutes and enable the frogs to make very long leaps

flying gecko *n* **:** a gecko (*Ptychozoon homalocephalum*) having membranous expansions along the sides of the body, head, limbs, and tail — called also *fringed gecko*

flying gurnard *n* **:** any of several marine fishes that resemble gurnards, constitute the family Dactylopteridae, and have very large pectoral fins which allow them to glide above the water for short distances — called also *flying robin*

flying herd *n, Brit* **:** a dairy herd kept only for milk production, all calves being sold or discarded and all replacements being brought in from other sources

flying horse *n* **1 :** HIPPOGRIFF **2 :** a mechanized seat in the shape of a horse (as on a merry-go-round)

flying jen·ny \ˌ=ˈjenē\ *or* **flying jin·ny** \-ˈjinē\ *n, chiefly South & Midland* **:** a usu. simple homemade merry-go-round

flying jib *n* **:** a sail set outside of the jib and on the flying jibboom — see SAIL illustration

flying jibboom *n* **:** an extension of a jibboom — see SHIP illustration

flying lemur *n* **:** either of two arboreal nocturnal mammals that are about the size of a cat, that have a broad fold of skin extending from the neck to the tail on each side so as to embrace the limbs and form a parachute used in making long sailing leaps, very fine soft fur, and largely frugivorous habits, and that are usu. considered to constitute a distinct order (Dermoptera) although they have sometimes been placed with the insectivores or primates or even included among the bats: **a :** an East Indian mammal (*Cynocephalus volans*) that somewhat suggests a large squirrel **b :** a very similar Philippine mammal (*C. philippinensis*)

flying level *n* **:** a hand level used by civil engineers for reconnaissance over a course (as of a projected road or canal)

flying lizard *n* **:** DRAGON 7a

fly·ing·ly *adv* **:** with flying colors

flying machine *n* **:** an apparatus for navigating the air ⟨began to look anxiously for a level place on which to land his *flying machine* —Tudor David⟩

flying mare *n* **:** a wrestling maneuver in which the aggressor seizes an opponent's wrist, turns about, and jerks him over his back

flying marmot *n* **:** TAGUAN; *broadly* **:** any of various large flying squirrels of the genus *Petaurista*

flying moor *n* **:** a mooring in which the first anchor is let go while the ship has enough way to carry it at least to the point for dropping the second anchor

flying mouse *n* **:** any of several tiny flying phalangers of the genus *Acrobates*

flying officer *n* **:** an air force officer (as in the British Royal Air Force) equivalent in rank to a lieutenant in the army

flying parry *n, in fencing* **:** a backward glide on an opponent's blade in the high line followed by a cutover return made to either the high or low line

flying pay *n* **:** FLIGHT PAY

flying phalanger *or* **flying opossum** *n* **:** any of various small phalangers of the Australian region (esp. of the genera *Petaurus* and *Acrobates*) that have a wide membrane like that of the flying squirrels connecting the forelegs and hind legs and similarly used — called also *flying squirrel, squirrel;* compare SUGAR SQUIRREL

flying ring *n* **:** one of a pair of metal rings covered with leather or rubber and suspended at the ends of swinging ropes for use in gymnastic exercises

flying robin *n* **:** FLYING GURNARD

flying sap *n* **:** a sap constructed well to the front under enemy fire and covered by using two gabions filled with earth and pushed forward side by side

flying saucer *n* **:** any of various unidentified moving objects repeatedly reported as seen in the air and usu. alleged to be saucer-shaped or disk-shaped — called also *flying disk*

flying shear *n* **:** blades that cut off hot strip steel while it is being rolled by moving with the strip at the moment of severing

flying shore *n* **:** a horizontal supporting shore

flying skip *n* **:** a skip (as in dancing) covering distance while in the air

flying snail *n* **:** PTEROPOD

flying snake *n* **:** a brilliant gold-and-black tree snake (*Chrysopelea ornata*) of the family Boigidae that is able to leap clear of the ground when striking and often planes from tree to tree in the manner of a flying squirrel for distances as great as eight feet

flying speed *n* **:** an airspeed sufficient to provide the lift necessary to support an airplane in level flight

flying spider *n* **:** a ballooning spider

flying spot *n* **:** a spot of light that is moved over an image so that light reflected from or transmitted by different parts of the image is translated into electrical signals for transmission (as in television)

flying squad *n* **:** a usu. small standby group of people ready to move or act swiftly; *esp* **:** a police unit formed to respond quickly in an emergency

flying squadron *n* **1 :** a naval squadron moving rapidly from place to place at a distance from the main command **2 :** FLYING SQUAD

flying squid *n* **:** any of various squids that are able to leap out of the water

flying squirrel *n* **1 :** any of various squirrels distinguished by folds of skin connecting the forelegs and hind legs that enable them to make very long gliding leaps; *esp* **:** a small large-eyed nocturnal No. American squirrel (*Glaucomys volans*) with very soft fur that is gray or brownish above and pure white below — see PETAURISTIDAE, TAGUAN **2** *Austral* **:** FLYING PHALANGER **3 :** an African scaletail

flying start *n* **:** a start in racing in which the signal is given while the competitors are in motion

flying switch *n* **:** a maneuver in which one or more railroad cars are disconnected from a locomotive while moving and as the locomotive pulls away are switched to another track to roll to a desired position under their own momentum

flying tackle *n* **1 :** a tackle in football in which the tackler dives or throws his body through the air at the ballcarrier **2 :** a professional wrestling maneuver in which a contestant lunges at his opponent from a distance and hits him with his shoulder at or near the waist

flying tail *n* **:** a horizontal stabilizer on a high-speed airplane that has its entire surface adjustable to correct longitudinal trim

flying wedge *n* **1 :** an offensive formation in football in which the players form up in a wedge with the ballcarrier at the center **2 a :** a formation (as of guards or police) resembling the football flying wedge **b :** something notably vigorous and determined in action

flying windmill *n, slang* **:** HELICOPTER

fly kick *n* **:** the act or an instance of fly-kicking in rugby

fly-kick \ˈ=ˌ=\ *vi* **:** to kick the ball in rugby without first catching it with the hands

fly ladder *n* **:** ²FLY 11

flyleaf \ˈ=ˌ=\ *n* [fr. ²*fly* + *leaf*] **1 :** a blank leaf at the beginning or end of a book or similar work; *specif* **:** the free inner leaf of the endpaper of a book **2 :** paper attached to the inner edge of a paper box that is used for decorative purposes or to cover the contents

fly·less \ˈflīləs\ *adj* **:** free from infestation with flies (as houseflies or blowflies) — **fly·less·ness** *n* -ES

fly line *n* **1 :** the habitual line of flight of a bird group in its migrations — compare FLYWAY **2 :** line for use in fly-fishing

fly loft *n* **:** the flies of a theater

fly·man \ˈflīmən, -ˌman\ *n, pl* **flymen 1 :** the driver of a fly **2 :** a worker in the flies of a theater who manipulates curtains and scenery

fly mold *n* **:** FLY FUNGUS 2

fly mushroom *n* **:** FLY AGARIC

fly·ness *n* -ES [³*fly* + *-ness*] **:** the quality or state of being knowing, wide-awake, or crafty

fly net *n* **:** a net to exclude or keep off insects (as from a harness horse)

fly netting *n* **:** fine cotton mesh formerly used for window screens

fly nut *n* **:** WING NUT

fly orchid *n* **:** a European orchid (*Listera muscifera*) whose flowers resemble flies

fly out *vi* **:** to be put out in baseball by hitting a fly ball that is caught ⟨*flied out* to left field⟩ ⟨*flied out* to the shortstop⟩

flyover \ˈ=ˌ==\ *n* -S [fr. *fly over*, v.] **1 :** a prearranged and usu. low-altitude flight over a public gathering or place by one or more airplanes **2** *Brit* **:** OVERPASS

fly page *n* [²*fly*] **:** one side of a flyleaf

flypaper \ˈ=ˌ==\ *n* **:** paper poisoned or coated with a sticky substance for killing flies

flypast \ˈ=ˌ=\ *n* -S [fr. *fly past*, v.] *Brit* **:** FLYOVER 1

¹flype \ˈflīp\ *vt* -ED/-ING/-S [ME *flipen*, prob. of Scand origin like ²*flype*] **1** *chiefly Scot* **:** to strip off by or as if by peeling **2** *chiefly Scot* **:** to turn or fold back (as a stocking)

²flype \ ″ \ *n* -S [of Scand origin; akin to Icel *flipi* lip of a horse, piece of skin or leather, *flipa* to wound, ON *fleipa* to gossip, OSw *flipa* to whimper and perh. to ON *flā* to flay — more at FLAY] *chiefly Scot* **:** a fold or flap (as of something turned back)

fly poison *n* **1 :** a bulbous herb (*Amianthium muscaetoxicum*) of the family Liliaceae of which the pounded bulb has been used as a poison for flies **2 :** any of several plants of the genus *Zigadenus* (esp. *Z. densus*)

fly press *n* **:** a fly-operated hand-screw press (as for embossing)

flyproof \ˈ=ˌ=\ *adj* **:** made tight or close enough to keep houseflies out

fly rail *n* **1 :** a bracket that turns out to support the hinged leaf of a table **2 :** a railing above the fly gallery of a theatrical stage bearing cleats or pins by which ropes may be made fast

fly reel *n* **:** a narrow-spool single-action fly-fishing reel

fly rod *n* **:** a light springy rod used with a reel and a heavily oiled or treated line in fly-casting

fly rollway *n* **:** a steep logging skidway on a slope

flysch \ˈflish\ *n* -ES *sometimes cap* [G dial. (Switzerland), lit., something that slides or flows; derivative fr. the root of OHG *fliozzan* to flow — more at FLEET] **:** a thick and extensive deposit largely of sandstone that is formed in a geosyncline adjacent to a rising mountain belt and is esp. common in the Alpine region of Europe

fly sheet *n* [¹*fly*] **1 :** a small loose advertising sheet **:** HANDBILL **2 :** a sheet of a folder, booklet, or catalog giving directions for the use of or information about the material that follows

fly shuttle *n* [¹*fly*] **:** a handloom shuttle operated by a cord or picker stick

¹flyspeck \ˈ=ˌ=\ *n* [⁵*fly* + *speck*] **1 :** a speck or stain made by the excrement of a fly; *broadly* **:** any insignificant dot **2 :** a disease of pome fruits caused by a fungus (*Leptothyrium pomi*) and marked by clusters of small black specks on the fruit

²flyspeck \ˈ=ˌ=\ *vt* **:** to soil with flyspecks

fly stone *n* **:** native cobalt arsenide used esp. formerly as a fly poison by being ground and added to sweetened water

fly-strike \ˈ=ˌ=\ *n* **:** infestation (as of the skin of sheep) with fly maggots (as of blowflies)

fly-struck \ˈ=ˌ=\ *adj* **:** infested with fly maggots

flyswatter \ˈ=ˌ==\ *also* **flyswat** \ˈ=ˌ=\ *n* **:** SWATTER

fly table *n* **:** BUTTERFLY TABLE

flyte \ˈflīt\ *var of* FLITE

fly tent *n* **:** a tent with a fly

fly·ti·er \ˈflīˌtī(ə)r, -īə\ *n* -S **:** a maker of flies for angling

flytime \ˈ=ˌ=\ *n* **:** the season of year during which a particular kind of fly (as the housefly or blowfly) is esp. troublesome

¹flyt·ing *var of* FLITING

²flyt·ing \ˈflīd·iŋ\ *n* -S [¹*flyting*] **:** a dispute or exchange of personal abuse or ridicule esp. in verse form between two characters in a poem (as an early epic) or between two poets (as of 16th century Scotland)

fly title *n* [²*fly*] *Brit* **:** HALF TITLE 1

flytrap \ˈ=ˌ=\ *n* **1 :** a trap for catching flies often having the form of a wire or glass cylinder with a conical cover and bottom in which is a small opening **2 a :** PITCHER PLANT **b :** DOGBANE 1 **c :** VENUS'S-FLYTRAP

¹fly-up \ˈ=ˌ=\ *adj* **1 :** arranged to open by flying upward ⟨a *fly-up* lid⟩ **2 :** arranged to be reached by flying ⟨the advantages of *fly-up* waterers in the poultry house⟩

²fly-up \ ″ \ *n* -S **:** a ceremony at which a brownie scout formally leaves her brownie troop and becomes a member of an intermediate girl scout troop

fly up *vi* [¹*fly* + *up*] **:** to become a member of an intermediate girl scout troop on leaving a brownie scout troop

fly-up-the-creek \ˌ=(ˌ)=ˌ=ˈ=\ *n* **1 :** GREEN HERON **2** *chiefly South & Midland* **:** a flighty person **3** *usu cap F&C* **:** FLORIDIAN — used as a nickname

flyway \ˈ=ˌ=\ *n* [²*fly* + *way*] **:** a geographic course along which birds customarily migrate between breeding and wintering areas; *broadly* **:** such a migration route together with the breeding and wintering areas that it connects

flyweight \ˈ=ˌ=\ *n* [⁵*fly* + *weight*] **1 a :** a boxer in a weight division having a maximum limit of 112 pounds — compare FEATHERWEIGHT **b :** something small or trivial of its kind **2 :** a weight (as on a closure or governor) having a flyball action

flywheel \ˈ=ˌ=\ *n* [²*fly* + *wheel*] **1 :** a heavy metal wheel for opposing and moderating by its inertia any fluctuation of speed in the machinery with which it revolves; *esp* **:** one on an engine crankshaft to counteract variable torque during the stroke and carry the engine over the dead centers **2 :** a wheel similar to a flywheel used for storing kinetic energy (as for motive power)

fly whisk *n* **:** a device that consists of a bundle of flexible fibers (as horsehairs) mounted in a handle, that is used primarily to brush away flies (as from a person or a horse), and that has often served as a symbol of high position or authority

flywire \ˈ=ˌ=\ *n* [⁵*fly* + *wire*] *Austral* **:** SCREEN 11

fm *abbr* **1** farm **2** fathom **3** form **4** from

FM *abbr* **1** face measurement **2** fan marker **3** field manual **4** field marshal **5** fine measurement **6** foreign mission **7** foundation member **8** frequency modulation

Fm *symbol* fermium

f major *n, usu cap F* **:** the major musical key having a signature of one flat

f minor *n, usu cap F* **:** the minor musical key having a signature of four flats

fmr *abbr* former

fn *abbr* **1** footnote **2** fusion

fnd *abbr* found

fndd *abbr* founded

fndg *abbr* founding

fndn *abbr* foundation

fndr *abbr* founder

f-number \ˈ=ˌ==\ *n* [*f*, symbol for *focal length*] **:** the ratio of the focal length to the entrance pupil diameter in an optical system or the objective of such a system; *specif* **:** a number following the symbol f/ that expresses the relative aperture of a camera lens, the smaller the number the brighter the image and therefore the shorter the exposure required ⟨the *f-number* of a lens with an f/8 relative aperture is 8⟩

fo *abbr* folio

FO *abbr* **1** field officer **2** firm offer **3** flag officer **4** flight officer **5** flying officer **6** foreign office **7** for orders **8** forward observer **9** free overside **10** fuel oil **11** full organ **12** full out

¹foal \ˈfōl\ *n* -S [ME *fole*, fr. OE *fola;* akin to OHG *folo* foal, ON *foli*, Goth *fula* foal, L *pullus* young of an animal, Gk *pōlos* foal, young of an animal, girl, Gk *paid-, pais* child — more at FEW] **1 :** the young of an animal of the horse family; *esp* **:** one under one year — compare COLT, FILLY **2** *obs* **:** the young of various animals — **in foal** *or* **with foal :** PREGNANT — used of a mare

²foal \ ″ \ *vb* -ED/-ING/-S [ME *folen*, fr. *fole*, n.] *vt* **:** to bring forth (a foal) ~ *vi* **:** to bring forth young — used of an animal of the horse family; often used with *down*

foalfoot \ˈ=ˌ=\ *n, pl* **foalfoots** [ME *folefot*, fr. *fole* + *fot*, *foot* foot; fr. the shape of the leaves] **:** COLTSFOOT a

foal·hood \ˈ=ˌhu̇d\ *n* **:** the period or state of being a foal

¹foam \ˈfōm\ *n* -S [ME *fom, fome, foom*, fr. OE *fām;* akin to OHG *feim* foam, Norw *feim* coating, L *spuma* foam, *pumex* pumice, Skt *phena* foam] **1 :** a light whitish mass of fine bubbles that is formed in or on the surface of a liquid by agitation (as of ocean waves) or fermentation or effervescence **:** a dispersion of a gas or vapor in a liquid **:** FROTH, SPUME — compare EMULSION 2a **2 :** the froth formed in the mouth of an animal by salivation or on the skin (as of a horse) by sweating **3 :** SEA **4 :** something like foam ⟨a fine ~ of lace at his wrists and throat —Max Peacock⟩ **5 :** a stabilized frothy substance generated either by a chemical reaction or by mechanical agitation for use in fighting esp. gasoline and oil fires by blanketing and smothering them **6 :** material in a lightweight cellular spongy or rigid form produced by foaming: as **a :** FOAM RUBBER **b :** EXPANDED PLASTIC

²foam \ ″ \ *vb* -ED/-ING/-S [ME *fomen*, fr. *fom, fome*, n.] *vi* **1 :** to gather or form foam **2 :** to froth at the mouth in anger **:** be angry **:** RAGE ⟨he ~*ed* and stormed and threatened⟩ **3 :** to gush out in foam ⟨blood ~*ing* from his mouth⟩ **4 :** to form a froth or scum on the water surface that entrains solids and prevents the liberation of steam — used of a steam boiler ~ *vt* **1 :** to cause to foam **:** cover with foam; *specif* **:** to cause air bubbles to form in (as concrete, mortar, or plaster) **2 :** to introduce gas bubbles into (as a plastic or resin) in order to form a lightweight cellular material **:** EXPAND, WHIP ⟨plastic is ~*ed* in place in a sandwich construction⟩

foam cell *n* **:** a swollen vacuolated reticuloendothelial cell filled with lipid inclusions and characteristic of certain conditions involving disturbance of lipid metabolism

foam concrete *or* **foamed concrete** *n* **:** concrete in which air bubbles have been formed primarily to reduce the weight

foamed plastic *also* **foam plastic** *n* **:** EXPANDED PLASTIC

foam·er \ˈfōmə(r)\ *n* -S **:** one that foams ⟨~*s* crashing on the shore⟩

foamflower \ˈ=ˌ==\ *n* **:** FALSE MITERWORT

foam glass *n* **:** a black opaque cellular glass material ⅕ the weight of glass that is made by firing crushed glass with powdered carbon and is used as a substitute for cork, balsa wood, or kapok in life preservers and as an insulating material

foam·i·ly \ˈfōməlē, -li\ *adv* **:** in a foamy manner

foam·i·ness \-mēnəs, -min-\ *n* -ES **:** the quality or state of being foamy

foam·ing \ˈfōmiŋ\ *adj* [ME *foming*, fr. pres. part. of *fomen* to foam — more at FOAM] **:** covered with foam **:** producing foam — **foam·ing·ly** *adv*

foaming agent *n* **:** a material used to produce foaming (as in concrete, mortar, plaster)

Foam·ite \ˈfōˌmīt\ *trademark* — used for a preparation consisting of two chemical solutions that on mixture generate a tough foam of carbon dioxide for extinguishing fires

foam·less \ˈ=ləs\ *adj* **:** having no foam **:** free from foam ⟨the blue line of a ~ sea —D.G.Rossetti⟩

foamlike \ˈ=ˌ=\ *adj* **:** having the appearance and texture of foam ⟨~ dresses⟩

foam rubber *n* **:** spongy rubber of fine texture made from latex by foaming (as by whipping) before vulcanization and used esp. in mattresses, cushions, and upholstery

foamy \ˈfōmē, -mi\ *adj* -ER/-EST [ME *fomy*, fr. OE *fāmig*, fr. *fām* foam + *-ig* -y — more at FOAM] **1 :** covered with foam **:** FROTHY **2 :** full of, consisting of, or resembling foam

¹fob \ˈfäb\ *vt* **fobbed; fobbed; fobbing; fobs** [ME *fobben* — more at FOP] **1** *archaic* **:** to impose on **:** DECEIVE, CHEAT **2** *archaic* **:** to obtain or to introduce by fraud or deceit **:** palm off **3 :** to fob off

²fob \ ″ \ *n* -S [ME] *archaic* **:** TRICK, SHAM

³fob \ ″ \ *n* -S [perh. akin to G dial. *fuppe* pocket, *fuppen* to pocket stealthily] **1** *also* **fob pocket :** a small pocket just below the front waistband of men's trousers **2** *also* **fob chain :** a short chain or ribbon connecting a watch carried in a fob pocket and an ornament hanging outside **3 a** (1) **:** an ornament (as a seal) attached to a fob chain (2) **:** a decorative device attached to a zipper, pin, or belt **b :** the watch carried in a fob pocket

⁴fob \ ″ \ *vt* **fobbed; fobbed; fobbing; fobs :** to put into one's fob **:** POCKET

FOB *abbr, often not cap* free on board

fob off *vt* [¹*fob*] **1 :** to put off with a deceit or with an inferior substitute for what is needed or expected ⟨the . . . patient thus denied effective examination is *fobbed off* with a bottle of medicine —*Spectator*⟩ **2 :** to pass or offer (something spurious) as genuine **:** palm off ⟨the pretentious phraseology with which they *fobbed off* their prophecies on the laity —Lancelot Hogben⟩ **3 :** to put aside

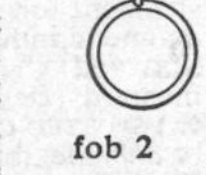

fob 2

: fend off ⟨a pleasant . . . gift of humor which he used to *fob off* laymen who wanted a simple explanation of relativity — G.R.Harrison⟩ : thrust away ⟨why do they now *fob off* what once they would have welcomed eagerly —Walter Lippmann⟩

FOC *abbr* **1** free of charge **2** free on car

fo·cal \ˈfōkəl\ *adj* [*focus* + *-al*] : of, relating to, or having a focus — **fo·cal·ly** \-kəlē, -li\ *adv*

focal area *n* : a region whose characteristic speech features are imitated in neighboring regions : a center from which linguistic changes spread — compare GRADED AREA, RELIC AREA

focal infection *n* : a persistent bacterial infection of some organ or region (as a tonsil or the root of a tooth); *esp* : one causing symptoms elsewhere in the body

fo·cal·iza·tion \ˌfōkələˈzāshən, -ˌlīz-\ *n* -s : the act of focalizing or the state of being focalized

fo·cal·ize \ˈfōkəˌlīz\ *vb* -ED/-ING/-s *vt* **1** : to bring to a focus : FOCUS **2** : to adjust the focus of (as a lens or the eye) **3** *med* : to confine to a limited area ⟨~ an infection⟩ ~ *vi* **1** : to come to a focus : CONVERGE, CONCENTRATE **2** *med* : to become confined to a limited area ⟨pullorum disease commonly ~s in the ovary of the adult bird⟩

focal length *n* : the distance from the principal point of a lens or concave mirror to the principal focus

focal plane *n* : a plane that is parallel to the plane of a lens or mirror and that passes through a principal focus

focal-plane shutter *n* : a camera shutter used chiefly for instantaneous exposures in which a slit in an opaque curtain is passed directly across and in front of the film near the focal plane, the width of the slit and the speed of its movement determining the duration of the exposure

focal point *n* **1** : PRINCIPAL FOCUS **2** : a center of activity or of interest : the point of convergence of lines of action or of argument ⟨the producer . . . is the *focal point*, the coordinator of all these creative forces —Rebecca Franklin⟩

focal spot *n* : the small area of the target of an X-ray tube on which the cathode rays are focused

focht \ˈfäkt\ *Scot var of* FOUGHT

fo·com·e·ter \fōˈkäməd·ə(r)\ *also* **fo·cim·e·ter** \-ˈsim-\ *n* [F *focomètre, focimètre,* fr. *foco-, foci-* (fr. NL *focus*) + *-mètre* -meter] : an instrument for measuring either the visual or the photographic focal length of an objective or of another optical system

fo'c'sle *var of* FORECASTLE

¹fo·cus \ˈfōkəs\ *n, pl* **focuses** \-ōkəsəz\ *or* **fo·ci** \-ōˌsī\ [NL, fr. L, fireplace, hearth; perh. akin to Arm *bosor* red, *bots* flame] **1** : a point at which rays (as of light, heat, sound) converge or from which they diverge or appear to diverge; *specif* : the point where the geometrical lines or their prolongations conforming to the rays diverging from or converging toward another point intersect and give rise to an image after reflection by a mirror or refraction by a lens or optical system **2 a** : FOCAL LENGTH ⟨a telescope of twenty-feet ~⟩ **b** : adjustment (as of the eye or an eyepiece) for distinct vision ⟨a telescope or microscope comes sharply to ~⟩ **c** : the position in which something must be placed (as in relation to a camera lens) for clearness of image or clarity of mental perception ⟨the whole scene was difficult to bring into ~⟩ ⟨brought into immediate ~ the meaning of the war⟩ **d** : the area that may be seen distinctly by the eye or resolved into a clear image by a lens ⟨wide-*focus* lens camera⟩ **3** : one of the points that with the corresponding directrix defines a conic section ⟨conic *foci*⟩ **4** : a localized area of disease or the chief site of a generalized disease or infection ⟨a tuberculous ~ in the lungs⟩ **5** [L] *archaic* : HEARTH, FIREPLACE **6** : a central point: as **a** : a center of activity or attraction or one drawing the greatest attention and interest ⟨Whitehall . . . was the ~ of political intrigue and of fashionable gaiety —T.B.Macaulay⟩ **b** : a point of concentration or of emanation ⟨a happy man or woman is . . . a radiating ~ of goodwill —R.L.Stevenson⟩ **c** : one aspect or area of a culture that is more complex and extensively elaborated than others **d** : FOCAL AREA **7** : the place of origin of an earthquake being a rather indefinite region that approaches nearest to a point in some volcanic earthquakes and nearest to a line or plane in some tectonic earthquakes **8** : the first-formed usu. central part of a fish scale **9** : a unit of classification in the Midwestern system for American archaeology constituting a group of components yielding artifacts almost identical in those features determinative of type — see ASPECT; compare PATTERN, PHASE **syn** see CENTER — **in focus** : having or giving the proper sharpness of outline due to good focalization— used of an optical instrument or its parts or of an image — **out of focus** : not in focus

²focus \"\ *vb* **focused** *also* **focussed**; **focused** *also* **focussed**; **focusing** *also* **focussing**; **focuses** *also* **focusses** *vt* **1 a** : to bring (as light rays) to a focus : CONCENTRATE **b** : to cause (an electron beam esp. in a television tube) to converge and give a small bright spot **2** : to cause to be concentrated ⟨the crime ~*ed* public attention on the problem of parole⟩ **3** : to adjust the focus of (as the eye or a lens) ⟨~*ing* the glasses on a distant ship⟩ **4** : to bring (as an image) into focus ⟨the most clearly ~*ed* picture yet available of the American conservative mind at work —Eric Goldman⟩ ~ *vi* **1** : to come to a focus : CONVERGE **2** : to adjust one's eye or a camera to a certain range ⟨newborn babies cannot ~ for several months⟩

fo·cus·able \-səbəl\ *adj* : capable of being focused or brought into focus

fo·cus·er \-sə(r)\ *n* -s : one that focuses or aids in focusing

focusing cloth *n* : an opaque dark cloth used to cover the rear of the camera and the head and shoulders of the photographer in order to exclude most of the light except that coming through the lens

focusing coil *n* : a coil that focuses an electron beam (as in a cathode-ray tube) by means of a magnetic field

focusing glass *n* : a small magnifying glass used for enlarging the image thrown on the ground glass of a camera as an aid in exact focusing

focus lamp *n* **1** : an incandescent lamp having a filament coiled or crumpled into a spiral or zigzag form so that the light, being concentrated in a small space, can be brought into the focus of a lens or mirror **2** : an arc lamp with feeding mechanism so constructed as to keep the arc in a constant position with reference to the optical system by means of which its rays are focused

fo·cus·less \ˈ==ləs\ *adj* : having no focus : not focusing

FOD *abbr* free of damage

¹fod·der \ˈfädə(r)\ *n* -s *often attrib* [ME, fr. OE *fōdor, foddor* — more at FOOD] **1** : FOOD, PROVISION — not now in formal use **2** : something fed to domestic animals; *esp* : coarse food (as hay, vegetables, corn fodder) for cattle, horses, and sheep ⟨~ plants⟩ ⟨~ trees⟩ — compare CONCENTRATE, ROUGHAGE **3** : something that is used to supply a constant demand : something to be consumed: as **a** *slang* : AMMUNITION **b** : raw material for artistic creation ⟨burlesques of animals, babies, and females are perennial clown ~ —Bill Ballantine⟩ ⟨the ~ of the middlebrow novelist —V.S. Pritchett⟩ **c** : human beings regarded for a certain purpose as an undifferentiated mass ⟨labor ~⟩ ⟨cannon ~⟩ ⟨factory ~⟩

²fodder \"\ *vt* **foddered**; **foddered**; **foddering** \-d(ə)riŋ\ **fodders** [ME *fodderen,* fr. ¹*fodder,* n.] **1** : to feed with or as if with fodder **2** *obs* : GRAZE

³fodder *var of* FOTHER

fodder beet *n* : a sugar beet used or grown for fodder

foddering *n* -s [¹*fodder* + *-ing*] : a portion or allowance of fodder

fod·der·less \ˈfädə(r)ləs\ *adj* : having no fodder ⟨~ and starving cattle⟩

fodg·el \ˈfäjəl\ *adj* [prob. fr. *fodge,* var. of ¹*fadge*] *Scot* : plump and well-built : BUXOM

fo·di·ent \ˈfōdēənt\ *adj* [L *fodient-, fodiens,* pres. part. of *fodere* to dig — more at BED] : fitted for digging or burrowing ⟨a ~ animal⟩

foe \ˈfō\ *n* -s [ME *fo, fa,* fr. OE *fāh, fā,* fr. *fāh, fā,* adj., hostile, outlawed; akin to OHG *gifēh* hostile, *fēhan* to hate, ON *feikn* terrible, horrible, Goth bi*faih* greediness, L *piget* it annoys, Skt *piśuna* malicious, treacherous] **1** : one who holds a grudge or personal enmity, hatred, or malice against another : ENEMY ⟨a political ~ of long standing⟩ **2** : an enemy in war : a hostile army or a member of a hostile force : ADVERSARY ⟨whispering, with white lips, "the ~! They come! they come!" —Lord Byron⟩ **3** : one who opposes on principle ⟨a ~ to religion⟩ ⟨a ~ of speculative theories⟩ **4** : something prejudicial or injurious ⟨a ~ to health⟩ **syn** see ENEMY

foe·de·ra·tus \ˌfedəˈrād·əs\ *n, pl* **foedera·ti** \-ˈäd·ˌī\ [L, fr. *foederatus,* adj., allied, federated — more at FEDERATE] : an auxiliary soldier serving the Roman Empire

foehn *or* **föhn** \ˈfərn, ˈfen, *Ger* fœ̄n\ *n* -s [G *föhn,* fr. OHG *phōnno,* fr. (assumed) VL *faonius,* fr. L *favonius* warm west wind; akin to L *fovēre* to warm — more at DAY] : a warm dry wind blowing down the side of a mountain — compare CHINOOK 3b

foehnlike \ˈ=,=\ *adj* : having the characteristics of a foehn

foe·less \ˈfōləs\ *adj* : having no enemy

foe·man \ˈfōmən\ *n, pl* **foemen** [ME *foman,* fr. OE *fāhman,* fr. *fāh* hostile + *man* — more at FOE, MAN] : an enemy in war : FOE ⟨and the stern joy which warriors feel in *foemen* worthy of their steel —Sir Walter Scott⟩

foe·nic·u·lum \fēˈnikyələm\ *n, cap* [NL, fr. L *foeniculum, faeniculum, feniculum* fennel — more at FENNEL] : a small genus of Eurasian herbs (family Umbelliferae) with pinnately compound leaves and yellow flowers — see FENNEL

foenngreek *or* **foenugreek** *var of* FENUGREEK

foenus *var of* FAENUS

foetid *var of* FETID

foeto- *or* **foeti-** — see FETO-

foetus *var of* FETUS

fo·far·raw \ˈfōfəˌrȯ\ *var of* FOOFARAW

¹fog \ˈfȯg, ˈfäg\ *n* -s [ME *fogge, fog* rank grass, winter grass, perh. of Scand origin; akin to Norw *fogg* tall, worthless grass, ON *fugja* mold, *fūll* rotten — more at FOUL] **1** *dial* **a** : dead or decaying grass on land in the winter **b** : a second growth of grass : AFTERMATH **2** *dial* **a** : MOSS **b** : VELVET GRASS

²fog \"\ *vb* **fogged**; **fogged**; **fogging**; **fogs** *vt* **1** *Brit* **a** : to pasture (animals) on fog **b** : to feed (cattle) with fog **2** *dial* : to leave (land) under fog ~ *vi, dial* : to become overgrown with fog

³fog \"\ *n* -s [prob. of Scand origin; akin to Shetland Norse *fjog, fjug* thin layer of cloud, dust, Dan *fog* spray, shower, driving rain, ON *fjūk* snowstorm, *fjūka* to be driven by the wind (used of snow), to snow violently; akin to MHG *fochen* to blow, L *pussula, pustula* blister, pimple, Gk *physan* to blow, inflate, *pygē* buttocks, Skt *puṣyati* he thrives, flourishes, nourishes, promotes; basic meaning: blowing, inflating] **1** : vapor condensed to fine particles of water suspended in the lower atmosphere that differs from cloud only in being near the ground and is sometimes distinguished from mist in being less transparent **2 a** : a murky or thick condition of the atmosphere **b** : a substance so diffused as to lessen the transparency of the atmosphere **c** : a suspension of fine droplets in a gas ⟨tar ~ in manufactured gas⟩ **3 a** : a fine spray of water or foam discharged from a fog nozzle used in fire fighting **b** : a fine spray of any substance (as an insecticide) **4** : a state of mental confusion, uncertainty, or obscurity : BEWILDERMENT ⟨I am in a complete ~ as to what to do next⟩ ⟨the subject is wrapped in ~s of vague thinking —H.A. Overstreet⟩ **5** *or* **fog blue a** : a variable color averaging a grayish blue that is redder and paler than electric, greener and paler than copenhagen, and redder, lighter, and stronger than Gobelin **b** : a nearly neutral slightly bluish light gray **6** : a general or local density in a developed photographic image that is not associated with the image-forming exposure and is caused by chemical action or stray radiation

⁴fog \"\ *vb* **fogged**; **fogged**; **fogging**; **fogs** *vt* **1 a** : to cover or envelop with or as if with fog ⟨a *fogged* landscape⟩ **b** : to obscure (as a view) with or as if with fog ⟨a heavy smoke *fogged* our view of the city⟩ — often used with *up* ⟨the smoke *fogged* up the road ahead⟩ **c** : to make blurred ⟨his eyes were still *fogged* with sleep⟩ **d** : to make fogbound — often used with *in* ⟨the airport was *fogged* in for two days⟩ **e** : to cover or treat with a substance (as insecticide or pesticide) in the form of spray ⟨thoroughly *fogged* the area with insecticide⟩ **2** : to make obscure or confusing to the intelligence or understanding ⟨~ an issue with too much talk⟩ ⟨a text *fogged* by generalities⟩ — often used with *up* ⟨the issue was *fogged* up during the debate⟩ **3** : to make confused (as a person or the mind) ⟨*fogged* by the examination⟩ ⟨arguments that only ~ the understanding⟩ **4** *dial* : DRIVE, CHASE **5** : to blur (a field of vision) with lenses that prevent a sharp focus in order to relax accommodation before testing vision **6** : to produce fog on (a photographic film or plate) during development ~ *vi* **1** : to become covered or thick with fog — often used with *up* ⟨the pilot could not return because the airfield had *fogged* up behind him⟩ **2 a** : to become blurred or beclouded by a covering of fog or mist ⟨his glasses *fogged* when he entered the warm room⟩ — often used with *up* ⟨the mirror *fogged* up with the steam⟩ **b** : to become indistinct through exposure to light or radiation **3** *chiefly West* : RUSH, HURRY, RUN, GALLOP ⟨cattle came *fogging* down the road⟩ **4** *Brit* : to put fog signals in place on a railway line **syn** see OBSCURE

fo·gas \ˈfōˌgäsh\ *n, pl* **fogas** [Hung] : an eastern European fish (*Lucioperca sandra*) resembling a perch; *esp* : one from Lake Balaton in Hungary that is highly esteemed as food

fogbank \ˈ=,=\ *n* : a mass of fog resting upon the sea

fog belt *n* : a region where fogs are frequent

fogbound \ˈ=,=\ *adj* **1** : covered with or surrounded by fog ⟨~ coast⟩ **2** : unable to move because of fog ⟨~ ship⟩ ⟨~ air passengers at an airport⟩

fog·bow \ˈ=,bō\ *n* : a nebulous arc or circle of white or yellowish light sometimes seen in a fogbank — called also *fogdog, fogeater, seadog*

fog buoy *n* **1** : a buoy bearing a warning bell or whistle **2** : a buoy towed by a ship in formation to indicate to the next astern her proper position — called also *position buoy, towing spar*

fogdog \ˈ=,=\ *n* : FOGBOW

fogeater \ˈ=,==\ *n* **1** : FOGBOW **2** : the full moon when rising in a fog

fogey *var of* FOGY

fog fever *n, Brit* : an acute pulmonary emphysema of cattle grazing on aftermath

fogfruit \ˈ=,=\ *n* : a plant of the genus *Lippia* (as *L. lanceolata* and *L. nodiflora*)

fog·gage \ˈfȯgij, ˈfäg-\ *n* -s [ME (Sc dial.) *fogage* winter grass, winter grazing, fr. *fog* winter grass + *-age* — more at FOG] *chiefly Scot* : ¹FOG 1a

fog·ga·ra \ˈfägərə\ *n* -s [Ar] : an underground conduit for water in desert country (as in the Sahara)

¹fog·ger \ˈfȯgə(r), ˈfäg-\ *n* -s [²*fog* + *-er*] *dial Eng* : a farm laborer chiefly engaged in caring for cattle

²fogger \"\ *n* -s [⁴*fog* + *-er*] : one that fogs: *esp* : an apparatus for spreading a fog of pesticide

fog·gie \ˈfägi\ *Scot var of* FOGY

fog·gi·ly \ˈfȯgəlē, ˈfäg-, -li\ *adv* : in a foggy manner : MISTILY

fog·gi·ness \-gēnəs, -gin-\ *n* -ES : the quality or state of being foggy

fogging *pres part of* FOG

fog grass *n* : ¹FOG 1

fog gun *n* : FIRE GUN 1

¹fog·gy \ˈfȯgē, ˈfägē, -gi\ *adj* -ER/-EST [¹*fog* + *-y*] **1** *dial Brit* : of, covered with, or resembling coarse grass **2** *chiefly Scot* : MOSSY

²foggy \"\ *adj* -ER/-EST [³*fog* + *-y*] **1** *obs* : BLOATED, FLABBY **2** *obs* : MARSHY, BOGGY **3 a** : filled or abounding with fog ⟨~ coast⟩ ⟨a ~ morning⟩ **b** : covered or made opaque by moisture or grime ⟨a ~ skylight⟩ **c** : FOGGED ⟨a ~ old snapshot⟩ **4** : not clear: as **a** : slightly hoarse or husky in tone ⟨her ~, appealing voice —*Time*⟩ **b** : VAGUE, MUDDLED, CONFUSED ⟨the ~ language of prophecy⟩ **c** : TENUOUS — used esp. in negative statements ⟨they haven't the *foggiest* notion of what they are voting for⟩

¹foghorn \ˈ=,=\ *n* [³*fog* + *horn*] **1** : a horn sounded as a fog signal **2** : a loud hoarse or insistent voice

²foghorn \"\ *vt* : to sound by or as if by a foghorn ⟨personal faults . . . we hear ~*ed* over the radio —Kay Hardy⟩

fogie *var of* FOGY

fo·gle \ˈfōgəl\ *n* -s [origin unknown] *slang* : a silk handkerchief or neckerchief

fogle hunter *or* **fogle heister** *n, slang* : PICKPOCKET

fog·less \ˈfȯgləs, ˈfäg-\ *adj* : marked by the absence of fog ⟨the first ~ morning in a week⟩

fog light *or* **fog lamp** *n* : a lamp or automotive headlight often yellow in color and specially designed to penetrate fog, dust, or smoke

fog nozzle *n* : a fire-hose nozzle that discharges a fine spray of water or foam

fo·go \ˈfō(ˌ)gō\ *n* -s [prob. alter. of *hogo*] *dial* : STENCH, STINK

fo·gón \fōˈgōn\ *n, pl* **fogo·nes** \-ˈgō(ˌ)nās\ [Sp, hearth, fireplace, prob. fr. Catal *fogó,* fr. *foc* fire, fr. L *focus* hearth, fireplace, fire — more at FOCUS] : a corner-set fireplace found in Indian and Spanish American architecture in southwestern U.S.

fo·gou \ˈfō(ˌ)gü\ *n* -s [Corn *fogo, fougo, ogo;* akin to W *gogof* cave, Bret *kougoñ*] *dial Eng* : CAVE

fo·gram *or* **fo·grum** \ˈfōgrəm\ *n* -s [origin unknown] : an antiquated person : FOGY

fog room *n* : a room for the curing of concrete into which water is sprayed in a fine mist

fogs *pres 3d sing of* FOG, *pl of* FOG

fo·gy *also* **fo·gey** *or* **fo·gie** \ˈfōgē, -gi\ *n, pl* **fogies** *also* **fogeys** [origin unknown] **1** : a person who is behind the times, overconservative, or slow — usu. used with *old* ⟨notorious old bore; regular old ~ —W.M.Thackeray⟩ **2** : one of the increases over base pay that are given after specified periods of military service

fo·gy·ish \-gēish\ *adj* : having old-fashioned views : OUT-OF-DATE : ANTIQUATED ⟨~ educators⟩ ⟨~ opinions⟩

fo·gy·ism \-gēˌizəm\ *n* -s : conservative or old-fashioned ideas or behavior

foh \ˈfō\ *archaic var of* FAUGH

föhn *var of* FOEHN

foi·ble \ˈfȯibəl\ *n* -s [obs. F (now *faible*), fr. obs. *foible,* adj. (now *faible*), weak, fr. OF *fleble, feble, foible* — more at FEEBLE] **1** : the part of a sword blade or foil blade between the middle and point — opposed to *forte* **2** : a minor flaw or shortcoming in personal character or behavior : FAILING, WEAKNESS ⟨longing for past ages is a human ~⟩ **3** : an eccentric or whimsical liking for or interest in something : FAD ⟨hi-fi looked like the private ~ of experts —Brooks Atkinson⟩ **syn** see FAULT

foie gras \fwägrä\ *n* [F] : fat liver esp. of a goose usu. in the form of a pâté, puree, or terrine

¹foil \ˈfȯil, *esp before pause or consonant* -ȯiəl\ *vt* -ED/-ING/-s [ME *foilen* to trample, full (cloth), modif. of MF *fouler* — more at FULL] **1** *obs* : to tread under foot : TRAMPLE **2** : to spoil (a trail or scent) by crossing or retracing **3 a** : to prevent (a person) from attaining a desired end : keep from achieving a goal : DEFEAT, REPULSE ⟨~*ed* at Council Bluffs . . . they turned toward the southwest —R.A.Billington⟩ **b** : to bring (as a scheme, an effort, an attack) to naught : make vain and ineffectual : BAFFLE ⟨intelligence as a means to ~ brute force —Lafcadio Hearn⟩ **syn** see FRUSTRATE

²foil \"\ *n* -s [ME *foyle,* fr. *foilen,* v.] **1** *archaic* : DEFEAT, CHECK, FRUSTRATION **2** *obs* : an incomplete fall in wrestling **3** *also* **foil·ing** \ˈfȯiliŋ\ *archaic* : the track or trail of an animal **4 a** : a fencing weapon that resembles an épée but has a flat guard which may be round, oval, rectangular, or figure-eight in outline and a lighter and more flexible blade of rectangular or square cross section tapering to a blunt point **b foils** *pl* : the art or practice of fencing with foils that limits the target to the trunk

³foil \"\ *n* -s [ME *foile, foil,* fr. MF *fuelle, fueille, foille* (fr. L *folia,* pl. of *folium*) & *fuel, fueil, foil,* fr. L *folium* — more at BLADE] **1** : a plant leaf — now used chiefly in compounds; compare SEXFOIL, TREFOIL **2 a** : one of several small curved indentations that meet and form points or cusps; *specif* : an indentation between cusps in Gothic tracery **b** : one of several arcs that enclose a complex figure ⟨the rim of a tray having eight ~s⟩ **3** *obs* **a** : a leaf of paper **b** : COUNTERFOIL **4 a** : a paper-thin material : TISSUE; *esp* : very thin metal for such purposes as providing decorative covering or moistureproof lining or wrapping **b** : a thin coat of tin or silver laid on the back of a looking glass to cause reflection **c** *or* **foil paper** : METALLIC PAPER 3 **5 a** *obs* : the setting of a jewel **b** : a thin piece of metal or other material put under a paste or inferior stone to add color or brilliancy **6** : something that serves by contrast of color or quality to set off another to advantage or sometimes to disadvantage ⟨everything was animated and gay . . . the men in their black coats were an admirable ~ —Victoria Sackville-West⟩ ⟨an artist and an intellectual, a ~ for her sentimental mother —B.R.Redman⟩ ⟨acting as a ~ for a stage comedian⟩

foils 2a

⁴foil \"\ *vt* -ED/-ING/-s **1** : to back or cover with foil **2** : to enhance or set off by contrast

foiled \ˈfȯi(ə)ld\ *adj* [³*foil* + *-ed*] *of an arch or window* : ornamented with foils : having curved indentations

foil·ing \ˈfȯiliŋ\ *n* -s [³*foil* + *-ing*] : ornamentation with foils

foils·man \ˈfȯilzmən\ *n, pl* **foilsmen** : one who fences with a foil : FENCER

¹foin \ˈfȯin\ *vi* -ED/-ING/-s [ME *foinen,* fr. *foin* fork for spearing fish, fr. MF *foisne, foine,* fr. L *fuscina*] *archaic* : to thrust with a sword or spear : LUNGE

²foin \"\ *n* -s [ME, fr. *foinen,* v.] **1 a** : a pass in fencing : LUNGE **b** : a wound made by a thrust **2** *archaic* : ²FOIL 4

³foin *n* -s [ME *foine, foin, fune,* fr. OF *foine, faine,* fr. (assumed) VL *fagina,* fr. L *fagus* beech + *-ina* (fr. fem. of *-inus* -ine) — more at BEECH] *obs* : the stone marten or its fur

foi·son \ˈfȯizᵊn\ *n* -s [ME *foisoun,* fr. MF *foison,* fr. L *fusion-, fusio* action of pouring, founding, melting, effusion — more at FUSION] **1** *archaic* : rich harvest : PLENTY, ABUNDANCE ⟨that from the seedness the bare fallow brings to teeming ~ —Shak.⟩ **2** *chiefly Scot* **a** : nourishment or sustenance esp. from food or drink **b** : physical energy or strength **c** : strength of mind or character

foi·son·less \-ləs\ *adj, dial Brit* : FUSHIONLESS

¹foist *n* -s [fr. earlier *fuste,* fr. MF, fr. *fust* wood, stick, beam, barrel, fr. L *fustis* cudgel] **1** *obs* : a light galley **2** *obs* : RIVERBOAT : BARGE

²foist \ˈfȯist\ *vb* -ED/-ING/-s [prob. fr. obs D *vuisten* to take into one's hand, fr. MD *vūsten, vuisten,* fr. *vūst, vuist* fist; akin to OE *fȳst* fist — more at FIST] *vt* **1** *obs* : to introduce when palmed : PALM — used of dice **2 a** : to introduce or insert surreptitiously or without warrant ⟨the comments of men . . . had been ~*ed* into Christian religion —Matthew Arnold⟩ **b** : to force another to accept esp. by stealth or deceit ⟨there are two nestlings unless a cowbird has ~*ed* its brat upon them —D.C.Peattie⟩ ⟨when the states . . . ~ unnecessary expenses on local taxpayers —T.C.Desmond⟩ **c** : to attribute wrongfully ⟨an author may try out a theory on paper and be dissatisfied with it. If by chance the document survives him it is unfair to ~ the doctrine upon him —R.I. Aaron⟩ ⟨a purely imaginary characteristic is ~*ed* on the universe and presented as an axiom of science —Herbert Dengle⟩ **3** : to pass off (something spurious) as genuine or worthy ⟨her novel is better written than many ~*ed* on the reading public —Harry Hansen⟩ ~ *vi* **1** *obs* : to practice cheating **2** *obs* : to pick pockets

³foist *n* -s **1** *obs* : FOISTER **2** *obs* : RASCALITY, SWINDLE

foist·er \ˈfȯistə(r)\ *n* -s [²*foist* + *-er*] **1** *archaic* : PICKPOCKET **2** *obs* : a palmer of dice : CHEAT, ROGUE

foisty \ˈfȯisti\ *adj* -ER/-EST [alter. of *fusty*] *dial Brit* : MUSTY, MOULDY

FOK *abbr* free of knots

fol *abbr* **1** folio **2** following

fo·la·cin \ˈfōləsən, ˈfäl-\ *n* -s [*folic acid* + *-in*] : FOLIC ACID 1

¹fold \ˈfōld\ *n* -s [ME *fold, fald,* fr. OE *falod, falud, fald;* akin to OS *faled* pen, enclosure, MLG *vālt* pen, enclosure, manure heap, MD *vaelt, vaelde,* and perh. to ON *fjǫl* plank, OHG *spaltan* to split — more at SPILL] **1 a** : an enclosure for sheep : PEN **b** *Brit* : a small portable wire enclosure that is commonly attached to a coop or hutch for moving poultry or rabbits about onto fresh grass **2 a** : a flock of sheep **b** : a group, institution, or organization providing spiritual salvation or paternal guidance, care, and protection : the company of the faithful or of the righteous : the adherents of a common religious or political belief ⟨the ~ of Protestantism⟩ ⟨a drift into the Republican ~⟩ **3** *dial Eng* : an enclosed area or yard adjoining or surrounding a house

²fold \"\ *vt* -ED/-ING/-S [ME *folden,* fr. ¹*fold,* n.] **1 :** to pen up or confine (as sheep) in a fold or on a crop to be grazed **2 a :** to pen sheep for the fertilization of (land) **b :** to pen grazing animals for the harvesting of (a crop)

³fold \"\ *vb* -ED/-ING/-S [ME *folden, falden,* fr. OE *fealdan;* akin to OHG *faldan* to fold, ON *falda* to fold, cover the head, Goth *falthan* to roll up, fold, L *duplus* double, Gk *diplasios* twofold, Skt *puṭati* he covers with, *puṭa* fold] *vt* **1 :** to lay one part over another part of **:** double upon itself **:** lay in pleats ⟨~ a length of cloth⟩ ⟨~ a letter⟩ ⟨~ printed sheets for binding⟩ ⟨~ over the edge to make a hem⟩ **2 :** to reduce the length or bulk of by doubling over or lapping over ⟨~ a tent⟩ ⟨~*ed* his long legs under the chair⟩ — often used with *up* ⟨the bedding was ~*ed* up and stowed away⟩ **3 :** to clasp together (as the hands) **:** ENTWINE ⟨~ your arms⟩ ⟨the bird ~*s* its wings⟩ **4 :** to clasp or enwrap closely **:** ENVELOP, EMBRACE, SURROUND ⟨~*ing* her son to her breast⟩ ⟨a village ~*ed* away in the hills⟩ **5 :** to bend (a surface or stratum) into folds **6 a :** to incorporate (a food ingredient) into a mixture by repeated overturnings without stirring or beating ⟨~ beaten egg whites into cake mix⟩ ⟨~ raisins into batter⟩ **b :** to incorporate closely **:** make a part of something (as by enveloping) ⟨all sorts of persons, places, and animals have been ~*ed* into this version of Tolstoy's vision —Philip Hamburger⟩ **7 :** ¹PLY 1b **8 a :** to turn (one's cards) facedown to concede defeat or indicate dropping **b :** to bring (as a business venture) to an end **:** close up ⟨after a few months he decided to ~ the magazine⟩ ~ *vi* **1 :** to become doubled or pleated **:** become flatter or smaller by doubling ⟨the bed ~*s* into a recess in the wall⟩ — often used with *up* ⟨watched him ~ up into the seat⟩ ⟨the map ~*s* up into a handy case⟩ **2 :** to fold up

⁴fold \"\ *n* -S [ME *fold, folde,* fr. *folden,* v.] **1 :** a doubling or folding over esp. of a flexible substance **:** the manner in which something is folded ⟨an accordion ~ is used for maps⟩ **2 :** a part doubled or laid over another part **:** PLEAT, BEND, PLICATION ⟨hidden in the ~*s* of the curtain⟩ ⟨~*s* of a banner⟩ **:** LAYER, COAT **3 :** a coil of a snake **4** *archaic* **:** one side of a double door or gate **:** LEAF **5 :** the pages or leaves of a book formed by folding one sheet of paper **6 a :** a bend or flexure into an arch or a trough produced in rock by forces operative after the depositing or consolidation of the rock — see ANTICLINE, SYNCLINE **b** *chiefly Brit* **:** an undulation in the landscape either upward (as a low rounded hill) or downward (as a hollow) **7** *anat* **:** a margin apparently formed by the doubling upon itself of a membrane or other flat structure **:** PLICA, RUGA ⟨neural ~*s*⟩ ⟨vocal ~*s*⟩ **8 :** PLY 2a **9 :** the crease made by folding a newspaper in half ⟨a headline should not be placed across the ~⟩ **10 :** FOLDER 2

-fold \ˌfōld\ *suffix* [ME *-fold, -fald,* fr. OE *-feald;* akin to OHG *-falt* -fold, ON *-faldr,* Goth *-falths;* derivatives fr. the root of E ³*fold*] **1 :** multiplied by (a specified number) **:** times — in adjectives ⟨a twelve*fold* increase⟩ and adverbs ⟨it will repay you ten*fold*⟩ **2 :** having (so many) laps, layers, or parts ⟨the three*fold* aspect of the problem⟩

fold·able \ˈfōldəbəl\ *adj* **:** that can be folded **:** FOLDING

fold·age \ˈfōldij\ *or* **fald·age** \ˈfōldij, ˈfal-\ *n* -S [ME *faldage,* fr. *fold, fald* + *-age*] *old English law* **:** the right of the lord of a manor to have his tenant's sheep graze on his land so as to manure it

foldaway \ˈ⸗ˌ⸗ˌ⸗\ *adj* [fr. *fold away,* v.] **:** designed to fold out of the way or out of sight ⟨~ doors⟩ ⟨~ bed⟩

foldboat \ˈ⸗ˌ⸗\ *n* [trans. of G *faltboot*] **:** FALTBOAT

foldboater \ˈ⸗ˌ⸗ˌ⸗\ *n* **:** a person operating a faltboat

foldboating \ˈ⸗ˌ⸗ˌ⸗\ *n* **:** traveling in a faltboat; *esp* **:** the sport of shooting rapids and cruising on swift water in a faltboat

fold breccia *n* **:** a breccia resulting from the folding of brittle rock strata

foldcourse \ˈ⸗ˌ⸗\ *n* [¹*fold* + *course*] **1** *English law* **a :** land to which foldage is incident **b :** the right of foldage **2 :** SHEEPWALK

folded dipole *n* **:** an antenna in the form of an elongated horizontal loop resembling a dipole in appearance with connections at the middle of one or both of the two parallel sides

folden *archaic past part of* FOLD

fold·er \ˈfōldə(r)\ *n* -S [fr. ³*fold* + *-er*] **1 :** one that folds: as **a :** an instrument or machine for folding paper, leather, or other flexible material **b :** a worker who folds or who operates a folding machine **c :** CLEANER 1e **2 :** a printed circular folded usu. so that the printed matter does not cross the fold ⟨advertising ~⟩ ⟨railroad timetable ~⟩ — compare BROADSIDE **3 :** a folded cover or large envelope for holding or filing loose papers **4 :** a cut and creased flat piece of paperboard or corrugated board designed to be folded and secured as a shipping case (as for a book)

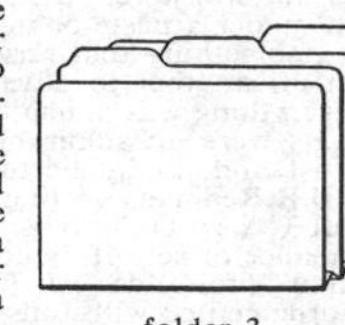
folder 3

fol·de·rol \ˈfäldəˌräl\ *also* **fal·de·ral** \ˈfaldəˌral\ *n* -S [fr. *fol-de-rol, fal-deral,* a refrain in old songs] **1 :** impractical, unnecessary, or excessive trimming, finery, or effects **:** pretty but flimsy or useless ornament **:** something that is unnecessary **:** TRIFLE, GEWGAW ⟨a gas or electric range and other ~*s* of an effete generation —Della Lutes⟩ ⟨the new collections of custom furs around town reveal plenty of ~, but there are practical things too —Lois Long⟩ **2 :** nonsensical talk or action **:** PIFFLE, NONSENSE ⟨the rest of the play . . . is a windy collection of improbable motives and costumed ~ —*Newsweek*⟩

¹folding *adj* [ME, fr. pres. part. of *folden* to fold — more at FOLD (to bend)] **1 :** capable of being folded up **:** COLLAPSIBLE ⟨~ chair⟩ ⟨~ table⟩ ⟨~ screen⟩ ⟨~ camera⟩ **2** *of paper and boards* **a :** safely foldable **b :** designed to be folded

²folding *n* -S [ME, action of penning livestock, fr. gerund of *folden* to fold — more at FOLD (to pen)] *Brit* **:** rotation grazing; *specif* **:** short-time intensive grazing of small areas of arable crops on which animals are confined by a portable fence

folding box *or* **folding carton** *n* **:** a container or carrier of paperboard that can be folded flat for shipment to the user

folding brake *n* **:** a device for folding over an edge on thin sheet metal

folding door *n* **1 :** a door in sections that can be folded back **:** an accordion door **:** DOUBLE DOOR **2 :** either of a pair of sliding doors between two rooms en suite

folding door 1

folding money *n* **:** ready or plentiful cash **:** money in sizable amounts **:** PAPER MONEY, BILLS — contrasted with *small change*

folding stair *n* **:** a movable stair (as to an attic) that can be folded or retracted out of the way

folding star *n* [²*folding;* fr. its rising at the time sheep were put into the fold] **:** EVENING STAR 1

folding strength *n* **:** the capacity of paper to withstand repeated folding without rupture

fold·less \ˈfōldləs\ *adj* [⁴*fold* + *-less*] **:** having no fold or crease

fold mountain *n* **:** a mountain whose rocks are predominantly folded

foldout \ˈ⸗ˌ⸗\ *n* -S [fr. *fold out,* v.] **:** an extra die-cut or folded leaf in a book, magazine, or other printed work

folds *pres 3d sing of* FOLD, *pl of* FOLD

fold soke *n* [ME *faldsok, faldsoken,* fr. *fald, fold* + *sok, soken* soke] **:** FOLDAGE

fold up *vi* **1 :** to give way **:** COLLAPSE, CRUMPLE ⟨at the first shot the deer stopped short, then suddenly *folded up*⟩ ⟨the old chair suddenly *folded up* under him⟩ **2 a :** to cease resistance or exertion **:** give up **:** FAIL, QUIT ⟨the horse *folded up* in the homestretch⟩ ⟨the defense *folded up* under the savage attack⟩ ⟨the weak just get crushed; you can't blame them for *folding up* —K.M.Dodson⟩ **b :** to stop production or operation for lack of funds, support, or business success **:** go bankrupt **:** close up **:** CLOSE ⟨small businesses were *folding up* right and left⟩

fold yard *n* [¹*fold*] *Brit* **:** an enclosure for sheep or cattle

fol·ger·ite \ˈfōljəˌrīt\ *n* -S [W.M.*Folger* †1928 Am. naval officer + E *-ite*] **:** PENTLANDITE

¹folia *pl of* FOLIUM

²fo·lia \fōˈlēə\ *n* -S [Pg, lit., folly, madness, fr. OPg, fr. OProv, fr. *fol* foolish, mad (fr. LL *follus*) + *-ia* -y (fr. L) — more at FOOL] **:** a noisy carnival dance of Portuguese origin

fo·li·a·ceous \ˌfōlēˈāshəs\ *adj* [L *foliaceus,* fr. *folium* leaf + *-aceus* -aceous — more at BLADE] **1 :** belonging to, consisting of, or having the texture or form of a foliage leaf ⟨~ sepal⟩ ⟨~ thallus⟩ ⟨~ inflorescence⟩ **2** *zool* **:** resembling a leaf in form or mode of growth **3 :** consisting of thin laminae of a mineral substance **:** having the form of a leaf or plate ⟨~ spar⟩

fo·li·a·ceous·ness *n* -ES **:** the quality or state of being foliaceous

fo·li·age \ˈfōl(ē)ij, -lyij\ *n* -S [alter. (influenced by L *folium*) of earlier *fuellage, foillage,* fr. MF *fuellage,* fr. *fuelle, fueille, foille* leaf + *-age* — more at FOIL] **1 :** the mass of leaves of a plant as produced in nature **:** LEAFAGE ⟨a tree with handsome ~⟩ **2 :** a cluster of leaves, flowers, and branches **3 :** a carved representation of leaves, flowers, and branches used for architectural ornamentation (as of capitals, friezes)

foliage brown *n* **:** FEUILLE MORTE

fo·li·aged \-jd\ *adj* **:** furnished or decorated with foliage **:** LEAVED ⟨the variously ~ mulberry⟩

foliage green *n* **:** a moderate yellow green that is greener and duller than average moss green and yellower and duller than average pea green or average apple green

foliage leaf *n* **:** an ordinary green leaf as distinguished from floral leaves, scales, and bracts

fo·li·a·geous \ˌfōlēˈājəs\ *adj* **:** containing representations of foliage

foliage plant *n* **:** a plant grown primarily for its decorative foliage (as members of the genera *Coleus* and *Philodendron*)

fo·li·al \ˈfōlēəl\ *adj* [L *folium* leaf + *-al*] **:** FOLIAR

fo·li·ar \ˈfōlēə(r)\ *adj* [F *foliaire,* fr. L *folium* leaf + F *-aire* -ar] **:** consisting of or relating to leaves

foliar bundle *n* **:** LEAF TRACE

foliar feeding *n* **:** the feeding of plants through leaves by spraying plant food on them

foliar gap *n* **:** LEAF GAP

foliar trace *n* **:** LEAF TRACE

¹fo·li·ate \ˈfōlēət, -ēˌāt, *usu* -d·+V\ *adj* [L *foliatus* leaved, fr. *folium* leaf + *-atus* -ate — more at BLADE] **1 :** shaped like a leaf ⟨~ sponge⟩ ⟨~ spearhead⟩ **2 :** furnished with or composed of leaves or leaflets **:** LAMINATED, FOLIATED, LEAFY ⟨~ stalk⟩ — used in combination ⟨3-*foliate*⟩ **3 :** FOLIOLATE

²foliate \"\ *n* -S **:** a rock displaying foliation

³foliate \-ēˌāt, *usu* -ād·+V\ *vb* -ED/-ING/-S [L *folium* + E *-ate* (v. suffix)] *vt* **1 :** to beat into a leaf or thin foil **2 :** to spread over (glass) with a thin coat of tin amalgam ⟨~ a mirror⟩ **:** FOIL **3 :** to number the leaves of (as a manuscript) — compare FOLIO, PAGE **4 a :** to form (as an arch) with foils **b :** to ornament (as a pedestal) with foliage ~ *vi* **1 :** to divide into laminae or leaves **2 :** to put forth leaves

fo·li·at·ed \ˈfōlēˌād·əd\ *adj* [L *foliatus* + E *-ed*] **1 :** produced or formed by foliating **:** characterized by foliation **:** ornamented with foils or with foliage **2 :** FOLIATE ⟨where weeds were as high and ~ as trees —Peggy Bennett⟩ **3 :** characterized by being separable into thin plates or folia ⟨graphite has a ~ structure⟩ **4** *of a joint in carpentry* **:** LAPPED, RABBETED

foliate papilla *n* **:** any of certain paired oval papillae of the lateral aspect of the posterior part of the tongue that are rudimentary in man but form the chief organs of taste of certain other mammals (as rabbits)

fo·li·a·tion \ˌfōlēˈāshən\ *n* -S [L *folium* + E *-ation*] **1 a :** the process of forming into a leaf **b :** the state of being in leaf **c :** VERNATION **2 a :** the act of foliating the leaves of a book or manuscript **b :** foliated numbers **3 :** the act of coating with tin amalgam (as in making mirrors) **4 a :** ornamentation with naturalistic or conventionalized foliage **b :** an ornament or decoration resembling a leaf **5 :** the enrichment of an opening by means of foils formed by cusps — compare TRACERY **6 :** the act of beating a metal into a thin plate, leaf, or foil **7 :** foliated texture **:** the process or property of dividing into plates or slabs due to the parallel arrangement or cleavage of the minerals **:** BANDED STRUCTURE

fo·lic acid \ˈfōlik-, ˈfäl-\ *n* [L *folium* leaf + E *-ic;* fr. its presence in green leaves] **1 :** a yellow or yellowish orange crystalline vitamin $C_{19}H_{19}N_7O_6$ of the vitamin B complex obtained esp. from leaves and from liver and also made synthetically and used chiefly in the treatment of nutritional megaloblastic anemia and sprue — called also *folacin, PGA, pteroylglutamic acid, pteroylmonoglutamic acid, vitamin B_c* **2 :** PTEROYLGLUTAMIC ACID 2

fo·lie à deux \(ˌ)fōˌlē(ˌ)äˈdə(r·), -dɶ\ *n, pl* **folies à deux** \-ē(ˌ)(z)ä-\ [F, lit., double madness] **:** the presence of the same or similar delusional ideas in two persons closely associated with one another; *esp* **:** the result of transmission of delusional ideas from one person to another

folie du doute \-ēdəˈdüt\ *n, pl* **folies du doute** \-ē(z)də-\ [F, lit., madness of doubt] **:** pathological indecisiveness esp. when extended to ordinarily simple choice situations

fo·lif·er·ous \fōˈlif(ə)rəs\ *also* **fo·li·if·er·ous** \ˌfōlēˈif(ə)rəs\ *adj* [L *folium* leaf + E *-ferous*] **:** producing leaves

fo·li·ic·o·lous \ˌfōlēˈikələs\ *adj* [ISV *folii-* (fr. L *folium* leaf) + *-colous*] **1 :** growing upon leaves ⟨~ liverworts⟩ **2 :** parasitic upon leaves ⟨~ fungi⟩

fo·li·i·form \ˈfōlēəˌfȯrm\ *adj* [ISV *folii-* + *-form;* prob. orig. formed as F *foliiforme*] **:** having the shape of a leaf

fo·lin·ic acid \fōˈlinik-\ *n* [*folic* + *-in* + *-ic*] **:** any of several natural or synthetic acids (as leucovorin) that are metabolically active forms of folic acid and support the growth of certain bacteria (as *Leuconostoc citrovorum*) — called also *citrovorum factor*

¹fo·lio \ˈfōlēˌō, -ōl, yō\ *n* -S [ME, fr. L, abl. of *folium* leaf of a tree, leaf of paper — more at BLADE] **1 a :** a leaf esp. of a manuscript or book **b :** a leaf number ⟨a school workbook in which writing is to appear on only one side of the leaf often has ~*s* on the right-hand pages⟩ **c :** a page number ⟨in books the even ~*s* are on the left-hand pages and the odd ~*s* on the right-hand pages⟩ **d :** an identifying reference in accounting used in posting to indicate source of entry and account to which entered **2 a :** a sheet of paper folded once **b :** a case or folder for loose papers **3 a :** the size or form of a folio book ⟨books in ~⟩ **b :** a folio book or publication **c :** a book of the largest size — see BOOK tables **d :** the size of a piece of paper cut two from a sheet; *also* **:** paper or a page of this size — abbr. *fo* or *f;* symbol *F;* see BOOK tables **4 :** a certain number of words taken as a unit or division in a document for purposes of measurement or reference (as in Great Britain and Ireland 72 or 90 and in the U.S. generally 100 by statutory provision) **5** *also* **folio post :** a certain size (as 17 x 22 inches) of a sheet of esp. writing or ledger paper

²folio \"\ *adj* **1 :** formed of sheets each folded once into two leaves or four pages ⟨a ~ edition⟩ ⟨a work in five volumes ~⟩ **2 a :** of the size of a folio book ⟨a ~ case⟩ ⟨a huge ~ atlas⟩ **b :** produced in folio ⟨to the bibliographer . . . a book made up in octavo format may be the same size as one in ~ format, depending on the size of the sheet used for the text —Edith Diehl⟩ **3 :** of full size and not folded — used of sheets and reams of paper

³folio \"\ *vt* -ED/-ING/-S **1 :** to put a serial number on each leaf or each page of (a manuscript or a book) — compare FOLIATE, PAGE **2** *law* **:** to mark with its number each folio in (as a pleading, brief, affidavit)

fo·lio·branch \ˈfōlēōˌbraŋk, -aiŋk\ *also* **fo·lio·bran·chi·ate** \ˌ⸗⸗⸗ˈbraŋkēət, -ēˌāt\ *adj* [*folio-* (fr. L *folium* leaf) + *-branch* or *branchiate*] **:** having gills that resemble leaves

fo·lio·cel·lo·sis \ˌfōlēōsəˈlōsə̇s\ *n, pl* **foliocello·ses** \-ōˌsēz\ [NL, fr. *folio-* + ISV *cell* + NL *-osis*] **:** MOTTLE-LEAF

fo·li·o·late \ˈfōlēəˌlāt, *usu* -ād·+V\ *adj* [*foliole* + *-ate*] **:** having leaflets **:** relating to or consisting of leaflets — usu. used in combination ⟨bi*foliolate*⟩

fo·li·ole \ˈfōlēˌōl\ *n* -S [F, fr. LL *foliolum,* dim. of *folium* leaf — more at BLADE] **1 :** LEAFLET **2 :** a small leaf-shaped organ or a part resembling a leaf

fo·li·o·lif·er·ous \ˌ⸗⸗⸗ˈlif(ə)rəs\ *adj* [*foliole* + *-i-* + *-ferous*] **:** bearing leaflets

fo·li·o·lose \ˈ⸗⸗⸗ˌlōs\ *adj* [*foliole* + *-ose*] **:** FOLIOLATE

fo·li·ose \ˈfōlēˌōs\ *or* **fo·li·ous** \-ēəs\ *adj* [L *foliosus,* fr. *folium* + *-osus* -ous, -ose] **1 :** LEAFY **2 :** resembling a leaf ⟨the ~ lichens are flat and thin —E.A.Bessy⟩

fo·li·ot \ˈfōlēət\ *n* -S [F, fr. MF, prob. fr. *folier* to play the fool, fr. *fol* foolish, mad — more at FOOL] **:** the earliest form of mechanical-clock escapement consisting of a crossbar with adjustable weights for regulating the rate of oscillation of a verge or vertical spindle

-folious \ˌfōlēəs\ *adj comb form* [L *foliosus*] **:** having (such or so many) leaves ⟨centi*folious*⟩

fo·li·um \ˈfōlēəm\ *n, pl* **fo·lia** \-ēə\ [NL, fr. L, leaf — more at BLADE] **1 :** one of the lamellae of the cerebellar cortex **2 :** a thin layer occurring esp. in metamorphic rocks **3 :** FOLIO 1

¹folk \ˈfōk\ *n, pl* **folk** *or* **folks** [ME, fr. OE *folc;* akin to OHG *folc* people, band of warriors, ON *folk* and perh. to Alb *plok, plogn* heap, OE *full* — more at FULL] **1** *pl folks, archaic* **a :** a group of kindred tribes forming a nation **:** PEOPLE ⟨the organization of each ~ . . . sprang mainly from war —J.R. Green⟩ **b :** an animal kind or species ⟨the conies are but a feeble ~ —Prov 30:26 (AV)⟩ **2** *pl folk* **:** the masses of people in a homogeneous social group as contrasted with the individual or with a selected class **:** the great proportion of the members of a people that determines the group character and that tends to preserve its characteristic form of civilization and its customs, arts and crafts, legends, traditions, and superstitions from generation to generation **3** *pl folk, archaic* **:** a mass or group of people in relation to a superior: as **a :** the subjects of a king **b :** the lay members of the church **:** LAITY **c :** the followers or retainers of a lord **d :** the domestics of a household **4** *folk or folks pl* **:** a certain kind or class of people — used with a qualifying adjective or phrase ⟨fine ~*s*⟩ ⟨parties for the young ~*s*⟩ ⟨protecting their women*folk*⟩ ⟨always ready to help ~*s* in trouble⟩ **5** *folks pl* **:** people indefinitely ⟨~*s* say the house is haunted⟩ **6** *folks pl* **a :** the persons of one's own family **:** RELATIVES **b :** persons without pretensions or free from formality of manner ⟨they like best the actors that they can feel easy with, that are just ~*s* —*Yale Rev.*⟩

²folk \"\ *adj* [trans. of G *volks-* (as in *volkslied* folk song), fr. gen. of *volk* people, common people, nation, fr. OHG *folc*] **1 :** originated or widely used among the common people as distinguished from the academic, the cosmopolitan, the modern and professional, or the sophisticated ⟨~ belief⟩ ⟨~ hero⟩ ⟨~ music⟩ ⟨~ remedy⟩ ⟨~ speech⟩ **2 :** of or relating to the common people or to the study of the common people ⟨~ sociology⟩

folk art *n* [prob. trans. of G *volkskunst*] **:** the traditional typically anonymous art of the people that is an expression of community life and is distinguished from academic or self-conscious or cosmopolitan expression — compare COURT ART

folkcraft \ˈ⸗ˌ⸗\ *n* **1 :** the art and tradition of management of public affairs by the common people — distinguished from *statecraft* **2 :** artisanship and artistry carried on by the common people

folk dance *n* [trans. of G *volkstanz*] **:** a dance that originates as ritual among and is characteristic of the common people of a country and that is transmitted from generation to generation with increasing secularization — distinguished from *court dance*

folk etymology *n* [trans. of G *volksetymologie*] **:** the transformation of words so as to give them an apparent relationship to other better-known or better-understood words (as the change of *asparagus* to *sparrowgrass* or the change of *chaise longue* to *chaise lounge*) — called also *popular etymology*

folkfree \ˈ⸗ˌ⸗\ *adj* [trans. of OE *folcfrī*] **:** having a free man's rights **:** having folkright

folk high school *n* [trans. of Dan *folkehøjskole*] **:** a school established in Denmark and elsewhere in the Scandinavian countries for liberal education for working adults

folk·ish \ˈfōkish\ *adj* **:** having a folk character ⟨a ~ orchestral suite⟩ ⟨~ comedy⟩ — **folk·ish·ness** *n* -ES

folkland \ˈ⸗ˌ⸗\ *n* [alter. of OE *folcland,* fr. *folc* folk, people, band of warriors + *land* — more at FOLK, LAND] **:** land held in early England by customary law without written title — opposed to *bookland*

folklike \ˈ⸗ˌ⸗\ *adj* **:** having the character of anonymous tradition **:** FOLKISH

folklore \ˈ⸗ˌ⸗\ *n* [trans. of G *volkskunde*] **1 :** traditional customs, beliefs, dances, songs, tales, or sayings preserved orally and unreflectively among a people or group **2 :** a comparative science that investigates the life and spirit of a people or of peoples as revealed in their traditional customs and tales — compare MYTHOLOGY **3 :** a widely held unsupported specious notion or body of notions

folk·lor·ic \ˈ⸗ˌlȯrik, -ˌlōr-, -rēk\ *adj* **:** of, resembling, or characteristic of folklore ⟨a ~ competition in which nearly a hundred couples dance the fandango —*Holiday*⟩ ⟨~ music⟩

folk·lor·ish \-rish,-rēsh\ *adj* **:** FOLKISH

folk·lor·ism \-ˌrizəm\ *n* -S **:** the study of folklore

folk·lor·ist \-rəst\ *n* -S **:** a student of folklore — **folk·lor·is·tic** \ˌ⸗ˌ⸗ˈistik, -tēk\ *adj*

folk medicine *n* **:** traditional medicine as practiced nonprofessionally by people isolated from modern medical services and involving esp. the use of vegetable remedies on an empirical basis and the retention of outmoded theories

folk·moot \ˈfōkˌmüt\ *or* **folk·mote** \-ˌmōt\ *n* -S [alter. of OE *folcmōt, folcgemōt,* fr. *folc* people + *mōt, gemōt* meeting — more at FOLK, MOOT] **:** an assembly of the people; *esp* **:** a general assembly, court, or council (as of a town, city, or shire) in early England — compare MOOT

folk nation *n* **:** a political unity of related tribes ⟨the Iroquois Confederacy was a *folk nation*⟩

folk psychology *n* [trans. of G *völkerpsychologie*] **1 :** the study of the mind and behavior esp. of primitive peoples through analysis of the human factors involved in their cultural and technological development **2 :** the mental traits common to or characteristic of a people

folkright \ˈ⸗ˌ⸗\ *n* [trans. of OE *folcriht*] **:** the right of the people under the customary laws and usages esp. in early England

folks *pl of* FOLK

folk's-glove \ˈ⸗ˌ⸗\ *n, pl* **folk's-gloves** [by folk etymology] **:** FOXGLOVE 1

folks·i·ly \ˈfōksəlē, -li\ *adv* **:** in a folksy manner

folks·i·ness \-sēnəs, -sin-\ *n* -ES **:** the quality of being folksy ⟨the ~ is exaggerated to an excruciating degree —Quentin Anderson⟩

folk singer *n* **:** a singer of folk songs

folk society *n* **:** a usu. small isolated illiterate society characterized as homogeneous in cultural tradition, as having a sacred rather than secular orientation, and as possessing a high degree of internal integration and group solidarity — contrasted with *urban society*

folk song *n* [trans. of G *volkslied,* trans. of E *popular song*] **1 :** a song originating in or traditional among the common people of a country or region and forming part of their characteristic culture — compare LIED, POPULAR SONG **2 :** a song having such qualities of folk song as stanzaic form, choral refrain, and simplicity of melody and accompaniment but written by a known composer — compare ART SONG

folk state *n* [trans. of G *volksstaat*] **:** a state embracing a racially homogeneous population **:** a state having ethnic unity

folk story *n* **:** FOLKTALE

folksy *also* **folks·ey** \ˈfōksē, -si\ *adj* **folksier; folksiest** [*folks* (pl. of ¹*folk*) + *-y*] **1 :** SOCIABLE, FRIENDLY, NEIGHBORLY ⟨find it hard to be ~ just after prayer —Christopher Morley⟩ **2 :** informal, casual, or familiar often artificially or excessively ⟨~ radio commentator —*Newsweek*⟩ ⟨~, saccharine radio programs —*Time*⟩ **3 :** relating to or having the character of folk arts or crafts or other aspects of popular culture ⟨~ musical composition⟩

folktale \ˈ⸗ˌ⸗\ *n* **:** a tale circulated by word of mouth among the common people; *esp* **:** a tale traditional among a people and characteristically anonymous, timeless, and placeless

folk tune *n* **:** a traditional popular vocal or instrumental melody; *specif* **:** the melody of a folk song

folkway \ˈ⸗ˌ⸗\ *n* **:** a mode of thinking, feeling, or acting common to a people or to a social group; *esp* **:** a social habit that has not been rationalized or given ethical force

foll *abbr* following

fol·ler \ˈfälər\ *dial var of* FOLLOW

folles *pl of* FOLLIS

fol·let·to \fəˈled·(,)ō\ *n, pl* **follet·ti** \-)ē\ [It, fr. OIt, fr. OF *folet* fool, goblin, fr. *fol* foolish, mad — more at FOOL] **:** IMP, GOBLIN, FAIRY; *esp* **:** a supernatural being who is a survival in popular form of an ancient Etruscan or Roman deity

fol·li·cle \ˈfälәkəl, -lēk-\ *n* -S [NL *folliculus*, fr. L, small bag, husk, pod, dim. of *follis* bag, sack — more at FOOL] **1 a :** a small cavity or deep narrow-mouthed depression ⟨a hair ~⟩; *esp* **:** a small simple or slightly branched gland **:** CRYPT **b :** a small lymph node — see GRAAFIAN FOLLICLE **2 :** a dry dehiscent one-celled, many-seeded, and monocarpellary fruit (as that of the peony, larkspur, or milkweed) differing from a pod or legume in opening along only one (as the inner or ventral) suture — see FRUIT illustration **3 :** an air sac (as on a sea plant)

follicle mite *n* **:** any of several minute mites of the genus *Demodex* that are parasitic in the hair follicles

follicle-stimulating hormone *n* **:** a hormone of protein-carbohydrate composition obtained from the anterior lobe of the pituitary gland that stimulates the growth of Graafian follicles in the female and activates the sperm-forming cells in the male —abbr. *FSH;* see LUTEINIZING HORMONE

fol·lic·u·lar \fəˈlikyələ(r), (ˈ)fä¦l-\ *adj* [NL *folliculus* + E *-ar*] **1 :** like, belonging to, or provided with follicles **:** consisting of or involving follicles **2 :** affecting follicles ⟨~ tonsillitis⟩

follicular hormone *n* **:** ESTRONE

follicular mange *n* **:** DEMODECTIC MANGE

fol·lic·u·late \fəˈlikyələt, (ˈ)fä¦l-, -ˌlāt\ *also* **fol·lic·u·lat·ed** \-ˌlād·əd\ *adj* [*folliculе* + *-ate, -ated*] **:** having or consisting of follicles

fol·li·cule \ˈfälə,kyül\ *n* -S [NL *folliculus* — more at FOLLICLE] **:** FOLLICLE

fol·lic·u·lin \fəˈlikyələn, fäˈ-\ *n* -S [NL *folliculus* + E *-in*] **:** ESTROGEN; *esp* **:** ESTRONE

fol·lic·u·li·na \ˌ=ˌ==ˈlīnə, -ˈlēnə-\ *n, cap* [NL, fr. L *folliculus* + NL *-ina*] **:** a genus (the type of the family Folliculinidae) of spirotrichous trumpet-shaped tube-dwelling chiefly marine ciliates related to *Stentor*

¹fol·lic·u·li·nid \=ˌ==¦līnəd, -¦lin-\ *adj* [NL *Folliculinidae*, fr. *Folliculina*, type genus + *-idae*] **:** of or relating to the genus *Folliculina* or the family Folliculinidae

²folliculinid \"\ *n* -S **:** a ciliate of the genus *Folliculina* or the family Folliculinidae

fol·lic·u·li·tis \=ˌ==ˈlīd·əs\ *n* -ES [NL, fr. *folliculus* + *-itis*] **:** inflammation of one or more follicles

fol·lic·u·lose \fəˈlikyə,lōs, (ˈ)fä¦l-\ *adj* [NL *folliculus* + E *-ose*] **1 :** containing follicles **2 :** resembling a follicle

fol·lic·u·lus \=ˈ==ləs\ *n, pl* **follicu·li** \-ˌlī, -ˌlē\ [NL — more at FOLLICLE] **:** FOLLICLE

follies *pl of* FOLLY

fol·lis \ˈfäləs, ˈfōl-\ *n, pl* **fol·les** \-ä,lēz, -ō,lās\ [LL, fr. L *follis* bag — more at FOOL] **1 :** a Roman bronze coin of the late Empire having a silver coating and a very small value **2 :** a large bronze coin current in the Byzantine Empire under Anastasius (A.D. 491-518) that was marked with a large M

¹fol·low \ˈfä(ˌ)lō, -lə, *often* -ləw+V\ *vb* -ED/-ING/-S [ME *folwen, folowen*, fr. OE *folgian;* akin to OE *fylgan* to follow, OFris *folgia, fulgia*, OS *folgōn*, OHG *folgēn*, ON *fylgja*, and perh. to W *ôl* mark, track, *olaf* last, Corn *ōl* mark, trace, track] *vt* **1 :** to go, proceed, or come after **:** move behind over the same path or course often as an attendant or retainer ⟨the bravest man I ever knew ~*ed* me up San Juan Hill —Theodore Roosevelt⟩ **2 a :** to go after in pursuit or in an effort to overtake ⟨fraud statutes, the principle of which is to ~ and punish the security swindler under the criminal law —Frank Parker⟩ **b :** to seek to attain **:** strive after ⟨yearning in desire to ~ knowledge —Alfred Tennyson⟩ **3 a :** to accept as authority **:** take as leader or master ⟨we have forsaken all, and ~*ed* thee —Mt 19:27 (AV)⟩ **b :** to act in accordance with **:** OBEY ⟨~ directions⟩ ⟨~ a policy⟩ **c :** to yield to and obey (the guidance of a dancing partner) ⟨the girl must learn to ~ the man's lead⟩ **4 a :** to copy after **:** take as an example **:** take after **:** IMITATE ⟨the new building ~*s* the facades and roof lines of the original buildings —Maxwell Mays⟩ **b :** to move or change in constant relation to **:** correlate with ⟨school enrollment ~*s* the birthrate⟩ ⟨the condition of the ionosphere has ~*ed* the course of the sun's activity —*London Calling*⟩ **5 a :** to walk or proceed along (as a road or course) ⟨~ a path through the woods⟩ **b :** to engage in (a profession, trade, or calling) **:** PURSUE ⟨those who ~ the sea⟩ ⟨a district where cotton raising is widely ~*ed*⟩ **6 a :** to attend the funeral of ⟨he ~*ed* his poor body to the grave⟩ **b** *dial* **:** ESCORT, ACCOMPANY ⟨he ~*ed* her home from the party⟩ **7 a :** to come or take place after in time, sequence, or order ⟨a juggling act ~*ed* the singer⟩ **b :** to cause to be followed **:** place in sequence **:** furnish with a successor ⟨~*ed* dinner with a liqueur⟩ ⟨~*ed* a fine first novel with an even finer one⟩ **8 a :** to come about or take place as a result, effect, or natural consequence of **:** ensue after ⟨the Nemesis that attends upon human pride, the vengeance that ~*s* crime —G.L.Dickinson⟩ **b :** to come to be existent or present at a place in consequence or as a result of ⟨the flag often ~*s* trade⟩ ⟨houses ~*ed* the factories⟩ **9 a :** to watch steadily (as a receding object) **:** keep the eyes fixed upon (something in motion) ⟨~*ed* the ball over the fence⟩ **b :** to keep the mind upon (something in progress) ⟨~ a speech⟩ ⟨~ a play⟩ **c :** to attend to the successive members or stages of ⟨~ a magazine serial⟩ **:** keep abreast of ⟨~*ed* the developments in his field⟩ ⟨his friends ~*ed* his career with interest⟩ **d :** to understand the logical force of (as an argument or line of thought) **:** keep up with ⟨I don't quite ~ you⟩ ~ *vi* **1 :** to go or come after a person or thing in place, time, or sequence ⟨if one sheep goes through the gate the rest will ~⟩ **2 :** to result or occur as a consequence, an effect from a cause, or as a valid inference from a premise ⟨as they were rich but it did not ~ that they had not made their money honestly —Margaret Deland⟩

syn SUCCEED, ENSUE, SUPERVENE: FOLLOW is a general term often interchangeable with SUCCEED or ENSUE. SUCCEED suggests following another in an office, rank, title, position, or role ⟨George III *succeeded* George II⟩ ⟨George III *succeeded* to the throne after George II⟩ It is likely to suggest a fixed, predictable, or likely order, although it does not always do so ⟨simplicity of concept *succeeds* complexity of calculation —E.T.Bell⟩ ⟨the anxieties of common life began soon to *succeed* to the alarms of romance —Jane Austen⟩ ENSUE means to follow; it is likely to indicate following as a consequence or plausible concomitant and is unlikely to be used with completely unusual or unexpected developments ⟨the riot which *ensued* on that damp evening —T.B.Costain⟩ ⟨if a leech is pulled off . . . he is liable to leave his jaws in the wound, and blood poisoning may *ensue* —C.S.Forester⟩ SUPERVENE indicates a taking place after or during something else of an additional, unlooked-for, unpredictable development which may change or counter expectations ⟨two worlds, two antagonistic ideals, here in evidence before him. Could a third condition *supervene*, to mend their discord —Walter Pater⟩ ⟨with this undue elevation of spirits had *supervened* an entire oblivion or contempt of those undefined apprehensions —Sheridan Le Fanu⟩

syn PURSUE, CHASE, TAG, TRAIL, TAIL: FOLLOW is the general term meaning to come behind after one in his path. It may be used to indicate performance of this action in any way or with any motive from loyal devotion of a retainer to a leader to malevolent intent to harm ⟨what was it that made men *follow* Oliver Cromwell and take at his hands that which they would not receive from any of his contemporaries —S.M.Crothers⟩ ⟨my man that shall . . . do all a hunter can to trace and *follow* and find and catch and crucify . . . all your crew —Robert Browning⟩ PURSUE indicates a persistent, determined, continuing following after in order to overtake or attain ⟨as lean dogs *pursue* some struck and sobbing fawn —P.B.Shelley⟩ ⟨he *pursues* his object with a pertinacity and ingenuity that does credit to his understanding —S.M.Crothers⟩ ⟨to *pursue* every tangle of thought to its final unravelment —A.N.Whitehead⟩ CHASE implies a rapid, active quest after something in flight or, sometimes, activity designed to put to flight ⟨and watch the fearless chamois-hunter *chase* his prey through tracts abrupt of desolate space —William Wordsworth⟩ ⟨the last defeated warrior was *chased* upon a reservation —R.A.Billington⟩ TAG, an informal word, may suggest close following, usu. without any intention, esp. malevolent intention, to overtake or injure ⟨they *tagged* happily after the mayor's secretary down the city-hall corridors —*Time*⟩ TRAIL indicates a close following of another's footsteps or track ⟨I tracked him, as I have *trailed* Coleridge, into almost every section of eight floors of a great library —J.L.Lowes⟩ In intransitive uses it may lack suggestions of intentness and connote aimless or casual following ⟨watch the miners troop home — small black figures *trailing* slowly in gangs across the white field —D.H.Lawrence⟩ TAIL, an informal term, suggests intent, stealthy following in order to observe but usu. not to overtake or capture ⟨sometimes *tailed* . . . by Army, Navy, or FBI cars —*Time*⟩

— **as follows :** as comes next — used impersonally ⟨their names are *as follows*⟩ — **follow copy :** to reproduce matter (as by typesetting or typewriting) exactly as it appears in copy — **follow one's nose 1 :** to go in a straight or obvious course ⟨just *follow your nose* until you get there; you can't miss it⟩ **2 :** to proceed without plan or reflection **:** to obey one's instincts — **follow suit 1 :** to play a card of the same suit as the card led **2 :** to follow an example set — **follow the hounds :** to hunt on horseback with hounds — **follow the string** *of an archery bow* **:** to become curved from use

²follow \"\ *n* -S **1 :** the act or process of following **2 a :** a stroking technique used by a billiard player consisting of striking the cue ball above its center; *also* **:** the forward spin so imparted to the ball **b :** FOLLOW SHOT **3 :** FOLLOW-UP 4

follow block *n* **1 :** a circular wooden block used in spinning sheet metal on a lathe **2 :** an adjustable block or plate used in a card file to keep the cards in upright position

followed *past of* FOLLOW

fol·low·er \ˈfäləwə(r), -lōə-\ *n* -S [ME *folwer, folower*, fr. OE *folgere*, fr. *folgian* to follow + *-ere* -er — more at FOLLOW] **1 a :** one in the service of another **:** RETAINER, ATTENDANT, SERVANT **b :** one that follows the opinions or teachings of another **:** ADHERENT, DISCIPLE **c :** one that imitates another **d :** a beau or admirer esp. of a maidservant **2** *archaic* **:** one that chases **:** PURSUER **3** *Brit* **:** a young domestic animal ⟨a herd of 34 Ayrshire cows and 36 ~*s*⟩ **4 a :** a disk of wood used to apply pressure to hooped cheese **b :** a short wooden piece placed on top of a pile so that the pile may be driven below the bottom limit of a pile driver or below a water surface **c** (1) **:** a short metal cylinder in the tubular magazine of a firearm between the spiral spring and the column of cartridges (2) **:** the short metal arm in a box magazine between the magazine spring and the cartridges **d :** the movable plate of a screw press **e :** a flange for holding piston rings in position **f :** a gland in a stuffing box **g** *or* **follower block :** FOLLOW BLOCK **h** *or* **follower plate :** the metal plate bearing against either end of a railroad-car draft gear and transmitting the stresses from the coupler to the draft gear and from the draft gear to the draft sill **5 :** a sheet of parchment or paper added to the first sheet of an indenture or other deed **6 :** a machine part (as a cogwheel) that receives motion from another part — see WHITWORTH'S QUICK RETURN illustration **7 :** a tool used during disassembly of a cylinder lock to keep the springs and drivers in place

follower rest *n* **:** FOLLOW REST

fol·low·er·ship \-ˌship\ *n* **1 :** the body of followers of a leader **:** FOLLOWING **2 :** the capability of following a leader or obeying authority ⟨statesmanship gives way to demagogy and leadership degenerates into ~ —L.J.Halle⟩

¹following *adj* [ME *folwing, folowing*, fr. pres. part. of *folwen, folowen* to follow — more at FOLLOW] **1 :** next after **:** SUCCEEDING, ENSUING ⟨the meeting was held on the ~ day⟩ **2 :** that immediately follows ⟨the ~ table shows the rate of increase⟩ ⟨trains will leave at the ~ times⟩ **3** *of a wind* **:** blowing in or running in the direction in which a ship is moving **4 :** being east of or having a greater right ascension than another celestial body so as to follow it in the field of a telescope by reason of diurnal motion — compare PRECEDING

²following *n* -S [ME *folwing, folowing*, fr. gerund of *folwen, folowen*] **1 :** the followers, adherents or partisans of one **2 a :** the regular readers of an author or publication **b :** the patrons of a sport or entertainment **c :** the admirers or supporters of a performer in the arts, sports, or entertainment **:** FANS

³following *prep* [¹*following*] **:** subsequent to **:** after in time ⟨~ the lecture the meeting was open to discussion⟩

following sea *n* **:** a sea moving in about the direction of a ship's heading — compare HEAD SEA, QUARTERING SEA

¹follow on *vi* **1** *of a batting side in cricket* **:** to go in for a second innings immediately after its first at the option of the opposing side and when behind by a certain number of runs (as 200 or 150) **2 :** to move on in the direction of a body going before (as of a billiard ball in a follow shot) ~ *vt* **:** to come after **:** SUCCEED

²follow on *n, pl* **follow ons** [¹*follow on*] **:** the act or an instance of following on

follow out *vt* **1 :** to follow to the end or to a conclusion ⟨*followed out* all the cross references⟩ **2 :** EXECUTE **:** carry out ⟨faithfully *followed out* his instructions⟩

follow rest *n* **1 :** a tool rest that travels with the slide rest of a lathe **2 :** a rest that is fixed as to position relative to a grinding wheel and used for supporting cylindrical work

follows *pres 3d sing of* FOLLOW, *pl of* FOLLOW

follow shot *n* **:** a billiard shot made by hitting the cue ball above the center that causes the cue ball to roll forward after contact with the object ball — compare DRAW SHOT

follow spot *n* **:** a spotlight for following a performer moving about a stage

follow-the-leader \ˌ===ˈ==\ *also* **follow-my-leader** \ˌ==-(ˌ)=ˈ==\ *n* **:** a game in which the players in single file must imitate all the actions of the leader

follow through *vi* **1 :** to continue a stroke or motion (as the swing of a bat, club, or racket) to the end of its arc **:** complete the swing **2 :** to press on in an activity or process beyond the initial or preparatory stages esp. to a conclusion ⟨after a bombardment the infantry failed to *follow through*⟩

follow-through \ˈ==ˌ=, ˌ==ˈ=\ *n* -S [*follow through*] **1 :** the act of following through (as in the swing of a bat, club, or racket); *also* **:** the part of the stroke following the striking of the ball **2 :** the act of following up a planned or initiated activity to a conclusion ⟨reports and recommendations will be submitted to the director of purchases for *follow-through* —*Management Rev.*⟩

follow up *vt* **1 :** to pursue closely and steadily ⟨*followed up* the wounded deer⟩ **2 a :** to follow (an act or achievement) with a similar or related act **b :** to strengthen the effect of by further action ⟨*followed up* victory with rapid advance⟩ **:** PURSUE, EXPLOIT ⟨*followed up* his initial effort⟩ ⟨*follow up* an early advantage⟩ **3 :** to seek further details about (a news story already printed or broadcast); *also* **:** to print or broadcast usu. on subsequent days one or more stories other than the first on (a news event) **4 :** to maintain constant or intermittent contact with (as a case) after diagnosis or therapy

¹follow-up \ˈ==ˌ=\ *adj* [*follow up*] **:** of or relating to renewed or repeated action: as **a :** relating to a second or subsequent offer or proposal (as to a possible customer) ⟨a *follow-up* letter⟩ ⟨a *follow-up* order⟩ **b :** serving to test or reinforce the effectiveness of previous action ⟨*follow-up* instruction⟩ **c :** relating to the study or treatment of persons after institutionalization ⟨*follow-up* care of the mentally ill⟩ ⟨*follow-up* survey of delinquent children⟩ ⟨*follow-up* study of the results of surgery⟩

²follow-up \"\ *n* -S [*follow up*] **1 :** a system of pursuing an initial effort (as in advertising or in the activity of a salesman) by supplementary action **2 :** a system of recording the steps taken in the collection of an overdue account **3 a :** reexamination of or maintenance of contact with a patient at a prescribed interval or intervals following a basic examination, a course of treatment, or surgery **b :** a patient or case so followed up **4 :** a news story presenting new information on or a new handling of a story printed or broadcast earlier; *also* **:** a news story of minor significance related and usu. attached to one of major significance

fol·ly \ˈfälē, -li\ *n* -ES [ME *folie*, fr. OF, fr. *fol* foolish, mad + *-ie* -y — more at FOOL] **1 :** lack of good sense or of normal prudence and foresight **:** weakness or triviality of intellect ⟨answer not a fool according to his ~ —Prov 26:4 (AV)⟩ ⟨~ has a louder voice than common sense —C.H.Grandgent⟩ **2 :** inability or refusal to accept existing reality or to foresee inevitable consequence ⟨the ~ of passing on hills and blind curves⟩ ⟨reformers . . . are prone to regard the existing order as sheer ~ or evil —H.J.Muller⟩ **3 :** a thoughtless act or irrational idea **:** an unconsidered or unwise procedure ⟨she had been guilty of the capital ~ of cutting herself off from her family —Arnold Bennett⟩ **4 a** *obs* **:** EVIL, WICKEDNESS; *esp* **:** LEWDNESS **b :** actions or conduct so misguided as to result in destruction or tragic consequence ⟨saints have preached . . . the ~ of human strife —M.R.Cohen⟩ **5 :** an excessively costly or unprofitable undertaking; *esp* **:** a ruinously costly often unfinished building **6 a :** a lapse from strict propriety or sobriety **:** INDULGENCE, WHIM, VANITY, FOOLERY ⟨let us go while we are in our prime; and take the harmless ~ of the time —Robert Herrick †1674⟩ ⟨*follies* of fashion⟩ **b :** a summerhouse or pavilion designed for picturesque effect or to suit a fanciful taste **7 follies** *pl* **:** a stage revue

fol·ly·er \ˈfälēə(r)\ *or* **vol·y·er** \ˈvälēə(r)\ *n* -S [fr. E dial. var. of *follower*] **:** a small lug-rigged often British boat used in seine fishing

folo *like* ²*follow*\ *n* -S [alter. of ²*follow*] **:** FOLLOW-UP 4

fol·som \ˈfōlsəm *also* -lts-\ *adj, usu cap* [fr. *Folsom*, N.M., its type station] **:** of or relating to a prehistoric culture of No. America on the east side of the Rocky mountains from Alberta, Canada, to southern New Mexico that is characterized esp. by a leaf-shaped flint projectile point having a concave base with side projections and a longitudinal groove on each face ⟨*Folsom* man⟩

fol·som·oid \-sə,mȯid\ *adj, usu cap* **:** resembling a Folsom projectile point

¹fo·ment \ˈfō,ment\ *n* -S [ME, fr. L *fomentum*, fr. (assumed) OL *fovementum*, fr. L *fovēre* to warm + *-mentum* -ment — more at DAY] **1 :** FOMENTATION **2 :** a state of excitation **:** FERMENT

²foment \(ˈ)=¦=\ *vt* -ED/-ING/-S [ME *fomenten*, fr. LL *fomentare*, fr. L *fomentum*] **1 :** to apply hot moist cloths to (the body) **:** treat with moist heat **2 :** to nurse to life or activity **:** promote the growth of **:** ROUSE, INCITE, ENCOURAGE, INSTIGATE ⟨a special need for ~*ing* exchanges of professors, students, and publications —D.D.Brand⟩ — usu. used in an unfavorable sense ⟨~ revolution⟩ ⟨~ riots⟩ **3** *obs* **:** EXCITE

syn see INCITE

fo·men·ta·tion \ˌfōmənˈtāshən, -ˌmen-\ *n* -S [ME *fomentacioun*, fr. LL *fomentation-, fomentatio*, fr. *fomentatus* (past part. of *fomentare*) + L *-ion-, -io* -ion] **1 :** the act of fomenting **:** EXCITATION, INSTIGATION, ENCOURAGEMENT **2 a :** the application of hot moist substances (as wet cloths) to the body for the purpose of easing pain **b :** the material thus applied **c :** POULTICE

fo·ment·er \(ˈ)fō¦mentə(r)\ *n* -S **:** one that foments ⟨a ~ of class antagonisms —D.M.Potter⟩

fo·mes \ˈfō(ˌ)mēz\ *n, cap* [NL, fr. L, touchwood, tinder; akin to L *fovēre* to warm] **:** a genus of bracket fungi (family Polyporaceae) usu. forming corky or woody perennial sporophores often of large size and including some fungi that cause destructive heartrots of timber and other trees

fomi·tes \ˈfämə,tēz, ˈfōm-\ *n pl* [NL, fr. L, pl. of *fomes*] **:** inanimate objects (as clothing, dishes, toys, books) that may be contaminated with infectious organisms and serve in their transmission

fo·mor \ˈfō,mȯ(ə)r, -ō,wȯ-\ *n* -S *cap* [obs. IrGael *fomór, fomorach* (now *fomhuireach*), fr. IrGael *fo* under (fr. OIr) + *muir* sea (fr. OIr); akin to L *sub* under and *mare* sea — more at OVER, MARINE] **:** FOMORIAN

fo·mor·i·an \(ˈ)fō¦mȯrēən,ˈ-ō¦wȯ-\ *n* -S *cap* [obs. IrGael *fomor* + E *-ian*] **:** one of a race of sea robbers in Celtic legend who were prob. orig. gods representing the powers of evil and darkness

fon \ˈfän\ *n, pl* **fon** *or* **fons** *usu cap* **1 a :** a Negro people of West Africa esp. in the region of Abomey, Benin **b :** a member of such people **2 :** the language of the Fon people that is closely related to or a dialect of Ewe

fonc·tion·naire \ˌfäŋ(k)shəˈna(a)(ə)r, F fōⁿksyȯneer\ *n, pl* **fonctionnaires** \-na(a)(ə)rz,-neer\ [F, fr. *fonction* function, office + *-aire* -ary — more at FUNCTION] **:** a French or French colonial government official

¹fond \ˈfänd\ *adj* -ER/-EST [ME *fonned, fond*, fr. *fonne* fool, dupe, buffoon + *-ed*] **1 :** FOOLISH, SILLY, INFATUATED ⟨~ scheme⟩ ⟨~ pride⟩ — used of persons now chiefly in dial. ⟨our John be right ~ about her⟩ **2 :** hopeful and credulous to an absurd degree ⟨a ~ promoter of visionary schemes⟩ ⟨grant I may never prove so ~ to trust man on his oath and bond —Shak.⟩ **3** *chiefly Scot* **:** EAGER, ANXIOUS — used with *to* ⟨very ~ to get the hay in before the fair⟩ **4 a :** having an affection or liking — used with *of* ⟨~ of his nephew⟩ ⟨~ of skating⟩ ⟨~ of music⟩ **b :** having a tendency or predisposition — used with *of* ⟨historians and biographers . . . are ~ of explaining him as "a man of his age" —Irving Kristol⟩ ⟨~ of painting big pictures —David Sylvester⟩ **5 a :** foolishly tender **:** weakly indulgent ⟨hopelessly spoiled by a ~ mother⟩ **b :** LOVING, AFFECTIONATE ⟨a ~ wife⟩ ⟨a ~ kiss⟩ **6 :** doted on **:** regarded with unreasoning affection **:** DEAR ⟨his ~*est* hopes fulfilled⟩ **:** clung to with strong attachment ⟨how are we to rid ourselves of our ~ prejudices and open our minds —James Ford⟩

²fond *vb* -ED/-ING/-S *vi, obs* **:** to be foolish **:** be fond **:** DOTE ~ *vt* **1** *obs* **:** BEFOOL, BEGUILE **2** *obs* **:** FONDLE, CARESS

³fond \ˈfänd\ *n* -S [F — more at FUND] **1 :** a background or foundation for added characteristics or aspects **:** GROUNDWORK, BASIS **2** *obs* **:** FUND **3 :** the ground of a lace usu. forming the background for a design

fon·da \ˈfändə\ *n* -S [Sp, prob. fr. Lingua Franca, fr. Ar *funduq* — more at FONDUK] **:** BOARDINGHOUSE, INN

fon·dant \ˈfändənt\ *n* -S [F, fr. pres. part. of *fondre* to melt — more at FOUND] **1 :** a soft creamy preparation of sugar, water, and flavorings that is used as a basis for candies or icings **2 :** a candy consisting chiefly of fondant

fon·dante potatoes \ˈfän,dant-\ *n pl* [F *fondante*, fem. of *fondant*, pres. part. of *fondre*] **:** potato balls or ovals that are first half cooked in water and then braised in butter

fond·ish \ˈfändish\ *adj* **:** somewhat fond

fon·dle \ˈfändᵊl\ *vb* **fondled**; **fondled**; **fondling** \-nd(ᵊ)liŋ, -lēŋ, ÷-nl-\ **fondles** [²*fond* + *-le*] *vt* **1** *obs* **:** to treat with doting indulgence **:** PAMPER, CODDLE **2 :** to handle tenderly, lovingly, or lingeringly **:** treat caressingly **:** CARESS ⟨the nurse *fondled* the child⟩ ⟨*fondled* her jewels⟩ ⟨*fondling* his favorite phrase⟩ ⟨*fondling* the memory of her past goodness to him —Liam O'Flaherty⟩ ~ *vi* **:** to show affection or desire by caressing

fon·dler \-d(ᵊ)lə(r)\ *n* -S **:** one that fondles

fond·ling \ˈfändliŋ, -lēŋ\ *n* -S [¹*fond* + *-ling*] **1** *obs* **:** FOOL, SIMPLETON, NINNY **2 :** a person or thing fondled or caressed **:** PET

fon·dling·ly \ˈfänd(ᵊ)liŋlē, -lēŋ-, -li\ *adv* **:** in a fondling manner **:** CARESSINGLY, AFFECTIONATELY

fond·ly \ˈfändlē, -li\ *adv* [ME *fonnedly, fondly*, fr. *fonned, fond* foolish + *-ly* — more at FOND] **1** *archaic* **:** FOOLISHLY ⟨make him speak ~ like a frantic man —Shak.⟩ **2 :** in a fond manner **:** AFFECTIONATELY, TENDERLY ⟨he was often spoken of ~ as "the old man"⟩ **3 :** in a willingly credulous manner ⟨the result was not what we ~ hoped⟩

fond·ness \ˈfän(d)nəs\ *n* -ES [ME *fonnednesse, fondnesse*, fr. *fonned, fond* foolish + *-nesse* -ness] **1** *obs* **:** FOOLISHNESS, FOLLY **2 :** doting affection **:** tender liking **3 :** APPETITE, PROPENSITY, RELISH ⟨he has a ~ for truffles⟩ ⟨~ for argument⟩

¹fon·du \(ˈ)fän¦d(y)ü\ *adj* [F, fr. past part. of *fondre* to melt — more at FOUND] **1 :** passing into each other by subtle gradations **:** BLENDED — used of colors or of the surface or material on which the colors are laid **2 :** MELTED — used of foods

²fon·du \(ˈ)fän¦d(y)ü, F fōⁿdü\ *n* -S [F, fr. past part. of *fondre*] **:** a lowering or sinking down of the body in ballet dancing by bending the knee of the supporting leg

fon·due *also* **fon·du** \(ˈ)fän¦d(y)ü\ *n* -S [F *fondue*, fr. fem. of *fondu*, past part. of *fondre*] **1 :** a preparation of melted cheese usu. flavored with wine or brandy **:** cooked cheese **2 :** a soufflé made with bread crumbs

fon·duk *or* **fon·douk** *or* **fun·duck** \ˈfän(ˌ)dək, ˈfən-, -ˌdük, -ˌdük\ *n* -S [Ar *funduq*, fr. Gk *pandokeion, pandocheion* inn, fr. *pandokos* all-receiving, common to all, fr. *pan-* + *-dokos* (fr. *dekesthai, dechesthai* to accept, receive, welcome); akin to Gk *dokein* to seem good, seem, think — more at DECENT] **1 :** a business establishment or commercial warehouse in northern Africa **2 :** an inn or hotel in northern Africa

f_1 layer \ˈef¦wən-\ *n, usu cap F* **:** the lower and usu. less densely ionized of the two layers into which the F region of the ionosphere splits in the daytime occurring at varying heights from about 90 to 150 miles above the earth's surface and being more densely ionized than the E layer

fo·nio \ˈfōnē,ō\ *n* -S [F, fr. a native name in northern Africa] **:** a crabgrass (*Digitaria exilis*) of northern Africa with seeds that are used as a cereal

fo·no \ˈfō(,)nō\ *n* -S [Samoan & Tongan] **:** a Samoan council of faipules constituting the central political structure of a village, district, or island

fons \ˈfänz, ˈfōn(t)s\ *n, pl* **fon·tes** \-än‚tēz, -ōn‚tās\ [L — more at FOUNT] **:** FOUNT, SOURCE

fons et ori·go \‚fōn(t),sed·əˈrē(‚)gō\ *n* [LL] **:** source and origin ⟨western Europe, which . . . is always dimly assumed as the *fons et origo* of all social forces —Donald Davidson⟩ **:** original cause ⟨that this survival of the family god was the *fons et origo* of Hebrew monolatry —*Times Lit. Supp.*⟩

¹font \ˈfänt\ *n* -S [ME *fant, font, funt*, fr. OE *fant, font*, fr. LL *font-, fons*, fr. L, fountain, spring, source — more at FOUNT] **1 :** a basin or vessel often mounted on a pedestal in which water is contained for baptizing ⟨that name was given me at the ~ —Shak.⟩ **2 :** a point from which something originates **:** FOUNTAIN, SPRING, SOURCE ⟨~ of botanical and geological information —Robert Bobrow⟩ **3 :** a receptacle for holy water **4 :** the oil reservoir of a lamp

font 1

²font \"\ *n* -S [MF *fonte*, fr. (assumed) VL *fundita*, fem. of (assumed) VL *funditus*, past part. of L *fundere* to found, pour — more at FOUND] **1 a :** the act or process of casting or founding **b :** a chamber for holding molten glass that is forced into a mold by pressure from a plunger **2 a :** an assortment of type, matrices, or characters of one size and style including a due proportion of all the letters in the alphabet, points, accents, and figures **b :** a set of any one sort of typographical material ⟨a ~ of brass rules⟩ ⟨a ~ of wood furniture⟩

³font \"\ *vt* -ED/-ING/-S **:** to arrange or make up (as type) into fonts **:** equip (as a type case or cabinet) with a font or fonts — often used with *up*

fon·tai·nea \fän·ˈtānēə\ *n, cap* [NL, after William M. *Fontaine* †1913 Am. geologist] **:** a genus of fossil dicotyledonous plants from the Cretaceous of No. America

font·al \ˈfäntᵊl\ *adj* [LL & L; LL *fontalis* baptismal, fr. L, of a fountain, spring or source, fr. *font-, fons* + *-alis* -al] **1 :** relating to a font, fountain, source, or origin **:** ORIGINAL, PRIMARY ⟨from the ~ light of ideas only can a man draw intellectual power —S.T.Coleridge⟩ **2 :** BAPTISMAL

fon·ta·nel *also* **fon·ta·nelle** \¦fäntᵊn¦el\ *n* -S [ME *fontinelle*, fr. MF *fontenele* little spring, fontanel, dim. of *fontaine* spring — more at FOUNTAIN] **1** *obs* **a :** an opening for the discharge of bodily secretions **b :** an ulcer or vent discharging secretions from the body **2 :** a membrane-covered opening in bone or between bones; *specif* **:** one of the intervals closed by membranous structures between the uncompleted angles of the parietal bones and the neighboring bones of a fetal or young skull

fon·tange *or* **fon·tanges** \fōⁿtäⁿzh\ *n, pl* **fontanges** \"\ [F *fontange*, after Marie Angélique de Scorraille de Roussilles, duchess of *Fontanges* †1681 Fr. mistress of Louis XIV] **:** COMMODE 1

fontes *pl of* FONS

fon·ti·na \fän·ˈtēnə, fōn-‚-\ *n* -S *often cap* [It] **:** a semisoft to hard ripened cheese of Italian origin that varies in flavor from mild to medium sharp

fon·ti·nal \ˈfäntᵊnᵊl\ *adj* [L *fontinalis* of or from a spring, irreg. fr. *font-, fons* spring + *-alis* -al] **:** growing in or near springs

fon·ti·na·la·ce·ae \‚fäntᵊnəˈlāsē‚ē\ *n pl, cap* [NL, fr. *Fontinalis*, type genus + *-aceae*] **:** a small family of aquatic mosses (order Isobryales) having long floating stems and capsules nearly covered by the surrounding leaf clusters — see DICHELYMA, FONTINALIS

fon·ti·nal·is \-ᵊnˈaləs, -ˈāl-, -ˈäl-\ *n* [NL, fr. L] **1** *cap* **:** the type genus of Fontinalaceae **2** -ES **:** any water moss of the genus *Fontinalis*

font name *n* **:** FIRST NAME, FORENAME

foo \(ˈ)fü\ *Scot var of* HOW

¹foo·chow \ˈfü¦jō, -¦chau̇\ *n* -S *cap* [fr. *Foochow*, China] **:** a dialect of Chinese spoken in and near Foochow in southeastern China

²foochow \"\ *adj, usu cap* [fr. *Foochow*, China] **:** of or from the city of Foochow, China **:** of the kind or style prevalent in Foochow

food \ˈfüd *sometimes* ˈfu̇d\ *n* -S *often attrib* [ME *fode*, fr. OE *fōda*; akin to OE *fōdor, foddor* food, fodder, OHG *fuotar* food, fodder, ON *fætha, fæthi* food, *fōthr* fodder, Goth *fodeins* food, L *pabulum* food, fodder, *panis* bread, *pascere* to pasture, feed, graze, Gk *pateisthai* to eat, OSlav *pasti* to graze] **1 a :** material consisting of carbohydrates, fats, proteins, and supplementary substances (as minerals, vitamins) that is taken or absorbed into the body of an animal in order to sustain growth, repair, and all vital processes and to furnish energy for all activity of the organism ⟨any population is limited by the available supply of ~⟩; *esp* **:** parts of the bodies of animals and plants consumed by animals **:** PROVENDER, PROVISIONS, VIANDS ⟨acres devoted to growing ~⟩ ⟨longing for the ~s of her homeland⟩ — compare METABOLISM, NUTRITION **b :** simple inorganic substances that are absorbed by plants in gaseous form (as carbon dioxide) or in solution in water (as nitrates, phosphates) **:** plant nutrients **c :** complex organic substances constructed within the bodies of green plants by photosynthesis or other processes for use directly as building material and as source of energy for growth and reproduction **2 a :** nutriment in solid form — opposed to *drink* **b :** the chief substance of regularly taken meals as distinguished from candy, appetizers, or condiments **3 a :** something that nourishes or develops ⟨spiritual ~⟩ ⟨intellectual ~⟩ or sustains ⟨praise was her favorite ~ —Eden Phillpotts⟩ **b :** something that supplies a process or activity ⟨~ for thought⟩ **4** *obs* **:** the act of eating **5 foods** *pl* **:** stocks or bonds of food companies

food ball *n* **:** HAIR BALL

food canal *n* **:** ALIMENTARY CANAL

food chain *n* **:** a sequence of organisms in an ecological community each of which uses the next usu. lower member of the sequence as a food source, plants being the ultimate basis of the sequence

food chopper *n* **:** a machine or implement that chops or grinds food

food color *n* **:** a dye or pigment permitted for use in foods — see DYE tables I and II

food conversion *n* **:** the rate at which an animal converts food into tissue usu. expressed as pounds of food consumed per pound of liveweight gained

food cycle *n* **:** a group of food chains constituting all or a significant part of the food relations that enable survival of the population of a community

food fish *n* **:** a fish used as human food — often distinguished from *game fish*; compare PANFISH

food-gatherer \ˈ=‚===\ *n* **:** one that lives upon food procured by hunting, fishing, and gathering rather than through agriculture or animal husbandry

food grain *n* **:** a grain (as wheat, rice, rye, or buckwheat) grown for human food

food·less \ˈ=ləs\ *adj* [ME *fodeles*, fr. *fode* food + *-les* — more at FOOD] **:** lacking food **:** barren of food — **food·less·ness** *n* -ES

foo dog *usu cap F, var of* FU DOG

food plant *n* **:** a plant (as wheat, potato, cabbage) some part of which provides food for human consumption

food poisoning *n* **1 :** either of two acute gastrointestinal disorders caused by bacteria or their toxic products: **a :** a rapidly developing intoxication marked by nausea, vomiting, prostration, and often severe diarrhea and caused by the presence in food of toxic products produced by bacteria (as certain staphylococci) **b :** a less rapidly developing infection esp. with salmonellas that has generally similar symptoms and that results from multiplication of bacteria ingested with contaminated food — called also *bacterial food poisoning;* compare BOTULISM, MUSSEL POISONING, SALMONELLOSIS **2 :** a gastrointestinal disturbance occurring after consumption of food which is contaminated with chemical residues (as from sprays) or food (as certain fungi) which is inherently unsuitable for human consumption

food press *n* **:** a perforated metal cone through which food is pressed by means of a wooden pestle

foodstuff \ˈ=‚=\ *n* **:** a substance with food value: as **a :** the raw material of food before or after processing ⟨a bountiful crop of cereal ~s⟩ ⟨a basket of ~s including flour⟩ ⟨green ~s from the garden⟩ **b :** an element of nutrition (as protein, carbohydrate, vitamin) ⟨the sponge obtains its necessary ~s from the plankton⟩

food tube *n* **:** ALIMENTARY CANAL

food unit *n* **:** a unit of 1701 calories that is used in nutritional research

food vacuole *n* **:** one of the usu. transitory vacuoles in the protoplasm of a protozoan in which digestion takes place — see AMOEBA illustration

food web *n* **:** the totality of interacting food chains in an ecological community

foo·fa·raw \ˈfüfə‚rȯ\ *also* **foo·foo·rah** \-fə‚rä, -rȯ\ *or* **fo·far·raw** \ˈfōf-\ *n* -S [origin unknown] **1 :** frills and flashy finery ⟨too much ~ on that dress to suit me⟩ **2 :** a disturbance or to-do over a trifle **:** FUSS ⟨what's the occasion for all this ~⟩

¹foo-foo \ˈfü(‚)fü\ *n* -S [perh. by alter. & redupl. fr. ¹*fool*] *slang* **:** FOOL, NINNY

²foo-foo \"\ *n* -S [of African origin; akin to Ewe *fu'fu'* food made from boiled and pounded yam, cassava, and coco, Wolof *fufu* food made from cassava meal] **:** a dough made from boiled and mashed plantains

¹fool \ˈfül\ *n* -S [ME *fol, fool*, fr. OF *fol*, fr. LL *follis*, fr. L, bellows, bag; akin to L *flare* to blow — more at BLOW] **1 :** a person lacking in judgment or prudence ⟨a ~ and his money are soon parted⟩ **:** one that acts stupidly or recklessly ⟨fortune favors ~s⟩ **2 a :** a retainer formerly kept in great households to provide casual entertainment and commonly dressed in motley with cap, bells, and bauble — called also *jester* **b :** one that is victimized or that is made to appear foolish **:** GULL, DUPE, BUTT ⟨a ~ of circumstances⟩ ⟨history has made ~s of many rash prophets⟩ ⟨he doesn't look very bright but he's nobody's ~⟩ **3 a :** a harmlessly deranged person or one lacking in common powers of understanding **:** NATURAL, IDIOT — now used chiefly in the phrase *born fool* **b :** one having a special weakness ⟨a ~ for women⟩ or fondness ⟨a ~ for candy⟩ **c :** one with a marked propensity or talent for a certain activity ⟨a letter-writing ~⟩ ⟨that horse is a running ~⟩ ⟨a ~ for luck⟩ **4 :** one that cannot stand comparison with another ⟨home's a ~ beside this-here place . . . let's dance another round —Elizabeth M. Roberts⟩ **5 a :** mashed fruit and cream **b :** a dessert made of pulped fruit covered with a custard and cream ⟨gooseberry ~⟩ **6 :** PLUM POCKET

syn FOOL, IDIOT, IMBECILE, MORON, SIMPLETON, and NATURAL are often applied popularly and interchangeably to anyone regarded as lacking sense or good judgment but can be more strictly applied to someone mentally deficient in a given degree. FOOL, the most general, can apply to anyone mentally deranged as well as mentally deficient, implying lack or loss of reason or intelligence; it may be used as an extremely offensive term of contempt ⟨*fools* rush in where angels fear to tread —Alexander Pope⟩ ⟨he was a *fool* and liable, as such, under the stress of bodily or mental disturbance, to spasmodic fits of abject fright which he mistook for religion —Norman Douglas⟩ ⟨I was a *fool*, if you like, and certainly I was going to do a foolish, overbold act —R.L.Stevenson⟩ ⟨to act like a *fool*⟩ IDIOT, IMBECILE, and MORON are technical designations for one mentally deficient. An IDIOT is incapable of connected speech or of avoiding the common dangers of life and needs constant attendance. An IMBECILE is incapable of earning a living but can be educated to attend to simple wants or avoid most ordinary dangers. A MORON can learn a simple trade but requires constant supervision in his work or recreation. In nontechnical use, IDIOT implies utter feeblemindedness; IMBECILE implies half-wittedness; MORON implies general stupidity ⟨comes like an *idiot*, babbling and strewing flowers —Edna S. V. Millay⟩ ⟨actually there never is a status quo, except in the minds of political *imbeciles* —Henry Miller⟩ ⟨even *morons* get college degrees —H.R.Warfel⟩ SIMPLETON, a term of indulgent contempt, implies silliness or lack of sophistication ⟨a sweet-natured *simpleton* who wrote lovely songs for children —S.F. Damon⟩ ⟨in spite of her experience of his lying, she had never suspected that that particular statement was a lie. What a *simpleton* she was! —Arnold Bennett⟩ NATURAL, now rare, once designated any congenitally feebleminded person ⟨the man is not a *natural;* he has a very quick sense, though very slow understanding —Richard Steele⟩

²fool \"\ *vb* -ED/-ING/-S [ME *folen*, fr. MF *foler*, fr. *fol* foolish] *vi* **1 a :** to spend time idly or aimlessly **:** waste time ⟨is this a time for ~*ing* —John Dryden⟩ — often used with *around* ⟨he hasn't been working at all, just ~*ing* around⟩ **b :** to meddle or tamper thoughtlessly or ignorantly **:** handle recklessly — used with *with* ⟨emotions are dangerous things to ~ with⟩ or *around with* ⟨don't ~ around with that gun⟩ **c :** to act or work tentatively or unsystematically or casually — often used with *around* ⟨~*ing* around in his home laboratory⟩ ⟨~*ing* around with new wing designs⟩ ⟨he ~*ed* with farm machinery so much that he just about didn't get any farming done —Danforth Ross⟩ **d :** to deal without serious intent **:** TRIFLE, PHILANDER — often used with *around* ⟨falls into the habit of ~*ing* around with a blond instead of going dutifully home —*Time*⟩ ⟨time to stop ~*ing* around and get married and settle down⟩ **2 a :** to play or improvise a comic role **:** make comedy ⟨a master maker of comedy, he could ~ excellently —Edith Hamilton⟩ ⟨he is serious, but she likes to ~⟩ **b :** to speak in jest **:** speak or act in playful deception **:** JOKE ⟨don't be frightened, I was only ~*ing*⟩ **3 a :** to contend or fight without serious intent or with less than full strength **:** TOY — used with *with* ⟨the champion ~*ed* with him for six rounds and then knocked him out⟩ ⟨a dangerous man to ~ with⟩ **b :** to go at less than full or normal speed **:** AMBLE, LOITER — used with *along* or *about* ⟨we didn't hurry, just ~*ed* along enjoying the scenery⟩ **~** *vt* **1 a :** to make a fool of **:** DECEIVE, DUPE ⟨to ~ rustlers . . . ranchers started putting brands in two or three different places —S.E.Fletcher⟩ ⟨his disguise didn't ~ anybody⟩ ⟨~*ing* the voters with large promises⟩ **b :** to take by surprise **:** exceed or disappoint the expectations of ⟨I don't think he is ready for work, but he may ~ me⟩ **2** *obs* **:** to make foolish **:** INFATUATE ⟨for, ~*ed* with hope, men favor the deceit —John Dryden⟩ **3 :** to spend on trifles or without advantage **:** FRITTER — used with *away* ⟨~*ed* the whole afternoon away⟩ ⟨~*ed* away his week's allowance in two days⟩

³fool \"\ *adj* [partly fr. ME *fol, fool*, fr. OF *fol*, fr. LL *follus*, fr. *follis*, n.; partly fr. ¹*fool*] **:** FOOLISH, SILLY, STUPID ⟨his ~ idea of rewriting the books of authors —Bennett Cerf⟩ ⟨the dog was barking his ~ head off⟩

fool duck *n* [so called fr. its tameness that allows it to be easily caught] **:** RUDDY DUCK

fool·er \ˈfülə(r)\ *n* -S **:** one that fools **:** JOKER ⟨these legal counterfeits are real ~s —J.C.Furnas⟩

fool·ery \-l(ə)rē, -ri\ *n* -ES **1 :** the habit or practice of folly or fooling **:** the behavior of a fool **:** ABSURDITY ⟨folly in fools bears not so strong a note, as ~ in the wise, when wit doth dote —Shak.⟩ **2 :** an act of folly or fooling **:** a foolish, absurd, or nonsensical performance, utterance, or belief ⟨the solemn ~ of scholarship for scholarship's sake —Aldous Huxley⟩

foolfish \ˈ=‚=\ *n* **1 :** FILEFISH **2 :** the eel-back flounder or a related fish

fool-happy *adj, obs* **:** lucky without judgment or contrivance

foolhardihood \ˈ=‚==‚=, =ˈ==‚=\ *n* **:** FOOLHARDINESS

foolhardily \ˈ=‚===\ *adv* [ME *folhardily*, fr. *folhardy* + *-ly*] **:** in a foolhardy manner ⟨tried ~ to attract attention to himself⟩

foolhardiness \ˈ=‚===\ *n* [ME *folhardinesse*, fr. *folhardy* + *-nesse* -ness] **:** the quality or state of being foolhardy ⟨courage . . . the mean between ~ and cowardice —G.L.Dickinson⟩

foolhardy \ˈ=‚==\ *adj* -ER/-EST [ME *folhardy, foolhardy*, fr. OF *fol hardi*, fr. *fol* foolish + *hardi* bold, brave — more at FOOL, HARDY] **:** daring but lacking judgment **:** foolishly adventurous and bold **:** exhibiting or characterized by lack of regard for foreseeable or avoidable danger ⟨a ~ dive into shallow water⟩ ⟨since I had been so ~ as to come ashore with these desperadoes —R.L.Stevenson⟩ **syn** see ADVENTUROUS

fool hay *n* **1 :** ROUGH BENT **2 :** WITCHGRASS 2

foolhearted \ˈ=¦==\ *adj* **:** having the heart of a fool **:** FOOLISH

fool hen *n* [fr. its stupidity that permits it to be easily caught] **:** a grouse that exhibits little alertness or fear of man: **a :** SPRUCE GROUSE **b :** FRANKLIN GROUSE

fool·ish \ˈfülish, -lēsh\ *adj, sometimes* -ER/-EST [ME *folish, foolish*, fr. *fol, fool* + *-ish*] **1 :** marked by folly **:** lacking in judgment, fit consideration, or intelligence: as **a :** lacking in intellect **:** IDIOTIC, FEEBLEMINDED, SIMPLE **b :** lacking in discretion or consideration of effects and consequences ⟨many changes that well might seem rash, mistaken, ~ and ill-advised —J.C.Powys⟩ **c :** lacking in sense or seriousness **:** NONSENSICAL ⟨obscurely and uselessly, like a ~ suggestion —Liam O'Flaherty⟩ **d :** lacking in significance, balance, fitness, or relevance ⟨a prince who should . . . not, like a subject, ~ matters mince —John Keats⟩ **e :** lacking in prowess, cunning, or strength ⟨the line which ~ birds are caught with —William Wordsworth⟩ **f :** idly and vainly enthusiastic or enamored **:** INFATUATED ⟨when you began to feel ~ about that man, I warned you he would not make you happy —Thomas Hardy⟩ **2 a :** ABSURD, RIDICULOUS ⟨a ~ little hat⟩ **b :** NONPLUSSED, ABASHED ⟨stood looking and feeling ~ —Arnold Bennett⟩ **c** *obs* **:** DIVERTING, AMUSING **3 :** absurdly paltry, insignificant, or inadequate **:** TRIFLING, HUMBLE ⟨we have a trifling, ~ banquet toward —Shak.⟩ ⟨all our ~ little paper knives and pincushions —Compton Mackenzie⟩

syn SILLY, ABSURD, PREPOSTEROUS: FOOLISH applies to what is marked by folly and nonsense, to what is not wise, sensible, or judicious ⟨only a *foolish* optimist can deny the dark realities of the moment —F.D.Roosevelt⟩ ⟨we need courage to look into our own heart and clear it of the *foolish* desires which make us sow vain hopes and devote needless toil and anxiety to raise bitter crops of disappointment —M.R.Cohen⟩ SILLY may indicate a fatuous lack of common sense, a witless, inane, or childish lack of reason ⟨how *silly* an ardent and unsuccessful wooer can be, especially if he's getting on in years —Dashiell Hammett⟩ ⟨a circle of *silly* young officers, who talked in bellicose and boastful terms —*Times Lit. Supp.*⟩ ABSURD may apply to what is flagrantly and ridiculously inconsistent with reason and common sense ⟨it is *absurd* to suppose that the shrewd traders . . . were moved by an abstract question of hereditary right —J.R.Green⟩ PREPOSTEROUS may indicate glaring, nonsensical lack of reasonableness ⟨if a man cannot see a church, it is *preposterous* to take his opinion about its altarpiece or painted window —T.H.Huxley⟩ ⟨a *preposterous* attempt to turn back the pages of history —V.L.Parrington⟩ ⟨a *preposterous* kind of resentment which endeavors to wreak itself on the beloved object —Nathaniel Hawthorne⟩ **syn** see in addition SIMPLE

foolish guillemot *n* **:** a common murre (*Uria aalge*) of northern seas

fool·ish·ly *adv* **:** in a foolish manner

fool·ish·ment \-mənt\ *n* -S *chiefly Midland* **:** FOOLISHNESS

fool·ish·ness *n* -ES [ME *folishnes*, fr. *folish* foolish + *-nes* -ness] **1 :** the quality or state of being foolish **:** FOLLY **2 :** a foolish practice **:** ABSURDITY

foolkiller \ˈ=‚==\ *n* **:** one that kills fools ⟨a sudden gale, a vicious north wind called the ~, which could blow a 40-foot boat to kingdom come —*Saturday Rev.*⟩; *esp* **:** an imaginary or legendary person whose business is destroying fools

fool·oc·ra·cy \fü'läkrəsē\ *n* -ES [¹*fool* + *-o-* + *-cracy*] **1 :** government by fools **2 :** a ruling class of fools

fool·om·e·ter \fü'lämәd·ə(r)\ *n* [¹*fool* + *-o-* + *-meter*] **:** a standard for measuring folly ⟨she was also useful as a touchstone, a ~ —Rose Macaulay⟩

foolproof \ˈ=‚=\ *adj* **1 :** so simple, plain, or strong as not to be liable to be misunderstood, damaged, or misused ⟨~ tools⟩ ⟨~ automatic washer⟩ **2 :** guaranteed to operate without breakdown or failure under any conditions ⟨~ elevator⟩ ⟨~ rule of thumb⟩ ⟨the system for reducing armaments must be ~ — that is, proof against cheating by any nation —*N.Y. Herald Tribune*⟩ — **fool·proof·ness** *n* -ES

fools *pl of* FOOL, *pres 3d sing of* FOOL

fools·cap *or* **fool's cap** \ˈfülz‚kap\ *n* **1 :** a cap or hood usu. with bells worn by jesters **2 :** DUNCE CAP **3** *usu* **foolscap** [so called fr. the watermark of a fool's cap formerly applied to such paper] **:** a size of paper differing somewhat in the various grades and typically about 16x13 inches for writing and drawing papers, 17x13 for printing papers and boards, and 18x14 for wrapping papers

foolscap 1

fool's-coat \ˈ=‚=\ *n, pl* **fool's-coats** [so called fr. its gaudy, multicolored plumage] **:** GOLDFINCH 1

fool's cress *n* **:** FOOL'S WATERCRESS

fool's errand *n* **:** a needless or profitless errand

fool's gold *n* **1 :** PYRITE **2 :** CHALCOPYRITE

fool's huckleberry *n* **:** a straggling shrub (*Menziesia ferruginea*) of northwestern No. America with glandular hirsute petioles and pedicels

fool's paradise *n* [ME *foles paradise*] **:** a state of delusory or deceptive success or happiness **:** a state of fatuous complacency based on unreal conditions or false expectations ⟨may go on living in a *fool's paradise* until they are caught in the final crash —M.B.Foster⟩

fool's parsley *n* **:** a European weed (*Aethusa cynapium*) of the family Umbelliferae that is naturalized in America and resembles parsley but causes nausea and poisoning when eaten

fool's-stones \ˈ=‚=\ *n pl but sing or pl in constr* [so called fr. the resemblance of the roots to testes] **:** any of several European orchids of the genus *Orchis*

fool's watercress *n* **:** a European perennial herb (*Apium nodiflorum*) with simple pinnate leaves and umbels of greenish white flowers

foon·er \ˈfünər\ *Scot var of* FOUNDER

¹foos·ter \ˈfüst(h)ər\ *n* -S [IrGael *fūstar*] *chiefly Irish* **:** FUSS, BUSTLE, TO-DO

²fooster \"\ *vi* -ED/-ING/-S *chiefly Irish* **:** to bustle around **:** FLUSTER; *esp* **:** to waste time by fussing and chattering ⟨you can't expect children to concentrate when everybody's gabbling and ~*ing* around them —Michael McLaverty⟩

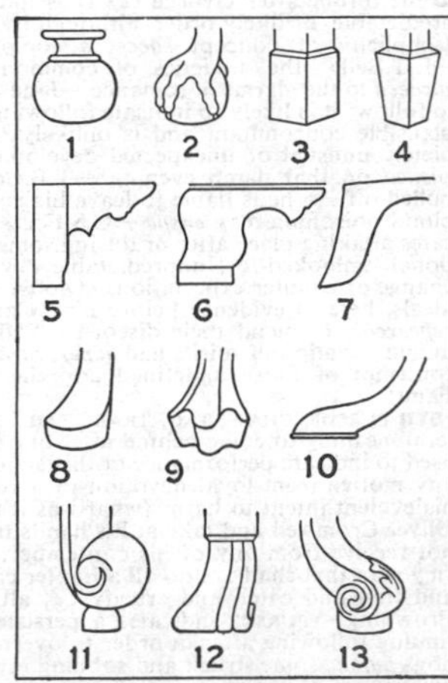

feet used in furniture: *1* ball, *2* claw and ball, *3* block, *4* spade, *5* straight bracket, *6* ogee bracket, *7* French bracket, *8* club, *9* drake, *10* snake, *11* flemish scroll, *12* Spanish scroll, *13* French scroll

¹foot \ˈfu̇t, *usu* -u̇d·+V\ *n, pl* **feet** \ˈfēt *usu* -ēd·+V\ *also* **foot** *see numbered senses, often attrib* [ME *fot, foot*, fr. OE *fōt*; akin to OHG *fuoz* foot, ON *fōtr*, Goth *fotus*, L *ped-, pes*, Gk *pod-, pous*, Skt *pad*]

1 : the terminal part of the vertebrate leg upon which an individual stands consisting in most bipeds (as man) and many quadrupeds (as the cat) of all the structures (as heel, arches, and digits) below the ankle joint or in digitigrade animals (as the horse or sheep) of the terminal parts of one or more digits often encased in a horny hoof **2 :** any of various invertebrate organs of locomotion or attachment: as **a :** a limb of an arthropod **b :** the ventral muscular surface or a ventral muscular process of a mollusk flattened for creeping in most gastropods or tapering for burrowing in many bivalves — compare PSEUDOPODIUM; see TUBE FOOT; CLAM illustration **3 :** any of various ancient and modern units of length based on the length of the human foot; *esp* **:** the unit used generally in English-speaking countries equal to ⅓ yard and comprising 12 inches ⟨a width of 16 *feet*⟩ ⟨a 5-*foot* tree⟩ ⟨six ~ tall⟩ — *pl foot* used preceded by a number and followed by a noun; *pl feet* or *foot* used preceded by a number and followed by an adverb ⟨10 *feet* tall⟩; see CAPE FOOT, GREEK FOOT, ROMAN FOOT; MEASURE table **4 :** the least bit of length, distance, or area ⟨payed out the rope to the last ~⟩ ⟨dragged along complaining every ~ of the way⟩ ⟨I'll starve ere I rob a ~ further —Shak.⟩ ⟨searched the grounds ~ by ~⟩ **5 a :** the basic unit of verse meter **:** a single instance of the recurring pattern which constitutes metrical rhythm **:** a group of syllables constituting a metrical unit **b :** the basic unit in a rhythmic series of any kind whether metrical or not — compare CADENCE, METER **6 a :** motion or power of walking or running **:** STEP, TREAD ⟨graceful and light of ~⟩ **b :** SWIFTNESS, SPEED ⟨the horse showed early ~ but tired before the end⟩ **7 :** something resembling a foot in position or use **:** the lowest supporting or structural part **:** BASE: as **a :** the lower end of the leg of a chair or table **b :** one of the areas of the base of a piece of printing type on each side of the groove; *also* **:** the corresponding area in type cast with no groove or in wood type — see TYPE illustration **c** (1) **:** the basal portion of the sporogonium in mosses embedded in the gametophyte and absorbing food from it (2) **:** a specialized outgrowth by which the embryonic sporophyte of many ferns and related plants and some seed plants absorbs nourishment from the gametophyte (3) **:** the basal portion of an epidermal hair lying within the epidermis and often differing in shape from adjacent epidermal cells **d :** the lowest part of an organ pipe **e :** a piece on a sewing machine that presses the cloth against the feed **f :** FOOTING 9 **8** *foot pl, chiefly Brit* **:** INFANTRY ⟨three regiments of ~ and two of cavalry⟩ ⟨the 41st *Foot*⟩ **9 :** the lower edge: as **a** *pl* **foots :** the bottom woven edge (as of a wicker basket) — see BASKET illustration **b :** the edge of a sail nearest the deck **c :** the bottommost part of a type page or printed page **d :** the lowermost edge of a book that is standing upright — compare BINDING EDGE, FORE EDGE, HEAD, TAIL **10 :** the lowest part **:** BOTTOM ⟨~ of a hill⟩ ⟨~ of a staircase⟩ **11 a :** the end that is lower or opposite the head ⟨~ of the bed⟩ ⟨~ of a lane⟩ ⟨~ of a line of dancers⟩ ⟨~ of the class⟩ **b :** the part that covers the foot ⟨the ~ of a stocking⟩ **12 :** something placed at the bottom: as **a** *obs* **:** the refrain of a song **b** *obs* **:** the sum of an account **13** *obs* **a :** FOOTING, BASIS, RANK **b :** customary value or price **:** standard rate of reckoning **14 :** the point of intersection of one line with another line or the point of contact with a plane **15 foots** *pl but sing or pl in constr* **:** material deposited esp. in aging or refining ⟨~s or soap stock precipitated in refining of fatty oils with alkali⟩ **:** SEDIMENT **:** DREGS **:** RESIDUE — compare ²BREAK 6d **16 :** FOOTWALL **17 foots** *pl* **:** FOOTLIGHTS — **at foot** *adv* **:** NEARBY **:** in the same enclosure (as for nursing) ⟨a mare with her colt *at foot*⟩ — **at one's feet :** under one's spell or influence **:** in subjection ⟨kept the audience *at her feet* for several seasons⟩ — **off its feet** *adv (or adj), of set type* **:** out of line with or inclined from the vertical (as from improper locking) — **off one's feet 1 :** in a sitting or lying position **:** not upright ⟨told by the doctor to stay *off his feet* as much as possible⟩ **2 :** beyond emotional self-control ⟨swept *off her feet* by a whirlwind courtship⟩ — **on foot** *adv* **1 :** in a walking or running state ⟨tour the campus *on foot*⟩ **2 :** under way **:** in progress ⟨plans to enlarge the campus are *on foot*⟩ — **on one's feet 1 :** in a standing position ⟨jumped and landed *on his feet*⟩ **2 :** in a position to go on ⟨the nomination put him *on his feet*⟩ **:** in an established position or state ⟨the business is finally *on its feet*⟩ **3 :** in a recovered condition (as from illness) **:** at a stage of being able to resume work or activity **4 :** without obvious deliberation or hesitation **:** EXTEMPORANEOUSLY ⟨a debater should be able to think *on his feet*⟩ — **put one's foot down :** to take a firm stand ⟨*put his foot down* on our staying out after midnight⟩ **:** give a clear or decisive order — **put one's foot into it :** to make a tactless or embarrassing blunder **:** get into trouble ⟨we can count on him to *put his foot into it* at the wrong moment⟩ — **with both feet** *adv* **:** HEAVILY, SOLIDLY, EMPHATICALLY ⟨came down *with both feet* against the proposal⟩

²foot \"\ *vb* -ED/-ING/-S [ME *foten*, fr. *fot*, *foot*] *vi* **1 :** to tread to music **:** DANCE, TRIP — often used with *it* ⟨~ it featly here and there —Shak.⟩ **2 :** to go on foot **:** WALK, RUN — contrasted with *ride*; often used with *it* ⟨~ it softly across the lambing fields —Roland Mathias⟩ ⟨a couple of men tearing up the path as tight as they could ~ it —Mark Twain⟩ **3** *of a falcon* **:** to seize prey with the talons **4** *of a sailboat* **:** to make speed or distance forward — contrasted with *point* ⟨under all sail . . . she ~s along in a light breeze —Luis Marden⟩ ~ *vt* **1 a :** to perform the movements of (a dance)⟨~ the saraband or some other intricate forgotten dance —Dixon Wecter⟩ **b :** to walk, run, or dance on, over, or through ⟨~ the greensward⟩ ⟨the moon . . . ~*ing* the treetops —C.E.S.Wood⟩ ⟨~*ing* his way to Paris —H.O.Taylor⟩ **2** *archaic* **a :** to kick with the foot **b :** REJECT, SPURN **c :** to seize or strike with the talons **3** *archaic* **:** to set on a basis **:** ESTABLISH **4 a :** to sum up (as numbers in a column) — sometimes used with *up* ⟨~ up an account⟩ **b :** to pay or stand credit for (a bill, expenses) ⟨~ the cost of a trip to the mountains⟩ **5 :** to make or renew the foot of (as a stocking) **6 :** TRACK 1 **7** *Irish* **:** to set (turf sods) on end in small heaps to dry ⟨~*ing* turf is a job —Bryan MacMahon⟩ **8 :** to splice (an arrow) with a footing **9 :** to hold the lower edge of (a stage flat) in place with the foot to facilitate raising to vertical position

foot·age \'fu̇d·|ij, -u̇t|, |ēj\ *n* -S **1 :** length or quantity expressed in feet: as **a :** BOARD FEET **b :** the total number of running feet of motion-picture film used for a complete story or for one or more scenes or for any subject **2 :** payment (as of miners) by the running foot of work; *also* **:** amount so paid

foot–and–mouth disease *n* **:** an acute contagious febrile disease affecting esp. cloven-footed animals, caused by a filtrable virus, and characterized by ulcerating vesicles in the mouth, about the hoofs, and on the udder and teats — called also *aphthous fever*

footback \'=,=\ *adv* [¹*foot* + *back* (as in *horseback*)] *dial* **:** on foot

footbacker \'=,==\ *n* -S *dial* **:** a person traveling on foot

¹football \'=,=\ *n, often attrib* [ME *fotbal*, *footbal*, fr. *fot*, *foot* + *bal* ball — more at FOOT, BALL] **1 :** any of several games played with a football on a rectangular field having two goalposts at each end by two teams whose object is to get the ball over a goal line or between goalposts: as **a** *Brit* **:** SOCCER **b** *Brit* RUGBY **c :** a game played between two teams of 11 players each in which the ball is in recognized possession of one side at a time and is advanced by running or passing, in which opposing players may stop the ballcarrier by tackling him, and in which teammates of the ballcarrier may precede him down the field to block off opponents — see AUSTRALIAN RULES FOOTBALL, CANADIAN FOOTBALL, GAELIC FOOTBALL, SIX-MAN FOOTBALL, TOUCH FOOTBALL **2 a :** an inflated oval ball made of a bladder encased usu. in leather, rubber, or plastic and used for throwing and kicking in the game of football **b** *Brit* **:** a soccer ball **3 a :** something that is tossed or kicked about **:** something or someone subjected to rough or irresponsible treatment ⟨sorry to see the GI made the ~ of politics —*N.Y. Herald Tribune*⟩ **b :** an item of merchandise priced to serve as a loss leader

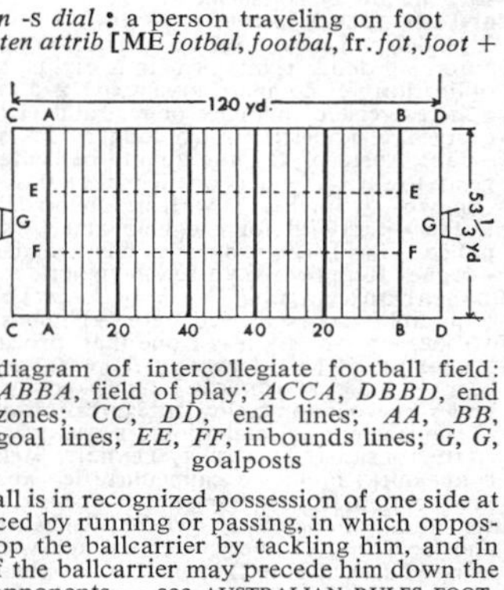

diagram of intercollegiate football field: *ABBA*, field of play; *ACCA*, *DBBD*, end zones; *CC*, *DD*, end lines; *AA*, *BB*, goal lines; *EE*, *FF*, inbounds lines; *G*, *G*, goalposts

²football \"\ *vb* -ED/-ING/-S *vi* **:** to play football ~ *vt* **:** to sell (an item of merchandise) below cost as a loss leader

footballer \'=,bȯlə(r)\ *n* **:** one that plays football or soccer

footband \'=,=\ *n* **1 :** a reinforcing strip of canvas on the afterpart of the foot of a sail — called also *footlining* **2 :** the bottom headband of a book — called also *tailband*

foot base *n* **:** a molding above a plinth

footbath \'=,=\ *n* **1 :** a bath for cleansing, warming, or disinfecting the feet (as at the entrance to an indoor swimming pool) ⟨a mustard ~ —Eric Knight⟩ **2 :** a small portable tub ⟨stepping into a ~ and washing upward —Flora Thompson⟩

footbeat \'=,=\ *n* **:** FOOTSTEP

foot–binding \'=,==\ *n* **:** the compressing of the feet of girls with tight bandages (as formerly in China) so as to keep the feet from being over three or four inches long

footblower \'=,==\ *n* **1 :** a bellows worked by foot **2 :** FOOTMAKER

footboard \'=,=\ *n* **1 :** a board or narrow platform on which one may stand or brace his feet: as **a :** the footrest of a coachman's box **b** (1) **:** FOOTPLATE (2) **:** a step slightly above track level on yard and freight locomotives for the use of train and yard personnel in yard operations **c :** a small platform at the rear of a carriage for a footman **d** (1) **:** the part of the front flooring in an automobile against which one's feet may rest (2) **:** RUNNING BOARD **2 :** a board forming the foot of a bed **3 :** TREADLE

foot bolt *n* **:** a bolt operated by foot pressure and attached to the bottom of a door to hold it in either open or closed position

footboy \'=,=\ *n* **:** a serving boy **:** PAGE, ATTENDANT

foot brake *n* **:** a brake operated by foot pressure

footbridge \'=,=\ *n* [ME *fotbrigge*, fr. *fot*, *foot* + *brigge*, bridge — more at BRIDGE] **:** a bridge for pedestrians

footcandle \'=,==\ *n* **:** a unit of illuminance on a surface that is everywhere one foot from a uniform point source of light of one candle and equal to one lumen per square foot

footcandle meter *n* **:** a direct-reading illuminometer calibrated in footcandles

foot carrier *n* **:** a postal carrier who makes his mail deliveries on foot

footcloth \'=,=\ *n* [ME *fotcloth*, fr. *fot*, *foot* + *cloth*] **1 :** an ornamental cloth draped over the back of a horse to reach the ground on each side and serve to indicate the state and dignity of the rider **2** *obs* **:** CARPET, RUG

foot couple *n* **:** the couple at the end of a double line of square dancers farthest from the music — compare HEAD COUPLE

foot cut *n* **:** a cut made at the low end of a rafter for proper seating on the wall plate

foot drop *n* **1 :** an extended position of the foot caused by paralysis of the flexor muscles of the leg — called also *toedrop* **2 :** a planter with a seed-dropping mechanism to be operated by the foot

foot·ed \'fu̇d·əd, -u̇təd\ *adj* [ME *foted*, *footed*, fr. OE *-fōted*, fr. *fōt* foot + *-ed*] **1 :** having a foot ⟨~ creatures⟩ ⟨~ candy dish⟩ **:** having such or so many feet ⟨black-*footed*⟩ ⟨four-*footed*⟩ **:** shaped in the foot ⟨claw-*footed*⟩ **2 :** having or capable of such a gait or tread **:** having such ability with the feet ⟨fleet-*footed*⟩ ⟨nimble-*footed*⟩ ⟨soft-*footed*⟩ **3 :** composed in meter ⟨good poetry . . . without rhyme or ~ rhythms —Michael Earls⟩ **4** *of an arrow* **:** having a footing of hardwood spliced to the fore end of the shaft

foot·ed·ness *n* -ES **:** the dominance of one foot over the other ⟨ambidexterity and mixture of eyedness, handedness, and ~ —J.R.Gallagher⟩

foote·ite \'fu̇d·,īt\ *n* -S [A.E. *Foote* †1895 Am. mineral collector + E *-ite*] **:** CONNELLITE

¹foot·er \'fu̇d·ə(r), -u̇tə-\ *n* -S [ME *foter*, *footer*, fr. *fot*, *foot* + *-er*] **1 :** one that goes on foot **:** PEDESTRIAN **2 :** a person or thing a (specified) number of feet in height, length, or breadth — used in combination ⟨the man is a six-*footer*⟩ ⟨the yacht was an 80-*footer*⟩ ⟨holed a 20-*footer* for par⟩ **3** *Brit* **:** RUGBY, SOCCER **4 :** the bowling mat used in lawn bowling **5 :** a hawk that seizes prey with the talons **6 a :** a machine for knitting feet on hosiery — compare LEGGER **b :** an operator of this machine **7 :** a mine worker who attaches and detaches tubs at the bottom of a haulage incline **8 :** FOOTING 7c

²foo·ter \'fu̇d·ə(r), -u̇tə-\ *var of* FOUTER

³foo·ter \"\ *vi* -ED/-ING/-S [F *foutre*, lit., to copulate — more at FOUTER] **:** FOOTLE

footfall \'=,=\ *n* **:** the sound of a footstep ⟨walked together with hushed ~s —Ida A. R. Wylie⟩

foot fault *n* **1 :** a fault called against a server in tennis by reason of his failure to keep both feet behind the base line or because of walking, running, or failure to maintain contact with the ground during the delivery of a service **2 :** the stepping over the end line in volleyball while serving or over the center line while playing

footfault \'=,=\ *vi* [*foot fault*] **:** to commit a foot fault

footfeed \'=,=\ *n* **:** the pedal operating the throttle in a motor vehicle

footfolk \'=,=\ *n* [trans. of G *fussvolk*] *archaic* **:** INFANTRY

foot front *n* **:** FRONT FOOT

footgear \'=,=\ *n* **:** covering for the feet (as shoes, boots, slippers)

footglove \'=,=\ *n* **1 :** a heavy stocking worn over the shoe **2 :** a close-fitting sock of soft material worn to protect the foot or the stocking against harsh shoe linings

footgrip \'=,=\ *n* **:** a surface (as of a stair tread) roughened or grained to prevent slipping

foot guard *n* **:** a guard for the foot: as **a :** a boot or pad for a horse's foot to prevent injury to the hoof by interfering or overreaching **b :** a filler placed in the space between converging railroad rails to prevent the feet of persons from becoming wedged between the rails

foothill \'=,=\ *n* **1 :** a hill at the foot of higher hills **2 foothills** *pl* **:** a hilly region at the base of a mountain range

foothill death camas *n* **:** an herb (*Zigadenus paniculatus*) of the western U.S. with greenish white racemose flowers and narrow leaves that are poisonous to cattle

foothills yellow pine *n* **:** PONDEROSA PINE

foothold \'=,=\ *n* **1 :** a hold for the feet **:** a place where one may tread or stand **:** a stable position of the feet **:** FOOTING ⟨a layer of wooden planking . . . affording a safe ~ to the crew in wet weather⟩ ⟨pine and balsam find a precarious ~ on the shaggy cliffs —*Amer. Guide Series: Minn.*⟩ **2 :** a position providing a base for further efforts to advance (as in a military invasion) ⟨effort to win a continental ~ —*Collier's Yr. Bk.*⟩ ⟨settlers struggling to secure a ~ in the new country —*Amer. Guide Series: Oregon*⟩ **3 :** a light rubber overshoe or sandal with only a strap around the heel — called also *tip*

foothook \'=,=\ *n* **:** FUTTOCK

foothot \'=|=\ *adv* [ME *fot hot*, *foot hot*] *archaic* **:** without delay **:** HASTILY

footie *var of* FOOTSIE

foot indian *n, usu cap I* **:** a South American Indian who travels by foot and not by canoe or horseback

foot·ing \'fu̇d·|iŋ, -u̇t|, |ēŋ\ *n* -S [ME *foting*, *footing*, fr. *fot*, *foot* + *-ing*] **1 :** a stable position of the feet **:** a surface or its condition with respect to one walking or running on it ⟨the loose stones made the ~ treacherous⟩; *specif* **:** the condition of a racetrack **2 :** the placing of the feet so as to ensure stability ⟨be careful of your ~ up here⟩ **:** ability to keep a grip with the feet on a surface so as to stay upright or move steadily forward ⟨lost her ~ and tumbled down the slope⟩ **3 :** FOOTLING **4 a :** a place or space for standing **:** basis for operations **:** FOOTHOLD ⟨a deliberate act of policy . . . in order to stake a claim for a ~ in Morocco —Wickham Steed⟩ **b :** established position **:** STATUS ⟨finally achieved a ~ at court⟩ ⟨placing the children of a former marriage on the same ~, with regard to inheritance —*Encyc. Americana*⟩ **c** *archaic* **:** payment exacted informally for entering upon a new status in a trade or profession **:** an initiation fee — used chiefly in the phrase *pay one's footing* **5 :** BASIS ⟨negotiating on a new ~ of mutual trust⟩ ⟨put the enterprise on a firm ~⟩ ⟨when the nation is on a war ~ —Zechariah Chafee⟩ **6 :** social relationship **:** terms of social intercourse ⟨tribes that are on a friendly ~ —Edward Sapir⟩ ⟨throwing our ideals overboard and meeting saints and dictators on the same ~ —*New Statesman and Nation*⟩ **7 a :** the substructure or bottom unit of a wall or column **:** BASE **b :** the part of a structure that is in contact with the soil or rock foundation **c :** an enlargement at the lower end of a foundation wall, pier, or column to distribute the load **8 a :** the straight side of an edging lace **b :** a very narrow lace or net used as an insertion, edging, or trimming **9 :** a piece of hardwood inserted into an arrow shaft and projecting into the pile **10 :** the amount or sum total of a column of figures

footing beam *n* **:** the tie beam of a roof

footing stone *n* **:** a broad flat stone for the base or lowest course of a wall

foot iron *n* **1 :** the step of a carriage **2 :** a bracket for securing scenery to the stage floor

foot jaw *n* **:** MAXILLIPED

footlambert \'=¦==\ *n* **:** a unit of luminance equal to the luminance of a perfectly diffusing surface that emits or reflects one lumen per square foot

foot landraker *n, obs* **:** FOOTPAD, TRAMP

foo·tle \'fu̇|d·ᵊl, 'fu̇|, |tᵊl\ *vi* **footled; footled; footling** \|d·ᵊliŋ, |t(ᵊ)liŋ\ **footles** [alter. of ³*footer*] **1 :** to waste time **:** TRIFLE, FOOL, POTTER — used with *around* or *about* **2 :** to talk or act foolishly

foo·tler \|d·ᵊlə(r), |t(ᵊ)lə-\ *n* -S **:** one that footles **:** TRIFLER ⟨unless a writer is quite ruthless with these amiable ~s —*N.Y. Herald Tribune*⟩

foot·less \'fu̇tləs\ *adj* [ME *fotles footles*, fr. *fot*, *foot* + *-les* -less] **1 a :** lacking a foot **:** having no feet **b :** lacking foundation **:** UNSUBSTANTIAL ⟨~ halls of air —J.G.Magee⟩ **2 :** CLUMSY, STUPID, INEPT, USELESS, FUTILE ⟨~ and vacillating foreign policy —Alvin Johnson⟩ — **foot·less·ly** *adv* — **foot·less·ness** *n* -ES

footlicker \'=,==\ *n* -S **:** SYCOPHANT, BOOTLICKER

footlight \'=,=\ *n* **1 :** a light that casts its illumination upward from foot level; *esp* **:** one of a row of lights set across the front of a stage floor — usu. used in pl. **2 footlights** *pl* **:** the stage as a profession

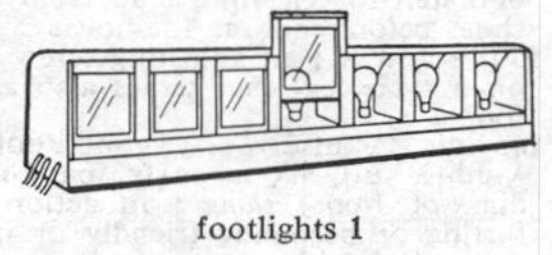

footlights 1

footlike \'=,=\ *adj* **:** resembling a foot

foot line *n* **1 :** the weighted line of a fishing net **2 :** a line at the foot of a type page that is sometimes blank and sometimes carries the page number or signature figure or letter **3 :** FOOT SCORE

¹foot·ling \'fu̇tliŋ\ *n* -S [fr. ¹*foot* + *-ling* (n. suffix)] **:** one of the fore-and-aft strips of wood secured to the frames in the bottom of a small boat **:** FLOORBOARD — called also *footing*

²footling \"\ *adv (or adj)* [¹*foot* + *-ling* (adv. suffix)] **:** with or having the feet foremost ⟨~ presentation at delivery⟩

³foo·tling \'fu̇|d·ᵊliŋ, 'fu̇|, |t(ᵊ)liŋ\ *adj* [fr. pres. part. of *footle*] **1 :** lacking judgment, intelligence, or experience **:** FOOLISH, SILLY ⟨~ amateurs who understand nothing —E.R. Bentley⟩ **2 :** lacking importance, use, or value **:** TRIVIAL, INSIGNIFICANT ⟨a pity that such an attractive young woman should be interested in such ~ things —Nevil Shute⟩

footlining \'=,==\ *n* **:** FOOTBAND

footlock \'=,=\ *n* **1 :** a grip secured by the feet in climbing a rope **2 :** a level or relatively level projection temporarily fastened to a roof to provide footing for a workman

footlocker \'=,==\ *n* [¹*foot* + *locker*] **:** a small flat trunk equipped with a lock and designed to be placed at the foot of a barracks bunk

footlog \'=,=\ *n, chiefly Midland & West* **:** a simple footbridge consisting often of a single log hewn flat on one side ⟨crossing the ~ over Marsh Run —Conrad Richter⟩

footloose \'=,=\ *adj* **:** able or accustomed to act and travel about freely **:** not tied **:** WANDERING, NOMADIC ⟨Americans, from frontier times downward, have been a ~ people, always moving on —G.R.Stewart⟩ ⟨~ bachelors⟩

foot louse *n* **:** a sucking louse (*Linognathus pedalis*) on sheep congregating and feeding chiefly on the hairy skin immediately above the hooves

footmaker \'=,==\ *n* **:** a member of a chair of glassworkers who gathers and blows glass and shapes it on a marver table

foot·man \'=mən\ *n, pl* **footmen** [ME *fotman*, *footman*, fr. *fot*, *foot* + *man*] **1 a** *archaic* **:** a traveler on foot **:** PEDESTRIAN **b** *obs* **:** FOOTPAD **c** *obs* **:** one who runs foot races **d :** FOOT SOLDIER **2 a :** a servant in livery formerly in attendance upon a rider or required to run before his master's carriage **b :** a house servant who assists the butler in serving at table, tending the door, carrying luggage and parcels, running errands **c :** DOORMAN 1a **d :** a policeman who rides in the back of a patrol wagon and supervises the transportation of prisoners (as from a police beat to a station house or jail) — called also *wagonman* **3 :** a metal stand for holding a plate or kettle near a fire to keep it warm **4 :** BOTTOMER c

foot mange *n* **:** CHORIOPTIC MANGE

footman moth *n* [so called fr. its coloration, reminiscent of a footman's livery] **:** any of numerous moths of the family Lithosiidae

foot·man·ship \'fu̇tmən,ship\ *n, archaic* **:** speed afoot **:** prowess in running and walking

foot mantle *n* [ME *fot mantel*] **1 :** a long garment formerly worn to protect the dress in riding **2 :** FOOTCLOTH

footmark \'=,=\ *n* **:** FOOTPRINT

foot–mouth \'=,=\ *n* [by shortening] **:** FOOT-AND-MOUTH DISEASE

¹footnote \'=,=\ *n* [¹*foot* + *note*] **1 :** a note of reference, explanation, or comment placed below the text on a printed page or underneath a table or chart — compare REFERENCE MARK **2 :** an utterance or action that is subordinated or added to a larger statement or event **:** COMMENTARY, AFTERTHOUGHT ⟨this novel is a ~ to recent history⟩ ⟨it has been said that all philosophy is a ~ to Plato —Lionel Trilling⟩

²footnote \"\ *vt* **:** to furnish with a footnote **:** ANNOTATE

foot of the fine *n, pl* **feet of the fines** [trans. of AF *pee de la fin*] **:** the part of a tripartite indenture made in case of a fine of land made for the court's records — compare CHIROGRAPH

footpace \'=,=\ *n* **1 :** a walking pace ⟨the coach proceeded at a ~⟩ **2** *obs* **:** CARPET, MAT **3 a :** an elevated platform **:** DAIS **b :** a landing on a staircase **c :** PREDELLA 1a

¹footpad \'=,=\ *n* [¹*foot* + *pad* (highwayman)] **:** one who robs a pedestrian **:** HOLDUP MAN

²footpad \"\ *n* [¹*foot* + *pad* (thick sole)] **:** PAD 4a(1) ⟨ancient bull elephant that glides on noiseless, 28-inch ~s —*Time*⟩

foot page *n* [ME *fot page*] **:** an errand boy **:** ATTENDANT, FOOTBOY

foot passenger *n* **:** PEDESTRIAN, PASSERBY

footpath \'=,=\ *n* **1 :** a narrow path for pedestrians **:** FOOTWAY; *specif, Brit* **:** SIDEWALK

foot pavement *n, chiefly Brit* **:** SIDEWALK

footpick \'=,=\ *n* **:** a pointed pole with handgrips and foot piece for digging in hard or stony ground

footplate \'=,=\ *n* **1 :** a carriage step **2 a :** a platform on early locomotives for the engineer to stand on **b** *Brit* **:** the floor of a locomotive cab **3 :** a wooden sill to distribute concentrated loads in a frame construction

foot post *n* **1 :** a postal carrier who travels on foot **:** FOOT CARRIER **2 :** a mail-delivery service employing exclusively foot carriers

footpost \'=,=\ *n* **:** one of the posts at the foot of a bed

foot–pound \'=¦=\ *n, pl* **foot–pounds 1 :** a unit of work in the fps system equal to the work done by a pound-force acting through a distance of one foot in the direction of the force **2 :** a unit of torque equal to the torque produced by a pound-force acting perpendicular to and at the end of a lever arm of one foot — called also *pound-foot*

foot–poundal \'=¦==\ *n* **:** the absolute unit of work in the fps system equal to the work done by a force of one poundal acting through a distance of one foot in the direction of the force

foot–pound–second \'=,=¦==\ *adj* **:** being or relating to a system of units based upon the foot as the unit of length, the pound as the unit of weight or mass, and the second as the unit of time — abbr. *fps*

footprint \'ˌ=ˌ=\ *n* **1 :** an impression of the foot on a surface **2 :** TRACE

foot pump *n* **1 :** a portable hand pump held in place by the foot : STIRRUP PUMP **2 :** a pump operated by a treadle

footrace \'ˌ=ˌ=\ *n* **:** a race run on foot

foot racer *n* **:** one that runs footraces

footrail \'ˌ=ˌ=\ *n* **1 :** a crosspiece (as between the legs of a table or chair or under a car seat) serving to support the feet **2 :** the crosspiece at the foot of a bed

footrest \'ˌ=ˌ=\ *n* **:** a support for the feet : FOOTRAIL : FOOTSTOOL

foot·rill \'fu̇·trəl, -u̇t·ˌril\ *n* [perh. alter. of *foot trail*] *Brit* **:** a level or inclined road giving entrance (as by a tunnel driven in a hillside) to a mine

footrope \'ˌ=ˌ=\ *n* **1 :** a rope rigged below a yard for men to stand on when reefing or furling — see SHIP illustration **2 :** the part of a boltrope sewed to the lower edge of a sail

foot rot *n* **1 a :** a disease (as mal di gomma of citrus) that rots the stem or trunk of an affected plant near the ground **b :** a disease of cereals (as wheat) in which the culm blackens and decays resulting in lodging — compare TAKE-ALL **2 :** a progressive inflammation of the tissues in the region of the feet (as between the digits) of sheep or cattle; *specif* **:** a necrobacillosis marked by sloughing, ulceration, suppuration, and sometimes loss of the hoof — called also *foul-foot*

foot rule *n* **:** a stick one foot long for measuring length or distance ⟨carpenter with *foot rule*, notebook, and pencil —May Sinclair⟩; *broadly* **:** a standard of measurement or judgment ⟨measured with the *foot rule* of the individual life —S.A. Coblentz⟩

foots \'fu̇ts\ *pl of* FOOT

foot scab *n* **:** CHORIOPTIC MANGE

footscald \'ˌ=ˌ=\ *n* **:** an injury (as from a hot shoe) to the sole of a horse's foot

foot score *n* **:** a line 12 feet behind the tee and at right angles to the length of a curling rink from which a player delivers his stone — called also *foot line;* see CURLING illustration

footscraper \'ˌ=ˌ=ˌ=\ *n* **:** a sharp-edged plate or bar fixed on a doorstep for cleaning mud from the shoes before entering the house

footscraper

foot screw *n* **:** an adjusting screw (as on a table leg) that serves also as a foot

foot·sie \'fu̇tsē, -si\ *also* **foot·ie** \-u̇d·|ē, -u̇t|, |i\ *n* -s [fr. baby-talk dim. of ¹*foot*] *slang* **:** an action of flirting or becoming friendly or intimate often with covertness and sometimes with duplicity — usu. used with the verb *play* ⟨play ~ under the table⟩ ⟨if she was playing ~ with somebody else, how'd she find the opportunity for it —Bob Wicks⟩

foot·slog \'ˌ=ˌ=\ *vi* **:** to march or tramp toilsomely through or as if through mud

foot·slog·ger \'ˌ=ˌ=ˌ=\ *n* **:** INFANTRYMAN

foot soldier *n* **:** a soldier who marches and fights on foot **:** INFANTRYMAN

footsore \'ˌ=ˌ=\ *adj* **:** having sore or tender feet (as by reason of much walking) — **footsoreness** *n* -ES

footstalk \'ˌ=ˌ=\ *n* **1 a :** PETIOLE 1 **b :** PEDUNCLE **2 :** the lower part of a millstone spindle

footstall \'ˌ=ˌ=\ *n* **1 :** the stirrup of a side saddle **2 :** the plinth, base, or pedestal of a pillar

footstep \'ˌ=ˌ=\ *n* [ME *fotstep, footstep,* fr. *fot, foot* + *step*] **1 a :** STEPPING, FOOTFALL, TREAD **b :** distance covered by a step **:** PACE **2 a :** the mark of the foot **:** TRACK **b :** TRACE, TOKEN ⟨the ~s of divine wisdom⟩ **3 :** a step on which to ascend or descend ⟨~ of a carriage⟩ **4** *or* **footstep bearing :** STEP BEARING

footstick \'ˌ=ˌ=\ *n* **:** a wooden or iron stick that when wedged with quoins secures the foot of a locked-up type page

footstock \'ˌ=ˌ=\ *n* **:** TAILSTOCK

footstone \'ˌ=ˌ=\ *n* **1 :** a single stone forming a kneeler at the foot of a gable slope to resist the thrust of the coping stones above **2 :** a stone placed at the foot of a grave

footstool \'ˌ=ˌ=\ *n* **1 :** a low stool to support the feet **:** OTTOMAN **2 :** a portable step (as for mounting a horse)

foot stove *n* **:** a box with a pan for hot coals to warm the feet

foot switch *n* **:** an electric switch operated by pressure of the foot

foot tender *n* **:** BOTTOMER C

foot–ton \'ˌ=ˌ=\ *n, pl* **foot–tons :** a unit of energy equal to the work done in raising one ton against standard gravity through the height of one foot

foot up *vt* [²*foot*] **:** to make a total of (as the cost) ~ *vi* **:** to amount to when added or reckoned — usu. used with *to* ⟨his debts *foot up* to a huge sum⟩

foot–up \'ˌ=ˌ=\ *n* -s [¹*foot*] **:** a lifting of the foot by a scrummager in rugby before the ball is fairly in the scrummage

foot valve *n* **:** a check valve at the lower end of a suction pipe (as in a well)

foot waling *n* **:** the inside bottom planks of a ship

footwalk \'ˌ=ˌ=\ *n* **1 :** a surface paved or constructed for walking along often with a handrail (as on a bridge or on a parapet) **2 :** SIDEWALK

footwall \'ˌ=ˌ=\ *n* **1 :** the lower or underlying wall of a vein, ore deposit, or coal seam in a mine **:** the wall upon which a miner stands **2 :** the lower wall of an inclined fault; *also* **:** the entire mass of rock below an inclined fault — opposed to *hanging wall*

foot warmer *n* **1 :** a contrivance to keep the feet warm **2 :** a warm covering (as a lined slipper) for the foot

foot washing *n* **:** a ceremonial cleansing of the feet preparatory to worship

footway \'ˌ=ˌ=\ *n* [ME *fotewey,* fr. *fot, foot* + *wey* — more at FOOT, WAY] **:** a footpath, sidewalk, or any way reserved for pedestrians

footwear \'ˌ=ˌ=\ *n* **:** wearing apparel for the feet (as shoes, boots, slippers, overshoes) usu. excluding hosiery

footwell \'ˌ=ˌ=\ *n* **:** a shallow well in the afterdeck of a sailboat

footwork \'ˌ=ˌ=\ *n* **1 :** the management of the feet and work done with them (as in boxing, football, tennis, dancing) **2 :** the activity of moving from place to place in the fulfillment of a task or purpose; *esp* **:** the activity of a news reporter in gathering news by direct investigation

foo·ty \'füd·ē, 'fü-\ *adj* [F *foutu,* fr. past part. of *foutre* to copulate — more at FOUTER] **1** *chiefly dial* **:** INSIGNIFICANT, PALTRY ⟨a ~ little town⟩ **2** *chiefly dial* **:** poorly kept **:** SHODDY ⟨a pair of ~ old boots⟩

foo yong \'fü'yȯŋ, -'yəŋ\ *n* -s [Chin (Pek) *fu²* *yung²*, lit., hibiscus] **:** a Chinese omelet made with bean sprouts, green pepper, and onion and fried in deep fat

¹foo·zle \'füzəl\ *vt* **foozled; foozled; foozling** \-z(ə)liŋ\ **foozles** [perh. fr. G dial. *fuseln* to work hurriedly or poorly] **:** to manage awkwardly **:** treat or play unskillfully **:** BUNGLE

²foozle \"\ *n* -s **:** act of foozling; *esp* **:** a bungling stroke (as in golf)

foo·zler \-z(ə)lə(r)\ *n* -s **:** one that foozles **:** BUNGLER

¹fop \'fäp\ *n* -s [ME *foppe, fop;* akin to ME *fobben* to deceive, cheat, MHG (Alemannic dial.) *voppen*] **1** *obs* **:** a foolish or silly person **:** a conceited pretender to wit or accomplishments **2 :** a man who is devoted to or vain of the exquisiteness or showiness of his dress **:** COXCOMB, DANDY, DUDE

²fop *vt* **fopped; fopped; fopping; fops** *obs* **:** FOOL, DUPE, CHEAT

fop·ling \'fäpliŋ\ *n* -s [¹*fop* + *-ling*] *archaic* **:** an insignificant or absurd man of fashion **:** PETIT MAÎTRE, LADIES' MAN

fop·pery \'fäp(ə)rē, -ri\ *n* -ES [¹*fop* + *-ery*] **1 :** foolish character or action **:** FOLLY, ABSURDITY, VANITY ⟨let not the sound of shallow ~ enter my sober house —Shak.⟩ **2 :** the behavior, dress, or other mark of a fop **:** COXCOMBRY, AFFECTATION

fop·pish \'fäpish, -pēsh\ *adj* **1** *obs* **:** FOOLISH, SILLY, STUPID **2 :** characteristic of a fop in dress or manners ⟨a ~ embroidered nightshirt —A. Conan Doyle⟩ — **fop·pish·ly** *adv* — **fop·pish·ness** *n* -ES

fop·py \'fäpē, -pi\ *adj* -ER/-EST **:** FOPPISH

fop's alley *n* **:** a fashionable promenade (as the passage through the center of the pit) in an 18th century theater or opera house

FOQ *abbr* free on quay

¹for \fə(r), (ˌ)fȯ(ə)r, (ˌ)fȯ(ə), *in R speech in the southern US also* (ˌ)fär\ *prep* [ME, fr. OE; akin to OHG *fora* before, *furi* before, for, ON *fyr,* Goth *faur* before, for, L *per* through, *pro* before, for, *prae* before, Gk *pro* before, ahead, Skt *pra-* before, forward, OE *faran* to travel, go — more at FARE] **1** *obs* **:** BEFORE **2 a :** as a preparation toward ⟨dressing ~ dinner⟩ or against ⟨storing nuts ~ the winter⟩ or in view of ⟨making plans ~ retirement⟩ ⟨studying ~ examinations⟩ **:** having as goal or object ⟨volunteered ~ the air force⟩ **b :** in order to be, become, or serve as ⟨originally built ~ a church⟩ ⟨ordered eggs ~ breakfast⟩ **c :** in order to bring about or further ⟨working ~ the good of humanity⟩ **d :** to supply the need of ⟨food ~ hungry mouths⟩ **e :** with the purpose or object of ⟨an instrument ~ measuring speed⟩ **f :** adapted to ⟨suits ~ tall men⟩ ⟨a calendar ~ 1960⟩ or prerequisite to ⟨a shelf ~ books⟩ ⟨mathematics ~ engineers⟩ **g :** in order to obtain ⟨write ~ a free catalog⟩ or gain ⟨work ~ a living⟩ **h :** in order to save (something in danger) ⟨on trial ~ his life⟩ ⟨could not tell ~ the life of me whether he was serious⟩ ⟨running ~ dear life⟩ or to remedy ⟨take something ~ his cough⟩ ⟨don't like to sell the house, but there is nothing else ~ it⟩ ⟨mud is good ~ bee stings⟩ **3 a** — used as a function word to indicate the object of a feeling ⟨hungry ~ praise⟩ ⟨longing ~ home⟩ or faculty ⟨a taste ~ spicy food⟩ ⟨an eye ~ color⟩ **b :** so as to secure as a result **:** conducive to ⟨telling you ~ your own good⟩ ⟨acting ~ the best in forbidding the trip⟩ **c** (1) **:** intending to go to or toward ⟨has just left ~ the office⟩ ⟨starting out ~ a trip across the country⟩ (2) **:** on the point of **:** having the intention of ⟨was just ~ going to bed⟩ ⟨wise men will have it that he meant these islands, and I am not ~ arguing the point —Norman Douglas⟩ **d** — used as a function word to indicate the person or thing that something is to be delivered to ⟨any letters ~ me⟩ or assigned to ⟨a slot ~ out-of-town mail⟩ or used by or in connection with ⟨are these the tires ~ this car⟩ **4 :** to the amount of ⟨a check ~ $100⟩ or extent of ⟨can see ~ miles from the hilltop⟩ or duration of ⟨waited ~ several hours⟩ ⟨won't be here ~ long⟩ or value of ⟨now pull ~ all you are worth⟩ **5 a :** in place of ⟨go to the store ~ me⟩ ⟨Doe now batting ~ Roe⟩ **:** in exchange as the equivalent of ⟨all that trouble ~ nothing⟩ ⟨my kingdom ~ a horse —Shak.⟩ or in requital of ⟨he gave blow ~ blow⟩ ⟨an eye ~ an eye⟩ **b :** in behalf of ⟨his lawyer will act ~ him in this affair⟩ **:** in support of ⟨let me carry that ~ you⟩ or in defense of ⟨fighting ~ their country⟩ **:** in favor of ⟨a prayer ~ those at sea⟩ ⟨which candidate are you ~⟩ — opposed to *against* **c :** in honor of **:** AFTER ⟨named ~ his grandfather⟩ **6 a** — used with a noun or pronoun followed by an infinitive to form an equivalent to such noun clauses as *that he should, that he might* ⟨~ him to confess would be painful⟩ ⟨shouted the news ~ all to hear⟩ ⟨~ you to have to pay for this is not fair⟩ ⟨here are some books ~ you to read⟩ **b** — used chiefly South & Midland redundantly after such verbs as *like, want, choose* ⟨I'd like ~ you to go⟩ **c** — used as a function word to introduce exclamations ⟨~ her to talk to her father like that⟩ or mild oaths ⟨~ God's sake hold your tongue and let me love —John Donne⟩ **7 a :** as being ⟨know ~ a fact⟩ ⟨do you take me ~ a fool⟩ ⟨take ~ granted⟩ ⟨mere noisy shouting often passes ~ comedy⟩ ⟨left ~ dead on the field⟩ **b** — used as a function word to indicate parenthetically an actual or implied enumeration or selection from an aggregate or series ⟨~ one thing, we have no money; ~ another, we have no time⟩ ⟨people don't buy it because, ~ one thing, the price is too high⟩ ⟨I ~ one will vote for him⟩ ⟨~ the last time, will you stop that noise⟩ ⟨be sensible ~ once⟩ **8 a :** because of ⟨shouted ~ joy⟩ **:** on account of ⟨decorated ~ bravery⟩ ⟨do it ~ my sake⟩ **b** *obs* **:** in order to prevent **:** for fear of ⟨here they shall not lie, ~ catching cold —Shak.⟩ **9** — used as a function word to indicate equality or proportion between numbers or quantities that are related, compared, or contrasted ⟨~ every good writer there are a dozen scribblers⟩ ⟨answered his argument point ~ point⟩ ⟨repeated the speech word ~ word⟩ ⟨the best fighter, weight ~ weight, in the country⟩ **10 a :** as regards **:** in respect to **:** CONCERNING ⟨a stickler ~ detail⟩ ⟨so much ~ that topic⟩ ⟨true ~ all I know⟩ ⟨safe ~ the present⟩ ⟨good country ~ deer⟩ **b :** in proportion to ⟨tall ~ his age⟩ **:** taking into account **:** CONSIDERING ⟨very cool ~ May⟩ ⟨that was a good score ~ him⟩ **c :** in spite of **:** NOTWITHSTANDING — usu. used with *all* ⟨you don't convince me ~ all your clever arguments⟩ ⟨the elephants ~ all their great size moved absolutely noiselessly —Jule Mannix⟩ ⟨a man's a man ~ a' that —Robert Burns⟩ — **for all me :** as far as I am concerned — **for all the world** — used to emphasize a likeness ⟨looked *for all the world* like a ship that had lost her foremast —Frank Yerby⟩ — **for itself 1** *of a being* **:** capable of functioning esp. in the epistemological process purely by relation to itself **:** SELF-DETERMINED **2** *of a notion* **:** related to itself or its own manifestations

²for \"\ *conj* [ME, fr. OE, fr. *for,* prep.] **1** *archaic* **:** by reason that **:** for the reason that **:** BECAUSE ⟨my foolish rival, that her father likes only ~ his possessions are so huge —Shak.⟩ **2 :** for this reason or on this ground **:** as indicated or shown by the following circumstance **:** in substantiation of which **:** witness the fact that — used to introduce a reason for something before advanced (as a cause, motive, explanation, justification, or proof, of an action related or a statement made) ⟨we believe that he will succeed, ~ he has talent⟩ ⟨the army should be reduced in numbers, ~ possession of large armies has led nations to war⟩ **3** *obs* **:** in order that ⟨and, ~ the time shall not seem tedious, I'll tell thee what befell me —Shak.⟩

³for \'fȯ(ə)r, 'fȯ(ə), *in R speech in the southern US also* 'fär\ *n* -s [¹*for*] **1 :** one who takes the affirmative side **2 :** what is said or felt in favor of someone or something **:** PRO

for- *prefix* [ME, fr. OE; akin to OHG *fir-, far-, fur-* for-, OS *for-,* Goth *fra-, fair-* for-, *faur-* for-, fore-, OE *for*] **1 :** so as to involve prohibition, exclusion, omission, failure, or refusal — almost exclusively in words coined before 1600 ⟨*forsay*⟩ ⟨*forheed*⟩ **2 :** destructively or detrimentally — almost exclusively in words coined before 1600 ⟨*forhang*⟩ ⟨*forstorm*⟩ **3 :** completely **:** excessively **:** to exhaustion **:** to pieces — almost exclusively in words coined before 1600 ⟨*forbruise*⟩ ⟨*forweary*⟩ ⟨*forspent*⟩

for *abbr* **1** foreign **2** forel **3** forest; forestry

FOR *abbr* free on rail

fora *pl of* FORUM

for a' \fə'rȯ\ *adv, Scot* **:** NEVERTHELESS, NOTWITHSTANDING ⟨she has a bonny face for a'⟩

¹for·age \'fȯrij, 'fär-, -rēj\ *n* -s *often attrib* [ME, fr. MF *fourage, forage,* fr. OF, fr. *forre, fuerre* fodder, straw, of Gmc origin; akin to OHG *fuotar* food, fodder — more at FOOD] **1 a :** vegetable food (as hay, grain) for domestic animals ⟨~ crop⟩ **b :** food that wild or domestic animals take for themselves **2** [²*forage*] **:** the act of foraging **:** search for provisions ⟨they skirt the land like scouts upon a ~ —Eileen Duggan⟩

²for·age \", *esp in pres part* -rəj\ *vb* -ED/-ING/-S [ME *foragen,* fr. MF *fourager,* fr. *fourage*] *vt* **1 a :** to strip of provisions **:** collect forage from **b** *archaic* **:** SPOIL, PLUNDER **2 :** to supply (as horses and cattle) with forage **3 :** to secure by foraging ⟨*foraged* a chicken for the feast⟩ ~ *vi* **1 :** to wander or rove in search of forage or food **2 :** to secure forage (as for horses and cattle) by stripping the country **3 :** RAVAGE, RAID **4 :** to make a search **:** RUMMAGE ⟨*foraging* in his pockets for a match⟩ ⟨went *foraging* for bedroom slippers, shaving mirrors, and stationery —Bill Davidson⟩

³for·age \'fȯrij\ *n* -s [by folk etymology] **:** FORE EDGE ⟨~ painting in bookbinding⟩

forage acre *n* **:** a unit of grazing value equivalent to one acre of land entirely covered with herbage that can be completely utilized by grazing animals — abbr. *F.A.*

forage cap *n* **:** a small military cap with a visor and a round flat crown to be worn with undress uniforms

forage density *n* **:** the proportion of the soil surface in a range or pasture that is covered by vegetation within the reach of animals

forage fish *n* **:** fish of value as food for other fishes more useful to man — compare FOOD FISH, GAME FISH, ROUGH FISH

forage grass *n* **:** grass used as feed for stock

forage harvester *n* **:** FIELD CHOPPER

forage poisoning *n* **:** staggers of domestic animals and birds due to toxic elements taken in with the food; *often* **:** BOTULISM

forage press *n* **:** BALER

for·ag·er \'fȯrəjə(r), 'fär-, -rēj-\ *n* -s [ME, fr. MF *fourageur,* fr. *fourager* + *-eur* -or] **1 :** one that forages **2 foragers** *pl* **a :** soldiers detailed to forage **b :** cavalrymen advancing in line with extended intervals **3 :** FORAGING ANT

forag·ing ant *n* **:** an ant (as the driver and army ant) that goes out in search of food in companies

for·a·lite \'fȯrəˌlīt\ *n* -s [L *forare* + E *-lite*] **:** a marking found in stratified rocks that resembles a worm's burrow

for·am \'fȯrəm\ *n* -s [NL *Foraminifera*] **:** one of the Foraminifera

fo·ra·men \fə'rāmən, fō'-\ *n, pl* **fo·ram·i·na** \-ramənə\ *or* **foramens** [L, fr. *forare* to bore, pierce — more at BORE] **1 :** a small opening, perforation, or orifice **:** FENESTRA **2** [NL, fr. L] **:** MICROPYLE 2

foramen mag·num \-'magnəm\ *n* [NL, lit., great opening] **:** the large opening in the occipital bone through which the medulla oblongata passes to become the spinal cord

foramen of ma·gen·die \-məˌzhän'dē\ *usu cap M* [after François *Magendie* †1855 Fr. physiologist] **:** a passage through the midline of the roof of the fourth ventricle of the brain which together with the foramina of Key and Retzius affords a passage for the cerebrospinal fluid from the ventricles to the subarachnoid spaces

foramen of mon·ro \-mən'rō\ *usu cap M* [after Alexander *Monro* †1817 Scot. anatomist] **:** the opening from each lateral ventricle into the third ventricle of the brain

foramen of wins·low \-'winz(ˌ)lō\ *usu cap W* [after Jakob B. *Winslow* †1760 Dan. anatomist] **:** EPIPLOIC FORAMEN

foramen ova·le \-ō'va(ˌ)lē, -'vā(-, -'vä(-\ *n* [NL, lit., oval opening] **1 :** an opening in the septum between the two atria of the heart that is normally open only in the fetus **2 :** an oval opening in the greater wing of the sphenoid for passage of the mandibular nerve

fo·ram·i·nal \fə'ramənᵊl\ *adj* [L *foramin-, foramen* + E *-al*] **:** of or occurring by way of a foramen ⟨~ block⟩

foramina of key and ret·zi·us \-ˌkāən'retsēəs\ *usu cap K&R* [after Ernst A. H. *Key* †1901 and Gustaf M. *Retzius* †1919 Swed. anatomists] **:** passages at the lateral recesses of the fourth ventricle of the brain — see FORAMEN OF MAGENDIE

fo·ram·i·nate \fə'ramə,nāt\ *or* **fo·ram·i·nat·ed** \-ˌād·əd\ *adj* [LL *foraminatus,* fr. L *foramin-, foramen* + *-atus* -ate, -ated] **:** having foramina **:** PERFORATED

for·a·min·i·fer \ˌfȯrə'minəfə(r)\ *n* -s [NL *Foraminifera*] **:** one of the Foraminifera

fo·ram·i·nif·era \fəˌramə'nif(ə)rə, ˌfȯrəmə'-\ *n pl* [NL, fr. L *foramin-, foramen* + NL *-i-* + *-fera* (fr. neut. pl. of L *-fer*)] **1** *cap* **:** an order of Rhizopoda comprising large chiefly marine protozoans that have one or more nuclei, that are generally enclosed in a typically calcareous shell having minute openings for slender branching pseudopodia and consisting of several successively formed communicating chambers each larger than the preceding, that have a complex life cycle in which sexual and asexual generations alternate, and that are so abundant that their shelly remains constitute a major part of various sedimentary limestones (as chalk) and serve to identify geologic horizons — compare INDEX FOSSIL; see BILOCULINA, GLOBIGERINA **2 :** organisms belonging to Foraminifera

fo·ram·i·nif·er·al \ˌ=ˌ=ˌ=nif(ə)rəl, ˌ=ˌ=ˌ=ˌnif(ə)rəl\ *adj* [NL *Foraminifera* + E *-al*] **:** of, derived from, or relating to the Foraminifera or their shells

¹fo·ram·i·nif·er·an \-rən\ *adj* [NL *Foraminifera* + E *-al*] **:** FORAMINIFERAL

²foraminiferan \"\ *n* -s **:** one of the Foraminifera

fo·ram·i·nif·er·ous \-rəs\ *adj* [NL *Foraminifera* + E *-ous*] **:** FORAMINIFERAL

fo·ram·i·nous \fə'ramənəs\ *adj* [L *foramin-, foramen* + E *-ous*] **:** having foramina **:** POROUS

fo·ram·i·nule \-məˌnyül\ *n* -s [L *foramin-, foramen* + E *-ule*] **:** a minute foramen

for and *conj, obs* **:** and also

for·as·much as \ˌfȯrəz'məch-, ˌfərəz'm-\ *conj* [ME *for as much as*] **:** in consideration that **:** seeing that **:** SINCE ⟨*forasmuch as* the earth cannot hold aught beside them, you have dedicated the earth . . . to wisdom, liberty —E.L.Masters⟩ ⟨*forasmuch as* transatlantic firms are glad to print cheap popular translations —Caroline Ticknor⟩

for·as·te·ro \ˌfȯrə'ste(ˌ)rō\ *n* -s [Sp, lit., stranger, fr. Catal *foraster, forester,* fr. OCatal, fr. OProv *forestier,* fr. *forest* hamlet, country house, fr. (assumed) VL *forestis,* fr. L *foris* outside — more at FORUM] **:** any of various very productive cacaos with thick hard shells and purple seeds — compare CRIOLLO

¹for·ay \'fȯˌrā, ='= *also* 'fä,- *or* 'fō,-\ *vb* -ED/-ING/-S [ME *forrayen,* fr. MF *forrer,* fr. *forre, fuerre* fodder, straw — more at FORAGE] *vt, archaic* **:** to ravage in search of spoils **:** PILLAGE ⟨he might ~ our lands —Sir Walter Scott⟩ ~ *vi* **:** to make a raid or brief invasion ⟨~*ed* briefly into enemy territory⟩ **:** FORAGE, PILLAGE

²foray \"\ *n* -s [ME *forray,* fr. *forrayen,* v.] **1 :** a sudden or irregular incursion for war or spoils **:** RAID ⟨abandoned its attacks against our principal ports except for attempted sneak and surprise ~s —D.D.Eisenhower⟩ **:** ATTACK ⟨these legislative ~s became tedious —*New Republic*⟩ **2** *obs* **:** spoils won in a foray **:** BOOTY

for aye *adv* [ME *for aye*] **:** ALWAYS, FOREVER, ETERNALLY

for·ay·er \-āə(r)\ *n* -s [ME *forrayer,* fr. *forrayen* + *-er*] **1 :** one that makes or joins in a foray **2** *obs* **:** one that goes before **:** HARBINGER

forb \'fȯrb\ *n* -s [Gk *phorbē* fodder, food, fr. *pherbein* to graze, pasture; akin to OE *beorgan, birgan* to taste, eat, ON *bergja* to taste] **:** an herb other than grass **:** a broadleaf herb **:** WEED

forbade *or* **forbad** *past of* FORBID

¹for·bear \fȯr'be(ə)r, fər-, -'ba(ə)r; fȯə'beə, fə'-, -'ba(ə)\ *vb* **for·bore** \-'bō(ə)r, -'bȯ(ə)r; -'bōə, -'bȯ(ə)\ *or archaic* **forbare** *\pronounced like* FORBEAR\ **forborne** \-'bō(ə)rn; -'bȯ(ə)n\ **forbearing; forbears** [ME *forberen,* fr. OE *forberan* (akin to OHG *firberan* to refrain from, abstain, Goth *frabairan* to endure), fr. *for-* + *beran* to bear — more at FOR-, BEAR] *vt* **1** *obs* **a :** to bear with **:** ENDURE **b :** to control (feelings) **2** *obs* **:** to leave alone **:** SHUN ⟨~ his presence —Shak.⟩ **3** *obs* **:** to do without **:** endure the privation of ⟨fruits . . . whose taste too long *forborne* —John Milton⟩ **4 :** to refrain from **:** abstain or desist from ⟨so poison-mean the marsh mosquitoes *forbore* to bite him —S.H.Adams⟩ ⟨could not ~ crying out⟩ ⟨wherever he has not the power to do or ~ any act —Frank Thilly⟩ **:** FORGO ⟨a merchant who could not ~ the fun of setting sail —*Times Lit. Supp.*⟩ ~ *vi* **1 :** to hold back **:** ABSTAIN, DECLINE ⟨~, my friends, and spare me this ovation —W.S.Gilbert⟩ ⟨I cannot ~ from expressing my surprise⟩ **2 :** to control oneself when provoked **:** be patient ⟨*forbore* with his friend's failings⟩ **syn** see FORGO, REFRAIN

²forbear *var of* FOREBEAR

for·bear·ance \-'berən(t)s, -'ba(ə)r-\ *n* -s [¹*forbear* + *-ance*] **1 :** a delay in enforcing or a suspension of or a refraining from enforcing debts, rights of action, rights, privileges, claims, or obligations — compare RENEWAL **2 :** the act of forbearing **:** the exercise of patience or restraint ⟨I believe you equal to every . . . domestic ~, so long as . . . you have an object —Jane Austen⟩ **3 :** the quality of being forbearing **:** indulgence toward offenders or enemies **:** LONG-SUFFERING, LENIENCY ⟨known . . . for her ~ with her incorrigible husband —Willa Cather⟩ ⟨grateful for the help and ~ shown to us by the police —Basil Thomson⟩ ⟨~ has broadened into unconcern —Agnes Repplier⟩ **syn** see PATIENCE

for·bear·ant \-nt\ *adj* [¹*forbear* + *-ant*] *archaic* **:** FORBEARING ⟨equitable, nay ~ if need were —Thomas Carlyle⟩

for·bear·er \-rə(r)\ *n* -s **:** one that forbears

forbearing *adj* [ME *forbering,* fr. pres. part. of *forberen* to forbear — more at FORBEAR] **:** marked by calm patience esp. under provocation **:** slow to expression of resentment or acts of punishment or retaliation **:** PATIENT

syn TOLERANT, CLEMENT, LENIENT, MERCIFUL, INDULGENT: FORBEARING implies a calm unruffled abstention, esp. under provocation, from judging harshly or taking due action against something or somebody ⟨where life shall be seemly and noble and *forbearing* . . . yet strong enough withal to resist aggression —Learned Hand⟩ TOLERANT emphasizes the acceptance, often negative but usu. generous, of what one would be or might be expected to object to or oppose ⟨it will make us *tolerant* and forgiving, patient with stubbornness and prejudice —A.C.Benson⟩ CLEMENT emphasizes a humaneness in the exercise of a power to judge or punish ⟨he was *clement* whenever he could be *clement* with safety, and he began to pardon the proscribed —John Buchan⟩ LENIENT emphasizes the mildness of the judgment or punishment ⟨she looked on his foibles with a *lenient* eye, for she had been accustomed to such all her life —Anthony Trollope⟩ MERCIFUL emphasizes the idea of compassionate treatment, esp. with the implication of forgiveness ⟨many have had the impression that he is not very *merciful* or sympathetic to sinners or enemies of the law —M.R.Cohen⟩ INDULGENT suggests strongly a laxness, an easygoingness, as from an absence of a precise standard, and often implies a weakness in the exercise of the power to judge, restrain, or punish ⟨a main criticism is that juries are now rigorous, now *indulgent*, prone to severity in cases involving attacks on property, but to leniency in cases of assault . . .; too often swayed by local prejudices or political feeling; too susceptible to the oratory of clever criminal lawyers —F.A.Ogg & Harold Zink⟩

for·bear·ing·ly *adv* **:** in a forbearing manner ⟨under her management all beginners were treated ~⟩

for·bear·ing·ness *n* -ES **:** FORBEARANCE

forbes·ite \'fȯrb,zīt\ *n* -S [David *Forbes* †1876 Brit. geologist + E *-ite*] **:** a mineral $H(Ni,Co)AsO_4.3\frac{1}{2}H_2O$ consisting of a grayish white hydrous fibrocrystalline nickel cobalt arsenate

forbes scale \'fȯrbz-\ *n, usu cap F* [after Stephen A. *Forbes* †1930 Am. entomologist] **:** a thin grayish armored scale (*Aspidiotus forbesi*) attacking fruit trees and resembling the San Jose scale but usu. much less destructive

¹for·bid \fȯr'bid, fə'-, fə(r)'-\ *vb* **for·bade** \-'bad, -'bād, -'baa(ə)d\ *or* **for·bad; for·bid·den** \-'bidᵊn\ *or archaic* **forbid; forbidding; forbids** [ME *forbidden*, alter. (influenced by *bidden* to entreat, pray, invite, command) of *forbeden*, fr. OE *forbēodan* (akin to OFris *urbiāda* to forbid, OHG *firbiotan*, Goth *faurbiudan*), fr. *for-* + *bēodan* to offer, proclaim, command — more at BID] *vt* **1 :** to command against or contrary to **:** INTERDICT ⟨~ the banns⟩ **:** PROHIBIT ⟨order . . . *forbidding* strikes of civil-service employees —*Collier's Yr. Bk.*⟩ ⟨the law ~*s* rich and poor alike to sleep under bridges⟩ ⟨God ~ that war should come⟩ **2 a :** to exclude or warn off from by express command ⟨I ~ you the house⟩ **b :** to bar from use ⟨*forbade* . . . movie cameras at House Committee hearings —*Americana Annual*⟩ ⟨running with the ball is *forbidden* in basketball⟩ **3 :** to hinder or prevent as if by an effectual command **:** make impossible or impracticable ⟨rocky rapids *forbade* further progress up the stream⟩ ⟨space ~*s* further treatment of the subject here⟩ ⟨modesty ~*s* telling what my part in the affair was⟩ ~ *vi* **:** to utter a prohibition **:** HINDER ⟨~ who will, none shall from me withhold longer thy offered good —John Milton⟩

syn FORBID, PROHIBIT, ENJOIN, INTERDICT, INHIBIT, and BAN can mean, in common, to debar (someone) from doing, using, entering, or otherwise acting or to order (something) not to be done, used, entered, or otherwise acted upon. The more or less familiar FORBID and the more formal PROHIBIT imply the exercise of authority or the existence of imperative conditions, FORBID suggesting an expected obedience or an absolute proscription, PROHIBIT applying more particularly to official and less autocratic proscriptions ⟨*forbid* a child to go out on a rainy day⟩ ⟨a law *forbidding* the sale of liquor on Sunday⟩ ⟨limitations of space *forbid* elaborately detailed treatments of these subjects —*Amer. Guide Series: N.H.*⟩ ⟨the act was wrong in the sense that it was *prohibited* by law —B.N.Cardozo⟩ ⟨condemned for not taking active steps toward *prohibiting* an armed group from organizing on its soil —*Collier's Yr. Bk.*⟩ ⟨implements of war would be *prohibited* and prevented —Vera M. Dean⟩ ENJOIN, a legal term implying a judicial order that forbids something under penalty, suggests a strong and compelling proscription or exhortation ⟨the president, under the war powers, seized the railroads and the courts *enjoined* the strike —*Collier's Yr. Bk.*⟩ ⟨a deed of filial duty *enjoined* upon him by his father's fearful command —Karl Polanyi⟩ ⟨immediately after he had concluded his lecture, someone was certain to *enjoin* him to relax —Bryan MacMahon⟩ INTERDICT implies prohibition by authority usu. for a given time and for a salutary purpose ⟨the navy has prohibited, the church has *interdicted* the defloration ceremony, formerly an inseparable part of the marriages of girls of rank —Margaret Mead⟩ ⟨alcohol and tobacco are *interdicted* —*Yr. Bk. of Medicine*⟩ ⟨to *interdict*, or at least discourage, his visits —George Meredith⟩ INHIBIT applies to the imposition of restraints or restrictions whether by authority or by circumstances or conditions ⟨signalized the opening of a new reign by *inhibiting* stage plays —A.T.Quiller-Couch⟩ ⟨stiff royalties — payable in dollars — have *inhibited* widespread production of U. S. plays —W.H. Whyte⟩ ⟨the destructive exchange practices which *inhibited* the flow of world trade —Eugene Meyer⟩ BAN implies civil or ecclesiastical prohibition and strongly connotes condemnation or disapproval ⟨these laws . . . were specific in naming the one weapon to be *banned* —R.W.Thorp⟩ ⟨the proscribed categories of persons *banned* from Federal employment —Benjamin Ginzburg⟩ ⟨authorities *banned* the rebuilding of wooden houses in the same area —Theodore Hsi-en Chen⟩

²forbid \"\ *adj* [fr. archaic past part. of ¹*forbid*] *archaic* **:** ACCURSED ⟨she becomes a leper herself . . . and lives for years in a cave hermitage, a thing ~ —*Nation*⟩ ⟨the sensitive plant, like one ~, wept —P.B.Shelley⟩

for·bid·dance \fȯ(r)'bidᵊn(t)s, fə(r)-\ *n* -S **:** the act of forbidding **:** a command or edict against something **:** PROHIBITION

for·bid·den \-dᵊn\ *adj* [ME, fr. past part. of *forbidden* to forbid — more at FORBID] **1 :** not allowed **:** not permitted **:** PROHIBITED ⟨the whole attraction of such knowledge consists in the fact that it is ~ —Bertrand Russell⟩ ⟨secretly enjoying a ~ cigar⟩ **:** TABOO ⟨~ meaning of a dream⟩ **2 :** not conforming to the usual selection rules — used of quantum phenomena ⟨~ transition⟩ ⟨~ radiation⟩ ⟨the line spectrum . . . would consist of only one line and be typically of a ~ —L.M.Branscomb⟩ — **for·bid·den·ly** *adv* — **for·bid·den·ness** *n* -ES

forbidden degree *n* **:** a degree of consanguinity or affinity within which marriage is forbidden — called also *prohibited degree;* compare LEVITICAL DEGREES

forbidden fruit *n* **1 :** an immoral pleasure (as illicit sexual intercourse) **2 a :** any of several varieties of citrus fruit; *esp* **:** a small shaddock **b :** the fruit of a Ceylonese tree (*Tabernaemontana dichotoma*) that has powerfully narcotic seeds **3** [fr. *Forbidden Fruit*, a trademark] **:** an American liqueur of orange color made from grape brandy flavored with shaddock

for·bid·der \-də(r)\ *n* -S [ME, fr. *forbidden* + *-er*] **:** one that forbids

for·bid·ding \-diŋ, -dēŋ\ *adj* [ME, fr. pres. part. of *forbidden*] **1 :** such as to make approach or passage difficult or impossible ⟨~ mountains⟩ ⟨~ walls⟩ ⟨~ terminology⟩ **2 :** DISAGREEABLE, REPELLENT ⟨desolate ~ countryside⟩ ⟨dark ~ ravines⟩ **3 :** MENACING, GRIM ⟨~ array of guns⟩ — **for·bid·ding·ly** *adv* — **for·bid·ding·ness** *n* -ES

forbids *pres 3d sing of* FORBID

for·biv·o·rous \(')fȯ(r)¦bivərəs\ *adj* [*forb* + *-i-* + *-vorous*] **:** feeding on forbs ⟨~ grasshoppers⟩

¹forbode *n* -S [ME *forbod, forbode*, fr. OE *forbod*, fr. *forbēodan* to forbid — more at FORBID] *archaic* **:** FORBIDDANCE, PROHIBITION

²forbode *var of* FOREBODE

forbore *past of* FORBEAR

forborne *past part of* FORBEAR

forbs *pl of* FORB

for·bush's sparrow \'fȯr,bu̇shəz-, -,bəsh-\ *n, usu cap F* [after Edward H. *Forbush* †1929 Am. ornithologist] **:** a sparrow (*Melospiza lincolnii gracilis*) of the Pacific coast closely related to the Lincoln's sparrow but browner

¹for·by *or* **for·bye** \fȯr'bī̄ä, fər-, -'bī\ *prep* [ME *forby*, prep. & adv., fr. *for-*, *fore-* fore- + *by*, prep. & adv. — more at BY] **1** *archaic* **a** *of motion* **:** PAST **b** *of position* **:** NEAR **c :** BY ⟨took her up ~ the lily hand —Edmund Spenser⟩ **2** *chiefly Scot* **:** as well as **:** BESIDES **3** *Scot* **:** EXCEPT ⟨left without a copper ~ some insurance⟩

²forby *or* **forbye** \"\ *adv* [ME *forby*] *chiefly Scot* **:** over and above **:** in addition **:** BESIDES ⟨you're a liar and a thief, lassie, and ~ ye tried to kill me too —Rose Macaulay⟩

³forby *or* **forbye** \"\ *adj, chiefly Scot* **:** UNUSUAL, UNCOMMON, REMARKABLE; *specif* **:** unusually good ⟨a ~ wife⟩

for·çat \fȯrsä\ *n* -S [F, fr. It *forzato*, fr. past part. of *forzare* to force, fr. (assumed) VL *fortiare* — more at FORCE] **:** a convict in France condemned to imprisonment with hard labor or formerly to the galleys

¹force \'fō(ə)rs, 'fȯ(ə)rs, 'fōəs, 'fȯ(ə)s\ *n* -S *often attrib* [ME, fr. MF *force*, fr. (assumed) VL *fortia*, fr. L *fortis* strong + *-ia* -y — more at FORT] **1 a :** strength or energy esp. of an exceptional degree **:** active power **:** VIGOR **b :** physical strength or vigor of a living being ⟨drained of all ~ by his mighty effort⟩ **c :** power to affect in physical relations or conditions ⟨the ~ of the blow was somewhat spent when it reached him⟩ ⟨the rising ~ of the wind⟩ **d :** moral or mental strength esp. when manifested as power of effective action (as in the overcoming of opposition) ⟨the ~ of his character had the impact of a physical pressure⟩ ⟨a man of great ~ and determination⟩ **e :** power or capacity to sway, convince, or impose obligation **:** VALIDITY, EFFECT ⟨the ~ of his arguments⟩ ⟨who could resist the ~ of such an appeal⟩; *often* **:** legal efficacy **:** operative effect ⟨that law is still in ~⟩ ⟨an agreement having the ~ of law⟩ **2 a :** might or greatness esp. of a prince or state; *often* **:** strength in or capacity for waging war ⟨the ~ of this lord was so great that no other would contest his right to rule⟩ **b** (1) **:** a group of individuals occupied with or ready for combat ⟨the entire ~ of the fortress⟩; *usu* **:** a body of troops, ships, airplanes, or combinations thereof esp. when assigned to a particular military purpose or necessity ⟨took a small ~ of infantrymen and searched the village⟩ ⟨the enemy assembled a great ~ for the spring offensive⟩ — see TASK FORCE (2) **forces** *pl* **:** the whole military strength (as of a nation) **:** ARMED FORCES **c :** a body of persons available for or serving a particular end ⟨a large available labor ~⟩; *often* **:** a more or less organized group or staff having a common responsibility or task ⟨a conscientious police ~⟩ ⟨the plantation ~ took a half-holiday⟩ **3 a :** power, violence, compulsion, or constraint exerted upon or against a person or thing ⟨conciliation may succeed where ~ completely fails⟩ ⟨those who will not respond to kindness must yield to ~⟩ **b :** strength or power of any degree that is exercised without justification or contrary to law upon a person or thing **c :** violence or such threat or display of physical aggression toward a person as reasonably inspires fear of pain, bodily harm, or death **4** *dial Eng* **:** a large part, quantity, or number **5 :** an agency or influence (as a push or pull) that if applied to a free body results chiefly in an acceleration of the body and sometimes in elastic deformation and other effects (as from overcoming cohesion or adhesion or sustaining weight) **6 :** the quality of conveying impressions intensely in writing or speech (as by vividness, cogency, or passion) ⟨a stimulating essay marked by ~ and cogency⟩ **7 :** an act (as of misdirection) or course (as of play) that forces the response of another (as in a play in a game) into a predetermined pattern ⟨sometimes a ~ is useful for locating honors in the opponents' hands⟩ **8 a :** the upper hollow embossing die **:** ⁵COUNTER 10b **b :** a specially formed bar or plate attached to the underside of the slide of a punch press chiefly for use in riveting and seaming **9 :** a billiards stroke made by striking a cue ball hard and just below the center so that it rebounds or stops sharply or goes off at a desired angle after striking the object ball

syn VIOLENCE, COMPULSION, COERCION, DURESS, CONSTRAINT, RESTRAINT: FORCE is a general term for exercise of strength or power, esp. physical, to overcome resistance ⟨there is the *force* used by parents when . . . they compel their children to act or refrain from acting in some particular way. There is the *force* used by attendants in an asylum when they try to prevent a maniac from hurting himself or others. There is the *force* used by the police when they control a crowd . . . there is the *force* used in war —Aldous Huxley⟩ VIOLENCE is applicable to dynamic power showing great strength, power, intensity, fury, destructiveness ⟨a wild nightmare of *violence*, noise, confusion, and pain —T.B.Costain⟩ ⟨force must not be confused with *violence* . . . the completely successful use of force implies the absence of *violence*, because those against whom force is used recognize the futility of resistance —P.M.Sweezy⟩ COMPULSION is applicable to any power or agency that compels, that makes an individual follow a will not his own ⟨*compulsion* exists where a being is inevitably determined by an external cause —Frank Thilly⟩ ⟨masterpieces I read under *compulsion* without the faintest interest —Bertrand Russell⟩ COERCION often suggests unethical, unjust compulsion, as by threat or deception ⟨a promise obtained by *coercion* is hardly binding⟩ ⟨the amiable trait in his character of an intense dislike to *coercion* —G.B.Shaw⟩ DURESS may suggest a stronger coercion in which the compelling is accomplished by confinement or violence, or dire threats of confinement or violence ⟨our *duress*, his arrogance, our awful servitude —Edna S. V. Millay⟩ ⟨a fake declaration of love by the heroine under *duress* —Dyneley Hussey⟩ CONSTRAINT may apply to the action of any agency enjoining unwilling performance or avoidance of an action ⟨the *constraint* of society had banished his former expression of easy good humor —G.B.Shaw⟩ ⟨prose is memorable speech set down without *constraint* of meter —A.T. Quiller-Couch⟩ RESTRAINT suggests an agency which checks free activity or expression or an atmosphere in which such restriction is likely or common ⟨long years of abstinence and *restraint* and an avoidance of physical contacts and emotional responses before marriage —A.C.Kinsey⟩ ⟨they rushed into freedom and enjoyment, into the unfettered use of their powers, with an energy proportional to their previous *restraint* —G.L. Dickinson⟩ **syn** see in addition POWER

— **by force of** *prep* [ME, trans. of OF *à force de*] **:** in virtue of **:** by means of **:** THROUGH ⟨*by force of* the authority vested in my present office⟩ — **in force 1 :** in great numbers **:** with many individuals ⟨the Indians invaded *in force* that winter⟩ **2 :** VALID, OPERATIVE, BINDING ⟨these antiquated laws have been *in force* since the 17th century⟩

²force \"\ *vb* -ED/-ING/-S [ME *forcen*, fr. MF *forcier*, *forcer* to attack, rape, compel, fr. (assumed) VL *fortiare*, fr. L *fortis* strong] *vt* **1 :** to do violence to; *esp* **:** RAPE ⟨a maiden *forced* by the intruder⟩ **2 :** to constrain or compel by physical, moral, or intellectual means or by the exigencies of circumstances ⟨*forced* by injuries to stay at home⟩ ⟨hunger *forced* him to forget his scruples⟩ ⟨such evidence ~*s* conviction on the mind⟩ ⟨financial weakness ~*s* many small businesses to the wall⟩ **3 :** to make, cause, make to be, or accomplish through natural or logical necessity ⟨~*s* the diameters to be equal —Josiah Royce⟩ **4 a :** to press, drive, attain to, or effect as indicated against resistance or inertia by some positive compelling force or action ⟨~ your way through⟩ ⟨much of the previously unobtainable oil is *forced* to the surface —*Amer. Guide Series: Pa.*⟩ ⟨basic problems *forced* on us by the age in which we live —J.B.Conant⟩ **b :** to press, impose, or thrust urgently, importunately, inexorably ⟨he *forced* his personality upon his little world by organizing an army —L.C.Powys⟩ ⟨~ his attentions on a woman⟩ **c :** to drive (as warm air) through or into a duct or channel by some impelling force (as a fan) ⟨~ the caulking compound into the crevices⟩ **5 :** to achieve or win by strength in struggle or violence: **a :** to win one's way into **:** storm successfully **:** enter in attack ⟨~ a castle⟩ **b :** to effect a passage through by overcoming defenses ⟨*forced* the mountain passes —O.L. Spaulding⟩ **c :** to break open or through ⟨~ a lock⟩ ⟨eventually the gate was *forced*⟩ **6 a :** to raise, accelerate, or heighten to the utmost ⟨*forcing* the pace⟩; *sometimes* **:** to intensify the action and pressure in (as a game) ⟨*forced* the game by a series of brilliant plays⟩ **b :** to give forth, emit, produce only with unnatural or unwilling effort, not freely, spontaneously ⟨the laughter was *forced* and unnatural —Sherwood Anderson⟩ **c :** to wrench, strain, use with marked unnaturalness and lack of ease **:** press to an unusual use, past a usual limit, or into an unusual meaning or interpretation ⟨to ~, to dislocate if necessary, language into his meaning —T.S.Eliot⟩ ⟨a *forced* interpretation of the passage⟩ **7 a :** to hasten the speed, growth, progress, developing, or maturing of (as through artificial means, maximum effort, close care, or individual attention) ⟨a *forced* march⟩ ⟨children *forced* into early maturity by heavy responsibilities⟩ **b :** to bring (plants or their wanted parts, as flowers or fruit) to maturity out of the normal season (as by the use of heat and special lighting) ⟨*forcing* lilies for the Easter trade⟩ **8 a** *archaic* **:** REINFORCE, MAN ⟨~ with soldiers⟩ **b :** to increase the intake of (as fluids) beyond the normal bodily requirement ⟨it is wise to ~ fluids when any systemic intoxication is present⟩ **9 a :** to cause (a person) to respond in a particular way in a game or trick usu. to one's own advantage (as by discarding a playing card that an opponent must take under the rules of the game) ⟨card tricks that depend on misdirection to ~ the helper to take the intended card⟩ **b :** to induce (as a particular bid or play by another player) in a card game by some conventional act, play, bid, or response ⟨doubled the opponent's bid to ~ a try for game from his partner⟩ ⟨hoped to ~ the trump ace out by leading the remaining club⟩ **10 a :** to cause (a runner in baseball) to be put out by compelling him (as by a hit) to vacate the base he has been occupying and attempt to advance to the next base **b :** to cause (a run) to be scored in baseball or (a runner) to score (as by giving a base on balls when the bases are full) **11 :** to develop (photographic material) to the limit either in time or by chemical means or both in order to obtain detail in the shadow portions of an underexposed negative or the highlights of an underexposed print ~ *vi* **1 :** to advance or progress by force ⟨our troops *forcing* ahead⟩ **2 :** to grow, advance, mature by being forced ⟨these plants ~ well⟩ **3 a :** to make a series of shots intended to put an opponent in a racket game out of position for a subsequent shot **b :** to make a bid or play in a card game that forces another player or a particular response

syn COMPEL, COERCE, CONSTRAIN, OBLIGE: FORCE is a general term indicating use of strength, power, weight, stress, duress in overcoming resistance ⟨the editors were *forced* to flee for their lives and the newspaper plant was burned —*Amer. Guide Series: Ark.*⟩ ⟨American pressure had been sufficient to *force* Germany to suspend unrestricted submarine warfare —C.E. Black & E.C.Helmreich⟩ ⟨those yield data and *force* the mind to put many queries —H.O.Taylor⟩ COMPEL may more strongly indicate irresistible overcoming of unwillingness or resistance ⟨yellow fever was raging in Charleston, and for this reason the Scots were *compelled* to remain on board —W.P. Webb⟩ ⟨the discovery of new facts *compels* the rational thinker to reexamine the adequacy of his previous generalizations —M.R.Cohen⟩ COERCE implies domineering and overriding resistance by notably unethical tactics like violence, intimidation, pressure, duress ⟨no one can claim that he was *coerced* by bribery. This is reserved for threats and direct pleas —W.D. Falk⟩ CONSTRAIN suggests forcing by something that either does or seems to constrict, press, confine, compress ⟨tied him to the wall, where he was *constrained* to stay till a kind passerby released him —John Galsworthy⟩ ⟨*constrained* through poverty to live in the houses of others —Edith Sitwell⟩ OBLIGE, although it may apply to any binding force, is common in situations involving ethical, social, or intellectual necessity, through the effect of codes or principles ⟨the Protestant missionary felt *obliged* to give the Indian a book religion —*Amer. Guide Series: Minn.*⟩ ⟨*obliged* to receive and grind grain for his fellow townsmen —*Amer. Guide Series: R.I.*⟩

— **force a safeguard :** to violate (as by overwhelming a protecting guard) protection accorded a person or property — **force one's hand :** to cause one to act precipitously ⟨his unexpected offer for the property *forced my hand*⟩ **:** force one who for diplomatic or tactical reasons is passive or noncommittal to act in a way that reveals his beliefs or purposes or intentions

³force \"\ *n* -S [ME *fors, force*, fr. ON *fors, foss*; akin to Skt *pr̥ṣat* drop, OSlav *prachŭ* dust] *dial* **:** WATERFALL, CASCADE

⁴force \"\ *vt* -ED/-ING/-S [alter. (influenced by ²*force*) of ¹*farce*] *archaic* **:** FARCE, STUFF ⟨malice *forced* with wit —Shak.⟩

force·able \-səbəl\ *adj* [by alter.] **:** FORCIBLE

force·ably \-blē, -li\ *adv* **:** FORCIBLY

force account *n* **1 :** the part of the expense account of a public body (as a municipality) resulting from the employment of a labor force (as for garbage collection and the maintenance of streets) usu. distinguished from the part resulting from contracting similar services with commercial agencies ⟨disadvantages of the *force-account* method of handling municipal maintenance⟩ **2 :** a labor force maintained under force account ⟨every public-works department requires a considerable *force account*⟩

force and arms *n* **:** VIOLENCE — used in old legal indictments and declarations in trespass

force and effect *n* **:** legal efficacy **:** the existing foundation of enforceable rights and duties ⟨the entrenched sections of the South Africa Act are still of *force and effect* —E.P.Dvorin⟩

force–break \'ₛ,ₛ\ *vt* **:** to train (as a horse or dog) by punishing faults rather than by rewarding success

force cup *n* **:** PLUNGER 2e

forced \'fō(ə)rst, 'fȯ(ə)rst, 'fōəst, 'fȯ(ə)st\ *adj* **1 :** compelled by force **:** INVOLUNTARY, COMPULSORY ⟨~ service⟩ ⟨a ~ landing⟩ **2 :** done or produced with or as if with notable effort, exertion, or pressure ⟨a ~ artificial style of writing⟩ ⟨a ~ laugh⟩ **3 :** produced by or subjected to forcing ⟨~ chrysanthemums⟩ ⟨*forced*-air heating⟩ ⟨furnaces of the *forced*-convection type⟩ — **forced·ly** \-sədlē, -stlē, -li\ *adv* — **forced·ness** \-sədnəs, -stnəs\ *n* -ES

forced draft *n* **:** a draft of air for use in combustion forced through a grate or other burner by or as if by a blower ⟨a *forced draft* heating unit⟩

forced heir *n* **:** an heir who cannot be disinherited except for good causes recognized by law and whose share in his ancestor's estate cannot be impaired by the will of the ancestor or even by gifts made inter vivos

forced landing *n* **:** an emergency airplane landing made under some compulsion of circumstance (as engine failure, adverse weather conditions) beyond the control of the pilot

forced march *n* **:** a march (as of a military force) greater in extent than the distance usu. covered and often carried out under difficulties (as increased pace or restricted halts)

forced oscillation *also* **forced vibration** *n* **:** an oscillation imposed upon a body or system by and with the frequency of some external vibrator of sensibly different frequency — opposed to *free oscillation*

forced saving *n* **1 :** involuntary saving by an individual resulting from restrictions imposed upon expenditures, deferred income, insurance, or other circumstances **2 :** involuntary transfer of purchasing power from consumers to investors by means of a money and credit expansion accompanied by a decrease in the value of money

forced ventilation *n* **:** mechanical ventilation

force–feed \'ₛ¦ₛ\ *vt* **force–fed** *or* **forced–fed; force–fed** *or* **forced–fed; force–feeding** *or* **forced–feeding; force–feeds** [*force feed*] **1 :** to feed (as an animal) by forcible administration of food ⟨necessary to *force-feed* the young birds by pushing food well back in the throat⟩ **2 :** to cause to take in or to expand vigorously ⟨the cities never became swollen until after the Civil War, which *force-fed* urban industry —*Times Lit. Supp.*⟩ ⟨*forced-fed* on propaganda, people turn from it with loathing —Eric Johnston⟩

force feed *n* **:** a lubricating system (as in an internal-combustion engine) in which the lubricant is supplied under pressure

force field *n* **:** FIELD OF FORCE

force fit *n* **:** PRESS FIT

force·ful \'fōrsfəl, 'fȯrs-,'fōəs-, 'fȯ(ə)s\ *adj* **:** possessing or filled with force **:** exerting or impelled by force **:** FORCIBLE, MIGHTY, EFFECTIVE ⟨a vigorous ~ personality⟩ ⟨his ~ presentation of the data⟩ ⟨won the Pulitzer prize for his ~ novel⟩ — **force·ful·ly** \-f(ə)lē, -li\ *adv* — **force·ful·ness** *n* -ES

force land *vi* [back-formation fr. *forced landing*] **:** to make a forced landing

force·less \-sləs\ *adj* **:** lacking force **:** FEEBLE, WEAK ⟨a ~ argument⟩ — **force·less·ness** *n* -ES

force main *n* **:** a principal conduit (as in a sewer system) through which water is pumped as distinguished from one through which it flows by gravity

force ma·jeure \-mä'zhər, -mə'-\ *n* [F, lit., superior force] **1 :** superior or irresistible force **2 :** an event or effect that cannot reasonably be anticipated or controlled — compare ACT OF GOD, INEVITABLE ACCIDENT, VIS MAJOR

forcemeat \'ₛ,ₛ\ *n* [⁴*force* + *meat*] **:** finely chopped and highly seasoned meat or fish that often has added eggs, cereal products, or other enrichments and is either served alone or used as a stuffing — called also *farce*

forcement *n* -s [²*force* + *-ment*] *obs* **:** an act of forcing **:** COMPULSION

for·ce·ne \ˈfȯrsəˌnā, (ˈ)fȯrˈsēn\ *adj* [F *forcené*, frantic, mad, insane, fr. OF *forsené*, past part. of *forsener* to be or become mad or furious, fr. *fors* out of, outside, except + *sen* mind, sense, of Gmc origin; akin to OHG *sin* sense, mind — more at FORECLOSE, SENSE] *of a heraldic representation of a horse* **:** depicted rearing

force of friction **:** the force required to initiate or to maintain relative motion against friction

force of habit **:** behavior made involuntary or automatic by repeated practice ⟨said no from *force of habit*⟩

force–out \ˈ⸗ˌ⸗\ *n* [fr. *force out*, v.] **:** FORCE PLAY

force play *n* **:** a baseball play in which the runner is automatically out unless he advances one base

force polygon *n* **:** a closed polygon whose sides taken in order represent in magnitude and direction a system of forces in equilibrium

for·ceps \ˈfȯrsəps, ˈfō(ə)s-, -ˌseps\ *n, pl* **forceps** \"\ *also* **forcepses** \-psəz\ *or* **forci·pes** \-ˌsəˌpēz\ [L, fr. *formus* hot + *-ceps* (fr. *capere* to take) — more at WARM, HEAVE] **1 :** an instrument for grasping, holding firmly, or exerting traction upon objects that it would be inconvenient or impracticable to seize with the fingers; *esp* **:** such an instrument for delicate operations (as of jewelers, surgeons, obstetricians, dentists) **:** PINCERS, TONGS — sometimes used with *pair* ⟨a pair of ~⟩ **2** [NL, fr. L] **:** a limb resembling a forceps; *esp* **:** a pair of curved hard movable appendages at the end of the abdomen of an insect (as the earwig)

for·ceps·like \-ps,līk\ *adj* **:** resembling a forceps esp. in having two opposable processes

force pump *n* **:** a pump with a solid piston for drawing and forcing through valves a liquid (as water) to a considerable height above the pump or under a considerable pressure

forceput \ˈ⸗ˌ⸗\ *n* [alter. of earlier *forced put*] *now chiefly dial* **:** an action that is made unavoidable or inevitable by circumstances ⟨this marry-me-quick business . . . looks too much like a *forceput* —B.A.Williams⟩

¹**for·cer** \ˈfōrsər, ˈfȯr-; ˈfōəsə(r, ˈfȯ(ə)s-\ *n* -s [ME, fr. OF *forcier*, fr. *force* — more at FORCE] *archaic* **:** COFFER, CHEST

²**for·cer** \"\ *n* -s [²*force* + *-er*] **1 :** one that forces (as by driving, compelling, or pressing); *esp* **:** a person that forces crops (as for out-of-season markets) **2 a :** the solid piston of a force pump **b :** a small hand pump (as for sinking pits or draining cellars) **c :** FORCE 8 a **3 :** a plant esp. adapted to forcing

forces *pl of* FORCE, *pres 3d sing of* FORCE

forces letter *n* [(*Armed*) *Forces*] *Brit* **:** an air-letter sheet for use in writing to a member of the armed forces

forchette *var of* FOURCHETTE

forc·ibil·i·ty \ˌfōrsəˈbiləd·ē, ˌfȯrs-, -ōəs-, -ȯ(ə)s-, -atˌ, |i\ *n* -ES **:** the quality or state of being forcible ⟨the ~ of his language⟩

forc·ible \ˈfōrsəbəl, ˈfȯrs-, ˈfōəs-, ˈfȯ(ə)s-\ *adj* [ME, fr. MF, fr. *force* + *-ible*] **1 :** effected by force used against opposition or resistance **:** obtained by compulsion or violence ⟨a ~ entry⟩ ⟨determined on ~ repatriation of the refugees⟩ **2 :** possessing force **:** characterized by force, efficiency, or energy **:** POWERFUL, EFFICACIOUS, IMPRESSIVE, CONVINCING ⟨expressed his views in very ~ words⟩ ⟨used ~ maneuvers to obtain the chairmanship⟩ — **forc·ible·ness** *n* -ES — **forc·ibly** \-blē, -li\ *adv*

forcible entry and detainer *n* **1 :** the entering upon and taking or the keeping possession of land or a tenement by actual force or by threats or display of force menacing life or limb without authority of law **2 :** the statutory proceeding to regain possession of property alienated by forcible entry and detainer

forcible–feeble \ˈ⸗⸗⸗ˈ⸗⸗\ *adj* [fr. *Forcible Feeble*, nickname of *Francis Feeble*, character in Shakespeare's *2 Henry IV* who was a woman's tailor turned soldier] **:** seemingly vigorous but really weak or insipid

forcing *pres part of* FORCE

forcing bed *n* **:** HOTBED

forcing cone *n* **:** the portion of the boring of a shotgun in which the chamber diameter decreases to bore diameter and which in section is a truncated cone

forcing ground *n* **:** HOTBED 2

forcing house *n* **1 :** a greenhouse in which plants are forced esp. in quantities for market **2 :** HOTBED 2

forc·ing·ly *adv* [fr. *forcing* (pres. part. of ²*force*) + *-ly*] **:** so as to force or exert pressure

forcing pump *n* **:** FORCE PUMP

forcing system *n* **:** CULBERTSON SYSTEM

for·ci·pate \ˈfȯ(r)səˌpāt\ *also* **for·ci·pat·ed** \-ˌād·əd\ *adj* [L *forcip-*, *forceps* + E *-ate*, *-ated* — more at FORCEPS] **:** shaped like a forceps **:** deeply forked

forcipes *pl of* FORCEPS

for·cip·i·form \(ˈ)fȯ(r)ˈsipəˌfȯrm\ *adj* [L *forcip-*, *forceps* + E *-iform*] **:** shaped like a forceps; *usu* **:** having or being forcipulate pedicellariae with two valves that cross when closed — compare FORFICIFORM

for·ci·pressure \ˈfȯ(r)sə+ˌ-\ *n* [blend of L *forcip-*, *forceps* and E *pressure*] **:** compression of a blood vessel with a forceps to arrest hemorrhage

for·cip·u·la·ta \fȯ(r)ˌsipyəˈläd·ə, -ˈlād·ə\ *n pl, cap* [NL, fr. *forcipula* (dim. of L *forcip-*, *forceps*) + *-ata*] **:** the most highly specialized order of starfishes, distinguished by possession of stalked forficulate pedicellariae with three ossicles

for·cip·u·late \(ˈ)fȯ(r)ˈsipyəˌlāt\ *adj* [NL *forcipula* + E *-ate*] **:** like a small forceps; *usu* **:** being or having stalked pedicellariae made up of a basal ossicle with two articulated blades — see FORCIPIFORM, FORFICIFORM; compare FORFICULATE

for·cip·u·lo·sa \fȯ(r)ˌsipyəˈlōsə\ [NL, fr. *forcipula* + *-osa* (fr. L, neut. pl. of *-osus* -ous)] *syn of* FORCIPULATA

forcive *adj* [¹*force* + *-ive*] *obs* **:** FORCIBLE

forclose *obs var of* FORECLOSE

¹**ford** \ˈfō(ə)rd, ˈfȯ(ə)rd, ˈfōəd, ˈfȯ(ə)d\ *n* -s [ME, fr. OE; akin to OFris *forda* ford, OS *ford*, OHG *furt* ford, ON *fjörthr* fjord, bay, W *rhyd* ford, L *portus* house door, port, *porta* gate, Av *pərətush* passage, ford, bridge, OE *faran* to travel, go — more at FARE] **1 :** a shallow and usu. narrow part of a river or other body of water that may be crossed by man or animal by wading; *broadly* **:** any shallows that may be passed through (as by a wheeled vehicle) **2** *archaic* **:** a body of water **:** STREAM

²**ford** \"\ *vb* -ED/-ING/-S *vt* **1 :** to pass or cross (as a river or other body of water) by a ford **2 :** to pass over (water) ⟨the plank that ~*ed* the creek⟩ ⟨~*ing* the river on rafts⟩ ~ *vi* **:** to cross a body of water by a ford

³**ford** \"\ *n* -s [after *Ford*, a popular low-priced automobile] *slang* **:** a highly successful fashion design; *often* **:** a low-priced copy of a successful high-priced style in women's dress

ford·able \-dəbəl\ *adj* **:** crossable by fording ⟨a ~ stream⟩

ford cup *n, usu cap F* [fr. the *Ford* Motor Company] **:** a viscometer used for testing paints, varnishes, and lacquers

fording *n* -s [fr. gerund of ²*ford*] **1 :** the act of crossing a ford **2 :** a fording place **:** FORD

ford·ism \-ˌdizəm\ *n* -s *usu cap* [Henry *Ford* †1947 Am. auto manufacturer + E *-ism*] **:** a technological system that seeks to increase production efficiency primarily through carefully engineered breakdown and interlocking of production operations and that depends for its success on mass production by assembly-line methods

ford·ize \-ˌdīz\ *vt* -ED/-ING/-S *often cap* [Henry *Ford* + E *-ize*] **1 :** to standardize in the interests of efficiency and mass production ⟨~ a plant⟩ ⟨~ the cotton industry⟩ **2 a :** to organize and control (people or their work) as if on an assembly line ⟨the medical profession cannot be *fordized* until human beings become robots —E.H.Cary⟩ ⟨an attempt to ~ high-school education —H.R.Linville⟩ **b :** to deprive of individuality ⟨can we ~ our minds as well as our motors —Glenn Frank⟩

ford·less \ˈ⸗ləs\ *adj* **:** lacking a ford **:** impossible to cross on foot ⟨a ~ tide⟩

for·do *or* **fore·do** \fȯrˈdü, fōr-\ *vt* **for·did** *or* **fore·did** \-ˈdid\ **for·done** *or* **fore·done** \-ˈdən\ **for·do·ing** *or* **fore·do·ing** \-ˈdüiŋ\ **for·does** *or* **fore·does** \-ˈdəz\ [ME *fordon*, fr. OE *fordōn*, fr. *for-* + *dōn* to do — more at DO] **1 a** *archaic* **:** to do away with **:** KILL, ABOLISH, DESTROY **:** UNDO, RUIN **b :** to bring to an end **:** TERMINATE ⟨subject to appraisal as an affair *fordone* —H.B.Alexander⟩ **2 :** to overcome with fatigue **:** EXHAUST — used only as past participle ⟨quite *fordone* with the heat⟩

for·dyce's disease \ˈfȯrˌdīsəz-\ *also* **for·dyce disease** \-ˌdīs-\ *n, usu cap F* [after John A. *Fordyce* †1925 Am. dermatologist] **:** a common anomaly of the oral mucosa in which misplaced sebaceous glands form yellowish white nodules on the lips or the lining of the mouth

¹**fore** \ˈfō(ə)r, ˈfȯ(ə)r, ˈfōə, ˈfȯ(ə)\ *adv* [ME, adv. & prep., fr. OE; akin to OHG *fora*, adv. & prep., before, Goth *faura*, adv. & prep., OE *for*, prep., for, before — more at FOR] **1** *obs* **:** at an earlier time or period **:** FORMERLY, PREVIOUSLY **2 :** in, toward, or adjacent to the front **:** FORWARD ⟨went ~ to check his instruments⟩ ⟨the bolt struck ~ of the mast⟩ — see FORE AND AFT

²**fore** *also* **'fore** \"\ *prep* [ME *fore*] **1** *now dial* **:** BEFORE **2 :** in the presence of — used chiefly in oaths

³**fore** \"\ *adj* [*fore-*] **1 :** prior in order of occurrence **:** PREVIOUS, FORMER, EARLIER ⟨during the ~ years of the last decade⟩ **2 :** situated in front of something else **:** FORWARD ⟨the ~ body of a whale⟩ — often contrasted with *back* and *hind*

⁴**fore** \"\ *n* -s **:** something that occupies a front or anterior position: as **a** (1) **:** FOREMAST (2) **:** ⁵BOW 1 **b** (1) **:** FOREQUARTER ⟨lamb ~*s* are cheap now⟩ (2) **:** FORELEG ⟨a horse lame in his off ~⟩ (3) **:** FORE WING ⟨markings on the hind wing more sober than those on the ~⟩ — **at the fore** *adv* (*or adj*) **:** on the foremast usu. at the masthead — used of a flag hoisted as a signal (as for sailing) — **to the fore** *adv* (*or adj*) **1 a :** within call **b :** in a still surviving state **:** ALIVE **2 :** in available or ready condition — used of money, credit, or other resources **3 :** in a position of prominence **:** FORWARD

⁵**fore** \"\ *interj* [prob. short for *before*] — used by a golfer to warn anyone within range of the probable line of flight of his ball

fore- \"\ *comb form* [ME *for-*, *fore-*, fr. OE *fore-*, fr. *fore*, adv.] **1 a :** at an earlier point in time **:** beforehand ⟨*foresee*⟩ ⟨*foretell*⟩ **b :** occurring at an earlier point in time **:** occurring beforehand ⟨*forepayment*⟩ ⟨*foreperiod*⟩ **c :** being an early part of (something stipulated) ⟨*foreday*⟩ ⟨*foresummer*⟩ **2 a :** situated at or toward the front **:** situated in front of something ⟨*foreleg*⟩ ⟨*foreporch*⟩ **b :** being the front part of (something stipulated) ⟨*forearm*⟩ ⟨*forepalate*⟩

fore and aft *adv* **1 :** lengthwise of a ship **:** from stem to stern — compare ¹ATHWART 1b **2 :** in, at, or toward both the bow and stern

fore–and–aft \ˌ⸗⸗ˈ⸗\ *adj* [*fore and aft*] **1 :** lying, running, or acting in the general line of the length of a ship or other construction (as a house or an airplane) **:** LONGITUDINAL ⟨a *fore-and-aft* shot⟩ — see FORE-AND-AFT SAIL **2** *of a sailing ship* **:** having no square sails — see FORE-AND-AFT RIG, SCHOONER, SLOOP **3** *of a hat or cap* **:** having peaks in front and back

fore–and–aft bridge *n* **:** a gangway that sometimes connects a ship's forward bridge and after bridge

fore–and–aft·er \ˌ⸗⸗ˈaftə(r)\ *n* -s [*fore-and-aft* (*rig*) + *-er*] **1 a :** a ship with a fore-and-aft rig; *esp* **:** SCHOONER **b :** something arranged fore and aft (as a longitudinal member dividing a hatchway) **2 :** a cocked hat worn with peaks in front and back

fore–and–aft rig *n* **1 :** a sailing-ship rig in which most or all of the sails are not attached to yards but are bent to gaffs or set on the masts or on stays in the midship line of the ship — compare SQUARE RIG **2** *slang Brit* **:** the uniform of a naval rating who wears a peak cap

fore–and–aft rigged *adj* **:** equipped with a fore-and-aft rig

fore–and–aft sail *n* **:** a sail not supported by a yard and usu. carried on a gaff or stay — see SAIL illustration

¹**forearm** \(ˈ)⸗ˈ⸗\ *vt* [*fore-* + *arm* (*v*)] **:** to arm in advance for attack or resistance; *broadly* **:** PREPARE ⟨we must ~ ourselves against the coming winter⟩

²**forearm** \ˈ⸗ˌ⸗\ *n* [*fore-* + *arm* (part of the body)] **1 :** the part of the arm or forelimb between the elbow and the wrist in a primate **:** ANTEBRACHIUM; *sometimes* **:** the corresponding part in other vertebrate animals — see HORSE illustration **2 :** FORE-END 2

forebay \ˈ⸗ˌ⸗\ *n* [*fore-* + *bay*] **1 :** a reservoir or canal from which water is immediately taken to run a waterwheel, turbine, or other equipment; *broadly* **:** the discharging end of a pond or millrace **2 :** the overhanging front of the upper story of a Pennsylvania Dutch barn

fore beam *n* **:** CLOTH BEAM

fore·bear *or* **for·bear** \ˈfōrˌbe(ə)r, ˈfȯr-, -ˌba(ə)(ə)r; ˈfōəˌbeə, ˈfȯ(ə)ˌ-, -ˌba(ə)ə\ *n* [ME (Sc dial.) *forebear*, fr. *fore-* + *-bear* one that is (fr. *been* to be + *-ar*, *-er* -er) — more at BE] **:** ANCESTOR, FOREFATHER — usu. used in pl. **syn** see ANCESTOR

forebitt \ˈ⸗ˌ⸗\ *n* [*fore-* + *bitt*] **:** one of the bitts near the foremast

foreboard \ˈ⸗ˌ⸗\ *n* [*fore-* + *board*] **:** the foredeck of a ship

fore·bode *or* **for·bode** \fōrˈbōd, fȯr'-, fə(r)'-, fōə'-, fȯ(ə)'-\ *vb* -ED/-ING/-S [*fore-* + *bode*] *vt* **1 :** FORETELL, PORTEND ⟨such heavy air ~*s* a storm⟩ **2 :** to be prescient of **:** have an inward conviction of (as coming ill or misfortune) **:** augur despondingly ~ *vi* **:** FORETELL, PRESAGE, AUGUR, PREDICT **syn** see FORETELL

fore·bod·er \-də(r)\ *n* -s **:** one that forebodes

¹**foreboding** *n* -s [fr. gerund of *forebode*] **:** the act of one who forebodes; *also* **:** a result of foreboding **:** a presage, prediction, or presentiment esp. of coming evil **:** PORTENT ⟨I have a sort of ~ about him —Henry James †1916⟩ **syn** see APPREHENSION

²**foreboding** *adj* [fr. pres. part. of *forebode*] **:** indicative of or marked by foreboding ⟨a ~ glance⟩ ⟨troubled ~ thoughts⟩ — **fore·bod·ing·ly** *adv* — **fore·bod·ing·ness** *n* -ES

forebody \ˈ⸗ˌ⸗⸗\ *n* [*fore-* + *body*] **1 a :** the part of a ship forward of the largest or midship cross section — compare AFTERBODY, MIDDLE BODY **b :** the part of a seaplane float or hull forward of the step; *specif* **:** the bottom surface forward of the step and below the chines **2 :** THORAX

foreboom \ˈ⸗ˌ⸗\ *n* [*fore-* + *boom*] **:** the boom of the foremast of a ship

foreboot \ˈ⸗ˌ⸗\ *n* [*fore-* + *boot*] **:** a receptacle in the front of a vehicle (as for the stowing of baggage)

forebrace \ˈ⸗ˌ⸗\ *n* [*fore-* + *brace*] **:** a brace for swinging a fore yardarm — see SHIP illustration

forebrain \ˈ⸗ˌ⸗\ *n* [*fore* + *brain*] **1 a :** the anterior of the three primary divisions of the developing vertebrate brain **b :** the part of the brain of the adult, comprising the telencephalon and diencephalon, that develops from the embryonic forebrain **c :** TELENCEPHALON **2 :** the protocerebrum of an invertebrate

forebreast \ˈ⸗ˌ⸗\ *n* [Sc *forebreist* front part, fr. ME *forebrest*, fr. *fore-* + *brest* breast — more at BREAST] **1 :** FOREFIELD 2 **2 :** the anterior part of the chest esp. of a quadruped

foreby *var of* FORBY

forecabin \ˈ⸗ˌ⸗⸗\ *n* [*fore-* + *cabin*] **:** a cabin in the forepart of a ship

forecaddie \ˈ⸗ˌ⸗⸗\ *n* [*fore-* + *caddie*] **:** a golf caddie who is stationed in advance of the players and who indicates the position of balls on the course

forecarriage \ˈ⸗ˌ⸗⸗\ *n* [*fore-* + *carriage*] **1 :** the forward part of the running gear of a four-wheeled vehicle when arranged so as to permit the two front wheels to turn independently of the rear wheels **2 :** a small usu. 2-wheeled carriage attached under the front end of the beam of a heavy-duty walking plow

¹**fore·cast** \ˈfōrˌkast, ˈfȯr-, ˈfōə-, ˈfȯ(ə)ˌ-, -ˌkaa(ə)st, -ˌkaist, -ˌkȧst *also* ˌ⸗ˈ⸗\ *vb* **forecast** *or* **forecasted; forecast** *or* **forecasted; forecasting; forecasts** [ME *forcasten*, *forecasten*, fr. *for-*, *fore-* fore- + *casten* to cast, contrive — more at CAST] *vt* **1** *archaic* **:** to plan ahead **:** SCHEME, FOREORDAIN **2 a :** to anticipate, calculate, or predict (some future event or condition) usu. as a result of rational study and analysis of available pertinent data ⟨it should be possible to ~ accurately swings in the business cycle⟩ ⟨the guide ~ good fishing if the weather held⟩; *esp* **:** to predict (weather conditions) usu. on the basis of correlated meteorological observations **b :** to indicate or hint at as likely to occur or ensue ⟨optimists are ~*ing* an immediate upswing in business⟩ **3 :** to serve as a forecast of **:** FORETELL, PRESAGE ⟨such events ~ war⟩ ~ *vi* **1** *obs* **:** to contrive or plan beforehand **2 :** to calculate the future **:** FORESEE, FORETELL ⟨if it turns out as I ~*ed*⟩ **syn** see FORETELL

²**forecast** \ˈ⸗ˌ⸗\ *n* [ME *forcast*, *forecast*, fr. *for-*, *fore-* fore- + *cast* cast, plan — more at CAST] **1** *obs* **a :** previous contrivance or determination **b :** PLAN, DESIGN **2** *archaic* **:** foresight of consequences and provision against them **:** PREVISION, FORETHOUGHT **3 :** a prophecy, estimate, or prediction of a future happening or condition ⟨waited for the noon weather ~⟩

fore·cast·er \-tə(r) *also* ⸗ˈ⸗⸗\ *n* **:** one that forecasts; *esp* **:** one that professionally forecasts the weather

fore·cast·ing·ly \(ˈ)⸗ˈ⸗⸗⸗\ *adv* **:** so as to form or formulate a forecast **:** with foresight

fore·cas·tle *or* **fo'c'sle** \ˈfōksəl *sometimes* ˈfōrˌkasəl *or* ˈfȯr-\ *n* -s [ME *forcastel*, *forecastel*, fr. *for-*, *fore-* fore- + *castel* castle — more at CASTLE] **1 a :** an ancient warship's short upper deck forward raised like a castle in order to command an enemy's decks **b :** the part of the upper deck of a ship forward of the foremast or of the fore channels **2 :** the forward part of a merchantman where the sailors live either under the deck or in a compartment above the deck

forecastle deck *n* **:** a partial deck above the main deck at the bow of a ship over a forecastle

fore·cas·tle·head \-lˌhed\ *n* **:** the forward part of a forecastle (sense 1b)

fore–chains \ˈ⸗ˌ⸗\ *n pl* **:** the forward chains of a ship

forecheck \ˈ⸗ˌ⸗\ *vi* **:** to check an opponent in ice hockey in his own defensive zone

fore·clos·able \fōrˈklōzəbəl, fȯr-\ *adj* **:** capable of being foreclosed **:** subject to foreclosure

fore·close \(ˈ)fōrˈklōz, fȯr-, fōə'-, fȯ(ə)'-\ *vb* [ME *forclosen*, fr. OF *forclos*, past part. of *forclore*, fr. *fors* outside, out of, except (fr. L *foris* outside) + *clore* to close — more at FORUM, CLOSE] *vt* **1 :** to shut out **:** DEBAR, PREVENT, HINDER, PRECLUDE ⟨refused to ~ the possibility of a third term⟩; *sometimes* **:** to bring to an end ⟨if he went back to his family he would ~ any chance for independent growth⟩ **2** *obs* **:** to close or block up **:** BAR **3 :** to hold exclusively **4 :** to deal with or close in advance ⟨the chairman cleverly *foreclosed* the question⟩ **5 a :** to bar or cut off (as one having an equity of redemption) for a default in payment of what is due on a mortgage **:** take away the equity of redemption from **b :** to subject to foreclosure proceedings **:** take away the right of (a mortgagor or lienor) to redeem property — see EQUITY OF REDEMPTION ~ *vi* **:** to foreclose a mortgage

fore·clo·sure \-lōzhə(r)\ *n* **:** an act or instance of foreclosing; *specif* **:** a legal proceeding that bars or extinguishes a mortgagor's right of redeeming a mortgaged estate

foreconceive *vt* [*fore-* + *conceive*] *obs* **:** PRECONCEIVE

foreconscious \ˈ⸗ˌ⸗⸗\ *n* [*fore-* + *conscious*; trans. of G (*das*) *vorbewusste*] **:** PRECONSCIOUS

forecourse \ˈ⸗ˌ⸗\ *n* [*fore-* + *course*] **:** FORESAIL 1

forecourt \ˈ⸗ˌ⸗\ *n* [*fore-* + *court*] **1 :** the outer or front court of a building or group of buildings **2 :** the forward part of a court; *esp* **:** the area between the service line and the net of a lawn tennis court

foredate \⸗ˈ⸗\ *vt* [*fore-* + *date*] **:** ANTEDATE

foredawn \ˈ⸗ˌ⸗\ *n* [*fore-* + *dawn*] **:** the time immediately before dawn

foredeck \ˈ⸗ˌ⸗\ *n* [*fore-* + *deck*] **:** the forepart of the main deck of a ship

foredeem *vb* [*fore-* + *deem* (to judge)] *obs* **:** to judge in advance **:** FORECAST

foredeep \ˈ⸗ˌ⸗\ *n* [*fore-* + *deep*] **:** a deep depression in the ocean bottom fronting a mountainous land area ⟨the Tuscarora ~ lies off the coast of Japan⟩

foredestine \⸗ˈ⸗⸗\ *vt* [ME *fordestinen*, *foredestinen*, fr. *for-*, *fore-* fore- + *destinen* to destine — more at DESTINE] **:** PREDESTINE

foredestiny *n* [*fore-* + *destiny*] **1** *obs* **:** FORECAST **2 :** PREORDINATION

foredo *var of* FORDO

foredone \(ˈ)⸗ˈ⸗\ *adj* [*fore-* + *done*] **:** previously done or made

¹**foredoom** \ˈ⸗ˌ⸗\ *n* [*fore-* + *doom* (n.)] *archaic* **:** consignment in advance to a particular fate **:** DESTINY

²**foredoom** \(ˈ)⸗ˈ⸗\ *vt* [*fore-* + *doom* (v.)] **1 :** to doom beforehand ⟨~*ed* by her unfortunate background⟩; *often* **:** to consign in advance to a particular fate ⟨efforts ~*ed* to failure⟩ **2** *archaic* **:** to predict as a doom or destiny **:** FORECAST, PRESAGE

foredoor \ˈ⸗ˌ⸗\ *n* [*fore-* + *door*] *now dial* **:** the front door of a house

foredune \ˈ⸗ˌ⸗\ *n* [*fore-* + *dune*] **:** a dune ridge (as at the landward margin of a beach) more or less completely stabilized by vegetation

fore edge *also* **fore·edge** \ˈ⸗ˌ⸗\ *n* [*fore-* + *edge*] **:** the edge of a book, book section, or illustration opposite the backbone

fore–edge painting *n* **:** the method or act of painting a picture on the fore edge of a book so that the picture is visible only when the pages are slightly fanned; *also* **:** a picture so painted

fore–eld·er \ˈfōrˌeldər\ *n* [ME *foreldre*, fr. *for-*, *fore-* fore- + *eldre* elder, ancestor — more at ELDER] *chiefly Scot* **:** ANCESTOR, FOREFATHER — usu. used in pl.

fore–end \ˈ⸗ˌ⸗\ *n* [ME *forende*, fr. *for-*, *fore-* fore- + *ende* end — more at END] **1 :** the anterior end or part **2 :** the part of the stock of a firearm under the barrel and forward of the trigger guard

fore–exercise \⸗ˈ⸗⸗ˌ⸗\ *n* [*fore-* + *exercise*] **:** a preliminary exercise; *esp* **:** one designed to acquaint students with the technique of a test about to be administered

foreface \ˈ⸗ˌ⸗\ *n* [*fore-* + *face*] **:** the part of the head of a quadruped that is in front of the eyes **:** MUZZLE

forefather \ˈ⸗ˌ⸗⸗\ *n* [ME *forfader*, *forefader*, fr. *for-*, *fore-* fore- + *fader* father — more at FATHER] **1 :** one that precedes another in a line of descent in any degree of consanguinity but usu. in a remote degree **:** ANCESTOR **2 :** a person of an earlier period and common heritage without necessarily a traceable genealogic relationship **:** FOREBEAR — usu. used in pl. **syn** see ANCESTOR

fore·fa·ther·ly *adj, archaic* **:** of or relating to a forefather

forefather's–cup \ˈ⸗ˌ⸗⸗ˌ⸗\ *n, pl* **forefather's–cups :** PITCHER PLANT a

¹**forefeel** \ˈ⸗ˈ⸗\ *vt* [*fore-* + *feel*] **:** to have a presentiment of **:** ANTICIPATE ⟨~*ing* their doom⟩

²**forefeel** \ˈ⸗ˌ⸗\ *n* **:** a presentiment or anticipatory sensation ⟨a ~ of winter in the air⟩

forefence *n* [*fore-* + *fence*] *obs* **:** a front defense

forefend *var of* FORFEND

forefield \ˈ⸗ˌ⸗\ *n* [*fore-* + *field*] **1 :** the nearest part of a field (as of view or of combat) **2** *Brit* **:** the face of a mine working — called also *forebreast*

forefinger \ˈ⸗ˌ⸗⸗\ *n* [ME *forfinger*, *forefinger*, fr. *for-*, *fore-* fore- + *finger*] **:** the finger next to the thumb **:** INDEX FINGER

¹**forefoot** \ˈ⸗ˌ⸗\ *n, pl* **forefeet** [ME *forfot*, *forefot*, fr. *for-*, *fore-* fore- + *fot* foot — more at FOOT] **1 :** one of the anterior feet of a quadruped or multiped **2 :** the forward part of a ship where the stem and keel meet

forefinger

²**forefoot** \"\ *vt, West* **:** to rope (an animal) by the forefeet

¹**forefront** \ˈ⸗ˌ⸗\ *n* [ME *forfrount*, *forefrount*, fr. *for-*, *fore-* + *frount* front — more at FRONT] **:** the foremost part or place **:** VANGUARD ⟨had lived in the ~ of her time —Virginia Woolf⟩ ⟨in the ~ of cultural civilization —G.B.Shaw⟩

²**forefront** \"\ *vt* **:** to provide with a forefront

foregain *or* **foregainst** *prep* [ME *forgain* (fr. *for-*, *fore-* fore- + *again* against) & *forgaines*, fr. *for-*, *fore-* + *againes* against — more at AGAIN, AGAINST] *obs* **:** OPPOSITE

fore·gang·er \ˈfōrˌgaŋər, ˈfȯr-\ *n* [*fore-* + *ganger*] **1** *obs* **:** one that goes before **2 a :** a short rope grafted on a harpoon (as of a whaler) to which the longer line is attached **b :** a length of rope or chain stouter than the rest of the cable and placed next to an anchor

foregate \ˈ⸗ˌ⸗\ *n* [ME *forgate*, *foregate*, fr. *for-*, *fore-* fore- + *gate*] *archaic* **:** a main entrance or front gate

foregather *var of* FORGATHER

foregift \ˈ⸗ˌ⸗\ *n* [*fore-* + *gift*] *Brit* **:** a premium paid for a lease by a tenant; *sometimes* **:** a payment in advance (as on a lease)

foreglance \'ˌ=ˌ=\ *n* [*fore-* + *glance*] **:** a glance forward or beforehand

foregleam \'ˌ=ˌ=\ *n* [*fore-* + *gleam*] **:** a premonitory gleam **:** FORECAST

foreglimpse \'ˌ=ˌ=\ *n* [*fore-* + *glimpse*] **:** a glimpse of the future **:** FOREGLEAM

[1]**fore·go** \fōrˈgō, fȯr-, fōə'-, fȯ(ə)'-\ *vt* **fore·went** \-'went\ **fore·gone** \-'gȯn\ **fore·go·ing** \-'gōiŋ\ **fore·goes** \-'gōz\ [ME *forgon, forgan*, fr. OE *foregān*, fr. *fore-* + *gān* to go — more at GO] **:** to go before **:** PRECEDE ⟨the story of his mishap *forewent* him⟩

[2]**forego** *var of* FORGO

fore·go·er \-'gōə(r)\ *n* [ME *forgoer, foregoer*, fr. *forgon* + *-er*] **:** one that goes before: as **a** *obs* **:** a messenger sent ahead (as a king's purveyor) **:** FORERUNNER **b :** one that leads or goes in the van **:** EXAMPLE **c :** PREDECESSOR, ANCESTOR **d :** the foreganger of a harpoon

fore·go·ing \(ˈ)=ˈgōiŋ, -ōeŋ\ *adj* [ME *forgoing*, fr. pres. part. of *forgon*] **:** prior in place, time, or arrangement **:** ANTECEDENT, PRECEDING ⟨the ~ paragraphs⟩

fore·gone \-ˈgȯn\ *adj* [fr. past part. of [1]*forego*] **:** PREVIOUS, PAST ⟨nostalgic dreams of ~ summers⟩ — **fore·gone·ness** \-n(n)əs\ *n* -ES

foregone conclusion *n* **1 :** a conclusion that has preceded argument or examination **:** a predetermined conclusion **2 :** an inevitable result **:** CERTAINTY ⟨under the circumstances his victory was a *foregone conclusion*⟩

foregrip \'ˌ=ˌ=\ *n* [*fore-* + *grip*] **:** the portion of a fishing rod butt lying between the forward edge of the reel seat and the forward end of the butt

foreground \'ˌ=ˌ=\ *n* [*fore-* + *ground*] **1 :** the part of a scene or representation that is or is depicted as being nearest to and in front of the spectator — compare BACKGROUND, DISTANCE, PERSPECTIVE **2 :** a position of prominence **:** FOREFRONT ⟨in the ~ of our activities⟩

foregut \'ˌ=ˌ=\ *n* [*fore-* + *gut*] **1 :** the anterior part of the primitive alimentary canal of a vertebrate embryo including those parts that develop into the pharynx, esophagus, stomach, and extreme anterior part of the intestine **2 :** the anterior part of the definitive alimentary canal of an invertebrate animal

forehall \'ˌ=ˌ=\ *n* [*fore-* + *hall*] **:** a front hall esp. in a large building

forehammer \'ˌ=ˌ=\ *n* [ME *forhamer, forehamer*, fr. *for-, fore-* fore + *hamer* hammer — more at HAMMER] **:** the hammer that strikes first when two hammers are used; *sometimes* **:** SLEDGEHAMMER

[1]**forehand** \'ˌ=ˌ=\ *n* [*fore-* + *hand*] **1** *archaic* **:** superior position **:** ADVANTAGE **2** *obs* **:** the chief or most important part **3 :** the part of a horse that is before the rider **4** *Brit* **:** a working foreman or supervisor; *esp* **:** one in charge of a process or apparatus in copper extracting **5 :** a forehand stroke (as in tennis or racquets) ⟨a player with an excellent ~⟩; *also* **:** the side on which such strokes are made ⟨he took the ball on his ~⟩ ⟨played to his opponent's ~⟩ — opposed to *backhand* **6** [trans. of G *vorderhand* lead] **:** the player in skat whose turn to bid comes first

forehand 5

[2]**forehand** \"\ *adv* **:** with a forehand stroke

[3]**forehand** \"\ *adj* [[2]*fore* + *hand*] **1** *obs* **:** done or given in advance **:** PRIOR, ANTICIPATIVE — see FOREHAND RENT **2** *of a stroke in racket games* **:** made on the side of the playing arm with the palm forward

forehanded \'=ˈhandəd, -aan-\ *adj* **1** *obs, of a horse* **:** having a forehand of an indicated sort **2 :** mindful of the future **:** THRIFTY, PRUDENT; *often* **:** having resources reserved for the future **3 :** FOREHAND 2

fore·hand·ed·ly *adv* **:** in a forehanded manner **:** THRIFTILY, PRUDENTLY

fore·hand·ed·ness *n* -ES **:** the quality or state of being ready and prepared (as for future need); *often* **:** THRIFT

forehand rent *n* **1** *Scots law* **:** rent made payable before the tenant's crop out of which it is to be paid has been harvested **2** *English law* **:** FOREGIFT

fore·head \ˈfȯrəd, ˈfärəd; ˈfōr,hed, ˈfȯr,h-, ˈfōə,h-, ˈfȯ(ə),h-; *sometimes* ˈfȯ,red *or* ˈfä,red\ *n* [ME *forheved, forhed*, fr. OE *forhēafod*, fr. *for-, fore-* fore + *hēafod* head — more at HEAD] **1 :** the part of the face above the eyes **:** BROW **2 :** the aspect or countenance as expressing emotion or personal qualities (as of assurance or effrontery or sometimes modesty) **3 :** the front or forepart of something ⟨flames in the ~ of the morning sky —John Milton⟩ **4 :** the face of a mine working

fore·head·ed \-dəd\ *adj* **:** having or characterized by a forehead — used in combination with a qualifying adjective ⟨a low-*foreheaded* race⟩

forehearth \'ˌ=ˌ=\ *n* [*fore-* + *hearth*] **1 :** the forward extension of the hearth of a blast furnace under the tymp; *also* **:** a similar extension of any smelting hearth **2 :** a steel furnace having an attachment in the front so as to dispense with the casting ladle **3 :** a separate receptacle taking the place of a hearth in front of a furnace for receiving molten material flowing out esp. to permit settling; *also* **:** a chamber at the end of a tank furnace from which glass is withdrawn for working

foreheater \'ˌ=ˌ==\ *n* [*fore-* + *heater*] **:** a shallow iron pan in which brine is boiled in the preparation of salt

forehold \'ˌ=ˌ=\ *n* [*fore-* + *hold*] **:** a hold in the forward part of a ship

forehoof \'ˌ=ˌ=\ *n, pl* **forehoofs** *also* **forehooves** [*fore-* + *hoof*] **:** the hoof of a forefoot (as of a horse)

forehook \'ˌ=ˌ=\ *n* [*fore-* + *hook*] **:** a piece of timber placed across the stem to unite the bows and strengthen the forepart of a ship **:** BREASTHOOK

[1]**for·eign** \ˈfȯrən, ˈfär-\ *adj* [ME *forein*, fr. OF *forain, forein*, fr. LL *foranus* situated on the outside, fr. L *foris* outside + *-anus* -an — more at FORUM] **1 :** situated outside a place or country: as **a :** situated outside one's own country ⟨~ nations⟩ ⟨~ cities⟩ **b :** situated outside a locality under consideration (as a private estate or a township) **2 :** born in, belonging to, derived from, intended for, or characteristic of some place or country (as nation) other than the one under consideration **:** not native or domestic ⟨our large ~ population⟩ ⟨~ art⟩ ⟨outgoing ~ mail⟩ ⟨incoming ~ mail⟩ **3 :** of, relating to, or proceeding from some other person, material thing, or substance than the one under consideration ⟨a man cannot save himself by ~ aid⟩ ⟨nothing is ~: parts relate to whole —Alexander Pope⟩ ⟨allergenic effects of ~ proteins⟩ ⟨the introduction of ~ genes in maize⟩ ⟨~ matter in milk⟩ **4 :** alien in character **:** not connected or pertinent **:** lacking congruity **:** INAPPROPRIATE ⟨~ to the plan⟩ ⟨this design is not ~ from some people's thoughts —Jonathan Swift⟩ **5 :** related to or dealing with other nations ⟨~ trade⟩ ⟨a ~ policy⟩ ⟨~ dividends⟩ **6 :** occurring in an abnormal situation in the living body and commonly introduced from without ⟨a sliver of wood under a fingernail or a coin in the esophagus are equally ~ bodies to the physician⟩ **7** *obs* **:** not belonging to or concerned with one's own household or family **8 a :** not being within the sphere of operation of the laws of a country under consideration — opposed to *domestic* **b :** not being within the sphere of operation of a locality (as a state or county) under consideration **9 a** *of a ship* **:** owned by a national of a foreign nation **b** *of the registry of a ship* **:** being under the flag of a nation other than that of which the owner is a national **syn** see EXTRINSIC

[2]**foreign** \"\ *n* -S [ME *forein*, fr. *forein*, adj.] **1** *obs* **:** FOREIGNER **:** a ship of foreign origin or registry **2** *obs* **:** an outlying part (as of a town or monastery) **3 :** a bond or other security originating in the jurisdiction of and usu. issued by a foreign governing body — usu. used in pl. ⟨~*s* drifted somewhat lower today⟩

foreign affairs *n pl* **:** matters relating to foreign countries **:** affairs other than domestic; *esp* **:** matters having to do with international relations and with the interests of the home country in foreign countries — see FOREIGN OFFICE

foreign aid *n* **:** economic or other assistance provided by one nation to another esp. as a tool in molding opinion in the recipient nation

foreign attachment *n* **:** a legal process by which the property of a foreign or absent debtor is attached within the jurisdiction for the satisfaction of a debt due from him to the plaintiff

foreign bill *n* **:** a bill of exchange not classified as an inland bill under the applicable law

foreign–born \'==ˈ=\ *adj* **:** born under an alien sovereignty **:** foreign by birth whether naturalized or not

foreign car *n* **:** a freight car that is not owned by the railroad upon which it is being used — contrasted with *home car*

foreign corporation *also* **foreign company** *n* **:** a corporation or other organization having the essential attributes of a corporation that is chartered under the laws of a state or government other than that in which it is doing business

foreign correspondent *n* **:** a correspondent employed to send from a foreign country or region news or comment for publication

foreign devil *n* [trans. of Chin (Pek) *fan*[1] *kuei*[2]] **:** a foreigner in China — usu. used disparagingly

for·eign·er \ˈfȯrənə(r), ˈfär-\ *n* -S [ME *foreiner*, fr. *forein*, adj. + *-er*] **1 :** a person belonging to or owing allegiance to a foreign country **:** ALIEN **2 :** something originating in another country; *esp* **:** a ship from abroad **3** *now dial* **:** STRANGER, OUTSIDER; *usu* **:** a nonresident or an unknown person in a community

foreign exchange *n* **1 :** a process of settling accounts or debts between persons residing in different countries **2 :** foreign coins and currency or current and short-term credit instruments payable in such currency

foreign factor *n* **:** an agent traveling on a ship and in charge of another's cargo with power to sell it for cash or exchange it for other property and to bring that property back to the port of embarkation — compare DOMESTIC FACTOR

foreign–flag \'==ˈ=\ *adj* **:** registered under a foreign flag — used of a ship or airplane or of its owner ⟨*foreign-flag* competitors⟩ ⟨*foreign-flag* lines flying into the country⟩

for·eign·ism \ˈfȯrə,nizəm, ˈfär-\ *n* -S **1 :** something peculiar to a foreign language or people **:** a foreign idiom or custom; *usu* **:** a feature of pronunciation or grammar or a word or word usage that is identified as foreign **2 :** imitation of foreign usage

for·eign·ize \-,nīz\ *vt* -ED/-ING/-S **:** to make foreign **:** give a foreign character or flavor to ⟨concealing fact under a *foreignized* terminology⟩

foreign jury *n* **:** a jury selected usu. because of local prejudice from a county other than that where a case is being tried

foreign legion *n* [trans. of F *légion étrangère*] **:** a volunteer corps of foreign citizens in the military service of a state

for·eign·ly *adv* **:** in a foreign manner

foreign minister *n* **:** a governmental minister for foreign affairs ⟨the *foreign minister* of the U.S. bears the title Secretary of State⟩

foreign mission *n* **:** a religious mission conducted outside the nation or national territory from which it is commissioned — compare HOME MISSION

for·eign·ness \ˈfȯrən(n)əs, ˈfär-\ *n* -ES **1 :** the quality or state of being foreign ⟨the ~ of his background⟩ **2 :** lack of relation or appropriateness **:** IRRELEVANCY ⟨the complete ~ of such an approach weakened the force of his thesis⟩

foreign office *n* **:** a government department (as a ministry or cabinet bureau) having to do with foreign affairs and usu. headed by a minister ⟨the British *Foreign Office*⟩ ⟨caused a stir in the *foreign offices* of the democracies⟩

foreign policy *n* **:** the underlying basic direction of the activity and relationships of a sovereign state in its interaction with other sovereign states typically manifested in peace, war, neutrality, and alliance or various combinations of or approaches to these

foreign relations *n pl* **:** the relations between sovereign states **:** the manifest result of foreign policy; *broadly* **:** the field of international interaction and reaction ⟨a specialist in *foreign relations*⟩

foreigns *pl of* FOREIGN

foreign service *n* **1** [trans. of ML *servitium forinsecum*] **:** forinsec service **2 :** the field force of a foreign office comprising diplomatic personnel concerned primarily with governmental relations and consular personnel concerned largely with individual and commercial matters **3 :** service in the armed forces of a nation performed outside the national or continental boundaries but not necessarily beyond the boundaries of its sovereignty

foreign shipment *n* **:** a railroad shipment originating on or passing to another line

foreign–trade zone *n* **:** an isolated policed area adjacent to a port of entry (as a seaport or airport) where foreign goods may be unloaded for immediate transshipment or stored, repacked, sorted, mixed, or otherwise manipulated without being subject to import duties

foreign voltage *n* **:** a voltage imposed (as for the purpose of control or by accident) on an electrical circuit from some other source than the regular source

foreign word *n* **1 :** a word of a foreign language **2 :** a word taken from another language, pronounced and written as alien, and in English usu. printed in italics **3 :** a word adopted from another language **:** LOANWORD

foreintend \ˌ==ˈ=\ *vt* [*fore-* + *intend*] **:** to plan in advance **:** intend to act or do as a result of deliberation

foreiron \'ˌ=ˌ==\ *n* [*fore-* + *iron*] **:** COLTER

[1]**fore·judge** *or* **for·judge** \fərˈjəj, fōr-, fȯr-\ *vt* [ME *forjuggen*, fr. MF *forjugier, forsjugier*, fr. *fors* outside + *jugier* to judge — more at FORECLOSE, JUDGE] **1 :** to expel, oust, or put out by judgment of a court — used with *from* or *of* or with a double object **2** *obs* **:** ADJUDGE, CONDEMN

[2]**forejudge** \fōrˈjəj, fȯr-\ *vt* [*fore-* + *judge*] **:** PREJUDGE

fore·judg·er *or* **for·judg·er** \fərˈjəjə(r), fōr-, fȯr-\ *n* -S [ME *forjugger*, fr. MF *forjugier, forsjugier* to forejudge] **:** a judgment under English law by which one is expelled, ousted, or put out

fore·judg·ment \-ˈjəjmənt\ *n* [*fore-* + *judgment*] **:** FOREJUDGER

fore·know \fōrˈnō, fȯr-\ *vt* [ME *foreknowen*, fr. *fore-* + *knowen* to know — more at KNOW] **:** to have previous knowledge of **:** know beforehand ⟨who would the miseries of man ~ —John Dryden⟩ **syn** see FORESEE

fore·know·able \-ōəbəl\ *adj* **:** being or capable of being known in advance ⟨a ~ verdict⟩

fore·know·er \-ōə(r)\ *n* **:** one that foreknows

fore·know·ing·ly *adv* **:** with foreknowledge

foreknowledge \(ˈ)=ˈ==\ *n* [*fore-* + *knowledge*] **:** knowledge of a thing before it happens or exists **:** PRESCIENCE, PRECOGNITION ⟨some of the tests seemed to indicate a definite ~ of what card would turn up next⟩ ⟨~ of human weakness⟩

for·el *also* **for·rel** \ˈfärəl\ *n* -S [ME *forel* case, sheath, fr. MF *forrel, fourrel*, dim. of *fuerre* sheath — more at FUR] **1 a** *now dial Eng* **:** SHEATH, CASE **b :** a sheath or slipcase for holding a book **2 :** an inferior parchment for book covers **3 :** BURSE 2c

forelady \'ˌ=ˌ==\ *n* [*fore-* + *lady*] **:** a woman employed to supervise a group of working women (as in a factory) — called also *floorlady, floorwoman*

fore·land \ˈfōrlənd, ˈfȯr-\ *n* [ME *forland, foreland*, fr. *for-, fore-* fore- + *land*] **1 :** PROMONTORY, HEADLAND **2 :** land lying in front or forming the forward margin of something ⟨the ~ of the oil region⟩ ⟨the ~ of a national boundary⟩ **3 :** a portion of the natural shore on the outside of an embankment or sea wall that receives the shock of waves and deadens their force **4 :** a region of comparatively undisturbed rocks adjacent to an orogenic belt

forelay \'ˌ=ˌ=\ *vb* **forelaid; forelaid; forelaying; forelays** [*fore-* + *lay*] *vt* **1** *now chiefly dial* **:** to lie in wait for **:** AMBUSH, WAYLAY **2** *archaic* **:** HINDER, OBSTRUCT **3** *dial* **:** to plan on **:** INTEND **~** *vi, dial* **:** to make arrangements beforehand

foreleech \'ˌ=ˌ=\ *n* [*fore-* + *leech* (edge of a sail)] **:** the luff of a fore-and-aft sail

foreleg \'ˌ=ˌ=\ *n* [ME *forlegge*, fr. *for-, fore-* fore- + *legge* leg — more at LEG] **1 :** either of the anterior pair of legs of a quadruped or multiped **2 :** a front leg of a legged inanimate object (as a chair)

forelimb \'ˌ=ˌ=\ *n* [*fore-* + *limb*] **:** an arm or a fin, wing, or leg of a vertebrate animal that is a foreleg of a quadruped or is homologous to it

[1]**forelock** \'ˌ=ˌ=\ *n* [ME *forlok, forelok*, fr. *for-, fore-* fore- + *lok* lock (fastening device) — more at LOCK] **:** COTTER PIN, SPLIT PIN, LINCHPIN

[2]**forelock** \"\ *vt* **:** to fasten with a forelock

[3]**forelock** \"\ *n* [*fore-* + *lock* (tuft of hair)] **:** a lock of hair that grows from the forepart of the head; *specif* **:** the part of a horse's mane that arises between the ears and hangs forward over the face — see HORSE illustration

forelock hook *n* **:** a hook by means of which a bunch of three yarns is twisted into a strand of rope

forelook \=ˈ=\ *vi* [*fore-* + *look*] **:** to look ahead or toward the future

[1]**fore·man** \ˈfōrmən, ˈfȯr-, ˈfōəm-, ˈfȯ(ə)m-\ *n, pl* **foremen** [ME *forman, foreman*, fr. *for- fore-* fore- + *man*] **:** a first or chief man: as **a** *obs* **:** a man who goes in advance **:** LEADER **b :** a member of a jury that acts as speaker, presides over deliberations, and conducts communication with the court **c** (1) **:** a chief and often specially trained workman who works with and commonly leads a gang or crew (2) **:** a representative of an owner or management in authority over a group of workers, a particular process or operation, a section of a plant or an entire organization ⟨the old-time ranch ~ had all the responsibilities and few of the benefits of ownership⟩ ⟨in the modern industrial plant the ~ is at once a link in the chain of management and a bridge between management and labor⟩

[2]**foreman** \"\ *vt* **foremaned** *or* **foremanned; foremaned** *or* **foremanned; foremaning** *or* **foremanning; foremans :** to supervise in the status of a foreman

fore·man·ship \-n,ship\ *n* **:** the office or occupation of a foreman ⟨took a course in ~⟩

fore·mast \ˈfōr,mast, ˈfȯr-, ˈfōə,-, ˈfȯ(ə),-, -,maast, -,mȧst, -məst\ *n* [*fore-* + *mast*] **:** the mast nearest the bow of a sailing ship — see SHIP illustration

fore·mast·man \-tmən\ *also* **fore·mast·hand** \-t,hand\ *n, pl* **foremastmen** *also* **foremasthands** *n* **:** a common sailor **:** a man before the mast

forematter \'ˌ===\ *n* [*fore-* + *matter*] **:** FRONT MATTER

foremilk \'ˌ=ˌ=\ *n* [*fore-* + *milk*] **1 :** the first-drawn milk (as of a cow) usu. poor in fat and contaminated with bacteria from the teat canal **2 :** COLOSTRUM

[1]**fore·most** \ˈfōr,mōst, ˈfȯr-, ˈfōə,-, ˈfȯ(ə),- *also* -,məst\ *adj* [alter. (influenced by *fore-* & *most*) of ME *formest*, adj. & adv., fr. OE *formest, fyrmest*, superl. of *forma* first; akin to OS *formo* first, OS & OHG *fruma* advantage, profit, ON *frum-* first, Goth *fruma*, OE *faran* to travel, go — more at FARE] **1 :** standing at the head, van, or front in a series or progression **:** most advanced in position **:** FIRST, HEADMOST ⟨was none who would be ~ to lead such dire attack —T.B.Macaulay⟩ **2 :** of first rank, position, influence, worth, reputation **:** leaving others behind **:** PREEMINENT ⟨great in council and great in war, ~ captain of his time —Alfred Tennyson⟩ ⟨unquestionably the ~ figure among Maine artists —*Amer. Guide Series: Maine*⟩ **syn** see CHIEF

[2]**foremost** \"\ *adv* [alter. of ME *formest*, adj. & adv.] **1 :** in the first place **:** FIRST ⟨put his best foot ~⟩ **2 :** most importantly ⟨first and ~⟩

fore·most·ly *adv* **:** before all **:** in the foremost place

foremother \'ˌ===\ *n* [*fore-* + *mother*] **:** a woman corresponding in relationship to a forefather **:** a female ancestor or forebear

forename \'ˌ=ˌ=\ *n* [*fore-* + *name*] **:** a name that precedes one's surname **:** a personal name by which an individual is distinguished from others with the same surname **:** a first or middle name ⟨a tendency to call men by the initials of their ~*s* —E.C.Smith⟩

fore·named \'=ˈnāmd\ *adj* [ME *fornamed, forenamed*, fr. *for-, fore-* fore + *named*, past part. of *namen* to name — more at NAME] **:** previously mentioned **:** named before

fore·nenst *or* **fore·nent** \fə(r)-\ *var of* FORNENT

fore·night \ˈfōr,nīt\ *or* **fore·nicht** \-,nikt\ *n* [*fore-* + *night* or *nicht*] *Scot* **:** the part of evening between twilight and bedtime

forenoon \'ˌ=ˌ=, =ˈ=\ *n* [ME *fornoon, forenoon*, fr. *for-, fore-* fore- + noon] **:** a part of day ending with noon; *usu* **:** the time between daylight or breakfast and noon

forenoon watch *n* **:** the watch on a ship from 8 a.m. to noon

forenotice \'ˌ=ˌ==\ *n* [*fore-* + *notice*] **:** notice or warning conveyed in advance

[1]**fo·ren·sic** \fəˈren(t)sik, (ˈ)fōrˈre-, (ˈ)fȯˈre-, -nz|, |ēk\ *adj* [L *forensis* of a market or forum, public, forensic (fr. *forum* market, forum) + E *-ic* — more at FORUM] **1 :** belonging to courts of judicature or to public discussion and debate **2 :** used in legal proceedings or in public discussions; *broadly* **:** ARGUMENTATIVE, RHETORICAL ⟨~ eloquence⟩ **3 :** of or relating to forensics ⟨an excellent ~ program⟩ — **fo·ren·si·cal·ly** \|əˈk(ə)lē, |ēk-, -li\ *adv*

[2]**fo·ren·sic** \fəˈre-, fōrˈe-, fȯˈre-\ *n* -S **1 :** an argumentative exercise in the form of a speech or thesis formerly much used as an exercise in American schools and colleges **2 forensics** *pl but sing or pl in constr* **:** the art or study of argumentative discourse; *sometimes* **:** DEBATE 2

fo·ren·si·cal \|əkəl\ *adj* [L *forensis* + E *-ical*] *archaic* **:** FORENSIC

forensic ballistics *n pl but sing or pl in constr* **:** ballistics applied in the determination of legal evidence esp. as concerned with the identification of firearms, ammunition, bullets, and cartridge cases

forensic chemistry *n* **:** chemistry applied to legal questions — called also *legal chemistry*

forensic medicine *n* **:** a science that deals with the relation and application of medical facts to legal problems — called also *medical jurisprudence*

forensic psychiatry *n* **:** the application of psychiatry in courts of law (as for the determination of criminal responsibility or liability to commitment for insanity)

fore–oath \'ˌ=ˌ=\ *n* [*fore-* + *oath*] **:** an oath required of a party bringing suit under old English law unless the cause of complaint were manifest

foreordain \ˌ=ˌ=ˈ=\ *vt* [ME *forordeinen*, fr. *for-, fore-* fore- + *ordeinen* to ordain — more at ORDAIN] **:** to dispose or appoint in advance **:** PREDESTINATE, PREDETERMINE ⟨this ~*ed* course of events⟩ ⟨~*ed* to perish as their fathers had⟩

foreordination \ˌ=ˌ==ˈ==\ *n* [*fore-* + *ordination*] **:** the quality or state of being foreordained; *esp* **:** PREDESTINATION 2

foreparent \'ˌ=ˌ==\ *n* [*fore-* + *parent*] *Midland* **:** ANCESTOR, FOREBEAR — usu. used in pl.

forepart \'ˌ=ˌ=\ *n* [ME *forpart, forepart*, fr. *for-, fore-* fore- + *part*] **1 :** the forward or anterior part of something **:** FRONT ⟨the ~ of a ship⟩: as **a :** the forward part of a shoe or last **b :** the part of a garment (as a jacket) that covers the chest; *sometimes* **:** either of the pieces of material that when assembled form one lateral half of the forepart of a garment **2 :** the earlier part of a period of time ⟨spent the ~ of the morning on the beach⟩

forepassed *or* **forepast** \=ˈ=\ *adj* [*fore-* + *passed, past*] **:** BYGONE

forepaw \'ˌ=ˌ=\ *n* [*fore-* + *paw*] **:** the paw of a foreleg

forepeak \'ˌ=ˌ=\ *n* [*fore-* + *peak*] **:** the extreme forward lower compartment or tank used for trimming or storage in a ship

forepiece \'ˌ=ˌ=\ *n* [*fore-* + *piece*] **:** a front piece: as **a :** the flap in the forepart of a sidesaddle that guards the rider's dress **b :** CURTAIN RAISER

forepillar \'ˌ=ˌ==\ *n* [*fore-* + *pillar*] **:** PILLAR 4d

fore plane *n* [[3]*fore*] **:** a carpenter's plane usu. about 18 inches long and intermediate between the jack plane and jointer

foreplay \'ˌ=ˌ=\ *n* [*fore-* + *play*] **:** sexual stimulation that normally tends to lead to sexual intercourse

forepleasure \'ˌ=ˌ==\ *n* [*fore-* + *pleasure*] **:** pleasurable excitement (as that induced by stimulation of erogenous zones) that tends to lead to or release a more intense emotional reaction (as in orgasm) — compare ENDPLEASURE

foreplot \=ˈ=\ *vt* [*fore-* + *plot*] **:** to work out in advance ⟨you can ~ the course of the story easily enough⟩

forepoint *vt* [*fore-* + *point*] *obs* **:** PREDESTINE, FORECAST

[1]**forepole** *also* **forepale** \(ˈ)=ˈ=\ *vt* [*fore-* + *pole* or *pale* (v.)] **:** to advance (an excavation) in quicksand or caving ground by driving poles, slabs, or sheathing into the ground ahead of the excavation or simultaneously with it

[2]**forepole** \'ˌ=ˌ=\ *n* [*fore-* + *pole* (n.)] **:** a piece of lagging, a heavy plank, or a pole, sharpened on one end and used in forepoling — called also *lath, spile, spiling*

forepost \ˈ=,=\ *n* [*fore-* + *post*] **:** OUTPOST

foreprise *or* **foreprize** *vt* -ED/-ING/-S [*forprise* fr. *fore-* + *-prise* (as in *apprise*); *foreprize* alter. of *foreprise*] *obs* **:** to determine, provide for, or deal with beforehand **:** take for granted or in advance

forepump \ˈ=,=\ *n* [*fore-* + *pump*] **:** a vacuum pump auxiliary to a more effective pump for which it supplies a first stage of exhaustion — called also *backing pump*

forequarter \ˈ=,==\ *n* [*fore-* + *quarter*] **:** a front quarter or part; *specif* **:** the front part of the lateral half of a carcass (as of beef, veal, lamb, or mutton) usu. divided between the 12th and 13th ribs

forereach \=ˈ=\ *vb* [*fore-* + *reach*] *vi, of a ship* **:** to gain ground in going about usu. by carrying more way while in stays ~ *vt* **1 :** to gain upon (as a ship) **2 :** to overhaul and go ahead of (a ship) when close-hauled

foreribs \ˈ=,=\ *n pl* [*fore-* + *ribs*] *Brit* **:** a cut of beef including the ribs immediately in front of the loin and forming one of the best roasting cuts **:** the prime ribs

fore rider *n* [ME *forerider*, fr. *fore-* + *rider*] **:** a rider in advance (as an outrider or scout)

¹fore·right \ˈfōr,rīt\ *adv* [ME, fr. *fore-* + *right* (adv.)] *now dial Eng* **:** straight ahead **:** directly forward

²foreright \"\ *adj* **1** *dial Eng* **:** going straight ahead **:** STRAIGHTFORWARD, DIRECT ⟨the ~ path⟩ **2** *dial* **:** HEADSTRONG, OBSTINATE

³foreright \"\ *prep, dial Eng* **:** directly opposite **:** across from

foreroom \ˈ=,=\ *n* [*fore-* + *room*] *dial* **:** LIVING ROOM, PARLOR

¹forerun \=ˈ=\ *vt* [ME *forrennen, forerennen*, fr. *for-, fore-* fore- + *rennen* to run — more at RUN] **1 :** to run before **:** be in advance of (something following) **:** PRECEDE **2 :** to come before as an earnest of something to follow **:** introduce as a harbinger **:** ANNOUNCE ⟨these signs ~ the death or fall of kings —Shak.⟩ **3 :** FORESTALL, ANTICIPATE

²forerun \ˈ=,=\ *or* **forerunning** \ˈ=,==\ *n* **:** the first part that comes over in a distillation **:** the most volatile portion of a distilland ⟨the ~s of citronella oil⟩ — often used in pl.

forerunner \ˈ=ˈ==\ *n* [ME *forrenner, forerenner*, fr. *for-, fore-* fore- + *renner* runner; prob. trans. of L *praecursor* — more at RUNNER] **1 :** one going or sent before to give notice of the approach of others **:** HARBINGER ⟨blustery March days that are ~s of spring⟩: as **a :** a premonitory sign or symptom ⟨a stuffy feeling that is often the ~ of a cold⟩ ⟨a sudden alteration in the cost of money is a frequent ~ of economic decline⟩ **b :** one or more skiers who run the course before the start of a downhill skiing race to break trail, establish a typical time for the course, or indicate hazards **2 :** PREDECESSOR, FOREBEAR, ANCESTOR ⟨colonial administrators who . . . like their ~s . . . dedicate their lives to arduous and largely unrecognized service —*Times Lit. Supp.*⟩ ⟨a ~ of present-day cartoonists⟩ **3 a :** a piece of cloth tied on a ship's log line some fathoms from the outboard end to mark the limit of drift line **b :** FOREGANGER 2a

fores *pl of* FORE

foresaddle \ˈ=,==\ *n* [*fore-* + *saddle*] **:** a wholesale cut of veal, lamb, or mutton consisting of the undivided forequarters of a carcass — compare HINDSADDLE

fore·said \ˈfōr,sed, ˈfȯr-\ *adj* [ME *foresaid, forsaid*, fr. OE *foresǣd*, fr. *fore-* + *gesægd, gesǣd*, past part of *secgan* to say — more at SAY] *archaic* **:** AFORESAID

fore·sail \ˈfōr,sāl, ˈfȯr-, ˈfōə,-, ˈfȯ(ə),-, -səl\ *n* [ME *foreseile*, fr. *for-, fore-* fore- + *seile, seile* sail — more at SAIL] **1 :** a sail that is carried on the foreyard of a square-rigged ship and that is the lowest sail on the foremast — called also *forecourse*; see SAIL illustration **2 :** the lower sail set abaft the foremast of a schooner — see SAIL illustration **3 :** FORESTAYSAIL

foresay \=ˈ=\ *vt* [ME *forseyen, foreseyen*, fr. OE *foresecgan*, fr. *fore-* + *secgan* to say — more at SAY] *archaic* **:** to tell in advance **:** PREDICT, FORETELL

fore·see \(ˈ)fōrˈsē, (ˈ)fȯr-, (ˈ)fōə-, (ˈ)fȯ(ə)-\ *vb* [ME *forseen, foreseen*, fr. OE *foresēon*, fr. *fore-* + *sēon* to see — more at SEE] *vt* **1 :** to see (as a future occurrence or development) as certain or unavoidable **:** look forward to with assurance ⟨should have *foreseen* the risk of economic collapse⟩ ⟨surely you can ~ what will happen next⟩ **2** *obs* **:** to provide esp. for or against **3** *obs* **:** to see, interview, or consider beforehand ~ *vi, obs* **:** to have or exercise foresight

syn FORESEE, FOREKNOW, DIVINE, APPREHEND, ANTICIPATE can mean to know or prophesy a future event or have knowledge of something prior to its manifestation. FORESEE in itself gives no hint of how the knowledge is derived or prophecy arrived at ⟨I had not *foreseen* the black depths of loneliness —Francis Stuart⟩ ⟨our failure to *foresee* all future problems —Vera M. Dean⟩ FOREKNOW, stressing the prior knowledge, usu., though not always, implies supernatural powers or the assistance of them, as divine revelation ⟨he cannot, however, *foreknow* how his opponent will behave in action —A.J.Toynbee⟩ ⟨they were willing to say that God *foreknows* the sin of those who are not elected to salvation —K.S.Latourette⟩ DIVINE, often indistinguishable from FORESEE, frequently suggests a gift, the assistance of a special power, or unusual discernment ⟨the military genius is the general who repeatedly succeeds in *divining* the unpredictable by guesswork or intuition —A.J. Toynbee⟩ ⟨impossible for him to *divine* the complexity and subtlety of these abstract mathematical ideas which were waiting for discovery —A.N.Whitehead⟩ ⟨whose talents for *divining* news and coordinating its coverage remain a matter of perpetual awe —Gladwin Hill⟩ APPREHEND often implies somewhat less certainty of what is foreseen than the previous words but a stronger emotional effect of the advance knowledge or the suspicion, often suggesting esp. a certain anxiety or dread ⟨she *apprehended*, not without good cause, that his kingdom might soon be extended to her frontiers —T.B. Macaulay⟩ ⟨his lips quivered, and she *apprehended* rather than heard what he said —Ellen Glasgow⟩ ANTICIPATE suggests an action of some kind in relation or seeming relation to the thing foreseen or prophesied, as the formulation of an historical hypothesis that makes the future event reasonable or seemingly inevitable, or an experiencing of prior joy or pain on account of the thing foreseen, or an interrelated move as one that forestalls, aggravates, or is motivated by the thing foreseen ⟨his leadership in the state has consisted of *anticipating* the thinking of the major groups of voters and following what he believes to be public opinion —Frank Tollman⟩ ⟨to *anticipate* charity by preventing poverty —Theodore Bienenstok⟩ ⟨sometimes we are able to *anticipate* a news event . . . but more often than not news breaks without any warning —S.W.Rumsam⟩ ⟨to *anticipate* the arrival of the next attack —H.G.Wells⟩

fore·see·abil·i·ty \(,)=,sēəˈbiləd·ē\ *n* **:** the quality or state of being foreseeable

fore·see·able \(ˈ)=ˈsēəbəl\ *adj* **1 :** being such as may reasonably be anticipated ⟨the ~ costs are well within the budget allowed⟩ ⟨~ problems⟩ **2 :** lying within the range for which forecasts are possible ⟨does not anticipate a tax cut in the ~ future⟩

fore·see·ing·ly \-ēiŋlē\ *adv* **:** with foresight

fore·se·er \(ˈ)=ˈsēə(r)\ *n* **:** one that foresees

¹foreset \=ˈ=\ *vt* [*fore-* + *set*] **:** to arrange beforehand

²foreset \ˈ=,=\ *adj* [*fore-* + *set* (past part. of *set*)] **:** of, relating to, or forming the steeper slope on the outer margin of a delta or the lee side of a dune or the sediments deposited on such a slope ⟨a silty ~ slope⟩

³foreset \"\ *also* **foreset bed** *n* **:** a foreset slope or layer (as of sediment or rock)

fore·sey \ˈfōrˈsī\ *n* -S [*fore-* + Sc *sey*] *Scot* **:** a cut of beef including the prime ribs and usu. some of the more anterior ribs

¹foreshadow \(ˈ)=ˈ==\ *vt* [*fore-* + *shadow* (v.)] **:** to shadow or typify beforehand **:** be the archetype or prototype of **:** PREFIGURE — **foreshadower** \(ˈ)=ˈ===\ *n* -S

²foreshadow \ˈ=,==\ *n* [*fore-* + *shadow* (n.)] **:** a shadow of a thing cast before; *broadly* **:** an indication of what is to come

foreshaft \ˈ=,=\ *n* [*fore-* + *shaft*] **:** the forward portion of the shaft of an arrow to which the footing is joined and to which the head is attached

foreshank \ˈ=,=\ *n* [*fore-* + *shank*] **:** SHIN 1b

foresheet \ˈ=,=\ *n* [*fore-* + *sheet*] **1 a :** one of the sheets of a foresail **b :** the rope by which the clew of a forecourse is held down — see SHIP illustration **2 foresheets** *pl* **:** the forward portion of an open boat

foreship \ˈ=,=\ *n* [ME *forship, foreship*, fr. OE *forscip*, fr. *for-, fore-* fore- + *scip* ship — more at SHIP] **:** the forward part of a ship

foreshock \ˈ=,=\ *n* [*fore-* + *shock*] **:** one of the accessory or minor tremors commonly preceding the principal shock of an earthquake

foreshore \ˈ=,=\ *n* [*fore-* + *shore*] **1 :** a strip of land margining a body of water (as a lake or stream) ⟨camped on the wooded ~ of the island⟩ ⟨the frozen gravel and clay thawed when exposed to the warm air, and soon innumerable small streams were running across the ~ —*Geog. Rev.*⟩ **2 :** the part of a seashore between the low-water line usu. at the seaward margin of a low-tide terrace and the upper limit of wave wash at high tide usu. marked by a beach scarp or berm ⟨under British law the ~ is ordinarily vested in the Crown⟩

foreshorten \=ˈ==\ *vt* [*fore-* + *shorten*] **1 :** to shorten (as a design) by proportionately contracting in the direction of depth so that an illusion of projection or extension in space is obtained **2 :** to make more compact **:** ABRIDGE, CONTRACT, SHORTEN ⟨distance and geography — though ~*ed* in the air age — still have strategical . . . meaning —H.W.Baldwin⟩ ⟨allows a long and scattered history to be gathered and ~*ed* —Susanne K. Langer⟩ ⟨dramatize and ~ the development of events —*Times Lit. Supp.*⟩

foreshortening *n* -S **:** the act of one that foreshortens or the state of being foreshortened; *often* **:** representation in art or literature in a foreshortened mode

foreshot \ˈ=,=\ *n* [*fore-* + *shot*] **:** the forerun in the distillation of whiskey

¹foreshow \=ˈ=\ *vt* [ME *forshewen, foreshewen*, fr. OE *foresceāwian*, fr. *fore-* + *scēawian* to show — more at SHOW] **1 a :** FORETELL **b :** to show beforehand **2** *obs* **:** BETOKEN, SHOW ⟨your looks ~ you have a gentle heart —Shak.⟩ — **foreshow·er** \"+ə(r)\ *n*

²foreshow *n* [*fore-* + *show*] *obs* **:** FORETOKEN

foreside \ˈ=,=\ *n* [ME *forside, foreside*, fr. *for-, fore-* fore + *side*] **:** the front side or part **:** FRONT

fore·sight \ˈfōr,sīt, ˈfȯr-, ˈfōə,-, ˈfȯ(ə),-, *usu* -īd.+V\ *n* [ME *forsight, foresight*, fr. *for-, fore-* fore- + *sight*] **1 :** an act or the power of foreseeing **:** PRESCIENCE, FOREKNOWLEDGE **2 :** an act of looking forward; *also* **:** a view forward **3 :** action in reference to the future **:** provident care **:** PRUDENCE, FORETHOUGHT **4 :** FRONT SIGHT **5 a :** a reading taken by a surveyor in leveling to determine the elevation of the point on which the rod rests when read — called also *minus sight* **b :** a sight or bearing taken in a forward direction by a compass or transit **syn** see PRUDENCE

fore·sight·ed \ˈ=ˈsīd·əd\ *adj* **:** having foresight; *esp* **:** provident for the future — **fore·sight·ed·ly** *adv* — **fore·sight·ed·ness** *n* -ES

fore·sight·ful \ˈ=,sītfəl\ *adj* **:** characterized by foresight ⟨~ plans⟩ **:** FORESIGHTED

fore·sight·less \ˈ=,=ləs\ *adj* **:** lacking in foresight — **fore·sight·less·ness** *n* -ES

foresignify \=ˈ===\ *vt* [*fore-* + *signify*] **:** to signify beforehand **:** FORESHOW, PREFIGURE

foreskin \ˈ=,=\ *n* [*fore-* + *skin*] **:** a fold of skin that covers the glans of the penis — called also *prepuce*

fore·slack *var of* FORSLACK

foresleeve \ˈ=,=\ *n* [ME *foresleve*, fr. *fore-* + *sleve* sleeve — more at SLEEVE] **:** an ornamental sleeve or part of a sleeve that can be slipped on or off

fore·slow *var of* FORSLOW

foresound \ˈ=,=\ *n* [*fore-* + *sound*] **:** one of the audible vibrations occas. noted immediately preceding or accompanying the first disturbance of the ground during an earthquake — usu. used in pl.

¹forespeak \=ˈ=\ *vt* [ME *forspeken, forespeken*, fr. *for-, fore-* fore- + *speken* to speak — more at SPEAK] **1 :** to speak of beforehand **:** FORETELL, PREDICT **2 :** to bespeak in advance ⟨all the rooms were *forespoken* weeks ago⟩

²fore·speak *var of* FORSPEAK

forespeaker \=ˈ==\ *n* [ME *forspeker*, fr. ¹*for* + *speker* speaker — more at SPEAKER] **1** *archaic* **:** one that speaks for another **2** [*fore-* + *speaker*] *obs* **:** one that speaks first

forespeaking *n* [fr. gerund of ¹*forespeak*] *obs* **:** PREDICTION

¹fore·spent *var of* FORSPENT

²forespent *adj, obs* **:** already spent **:** gone by **:** PAST

forespore \ˈ=,=\ *n* [*fore-* + *spore*] **:** a precursor of a spore; *specif* **:** a form preceding the endospore in some bacteria and characterized by diffuse response to chromatin stains

¹for·est \ˈfȯrəst, ˈfär-\ *n* -S *often attrib* [ME, fr. OF, fr. ML *forestis*, fr. L *foris* outside — more at FORUM] **1 a :** a tract of more or less wooded land formerly set apart in England primarily for the keeping and hunting of game though often including inhabited areas, usu. belonging to the sovereign, and having its own distinctive laws, courts, and officers — compare CHASE, PARK, WARREN **b** *Scot* **:** a tract of usu. treeless upland set apart for the keeping and hunting of deer **2 a :** a dense growth of trees and underbrush covering a large tract of land; *specif* **:** an extensive plant community of shrubs and trees in all stages of growth and decay with a closed canopy having the quality of self-perpetuation or of development into an ecological climax **b :** such a growth or community together with the land on which it stands **3** *archaic* **:** an uncultivated or waste area **4** *Brit* **:** a district once wooded but now under cultivation — used chiefly in place names **5** *usu cap* **:** a usu. dense and often hilly wooded region (as in equatorial Africa) inhabited by a people whose culture has become characteristic of the region ⟨~ Pygmies⟩ — contrasted with *bush* and *jungle* **6 :** something felt to resemble a forest: as **a :** a large number of upright objects ⟨a ~ of masts⟩ **b :** a great quantity ⟨from the ~ of answers received⟩ ⟨creating whole ~s of abstract terms in striving for a narrow precision of expression⟩

²forest \"\ *vt* -ED/-ING/-S **1 :** to cover with trees or forest **:** AFFOREST, REFOREST ⟨~*ed* with pine and spruce —*Amer. Guide Series: Minn.*⟩ **2 :** to place or hide in a forest

forestaff \ˈ=,=\ *n* [*fore-* + *staff*] **:** CROSS-STAFF 2

forestage \ˈ=,=\ *n, often attrib* [*fore-* + *stage*] **:** a part of a theater stage nearest the audience and usu. projecting beyond the curtain **:** APRON ⟨the stage is to be forty feet deep at the center, and there will be two small ~ areas at either side and forward of the proscenium —Alice Griffin⟩

forestair \ˈ=,=\ *n* [*fore-* + *stair*] *Scot* **:** an open outside staircase

for·est·al \ˈfȯrəstᵊl, ˈfär-\ *adj* **:** of, relating to, or being a forest ⟨~ resources⟩

¹fore·stall \ˈfōr,stȯl, ˈfȯr-, ˈfōə,-, ˈfȯ(ə),-\ *n* -S [ME *forstall, forestall*, fr. OE *foresteall*, fr. *fore-* + *steall* position, stall — more at STALL] **1 :** an offense under old English law of feloniously waylaying on the highway; *also* **:** the feudal franchise of jurisdiction over this offense **2 a :** FRONTSTALL **b :** FRONT 2d(2)

²forestall \=ˈ=\ *vt* -ED/-ING/-S [ME *forstallen, forestallen*, to ambush, intercept, fr. *forstall, forestall*, n.] **1** *archaic* **:** to intercept, lie in wait for, or stop the passage of (a person or thing) esp. on the road or highway and for a felonious purpose **2 :** to exclude, hinder, or prevent by prior occupation or by measures taken in advance **3 a :** to get ahead of **:** act in advance of **:** take or think of beforehand **b** *obs* **:** to take possession of in advance of someone or something else esp. to the exclusion or detriment of the latter **:** deprive by prior action **4** *obs* **:** OBSTRUCT, BESET ⟨~ a road⟩ **:** prevent ingress (as of a tenant) to (rented premises) **5 :** to anticipate or prevent the normal trading in (as a market) by buying or contracting for merchandise or provisions on their way to the market with the intention of reselling at a higher price, by dissuading persons from bringing merchandise or provisions to market, or by persuading those who have brought merchandise or provisions to market to raise the price ⟨~*ing* the wheat harvest and selling it at three times its cost —G.B.Shaw⟩ **syn** see PREVENT

fore·stall·er \-lə(r)\ *n* -S [ME *forstaller, forestaller*, fr. *forstallen, forestallen* + *-er*] **1 :** one that forestalls; *broadly* **:** MIDDLEMAN 3a **2 :** the act or offense of forestalling

fore·stall·ment \-lmənt\ *n* -S [ME *forstallment, forestallment*, fr. *forstallen, forestallen* + *-ment*] **:** an act of forestalling or the result of this **:** ANTICIPATION ⟨disheartened at the ~ of his invention⟩

forestarling \ˈ=,==\ *n* [*fore-* + *starling*] **:** an icebreaker in front of a bridge starling

for·est·a·tion \,fȯrəˈstāshən, ,fär-\ *n* -S [¹*forest* + *-ation*] **:** the establishment of a forest

forestay \ˈ=,=\ *n* [ME *forstay, forestay*, fr. *for-, fore-* fore- + *stay*] **:** a support in front or directed to the front; *specif* **:** a stay from the foremast head to the deck of a ship which supports the foremast in a fore-and-aft direction and to which the forestaysail is secured by hanks — see SHIP illustration

fore·stay·sail \=ˈ=,sāl, -,səl\ *n* **:** the aftermost headsail of a schooner, ketch, or yawl that is triangular in shape and set on hanks on the forestay — called also *foresail*; see SAIL illustration

forest bat *n* **:** any of several brightly marked vespertilionid bats (genus *Kerivoula*) of African forests — called also *painted bat*

forest cover *n* **:** land cover consisting of forest **:** the plants of a forest together with the products of their decay

for·est·ed \ˈfȯrəstəd, ˈfär-\ *adj* **:** covered with forest **:** WOODED

forestem \ˈ=,=\ *n* [ME *forstem, forestem*, fr. *for-, fore-* fore- + *stem*] *Scot* **:** STEM 2a(1)

for·est·er \ˈfȯrəstə(r), ˈfär-\ *n* -S [ME *forster, forester*, fr. OF *forestier* fr. *forest* + *-ier* -er — more at FOREST] **1 :** an officer formerly charged with the watching of a royal forest in Great Britain and with the preserving of its plants and game animals **2 a :** a person in charge of growing timber (as on an estate) **b :** a person who supervises the development, care, and management of forest land or forest parkland **3 :** an inhabitant or frequenter of the forest: as **a :** a half-wild English pony of the New Forest area **b** *also* **forester moth** (1) **:** any of various moths of the family Agaristidae — see EIGHT-SPOTTED FORESTER (2) **:** any of several brightly colored European moths of the family Zygaenidae **c** *Austral* **:** GIANT KANGAROO; *esp* **:** a male giant kangaroo **4** *usu cap* **:** a member of one of the major benevolent and fraternal orders

for·est·er·ship \-(r),ship\ *n* **:** the office of or an appointment as forester

forest fire *n* **:** an uncontrolled fire in a wooded area — see CROWN FIRE, GROUND FIRE

forest floor *n* **:** the richly organic layer of soil in a forest consisting of the more or less decayed debris (as fallen leaves and branches) that makes up the litter, duff, and leaf mold and commonly including the A-horizon, B-horizon, and C-horizon of the soil proper

forest fly *n* **:** a winged blood-sucking fly (*Hippobosca equina*) that is related to the sheep ked and that bites horses and cattle

forest green *n* **1 :** a dark green that is yellower and stronger than evergreen or average bottle green **2 :** a moderate olive green that is greener and deeper than holly green (sense 2), yellower, lighter, and stronger than cypress, and greener, stronger, and slightly darker than Lincoln green

forest hog *or* **forest pig** *n* **:** a large dark-colored wild pig (*Hylochoerus meinertzhageni*) native to the forested region of tropical Africa and closely related to the babirusa

fo·res·tial \fəˈrestēəl, -s(h)chəl\ *adj* [¹*forest* + *-ial*] **:** FORESTAL

forestick \ˈ=,=\ *n* [*fore-* + *stick*] **:** the front log of an open log fire (as in a fireplace) in which the main logs are parallel in arrangement

for·es·ti·e·ra \,fȯrəstēˈirə, ,fär-, -ēˈerə, -ˈstirə\ *n* [NL, after Pierre Gaspard *Forestier* †1847 Fr. physician] **1** *cap* **:** a genus of sometimes spiny American shrubs or trees (family Oleaceae) with simple opposite leaves and inconspicuous flowers followed by single-seeded drupes **2** -S **:** any plant of the genus *Forestiera* — see TANGLEBUSH

foresting *pres part of* FOREST

forest law *n* **:** a law (as for the protection of game or preservation of timber) that is peculiarly applicable in a forest; *esp* **:** one of several laws enacted by William I and other Norman English kings for the protection of the royal forests

for·est·less \ˈfȯrəstləs, ˈfär-\ *adj* **:** having no forests **:** lacking wooded areas ⟨the wide ~ plains⟩

forestlike \ˈ=,=\ *adj* **:** like or like that of a forest

forest mahogany *n* **:** any of several Australian trees of the genus *Eucalyptus*: as **a :** TALLOWWOOD **b :** RED MAHOGANY **c :** RED GUM

forest mole *n* **:** a very large partially diurnal forest-dwelling southern African mole (*Chrysospalax trevelyani*) closely related to the golden moles

forest negro *n, often cap F, cap N* **:** an African characterized by possession of all the typical negroid traits highly developed and supposed to be most common in the forests of tropical West Africa including much of the Niger and Congo basins

forest oak *n, Austral* **:** a she-oak (esp. *Casuarina torulosa*)

forestock \ˈ=,=\ *n* [*fore-* + *stock*] **:** FORE-END 2

forest of dean red *often cap F&D* [fr. *Forest of Dean*, a kind of sandstone, fr. *Forest of Dean*, Gloucestershire, Eng.] **:** ENGLISH RED 2a

forestomach \ˈ=,==\ *n* [*fore-* + *stomach*] **:** the cardiac part of the stomach

forest pathology *n* **:** a branch of plant pathology that deals with diseases of trees

forest ranger *n* **:** an officer charged with the duty of patrolling and guarding a forest; *esp* **:** one in charge of the management and protection of a portion of a public forest

forest red gum *n* **:** a broad-leaved Australian eucalypt (*Eucalyptus tereticornis*) yielding a heavy durable dark red timber

forestroke \ˈ=,=\ *n* [*fore-* + *stroke*] **:** a forward stroke (as in various games)

for·est·ry \ˈfȯrəstrē, ˈfär-, -ri\ *n* -ES *often attrib* [MF *foresterie*, fr. *forest* + *-erie* -ery] **1** *Scots law* **:** a right to the privileges of a royal forest; *also* **:** a tract over which such privileges are enjoyed **2 :** forest land **:** FOREST **3 :** a science of developing, caring for, or cultivating forests **:** the management of growing timber

forests *pl of* FOREST, *pres 3d sing of* FOREST

forest school *n* **:** a school of forestry

forest shrew *n* **:** any of several small shrews (genus *Sylvisorex*) found in forests at high elevations in tropical Africa

forest tea *n* **:** a Philippine plant (*Ehretia microphylla*) used as a substitute for tea in the Philippines esp. by resident Chinese

forest tent caterpillar *n* **:** a hairy orange-striped and orange-spotted bluish tent caterpillar (*Malacosoma disstria*) that is gregarious, spins a carpet rather than a tent, and is sometimes a serious defoliator of deciduous trees

forest type *n* **:** similarity of composition and development (as in two or more stands of trees) due to the impact of corresponding physical and biological factors; *sometimes* **:** a forest association

for·esty \ˈfȯrəstē, ˈfär-\ *adj* **:** covered with or abounding in forests

forest yaws *n* **:** ESPUNDIA

foreswear *var of* FORSWEAR

foretack \ˈ=,=\ *n* [*fore-* + *tack*] **:** a rope by which the tack of a square foresail is hauled and held

foretackle \ˈ=,==\ *n* [*fore-* + *tackle*] **:** the tackle that hooks on to the pendant on the foremast

foretake *vt* [*fore-* + *take*] *obs* **:** ANTICIPATE, PRESUPPOSE

foretalk \ˈ=,=\ *also* **foretalking** \ˈ=ˈ==\ *n* **:** PREFACE

¹foretaste \ˈ=,=\ *n* [ME *fortaste, foretaste*, fr. *for-, fore-* fore- + *taste*] **1 :** something that serves to indicate or warn of what is to come ⟨the drill had a ~ of rain⟩ **2 :** a taste or trial in advance **:** a small anticipatory sample ⟨those brilliant February days that sometimes come as a ~ of spring⟩ ⟨a journey like this was only a ~, too rewarding not to be repeated —Van Wyck Brooks⟩

²foretaste \=ˈ=\ *vt* [ME *fortasten, foretasten*, fr. *for-, fore-* fore- + *tasten* to taste — more at TASTE] **:** to taste beforehand **:** have a foretaste of **:** ANTICIPATE ⟨*foretasting* his discharge from the army on a few weekend pass⟩

fore·tast·er \"+ə(r)\ *n* **:** one that foretastes

fore·tell \(ˈ)fōrˈtel, (ˈ)fȯr, (ˈ)fōə-, (ˈ)fȯ(ə)-\ *vb* [ME *fortellen, foretellen*, fr. *for-, fore-* fore- + *tellen* to tell — more at TELL] *vt* **1 :** to tell of from foreknowledge **:** PREDICT, PROPHESY **2** *obs* **:** to tell, acquaint, or command beforehand ~ *vi, obs* **:** to utter prediction **:** PROPHESY

syn PREDICT, FORECAST, PROPHESY, PROGNOSTICATE, AUGUR, PRESAGE, PORTEND, FOREBODE: FORETELL applies to telling of the coming of some future event by any procedure or source of information ⟨some sorcerer . . . had *foretold* —Alfred Tennyson⟩ ⟨the marvelous exactness with which eclipses are *foretold* —K.K.Darrow⟩ PREDICT is closely synonymous with FORETELL; it may be preferred in today's English to suggest or apply to inference from facts and laws of nature ⟨if we can trace certain changes slowly at work in the period preceding our own we may be able to *predict* with some probability that these changes will continue for some time at least to operate in the same direction —W.R.Inge⟩ ⟨astronomers, who developed mathematics to such a degree that it could *predict* the wanderings of the planets and their satellites —K.K.Darrow⟩ FORECAST may suggest concomitant anticipation, consideration of effects, and provision for one's needs ⟨he *forecast* the war, announced in his message the intention to put the state militia on a war footing —*Encyc. Americana*⟩ PROPHESY may imply mystic inspiration, real or pretended, supernatural machinery, or augury or pontifical assurance ⟨ancestral voices *prophesying* war —S.T.Coleridge⟩ ⟨professional astrologists make a practice of *prophesying* the presidency for budding statesmen —S.H.Adams⟩ PROGNOSTICATE may indicate learned or skilled use of symptoms and signs; it is applicable to a physician's procedure ⟨*prognosticating* a quick recovery⟩ ⟨the slight moisture resolved itself into a monotonous smiting of earth by heaven, in torrents to which no end could be *prognosticated* —Thomas Hardy⟩ AUGUR may indicate foreknowing the future by interpreting omens; used in relation to things and conditions, it indicates presentation as an omen of good or evil ⟨the morrow brought a very sober-looking morning; the sun making only a few efforts to appear; and Catherine *augured* from it everything most favorable to her wishes —Jane Austen⟩ PRESAGE and PORTEND, the latter usu. used of evil things or adverse developments, may apply to foreshadowing or suggesting a coming event or indicating its likelihood, sometimes by occult procedures ⟨they think that the sight of a meteor *presages* some misfortune —J.G.Frazer⟩ ⟨the yellow and vapory sunset . . . had *presaged* change —Thomas Hardy⟩ ⟨all the signs, the position of the stars, and the very disposition of nature *portended* war and disaster⟩ ⟨the appearance of these spectral flames, it is claimed, is not exclusively confined to *portending* the demise of someone already ill —*Irish Digest*⟩ FOREBODE indicates a feeling, indefinable, perhaps ill-based, but insistent and worrisome, or an indication calling forth worrisome or dread feeling ⟨his heart *forebodes* a mystery —Alfred Tennyson⟩ BODE applies to indication of future probability, often indefinite and often dire ⟨an eternal nightmare which, even for the richest and safest of nations, *bodes* catastrophes —A.L.Guérard⟩ ⟨the mood of quiet, grim resolution which here prevails *bodes* ill for those who conspired and collaborated to murder world peace —F.D.Roosevelt⟩ ⟨the dynamics of social change, which is *foreboded* in the emotional tensions of individuals —Franz Alexander⟩

fore·tell·able \(')=¦teləbəl\ *adj* **:** being of a kind that may be anticipated and foretold ⟨a ~ disaster⟩

fore·tell·er \(')=¦telə(r)\ *n* **:** one that foretells **:** a predictor or prophet

forethigh \'=,=\ *n* [*fore-* + *thigh*] **:** the part of the forelimb of a quadruped (as a horse) lying between elbow and knee

forethink \=¦=\ *vb* [ME *forthinken, forethinken, forthenken, forethenken*, fr. OE *forethencan*, fr. *fore-* + *thencan* to think — more at THINK] *vt* **:** to consider (something) beforehand; *broadly* **:** to anticipate in the mind **:** PROGNOSTICATE ~ *vi, obs* **:** to think beforehand **:** PLAN

fore·think·er \"+ə(r)\ *n* **:** one that forethinks

[1]**fore·thought** \'fōr,thȯt, 'fȯr-, 'fōə-, 'fȯ(ə),-, *usu* -ȯd.+V\ *n* [ME *forthought, forethought*, fr. *for-, fore-* + *thought*, n.] **1 :** a thinking or planning out in advance **:** PREMEDITATION ⟨this was no spontaneous crime but a product of careful ~⟩ **2 :** prior thought **:** CONSIDERATION ⟨turned without ~ and offered his hand⟩ **3 :** prudent thought or consideration for the future **:** provident care ⟨her ~ saw that we never lacked anything we really needed⟩ **syn** see PRUDENCE

[2]**forethought** \"\ *adj* [ME *forthought, forethought*, fr. past part. of *forthinken, forethinken*] **:** thought of or planned beforehand **:** AFORETHOUGHT; *often* **:** DELIBERATE

fore·thought·ed \-ȯdəd\ *adj* **:** having or marked by forethought ⟨a ~ person who is never at a loss for the next step⟩ — **fore·thought·ed·ly** *adv*

fore·thought·ful \(')=¦thȯtfəl\ *adj* **:** full of or having forethought **:** PROVIDENT ⟨careful ~ planning⟩ — **fore·thought·ful·ly** \-fəlē, -li\ *adv* — **fore·thought·ful·ness** *n* -ES

fore·thought·less \'=,=ləs\ *adj* **:** lacking forethought

foretime \'=,=\ *n* [*fore-* + *time*] **:** former or past time **:** the time before the present ⟨the heroic ~ of our remotest fathers⟩

foretimed \(')=¦=\ *adj* [*fore-* + *timed*] **:** existing too soon **:** ANTEDATED ⟨a man ~ by a century⟩

[1]**foretoken** \'=,==\ *n* [ME *fortoken, foretoken*, fr. OE *foretācn*, fr. *fore-* + *tācn* token, sign — more at TOKEN] **:** a premonitory sign or warning

[2]**foretoken** \=¦==\ *vt* [ME *fortokenen, foretokenen*, fr. *fortoken, foretoken*, n.] **:** to serve as advance warning of **:** FORESHOW, PROMISE ⟨the clear air and bright sunset seemed to ~ good weather⟩

fore-tooth \'=,=\ *n* [*fore-* + *tooth*] **:** one of the teeth in the forepart of the mouth **:** INCISOR

fore·top \'fōr,täp, 'fȯr-, 'fōə-, 'fȯ(ə),-, *or in sense 3* -,təp\ *n* [ME *fortop, foretop*, fr. *for-, fore-* fore- + *top*] **1** *archaic* **:** the front of the crown of the head; *also* **:** the crown of the head **2 :** hair on the forepart of the head: as **a** *archaic* **:** an ornamental arrangement of the front of a wig or hairdo **b :** the forelock of a horse **3 a :** the platform at the head of a ship's foremast — see SHIP illustration **b :** FORETOPMAN

fore-topgallant \¦=,täp¦galənt, -,tə(p)¦-\ *adj* [*fore-* + *topgallant*] **:** of, relating to, or being a part (as a mast, sail, or yard) next above the fore-topmast ⟨the *fore-topgallant* sail⟩ — see SAIL illustration

fore·top·man \'=¦täpmən, '=,täpmən, -,təp-\ *n, pl* **foretopmen** [*foretop* + *man*] **:** a member of a ship's crew on duty on the foremast and above

fore-topmast \=¦=,mast, -,maa(ə)st, -,mȧst, -,məst\ *n* [*fore-* + *topmast*] **:** a ship's mast next above the foremast

fore-topsail \-,sāl, -,səl\ *n* [*fore-* + *topsail*] **:** the sail above the foresail set on the fore-topmast — see SAIL illustration

foretruck \'=,=\ *n* [*fore-* + *truck*] **:** the truck at the head of a foremast

foreturn \'=,=\ *n* [*fore-* + *turn*] **:** the twist of the yarns or wires composing a strand of a rope — compare AFTERTURN

[1]**for·ev·er** \fə'revə(r), fō'- *sometimes* fə'evə *or* fō'evə\ *adv* [ME *for ever*] **1 :** for a limitless time or endless ages **:** EVERLASTINGLY, ETERNALLY **2 :** at all times **:** ALWAYS, CONTINUALLY, INCESSANTLY

[2]**forever** \"\ *n* -S **:** ETERNITY

for·ev·er·more \fə,revər'mō(ə)r, fō,-, -'mȯ(ə)r; fə,revə'mōə, fō,-, -'mȯ(ə) *sometimes* fə,e- *or* fō,e-\ *adv* [¹*for* + *evermore*] **:** FOREVER

for·ev·er·ness *n* -ES **:** ETERNITY; *often* **:** a seemingly interminable duration ⟨will never forget the ~ of that day of waiting⟩

forewarm \=¦=\ *vt* [*fore-* + *warm*] **:** PREHEAT — **forewarmer** \'=,==\ *n*

fore·warn \fōr'wȯ(ə)rn, fȯr-; fōə'wȯ(ə)n, fȯ(ə)'-\ *vt* [ME *forwarnen, forewarnen*, fr. *for-, fore-* fore- + *warnen* to warn — more at WARN] **:** to warn in advance: as **a :** to give previous notice or information to ⟨we were ~*ed* to expect you before dark⟩ **b :** to caution in advance esp. in the form of an admonition ⟨let me ~ you, young man, you'll be sorry if you are late for supper⟩ **syn** see WARN

fore·warn·er \-nə(r)\ *n* [ME *forwarner, forewarner*, fr. *forwarnen, forewarnen* + *-er*] **:** one that forewarns

fore·warn·ing·ly \-niŋlē\ *adv* **:** so as to forewarn

forewaters \'=,==\ *n pl* [*fore-* + *waters*] **:** AMNIOTIC FLUID

forewent *past of* FOREGO

fore wing *n* [³*fore*] **:** either member of the anterior pair of wings of a 4-winged insect

forewoman \'=,==\ *n, pl* **forewomen** [*fore-* + *woman*] **:** FORELADY

fore·word \'fōr,wərd, 'fȯr-, -,wərd; 'fōə,wəd, 'fȯ(ə),-, -,wəd\ *n* [*fore-* + *word*; prob. trans. of G *vorwort*] **:** PREFACE; *often* **:** front matter likely to be of interest but not necessarily essential for the understanding of the text of a book and commonly written by someone other than the author of the text

foreworld \'=,=\ *n* [*fore-* + *world*; prob. trans. of G *vorwelt*] **:** the primeval or ancient world

foreworn *var of* FORWORN

[1]**foreyard** \'=,=\ *n* [ME *foryerd, foreyerd*, fr. *for-, fore-* fore- + *yerd* yard — more at YARD (enclosure)] **:** a yard in front

[2]**foreyard** \"\ *n* [³*fore-* + *yard* (spar)] **:** the lowest yard on a foremast — see SHIP illustration

for·fairn \fər'färn\ *adj* [ME *forfaren*, past part. of *forfaren* to perish, destroy, go astray, fr. *for-* + *faran* to travel, go — more at FARE] **1** *Scot* **:** FORLORN, BEREFT **2** *Scot* **:** worn out and decrepit (as with age) **:** EXHAUSTED

for·far \'fȯrfər\ *also* **for·fars** \-rz\ *n, pl* **forfars** [fr. *Forfar*, county and town in Scotland where it was first made] **:** a coarse heavy linen cloth

for·far·shire \'==,shi(ə)r, -iə-, -shə(r)\ *or* **forfar** *adj, usu cap* [fr. *Forfarshire* or county of *Forfar*, Scotland] **:** ANGUS

for·fault \'fȯrfȯt\ *archaic Scot var of* FORFEIT

[1]**for·feit** \'fȯrfət, -ô(ə)f-, *usu* -əd.+V\ *n* -S [ME *forfait, forfet*, fr. MF, fr. past part. of *forfaire* to commit a crime, lose possession because of a crime committed, prob. fr. *for, fors* outside, out of + *faire* to make, do, fr. L *facere* — more at FORECLOSE, DO] **1** *obs* **:** MISDEED, CRIME, HARM **2 :** something which is lost or the right to which is alienated by a crime, offense, neglect of duty, or breach of contract **:** a thing forfeit or forfeited; *often* **:** FINE, MULCT, PENALTY ⟨he who murders pays the ~ of his life⟩ **3 :** forfeiture esp. of civil rights **4 a :** something deposited (as for making some mistake in a game) and then redeemed on payment of a fine **b forfeits** *pl but sing in constr* **:** a game in which forfeits are exacted

[2]**forfeit** \"\ *vb* -ED/-ING/-S [ME *forfaiten, forfeten*, fr. *forfait, forfet*, n.] *vi* **1** *obs* **:** to be guilty of a misdeed **2 :** to yield or be subject to a forfeit ⟨if they fail or refuse to make delivery by the 15th they must ~⟩ ~ *vt* **1 :** to lose or lose the right to by some error, fault, offense, or crime **:** alienate the right to possess by some neglect or crime **:** have to pay as a forfeit ⟨~*ed* his estate by treason⟩ ⟨~*ing* respect by his actions⟩ **2 a :** to subject (as property) to confiscation as a forfeit **b** *archaic* **:** to subject to forfeiture of property **:** confiscate the estate or possessions of — used of government action **3** *obs* **:** to cause the forfeiture or loss of

[3]**forfeit** \"\ *adj* [ME *forfait, forfet*, fr. MF, fr. past part. of *forfaire*] **:** lost or alienated for an error, fault, offense, breach of condition or legal duty, or crime ⟨thy wealth being ~ to the state —Shak.⟩

for·feit·able \-fəd·əbəl\ *adj* [ME *forfaitable, forfetable*, fr. *forfaiten, forfeten* + *-able*] **:** capable of being forfeited **:** subject to forfeiture — **for·feit·able·ness** *n* -ES

for·feit·er \-fəd·ə(r)\ *n* -S [ME *forfaitour, forfetour*, fr. MF *forfaiteur, forfetour*, fr. *forfait, forfet* + *-eur* -or] **:** one that forfeits

for·feit·ure \-fə,chu̇(ə)r, -,chüə, -chə(r), -,tyu̇-, -,tu̇-\ *n* -S [ME *forfaiture, forfeture*, fr. MF, fr. *forfait, forfet* + *-ure*] **1 a :** the divesting of the ownership of particular property of a person on account of the breach of a legal duty and without any compensation to him **:** the loss of property or money on account of one's breach of the terms of an agreement, bond, or other legal obligation **b :** loss of some right, privilege, estate, honor, office, or effects in consequence of a crime, offense, breach of condition, or other act **2 :** the loss of something through one's own act ⟨repeated roughness leads to ~ of the game⟩ ⟨by his trickery he gained only complete ~ of his father's trust⟩ **3 :** something (as property or money) lost as a forfeit

forfeiture bond *n* **:** a bond providing for forfeiture of the full penalty upon breach of the condition of the bond

for·fend \(')fȯr'fend, 'fȯ(ə)'-\ *also* **fore·fend** \(')fōr-, -ȯr'-, -ōə-,-ȯ(ə)'-\ *vt* [ME *forfenden*; fr. *for-* + *fenden* to fend — more at FEND] **1 a** *archaic* **:** FORBID, PROHIBIT **b :** to ward off **:** AVERT, PREVENT ⟨may God ~ such an unhappy fate⟩ ⟨~ the crash of civilization —*Saturday Rev.*⟩ ⟨may Heaven ~ that she should die so young⟩ **2 :** PROTECT, PRESERVE, SECURE ⟨gathered in an isolated area to ~ themselves from the epidemic⟩

for·fi·ca·tion \,fȯ(r)fə'kāshən\ *n* -S [L *forfic-, forfex* scissors, shears (perh. alter. of *forcip-, forceps*) + E *-ation* — more at FORCEPS] **:** a deep furcation

for·fic·i·form \fȯr'fisə,fȯrm\ *adj* [L *forfic-, forfex* + E *-iform*] **:** shaped like a scissors; *usu* **:** having or being forcipulate pedicellariae with two valves that do not cross when closed — compare FORCIPIFORM

for·fic·u·la \-'fikyələ\ *n, cap* [NL, fr. L, small scissors, dim. of *forfic-, forfex*] **:** a genus (the type of the family Forficulidae) of earwigs that are sometimes destructive to cultivated bulbs

for·fic·u·late \-lət, -,lāt\ *adj* [L *forficula* + E *-ate*] **:** FORKED, FURCATE — used esp. of plant or animal parts (as certain pedicellariae); compare FORCIPULATE

for·fi·cu·li·dae \,fȯrfə'kyüləˌdē\ *n pl, cap* [NL, fr. *Forficula*, type genus + *-idae*] **:** a large cosmopolitan family of insects (order Dermaptera) that have the abdomen depressed and the forceps flattened or cylindrical and that comprise the typical earwigs — see FORFICULA

for·fough·en *or* **for·fouch·en** \fər'fōkən, -ăk-, -ōk-\ *or* **for·fought·en** \-ktən\ *adj* [ME *forfoughten*, fr. *for-* + *foughten*, past part. of *fighten* to fight — more at FIGHT] *chiefly Scot* **:** worn out and depressed **:** EXHAUSTED

for·gainst \fər'gān(t)st, -gen-\ *prep* [ME *forgaines, forgenes*, fr. *fore-* + *againes, agenes* against — more at AGAINST] *chiefly Scot* **:** AGAINST

forgat *archaic past of* FORGET

for·gath·er \(')fȯr'gaḵthə(r), -ȯ(ə)'-, ¦eth-\ *or* **fore·gath·er** \(')fōr'-, -ȯr'-, -ōə'-, -ȯ(ə)'-\ *vi* [ME (Sc dial.) *forgadderen*, fr. *for-* + *gadderen* to gather — more at GATHER] **1 a :** to come together ⟨these two old buzzards have got to *foregather* in secret —P.G.Wodehouse⟩ **:** CONVENE, ASSEMBLE ⟨where young musicians could ~ for stimulus and instruction —*Atlantic*⟩ **b :** to come together in a social group **:** consort socially ⟨~*s* with a squad of his admirers for lunch —H.H.Martin⟩ **2 :** to meet someone usu. incidentally ⟨~*ed* with many a homespun philosopher in his travels⟩

forgave *past of* FORGIVE

[1]**forge** \'fō(ə)rj, -ȯ(ə)rj,-ōəj,-ȯ(ə)j\ *n* -S [ME, fr. OF, fr. L *fabrica* workshop of an artisan who works in hard materials, smithy, fr. *fabr-, faber* artisan, smith + *-ica* (fr. fem. of *-icus* -ic) — more at DAFT] **1 a :** a place or establishment where iron or other metal is wrought by heating and hammering; *usu* **:** a furnace or a shop with its furnace where metal is heated and wrought **:** SMITHY **b :** a workshop where wrought iron is produced directly from the ore or where iron is rendered malleable by puddling and shingling **:** SHINGLING MILL, BLOOMERY **2** *obs* **:** MANUFACTURE, FABRICATION, PRODUCTION; *sometimes* **:** the act of forging

forge 1a

[2]**forge** \"\ *vb* -ED/-ING/-S [ME *forgen*, fr. MF *forgier*, fr. L *fabricare*, *fabricari* to fashion, construct, forge, fr. *fabrica*] *vt* **1 a :** to form by heating and hammering **:** beat (as a metal) into a particular shape ⟨Mars's armor *forged* for proof eterne —Shak.⟩ **b :** to form (metal) by a mechanical or hydraulic press with or without heat **2 :** to form or shape out in any way **:** FASHION, MAKE, PRODUCE ⟨attempting to ~ an agreement between the conflicting groups⟩ ⟨a man who has chosen to ~ himself a coherent outlook sooner than surrender to disruptive tendencies —Cecil Sprigge⟩ **3 :** to make or imitate falsely ⟨did not hesitate to ~ his own character references⟩ ⟨*forged* rare postage stamps that fooled expert philatelists⟩; *specif* **:** to alter (a writing) in respect of a material matter with intent to defraud ⟨he *forged* a check for $20⟩ ~ *vi* **1 :** to work at a forge **:** do forging **2 :** to commit forgery ⟨living by trickery and *forging*⟩ **3** *of a horse* **:** to make a clicking noise by overreaching so that a hind shoe hits a fore shoe **syn** see MAKE

[3]**forge** \"\ *vi* -ED/-ING/-S [origin unknown] **1 a :** to move forward or ahead steadily but slowly or gradually ⟨the ship continued to ~ ahead after the sails were furled⟩ **b :** to move with a sudden increase of speed and power ⟨the ship *forged* ahead as the breeze filled her sails⟩ ⟨the runner *forged* into the lead in the stretch⟩ **2 :** PROGRESS, ADVANCE ⟨companies that *forged* to prominence on a single basic invention⟩

forge·a·bil·i·ty \,=ə'biləd·ē, -ətē, -i\ *n* **:** suitability for being forged ⟨some alloys exhibit greater ~ than others⟩

forge·able \'=əbəl\ *adj* **:** capable of or suitable for being forged — used chiefly of metals

forge·man \'=mən\ *n, pl* **forgemen** **:** SMITH 1a

for·ger \'fōrjə(r), -ōrj-, -ōəj-, -ȯ(ə)j-\ *n* -S [ME *forger, forgeour*, fr. MF *forgeur*, fr. *forgier* + *-eur* -or] **1 a** *obs* **:** an author or maker **b :** FALSIFIER; *specif* **:** a creator of false tales **c :** a person guilty of forgery (as of a document) **2 :** one that forges metals; *esp* **:** a person whose work is to forge a specified thing or material ⟨an iron ~⟩ ⟨experienced axle ~*s*⟩

for·gery \-j(ə)rē, -ri\ *n* -ES [²*forge* + *-ery*] **1** *obs* **:** the act or art of forging metal **2** *archaic* **:** the act of inventing or devising **:** INVENTION; *often* **:** FEIGNING, FICTION **3 :** an act of forging; *usu* **:** the crime of falsely and with fraudulent intent making or altering a writing or other instrument that if genuine might apparently be of legal effect on the rights of another — see FALSI CRIMEN **4 :** something produced by forging, fabricating, or counterfeiting ⟨17th century *forgeries* of medieval documents⟩ ⟨the *forgeries* of jealousy —Shak.⟩

forgery bond *n* **:** insurance against loss from forgery or alteration of negotiable instruments or evidences of debt or ownership

[1]**for·get** \fə(r)'get *also* fō(r)'-, *usu* -ed.+V\ *vb* **for·got** \-gät, *usu* -äd.+V\ *or archaic* **for·gat** \-gat, *usu* -ad.+V\ **for·got·ten** \-gätᵊn\ *or* **forgot**; **forgetting**; **forgets** [ME *forgeten, foryeten*, fr. OE *forgietan, forgeotan, forgitan* (akin to OS *fargetan* to forget, OHG *firgezzan*), fr. *for-* + *-gietan, -geotan, -gitan* (akin to ON *geta* to get) — more at GET] *vt* **1 a :** to lose the remembrance of **:** let go from the memory **:** be unable to think of or recall ⟨soon *forgot* her father's warning⟩ ⟨*forgetting* past favors and old friends⟩ **b** *obs* **:** to lose the power or use of **:** cease from doing **2 :** to omit or disregard unintentionally **:** NEGLECT ⟨I *forgot* to close the door⟩ **3 :** to treat with inattention or disregard **:** SLIGHT ⟨the successful leader does not ~ his subordinates⟩ ⟨*forgot* her lessons until bedtime⟩ ⟨lend a hand and I'll not ~ you when I'm paid⟩ **4 :** to disregard intentionally **:** OVERLOOK — usu. used in the imperative ⟨~ it⟩ ~ *vi* **1 :** to cease remembering or noticing ⟨she *forgot* about the note to her mother⟩ ⟨if we forgive and ~ we may hope to be forgiven⟩ **2 :** to fail to become mindful at the intended or proper time ⟨*forgot* about paying the bill until the discount date was past⟩ ⟨if you ~ about turning down the oven you will burn the roast⟩ **syn** see NEGLECT — **forget oneself :** to do something or behave in a manner unworthy of one **:** lose one's dignity, temper, or self-control

[2]**forget** \"\ *n* -S **:** an act of forgetting

[3]**for·get** \fə(r)jət, -,jet\ *n* -S [by alter.] **:** FOURCHETTE 2

for·get·ful \fə(r)'getfəl *also* fō(r)'-\ *adj* [ME *forgetful, foryetful*, fr. *forgeten, foryeten* + *-ful*] **1 :** apt to forget **:** having a poor memory ⟨he was so ~ that he constantly missed appointments⟩ **2 :** characterized by or indulging in heedless or negligent failure to remember or pay attention ⟨~ of her responsibilities⟩ **3 :** inducing oblivion **:** causing an end to awareness or consideration ⟨lulled by ~ sleep⟩

syn OBLIVIOUS, UNMINDFUL: FORGETFUL may describe a tendency not to remember through defective memory; it may imply a negligent or heedless failure to keep in mind something that should be remembered ⟨so *forgetful* as to be duped into making "deals" at the expense of our allies —F.D.Roosevelt⟩ OBLIVIOUS may suggest a failure to notice, an inability to remember due to exterior forces or conditions, or a determination to hold from one's cognition; the word is sometimes a synonym of *unconscious* and *unaware* ⟨those who hope to render themselves, through absorption in the mere habit and technique of writing poetry, *oblivious* to the harsh interruptions of reality —C.D.Lewis⟩ ⟨I was often seasick but that semicomatose condition has its advantage—it makes one *oblivious* to danger —Herbert Hoover⟩ ⟨he is *oblivious* of all distractions when he is wrapped up in his work —E.J.Kahn⟩ UNMINDFUL may be close to FORGETFUL; it may suggest inattention and heedlessness; it may indicate deliberate purposive ignoring and thrusting from the mind ⟨totally *unmindful* of their mutual dependence —*Amer. Guide Series: Minn.*⟩ ⟨we sat about *unmindful* of the winds and the snow —H.A. Chippendale⟩

for·get·ful·ly \-fəlē, -li\ *adv* **:** in a forgetful manner

for·get·ful·ness *n* -ES [ME *forgetfulnesse, foryetfulnesse*, fr. *forgetful, foryetful* + *-nesse* -ness] **:** the act or state of being forgetful

for·ge·tive \'fōrjə|d·iv, -ōj-|, tiv\ *adj* [prob. fr. ²*forge* + *-tive* (as in *inventive*)] **:** INVENTIVE, PRODUCTIVE, IMAGINATIVE

forget-me-not \=¦=(,)=,=\ *n* -S **1 a :** any of several small herbaceous plants constituting the genus *Myosotis*, having usu. bright blue or white flowers arranged in a scorpioid raceme, and including some that are cultivated as ornamentals; *esp* **:** a perennial herb (*M. scorpioides*) with angular succulent stems, rough pubescent leaves, and sky-blue flowers with yellow centers that is prob. native to Europe but now widely distributed in temperate No. America **b :** any of various plants resembling the forget-me-nots esp. in clear blue color of flowers — usu. used with a qualifying term; see CAPE FORGET-ME-NOT, CHINESE FORGET-ME-NOT **2** *or* **forget-me-not blue a :** a variable color averaging a light blue that is greener and paler than average della Robbia blue **b :** a pale to grayish blue that is greener and less strong than Alice blue — called also *myosotis blue*

forgets *pres 3d sing of* FORGET, *pl of* FORGET

for·get·ta·ble \fə(r)'ged·əbəl, -etəb- *also* fō(r)'-\ *adj* [¹*forget* + *-able*] **:** fit or likely to be forgotten — **for·get·ta·ble·ness** *n* -ES

for·get·ter \-'ged·ə(r), -etə-\ *n* -S [ME *forgeter, foryeter*, fr. *forgeten, foryeten* to forget + *-er*] **:** one that forgets esp. habitually or deliberately

for·get·tery \-ed·ərē, -etə-, -ri\ *n* -ES [¹*forget* + *-ery*] **:** a faculty for forgetting **:** a poor memory ⟨a remarkable ~ for those irksome little chores⟩ ⟨a well-managed ~ is often as important as a good memory⟩

forgetting *pres part of* FORGET

for·get·ting·ly *adv* **:** by forgetting **:** ABSENTMINDEDLY

forge water *n* [¹*forge*] **:** a tonic formerly popular consisting of water in which heated irons have been thrust

forge welding *n* **:** the uniting of two pieces of hot metal by hammering them together on an anvil

for·gie \fər'gē\ *Scot var of* FORGIVE

forging *n* -S [ME, fr. gerund of *forgen* to forge — more at FORGE] **1 :** the act of one that forms by heating and hammering **2 a :** a piece of forged work (as in iron) **3 :** FORGERY 3

forging machine *n* **:** a forging press that operates in a horizontal position (as for the upsetting of bolts)

forging press *n* **:** a punch press that forges metal by subjecting it to heavy pressure between dies

forging roll *n* **:** a rolling mill that forges comparatively uniform shapes by rolls of variable radii around the circumference

for·giv·able \fə(r)'givəbəl *also* fōr'-\ *adj* **:** being of a kind that can be forgiven ⟨a ~ error⟩ — **for·giv·able·ness** \-nəs\ *n* -ES

for·giv·ably \-əblē, -li\ *adv* **:** in a forgivable manner

for·give \fə(r)'giv *also* fō(r)'-\ *vb* **for·gave** \-'gāv\ **for·giv·en** \-'givən, -ibᵊm\ **forgiving; forgives** [ME *foryeven, foryiven, forgeven, forgiven*, fr. OE *forgiefan, forgifan* (akin to OS *fargeban* to give, forgive, promise, OHG *firgeban* to give, forgive, Goth *fragiban* to forgive), fr. *for-* + *giefan, gifan* to give — more at GIVE] *vt* **1 :** to cease to feel resentment against on account of wrong committed **:** give up claim to requital from or retribution upon (an offender) **:** ABSOLVE, PARDON ⟨Father, ~ them, for they do not know what they are doing —Lk 23:34 (NCE)⟩ **2 a :** to give up resentment of or claim to requital for (an offense or wrong) **:** remit the penalty of ⟨and their sins should be *forgiven* them —Mk 4:12 (AV)⟩ **b :** to grant relief from **:** refrain from exacting ⟨*forgave* his tenants thousands of dollars in back rent⟩ ⟨a loophole in the tax law that ~*s* all if a taxpayer is out of the U.S. —*Time*⟩ ~ *vi* **:** to grant forgiveness **syn** see EXCUSE

for·give·ness *n* -ES [ME *foryevenesse, foryivenesse, forgevenesse, forgivenesse*, fr. OE *forgifnes, forgifenes*, fr. *forgifen* (past part. of *forgiefan, forgifan*) + *-nes* -ness] **1 :** an act of forgiving or state of being forgiven; *often* **:** REMISSION ⟨the ~ of the tax liability . . . should not result in such a serious disturbance to the revenues —*Jour. of Accountancy*⟩ **2** *archaic* **:** disposition to pardon **:** willingness to forgive

for·giv·er \fə(r)ˈgivə(r) *also* fȯrˈ-\ *n* -s [ME *foryever, foryiver, forgever, forgiver,* fr. *foryeven, foryiven, forgeven, forgiven* + *-er*] **:** one that forgives

forgiving *adj* **:** willing or able to forgive **:** characterized by forgiveness ⟨a kindly ~ nature⟩ ⟨said a ~ word of welcome to his erring son⟩ — **for·giv·ing·ly** *adv* — **for·giv·ing·ness** *n* -es

for·go \(ˈ)fȯrˈgō, ˈfȯ(ə)ˈ-\ *also* **fore·go** \(ˈ)fōrˈ-, -ȯrˈ-,-ōəˈ-, -ȯ(ə)ˈ-\ *vt* **for·went** *also* **fore·went** \-ˈwent\ **for·gone** *also* **fore·gone** \-ˈgȯn\ **for·go·ing** *also* **fore·go·ing** \-ˈgōiŋ\ **forgoes** *also* **foregoes** [ME *forgon, forgan,* fr. OE *forgān* to pass by, forgo (akin to OS *fargangan* to pass away, OHG *firgangan* to pass away, Goth *faurgaggan* to go by), fr. *for-* + *gān* to go — more at GO] **1** *archaic* **:** to depart from **:** QUIT, LEAVE, FORSAKE **2 :** to abstain from **:** let slip or pass **:** relinquish the enjoyment or advantage of **:** give up **:** RESIGN, RENOUNCE ⟨never *forwent* an opportunity of honest profit —R.L.Stevenson⟩ ⟨decided to ~ dessert for a few days⟩

syn ABNEGATE, ESCHEW, FORBEAR, SACRIFICE: FORGO is usu. used when one abstains from or gives up an available pleasure or advantage on the grounds of policy or expediency ⟨he agreed . . . to *forgo* all remuneration until his apprenticeship was completed —Van Wyck Brooks⟩ ⟨he has asked his people to forsake all narrow views of their own security and prosperity and . . . to *forgo* many immediate benefits —*Economist*⟩ ⟨to *forgo* wartime profits —*New Republic*⟩ ⟨this is a book no theater lover should lightly *forgo* —*Spectator*⟩ ABNEGATE is usu. used when one surrenders, relinquishes, or renounces on grounds of policy, expediency, or sometimes principle, something that one already has, the idea of self-denial often being strongly implied ⟨*abnegate* all rights to a property⟩ ⟨smile in a self-*abnegating* way⟩ ESCHEW suggests a more all-out abstinence from, often a positive avoidance of, something, usu. something inadvisable or distasteful, or something wrong but tempting ⟨the normal vegetarian only *eschews* fish, flesh, and fowl —N.C.Wright⟩ ⟨the laudable aim of *eschewing* controversial philosophical issues in a textbook —G.B.Keene⟩ ⟨it *eschews* cartoon, illustration, graph, or any device to attract attention —*Marketing*⟩ ⟨the emotions are *eschewed* as distorters of true knowledge —S.J.Beck⟩ FORBEAR is used when one exercises patient self-restraint in refraining from some action on grounds of prudence or high resolve ⟨she had forgotten several things . . . but she *forbore* to mention it —Elizabeth Goudge⟩ ⟨*forbear* to complain even though treated unjustly⟩ SACRIFICE implies and has generally implied a self-denial, a renunciation of an advantage, usu. immediate, in the interests of a future advantage or of someone or something else, as a religious or ethical value, but has come to apply more frequently to the giving up of something of value in the interests of something else, often of less value ⟨the individual will gladly *sacrifice* both time and money in the party interest —*Nation's Business*⟩ ⟨*sacrificed* their fortune in the world for theology's sake —H.O.Taylor⟩ ⟨significantly important news is often *sacrificed* for whatever can be depended on to make headlines —F.L.Mott⟩ ⟨a writer who, at times, *sacrificed* his talents to his ambition and pursuit of power —Daniel George⟩

for·go·er \-ˈgō(ə)r\ *n* -s **:** one that forgoes

for good *adv* **:** PERMANENTLY ⟨I certainly hope they are gone *for good*⟩

forgot *past of* FORGET

forgotten *past part of* FORGET

forgotten man *n* **:** a person or category of persons that receives less consideration or attention than is merited ⟨one of the *forgotten men* of American literature —Jay Leyda⟩ ⟨the ultimate consumer has become a *forgotten man* to industrial designers⟩

for–hire \ˌ=ˈ=\ *adj* [fr. the phrase *for hire*] **:** available or offered for rent ⟨*for-hire* vehicles⟩

for·hoo \fərˈhü\ *or* **for·hoo·ie** \-ˈhü·ē\ *vt* [ME *forhowen, forhohien* to despise, reject, abandon, fr. OE *forhogian* (akin to OS *farhuggian* to despise, OHG *farhuggen*), fr. *for-* + *hogian* to care for, think about; akin to OE *hycgan* to think, consider, understand — more at HUG] *Scot* **:** to forsake or abandon

fo·rin·sec \fəˈrin(t)sək\ *adj* [ML *forinsecus,* fr. L, from outside, fr. *foris* outside + *-insecus* (as in *extrinsecus* on the outside) — more at FORUM, EXTRINSIC] *of obligations under feudal law* **:** extraordinary in nature or performed away from the holding of a mesne lord for his superior ⟨~ service included foreign military service, the supplying of labor, and certain payments⟩

fo·rint \ˈfō(ˌ)rint\ *n* -s [Hung, fr. It *fiorino* florin — more at FLORIN] **1 :** a Hungarian florin **2 a :** the basic monetary unit of Hungary as established in 1946 — see MONEY table **b :** a coin representing one forint unit

fo·ris·fa·mil·i·ate \ˌfōrəsfəˈmilēˌāt\ *vb* -ED/-ING/-S [ML *forisfamiliatus,* past part. of *forisfamiliare,* fr. L *foris* outside + *familia* family — more at FORUM, FAMILY] *vt, Scots law* **:** to portion off so as to exclude further claim of inheritance **:** emancipate from paternal authority ~ *vi* **:** to renounce a legal title to a further share of paternal inheritance — **fo·ris·fa·mil·i·a·tion** \-ˌmilēˈāshən\ *n* -s

for·jes·ket *or* **for·jes·kit** \fərˈjeskət\ *or* **for·jas·kit** \-ˈjaskət\ *adj* [alter. (influenced by *for-*) of *disjaskit*] *Scot* **:** weary or broken down **:** EXHAUSTED ⟨~ sair, with weary legs —Robert Burns⟩

forjudge *var of* FOREJUDGE

¹fork \ˈfȯ(ə)rk, ˈfȯ(ə)k\ *n* -s *often attrib* [ME *forke,* fr. OE & ONF; OE *force, forca,* fr. L *furca;* ONF *forque,* fr. L *furca;* perh. akin to Lith *žirklės* scissors] **1 a :** an instrument or implement consisting of a handle with a shank terminating in two or more prongs used for piercing, holding, taking up, pitching, or digging something **b :** a small instrument of this description for use in manipulating food esp. in serving and eating — see DESSERT FORK, DINNER FORK, OYSTER FORK, SALAD FORK **c :** any of various pronged grappling devices often with automatic trip arrangements that are used in conjunction with a tackle for handling loose bulky material (as hay or straw) **d :** FORKLIFT **2 a :** a forked part, tool, or piece of equipment (as a tuning fork): as **a** *obs* **:** GALLOWS 1a **b :** a barbed point (as of an arrow) **c :** the lower part of the human body where the legs diverge from the trunk usu. including the legs **d :** CRUTCH 4a **e :** the end of the pallet lever of a lever-escapement watch that consists of a slot, two horns, and a guard finger and that imparts an impulse to the balance roller **f :** the front part of a saddletree **g :** FILLING FORK **h :** a long iron or steel rod with a forked end used in glass manufacturing for carrying finished articles to the lehr **i :** a forked electrical fitting for holding an insulator **j :** a 2-pronged support (as for the axle of a wheel or caster) ⟨the front ~ of a bicycle⟩ — see BICYCLE illustration **3 a :** a division into branches or the place where something divides into branches ⟨came to a ~ in the road⟩ ⟨the ~ of a fish's tail⟩ ⟨pruning should eliminate weak ~*s* at which a tree may later split⟩ **b :** a place where two or more streams flow together to form a larger waterway **:** CONFLUENCE; *often* **:** an area of land or a settlement bounded by or adjoining such a fork — often used in pl. and in place names ⟨stopped for the night at Miller's *Forks*⟩ **4 a :** one of the branches into which something forks ⟨take the left ~ at the crossroads⟩ **b :** an alternative or choice ⟨after certain basic training the student specializes in one of two ~*s*⟩ **5 a :** an attack by one chess piece (as a pawn or knight) on two pieces simultaneously **b :** TENACE **6 :** a change in elevation of artillery capable of producing a change in the range equal to four range probable errors

²fork \"\ *vb* -ED/-ING/-S [ME *forken,* fr. *forke,* n.] *vi* **1 :** to divide into two or more branches ⟨just over the hill the road ~*s*⟩ **2** *of lightning* **:** to play in zigzag or forked streaks **3 a :** to use a fork ⟨he could ~ all day against any two men in the crew⟩ **b :** to make a turn into or travel a fork ⟨the car ~*ed* to the left⟩ ~ *vt* **1 :** to give the form of a fork to **:** cause to be forked ⟨~*ing* her fingers⟩ **2 :** to raise or pitch (as hay or earth) with a fork ⟨~*ed* down a manger of hay⟩ **3 :** to attack (two chessmen) simultaneously (as with a knight or pawn) **4** *chiefly West* **:** to mount (a horse) esp. with a quick swing ⟨he jumped out of the buggy, ~*ed* his horse, and took after her —J.F.Dobie⟩ **5 :** to pay or contribute — used with *over, out,* or sometimes *up* ⟨he had to ~ over $5000 to keep the matter quiet⟩ ⟨not everybody can afford to ~ out a premium to get a new car⟩ **syn** see BRANCH

fork·able \-kəbəl\ *adj* **:** fit to handle or transport with a fork

fork ball *n* **:** a pitched ball in baseball that is gripped between the forked index and second fingers with the thumb underneath and delivered with a snap of the wrist

fork beam *n* **:** BEAM ARM 1

forked \ˈfȯ(ə)rkt, ˈfȯ(ə)kt, -kəd\ *adj* [ME, fr. past part. of *forken* to fork] **1 a :** resembling a fork esp. in having one end divided into two or more branches or points ⟨a bird with a ~ tail⟩ ⟨~ lightning⟩ **b :** having or distinguished by a fork or a forked part ⟨a ~ road⟩ ⟨the long-*forked* chimney swifts⟩ **2** *obs* **a :** having a double meaning **:** AMBIGUOUS, EQUIVOCAL **b :** HORNED; *often* **:** CUCKOLDED — **fork·ed·ly** \-kədlē, -li\ *adv* — **fork·ed·ness** *n* -es

forked catchfly *or* **forking catchfly** *n* **:** a European weedy annual herb (*Silene dichotoma*) having flowers with notched petals

forked chain *n* **:** BRANCHED CHAIN

forked chickweed *n* **:** any of various plants of the genus *Paronychia; esp* **:** a slender small branching weed (*P. canadensis*)

forked leaf *also* **fork–leaf blackjack** *n* **:** TURKEY OAK b

forked worm *n* **:** GAPEWORM

for keeps *adv* **:** PERMANENTLY

fork·er \ˈfȯrkər, ˈfȯ(ə)kə(r\ *n* -s **1 :** one that forks; *esp* **:** a workman who lifts, transfers, or holds with a fork **2** *obs* **:** something forked

fork·ful \ˈ=ˌfu̇l\ *n, pl* **fork·fuls** \-lz\ *or* **forks·ful** \-ks,fu̇l\ **:** as much as a fork will hold

forkhead \ˈ=ˌ=\ *n* -s **1 :** an arrowhead with two or occas. three prongs pointing forward **2 :** a forked end of a rod

fork·i·ness \ˈfȯrkēnəs, -ȯ(ə)k-, -kin-\ *n* -ES **:** the quality or state of being forky

forking *pres part of* FORK

fork length *n* **:** the length of a fish measured from the most anterior part of the head to the deepest point of the notch in the tail fin

fork·less \ˈ=ləs\ *adj* **:** having no fork

forklift \ˈ=ˌ=\ *n* **:** a machine for hoisting heavy objects (as boxes, bales, or metal bars) by means of a row of steel fingers inserted under the load and drawn up a vertical guide to the required level usu. by hydraulic means

forklike \ˈ=ˌ=\ *adj* **:** resembling a fork or functioning like the tines of a fork

fork·man \ˈ=mən\ *n, pl* **forkmen :** FORKER 1; *usu* **:** a metalworker who with a fork or hook guides the bloom through the roughing mill or billets of nonferrous metals from furnace to extruding press

forks *pl of* FORK, *pres 3d sing of* FORK

forktail \ˈ=ˌ=\ *n* **:** any of various fork-tailed animals (as birds or fishes): as **a :** SWORDFISH **b :** KITE **c :** GRILSE **d :** any of various chiefly black and white thrushes (genus *Enicurus*) widely distributed in the Oriental region and having long deeply forked tails

forktail cat *n* **:** BLUE CATFISH

fork–tailed \ˈ=ˈ=\ *or* **forktail** \ˈ=ˌ=\ *adj* **:** having the tail or posterior end of the body deeply cleft ⟨a *fork-tailed* schistosome cercaria⟩; *usu* **:** having the outer feathers or rays of the tail much longer than the central ones — used of birds and fishes

fork–tailed flycatcher *n* **:** a tropical American flycatcher (*Muscivora tyrannus*) that is rather like a swallow in appearance, with a black head and a long deeply forked black tail

fork–tailed gull *n* **:** SABINE'S GULL

fork–tailed kite *n* **:** SWALLOW-TAILED KITE

fork–tailed petrel \ˈ=ˌ=-\ *also* **forked–tailed petrel** \ˈ=ˌ=-\ *n* **:** a bluish gray white-marked petrel (*Oceanodroma furcata*) that has a deeply forked tail and is widely distributed in the northern Pacific; *also* **:** any of several closely related birds with more or less forked tails

forktail perch *n* **:** either of two commercially important embiotocid food fishes (*Damalichthys vacca* and *Phanerodon furcatus*) of the Pacific coast of No. America

fork–tongued \ˈ=ˈ=\ *or* **forked–tongued** \ˈ=ˈ=\ *adj* **:** given to prevarication

fork truck *or* **forklift truck** \ˈ=ˌ=-\ *n* **:** a lift truck equipped with a forklift

forky \ˈfȯrkē, -ȯ(ə)kē, -ki\ *adj, often* -ER/-EST **:** divided into or terminating in two or more branches **:** FORKED ⟨a ~ beard⟩

for·la·na \fȯrˈlänä, -nə\ *also* **fur·la·na** \fu̇rˈ-\ *n, pl* **forla·ne** \-(ˌ)nā\ *or* **forlanas** [It, fr. fem. of *forlano, furlano,* adj., var. of *friulano* Friulian, fr. *Friuli,* former duchy in northeastern Italy] **1 :** a lively old Italian dance in ⁶⁄₈ or ⁶⁄₄ time **2 :** the music for a forlana

¹for·lorn \fə(r)ˈlȯ(ə)rn, -ȯ(ə)n\ *adj, often* -ER/-EST [ME *forloren, forlorn* (past part. of *forlesen, forleosen* to lose), fr. OE *forloren,* past part. of *forlēosan* to lose (akin to OS *farliosan* to lose, OHG *furliosan,* Goth *fraliusan*), fr. *for-* + *lēosan* to lose — more at LOSE] **1** *obs* **:** LOST, ASTRAY **:** **a :** morally abandoned **b :** RUINED, DOOMED **2 a :** FORSAKEN, DESTITUTE, BEREFT — usu. used postpositively and with *of* ⟨a person ~ of hope⟩ **b :** deserted and desolate **:** sad and lonely esp. by reason of emptiness or abandonment ⟨a ~ huddle of sagging buildings⟩ **3 a :** being in poor condition **:** MISERABLE, DISORDERED, BEDRAGGLED, WRETCHED ⟨a few ~ chickens scratched about the muddy yard⟩ ⟨never did I see such a ~ woebegone face⟩ **b :** pathetic or pitiable esp. as indicative of loneliness, distress, or sorrow ⟨a ~ cry⟩ ⟨~ hungry-looking waifs⟩ **4 :** having but the barest plausibility or promise **:** nearly hopeless ⟨one final ~ attempt to reach the sinking ship in time to rescue the crew⟩ **syn** see ALONE, DESPONDENT

²forlorn \"\ *n* -s **1** *archaic* **:** one who is forlorn **2** *obs* **a :** a forlorn hope or a member of one **b :** VANGUARD

forlorn hope *n* [by folk etymology fr. D *verloren hoop,* lit., lost band] **1 a :** a body of men selected usu. from volunteers to attempt a breach, scale a wall, or perform other perilous service esp. in advance of the main force **b :** a member of such a body **2 :** a desperate or extremely difficult enterprise **:** an undertaking unlikely to be completed successfully or without great hazard **3 a :** a vain or faint hope **b :** something unlikely to succeed

for·lorn·i·ty \-nəd·ē, -ətē, -i\ *n* -ES **1 :** forlorn quality or state **2 :** a forlorn thing or person

for·lorn·ly *adv* **:** in a forlorn manner

for·lorn·ness \ˈ=ˈnəs\ *n* -ES [ME *forlorennesse,* fr. *forloren, forlorn* + *-nesse* -ness] **:** forlorn quality or state; *esp* **:** desolate isolated condition or location ⟨the complete ~ of the scene⟩

¹form \ˈfȯ(ə)rm, -ȯ(ə)m\ *n* -s *often attrib* [ME *forme, fourme,* fr. OF, fr. L *forma,* perh. modif. of Gk *morphē*; perh. akin to Gk *marmairein* to flash, sparkle — more at MORN] **1** *obs* **:** IMAGE, REPRESENTATION **2 a :** the shape and structure of something as distinguished from the material of which it is composed ⟨the carefully graded ~ of the curves⟩ **b :** a body esp. of a human being as distinguished (1) by external appearance or (2) from the countenance or visage **:** FIGURE ⟨the dress displayed her ~ to advantage⟩ **c** *archaic* **:** pleasing external appearance **:** BEAUTY ⟨he had no ~ or comeliness —Isa 53:2 (RSV)⟩ **3 a :** the ideal or intrinsic character of anything or something that imposes this character; *sometimes* **:** a pattern or schema **b** *in metaphysics* **:** the essential nature of a thing as distinguished from the matter in which this is embodied: as (1) *in Platonic philosophy* **:** a transcendent idea, universal essence, or subsistent entity (2) *in Aristotelian or scholastic philosophy* **:** the component of a thing that determines it in its kind or species **:** FORMAL CAUSE — often distinguished from *matter* (3) *in Baconian philosophy* **:** the basis constituting the condition for the existence of any given nature or quality (as density, heat, or color) **c** *in Kantian philosophy* **:** one of the formative modes of perception and cognition regarded as a subjective factor molding reality as given in sensation into systematic experience esp. as regards spatial and temporal order **4 a** *obs* **:** manner, method, or style (as of proceeding) **b :** established method of expression or practice **:** fixed or formal way of proceeding **:** procedure according to rule or rote **c :** a prescribed and usu. set order of words **:** FORMULA ⟨the ~ of the marriage service in the prayer book⟩ **d** *obs* **:** RECIPE, PRESCRIPTION **e** (1) **:** a printed or typed document with blank spaces for insertion of required or requested specific information ⟨a ~ for a deed⟩ ⟨be sure to fill all blanks on your tax ~⟩ (2) **:** a document of this kind which is attached to and forms an endorsement of a property insurance policy and in which is filled in a description of the property insured; *broadly* **:** such an endorsement containing alterations or modifications of the provisions of a standard policy **5 a :** conduct regulated by extraneous controls (as of custom or etiquette) **:** CEREMONY, CONVENTIONALITY, FORMALITY; *sometimes* **:** show without substance **:** empty pretentious appearance or ceremony **b :** a prescribed manner of behaving (as in society) ⟨the rigid ~ of the imperial court⟩ **:** an act of conduct or mode of procedure prescribed (as by custom or a code of etiquette) ⟨the complex ~*s* and taboos of the savage⟩ **:** FORMALITY, CEREMONY, CONVENTIONALITY ⟨knew all the ~*s* for wooing a proper young miss⟩ **c :** manner or conduct as tested by a prescribed or accepted standard — used with a qualifying adjective ⟨his behavior was often bad ~⟩ ⟨such poor ~ is to be deplored⟩ **d :** manner or style of performing or accomplishing something esp. when recognized standards of technique exist ⟨he is a strong swimmer but weak on ~⟩ **6 a :** the resting place of a hare or occas. of another animal **b :** a long seat **:** JOINT STOOL, BENCH ⟨seated on a low ~ against the wall⟩ **c :** a supporting frame model of the human figure or other device used for displaying merchandise in a store; *also* **:** a proportioned and often adjustable model for fitting clothes **d :** something that holds, supports, and gives or determines shape; *esp* **:** a mold in which concrete is placed to set **7** *obs* **a :** degree of quality, dignity, eminence, or excellence **b :** a class or rank esp. in society or official life **8 a :** the total combination of the letterpress matter imposed and locked up in a chase with the furniture, quoins, and the chase itself **b :** set-up type ⟨how to move ~*s* from the galley to the stone⟩ ⟨wind the cord clockwise around the ~⟩ **9 a :** one of the different modes of existence, action, or manifestation of a particular thing or substance **:** KIND, MODIFICATION, SPECIES, VARIETY ⟨the diamond, graphite, and soot are allotropic ~*s* of carbon⟩ ⟨the democratic ~ of government⟩ ⟨one ~ of respiratory disorder⟩ ⟨the ~ of vegetation typical of xerophytic areas⟩ **b** *also* **for·ma** \-mə\ **:** a botanical taxonomic category ranking below a variety and consisting of individuals that differ from those of related forms in one or very few characters ⟨the *discretiflorus* ~ of the rush *Juncus tenuis*⟩; *also* **:** a member of such a category **c :** a distinguishable group of organisms — commonly used by zoologists to avoid taxonomic implications ⟨the southern ~ of the hairy woodpecker⟩ **10 a :** orderly arrangement or method of arrangement (as in the presentation of ideas) **:** manner of coordinating elements (as of an artistic production or course of reasoning); *sometimes* **:** a particular kind or instance of such arrangement ⟨the sonnet is a poetical ~⟩ **b** *in logic* (1) **:** the structure, pattern, or schema possessed in common by different logical statements esp. as disclosed through the substitution of variables for different descriptive terms so that the manner in which the terms are interrelated becomes apparent (2) **:** the structure of an argument or an inference as symbolized by the use of variables (3) **:** the logical properties of a word, expression, or symbol as exhibited by its contribution to the logical form of statements in which it may properly occur **c :** the structural element, plan, or design of a work of art; *specif* **:** the combinations and relations to each other of various components (as lines, colors, and volumes in a visual work of art or themes and elaborations in an aural work of art) ⟨~ consists in a pattern of relationships that gives unity to a complex of perceptual elements —F.S.Haserot⟩ — often contrasted with *content* **d :** a relationship between or among elements of raw subject matter (as in a painting) which is sensed and made structural by the artist; *also* **:** a visible and measurable unit defined by a contour **:** a bounded surface or volume or a system of visible elements **e** (1) **:** the structural pattern of a musical composition (2) **:** a specific type (as fugue, rondo, sonata) of such pattern **11 :** a class or grade in a British secondary school or in certain American private schools — see SIXTH FORM **12 a :** the past performance of a race horse; *often* **:** a table giving details relating to a horse's past performance (as handicaps, jockeys, odds) used by bettors in making selections ⟨a ~ sheet⟩ ⟨a racing ~⟩ ⟨~ players⟩ **b :** CONDITION, FITNESS ⟨preseason workouts to get in ~ for the regular season⟩; *often* **:** known ability to perform ⟨a batter off his ~ at the plate⟩ ⟨a musician playing at the top of his ~⟩ **13 :** the combination of faces included under a general crystallographic symbol and necessary to satisfy the symmetry of the crystal ⟨a single crystal often exhibits faces of two or more crystal ~*s* which supplement one another or truncate one another's edges or corners⟩ **14 a :** LINGUISTIC FORM **b :** one of the different aspects a word may take as a result of inflection or change of spelling or pronunciation ⟨obsolete, participial, or verbal ~*s*⟩ **15** *math* **:** a rational integral homogeneous function of a set of variables **16 :** the immature flower bud of the cotton plant **17 :** BOOK 1d(1) **18 :** the profile of a screw thread

syn FORMALITY, CEREMONY, CEREMONIAL, RITE, RITUAL, LITURGY: FORM is a general word and usu. lacks any special connotation ⟨there had been no fixed order for the coronation of an English king, and the *form* which was observed at Bath was reached only after . . . two experimental drafts —F.M.Stenton⟩ ⟨his inclinations toward the *forms* of the Church of England —G.H.Genzmer⟩ ⟨made his declaration in *form* —Jane Austen⟩ Modified, as by *good* or *bad,* FORM indicates the degree of conformity to established usage or custom ⟨it was accepted poetic good *form* that the lover, writing of his lady, should inventory her charms from top to toe —J.L.Lowes⟩ ⟨nothing could be worse *form* . . . than any display of temper in a public place —Edith Wharton⟩ FORM may indicate a traditional or sanctioned procedure lacking force, significance, or real vitality ⟨if congress remains at liberty to give this court appellate jurisdiction . . . the distribution of jurisdiction made in the Constitution is *form* without substance —John Marshall⟩ FORMALITY applies either to a prescribed procedural detail, often one done perfunctorily and lacking in import, or to an attitude of punctilious, reserved stiffness ⟨the first reading of a public bill is a *formality* and is in effect little more than information given to the House that the bill is on its way —R.M.Dawson⟩ ⟨the cold *formality* of the duchess's court⟩ CEREMONY is likely to suggest dignified, impressive, elaborate, or punctilious performance of actions ranging from those of deep spiritual significance to trifling everyday courtesies or routine actions ⟨the *ceremonies* at the investiture of a pope⟩ ⟨*ceremonies* in honor of the martyred king⟩ ⟨the beauty of an inherited courtesy of manners, of a thousand little *ceremonies* flowing out of the most ordinary relations and observances of life —Laurence Binyon⟩ CEREMONIAL, occas. a synonym for CEREMONY, is more likely to suggest a system or code of prescribed ceremonies ⟨the gorgeous *ceremonial* of the Burgundian court —W.H.Prescott⟩ RITE indicates the prescribed speech and action of a special formal occasion, esp. a very significant or unusual one, an ordinary event treated as though of major importance, or an esoteric practice ⟨had gone through this formality as resignedly as through all the others which made of a nineteenth century New York wedding a *rite* that seemed to belong to the dawn of history —Edith Wharton⟩ ⟨the semipagan *rites* peculiar to the burial of the dead in middle-class houses —Rudyard Kipling⟩ ⟨abhorred *rites* to Hecate in their obscured haunts —John Milton⟩ RITUAL in its older sense indicates the totality of the rites of service or faith ⟨the Roman *ritual* had always a great attraction for him —Oscar Wilde⟩ More frequently today it designates any series of actions given an unusual importance and a prescribed order or manner ⟨the *ritual* of asepsis today is the same the world over —Harvey Graham⟩ ⟨it was essential to reach a cave around the next headland where she would sit down facing the sea before she thought about anything — thus making a little *ritual* against despair —Audrey Barker⟩ Where it is not an equivalent for RITUAL or RITE, LITURGY may indicate the prescribed form for an act or session of worship as written and accepted ⟨he [Henry VIII] insisted on . . . the maintenance of full ritual in the *liturgy* —Hilaire Belloc⟩

syn FIGURE, SHAPE, CONFORMATION, CONFIGURATION: FORM may suggest an appearance in which both clear outline and also structure and orderly disposition of details are presented or suggested ⟨appearing in book *form*⟩ ⟨the republican *form* of government⟩ ⟨a sense of interdependence and interrelated unity that gave *form* to intellectual stirrings that had been previously inchoate —John Dewey⟩ ⟨school architecture throughout the state is highly specialized. Rigid state laws for heating, ventilation, and lighting offer little opportunity for variation on standard *form* —*Amer. Guide Series: N.J.*⟩ FIGURE is likely to call attention to outlines, to bounding, enclosing circumference or outer lines ⟨a geometrical *figure*⟩ ⟨the *figures* of a dance⟩ ⟨the cloud *figures* in the sky —Sylvia Berkman⟩ ⟨the president rose to his great height, a somber, towering *figure* in black —Sir Winston Churchill⟩ SHAPE may sometimes suggest both outline and also content, mass, body, bulk, or detail ⟨hat *shapes* of beaver, coon, otter, and other skins —*Amer. Guide Series: Conn.*⟩ ⟨the construction of a play sets up its *shape*, and builds its skeleton —John Van Druten⟩ ⟨the *shape* of an idea emerged gradually out of the fog of words —Ellen Glasgow⟩ ⟨whole stone logs are found, some wonderfully and delicately colored, in the *shape* of the Asiatic gingko tree —*Amer. Guide Series: Wash.*⟩ CONFORMATION is usable in reference to whole complicated structure or to detailed arrangement or presentation ⟨they failed to find any relation between altitude tolerance and body stature or *conformation* —H.G.Armstrong⟩ ⟨a culture acquires its *conformation* and specificity from the uniqueness of its institutions —Abram Kardiner⟩ CONFIGURATION is applicable to a detailed outline or statement of the nature and disposition or arrangement of various parts ⟨he used to wake up and not know where he was, but the *configurations* of a dream could easily have taken on such a shape as this — the dining room of the Marlborough in the shadowy light of early morning —Hamilton Basso⟩ ⟨though the main street is wide and lined with stores, most of the others fit crookedly into the *configurations* of the valley —*Amer. Guide Series: Pa.*⟩

syn USAGE, CONVENTION, CONVENANCE: these nouns all have in common the sense of a fixed or accepted way of doing something. FORM can apply to a prescribed or approved way of behaving, method of procedure, or technique in any sphere of activity where correctness or uniformity of method or manner is thought essential ⟨the *forms* of good conduct⟩ ⟨the *forms* of worship⟩ ⟨good *form* in swimming⟩ ⟨a *form* of address⟩ USAGE implies the sanction of precedent or tradition, often designating a form preserved out of respect for a class, profession, or religion ⟨descriptions of *usages* presuppose descriptions of uses, that is, ways or techniques of doing the thing the more or less widely prevailing practice of doing which constitutes the usage —Gilbert Ryle⟩ ⟨to bury in the first furrow certain fruits of a particular structure, such as figs, pomegranates, and locust beans, is a *usage* frequently observed —J.G.Frazer⟩ CONVENTION, often interchangeable with FORM, esp. in application to social behavior, stresses general agreement and therefore applies to some set way of doing or saying something that is sanctioned or believed to be sanctioned only by general unquestioning acceptance ⟨this music followed *conventions* perfectly understood by the contemporaries —P.H.Lang⟩ ⟨certain parliamentary *conventions* which exist to supplement the rules of procedure —T.E.May⟩ ⟨this genius who was too wild and elemental ever to conform to any aesthetic *convention* —H.M.Ledig-Rowohlt⟩ CONVENANCE, a literary term still retaining some of its character as a loanword, applies only to social conventions especially regarded as essential to propriety or decorum ⟨disregarding the social *convenances*, continued to chatter on —R.H.Sampson⟩ ⟨the *convenances* of life —A.C.Benson⟩

²**form** \"\ *vb* -ED/-ING/-S [ME *formen, fourmen*, fr. OF *former, fourmer*, fr. L *formare*, fr. *forma*, n.] *vt* **1 a** : to give form or shape to : FRAME, CONSTRUCT, MAKE, FASHION ⟨man, ~*ed* of earth, to earth returns⟩ ⟨the skilled craftsman ~*s* and finishes the rough stone to a thing of beauty⟩ **b** : to constitute by nominating or appointing individuals to governmental positions usu. associated with membership in a cabinet or government ⟨asked to ~ a new cabinet —M.S.Stewart⟩ ⟨was called upon to ~ a government —Kenneth Lawson⟩ **2 a** : to give a particular shape to : shape, mold, or fashion into a certain state or condition or after a particular model : ARRANGE, ADJUST ⟨~ the paste into lozenges and roll them in sugar⟩ ⟨a state ~*ed* after the Roman republic⟩ **b** : to model by instruction and discipline : mold esp. by influence ⟨'tis education ~*s* the common mind —Alexander Pope⟩ **3** : DEVELOP, ACQUIRE, CONTRACT ⟨~ a habit⟩ **4** : to serve to make up or constitute : be a usu. essential or basic element of ⟨bonds ~*ed* the bulk of his estate⟩ ⟨her hat was ~*ed* of feathers⟩ **5 a** : to treat (plates) for use in an electrical storage battery by coating the positive plate with lead dioxide and the negative plate with spongy lead **b** : to treat (mercury arc rectifiers) to remove all moisture and gas after a period of idleness or after opening the tank **6 a** : to have (as a tense) expressed ⟨~*s* the past tense in -*ed*⟩ **b** : to combine to make (a compound word) **c** : to make up : CONSTITUTE ⟨~ a clause or sentence⟩ **7** : to arrange in order : draw up ⟨the battalion advanced as soon as its lines were ~*ed*⟩ **8** : to bend or stretch (metal) to conform to the shape of a die or other tool ~ *vi* **1** : to become formed or shaped ⟨a clot ~*ed* gradually over the cut⟩ **2** : to take form : come into existence : ARISE ⟨popular protest ~*ed* steadily⟩ ⟨thunderheads were ~*ing* over the hills⟩ **3** : to take on a definite form, shape, or arrangement ⟨the infantry ~*ed* in columns⟩ **4** *of a hare* : to run to or crouch in a form **syn** see MAKE

— **form on** : to take up a formation next to ⟨ordered the group to *form on* the last platoon⟩

form- *or* **formo-** *comb form* [*formic* (*acid*)] : formic acid : formyl ⟨*form*anilide⟩ ⟨*formo*toluidide⟩

-form \ˌfȯrm\ *adj comb form* [MF and L; MF *-forme*, fr. L *-formis*, fr. *forma* form — more at FORM] : in the form or shape of : resembling : -MORPHOUS — preceded by *i* ⟨calci*form*⟩ ⟨ovi*form*⟩

for·ma \ˈfȯrmə, -ȯ(ə)mə\ *n, pl* **for·mae** \-ˌmē\ *also* **formas** [NL, fr. L, form] : FORM 9b

form·abil·i·ty \ˌ⸗ə'bilədē, -ətē, -i\ *n* : capacity for being formed into new shapes ⟨the excellent ~ of modern plastics⟩

form·able \'⸗əbəl\ *adj* [ME, fr. LL *formabilis*, fr. L *formare* to form + *-abilis* -able — more at FORM] : capable of being formed : suitable for forming ⟨~ sheet metal⟩

form·ably \-əblē, -li\ *adv* : so as to be formable

for·ma·gen \'fȯrməjən, -ˌjen\ *n* -S [L *forma* form + E *-gen*] : a substance having a formative effect on plants; *esp* : one that modifies the shape, size, or arrangement of organs — **for·ma·gen·ic** \¦⸗⸗'jenik\ *adj*

¹**for·mal** \'fȯrməl, -ȯ(ə)m-\ *adj* [ME *formal, formel*, fr. OF & L; OF, fr. L *formalis*, fr. *forma* form + *-alis* -al] **1 a** : belonging to or being the essential constitution of a thing as distinguished from the matter composing it ⟨the ~ nature of a square is a relation of lines and angles rather than a matter of space or solidity⟩; *often* : having power to make a thing what it is : CONSTITUTIVE, ESSENTIAL ⟨divine goodwill is the ~ cause of human aspiration⟩ **b** : relating to, concerned with, or constituting the outward form, superficial qualities, or arrangement of something as distinguished from its content: as (1) : of, relating to, or preoccupied with the material or compositional factors in art or emphasizing these over other factors (as subject matter or content) ⟨a ~ style in painting⟩; *often* : having a symmetrical arrangement of elements ⟨~ balance in design⟩ ⟨a ~ composition⟩ (2) : consisting of, based upon, evidenced by, or considering observable similarities and differences in linguistic form as distinguished from logical, a priori, semantic, comparative, or historical similarities and differences ⟨the ~ approach to comparative linguistics⟩ ⟨a ~ classification of language⟩ (3) : of, relating to, or constituting logical, epistemological, or ontological forms; *also* : belonging to a formalized system : SYNTACTICAL **2 a** : following or according with established form, custom, or rule : not deviating from what is usual or generally acceptable : CONVENTIONAL ⟨still in constraint your suffering sex remains or bound in ~ or in real chains —Alexander Pope⟩ ⟨paying ~ attentions to his hostess⟩ **b** : done in due form : carried out with solemnity : CEREMONIAL ⟨no noble rite nor ~ ostentation —Shak.⟩ ⟨received a ~ rebuke before the whole congregation⟩ **c** *obs* : characterized by or formed in due order : REGULAR **3 a** : based on forms and rules, esp. such as are accepted by convention : of or following a prescribed form ⟨a ~ exposition⟩ ⟨~ landscape architecture⟩ ⟨a ~ reception⟩ **b** : characterized by punctilious respect for form : EXACT, METHODICAL, ORDERLY ⟨a man very ~ in all his dealings⟩; *often* : constrained by reason of excessive devotion to form : PRIM, RIGID, STIFF, CEREMONIOUS ⟨those stern ~ even formidable ancestors locked in their rigid armor of propriety⟩ **c** *of a legal procedure* : requiring special or stipulated solemnities or formalities to become effective (as in the creating of a legal relationship) **4** *obs* **a** : sound in mind : SANE **b** : CIRCUMSTANTIAL **5** : having the appearance without the substance : being or subject to being so construed only as a matter of form ⟨~ Christians who go to church on Easter Sunday to show off their new clothes⟩ : NOMINAL ⟨a purely ~ requirement that can be waived without trouble⟩ ⟨a ~ party to a suit⟩ **syn** see CEREMONIAL

²**formal** \"\ *n* -S : something formal in character: as **a** : a social affair (as a dance) requiring formal evening dress **b** (1) : EVENING DRESS (2) : a man's formal evening costume

³**for·mal** \fȯr'mal\ *n* -S [ISV, fr. *formaldehyde*] **1** : METHYLAL **2** : any acetal derived from formaldehyde and an alcohol ⟨butyl ~⟩ ⟨polyvinyl ~⟩

⁴**for·mal** \'fȯrməl\ *adj* [*formula* + *-al*] : ³MOLAR 2 ⟨~ concentration of a solution⟩

formal cause *n, in Aristotelianism* : the structure, essence, or pattern that a fully realized thing embodies

formal contract *n* **1** : a contract under seal or by statute having that effect : SPECIALTY CONTRACT **2** : RECOGNIZANCE **3** : a negotiable instrument

form·al·de·hyde \fȯrm+\ *n* [ISV *form-* + *aldehyde*; orig. formed as G *formaldehyd*] : a very reactive aldehyde HCHO that has a tendency to polymerize, that is a colorless pungent irritating combustible gas when pure but is conveniently handled in the form of aqueous solutions or solid polymers (as paraformaldehyde), that is usu. made by oxidation of methanol or of gaseous hydrocarbons, and that is used chiefly as a disinfectant and preservative, as a hardening and insolubilizing agent esp. for proteins, and in the synthesis of other compounds (as pentaerythritol) and of phenolic and other synthetic resins — called also *formic aldehyde, methanal*

formaldehydesulfoxylate \⸗'⸗⸗,⸗(,)⸗'⸗⸗,⸗\ *n* [*formaldehyde* + *sulfoxylate*] : a salt of formaldehydesulfoxylic acid

formaldehydesulfoxylic acid \⸗'⸗⸗,⸗,⸗,⸗'⸗⸗-\ *n* [ISV *formaldehyde* + *sulfoxylic*] : an unstable acid $HOCH_2SO_2H$ known only in the form of salts (as sodium formaldehydesulfoxylate) that are strong reducing agents

formaldehyde tanning *n* : tanning with formaldehyde solutions esp. in the preparation of white leathers

for·mal·de·hy·do·gen·ic \⸗¦⸗⸗,hī,dō¦jenik\ *adj* [*formaldehyde* + *-o-* + *-genic*] : yielding formaldehyde ⟨~ steroids⟩

formal discipline *n* : disciplinary training supposedly imparted by the form of a study (as mathematics) as distinguished from its content value; *also* : the study itself

formal fallacy *n* : a violation of any rule of formal inference — called also *paralogism*; contrasted with *material fallacy* and *verbal fallacy*; compare AFFIRMATION OF THE CONSEQUENT, DENIAL OF THE ANTECEDENT, IGNORATIO ELENCHI, ILLICIT PROCESS, PETITIO PRINCIPII

formal garden *n* : a garden laid out with complete regularity on formal lines and in accord with the methods of classic design, the plantings being in symmetrically arranged rows or geometrical figures

For·ma·lin \'fȯrmələn\ *trademark* — used for a clear aqueous solution of formaldehyde that usu. contains about 37 percent formaldehyde by weight or 40 percent by volume together with a small amount of methanol for inhibiting polymerization

for·ma·lin·ize \-lə,nīz\ *vt* -ED/-ING/-S *see -ize in Explan Notes* : FORMOLIZE

for·mal·ism \'fȯrmə,lizəm, -ȯ(ə)m-\ *n* -S [¹*formal* + *-ism*] **1 a** : the practice or the doctrine of strict adherence to or dependence on prescribed or external forms ⟨the rigid ~ of the royal court⟩; *also* : an instance of this ⟨the petty ~*s* with which he filled his life⟩ **b** : the using or observance of external religious forms without the life and spirit of religion **c** (1) : any theory (as that of Kant) holding that the nature of duty is determined by purely formal principles (as the categorical imperative) rather than by a consideration of the consequences of actions (2) : INTUITIONISM 1 **d** : a philosophy of mathematics that seeks to establish the consistency of mathematics by metamathematical methods — compare INTUITIONISM **2 a** : emphatic or predominant attention to arrangement, style, or artistic means (as in graphic art, literature, or music) usu. with corresponding de-emphasis of content; *often* : strict adherence to traditional or prescribed rules and methods in the arts **b** : dramatic representation in which all the elements of production are conventionalized into simple and arbitrary terms

¹**for·mal·ist** \-ləst\ *n* -S [¹*formal* + *-ist*] **1** : a person who adopts as a matter of form the current opinions and modes of action : TIMESERVER **2 a** : one overattentive to forms or too much confined to them **b** : one given to formalism : a formal person; *often* : an advocate or proponent of a theory of formalism **3** : one that gives form : a form-giving power or element ⟨the sun and moon, the great ~*s* in the sky —R.W. Emerson⟩

²**formalist** \"\ *adj* : of or relating to formalists : FORMALISTIC

for·mal·is·tic \¦⸗mə¦listik\ *adj* : concerned with or characterized by formalism ⟨the ~ approach to the study of society —C.V.Woodward⟩; *often* : employing or advocating formalism (as in ethics) — **for·mal·is·ti·cal·ly** \-ək(ə)lē\ *adv*

for·mal·i·ter \fȯr'malədˌər\ *adv* [LL, fr. L *formalis* formal — more at FORMAL] : FORMALLY; *esp* : with reference to Aristotelian form

for·mal·i·ty \fȯ(r)'malədē, -ətē, -i\ *n* -ES [MF *formalité*, fr. *formal* + *-ité* -ity — more at FORMAL] **1** : the quality or state of being formal: as **a** *obs* : the practice or exhibition of formalism in art or music **b** : strictly ceremonious quality or state : precise stiff regularity or conformance **2** *archaic* : the distinctive quality that makes a thing what it is or defines its nature : ESSENCE **3** : compliance with formal or conventional rules : conformity to established form or method of procedure (as in law) : FORM, CEREMONY, CONVENTIONALITY **4** : the dress or insignia prescribed for academic, municipal, or sacerdotal office — usu. used in pl. ⟨the lord mayor in his *formalities* headed the procession⟩ **5 a** : an established form or formal procedure that is required or conventional esp. in religious, legal, courtly, or social matters **b** : a customary ceremony without much real significance ⟨he was installed with all the usual *formalities* —Conyers Middleton⟩ **6** *obs* **a** : ceremonious attention **b** : formal aspect **c** : invariable practice : ORDER, REGULARITY **d** : external appearance or form; *often* : form without substance **7** *in scholasticism* **a** : the manner in which a thing is conceived or constituted by an act of human thinking **b** : the result of such an act **syn** see FORM

for·mal·iz·able \¦fȯrmə¦līzəbəl, ¦fȯ(ə)m-\ *adj* : capable of being formalized

for·ma·li·za·tion \ˌ⸗mələ'zāshən, -ˌlī'z-\ *n* -S : an act of formalizing or the state of being formalized — compare AXIOMATIZATION

¹**for·mal·ize** \'fȯrmə,līz, 'fȯ(ə)m-\ *vb* -ED/-ING/-S *see -ize in Explan Notes* [*formal* + *-ize*] *vt* **1** *obs* : to give form or formal existence to : ANIMATE **2** : to give a certain or definite form to : SHAPE, MOLD **3 a** : to render formal; *often* : STYLIZE **b** : to state precise rules for the combination and transformation of (as expressions or language) usu. by replacing the original words by symbols that can be discussed without reference to their meaning — compare FORMATION RULE, TRANSFORMATION RULE **c** : to give formal status or approval to (as a decision, plan, or proposal) **4** *obs* : to take exception to : cavil at ~ *vi* **1** : to be formal : affect formality **2** *obs* : to object without good reason : CAVIL, SCRUPLE — **for·mal·iz·er** \-ˌlīzə(r)\ *n* -S

²**formalize** \"\ *vt* -ED/-ING/-S [*formal*in + -ize] : FORMOLIZE

formal logic *n* : a system of logic (as Aristotelian logic or symbolic logic) that abstracts the forms of thought from its content to establish abstract criteria of consistency — contrasted with *material logic*

for·mal·ly \'⸗məlē, -li\ *adv* [ME, fr. *formal* + *-ly*] : in a formal manner: as **a** : with respect to or according to form **b** : EXPRESSLY, EXPLICITLY **c** : in prescribed or customary form **d** : with formality : CEREMONIOUSLY ⟨inspection of the new hotel . . . which will be ~ opened for dinner this evening —D.D.Martin⟩

formal matter *n* : MATTER OF A PROPOSITION b

formal mode *n* : language that makes statements about linguistic signs without reference to their meaning or denotation — contrasted with *material mode*

for·mal·ness *n* -ES : the quality or state of being formal : FORMALITY

formal proposition *n* : a proposition in which no specific content is designated or a principle is stated in the manner of a formula (as "if all A is B, then no A is not B")

formals *pl of* FORMAL

formal sociology *n* : a branch of sociology concerned with the modes of recurrent social relationships (as competition, division of labor, supraordination, and subordination) that are conceived to exist in any type of human association

formal subject *n* : GRAMMATICAL SUBJECT

formal truth *n* : the true elaboration of concepts, meanings, or implications that is relatively independent of external existence or nonexistence ⟨the *formal truth* of a definition⟩ ⟨the truth that certain premises give a certain conclusion is a *formal truth*⟩ — called also *logical truth*

form·amide \fȯrm+\ *n* [ISV *form-* + *amide*] : a colorless hygroscopic liquid $HCONH_2$ made in various ways (as from ammonia and a formic ester or from ammonia and carbon monoxide under pressure) and used chiefly as a solvent and softening agent; the amide of formic acid

form·am·i·dine \fȯr'mamə,dēn, -dən\ *n* -S [ISV *formamide* + *-ine*] : an unstable base $HC(=NH)NH_2$ known only in the form of its salts and other derivatives

formamido- *comb form* [*formamide*] : containing the univalent radical HCONH— derived from formamide ⟨*para-form-amido*benzoic acid⟩

for·man·ite \'fȯrmə,nīt\ *n* -S [Francis G. *Forman*, 20th cent. Australian geologist + E *-ite*] : a mineral $(U,Zr,Th,Ca)(Ta,Nb)O_4$ consisting essentially of an oxide of uranium, zirconium, thorium, calcium, tantalum, and niobium with some rare-earth metals and isomorphous with fergusonite

for·mant \'fȯrmənt, -ȯ(ə)m-, -ˌmant, -aa(ə)nt\ *n* -S [G, fr. L *formant-*, *formans*, pres. part. of *formare* to form — more at FORM] **1** : a characteristic component of the quality of a speech sound; *specif* : any of several resonance bands which are regarded as together determining the phonetic quality of a vowel **2 a** : ²DETERMINATIVE 3 **b** : a derivational affix

formas *pl of* FORMA

for·mat \'fȯr,mat, -ȯ(ə)m-, *usu* -ad·+V\ *n* -S [F or G; F, fr. G, fr. L *formatus*, past part. of *formare* (prob. in such contexts as NL *liber in quarto formatus* volume formed in quarto)] **1 a** : the shape and size of a publication as determined by the number of times each constituent sheet has been folded ⟨in octavo ~ each sheet is folded 3 times to produce 8 leaves⟩ — compare BOOK tables **b** : the general makeup or style of a publication ⟨a double-column ~⟩ ⟨loose-leaf ~⟩ **2** : general plan of physical organization or arrangement (as of a television show or the design of a coin) ⟨the ~ of the new show included a careful balance of music and comedy⟩ ⟨students are given practice exercises to acquaint them with the ~ of the tests⟩ **3** : SIZE, SHAPE, PROPORTION ⟨a rare stamp of triangular ~⟩ ⟨cameras employing ~*s* up to 24 by 36 millimeters⟩ ⟨the exceptionally tall ~ of the panels⟩

¹**for·mate** \'fȯr,māt, *usu* -ād·+V\ *n* -S [*form-* + *-ate*] : a salt or ester of formic acid

²**formate** \"\ *vi* -ED/-ING/-S [back-formation fr. *formation*] *of aircraft* : to fly in or join a formation

for·ma·tion \fȯr'māshən, -ȯ(ə)'-\ *n* -S [ME *formacioun*, fr. MF or L; MF *formation*, fr. L *formation-*, *formatio*, fr. *formatus* + *-ion-*, *-io* -ion] **1** : an act of giving form or shape to something or of taking form : PRODUCTION, DEVELOPMENT ⟨planned the ~ of a social club⟩ ⟨the ~ of good habits⟩ **2** : something that is formed ⟨new word ~*s*⟩ ⟨a greenish ~ of mold on bread⟩ **3** : the manner in which a thing is formed : STRUCTURE, CONSTRUCTION, FORM ⟨the peculiar ~ of the heart⟩ **4 a** : the largest unit in ecological community organization comprising two or more associations together with the successional communities that lead to their establishment, the unit as a whole corresponding in area with a region of essentially uniform climate ⟨the grassland ~⟩ — compare BIOME **b** : a group of associations bound together by close similarity in life forms or habits and by dependence upon closely similar climates — compare CLIMAX 4 **5 a** : any particular mineral aggregate or rock — not often used technically **b** : any igneous, sedimentary, or metamorphic rock represented as a unit in geological mapping : a cartographic unit **c** : any sedimentary bed or consecutive series of beds sufficiently homogeneous or distinctive to be regarded as a unit ⟨the Trenton ~⟩ **6 a** : an arrangement of a body of troops in line, column, or other prescribed manner **b** : an arrangement of football players at the start of a play; *esp* : the deployment of the offensive backfield at the start of a play from scrimmage — usu. used in combination; see A FORMATION, DOUBLE WINGBACK FORMATION, I FORMATION, PUNT FORMATION, SINGLE WINGBACK FORMATION, SPLIT T, SPREAD FORMATION, T FORMATION **c** : an arrangement of two or more airplanes flying as a unit and for a particular purpose (as attack, protection, or review) **7** : the arrangement of the fibers in a sheet of paper ⟨a well closed, or regular, ~⟩ ⟨a wild, or irregular, ~⟩

for·ma·tion·al \-shənᵊl, -shnəl\ *adj* : of or concerned with formation or a formation ⟨~ contrasts in geologic strata⟩ ⟨the ~ aspects of character building⟩ — **for·ma·tion·al·ly** \-ᵊlē, -əlē, -li\ *adv*

formation rule *n* : a principle in logic for establishing permissible combinations of signs (as for determining how to construct statements or formulas in a formalized language or calculus) — contrasted with *transformation rule*

¹**for·ma·tive** \'fȯ(r)məd·iv\ *adj* [MF *formatif*, fr. L *formatus* + MF *-if* -ive] **1 a** : capable of giving form : tending to give form : CONSTRUCTIVE ⟨a ~ influence⟩ ⟨farm animals . . . were brought to the colonies as a basic element of ~ equipment —E.D.Ross⟩ **b** *of an affix or other word element* : used in word formation or inflection **2** : capable of or subject to alteration by growth and development; *usu* : producing new cells and tissues : MERISTEMATIC, PLASTIC ⟨a ~ zone in developing bone⟩ ⟨the ~ cambium of a woody stem⟩ **3 a** : of, relating to, or characterized by formative effects or formation : CREATIVE ⟨the ~ period in the life of a child⟩ ⟨~ years⟩ ⟨the ~ arts⟩ **b** *usu cap* : of or belonging to the period of prehistoric cultural development in Peru and Central America during which the characteristic techniques and styles were forming — compare CLASSIC, FLORESCENT — **for·ma·tive·ly** \-ə̇vlē, -li\ *adv* — **for·ma·tive·ness** *n* -ES

²**formative** \"\ *n* -S : the element (as a prefix or termination) in a word that serves to give the word appropriate form and is no part of the base

for·ma·to·re \ˌfȯrmə'tō(ˌ)rā\ *n* -S [It, fr. L *formator* one that forms, fr. *formatus* + *-or*] : a molder or modeler (as of plaster or wax)

formatrix *n, pl* **formatrixes** *or* **formatrices** [LL, fem. of L *formator*] *obs* : a formative agent

form·a·zan \'fȯrmə,zan\ *n* -S [*form-* + *az-* + *-an*] : a hypothetical hydrazone $HN{=}NCH{=}NNH_2$ related to formic acid and known only in the form of intensely colored derivatives (as triphenyl-formazan) that are obtained either from hydrazones by coupling with diazonium compounds or from colorless tetrazolium compounds by the reducing action of living tissues, in the latter case serving as indicators of viability as a result of color production; *also* : any of these derivatives

form block *n* : a temporary die made of wood or plastic and used for forming a few experimental samples of embossed work (as of metal foil or paper)

form board *n* : a small board with spaces for the insertion of blocks of different shapes and sizes that is used to test an individual's speed and accuracy of insertion and his approach to the problem

form class *n* : a class of linguistic forms that can be used in the same position in a construction and that have one or more morphological or syntactical features in common ⟨*book, hat, going, deceased, little one*, and *rapidly flowing stream* belong to the same *form class* as shown by the fact that each can be used in the same position in the construction *the — is*⟩ ⟨*books* and *hats* belong to the *form classes* of nouns and of plurals⟩ ⟨*opened* and *walked* belong to the *form classes* of verbs and of past tenses⟩ — see MAJOR FORM CLASS

form critic *n* **:** a specialist in form criticism

form criticism *n* **:** a method of biblical criticism that seeks to classify units of scripture into literary patterns (as love poems, parables, sayings, elegies, legends) and that attempts to trace each type to its period of oral transmission in an effort to determine the original form and the relationship of the life and thought of the period to the development of the literary tradition

form cutter *n* **:** a cutting tool having its edge shaped to the profile to be imparted to the work

forme \ˈfō(ə)rm, -ō(ə)m\ *n* -s [F, lit., form — more at FORM] **1** *Brit* **:** ¹FORM 8 **2 a :** a pattern of an upper of a shoe **b :** a low bench on which shoemakers formerly sat when working

formed \ˈfō(ə)rmd, -ō(ə)md\ *adj* [ME, fr. past part. of *formen* to form — more at FORM] **1 :** clearly defined **:** SETTLED, DEFINITE ⟨I have no ~ opinion about the chances of success⟩ **2 :** fully developed (as by discipline or training) **:** MATURED ⟨a ~ opposition arose over the terms of the agreement⟩ ⟨a graceful but not yet fully ~ literary style⟩ **3 :** being or having the characteristics of living matter **:** ORGANIZED ⟨~ ferments extracted from the gastric mucosa⟩ ⟨~ elements of the blood⟩ **4 :** shaped (as by pressure or carving) to fit ⟨~ plastic snugly encloses the assembly⟩ ⟨a ~ handgrip on a grease gun⟩

formed coil *n* **:** an electric coil wound by a machine upon a form and transferred afterward to an armature as distinguished from a coil wound directly on the armature

for·me·don \ˈfȯrmə͵dän\ *n* -s [ME, fr. AF, fr. ML *forma doni*, lit., form of a gift] **:** a former writ of right for recovering per formam doni entailed property under English law

for·mée *also* **for·mé** \ˈfȯr͵mā\ *or* **formy** \-͵mē\ *adj* [ME *forme*, fr. MF *formé, fourmé*, past part. of *former, fourmer* to form — more at FORM] *of a cross* **:** having the arms narrow at the center and expanding toward the ends, the sides of the arms being either straight or concave lines and the ends of the arms cut off square or very slightly concave **:** PATTÉE — compare MALTESE CROSS 1; see CROSS illustration

forme fruste \fȯrmfrüest\ *n, pl* **formes frustes** \"\ [F, lit., worn-down form] **:** an atypical and usu. abortive manifestation of a disease

for·men·kreis \ˈfȯrmən͵krīs\ *n, pl* **formenkrei·se** \-īzə\ *or* **formenkreis·es** \-īsəz\ [G, lit., cycle of forms, fr. *formen*, pl. of *form* (fr. MHG *forme*, fr. L *forma*) + *kreis* circle, cycle — more at FORM, ARTENKREIS] **:** a polytypic species (as of birds)

¹form·er \ˈfȯrmər, ˈfō(ə)mə(r\ *n* -s [ME, fr. *formen* to form + *-er* — more at FORM] **1 :** one that forms **:** MAKER, CREATOR, SHAPER ⟨discipline is a ~ of character⟩ **2 :** a worker who forms materials into products or products from materials (as by cutting, pressing, bending, molding, or other hand or machine operation) — often used in combination with an attributive noun indicating the material acted on or the product produced ⟨a coil ~⟩ ⟨expert felt ~*s*⟩ **3 :** a device, tool, or machine used to form some material or product: as **a :** a shape around or by which an article is to be shaped, molded, woven, wrapped, pasted, or otherwise constructed ⟨the ~ on which paper bags are pasted⟩ **b :** a templet, pattern, gauge, guide, or block by which an article is shaped or bent **c :** FORMING DIE **d :** a device or machine for bending sheet metal into various forms (as tubes or cylinders) **e :** a machine used in ropemaking for twisting yarn into strands **4** [¹*form* + *-er*] *chiefly Brit* **:** a member of a school form — usu. used in combination ⟨sixth *formers*⟩ ⟨invited the lower *formers* on a picnic⟩

²for·mer \"\ *adj* [ME, fr. *forme* first (fr. OE *forma*) + *-er* — more at FOREMOST] **1 a :** preceding in order of time; *usu* **:** of, relating to, or occurring in the past **:** ANTECEDENT, PREVIOUS, PRIOR, EARLIER ⟨recovered some of her ~ ease⟩ ⟨as we agreed in ~ correspondence⟩ **b** *obs* **:** being far distant in time **:** ANCIENT **2 :** near the beginning **:** PRECEDING ⟨the ~ part of a discourse or argument⟩ **3 :** first mentioned or in order of two things mentioned or understood ⟨of these two evils the ~ is the lesser⟩ **4** *obs* **:** anterior in place or situation **:** FRONT, FOREMOST **5 :** having been at some previous time **:** ONETIME, SOMETIME ⟨~ president of his fraternity⟩ ⟨~ members of the legislature⟩

former adjudication *n* **:** RES JUDICATA

for·mer·et \ˈfȯrmə͵ret\ *n* -s [F, fr. MF, fr. *forme* form, large window in a church — more at FORM] **:** a wall rib in a roof vaulted with ribs

former jeopardy *n* **:** JEOPARDY 3

for·mer·ly \ˈfȯrmə(r)lē, -ō(ə)məlē, -li\ *adv* [²*former* + *-ly*] **1** *obs* **a :** in time immediately preceding **:** just before **b :** BEFOREHAND, FIRST **2 :** in time past **:** in the time of an earlier or previous period **:** ONCE, HERETOFORE, PREVIOUSLY ⟨~ there were giants in the world⟩ ⟨we ~ lived in the country⟩ ⟨a ~ prosperous area⟩

-for·mes \ˈfȯr͵mēz\ *n pl comb form* [NL, fr. L, pl. of *-formis* -form] **:** ones having (such a) form **:** ones resembling — in names of zoological orders and certain other groups of higher rank than family ⟨Galli*formes*⟩ ⟨Passeri*formes*⟩

form factor *n* **:** the ratio between the volume of a tree and that of a geometric solid (as a cylinder) having the same diameter and height

formfitting \ˈ=ˌ==\ *adj* **:** conforming to the outline of the body **:** CLOSE-FITTING ⟨a ~ sweater⟩ ⟨a comfortably ~ armchair⟩

form·ful \ˈ=fəl\ *adj* **:** exhibiting or notable for form (as in a sport) ⟨a ~ jump —*Time*⟩

form genus *n* **:** an artificial taxonomic category established for organisms of which the true relationships are obscure due to incomplete knowledge of structure (as in some fossils) or of development or life history (as in Fungi Imperfecti and various animal parasites)

form grinder *n* **:** a grinding wheel shaped to the contour to be imparted to the work — compare FORM CUTTER

for·mic \ˈfȯrmik, -ōəm-\ *adj* [irreg. fr. L *formica* ant — more at PISMIRE] **1 :** of or relating to ants **2 :** being or derived from formic acid

for·mi·ca \fȯrˈmīkə\ *n, cap* [NL, fr. L, ant] **:** a genus of hymenopterous insects formerly including all the ants but now restricted to various typical ants (as the mound-building ants and the sanguinary ant)

For·mi·ca \(ˈ)fȯrˈmīkə, fərˈm-\ *trademark* — used for various laminated plastic products used esp. in furniture (as for tabletops) and in building (as for wallboards)

formic acid *n* **:** a colorless pungent fuming vesicatory liquid acid HCOOH that occurs naturally in most ants and some other insects and in many plants, that is usu. made by acidification of sodium formate, and that is used chiefly in dyeing and finishing textiles as an acidifying or reducing agent — called also *methanoic acid*

formic aldehyde *n* **:** FORMALDEHYDE

for·mi·can \fȯrˈmīkən\ *adj* [L *formica* + E *-an*] **:** of or relating to ants

for·mi·ca·ri·idae \͵fȯrməkəˈrīə͵dē\ *n pl, cap* [NL, fr. *Formicarius*, type genus (fr. L *formica* + *-arius* -ary) + *-idae*] **:** a large family (suborder Tyranni) comprising the typical antbirds of tropical America — compare FURNARIIDAE — **for·mi·car·i·oid** \-ˈka(a)rē͵ȯid\ *adj or n* — **for·mi·car·oid** \-ˈka(a)͵rȯid\ *adj*

for·mi·car·i·um \-ˈkerēəm, -ˈa(a)r-, -ˈār-\ *n, pl* **formicar·ia** \-rēə\ [ML] **:** FORMICARY; *specif* **:** an artificial ant nest arranged for observation or study of the activities of the insects

for·mi·cary \ˈfȯrmə͵kerē, -i\ *n* -ES [ML *formicarium*, fr. L *formica* ant + *-arium* -ary] **:** the dwelling of a colony of ants **:** an ant hill or ant nest

for·mi·ca·tion \͵==ˈkāshən\ *n* -s [L *formication-, formicatio*, fr. *formicatus* (past part. of *formicare* to crawl like an ant, fr. *formica* ant) + *-ion-, -io* -ion — more at PISMIRE] **:** an abnormal sensation resembling that made by insects creeping in or on the skin

for·mic·i·dae \fȯrˈmisə͵dē\ *n pl, cap* [NL, fr. *Formica*, type genus + *-idae*] **:** a family of hymenopterous insects including all the ants

for·mi·cide \ˈfȯrmə͵sīd\ *n* -s [L *formica* ant + E *-cide*] **:** a substance used for destroying ants

¹for·mi·cine \-͵sīn, -sən\ *adj* [L *formicinus*, fr. *formica* ant + *-inus* -ine] **1 :** of, relating to, or resembling an ant **2** [NL *Formicinae* group of ants, fr. L, fem. pl. of *formicinus*] **:** belonging to a group of ants that resemble and are closely related to those of the genus *Formica*

²formicine \"\ *n* -s **:** a formicine ant

for·mi·civ·o·rous \ˈ==ˈsiv(ə)rəs\ *adj* [L *formica* ant + E *-i-* + *-vorous*] **:** feeding on ants

for·mi·coi·dea \͵==ˈkȯidēə\ *n pl, cap* [NL, fr. *Formica* + *-oidea*] **:** a superfamily of aculeate hymenopterous insects consisting of the ants and being coextensive with Formicidae

for·mi·col·o·gist \-ˈkäləjəst\ *n* -s [L *formica* ant + E *-o-* + *-logist*] **:** MYRMECOLOGIST

for·mi·da·bil·i·ty \͵fō(r)mədəˈbilədē, -ətē, -i\ *n* -ES **:** formidable quality ⟨a ~, in both size and substance, which must have deterred many readers —*Times Lit. Supp.*⟩

for·mi·da·ble \ˈfō(r)mədəbəl, fō(r)ˈmid-\ *adj* [ME, fr. L *formidabilis*, fr. *formidare* to fear, dread (fr. *formido* fear, terror) + *-abilis* -able; akin to Gk *mormō* she-monster, bugbear, *mormoros* fear] **1 :** exciting fear, dread, or apprehension ⟨a grim and ~ foe⟩ ⟨a ~ prospect⟩ ⟨the first attack was dangerous, but a second must be more ~ still —William Cowper⟩ **2 :** able seriously to impede a projected interaction or course of action usu. by interposing difficulties, hardships, or obstructions ⟨the mountains were a ~ barrier to our progress⟩ ⟨these qualities . . . made the Miltonic sentence a ~ construction —R.M.Weaver⟩; *broadly* **:** DIFFICULT ⟨~ coloratura passages⟩ **3 :** tending to inspire awe or wonder usu. by reason of notable size, quantity, superiority, or excellence ⟨had a ~ array of compositions to his credit —Joseph Wechsberg⟩; *broadly* **:** LARGE, SUPERIOR, OUTSTANDING ⟨in a society based on oral tradition the memory of the elders is ~⟩ ⟨a social lioness of ~ glamour⟩ ⟨his ~ accomplishments in art⟩ — **for·mi·da·ble·ness** \-nəs\ *n* -ES — **for·mi·da·bly** \-əblē, -li\ *adv*

forming *pres part of* FORM

forming die *n* **:** a die resembling a drawing die but lacking a blank holder

forming press *n* **:** a punch press used for forming (as metal parts)

forming punch *n* **:** a punch that operates with a forming die

forming rolls *n pl* **:** a set of rolls shaped to give a predetermined contour of cross section to work run through them

forming tool *n* **1** *or* **form tool :** a tool or machine accessory so shaped that it imparts a predetermined contour or profile to the work **2 :** a pair of light tongs with broad flat ends used in manipulating and shaping softened glass

form·ism \ˈfō(r)͵mizəm\ *n* -s [¹*form* + *-ism*] **:** a philosophical theory (as Platonism or Aristotelianism) assigning a preeminent place to metaphysical forms

form·ist \-͵məst\ *n* -s **:** one who advocates strict adherence to forms — **form·is·tic** \(͵)=ˈmistik\ *adj*

form·less \ˈ=ləs\ *adj* **:** deficient in or lacking form: as **a :** having no regular or inherent shape ⟨fluids are ~, taking the shape of their container⟩ **b :** SHAPELESS 2 ⟨a ~ old dress⟩ **c :** lacking order or arrangement **:** INCHOATE ⟨the ~ welter of his prose works —George Saintsbury⟩ **d :** having no physical existence **:** IMMATERIAL ⟨the primitive society exists in a world filled with taboos, mysteries, and ~ but often malevolent beings⟩ — **form·less·ly** *adv* — **form·less·ness** *n* -ES

form letter *n* **:** a letter on a subject of frequent recurrence (as in a business house) that can be sent to different persons without essential change other than in the address

form line *n* **:** a line drawn on a map to depict surface configuration in a generalized manner and usu. without indicating elevations — compare CONTOUR LINE

form master *n* **:** a teacher in charge of a form esp. in an English secondary school

formo- — SEE FORM-

form of action : one of the personal actions formerly brought at common law (as assumpsit, detinue, replevin)

form of address : a formula generally accepted as proper or suitable for addressing an individual of a particular rank or status either orally or in writing

form of discourse : one of the types into which discourses are classified according to function and which comprise exposition, argument, description, and narration

form of forms : FIRST CAUSE

form oil *n* **:** oil with which concrete forms esp. of metal are sometimes treated to prevent sticking upon removal

For·mol \ˈfȯr͵mōl, -ōl\ *trademark* — used for an aqueous solution of formaldehyde

for·mol·ize \-͵līz\ *vt* -ED/-ING/-S *see -ize in Explan Notes* [*Formol* + *-ize*] **:** to treat (as a serum) with a dilute formaldehyde solution esp. for the purpose of attenuating a virus or toxin

for·mo·ni·trile \fȯr͵mō+\ *n* -s [ISV *form-* + *nitrile*] **:** HYDROGEN CYANIDE

for·mo·sa \fō(r)ˈmōsə, -zə\ *adj, usu cap* [fr. *Formosa*, island in the China Sea] **:** of or from the island of Formosa ⟨*Formosa* tea⟩ **:** of the kind or style prevalent in Formosa **:** FORMOSAN

formosa camphor *n, usu cap F* **:** dextrorotatory camphor

¹for·mo·san \-sᵊn, -zᵊn\ *adj, usu cap* [*Formosa* + E *-an*] **1 :** of or relating to the island of Formosa or its inhabitants **2 :** of, relating to, or in the Formosan language

²formosan \"\ *n* -s *cap* **1 a :** a native or inhabitant of Formosa **b :** a member of one of the largely uncivilized groups of mixed Mongolian and Indonesian descent that live in the interior of the island **2 a :** the Indonesian languages of the Formosan people **b :** any of these languages

formosan pheasant *n, usu cap F* **:** a rather light-colored pheasant native to Formosa that is probably a variety of the ring-necked pheasant with which it freely interbreeds and that like the latter has been widely introduced in No. America

for·mos·i·ty \fȯrˈmäsəd-ē, -ətē, -i\ *n* -ES [ME *formosite*, fr. L *formositas*, fr. *formosus* beautiful (fr. *forma* form, beauty + *-osus* -ous) + *-itas* -ity — more at FORM] *archaic* **:** beauty or a beautiful thing

form quotient *n* **:** the ratio of the breast-high diameter of a tree to the diameter at some higher point

forms *pl of* FORM, *pres 3d sing of* FORM

form species *n* **:** a taxonomic species placed in a form genus

for·mu·la \ˈfȯrmyələ, -ō(ə)m-\ *n, pl* **formu·las** \-ləz\ *also* **formu·lae** \-͵lē, -͵lī\ *often attrib* [L, dim. of *forma* form] **1 a :** a set form of words for use in a ceremony or ritual **b :** a formal statement of religious doctrine or a written confession of faith **c :** a conventionalized statement intended to express some fundamental truth or principle esp. as a basis for negotiation, discussion, or action ⟨the two nations sought a ~ that would allow settling of the border dispute⟩ ⟨the ~ "54–40 or fight"⟩ **2 a :** a recipe or prescription giving method and proportions of ingredients for the preparation of some material (as a medicine, a blend of coffee, or a caulking compound) **b :** a milk mixture or substitute for feeding an infant typically consisting of prescribed proportions and forms of cow's milk, water, and sugar; *often* **:** a batch of this made up at one time to meet an infant's future requirements (as during a 24-hour period) **3 a :** a general fact, rule, or principle expressed in symbols ⟨certain earlier workers attempted to differentiate nematodes by a ~ of numerical ratios⟩ **b :** a symbolic expression showing the composition or constitution of a chemical substance and consisting of symbols for the elements present and subscripts to indicate the relative or total number of atoms present in a molecule ⟨the ~*s* for water, sulfuric acid, and ethyl alcohol are H_2O, H_2SO_4, and C_2H_5OH respectively⟩ — see EMPIRICAL FORMULA, GENERAL FORMULA, MOLECULAR FORMULA, STRUCTURAL FORMULA **c :** a group of symbols (as numbers, letters, or arbitrary signs) associated to express briefly a single concept; *also, in logic* **:** any combination of signs in an uninterpreted calculus **d** *in logic* **:** an expression (as a statement or matrix) stipulated to be meaningful by the rules of the calculus to which it belongs; *esp* **:** such an expression containing only variables **4 :** a prescribed or set form **:** a fixed or conventional method (as of acting, arranging, or speaking) **:** an established rule or custom — often used somewhat derogatorily ⟨many of the paintings were unimaginative ~ works⟩ ⟨the limitations of ~ fiction —Coleman Rosenberger⟩ **5 :** any of the various written forms by which the praetors of ancient Rome referred causes to judges or arbitrators for hearing and adjudication upon a summons of the defendant into court by the plaintiff

for·mu·lable \-ləbəl\ *adj* [*formulate* + *-able*] **:** capable of being formulated

for·mu·la·ic \ˈ==ˈlā·ik\ *adj* [*formula* + *-ic*] **:** characterized by or made up of formulas **:** constituting a formula ⟨~ expression of ideas⟩ ⟨a ~ phrase⟩ — **for·mu·la·i·cal·ly** \-ək(ə)lē\ *adv*

for·mu·lar·ism \ˈfȯrmyələ͵rizəm\ *n* -s [¹*formulary* + *-ism*] **:** the practice of depending on or adhering strictly to set formulas — **for·mu·lar·is·tic** \ˈ===ˈristik\ *adj*

for·mu·la·ri·zable \ˈ==ˈrīzəbəl\ *adj* **:** capable of being reduced to a formula **:** FORMULABLE

for·mu·lar·iza·tion \͵===rəˈzāshən, -͵rīˈz-\ *n* -s **:** an act or a product of formularizing

for·mu·lar·ize \-͵rīz\ *vt* -ED/-ING/-S [¹*formulary* + *-ize*] **1 :** to state in or reduce to a formula **:** FORMULATE **2 :** to bind or circumscribe the action of by formulas ⟨men tricked by their own ingenuity into becoming *formularized* slaves of the machines they created⟩ — **for·mu·lar·iz·er** \-zə(r\ *n* -s

¹for·mu·lary \ˈ==͵lerē, -ri\ *n* -ES [MF *formulaire*, fr. *formule* formula (fr. L *formula*) + *-aire* -ary] **1 :** a book or other collection of stated and prescribed forms (as of oaths, declarations, or prayers) **:** a system of formulas ⟨a liturgical ~⟩ **2 :** a prescribed form or model **:** FORMULA **3 :** a book containing a list of medicinal substances and formulas for making medicines

²formulary \"\ *adj* [*formula* + *-ary*] **1 :** of or relating to formulas or to a formulary system **2 :** constituting a formula ⟨a ~ solution of a problem⟩ **3 :** preoccupied with or adhering to formulas ⟨a stiff ~ man⟩

formulas *pl of* FORMULA

for·mu·lat·able \ˈ==͵lād·əbəl\ *adj* **:** capable of being formulated

for·mu·late \-͵lāt, *usu* -ād·+V\ *vt* -ED/-ING/-S [*formula* + *-ate*] **1 a :** to reduce to or express in or as if in a formula **:** put into a systematized statement or expression **b :** to plan out in orderly fashion **:** DEVISE ⟨*formulating* expedients to meet the emergency⟩ **2 a :** to develop a formula for the preparation of (as a soap or a plastic) **:** standardize by formula **b :** to make or prepare in accord with a formula

for·mu·la·tion \͵==ˈlāshən\ *n* -s **:** an act or the product of formulating ⟨his ~ of the data was clear and concise⟩ ⟨a new varnish ~⟩

for·mu·la·tive \ˈ==͵lād·iv, -ātiv, -ēv\ *adj* **:** tending to effect formulation ⟨exerting ~ influences on the student's thought processes⟩

for·mu·la·tor \-͵lād·ə(r), -ātə-\ *n* -s **:** one that formulates; *esp* **:** a developer of commercial and industrial formulas

for·mu·la·to·ry \-͵lə͵tōrē, -͵ōr-\ *adj* **:** of or relating to formulation

for·mule \ˈfȯr(͵)myül\ *n* -s [F, fr. L *formula* — more at FORMULA] **:** FORMULA

for·mu·lism \-͵myə͵lizəm\ *n* -s [*formula* + *-ism*] **:** attachment to or reliance on formulas

for·mu·lis·tic \ˈ==ˈlistik\ *adj* **:** based on or characterized by a formula

for·mu·li·za·tion \͵==ləˈzāshən, -͵līˈz-\ *n* -s **:** FORMULATION

for·mu·lize \ˈ==͵līz\ *vt* -ED/-ING/-S [*formula* + *-ize*] **:** FORMULATE 1

form up *vi* **:** to assume or participate in an orderly arrangement ⟨the waiting crowd *formed up* in a long line⟩ ⟨the planes *formed up* over the airfield⟩

Form·var \ˈfȯrm͵vär\ *trademark* — used for various thermoplastic resins that are formals of polyvinyl alcohol and are used esp. in coatings, adhesives, and molding materials

form word *n* **:** FUNCTION WORD

formwork \ˈ=͵=\ *n* **:** a set of forms in place for the reception of concrete

formy *var of* FORMÉE

for·myl \ˈfȯr͵mil, -͵məl\ *n* -s [ISV *form-* + *-yl*] **:** the radical HCO– of formic acid that is also characteristic of aldehydes

for·myl·ate \-͵mə͵lāt\ *vt* -ED/-ING/-S [*formyl* + *-ate*] **:** to introduce formyl into (a compound) — **for·myl·a·tion** \͵==ˈlāshən\ *n* -s

formyl violet S4B *n, usu cap F&V* **:** an acid dye — see DYE table I (under *Acid Violet 17*)

for·nent \fə(r)ˈnent\ *or* **for·ninst** \-ˈninzt, -ˈnin(t)st\ *also* **for·nenst** \-ˈnenzt, -ˈnen(t)st\ *prep* [ME (Sc dial.) *fornent, forenent, forentis*, fr. ME *for-, fore-* fore + *anent* or *anentes* anenst — more at ANENT, ANENST] **1** *dial* **:** in front of **:** OPPOSITE ⟨a little square ~ the church⟩ **2** *dial* **:** near to **:** alongside of **:** BESIDE, AGAINST ⟨left the shovel ~ the fence⟩

¹for·ni·cate \ˈfō(r)nə͵kāt, *usu* -ād·+V\ *vb* -ED/-ING/-S [LL *fornicatus*, past part. of *fornicare, fornicari*, fr. L *fornic-, fornix* arch, vault, arched basement (inhabited by people of the lower classes), brothel, prob. fr. *fornus, furnus* oven — more at FURNACE] *vi* **:** to commit fornication ~ *vt* **:** to engage in fornication with

²for·ni·cate \-nəkət, -nə͵kāt\ *also* **for·ni·cat·ed** \-nə͵kād·əd\ *adj* [L *fornicatus*, fr. *fornic-, fornix* arch, vault + L *-atus* -ate, -ated] **1 :** having an arched or vaulted form ⟨a small mollusk with an abruptly ~ shell⟩ ⟨broad ~ leaves⟩ **2** *of plants* **:** having fornices

¹for·ni·ca·tion \͵fō(r)nəˈkāshən\ *n* -s [ME *fornicacioun*, fr. MF & LL; MF *fornication*, fr. LL *fornication-, fornicatio*, fr. *fornicatus* (past part.) + L *-ion-, -io* -ion] **1 :** human sexual intercourse other than between a man and his wife **:** sexual intercourse between a spouse and an unmarried person **:** sexual intercourse between unmarried people — used in some translations (as AV, DV) of the Bible (as in Mt 5:32) for *unchastity* (as in RSV) or *immorality* (as in NCE) to cover all sexual intercourse except between husband and wife or concubine **2 :** sexual intercourse on the part of an unmarried person accomplished with consent and not deemed adultery — compare INCEST, RAPE

²fornication \"\ *n* -s [L *fornication-, fornicatio*, fr. *fornicatus* vaulted + *-ion-, -io* -ion] **:** a vaulting or arching **:** vaulted construction (as of a cloister)

for·ni·ca·tor \ˈfō(r)nə͵kād·ə(r), -ātə-\ *n* -s [ME *fornicatour*, fr. LL *fornicator*, fr. *fornicatus* (past part.) + L *-or*] **:** a person guilty of fornication — sometimes used to distinguish the male participant in such conduct; compare FORNICATRIX

for·ni·ca·to·ry \ˈfō(r)nəkə͵tōrē, fō(r)ˈnik-\ *adj* [*fornicate* + *-ory*] **:** of or relating to fornication ⟨~ literature⟩

fornicatress *n* -ES [*fornicator* + *-ess*] *obs* **:** FORNICATRIX

for·ni·ca·trix \͵fō(r)nəˈkā·triks\ *n, pl* **fornicatri·ces** \-kəˈtrī͵sēz\ [LL, fem. of *fornicator*] **:** a woman guilty of fornication — compare FORNICATOR

for·nic·i·form \(ˈ)fȯrˈnisə͵fȯrm\ *adj* [L *fornic-, fornix* + E *-iform*] **:** FORNICATE

for·nix \ˈfȯrniks, -nēks\ *n, pl* **forni·ces** \-nə͵sēz\ [NL, fr. L, arch, vault — more at FORNICATE] **1** *anat* **:** an arch or fold or an arched or folded structure: as **a :** the vault of the cranium **b :** the part of the conjunctiva overlying the cornea **c :** a body of nerve fibers lying beneath the corpus callosum with which they are continuous posteriorly and serving to integrate the hippocampus with other parts of the brain **d :** the vaulted upper part of the vagina surrounding the uterine cervix **e :** the fundus of the stomach **f :** the vault of the pharynx **2 :** one of the small arched scales in the throat of the corolla of some plants (as members of the genus *Myosotis*)

for·pine \fə(r)ˈpīn\ *vb* -ED/-ING/-S [ME *forpinen*, fr. *for-* + *pinen* to pine — more at PINE] *archaic* **:** to waste or pine away (as from anguish or suffering)

for·pit *or* **for·pet** \ˈfōrpət\ *n* -s [alter. of *fourth part*] *chiefly Scot* **:** ¼ peck

for·rad *or* **for·rard** \ˈfȯrə(r)d\ *dial var of* FORWARD

for·rad·er *also* **for·rard·er** \-də(r)\ *chiefly dial comparative of* FORWARD

for real *adv* **1 :** in earnest **:** SERIOUSLY ⟨this was no casual scuffling: they were fighting *for real*⟩ **2** *slang* **:** REALLY ⟨now you've messed things up *for real*⟩

forrel *var of* FOREL

for·rit \ˈfȯrət\ *chiefly Scot var of* FORWARD

for·rit·some \-tsəm\ *adj* [*forrit* + *-some*] *Scot* **:** BOLD, IMPUDENT, FORWARD

fors *pl of* FOR

for·sake \fə(r)ˈsāk, fȯrˈ-, fō(ə)ˈ-\ *vt* **for·sook** \-ˈsu̇k\ **for·saken** \-ˈsākən\ **forsaking; forsakes** [ME *forsaken* to reject, forsake, fr. OE *forsacan*, fr. *for-* + *sacan* to dispute, Goth *sakan* to quarrel — more at SAKE] **1 :** to renounce or surrender (as a custom or practice formerly held dear) ⟨promised to ~ his bad habits if she would marry him⟩ **2 :** to quit or leave entirely **:** depart or withdraw from **:** LEAVE, DESERT, ABANDON ⟨false friends ~ us in adversity⟩ ⟨*forsook* the theater for a career in politics⟩

forsaken *adj* [ME, fr. past part. of *forsaken*] **:** left desolate or empty **:** DESERTED ⟨the ~ slopes where children once played on their way from school⟩; *often* **:** miserable and forlorn as if deserted ⟨the conviction that where one was born and lives is the best place in the world no matter how ~ a hole it may appear to an outsider —E.L.Ullman⟩ — see GODFORSAKEN — **for·sak·en·ly** *adv* — **for·sak·en·ness** \-kən(n)əs\ *n* -ES

for·sak·er \-kə(r)\ *n* -S [ME, fr. *forsaken* to forsake + *-er*] **:** one that forsakes

forslack *vt* [*for-* + *slack*] *obs* **:** to be remiss in **:** NEGLECT

for·slow \fə(r)'slō\ *vb* [ME *forslewen* to be slow, delay, fr. OE *forslǣwan, forslāwian*, fr. *for-* + *-slǣwan, slāwian* to be slow, fr. *slāw* slow — more at SLOW] *archaic* **:** to put off **:** DELAY

forsook *past or obs past part of* FORSAKE

for·sooth \fə(r)'süth\ *adv* [ME *for soth, for sothe*, fr. OE *forsōth*, fr. *for* + *sōth* truth — more at SOOTH] **:** in truth **:** CERTAINLY, INDEED — now often used to imply contempt or doubt ⟨a pretty story ~⟩

for·speak \fə(r)'spēk\ *vt* [ME *forspeken* to cast a bad spell over, speak evil of, fr. OE *forspecan, forsprecan* to speak in vain, deny, denounce, fr. *for-* + *specan, sprecan* to speak — more at SPEAK] **1** *now dial Brit* **:** to cast a bad spell over **:** bewitch esp. by immoderate praise ⟨don't boast about the child, lest you ~ him⟩ **2** *obs* **:** to speak against **:** ASPERSE

for·spent \fə(r)'spent\ *adj* [*for-* + *spent*] *archaic* **:** worn out **:** EXHAUSTED ⟨~ with speed —Shak.⟩

forss·man antibody \'fȯrsmən-\ *n, usu cap F* [after John *Forssman* †1947 Swedish pathologist] **:** an antibody (as heterophile antibody) active against a Forssman antigen

forssman antigen *n, usu cap F* [after J. *Forssman*] **:** an antigenic constituent occurring in animals without regard to biologic relationship (as one present in guinea pigs and sheep but absent from rabbits and cattle) **:** a heterophile antigen

for·ster·ite \'fȯ(r)stə,rīt\ *n* -S [Johann R. *Forster* †1798 Ger. traveler + E *-ite*] **:** a mineral consisting of magnesian olivine; *specif* **:** magnesium silicate Mg_2SiO_4 constituting the essential component of some refractories

forster's tern *n, usu cap F* [after Johann R. *Forster*] **:** a black-capped tern (*Sterna forsteri*) that is related to the common tern, breeds chiefly in marshes and on the interior lakes of No. America, and migrates southward in winter

forst·ner bit \'fȯrstnər-\ *n, usu cap F* [fr. the name *Forstner*] **:** a spurless wood-drilling bit used esp. for drilling blind holes

for sure *adv* **:** CERTAINLY, INEVITABLY

for·swear *or* **fore·swear** \fȯr'swe(ə)r, -wa(a)(ə)r; fō(ə)'sweə, -wa(a)ə\ *vb* **for·swore** *or* **fore·swore** \fȯr'swō(ə)r, -wȯ(ə)r; fō(ə)'swōə, -wȯ(ə)\ **forsworn** *or* **foresworn** \fȯr'swō(ə)rn, fō(ə)'swȯ(ə)n\ **forswearing** *or* **foreswearing**; **forswears** *or* **foreswears** [ME *forsweren*, fr. OE *forswerian* (akin to OS *farswerian* to swear falsely, OHG *farsweren* to abjure), fr. *for-* + *swerian* to swear — more at SWEAR] *vt* **1 :** to reject or renounce upon oath; *broadly* **:** to renounce earnestly, determinedly, or with protestations — sometimes used with an infinitive as object ⟨she had *forsworn* to wed again⟩ **2 :** to deny upon oath ⟨*forswore* the debt⟩ **3 a** *archaic* **:** to swear to (as a matter of fact) falsely **b :** PERJURE ⟨~ himself⟩ ~ *vi* **:** to swear falsely **:** commit perjury **syn** see ABJURE

forsworn *or* **foresworn** *adj* [ME, fr. OE *forsworen*, past part. of *forswerian*] **:** PERJURED

for·syth·ia \fə(r)'sithēə, fȯ(r)- *sometimes* -ithēə\ *n* [NL, fr. William *Forsyth* †1804 Brit. botanist + NL *-ia*] **1** *cap* **:** a small genus of ornamental Asian and European shrubs (family Oleaceae) with opposite leaves and bright yellow bell-shaped flowers which appear before the leaves in early spring **2** -S **:** any plant of the genus *Forsythia* **3** -S *often cap* **a :** a moderate orange yellow **b :** a brilliant yellow

¹fort \'fō(ə)r|t, -ō(ə)r|, -ōə|, -ō(ə)|, *usu* |d·+V\ *n* -S [ME *forte*, fr. MF *fort*, fr. *fort* strong, fortified, fr. L *fortis* strong, fr. OL *forctis*; prob. akin to OHG *berg* mountain — more at BARROW] **1 :** a strong or fortified place: as **a :** a fortified place occupied only by troops and surrounded with such works as a ditch, rampart, and parapet **:** FORTIFICATION **b :** an enclosed work possessing bastions **c :** a permanent army post of the U.S. — often used in place names **2 :** a trading post on the No. American frontier

²fort \"\ *vb* -ED/-ING/-S *vt* **1 :** to protect by or station or gather in a fort **2 :** to enclose by fortifications **:** FORTIFY ~ *vi* **1** *archaic* **:** to construct fortifications **2 :** to gather in a strong or fortified place (as for defense)

fort *abbr* fortification; fortified

for·ta·le·za \,fȯ(r)d·ə'lāzə\ *adj, usu cap* [fr. *Fortaleza*, Brazil] **:** of or from the city of Fortaleza, Brazil **:** of the kind or style prevalent in Fortaleza

for·ta·lice \'fȯ(r)d·ələs\ *n* -S [ME, fr. ML *fortalitia* — more at FORTRESS] **1** *archaic* **:** FORTRESS **2** *archaic* **:** a small fort or an outwork of a fortification

fort ancient *adj, usu cap F&A* [fr. *Fort Ancient*, Warren county, Ohio] **:** of or belonging to a late prehistoric aspect of the upper Mississippi culture centered in southern Ohio and Indiana and extending into Kentucky and West Virginia

¹forte \'fō(ə)r|t, -ō(ə)r|, -ōə|, -ō(ə)|, *usu* |d·+V *also* 'fȯr|d·-(,)ā, -ō(ə)|, |(,)tā\ *n* -S [earlier *fort*, fr. MF, fr. *fort*, adj., strong — more at FORT] **1 :** one's strong point **:** that in which one excels ⟨writing is his ~⟩ **2 :** the stronger part of the blade of a sword **:** the part or half of a sword nearest the hilt — opposed to *foible*

²for·te \'fȯr|d·(,)ā, 'fō(ə)|, (,)tā; *also* 'fȯr|d·|ē, |t|, |i\ *adv (or adj)* [It, strongly, loudly, fr. *forte*, adj., strong, loud, fr. L *fortis* strong — more at FORT] **:** LOUDLY, POWERFULLY — used as a direction in music; opposed to *piano*; abbr. *f* or *F*

³forte \"\ *n* -S **:** a tone or passage played forte

for·te·men·te \,fȯrd·ə'men·(,)tā\ *adv* [It, fr. *forte*, adj.] **:** STRONGLY, LOUDLY — used as a direction in music

for·te·pi·a·no \,fȯ(r)d·ə'pyä(,)nō\ *n* [F or It; F, fr. It, fr. *forte* loud + *piano* soft] *archaic* **:** PIANOFORTE

forte-piano \¦=¦=(,)=\ *adj* [It, lit., loud-soft] **:** loud then immediately soft — used as a direction in music; abbr. *fp*

fortes *pl of* FORTIS

for·tes·cue \'fȯrd·ə,skyü\ *also* **for·tes·cure** \-yůr\ *or* **for·tes·que** \-yü\ *n* -S [alter. (influenced by the proper name *Fortescue*) of *forty-skewer*] **:** an Australian scorpion fish (*Centropogon australis*) having along the back venomous erectile spines capable of inflicting painful wounds — called also *forty-skewer, scorpion*

¹forth \'fō(ə)rth, 'fȯ(ə)rth, 'fōəth, 'fȯ(ə)th\ *adv* [ME, adv. & prep., fr. OE; akin to OFris & OS *forth* forward, further, MHG *vort*, and to OE *for*, prep., for, before — more at FOR] **1 :** onward in time, place, or order **:** in advance from a given point **:** on to or toward the end **:** FORWARD ⟨from that day ~⟩ ⟨one, two, three, and so ~⟩ ⟨swaying back and ~⟩ **2 :** out esp. from a state of concealment, retirement, confinement, or nondevelopment **:** out into notice or view ⟨the plants in spring put ~ leaves⟩ ⟨invites them ~ to labor in the sun —John Dryden⟩ ⟨a spring issuing ~ from the hill⟩ **3** *obs* **:** beyond a certain boundary **:** AWAY, ABROAD ⟨I have no mind of feasting ~ tonight —Shak.⟩

²forth \"\ *prep* [ME] **1** *obs* **:** forward or onward to **2** *archaic* **:** forth from **:** out of

³forth *n* -S [ME, fr. ¹*forth*] *obs* **:** free course **:** WAY — used chiefly in the phrase *have one's forth*

for that *conj, archaic* **:** BECAUSE

forthbringer \(')=¦==\ *n* -S [¹*forth* + *bringer*] **:** one that brings forth

forth·come \(')=¦kəm\ *vi* [back-formation fr. *forthcoming*] **:** to be forthcoming

forth·com·er \-mə(r)\ *n* -S **:** one that comes forth

¹forth·com·ing \(')=¦kəmiŋ, -mēŋ\ *adj* [fr. pres. part. of obs. *forthcome* to come forth, fr. ME *forthcomen*, fr. ¹*forth* + *comen* to come — more at COME] **1 :** about to appear **:** APPROACHING ⟨the ~ holidays⟩ ⟨a new edition is reported to be ~ in the fall⟩ **2 a :** readily available ⟨new funds will be ~ after the election⟩ **b :** AFFABLE, APPROACHABLE, SOCIABLE ⟨a pleasingly ~ manner⟩

²forthcoming \"\ *n* [fr. gerund of obs. *forthcome*] **1 :** a coming forth **:** APPROACH **2** *or* **furth·com·ing** \fərth'kəmiŋ\ **:** an action under Scots law by which an arrestment is perfected by sentence ordering the debt to be paid or the goods to be delivered to the creditor

forthcoming bond *n* **:** a bond given to a sheriff conditioned to duly produce the property levied upon

forth·com·ing·ness *n* -ES **:** the quality or state of being forthcoming; *usu* **:** APPROACHABILITY, SOCIABILITY

forthfaring \=¦==\ *n* -S [¹*forth* + *faring*, gerund of ¹*fare*] **:** an act or instance of going out **:** a journey forth

forthgaze \=¦=\ *vi* **:** to gaze forth

forthgoer \=¦==\ *n* [¹*forth* + *goer*] **:** one that goes forth (as from a home place or group of associates)

¹forthgoing \(')=¦gōiŋ, -ōēŋ\ *n* [ME, fr. gerund of *forthgon* to go forth, fr. ¹*forth* + *gon* to go — more at GO] **:** a going forth (as a departure) **:** something that goes forth (as an utterance)

²forthgoing \"\ *adj* **:** ENTHUSIASTIC, GRACIOUS

for·think \fər'thiŋk\ *vb* **for·thought** \-'thȯt\ **forthought; forthinking; forthinks** [ME *forthinken, forthenken* to regret, repent, displease, be displeased; partly fr. *for-* + *thinken* to seem; partly fr. OE *forthencan* to mistrust, despise, despair, fr. *for-* + *thencan* to think — more at THINK] *vt, now chiefly Scot* **:** to change the mind of (oneself); *often* **:** REGRET ~ *vi, now chiefly Scot* **:** to have a change of mind or a feeling of regret

forth of *prep* [¹*forth*] **:** out of **:** out from ⟨the lion came *forth of* his den⟩

forth on *adv* [ME, fr. ¹*forth* + *on* (adv.)] *obs* **:** ONWARD, FORTHWITH

¹forthputting \(')=¦==\ *adj* [¹*forth* + *putting*, pres. part. of *put*] **:** BOLD, FORWARD

²forthputting \"\ *n* [¹*forth* + *putting*, gerund of *put*] **1 :** an act of putting forth ⟨his determined ~ of effort⟩ **2 :** forward or aggressive conduct

¹forth·right \(')=¦=\ *adv* [ME, fr. ¹*forth* + *right* (adv.)] **1 a :** directly forth or ahead **:** unswervingly forward **b :** without hesitation **:** FRANKLY ⟨spoke ~ and to the point⟩ **2** *archaic* **:** STRAIGHTWAY, STRAIGHTFORWARD, IMMEDIATELY

²forthright \"\ *adj* [ME, fr. ¹*forth* + *right* (adj.)] **:** proceeding straight on; *usu* **:** lacking ambiguity **:** DIRECT, STRAIGHTFORWARD ⟨a ~ man⟩ ⟨a ~ approach to a problem⟩ — **forth·right·ly** *adv* — **forth·right·ness** *n* -ES

³forthright \'=,=\ *n* **:** a straight path or direct course (as of action)

forthsetting \=¦==\ *n* [¹*forth* + *setting*, gerund of *set*] *archaic* **:** an exhibition or setting forth

forthtell \=¦=\ *vt* [¹*forth* + *tell*] **:** to make public **:** PUBLISH — **forth·tell·er** \"+ə(r)\ *n*

forth·ward \'fōrthwərd, 'fȯr-\ *adv* [ME, fr. OE *forthweard* forward, continually, henceforth, fr. ¹*forth* + *-weard* -ward] *archaic* **:** FORWARD

forthwith \'=,=\ *adv* [ME, fr. ¹*forth* + *with*] **1 :** with dispatch **:** without delay **:** within a reasonable time ⟨you are to proceed ~ to your home⟩ **:** IMMEDIATELY **2 :** immediately after some preceding event **:** THEREUPON ⟨when students . . . are suspended, they must ~ leave Williamsburg —*College of William & Mary Catalog*⟩ ⟨the legislature left the capital and that city ~ became less important to the revolutionary forces⟩ ⟨immediately there fell from his eyes as it had been scales: and he received sight ~ —Acts 9:18 (AV)⟩

for thy *adv* [ME *forthy*, fr. OE *forthȳ*, fr. *for* + *thȳ*, instr. of *thæt* it, that — more at THAT] *obs* **:** on this account **:** THEREFORE ⟨have no care *for thy* —Edmund Spenser⟩

forthy \'fōrthi\ *adj* [¹*forth* + *-y*] **1** *dial Brit* **:** forward and enterprising **:** inclined to be officious **2** *dial Brit* **:** open and friendly in nature and disposition **:** AFFABLE

forties *pl of* FORTY

¹for·ti·eth \'fȯ(r)d·|ēəth, -(r)t|, |iəth\ *adj* [ME *fourtithe*, adj. & n., fr. OE *fēowertigotha*, fr. *fēowertig* forty + *-otha, -tha* -th — more at FORTY] **1 :** being number 40 in a countable series ⟨the ~ day⟩ — see NUMBER table **2 :** being one of 40 equal parts into which something is divisible ⟨a ~ share of the money⟩

²fortieth \"\ *n* -S [ME *fourtithe*] **1 :** number 40 in a countable series **2 :** the quotient of a unit divided by 40 **:** one of 40 equal parts of something ⟨one ~ of the total⟩

for·ti·fi·able \'fȯ(r)d·ə,fīəbəl\ *adj* **:** capable of or suitable for being fortified

for·ti·fi·ca·tion \,fȯ(r)d·əfə'kāshən, -)təf-\ *n* -S [ME *fortificacioun*, fr. MF *fortification*, fr. LL *fortification-, fortificatio*, fr. *fortificatus* (past part. of *fortificare*) + L *-ion-, -io* -ion] **1 :** an act or process of fortifying: as **a :** a strengthening by corroboration (as of a statement) or by reinforcement (as of a structure) **b :** the act of furnishing (as a military post) with defensive works; *also* **:** the art or science of fortifying places or positions **c :** increase in the content of an ingredient (as alcohol in wine or vitamins in flour) by addition **:** ENRICHMENT **2 :** something that fortifies, defends, or strengthens; *esp* **:** works erected to defend a place or position

fortification agate *n* **:** agate having angular markings resembling the plan of a fortification

fortified wine *n* **:** a wine (as most dessert wines) to which alcohol usu. in the form of grape brandy has been added during or after fermentation — used descriptively but not permitted in labeling or advertising in the U.S.

for·ti·fi·er \'fȯrd·ə,fī(ə)r, -rtə,-; 'fȯd·ə,fīə, -ōtə,-\ *n* -S **:** one that fortifies

for·ti·fy \-,fī\ *vb* -ED/-ING/-ES [ME *fortifien*, fr. MF *fortifier*, fr. LL *fortificare*, fr. L *fortis* strong + *-ficare* -fy — more at FORT] *vt* **1 :** to make strong **:** STRENGTHEN: as **a :** to strengthen and secure (as a town) by forts or batteries or by surrounding with fortifications **b** *obs* **:** to equip and supply (as a garrison or fortress) **c :** to add strength by reinforcing the structure of ⟨~*ing* the dam with riprap⟩ **d :** to give physical strength, courage, or endurance to **:** INVIGORATE, REFRESH ⟨a balanced diet *fortifies* the system against infection⟩ ⟨*fortified* himself with a glass of wine⟩ **e :** to add mental or moral strength to **:** furnish with resistant power **:** help to endure **:** ENCOURAGE, CONFIRM ⟨their spirits *fortified* with prayer⟩ ⟨*fortified* by initial successes he determined to carry out his plan⟩ ⟨let thy spirit ~ me in times of trouble⟩ **2** *obs* **:** to make (as a way) passable **3 :** to add material to for the purpose of strengthening or improving: as **a :** to add ethyl alcohol to (as wines) **b :** to enrich (as a foodstuff or diet) by increasing the content of material usu. present (as minerals or vitamins) or by adding something not normally present (as an antibiotic) **c :** to bring (as a weak or spent solution) to the proper concentration by addition of a deficient substance ⟨~*ing* spent nitric acid recovered from the nitrating of cellulose with concentrated nitric acid⟩ ~ *vi* **1** *obs* **:** to grow or become strong **2 :** to erect fortifications **:** prepare military defenses **syn** see STRENGTHEN

for·ti·fy·ing·ly *adv* **:** so as to fortify **:** with or for a fortifying effect

for·tin \'fȯrd·ən\ *n* -S [F, fr. It *fortino*, dim. of *forte* fort, prob. fr. F *fort* — more at FORT] **:** a little fort

for·tin barometer \(')fȯr'taⁿ-\ *also* **fortin's barometer** *n, usu cap F* [after Jean *Fortin* †1831 Fr. physicist and engineer, its inventor] **:** a cup barometer having an adjustable cistern

forting *pres part of* FORT

¹for·tis \'fȯr|d·əs, 'fȯ(ə)|, |təs\ *adj* [NL, fr. L, strong — more at FORT] *of one of two homorganic consonants* **:** produced with greater articulatory tenseness and stronger expiration ⟨\t\ in *toe* is ~, \d\ in *doe* is lenis⟩

²fortis \"\ *n, pl* **fortes** \|d·(,)ēz, |,tēz\ [NL, fr. *fortis*, adj.] **:** a fortis consonant

For·ti·san \'fȯ(r)d·ə,san, -,zan\ *trademark* **1** — used for a strong filament yarn made from regenerated cellulose **2 :** a lightweight fabric made from Fortisan yarn and used for parachutes, clothing, curtains, bandages, and various industrial purposes

¹for·tis·si·mo \(')fȯ(r)¦tisə,mō\ *adv (or adj)* [It, fr. L *fortissimus*, superl. of *fortis* — more at FORT] **:** very loud — used as a direction in music; abbr. *ff*

²fortissimo \"\ *n, pl* **fortissimos** \-,mōz\ *or* **fortissi·mi** \-,mē\ [It, fr. *fortissimo*, adj.] **:** a very loud passage, sound, or tone

for·tis·sis·si·mo \¦fȯ(r)d·ə¦sisə,mō\ *adv (or adj)* [It, fr. *fortissimo* (by reduplication of the *-iss-* of the superl. suffix)] **:** with greatest loudness — used as a direction in music; abbr. *fff*

for·ti·tude \'fȯ(r)d·ə,tüd, -)tə,-, -ə,tyüd\ *n* -S [ME, fr. L *fortitudo*, fr. *fortis* strong + *-tudo* -tude — more at FORT] **1** *obs* **:** STRENGTH, IMPREGNABILITY ⟨the ~ of the place is best known to you —Shak.⟩ **2 :** the strength or firmness of mind that enables a person to encounter danger with coolness and courage or to bear pain or adversity without murmuring, depression, or despondency **:** passive courage **:** resolute endurance ⟨had borne her mother's death . . . with quiet ~ —Ellen Glasgow⟩ ⟨the temporary ~ they had gained from the jug —Irwin Shaw⟩

syn GRIT, BACKBONE, PLUCK, GUTS, SAND. Although these terms are often used interchangeably, the following distinctions may be made: FORTITUDE usu. indicates blended resolute courage, firm behavior, and power of prolonged endurance under duress ⟨a life of unremitting physical toil and mental anxiety combined with miserable health . . . no small test of *fortitude* —John Buchan⟩ ⟨deepest admiration of Welch's *fortitude* and indomitable spirit during these months when he was slowly dying of cancer —Eleanor M. Sickels⟩ GRIT usu. blends strength, mental firmness, and a hard or indomitable endurance of deprivation or distress ⟨the foot soldier will still have to advance against strongly entrenched and fanatical troops, through sheer *grit* and fighting skill —H.S. Truman⟩ BACKBONE may indicate resolute ability and determined independence in confronting opposition or difficulty without quailing ⟨the man's *backbone* and perseverance did not fail him once in all the years of poverty and discouragement⟩ ⟨like conscience-stricken dogs they lost *backbone*, and visibly were in a condition to submit to anything —Kenneth Roberts⟩ PLUCK usu. applies to game stoutheartedness in the face of danger or willingness to continue fighting against odds ⟨the energy, fortitude, and dogged perseverance that we technically style *pluck* —E.G.Bulwer-Lytton⟩ ⟨what indomitable courage he had, how fearless he was in the midst of danger, how keen and wary in his dealing with an enemy, and how full of resources and *pluck* when difficulties arose —H.E.Scudder⟩ GUTS, usu. forceful and sometimes considered vulgar, indicates vigorous stamina in confronting and coping with what alarms, repels, discourages, or enervates ⟨he could tell by the set of Bill's mouth that sheer *guts* was all that kept him hanging to that bull's head now —F.B.Gipson⟩ ⟨what bothered him was not the superzealot attackers so much as the lack of plain old-fashioned *guts* on the part of the people who give in to them —Elmer Davis⟩ SAND is a close synonym of GRIT, occas. somewhat weaker in its implications ⟨a fine personality, the teacher type; needs more *sand* in his blood; inclined to be apologetic —H.H.Arnold & I.C.Eaker⟩

for·ti·tu·di·nous \¦=¦tüdənəs, -¦tyü-\ *adj* [L *fortitudin-, fortitudo* + E *-ous*] **:** having or marked by fortitude **:** COURAGEOUS ⟨~ heroes —Edward Gibbon⟩

fort–lamy \¦fȯ(r)lə¦mē\ *adj, usu cap F&L* [fr. *Fort-Lamy*, Republic of Chad] **:** of or relating to Fort-Lamy, capital of the Republic of Chad **:** of the kind or style prevalent in Fort-Lamy

fort·let \'=lət\ *n* -S [ME *fortelet*, fr. *forte* fort + *-let* — more at FORT] **:** a small or rudimentary fort

fortlike \'=,=\ *adj* **:** resembling a fort esp. in grim solidity or in well-defended state ⟨a square ~ house⟩ ⟨secure ~ vaults⟩

fort·night \'fōrt,nīt, 'fȯr-, 'fōət-, 'fȯ(ə)t-\ *n* [ME *fourtenight*, fr. earlier *fourtene night*, fr. OE *fēowertȳne niht* fourteen nights] **:** the space of fourteen days **:** two weeks

¹fort·night·ly *adj* [*fortnight* + *-ly* (adj. suffix)] **:** occurring, appearing, or being made, done, or acted upon once in two weeks or every two weeks ⟨~ meeting⟩ ⟨~ letters⟩ ⟨~ tasks⟩

²fort·night·ly *adv* [*fortnight* + *-ly* (adv. suffix)] **:** once in a fortnight **:** every fortnight

³fort·night·ly *n* -ES [¹*fortnightly*] **:** a publication issued fortnightly

fort·nit·er *or* **fort·night·er** \-,nīd·ə(r)\ *n* -S [fr. *Fortniter*, a trademark] **:** a large traveling bag with hangers in the lid for garments and compartments in the bottom for accessories (as shoes)

for to *prep* [ME, fr. ¹*for* + *to*] *now chiefly dial* **:** TO ⟨he did go down to the meadow *for to* mow —*Ballad Book*⟩

for·tress \'fȯrtrəs, 'fō(ə)t-\ *n* -ES *often attrib* [ME *forteresse, fortresse*, fr. MF *fortelesce, forteresce*, fr. ML *fortalitia*, fr. L *fortis* strong — more at FORT] **1 :** a fortified place **:** STRONGHOLD; *esp* **:** a large and permanent fortification sometimes including a town **2 :** a center or source of assurance or protection **:** a refuge or support ⟨they meet in freedom and in peace, and, meeting so, are an earnest and a prayer and . . . a ~ —Bernard DeVoto⟩ **:** a region (as central Europe) dominated by a single military power and regarded as an impregnable stronghold

²fortress \"\ *vt* -ED/-ING/-ES **:** to furnish or protect with or as if with a fortress **:** FORTIFY

fort royal *n* [¹*fort* + *royal* (adj.)] *obs* **:** a fort of great magnitude

forts *pres 3d sing of* FORT, *pl of* FORT

for·tu·i·tism \fȯ(r)'tüə,tizəm, fə(r)-, -)·'tyü-\ *n* -S [*fortuitous* + *-ism*] **:** the doctrine or belief that evolutionary adaptations and progress are chance results rather than determined consequences of natural law or the outcome of teleology — compare TYCHISM

for·tu·i·tist \-üəd·əst, -üətəs\ *n* -S [*fortuitous* + *-ist*] **:** a believer in fortuitism

for·tu·i·tous \-üəd·əs, -üətəs\ *adj* [L *fortuitus*, derivative fr. the root of *fort-, fors* chance, luck — more at FORTUNE] **1 :** occurring by chance without evident causal need or relation or without deliberate intention ⟨the ~ rencounters, the strange accidents of fortune —Henry Miller⟩ ⟨by which the events of life are no longer regarded as isolated and ~ moments —P.E.More⟩ **2 :** LUCKY **syn** see ACCIDENTAL

for·tu·i·tous·ly *adv* **:** in a fortuitous manner **:** by chance

for·tu·i·tous·ness *n* -ES **:** FORTUITY

for·tu·i·ty \-üəd·ē, -üətē, -i\ *n* -ES [irreg. fr. *fortuitous* + *-y*] **1 :** fortuitous quality or state or an appearance of this **2 :** a chance event or occurrence

¹for·tu·nate \'fȯ(r)chənət, -chnət, *usu* -əd·+V\ *adj* [ME *fortunat*, fr. L *fortunatus*, fr. past part. of *fortunare* to make prosperous, fr. *fortuna*] **1 :** coming by good luck or favorable chance **:** bringing some good thing not foreseen as certain **:** presaging happiness **:** AUSPICIOUS ⟨a ~ event⟩ ⟨made a ~ investment⟩ **2 :** receiving some unforeseen or unexpected good or some good not dependent on one's own efforts **:** LUCKY ⟨how ~ we are to get such a nice room⟩ **3** *of a sign of the zodiac* **:** having a fortunate influence **syn** see LUCKY

²fortunate \"\ *n* -S **:** one that is fortunate

for·tu·nate·ly *adv* **:** in a fortunate manner **:** LUCKILY

for·tu·nate·ness *n* -ES **:** the quality or state of being fortunate

¹for·tune \'fȯr|chən, 'fȯ(ə)|, |(,)chün\ *n* -S *often attrib* [ME, fr. MF, fr. L *fortuna*, derivative fr. the root of *fort-, fors* chance, luck; akin to L *ferre* to carry — more at BEAR] **1 a :** a hypothetical force or power that unpredictably or capriciously determines events and issues favorably or unfavorably for persons or causes ⟨more by ~, lady, than by merit —Shak.⟩ — often personified as a mythical being and then usu. cap. ⟨turn, *Fortune*, and help thy devoted servant⟩ **2** *obs* **:** something that befalls one **:** ACCIDENT, MISHAP **3 a :** good luck **:** favorable issue **:** SUCCESS **:** prosperity attained partly through luck ⟨~ attended the general's campaign⟩ **b :** a turn or course of good or bad luck falling to one either by pure chance or incidentally in the course of some undertaking ⟨it was my good ~ to be present —A.N.Whitehead⟩ **c fortunes** *pl* **:** the turns and courses of luck accompanying the progress of an individual (as through life or toward ultimate success) ⟨following the ~*s* of a typical rags-to-riches hero in the comics⟩ ⟨his ~*s* varied but he never gave up his main objective⟩ **4 :** what is to befall one **:** DESTINY, FATE ⟨read his ~ in his palm⟩ ⟨it may be my ~ to succeed or fail but I will not hesitate to try⟩ **5 a :** condition in life as determined by material possessions **:** large possessions **:** RICHES, WEALTH ⟨a man of ~⟩ **b :** a store of material possessions or wealth owned (as by an individual or a family) ⟨was left a ~ by his uncle⟩ — often used in pl. ⟨the family ~*s* had declined greatly since his grandfather's day⟩ **6** *archaic* **:** a woman of wealth and substance **:** HEIRESS **7 :** one of the benevolent planets (Jupiter, Venus) in a favorable aspect **syn** see CHANCE

²fortune \"\ *vb* -ED/-ING/-S [ME *fortunen*, fr. MF *fortuner*, fr. L *fortunare*, to make prosperous] *vt* **1** *obs* **:** to give or ascribe either good or bad fortune to **:** ordain the fortune of **2** *archaic* **:** to provide with a fortune esp. as a dower ~ *vi*, *archaic* **:** to fall out **:** HAPPEN, CHANCE

fortune hunter *n* **:** a person that seeks to acquire wealth esp. by marriage

for·tune·less \-nləs\ *adj* **1 :** lacking in or not conducive to good fortune **:** UNFORTUNATE ⟨this ~ encounter⟩ **2 :** lacking wealth **:** POOR, IMPOVERISHED; *esp* **:** having no marriage portion ⟨but who would marry a ~ girl⟩

fortune line *n* **:** LINE OF THE SUN
for·tu·nel·la \ˌfȯ(r)chəˈnelə\ *n, cap* [NL, fr. Robert *Fortune* †1880 Scot. traveler and botanist + NL *-ella*] **:** a genus of Asiatic evergreen citrus shrubs or small trees comprising the kumquats and being often included in the genus *Citrus* from which it is distinguished by small acid fruits with a sweet pulpy edible skin and only three to seven fruit segments
fortune-tell \ˈ==ˌ=\ *vt* [back-formation fr. ¹*fortune-telling*] **:** to tell the fortune of ⟨I'll conjure you, I'll *fortune-tell* you —Shak.⟩
fortune-teller \ˈ==ˌ==\ *n* [¹*fortune* + *teller*] **:** one that tells fortunes; *esp* **:** a person who for payment predicts what are claimed to be future events or influences in the life of another
¹fortune-telling \ˈ==ˌ==\ *n* [¹*fortune* + *telling*, gerund of *tell*] **:** the art or practice of telling fortunes
²fortune-telling \"\ *adj* [¹*fortune* + *telling*, pres. part. of *tell*] **:** engaged in or practicing fortune-telling **:** serving to tell fortunes
fort wayne \-ˈwān\ *adj, usu cap F&W* [fr. *Fort Wayne*, Ind.] **:** of or from the city of Fort Wayne, Ind. ⟨a *Fort Wayne* hotel⟩ **:** of the kind or style prevalent in Fort Wayne
fort worth *adj, usu cap F&W* [fr. *Forth Worth*, Tex.] **:** of or from the city of Fort Worth, Texas ⟨the *Fort Worth* stockyards⟩ **:** of the kind or style prevalent in Fort Worth
¹for·ty \ˈfȯr|d·ē, ˈfȯr|, ˈfō(ə)|, ˈfōə|, |t|, |i\ *adj* [ME *fourty*, fr. OE *fēowertig*, fr. *fēowertig*, n., group of 40, fr. *fēower* four + *-tig* group of 10 — more at FOUR, EIGHTY] **:** being one more than 39 in number ⟨~ years⟩ — see NUMBER table
²forty \"\ *pron, pl in constr* [ME *fourty*, fr. *fourty*, adj.] **:** 40 countable persons or things not specified but under consideration and being enumerated ⟨~ are here⟩ ⟨~ were found⟩
³forty \"\ *n* -ES **1 :** four tens **:** twice 20 **:** five times eight **:** two twenties **:** eight fives **:** two score **2 a :** 40 units or objects ⟨a total of ~⟩ **b :** a group or set of 40 ⟨arranged by *forties*⟩ **3 :** the numerable quantity symbolized by the arabic numerals 40 **4 :** the 40th in a set or series; *esp* **:** an article of clothing of the 40th size ⟨wears a ~⟩ **5 :** something having as an essential feature 40 units or members **6 :** a 40-acre plot of land **:** one sixteenth of a section of land **:** a rectangular block of land with quarter-mile sides **7 :** a boat of 40 tons burden **8 :** three points won in a game of tennis **9 forties** *pl* **a :** the numbers 40 to 49 inclusive ⟨a score in the *forties*⟩ ⟨low grades in the *forties*⟩ **b :** the members of a series or set of successive numbers that end in 40 to 49 inclusive ⟨the *forties* of the preceding century⟩ ⟨lives in the *forties* in the next block⟩ **c :** the portion of a continuum lying between 40 and 50 on a scale of measurement or segmentation ⟨temperatures in the *forties* tomorrow⟩ ⟨a man in his *forties*⟩ ⟨dresses selling in the *forties*⟩ ⟨in the latitude of the *forties*⟩
¹forty-eight \¦==¦=\ *adj* **:** being one more than 47 in number ⟨*forty-eight* years⟩ — see NUMBER table
²forty-eight \"\ *pron, pl in constr* **:** 48 countable persons or things not specified but under consideration and being enumerated ⟨*forty-eight* are here⟩ ⟨*forty-eight* were found⟩
³forty-eight \"\ *n* **1 :** eight and 40 **:** three times 16 **:** four times 12 **:** six times eight **:** four dozen **2 a :** 48 units or objects ⟨a total of *forty-eight*⟩ **b :** a group or set of 48 **3 :** the numerable quantity symbolized by the arabic numerals 48 **4 :** the 48th in a set or series; *esp* **:** an article of clothing of the 48th size ⟨wears a *forty-eight*⟩ **5 :** FORTY-EIGHTMO **6 :** a 48-hour leave (as from military duties)
forty-eighter \ˌfō(r)d·ēˈād·ə(r)\ *n* -S [(*eighteen*) *forty*= *eight* + *-er*; trans. of G *achtundvierziger*] **:** a German who participated in the revolution of 1848; *specif* **:** one of these revolutionists who subsequently fled to the U.S.
¹forty-eighth \¦==¦=\ *adj* **1 :** being number 48 in a countable series ⟨the *forty-eighth* day⟩ — see NUMBER table **2 :** being one of 48 equal parts into which something is divisible ⟨a *forty-eighth* share of the money⟩
²forty-eighth \"\ *n* **1 :** number 48 in a countable series **2 :** the quotient of a unit divided by 48 **:** one of 48 equal parts of something ⟨one *forty-eighth* of the total⟩
forty-eightmo \ˌfō(r)d·ēˈāt(ˌ)mō\ *n* -S [*forty-eight* + *-mo*] **:** the size of a piece of paper cut 48 from a sheet; *also* **:** paper or a page of this size — abbr. *48mo;* symbol *48°*; see BOOK tables
¹forty-fifth \¦==¦=\ *adj* **1 :** being number 45 in a countable series ⟨the *forty-fifth* day⟩ — see NUMBER table **2 :** being one of 45 equal parts into which something is divisible ⟨a *forty-fifth* share of the money⟩
²forty-fifth \"\ *n* **1 :** number 45 in a countable series **2 :** the quotient of a unit divided by 45 **:** one of 45 equal parts of something ⟨one *forty-fifth* of the total⟩
¹forty-first \¦==¦=\ *adj* **1 :** being number 41 in a countable series ⟨the *forty-first* day⟩ — see NUMBER table **2 :** being one of 41 equal parts into which something is divisible ⟨a *forty-first* share of the money⟩
²forty-first \"\ *n* **1 :** number 41 in a countable series **2 :** the quotient of a unit divided by 41 **:** one of 41 equal parts of something ⟨one *forty-first* of the total⟩
¹forty-five \¦==¦=\ *adj* **:** being one more than 44 in number ⟨*forty-five* years⟩ — see NUMBER table
²forty-five \"\ *pron, pl in constr* **:** 45 countable persons or things not specified but under consideration and being enumerated ⟨*forty-five* are here⟩ ⟨*forty-five* were found⟩
³forty-five \"\ *n* **1 :** five and 40 **:** five times nine **:** nine fives **:** three fifteens **2 a :** 45 units or objects ⟨a total of *forty-five*⟩ **b :** a group or set of 45 **3 :** the numerable quantity symbolized by the arabic numerals 45 **4 :** the 45th in a set or series; *esp* **:** an article of clothing of the 45th size ⟨wears a *forty-five*⟩ **5 :** a 45 caliber pistol — usu. written .45 **6 :** a variation of spoil five in which points are scored on every deal and 45 points are game **7 :** a microgroove phonograph record designed to be played at 45 revolutions per minute — usu. written 45
¹forty-four \¦==¦=\ *adj* **:** being one more than 43 in number ⟨*forty-four* years⟩ — see NUMBER table
²forty-four \"\ *pron, pl in constr* **:** 44 countable persons or things not specified but under consideration and being enumerated ⟨*forty-four* are here⟩ ⟨*forty-four* were found⟩
³forty-four \"\ *n* **1 :** four and 40 **:** four times 11 **2 a :** 44 units or objects ⟨a total of *forty-four*⟩ **b :** a group or set of 44 **3 :** the numerable quantity symbolized by the arabic numerals 44 **4 :** the 44th in a set or series; *esp* **:** an article of clothing of the 44th size ⟨wears a *forty-four*⟩ **5 :** a 44 caliber pistol — usu. written .44
¹forty-fourth \¦==¦=\ *adj* **1 :** being number 44 in a countable series ⟨the *forty-fourth* day⟩ — see NUMBER table **2 :** being one of 44 equal parts into which something is divisible ⟨a *forty-fourth* share of the money⟩
²forty-fourth \"\ *n* **1 :** number 44 in a countable series **2 :** the quotient of a unit divided by 44 **:** one of 44 equal parts of something ⟨one *forty-fourth* of the total⟩
for·ty·ish \ˈfō(r)d·ēish\ *adj* **:** approaching or being about 40 years old ⟨a pleasant ~ man⟩
forty-knot \ˈ==ˌ=\ *n* **:** a prostrate tropical American herb (*Achyranthes repens*) with many-jointed stems
forty-legs \ˈ==ˌ=\ *n pl but sing or pl in constr, Brit* **:** CENTIPEDE
forty-leven \¦==¦=\ *adj* [*forty* + *leven*, short for *eleven*] *dial* **:** extremely numerous **:** INNUMERABLE ⟨asked *forty-leven* questions⟩
¹forty-nine \¦==¦=\ *adj* **:** being one more than 48 in number ⟨*forty-nine* years⟩ — see NUMBER table
²forty-nine \"\ *pron, pl in constr* **:** 49 countable persons or things not specified but under consideration and being enumerated ⟨*forty-nine* are here⟩ ⟨*forty-nine* were found⟩
³forty-nine \"\ *n* **1 :** nine and 40 **:** seven sevens **:** the square of seven **2 a :** 49 units or objects ⟨a total of *forty-nine*⟩ **b :** a group or set of 49 **3 :** the numerable quantity symbolized by the arabic numerals 49 **4 :** the 49th in a set or series; *esp* **:** an article of clothing of the 49th size ⟨wears a *forty-nine*⟩
forty-nine dance *n* **:** an American Indian round dance developed under the influence of white couple dances
forty-niner \ˌfō(r)d·ēˈnīnə(r), ˌfō(r)|, |t|, |i\ *n* -S [(*eighteen*) *forty-nine* + *-er*] **1 :** one who went to California in the rush for gold in 1849 **2 :** an enthusiastic seeker of valuable minerals; *esp* **:** one who participates in a rush to the site of a new strike
¹forty-ninth \¦==¦=\ *adj* **1 :** being number 49 in a countable series ⟨the *forty-ninth* day⟩ — see NUMBER table **2 :** being one of 49 equal parts into which something is divisible ⟨a *forty-ninth* share of the money⟩
²forty-ninth \"\ *n* **1 :** number 49 in a countable series **2 :** the quotient of a unit divided by 49 **:** one of 49 equal parts of something ⟨one *forty-ninth* of the total⟩
¹forty-one \¦==¦=\ *adj* **:** being one more than 40 in number ⟨*forty-one* years⟩ — see NUMBER table
²forty-one \"\ *pron, pl in constr* **:** 41 countable persons or things not specified but under consideration and being enumerated ⟨*forty-one* are here⟩ ⟨*forty-one* were found⟩
³forty-one \"\ *n* **1 :** one and 40 **2 a :** 41 units or objects ⟨a total of *forty-one*⟩ **b :** a group or set of 41 **3 :** the numerable quantity symbolized by the arabic numerals 41 **4 :** the 41st in a set or series; *esp* **:** an article of clothing of the 41st size ⟨wears a *forty-one*⟩ **5 :** a 41 caliber pistol — usu. written .41 **6** *or* **forty-one pool :** a pool game played with a cue ball and 15 object balls in which each player attempts to score sufficient points to total exactly 41 when added to his private number
forty-rod \ˈ==ˌ=\ *n* [so called fr. its alleged ability to kill at forty rods] *dial* **:** whiskey esp. when cheap and strong
¹forty-second \¦==¦==\ *adj* **1 :** being number 42 in a countable series ⟨the *forty-second* day⟩ — see NUMBER table **2 :** being one of 42 equal parts into which something is divisible ⟨a *forty-second* share of the money⟩
²forty-second \"\ *n* **1 :** number 42 in a countable series **2 :** the quotient of a unit divided by 42 **:** one of 42 equal parts of something ⟨one *forty-second* of the total⟩
forty-second cousin *n* **:** a distant relative ⟨he's some sort of a *forty-second cousin* on my father's side⟩
¹forty-seven \¦==¦==\ *adj* **:** being one more than 46 in number ⟨*forty-seven* years⟩ — see NUMBER table
²forty-seven \"\ *pron, pl in constr* **:** 47 countable persons or things not specified but under consideration and being enumerated ⟨*forty-seven* are here⟩ ⟨*forty-seven* were found⟩
³forty-seven \"\ *n* **1 :** seven and 40 **2 a :** 47 units or objects ⟨a total of *forty-seven*⟩ **b :** a group or set of 47 **3 :** the numerable quantity symbolized by the arabic numerals 47 **4 :** the 47th in a set or series; *esp* **:** an article of clothing of the 47th size ⟨wears a *forty-seven*⟩
¹forty-seventh \¦==¦==\ *adj* **1 :** being number 47 in a countable series ⟨the *forty-seventh* day⟩ — see NUMBER table **2 :** being one of 47 equal parts into which something is divisible ⟨a *forty-seventh* share of the money⟩
²forty-seventh \"\ *n* **1 :** number 47 in a countable series **2 :** the quotient of a unit divided by 47 **:** one of 47 equal parts of something ⟨one *forty-seventh* of the total⟩
¹forty-six \¦==¦=\ *adj* **:** being one more than 45 in number ⟨forty-six years⟩ — see NUMBER table
²forty-six \"\ *pron, pl in constr* **:** 46 countable persons or things not specified but under consideration and being enumerated ⟨*forty-six* are here⟩ ⟨*forty-six* were found⟩
³forty-six \"\ *n* **1 :** six and 40 **:** 23 times two **2 a :** 46 units or objects ⟨a total of *forty-six*⟩ **b :** a group or set of 46 **3 :** the numerable quantity symbolized by the arabic numerals 46 **4 :** the 46th in a set or series; *esp* **:** an article of clothing of the 46th size ⟨wears a *forty-six*⟩
¹forty-sixth \¦==¦=\ *adj* **1 :** being number 46 in a countable series ⟨the *forty-sixth* day⟩ — see NUMBER table **2 :** being one of 46 equal parts into which something is divisible ⟨a *forty-sixth* share of the money⟩
²forty-sixth \"\ *n* **1 :** number 46 in a countable series **2 :** the quotient of a unit divided by 46 **:** one of 46 equal parts of something ⟨one *forty-sixth* of the total⟩
forty-skewer \ˈ==ˌ==\ *n* **:** FORTESCUE
forty-spot \ˈ==ˌ=\ *n* **:** a Tasmanian diamond bird (*Pardalotus quadragintus*) having the plumage spotted with white
¹forty-third \¦==¦=\ *adj* **1 :** being number 43 in a countable series ⟨the *forty-third* day⟩ — see NUMBER table **2 :** being one of 43 equal parts into which something is divisible ⟨a *forty-third* share of the money⟩
²forty-third \"\ *n* **1 :** number 43 in a countable series **2 :** the quotient of a unit divided by 43 **:** one of 43 equal parts of something ⟨one *forty-third* of the total⟩
¹forty-three \¦==¦=\ *adj* **:** being one more than 42 in number ⟨*forty-three* years⟩ — see NUMBER table
²forty-three \"\ *pron, pl in constr* **:** 43 countable persons or things not specified but under consideration and being enumerated ⟨*forty-three* are here⟩ ⟨*forty-three* were found⟩
³forty-three \"\ *n* **1 :** three and 40 **2 a :** 43 units or objects ⟨a total of *forty-three*⟩ **b :** a group or set of 43 **3 :** the numerable quantity symbolized by the arabic numerals 43 **4 :** the 43d in a set or series; *esp* **:** an article of clothing of the 43d size ⟨wears a *forty-three*⟩
¹forty-two \¦==¦=\ *adj* **:** being one more than 41 in number ⟨*forty-two* years⟩ — see NUMBER table
²forty-two \"\ *pron, pl in constr* **:** 42 countable persons or things not specified but under consideration and being enumerated ⟨*forty-two* are here⟩ ⟨*forty-two* were found⟩
³forty-two \"\ *n* **1 :** two and 40 **:** three times 14 **:** six times seven **2 a :** 42 units or objects ⟨a total of *forty-two*⟩ **b :** a group or set of 42 **3 :** the numerable quantity symbolized by the arabic numerals 42 **4 :** the 42d in a set or series; *esp* **:** an article of clothing of the 42d size ⟨wears a *forty-two*⟩ **5 :** a game played with dominoes but resembling the card game pitch and having the sum of the counters equal 42
forty winks *n pl but sing or pl in constr* **:** a short sleep **:** NAP
fo·rum \ˈfōrəm, ˈfȯr-\ *n, pl* **forums** \-mz\ *also* **fo·ra** \-rə\ [L; akin to L *foris, foras* outside, *foris, fores* door — more at DOOR] **1 :** the marketplace or public place of an ancient Roman city consisting of an open place or square surrounded by shops or in later times by public buildings or ornamental structures (as colonnades) and forming the center of judicial and public business **2 :** a judicial body or assembly **:** COURT, TRIBUNAL ⟨in the ~ of one's own conscience⟩; *often* **:** the particular court before which a case can be or is being tried **3 a :** an organization that holds public meetings for the discussion of subjects of current interest **b :** a meeting that is held by such an organization and is frequently in the form of a question period following a lecture; *broadly* **:** a lecture followed by audience discussion and questioning of the lecturer **c :** a program (as on radio or television) involving discussion of a problem usu. by several authorities under the supervision of a chairman or moderator and usu. providing no means of audience participation **4 a :** a public meeting place for open discussion ⟨this busy intersection had been the town's ~ for generations⟩ **b :** a medium of open discussion ⟨aims of the publication are . . . to act as a ~ in which controversial issues . . . can be discussed —*Biol. Abstracts*⟩
forum non con·ve·ni·ens \-ˌnänkənˈvēnēˌen(t)s\ [NL, lit., unsuitable tribunal] **:** a doctrine whereby a court of law having full jurisdiction over a case brought in a proper venue or district declines to determine the case on its merits because justice would be better served by the trial of the case in another jurisdiction or district
for·wan·der \fə(r)ˈwändə(r)\ *vi* [ME *forwandren*, fr. *for-* + *wandren* to wander — more at WANDER] *archaic* **:** to wander far **:** become weary from wandering
¹for·ward \ˈfȯrwərd, ˈfō(ə)wəd *also in the South* ˈfärwərd, ˈfäwəd *sometimes* ˈfȯrəd\ *adj, sometimes* -ER/-EST [ME *forward, foreward*, fr. OE *foreweard* fore, former, toward the front, fr. *fore-* + *-weard* -ward] **1 a :** near, at, or belonging to the forepart ⟨the ~ gun in a ship⟩ **b :** situated in advance ⟨baggage is carried in the ~ cars⟩ **c :** of, being, or situated in or near the immediate vicinity of an area of actual opposition or conflict of military forces ⟨arranging ~ transport⟩ ⟨a ~ area⟩ **2 a :** strongly inclined **:** ANXIOUS, EAGER, READY ⟨always ~ to criticize his neighbors⟩ **b** *archaic* **:** ARDENT, SPIRITED, ZEALOUS **c :** tending to push oneself forward **:** lacking proper modesty and reserve **:** BRASH, BOLD, INDECOROUS ⟨badly disciplined children are often distressingly ~⟩ ⟨a flashy ~ young woman⟩ **3 :** notably advanced or developed **:** PRECOCIOUS ⟨the child was very ~ at walking⟩**: a** (1) *of vegetation* **:** advanced in growth beyond what is normal for the season ⟨a location sheltered from late sun avoids too ~ blossom which might be nipped by frost⟩ (2) *of a season* **:** advanced beyond what is usual **:** EARLY ⟨spring was very ~ that year⟩ **b** *of a female animal* **:** far-advanced in pregnancy ⟨bring only ~ ewes into the lambing pen⟩ **c** (1) *of an animal* **:** large and well-grown for its age ⟨fattening ~ stocks for market⟩ (2) *of a two-year-old registered horse* **:** born early in the year so that when officially two years old on January first it will be nearly three years old in chronological fact ⟨the demand for ~ two-year-olds necessitates a short breeding season . . . and the months most favorable for . . . regular ovulations are lost —*Veterinary Bull.*⟩ **4 a :** moving, tending, or leading toward a position in front ⟨picked her ~ way down the cluttered aisle⟩ ⟨checked a sudden ~ movement of the dog with a word⟩ **b :** more nearly ahead of the extended line of the popping crease than usual — used of a cricket fieldsman or his position ⟨~ short leg⟩ ⟨~ point⟩ **5 a :** supporting or advocating an advanced policy or energetic action in the direction of what is considered progress ⟨~ statesmen⟩ ⟨a firm ~ policy⟩ **b :** EXTREME, RADICAL, ULTRA ⟨on the ~ fringe of liberalism⟩ **6 :** of, relating to, or for the future **:** relating to or for future delivery ⟨~ buying of produce⟩
²forward \"\ *adv, sometimes* -ER/-EST [ME, fr. OE *forewearde*, fr. *forweard*, adj.] **:** to or toward what is before or in front: as **a :** toward, into, or through the future ⟨from that time ~⟩ ⟨looking ~ to the time I retire⟩ **b :** in a forward direction ⟨they went slowly ~ through the mud⟩ **c :** to or into the fore part of a ship — opposed to *aft* ⟨sent the sailors ~⟩ **d :** into prominence ⟨he first came ~ with the adoption of his control plan⟩ ⟨the brush and rocks came ~ as we approached and we saw it was no easy climb⟩ **e :** to the front of the church as a sign of conversion ⟨came ~ when the evangelist gave the invitation⟩ ⟨went ~ on the first evening of the revival⟩
³forward \"\ *n* -S **1 :** the forepart of a ship **2 a :** one of the players in certain games (as soccer, hockey, basketball, or water polo) who is stationed at or relatively near the front of his side or team and whose chief duty is to carry on the offensive play — see VOLLEYBALL illustration **b :** a defensive or offensive lineman in football — compare ¹BACK 5a
⁴forward \"\ *vt* -ED/-ING/-S [²*forward*] **1 :** to help onward **:** ADVANCE, PROMOTE, HASTEN ⟨~*ing* the growth of a plant with proper lighting⟩ ⟨his good work should ~ him in rank⟩ **2 a :** to send forward **:** send toward the place of destination **:** TRANSMIT ⟨I shall ~ the bill of lading this afternoon⟩ ⟨we will ~ the goods on receipt of your check⟩ **b :** to send or ship onward from an intermediate post or station in transit (as from one carrier to another or from the post office of address to another) ⟨left before your letter came but I ~*ed* it to her new address⟩ ⟨prepared to receive and ~ foreign shipments at minimum cost⟩ **3 :** to perform on (a book) the construction operations following sewing **syn** see ADVANCE, SEND
forward air controller *n* **:** the person either on the ground or in the air near the front lines who in close air-support operations spots enemy troops, guns, tanks, and other targets and by radio directs fighter-bombers in attacks on these targets
for·ward·al \-dᵊl\ *n* -S **:** FORWARDING
forward allowance *n, Brit* **:** ²LEAD 3g
forward echelon *n* **:** an advance element of a military headquarters or unit **:** an advance command post — compare REAR ECHELON
for·ward·er \-də(r)\ *n* -S [⁴*forward* + *-er*] **:** one that forwards: as **a :** an agent who performs services (as clearing of customs, receiving, assembling, transshipping, or delivering) designed to assure and facilitate the passage of goods of his principal to their destination — called also *freight forwarder* **b :** a bindery worker who performs any of the construction operations following sewing
forward exchange *n* **:** a draft or other form of foreign exchange to be delivered at a specified future date
for·ward·ing *n* -S **:** the act of one that forwards; *esp* **:** the business of a forwarder of goods
forward-looker \ˌ=ˈ==ˌ==\ *n* **:** one that looks to the future esp. for improvement of the world and man **:** VISIONARY
forward-looking \¦==¦==\ *adj* **:** concerned with or planning for the future ⟨*forward-looking* industrialists build up reserves in times of expansion⟩
¹for·ward·ly *adv* [¹*forward* + *-ly* (adv. suffix)] **1 a** *archaic* **:** with readiness, eagerness, or self-assurance **b :** in a forward manner **:** BOLDLY, PRESUMPTUOUSLY ⟨the pert child answered very ~⟩ **2 :** at or toward the front or forward part ⟨a ~ displaced upper molar⟩
²forwardly *adj* [¹*forward* + *-ly* (adj. suffix)] *obs* **:** READY, EAGER, ADVANCED, EARLY
for·ward·ness *n* -ES **:** the quality or state of being forward: as **a :** READINESS, EAGERNESS, ZEAL ⟨~ in propagating the gospel⟩ **b :** an advanced stage of progress or of preparation **:** EARLINESS, PRECOCITY ⟨the ~ of spring⟩ ⟨~ of a pupil⟩ **c :** BOLDNESS, CONFIDENCE; *often* **:** excessive boldness **:** PRESUMPTION
forward observer *n* **:** an observer operating with front-line troops who is trained and equipped to adjust supporting artillery fire
forward of the beam : a ship's relative bearing of less than 90 or more than 270 degrees
forward pass *n* **:** a pass in football made in the direction of the opponents' goal
forward play *n* **:** batting in cricket in which the batsman steps forward and plays the ball near or forward of the popping crease — contrasted with *back play*
for·wards *pronunc at* FORWARD + z\ *adv* [ME *forwardes, forewardes*, fr. *forward, foreward* forward + *-es* -s (adv. suffix)] **:** FORWARD — now used chiefly to indicate an actual direction (as of a movement)
for·warn \fərˈwō(ə)rn\ *vt* [ME *forwernen*, fr. OE *forwiernan*, fr. *for-* + *wiernan* to forbid — more at FOR-, WARN] *archaic* **:** FORBID, PROHIBIT
forwaste *vt* [*for-* + *waste*] *obs* **:** to lay waste **:** make desolate
for·wea·ried \fə(r)ˈwirēd\ *adj* [ME *forweried*, fr. *for-* + *weried*, past part. of *werien* to weary — more at WEARY] *archaic* **:** EXHAUSTED
forwent *past of* FORGO
for what *conj* **:** for anything **:** for all **:** as far as ⟨they may all be dead, *for what* we know⟩
¹for·why \fȯr'(h)wī, fō(ə)'-\ *adv* [ME, fr. OE *for hwī, for hwȳ*, fr. ¹*for* + *hwī, hwȳ*, instr. of *hwæt* what — more at WHAT] *chiefly dial* **:** WHY, WHEREFORE
²forwhy \"\ *conj* [ME, fr. *forwhy*, adv.] *archaic* **:** BECAUSE, FOR, SINCE
for·worn \fərˈwō(ə)rn, -ˈwȯ(ə)rn\ *also* **fore·worn** \fōr'-\ *adj* [fr. past part. of obs. *forwear, forewear* to wear out, exhaust, fr. ME *forweren, forwerien*, fr. *for-* + *weren, werien* to wear — more at WEAR] **1** *obs* **:** worn out by use **:** old and worn **:** TATTERED **2 :** exhausted by effort or labor **:** greatly tired ⟨~ by the long walk under a hot sun⟩
for·zan·do \(ˈ)fȯrˈtsän(ˌ)dō\ *adj (or adv)* [It, verbal of *forzare* to force, fr. (assumed) VL *fortiare* — more at FORCE] **:** SFORZANDO — abbr. *fz*
for·za·to \(ˈ)fȯrˈtsäd·(ˌ)ō, -ä(ˌ)tō\ *adj (or adv)* [It, past part. of *forzare*] **:** SFORZANDO
FOS *abbr* free on steamer
fosh \ˈfōsh\ *Scot past of* FETCH
fo·sha·gite \ˈfōshəˌgīt\ *n* -S [William F. *Foshag* †1956 Am. geologist + E *-ite*] **:** a mineral $Ca_5Si_3O_{10}(OH)_2.2H_2O$ consisting of a basic hydrous calcium silicate
¹fos·sa \ˈfäsə, ˈfōsə\ *n, pl* **fos·sae** \-ˌsē, -ˌsī\ [L, cavity, ditch, trench, fr. fem. of *fossus*, past part. of *fodere* to dig — more at BED] *anat* **:** PIT, CAVITY, DEPRESSION ⟨the temporal ~ of the skull⟩ ⟨the ~ of the vena cava⟩ ⟨the nasal *fossae*⟩
²fossa \"\ *n* [Malagasy] **1** *also* **fous·sa** \ˈfüsə\ -S **a :** a slender lithe mammal (*Cryptoprocta ferox*) that is the largest carnivore of Madagascar and is intermediate in some respects between cats and civets although classed with the latter **b :** FANALOKA **2** *cap* [NL, fr. Malagasy] **:** a monotypic genus of Malagasy civets closely related to the Asiatic palm civets and including only the fanaloka
fos·sar·ia \fäˈsa(a)rēə\ *n, cap* [NL, fr. L *fossa* ditch + NL *-aria*] **:** a widely distributed genus of small freshwater pulmonate snails (family Lymnaeidae) including important intermediate hosts of liver flukes and possibly of other trematode worms of medical or veterinary importance
fos·sar·i·an \fäˈ==\ *n* -S [LL *fossarius* fossor (fr. L *fossa* + *-arius* -ary) + E *-an*] **:** FOSSOR
fos·sate \ˈfäˌsāt\ *adj* [¹*fossa* + *-ate*] **:** having a pit ⟨primitive ~ tapeworms⟩
fosse *or* **foss** \ˈfäs, ˈfōs\ *n, pl* **fosses** [ME *fosse*, fr. OF, fr. L *fossa*] **1 :** CANAL, DITCH, TRENCH: as **a :** a ditch serving

as a barrier against an enemy — see CASTLE illustration **b :** a moat surrounding a castle **c :** a depression between a glacier and a moraine **2** *archaic* **:** a hole dug in the ground **:** PIT **3 :** FOSSA

fos·sette \(')fä¦set, (')fȯ¦-\ *n* -s [F, small cavity, dimple, fr. OF *fossete*, fr. *fosse* + *-ete* -ette] **:** a small fossa **:** a little hollow: *specif* **:** a depression for the resilium in bivalve shells

fosse-way \'=,=\ *n, usu cap F* [so called fr. the ditch along each side] **:** any of the principal Roman roads in Britain

fos·sick \'fäsik\ *vb* -ED/-ING/-S [E dial. *fussick, fussock* to potter over one's work, bustle about, irreg. fr. E *fuss*] *vi* **1** *Austral* **:** to search for gold typically by picking over abandoned workings **2** *chiefly Austral* **:** to search about **:** RUMMAGE, PROSPECT ~ *vt, chiefly Austral* **:** to search for by or as if by rummaging **:** ferret out

fos·sick·er \-kə(r)\ *n* -s *chiefly Austral* **:** one that fossicks **:** PROSPECTOR

fos·si·form \'fäsə,fȯrm, 'fȯs-\ *adj* [¹*fossa* + *-iform*] **:** having the form of a fossa **:** DEPRESSED, GROOVED

¹fos·sil \'fäsəl *also* 'fȯs- *sometimes* -(,)sil\ *n* -s [L *fossilis*, adj., dug up] **1** *archaic* **:** a rock, mineral, or other substance dug out of the earth **2 :** any remains, impression, or trace of an animal or plant of past geological ages that has been preserved in the earth's crust ⟨the tangible evidences of paleobotany are ~*s* —W.C.Darrah⟩ **3 a :** a person whose views are outmoded **:** one whose interests are in the past ⟨one of the ~*s* of the old abolition party —*N. H. Patriot & State Gazette*⟩ **b :** something that has become rigidly fixed ⟨aesthetic theories are filled with ~*s* of antiquated psychologies —John Dewey⟩ **4 a :** a word or sense once in common use but now obsolete except in certain idioms and phrases (as *fro* in *to and fro*) **b :** a linguistic form no longer productive but preserved in certain words (as the prefix *a* in *aloft, away*)

²fossil \"\ *adj* [L *fossilis* dug up, fr. *fossus* (past part. of *fodere* to dig) + *-ilis* -ile — more at BED] **:** having the characteristics of a fossil: as **a :** extracted from the earth ⟨the main sources of concentrated energy available to man were the ~ fuels such as coal, oil, and natural gas —E.V.Murphree⟩ **b :** preserved in an identifiable and commonly more or less mineralized or petrified form through geologic ages **c :** dead to change or progress **:** rigidly fixed **:** ANTIQUATED

fossil copal *n* **:** COPALITE

fossil flour *n* **:** ground diatomite

fos·sil·if·er·ous \¦fäsə¦lif(ə)rəs *also* ¦fȯs-\ *adj* [ISV ¹*fossil* + *-i-* + *-ferous*] **:** containing fossils

fos·sil·i·fi·ca·tion \fäsə,lifə'kāshən *also* fȯ,-\ *n* -s [¹*fossil* + *-i-* + *-fication*] **:** FOSSILIZATION

fos·sil·i·fy \=ˈ==,fī\ *vb* -ED/-ING/-ES [¹*fossil* + *-i-* + *-fy*] **:** FOSSILIZE

fos·sil·ist \'fäsələst *also* 'fȯs-\ *n* -s **:** PALEONTOLOGIST

fossil ivory *n* **:** ivory that has been buried long enough to become yellowish, variegated, sepia, or black in color — see OLD BERING SEA

fos·sil·iza·tion \,==lə'zāshən, -,lī'z-\ *n* -s [ISV *fossilize* + *-ation*] **:** the process of fossilizing or becoming fossilized

fos·sil·ize \'==,līz\ *vb* -ED/-ING/-S *see -ize in Explan Notes* [ISV ¹*fossil* + *-ize*] *vt* **1 :** to turn into a fossil ⟨their *fossilized* remains, recovered from some limestone that they helped to build, are often wonderfully attractive —W.E.Swinton⟩ **2 :** to preserve as if in fossil form **:** make outmoded, rigid, or fixed ⟨"no" as clearly stamps one as retrogressive, *fossilized*, probably isolationist or worse —Irving Kolodin⟩ ~ *vi* **:** to become changed into a fossil ⟨not all plant materials ~ equally well —*Science News Letter*⟩

fossil man *n* **:** man known only from fossilized skeletal remains

fos·sil·o·gy \fä'siləjē *also* fȯ'-\ *or* **fos·sil·ol·o·gy** \,fäsə'läləjē *also* ,fȯs-\ *n* -ES [*fossilogy* fr. *fossil* + *-logy*; *fossilology* fr. *fossil* + *-o-* + *-logy*] *archaic* **:** PALEONTOLOGY

fossil oil *n* **:** PETROLEUM

fossil ore *n* **:** a fossiliferous ore in which the fossil fragments have turned into some compound of iron

fossil resin *n* **:** any of various hard natural resins (as amber or some copals) usu. found in the earth as exudates of trees long dead

fossil turquoise *n* **:** ODONTOLITE

fos·sor \'fäsə(r) *also* 'fȯs-\ *n* -s [LL, fr. L, digger, fr. *fossus* (past part. of *fodere* to dig) + *-or*] **:** a gravedigger in the early church

fos·so·ri·al \(')fä¦sȯrēəl, -sȯr- *also* (')fȯ¦-\ *or* **fos·so·ri·ous** \-ēəs\ *adj* [ML *fossorius* adapted to digging (fr. L *fossus* + *-orius* -ory) + E *-al* or *-ous*] **:** adapted to digging ⟨a ~ foot⟩ ⟨a ~ mammal⟩ — opposed to *cursorial*

fos·su·late \'fäs(y)ələt, -,lāt *also* 'fȯs-\ *adj* [NL *fossula* small fossa (fr. L, small ditch, fr. *fossa* cavity, ditch, trench + *-ula*) + E *-ate* — more at ¹FOSSA] *zool* **:** slightly hollowed or grooved

¹fos·ter \'fȯstər\ *n* -s [ME, foster child, offspring, food, fr. OE *fōstor* food, feeding; akin to ON *fōstr* action of bringing up; derivative fr. the root of E *food*] *Scot* **:** a foster child

²fos·ter \'fȯstə(r), 'fäs-\ *n* -s [ME *foster, fostre*, fr. OE *-fōstre* nurse; akin to ON *fōstra* nurse; derivative fr. the root of E ¹*foster*] *archaic* **:** a foster parent

³fos·ter \"\ *vt* **fostered; fostered; fostering** \-t(ə)riŋ\ **fosters** [ME *fostren, fostrien*; akin to ON *fōstra* to raise, bring up; derivative fr. the root of E ¹*foster*] **1** *obs* **:** to supply with food or nourishment ⟨one bred but of alms and ~*ed* with cold dishes —Shak.⟩ **2 a** *obs* **:** to bring up with parental care **b :** to bring up under fosterage ⟨the young prince was ~*ed* in the home of the duke⟩ **3 :** to keep warm **:** WARM ⟨what a viper have I been ~*ing* in my bosom —Oliver Goldsmith⟩ **4 :** to promote the growth or development of **:** promote and sustain **:** ENCOURAGE, CULTIVATE ⟨the type of civilization which ~*ed* the minstrel —C.D.Lewis⟩ ⟨~ the use of radioactive isotopes —L.V.Joseph⟩ **syn** see NURSE

⁴foster \"\ *adj* [ME *foster, foster-* (as first constituent in such terms as *foster moder, fostermoder* foster mother, *foster child, fosterchild* foster child), fr. OE *fōstor-*, fr. *fōstor* food, feeding] **:** affording, receiving, or sharing nourishment, upbringing, or parental care though not related by blood or legal ties: as **a :** rearing the child of another ⟨a ~ parent⟩ **b :** brought up by someone other than one's natural parent ⟨a ~ child⟩ **c :** reared in the same family but not of the same parentage ⟨~ brothers⟩

⁵foster *n* -s [ME, alter. of *forster* — more at FORESTER] *obs* **:** FORESTER

fos·ter·age \'fȯstərij, 'fäs-\ *n* -s [³*foster* + *-age*] **1 a :** the care of a foster child **b :** the state of being a foster child **2 :** the custom once widely prevalent in Ireland, Wales, and Scotland of entrusting one's child to foster parents to be nursed and brought up ⟨the ties of clanship were strengthened by ~⟩ **3 :** the act of encouraging or promoting development

foster care *n* **:** supervised care for orphaned, neglected, or delinquent children or for persons mentally ill in a substitute home or an institution on either a full-time or day-care basis

fos·ter·er \-tərə(r)\ *n* -s [ME *fosterere*, fr. *fostren* to foster + *-ere* -er] **1 :** one that fosters **2** *archaic* **:** a foster brother

foster home *n* **:** a household in which an orphaned, neglected, or delinquent child or a person mentally ill is placed for care usu. with the approval of the government or of a social-service agency

fostering *n* -s [ME *fostringe, fostring*, fr. *fostren* to foster + *-inge, -ing* -ing] **1 :** the act of one that fosters **2 :** FOSTERAGE 2

fosterland \'==,=\ *n* [OE *fōstorland*, fr. *fōstor* food, feeding + *land* — more at ¹FOSTER, LAND] **:** land allotted under old English law for the maintenance esp. of monks

fos·ter·ling \'fȯstə(r)liŋ, 'fäs-\ *n* -s [ME, fr. OE *fōstorling*, fr. *fōstor* + *-ling*] **:** a foster child

¹foster-mother \'==¦==\ *n* [*foster mother* (noun phrase) woman that feeds or brings up another's child, fr. ME *foster moder, fostermoder*, fr. OE *fōstormōdor*; akin to ON *fōstrmōthir* woman that feeds or brings up another's child; both fr. a prehistoric NGmc-WGmc compound whose first and second constituents respectively are represented by OE *fōstor* food, feeding and by OE *mōdor* mother — more at ¹FOSTER, MOTHER] *Brit* **:** a device intended to foster young animals: as **a :** a completely enclosed movable heated house and attached run for starting young chicks without a hen **b :** a many-nippled nursing bottle for feeding litters of puppies or pigs

²foster-mother \"\ *vt* [*foster mother* (noun phrase) woman that feeds or brings up another's child] **:** to serve as the mother of ⟨*foster-mother* three little children —Dorothy C. Fisher⟩

FOT *abbr* free on truck

fotch \'fäch\ *vb* **fotched** *or* **fotch; fotched** *or* **fotch; fotching; fotches** [ME *focchen*, alter. of *fecchen* to fetch — more at FETCH] *South & Midland* **:** FETCH

¹foth·er \'fäthə(r)\ *or* **fod·der** \-ädə-\ *n* -s [ME, fr. OE *fōther*; akin to OHG *fuodar* cartload, OE *fæthm* embracing or outstretched arms — more at FATHOM] **1** *now dial Eng* **:** LOAD; *esp* **:** WAGONLOAD **2 :** any of various units of weight for lead; *esp* **:** a modern unit equal to 19½ hundredweights

²fother \"\ *dial var of* FODDER

³fother \"\ *vt* -ED/-ING/-S [prob. modif. of LG *fodern* to line, fr. MLG *vōderen*, fr. *vōder* lining; akin to Goth *fodr* sheath — more at FUR] **:** to cover (a sail or piece of canvas) esp. with oakum or rope yarn for use in temporarily stopping a leak in the hull of a ship

foth·er·gil·la \,fäthə(r)'gilə\ *n* [NL, fr. John *Fothergill* †1780 Brit. physician and botanist] **1** *cap* **:** a small genus (family Hamamelidaceae) of deciduous shrubs of the southeastern U.S. that have alternate coarsely toothed leaves with petioles and stipules and bear white apetalous flowers in terminal heads or spikes **2** -s **:** any plant of the genus *Fothergilla* — called also *witch alder*

fo·tui \'fūd·ē, fō'tüē\ *n* -s [native name in British Guiana] **:** a tropical So. American timber tree (*Jacaranda copaia*) yielding a moderately light soft whitish wood

¹fou \'fü\ *adj* [ME (Sc) *fow* full, fr. ME *ful, full* — more at FULL] *Scot* **:** DRUNK

²fou \"\ *n* -s [Sc *fou*, adj., full, fr. ME (Sc) *fow*] *Scot* **:** BUSHEL

fou·cault current \(')fü¦kō-\ *n, usu cap F* [after Jean B.L.*Foucault* †1868 Fr. physicist] **:** EDDY CURRENT

foucault pendulum *n, usu cap F* [after J.B.L. *Foucault*] **:** a freely swinging pendulum that consists of a heavy mass suspended by a long line, that oscillates for long periods in the original plane of motion, and that is used to demonstrate the rotation of the earth

foud *or* **fowd** \'fau̇d\ *n* -s [ME (Sc) *fowde*, fr. ON *fōguti* bailiff, fr. MLG *voget*, fr. ML *vocatus* legal representative, fr. L *advocatus* advocate — more at ADVOCATE] **:** a magistrate, sheriff, or bailiff in the Orkney, Shetland, and Faroe islands

fou·droy·ant \(')fü¦drȯi(y)ənt\ *adj* [F, pres. part. of *foudroyer* to strike (as lightning), blast, thunder, fr. OF *foudroier* to strike (as lightning), fr. *foudre* lightning, fr. L *fulgur*; akin to L *flagrare* to burn — more at BLACK] **1 :** THUNDERING, DAZZLING **2** *med* **:** FULMINATING, FULMINANT

fouet·té \(')fwe¦tā\ *n* -s [F, fr. past part. of *fouetter* to whip, fr. MF, fr. *fouet* whip, fr. OF, fr. *fou* beech (fr. L *fagus*) + *-et* — more at BEECH] **:** a quick whipping movement of the raised leg in ballet dancing often accompanied by continuous turning on the supporting leg

fou·gade \(')fü¦gäd\ *n* -s [F, modif. of It *fogata* chase, pursuit, light surface mine, fr. fem. of *fogato*, past part. of *fogare* to put to flight, fr. L *fugare*, fr. *fuga* flight; akin to L *fugere* to flee — more at FUGITIVE] **:** FOUGASSE

fou·gasse \-gas,-gäs\ *n* -s [F, alter. of *fougade*] **:** a land mine in which the charge is overlaid by stones or other missiles so placed as to be hurled in the desired direction

fought *past of* FIGHT

¹fought·en \'fȯtᵊn\ *now dial past part of* FIGHT

²fought·en \'fōktən\ *adj, chiefly Scot* **:** worn out **:** exhausted esp. from fighting

foughten field *n, archaic* **:** BATTLEGROUND

fough·ty \'fōti\ *adj* [origin unknown] *dial Eng* **:** MUSTY, MOLDY

foujdar *var of* FAUJDAR

¹foul \'fau̇l, *esp before pause or consonant* -au̇əl\ *adj, usu* -ER/-EST [ME, fr. OE *fūl*; akin to OHG *fūl* rotten, ON *fūll* foul, Goth *fūls* stinking, L *pus* pus, *putēre* to stink, Gk *pyon* pus, *pythein* to cause to rot, Skt *pūyati* it stinks] **1 a :** offensive to the senses **:** LOATHSOME ⟨in their ~ homes of dirt and rag —Bernard Gutteridge⟩ **b :** charged with offensive matter **:** ROTTEN, PUTRID ⟨the contents of the bowl are ~ and stinking —J.G.Frazer⟩ **2 :** full of dirt or mud **:** MUDDY **3 a :** morally or spiritually odious **:** WICKED ⟨how ~ are all impulses of prejudice —J.H.Holmes⟩ **b :** notably unpleasant or distressing ⟨if my day has been ~, I can turn on my . . . radio and everything's mellow —Adrian Dove⟩ **4 a :** OBSCENE, PROFANE ⟨much of this most tedious and lengthy book is ~, lewd, and revolting —Hartley Shawcross⟩ **b :** ABUSIVE ⟨it was hard for me to take all the ~ names he called me —H.A. Chippendale⟩ **c** *dial Eng* **:** bad-tempered **:** UNFRIENDLY **5 a :** wet and stormy **:** DISAGREEABLE ⟨~ weather⟩ ⟨a ~ sky⟩ **b :** obstructive to navigation **:** UNFAVORABLE, DANGEROUS ⟨we had a ~ tide —Peter Heaton⟩ ⟨always presume your course to be ~ unless you know it to be clear —H.A.Calahan⟩ **6 a** *now dial Brit* **:** not attractive **:** HOMELY, UGLY ⟨I don't look too ~ do I —A.J.Cronin⟩ **b** *of a feather or plumage* **:** of any color not accepted as standard for birds of a particular variety or breed **7 a :** grossly unfair **:** TREACHEROUS, DISHONORABLE ⟨competition was stifled by fair means or ~ —Grace L. Nute⟩ **b :** characterized by harshness, roughness, or violence ⟨war is a ~ game —R.W.Emerson⟩ **c :** constituting an infringement of rules in a game or sport ⟨a ~ hand in poker⟩ ⟨a ~ blow in boxing⟩ **8 a :** marked up **:** defaced by changes ⟨a ~ galley proof⟩ ⟨a ~ manuscript⟩ **b** *of a proof in printing* **:** pulled before the latest alterations were made in type **9 a :** encrusted, clogged, or choked with a foreign substance ⟨a ~ ship bottom⟩ ⟨a ~ chimney⟩ ⟨on ~ land weeds may get the better of clover —E.V.Wilcox⟩ **b :** littered esp. with matter that should have been put away ⟨a ~ stone in printing⟩ **10 a :** odorous and impure **:** POLLUTED ⟨a ~ air⟩ ⟨~ water⟩ **b** *archaic* **:** DISCOLORED ⟨we make ~ the clearness of our deservings —Shak.⟩ **11 :** hindered from freedom of motion by collision or entanglement **:** ENTANGLED ⟨a ~ fishline⟩ **12 :** eating coarse food or carrion — used esp. in the phrase *foul feeder* **13** *of a typecase* **:** containing many missorted characters **14 :** outside the foul lines in baseball — compare FOUL BALL, FOUL LINE **syn** see DIRTY

²foul \"\ *n* -s [ME, fr. OE *fūl*, fr. *fūl*, adj. — more at ¹FOUL] **1** *archaic* **:** something that is foul ⟨the ~ befall the man who ever lays a snare in its way —Laurence Sterne⟩ **2 :** FOOT ROT 2 **3 :** an entanglement or collision esp. in angling or sailing **4 a :** an infringement of the rules in a game or sport (as in basketball) for which a penalty is levied against the offending person or team — see PERSONAL FOUL, TECHNICAL FOUL, VIOLATION **b :** FREE THROW **5 :** FOUL BALL

³foul \"\ *adv* [ME *foule*, fr. OE *fūle*, fr. *fūl*, adj.] **:** FOULLY

⁴foul \"\ *vb* -ED/-ING/-S [ME *foulen*, fr. OE *fūlian*, fr. *fūl*, adj.] *vi* **1 :** to become or be foul: as **a :** to become odorous **:** DECOMPOSE, ROT ⟨it is this organic refuse which alone is ~*ing* —Emily Holt⟩ **b :** to become encrusted, clogged, or choked with a foreign substance ⟨a gun ~*s*⟩ **c :** to become entangled or come into collision ⟨this may cause . . . the suspension lines of the parachute to ~ —H.G.Armstrong⟩ **2 :** to commit a foul in a sport or game **3 :** to make an out in baseball by hitting a foul ball that is caught by a member of the opposing team ⟨the batter ~*ed* to the first baseman⟩ ~ *vt* **1 :** to make foul: as **a :** to make dirty **:** SOIL, POLLUTE ⟨air was ~*ed* and darkened by factory soot —J.D.Hart⟩ **b :** to become entangled or come into collision with ⟨a raveled rope ~*ed* a pulley —L.C.Douglas⟩ ⟨the propeller ~*ed* a treetop —T.E.McKitterick⟩ **c :** to encrust with a foreign substance ⟨when a ship's bottom is ~*ed* from sea grass and barnacles it often takes 10 percent more fuel to keep her going at normal speed —*Nat'l Geographic*⟩ **d :** OBSTRUCT, BLOCK ⟨the carrier's flight deck was ~*ed* by a crashed plane⟩ **e** *of a bird* **:** to mark with areas of plumage of a color not accepted as standard **2 :** to bring into disgrace **:** DISHONOR, DISCREDIT ⟨it is senseless to ~ our municipal personnel with unproved charges —Robert Moses⟩ **3 :** to commit a foul against (as in basketball) **4 :** to hit (a baseball) foul ⟨he ~*ed* the first pitch⟩

foul anchor *or* **fouled anchor** *n* **1 a :** an anchor whose cable has become twisted around the stock or fluke **b :** an anchor that has hooked or become entangled with another anchor **2 :** a conventionalized anchor with a section of cable entwined about its shank or hanging from its ring used on nautical insignia, seals, or pennants

foul anchor 2

fou·lard \(')fü¦lärd, fə'l-, (')fü¦l-, -läd\ *n* -s [F] **1 a :** a lightweight plainwoven or twilled silk usu. printed with a small neat evenly spaced pattern **b :** an imitation of this fabric made usu. of rayon, cotton, wool, or nylon **2 :** an article of clothing (as a tie, scarf, or handkerchief) that is made of foulard

foul ball *n* **:** a batted baseball that rolls outside an infield foul line or that lands in foul territory — compare FAIR BALL, FOUL TIP

foul berth *n* **:** a berth in which an anchored ship cannot swing without fouling another ship or in which it becomes grounded at low tide

foul bill *n* **:** FOUL BILL OF HEALTH

foul bill of health : a certificate given to a ship's master at the time of leaving port indicating that there was an epidemic at the place of departure when the ship left — compare CLEAN BILL OF HEALTH

foul bill of lading : a bill of lading with notations as to shortages or condition of goods that limits the rights of the holder — compare CLEAN BILL OF LADING

foulbrood \'=,=\ *n* **:** any of three destructive bacterial diseases of the larvae of the honeybee: **a :** AMERICAN FOULBROOD **b :** EUROPEAN FOULBROOD **c :** PARAFOULBROOD

fouldcourse *var of* FOLDCOURSE

foulder *vi* -ED/-ING/-S [obs. *foulder*, n., lightning, fr. ME *fouldre, foudre*, fr. MF — more at FOUDROYANT] *obs* **:** FLASH ⟨loud thunder . . . did rend the rattling skies with flames of ~*ing* heat —Edmund Spenser⟩

fou·le \(')fü¦lā\ *n* -s [F *foulé*, past part. of *fouler* to full — more at FULL] **:** a cloth treated by fulling

fouled-up \'=¦=\ *adj* [*fouled* fr. past part. of ⁴*foul*] **:** characterized by total confusion or disorganization **:** CONFUSED, SNAFU ⟨a fantastically *fouled-up* operation —H.H.Martin⟩ ⟨an impossibly *fouled-up* bungle —Cameron Hawley⟩

¹fouler *comparative of* FOUL

²foul·er \'fau̇lə(r)\ *n* -s [⁴*foul* + *-er*] **1 :** one that fouls **2 :** FOULING SHOT

foulest *superlative of* FOUL

foul-foot \'=,=\ *n* **:** FOOT ROT 2

foul hawse *n* **:** an arrangement of starboard and port anchor cables in which the cables cross or twist with the swinging around of the ship — compare OPEN HAWSE

foul-hook \'=¦=\ *vt* **:** to hook (a fish) elsewhere than in the mouth

fouling *n* -s [fr. gerund of ⁴*foul*] **1 :** an accumulation of deposits **:** INCRUSTATION ⟨~ in sewage pipes⟩ ⟨marine ~⟩ **2 :** a deposit left in the bore of a gun after firing that consists of the powder residue and in small arms of a thin plating of the bullet metal

fouling organism *n* **:** any of various aquatic organisms with free-swimming larvae and sedentary adult stages that cause fouling of ships and underwater structures

fouling point *n* **1 :** the point at a railroad switch or turnout beyond which cars must be placed to prevent their being struck by cars running on the line from which the switch diverges **2 :** the point at a turnout back of the frog in signaled track where insulated joints are placed

fouling shot *n* **:** one of several rounds fired before a rifle match to warm the barrel and to furnish some fouling in order that the initial rounds of record fire pass through the bore under conditions similar to those obtaining for later rounds

foul line *n* **1 :** either of two straight lines extending from the rear corner of home plate through the outer corners of first and third base respectively and prolonged to the boundary of a baseball field — see BASEBALL illustration **2 :** a line across a bowling alley 60 feet from the center of the number 1 pin spot across which a player must not step when delivering the ball

foul·ly \'fau̇l(l)ē, -)i\ *adv* [ME, fr. OE *fūllice, fūllīce*, fr. *fūllic, fūllic*, adj., foul, fr. *fūl* foul + *-lic, -lic* -ly (adj. suffix)] **:** in a foul manner: as **a :** in an obscene manner **:** LEWDLY **b :** in a shameful manner **:** WICKEDLY ⟨last June two constables were ~ murdered —Robert Sherrod⟩ **c** *archaic* **:** FETIDLY **d** *archaic* **:** GRIEVOUSLY **e :** in a coarse manner **:** INSULTINGLY ⟨an internationally honored teacher, scholar, and philosopher was ~ condemned —M.R.Cohen⟩ **f** *archaic* **:** in an ugly manner **:** HIDEOUSLY

foulmouthed \'=¦=\ *adj* **:** given to the use of obscene, profane, or abusive language ⟨so he went off cursing like the ~ blackguard that he was —A. Conan Doyle⟩ ⟨nowhere is cant at once so ~ and so tight-laced as in the penny, two-penny, threepenny, or sixpenny press —Herbert Read⟩

foul·ness *n* -ES [ME *foulnesse*, fr. OE *fūlnes*, fr. *fūl* foul + *-nes* -ness] **1 :** the quality or state of being foul: as **a** *obs* **:** physical repulsiveness ⟨the fury . . . with new methods tried the ~ of the infernal form to hide —John Dryden⟩ **b :** a deposit of foul matter **:** FILTH ⟨the floors were made of serpents encased in ~ —R.B.Anderson⟩ **c :** moral impurity, obscenity, or vulgarity ⟨the cheapness of his person and the ~ of his tongue —Hamilton Basso⟩ **d :** UNCLEANNESS, POLLUTION ⟨a medicine . . . useful in . . . ~*es* of the blood —George Berkeley⟩ **e :** an unfavorable state (as of weather) **2 :** FIREDAMP

foul out *vi* **1 :** FOUL *vi* 3 **2 :** to be put out of a basketball game for exceeding the number of fouls permitted

foul play *n* **:** unfair, dishonest, or treacherous conduct or dealing; *specif* **:** VIOLENCE ⟨met with *foul play*⟩ ⟨a victim of *foul play*⟩ — compare FAIR PLAY

fouls *pl of* FOUL, *pres 3d sing of* FOUL

foul shot *n* **:** FREE THROW

foul·some \'fü(l)səm\ *adj* [ME *foulsom*, alter. (influenced by ¹*foul*) of *fulsom* fulsome] *chiefly Scot* **:** DISGUSTING, FULSOME

foul-spoken \'=¦==\ *adj* **:** FOULMOUTHED

foul strike *n* **:** a foul that counts as a strike in baseball

foul tip *n* **:** a pitched ball in baseball that is slightly deflected by the bat; *specif* **:** a tipped pitch legally caught by the catcher and counting as a full strike with the ball remaining in play

foul up *vt* **1 :** to make dirty **:** CONTAMINATE ⟨the ranchers used water out of open creek holes that was sometimes alkali and *fouled up* by stock —Bruce Siberts⟩ **2 :** to spoil by making mistakes or using poor judgment **:** CONFUSE ⟨no army would risk *fouling up* a major landing —Linnell Jones⟩ **3 :** to have a depressing effect on **:** DARKEN **:** LOWER ⟨a sad sack like that one only *fouls up* the spirit of the ward —*Atlantic*⟩ **4 :** ENTANGLE, CHOKE, BLOCK ⟨in two or three years the ivy should have been *fouling up* the television aerial —R.M. Yoder⟩ ⟨a big car trying to get into a small parking space *fouled up* traffic —Bill Hatch⟩ ~ *vi* **:** to become confused **:** get into difficulty **:** BUNGLE ⟨he couldn't shake the feeling that it was his fault. He had *fouled up* —Pat Frank⟩

foul-up \'=,=\ *n* -s [*foul up*] **1 :** a state of confusion brought on by ineptitude or mismanagement **:** MIX-UP ⟨as with all transportation there are occasional *foul-ups* which gratify nobody —Richard Thruelsen⟩ **2 :** a mechanical difficulty ⟨the added complication of a *foul-up* in the steering mechanism in her motor pilot boat —*Springfield (Mass.) Union*⟩

fou·mart *also* **foul·mart** \'fümərt, -,märt\ *n* -s [ME *fulmard, fulmarde, folmarde, folmert*, prob. fr. ¹*foul* + (assumed) ME *marth* marten, fr. OE *mearth* — more at MARTEN] **1 :** the European polecat **2 :** a contemptible person — used as a general term of abuse

¹found *past of* FIND

²found \'fau̇nd\ *n* -s **:** free food and lodging in addition to wages ⟨they're paid $175 a month and ~ —*New Yorker*⟩

³found \"\ *vb* -ED/-ING/-S [ME *founden*, fr. OF *fonder*, fr. L *fundare*, fr. *fundus* bottom — more at BOTTOM] *vt* **1 :** to take the first steps or measures in building **:** build for the first time ⟨~*ed* palaces and planted bowers —Matthew Prior⟩ **2 :** to lay the base or foundation of **:** set on something solid for support ⟨the winds blew and beat upon that house but it did not fall because it had been ~*ed* on the rock —Mt 7:25 (RSV)⟩ **3 :** to establish (as an institution) often with provision for future maintenance **:** ORIGINATE, INITIATE ⟨this school was ~*ed* by a bequest of . . . $1,250,000 —C.W.Dabney⟩ ⟨he had ~*ed* prizes and scholarships and endowed hospital beds and charities —Osbert Lancaster⟩ **4 a :** to establish on a firm basis **:** fix firmly ⟨the single vital principle on which the true republic must ~ itself . . . is the principle of goodwill —V.L. Parrington⟩ ⟨all his imaginative work is ~*ed* on personal reminiscences of actual incidents and people —R.W.Stallman⟩ **b :** to serve as a basis for ⟨is enough to ~ my notion of their

having . . . the relation of brothers —John Locke⟩ **~** *vi* **:** to have a foundation **:** DEPEND — used with *on* or *upon* ⟨all delineation . . . must either ~ on belief and provable fact or have no foundation at all —Thomas Carlyle⟩
syn ESTABLISH, INSTITUTE, ORGANIZE: FOUND applies to the first steps, usu. the devising of the project or providing funds for it, taken to set up a business, colony, institution, city, or the like ⟨a lottery by which $40,000 was raised to *found* the College of Medicine —*Amer. Guide Series: Md.*⟩ ⟨the Conservatory of Music, *founded* by two distinguished dancers from Latvia —*Report: (Canadian) Royal Commission on Nat'l Development*⟩ ⟨*founding* a race, a whole descent, a whole line . . . which had gone on unbroken since before the time of William the Conqueror —Louis Bromfield⟩ ⟨the baronet looked down on the generous future he thus *founded* —George Meredith⟩ ESTABLISH usu. adds to FOUND the idea of bringing into enduring existence ⟨the power which in 1644 *established* itself as the Ch'ing dynasty in Peking —C.A.Fisher⟩ ⟨follows a route to California *established* by James Beckwourth —*Amer. Guide Series: Nev.*⟩ ⟨to *establish* a business⟩ INSTITUTE stresses an origination, a taking of the first steps in establishing something, but applies more widely than FOUND or ESTABLISH, for it comprises things that do and things that do not have a long life, as, respectively, a method of teaching and a course of lectures ⟨the office of prime minister was formally *instituted* in the Gold Coast —*Americana Annual*⟩ ⟨*institute* the first large-scale reforestation project in the U. S. —*Amer. Guide Series: N.C.*⟩ ⟨the act provided that no appeal could be *instituted* at a time later than twenty-eight days after the date upon which the magistrate made his decision or order⟩ ORGANIZE can imply founding but stresses the steps taken to establish also a proper functioning of something, as by the establishing of a separation and interrelationship of necessary operations or responsibilities ⟨he determined to take upon his own shoulders the responsibility of *organizing* some amusements —Thomas Hardy⟩ ⟨a small class of 15 children was *organized* —*Amer. Guide Series: Minn.*⟩ ⟨he *organized* the Harmonia Society and presented Haydn's *The Seasons* —*Amer. Guide Series: N.Y.*⟩ ⟨the development of trade had been well begun before the town itself was *organized* —*Amer. Guide Series: La.*⟩ **syn** see in addition BASE

⁴found \'fün(d)\ *n* -s *Scot* **:** BASE, FOUNDATION

⁵found \'fau̇nd\ *vt* -ED/-ING/-S [ME *founden* to mix, fr. MF *fondre* to mix, pour, melt, fr. L *fundere* to found, pour; akin to OE *gēotan* to pour, OHG *giozzan* to pour, ON *gjōta* to bring forth (young), Goth *giutan* to pour, Gk *chein* to pour, Skt *juhoti* he pours into the fire, sacrifices] **1 a :** to melt (metal) and pour into a mold **b :** to make (a metal object) in this way **:** CAST **2 a :** to cause (ingredients for making glass) to melt or fuse **b :** to make (glass) by this method

⁶found \"\ *n* -s *archaic* **:** an act or process of founding **:** CASTING

¹foun·da·tion \fau̇n'dāshən\ *n* -s [ME *foundacioun*, fr. MF *fondation*, fr. L *fundation-, fundatio*, fr. *fundatus* (past part. of *fundare* to found) + *-ion-, -io* -ion] **1 :** the act of founding: as **a :** the act of taking the first steps in building or of building for the first time ⟨thy love for me before the ~ of the world —Jn 17:24 (RSV)⟩ **b :** the act of establishing on a permanent basis typically with provision for future maintenance ⟨his piety was evidenced by his ~ of several religious houses⟩ **2 a :** the basis on which something is founded **:** the basis upon which something stands or is supported ⟨is very little ~ for this objection either in reason or good taste —William Hazlitt⟩ **b** *archaic* **:** a basis of agreement **:** UNDERSTANDING ⟨the English might again repair to their respective houses and trade on the old ~ —Alexander Hamilton⟩ **3 a :** funds given for the permanent support of an institution or cause **:** ENDOWMENT ⟨we are anxious to establish scholarships and endowments; hence we solicit such ~*s* from our friends —*Bull. of Mt. Saint Mary's College*⟩ **b :** an organization or institution established by endowment ⟨the citizen taxpayer has succeeded the philanthropic ~ as the principal underwriter of the costs of science —*Scientific American Reader*⟩ or otherwise established with provision for future maintenance ⟨the Benedictine order is a religious ~ dating from the sixth century⟩ **4 a :** an underlying natural or prepared base or support ⟨the terrain . . . has a gracefully undulating surface over a limestone ~ —J.T.Dorris⟩ ⟨~ for the boilers and engines of a ship⟩ **b :** a means of transferring building loads to the soil below: (1) **:** the supporting part of a wall or structure usu. below ground level and including footings (2) **:** the whole masonry substructure of a building **5 :** a body or ground upon which something is built up or overlaid: as **a :** a stiffening or backing piece in an article of clothing **b :** a basic stitch or pattern **c :** the form on or over which a manufactured article is constructed ⟨allow woven rush baskets to dry thoroughly before you remove them from the ~ as in this way the shape becomes properly set —F.J.Christopher⟩ **d** *or* **foundation garment :** a woman's supporting undergarment **:** CORSET, CORSLET, GIRDLE **e :** a cosmetic in liquid, cream, or cake form usu. used as a base for makeup **f :** a priming coat of pigment sometimes laid over canvas as a ground for oil painting **g :** a thin sheet of pressed beeswax imitating the bottoms of natural honeycomb cells that is placed in a frame or section to shorten the time for and increase uniformity in comb building by hived bees **h :** a card of a prescribed rank placed face up as the starter for a sequence in solitaire — **on the foundation** *Brit* **:** belonging to an endowed institution or holding an endowed scholarship or other emolument

foundation 5d

²foundation \"\ *vt* -ED/-ING/-S **:** ³FOUND

foun·da·tion·al \(')fau̇n¦dāshənᵊl, -shnəl\ *adj* **:** forming or serving as a foundation **:** FUNDAMENTAL — **foun·da·tion·al·ly** \-ᵊlē, -əl, ¦i\ *adv*

foun·da·tion·ary \fau̇n'dāshə,nerē, -ri\ *adj* **:** of or relating to a foundation

foundation bed *n* **:** the soil immediately beneath the foundation of a building **:** bearing soil

foundation day *n, usu cap F&D* **:** AUSTRALIA DAY — used esp. in Victoria

foun·da·tion·er \fau̇n'dāsh(ə)nə(r)\ *n* -s *Brit* **:** one who derives support from the funds or foundation of a college or school

foun·da·tion·less \-shənləs\ *adj* **:** lacking foundation **:** BASELESS

foundation mat *n* **:** FLOATING FOUNDATION

foundation member *n, Brit* **:** CHARTER MEMBER

foundation planting *n* **:** a group of plants used in landscape design to blend a building with its setting and obscure any undesirable features of the foundation

foundation seed *n* **:** pure seed stocks grown by or under the supervision of a public agency for use in the production of registered and certified seed

foundation stock *n* **:** stock directly ancestral to a herd, strain, or breed ⟨although fourteen . . . animals made up the *foundation stock* only six of these have actually made a permanent contribution to the line —David England⟩

foundation stone *n* **1 :** a stone in the foundation of a building; *specif* **:** such a stone laid with public ceremony in celebration of the beginning of erection — compare CORNERSTONE **2 :** BASIS, GROUNDWORK ⟨absolute fear of magic powers . . . was the *foundation stone* of all . . . ceremonies of oath taking —L.S.B.Leakey⟩

foundation stop *n* **1 :** a stop in a pipe organ whose pipes are in unison with or one or more octaves higher or lower than the piano strings sounded by the corresponding keys — compare MUTATION STOP **2 :** any one of the fundamental flue stops (as the diapasons) as contrasted with reed stops or mixture stops

founded *past of* FOUND

¹found·er \'fau̇ndə(r)\ *n* -s [ME *foundere*, alter. (influenced by ME *-ere* -er) of *foundour, foundeour*, fr. OF *fondeor*, fr. L *fundator*, fr. *fundatus* (past part. of *fundare* to found) + *-or* — more at FOUND] **:** one that founds, establishes, or builds ⟨the ~*s* of the college⟩

²foun·der \"\ *vb* **foundered; foundered; foundering** \-d(ə)riŋ\ **founders** [ME *foundren* to strike down, knock to the ground, fall to the ground, fr. MF *fondrer* to send to the bottom, fall to the ground, fr. (assumed) VL *fundorare*, fr. (assumed) VL *fundor-, fundus* bottom, alter. of L *fundus* — more at BOTTOM] *vi* **1 :** to become disabled: as **a :** to break down or go lame ⟨his horse ~*ed* while he was still five miles from home⟩ **b :** to become stuck ⟨the sheep ~*ed* in the deep snow⟩ **c :** to become stiff or sick from overeating ⟨the old horse ~*ed* on green corn⟩ **2 a :** to give way **:** COLLAPSE ⟨the palatial hotel . . . swayed and plunged then ~*ed*, turning its desk register into a death toll —*Time*⟩ **b :** to sink or slip sideways ⟨large masses of the Grenville ~*ed* and were engulfed in the granite magma —C.O.Dunbar⟩ **3 :** to sink below the surface of the water ⟨a squall came up the next day and imminent was the danger that the boat would ~ —B.N. Cardozo⟩ **4 a :** to come to grief **:** FAIL ⟨their efforts either ~*ed* in the committees of the state legislature or were voted down at the polls —Dwight Macdonald⟩ **b :** to break down because of an immaterial obstacle ⟨the idea of the five-power conference . . . had ~*ed* up to now on the point whether it should be held before or after implementation of the . . . declaration —Arnaldo Cortesi⟩ **~** *vt* **1 a :** WRECK, DAMAGE ⟨how often have we ~*ed* progress to save some sterile principle —Richard Christopherson⟩ **b :** to cause to become disabled or lame; *esp* **:** to cause (an animal) to founder by overfeeding **2 :** to send (a ship) to the bottom **:** SINK

³foun·der \"\ *n* -s **1 :** laminitis esp. when of digestive origin **2 :** CHEST FOUNDER

⁴found·er \"\ *n* -s [ME *foundour, founder*, fr. MF *fondeur*, fr. OF *fondeor*, fr. *fondre* to pour, melt + *-eor* -or — more at FOUND] **1 :** one who founds metal or glass; *specif* **:** TYPEFOUNDER **2 :** the foreman who immediately directs the operation of an iron blast furnace

foun·der·ous *or* **foun·drous** \'fau̇nd(ə)rəs\ *adj* **:** likely to cause one to founder **:** MIRY, SWAMPY ⟨if a way becomes ~ the public may have a right to deviate —F.D.Smith & Barbara Wilcox⟩

founders' shares *n pl* [¹*founder*] *chiefly Brit* **:** stock issued to the organizers of a public company or corporation and carrying certain special privileges — compare MANAGEMENT SHARES

founders' type *n* [⁴*founder*] **:** FOUNDRY TYPE

founding *n* -s [fr. gerund of ⁵*found*] **:** the art of melting and casting

founding father *n* [*founding* fr. pres. part. of ³*found*] **:** the originator of an institution or movement **:** FOUNDER; *specif, usu cap both Fs* **:** a member of the American Constitutional Convention of 1787 ⟨Benjamin Franklin, the oldest and perhaps the wisest of our *Founding Fathers* —J.F.Hopkins⟩

found·ling \'fau̇ndliŋ, -lēŋ\ *n* -s [ME *foundling, foundeling*, fr. *founde, founden* found (past part. of *finden* to find) + *-ling* — more at FIND] **:** an infant found after its unknown parents have deserted it **:** a baby deserted by unknown parents

foundling hospital *n* **:** an institution for foundlings

found·ress \-drəs\ *n* -ES [ME *founderesse*, fr. *foundere* founder + *-esse* -ess] **:** a female founder

found·ry \'fau̇ndrē, -ri\ *n* -ES *often attrib* [F *fonderie*, fr. MF, fr. *fondre* to pour, melt + *-erie* -ery] **1 a :** the act, process, or art of casting metals **b :** articles produced by founders **:** CASTINGS **2 :** a building or establishment where metal or glass founding is carried on **3 a :** a place where stereotyping or electrotyping is done **b :** TYPEFOUNDRY **c :** a department in a printing works for the melting down of composing machine type or slugs

foundry facing *n* **:** a usu. carbonaceous material applied to the surface of a sand mold to prevent the molten metal from penetrating and reacting with the sand of the mold

foundry iron *or* **foundry pig** *n* **:** pig iron suitable for making castings

found·ry·man \-mən\ *n, pl* **foundrymen :** a foundry worker

foundry proof *n* **:** a proof taken from a form that has been locked up and made ready for plating

foundry scrap *n* **:** IRON SCRAP 2

foundry type *n* **:** type cast by a typefounder esp. as distinguished from type cast by a typesetting machine

founds *pl of* FOUND, *pres 3d sing of* FOUND

¹fount \'fau̇nt\ *n* -s [ME, baptismal font, source, fr. OF *font*, fr. L *font-, fons* fountain, spring; prob. akin to Skt *dhanvati* it flows] **1 a :** a fountain or spring **b :** a reservoir for liquids: as (1) **:** the oil reservoir of a lamp (2) **:** INKWELL (3) **:** a drinking vessel for poultry; *esp* **:** one maintaining a constant water level by gravity feed **2 :** something that resembles a spring or reservoir **:** SOURCE ⟨the people were sovereign, the sole ~ of power —John Buchan⟩

²fount \'fänt, 'fau̇nt\ *n* -s [F *fonte*, fr. MF, act or process of casting or founding — more at FONT] *Brit* **:** a font of type

¹foun·tain \'fau̇ntᵊn, -tən\ *n* -s *often attrib* [ME *fountaine*, fr. MF *fontaine*, fr. LL *fontana*, fr. L, fem. of *fontanus* of a spring, fr. *font-, fons* spring + *-anus* -an] **1 a** (1) **:** a spring of water issuing from the earth ⟨the greatest objection to this country is the want of ~*s* and running streams —H.M.Brackenridge⟩ (2) **:** the point of origin or head of a stream ⟨making rivers to ascend to their ~*s* —John Ray⟩ **b :** something that resembles a flowing spring ⟨with purple ~*s* issuing from your veins —Shak.⟩ **2 :** the source from which something proceeds or from which it is supplied ⟨he is the ~ of honor and all titles spring from his power of conferment —W.A.Robson⟩ **3 a :** an artificially produced jet of water **b :** the structure from which such a jet of water rises or flows **c :** DRINKING FOUNTAIN **d :** an upward jet or downward shower of something other than water ⟨spectacular ~*s* of lava —Howel Williams⟩ **e :** a pyrotechnic device that emits a shower of sparks in imitation of water falling from a fountain **4** *heraldry* **:** a roundel barry-wavy of six argent and azure **5 :** a reservoir containing a liquid or other substance that can be conducted or drawn off as needed for use ⟨the ink ~ in a printing press⟩ **6 :** SODA FOUNTAIN

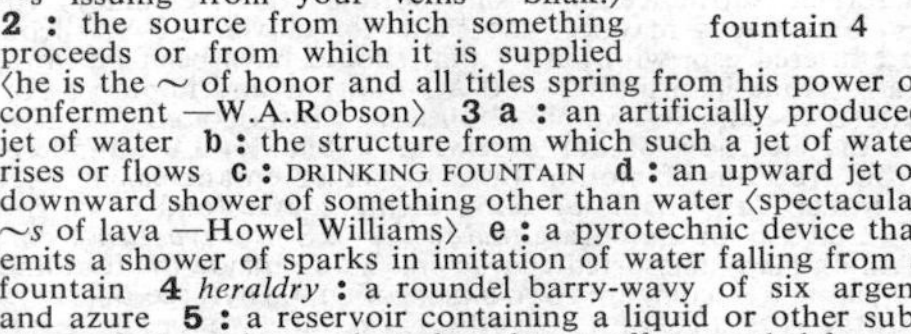
fountain 4

²fountain \"\ *vb* -ED/-ING/-S *vi* **:** to flow or spout like a fountain **~** *vt* **:** to cause to flow like a fountain

fountain brush *n* [*fountain (pen)*] **:** a marking or painting brush with a reservoir in its handle for ink or paint

foun·tained \-ᵊnd,-ənd\ *adj* [¹*fountain* + *-ed*] **:** having a fountain

foun·tain·eer \¦fau̇ntᵊn¦i(ə)r, -tə¦ni-\ *n* -s [F *fontenier*, fr. MF, fr. *fontaine* fountain + *-ier* -eer] **1** *obs* **:** one in charge of a fountain **2** [¹*fountain* + *-eer*] **:** SODA JERK

fountain grass *n* **:** an ornamental grass (*Pennisetum ruppelii*) with long nodding or curving spikes of flowers that have prominent bristles extending beyond the spikelets

fountainhead \'⸗⸗,⸗\ *n* **1 :** a fountain or spring that is the head or source of a stream **2 :** a place of origin or issue **:** principal source ⟨theory serves as a ~ of inspiration to action —John Dewey⟩

foun·tain·less \'⸗⸗ləs\ *adj* **:** being without sources of water ⟨barren desert ~ and dry —John Milton⟩

fountain moss *n* **1 :** a moss of the genus *Fontinalis* (esp. *F. antipyretica*) **2 :** a highly variable No. American moss (*Philonotis fontana*) that grows about springs and seeps and often forms dense thick mats

fountain of honor *or* **fountain of justice** *often cap F&H&J* **:** the British crown conceived as the source of all justice, honors, dignities, titles, peerages, and privileges ⟨arms and honors have always proceeded from the sovereign as the *fountain of honor* —L.G.Pine⟩

foun·tain·ous \'fau̇nt(ᵊ)nəs, -tən-\ *adj* **1 :** of, relating to, or having the characteristics of a fountain **2 :** full of or containing fountains

fountain pen *n* **:** a pen containing a reservoir that automatically feeds the writing point with ink

fountain plant *n* **1 :** a garden amaranth (*Amaranthus tricolor angustior*) **2 :** a Mexican shrub or woody herb (*Odontonema cuspidatum*) of the family Acanthaceae

fountain shell *n* **:** a king conch (*Strombus gigas*) sometimes used for a garden ornament

fountain syringe *n* **:** a syringe for introducing fluid into a body space under gravity flow

fountain tree *n* [so called fr. the water obtained fr. its leaves] **1 :** WATER VINE 1 **2 :** DEODAR

fount·ful \'fau̇ntfəl\ *adj, archaic* **:** full of springs or fountains

fou·qui·e·ria \fü'kirēə, ,fükē'ir-, ,fükē'er-\ *n, cap* [NL, fr. Pierre Eloi *Fouquier* †1850 Fr. physician + NL *-ia*] **:** a small genus of scarlet-flowered shrubs or low trees (family Fouquieriaceae) with brittle wood and spiny stems that are leafless for most of the season — see OCOTILLO

fou·qui·e·ri·a·ce·ae \(,)fü,kirē'āsē,ē, ,fükē,ir-, ,fükē,er-\ *n pl, cap* [NL, fr. *Fouquieria*, type genus + *-aceae*] **:** a small family of spiny shrubs or trees (order Parietales) of southwestern No. America

¹four \'fō(ə)r, -ȯ(ə)r, -ōə, -ȯ(ə)\ *adj* [ME *four, foure*, fr. OE *fēower;* akin to OHG *fior* four, ON *fjōrir*, Goth *fidwor*, L *quattuor*, Gk *tettares, tessares*, Skt *catur*] **:** being one more than three in number ⟨~ years⟩ — see NUMBER table

²four \"\ *pron, pl in constr* [ME *four, foure*, fr. OE *fēower*, adj.] **:** four countable persons or things not specified but under consideration and being enumerated ⟨~ are here⟩ ⟨~ were found⟩

³four \"\ *n* -s [ME *four, foure*, fr. *four, foure*, adj. & pron.] **1 :** twice two **:** two times two **:** two twos **:** the square of two **2 a :** four units or objects ⟨a total of ~⟩ **b :** a group or set of four ⟨arranged by ~*s*⟩ **3 a :** the numerable quantity symbolized by the arabic numeral 4 **b :** the figure 4 **4 :** four o'clock — compare BELL table, TIME illustration **5 :** the fourth in a set or series: as **a :** a playing card marked to show that it is fourth in a suit **b :** a domino with four spots on one of its halves **c :** a die with four spots on the side uppermost **d :** an article of clothing of the fourth size ⟨wears a ~⟩ **6 :** something having as an essential feature four units or members: as **a** *cricket* (1) **:** a hit that counts four runs (2) **:** a hit from which four runs are scored **b** (1) **:** a 4-oared racing boat (2) **:** the crew of such a boat (3) **fours** *pl* **:** races for 4-oared boats **c :** four cards of a kind (as in poker) — usu. used in pl. **d fours** *pl* **:** QUARTO ⟨a book printed in ~*s*⟩ **e :** a 4-cylinder engine or automobile **f :** a set of four players or contestants (as a table at bridge) **7 fours** *pl* **:** the four feet or the hands and feet or knees — see *on all fours* at ALL FOURS

four ale *n* [so called fr. its being orig. sold at fourpence a quart] *Brit* **:** a cheap mild ale

four back *n* **:** a bowling game in which only the four back pins are spotted

four-bag·ger \'⸗'bagə(r), -aag-, -aig-\ *n* [¹*four* + *bag* + *-er*] **:** HOME RUN

four-ball \'⸗,⸗\ *or* **four-ball match** *n* **1 :** BEST-BALL FOURSOME **2 :** a golf match in which four players tee off and partners select the better drive and alternate in striking the ball

fourbe *or* **fourb** *n* -s [F *fourbe*, fem., trick & *fourbe*, masc., swindler, fr. MF, fr. *fourbir* to polish, clean, steal — more at FURBISH] **1** *obs* **:** TRICK **2** *obs* **:** IMPOSTOR

four·be·rie \¦fu̇rbə¦rē\ *n* -s [F, fr. *fourbe* + *-erie* -ery] **:** TRICKERY, DECEPTION

¹four·ble \'fōrbəl, 'fȯr-\ *adj* [¹*four* + *-ble* (as in *double*)] *dial* **:** QUADRUPLE, FOURFOLD

²fourble \"\ *n* -s **:** a unit of pipe for drilling oil consisting of four lengths coupled together

fourble board *n* **:** a platform at a height of 80 feet or more above the floor of an oil derrick

four·cault process \(')fu̇|(ə)r¦kō-, (')fō|\ *n, usu cap F* [after Émile *Fourcault*, 20th cent. Belg. inventor] **:** a process of drawing molten glass vertically upward in sheet form ⟨the *Fourcault process* produces flat glass for windows —E.R.Riegel⟩

four-centered arch \'⸗¦⸗⸗-\ *n* **:** an arch whose intrados curve is described from four centers — compare TUDOR ARCH

four·chée *also* **four·ché** \(')fu̇(ə)r¦shā\ *or* **four·chy** \'fu̇(ə)r-shē\ *adj* [F *fourchée* (fem.) & *fourché* (masc.), fr. OF *forchiée* (fem.) & *forchié* (masc.), fr. *forchié*, past part. of *forchier* to fork, fr. *forche* fork, fr. L *furca* — more at FORK] **1** *heraldry* **:** having the end of each arm divided so as to terminate in a V — used of a cross; see CROSS illustration **2** *heraldry* **:** divided near the end into two parts ⟨a lion rampant, tail ~⟩

¹four·chette \(')fu̇(ə)r¦shet\ *n* -s [F, lit., fork, fr. MF *forchete*, fr. *forche* + *-ete* -ette] **1 a :** a small fold of membrane connecting the labia minora in the posterior part of the vulva **b :** WISHBONE **c :** FROG 2 **2** *or* **for·chette** \(')fȯ(ə)r-\ **:** the strip or shaped piece used for the sides of the fingers of a glove — see GLOVE illustration **3 :** TENACE

²four·chet·té \¦fu̇rshə¦tā\ *adj* [modif. of F *fourcheté*, fr. *fourchette* fork] **:** FOURCHÉE

four-color \'⸗¦⸗⸗\ *adj* **1 :** having four colors **2** *of process printing* **:** using the four colors red, yellow, blue, and black — compare COLOR PHOTOGRAPHY

four-cornered \'⸗¦⸗⸗\ *adj* [ME, fr. *four, foure* four + *cornered*] **1 :** QUADRANGULAR **2 :** having four participants ⟨a *four-cornered* fight⟩

four corners *n pl* **1** *sing in constr* **:** the intersection of two roads or the meeting of four roads **:** CROSSROADS ⟨a little grocery at the *four corners* —John Dos Passos⟩ **2 :** the entire area comprising something ⟨in the *four corners* of the political, social, cultural, and religious horizon —A.L. Guérard⟩ **3** *sing in constr* **:** a skittles game with four pins

four-coupled locomotive \'⸗¦⸗⸗-\ *n* **:** a locomotive with two pairs of driving wheels which are connected together by coupling rods

four·croya \fu̇r'krȯi(y)ə, fōr-\ [NL, fr. Count Antoine F. de *Fourcroy* †1809 Fr. chemist] *syn of* FURCRAEA

four-cycle \'⸗¦⸗⸗\ *adj* **:** having a four-stroke cycle ⟨a *four-cycle* internal combustion engine⟩

four-decker \'⸗¦⸗⸗\ *n* **:** a ship with four decks

four-dimensional \¦⸗⸗¦(⸗)⸗\ *adj* **:** having or relating to four dimensions; *esp* **:** involving or relating to the fourth dimension

four-door \'⸗¦⸗\ *adj, of an automobile* **:** having two seating compartments each provided with two doors

four·drin·i·er \fu̇r'drinēər, -ē,ā\ *or* **fourdrinier machine** *n* -s *often cap F* [after Henry *Fourdrinier* †1854 and Sealy *Fourdrinier* †1847 Eng. papermakers and inventors] **:** a paper machine in which the web of paper is formed on an endless traveling wire screen that passes under a dandy roll, over suction boxes, through presses, and over dryers to the calenders and reels — compare CYLINDER MACHINE

fourdrinier wire *n, often cap F* **:** a continuous screen of fine wire cloth used for draining pulp in a fourdrinier machine

four-em space *n* [contr. of *four-to-em space*] **:** a space in printing that is ¼ of an em in thickness

four-eyed \'⸗¦⸗\ *adj* **1 :** having or appearing to have four eyes **2 :** wearing glasses ⟨getting tired of being called a *four-eyed* weakling⟩

four-eyed fish *n* **:** a fish of the genus *Anableps*

four-eyed opossum *n* **:** any of various So. American opossums that are distributed between two genera (*Metachirops* and *Metachirus*) and are distinguished by a patch of light hair above each eye

four-eyes \'⸗,⸗\ *n pl but sing in constr* **1 :** FOUR-EYED FISH **2 :** a person who wears glasses

4-f \'⸗¦⸗\ *n, pl* **4-f's** *usu cap F* [so called fr. the arbitrary official designation of the class of registrants consisting of those men found unfit for military service under the Selective Service System established by the U.S. during World War II] **:** one who is rejected for military service because of a physical, mental, or moral disability

four-five-six \¦⸗¦⸗¦⸗\ *n* **:** a game played with three dice in which 4-5-6 is one of the winning casts

four flush *n* [³*four* + *flush*] **:** four cards of the same suit in a five-card poker hand

four-flush \"\ *vi* [*four flush*] **:** to make a false claim **:** BLUFF ⟨no beating around the bush and pretending and *four-flushing* —*Amer. Mercury*⟩

four-flusher \'⸗¦⸗ə(r)\ *n* **:** one that cannot back up his pretensions **:** BLUFFER ⟨did you ever see a *four-flusher* that went on holding people's confidence —Sinclair Lewis⟩

¹four·fold \'⸗¦fōld\ *adj* [ME *fourfold, fourefold*, fr. OE *fēowerfeald*, fr. *fēower* four + *-feald* -fold] **1 :** having four parts or aspects **:** QUADRUPLE **2 :** being four times as large, as great, or as many as some understood size, degree, or amount ⟨a ~ increase⟩ **3 :** TETRAD

²fourfold \"\ *adv* [ME *fourfold, fourefold*, fr. *fourfold, fourefold*, adj.] **:** to four times as much or as many **:** by four times ⟨increased ~⟩

four-foot \'=,=\ *adj* [ME *fourfote, fourefote*, fr. OE *fēowerfōte*, fr. *fēower* four + *-fōte* (fr. *fōt* foot)] **1 :** FOUR-FOOTED **2 :** having a dimension of four feet

four-footed \'=¦==\ *adj* [ME *fourfoted, fourefoted*, fr. OE *fēowerfōted*, fr. *fēower* four + *-fōted* footed] **1 :** having four feet : QUADRUPED **2 :** of, relating to, or characteristic of quadrupeds

four-footed butterfly *n* **:** a butterfly of the family *Nymphalidae*

four-foot octave *n* **:** SMALL OCTAVE

four-foot pitch *n* **:** the pitch of a 4-foot stop on a pipe organ

four-foot stop *n* **:** a pipe-organ stop sounding pitches an octave higher than the notes indicate — compare EIGHT-FOOT STOP

four-four \'=ˈ=\ *or* **four-four time** *n* **:** the rhythmic content per measure as indicated 4/4 in a musical composition consisting of four quarter notes or tones or their equivalent

four freedoms *n pl, often cap both Fs* **:** the four basic human freedoms identified by F.D. Roosevelt as freedom of speech and expression, freedom of worship, freedom from want, and freedom from fear

four gents chain *or* **four ladies chain** *n* **:** a crossover in a square dance in which all four men or all four women join hands in the center of the set

four·gon \fürgōⁿ\ *n, pl* **fourgons** \-ōⁿ(z)\ [F, wagon for carrying baggage, poker, fr. OF *forgon* poker, fr. *forgier, furgier* to search, rummage, fr. (assumed) VL *furicare*, irreg. fr. L *fur* thief — more at FURTIVE] **:** a wagon for carrying baggage ⟨you look through the glassed-in windows of the promenade and see the last ~*s* loaded —Christopher Morley⟩

4-h \'=ˈ=\ *adj, usu cap H* [so called fr. the fourfold aim of improving the head, heart, hands, and health] **:** of or relating to the 4-H club or the 4-H club program

four-hand \'=,=\ *adj* **:** FOUR-HANDED

four-handed \'=¦==\ *adj* **1 :** having four hands **:** QUADRUMANOUS **2 :** designed for execution by four hands ⟨a piano duet is a *four-handed* musical composition⟩ **3 :** requiring the participation of four persons ⟨a *four-handed* game⟩ ⟨*four-handed* reel⟩

4-h'er \'=¦āchə(r)\ *n, usu cap H* **:** a member of a 4-H club established by the U.S. Dept. of Agriculture to instruct young people esp. in rural areas in modern farm practices and the fundamentals of good citizenship

four-hol·er \'=¦hōlə(r)\ *n* [¹*four* + *hole* + *-er*] **:** a privy with four openings

four-horned antelope \'=,=-\ *n* **:** an Indian antelope (*Tetracerus quadricornis*) the male of which has two pairs of horns — called also *bekra, bhokra, doda*

four horsemen *n pl* **1** *usu cap F&H* **:** war, famine, pestilence, and death personified as the four major plagues of mankind ⟨the *Four Horsemen* still darken the skies —Harrison Smith⟩ — with reference to Apoc 6:2–7(NCE) **2 :** four threatening forces of any kind ⟨the *four horsemen* . . . scarcities, subsidies, doles, and inflation —Raymond Moley⟩

four hundred *or* **400** *n, usu cap F&H* [so called fr. the idea that a social elite must necessarily be small in number] **:** the exclusive social set of a community — used with *the* ⟨a crystal= chandelier background that provided her with relatives and friends in the *400* —Marjorie B. Snyder⟩

four-hundred-day clock *n* [trans. of G *vierhunderttageuhr*] **:** ANNIVERSARY CLOCK

fou·ri·er analysis \¦fürē¦ā-\ *n, usu cap F* [after Baron Jean Baptiste Joseph *Fourier* †1830 Fr. geometrician and physicist] **:** the fitting of terms of a Fourier series to periodic data

fou·ri·er·ism \'fürēə,rizəm, 'fȯr-,'fyür-\ *n* -s *usu cap* [F *fouriérisme*, fr. F. M. Charles *Fourier* †1837 Fr. social scientist and reformer + F *-isme* -ism] **:** a plan for the reorganization of society into cooperative communities of small groups living in common — called also *phalansterianism*

fou·ri·er·ist \-ərəst\ *or* **fou·ri·er·ite** \-ə,rīt\ *n* -s *usu cap* [*fourierist* fr. F *fouriériste*, fr. F. M. Charles *Fourier* †1837 + F *-iste* -ist; *fourierite* fr. F. M. Charles *Fourier* †1837 + E *-ite*] **:** an advocate of Fourierism

fou·ri·er·is·tic \¦===¦ristik\ *adj, usu cap* [*fourierist* + *-ic*] **:** of, relating to, or resembling Fourierism

fou·ri·er series \¦fürē¦ā-\ *n, usu cap F* [after Baron Jean Baptiste Joseph *Fourier* †1830] *math* **:** an infinite series of the form $a_0/2+a_1\cos x+b_1\sin x+a_2\cos 2x+b_2\sin 2x+\cdots$ that may be used to approximate a function or to fit a given set of data (as periodic data)

fou·ri·er's theorem \-ē¦āz-\ *n, usu cap F* [after Jean Baptiste Joseph *Fourier* †1830] **:** a theorem in mathematics: any periodic function may be resolved into sine and cosine terms involving known constants

four-in-hand \'==,=\ *n* **1 a :** a team of four horses driven by one person **b :** a vehicle drawn by such a team **2 :** a necktie cut on the bias and often made with a lining and tied in a slipknot so that the long flared ends overlap vertically in front

four-in-hand 2

four-leaf clover \'=,=-\ *n* **1** *also* **four-leafed clover** \'=,=-\ **:** an atypical clover leaf with four leaflets often believed to be an omen of good luck **2 :** a closed circle of four square dancers with overlapping arms

four-letter word *n* **:** any of a group of vulgar or obscene words typically made up of four letters ⟨books which rely for their appeal upon sensation and *four-letter words* —Louis Bromfield⟩ ⟨*four-letter words* used across the tracks —Lou Richter⟩

four-lined plant bug *also* **four-lined leaf bug** \'=,=-\ *n* **:** a yellow or orange leaf bug (*Poecilocapsus lineatus*) that is widespread in eastern and central No. America, that has four longitudinal black stripes down the back, and that feeds on various wild and cultivated plants

four-line octave *n* [so called fr. the four accent marks of the symbol C'''' representing the third C above middle C] **:** the musical octave that begins on the third C above middle C — see PITCH illustration

four·ling \'=liŋ\ *n* -s [³*four* + *-ling*] **:** a twin crystal consisting of four individuals

four·mar·i·er·ite \fùr'marēə,rīt\ *n* -s [F *fourmariérite*, fr. Paul *Fourmarier*, 20th cent. Belg. geologist + F *-ite*] **:** a mineral $PbU_4O_{13}.5H_2O(?)$ consisting of a hydrous oxide of lead and uranium

four-masted bark \'=,==-\ *n* **:** a 4-masted ship that is fore= and-aft rigged on the aftermost mast and square-rigged on the other three masts

four-mast·er \'=¦=ə(r)\ *n* -s **:** a 4-masted ship

four-minute man *n* **:** one of a body of men who during World War I made short speeches esp. to promote the sale of government bonds

four noble truths *n pl, usu cap F&N&T* **:** the basic doctrines of Buddhism specifying that all life is subject to suffering, that the desire to live is the cause of repeated existences, that only the annihilation of desire can give release, and that the way of escape is the elimination of selfishness by means of the Eightfold Path

four-oar \'=,=\ *n* **:** a four-oared boat

four-oared \'=¦=\ *adj* **1 :** provided with or rowed by four oars with one man to an oar **2 :** participated in by four-oared boats

four-o'clock \'==,=\ *n* **1 :** a plant of the genus *Mirabilis:* as **a :** a common garden plant (*M. jalapa*) with fragrant yellow, red, or white flowers that open late in the afternoon — called also *marvel-of-Peru* **b :** a California plant (*M. laevis*) with red flowers **2** [so called fr. its cry] **:** FRIARBIRD

four-o'clock family *n* **:** NYCTAGINACEAE

four of a kind : four playing cards of the same rank — called also *double pair royal;* see POKER illustration

four paws *n pl but usu sing in constr* **:** four short chains terminating in hooks at one end and welded at the other end to a single ring for use in skidding logs — called also *four-paw grab*

four·pence *Brit* '=,pən(t)s, *US* " *or* '=,pen-\ *n, pl* **fourpence** *or* **fourpences 1 :** the sum of four usu. British pennies **2 :** a British silver coin worth four pennies now used only as maundy money **:** GROAT **3 :** FIPPENNY BIT

fourpence ha' penny *n* **:** FIPPENNY BIT

¹four·pen·ny \-nē,-ni, *Brit sometimes* 'fȯpni\ *adj* [ME *fourepeny-* (in *fourepenynail*), fr. *four, foure* four + *peny* penny] **:** amounting to, worth, or costing fourpence

²fourpenny \"\ *n* **:** FOURPENCE

fourpenny nail *n* [ME *fourepenynail* nail costing fourpence per hundred, fr. *fourepeny-* fourpenny + *nail*] **:** a nail 1⅜ inches long by 15½ gauge

four-pip·er \'=¦pīpə(r)\ *n* [¹*four* + *pipe*, n. + *-er*] **:** FOUR= STACKER

four-post·er \'=¦pōstə(r)\ *n* [¹*four* + *post*, n. + *-er*] **:** a bed whose tall often carved corner posts were orig. designed to support curtains or a canopy

four-poster

four·pound·er \'=¦paùndə(r)\ *n* **:** a gun throwing a 4-pound projectile

four-quarter plan *n* **:** the plan of dividing the academic year into four quarters of approximately 12 weeks each

four questions *n* **:** the four questions concerning the meaning of Seder customs asked usu. by the youngest participant at the beginning of the Passover Seder service prompting recital of the Haggada

four·ra·gère \¦fùrə¦zhe(ə)r\ *n* -s [F, fr. fem. of *fourrager*, adj., connected with or yielding forage, fr. *fourrage* forage, fr. OF *forage* — more at FORAGE] **:** a braided cord worn usu. around the left shoulder; *esp* **:** such a cord awarded as a decoration to a military unit for distinguished service or conspicuous gallantry in war — compare AIGUILLETTE

four·ri·er \'fùrēə(r)\ *n* -s [MF, forager, fr. OF *forrier*, fr. *forre, fuerre* fodder, straw — more at FORAGE] **:** one that goes before **:** FORERUNNER, PRECURSOR

four-rowed barley \'=,=-\ *n* **:** a barley in which the overlapping of the lateral members of each cluster of three fertile spikelets makes the spike appear to have four rows — compare SIX-ROWED BARLEY, TWO-ROWED BARLEY

fours \'fō(ə)rz, -ȯ(ə)rz,-ōəz,-ȯ(ə)z\ *or* **fours·es** \-zəz\ *n pl but usu sing in constr* [*fours* fr. pl. of ³*four; fourses* fr. *fours* + *-es* (suffix forming plural of nouns)] *dial Eng* **:** a light meal served in the afternoon esp. to harvest workers

fourscore \'=¦=\ *adj* [ME *fourscore, fourescore*, fr. *four, foure* four + *score*] **:** being 80 in number

fourscorth *adj* [*fourscore* + *-th*] *obs* **:** EIGHTIETH

¹four·some \'=səm\ *n* -s [ME *foursum*, fr. (assumed) ME *foure sum* one of four, fr. OE *fēowra sum*, fr. *fēowra* (gen. of *fēower* four) + *sum* some, one — more at FOUR, SOME] **1 a :** a group of four **:** QUARTET **b :** two couples each of which consists of a man and a woman **2 a :** a golf match between two pairs of partners each of whom plays his own ball — compare FOUR= BALL **b :** a similar match with each side playing one ball and partners striking alternately — called also *Scotch foursome*

²foursome \"\ *adj* **1** *Scot* **:** suitable for four persons **2** *Scot* **:** requiring four participants

four-spined stickleback \'=,=-\ *n* **:** a stickleback (*Apeltes quadracus*) that occurs along the New England coast

four-spot \'=,=\ *n* **1 :** a four in cards or dice **2** *or* **fourspot flounder** \'=,=-\ *also* **four-spotted flounder** \'=,==-\ **:** a flatfish (*Paralichthys oblongus*) of the eastern coast of the U.S.

¹foursquare \'=¦=\ *adj* [ME *foursquare, fouresquare*, fr. *four, foure* four + *square*] **1 a :** having four equal sides and four right angles **:** SQUARE ⟨a large ~ Victorian mansion —Osbert Lancaster⟩ **b :** arranged in a square ⟨a stockyard where thatched cowhouses . . . cart sheds and a great old barn . . . huddle ~ —J.W.Day⟩ **2 :** characterized by boldness and conviction **:** sound and unswerving **:** FORTHRIGHT ⟨they are . . . ~ and simple and staunch —H.S.Commager⟩ **3** *usu cap* **:** of or relating to a fundamentalist religious cult or sectarian movement originating in southern California after World War I ⟨*Foursquare* churches⟩ ⟨the *Foursquare* technique⟩ ⟨a *Foursquare* choir⟩

²foursquare \'=¦=\ *adv* **1 :** in a square position **:** SOLIDLY ⟨their monuments stand ~ —J.E.M.White⟩ **2 :** in an unequivocal manner **:** FORTHRIGHTLY ⟨he stood ~ for religious liberty and toleration —C.G.Bowers⟩

³foursquare \'=,=\ *n, archaic* **:** a figure with four equal sides and four right angles ⟨of a shape between a circle and a ~ —William Upton⟩

four-square·ness \'=¦=nəs\ *n* -ES **:** lack of refinement **:** BLUNTNESS

four-stack·er \'=¦stakə(r)\ *n* [¹*four* + *stack*, n. + *-er*] **:** a destroyer of World War I design with four smokestacks

four-star *or* **four-starred** \'=¦=\ *adj* **1 :** of a high degree of excellence **2 :** having the military rank of general or admiral

fourstrand \'=,=\ *or* **four-stranded** \'=¦==\ *adj* [*fourstrand* fr. ¹*four* + *strand*, n.; *four-stranded* fr. ¹*four* + *strand*, n. + *-ed*] **:** having four strands; *specif, of a rope* **:** having four strands laid up right-handed with a core in the center

four-strip·er \'=¦strīpə(r)\ *n* [so called fr. the four gold stripes worn on the sleeve of his uniform] **:** a captain in the U.S. Navy

four-stroke cycle *n* **:** a cycle in which air or an explosive mixture is drawn into the cylinder of an internal-combustion engine on a suction stroke, is compressed and ignited on a compression stroke, burns and performs useful work on an expansion stroke, and expels the products of combustion on an exhaust or scavenging stroke

¹four·teen \(')fō(ə)r|(t)¦tēn, -ȯ(ə)r|, -ōə|, -ȯ(ə)| *sometimes* |d-¦tēn\ *adj* [ME *fourtene*, fr. OE *fēowertīene, fēowertȳne, fēowertēne* (akin to OHG *fiorzehan* fourteen, ON *fjōrtān*, Goth *fidwortaihun*), fr. *fēower* four + *-tīene, -tȳne, -tēne* (fr. *tīen, tȳn, tēn* ten) — more at FOUR, TEN] **:** being one more than 13 ⟨~ years⟩ — see NUMBER table

²fourteen \"\ *pron, pl in constr* [ME *fourtene*, fr. OE *fēowertīene, fēowertȳne, fēowertēne*, fr. *fēowertīene, fēowertȳne, fēowertēne*, adj.] **:** 14 countable persons or things not specified but under consideration and being enumerated ⟨~ are here⟩ ⟨~ were found⟩

³fourteen \"\ *n* -s [ME *fourtene*, fr. OE *fēowertīene, fēowertȳne, fēowertēne*, fr. *fēowertīene, fēowertȳne, fēowertēne*, adj.] **1 :** 10 and four **:** twice seven **:** seven times two **2 a :** 14 units or objects ⟨a total of ~⟩ **b :** a group or set of 14 **3 :** the numerable quantity symbolized by the arabic numerals 14 **4 :** the 14th in a set or series; *esp* **:** an article of clothing of the 14th size ⟨wears a ~⟩

four·teen·er \-nə(r)\ *n* -s **1 :** a poetic line of 14 syllables; *esp* **:** such a line consisting of seven iambic feet **2 :** a mountain peak 14,000 or more feet above sea level

fourteen-one continuous *n* **:** the championship game of pocket billiards in which the balklines are located fourteen inches from the cushions, a player being permitted only one shot from balk, and in which a player must call his shots and amass 150 points to win

fourteen step *n* **:** an ice-skating step combination of waltz and various turns

¹four·teenth \-n(t)th\ *adj* [ME *fourtenthe*, adj. & n., alter. (influenced by *fourtene* fourteen) of *fourtethe*, fr. OE *fēowertēotha* (akin to ON *fjōrtāndi* fourteenth), fr. *fēowertīene, fēowertȳne, fēowertēne* fourteen + *-otha, -tha* -th] **1 :** being number 14 in a countable series ⟨the ~ day⟩ — see NUMBER table **2 :** being one of 14 equal parts into which something is divisible ⟨a ~ share of the money⟩

²fourteenth \"\ *n, pl* **fourteenths** \-n(t)s,-n(t)ths\ [ME *fourtenthe*] **1 :** number 14 in a countable series ⟨the ~ of the month⟩ **2 :** the quotient of a unit divided by 14 **:** one of 14 equal parts of something ⟨one ~ of the total⟩ **3 :** a musical interval comprising an octave and a seventh

fourteen-two balkline *n* **:** a carom billiards game in which balklines are located 14 inches from the cushions and two shots are permitted from balk

¹fourth \'fō(ə)rth, -ȯ(ə)rth,-ōəth,-ȯ(ə)th\ *adj* [ME *fourthe*, adj. & n., alter. (influenced by *four, foure* four) of *ferthe*, fr. OE *fēortha, fēowertha* (akin to OHG *fiordo* fourth, ON *fjōrthi*), fr. *fēower* four + *-tha* -th — more at FOUR] **1 :** being number four in a countable series ⟨the ~ day⟩ — see NUMBER table **2 :** being one of four equal parts into which something is divisible ⟨a ~ share of the money⟩ **3** *in certain motor vehicles* **:** being the forward gear or speed next higher than third

²fourth \"\ *n* -s [ME *fourthe*] **1 :** number four in a countable series ⟨the ~ of the month⟩ **2 :** the quotient of a unit divided by four **:** one of four equal parts of something ⟨one ~ of the total⟩ **3 a :** the musical interval embracing four diatonic degrees **b :** the tone at this interval; *specif* **:** SUBDOMINANT **c :** the harmonic combination of two tones a fourth apart **4 :** the fourth forward gear or speed of a motor vehicle **5 a** *usu cap* **:** INDEPENDENCE DAY — used with preceding *the* **b** *Brit* **:** the day on which bills dated the first of the month become due — used in the phrase *fourth of the month* **6 :** QUARTE

³fourth \"\ *adv* **1 :** in the fourth place **2 :** with three exceptions ⟨the nation's ~ largest city⟩

fourth class *n* **1 :** a class or group ranking fourth in a series **2 a :** a class of mail in the U.S. that comprises merchandise and non-second-class printed matter weighing over 8 oz. and not sealed against inspection **b :** a class of mail in Canada that comprises merchandise and printed matter exceeding certain weights

fourth cranial nerve *or* **fourth nerve** *n* **:** TROCHLEAR NERVE

fourth day *n, usu cap F* **:** WEDNESDAY — used chiefly by the Friends

fourth deck *n* **:** the lowest deck in a typical merchant ship of many decks; *sometimes* **:** ORLOP DECK — see DECK illustration

fourth dimension *n* [prob. trans. of NL *quarta dimensio*] **1 :** a dimension in addition to the three dimensions length, breadth, and thickness that is assumed to exist in order to satisfy certain mathematical analogies and that in the theory of relativity constitutes the time coordinate used along with the rectangular coordinates *x, y, z* to locate a point (as for recording an event) **2 :** something outside the range of ordinary experience ⟨a *fourth dimension* of meaning that transcends . . . the issue of clarity versus obscurity —Peter Viereck⟩

fourth-dimensional \¦=(,)=¦=(=)=\ *adj* **:** relating to the fourth dimension

fourth estate *n, often cap F&E* **:** a group other than the clergy, nobility, or commons that wields political power; *specif* **:** the public press ⟨the *Fourth Estate* . . . has genuine being in Congress and in national politics generally —W.S.White⟩ — compare ESTATE 3, FIFTH ESTATE

fourth hand *n* **:** the fourth player in various card games to have the right to bid or to play to any trick

fourth·ly *adv* **:** in the fourth place

fourth of july *usu cap F&J* **:** INDEPENDENCE DAY

fourth-rate \'=¦=\ *adj* **1 :** belonging or relating to a fourth rank or grade (as in order of excellence) **2 :** of negligible worth — **fourth-rat·er** \'=¦rād·ə(r)\ *n*

fourth ventricle *n* **:** a somewhat rhomboidal ventricle of the posterior part of the brain that connects at the front with the third ventricle through the aqueduct of Sylvius and at the back with the central canal of the spinal cord

four-times accented octave *n* **:** FOUR-LINE OCTAVE

four-toed \'=¦=\ *adj* **:** having four toes; *specif* **:** having four toes on each foot

four-tooth \'=,=\ *n, pl* **four-tooths :** a 2-year-old sheep

four-way \'=¦=\ *adj* **1 :** allowing passage in any of four directions ⟨a *four-way* valve⟩ ⟨a *four-way* traffic light⟩ **2 :** including four participants ⟨a *four-way* talk⟩

four-way cock *n, mech engin* **:** a cock connected with four pipes or ports and having two or more passages in the plug by which the adjacent pipes or ports may be made to communicate

four-way switch *n* **:** an electric switch used in house wiring so that a light may be turned on or off at three or more places

four-wheel *or* **four-wheeled** \'=¦=\ *adj* **1 :** having four wheels ⟨a *four-wheel* carriage⟩ **2 :** acting on or by means of four wheels of an automotive vehicle ⟨*four-wheel* drive⟩ ⟨*four-wheel* brakes⟩

four-wheeled scraper *n* **:** a scraper with four wheels and a metal scoop suspended from an axle that can be raised to clear the ground after loading

four-wheel·er \'=¦(h)wēlə(r)\ *n* **:** a vehicle with four wheels; *specif* **:** a one-horse carriage with four wheels

fous *pl of* FOU

foussa *var of* FOSSA

fout \'faùt, 'fōt\ *dial past of* FIGHT

fou·ter \'füd·ər, -ütə-\ *or* **fou·tra** \-ü·trə\ *n* -s [MF *foutre* to copulate with, copulate, fr. L *futuere;* prob. akin to L *-futare* to beat — more at BEAT] **1** *archaic* **:** something of little value **:** FIG ⟨a *foutra* for the world and worldlings base —Shak.⟩ **2 a** *chiefly Scot* (1) **:** an objectionable or tedious person (2) **:** a worthless or bungling person **b** *Scot* **:** CHAP, FELLOW

fouth \'füth\ *n* -s [ME (Sc), fr. ME *fulth* fullness — more at FULTH] *chiefly Scot* **:** ABUNDANCE, PLENTY

fo·vea \'fōvēə\ *n, pl* **fove·ae** \-vē,ē, -vē,ī\ [L, small pit] **:** a small depression or pit **:** FOSSA; **a** [NL, fr. L] **:** the hollowed leaf base in the quillwort containing a sporangium **b** *or* **fovea cen·tra·lis** \-,sen·'tralǝs, -rāl-,-räl-\ [*fovea* fr. NL, fr. L; *fovea centralis* fr. NL, central fovea] **:** a small rodless area of the retina affording acute vision — see EYE illustration

fo·ve·al \-vēəl\ *adj* **:** of or relating to a fovea (as the retinal fovea) **:** situated in or mediated through the fovea — **fo·ve·al·ly** \-əlē\ *adv*

fo·ve·ate \-vē,āt, -ēət\ *or* **fo·ve·at·ed** \-ē,ād·əd\ *adj* [*foveate* fr. NL & L *fovea* small pit + E *-ate; foveated* fr. NL & L *fovea* + E *-ate* + *-ed*] **:** having foveae **:** PITTED

fo·ve·a·tion \,fōvē'āshən\ *n* -s [*foveate* + *-ion*] **1 :** the act or process of forming pits **2 :** the state of being pitted

fo·ve·i·form \'fōvēə,fȯrm, fō'v-\ *adj* [ISV *fovea* (fr. NL & L) + *-iform*] **:** like a fovea

fo·ve·o·la \fō'vēələ\ *n, pl* **foveo·lae** \-,lē\ *or* **foveolas** [NL, dim. of *fovea*] **:** a small pit; *specif* **:** one of the pits in the embryonic gastric mucosa from which the gastric glands develop — **fo·ve·o·lar** \-lə(r)\ *adj*

fo·ve·o·lar·i·ous \¦fōvēə¦la(a)rēəs\ *adj* [prob. fr. (assumed) NL *foveolarius*, fr. NL *foveola* + L *-arius* -ary] **:** FOVEATE

fo·ve·o·late \'fōvēə,lāt, fō'vēələt\ *or* **fo·ve·o·lat·ed** \-ēə,lād·əd\ *adj* [*foveolate* prob. fr. (assumed) NL *foveolatus*, fr. NL *foveola* + L *-atus* -ate; *foveolated* prob. fr. (assumed) NL *foveolatus* + E *-ed*] **:** FOVEATE

fo·ve·ole \'fōvē,ōl\ *or* **fo·ve·o·let** \¦fōvēə¦let, fō'vēələt\ *n* -s [*foveole* fr. NL *foveola; foveolet* fr. *foveole* + *-et*] **:** FOVEOLA

¹fow \'fü\ *dial Brit var of* FULL

²fow \"\ *var of* FOU

³fow \'faù, 'fō\ *dial Brit var of* FOUL

FOW *abbr* **1** first open water **2** free on wagon

fowd *var of* FOUD

fow·er \'faù(ə)r\ *Scot var of* FOUR

fowk \'faùk\ *chiefly Scot var of* FOLK

¹fowl \'faùl, *esp before pause or consonant* -aùəl\ *n, pl* **fowl** *or* **fowls** [ME *foul*, fr. OE *fugel;* akin to OHG *fogal* bird, ON *fugl*, Goth *fugls*, and prob. to OHG *fliogan* to fly — more at FLY] **1 :** a bird of any kind ⟨dominion over . . . the ~ of the air —Gen 1:28 (AV)⟩ ⟨watch the hungry ocean ~ breast its way southward —Llewelyn Powys⟩ **2 a :** a domestic cock or hen **:** CHICKEN; *esp* **:** an adult hen — see DOMESTIC FOWL **b :** any of several domesticated or wild gallinaceous birds ⟨jungle ~⟩ ⟨guinea ~⟩ **3 :** the meat of fowls used as food; *esp* **:** the meat of domestic fowls

²fowl \"\ *vi* -ED/-ING/-S [ME *foulen*, fr. OE *fuglian*, fr. *fugel*] **:** to seek, catch, or kill wild fowl for sport or food ⟨such persons as may lawfully hunt, fish, or ~ —William Blackstone⟩

fowl cholera *n* **:** an acute contagious septicemic disease of birds marked by fever, weakness, diarrhea, and petechial hemorrhages in the mucous membranes, caused by a bacterium (*Pasteurella multocida* syn. *avicida*), and highly destructive of all types of domestic poultry and most wild birds — compare FOWL PLAGUE

fowl·er \'faùlə(r)\ *n* -s [ME *foulere*, fr. OE *fuglere*, fr. *fugel* + *-ere* -er] **:** one that hunts wild fowl for sport or food

fow·ler flap \"-\ *n, usu cap 1st F* [after Harlan D. Fowler, 20th cent. Am. aeronautical designer] **:** an extensible trailing= edge flap that in the deflected position exposes a slot in the airplane wing

fow·ler·ite \'faùlə,rīt\ *n* -s [Samuel *Fowler* †1844 Am. physician and mineralogist + E *-ite*] **:** a mineral consisting of a zinc-bearing rhodonite

fow·ler's solution \'faùlə(r)z-\ *n, usu cap F* [after Thomas *Fowler* †1801 Eng. physician] **:** an alkaline aqueous solution of potassium arsenite used in medicine (as in treating some diseases of the blood or skin)

fowler's toad *n, usu cap F* [after Samuel Page *Fowler* †1888 Am. antiquarian and naturalist] **:** a No. American toad (*Bufo fowleri*) with long postorbital and parallel frontoparietal crests

fowling piece *n* [*fowling* fr. gerund of ²*fowl*] **:** a light gun for shooting birds or small quadrupeds

fowl leukemia *also* **fowl leukosis** *or* **fowl leukosis complex** *n* : AVIAN LEUKOSIS COMPLEX
fowl meadow grass *or* **fowl grass** *n* : a slender pasture grass (*Poa palustris*) of Europe and America
fowl mite *n* **1** : CHICKEN MITE **2** : NORTHERN FOWL MITE
fowl paralysis *n* : NEUROLYMPHOMATOSIS
fowl pest *n* **1** : FOWL PLAGUE **2** : NEWCASTLE DISEASE
fowl plague *n* : a highly fatal virus disease of domestic poultry excepting pigeons and of many kinds of wild birds — compare FOWL CHOLERA
fowl pox *n* : either of two forms of a virus disease of chickens, turkeys, and various other birds characterized by head lesions: **a** : a cutaneous form marked by pustules, warty growths, and scabs esp. on the unfeathered skin — called also *sorehead* **b** : a more serious form occurring as cheesy lesions of the mucous membranes of the mouth, throat, and eyes that sometimes coalesce into a false membrane — called also *avian diphtheria*
fowl spirochetosis *n* : a severe febrile disease of poultry that is marked by enteritis and diarrhea and by congestion and often localized necrosis or ecchymoses in the liver and spleen and that is caused by a spirochete (*Borrelia anserina*) which is transmitted either directly or by a biting arthropod (as the chicken tick) — compare ARGAS
fowl tick *n* : CHICKEN TICK
fowl typhoid *n* : an infectious disease of poultry characterized by diarrhea, anemia, and great prostration and caused by a bacterium (*Salmonella gallinarum*)
[1]**fox** \'fäks\ *n, pl* **foxes** *or* **fox** *often attrib* [ME, fr. OE; akin to OLF *vus* fox, OHG *fuhs* fox, *foha* she-fox, ON *fōa* fox, Goth *fauho* fox, Skt *puccha* tail] **1** : any of various alert carnivorous mammals of the family Canidae related to the wolves but smaller, with shorter legs, more pointed muzzle, large erect ears, and long bushy tail and now placed in *Vulpes* and several other genera represented by one or more species in most parts of the world — see ARCTIC FOX, FENNEC, GRAY FOX, SILVER FOX; compare COLOR PHASE **2** : the fur of a fox **3** : a clever crafty man : a sly fellow ⟨the ~*es* live by their wits and rely on fraud —J.H.Hallowell⟩ **4** *archaic* : SWORD ⟨thou diest on the point of ~ —Shak.⟩ **5** : a moderate yellowish brown that is stronger and slightly yellower and lighter than Bismarck brown and yellower and deeper than maple sugar — called also *antique drab, Dresden brown* **6** *usu cap* **a** (1) : an Indian people near Lake Winnebago and in the Fox river valley of Wisconsin (2) : a member of such people **b** : an Algonquian language of the Fox, Sauk, and Kickapoo peoples **7 a** : two or more tarred rope yarns hand twisted by sailors to make small cordage used for lashings or for weaving mats — compare SEIZING **b** : a single rope yarn twisted up against its lay for similar use — called also *Spanish fox* **8** : a longitudinal bar to which the tool carriage of a fox lathe is fastened and which receives motion from gearing in the headstock

red fox

[2]**fox** \"\ *vb* -ED/-ING/-ES *vt* **1 a** : to trick by ingenuity or cunning : FOOL, OUTWIT ⟨we would ~ him into withdrawing vitally needed strength —E.E.S.Montagu⟩ **b** : CONFUSE, BEWILDER, BAFFLE ⟨some survivors . . . were completely ~*ed* by the tragedy —Alan Villiers⟩ **2** *obs* : to make drunk : INTOXICATE ⟨I drank . . . so much wine that I was even almost ~*ed* —Samuel Pepys⟩ **3 a** : to repair (a shoe) by renewing the upper **b** : to add a strip of something to; *specif* : to trim (a shoe) with a strip of leather ~ *vi* : to act like a fox : DISSEMBLE ⟨you never know — he may be ~*ing* —Guthrie Wilson⟩
[3]**fox** \"\ *usu cap* — a communications code word for the letter *f*
fox and geese *n* **1 a** : a board game in which pegs or pieces representing geese can be moved only forward in their attempt to corner the fox while the piece representing the fox can move in any direction and can remove geese from the board by jumping them **b** : a similar game played on a checkerboard in which four pieces representing geese are moved forward one space at a time to try to corner the fox who can be moved one space at a time forward or back but cannot jump — called also *devil and the tailors* **2** : a game usu. played in the snow in which one player representing the fox tries to catch one of the others representing the geese as they run around the rim and through the spokes of a wheel-shaped figure

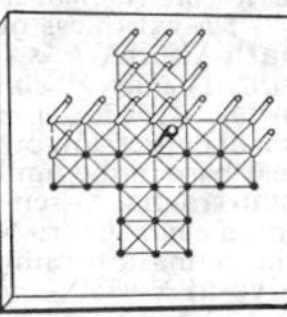
fox and geese 1a

foxbane \'=,=\ *n* : a wolfsbane (*Aconitum lycoctonum*)
fox bat *n* : FRUIT BAT
fox·ber·ry \'fäks — *see* BERRY\ *n* **1** : a bearberry (*Arctostaphylos uva-ursi*) **2** : MOUNTAIN CRANBERRY
fox bolt *n* : an anchor bolt with a split end to receive a fox wedge for use in blind holes
fox dog *n* **1** : FOXHOUND **2** : Azara's dog or various related So. American wild dogs **3** : LONG-EARED FOX
foxed \'fäkst\ *adj* [[1]*fox* + *-ed*] : discolored with yellowish brown stains due to dampness, fungus activity, metallic impurities, or incipient decay ⟨~ leaves of old books⟩
fox encephalitis *n* : a virus disease of foxes, dogs, and related animals that is marked by virus invasion of endothelial tissues esp. of smaller blood vessels resulting in local hemorrhage which damages the tissues of the affected area and leads to inflammation of the brain or other organs
fox·er \'fäksə(r)\ *n* -s : a worker who foxes shoes or rubbers
foxfeet \'=,=\ *n pl but sing in constr* : FIR CLUB MOSS
fox fire *n* [ME *foxfire*, fr. [1]*fox* + *fire*] **1** : an eerie phosphorescent light; *esp* : the luminescence of decaying wood **2** : any of various luminous fungi (as *Armillaria mellea*) that cause decaying wood to glow
foxfish \'=,=\ *n* : the European dragonet
fox geranium *n* : HERB ROBERT
foxglove \'=,=\ *n* [ME, alter. of *foxesglove*, fr. OE *foxes glōfa*, fr. *foxes* (gen. of [1]*fox*) + *glōfa*, *glōf* glove, pouch — more at GLOVE] **1** : a plant of the genus *Digitalis*; *esp* : a common European biennial or perennial (*D. purpurea*) with long clusters of dotted whitish or purple tubular flowers — called also *fairy bell, fingerflower, fingerroot* **2** : any of several other plants: as **a** *dial Eng* : MULLEIN **b** : TRUMPET CREEPER **c** : PITCHER PLANT **d** : POKEWEED
foxglove aphid *n* : an aphid (*Acyrthosiphon solani*) that is an economic pest of various cultivated plants (as potatoes) in temperate regions
fox grape *n* : any of several native grapes of eastern No. America with foxy fruit of sour or musky flavor: as **a** : MUSCADINE 2 **b** : CHICKEN GRAPE **c** : a tall-growing grape (*Vitis labrusca*) that has heavily tomentose young growth and compact thyrses of bluish black to pink or greenish white fruits which are sharp and acid until fully ripe and that is an ancestor of most hardy American cultivated grapes
foxhole \'=,=\ *n* : a pit usu. dug hastily during combat for individual cover against enemy fire, sometimes large enough for two or three men, and elaborated in construction as the situation demands and materials available permit
foxhound \'=,=\ *n* : any of certain large swift powerful hounds of great endurance that are used in hunting foxes, that are considered to form several breeds and many distinctive strains, and that are from 21 to 25 inches high with a dense hard glossy coat usu. of black, tan, and white, long ears, straight forelegs, heavy hind legs, and the tail carried gaily over the back — see AMERICAN FOXHOUND, ENGLISH FOXHOUND
foxier *comparative of* FOXY
foxiest *superlative of* FOXY
fox·i·ly \'fäksəlē, -li\ *adv* : in a foxy manner : CRAFTILY, TRICKILY
fox·i·ness \'fäksēnəs, -sin-\ *n* -ES : the quality or state of being foxy
fox·ing \'fäksiŋ\ *n* -s [fr. *foxed*, after such pairs as E *colored: coloring*] **1** : DISCOLORATION; *esp* : brownish spots in the paper of old books **2** [fr. gerund of [2]*fox*] **a** : a piece of material applied to the upper or extending around the outsole of a boot or shoe **b** : a piece of leather ornamenting the lower part of the quarter of a shoe, covering the counter, and sometimes extending to the vamp — see SHOE illustration
fox key *n* : a cotter secured by a fox wedge
fox lathe \'fäks-\ *n* [perh. after James *Fox fl*1821 Eng. toolmaker] : a lathe with or without a turret having a chasing bar and leaders for thread cutting and being used for turning brass
fox maggot *n* : a screwworm (*Wohlfahrtia opaca*) developing in the flesh of various mammals and esp. destructive to young ranch mink and foxes
fox mark *n* [*fox* (as in *foxed*) + *mark*] : a brownish spot; *esp* : a discoloration of old paper
fox moth *n* : a grayish brown European moth (*Macrothylacia rubi*) of the family Lasiocampidae
fox plum *n* : a bearberry (*Arctostaphylos uva-ursi*)
fox poison *n* : SPURGE LAUREL 1
fox shark *n* : THRESHER SHARK
fox snake *n* : a common rodent-eating colubrid snake (*Elaphe vulpina*) of the upper Mississippi valley
fox sparrow *n* : a large American sparrow (*Passerella iliaca*) typically rich chestnut above and striped below
fox squirrel *n* : a large stout-bodied arboreal squirrel (*Sciurus niger*) that is now rare over much of its range from the Mississippi valley and the southeastern U.S. north to New Jersey and central New York and is represented by several varieties differing chiefly in color — see BLACK SQUIRREL, CAT SQUIRREL
foxtail \'=,=\ *n* [ME *fox tail*, fr. [1]*fox* + *tail*] **1 a** : the tail of a fox **b** : something resembling the tail of a fox ⟨there were ~*s* white and wispy all over the sky —David Walker⟩ **2 a** *or* **foxtail grass** : any of several grasses esp. of the genera *Alopecurus, Hordeum,* and *Setaria* with spikes resembling brushes — compare BRISTLE GRASS **b** : any of several ground pines; *esp* : a widely distributed ground pine (*Lycopodium alopecuroides*) of barren sandy or peaty moist coastal regions of eastern and southeastern U.S. that has numerous erect fertile branches thickly clothed with usu. bristly ciliate leaves **3** : the last cinder obtained in the fining of metal
foxtail barley *n* : SQUIRRELTAIL
foxtail lily *n* : a plant of the genus *Eremurus*
foxtail millet *n* : a coarse drought-resistant but frost-sensitive annual grass (*Setaria italica*) with a thick heavy elongated spicate inflorescence that is probably derived from an Old World bristle grass (*S. viridis*), has differentiated into a number of varieties under cultivation, and is grown for grain, hay, and forage in the Old World and chiefly for green fodder and silage in the U. S. — called also *Hungarian grass, Italian millet;* see GERMAN MILLET, SIBERIAN MILLET
foxtail pine *n* : any of several American pines with a dense head of foliage: as **a** : a moderate to large pine (*Pinus balfouriana*) of upland western No. America that is initially pyramidal but becomes irregular and open with age and that has stiff crowded persistent leaves, short-stalked dark brown pendulous cones, and bark initially milk white but becoming reddish brown and deeply fissured with age **b** : BRISTLECONE PINE **c** : LOBLOLLY PINE 1
foxtail wedging *n* : the process of fastening by fox wedges — called also *fox wedging*
fox terrier *n* : either of two small-sized high-spirited terriers that were formerly used to dig out foxes, that weigh about 16 to 18 pounds, and that have a flat moderately narrow skull, very little stop, a long muzzle, small V-shaped ears which droop forward close to the cheek, straight forelegs, and muscular hindquarters without any tendency to droop or crouch: **a** : such a dog with a close smooth dense coat — called also *smooth fox terrier* **b** : such a dog with a harsh wiry coat of moderate length — called also *wirehaired fox terrier*

wirehaired fox terrier

[1]**fox-trot** \'=,=\ *n* **1** : a short broken slow trotting gait in which the hind foot of the horse hits the ground a trifle before the diagonally opposite forefoot and the head nods in time to the movement **2 a** : a ballroom dance in duple time that includes slow walking steps, quick running steps, and two-steps **b** : an ice dancing step **3** : the music to which a fox-trot is danced : jazz in duple rhythm fast or slow — compare BLUES, CHARLESTON
[2]**fox-trot** \"\ *vi* [[1]*fox-trot*] : to dance the fox-trot
foxtrot \"\ *usu cap* [[1]*fox-trot*] — a communications code word for the letter *f*
fox wedge *n* : a wedge for expanding the split end of a bolt, cotter, dowel, tenon, or other piece in order to fasten the end in a hole or mortise and prevent withdrawal
fox wolf *n* : any of several So. American wild dogs (as Azara's dog and the crab-eating fox)
foxy \'fäksē, -si\ *adj, usu* -ER/-EST [[1]*fox* + *-y*] **1 a** : resembling a fox in appearance or disposition : SLY, WILY ⟨a strain of ~ secretiveness —Edgar Johnson⟩ **b** : alert and knowing : smart in appearance and behavior : CLEVER ⟨this ~ publicity man turned fumbling poet —Sherwood Anderson⟩ **2 a** : having the color of a fox : being of the color fox **b** : characterized by excessive use of reddish tints — used esp. of an oil painting ⟨such an excessive brownness in their shadows as to make them sometimes perfectly ~ —W.M.Craig⟩ **3** : defective in color or quality esp. from age or dampness : FOXED ⟨this book . . . when it is old and ~ —R.L.Stevenson⟩ **4** : having the flavor of native American grapes (as the fox grape) ⟨we say the wine tastes "grapey"; wine makers call it a ~ taste —Frank Schoonmaker & Tom Marvel⟩ **syn** see SLY
foy \'fȯi\ *n* -s [D dial. *fooi* feast given by a farmer to his laborers at the end of the harvest, fr. MD *foye, voye* journey, way, parting entertainment, fr. OF *voie* journey, way, fr. L *via* way — more at VIA] *chiefly Scot* : a farewell entertainment or feast (as at the end of a harvest or just before a marriage)
foya·ite \'fȯi(y)ə,īt, 'fōyə-\ *n* -s [G *foyait*, fr. *Foya* (La Foia), mountain in Algarve province, Portugal + G *-it* -ite] **1** : a coarse-grained hornblende-nepheline-syenite rock **2** : a nephelite-syenite rock with trachytoid texture — **fo·ya·it·ic** \¦=¦=¦id·ik\ *adj*
foy boat \'fȯi-\ *n* [*foy* (origin unknown) + *boat*] : a pilot boat used in and about the river Tyne
foy·er \'fȯi(y)ə(r) *also* 'fȯi,(y)ā *sometimes* fȯi'(y)ā\ *n* -s [F, lit., fireplace, fr. ML *focarius* fireplace, fr. L *focus* fireplace, hearth + *-arius* -ary — more at FOCUS] **1 a** : an anteroom or lobby esp. of a theater, library, or other public building — compare GREENROOM **b** : an entrance hallway or vestibule leading typically to stairs or to the interior of private living quarters **2 a** : a gathering place : CENTER ⟨a student ~ . . . where they can eat meals composed principally of soup and starches for . . . about twenty cents —Paul Bowles⟩ **b** : a focal point : center of concentration ⟨intended that the university . . . should become the ~ of Hellenism in a very practical sense —H.A.Gibbons⟩ **3** : a crucible for molten metal in a furnace
fo·zi·ness \'fōzinəs\ *n* -ES *chiefly Scot* : the quality or state of being fozy: **a** : SPONGINESS **b** : OBESITY **c** : FATHEADEDNESS
fo·zy \-zi\ *adj, usu* -ER/-EST [D *voos* spongy and light-textured + E *-y*; akin to ON *fauskr* rotten log, OE *fūl* foul — more at FOUL] **1** *chiefly Scot, of a vegetable* : spongy and light-textured : OVERGROWN **2** *chiefly Scot, of a person* **a** : fat and bloated : OBESE **b** : dull-witted and insipid : FATHEADED
fp *abbr* freezing point
FP *abbr* **1** field punishment **2** fine paper **3** fireplace **4** fireplug **5** flash point **6** floating policy **7** foot-pound **8** [It *fortepiano*] loud, then soft **9** freight and passenger **10** fully paid
FPA *abbr* free of particular average
FPAAC *abbr* free of particular average, American conditions
FPAEC *abbr* free of particular average, English conditions
FPC *abbr* for private circulation
FPM *abbr* feet per minute
FPO *abbr* **1** field post office **2** fleet post office
fprf *abbr* fireproof
FPS *abbr* **1** *often not cap* feet per second **2** *usu not cap* foot-pound-second **3** *often not cap* frames per second
fqcy *abbr* frequency
fqt *abbr* frequent
fr *abbr* **1** *often cap* father **2** fragment **3** frame **4** franc **5** *often cap* [L *frater*] brother **6** frequent **7** *often cap* friar **8** from **9** front **10** fruit
FR *abbr* **1** fire resistant; fire retardant **2** freight release
Fr *symbol* francium
[1]**fra** \'frä\ *prep* [ME (northern dial.) *fra, fro*, fr. ON *frā* — more at FROM] *Scot* : FROM
[2]**fra** \'frä\ *n* -s *usu cap* [It, short for *frate* brother, monk, fr. L *frater* brother — more at BROTHER] : BROTHER — often used as a title preceding the name of an Italian monk or friar ⟨*Fra* Angelo⟩ ⟨*Fra* Dominic⟩
fra·ca \frə'kä\ *n* -s [F *fracas*] *Scot* : FRACAS
fra·cas \'frākəs *also* 'frak-, *Brit usu* 'fra(,)kä\ *n, pl* **fracases** \-səz\ *or Brit* **fracas** \-äz\ [F, din, hubbub, row, fr. MF, fr. OIt *fracasso*, fr. *fracassare* to break into pieces, shatter, destroy, fr. (assumed) VL, blend of L *frangere* to break and *quassare* to shake, break into pieces — more at BREAK, QUASH] : a noisy quarrel : BRAWL, FIGHT, ALTERCATION ⟨there was suddenly a ~, and one of them clenched his fists and hit another full in the face —E.V.Lucas⟩ ⟨the most violent ~ in . . . parliamentary history resulted in hurled benches and three injuries —*Collier's Yr. Bk.*⟩ **syn** see BRAWL
frack \'frak\ *var of* FRECK
fract·ed \'fraktəd\ *adj* [L *fractus*, (past part.) + E *-ed*] **1** *obs* : BROKEN **2** *of a heraldic ordinary* : having a part displaced as if the charge were broken
[1]**frac·tion** \'frakshən\ *n* -s [ME *fraccioun*, fr. LL *fraction-, fractio* action of breaking, fr. L *fractus* (past part. of *frangere* to break) + *-ion-, -io* -ion — more at BREAK] **1** : a part of a whole: as **a** : the indicated quotient of one expression divided by another — see NUMBER table **b** (1) : a piece broken off : FRAGMENT, SCRAP (2) : a discrete unit : PORTION, SECTION ⟨a minute ~ of the voters⟩ **c** : a part less than a point in a security quotation ⟨the price of U.S. steel declined a ~⟩ **2** *archaic* **a** : a rupture in relations : DISCORD, DISSENSION, DISHARMONY **b** : a breach of peace : FRACAS, RUCTION **3 a** : a breaking up : BREAKING; *specif, often cap* : the breaking of the bread by the priest before the communion in Eastern and Western Christian liturgies **b** *obs* : a broken place : FRACTURE, RUPTURE, BREACH, BREAK **4** : LITTLE, BIT ⟨a ~ closer⟩ **5** : one of several portions (as of a distillate or precipitate) separable by fractionation and consisting either of mixtures or of pure chemical compounds : CUT ⟨petroleum ~*s*⟩ ⟨gamma globulin is a ~ of blood plasma⟩ **6** : a type character representing a mathematical fraction — see PIECE FRACTION **7** : a group of Communists who work for reform within a non-Communist organization — compare CELL 9 **syn** see PART
[2]**fraction** \"\ *vt* -ED/-ING/-S : to separate or divide into portions, separable units, or discrete components; *specif* : FRACTIONATE 1
[1]**frac·tion·al** \-shən^əl, -shnəl\ *adj* **1** : of or relating to a fraction : being or constituting a fraction; *esp* : having to do with only a small portion of a possible whole, total, or entirety ⟨showing only ~ allegiance to his country⟩ **2** : relatively small : INCONSIDERABLE, INSIGNIFICANT ⟨waited only a ~ part of the time allowed⟩; *also* : very short ⟨spoke after a ~ pause⟩ **3** : of, relating to, or being fractional currency ⟨a ~ coin⟩ **4** : of or relating to any process used to separate the components of a mixture through differences in physical or chemical properties (as volatility or solubility) ⟨~ distillation of petroleum⟩ ⟨~ crystallization of the rare earths⟩
[2]**fractional** \"\ *n* -s [by shortening] : FRACTIONAL TIME
fractional burial *n* : a burial in which only part (as the head) of a body is interred
fractional currency *n* **1** : paper money in denominations of less than one dollar issued by the U.S. 1863–76 **2** : currency in denominations less than the basic monetary unit
fractional equation *n* : an equation containing the unknown in the denominator of one or more terms (as $\frac{a}{x}+\frac{b}{x+1}=c$)
frac·tion·al·ism \-shən^əl,izəm, -shənə,li-\ *n* -s **1** : the state of consisting of separate usu. nonhomogeneous or inharmonious units ⟨the ~ of a modern society striving toward unity⟩ **2** : the action of forming or encouraging the formation of a fraction within the Communist party
frac·tion·al·iza·tion \,frakshən^ələ'zāshən, -shnələ-\ *n* -s : the act or process of fractionalizing or the state of being fractionalized ⟨stimulates division of leadership and ~ within the electorate —V.O.Key⟩
frac·tion·al·ize \'frakshən^əl,īz, -shnə,līz\ *vt* -ED/-ING/-S [[1]*fractional* + *-ize*] : to break up into fractions or subdivisions ⟨the *fractionalizing* of the empire into many independent nations⟩ ⟨trying to unify a *fractionalized* congress⟩
fractional lot *n* : ODD LOT
frac·tion·al·ly \-shən^əlē, -shnəlē, -li\ *adv* : in a fractional manner : by a fraction : to the extent of a fraction ⟨the stock had declined ~⟩ : by fractions ⟨squirming on his belly like a lizard, moving ~ . . . one shoulder came forward, a pause, then the other —Alan Sullivan⟩ : to a small or insignificant extent ⟨the area had been only ~ explored⟩
fractional note *n* **1** : a piece of postal currency **2** : a piece of fractional paper money of government or private issue esp. in the U.S. and Canada — called also *shinplaster;* compare FRACTIONAL CURRENCY
fractional sterilization *n* : sterilization by repeated exposure to flowing steam at such intervals as would permit bacterial or other spores present to pass into the nonresistant negative stage between exposures
fractional substitution *n* : encipherment beginning with fractionating, continued by transposing the units singly, and completed by recombining the units according to the resulting juxtapositions and replacing them by letters again
fractional time *n* : the time made by a contestant in a race at the end of a fractional part (as a lap or a quarter mile) of the total distance covered
frac·tion·ary \-shə,nerē\ *adj* **1** : FRACTIONAL **2** : concerned with or done by fractions or piecemeal
frac·tion·ate \-shə,nāt, *usu* -ād·+V\ *vt* -ED/-ING/-S [[1]*fraction* + *-ate*] **1 a** : to separate (a mixture) into different portions (as by distillation, precipitation, or screening) : subject to fractional distillation, fractional crystallization, or other fractional process **b** : to divide or break up (a whole or unit) into component parts or smaller units : separate into divisions, parts, sections, or fragments ⟨practically all the lands have been . . . *fractionated* through allotment —Laura Thompson⟩ ⟨suggest . . . we ~ our problem by first looking for a criterion of meaning —Gustav Bergmann⟩ **2** : to replace (letters) by bifid or trifid substitutes
frac·tion·a·tion \,frakshə'nāshən\ *n* -s : the act or process of fractionating or the state of being fractionated ⟨a mass of material (15 loose-leaf binders containing 3000 typewritten pages) which has been subjected . . . to ~ —*New Republic*⟩ ⟨land ~⟩ ⟨~ of the culture —C.P.Shaw⟩ ⟨~ of blood plasma by precipitation of proteins⟩; *specif* : the crystallization with falling temperature of successive minerals from a silicate magma
frac·tion·a·tor \'==,nād·ə(r)\ *n* -s : an apparatus for fractionating esp. by fractional distillation
fractioned *past of* FRACTION
fractioning *pres part of* FRACTION
frac·tion·ize \-,nīz\ *vt* -ED/-ING/-S *see -ize in Explan Notes* : FRACTIONATE 1b
fractions *pl of* FRACTION, *pres 3d sing of* FRACTION
frac·tious \'frakshəs\ *adj* [[1]*fraction* + *-ous*] **1** : tending to cause trouble (as by disobedience or opposition to an established order) : hard to manage or unmanageable : REFRACTORY, UNRULY ⟨a ~ horse⟩ ⟨a ship with a ~ crew threatening mutiny throughout the trip⟩ **2** : not smooth or free of trouble in operation : likely to function in unpredictable and

troublesome ways ⟨rockets and guided missiles are much too ~ to be tested anywhere near a thickly populated area —*Time*⟩ ⟨loudspeakers remain the most ~ of all high-fidelity components —J.M.Conly⟩ **3 a :** QUARRELSOME, CONTRARY ⟨at the beginning the crowd was captious and ~, owing to delays and bad arrangements —Arnold Bennett⟩ **b :** PEEVISH, IRRITABLE ⟨a ~ child⟩ ⟨like a ~ mother hen rounding up a brood of willful chicks —H.J.Higdon⟩ **syn** see IRRITABLE

frac·tious·ly *adv* : in a fractious manner

frac·tious·ness *n* -ES : the quality or state of being fractious

fracto- *comb form* [L *fractus*] : broken up and ⟨*fracto*cumulus⟩ : fracture ⟨*fracto*graph⟩

frac·to·graph \ˈfraktəˌgraf\ *n* [*fracto-* + *-graph*] : a fractographic photograph

frac·to·graph·ic \ˌ==ˈgrafik\ *adj* : of, used in, or relating to fractography — **frac·to·graph·i·cal·ly** \-fək(ə)lē\ *adv*

frac·tog·ra·phy \frakˈtägrəfē\ *n* -ES [*fracto-* + *-graphy*] : the microscopic study of fractured surfaces of metals at high magnification

1**fractur** *usu cap, var of* FRAKTUR

2**frac·tur** \fräkˈtü(ə)r, -üə\ *or* **fractur painting** *also* **fraktur** \"\ *or* **fraktur painting** *n* -S [PaG *fraktur*, fr. G *fraktur* (formerly spelled *fractur*), a Gothic script — more at FRAKTUR] : illuminated writing featuring decorative motifs (as tulips, birds, and scrolls) and used by Pennsylvania Germans on documents (as wedding, birth, and baptismal certificates) often framed and hung

frac·tur·able \ˈfrakchərəbəl, -ksh-\ *adj* : capable of being fractured : BREAKABLE

frac·tur·al \-kchərəl, -ksh(ə)rəl\ *adj* : of, relating to, being, or due to fracture

1**frac·ture** \ˈfrakchə(r), -ksh-\ *n* -S [ME, fr. L *fractura*, fr. *fractus* (past part. of *frangere* to break) + *-ura* -ure — more at BREAK] **1 a :** the act or process of breaking or the state of being broken : rupture by a break through the entire thickness of a material : BREACH; *specif* : the breaking of hard tissue (as a bone, tooth, or cartilage) **b :** the rupture (as by tearing) of soft tissue ⟨kidney ~⟩ **2 :** the product or result of fracturing : BREAK, CRACK, CLEFT **3 :** the texture or general appearance of the freshly broken surface of a mineral ⟨a rock with a conchoidal ~⟩ **4 :** BREAKING 1

2**fracture** \"\ *vb* **fractured; fractured; fracturing** \-kchəriŋ, -ksh(ə)r-\ **fractures** *vt* **1 a :** to cause a fracture in : BREAK ⟨~ a rib⟩ ⟨the bump in the road *fractured* a spring on the car⟩ **b :** RUPTURE, TEAR, LACERATE ⟨a blow that *fractured* a kidney⟩ **2 a :** to damage or destroy as if by rupturing or tearing apart ⟨~ the newfound unity of the two parties⟩ ⟨may seriously ~ himself as he tries to patch up the rifts in the . . . party —Sidney Hyman⟩ **b :** to break into pieces : cause great disorder in ⟨a scream that *fractured* the peace of the night⟩ ⟨conspiracy to ~ their sensibilities —*Time*⟩ **c :** to break up : FRACTIONATE ⟨by *fracturing* and dispersing senatorial power —W.V.Shannon⟩ ⟨most world movements and agencies . . . have been *fractured* or assimilated by national interests in one way or another —Liston Pope⟩ **d :** to show disregard for (as a law or rule) : VIOLATE ⟨declared the principle of the separation of church and state *fractured* by the agreement⟩ ⟨he *fractured* many of the laws of probability —Sheldon Cheney⟩ ~ *vi* : to undergo fracture : break esp. through a total thickness ⟨under the blow the thighbone *fractured*⟩

fracture cleavage *n* : geologic cleavage independent of the orientation of mineral grains but due to the presence of many closely spaced fractures or incipient fractures

fracture plane *n* : a point in an arthropod appendage that is modified for the ready occurrence of autotomy (as by the presence of special muscles and mechanisms to prevent loss of body fluid)

frad·i·cin \ˈfradəsən\ *n* -S [NL *fradia* (specific epithet of *Streptomyces fradiae*) + E *-cin* (as in *actinomycin*)] : a crystalline antibiotic active against fungi that is produced by an actinomycete (*Streptomyces fradiae*) — compare NEOMYCIN

frae \ˈfrā\ *prep* [ME (northern dial.) *fra, frae, fro*, fr. ON *frā* — more at FROM] *Scot* : FROM

fraenulum *var of* FRENULUM

fraenum *var of* FRENUM

frag \ˈfrag\ *n* -S [by shortening] : FRAGMENTATION BOMB

frag *abbr* **1** fragile **2** fragment; fragmentation

fra·gar·ia \frəˈga(a)rēə\ *n, cap* [NL, fr. L *fragum* strawberry + NL *-aria*] : a small genus of low perennial herbs (family Rosaceae) that comprise the strawberries, have trifoliate leaves, cymose white flowers, and long slender runners, and are represented in cultivation mainly by horticultural forms derived from several wild species (as *F. vesca, F. virginiana, F. chiloensis, F. moschata*) and including many hybrids of these — see CHILEAN STRAWBERRY, STRAWBERRY, WOOD STRAWBERRY

fra·ge \ˈfrägə, ˈfrāg\ *n* -S [G, lit., question, fr. OHG *frāga* — more at PRAY] : the lowest bid in a card game (as frog or skat)

frag·i·lar·ia \ˌfrajəˈla(a)rēə\ *n, cap* [NL, fr. L *fragilis* frail + NL *-aria*] : a genus (the type of the family Fragilariaceae of the order Pennales) of rectangular diatoms forming irregular colonies

frag·ile \ˈfrajəl, *US also & Brit usu* -aˌjīl\ *adj* [MF, fr. L *fragilis* — more at FRAIL] **1 a :** easily broken or destroyed : FRAIL ⟨the ~ stem of the tall flower⟩ ⟨a person of ~ moral convictions⟩ **b :** delicate of constitution or of health : barely able or unable to endure without harm the normal day-to-day physical demands of existence : unusually susceptible to ill health or physical harm ⟨a ~ and tottering old man⟩ ⟨too ~ to stand the Vermont winter —Sinclair Lewis⟩ **c :** giving the impression of or having qualities suggesting someone that is fragile of body or health ⟨a ~ soprano⟩ ⟨a ~ gesture⟩ ⟨~ hands⟩ **2 a :** WEAK, TENUOUS, UNSUBSTANTIAL ⟨a ~ connection with great men⟩ ⟨the ground of his faith . . . seemed to me so ~ —H.J.Laski⟩ **b :** thin and transparent ⟨a ~ skin⟩ : extremely light and evanescent ⟨a ~ tone⟩ : DIAPHANOUS ⟨a ~ taffeta⟩ **c :** extremely subtle or fine : calling for an extremely fine perception ⟨a ~ wine⟩ ⟨the tantalizing, ~ taste of fresh blue crab —Hugh Cave⟩ **d :** SHORT-LIVED, EVANESCENT ⟨a ~ moment⟩ **syn** see WEAK

fragile fern *n* : a delicate fern (*Cystopteris fragilis*) widely distributed in Europe, Asia, and No. America with 2 or 3 thin pinnatifid fronds, creeping rootstocks, and slender brittle stems — called also *brittle fern*

frag·ile·ly \-əl(l)ē, -īllē, -il\ *adv* : in a fragile manner

fra·gi·li·tas os·si·um \frəˈjiləˌtasˈäsēəm\ *n* [NL, lit., fragility of bones] : a familial disease marked by extreme brittleness of the long bones and a bluish color of the whites of the eyes

fra·gil·i·ty \frəˈjiləd·ē, -ətē, -i\ *n* -ES [ME *fragilite*, fr. MF *fragilité*, fr. L *fragilitat-, fragilitas*, fr. *fragilis* + *-itat-, -itas* -ity] **1 :** the quality or state of being fragile ⟨the extreme ~ of public order —G.W.Johnson⟩ ⟨most men's touching illusion as to the frailness of women and their spiritual ~ —Joseph Conrad⟩ ⟨worried because of the ~ of the vase⟩ **2 :** something fragile ⟨rooms . . . heavy with *fragilities* —Natacha Stewart⟩

fragility test *n* : a test of the relative fragility of red blood cells made by exposing them to hypotonic solutions and determining the point at which they rupture

fra·gil·o·cyte \frəˈjiləˌsīt\ *n* -S [L *fragilis* + E *-o-* + *-cyte*] : an exceptionally fragile red blood cell (as in congenital hemolytic jaundice)

fra·gil·o·cy·to·sis \frəˌjilō(ˌ)sīˈtōsəs\ *n, pl* **fragilocyto·ses** \-ˈtōˌsēz\ [NL, fr. ISV *fragilocyte* + NL *-osis*] : an abnormal state characterized by the presence of fragilocytes in the blood

1**frag·ment** \ˈfragmənt\ *n* -S [ME, fr. L *fragmentum*, fr. *frag-* (stem of *frangere* to break) + *-mentum* -ment — more at BREAK] **1 :** a part broken off : a small detached portion : an imperfect or incomplete part ⟨pieces of pottery and ~s that can be reconstructed —*Amer. Guide Series: N.J.*⟩ ⟨enchanting ~s of Irish life —John McNulty⟩ ⟨only ~s remain of the covered-wagon ballads —*Amer. Guide Series: Oregon*⟩ **2 :** something that is small and usu. insignificant ⟨a ~ of silence —Guy Fowler⟩ **syn** see PART

2**frag·ment** \ˈfragˌment, =ˈ=\ *vb* -ED/-ING/-S *vi* : to break into fragments : FRAGMENTIZE ⟨the vase fell and ~*ed* into small pieces⟩ ⟨this pluralized and ~*ing* society —Walter Lippmann⟩ ~ *vt* : to break or divide into disorganized or not unified pieces ⟨a foreign policy that is ~*ed* rather than organized to a focal purpose⟩ ⟨an old woman's ~*ed* memory —Meridel Le Sueur⟩; *esp* : to destroy by such breaking or dividing up ⟨the remaining hopes of control of weapons have been ~*ed* by the new bomb —M.W.Straight⟩

frag·men·tal \(ˈ)fragˈmentᵊl\ *adj* : FRAGMENTARY : consisting of fragmentary or detrital material (as conglomerate, sandstone, shale, or tuff) — compare CLASTIC 2 — **frag·men·tal·ly** \-ᵊlē\ *adv*

frag·men·tal·ize \fragˈmentᵊlˌīz\ *vt* -ED/-ING/-S : FRAGMENTIZE ⟨his rapid oscillations of style and plot . . . ~ the American myth and destroy the cohesiveness of the allegory —Harvey Swados⟩

frag·men·tar·i·ly \ˌfragmənˈterəlē, -li\ *adv* : in a fragmentary manner ⟨the dim light penetrated only ~ into the drifting mist⟩

frag·men·tar·i·ness \-rēnəs, -rin-\ *n* -ES : the quality or state of being fragmentary ⟨the ~ of our approach and the unsystematic nature of our categories —Anna G. Hatcher⟩ ⟨exasperated by the ~ of the facts at my disposal —W.S.Maugham⟩

frag·men·ta·rism \ˈfragməntəˌrizəm\ *n* -S [*fragmentary* + *-ism*] : FRAGMENTARINESS

frag·men·tary \ˈfragmənˌterē, -ri\ *adj* **1 :** consisting of or composed of fragments ⟨large leg bones, and other ~ remains of an elephant —*Amer. Guide Series: Nev.*⟩ ⟨the sampling of most authors is necessarily ~ —Uriel Weinreich⟩ ⟨historical links between certain of the more ~ letters —Robert Lawrence⟩ : consisting of disconnected and incomplete parts ⟨had only a ~ education⟩ : INCOMPLETE, PARTIAL ⟨gave only a ~ account of the incident⟩ ⟨~ and inconclusive knowledge —*Current Biog.*⟩ ⟨this viewpoint may prove to be optimistic, but ~ evidence so far has not suggested that it is —J.A.Morris b. 1904⟩ : DISORGANIZED ⟨our approach to the problem is still ~ —*N.Y.Times*⟩ ⟨we need wholeness, but he is ~ —E.R.Bentley⟩ **2 :** dealing in or being only a fragment of a whole ⟨every ~ science of man, such as economics —Edward Sapir⟩ **3 :** FRAGMENTAL

frag·men·tate \-ˌtāt\ *vb* -ED/-ING/-S [back-formation fr. *fragmentation*] : to break into pieces esp. explosively : FRACTIONATE, FRAGMENTIZE ⟨they were sure the master rods on the engines were all *fragmentating* —David Beaty⟩ ⟨permits the . . . artist to ~ a single small idea into a limitless string of daily episodes —C.W.Morton⟩

frag·men·ta·tion \ˌ==ˈtāshən\ *n* -S [F, fr. *fragmenter* to divide into fragments (fr. *fragment*, n., fr. L *fragmentum*) + *-ation*] **1 :** the act or process of fragmenting or fractionating or the state of being fragmentated or fractionated ⟨the constant ~ of landholdings —J.H.Steward⟩ ⟨cried for the ~ of India —*Time*⟩ ⟨the growing ~ of the corporation into a multitude of divisions and departments —W.H.Whyte⟩ : the act or process of making fragmentary or the state of becoming or being fragmentary ⟨the contemporary pursuit of brevity, with its inevitable consequence of ~, in all fields of communication is alarming —F.L.Mott⟩ ⟨the ~ of the past was to be overcome by integration —*Amer. Anthropologist*⟩; *esp* : a shattering into numerous and widely scattered fragments (as of a fragmentation bomb) **2 :** the fragments from the fragmentation of a shell, grenade, or bomb ⟨the explosion rained ~ all about them⟩ **3 :** disorganization of mind or behavior : a breakdown of the usual pattern of thought or action

fragmentation bomb *or* **fragmentation shell** *n* : a bomb or shell whose relatively thick casing is splintered upon explosion and thrown in fragments in all directions at high speed and temperature

frag·ment·ist \ˈfragməntəst\ *n* -S [G, fr. *fragment* (fr. L *fragmentum*) + *-ist*] : a writer of a literary fragment

frag·ment·iza·tion \ˌfragməntəˈzāshən\ *n* -S : the act or process of fragmentizing or the state of being fragmentized ⟨up in arms against a ~ of their native land —Sidney Wallach⟩

frag·ment·ize \ˈfragmənˌtīz\ *vb* -ED/-ING/-S *vt* : to break up or apart or into pieces, sections, or fragments : FRACTION, FRACTIONATE 1b ⟨the barriers of race, color, nationality, economic strife, religious belief, and political ideology which ~ our world —*Christian Science Monitor*⟩ ~ *vi* : to fall apart : break up or separate into pieces, parts, or fragments ⟨watched the bridge ~ before his eyes⟩

fra·grance \ˈfrāgrən(t)s\ *n* -S [F or L; F, fr. L *fragrantia*, fr. *fragrant-, fragrans* + *-ia* -y] **1 :** the quality or state of having a sweet or pleasing odor : sweetness or pleasantness of smell ⟨the ~ of flowers⟩ ⟨the ~ of balsam⟩ **2 a :** a sweet smell or pleasing odor esp. delicate or evanescent ⟨a ~ not unpleasant to the nostrils⟩ **b :** the odor of perfume, cologne, or toilet water ⟨as close as ~ clings to a woman's robe —John Galsworthy⟩ **3 a :** a quality resembling a perfume (as in pleasantness, delicacy, or evanescence or in seeming to be an emanation) ⟨a relationship that gave something of ~ to an occupation much in need of it —L.C.Douglas⟩ ⟨she inhaled the sharp ~ of those days —Maurice Hewlett⟩ ⟨to handle a first edition of Montaigne . . . was not without its poetic ~ —H.J.Laski⟩ **b :** something having such a quality ⟨literature represents the ~ of culture —W.P.Webb⟩

syn FRAGRANCE, PERFUME, SCENT, INCENSE, REDOLENCE, and BOUQUET agree in signifying a sweet or pleasant odor. FRAGRANCE usu. suggests the odor of flowers or a like pleasing and usu. delicate emanation ⟨the soft wind from across the bayou brought in the garden *fragrance* —Stark Young⟩ ⟨their subtle *fragrance* of sandalwood, aloes, musk, cassia, and sweet calamus —Elinor Wylie⟩ ⟨none can resist the *fragrance* of pines, firs, and spruces in the forest —A.C.Morrison⟩ PERFUME differs little from FRAGRANCE except in possibly suggesting a less delicate odor and commonly implying the odor of a liquid specially manufactured to emit it ⟨the *perfume* of lilies had overcome the scent of books —John Galsworthy⟩ ⟨the strong *perfume* of orange blossoms⟩ ⟨her *perfume* was heavy and cloying⟩ SCENT in being often interchangeable with *odor* is more neutral in its connotations than FRAGRANCE or PERFUME, but in being also often interchangeable with PERFUME, esp. in British use, can apply to the fragrance as of flowers or any delicately perceived, usu. pleasant, odor ⟨the still nights in the small harbors, with a *scent* of seaweed abroad —William Black⟩ ⟨the *scent* of the apples —Robert Frost⟩ ⟨a delicate *scent* of apricots lingered in the flask at his side —Elinor Wylie⟩ INCENSE applies to the agreeably odorous smoke of burning spices or aromatic gums or to any similar penetrating odor, often, because of the association of incense with religious rites, suggesting a spiritually uplifting effect ⟨*incense*-breathing morn —Thomas Gray⟩ ⟨the *incense* of mown fields⟩ REDOLENCE now usu. suggests a mixture of fragrant, often pungent odors ⟨the *redolence* of the forest⟩ ⟨the kitchen *redolence* of Christmas cooking and baking⟩ BOUQUET in this comparison commonly applies to the distinctive and esp. delicate and agreeable odor of a good wine or liquor but can extend to any odor, as of a food, suggesting this ⟨some of the vocabulary of the winetaster has crept in, like the word *bouquet*, which means smell or scent, and yet is more descriptive of what the nose gets from a wine than either smell or scent —Mary Mabon⟩ ⟨duck that has been hung a long time, so you can smell the *bouquet* —*Time*⟩ ⟨the grateful smell of cooking pork grew every moment more perfect in *bouquet* —Ethel Anderson⟩

fra·gran·cy \-nsē, -si\ *n* -ES [L *fragrantia*] *archaic* : FRAGRANCE

fra·grant \-nt\ *adj* [ME *fragraunt*, fr. L *fragrant-, fragrans*, pres. part. of *fragrare* to give off an odor, be fragrant; akin to MHG *bræhen* to smell] : having a fragrance : marked by fragrance ⟨an air ~ with sweetest flowers —H.O.Taylor⟩ ⟨fresh and ~ as meadow hay —Herman Melville⟩ ⟨my sojourn in the garden of Africa has left so many ~ memories —R.S.B. Baker⟩ ⟨people talk of matters which . . . communicate a rich color, a ~ sentiment to them —A.C.Benson⟩ — **fra·grant·ly** *adv* — **fra·grant·ness** *n* -ES

fragrant balm *n* **1 :** OSWEGO TEA **2 :** BEE BALM 2b

fragrant bedstraw *n* : a bedstraw (*Galium triflorum*) that has small white flowers and is fragrant when drying

fragrant goldenrod *n* : BLUE MOUNTAIN TEA

fragrant shield fern *or* **fragrant cliff fern** *or* **fragrant wood fern** *n* : a stout pinnate-leaved fern (*Dryopteris fragrans*) of northern regions

fragrant sumac *n* : a sweet-scented sumac (*Rhus aromatica*) with ternate leaves, yellowish green flowers in spikes resembling catkins, and red hairy fruits

frags *pl of* FRAG

fraid \ˈfrād\ *adj* [by shortening] *dial* : AFRAID

fraidy·cat \ˈfrādēˌkat, -di,-, *usu* -ad·+V\ *or* **fraid·cat** \-d,k-\ *n* [*fraidy* (fr. *fraid* + *-y*) or *fraid* + *cat*] : one that is timid or easily frightened — used chiefly among children or of children

1**fraik** \ˈfrāk\ *n* -S [alter. of 1*freak*] **1** *Scot* : 1FREAK **2** *Scot* : FLATTERY

2**fraik** \"\ *vi, Scot* : to make flattering remarks : CAJOLE

1**frail** \ˈfrāl, *esp before pause or consonant* -āəl\ *n* -S [ME *frayel, freyel*, fr. MF *fraiel, freel, frael*, perh. fr. *fraiel, freel, frael* piece of a vine with grapes attached, alter. of *flaiel, flael* flail, whip, piece of a vine with grapes attached — more at FLAIL] **1 :** a basket typically made of rushes and used for shipping (as of figs or raisins) **2 :** the quantity (as 32, 56, or 75 pounds) of raisins contained in a frail

2**frail** \"\ *adj* -ER/-EST [ME *frele, freel, frail*, fr. MF *fraile, frele*, fr. L *fragilis*, fr. *frag-* (stem of *frangere* to break) + *-ilis* -ile — more at BREAK] **1 a :** easily led into evil : morally weak ⟨a fiery sermon delivered to all of ~ humanity⟩ **b :** easily led from one's chosen course : lacking in general strength of character or purpose ⟨~ enough to give in if subjected to any pressure⟩ **2 a :** easily broken : not firm or durable ⟨a bridge with ~ construction⟩ ⟨a small and ~ ship⟩ **b :** easily destroyed : likely to fail or die quickly ⟨a ~ flower⟩ ⟨a ~ and very old woman⟩ **c :** unusually susceptible to disease or other infirmity ⟨a man of ~ constitution⟩ **3 a** (1) **:** lacking even normal strength or force ⟨their voices were weak and ~ —Humayun Kabir⟩ (2) **:** weak and small ⟨his steady, workman's hands looking enormous around the ~ tube of tobacco —Irwin Shaw⟩ **b** (1) **:** lacking significant substance ⟨a charming, ~, breathless book —*New Yorker*⟩ ⟨smiled a minute ~ smile —Raymond Chandler⟩ ⟨his lyrics are ~ and derivative —F.B.Millett⟩ (2) **:** tenuous and thin ⟨only ~ hope of finding more survivors existed —*N.Y. Times*⟩ ⟨how ~ the barrier between civilization and the primal jungle —Oscar Handlin⟩ ⟨the love of truth is pitifully ~ —M.R.Cohen⟩ **syn** see WEAK

3**frail** \"\ *dial var of* FLAIL

frai·le·jón \ˌfrälāˈhōn\ *n, pl* **frailejo·nes** \-ōˌnās\ [AmerSp, aug. of Sp *fraile* friar, fr. OSp *fraire*, fr. OProv, brother, friar, fr. L *fratr-, frater* brother — more at BROTHER] **1 :** any of several xerophytic plants of the genus *Espeletia* (family Compositae) of the higher Andes (esp. *E. grandiflora*) **2 :** the tomentum of the stem and leaves of frailejón resembling wool

frail·ly \ˈfrāl(l)ē, -i\ *adv* [ME *frelly*, fr. *frele* frail + *-ly*] : in a frail manner ⟨paint scenes of Venice drained of its water, with the buildings ~ poised on the oaken pilings that are their principal foundations —R.M.Coates⟩

frail·ness *n* -ES [ME *frelenesse, freelnesse, frailnesse*, fr. *frele, freel, frail* + *-nesse* -ness] : the quality or state of being frail ⟨the ~ of the child from birth made her susceptible to every prevailing illness⟩ ⟨a ~ of character, a tendency to give up easily⟩

frail·ty \ˈfrā(ə)ltē, -ti\ *n* -ES [ME *frelete, freelte, frailte*, fr. MF *frailete, freleté*, fr. L *fragilitat-, fragilitas*, fr. *fragilis* + *-itat-, -itas* -ity] **1 :** the quality or state of being frail ⟨declaim against the ~ of human flesh⟩: **a :** INSUBSTANTIALITY ⟨a novel marked by ~ of subject matter⟩ **b :** TENUOUSNESS ⟨the ~ of the connection between the two sides of the family⟩ **c :** INFIRMITY ⟨always concerned for the ~ of his physical being⟩ **d :** SUSCEPTIBILITY ⟨the ~ of young lads to the charms of young ladies⟩ **2 :** an inadequacy, a fault, or a sin resulting from weakness (as of constitution or moral character) **syn** see FAULT

fraim \ˈfrām\ *var of* FREMD

fraischeur *n* -S [MF *fraischeur, fraicheur*, fr. *fraische, fraiche*, fem. of *frais* fresh — more at FRESH] *obs* : FRESHNESS, COOLNESS

1**fraise** \ˈfrāz\ *n* -S [alter. of *phrase*] **1** *or* **frase** *dial Brit* : a noisy confusion : HUBBUB **2** *Scot* : FLATTERY, CAJOLERY : empty talk

2**fraise** \"\ *vt* -ED/-ING/-S : FLATTER, CAJOLE

3**fraise** \"\ *n* -S [F, lit., mesentery of a calf or lamb, fr. MF, fr. *fraiser* to unwrap, shell (as a bean), fr. (assumed) VL *fresare*, fr. L *fresa* (in the term *faba fresa* ground bean), fem. of *fresus*, past part. of *frendere* to gnash, crush, grind — more at GRIND] **1 :** an obstacle used in fortification consisting of pointed stakes driven into the ramparts in a horizontal or inclined position **2 :** a style of neck ruff **3 :** a fluted reamer for enlarging holes in stone **4 :** a cutting tool for correcting the shape of the teeth of timepiece wheels

4**fraise** \"\ *vt* -ED/-ING/-S **1 :** to ream out and enlarge (as a hole in stone) **2 :** to shape or dress with a fraise

5**fraise** \"\ *n* -S [F, strawberry, fr. OF *fraise, frese*, irreg. (perh. influence of the *-s-* in *framboise* raspberry) fr. LL *fraga*, fr. L, pl. of *fragum*] **1** *also* **frase :** a heraldic representation of a strawberry blossom often not distinguished from a cinquefoil — called also *fraser* **2 :** strawberry color

frake \ˈfrāk\ *n* -S [prob. native name in Africa] : LIMBA

1**frak·tur** *also* **frac·tur** \fräkˈtü(ə)r, -üə\ *n* -S *usu cap* [G *fraktur* (formerly spelled *fractur*), an ornate kind of handwriting developed in the 16th cent., fraktur, fr. L *fractura* action of breaking; fr. the curlicues that broke up the continuous line of a word — more at FRACTURE] : a German style of black-letter text type

2**fraktur** *or* **fraktur painting** *var of* FRACTUR

fram \ˈfram\ *vb* **frammed; frammed; framming; frams** [origin unknown] *South & Midland* : POUND, BEAT

fram·able *or* **frame·able** \ˈfrāməbəl\ *adj* : capable of being framed

fram·be·sia *also* **fram·boe·sia** \framˈbēzh(ē)ə, -zēə\ *n* -S [NL, fr. F *framboise* raspberry; fr. the raspberry appearance of the excrescences] : YAWS

fram·boise \fräⁿˈbwaz\ *n* -S [F, fr. OF, prob. modif. (perh. influenced by the *f-* in *fraise* strawberry) of a WGmc word represented by D *braambes* blackberry, MLG *brāmber*, OHG *brāmberi*, all fr. a prehistoric WGmc compound whose first constituent is represented by OHG *brāma, brāmo* bramble and whose second constituent is represented by D *bes* berry, OHG *beri* — more at BROOM, BERRY] **1 :** raspberry color **2 :** raspberry brandy usu. unsweetened

1**frame** \ˈfrām\ *vb* -ED/-ING/-S [ME *framien, framen* to benefit, comfort, construct, fr. OE *framian, fromian* to avail, benefit, make progress; akin to OFris *framia* to carry out, further, OS *gifram̄on*, ON *frama*, all fr. a prehistoric WGmc-NGmc verb derived fr. a word represented by ON *fram* forward — more at FROM] *vi* **1 a** *obs* : to get on : FARE **b** *archaic* : PROCEED, GO ⟨~ upstairs and make little din —Emily Brontë⟩ **2 a** *now dial Eng* : to show promise and adaptability **b** *archaic* : CONTRIVE, MANAGE ~ *vt* **1** *obs* : to prepare (wood) for a building (as by hewing out timbers) **2 a :** PLAN, DEVISE, CONTRIVE ⟨the committee *framed* a new method of achieving their purpose⟩ **b :** to give expression to : FORMULATE ⟨~ a rule that brings order into our perceptions —Virginia Woolf⟩ ⟨the specific problems . . . are still the persistent and central problems of philosophy, although perhaps not now *framed* in just his terminology —Alice Ambrose⟩ ⟨the poignancy of the hero's failure is *framed* in the plaint of that ubiquitous figure of Italian life, the sorrowing mother —C.W.White⟩ **c :** SHAPE, FASHION, FORM ⟨~ a figure out of clay⟩ : MAKE, CONSTRUCT ⟨a series of questions so *framed* as to involve by way of answer the plain alternative of yes or no —N.H.Snaith⟩ **d :** INVENT, FABRICATE ⟨*framed* a series of new characters for a radio drama series⟩ ⟨*framed* a device for eliminating rattles in a car⟩ **e :** CONCEIVE, IMAGINE ⟨could not ~ the man in my mind from the inadequate description⟩ **f :** to make a draft of or draw up (as a law or constitution) ⟨~ a plan for combating inflation —*Current Biog.*⟩ ⟨it was once my duty to ~ a case against a manifest thief —R.W.Chapman⟩ ⟨a subcommittee which *framed* the so-called tidelands oil bill —W.A. Clark⟩ ⟨when the Bolsheviks' five-year plan was being *framed* —G.N.S.Raghavan⟩ **3 :** to fit or adjust esp. to something or for an end : REGULATE, ARRANGE ⟨and ~ my face to all occasions —Shak.⟩ ⟨the professional training is *framed* to teach the student what children are like at different stages —*Choice of Careers: Local Gov't*⟩ ⟨he *framed* his model exordium to the middle-class youth in these words —Roy Lewis & Angus Maude⟩ ⟨required to pass tests which are *framed* to be within the power of a normal girl at each stage of her growth

—*Girl Guiding & The Church*⟩ **4 :** to bring about **:** CAUSE, PRODUCE ⟨fear ~*s* disorder and disorder wounds —Shak.⟩ ⟨struggling to ~ an alliance to secure southeast Asia —Benjamin Welles⟩ **5** *archaic* **:** to give direction to **:** start out on (a journey) **6 :** to put together the frame of **:** construct by fitting and uniting the parts of the skeleton of (a structure) ⟨*framed* a house at Steilacoom in 1860 and shipped it by steamer to be set up in the new settlement —*Amer. Guide Series: Wash.*⟩ ⟨*framed* a boat in the cellar and completed it outside⟩; *specif* **:** to erect the frames of (a ship) on the building ways **7 a :** UTTER, ARTICULATE ⟨*framed* a reply in words as flattering as the question⟩ **b :** to form the mouth and lips into the form for uttering but without making a vocal sound ⟨their lips ~ the words, "We're pleased to see you" —Richard Harrison⟩ ⟨tremulous lips *framed* an affirmative, but never uttered it —Zane Grey⟩ **8 a :** to provide with a frame **:** enclose in a frame ⟨~ a picture⟩; *also* **:** to enclose as if in a frame ⟨a face *framed* in a wealth of auburn hair⟩ ⟨he had had the entire lobby *framed*, at a height of about 15 feet, by slender boxes of hanging ivy and various nondescript plants —Douglas Woolf⟩ ⟨his eyes were *framed* above with unusually long eyelashes and below with the blue semicircle of ill health —Scott Fitzgerald⟩ **b :** to serve as a frame for ⟨the window *framed* a view of the lake⟩ **9 :** to run (crutched soap) into a frame to cool and solidify **10 a :** to devise falsely (as a criminal charge against an innocent man) ⟨~ a case against a neighbor to get rid of him⟩ — often used with *up* **b :** to contrive the evidence against (an innocent man) so that a verdict of guilty is assured ⟨many of the so-called anarchists . . . had been *framed* by courts and prosecutors —F.P.Adams⟩ ⟨innocent women were frequently *framed* by a ring consisting of police officers, stool pigeons, bondsmen, and lawyers —Morris Ploscowe⟩ **c :** to prearrange (as a contest or an incrimination) so that a particular outcome is assured ⟨the wrestling matches were *framed*⟩ — often used with *up* **11 :** to bring (a projected image) into register with the aperture of a motion-picture projector so that the horizontal frame line does not appear on the screen **syn** see BUILD, CONTRIVE

2frame \"\ *n* -s [ME, fr. *framien, framen*, v.] **1 a** *archaic* **:** something composed of parts fitted together and united **b** *archaic* **:** BUILDING; *esp* **:** a wooden building **c :** the form in which something is fashioned **:** SYSTEM ⟨a ~ of government⟩ ⟨how fine if we had an intimate theater . . . to produce certain works that call for a small ~ —Howard Taubman⟩; *esp* **:** the bodily structure **:** the physical construction or constitution **:** BODY, FIGURE ⟨he is distinctly, almost nobly handsome, with stalwart ~ —S.H.Adams⟩ ⟨sobs swept at intervals through her ~, shaking it —Arnold Bennett⟩ **d** *archaic* **:** a proper or correct form, order, or shape ⟨before the hills in order stood, or earth received her ~ —Isaac Watts⟩ **e :** a standardized form or shape ⟨the artistry of a low comedian . . . stands out in splendid relief from the ~ of a dull musical comedy —E.R. Bentley⟩ ⟨the mock-heroic ~ is intermittent —Austin Warren⟩ **2 a :** the constructional system that gives shape or strength (as to a building) **:** an underlying structure or skeleton ⟨his enormous weight broke the ~ of the sofa⟩; *specif* **:** the arrangement of supporting girders, beams, columns, joists, or trusses forming the main support (as of a building) ⟨the ~ of the roof had begun to sag⟩ **b :** such a skeleton or outline not filled in or covered (as by the other constituents of the whole of which it is a part) ⟨the fire left only the steel ~ of the building standing⟩ **c :** a basic structural unit onto or into which other constituents of a whole are fitted, to which they attach, or with which they are integrated: as (1) **:** the basic unit of a handgun which serves as a mounting for the barrel and operating parts of the arm — compare RECEIVER (2) **:** any of the skeleton structures forming the athwart ribs of a ship — see CANT FRAME, SQUARE FRAME (3) AIRFRAME; *also* **:** a structural piece supporting the longitudinal members or skin of the fuselage, float, or hull of an airplane **d** *dial* **:** an emaciated person or animal **:** SKELETON **3 a :** an open case or structure made for admitting, enclosing, or supporting something (as one that encloses a window, door, or picture) **b :** something on, in, or across which something else is held or stretched: as (1) *archaic* **:** LOOM 3 (2) **:** a machine built upon or within a framework and used esp. in manufacture of yarn and textiles ⟨a spinning ~⟩ (3) **:** an adjustable structure of four bars forming an open square or rectangle for holding cloth (as for embroidery or quilting) — compare CURTAIN STRETCHER (4) **:** a rack used in carpet manufacturing for holding yarn packages used in the pile **c :** a foundry molding box or flask that being filled with sand around a pattern serves as a mold for castings **d :** the covered lattice structure used on the arms of a windmill **e :** the skeleton structure supporting the boiler and machinery of a locomotive upon its wheels or either of the two structures containing the axle boxes and supporting the upper part of an electric car **f :** a structural unit in an automobile chassis supported on the axles and supporting the rest of the chassis and the body **g :** the ribs and stretchers of an umbrella or similar structure with a fabric covering **h :** an openwork wooden structure usu. enclosing a sheet of foundation placed in a beehive to encourage bees to build honeycomb in an orderly fashion **i :** a board for holding coins, medals, or stamps on exhibition **j :** a stand to support printers' type cases **k** (1) **:** SAW GATE (2) **:** a piece shaped like a yoke and resembling a saw gate ⟨the ~ of a micrometer⟩ ⟨the ~ of a C-clamp⟩ **l :** a large shallow rectangular metal pan having removable sides used for the cooling and solidifying of liquid soap in soap manufacture **m** (1) **:** a part of a pair of glasses that holds one of the lenses (2) **frames** *pl* **:** the constituent of a pair of glasses other than the lenses **4 a** *obs* **:** the act of framing, constructing, or devising **b** *archaic* **:** the manner or method in which something is fashioned **5 a :** a particular state or disposition (as of the mind) ⟨left the shop in a very puzzled ~ of mind —F.W.Crofts⟩ **b** *archaic* **:** attitude of mind **:** state of feeling **:** HUMOR, MOOD ⟨we have sent him to you in the best health and in the happiest ~ —Charles Dickens⟩ **6 a :** an enclosing usu. rectangular and esp. ornamental border or a physical limitation suggesting such a border: (1) **:** a single line or an ornamental band bordering a stamp (2) **:** the lines around boxed matter in a newspaper (3) **:** the boundary of the gate of a motion-picture camera, printer, or projector (4) **:** FALSE PROSCENIUM **b :** the matter or area enclosed in such a border or as if in such a border: as (1) **:** one of the squares in which scores for each round are recorded (as in bowling); *also* **:** a round in bowling (2) **:** boxed matter in a newspaper; *esp* **:** a box of a comic strip (3) **:** one picture of the series on a length of motion-picture film or on a filmstrip or microfilm (4) **:** a complete picture or image being transmitted by television **c :** a playing unit of a game (as an inning in baseball) **d :** an abstract set of limitations (as of circumstances or considerations) within which a thing or a group of things is contained, in relation to which they are unified, or within which they acquire a usu. particular or a typical significance or expression **:** a limiting, typical, or esp. appropriate set of circumstances ⟨a joke that can be told . . . out of ~ —James Burnham⟩ ⟨within the ~ of business-as-usual —*New Republic*⟩ ⟨the ~ of experience in which the American strategic problem in the atomic age is set —H.W.Baldwin⟩ ⟨clinical studies carried on within the ~ of our own society and culture —Ralph Linton⟩ **e :** an event or set of events or circumstances that form the background for the action of a novel or dramatic work ⟨the main ~ of action of the novel is the week of a false armistice in 1918 —Carvel Collins⟩ **f :** a literary device used in a story or dramatic work to bring together into a unity the matter of the story or drama or to provide a plausible excuse for relating or presenting it; *esp* **:** such a device not essential to the story or dramatic action itself ⟨the story uses a ~ purporting to be told to the writer 20 years after the events⟩ **g :** a part of a syntactical or morphological linguistic construction that remains unchanged even though the remainder may be altered by the substitution of new items

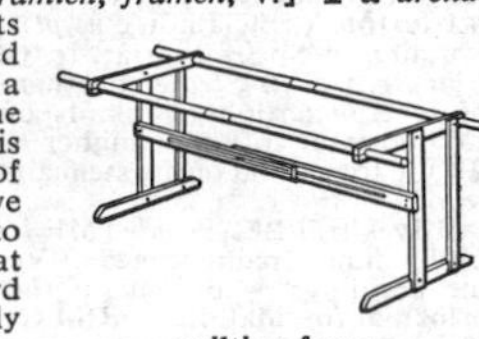

quilting frame

7 : COLD FRAME **8** *slang* **:** FRAME-UP **9 :** SLATE 3d **10 :** a listing or other scheme in statistics for identification of the elementary sampling units that constitute a population

3frame \"\ *also* **framed** \-md\ *adj* **:** having a wood frame ⟨a ~ building with brick siding⟩ ⟨inexpensive ~ houses⟩ **:** having a frame (of a specified material) ⟨a steel-*frame* office building⟩ ⟨reinforced concrete ~ construction⟩

fra·mea \ˈfrāmēə\ *n, pl* **frame·ae** \-ē,ē\ [L, prob. fr. a Gmc word derived fr. a word represented by OHG *fram* forward, further — more at FROM] **:** a spear with a long shaft and iron head used by the ancient Teutons

frameable *var of* FRAMABLE

framed *past of* FRAME

frame frequency *n* **:** the number of times per second that the frame area in television is completely scanned — compare LINE FREQUENCY

frame·less \ˈfrāmləs\ *adj* **:** having no frame ⟨a ~ picture⟩

frame·man \ˈ=mən\ *n, pl* **framemen :** a telephone worker who connects the terminals of trunk and local lines on a wire= distributing frame

frame of reference 1 : an arbitrary set of usu. orthogonal axes with reference to which the position or motion of a point, body, or group of bodies is described or with reference to which physical laws are formulated **2 a :** a usu. systematic set of principles, rules, or presuppositions or a system of laws, mores, or values or an interlocking group of facts or ideas serving to orient or give particular meaning (as to a fact, statement, or point of view) or serving as a matrix for behavior or for the formation of attitudes; *broadly* **:** VIEWPOINT, THEORY ⟨give me some *frame of reference* in which to discuss his contention —*N. Y. Times*⟩ ⟨each of us views the problem from his particular and limited *frame of reference* —S.G. DiMichael⟩ ⟨the most common *frames of reference* that the term evokes — economic theories or political loyalties, specific industries or all industries, all foreign countries or particular ones —S.L.Payne⟩ **b :** the characteristics of a ground which influence or determine the perception of a figure against it

fram·er \ˈfrāmə(r)\ *n* -s **1 :** one that frames: as **a :** INVENTOR, CONTRIVER, FORMULATOR ⟨a ~ of an intricate poetic stanza⟩ ⟨a ~ of the constitution⟩ ⟨a ~ of witty turns of phrase⟩ **b :** a worker who makes frames (as of boxes) or assembles framework (as of furniture to be upholstered) **c :** a worker who puts on frames (as on pictures) **2 :** FRAME SPINNER

frames *pres 3d sing of* FRAME, *pl of* FRAME

frame spacing *n* **:** the fore-and-aft distance between the heels of two consecutive frames of a ship

frame spinner *n* **:** an operator of a frame spinning machine

frame spinning *n* **:** yarn spinning on a frame as distinguished from spinning on a mule **:** RING SPINNING

frame story *or* **frame tale** *n* [trans. of G *rahmenerzählung*] **:** a story told within a frame or a story constituting a frame for another story or a series of other stories

frame–up \ˈ=,=\ *n* -s [*frame up*] **1 :** an act or series of actions in which someone is framed ⟨points an accusing finger at overzealous prosecutors, avenging witnesses, concealment of evidence of innocence, and ruthless *frame-ups* —*Nation*⟩ **2 :** an action that is framed ⟨looked legitimate enough but at the investigation it was proved to be a *frame-up*⟩

1framework \ˈ=,=\ *n* [*2frame + work*] **1 a** (1) **:** a skeletal or structural frame ⟨the ~ of the ship⟩ (2) **:** an openwork frame ⟨the vines climbed a ~⟩ (3) **:** a basic ideational or narrative structure ⟨the ~ of the political theory⟩ ⟨the ~ of the novel⟩ (4) **:** a systematic set of relationships ⟨the family was so large he had difficulty keeping the ~ of kinship clear in his mind⟩ **b :** frames or a system of frames ⟨the ~ he had constructed for a gallery of pictures⟩ **2 :** work done in or by means of a frame **3 :** a conceptual scheme, structure, or system **:** the limits or outlines esp. of a particular set of circumstances **:** FRAME OF REFERENCE **4 :** the larger branches of a tree that together determine its shape and symmetry

2framework \"\ *vt* **:** to graft scions of another variety on the framework of (as a fruit tree) after removal of all smaller laterals usu. to obtain more desirable fruit — compare TOPWORK

fram·ing \ˈfrāmiŋ, -mēŋ\ *n* -s [ME, fr. gerund of *framien, framen* to frame — more at FRAME] **:** FRAME, FRAMEWORK ⟨the ~ of the dormitories is reinforced concrete with buff-colored brick facing —*Current Biog.*⟩ ⟨the huge stone chimney and part of the ~ are probably all that is left of an original one= room house —*Amer. Guide Series: Conn.*⟩

framing chisel *n* **:** a long sturdy chisel designed for rough carpentry work

framing square *n* **:** a large carpenter's square graduated with scales typically for use in cutting off and notching (as rafters or stair joists)

frammed *past of* FRAM

framming *pres part of* FRAM

fram·mit \ˈframət\ *var of* FREMD

frampold *adj* [origin unknown] **1** *obs* **:** PEEVISH, CROSS, VEXATIOUS, QUARRELSOME **2** *obs, of a horse* **:** FIERY, SPIRITED

frams *pres 3d sing of* FRAM

franc \ˈfraŋk\ *n* -s [ME *frank*, fr. MF *franc*, fr. ML *Francus* Frenchman (in *Francorum rex* king of the French, the device on the 14th cent. francs), fr. LL, Frank — more at FRANK] **1 a :** an old French gold coin first struck in 1360 **b :** an old French silver coin issued from 1575 to 1641 **2 a** (1) **:** the basic monetary unit of modern France established during the Revolution — see MONEY table (2) **:** a coin representing this unit **b :** any of numerous monetary units (as of Belgium, Luxembourg, or Switzerland) or their corresponding coins orig. equivalent to the French franc — see MONEY table **c** [Alb *frëngë*, fr. F *franc*] **:** the former monetary unit of Albania **3 a :** any of numerous monetary units of specified French dependencies **b :** a coin representing one of these units **4 :** a monetary unit of Morocco equivalent to 1/100 dirham — see MONEY table

france \ˈfran(t)s, -aa(ə)n-, -ain-, -än-\ *adj, usu cap* [fr. *France*, country in Europe] **:** of or from France **:** of the kind or style prevalent in France **:** FRENCH

france rose *n, often cap F* **:** a deep pink to purplish pink that is deeper than arbutus

fran·chis·al \ˈfran,chīzəl, -raan- *sometimes* -īsəl\ *adj* [*franchise* + *-al*] **:** of, relating to, or having the characteristics of a franchise

1fran·chise \ˈfran,chīz, -raan- *sometimes* -īs\ *n* -s [ME, fr. OF, fr. *franchir* to free, fr. *franche* (fem. of *franc* free) + *-ise* -ice — more at FRANK] **1** *obs* **:** freedom from servitude or restraint **2 a :** freedom or immunity from some burden, exaction, restriction, or superior jurisdiction vested either in a natural or an artificial person or a particular class or order of persons **:** EXEMPTION — compare CHARTER 2b **b** *archaic* **:** the jurisdiction over which such a freedom extends **:** the limits of such an immunity **3 a :** a right or privilege conferred by grant from a sovereign or a government and vested in an individual or a group; *specif* **:** a right to do business conferred by a government — see FRANCHISE TAX **b :** a constitutional or statutory right or privilege; *esp* **:** the right to vote — usu. used with *the* **c** (1) **:** the right granted to an individual or group to market a company's goods or services in a particular territory (2) **:** the territory involved in such a right **d :** a contract for public works or public services granted by a government to an individual or company **e** (1) **:** the right of membership granted by certain professional sports leagues (2) **:** such membership itself (3) **:** a team and the professional organization operating it having such membership **f :** the right to present, broadcast, or televise the events put on by a sports league or organization **4 a :** an amount of liability (as a percentage or a sum) specified in an insurance contract below which an underwriter claims only partial liability or disclaims liability and often above which the underwriter assumes total liability **b :** group coverage insurance of fewer than the minimum number of participants required by state law for such coverage

2franchise \"\ *vt* -ED/-ING/-S [ME *fraunchisen*, fr. MF *fraunchiss-*, stem of *franchir*] **1** *archaic* **:** to set free **2 :** to grant a franchise or the franchise to **:** ENFRANCHISE ⟨an amendment *franchising* adults over 18⟩ ⟨these firms are now being *franchised* to handle this manufacturer's line —*Distribution Age*⟩

franchise bond *n* **:** a surety bond that insures a government or state against loss due to a franchise holder's failure to complete work specified in the franchise grant

fran·chise·ment \-mənt, -,chəzm- *sometimes* -,chəsm- *or* fra(a)n'chī-\ *n* -s [MF, fr. OF *franchissement*, fr. *franchiss-* + *-ment*] **:** ENFRANCHISEMENT

fran·chiser \ˈfran,chīzə(r), -raan- *sometimes* -īsə-\ *n* -s [*1franchise* + *-er*] **:** one that holds a franchise ⟨a four-page tabloid . . . designed to keep carbonated beverage packers and their ~*s* abreast of news in the canned soft-drink field —*Modern Packaging*⟩

franchise stamp *n* **:** a postage stamp issued by some countries for use on free mail (as that of a charitable institution)

franchise tax *n* **:** a business tax imposed upon various corporations granted a franchise

fran·cic \ˈfran(t)sik\ *adj, usu cap* [ML *Francicus*, fr. LL *Francus* Frank + L *-icus* -ic — more at FRANK] **:** FRANKISH

fran·cien \frāⁿsyaⁿ\ *n* -s *usu cap* [F, fr. *Île-de-France* + *-ien* -ian] **:** the dialect of French used in the middle ages in Île-de-France that furnishes the basis for the literary and official form of the modern French language

1fran·cis·can \(ˈ)fran¦siskən, -raan-\ *adj, usu cap* [ML *Franciscus* (St. Francis of Assisi) †1226 Ital. monk & preacher + E *-an*] **:** of or relating to St. Francis of Assisi, to the Order of St. Francis, or to the Franciscans

2franciscan \"\ *n* -s *usu cap* **:** a member of one of various religious foundations established by St. Francis of Assisi in the early 13th century including the Friars Minor, the Poor Clares, and the Franciscan tertiaries

fran·cis·can·ism \=ˈ=kə,nizəm\ *n* -s *often cap* **:** Franciscan beliefs or practices

fran·ci·um \ˈfran(t)sēəm\ *n* -s [NL, fr. *France* + NL *-ium*] **:** a radioactive element of the alkali-metal group discovered as a disintegration product of actinium and obtained artificially by the bombardment of thorium with protons — symbol *Fr;* see ACTINIUM SERIES, ELEMENT table

franck–con·don principle \ˈfraŋkˈkändən-, -rän-\ *n, usu cap F&C* [after James *Franck* †1964 Am. physicist born in Germany and Edward U. *Condon* b1902 Am. physicist] **:** a principle in spectroscopy: the intensities of molecular spectral bands due to electronic transitions are consistent with the assumption that the relatively large mass of the atomic nuclei in the molecule prevents appreciable change in their configuration during such transitions

franck·e·ite \ˈfräŋkə,īt\ *n* -s [G *franckeit*, fr. Carl and Ernest *Francke*, 19th cent. Ger. mining engineers + G *-it* -ite] **:** a mineral consisting of a dark gray or black massive lead antimony tin sulfide (sp. gr. 5.55)

fran·co \ˈfräŋ(,)kō\ *adj* [It (*porto*) *franco* free carriage, fr. *porto* carriage + *franco* free, fr. ML *francus* — more at FRANK] **:** free of charge **:** FRANKED: **a :** postage free **b :** delivered free

franco- *comb form, usu cap* [ML, fr. *Francus* Frenchman, fr. LL, Frank — more at FRANK] **:** French and ⟨*Franco*-Swiss⟩ **:** French ⟨*Franco*phile⟩

fran·co·ism \ˈfraŋkō,izəm, -rän-\ *n* -s *usu cap* [Francisco *Franco* b1892 Span. soldier and dictator of Spain + E *-ism*] **1 :** the political or social policies advocated or put into effect by the dictator Franco **2 :** the advocacy of or allegiance to Franco's policies

fran·çois pre·mier \frāⁿˈswä·prəˈmyā\ *n, usu cap F&P* [F, after *François premier* (Francis I) †1547 king of France] **:** a furniture style modeled on that of the Italian Renaissance and introduced into France under Francis I

fran·co·ist \ˈfraŋkōəst, -räŋ-\ *n* -s *usu cap* [Francisco *Franco* + E *-ist*] **1 :** a member of General Franco's forces in the Spanish civil war **2 :** an advocate of or adherent to Francoism

fran·co·lin \ˈfraŋkələn, -kəl-\ *n* -s [F, fr. OF, fr. OIt *francolino*] **:** any of numerous partridges of southern Asia and Africa constituting *Francolinus* and related genera — see BLACK PARTRIDGE

1fran·co·ni·an \(ˈ)fran¦kōnēən, -an¦-, -nyən\ *adj, usu cap* [*Franconia*, former duchy of Germany + E *-an*] **1 :** of or relating to Franconia **2 :** of, relating to, or being a Franconian dialect or the Franconian dialects

2franconian \"\ *n* -s *cap* **:** the West Germanic language of the Franks esp. as represented by a group of dialects, partly Low German and partly High German, attested by written documents of which the earliest belong to the late 8th or early 9th century over an area extending from the lowest part of the Rhine as far south as the northern border of Alsace and as far east as the region around Bamberg in northern Bavaria and continuing in oral use to the present day — compare FRANKISH, LOW FRANCONIAN

fran·co·nia potatoes \-nēə-, -nyə-\ *n pl, usu cap F* **:** potatoes cooked with a roast and often basted with the drippings

1fran·co·phile \ˈfraŋkə,fīl, -kō,-\ *or* **fran·co·phil** \-,fil\ *adj, usu cap* [*Franco-* + *-phile, -phil* (adj. comb. form)] **:** markedly friendly or attracted toward France or French culture or customs

2francophile \"\ *or* **francophil** \"\ *n* -s *usu cap* [*Franco-* + *-phile, -phil* (n. comb. form)] **:** a Francophile person

fran·co·phil·ia \,==ˈfilēə, -lyə\ *n* -s *usu cap* [NL, fr. *Franco-* + *philia*] **:** the quality or state of being Francophile

1fran·co·phobe \ˈ==,fōb\ *adj, usu cap* [*Franco-* + *-phobe* (adj. comb. form)] **:** marked by a fear or strong dislike of France or French culture or customs

2francophobe \"\ *n* -s *usu cap* [*Franco-* + *-phobe* (n. comb. form)] **:** a Francophobe person

fran·co·pho·bia \,==ˈfōbēə\ *n* -s *usu cap* [NL, fr. *Franco-* + *-phobia*] **:** the quality or state of being Francophobe

1franco–provençal \¦fraŋ(,)kō+\ *adj, usu cap F&P* [*Franco-* + *Provençal*; trans. of It *franco-provenzale*] **:** of, relating to, or constituting Franco-Provençal

2franco–provençal \"\ *n, cap F&P* **:** a group of southeastern French dialects spoken in western Switzerland and the adjacent parts of France bordering on the Provençal dialect area

franc–ti·reur \,frāⁿtēˈrər, +V -ər·\ *n* -s [F, fr. *franc* free + *tireur* shooter, fr. MF, fr. *tirer* to pull, shoot + *-eur* -or — more at FRANK] **:** a civilian esp. French guerrilla fighter or sniper

FR and CC *abbr* free of riot and civil commotion

fran·gi·bil·i·ty \,franjəˈbiləd·ē\ *n* -ES **:** the quality or state of being frangible

fran·gi·ble \ˈfranjəbəl\ *adj* [ME, fr. MF & ML; MF, fr. ML *frangibilis*, fr. L *frangere* to break + *-ibilis* -ible — more at BREAK] **:** capable of being broken **:** BREAKABLE, BRITTLE, FRAGILE ⟨a fire-extinguishing fluid in a ~ container⟩ ⟨these ladies' dainty and ~ shoulder blades must not be burdened by so deplorable an event —Elinor Wylie⟩ — **fran·gi·ble·ness** *n* -ES

frangible bullet *n* **:** a bullet used in firing practice that breaks into powder or fragments upon contact with the target and does not penetrate

fran·gi·pane \ˈfranjə,pān, -raan-, frāⁿzhēpän\ *n* -s [F & It.; F, fr. It *frangipane*, a kind of perfume orig. used to perfume gloves, after the Marquis Muzio *Frangipane* or *Frangipani*, 16th cent. Ital. nobleman] **1 :** FRANGIPANI **2 a :** a dessert of almond cream flavored with frangipani or jasmine perfume **b :** a custard cream flavored with almonds and used as a tart filling

fran·gi·pani *also* **fran·gi·pan·ni** \,==ˈpanē, -ˈpänē\ *n, pl* **frangipani** *or* **frangipanis** *also* **frangipanni** *or* **frangipannis** [modif. of F & It *frangipane*] **1 :** a perfume derived from or imitating the odor of the flower of the red jasmine **2 :** any of various tropical American shrubs or small trees of the genus *Plumeria* (as red jasmine)

fran·gu·la \ˈfraŋgyələ\ *n* -s [NL, fr. L *frangere* to break + *-ula*; fr. the frangibility of its wood] **1 :** ALDER BUCKTHORN **2 :** the bark of frangula used in medicine for its laxative properties

frangula emodin *n* **:** EMODIN

fran·gu·lin \-lən\ *n* -s [ISV *frangul-* (fr. NL *frangula*) + *-in*; orig. formed in G] **:** an orange crystalline glycoside $C_{21}H_{20}O_9$ obtained esp. from the bark of the alder buckthorn and yielding emodin and rhamnose on hydrolysis

franion *n* -s [origin unknown] *archaic* **:** an habitual pleasure seeker or merrymaker **:** IDLER, REVELER

1frank \ˈfraŋk, -aiŋk\ *n* -s *cap* [ME *Frank, Franc*, partly fr. OE *Franca*; partly fr. OF *Franc*, fr. LL *Francus*, of Gmc origin; akin to OHG *Franko* Frank, OE *Franca*] **1 :** a member of one of the West Germanic peoples entering the Roman provinces in A.D.253, occupying the Netherlands and most of Gaul, and shortly afterward establishing themselves in two divisions along the lower and middle Rhine **2 :** a western European ⟨Europeans are still called *Franks* in the Levant —Emil Lengyel⟩

²frank \"\ *adj* -ER/-EST [ME, fr. OF *franc*, fr. ML *francus*, fr. LL *Francus*, n., Frank] **1** *obs* **a :** free from bondage or restraint **b :** free of charge or other conditions **:** UNCONDITIONAL **2** *archaic* **:** LIBERAL, GENEROUS, PROFUSE **3** *obs* **a :** superior in quality or strength **b :** LUXURIANT, RANK, VIGOROUS **4 a :** marked by free unrestrained willing expression of facts, opinions, or feelings without reticence, inhibition, or concealment ⟨forthright comments from a ~ critic⟩ ⟨a kindly but ~ warning⟩ ⟨most ~ in his confession of entire disbelief in the legends which . . . almost all thought it decent to pretend to credit —J.A.Froude⟩ **b :** marked by or suggestive of freedom and honesty in expression **:** lacking concealment, dissembling, or guile ⟨suspicion or hostility dispelled by a ~ smile⟩ **5 a :** lacking disguise or masking **:** bluntly or honestly avowed **:** downright and clearly obvious **:** sheer and utter without reservation, mitigation, or inhibition ⟨the mixture of the idea of evolution with the ~ materialism of Haeckel and the subtle agnosticism of Huxley —R.W.Murray⟩ ⟨her mouth was painted ripely with mauve as if in ~ appeal to be kissed —Edmund Wilson⟩ **b** *med* **:** UNMISTAKABLE, MANIFEST **:** clinically evident ⟨~ pus⟩ ⟨~ anemia⟩

syn CANDID, OPEN, PLAIN: FRANK may suggest a willingness to express oneself in a free and forthright way, without reservations or modifications brought about by timidity, evasiveness, or tact ⟨intelligent enough to realize just what all the theorists of his age were actually doing, and *frank* enough to announce it openly —J.H.Randall⟩ ⟨I have now told you everything without an attempt of circumlocution or concealment. Do you in your turn be as *frank* with me —A. Conan Doyle⟩ ⟨his notorious comment — which the American democrat has never forgiven him, "The people! — the people is a great beast!" — was characteristically *frank* —V.L.Parrington⟩ CANDID may suggest a sincerity and honesty marked by straightforward expression without evasion or expedient reservation ⟨I am sure that he was *candid* with me. I am certain that he had no guile —W.A.White⟩ ⟨as a leader of our party for 10 years I have never lacked *candid* critics in my own ranks —Clement Attlee⟩ OPEN may imply an inclination to ready, free, natural, honest expression lacking concealment or reserve ⟨wished her children would be more *open* with her and not have so many secrets among themselves⟩ ⟨the absurdity of her remark moved him to *open* taunts⟩ PLAIN may stress simple straightforward expression not mollified by tact or complicated by erudite language ⟨the admiral . . . made the following signal in *plain* language: "Will be compelled to return fire" —Emil Lengyel⟩ ⟨the difference between ordinary phraseology that makes its meaning *plain* and legal phraseology that makes its meaning certain —Ernest Gowers⟩

³frank \"\ *vt* -ED/-ING/-S **1 a :** to mark (a piece of mail) with an official signature indicating the right of the sender to free mailing **b :** to mark (mail) with a sign indicating the right of the sender to exemption from postage **c :** to send by mail at no expense to the sender **d :** to affix to (mail) a stamp or a marking indicating the payment of postage **:** put a postage stamp on ⟨a cover *~ed* with two 3-cent stamps⟩ ⟨he *~ed* his business mail with meter impressions⟩ **e :** to label (mail) as having the postage paid ⟨a commemorative stamp *~ed* the letter⟩ **f :** to mark (mail) with a postal marking of any kind **2 :** to facilitate the passage of **:** help forward **:** enable to pass or go freely or easily **3 :** to make immune (as by a pass inscribed with an official signature) **:** EXEMPT, FREE ⟨court functionaries drew up in motorcars to my hotel, and presented me with a case all over seals and imperial devices *~ing* me through the customs houses of the universe —W.J.Locke⟩

⁴frank \"\ *n* -S [³*frank*] **1 a :** the signature of the sender on a piece of franked mail serving in place of a postage stamp **b :** a mark or stamp on a piece of mail indicating postage paid ⟨a meter ~ on business mail⟩ **c :** a franked envelope or cover **2 :** the privilege of sending mail free of charge

⁵frank *n* -S [ME, fr. MF *franc* pigsty, fr. OLF *hranne, chramne*; akin to OS *hrama* frame, and perh. to Gk *kremannynai* to hang — more at CREMASTER] *obs* **:** a sty for boars

⁶frank *vt* -ED/-ING/-S [ME *franken*, fr. ⁵*frank*] *obs* **:** to shut up (a boar) in a frank esp. for fattening

⁷frank *n* -S [⁶*frank*; fr. its fattening properties] *obs* **:** SPURRY

⁸frank \ˈfraŋk, -raaŋk\ *n* -S [imit. of its cry] *dial Brit* **:** a common European heron (*Ardea cinerea*)

⁹frank \"\ *vt* -ED/-ING/-S [origin unknown] **:** to join or frame together (as molded sash bars) by mitering to the depth of the molding and cutting off the rest of each abutting piece square or finishing with a mortise-and-tenon joint

¹⁰frank \"\ *n* -S [G & Flem, fr. F *franc* — more at FRANC] **:** FRANC 2 b

¹¹frank *n* -S [by shortening] **:** FRANKFURTER

frank·al·moign *or* **frank·al·moin** *also* **frank·al·moigne** \ˈfraŋkal,mȯin, ⸗ˈ⸗⸗, ,⸗⸗ˈ⸗\ *n* -S [*frank* + *almoign, almoin*; trans. of ML *eleemosyna libera*] **:** a tenure in English law by which a religious corporation holds lands given to them and their successors forever usu. on condition of praying for the soul of the donor and his heirs — compare LAY FEE

frank bank *n* [trans. of ML *francus bancus*] *obs* **:** FREE BENCH

fran·ke·nia \fraŋˈkēnēə, -anˈ-\ *n, cap* [NL, after Johan *Frankenius* (Franke) †1661 Swed. professor of anatomy and botany] **:** a genus (the type of the family Frankeniaceae) of perennial herbs or undershrubs with opposite leaves and solitary pink, violet, or red flowers usu. in the forks of the branches — **fran·ke·ni·a·ceous** \⸗ˌ⸗nēˈāshəs\ *adj*

fran·ke·ni·a·ce·ae \⸗ˌ⸗⸗ˈāsē,ē\ *n pl, cap* [NL, fr. *Frankenia*, type genus + *-aceae*] **:** a family of perennial herbs or low-growing evergreen woody plants (order Parietales) native to seacoasts in temperate and subtropical regions and sometimes used as border or ground carpet plants in light sandy soil or in rockeries — see FRANKENIA

frank·en·stein \ˈfraŋkən,stīn *sometimes* -tēn\ *n* -S *usu cap* [after Baron *Frankenstein*, hero of the novel *Frankenstein* (1818) by Mary W. Shelley †1851 Eng. novelist, whose life is ruined by a monster he created from parts of corpses and endowed with life; fr. his name being taken to be the name of the monster he created] **1 :** a monster in the shape of a man; *esp* **:** one resembling the man-made monster of the novel *Frankenstein* ⟨he learned the art of making theatrical masks with plastic materials . . . would appear before his mother or guests as a *Frankenstein* with a bloody hole in his forehead, from which protruded a spike —Victor Eisenstein⟩ **2 :** a work or agency that proves troublesomely uncontrollable esp. to its creator; *esp* **:** one that ultimately destroys or ruins its creator ⟨warfare has ever been the creature of man's ingenuity and has today become the *Frankenstein* that may indeed destroy the human race —A.M.Prentiss⟩ ⟨if the scientific method . . . is not to become a consuming *Frankenstein*, it must be extended to the admittedly more complex and baffling problems of human relationships —C.F.Richards⟩

fran·ken·stein·i·an \ˌ⸗⸗ˈstīnēən -tin-\ *adj, usu cap* **:** of, relating to, or resembling a Frankenstein ⟨a sort of *Frankensteinian* phobia created by factions who would have people everywhere believe there is no room in one world for more than one economic and social system —Norman Corwin⟩

frankenstein monster *also* **frankenstein's monster** *n, usu cap F* **:** FRANKENSTEIN ⟨a *Frankenstein monster* that would stand before a typecase and pluck out letters and click them into a composing stick —T.W.Duncan⟩ ⟨bureaucracy . . . become a *Frankenstein monster*, a law unto itself, interested largely in its own perpetuation and expansion —E.S.Griffith⟩ ⟨French fears that a rearmed Germany might prove to be a *Frankenstein's monster* which would turn on its creators —O.N.Bradley⟩

fran·ken·thal \ˈfraŋkən,thȯl, ˈfräŋkən,täl *n* -S *usu cap* [fr. *Frankenthal*, city in Bavaria, Germany where it was produced] **:** faience and hard-paste porcelain produced at Frankenthal, Bavaria during the second half of the 18th century and noted for well-modeled figures

frank·er \ˈfraŋkə(r)\ *n* -S [³*frank* + *-er*] **:** one that franks; *esp* **:** a machine for franking mail

frank·fort \ˈfraŋkfə(r)t, *usu* -d·+V\ *adj, usu cap* **1** *or* **frankfurt** \", ˈfräŋk,fu̇rt\ [fr. *Frankfurt* am Main, Germany] **:** of or from the city of Frankfurt am Main, Germany **:** of the kind or style prevalent in Frankfurt am Main **2** *or* **frankfurt** [fr. *Frankfurt* an der Oder, Germany] **:** of or from the city of Frankfurt an der Oder, Germany **:** of the kind or style prevalent in Frankfurt an der Oder **3** [fr. *Frankfort*, Ky.] **:** of or from Frankfort, the capital of Kentucky ⟨a *Frankfort* residence⟩ **:** of the kind or style prevalent in Frankfort

frankfort black *n, usu cap F* **:** a pigment made usu. by charring vegetable material (as vine twigs or the lees of wine) — called also *drop black*

frank·furt·er *or* **frank·fort·er** \R ˈfraŋkfə(r)|d·ər, -k,fər|, |tər -R -kfə|d·ə(r, -k,fə|, |tə(r\ *or* **frank·furt** *or* **frank·fort** \ˈfraŋkfə(r)t, *usu* -d·+V\ *n* -S [*frankfurter, frankforter* fr. G *Frankfurter* of Frankfurt, fr. *Frankfurt* am Main, Germany; *frankfurt, frankfort* short for *frankfurter, frankforter*] **:** a sausage (as of beef or beef and pork or a mixture of meats and poultry) that is cured and cooked and stuffed in a casing or skinless

frankfurt horizontal *or* **frankfort horizontal** *or* **frankfurt plane** *or* **frankfort plane** *n, usu cap F* [*Frankfurt* am Main] **:** EYE-EAR PLANE

frankhearted \ˈ⸗ˌ⸗⸗\ *adj* **:** having an open or honest heart

frank·in·cense \ˈfraŋkən,sen(t)s\ *n* -S [ME *fraunk encens*, fr. *fraunk, frank* free, pure + *encens* incense — more at FRANK, INCENSE] **1 :** a gum resin containing volatile oil obtained from various chiefly East African or Arabian trees of the genus *Boswellia*, valued in ancient times in worship and for embalming and fumigation, and still an important incense resin — called also *Indian frankincense* **2 :** GUM THUS 2

frankincense pine *n* **:** LOBLOLLY PINE 1

franking *n* -S [fr. gerund of ³*frank*] **1 :** the stamp or other indication relating to postage on a cover — see MIXED FRANKING **2 :** the mailing charge ⟨~ was paid by a 2-shilling stamp —L.A.Wolf⟩ **3 :** the sending of mail free of charge (as by frank)

¹frank·ish \ˈfraŋkish, -raiŋ-, -kēsh\ *adj, usu cap* [¹*Frank* + *-ish*] **:** of or relating to the Franks

²frankish \"\ *n* -ES *cap* **:** the West Germanic language of the Franks esp. as represented by a large and early stratum of Germanic elements in the vocabulary of French — compare FRANCONIAN

frank·lin \ˈfraŋklən\ *n* -S [ME *frankeleyn, fraunkeleyn*, fr. AF *fraunclein*, fr. OF *franc, fraunc* free + *-lenc, -layn, -lein* -ling — more at FRANK, CHAMBERLAIN] **:** a substantial landowner of 14th and 15th century England who is of free but not noble birth

franklin grouse *or* **franklin's grouse** *n, usu cap F* [after Sir John *Franklin* †1847 Eng. explorer] **:** a grouse (*Canachites franklinii*) of northwestern evergreen forests closely related to or included among the spruce grouses

¹frank·lin·ia \fraŋkˈlinēə\ [NL, fr. Benjamin *Franklin* †1790 Am. statesman, scientist, and philosopher + NL *-ia*] *syn of* GORDONIA

²franklinia \"\ *n* -S [NL, fr. Benjamin *Franklin* + NL *-ia*] **:** a plant of the genus *Gordonia*; *esp* **:** FRANKLIN TREE

frank·lin·i·an \(ˈ)⸗ˈ⸗nēən\ *adj, usu cap* [Benjamin *Franklin* + E *-ian*] **:** of, relating to, or having the characteristics of Benjamin Franklin

frank·lin·i·el·la \ˌfraŋk,linēˈelə\ *n, cap* [NL, prob. fr. Henry James *Franklin* †1958 Am. zoologist and entomologist + NL *-i-* + *-ella*] **:** a large genus of thrips including numerous serious pests of cultivated plants some of which are vectors of virus diseases — see FLOWER THRIPS, TOBACCO THRIPS

frank·lin·ite \ˈfraŋklə,nīt\ *n* -S [*Franklin*, N.J. + E *-ite*] **:** an iron-black slightly magnetic mineral $ZnFe_2O_4$ consisting of an oxide of iron and zinc occurring in octahedral crystals or massive and constituting a member of the magnetite series

franklin's gull *n, usu cap F* [after Sir John *Franklin*] **:** a small black-headed gull (*Larus pipixan*) that breeds in the western interior of No. America

franklin stove *also* **franklin** *n, usu cap F* [after Benjamin *Franklin*, its inventor] **1 :** a metal heating stove resembling an open fireplace but designed to be set out in a room so as to conserve heat and to distribute it evenly **2 :** an enclosed metal heating stove designed to be set out in a room

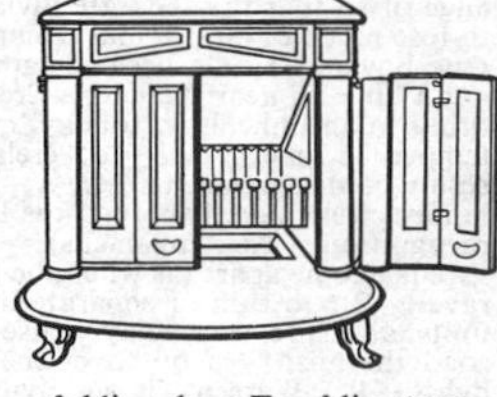

folding door Franklin stove

franklin tree *n, usu cap F* [after Benjamin *Franklin*] **:** a shrub or small tree (*Gordonia alatamaha*) frequently cultivated for its foliage and solitary showy white flowers

frank·ly *adv* [²*frank* + *-ly*] **1 :** in a frank manner: **a :** GENEROUSLY, UNRESERVEDLY ⟨wishing to repay the money so ~ offered to him in his need⟩ **b :** without concealment **:** OPENLY, PLAINLY, CLEARLY ⟨the ordeals he and his companions underwent are ~ harrowing —*Geoffrey Bles Annual List*⟩ ⟨the avenue now had a building that was ~ commercial as well as dignified —*Amer Guide Series: N.Y. City*⟩ ⟨the bottle was ~ enormous —Margery Allingham⟩ **c :** FORTHRIGHTLY, BLUNTLY ⟨the bold types ~ surround the table and heap up their plates with everything close at hand —*Sydney (Australia) Bull.*⟩ ⟨one needs then ~ to face oneself and to observe the particular kind of folly one is committing —H.A.Overstreet⟩ **2 :** INDEED **:** to tell the truth **:** to be sure **:** UNDOUBTEDLY ⟨~ . . . we could afford to give them the materials free —*Monsanto Mag.*⟩

frankmarriage \ˈ⸗ˌ⸗⸗\ *n* [ME *franke mariage*, fr. AF *fraunk mariage*, lit., free marriage] **:** the tenure in feudal law by which a man and his wife held an estate granted by a blood relative of the wife in consideration of their marriage, whether before or after it, to be held of the donor by the issue of the marriage to not less than the fourth generation and without other service than fealty — called also *liberum maritagium*

frank·ness *n* -ES **:** the quality or state of being frank ⟨charmed by the ~ of the boy's reply⟩ ⟨told people what he thought with ~ that bordered on discourtesy⟩

frankpledge \ˈ⸗ˌ⸗\ *n* [ME *frankplegge, fraunkplegge*, fr. AF *fraunc plege* (intended as trans. of ME *friborg*, alter. — influenced by ME *fri, fre* free — of assumed OE *frithborh*), fr. OF *fraunc, franc* free + *plege* pledge — more at FRITHBORH, FRANK, PLEDGE] **:** the system or condition in Old English law under which with certain exceptions each male member of a tithing of 12 years of age or upward was responsible for the good conduct of and for the damage done by other members of the tithing; *also* **:** the member himself or the tithing

franks *pl of* FRANK, *pres 3d sing of* FRANK

frank tenant *n* [AF *franc tenant*, fr. OF *franc* free + *tenant* tenant — more at TENANT] *Old Eng law* **:** one that holds a freehold estate

frank tenement *n* [ME, fr. AF *fraunc tenement*, fr. OF *franc, fraunc* free + *tenement* — more at TENEMENT] **:** a freehold estate

frank tenure *n* **:** a freehold tenure

fran·se·ria \franˈsirēə\ *n* [NL, fr. Antonio *Franseri*, 18th cent. Span. physician and botanist + NL *-ia*] **1** *cap* **:** a genus of annual or perennial herbs or shrubs of the family Compositae having alternate leaves and inconspicuous greenish flowers in discoid heads with pistillate heads in the axils of the upper leaves at the bases of nodding spikes or racemes of staminate heads **2** -S **:** any plant of the genus *Franseria* — called also *bur-ragweed*

¹fran·tic \ˈfrantik, -raan-, -tēk\ *adj* [ME *frenetik, frentik, frantik* — more at FRENETIC] **1 a** *archaic* **:** mentally deranged **:** DELIRIOUS, INSANE, MAD ⟨sorrows, and grief of heart, makes him speak . . . like a ~ man —Shak.⟩ **b :** almost mentally deranged **:** nearly mad ⟨at the beach outside Venice they drove the caretaker ~ by demanding, one after the other, an adequately large bathing suit —Robert Berkelman⟩ **c :** emotionally out of control **:** overwhelmed with feeling to the point of wildness **:** FRENZIED ⟨~ with anger and frustration⟩ **2 a :** marked by fast and nervous, disordered, or anxiety-driven activity ⟨this almost ~ search for new writers —J.T. Farrell⟩ ⟨the most ~ dancers in the world —Wolcott Gibbs⟩ ⟨did a tumbling act, spinning across the stage in a series of ~ cartwheels as though she were made of springs —Winifred Bambrick⟩ ⟨tornadoes and ~ thunderstorms —*Springfield (Mass.) Union*⟩ ⟨there was something desperate and ~ in this gaiety —B.A.Williams⟩ **:** wild or out of control esp. with fear and anxiety ⟨after longer periods without water they sometimes become ~ —*Amer. Guide Series: Ariz.*⟩ ⟨clasping me in desperation like a person ~ with drowning —R.P.Warren⟩ ⟨destroyed the bridges . . . in spite of ~ protests from the townspeople —*Amer. Guide Series: Tenn.*⟩ **b :** noisy or active in an uncontrolled way ⟨~ applause at the end of the opera⟩ ⟨the batsman, making a ~ attempt to cover himself —Dorothy Sayers⟩ **3** *of an emotion* **:** intense to the point of hysteria ⟨~ fear and fanatical hatred —M.R.Cohen⟩ ⟨a child, playing on a damp beach, suddenly finds he can repeat, over and over, the imprint of his hand . . . will do this, then, in ~ joy —Roger Burlingame⟩ **4 :** of or befitting one that is frantic ⟨the forest seemed a vast hive of men buzzing about in ~ circles —Stephen Crane⟩ ⟨protests with ~ words and gestures that he has only desired peace —Sir Winston Churchill⟩ ⟨our ~ zeal to extend the frontiers of knowledge —E.S.McCartney⟩ ⟨the ~ beat of hoofs down the road —T.B.Costain⟩ **5 :** very great **:** EXTREME ⟨in a ~ hurry to get home⟩ — **fran·ti·cal·ly** \-tək(ə)lē, -tēk-, -li\ *adv* — **fran·tic·ly** *adv* — **fran·tic·ness** *n* -ES

²frantic *n* -S [ME *frenetik, frentik, frantik*, fr. *frenetik, frentik, frantik*, adj.] *archaic* **:** LUNATIC

fran·zy \ˈfranzē\ *dial var of* FRENZY

frap \ˈfrap\ *vt* **frapped; frapped; frapping; fraps** [ME *frapen, frappen*, fr. MF *fraper*, prob. of imit. origin] **1** *dial Eng* **:** STRIKE, BEAT **2 :** to draw tight **:** strengthen with bonds (as a ship by passing cables around it) **:** bind, draw together, or secure with ropes

frap·le \ˈfrapəl\ *vi* -ED/-ING/-S [perh. freq. of *frap*] *archaic* **:** BLUSTER, WRANGLE — **frap·ler** \-p(ə)lə(r)\ *n* -S

¹frap·pé *or* **frappe** \fraˈpā\ *adj* [F *frappé*, fr. past part. of *frapper* to strike, chill, fr. OF *fraper* to strike, beat — more at FRAP] *of a food or beverage* **:** ICED, FROZEN ⟨wine ~⟩

²frappé \"\ *or* **frappe** \ˈfrap\ *n* -S **1 :** an iced and flavored semiliquid mixture served in glasses **2** *usu frappé* **:** an after-dinner drink of liqueur served in a cocktail glass over shaved ice **3** *usu frappe* **:** a thick milk shake

³frap·pé \fraˈpā\ *vt* **frappéed; frappéed; frappéing; frappés** **:** to freeze to a soft mush

⁴frappé \"\ *n* -S [F, fr. past part. of *frapper*] **:** a movement in ballet in which the free foot beats against the ankle of the supporting foot

frapping *n* -S [fr. gerund of *frap*] **:** a lashing that binds tightly or binds things together

frasch process \ˈfräsh-\ *or* **frasch method** *n, usu cap F* [after Herman *Frasch* †1914 Am. chemist born in Germany, its inventor] **:** a method of mining deep-lying sulfur by forcing into the deposit very hot water and pumping out the sulfur thereby melted

¹frase \ˈfrāz\ *Scot var of* PHRASE

²frase *var of* FRAISE

fra·ser \ˈfrāzə(r)\ *n* -S [F *fraisier* strawberry plant, fr. *fraise* strawberry, fr. OF *fraise, frese* — more at FRAISE] **:** ⁵FRAISE

fraser fir *n, usu cap 1st F* [after John *Fraser* †1811 Brit. botanist] **:** an evergreen tree (*Abies fraseri*) of the southern Alleghenies similar to the balsam fir but having leaves rarely more than ¾ inch long and rounded and notched at the apex

fras·ni·an \ˈfrasnēən\ *adj, usu cap* [*Frasnian*, subdivision of the Devonian, fr. *Frasne*, France + E *-ian*] **:** of or relating to a subdivision of the European Devonian — see GEOLOGIC TIME table

frass \ˈfras\ *n* -ES [G, lit., food, feed, fr. OHG *frāz* food, fr. OHG *frezzan* to eat voraciously, devour — more at FRET] **:** debris or excrement produced by insects

¹frat \ˈfrat, *usu* -ad·+V\ *n* -S [by shortening] **:** FRATERNITY

²frat \"\ *vi* **fratted; fratted; fratting; frats** [short for *fraternize*] **:** to associate on friendly terms **:** FRATERNIZE

¹fratch \ˈfrach\ *vi* -ED/-ING/-ES [ME *fracchen* to creak, prob. of imit. origin] *dial Eng* **:** QUARREL, WRANGLE

²fratch \"\ *n* -ES *dial Eng* **:** DISAGREEMENT, QUARREL

fratched *adj, dial Brit* **:** IRRITATED, PEEVED

fratchy \ˈfrachi\ *adj* -ER/-EST *dial Brit* **:** irritable and argumentative **:** PEEVISH

fra·te \ˈfrä(,)tā\ *n, pl* **fra·ti** \-tē(,)\ [It, lit., brother — more at FRA] **:** FRIAR — often used as a title

¹fra·ter \ˈfrād·ə(r)\ *n* -S [ME *fraytour, frater*, fr. OF *fraitur*, short for OF *refraitur, refaitur*, fr. ML *refectorium* — more at REFECTORY] **:** a refectory of a monastery

²fra·ter \ˈfrä|d·ə(r), -rā|, |tə-\ *n* -S [ML, fr. L, brother — more at BROTHER] **1 :** a member of certain religious orders (as the Benedictine order) who is studying for the priesthood — often used as a title or form of address esp. among members of the same or similar orders **2 a :** a fraternity brother **b :** a brother Freemason in certain Masonic orders

¹fra·ter·nal \frəˈtərnᵊl, -ˈtən-\ *adj* [ME, fr. ML *fraternalis*, fr. L *fraternus* (fr. *frater*) + *-alis* -al] **1 a :** of, relating to, or involving brothers ⟨trying to improve the ~ relationship between the two boys even though their father did not care⟩ **b :** of, relating to, or being a fraternity or confederation ⟨a ~ order⟩ ⟨a ~ chapter house⟩ ⟨a ~ delegate to national meetings⟩ **c :** of, relating to, or being one of many men's or sometimes women's clubs or associations usu. having secret rites, restricted membership, and religious, social, charitable, or professional purposes **2** *of twins* **:** derived from two ova **:** DIZYGOTIC **3 :** FRIENDLY, BROTHERLY ⟨so we shall have ~ nations . . . instead of warring, organized interests —H.J. Mackinder⟩ — **fra·ter·nal·ly** \-ᵊlē, -ᵊli\ *adv*

²fraternal \"\ *n* -S **1 :** a member of a fraternal order **2 :** a society providing fraternal insurance

fraternal benefit society *n* **:** a fraternal order or association providing fraternal insurance

fraternal insurance *n* **:** insurance issued by a fraternal order or association to its members, formerly meeting its obligations by assessments upon members at the time obligations arose but now generally by a legal reserve

fra·ter·nal·ism \-nᵊl,izəm, -nə,li-\ *n* -S **1 a :** the state of being fraternal **b :** fraternal feeling **2 :** the theoretic justification of fraternal societies or their practices; *also* **:** the advocacy of fraternal societies

fra·ter·nal·ist \-nᵊləst, -nələ-\ *n* -S **:** a person who practices or advocates fraternalism

fraternal polyandry *n* **:** polyandry in which several brothers share one wife — contrasted with *sororal polygyny*

fraternal worker *n* **:** a person engaged professionally in the work of a church who comes from and is usu. supported by a church in another country

fra·ter·ni·ty \frəˈtərnəd·ē, -ˈtən-, -ətē, -i\ *n* -ES [ME *fraternite*, fr. MF & L; MF *fraternite*, fr. L *fraternitat-, fraternitas*, fr. *fraternus* + *-itat-, -itas* -ity] **1 :** a group of people associated or formally organized for a common purpose, interest, or pleasure: as **a :** a religious or ecclesiastical brotherhood **b :** a usu. organized group of men of the same class, occupation, interest, or pursuit **:** COMPANY, GUILD **:** fraternal order **c :** a national or local men's student organization formed chiefly for social purposes having secret rites and a name consisting of usu. three Greek letters; *also* **:** an organization of alumni who were members of such an organization **d :** a student organization for scholastic, professional, or extracurricular activities; *esp* **:** a national honorary organization including students and alumni ⟨an honorary ~⟩ ⟨a debating ~⟩ **2 a :** the quality or state of being a brother or being brothers **:** the relationship of a brother or of brothers **b :** the quality or state of being brotherly or very friendly **:** BROTHERLINESS **c :** a brotherly commonness (as of occupation) ⟨men with a ~ of interests⟩ **3 :** men of the same class, profession, occupation, character, or tastes ⟨the legal ~⟩ ⟨the racetrack ~⟩ ⟨the despised ~ of armchair historians —T.S.Brown⟩ **4 a :** the entire progeny of a single mating **b :** a group of siblings

frat·er·ni·za·tion \ˌfrad·ə(r)nəˈzāshən, -atə(-, -nīˈ-\ *n* -S **:** the act of fraternizing

frat·er·nize \ˈfrad·ə(r),nīz, -atə-\ *vb* -ED/-ING/-S *see -ize in Explan Notes* [F *fraterniser*, fr. ML *fraternizare*, fr. L *fraternus* brotherly (fr. *frater* brother) + ML *-izare* -ize — more at BROTHER] *vi* **1 a :** to associate or mingle as brothers or on fraternal terms **:** engage in comradely social intercourse ⟨he sent a detachment of cavalry to reconnoiter the route again and ~ with the Indians —Bernard De Voto⟩ ⟨guest of honor at a dinner . . . where he *fraternized* with seven prominent hoodlums —Polly Adler) ⟨the militiamen were persuaded to lay down their arms and ~ with the strikers —*Amer. Guide Series: Md.*⟩ ⟨greater opportunities for the people of the western nations to mingle and ~ with each other —*Saturday Rev.*⟩ **b :** to associate on intimate terms with members of a hostile group (as civilians of an occupied country) esp. when contrary to military orders ⟨caught the men *fraternizing*⟩ ⟨the crime of *fraternizing* with foreigners —H.W.Carter⟩; *esp* **:** to have sexual intercourse with a woman of an occupied country ⟨by the first few weeks of occupation 70 percent of our troops had *fraternized* in husbandly fashion —John McPartland⟩ **c :** to be friendly or amiable **2** *of animals* **:** to mingle, live together, or inhabit the same area without hostility ⟨after mating, it is believed that the male lives alone and does not ~ even with others of his own sex, while the female orang retires to bear her young alone —Weston La Barre⟩ ⟨still a few antelope in the cattle country; they ~ easily with the domestic beasts —Tom Marvel⟩ **~** *vt, archaic* **:** to bring into a fraternal or friendly sympathetic relationship — **frat·er·niz·er** \-zə(r)\ *n* -s

fraters *pl of* FRATER

frati *pl of* FRATE

frat·i·cel·li \ˌfrad·ə'chelē\ *n pl, cap* [It, pl. of *fraticello*, lit., little brother, dim. of *frate* brother — more at FRA] **:** any of several small Christian sects existing chiefly in Italy from the 13th to the 15th centuries and having some connection with the Franciscans: as **a :** a band of seceders from the Franciscan order under the leadership of Angelo de Clareno (1247–1337) **b :** the Spirituals or Spiritual Franciscans who revolted against the order and defied many popes **c :** the followers of Michael of Cesena (1270–1342) who defended a theory of poverty and property for monks and ecclesiastics generally

fra·tor·i·ty \frə'tärəd·ē, -'tȯr-\ *n* -ES [*fraternity* + *sorority*] **:** a society or club including both men and women or boys and girls

frat·ri·ci·dal \ˌfra·trə¦sīdᵊl *sometimes* -rāt-\ *adj* **:** of, relating to, being, or resulting in fratricide ⟨the outbreak of one of the bloodiest, most ~ wars in Irish history —Paul Blanshard⟩

frat·ri·cide \'==ˌsīd\ *n* -s [in sense 1, fr. ME, fr. MF or L; MF, fr. L *fratricida*, fr. *fratr-, frater* brother + *-cida* -cide (killer); in sense 2, fr. MF or L; MF, fr. L *fratricidium*, fr. *fratr-, frater* + *-cidium* -cide (killing) — more at BROTHER] **1 :** one that murders or kills his own brother or sister or some person (as a countryman) who stands in a relationship resembling that of a brother or sister ⟨besides being a great lady she is also a ~, a moral coward and a tosspot —*Time*⟩ **2 :** the act of a fratricide

fra·try \'frā·trē\ *also* **fra·tery** \-ād·ərē\ *n* -ES [prob. fr. 1*frater* + *-y*] **1 :** a refectory of a monastery **2 :** the residential quarters of a monastery

frats *pl of* FRAT, *pres 3d sing of* FRAT

fratted *past of* FRAT

fratting *pres part of* FRAT

frau \'fraů\ *n* [G, woman, married woman, wife, fr. OHG *frouwa* mistress, lady; akin to OE *frēa* lord, master, OS *frūa* mistress, lady, *frao* lord, master, OHG *frō* lord, master, ON *freyja* mistress, lady, Goth *frauja* lord, master, OE *faran* to travel, go — more at FARE] **1** *pl* **frauen** \-aůən\ *usu cap* **:** MRS. — usu. used preceding the name of a German married woman **2** -s **:** WIFE, HOUSEWIFE — sometimes used disparagingly

fraucht \'frȯkt, -räkt\ *Scot var of* FRAUGHT

fraud \'frȯd\ *n* -s [ME *fraude*, fr. MF, fr. L *fraud-, fraus*; akin to Skt *dhūrvati* he injures, *dhūrta* fraudulent, and prob. to OHG *triogan* to deceive, ON *draugr* ghost, Skt *droha* injury, treachery] **1 a :** an instance or an act of trickery or deceit esp. when involving misrepresentation **:** an act of deluding **:** DELUSION ⟨the presumed guarantee of standards is really a ~ —Walter Moberley⟩: as (1) *or* **fraud in fact :** an intentional misrepresentation, concealment, or nondisclosure for the purpose of inducing another in reliance upon it to part with some valuable thing belonging to him or to surrender a legal right **:** a false representation of a matter of fact by words or conduct, by false or misleading allegations, or by the concealment of what should have been disclosed that deceives or is intended to deceive another so he shall act upon it to his legal injury — called also *actual fraud* (2) *or* **fraud in equity :** an act, omission to act, or concealment by which one person obtains an advantage against conscience over another or which equity or public policy forbids as being prejudicial to another (as an act in violation of a relationship of trust and confidence) — called also *equitable fraud, legal fraud;* see CONSTRUCTIVE FRAUD **b :** a means used in trickery **:** a dishonest stratagem or a spurious thing passed off as genuine **:** TRICK, HOAX ⟨who worked the big ~ on the . . . bank —Rudyard Kipling⟩ **2 :** the quality of being deceitful **:** the disposition to deceive ⟨the dross of ~ and charlatanism —Lewis Mumford⟩ **3 :** the condition of being defrauded or beguiled **4 a :** a person who is not what he pretends to be **:** PRETENDER, HUMBUG, HYPOCRITE ⟨the pretentious ~ who assumes a love of culture that is alien to him —Richard Watts⟩ **b :** one who defrauds **:** CHEAT ⟨the ~ is simply another variety of confidence man who pretends to have influence —G.A.Graham⟩ **syn** see DECEPTION, IMPOSTURE

fraud·ful \-dfəl\ *adj* [ME, fr. *fraude* + *-ful*] *archaic* **:** marked by fraud **:** FRAUDULENT — **fraud·ful·ly** \-fəlē, -li\ *adv, archaic*

fraud in equity 1 : FRAUD 1a(2) **2 :** fraud for which a court of equity grants a remedy

fraud order *n* **:** an order issued by the U. S. postmaster general forbidding the use of the mails to a person who has used them fraudulently

fraud·u·lence \'frȯjələn(t)s\ *n* -s [ME, fr. L *fraudulentia*, fr. *fraudulentus* fraudulent + *-ia* -y] **:** the quality or state of being fraudulent **:** deliberate deceit **:** DECEITFULNESS, FRAUD

fraud·u·len·cy \-nsē\ *n* -ES [L *fraudulentia*] *archaic* **:** FRAUDULENCE, FRAUD

fraud·u·lent \-nt\ *adj* [ME, fr. MF, fr. L *fraudulentus*, fr. *fraud-, fraus*] **1 :** belonging to or characterized by fraud ⟨throw off the yoke of superstition, of ~ priests and tyrannous rulers —M.R.Cohen⟩ **:** founded on fraud ⟨I should be very sorry to think that there was anything fishy or ~ about the . . . institution of Private Property —L.P.Smith⟩ **:** FALSE ⟨~ claims for unemployment compensation —*Wall Street Jour.*⟩ **:** obtained or performed by fraud ⟨~ land grants —E.G.Gudde⟩ ⟨beset with charges of ~ voting —*Amer. Guide Series: N.J.*⟩ **2** *of a legal conveyance* **:** made in fraud of others' rights; *specif* **:** made without adequate consideration in violation of the rights of creditors or made to hinder or delay them — **fraud·u·lent·ly** *adv* — **fraud·u·lent·ness** *n* -ES

fraudulent preference *n* **:** a payment to or advantage conferred on one creditor in fraud of the rights of other creditors by an insolvent debtor

fraudulent representation *n* **:** a representation that a past or present material fact is true which is made in any manner or form with the intention of inducing someone to act thereon and by one who either knows of its falsity or is ignorant of its truth or falsity or who acts recklessly without regard to its truth and which in some jurisdictions requires an actual intention to deceive for one to be held liable for damages but which is even without such intention sometimes fraudulent in law and ground for avoiding a contract — compare DECEIT, MISREPRESENTATION, WARRANTY

frauen *pl of* FRAU

1fraught \'frȯkt, -räkt\ *n* -s [ME, fr. MD or MLG *vracht, vrecht*, prob. fr. an (assumed) OFris word akin to OHG *frēht* reward, earnings, fr. *fir-, fur-* for- + *ēht* property — more at AUGHT] **1** *chiefly Scot* **:** FREIGHT, PASSAGE **2** *now chiefly Scot* **a :** LOAD, CARGO **b :** the amount one person can carry at a time ⟨carry a ~ of water to the manse —J.M.Barrie⟩

2fraught \"\ *vt* **fraughted** *or* **fraught; fraughted** *or* **fraught; fraughting; fraughts** [ME *fraughten*, fr. *fraught*, n.] *now chiefly Scot* **:** LOAD, FREIGHT, FILL

3fraught \'frȯt, *usu* -ȯd·+V\ *adj* [ME, fr. past part. of *fraughten*] **1** *archaic* **:** carrying as a load **:** LADEN, FREIGHTED **2 a :** burdened or menaced with ⟨the long, danger-*fraught* wait before the . . . invasion —*Manchester Guardian Weekly*⟩ ⟨an extrahazardous occupation ~ with dangers —R.M. Hutchins⟩ **:** ENDANGERED, THREATENED ⟨the changed times were ~ with other obstacles than these —Charles Dickens⟩ **b :** giving promise or prospect — used with *with* ⟨opinions that we loathe and believe to be ~ with death —O.W.Holmes †1935⟩ ⟨achievements . . . ~ with happy consequences for the future —John Buchan⟩ **c :** ACCOMPANIED, ATTENDED — used with *with* ⟨a great event which might be ~ with strange consequences —Robert Hichens⟩ ⟨the speaking of words ~ with deep emotional significance —A.T.Weaver⟩ ⟨here . . . every footstep is ~ with memories —Norman Douglas⟩

fraught·age \-ȯd·ij\ *n* -s [ME, fr. 1*fraught* + *-age*] *archaic* **:** FREIGHT

fräu·lein \'frȯiˌlīn *sometimes* -raů,- *or* -rō,-\ *n* -s [G, fr. MHG *vrouwelīn* young lady, dim. of *vrouwe* lady, mistress, fr. OHG *frouwa* — more at FRAU] **1** *usu cap* **:** MISS — usu. used before the name of an unmarried German girl or woman **2 a :** a usu. young unmarried woman esp. of Germany ⟨an operetta about the love of an American GI for a ~ —Percy Winner⟩ ⟨a German ~ with bare and sunburned legs and plaited hair —Negley Farson⟩ **b :** a German governess ⟨the parties of children that used to be seen hurrying along the avenue at the close of the afternoon, in the care of nannies or mademoiselles or ~s —Rebecca West⟩

fraun·ho·fer lines \'fraůnˌhōfə(r)\ *n, usu cap F* [after Joseph von *Fraunhofer* †1826 Bavarian optician and physicist] **:** any of the dark lines in the spectrum of sunlight

fra·va·shi \frə'väshē\ *n* -s [Av *fravashay-*] *Persian religion* **:** an immortal preexisting spiritual guardian or genius of each individual **:** the heavenly image and celestial archetype of each creature; *collectively* **:** the ministering angels of divine heavenly beings

frawn \'frȯn\ *n* -s [IrGael *fraochān*] **:** WHORTLEBERRY 1

frax·e·tin \'fraksəd·ən\ *n* -s [ISV *fraxin* + *-etin*] **:** a yellow crystalline compound $C_{10}H_8O_5$ derived from coumarin and obtained by hydrolysis of fraxin

frax·in \'fraksən\ *n* -s [ISV *frax-* (fr. L *fraxinus*) + *-in;* orig. formed in G] **:** a bitter yellowish crystalline glucoside $C_{16}H_{18}O_{10}$ found esp. in the bark of the ash and the horse chestnut

frax·i·nel·la \ˌfraksə'nelə\ *n* -s [NL, dim. of L *fraxinus;* fr. the similarity of its leaves to those of an ash] **:** a Eurasian perennial herb (*Dictamnus albus*) of the family Rutaceae with flowers which exhale a flammable vapor in hot weather and were formerly reputed to have the power to expel arrows from the body — called also *burning bush, gas plant*

frax·i·nus \'fraksənəs\ *n, cap* [NL, fr. L, ash — more at BIRCH] **:** a genus of trees or sometimes shrubs (family Oleaceae) comprising the ashes, being natives of the north temperate zone, and having thin furrowed bark, opposite pinnate leaves, and small apetalous flowers followed by fruits that are samaras

1fray \'frā\ *vb* -ED/-ING/-S [ME *fraien*, short for *afraien, affraien* — more at AFFRAY] *vt* **1** *archaic* **:** FRIGHTEN, SCARE, TERRIFY **2** *archaic* **:** to frighten away **:** DISPEL **~** *vi, archaic* **:** BRAWL, QUARREL, FIGHT

2fray \"\ *n* -s [ME, short for *afray, affray* — more at AFFRAY] **1** *now chiefly Scot* **:** APPREHENSION, FRIGHT, TERROR **2 a :** COMMOTION, TUMULT **b :** QUARREL, BRAWL ⟨authority to quell all quarrels, ~s, and disorders among persons subject to this code —*U.S. Code*⟩ ⟨sometimes those cold ornery guys turned very dangerous in a ~ . . . used knucks, even knives —T.W. Duncan⟩ **c :** SKIRMISH, COMBAT, FIGHT ⟨who began this bloody ~ —Shak.⟩ ⟨picked up a club and threw himself into the ~⟩ **d :** DISPUTE, DEBATE ⟨the editor took a side opposite to the local faculty in the ~⟩ ⟨known for his scientific-political ~s as well as his chemistry —*Newsweek*⟩ **syn** see CONTEST

3fray \"\ *vb* -ED/-ING/-S [MF *frayer, froyer* to rub, fr. L *fricare* — more at BRINE] *vt* **1 a :** to rub against something ⟨a deer ~s his antlers to remove the velvet⟩ **b :** to wear (as an edge of cloth or an end of rope) or wear off by or as if by rubbing **:** FRET ⟨the friction ~*ed* the edge of the polishing cloth⟩ **c :** to separate the strands or threads at the edge or end of (as a piece of fabric or rope); *also* **:** to divide an end or edge so that the separate divisions fan out **2 a :** to cause to lose much of an original strength, force, or essential quality ⟨the boy's gratitude became rapidly ~*ed*⟩ ⟨his boyish charm got a bit ~*ed* near the end —Crary Moore⟩ **b :** to strain and bring to an unhealthy, touchy, or inauspicious condition ⟨his temper became a bit ~*ed*⟩ ⟨relations . . . already ~*ed* as a result of disagreements —*N.Y. Times*⟩ ⟨excursions from the family circle have benefited his health and ~*ed* nerves out of recognition —Rex Ingamells⟩ **~** *vi* **1 :** to wear out or into shreds **:** come apart (as when the threads of a fabric loosen and ravel) **2 :** to thin or separate into shreds, parts, or separate units, and spread or splay — used with *out* ⟨in the dips of the road the mist ~*ed* out over the slab and blunted the headlights —R.P.Warren⟩ ⟨is our civilization widening and deepening, or is it ~*ing* out —Douglas Stewart⟩ ⟨white pelicans . . . rise, ~*ing* out, peeling off, in a slow roar of aroused wings —Marjory S. Douglas⟩ ⟨feathered lines that ~*ed* out upon the skin —Elizabeth M. Roberts⟩

4fray \"\ *n* -s **:** a raveled place or worn spot (as on fabric)

5fray \'frī\ *n* -s [Sp, short for *fraile*, alter. of OSp *fraire*, fr. OProv, brother, monk, fr. L *fratr-, frater* brother — more at BROTHER] **:** BROTHER — a title of a clergyman of various religious orders in Spanish countries

frayed·ly *adv* **:** in the manner of one that is frayed

frayed·ness *n* -ES **:** the quality or state of being frayed

fraying *n* -s [fr. gerund of 3*fray*] **:** something rubbed or worn off by fraying: as **a :** the velvet that a deer frays from his antlers **b :** pieces of fabric worn off

frayn *or* **frayne** \'frān\ *vb* -ED/-ING/-S [ME *freynen, fraynen*, fr. OE *fregnan, frignan* — more at PRAY] *vt, archaic* **:** to inquire of **:** ASK **~** *vi, obs* **:** ASK, INQUIRE

1fraze \'frāz\ *n* -s [F *fraise*, fr. *fraise*, a kind of ruff; fr. the shape of some cutters — more at FRAISE] **1 a :** a small milling cutter used to cut down the ends of canes or rods to receive a ferrule **b :** the end of a cane or rod shaped as if by a fraze **2** [2*fraze*] **:** the unevenness caused by rough edges or burs

2fraze \"\ *vt* -ED/-ING/-S **:** to smooth by or as if by removing fraze; *specif* **:** to cut or shape (the end of something) to receive a ferrule — **fraz·er** \-zə(r)\ *n* -s

fra·zil \'frāzəl, frə'zil\ *or* **frazil ice** *n* -s [CanF *frasil, frazil, fraisil*, fr. F *fraisil* coal cinders, alter. of OF *faisil*, fr. (assumed) VL *facilis*, fr. L *fac-, fax* torch + *-ilis* -ile] **:** ice crystals or granules sometimes resembling slush that are formed in turbulent water

1fraz·zle \'frazəl\ *vb* **frazzled; frazzled; frazzling** \-z(ə)liŋ\ **frazzles** [alter. (prob. influenced by 3*fray*) of E dial. *fazle* to tangle, fray, fr. ME *faselen* to fray, fr. *fasel*, n., fringe, frayed edge, dim. of *fas* fringe, fr. OE *fæs* — more at FASH] *vt* **1 :** 3FRAY ⟨a bedside lamp with a *frazzled* cord and torn shade —Hamilton Basso⟩ **2 a :** to reduce to a state of extreme physical or nervous fatigue ⟨as if all of these projects weren't enough to ~ him —Diane Disney Miller⟩ ⟨finally arrived . . . *frazzled* and miserable —Joseph Wechsberg⟩ **b :** to disturb greatly **:** UPSET ⟨he has probably helped to open as many curious minds as he has helped to ~ unstable ones —*Time*⟩ **~** *vi* **:** to become frazzled **:** FRAY, WEAR ⟨a thin ribbon of gray smoke . . . *frazzled* into nothingness —J.B.Clayton⟩ ⟨guaranteed not to rip in the seams or ~ at the sleeves —J.C.Harris⟩ ⟨I think he rather *frazzled* out —G.W.Johnson⟩

2frazzle \"\ *n* -s **1 :** the state of being frazzled **2 a :** a frayed or tattered end or edge **b :** a condition of fatigue or nervous exhaustion suggesting such an end or edge ⟨worn to a ~⟩

1freak \'frēk\ *n* -s [perh. fr. obs. *freak* man-at-arms, human being, extraordinary or supernatural creature (in such phrases as *the freaks of Fortune*, lit., the minions of Fortune), fr. ME *freke*, fr. OE *freca* warrior, hero, fr. *frec* greedy, eager, bold, dangerous; akin to OHG *freh* untamed, greedy, ON *frekr* greedy, harsh, severe, Goth *faihufriks* covetous, greedy for money, Pol *pragnąć* to desire, Czech *prahnouti*] **1 a :** a sudden apparently causeless turn of the mind **:** WHIM, FANCY, CAPRICE ⟨the condition of the mare, and the young gentleman's strange ~ in riding her out all night —George Meredith⟩ ⟨his spurts of action are not mere ~s of a temperament that alternates between feverish exploits and slothful lethargy —Karl Polanyi⟩ ⟨you should be able to stop and go on, and follow this way or that, as the ~ takes you —R.L.Stevenson⟩; *also* **:** an odd or whimsical idea or preconception ⟨a bishop arrived who'd some strange ~s about meditation —George Bellairs⟩ **b :** an odd, unexpected, or seemingly capricious action or event ⟨by a ~ of wind the smoke had been blown high —Wallace Stegner⟩ ⟨stories about ~s of the weather, floods, and great droughts —*Amer. Guide Series: Ind.*⟩ ⟨a ~ of good fortune —*New Yorker*⟩ **2** *archaic* **:** a freakish quality or disposition **:** CAPRICIOUSNESS, WHIMSICALITY **3 a :** a product of freakish thought or action or of a freakish process **:** something markedly unusual or abnormal ⟨~s of this storm include a shingle driven through a fence post, a flock of chickens picked clean, and the walls of a house carried away bodily, leaving a cupboard full of unbroken china —*Amer. Guide Series: Minn.*⟩ ⟨the ~s of contemporary fashion —O. Elfrida Saunders⟩ ⟨no individual ~, but a confirmed habit of the species —James Stevenson-Hamilton⟩ **b :** something markedly abnormal mentally or physically esp. to the point of shocking usual expectations; *esp* **:** one with a physical oddity who appears in a circus sideshow or similar exhibition — compare MUTATION, SPORT 6 **4** *Brit* **:** a wild card in poker; *esp* **:** a wild deuce

2freak \"\ *adj* **:** having the character of a freak **:** diverging from what is natural or normal ⟨when rain comes it is often in ~ deluges —Keith Ellis⟩ ⟨the range of the four main voices, . . . is not more than four octaves . . . except in the case of Russian basses and ~ sopranos —Ralph Vaughan Williams⟩ ⟨grotesque sandstone formations, tooled by centuries of wind and weather into ~ shapes —*Amer. Guide Series: Calif.*⟩

3freak \"\ *vt* -ED/-ING/-S **:** to streak esp. with color ⟨silver and mother-of-pearl ~*ing* the intense azure —Robert Bridges †1930⟩

freaked *adj* [fr. past part. of 3*freak*] **:** marked by streaks ⟨here tall bare fells, capped and ~ with snow —John Brophy⟩; *esp* **:** colorful or vivid with contrasting streaks of color occurring capriciously ⟨the rarest moths, those ~ with azure and the deepest crimson —L.P.Smith⟩ **syn** see VARIEGATED

freak·ish \-kish, -kēsh\ *adj* **1 :** marked by freak turns of mind or actions **:** produced by such turns of mind or actions **:** WHIMSICAL, CAPRICIOUS ⟨a ~ spirit even in his kindness —Glenway Wescott⟩ ⟨a frenzied kind of person, acting on ~ impulses —Peggy Bennett⟩ ⟨a ~ structure with elaborate porches and odd-shaped windows —*Amer. Guide Series: Conn.*⟩ **2 :** being or befitting a freak **:** markedly odd or abnormal ⟨a ~ person with a great head and diminutive body⟩ ⟨a ~ gift for remembering thousands of unrelated facts⟩ ⟨how queer . . . must seem this ~ bookworm —Jean Stafford⟩ — **freak·ish·ly** *adv* — **freak·ish·ness** *n* -ES

freak of nature : FREAK 3b ⟨these *freaks of nature* include giants, dwarfs, . . . and numerous others upon whom nature has played queer tricks —A.M.Smith⟩

freakpot \'=ˌ=\ *n* **1** *Brit* **:** a deal in poker with deuces wild **2 freakpots** *n pl but sing in constr, Brit* **:** a game in which deuces are always wild

freak show *n* **:** an exhibition (as a sideshow) featuring freaks of nature

freaky \'frēkē\ *adj* -ER/-EST **:** FREAKISH

fream \'frēm\ *vi* -ED/-ING/-S [perh. modif. of L *fremere* to roar, murmur — more at FREMITUS] *of a boar* **:** to make the roaring cry characteristic of rutting

freat \'frēt\ *var of* FREIT

1freath \'frēth\ *vi* -ED/-ING/-S [prob. alter. of 2*froth*] *Scot* **:** to froth and foam ⟨see the ale ~⟩

2freath \"\ *n* -s [prob. alter. of 1*froth*] *Scot* **:** FOAM

freck \'frek\ *adj* [ME *frek*, fr. OE *frec* greedy, eager, bold, dangerous — more at FREAK] **1** *dial Brit* **a :** EAGER, READY **b :** FORWARD, IMPETUOUS **2** *now chiefly Scot* **:** stout and strong **:** HEARTY

freck·en \'frekən\ *n* -s [ME *freken, fraken*] *now dial* **:** FRECKLE

1freckle \'frekəl\ *n* -s [ME *frekel, frakel*, alter. of *freken, fraken*, of Scand origin; akin to ON *freknōttr* freckled, Icel & Norw dial. *frekna* freckle; akin to MHG *sprinkel, sprenkel* spot, OE *spearca* spark — more at SPARK] **1 a :** a small brownish spot in the skin usu. due to precipitation of pigment on exposure to sunlight — called also *ephelis;* compare LENTIGO **b :** any spot or small bit of coloring or discoloration ⟨you felt that the sun would . . . send little ~s of light to dance upon her —Edith Sitwell⟩; *specif* **:** a superficial spot on the skin of fruits (as in peach scab) **2 :** an instance of freckling or a spotted condition produced by or resembling freckles ⟨a shadowy ~ had strewn itself throughout her ivory skin —Glenway Wescott⟩ ⟨the ~ of red villas on the coast —Virginia Woolf⟩

2freckle \"\ *vb* **freckled; freckled; freckling** \-k(ə)liŋ\ **freckles** *vt* **:** to sprinkle or mark with freckles or small spots **:** SPOT ⟨the tiny, black spots (actually, a species of mushroom) that ~ their walls —P.E.Deutschman⟩ ⟨watching the lights from outside my window ~ the ceiling with color —E.L. Wallant⟩ **~** *vi* **:** to become covered or marked with freckles ⟨a skin that ~s but does not tan in the sun⟩

freck·led \-ld\ *adj* [ME *frekled, frakled*, fr. *frekel, frakel* + *-ed*] **:** spotted with or as if with freckles **:** SPECKLED ⟨a ~ face⟩ ⟨two damp rooms with lichen-*freckled* walls —Anne S. Mehdevi⟩ — **freck·led·ness** *n* -ES

freckled duck *n* **:** an Australian and Tasmanian duck (*Stictonetta naevosa*) with speckled white-and-brown markings

freckle–faced \¦==¦=\ *adj* **:** having a noticeably freckled face ⟨a *freckle-faced* boy⟩

freckling *n* -s [fr. gerund of 2*freckle*] **1 :** a marking like a freckle ⟨a face covered with lines and ~s⟩ **2 :** a spotted condition; *also* **:** an area marked by freckles ⟨terrapins . . . with the thick ~ of golden pinhead spots —Gerald Durrell⟩

freck·ly \'frek(ə)lē, -li\ *adj, often* -ER/-EST **:** marked with freckles **:** FRECKLED ⟨a ~ face⟩ ⟨a ~ skin⟩

fred·do \'frā(ˌ)dō\ *adj (or adv)* [It, fr. L *frigidus* — more at FRIGID] **:** COLD, PASSIONLESS — used as a direction in music

fred·er·icks·burg \'fred(ə)riks,bərg\ *adj, usu cap* [*Fredericksburg*, subdivision of the Comanchean, fr. *Fredericksburg*, Texas] **:** of or relating to a subdivision of the Comanchean — see GEOLOGIC TIME table

fred·er·ic·ton \'fred(ə)riktən\ *adj, usu cap* [fr. *Fredericton*, New Brunswick, Canada] **:** of or from Fredericton, the capital of New Brunswick **:** of the kind or style prevalent in Fredericton

frederik *or* **fred·er·ik d'or** \'fred(ə)rik'dȯ(ə)r\ *n* -s [*frederik* fr. Dan, fr. *Frederik* VI †1839 king of Denmark; *frederik d'or* fr. Dan *frederikdor*, fr. *Frederik* VI + F *d'or* of gold] **:** a gold coin of Frederick VI of Denmark

fred·er·iks·berg \'fred(ə)riks,bərg\ *adj, usu cap* [fr. *Frederiksberg*, Denmark] **:** of or from the city of Frederiksberg, Denmark **:** of the kind or style prevalent in Frederiksberg

1free \'frē\ *adj* **fre·er** \'frēə(r), 'fri(ə)r, -iə\ **fre·est** \'frēəst\ [ME *fre, free*, fr. OE *frēo;* akin to OHG *frī* free, ON *frjāls*, Goth *freis*, W *rhydd* free, Gk *prays* mild, gentle, Skt *priya* (adj.) dear, *priya* (n.) friend, husband; basic meaning: dear, hence, belonging to one's own family or clan, not being a slave] **1 a :** not being in the position of a slave or serf **:** having the freedom of action and the legal and political rights of a citizen ⟨an edict setting the slave ~⟩ **b :** not subject to a particular ruling, authority, or obligation **:** enjoying a special privilege or immunity **c** (1) **:** not being under an arbitrary, despotic, or totalitarian government **:** subject only to reasonably fixed laws that defend from encroachments upon natural or acquired rights **:** enjoying civil and political liberty ⟨~ citizens⟩ ⟨a ~ people⟩ ⟨the ~ world⟩ (2) **:** defending individual rights against encroachment **:** assuring or maintaining individual liberty **:** not arbitrary or despotic **:** maintained by a politically independent people ⟨a ~ country⟩ ⟨a ~ government⟩ **d :** enjoying political independence or freedom from outside domination ⟨a ~ city⟩ ⟨a ~ nation⟩ **e :** not subject to a parent or guardian **:** not being under guardianship, manus, or potestas **f :** SELF-RELIANT, INDEPENDENT ⟨my young friend, who seems to have as ~ and erect a mind as any I have ever met —R.W.Emerson⟩ ⟨endowed with a mind that was extraordinarily subtle, ~, and fertile in general ideas —M.R.Cohen⟩ **2 a :** not determined by anything beyond its own nature or being: as (1) **:** originating in the soul, personality, or pure ego **:** being without compulsion from the passions or habit or from the organism or environment **:** choosing or capable of choosing for itself ⟨a ~ agent⟩ (2) **:** determined by the choice of the actor or by his wishes ⟨~ actions⟩ ⟨~ choices⟩ (3) **:** determined by intrapsychic needs rather than by the objective demands of the stimulus situation **b :** made, done, or given voluntarily or spontaneously **:** SPONTANEOUS ⟨a ~ offer⟩ ⟨gave his ~ consent⟩ **3** *obs* **a :** of or marked by gentle birth and breeding **:** NOBLE **b :** magnanimous or generous in conduct or character **4 a** (1) **:** clear, exempt, relieved, or released esp. from a burdensome, noxious, oppressive, or deplorable condition or obligation ⟨~ from pain⟩ ⟨~ from disease⟩ ⟨a duty-*free* import⟩ ⟨~ from impurities⟩ ⟨the only spot where he was ~ from hay fever —S.H.Holbrook⟩ **:** RID ⟨she was glad to be ~ of old Matthew —Ellen Glasgow⟩ (2) **:** UNTOUCHED, UNTAINTED — usu. used with *from* ⟨interested in keeping local government ~ from profit —W.E.Jackson⟩ (3) **:** not bothered — usu. used with *from* ⟨at this stage the herring is ~ from invertebrate predators —W.H.Dowdeswell⟩ **b :** not bound, confined, imprisoned, or detained by or as if by force ⟨the prisoner was now ~⟩ ⟨cattle left ~ to range⟩ ⟨upon opening the skull a considerable amount of ~ blood is noted —H.G.Armstrong⟩ **c :** invested with a particular freedom or franchise **:** enjoying particular immunities or privileges — usu. used with *of* **d** (1) **:** having no trade restrictions **:** open for commercial purposes to everyone **:** exempt from liability to duty, tax, or toll (2) **:** duty free ⟨the refineries had an interest in ~ sugar —F.L.Paxson⟩ **e** (1) **:** not subject to government regulation except in legally designated areas — see FREE ECONOMY (2) **:** entailing, arising from, or being under no compulsion or coercion recognized by the courts ⟨no reasonable ground for interfering with . . . the right of ~ contract by determining the hours of labor —R.F.Peckham⟩ ⟨the employee was ~ to agree to working conditions injurious to his health⟩ (3) *of foreign exchange* **:** not subject to restriction or official control **f** (1) **:** having no obligations (as to work) or commitments (as to duty or custom) **:** not given over to one's customary employment or occupation ⟨the foreman of a trail herd allowed his cowhands a ~ evening when they camped for the night near a large town —*Amer. Guide Series: Nev.*⟩ (2) **:** untrammeled by duties or obligations ⟨she would, like most girls, like a year or two ~ before she entered upon motherhood —Ruth Park⟩ ⟨thought that the life of a bachelor would be *freer* than that of a married man⟩ **g :** LOOSE, INEXACT ⟨population in 1940 was only 18,000 and the current estimate is 58,000 with ~ talk of 100,000 by 1960 —*Newsweek*⟩ ⟨a scherzo is a ~ term for something rather humorous and sprightly that goes at a good clip —Ross Parmenter⟩ **h :** not being part of the time for which one is paid ⟨whether within or outside the plant, on ~ or on paid time —*Dun's Rev.*⟩ **5 a** (1) **:** not obstructed or impeded **:** OPEN, CLEAR ⟨raced the car along the ~ and open highway⟩ ⟨the boat had ~ passage along the channel⟩ ⟨a considerable amount of ~ floor space in addition to the space required for equipment —H.G.Armstrong⟩ ⟨the side with the *freest* access to its resources should be the ultimate victor —Michael Scully⟩ (2) **:** not being used or occupied ⟨tried to telephone five times before he got a ~ circuit⟩ ⟨lying on her bed waiting for the bathroom to be ~ —Charles Ingle⟩ ⟨a ~ position in a molecule or crystal⟩ **b :** not impeded, hampered, or restricted in its natural or normal operation **:** LOOSE, UNFETTERED ⟨the movement of the motor shaft seemed ~ enough⟩ ⟨found his hands ~ of the chains⟩ ⟨the runner fell into a ~ easy jog⟩ ⟨wheeled the cylinders to make certain they were turning ~ and fast —S.H.Holbrook⟩ ⟨flying from out of the jungle with a great ~ flapping of wings —Jack McLaren⟩ **c :** having liberty by reason of not being restrained, hindered, or compelled by an outward force ⟨~ to tell the truth as he sees it⟩ ⟨any member is ~ to raise any topic —*London Calling*⟩ ⟨she was ~ . . . to go where she liked and do what she liked . . . had no responsibilities, no cares —Arnold Bennett⟩ **d :** not interfered with by autocratic restrictions or autocratically compelling forces or agencies **:** engaged in by men who are politically and socially free ⟨~ elections⟩ **e :** executed or allowed to be executed without interference from the opposing side — used of a kick, throw, or hit in competitive sports **f** (1) **:** not fixed **:** not fastened ⟨one end of the rope was left ~ and trailed in the water behind the boat⟩ ⟨rising like a toy balloon that had slipped ~ of a child's fingers —Horace Sutton⟩ (2) **:** not supported ⟨the cantilever construction allowed the ~ end of the beam to project over 15 feet⟩ (3) **:** not confined to a particular position or place **:** free moving ⟨in twelve-tone music, no note is wholly ~ for it must hold its place in the series —J.L.Stewart⟩ (4) *of a particle or mass in physics* **:** capable of moving or turning in any direction **g** *of a foot or hand* **:** not being used in a particular operation ⟨while he was skating on one foot he held the ~ foot up in front of him⟩ ⟨held the chair tilted with one hand and pointed under it with his ~ hand⟩ **h** *of a missile* **:** not guided **:** not capable of being directed while in flight **i** *gymnastics* **:** performed without apparatus **6** *obs* **:** of, relating to, or located on a freehold **7 :** acting or prone to act in a way that is copious, ample, or profuse or that lacks constraint, restraint, or reserve: as **a :** not parsimonious with one's possessions **:** LIBERAL, OPENHANDED, LAVISH ⟨pretty ~ with his money⟩ ⟨the evidence of high living standards and ~ spending in New York —Dixon Wecter⟩ **b :** marked by freedom of expression **:** spoken or uttered without reserve or restraint **:** OUTSPOKEN **c :** availing oneself of or using without stint or reserve — now usu. used with *with* **d :** unconstrained by timidity or reserve **:** FRANK, OPEN ⟨most of these women of distinction were courtesans, ~ in spirit, manners, and finances —H.M.Parshley⟩ **e** *archaic* **:** READY, EAGER, PRONE **f :** observing or marked by few if any responsibilities or limitations ⟨the professor had made ~ use of cracks and weather marks on the stone, combining them with the hieroglyphics to make the translation come out right —Martin Gardner⟩ **g :** overly familiar or forward in action or attitude ⟨a young man who had been much too ~ with the ladies of the town —Harvey Graham⟩ **h :** going beyond decorous bounds **:** IMMODERATE, LICENTIOUS ⟨indulging in inexcusably ~ talk before the ladies⟩ ⟨resting her chin on her clasped hands, her elbows on the table, in an attitude which the older women thought shockingly ~ —Edith Wharton⟩ **i** *chiefly Brit, of a graft stock* **:** SEEDLING **8 :** individual and exclusive in nature as opposed to common — used of certain franchises **9 a :** not costing or charging anything ⟨a ~ school⟩ **b :** given or furnished without cost or payment **:** GRATUITOUS ⟨~ admission⟩ ⟨a ~ ticket to a circus⟩ **c :** admitted without payment ⟨the dance hall was largely filled with ~ customers⟩ **10 :** easily or readily worked or wrought **:** having a texture or structure that is loose, soft, malleable, or lacking in firm cohesiveness **11 a :** PERMISSIBLE ⟨it is ~ for him to think so⟩ **b :** being or feeling at liberty to use or enjoy — used with *of* ⟨made his friends ~ of his land and possessions⟩ ⟨made their children ~ of every novel in the house —*Times Lit. Supp.*⟩ ⟨he was ~ of the house, and might be found at any moment, in the hall or patio, or sitting at ease in the study —R.P. Warren⟩ **12** *obs* **:** GUILTLESS, INNOCENT **13 a :** not united or combined with something else **:** SEPARATED, UNATTACHED ⟨a ~ ore⟩ ⟨a ~ column⟩ ⟨electrons . . . quite a number of them are ~, that is, they are not attached to any particular atom —*Magic of Communication*⟩ **b :** DISTINCT, SEPARATE ⟨having flowers with ~ whorls⟩ ⟨a vine with ~ stipules⟩ **c** (1) **:** uncombined with or not present as an element in other substances ⟨turkeys require ~ water for drinking purposes —R.E. Trippensee⟩ ⟨the slower flowing watercourses retain water, either ~ or in sand, all the year round —*Geog. Jour.*⟩ (2) **:** chemically uncombined or readily obtainable in uncombined form (as by heating) **:** AVAILABLE 6b **:** NATIVE 11a ⟨~ oxygen⟩ ⟨~ acids⟩ — opposed to *bound* **d :** not permanently attached **:** able to move about ⟨the ~ zooids of some bryozoans⟩ **e** *of a vowel* **:** not followed by a consonant in the same syllable — opposed to *checked* **f** *of accent in speech* **:** not occurring on the same syllable in all words **:** not fixed ⟨accent in English is ~⟩ **g** *of a linguistic form* **:** capable of being used alone with meaning ⟨the word *hats* is a ~ form⟩ — opposed to *bound* **14 a :** departing somewhat from faithfulness to an original form ⟨a ~ version of a Greek play⟩ ⟨a ~ rendering of a piano concerto⟩ **:** not literal or exact ⟨a ~ translation⟩ **b :** not determined or restricted by or observing or conforming to conventional or established forms ⟨a ~ use of the dance steps he had learned⟩ ⟨was considered her superior at ~ skating —*Current Biog.*⟩ ⟨his subjects were chiefly historical and marine, done in ~ and incisive lines —*Amer. Guide Series: Oreg.*⟩ ⟨~ rhythms⟩ ⟨the stone-cut inscriptions of today which employ *freer* forms —F.W.Goudy⟩ — see FREE VERSE **c :** of or relating to a free church ⟨a church that belongs to the ~ tradition⟩ ⟨whether that church is established or ~⟩ **15 :** FAVORABLE — used of a wind blowing from a direction more than six points from straight ahead **16 a :** of, relating to, or characterized by free men or freedom **:** resulting from freedom **:** produced by free men ⟨~ labor⟩ ⟨if we do not take such action, the ~ Pacific will be lost —*Time*⟩ **b :** not allowing slavery **:** making slavery illegal ⟨the territory of Iowa was shortly to be admitted to the Union as a ~ state —Marjory S. Douglas⟩ **17 a :** FREE-FOR-ALL ⟨a ~ competition⟩ ⟨that most pleasurable of Anglo-Saxon pastimes, a ~ fight —Winston Churchill⟩ **b** *of firearms* **:** being under few limitations for match firing with regard to the specifications of the arm ⟨a ~ rifle⟩ ⟨a ~ pistol⟩ **18 a :** not having or using **:** LACKING — usu. used in combination or with *from* or *of* ⟨footloose and fancy-*free*⟩ ⟨a germ-*free* atmosphere⟩ ⟨~ of imperfections⟩ ⟨a face ~ of makeup⟩ ⟨a statement ~ of any insulting implication⟩ ⟨a night ~ from terrors⟩ **b :** being outside ⟨the house was set up to be ~ of the prison confines⟩ **19** *of wool* **:** that has no defects **20 a** *of paper pulp* **:** that parts with its water readily — compare SLOW **b** *of a sheet of paper* **:** not containing groundwood pulp **21 a** *of a bid in bridge* **:** not made for the purpose of keeping the bidding open — used of a raise, response, or rebid that is just sufficient to overcall a preceding bid by the bidder's right-hand opponent **b** *of a double in bridge* **:** made when the opponent's bid is sufficient for game at its undoubled value

syn INDEPENDENT, SOVEREIGN, AUTONOMOUS, AUTARCHIC (or AUTARCHICAL, AUTARKIC, AUTARKICAL): FREE, applied to a state or people, stresses complete absence of external rule, control, or guidance with the full right to make all of one's own decisions ⟨the U.S. became a *free* country after the American Revolution⟩ ⟨for liberty is to be *free* from restraint and violence from others, which cannot be where there is no law —John Locke⟩ ⟨freedom makes a man to choose what he likes; that is, makes him *free* —A.T.Quiller-Couch⟩ INDEPENDENT may describe that which stands alone without relation or connection ⟨words have a meaning *independent* of the pattern in which they are arranged —Aldous Huxley⟩ Applied to nations, it indicates lack of connection with any state or government having power to rule or control ⟨the colony became a dominion and then, severing all ties with the motherland, became *independent*⟩ Applied to persons it indicates a disposition to stand alone and apart with self-reliance and without binding attachment or applies to one who has taken such a stand or stands as if in such a way ⟨in America it seems that almost one third of the voters classify themselves as *independent* and a large number of others do not hesitate to cross party lines to vote for candidates of the other party —E.S.Griffith⟩ SOVEREIGN implies both absence of a superior power over the thing described and unquestioned supremacy within its own sphere ⟨Puerto Rico . . . is a self-governing commonwealth under the American flag. It is *sovereign*, independent, and equal, but has of its own free choice, and for sound and practical reasons, entrusted its foreign and defense policy to the government in Washington —J.C.Harsch⟩ ⟨the alternative purpose proposed by the Scottish Nationalists — namely, the creation of a *sovereign* Scottish nation —*Scotsman*⟩ AUTONOMOUS may indicate an independence of a government in local matters but a degree of control over that government in others ⟨*autonomous* communities within the British Empire, equal in status, in no way subordinate one to another in any aspect of their domestic or external affairs, though united by a common allegiance to the Crown, and freely associated as members of the British Commonwealth of Nations —*Statute of Westminster*⟩ ⟨ANDORRA. An *autonomous* state on the south slope of the eastern Pyrenees, nominally under the joint sovereignty of France and the Spanish bishop of Urgel —*Americana Annual*⟩ AUTARCHIC and its variants now stress economic self-sufficiency more than political independence ⟨all of the countries of the Soviet bloc operate an *autarchical* type of economy. Striving for self-sufficiency, they buy only the barest minimum of goods from abroad —Clifton Daniel⟩ — **for free :** at no cost **:** for nothing **:** GRATIS, GRATUITOUS ⟨bought the entire stock and distributed them to all hands *for free* —Fletcher Pratt⟩ ⟨just across the river is an outdoor movie, with children hanging on the parapet trying to see *for free* —Claudia Cassidy⟩ ⟨where most of the best things in life are *for free* —Budd Schulberg⟩ ⟨publicity *for free* was not his motive either —Carl Jonas⟩ — **free in and out** *of cargo assigned to a chartered vessel* **:** loaded, stowed, trimmed, and discharged at the expense of the charterer or of the charterer and the consignee without cost to the shipowner — **with a free hand :** LIBERALLY, GENEROUSLY, LAVISHLY ⟨the company gave out gifts *with a free hand* at Christmas⟩

²free \"\ *vt* **freed; freed; freeing; frees** [ME *freen*, fr. OE *frēogan, frēon* to free, love; akin to MHG *vrīen* to free, woo, ON *frjā* to love, Goth *frijōn* to love, Skt *priyāyate* he makes friends with; derivative fr. the root of E ¹*free*] **1 a :** to cause to be free **:** set at liberty ⟨~ the slaves⟩ ⟨~ her husband to marry again⟩ **b :** to relieve or rid of something that confines, limits, oppresses, upsets, or embarrasses ⟨*freed* him of his chains⟩ ⟨~ a party of an obnoxious bore⟩ ⟨an Irish brogue from which she later found it difficult to ~ herself —*Current Biog.*⟩ ⟨human sensibility must be *freed* from the dust of erudition and the weight of tradition —Clive Bell⟩ ⟨~ another large portion of her import trade from quantitative restrictions —H.F.Tysser⟩ **c :** RELEASE ⟨~ a stuck door by throwing his weight against it⟩ ⟨*freed* rayon cloth distribution from control —*Times Rev. of Industry*⟩ **d :** to make immune or secure — used with *from* ⟨~ a child from danger⟩ ⟨good health can ~ the body from infection⟩ **e :** DISENTANGLE, CLEAR, DISENCUMBER ⟨~ a fishline from overhead branches⟩ ⟨~ a passage of refuse and debris⟩ ⟨the orange, peeled, carefully *freed* of every shred of white rind —Marcia Davenport⟩ **f :** to let loose **:** allow to go freely ⟨flower scents, that only nighttime ~*s* —Amy Lowell⟩ **2** *obs* **:** to get rid of **:** REMOVE, BANISH

syn RELEASE, LIBERATE, EMANCIPATE, MANUMIT, AFFRANCHISE, ENFRANCHISE, DELIVER, DISCHARGE: FREE is a general term often interchangeable with many of the following; it applies to setting at liberty from whatever binds, as dependence, restraint, obligation, oppression, or suppression ⟨*freed* from debt⟩ ⟨speculation could not *free* itself from the moving principles of Christian theology —H.O.Taylor⟩ ⟨the more progressive lawyers are trying to *free* their own writing from archaic terminology —Milton Hall⟩ ⟨*freed* from the tyranny of the classroom —Allen Johnson⟩ RELEASE may suggest more forcefully than FREE the action of unloosing from a confined or constrained situation without, however, necessarily implying the permanent liberation that FREE usu. does ⟨state institutions *released* on parole or some other form of conditional release a total of 34,032 prisoners —R.S.Banay⟩ ⟨it gave him the feeling that she had reclaimed, reappropriated him. No! That she had never for a moment *released* him —S.H.Adams⟩ ⟨only by indulging a deep impulse towards sermonizing could he *release* those other impulses which made him the great writer he was —C.H.Sykes⟩ LIBERATE may suggest the process or act of freeing or disengaging from bondage, restraint, or constriction, usu. with resulting liberty ⟨to *liberate* a certain group of individuals, those concerned in new forms of industry, commerce, and finance, from shackles inherited from feudalism —John Dewey⟩ ⟨to *liberate* Victorian women from the confining clothes of the period —Lois Long⟩ ⟨the central idea of Goethe's drama is that Orestes can be reconciled with fate and *liberated* from the furies of his conscience —W.A.Kaufmann⟩ EMANCIPATE may refer to the formal process of setting free after slavery; it may refer to a freeing or becoming free from previous restraints or shackles and attaining to independence of action ⟨the descendants of such slaves, when they shall be *emancipated*, or who are born of parents who had become free before their birth —R.B. Taney⟩ ⟨a Greek education which *emancipated* him from the superstitions of his countrymen —J.G.Frazer⟩ ⟨the vital necessity of education and its power to *emancipate* the working classes, mentally, socially, and politically —Alfred Plummer⟩ MANUMIT may refer to the formal conferring of freedman status on slave or serf, usu. by his owner ⟨it appears from the report, that Darnall was born in Maryland, and was the son of a white man by one of his slaves, and his father executed certain instruments to *manumit* him —R.B.Taney⟩ ⟨a master may *manumit* his slave in the church, or outside of it, before a judge or other person, by testament, or by letter; but he must do this in person —*Political Science Quarterly*⟩ AFFRANCHISE and the more common ENFRANCHISE imply freeing from subjection or other condition marked by lack of personal or political liberty, the latter usu. implying admission to full political rights ⟨every slave, after fifteen years, should be *affranchised* —W.S.Landor⟩ ⟨American Negroes emancipated by the proclamation of President Lincoln in 1863 but not *enfranchised* until the Fifteenth Amendment went into effect in 1870⟩ DELIVER still occasionally shows evidence that it is etymologically a cognate of LIBERATE ⟨from the fury of the Norsemen, Good Lord *deliver* us⟩ ⟨a rescue party was in time to *deliver* him with his head still on his shoulders —A.M. Young⟩ Similarly, DISCHARGE in some uses may indicate release from confinement, restraint, or constriction ⟨*discharge* a prisoner⟩ ⟨an honorably *discharged* veteran⟩ ⟨no person held to service or labor in one State, under the laws thereof, escaping into another, shall, in consequence of any law or regulation therein, be *discharged* from such service or labor —*U.S. Constitution*⟩

³free \"\ *adv* [ME *fre, free*, fr. *fre, free*, adj. — more at ¹FREE] **1 :** FREELY ⟨the high overtone of the saw penetrates every corner of the mill, singing when it runs ~ —*Amer. Guide Series: Ark.*⟩ ⟨a ~ moving joint⟩ **2 :** without charge ⟨children admitted ~⟩ ⟨people have traditionally been able to walk into museums ~ —Huntington Hartford⟩ **3 :** with the wind more than six points from dead ahead **:** not close-hauled ⟨a yacht sailing ~⟩

free air *n* **:** air not under restraint (as by pressure or flow) **:** normal atmospheric air; *specif* **:** all of the atmosphere usu. above 100 feet from the earth that is not greatly bound or restricted in its movements by surface friction of the earth and the resulting turbulence

free alms *n pl* [ME *fre almes*, trans. of ML *eleemosyna libera*] **:** FRANKALMOIGN

free alongside ship *or* **free alongside vessel** *adv (or adj)* **:** with delivery at the side of the ship free of charges, the buyer's liability then beginning

free and clear *adv (or adj)* **:** without liens or other legal claims ⟨after only a few months the property was *free and clear*⟩ ⟨they owned it and owned it *free and clear*⟩

free and common socage *n* **:** FREE SOCAGE

¹free and easy *adj* **1 :** marked by casualness, informality, and total lack of constraint ⟨a *free and easy* laugh⟩ ⟨the *free and easy*, open-air life of the plains —Allan Murray⟩ ⟨a *free and easy* relationship between the older and younger members of the family⟩ **2 :** not observant of strict demands ⟨a *free and easy* way with his literary judgments⟩ ⟨his reputation had been no worse than that of his *free and easy* young associates —S.H.Adams⟩ ⟨the incumbent had got fat by being *free and easy* with union money —Kermit Eby⟩ ⟨the fair, *free and easy* daughter of the leading publican —S.E.Morison & H.S.Commager⟩ ⟨too *free and easy* a community to put up with reformers or longhairs —W.S.Campbell⟩

²free and easy *n, pl* **free and easies 1 a :** a convivial party esp. in a public house **b :** a usu. somewhat disreputable music hall or tavern providing entertainment **2 :** a Salvation Army praise meeting at which joyousness and informality are esp. encouraged

³free and easy *adv* **:** in a free and easy manner ⟨a crew of young bloods who lived *free and easy* and were inclined to damn the consequences of most any act they took a notion to perform —F.B.Gipson⟩

free association *n* **1 a :** the verbal or written expression of all the content of consciousness without censorship or intellectual control as an aid in gaining access to unconscious processes esp. in psychoanalysis **b :** the reporting of the first thought that comes to mind in response to a given stimulus (as in the word association test) **2 :** an idea or image elicited by free association **3 :** a method using free association

free astray *n* **:** a shipment that is miscarried or unloaded at a wrong destination and then forwarded correctly free of extra charge because of being astray

free ball *n* **:** a ball other than a legal forward pass that is not dead and not in the possession of any player in a football game and that may be recovered by either side

free balloon *n* **:** a balloon which can be made to ascend by the use of ballast and to descend by the release of gas but which cannot be guided in flight

free-banking system *n* **:** a system under which all applicants are permitted to organize banking corporations or associations and under prescribed conditions issue notes (protected by deposited securities)

free baptist *n, cap F&B* **:** a freewill Baptist of the original group founded in No. Carolina in 1729

free bench *or* **free bank** *n* [trans. of ML *francus bancus*] **:** the interest formerly held in English law by a widow or sometimes a widower in the copyhold or customary lands of the deceased spouse — compare DOWER 1

free-blown \ˈ=ˌ=\ *adj, of glass* **:** blown without the assistance of a mold and with the use only of blowpipe and punty

freeboard \ˈ=ˌ=\ *n* **1 a :** the distance between the waterline and the freeboard deck of a ship **b :** the height that is above the recorded high-water mark of a structure associated with a body of water (as a dam, seawall, or culvert) and that is an allowance against overtopping by waves or other transient disturbances **2 :** the space between the surface of the ground and the undercarriage of an automobile

freeboard deck *n* **:** the deck up to which a ship's freeboard is measured and below which all bulkheads are made watertight — see DECK illustration

free·boot \ˈfrē,büt\ *vi* [back-formation fr. *freebooter*] **:** to act as a freebooter **:** PLUNDER

free·boot·er \ˈfrē,büd·ə(r), -ütə-\ *n* [part trans. of D *vrijbuiter*, fr. *vrijbuit* plunder (fr. *vrij* free — akin to OHG *frī* free — + *buit* booty, fr. *buiten* to exchange, plunder, fr. MD *būten*, fr. MLG) + *-er* (akin to OE *-ere* -er); akin to MLG *būte* exchange, distribution — more at FREE, BOOTY, -ER] **:** one that goes about plundering without the authority of national warfare **:** a member of a predatory band **:** PILLAGER, PIRATE

freebooty *n* [blend of *freebooter* and *booty*] *obs* **:** PLUNDER

free boring *n* **:** a milling of the rifling from a section of the bore of a firearm immediately forward of the chamber

freeborn \ˈ=ˈ=\ *adj* [ME *freborn, freeborn*, fr. *fre, free* free + *born*] **1 :** not born in vassalage or slavery **2 :** belonging to or befitting one that is freeborn

free capital *n* **1 :** capital that has numerous possible or actual uses as opposed to capital confined to a specialized use **2 :** capital available for investment

free cell formation *n* **:** a process of cell formation that is frequent in endosperm development and in spore formation in many fungi (esp. ascomycetes) and in which successive nuclear divisions are followed by the nuclei each appropriating a portion of cytoplasm and usu. simultaneously becoming invested with a cell wall and leaving a surplus of cytoplasm — compare CLEAVAGE 4c, EPIPLASM

free central *adj* **:** having the placentas on a central column of tissue that is not connected by partitions to the wall of the ovary

free chant *n* **:** a recitative for psalms and canticles having a 2-chord phrase for each hemistich

free chapel *n, Eng eccl law* **:** an English chapel not subject to the jurisdiction of the ordinary as a result of having been founded by the king or by a subject specially authorized

free charge *n* **:** the part of the electric charge on a conductor that escapes to earth when the conductor is grounded

¹free-choice \ˈ=ˈ=\ *adj* **:** of, relating to, or supplied according to the method of free-choice feeding ⟨fed solely on *free-choice* grains and meals —*Poultry Farming*⟩

²free-choice \"\ *adv* **:** by free-choice feeding ⟨salt may be fed *free-choice* —C.F.Rooks⟩ ⟨hogs fed *free-choice* on minerals, corn, and supplement⟩

free-choice feeding *n* **:** a method of feeding livestock in which various feeds are kept constantly available and the feeders are allowed to balance their own diet

free church *n* **1 :** a church whose sittings are for all and without charge **2** *often cap F&C* **:** a church not established or under state control: **a** *cap F&C, in Scotland* **:** the church organized by those who left the Church of Scotland in 1843 to be free from state control in spiritual matters — called also *Free Kirk* **b** *cap F&C, in England* **:** a nonconformist church

free-church \'⸗¦⸗\ *adj* [*free church*] **:** of or relating to a church that is not an established church ⟨the American *free-church* system⟩ — **free-church·ly** *adv*

free churchman *n, often cap F&C* [*free church* + *man*] **:** a member of a free church

free city *n* **:** a self-governing city or city-state usu. possessing sovereign power: as **a :** an Italian city-state of the 11th century and later **b :** certain cities of Germany since the 13th century having free institutions **c :** a territorial unit (as formerly Danzig) comprising a city and often adjacent areas that functions as a semiautonomous political entity under the authority of an international organization — compare CITY 2f

free classic *n* **:** an architectural style in England at the close of the 19th century characterized by an unconventional use of classical or baroque elements

free coinage *n* **1 a :** the conversion of bullion of any specified metal into legal-tender coins for any person who chooses to bring it to the mint **b :** such coinage when done at a certain fixed charge proportionate to the cost of the operation — compare BRASSAGE, SEIGNORAGE **2 :** legal-tender coins made by free coinage

free companion *n* **:** one of a band of medieval mercenaries available for hire by a prince or country **:** CONDOTTIERE

free company *n* **:** a band of free companions

free corps *n* [trans. of G *freikorps*] **:** a corps of usu. German volunteer soldiers

free counterpoint *n* **:** counterpoint freed from the harmonic and melodic limitations of strict counterpoint

free crushing *n* **:** a method of crushing ore in which the rate of feed is such that the crushed material passes freely through the crushing unit

free currency *n* **:** a currency not based on metal **:** inconvertible paper currency — compare NORMATIVE CURRENCY

freed *past of* FREE

free democrat *n, usu cap F&D* [trans. of G *freier demokrat*] **:** a member of a conservative and Protestant political party formed in West Germany that stresses individual freedom esp. in economics

free diver *n, Brit* **:** SKIN DIVER

free diving *n, Brit* **:** SKIN DIVING

freed·man \'frēdmən, -,man, -,maa(ə)n\ *n, pl* **freedmen :** a man who has been a slave and has been set free; *specif* **:** an American Negro freed from slavery as a result of the Civil War

free·dom \'frēdəm\ *n* -s [ME *fredom*, fr. OE *frēodōm*, fr. *frēo* free + *-dōm* -dom] **1 :** the quality or state of being free: as **a :** the quality or state of not being coerced or constrained by fate, necessity, or circumstances in one's choices or actions ⟨the philosophical implications of the play theory are found in its opposition of ~ and necessity, of spontaneity and order —John Dewey⟩ **b** (1) **:** the status of the will as an uncaused cause of human actions **:** the absence of antecedent causal determination of human decisions (2) **:** self-realization or spiritual self-fulfillment that is not incompatible with the existence of natural causes of the will-act **:** SELF-DETERMINATION ⟨the Stoic conception of ~ is one of rational self-determination; free acts are those which are in conformity with a man's rational nature and, ultimately, with the rational nature of the universe —Frank Thilly⟩ **c** (1) **:** exemption or liberation from slavery, imprisonment, or restraint or from the undue, arbitrary, or despotic power and control of another **:** LIBERTY, INDEPENDENCE (2) **:** the ability or capacity to act without undue hindrance or restraint **d :** the quality or state of being exempt or released ⟨~ from care⟩ ⟨~ from annoyance⟩ ⟨~ from taxes⟩ **e :** GENEROSITY, LARGENESS, MAGNANIMITY ⟨betray him and announce either the ~ and nobility of his soul or its meanness and limitation —Laurence Binyon⟩ **f** (1) **:** EASE, FACILITY ⟨able to speak the foreign language with ~⟩ (2) **:** the quality or state of running or operating smoothly and without impediment ⟨the machine ran with greater ~ after greasing⟩ **g :** the quality of being frank, open, unreserved, or outspoken **h :** improper familiarity **:** undue social liberty **:** violation of the strict dictates of decorum or decency **i :** boldness or vigor of conception or execution **j :** unrestricted use ⟨give a friend the ~ of the house⟩ ⟨gave the visitor the ~ of the club⟩ **2 :** RIGHT, PRIVILEGE, FRANCHISE ⟨follow the . . . political line as a price for their limited ~ to preach and teach —T.P.Whitney⟩: as **a :** the right of participating as a member or a citizen often conferred as a mark of honorary distinction upon one who is not a member or a citizen **b :** a right or liberty guaranteed by a constitution or fundamental law ⟨formulated in their first civil contract certain ~s as essential to a happy people⟩ or granted by one in authority ⟨given the ~ to enter without showing his pass⟩ or assured by convention or popular sentiment ⟨no one cared if the beloved old man was allowed a ~ denied to law-abiding citizens⟩ **c :** the right or privilege of availing oneself of speech or of acting according to the dictates of conscience or utilizing, supporting, and acting according to one's own view of religion without undue restraints or within reasonably formulated and legally specified limits **3 :** a share of common land formerly allotted in Scotland to a freeman

free·dom·ism \'frēdə,mizəm\ *n* -s **:** the doctrine that man has freedom of choice in his actions **:** INDETERMINISM — opposed to *determinism*

free·dom·ist \-məst\ *n* -s **:** an advocate or adherent of freedomism

free·dom·is·tic \¦frēdə¦mistik\ *adj* **:** of, relating to, or having the characteristics of freedomism

free·dom·ite \'frēdə,mīt\ *n* -s *usu cap* [prob. trans. of Russ *svobodnik*] **:** a member of a Doukhobor sect emigrating from Russia to Canada at the end of the 19th century

freedom of contract : a power of freely contracting and freely determining the provisions of contracts without arbitrary or unreasonable legal restrictions guaranteed as a natural right by U.S. federal and state constitutions — called also *liberty of contract*

freedom of navigation 1 : the right recognized in international law esp. by treaties or agreements for vessels of one or all states to navigate streams passing through two or more states **2 :** FREEDOM OF THE SEAS

freedom of speech : the right to express facts and opinions subject only to reasonable limitations (as the power of the government to protect itself from a clear and present danger) guaranteed by the 1st and 14th amendments to the U.S. Constitution and similar provisions of some state constitutions

freedom of the press : the right of publishing books, pamphlets, newspapers, or periodicals without restraint or censorship subject only to the existing laws against libel, sedition, and indecency

freedom of the seas : the right of a merchant ship of any nation to travel any waters except territorial waters either in peace or war

¹free-drop \'⸗¦⸗\ *n* **1 :** a dropping (as of supplies) from airplanes to the ground without parachutes **2 :** something dropped by free-drop

²free-drop \"\ *vt* **:** to drop (as supplies) by a free-drop ⟨lumber and a few other items were *free-dropped* from 100 feet —P.A.Siple⟩

freedwoman \'⸗,⸗⸗\ *n, pl* **freedwomen :** a woman freed from slavery

free economy *n* **:** an economy that is based upon the principles of private enterprise and has a minimum of governmental restrictions — compare FREE ENTERPRISE; PLANNED ECONOMY

free electron *n* **1 :** an electron within a conducting substance (as a metal) but not permanently attached to any atom **2 :** an electron moving in a vacuum

free endpaper *n* **:** the inner leaf of an endpaper secured at its binding edge to the first or last page of a book and forming a flyleaf

free energy *n* **1 :** the part of the energy of a portion of matter that may be changed without change of volume **:** internal thermodynamic potential **2 :** AVAILABLE ENERGY

free enterprise *n* **1 :** an economic system in which primary reliance is placed upon private business operating in competitive markets to satisfy consumer demands and to maintain equilibrium in the national economy and in which government action in this respect is restricted to protecting the rights of individuals rather than acting as a directing economic force **2 :** a business enterprise operating under free enterprise

free fall *n* **1 a :** the fall through the air of a body free from guidance or restraint in falling (as from a parachute) **b :** the part of a parachute jump before the parachute opens **2 :** the condition of unrestrained motion in a gravitational field (as when the power that drives a rocket in flight is shut off)

free fantasia *n* **:** the development section of a piece of music composed in the sonata form

free field *n* **:** a sound-wave field devoid of obstacles causing reflection, refraction, or diffraction

free fishery *n* **:** an exclusive privilege of fishing in public waters that is derived from governmental grant and is independent of the soil

free flight *n* **:** the flight (as of a rocket) after the power is shut off

free-floating \'⸗¦⸗⸗\ *adj* **1 a :** relatively unattached or attached by a device that allows relatively free movement **:** moving or capable of moving in almost any direction ⟨a *free-floating* tone arm on a phonograph⟩ **b :** relatively uncommitted (as to a system of ideas or a particular purpose) ⟨was not sure how any of the *free-floating* intellectuals would vote⟩ **2 :** felt as an emotion without apparent cause ⟨*free-floating* anxiety⟩

¹free-for-all \¦frēfə¦(r)ȯl\ *adj* **1 :** unrestricted as to entries, participants, or users ⟨a *free-for-all* race⟩ ⟨a *free-for-all* discussion⟩ ⟨*free-for-all* use of patents during wartime⟩ **2 a :** constituting a free-for-all ⟨a *free-for-all* fight waged for several days over the passage of the law⟩ **b :** observing no rules or restrictions ⟨the game was *free-for-all* with no holds barred⟩

²free-for-all \'⸗⸗,⸗\ *n* -s **1 :** a discussion, fight, or brawl unrestricted as to participants and usu. bound by no special rules ⟨the debate on the controversial bill was a *free-for-all*⟩ ⟨got into a *free-for-all* in a back alley with some thugs and had a tooth knocked out⟩ **2 :** an altercation that has got out of control ⟨the moderator at the town meeting raised the controversial issue and in five minutes the discussion became a *free-for-all*⟩

free form *n* **:** an asymmetrical biomorphic and usu. nonrectilinear shape used in works of art or of design esp. of the 20th century and found typically in the works of the 20th century painters Hans Arp and Joan Miró

free-form \'⸗¦⸗\ *adj* **:** of, relating to, or having the characteristics of a free form ⟨a *free-form* contour⟩ ⟨*free-form* art⟩ ⟨a *free-form* coffee table⟩ ⟨a *free-form* swimming pool⟩

free frank *n* **:** a postal frank indicating free postage

free gold *n* **:** gold held in excess of legal reserve requirements or gold certificates held by the U. S. Federal Reserve system over the required minimum set as backing for Federal Reserve notes and member-bank deposits

free goods *n pl* **1 :** goods admitted into a country free of duty **2 :** goods not subject to seizure in time of war **3 :** goods having utility but accessible in such abundance as to possess no economic value

free gratis *adv (or adj)* **:** without cost **:** FREE, GRATIS — not often in formal use ⟨the car was given *free gratis* to anyone guessing the right number⟩ ⟨souvenirs were *free gratis*⟩

free gunnery *n* **:** FLEXIBLE GUNNERY

¹freehand \'⸗,⸗\ *adj* [¹*free* + *hand*] **1 :** executed without mechanical aids or devices ⟨a ~ sketch of a child⟩ ⟨took a course in ~ drawing⟩ ⟨~ grinding⟩ ⟨~ lettering⟩ **2 a :** not conforming strictly to an established or conventional form or pattern **:** FREE ⟨matching ribbon four inches wide makes a vast ~ X under one side of the bosom —Lois Long⟩ ⟨the procedure he used was a ~ adaptation of the one he had developed in his most recent experiments with dogs —Berton Roueché⟩ **b :** UNRESTRAINED ⟨the wealth of inspiration in the ~ imagination and fantasy of these mountaineers —Sacheverell Sitwell⟩ ⟨settled down to ~ drinking —Martin Quigley⟩

²freehand \"\ *adv* [¹*freehand*] **:** in a freehand manner ⟨drew a sketch ~⟩

free hand \'⸗¦⸗\ *n* [¹*free* + *hand*] **:** freedom of action or decision ⟨gave him a *free hand* in running the business⟩

freehanded \'⸗¦⸗⸗\ *adj* **1 :** OPENHANDED, LIBERAL, GENEROUS ⟨for he was as ~ a young fellow as any in the army —W.M. Thackeray⟩ **2 :** FREEHAND ⟨a ~ drawing of a child⟩ ⟨dealing in pretty ~ overstatement⟩ — **free·hand·ed·ly** *adv*

free handicap *n* **:** a handicap in horse racing in which no liability for entrance money, stake, or forfeit is incurred until the weight assigned has been accepted explicitly or by default

freehearted \'⸗¦⸗⸗\ *adj* [ME *fre herted*, fr. *fre* free + *herted* hearted] **1 :** FRANK, OPEN, UNRESERVED **2 :** GENEROUS, LIBERAL — **free·heart·ed·ly** *adv*

¹freehold \'⸗,⸗\ *n* [ME *frehold* (trans. of AF *fraunc tenement* frank tenement), fr. *fre* free + *hold* (n.)] **1 a :** a tenure of real property by which an estate of inheritance in fee simple or fee tail or for life is held **b :** an estate held by such tenure — compare ²FEE 1 **2 :** a tenure of an office or dignity similar to a freehold

²freehold \"\ *adv* **:** by freehold ⟨he owns, ~, an estate which is rich, though unimproved —Ian Watt⟩

free·hold·er \'⸗,⸗ə(r)\ *n* [ME *freholder* (trans. of AF *fraunc tenaunt* frank tenant), fr. *fre* free + *holder*] **1 :** the owner of a freehold **2 :** a public officer in New Jersey serving on a board that has charge of the property, finances, and affairs of a county and being similar to a county commissioner or supervisor

free house *n* **:** a British inn or public house not committed to the purchase of supplies from a particular brewery

free-in-county \¦⸗⸗¦⸗⸗\ *adj* **:** mailable free of postage when sent to an address within the county where printed — used of second-class mail matter and specif. newspapers

freeing *pres part of* FREE

freeing port *n* [fr. gerund of *free*] **:** an opening covered by a hinged plate in the lower part of the bulwarks of a ship to allow deck water to run overboard

free kick *n* **:** a kick in football (as after a safety) that the opponents may not block but may run back after receiving

free kirk *n, cap F&K, Scot* **:** FREE CHURCH 2a

free kirker *n, usu cap F&K* **:** a member or adherent of the Free Church of Scotland

free·lage \'frēlij\ *n* -s [ME (Sc) *frelage*, fr. ME *fre* free + ME (northern dial.) *-lage* (as in *knawlage*, n., knowledge)] *dial Brit* **:** FREEDOM, FRANCHISE

free lance *n* [¹*free* + *lance*] **1 a :** a knight or roving soldier available for hire by a state or commander **:** FREE COMPANION, CONDOTTIERE **b :** one who acts on his own responsibility without regard to party lines or deference to authority **2 :** one who pursues a profession or occupation usu. in the arts under no long-term contractual commitments to any one employer or company ⟨the *free lance* works from his own studio, contacting his clients when necessary . . . is paid by the job, and the number and importance of his jobs depends largely on the reputation he has built —*Design*⟩; *esp* **:** a writer who writes stories or articles for the open market with long-term commitments to no one publisher or periodical

¹free-lance \'⸗¦⸗\ *adj* [*free lance*] **:** of, relating to, or befitting a free lance ⟨*free-lance* factual articles —*Americana Annual*⟩ ⟨sold . . . *free-lance* material to newsreel companies —*Current Biog.*⟩ ⟨*free-lance* illustrating —*Print*⟩; *esp* **:** independent or being under no long-term esp. contractual commitment to any person, company, group, or ideology ⟨a *free-lance* writer⟩ ⟨a *free-lance* designer of window displays —*Current Biog.*⟩ ⟨the alliance in this country between *free-lance* intellect and formal political power —*Times Lit. Supp.*⟩ ⟨left shortly for a period of *free-lance* missionary work in Chicago —Carey McWilliams⟩ ⟨a *free-lance* wearing-apparel salesman —*N.Y. Times*⟩ ⟨the *free-lance* or lone-wolf gambler is a survival of the old frontier days —D.W.Maurer⟩

²free-lance \"\ *vb* [*free lance*] *vi* **:** to act as a free lance ⟨spent ten years on the *Times*, until 1924, when he left to *free-lance*; has written novels; has contributed to magazines —Bernard Kalb⟩ **~** *vt* **:** to offer or contract for the purchase of in the manner of a free lance ⟨tried *free-lancing* his sketches in New York and London⟩ ⟨the others still *free-lance* their instrumental talents or sing at churches and with choral groups —Martin Mayer⟩; *esp* **:** to write and submit for publication in the manner of a free-lance writer ⟨he *free-lanced* pieces for British publications⟩

free-lanc·er \"+ə(r)\ *n* [²*free-lance* + *-er*] **:** FREE LANCE; *esp* **:** a free-lance writer

free list *n* **:** a list of persons or things for which no charge is made in circumstances when a charge is usual; *specif* **:** a schedule of commodities admitted to a country free of duty

free-liv·er \'frē'livə(r)\ *n* **:** one who lives with more than usual freedom in the gratification of physical appetites

free-living \'⸗¦⸗⸗\ *adj* **1 :** marked by more than usual freedom in the gratification of physical appetites **2** *biol* **a :** not fixed to a substrate **:** capable of motility **b :** metabolically independent — compare PARASITIC, SYMBIOTIC

freeload \'⸗¦⸗\ *vi* **1 :** to impose upon another's generosity or hospitality (as in entertaining) without sharing in the cost or responsibility involved or without making an effort to return the favor or remove the obligation ⟨big parties attended by ~*ing* pseudo opera stars —John Brooks⟩ **2 :** to take advantage of an opportunity to use without obligation property or facilities belonging to another (as a club) ⟨~*ing* public servants who dote on hauling their relatives all over the lot at public expense —*Time*⟩ — **free·load·er** \"+ə(r)\ *n* -s

freeloading *n* [fr. gerund of *freeload*] **:** the activity or practice of one that freeloads ⟨undertakes to instruct the narrator in the arts of ~ and benign swindling —*New Yorker*⟩

free love *n* **1 :** sexual intercourse or cohabitation without a legal wedding — compare COMMON-LAW MARRIAGE **2 :** the doctrine that advocates the legalization of free love

free lunch *n* **:** a buffet lunch formerly available in certain bars or saloons to those buying drinks

free·ly *adv* [ME *frely*, fr. OE *frēolīce*, fr. *frēolic*, adj., free, freeborn, noble, fr. *frēo* free + *-lic* -ly] **:** in a free manner: as **a :** of one's own accord **:** WILLINGLY ⟨he ~ shared his supply with the needy settlers about him —*Amer. Guide Series: N.H.*⟩ ⟨asserts its intention to become a member of the international organizations of the free world and ~ undertakes to participate in the European Defense Community —*Current History*⟩ **b** (1) **:** not in bondage **:** in freedom (2) **:** by free men ⟨~ elected governments —C. E. Black & E. C. Helmreich⟩ **c** (1) **:** without restraint or reserve **:** PLENTIFULLY, ABUNDANTLY ⟨a ~ growing plant⟩ ⟨gave out largesse ~⟩ (2) **:** OPENLY, FRANKLY ⟨sometimes spoken my opinion of him, and to him, too ~ —Jane Austen⟩ ⟨he came to admit ~ that the future belonged to the man of statistics and economics —M.R.Cohen⟩ **d :** without hindrance **:** UNCONSTRAINEDLY ⟨its doors swing ~ open to all who come —*Amer. Guide Series: N.H.*⟩ ⟨within a few years the world's major currencies would be ~ convertible, freed from exchange restrictions —Fritz Machlup⟩ ⟨the wood burns fiercely and ~ in a pile —*Sydney (Australia) Bull.*⟩ **e :** with freedom from strict observance of any model, pattern, convention, or rule ⟨the detail is ~ executed —*Amer. Guide Series: Minn.*⟩ ⟨a ~ flowing line⟩

free·man \'frēmən, -,man, -,maa(ə)n\ *n, pl* **freemen** [ME *freman*, fr. OE *frēoman*, fr. *frēo* free + *man*, *mann* man] **1 a :** one not subject to the will of another; *specif* **:** one not a slave or vassal **b :** one enjoying civil or political liberty **2 :** one having the freedom of a company or municipality **:** a member of a corporation or company or one with the full rights of a citizen

free market *n* **:** an economic market operating by free competition **:** an economic condition of unrestricted buying and selling

free·mar·tin \'frē,mär|tᵊn, -mȧ|, |d·ən, |tən\ *n* [prob. fr. ¹*free* + *-martin* (perh. alter. of *mart* beef animal fattened for slaughter) — more at MART] **:** a sexually imperfect usu. sterile female calf twinborn with a male; *also* **:** a similar female of another species

free·ma·son \'frē¦māsᵊn\ *n* [ME *fremason*, fr. *fre* free + *mason*] **1** *obs* **:** one of a class of itinerant skilled masons of medieval and early modern times who formed associations and had secret signs as means of recognition **2** *usu cap* **:** a member of a widespread secret society called Free and Accepted Masons made up of persons who are united for fraternal purposes — called also *Mason*

free·ma·son·ry \-nrē, -ri\ *n* [ME *fremasonry*, fr. *fremason* + *-ry*] **1** *obs* **:** the craft or labor of a freemason **2** *usu cap* **:** the principles, institutions, or practices of Freemasons — called also *Masonry* **3 :** natural or instinctive fellowship or sympathy ⟨that feeling of participation in the ~ of the sea that sets the seaman apart from the ordinary chap —Peter Heaton⟩ ⟨there is no ~ like the passion for books, unless it be that of love —J.C.Snaith⟩

free methodist *n, usu cap F&M* **:** a member of a fundamentalist Methodist group organized in 1860 and dedicated to Wesleyan simplicity and an experience by each member of complete renewal in holiness

¹free milling *n* **:** the treatment of gold or silver ore by crushing and amalgamation

²free milling *adj, of gold or silver ore* **:** lending itself to free milling **:** in native form and easily amalgamated or cyanided

free-minded \'⸗¦⸗⸗\ *adj* **:** having a mind free from care

free miner *n* **:** a person or association holding a purchased, limited, revocable, and renewable mining license under Canadian Dominion laws and British Columbia provincial laws and thereby authorized to prospect on unoccupied lands and to carry on mining operations subject to other conditions imposed by the law

freend \'frēnd\ *Scot var of* FRIEND

free·ness *n* -ES [ME *frenesse*, fr. *fre* free + *-nesse* -ness] **:** FREEDOM

free nuclear stage *n* **:** an early stage in the development of a female gametophyte or an embryo of most gymnosperms in which repeated nuclear divisions occur without cell-wall formation

free on board *adv (or adj)* **:** without charge for delivery to and placing on board a carrier at a specified point — abbr. *f.o.b.*

free oscillation *n* **1 :** the oscillation of a body or system with its own natural frequency and under no external influence other than the impulse that initiated the motion — called also *free vibration;* opposed to *forced oscillation* **2 :** damped alternating current produced by an electric impulse in a circuit but flowing while no external electromotive force is being applied

free overside *or* **free overboard** *adv (or adj)* **:** EX SHIP

free paper *n* **:** a certificate of manumission issued to freed slaves — usu. used in pl.

free part *n* **:** an independent part of a canon or fugue added to fill out the harmony

free pass *n* **:** ³PASS 4d

free path *n* **:** MEAN FREE PATH

free perspective *n* **:** intentional falsification of perspective (as in painting or stage designing) for a particular effect such as the illusion of great depth or distance

free piston *n* **:** a combination of two pistons that are usu. of different diameters, are rigidly attached to the same piston rod, work in different cylinders without external connection, and are used in some pumps and pressure gauges

free place *n* **:** a scholarship granting free tuition in a British secondary school

free plac·er \'frē¦plāsə(r)\ *n* [*free place* + *-er*] **:** a secondary-school student holding a free place

free play *n* **:** unrestricted movement, activity, or interplay ⟨*free play* was being given to private enterprise and individual initiative —*Americana Annual*⟩

free port *n* **:** FOREIGN-TRADE ZONE

¹freer *comparative of* FREE

²freer \'fre(ə)r\ *archaic Scot var of* FRIAR

³fre·er \'frēə(r), 'fri(ə)r, -iə\ *n* -s [²*free* + *-er*] **:** one that frees ⟨the ~ of the slaves⟩

free radical *n* **:** an atom or a group of atoms [as triphenylmethyl $(C_6H_5)_3C\cdot$ or hydroxyl $OH\cdot$] characterized by the presence of at least one unpaired electron and held to participate in many reactions (as polymerization and reactions in biological systems)

free rate *n* **:** the quotation established for a currency in the free foreign-exchange market as distinguished from the restricted or official rate

free reach *n* **:** a sailing reach with the wind abaft the beam

free reed *n* **:** a reed in a musical wind instrument whose edges do not overlap the edges of the opening over which it is fixed and that is used typically in the harmonium or concertina — compare BEATING REED

free rein *n* **:** unrestricted liberty of action or decision ⟨the dictator had *free rein* to do as he pleased⟩

free ride *n* **1 :** a benefit (as food, entertainment, or acclaim) gained or accepted at another's expense or without cost to or effort by the one benefiting **2 a :** a subscription to a new security offering with the hope that the bonds or shares allotted can be sold out at a profit before actual payment is made **b :** a speculation on a very thin margin or where a quick profit seems assured by government or other action **3 :** the right to receive another card in stud poker without putting any chips in the pot

free rider *n* **:** one who gets or tries to benefit by a free ride ⟨tried to run a restaurant but failed because of too many friends who were *free riders*⟩; *specif* **:** a worker who enjoys the benefits derived from a union contract and activities without becoming a member of the union

free run *also* **free run wine** *n* **:** wine consisting of juice that ran freely from the pomace after fermentation without being pressed out

frees *pres 3d sing of* FREE

free sample *n* **:** a usu. small and packaged portion of merchandise distributed free esp. as an introduction to potential customers

free service *n* [ME *fre service* (trans. of ML *liberum servitium*), fr. *fre* free + *service, servise* service] *old English law* **:** one of such feudal services as were not unbecoming the character of a soldier or a freeman to perform (as to serve under his lord in war) — usu. used in pl.

free ship *n* **:** a ship of a neutral nation free from capture in time of war even though carrying an enemy's goods — compare CONTRABAND OF WAR

free·sia \ˈfrēzh(ē)ə, -zēə\ *n* [NL, fr. F.H.T.*Freese* †1876 Ger. physician + NL *-ia*] **1** *cap* **:** a genus of sweet-scented African herbs (family Iridaceae) with bulbous tunicate corms and narrow funnelform or tubular red, white, or yellow flowers **2** -s **:** any plant of the genus *Freesia*

free silver *n* **1 :** the free coinage of silver often at a fixed ratio with gold **2 :** the advocacy of or political philosophy favoring free silver

free skating *n* **:** figure skating esp. in competition in which the skater executes skating figures or steps in an arrangement of his own devising to music of his own choice

free socage *n* [ME *fre socage* (trans. of ML *socagium liberum*), fr. *fre* free + *socage*] **:** a free tenure of land held by services of an honorable but not spiritual, military, or serviential nature — called also *free and common socage*

free soil *n* [¹*free* + *soil*] **1 :** an area in which slavery is prohibited; *esp* **:** U. S. territory where prior to the Civil War slavery was prohibited — compare SLAVE STATE **2 :** free-soil principles or beliefs

free-soil \ˈ=ˌ=\ *adj* [*free soil*] **1 :** of, relating to, or advocating the prohibiting of the extension of slavery to the territories of the U. S. prior to the Civil War **2** *usu cap F&S* **:** of or belonging to the Free-Soil party which was active during the period 1848–54 in opposing the extension of slavery to the territories of the U. S. and the admission of slave states into the Union

free-soil·er \ˈ=ˈsȯilə(r)\ *n, usu cap F&S* [*free soil* + *-er*] **:** one that is in favor of free soil or a member of the Free-Soil party

free-soil·ism \-ˌlizəm\ *n* -s *usu cap F&S* [*free soil* + *-ism*] **:** the advocacy of free soil

free speech *n* **:** FREEDOM OF SPEECH ⟨the first amendment to the Constitution guarantees *free speech*⟩

free-spoken \ˈ=ˈ==\ *adj* **:** speaking freely **:** OUTSPOKEN

free spool *n* **:** the spool of a fishing reel equipped with a device that allows the spool to revolve without any tension on the line (as in the process of casting or trolling)

free-spool \ˈ=ˈ=\ *vt* **:** to set a device controlling the free spool of (a fishing reel) to permit the line to unreel without tension

freest *superlative of* FREE

freestanding \ˈ=ˈ==\ *adj* **:** standing alone and on its own foundation free of architectural or supporting frame or attachment ⟨a ~ wall⟩ ⟨a ~ stairway⟩ ⟨a piece of ~ sculpture⟩

free state *n, usu cap F&S* **:** a state of the U.S. in which slavery was prohibited before the Civil War

free-state man *n* **:** a resident of Kansas who was opposed to slavery in the territory before its admission to the union

free stater \ˈ=ˌstād·ə(r), -ātə-\ *n, cap F&S* **1 :** a native or resident white of the former Orange Free State **2 a :** a native or inhabitant of the Irish Free State **b :** one professing allegiance to the Irish Free State rather than to an Irish republic **3 :** MARYLANDER

¹**freestone** \ˈ=ˌ=\ *n* [ME *freston*, fr. *fre* free + *stoon, ston* stone] **1 :** a stone (as sandstone or limestone) that may be cut freely in any direction without splitting **2** [¹*free* + *stone*] **a :** a fruit stone to which (as in certain varieties of peach, plum, or cherry) the flesh does not cling **b :** a fruit having such a stone — compare CLINGSTONE **3 :** a pale orange yellow that is yellower, less strong, and slightly lighter than sunset and yellower and less strong than peachblow — called also *Bath stone, Caen stone*

²**freestone** \"\ *or* **freestone water** *n* **:** water containing little or no dissolved substances (as calcium)

freestyle \ˈ=ˌ=\ *n, often attrib* **:** a race in which a contestant uses a style (as of swimming) of his choice instead of a specified style (as a breaststroke) to be used by all entrants ⟨the one-mile ~⟩ ⟨the prestige of winning the ~ —Shelley Mann⟩ ⟨~ skating⟩

free·styl·er \ˈ=ˌstīlə(r)\ *n* **:** a competitive swimmer noted for his ability in freestyle events

free-swimming \ˈ=ˈ==\ *adj* **:** able to swim about **:** not attached

free-swinging \ˈ=ˈ==\ *adj* **:** bold, forthright, and heedless of personal consequences or feelings ⟨a *free-swinging* soldier of fortune —Will Herberg⟩ ⟨an energetic, *free-swinging* examination of every facet of the present American educational system —*Saturday Rev.*⟩ ⟨a wrathful, indignant, and *free-swinging* account of the town's crime —Herman Kogan⟩

¹**freet** \ˈfrāt, ˈfrēt\ *var of* FREIT

²**freet** \ˈfrēt\ *dial Brit var of* ¹FRET 1

free-tailed bat \ˈ=ˌ=-\ *n* **:** a bat of the families Emballonuridae or Molossidae in which the tail is more or less independent of the posterior portion of the flight membrane

free tenement *n* [ME *fre tenement* (trans. of AF *fraunc tenement* frank tenement), fr. *fre* free + *tenement*] *English law* **:** a freehold tenement

freethinker \ˈ=ˈ==\ *n* **1 :** one that forms opinions (as about religious matters) on the basis of reason independently of authority; *esp* **:** one whose beliefs differ markedly from those of an established religion usu. in the direction of skepticism or denial of established belief ⟨was far from being a religious skeptic ⟨he scorned ~s, and was passionately devoted to the example of Christ —*Time*⟩ **2 :** AGNOSTIC **syn** see AGNOSTIC

¹**freethinking** \ˈ=ˈ==\ *n* [¹*free* + *thinking*, n.] **:** the beliefs of a freethinker ⟨seduced by the intellectual charms of utopian socialism and atheistic ~ —G.L.Kline⟩

²**freethinking** \"\ *adj* [³*free* + *thinking*, adj.] **:** holding the beliefs or engaging in the reasoning of a freethinker ⟨discoveries made and offered to a ~ democracy are the basis of tomorrow's decisions —A.A.Berle⟩ ⟨reared in liberal and ~ circles —*Amer. Guide Series: Tenn.*⟩ ⟨under both church and ~ auspices —Oscar Handlin⟩

free thought *n* **:** free thinking or unorthodox thought; *specif* **:** 18th century deism ⟨the line between tutelage and *free thought* varies from individual to individual —G.B.Shaw⟩ ⟨heresies naturally grew also; orthodox thought was followed by *free thought* —G.G.Coulton⟩

free throw *n* **:** an unhindered shot in basketball that is made from behind a line established for the purpose and usu. because of a foul by an opponent and that if successful counts one point — compare BASKET; see BASKETBALL illustration

free time *n* **:** a period allowed shippers or consignees to load or unload cargo before demurrage or storage charges accrue

free trade *n* **1 a :** trade based upon the unrestricted international exchange of goods with tariffs used only as a source of revenue not as instruments to influence the quantity, direction, or price of goods traded **b :** the principles or policy advocating such unrestricted trade — compare PROTECTION 4b **2** *chiefly Scot* **:** SMUGGLING

free trader \ˈ=ˈtrādə(r)\ *n* [¹*free* + *trader*] **1 :** a trader among the American Indians who was not in the service of a trading company **2** [*free trade* + *-er*] **:** one that practices, supports, or advocates free trade

free-trade zone *n* **:** FOREIGN-TRADE ZONE

free union *n* [trans. of F *union libre*] **:** cohabitation without marriage

free variable *n* **:** a variable whose range is not restricted by quantification

free variation *n* **:** use or usability in the same environment by different speakers or in different utterances of linguistic items that are perceptually different but semantically the same and idiomatically normal (as using either an unreleased or a released \t\ in *cat* or using either \wit͟h\ or \with\ for *with*)

free verse *n* [trans. of F *vers libre*] **:** verse whose meter is irregular in some respect or whose rhythm is not metrical

free vibration *n* **:** FREE OSCILLATION

free water *n* **:** water that is free: **a :** water that will settle from oil rapidly **b :** water in ore analysis that is not in chemical combination with mineral matter **c :** ground water free to move in response to gravity — called also *gravitational water*

freeway \ˈ=ˌ=\ *n* **1 :** an expressway with fully controlled access **2 :** a toll-free highway — compare PARKWAY, TURNPIKE

¹**freewheel** \ˈ=ˈ=\ *n* **1 :** a power-transmission system in a motor vehicle comprising an overrunning clutch that is interposed between the gearbox mechanism and the final drive and that makes the connection for a positive drive between the engine shaft and propeller shaft but permits the propeller shaft to run freely when its speed is greater than that of the engine shaft **2 :** a clutch that is fitted in the rear hub of a bicycle and that engages the rear sprocket with the rear wheel when the pedals are rotated forward and permits the rear wheel to run on free from the rear sprocket when the pedals are stopped or rotated backward — compare COASTER BRAKE

²**freewheel** \"\ *vi* **1 a :** to run freely independently of a gear by the use of a freewheel — used of a bicycle, bicyclist, or motor vehicle ⟨he ~ed down the long hill —Bruce Marshall⟩ **b** *of a clutch* **:** to operate like a freewheel **2 :** to move, act, live, or drift along freely, independently, or irresponsibly or heedless of rules, responsibilities, or consequences

free·wheel·er \"+ə(r)\ *n* **:** one that freewheels; *esp* **:** a freewheeling bicycle or motor vehicle

¹**freewheeling** *n* [fr. gerund of ²*freewheel*] **:** the action of one (as a bicycle) that freewheels

²**freewheeling** *adj* [fr. pres. part. of ²*freewheel*] **:** befitting one that freewheels **:** relatively heedless of forms, rules, responsibilities, or consequences ⟨a ~ logic —Stanley Newman⟩ ⟨reverting to . . . ~ foolishness —*Time*⟩ ⟨roams about the West in ~ style —John McCarten⟩ ⟨~ generalities —*New Yorker*⟩ ⟨a God-sent warning of his ~ grammar and spelling —Bice Clemow⟩ — **freewheelingness** *n* -ES

free will *n* [ME *fre wil*, fr. *fre* free + *wil, will* will, n.] **1 :** the power asserted of moral beings of willing or choosing within certain limitations or with respect to certain matters without the restraints of physical or divinely imposed necessity or outside causal law **:** spontaneous will or partially causeless volition **2 :** the ability to choose between alternative possibilities in such a way that the choice and action are to some extent creatively determined by the conscious subject at the time

freewill \ˈ=ˈ=\ *adj* [*free will*] **1 :** of or belonging to free will **:** VOLUNTARY, SPONTANEOUS ⟨a ~ offering⟩ **2** *cap* **:** of or relating to Freewill Baptists ⟨*Freewill* churches⟩

freewill baptist *n, usu cap F&B* **:** a member of one of three Baptist groups including an original group and dissenting Bullockites and United American Freewill Baptists that hold Arminian doctrines and observe open communion and except among the Bullockites usu. foot washing and anointing

free-will·er \ˈ=ˈwilə(r)\ *n* **1 :** a believer in or advocate of a doctrine of free will **:** LIBERTARIAN **2 :** FREEWILL BAPTIST

free-will·ist \-ləst\ *n* -s **:** FREE-WILLER 1

freewill offering *n* **:** a voluntary religious offering made in addition to what is required by a vow, tithe, or pledge ⟨she preached on shipboard and a *freewill offering* from the passengers enabled her to get back east —M.L.Bach⟩

freez·able \ˈfrēzəbəl\ *adj* **:** capable of or susceptible to being frozen

¹**freeze** \ˈfrēz\ *vb* **froze** \ˈfrōz\ *or dial* **friz** \ˈfriz\ **fro·zen** \ˈfrōzᵊn\ *or chiefly dial* **froze** *or dial* **friz**; **freezing**; **freezes** [ME *fresen*, fr. OE *frēosan*; akin to OHG *friosan* to freeze, ON *frjōsa* to freeze, Goth *frius* coldness, L *pruina* hoarfrost, Skt *pruṣvā* drop of water, ice] *vi* **1 a :** to become congealed into ice by cold ⟨fresh water ~s at 32° Fahrenheit⟩ **b :** to become hardened into a solid body by the abstraction of heat ⟨the melting was done in an Arsem vacuum furnace and the molten metal allowed to ~ slowly —*Jour. of Research*⟩ **2 a :** to become chilled with cold **:** be very cold ⟨the furnace went out and we *froze* trying to get it going again⟩; *also* **:** to suffer loss of animation or life by lack of heat ⟨the lost climber became exhausted and almost *froze* to death⟩ **b :** to become coldly formal in manner **:** act coldly ⟨the hostess *froze* and avoided us during the party⟩ **c :** to cause loss of sensitivity in or to anesthetize a part esp. by cold ⟨some dentists prefer *freezing* to the administering of gas before tooth extraction⟩ **3 a :** to remain solidly in contact or affixed by reason of freezing — used with *to* ⟨the damp clothes *froze* to the clothesline⟩ **b :** to adhere solidly or stay immovably fixed — used with *to* ⟨the brake shoe *froze* to the brake drum⟩ ⟨a large nut to be removed had *frozen* to its bolt —G.F.Burnley⟩ ⟨under pressure and movement, two clean metal surfaces . . . will weld or ~ together, often with severe consequences —C.H. Hack⟩ **c :** to grip very tightly (as from fear) — used with *to* ⟨the terrified driver *froze* to the wheel⟩ **d** (1) *of a billiard or pool ball* **:** to come to rest in contact with another ball or with a cushion (2) *of a curling stone* **:** to come to rest against another stone **4 a :** to have its liquid content freeze **:** become clogged with ice ⟨in the winter the water pipes *froze*⟩ ⟨so cold the car radiator *froze*⟩ **b** *of a car* **:** to have the radiator liquid freeze ⟨we left the car out all night and it *froze*⟩ **5 :** to become motionless as if suddenly frozen: **a :** to stand or remain without movement or activity of any kind ⟨at the least sign of alarm, ~ in your tracks and don't move a muscle —*Boy Scout Handbook*⟩; *esp* **:** to become incapable of acting or speaking (as from fright) ⟨when I put a mike in front of her she'd ~ —Pete Martin⟩ — often used with *up* **b :** to become fixed and unalterable ⟨a perceptible tendency for the techniques of microprinting to ~ at present levels —H.M.Silver⟩ **c** *of a mechanism or moving part* **:** to cease to function or to resist movement by reason of jamming, locking, or damage **:** stick in operation ⟨the intense heat caused too great an expansion and the piston *froze* in the cylinder⟩ ⟨the speedometer *froze* at 90 miles an hour when the car overturned⟩ **6 :** to become fixed and motionless or unalterable as if by freezing ⟨the whole crowd had *frozen* into fascinated attention —Dorothy Sayers⟩ ⟨his anger *froze* in his face⟩ ⟨smiles which readers prepare for his latest effort may ~ on their faces —Laurent LeSage⟩ ~ *vt* **1 a :** to harden into ice **:** convert from a liquid to a solid by cold ⟨the low temperature *froze* the water in the birdbath⟩ **b :** to clog with ice ⟨the intense cold *froze* the water pipes⟩ **c** (1) **:** to subject in storage to a temperature below freezing ⟨~ meat to preserve it during the summer⟩ (2) **:** to subject (food packages) to intense cold and solidification into a block like ice for preservation ⟨patrons prepared and wrapped meats at home and *froze* them in their lockers —*Pa. State Bull. 433*⟩ **2 a :** to make extremely cold **:** give a sensation of extreme cold or an all-embracing sense of coldness to **:** CHILL ⟨the spectators at the game were *frozen* by the unseasonably low temperature⟩ **b :** to act toward in a stiff and formal unfriendly way **:** discourage or dampen the enthusiasm of by coldness of demeanor ⟨conducted herself with hauteur and *froze* her neighbors⟩ ⟨the director tended to ~ newcomers who stepped out of line⟩ **c :** to cause to act adversely **:** ALIENATE ⟨the object of this book being largely to persuade the prospective reader, and not to ~ him with assumptions of his mental inadequacy —C.D.Lewis⟩ **3 a :** to harden, damage, kill, or have other effect upon by the action of frost ⟨one night of frost *froze* the ground surface solid⟩ ⟨found her annuals in the garden *frozen* and blackened in the morning after the cold night⟩ **b :** to cause loss of animation or life in from lack of heat ⟨the winter struck early and *froze* several tramps sleeping in alleyways⟩ **c :** to anesthetize (a part) by or as if by cold ⟨had the inflamed appendix *frozen* —*Current Biog.*⟩ ⟨a face nicely *frozen* from injections —Monica Stirling⟩ **4 a :** to cause to adhere by or as if by the effect of intense cold ⟨the low temperature *froze* the damp clothes to the line⟩ ⟨the heat of friction *froze* the two metal surfaces together⟩ **b :** to cause (a billiard or pool ball) to come to rest in contact with another ball or with a cushion **c :** to cause to grip tightly or remain in immovable contact as if paralyzed ⟨fear *froze* the pilot to the controls⟩ **5 :** to make or cause to become fixed, immovable, inflexible, or unalterable: as **a :** to cause to stand or remain rigidly motionless ⟨the sudden noise *froze* the animal in an attitude of fright⟩ ⟨the sound of her name . . . *froze* her on the bottom step —Berton Roueché⟩ ⟨it isn't fear-paralysis that keeps a rabbit *frozen* in its squat at the sound of a shot —*Sydney (Australia) Bull.*⟩ **b :** to fix securely, permanently, or irremovably ⟨premature choices tend to lead you into, and ~ you in, occupations which will be inadequately rewarding spiritually —H.M.Wriston⟩ ⟨he had concluded that the city-manager plan would tend to ~ in office whoever won the first election —Darrell Garwood⟩ **c :** to harden into inflexibility or convert as if by hardening into a rigid unchanging form ⟨his mind shut hard . . . upon his first impressions and *froze* them to unalterable convictions —Virginia Woolf⟩ ⟨most social planning to date aims essentially to ~ most of the existing cultural values —A.L.Kroeber⟩ ⟨a scholastic tendency to ~ our concepts of a writer's life —Jay Leyda⟩ ⟨tend to ~ his message into an orthodoxy —André Martinet⟩ **d :** to fix so as to maintain unaltered in form, condition, or relationship: (1) **:** to stop any further alteration in ⟨a system of rules which ~s a social position and keeps one class or race on top of another —Philip Mason⟩ ⟨~ designs and go into production on current aircraft models —*Newsweek*⟩ ⟨that all unresolved problems . . . be *frozen* for ten years during which concerted efforts would be made to seek permanent peaceful solutions —*N.Y. Times*⟩ ⟨*freezing* the status quo —A.H.Vandenberg †1951⟩ (2) **:** to fix inflexibly (as by executive order) at a point or in a status governing or prevailing on a particular day ⟨~ the price on essential commodities⟩ ⟨~ wages as of the last pay period⟩ (3) **:** to forbid further manufacture, use, or sale of (a raw material) (4) **:** to immobilize by governmental regulation or legislation the expenditure, withdrawal, or exchange of (foreign-owned bank balances) — compare BLOCK *vt* 1h (5) **:** to forbid (a worker) to leave or change a job (6) **:** to counteract the growth, expansion, or development of ⟨the older generation was trying to ~ the country and make it static —Hugh MacLennan⟩ (7) **:** to prevent the use of (money) by tying up (as in capital stock or inventory) ⟨the amount of additional capital *frozen* into the inventory of every tire or oil outlet by the new taxes —T.H.White b. 1915⟩ ⟨another step to *free frozen* money —P.J.O'Brien⟩ **6 a :** to make (as the face) expressionless ⟨with instructions to recognize no one; and in fact he did ~ his face up when an old acquaintance hailed him —Fletcher Pratt⟩ ⟨a look of incredulity *froze* his face . . . and his eyes went blank with surprise —Hamilton Basso⟩ **b :** to preserve rigidly a particular expression on ⟨he still sat, his face *frozen* in shame and misery —Agnes S. Turnbull⟩ **7 :** to make inaccessible **:** prevent access to or use of ⟨police chiefs here and there are constantly *freezing* their records to protect someone —*Quill*⟩ **8 a :** to photograph as static a single point in (fast action) or in the action of (something in fast motion) ⟨pictures made with speedlights . . . ~ action completely —Bruce Downes⟩ ⟨the camera . . . is capable of *freezing* the whirring of a moving fan blade —*Science News Letter*⟩ ⟨high speed photography that *freezes* bullets in flight —*Time*⟩ **b :** to preserve in a relatively permanent and unalterable form ⟨the tape could ~ the speech of a native and repeat it as often as desired —N.A.McQuown⟩ **9 :** to attempt to keep possession of (a ball or puck) in the closing minutes of play (as in a basketball or hockey game) without an attempt to score in order to protect a small lead ⟨they decided to play a defensive game and ~ the ball —A.J.Liebling⟩ **10 :** to play a wild card on (the discard pile) in canasta and related games — compare FROZEN 2e

²**freeze** \"\ *n* -s [ME *frese*, fr. *fresen*, v. — more at ¹FREEZE] **1 :** a state of weather marked by unusually low temperature esp. when below the freezing point ⟨the ~ . . . destroyed the citrus groves —*Amer. Guide Series: Fla.*⟩ **2 :** an act or instance of freezing **:** the state of being frozen **3 a :** a legislative or administrative and usu. emergency action intended to restrict or forbid something (as the use or manufacture of goods needed in a war effort) or prevent alteration (as in wages, prices, job positions, or manufacturing quotas) ⟨clamped a ~ on certain steel stocks, ordered warehouses to ship them only to defense contractors —*Time*⟩ ⟨the military ~ on multiengine helicopter production —F.B.Lee⟩ ⟨a three-and-a-half-year Federal ~ on station building —*Newsweek*⟩ ⟨a ~ is the logical first technique in price control —T.B.Worsley⟩ ⟨the 60-day temporary ~ of food prices —*Business Week*⟩ **b** *slang* **:** cold and unfriendly treatment **c :** a keeping possession of the ball or puck (as in basketball or hockey) with no effort at scoring often in the last minutes of play in order to prevent scoring by one's opponent ⟨one never knows when the ~ will be needed to stave off the last-minute rally of an opponent —*Athletic Jour.*⟩

freeze-dry \ˈ=ˈ=\ *vt* **:** to dry in a frozen state under high vacuum so that ice or other frozen solvent sublimes rapidly and a porous solid remains **:** LYOPHILIZE

freeze dryer *n* **:** an apparatus used for freeze-drying

freeze-drying *n* -s [fr. gerund of *freeze-dry*] **:** the process by which matter is freeze-dried **:** LYOPHILIZATION

freeze·me·ter \ˈfrēzˌmēd·ə(r)\ *n* [*freeze* + *-meter*] **:** a hydrometer designed to test the strength of antifreeze solutions in automobile radiators

freeze out *vt* [¹*freeze* + *out*] **1 a :** to drive out or exclude by cold ⟨the drop in temperature when the furnace went out *froze out* the club meeting⟩ **b :** to drive out or eliminate from competition or eliminate or exclude from a position of intimacy, significance, influence, or authority esp. by stratagem, by coldly formal rejection, or by force ⟨the depression *froze out* most of his competitors⟩ ⟨the majority stockholders *froze out* the minority and took over the business⟩ ⟨tended to *freeze* out newcomers until their family and educational backgrounds had been ascertained⟩ **2 :** to eliminate from a game of freeze-out

freeze-out \ˈ=ˌ=\ *n* -s [*freeze out*] **1 :** elimination or exclusion by freezing out **2 :** a method of playing poker by which the players start with agreed-upon capital to which they cannot add or from which they can withdraw nothing, each player being forced to drop out of the game as soon as his capital is lost and all stakes thus going to the last remaining player; *also* **:** a poker game played by this method

freeze over *vb* [¹*freeze* + *over*] *vi* **:** to become covered with a layer of ice ⟨the pond *froze over* as early as October⟩ ~ *vt* **:** to cause to become covered with a layer of ice ⟨a single night's cold was enough to *freeze over* the pond⟩

freeze-over \ˈ=ˌ=\ *n* -s [*freeze over*] **:** an instance of freezing over ⟨going skating at the first *freeze-over* on the pond⟩

freeze-proof \ˈ=ˌ=\ *vt* [²*freeze* + *-proof* (as in *waterproof*, v.)] **:** to protect (as shipments of coal) from forming a hard solid mass in cold weather

freez·er \ˈfrēzə(r)\ *n* -s **1 :** one that freezes or keeps very cold: **a :** a hand-operated machine that freezes ice cream **b :** an operator of an ice-cream freezing machine **c :** a railroad refrigerator car **d** (1) **:** an insulated compartment or room equipped to freeze perishable foods rapidly at a temperature of −10° to −30° F to prepare them for storage in a locker at subfreezing temperature (2) **:** a cabinet equipped with both a quick-freezing unit and a storage locker or a single compartment for both quick-freezing and storage esp. for the use of one family — called also *home freezer* (3) **:** a refrigerated room **e :** a food processor who operates a food-freezing plant **2** *Austral* **:** a sheep bred and raised for export as frozen meat **3 :** a tool used in metalcraft for retouching castings **4** *slang* **:** PRISON, JAIL

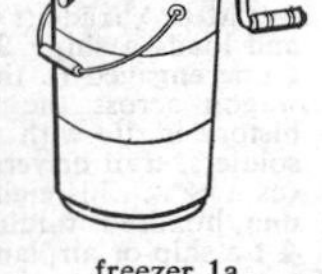
freezer 1a

freezer burn *n* **:** light-colored spots developed in frozen foods (as poultry and meat) as a result of surface evaporation and drying when improperly or inadequately wrapped or packaged

freezer locker *n* **:** a storage unit in a commercial food-freezing plant

freez·er·ship \ˈ==,ship\ *n* **:** a ship designed for the transporting of frozen fish

freezes *pres 3d sing of* FREEZE, *pl of* FREEZE

freeze-up \ˈ=,=\ *n* -S [*freeze up* (verb phrase), fr. ¹*freeze* + *up*] **1 :** a freezing over of a body of water esp. when marking the onset of winter ⟨goes on duty in April, just before the swans arrive, and stays with them until they leave at *freeze-up* —Lyn Harrington⟩ **2 :** a period during which the bodies of water in an area are frozen over ⟨the *freeze-up* lasted six weeks last year⟩ ⟨before the *freeze-up* sets in —V.E.Fuchs⟩ ⟨all their food for seven months had to be taken to camp before the winter *freeze-up* —Bill Wolf⟩

¹**freezing** *adj* [fr. pres. part. of ¹*freeze*] **1 :** being at or below freezing point ⟨the temperature is ~⟩ **2 :** very cold ⟨hurry up and let's get indoors because I'm ~⟩ **3** *of precipitation* **:** falling to earth in a liquid state and then usu. partially freezing on exposed surfaces ⟨a ~ drizzle⟩ ⟨a ~ rain⟩ — **freez·ing·ly** *adv*

²**freezing** *adv* **:** to a freezing degree ⟨~ cold weather⟩

³**freezing** *n* -S [fr. gerund of ¹*freeze*] **:** the method by which foods are frozen to preserve them

freezing mixture *n* [*freezing* fr. gerund of ¹*freeze*] **:** a mixture (as of salt and ice or of dry ice and acetone) for producing intense cold

freezing point *n* [*freezing* fr. gerund of ¹*freeze*] **:** the temperature at which a liquid solidifies; *specif* **:** the temperature at which the liquid and solid states of the substance are in equilibrium at atmospheric pressure **:** MELTING POINT ⟨the *freezing point* of water is 0°C or 32°F⟩

freezing-point law *n* **:** a law of physical chemistry: the freezing point of a dilute binary solution is lower than that of the pure solvent by an amount proportional to the concentration of the solute

freezing process *n* [*freezing* fr. gerund of ¹*freeze*] **1 :** a process of excavating shafts or tunnels in unstable material (as quicksand) by freezing an area larger than the intended work and excavating in the frozen earth **2 :** a method of sinking a shaft through watery strata during the winter by thawing part way through the frozen surface with fire, digging out the softened earth, and then allowing another frozen crust to form and repeating the operations as needed

free zone *n* **:** FOREIGN-TRADE ZONE

freezy \ˈfrēzē\ *adj* -ER/-EST [¹*freeze* + -*y*] *slang* **:** FREEZING

fre·ga·tae \frəˈgā,tē\ *n pl, cap* [NL, fr. pl. of *Fregata*] **:** a suborder of the order Pelecaniformes that is coextensive with the family Fregatidae

fre·gat·i·dae \frəˈgad·ə,dē\ *n pl, cap* [NL, fr. *Fregata*, type genus (fr. F *frégate* frigate bird, frigate) + -*idae*] **:** a family of web-footed sea birds comprising the frigate birds — see FREGATAE

fre·ge·an \ˈfrāgēən\ *adj, usu cap* [Friedrich Ludwig Gottlob *Frege* †1925 Ger. mathematician + E -*an*] **:** of or relating to F. L. Gottlob Frege or his contributions to the development of symbolic logic and the foundations of arithmetic

f region *n, cap F* [¹*f* + *region*] **:** the highest region of the ionosphere occurring from 90 to more than 250 miles above the earth's surface and often splitting in the daytime into two layers whose heights vary — see F_1 LAYER, F_2 LAYER

frei·berg·ite \ˈfrī,bərˌgīt\ *n* -S [G *freibergit*, fr. *Freiberg*, Saxony, Germany, its locality + G -*it* -ite] **:** argentian tetrahedrite

frei·burg \ˈfrī,bərg, -ȯg, *Ger* -bu̇rk\ *adj, usu cap* [*Freiburg* im Breisgau, Germany] **:** of or from the city of Freiburg im Breisgau, Germany **:** of the kind or style prevalent in Freiburg

frei·es·le·ben·ite \ˌfrīəsˈlābə,nīt\ *n* -S [G *freieslebenit*, fr. Johann K. *Freiesleben* †1846 Ger. mineralogist + G -*it* -ite] **:** a mineral $Pb_3Ag_5Sb_5S_{12}$ consisting of a gray metallic-looking sulfide of antimony, lead, and silver

¹**freight** \ˈfrāt, *usu* -ād·+V\ *n* -S *often attrib* [ME, fr. MD or MLG *vracht, vrecht* — more at FRAUGHT] **1 :** the compensation paid for the transportation of goods or for the use of all or part of a ship, train, plane, or other means of such transportation — called also *freightage* **2 a :** something that is loaded for transportation **:** CARGO ⟨an airplane carrying a very heavy ~⟩ — see AIRFREIGHT **b :** LOAD, BURDEN ⟨a man staggering under a ~ of small logs in a basket⟩ ⟨burdened by a ~ of woes⟩ ⟨the silvery blue larkspur bending under a ~ of bees —D.C.Peattie⟩ **3 a :** freight transportation; *specif* **:** the ordinary transportation of goods afforded by a common carrier and distinguished from express usu. by lower rates, deferred dispatch, extra charge for pickup and delivery, or larger volume minimum ⟨~ is less expensive than express⟩ ⟨a ~ charge⟩ ⟨~ service⟩ **b :** a train designed or used for such transportation ⟨a 100-car ~ pounding the rails beside us —Richard Bissell⟩

²**freight** \"\ *vt* -ED/-ING/-S [ME *freighten*, fr. *freight*, n.] **1 a :** to load (as a ship or plane) with goods for transportation **:** furnish with freight ⟨a ship being ~*ed* at the dockside⟩ **b :** to weigh down **:** LOAD, BURDEN ⟨a time . . . so ~*ed* with conflicting and violent emotion —Marya Mannes⟩ ⟨~*ed* with the . . . fears of millions of mankind —A.E.Stevenson †1965⟩ **:** CHARGE ⟨persistent delinquency . . . heavily ~*ed* with neurotic complications —Edwin Powers & Helen Witmer⟩ ⟨every word he spoke was ~*ed* with meaning for the American way of self-government —C.A.Beard⟩ ⟨~*ed* with dark torment and intimate self-revelation —A.M.Schlesinger b.1917⟩; *esp* **:** to charge or burden (as a piece of writing) with significance or meanings esp. too heavily ⟨his gaiety was serious . . . his comedy was ~*ed* —Francis Hackett⟩ ⟨there is a minimum of ~*ed* sermonizing, which usually bores the reader and consequently wastes the message —Siegfried Mandel⟩ ⟨those oddly associated adjectives were ~*ed* for him beyond their usual connotations —F.O.Matthiessen⟩ ⟨his means of expression are so elaborate and so heavily ~*ed* —Winthrop Sargeant⟩ **c :** to make rich (as in hope or joy) ⟨their counsel is ~*ed* with the rich experience of many years of successful work —J.A.O'Brien⟩ ⟨he is ~*ed* with honors which he wears invisibly —Lucien Price⟩ **2 :** to hire or let for transportation of goods or passengers **3 :** to transport, carry, or ship by freight ⟨boats ~*ed* hogsheads of tar to the canal communities —S.H.Adams⟩ ⟨beef, pork, mutton, butter, cheese, and grain were ~*ed* out in winter on sleds —*Amer. Guide Series: Vt.*⟩

³**freight** *adj* [ME, past part. of *freighten* to freight] *obs* **:** LADEN, FRAUGHT

freight·age \ˈfrād·|ij, -āt|, |ēj\ *n* -S **:** FREIGHT

freight agent *n* **:** a carrier employee who receives, forwards, or delivers goods or who represents or directs locally the freight functions of a carrier

freight bill *n* **:** a bill rendered by a carrier to a consignee of freight and containing an identifying description of the freight, the name of the shipper, the point of origin of the shipment, its weight, and the amount of charges

freight bureau *or* **freight conference** *n* **:** a regional organization of carriers that represents all of the participating members in rate and tariff matters and in the publication of tariffs

freight car *n* **:** a railroad car for the transportation of freight

freight claim *n* **:** a demand by a shipper or consignee upon a carrier (as for reimbursement of an overcharge or for loss or damage to goods accepted for transportation)

freight·er \ˈfrād·ə(r), -ātə-\ *n* -S **1 :** one that loads or charters and loads a ship **2 :** one whose business is freighting; *esp* **:** one engaged in the former business of shipping goods by wagon across the western plains of the U.S. ⟨the city's history is rife with stories of the wild behavior of cowboys, soldiers, trail drivers, and ~*s* —*Amer. Guide Series: Texas*⟩ ⟨as a ~ . . . his eight-mule wagon was held up by a band of one hundred raiding Sioux —S.H.Adams⟩ **3 :** SHIPPER **4 :** a ship or airplane used chiefly to carry freight ⟨makes air ~*s* out of conventional commercial aircraft —*N.Y. Times*⟩

freight house *n* **:** a facility owned and operated by a railroad for receiving, delivering, or dispatching freight

freighting *n* -S [ME, fr. *freighten* to freight + -*ing*] **:** the transporting of freight as a business or occupation

freight insurance *n* **:** insurance for indemnifying the policyholder against loss of the freight money if the shipowner cannot complete his contract of carriage because of unavoidable peril

freight rate *n* **:** the charge per unit (as per hundred pounds or per ton) by a carrier for the transportation of cargo generally published in a freight tariff

frei·jo \ˈfrā,jō, (ˈ)frāˈzhō\ *n* -S [modif. of Pg *Frei-Jorge*, lit., friar George, fr. *frei* brother, friar (short for *freire*, fr. OProv *fraire*, fr. L *frater* brother) + *Jorge* George — more at BROTHER] **1 :** the hard strong wood of a timber tree (*Cordia goeldiana*) of the lower Amazon used in pails and casks — called also *Jenny wood* **2 :** the tree that yields freijo

frei·ri·nite \ˈfrāˈrē,nīt\ *n* -S *often cap* [*Freirina*, north central Chile, its locality + E -*ite*] **:** a mineral $Na_3Cu_3(AsO_4)_2(OH)_3.H_2O$ consisting of a basic hydrous arsenate of sodium and copper

freit \ˈfrāt, ˈfrēt\ *n* -S [ME *frete* divination, fr. ON *frētt* news, inquiry; akin to ON *fregna* to inquire, find out — more at PRAY] **1** *chiefly Scot* **:** a superstitious observance or idea ⟨an idle ~⟩ **2** *chiefly Scot* **:** a saying or saw conveying a superstition ⟨an old ~ about the weather⟩ **3** *chiefly Scot* **:** an omen esp. of misfortune

frei test \ˈfrī-\ *n, usu cap F* [after Wilhelm Siegmund *Frei* †1943 Ger. dermatologist] **:** a serologic test for the identification of lymphogranuloma venereum — called also *Frei skin test*

freity \ˈfrād·i, -ēd·i\ *adj* -ER/-EST [*freit* + -*y*] *chiefly Scot* **:** SUPERSTITIOUS

fremd \ˈfremd\ *adj* [ME *fremd, fremde*, fr. OE *fremde*; akin to OHG *fremidi, framadi* strange, Goth *framatheis* strange, belonging to someone else, alienated; all fr. a prehistoric EGmc-WGmc adjective derived from a word represented by OE *fram* from, away — more at FROM] **1** *now chiefly Scot* **:** FOREIGN, UNFAMILIAR **2** *now chiefly Scot* **:** not belonging to one's own family or household **:** UNRELATED — **fremd·ly** *adv* — **fremd·ness** *n* -ES

frem·i·tus \ˈfreməd·əs\ *n* -ES [L, murmur, roar, fr. *fremitus*, past part. of *fremere* to murmur, roar; akin to OE *bremman* to roar, OHG *breman* to murmur, Skt *bhramara* bee] **:** a sensation felt by the hand when it is placed on a part of the body (as the chest) that vibrates during speech

fre·mont cottonwood \ˈfrē,mänt-\ *n, usu cap F* [after John *Frémont* †1890 Am. explorer] **:** a poplar (*Populus fremontii*) of the southwestern U.S. and esp. California and Arizona with whitish bark and deltoid orbicular yellowish green leaves

fre·mon·tia \frəˈmäntēə, frē-, -änch(ē)ə\ *n* [NL, fr. John C. *Frémont* †1890 + NL -*ia*] **1** *cap* **:** a genus of Californian and Mexican shrubs (family Sterculiaceae) with alternate leaves and showy yellow flowers **2** -S **:** any plant of the genus *Fremontia* — see FLANNELBUSH

fre·mon·to·den·dron \frə,män·,tōˈdendrən, frē,-\ [NL, fr. John C. *Frémont* †1890 + NL -*o-* + -*dendron*] *syn of* FREMONTIA

fremont's pine *or* **fremont's nut pine** *n, usu cap F* **:** a pine (*Pinus monophylla*) of the western U.S. with leaves usu. solitary or in pairs

fremont's squirrel *n, usu cap F* **:** a Rocky mountain squirrel (*Sciurus fremonti*) with a conspicuously white-fringed tail

frena *pl of* FRENUM

fre·nal \ˈfrēnᵊl\ *adj* [ISV *fren*um + -*al*] **1 :** of or relating to a frenum **2 :** LORAL

fre·na·tae \ˈfrēnə,tē\ *n pl, cap* [NL, fem. pl. of *frenatus*, having a frenum or frenulum] *in some classifications* **:** a group of Lepidoptera comprising most that have a frenulum and including the butterflies and the majority of the moths

¹**fre·nate** \ˈfrē,nāt\ *adj* [NL *frenatus*, fr. L, bridled, past part. of *frenare* to bridle, fr. *frenum* bridle — more at FRENUM] **:** having a frenum or frenulum

²**frenate** \"\ *adj* [NL *Frenatae*] **:** of or relating to the Frenatae

³**frenate** \"\ *n* -S [NL *Frenatae*] **:** a butterfly or moth of the group Frenatae

¹**french** \ˈfrench\ *adj, usu cap* [ME *french, frensh*, fr. OE *frencisc*, fr. *Franca* Frank + -*isc* -ish] **1 a :** of or belonging to the people, the culture, or the civilization of France ⟨the *French* nation⟩ ⟨the *French* army⟩ ⟨the *French* countryside⟩ **b :** befitting, derived from, or suggesting the people or the culture of France ⟨*French* cooking⟩ ⟨*French* attitudes⟩ **:** made in France or copied from articles designed in or associated with France ⟨a *French* hat⟩ ⟨a *French* fabric⟩ **:** settled by the French ⟨a *French* section of the territory⟩ or made up of French people ⟨a *French* group⟩ **2 :** of, belonging to, or in French ⟨a *French* lesson⟩ ⟨a *French* book⟩ **3 :** of or belonging to the overseas descendants of the French people (as the French Canadians) — **french·ly** *adv, usu cap* — **french·ness** *n* -ES *usu cap*

²**french** \"\ *n, cap* [ME *french, frensh*, fr. OE *frencisc*, fr. *frencisc*, adj.] **1** -ES **:** a Romance language that developed out of the Vulgar Latin of all of Transalpine Gaul except the southern part and that is the vehicle of an important literature at first in a wide variety of dialects with the earliest texts dating from the 9th century and that became in a form based on the Francien dialect the literary and official language of France — see ANGLO-FRENCH, MIDDLE FRENCH, OLD FRENCH, OLD NORTH FRENCH; compare PROVENÇAL **2** *pl in constr* **:** the French people

³**french** \"\ *vb* -ED/-ING/-ES *often cap* [¹*french*] *vt* **1 :** to make French in form **2 :** to prepare in a French manner: as **a :** to cut (snap beans) in strips lengthwise before cooking **b :** to cut off the strip of meat along the bone of (a rib chop) **c :** to cut (a tenderloin) into slices and pound the slices flat before cooking **3** *slang* **:** to engage (someone) in cunnilingus or fellatio ~ *vi* **:** to undergo frenching

french anemone *n, usu cap F* **:** one of several horticultural varieties of the poppy anemone

french arch *n, usu cap F* **:** a masonry construction that consists of bricks laid sloping on each side so as to meet in the center at an angle and that is used instead of a true flat arch

french bean *n, usu cap F* **1** *chiefly Brit* **:** a bean of which the whole young pod is eaten (as a green bean, wax bean) **:** SNAP BEAN **2** *chiefly Brit* **:** KIDNEY BEAN

french beaver *n, usu cap F* **:** European rabbit fur processed to simulate nutria or beaver

french bed *n, usu cap F* **1 :** a bedstead with head and foot rolled outward in scroll form **2 :** a short-sheeted bed

french beige *n, often cap F* **:** a light brown that is darker and slightly yellower than blush, deeper and slightly yellower than alesan, and redder and slightly darker than cork — called also *hopi, sunburn*

french berry *n, usu cap F* **:** AVIGNON BERRY

french blue *n, often cap F* **1 :** a strong purplish blue that is the color of ultramarine prepared artificially — called also *artificial ultramarine, French ultramarine, Gmelin's blue, Guimet's blue, lime blue, new blue, permanent blue* **2 :** ULTRAMARINE 1b

french boston *n, usu cap F* **:** a card game consisting of a variety of boston in which the bidder can either have a partner or play alone

french bowline *n, usu cap F* **:** PORTUGUESE BOWLINE

french bracken *n, usu cap F* **:** ROYAL FERN

french bracket foot *n, usu cap 1st F* **:** a bracket foot marked by simple long S-curve inner lines and slightly concave vertical outer line — see FOOT illustration

french bread *n, usu cap F* [ME *frensh breed*] **1 :** a bread with a crisp crust and little crumbling made with flour, water, salt, and leaven and baked in a stick about 18 inches long **2 :** any of various fancy-shaped breads (as French rolls and crescents)

french brier *n, usu cap F* **:** the root of brier used in pipe manufacturing

french bulldog *n* **1** *usu cap F* **:** a breed of small bat-eared dog that was developed in France supposedly from a crossing of small English bulldogs with native dogs, that is active, muscular, heavy-boned, compactly built, and weighs up to 28 pounds, and that has a large square head with well-defined stop, short nose, and a less prominent underjaw than the English bulldog **2** *often cap F* **:** a dog of the French bulldog breed

french canadian *n, usu cap F&C* [¹*french* + *canadian*, n.] **1 a :** a French settler in Canada — compare ACADIAN, HABITANT **b :** one of the descendants of French settlers in lower Canada now predominating in the population of the province of Quebec but found throughout Canada as well as in New England and along the northern border of the U.S. **2 :** French as spoken in Canada **:** CANADIAN FRENCH

french-canadian *adj, usu cap F&C* [*french canadian*] **1 :** of, relating to, or characteristic of the French Canadians **2 :** of, relating to, or characteristic of the Canadian-French language

french canadianism *n, usu cap F&C* [*french canadian* + -*ism*] **:** the movement advocating the political independence of French Canada and its culture

french canna *n, usu cap F* **:** any of various large-flowered dwarf cannas that are used extensively as ornamental bedding plants

french chalk *n, usu cap F* **:** a soft white granular variety of steatite used as a grease remover in dry cleaning or for drawing lines on cloth or other special uses

french chestnut *n, usu cap F* **:** SPANISH CHESTNUT

french chippendale *n, usu cap F&C* **:** a Chippendale furniture with elaborate detail like Louis Quatorze and Louis Quinze furniture

french chop *n, usu cap F* **:** a rib chop with the meat trimmed from the end of the rib

french cleaner *n, usu cap F* **:** DRY CLEANER

french cleaning *n, usu cap F* **:** DRY CLEANING

french clover *n, usu cap F* **:** CRIMSON CLOVER

french cocklebur *n, usu cap F* **:** CAESAR WEED

french column *n, usu cap F* **:** an apparatus that is used for effecting fractional condensation and that consists of a chambered column or dephlegmator with which is connected a series of U-tubes

french combing wool *n, usu cap F* **:** wool having a staple length intermediate between that of clothing wool and combing wool

french crown *n, usu cap F, obs* **:** ECU 1

french cuff *n, usu cap F* **:** a soft double cuff that is made by turning back part of a wide cuff band and that fastens by cuff buttons or cuff links — distinguished from *barrel cuff*

French cuff

french curve *n, often cap F* **:** a curved piece of flat material (as wood, ebonite, celluloid) often in the form of a scroll and used as an aid in drawing noncircular curves

french disease *n, usu cap F, archaic* **:** SYPHILIS

french door *n, usu cap F* **:** a light door in which the area included between the outer stiles and rails is divided by muntins into rectangular units provided with panes of glass; *also* **:** one of a pair of such doors mounted in a single frame

french doughnut *n, usu cap F* **:** a doughnut shaped of cream-puff dough and fried in deep fat

french drain *n, usu cap F* **:** a drain consisting of an underground passage made by filling a trench with loose stones and covering with earth — called also *rubble drain*

french dressing *n, usu cap F* **:** a salad dressing of oil and vinegar or lemon juice seasoned with salt, pepper, mustard, or other condiments

french drip *n, often cap F* **:** DRIP COFFEE

frenched *adj* [fr. past part. of ³*french*] *of a plant* **:** affected by frenching

french endive *n, usu cap F* **:** ENDIVE 2

french·er \ˈfrenchə(r)\ *n* -S *cap* [¹*french* + -*er*] *archaic* **:** FRENCHMAN — usu. used disparagingly

frenches *pl of* FRENCH, *pres 3d sing of* FRENCH

french fake *n, usu cap 1st F* **:** a mode of coiling a rope by running it backward and forward in parallel bends; *also* **:** a modification of a Flemish coil

french flat *n, usu cap 1st F, archaic* **:** APARTMENT 1

french fold *n, often cap 1st F* **:** a folding of a sheet printed on one side into four or more leaves so that the outside pages read consecutively; *also* **:** a sheet folded in this manner

french folio *n, usu cap 1st F* **:** a lightweight writing paper often used in manifolding and for printers' proofs

french foot *n, usu cap 1st F* **1 :** a hosiery foot used in full-fashioned stockings in which the back seam of the leg is continued through the middle of the sole — compare ENGLISH FOOT **2 :** FRENCH BRACKET FOOT

french fried potato *n, often cap 1st F* [¹*french* + *fried potato* (noun phrase)] **:** FRENCH FRY — usu. used in pl.

¹**french fry** *vt, often cap 1st F* [back-formation fr. *french fried* (in *french fried potato*)] **1 :** to fry strips of (potato) in deep fat until brown **2 :** to cook by frying in deep fat until brown ⟨*french fried* onions⟩ ⟨*french fried* shrimp⟩

²**french fry** *also* **french fried** *n, pl* **french fries** *also* **french frieds** *often cap 1st F* [short for *french fried potato*] **:** one of the strips of a potato that has been cut into long strips of triangular or rectangular cross section and fried in deep fat until brown — usu. used in pl.

french fryer *n, often cap 1st F* [¹*french fry* + -*er*] **:** a deep open pan or kettle fitted with a wire basket in which food is placed for deep-fat frying

french fryer

french gray *n, often cap F* **:** a light greenish gray that is bluer and duller than ash gray or lichen green

french green *n, often cap F* **:** a moderate yellowish green that is greener and darker than tarragon, greener and duller than malachite green, and duller and slightly greener than verdigris

french grunt *n, usu cap F* **:** a grunt (*Haemulon flaveolineatum*) of Florida and the West Indies — called also *openmouthed grunt*

¹**french guianese** *also* **french guianan** *adj, usu cap F&G* [*French Guiana*, French overseas department on northeast coast of So. America + E -*ese* or -*an*] **1 :** of, relating to, or characteristic of French Guiana **2 :** of, relating to, or characteristic of the people of French Guiana

²**french guianese** *also* **french guianan** *n, usu cap F&G* **:** a native or inhabitant of French Guiana

french hand work *n, usu cap F* **:** a laundry service in which fancy articles are washed and ironed by hand

french harp *n, usu cap F, chiefly Midland* **:** HARMONICA 3

french-headed \ˈ=;==\ *adj, usu cap F* **:** provided with pinch pleats ⟨full *French-headed* flounces⟩ ⟨*French-headed* curtains⟩

french heading *n, usu cap F* **:** PINCH PLEAT

french heath *n, usu cap F* **:** FRENCH BRIER

french heel *n, usu cap F* **1 :** a woman's shoe heel that is usu. high and pitched well forward and has a back line and breast line with a pronounced curve — see LOUIS HEEL **2 :** a narrow heel reinforcement for hosiery

french hem *n, usu cap F* **:** a small hem similar to a French seam

french honeysuckle *n, usu cap F* **1 :** SULLA **2 :** RED VALERIAN

french hood *n, usu cap F* **:** a 16th century woman's headdress covering the hair except in front and having a jeweled crescent-shaped framework sometimes with a fall of cloth and set back on the head

french horn *n, usu cap F* **1 :** a brass wind musical instrument derived from the hunting horn and consisting of a long conical tube with a narrow funnel-shaped mouthpiece at one end, a flaring bell at the other, and keys or valves and having a range in pitch of more than three octaves upward from two octaves below middle C **2 :** an 8-foot pipe-organ reed stop having a quality similar to that of a French horn

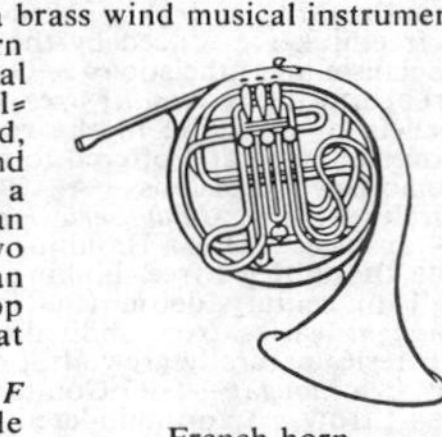

French horn

french ice cream *n, usu cap F* **:** a frozen yellow custard made with cream and egg yolks

frenchier *comparative of* FRENCHY

frenchies *pl of* FRENCHY

frenchiest *superlative of* FRENCHY

french·i·fi·ca·tion \ˌfrenchəfəˈkāshən\ *n* -S *often cap* [fr. *frenchify*, after such pairs as E *amplify: amplification*] **:** the act of frenchifying or the state of being frenchified

french·i·fy \ˈfrenchə,fī\ *vb* -ED/-ING/-ES *often cap* [¹*french* + -*i-* + -*fy*] *vt* **1 a :** to make French in qualities, traits, or typical ideas or practices ⟨his residence in Paris *frenchified* him in many ways⟩ ⟨the foreign intelligence agent *frenchified* his behavior and accent⟩ **b :** to make over to accord with French policies or organizational plan ⟨~ the schools of the colony⟩ **:** subject to French civil or cultural control ⟨~ the islands⟩ **2 a :** to make superficially or spuriously French in qualities or actions ⟨*frenchified* bistro entertainers⟩ **b :** to make affected or somewhat effeminate **:** DANDIFY ⟨a mincing *frenchified* walk⟩ **3 :** to make (a linguistic form) accord with typical French linguistic forms ⟨*frenchified* his name from Thomas Becket to Thomas à Becket⟩ **:** change (a linguistic form) to a French equivalent ⟨*frenchified* his name from Jacob to Jaques⟩ **~** *vi* **:** to acquire French qualities, traits, or ideas

french·i·ly \-ələ̄\ *adv, usu cap F* [*frenchy* + *-ly*] **:** in a Frenchy manner ⟨a *Frenchily* farcical situation —S.H.Adams⟩

french indian *n, cap F&I* **:** an Indian who was friendly to or strongly influenced by the French in prerevolutionary America

french·i·ness \'frenchēnə̇s, -chin-\ *n* -ES *usu cap* [*frenchy* + *-ness*] **:** the quality or state of being French or Frenchy

frenching *n* -S [fr. gerund of ³*french*] **1 :** a narrowing, thickening, and crinkling of leaves characteristic of various plant diseases of which virus, nutritional deficiency, or physiological factors may be the cause **2** *in Florida* **:** MOTTLE-LEAF

french·ism \'fren,chizəm\ *n* -S *usu cap F* **:** GALLICISM 1

french·ize \-,chīz\ *vt* -ED/-ING/-S *often cap* **:** FRENCHIFY; *esp* **:** to alter in linguistic or literary form to approximate that of the French language ⟨"riding coat" *frenchized* to "redingote"⟩

french kid *n, usu cap F* **:** fine kidskin leather that is alum tanned or vegetable tanned and finished to resemble leather orig. made in France

french kiss *n, sometimes cap F* **:** DEEP KISS

french knot *n, usu cap F* **:** a decorative stitch made by winding the thread one or more times around the needle and drawing the needle back through the material at the point where it came out

french lavender *n, usu cap F* **1 :** a shrubby grayish lavender (*Lavandula stoechas*) native to southwestern Europe **2 :** SPIKE LAVENDER

french leave *n, usu cap F* [so called fr. an 18th century French custom of leaving a reception without taking leave of the host or hostess] **:** an informal, hasty, or secret departure; *esp* **:** the leaving of a place without paying one's debts

french leg *n, usu cap F* **:** a cabriole leg that is light in construction and terminates without enlargement or with a slight bulk above the foot

french letter *n, usu cap F, slang Brit* **:** CONDOM

french lug *n, usu cap F* **:** BALANCE LUGSAIL

french·man \'-mən\ *n, pl* **frenchmen** [ME *Frenshman, frensh man,* fr. OE *frencisc man,* fr. *frencisc* French + *man, mann* man] **1** *cap* **a :** a native or inhabitant of France **b :** one that is of French descent **2** *usu cap* **:** a French ship **3** *usu cap* **:** a frenched plant (as of tobacco) **4** *usu cap, Brit* **:** RED-LEGGED PARTRIDGE

french marigold *n, usu cap F* **:** a strong-scented bushy annual herb (*Tagetes patula*) having flower heads usu. about 1½ inches across and marked with red

french molt *n, usu cap F* **:** an irregular and atypical molt of young cage birds by some attributed to dietary deficiency and by others to the attack of an unidentified mite

french morocco *n, usu cap F* **:** a morocco made from sheepskin

french mulberry *n, usu cap F* **1 :** a shrub (*Callicarpa americana*) of the southern U.S. with clusters of small pink flowers and purple berries that is often used as an ornamental **2 :** WHITE MULBERRY

french nude *n, often cap F* **:** ALESAN

french ocher *n, often cap F* **:** YELLOW OCHER

french order *n, usu cap F* **:** a style of architecture characterized esp. by the use of rusticated columns and introduced by the French architect Delorme (1515–70)

french partridge *n, usu cap F* **:** RED-LEGGED PARTRIDGE

french pastry *n, usu cap F* **:** fancy pastry made usu. of puff paste baked in individual portions varying in shape and filled (as with custard or preserved fruit)

french pea *n, usu cap F* **:** PETITS POIS

french pink *n, usu cap F* **1 :** CORNFLOWER 1b **2 :** THRIFT 6

french pitch *n, usu cap F* **:** DIAPASON NORMAL

french plague *or* **french pox** *n, usu cap F, obs* **:** SYPHILIS

french polish *n, usu cap F* **1 :** a rubbed and polished finish for furniture using oil and shellac; *also* **:** the glossy surface of such a finish **2 :** a preparation usu. of shellac and oil used as a furniture polish

french provincial *n, usu cap F & often cap P* **:** a style of furniture, architecture, or fabric design originating in the 17th and 18th century French provinces or a style derived from or associated with this

french pusley *n, usu cap F* **:** a portulaca (*Portulaca grandiflora*)

french reef *n, usu cap F* **:** a reef in a square sail made with a jackstay on the reef band and a becket on the yard

french roast *n, usu cap F* **:** coffee of a darker roast than is usual in the U.S. but not as dark as Italian roast

french roll *n, usu cap F* **:** a roll resembling French bread in texture and oval in shape

french roof *n, usu cap F* **:** a curb roof much like the mansard

french rose *n, usu cap F* **:** a common red rose (*Rosa gallica*) the petals of which are the source of an oil used chiefly in perfumery

french sage *n, usu cap F* **:** JERUSALEM SAGE

french sash *n, usu cap F* **:** a casement swinging on hinges — compare FRENCH WINDOW

french scarlet *n, often cap F* **:** SCARLET 2b

french scroll *n, usu cap F* **:** a ball-shaped furniture scroll with spirals nearly horizontal in position — see FOOT illustration

french seal *n, usu cap F* **:** rabbit fur processed to simulate seal

french seam *n, usu cap F* **:** a standing seam made by stitching on the right side, trimming closely, turning, and stitching on the wrong side so as to enclose all raw edges

French seam

french sennit *n, usu cap F* **:** a sennit more open than flat and braided of an odd number (as five or seven) of rope yarns

french 75 *n, pl* **french 75's** *usu cap F* **:** a cocktail consisting of lemon juice, gin, angostura bitters, and sugar added to a base of chilled champagne

french silver *n, usu cap F & often cap S* **:** a breed of large domestic rabbits of French origin having the undercoat blue with a mingling of black and white hairs and a silvery outer coat

french sixth *n, usu cap F* **:** an augmented sixth chord consisting of a major third, an augmented fourth, and an augmented sixth above the lowest tone (as A♭, C, D, F♯)

french sole *n, usu cap F* **:** a European sole (*Solea pegusa*)

french sorrel *n, usu cap F* **1 :** a wood sorrel (*Oxalis montana*) **2 :** a European garden sorrel (*Rumex scutatus*)

french spinach *n, usu cap F* **:** RED GOOSEFOOT

french spun *n, pl* **french spuns** *usu cap F* **:** soft worsted yarn made by the French system

french square *n, usu cap F* **:** a square bottle with flattened corners used in the dispensing of liquid medicines

french system *n, usu cap F* **:** a method of spinning worsted yarn esp. for wools shorter than three inches — called also *continental system;* compare BRADFORD SYSTEM

french tack *n, usu cap F* **:** a loose invisible joining between two parts of a garment that consists of blanket stitches worked across several threads to form a bar

french tamarisk *n, usu cap F* **:** a Eurasian shrub or small tree (*Tamarix gallica*) with white or pink flowers that is often found as an escape in the southern U.S.

french tea *n, usu cap F* **1 :** an aromatic herb (*Micheliella anisata*) of the mint family of the southeastern U.S. **2 :** a tea made from a sage (*Salvia officinalis*) of southern France — called also *Greek tea*

french telephone *n, usu cap F* **:** HANDSET

french tip *n, usu cap F* **:** a guard formed in bookbinding by folding a narrow strip of the binding edge of an insert and tipped in by wrapping but not pasting around a fold of a signature

french toast *n, usu cap F* **:** bread dipped in a mixture of egg and milk and then sautéed

french toe *n, usu cap F* **:** a toe of a shoe having a square tip

french trumpet *n, usu cap F* **:** an 8-foot reed pipe-organ stop of brilliant tone

french ultramarine *n, often cap F* **:** FRENCH BLUE

french varnish *n, usu cap F* **:** FRENCH POLISH

french vermilion *n, often cap F* **:** a strong to vivid reddish orange that is redder and darker than mikado — called also *cadmium red*

french vermouth *n, usu cap F* **:** dry vermouth

french veronese green *n, often cap F&V* **:** VIRIDIAN 2

french walnut *n, usu cap F* **:** ENGLISH WALNUT

frenchweed \'=,=\ *n, usu cap* **1 :** PENNYCRESS **2 :** a tropical American plant (*Galinsoga parviflora*) naturalized and troublesome as a weed in Europe and No. America

french willow *n, usu cap F* **1 :** ALMOND WILLOW 1 **2 :** FIREWEED b

french window *n, usu cap F* **1 :** a French door placed in an exterior wall and opening usu. onto a porch or terrace **2 :** CASEMENT 2b

French window 1

frenchwoman \'=,==\ *n, pl* **frenchwomen** *cap* **:** a woman who is French

¹**frenchy** \'frenchē, -chi\ *adj, often* -ER/-EST *usu cap* [¹*french* + *-y*] **:** French in quality ⟨the little daughter of a very *Frenchy* lady —William Soskin⟩ ⟨a score that briskly sets about creating a *Frenchy* atmosphere —Douglas Watt⟩; *esp* **:** markedly, affectedly, or spuriously French in quality or French in a superficial usu. frivolous sense

²**frenchy** \"\ *n* -ES *cap* **:** a Frenchman or French woman

french yellow *n, often cap F* **:** a brownish orange to strong yellowish brown — called also *Cathay, Mexican, Yucatan*

fre·net·ic \frə̇'ned·ik, -etik\ *adj* [ME *frenetik* insane, fr. MF *frenetique,* fr. L *phreneticus,* modif. of Gk *phrenitikos,* fr. *phrenitis* inflammation of the brain (fr. *phren-, phrēn* mind + *-itis*) + *-ikos* -ic; akin to ON *grunr* suspicion] **1 a :** FRENZIED, FRANTIC, HECTIC ⟨a ~ but unsuccessful attempt to beat a deadline⟩ ⟨a woman who let out ~ screams after a car accident⟩ ⟨the ~ bustle on the stock-market floor following a sharp decline in stocks⟩ **b :** wild and excited ⟨a noisy ~ celebration⟩ ⟨~ cheering⟩ **2 :** tense and marked by a tendency to overexcitement ⟨a thin ~ woman —C.O.Gorham⟩ — **fre·net·i·cal·ly** \-ə̇k(ə)lē, -ēk-, -li\ *adv*

fre·net·i·cal \-ə̇kəl\ *adj* [*frenetic* + *-al*] *archaic* **:** FRENETIC

fren·tón \'fren,tän, =ˈ=\ *n, pl* **fren·to·nes** \fren'tōnēz\ *usu cap* [AmerSp, fr. Sp *frentón,* adj., having a large forehead, aug. of *frente* forehead, fr. L *front-, frons* — more at BRINK] **:** a member of an Indian people constituting a division of the Guaicuru and comprising the Mocoví and Toba and formerly the Abipón

fren·u·lar \'frenyələ(r)\ *adj* [*frenulum* + *-ar*] **:** of or relating to a frenulum

fren·u·lum \'frenyələm\ *also* **frae·nu·lum** \'frēnyə-, 'frenyə-\ *n, pl* **frenu·la** *also* **fraenu·la** \-lə\ [NL, dim. of L *frenum, fraenum*] **1 :** a frenum esp. when small; *specif* **:** a narrow band of white matter in the brain running between the upper surface of the anterior medullary velum and the corpora quadrigemina **2 :** a bristle or group of bristles on the front edge of the posterior wings of many lepidopterous insects that interlocks with a process on the front wings and thus unites the wings

fre·num *also* **frae·num** \'frēnəm\ *n, pl* **fre·nums** \-nəmz\ *or* **fre·na** \-nə\ [L, lit., bridle; akin to L *fretus* relying, *firmus* firm — more at FIRM] **1 :** a connecting fold of membrane serving to support or restrain (as the underside of the tongue) **2 :** a fold or ridge extending from the scutellum of an insect to the base of each anterior wing **3 :** a stripe of color on the cheek

frenzical *adj* [obs. E *frenzic* insane, delirious (fr. E ¹*frenzy* + *-ic*) + E *-al*] *obs* **:** INSANE, DELIRIOUS ⟨a certain ~ malady they call love —Philip Sidney⟩

fren·zied \'frenzēd, -zid\ *adj* [¹*frenzy* + *-ed*] **:** marked by frenzy **:** giving evidence of abnormal excitement or emotional disturbance **:** extremely stirred up **:** HECTIC ⟨could hear the prosecutor's ~ denunciations of the accused —H.W.Carter⟩ ⟨a ~ look in the eye⟩: as **a :** marked by extreme tense persistent and often disorderly activity ⟨a ~ buying on the stock exchange⟩ ⟨the last few ~ moments of rehearsals —*Amer. Guide Series: Calif.*⟩ ⟨wrote with a ~ facility —V.S. Pritchett⟩ **b :** loud and insistent ⟨a ~ clamor⟩ ⟨~ applause⟩ — **fren·zied·ly** *adv*

¹**fren·zy** *or* **phren·sy** \-zē, -zi\ *n* -ES [ME *frenesie,* fr. MF, fr. ML *phrenesia,* alter. of L *phrenesis,* fr. *phreneticus,* after such pairs as L *poeticus* poetic: *poesis* poetry, poesy] **1 a :** a temporary madness or insane derangement **:** a paroxysm from a mania ⟨was generally docile but became uncontrollable in his *frenzies*⟩ ⟨in a rage amounting to a ~⟩ **b :** a strong mental disturbance resembling such a derangement and usu. resulting in a violent passion ⟨the old man's drunken *frenzies* and the way his mulatto brood ran shrieking . . . when he turned on them with a horsewhip —Ellen Glasgow⟩ **c :** a violent mental or emotional agitation **:** abnormal or unusual excitement ⟨a disturbing air of ~ about his writing⟩ ⟨a ~ of delight⟩ ⟨the sexual ~ —E.A.Armstrong⟩ ⟨a ~ of resentment —*Amer. Guide Series: Oregon*⟩ ⟨a ~ of mystical exaltation —C.S. Kilby⟩ **2 a :** the activity of one that is frenzied ⟨a ~ of skiing⟩ ⟨small watercourses race in a white-capped ~ down mountain and forest slope —*Amer. Guide Series: Oregon*⟩; *esp* **:** intense persistent usu. wild and often disorderly compulsive or agitated activity ⟨the wild ~ of religious camp meetings —J.T.Adams⟩ ⟨the ~ of the geysers —Margaret Clarke⟩ **b :** an activity of this kind ⟨until the imagination is tortured into a ~ of baffled guessing —J.W.Beach⟩ ⟨a ~ of high living —Arnold Bennett⟩ ⟨the ~ of wartime production —*Amer. Guide Series: Mich.*⟩ ⟨a ~ of abuse⟩ **c :** intensity of effort ⟨in order to wrest a living from the soil . . . had to toil with a ~ approaching desperation —D.L.Cohn⟩ **syn** see MANIA

²**frenzy** \"\ *adj* -ER/-EST *dial Eng* **:** ANGRY

³**frenzy** \"\ *vt* -ED/-ING/-ES **:** to affect with frenzy **:** drive to madness ⟨the sport which *frenzies* our colleges each autumn —Frederic Morton⟩

Fre·on \'frē,än\ *trademark* — used for any of a series of nonflammable gaseous and liquid paraffin hydrocarbons that contain one or more fluorine atoms in the molecule and are used chiefly as refrigerants and as propellants for aerosols

freq *abbr* frequency; frequent; frequentative

fre·quence \'frēkwən(t)s\ *n* -S [ME, crowd, fr. L *frequentia*] **1** *archaic* **:** crowded state **:** CONCOURSE, CROWD **2 a** *obs* **:** frequent use or practice **:** FAMILIARITY **b :** FREQUENCY 1b

fre·quen·cy \'nsē, -si\ *n* -ES [L *frequentia* crowd, fr. *frequent-, frequens* crowded, frequent + *-ia* -y] **1 :** the quality or state of being frequent: as **a** *obs* **:** frequent use or practice **:** FAMILIARITY **b :** the fact or condition of occurring frequently **:** occurrence often repeated **:** common occurrence ⟨the ~ of crimes has aroused the public⟩ **2 a :** the number of times that a periodic function takes on the same sequence of values as the independent variable (as one that represents time) varies through one unit **:** the reciprocal of the period **b :** the number of individuals falling within a single class when objects are classified according to variations in a set of one or more specified attributes **3 :** the number of repetitions of a periodic process in a unit of time: as **a :** the number of complete alternations per second of an alternating electric current **b :** the number of sound waves per second produced by a sounding body (as a tuning fork) **c :** the number of complete oscillations per second of the electric or magnetic component of an electromagnetic wave

frequency band *n* **:** one of a succession of acoustic, radio, or spectral frequency ranges each beginning where the preceding one leaves off — compare RADIO FREQUENCY

frequency changer *or* **frequency converter** *n* **:** a motor generator used to change the frequency of an alternating-current circuit with or without a phase or voltage change

frequency curve *n* **:** a curve that graphically represents a frequency distribution

frequency distribution *n* **:** a systematic arrangement of statistical data that exhibits the division of the values of the variable into classes and that indicates the frequencies or relative frequencies that correspond to each of the classes

frequency indicator *n* **:** a one-point frequency meter that measures one frequency only and that is used in transmitting stations to maintain constant frequency

frequency meter *n* **:** an instrument for measuring the frequency in cycles per second of an alternating current or of a radio wave

frequency-modulated \'===,==,==\ *adj* **:** modulated by frequency modulation **:** of, using, or relating to waves so modulated

frequency modulation *n* **:** modulation of the frequency of the carrier wave in accordance with speech or a signal; *specif* **:** the system of broadcasting using this method of modulation — abbr. *FM;* compare AMPLITUDE MODULATION

frequency multiplier *n* **:** a device (as a frequency changer) for multiplying by an integer the frequency of a circuit

frequency polygon *n* **:** a frequency curve made up of straight lines

frequency rate *n* **:** the number of disabling injuries of given types resulting from industrial accident per million man-hours worked

frequency response *n* **:** a response depicting the output-to-input ratio of a transducer as a function of frequency

frequency shift *n* **:** a method of communication in radiotelegraphy based on slight shifts in the carrier frequency in accordance with the code signals

¹**fre·quent** \'frēkwənt\ *adj, sometimes* -ER/-EST [ME, ample, abundant, fr. MF or L; MF, crowded, fr. L *frequent-, frequens* crowded, frequent; prob. akin to L *farcire* to stuff — more at FARCE] **1** *obs* **a :** FILLED, THRONGED — used of a place **b :** FULL, NUMEROUS — used of an attendance or assembly **2 a :** COMMON, FAMILIAR, CURRENT, USUAL ⟨cannibalism is not a ~ practice among these Indians⟩ ⟨degenerative changes are somewhat *frequenter* in patients with backache —*Jour. Amer. Med. Assoc.*⟩ **b :** happening or found at short intervals **:** often repeated or occurring ⟨~ visits⟩ ⟨the inns are very ~ on this road⟩ ⟨bootleg coal workings are ~ —*Amer. Guide Series: Pa.*⟩ **3 :** given to some practice **:** HABITUAL, PERSISTENT ⟨were not ~ at visiting —Pearl Buck⟩ ⟨a ~ guest at my house⟩ **4** *archaic* **:** familiarly associated (as in friendship or understanding) **:** INTIMATE, VERSED

²**fre·quent** \(')frē¦kwent, 'frēkwənt\ *vb* -ED/-ING/-S [ME *frequenten,* fr. MF or L; MF *frequenter,* fr. L *frequentare,* fr. *frequent-, frequens*] *vt* **1 a :** to associate with, be in, or resort to often or habitually **:** visit often ⟨gray and white herons ~ the marshes —*Amer. Guide Series: Fla.*⟩ ⟨many ships ~ the port⟩ ⟨when I first began to ~ her house —W.B.Yeats⟩ **b :** to read systematically or habitually **:** familiarize oneself with the thought or writings of ⟨the lessons he proposes as the profit of *~ing* Milton would . . . be more reasonably sought elsewhere —F.R.Leavis⟩ **2** *obs* **:** to use, practice, celebrate, or partake of frequently **3** *obs* **:** to crowd or fill **4** *obs* **a :** FAMILIARIZE **b :** to furnish abundantly **~** *vi, archaic* **:** to visit regularly or frequently ⟨nor track nor pathway might declare that human foot *~ed* there —Sir Walter Scott⟩

fre·quen·ta·tion \,frēk,wen'tāshən, -wən-\ *n* -S [ME *frequentacioun* frequent gathering, fr. LL *frequentation-, frequentatio,* fr. L, action of crowding or packing together, fr. *frequentatus* (past part. of *frequentare* to frequent, crowd) + *-ion-, -io* -ion] **1 a :** the act, habit, or an instance of frequenting or visiting often ⟨my ~ of the late major all the time he has been living here —Glenway Wescott⟩ ⟨his *~s* among the scum . . . were . . . distinctly insalubrious —Augustus John⟩ **b :** systematic or habitual reading ⟨only the ~ of the old masters enables us to judge the new —Meyer Schapiro⟩ ⟨one whose mind is trained by the ~ of newspaper columns —Pier-Maria Pasinetti⟩ **2** *archaic* **:** frequent use, practice, or celebration

¹**fre·quen·ta·tive** \frē'kwentəd·iv, -ətiv\ *adj* [L *frequentativus,* fr. *frequentatus* (past part. of *frequentare* to frequent, crowd, do repeatedly) + *-ivus* -ive] **:** denoting repeated or recurrent action or state — used of a verb aspect, verb form, or meaning; compare ITERATIVE

²**frequentative** \"\ *n* -S **:** a frequentative verb or verb form

fre·quent·er \frē'kwentə(r), 'frēkwən-\ *n* -S **:** one that frequents

fre·quent·ly *adv* **:** at frequent or short intervals

fre·quent·ness *n* -ES **:** the quality or state of being frequent **:** FREQUENCY

fres·cade \fres'kād, -äd\ *n* -S [obs. F, fr. MF, prob. fr. (assumed) OProv *frescada* cool of the evening, cool drink (whence Prov *frescado*), fr. OProv *fresc* fresh, of Gmc origin; akin to OHG *frisc* fresh] **:** a cool walk **:** shady place ⟨where each ~ rings with melodious booing —W.H.Auden⟩

¹**fres·co** \'fres,kō\ *n, pl* **frescoes** *or* **frescos** [It, fresh plaster on which one may paint, coolness, fr. *fresco,* adj., cool, fresh, of Gmc origin; akin to OHG *frisc* fresh] **1 a** (1) **:** the art of painting on freshly spread moist lime plaster with pigments suspended in a water vehicle — called also *buon fresco* (2) **:** a painting so executed **b :** SECCO **c :** mural painting; *also* **:** MURAL **2** *obs* **:** cool refreshing air **:** SHADE

²**fresco** \"\ *vt* -ED/-ING/-ES **1 :** to paint in fresco ⟨a ceiling decoration for the . . . Louvre has just been *~ed* —Janet Flanner⟩ **2 :** to cover (a vertical surface) **:** decorate heavily ⟨walls *~ed* with little drawings in heavy frames⟩

fresco secco *n* [It, dry fresco] **:** SECCO

¹**fresh** \'fresh\ *adj* -ER/-EST [ME *fresh, fersh,* fr. OE & OF; OE *fersc* fresh, not salt, unsalted; akin to OFris *fersk* fresh, MD *versch,* OHG *frisc* fresh, and perh. to Russ *presnyĭ* fresh, sweet, unleavened; OF *freis* fresh (fem. *fresche*), of Gmc origin; akin to OHG *frisc* fresh] **1 a :** not containing or composed of salt water **:** not salt ⟨sediment . . . is carried out to sea much farther than if the ocean were ~ —G.E. & Nettie MacGinitie⟩ ⟨~ water⟩ **b** (1) **:** having or conveying no taint **:** PURE, INVIGORATING, LIVELY, BRISK ⟨how sweet it was to breathe the ~ air —Bram Stoker⟩ ⟨a ~ dewy morning⟩ (2) *of wind* **:** STRONG — see FRESH BREEZE, FRESH GALE (3) *chiefly Scot* **:** free from frost **:** OPEN ⟨our winters have been ~ of late⟩ **2 a :** newly produced, gathered, or made **:** not altered by processing (as by canning, pickling in salt or vinegar, or refrigeration) ⟨~ vegetables⟩ ⟨~ fruit⟩ **b :** having its original qualities unimpaired: as (1) **:** not exhausted or fatigued **:** full of or renewed in vigor or readiness for action **:** FRESHENED, REFRESHED, ACTIVE ⟨next morning he was ~ and gay, all his weariness gone⟩ ⟨had I been as ~ as when I arose —R.L.Stevenson⟩; *specif, of land* **:** not depleted of its fertility **:** recently put into cultivation ⟨New England had its troubles . . . when . . . the greater product of *fresher* lands came flooding eastward —Russell Lord⟩ (2) **:** not stale, sour, decayed, or deteriorated in any way ⟨meat kept ~ by refrigeration⟩ ⟨~ bread⟩ (3) **:** not faded or tarnished **:** not dim **:** BRIGHT, ALIVE ⟨the beams and paint are as ~ as spring —Sacheverell Sitwell⟩ ⟨the big trucks are painted a ~ white —J.K.Howard⟩ ⟨his memory is still ~ in the hearts of his people⟩ **:** not worn or rumpled **:** SPRUCE ⟨he always keeps his clothes ~ and tidy⟩ ⟨made herself ~ and recombed her hair —Agnes S. Turnbull⟩ (4) *of rock* **:** unaltered by surface agencies (as rain, wind, or frost) (5) *chiefly Scot* **:** not under the influence of drink **:** SOBER — used esp of someone who has just sobered up **3 a** (1) **:** experienced newly or anew **:** not known or experienced before **:** NEW ⟨a considerable number of ~ Lincoln letters were turned up —Bernard Kalb⟩ ⟨I got a ~ cold in my head —Tobias Smollett⟩ **:** ADDITIONAL, ANOTHER, DIFFERENT ⟨we must make a ~ start⟩ ⟨begin a ~ paragraph⟩ (2) **:** not trite or hackneyed **:** ORIGINAL, STRIKING, VIVID, NOVEL, VITAL ⟨can anyone hope to say anything not new, but even ~, on a topic so well worn? —H.S.Bennett⟩ ⟨language and metaphor that are . . . ~ and . . . singular today —H.V. Gregory⟩ ⟨his material is familiar; his handling of it, however, is notably ~ —M.A.Hamilton⟩ **b :** newly or recently made or received **:** RECENT ⟨the news he brought was not very ~⟩ ⟨those scratches are all ~ —Erle Stanley Gardner⟩ ⟨a ~ wound⟩ ⟨on striking ~ lion spoor the trackers follow on it —James Stevenson-Hamilton⟩ **c :** having little or no experience **:** INEXPERIENCED, RAW, GREEN ⟨coming ~ to the job —Helen Howe⟩ **d :** newly or just come or arrived ⟨the engineer, ~ out of college —Richard Joseph⟩ ⟨a new car ~ from the assembly line —F.L.Allen⟩ ⟨weekly newspaper ~ off the press —Lewis Nordyke⟩ **e** *of a cow or other female mammal* (1) **:** having the milk flow recently established (2) **:** having recently calved (3) **:** giving milk **f** *of a bird* **:** newly molted **:** having the feathers unworn and unmarred **4** [prob. by folk etymology fr. G *frech,* fr. OHG *freh* untamed, greedy — more at FREAK] **:** disposed to take liberties **:** SAUCY, IMPUDENT,

IMPERTINENT, RUDE ⟨he was ~ with the nurses while on duty —Greer Williams⟩ ⟨his teacher reprimanded him for being ~ —Priscilla Noddin⟩ ⟨don't get ~ with mother⟩ **syn** see NEW

[2]**fresh** \"\ *vb* -ED/-ING/-ES [ME *freshen*, fr. *fresh, fersh*, adj.] *vt* **:** to make fresh or spruce **:** FRESHEN, REFRESH, RENEW — often used with *up* ⟨back to the hotel to ~ himself up⟩ ~ *vi* **1 :** to become fresh — often used with *up* ⟨the sea was beginning to ~ up⟩ **2 :** to make oneself fresh — often used with *up* ⟨going to ~ up⟩

[3]**fresh** \"\ *adv* [ME *freshe*, fr. *fresh, fersh*, adj.] **:** just recently **:** just now **:** FRESHLY ⟨stocking his cigar case from a bundle ~ in —John Galsworthy⟩ ⟨we're ~ out of tomatoes⟩ ⟨the circus was ~ out of funds —Henry LaCossitt⟩ ⟨a ~ laid egg⟩ ⟨a ~ caught fish⟩ ⟨the sheepskin was ~ dried —Ernest Hemingway⟩

[4]**fresh** \"\ *n* -ES [[1]*fresh*] **1 a :** an increased flow or rush of water **:** FRESHET, FLUSH **b :** a stream, spring, or pool of fresh water **c** (1) **:** a stream of fresh water running into salt water **:** the mingling of fresh and salt waters (2) **:** the part of a river or its shores above the flow of tidal seawater **2** *chiefly Scot* **:** a period of open weather ending a frost **:** THAW **3 :** the early or beginning part of a duration (as a day, a year, or a lifetime)

fresh air *adj* [fr. *fresh air* (noun phrase)] **:** relating to a movement, place, or activity providing rural or outdoor facilities (as for health or recreation) esp. for underprivileged children ⟨a *fresh air* farm for convalescent children —M.V. Merrick⟩ ⟨*fresh air* work —J.T.McDonnell⟩

fresh breeze *n* **:** wind having a speed of 19 to 24 miles per hour — see BEAUFORT SCALE table

fresh·en \ˈfreshən\ *vb* **freshened; freshened; freshening** \-sh(ə)niŋ\ **freshens** *vi* **1 :** to grow or become fresh: as **a** *of wind* **:** to increase in strength **:** grow more brisk ⟨the wind ~*ed* from the north quarter⟩ **b :** to become fresh in appearance **:** become brighter, more vivid, or stronger in color or vitality ⟨the flowers ~*ed* after a good watering and some warm weather⟩ ⟨at the compliment, the young girl's face ~*ed*⟩ **c** *of water* **:** to lose saltiness ⟨the water ~*s* quickly as one moves upstream from the sea⟩ **2 a** *of a cow or other milch animal* **:** to come into milk **b :** to give birth to young **3 :** to wash the hands and face, take a shower, put on clean clothes, or perform other operations designed to improve one's appearance or encourage a sense of well-being — usu. used with *up* ⟨went back to the hotel to ~ up before going out to dinner⟩ ⟨went to her room to ~ after the long night and day journey —James Reynolds⟩ ~ *vt* **1 :** to make fresh: as **a :** to separate (as water) from saline ingredients **:** make less salty ⟨~ salt fish⟩ **b :** to make fresher, newer, or more interesting in appearance or constitution **:** make brighter, more vivid, or stronger in color or vitality — sometimes used with *up; also* **:** REFRESH, REVIVE ⟨like a wind of morning rising from the sea, it stirred his hair and ~*ed* him —R.O.Bowen⟩ ⟨in season pink and white dogwood ~ the scene —*Amer. Guide Series: Pa.*⟩ ⟨the sun departed, leaving the soothing fingers of the darkness to ~ up the herbage and cool down the hot sands —Myrtle R. White⟩ ⟨crews of painters are now ~*ing* up several of the buildings —*Springfield (Mass.) Daily News*⟩ ⟨the gown that she wore . . . was very old, though some attempt had been made to ~ it —Edith Sitwell⟩ **c :** to give (tissues) a fresh raw surface (as by scraping fibrous tissue from a fracture site) esp. to promote union and healing **d :** to improve (a stale drink) by adding fresh matter ⟨poured some more coffee in the cup to ~ it⟩ ⟨~ the highball with more ice⟩ **2 :** to put (as oysters or clams) in fresher water **3 a :** to relieve (as a rope) by change of place or position where friction causes wear **b :** SHIFT, REDISTRIBUTE ⟨~ a ship's ballast⟩ **4 :** to improve the appearance or restore or increase the sense of well-being of (oneself) by freshening — usu. used with *up*

fresh·en·er \-sh(ə)nə(r)\ *n* -S **:** one that freshens: as **a :** a drink that revives or cheers **b :** an astringent lotion for cleansing the skin

[1]**fresher** *comparative of* FRESH

[2]**fresh·er** \-shə(r\ *n* -S [[1]*fresh* + -*er*] *Brit* **:** FRESHMAN

freshest *superlative of* FRESH

fresh·et \ˈfreshət, *usu* -əd.+V\ *n* -S [[4]*fresh* + -*et*] **1 a** *archaic* **:** a stream of fresh water **b :** a stream or current of fresh water that flows into the sea **2 a :** a great rise or a flood or overflowing of a stream caused by heavy rains or melted snow **:** a sudden inundation **b :** something resembling or suggesting a freshet esp. in being in sudden large supply ⟨rewarded handsomely by ~*s* of applause —Douglas Watt⟩ ⟨this quickened interest is shown in a ~ of publications —*Amer. Polit. Sci. Rev.*⟩ ⟨the almost endless and endlessly varied ~ of letters —*New Yorker*⟩ ⟨the ~*s* of welcome —Clemence Dane⟩

fresh gale *n* **:** wind having a speed of 39 to 46 miles per hour — see BEAUFORT SCALE table

freshing *n* -S [fr. gerund of [2]*fresh*] **:** the recutting of worn rifling in the barrel of a firearm — often used with *out* ⟨the barrel needs ~ out⟩

fresh·ly *adv* [ME, fr. *fresh, fersh* fresh + -*ly*] **:** in a fresh manner: as **a :** NEWLY, RECENTLY ⟨a ~ cleaned floor⟩ ⟨a ~ acquired egg⟩ **b :** STRONGLY, VIGOROUSLY ⟨a ~ blowing breeze⟩ **c :** BRIGHTLY, VIVIDLY ⟨a ~ green leaf⟩ **d :** STRIKINGLY ⟨a ~ original poem⟩ **e :** IMPUDENTLY ⟨a ~ forward remark⟩

fresh·man \ˈ=mən\ *n, pl* **freshmen** *often attrib* **1 :** one having as yet only the rudiments of knowledge esp. in a particular field or occupation **2 a :** a student in his first year or having chiefly first-year standing at a college or university **b :** a student in his first year in a secondary school **3 :** a newcomer in an occupation or activity requiring expert skill ⟨the tradition that Senate *freshmen* should be seen and not heard —*Time*⟩ ⟨a busy Congress, with a large contingent of *freshmen* —*Congressional Highlights*⟩ ⟨his ~ year in the major leagues⟩ ⟨made her ~ appearances in silent films⟩

freshman composition *n* **1 :** an elementary composition course usu. required in most colleges **2 :** a composition written as an assignment in a freshman course

fresh·man·ic \(ˈ)fresh'manik\ *adj* **:** of, belonging to, or befitting a freshman (as in college) ⟨a ~ innocence of outlook⟩

fresh·man·ship \ˈfreshmən,ship\ *n* **:** the quality or state of being a freshman

freshman week *n* **:** a week usu. just before the beginning of the college year given over to activities intended to orient entering students

fresh meadow *n* **:** a low-lying meadow made marshy or subject to inundation by fresh water

fresh·ness *n* -ES [ME *freshnesse*, fr. *fresh, fersh* fresh + -*nesse* -ness] **:** the quality or state of being fresh

fresh pursuit *or* **fresh suit** *n* [*fresh pursuit* prob. trans. of AF *fresche sute; fresh suit* fr. ME *vers suite* (trans. of AF *fresche sute*), fr. *fresh, fersh, vers* fresh + *suite* pursuit — more at SUIT] **:** a pursuit undertaken immediately or while the circumstances still indicate a reasonable chance for success to recapture property illegally taken or being moved in violation of law, to claim property in something not yet reduced to ownership, or to capture someone detected in a violation of law

fresh-run *adj, of an anadromous salmon* **:** recently returned to fresh water

[1]**freshwater** \ˈ=¦==\ *n* [ME *fresh water* (noun phrase), fr. *fresh, fersh* fresh + *water*] **:** a freshwater pond, lake, stream, or river

[2]**freshwater** \"\ *adj* [ME *fresh water* (noun phrase used attributively), fr. *fresh water* (noun phrase)] **1 :** of or belonging to water that is not salt **:** living in or taken from fresh water or a body of fresh water ⟨~ fish⟩ ⟨~ mussels⟩ **:** consisting of fresh as opposed to salt water ⟨a ~ stream⟩ **:** marked by bodies of fresh as opposed to salt water ⟨~ areas⟩ **:** taking place in a body of fresh water ⟨~ battles —Martin Levin⟩ **2 a :** accustomed to navigating only in freshwaters ⟨a ~ sailor⟩ **b** *obs* **:** UNTRAINED, UNSKILLED **3 :** inland and usu. provincial ⟨a small ~ town —G.Patton⟩ ⟨a ~ college⟩

freshwater catfish *n* **:** an Australian catfish (*Tandanus tandanus*) that is sometimes smoked and is also an excellent hardy aquarium fish — see NEW ZEALAND BLUE COD

freshwater clam *n* **:** MUSSEL 2

freshwater cod *or* **freshwater cusk** *n* **:** BURBOT

freshwater crab *n* **:** a small crab (*Sesarma bidentatum*) from upland streams of Jamaica

freshwater drum *n* **:** a croaker (*Aplodinotus grunniens*) of the Great Lakes and Mississippi valley that sometimes attains a weight of 50 pounds or more — called also *bubbler*

freshwater flying fish *n* **:** FLYING FISH 2

freshwater herring *n* **:** any of various fishes (as the Australian grayling or the Columbia chub) not closely related to herrings but likened to the herring in size or appearance or food qualities

freshwater limpet *n* **:** any minute conical gastropod (family Ancylidae) superficially resembling a limpet but living and feeding on freshwater plants — called also *river limpet*

freshwater medusa *n* **:** a jellyfish of the genus *Craspedacusta*

freshwater mussel *n* **:** MUSSEL 2

freshwater polyp *n* **:** HYDRA

freshwater shipworm *n, Austral* **:** a voracious and destructive shipworm (*Nausitora meselli*) inhabiting fresh and brackish waters

freshwater shrimp *n* **1 :** a member of the malacostracan order Amphipoda; *esp* **:** a member of a common genus (*Talitrus*) of relatively large amphipods **2** *Austral* **:** a small translucent decapod (*Paratypa australiense*) common in backwaters of the Murray river

freshy \ˈfreshē, -shi\ *n* -ES [*fresh*man + -*y*] *slang* **:** a freshman in a college, university, or secondary school

fres·nel \frāˈnel\ *n* -S [after Augustin J. *Fresnel* †1827 Fr. physicist] **:** a unit of frequency equal to one trillion cycles per second

fresnel biprism *n, usu cap F* **:** BIPRISM

fresnel lens *n, usu cap F* **:** a lens that has a surface consisting of a concentric series of simple lens sections so that a thin lens with a short focal length and large diameter is possible and that is used esp. in searchlights and viewing devices

fresnel mirrors *n, usu cap F* **:** two plane mirrors hinged so that there is no gap between the edges and so that the two planes make an angle with each other of nearly 180 degrees and used in demonstrating interference phenomena

fresnel rhomb *n, usu cap F* **:** a rhombic prism of glass used to transform plane polarized light into circularly polarized or elliptically polarized light

fres·no scraper \ˈfrez,nō-\ *or* **fresno** *n* -S *sometimes cap F* [*Fresno* Agricultural Works, Fresno, California, where it is made] **:** BUCK SCRAPER

fres·son process \freˈsōⁿ-\ *n, usu cap F* [after Henri T. *Fresson* †1951 Fr. agricultural engineer] **:** a printing process in photography which is similar to the carbon process but with no transferring and in which development of the image occurs when pigment is removed from the unexposed portions of the image by washing the print surface with finely divided wet sawdust

[1]**fret** \ˈfret, *usu* -ed.+V\ *vb* **fretted; fretted; fretting; frets** [ME *freten*, fr. OE *fretan*; akin to OHG *frezzan* to devour, Goth *fraitan*; all fr. a prehistoric EGmc-WGmc compound whose first and second constituents respectively are represented by Goth *fra-* for- and by Goth *itan* to eat — more at FOR-, EAT] *vt* **1 a** *obs* **:** EAT, DEVOUR **b** *archaic* **:** CONSUME ⟨our thin wardrobe eaten and *fretted* . . . by moths —Charles Lamb⟩ **2 a :** to cause to suffer emotional wear and tear **:** trouble persistently **:** VEX, TORMENT, WORRY ⟨misgiving *fretted* him —Carson McCullers⟩ ⟨don't you ~ yourself about me —J.C. Powys⟩ **b :** to bring by bothering or tormenting ⟨*fretted* to irritation by the remarks⟩ ⟨*fretted* out of her coma by a violent thirstiness —Florence Gould⟩ **3 a :** to eat into or wear away **:** CORRODE ⟨the acid *fretted* the metal⟩ ⟨the river *fretted* the soft banks⟩ ⟨rainwater ~*s* the rocks⟩; *also* **:** to make irregular esp. along an edge as if by eating **:** FRAY, RAVEL ⟨the horizon was *fretted* by long thin lines of spruce and fir —O.S.J.Gogarty⟩ ⟨honeycombed and *fretted* and pocked —M.S.Douglas⟩ **b :** RUB, CHAFE, GALL ⟨a harness strap was *fretting* the horse so that he became almost unmanageable⟩ **c :** to diminish or lessen by slow consumption or using up ⟨his *fretted* fortunes gave him hope and fear —Shak.⟩ **d :** to make by wearing away a substance ⟨the stream *fretted* a channel for itself through the soft earth⟩ **4 :** to pass, occupy, or waste (as time or life) in fretting ⟨a poor player that struts and ~*s* his hour upon the stage —Shak.⟩ — often used with *away* or *out* **5 :** ROUGHEN, AGITATE, DISTURB **:** cause to ripple ⟨~ the surface of the lake⟩ ~ *vi* **1 a :** to eat into something **:** make a way by wearing away or off or by corrosion **b :** RANKLE ⟨the insult *fretted* in his breast for some time⟩ **c :** to affect something as if by gnawing or biting **:** GRATE ⟨the . . . urgent voice *fretted* at his nerves —Graham Greene⟩ ⟨the familiar objects *fretted* on his mood —S.E.White⟩ **2 :** WEAR, CORRODE ⟨marble one expects to ~ away, for it is merely fused limestone, very subject to the solvent action of rain —*Sydney (Australia) Bulletin*⟩ **:** CHAFE ⟨his back where the harness rubbed began to ~⟩ **:** FRAY, RAVEL **3 a :** to become vexed, worried, impatient, or irritated ⟨*fretting* over the high cost of feeding their families —Vance Packard⟩ ⟨when I *fretted* with impatience —Isaac Rosenfeld⟩ **b** *of running water* **:** to become agitated ⟨a brook *fretting* over rocks⟩ **c :** to occupy oneself fretfully or impatiently **:** FUSS ⟨the cook had dinner simmering on the stove . . . and *fretted* with brooms, linens, mops —Frederick Way⟩ **d :** to feel impatient or irritated and usu. passive opposition ⟨tribes of hostile Indians who *fretted* against forward thrust of settlement —V.L.Parrington⟩ ⟨the younger son, *fretting* against parental opposition —C.D.Lewis⟩ **4** *now dial Eng* **:** FERMENT, WORK ⟨sweet wine is liable to ~⟩ **syn** see WORRY

[2]**fret** \"\ *n* -S [ME, action of gnawing, fr. *freten* to eat, devour, gnaw — more at [1]FRET] **1 a :** the action of eroding **:** a wasting away or being wasted away as if by being gnawed or eaten **b :** a worn or eroded spot (as in an asphalt highway or the insulation of an electric wire) **c** *obs* **:** a spot of decay **:** ULCER **2 a :** an agitation of mind marked by complaint and impatience **:** IRRITATION, FRETTING ⟨the cook was in a marked ~ because the potatoes had burned⟩ ⟨trying to curb his constant worry and ~⟩ **b :** something that frets the mind or temper ⟨one of those still moments when the small ~*s* vanish —D.H.Lawrence⟩ ⟨the great peace beyond all this turmoil and ~ —L.P. Smith⟩ ⟨relief from domestic ~*s* —S.H.Adams⟩ **3** *obs* **:** FLURRY, SQUALL **4 :** fermentation effervescence (as of liquor) **5 :** CHRYSAL

[3]**fret** \"\ *vt* **fretted; fretted; fretting; frets** [ME *fretten*, fr. MF *freter* to decorate with interlaced designs, bind with a ferrule, fr. OF, fr. *frete* ferrule] **1 a :** to decorate with interlaced designs **:** embroider with gold or silver **b :** to mark decoratively esp. with a network of things **:** form a pattern or design upon ⟨the air was *fretted* with a kaleidoscopic network of swifts —William Beebe⟩ **2 :** to enrich (as a ceiling) with embossed or pierced carved patterns

[4]**fret** \"\ *n* -S [ME, fr. MF *frete* interlaced design on a shield, fr. *freter* to decorate with interlaced designs] **1 :** an ornamental network; *esp* **:** a medieval net of gold, silver, or jewels for a woman's headdress **2 :** an ornament or ornamental work often in relief consisting of small straight bars intersecting one another in right or oblique angles or often of solid slats intersecting each other **3 a :** a heraldic device consisting of narrow bends crossed saltirewise and interlaced **b :** a heraldic device consisting of two narrow bends in saltire interlaced with a voided lozenge

fret 2: *1, 2, 3, 4,* Greek frets; *5* Japanese fret

[5]**fret** \"\ *n* -S [prob. fr. MF *frete* ferrule, fr. OF, prob. of Gmc origin; akin to OE *fetor* fetter — more at FETTER] **:** one of a series of ridges of metal, ivory, or other material fixed across the fingerboard of a guitar or similar instrument

[6]**fret** \"\ *vt* **fretted; fretted; fretting; frets :** to furnish with frets (as a stringed instrument)

[7]**fret** \"\ *n* -S [L *fretum* — more at FRETUM] *archaic* **:** STRAIT

fret·ful \ˈfretfəl\ *adj* [[1]*fret* + -*ful*] **1** *obs* **:** GNAWING, CORROSIVE, IRRITATING **2 a :** disposed to fret ⟨a ~ baby⟩ **:** PEEVISH ⟨a ~ and cantankerous old man⟩ **:** IMPATIENT, RESTLESS ⟨turned a ~ hungry eye upon the calendar, counting the days that intervened —A.J.Cronin⟩ ⟨a constant ~ stamping of hoofs upon splintery planks —Kenneth Roberts⟩ **b :** ILL-HUMORED, ANGRY ⟨weary days of ~ argument —C.A. & Mary Beard⟩ **3 a** *of water* **:** showing agitation **:** TROUBLED ⟨the ~ waters of the Rogue river —*Amer. Guide Series: Oregon*⟩ **b** *of wind* **:** coming brokenly **:** GUSTY **syn** see IRRITABLE

fret·ful·ly \-fəlē, -li\ *adv* **:** in a fretful manner

fret·ful·ness *n* -ES **:** the quality or state of being fretful

fretize *vt* -ED/-ING/-S [perh. fr. [4]*fret* + -*ize*] *obs* **:** to ornament with fretwork

fret·less \ˈfretləs\ *adj* **:** having no frets

frets *pres 3d sing of* FRET, *pl of* FRET

fretsaw \ˈ=,=\ *n* [[4]*fret*] **:** a narrow-bladed fine-toothed saw held under tension in a frame and used for cutting frets, scrolls, and other curved outlines; *also* **:** COMPASS SAW, COPING SAW

fret·some \ˈfretsəm\ *adj* [[1]*fret* + -*some*] **:** ANNOYING, IRRITATING, BOTHERSOME

fretted *adj* [fr. past part. of [3]*fret*] *of heraldic charges or ordinaries* **:** interlaced with one another — see PARTED AND FRETTED

fret·ter \ˈfred·ə(r), -etə-\ *n* -S [[1]*fret* + -*er*] **:** one that frets

[1]**fretting** *n* -S [ME *freting*, fr. *freten* to eat, devour, gnaw + -*inge*, -*ing* -ing — more at FRET] **:** damage caused by rubbing, chafing, or wearing away

[2]**fretting** *n* -S [ME *freting*, fr. *freten, fretten* to decorate with interlaced designs + -*inge*, -*ing* -ing — more at FRET] **:** FRETWORK

fret·ting·ly *adv* [ME *fretingly*, fr. *freting* (fr. *freten* to fret, devour + -*ing*, adj. suffix used to form the present participle) + -*ly* — more at FRET] **:** in the manner of one that frets ⟨hung around the house ~ occupying himself with trivialities⟩

[1]**fret·ty** \ˈfred·ē, -etē, -i\ *adj* [ME *frette*, fr. MF *freté*, fr. OF, past part. of *freter* to decorate with interlaced designs — more at FRET] **1** *heraldry* **:** covered with narrow bands interlacing saltirewise **2** *heraldry* **:** FRETTED

[2]**fretty** \"\ *adj* -ER/-EST [[1]*fret* + -*y*] **:** FRETFUL ⟨baby made ~ resentful sounds —Ethel Wilson⟩

fre·tum \ˈfrēd·əm, -ētəm\ *n, pl* **fre·ta** \-ēd·ə, -ētə\ [L; prob. akin to L *fervēre* to boil — more at BURN] **:** an arm of the sea **:** STRAIT

fretwork \ˈ=,=\ *n* [[4]*fret* + *work*] **1 a :** decoration consisting of work carved, pierced, or otherwise adorned with frets **b :** ornamental openwork or work in relief esp. when elaborate or intricate **2 :** something suggesting intricate fretwork ⟨the ~ of shade and sunshine —T.B.Macaulay⟩ ⟨the ~ of trees —Ellen Glasgow⟩

fretworked \ˈ=¦=\ *adj* **:** decorated with fretwork ⟨a ~ handle on the box⟩ **:** done in fretwork ⟨a ~ motto on the postcard⟩

[1]**freud·i·an** \ˈfrȯidēən\ *adj, often cap* [Sigmund *Freud* †1939 Austrian neurologist, founder of psychoanalysis + E -*ian*] **1 :** of, relating to, or according with the theories or practices of Sigmund Freud and his system of psychoanalysis ⟨~ theories⟩ ⟨~ repressions⟩ **2 a :** readily interpretable in psychoanalytic terms **:** characterized by thinly veiled psychodynamics ⟨a clear ~ reason for his action⟩ ⟨a ~ slip of the tongue⟩ **b :** arising from or belonging to repressed libidinal impulses ⟨a ~ compulsion⟩ **c :** SEXY, SMUTTY ⟨a bit too ~ in his remarks for polite society⟩ — **freud·i·an·ism** \-ə,nizəm\ *n* -S *usu cap*

[2]**freudian** \"\ *n* -S *usu cap* **:** an adherent of the Freudian school of psychoanalysis **:** an orthodox psychoanalyst

freud·ism \-,dizəm\ *n* -S *usu cap* **:** FREUDIANISM

freund's adjuvant \ˈfrȯin(d)z-\ *n, usu cap F* [after Jules T. *Freund* *b*1890 Am. immunologist] **:** any of various substances (as lanolin, paraffin oil, or killed tubercle bacilli) added to an antigen to enhance its antigenicity

frey·ci·ne·tia \,frāsəˈnēsh(ē)ə\ *n* [NL, fr. Louis C. de Saulces de *Freycinet* †1842 Fr. naval officer + NL -*ia*] **1** *cap* **:** a genus of Asiatic evergreen woody climbers (family Pandanaceae) with fleshy often brightly colored bracts and red berries **2** -S **:** any plant of the genus *Freycinetia*

fri·a·bil·i·ty \,frīəˈbiləd·ē, -ətē, -i\ *n* -ES **:** the condition of being friable

fri·a·ble \ˈfrīəbəl\ *adj* [MF or L; MF, fr. L *friabilis*, fr. *friare* to rub, crumble + -*abilis* -able — more at FRICTION] **:** easily crumbled, pulverized, or reduced to powder ⟨~ sandstone⟩ ⟨~ carcinomatous tissue⟩ ⟨~ curds formed in the stomach⟩ — **fri·a·ble·ness** *n* -ES

fri·and \ˈfrē,änd, *F* frēäⁿ\ *adj* [F, fr. OF *friant*, fr. pres. part. of *frire* to fry, roast — more at FRY] *archaic* **:** dainty or fond of dainties

fri·ar \ˈfrī(ə)r, -īə\ *n* -S [ME *frere, fryer*, fr. OF *frere*, lit., brother, fr. L *fratr-, frater* — more at BROTHER] **1 a :** a member of a mendicant order **b :** MONK **2 :** SILVERSIDES **3** *archaic* **:** a white or pale patch on a printed sheet caused by insufficient deposition of ink — compare MONK **4 :** PILGRIM BROWN

friarbird \ˈ=,=\ *n* [so called fr. its bare head and neck] **1 :** an Australian honey eater (*Philemon corniculatus*) having the head black and destitute of feathers — called also *four-o'clock* **2 :** any of various birds of Australia, New Guinea, and the southwest Pacific islands that are related to the friarbird

fri·ar·ly \-ī(ə)rlē, -īəl-, -li\ *adj* **:** like a friar **:** relating to friars

friar minor *n, pl* **friars minor** *usu cap F&M* [ME *frere menour*, fr. OF *frere meneur*] **:** a friar belonging to a division of the Franciscan order that follows the unmodified rule of St. Francis

friar minor conventual *n, pl* **friars minor conventual** *usu cap F&M&C* **:** a friar belonging to a division of the Franciscan order that follows a modified rule of St. Francis

friar preacher *n, pl* **friars preachers** *or* **friar preachers** *usu cap F&P* [ME *frere prechour*, fr. OF *frere preecheur*] **:** DOMINICAN

friar's balsam *n* **:** an alcoholic solution containing essentially benzoin, storax, balsam of Tolu, and aloes used chiefly as a local application (as for small fissures) and after addition to hot water as an inhalant in bronchitis — called also *compound benzoin tincture*

friar's chicken *n, Scot* **:** chicken broth with eggs in it

friar's cloth *n* **:** MONK'S CLOTH

friar's-cowl \ˈ=¦=¦=\ *n, pl* **friar's-cowls :** any of several plants having a cowled flower or inflorescence: as **a :** a European arum (*Arisarum vulgare*) with a cowl-shaped spathe **b :** CUCKOOPINT **c :** a common Old World monkshood (*Aconitum napellus*) having flowers with the helmet convex to hemispherical or arched

friar skate *n* **:** a European skate (*Raja alba*) or related fish

fri·ary \ˈfrī(ə)rē, -ri\ *n* -ES [alter. (influenced by *friar*) of earlier *frary* friary, brotherhood, fr. ME *frarie, frerie*, fr. MF *frarie, frairie, frerie*, fr. ML *fratria*, fr. *fratr-, frater* friar, monk (fr. L, brother) + L -*ia* -y — more at BROTHER] **:** a convent or brotherhood of friars **:** MONASTERY

frib \ˈfrib\ *n* -S [origin unknown] **:** a short small dirty lock of wool

[1]**frib·ble** \ˈfribəl\ *vb* **fribbled; fribbled; fribbling** \-b(ə)liŋ\ **fribbles** [origin unknown] *vi* **1 :** to act in a trifling or foolish manner **:** act frivolously **2** *obs* **:** TOTTER, STAMMER, FALTER ~ *vt* **:** to trifle or fool away

[2]**fribble** \"\ *n* -S **:** a frivolous person, thing, or idea **:** TRIFLER ⟨a man whom he pilloried as a ~ and a dilettante —Leonard Bacon⟩

[3]**fribble** \"\ *adj* **:** FRIVOLOUS, TRIFLING ⟨a ~ fellow who orders his dressing gown to match his sheets —*Time*⟩

fribbling *adj* **:** FRIVOLOUS, TRIFLING, CAPTIOUS ⟨~ banalities —P.A.Samuelson⟩

frib·by \ˈfribē\ *adj* -ER/-EST [*frib* + -*y*] *chiefly Brit* **:** SMALL, SHORT — used of locks of wool

fri·bourg \ˈfrē,bu̇(ə)r\ *n, usu cap* [fr. *Fribourg*, canton of Switzerland] **:** a Swiss breed of black and white cattle used for dairy, meat, and draft

fric·an·deau *also* **fric·an·do** \ˈfrikən,dō, ,==ˈ=\ *n, pl* **fricandeaux** \-ōz\ *or* **fricandeaus** \-ōz\ *also* **fricandoes** [F *fricandeau*, fr. MF, irreg. fr. *fricasser*] **:** larded veal roasted and glazed in its own juices

[1]**fric·as·see** \ˈfrikə,sē, ,==ˈ= *sometimes* ˌzē\ *n* -S [MF, fr. fem. of *fricassé*, past part. of *fricasser* to fricassee, perh. fr. *frire* to fry + *casse* ladle, dripping pan, kettle — more at FRY, CASSEROLE] **1 :** a stew formerly of light-colored meat (as veal or chicken) in a light gravy **2 :** a stew of meat or other foods in light or brown gravy

[2]**fricassee** \"\ *vt* **fricasseed; fricasseed; fricasseeing; fricassees :** to cook as a fricassee

fri·ca·tion \friˈkāshən\ *n* -S [ME *fricacioun*, fr. L *frication-*, *fricatio*, fr. *fricatus* (past part. of *fricare* to rub) + *-ion-*, *-io* -ion — more at FRICTION] 1 *obs* : FRICTION; *specif* : a rubbing of the body with the hands 2 a : a fricative sound b : the frictional rustling of a fricative sound

¹fric·a·tive \'frikəd·iv, -ətiv\ *adj* [L *fricatus* + E *-ive*] : characterized by frictional passage of the expired voiced or voiceless breath against a narrowing at some point in the vocal tract ⟨\f v th t͟h s z sh zh h\ are ~⟩ — compare SPIRANT

²fricative \"\ *n* -s : a fricative consonant

fric·a·trice \'frikə·trəs\ *n* -s [MF, female homosexual, fr. L *fricare* to rub + MF *-trice* -trix (fr. L *tric-*, *-trix*); trans. of L & Gk *tribas* — more at TRIBADE] *archaic* : a lewd woman : HARLOT; *specif* : a female homosexual

fricht \'frikt\ *Scot var of* FRIGHT

fricht·some \-səm\ *adj* [*fricht* + *-some*] *Scot* : FRIGHTFUL, TERRIBLE ⟨a ~ rain storm⟩

¹fric·tion \'frikshən\ *n* -s [MF or L; MF, fr. L *friction-*, *frictio*, fr. *frictus* (past part. of *fricare* to rub) + *-ion-*, *-io* -ion; akin to L *friare* to rub, crumble, OIr *brissim* I break, Skt *bhrīṇanti* they injure, hurt] 1 a : the act of rubbing one body against another : ATTRITION; *specif* : the act of rubbing the body esp. to stimulate the skin ⟨after the haircut, I had a shampoo, some ~, a little brilliantine —O.F.Karaka⟩ b : resistance to the relative motion of one body sliding, rolling, or flowing over another with which it is in contact c : the clashing between two persons or parties of opposed views : disagreement tending to prevent or retard progress 2 : rubber forced into textile fabric by calendering 3 : nonvibratory sound produced by impingement of air against some part of the respiratory tract

²friction \"\ *vt* -ED/-ING/-S : to impregnate (textile fabric) with rubber by calendering : RUBBERIZE

fric·tion·al \-shən°l, -shnəl\ *adj* : relating to friction : moved by friction : produced by friction ⟨~ electricity⟩ — **fric·tion·al·ly** \-°lē, -əlī, |ī\ *adv*

frictional gearing *n* : FRICTION GEARING

frictional unemployment *n* : the temporary unemployment of resources (as labor) resulting from job changes, imbalance of factors of production, or short term lack of mobility preventing continuous employment

friction bearing *n* : a solid bearing on a railroad freight car usu. of brass construction with babbitt lining whose interior surface is in direct contact with the surface of the axle end which it supports

friction board *n* : a heavy compressed impregnated solid paperboard used for making pulleys usu. by cutting into disks that are then compacted together coaxially

friction brake *n* 1 : a brake operating by friction 2 : an absorption dynamometer that absorbs energy by friction

friction breccia *n* : a breccia composed of rocks shattered and crushed under friction

friction calender *n* : a calender used for friction glazing — compare SUPERCALENDER

friction clamp *n* : a clamp that holds or supports by friction alone without indentation or deformation of the bodies concerned

friction clutch *n* : a clutch in which connection is made through sliding friction

friction composition *n* : a composition that readily ignites by friction — compare ³MATCH 3

friction crack *n* : a short crack in glaciated rock that is transverse to the direction of ice movement and that presumably results from local increase in friction between ice and rock

friction drive *n* : an automobile power-transmission system in which the gearbox is replaced by a friction gearing the driver and follower of which are arranged so that by varying their position relative to one another a full range of variation in desired speed ratios may be obtained

friction gearing *also* **friction gear** *n* : a gearing for transmitting motion by surface friction instead of by teeth

friction–glazed \'ˌ=ˌ=\ *adj, of paper* : glazed by being passed in a continuous sheet between two calender rolls one of which by revolving faster than the other burnishes the surface — compare FLINT-GLAZED — **friction glazing** *n*

friction head *n* : the head (sense 14a) lost by flowing water as a result of friction between the moving water and the walls of its conduit plus intermolecular disturbances

friction horsepower *n* : power lost esp. in an internal-combustion engine through friction between parts of the machine itself

fric·tion·ize \'frikshəˌnīz\ *vt* -ED/-ING/-S : to act upon by friction or rubbing

friction jewel *n* : a bearing jewel that is pressed-fit into place in a watch plate

fric·tion·less \'frikshənləs\ *adj* 1 : devoid of friction ⟨a ~ connection between the two moving parts⟩ : operating without significant friction ⟨a ~ bearing⟩ 2 : AMICABLE ⟨a totally ~ relationship existed between the two people⟩ — **fric·tion·less·ly** *adv*

friction match *n* : a match that is ignited by friction and has a tip usu. containing phosphorus sulfide mixed with other combustibles and with oxidizing material (as potassium chlorate, saltpeter, or red lead)

friction primer *n* : a device operating by friction used for igniting the charge in a cannon

friction ridge *n* : one of the corrugated ridges characteristic of the skin of the palmar and plantar surfaces of primates

frictions *pl of* FRICTION, *pres 3d sing of* FRICTION

friction saw *n* : a toothless circular saw used for cutting metals or other materials by fusion in the cut due to frictional heat — **friction sawing** *n*

friction slip *n* : a slipping friction clutch or coupling

friction socket *n* : a tool used for recovering tools of small diameter from a well

friction sound *n* : an auscultatory sound caused by the rubbing together of two inflamed serous surfaces (as of the pleural membranes in pleurisy)

friction tape *n* : cotton tape impregnated with water-resistant insulating material and an adhesive and used esp. to protect, insulate, and support electrical conductors — called also *electric tape*

friction–tight \'ˌ=ˌ=\ *adj* : tight enough to operate by means of friction

friction top *n* : a top for a container held in place by friction between the mating parts

friction wheel *or* **friction pulley** *n* : a wheel operating by friction (as in a friction gearing)

fri·day \'frīdē, -di *also* -(ˌ)dā\ *n* -s *usu cap* [ME, fr. OE *frīgedæg*; akin to OFris *frīadei*, *frīgendei* Friday, OHG *frīatag*; all fr. a prehistoric WGmc compound formed from components represented by OHG *Fria*, the Germanic goddess of love, and *tag* day; trans. of L *Veneris dies*, lit., day of Venus (the Roman goddess of love and the planet Venus) — more at DAY] : the sixth day of the week : the day following Thursday

fri·days \"+z\ *adv, usu cap* : on Friday repeatedly : on any Friday

¹fridge \'frij\ *vb* -ED/-ING/-S [prob. alter. of ¹*frig*] *vt, dial Eng* : RUB, FRAY, IRRITATE ~ *vi, dial Eng* : FIDGET, CHAFE

²fridge \"\ *n* -s [by shortening and alter.] *chiefly Brit* : REFRIGERATOR

fridstool *var of* FRITHSTOOL

fried \'frīd\ *adj* [ME, fr. past part. of *frien* to fry — more at FRY] 1 *of food* : cooked by frying 2 : INTOXICATED ⟨he was plenty ~ when he left here —William Ward⟩

friedcake \'ˌ=ˌ=\ *n* : a cake in the form of a ring, twist, ball, or strip fried in deep fat : DOUGHNUT, CRULLER

frie·del–crafts reaction \frē¦del'kraf(t)s-, ¦frē,del¦-\ *n, usu cap F&C* [after Charles *Friedel* †1899 Fr. chemist & James M. *Crafts* †1917 Am. chemist] : a synthetic reaction in organic chemistry in which anhydrous aluminum chloride acts as the typical catalyst: as a : the synthesis of a hydrocarbon (as ethylbenzene) by alkylation of an aromatic hydrocarbon with an alkyl halide b : the synthesis of a ketone (as benzophenone) by acylation of an aromatic hydrocarbon with an acyl chloride or acid anhydride

frie·del·in \frē'delən\ *n* -s [Charles *Friedel* + E *-in*] : a crystalline triterpenoid ketone $C_{30}H_{50}O$ extracted esp. from cork

frie·del·ite \-ˌlīt\ *n* -s [F, fr. Charles *Friedel* + F *-ite*] : a mineral $Mn_8Si_6O_{18}(OH, Cl)_4.3H_2O$ consisting of a rose-red manganese silicate containing chlorine (hardness 4–5, sp. gr. 3.07)

fried·länd·er's bacillus \'frēt|ˌlendə(r)z-, -ēd|\ *also* **fried·länder bacillus** *or* **friedländer's pneumobacillus** *n, usu cap F* [after Carl *Friedländer* †1887 Ger. pathologist] : PNEUMOBACILLUS

fried·man test \'frēdmən-\ *also* **friedman's test** *n, usu cap F* [after Maurice H. *Friedman* b1903 Am. physiologist] : a modification of the Aschheim-Zondek test for pregnancy using rabbits as test animals

fried pie *n* : a turnover fried in deep fat

fried·reich's ataxia \'frē,drīks-, -īks\ *also* **friedreich's disease** *n, usu cap F* [after Nikolaus *Friedreich* †1882 Ger. physician] : a recessive hereditary anomaly marked by muscular incoordination and twitching and usu. becoming manifest in the adult

fried·richs·dor \'¦frēdriks¦dȯ(ə)r, -iks-\ *n* -s [G, fr. *Friedrich* Frederick II †1786 king of Prussia + F *d'or* of gold] 1 : a former gold coin of Prussia equal to five silver talers first struck by Frederick II 2 : FREDERIK

¹friend \'frend\ *n* -s [ME *frend*, fr. OE *frēond*; akin to OHG *friunt* friend, relative, ON *frændi* blood relative, friend, Goth *frijonds* friend; all fr. the pres. part. of a Gmc verb represented by OE *frēogan*, *frēon* to love, OS *friohan*, *friehan*, ON *frjā*, Goth *frijon*; akin to OE *frēo* free — more at FREE] 1 a : one that seeks the society or welfare of another whom he holds in affection, respect, or esteem or whose companionship and personality are pleasurable : an intimate associate esp. when other than a lover or relative — often used as a form of address b : ACQUAINTANCE 2 a : one not hostile or not an enemy b : one that is of the same nation, party, or other group and whose friendly feelings are assumed or from whom sympathy or cooperation is expected 3 : one that gives assistance or that favors or promotes something (as a cause, institution, or project) ⟨~s of divorce and birth control, or critics of denominational education —Paul Blanshard⟩ ⟨the inexhaustible ~ of all good causes —Van Wyck Brooks⟩ ⟨this trend has alarmed ~s of the liberal arts —Raymond Walters b. 1885⟩ ⟨nature is still the painter's nearest ~ —F.J.Mather⟩ 4 *now chiefly Scot* : KINSMAN 5 a *obs* : PARAMOUR b : a favored date : a boyfriend or girlfriend : SWEETHEART 6 *cap* : one of a religious group of Christians that lay special stress on the guidance of the Holy Spirit, that reject outward rites and an ordained ministry, that practice simplicity of dress and speech, and that have a long tradition of actively working for peace and opposing war — called also *Quaker* 7 : a troublesome acquaintance : one causing or likely to cause annoyance ⟨has your ~ been up bothering you lately⟩

syn ACQUAINTANCE, INTIMATE, CONFIDANT: FRIEND applies to a person one has regarded with liking and a degree of respect and has known for a time in a pleasurable relationship neither notably intimate nor dependent wholly on business or professional ties ⟨a *friend* is one who knows all about us, but is loyal to us just the same —C.A.Dial⟩ ⟨a companion loves some agreeable qualities which a man may possess, but a *friend* loves the man himself —James Boswell⟩ ACQUAINTANCE is likely to indicate one known, usu. not unfavorably, with less familiarity, closeness, fellowship, and well-wishing than FRIEND ⟨you understand that I am not their friend. I am only a holiday *acquaintance* —Joseph Conrad⟩ INTIMATE implies a closeness precluding reserve or reservation ⟨a few *intimates* in whose critical judgment he had confidence —Allen Johnson⟩ CONFIDANT (applicable to persons of either sex, although the feminine form *confidante* is still used) indicates a person in whom one confides secrets, usu. but not necessarily an intimate ⟨the same detective and his friend and *confidant*, Dr. Watson —A.C.Ward⟩ ⟨could she make a *confidant* of such a man? Something in her yearned to unburden itself in a torrent of pitiful words —J.C.Powys⟩

— **be friends with** : to have friendly relations with ⟨making an effort to *be friends with* people they essentially disliked⟩ — **make friends with** : to become friendly with : establish friendly relations with ⟨advised the child to *make friends with* as many of his classmates as possible⟩ — compare MAKE *vt* 24a

²friend \"\ *vt* -ED/-ING/-S [ME *frenden*, fr. *frend*, n.] 1 *obs* : to make friends of : join as friends 2 : to act as the friend of : BEFRIEND, AID, SERVE ⟨and I will ~ you, if I may, in the dark and cloudy day —A.E.Housman⟩

friend at court *or* **friend in court** [ME *frend in court*] : one in a position of importance or influence who is disposed to act in one's behalf

friend·ed \-dəd\ *adj* [ME *frended*, fr. past part. of *frenden*] *archaic* : provided with friends

friending *n* -s [fr. gerund of ²*friend*] *obs* : FRIENDLINESS

friend·less \'frendləs, *rapid* -nl-\ *adj* [ME *frendles*, fr. OE *frēondlēas*, fr. *frēond* friend + *-lēas* -less] : having no friends — **friend·less·ness** *n* -ES

friend·li·ly \-lələ, -ləli\ *adv* [¹*friendly* + *-ly*] : in a friendly manner

friend·li·ness \'frendlēnəs, -lin-, *rapid* -enl-\ *n* -ES [ME *frendlinesse*, fr. *frendly* + *-nesse* -ness] : the quality or state of being friendly ⟨a certain indescribable kindliness or ~ of spirit —P.E.More⟩

¹friend·ly \-lē, -li\ *adj* -ER/-EST [ME *frendly*, fr. OE *frēondlic*, fr. *frēond* friend + *-lic* -ly — more at FRIEND] 1 : of, relating to, befitting, or typical of a friend, of friends, or of friendship: as a : showing or marked by the disposition or attitude of one that is or wishes to be a friend : manifesting or disposed to goodwill, kindly interest, pleasant warmth, or familiar sociability ⟨~ neighbors⟩ ⟨a ~, approachable person —C.H. Voss⟩ ⟨wished to be ~ to even the worst members of the club⟩ : prone to favor, support, or aid ⟨a teacher not too ~ toward independent students⟩ ⟨an administration ~ to experimentation⟩ ⟨a ~ correspondence with a former rival⟩ b : not hostile or antagonistic ⟨a ~ state⟩ ⟨~ Indians⟩; *specif* : belonging to one's own country's forces or those of an ally ⟨~ planes⟩ ⟨in ~ territory⟩ ⟨an unduly heavy price in ~ casualties —*N.Y. Times*⟩ ⟨fell victim to a ~ destroyer which . . . would not listen to her frantic signals —E.L.Beach⟩ c (1) : warm and comforting or cheerful ⟨sitting in the ~ glow of the fire⟩ ⟨came out of a drab side street into the ~ lights of the theater district⟩ (2) : having qualities that attract and none that are forbidding in any way ⟨~ and charming hills —Mark Saxton⟩ (3) : conducing to amicable feeling and goodwill ⟨the ~ rooms of the club⟩ 2 : serving a beneficial or helpful purpose : FAVORABLE, PROPITIOUS ⟨a ~ breeze finally drove the boat into harbor⟩ ⟨official attitudes that are ~ to private investors —*U.S.News & World Report*⟩ 3 : marked by a lack of fierce zeal for victory : engaged in for sport or recreation rather than for stakes or prizes : not bitterly, savagely, or hotly contested ⟨a ~ game of tennis⟩ ⟨a ~ game of poker with a maximum raise of two cents⟩ 4 *usu cap* : of or relating to the Friends **syn** see AMICABLE

²friendly \"\ *adv, usu* -ER/-EST [ME *frendly*, fr. OE *frēondlice*, fr. *frēondlic*, adj.] : in a friendly manner : AMICABLY, FRIENDLILY ⟨he was . . . ~ disposed toward the British —W.G. Harmon⟩

³friendly \"\ *n* -ES [¹*friendly*] : one that is friendly; *esp* : a native who is friendly to settlers or invaders ⟨but bands began to form and the cry rose, "Kill the whites! Kill the *friendlies!*" —Meridel Le Sueur⟩

friendly crab *n* : WOOD CRAB

friendly fire *n* : a fire contained within the receptacle provided for it (as a boiler or heater), no liability being assumed in a fire insurance contract by the underwriter for property destroyed by the fire while thus contained — compare HOSTILE FIRE

friendly society *n, Brit* : BENEFIT SOCIETY

friend of god *usu cap F&G* [trans. of G *gottes freund*] : a clerical or lay mystic of a 14th century Rhenish and Swiss movement that sought holiness not in ceremonies and creeds but in a direct personal relationship with God

friend of the court 1 : AMICUS CURIAE 2 : a public officer in Michigan who assists the court, aids in carrying out its orders and decrees, and advises the public in many matters (as those involving domestic relations)

friends *pl of* FRIEND, *pres 3d sing of* FRIEND

friend·ship \'fren(d)ˌship, -nˌship\ *n* [ME *frendship*, fr. OE *frēondscipe*, fr. *frēond* friend + *-scipe* -ship] 1 a : the state of being friends ⟨the two men valued their long-standing ~⟩ : the state of being in a friendly relationship ⟨the two countries made enough concessions to each other so that their ~ was not endangered by the crisis⟩ b : the state of being a friend ⟨the man valued his neighbor's ~⟩ 2 : friendly feeling : FRIENDLINESS ⟨felt encouraged by the ~ his fellow employees showed him⟩ 3 *obs* : AID, HELP, ASSISTANCE

friendship sloop \"-\ *n, usu cap F* [fr. *Friendship*, Maine] : a sloop-rigged centerboard fishing boat typically about 30 feet overall that has a clipper bow and strong sheer and that is popular along the Maine coast

frier *var of* FRYER

fries *pl of* FRY, *pres 3d sing of* FRY

¹frie·sian \'frēzhən *also* -zhēən\ *usu cap, var of* FRISIAN

²friesian \"\ *n* -s *usu cap, chiefly Brit* : HOLSTEIN-FRIESIAN

fries·land \'frēz|lənd, -ēsl-, -ˌland\ *n, often cap* [fr. *Friesland*, province in the Netherlands] *southern Africa* : HOLSTEIN-FRIESIAN

fries reaction \'frēs-, -ēz-\ *n, usu cap F* [after Karl *Fries* b1875 Ger. chemist] : the isomerization of an aryl ester of a carboxylic acid into a phenolic ketone by means of anhydrous aluminum chloride

¹frieze \'frēz, frē'zā, frə'zā\ *n* -s [ME *frise*, fr. MF *frise*, fr. MD *friese*, *vriese* — more at FRIZZLE] 1 a : a heavy durable fabric with a rough surface that is woven of coarse wool and shoddy in gray or mixed colors and is made esp. in Ireland for overcoats b : a wiry upholstery fabric with patterns in cut and uncut loops that is made with a cotton backing and a wool, mohair, or rayon pile 2 a : a pile surface of uncut loops or of patterned cut and uncut loops; *also* : the yarn used for such a surface b : a carpet having a pile of tightly twisted yarn

²frieze \'frēz\ *vt* -ED/-ING/-S [ME *frisen*, fr. *frise*, n.] : to make a nap on (cloth)

³frieze \'frēz\ *n* -s [MF *frise*, perh. fr. ML *phrygium*, *frigium*, *frisium* embroidery, embroidered cloth, fr. L *Phrygium*, neut. of *Phrygius* Phrygian, fr. *Phrygia*, noted for its fine embroidery; fr. the fancy decorations reminiscent of embroidery on some friezes] 1 a : the part of an entablature that is between the architrave and the cornice b : a sculptured or richly ornamented band (as on a building or a piece of furniture) — see ENTABLATURE illustration 2 : a band, line, or series suggesting a frieze ⟨a ~ of willows —C.B.Firestone⟩ ⟨a constant ~ of visitors wound its way around the . . . ruins —Mollie Panter-Downes⟩ ⟨an interminable ~ of sobbing boys, dying dogs and disabled children —*Time*⟩

⁴frieze \"\ *vt* -ED/-ING/-S : to adorn with a frieze

frieze rail *n* [³*frieze*] : the rail below a frieze panel

friez·ing \'frēziŋ\ *n* -s [³*frieze* + *-ing*] : a frieze esp. along a ship's quarter

friezy \-zē\ *adj* -ER/-EST [¹*frieze* + *-y*] : made of frieze or of a rough cloth resembling frieze ⟨a ~ coat⟩ : resembling frieze ⟨a ~ cloth⟩

¹frig \'frig\ *vb* **frigged**; **frigged**; **frigging**; **frigs** [ME *friggen*] *vi, now dial Eng* : WRIGGLE ~ *vt, dial chiefly Eng* : RUB, CHAFE

²frig \"\ *vb* **frigged**; **frigged**; **frigging**; **frigs** [prob. fr. ¹*frig*] *vt* : to copulate with — usu. considered vulgar ~ *vi* 1 : COPULATE — usu. considered vulgar; in its *-ing* form often in speech a meaningless intensive 2 : to waste time in a futile or fooling manner — often used with *around*

³frig \'frij\ *n* -s [by shortening] *Brit* : REFRIGERATOR

frig·ate \'frigət, *usu* -əd·+V\ *n* -s [MF *frigate*, fr. It *fregata*] 1 : a light boat propelled orig. by oars but later by sails 2 : a ship of a former class of ship-rigged war vessels intermediate between corvettes and ships of the line usu. with a full battery on the gun deck and a light battery on the spar deck 3 : a British or Canadian escort ship between a corvette and a destroyer in size and corresponding to a U. S. destroyer escort 4 : a ship of a class of U. S. warships of 5000 to 7000 tons that is smaller than a cruiser and larger than a destroyer

frigate 2

frigate bird *n* : any of several long-winged strong-flying sea birds chiefly of tropical seas (family Fregatidae) that are noted for their rapacious habits and obtain much of their diet of chiefly fish by robbing other birds — called also *man-o'-war bird*

frigate–built \'ˌ=ˌ=\ *adj, of a ship* : built with a raised quarter-deck and forecastle

frigate mackerel *n* : a small scombroid fish (*Auxis thazard*) that is bluish green above and silvery beneath and often marked with black spots or wavy bars and that is very oily and little sought for food or game though widely available in warm seas

frigefact *vt* -ED/-ING/-S [L *frigefactare*, fr. *frigēre* to be cold, freeze + *factare* to make, do, freq. of *facere* to make, do — more at FRIGID, DO] *obs* : CHILL — **frigefaction** *n* -s *obs* — **frigefactive** *adj, obs*

frig·gle \'frigəl\ *vi* -ED/-ING/-S [freq. of ¹*frig*] *dial Brit* : to fuss over trifles : PUTTER

¹fright \'frīt, *usu* -īd·+V\ *n* -s [ME, fr. OE *fyrhto*, *fryhto* fear, fright; akin to OE *forht* afraid, fearful, OFris *fruchte* fear, OS & OHG *forht*, *foraht* afraid, *forhta* fear, Goth *faurhts* afraid, *faurhtei* fear, and perh. to Toch A *pärsk-*, *prask-* to fear, *praski* fear, Toch B *pärsk-*, *präsk-* to fear, *prosko*, *proskye* fear] 1 a : terror excited by sudden danger : sudden and violent fear usu. of short duration : ALARM ⟨familiarity rubbed away the ~ at the strangeness and dissipated the prejudice born of ignorance —Oscar Handlin⟩ b : an instance of such terror, fear, or alarm ⟨the sudden apparition gave him a ~⟩ c : FEAR ⟨incessant ~ of the future —Oscar Handlin⟩ 2 : something strange, ugly, unsightly, or shocking ⟨he was a bundle of rags, his hair had grown prodigiously, his beard was a ~ —I.L.Idriess⟩ **syn** see FEAR

²fright \"\ *vt* -ED/-ING/-S [ME *frighten*, fr. OE *fyrhtan*, *fryhtan*; akin to OE *forhtian* to fear, OFris *fruchtia*, OS *forhtian*, OHG *furhten*, *forhten*, Goth *faurhtjan* to fear, OE *fyrhto*, *fryhto*, n.] : to alarm suddenly : SCARE, FRIGHTEN ⟨are not easily ~*ed* by politics —*Kiplinger Washington Letter*⟩ **syn** see FRIGHTEN

fright disease *n* : CANINE HYSTERIA

fright·en \'frīt°n\ *vb* **frightened**; **frightened**; **frightening** \-t(°)niŋ\ **frightens** [¹*fright* + *-en*] *vt* 1 : to markedly disturb with fear : throw into a state of alarm : make afraid : TERRIFY ⟨the mask ~*ed* the child⟩ 2 a : to impel or drive by frightening ⟨~*ed* the boy into confessing his crime⟩ ⟨~*ed* the prowler away⟩ b : to evoke by the use of frightening methods ⟨~ the secret out of the man⟩ 3 *dial Eng* : to take by surprise : AMAZE ⟨I shouldn't be ~*ed* if it rained today⟩ ~ *vi* 1 : to produce fright : SCARE, TERRIFY ⟨a costume designed to ~⟩ 2 : to become frightened ⟨not a man who ~*s* easily⟩

syn FRIGHT, SCARE, ALARM, TERRIFY, TERRORIZE, STARTLE, AFFRAY, AFFRIGHT: these verbs have in common the meaning of to fill with fear or dread. FRIGHTEN, perhaps the most general, may apply to a momentary reaction of mild or acute apprehension or to a long-standing state of mind in which fear or dread prevails, although more frequently implying a shortish reaction of acute apprehension and generally suggesting a paralyzing effect upon the body or the will ⟨children *frightened* by thunder⟩ ⟨the silence of the house for a long time *frightened* Clara —Sherwood Anderson⟩ ⟨when I started down that precipice I was *frightened*, literally scared numb and stiff —W.A.White⟩ FRIGHT is an older and now almost solely literary or dialect form of FRIGHTEN ⟨you have Death perpetually before your eyes, only so far removed as to compose the mind without *frighting* it —Thomas Gray⟩ Often equivalent to FRIGHTEN in conversational use, SCARE usu. implies a quick fear that causes one to run, shy, or tremble ⟨the near approach of death *scared* him into sincerity —T.B. Macaulay⟩ ⟨sensational books commonly try to *scare* the reader —C.E.Kellogg⟩ ALARM, in modern use, stresses apprehension or anxiety ⟨they had been *alarmed* during the night by loud noises that must have been demolitions of some kind —Eric Linklater⟩ ⟨my mother, *alarmed* by the cries and fighting, came running downstairs to help me —R.L.Stevenson⟩ TERRIFY puts stress upon acute fear and agitation, usu. suggesting a state of mind in which self-control or self-direction are impossible ⟨something in his face and in his voice *terrified* her heart —Robert Hichins⟩ ⟨these things *terrified* the people to the last degree —Daniel Defoe⟩ TERRORIZE, as distinct from TERRIFY, often implies an intentional affecting with terror ⟨a band of cutthroats and thieves that *terrorized* the lower Mississippi valley —*Amer. Guide Series: Tenn.*⟩ ⟨he delighted in *terrorizing* the guests by his bullying and swaggering ways —E.V.Buckholder⟩ STARTLE always implies surprise or a sudden usu. light shock that causes one to jump or shrink ⟨an infant is *startled* by a loud noise —Morris Fishbein⟩ ⟨suddenly she was *startled* into an upright position, with her eyes staring and her mouth wide open —Liam O'Flaherty⟩ AFFRAY and AFFRIGHT are now archaic and found usu. in poetic works; AFFRAY is very close to TERRIFY, AFFRIGHT close to FRIGHTEN ⟨blastings and blightings of hope and love, and rude shocks that *affray* —Robert Bridges †1930⟩ ⟨I was *affrighted* by that impossible novel —W.B.Yeats⟩ ⟨a picture of Purgatory which made the hair of those who gazed on it stand on end in terror, and so *affrighted* the butchers and the fishmongers that they abandoned their trade of taking life —Laurence Binyon⟩

fright·en·able \-t(ᵊ)nəbəl\ *adj* : capable of being frightened ⟨a child too easily ~⟩

frightened *adj* : affected with fright : made afraid : SCARED ⟨a ~ child⟩ ⟨~ of doing wrong⟩ **syn** see AFRAID

fright·ened·ly \-t(ᵊ)n(ə)dlē, -li\ *adv* : in a frightened manner

frightening *adj* : tending to frighten : exciting alarm ⟨a ~ display of air power⟩ ⟨a ~ apparition⟩ — **fright·en·ing·ly** *adv*

fright·ful \ˈfrītfəl\ *adj, sometimes* **frightfuller**; **frightfullest** [ME, fr. ¹*fright* + *-ful*] **1 a** *archaic* : tending to frighten easily : TIMID **b** *dial chiefly Eng* : ALARMED, FRIGHTENED **2** : conducive to fright : likely to arouse the emotions of fright, fear, or alarm ⟨the gods, as they appear to men, are radiant . . . the demons are ~, producing perturbation and terror —H.O. Taylor⟩ ⟨seeing some ~ specter —Charles Lamb⟩ **3** : egregious, startling, objectionable, or terrible (as because of enormity, outrageousness, or grotesqueness) and likely to shock, alarm, revolt, or stun ⟨its cost in money, property loss, and lives was ~ —Allan Nevins & H.S.Commager⟩ ⟨they talked most ~ scandal —George Meredith⟩ ⟨regard the most ~ things as normal —H.M.Parshley⟩ **4** : EXTREME, AWFUL ⟨a ~ thirst⟩ ⟨a ~ snob⟩ **syn** see FEARFUL

fright·ful·ly \-f(ə)lē, -li\ *adv* : in a frightful manner: as **a** : ALARMINGLY ⟨worried by the ~ fast movement of the car over the dark road⟩ **b** : EGREGIOUSLY, SHOCKINGLY ⟨the ~ cruel treatment of the animal⟩ **c** : VERY, EXTREMELY ⟨I'm ~ sorry I inconvenienced you⟩

fright·ful·ness \-fəlnəs\ *n* -ES **1** : the quality or state of being frightful **2** [trans. of G *schrecklichkeit*] : action or policy intended to terrorize esp. in warfare

frighting *pres part of* FRIGHT

frights *pl of* FRIGHT, *pres 3d sing of* FRIGHT

fright wig *n* : a costume wig with hair that stands out from the head or that may be made to stand out when the wearer wants it to

frig·id \ˈfrijəd\ *adj* [L *frigidus*, fr. *frigēre* to be cold; akin to L *frigus* frost, cold, Gk *rhigos*] **1 a** : very cold : markedly lacking heat or warmth ⟨a ~ climate⟩ ⟨a ~ day⟩ ⟨natural caves where the ~ water coats the surroundings with ice —*Amer. Guide Series: N.H.*⟩ **b** : lacking warmth, ardor, or vivacity of feeling : forbidding in manner : stiff and formal **c** : indifferent or hostile ⟨felt ~ toward the plan⟩ **2** : lacking imaginative qualities : INSIPID, PLODDING, DULL ⟨an artist's ~ conception⟩ ⟨writing a precise and ~ poetry⟩; *also* : POINTLESS, SENSELESS **3 a** : abnormally averse to sexual intercourse — used esp. of women **b** *obs* : lacking sexual vigor : IMPOTENT **c** *of a female* : unable to achieve orgasm during sexual intercourse — **frig·id·ly** *adv* — **frig·id·ness** *n* -ES

Frig·i·daire \ˌfrijəˈda(a)(ə)r, -deˌ, |ə\ *trademark* — used for a mechanical refrigerator

frig·i·dar·i·um \ˌfrijəˈda(a)rēəm\ *n, pl* **frigidar·ia** \-ēə\ [L, fr. *frigidus* + *-arium*] : a room of the ancient Roman thermae furnished with a cold bath and used for cooling off

fri·gid·i·ty \frəˈjidəd·ē, -ətē, -i\ *n* -ES [ME *frigidite*, fr. LL *frigiditas*, fr. L *frigidus* + *-itas* -ity] : the quality or state of being frigid; *specif* : marked or abnormal sexual indifference esp. in a woman

frigid zone *n* : the area or region between the arctic circle and the north pole or between the antarctic circle and the south pole — see ZONE illustration

frigo- *comb form* [ISV, fr. L *frigus* frost, cold] : cold ⟨*frigo*stable⟩ ⟨*frigo*therapy⟩

frig·o·rif·ic \ˌfrigəˈrifik\ *adj* [L *frigorificus*, fr. *frigor-*, *frigus* frost, cold + *-i-* + *-ficus* -fic — more at FRIGID] : causing cold : COOLING, CHILLING

fri·go·ri·fi·co \ˌfrigəˈrifəˌkō\ *n* -S [AmerSp *frigorifico*, fr. Sp, adj., chilling, fr. L *frigorificus*] **1** : a So. American meat-packing plant primarily for the exportation of frozen meat **2** *or* **frigorifico hide** : a So. American cattle hide from a frigorifico

frig·o·rim·e·ter \ˌfrigəˈrimədə(r)\ *n* [L *frigor-*, *frigus* coldness + E *-i-* + *-meter*] : a low-temperature thermometer

frigs *pres 3d sing of* FRIG, *pl of* FRIG

fri·jol \(ˈ)frēˈhōl, -ˈhōl\ *also* **fri·jole** \ˈ", frēˈhōlē\ *n, pl* **fri·jo·les** \frēˈhōlēz, -ˈhōˌlās, -ˈhōˌlās\ [Sp *frijol*, fr. earlier *fesol*, *fresol*, fr. Pg *feijão* or Pg dial. (Galicia) *freixó*, *feixoo*, fr. L *phaseolus* kidney bean, dim. of *phaselus*, fr. Gk *phasēlos*] *chiefly Southwest* : BEAN 1b: as **a** : KIDNEY BEAN **b** : COWPEA 1b

fri·jo·li·llo \ˌfrē(h)əˈlē(ˌ)(y)ō\ *n* -S [AmerSp, dim. of Sp *frijol*] : any of several leguminous herbs or trees: as **a** : CORAL BEAN 2 **b** : LOCOWEED

¹**frill** \ˈfril\ *vb* -ED/-ING/-S [perh. fr. Flem *frullen*, fr. *frul*, n.] *vt* **1 a** : to provide or decorate with a frill ⟨~ a cap⟩ : crimp or pleat an edge of **b** : to serve as a frill for ⟨if you look up . . . you see that clouds ~ the sky —Leo Sinden⟩ **2** *Austral* : to ring (a tree) with a frill : FRILL-BARK ~ *vi, of a photographic emulsion* : to wrinkle and loosen from the film or plate support

²**frill** \ˈ"\ *n* -S [perh. fr. Flem *frul*] **1** : an ornamental flared or ruffled edge: as **a** : a gathered, pleated, or bias-cut fabric edging used on clothing **b** : a strip of paper curled at one end and rolled to be slipped over the bone end (as of a chop) in serving **2** : something resembling a frill ⟨a ~ of white beard edging his face —Victoria Sackville-West⟩ as: **a** : a fold of hair or feathers about the neck of an animal **b** : an architectural ornamental trimming ⟨gables decorated with jigsaw ~s —*Amer. Guide Series: Tenn.*⟩ ⟨varicolored houses often ornamented with little baroque ~s in white —Christopher Rand⟩ **c** : AFFECTATION, AIR — usu. used in pl. ⟨an honest, just, ever generous man who had no ~s, no side, no nonsense about him —W.A.White⟩ **d** : something that has only decorative significance and can be dispensed with : something refined, tasty, or elegant but insubstantial : something not essential : SUPERFLUITY, EXTRAVAGANCE, DAINTY, DELICACY, LUXURY ⟨the elimination of typographic ~s and unnecessary elaboration —*Linotype News*⟩ ⟨one man's fundamentals may be another man's ~s —Bice Clemow⟩ ⟨detestation of anything resembling ~s and fancies in food and drink and clothing⟩ **3** *Austral* : a border made by forcing back a narrow strip of bark below a groove cut around the trunk of a tree **4** *often cap* : a canary of a domestic variety marked by frilled and curled feathers

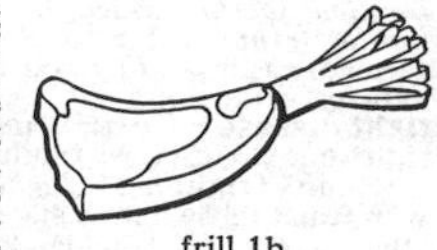
frill 1b

frill–bark \ˈ≈,≈\ *vt, Austral* : to ring (a tree) with a frill

frilled lizard *n* : a large Australian agamoid lizard (*Chlamydosaurus kingii*) having a broad frill on each side of the neck

frilled shark *or* **frill shark** *n* : an eel-shaped shark (*Chlamydoselachus anguineus*) found in deep water off the coast of Japan and in parts of the Atlantic that has six pairs of gill slits with broad frilled margins and a terminal mouth

frill·ery \ˈfrilərē\ *n* -ES [²*frill* + *-ery*] : an arrangement of frills (as on a dress) : FRILL

frill·ies \ˈfrilēz\ *n pl* [*frilly* + *-es* (pl. suffix)] : women's clothing with ruffles : TRIMMINGS; *esp* : frilled lingerie

frill·i·ness \ˈfrilēnəs, -lin-\ *n* -ES : the quality of being frilly

frill·ing \ˈfriliŋ\ *n* -S : a frill or arrangement of frills : an edging gathered into a frill

frilly \ˈfrilē, -li\ *adj* -ER/-EST : having or resembling a frill : NONESSENTIAL, ORNAMENTAL, FRIVOLOUS, TRIFLING ⟨get out of my field clothes and sun helmet into something ~ —Eve Langley⟩ ⟨like her earlier writing, it is . . . rather ~ here and there —E.A.Speiser⟩ ⟨~ cakes coated with icing —*New Yorker*⟩

frim \ˈfrim\ *adj* [ME, abundant, flourishing, prob. fr. OE *freme* good, excellent; akin to OE *fram* bold, strong, ON *framr* foremost, *fram* forward — more at FROM] **1** *dial Eng* : marked by good physical condition : FLOURISHING ⟨a ~ calf⟩ **2** *dial Eng* : tender and succulent ⟨in the spring when the grass is young and ~⟩

¹**fringe** \ˈfrinj\ *n* -S *often attrib* [ME *frenge*, fr. MF *frenge*, *frange*, *fringe*, fr. (assumed) VL *frimbia*, fr. L *fimbria*] **1** : an ornamental border (as for clothing, upholstery, curtains) consisting of short lengths of straight or twisted thread, cord, or leather hanging from cut or raveled edges of garments or from a separate band and often grouped or knotted in various designs **2** : something resembling a fringe : BORDER, EDGING, MARGIN, PERIPHERY ⟨the . . . people who lived just outside the ~ of the drought area —R.W.Murray⟩ ⟨a narrow ~ of continental coast —*Encyc. Americana*⟩: as **a** : a growth like a fringe (as of hair or bristles) ⟨hair forming a ~ around his bald head —Frances H. Eliot⟩ **b** : ⁵BANG **c** : a fimbriate border (as that of certain petals); *specif* : the peristome of a moss **d** : the confused double outline produced by lack of registration between two or more component pictures of a color photograph **e** : one of various light or dark bands produced by the interference or diffraction of light **f** : vague images and feelings attending a definite idea or sometimes present when the idea cannot be recalled **3 a** : something that is marginal, borderline, or introductory in relation to some activity, process, or subject matter : something that is secondary or supplementary to what is basic or central in importance or value ⟨this is an enormous field of which I can here touch only the ~ —G.G.Coulton⟩ ⟨education for an age in which leisure is the center rather than the ~ —John Diebold⟩ **b** : a group of persons occupying a marginal, extremist, or markedly deviant position (as economically, socially, politically, or culturally) ⟨an unwashed child from the criminal ~ of town —Frances G. Patton⟩ ⟨the ~s of Salem society were superstitious —Van Wyck Brooks⟩ ⟨this attack has been well organized by ~ groups —*New Republic*⟩ ⟨that is what they talk about in the ~ sects, not in proper congregations —*Time*⟩ ⟨the ~ types — the pathological and near pathological —John McPartland⟩ — see LUNATIC FRINGE **c** : FRINGE BENEFIT ⟨most unions want higher pensions, health and welfare, other ~s —*Kiplinger Washington Letter*⟩

²**fringe** \ˈ"\ *vb* -ED/-ING/-S *vt* **1** : to furnish or adorn with or as if with a fringe ⟨the cloth over the tea table is *fringed* with blue elephants —*New Yorker*⟩ ⟨~ a rug⟩ **2** : to serve as a fringe for ⟨grass *fringed* the stream⟩ ~ *vi* : to spread out like a fringe ⟨in that medieval time the cathedral *fringed* out into the university —Francis Hackett⟩

fringe area *n* : a region in which reception from a given broadcasting station is weak or subject to serious distortion due to distance, obstructions, or other causes

fringe benefit *n* : an employment benefit (as a pension, a paid holiday, or health insurance) granted by an employer that involves a money cost without affecting basic wage rates

fringe bush *n* : FRINGE TREE

fringe cup *n* **1** : MITERWORT 1 **2** *also* **fringe cups** *pl but sing or pl in constr* : FALSE ALUMROOT

fringed \ˈfrinjd\ *adj* [ME *frenged*, fr. *frenge* + *-ed*] : furnished with a fringe

fringed fern *n* : CLIMBING FERN

fringed gecko *n* : FLYING GECKO

fringed gentian *n* : any of several No. American herbs of the genus *Gentiana* having the margin of the corolla lobes fringed: as **a** : a widely but irregularly distributed annual or biennial herb (*G. crinita*) of eastern and central No. America that has violet-blue or white fringed flowers **b** : a similar but somewhat smaller blue-flowered plant (*G. procera*) of central and western No. America

fringed heath *n* : a prostrate European shrub (*Erica ciliaris*) with small rosy purple flowers and glandular-ciliate leaves

fringed loosestrife *n* : a perennial leafy herb (*Lysimachia ciliatum*) of eastern No. America having ciliate leaves and yellow flowers

fringed gentian a

fringed orchis *also* **fringed orchid** *n* : any of several summer-flowering American orchids of the genus *Habenaria* distinguished by a fringed or lacerated lip

fringed pink *n* **1** : any of several pinks with laciniate petals; *esp* : a Eurasian perennial herb (*Dianthus superbus*) sometimes cultivated for its showy fragrant lilac or rose flowers with deeply fringed margins **2** : a low wiry-stemmed branching herb (*Linanthus dianthiflorus*) of southern California with fringed pink flowers

fringed polygala *n* : GAYWINGS

fringed poppy mallow *n* : a poppy mallow (*Callirhoë digitata*) of the Great Plains

fringed tapeworm *n* : a cyclophyllidean tapeworm (*Thysanosoma actinioides*) found in the intestine and bile ducts of sheep and goats esp. in the western U.S. and having the hinder margin of each segment fringed

fringeflower \ˈ≈,≈\ *n* : BUTTERFLY FLOWER

fringefoot \ˈ≈,≈\ *n, pl* **fringefoots** : any of numerous iguanid lizards (genus *Uma*) living in desert areas of the southwestern U.S. and adjacent Mexico and having the feet modified for movement over loose sand by elongated pointed scales fringing the digits

fringepod \ˈ≈,≈\ *n* : a plant of the genus *Thysanocarpus*

fring·er \ˈfrinjə(r)\ *n* -S **1** : one that fringes or makes a fringe **2** : one who is a member of a fringe ⟨made himself just as unpopular with ~s on the right as with those on the left —*Time*⟩

fringes *pl of* FRINGE, *pres 3d sing of* FRINGE

fringetail \ˈ≈,≈\ *n* : a goldfish with some of the fins long and fringed

fringe tree *n* : a small tree or shrub of the genus *Chionanthus*; *esp* : a small tree (*C. virginica*) occurring in the southern U.S. but used as an ornamental further north esp. in sheltered locations and having clusters of white flowers — called also *fringe bush*

fringe–tree bark *n* : the dried root bark of the fringe tree (*Chionanthus virginica*) formerly used as a diuretic

frin·gil·la \frinˈjilə\ *n, cap* [NL, fr. L *fringilla*, *fringuilla* chaffinch] : a genus (the type of the family Fringillidae) of singing birds including the chaffinch, brambling, and related forms

¹**frin·gil·lid** \(ˈ)frinˈjiləd\ *adj* [NL *Fringillidae*] : of or relating to the Fringillidae or a finch

²**fringillid** \ˈ"\ *n* -S : one of the Fringillidae : FINCH

frin·gil·li·dae \frinˈjiləˌdē\ *n pl, cap* [NL, fr. *Fringilla*, type genus + *-idae*] : a family of small seed-eating passerine birds that comprise the finches, that have strong bills which are short and usu. thick at the base, and that often exhibit well-marked sexual dimorphism with the juveniles resembling the females

fringing *adj* : forming a fringe ⟨that same rugged west coast with its deep fiords and its innumerable ~ islands —L.D. Stamp⟩

fringing forest *n* : a forest growing along a watercourse in a region otherwise devoid of trees

fringing reef *n* : a coral reef that borders the land

fringy \ˈfrinjē, -ji\ *adj* -ER/-EST : adorned with fringes : resembling fringe ⟨the gracefullest little ~ films of lace —Mark Twain⟩

frip·per \ˈfripə(r)\ *also* **frip·per·er** \-pərə(r)\ *n* -S [*fripper* fr. MF *fripier*, fr. OF *frepier*, fr. *frepe* + *-ier* -er; *fripperer* fr. MF *fripier* + E *-er*] *archaic* : one who deals in frippery or in old clothes

¹**frip·pery** \ˈfrip(ə)rē, -ri\ *n* -ES [MF *friperie* rags, old clothes, fr. OF *freperie*, fr. *frepe*, *ferpe*, *feupe* rag, old garment (fr. ML *faluppa* piece of straw, splinter) + *-erie* -ery] **1** *obs* **a** : castoff clothes **b** : a place where old clothes are sold **2 a** : a piece of finery : FINERY; *esp* : a showy nonessential article of dress that may be cheap and tawdry, excessively detailed and ornamented, or elegant and rich ⟨the *fripperies* of her elegant bonnet trembling —Arnold Bennett⟩ **b** : affected elegance : OSTENTATION

²**frippery** \ˈ"\ *adj* : TRIFLING, CONTEMPTIBLE

friscal *n* -S [prob. alter. of ¹*frisk* + *-al*] *obs* : FRISK, CAPER

¹**frisco** *n* -ES [prob. alter. of ¹*frisk* + *-o* (common Sp & It n. ending)] *obs* : FRISCAL

²**fris·co** \ˈfri(ˌ)skō\ *adj, usu cap* [fr. *Frisco*, short for *San Francisco*, Calif.] *slang* : of or relating to the city of San Francisco, Calif. ⟨the *Frisco* convention⟩

fri·sé \frēˈzā, frəˈ-\ *n* -S [F, fr. past part. of *friser* to curl, frieze — more at FRIZZ] : FRIEZE 1b, 2a

frise aileron \ˈfrēz-\ *n, usu cap F* [after Leslie G. *Frise b* 1897 Eng. engineer] : an aileron having a nose portion projecting ahead of the hinge axis and a lower surface in line with the lower surface of the wing so that when the trailing edge of the aileron is raised the nose portion protrudes below the lower surface of the wing thus increasing the drag

fri·sette \frēˈzet, frəˈ-\ *n* -S [F, fr. *friser* to curl + *-ette* — more at FRIZZ] *archaic* : a fringe of hair or curls worn on the forehead by women

fri·seur \frēˈzər\ *n* -S [F, fr. *friser* + *-eur* -or] : HAIRDRESSER

¹**fri·sian** \ˈfrizhən, ˈfrē| *also* |zhēən\ *adj, usu cap* [L *Frisii* + E *-an*] **1 a** : of, relating to, or characteristic of Friesland **b** : of, relating to, or characteristic of the Frisians. **2** : of, relating to, or characteristic of the Frisian language

²**frisian** \ˈ"\ *n* -S *cap* **1 a** : a member of the Frisii **b** : one of the modern descendants of the Frisii that inhabit principally the Netherlands province of Friesland and the Frisian islands in the North sea **2** : the West Germanic language of the Frisian people — see INDO-EUROPEAN LANGUAGES table

fri·sii \ˈfriz(h)ēˌī, -zēˌē\ *n pl, cap* [L] : a Germanic people that settled along the coast of the North sea in prehistoric times

¹**frisk** \ˈfrisk\ *vb* -ED/-ING/-S [obs. *frisk*, adj., lively, brisk, fr. ME, fr. MF *frisque*, *frique*, of Gmc origin; akin to OHG *frisc* fresh, lively — more at FRESH] *vi* : to leap, skip, dance, or gambol esp. in frolic : move briskly and sportively or playfully ⟨the innocent voices laughing in the evening, the dogs ~*ing* —T.H.White b.1915⟩ ⟨filling in the time . . . by ~*ing* about —T. B.Costain⟩ ~ *vt* **1** : to move in a frisking manner ⟨a milk-cart pony rattles down the street, ~*ing* his mane —*Times Lit. Supp.*⟩ ⟨~*ing* about the hem of her skirt —T.B.Costain⟩ **2 a** : to search or go through esp. for concealed weapons or stolen articles ⟨they'd used this fake bell boy to ~ my coat while I was washing —Erle Stanley Gardner⟩ ⟨~*ing* the ladies' cabins in their absence —*New Yorker*⟩; *esp* : to search (a person) for such purpose usu. by running the hand rapidly over the clothing and through the pockets ⟨I went behind him and ~*ed* him carefully —Hartley Howard⟩ **b** : to take or steal from esp. by such frisking ⟨a certain soldier was ~*ed* of $800 when boarding the train for home —Dixon Wecter⟩

²**frisk** \ˈ"\ *n* -S **1 a** *archaic* : CARACOLE, CAPER, JIG **b** : a frolicking movement : GAMBOL, ROMP ⟨in a few minutes . . . she was exploring the yard with ~s of pleasure —Mary Mian⟩ **c** : a gay time : FROLIC, DIVERSION ⟨so come . . . it will be a ~ that will do you good —Mary W. Shelley⟩ **2** : a frisking esp. for concealed weapons or stolen articles ⟨a quick ~ of the coats in the coatroom of the hall —W.L.Gresham⟩

frisk·er \-kə(r)\ *n* -S [*frisk* + *-er*] : one that frisks

fris·ket \ˈfriskət\ *n* -S [F *frisquette*, fr. MF, fr. fem. of *frisquet* vivacious, flirtatious, fr. *frisque*, *frique* lively — more at FRISK] **1** : a light frame to hold the sheet of paper to the tympan in printing on a hand press; *also* : a sheet stretched in a frame with parts cut out to lay over an inked form so that only certain parts shall be printed **2** : a masking device comparable to a frisket used in photography and photoengraving

frisk·i·ly \ˈfriskəlē, -li\ *adv* : in a frisky manner ⟨moves about ~ despite his age⟩

friskin *n* -S [prob. alter. of *frisking*, gerund of ¹*frisk*] *obs* : a frisky action or person

frisk·i·ness \ˈfriskēnəs, -kin-\ *n* -ES : the quality or state of being frisky ⟨the ~ of young colts just put out to pasture⟩

frisk·ing·ly *adv* : in a frisking manner

frisky \ˈfriskē, -ki\ *adj* -ER/-EST [obs. *frisk* lively, frisk + *-y* — more at FRISK] : inclined to frisk : FROLICSOME, GAY, PLAYFUL ⟨still dancing with ~ step —Nathaniel Hawthorne⟩ ⟨the mood of the picture is ~ —Bosley Crowther⟩ ⟨too ~ for an old man —Francis Jeffrey⟩

fri·so·lée \ˌfrēzəˈlā\ *n* -S [F *frisolée*, *friselée*, fr. fem. of *friselé*, past part. of *friseler* to curl, fr. *friser* — more at FRIZZ] : MOSAIC

fri·son \frēˈzōⁿ\ *n* -S [F, fr. *friser* to curl] : waste silk usu. taken from the outside of the cocoon

friss \ˈfrish\ *also* **frisz·ka** \ˈfrishkə\ *n, pl* **frisses** *also* **friszkas** [*friss* fr. Hung; *friszka* fr. Pol, fr. Hung *friss*] : the fast section of a czardas — contrasted with *lassú*

fris·son \frēˈsōⁿ\ *n, pl* **frissons** \-ōⁿ(z)\ [F, fr. LL *friction-*, *frictio*, irreg. (influence of L *friction-*, *frictio* friction), fr. L *frigēre* to be cold + *-ion-*, *-io* -ion — more at FRIGID] : SHUDDER, QUIVER, CHILL, TINGLE ⟨and again a ~ of surprise shot through him —Kathleen Freeman⟩ ⟨a little ~ of fear — Kathryn Hulme⟩; *esp* : a pleasurable sensation of fright or gloom : THRILL ⟨made a lucrative living from thrillers with a certain psychological ~ —Vernon Young⟩

fri·sure \ˈfrizhər, frəˈzhu̇(ə)r\ *n* -S [F, fr. *friser* to curl + *-ure* — more at FRIZZ] : a style of curling or dressing the hair : HAIRDRESSING, HAIRDO

¹**frit** \ˈfrit\ *n* -S [It *fritta*, fr. fem. of *fritto*, past part. of *friggere* to fry, fr. L *frigere* — more at FRY] **1** : the materials of which glass is made after having been calcined or partly fused in a furnace but before vitrification **2** : glass variously compounded that is quenched and ground as a basis for glazes or enamels

²**frit** \ˈ"\ *vt* **fritted**; **fritted**; **fritting**; **frits** : to prepare (materials for glass) by heat : FUSE

³**frit** \ˈ"\ *adj* [fr. E dial. past part. of ²*fright*] *dial Eng* : FRIGHTENED

frit fly \ˈ≈-\ *n* [origin unknown] : a fly of the family Chloropidae (esp. *Oscinella frit*) injurious to grain in Europe

¹**frith** \ˈfrith\ *n* -S [ME, fr. OE *fyrhthe* wooded country] **1** *dial Eng* **a** : a tract of land grown with copsewood : COPPICE **b** : a clearing within a wooded area **2** *dial Eng* **a** : BRUSHWOOD, UNDERWOOD; *esp* : brushwood suitable for wattling **b** : HURDLE, HEDGE; *esp* : one made or mended with wattled brushwood

²**frith** \ˈ"\ *n* -S [alter. of *firth*] : a narrow arm of the sea : the opening of a river into the sea : FIRTH

frithborh *also* **frithborgh** *n* [ME *frithborg*, fr. (assumed) OE *frithborh*, fr. *frith* peace + *borh* pledge; akin to OE *frithu* peace, OHG *fridu*, ON *frithr* peace, Goth *gafrithon* to reconcile, OE *frēo* free — more at FREE, BORROW] *obs* : FRANKPLEDGE

frith·stool \ˈfrithˌstu̇l\ *also* **frid·stool** \ˈ", -idˌs-\ *n* [OE *frithstōl* place of safety or refuge, fr. *frith* peace + *stōl* chair, seat — more at STOOL] : a seat of sanctuary or refuge placed in ancient times in some English churches

frit·il·lar·ia \ˌfridᵊlˈa(a)rēə\ *n* [NL, fr. L *fritillus* dice-cup + NL *-aria*; fr. the checkered markings of the petals] **1** *cap* : a genus of bulbous herbs (family Liliaceae) of north temperate regions having mottled or checkered nodding flowers — see CHECKERED LILY, CROWN IMPERIAL **2** -S : any plant, bulb, or flower of the genus *Fritillaria*

frit·il·lary \ˈfridᵊlˌerē, *chiefly Brit* frəˈtiləri\ *n* -ES [NL *Fritillaria*] **1** : a plant of the genus *Fritillaria* **2** : any of numerous butterflies of *Speyeria*, *Argynnis*, and related genera — compare SILVERSPOT

Fri·tos \ˈfrē(ˌ)tōz, -ōs\ *trademark* — used for corn chips

¹**frit·ter** \ˈfrid·ə(r), -itə-\ *n* -S [ME *fritour*, *fritur*, *frutour*, *frutur*, fr. MF *friture*, fr. (*assumed*) VL *frictura*, fr. L *frictus* (past part. of *frigere* to roast, fry) + *-ura* -ure] **1** : a small quantity of batter often containing fruit or meat and fried in deep fat or sautéed ⟨apple ~s⟩ ⟨corn ~s⟩ ⟨clam ~s⟩ **2** *New Eng* : GRIDDLE CAKE

²fritter \"\ *n* -s [alter. of *fitter*] : FRAGMENT, SHRED ⟨each . . . morsel, crumb, scrag and ~ from the bins —Edith Sitwell⟩
³fritter \"\ *vb* -ED/-ING/-S *vt* **1** : to reduce or waste piecemeal : DIMINISH, CONSUME, DISSIPATE — used chiefly with *away* ⟨foolishly ~*ing* away time and energy⟩ ⟨~*ing* our time and thoughts away on trivial things —Dorothy C. Fisher⟩ **2** : to cut or break into small pieces or fragments : DISPERSE ⟨the responsibility for measures is ~*ed* and divided among a triad of authorities —Ernest Barker⟩ ~ *vi* **1** : to break up : divide into fragments ⟨there is formed . . . a slag which ~*s* on cooling —*Chem. Abstracts*⟩ **2** : to dissipate itself : DWINDLE ⟨the threat of economic sanctions ~*ed* into impotent "moral" protest —*Fortune*⟩ ⟨the conspiracy ~*ed* away to an ignominious conclusion —*Amer. Guide Series: Ind.*⟩ **syn** see WASTE
frit·ter·er \-ıd·ərə(r), -ıtə-\ *n* -s : one that fritters
fritting *n* -s [fr. gerund of ²*frit*] **1** : the act or process of quenching from a molten condition in preparation of a frit for glaze or enamel **2** : the act or process of fusing into a glass the otherwise soluble components of a glaze or enamel
frit·to mi·sto \ˌfrētō'mē(ˌ)stō\ *n* [It, mixed fried food] : MIXED GRILL
fritz \'frits\ *n* -ES *usu cap* [G, nickname for *Friedrich* (Frederick), a common German given name] : GERMAN ⟨it was the first I'd seen since the *Fritzes* cleared out —Kay Boyle⟩ — usu. used disparagingly — **on the fritz** *adv (or adj)* [origin unknown] : in a state of disrepair — usu. used with *go* ⟨his supercharger had gone *on the fritz* —G.P.Elliott⟩
fri·u·li·an \(ˈ)frē¦ülēən\ *n* -s *cap* [*Friuli*, district in Italy + E *-an*] **1** : a member of a people in northeastern Italy of the district of Friuli — called also *Furlan* **2** : the Rhaeto-Romanic dialect of the Friulians
¹friv·ol \'frivəl\ *vi* **frivoled** *or* **frivolled**; **frivoled** *or* **frivolled**; **frivoling** *or* **frivolling** \-v(ə)liŋ\ **frivols** [back-formation fr. *frivolous*] : to act frivolously : TRIFLE ⟨a man of weight . . . does not come and ~ in the typists' room —Dorothy Sayers⟩ — **friv·ol·er** *or* **friv·ol·ler** \-v(ə)lə(r)\ *n* -s
²frivol \"\ *n* -s [back-formation fr. *frivolous*] : something that is frivolous : TRIFLE ⟨a restful holiday may be spent away from fashions and ~*s* —Napier Devitt⟩
frivol away *vt* : to spend frivolously : fritter away ⟨you who would *frivol* life away in charming play —Ethna MacCarthy⟩
fri·vol·i·ty \frə'välәd·ē, -ətē, -i\ *n* -ES [F *frivolité*, fr. *frivole* frivolous (fr. L *frivolus*) + *-ité* -ity] **1** : the quality or state of being frivolous : the fact or habit of trifling : lack of seriousness : unbecoming levity ⟨greatness can never be founded upon ~ and corruption —Matthew Arnold⟩ **2** : an act or thing that is frivolous ⟨free from the vices and *frivolities* of the Court —Max Peacock⟩ ⟨nosegays and other *frivolities* for Easter —*New Yorker*⟩
friv·o·lous \'friv(ə)ləs\ *adj* [ME, fr. L *frivolus*, prob. fr. *friare* to rub, crumble — more at FRICTION] **1** : of little weight or importance : having no basis in law or fact : LIGHT, SLIGHT, SHAM, IRRELEVANT, SUPERFICIAL ⟨the procedure encourages ~ cases —David Fellman⟩ ⟨is it not possible to screen out ~ charges —A.F.Westin⟩ ⟨a ~ argument⟩ **2** : given to trifling or unbecoming levity : not grave or serious in demeanor, purpose, or acts : LIGHT-MINDED ⟨as ~ as his eldest son —C.H. Sykes⟩ ⟨she spends . . . too much time at soda fountains . . . it makes her appear ~ —Ellen Glasgow⟩ ⟨the . . . ~ existence of a public official mingling in corrupt social circles —*Encyc. Americana*⟩ : not serious or practical (as in content or form) : LIGHT, GAY, PLAYFUL ⟨this letter is, on the whole, ~ in its temper —Irving Kristol⟩ ⟨some ~ lapel pins . . . in the form of heads of young girls —*New Yorker*⟩ — **friv·o·lous·ly** *adv*
friv·o·lous·ness *n* -ES : the quality or state of being frivolous : FRIVOLITY
friz *dial past of* FREEZE
frize \'frēz\ *archaic var of* FRIZZ
friz·er *also* **frizz·er** \'frizə(r)\ *n* -s : one that frizzes
¹frizz *also* **friz** \'friz\ *vb* **frizzed**; **frizzed**; **frizzing**; **frizzes** [alter. (influenced by *frizzle*) of F *friser* to shrivel up (as meat when fried), curl, crimp, prob. fr. *fris-*, stem of *frire* to fry — more at FRY] *vt* **1** : to form into small tight curls : CURL ⟨plays a ~*ed* girl of the 20s —*Time*⟩ — often used with *up* ⟨a young girl ~*ing* up her hair in preparation for a date⟩ **2** : to remove a thin layer of the grain side of (a skin) in leather manufacture (as by rubbing with pumice stone or a blunt instrument after prolonged liming); *also* : to pare off with a sharp knife (as in the making of glove leather) ~ *vi*, *of hair* : to be in or form into a mass of tight curls
²frizz *also* **friz** \"\ *n* -ES **1** : a tight curl or curls ⟨she took a pencil from the *frizz* behind her ear —Elizabeth Taylor⟩ **2** : hair that is tightly curled
³frizz \"\ *vb* -ED/-ING/-ES [alter. (influenced by *sizzle*) of ¹*fry*] : to fry, cook, or sear with a sizzling noise : SIZZLE
friz·zen \'friz°n\ *n* -s [alter. of earlier *frizzle*, of unknown origin] : the pivoted metal upright of the action of a flintlock against which the flint strikes upon firing
frizz·i·ly \-zəlē, -li\ *adv* : in a frizzy manner ⟨a head of hair curled a little too ~⟩
frizz·i·ness \-zēnəs, -zin-\ *n* -ES : the quality or state of being frizzy ⟨had trouble combing out the ~ of the dog's coat⟩
¹friz·zle \'frizəl\ *vb* **frizzled**; **frizzled**; **frizzling** \-z(ə)liŋ\ **frizzles** [prob. akin to OE *fris* curly, OFris *frīsle*, *frēsle* curl, lock of hair] *vt* : to curl or crisp (as the hair) usu. with heat : FRIZZ — often used with *up* ⟨*frizzled* up her locks for the occasion⟩ ~ *vi* : CURL, CRISP — used esp. of hair; often used with *up*
²frizzle \"\ *n* -s **1 a** : a crisp curl or curls **b** : the state of being frizzed **2** *often cap* : a domestic fowl having the feathers curled backward that is in some areas regarded as constituting a separate breed but prob. represents a simple genetic variation
³frizzle \"\ *vb* -ED/-ING/-S [blend of ¹*fry* and *sizzle*] *vt* **1** : to fry until crisp and curled ⟨*frizzled* beef⟩ **2** : to burn, scorch, or sear by the application of heat ⟨if you touch a turbine in the wrong place, you get *frizzled* —Ann Bridge⟩ ⟨sometimes the brown grass was dark and *frizzled* with heat —Eve Langley⟩ ~ *vi* : to cook with a sizzling noise ⟨I could smell the bacon *frizzling* downstairs —E.L.Thomas⟩
⁴frizzle \"\ *n* -s : the act or noise of frizzling ⟨letting escape the sudden ~ and fragrance of the roast —Adrian Bell⟩
friz·zly \'friz(ə)lē\ *adj*, *sometimes* -ER/-EST : FRIZZY ⟨~ hair⟩
frizzy \'frizē -zi\ *adj* -ER/-EST **1** *of hair* : tightly curled ⟨the aborigine's mass of short ~ hair⟩ **2** : FRILLED
frl *abbr* fractional
frm *abbr* **1** frame; framing **2** from
¹fro \frə, (ˈ)frō\ *prep* [ME *fra*, *fro*, fr. ON *frā* — more at FROM] *dial Brit* : FROM
²fro \'frō\ *adv* [ME *fra*, *fro*, fr. *fra*, *fro*, prep.] : BACK, BACKWARD, FROM, AWAY — used correlatively with *to* in the phrase *to and fro*
¹frock \'fräk\ *n* -s [ME *frok*, *frokke*, fr. MF *froc*, of Gmc origin; akin to OS *hroc* mantle, coat, OFris *hrock*, OHG *hroch*, and prob. to OE *rocc*, OS *rok*, OHG *roc*, *roch*, OIr *rucht*, MW *rhuch*] **1** : an outer garment worn chiefly by monks and friars : HABIT **2** : an outer garment worn chiefly by men: **a** : a long loose mantle **b** : COAT OF MAIL **c** : a workman's outer shirt; *esp* : SMOCK FROCK **d** : a woolen jersey worn esp. by sailors **e** : FROCK COAT; *also* : a military coat of similar cut **3 a** : a woman's dress **b** : a dress worn by a girl and formerly by both boys and girls
²frock \"\ *vt* -ED/-ING/-S **1** : to clothe in a frock ⟨~*ed* in dusty pink with a musquash coat —*Perth (Australia) Sunday Times Mag.*⟩ **2** : to make a cleric of — compare UNFROCK
frock coat *n* : a man's usu. double-breasted coat having knee-length skirts front and back
frock·ing \-kiŋ\ *n* -s [¹*frock* + *-ing*] : cloth suitable for a frock
froe *or* **frow** \'frō\ *n* -s [alter. of *frower*] **1** : a cleaving tool with handle at right angles to the blade for splitting cask staves and shingles from the block **2** : a steel wedge for splitting logs
¹froe·be·lian \(ˈ)frā¦bēlēən, (ˈ)frō¦-, (ˈ)frǣ¦-, -bel-, -lyən\ *adj*, *usu cap* [Friedrich *Froebel* †1852 Ger. educator who founded the kindergarten system + E *-ian*] : relating to or derived from Friedrich Froebel or his kindergarten system of education
²froebelian \"\ *n* -s *usu cap* : a person who teaches by or favors the Froebelian system
froehlich's syndrome *usu cap F*, *var of* FRÖHLICH'S SYNDROME
froe·man \'frōmən\ *n*, *pl* **froemen** [*froe* + *man*] : ²RIVER
FROF *abbr* fire risk on freight

¹frog \'frȯg, 'fräg\ *n* -s [ME *frogge*, fr. OE *frogga*; akin to OE *frosc*, *frox*, *forsc* frog, OHG *frosk*, ON *frauki* & *froskr* frog, Skt *pravate* he jumps up, *plava* frog; basic meaning: jumping, hopping] **1 a** : any of various smooth-skinned web-footed tailless agile leaping amphibians (as of the suborder Diplasiocoela) being largely aquatic, feeding chiefly on insect larvae, small fishes, and other water dwellers, and laying eggs in clusters enclosed in a gelatinous matrix from which hatch the tailed gilled limbless larvae that later metamorphose into 4-limbed adults without tails or gills : one of the more aquatic members of the order Salientia as distinguished from the more terrestrial toads — compare BUFO, RANA, TADPOLE **b** : an amphibian of the order Salientia **c** [so called fr. their reputation for eating frogs] : FRENCHMAN — usu. taken to be offensive **d** : a throat condition that produces hoarseness — often used in the phrase *frog in the throat* **2** : the triangular elastic horny pad in the middle of the sole of the foot of the horse and related animals — see FRUSH **3 a** (1) : a looped device attached to a belt for holding a weapon or tool (2) : a front fastening for a garment (as a coat, jacket, dress) that is made usu. of braid in an ornamental looped design with a bar-shaped button or thick knot on one edge of the opening to fit into a loop on the other **b** : a device made of rail sections constructed and assembled to permit the wheels on one rail of a track to cross another rail of an intersecting track **c** : a shallow place for mortar in the upper face of a brick **d** : the frame or block to which the share, moldboard, landside, or beam of a plow are secured **e** : the nut of a violin bow : HEEL — see BOW illustration **f** (1) : the junction of two branches of a flume (2) : a guiding timber at the mouth of a slide **g** : a device for supporting and mutually insulating trolley wires that cross each other **h** : the seat for the plane iron in the stock of a carpenter's plane **i** : a loom device that actuates a stop motion when the shuttle is out of position **4** : an imperfectly ripened prune of inferior quality **5** [by folk etymology fr. *frage*] **a** : a card game developed from tarok and popular esp. in Mexico **b** : the lowest bid in this and similar games — compare CHICO, FRAGE

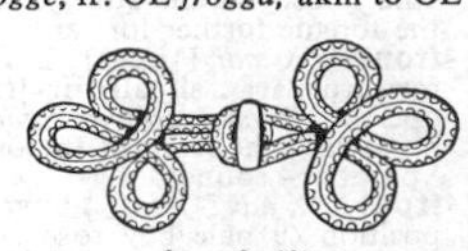
frog 3a(2)

²frog \"\ *vi* **frogged**; **frogged**; **frogging**; **frogs** : to catch or look for frogs
frogbit *or* **frog's-bit** \'ˌ=ˌ=\ *n*, *pl* **frogbits** *or* **frog's-bits** **1** : a European aquatic floating herb (*Hydrocharis morsus-ranae*) with roundish heart-shaped leaves and small white flowers **2** : an American aquatic plant (*Limnobium spongia*) with round-cordate or reniform leaves and sessile or short-stalked spathes
frogbit family *or* **frog's-bit family** *n* : HYDROCHARITACEAE
frog boot *n* : a cushion (as of rubber or leather) fitted around the frog of a horse's foot to prevent shock — called also *frog pad*
frog breathing *n* : a technique using mouth and tongue to force air into the lungs that was developed by some patients suffering from poliomyelitic paralysis of respiratory muscles
frog cheese *n* : a young puffball
frog crab *n* : any of numerous crabs constituting the family Raninidae, having an elongated carapace, flattened legs, and a stance like that of a frog, and being widely distributed in shallow or moderately deep tropical seas
frog duck *n* : HOODED MERGANSER
frogeater \'=ˌ==\ *n* **1** : one that eats frogs **2** *usu cap* : FRENCHMAN — usu. taken to be offensive
frogeye \'=ˌ=\ *n* : any of numerous leaf diseases characterized by the concentric rings about the diseased spots: as **a** (1) : a disease of growing tobacco caused by a parasitic fungus (*Cercospora nicotianae*) (2) : a similar and often severely defoliating disease of soybeans caused by a related fungus (*Cercospora diazu*) **b** : a phase of black rot of apples in which the leaves are so spotted — **frog-eyed** \'=ˌ=\ *adj*
frogface \'=ˌ=\ *n* : a face resembling a frog's; *specif* : one with the nose broadened by polyps
frogfish \'=ˌ=\ *n* **1** : a fish (as the angler) of the family Antennariidae; *broadly* : one of the order Pediculati **2** : TOADFISH 1
frogged \'frȯgd, 'frägd\ *adj* [¹*frog* + *-ed*] : decorated or fastened with frogs
frog·ger \-g-ə(r)\ *n* -s [¹*frog* + *-er*] **1** : a logger who helps to load logs and timber on sleds or drays for removal from the forest — called also *trailer*, *zoogler* **2** : CHASER 3a
frog·gery \-gərē\ *n* -ES [¹*frog* + *-ery*] : a gathering of frogs; *also* : a place where frogs abound
frog·ging \-giŋ\ *n* -s [¹*frog* + *-ing*] : FROG 3a(2) : an ornamentation with frogs
frog·gish \-gish\ *adj* : characteristic of a frog
frog·gy \-gē,-gi\ *adj* -ER/-EST : abounding in frogs : of, relating to, or resembling frogs ⟨his gruff, ~ voice —E.J.Kahn⟩
froghopper \'=ˌ==\ *n* : a member of the Cercopidae : SPITTLE INSECT
frog kick *n* : the breaststroke kick when it is executed with the hip joints in a position with the knees apart
frog·let \-glət\ *n* -s [¹*frog* + *-let*] **1** : a small or young frog **2** : a small tree toad (as *Crinia laevis* of Tasmania)
frog lily *n* **1** : SPATTERDOCK **2** : a plant of the genus *Potamogeton*
frog·ling \-gliŋ\ *n* -s [¹*frog* + *-ling*] : a small or young frog : FROGLET
frog·man \-ˌman, -ˌmən, -ˌmaa(ə)n\ *n*, *pl* **frogmen** : a person equipped with a face mask, flippers, a rubber suit, or other devices for swimming under water for extended periods; *esp* : a person so equipped for military reconnaissance and demolition of underwater obstacles
frog-march \'=ˌ=\ *vt* : to carry (as a resisting prisoner) face downward by the arms and legs
frogmouth \'=ˌ=\ *n* : any of various birds of Oriental and Australian regions related to the goatsuckers and constituting the family Podargidae
frog orchis *or* **frog orchid** *n* : any of several green-flowered orchids of the genus *Habenaria*
frog pad *n* : FROG BOOT
frog plant *n* : ORPINE
frogs *pres 3d sing of* FROG, *pl of* FROG
frog's-bit *var of* FROGBIT
frog's-bladder \'=ˌ==\ *n*, *pl* **frog's-bladders** : ORPINE
frog shell *n* : any of numerous chiefly tropical gastropod mollusks (family Cymatiidae) that resemble the related tritons but have notably thick heavy rugose or tuberculated shells; *also* : a shell of one of these mollusks
frogskin \'=ˌ=\ *n* [so called fr. the green back] *slang* : a piece of paper money; *esp* : a dollar bill
frog spawn *n* **1** : a red alga of the genus *Batrachospermum* **2** : FROG SPIT 2
frog spit *or* **frog spittle** *n* **1** : CUCKOO SPIT 1a **2** : an alga (as of the family Chlorophyceae) that forms slimy masses on ponds or other quiet water
frogsticker \'=ˌ==\ *n*, *Midland* : POCKETKNIFE
frogstool \'=ˌ=\ *n* : TOADSTOOL
froh·berg·ite \'frō,bər,gīt\ *n* -s [Max H. *Frohberg* b1901 Canadian geologist born in Germany + E *-ite*] : a mineral $FeTe_2$ consisting of a telluride of iron and belonging to the marcasite group
fröh·lich \'frœlik\ *adj* [G, fr. OHG *frōlīh*, fr. *frō* happy, cheerful + *-līh* -ly — more at FROLIC] *adj* : JOYOUS, HAPPY — used as a direction in music
fröh·lich's syndrome *or* **froeh·lich's syndrome** \'frā¦lik(s)-, 'frēl, 'frœl-, -ik(s)-\ *n*, *usu cap F* [after Alfred *Fröhlich* †1953 Austrian neurologist] : ADIPOSOGENITAL DYSTROPHY
froise \'frȯiz\ *n* -s [ME] *dial Eng* : a large thick pancake often served with bacon
¹frol·ic \'frälik, -lēk\ *adj* [D *vroolijk*, fr. MD *vrolijc*, fr. *vro* happy, joyful + *-lijc* -ly (akin to OHG *-līh*); akin to OFris *frō* happy, OS *frā*, *frō*, *fraho*, OHG *frō* happy, ON *frār* swift, OE *frogga* frog — more at FROG] : full of fun or mirth : dancing, playing, or frisking about : GAY, MERRY ⟨contrasting the stern anxiety of his present mood with the ~ spirit of the preceding year —Nathaniel Hawthorne⟩ — **frol·ic·ly** \-ləklē, -li\ *adv*
²frolic \", *chiefly in pres part* -lək\ *vi* **frolicked**; **frolicked**; **frolicking**; **frolics** : to amuse oneself : make merry : make fun : DISPORT, REVEL ⟨who has *frolicked* with him the night before and little dreams that he is to leave her —*Encyc. Americana*⟩ **2** : to move gaily or sportively : play about happily : ROMP, CAPER, GAMBOL ⟨two white pigeons *frolicking* on the green lawn —*N.Y. Times*⟩ ⟨a young daughter who . . . *frolicked* around the bar, the storerooms, and the wine cellars —*New Yorker*⟩ **syn** see PLAY
³frolic \"\ *n* -s [²*frolic*] **1** : a playful, sportive, or gaily mischievous action : a good time : PRANK, LARK ⟨would ask a visitor if she wanted onions in her cocoa . . . had always been up to some ~ like that —Jean Stafford⟩ ⟨boys bent on a ~ —Margaret Mead⟩ ⟨for the first ten months the klan existed mainly as a ~ —Dixon Wecter⟩ **2 a** : FUN, MERRIMENT, GAIETY ⟨their sedateness is as comical as their ~ —George Meredith⟩ ⟨can read and enjoy him for his lively sense of adventure and ~ —Richard McLaughlin⟩ ⟨expecting to indulge in an evening of lightsome ~ —Theodore Dreiser⟩ **b** : an occasion or scene of gaiety and mirth : DANCE, PARTY, PICNIC ⟨working in behalf of the seventh annual spring ~, a tea dance —*N.Y. Times*⟩ ⟨~*s* at the officers' club —H.H. Martin⟩: as (1) *dial* : BEE 3 ⟨quilting ~⟩ (2) *dial* : a lively country party usu. with dancing and games **syn** see ²PLAY
frol·ic·some \-səm\ *adj* : full of gaiety and mirth : given to pranks : SPORTIVE, PLAYFUL ⟨treated the whole affair as a ~ adventure —Herman Melville⟩ ⟨a ~ young thing⟩ — **frol·ic·some·ly** *adv* — **frol·ic·some·ness** *n* -ES
from \ˌf(r)əm, ˌfᵊm, ¦främ, ¦frəm, ˌfräm\ *prep* [ME *fram*, *from*, fr. OE; akin to OE & OHG *fram*, adv., forth, away, forward, ON *frā*, prep., from, *fram*, adv., forward, Goth. prep., from, OE *faran* to travel, go — more at FARE] **1** — used as a function word to indicate a starting point: as (1) a point or place where an actual physical movement (as of departure, withdrawal, or dropping) has its beginning ⟨he set out ~ town this morning⟩ ⟨held the funeral ~ the funeral parlor —R.O.Bowen⟩ ⟨shrinking ~ his touch⟩ ⟨a fall ~ a horse⟩ ⟨the first pigeon race . . . ever held ~ this city —*Springfield (Mass.) Daily News*⟩ ⟨he comes ~ beyond the sea⟩ ⟨came out ~ under the table⟩ ⟨five tanks were shot ~ under him —*Current Biog.*⟩; (2) something that is taken as a starting point in measuring or reckoning or in a statement of limits ⟨it is 20 miles ~ here to the nearest town⟩ ⟨three years ~ that day⟩ ⟨ready to go home within a fortnight ~ the operation —*Lancet*⟩ ⟨~ five to ten years are needed for the project⟩ ⟨~ childhood he displayed great ability⟩ ⟨frames and trays range ~ $1 —*N.Y. Herald Tribune*⟩; (3) the starting or focal point of any activity or movement ⟨will fight you ~ our beaches and ~ our ruined homes⟩ ⟨looked at me ~ under her glasses⟩ ⟨~ one point of view you are right⟩ ⟨I speak ~ the heart⟩ ⟨shot straight ~ the hip⟩; often used with words that express the condition of being suspended or pendent ⟨ornaments hanging ~ a Christmas tree⟩ **2** — used as a function word to indicate (1) the fact or condition of spatial or physical absence, separation, remoteness, or disjunction ⟨an ocean separates America ~ Europe⟩ ⟨the wind was ~ them⟩ ⟨a dunlin, disturbed ~ its young, creeps along the ground —E.A.Armstrong⟩; often used, chiefly Brit., in the phrase *from home* ⟨seemed to discover a home ~ home in our house —Adrian Bell⟩ ⟨he had been ~ home . . . during most of the period mentioned —F.W. Crofts⟩; also in obs. usage to indicate qualitative remoteness or unlikeness; (2) the act, fact, or condition of removal, withdrawal, abstention, separation, dissent, discrimination, qualification, or differentiation of any kind ⟨the most extensive file . . . lacks only five numbers ~ being complete —B.A.Botkin & A.F.Harlow⟩ ⟨asked him to refrain ~ interrupting⟩ ⟨exclude a man ~ membership⟩ ⟨he differs ~ his brother in every particular⟩ ⟨purging its abuses ~ the faith⟩ ⟨put his wife ~ him⟩ ⟨set men free ~ superstition⟩; (3) change or transition from one state or condition to another or replacement of one thing by another ⟨~ the defense they sprang to the attack⟩ ⟨things go ~ bad to worse⟩ ⟨transformed ~ wretched serfs into proud freemen⟩ ⟨turned ~ their books to the grim business of war⟩ **3** — used as a function word to indicate the source or original or moving force of something: as (1) the source, cause, means, or ultimate agent of an action or condition ⟨all his misfortunes spring ~ that piece of folly⟩ ⟨you will hear ~ my lawyer⟩ ⟨he holds his appointment ~ the trustees⟩ ⟨smoking a cigarette ~ one hand and sipping chocolate ice-cream soda . . . ~ the other —Frances Perkins⟩ ⟨emissaries ~ a barbarian king⟩ ⟨these lakes . . . are, ~ their low temperature, entirely destitute of fish —*Encyc. Americana*⟩ ⟨tea time when visits ~ her family usually occurred —Osbert Lancaster⟩; (2) the ground, reason, or basis (as of a judgment, belief, finding, or action) ⟨its composition appears to be uncertain ~ the physical facts —W.E.Swinton⟩ ⟨cannot generalize ~ the state of the weather in Great Britain and Ireland —Geoffrey Jefferson⟩ ⟨negotiations ~ strength⟩; (3) descent, ancestry, or birth ⟨descended ~ a long line of kings⟩ ⟨two colts ~ the same dam⟩; (4) the place of origin, source, or derivation of a material or immaterial thing ⟨all creation is ~ conflict —W.B.Yeats⟩ ⟨assigned two chapters ~ the text⟩ ⟨took a dime ~ his pocket⟩; (5) the model or original (as of a work of art) ⟨painting done directly ~ nature⟩ ⟨the church was built ~ his plans⟩; also used to indicate a person or thing that another is named for ⟨the name was soon changed to Jamaica, ~ the Jameco Indians, the aboriginal settlers —*Amer. Guide Series: N.Y. City*⟩; (6) the fact or condition of being suspended or pendent ⟨wear it ~ the principal masthead when the yacht is in commission —Peter Heaton⟩; (7) selection out of a number of individuals ⟨chosen ~ a large number of competitors⟩; (8) the fact or condition of being native to or a resident of ⟨people ~ Ohio are often called Buckeyes⟩ — **from . . . to . . .** — used (1) with a repeated noun to indicate recurrence or continued succession ⟨beg *from* door *to* door⟩ ⟨a ration issued *from* day *to* day⟩ and (2) with extremes or extremely unlike objects to indicate a wide range ⟨known *from* Maine *to* California⟩ ⟨a noncommittal word that might be used of anything *from* babies *to* furnaces —J.C.Swaim⟩
¹from·ward \'främwə(r)d\, 'frəm-\ *also* **from·wards** \-dz\ *adv* [ME *fromward*, *framward*, fr. OE *framweard*, *framweardes*, fr. *fram* from + *-weard*, *-weardes* -ward, -wards] *now dial Eng* : away from : AWAY
²fromward \"\ *also* **fromwards** \"\ *prep* [ME *fromward*, *framward*, fr. *fromward*, *framward*, adv.] *now dial Eng* : FROM
frond \'fränd\ *n* -s [L *frond-*, *frons* leafy branch, foliage — more at BRIM] **1** : LEAF; *esp* : the leaf of a palm ⟨beyond the dim, stirring ~*s* of the palm trees —*Omnibook*⟩ **2 a** : a foliaceous thallus or thalloid shoot ⟨the ~ of a lichen⟩ ⟨the ~*s* of duckweed⟩ **b** : the leaf of a fern whether a foliage leaf or a sporophyll — see CIRCINATE, CROSIER 3 **3** : something resembling a frond ⟨the sensitive ~*s* of some complex insect antennae⟩ ⟨the ~*s* of his hair were all dabbled and stiff —Edith Sitwell⟩

frond of a fern

frond·age \-dij\ *n* -s [*frond* + *-age*] : a collection of fronds : leafy foliage
frond·ed \-dəd\ *adj* : furnished with fronds ⟨~ palms⟩
fron·del·ite \frän'de,līt\ *n* -s [Clifford *Frondel* b1907 Am. mineralogist + E *-ite*] : a mineral $MnFe_4(PO_4)_3(OH)_5$ consisting of a basic phosphate of manganese and iron and isomorphous with rockbridgeite
fron·dent \'fränd°nt\ *adj* [L *frondent-*, *frondens*, pres. part. of *frondēre* to be in leaf, put forth leaves, fr. *frond-*, *frons*] : having fronds
fron·des·cence \frän'des°n(t)s\ *n* -s [NL *frondescentia*, fr. L *frondescent-*, *frondescens* pres. part. of *frondescere* to become leafy, incho. of *frondēre*] + *-ia* -y — more at FROND] **1** : the condition or period of unfolding of leaves **2** : FOLIAGE — **fron·des·cent** \(ˈ)frän¦des°nt\ *adj*
fron·deur \frōⁿdœr\ *n*, *pl* **frondeurs** \-r(z)\ [F, slinger, participant in a 17th cent. French revolt in which parliamentarians were compared to schoolboys who use their slings only when the teacher is not looking, rebel, malcontent, fr. *fronde* sling (fr. OF *fonde*, *fronde*, fr. — assumed — VL *fundula*, dim. of L *funda*) + *-eur* -or] : REBEL, MALCONTENT, DISSIDENT ⟨he did exhibit the spirit of a ~ —H.A.Gibbons⟩

fron·dif·er·ous \(ˈ)frän¦dif(ə)rəs\ *adj* [L *frondifer*, fr. *frond-*, *frons* leaf + *-i-* + *-fer* -ferous] : bearing fronds or leaves

frond·let \ˈfrändlət\ *n* -s : a small frond

fron·dose \ˈfrän,dōs\ *adj* [L *frondosus*, fr. *frond- frons* + *-osus* -ose] : bearing fronds : resembling a frond : THALLOID — **fron·dose·ly** *adv*

frons \ˈfränz\ *n, pl* **fron·tes** \-n·,tēz\ [L] **1** : FOREHEAD **2** [NL, fr. L] : the upper anterior part of the head capsule of an insect usu. consisting of a separate sclerite between the epicranium and clypeus

1front \ˈfrənt\ *n* -s [ME *frount, front*, fr. OF *front*, fr. L *front-, frons* — more at BRINK] **1 a** : FOREHEAD, BROW ⟨slavery will be branded on our ~ —W.E.Channing⟩; *also* : the whole face ⟨tears ran down that noble ~⟩ **b** (1) : countenance, demeanor, bearing, or posture esp. in the face of danger or other trial ⟨let us . . . take with unshaken ~ what comes —Theodore Roosevelt⟩ ⟨appeared with dauntless ~, accompanied by his paramour —T.B.Macaulay⟩ (2) : the outward, visible, or feigned bearing or behavior of a person as contrasted with his true or essential character, feelings, or condition ⟨the brave ~ she had maintained so long —T.B.Costain⟩ ⟨has good within him, behind a perfectly abominable ~ —Irving Stone⟩ ⟨a perpetually phony ~ of good fellowship is maintained —V.A. Young⟩ ⟨was putting up a ~ . . . in order not to distress this girl —Mary R. Rinehart⟩; *also* : external and often feigned appearance (as of material prosperity or high social position) ⟨very good clothes at bargain prices — important to a man who must maintain a ~ —R.M.Yoder⟩ (3) : an artificial, affected, or self-important manner : show of vanity or haughtiness : AIRS ⟨he was very humble and had no ~ for a prince —*Time*⟩ (4) : stand or posture in reference to some issue or problem : POINT OF VIEW, OUTLOOK, POLICY, POSITION — chiefly used with *change* ⟨a change of ~ was signaled by his offer to come to terms⟩ ⟨suddenly changed ~ and threw in with the opposition⟩ **c** (1) : the foremost rank (as of an army) : VAN (2) : a line of battle (3) *often cap* : a zone of conflict esp. between armies ⟨a division going up to the ~⟩ (4) : lateral space occupied by a military unit (5) — used as a military command of execution for individuals to turn their heads straight forward (as after dressing to the right) ⟨ready, ~!⟩ (6) — used as a call by a hotel desk clerk in summoning a bellboy (7) : a sphere or area of conflict or activity ⟨while men are always on fire over their opinions, they are rarely so on more than one ~ at a time —Curtis Bok⟩ ⟨the four ~s are military, economic, political, and psychological —*Congressional Record*⟩ ⟨progress on the educational ~⟩ ⟨a fairly quiet month on the athletic ~ —*Dartmouth Alumni Mag.*⟩ **d** (1) : a coalition or movement linking persons, elements, or groups often of diverse political, ideological, or other tendency in an effort to achieve certain common objectives ⟨common unity and a common ~ are surely a pressing political need —Christopher Fremantle⟩ ⟨announced his purpose to be the erection of a solid ~ . . . a hemisphere wholly prepared to consult together for our mutual safety —R.W. Van Alstyne⟩ ⟨a united psychiatric ~ to frustrate the drive of courts and lawyers to make psychiatric testimony conform to antiquated concepts —Edward de Grazia⟩; *specif* : a coalition of political parties of diverse ideological or other tendency for the achievement of certain common objectives — usu. used with a qualifier ⟨and to create a popular democratic ~ —*Collier's Yr. Bk.*⟩ ⟨the people's ~s represented an intermediate stage between Western and Soviet forms of democracy —Taylor Cole⟩ (2) : a person, group, or thing that is used to cover up or mislead concerning the identity or the usu. illegal, harmful, or self-serving true character, purpose, or activity of the actual controlling or directing agent : FACADE ⟨uses her as a ~ for his sinister machinations —*N.Y.Times Bk. Rev.*⟩ ⟨operated a florist shop as a ~ —Robert Shaplen⟩ ⟨assailed the . . . nominees as ~s for a party of privilege —*Collier's Yr. Bk.*⟩ ⟨all political groups and mass organizations are useful ~s to strengthen the party's influence —N.D.Palmer & S.C.Leng⟩ (3) : a person who serves as the official though often only nominal head or spokesman of an enterprise or group to lend it prestige : FIGUREHEAD ⟨a retired general with an impressive war record made an excellent ~ for the company⟩ **2** : something that confronts or faces forward: as **a** (1) : a face of a building; *esp* : the face that contains the principal entrance (2) : the part of a theater in front of the curtain; *also* : the personnel engaged to work there (3) : the faceplate of a mortise lock through which the ends of the bolt are projected (4) : the part of a crab's carapace between the eyes (5) : FRONS 2 (6) : the forepart of the chest and forelegs in a quadruped (7) : the forepart of a garment ⟨a book . . . propped against his meager ~ of tweed —James Stern⟩ (8) : SHIRTFRONT (9) : DICKEY (10) : the part of the human figure opposite to the back ⟨lying on his ~⟩ **b** (1) : the part or surface of something that seems to look out or be directed forward : the fore or forward part ⟨a grasshopper's back is really his ~ —J.B.S.Haldane⟩ (2) : land that faces or abuts (as on a body of water, a river, a road) : FRONTAGE ⟨a lake ~⟩; *also* : a promenade along the beach at a seaside resort ⟨they walked on the ~ together —W.S.Maugham⟩ (3) : a relatively narrow zone of rock characterized by concentration of some elements or scarcity of others relative to adjacent zones (4) : the end of a dynamo or motor shaft opposite to the end that carries the pulley or other coupling member (5) : the side of a paper machine from which it is operated (6) : the boundary between two dissimilar air masses — see COLD FRONT, WARM FRONT (7) : the part of the upper surface of the tongue behind the blade that lies opposite the hard palate when the tongue is at rest (8) : BELLY 5d **c** : the first part of something: as (1) *archaic* : the first part of a season or other unit of time : BEGINNING (2) **fronts** *pl* : the first portion of a distillate ⟨benzene ~s⟩ **d** : something attached to the forepart: as (1) : false hair worn over the forehead by a woman (2) : the part of a bridle that crosses the forehead — see BRIDLE illustration **3 a** : a position directly before or ahead of a person or before the foremost part of a thing ⟨with six seconds to go he forged out in the ~ of his rivals⟩ ⟨a tree stood in the ~ of the yard⟩ **b** : a position of leadership, advantage, or superiority in any field ⟨an indefatigable worker, he rapidly made his way to the ~ of his profession⟩ — **front and center 1** — used as a preparatory military command before "march" for certain designated individuals to march to the front of the center of a formation **2** — used as a call for someone not in sight to come forward — **in front of** *prep* : directly before : before the foremost part of : ahead of ⟨watching the road *in front of* him⟩ ⟨a tree stood *in front of* the house⟩ ⟨frightened of what lies *in front of* them —*Isis*⟩ ⟨*in front of* him were two Union lines —G.J.Fiebeger⟩ — **out front** *adv* : in the audience

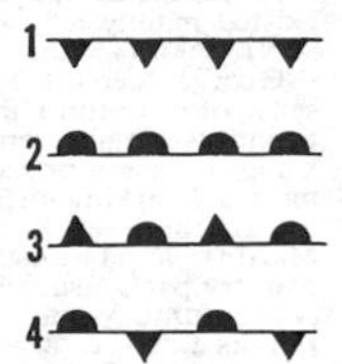

front 2b(6): symbols used on weather maps to indicate *1* cold front, *2* warm front, *3* occluded front, *4* stationary front

2front \"\ *vb* -ED/-ING/-S [partly fr. MF *fronter*, fr. *front*, n.; partly fr. 1*front*] *vi* **1** : to have or turn the face or front in a specified direction : FACE ⟨the house ~s toward the east⟩ **2 a** : to act as a sponsor, advocate, or spokesman ⟨the persons who had gotten them jobs ~*ed* for them in time of stress —C.R.Cooper⟩ ⟨his ability to . . . ~ for the U. S. in world affairs —*Time*⟩ **b** : to serve as a front ⟨~*ing* for oil interests —*Current Biog.*⟩ ⟨the top men in the community have little time for committee meetings; they send a lesser man to ~ for them —O.S.Strong⟩ ~ *vt* **1 a** : to face up to : CONFRONT ⟨went to the woods because I wished . . . to ~ only the essential facts of life —H.D.Thoreau⟩ ⟨loses his job . . . and with it his ability to ~ life benignly —J.P.Bishop⟩ **b** : to appear before : meet face-to-face ⟨daily ~*ed* him in some fresh splendor —Alfred Tennyson⟩ **2 a** : to stand in front of : serve as a front to ⟨a lawn ~*ing* a house⟩ **b** : to be the leader of (a dance orchestra) ⟨appeared as soloist in reviews, in addition to ~*ing* bands —*Esquire's Jazz Bk.*⟩ **3** *obs* : BEGIN, INTRODUCE, PREFACE **4** : to supply a front to : put a facing upon ⟨~*ed* the building with brick⟩ **5** : to face or look toward : have the front toward, opposite, or over against ⟨the house ~s the street⟩ **6** : to articulate (a sound) with the tongue further forward

3front \"\ *adj* [1*front*] **1** : of or relating to the front or forward part : situated in front ⟨a ~ view⟩ ⟨~ seats at the opera⟩ **2** *comparative sometimes* **fronter** : articulated at or toward the front of the oral passage ⟨\ē\, \a\, \s\, and \p\ are ~ sounds⟩

4front \"\ *adv* [1*front*] : toward, in, or at the front or forward position ⟨a pale boy rose and came ~ of the class —Willa Cather⟩ ⟨those who are older and sit farther ~ than I do —Henry Hewes⟩ — often used in the phrases *up front* and *out front* ⟨a few riflemen might be needed up ~ later —*Combat Forces Jour.*⟩ ⟨way out ~ in the race —T.M.Pryor⟩

front *abbr* frontispiece

front·ad \ˈfrənt,ad, -n·,tad\ *adv* [1*front* + *-ad*] : toward the front ⟨outside the eye the infraorbital line runs ~ —Nils Holmgren⟩

front·age \ˈfrəntij, -tēj\ *n* -s [1*front* + *-age*] **1 a** : a portion of land that fronts (as on a stream, body of water, or road) ⟨the Romans won . . . a ~ on the Atlantic ocean —A.J. Toynbee⟩ ⟨states of the Union . . . which have a salt-water ~ —*Congressional Record*⟩; *also* : the extent of front ⟨has a lake ~ of approximately two miles —*Amer. Guide Series: La.*⟩ **b** : the land between the front of a building and the street **2** : the front part or face of a building ⟨dirty plaster ~s embossed with scrollwork and heraldic devices —Christopher Isherwood⟩ ⟨the pillars of its colonnaded ~ —Claud Cockburn⟩ **3** : the act or fact of facing a given way : EXPOSURE **4** : something that belongs to, is part of, or appears in or on a front ⟨a dazzling ~ of flowers and faces —Leonard Merrick⟩ **5** : the lateral extent of responsibility of a military unit : the width of a zone of military action in an attack : the width of a military sector in defense

front·ag·er \-jə(r)\ *n* -s : one that holds the frontage (as on a road or on water)

frontage road *n* : a local street or road generally paralleling an expressway or through street on one or both of its sides to collect local traffic and provide access to property isolated from the expressway through access controls — called also *service road*

1fron·tal \ˈfrənt°l *sometimes* -rän-\ *n* -s [in sense 1, fr. ME *frountel, frontel*, fr. MF *frontel*, fr. L *frontale*, fr. *front-, frons* + *-ale* (neut. of *-alis* -al); in sense 2, fr. ME *frountel, frontel*, fr. ML *frontellum*, dim. of L *front-, frons;* in other senses, fr. 2*frontal*] **1** : something worn across the forehead; *specif* : an ornamental band often of jewels **2** : a movable decorative piece (as of rich stuff or embroidery) covering the front of an altar in a church **3** : FACADE **4 a** : FRONTAL BONE **b** : a frontal scale or plate

2frontal \"\ *adj* [NL *frontalis*, fr. L *front-, frons* forehead + *-alis* -al — more at BRINK] **1 a** : of or relating to the forehead or the frontal bone **b** : of or being a scale or plate lying between the eyes and over the frontal bone in a reptile **2 a** : belonging to the front part ⟨a ~ appendage⟩ **b** : of or relating to the front : taking place from or at the front ⟨to cease all ~ resistance and to limit its activity to guerrilla warfare —D.J. Dallin⟩ **c** : directed against the front : delivered upon the main or essential point or issue : DIRECT ⟨a ~ assault on the enemy⟩ ⟨~ attack . . . on broad problems of human nature —F.A.Geldard⟩ **3 a** : parallel to the main axis of the body and at right angles to the sagittal plane **b** : having or showing frontality **4** : of or relating to a meteorological front **5** : FRONT 2 — **fron·tal·ly** \-°lē,-°li\ *adv*

frontal angle *n* : the angle formed by the intersection of lines from the bregma and glabella to the auricular point

frontal apron *n* : APRON 5

frontal artery *n* : one of the terminal branches of the ophthalmic artery

frontal bone *n* : one of a pair of membrane bones of the upper front part of the cranium next anterior to the parietals, in man becoming united into a single bone that forms the forehead and upper part of the orbits

frontal convolution *or* **frontal gyrus** *n* : any of the convolutions of the outer surface of the frontal lobe of the brain

frontal crest *n* : a median ridge on the internal surface of the vertical part of the human frontal bone

frontal eminence *n* : the prominence of the human frontal bone above each superciliary ridge

frontal gibbosity *n* : a protuberance on the head of certain male fishes prominent as sexual maturity is reached

frontal index *n* : the ratio of the least breadth of the forehead to its greatest breadth multiplied by 100

fron·ta·lis \,frən·ˈtaləs, frän-, -tāl-,-tāl-\ *n* -ES [NL, fr. *frontalis* frontal] : the muscle of the forehead that forms part of the occipitofrontalis

fron·tal·i·ty \,frən·ˈtaləd·ē, frän-\ *n* -ES **1** *in sculpture* : a schematic composition of the front view that is complete without lateral movement **2** *in the pictorial arts* : an arrangement of one or more planes parallel to the picture plane

frontal lobe *n* : the anterior division of each cerebral hemisphere having its lower part in the anterior fossa of the skull and being bordered behind by the central sulcus

frontal nasal spine *n* : a median process projecting down from the frontal bone and articulating with the two nasal bones — called also *superior nasal spine*

frontal nerve *n* : a branch of the ophthalmic nerve supplying the forehead, scalp, and adjoining parts

frontal shield *also* **frontal plate** *n* : a platelike prolongation of the base of the upper mandible over the forehead that is a characteristic feature of the coots and gallinules

frontal sinus *n* : either of two air spaces lined with mucous membrane that lie within the frontal bone above the orbit on each side

frontal vein *n* : a vein of the middle of the forehead that unites with the supraorbital to form the angular vein near the inner angle of the orbit

front bench *n* : either of the two benches nearest the chair in the British House of Commons or House of Lords occupied by government and opposition spokesmen — compare BACK BENCH

front bencher *n* : a government or opposition spokesman in the British House of Commons or House of Lords

front–connected switch \¦=¦==-\ *n* : a switch in which the conductors are fastened to terminals in front of the mounting

front court *n* : a basketball team's offensive half of the court

front dive *n* **1** : a dive in which for the takeoff the diver faces the water **2** : one of several competitive dives including those in which the body rotates forward from a front takeoff — compare BACK DIVE, INWARD DIVE, REVERSE DIVE, TWIST DIVE

front door *n* **1** : the main entrance to a dwelling or apartment having more than one entrance : a doorway fronting on or giving direct access to a street or road **2 a** : a place or area affording the main or best approach or access (as to a country) ⟨the war would then be brought directly to the *front door* of the Americas —Emil Lengyel⟩ **b** : an open direct forthright approach or a legal approach toward gaining some object ⟨should do it directly and openly, through the *front door* —*Yale Rev.*⟩

front drop *n* : a fundamental trampoline stunt consisting of dropping to a prone position on the bed with the head up and then rebounding to a standing position

front·ed \¦frəntəd\ *adj* : having or furnished with a front of a specified kind or quality ⟨plaster-*fronted* houses . . . painted in garish colors —James Reach⟩ ⟨a tuck-*fronted* shirt —*New Yorker*⟩

1fronter *comparative of* FRONT

2fronter *n* -s [1*front* + *-er*] : one who is a member of an organization which is or is alleged to be a front ⟨a Communist ~ —Hillel Silver⟩

frontes *pl of* FRONS

front–fanged \ˈ=¦=\ *adj* : having grooved or perforated venom-conducting teeth in the front of the mouth — used chiefly of members of the Proteroglypha; compare BACK-FANGED, PIT VIPER

front flap *n* : the part of a book jacket that folds over and onto the inside of the front board

front foot *n* : a foot measured along the front of a piece of property — called also *foot front*

front–foot rule *n* : a method of property assessment based upon the length of frontage of the property

1fron·tier \,frən·ˈti(ə)r, -ˈtiə, ˈ=,= *also* frän·ˈ- *or* ˈfrän·,- *sometimes* ,frən·ˈ-, *chiefly Brit* ˈ=,tiə(r *or* ˈ=,tyə(r\ *n* -s [ME *frounter, fronter*, fr. MF *frontiere*, fr. *front* — more at FRONT] **1 a** (1) : a part of a country that fronts or faces another country ⟨the inhabitants of the ~ between Canada and the U.S.⟩; *specif* : a demarcated boundary between countries ⟨crossed the ~ into Mexico⟩ (2) : a boundary between territorial units ⟨lived on the edge of the river that defined the ~ between the two counties⟩ **b** *obs* : BARRIER, DEFENSE; *specif* : a stronghold upon a border province or frontier **2 a** : a typically shifting or advancing zone or region esp. in No. America that marks the successive limits of settlement and civilization : a zone or region that forms the margin of settled or developed territory ⟨the ~, where people . . . lead rough lives and seldom meet together for pleasure —Willa Cather⟩ **b** : an area (as of thought or investigation) that constitutes the most advanced, obscure, or unexploited field or line of inquiry with respect to a particular subject : the farthermost limits of knowledge or achievement ⟨the latest ~s of linguistic research⟩ ⟨the study advances appreciably the ~ of political analysis —R.M.Goldman⟩ ⟨progress on the atomic ~ last week —*Time*⟩ ⟨work on one of the ~s of modern science—the geology of the deeper parts of the earth's crust —W.H.Bucher⟩ **c** : a line of division between different or opposed things ⟨the ~ of drama and melodrama is vague —T.S.Eliot⟩ **d** : a new or relatively unexploited field that offers scope for large exploitative or developmental activity ⟨a large economic ~ right at home —T.J.Kreps⟩ ⟨is television destined to become a great new educational ~ —*Mich. Alumnus*⟩ ⟨the ~s of the future are marketing ~s —Bud Wilson⟩

2frontier \"\ *adj* **1** : situated on a frontier between countries : BORDERING, CONTERMINOUS ⟨all ~ garrisons were ordered withdrawn⟩ **2** : of or relating to a frontier esp. in No. America : characteristic of people living on such a frontier ⟨turning to the task with typical ~ ingenuity —R.A.Billington⟩ ⟨the hardships of ~ life⟩ ⟨one of the last real ~ towns⟩ **3** : advancing or pushing back the frontiers of knowledge or achievement : EXPLORATORY, PIONEERING ⟨~ research in the humanities —C.E.Odegaard⟩ ⟨a ~ report in the field⟩

3frontier \"\ *vt* -ED/-ING/-S *archaic* : BORDER, FACE

fron·tiers·man \-rzmən, -əz-\ *n, pl* **frontiersmen** : a man living on the frontier

fronting *pres part of* FRONT

fron·tis \ˈfrəntəs *sometimes* -rän-\ *n* -ES [by shortening] : FRONTISPIECE

1fron·tis·piece \ˈfrəntə,spēs *sometimes* -rän-\ *n* -s [alter. (influenced by *piece*) of earlier *frontispice*, fr. MF, fr. LL *frontispicium* front of a building, lit., view of the front, fr. L *front-, frons* forehead, brow, front + *-i-* + *-spicium* (fr. *specere* to look, look at) — more at FRONT, SPY] **1 a** : the principal front of a building; *esp* : the entryway of a building when decoratively treated **b** : an ornamental or decorated pediment (as over a portico or window); *also* : a sculptured panel (as of a door) **2 a** *obs* : TITLE PAGE **b** *archaic* : an ornamental figure or illustration on the first page of a book or pamphlet; *also* : the page itself **c** : an illustration preceding and usu. facing the title page of a book or magazine or of a major section of a book; *also* : the page itself **3** : an architectural drawing in which details are assembled and presented in an attractive way

2frontispiece \"\ *vt* -ED/-ING/-S : to supply with, show on, or act as a frontispiece

front·less \ˈfrəntləs\ *adj* **1** : being without face or front **2** *archaic* : SHAMELESS

front·let \-lət, *usu* -ləd.+V\ *n* -s [in sense 1, fr. ME *frontlette*, fr. MF *frontelet*, dim. of *frontel;* in other senses, fr. 1*front* + *-let* — more at FRONTAL] **1 a** : FRONTAL, BROWBAND ⟨a black velvet ~ just visible as a loop on the forehead —Doreen Yarwood⟩ **b** : PHYLACTERY ⟨~s between thine eyes —Deut 6:8(AV)⟩ **2** : a fronting piece: as **a** : an architectural facade **b** : SUPERFRONTAL; *also* : a short valance over an altar frontal **3 a** : the forehead esp. of a quadruped mammal **b** : the forehead of a bird when distinguished by a different color or texture of plumage

frontlighting \ˈ=¦==\ *n* : the broad basic lighting of a photographic subject from the front or the side toward the camera

front line *n* **1** : a military line formed by the most advanced tactical units in a combat situation; *also* : the line or zone of contact with an enemy : FRONT **2** : the most advanced, responsible, or vanguard position in any field of activity or struggle ⟨constantly in the *front line* of antislavery agitation —F.S.Philbrick⟩

frontline \ˈ=¦=\ *adj* [*front line*] : situated or suitable for use at the front ⟨a new ~ ambulance —*Army Reserve Training Bull.*⟩ : relating to advance activity or procedure ⟨~ agricultural news —*Atlantic*⟩ ⟨in the cultural struggle . . . the schools are the ~ trenches —Paul Blanshard⟩

front man \ˈ=,=\ *n, pl* **front men** [1*front*] **1** : FRONT ⟨would almost certainly be used as a *front man* by whatever group succeeded in capturing him —R.C.Doty⟩ ⟨the *front men* of the leading law firms . . . are usually chosen . . . for their glamour or histrionic abilities —*Harper's*⟩ ⟨does business anonymously through *front men*⟩ ⟨has had a long career as a professional *front man* with no power —E.D.Canham⟩ **2 a** : a barker esp. for a show or circus ⟨also acted for a short time as *front man* for a magician —*Current Biog.*⟩ **b** : one who leads a dance orchestra ⟨big bands used to take their personality from the improvisations of the *front men* —*Time*⟩

front matter *n* : matter preceding the main text of a book — called also *preliminaries;* compare BACK MATTER

fronto- *comb form* [ISV, fr. L *front-, frons* forehead, brow, front — more at BRINK] **1** : frontal bone and ⟨*fronto*parietal⟩ : frontal lobe and ⟨*fronto*pontine⟩ **2** [1*front* + *-o-*] : boundary of an air mass ⟨*fronto*genesis⟩

front office *n* : the head or executive office; *specif* : the policy-making staff ⟨play the genial host while . . . worrying about what the *front office* will say when they turn in the liquor bill —R.D.Altick⟩

fron·to·genesis \¦frəntō, -rän-+\ *n* [NL, fr. *fronto-* + L *genesis*] : the coming together of two dissimilar masses or currents of air in such a way that a distinct front is formed or sharpened between them and that they commonly react upon each other to induce cloud and precipitation

front·o·ly·sis \,frənt·ˈäləsəs, ,frən·tä-, -frənt·ˈtä-\ *n, pl* **frontoly·ses** \-ə,sēz\ [NL, fr. *fronto-* + *-lysis*] : a process tending to destroy a meteorological front (as by horizontal mixing and divergence of the air)

1fron·ton \,frən·ˈtōn, frän-\ *n, pl* **frontons** \-tōn(z)\ [F, fr. It *frontone*, aug. of *fronte* forehead, front, fr. L *front-, frons*] : a pediment esp. over a door or window : FRONTAL

2fron·ton \ˈfrän,tän, =ˈ=\ *n* -s [Sp *frontón*, irreg. aug. (influence of L *front-, frons*) of *frente* forehead, front, fr. L *front-, frons* — more at BRINK] : a court or building for the game of jai alai

fron·to–occipital \¦frəntō, -rän-+\ *adj* [*fronto-* + *occipital*] : of or pertaining to the forehead and occiput

fron·to·parietal \"+\ *adj* [*fronto-* + *parietal*] : of, relating to, or involving both frontal and parietal bones of the skull

frontoparietal suture *n* : CORONAL SUTURE

fron·to·pontine \"+\ *adj* [*fronto-* + L *pont-, pons* bridge + E *-ine*] : of or relating to both the frontal lobe and the pons

frontopontine tract *n* : a neural tract beginning in the frontal cortex and ending in the pons

1front–page \ˈ=¦=\ *adj* [*front page*] : of, relating to, or appearing on the front page of a newspaper : very newsworthy ⟨*front-page* news⟩ — opposed to *back-page*

2front–page \"\ *vt* [*front page*] : to print (news) or report (an event) on the front page of a newspaper or periodical ⟨every newspaper in the world *front-paged* the story —Walter White⟩

frontpiece \ˈ=¦=\ *n* : the piece or part in or at the front of something

front–porch campaign *n* : a presidential campaign in which the candidate instead of stumping the country stays at home issuing written statements and making most of his speeches in his home community (as from his front porch)

front–rank \ˈ=¦=\ *adj* [*front rank*] : being in the front rank : ranking among the best : of the first quality or importance : FIRST-RATE ⟨emerges as a figure of *front-rank* importance in

the American social sciences —Eric Goldman⟩ ⟨a *front-rank* university⟩
front room *n* : LIVING ROOM, PARLOR
front-runner \ˈ=ˌ==\ *n* **1** : a contestant who runs best when in the lead; *also* : one who can set his own fast pace **2** : the leading contestant or one of the leading contestants in any rivalry or competition ⟨the *front-runner* . . . on two ballots —T.L.Stokes⟩ ⟨one of the *front-runners* in the postwar frozen-orange-juice derby —E.J.Kahn⟩
fronts *pres 3d sing of* FRONT, *pl of* FRONT
front sight *n* : the sight of a weapon nearest the muzzle
frontstall \ˈ=ˌ=\ *n* : a plate of armor attached to a horse's bridle with holes for the eyes and nostrils
front string *n* : an exposed stair stringer
front vault *n* : a vault in gymnastics executed to the right or left in which the body is raised sideward and then rotated a quarter turn inward so that the front of the body passes over the apparatus
front wall *n* : the wall against which the ball is served in a rackets game and from which every fair hit must rebound
front·ward \ˈfrəntwə(r)d\ *also* **front·wards** \-dz\ *adv* : toward the front : in a frontal direction ⟨a strip reaching . . . *frontwards* over a distance of hundreds of miles —Bruce Bliven b.1889⟩ ⟨practice sewing backward as well as ~ —Clarence Poulin⟩
front·ways \-ˌwāz\ *adv* : from the front ⟨looked at the statue first sideways and then ~⟩
front-wheel \ˈ=ˌ=\ *adj* [*front wheel*] : operative on the front wheels of a vehicle ⟨*front-wheel* drive⟩ ⟨*front-wheel* brake⟩
front yard *n* : an area in front of a house
frop·pish \ˈfräpish\ *adj* [alter. of earlier *frappish*, fr. *frap* + *-ish*] *archaic* : PEEVISH, FRETFUL
frore \ˈfrō(ə)r, -ō(ə)r, -ōə, -ōə\ *adj* [ME *froren*, fr. OE, past part. of *frēosan* to freeze — more at FREEZE] : FROSTY, COLD, FROZEN ⟨the evenings, whatever they be — frosty and ~, warm and wet —C.G.Glover⟩ ⟨stood in a ~ and fearful silence —Eric Linklater⟩
frory \-ōrē, -ōrē, -ri\ *adj* [*frore* + *-y*] *archaic* : FROZEN, FROSTY
¹frosh \ˈfräsh\ *also* **frosk** \-sk\ *n* [ME *frosk*, *frosh*, *frush*, *frosse*, fr. OE *frosc*, *frox*, *forsc* & ON *froskr* — more at FROG] *now dial Eng* : FROG
²frosh \ˈfräsh\ *n, pl* **frosh** [by shortening & alter.] : FRESHMAN
¹frost \ˈfrȯst *also* -äst\ *n* -s [ME *frost*, *forst*, fr. OE; *akin to* OS, OHG, & ON *frost*; derivatives fr. the root of E *freeze*] **1 a** : the process of freezing : congelation of fluids, esp. water **b** (1) : the condition or temperature of the air that causes the freezing of water : freezing weather (2) : a frozen condition **c** (1) : a covering of minute ice crystals on a cold surface that is formed by the condensation of atmospheric vapor at temperatures below freezing — called also *hoarfrost*, *white frost*; compare BLACK FROST (2) : the cause of such crystallization and freezing regarded as a special agency — compare JACK FROST **2 a** : coldness of deportment or temperament : an indifferent, reserved, or unfriendly manner ⟨our friends have . . . a slight ~ or tartness in their speech —F.A.Swinnerton⟩ **b** : something that meets with a cold reception : FIASCO, FAILURE ⟨one small meeting can be a ~ and another a crashing success —R.H.Rovere⟩ ⟨the trip proved to be a ~ —R.L. Taylor⟩ ⟨the play was . . . a most dreadful ~ —Arnold Bennett⟩
²frost \"\ *vb* -ED/-ING/-S *vt* **1** : to roughen or sharpen (as the nailheads or calks of horseshoes) so as to prevent slipping on ice **2 a** : to cover with or as if with frost or a surface resembling frost; *esp* : to put icing on (cake) ⟨white pleated panels ~ a pastel dress —*McCall's Needlework*⟩ ⟨a face mask . . . tends to produce fogging of the goggles . . . and to ~ them over below —10°F —H.G.Armstrong⟩ **b** : to produce on (as metal or glass) a fine-grained sparkling slightly roughened surface with a distinctive pattern **c** : to pit or etch (a rock) by wind action **3 a** : to injure by frost : FREEZE ⟨froze to death 2000 of their birds and ~*ed* the remaining 1000 . . . badly —John Bird⟩ **b** : to freeze so as to kill (as plants) or cause to drop (as buds) ~ *vi* **1** : to become frosted : FREEZE ⟨I've had tumblers ~*ing* all day —Eugene Walter⟩ ⟨the fur parka . . . began to ~ up —Robert Murphy⟩ ⟨I have on various evenings hugged the open fire . . . to keep my bones from ~*ing* —W.A. Krauss⟩ — often used with *over* ⟨all of the cabin windows will ~ over —H.G.Armstrong⟩ **2** : to dry with the appearance of a frosty window — used esp. of varnish and oil films
frostbird \ˈ=ˌ=\ *n* : any of various migratory birds that appear at about the time of the first frost; *esp* : GOLDEN PLOVER
¹frostbite \ˈ=ˌ=\ *vt* **frostbit**; **frostbitten** *also* **frostbit**; **frostbiting**; **frostbites** : to blight or nip with frost : damage by freezing
²frostbite \"\ *n* : the freezing or the local effect of a partial freezing of some part of the body (as the ears or nose)
frostbitten \ˈ=ˌ==\ *adj* : injured, nipped, or withered by frost or freezing ⟨~ grapes unsalable as fresh fruit —*Time*⟩
frost-blite \ˈ=ˌ=\ *n* **1** : LAMB'S-QUARTERS **2** : a plant of the genus *Atriplex*
frost boil *n* : a defective spot in the surface of a pavement due to the pulverizing and swelling action of frost
frostbow \ˈ=ˌ=\ *n* : a white arc in the sky that occurs in frosty weather and is formed by reflection of sunlight from floating ice crystals : the parhelic circle that has its center at the zenith and is not to be confused with the white rainbow
frost crack *n* : a split in a tree trunk due to uneven shrinkage during severe frost
¹frost·ed \-təd\ *adj* [fr. past part. of ²*frost*] **1 a** : covered with hoarfrost or something like hoarfrost ⟨a ~ windowpane⟩ **b** : ornamented with frosting ⟨a ~ cake⟩ **c** : FROSTBITTEN **2** : etched with or as if with sand ⟨a ~ electric light bulb⟩ **3** : made white or dim by age ⟨a wild red mustache, ~ now —Judson Philips⟩ ⟨his eyes were at moments ~ by age —John Mason Brown⟩ **4** : cold or distant in manner or temperament : ARROGANT, STUCK-UP ⟨they . . . come back as ~ little snobs —*Time*⟩ **5** : quick-frozen for preservation and commercial distribution ⟨~ vegetables⟩
²frosted \"\ *n* -s : ice cream added to a liquid (as milk and chocolate syrup) and shaken or stirred until almost melted ⟨chocolate ~⟩ — compare FLOAT 14
frosted bat *n* : any of various bats having the basic fur color obscured by intermingled white or white-tipped hairs; *esp* : a common Eurasian bat (*Vespertilio murinus*)
frosted rustic *adj* : having the margins of the stones cut to a plane parallel to the plane of the wall with the intermediate part having an irregular surface — used esp. in the phrase *frosted rustic work*
frosted scale *n* : an unarmored scale (*Lecanium pruinosum*) that has a body covered with a frosting of wax and is a pest on peach and apricot trees
frost·er \-tə(r)\ *n* -s **1** : one that frosts: as **a** : a sand blaster who produces a frosted appearance on glass **b** : one who frosts baked goods by hand or by machine **2** : one who roughs out the ground for a wood carving with a punch
frostfish \ˈ=ˌ=\ *n* **1** : TOMCOD 1a **2** : SMELT 1a(1) **3** *New Zeal* : a scabbard fish (*Lepidopus caudatus*)
frost flower *n* **1 a** : a small bulbous herb (*Milla biflora*) of Mexico and the southwestern U.S.; *also* : its star-shaped flower — called also *floating star* **b** : a plant of the genus *Aster* **c** : FROSTWEED **2** : an ice crystal resembling a flower; *esp* : one formed on the ground or in the subsoil
frost grape *n* **1** : CHICKEN GRAPE **2** : RIVERBANK GRAPE
frost gray *n* : a nearly neutral slightly purplish medium gray that is very slightly bluer than Quaker drab — called also *chateau gray*
frost gull *n* : BONAPARTE'S GULL
frost heave *or* **frost heaving** *n* : an upthrust of ground caused by freezing of moist soil (as under a footing or pavement)
frost·i·ly \-təlē, -li\ *adv* : to a frosty or chilling degree : in a chilly, reserved, or distant manner ⟨he smiled ~⟩
frost·i·ness \-tēnəs, -tin-\ *n* -ES : the quality or state of being frosty or frigid ⟨often criticized for his excessive ~ toward modern art —*Newsweek*⟩
frost·ing \-tiŋ, -tēŋ\ *n* -s **1 a** : ICING **b** : a trimming on a garment ⟨white angora ~ on cuffs and collar of a box jacket —*McCall's Needlework*⟩ **2** : lusterless finish of metal or glass : MAT **3** : a finely pulverized glass used with a mixture of varnish and glue esp. to frost paper shades **4** : a light tracery of lines or scratches machined on polished machine parts for ornamental effect and sometimes also for better retention of lubricant
frost·less \-tləs\ *adj* : not marked or hardened by frost ⟨a ~ night⟩ ⟨the water was soaking into the ~ ground —J.P. Marquand⟩
frost line *n* : the depth to which frost penetrates the soil
frost necrosis *n* : death of plant tissue due to low temperature
frost plant *n* : FROSTWEED
frost pocket *n* : a small low area that has poor aerial drainage and is subject to frequent frosts
frost rib *or* **frost ridge** *n* : a ridge on a tree trunk caused by the healing and recurrence of frost cracks
frost ring *n* : a false annual ring in the trunk of a tree that is often evident only as a brownish line of collapsed or abnormal cells and is caused by defoliation due to frost and subsequent leafing out again
frostroot \ˈ=ˌ=\ *n* : SKEVISH
frosts *pres 3d sing of* FROST, *pl of* FROST
frost smoke *n* : frozen fog over water esp. in polar regions
frost snipe *n* **1** : STILT SANDPIPER **2** : RED-BACKED SANDPIPER
frost thrusting *n* : the movement of rock fragments by frost action; *also* : the result of such movement
frost valve *n* : a valve to drain the part of a pipe, hydrant, or pump where water would be liable to freeze
frostweed \ˈ=ˌ=\ *n* : any of several plants upon which ice crystals form during the first frosts: as **a** : an American plant of the genus *Helianthemum* — see FROSTWORT **b** : a salt-marsh fleabane (*Pluchea camphorata*)
frostweed aster *n* : HEATH ASTER
frostwork \ˈ=ˌ=\ *n* **1** : the figures that moisture sometimes forms in freezing (as on a windowpane) **2** : ornamentation (as on silver, glass, paper) imitative of frost figures
frostwort \ˈ=ˌ=\ *n* : a shrubby frostweed (*Helianthemum canadense*) of northeastern No. America with solitary terminal petalous flowers and few apetalous cleistogamous flowers
frosty \ˈfrȯstē, -ti *also* -räs-\ *adj* -ER/-EST [ME, fr. *frost* + *-y*] **1** : attended with or producing frost : having power to congeal water : COLD, FREEZING ⟨a ~ night⟩ **2 a** : covered with or as if with hoarfrost : HOARY; *esp* : GRAY ⟨ran his thin brown fingers through his ~ hair —Elinor Wylie⟩ **b** : of a pure or glistening white : producing an effect of crispness or coolness ⟨the brice . . . was the traditional vision in white satin and . . . ~ lace veil —James Reynolds⟩ **3** : marked by coolness or extreme reserve in manner : SEVERE, FRIGID, CHILL, UNFRIENDLY ⟨he got a ~ reception from the Senate group —*N.Y. Times*⟩ ⟨his smile was distinctly ~ —Erle Stanley Gardner⟩ ⟨the night superintendent was a man ~ and suspicious —Sinclair Lewis⟩
frosty-beak \ˈ==ˌ=\ *n* : MALLARD 1
frosty green *n* : NICKEL GREEN
frosty mildew *n* : a leaf spot of various plants caused by fungi of the genus *Cercosporella* and characterized by pale to white usu. circumscribed lesions on affected foliage
¹froth \ˈfrȯth *also* -ä-\ *n, pl* **froths** \-ths, -thz\ [ME *froth*, *frooth*, fr. ON *frotha*; akin to ON *frauth* froth, *frȳsa* to snort, OE *āfrēothan* to froth, Gk *prēthein* to blow up, Skt *prothati* he snorts] **1 a** : an aggregation of bubbles formed in or on a liquid (as by fermentation or agitation) : FOAM, SPUME, SCUM **b** : a foamy slaver sometimes accompanying disease (as rabies) or exhaustion **2** : something light, unsubstantial, or of little value ⟨it is common belief that ~ must be offered to viewers in the summer —*N.Y. Times*⟩ ⟨the writing of some folk is nothing but a ~ of words —G.D.Brown⟩
²froth \-th, -th\ *vb* -ED/-ING/-S [ME *frothen*, fr. *froth*, n.] *vt* **1** : to cause to foam : cause froth on the surface of ⟨with which to ~ chocolate, a favorite drink —*Amer. Guide Series: Texas*⟩ **2** : VENT, VOICE ⟨belligerently ~*ing* a rush of hasty and intemperate words⟩ ⟨came out of classes ~*ing* ideas —*Time*⟩ **3** : to cover with froth ⟨a horse ~*s* his chain⟩ ~ *vi* : to foam at the mouth ⟨it hit him square and he died ~*ing* —Richard Bissell⟩ **2** : to throw froth out or up : FOAM ⟨liquids which ~ to a troublesome extent during distillation —*Pharmacopoeia of the U.S.A.*⟩ ⟨surging, ~*ing*, heaving water —Gavin Casey⟩
froth·er \-thə(r), -th-\ *n* -s [²*froth* + *-er*] : an agent (as pine oil or cresol) that is active in froth flotation through its ability to change the surface tension of a liquid and consequently decrease the wettability of the particles to be recovered
froth flotation *n* : flotation in which air bubbles are introduced into a mixture of finely divided ore or other material with water and a chemical that aids attachment of the bubbles to the particles of the desired material and its recovery as a froth
froth·i·ly \-thəlē, -th-, -li\ *adv* : in a frothy manner
froth·i·ness \-thēnəs, -th|, |in-\ *n* -ES : the quality or state of being frothy
froth insect *also* **froth hopper** *or* **froth worm** *n* : SPITTLE INSECT
froth pit *n* : a minute depression in the surface of a coated paper caused by froth in the coating mixture used
frothy \-th|ē, -th|, |i\ *adj* -ER/-EST **1** : full of or consisting of foam, froth, or light bubbles : SPUMOUS, FOAMY ⟨~ waves⟩ **2 a** : gaily frivolous, superficial, or light in content or treatment : INSUBSTANTIAL, SHALLOW ⟨a ~ comedy⟩ ⟨the symphony . . . is ~, brilliant, without much thematic development —E.T. Canby⟩ ⟨a ~ and rhetorical exposition of meager doctrine without pretense of scholarship —H.J.Laski⟩ **b** : made of light thin material : having frilly trimmings ⟨~ garments lying all about on chairs and in the box —Arnold Bennett⟩ ⟨a ~ creation of white nylon tulle —*New Yorker*⟩
frot·tage \frōˈtäzh, frə-\ *n* -s [F, fr. *frotter* to rub + *-age*] **1** : RUBBING, POLISHING ⟨gasoline . . . is applied with gauze . . . by ~ to each local itching area —*Jour. Amer. Med. Assoc.*⟩ **2 a** : the artistic process of composing directly on paper a variety of shapes and motifs produced from rubbings **b** : a composition made by this process **c** : a drawing or painting modeled on images produced from rubbings **3** : masturbation by rubbing against another person
frot·to·la \ˈfrōd·ələ, ˈfräd-, *It* ˈfrȯttōlä\ *n, pl* **frotto·le** \-ᵊl,ā, -ōlā\ [It, fr. OIt, fr. *frotta* crowd, multitude, fr. MF *flote*, fr. OF, fr. (assumed) OIt *flotta*, alter. of (assumed) *flotto*, fr. L *fluctus* action of flowing, flood, wave — more at FLUCTUATE] : a secular part-song of Italy of the 15th and 16th centuries that is largely homophonic and has the music repeated with each verse
frot·ton \(ˈ)frō¦tōⁿ\ *n, pl* **frottons** \-ōⁿ(z)\ [F, fr. *frotter* to rub] : a burnisher for rubbing the back of paper in block printing
frou·frou \ˈfrüˌfrü\ *n* -s [F, of imit. origin] **1** : a rustling esp. of a woman's skirts **2** : frilly trimming; *esp* : abundant or excessive ornamentation (as ruffles, beading, flowers, veiling) in women's clothing **3** : fussy details or showy accessories and amenities esp. in a social setting ⟨the ~ of Victorian decor⟩
frough *also* **frow** *adj* [ME] *obs* : BRITTLE, FRAGILE
frounce \ˈfrau̇n(t)s\ *vt* -ED/-ING/-S [ME *frouncen*, fr. MF *froncir*, of Gmc origin; akin to OHG *runzala* wrinkle, ON *hrukka*] *archaic* : CURL, FRIZZLE ⟨not tricked and *frounced* —John Milton⟩
¹frow \ˈfrau̇, ˈfrō\ *n* -s [ME *frowe*, fr. MD *vrouwe* lady, woman; akin to OHG *frouwa* mistress, lady — more at FRAU] **1 a** : a Dutch or German woman **b** : WOMAN, WIFE, HOUSEWIFE ⟨I'm not going to settle down into a ~ until I've had some fun —Joyce Cary⟩ ⟨a crocodile-hided . . . old ~ —A.M. Mizener⟩ **2 a** *obs* : MAENAD, BACCHANTE **b** *dial Brit* : an untidy messy woman; *specif* : one of loose morals
²frow \ˈfrō\ *var of* FROE
fro·ward \ˈfrō(w)ə(r)d, -ōrd\ *adj* [ME *froward*, *fraward*, fr. *fra*, *fro* from + *-ward* — more at FRO] **1** : habitually disposed to disobedience and opposition : PERVERSE ⟨of a vehement and untamable mind, ~ beyond control —John Bennett⟩ **2** *archaic* ADVERSE, UNFAVORABLE **syn** see CONTRARY
fro·ward·ly *adv* : in a froward manner
fro·ward·ness *n* -ES : the quality or state of being froward
frow·er \ˈfrō(ə)r, -ōə\ *n* -s [perh. alter. of obs. *froward* turned away, fr. *fro* + *-ward*; fr. the position of the handle] : FROE
¹frown \ˈfrau̇n\ *vb* -ED/-ING/-S [ME *frounen*, fr. MF *froignier*, *frogner* to snort, turn up one's nose, frown, of Celt origin; akin to MBret *froan* nostril, W *ffroen* nostril, OIr *srōn* nose] *vi* **1 a** : to contract the brow (as in displeasure, sternness, or concentration) : put on a stern, grim, or surly look : SCOWL ⟨she looked away, ~*ing* —Richard Llewellyn⟩ ⟨he ~*ed* in astonishment —Louis Auchincloss⟩ **b** : to present a somber or menacing appearance — used of inanimate objects ⟨grim gray towers . . . ~ down upon this dignified old town —*Amer. Guide Series: Texas*⟩ **2 a** : to give evidence of displeasure or disapproval by facial expression — used chiefly with *at* ⟨his neighbors ~*ed* at him with impatience —Margaret Deland⟩ **b** : to give evidence of displeasure or disapproval by other means — used chiefly with *on* or *upon* ⟨his religion ~*s* upon smoking, drinking, and modern faddism —*Current Biog.*⟩ ⟨society ~*s* on such deviations from good taste⟩ ~ *vt* : to show displeasure with or disapproval of by facial expression or other means ⟨I will be neither ~*ed* nor ridiculed into error —Noah Webster⟩
²frown \"\ *n* -s **1** : a wrinkling of the brow (as in displeasure or concentration) : a severe, reproving, or stern look : SCOWL ⟨looked about him with a ~⟩ **2** : an expression of displeasure ⟨the book received critical ~*s*⟩
frown·er \-nə(r)\ *n* -s [ME *frouner*, fr. *frounen* + *-er*] : one that frowns
frown·ing·ly *adv* : in a frowning manner ⟨meditated ~ over a cup of tea⟩
¹frowst \ˈfrau̇st\ *n* -s [back-formation fr. *frowsty*] *chiefly Brit* : stale stuffy atmosphere : offensive or musty odor ⟨the ~ that rose . . . from my bedding —Monica Baldwin⟩ ⟨the ~ of a third-class carriage full of sleepy travelers —John Buchan⟩
²frowst \"\ *or* **froust** \"\ *vi* -ED/-ING/-S *Brit* : to loll or lounge esp. indoors ⟨why should one ~ within four walls on such a night —J.C.Snaith⟩
frows·ty *or* **frous·ty** \-ti\ *adj* -ER/-EST [alter. of *frowsy*] *chiefly Brit* : musty and stuffy : having an unpleasant smell ⟨cool night air rushed into the ~ little room —Carol Bache⟩
frow·sy *also* **frow·zy** \ˈfrau̇zē, -zi\ *adj* -ER/-EST [origin unknown] **1** : having a slatternly, slovenly, unkempt, or uncared-for appearance : SHABBY, MEAN, SQUALID, DISHEVELED ⟨filled the entrance with her ~ bulk —Arthur Morrison⟩ ⟨~ white hair⟩ ⟨a ~ old office⟩ ⟨reduced to a daily diet of ~ economy —F.A.Swinnerton⟩ **2** : MUSTY, STALE ⟨a ~ smell of stale beer and stale smoke —W.S.Maugham⟩ ⟨this must render the air moist, ~, and even putrid —Tobias Smollett⟩ **syn** see SLATTERNLY
frowy \ˈfrau̇ē\ *adj* [*frough*, *frow* + *-y*] *chiefly New Eng* : STALE, RANCID
frowze *n* -s [origin unknown] *obs* : frizzed hair; *specif* : a frizzed wig
frow·zled \ˈfrau̇zəld\ *also* **frow·zly** \-z(ə)lē\ *adj* [blend of *frowzy* and *tousled*] : FROWSY, DISHEVELED, UNKEMPT ⟨powder-smeared and ~ —Stephen Crane⟩
froze *past or chiefly dial past part of* FREEZE
fro·zen \ˈfrōzᵊn\ *adj* [ME *frosen*, alter. (influenced by *fresen* to freeze) of *froren*, fr. past part. of *fresen* to freeze — more at FREEZE] **1 a** : congealed by cold : affected or crusted over by freezing ⟨a ~ brook⟩ **b** : subject to frost or to long and severe cold : CHILLY ⟨the ~ north⟩ **c** (1) : clogged with ice ⟨~ water pipes⟩ (2) : injured or killed by cold ⟨~ plants⟩ **d** : CHILLED, REFRIGERATED — used of foods prepared for the table ⟨~ custard⟩ ⟨~ fruit salad⟩ **2 a** (1) : not susceptible or responsive to feeling : drained or incapable of emotion : BENUMBED ⟨~ and bitter and visibly tortured by loneliness —Marcia Davenport⟩ (2) : expressing coldness or unfriendliness : not heartfelt or sincere : IMPASSIVE, FRIGID, MECHANICAL, STIFF ⟨friends give you that ~ look —Clyde Martin⟩ **b** : incapable of being changed, moved, or undone : not subject to change or movement : not flexible, dynamic, or plastic : IMMOBILE, RIGID, PETRIFIED, FIXED ⟨in the United States today institutions are not ~ —Zechariah Chafee⟩ ⟨a ~ social system⟩ ⟨stood ~ with terror⟩ ⟨thinks there should be no ~ agenda for any meeting —*Kiplinger Washington Letter*⟩; *specif* : debarred from change in status or from movement by law or other official action ⟨workers are ~ in their jobs for the duration of the war⟩ ⟨prices and wages are ~ for the emergency⟩ **c** : not available for present use : not liquid ⟨~ inventories⟩ ⟨~ capital⟩ **d** *of a billiard ball* : resting against another ball or a cushion **e** : not subject to being taken unless a player holds a pair to match the top card in rank — used of the discard pile in canasta and related games — **fro·zen·ly** \-ᵊnlē, -li\ *adv* — **fro·zen·ness** \-ᵊn(n)əs\ *n* -ES
frozen account *n* : a bank, trust-company, or brokerage account from which withdrawals are barred by court or government order
frozen asset *n* : an asset that cannot readily be turned into cash without heavy loss
frozen credit *n* : extended credit on a loan that cannot be paid off when due or in the foreseeable future
frozen daiquiri *n* : a daiquiri beaten into shaved ice to a consistency resembling that of a sherbet and drunk through straws
frozen food *n* : food that has been subjected to rapid freezing and is kept frozen until used
frozen-pack \ˈ==ˌ=\ *n* : the preserving of food (as fruits and vegetables) by packaging and quick-freezing
frozen pudding *n* : a rich frozen custard containing nuts and candied fruit and sometimes flavored with rum or sherry
frozen shoulder *n* : a shoulder afflicted with severe pain and stiffening
frozen sleep *n* : local or systemic reduction of temperature in an unconscious patient (as for the relief of pain in inoperable cancer)
frt *abbr* freight
fruct·ed \ˈfrəktəd, -rük-, -rük-\ *adj* [L *fructus* fruit + E *-ed* — more at FRUIT] : bearing fruit — used of a heraldic tree or plant
fruc·tes·cence \ˌfrəkˈtesᵊn(t)s, frük-, -rük-\ *n* -s [NL *fructescentia*, fr. L *fructescent-*, *fructescens*, pres. part. of *fructescere* to produce fruit, fr. *fructus* fruit] : the period of maturing of fruit — **fruc·tes·cent** \¦frək¦tesᵊnt, (ˈ)frük-, (ˈ)frük-\ *adj*
fructi- *comb form* [L, fr. *fructus* — more at FRUIT] : fruit ⟨*fructi*colous⟩
fruc·tif·er·ous \¦frəkˈtif(ə)rəs, (ˈ)frük-, (ˈ)frük-\ *adj* [L *fructifer*, fr. *fructi-* + *-fer* -ferous] : bearing or producing fruit — **fruc·tif·er·ous·ly** *adv*
fruc·ti·fi·ca·tion \ˌfrəktəfəˈkāshən, ˌfrük-, ˌfrük-\ *n* -s [LL *fructification-*, *fructificatio*, fr. L *fructificatus* (past part. of *fructificare* to bear fruit) + *-ion-*, *-io* -ion — more at FRUCTIFY] **1** : the action of forming or producing fruit : FRUITING **2 a** : the ripened plant ovary and its appendages : FRUIT **b** : a sporophore or sporogenous structure ⟨the ~ of a fungus⟩
fruc·ti·fi·ca·tive \ˈ=ˌ==ˌkād·iv, ¦frək¦tifəkəd-, (ˈ)frük¦-, (ˈ)frük¦-\ *adj* [*fructification* + *-ive*] : having the capacity for fructification
fruc·ti·fi·er \ˈ=ˌtəˌfī(ə)r\ *n* -s : something that fructifies ⟨the local deities . . . ~*s* of the soil —A.P.Davies⟩
fruc·ti·form \-ˌfȯrm\ *adj* [*fructi-* + *-form*] : having the form of a fruit
fruc·ti·fy \ˈfrəktəˌfī, -rük-, -rük-\ *vb* -ED/-ING/-ES [ME *fructifien*, fr. MF *fructifier*, fr. L *fructificare*, fr. *fructi-* + *-ficare* -fy] *vi* : to bear fruit ⟨its seeds shall ~ —Amy Lowell⟩ ~ *vt* : to make fruitful : make productive ⟨then he kisses the earth she *fructifies* —Francis Yeats-Brown⟩
fruc·tiv·o·rae \ˌfrəkˈtivəˌrē, frük-, frük-\ [NL, fr. *fructi-* + L *-vorae* (fem. pl. of *-vorus* -vorous)] *syn of* MEGACHIROPTERA
fruc·tiv·o·rous \¦frək¦tivərəs, (ˈ)frük-, (ˈ)frük-\ *adj* [*fructi-* + *-vorous*] : FRUGIVOROUS
fruc·tol·y·sis \ˌfrəkˈtäləsəs, frük-, frük-\ *n, pl* **fructoly·ses** \-ləˌsēz\ [NL, fr. L *fructus* fruit + NL *-o-* + *-lysis* — more at FRUIT] : the breakdown of fructose esp. in the metabolism of stored sperm
fruc·to·san \ˈfrəktəˌsan, -rük-, -rük-\ *n* -s [*fructose* + *-an*] : a polysaccharide (as inulin) yielding primarily fructose on hydrolysis
fruc·tose \-ˌtōs *also* -ōz\ *n* -s [ISV *fruct-* (fr. L *fructus* fruit) + *-ose*] : a ketose sugar $HOCH_2(CHOH)_3COCH_2OH$ known in levorotatory, dextrorotatory, and racemic forms; *esp* : the very sweet soluble levorotatory D-form that occurs esp. in fruit juices and honey and combined in many disaccharides and polysaccharides — see INVERT SUGAR, LEVULOSE, SUCROSE
fruc·to·side \-təˌsīd\ *n* -s [*fructose* + *-ide*] : a glycoside that yields fructose on hydrolysis — **fruc·to·sid·ic** \ˌ==ˈsidik\ *adj*
¹fruc·tu·ary \ˈfrəkchəˌwerē, -ksh-\ *n* -ES [LL *fructuarius*, fr. *fructuarius*, adj.] : USUFRUCTUARY

²fructuary \"\ *adj* [LL *fructuarius*, fr. L, of fruit, fruit-bearing, fr. *fructus* + *-arius* -ary] **:** of or relating to a usufruct — used of a stipulation in Roman and civil law

fruc·tu·ous \-chəwəs, -sh-\ *adj* [ME, fr. MF & L; MF *fructueux*, fr. L *fructuosus*, fr. *fructus* fruit + *-osus* -ous] **:** FRUITFUL, PRODUCTIVE, PROFITABLE ⟨a ~ land⟩ — **fruc·tu·ous·ly** *adv* — **fruc·tu·ous·ness** *n* -ES

fruc·tus in·dus·tri·a·les \'frùktə,sin,dùstrē'ä,lās\ *n pl* [NL] **:** crops (as wheat, corn) produced by labor on the part of man — distinguished from *fructus naturales*

fruc·tus nat·ur·a·les \-,nüd-ə'rä,lās\ *n pl* [NL, lit., natural fruits] **:** crops produced without any substantial assistance from man — distinguished from *fructus industriales*

fru·gal \'frügəl\ *adj* [MF or L; MF, fr. L *frugalis*, back-formation fr. *frugaliter*, adv., economically, frugally, fr. *frugi* fit, economical, frugal, fr. dat. of *frux* fruit, produce, value (in such phrases as *esse frugi bonae* to be capable of a good harvest or revenue); akin to L *frui* to enjoy, have the use and enjoyment of — more at BROOK] **1 :** economical in the use or expenditure of resources **:** not wasteful or lavish **:** SAVING, THRIFTY ⟨the cost of the war was appalling to his ~ mind —C.S.Forester⟩ ⟨a ~ farm family⟩ **2 :** reflecting or displaying economy in the use or expenditure of resources **:** SCANTY, MEAN ⟨a small and ~ apartment —T.B.Costain⟩ ⟨insistence on a ~ diet —Lillian Smith⟩ **syn** see SPARING

fru·gal·i·ty \frü'galəd-ē, -ətē, -i\ *n* -ES [L *frugalitas*, fr. *frugalis* + *-itas* -ity] **:** the quality or state of being frugal **:** careful management of resources **:** THRIFT ⟨lived with great ~⟩

fru·gal·ly \'frügəlē, -li\ *adv* **:** in a frugal manner

fru·gal·ness \-əlnəs\ *n* -ES **:** the quality or state of being frugal

fru·giv·o·ra \frü'jivərə\ [NL, fr. L *frugi-* (fr. *frug-*, *frux*) + NL *-vora*] *syn of* MEGACHIROPTERA

fru·giv·o·rous \(')=¦==rəs\ *adj* [L *frugi-* + E *-vorous*] **1 :** feeding on fruit **2 :** of or relating to the Megachiroptera

¹fruit \'früt, *usu* -üd·+V\ *n* -S *often attrib* [ME, fr. OF, fr. L *fructus* use, enjoyment, product, fruit, fr. *fructus*, past part. of *frui* to enjoy, have the use and enjoyment of — more at BROOK] **1 a :** a product of plant growth useful to man or animals (as grain, vegetables, cotton, flax) — usu. used in pl. ⟨the ~s of the field⟩ **b** (1) **:** the reproductive body of a seed plant consisting of one or more seeds and usu. various protective and supporting structures — used esp. of edible bodies ⟨squash vines full of green ~s that will be killed by frost⟩ (2) **:** such a fruit having an edible more or less sweet pulp associated with the seed and usu. being used as or in a dessert or sweet course ⟨apples, peaches, plums, and berries are among our best native ~s⟩ — contrasted with *vegetable* ⟨pears and cherries are ~s while squashes and beans are vegetables⟩ (3) **:** a succulent plant part used chiefly in a dessert or sweet course ⟨rhubarb though actually the petiole of a leaf is considered a ~⟩ **c :** a dish, selection, or diet of fruits ⟨pass the ~⟩ ⟨live on ~⟩ **d :** a product of fertilization in a plant with its modified envelopes or appendages (as the cystocarp in various algae or the sporogonium of a moss); *specif* **:** the ripened ovary of a seed plant and its contents including such adjacent tissues as may be inseparably connected with it (as the pod of a pea or the capsule of many annuals) — compare SEED **2 :** OFFSPRING, YOUNG, PROGENY ⟨the ~ of the womb⟩ **3 :** the effect or consequence of an action or operation **:** ISSUE, RESULT ⟨that policy bore ~⟩ ⟨the ~s of crime⟩ ⟨the ~s of sound instruction⟩ **4** *slang* **:** HOMOSEXUAL

²fruit \"\ *vb* -ED/-ING/-S [ME *fruiten*, fr. *fruit*, n.] *vi* **:** to bear or produce fruit **:** come to fruition ⟨a tree that ~s annually⟩ ⟨some of the tomatoes blossomed but didn't ~⟩ ⟨the culture he served . . . never ~*ed* in wisdom —V.L.Parrington⟩ ~ *vt* **:** to cause to bear fruit **:** develop fruit upon ⟨~*ed* the seedlings⟩

fruit·age \'früd-|ij, -üt|, |ēj\ *n* -S [MF, fr. *fruiter* to bear fruit (fr. *fruit*, n.) + *-age*] **1 a :** the condition or process of bearing fruit **b :** a quantity of fruit ⟨a tree bending with ~⟩ **:** yield of fruit ⟨the bark of this tree is so beautiful itself that it would be worth planting if there were not the rich ~ —*Horticulture*⟩ **c :** OFFSPRING, PROGENY ⟨their marriage had five children as its ~⟩ **2 :** the product or result of an action **:** good or bad effect ⟨seldom is it given to any man to see . . . the ~ of his life —*Christian Century*⟩

fruit·ar·i·an \früd-'erēən, -ü't|, |a(a)r-, |är-\ *n* -S [¹*fruit* + *-arian* (as in *vegetarian*)] **:** one who lives chiefly on fruit

fruit bark beetle *n* **:** SHOT-HOLE BORER

fruit bat *n* **:** any of numerous large bats that constitute the suborder Megachiroptera, are confined to the warm parts of the Old World, and feed on fruit — called also *flying fox*

fruit body *n* **:** FRUITING BODY

fruit bud *n* **1 :** a bud that produces flowers and, if fertilized, fruit **2 :** a bud that produces both leaves and flowers (as in the apple, pear, and blackberry) — compare MIXED BUD

fruitcake \'=,=\ *n* **:** a rich light or dark cake that usu. contains a variety of nuts and dried or candied fruits and is often highly spiced

fruit cocktail *n* **:** a mixture of usu. tart and sweet fruits sometimes flavored with a liquor (as sherry) and served in a small stemmed glass as a first course — compare FRUIT CUP

fruit cup *n* **:** a mixture of fruits sometimes topped with a small ball of fruit ice and served in a medium-sized stemmed glass as a dessert course — compare FRUIT COCKTAIL

fruit dot *n* **:** SORUS

fruit dove *n* **:** any of numerous small brightly colored fruit-eating pigeons that have bright red or yellow feet and legs, that are usu. made a subfamily of Columbidae but sometimes a separate family, and that are found mainly in an area extending from India to Polynesia and south to Australia — called also *fruit pigeon*

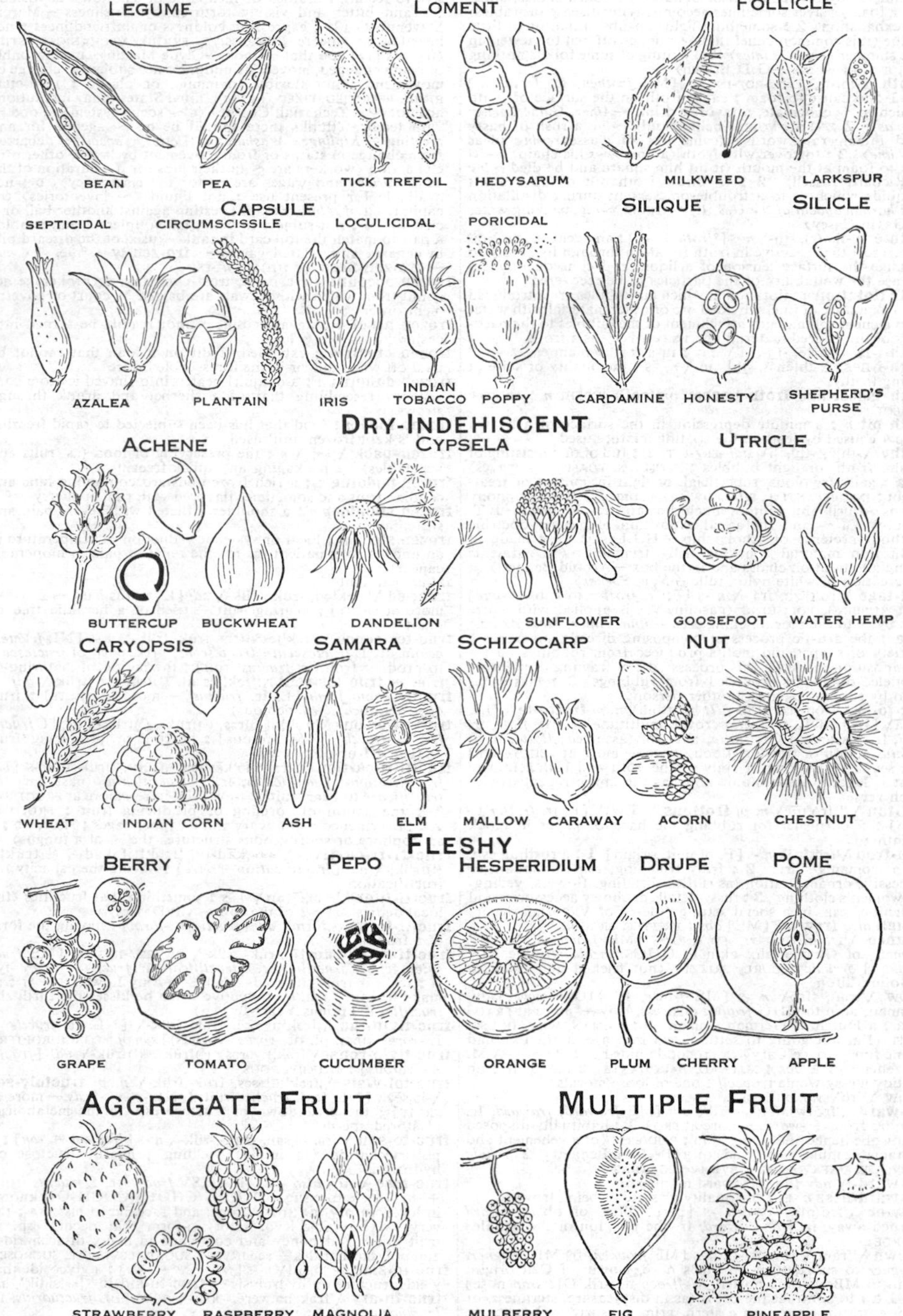

fruit·ed \'früd-əd, -ütəd\ *adj* **1 :** bearing fruit ⟨a heavily ~ plant⟩ **2 :** having fruit added ⟨~ cereal⟩ ⟨~ jello⟩

fruit·er \-üd-ə(r), -ütə-\ *n* -S [¹*fruit* + *-er*] **1 :** a ship for carrying fruit **2 :** a tree or plant that bears fruit

fruit·er·er \-üd-ərə(r), -ütə-\ *n* -S [ME, fr. *fruiter* fruiterer (fr. MF *fruitier*, fr. *fruit* + *-ier* -er) + *-er*] **:** one who deals in fruit **:** a seller of fruits

fruit·er·ess \-üd-ərəs, -ütə-\ *n* -ES **:** a female seller of fruit

fruit·ery \-üd-ərē, -ütə-\ *n* -ES [¹*fruit* + *-ery*] *archaic* **:** FRUIT

fruit fly *n* **:** any of various small acalyptrate flies whose larvae feed on fruit or decaying vegetable matter: as **a :** a member of the genus *Drosophila* **b :** any of various members of the family Trypetidae (as the Mediterranean fruit fly)

fruit·ful \'frütfəl\ *adj, sometimes* **fruitfuller**; *sometimes* **fruitfullest** [ME, fr. ¹*fruit* + *-ful*] **1 a** (1) **:** yielding or producing fruit ⟨a ~ soil⟩ ⟨a ~ womb⟩ (2) **:** conducive to an abundant yield ⟨a ~ rain⟩ **b** *obs* **:** COPIOUS, ABUNDANT **2 :** abundantly productive ⟨regarded as the great waster, the ~ mother of social misery —V.L.Parrington⟩ ⟨a ~ writer⟩; *esp* **:** abundantly productive of desirable results ⟨a brilliant culmination of a rich and ~ career —F.E.Egler⟩ ⟨a ~ discussion⟩ ⟨made a number of ~ suggestions⟩ **syn** see FERTILE

fruit·ful·ly \-fəlē, -li\ *adv* [ME, fr. *fruitful* + *-ly*] **:** in a fruitful manner

fruit·ful·ness *n* -ES [ME *fruitfulnes*, fr. *fruitful* + *-nes* -ness] **:** the quality or state of being fruitful ⟨the ~ of this type of research —Edward Sapir⟩

fruit head *n* **:** a capitate inflorescence (as of the hop) in the fruiting stage

fruitier *comparative of* FRUITY

fruitiest *superlative of* FRUITY

fruit·i·ness \'früd-|ēnəs, -üt|, |in-\ *n* -ES **:** the quality or state of being fruity

fruiting *pres part of* FRUIT

fruiting body *n* **:** an organ (as an apothecium or the sporophore of mushrooms, mosses, liverworts) specialized for producing spores — called also *spore fruit*

fruiting calyx *n* **:** a calyx subtending a mature ovary; *esp* **:** one modified to form part of the fruit

fru·i·tion \frü'ishən\ *n* -S [ME *fruicioun*, fr. MF or LL; MF *fruition*, fr. LL *fruition-*, *fruitio*, fr. L *fruitus* (alter. of *fructus*, past part. of *frui* to enjoy, have the use and enjoyment of) + *-ion-*, *-io* -ion — more at BROOK] **1 :** the pleasurable use or possession of something **:** ENJOYMENT ⟨the sweet ~ of an earthly crown —Christopher Marlowe⟩ **2** [influenced in meaning by ¹*fruit*] **a :** the state of bearing fruit ⟨the fields needed rain for ~ —Pearl Buck⟩ **b :** REALIZATION, ACCOMPLISHMENT, CONCLUSION ⟨the ~ of a farsighted policy —Marquis James⟩ ⟨carry that mission to a successful ~ —J.C. Lincoln⟩ **syn** see PLEASURE

fru·i·tive \'früəd-iv\ *adj* [ML *fruitivus*, fr. L *fruitus* + *-ivus* -ive] **1 :** ENJOYING, POSSESSING **2** [*fruition* + *-ive*] **:** capable of producing fruit **:** FRUITFUL ⟨the big garden lying warm and brown and ~ in the sun —Nancy Hale⟩

fruit knife *n* **:** a small knife usu. with a fancy handle and a blade sharp enough to pare and cut fruit at table

fruit·less \'frütləs\ *adj* [ME, fr. ¹*fruit* + *-less*] **1 :** lacking or not bearing fruit **:** BARREN ⟨a ~ tree⟩ **2 :** productive of no advantage or good effect **:** VAIN, UNSUCCESSFUL, UNPROFITABLE ⟨a ~ effort⟩ ⟨~ negotiations⟩ — **fruit·less·ly** *adv* — **fruit·less·ness** *n* -ES

fruit·let \-lət\ *n* -S [¹*fruit* + *-let*] **1 :** a fruit of small size **2 :** a unit or member of a collective fruit

fruit liqueur *n* **:** a liqueur made chiefly by a maceration process from fruit and neutral spirits or brandy — compare PLANT LIQUEUR

fruit pigeon *n* **1 :** FRUIT DOVE **2 :** GREEN PIGEON

fruit pit *n* **:** BITTER PIT

fruit pox *n* **:** a nonparasitic disease of unknown origin characterized by dark green dots that later become sunken and sometimes coalesce to form streaks esp. on greenwrap tomato fruits

fruits *pl of* FRUIT, *pres 3d sing of* FRUIT

fruit salad *n, slang* **:** military service ribbons and decorations ⟨peeking up at three rows of *fruit salad* on his chest —K.M. Dodson⟩ ⟨twenty thousand medals for . . . one year of combat is a lot of *fruit salad* —John Ciardi⟩

fruit-set \'=,=\ *n* **:** SET 17d

fruit spot *n* **:** any of various diseases of plants characterized by the occurrence of sunken, pithy, or discolored local lesions on the fruits and commonly caused by parasitic fungi — see CYLINDROSPORIUM

fruit spur *n* **:** a short stout twig that bears the fruit buds in a fruit tree (as the apple or pear)

fruitstalk \'=,=\ *n* **:** PEDUNCLE

fruitsucker \'=,==\ *n* **:** GREEN BULBUL

fruit-tree bark beetle *n* **:** SHOT-HOLE BORER

fruit-tree leaf roller *n* **:** a small tortricid moth (*Archips argyrospila*) having larvae that are leaf rollers feeding on apple and other fruit trees

fruit wine *n* **:** a wine fermented from fruit other than grapes

fruitwood \'=,=\ *n* **1 :** the wood of a fruit tree; *esp* **:** the wood of such a tree used for furniture **2 :** the twigs or shoots of a plant that produce flower buds as distinguished from those that bear only leaf buds

fruitworm \'=,=\ *n* **:** any of numerous insect larvae mainly of the orders Diptera and Lepidoptera that feed on or in fruits

fruit wrap *or* **fruit wrapper** *n* **:** a strong thin paper sometimes treated for use as a protective covering for fruit

fruity \'früd-|ē, -üt|, |i\ *adj* -ER/-EST **1 a :** relating to a fruit **:** resembling or suggesting a fruit (as in taste or odor) **:** rich with or as if with fruits or fruit flavor ⟨the ~ fragrance always surprised them —Jean Stafford⟩ ⟨a ~ cake⟩ ⟨a ~ scent, possibly orange —*New Yorker*⟩ **b :** retaining the flavor and fragrance of the grape **:** rich in flavor — used of wines **2 a :** having a rich, strong, or spicy quality **:** extremely effective, interesting, or enjoyable **:** JUICY, ATTRACTIVE ⟨described postmortems, good rich ~ ones —Thomas Wood †1950⟩ ⟨dialogue . . . highly characterized in a finely ~ southern vein —E.R.Bentley⟩ ⟨his comparisons are not only humorous but ~ and unfaded —R.F.Adams⟩ **b :** sweet or sentimental esp. to excess **:** SYRUPY ⟨his voice was rich and arrogant, with a mellow ~ note —George Bellairs⟩ ⟨an educational bureaucrat . . . from his cameo ring to his ~ smile —*Time*⟩ ⟨~ bits of poetry —David Swift⟩ **c** *slang* **:** mentally unbalanced **:** CRAZY, NUTTY, SILLY, WACKY ⟨knocked me *fruitier* than a nutcake —E.J.Kahn⟩ ⟨I tell you he's ~ —J.T.Farrell⟩ ⟨the drugstore man thought I was ~ —C.C.Dewey⟩ **d** *slang* **:** HOMOSEXUAL

frum \'frùm, 'frəm\ *var of* FRIM

fru·men·ta·ceous \¦frümən-¦tāshəs\ *adj* [LL *frumentaceus*, fr. L *frumentum* grain (fr. *frui* to enjoy) + *-aceus* -aceous — more at BROOK] **:** made of or resembling wheat or other grain

fru·men·ty \'früməntē, 'frùm-\ *or* **fur·men·ty** \'fərm-\ *or* **fur·me·ty** *or* **fur·mi·ty** \-məd-ē\ *n* -ES [ME *furmente*, *frumente*, *frumenty*, fr. MF *furmentee*, *formentee*, *frumentee*, *fromentee*, fr. *furment*, *forment*, *frument*, *froment* grain, wheat, fr. L *frumentum*] **1 :** a dish of wheat boiled in milk and usu. flavored with sugar, spice, and raisins **2 :** a cereal dessert set in a mold

frum·er·ty *or* **frum·e·ty** \'frùmə(r)d·i, 'frəm-\ *dial Eng var of* FRUMENTY

¹frump \'frəmp\ *vb* -ED/-ING/-S [perh. short for *frumple*; fr. the distortion of the face in a sneer] *vt* **1** *archaic* **:** INSULT, FLOUT, MOCK, SNUB **2** *archaic* **:** PROVOKE, IRRITATE, VEX ~ *vi, archaic* **:** SULK

²frump \", *dial Brit* " *or* 'frùmp\ *n* -S **1 frumps** *pl, dial Brit* **:** a cross mood **:** SULKS **2** [short for *frumple*] **a :** a dowdy, unattractive, or generally uninteresting girl or woman ⟨a terribly plain little ~ —Jessamyn West⟩ ⟨weighs about two hundred pounds, doesn't know how to dress, and, briefly, is an awful ~ —Olive H. Prouty⟩ **b :** a staid, drab, old-fashioned person ⟨representing the New England founding fathers as the usual reputable ~s —John McCarten⟩

frump·i·ly \-pəlē, -li\ *adv* **:** in a frumpy manner

frump·i·ness \-pēnəs, -pin-\ *n* -ES **:** the quality or state of being frumpy

frump·ish \'frəmpish, -pēsh\ *adj* **1** *archaic* **:** CROSS, SCORNFUL **2 :** generally uninteresting or unattractive **:** DOWDY, DULL, OLD-FASHIONED ⟨nothing is so ~ as last year's gambling game —Nancy Mitford⟩ — used esp. of a woman ⟨a ~ middle-aged spinster —Carol Field⟩ ⟨~ in a lacy old-fashioned way —Edmund Wilson⟩ ⟨a ~ old maid —Louis Bromfield⟩ — **frump·ish·ly** *adv* — **frump·ish·ness** *n* -ES

frum·ple \ˈfrümpəl, ˈfrəm-\ *vt* -ED/-ING/-S [ME *fromplen*, fr. MD *verrompelen*, fr. *ver-* for- (akin to OHG *fir-*) + *rompelen* to wrinkle — more at RUMPLE] *dial Brit* : WRINKLE, CRUMPLE

frumpy \ˈfrəmpē, -pi\ *adj* -ER/-EST : DULL, FRUMPISH, DOWDY, DRAB ⟨a dull ~ Victorian society —Anita Leslie⟩ ⟨enraged all the ~ bluestockings by the smartness of her toilet —V.L. Parrington⟩

¹frush \ˈfrəsh\ *n* -ES [perh. alter. of ¹*frosh*] **1** : the frog of a horse's foot **2** : a discharge from the frog of a horse's foot; *also* : THRUSH

²frush \ˈfrüsh, ˈfrəsh\ *adj* [perh. alter of *frough*] **1** *dial Brit, of timber or cloth* : decayed to the point of brittleness : lacking tensile strength **2** *dial Brit, of soil* : friable and mellow

frusta *pl of* FRUSTUM

frus·to·conical \ˌfrə(ˌ)stō+\ *adj* [*frustum* + *-o-* + *conical*] : of the shape of a frustum of a cone

frustra *pl of* FRUSTRUM

frus·tra·ne·ous \ˌfrəˈstrānēəs, ˌfrəˈs-\ *adj* [L *frustra* + E *-aneous* (as in *extraneous*)] : leading to frustration : VAIN, UNPROFITABLE

¹frus·trate \ˈfrəˌstrāt, *chiefly Brit* (ˌ)ˌ=ˈ=; *usu* -ād·+V\ *vt* -ED/-ING/-S [ME *frustraten*, fr. L *frustratus*, past part. of *frustrare, frustrari* to deceive, disappoint, frustrate, fr. *frustra* in error, in vain; akin to L *fraud-, fraus* deception, fraud — more at FRAUD] **1 a** : to check, balk, or defeat in an endeavor or purpose : prevent from attaining ⟨*frustrated* by army routine —Darrell Berrigan⟩ ⟨*frustrated* by a blank wall of suspicion . . . and bureaucratic inertia —H.W.Carter⟩ **b** : to induce feelings of frustration or discouragement in ⟨brought the short story to a harsh perfection that ~*s* contemporary short-story writers —Alfred Kazin⟩ ⟨the story of a personality *frustrated* by the practical temper of America —J.D.Hart⟩ **2 a** : to make ineffectual : bring to nothing : DEFEAT, BAFFLE, FOIL ⟨nature . . . supports as well as ~*s* our lofty aspirations —H.J. Muller⟩ ⟨illness *frustrated* his plans for college⟩ ⟨did all they could to ~ . . . the inquiry —William McFee⟩ **b** : to make null or ineffectual : make invalid or of no effect : NULLIFY

syn THWART, BALK, FOIL, BAFFLE, OUTWIT, CIRCUMVENT: FRUSTRATE indicates a check, repelling, defeating of a sort that makes efforts vain, ineffectual, often with ego depreciation ⟨if waves of black pessimism swept over him in those unhappy later years when his ambitions were hopelessly *frustrated*, there was provocation enough —V.L.Parrington⟩ THWART may suggest a defeating, checking, or frustrating by obstructing one's course with some block or barrier ⟨his hatred of pioneer life and all its conditions, those conditions that were *thwarting* his creative life —Van Wyck Brooks⟩ ⟨I was anxious about her but I did not like to *thwart* her in her present mood —Rose Macaulay⟩ BALK likewise indicates frustrating by obstacles and obstructions, esp. those that hamper or hobble ⟨these regulations frequently *balked* the efforts of our Intelligence Corps to pry vital information from prisoners —*Saturday Rev.*⟩ ⟨I've always been *balked* or bullied out of having what I wanted —Ellen Glasgow⟩ FOIL indicates checking or defeating with galling or disheartening discomfiture ⟨*foiled*, he sank down again —Robert Browning⟩ BAFFLE indicates frustrating defeat by something confusing, perplexing, and vexing ⟨such knotty problems of alleys . . . such sphinx's riddles of streets . . . as must, I conceive, *baffle* the audacity of porters —Thomas De Quincey⟩ ⟨all these complexities and bonds that *baffled* him —James Boyd⟩ OUTWIT and CIRCUMVENT are more likely to stress the fact of defeat or escape by greater wit, craft, ingenuity, perception, or stratagem and less likely to suggest resulting disposition or attitude ⟨the skill with which she had hoodwinked and *outwitted* every statesman in Europe during fifty years —J.R.Green⟩ ⟨the *Defiance* was an opposition boat and had been refused a license to carry passengers on San Francisco Bay. But her captain had a plan to *circumvent* the dastardly port officials —Julian Dana⟩

²frustrate \"\ *adj* [ME *frustrat*, fr. L *frustratus*, past part.] **1 a** : balked in some endeavor, purpose, or action : FRUSTRATED, BAFFLED ⟨tore at the lock, ~ in fear —G.D.Brown⟩ ⟨~ and unhappy lovers —Elinor Wylie⟩ **b** : reflecting or indicating frustration ⟨turned a ~ eye upon me⟩ ⟨gave him a ~ look⟩ **2** : of no effect : VAIN, UNPROFITABLE, NULL ⟨makes love itself seem ~, vulgar, or disgusting —W.Y.Tindall⟩ ⟨his ~ and unhopeful quest —M.G.Bishop⟩

³frustrate \ˈ=,=\ *n* -S : a person who is frustrated

frustrated *adj* **1 a** : balked in some endeavor or purpose : THWARTED, DISAPPOINTED ⟨the Irish writer is a ~ talker —H.M.Reynolds⟩ ⟨a ~ jail break⟩ **b** : reflecting or indicating frustration ⟨gave a ~ shrug —Winifred Bambrick⟩ ⟨the venom with which he was attacked . . . may be attributed to their ~ rage —J.H.Plumb⟩ **c** : filled with a sense of frustration : filled with a deep chronic sense of insecurity, discouragement, and dissatisfaction as a result of thwarted desires, inner conflicts, or other unresolved problems ⟨a ~ man, divided against himself —P.M.Clyde⟩ ⟨a morbid, ~, sensitive . . . man —William Phillips b. 1907⟩ ⟨~ because . . . constantly worried about being fired —*Time*⟩ ⟨the world is full of anxious, frightened, ~, hurt people —*Episcopal Churchnews*⟩ **2** : delayed in or prevented from being shipped for any reason — used of cargo, goods, or supplies ⟨bogus documents describing the goods as rejected or ~ exports —*Criminal Law Rev.*⟩ ⟨permission recently given to manufacturers to sell ~ export garments . . . on the home market —*Times Rev. of Industry*⟩

frus·trat·er \ˈ=,strād·ə(r), -ātə-, *chiefly Brit* (ˌ)=ˈ==\ *n* -S : one that frustrates ⟨a city need not be a ~ of life —Julian Huxley⟩

frus·trat·ing·ly *adv* : in a frustrating manner ⟨~ unresolved and inconclusive —W.W.Taylor⟩

frus·tra·tion \(ˌ)frəˈstrāshən\ *n* -S [ME *frustracioun*, fr. L *frustration-, frustratio* deception, disappointment, frustration, fr. *frustratus* + *-ion-, -io* -ion] **1 a** : the act of frustrating ⟨will make parliamentary alliances . . . with a view to obstruction and ~ —A.E.Stevenson b. 1900⟩ ⟨the ~ of creative instinct is a notorious evil of the machine age —*Times Lit. Supp.*⟩ **b** (1) : the condition or an instance of being frustrated in some purpose : DISAPPOINTMENT, DEFEAT ⟨cruel ~*s* had eaten away that confidence —Oscar Handlin⟩ ⟨you've never experienced ~ until you watch a one-channel television set —Goodman Ace⟩ ⟨life became for him a series of great ~*s*⟩ ⟨the life of the admiral closed on a note of ~ —S.E.Morison⟩ (2) : a deep chronic sense or condition of insecurity, discouragement, and dissatisfaction arising from thwarted desires, inner conflicts, or other unresolved problems ⟨~ brought about by the constant inner conflict between the desire to possess and the yearning to renounce —*Orient Bk. World*⟩ ⟨the child seeks to retaliate for ~ by biting —G.S.Blum⟩ ⟨loneliness and ~: those are two constant themes in American literature —Malcolm Cowley⟩ ⟨the gusto and excitement concealed a certain ominous shallowness and ~ —Richard Watts⟩ ⟨a lifelong ~ —H.S.Canby⟩ **c** : something that frustrates ⟨as a work of serious reference the volume is full of ~*s* —*Saturday Rev.*⟩ ⟨escape lodges, women's clubs, bridge clubs, and other modern ~*s* —*Current Biog.*⟩ ⟨postwar Britain was a ~ . . . to the advertising man —E.S.Turner⟩ **2** : a doctrine in the law of contracts whereby courts depart from the general rule that impossibility does not excuse performance and does not terminate contracts and instead adjust equitably conflicting rights as if the original state of affairs had continued although the value of an expected performance has been destroyed by fortuitous circumstances which the parties were not negligent in failing to guard against or by a radical change in the state of affairs (as war, government orders, cancellation of unique events) which the parties were not bound to have foreseen

frus·tra·tive \ˈfrəˌstrāḍ·|iv, ˈfrəstrə|, (ˌ)frəˈstrā|, |t|, |ēv\ *adj* : tending to frustrate

frus·tu·la·tion \ˌfrəschəˈlāshən\ *n* -S [NL *frustul*um bud from a hydroid (fr. L, small piece) + E *-ation*] : constriction of small buds that settle down and grow into new hydranths from a hydroid

frus·tule \ˈfrəsˌchül\ *n* -S [F, fr. L *frustulum* small piece] : the siliceous shell of a diatom composed of two valves that overlap; *often* : the siliceous shell of a diatom together with the protoplast — see EPITHECA

frus·tu·lum \ˈfrəschələm\ *n, pl* **frustu·la** \-lə\ [NL, fr. L, small piece] : a light breakfast allowed on fast days in the Roman Catholic Church

frus·tum \ˈfrəstəm\ *also* **frus·trum** \-trəm\ *n, pl* **frustums** \-təmz\ *or* **frus·ta** \-tə\ *also* **frustrums** \-trəmz\ *or* **frus·tra** \-trə\ [NL, fr. ML & L; ML *frustrum* piece, bit, alter. of L *frustum* — more at BRUISE] **1** : the part of a cone-shaped solid next to the base and formed by cutting off the top by a plane parallel to the base; *also* : the part of a solid (as a cone or pyramid) intersected between two planes that are either parallel or sometimes inclined to each other **2** : one of the drums of the shaft of a column

frustums 1

fru·tes·cence \früˈtesᵊn(t)s\ *n* -S : the quality or state of being frutescent

fru·tes·cent \(ˈ)früˈtesᵊnt\ *adj* [L *frutex* shrub, bush + E *-escent*] : having or approaching the appearance or habit of a shrub : SHRUBBY

fruti- *comb form* [L *frutic-, frutex*] : shrub ⟨*fruti*colous⟩

fru·ti·ce·tum \ˌfrüd·əˈsēd·əm\ *n, pl* **frutice·ta** \-ēd·ə\ [NL, fr. L, place full of shrubs, fr. *frutic-, frutex* + *-etum*] : a collection of shrubs grown for ornament or study (as in a botanical garden) — compare ARBORETUM

fru·ti·cose \ˈfrüd·əˌkōs\ *adj* [L *fruticosus*, fr. *frutic-, frutex* shrub — *-osus* -ose; akin to MHG *briezen* to bud, swell, OHG *broz* bud, sprout, OIr *broth* whisker, hair] : occurring in the form of or resembling a shrub : SHRUBBY ⟨a ~ chrysanthemum⟩ ⟨herbaceous or sometimes ~ perennials⟩; *esp, of a lichen* : having a shrubby bushy thallus with flattened or cylindrical branches

fru·tic·u·lose \früˈtikyəˌlōs\ *adj* [L *frutic-, frutex* + *-ulus* (dim. suffix) + E *-ose*] : resembling a small shrub

fru·ti·lla \früˈtē(y)ə\ *n* -S [Sp, dim. of *fruta* edible fruit, fr. ML *fructa*, pl. of *fructum*, alter. of L *fructus* — more at FRUIT] : CHILEAN STRAWBERRY

frwy *abbr* freeway

¹fry \ˈfrī\ *vb* **fried; fried; frying; fries** [ME *frien*, fr. OF *frire*, fr. L *frigere* to roast, fry; akin to Gk *phrygein* to roast, fry, Skt *bhṛjjati* he roasts] *vt* : to cook in a pan or on a griddle by heating over a fire esp. with the use of fat : cook in hot fat ⟨~ fish⟩ — compare BROIL ~ *vi* **1** : to undergo the process of frying : become subject to the action of heat in a frying pan or on a griddle **2** *slang* : to suffer execution in the electric chair ⟨if I burn, you'll ~ along with me —Barton Black⟩

²fry \"\ *n* -ES **1 a** (1) : a dish of something fried ⟨a mixed ~ of . . . tiny crayfish and squid —P.E.Deutschman⟩ (2) : FRENCH FRY **b** : a social gathering or picnic at which food is fried and eaten ⟨a fish ~⟩ ⟨a steak ~⟩ ⟨organized a ~⟩ **c** *or* **fry meat** *chiefly Midland* (1) : a portion of fried meat (2) : meat suitable for frying **2** : an internal part or organ of an animal (as pig's liver, calf's pluck) that is usu. eaten fried — usu. used in pl. **3** : a state of excitement ⟨he was in an awful ~⟩

³fry \"\ *n, pl* **fry** [ME *frie, fry*, prob. fr. ONF *fri*, fr. OF *froyer, frayer, frier* to rub, spawn — more at FRAY] **1 a** : young or recently hatched fishes — compare FINGERLING **b** : the young or brood of other animals (as oysters or birds) **c** *obs* : human offspring **2** : very small adult fishes; *esp* : those (as various anchovies) that swim in schools **3** : members of a group or class : PERSONS, INDIVIDUALS — often used disparagingly ⟨a great part of the earth is peopled with these ~ —Katherine Mansfield⟩ or with a qualifier indicating smallness, youth, or insignificance ⟨the lesser ~ of the expedition march side by side with natives —Gordon Nares⟩ ⟨small ~ such as voles and field mice —Douglas Carruthers⟩ ⟨sturdy school shoe for the young ~ —*Footwear News*⟩ ⟨so beautifully illustrated that you and the young ~ will read it like a book —*Parents' Mag.*⟩

fry cook *n* : a cook who specializes in fried foods

fry·er *also* **fri·er** \ˈfrī(ə)r, -īə\ *n* -S **1** : one that fries **2** : something intended for or used in frying: as **a** : a young chicken; *esp* : one weighing between 2½ and 4 pounds — compare BROILER **b** : a rabbit of 2½ to 3 months of age **c** : a deep utensil for frying foods sometimes with a cover and fitted with a basket

frying pan *n* [ME, fr. *frying* (gerund of *frien* to fry) + *pan*] : a metal pan with a handle used for frying foods : SPIDER — **out of the frying pan into the fire** : clear of one difficulty only to fall into a greater one

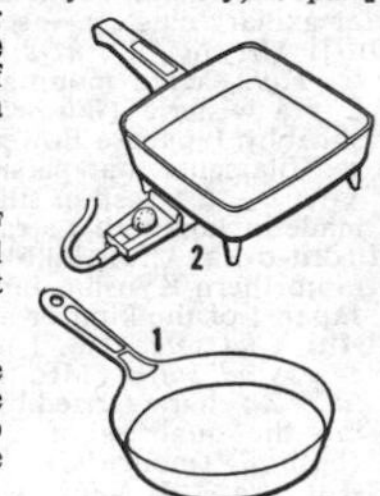

frying pans: *1* used over source of heat; *2* heated electrically

frypan \ˈ=,=\ *n* : FRYING PAN

fs *abbr* facsimile

FS *abbr* **1** factor of safety **2** [F *faire suivre*] please forward **3** field service **4** filmstrip **5** final statement **6** financial secretary

f's *or* **fs** *pl of* F

FSH *abbr* follicle-stimulating hormone

f sharp \ˈ=ˈ=\ *n, usu cap F* **1** : the keynote of F-sharp major or F-sharp minor **2** : the tone a half step above F

f-sharp major \ˈ=,=ˈ==\ *n, usu cap F* : the major musical key having a signature of six sharps

f-sharp minor \ˈ=,=ˈ==\ *n, usu cap F* : the minor musical key having a signature of three sharps

fspc *abbr* frontispiece

fst *abbr* fast

f star *n, usu cap F* : a star of spectral type F — see SPECTRAL TYPE table

f-stop \ˈ=,=\ *n* [*f* (symbol for *focal length*)] : a camera lens aperture setting indicated by an f-number

f-system \ˈ=,==\ *n* [*f* (symbol for *focal length*)] : a system of camera lens aperture markings that uses f-numbers

ft *abbr* **1** [L *fiat*] let it be done; let it be made **2** foot; feet **3** forint **4** fort; fortification; fortified

FT *abbr* **1** full terms **2** fume tight

ftd *abbr* fortified

fth *or* **fthm** *abbr* fathom

FTI *abbr* federal tax included

ft *abbr* **1** fighter **2** fitter

f_2 layer \ˈefˌtü-\ *n, cap F* : the upper and usu. more densely ionized of the two layers into which the F region of the ionosphere splits in the daytime, occurring at varying heights from about 150 to 250 miles or more above the earth's surface

fu' \ˈfü\ *chiefly Scot var of* FULL

Fu·a·din \ˈfyüədᵊn\ *trademark* — used for stibophen

fub \ˈfəb\ *archaic var of* FOB

fub·sy \ˈfübsi, ˈfəb-\ *adj* [obs. E *fubs* chubby person + E *-y*] *dial chiefly Eng* : chubby and somewhat squat

fuc- *or* **fuco-** *or* **fuci-** *comb form* [NL, fr. *Fucus*] **1** : derived from or related to the alga fucus ⟨*fuc*ic acid⟩ ⟨*fuci*phagous⟩ **2** : fucose ⟨*fuc*oside⟩ ⟨*fuco*pyranoside⟩

fu·ca·ce·ae \fyüˈkāsēˌē\ *n pl, cap* [NL, fr. *Fucus*, type genus + *-aceae* — more at FUCUS] : a small family of brown algae (order Fucales) including the gulfweeds and rockweeds

fu·ca·ceous \(ˈ)=ˈ=shəs\ *adj* [NL *Fucaceae* + E *-ous*] : of or relating to the Fucaceae

fu·ca·le·an \(ˈ)fyüˈkālēən\ *adj* [NL *Fucales* + E *-an*] : of or relating to the Fucales

fu·ca·les \fyüˈkā(ˌ)lēz\ *n pl, cap* [NL, fr. *Fucus* + *-ales*] : an order of brown algae coextensive with the family Fucaceae and including exclusively diploid plants — compare LAMINARIALES

fuch·sia \ˈfyüshə *sometimes* -üshēə *or* -ükṣēə\ *n* [NL, fr. Leonhard *Fuchs* †1566 Ger. botanist + NL *-ia*] **1** *cap* : a genus of decorative shrubs (family Onagraceae) with pendulous tetramerous flowers found chiefly in tropical America but often cultivated as pot plants **2** -S : any plant of the genus *Fuchsia* **3** -S : a vivid reddish purple — compare FUCHSIA PURPLE

fuchsia pink *n* : a moderate purplish pink that is bluer and deeper than Vassar rose (sense 2)

fuchsia purple *n* : a variable color averaging a strong reddish purple that is redder and less strong than purple orchid and redder and duller than phlox purple — compare FUCHSIA

fuchsia red *n* : a moderate to deep purplish red — called also *magenta*

fuchsia rose *n* : a variable color averaging a moderate purplish red that is bluer and deeper than average rose, redder and deeper than violine pink, redder, lighter, and stronger than magenta rose, and bluer and stronger than solferino

fuch·sine *or* **fuch·sin** \ˈfyüks|ən, -kˌs|ēn *also* ˈfyü(ˌ)sh| *or* ˈfük(ˌ)s|\ *n* -S [F *fuchsine*, prob. fr. *fuchsia* (fr. NL *Fuchsia*) + *-ine*; fr. its color] **1** *often cap* : a triphenylmethane dye that is made usu. in the form of the chloride by oxidation of a mixture of aniline and toluidines, that gives a brilliant bluish red solution and dyes wool or silk directly or mordanted cotton, but is used chiefly in coloring paper and as a biological stain — called also *magenta, rosaniline*; see DYE table I (under *Basic Violet 14* and *Solvent Red 41*); compare ACID FUCHSINE, NEW FUCHSINE, PARA FUCHSINE **2** : FUCHSIA 3

fuch·sin·o·phil \f(y)ükˈsinəˌfil\ *also* **fuch·sin·o·phile** \-fīl\ *or* **fuch·si·no·phil·ic** \(ˌ)f(y)ükˌsinəˈfilik\ *adj* [*fuchsinophil*, *fuchsinophile* fr. ISV *fuchsine* + *-o-* + *-phil, -phile; fuchsinophilic* fr. *fuchsinophil, fuchsinophile* + *-ic*] : having an affinity for the acid dye fuchsine ⟨~ cytoplasmic granules⟩ or depending on such an affinity ⟨the ~ mitochondrial reaction⟩

fuchs·ite \ˈf(y)ükˌsīt\ *n* -S [G *fuchsit*, fr. Johann N. von *Fuchs* †1856 Ger. mineralogist + G *-it* -ite] : a mineral consisting of a common mica containing chromium

¹fu·coid \ˈfyüˌkȯid\ *or* **fu·coi·dal** \(ˈ)fyüˈkȯidᵊl\ *adj* [*fucoid* prob. fr. (assumed) NL *fucoides*, fr. NL *Fucus* + L *-oides* -oid; *fucoidal* fr. *fucoid* + *-al*] **1 a** : of, relating to, or resembling algae of the order Fucales **b** : resembling or having the nature of seaweeds **2** : of, relating to, or containing impressions of fossil fucoids or markings that resemble such impressions

²fucoid \"\ *n* -S [prob. fr. NL *fucoides*, fr. (assumed) NL *fucoides*, adj.] **1** : a seaweed of the order Fucales **2** : a fossil of an alga or a plant resembling an alga

fu·coi·din \fyüˈkȯidᵊn\ *n* -S [ISV ²*fucoid* + *-in*] : a sulfuric ester of fucosan obtained from various brown algae (as those of the genus *Fucus*)

fu·co·san \ˈfyükəˌsan\ *n* -S [prob. ISV *fucose* + *-an*] : a polysaccharide occurring in various brown algae (as those of the genus *Fucus*) and yielding fucose on hydrolysis

fu·cose \ˈfyüˌkōs\ *n* -S [ISV *fuc-* + *-ose*] : an aldose sugar $CH_3(CHOH)_4CHO$ occurring combined in the dextrorotatory D-form in various glycosides (as jalapin) and in the levorotatory L-form in fucosan, fucoidin, and polysaccharides typical of some blood groups; 6-deoxy-galactose — compare GLUCOSE

fu·cos·ter·ol \fyüˈkästəˌrōl, -ˌrōl\ *n* [*fuc-* + *sterol*] : a crystalline sterol $C_{29}H_{47}OH$ occurring in various algae (as *Fucus vesiculosus*)

fu·co·xanthin \ˌfyükō+\ *n* [ISV *fuc-* + *xanthin*] : a brown crystalline carotenoid pigment $C_{40}H_{60}O_6$ occurring esp. in the ova of brown algae

fu·cus \ˈfyükəs\ *n* [L, archil, red dye, rouge, deceit, fr. Gk *phykos* seaweed, rouge, of Sem origin; akin to Heb *pūk* antimony used as a cosmetic] **1** -ES *obs* **a** : a face paint or complexion aid : COSMETIC **b** : outward show : FACADE ⟨God . . . sees through all the daubings and ~*es* of hypocrisy —John Scott⟩ **2** [NL, fr. L] *cap* : a genus (the type of the family Fucaceae) of cartilaginous dichotomously branched brown algae that are blackish brown to olive green in color, have the reproductive cavities restricted to the bladder-shaped branch buds, and are used in the kelp industry and as a source of algin — compare ASCOPHYLLUM **3** -ES : any of various brown algae; *esp* : any plant of the genus *Fucus*

fu·cused \-st\ *adj, archaic* : artificially embellished

fud \ˈfəd\ *n* -S [perh. of Scand origin; akin to ON *futh* vulva, Norw dial. *fud* buttocks; akin to MHG *vut* vulva, Skt *puta* buttock, OE *fūl* foul — more at FOUL] **1** *chiefly Scot* **a** : BUTTOCKS, RUMP **b** : the tail of an animal (as a rabbit or hare) **2** [perh. alter. of *food*] *chiefly Brit* : waste from wool carding **3** [by shortening] : FUDDY-DUDDY ⟨old ~*s* like that never . . . retire —R.L.Scott⟩

¹fud·dle \ˈfədᵊl\ *vb* **fuddled; fuddled; fuddling** \-d(ᵊ)liŋ\ **fuddles** [origin unknown] *vi* : to take part in a drinking bout : TIPPLE ⟨then there's *fuddling* about in the public houses, and drinking bad spirits —Thomas Hughes⟩ ~ *vt* **1** : to make drunk : INTOXICATE ⟨she would ~ herself every night with ale and whiskey —Richard Free⟩ **2** : to make confused : MUDDLE ⟨corridors, archways, recesses . . . combined to ~ any sense of direction —Elizabeth Bowen⟩ **3** : to make (a fish) torpid : STUPEFY ⟨catch a trout by *fuddling* him —A.A.Horn⟩

²fuddle \"\ *n* -S **1** *obs* : LIQUOR ⟨we sipped our ~ —Ned Ward⟩ **2** : INTOXICATION ⟨a venerable toper . . . whom the oldest inhabitant had never seen otherwise than in a state of benevolent ~ —Norman Douglas⟩ **3** *chiefly Brit* : a prolonged drinking spell — used esp. in the phrase *on the fuddle* **4** : a confused mixture : JUMBLE ⟨in front of a side altar a ~ of candles burned —Bruce Marshall⟩

fud·dler \ˈfəd(ᵊ)lə(r)\ *n* -S : DRUNKARD

¹fuddy–duddy \ˈfədēˌdədē, ˈfədiˌdədi, ˌ==ˈ==\ *n* -ES [perh. redupl. of Sc *fuddy, fuddie* tail of an animal, short-tailed animal, fr. *fud* buttocks, tail of an animal + E *-y*] **1** : one who is old-fashioned or ultraconservative : FOGY ⟨anybody over thirty has to . . . ask himself just how much of a *fuddy-duddy* he really is —Alistair Cooke⟩ **2** : one who is pompous and unimaginative : STUFFED SHIRT ⟨the general impression . . . that anyone from a colonel up is a frozen-faced *fuddy-duddy* —Fletcher Pratt⟩ **3** : one who is concerned about trifles : FUSSBUDGET ⟨an academic *fuddy-duddy* counting the semicolons —S.E.Hyman⟩

²fuddy–duddy \"\ *adj* **1** : prim and conservative : FUSSY ⟨a *fuddy-duddy* professor in a classroom of rowdy boys —*Time*⟩ **2** : OLD-FASHIONED, OUTDATED ⟨the atom bomb is already *fuddy-duddy* —Ellery Queen⟩

¹fudge \ˈfəj\ *vb* -ED/-ING/-S [prob. alter. of ²*fadge*] *vi* **1** *archaic* : to work out : RESULT ⟨we will see how this will ~ —Sir Walter Scott⟩ **2 a** : to act dishonestly : CHEAT; *specif* : to move a taw forward beyond the proper limits when starting to shoot in a game of marbles ⟨you *fudged* a mile —W.D.Steele⟩ **b** : to fail to live up to something : WELSH ⟨a man who would ~ on his oath of office —Harold Benjamin⟩ **3** : to insert a last-minute newspaper item **4** : to move slowly or cautiously ⟨you keep *fudging* along —K.M.Dodson⟩ **5** : to avoid commitment : HEDGE ⟨we object to that kind of *fudging* off and whitewashing —R.E.Danielson⟩ ~ *vt* **1 a** : to devise as a substitute : contrive without adequate basis : FAKE ⟨it is not necessary to ~ anecdotes when there are so many of them —A.J.Liebling⟩ **b** : EMBELLISH, DISTORT ⟨used to ~ the accounts to the credit of the latter —J.V.DeMorgan⟩ **c** : to spoil the line of : BLUR ⟨the outlines of lips and nostrils had been *fudged* in the drawing —Oliver La Farge⟩ **2** : to squeeze in belatedly : INTERPOLATE; *specif* : to insert (a news item) at the last minute **3** : to fail to come to grips with : DODGE ⟨has too often blessed war, condoned injustice, *fudged* the racial issue, and shared the profits of acquiescence —M.A. Kapp⟩

²fudge \"\ *n* -S **1** : a piece of foolish nonsense : BUNKUM, TWADDLE — often used interjectionally to express annoyance, disappointment, or disbelief ⟨oh, ~, she says they can't come⟩ **2** : an item (as a news flash received too late for plating) typeset and inserted directly on the printing press — compare STOP PRESS **3** : a soft candy made typically of sugar, milk, butter, and chocolate cooked together and beaten to a creamy consistency **4** : RUSSIAN CALF

fudge box *n* **1** : the metal container in a newspaper printing press for holding fudge matter **2** : newspaper space left blank for the insertion of last-minute items

fudge edge *n* : a shoe sole or sole edge stitched and trimmed very close to the upper

fudg·er \ˈfəjə(r)\ *n* -S : a worker in a shoe factory who finishes the edge of a sole

fudge wheel *n* : a tool used in shoe manufacturing to ornament the edge of a sole or welt in imitation of welt stitching

fu dog *or* **foo dog** \ˈfü-\ *n, usu cap F* [Chin *fu²* happiness] : a mythical lion-dog used as a decorative motif in Far Eastern art — called also *Fu lion*

fue·gi·an \f(y)üˈāgēən, ˈfwāg-\ *n* -S *usu cap* [Tierra del *Fuego*, archipelago at southern end of So. America + E *-ian*] **1** : an Indian people of Tierra del Fuego — compare ALACALUF, ONA, YAHGAN **2** : a member of the Fuegian people

fuehrer *sometimes cap, var of* FÜHRER

[1]fu·el \'fyü|əl, -ü|əl *also* -ü|l, *chiefly Brit* |(,)il\ *n* -s *often attrib* [ME *fewel*, fr. OF *fouaille, fuaille*, fr. *feu* fire, fr. LL *focus*, fr. L, hearth — more at FOCUS] **1 a :** a material (as coal, coke, gas, oil, peat, wood) used to produce heat or power by burning **:** something that feeds fire **b :** nutritive material **:** FOOD **:** ALIMENT ⟨animals take food to obtain ~ or energy to carry on all their life activities —G.E. & Nettie MacGinitie⟩ **c :** any material from which atomic energy can be liberated; *esp* **:** fissionable material used in a nuclear reactor — called also *nuclear fuel* **2 :** a source of sustenance or additional incentive **:** REINFORCEMENT ⟨public opinion . . . ought to provide the ~ to carry American foreign policy forward —H.J. Morgenthau⟩

[2]fuel \"\ *vb* **fueled** *or* **fuelled; fueled** *or* **fuelled; fueling** *or* **fuelling; fuels** *vt* **1 :** to provide with material for burning ⟨the virgin stand of big trees . . . went long ago . . . to ~ the furnaces —J.W.Schaefer⟩ **2 :** SUPPORT, STIMULATE ⟨the country might be on its way to self-sufficiency in petroleum instead of . . . scrabbling for supplies to ~ its industrial development —S.G.Hanson⟩ ~ *vi* **:** to take in fuel **:** become provided with fuel — often used with *up* ⟨the plane's ~*ing* up —Kay Boyle⟩

fuel dope *n* **:** DOPE 2d

fu·el·er *or* **fu·el·ler** \-lə(r)\ *n* -s [ME *fewelere*, fr. *fewel* fuel + *-ere* -er] **:** one that supplies fuel or feeds fires

fuel filter *n* **:** an attachment to the fuel line of an automotive internal-combustion engine that filters the liquid before it enters the carburetor

fuel injector *n* **:** a pump and valve mechanism that sprays liquid fuel intermittently into the cylinder of a diesel engine

fuel–mixture indicator *n* **:** EXHAUST-GAS ANALYZER

fuel oil *n* **:** an oil used for fuel esp. in a furnace or heater and usu. having a flash point higher than that of kerosine

fuel pump *n* **:** a pump in a motor vehicle that propels liquid fuel from the tank to the carburetor

fuerth *usu cap, var of* FÜRTH

[1]fuff \'fəf\ *vb* -ED/-ING/-S [imit.] *vi* **1** *chiefly Scot* **a :** to puff and blow **:** PANT **b :** to give off puffs of vapor **2** *chiefly Scot* **:** to spit and hiss **3** *chiefly Scot* **:** to fly into a rage **:** have a fit of temper ~ *vt, chiefly Scot* **:** to cause to give off puffs; *specif* **:** SMOKE

[2]fuff \"\ *n* -s **1** *chiefly Scot* **:** a gust or puff esp. of wind **2** *chiefly Scot* **:** an outburst of temper **:** RAGE

fuf·fle \'fəfəl\ *vb* -ED/-ING/-S [perh. freq. of [1]*fuff*] *vi, Scot* **:** to become disheveled or mussed up ~ *vt, Scot* **:** DISARRAY, MUSS

[1]fug \'fəg\ *n* -s [by alter.] *Scot* **:** [1]FOG

[2]fug \"\ *n* -s [prob. alter. of [3]*fog*] **:** an odorous emanation; *esp* **:** the stuffy atmosphere of a hot crowded poorly ventilated space ⟨cooking and breathing soon produced a pleasant ~ in the tents —J.R.Ullman⟩

[3]fug \"\ *vb* **fugged; fugged; fugging; fugs** *vi* **:** to loll indoors in a stuffy atmosphere ⟨we retired . . . to steam and ~ for fourteen long hours —Frank Hurley⟩ ~ *vt* **:** to make stuffy and odorous ⟨the small tent was *fugged* —Walter Macken⟩

fu·ga \'fügə\ *n* -s [It — more at FUGUE] **1 :** FUGUE **2 :** a canon in medieval music

fu·ga·cious \(')fyü¦gāshəs\ *adj* [L *fugac-, fugax* swift, fleeting (fr. *fugere* to run away) + E *-ious* — more at FUGITIVE] **1 a :** of an unsubstantial nature **:** lasting a short time **:** EVANESCENT ⟨the painter's fame is based on the most ~ of substances — public favor —Frederic Taubes⟩ **b** *also* **fugaceous :** falling off or disappearing before the usual time — used chiefly of plant parts other than floral organs (as stipules or moss calyptras); opposed to *persistent;* compare CADUCOUS, DECIDUOUS **2 :** not fixed in a certain place **:** WANDERING ⟨unlike other minerals . . . oil and gas are . . . ~ —Robert Kratovil⟩

fu·ga·cious·ness *n* -ES **:** the quality or state of being fugacious

fu·gac·i·ty \fyü'gasəd·ē\ *n* -ES [fr. *fugacious*, after such pairs as E *capacious: capacity*] **1 :** lack of enduring qualities **:** TRANSIENCE ⟨that the fresh bloom of the carol was evanescent . . . I always knew; but never realized its extreme ~ until five years ago —A.T.Quiller-Couch⟩ **2 a :** the vapor pressure of a vapor assumed to be an ideal gas obtained by correcting the determined vapor pressure and useful as a measure of the escaping tendency of a substance from a heterogeneous system **b :** a correction for the deviation in the behavior of an actual solution from that of an ideal solution — compare ACTIVITY 6b

fu·gae warrant *also* **fu·gie warrant** \'f(y)ü(,)jē-\ *n* [*fugae* prob. alter. (influenced by L *fugae* of running away — in the Scots law phrase used in reference to an absconding debtor NL *in meditatione fugae* in contemplation of running away — gen. of *fuga* flight, running away) of *fugie*, prob. by shortening & alter. fr. [2]*fugitive*] *Scots law* **:** a warrant to attach an absconding debtor

fu·gal \'fyügəl\ *adj* [[1]*fugue* + *-al*] **:** of, relating to, or in the style of a musical fugue — **fu·gal·ly** \-əlē,-əli\ *adv*

-fu·gal \ˌfyə|gəl, ˌfə|g-, ˌfē|g-, |k-, *chiefly Brit* ¦fyügəl\ *adj comb form* [prob. fr. (assumed) NL *-fuga* -fuge + E *-al*] **:** fleeing **:** passing from ⟨centri*fugal*⟩ — **-fu·gal·ly** \gəlē, -li\ *adv comb form*

fu·ga·ra \fü'gärə\ *n* -s [It, fr. Pol *fujara* shepherd's flute] **:** a labial pipe-organ stop of 8-foot or 4-foot pitch and of string quality

[1]fu·ga·to \fü'gäd·(,)ō\ *adv (or adj)* [It, fr. past part. of *fugare* to compose as a fugue, fr. *fuga* fugue — more at FUGUE] **:** in the style of but not strictly in the form of a musical fugue

[2]fugato \"\ *n* -s [It, fr. past part. of *fugare* to compose as a fugue] **:** a musical passage in fugato style

fuge \'fyüg\ *n* -s [earlier spelling of [1]*fugue*] **:** FUGUING TUNE

-fuge \ˌfyüj\ *n comb form* -s [F, prob. fr. (assumed) NL *-fuga*, fr. LL *-fuga, -fugia* (in *febrifuga, febrifugia* centaury), fr. L *fugare* to put to flight, fr. *fuga* flight — more at FUGUE] **:** one that drives away ⟨dolori*fuge*⟩ ⟨vermi*fuge*⟩

fug·gy \'fəgē\ *adj, usu* -ER/-EST [[2]*fug* + *-y*] **:** stuffy and smelly ⟨the air was ~; the light dim —Virginia Woolf⟩

fu·ghet·ta \f(y)ü'ged·ə\ *n* -s [It, dim. of *fuga* fugue] **:** a short or condensed fugue

fugi *var of* FUJI

fu·gie \'fyüjē\ *n* -s [prob. by shortening & alter.] **1** *Scot* **:** FUGITIVE **2** *Scot* **a :** a fighting cock that will not fight **b :** a cowardly person

fu·gi·tate \'fyüjə,tāt\ *vb* -ED/-ING/-S [[1]*fugit*ive + *-ate* (v. suffix)] *vt, Scots law* **:** to declare judicially to be a fugitive from justice and thereby cause the escheat of the fugitive's movable property to the crown **:** OUTLAW ~ *vi* **:** to run away

fu·gi·ta·tion \ˌ==ˈtāshən\ *n* -s [*fugitate* + *-ion*] **1** *Scots law* **:** a judicial declaration of outlawry **2 :** the act of fleeing

[1]fu·gi·tive \'fyüjəd·iv, -ətiv\ *adj* [ME *fugitif, fugitive*, fr. MF & L; MF *fugitif*, fr. L *fugitivus*, fr. *fugere* to run away, flee; akin to Gk *pheugein* to run away, flee, Lith *baugus* timorous, and prob. to OHG *biogan* to bend — more at BOW] **1 :** running away or intending flight (as from an enemy, a master, duty, or justice) **:** FLEEING ⟨a ~ slave⟩ ⟨a ~ debtor⟩ ⟨the new note served notice that neither the ~ . . . diplomat nor his wife would be handed over —*Wall Street Jour.*⟩ **2 :** moving from place to place **:** WANDERING ⟨a ~ theatrical company⟩ ⟨the ~ clouds of the sky —K.K.Darrow⟩ **3 a :** being of short duration **:** FLEETING ⟨the journalist . . . is concerned only with the ~ moment —A.L.Guérard⟩ **b :** difficult to grasp or retain **:** ELUSIVE ⟨thought is clear or muddy, graspable or ~, according to the purity of the medium —J.M.Barzun⟩ **c :** likely to evaporate **:** VOLATILE ⟨~ elements escape from the magma in rock crystallization⟩ **d :** likely to deteriorate **:** PERISHABLE ⟨a great deal of valuable material is mounted on ~ cardboard —*All The King's Horses*⟩ **e :** subject to change **:** not fixed ⟨its membership is ~ but the institution . . . requires continuity —O.W.Phelps⟩; *specif* **:** fading when exposed to light ⟨many of these dyes . . . are so ~ to light that dyed material if left uncovered in a mill room during a weekend . . . may be found to have faded —C.M.Whittaker & C.C.Wilcock⟩ **f :** likely to disappear or fall away; *specif* **:** not permanently established — used esp. of a botanical species **4 a :** SCATTERED, INFREQUENT, OCCASIONAL ⟨he has only to collect his ~ pieces to have . . . a book of deep significance —T.V.Smith⟩ **b :** being of transient interest **:** EPHEMERAL ⟨the press ranges from the superficiality of fragmentary items in the most ~ tabloid to the rich fare of the *New York Times* —William Albig⟩ **syn** see TRANSIENT

[2]fugitive \"\ *n* -s [ME *fugitif, fugitive*, fr. MF & L; MF *fugitif*, fr. L *fugitivus*, fr. *fugitivus*, adj.] **1 :** one who flees or tries to escape: as **a :** one who runs away from a master or employer or from uncongenial surroundings ⟨a ~ from a sweatshop —A.E.Stevenson b.1900⟩ **b :** one who tries to elude justice ⟨surrender of the ~ for trial —R.G.Neumann⟩ **c :** one who flees or is forced to leave his country **:** EXILE, REFUGEE ⟨for the doubtful benefit of the political ~ —Alona Evans⟩ **2 :** one who goes from place to place usu. without a fixed purpose or direction **:** WANDERER **3 :** something elusive or hard to find ⟨what muse but his can nature's beauties hit, or catch that airy ~ called wit —Walter Harte⟩ **4 a :** a dye that is not fast **b :** an article colored with such a dye ⟨cotton ~*s* are simply dyed with alkali and common salt —G.H.Johnson⟩

fugitive from justice : one who having committed or being accused of a crime in one jurisdiction is absent for any reason from that jurisdiction; *specif* **:** one who flees to avoid punishment

fu·gi·tive·ly \-d·əvlē, -tə-, -li\ *adv* **:** in a fugitive manner **:** in the manner of a fugitive

fu·gi·tive·ness \-d·ivnəs, -ti-\ *n* -ES **:** the quality or state of being fugitive

fugitive warrant *n* **:** a warrant providing for the arrest and detention of an alleged fugitive from justice pending the extradition proceeding

fu·gi·tiv·i·ty \ˌfyüjə'tivəd·ē\ *n* -ES **:** FUGITIVENESS

fu·gle \'fyügəl\ *vi* -ED/-ING/-S [back-formation fr. *fugleman*] *archaic* **:** to act as fugleman

fu·gle·man \-mən, -ˌman\ *also* **flu·gel·man** \'flü-\ *n, pl* **fuglemen** *also* **flugelmen** [modif. of G *flügelmann*, fr. *flügel* wing (fr. MHG *vlügel*) + *mann* man, fr. OHG *man;* akin to OHG *fliogan* to fly — more at FLY, MAN] **1 :** a trained soldier formerly posted in front of a line of men at drill to serve as a model in their exercises **2 :** one who heads a group **:** LEADER ⟨their ~ was an accomplished man of letters but in his followers his . . . virtues disappeared —John Buchan⟩; *specif* **:** a political manager ⟨the politician in the frock coat who was the . . . chief ~ —Robert Grant †1940⟩

fugs *pl of* FUG, *pres 3d sing of* FUG

fu·gu \'fü(,)gü\ *n* -s [Jap] **:** any of various globefishes that contain a heat-stable toxic principle resembling curare and are sometimes eaten in Japan with suicidal intent

[1]fugue \'fyüg\ *n* -s [alter. (influenced by F *fugue*, fr. It *fuga*) of earlier *fuge*, prob. fr. It *fuga* fugue, act of running away, flight, fr. L, act of running away, flight; akin to L *fugere* to run away, flee — more at FUGITIVE] **1 :** a contrapuntal musical composition in which one or two melodic themes are repeated or imitated by the successively entering voices and developed in a continuous interweaving of the voice parts into a well-defined single structure — compare CANON **2 :** something having a thematic structure that is suggestive of a musical fugue ⟨it was an immense, dissonant ~ in black with incidental color —Alfred Frankenstein⟩ **3 :** a pathological disturbance of consciousness during which the patient performs acts of which he appears to be conscious but of which on recovery he has no recollection

[2]fugue \"\ *vb* -ED/-ING/-S *vi* **:** to compose or perform a musical fugue ~ *vt* **:** to make a fugue of

fuguing tune *or* **fuguing piece** *n* [*fuguing* fr. gerund of [2]*fugue*] **:** an early 19th century hymn characterized by polyphony and imitation — called also *fuge*

fugu·ist \'fyügəst\ *n* -s **:** one who composes or performs fugues

füh·rer *or* **fueh·rer** *also* **fuh·rer** \'fyůrə(r), 'fir-, *G* 'fūerər\ *n* -s *sometimes cap* [G *führer* leader, guide, fr. MHG *vüerer* wagoner, bearer, fr. *vüeren* to lead, drive, bear (fr. OHG *fuoren* to lead, set in motion) + *-er* -er, fr. OHG *-āri;* akin to OE *fēran* to go, ON *fœra* to bring; derivative fr. the root of OE *faran* to go — more at FARE] **:** one in a position of authority **:** LEADER; *esp* **:** TYRANT ⟨an epoch of ~*s* and generalissimos backed by . . . unprecedented instruments of coercion —Leland Stowe⟩

fui·dhir \'fwi,thi(ə)r\ *n* -s [MIr *fuidir*] **:** a stranger or refugee in ancient Ireland placing himself under the protection of a chief and becoming his tenant

fuil \'fœl, 'fūel\ *Scot var of* FOOL

fu·i·re·na \ˌfyüə'rēnə\ *n, cap* [NL, fr. Georg *Fuiren* †1628 Dan. physician] **:** a genus of sedges (family Cyperaceae) with leafy culms and many-flowered terete spikelets in terminal or axillary clusters — see UMBRELLA GRASS c

fu·ji \'f(y)ü(,)jē\ *n* -s [in sense 1, fr. Jap; in other senses, fr. *Fuji*, sacred mountain in south central Honshu, Japan] **1 :** a wisteria (*Wistaria sinensis*) **2** *also* **fugi cherry :** a shrubby Japanese flowering cherry with pale pink petals and red filaments that persist after the petals fall **3** *also* **fu·gi** \-(,)jē\ **a :** a spun silk clothing fabric in plain weave orig. made in Japan **b :** a rayon imitation of this fabric

fu·ku·o·ka \¦fü(,)kü¦ōkə\ *adj, usu cap* [fr. *Fukuoka*, city in northern Kyushu, Japan] **:** of or from the city of Fukuoka, Japan **:** of the kind or style prevalent in Fukuoka

[1]-ful \ˌfəl *sometimes* (,)fůl *esp when an unstressed vowel precedes*\ *adj suffix* [ME, fr. OE, fr. *full*, adj.] **1 :** full of ⟨event*ful*⟩ **2 :** characterized by **:** -OUS ⟨peace*ful*⟩ ⟨boast*ful*⟩ **3 :** having the qualities of **:** resembling ⟨master*ful*⟩ **4 :** -ABLE ⟨bash*ful*⟩ ⟨mourn*ful*⟩

[2]-ful *also* **-full** \ˌfůl\ *n suffix* -s [ME *-ful*, fr. OE *-ful, -full*, fr. *full*, adj.] **:** number or quantity that fills or would fill ⟨cup*ful*⟩ ⟨room*ful*⟩ ⟨belly*ful*⟩ — sometimes after pl. nouns ⟨bags*ful*⟩

fu·la *or* **fu·lah** \'fülə, 'fůlə\ *also* **ful** \'fül, 'fůl\ *n, pl* **fula** *or* **fulas** *or* **fulah** *or* **fulahs** *also* **ful** *or* **fuls** *usu cap* **1 a :** a Sudanese people of African Negroid stock and Mediterranean Caucasoid admixture with highly variable skin color that is often reddish brown, hair wavy to crisp, and slender figure — called also *Fellata, Fulani, Fulbe* **b :** a member of such people **2 :** FULANI 2a

fu·la·ni \'fü,länē, fü'l-\ *n, usu cap* **1** *pl* **fulani** *or* **fulanis a :** FULA 1a; *esp* **:** the Fula of northern Nigeria and adjacent areas **b :** a member of such people **2** *pl* **fulani** *or* **fulanis a :** the language of the Fula people now classified as West-Atlantic and most closely related to Serer — called also *Fula, Fulfulde, Peul* **b :** a trade language used by other tribes in many areas of West Africa **3 a :** a West African breed of large white-coated black-skinned humped cattle with horns rising in a lyre-shaped curve **b** *pl* **fulani** *or* **fulanis :** an animal of this breed

ful·be \'fül(,)bā\ *n, pl* **fulbe** *or* **fulbes** *usu cap* **:** FULA 1

ful·bright \'fůl,brīt, *usu* -īd·+V\ *n* -s *usu cap* [after James William *Fulbright* b1905 U.S. senator] **:** a grant awarded under the Fulbright Act that makes U.S. surplus property in foreign countries available to finance lectures or research abroad by American students and professors

ful·chronograph \(')fůl, ¦fəl+\ *n* [L *ful*gur lightning (fr. *fulgēre* to shine, flash) + E *chronograph*] **:** a lightning-recording device that consists of a revolving aluminum disk having on its rim several hundred steel fins which, as they pass successively every forty-millionth of a second between two coils carrying the surge current of a lightning stroke, become proportionately magnetized and register the duration and intensity of the strokes

ful·ci·ment \'fůlsəmənt, 'fəl-\ *n* -s [L *fulcimentum*, fr. *fulcire* to prop + *-mentum* -ment] *archaic* **:** PROP

ful·cral \'fůlkrəl, 'fəl-\ *adj* [*fulcr*um + *-al*] **:** of or relating to a fulcrum

ful·crate \-ˌkrāt\ *adj* [prob. fr. (assumed) NL *fulcratus*, fr. NL *fulcrum* + L *-atus* -ate] *biol* **:** having a fulcrum

[1]ful·crum \'fůlkrəm, 'fəl-\ *n, pl* **fulcrums** \-mz\ *or* **ful·cra** \-rə\ [LL, fr. L, bedpost, fr. *fulcire* to prop — more at BALK] **1 a :** PROP, SUPPORT; *specif* **:** the support about which a lever turns ⟨an oar rests against some kind of ~ on the boat —*Notes & Queries on Anthropology*⟩ — see LEVER illustration **b :** one that supplies leverage for action ⟨he is . . . the reader's eyes and ears and the ~ of his judgment —Bernard De Voto⟩ **2** [NL, fr. LL] **:** a part of an animal that serves as a hinge or support: **a :** one of the small modified scales or spines on the anterior edge of the fins of many ganoid and a few teleost fishes **b :** the horny inferior surface of the ligula of various insects; *specif* **:** a chitinous framework at the base of the proboscis of insects of the order Diptera **c :** the stem or median part of the incus of the mastax of certain rotifers

[2]fulcrum \"\ *vt* -ED/-ING/-S **:** to furnish with a fulcrum **:** apply a fulcrum to **:** make a fulcrum of

fule \'fūel\ *Scot var of* FOOL

ful·fill *or* **ful·fil** \(')fůl¦fil *sometimes* fəl'f-, *rapid sometimes* fů'f- *or* fə'f- *by l-dissimilation*\ *vt* **fulfilled; fulfilled; fulfilling; fulfills** *or* **fulfils** [ME *fulfillen*, fr. OE *fullfyllan*, fr. [1]*full* + *fyllan* to fill — more at FULL, FILL] **1** *archaic* **:** to make full **:** FILL ⟨the world has received animals . . . and is ~*ed* with them —Benjamin Jowett⟩ ⟨her subtle, warm, and golden breath . . . ~*s* him with beatitude —Alfred Tennyson⟩ **2 :** to supply the missing parts of **:** make whole **:** INTEGRATE ⟨admirable though the illustrations are, their virtue is . . . that they ~ the text —*Times Lit. Supp.*⟩ **3 a :** to carry out **:** ACCOMPLISH, EXECUTE ⟨he had struck out into the wilderness . . . partly for reasons of his own, partly to ~ an order of his superior —Vicki Baum⟩ **b :** to finish out **:** bring to an end ⟨she came to install herself and ~ her time at the house —Willa Cather⟩ **c :** to come up to (as a requirement) **:** MEET, ANSWER, SATISFY ⟨this work ~*s* a need that lawyers have felt for many years —*Columbia Univ. Press Books*⟩ **4 a :** to measure up to **:** convert into reality ⟨pioneering courage balanced by a sense of the failure of life to ~ its ultimate expectations —Leslie Rees⟩ **b :** to realize the full potentialities of **:** develop completely **:** CONSUMMATE ⟨the inalienable right of a man to realize his potentialities, to ~ himself, to enter upon his destiny —August Heckscher b. 1913⟩ **syn** see PERFORM, SATISFY

ful·fill·er \-lə(r)\ *n* [ME, fr. *fulfillen* + *-er*] **:** one that fulfills

ful·fill·ment *or* **ful·fil·ment** \=ˈ=mənt\ *n* -s **1 :** the act or process of fulfilling **:** EXECUTION ⟨participation in the ~ of mother's dreams —C.S.Hill⟩ **2 :** the quality or state of being fulfilled **:** COMPLETION ⟨a patchwork quilt which I was well aware would never reach ~ —Agnes Repplier⟩

ful·ful·de \fůl'fůldē\ *n, pl* **fulfulde** *or* **fulfuldes** *usu cap* **:** FULANI 2a

ful·gence \'fůljən(t)s, 'fəl-\ *or* **ful·gen·cy** \-nsē\ *n, pl* **fulgences** *or* **fulgencies** [*fulgence* fr. ME, fr. *fulgent*, after such pairs as ME *excellent: excellence; fulgency* fr. *fulgent* + *-cy*] **:** brilliant luster **:** RESPLENDENCE

ful·gen·ic acid \(')fů¦l¦jenik-, ¦fə|\ *n* [*fulgenic* fr. G *fulgen-* (fr. L *fulgens* fulgent) + E *-ic*] **:** a dicarboxylic acid $[CH_2=C(COOH)-]_2$ known in the form of derivatives

ful·gent \'fůljənt, 'fəl-\ *adj* [ME, fr. L *fulgent-, fulgens*, pres. part. of *fulgēre* to shine, flash; akin to L *flagrare* to burn — more at BLACK] **:** dazzlingly bright **:** RADIANT ⟨the sun was ~ —Dan Levin⟩ ⟨lilac and wistaria . . . ~, with a burning scent —William Faulkner⟩ — **ful·gent·ly** *adv*

ful·gid \-jəd\ *adj* [L *fulgidus*, fr. *fulgēre*] **1** *archaic* **:** shining brightly **:** GLITTERING ⟨the ~ sunbeams spread abroad their animating light —William Bartram⟩ **2** *zool* **:** fiery red with metallic reflections

ful·gide \-ˌjīd, -ˌjəd\ *n* -s [G *fulgid*, fr. *fulg-* (fr. L *fulgēre*) + *-id* -ide] **1 :** the anhydride $C_6H_4O_3$ of fulgenic acid **2 :** a derivative of fulgenic acid (as some aryl derivatives used in photography to produce removable light images in blue and black tones)

ful·gor \'fůlgər, 'fəl-, -ˌgȯ(ə)r\ *or* **ful·gour** \-ˌgər\ *n* -s [L *fulgor*, fr. *fulgēre*] *archaic* **:** dazzling brightness **:** SPLENDOR — **ful·gor·ous** \-ˌgərəs\ *adj*

ful·go·ra \'fůlgərə, 'fəl-\ *n, cap* [NL, fr. L *Fulgora*, goddess of lightning] **:** the type genus of the family Fulgoridae

[1]ful·go·rid \-rəd, -ˌrid\ *adj* [NL *Fulgoridae*] **:** of or relating to the Fulgoridae

[2]fulgorid \"\ *n* -s [NL *Fulgoridae*] **:** an insect of the family Fulgoridae

ful·gor·i·dae \fůl'gȯrə,dē, ˌfəl-\ *n pl, cap* [NL, fr. *Fulgora*, type genus + *-idae*] **:** a family of chiefly tropical often grotesquely formed plant-feeding insects (superfamily Fulguroidea) that have the beak obviously arising from the base of the head and the ocelli near or below the eyes — see LANTERN FLY

ful·go·roi·dea \ˌfůlgə'rȯidēə, ˌfəl-\ *n pl, cap* [NL, fr. *Fulgora* + *-oidea*] **:** a superfamily of insects (suborder Homoptera) that usu. have ocelli in cavities of the cheeks and the anal veins of the fore wings fused apically to form a Y — see LANTERN FLY

ful·gu·ral \'fůlg(y)ərəl, 'fəl-\ *adj* [L *fulguralis*, fr. *fulgur* lightning + *-alis* -al] *archaic* **:** of or relating to lightning

ful·gu·rant \-rənt\ *adj* [L *fulgurant-, fulgurans*, pres. part. of *fulgurare*] **:** flashing like lightning **:** DAZZLING ⟨these great best canvases still look as astonishing and as invitingly new as they did . . . when . . . his ~ popularity was in full growth —Janet Flanner⟩

ful·gu·rate \-ˌrāt\ *vb* -ED/-ING/-S [L *fulguratus*, past part. of *fulgurare* to lightning, flash like lightning, fr. *fulgur* lightning, fr. *fulgēre* to shine, flash] *vi, obs* **:** to flash like lightning ~ *vt* **1 :** to emit flashes of ⟨he is said to have been conspicuously handsome: well built, of soldierly bearing, with . . . blue eyes that *fulgurated* . . . terror, love, or hate —*New Yorker*⟩ **2 :** to perform electrodesiccation on **:** remove or destroy by means of electrodesiccation ⟨relieved the patient's discomfort by *fulgurating* the uterine mass⟩

ful·gu·ra·tion \ˌ=='rāshən\ *n* -s [L *fulguration, fulguratio* sheet lightning, fr. *fulguratus* + *-ion-, -io* -ion] **1 a :** the act or process of flashing like lightning **:** a lightning flash ⟨it was pleasant to be sitting there while the sultriest ~*s*, flickering, cast corners in the glass —Wallace Stevens⟩ **b :** a spiritual radiation or divine manifestation **c :** *Leibnizianism* **:** the monads that are coeternal with God **2 :** the sudden brightening of a fused globule of gold or silver when the last film of oxide of lead or copper leaves its surface in assaying **3 :** ELECTRODESICCATION

ful·gu·rite \'==,rīt\ *n* -s [ISV *fulgur-* (fr. L *fulgur*) + *-ite*] **:** an often tubular vitrified crust produced by the fusion of sand or rock by lightning

ful·gu·rous \-ˌrəs\ *adj* [L *fulgur* + E *-ous*] **:** charged with or emitting flashes of or like lightning ⟨adventures related often with raffish gusto, in style both vivid and ~ —Idwal Jones⟩

ful·ham \'fůləm\ *n* -s [perh. by folk etymology (influence of *Fulham*, London borough formerly much frequented by professional gamblers) fr. earlier *fullan*, perh. fr. [1]*full* + *one*, n.] *archaic* **:** a loaded die ⟨there is no loading of the dice or throwing of ~*s* —A. Conan Doyle⟩

fu·li·ca \'fyüləkə\ *n, cap* [NL, fr. L, coot — more at BALD] **:** a genus of aquatic birds (family Rallidae) comprising the coots and being distinguished from the typical rails by the presence of a frontal shield and lobed toes — compare GALLINULE

fu·li·cine \-lə,sīn, -ˌsən\ *adj* [NL *Fulicinae* subfamily comprising the coots, fr. *Fulica* + *-inae*] **:** of or relating to the genus *Fulica*

fu·lig·i·nos·i·ty \(,)fyü,lijə'näsəd·ē\ *n* -ES [F *fuliginosité*, fr. MF, fr. LL *fuliginosus* sooty + MF *-ité* -ity] **:** the quality or state of being fuliginous

fu·lig·i·nous \(')fyü¦lijənəs\ *adj* [LL *fuliginosus* sooty, fr. L *fuligin-, fuligo* soot + *-osus* -ose; akin to MIr *dūil* wish, Lith *dulsvas* smoke-colored, L *fumus* smoke — more at FUME] **1** *obs* **:** of or relating to certain noxious bodily vapors formerly held to be produced by organic processes ⟨it is not amiss to bore the skull with an instrument to let out the ~ vapors —Robert Burton⟩ **2 a :** of, relating to, or containing soot **:** SOOTY ⟨plenty of Londoners who are fed up with the current spell of ~, choking weather —Mollie Panter-Downes⟩ **b :** CLOUDED, OBSCURE, MURKY ⟨a ~ sense of ironical humor —W.J.Locke⟩ **3 :** having the color of soot **:** DARK, DUSKY — **fu·lig·i·nous·ly** *adv*

fu·li·go \fyü'lī(,)gō, fü'lē(-\ *n, cap* [NL, fr. L, soot] **:** a widely distributed genus of large slime molds with the sporangia gathered in an aethalium and the plasmodium commonly bright yellow

fu lion *n, usu cap F* [Chin fu^2 happiness] **:** FU DOG

fulk \'fəlk, 'fůlk\ *vi* -ED/-ING/-S [origin unknown] **:** to move the hand unfairly in shooting marbles

[1]full \'fůl\ *adj* -ER/-EST [ME *ful, full*, fr. OE *full;* akin to OHG *fol* full, ON *fullr*, Goth *fulls*, L *plenus* full, *plēre* to fill, Gk *plērēs* full, *plēthein* to be full, Skt *pūrṇa* full] **1 a :** containing all that possibly can be placed or put within ⟨a ~ hamper⟩ ⟨a ~ magazine⟩ — often used with *of* ⟨a bin ~ of corn⟩ **b :** having the normal or intended capacity supplied or accommodated : entirely occupied ⟨a ~ bus⟩ ⟨a ~ house⟩ **c** : occupying completely the requisite space ⟨a ~ cargo⟩ ⟨a ~ audience⟩ **d** : possessed of the appropriate or normal complement ⟨a ~ dramatic company⟩ ⟨a ~ jury⟩ **e** : regularly allotted : normally apportioned ⟨more than its ~ share of lovely old American houses —Jerome Weidman⟩ **f** *of an ablaut grade* : NORMAL **2 a** (1) : lacking restraint or check : PRECIPITOUS, HEADLONG ⟨~ retreat⟩ (2) : being without reservation : UNQUALIFIED ⟨~ supporters of a policy⟩ **b** : possessing the maximum strength or force ⟨a ~ gale⟩ **c** (1) : followed to the greatest extent feasible : all possible ⟨making ~ use of a library's resources⟩ (2) : greatest or highest potential ⟨a ship going at ~ speed⟩ ⟨a machine operating at ~ capacity⟩ (3) : being at or of the greatest or highest degree : MAXIMUM ⟨~ strength⟩ ⟨~ potency⟩ **3 a** : rounded in outline ⟨a ~ face⟩ : well filled out : PLUMP ⟨a ~ figure⟩ : generously formed : SWELLING ⟨~ lips⟩ **b** (1) : filled or distended by wind ⟨~ sails⟩ (2) *of a ship* : having the sails filled with wind **c** : big with young or eggs **d** : having an abundance of material esp. in the form of gathered, pleated, or flared parts ⟨a ~ skirt⟩ **e** (1) : slightly oversize, projecting, or standing out usu. so as to require more tooling (2) : risen above the normal level : SWOLLEN ⟨in spring when the rivers and streams are ~⟩ **4 a** : possessing, containing, or furnished with an abundance or great number — used with *of* ⟨a face ~ of wrinkles⟩ ⟨a city ~ of soldiers⟩ ⟨a room ~ of pictures⟩ **b** : possessing all particulars : completely familiar or expert — used with *of* ⟨he is ~ of his subject and our foremost authority —W.O.Douglas⟩ **c** : packed with variety of experience ⟨a ~ life⟩; *also* : possessing much knowledge ⟨education having made him a ~ man⟩ **5 a** : satisfied esp. with food or drink : REPLETE **b** : large enough so as to satisfy ⟨a ~ meal⟩ **6 a** (1) : enjoying or possessed of all recognized or authorized prerogatives, rights, and privileges : not temporary, substitute, or provisional ⟨a ~ member⟩ (2) : being without reduction or subtraction : REGULAR ⟨working only half time but drawing ~ salary⟩ ⟨maintaining ~ diplomatic relations with a foreign country⟩ ⟨a ~ term of office⟩ (3) : being without truncation : UNABBREVIATED ⟨~ words⟩ **b** (1) : containing all details : COMPLETE ⟨a ~ statement⟩ ⟨a ~ report⟩ (2) : not lacking in any feature, quality, or accomplishment : PERFECT ⟨quite old but in ~ possession of his faculties⟩ **7** *archaic* : completely weary : utterly sick — used with *of* **8** : filled with emotion ⟨a ~ heart⟩ **9 a** : having the limit or near limit — used with *of* ⟨a man weary and ~ of years⟩ **b** (1) : being at the height of development ⟨a flower in ~ bloom⟩ ⟨the tide at ~ flood⟩ ⟨a moon nearly ~⟩ (2) : MATURE, ADULT ⟨men and women of ~ age⟩ **10** : having the same parents ⟨~ sisters⟩ **11** *of a color* : PURE **12 a** : carried to the greatest practical extent ⟨a shotgun with a ~ choke⟩ **b** : extended to or occupying the largest possible space, area, or dimensions ⟨a ~ basement⟩ **c** : completely covering the boards and backbone ⟨a book bound in ~ crushed blue morocco with gilt edges and blind tooling⟩ — compare HALF **13 a** : having marked volume or depth ⟨a ~ voice⟩ ⟨a ~ tone⟩ **b** *of a vowel* : BACK 1c **14 a** : squarely facing ahead ⟨a *full*-face portrait⟩ **b** : being in dead center : DIRECT ⟨a cue ball making a ~ hit on the object ball⟩ **15** : completely occupied : ENGROSSED — used with *of* ⟨I have been ~ of work since I wrote last —H.J.Laski⟩ **16** : being the rank of the three of a kind in a full house in poker — used postpositively ⟨jacks ~⟩ **17** : possessing a rich or pronounced quality ⟨a wine of ~ body⟩ ⟨a food of ~ flavor⟩

²full \"\ *adv* [ME *ful, full*, fr. OE *full*, fr. *full*, adj.] **1 a** : VERY, EXTREMELY ⟨I knew ~ well he had lied to me⟩ **b** : ENTIRELY, COMPLETELY, QUITE ⟨it was ~ dark by then —A.J.Liebling⟩ ⟨swung ~ around —Morley Callaghan⟩ **2** : to the full : to the utmost extent : to the highest degree, state, or condition ⟨the sun was ~ on the suburb —Herbert Gold⟩ **3 a** *of a position* : EXACTLY ⟨~ in the center of the sacred wood —Joseph Addison⟩ **b** *of a direction* : STRAIGHT, SQUARELY ⟨the blow hit him ~ in the face⟩ ⟨he turned and looked ~ at me —Nigel Balchin⟩

³full \"\ *n* -S [ME *fulle*, fr. OE *fulla*, fr. *full*, adj.] **1 a** : the utmost extent ⟨enjoy a book to the ~⟩ **b** : the highest or fullest state, condition, or degree ⟨the ~ of the moon⟩ ⟨the ~ of the tide⟩ ⟨when the moon is at ~⟩ **2** : a satiating or glutting share or portion — often used with the possessive adjective ⟨had his ~ of that job⟩ **3** : the requisite or complete amount — often used with *in* ⟨paid in ~⟩ **4** *Brit* : BEACH RIDGE **5** : FULL HOUSE

⁴full \"\ *vb* -ED/-ING/-S [ME *fullen* to become full, fill, fr. *ful, full*, adj. — more at ¹FULL] *vi, of the moon* : to become full ~ *vt* **1** : to make full in sewing esp. by gathering or pleating **2** : to distribute (fullness) by fitting a longer edge to a shorter edge smoothly in sewing — often used with *on*

⁵full \"\ *vt* -ED/-ING/-S [ME *fullen*, fr. MF *fouler*, fr. (assumed) VL *fullare*, fr. L *fullo* fuller; perh. akin to Skt *bhāla* luster — more at BALD] : to shrink and thicken (woolen cloth) by fulling

-full — see -FUL

full age *n* [ME *ful age, full age*] : mature age or legal majority; *specif* : the time of life at which one attains full personal rights and capacities, which under common law is attained upon the last day of completing 21 years or specif. on the first instant of the day preceding the 21st birthday and under civil law is attained upon completing 25 years, and which in some states is attained by women upon completing 18 years

fullam *var of* FULHAM

full and by *also* **full and bye** *adj* [ME *full and by*] : sailing with all sails full and lying as near the wind as possible : CLOSE-HAULED

full and down *adj, of a ship* : having all cargo space filled and being so weighted as to have the hull down exactly to the Plimsoll mark

full anthem *n* : an anthem entirely of chorus parts — compare VERSE ANTHEM

full automatic *adj* : AUTOMATIC 5

fullback \'=,=\ *n* [¹*full* + *back*, n.] **1** : a football back who is used primarily for line plunges and blocking on offense and who usu. backs up the line on defense **2** : a primarily defensive member of a team usu. stationed near the defended goal (as in soccer, speedball, field hockey, rugby)

full binding *n* : a book binding wholly of leather — called also *whole binding*; compare HALF BINDING, QUARTER BINDING, THREE-QUARTER BINDING

full blast *adv* : at full capacity : with great intensity

full blood *n* **1** : descent from parents both of one pure breed — called also *whole blood*; compare BLOOD 2g, PUREBRED **2** : a person or animal of full blood

full-blooded \'=¦==\ *adj* **1** : of unmixed ancestry : PUREBRED ⟨*full-blooded* Indians⟩ **2** : FLORID, RUDDY ⟨a *full-blooded* face⟩ **3 a** : SANGUINE, ARDENT ⟨a *full-blooded* personality⟩ ⟨*full-blooded* generosity⟩ **b** : IMPELLING, FORCEFUL ⟨a *full-blooded* argument⟩ ⟨a *full-blooded* prose style⟩ **4 a** : lacking no particulars : GENUINE ⟨a *full-blooded* war⟩ ⟨a *full-blooded* socialist⟩ **b** : extremely thorough or complete ⟨a *full-blooded* analysis⟩ **c** : containing fullness of substance : RICH ⟨a *full-blooded* narrative⟩ — **full-blood·ed·ness** *n* -ES

full-blown \'=¦=\ *adj* **1 a** : being at the height of bloom ⟨a *full-blown* rose⟩ **b** : fully ripe, mature, or mellow : LUSH ⟨a woman of *full-blown* charms⟩ **2** : possessing all the usual or necessary features, attributes, or qualities ⟨a *full-blown* scandal⟩ ⟨a *full-blown* atomic power plant⟩ ⟨ideas that did not emerge *full-blown* but took years to develop⟩

full-bod·ied \'=¦bädēd, -did\ *adj* **1** : having a large body : STOUT, CORPULENT ⟨his mother, *full-bodied*, with a mop of thick dark hair —Crichton Porteous⟩ ⟨dangerously *full-bodied*⟩ **2 a** : marked by richness and fullness of flavor ⟨a *full-bodied* red wine⟩ **b** : marked by fullness of body ⟨*full-bodied* ink⟩ ⟨*full-bodied* varnish⟩ **3** : marked by breadth of scope, excellence of texture, or richness of tone : SUBSTANTIAL ⟨this *full-bodied* novel, fresh, dramatic, violent —R.L.Blakesley⟩ ⟨the brilliant *full-bodied* numbers that our modern composers turn out —Deems Taylor⟩ **4** : having importance, significance, or meaningfulness ⟨the U.S. played a *full-bodied* role in the world and did not attempt to secede from it —Roscoe Drummond⟩

full-bodied money *n* : money which has a face value not in excess of its intrinsic value as a commodity

full-boled \'=¦=\ *adj, of a tree trunk or log* : having the same or nearly the same diameter from one end to the other

full bond *n* : a bond in masonry where all bricks are laid as headers

full-bosomed \'=¦==\ *adj* : having an amply developed bosom ⟨a pretty, *full-bosomed*, physically and emotionally precocious schoolgirl —S.H.Adams⟩

full bottom *n* : a full-bottomed wig worn esp. by some barristers

full-bot·tomed \'=¦bäd·əmd, -ätə-\ *adj* [¹*full* + *bottom*, n. + *-ed*] **1** *of a wig* : large and having curled sections falling below the shoulders **2** : of great capacity below the waterline (as a ship having a small rise of floor)

full-bound \'=¦=\ *adj* **1** *of a book* : having full binding **2** *carpentry* : having an equal amount of wood in all rails — used of sashes

full cadence *n* : PERFECT CADENCE

full capping *n* [*capping* fr. gerund of ²*cap*] : the application of camelback to the entire area of a worn tire tread including the shoulders — compare TOP CAPPING

full-cell process *or* **full-cell treatment** *n* : a method of treating wood so that a preservative chemical partially or completely fills the cells in the treated portion (as in the Bethell process) — compare EMPTY-CELL PROCESS

full cock *n* : the position of the hammer of a firearm when fully retracted and ready to be released by the sear — compare HALF COCK

full-court press *n* : a press employed in basketball on both halves of the court — called also *all-court press*

full cousin *n* : COUSIN 1b

full coverage *n* : insurance that provides payment for all losses up to the limit of the policy without any deductions

full-cream cheese *n* : cheese made from unskimmed milk

full-crew law *n* : a law establishing standards about the number of employees to be used on trains

full-crown fender *n* : an automobile fender arched across its entire width

full cry *n* : eager chase — used of hounds that have caught the scent and give tongue together

full dress *n* : the style of dress prescribed by fashion or governmental regulation for ceremonial or formal social occasions — compare EVENING DRESS, FULL-DRESS UNIFORM

full-dress \'=¦=\ *adj* [*full dress*] **1** : complete down to the last formal detail ⟨a *full-dress* welcome⟩ ⟨a *full-dress* biography⟩ **2** : carried out by all possible means or from all possible approaches ⟨a *full-dress* investigation⟩

full-dressed \'=¦=\ *adj* **1** *of poultry* : dressed completely with feathers, viscera, and usu. head and feet removed — compare NEW YORK DRESSED **2** *of a ship* : dressed with ensigns and a line of pennants — compare *dress ship* 1 at ¹DRESS

full dress ship *n* : a ship dressed with ensigns and a line of pennants — compare *dress ship* 1 at ¹DRESS

full-dress uniform *n* : the military or naval uniform established by regulations for wear on a ceremonial occasion — compare DRESS UNIFORM

fulled *past of* FULL

¹full·er \'fulə(r)\ *n* -S [ME *fullere*, fr. OE, fr. L *fullo* fuller + OE *-ere* -er — more at ⁵FULL] **1** : one that fulls cloth **2** : WEIGHTER

²ful·ler \"\ *vt* -ED/-ING/-S [prob. fr. the name *Fuller*] : to form a groove or channel in ⟨~ a bayonet⟩

³ful·ler \"\ *n* -S **1** : a blacksmithing set hammer with a longitudinally half-round peen or a form of bottom tool with a similar working end sometimes used in conjunction with the first for grooving and spreading iron; *also* : a groove made by such a tool or any groove or fluting **2** : the portion of a forging die that reduces the cross-sectional area between the ends of the stock and permits the metal to move outward during preliminary forging

fuller 1

ful·ler·board \'==,=\ *n* [prob. fr. the name *Fuller*] : a paperboard which may be pressed into various forms and used as an electrical insulator in low-voltage work — called also *pressboard*

fuller faucet *also* **fuller bibcock** *or* **fuller cock** *n* [fr. *Fuller*, a trademark] : a faucet opened and closed by means of a lever and eccentric

ful·ler·ing tool *n* [*fullering* fr. gerund of ²*fuller*] : a blacksmith's fuller; *also* : a tool for caulking metal plates

ful·ler rose beetle *or* **fuller's rose weevil** *n, usu cap F* [perh. after Andrew S. *Fuller* †1896 Am. horticulturist] : a small broad-snouted grayish weevil (*Pantomorus godmani*) feeding on the leaves of numerous cultivated plants and being esp. destructive to citrus and certain ornamentals

full·er's card *n* [*fuller's* (poss. of ¹*fuller*) + *card*] : WILD TEASEL

full·er's earth *n* [ME *fulleres erthe*] : a white to brown naturally occurring earthy substance resembling potter's clay but lacking in plasticity, consisting chiefly of the clay minerals montmorillonite and attapulgite, and used in fulling cloth and now esp. as an adsorbent (as in refining and decolorizing oils and fats) and as a catalyst

full·er's herb *n* [so called fr. its former use in removing stains from cloth] : SOAPWORT

full·er's teasel *n* [ME *fulleres tesel*] : a teasel (*Dipsacus fullonum*) having heads with curved barbed bracts that are used in the woolen industry for gigging and napping

full·er's thistle *n* : TEASEL 1

fullface \'=,=\ *n* : BOLDFACE 2

full faith and credit *n* : an obligation under the U.S. Constitution of one state to recognize and give effect to the public acts, records, and judicial proceedings of her sister states

full-fashioned \'=¦==\ *also* **fully fashioned** *adj* : employing or produced by a flat-knit process for shaping to conform to body lines ⟨*full-fashioned* knitting⟩ ⟨*full-fashioned* hosiery⟩

full-feathering \'=¦=(=)=\ *adj, of an airplane propeller* : capable of being feathered in flight to a pitch angle of approximately 90 degrees so that the drag is a minimum and there is no tendency to rotate

full-feed \'=¦=\ *vt* : to feed (an animal) to the full extent of its needs

full-fledged \'=¦=\ *adj* **1** : fully developed : MATURE **2** *of a bird* : fully fledged **3** : having attained complete status : GENUINE ⟨a *full-fledged* lawyer⟩

full force and effect *n* : FORCE AND EFFECT

full-form insurance *n* : marine insurance covering partial as well as total loss

full frame *n* : BRACED FRAME

full framing *n* : BRACED FRAMING

full gainer *n* : GAINER

full gate *n* : the adjustment of a water turbine to utilize its full capacity ⟨working at *full gate*⟩

full gear *n* : the condition of a steam engine with valves worked by a link motion where the link motion operates the valve to the fullest extent

full gilt *n* : a book having gilt on all three edges

full gospel *n, usu cap F&G* : an American fundamentalistic sect originating in the South about 1935

full grain *or* **full grain leather** *n* : leather retaining original grain surface with only hair and associated epidermis removed

full-grooved ax \'=,=-\ *n* : a prehistoric grooved ax having the groove completely encircling the area where the ax handle was attached

full-grown \'=¦=\ *adj* : having reached full growth or development : MATURE

full gum *n* : ORIGINAL GUM

full habit *n* : a condition of the body characterized by congestion of the visible blood vessels and tendency to stoutness — compare ENDOMORPHIC, HABIT

fullhearted \'=¦==\ *adj* : having a heart full of courage or confidence or understanding ⟨~ support⟩ ⟨~ recognition of the 19th century and its greatness —*Times Lit. Supp.*⟩ — **full·heart·ed·ly** *adv* — **full·heart·ed·ness** *n* -ES

full house *or* **full hand** *n* : a poker hand containing three of a kind and a pair (as three aces and two tens) and ranking above a flush and below four of a kind — see POKER illustration

full·ing \'fu̇liŋ, -lēŋ\ *n* -S [ME *fullinge*, fr. *fullen* to full + *-inge* -ing — more at ⁵FULL] : the process of shrinking and thickening woolen fabric by application of moisture, heat, friction, and pressure that causes the fibers to felt

fulling mill *n* [ME *fullinge mille*] **1** : a machine for fulling cloth **2** : a factory where cloth is fulled

fulling stock *n* **1** : a wooden beater for fulling cloth **2 a** : a mallet for beating oil into hides **b** : a machine in which such mallets form the essential feature — usu. used in pl.

full-jacket \'=¦==\ *or* **full-jacketed** \'=¦===\ *adj, of a bullet* : having the core covered with a jacket

full-length \'=¦=\ *adj* **1** : having the full or usual length of its kind : not curtailed or skimpy ⟨a *full-length* play⟩ ⟨a *full-length* book⟩ **2** : having, accommodating, or representing the full height of the human figure ⟨a *full-length* mirror⟩

full lot *n* : BOARD LOT

full marks *n pl* : complete credit : due commendation ⟨*full marks* must be given the victor⟩

full moon *n* [ME *ful mone, ful moone*, fr. OE *full mōna*] **1 a** : the moon with its whole apparent disk illuminated appearing when the moon is in opposition to the sun — see MOON illustration **b** : the time when the moon is full **2** : the 14th day of the moon occurring regularly according to a set of calendar rules without regard to the real moon of the sky

full-moon maple *n* : JAPANESE MAPLE

fullmouth \'=,=\ *n* : a fullmouthed animal (as a sheep or cow); *also* : the mouth of such an animal

fullmouthed \'=¦=\ *adj* **1** : having a full mouth; *esp* : having a full complement of teeth — used esp. of sheep and cattle **2** : uttered as with full power or sound : LOUD, NOISY ⟨a ~ welcome⟩

full nelson *n* : a hold gained by a wrestler who from a position behind his opponent places both arms under his opponent's arms and clasps his hands or wrists behind the opponent's neck — compare HALF NELSON, QUARTER NELSON, THREE-QUARTER NELSON

full·ness *also* **ful·ness** \'fu̇lnəs\ *n* -ES [ME *fulnesse*, fr. *ful, full* full + *-nesse* -ness] : the quality or state of being full

full of the moon [ME *fulle of the mone*] : the time or condition of complete illumination of the lunar disk

full-orbed \'=¦ȯ(ə)rbd\ *adj* : having or forming a full orb ⟨the *full-orbed* moon⟩ ⟨the *full-orbed* pumpkins —Van Wyck Brooks⟩

full organ *adv* (*or adj*) : with all or most of the stops drawn so that the full power of the instrument is heard — often used as a direction in music

full-out \'=¦=\ *adj* **1** : flush left — used of a typeset or typewritten line **2** : COMPLETE, TOTAL ⟨a *full-out* war effort⟩

full-paid \'=¦=\ *adj* : FULLY PAID

full-patch \'=¦=\ *adj* : FULL-JACKET

full-pitch winding *n* : the winding of an armature in which the two sides of the armature coil span a distance equal to the pole pitch

full plate *n* : a watch having all its train wheels and escapement under one plate with only the balance exposed

full position *n* : the position of an advertisement that has reading matter on two sides or that is at the top of a column and has reading matter on at least one side

full reporting clause *n* : a clause in an insurance policy that provides that the indemnity will not exceed that proportion of loss which the last reported value of the property bears to the actual value

full-rigged \'=¦=\ *adj* **1** : having all the sails and rigging necessary; *esp* : having three or more masts each with its full complement of square sails ⟨a *full-rigged* ship⟩ — see SAIL illustration **2** : completely equipped

full-rig·ger \'=¦rigə(r)\ *n* [*full rig* (noun phrase) + *-er*] : a ship having a full rig

full rudder *n* : the maximum angle with the keel to which the rudder of a boat may be moved

full run *n* : a contract purchased from an advertising agency whereby a card of a type suitable for bus, subway, or train advertising is required to be placed in every car in a specified district

fulls *pl of* FULL, *pres 3d sing of* FULL

-fulls *pl of* -FULL

full-scale \'=¦=\ *adj* **1** : identical to an original in proportion and size ⟨a *full-scale* drawing⟩ **2 a** : ABSOLUTE, COMPLETE ⟨help them . . . towards *full-scale* success in the larger theatre —Leslie Rees⟩ **b** : involving full use of available resources ⟨a *full-scale* civil war⟩ ⟨started *full-scale* production⟩

full score *n* : a musical score in which all the parts of a composition are given; *esp* : one in which each vocal or instrumental part is on a separate staff

full sea *n, archaic* : FLOOD TIDE

full seamark *n* : the limit of flood tide

full service *n* : a musical setting of all the canticles used in the liturgy of the Anglican church esp. for chorus only with no solo parts — compare FULL ANTHEM

full-shroud \'=¦=\ *vt* : to provide (a gear wheel) with shrouds extending to the tops of the teeth

full sight *n* : a sight or aim in which all the front sight of a gun is seen in the notch of the rear sight

full snipe *n* : a common European snipe (*Capella gallinago*)

full speed *n* : top or utmost speed; *specif* : a speed one eighth more than standard speed

full stop *or* **full point** *n* : PERIOD 5a

full-summed \'=¦=\ *adj* : FULL-FLEDGED 2

full swell *adv* (*or adj*) : with all stops on the swell manual drawn — often used as a direction in music

full-term \'=¦=\ *adj, of an infant* : retained in the uterus for the entire normal gestation period

full tilt *adv* [¹*full* + *tilt* (single combat between mounted men)] : at high speed : with a rush

full time *n* : the amount of time considered the normal or standard amount for working during a given period (as a day, week, or month)

full-time \'=¦=\ *adj* [*full time*] **1** : employed for or working the amount of time considered customary or standard ⟨*full-time* clerks⟩ **2** : involving or operating the amount of time considered customary or standard ⟨*full-time* teaching⟩

full to fifteenth : full organ excepting reeds and mixtures — used as a direction in organ music

full toss *or* **full pitch** *or* **full volley** *n* : a bowled ball in cricket so pitched that it will if left alone hit or land close to the stumps before touching the ground

full-track vehicle *n* : a vehicle (as a tank) that is entirely supported, driven, and steered by a caterpillar tread

full trailer *n* : a trailer whose weight is carried entirely on its own wheels — compare SEMITRAILER

full twist *n* : a front or back dive in which the diver executes a complete turn of the body on a vertical axis without bending the body — compare HALF TWIST

full vamp *n* : a one-piece upper seamed at the center of the heel

full verb *n* : a verb with full meaning — compare LINK VERB

full-wave rectifier *n* : a rectifier that converts alternating current into continuous current and that utilizes both halves of each cycle of the alternating current

full word *n* : a word conveying an idea or image : SEMANTEME — compare FUNCTION WORD

ful·ly \'fu̇l(l)ē, |i, *when emphatic also* 'fu̇l|l\ *adv* [ME, fr. OE *fullīce*, fr. OE *full* + *-līce* -ly — more at FULL] **1** : in a full manner : to a full degree : COMPLETELY, ENTIRELY, THOROUGHLY **2** : at least ⟨~ half the class⟩

fully fashioned *var of* FULL-FASHIONED

fully fledged *adj, chiefly Brit* : FULL-FLEDGED

fully found *adj, of a boat* : completely equipped for service

fully insured *adj, under old age and survivors insurance* : having at age 65 or at death at least one quarter of coverage for each two calendar quarters since December 31, 1950, or since reaching age 21, whichever is later, at least six quarters of coverage being required

fully insured for life *under old age and survivors insurance* : having 40 quarters of coverage

fully paid *adj, of corporate shares* : paid for at full face value with no further money due from the stockholder

ful·mar \'fu̇lmər, -,mär\ *also* **fulmar petrel** *n* -S [of Scand origin; akin to ON *fúlmār*, fr. *fúll* foul + *mār* gull — more at FOUL, MEW] **1** : an Arctic sea bird (*Fulmarus glacialis*) that is closely related to the petrels, resembles the herring gull in size and color, is very abundant on the northern No. Atlantic, breeds on cliffs, feeds chiefly on fish and floating offal and is esp. fond of whale blubber, and is valued for its eggs, oil, and feathers and for the strong-scented flesh of young birds which

is sometimes used as food **2 :** any of several birds of southern seas that are related to the fulmar
ful·mi·nant \ˈfu̇lmənənt *also* ˈfəl-\ *adj* [L *fulminant-, fulminans,* pres. part. of *fulminare* to lightning] **:** FULMINATING 3
¹ful·mi·nate \-ˌnāt, *usu* -ād.+V\ *vb* -ED/-ING/-S [ME *fulminaten,* fr. ML *fulminatus,* past part. of *fulminare,* fr. L, to lightning, strike with lightning, fr. *fulmin-, fulmen* lightning, stroke of lightning; akin to L *fulgēre* to shine, flash, *flagrare* to burn — more at BLACK] *vt* **1 :** to utter or send out with denunciation or censures ⟨~ a decree⟩ **2 :** to cause to explode ~ *vi* **1 :** to issue or send forth censures or invectives menacingly or authoritatively **2 :** to make a sudden loud noise **:** DETONATE, EXPLODE **3** *of a disease* **:** to come on suddenly and intensely
²fulminate \"\ *n* -S [ISV *fulmin-* (fr. L *fulmin-, fulmen* lightning) + *-ate*] **:** a salt of fulminic acid; *esp* **:** MERCURY FULMINATE
fulminate of mercury : MERCURY FULMINATE
fulminating *adj* [fr. pres. part. of ¹*fulminate*] **1 :** exploding with a vivid flash **:** THUNDERING **2 :** hurling denunciations, menaces, or censures ⟨a ~ bishop⟩ **3 :** coming on suddenly with great severity **:** characterized by a rapid and severe course ⟨a ~ disease⟩
fulminating gold *n* **:** any of several explosive substances containing gold and nitrogen (as a powder obtained by the action of ammonia on gold oxide)
fulminating material *n* **:** a detonating substance that appears during thunderstorms as luminous balls
fulminating mercury *n* **:** MERCURY FULMINATE
fulminating silver *n* **1 :** a black crystalline explosive substance obtained by the action of ammonia on silver oxide **2 :** SILVER FULMINATE
ful·mi·na·tion \ˌfu̇lməˈnāshən *also* ˌfəl-\ *n* -S [MF, pronouncement of an ecclesiastical sentence or censure, fr. L *fulmination-, fulminatio* lightning, fr. *fulminatus* (past part. of *fulminare* to lightning) + *-ion-, -io* -ion] **1 :** vehement menace or censure ⟨uncowed by police ~⟩ **2 :** something that is thundered forth ⟨ecclesiastical ~s⟩ **3 :** the act or action of exploding
ful·mi·na·tor \ˈ⸗⸗ˌnād·ə(r), -ātə-\ *n* -S [L, hurler of lightning, fr. *fulminatus* (past part. of *fulminare* to lightning, strike with lightning) + *-or*] **:** one that fulminates
ful·mine \ˈfu̇lmən, ˈfəl-\ *vb* -ED/-ING/-S [MF *fulminer,* fr. L *fulminare*] *archaic* **:** FULMINATE
ful·min·e·ous \(ˈ)fu̇lˈminēəs, ¦fəl¦-\ *adj* [L *fulmineus,* fr. *fulmin-, fulmen* lightning + *-eus* -eous] **:** FULMINOUS
ful·min·ic acid \(ˈ)fu̇l¦minik-, ¦fəl¦\ *n* [*fulminic* ISV *fulmin-* (fr. L *fulmin-, fulmen* lightning) + *-ic*] **:** an unstable acid CNOH isomeric with cyanic acid and known only in solution (as ether, in which it polymerizes rapidly) and in the form of highly explosive salts
ful·mi·nous \ˈfu̇lmənəs, ˈfəl-\ *adj* [L *fulmin-, fulmen* + E *-ous*] **:** of, relating to, or resembling thunder and lightning
ful·min·uric acid \ˌfu̇l¦mə¦n(y)u̇rik-, ¦fəl\ *n* [*fulminuric* ISV *fulmin-* (as in *fulminic*) + *uric*] **:** a white crystalline explosive acid $NCCH(NO_2)CONH_2$ structurally related to nitromethane and obtainable in the form of salts by boiling mercury fulminate with potassium chloride solution
fulness *var of* FULLNESS
ful·nio \ˈfu̇lnēˌō\ *n, pl* **fulnio** *or* **fulnios** *usu cap* **1 a :** a people of the state of Pernambuco, Brazil **b :** a member of such people **2 :** the language of the Fulnio people
fü·löpp·ite *also* **ful·lopp·ite** *or* **ful·opp·ite** \ˈfu̇ləˌpīt, ˈfil-\ *n* -S [Bela *Fülöpp,* 20th cent. Hung. mineral collector + E *-ite*] **:** a lead-gray mineral $Pb_3Sb_8S_{15}$ consisting of lead, antimony, and sulfur
fuls *pl of* FUL
-fuls *pl of* -FUL
ful·some \ˈfu̇lsəm *also* -lts-\ *adj* [ME *fulsom,* fr. *ful, full* full + *-som* -some — more at FULL (adj.)] **1 a :** COPIOUS, ABUNDANT **b** *obs* **:** PLUMP, FAT **2** *obs* **:** LUSTFUL, WANTON **3 a :** offensive to sense or appetite **:** NAUSEATING, SICKENING ⟨~ richness of the food⟩ **b :** offensive to moral or aesthetic sensibility **:** REPULSIVE, DISGUSTING ⟨~ prejudices⟩ ⟨~ language⟩ **c :** offensive from insincerity or baseness of motive ⟨~ politeness⟩ ⟨~ praise⟩ ⟨~ compliments⟩ ⟨trying not to be ~ to make up for his coldness at the governor's party —C.S.Forester⟩ **4 :** counter to the norms of propriety or social usage **:** displaying bad taste ⟨the ~ chromium glitter of the escalators —Lewis Mumford⟩ ⟨a ~ prose style⟩ — **ful·some·ly** *adv* — **ful·some·ness** *n* -ES
fulth \ˈfu̇l(t)th\ *n* -S [ME *fulthe, fulth,* fr. *ful, full* full + *-the, -th* -th] *now dial Eng* **:** FULLNESS, REPLETION
ful·ton cat \ˈfu̇ltᵊn-\ *n, usu cap F* [prob. fr. the name *Fulton*] **:** WILLOW CAT
fulup *usu cap, var of* FELUP
ful·vene \ˈfu̇lˌvēn, ˈfəl-\ *n* -S [G *fulven,* fr. L *fulvus* tawny + G *-en* -ene] **:** an unstable yellow hydrocarbon C_6H_6 that is a methylene derivative of cyclopentadiene; *also* **:** any of a series of its derivatives
ful·ves·cent \(ˈ)fu̇l¦vesᵊnt, ¦fəl¦-\ *adj* [L *fulvus* + E *-escent*] **:** somewhat fulvous
ful·vid \ˈfu̇lvəd, ˈfəl-\ *adj* [LL *fulvidus,* fr. L *fulvus*] **:** FULVOUS
ful·vous \-vəs\ *adj* [L *fulvus;* perh. akin to L *flavus* yellow — more at BLUE] **:** dull brownish yellow **:** TAWNY ⟨my neighbor's field turned to a stretch of ~ stubble —Lori Petri⟩ ⟨staining the clearness with its ~ storm water —Victor Canning⟩
fulvous tree duck *n* **:** a long-legged long-necked brownish duck (*Dendrocygna bicolor*) known from several widely separated populations in the Americas, India, and eastern Africa
ful·yie *or* **ful·zie** \ˈfül(y)ē\ *n* -S [ME (Sc) *fulȝe* dung] *Scot* **:** DIRT, FILTH; *specif* **:** street sweepings
fum \ˈfəm\ *n* -S **:** FENG HUANG
fumadiddle *var of* FLUMMADIDDLE
fu·ma·gil·lin \ˌfyüməˈjilən\ *n* -S [*fumagill-* (rearrangement of some of the letters of the species name NL *Aspergillus fumigatus,* fr. *Aspergillus,* genus name + *fumigatus,* specific epithet, fr. L, past part. of *fumigare* to fumigate) + *-in* — more at ASPERGILLUS, FUMIGATE] **:** a crystalline orally effective antibiotic ester of an unsaturated acid produced by a soil fungus (*Aspergillus fumigatus*) and used in the treatment of amebiasis
fu·ma·gine \ˈfyüməˌjēn\ *n* -S [F, fr. NL *Fumagin-, Fumago,* former genus name, fr. L *fumus* smoke] **:** a dark-colored sooty mold found chiefly on greenhouse plants or in southern latitudes and caused by various fungi of the order Erysiphales
fumar- *or* **fumaro-** *comb form* [ISV, fr. NL *Fumaria*] **:** fumaric acid ⟨*fumar*amide⟩ ⟨*fumaro*nitrile⟩
fu·ma·rase \ˈfyüməˌrās, -āz\ *n* -S [ISV *fumar-* + *-ase*] **:** a crystalline enzyme occurring in many animal and plant tissues that accelerates the interconversion of fumaric acid and L-malic acid by hydration and dehydration (as in the Krebs cycle)
fu·ma·rate \-ˌrāt, -rət\ *n* -S [ISV *fumar-* + *-ate*] **:** a salt or ester of fumaric acid
fu·mar·ia \fyüˈma(a)rēə\ *n* [NL, fr. LL, fumitory, fr. L *fumus* smoke + *-aria*] **1** *cap* **:** a genus of annual herbs (family Fumariaceae) with only one petal spurred at the base and a one-seeded globose capsule **2** *pl* **fumari·ae** \-ēˌē\ **:** an extract or dried leaves of the common fumitory formerly used as a tonic and alterative
fu·mar·i·a·ce·ae \fyüˌma(a)rēˈāsēˌē\ *n pl, cap* [NL, fr. *Fumaria,* type genus + *-aceae*] **:** a family of erect or climbing herbs (order Papaverales) of the northern hemisphere and southern Africa with basal or alternate dissected leaves, irregular spurred flowers, and capsular fruit — **fu·mar·i·a·ceous** \⸗¦⸗¦āshəs\ *adj*
fu·mar·ic acid \(ˈ)fyü¦marik-\ *n* [*fumaric* ISV *fumar-* + *-ic*] **:** a crystalline unsaturated dicarboxylic acid HOOCCH=CHCOOH that is found in fumitory and many other plants and is formed from succinic acid as an intermediate in the Krebs cycle, that is made synthetically (as by heating maleic acid), and that is used chiefly in making polyester resins; *trans*-butene-dioic acid — see CIS-TRANS ISOMERISM a
fu·ma·rine \ˈfyüməˌrēn, -rən\ *n* -S [prob. fr. F, fr. NL *Fumaria* + F *-ine*] **:** PROTOPINE
fu·ma·role *also* **fu·me·role** \ˈfyüməˌrōl\ *n* -S [It *fumarola,* modif. of LL *fumariolum* vent, smoke hole, dim. of *fumarium* vent, smoke hole, fr. L, smoke chamber for aging wine, fr. *fumus* smoke + *-arium* -ary] **:** a hole in a volcanic region and usu. in lava from which issue gases and vapors at high temperature — **fu·ma·rol·ic** \¦⸗⸗¦rōlik, -¦räl-\ *adj*
fu·mar·o·yl \fyüˈmarəˌwil\ *or* **fu·ma·ryl** \ˈfyüməˌril\ *n* -S [ISV *fumar-* + *-oyl* or *-yl*] **:** the radical —COCH=CHCO— of fumaric acid
fu·ma·to·ri·um \ˌfyüməˈtōrēəm\ *n* -S [NL, fr. L *fumatus* (past part. of *fumare* to smoke, fr. *fumus* smoke) + *-orium* -ory] **:** an airtight compartment in which vapor may be generated to destroy fungous or insect pests (as on growing plants) **:** a fumigation chamber
¹fum·ble \ˈfəmbəl\ *vb* **fumbled; fumbled; fumbling** \-b(ə)liŋ\ **fumbles** [prob. of Scand origin; akin to Sw *fumla* to fumble, bungle, Norw dial. *fumla*] *vi* **1 a :** to grope for or handle something clumsily, perplexedly, or aimlessly ⟨*fumbled* nervously with her necklace before she answered⟩ **b :** make awkward attempts to do or find something ⟨his numb hands ~ with the shoestring⟩ ⟨*fumbled* in his pocket for a coin⟩ **c :** search by trial and error ⟨a generation that ~s after a fresh outlook on life⟩ **d :** BLUNDER ⟨just when the whole scheme hung in balance he *fumbled*⟩ **2** *archaic* **:** to be impotent in sexual relations **3 :** to speak gropingly or indistinctly ⟨he *fumbled* in answering and made them suspicious⟩ **:** MUMBLE ⟨shyness made his tongue ~⟩ **4 :** to feel one's way or move awkwardly ⟨they *fumbled* along the dark path⟩ ⟨*fumbled* about until the admiral indicated where he was to sit —J.A.Michener⟩ **5 a :** to drop or juggle or fail to play cleanly a ground ball — compare MUFF **b :** to lose hold of a football while handling or running with it ~ *vt* **1 :** to accomplish or bring about by clumsy or groping manipulation ⟨*fumbled* the door open⟩ **2 a :** to feel of or handle gropingly or clumsily ⟨his toes *fumbling* the rough edge of a big rip in the carpet —Raymond Chandler⟩ ⟨he *fumbled* the pages looking for the place⟩ **b :** to deal with in an awkward or blundering way **:** BUNGLE ⟨where adept decisive action is needed he ~s the problem⟩ ⟨he *fumbled* a chance to take the fort by surprise⟩ **3 :** to utter in a groping, indistinct, or blundering way ⟨startled into confusion, he ~s out a few broken sentences⟩ ⟨made to feel inferior if we ~ an unusual word —G.A.Miller⟩ **4** *archaic* **:** to bundle cumbrously or confusedly ⟨send them forth so covered, veiled, and *fumbled* up —John Molle⟩ ⟨~ this, next, and last week's devotion all in a prayer —Thomas Fuller⟩ **5 :** to make (one's way) in a clumsy or groping manner ⟨the baby turtles will ~ their way down to the water's edge —Alan Moorehead⟩ ⟨watch a growing community ~ its way to maturity —T.H. White b.1915⟩ **6 a :** MISPLAY ⟨~ a ground ball⟩ **b :** to lose hold of (a football) while handling or running
²fumble \"\ *n* -S **1 :** an act or instance of fumbling ⟨a long evolution that begins with the ~s, trials and errors of practical men —Charles Frankel⟩ ⟨safe on the shortstop's ~⟩ **2 :** a fumbled ball ⟨fell on the quarterback's ~⟩
fum·bler \ˈfəmb(ə)lə(r)\ *n* -S **:** one that fumbles
fumbling *adj* [fr. pres. part. of *fumble*] **:** marked by groping or clumsiness ⟨a writer . . . so preoccupied with his matter as to be careless and ~ in his manner —Brand Blanshard⟩ — **fum·bling·ly** *adv*
fum·bling·ness *n* -ES **:** the quality or state of being fumbling ⟨was entirely self-taught, and his earliest paintings reveal a certain ~ —R.M.Coates⟩
¹fume \ˈfyüm\ *n* -S [ME, fr. MF *fum,* fr. L *fumus;* akin to OHG *toumen* to be fragrant, Gk *thymos* spirit, mind, courage, Skt *dhūma* smoke] **1 a :** a gaseous emission (as from a burning or evaporating substance) that is usu. odorous and sometimes noxious **:** SMOKE ⟨a thin ~ rising from his pipe and scenting the library⟩ **:** VAPOR ⟨the rain . . . sprang back on itself and the ground was hidden by a white ~ —Audrey Barker⟩ **:** ODOR ⟨noticed the ~s of whiskey when he talked⟩ **b :** an often noxious suspension of particles in air or gas that may be formed in various ways (as by condensation of vapors or by chemical reaction) ⟨the air pollution aspects of smoke and ~s⟩ — usu. used in pl. and sometimes only of suspensions of solid particles in distinction from *mist* **c :** solid material deposited by condensation of fumes ⟨the baghouse ~ in lead smelting⟩ **2 a :** a noxious vapor formerly supposed to rise to the brain from the stomach (as from alcoholic drinks) ⟨a day's idleness to let the ~s of rum-punch . . . get out of his head —David Garnett⟩ **b :** something (as an emotion) that impairs one's reasoning ⟨until the ~s of passion cleared away⟩ **3 :** a state of excited irritation or anger — usu. used in the phrase *in a fume* ⟨might go away in a ~ muttering —Thomas Wood †1950⟩ **4 :** something like a fume in being transient or unsubstantial and noxious or offensive ⟨the all-pervading ~s of sanctimoniousness —Max Ascoli⟩
²fume \"\ *vb* -ED/-ING/-S [ME *fumen,* fr. MF *fumer* to smoke, expose to fumes, fr. L *fumare* to smoke, fr. *fumus*] *vt* **1 a :** to expose to fumes ⟨~ a fabric with acid vapors to develop color effects⟩ **b :** to fill or permeate with fumes (as of incense) **c** *obs* **:** PERFUME ⟨sheets *fumed* with violets —John Marston⟩ **2 :** to give off in or as if in fumes ⟨the freighter was *fuming* thick black smoke⟩ ⟨an itinerant agitator who *fumed* race hatred⟩ **3 a :** to cause (a substance) to emit fumes (as by heating) ⟨~ the slag in a furnace to recover the lead contained⟩ **b :** to produce by fuming; *esp* **:** SUBLIME 1a — usu. used as a past participle ⟨*fumed* litharge⟩ ~ *vi* **1 a :** to emit fumes (as in combustion or chemical action) ⟨hydrogen chloride ~s in moist air⟩ **:** SMOKE, REEK ⟨a cigarette ~s forgotten in the ash tray⟩ ⟨the refinery area ~s with oil⟩ **b :** to act as if generating fumes: as (1) **:** to be in a state of excited irritation or anger ⟨he fretted and *fumed* over the delay⟩ (2) **:** to speak in a fuming manner ⟨he *fumed* at his opponent in an arm-waving, name-calling harangue⟩ **2 :** to rise and pass away in or as if in fumes ⟨a cloud of incense ~s from the censer⟩ ⟨their happiness had suddenly *fumed* away⟩ — **fum·er** \-mə(r)\ *n* -S
fume chamber *or* **fume cupboard** *n, chiefly Brit* **:** a chamber with forced draft used for eliminating undesirable fumes — compare HOOD 3d (2)
fumed oak *n* [*fumed* fr. past part. of ²*fume*] **:** oak given a weathered appearance by exposure to fumes of ammonia
fume·less \ˈfyümləs\ *adj* **:** free from fumes
fumerole *var of* FUMAROLE
¹fu·met \ˈfyümət\ *n* -S [prob. alter. of ME *fume,* fr. MF *fumee,* fr. OF, excrement, fr. fem. of *fumé, femé,* past part. of *fumer, femer* to fertilize with dung, discharge excrement, fr. ML *fimare* to fertilize with dung, fr. L *fimus* dung; prob. akin to L *fumus* smoke] *archaic* **:** the dung of deer
²fumet \"\ *also* **fu·mette** \(ˈ)fyü¦met\ *n* -S [F *fumet* odor, fume of wine or meat, fr. MF, fr. *fumer* to smoke, expose to fumes] **:** a concentrated essence of game or fish, herbs, and spices used in flavoring a sauce
fumewort *or* **fumeroot** \ˈ⸗,⸗\ *n* **:** FUMITORY; *broadly* **:** any of several plants closely related to the fumitories (as some members of the genus *Corydalis*) — usu. used in combination ⟨the yellow and slender ~s⟩
fumid *adj* [L *fumidus* smoky, fr. *fumus* smoke] *obs* **:** SMOKY, VAPOROUS
fu·mig·a·cin \fyüˈmigəsən\ *n* -S [*fumiga-* (fr. NL *fumigatus,* specific epithet of *Aspergillus fumigatus*) + *-cin* (as in *actinomycin, streptothricin*) — more at FUMAGILLIN] **:** a crystalline antibiotic acid $C_{32}H_{44}O_8$ obtained from a soil fungus (*Aspergillus fumigatus*) — called also *helvolic acid*
fu·mi·gant \ˈfyüməgənt, -mēg-\ *n* -S [*fumigate* + *-ant*] **:** a gaseous or readily volatilizable chemical (as hydrogen cyanide or paradichlorobenzene) used as a disinfectant or pesticide — compare AEROSOL 2
fu·mi·gate \ˈfyüməˌgāt, *usu* -ād.+V\ *vt* -ED/-ING/-S [L *fumigatus,* past part. of *fumigare,* fr. *fumus* smoke + *-igare* (akin to L *agere* to drive) — more at AGENT] **1 :** to apply smoke, vapor, or gas to ⟨tribes that ~ bodies to dry and preserve them⟩: as **a** *archaic* **:** to scent with incense or perfume ⟨with fragrant thyme the city ~ —John Dryden⟩ **b :** to treat (as a house or room) with a gas for the purpose of disinfecting or of destroying pests **c :** to make an odor imperceptible in (as a room) esp. by permeation with aromatic fumes **2 :** to remove or conceal what is offensive in ⟨the descriptions of . . . illnesses might very well have been *fumigated* —Clifton Fadiman⟩
fu·mi·ga·tion \ˌfyüməˈgāshən\ *n* -S [ME *fumigacioun,* fr. MF *fumigation,* fr. LL *fumigation-, fumigatio,* fr. L *fumigatus* + *-ion-, -io* -ion] **:** the act or process of fumigating ⟨~ of infested but irreplaceable trees⟩ ⟨jeered at the preliminary charity bout as crass ~⟩
fu·mi·ga·tor \ˈfyüməˌgād·ə(r), -ātə-\ *n* -S [ISV *fumigate* + *-or*] **:** one that fumigates: as **a :** a device or apparatus that generates a gas or vapor for use as a fumigant **b :** FUMIGANT **c** (1) **:** EXTERMINATOR a (2) **:** one who kills insect pests on trees or shrubs by treatment with poisonous gas (3) **:** one who cleans and moth-proofs rugs and upholstered furniture and fumigates them by placing them in an airtight chamber with disks impregnated with hydrocyanic acid
fu·mi·ga·to·ri·um \ˌfyüməgəˈtōrēəm\ *n* -S [NL, fr. L *fumigatus* + *-orium* -ory] **:** FUMATORIUM
fu·mi·ga·to·ry \ˈfyüməgəˌtōrē, -mēg-, -tȯr-, -ri\ *adj* [*fumigate* + *-ory*] **:** having the quality of fumigating
fum·i·ly \ˈfyüməlē\ *adv* **:** in a fumy manner
fum·ing·ly *adv* [*fuming* (pres. part. of ²*fume*) + *-ly*] **:** in a fuming manner **:** ANGRILY ⟨exclaimed ~ that he was not accustomed to such treatment⟩
fuming nitric acid *n* **:** concentrated nitric acid containing dissolved nitrogen oxides prepared as either a colorless to pale yellow or a red to brown corrosive poisonous liquid and used esp. as a nitrating agent and as a powerful oxidizing agent (as in rocket propellants)
fuming sulfuric acid *n* **:** OLEUM 2
fum·ish \ˈfyümish\ *adj, obs* **1 :** emitting or having the character of fumes **:** SMOKY **2 :** tending to fume **:** CHOLERIC
fu·mi·to·ry \ˈfyüməˌtōrē\ *n* -ES [alter. (influenced by E *-ory*) of earlier *fumeterre,* fr. ME *fumetere,* fr. MF, fr. ML *fumus terrae,* fr. L *fumus* smoke + *terrae,* gen. of *terra* earth — more at TERRACE] **:** a plant of the genus *Fumaria; esp* **:** a common European herb (*F. officinalis*)
fumitory family *n* **:** FUMARIACEAE
fumosity *n* -ES [ME *fumosite,* fr. MF & ML; MF *fumosité,* fr. ML *fumositat-, fumositas,* fr. L *fumosus* + *-itat-, -itas* -ity] **1** *obs* **:** the quality or state of having or emitting fumes **2** *obs* **:** a fumy exhalation
fumous *also* **fumose** *adj* [ME, fr. L *fumosus,* fr. *fumus* smoke + *-osus* -ose] *obs* **:** producing, full of, or consisting of fumes **:** SMOKY
fums *pl of* FUM
fu·mu·lus \ˈfyümyələs\ *n* -ES [NL, fr. L *fumus* smoke + NL *-ulus*] **:** a thin cloud resembling a veil and forming at any level
fumy \ˈfyümē\ *adj* **fumier; fumiest** [¹*fume* + *-y*] **:** producing or full of fumes ⟨a bottle of ~ household bleach⟩ ⟨a ~ café⟩
¹fun \ˈfən\ *vb* **funned; funned; funning; funs** [perh. alter. of ME *fonnen* to fool, make a fool of, fr. *fonne* fool, dupe] *vt, now dial* **:** HOAX, TEASE, TRICK, KID ~ *vi* [fr. ²*fun*] **:** to indulge in banter or play **:** speak or act in fun **:** JOKE, FOOL ⟨*funning* about the marriage⟩ ⟨passed the time *funning* till others tired of his horseplay⟩
²fun \"\ *n* -S **1** *obs* **:** a practical joke **:** TRICK, HOAX **2 :** what provides amusement or enjoyment ⟨a book that is ~ to read⟩ ⟨a fellow who is ~ to have around⟩ **:** enjoyable activity ⟨the game was no ~⟩ ⟨picnics are great ~⟩ ⟨didn't know hard study could be so much ~⟩ ⟨sitting on the ground was part of the ~⟩; *specif* **:** playful often boisterous action or speech **:** JOCULARITY **:** RIDICULE ⟨made myself a fine figure of ~ for someone outside —Arthur Grimble⟩ **3 :** the disposition or mood to find or make a cause for amusement **:** PLAYFULNESS ⟨a carefree man who was always full of ~⟩ ⟨has a lot of ~ in him⟩ ⟨don't say that even in ~⟩ **4 :** AMUSEMENT, ENJOYMENT ⟨play cards for ~⟩ ⟨have ~ at the party⟩ ⟨the baby had a lot of ~ with the blocks⟩ ⟨robbed him just for the ~ of it⟩ ⟨never got any ~ out of listening to serious music⟩ **5 :** violent or excited activity or argument **:** FIREWORKS ⟨a rabbit stampeded the herd and then the ~ began⟩ ⟨just toss in the South as a conversation piece and watch the ~ —James Street⟩
syn FUN, JEST, SPORT, GAME, and PLAY agree in designating what provides diversion or amusement or is intended to arouse laughter. FUN implies amusement or an engagement in what interests as an end in itself or applies to what provides this amusement or interest, often also implying a propensity for laughing or for finding a usu. genial cause for laughter or amusement ⟨had such a zest for everything and thought it all such *fun* —O.E.Rölvaag⟩ ⟨make living more *fun,* life more complete —*Printers' Ink*⟩ ⟨a man full of *fun*⟩ JEST occurs in phrases (as *in jest*) or applies to activity or utterance not to be taken seriously, sometimes carrying an implication of ridicule or hoaxing ⟨a man given to making his most significant remarks in *jest*⟩ ⟨make *jest* of very serious problems⟩ SPORT, often interchangeable with FUN ⟨there is a good deal of *sport* in many serious activities⟩ or JEST ⟨play a trick on a friend for the *sport* of it⟩ or GAME, although here usu. generic or applying to activity calling for a certain skill ⟨go at *sport* as if it were a way of life⟩ ⟨the *sport* of fly casting⟩ ⟨the *sport* of tennis⟩ can also imply amusement or provoking of laughter by putting someone or something up to gentle or malicious ridicule ⟨make *sport* of a suggestion⟩ ⟨make a good deal of *sport* out of someone else's misfortune⟩ GAME in a now rare earlier sense of FUN implies a certain ridicule ⟨make *game* of an unfortunate rival⟩ More commonly today it applies to any activity engaged in for fun ⟨a *game* of tennis⟩ ⟨*games* to keep children amused⟩ PLAY, a generic term for all games or amusements, stresses in all senses an opposition to *earnest,* carrying no suggestion of anything but an intent to divert or be diverted ⟨*play* time in a nursery⟩ ⟨made his work *play* by enjoying it thoroughly⟩ ⟨pretend to spank a child in *play*⟩
³fun \"\ *adj* [²*fun*] **1 :** providing fun, entertainment, or amusement ⟨a ~ party⟩ ⟨~ hat⟩ **2 :** full of fun **:** PLEASANT ⟨a ~ night⟩ ⟨have a ~ time⟩
⁴fun \"\ *n* -S [alter. of *whin*] *Scot* **:** FURZE
⁵fun \ˈfün, -üŋ\ *n, pl* **fun** [Jap] **:** a Japanese unit of weight equal to ¹⁄₁₀ momme, .375 grams, or 5.79 grains
fu·nam·bu·la·tion \(ˌ)fyüˌnambyəˈlāshən\ *n* -S [prob. fr. *funambulator,* after such pairs as E *perambulator: perambulation*] **:** ROPEDANCING
fu·nam·bu·la·tor \⸗ˈ⸗⸗ˌlād·ə(r)\ *n* -S [perh. fr. obs. E *funambule,* v., to walk or dance on a rope (prob. fr. L *funambulus,* n., funambulist) + E *-ator*] **:** FUNAMBULIST
fu·nam·bu·la·to·ry \-ˌlə,tōrē\ *adj* [prob. fr. *funambulator,* after such pairs as E *auditor: auditory*] **1 :** relating to or resembling ropedancing **2 :** performing as or as if a ropedancer
fu·nam·bu·list \-ləst\ *n* -S [prob. fr. L *funambulus* funambulist (fr. *funis* rope + *-ambulus* — fr. *ambulare* to walk) + E *-ist* — more at FUNICULUS, AMBLE] **:** ROPEWALKER, ROPEDANCER
fu·nam·bu·lo \-ˌlō\ *n* -ES [It *funambolo, funambulo,* fr. L *funambulus*] **:** FUNAMBULIST
funambulus *n, pl* **funambuli** [L] *obs* **:** FUNAMBULIST
fu·nar·ia \fyüˈna(a)rēə\ *n, cap* [NL, fr. L *funis* rope + NL *-aria*] **:** the type genus of Funariaceae comprising the cord mosses and being characterized by filamentous setae, a gibbous obtusely pyriform capsule, and usu. a double peristome of 16 teeth
fu·nar·i·a·ce·ae \fyüˌna(a)rēˈāsēˌē\ *n pl, cap* [NL, fr. *Funaria* + *-aceae*] **:** a family of acrocarpous true mosses (order Funariales) with annual or biennial erect gametophores — see FUNARIA — **fu·nar·i·a·ceous** \⸗¦⸗¦āshəs\ *adj*
fu·nar·i·a·les \-ēˈā(ˌ)lēz\ *n pl, cap* [NL, fr. *Funaria* + *-ales*] **:** an order of usu. acrocarpous mosses having erect gametophores with an apical rosette of leaves
¹func·tion \ˈfəŋ(k)shən\ *n* -S [L *function-, functio* performance, fr. *functus* (past part. of *fungi* to perform) + *-ion-, -io* -ion; prob. akin to Skt *bhuṅkte* he enjoys] **1 a :** professional or official position **:** OCCUPATION ⟨big business has elevated the ~ of management to the status of the learned professions —*Nation's Business*⟩ ⟨a man combining the dual ~s of chief and sorcerer —J.G.Frazer⟩ **b** *obs* **:** those engaged in an occupation ⟨the scribes are not a sect but a ~ —Samuel Purchas⟩ **2 :** the action for which a person or thing is specially fitted, used, or responsible or for which a thing exists **:** the activity appropriate to the nature or position of a person or thing **:** ROLE, DUTY, WORK ⟨the ~ that older people can perform in city life today⟩ ⟨it is the ~ of stockholders to assume the risk⟩ ⟨outlined the required and permitted ~s vested in the committee⟩ ⟨discharged the ~s of his office with distinction⟩ **:** USE ⟨form follows ~⟩ ⟨glass has an important ~ in modern architecture⟩ **:** PURPOSE ⟨literary criticism serves complex psychological and sociological ~s⟩ ⟨poetry fulfills its ~ when it introduces us to life⟩ **3** *obs* **:** bodily or mental action **:** BEHAVIOR, PERFORMANCE ⟨~ is smothered in surmise —Shak.⟩ **4 a :** an impressive and elaborate religious ceremony **b :** an often formal public or social ceremony or gathering (as a

dinner or reception) ⟨seating notables at official diplomatic ~s⟩ **5 :** one of a group of related actions contributing to a larger action **:** OPERATION ⟨marketing involves the propaganda ~⟩ ⟨the higher human ~s of interpretation and decision⟩: as **a :** the normal and specific contribution of any bodily part (as a tissue, organ, or system) to the economy of a living organism ⟨the primary ~ of any gland is secretion⟩ **b :** syntactic relation (as subject, predicate, qualifier) ⟨*round* has a qualifying ~ in "round eyes"⟩ **c :** a feature of meaning distinguished as characteristic of a type of word ⟨number is a ~ of nouns; tense, of verbs⟩ **d :** the contribution (as of an element, trait, activity) to the consistency or equilibrium of a culture **6 :** either of two magnitudes so related to each other that to values of one there correspond values of the other **:** a correspondence that associates a unique number represented symbolically by $f(x, y, z \ldots)$ with every ordered set of numbers $(x, y, z \ldots)$ each over its domain ⟨the area of a circle is a ~ of its radius because to every value of the radius r there corresponds a unique value of the area A⟩ **7 :** any quality, trait, or fact so related to another that it is dependent upon and varies with it ⟨sand height is not a ~ of sea-level height —*Science*⟩ **8 a :** an expression which contains a variable term and whose meaning or truth is determined when concrete values of the variable are specified **b :** a propositional or sentential function — compare PREDICATE 1b **c :** the rule, law, relation, or operation denoted by such an expression **9 :** characteristic behavior of a compound due to the presence of a particular atom, group of atoms (as an amino group), or mode of union of atoms (as a double bond); *also* **:** the atom, group, or arrangement causing such behavior ⟨a compound of simple ~ is one containing only one kind of ~ —*Chem. Abstracts*⟩ **10 :** the performance or fulfillment of a function **:** FUNCTIONING ⟨the bubbles in the tissues . . . causing altered sensory or motor ~s —H.G.Armstrong⟩ **11 :** an organizational unit performing a group of related acts and processes **:** ACTIVITY ⟨directed all ~s of the department to effect a reduction in force⟩

syn FUNCTION, OFFICE, DUTY, and PROVINCE can signify in common the acts, activity, or operations expected of a person or thing by virtue of his or its nature, structure, status, or position. FUNCTION can apply very comprehensively to person or thing ⟨to fulfill one's *function* as a human being⟩ ⟨one of the *functions* of a chairman is to preside over meetings⟩ ⟨the *function* of the appendix is unknown⟩ ⟨the main *function* of a language is to communicate ideas or feelings⟩ OFFICE, often close to FUNCTION in application to things, usu. applies to the function or work expected of a person by virtue of his trade, profession, or position in relation to others ⟨the *office* of books is not to create bookworms, but independent souls —Howard M. Jones⟩ ⟨the view here taken of the work and *office* of philosophy —John Dewey⟩ ⟨for all these the good *offices* of an editor are needed —*Times Lit. Supp.*⟩ ⟨the hangman addressed himself to his *office* —T.B.Macaulay⟩ ⟨performing the *office* of president in his absence⟩ ⟨it is not the *office* of a friend to meddle too much⟩ DUTY, in this connection, applies to a task one is expected to perform by reason of the obligation inherent in one's position, relationship, or calling ⟨one's *duty* as a citizen is to vote intelligently⟩ ⟨the *duties* of a school principal⟩ ⟨the *duty* of the vicar as a husband and father should not clash with his *duties* as a clergyman⟩ ⟨the *duties* of a clerk⟩ PROVINCE may apply to any duty or function falling under one's jurisdiction, power, competence, and so on ⟨the historian takes for his *province* those human activities which flow from thought —E.J.Tapp⟩ ⟨a question of universal interest which lies in the *province* of the biologist, How did life make its appearance on our planet? —W.J.V.Osterhout⟩ ⟨such issues are deemed beyond the *province* of a court —Felix Frankfurter⟩

2function \"\ *vi* **functioned; functioned; functioning** \-sh(ə)niŋ\ **functions 1 :** to have a function **:** SERVE ⟨shivering ~s to maintain the heat of the body⟩ ⟨an attributive noun ~s as an adjective⟩ **2 :** to carry on a function or be in action **:** OPERATE, WORK ⟨a government ~s through numerous divisions⟩ ⟨war was, when seen ~*ing*, senseless and horrible —Rose Macaulay⟩ ⟨a conductor who ~*ed* also for a time as a music critic —Harriett Johnson⟩ **syn** see ACT

functionaire *var of* 1FUNCTIONARY

func·tion·al \ˈfəŋ(k)shənᵊl, -shnəl\ *adj* **1 a :** of, connected with, or being a function ⟨replace the foreman who supervised all aspects of work with several ~ foremen⟩ ⟨a manager who has ~ authority over a specified process through the several departments⟩ **:** dependently related ⟨many similarities, some ~ to the pastoral nomadic way of life, some due to historical relationship —Elizabeth Bacon⟩ **b :** of, relating to, or based on function or functioning ⟨the problem now is not a constitutional one, it is a ~ one . . . to make the machinery established at San Francisco work —C.M.Eichelberger⟩ ⟨a ~ expert, available to keep the administrative organization . . . in good running order —F.R.M.de Paula⟩ ⟨a ~ presentation of government activities that groups related items regardless of agency or location⟩: as (1) **:** affecting functions but not structure — compare ANATOMIC, ORGANIC, PSYCHOGENIC (2) **:** of or selected by functional representation ⟨delegates elected on a ~ rather than geographical basis⟩ **:** OCCUPATIONAL (3) **:** of or affecting the adaptation of a property (as equipment or a building) to prevailing standards or use ⟨the air-conditioned coach resulted in the ~ obsolescence of the old day coach⟩ **2 :** existing or used to contribute to the development or maintenance of a larger whole **:** having a useful function ⟨a style of writing in which every word is ~⟩ ⟨its trunk and branches were a ~ part of the tree house⟩: as **a :** designed or developed chiefly from the point of view of use **:** UTILITARIAN ⟨~ architecture⟩ ⟨~ fabrics⟩ ⟨the play's dialogue was strictly ~⟩ **b :** relating directly to everyday needs and interests **:** concerned with application in activity **:** PRACTICAL ⟨~ education selects knowledge that is concrete and usable, not abstract and theoretical⟩ **c :** carrying out or consisting of a group of related activities **:** performing a specialized service ⟨the European Defense Community and other ~ arms of the emerging political structure —*New Republic*⟩ ⟨whether ~ cooperation would lead to structural union⟩ **3 :** performing or able to perform its regular function **:** in a functioning condition ⟨vision that is ~ only in bright light⟩ **:** WORKING ⟨the flashlight was still ~ after being dropped⟩ **4 :** placing related functions in an industry or business under the direction of a specialist **:** having specialized administration ⟨~ organization⟩ ⟨~ management⟩ **5 :** FUNCTIONALIST **6 :** relating or attempting to demonstrate the relatedness of any single aspect of culture to the maintenance of an integrated sociocultural whole ⟨in our western civilization the personal life and the ~ life have fallen apart —P.C.W.Gutkind⟩ ⟨~ sociology⟩ **7 :** having no neurological or organic pathology ⟨a ~ psychosis caused by maladjustment⟩ ⟨in the ~ . . . disorders the amount of organ pathology which is discovered, even with careful and thorough examination, is neither sufficient nor impressive enough to account for the symptoms —E.A.Strecker⟩

functional calculus *n* **:** a branch of symbolic logic that utilizes quantifiers in order to deal with propositional functions in addition to the unanalyzed propositions of propositional calculus — called also *predicate calculus;* see HIGHER FUNCTIONAL CALCULUS, LOWER FUNCTIONAL CALCULUS

functional determinant *n* **:** a determinant whose constituents are partial derivatives of one set of variables as to another set, each row containing derivatives of only one variable and each column derivatives as to only one variable

functional finance *n* **:** management of the public debt of a country designed to balance its economy

functional group *n* **:** 1FUNCTION 9

functional illiterate *n* **:** a person unable to read and understand directions ⟨Selective Service ruled that all examinees with less than five years of schooling were *functional illiterates*⟩

func·tion·al·ism \-shənᵊl,izəm, -shnə,li-\ *n* -s **1 :** a psychology in which mental or behavioral processes are viewed as adaptive responses of the whole organism **:** instrumental psychology **2 a :** a philosophy of design (as in architecture) holding that form should be adapted to use, material, and structure **b :** design in which the functionalist principle dominates **3 :** a theory of culture which analyzes the interrelatedness and interdependence of patterns and institutions within a cultural complex or social system and which emphasizes the interaction of these forms in the maintenance of sociocultural unity or in meeting biosocial requirements **4 :** any doctrine or practice that emphasizes practical utility or functional relations ⟨the prevailing outlook of ~ in which a man asks of a thing only "What's it good for?"⟩ **5 :** a system of functional organization or representation **6 :** the theory or practice of achieving cooperation or union between governmental units by gradual integration of economic and other functions rather than immediate political federation ⟨~ in contrast to federalism as a road to European unity —D.C.Stone⟩

1func·tion·al·ist \-shənᵊləst, -shnəl-\ *n* -s **:** one who advocates or employs functionalism

2functionalist \"\ *or* **func·tion·al·is·tic** \ˌfəŋ(k)shənᵊlˈistik, -shnəˈli-\ *adj* [*functionalist* fr. 1*functionalist; functionalistic* fr. 1*functionalist* + *-ic*] **:** of or relating to functionalism (as in architecture or sociology) ⟨the ~ theory of mind⟩

func·tion·al·i·ty \ˌfəŋ(k)shəˈnalədē\ *n* -ES **:** the quality, state, or relation of being functional **:** UTILITY **:** INTERRELATION

func·tion·al·iza·tion \ˌfəŋ(k)shənᵊləˈzāshən, -shnəl-, -ᵊl,īˈz-, -ə,līˈz-\ *n* -s **1 :** the act or process of functionalizing **2 :** the quality or state of being functionalized

func·tion·al·ize \ˈfəŋ(k)shənᵊl,īz, -shnə,līz\ *vt* -ED/-ING/-S **1 :** to cause to be functional **2 :** to organize (as work or management) into units performing specialized tasks

functional load *also* **functional burden** *or* **functional burdening** *n* [prob. trans. of G *funktionelle belastung*] **:** the measure of the actual functioning of a usu. phonemic difference as the sole distinction between two otherwise identical elements (as morphemes or words) of a language

func·tion·al·ly \ˈfəŋ(k)shənᵊlē, -shnəl|, |i\ *adv* **1 :** as regards function ⟨ornamental columns that were ~ unnecessary⟩ **2 :** in a functional manner ⟨a ~ designed auditorium⟩

functional middleman *n* **:** AGENT MIDDLEMAN

functional psychology *n* **:** FUNCTIONALISM 1

functional representation *n* **:** representation in legislative or other political bodies based on the economic and social groups of a community

functional shift *or* **functional change** *n* **:** the process by which a word or form comes to be used in a second or third grammatical function (as a noun used in a verb function) — compare CLASS CLEAVAGE

functional yield *n* [prob. trans. of F *rendement fonctionnel*] **:** FUNCTIONAL LOAD

func·tion·a·rism \ˈfəŋ(k)sh(ə)nə,rizəm\ *n* -s [*functionary* + *-ism*] **:** administration by functionaries **:** OFFICIALISM

1func·tion·ary \ˈfəŋ(k)shə,nerē, -ri\ *also* **func·tion·aire** *or* **func·tion·naire** \ˌ⸗⸗ˌna(a)(ə)r, -ˌne|, |ə\ *n, pl* **functionaries** *also* **functionaires** *or* **functionnaires** [*functionary* (trans. of F *fonctionnaire*) fr. 1*function* + *-ary* (n. suffix); *functionaire, functionnaire* modif. (influenced by E 1*function*) of F *fonctionnaire*, fr. *fonction* function (fr. L *function-, functio* performance) + *-aire* -ary — more at FUNCTION] **:** one who serves in a certain function ⟨characters in melodrama . . . are rather *functionaries* in a preconceived plot —Roger Manvell⟩ ⟨the *functionaries* who summon motorcars for the clubhouse patrons —Frank Sullivan⟩; *esp* **:** one holding a paid position or office in a government or party **:** CIVIL SERVANT ⟨the bureaucracy . . . includes a number of functionaries . . . 1 court clerk . . . 1 forest guard . . . 1 market sweeper —Mary Tew⟩ **:** OFFICIAL ⟨the distinction between members of the Communist party and *functionaries* —Sidney Hook⟩

2functionary \"\ *adj* [1*function* + *-ary* (adj. suffix)] **:** FUNCTIONAL 1b

func·tion·ate \ˈ⸗⸗,nāt\ *vi* -ED/-ING/-S **:** to carry on a natural esp. organic function ⟨interferes with the normal action of the auricle, rendering it . . . powerless to ~ properly —F.A. Faught⟩ — **func·tion·a·tion** \ˌ⸗⸗ˈnāshən\ *n* -s

functioned *past of* FUNCTION

functioning *pres part of* FUNCTION

func·tion·less \ˈfəŋ(k)shənləs\ *adj* **:** having no useful function

functions *pl of* FUNCTION, *pres 3d sing of* FUNCTION

function word *n* **:** a word expressing primarily grammatical relationship (as a preposition, auxiliary verb, conjunction, conjunctive adverb, or relative) — called also *empty word, form word;* compare FULL WORD

func·tor \ˈfəŋ(k)tə(r)\ *n* -s [NL, fr. L *functus* (past part. of *fungi* to perform) + NL *-or* — more at FUNCTION] **1 :** something that performs a function or operation **2 :** a sign for a nonpropositional function; *esp* **:** a syncategorematic sign used to indicate operations in symbolic logic — **func·to·ri·al** \ˌfəŋ(k)ˈtōrēəl\ *adj*

func·tus of·fi·cio \ˌfəŋ(k)təsəˈfishē,ō\ *adj* [L, having performed his duty, having served its purpose] **:** of no further official authority or legal efficacy — used of an officer no longer in office or of an instrument, power, or agency that has fulfilled the purpose of its creation ⟨once exercised, their power of approval or disapproval is *functus officio* —*U.S. Fed. Supp.*⟩

1fund \ˈfənd\ *n* -s [F & L; F *fond* bottom, innermost part, basis & F *fonds* stock or capital, piece of landed property, fr. L *fundus* bottom, piece of landed property — more at BOTTOM] **1** *obs* **a :** the lowest or innermost part **:** BOTTOM **b :** BASIS 3 ⟨what may afford ~ enough for ridicule —Joseph Butler⟩ **2** *obs* **:** FONT **3 a :** a quantity of material resources maintained or available as a source of supply ⟨of a large ~ of land and of a considerable reserve of labor seeking employment in agriculture —Peter Struve⟩ **b :** a supply of intangible resources (as of information, stories, wisdom, goodwill) **4 :** an appropriation (as of permanent revenue) or a deposit or collection of money or its equivalent used as a resource or security: **a :** a sum of money or other resources the principal or interest of which is set apart for a specific objective or activity ⟨a ~ for retirement of bonds⟩ ⟨a campaign ~⟩; *specif* **:** a reserve or accumulation set up by a self-insurer or some public body (as the federal or a state government) for the assumption of certain risks **b :** money on deposit which is held at a specified place and on which checks or drafts can be drawn — usu. used in pl. ⟨prefers payment from foreign concerns in New York ~s⟩ **c :** STOCK, CAPITAL ⟨the ~ of a bank⟩ **d funds** *pl* **:** the stock of the British national debt — called also *public funds;* usu. used with *the* ⟨the holdings of these men in the ~s —W.O. Aydelotte⟩ **5 funds** *pl* **:** available pecuniary resources ordinarily including cash and negotiable paper that can be converted to cash at any time without loss ⟨will be in ~s again after payday⟩ **6 :** an organization administering a special fund ⟨the International Monetary *Fund* . . . conferred with its members —*Britannica Bk. of the Yr.*⟩

2fund \"\ *vt* -ED/-ING/-S **1 a :** to provide and appropriate a fund or permanent revenue to pay the interest of **:** make permanent provision of resources for discharging the interest or principal of ⟨a pledge of customs revenue to ~ government notes⟩ ⟨~ employees' pensions⟩ **b :** to make provision for meeting (a recurrent future liability) by systematic accumulation of a fund ⟨~ a pension plan⟩ **2 :** to place in a fund **:** store up **:** ACCUMULATE ⟨a background of . . . ~*ed* notions of the beautiful —F.J.Mather⟩ **3 :** to convert (a floating or short-time debt or a number of different debts) into a debt that is payable either at a distant date usu. with an option to the debtor to redeem after a certain time or at no definite date and that bears a fixed interest **4 :** to invest (money) in the British public funds

fun·dal \ˈfəndᵊl\ *adj* [*fundus* + *-al*] **:** FUNDIC

fun·da·ment \ˈfəndəmənt\ *n* -s [ME, foundation, alter. (influenced by L *fundamentum*) of *foundement, fundement,* fr. OF *fondement,* fr. L *fundamentum,* fr. *fundare* to found (fr. *fundus* bottom) + *-mentum* -ment] **1 a** *obs* **:** the base on which a structure (as a building or wall) is erected **b :** an underlying ground or theory **:** basic principle ⟨relations between countries based on the ~s of mutual respect and neighborliness⟩ **:** FOUNDATION ⟨archaeology and history are giving us a firm ~ of facts —W.W.Hill⟩ **2 a :** the part of the body on which one sits **:** BUTTOCKS **b :** ANUS **3** *biol* **:** ANLAGE **4 :** the part of a land surface that has not been altered by human activities

1fun·da·men·tal \ˌfəndəˈmentᵊl\ *adj* [ME, fr. LL *fundamentalis* of a foundation, fr. L *fundamentum* + *-alis* -al] **1 :** producing, supporting, regulating, or conditioning something (as a development or system) **:** BASIC, UNDERLYING — often used with *to* ⟨responsibility is ~ to democracy⟩: **a :** serving as an original or generating source **:** being the one from which others are derived **:** PRIMARY ⟨the chronicle is the ~ account of the era from which all later historians drew⟩ **:** FORMATIVE ⟨the various theories developed from that ~ idea⟩ **b :** serving as a basis supporting existence or determining essential structure or function **:** forming the foundation on which something immaterial is built ⟨the productivity ~ to a sound economy⟩ ⟨the ~ rules governing all scientific experiments⟩ **c :** constituting a necessary or elemental quality, part, or condition **:** INDISPENSABLE ⟨American business sagacity had been ~ in that triumph —Bernard DeVoto⟩ **:** IRREDUCIBLE ⟨considered the atom the ~ unit of matter⟩ **2 a :** of or extending or relating to essential structure, function, or facts **:** going to the root of the matter ⟨naive as the child's questions may sound, they are ~ —W.K.Livingstone⟩ **:** RADICAL ⟨distinguish ~ from superficial differences⟩ ⟨monarchy had undergone ~ changes beneath its continuing forms⟩ **:** ELEMENTARY ⟨less ~ and general instruction and more advanced and specialized study⟩; *specif* **:** of or dealing with general principles (as of a chemical or electrical process) rather than practical application **:** PURE ⟨~ science⟩ **b :** concerned with fundamentals (as of life or religion); *specif* **:** FUNDAMENTALIST ⟨replace modernist with ~ Bible lessons⟩ ⟨a preacher who is evangelical, Bible-teaching, and ~⟩ **3 :** serving as or employing an arbitrarily established standard, reference point, or basis of reckoning ⟨~ units of measurement⟩ ⟨taking the equator as the ~ circle⟩ **4 a** *of a musical chord or its position* **:** having the root in the bass **b :** of, relating to, or produced by the lowest component of a complex vibration **5 :** being or constituting the lowest geological formation **:** BASAL ⟨the ~ gneiss of the British isles⟩ **6 :** of central importance **:** PRINCIPAL ⟨lost sight of his ~ purpose in the pursuit of secondary aims⟩ **:** VITAL ⟨such ~ events as birth, marriage, and death⟩ **7 :** forming a sustained or recurring element **:** serving as a background or starting point ⟨used black jute as the ~ material with patterns in colored thread⟩ ⟨in the ~ position the boxer's right arm is leading, his left guarding⟩; *specif* **:** forming the underlying pattern or image in a work of art ⟨the conductor feels . . . doubt as to whether he should beat auxiliary beats or ~ beats —Warwick Braithwaite⟩ ⟨obscures the ~ image of his poem with ornate metaphor⟩ **8 :** belonging to one's innate or ingrained characteristics **:** DEEP-ROOTED ⟨fatigue nor worry nor professordom could extinguish his ~ gaiety —John Mason Brown⟩ **syn** see ESSENTIAL

2fundamental \"\ *n* -s **1 :** something fundamental; *esp* **:** one of the minimum constituents without which a thing would not be what it is or on which all further development is founded — often used in pl. ⟨reading, writing, spelling, and arithmetic are ~s of education⟩ **2 a :** the prime tone of any given harmonic series that gives the heard pitch of the tone sounded — compare OVERTONE **b :** the root of a chord **3 :** the harmonic component of a complex vibration or wave train (as a sound wave) that has the lowest frequency and commonly the greatest amplitude **syn** see PRINCIPLE

fundamental bass *n* **1 :** the root note of a musical chord **2 :** the generating tone of a series of harmonics **3 :** a bass formed of the roots of a succession of harmonics

fundamental complex *n* **1 :** a widespread complex assemblage of highly metamorphic rocks that is the foundation of the geological column **:** the Archean rocks **2 :** an assemblage of metamorphic rocks in any region and of any age that unconformably underlies the sedimentary or unmetamorphosed rocks of the region

fundamental education *n* **:** preparation of children or adults without opportunity for traditional formal schooling (as in underdeveloped areas) for effective participation in community life through instruction in basic facts and skills (as of literacy, agriculture, homemaking, hygiene, citizenship)

fun·da·men·tal·ism \ˌ⸗⸗ˈmentᵊl,izəm\ *n* -s [1*fundamental* + *-ism*] **1 a** *often cap* **:** a militantly conservative movement in American Protestantism originating around the beginning of the 20th century in opposition to modernist tendencies and emphasizing as fundamental to Christianity the literal interpretation and absolute inerrancy of the Scriptures, the imminent and physical second coming of Jesus Christ, the virgin birth, physical resurrection, and substitutionary atonement **b :** the beliefs on which this movement was founded **c :** adherence to the attitude opposing modernism and to the literalist doctrines of fundamentalism ⟨a minister noted for his strict ~⟩ **2 :** a movement or attitude similar in a significant respect (as literalism or strict adherence to traditional beliefs) to the American religious fundamentalism ⟨Muslim ~⟩ ⟨~ in education stresses the three R's⟩

1fun·da·men·tal·ist \-ᵊləst\ *n* -s [1*fundamental* + *-ist*] **1** *sometimes cap* **:** an adherent or proponent of Protestant fundamentalism **2 :** an extreme conservative; *esp* **:** one who attacks any deviation from certain doctrines and practices he considers essential (as to a religious, political, or educational system) ⟨a political ~ . . . could reduce the shadings of any political controversy into a black-and-white conflict between free enterprise and socialism —*Time*⟩ **3** *often cap* **:** a member of a small dissident Mormon sect continuing to practice polygamy after its outlawry in 1890

2fundamentalist \ˌ⸗⸗ˌ⸗⸗⸗\ *or* **fun·da·men·tal·is·tic** \ˌ⸗⸗ˌ⸗⸗ˈistik, -tēk\ *adj* [2*fundamentalist* fr. 1*fundamentalist; fundamentalistic* fr. 1*fundamentalist* + *-ic*] **:** of, adhering to, or marked by fundamentalism ⟨comparing the neoorthodox with the ~ position⟩ ⟨a ~ revival preacher⟩ ⟨an economic outlook strongly ~ in tone⟩

fun·da·men·tal·i·ty \ˌfəndə,menˈtalədē, -,mən-\ *n* -ES **:** the quality or state of being fundamental

fundamental law *n* **:** the organic or basic law of a state or political subdivision with which all departments of government including the lawmaking body must conform **:** CONSTITUTION ⟨judged the statute passed by the legislature to be contrary to the *fundamental law* of the land⟩

fun·da·men·tal·ly \ˌfəndəˈmentᵊlē, -ᵊli *sometimes* ⸗-tlē *or* ⸗-tli\ *adv* [ME *fundamentalli,* fr. *fundamental* + *-li* -ly] **:** in a fundamental manner **:** in the manner of a primary source ⟨animals are ~ dependent on plant life⟩ **:** in essential structure or function ⟨systems ~ different⟩ ⟨~ all forms of mathematics are short cuts for the operations of grade-school arithmetic —Robert Bendiner⟩ **:** in fundamental disposition ⟨a ~ honest person⟩ **:** BASICALLY

fun·da·men·tal·ness \ˌ⸗⸗ˈmentᵊlnəs\ *n* -ES **:** the quality or state of being fundamental

fundamental particle *n* **:** ELEMENTARY PARTICLE

fundamental tissue *n* **:** plant tissue other than dermal and vascular tissues that consists typically of relatively undifferentiated parenchymatous and supportive cells

fundamental tone *n* **:** FUNDAMENTAL 2

fundaments *pl of* FUNDAMENT

fun·da·men·tum \ˌfəndəˈmentəm\ *n* -s [L, lit., foundation — more at FUNDAMENT] **:** a logical basis or ruling principle **:** GROUND

fun·da·tri·ge·nia \ˌfən,dā·trəˈjēnyə, -nēə\ *n, pl* **fundatrigeni·ae** \-nē,ē\ [NL, fr. *fundatri-* (fr. *fundatrix*) + *-genia* (irreg. fr. Gk *-genēs* born) — more at -GEN] **:** a viviparous parthenogenetic wingless female aphid produced by a fundatrix and giving rise to further wingless forms or to migrants — **fun·da·tri·gen·ic** \ˌ⸗ˌ⸗⸗ˈjenik\ *adj*

fun·da·trix \ˌfənˈdā·triks\ *n, pl* **fundatri·ces** \ˌfənˈdā·trə,sēz, fəndəˈtrī(,)sēz\ [NL, fr. LL, foundress, fem. of L *fundator* founder, fr. *fundatus* (past part. of *fundare* to found, fr. *fundus* bottom) + *-or* — more at BOTTOM, -TRIX] **:** a viviparous parthenogenetic winged or wingless female aphid produced on the primary host plant from an overwintering fertilized egg

funded *past of* FUND

funded debt *also* **funded liability** *n* [*funded* fr. past part. of 2*fund*] **:** FIXED LIABILITY; *specif* **:** BONDED DEBT

fundholder \ˈ⸗,⸗⸗\ *n* **1 :** one that has money invested in the British public funds **2 :** one that holds stocks, bonds, or other funds as a mere investment

1fundi *pl of* FUNDUS

2fun·di \ˈfəndē\ *n* -s [perh. fr. Limba *fandi ha* grass] **:** a tropical African grass (*Digitaria exilis*) cultivated for its seed that resembles millet

fun·dic \ˈfəndik\ *adj* [*fundus* + *-ic*] **:** of or relating to a fundus

fundic gland *n* **:** one of the tubular glands of the fundus of the stomach secreting pepsin and mucus — compare CHIEF CELL 1, PARIETAL CELL

funding *pres part of* FUND
fund·less \'fəndləs\ *adj* **:** being without funds
fun·do \'fün(,)dō\ *n* -s [Sp, country estate, fr. L *fundus* bottom, piece of landed property] **:** a large agricultural estate in Chile
funds *pl of* FUND, *pres 3d sing of* FUND
funduck *var of* FONDUK
fun·du·line \'fəndə,līn, 'fənjə-\ *adj* [NL *Fundulinae* subfamily of fishes including the common killifishes, fr. *Fundulus*, type genus + *-inae*] **:** of or relating to the genus *Fundulus*
fun·du·lus \-ləs\ *n* [NL, fr. L *fundus* bottom + NL *-ulus*] **1** *cap* **:** a genus of carnivorous cyprinodont fishes including the common killifishes **2** *pl* **fundulus :** any fish of the genus *Fundulus*
fun·dus \'fəndəs\ *n, pl* **fun·di** \-,dī\ [NL, fr. L, bottom, piece of landed property — more at BOTTOM] **1 :** the bottom of or part opposite the aperture of the internal surface of a hollow organ of the body: as **a :** the greater curvature of the stomach **b :** the lower back part of the bladder **c :** the large upper end of the uterus **d :** the part of the eye opposite the pupil **2** [L] *Roman & civil law* **:** LAND, BUILDINGS **:** land with buildings affixed thereto **:** REAL ESTATE
fun·du·scop·ic *also* **fun·do·scop·ic** \ˌfəndə¦skäpik\ *adj* [*funduscopic* fr. *fundus* + *-scopic* (as in *microscopic*); *fundoscopic* fr. *fundo-* (fr. *fundus*) + *-scopic* (as in *microscopic*)] **:** of, relating to, or by means of funduscopy
fun·dus·co·py \,fən'dəskəpē\ *also* **fun·dos·co·py** \-dä̇s-\ *n* -ES [*funduscopy* fr. *fundus* + *-scopy*; *fundoscopy* fr. *fundo-* (fr. *fundus*) + *-scopy*] **:** ophthalmoscopic examination of the fundus of the eye
fu·ne·bri·al \(')fyü¦nēbrēəl, -neb-\ *adj* [L *funebris* funereal (fr. *funus* funeral) + E *-al*] **:** FUNEREAL
funebrious *or* **funebrous** *adj* [*funebrious* fr. L *funebris* + E *-ous*; *funebrous* fr. L *funebris* + E *-ous*] *obs* **:** FUNEREAL
¹fu·ner·al \'fyün(ə)rəl\ *adj* [ME, fr. LL *funeralis*, fr. L *funer-*, *funus* funeral (n.) + *-alis* -al; perh. akin to ON *deyja* to die — more at DIE] **1 :** of, relating to, or constituting a funeral ⟨~ notices in the newspaper⟩ ⟨made the ~ arrangements⟩ ⟨attended his ~ service⟩ **2 :** forming part of, connected with, or used in connection with a funeral or related observances ⟨preached the ~ sermon⟩ ⟨marched in the ~ procession⟩ ⟨a grave covered with ~ flowers⟩ ⟨insurance covered all the ~ expenses⟩ **3 :** FUNEREAL 2 ⟨a sky that was dull and ~⟩
²funeral \"\ *n* -s [ME *funerelles* (pl.), fr. MF *funerailles* (pl.), fr. ML *funeralia* (pl.), fr. LL *funeralia*, neut. pl. of *funeralis*, adj.] **1 a :** the observances held in honor or on behalf of one who has died ⟨dances held on the occasion of a chieftain's ~⟩ ⟨Egyptian animals had their ranks . . . and their ~s sometimes rivaled in magnificence those of the pharaohs —Elizabeth Lee⟩; *esp* **:** a rite or service for a dead person held ordinarily in the presence of the body before burial or cremation ⟨a church ~ with a Scripture reading and a eulogy⟩ ⟨a ~ conducted by his fellow Masons⟩ ⟨given a military ~ in the fort⟩ — compare COMMITTAL, MEMORIAL SERVICE, REQUIEM **b funerals** *pl, obs* **:** a funeral ceremony or sermon **:** OBSEQUIES ⟨his ~s were performed very solemnly in the collegiate church at Westminster —Thomas Fuller⟩ **2** *now dial* **:** a funeral sermon ⟨after preaching a man's ~ he walked down to pay his respects to the departed —A.W.Long⟩ **3 :** a funeral party on its way to the funeral or committal **:** a funeral procession ⟨the ~ is expected to reach the cemetery at 1:30⟩ **4 a :** the end of the existence of something ⟨planning the ~ of the opposition party⟩ **b** *obs* **:** DEATH **5 :** a matter of concern to one **:** a problem that one must solve **:** LOOKOUT ⟨I didn't see how the prom committee could handle it, but it wasn't my ~ —Albert Halper⟩
funeral car *or* **funeral coach** *n* **:** HEARSE 4
funeral certificate *n* **:** a certificate filed in 16th and 17th century England and Ireland by an officer of arms attesting the use of only authorized arms at the funeral of an armigerous person and now valued as a source of detailed genealogical and armorial information
funeral chapel *n* **1 :** a room in a funeral home used for funerals and often for the viewing of the deceased by mourners **2 :** a building containing a funeral chapel **:** FUNERAL HOME
funeral director *n* **:** one whose profession is the management of funeral and burial preparations and observances and who is usu. an embalmer — called also *mortician, undertaker*
funeral home *or* **funeral parlor** *n* **:** an establishment with facilities for the preparation of the dead for burial or cremation, for the viewing of the body, and for funerals
fu·ner·al·ize \'fyün(ə)rə,līz\ *vt* -ED/-ING/-S *dial* **:** to hold a funeral or memorial service for ⟨put off *funeralizing* him⟩
funeral pie *n* [prob. so called fr. a Pennsylvania Dutch custom of serving it at funerals] **:** pie made of raisins
fu·ner·ary \'fyünə,rerē, -eri\ *adj* [L *funerarius*, fr. *funer-*, *funus* + *-arius* -ary] **:** of, used for, or associated with burial **:** FUNERAL ⟨the ~ rites of the deceased ruler⟩ **:** MORTUARY ⟨a ~ monument⟩ **:** BURIAL ⟨a pharaoh's ~ chamber⟩
fu·ne·re·al \(')fyü¦nirēəl, -nēr-\ *adj* [L *funereus* funereal (fr. *funer-*, *funus* + *-eus* -eous) + E *-al*] **1 :** of or belonging to a funeral ⟨organ works . . . suited to both marital and ~ occasions —Virgil Thomson⟩ **2 :** befitting or suggesting a funeral (as in appearance or mood) ⟨an almost ~ gloom seemed to have descended —Jack London⟩ ⟨the ~ pace of the bullock carts —E.E.Shipton⟩ **:** oppressively solemn ⟨the butler . . . admitted us with silent ~ dignity —W.H.Wright⟩ **:** GLOOMY ⟨a large dark room furnished in a ~ manner with black horsehair —Charles Dickens⟩ — **fu·ne·re·al·ly** \-əlē, -li\ *adv*
fu·nest \(')fyü¦nest\ *adj* [F *funeste*, fr. L *funestus*, fr. *funer-*, *funus*] **:** portending death or evil **:** FATAL, DIRE, DOLEFUL
fun fair *n, chiefly Brit* **:** AMUSEMENT PARK
funfest \'₌,₌\ *n* **:** a gathering for amusements ⟨turned the monthly meeting of their dance group into a public ~⟩ ⟨the town's annual ~ attracts crowds of tourists⟩
¹fung \'fəŋ\ *Scot var of* FUNK
²fung \'fu̇ŋ\ *also* **funj** \'nj\ *or* **fun·ji** \'n(,)jē\ *n, pl* **fung** *or* **fungs** *also* **funj** *or* **funjes** *or* **funji** *or* **funjis** *usu cap* **1 a :** a Negroid people dominant in Sennar **2 :** a member of such people **3 :** the language of the Fung people
¹fun·gal \'fəŋgəl\ *adj* [NL *Fungales*] **1 :** FUNGOUS **2 :** consisting of fungi
²fungal \"\ *n* -s [NL *Fungales*] **:** FUNGUS
fun·ga·les \,fəŋ'gā(,)lēz\ *n pl, cap* [NL, fr. L *fungus* + NL *-ales*] *in some esp former classifications* **:** a group coextensive with Fungi
fun·gate \'fəŋ,gāt\ *vi* -ED/-ING/-S [*fungus* + *-ate*] **:** to assume a fungous form or grow rapidly like a fungus — **fun·ga·tion** \,fəŋ'gāshən\ *n* -s
fung-hwang *var of* FÊNG HUANG
¹fungi *pl of* FUNGUS
²fun·gi \'fən,jī, 'fəŋ,gī\ *n pl, cap* [NL, fr. L, pl. of *fungus* — more at FUNGUS] **:** a division or other major group of lower plants that is often included in Thallophyta coordinate to Algae, that includes a varied assemblage of saprophytic and parasitic plants which lack chlorophyll, and that comprises the classes Phycomycetes, Ascomycetes, Basidiomycetes, and Fungi Imperfecti, and usu. also the Myxomycetes and Schizomycetes
fungi- *comb form* [perh. fr. NL, fr. L *fungus*] **:** fungus ⟨*fungicolous*⟩ ⟨*fungiform*⟩
fun·gia \'fənjēə, 'fəŋgēə\ *n, cap* [NL, fr. L *fungus* + NL *-ia*] **:** a genus (the type of the family Fungiidae) of madrepores comprising the typical mushroom corals — **fun·gi·an** \-ēən\ *adj or n*
fun·gi·bil·i·ty \,fənjə'biləd·ē\ *n* -ES **:** the quality or state of being fungible
¹fun·gi·ble \'fənjəbəl\ *n* -s [NL *fungibilis*, adj., fungible] **:** goods that are fungible — usu. used in pl. ⟨~s loaned under a contract of mutuum⟩
²fungible \"\ *adj* [NL *fungibilis*, fr. L *fungi* to perform + *-ibilis* -ible — more at FUNCTION] **1 :** of such a kind or nature that one specimen or part may be used in place of another specimen or equal part in the satisfaction of an obligation — used of things that can be counted, weighed, or measured and are consumed or alienated by use (as food, coal, oil, lumber) ⟨~ goods enjoyed under the usufruct of property⟩ **2 :** capable of mutual substitution **:** INTERCHANGEABLE
fun·gic \'fənjik, 'fəŋgik\ *adj* [ISV *fung-* (fr. L *fungus*) + *-ic*; orig. formed as F *fongique*] **:** of or relating to fungi
fun·gi·ci·dal \¦fənjə¦sīdᵊl, ¦fəŋgə-\ *adj* [*fungicide* + *-al*] **1 :** destroying fungi ⟨a ~ compound for use in skin infections⟩; *broadly* **:** preventing further ravage (as of plants, cloth, or wood) by a fungus by killing or inactivating it ⟨the ~ action of the solution in the timber⟩ **2 :** of or relating to a fungicide — compare FUNGISTATIC — **fun·gi·cid·al·ly** \-ᵊlē, -ᵊli\ *adv*
fun·gi·cide \'₌₌,sīd\ *n* -s [ISV *fungi-* + *-cide*] **:** an agent that destroys fungi; *broadly* **:** an agent hostile to fungi (as a fungistat or seed disinfectant)
fun·gi·cid·in \¦₌₌¦sīdᵊn\ *n* -s [*fungicide* + *-in*] **:** NYSTATIN
¹fun·gid \'fənjəd, 'fəŋgəd\ *adj* [prob. irreg. fr. NL *Fungiidae*, fr. *Fungia* + *-idae*] **:** of or relating to the genus *Fungia* or the family Fungiidae
²fungid \"\ *n* -s [prob. irreg. fr. NL *Fungiidae*] **:** a madrepore of the genus *Fungia* or the family Fungiidae
fun·gi·form \'fənjə,fȯrm 'fəŋgə-\ *adj* [prob. fr. NL *fungiformis*, fr. *fungi-* + *-formis* -form] **:** shaped like a mushroom
fungiform papilla *n* [prob. trans. of NL *papilla fungiformis*] **:** any of numerous papillae on the upper surface of the tongue that are flat-topped and noticeably red from the richly vascular stroma and that usu. contain taste buds
fungi im·per·fec·ti \-,impə(r)'fek,tī\ *n pl, cap F&I* [NL, lit., imperfect fungi] **:** a large and heterogeneous group of fungi comprising forms whose life cycle is imperfectly known or lacks the sexual stage, including many that are undoubtedly ascomycetes or more rarely basidiomycetes for which the perfect stage exists but has not been identified, and being usu. divided among the orders Sphaeropsidales, Melanconiales, Moniliales, and Mycelia sterilia
fung·inert \'fənjə,nərt, 'fəŋgə-, ,₌₌'₌\ *adj* [*fungus* + *inert*] **:** not supporting fungous growth
fun·gi·sta·sis \,fənjə'stāsəs, ,fəŋgə-, -'stasəs, ,fən'jistəsəs, ,fəŋ'gi-\ *n* [*fungi-* + *-stasis*] **:** fungistatic action
fun·gi·stat \'fənjə,stat, 'fəŋgə-\ *n* -s [*fungi-* + *-stat*] **:** a fungistatic agent
fun·gi·stat·ic \¦₌₌¦stad·ik\ *adj* [*fungi-* + *static*] **:** capable of inhibiting the growth of fungi without destroying them — compare FUNGICIDAL — **fun·gi·stat·i·cal·ly** \-d·ək(ə)lē\ *adv*
fun·gi·tox·ic \-¦täksik\ *adj* [*fungi-* + *toxic*] **:** toxic to fungi — **fun·gi·tox·ic·i·ty** \,₌₌,täk'sisəd·ē\ *n*
fun·giv·o·rous \¦fən¦jivərəs, ¦fəŋ¦gi-\ *adj* [prob. fr. (assumed) NL *fungivorus*, fr. NL *fungi-* + L *-vorus* -vorous] **:** feeding customarily on or in fungi **:** MYCETOPHAGOUS
fun·go \'fəŋ(,)gō\ *n, pl* **fungoes** [origin unknown] **1 :** a fly ball hit for practice purposes by a player who tosses the ball into the air and bats it as it comes down **2** *or* **fungo bat :** a lightweight bat that is longer and thinner than the ordinary bat and is used for fungo hitting
¹fun·goid \'fəŋ,gȯid\ *adj* [prob. fr. (assumed) NL *fungoides*, fr. L *fungus* + NL *-oides* -oid] **1 :** resembling a fungus: as **a :** having a mushroom shape or spongy or fleshy texture ⟨a ~ ulcer⟩ **b :** growing rapidly ⟨the ~ growth of bureaucracy —Eric Partridge⟩ **2** *chiefly Brit* **:** FUNGOUS 1a, 1b ⟨dampness promotes a ~ growth⟩
²fungoid \"\ *n* -s **:** a fungoid growth
fun·gol·o·gist \,fəŋ'gäləjəst\ *n* -s [*fungology* + *-ist*] **:** MYCOLOGIST
fun·gol·o·gy \-jē\ *n* -ES [*fungus* + *-o-* + *-logy*] **:** MYCOLOGY
fun·gose \'fəŋ,gōs\ *adj* [L *fungosus*] **:** FUNGOUS
fun·gos·i·ty \,fəŋ'gäsəd·ē\ *n* -ES [prob. fr. (assumed) NL *fungositat-*, *fungositas*, fr. L *fungosus* fungous + *-itat-*, *-itas* -ity] **1 :** the quality or state of being fungous **2 :** a fungous excrescence
fun·gous *also* **fun·gus** \'fəŋgəs\ *adj* [*fungous* fr. ME, fr. L *fungosus*, fr. *fungus* + *-osus* -ose; *fungus* alter. (influenced by *fungus*, n.) of *fungous*] **1 a :** of, relating to, or having the characteristics of a fungus or the Fungi ⟨an old stump with a flourishing ~ growth⟩ **b :** caused by a fungus ⟨a ~ disease⟩ **c :** infected by a fungus ⟨a dangerous shower stall with . . . *fungus* walls —Jean Stafford⟩ **2 :** FUNGOID 1
¹fun·gus \'fəŋgəs\ *n, pl* **fun·gi** \'fən,jī, 'fəŋ,gī\ *also* **funguses** [L, prob. modif. of Gk *spongos* sponge, prob. of non-IE origin; akin to the source of Arm *sung* sponge] **1 :** any of numerous chiefly saprophytic or parasitic plants that constitute the division Fungi; lack true chlorophyll; have a body made up of single cells or of filamentous coenocytic or septate hyphae arranged in a soft mycelium or in some cases partially disposed in complex highly specialized and characteristic fruiting bodies; often exhibit complex alternation of generations with very distinct sexual and asexual phases; include the molds, mildews, rusts, smuts, mushrooms, toadstools, and puffballs, and usu. the yeasts, bacteria, and slime molds; and are often destructive pathogens of plants, man, and lower animals but have representatives that are used for food or are greatly valued for the organic fermentations that they produce ⟨a cellar wall covered with ~⟩ ⟨a *fungus*-proof coating for leather⟩ ⟨edible ground *fungi*⟩ **2** [LL or obs. F; obs. F, fr. MF, fr. LL, fr. L, fungus (plant)] **:** an abnormal spongy growth; *esp* **:** a mass of spongy granulations **3 :** infection with a fungus or disease caused by it; *specif* **:** a serious highly contagious skin disease of freshwater fishes esp. in hatcheries and aquaria caused by a mold (*Saprolegnia ferax*) **4 :** something resembling a fungus ⟨the blighting of everything fair . . . with the garish ~ of greed —Herman Wouk⟩
²fungus \"\ *vi* -ED/-ING/-ES **:** to become infected with a fungus ⟨a few impounded Chinook, however, ~*ed* rapidly and . . . usually died —*Scientific American*⟩
fungused *adj* [fr. past part. of ²*fungus*] **:** infected with or affected by fungus **:** having a fungous growth
fungus gall *n* **:** a malformation of a plant resulting from an attack of a parasitic fungus
fungus garden *n* **:** a growth of fungus in the nests of various ants and beetles that is tended and used by them for food — compare AMBROSIA BEETLE, BROMATIUM
fungus gnat *n* **:** any of numerous small two-winged flies constituting the families Mycetophilidae and Sciaridae and having larvae that feed on fungi
fungus root *n* **:** MYCORRHIZA
fun house *n* **:** a building in an amusement park containing various devices designed to startle or amuse (as distorting mirrors, unexpected air blasts, fantastic lighted scenes) and arranged along a passage through which patrons walk
fu·nic \'fyünik\ *adj* [*funis* + *-ic*] **:** of, relating to, or originating in the umbilical cord
fu·ni·cle \'fyünəkəl\ *n* -s [NL *funiculus*] **:** FUNICULUS
¹fu·nic·u·lar \(')fyü¦nikyələ(r), f(y)ə'n-\ *adj* [L *funiculus* + E *-ar*] **1 :** dependent on the tension of a cord or cable **2 :** having the form of or associated with a cord **3** [NL *funiculus* + E *-ar*] **:** of or consisting of a funiculus
²funicular \"\ *or* **funicular railway** *also* **fu·nic·u·laire** \₌¦₌₌¦la(a)(ə)r, -¦le|, |ə\ *n* -s [²*funicular* (trans. of F *funiculaire*, n.) fr. ¹*funicular*; *funicular railway* (prob. trans. of F *chemin de fer funiculaire*) fr. ¹*funicular* + *railway*; *funiculaire* fr. F *funiculaire*, n., fr. *funiculaire*, adj., funicular, fr. L *funiculus* + F *-aire* -ary (fr. L *-arius*)] **:** a cable railway ascending a mountain; *esp* **:** one having the weight of an ascending car partly or wholly counterbalanced by the weight of a descending car
funicular polygon *n* **1 :** an open or closed figure that is not necessarily plane and that is formed by a rope or cord acted upon at a number of points by forces acting in various directions **2 :** a figure representing lines of resultant stress in a rigid body acted upon at various points by forces that may or may not be concurrent and may or may not be coplanar
fu·nic·u·li·tis \₌,₌₌'līd·əs\ *n* -ES [NL, fr. *funiculus* + *-itis*] **:** inflammation of the spermatic cord
fu·nic·u·lus \fyü'nikyələs, f(y)ə'n-\ *n, pl* **funicu·li** \-,lī, -,lē\ [NL, fr. L, small rope, dim. of *funis* rope; perh. akin to Gk *thōminx* cord] **1 :** any of various bodily structures more or less like a cord in form: **a :** UMBILICAL CORD **b :** one of the small bundles of fibers of which large nerves are made up **c :** any of certain bands of white matter in the brain and spinal cord; *specif* **:** COLUMN 6c(1) **d :** SPERMATIC CORD **2 a :** the stalk of an ovule **b :** the hyphal cord attaching the peridiole to the peridium in certain fungi of the family Nidulariaceae **3 a :** a band of mesoblastic tissue extending from the stomach to the body wall in bryozoans **b :** the part of the antenna of an insect situated between the pedicel and the club **c :** a dorsal ligament connecting the petiole and propodeum of certain hymenoptera
fu·ni·pendulous \¦fyünə+\ *adj* [L *funis* rope + E *pendulous*] **:** suspended by a rope or cord
fu·nis \'fyünəs\ *n* -ES [NL, fr. L, rope] **:** UMBILICAL CORD
funj *or* **funji** *var of* FUNG
¹funk \'fəŋk\ *n* -s [prob. of F dial. origin; akin to F dial. (French Flanders) *funquer* to give off smoke, F dial. (Picardy) *funquer, finquer*; these fr. ONF *funkier* to give off smoke, fr. (assumed) VL *fumicare*, alter. (influenced by such words as L *communicare* to share, impart, communicate) of L *fumigare* to give off smoke, fumigate — more at FUMIGATE] **:** a strong offensive smell
²funk \"\ *vb* -ED/-ING/-S [prob. of F dial. origin; akin to F dial. (French Flanders) *funquer* to give off smoke, F dial. (Picardy) *funquer, finquer*] *vt* **1 :** to subject to offensive smell or smoke **2 :** to use (as a pipe) in smoking ~ *vi* **:** to emit an offensive smell or smoke
³funk \'fu̇ŋk, 'fəŋk\ *n* -s [perh. fr. (assumed) obs. E *funk* spark, fr. ME *funke*, prob. fr. MD *vonke, vunke*; akin to OHG *funcho* spark, ON *funi* fire, Goth *fon*, OPruss *panno*, OHG *fiur* — more at FIRE] *dial Brit* **:** ³PUNK 2
⁴funk \'fəŋk\ *vi* -ED/-ING/-S [prob. imit.] **1** *chiefly Scot* **:** ¹KICK 1 **2** *chiefly Scot* **:** to give vent to a rage or temper
⁵funk \", *dial Brit* " *or* 'fu̇ŋk\ *n* -s **1** *dial Brit* **:** BLOW; *specif* **:** ²KICK 1 **2 :** a fit of ill humor **:** RAGE
⁶funk \'fəŋk\ *n* -s [prob. fr. obs. Flem *fonck* perturbation] **1 a :** a state of paralyzing fear or timidity ⟨the man was in such a ~ that he would not use his legs —Sinclair Lewis⟩ ⟨pure nerve and bluff on his part and pure ~ on the part of his opponents then saved him —*Nation*⟩ **b :** a depressed state of mind ⟨in a deep, blue ~ about life in the city . . ., she wanted to flee —Bill Hosokawa⟩ **2** [⁷*funk*] **:** one that funks **:** SHIRKER, COWARD ⟨he must be a bit of a ~ . . . to be afraid of a poor old lady —L.P.Hartley⟩
⁷funk \"\ *vb* -ED/-ING/-S [prob. fr. ⁶*funk*] *vi* **:** to become frightened and shrink back **:** FLINCH, PANIC ⟨often . . . I have ~*ed* completely, such as the time I went up to the top of the 30-foot Olympic diving tower —Paul Gallico⟩ ~ *vt* **:** to funk at: **a :** to be afraid of **:** DREAD ⟨the seventeen-year-old . . . ~s riding the black horse but takes it on to please his dad —Leslie Rees⟩ ⟨it isn't a natural thing for a boy to ~ water —*Strand Mag.*⟩ **b :** to shrink from undertaking or facing ⟨every officer had either bungled or had ~*ed* the fight —R.H. Davis⟩ ⟨if the colleges ~ their job of turning out fully educated men —*New Yorker*⟩
⁸funk \"\ *n* -s *usu cap* [*Funk* (surname of *Peter Funk*) — more at PETER FUNK] **:** PETER FUNK
funk·er \'fəŋkə(r)\ *n* -s [⁷*funk* + *-er*] **:** ⁶FUNK 2
funk hole *n* [⁶*funk*] **1 :** DUGOUT 2 **2 :** a place of safe retreat ⟨*funk holes* on the bridge and below decks plated with armor —Hanson W. Baldwin⟩ ⟨joined a volunteer corps as a *funk hole* to evade real military service —*Times Hist. of the War*⟩
¹fun·kia \'fəŋkēə, 'fu̇ŋ-\ [NL, irreg. fr. C. H. *Funck* †1839 Ger. druggist and botanist + NL *-ia*] *syn of* HOSTA
²funkia \"\ *n* -s [NL *Funkia*] **:** PLANTAIN LILY
funk·i·ness \'fəŋkēnəs\ *n* -ES **:** the quality or state of being funky
funk money *n* [⁶*funk*] *Brit* **:** HOT MONEY
¹funky \'fəŋkē\ *adj* -ER/-EST [⁶*funk* + *-y*] **:** being in a state of funk **:** PANICKY ⟨if he did not give up to you like a ~ traveler to a highwayman —George Meredith⟩
²funky \"\ *adj* -ER/-EST [¹*funk* + *-y*] **1 :** MUSTY 2 **2 :** having an offensive odor **:** FOUL ⟨the ~ smell of stale bedclothes —James Jones⟩
funmaker \'₌,₌₌\ *n* **1 :** one that is given to playing jokes or setting up humorous situations ⟨evinced some disdain for the ~s —Walter Goodman⟩ **2 :** HUMORIST, COMEDIAN
funned *past of* FUN
¹fun·nel \'fənᵊl\ *n* -s *often attrib* [ME *fonel, funel*, fr. OProv *fonilh*, fr. ML *fundibulum*, short for L *infundibulum*, fr. *infundere* to pour in, fr. *in* + *fundere* to pour — more at IN, FOUND] **1 a :** a utensil that has typically the shape of a hollow cone with a tube extending from the point, is designed to catch and direct a downward flow of liquid or some other substance, and is sometimes fitted or combined with a strainer or filter — see SEPARATORY FUNNEL **b :** something shaped like a funnel (as a conical part, passage, or hole); *specif* **:** the swimming funnel of a cephalopod **c :** one that serves as a constricted channel or central agent or organization through which something passes or is transmitted **2 :** a stack or flue for the escape of smoke or for ventilation; *specif* **:** the stack of a ship **3 :** a cylindrical band of metal; *esp* **:** one around the top of an upper mast around which the rigging fits **4 :** RUNNING GATE **5 :** FUNNEL CLOUD **6 :** a black usu. cylindrical metal hood attached to a spotlight to prevent the spill of light outside the illuminated area of a stage

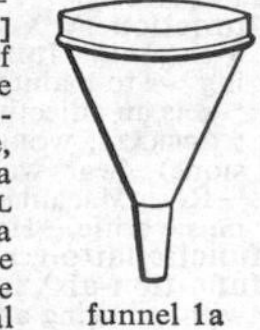
funnel 1a

²funnel \"\ *vb* **funneled** *also* **funnelled; funneled** *also* **funnelled; funneling** *also* **funnelling; funnels** *vi* **1 :** to have or take the shape of a funnel **:** NARROW, WIDEN ⟨a shallow, rounded valley bottom ~s into a miniature gorge with steep bluffs —*Jour. of Geol.*⟩ **2 :** to move to or from a focal point or into a central channel ⟨the gang . . . ~*ed* onto the end of the jetty off the slope —R.O.Bowen⟩ ⟨orders were ~*ing* out to the ships from the flagship —Alexander Griffin⟩ **3 :** to pass through or as if through a funnel; *specif* **:** to move through a constricted passage or central medium ⟨the fierce winds which ~*ed* up the valley center —John Steinbeck⟩ ⟨through the great port ~s much of the overseas commerce —*Newsweek*⟩ ⟨thousands of pictures . . . ~*ed* back to the press and public through the public-relations division —Robert Moora⟩ ~ *vt* **1 :** to cause to funnel: **a :** to form into the shape of a funnel ⟨~s his hands and shouts through them⟩ **b :** to cause to move to or from a focal point or into a central channel ⟨traffic is ~*ed* into consolidation stations . . . and fanned out to destinations —*Distribution Age*⟩ ⟨airlift's traffic pattern ~s planes from widely separated . . . bases into two 20-mile-wide corridors —*Nat'l Geographic*⟩ **c :** to direct to a single recipient or distribute from a single source ⟨impurities ~*ed* into the air by automobiles, backyard bonfires, and factory chimneys —*N.Y. Times*⟩ ⟨~ the kerosine into the tank⟩ **d :** to send or direct through a narrow passage or central medium ⟨pass . . . through which were ~*ed* troops and supplies —F.T.Chapman⟩ ⟨cupped her hands over the lens of the flashlight, ~*ing* the light through a small opening —E.S. Gardner⟩ ⟨if a bank ~s its news through a public-relations firm —*Banking*⟩ **2 :** to serve as a means for the transmission or direction of ⟨accused the press of ~*ing* secret military information to Soviet Russia —*Newsweek*⟩ ⟨~ . . . high-caliber young people to the agency business —*Printers' Ink*⟩
³fun·nel \'fünᵊl, 'fən-\ *n* -s [origin unknown] *dial Eng* **:** HINNY
funnel chest *also* **funnel breast** *n* **:** a depression of the anterior wall of the chest produced by a sinking in of the sternum
funnel cloud *n* **:** a funnel-shaped cloud that hangs below the greater thundercloud mass of a tornado
fun·nel·form \'fənᵊl,fȯrm\ *adj, of a corolla of a flower* **:** INFUNDIBULIFORM
funnel tube *n* **:** a long usu. glass tube that has a conical or bulging thistle-shaped top and sometimes a bulb with or without bulbs serving as a safety trap and that is used esp. in the chemical laboratory for pouring liquid into an apparatus

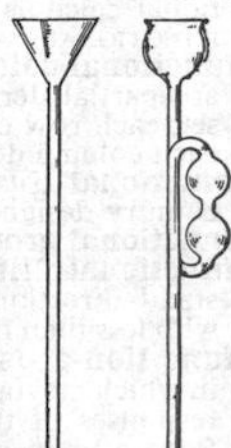
funnel tubes

fun·ni·ly \'fənᵊlē, -nəl, |i\ *adv* **:** in a funny manner **:** ODDLY, LAUGHABLY ⟨~ enough I've wanted to talk to you for a month —Eden Phillpotts⟩
fun·ni·ment \-nēmənt, -nim-\ *n* -s **:** a funny saying or action
fun·ni·ness \-nēnəs, -nin-\ *n* -ES **:** the quality or state of being funny
funning *pres part of* FUN
¹fun·ny \'fənē, -ni\ *adj* -ER/-EST [²*fun* + *-y*] **1 a :** affording light mirth and laughter typically by means of absurdity or oddness without much subtlety **:** AMUSING ⟨when they laughed it was not because they thought it was ~ but out of embarrassment —Barnaby Conrad⟩ ⟨he is the *funniest* writer in the world, with more kinds of fun than any other,

from the broadest burlesque . . . to the final subtlety of the tear-stained smile —Robert Morse⟩ **b :** seeking or intended to amuse **:** FACETIOUS, TRIFLING ⟨don't take him so seriously; he was just being ~⟩ ⟨cut out the ~ business and get to work⟩ ⟨a tactical mistake — to . . . get ~ with an official —*Irish Digest*⟩ **2 a :** differing from the ordinary in a suspicious, perplexing, quaint, or eccentric way **:** QUEER, ODD, FISHY ⟨they'd surely think it ~ if we shot up the price now —C.G. Benjamin⟩ **b :** ILL ⟨came to the doctor with the vague complaint that he felt ~ all over⟩ ⟨he had been a bit ~ in the top story —Norman Lewis⟩ **c :** INTOXICATED **3 :** involving trickery or deception **:** SPURIOUS, UNDERHANDED ⟨warned them he would shoot if they tried any ~ stuff⟩ ⟨fake bidding and other ~ business at the auction⟩ **4 :** COMIC 3 ⟨reading the ~ page in a daily paper⟩ **syn** see LAUGHABLE

²funny \"\ *n* -ES [perh. fr. ¹*funny*] **:** a narrow clinker-built British scull with one pair of outriggers for the oarlocks

³funny \"\ *n* -ES [¹*funny*] **1 :** one that is funny ⟨cast him as one of the *funnies* —Robertson Davies⟩ **2 :** a comic strip or comic section of a newspaper or periodical — usu. used in pl. ⟨follow their adventures in the *funnies*⟩ ⟨look at the *funnies*⟩

⁴funny *adv* **:** in an odd or amusing way ⟨made them suspicious when he began acting ~⟩

funny bone *n* [so called fr. the tingling felt when it is struck] **1 :** the place at the back of the elbow where the ulnar nerve rests against the medial condyle of the humerus **:** OLECRANON — called also *crazy bone* **2 :** SENSE OF HUMOR ⟨a joke that tickled his *funny bone*⟩

funny book *n* **:** COMIC BOOK

fun·ny·man \'==,man, -,maa(ə)n\ *n, pl* **funnymen :** a man with a reputation for humor **:** JOKER; *esp* **:** a professional humorist or comedian

funny–money \'==,==\ *n* **:** inflated currency; *esp* **:** currency inflated or otherwise manipulated for political or social purposes ⟨his opposition to the *funny-money* manipulations . . . brought him into disfavor —*Newsweek*⟩

funny paper *n* **:** FUNNY 2

fu·no·ri \fü'nōrē\ *n* -S [Jap] **1 :** any of several succulent marine algae esp. of the genus *Gloiopeltis* that furnish a tough glue **2** *or* **fu·no·rin** \-rən\ **:** a glue made from funori and used in the Orient as a size for textiles and paper

funs *pres 3d sing of* FUN, *pl of* FUN

fun·ster \'fənztə(r), -n(t)st-\ *n* -S **:** a person who seeks to amuse others **:** COMEDIAN, HUMORIST

fun·tu·mia \,fən·'t(y)ümēə\ *n* [NL, prob. fr. Ewe dial. *funtum* funtumia + NL *-ia*] **1** *cap* **:** a small genus of tropical African trees (family Apocynaceae) with opposite leaves and small axillary cymes of yellowish white flowers — see LAGOS RUBBER **2** -S **:** any tree of the genus *Funtumia*

¹fur *R* 'fər, + *vowel* 'fər·; *-R* 'fə, + *suffixal vowel* 'fər· *also* 'fər, + *vowel in a following word* 'fər· *or* 'fə *also* 'fər\ *dial var of* FAR

²fur \"\ *vb* **furred; furred; furring; furs** [ME *furren*, fr. MF *fourrer* to line a garment, fr. OF *forrer*, fr. *fuerre* sheath, of Gmc origin; akin to OE *fōdder* case, sheath, OFris *fōder* lining of a coat, OHG *fuotar* case, sheath, Goth *fodr* sheath; akin to Gk *pōy* herd, flock, Skt *pāti* he watches over, protects; basic meaning: guarding cattle] *vt* **1 :** to cover, line, or trim with fur or a fabric resembling fur ⟨russet velvet *furred* with sables —Francis Hackett⟩ **2 a :** to clothe with fur — usu. used in passive ⟨it was the 29th May . . . and still the fair were *furred* —*Tinsley's Mag.*⟩ **b :** to facilitate the growth of fur on (an animal) ⟨the same house will be used in September through November for *furring* about 600 mink —*Nat'l Fur News*⟩ **3 :** to coat or clog as if with fur ⟨dust had *furred* the beams and lodged on ridges in the plaster —Clemence Dane⟩ **4** *carpentry* **:** to apply furring to **:** support on furring — often used with *down, out, up* ⟨~ down a ceiling⟩ ~ *vi* **1 a :** to become coated or clogged as if with fur ⟨the pipes . . . *furred* up with lime —*English Digest*⟩ **b :** to become fluffy ⟨her tail *furred* out, her hair rose, and she assumed the typical attitude of a cat close-cornered by a dog —Archibald Rutledge⟩ **2 :** to grow fur ⟨mink ~ better in cool regions⟩

³fur \"\ *n* -S *see sense 4b* [ME *furre*, prob. fr. *furren*, v.] **1 :** a piece of the dressed pelt of an animal (as ermine, rabbit, seal) used as a material to make, trim, or line wearing apparel or other articles ⟨advertisers should invariably indicate by suitable descriptive matter . . . just what the ~ is —*Chamber of Commerce Bull.*⟩ **2 a :** an article of clothing made of fur ⟨her new ~ was a full-length muskrat coat⟩ **b :** one or more dressed pelts fashioned into a woman's neckpiece — usu. used in pl. ⟨a set of ~*s*⟩ **c :** a trimming or lining of fur on a garment worn as a mark of office or state or as a badge of a university degree ⟨add . . . wisdom to the ~*s* of power —William Shenstone⟩ **3 :** the fine soft thick hairy covering of a mammal usu. consisting of a double coating of hair that includes a layer of comparatively short soft curly barbed hairs that next to the skin protected by longer smoother stiffer hairs that grow up through these — compare HAIR 2, PELAGE, WOOL 1 **4 a furs** *pl* **:** the skins of animals with the fur attached **:** PELTRY ⟨a cargo of ~*s*⟩ **b** *pl usu* **fur :** fur-bearing animals ⟨many trainers break their retrievers of ~ altogether, not allowing them to see or carry rabbits for at least the first two seasons —P.R.A.Moxon⟩ **5 :** any of several patterns used in heraldry that are conventionally classified as tinctures **6 :** a coating resembling or suggesting fur: as **a :** a coat of epithelial debris on the tongue **b :** a deposit formed on the interior of boilers and other vessels by hard water and composed chiefly of carbonates **c :** the thick pile of a fabric (as chenille) **d :** the rough surface of lumber after sawing **7 :** a piece of wood nailed on a wall or ceiling to serve as base for a finished surface — compare FURRING 3b(1)

⁴fur \"\ *adj* **:** of or relating to fur

⁵fur \"\ *n* -S [ME, var. of *furgh, forwe, forow* — more at FURROW] *dial Brit* **:** FURROW

fur- *or* **furo-** *comb form* [ISV, fr. *furfural*] **1 :** related to furan ⟨*fur*odiazole⟩, furfural ⟨*fur*oin⟩, or furoic acid ⟨2-*fur*amide⟩ **2 :** containing a furan ring fused on one side to one side of another ring ⟨*furo*quinoline⟩

fur *abbr* **1** furlong **2** furlough **3** further

Fu·ra·cin \'fyùrəsən\ *trademark* — used for nitrofurazone

fu·ra·cious \fyə'rāshəs\ *adj* [L *furac-, furax* thievish (fr. *fur* thief) + E *-ious* — more at FURTIVE] *archaic* **:** given to theft **:** THIEVISH

fu·ral \'fyù,ral\ *n* -S [ISV *fur-* + *-al*] **:** FURFURYLIDENE

fur·al·de·hyde \fyə'r, (')fyù|r+,\ *n* [alter. of *furfuraldehyde* — more at FURFURAL] **:** FURFURAL 1

fu·ran \'fyù,ran, fyə'r-\ *also* **fu·rane** \-rān\ *n* -S [*furan, furane*, ISV *fur-* + *-an* or *-ane*] **1 :** a flammable liquid compound C_4H_4O that contains four carbon atoms and one oxygen atom in a ring, that is obtained from wood oils of certain pines but is usu. made synthetically from furfural by catalytic removal of the aldehyde group, and that is used chiefly in making tetrahydrofuran and other intermediates for the manufacture of nylon — compare STRUCTURAL FORMULA **2 :** a derivative of furan containing the furan ring

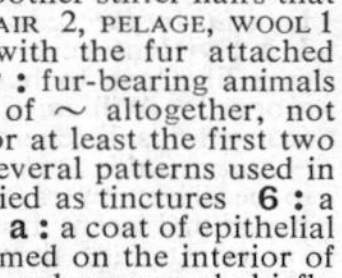

furan

fu·ra·noid \'fyùrə,nòid\ *also* **fu·roid** \-ù,ròid\ *adj* [*furan* or *fur-* + *-oid*] **:** resembling furan in chemical structure **:** characterized by the presence of the furan ring

fu·ra·nose \'fyùrə,nōs *also* -ōz\ *n* -S [*furan* + *-ose*] **:** a glycose sugar in the form of a cyclic hemiacetal containing a 5-member ring

fu·ran·o·side \fyə'ranə,sīd, -,səd\ *n* -S [*furanose* + *-ide*] **:** a glycoside containing the ring characteristic of a furanose

furan resin *n* **:** any of numerous resins made from derivatives of furan (as furfuryl alcohol or furfural) and used chiefly in adhesives and in impregnating and coating compositions

furbearer \'=,==\ *n* **:** an animal that bears fur esp. of a commercially desired quality

¹fur·be·low \'fərbə,lō, 'fəb-, 'fəib-\ *n* -S [by folk etymology fr. F dial. *farbella, ferbela*] **1 a :** a pleated or gathered piece of material **:** RUFFLE; *specif* **:** a flounce on women's clothing ⟨your slip . . . uncluttered by the conventional ~*s* of women's dresses —Lois Long⟩ **b :** something that resembles or suggests a furbelow esp. in being showy or superfluous ⟨its plate glass and the intricate ~*s* of its facade testified to suddenly acquired money —Jean Stafford⟩ ⟨dealt with . . . all phases and facets and ~*s* of our literary effort —Harvey Breit⟩ **2** *dial Eng* **:** a sea tangle (*Laminaria bulbosa*)

²furbelow \"\ *vt* -ED/-ING/-S **:** to trim with or as if with a furbelow ⟨it is the same old capitalist dog ~*ed* in bright nationalist ribbons —John Gunther⟩

fur·bish \'fərbish, 'fəb-, 'fəib-, -bēsh, *chiefly in pres part* -bəsh\ *vt* -ED/-ING/-ES [ME *furbisshen*, fr. MF *fourbiss-*, stem of *fourbir* to polish, of Gmc origin; akin to OHG *furben* to clean, sweep, polish] **1 :** to make lustrous **:** BURNISH, POLISH ⟨his coat of mail, ~*ed* so recently and so zealously that it shone like glass —T.B.Costain⟩ ⟨where the Bible is being revised . . . the church has reached maturity and seeks to improve and ~ its own weapons —Eric Fenn⟩ **2 :** to give a new look to **:** RENOVATE, REVIVE — often used with *up* ⟨aim of the restoration has been . . . to ~ up an old town —J.P.Bishop⟩ ⟨I am convinced we should take out the copybooks and ~ up their maxims —E.F.Mohler⟩

fur·bish·er \-shə(r)\ *n* -S [ME *furbissher*, fr. *furbisshen* + *-er*] *archaic* **:** one that furbishes; *esp* **:** one that furbishes arms and armor

fur breeder *n* **:** one that breeds fur-bearing animals esp. for commercial purposes

fur·ca \'fərkə\ *n, pl* **fur·cae** \-r,kī, -r,sē\ [NL, fr. L *furca*, fork — more at FORK] **:** a forked process: **a :** an internal skeletal projection from the ventral thoracic wall in certain insects **b :** a chitinous structure in the proboscis of certain flies **c :** the two-forked last abdominal segment of certain crustaceans **d :** FORCEPS 2

fur·cal \-rkəl\ *adj* [L *furca* + E *-al*] **:** FORKED, FURCATE — used chiefly of anatomical structures

fur·ca·ster·num \,fərkə+\ *n, pl* **furcasterna** *or* **furcasternums** [NL, fr. *furca* + *sternum*] **1 :** a part of the insect sternum bearing the furca **2 :** the posterior plate of an insect sternum **:** STERNELLUM

¹fur·cate \'fər,kāt, -,kət\ *adj* [LL *furcatus*, fr. L *furca* + *-atus* -ate] **:** branching like a fork **:** FORKED — **fur·cate·ly** *adv*

²fur·cate \-,kāt\ *vi* -ED/-ING/-S [ML *furcatus*, past part. of *furcare*, fr. L *furca*] **:** to branch like a fork **syn** see BRANCH

fur·ca·tion \,fər'kāshən\ *n* -S [ML *furcation-, furcatio*, fr. *furcatus* + L *-ion-, -io* -ion] **1 :** something that is branched **:** FORK **2 :** the act or process of branching

fur·cel·lar·ia \,fərsə'la(a)rēə\ *n, cap* [irreg. fr. L *furcilla* small fork (dim. of *furca*) + NL *-aria*] **:** a genus of red algae of the family Nemastomaceae whose only known species (*F. fastigiata*) is common in the No. Atlantic

fur·cel·late \'fərsə,lāt, ,fər'selət\ *adj* [irreg. fr. L *furcilla* + E *-ate*] **:** minutely or slightly furcate

fur·cif·er·ous \,fər'sif(ə)rəs\ *adj* [L *furci-* (fr. *furca* fork) + E *-ferous* — more at FORK] **:** having a forked appendage — used esp. of certain lepidopterous larvae

fur·ci·form \'fərsə,fòrm\ *adj* [L *furci-* + E *-form*] **:** FORKED

fur·cil·ia \,fər'silēə\ *n* -S [NL, fr. L *furca*] **:** an intermediate larva of a euphausid in which eye development is nearly adult but biramous swimming appendages are retained

fur·co·cer·cous \,fərkō|sərkəs\ *adj* [*furco-* (fr. L *furca*) + *-cercous* (fr. Gk *kerkos* tail)] *of a cercaria* **:** having the tail forked

fur·craea \,fər'krēə, '==\ *n, cap* [NL, after Count Antoine F. de *Fourcroy* †1809 Fr. chemist] **:** a small genus of tropical American plants (family Amaryllidaceae) closely related to and resembling *Agave* but distinguished by rotate white flowers — see CAJUN

fur·cu·la \'fərkyələ\ *n, pl* **furcu·lae** \-,lē\ [NL, fr. L, forked prop, dim. of *furca* fork — more at FORK] **1 :** a forked process or structure; *specif* **:** WISHBONE **2 :** an elevation on the embryonic floor of the pharynx from which the epiglottis develops **3 :** any of various appendages of insects; *specif* **:** the forked leaping appendage arising from the fourth abdominal segment of a collembolan — **fur·cu·lar** \-lə(r)\ *adj*

fur·cu·lum \-ləm\ *n, pl* **furcu·la** \-lə\ [NL, fr. L *furca* + *-ulum* (neut. dim. suffix)] **:** FURCULA; *esp* **:** WISHBONE

fur·dle \'fərdᵊl\ *vt* -ED/-ING/-S [modif. of MF *fardeler* to pack up — more at FARDEL] *now dial Eng* **:** to fold up **:** FURL

fur fabric *n* **:** a fabric usu. woven or knitted from rayon, wool, or cotton and made with a pile that is dyed and finished to resemble an animal's fur

fur farm *n* **:** a farm devoted to the raising of fur-bearing animals in a state of semidomestication typically in pens or on protected islands

fur farming *n* **:** the act or process of raising fur-bearing animals commercially for their pelts

fur·fur \'fərfər\ *n* -ES [L (also, bran); akin to L *frendere* to crush, bruise, grind — more at GRIND] **1 :** an exfoliation of a surface esp. of the epidermis **:** DANDRUFF, SCURF **2 fur·fu·res** \-rf(y)ə,rēz\ *pl* **:** flaky particles (as of scurf)

fur·fu·ra·ceous \,fərf(y)ə|rāshəs\ *adj* [LL *furfuraceus*, fr. L *furfur* + *-aceus* -aceous] **:** consisting of or covered with flaky particles **:** SCALY, SCURFY

fur·fu·ral \'fərf(y)ə,ral\ *n* [*furfural*, ISV, short for *furfuraldehyde*, fr. L *furfur* bran + ISV *aldehyde*] **1** *also* **fur·fur·aldehyde** \,fərf(y)ə|r+-\ **:** a liquid aldehyde C_4H_3OCHO that turns yellow to brown in air and has a penetrating odor, that is usu. made from corncobs, oat hulls, cottonseed hulls, or other materials containing pentosans by digestion with acid, and that is used chiefly in making furan and its derivatives (as intermediates for the manufacture of nylon), in making phenolic resins, and as a solvent (as for refining oils from petroleum) — called also *furaldehyde, 2-furaldehyde* **2 :** FURFURYLIDENE

fur·fu·ran \'fərf(y)ə,ran\ *n* [ISV *furfural* + *-an*] **:** FURAN

fur·fu·ra·tion \,fərf(y)ə'rāshən\ *n* -S [L *furfur* scurf + E *-ation*] **:** a scaling off (as of dandruff) **:** DESQUAMATION

fur·fu·rous \'fərf(y)ərəs\ *adj* [L *furfurosus* resembling bran, fr. *furfur* + *-osus* -ous] *archaic* **:** FURFURACEOUS

fur·fu·ryl \'fərf(y)ərəl, -)ə(,)ril\ *n* [ISV *furfural* + *-yl*] **:** the univalent radical $C_4H_3OCH_2$ derived from furfuryl alcohol by removal of the hydroxyl group; 2-furyl-methyl

furfuryl alcohol *n* **:** a liquid $C_4H_3OCH_2OH$ that turns amber to black in air, that occurs in the oil of roasted coffee and in cloves and is made by catalytic hydrogenation of furfural, and that is used chiefly in making dark corrosion-resistant resins and as a solvent; 2-furan-methanol

fur·fu·ryl·i·dene \,fərf(y)ə'rilə,dēn\ *n* -S [ISV *furfuryl* + *-idene*] **:** the bivalent radical $C_4H_3OCH<$ derived from furfural by removal of the aldehydic oxygen atom

fu·ri·ant \'f(y)ùrē,änt, ,==='=\ *n* -S [G & Czech, fr. L *furiant-, furians* pres. part. of *furiare* to enrage, fr. *furia* madness, fury — more at FURY] **:** a spirited Bohemian dance tune in ¾ time with shifting accents

fu·ri·bund \'fyùrə(,)bənd\ *adj* [L *furibundus*, fr. *furere* to be mad, rage — more at DUST] **:** full of fury **:** FRENZIED, RAGING

furies *pl of* FURY

fu·rio·sa·men·te \,fyùrē,ōsə'men·(,)tā, (,)fyùr,yō\ *adv* [It, fr. *furioso*] **:** FURIOUSLY — used as a direction in music

fu·ri·os·i·ty \,fyùrē'äsəd·ē\ *n* -ES [ME *furiosite*, fr. MF or LL; MF *furiosité*, fr. LL *furiositat-, furiositas*, fr. L *furiosus* + *-itat-, -itas* -ity] **1** *Scots law* **:** INSANITY **2 :** the quality or state of being furious **:** FURY

¹fu·ri·o·so \,fyùrē'ō(,)sō, fyùr'yō-\ *n* -S [It, fr. *furioso*, adj.] **:** a furious or insane man **:** FANATIC

²furioso \"\ *adj (or adv)* [It, fr. L *furiosus*] **:** with great force or vigor — used chiefly as a direction in music

fu·ri·ous \'fyùrēəs, -ùr-\ *adj* [ME, fr. MF *furieus*, fr. L *furiosus*, fr. *furia* madness, rage, fury + *-osus* -ous — more at FURY] **1 a :** exhibiting or goaded by anger or passion **:** FIERCE, VIOLENT ⟨fully expects a ~ renewal of the attacks against him —Howard Rushmore⟩ ⟨makes me ~ to think what slaves we were —Corra Harris⟩ **b :** appearing or moving as if angry **:** STORMY, TURBULENT ⟨the ~ outbursts of swirling flame from the palaces which have been set on fire —Laurence Binyon⟩ **c :** full of noise and excitement **:** BOISTEROUS ⟨ducking one another, dashing water with cupped hands, the fun was fast and ~ —C.P.Conigrave⟩ **d :** full of activity **:** ENERGETIC, VIGOROUS ⟨this loading job normally consumed for the . . . crew a leisurely day — or a ~ half of one —Wirt Williams⟩ **2 a :** existing in the height of its distinctive character **:** INTENSE ⟨everywhere the ecstatic green of California's brief and ~ spring —Wallace Stegner⟩ **b :** characterized by excess **:** EXTRAVAGANT ⟨lost such ~ sums —Mary W. Montagu⟩ **3 a** *Scots law* **:** mentally deranged **:** INSANE **b :** characterized by unreasoned enthusiasm **:** FANATICAL ⟨gradually formulated a theory to support his ~ conviction —*Time*⟩

furious fits *n pl but sing in constr* **:** CANINE HYSTERIA

fu·ri·ous·ly *adv* [ME, fr. *furious* + *-ly*] **1 a :** in an impassioned manner **:** ANGRILY, HOTLY ⟨an alarm is raised and a number of Moors on horseback ~ pursue them —Bernard De Voto⟩ **b :** in a turbulent manner **:** WILDLY ⟨the wind ran ~, tearing leaves off trees, carrying great volumes of dust before it —Sherwood Anderson⟩ **2 :** in a lively manner **:** ENERGETICALLY ⟨she would heave her huge body onto the saddle and go pedaling ~ up the narrow street —Arnold Hill⟩ **3 :** in an intensive manner or degree **:** EXTREMELY ⟨decorated with ~ modern murals —Frederic Morton⟩ ⟨a ~ colorful futurist study —S.E.Hyman⟩

fu·ri·ous·ness *n* -ES *archaic* **:** the quality or state of being furious

furious rabies *n* **:** rabies characterized by spasm of the muscles of throat and diaphragm, choking, salivation, extreme excitement, and evidence of fear often manifested by indiscriminate snapping at objects — compare DUMB RABIES

fu·ri·son \'fyùrəsən, -rəzən\ *n* -S [LG *vūrīsern*, fr. MLG, fr. *vūr* fire (akin to OHG *fiur*) + *īsern* iron; akin to OHG *īsan, īsarn* — more at FIRE, IRON] **:** an iron used to strike fire from a flint — used esp. in heraldry

¹furl \'fərl, *esp before pause or consonant* 'fər·əl; 'fəl, 'fəil\ *vb* -ED/-ING/-S [MF *ferler*, fr. ONF *ferlier* to tie tightly, fr. OF *fer, ferm* tight, fast (fr. L *firmus* firm) + *lier* to tie (fr. L *ligare*) — more at FIRM, LIGATURE] *vt* **1 a :** to roll up or gather in (a sail) and fasten close to a yard or mast **b :** to draw in (a flag) and secure to a staff **c :** to roll up as if furling a sail or a flag ⟨he was supposed to ~ the side flaps in the morning and let them down at night —Norman Mailer⟩ **2 :** to draw into ripples or folds **:** CURL, WRINKLE ⟨it shrivels behind ~*ed* leaves —Clive Arden⟩ **3 :** COVER, WRAP, ENFOLD ⟨the peacock . . . was itself ~*ed* into the night and the blackness closed in on them again —Rebecca West⟩ ~ *vi* **1 :** to curl or fold spirally ⟨she looked at the trees and at the ~*ing* blooms of the iris —Millen Brand⟩ **2 :** to roll away ⟨years of misery and sin ~ off and leave her heaven blue —J.R.Lowell⟩

²furl \"\ *n* -S **:** the act of furling or state of being furled **:** something that is furled

fur·lan \'fù(ə)rlən, fùr'län\ *n* -S *cap* [It *furlano, forlano, friulano*, fr. *Friuli*, district in Italy + It *-ano* -an] **:** FRIULIAN

furlana *var of* FORLANA

furl·er \'fərlər; 'fəla(r, 'fəil-\ *n* -S **:** one that furls

fur·less \'fərləs, 'fəl-\ *adj* **:** lacking fur ⟨a ~ animal⟩

fur·long \'fər,lòŋ, 'fə,l-, 'fəi,l- *also* -läŋ\ *n* -S [ME, fr. OE *furlang*, fr. *furh* furrow + *lang* long — more at FURROW, LONG] **1 a :** a unit of distance equal to ⅛ statute mile, 40 rods, 220 yards, or 201.17 meters **b :** SQUARE FURLONG **2** *now dial Eng* **:** a division of an unenclosed field **b :** a strip of newly plowed land between main furrows

¹fur·lough \'fər(,)lō, 'fə(-, 'fəi(-\ *n* -S [D *verlof*, lit., permission, fr. MD *verlof*, fr. *ver-* for- (akin to OHG *fir-*) + *lof* permission; akin to MHG *loube* permission — more at LEAVE] **1 a :** a leave of absence granted to a governmental or institutional employee (as a soldier, civil servant, or missionary) **b :** a document authorizing such a leave of absence **2 a :** a leave of absence granted by an employer to an employee; *esp* **:** a leave of absence granted at the employee's request **b :** a temporary lack of employment due to economic conditions **:** LAYOFF

²furlough \"\ *vb* -ED/-ING/-S *vt* **1 :** to grant a leave of absence to ⟨it is doubtful that the army will cooperate in extending deferments or in ~*ing* skilled workers —*Atlantic*⟩ **2 :** to subject to an enforced leave of absence **:** lay off ⟨the railroad recently announced it would ~ more than 2250 employees for five days . . . because of a continued decline in business —*Wall Street Jour.*⟩ ~ *vi* **:** to spend a furlough ⟨throngs of ~*ing* service people and chippies on . . . Broadway and Times Square —R.A.Gunnison⟩

furm \'fürm\ *Scot var of* ¹FORM 6b

furmenty *or* **furmety** *or* **furmity** *var of* FRUMENTY

furn *abbr* **1** furnished **2** furniture

¹fur·nace \'fərnəs, 'fən-, 'fəin-\ *n* -S *often attrib* [ME *furneis, furnas*, fr. OF *fornaise, fournaise*, fr. L *fornac-, fornax;* akin to L *formus* warm — more at WARM] **1 :** an apparatus for the production or application of heat: as **a :** an enclosed structure for reducing ore or melting or heat-treating metal by the application of intense heat produced typically by full combustion — compare HEARTH **b :** an oven for firing pottery **:** KILN **c :** an apparatus usu. consisting of a firepot and a system of pipes to carry heat to all parts of a building **d :** an atomic reactor **2** *archaic* **:** a boiler or crucible **3 :** something that resembles or has the effect of a furnace ⟨the immense ~*s* of the stars —J.A.Thomson & Patrick Geddes⟩ ⟨as gold is refined in the crucible so do the great Christian virtues . . . flow from all their purity from the ~ of man's affliction —W.F.Hambly⟩

²furnace \"\ *vt* -ED/-ING/-S **1** *obs* **:** to give forth like a furnace ⟨he ~*s* the thick sighs from him —Shak.⟩ **2 a :** to subject to heat ⟨a mixture of extremely fine silica and . . . lead oxide is *furnaced* for two hours at 625°C —E.R.Riegel⟩ **b :** to appear to heat **:** make glow ⟨the Indian House stood *furnaced* in melancholy red by a September sunset —William Sansom⟩

furnace black *or* **furnace combustion black** *n* **:** a carbon black made by the partial combustion of liquid and gaseous hydrocarbons (as petroleum distillates or refinery residues, natural gas, or a mixture of gas and oil) in a closed furnace or retort

fur·nace·man \-,man, -,mən\ *n, pl* **furnacemen 1 :** one who installs and repairs hot-air furnaces **2 :** a man who tends a furnace esp. a metallurgical furnace

furnace oil *n* **:** a fuel oil that can be burned in an atomizing burner and that is usu. a distilled product having a gravity of from 36° to 40° Bé

Fur·nace·stat \-nə(s)stat\ *trademark* — used for a thermostatic control for a hot-air-furnace fan to ensure delivery of properly heated air

furnace thermal black *n* **:** THERMAL BLACK

fur·nage \'fərnij\ *n* -S [ME, fr. MF *fornage*, fr. *forn, for, four* oven (fr. L *furnus*) + *-age;* akin to L *formus* warm — more at WARM] **:** a price paid for the use of an oven; *specif* **:** the fee paid a feudal lord by his tenants for the right to bake in his oven

fur·na·ri·idae \,fərnə'rīə,dē\ *n pl, cap* [NL, fr. *Furnarius*, type genus (fr. L *furnarius* baker, fr. *furnus* + *-arius* -ary) + *-idae*] **:** a family of tropical American birds comprising the ovenbirds and related forms and with the woodhewers, the antbirds, and several other tropical American birds forming a superfamily of the Tyranni

¹fur·nish \'fərnish, 'fən-, 'fəin-, -nēsh, *chiefly in pres part* -nəsh\ *vb* -ED/-ING/-ES [ME *furnisshen*, fr. MF *furniss-, fourniss-, forniss-*, stem of *furnir, fournir, fornir* to complete, carry out, equip, of Gmc origin; akin to OHG *frummen* to carry out, complete, OS *frummian;* causative-denominatives fr. the n. represented by OHG *fruma* advantage, profit — more at FOREMOST] *vt* **1 a :** to provide or supply with what is needed, useful, or desirable **:** EQUIP ⟨'tis now but four o'clock. We have two hours to ~ us —Shak.⟩ — usu. used with following *with* ⟨the wary collector sends for someone who can ~ him with . . . evidence of the authenticity of his picture —Clive Bell⟩ ⟨fins . . . ~*ed* with strong pointed spines — Richard Semon⟩ **b :** to supply (as a room or building) with furniture or appliances **:** equip for use ⟨a luxuriously ~*ed* reception room —John Pudney⟩ **2** *obs* **:** to fit out for work or active service ⟨Bucephalus . . . being saddled and ~*ed* . . . could endure none but Alexander —Edward Topsell⟩ **3** *obs* **:** ORNAMENT, DECORATE ⟨I'll show thee some attires and have thy counsel which is the best to ~ me tomorrow —Shak.⟩ **4 :** to make a gift of (something needed or desirable) **:** CONTRIBUTE, AFFORD, YIELD ⟨the southeast trade winds and the tropical foliage ~ alleviating coolness —H.A.Chippendale⟩ ~ *vi* **1 :** to equip living quarters with furniture and appliances ⟨the modern young couple about to ~ —R.D.Benn⟩ **2** *chiefly dial Brit* **:** to gain strength and weight **:** become fully developed **:** MATURE: as **a** *of a horse* **:** to gain strength and stamina

b : to have a fully developed comb, hackle, saddle, and tail ⟨in White Leghorns . . . there is the type which ~*es* slowly, the comb being slow in the growing and the feathering long —*Australasian*⟩

syn EQUIP, OUTFIT, APPOINT, ARM, ACCOUTER: FURNISH is a general term indicating supplying and providing; it may apply to anything supplied ⟨music was *furnished* by the United States Army Band —*Amer. Guide Series: Oreg.*⟩ ⟨such education as the local schools could *furnish* —G.F.Smythe⟩ but is used typically with tangible more or less permanent articles for use ⟨to *furnish* a room⟩ EQUIP, likewise wide in application ⟨*equip* oneself to practice law⟩, applies often to the provision of specific things making for greater convenience or utility ⟨the house is three stories high, and is *equipped* with a conservatory —*Amer. Guide Series: N. J.*⟩ ⟨delightful picnic spots along the way, *equipped* with outdoor fireplaces, lunch tables, and springwater —*Amer. Guide Series: Vt.*⟩ OUTFIT suggests provision of various things needed for a journey, expedition, or occasion ⟨it took several days to *outfit* me for my journey to Washington —Willa Cather⟩ ⟨an English ship *outfitted* by Raleigh arrived with supplies and reinforcements —*Amer. Guide Series: N. C.*⟩ APPOINT may suggest elegant equipment; the word is less used today in this sense than previously ⟨the interior has been *appointed* with pieces associated with the Colonial period —*Amer. Guide Series: N. Y. City*⟩ ⟨it has beautifully *appointed* lounges, cafeteria, dining room, meeting rooms —*Amer. Guide Series: Mich.*⟩ ARM often applies to supplying or furnishing that which adds to strength or security, to means of defense or offense ⟨ever youthful in ardor, and *armed* with the shining sword of truth, he fought and killed many ogres who oppressed the children of the light —M.R.Cohen⟩ ⟨*armed* with wide powers and unlimited resources —T.D.McCormick⟩ ACCOUTER indicates the providing of dress, personal equipment, and weapons for combat or as if for combat ⟨lying hidden in her bosom was a loaded pistol. Lying hidden at her waist was a sharpened dagger. Thus *accoutered* . . . Madame Defarge took her way —Charles Dickens⟩ ⟨the fully *accoutered* members of a Wild West show —*Saturday Rev.*⟩ **syn** see in addition PROVIDE

²furnish \"\ *n* -ES **1 :** an act or instance of furnishing **2 :** something furnished: as **a :** the raw materials placed in a beater for making paper pulp **b** *South* **:** groceries and supplies provided on credit to a plantation tenant by the owner

furnished *adj* [ME *furnisshed*, fr. past. part. of *furnisshen*] **1 :** provided with essentials **:** EQUIPPED ⟨a completely ~ toolbox⟩ **2** *obs* **:** possessing a quantity **:** STOCKED ⟨these rivers are very well ~ with fish —Daniel Denton⟩ **3 :** containing furniture ⟨the tenant of a ~ house —F.M.Ford⟩ **4** *heraldry* **:** provided with equipment ⟨a horse passant ~⟩

fur·nish·er \-shə(r)\ *n* -S **1 :** one that furnishes; *specif* **:** a dealer in men's furnishings **2 :** a revolving brush or roller that supplies the color used in printing textiles

furnishing *n* -S [ME *furnisshing*, fr. gerund of *furnisshen*] **1 :** the act or process of supplying furniture or equipment ⟨rudder irons . . . of this company's ~ —Thomas Hale⟩ **2 a :** an article or accessory of dress; *specif* **:** HABERDASHERY — usu. used in pl. ⟨a sale on dress shirts and other ~*s* for men⟩ **b :** an ornamental appendage of an animal ⟨the unusual butterfly comb, the crest and muffled face, look quite attractive . . . but such ~*s* do not appeal to the usual run of commercial poultry keepers —*Farmer's Weekly* (*So. Africa*)⟩ **3 :** an object or fixture that tends to increase comfort or utility ⟨dead bodies . . . surrounded by all the ~*s* they had made use of in life —Edith Hamilton⟩ ⟨a remarkable ability to . . . depict the ~*s* of a small town —J.D.Hart⟩; *specif* **:** an article of furniture for the interior of a building — usu. used in pl. ⟨a variety of ~*s*, among them such important upholstered pieces as an elegant long couch with loose down cushions —*New Yorker*⟩

fur·nish·ment \-shmənt\ *n* -S **1 a :** the act or process of furnishing **b :** the quality or state of being furnished **2 furnishments** *pl, archaic* **:** necessary equipment and supplies; *specif* **:** MUNITIONS ⟨purveyor for the army . . . vastly rich; grown so as contractor of ~*s* which he never furnishes —Lew Wallace⟩

furnish out *vt* **1 :** to provide a supply of (what is needed) **:** COMPLETE ⟨from among the impoverished citizens he *furnished out* masses of colonists to repair the decay of ancient cities —J.A.Froude⟩ **2 :** to provide material for **:** SUPPLY ⟨the assorted sins and failings which *furnish out* so many of the pages in . . . biographies —F.L.Mott⟩ **3** *obs* **:** to outfit esp. for military action **:** EQUIP

fur·ni·ture \'fərnəchə(r), 'fərnəchə(r, -nēch- *sometimes* -,chü(ə)r *or* -üə\ *n* -S *often attrib* [MF *fourniture*, fr. *fournir*, *furnir*, *fornir* to complete, carry out, equip — more at FURNISH] **1** *obs* **a** (1) **:** the act of furnishing or decorating (2) **:** an article of decoration **:** ORNAMENT ⟨see the barge be ready and fit it with such ~ as suits the greatness of his person —Shak.⟩ **b :** the execution of a plan ⟨toward the ~ of his hostile designs he had extraordinary subsidy —John Speed⟩ **2 a** *obs* **:** STOCK, STORE, SUPPLY ⟨we were particularly searched to the effect we carried in no ~ of arms nor powder —William Lithgow⟩ **b :** that by which something is filled **:** CONTENTS ⟨the Constitution has the normal ~ of all constitutions—provisions for amendment, for admitting member states —T.H.White *b*1915⟩ **3 :** something that is necessary, useful, or desirable: as **a** *archaic* **:** the harness and trappings esp. of a horse ⟨the saddles and rich ~ of the cavalry —Edward Gibbon⟩ **b :** a fund of ideas or information **:** mental equipment ⟨my intellectual ~ consists of an assortment of general propositions —O.W.Holmes †1935⟩ **c** *obs* **:** personal belongings **:** CLOTHING, ARMOR ⟨the king would find himself incommoded with all that ~ upon his back —Andrew Marvell⟩ **d :** articles of convenience or decoration used to furnish living quarters, offices, public and private buildings — usu. used of movable articles (as tables and chairs) as distinguished from such permanent installations as bathroom fixtures **e :** equipment needed for work or active service; *specif* **:** the tackle of a ship **f :** a mixture stop in a pipe organ **4** *archaic* **:** the state of being equipped **:** readiness for action ⟨you will inform yourself of the ~ of the French on the Mediterranean seas —John Evelyn⟩ **5 :** useful or decorative appendages **:** ACCESSORIES: as **a :** the mountings of a gun **b :** pieces of wood or metal less than type high that are placed in printing forms to fill in blank spaces or used with quoins to fasten matter in a chase **c :** HARDWARE; *specif* **:** the metal trimmings on a coffin **d :** background details ⟨mere ~ counts for a good deal in the best romances, and they are full of descriptions of riches and splendors —W.P.Ker⟩

furniture beetle *also* **furniture borer** *n* **:** a small borer beetle (*Anobium punctatum*) resembling a powder-post beetle but having the head bent under the thorax and feeding on both sapwood and heartwood of seasoned timber; *broadly* **:** a beetle of the family Anobiidae

furniture worker *n* **:** a worker who constructs wooden furniture and accessories to be installed in airplanes

furo- — see FUR-

fu·ro·ate \'fyürə,wāt\ *n* -S [*fur-* + *-ate*] **:** a salt or ester of furoic acid

fu·ro·ic acid \(')fyü¦rōik-\ *n* [*fur-* + *-ic*] **:** either of two crystalline monocarboxylic acids C_4H_3OCOOH derived from furan; *esp* **:** the alpha or 2-derivative obtained by oxidation of furfural and used chiefly as a preservative

furoid *var of* FURANOID

fu·role \'fyü,rōl, ⸗'⸗\ *n* -S [F, fr. MF *fuirole*, prob. of Gmc origin; akin to OE *fȳr* fire — more at FIRE] *archaic* **:** SAINT ELMO'S FIRE

fu·ror \'fyü,rȯ(ə)r, 'fyü,-, -,rō(ə)r, -,rȯ(ə), -,rōə *sometimes* f(y)ə'- *or* fyü'- *or* 'fyürə(r) *or* 'fyürə(r)\ *n* -S [MF & L; MF *fureur*, *furor*, fr. L *furor*, fr. *furere* to be mad, rage + *-or* — more at DUST] **1 :** an angry or maniacal fit **:** RAGE ⟨~ of the god of war —Henry Fuseli⟩ **2 :** a state of exaltation or inspiration **:** FRENZY ⟨the poetic ~ may have betrayed me into some indecency —Samuel Foote⟩ **3 :** a fashionable craze **:** VOGUE ⟨her singing . . . made her the ~ of Paris overnight —Janet Flanner⟩ **4 a :** furious or hectic activity **:** EXCITEMENT ⟨had not let the ~ of the catch distract him from the other whales —R.B.Robertson⟩ **b :** an outburst of public excitement or indignation **:** UPROAR ⟨the ~ over corruption in the executive departments —R.H.Rovere⟩ ⟨the sale of the plant had created a ~ in the town —Sherwood Anderson⟩ **c :** extreme turbulence **:** TEMPESTUOUSNESS ⟨strong dikes defend the land against the ~ of winter storms —Samuel Van Valkenburg & Ellsworth Huntington⟩

fu·rore \", *chiefly Brit* fyü'rōri\ *n* -S [It, fr. L *furor*] **1 :** FUROR 3 ⟨creating quite a ~ in vaudeville —*Music Trade News*⟩ **2 :** FUROR 4b ⟨~ about simplified spelling —D.B.Chidsey⟩

fur·phy \'fərfē\ *n* -ES [fr. *Furphy* (*carts*), water and sanitation carts used during World War I in Australia, fr. the *Furphy* manufacturing company, Shepparton, Victoria, Australia] *slang Austral* **:** a false report **:** RUMOR

furr \'fər, 'fə(r\ *n* -S [ME *fur* — more at FUR (furrow)] *dial Brit* **:** FURROW

furr-ahin \,fə·rə¦hin\ *n* -S [*furr* + Sc *ahin* behind, alter. of *ahind*] *Scot* **:** the right-hand hindmost horse that walks in the furrow in plowing

furred \'fərd, 'fəd\ *adj* [ME, fr. past part. of *furren* to line with fur — more at FUR] **1 :** lined, trimmed, or faced with fur ⟨the original painted by himself with a black cap and ~ gown —Horace Walpole⟩ **2 :** coated as if with fur; *specif* **:** having a coating consisting chiefly of mucus and dead epithelial cells ⟨a ~ tongue⟩ **3 a :** covered with or bearing fur ⟨~ animals thrive in cold climates⟩ **b :** wearing fur ⟨~ ladies in ermine and sable⟩ **4** *archit* **:** provided with furring

¹fur·ri·er \'fər·ēə(r *also* 'fə·rē·\ *n* -S [alter. of ME *furrer*, fr. AF *furrere*, fr. OF *forrer*, *fourrer* to fur + *-ere* -er — more at FUR] **1 :** one that buys and sells furs or fur products **:** fur dealer **2 a :** one that dresses furs **b :** one that makes, repairs, alters, or cleans fur garments

²furrier *comparative of* FURRY

fur·ri·ery \-ēərē, -ri\ *n* -ES **1 furrieries** *pl, archaic* **:** FURS **2 a :** the fur business **:** trade in furs **b :** the furrier's art **:** fur craftsmanship

furriest *superlative of* FURRY

fur·rin·er \'fər·ənə(r), 'fə·rə·\ *n* -S [by alter.] *dial* **:** FOREIGNER; *specif* **:** a person not a native of a given locality ⟨a mountain neighbor in a community that didn't take kindly to ~*s* —Frances Witherspoon⟩

fur·ri·ness \'fər·ēnəs, -r·in-\ *n* -ES **:** the quality or state of being furry

fur·ring \'fər·|iŋ, |ēŋ *also* 'fə·r|\ *n* -S [ME, fr. gerund of *furren* to trim or line with fur — more at FUR] **1 :** a fur trimming or lining ⟨among the clergy of the lower grade in a cathedral there was a distinction marked by the ~ of the amice —Daniel Rock⟩ **2 a :** the process of incrustation or of clogging as if with fur ⟨the ~ of the mouth and the throat in fevers —John Woodall⟩ **b :** a coating of or as if of fur; *specif* **:** a deposit from water that collects on the inside of a boiler **3 a** (1) **:** the process of double-planking a ship's sides (2) **:** the material used in this process (3) **:** strips of wood fastened to the frames or joists of a ship to shape or level them for the attachment of a finished surface (as sheathing) **b** (1) **:** the application of thin wood, brick, or metal pieces to the joists, studs, or walls of a building to form a level surface (as for lathing, plastering, or attaching wallboard), to form an air space, or to make the wall look thicker and the window jambs deeper — called also *firring* (2) **:** the material used in this process

furring brick *n* **:** a hollow brick large enough to bond and grooved to afford a key for plastering

furring insert *n* **:** a wire device inserted into concrete or masonry that serves as an anchor for the attachment of furring

furring strip *n* **:** a strip of wood or very light steel channel to support lath esp. in furring masonry walls

furring tile *n* **:** a structural clay tile that is used for lining the inside of a wall and carries no superimposed load

¹fur·row \'fər·(,)ō, 'fə·(,)rō, -ər·ə,-ə·rə, *often* -ər·əw *or* -ə·rəw +V\ *n* -S *often attrib* [ME *furgh*, *forwe*, *forow*, fr. OE *furh*; akin to OHG *furuh* furrow, ON *for* furrow, drainage ditch, L *porca*, and perh. to Skt *parśāna* precipice, chasm] **1 a :** a trench in the earth made by a plow ⟨twites nest under ~*s* and ringed plovers amid rows of potato plants —*Brit. Birds in Colour*⟩ **b :** a plowed field or farm ⟨artists frequently spring from sidewalks and ~*s* —A.W.Long⟩ **c :** something that resembles the track of a plow ⟨plowing a ~ across the Atlantic ocean —*N.Y. Times*⟩ **d** *Scot* **:** the earth turned over in plowing ⟨till crushed beneath the ~'*s* weight shall be thy doom —Robert Burns⟩ **2** *now chiefly Africa* **:** a natural or artificial watercourse for drainage or irrigation ⟨when leading water in concrete ~*s* it will run twice as quickly for the same fall as in an earth ~ —*Farmer's Weekly* (*So. Africa*)⟩ **3 :** a long and narrow indentation: as **a :** natural depression **:** GROOVE, CHANNEL ⟨tracing a fingernail along a ~ in the corduroy of her housecoat —Douglass Wallop⟩ ⟨major tectonic ~*s* or fault angles —C.A.Cotton⟩; *specif* **:** a groove in the face of a millstone **b :** a deep wrinkle on the face ⟨leathery folds and humorous wrinkles about his eyes deepening into a hundred crevices and ~*s* —J.C.Powys⟩ **c :** a crease in a plant or one of its parts ⟨seed single . . . marked with a ~ lengthwise —William Withering⟩ **d :** an indentation from the top of a dog's skull to the stop dividing the forehead into two lateral halves

²furrow \"\ *vb* -ED/-ING/-S *vt* **1 a :** to make a furrow in (earth) **:** PLOW **b :** to till as if with a plow **:** CULTIVATE ⟨plows literary ground that has been ~*ed* on innumerable occasions in the past —R.L.Neuberger⟩ **2 a** (1) **:** to make a channel in **:** SCORE ⟨the rocket ~*s* the dark and falls —C.P.Aiken⟩ (2) **:** to make streaks in ⟨fair cheeks were ~*ed* with hot tears —Lord Byron⟩ **b :** to shape into alternate ridges and grooves ⟨one of the thousands of canyons that ~ the wide coast range —Frank Cameron⟩; *specif* **:** to make wrinkles in (the brow) ⟨he may sweat and ~ his brow —J.N. Leonard⟩ ~ *vi* **1 :** to make a furrow **:** PLOW **2 :** to make a channel **:** COURSE ⟨without warning the tears began to ~ down his cheeks —Margaret O. R. Cole⟩ **3 :** to make an indentation or groove **:** WRINKLE ⟨any educator's brow will automatically ~, contemplating the sober prediction —*Newsweek*⟩

furrow drill *n* **:** a grain drill that opens furrows at intervals of 10 to 18 inches and deposits seed in them

furrowed *adj* **:** having furrows **:** WRINKLED, CORRUGATED ⟨his ~ face is occasionally lit by a warming smile —Colm Brogan⟩

furrowed prawn *n* **:** an Australian prawn (*Peneus latisulcatus*) that attains a length of nine inches and sometimes appears on the market as shrimp

fur·row·er \'fər·əwə(r), 'fə·rəw-; 'fər·ōə(r), 'fə·rō\ *n* -S **:** one that furrows

furrowing *n* -S **:** a process of cell division in certain plants in which cleavage furrows begin at the existing cell wall and progress inwardly until they meet (as in spore formation in certain algae and fungi and development of the endosperm in certain seed plants)

furrow irrigation *n* **:** irrigation of farmland by water run in furrows between the crop rows

furrow pan *n* **:** PLOW SOLE

furrow press *n* **:** a heavy wheel or bar attached to the rear of a plow to travel in the furrow and firm the seedbed

furrow slice *n* **:** the ridge of earth turned by a plow ⟨this plow may be adjusted to set the *furrow slice* on edge —A.F.Gustafson⟩

fur·rowy \'fər·əw|ē, 'fə·rəw|, 'fər·ō|, 'fə·rō|, |i\ *adj* **:** FURROWED

furrs *pl of* FURR

fur·ry \'fər·|ē, |i *also* 'fə̄r|\ *adj* -ER/-EST [²*fur* + *-y*] **1 :** consisting of or resembling fur ⟨one of those beautiful storms that wrap Denver in dry ~ snow —Willa Cather⟩ ⟨a lush ~ growth made up of algae, sea moss, tube worms, barnacles —Joseph Mitchell⟩ **2 :** covered with or as if with fur ⟨the ~ bulk of the bear —C.G.D.Roberts⟩ **3 :** clogged as if with fur ⟨his voice was husky and ~ —Frederic Prokosch⟩

furry dance \"-\ *n* [perh. by folk etymology fr. Corn *fēr* fair, market, fr. ML *feria* — more at FAIR] **:** a springtime serpentine dance through the streets of Helston, Cornwall

furs *pres 3d sing of* FUR, *pl of* FUR

fur seal *n* **:** any of various eared seals that have a double coat with a dense soft underfur highly valued for clothing and trimmings and that are now nearly extinct except at a few protected breeding places: **a :** a seal of the genus *Arctocephalus* **b :** a seal of the genus *Callorhinus*; *specif* **:** a seal (*C. alascanus*) that breeds on the Pribilof islands

furta *pl of* FURTUM

furta usus *pl of* FURTUM USUS

¹furth \'fərth\ *Scot var of* FORTH

²fürth *or* **fuerth** *or* **furth** \'fi(ə)rt, *Ger* 'fœrt\ *adj, usu cap* [fr. *Fürth*, Germany] **:** of or from the city of Fürth, Germany **:** of the kind or style prevalent in Fürth

furthcoming *var of* FORTHCOMING

¹fur·ther \'fərthər, 'fəthə(r, 'fəithə(r, *in Southern US often* 'fəthə(r *or* 'fəthər\ *adv* [ME, fr. OE *furthor*; akin to OHG *furthar*, *furdir* further, OS *furthor*; comparative fr. the root of E *forth*] **1 :** ¹FARTHER 1 **2 :** ¹FARTHER 2 **3 :** in addition **:** MOREOVER ⟨if we ~ suppose —C.H.Sykes⟩ ⟨~, when writing was finally popularized —A.N.Whitehead⟩ ⟨he felt ~ that it was his place to be there —Ira Wolfert⟩ ⟨the soil is ~ enriched by abundant applications of sheep manure —Tom Marvel⟩ **4 :** ¹FARTHER 4

²further \"\ *adj* [ME, fr. OE *furthra*, fr. *furthor*, adv.] **1 :** ²FARTHER 1 **2 :** going or extending beyond what exists **:** ADDITIONAL ⟨a ~ volume —Carl Van Doren⟩ ⟨she may obtain ~ education on the side —J.B.Conant⟩ ⟨people can have no ~ illusions about it —F.D.Roosevelt⟩ ⟨I know nothing ~ of them —Pearl Buck⟩ **3 :** ²FARTHER 3

³further \"\ *vb* **furthered**; **furthered**; **furthering** \-th(ə)riŋ\ **furthers** [ME *furtheren*, alter. (influenced by ¹*further* and ²*further*) of OE *fyrthrian*, fr. *furthor*] *vt* **:** to help forward **:** PROMOTE, ADVANCE ⟨does the music ~ the dramatic purpose —Irving Kolodin⟩ ~ *vi, now chiefly Scot* **:** to go on **:** make progress **syn** see ADVANCE

⁴further \"\ *n* -S *dial Brit* **:** good fortune **:** SUCCESS

fur·ther·ance \-th(ə)rən(t)s\ *n* -S [ME *furtheraunce*, fr. *furtheren* + *-aunce* -ance] **:** a helping forward **:** ADVANCEMENT, PROMOTION ⟨the elimination of poverty and the ~ of social justice —Oscar Handlin⟩

further education *n, Brit* **:** ADULT EDUCATION

fur·ther·er \-thərə(r)\ *n* -S [ME, fr. *furtheren* + *-er*] **:** one that furthers

fur·ther·ly \-thə(r)lē\ *adj, now dial Eng, of crops* **:** EARLY, FORWARD

fur·ther·more \'⸗⸗,⸗, ,⸗⸗'⸗\ *adv* [ME, fr. *further* + *more*] **:** in addition to what precedes **:** BESIDES, MOREOVER

fur·ther·most \'⸗⸗,mōst\ *adj* **:** most distant **:** FARTHEST

fur·ther·some \-ˌsəm\ *adj* [³*further* + *-some*] **1** *archaic* **:** encouraging advance **:** BENEFICIAL, USEFUL **2** *Scot* **:** VENTURESOME, RASH

fur·thest \-thəst\ *adv* (*or adj*) [ME, fr. *further* + *-est*] **:** FARTHEST

furthy \'fərthi\ *Scot var of* FORTHY

fur·tive \'fərd·iv, 'fə̄|, 'fəi|, |t|, |ēv\ *adj* [F or L; F *furtif*, fr. L *furtivus*, fr. *furtum* theft (fr. *fur* thief) + *-ivus* -ive; akin to Gk *phōr* thief, L *ferre* to carry — more at BEAR] **1 a :** done by stealth **:** SECRET, SURREPTITIOUS ⟨a ~ glance told her worlds —Mark Twain⟩ **b :** expressive of stealth **:** SNEAKY, SLY ⟨the ~ look of those who know they ought to be doing something else —Alan Ross⟩ **2 a :** obtained underhandedly **:** STOLEN **b :** given to stealing **:** THIEVISH ⟨the farmers were so much plagued by the ~ bird —J.H.Burton⟩ **syn** see SECRET

fur·tive·ly \|əvlē, -li\ *adv* **:** in a furtive manner

fur·tive·ness \|ivnəs, |ēv-\ *n* -ES **:** the quality or state of being furtive

fur·tum \'fərd·əm\ *n, pl* **fur·ta** \-d·ə\ [L] *Roman & civil law* **:** the unauthorized making of a profit from or appropriation to one's use of another's property **:** a trespass on movable property **:** THEFT

furtum usus \-'yüsəs\ *n, pl* **furta usus** [L, theft of use] *Scots law* **:** a trespass by temporarily depriving an owner of his movable property

fu·run·cle \'fyü,rəŋkəl\ *n* -S [L *furunculus* petty thief, secondary branch of a vine (that robs the main branches of sap), knob on a vine, furuncle, dim. of *furon-*, *furo* ferret, thief, fr. *fur* thief — more at FURTIVE] **:** a localized inflammatory swelling of the skin and underlying tissues that is caused by infection by a bacterium (esp. *Staphylococcus aureus*) in a hair follicle or skin gland and that discharges pus and a central core of dead tissue — called also *boil*; compare CARBUNCLE

fu·run·cu·lar \fyə'rəŋkyələ(r), (')fyü¦r-\ *or* **fu·run·cu·lous** \-ləs\ *adj* [L *furunculus* + E *-ar* or *-ous*] **1 :** having or tending to produce furuncles **2 :** resembling a furuncle

fu·run·cu·loid \-,lȯid\ *adj* [L *furunculus* + E *-oid*] **:** resembling a furuncle

fu·run·cu·lo·sis \fyə,rəŋkyə'lōsəs, (,)fyü,r-\ *n, pl* **furunculoses** \-ō,sēz\ [NL, fr. L *furunculus* + NL *-osis*] **1 :** the condition of having or tending to develop multiple furuncles **2 :** a highly infectious disease of the salmons and related fishes that is caused by a bacterium (*Bacterium salmonicida*), is characterized by purplish blotches followed by deep erosive ulcers of the skin and subcutaneous tissues, and is esp. virulent in hatcheries or other areas of heavy fish population

fu·run·cu·lus \fyə'rəŋkyələs, fyü'r-\ *n, pl* **furunculi** \-,lī\ [L] **:** FURUNCLE

fu·ry \'fyürē, 'fyür-, -ri\ *n* -ES [ME *furie*, fr. MF & L; MF, fr. L *furia*, fr. *furere* to be mad, rage + *-ia* -y — more at DUST] **1 a :** violent anger **:** extreme wrath **:** RAGE ⟨heaven has no rage like love to hatred turned, nor hell a ~ like a woman scorned —William Congreve⟩ **b :** a passionate fit **:** FRENZY ⟨roused his listeners to a ~ of compassionate indignation —*Amer. Guide Series: N.Y. City*⟩ **c :** something that appears to be driven by rage **:** violent turbulence ⟨the first ~ of the storm had spent itself —E.A.Poe⟩ **d :** the savagery of an animal ⟨taught them how to match their skill against the cunning and fierce ~ of the fastest of the ocean denizens —T. C.Roughley⟩ **2** [ME *furie*, fr. MF or L; MF, fr. L *Furiae*, fr. pl. of *furia*] **a** *usu cap* **:** an avenging deity of ancient Greece and Rome **b :** an avenging or infernal spirit ⟨liberated from the *furies* of his conscience —W.A.Kaufmann⟩ **c :** one who resembles an avenging or infernal spirit; *esp* **:** a malicious or spiteful woman ⟨sometimes she behaves like . . . a vindictive ~ —Rosemary Benét⟩ **3 :** extreme impetuosity or violence **:** unrestrained force ⟨attacked with ~ and precision —T.R. Hay⟩ **4 :** a state of inspired exaltation **:** AFFLATUS ⟨in an age of formalism, poetic ~ itself became a formal requirement —Irving Babbitt⟩ **syn** see ANGER — **like fury :** to an intense or extreme degree or extent ⟨kicked and plunged *like fury* —Henry Wynmalen⟩

fu·ryl \'fyürəl, -(,)ril\ *n* -S [ISV *fur-* + *-yl*] **:** either of two univalent radicals C_4H_3O derived from furan by removal of one hydrogen atom; *esp* **:** the alpha or 2-radical

furze \'fərz\ *n* -S [ME *firse*, *furse*, fr. OE *fyrs*; akin to Gk *pyros* wheat, *pyrēn* pit (of fruit), Lith *pūrai* winter wheat, OSlav *pyro* spelt] **:** any of several plants of the genera *Ulex* and *Genista*; *esp* **:** a spiny evergreen shrub (*U. europaeus*) with yellow flowers that is very common throughout Europe and is often used for fuel and fodder — called also *gorse*, *whin*

furzechat \'⸗,⸗\ *n* [*furze* + *chat* (bird)] **1 :** WHINCHAT **2 :** STONECHAT

furze lark *n* **:** MEADOW PIPIT

furze·ling \-,liŋ\ *n* -S [*furze* + *-ling*] **:** DARTFORD WARBLER

furze wren *n* **:** DARTFORD WARBLER

furzy \'fərzē\ *adj* -ER/-EST **:** abounding in or overgrown with or as if with furze ⟨his ~ brown chest half bare —J.R.Lowell⟩

fus *abbr* **1** fuselage **2** fusilier

fu·sain \'fyü,zān, ⸗'⸗\ *n* -S [F, spindle tree, charcoal made from spindle-tree wood, fusain, fr. (assumed) VL *fusagin-*, *fusago*, fr. L *fusus* spindle; fr. the fact that the wood of the tree was used for spindles] **:** a dull constituent closely resembling charcoal that is present in banded bituminous coals and causes much of the dust in coal mines — compare CLARAIN, DURAIN, VITRAIN

fu·sar·i·al \(')fyü¦za(a)rēəl\ *adj* [NL *Fusarium* + E *-al*] **:** of or relating to a fungus of the genus *Fusarium*

fu·sar·i·um \⸗'⸗⸗əm\ *n* [NL, fr. L *fusus* spindle + NL *-arium*] **1** *cap* **:** a form genus of fungi (family Tuberculariaceae) having a microconidium and a crescent-shaped or fusiform macroconidium — see DRY ROT 2b **2** *pl* **fusar·ia** \-ēə\ **:** any fungus of the genus *Fusarium*

fusarium wilt *n* **:** any of various plant wilt diseases caused by fungi of the genus Fusarium — compare DRY ROT

fu·sa·role \'fyüzə,rōl\ *n* -S [F *fusarolle*, *fusarole*, fr. obs It. *fusarola* (now *fusaiuola*), fr. *fuso* spindle, shaft of a column, fr. L *fusus* spindle] **:** a rounded usu. beaded convex molding placed under the echinus of capitals in the Doric, Ionic, and Corinthian orders

fu·sate \'fyü,zāt\ *adj* [L *fus*us + E *-ate*] : FUSIFORM

fusco- *comb form* [ISV, fr. L *fuscus*] : having a dark color : tawny ⟨*fusco*chlorin⟩ ⟨*fusco*ferruginous⟩

fus·cous \'fəskəs\ *adj* [L *fuscus* — more at DUSK] : of any of several colors averaging a brownish gray which is lighter than taupe (sense 1), lighter and less strong than average chocolate, and less strong and slightly redder than mouse gray

¹fuse \'fyüz\ *n* -S *often attrib* [It *fuso* spindle, fr. L *fusus*] **1** : a continuous train of explosive enclosed in a flexible waterproof cord or cable for setting off a charge (as dynamite) by communication of either fire or detonation ⟨detonating ~*s*⟩ — see SAFETY FUSE 1 **2** *usu* **fuze** \"\ : a detonating device for setting off (as by percussion) the bursting charge of a projectile, bomb, or torpedo ⟨our new proximity ~ which enabled artillery shells to burst automatically —F.E.Fox⟩

²fuse *or* **fuze** \"\ *vt* -ED/-ING/-S [¹*fuse* & ⁴*fuse*] : to equip with a fuse

³fuse \"\ *vb* -ED/-ING/-S [L *fusus*, past part. of *fundere* to pour, to melt — more at FOUND] *vt* **1 a** : to reduce to a liquid or plastic state by heat : DISSOLVE, MELT ⟨the thunderstorm had *fused* the electric mains —C.K.Finlay⟩ **b** : to blend by melting together : unite by heating ⟨foundries which ~ zinc and copper into hard, bright brass —*Newsweek*⟩ **c** *archaic* : to thin or dilute (the blood) ⟨purgatives are . . . to ~ and thin the blood —George Cheyne⟩ **2** : to unite as if by melting together : BLEND, INTEGRATE ⟨~*s* the clutter of detail into a rich and fascinating narrative —A.M.Schlesinger b.1917⟩; *specif* : to join (two adjacent bony surfaces) by surgery ~ *vi* **1** : to become fluid with heat : LIQUEFY, MELT ⟨acetate rayon tends to ~ if pressed at too high a temperature —W.L.Carmichael⟩; *specif* : to fail because of the melting of a link in an electrical circuit ⟨all the lights in the house have *fused* —*Christian Science Monitor*⟩ **2** : to become integrated : UNITE, MERGE ⟨the passion for service must ~ with the passion for knowledge —C.W.Eliot⟩ **syn** see MIX

⁴fuse \"\ *n* -S : a wire, bar, or strip of metal with a very low melting point that melts and breaks the circuit when an electric current exceeds a specified amperage ⟨plug ~*s* . . . have transparent windows at the top which enable the home-owner to see when they are blown —Bernard Gladstone⟩

fu·seau \(')fyü¦zō\ *n, pl* **fu·seaux** \-ōz\ [F, lit., spindle, fr. OF *fusel*, dim. of *fus*, fr. L *fusus*] : a fusiform multicellular body that resembles a spore and that is characteristic of various fungi of the genus *Trichophyton*

fuse block *n* **1** : FUSE GAUGE **2** *also* **fuse cutout** : a block of porcelain, slate, or other refractory material supporting a mounting for an electrical fuse

fuseboard \'=,=\ *n* : a slab of incombustible insulating material on which electrical safety fuses are mounted

fuse box *or* **fuse cabinet** *n* : CUTOUT BOX

fuse clip *n* : a spring clip supporting one end of a cartridge fuse and providing electrical connection with it

fused \'fyüzd\ *adj* **1 a** : melted together : united by heating; *specif, of a shirt collar* : stiffened by bonding an acetate interlining to the outside layers ⟨cotton broadcloth with ~ collar that does not need starching —*Eaton's Catalogue*⟩ **b** : reduced to liquid by heat : MOLTEN ⟨plating . . . consists in enveloping the metal with the higher melting point by the ~ bath of the metal with the lower melting point —*Scientific American*⟩ **c** : having atoms in common — used of ring systems in chemical compounds (as benzanthracene) **2** : MINGLED, BLENDED, INTEGRATED ⟨two sentences ~ into one⟩ ⟨a meandering fancy rather than a ~ vision —*Time*⟩

fused quartz *or* **fused silica** *n* : VITREOUS SILICA

¹fu·see *or* **fu·zee** \(')fyü¦zē\ *n* -S [F *fusée*, lit., spindleful of yarn, fr. OF *fusee*, fr. *fus* spindle, fr. L *fusus*] **1** : a conical spirally grooved pulley in a timepiece from which a cord or chain unwinds onto a barrel containing the spring, the increasing diameter of the pulley compensating for the lessening power of the spring **2** : ¹FUSE 1 **3** *obs* : a bony growth on the leg of a horse **4 a** : a wooden match with a bulbous head not easily blown out when ignited **b** : a paper match impregnated with niter and tipped with sulfur **5** : a red signal flare used esp. for protecting stalled trains and trucks

²fusee *or* **fuzee** \"\ *n* -S [modif. of F *fusil* — more at FUSIL] **1** : a flintlock gun : FIRELOCK **2** : FUSILIER

fuse gauge *also* **fuse cutter** *n* : an instrument for cutting fuses that consists of a block with a brass scale on one side and a hinged knife — called also *fuse block*

fu·se·lage \'fyüsə,läzh, -làzh *also* -üzə- *or* -läj *or* -làj *or* ,==' *sometimes* '==,lij *or* 'fyü(,)sl- *or* -fyüz(,)l-\ *n* -S [F, fr. *fuselé* spindle-shaped (fr. MF, fr. *fusel* spindle + *-é* -ate, fr. L *-atus*) + *-age* — more at FUSEAU] : the central body portion of an airplane designed to accommodate the crew and the passengers or cargo

fu·sel oil \'fyüzəl-\ *n* [G *fusel* bad liquor] **1** : an acrid oily liquid that has an unpleasant odor, that is obtained in small amounts as a by-product in alcoholic fermentation (as of potatoes, grain, or molasses), that consists of a mixture chiefly of alcohols (as isopentyl, active amyl, isobutyl, and normal propyl alcohols), and that is used esp. as a source of alcohols and as a solvent **2** : AMYL ALCOHOL 2a

fuseplug \'=,=\ *n* **1** : a plug fitted to the fuse hole of a military projectile to hold the fuse **2** : PLUG FUSE

fuses *pl of* FUSE, *pres 3d sing of* FUSE

fushion \'füzhən\ *var of* FOISON

fu·shion·less \-ləs\ *adj* **1** *Scot, of food or drink* : lacking in flavor or nourishment : INSIPID **2** *Scot, of a person* **a** : physically weak : lacking energy **b** : mentally or spiritually dull

fu·shun \'fü¦shün\ *adj, usu cap* [fr. *Fushun*, Manchuria] : of or from the city of Fushun, Manchuria : of the kind or style prevalent in Fushun

fusi- *comb form* [L *fusus* spindle] : spindle ⟨*fusi*form⟩ : spindle-shaped ⟨*Fusi*coccum⟩

fu·si·bil·i·ty \,fyüzə'biləd·ē, -ətē, -i\ *n* -ES [F *fusibilité*, fr. MF, fr. *fusible* + *-ité* -ity] : the quality, state, or degree of being fusible

fu·si·ble \'fyüzəbəl\ *adj* [F or ML; F, fr. MF, fr. ML *fusibilis*, fr. L *fusus* (past part. of *fundere* to pour, melt) + *-ibilis* -ible — more at FOUND] : capable of being fused; *esp* : capable of being liquefied by heat

fusible metal *or* **fusible alloy** *n* : a metal or alloy (as of bismuth, lead, and tin or of these three metals and cadmium or indium) having a low melting point usu. below 300°F and used typically for dies, fixtures, molds, patterns, boiler safety plugs, and automatic-sprinkler fuses

fu·si·cla·di·um \,fyüzə'klādēəm\ *n, cap* [NL, fr. *fusi-* + Gk *kladion* twig, shoot, dim. of *klados* branch, shoot — more at GLADIATOR] : a form genus of imperfect fungi (family Dematiaceae) that produces one-celled or once-septate spores on short conidiophores usu. in extensive groups

fu·si·coc·cum \-'käkəm\ *n, cap* [NL, fr. *fusi-* + *-coccum* (fr. Gk *kokkos* grain, seed, kermes berry)] : a form genus of imperfect fungi (family Sphaeropsidaceae) that have hyaline unicellular fusiform spores in several-chambered pycnidia

fu·si·form \'fyüzə,fȯrm\ *adj* [*fusi-* + *-form*] : shaped like a spindle : tapering toward each end — see ROOT illustration

fusiform bacillus *n* : a rod-shaped bacterium (*Fusobacterium fusiforme* or *Fusiformis plauti-vincenti*) having one blunt and one pointed end and being typically associated in pairs with the blunt ends apposed forming a fusiform figure — see VINCENT'S INFECTION

fusiform initial *n* : an elongated tapering cell in the cambium that through repeated division gives rise to vertically arranged cells — compare RAY INITIAL

fu·si·for·mis \,==='fȯrməs\ *n, cap* [NL, fr. ISV *fusiform*] *in some classifications* : a genus of parasitic anaerobic or microaerophilic nonmotile bacteria (family Bacteroidaceae) that stain unevenly, form no spores, and are often associated with purulent lesions

fusiform rust *n* : a rust esp. of loblolly and Caribbean pine seedlings caused by a fungus (*Cronartium fusiforme*) that produces distinctive spindle-shaped cankers on the stems

¹fu·sil \'fyüzəl\ *or* **fu·sile** \", -ü,zīl, -,sīl\ *adj* [ME *fusil*, fr. L *fusilis*, fr. *fusus* (past part. of *fundere* to pour, melt) + *-ilis* -ile — more at FOUND] **1** *archaic* **a** : made by melting and pouring into forms : CAST ⟨wrought ~ or graven in metal —John Milton⟩ **b** : liquefied by heat : melted and flowing ⟨o'er the silver pours the ~ gold —Alexander Pope⟩ **2** *archaic* : susceptible to melting : FUSIBLE

²fu·sil \'fyüzəl\ *n* -S [ME, fr. MF *fusel, fusil* spindle — more at FUSEAU] **1** : a rhomboidal heraldic bearing longer in proportion to its width than a lozenge **2** : a spindle-shaped siliceous concretion

fusil 1

³fusil \"\ *also* **fu·zil** \"\ *n* -S [F *fusil* steel for striking fire, musket, fr. OF *foisil, fuisil* steel for striking fire, fr. (assumed) VL *focilis*, fr. LL *focus* fire (fr. L, fireplace, hearth) + L *-ilis* -ile — more at FOCUS] : a light flintlock musket

fu·si·lier *or* **fu·si·leer** \¦fyüzə¦li(ə)r, -iə\ *n* -S [F *fusilier*, fr. *fusil* + *-ier* -er] **1** : a soldier armed with a fusil **2** : a member of one of the British regiments that were formerly armed with fusils

¹fu·sil·lade \'fyüsə,lād, -üzə-, -äd, -àd, ,==¦=\ *n* -S [F, fr. *fusiller* to shoot (fr. *fusil*) + *-ade*] **1 a** : a number of shots fired simultaneously or in rapid succession esp. with small arms : VOLLEY ⟨a ~ of buckshot —Horace Sutton⟩ **b** : FIRING SQUAD ⟨he was condemned to death . . . and died by the ~ —W. O.Scroggs⟩ **2** : a spirited outburst of any sort ⟨a ~ of marimba music —Maud Oakes⟩; *specif* : a barrage of criticism ⟨never . . . has a new head of government come under such a ~ from his own party —*Atlantic*⟩

²fusillade \"\ *vt* -ED/-ING/-S : to attack or shoot down by simultaneous or rapidly successive gunfire

fu·sil·ly \'fyüzəlē\ *adj* [ME *fusile*, fr. *fusil*] **1** : divided into fusil-shaped compartments — used of a heraldic field or bearing **2** : made of a row of fusils — used of a heraldic bearing

fusing *pres part of* FUSE

fusing disk *n* : a steel disk that causes fusion by the heat from its rapid rotation and is used to cut metal

fu·si·nite \'fyüzᵊn,īt\ *n* -S [alter. of *fusain* + *-ite*] : the opaque carbonized cell structure found in fusain and sometimes considered a mineral

fu·si·ni·za·tion \,fyüzᵊnə'zāshən, -,nī'z-\ *n* -S [alter. of *fusain* + *-ization*] : the transformation of plant material to fusain

fu·sion \'fyüzhən\ *n* -S *often attrib* [L *fusion-, fusio*, fr. *fusus* (past part. of *fundere* to pour, melt) + *-ion-* *-io* -ion — more at FOUND] **1 a** : the act or process of liquefying or rendering plastic by heat : transition of a substance from a solid to a liquid : MELTING ⟨welds accompanied by ~ are by far the most common —*Welding Handbook*⟩ **b** : the quality or state of flowing induced by this process ⟨that degree of heat must be employed which will give perfect ~ to the glaze —G.R. Porter⟩ **2** : a union by or as if by melting: as **a** : a merging of diverse elements into a unified whole : SYNTHESIS ⟨opera is the ~ of five arts into a composite whole —Warwick Braithwaite⟩; *specif* : the blending of retinal images in binocular vision **b** : a combination of ingredients achieved by heating and mixing together ⟨cement is a ~ formed from exact proportions of shale and limestone —E.S.Perry⟩ **c** : a political partnership : COALITION ⟨a ~ of Democrats and independent Republicans —*N.Y. Times*⟩ ⟨elected on a ~ ticket —F. H. LaGuardia⟩ **d** (1) : a blend of sensations, perceptions, ideas, or attitudes such that the component elements can seldom be identified by introspective analysis (2) : the perception of light from a source that is intermittent above a critical frequency as if the source were continuous — contrasted with *flicker;* see CRITICAL FLICKER FREQUENCY **e** : a coalescence into a solid unit : WELDING; *specif* : the surgical immobilization of a joint ⟨spinal ~⟩ **f** : coalescence between root and affix in a language (as in Latin *pēs* "foot" from assumed earlier *peds* with the root *ped-* and the nominative singular ending *-s*) — compare INFLECTIONAL **g** : the union of atomic nuclei to form heavier nuclei resulting in the release of enormous quantities of energy when certain light elements unite (as in the combination of heavy-hydrogen nuclei to form helium nuclei that takes place in the sun or in a hydrogen bomb) — called also *nuclear fusion;* contrasted with *fission*

fu·sion·al \-zhənᵊl, -zhnəl\ *adj* : relating to or characterized by fusion; *specif* : being or relating to a process, language, or type of linguistic structure in which fusion occurs

fusion bomb *n* : a bomb in which nuclei of a light chemical element unite to form nuclei of heavier elements with a release of energy; *esp* : HYDROGEN BOMB — compare ATOM BOMB

fusion frequency *n* : CRITICAL FLICKER FREQUENCY

fu·sion·ist \-zh(ə)nəst\ *n* -S [F *fusionniste*, fr. *fusion* (fr. L *fusion-, fusio*) + *-iste* -ist] : one who promotes or takes part in a coalition esp. of political parties

fu·sion·less \'füzhənləs\ *var of* FUSHIONLESS

fusion nucleus *n* **1 a** : PRIMARY ENDOSPERM NUCLEUS **b** : the triploid nucleus resulting from double fertilization that produces the endosperm nuclei in seed plants **2 a** : SYNKARYON **b** : ZYGOTE

fusion point *n* : MELTING POINT

fusion welding *n* : the welding of metals in a molten state without mechanical pressure or pounding

fu·site \'fyü,zīt\ *n* -S [*fusain* + *-ite*] : FUSINITE

fuso- *comb form* [L *fusus* spindle] **1** : shaped like a spindle ⟨*fuso*cellular⟩ **2** : fusiform bacillus and ⟨*fuso*spirillar⟩ ⟨*fuso*spirochetal⟩

fu·so·bacterium \¦fyü(,)zō+\ *n* [NL, fr. *fuso-* + *bacterium*] **1** *cap* : a genus of gram-negative anaerobic strictly parasitic rod-shaped bacteria usu. placed among the Bacteroidaceae and sometimes included in *Fusiformis* — see FUSIFORM BACILLUS **2** *pl* **fusobacteria** : any organism of the genus *Fusobacterium*

fu·so·cellular \"+\ *adj* [ISV *fuso-* + *cellular*] : composed of fusiform cells

fu·soid \'fyü,zȯid\ *adj* [L *fus*us spindle + E *-oid*] : FUSIFORM

fu·so·spirochetal \¦fyü(,)zō+\ *adj* [*fuso-* + *spirochetal*] : of, relating to, or caused by the fusiform bacillus and spirochetes — compare VINCENT'S INFECTION

fu·so·spirochete \"+\ *n* -S [ISV *fuso-* + *spirochete*] : the associated bacterium and spirochete that are typically present together in Vincent's infection

fu·so·spirochetosis \"+\ *n, pl* **fusospirochetoses** [NL, fr. ISV *fusospirochete* + NL *-osis*] : VINCENT'S INFECTION

¹fuss *n* -ES [origin unknown] *obs* : FUSSOCK

²fuss \'fəs\ *n* -ES [perh. of imit. origin] **1 a** : needless bustle or excitement : COMMOTION ⟨he found a point of vantage and settled himself with all the ~ of an audience in a theater —Audrey Barker⟩ **b** : effusive praise : TO-DO ⟨stand by this old man and make a big ~ over his ability to cook beans —L.C.Douglas⟩ **2 a** : a state of agitation esp. over a trivial matter ⟨in a ~ and a stew all afternoon —Molly L. Bar-David⟩ **b** : COMPLAINT, OBJECTION, PROTEST ⟨no ~ was made in his day if a new writer took from an old one whatever material he found congenial —C.E.Montague⟩ **c** : an angry dispute : QUARREL ⟨as a dying phase of the ~ they are raising a controversy over certain words and phrases —B.J.Hendrick⟩ **3** : an ornamental flourish : DECORATION ⟨printed in Caslon without ~ —*Times Lit. Supp.*⟩ **syn** see STIR

³fuss \"\ *vb* -ED/-ING/-ES *vi* **1 a** : to create or be in a state of restless activity : BUSTLE ⟨a fleet of small tugs . . . ~*ed* up and down continually —Leslie Richardson⟩; *specif* : to shower flattering attentions — usu. used with *over* ⟨the children kissed me and patted me and ~*ed* over me —Polly Adler⟩ **b** : to pay undue attention to small details : PUTTER ⟨~ with his clothes —J.B.Benefield⟩ **2** *slang* : to court a girl : DATE ⟨have the best time in college: dramatics and basketball and ~*ing* and dancing —Sinclair Lewis⟩ **3 a** : to become upset : FRET, WORRY ⟨I know I'm an idiot to ~ but they're two hours late —David Walker⟩ **b** (1) : NAG, COMPLAIN : ARGUE, PROTEST ⟨tears and ~*ing* are hard for a parent to take but some release is better for a child than attempts at Spartan bravery —Dorothy Barclay⟩ (2) *dial* : SCOLD, CHIDE — usu. used with *at* ⟨I don't like to be ~*ed* at in public —Eudora Welty⟩ ~ *vt* **1** : to stir up : ANNOY, AGITATE, UPSET ⟨she ~*ed* one; she was always in a state of emotion —Virginia Woolf⟩ **2** *slang* : COURT, DATE

fuss and feathers *n pl but usu sing in constr* : fanfare and ostentation ⟨official holidays . . . were celebrated with a maximum of *fuss and feathers* —A.T.Bouscaren⟩

fuss·budg·et \'fəs,bəjət, *usu* -əd·+V\ *n* -S : one who fusses or frets about trifles ⟨funny old ~*s* without much practical sense —M.M.Mathews⟩ — **fuss·budg·ety** \-əd·ē\ *adj*

fuss·er \'fəsə(r)\ *n* -S : one that fusses

fuss·i·ly \'fəsəlē, -li\ *adv* : in a fussy manner

fuss·i·ness \-sēnəs, -sin-\ *n* -ES : the quality or state of being fussy

fus·sle \'fəsəl\ *Scot var of* WHISTLE

fuss mill *n* : ATTRITION MILL

fus·sock \'fəsək, 'fəs-\ *n* -S [origin unknown] *dial Eng* **1** : DONKEY **2** : a pudgy or stupid person

fuss·pot \'fə,spät\ *n* -S : FUSSBUDGET

fuss up *vt, dial* : to make pretty : EMBELLISH ⟨*fuss up* the stage with superfluous people and superfluous action —*N.Y. Times*⟩

fussy \'fəsē, -si\ *adj* -ER/-EST **1 a** : nervous or easily upset : IRRITABLE ⟨a ~ manner that covered a nervousness he had never been able to conquer —J.D.Beresford⟩ **b** : full of commotion : BUSTLING ⟨~ . . . locomotives snort and wheeze as they drag heavily laden cane trucks to sugar factories —J.W.Coulter⟩ **2** : provided with an abundance of decorative detail : ORNATE ⟨the white curtains starched and all the ~ gilt handles rubbed up —Helen Shaw⟩ **3 a** : requiring or giving close attention to petty details : METICULOUS ⟨looked like a natural for the ~ bookkeeping routine of an orderly room —Earle Birney⟩ **b** : revealing a finicky concern for niceties : FASTIDIOUS, CHOOSY ⟨a man who was ~ about his food⟩ **syn** see NICE

¹fust \'fùst, 'fəst\ *n* -S [back-formation fr. *fusty*] *dial Brit* : a strong musty smell : MUSTINESS

²fust \"\ *vi* -ED/-ING/-S **1** *archaic* : to become moldy through disuse ⟨sure he that made us . . . gave us not that capability and godlike reason to ~ in us unused —Shak.⟩ **2** *archaic, of food or drink* : to taste or smell moldy or stale

³fust \'fəst\ *n* -S [It *fusto*, lit., trunk (of a tree), fr. L *fustis* club, staff — more at BEAT] : the shaft of a column or pilaster

⁴fust \"\ *dial var of* FIRST

fus·ta·nel·la \,fəstə'nelə, ,füs-\ *n* -S [It, fr. NGk *phoustanella*, dim. of *phoustani* woman's dress, fr. It *fustagno* fustian, fr. ML *fustaneum* — more at FUSTIAN] : a short full skirt of stiff white linen or cotton worn by men (as the evzones) in some Balkan countries

fus·tet \¦fə¦stet\ *n* -S [F, fr. MF *fustet, fustel*, fr. OProv, prob. fr. OCatal *fustet*, fr. Ar *fustaq, fustuq* — more at FUSTIC] **1** : SMOKE TREE 1a **2** : the yellow dyewood of the European smoke tree — called also *young fustic*

¹fus·tian \'fəschən, *chiefly Brit* -stiən *or* -styən\ *n* -S [ME *fustane, fustian*, fr. OF *fustane, fustaine*, fr. ML *fustaneum*, prob. fr. ML *fustis* tree trunk, fr. L, club, staff; trans. of Gk *xylinon* cotton, fr. neut. of *xylinos* wooden, fr. *xylon* wood, club] **1 a** : a strong cotton and linen fabric used for clothing and bedding **b** : a class of cotton fabrics usu. having a pile face and twill weave ⟨corduroys and velveteens belong to a group of filling-faced fabrics known by the old term ~ —John Hoye⟩ **2** : pretentious writing or speech : an inflated style : BOMBAST ⟨pure ~ — an appropriate accompaniment for some melodramatic stage spectacle —Winthrop Sargeant⟩ — often used interjectionally to express disbelief or disdain ⟨nonsense! ~! Good day to you! —S.H.Adams⟩ **syn** see BOMBAST

²fustian \"\ *adj* **1** : made of fustian ⟨a ~ coat⟩ **2** : pompous and overdone : EXAGGERATED ⟨~ antique heroes —H.O. Taylor⟩ **3** : GOOD-FOR-NOTHING, WORTHLESS ⟨a ~ rascal —Leslie Hotson⟩

fus·tic \'fəstik\ *n* -S [ME *fustik*, fr. MF *fustoc*, fr. Ar *fustuq, fustaq*, fr. Gk *pistakē* pistachio tree — more at PISTACHIO] **1** : any of several dyewoods: as **a** : the yellow wood of a common tropical American tree (*Chlorophora tinctoria*) — called also *dyer's mulberry, old fustic* **b** : FUSTET 2 **2** : the tree that yields old fustic — called also *dyer's mulberry* **3** : the yellow coloring matter extracted from old fustic and used esp. in dyeing wool — see DYE table I (under *Natural Yellow 11*) **4** : ⁶LIME 3

fus·ti·gate \'fəstə,gāt\ *vt* -ED/-ING/-S [LL *fustigatus*, past part. of *fustigare*, fr. L *fustis* club, staff + *-igare* (akin to *agere* to drive, act, do) — more at BEAT, AGENT] **1** : to beat with a stick : CUDGEL **2** : to criticize severely : CASTIGATE — **fus·ti·ga·tion** \,=='gāshən\ *n* -S

fus·ti·ga·tor \'==,gād·ə(r)\ *n* -S : one that fustigates

fus·ti·lugs \'fəstē,ləgz\ *n, pl* **fustilugs** [*fusty* + *lugs*, pl. of *lug*] *archaic* : a ponderous clumsy person; *esp* : a fat and slovenly woman

fus·ti·ly \'fəstəlē, -li\ *adv* : in a fusty manner

fus·tin \'fəstən\ *n* -S [G, fr. F *fustet* + G *-in*] : a crystalline compound $C_{15}H_{12}O_6$ obtained from the wood of various plants (as the smoke tree); dihydro-fisetin

fus·ti·ness \'fəstēnəs, -tin-\ *n* -ES : the quality or state of being fusty

fus·tle \'fùsəl, 'fəs-\ *vi* -ED/-ING/-S [blend of *fuss* and *bustle*] *dial Brit* : to fuss and bustle

fus·ty \'fəstē, -ti\ *adj* -ER/-EST [ME, fr. *fust* wine cask (fr. MF, club, stick, tree, cask, fr. L *fustis* club, staff) + *-y* — more at BEAT] **1** *Brit* : impaired by age or dampness : MOLDY ⟨~ hay⟩ **2** : saturated with dust and stale odors : MUSTY ⟨rummage into ~ rooms —Howard Griffin⟩ **3** : old-fashioned or rigidly conservative : ANTIQUATED ⟨a ~ elderly gentleman in a threadbare morning coat —George Bellairs⟩

fu·su·la \'fyüzələ\ *n, pl* **fusu·lae** \-,lē, -,lī\ *or* **fusulas** [NL, fr. L *fusus* spindle + *-ula* (fem. dim. suffix)] : a terminal projection of the spinneret of a spider through which the silk gland opens

fu·su·li·na \,fyüzə'līnə, -lēnə\ *n* [NL, fr. L *fusus* spindle + *-ulus* (dim. suffix) + NL *-ina*] **1** *cap* : a genus (the type of the family Fusulinidae) of large fossil spindle-shaped foraminiferans having a test with 4-layered walls and deeply folded septa and serving as an index fossil in various Lower and Middle Pennsylvanian rocks **2** -S : an animal or fossil of *Fusulina* or a related genus

¹fu·su·lin·id \¦==¦nəd, -¦linəd\ *adj* [NL *Fusulinidae*] : of or relating to the family Fusulinidae

²fusulinid \"\ *or* **fu·su·line** \'fyüzə,līn\ *n* -S : an animal or fossil of the family Fusulinidae

fu·su·lin·i·dae \,fyüzə'linə,dē\ *n pl, cap* [NL, fr. *Fusulina*, type genus + *-idae*] : a large family of Paleozoic foraminiferans known from their tests which form a major component of one widely distributed kind of Carboniferous limestone

fu·su·ma \'füsə,mä\ *n* -S [Jap] : a framed and papered sliding door used to partition off rooms in a Japanese house

fut *abbr* future; futures

futch·el *or* **futch·ell** \'fəchəl\ *n* -S [origin unknown] : one of the pieces of wood or metal forming a socket for the pole of a carriage and uniting the splinter bar and the fore axletree

fu·thark \'fü,thärk\ *also* **fu·thorc** *or* **fu·thork** \-thȯrk\ *n* -S [*futhark* fr. the first 6 letters (including *thorn* for *th*) of the Scandinavian and continental runic alphabets; *futhorc, futhork* fr. the first 6 letters of the Anglo-Saxon runic alphabet] : RUNIC ALPHABET

fu·tile \'fyüd·ᵊl, -ütᵊl, *also* -ü,tīl *sometimes* -ü(,)til\ *adj* [MF or L; MF *futile*, fr. L *futtilis, futilis* that easily pours out, vain, worthless, fr. *futt-, fut-* (fr. *fundere* to pour, melt) + *-ilis* -ile — more at FOUND] **1** : serving no useful purpose : INEFFECTIVE, FRUITLESS ⟨opposition . . . had been so ~ that surrender seemed the only course open —C.L.Jones⟩ **2** : occupied with trifles : FRIVOLOUS ⟨a ~ vain man —John Buchan⟩ — **fu·tile·ly** \-ᵊl(l)ē, -ᵊll, -il(l)ē, |i\ *adv* — **fu·tile·ness** \-lnəs, -īln-, -iln-\ *n* -ES

¹fu·ti·li·tar·i·an \(,)fyü,tilə'terēən, -'ta(ə)r-, -'tār-\ *n* -S [blend of *futile* and *utilitarian*] **1** : one who engages in futile pursuits **2** : one who believes in the futility of human striving and aspiration — **fu·til·i·tar·i·an·ism** \-ēə,nizəm\ *n* -S

²futilitarian \(;)=;=¦===\ *adj* : exhibiting or based on an attitude of futility ⟨~ defeatism of the . . . recent posthumous volume —Fred Rodell⟩

fu·til·i·ty \fyü'tiləd·ē, -ətē, -i\ *n* -ES [MF *futilité*, fr. L *futilitas*, fr. *futilis* + *-itas* -ity] **1** : the quality or state of being futile : USELESSNESS ⟨the economic ~ of military power —Norman Angell⟩ **2** : an abortive attempt or useless gesture ⟨as startling as the aptness of flower and insect symbiosis are their unsuccesses and *futilities* —D.C.Peattie⟩ ⟨the *futilities* of debate for its own sake —W.A.White⟩ **3** : a lack of serious purpose : FRIVOLITY ⟨the pure *futilities* and unmitigated flirtations of an aristocracy —Walter Bagehot⟩

futilous *adj* [L *futil*is + E *-ous*] *obs* : FUTILE

fut·tock \ˈfəd·ək, -ətək\ *n* -s [prob. alter. of *foothook*] **:** one of the curved timbers scarfed together to form the lower part of the compound rib of a ship; *esp* **:** one of the transverse framing timbers passing across the keel — see SHIP illustration
futtock hoop *or* **futtock band** *n* **:** an iron band located near the top of a lower mast and to which the futtock shrouds are secured
futtock plate *n* **:** an iron plate fastened to the top of a lower mast and equipped with deadeyes to which the topmast rigging and the upper ends of the futtock shrouds are secured
futtock shroud *n* **:** a short iron rod leading from the futtock hoop to the futtock plate and connecting the topmast rigging with the lower mast — see SHIP illustration
futtock staff *n* **:** a short wooden or iron bar covered with leather or canvas and seized across the topmast rigging above the top
futtock stave *n, obs* **:** a short rope used to confine shrouds near a masthead

futtock plate

fu·tu·nan \fəˈtünən, füˈ-\ *n* -s *usu cap* [*Futuna* islands, southwestern Pacific + E *-an*] **1 a :** a Polynesian people of the Futuna islands **b :** a member of such people **2** *also* **futuna :** the Polynesian language of the Futunan people — compare AUSTRONESIAN
fu·tu·rama \ˌfyüchəˈramə, -rämə\ *n* -s [fr. *Futurama,* an exhibit at the New York World's Fair (1939-40)] **:** a preview of something that is not yet a reality **:** indication of potential ⟨a model, a full-scale ~ of what a democratic city should be —Alden Stevens⟩
fu·tu·ram·ic \ˌ≠≠ˈramik\ *adj* **:** of advanced design ⟨a ~ car⟩
¹fu·ture \ˈfyüchə(r)\ *adj* [ME, fr. OF & L; OF *futur,* fr. L *futurus* about to be (suppletive fut. part. of *esse* to be) — more at BE] **1 :** that is to be **:** still to come ⟨some ~ day⟩; *specif* **:** existing after death ⟨doctrine of a ~ life —John Kenrick⟩ **2 :** of, relating to, or constituting the future tense ⟨a ~ auxiliary⟩ **3 :** existing or occurring at a later time **:** SUBSEQUENT ⟨at 18 the ~ chairman of the board joined the company as a shipping clerk⟩
²future \ˈ"\ *n* -s [ME, fr. *future,* adj.] **1 a :** time that is to come ⟨car of the ~⟩ ⟨do better in ~⟩ ⟨be more tidy in ~ —*Blackwood's*⟩ **b :** what is going to happen ⟨the past determines the ~⟩ ⟨never tell the ~ —Graham Greene⟩ **2 a :** a prospective usu. improved condition ⟨expectation of a ~ worthy of the past⟩; *specif* **:** one held to follow mortal life **b :** an expectation of advancement **:** prospect for progressive development ⟨man with a ~⟩ ⟨discussed the ~ of electronics⟩ **3 a :** a stock or commodity bought and sold for delivery at a future time — usu. used in pl. ⟨speculated heavily in soybean ~*s* —Douglass Cater⟩ **b :** a contract for the purchase or sale of something to be delivered at a definite future time and at a specified price **4** [ML *futurum,* fr. neut. of L *futurus*] **:** the future tense of a language **:** a verb form in the future tense
³future *vb* -ED/-ING/-S *obs* **:** POSTPONE, DELAY
future farmer *n, usu cap both Fs* **:** a member of the national organization of boys enrolled in vocational agriculture courses in high schools in the U.S. called Future Farmers of America
future interest *or* **future estate** *n* **:** an interest or estate in property limited or created so that its owner will come into the use, possession, or enjoyment of it at some future time **:** ESTATE IN EXPECTANCY
fu·ture·less \ˈfyüchə(r)ləs\ *adj* **:** lacking the prospect of a future
futurely *adv, obs* **:** in future
fu·ture·ness *n* -ES **:** the quality or state of existing in the future
¹future perfect *adj* **:** of, relating to, or constituting a verb tense that is traditionally formed in English with *will have* and *shall have* and that expresses completion of an action by a specified time that is yet to come ⟨*will have left* in "they will have left before we arrive" is a *future perfect* tense⟩
²future perfect *n* **:** the future perfect tense of a language **:** a verb form in the future perfect tense
future price *n* **:** the price of a stock or commodity on a futures contract — contrasted with *spot price*
future service benefit *n* **:** a pension benefit based on length of prospective service between employment date and retirement age and payable out of funds contributed by the employer, the employee, or both
future tense *n* **:** a verb tense traditionally formed in English with *will* and *shall* and expressive of time yet to come
fu·tur·ism \ˈfyüchəˌrizəm\ *n* -s [It *futurismo,* fr. *futuro* future (fr. L *futurus*) + *-ismo* -ism] **1 :** a point of view that seeks life's meaning or fulfillment in the future rather than in the past or present **:** UTOPIANISM — compare ARCHAISM 3c **2 :** a movement in art, music, and literature begun in Italy about 1910 and marked esp. by violent rejection of tradition and an effort to give formal expression to the dynamic energy and movement of mechanical processes
fu·tur·ist \-ˌrəst\ *n* -s [It *futurista,* fr. *futuro* + *-ista* -ist] **1 :** one who holds that the prophecies of the Bible are still to be realized — compare PRESENTIST, PRETERIST **2 :** one who practices or advocates futurism
fu·tur·is·tic \ˌfyüchəˈristik, -tēk\ *adj* **:** of or relating to the future or to futurism ⟨the scene of the most ~ battle of the last war —Alan Moorehead⟩ — **fu·tur·is·ti·cal·ly** \-tək(ə)lē, -tēk-, -li\ *adv*
futuristic garden *n* **:** a garden design based on the volume of foliage and architectural masses and the air masses between them and uniting all three into a single pattern
fu·tu·ri·tion \ˌfyüchəˈrishən\ *n* -s [ML *futurition-, futuritio,* fr. L *futurus* about to be + *-ition-, -itio* -ition — more at BE] **1** *archaic* **:** future existence **:** FUTURITY ⟨the ~ of salvation —John Pearson⟩ **2** *archaic* **:** assurance of a future ⟨had a fixed ~ from eternity —Jonathan Edwards⟩
fu·tu·ri·ty \fyüˈt(y)u̇rəd·ē, fyüˈty|, fyüˈch|, |ür-, -ətē, -i\ *n* -ES [¹*future* + *-ity*] **1 :** time to come **:** FUTURE ⟨neither service past, nor present sorrows, nor purposed merit in ~ can ransom me into his love again —Shak.⟩ **2 :** the quality or state of being future ⟨~ of current architecture⟩ **3 a futurities** *pl* **:** future events or prospects ⟨the reader whose scholarship is still among his *futurities* —Thomas De Quincey⟩ **b :** what will exist or happen in the future ⟨gazing . . . into ~ across the groom's shoulder —Marguerite Steen⟩; *specif* **:** POSTERITY **c :** a prospective future state; *specif* **:** life after death ⟨from this earth set free in some remote ~ —Walter de la Mare⟩ **4 :** FUTURITY RACE
futurity cocktail *n* **:** a cocktail made of sloe gin, vermouth, and sometimes rum and flavored with lemon juice, grenadine, and bitters
futurity race *n* **1 :** a horse race usu. for two-year-olds in which the competitors are nominated at birth or before — compare PRODUCE RACE **2 :** a race or competition (as a field trial) for which entries are made well in advance of the event
fuze *var of* FUSE
fuzee *var of* FUSEE
fuzil *var of* FUSIL
¹fuzz \ˈfəz\ *n* -ES [prob. back-formation fr. *fuzzy*] **1** *obs* **:** PUFFBALL 1 **2 :** a mass of fluffy particles or fibers: as **a :** the short hairs remaining on the seed of most cotton varieties after removal of the longer lint fibers **b :** fibers that project from the surface of a sheet of paper or are not firmly incorporated into it **c :** the beard of an adolescent boy ⟨although a little ~ had recently begun to appear, had no real excuse for shaving —J.R.Gallagher⟩ **3 :** a blurred effect ⟨the rainbow-colored ~ of streetlight nebula —MacKinlay Kantor⟩ **4** *slang* **:** an officer of the law **:** POLICEMAN
²fuzz \ˈ"\ *vb* -ED/-ING/-ES *vi* **:** to fly off in or become covered with fluffy particles **:** become fuzzy ⟨angora tends to ~⟩ — often used with *out* ⟨watch the cat's tail ~ out when she's angry⟩ ⟨~*ing* out of the legal concept . . . to comprise another new crime —Gerard Piel⟩ ~ *vt* **1 :** to cover with fluff **:** make fuzzy ⟨the land was ~*ed* with buffalo grass —W.A.White⟩ **2 :** to envelop in a haze **:** BLUR ⟨my head was still badly ~*ed* from the drink —Ralph Ellison⟩ — usu. used with *up* ⟨~ up the argument⟩ ⟨if a little haze ~*es* up the lamps they say it's all closed in —C.A.Lindbergh b.1902⟩
fuzzball \ˈ≠,≠\ *n, dial chiefly Eng* **:** PUFFBALL 1
fuzz·i·ly \ˈfəzəlē, -li\ *adv* **:** in a fuzzy manner
fuzz·i·ness \-zēnəs, -zin-\ *n* -ES **:** the quality or state of being fuzzy
fuzz stick *n* **:** a short stick of dead wood with the wet outer layer cut away and the dry center trimmed down into feathers that is used by campers to start a fire when the fuel is damp
fuzztail \ˈ≠,≠\ *n* -s *West* **:** a wild horse — compare BROOMTAIL
¹fuzzy \ˈfəzē, -zi\ *adj* -ER/-EST [perh. fr. LG *fussig* loose, light, spongy; akin to D *voos* spongy, ON *fauskr* rotten wood, OHG *fūl* rotten — more at FOUL] **1** *now dial Eng* **:** not firm **:** SPONGY **2 :** having a furry or downy appearance **:** covered with fuzz ⟨deep-piled ~ felts —Lois Long⟩ ⟨an inviting carpet of ~ green moss —Tom Marvel⟩ **3 :** lacking in clarity or definition: as **a :** indistinct in outline **:** not in focus **:** BLURRED ⟨camera movement is a very likely cause of ~ photos —*Kodak Photo Notes*⟩; *specif* **:** lacking in musical clarity ⟨the loud fugue gets ~ towards end —*Saturday Rev.*⟩ **b :** VAGUE, INCONCLUSIVE, INDEFINITE ⟨like many crusaders . . . vehement in assault but ~ as to the nature of his reforms —Charles Lee⟩ **c :** CONFUSED, INCOHERENT, MUDDLED ⟨when a man's thinking is ~ or involved, so will his writing be —W.R.Parker⟩; *specif* **:** muddled by drink ⟨drank faster than anybody else without becoming ~ —Herman Wouk⟩ **4 :** CURLED, CRISPED, FRIZZY ⟨~'red wigs stuck with jewels —G.W.Thornbury⟩
²fuzzy \ˈ"\ *n* -ES **1 :** FUZZY-WUZZY **2 :** FUZZTAIL
fuzzy-guzzy \ˌ≠≠ˈgəzē\ *n* -s [redupl. & alter. of ¹*fuzzy*] **:** a balsamweed (*Gnaphalium obtusifolium*) with glandular villous stem
fuzzy-headed \ˌ≠≠ˈ≠≠\ *adj* **1 :** having a head with a woolly or downy surface ⟨*fuzzy-headed* dandelion⟩ **2 :** FUZZY 3c
fuzzy-wuzzy \ˌ≠≠ˈwəzē\ *n* -ES *usu cap F&W* [redupl. & alter. of ¹*fuzzy*] **1 :** a Negro of the Republic of the Sudan **2 :** a native of New Guinea or the Solomon islands
FV *abbr* [L *folio verso*] on the back of the page
f–value \ˈ≠,≠≠\ *n* **:** F-NUMBER
FW *abbr* fresh water
FWB *abbr* four-wheel brake
FWD *abbr* **1** four-wheel drive **2** freshwater damage
fwd *abbr* forward
fwdd *abbr* forwarded
FWE *abbr* finished with engines
fx *abbr* foxed
FX *abbr* foreign exchange
fx station *n, usu cap F&X* **:** FIXED STATION
-fy \-ˌfī\ *vb suffix* -ED/-ING/-ES [ME *-fien,* fr. OF *-fier,* fr. L *-ficare,* fr. *-ficus* -fic] **1 :** make **:** form into ⟨dandi*fy*⟩ ⟨gaudi*fy*⟩ **2 :** invest with the attributes of **:** make similar to ⟨citi*fy*⟩
fy *abbr* ferry
FY *abbr* fiscal year
fyce \ˈfīs\ *var of* FEIST
FYI *abbr* for your information
¹fyke \ˈfīk\ *var of* FIKE
²fyke \ˈ"\ *or* **fike** \ˈ"\ *n* -s [D *fuik* bow net, fr. MD *fūke, fuycke*] **:** a long bag net kept open by a series of hoops
fyke net *n* **:** FYKE; *esp* **:** a fyke equipped with one or more cork-floated wing nets designed to direct the fish toward the mouth of the fyke proper
fykie *var of* FIKIE
fyle *Scot var of* ³FILE
fyl·fot \ˈfilˌfät\ *n* -s [ME, painted device to fill the lower part of a painted window, fr. *fillen* to fill + *foot*] **:** SWASTIKA 1
fyrd \ˈfərd, ˈfi(ə)rd\ *n* -s [OE *fierd, fyrd* (also, campaign, camp); akin to OHG *fart* journey, ON *ferth,* Goth *usfartho* departure; derivatives fr. the root of E *fare*] **1 :** the national militia in England prior to the Norman Conquest ⟨men of the ~ were mustered and their weapons counted —Hope Muntz⟩ **2 :** the duty to serve in the fyrd
fytte \ˈfit\ *archaic var of* ¹FIT
fz *abbr* [It *forzando; forzato*] accented

¹g \ˈjē\ *n, pl* **g's** *or* **gs** \ˈjēz\ *often cap, often attrib* **1 a :** the seventh letter of the English alphabet **b :** an instance of this letter printed, written, or otherwise represented **c :** a speech counterpart of orthographic *g* (as hard *g* in *go, sagged,* or soft *g* in *gem*) **2 a :** the keynote of G major or G minor **b :** the tone G **3 :** a printer's type, a stamp, or some other instrument for reproducing the letter *g* **4 :** someone or something arbitrarily or conveniently designated *g* esp. as the seventh in order or class **5 :** something having the shape of the letter G **6 :** a unit of force applied to a body at rest equal to the force exerted on it by gravity **:** one of several such units applied to a body when accelerated (as when an airplane pulls out of a dive or makes a sharp turn) **7 a :** a general factor in intelligence **b** [symbol for *general ability*] **:** ABILITY 2 **8** *slang* **:** a sum of 1000 dollars

²g *abbr, often cap* **1** game **2** garage **3** [F *gauche*] left **4** gauge **5** gauss **6** gelding **7** gender **8** general **9** genitive **10** German **11** gilbert **12** gilt **13** glider **14** gloom **15** goal; goalie **16** gold **17** good **18** gourde **19** government **20** grain **21** gram **22** grand **23** gravity; acceleration of gravity **24** great **25** green **26** Greenwich time **27** grid **28** groschen **29** gross **30** group **31** guard **32** guardian **33** guide **34** guilder **35** guinea **36** gulden **37** gulf

³g *symbol, often cap* conductance

-g *abbr* -ing — used esp. in standard abbreviations of the present participle forms of verbs (as *actg* for *acting*)

ga \ˈgä\ *n, pl* **ga** \"\ *or* **gas** \ˈgäz\ *usu cap* **1 a :** a people of Ghana linguistically and culturally related to the Ashanti and others of the region — called also *Akra, Incra* **b :** a member of such people **2 :** a Kwa language of the Ga people

ga' \ˈgä\ *Scot var of* GALL

ga *abbr* gauge

GA *abbr* **1** general agent **2** general assembly **3** general assistance **4** general average

Ga *symbol* gallium

¹gab \ˈgab\ *n* -s [prob. alter. of ²*gob*] **1** *chiefly Scot* **a :** MOUTH **b :** TONGUE **2** *chiefly Scot* **:** TASTE

²gab \ˈgab, ˈgaa(ə)b\ *vi* **gabbed; gabbed; gabbing; gabs** [prob. short for *gabble*] **:** to talk in an idle, rapid, or thoughtless manner **:** CHATTER ⟨*gabbed* . . . about his six kids —*Time*⟩ ⟨she'll probably ~ about it tomorrow at the office until I have to shut her up —Edna Ferber⟩

³gab \"\ *n* -s **:** TALK; *esp* **:** idle talk ⟨luncheon ~ among women —John Portz⟩

⁴gab \"\ *n* -s [prob. fr. Flem *gabbe* notch, gash] **:** a hook or notch (as in an eccentric rod for a valve motion) designed to drop over a rod or lever to make a temporary connection

⁵gab \"\ *vi* **gabbed; gabbed; gabbing; gabs** [F *gaber*, fr. ON *gabba*; akin to ME *gabben* to scoff, lie, D *gabberen* to joke, and perh. to OE *geonian, ginian* to yawn — more at YAWN] *archaic* **:** BOAST

⁶gab \"\ *n* -s [by shortening] **:** GABARDINE

ga·bar \ˈgäbər\ *n* -s *usu cap* [Per, fr. Ar *kāfir* unbeliever] **:** a Zoroastrian of Iran — compare PARSI

gab·ar·dine \ˈgabə(r),dēn, ˌ≈≈ˈ≈\ *n* -s [MF *gaverdine, galvardine*] **1 :** GABERDINE **2 :** a garment of gabardine; *esp* **:** a gabardine coat or suit **3 :** a firm durable fabric with a steep twill weave forming fine distinct diagonal ribs on the right side that is given a smooth hard finish with or without sheen and is made of various fibers and in many weights for clothing

ga·ba·rit \ˌgabəˈrē\ *n* -s [F, fr. Prov *gabarrit* ship's model, blend of *gabarro* ship (fr. OProv *gabarra*, prob. modif. of LL *carabus* boat resembling a coracle) and *garbi* ship's model, form, of Gmc origin; perh. akin to OHG *garawen* to prepare — more at CARAVEL, YARE] **1 :** an outline on a drawing of an object (as a machine part) intended to move showing the space necessary to permit its motion **2 :** an outline on a drawing of a stationary object showing the space that must be kept clear for necessary access to it

gab·bai \ˈgäˈbī, ˈ≈,≈\ *n, pl* **gab·ba·im** \-īəm,-ī(,)ēm\ *also* **gabbais** [Heb *gabbay* collector, treasurer] **1 :** a collector of charitable gifts or of taxes among the Jews in talmudic times **2 :** a synagogue official; *esp* **:** a treasurer or administrator of synagogue funds

gab·bard \ˈgabərd\ *or* **gab·bart** \-rt\ *n* -s [modif. (influenced by *-ard, -art*) of MF *gabarre*, *gabarre* ship, fr. OProv *gabarra*] **:** a small ship (as a lighter or barge) formerly much used in inland navigation in Scotland

¹gab·ber \ˈgabə(r)\ *vb* [prob. of imit. origin] *archaic* **:** JABBER

²gabber \"\ *n* -s [¹*gabber*] *archaic* **:** fast and incoherent or unintelligible talk

³gabber \", ˈgaab-\ *n* -s [²*gab* + *-er*] **:** one that talks much, habitually, and usu. idly **:** CHATTERER

¹gab·ble \ˈgabəl\ *vb* **gabbled; gabbled; gabbling** \-b(ə)liŋ\ **gabbles** [prob. of imit. origin] *vi* **1 :** to talk fast, idly, foolishly, or without meaning **:** JABBER, CHATTER ⟨with a mighty throat clearing, he would ~ through his prayer —Ernest Beaglehole⟩ ⟨he loves to ~ with housewives at church suppers —Andrew Hamilton⟩ ⟨spent his time *gabbling* in bars⟩ ⟨the clerk had *gabbled* about a fee due⟩ ⟨saying nothing comprehensible, just babbling and *gabbling*, half unconsciously —Arnold Bennett⟩ **2 :** to utter inarticulate sounds (as of a chicken) rapidly ⟨a skein of duck came across, *gabbling* softly to themselves in the high air —Naomi Mitchison⟩ ~ *vt* **:** to say with incoherent rapidity **:** BABBLE ⟨our excitement exploded and we *gabbled* the story over and over —Santha Rama Rau⟩

²gabble \"\ *n* -s **1 :** loud or rapid talk with little or no meaning **:** nonsense talk ⟨subjected to ~ about fifteenth-century politics —John McCarten⟩ **2 :** meaningless sounds rapidly uttered (as by chickens) or given out (as by a stream running over rocks) ⟨discriminating between music and ~ —R.L.Ives⟩ ⟨listening to the avid ~ of water running from a gargoyle at the corner of the schoolhouse —Eve Langley⟩

gab·ble·ment \-bəlmənt\ *n* -s *archaic* **:** GABBLE

gab·bler \ˈgab(ə)lə(r)\ *n* -s **:** one that gabbles

gab·ble rat·chet \ˈgabəl,rachət\ *or* **gabble rack·et** \-,rakət\ *var of* GABRIEL RATCHET

gab·bro \ˈga(,)brō\ *n* -s [It, prob. modif. of L *glaber* bare, smooth — more at GLAD] **:** a rock of a family of granular igneous rocks composed essentially of calcic plagioclase (as labradorite), a ferromagnesian mineral (as augite, hypersthene, olivine, or hornblende), and accessory minerals (as apatite, magnetite, ilmenite) — **gab·bro·ic** \(ˈ)gaˈbrōik\ *adj* — **gab·bro·it·ic** \ˌ≈(,)≈ˈid·ik\ *adj*

gab·broid \ˈga,brȯid\ *adj* [*gabbro* + *-oid*] **:** resembling gabbro

gab·by \ˈgabē, ˈgaab-, -bi\ *adj* -ER/-EST **:** fond of talking **:** TALKATIVE, GARRULOUS ⟨kept from his duties by ~ colleagues⟩ ⟨always liked a ~ team in practice, a team that shouted as it ran signals —Harry Sylvester⟩

ga·belle \gəˈbel\ *n* -s [ME, fr. MF, fr. OIt *gabella*, fr. Ar *qabālah*] **:** TAX; *specif* **:** an impost on salt (as in France for several centuries prior to 1790)

gab·er·dine \ˈgabə(r),dēn, ˌ≈≈ˈ≈\ *n* -s [MF *gaverdine*] **1 a :** a coarse long coat or smock worn chiefly by Jews in medieval times **b :** a loose garment like a smock worn by English laborers **c :** something that covers and protects **2** *dial Eng* **:** PINAFORE **3 :** GABARDINE

gab·er·lun·zie \ˌgabərˈlənzi, -lin-, *archaic* -lün(y)i\ *n* -s [earlier *gaberlungy*] **1** *Scot* **:** BEGGAR, MENDICANT; *esp* **:** a former licensed professional beggar **2** *Scot* **:** a wandering ne'er-do-well

gab·fest \ˈ≈,fest\ *n* -s [³*gab* + G *fest* festival — more at -FEST] **:** an occasion marked chiefly by conversation (as gab) ⟨the inevitable and excited curbstone political ~*s* —*World Report*⟩ ⟨his own drugstore — where the teenagers gather for a soda and a ~ —W.F.McDermott⟩

gab gab \ˈgäb,gäb, ˈgab,gab\ *n* [Chamorro] **1 :** CORAL TREE a **2 :** PIA

ga·bi *or* **ga·be** \ˈgäbē\ *n* -s [Tag *gabi*] *Philippines* **:** TARO

gabies *pl of* GABY

ga·bi·on \ˈgābēən, ˈgab-\ *n* -s [MF, fr. OIt *gabbione*, lit., large cage, aug. of *gabbia* cage, fr. L *cavea* — more at CAGE] **1 :** a hollow cylinder of wickerwork or strap iron like a basket without a bottom that is filled with earth and used in building fieldworks or in mining as revetments or as shelter from an enemy's fire **2 :** a contrivance like a gabion filled with stones and sunk to assist in forming a bar, dike, or similar structure (as in harbor works)

ga·bi·o·nade \ˌgābēəˈnād, -nȧd\ *n* -s [F *gabionnade*, fr. MF, fr. OIt *gabbionata*, fr. *gabbione* gabion + *-ata* -ade] **1 :** a work of fortification thrown up with gabions **2 :** a structure of gabions sunk in lines as a core for a sandbar in harbor improvements

ga·bi·oned \ˈgābēənd\ *adj* **:** furnished with gabions

ga·ble \ˈgābəl\ *n* -s [ME, fr. MF, fr. ONF, of Gmc origin; akin to ON *gafl* gable — more at CEPHALIC] **1 a :** the vertical triangular portion of the end of a building from the level of the cornice or eaves to the ridge of the roof **b :** a similar end when not triangular in shape (as of a gambrel roof) **c :** the end wall of a building as distinguished from the front or rear side **2 :** something resembling or suggesting a gable esp. in shape ⟨an immense mountain mass with three ~*s* fronting the valley —John Muir †1914⟩: *as* **a :** a decorative usu. triangular member (as on a piece of furniture or above a Gothic doorway arch) — see BELL GABLE **b** *or* **gable hood :** a heavy hooded headdress made with a peaked band similar to a gable framing the face and worn by women during Henry VIII's reign

1 gables

gableboard \ˈ≈≈,≈\ *n* **:** BARGEBOARD

ga·bled \-bəld\ *adj* **:** furnished or constructed with a gable ⟨a ~ house⟩ ⟨a ~ roof⟩ ⟨a ~ lintel⟩

gable end *n* [ME *gable ende*, fr. *gable* + *ende* end — more at END] **:** a gabled end wall (as of a wing of a building)

gable roof *n* **:** a double-sloping roof that forms a gable at each end — see ROOF illustration

ga·blet \ˈgāblət\ *n* -s [ME, fr. AF, dim. of ONF *gable*] **:** a small gable or canopy shaped like a gable (as over a tabernacle, niche, buttress)

gable wall *n* **:** a wall surmounted by a gable

gable window *n* **1 :** a window in a gable **2 :** a window with a gable

gab·lock \ˈgablək\ *var of* GAVELOCK

ga·bon \gəˈbōn, -bän\ *adj, usu cap* [fr. *Gabon* Republic in Africa] **:** of or relating to Gabon **:** of the kind or style prevalent in Gabon

gab·o·nese \ˌgabəˈnēz, ¦gab-, -ēs\ *n, pl* **gabonese** *cap* [*Gabon* + *-ese*] **:** a native or inhabitant of Gabon

¹ga·boon *or* **ga·bun** \gəˈbün, (ˈ)ga¦b-, (ˈ)gä¦b-\ *n* -s **1** *cap, in former classifications* **:** any of the Negro people of the Gabon Republic **2 a** *or* **gaboon mahogany** (1) **:** a light soft attractively grained pink to pinkish brown African wood (2) **:** a tree yielding gaboon (esp. *Aucoumea klaineana* and *Canarium schweinfurthii*) **b :** a high-grade black ebony obtained chiefly from the Gabon region of Africa

²ga·boon \(ˈ)gä¦bün, gəˈb-\ *n* -s [alter. of ¹*gob* (lump of tobacco) + *-oon* (as in *spittoon*)] *dial* **:** CUSPIDOR, SPITTOON

gaboon chocolate *n, usu cap G* **:** DIKA BREAD

gaboon viper *n, usu cap G* **:** a large heavy-bodied brilliantly marked extremely venomous West African viper (*Bitis gabonica*) of sluggish and unaggressive disposition

ga·bri·e·li·no *or* **ga·bri·e·le·no** \ˌgäbrēəˈlē(,)nō\ *n, pl* **gabrielino** *or* **gabrielinos** *or* **gabrieleno** *or* **gabrielenos** *usu cap* [Sp *gabrieleño*, fr. San *Gabriel*, a mission in Los Angeles county, Calif. + Sp *-eño* (suffix added to place names to form names of inhabitants)] **1 a :** a Shoshonean people of Los Angeles and Orange counties, California **b :** a member of such people **2 :** the language of the Gabrielino people

ga·bri·el rat·chet \ˈgābrēəl,rachət\ *n* [ME *Gabrielle rache*, fr. *Gabriel*, one of the seven archangels, the herald of good tidings (Lk 1), thought of as blowing a trumpet on Judgment Day + *rache* hound — more at RACH] *dial* **:** the cries of migrating wild geese flying by night which are often popularly explained as the baying of a supernatural pack of hounds and to which various superstitious significances (as forebodings of evil) are attributed

gabs *pl of* GAB, *pres 3d sing of* GAB

gab session *n, slang* **:** GABFEST

ga·by \ˈgābi, ˈgōbi\ *n* -ES [perh. of Scand origin; akin to Icel *gapi* reckless or frivolous person, fr. *gapa* to gape — more at GAPE] *now dial Eng* **:** SIMPLETON ⟨still whimpering after that ~ of a husband —W.M.Thackeray⟩

ga·chu·pin \ˌgächüˈpēn\ *n* -s [AmerSp *gachupin, cachupin*, fr. obs. Sp *cachopin* block, trunk, blockhead, fr. *cachopo* hollow or dry trunk of a tree, fr. *cacho* pot, shard — more at CACHUCHA] *chiefly Southwest* **:** a Spanish settler in America who immigrated from Spain — sometimes used disparagingly

g acid *n, usu cap G* **:** an acid $HOC_{10}H_5(SO_3H)_2$ made by sulfonating beta-naphthol and used as an intermediate for azo dyes; 2-naphthol-6,8-disulfonic acid

¹gad \ˈgad, ˈgaa(ə)d\ *n* -s [ME *gad, gadd*, fr. ON *gaddr* spike, sting — more at YARD (measure)] **1 a** *obs* **:** a sharp-pointed metal rod or stylus **b** *archaic* **:** SPEAR **c :** a chisel or pointed or wedge-shaped bar of iron or steel for breaking or loosening ore or rock **d** *West* **:** SPUR **2 a** *archaic* **:** a bar or ingot of metal **b :** a heraldic bearing supposed to represent such a gad sometimes depicted as a plain rectangle with the vertical dimension greater than the horizontal one and sometimes with a third dimension showing along the edge **3** *dial* **:** ROD, STICK: as **a :** a stiff whip or switch **b** *chiefly Scot* **:** FISHING ROD

²gad \"\ *vb* **gadded; gadded; gadding; gads** *vi* **:** to use a gad ~ *vt* **:** to break or loosen (as rock) with a gad in mining

³gad \"\ *vi* **gadded; gadded; gadding; gads** [ME *gadden*] **1 a :** to go or wander about esp. idly or for trivial purposes (as to gossip) — often used with *about* ⟨the women were *gadding* about gossiping instead of spending the day industriously —Ernest Beaglehole⟩ ⟨*gadding* about at political meetings —H.M.Parshley⟩ **b** *obs* **:** to run wild **:** dash about in an uncontrolled manner **2** *of an arrow* **:** to fly erratically

⁴gad \"\ *n* -s **:** the act of gadding **:** a wandering about usu. on rather trivial errands — now used chiefly in the phrases *on the gad* and *upon the gad*

⁵gad \"\ *interj* [euphemism for *God*] **:** a mild oath

⁶gad \"\ *n* -s [IrGael, fr. MIr *gat* willow twig — more at YARD (measure)] **:** a band or rope made of twisted straw or osiers

gad·a·ba \ˈgadəbə\ *n* -s *usu cap* **1 :** one of a people of primitive hoe cultivators in eastern India **2 :** the Munda language of the Gadabas

¹gadabout \ˈ≈≈,≈\ *adj* [fr. *gad about*, v., fr. ³*gad*] **:** being a gadabout ⟨a ~ brother who refused to settle down⟩

²gadabout \"\ *n* -s [fr. *gad about*, v.] **:** one that moves or wanders from place to place often with somewhat trivial purposes **:** GADDER ⟨social whirlers are of two kinds, the ones who concentrate on doing a lot of entertaining at home, and the ones who are ~*s* —A.C.Spectorsky⟩

gad·a·rene \ˈgadə,rēn, ˌ≈≈ˈ≈\ *adj* [LL *Gadarenus*, fr. Gk *Gadarēnos* inhabitant of Gadara, fr. *Gadara*, ancient town near the Sea of Galilee in northern Palestine] **1** *usu cap* **:** of or relating to Gadara or its inhabitants **2** *often cap* [fr. the *Gadarene* swine (Mt 8: 28) that rushed into the sea and drowned when Jesus sent into them demons exorcised from a demoniac person] **:** rushing precipitously forward **:** engaged in headlong flight ⟨watching the *Gadarene* swarms surging along the pavements of cities —Bruce Marshall⟩ ⟨perceiving this pitfall and attempting to prevent his ardent followers from making a ~ plunge into it —Bergen Evans⟩

gad·a·ria \gəˈdərēə\ *n* -s *usu cap* [Hindi *gadariyā*, fr. *gādar* sheep] **:** one of a caste of shepherds of central and northeastern India

gad·dang \ˈgä,däŋ, ≈ˈ≈\ *n, pl* **gaddang** *or* **gaddangs** *usu cap* [native name in the Philippines] **1 a :** a people inhabiting northern Luzon in the Philippines **b :** a member of such people **2 :** the Austronesian language of the Gaddang people

¹gad·der \ˈgadə(r), -aad-\ *n* -s [³*gad* + *-er*] **:** one that travels about habitually, restlessly, or with chiefly social purposes

²gadder \"\ *n* -s [²*gad* + *-er*] **:** a traveling drilling machine used in quarrying to make a line of holes into which gads are driven to break out the stone

¹gad·di *or* **ga·di** \gəˈdē, ˈ≈≈\ *n* -s [Hindi *gaddī*] **1** *India* **a :** a cushion esp. for a throne **b :** THRONE ⟨the succession to the ~ was not in all cases hereditary —*White Paper on Indian States*⟩ ⟨succeeded to the ~ in 1899 —*Statesman's Yr. Bk.*⟩ **2** *India* **:** a high ruling position ⟨helping the smaller ones of his tribe into ministerial ~*s* —*Weekly Observer*⟩

²gaddi \"\ *n, pl* **gaddi** *or* **gaddis** *usu cap* **1 :** a low-caste chiefly shepherd people in Kashmir **2 :** a member of the Gaddi people

gade \ˈgād\ *n* -s [NL *Gadus*, genus name] **:** a gadoid fish; *esp* **:** ROCKLING

gadfly \ˈ≈,≈\ *n* [¹*gad* + *fly*] **1 :** any of various flies (as a tabanid, botfly, or warble fly) that bite or annoy livestock **2 :** a usu. purposely annoying or provoking person; *esp* **:** one that stimulates or provokes to activity and esp. to the analysis and defense of ideas by persistent criticism esp. of an irritating pointed kind ⟨an immensely busy writer on various subjects, a ~ to the respectable —Carl Van Doren⟩ ⟨a ~, buzzing with ideas both for political strategy and the improvement of things in Oregon —*U. S. News & World Report*⟩

gadge \ˈgaj, -äj\ *dial Brit var of* GAUGE

¹gad·get \ˈgajət, *usu* -əd·+V\ *n* -s [origin unknown] **1 :** a usu. small and often novel mechanical or electronic device or contrivance esp. on a piece of machinery ⟨the garden tools and ~*s* which make gardening so much more fun —Una Van der Spuy⟩ ⟨radio was one of our greatest ~*s* —M.C.Faught⟩ ⟨relatively complicated ~*s*, like hay-loaders and elevators —G.E.Fussell⟩ ⟨swings, pushcarts, car seats, or any kind of ~ in which a baby may be left sitting —*Infant Care*⟩ ⟨interesting social ~*s*, the crèche, where the women workers' babies were cared for, the hospitals, the showers and the gymnasium —W.A.White⟩ ⟨promised to bring the fire truck to school to explain the purpose and use of various ~*s* and devices on the truck —*Deerfield (Wisc.) Independent*⟩ **2 :** a spring clip attached to the end of a punty in glass manufacturing

²gadget \"\ *vt* -ED/-ING/-S **:** to equip with or as if with gadgets ⟨our homes, ~*ed* to the last push button —James Street⟩

gad·ge·teer \ˌgajəˈti(ə)r, -iə\ *n* -s **:** one markedly fond of devising or employing gadgets ⟨an incorrigible ~, a manipulator and inventor of small marvels —G.W.Brace⟩ ⟨a short, stocky, energetic ~ . . . had an early flair for electrical devices —*Newsweek*⟩ ⟨the ~*s* who ride on our trains fascinate me, especially the compass carriers, who have to check every so often which way the train is going —F.J.Taylor⟩

gad·ge·teer·ing \-iriŋ\ *n* -s **:** the devising of gadgets ⟨spent his life at ~⟩ ⟨first step in tin can ~ is finding the right size cans —*Boy Scout Handbook*⟩

gad·get·ry \ˈgajətrē, -ri\ *n* -ES **1 :** GADGETEERING ⟨the ~ of science costs huge sums —W.A.Noyes b. 1898⟩ **2 :** GADGETS ⟨a world of mechanical ~ —A.C.Fisher⟩ ⟨the marvels of modern ~ that could reduce hard work to a minimum of effort —James Aldredge⟩ ⟨labor-saving ~ —J.I.Rodale⟩

gad·gety \-jəd·ē, -ət¦, ¦i\ *adj* **1 :** of or relating to a gadget ⟨the ~ handiness of a folding stool⟩ **:** consisting of or being a gadget ⟨~ merchandise —*Amer. Perfumer*⟩ **:** having the qualities of a gadget ⟨recommended . . . as the most compact, the simplest, the least ~ —E.T.Canby⟩ ⟨a very ~ gold pen —Cyril Ray⟩ **2 :** fond of gadgets or gadgeteering ⟨so ~ have we become, a new magazine is started to keep us informed on latest gadgets —*N.Y.Daily News*⟩ ⟨a ~ old gentleman who fiddled with rotary steam engines —W.S.Lynch⟩

ga·dhel·ic \gəˈdelik, (ˈ)ga¦d-\ *adj, usu cap* [ScGael *Gàidheal* & IrGael *Gaedheal* Gael + E *-ic* — more at GAEL] **:** GOIDELIC

²gadhelic \"\ *n* -s *cap* **:** GOIDELIC

¹gadid \ˈgādəd, ˈgad-\ *adj* [NL *Gadidae*] **:** of or relating to the Gadidae

²gadid \"\ *n* -s **:** a fish of the family Gadidae

gad·i·dae \ˈgadə,dē\ *n pl, cap* [NL, fr. *Gadus*, type genus + *-idae*] **:** a large family of soft-finned fishes of the order Anacanthini including many important food fishes (as the cod, haddock, tomcods, pollacks) that are chiefly marine although one genus (*Lota*) is confined to fresh water and that have a rather elongated body, small cycloid scales, a large mouth, wide gill openings, and usu. a barbel on the chin

gad·i·for·mes \ˌgadəˈfȯr,mēz\ *n pl, cap* [NL, fr. *Gadus* + *-iformes*] *in some classifications* **:** an order or other division of teleost fishes including the cods and closely related forms but usu. more restricted than the order Anacanthini to which it is partially equivalent

ga·di·tan \ˈgadətən, -atᵊn, -ə,tan\ *also* **gad·i·tane** \-,tān\ *adj, usu cap* [L *Gaditanus*, fr. *Gades* Cádiz, Spain, after such forms as L *Neapolis* Naples: *Neapolitanus* Neapolitan] **:** of or relating to Cádiz (anciently Gadir), in Spain

gad·ite \ˈga,dīt\ *n* -s *usu cap* [*Gad*, 7th son of Jacob (Gen 30:11), the eponymous ancestor of the Gadites (Josh 1:12) + E *-ite*] **:** a member of the Hebrew tribe of Gad **:** a descendant of Gad

gad·man \ˈgadmən\ *n, pl* **gadmen** [ME, fr. ¹*gad* + *man*] *dial Brit* **:** GOADMAN

¹gadoid \ˈgā,dȯid, ˈga,-\ *adj* [NL *Gadus*, genus name + E *-oid*] **:** resembling or relating to the Gadidae

²gadoid \"\ *n* -s **:** a gadoid fish

gad·o·le·ic acid \ˌgadəˈlēik-\ *n* [NL *Gadus* + E *oleic*] **:** an unsaturated fatty acid $C_{19}H_{37}COOH$ occurring in the form of glycerides in whale oil and many fish oils

gad·o·lin·ite \ˈgadᵊlə,nīt\ *n* -s [G *gadolinit*, fr. Johann *Gadolin* †1852 Finn. chemist + G *-it* -ite] **:** a mineral mainly $Be_2FeY_4Si_2O_{10}$ that is a source of rare earths and consists of a black or brown vitreous silicate of iron, beryllium, yttrium, cerium, and erbium (hardness 6.5–7, sp. gr. 4–4.5)

gad·o·lin·i·um \ˌgadᵊlˈinēəm\ *n* -s [NL, fr. *J.Gadolin* + NL *-ium*] **:** a trivalent magnetic metallic element of the rare-earth group occurring in combination in gadolinite, samarskite, and certain other minerals — symbol *Gd;* see ELEMENT table

ga·dop·sis \gəˈdäpsəs\ *n, cap* [NL, fr. *Gadus* + *-opsis*] **:** a genus of Australian and Tasmanian percoid freshwater fishes that resemble the cods

¹ga·droon \gəˈdrün\ *n* -s [F *godron* round plait, gadroon, fr. MF *goderon*, perh. dim. of OF *godet* drinking cup] **1 :** an ornament produced by notching or carving a rounded molding **2 :** a fluting or reeding that is usu. short in proportion to its width and often approaches an oval form and that is used decoratively (as in silverware, furniture, glassware, porcelain) — **ga·droon·ing** \-niŋ\ *n* -s

²gadroon \"\ *vt* -ED/-ING/-S **:** to decorate with gadroons

gads *pl of* GAD, *pres 3d sing of* GAD

gads·bod·i·kins \(ˈ)gadzˈbädəkənz, -dēk-\ *interj, often cap* [euphemism for *God's bodykins*] — a mild oath

ga·dus \ˈgādəs\ *n, cap* [NL, fr. Gk *gados*, a fish] **:** the type genus of the family Gadidae consisting of the typical codfishes

gad·wall \ˈga,dwȯl\ *also* **gad·wale** \-wāl\ *or* **gad·well** \-wel\ *n, pl* **gadwalls** *or* **gadwall** [origin unknown] **:** a grayish brown dabbling duck (*Anas strepera* or *Chaulelasmus streperus*) of approximately the size of the mallard

gad·zooks \gadˈzüks, -üks\ *interj, often cap* [*gads* (euphemism for *God's*) + *zooks*, origin unknown] *archaic* — a mild oath

gae \ˈgā, ˌgə\ *vi* **gaed** \ˈgād\ **gane** \ˈgān\ **gaun** \ˈgȯn\ **gaes** [ME (northern dial.) *gan* — more at GO] *Scot* **:** GO

-gaea *or* **-gea** \ˈjēə\ *n comb form* -s [NL, fr. Gk *gaia* land, earth] **:** a (specified) geographical area ⟨*Afrogaea*⟩ ⟨*Neogaea*⟩

gae·down \ˈgā,dün, ˈ≈,≈\ *n* -s [*gae* + *down*] *archaic Scot* **:** a drinking bout

gael \ˈgāl, *esp before pause or consonant* -āəl\ *n* -s *cap* [ScGael *Gàidheal* & IrGael *Gaedheal*, fr. or akin to MIr *Gōidel*] **1 :** a Scottish Highlander **2 a :** a Celtic esp. Gaelic-speaking inhabitant of Ireland, Scotland, or the Isle of Man **:** a member of the Gaelic-speaking division of the Celts esp. as opposed to the Cymric or Gallic Celts of Great Britain and the European continent **b :** IRISHMAN **c :** SCOTCHMAN 1

gael·dom \-dəm\ *n* -s *usu cap* **:** the realm or social order of the Gael or Gaelic civilization

¹gael·ic \ˈgālik, ˈgal-, ˈgäl-, -lēk\ *adj, usu cap* [ScGael *Gàidhealach* (fr. *Gàidheal*) & IrGael *Gaedhealach*, fr. *Gaedheal*] **1 :** of, relating to, or characteristic of the Gaels or esp. the Celtic Highlanders of Scotland — compare GOIDELIC **2 :** of, relating to, or characteristic of the language of the Gaels or esp. of the Celtic Highlanders of Scotland

²gaelic \"\ *n* -s *cap* [ScGael *Gàidhlig* (fr. *Gàidheal*) & IrGael *Gaedhealg, Gaedhilge*, fr. *Gaedheal*] **:** the Goidelic speech of the Celts in Ireland, the Isle of Man, and esp. in the Highlands of Scotland, the Hebrides, and other Scottish islands — compare IRISH, IRISH GAELIC, MANX, SCOTTISH GAELIC

gaelic football *n, usu cap G* **:** football played chiefly in Ireland between teams of 15 players who are permitted to dribble, kick, punt, or punch the ball with the fists but may not throw it or run with it

gael·i·cist \ˈgāləsəst\ *n* -s *usu cap* **1 :** an expert in Gaelic study **2 :** an advocate of Gaelic as a living tongue

gael·i·cize \-ˌsīz\ *vt* -ED/-ING/-S *sometimes cap* **:** to make Gaelic in form, quality, or customs

gael·tacht \ˈgā(ə)lˌtəkt\ *n* -s *cap* [IrGael *Gaedhealtacht*, fr. *Gaedheal* Gael] **1 :** the state of being Gaelic **2 a :** the Gaelic-speaking or Irish-speaking districts **b :** the population of such districts **3 :** the native race of Ireland

gae·tu·li \jēˈtüˌlī, jēˈtyü-, gīˈtü(ˌ)lē\ *n pl, cap* [L] **:** a Berber people living in ancient times to the south of Mauretania and Numidia

1**gae·tu·li·an** \(ˈ)≈ˈ≈lēən\ *adj, usu cap* [*Gaetuli* + *-an*] **1 :** of, relating to, characteristic of, or being a member of the Gaetuli **2 :** of, relating to, characteristic of, or derived from Gaetulia, the region inhabited by the Gaetuli

2**gaetulian** \"\ *n* -s *usu cap* **:** a member of the Gaetuli

ga·fat \gəˈfät\ *n* -s *usu cap* **:** a Semitic language formerly spoken in western Ethiopia but now replaced by Amharic

1**gaff** \ˈgaf, -äf\ *n* -s [prob. of imit. origin] *chiefly Scot* **:** a loud laugh **:** GUFFAW

2**gaff** \"\ *vi* -ED/-ING/-S [1*gaff*] *chiefly Scot* **:** to laugh loudly

3**gaff** \ˈgaf, -aa(ə)f,-aif\ *n* -s [F *gaffe*, fr. Prov *gaf*] **1 a :** a barbed spear or spearhead for taking fish or turtles **b :** an iron hook with a handle for holding or lifting heavy fish (as into a boat) **c :** the steel point of a pole used in logging **d :** a metal spur for a gamecock **e :** a butcher's hook **f** (1) **:** a climbing iron used by a telephone lineman (2) the steel point or the shank and steel point of such a climbing iron **2 a :** the spar upon which the head of a fore-and-aft sail is extended **b :** a similar spar on a ship without sails sometimes used when under way for hoisting colors **3 a :** HOAX, FRAUD **b :** GIMMICK, TRICK ⟨professional gamblers can be trusted to work out some sort of ~ to loosen up the percentage on any game of chance —C.B.Davis⟩ **4 a :** something painful or difficult to bear **:** ORDEAL ⟨was forced to drop out of competition because he couldn't stand the ~⟩; *esp* **:** persistent raillery or criticism **b :** wear and tear **:** roughness of treatment **:** ABUSE ⟨fabric that could take a great deal of ~ and still hold up⟩ **5 :** GAFFE

gaff 1b

4**gaff** \"\ *vt* -ED/-ING/-S [3*gaff*] **1 a :** to strike or secure with a gaff ⟨~ a salmon⟩ **b :** to fit or provide (as a gamecock) with a gaff **2 :** DECEIVE, TRICK; *also* **:** FLEECE **3 :** to tamper with for the purpose of cheating **:** FIX, GIMMICK ⟨gaming wheels and dice are often ~*ed* so that the player cannot win⟩

5**gaff** \"\ *n* -s [origin unknown] *Brit* **:** a cheap place of amusement; *esp* **:** a low-class theater or music hall — called also *penny gaff*

6**gaff** \"\ *vi* -ED/-ING/-S [origin unknown] *slang Brit* **:** to gamble esp. by tossing coins

7**gaff** \"\ *n* -s [origin unknown] **1 :** talk esp. when idle or foolish ⟨wasn't going to take any of his ~ —William Ornstein⟩ **2 :** OUTCRY, CLAMOR — **blow the gaff** *slang* **:** to give away a secret **:** BLAB

gaffe \ˈgaf, -aa(ə)f,-aif\ *n* -s [F, gaff, gaffe — more at 3GAFF] **:** a marked esp. social or diplomatic blunder or clumsy mistake **:** FAUX PAS ⟨mere social ~*s* and unfortunate encounters of the sort which used to provide copy for . . . society jokes —*Times Lit. Supp.*⟩ ⟨his attention to detail is really remarkable and seldom permits a major ~ —W.F.Albright⟩ ⟨like all newspapers it sometimes commits a ~ —Stuart Keate⟩

gaf·fer \ˈgafə(r)\ *n* -s [prob. contr. of *godfather*] **1 :** old man **:** old fellow ⟨old men's recollections . . . are not regarded by historians as good sources of history, but this *gaffer's* estimate of the situation is supported by a contemporary report —S.E.Morison⟩ — often used formerly as a form of friendly address **2** *Brit* **a :** EMPLOYER **b :** FOREMAN, OVERSEER **3 :** the master glass blower in charge of a shop in glassworking **4 :** an electrician in charge of the lighting of motion-picture or television sets

gaff–headed \ˈ≈ˈ≈≈\ *adj* [3*gaff*] *of a sail* **:** having four sides with the head laced along a gaff — compare JIB-HEADED

gaff·kya \ˈgafkēə\ *n, cap* [NL, after Georg *Gaffky* †1918 Ger. bacteriologist] *in some classifications* **:** a genus of parasitic gram-positive bacteria (family Micrococcaceae) that are now usu. placed in *Micrococcus*

gaffle *n* -s [ME *gaffolle*, fr. MD *gaffel*, *gafel* fork; akin to OE *gafol*, *geafel* fork, OHG *gabala*, OS *gafala* fork, OIr *gabul* forked branch, fork, vulva] *obs* **:** a steel lever used to bend a crossbow

gaff–rigged \ˈ≈ˌrigd\ *adj, of a boat* **:** having a gaff-headed mainsail and sometimes other gaff-headed sails

gaff·sail \ˈ≈ˌsāl, -ˌsəl\ *n* [3*gaff* + *sail*] **:** a fore-and-aft sail suspended from a gaff

gaff–topsail \ˈ≈ˈ≈(ˌ)≈, ˈ≈ˌ≈≈\ *n* **1 :** a usu. triangular topsail with its foot extended upon the gaff and its luff upon the topmast — see SAIL illustration **2 :** GAFF-TOPSAIL CATFISH **3** *or* **gaff–topsail pompano :** LONGFIN POMPANO

gaff–topsail catfish *n* **:** a sea catfish (*Bagre marina* syn. *Felichthys felis*) of the Atlantic and Gulf coasts of the U.S.

1**gag** \ˈgag, -aa(ə)g, -aig\ *vb* **gagged; gagged; gagging; gags** [ME *gaggen* to strangle, of imit. origin] *vt* **1 :** to apply a gag to: **a :** to stop the mouth of by thrusting something in it in order to hinder or prevent speaking or outcry **b :** to pry or hold open by means of a gag **c :** to silence by the force of authority or violence **:** prevent from exercising freedom of speech or expression ⟨the dictator's first act was to ~ all newspapers⟩ ⟨the opposition refused to be *gagged* and found new means of putting their ideas across to the public⟩ **2 :** to cause to heave (as with nausea) **:** cause to retch **3 :** OBSTRUCT, CHOKE ⟨~ a valve⟩ ⟨was struck by a sudden terror which transfixed him on the spot and *gagged* his throat —S.B. Kaiser⟩ **4 :** to straighten (rails) with a gag **5 :** to introduce gags into **:** provide gags for **:** fill with remarks or situations intended to arouse laughter ⟨an amply *gagged* musical comedy⟩ ⟨asked to ~ a new movie by a famous producer⟩ — often used with *up* ~ *vi* **1 :** HEAVE, RETCH **2 :** to be unable to endure something **:** BALK ⟨*gagged* at the sort of painting she was being taught, went off to earn her living in various advertising agencies —*Time*⟩ ⟨the defense was cunning beyond belief, and unscrupulous in its use of propaganda — they *gagged* at nothing —Maxwell Anderson⟩ **3 :** to make gags **:** engage in an interchange intended to arouse laughter ⟨there were no false notes in his testimony, no mugging and *gagging* —*New Republic*⟩ ⟨*gagging* with his mates —*Life*⟩

2**gag** \"\ *n* -s [1*gag*] **1 :** something thrust into the mouth to keep it open; *specif* **:** a medical device for keeping the mouth open **2 a :** something thrust into the mouth or throat to prevent or hinder speaking or outcry **b :** CLOTURE **c :** a device or action that hinders or prevents free expression of ideas **3 :** a laugh-provoking remark, story, device, or action or one intended to amuse or arouse laughter: **a :** an interpolation orig. of an amusing local or topical allusion or bit of byplay by an actor in his lines **b :** a clever, witty, or comic remark, stunt, trick, or piece of action or construction (as in a stage, motion-picture, radio, or television presentation or in a work of literature or art) esp. designed to arouse quick and broad laughter ⟨two comedians with dialogue full of fast ~*s*⟩ ⟨a partygoer who insists on wearing a lampshade for a hat as a ~⟩ ⟨improvise dialogue, ~*s*, and situations as they go along —*Current Biog.*⟩ ⟨his standard of humor was set by the ~*s* of the variety shows —S.H.Adams⟩ ⟨many a glamour girl got in a WAC recruiting line just for the ~ —*Time*⟩ **4 a :** a made-up story told plausibly or a contrived action to hoax or impose upon someone or to provide a pretext (as for evading something) ⟨when he picked up the telephone and demanded the general manager I thought it was just a ~ —Henry Miller⟩ **b :** a story of this kind used so frequently as to have become hackneyed ⟨the office boy's ~ about a death in the family so he can get a day off⟩ **c :** a trick of imposture or deception (as for making someone ridiculous or for gaining publicity) ⟨got himself arrested falsely as a ~ to get his name in the papers⟩ **5 :** a bit with rings at each end through which the cheekpiece of the bridle is continuous with the reins used to keep the horse's head properly up; *esp* **:** a light snaffle of this kind **6 :** a fuller used to straighten railway rails **7 :** a hand-controlled attachment used to prevent the operation of a punch when a hole is to be omitted **syn** see JOKE

3**gag** \"\ *n* -s [origin unknown] **:** a small grouper (*Mycteroperca microlepis*) of the coasts of the southern U.S. highly esteemed for food; *also* **:** any of several related fishes (as the yellowfin grouper)

ga·ga \ˈgäˌgä, ˈgaˌga, ˈgȧˌgȧ, ˌgə\ *adj* [F, fr. *gaga*, n., fool, dodderer, of imit. origin] **1 a :** mentally foolish **:** CRAZY, DOTING ⟨slowly becoming ~ . . . becoming a senile imbecile —Aldous Huxley⟩ **b :** characterized by a marked and interesting or foolish variation from a conventional or expected pattern **:** marked by interesting or foolish incongruities or surprises (as in quality or action) ⟨a ~ comedian⟩ ⟨~ misadventures that, on stage and screen, forever befall high-school or college youths —*Life*⟩ **2 :** markedly or wildly and often foolishly enthusiastic (as from love or infatuation) ⟨a hatcheck girl went simply ~ over the clothes —*Star Detective Cases*⟩ ⟨had been so ~ about him at first —Dawn Powell⟩

1**gage** \ˈgāj\ *n* -s [ME, fr. MF, of Gmc origin; akin to Goth *wadi* pledge — more at WED] **1 :** a personal pledge that one will appear to support by combat his assertions or claims; *esp* **:** a glove, cap, or other personal belonging cast on the ground to be taken up by an opponent as a pledge of combat **2 :** something deposited or given to or taken by another as a security for the performance of some act by the person depositing it or giving it up and forfeited by nonperformance **:** SECURITY; *also* **:** the transaction by which the security is given or taken — compare MORTGAGE, PLEDGE — **throw down the gage :** CHALLENGE, DEFY

2**gage** \"\ *vt* -ED/-ING/-S [MF *gager*, fr. OF *gagier*, fr. *gage*, n.] **1** *archaic* **:** to give or deposit as a gage **:** give as security for some act **:** offer as a forfeit **:** PLEDGE **2** *archaic* **:** STAKE, RISK

3**gage** *var of* GAUGE

4**gage** \ˈgāj\ *n* -s [by shortening] **:** GREENGAGE

gage block *n* **:** a hardened steel block that is used by machinists for extremely accurate measurement and has two opposite surfaces ground and lapped plane and parallel to a thickness within a few millionths of an inch of its designated size and usu. forms one of a graduated set of which two or more are often used in combination — called also *precision block, size block*

gage green *n* [4*gage*] **:** a grayish to moderate yellow green that is yellower and darker than mytho green and greener and very slightly darker than pois green

gage·ite \ˈgāˌjīt\ *n* -s [R. B. *Gage*, 20th cent. Am. collector of specimens in N.J. + E *-ite*] **:** a mineral $(Mn,Mg,Zn)_8Si_3O_{14}.2$(or 3?)H_2O consisting of a hydrous silicate of manganese, magnesium, and zinc

gage plate *n* **:** a metal plate placed between parallel running rails to maintain the gage on a railroad track

1**gag·er** \ˈgājə(r)\ *n* -s [prob. fr. MF, lit., to gage, fr. OF *gagier*] **:** the transaction of giving a gage **:** the action of providing security for a pledge

2**gager** *var of* GAUGER

gagged *past of* GAG

gag·ger \ˈgagə(r), -aag-,-aig-\ *n* -s **1 :** one that gags; *specif* **:** a workman who takes the bends out of rails at a straightening press with a steel gag **2 a :** a foundry lifter **b :** a piece of iron used in a foundry mold to keep the sand or a core in place **3 :** one that thinks up gags **:** JOKER, GAGMAN

gagging *pres part of* GAG

1**gag·gle** \ˈgagəl, ˈgaig-\ *vi* **gaggled; gaggled; gaggling** \-g(ə)liŋ\ **gaggles** [ME *gagelen*; prob. of imit. origin like MHG *gāgen* to gaggle, ON *gaga* to mock, *gagl* wild goose] **:** to make a noise like that of a goose **:** CACKLE, GABBLE

2**gaggle** \"\ *n* -s [ME *gagyll*, fr. *gagelen*, v.] **1 :** a flock of geese esp. when on the water — compare SKEIN **2 :** a group of people bonded because of some common element **:** BUNCH, GANG ⟨confronted by a whole ~ of photographers and reporters⟩ ⟨a ~ of gossiping women⟩ **3 :** a number of disorganized but related things ⟨a ~ of eponyms, synonyms, and terms that confront the medical student⟩ ⟨a ~ of little railroads between cities⟩

gag law *n* **:** a law or ruling prohibiting free debate or expression of opinion (as in a deliberative body) **:** CLOTURE; *also* **:** legislation restricting freedom of the press

gag line *n* **:** a remark or line (as in a comic cartoon) that constitutes a gag or is the climax of one

gag·man \ˈ≈ˌman, -ˌmaa(ə)n\ *n, pl* **gagmen 1 :** one who contrives gags for comedians or other entertainers **2 :** a comedian often good at ad-libbing whose act consists chiefly of laugh-provoking remarks

gag rein *n* **:** a rein for use with a gag — **gag–reined** \ˈ≈ˈ≈\ *adj*

gag resolution *n* **:** one of several resolutions passed in Congress between 1836 and 1844 providing in effect that no petition against slavery should be received or heard by the House

gagroot \ˈ≈ˌ≈\ *n* [so called fr. its use as an emetic] **:** INDIAN TOBACCO

gag rule *n* **:** GAG LAW, GAG RESOLUTION; *also* **:** ruling by gag law

gags *pres 3d sing of* GAG, *pl of* GAG

gag·ster \ˈgagztə(r), ˈgaa|, ˈgai|, |gst-\ *n* -s **:** GAGMAN; *also* **:** PRACTICAL JOKER

gagtooth \ˈ≈ˌ≈\ *n, pl* **gagteeth** [E dial. *gag* to project, stick out (of Scand origin; akin to ON *gaghals* having the head thrown back, Icel *gagur* bent backward, turned askew, Norw *gag* bent back, *gaga* to bend back) + *tooth*; akin to OE *gēagl* throat, jaws, MHG *gagen* to fidget and perh. to OE *geonian*, *ginian* to yawn — more at YAWN] **:** a projecting tooth — **gagtoothed** \ˈ≈ˌ≈\ *adj*

ga·he \ˈgä(ˌ)hā\ *n pl* [Apache] **:** grotesque masked dancers with yucca crowns representing mountain spirits in Apache Indian ceremonies — called also *crown dancers*; see APACHE DEVIL DANCE

gahn·ite \ˈgäˌnīt\ *n* -s [G *gahnit*, fr. Johan G. *Gahn* †1818 Sw. chemist + G *-it* -ite] **:** a usu. dark green mineral $ZnAl_2O_4$ consisting of an oxide of zinc and aluminum and constituting a member of the spinel series

gaiac *var of* GUAIAC

gai·as·sa \gīˈasə\ *n* -s [Ar *qayyāsah*, a kind of barge] **:** a Nile cargo boat with high stem and lateen rig

gai·ety *or* **gay·ety** \ˈgāəd·ē, -ətē, -i\ *n* -ES [F *gaieté*, fr. OF, fr, *gai* gay + *-té* -ty — more at GAY] **1 a :** MERRYMAKING, ENTERTAINMENT, FESTIVITY ⟨did not feel like joining in the ~ of the season⟩ ⟨paper bags filled with water dropped from windows, and other freshman *gaieties* marked the convention's sideshow —C.W.Ferguson⟩ **b :** the quality or state of being gay ⟨the face was in profile but the visible eye seemed to have ~ in it —Raymond Chandler⟩ **:** high spirits **:** MERRIMENT ⟨the high ~ of cocktail parties —R.L.Taylor⟩ **:** marked liveliness or cheerfulness ⟨a jumble of unmatched colors, which are said to lend ~ to the table —*New Yorker*⟩ **2 a :** FINERY, ELEGANCE ⟨a ~ of dress and manner⟩ **b :** an instance of such finery (as in dress) ⟨youthful *gaieties*, such as a raspberry fleece greatcoat with low patch pockets and a deep oblong collar in back —Lois Long⟩ **3 :** BEGONIA 3

gail *var of* GYLE

gaillard *var of* GALLIARD

gail·lar·dia \gəˈlärdēə, ≈ -dyə\ *n* [NL, fr. *Gaillard* de Marentonneau, 18th cent. Fr. botanist + NL *-ia*] **1** *cap* **:** a genus of chiefly western American herbs (family Compositae) having hairy foliage and long stalked flower heads with showy yellow, purple, or variegated rays **2** -s **:** any plant or flower of the genus *Gaillardia*

gai·ly *or* **gay·ly** \ˈgālē, -li\ *adv* [ME *gayly*, fr. *gay* + *-ly*] **1 :** in a gay manner: **a :** with marked liveliness, cheerfulness, or high spirits ⟨she then ran ~ off, rejoicing —Jane Austen⟩ **:** MERRILY **b :** with finery, elegance, or showiness (as of dress) ⟨ladies ~ dressed⟩ **c :** in a manner that is colorful and tends to arouse gaiety ⟨~ decorated floats⟩ **2** *chiefly Scot* **:** pretty much **:** to a considerable extent or degree

1**gain** \ˈgān\ *adj* -ER/-EST [ME *gayn*, *geyn*, fr. OE *gēn*, fr. ON *gegn* — more at AGAIN] **1** *dial Brit, of a route* **:** direct and straight ⟨the ~*est* way to the glen⟩ **2** *dial Brit* **:** useful and convenient **:** HANDY ⟨a ~ tool⟩

2**gain** \"\ *adv* -ER/-EST [ME *gayn*, fr. *gayn*, adj.] *dial Brit* **:** NEARLY, APPROXIMATELY

3**gain** *vi* -ED/-ING/-S [ME *gaynen*, *geinen*, fr. ON *gegna*, fr. *gegn*, adj.] **:** to be of advantage or help **:** be suitable or sufficient

4**gain** \ˈgān\ *n* -s [ME *gayne*, fr. MF *gain* (fr. OF *gaaing*, fr. *gaaignier* to gain) & *gaigne*, fr. OF *gaaigne*, fr. *gaaignier*] **1 :** an increase in or addition to what is of profit, advantage, or benefit **:** resources or advantage acquired or increased **:** PROFIT ⟨the moral and cultural ~*s* of the last 1000 years⟩ ⟨a lottery for private ~⟩ ⟨the practice resulted in quite a ~ in confidence in the driver⟩ ⟨the difficulties encountered, the compromises reached, the ~*s* achieved —Vera M. Dean⟩: as **a :** an increase of value (as from business transactions or increase in capital) ⟨the loss or ~ in a company's assets⟩ **b :** an increase in resources or business advantages resulting from business transactions or dealings **c :** a profit in the form of a sum of money, an acquired asset, or a reduction in liability arising from business transactions but not including mere advances in value — usu. used in pl. ⟨capital ~*s* to be entered separately on the income-tax form⟩ **2 :** the act of gaining something; *esp* **:** the act of obtaining or accumulating profit or valuable possessions **3 a :** an increase in amount, magnitude, or degree ⟨the ~ in weight of the cattle over a period of weeks was recorded⟩ ⟨the ~ in efficiency is more than worth the heat loss —*Modern Industry*⟩ ⟨sales aggregated 84,293,729 barrels, a ~ of 1.3 percent over 1951 —*Americana Annual*⟩ ⟨its absence would mean . . . more loss than ~ in social relations —W.C.Brownell⟩ **b :** the ratio of increase of output current, power, or voltage over input (as in an amplifier)

5**gain** \"\ *vb* -ED/-ING/-S [MF *gaigner*, fr. OF *gaaignier* to till, earn, win, gain, of Gmc origin; akin to OHG *weidanōn* to hunt, search for food; akin to OE *wāth* hunt, wandering, OHG *weida* pasture, fodder, food, ON *veithr* hunt, hunting, fishing, L *vis* power, force — more at VIM] *vt* **1 a :** to get or attain to possession, control, use, or benefit of (as an advantage) by industry, initiative, merit, or craft **:** OBTAIN, PROCURE, SECURE ⟨~ a sum of money⟩ ⟨~ a good reputation⟩ ⟨~ recognition⟩ ⟨~ admittance⟩ ⟨~ popularity⟩ ⟨~ a livelihood⟩ ⟨~ insight⟩ ⟨after climbing all the morning he had failed to ~ another glimpse of the great brown ram —C.G.D.Roberts⟩ ⟨~ the goodwill of the people —H.C.Atyeo⟩ ⟨a great aid to us in ~*ing* an inspection of the grounds —A.W.O'Neil⟩ **b** (1) **:** to get in competition ⟨~ a prize in a tennis match⟩ (2) **:** to come off winner or victor in ⟨~ a battle⟩ ⟨~ a suit at law⟩ **c :** to get or incur by a natural development, advance, or increment or by the normal exercise of one's function **:** come to have **:** RECEIVE ⟨the invalid ~*ed* strength under the doctor's care⟩ ⟨the writing was such that the reader actually ~*ed* the illusion of a cruise⟩ ⟨the false story ~*ed* credence⟩ ⟨the impression was ~*ed* that the divisional heads would hold key positions —*Farmer's Weekly (So. Africa)*⟩ ⟨the child is ~*ing* a sense of rhythm and balance —*Handwriting Today*⟩ **d :** to obtain by reclamation ⟨land ~*ed* from the sea⟩ **e :** to make or acquire (as a friend) ⟨~ an acquaintance⟩ **f :** to advance to the distance of by striving against odds or an opposing force ⟨the football team ~*ed* forty yards in the first three plays⟩ **g :** SUFFER ⟨~*ed* a black eye for his trouble⟩ ⟨the participants ~*ed* only ignominy and unhappiness⟩ **2 :** to draw to one's particular interest or party **:** win to one's side **:** PERSUADE ⟨~ adherents for his religious doctrines⟩ — often used with *over* ⟨had been ~*ed* over to urge this fatal course by a gift —*Encyc. Americana*⟩ **3 :** to arrive at ⟨the first ones to ~ the top of the mountain held it against attack⟩ ⟨~ a goal⟩ **:** REACH, ATTAIN ⟨he ~*ed* his car and he was safe —Jean Stafford⟩ **4 :** to cause to be obtained or given **:** AROUSE ⟨misfortune ~*s* the sympathy of friends⟩ ⟨~ the audience's attention⟩ **5 :** to increase in ⟨~ momentum⟩ ⟨~ impetus⟩ ⟨does not mean that the actual aesthetic experience ~*s* nothing when it is studied in the context of our total experience —Hunter Mead⟩ **6 :** to establish or reestablish a usual or normal use or position of ⟨~*ed* his feet after a fall⟩ ⟨~ my equilibrium⟩ **7** *of a timepiece* **:** to run fast by the amount of ⟨~*s* a minute a day⟩ ~ *vi* **1 :** to secure advantage or profit **:** acquire gain ⟨the man supplying the capital expected to ~ considerably by the enterprise⟩ **2 a :** INCREASE ⟨the child ~*ed* in weight⟩ ⟨~ in influence⟩ ⟨~ in reputation⟩ ⟨the day was ~*ing* in warmth⟩ **b :** to increase in weight ⟨despite her diet the woman continued to ~⟩ **c :** to improve in health ⟨the patient ~*ed* daily⟩ **d :** to become greater ⟨the water ~*ed* so frightfully in the ship that it seemed certain she would sink —Fletcher Pratt⟩ **3** *of a timepiece* **:** to run so that it is fast **:** register a time ahead of the correct time ⟨~*s* by an hour a day⟩ **syn** see GET, REACH — **gain a point :** to make a point — **gain face :** to establish or increase one's authority, influence, or reputation ⟨a petty official trying to *gain face* by treating his subordinates arrogantly⟩ ⟨she had *gained face*, for the time being, from the length of her conversation with Colonel Pole; three or four more of the family, after that, had bowed or briefly spoken to her —Elizabeth Bowen⟩ — **gain ground :** to make progress **:** improve esp. by getting larger, more valuable, or healthier ⟨stocks *gained ground* during the morning's trading⟩ ⟨the patient *gained ground* daily⟩ — **gain on** *or* **gain upon 1** *archaic* **:** to obtain influence or favor with **2 :** to encroach upon ⟨where the sea *gains on* the land⟩ **3 a :** to come nearer to by running faster than (one ahead in a race) **b :** to increase the distance from by running faster than (one behind in a race) ⟨his quarry was *gaining on* him every minute —Dale Van Every⟩ — **gain the wind :** to reach the windward side (as of another boat) when beating — **gain time :** to obtain or effect a delay in an action (as by pretexts)

6**gain** \"\ *n* -s [origin unknown] **1 :** a beveled shoulder above a tenon in carpentry **2 :** a notch, mortise, or groove (as in a timber or wall) for a girder or joist

gaincope *vt* -ED/-ING/-S [ME *geynecowpen*, fr. *geyne-* against (fr. OE *gēan-*, *gēn-* against, again) + *cowpen*, *copen* to strike — more at AGAIN, COPE (strike)] *obs* **:** to meet or intercept by a short cut

gaine \ˈgān\ *n* -s [F, lit., sheath, fr. OF, fr. L *vagina* — more at VAGINA] **1 :** the part of a term or similar support below a sculptured bust or head commonly in the form of a quadrangular pillar diminishing toward the base **2 :** the term-shaped lower part or body of a caryatid

gained *past of* GAIN

1**gain·er** *comparative of* GAIN

2**gai·ner** \ˈgānə(r)\ *n* -s **1 :** a fancy dive in which the diver from a forward approach rotates backward in tuck, pike, or layout position and enters the water feet first and facing away from the board — called also *full gainer* **2 :** one of a former group of competitive dives including reverse dives

gainest *superlative of* GAIN

gain·ful \ˈgānfəl\ *adj* **1 :** productive of gain **:** PROFITABLE, REMUNERATIVE; *esp* **:** providing an income ⟨a ~ occupation⟩ **2 :** customarily employed at a gainful occupation ⟨a ~ worker⟩ — **gain·ful·ly** \-fəlē, -li\ *adv* — **gain·ful·ness** *n* -ES

gain·giv·ing \ˈgānˌ≈≈, (ˈ)≈ˈ≈≈\ *n* [*gain-* (fr. ME *gayn-*, *geyne-* against) + *giving* (fr. gerund of *give*)] *archaic* **:** MISGIVING

gaining *pres part of* GAIN

gaining machine *n* [6*gain* + *-ing*] **:** a machine for cutting a gain

gain·less \ˈgānləs\ *adj* [4*gain* + *-less*] **1 :** not producing gain **:** UNPROFITABLE, UNAVAILING **2 :** making no advances **:** achieving no gains ⟨a saving and ~ life —John Cheever⟩ — **gain·less·ness** *n* -ES

1**gain·ly** \ˈgānlē, -li\ *adv* -ER/-EST [1*gain* + *-ly*] **1** *chiefly dial* **:** VERY, COMPLETELY **2** *chiefly dial* **:** NEARLY, HANDILY ⟨the birds singing ~ that came at my call —J.H.Payne⟩

2**gainly** \"\ *adj* [1*gain* + *-ly*] **1** *chiefly dial* **:** SUITABLE, BECOMING ⟨a ~ word⟩ **2 :** graceful and generally pleasing ⟨~ conduct⟩ ⟨a ~ youth with dark hair and eyes⟩

gai·nor \ˈgānə(r)\ *n* -s [AF *gainour*, fr. OF *gaaigneure*, fr. *gaaignier* to till, gain + *-eure* -ure — more at GAIN (obtain)] *Old Eng law* **:** TILLAGE, HUSBANDRY ⟨land in ~⟩

gains *pres 3d sing of* GAIN, *pl of* GAIN

gain·say \(ˈ)gān¦sā\ *vt* **gain·said** \-sād,-sed\ **gainsaid** \"\ **gainsaying** \-sāiŋ\ **gain·says** \-sāz,-sez\ [ME *gaynsayen*, fr. *gayn-* against + *sayen* to say — more at SAY] **1 :** DENY ⟨that capitalism had long existed in rudimentary form cannot be *gainsaid* —W.P.Webb⟩ ⟨a churlish critic who would ~ people the solace of fairy tales —W.H.Whyte⟩ **2 :** to speak against **:** CONTRADICT, CONTROVERT ⟨though I disagree with him, I will not ~ him⟩ **3 :** OPPOSE, RESIST ⟨standing armies that will permit us to grasp whatever we may desire, because no other nation or combination of nations is strong enough to ~ us —F.D.Roosevelt⟩ ⟨the development of a manner . . . that ~s the very purpose of criticism —F.R.Leavis⟩; *also* : SUBVERT ⟨his mother, whom he could not ~, was unconsciously but inflexibly set against his genius —Van Wyck Brooks⟩ **syn** see DENY

gainst *prep* [by shortening] *obs* : AGAINST

gain·stand \(ˈ)gān¦stand, -taa(ə)nd\ *vt* [ME *gaynstanden*, fr. *gayn-* against + *standen* to stand — more at STAND] *chiefly Scot* : WITHSTAND, RESIST

gain twist *n* [⁵*gain*] : a twist that is more rapid at the muzzle of a firearm than at the breech in order to increase gradually the rapidity of rotation of a projectile

¹**gair** \ˈgar\ *n* -s [ME (northern dial.) *gare*, fr. OE *gāra* — more at GORE] *Scot* : ²GORE 1a

²**gair** \ˈ"\ *adj* -ER/-EST [of Scand origin; akin to ON *gerr* greedy; prob. akin to ON *gjarn* eager, greedy — more at YEARN] **1** *Scot* : GREEDY, COVETOUS **2** *Scot* : PARSIMONIOUS, STINGY

gaird \ˈgärd\ *Scot var of* GUARD

gair·den \ˈgärdᵊn, ˈger-\ *Scot var of* GARDEN

gair·ten \ˈgärtᵊn, ˈger-\ *var of* GARTEN

gais·ling \ˈgāzlən, -liŋ\ *n* -s [ME *geslyng*, prob. fr. ON *gæslingr*, fr. *gās* goose + *-lingr* -ling — more at GOOSE] *Scot* : GOSLING

gaist \ˈgāst\ *Scot var of* GHOST

¹**gait** \ˈgāt, *usu* -ād·+V\ *n* -s [ME *gait, gate* — more at GATE (way)] **1** *archaic* : ³GATE 1 **2** *now dial* : ³GATE 2 **3** *Scot* : ³GATE 3 **4 a** : the manner of walking, running, or moving on foot ⟨a fast ~⟩ ⟨an awkward ~⟩ ⟨the ~ of a cowboy —*Current Biog.*⟩ **b** : any of the sequences of foot movement (as the walk, trot, pace, or canter) by which a horse moves forward **c** : the manner of moving forward in a vehicle ⟨everything swayed and veered in obedience to the ~ of the train —Nadine Gordimer⟩ ⟨step up our ~ to near the posted speed limit of 55 —*Sat. Eve. Post*⟩ **5 a** : the general speed or rate at which life proceeds or at which activities are pursued ⟨life in the summer slowed down to a leisurely ~⟩ **b** : the speed or rate of performance or accomplishment (as of production) ⟨after the speedup, the ~ was 300 airplanes a month⟩

²**gait** \ˈ"\ *vt* -ED/-ING/-S **1** : to train (a horse) to use a particular gait or set of gaits **2** : to lead (a show dog) before a judge to display carriage and movement

³**gait** \ˈ"\ *n* -s [prob. alter. of ¹*gate*] **1** : the distance between two adjoining carriages of a lace frame in textile manufacturing **2** *Brit* : a full repeat of a pattern in harness weaving — used in the woolen trade

⁴**gait** \ˈ"\ *vt* -ED/-ING/-S [by alter.] : ²GATE 3

gait·ed \ˈgād·əd, -ātəd\ *adj* **1 a** : having a particular kind of gait — used in combination ⟨a stiff-*gaited* man⟩ ⟨a slow-*gaited* life⟩ **b** *of a horse* : trained to use particular gaits — often used in combination ⟨a 3-*gaited* bay gelding⟩ **2** : specially fitted, trained, adjusted, or conditioned ⟨the sort of story that television is ~ to handle well —Douglas Mackenzie⟩ ⟨better ~ for the slower, more intimate aspects of Schumann than she is for such movement as the sonata opening —Irving Kolodin⟩ ⟨men who aren't ~ to decorating a house —Debs Myers⟩ ⟨the subject matter is ~ to the boy's expanding interests —O.W.Bennett⟩

gai·ter \ˈgād·ə(r), -ātə-\ *n* -s [F *guêtre*, fr. MF *guestre, guiestre*, prob. of Gmc origin; akin to OE *wrist* — more at WRIST] **1** : a cloth or leather leg covering reaching from the instep to ankle, mid-calf, or knee, usu. fastened by buttons or buckles, and held by a strap under the shank of the shoe ⟨bishops and archdeacons, as well as deans, wear aprons and ~s —F.C. Happold⟩ **2 a** : an ankle-high shoe with elastic gores in the sides — compare CONGRESS GAITER, ROMEO **b** : an overshoe reaching to the ankle or above and having a fabric upper — compare ARCTIC **3** : a protective covering (as for a leaf spring or over a weak spot in a fire hose)

gaiter 2a

gai·ter·less \-ləs\ *adj* : not wearing or not having gaiters ⟨a ~ farmer⟩ ⟨a ~ leg⟩

gai·ther \ˈgat͟hər\ *Scot var of* GATHER

¹**gal** \ˈgal\ *n* -s [by alter.] : GIRL

²**gal** \ˈ"\ *n* -s [after *Galileo* †1642 Ital. astronomer and physicist] : a unit of acceleration equivalent to one centimeter per second per second — used esp. for values of gravity

gal *abbr* **1** gallery **2** galley **3** gallon

¹**ga·la** \ˈgālə *also* ˈgalə *sometimes* ˈgälə *or* ˈgälə\ *n* -s [It, fr. MF *gale* merrymaking, festivity, pleasure — more at GALLANT] **1** *archaic* **a** : festive dress or decoration **b** : FESTIVITY, GAIETY **2 a** : a gay and lively celebration : a festive entertainment : FESTIVAL, FAIR; *specif* : an entertainment or entertaining presentation constituting a special occasion ⟨a grand ~ at Symphony Hall marking the city's bicentennial⟩ **b** *Brit* : an athletic meet esp. marking a special occasion **3** : a gay and lively group ⟨a ~ of actresses and society women with a flair for dress —*Brit. Bk. News*⟩

²**gala** \ˈ"\ *adj* : belonging to, deserving, or attended by festivities : suitable for festivity ⟨a ~ dress⟩ ⟨a ~ day⟩ ⟨a ~ occasion⟩

³**gala** *usu cap, var of* GALLA

gala- *or* **galacto-** *comb form, usu ital* [ISV, fr. *galactose*] : having the stereochemical arrangement of atoms or groups found in galactose ⟨*L-gala*-heptulose⟩

gal·a·bia *or* **gal·a·bi·eh** *or* **gal·a·be·ah** *or* **gal·la·bi·ya** \ˌgaləˈbē(y)ə\ *n* -s [Ar *jallabīyah*] : a loose cloak or robe usu. of homespun worn by the poorer people of Arabic-speaking countries of the Mediterranean

galact- *or* **galacto-** *comb form* [*galact-* fr. MF or L; MF *galact-*, fr. L, fr. Gk *galakt-*, fr. *galakt-, gala; galacto-* fr. Gk *galakto-*, fr. *galakt-, gala* — more at GALAXY] **1** : milk, milky fluid ⟨*galact*idrosis⟩ ⟨*galact*emia⟩ ⟨*galacto*rrhea⟩ **2** [ISV, fr. *galactose*] : related to galactose ⟨*galacto*pyranose⟩ — compare GALA- **3** [*galactic*] : galaxy; *specif* : the Milky Way galaxy ⟨*galacto*centric⟩

¹**ga·lac·ta·gogue** *or* **ga·lac·to·gogue** \gəˈlaktəˌgäg *sometimes* -gȯg\ *adj* [prob. fr. NL *galactagogus*, fr. *galact-* + *-agogus* -agogue] : promoting secretion of milk

²**galactagogue** *or* **galactogogue** \ˈ"\ *n* -s : a galactagogue agent

ga·lac·tan \gəˈlaktən, -ˌtan\ *n* -s [ISV *galact-* + *-an*] : any of several polysaccharides of plant or animal origin (as agar, arabogalactans, and the galactan occurring in the albumin glands of the snail *Helix pomatia*) that yield galactose on hydrolysis

ga·lac·tia \gəˈlakshēə, -ktēə\ *n, cap* [NL, fr. *galact-* + *-ia*] : a large genus of twining herbs or erect shrubs (family Leguminosae) that are found chiefly in warm regions and have pinnately trifoliate leaves and purple racemose flowers — see MILK PEA

ga·lac·tic \gəˈlaktik, -tēk\ *adj* [LL *galacticus* milky, fr. LGk *galaktikos*, fr. Gk *galakt-, gala* milk + *-ikos* -ic] **1** : of or relating to a galaxy (as the Milky Way) **2** : extremely great : HUGE ⟨a ~ profusion of merchandise —*Steelways*⟩ ⟨the ~ figure of one trillion, 370 billion francs —*Time*⟩

galactic coordinate *n* : a member of a system of celestial coordinates based on the equatorial plane of the Milky Way galaxy

galactic equator *n* : the great circle of the celestial sphere halfway between the galactic poles parallel to and about 1 degree north of the center line of the Milky Way and inclined about 62 degrees to the celestial equator

galactic latitude *n* : latitude in the system of galactic coordinates measured as distance north or south of the galactic equator

galactic longitude *n* : longitude in the system of galactic coordinates measured in degrees eastward from the point where the galactic equator crosses the celestial equator in the constellation Aquila

galactic noise *n* : unidentified radio-frequency radiation coming from the Milky Way — compare RADIO STAR

galactic pole *n* : either of the two opposite points of the celestial sphere that are at the greatest average distance from the Milky Way and are located one in the constellation of Coma Berenices and the other in the constellation of Sculptor — called also respectively *north galactic pole, south galactic pole*

ga·lac·tin \gəˈlaktən, -(ˌ)tin\ *n* -s [*galact-* (fr. Gk *galakt-, gala* milk) + *-in*] : LACTOGENIC HORMONE

ga·lac·tite \gəˈlakˌtīt\ *n* -s [MF or L; MF *galactite*, fr. L *galactites*, fr. Gk *galaktitēs* (*lithos*) stone that makes water milky, fr. *galakt-, gala* milk] : an unidentified soluble stone possibly of calcium nitrate whose milky solution gave rise to many legends and superstitions in medieval times

galacto- — see GALA-, GALACT-

ga·lac·to·cele \gəˈlaktəˌsēl\ *n* -s [prob. fr. NL *galactocele*, fr. *galact-* + *-cele*] : a cystic tumor containing milk or a milky fluid; *esp* : a tumor of this character in a mammary gland

ga·lac·to·cen·tric \gə¦laktə¦sen·trik\ *adj* [*galact-* + *-centric*] : having or relating to the Milky Way as the center ⟨a ~ universe⟩

ga·lac·to·lip·id *also* **ga·lac·to·lip·ide** *or* **ga·lac·to·li·pin** \gə¦laktə+\ *n* [*galact-* + *lipid* or *lipide* or *lipin*] : a glycolipid that yields galactose on hydrolysis — compare CEREBROSIDE

ga·lac·to·man·nan \ˈ"+\ *n* [*galact-* + *mannan*] : any of several polysaccharides that occur esp. in seeds (as locust beans) and yield galactose and mannose on hydrolysis

gal·ac·ton·ic acid \¦galˌak¦tänik-\ *n* [ISV *galact-* + *-onic*] : a crystalline acid $HOCH_2(CHOH)_4COOH$ obtained by oxidation of galactose

ga·lac·to·phore \gəˈlaktəˌfō(ə)r\ *n* -s [*galact-* + *-phore*] : a duct carrying milk

gal·ac·toph·o·rous \ˌgaˌlak¦täf(ə)rəs\ *adj* [Gk *galaktophoros*, fr. *galakt-* galact- + *-phoros* -phorous] : conveying milk ⟨a ~ duct⟩

ga·lac·to·poi·e·sis \gəˌlaktəˌpȯiˈēsəs\ *n, pl* **galactopoie·ses** \-ēˌsēz\ [NL, fr. *galact-* + *-poiesis*] : formation and secretion of milk

¹**ga·lac·to·poi·et·ic** \⸗¦⸗⸗¦ed·ik\ *adj* [*galact-* + *-poietic*] : inducing galactopoiesis

²**galactopoietic** \ˈ"\ *n* -s : a galactopoietic agent

ga·lac·tor·rhea *or* **ga·lac·tor·rhoea** \gəˌlaktəˈrēə\ *n* -s [NL, fr. *galact-* + *-rrhea* or *-rrhoea*] : a spontaneous flow of milk from the nipple

ga·lac·tos·amine \gəˌlakˈtōsəˌmēn, ˌgaˌl-, (ˌ)⸗¦⸗⸗¦⸗; gəˌlak(ˌ)tōˈsamən\ *n* [*galactose* + *amine*] : a crystalline amino derivative $HOCH_2(CHOH)_3CH(NH_2)CHO$ of galactose occurring in the D-form as chondrosamine; 2-deoxy-2-amino-galactose

ga·lac·tose \gəˈlakˌtōs *also* -ōz\ *n* -s [F, fr. *galact-* + *-ose*] : an aldose sugar $HOCH_2(CHOH)_4CHO$ that is less soluble and less sweet than glucose and that is known in dextrorotatory, levorotatory, and racemic forms of which the dextrorotatory D-form is obtained by hydrolysis of lactose melibiose, raffinose, or certain polysaccharides (as agar and pectin) and the levorotatory L-form by hydrolysis of flaxseed mucilage — compare GLUCOSE illustration

ga·lac·tos·emia \gəˌlak(ˌ)tōˈsēmēə\ *n* -s [NL, fr. ISV *galactose* + NL *-emia*] : galactose in the blood of infants due to an inability to utilize galactose because of a congenital absence of an enzyme that normally changes the galactose of galactose-containing foods into glucose

ga·lac·to·sid·ase \gəˌlaktəˈsīˌdās, -āz\ *n* -s [*galactoside* + *-ase*] : an enzyme (as lactase) that hydrolyzes a galactoside

ga·lac·to·side \gəˈlaktəˌsīd, -sə̇d\ *n* -s [*galactose* + *-ide*] : a glycoside that yields galactose on hydrolysis ⟨methol ~⟩

gal·ac·to·sis \ˌgaˌlakˈtōsəs\ *n, pl* **galacto·ses** \-ōˌsēz\ [NL, fr. Gk *galaktōsis* act of changing into milk, fr. *galaktousthai* to become milk (fr. *galakt-, gala* milk) + *-ōsis* -osis — more at GALAXY] : a secretion of milk

ga·lac·tos·uria \gəˌlak(ˌ)tōˈs(h)u̇rēə, -ōsˈyu̇-\ *n* -s [NL, fr. ISV *galactose* + NL *-uria*] : an excretion of urine containing galactose

ga·lac·to·syl \gəˈlaktəˌsil\ *n* -s [*galactose* + *-yl*] : a glycosyl radical $C_6H_{11}O_5$ that is derived from galactose — compare LACTOSE

ga·lac·tu·ron·ic acid \gə¦laktyə¦ränik-\ *n* [ISV *galact-* + *-uronic*] : a crystalline aldehyde-acid $HOOC(CHOH)_4CHO$ that is obtainable from pectic substances by hydrolysis or from methyl galactoside by oxidation and that is oxidizable to mucic acid

ga·la·fa·te \ˌgaləˈfä(ˌ)tā\ *n* -s [AmerSp (Cuba)] : a black oldwife (*Melichthys piceus*) of the western Atlantic from the West Indies to Brazil

ga·la·go \gəˈlä(ˌ)gō, -ˈlā(-; ˈgaləˌgō, ˈgälə-\ *n* [NL, perh. fr. Wolof *golokh* monkey] **1** *cap* : a genus of small actively nocturnal African primates (family Lorisidae) with elongated hind limbs that enable them to leap with great agility **2** -s : any primate of *Galago* or a closely related genus which genera together often form a subfamily of the family Lorisidae

ga·lah \gəˈlä\ *n* -s [native name in Australia] **1** : an Australian cockatoo (*Kakatoë roseicapilla*) that has the back, wings, and tail gray and the head and underparts various shades of rosy pink, that feeds on seeds and bulbous roots, that often is a destructive pest in wheat-growing areas, and that is often kept as a cage bird **2** *slang Austral* : FOOL, SIMPLETON

Gal·a·had \ˈgaləˌhad, -haa(ə)d\ *n* -s *usu cap* [after *Sir Galahad*, a knight in Arthurian legend who achieved the quest of the Holy Grail] : a man marked by unusual purity and self-sacrificing devotion to a noble cause

Gal·a·lith \ˈgaləˌlith\ *trademark* — used for a hornlike plastic made from casein and formaldehyde and used esp. in making small molded objects (as buttons, beads, or combs)

ga·la·nas \gäˈlänəs\ *n* -ES [W, murder] : a fine for murder in early Welsh law assessed upon the slayer and his kinsfolk and measured in cattle or money — compare ERIC

gal·an·ga \gəˈlaŋgə\ *n* -s [ME *galonga, galinga*, fr. ML *galanga, galinga*, fr. Ar *khalanjān*] : GALINGALE 1

galangal *or* **galengale** *var of* GALINGALE

galan·gin \gəˈlanjən, gəˈlaŋgən, ˈgalənjən\ *n* -s [*galanga* + *-in*] : a yellowish crystalline flavone pigment $C_{15}H_{10}O_5$ found in galingale

ga·lant \gəˈlänt, -ˈlȧnt\ *adj* [F, galant, gallant — more at GALLANT] : of, relating to, or composed in the galant style of musical composition

ga·lante *like* ²GALLANT 4\ *adj* [F, fem. of *galant*] : GALLANT 4

ga·lan·te·rie \gə¦läntə(ˌ)rē, -lȧn-\ *n, pl* **galanteri·en** \⸗,⸗⸗-ˈrēən\ *or* **galanteries** [G & F; G, lit., gallantry, courtesy, fr. F — more at GALLANTRY] : a nonessential movement added to or inserted in the classical musical suite (as minuet, loure, air)

ga·lan·thus \gəˈlan(t)thəs\ *n, cap* [NL, fr. Gk *gala* milk + NL *-anthus*; fr. its white flowers — more at GALAXY] : a small genus of European bulbous herbs (family Amaryllidaceae) comprising the snowdrops and having solid scapes and nodding flowers with three larger outer perianth segments and three smaller inner ones with 2-lobed tips

gal·an·tine *also* **gal·a·tine** \ˈgalə(n·)ˌtēn, ˌ⸗⸗ˈ⸗\ *n* -s [F *galantine*, fr. OF *galentine, galatine* fish sauce, fr. ML *galatina* prob. of L *gelatus*, past part. of *gelare* to freeze, congeal — more at COLD] : a dish of poultry, fish, game, or other meat boned, stuffed with forcemeat, cooked, pressed, covered with aspic, and served cold

galant style *n* [trans. of F *style galant*] : a light and elegant free homophonic style of musical composition in the 18th century with rococo ornamentation as contrasted with the serious fugal style of the baroque era

ga·lan·ty show \gəˈlantē-\ *n* [perh. fr. It *galante* gallant, fr. MF *galant* — more at GALLANT] : an entertainment consisting of the telling of a story by means of the shadows of miniature figures thrown on a wall or screen

ga·la·pa·go \gəˈläpəˌgō, -lap-\ *n, pl* **galapagos** \-ˌgəs, -ˌgōz\ [Sp *galápago*] : TORTOISE; *specif* : one of the very large land tortoises of the Galápagos Islands

galas *pl of* GALA

gal·a·tea \ˌgaləˈtēə\ *n* -s [after the *Galatea*, a 19th cent. British man-of-war; fr. its being originally used for children's sailor suits] : a striped cotton cloth in twill weave similar to a lightweight denim and formerly popular for uniforms and playclothes

ga·la·ti \gəˈläts(ē)\ *adj, usu cap* [fr. *Galati*, Romania] : of or from the city of Galati, Romania : of the kind or style prevalent in Galati

¹**ga·la·tian** \gəˈlāsh(ē)ən\ *n* -s *cap* [*Galatia*, ancient country in Asia Minor (fr. L) + E *-an*] : a native or inhabitant of Galatia in Asia Minor; *esp* : a member of a people believed to have been Gauls who conquered and settled Galatia in the 3d century B.C. or of the descendants of such people

²**galatian** \ˈ"\ *adj, usu cap* : of or relating to the Galatians or to Galatia

ga·la·tic \gəˈlad·ik\ *adj, usu cap* [L *Galaticus*, fr. Gk *Galatikos*, fr. *Galatai* Galatians + *-ikos* -ic] : GALATIAN

galavant *var of* GALLIVANT

ga·lax \ˈgāˌlaks\ *n* [NL, prob. fr. Gk *galaxias* Milky Way galaxy] **1** *cap* : a monotypic genus of evergreen herbs (family Diapensiaceae) of the southeastern U.S. with round to heart-shaped leaves that turn maroon, coppery, or purplish in the fall and are much used for funeral and other decorations **2** -ES : any plant of the genus *Galax*

ga·lax·i·al \gəˈlaksēəl\ *or* **ga·lax·i·an** \-ēən\ *adj* [*galaxy* + *-al* or *-an*] : GALACTIC

ga·lax·i·as \gəˈlaksēəs\ *n, cap* [NL, fr. Gk, a kind of fish (also, Milky Way galaxy)] : the type genus of the Galaxiidae

gal·ax·i·idae \ˌgalәkˈsīəˌdē, ˌgaˌlak-\ *n pl, cap* [NL, fr. *Galaxias*, type genus + *-idae*] : a family of scaleless freshwater and marine salmonoid fishes of the southern hemisphere

ga·lax·ite \ˈgāˌlakˌsīt, -lək-\ *n* -s [*Galax*, Va., its locality + E *-ite*] : a black mineral $MnAl_2O_4$ consisting of an oxide of manganese and aluminum and constituting a member of the spinel series

gal·axy \ˈgaləksē, -si *sometimes* ˈgāl-\ *n* -ES [ME *galaxie, galaxias*, fr. ML & L; ML *galaxia*, fr. L *galaxias*, fr. Gk, fr. *galakt-, gala* milk; akin to L *lac* milk] **1 a** *often cap* : MILKY WAY GALAXY **b** : one of billions of large systems of stars including not only stars but nebulae, star clusters, globular clusters, and interstellar matter that make up the universe — called also *extragalactic nebula* **2** : an assemblage of brilliant, noted, or notable persons or things ⟨a ~ of foreign diplomats⟩ ⟨a ~ of fireworks went up —J.M.Flagler⟩ **3** : GALAX 2

¹**gal·ba** \ˈgalbə, ˈgȯl-\ *n, cap* [NL, fr. L, a small worm, ash borer, fat man, fr. Gaulish, fat man — more at CALF] : a widely distributed genus of freshwater snails (family Lymnaeidae) that include important Old World hosts of the liver fluke (*Fasciola hepatica*) and that are sometimes considered indistinguishable from the genus *Lymnaea*

²**galba** \ˈ"\ *n* -s [alter. of *calaba*] : SANTA MARIA TREE

gal·ba·num \ˈgalbənəm, ˈgȯl-\ *n* -s [ME, fr. L, fr. Gk *chalbanē*, fr. Heb *ḥelbĕnāh*] : a yellowish to green or brown aromatic bitter gum resin that contains also some essential oil, that is derived from several Asiatic plants (as *Ferula galbaniflua*), and that resembles asafetida and has been used for similar medicinal purposes and also in incense

gal·bu·la \-byələ\ *n, cap* [NL, fr. L, a small bird, prob. of Celt origin; akin to OIr *gel* white — more at YELLOW] : the type genus of Galbulidae including certain typical jacamars

gal·bu·lae \-ˌlē\ *n pl, cap* [NL, fr. L, pl. of *galbula*] : a suborder of Piciformes consisting of the jacamars, puffbirds, toucans, barbets, and honey guides

gal·bu·li·dae \⸗ˈbyüləˌdē\ *n pl, cap* [NL, fr. *Galbula*, type genus + *-idae*] : a family of brightly colored, long-billed, tropical American birds (order Piciformes) containing the jacamars, and in some classifications the puffbirds — compare BUCCONIDAE

gal·bu·lus \ˈgalbyələs, ˈgȯl-\ *n, pl* **galbu·li** \-ˌlī\ [L; perh. akin to L *galba* fat man, ash borer] : a spherical closed fleshy cone of thickened or fleshy peltate scales (as in the cypress)

gal·cha \ˈgalchə, ˈgȯl-\ *n, pl* **galcha** *or* **galchas** *usu cap* **1 a** : an Iranian people constituting a division of the Tajik and living in the Pamirs and on the slopes of the Hindu Kush **b** : a member of such people **2** : the language of the Galcha — **gal·chic** \-chik\ *adj, usu cap*

¹**gale** \ˈgāl, *esp before pause or consonant* -āəl\ *n* -s [origin unknown] **1 a** : a strong current of air; *specif* : a wind having a speed from 32 to 63 miles per hour — see FRESH GALE, MODERATE GALE, STRONG GALE, WHOLE GALE; BEAUFORT SCALE table **b** *archaic* : a mild wind or current of air : BREEZE **2 a** : an emotional outburst (as of laughter) ⟨a ~ of merriment⟩ ⟨~s of hysterical patriotism —W.L.Sperry⟩ ⟨a ~ of excited conjecture —Carol Bache⟩ **b** : a strong continuous outpouring suggesting a gale ⟨earnestly shouted . . . into the teeth of the ~ of prevailing public opinion —Wendell Johnson⟩ ⟨~s of talk⟩ **syn** see WIND

²**gale** \ˈ"\ *n* -s [prob. alter. of ¹*gavel*] **1 a** *Brit* : an amount paid periodically as rent **b** : the royalty paid in English law for the right to work a mine; *also* : the right itself **2** : a grant of land in English law; *also* : the land granted

ga·lea \ˈgālēə\ *n* -s [NL, fr. L, leather helmet, helmet, fr. Gk *galē, galeē* weasel, ferret; perh. akin to L *glis* dormouse] **1 a** : CASQUE 3 **b** : ¹CAUL 2b **c** *or* **galea apo·neu·ro·ti·ca** \-ˌapōn(y)əˈräd·əkə\ : a cap or a membrane fitting like a helmet; *esp* : the aponeurosis underlying the scalp and linking the frontalis and occipitalis muscles **2** : a helmet-shaped part of a calyx or corolla; *esp* : the upper lip of a ringent or labiate corolla — compare LABIUM **3 a** : the outer or lateral lobe of the maxilla in mandibulate insects **b** : the spinneret on the movable finger of the chelicera of a pseudoscorpion

gale·age \ˈgālij\ *n* -s [²*gale* + *-age*] : ²GALE 2

ga·le·ate \ˈgālēˌāt, -ēət\ *also* **ga·le·at·ed** \-ēˌād·əd\ *adj* [L *galeatus* helmeted, fr. *galea* helmet + *-atus* -ate (adj. suffix)] : helmet-shaped : having a galea : HOODED

gale day *n, Brit* : the day on which rent or interest is due

ga·lee·ny \gəˈlēnē\ *n* -ES [Sp *gallina* (*morisca*), lit., Moorish hen, fr. L *gallina* hen, fr. *gallus* cock — more at GALLUS] *dial Eng* : GUINEA FOWL

ga·le·ga \gəˈlēgə\ *n, cap* [NL, prob. fr. It, fr. ML (*herba*) *Gallica*, lit., Gallic herb, fr. fem. of L *Gallicus* Gallic — more at GALLIC] : a small genus of tall perennial Eurasian herbs (family Leguminosae) with compound leaves and racemose blue or white flowers — see GOAT'S RUE 1

ga·le·gine \gəˈlējən, -ˌjēn\ *n* -s [ISV *galeg-* (fr. NL *Galega*) + *-ine*] : a bitter crystalline base $C_5H_9NHC(=NH)NH_2$ that is derived from guanidine and is obtained esp. from European goat's rue

ga·lei \ˈgālēˌī\ [NL, pl., fr. Gk *galeos* dogfish, shark] *syn of* PLEUROTREMATA

¹**ga·le·id** \-ēəd\ *adj* [NL *Galeidae*] : of or relating to the Carcharhinidae

²**galeid** \ˈ"\ *n* -s : a shark of the family Carcharhinidae

ga·le·idae \gəˈlēəˌdē, gāˈ-\ [NL, fr. *Galeus* + *-idae*] *syn of* CARCHARHINIDAE

ga·le·iform \gəˈlēəˌfȯrm, gāˈlē-ˌgāˈlē-\ *adj* [prob. fr. F *galéiforme*, fr. L *galea* helmet + F *-iforme* -iform] **1** : shaped like a helmet **2** [NL *Galeus* + E *-iform*] : resembling one of the Carcharhinidae : like a typical shark

ga·le·na \gəˈlēnə\ *n* -s [L, lead ore, dross that remains after melting lead] : a mineral PbS consisting of native lead sulfide occurring in cubic or octahedral crystals or massive, bluish gray in color with metallic luster, showing highly perfect cubic cleavage, and constituting the principal ore of lead

ga·le·ni·an \(ˈ)gā¦lēnēən, gəˈl-\ *adj, usu cap* [*Galen*, Greek physician + E *-ian*] : GALENIC

galenian figure *n, usu cap G* [so called fr. the fact that it was reputedly added by Galen to the three figures formulated by Aristotle †322 B.C. Greek philosopher] : the fourth syllogistic figure in logic

¹**ga·len·ic** \(ˈ)gā¦lenik, gəˈl-, -nēk\ *also* **ga·len·i·cal** \-nəkəl, -nēk-\ *adj* [*Galen fl* 2d cent. A.D. Greek physician and medical writer + E *-ic, -ical*] **1** *usu cap* : of or relating to Galen or his medical principles or method **2** : constituting a galenical

²**ga·le·nic** \gəˈlēnik, -len-, -nēk\ *or* **ga·le·ni·cal** \-nəkəl, -nēk-\ *adj* [*galena* + *-ic, -ical*] : belonging to or containing galena

ga·len·i·cal \gāˈlenəkəl, gəˈ-, -nēk-\ *n* -s [¹*galenical* (adj.)] : a standard medicinal preparation (as extract, tincture) containing usu. one or more active constituents of a plant and made by a process that leaves the inert and other undesirable constituents of the plant undissolved

galenic pharmacy *n, usu cap G* : the preparation of galenicals

ga·len·ism \ˈgāləˌnizəm\ *n, usu cap* : the Galenic system of medical practice

ga·len·ist \-nəst\ *n* -s *usu cap* : a follower or disciple of the ancient physician Galen

ga·le·nite \gəˈlēˌnīt\ *n* -s [G *galenit*, fr. L *galena* lead ore + G *-it* -ite] : GALENA

ga·le·no·bis·mu·tite \gə¦lēnō+\ *n* [ISV *galena* + *-o-* + *bismutite*; orig. formed as Sw *galenobismutit*] **:** a mineral $PbBi_2S_4$ consisting of a lead-gray or tin-white lead bismuth sulfide (sp. gr. 6.9)

ga·le·noid \gə'lē,nȯid\ *adj* [*galena* + *-oid*] **:** resembling galena

gal·en·so·ga *n, pl* **galensoga** [by alter.] **:** GALINSOGA 2

ga·len's vein \'gālənz-\ *n, usu cap G* [after *Galen*, Greek physician] **1 :** either of a pair of veins in the roof of the third ventricle that drain the interior of the brain **2 :** GREAT CEREBRAL VEIN

ga·le·o·cer·do \,gālēō'sər(,)dō\ *n, cap* [NL, fr. Gk *galeos* dogfish, shark + *kerdō* wily one, fox; akin to Gk *kerdos* profit — more at CAIRD (tinker)] **:** a genus of sharks (family Carcharhinidae) comprising the tiger shark

¹ga·le·oid \'gālē,ȯid\ *adj* [NL *Galeoidea*] **:** of or relating to the Galeoidea

²galeoid \"\ *n* -s **:** a shark of the suborder Galeoidea

ga·le·oi·dea \,gālē'ȯidēə\ *n pl, cap* [NL, fr. *Galeus* + NL *-oidea*] **:** a suborder of Pleurotremata comprising typical active predaceous fusiform sharks with the spiracle small or absent and an anal fin always present

ga·leo·pi·the·cus \,gālē(,)ōpə'thēkəs, -'pithəkəs\ [NL, fr. *galeo-* (fr. Gk *galeē* weasel) + *-pithecus* — more at GALEA] *syn of* CYNOCEPHALUS 2

ga·le·op·sis \,gālē'äpsəs\ *n, cap* [NL, fr. L, a nettle, fr. Gk *galeōpsis*, fr. *galē*, *galeē* weasel + *-opsis*] **:** a small genus of coarse annual Old World herbs (family Labiatae) distinguished by the calyx that has 5 to 10 nerves and the transversely 2-valved anther sacs — see HEMP NETTLE

ga·le·o·rhin·i·dae \,gālēō'rinə,dē\ *n pl, cap* [NL, fr. *Galeorhinus*, type genus + *-idae*] **1** *in some classifications* **:** a family of sharks equivalent to or more inclusive than Carchariidae **2** *in some classifications* **:** a family of sharks comprising the smooth dogfishes and related forms

ga·le·o·rhi·nus \-'rīnəs\ *n, cap* [NL, fr. Gk *galeos* dogfish, shark + NL *-rhinus* (fr. Gk *rhinē*, a shark)] **1 :** a genus of sharks including the topes and soupfin sharks **2** *in some classifications* **:** a genus of sharks comprising the smooth dogfishes

ga·le·ra \gə'lirə\ *n* [NL, fr. L, helmet, helmetlike cap of undressed skin, fr. *galea* helmet — more at GALEA] **1** *cap* **:** a genus of the family Viverridae comprising the tayra **2** -s **:** TAYRA

ga·lère \gə'le(ə)r\ *n* -s [F, lit., galley, slave ship, fr. MF, fr. OCatal *galera* galley, alter. of *galea* — more at GALLEY] **:** a group of people having a marked common quality or relationship

ga·le·rie \galə'rē\ *n* -s [AmerFr (Miss. Valley), fr. F, gallery — more at GALLERY] **:** GALLERY, VERANDA, PORCH — often used in areas of the South where French or creole dialect is spoken

gal·e·ru·ci·dae \,galə'rüsə,dē\ *n pl, cap* [NL, fr. *Galeruca*, type genus + *-idae*] **:** a small but widely distributed family of leaf-eating beetles formerly usu. included in Chrysomelidae

gales *pl of* GALE

gal·e·saur \'galə,sȯ(ə)r\ *n* -s [NL *Galesaurus*] **:** a reptile of the genus *Galesaurus* or the family Galesauridae

¹gal·e·sau·rid \¦==¦sȯrəd\ *adj* [NL *Galesauridae*, a family of reptiles, fr. *Galesaurus*, type genus + *-idae*] **:** of or relating to the genus *Galesaurus* or the family Galesauridae

²galesaurid \"\ *n* -s **:** GALESAUR

gal·e·sau·rus \,==¦sȯrəs\ *n, cap* [NL, fr. Gk *galeos* dogfish, shark + NL *-saurus*] **:** a genus (the type of the family Galesauridae) of advanced cynodont reptiles of the Karroo formation that have teeth suggesting those of a carnivorous mammal

¹ga·let \'galət\ *n* -s [modif. of Gk *galeē*, *galē* weasel, ferret] **:** ²FOSSA

²gal·et \'galət\ *var of* GALLET

ga·lette \gə'let\ *n* -s [F, fr. MF, fr. OF *galete*, fr. *galet* pebble — more at GALLET] **:** a flat round cake of pastry usu. sprinkled with sugar before baking

ga·le·us \'gālēəs\ *n, cap* [NL, fr. Gk *galeos* dogfish, shark] **1** *in some classifications* **:** a genus of sharks including the topes and related forms and being nearly coextensive with *Galeorhinus* **2** *in some classifications* **:** a genus of sharks including dogfishes that are usu. placed in *Mustelus*

ga·li·bi \gə'lēbē\ *n, pl* **galibi** *or* **galibis** *usu cap* [Carib *galibi* Caribs — more at CANNIBAL] **1 a :** a Carib people of French Guiana **b :** a member of such people **2 :** the language of the Galibi people

¹ga·li·cian \gə'lishən\ *n* -s *cap* [*Galicia*, region and ancient kingdom in northwest Spain + E *-an*] **1 :** a native or inhabitant of Spanish Galicia **2 :** the language of the Galicians

²galician \"\ *adj, usu cap* **1 :** of or relating to Galicia, a division of Spain north of Portugal, or to the Galicians **2 :** of, relating to, or being the Galician language

³galician \", gə'letsēən\ *adj, usu cap* [*Galicia*, former Austrian crownland in east central Europe + E *-an*] **:** of or relating to Galicia, a former province of the Austro-Hungarian empire now a region of southwestern Poland and western U.S.S.R.

⁴galician *like* ³GALICIAN\ *n* -s *cap* **1 :** a native or inhabitant of the former Austrian crownland Galicia **2 :** a Galician Jew of Poland **:** a speaker of one of the several Yiddish dialects among eastern European Jews

ga·lic·tis \gə'liktəs\ *n, cap* [NL, fr. Gk *galē* weasel + *iktis* yellow-breasted marten — more at GALEA] *in some classifications* **:** a genus of Mustelidae comprising the grison and the tayra of So. America

ga·lid·ia \gə'lidēə\ *n, cap* [NL, fr. Gk *galideus* young weasel (dim. of *galeē* weasel) + NL *-ia*] **:** a genus of Malagasy mongooses comprising a single species (*G. elegans*) distinguished by a black-ringed tail

gal·i·dic·tis \,galə'diktəs\ *n, cap* [NL, fr. Gk *galideus* young weasel + *iktis* yellow-breasted marten] **:** a genus of Malagasy mongooses marked with dark longitudinal stripes

¹gal·i·le·an *also* **gal·i·lae·an** \,galə'lēən\ *n* -s *cap* [L *Galilaea* Galilee, Roman province in northern Palestine (fr. Gk *Galilaia*, hilly region of northern Palestine) + E *-an*] **:** a native or inhabitant of Galilee

²galilean *also* **galilaean** \¦==¦==\ *adj, usu cap* **:** of or relating to Galilee, the northern province of Palestine under the Romans

³gal·i·le·an \", -lāən\ *adj, usu cap* [*Galileo* †1642 Ital. astronomer and physicist + E *-an*] **:** of or relating to Galileo Galilei, founder of experimental physics and astronomy

galilean glass *n, usu cap 1st G* **:** a Galilean telescope usu. binocular in form

galilean telescope *n, usu cap G* [³*galilean*] **:** the first form of refracting telescope including a positive objective lens and a negative eye lens and giving an erect image and a restricted field of view

gal·i·lee \'galə,lē\ *n* -s [AF, fr. ML *galilaea* porch of a church, prob. fr. L *Galilaea* Galilee] **:** a chapel or porch at the entrance of an English church (as at Durham, Ely, and Lincoln) used in various ways as an accessory room

gal·i·ma·ti·as \,galə'māshēəs, -'madē-, ¦==ma·¦tyä\ *n* -ES [F, fr. MF] **:** confused and meaningless talk **:** NONSENSE, GIBBERISH

gal·in·gale \'galən,gāl, -liŋ,-\ *also* **gal·an·gal** \-lən,gal, -liŋ,-\ *or* **gal·an·gale** \-,gāl\ *or* **cal·an·gall** \'kalən,gȯl, -liŋ,-\ *n* -s [ME *galyngale*, fr. MF *galingal*, *garingal*, fr. OF, fr. Ar *khalanjān*] **1 a :** a pungent aromatic rhizome produced in eastern Asia by plants related to the true ginger and formerly used in medicine and cookery **b :** either of two plants of the family Zingiberaceae that yield galingale: (1) **:** a Chinese perennial herb (*Alpinia officinalis*) with pyramidal racemes of rose-veined white flowers (2) **:** a stemless perennial herb (*Kaempferia galanga*) of southeastern Asia with fragrant short-lived largely white flowers **2 :** an Old World sedge (*Cyperus longus*) with a root having properties like and sometimes used in place of galingale; *broadly* **:** a plant of the genus *Cyperus*

gal·in·so·ga \,galən'sōgə\ *n* [NL, after Mariano M. de *Galinsoga* †1797 Span. botanist] **1** *cap* **:** a small genus of weedy tropical American herbs (family Compositae) with opposite leaves and small heads of yellowish flowers some of which have become naturalized in Europe and No. America — see FRENCHWEED 2 **2** *pl* **galinsoga :** any plant of the genus *Galinsoga*

gal·ion·gee \'galyən,jē, -lēə-, ¸==(=)'=\ *n* -s [Turk *kalyoncı* man-of-war's man, fr. *kalyon* man-of-war, galleon, fr. It *galeone*, fr. OSp *galeón* — more at GALLEON] **:** a Turkish sailor

galiot *var of* GALLIOT

gal·i·pine \'galə,pēn, -,pən\ *n* -s [ISV *galip-* (fr. NL *Galipea*, genus of So. American evergreen plants + *-ine*] **:** a crystalline alkaloid $C_{20}H_{21}NO_3$ derived from quinoline and found in angostura bark

gal·i·pot \'galə,pät, -,pō\ *n* -s [F] **:** the crude turpentine oleoresin formed as an exudation upon the bark of the cluster pine in southern Europe (as in France) — called also *Bordeaux turpentine*

ga·lise creek indian *or* **ga·lice creek indian** \gə'lēs-\ *n, usu cap G&C&I* [after *Galise Creek* or *Galice Creek*, Oregon] **:** TALTUSHTUNTUDE

ga·li·um \'gālēəm\ *n, cap* [NL, fr. Gk *galion* bedstraw, prob. fr. *gala* milk; fr. its use to curdle milk] **:** a large genus of cosmopolitan usu. trailing herbs (family Rubiaceae) with angled stems, opposite or whorled leaves, and small flowers — see CLEAVERS, WILD LICORICE

gal·joen \gal'yün\ *n* -s [Afrik, galleon, galjoen, fr. D, galleon, fr. MD *galioen*, prob. fr. MF *galion* — more at GALLEON] **:** a compressed deep-bodied percoid food and sport fish (*Dichistius capensis*) common in shallow water and surf along the coasts of southern Africa; *also* **:** any of several related fishes — often used with a qualifying term

¹gall \'gȯl\ *n* -s [ME, fr. OE *gealla*; akin to OHG *galla* gall, bile, ON *gall*, L *fel*, Gk *cholē*, *cholos* gall, bile, OE *geolu* yellow — more at YELLOW] **1 a :** BILE; *esp* **:** bile obtained from the gallbladder of an animal (as the ox) for use in the arts and in medicine **b :** something bitter to endure ⟨the ~ of repentance⟩ **c :** bitterness of spirit **:** RANCOR **2 :** GALLBLADDER **3 :** brazen boldness with impudent assurance and rankling insolence ⟨the small stockholder who . . . has the ~ to ask questions about the management —D.L.Cohn⟩ **4 :** GLASS GALL **syn** see TEMERITY

²gall \"\ *n* -s [ME *galle*, fr. OE *gealla*, fr. L *galla* gallnut] **1 a :** a sore or a granulating wound of the skin caused by chronic irritation (as on the back or withers of a horse due to rubbing or chafing of saddle or harness) — see SADDLE SORE **b** (1) **:** something that irritates or causes carking exasperation (2) **:** a state of irritation or exasperation (3) **:** the inner source or spring of such irritation or exasperation **2 a** *archaic* **:** a bare or weak spot (as on a string) **:** FLAW, BLEMISH; *also* **:** a lesion in wood (as around a knot) used in or intended for use in archery **b** *dial* **:** an unfertile or barren spot where the topsoil has been removed by erosion

³gall \"\ *vb* -ED/-ING/-S [ME *gallen*, fr. *galle* gall, sore] *vt* **1 a :** to fret and wear away by friction **:** hurt or break the skin of by rubbing **:** CHAFE ⟨a saddle often ~s the back of a horse⟩ ⟨constant friction against the ship's side soon ~ed the cable⟩ **b :** FRET, ANNOY, IRRITATE ⟨be ~ed by sarcasm⟩ **2 :** to harass by shooting at ⟨~ed by enemy fire⟩ ~ *vi* **1 :** to become sore or worn by rubbing **2 :** SEIZE *vi* 2

⁴gall \"\ *n* -s [ME *galle*, fr. MF, fr. L *galla* gallnut, gall on a plant; perh. akin to Gk *ganglion* cystic tumor, mass of nerve tissue, Skt *glau* round lump; basic meaning: ball, rounded object] **1 :** a swelling or excrescence of the tissues of a plant that results usu. from the attacks of parasites (as fungi, bacteria, insects), is often distinguished by characteristic shape or color, and in some instances forms an important source of tannin — see ALEPPO GALL, BLUE GALL, GREEN GALL; NUTGALL, OAK APPLE; GALL MIDGE **2 :** a small generally flattened pellet of clay found in some sandstones and sandy shales — called also *clay gall*

⁵gall \"\ *vb* -ED/-ING/-S *vt* **:** to cause galls to form on (as a tree) ~ *vi* **:** to form galls

gall- *or* **gallo-** *comb form* [*gallic acid*] **:** gallic acid ⟨*gall*aldehyde⟩

¹gal·la \'galə, 'gȯlə\ *n* -s [L] **:** any of certain nutgalls from oaks that are used in pharmacy for their astringent properties

²gal·la *or* **ga·la** \'galə, 'gälə\ *n, pl* **galla** *or* **gallas** *or* **gala** *or* **galas** *usu cap* [perh. fr. Ar *ghalīz* rough, wild] **1 a :** any of several groups of Cushitic-speaking peoples occupying British East Africa and southern Ethiopia **b :** a member of any of these groups **2 :** the Cushitic language of the Galla

gallabiya *var of* GALABIA

gall·acetophenone \(¦)gal, (¦)gȯl+\ *n* [ISV *gall-* + *acet-* + *phenyl* + *-one*; prob. orig. formed as G *gallazetophenon*] **:** a yellow crystalline compound $C_6H_2(OH)_3COCH_3$ formerly used as a mordant dye and also locally as an antiseptic; 2,3,4-trihydroxy-acetophenone — called also *Alizarine Yellow C*

gal·lah *also* **gal·lach** \'gäləK, gä'läK\ *n, pl* **gallahim** *also* **galla·chim** \gä'lōKəm, -Kēm, ,gälō'Kēm\ [Heb *gallāh*, lit., one who shaves] *among the Jews* **:** a Christian minister or cleric; *esp* **:** a Roman Catholic priest or monk

gal·la·mine triethiodide \'galə,mēn-\ *n* [*gallamine* fr. pyrogallol + *amine*] **:** a substituted ammonium salt $C_6H_3[OCH_2CH_2N(C_2H_5)_3]_3I_3$ derived from pyrogallol and used to produce muscle relaxation esp. during anesthesia

gall·anilide *also* **gall·anilid** \(')gal, (')gȯl+\ *n* [ISV *gall-* + *anilide*; orig. formed as G *gallanilid*] **:** the anilide $C_{13}H_{11}NO_4$ of gallic acid used locally for skin diseases

¹gal·lant *in current senses usu* ='= — *see* ²GALLANT\ *n* -s [ME *galaunt*, fr. MF *galant*, fr. *galant*, adj.] **1 a** (1) **:** a man of fashion **:** a young blood (2) *archaic* **:** GENTLEMAN — usu. used in pl. as a noun of address ⟨good morrow ~s! Want ye corn for bread? —Shak.⟩ **b** *obs* **:** a fashionably dressed woman **2 :** one who is gallant to ladies: **a :** ESCORT, DATE ⟨her ~ was now more than an hour overdue —Dorothy Barclay⟩ **b :** SUITOR **c :** LOVER

²gal·lant \'galənt *in sense 4 usu* gə'lant *or* ga'- *or* -'länt *or* -'laa(ə)nt *or* -'lànt\ *adj* [ME *galaunt*, fr. MF *galant*, fr. OF *galant*, pres. part. of *galer* to rejoice, have a good time, fr. *gale* pleasure, merrymaking, of Gmc origin; akin to OE *wela* weal — more at WEAL] **1 a :** marked by show, color, smartness, or splendor esp. in dress ⟨a ~ figure, with his sword, his rich-laced uniform, his cocked hat and powdered queue —C.B.Nordhoff & J.N.Hall⟩ ⟨the loveliest, the most ~ and dashing of the beauties of the end of Queen Victoria's reign —W.S.Maugham⟩ **b** *obs, of a woman* **:** HANDSOME **2** *archaic* **:** FINE, WONDERFUL, EXCELLENT — a generalized expression of admiration **3 a :** marked by dash and valor or by the promise or show of lively, valiant, or resolute performance; *broadly* **:** SPLENDID, STATELY ⟨command of a tall and ~ ship speeding over blue water —S.E.Morison⟩ **b :** marked by a blend of the high-spirited, brave, dashing, and chivalrous **:** inspiring admiration **:** showing courageous fortitude and ready resolution esp. in the face of defeat ⟨Pickett's desperate charge . . . facing a terrific fire, was one of the most ~ efforts —Allan Nevins & H.S.Commager⟩ ⟨losing a ~ fight for life⟩ **c :** noble, chivalrous, and often self-sacrificing ⟨a ~ white lie . . . that brings a measure of understanding to the estranged husband and wife —*Newsweek*⟩ **d** *in British parliamentary and formal use* **:** distinguished by being in the armed services ⟨the honorable and ~ member from Kent⟩ **4** [F *galant*, fr. It *galante* courteous, attentive to women, fr. MF *galant* dashing, lively, bold] **a :** notably marked by courtesy and attentiveness to women esp. in a spirited and dashing or elaborate way ⟨a ~ escort⟩ **b :** given to amorous quest and intrigue **:** concerned with amatory ventures ⟨~ enough to have made a distinguished marriage by an elopement —G.B.Shaw⟩ **syn** see CIVIL

³gallant *usu* ='=\ *vb* -ED/-ING/-S *vt* **1 :** to bestow gallant attentions on (a lady) **:** pay court to **:** act as a suitor or lover toward **2 a :** to act as an escort to or attend upon (a lady) **b :** ESCORT, CONDUCT **3** *obs* **:** to handle or manipulate (a fan) in a modish manner ~ *vi* **1 :** to act in the manner of a gallant **:** pay court **:** FLIRT **:** make love ⟨spent his evenings ~*ing* with the ladies of the town⟩ **2 :** to gad about or gallivant esp. with the opposite sex

gal·lant·ize \-n-,tīz, -nt-,īz; *stressed* ='=,= *or* '==,=\ *vt* -ED/-ING/-S **:** to act as a gallant toward **:** pay special courteous or amorous attention to

gal·lant·ly *adv* **:** in a gallant manner ⟨~ offering his seat to a lady⟩ ⟨~ fighting a losing battle⟩ ⟨sailing ~ into battle⟩

gal·lant·ness *n* -ES [ME *galantnesse*, fr. *galant*, *galaunt* gallant, adj. + *-nesse* -ness] **:** the quality or state of being gallant ⟨the ~ of the futile charge against the enemy⟩ ⟨said he had no use for ~ or other useless courtesy⟩

gal·lant·ry \'galəntrē, -ri\ *n* -ES [partly fr. *gallant*, adj. & n. + *-ry* and partly fr. F *galanterie*, fr. MF, fr. *galant*, adj. & n., gallant + *-erie* -ery] **1** *obs* **:** GALLANTS ⟨all the ~ of Troy —Shak.⟩ **2** *archaic* **:** gallant appearance **:** fine or ostentatious display **:** SPLENDOR **3 :** a markedly civil or courteous act or statement **4 :** the conduct of a gallant: as **a :** marked civility or markedly courteous attention to a lady ⟨his vivacious ~ stole away the hearts of all the women —T.B.Macaulay⟩ **b :** markedly amorous attention to a female; *esp* **:** such attention designed to win sexual favors **5 a :** bravery, intrepidity, or fortitude (as against great odds) esp. marked by dashing or heroic acts ⟨the desperate ~ of our naval task forces —G.C.Marshall⟩ ⟨~ in action⟩ **b :** an instance of this ⟨eyewitness's accounts of the rearguard *gallantries* and counterattacks . . . in the great retreat to the coast —*Times Lit. Supp.*⟩

gallant soldier *n* [by folk etymology fr. NL *Galinsoga*] **:** an annual So. American composite herb (*Galinsoga parviflora*) now a cosmopolitan weed with an erect much-branched stem, opposite leaves, and flower heads in clusters with their branches nearly opposite and equal

gall aphid *n* **:** an aphid that causes the formation of a gall on the plant on which it lives; *esp* **:** a member of the family Psyllidae

gallas *pl of* GALLA

gal·late \'ga,lāt, 'gȯ,-\ *n* -s [*gall-* + *-ate*] **:** a salt or ester of gallic acid

gallavant *var of* GALLIVANT

gall·ber·ry \'gȯl- — *see* BERRY\ *n* [⁴*gall* + *berry*] **:** INKBERRY 1

gallbladder \'=,==\ *n* [¹*gall* + *bladder*] **:** a membranous muscular sac present in most vertebrates in which the bile from the liver is stored until required, in man being pear-shaped and lodged in a fossa on the undersurface of the right lobe of the liver and opening by the cystic duct which joins the hepatic duct to form the common bile duct — see DIGESTION illustration

gal·le·ass *also* **gal·li·ass** \'galēəs, -ē,as\ *n* -ES [MF *galeasse*, *galiace*, fr. OIt *galeazza*, lit., large galley, aug. of *galea* galley, fr. ML, fr. MGk — more at GALLEY] **:** a large fast galley propelled by both sails and oars and mounting guns; *esp* **:** such a ship used by nations of southern Europe in the 16th and 17th centuries

galled \'gȯld\ *adj* [ME, fr. OE *geallede*, fr. *gealla* gall, sore + *-ede* -ed — more at GALL (sore)] **1 :** subjected to galling **:** having galls **2 :** sterile from exhaustion or removal of soil; *also* **:** rendered infertile by erosion

galle·gan \gə(l)'yāgən, gə'lēg-\ *adj, usu cap* [*gallego* + *-an*] **:** ²GALICIAN

galle·go \gə(l)'yā(,)gō\ *n* -s *cap* [Sp, n. & adj., Galician, fr. L *Gallaicus* of the Gallaeci, fr. *Gallaeci*, an ancient people in western Spain] **:** ¹GALICIAN

gal·le·in \'galēən, 'gȯl-\ *n* -s [ISV *gall-* + phthal*ein*; orig. formed in G] **:** a metallic-green crystalline phthalein dye $C_{20}H_{12}O_7$ made from phthalic anhydride and gallic acid or pyrogallol and used esp. in dyeing violet and as an indicator

gal·leon \'galēən, 'lyən\ *n* -s [OSp *galeón*, fr. MF *galion* large war galley, fr. OF *galie* galley — more at GALLEY] **1 :** a heavily built chiefly square-rigged sailing ship of the 15th to early 18th centuries usu. having a high, fortified, and sometimes elaborately decorated forecastle and poop and often three or four decks and being used for war or commerce esp. by the Spanish as treasure ships in their American trade **2 :** a large esp. stately sailing ship suggesting a galleon

gal·le·ri·an \gə'lirēən ga'-\ *n* -s [F *galérien*, fr. *galère* galley + *-ien* -an] *archaic* **:** GALLEY SLAVE

gal·ler·ied \'gal(ə)rēd, -rid\ *adj* **:** provided or decorated with a gallery ⟨~ country houses⟩ ⟨the fortified, ~ and intimidating great rock —Rose Macaulay⟩

gal·lery \'gal(ə)rē, -ri\ *n* -ES [MF *galerie*, fr. ML *galeria*, prob. alter. of *galilea*, *galilaea* galilee — more at GALILEE] **1 a :** a covered space more or less open at the sides for walking **:** a roofed promenade **:** AMBULATORY, PORTICO, COLONNADE **b :** a main corridor with windows running continuously on one side in an English country house **2 a :** a platform or passageway above ground level resembling a corridor, projecting from an outside wall, and open at the outer edge or having there only a rail or balustrade **:** BALCONY; *also, South & Midland* **:** PORCH, VERANDA **b :** a similar raised platform or passageway on the roof of a building **c** (1) **:** a platform at the quarter or around the stern of a ship — see QUARTER GALLERY, STERN GALLERY (2) **:** a gun platform or gun emplacement on a ship or aircraft carrier **d :** a raised usu. railed walk (as around the upper part of a large engine) to facilitate oiling or inspection **3 a :** a long and narrow passage, apartment, or corridor **b :** a horizontal or nearly horizontal subterranean passageway (as in a cave or excavated part of a military mining system); *also* **:** a working drift or level in mining **c :** a sunk or cut passageway in a fortification that is covered overhead as well as at the sides **d :** a passageway either within the thickness of a wall or projecting on corbels or between a main wall and an arcade (as in the front or flank of a Gothic church) **e :** a passage made underground by an animal (as a mole or ant) or in wood by an insect (as a beetle larva) **f :** BURROW 2 **g :** an artificial chamber provided for the collection of groundwater **4 a :** a room, series of rooms, wide corridor, or building devoted to the exhibition of works of art ⟨sculpture displayed in the north ~⟩; *also* **:** a long room or unusually wide corridor used for exhibitions or special ceremonials **b :** an institution devoted to the collection and exhibition of works of art ⟨the National *Gallery*⟩ **c :** a business establishment devoted to the exhibition and sale of works of art ⟨a new ~ showing modern prints⟩ **d :** ROGUES' GALLERY **e :** a collection or aggregation (as of varied specimens of one kind of thing) worthy of being put on display as if in a gallery ⟨what a ~ of men these are who line Ireland's Hall of Fame —*Saturday Rev.*⟩ ⟨the rich ~ of characters in this novel —H.S.Canby⟩ ⟨the world's ~ of attractive animals —W.E.Swinton⟩ ⟨in portraying his ~ of grotesques —Bergen Evans⟩ ⟨cameramen pick up a ~ of faces of every age, shade, and nationality —*Newsweek*⟩ ⟨his ~ of humors varies —*Encyc. Americana*⟩ **5 a :** a platform projecting from one or more interior walls (as of a church or theater) for additional accommodation (as of a part of a congregation or audience) or for special use; *esp* **:** the highest of such platforms in a theatre commonly having the cheapest seats **b :** the occupants of a gallery; *esp* **:** the part of a theater audience that is seated in the top gallery or in the cheapest seats **c :** a part of the general public lacking the discriminating taste of the connoisseur **d :** a body of spectators (as at a tennis match) or listeners (as at a debate) **6 :** any of several netted openings in court tennis below the side penthouse — see WINNING GALLERY **7 a :** a small ornamental barrier or railing (as along the edge of a table or shelf) **b :** an often ornamental ring to support a lampshade or globe **c :** a band-like jewelry setting usu. with a pierced or raised design **8 :** SHOOTING GALLERY; *esp* **:** an indoor shooting range **9 :** a photographer's studio **10 :** an upper-floor area open to and projecting over a lower-floor area of a house **syn** see BALCONY

gallery 7a

gallery car *n* **:** a double-decked railroad car used in suburban service

gallery deck *n* **:** a gallery or bay for gun emplacements on a ship or aircraft carrier

gallery forest *n* **:** FRINGING FOREST

gallery god *n* **:** an occupant of the gallery of a theater

gal·lery·ite \'gal(ə)rē,īt\ *n* -s **:** an occupant of a gallery esp. of a theater

gallerylike \'=(=)=,=\ *adj* **:** resembling a gallery

gallery load *n* **:** a cartridge designed for firing in a gallery

gallery organ *n* **:** a division of a pipe organ placed at the end of the nave in a gallery

¹gal·let *also* **gal·et** \'galət\ *n* -s [F *galet* pebble, fr. MF, fr. OF, dim. of *gal*, prob. of Celt origin; akin to OIr *gall* stone pillar] **:** a chip of stone **:** SPALL

²gallet *also* **galet** \"\ *vt* -ED/-ING/-S **:** to fill in the fresh mortar joints of (rubble masonry) with gallets

galle·ta grass *also* **galleta** \gə(l)'yed·ə, gī'|, |äd·ə\ *n* -s [Sp *galleta* hardtack, fr. F *galette* flat round cake of pastry, hardtack — more at GALETTE] **:** either of two perennial forage grasses (*Hilaria rigida* and *H. jamesii*) used for hay in southwestern U.S. and Mexico

gal·ley \'galē, -li\ *n* -s *often attrib* [ME *galeie,* fr. OF *galee, galie,* prob. fr. OCatal or fr. OProv *galea,* fr. MGk, prob. fr. Gk *galeē, galē* weasel, marten, a small fish — more at GALEA] **1 a :** a large low usu. one-decked ship propelled by both sails and oars, typically being 100 to 200 feet long, often having 20 oars on each side with many rowers to each oar, 2 or 3 masts rigged with lateen sails, guns at prow and stern, and a complement of 1000 to 1200 men, and used throughout medieval times esp. in the Mediterranean for war, trading, ceremonial, and pleasure purposes — see GALLEASS, GALLIOT, QUARTER GALLEY; compare GALLEON **b :** LYMPHAD 2 **2 :** a short crescent-shaped seagoing ship of classical antiquity propelled chiefly by oars though generally having a mast carrying an oblong sail — compare BIREME, PENTECONTER, QUADRIREME, QUINQUEREME, TESSARACONTER, TRIACONTER, TRIREME **3 :** a large open rowing boat formerly used in England by customs officers or press-gangs, by captains of warships, and as a river pleasure boat **4 a :** the kitchen and cooking apparatus of a ship, airplane, or trailer — see ¹CABOOSE 1a **b :** COOKHOUSE, KITCHEN **5 a :** an oblong tray commonly of pressed steel with upright sides to hold set type **b :** GALLEY PROOF **6 :** an inward circle made with the free foot during a hop in Cotswold morris dancing — **in this galley** *adv* **:** in this markedly incongruous place or group

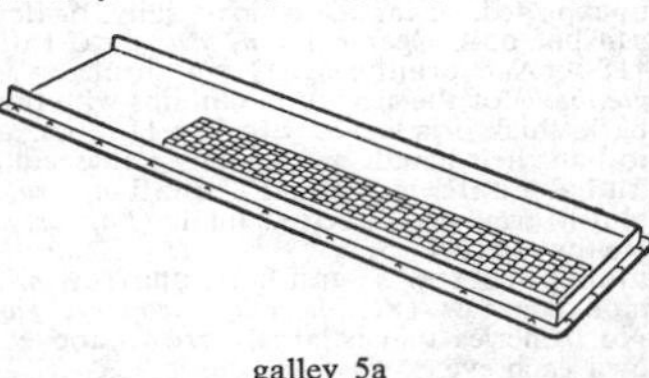

galley 5a

galley halfpenny *n* [ME *galey halfpeni,* fr. *galey, galeie* galley + *halfpeni* halfpenny; fr. its alleged introduction to London by Genoese traders — more at HALFPENNY] **:** a small base silver denier from the Continent that circulated in England in the 13th and 14th centuries

galley line *n* **:** an identifying line at the top of a galley of typeset matter

gal·ley·man \'==mən\ *n, pl* **galleymen** [ME *galay man,* fr. *galay, galeie* galley + *man*] **1 :** one who rows, works, or carries on trade in a galley **2 :** a utility man on a ship

galley method *n* [prob. fr. It *galea* galley, fr. ML, fr. MGk; fr. the supposed resemblance of the outline of the figures to a galley] **:** SCRATCH DIVISION

galley operator *n* **:** a regional wholesaler engaged in distributing or reshipping books and periodicals to individual dealers in rural or suburban areas

galley proof *n* **:** a proof from type on a galley before it is made up in pages

galley punt *n* **:** a clinker-built open boat with dipping lugsail and oars used esp. by English pilots

galley slave *n* **1 a :** a slave acting as a rower on a galley **b :** a criminal condemned to row on a galley **2 :** DRUDGE 1

galley slug *n* **:** SLUG 2b

galley–tile *n* [so called fr. its being originally transported by galley] *obs* **:** a tile of glazed earthenware

gal·ley-west \,galē'west\ *adv* [prob. alter. of E dial. *collywest, collyweston* in an opposite direction, badly askew, awry, perh. fr. a personal name] **:** into a condition of total disorder, destruction, confusion, or uselessness — used in the phrase *to knock galley-west* ⟨the trade was knocked *galley-west* when the government struck at its roots, jailed 30 of the biggest smugglers —*Today*⟩ ⟨hit him as hard as he could and knocked him *galley-west*⟩

gall fig *n* [⁴*gall*; fr. the fact that the fig wasp develops in galls produced in these figs] **:** CAPRIFIG

gallflower \'=,=\ *n* **:** a degenerate pistillate flower that occurs in some cultivated figs and is characterized by an aborted ovary incapable of developing seeds

gallfly \'=,=\ *n* **:** an insect that deposits its eggs in plants and causes galls in which the larvae feed

gall gnat *n* [⁴*gall*] **:** GALL MIDGE

gal·li \'ga,lī\ *n pl, cap* [NL, fr. L, pl. of *gallus* cock — more at GALLUS] **:** a suborder of Galliformes consisting of the megapodes, curassows, and pheasants and related birds (as the turkey)

¹gal·li·am·bic \,galē'ambik\ *n* -s [L *galliambus,* a song of the priests of Cybele, ancient nature goddess of Anatolia (fr. *Gallus,* eunuch priest of Cybele — fr. Gk *Gallos* — + L *iambus*) + E *-ic*] **:** a galliambic verse or meter

²galliambic \;==;==\ *adj, in classical prosody* **:** consisting of two iambic dimeters catalectic of which the last lacks the final syllable **:** consisting of four Ionic a minore feet varied by resolution or contraction

gallian *adj, cap* [L *Gallia* Gaul + E *-an*] *obs* **:** GALLIC, FRENCH

¹gal·liard *also* **gail·lard** \'galyə(r)d\ *adj* [ME *gaillard, galiard,* fr. MF *gaillard,* fr. OF, prob. of Celt origin; akin to OIr *gal* bravery, Corn *gallos* power, W *gallu* to be able; akin to Lith *galėti* to be able] **1** *archaic* **:** gay in spirits or appearance **:** LIVELY **2** *archaic* **:** HARDY, VALIANT

²galliard *also* **gaillard** \"\ *n* -s **1** *archaic* **:** a galliard man **2 a** [MF *gaillarde,* fem. of *gaillard,* adj.] **:** a gay dance with five steps to a phrase popular in the 16th century as a sequel to the stately pavane **b :** a 16th century dance tune in moderately quick triple time with or without an upbeat

gal·liar·dise \'galyə(r),dīz, -dēz\ *n* -s [MF *gaillardise,* fr. *gaillard* (adj.) + *-ise* -ice] *archaic* **:** extreme gaiety **:** MERRIMENT

galliass *var of* GALLEASS

gal·lic \'galik, -lēk\ *adj, usu cap* [ML *Gallicus,* fr. L, of the Gauls] **1 :** French esp. in quality ⟨*Gallic* wit and sophistication⟩ **2** [L *Gallicus,* fr. *Galli* Gauls, inhabitants of Gaul, *Gallia* Gaul, ancient country of Europe + *-icus* -ic] **a :** of or relating to Gaul ⟨Caesar . . . received the *Gallic* military post as a reward for party services —*Current History*⟩ **b :** of or relating to the Gauls — **gal·li·cal·ly** \-lək(ə)lē, -lēk-, -li\ *adv, usu cap*

gal·lic acid \'ga\|lik-, 'gȯ\|, \|lēk-\ *n* [part trans. of F *acide gallique,* fr. *acide* acid + *gallique* of gall, derived from gall, fr. *galle* gall + *-ique* -ic — more at GALL (excrescence)] **:** a white crystalline acid $C_6H_2(OH)_3COOH.H_2O$ that occurs widely in plants both in the free form (as in galls and in tea leaves) and combined in tannins from which it can be obtained by the action of molds or alkali and that is used chiefly in making pyrogallol, dyes, and writing ink and as a photographic developer; 3,4,5-trihydroxy-benzoic acid

¹gal·li·can \'galəkən, -lēk-\ *adj* [in sense 1, fr. L *Gallicanus* of the Roman province of Gaul, fr. *Gallicus* Gallic + *-anus* -an; in sense 2, fr. ML *Gallicanus* French, fr. L] **1** *usu cap* **:** GALLIC **2** *often cap* **:** of or relating to Gallicanism **:** marked by Gallicanism **:** advocating Gallicanism

²gallican \"\ *n* -s *usu cap* **:** one that advocates Gallicanism

gal·li·can·ism \-,nizəm\ *n* -s *usu cap* [F *gallicanisme* theory advocating administrative independence from papal control for the Roman Catholic Church in France, fr. MF *gallican* of the Roman Catholic Church in France, French (fr. ML *Gallicanus* French) + *-isme* -ism] **1 :** a theory orig. formulated in France advocating administrative independence from papal control for the Roman Catholic Church in each nation — compare ULTRAMONTANISM **2 :** advocacy of or devotion to Gallicanism or the independence it is designed to achieve

gal·li·cism \'galə,sizəm\ *n* -s *often cap* [F *gallicisme,* fr. MF, fr. ML *Gallicus* Gallic + MF *-isme* -ism] **1 a :** a word, expression, or grammatical construction distinctive of French appearing esp. in a context in another language ⟨an English novel full of ~s⟩ **b :** a word or expression that is adapted to another language from French by translation and that retains a distinctively French construction or word sense (as in *attorney general* or *it is to laugh* [from *c'est à rire*]) **2 a :** a mode of thought or an outlook that is distinctive of the French ⟨the ~ in French-Canadian novels⟩ **b :** a distinctively French action ⟨cheek kissing is a ~⟩

gal·li·ci·za·tion \,galəsə'zāshən, -,sī'z-\ *n* -s *usu cap* **:** the process or result of gallicizing or being gallicized

gal·li·cize \'galə,sīz\ *vb* -ED/-ING/-S *sometimes cap* [*gallic* + *-ize*] *vt* **1 :** to cause to acquire French quality or qualities or traits ⟨~ American architecture⟩ ⟨~ an English writer⟩; *also* **:** to cause to adopt French customs or modes of thought or conduct ⟨*gallicized* by an education in France⟩ **2 :** to make (a foreign word or phrase) French by adapting to French spelling or pronunciation ⟨Napoleon *gallicized* his Corsican name⟩ or by substituting a closely equivalent French word or phrase ⟨Walker *gallicized* his name to Marcheur⟩ ~ *vi* **:** to become French or adapt to French ways in speech, thought, or outlook

gal·lic·o·la \gȯ'likələ, ga'-,gə'-\ *n* -s [NL, fr. *galli-* (fr. L *galla* gall) + *-cola* — more at GALL (excrescence)] **:** the stage or an individual of some gall aphids and phylloxerans that produces leaf galls

gal·lic·o·lous \(')gȯ\|likələs, (')ga\|l-, gə'l-\ *adj* [L *galla* gall + E *-i-* + *-colous*] **:** producing and inhabiting galls

gal·li·crow \'galə,krō\ *n* [²*gally* + *crow* (bird)] *dial Eng* **:** SCARECROW

gallied *past of* GALLY

gallies *pres 3d sing of* GALLY

gal·li·form \'galə,fȯrm\ *adj* [NL *Galliformes*] **:** of or relating to the Galliformes

gal·li·for·mes \,==:'fȯr,mēz\ *n pl, cap* [NL, fr. *galli-* (fr. *Gallus*) + *-formes*] **:** an order of birds of largely terrestrial habits that are mostly rather large and heavy-bodied with short wings, legs adapted for running and scratching the ground where most of their food (as seeds or worms) is found, a large crop, and a muscular gizzard, that nest usu. on the ground, that produce numerous eggs and young which are precocial, and that include the pheasants, turkeys, grouse, partridges, quails, and related birds (as the common domestic fowl, the megapodes and curassows, and the hoatzins) — see GALLI, OPISTHOCOMI

gal·li·gas·kins \,galə'gaskənz, -lē'g-\ *n pl* [prob. modif. of MF *garguesques, greguesques,* fr. OSp *gregüescos,* fr. *griego* Greek, fr. L *Graecus* — more at GREEK] **1 a :** loose wide hose or breeches worn in the 16th and 17th centuries **b :** very loose trousers **2** *chiefly Scot* **:** LEGGINGS

gal·li·mau·fry \,galə'mȯfrē\ *n* -ES [MF *galimafree, calimafree* ragout, hash] **:** MEDLEY, MIXTURE, HODGEPODGE, JUMBLE ⟨written in a remarkable ~ of languages —*Times Lit. Supp.*⟩ ⟨a unique ~ of contestants —H.W.Wind⟩ ⟨a ~ of didactic speeches, romantic flourishes and characters for several unrelated kinds of plays —*Time*⟩

gal·li·na \gə'lēnə, gī'ēnə\ *adj, usu cap* [fr. *Gallina,* N.M.] **:** of or relating to an ancient culture in New Mexico contemporaneous with Anasazi and characterized by unpainted pottery resembling the Shoshoni utility types, painted pottery similar to Anasazi types, and leaf-shaped stone blades having a notch on each side halfway between the point and the base

gal·li·na·cean \,galə'nāshən\ *n* -s [NL *Gallinaceae,* a group of birds (fr. L *gallinaceae,* fem. pl. of *gallinaceus*) + E *-an*] **:** a gallinaceous bird

gal·li·na·ceous \;==;=shəs\ *adj* [L *gallinaceus* of domestic fowl, fr. *gallina* hen (fr. *gallus* cock) + *-aceus* -aceous — more at GALLUS] **1 :** resembling a bird (as a domestic fowl) of the order Galliformes ⟨~ pigeon⟩ **2 :** of or relating to the Galliformes ⟨~ birds⟩

gal·li·nae \gə'lī,nē\ *n pl* [NL, fr. L *gallinae,* pl. of *gallina* hen] **1** *usu cap* **:** a group of birds usu. nearly equivalent to Galliformes **2** *often cap* **:** wild birds (as wild turkey, grouse, pheasant, partridge, and quail) of the order Galliformes that are fit or lawful for hunting

galli·na·zo \,gä(y)ē\|nä(,)sō\ *adj, usu cap* [Sp, turkey buzzard, fr. *gallina* hen, fr. L] **:** of or relating to an ancient culture of the Viru valley in northern Peru characterized esp. by negative-painted pottery, irrigation, textiles, and limited metallurgy

gal·line \'ga,līn\ *adj* [L *gallus* cock + E *-ine*] **:** GALLINACEOUS

gal·li·ney \gə'lēnē\ *var of* GALEENY

¹galling *n* -s [fr. the gerund of ³*gall*] **:** the action or the results of galling ⟨resistance of stainless steel . . . to erosion, ~, and scoring —*Crane Co. Catalogue*⟩

²galling *adj* [fr. the pres. part. of ³*gall*] **:** of such a character as to gall **:** markedly irritating **:** CHAFING ⟨he has borne these assaults with a dignity ~ to his enemies —*New Republic*⟩ ⟨the attempts . . . to exchange the ~ status of wards for the honorable role of trading partners —D.L.Hurwood⟩ — **gall·ing·ly** *adv* — **gall·ing·ness** *n* -ES

gal·li·nip·per *also* **gal·ly·nip·per** \'galə,nipə(r), -lē,-\ *n* -s [origin unknown] **:** a biting insect: as **a :** a very large American mosquito (*Psorophora ciliata*) **b :** BEDBUG

gal·li·nule \'galə,n(y)ül\ *n* -s [NL *Gallinula,* genus of birds, fr. L *gallinula* pullet, chicken, dim. of *gallina* hen] **:** any of several aquatic birds that constitute a subfamily of the family Rallidae, are distinguished from the coots by the unlobed feet and from the rails by the presence of a frontal shield, and resemble a small domestic hen in general proportions and carriage — called also *marsh hen, swamphen, water hen*

gal·lio \'galē,ō\ *n* -s *usu cap* [after Junius Annaeus *Gallio* †*ab* A.D. 65 Roman proconsul of Achaia who dismissed the Jews' accusation against Paul (Acts 18:12-17), fr. L] **:** one that is Gallionic

gal·li·on·ic \;==;änik\ *adj, usu cap* [L *Gallion-, Gallio* + E *-ic*] **:** marked by indifference or easygoing carelessness or irresponsibility

gal·li·ot *or* **gal·i·ot** \'galēət, -ē,ät\ *n* -s [in sense 1, fr. ME *galiote,* fr. MF, fr. ML *galeota,* dim. of *galea* galley, fr. MGk; in sense 2, fr. D *galjoot,* fr. MD *galiote,* fr. MF *galiote* — more at GALLEY] **1 :** a small swift galley formerly used in the Mediterranean and moved both by sails and oars **2 :** a long narrow light-draft Dutch merchant ship carrying a mainmast and a jigger with a mainsail having a long foot and short gaff

gal·liph·a·gous \(')ga\|lifəgəs, (')ga\|-\ *adj* [L *galla* gall + E *-i-* + *-phagous* — more at GALL (excrescence)] **:** GALLIVOROUS

gal·li·pot \'galə,pät\ *n* [ME *galy pott,* prob. fr. *galy, galeie* galley + *pott* pot; fr. its being originally transported by galley — more at GALLEY, POT (earthen vessel)] **1 :** a small usu. ceramic vessel with a small mouth; *esp* **:** one used by apothecaries to hold medicines **2 :** DRUGGIST

gal·li·um \'galēəm\ *n* -s [NL, fr. L *gallus* cock (intended as trans. of Paul *É. Lecoq* de Boisbaudran †*ab* 1912 Fr. chemist, its discoverer) + NL *-ium*] **:** a rare bluish white usu. trivalent metallic element that is hard and brittle at low temperatures but melts just above room temperature and expands on freezing and that is obtained usu. as a by-product in the extraction of aluminum from bauxite or of zinc from zinc ores — symbol *Ga;* see ELEMENT table

gal·li·vant *also* **gal·a·vant** *or* **gal·la·vant** \'galə,vant, -vaa(ə)nt *sometimes* ,==:'=\ *vi* -ED/-ING/-S [perh. alter. of ³*gallant*] **1 :** to act as a gallant **:** attend gallantly or amorously upon a member of the opposite sex **:** go about usu. ostentatiously or indiscreetly with members of the opposite sex ⟨left his wife to go ~*ing* with other women⟩ **2 a :** to travel or roam for mere pleasure ⟨~*ed* around Europe —Louis Auchincloss⟩ **b :** MOVE, GO, TRAVEL ⟨the porters . . . ~*ed* along like a cheerful bunch of boys —Edmund Hillary⟩ ⟨the flames ~*ing* up the chimney —Helen Shaw⟩

gal·li·vat \'galə,vat\ *n* -s [prob. modif. of Pg *galeota* galliot, fr. Sp, fr. ML] **:** an East Indian ship propelled by sails and oars and often armed and used by pirates

gal·liv·o·rous \(,)gȯ\|livərəs, (')ga\|-\ *adj* [L *galla* gall + E *-i-* + *-vorous*] **:** feeding on galls or gall tissue (as the larvae of gall insects)

gal·li·wasp \'galə,wäsp, -wȯsp\ *n* [origin unknown] **:** a harmless lizard (*Diploglossus monotropis*) of eastern Central America; *also* **:** either of two similar related lizards of Jamaica

gall midge *n* **:** any of numerous minute two-winged flies of the family Cecidomyiidae most of which cause gall formation on various plants — called also *gall gnat*

gall mite *n* **:** any of various minute 4-legged mites that form galls on plants and are members of the family Eriophyidae — compare BLISTER MITE

gallnut \'=,=\ *n* [⁴*gall*] **:** a gall resembling a nut

¹gallo- *comb form* [L *Gallo-* Gaulish, fr. *Gallus* Gaul, inhabitant of ancient Gaul] **1** *cap* **:** Gaulish and ⟨*Gallo*-Roman⟩ **2** *cap* **:** French and ⟨*Gallo*-Briton⟩ **3** *often cap* **:** France ⟨*gallo*centric⟩

²gallo- — see GALL-

gall oak *n* **:** an oak producing gallnuts; *esp* **:** a Spanish and Portuguese oak (*Quercus lusitanica*) that produces gallnuts

gal·lo·cy·a·nine \,ga(,)lō'sīə,nēn, ,gȯ(-, -,nən\ *n* [ISV *gall-* + *cyan-* + *-ine*] **:** an oxazine dye $C_{15}H_{12}N_2O_5$ made from gallic acid and a nitroso derivative of aniline and used in dyeing mordanted wool and cotton bluish violet — see DYE table I (under *Mordant Blue 10*)

gall of the earth [earlier *gall of the earth* lesser centaury (trans. of MF *fiel de terre,* trans. of L *fel terrae*), fr. ¹*gall*] **1 :** a lion's foot of the genus *Prenanthes; esp* **:** a common perennial herb (*P. serpentaria*) that is widely distributed in the southern and eastern U.S. and has thick variable basal leaves and clusters of pink to white flower heads **2 :** a wild plant of the genus *Lactuca* **3 :** PINEDROPS 1

galloglass *archaic var of* GALLOWGLASS

gal·lo·man \'galō,man\ *n, pl* **gallo·men** \-,men\ *usu cap* [¹*Gallo-* + *-man* maniac (fr. F *-mane,* back-formation fr. *manie* mania) — more at BIBLIOMANIA] **:** FRANCOPHILE

gal·lo·ma·nia \,galō'mānēə, -nyə\ *n, usu cap* [F *gallomanie,* fr. ¹*Gallo-* + *manie* mania] **:** a strong prejudice in favor of what is French — **gal·lo·ma·ni·ac** \-nē,ak\ *n, usu cap*

gal·lon \'galən\ *n* -s *often attrib* [ME *galon, galun,* a liquid measure, fr. ONF *galon;* akin to OF *jalaie,* a measure of capacity; both directly or indirectly fr. ML *galeta* jug, pail, a liquid measure] **1 :** any of various units of capacity: as **a :** a unit of liquid capacity equal to 231 cubic inches ⟨a ~ jug⟩ **b :** a British unit of liquid and dry capacity equal to 277.42 cubic inches — called also *imperial gallon;* see ALE GALLON, WINE GALLON; MEASURE table **2 :** an extremely large quantity or number — usu. used in pl. ⟨~s of tea, which seems to have no effect on the nerves here —Fanny K. Wister⟩ ⟨in North America there are ~s of language families, each with one or two ~s of languages —C.F.Voegelin & T.A.Sebeok⟩

gal·lon·age \-nij\ *n* -s **:** amount in gallons

gal·loon \gə'lün\ *n* -s [F *galon,* fr. MF, fr. OF *galonner* to adorn with galloons] **:** a narrow ornamental fabric for trimming or finishing clothes or upholstery; *esp* **:** a braid with gold or silver threads or a strip of lace or embroidery with both edges scalloped or indented

gal·looned \-nd\ *adj* **:** trimmed or ornamented with galloon ⟨~ watchcases⟩

¹gal·lop \'galəp\ *n* -s [MF *galop,* fr. OF, prob. fr. *galoper,* v.] **1 a :** a springing gait of various quadrupeds; *specif* **:** a fast natural 3-beat gait of the horse in which one or two feet touch the ground in the order of one hind foot, diagonal biped including opposite hind foot, remaining forefoot — compare CANTER, RUN **b :** a ride or run at a gallop **c :** a stretch of land used for galloping horses ⟨horses, trained in seclusion on private ~s —A.J.Liebling⟩ **2 :** a rapid rate or pace ⟨the child went at a ~ to get his ice-cream cone⟩ ⟨this is not a book to be read at a ~ —Hal Lehrman⟩

²gallop \"\ *vb* -ED/-ING/-S [MF *galoper,* fr. OF] *vi* **1 a :** to move or run in a gallop (as of a horse) **b :** to ride at a gallop **:** ride at full speed ⟨~*ing* over the moors on a stallion⟩ **2 :** to go at great speed or as fast as possible ⟨dawdle to school but ~ home⟩ ⟨he ~*ed* over the dunes barefoot —Mary H. Vorse⟩ ~ *vt* **1 :** to cause to gallop ⟨~ a horse for miles⟩ **2 :** to transport at a gallop ⟨~*ed* the general over to headquarters⟩ ⟨we are ~*ed* to them over every obstacle on the pounding hoofs of rhapsodical prose —Virginia Woolf⟩ **3 :** to ride over at a gallop ⟨each knight must ~ the course three times —*Amer. Guide Series: Md.*⟩

¹gal·lo·pade *also* **gal·o·pade** \'galə\|pād, -päd\ *n* -s [F *galopade,* lit., act of galloping, fr. *galoper* to gallop + *-ade*] **:** GALOP

²gallopade *also* **galopade** \"\ *vi* -ED/-ING/-S **:** to dance a gallopade

gal·lop·er \'galəpə(r)\ *n* -s **1 :** a horseman that gallops **2 :** a horse that gallops fast **3 a :** a light fieldpiece on a carriage drawn without a limber that was formerly used by English regiments **b :** the carriage of such a gun **4** *Brit* **:** a military aide

¹gal·lo·phile \'galə,fīl\ *n* -s *usu cap* [¹*gallo-* + *-phile*] **:** ²FRANCOPHILE

²gallophile \"\ *adj, usu cap* **:** ¹FRANCOPHILE

gal·lo·phobe \-,fōb\ *n* -s *usu cap* [¹*gallo-* + *-phobe*] **:** FRANCOPHOBE

gal·lo·pho·bia \,==:'fōbēə\ *n, usu cap* [NL, fr. ¹*Gallo-* + *-phobia*] **:** FRANCOPHOBIA

galloping *adj* **1 :** marked by a motion like that of one galloping **:** fast moving **:** rapidly developing or increasing ⟨the ~ trend toward federal monopoly of power and other industries —Ray Tucker⟩ ⟨a ~ case of nerves —*Newsweek*⟩ ⟨~ inflation⟩ **2** *of a disease* **:** progressing rapidly toward a fatal conclusion ⟨~ consumption⟩ — **gal·lop·ing·ly** *adv*

galloping dominoes *or* **galloping ivories** *n pl, slang* **:** DICE

gallop rhythm *also* **gallop** *n* -s **:** an abnormal heart rhythm marked by the occurrence of three distinct sounds in each heartbeat like the sound of a galloping horse

gallo–roman \\|ga(,)lō+\ *adj, usu cap G&R* [¹*Gallo-* + *Roman*] **:** of or relating to Gaul under Roman rule

gallo–romance \"+\ *n, cap G&R* [¹*Gallo-* + *Romance*] **:** the Romance speech that developed out of Vulgar Latin in Transalpine Gaul — compare FRENCH, PROVENÇAL

gal·lo·tannic acid \\|galō, \|gȯlō+ . . . -\ *n* [*gallo-* (fr. L *galla* gall) + *tannic* — more at GALL (excrescence)] **:** GALLOTANNIN

gal·lo·tannin \"+\ *n* [*gallo-* (fr. L *galla* gall) + *tannin*] **:** a tannin occurring esp. in extracts from gall and yielding gallic acid on hydrolysis

gallous *var of* GALLOWS

¹gal·lo·vid·i·an \\|galə\|vidēən\ *adj, usu cap* [ML *Gallovidia* Galloway (district in southwestern Scotland) + E *-an*] **:** GALWEGIAN

²gallovidian \"\ *n* -s *cap* **:** GALWEGIAN

gal·low \'galə\ *var of* ²GALLY

gal·lo·way \'galə,wā\ *n* [fr. *Galloway,* a district in Scotland] **1** *often cap* **a :** a breed of small hardy horses of former times originating in Galloway, Scotland **b** -s **:** a large pony or small horse **2** *usu cap* **:** a breed of hardy medium-sized hornless chiefly black beef cattle native to southwestern Scotland and distinguished from the Aberdeen Angus chiefly by the very heavy curly coat

gal·low·glass \'galō,glas\ *n* -ES [IrGael *gallōglach,* fr. *gall* foreigner + *ōglach* servant, soldier, youth, fr. *ōclach* youth, fr. *ōac* young; akin to W *ieuanc* young, OE *geong* — more at YOUNG] **1 :** one of a class of soldiers (as mercenaries or retainers) formerly maintained by an Irish chief **2 :** a heavily armed Irish foot soldier — compare KERN

gal·low-grass \'galō+,-\ *n* [obs. *gallow* gallows (fr. ME *galwe*) + *grass;* fr. its use for making ropes] **:** HEMP

¹gal·lows \'ga(,)lōz, -ləz, *in sense 3 & archaic or dial in other senses* -ləs\ *n, pl* **gallows** *or* **gallowses** [ME *galwes,* pl. of *galwe,* fr. OE *galga, gealga;* akin to OHG *galgo* gallows, ON *galgi* gallows, Goth *galga* cross, Arm *jatk* twig] **1 a :** a frame usu. of two upright posts and a crossbeam from which is suspended the rope with which criminals are executed by hanging — compare GIBBET **b :** the punishment of hanging ⟨a crime worthy of the ~⟩ **c :** GALLOWS BIRD **2 :** a structure consisting of an upright frame with a crosspiece: as **a :** a rest for the tympan of a hand printing press when raised **b :** GALLOWS BITT **c** *or* **gallows frame :** the headframe of a mine **d :** a timber structure for butchering cattle **3 :** ³GALLUS

²gallows \"\ *or* **gal·lous** *or* **gal·lus** \-ləs\ *adj* [ME *gallowus,* fr. *galwes,* n.] **1 :** deserving the gallows **2** *now dial chiefly Brit* **a :** wild and villainous **b :** MISCHIEVOUS, RASCALLY

gallows bird *n* **:** one who deserves hanging

gallows bitt *also* **gallows frame** *n* **:** one of two or more frames amidships to support spare spars

gallows tree *or* **gallow tree** *n* [*gallows tree* fr. earlier *gallow tree,* fr. ME *galwe tree,* fr. OE *galgatrē, galgtrēow,* fr. *galga* + *trē, trēow* tree — more at TREE] **:** GALLOWS

galls *pres 3d sing of* GALL, *pl of* GALL

gallsick \'=,=\ *adj* [¹*gall* + *sick;* trans. of Afrik *galsiek*] **1 :** suffering from gall sickness ⟨a herd of ~ cattle⟩ **2 :** producing or having the conditions to produce gall sickness⟩ ⟨~ pastureland⟩

gall sickness *n* [¹*gall;* trans. of Afrik *galsiekte*] **:** ANAPLASMOSIS

gallstone \'=,=\ *n* [¹*gall* + *stone*] **1 :** calculus formed in the gallbladder or biliary passages — called also *biliary calculus* **2 :** LIGHT CHROME YELLOW

gallumph *var of* GALUMPH

gal·lup poll \'galə(p)\|pōl\ *n, usu cap G* [after George H.

Gallup †1901 Am. statistician] **:** a sampling of public opinion on a particular issue or of the degree of information among the public about a particular thing or of opinion or information in a particular group taken by questioning a representative cross section ⟨belongs certainly among the most remarkable stars visible with the naked eye; a *Gallup poll* among amateurs and professional astronomers alike would undoubtedly confirm this —*Sky & Telescope*⟩ ⟨contests of all kinds, questionnaires, and *Gallup polls* have become enormously popular —*Westralian Farmers Co-op. Gazette*⟩ ⟨we can . . . find out who are the supporters only by organized inquiries and *Gallup polls* —Barbara & Robert North⟩ ⟨an amateur *Gallup poll* to discover what modern American short-story writers are well known to the intelligent reading public in England —*Times Lit. Supp.*⟩

gal·lup·tious \gə'ləpshəs\ *adj* [fr. earlier *galoptious*, perh. alter. of *voluptuous*] *slang* **:** WONDERFUL, DELIGHTFUL, DELICIOUS

1gal·lus \'galəs\ *n, cap* [NL, fr. L, cock; perh. akin to ON *kalla* to call — more at CALL] **:** a genus of birds (family Phasianidae) that consists of the common domestic fowl and related wild birds — see JUNGLE FOWL

2gallus *var of* GALLOWS

3gal·lus \'galəs\ *n* -ES *often attrib* [alter. of *1gallows*] *chiefly dial* **:** SUSPENDER 2a ⟨worn close to the left-hand ~ —J.C. Furnas⟩ — usu. used in pl.

gal·lused \-st\ *adj, chiefly dial* **:** wearing galluses ⟨a coatless, ~ man —*Nation*⟩ ⟨~, austere farmers —David Roman⟩

gall wasp *n* [*4gall*; fr. the fact that it lives in galls] **:** one of the Cynipidae **:** a hymenopterous gallfly

1gally \'gȯlē\ *adj* [*2gall* + *-y*] **:** marked by bare spots or areas lacking vegetation (as from excessive wetness or erosion)

2gal·ly \'galē\ *vt* -ED/-ING/-ES [origin unknown] **1** *now chiefly dial* **:** FRIGHTEN, TERRIFY ⟨we've been *gallied* at a terrible affliction —Thomas Hardy⟩ **2 :** to put to flight (a whale) by frightening ⟨don't want to ~ those critters till we're fast to them —A.B.C.Whipple⟩

gallynipper *var of* GALLINIPPER

gal·ly·ware \'galē+,-\ *n* [perh. fr. *galley* + *ware*] **:** earthenware usu. tin-glazed

ga·lois theory \'gal,wä-\ *n, usu cap G* **:** a part of the theory of mathematical groups that is applied esp. to showing which algebraic equations can be solved by sequences of rational operations and by the extraction of integral roots of already known quantities and to proving that a quintic equation exists that cannot be solved by such procedures

1ga·loot \gə'lüt, *usu* -üd-+V\ *n* -S [origin unknown] **:** ROSS'S GOOSE

2galoot \"\ *n* -S [origin unknown] *slang* **:** FELLOW, PERSON; *esp* **:** a man who is strange, odd, or foolish ⟨such a simple-minded, honest kind of ~ —Robert Lowry⟩ ⟨till that crazy ~ . . . caught up with me —Earle Birney⟩ ⟨a man of any size feels like a ~ in that tomfool outfit —Jean Stafford⟩ ⟨tell me to my face that I'm a ~ . . . and a hick —Sinclair Lewis⟩

1gal·op \'galəp, (')ga¦lō\ *n* -S [F — more at GALLOP] **:** a lively dance in duple measure performed with sliding steps from side to side and popular in the 19th century; *also* **:** music for this dance

2galop \"\ *vi* -ED/-ING/-S **:** to dance a galop

galopade *var of* GALLOPADE

gal·o·pin \'galə,pan\ *n* -S [MF, fr. OF, one that gallops, fr. *galoper* to gallop] *archaic* **:** a kitchen helper **:** SCULLION

gal·lop·tious \gə'läpshəs\ *or* **ga·lup·tious** \-'ləp-\ *var of* GALLUPTIOUS

ga·lore \gə'lō(ə)r, -ō(ə)r, -ōə, -ȯ(ə)\ *adj* [IrGael *go leor* enough, fr. *go* to (fr. OIr *co, cu*) + *leor* enough (fr. OIr *lour, loor*); akin to W *llawer* much, many, OIr *lōg* reward, price — more at LUCRE] **:** ABUNDANT, PLENTIFUL, PROFUSE — used postpositively ⟨bargains ~ for sharp-eyed buyers —H.T. Simmons⟩ ⟨women's clubs and lodges, and other organizations ~ —F.L.Mott⟩ ⟨Philadelphia, which boasts history ~ —Lewis Mumford⟩

1ga·losh \gə'läsh\ *n* -ES [ME *galoche*, fr. MF, perh. alter. of *galette* flat round cake — more at GALETTE] **1** *obs* **:** a clog, patten, or shoe with a heavy sole **2 :** an overshoe designed to protect the shoe in wet weather or in wet areas and usu. made with a rubber or water-repellent fabric upper reaching to the ankle or somewhat higher **:** 2ARCTIC **3 :** a strip of material (as leather) running around a shoe at and above the sole for protection or ornament

2galosh \"\ *vt* -ED/-ING/-ES **:** to put a galosh on ⟨~ a shoe⟩; *also* **:** provide with a galosh

ga·lou·bet \,ga(,)lü¦bā\ *n* -S [F, fr. Prov] **:** PIPE 1a(1)

galravage *var of* GILRAVAGE

gals *pl of* GAL

gal·siek·te \'gäl,sēktə\ *n* -S [Afrik, fr. *gal* gall, bile (fr. MD *galle*) + *siekte* sickness (fr. MD *siecte*, fr. *siec* sick); akin to OHG *galla* gall, bile — more at GALL (bile), SICK] *Africa* **:** ANAPLASMOSIS

1galt \'gält, 'gȯ(l)t\ *n* -S [ME, fr. ON *göltr, galti*; akin to ON *gyltr* young sow — more at GILT] *dial Eng* **:** 1HOG 1; *usu* **:** a gelded male swine **:** BARROW

2galt *var of* GAULT

gal·ton bar \'gȯltᵊn-\ *n, usu cap G* [after Sir Francis *Galton* †1911 Eng. scientist, its inventor] **:** an instrument used in tests of the accuracy of estimate of visible lengths that consists of a horizontal bar to be bisected by an adjustable vertical line

gal·to·nia \gȯl'tōnēə\ *n* [NL, fr. Sir Francis *Galton* + NL *-ia*] **1** *cap* **:** a small genus of southern African bulbous plants (family Liliaceae) that was formerly included in *Hyacinthus* but is distinguished by the large two to three foot long somewhat fleshy leaves and larger flowers in long loose racemes — see SUMMER HYACINTH **2** -S **:** any plant of the genus *Galtonia*

gal·to·ni·an \(')≡¦≡≡ən\ *adj, usu cap* [Sir Francis *Galton* + E *-ian*] **:** of or relating to the English scientist Francis Galton or his work

galton's law of inheritance *or* **galton's theory of inheritance** *usu cap G* [after Sir Francis *Galton*, its formulator] **:** a theory in genetics: the parents of an individual together contribute on an average 50 percent of the total inherited characters, the 4 grandparents together 25 percent, the 3d generation of ancestors together 12.5 percent, etc. — compare MENDEL'S LAW

galton whistle *n, usu cap G* [after Sir Francis *Galton*, its inventor] **:** a whistle of variable high pitch used to test the upper limit of audibility

gal·trap \'galtrəp, 'gȯl-\ *var of* CALTRAP

ga·lu·chat \¦ga(,)lü¦shä\ *n* -S [F, fr. Jean-Claude *Galluchat* †1774 Fr. leather craftsman] **:** an ornamented shagreen

ga·lumph *or* **gal·lumph** \gə'ləm(p)f\ *vi* -ED/-ING/-S [prob. alter. of *2gallop*] **:** to move or progress with a clumsy bumping thudding heavy tread ⟨the elephant paid no heed to her calls and ~*ed* off again —*Newsweek*⟩ ⟨~*ing* along the bridle path on their mounts —Mollie Panter-Downes⟩ ⟨several pairs of feet ~*ed* down the passage —Monica Stirling⟩; *also* **:** to act in a way suggesting such a manner of moving ⟨my heart ~*ing* as I stood up —Vincent McHugh⟩

ga·luth *or* **ga·lut** \gä'lüt(h), 'gōləs\ *n, often cap* [Heb *gālūth* exile] **:** exile of the Jews from Palestine **:** DIASPORA

galv *abbr* galvanic; galvanism; galvanized

gal·van·ic \(')gal¦vanik, -nēk\ *adj* [F or It; F *galvanique*, fr. It *galvanico*, fr. Luigi *Galvani* + It *-ico* -ic] **1 a :** of, relating to, or producing galvanism **:** VOLTAIC — distinguished from *faradic* ⟨~ electricity⟩ ⟨~ battery⟩ ⟨~ current⟩ ⟨~ cell⟩ **b :** caused by galvanism — used esp. of the corrosion of metallic objects in damp earth as a result of electrolytic action **2 a :** having a sharp, marked, or jolting effect suggesting that of an electric shock **:** markedly engaging the interest, arousing to activity, or stimulating vitality ⟨a ~ speech⟩ ⟨a ~ personality⟩ ⟨made no secret in private of the ~ effect Napoleon's coronation worked in him —Lee Ellerich⟩ ⟨the most ~ religious music ever recorded —*Saturday Rev.*⟩ ⟨the product of mental energy and a ~ temperament —R.L.Cook⟩ **b :** produced as if by an electric shock ⟨a ~ reaction⟩ — **gal·van·i·cal·ly** \-nək(ə)lē, -nēk-, -li\ *adv*

galvanic couple *n* **:** a pair of dissimilar substances (as metals) capable of acting together as an electric source when brought in contact with an electrolyte

gal·va·nism \'galvə,nizəm\ *n* -S [F or It; F *galvanisme*, fr. It *galvanismo*, fr. Luigi *Galvani* †1798 Ital. physician and physicist who first described it + It *-ismo* -ism] **1 :** a direct current of electricity; *esp* **:** such a current produced by chemical action (as in a storage battery) **2 :** the therapeutic use of direct electric current **3 :** vital or forceful activity suggesting activation by a strong and continuous electric current

gal·va·ni·za·tion \,galvənə'zāshən, -,nī'z-\ *n* -S **:** the act or process of galvanizing; *specif* **:** the application of an electric current to the human body for medical purposes

gal·va·nize \'galvə,nīz\ *vt* -ED/-ING/-S [F *galvaniser*, fr. Luigi *Galvani* + F *-iser* -ize] **1 a :** to subject to the action of an electric current **b :** to arouse, stimulate, or excite as if by the application of an electric current ⟨the news *galvanized* the campers into a fury of activity⟩ ⟨~ the alliance, restore its confidence, and lead it to move and act in unison —*Newsweek*⟩ ⟨~ the government into vehement and extraordinary preparation —Sir Winston Churchill⟩ **2 :** to coat (iron or steel) with zinc — compare ELECTROGALVANIZE

galvanized iron *n* **:** iron or steel coated with zinc to protect it from rust

gal·va·niz·er \-zə(r)\ *n* -S **:** one that galvanizes ⟨serve as the chief ~ and spokesman —F.L.Allen⟩; *specif* **:** a worker who coats iron or steel with zinc

galv·an·neal \¦galv+,+\ *vt* [blend of *galvanize* and *anneal*] **:** to coat with an alloy of iron or steel and zinc produced by heating a surface already galvanized with zinc ⟨~*ed* wire⟩

galvano- *comb form* [*galvanic* + *-o-*] **:** galvanic current ⟨*galvanometer*⟩ **:** using or produced by galvanic current ⟨*galvanocautery*⟩ ⟨*galvanoplastics*⟩

gal·vano·graph \gal'vanə,graf, 'galvənē,-, -rȧf\ *n* [*galvano-* + *-graph*] **:** a copperplate engraving produced by galvanography; *also* **:** a picture printed from such a plate — **gal·vano·graph·ic** \(¦)gal¦vanə¦grafik, ¦galvənō¦-\ *adj*

gal·va·nog·ra·phy \,galvə'nägrəfē\ *n* -ES [ISV *galvano-* + *-graphy*] **:** a method similar to electrotyping of producing an intaglio-printing plate on copper

gal·vano·luminescence \¦galvə(,)nō, gal¦va-+\ *n* [*galvano-* + *luminescence*] **:** luminescence arising at the anode in an electrolytic cell (as with aluminum electrodes in sodium bicarbonate solution)

gal·vano·magnetic \"+\ *adj* [ISV *galvano-* + *magnetic*] **:** ELECTROMAGNETIC

gal·va·nom·e·ter \,galvə'nämәd·ə(r)\ *n* [*galvano-* + *-meter*] **:** an instrument for measuring a small electric current or for detecting its presence or direction by means of the movements of a magnetic needle or of a coil in a magnetic field that registers usu. on a scale or by a moving beam of light reflected from a mirror attached to the needle or the coil

gal·vano·met·ric \¦galvənō¦me·trik, (¦)gal¦van-\ *adj* [*galvano-* + *-metric*] **:** measured by a galvanometer

gal·vano·plastics \¦galvə(,)nō, gal¦va(-+\ *n pl but sing in constr* [*galvano-* + *plastics*] **:** a science of electroforming

gal·vano·plas·ty \gal'vanə,plastē, 'galvənō,-\ *n* -ES [*galvano-* + *-plasty*] **:** GALVANOPLASTICS

gal·vano·scope \-,skōp\ *n* [*galvano-* + *-scope*] **:** an instrument for detecting the presence and direction of an electric current (as of feeble intensity) by the deflection of a magnetic needle — compare GALVANOMETER

gal·vano·tac·tic \¦galvənō¦taktik, gal¦van-\ *adj* [*galvano-* + *-tactic*] **:** of, relating to, or being galvanotaxis

gal·vano·tax·is \-¦taksəs\ *n* [NL, fr. *galvano-* + *-taxis*] **:** a taxis in which a direct electric current is the directive factor

gal·vano·trop·ic \-¦träpik\ *adj* [ISV *galvano-* + *-tropic*] **:** characterized by galvanotropism

gal·va·not·ro·pism \,galvə'nä·trə,pizəm\ *n* [ISV *galvano-* + *-tropism*] **:** a tropism in which electricity is the stimulus

gal·ves·to·nian \,galvə'stōnēən, -nyən\ *n* -S *cap* [*Galveston*, Texas + E *-ian*] **:** a native or resident of Galveston, Texas

gal·way \'gȯl,wā\ *adj, usu cap* [fr. *Galway*, urban district and county in Ireland] **1 :** of or from the urban district of Galway, Ireland **:** of the kind or style prevalent in Galway **2 :** of or from County Galway, Ireland **:** of the kind or style prevalent in County Galway

galway hooker *n, usu cap G* [fr. *Galway*, seaport in Ireland] **:** a small Irish coasting cutter-rigged boat

gal·ways \-āz\ *n pl, often cap* [prob. fr. County *Galway*, Ireland] **:** whiskers following the line of the chin

1gal·we·gian \(')gal¦wēj(ē)ən\ *adj, usu cap* [irreg. (influence of *Norwegian*) fr. ML *Galwedia* Galloway (district in southwestern Scotland) + E *-an*] **:** of or relating to the district of Galloway, Scotland

2galwegian \"\ *n* -S *cap* **:** a native or resident of Galloway, Scotland

gal·yak *also* **gal·yac** \'gal,yak, 'gȯl,-, gəl'yak\ *n* -S [native name in Uzbekistan, U.S.S.R.] **:** a short-haired flat or slightly moiré fur derived from the pelt of a stillborn lamb, kid, or sometimes other hoofed mammal

gal·ziek·te \'gäl,zēktə, -,sē-\ *n* -S [obs. Afrik (now *galsiekte*) — more at GALSIEKTE] **:** ANAPLASMOSIS

1gam \'gam\ *n* -S [origin unknown] **1** *Scot* **:** TOOTH; *esp* **:** a large or crooked tooth **2** *Scot* **:** MOUTH

2gam \'gam, 'gaa(ə)m\ *n* -S [prob. fr. F dial. (northern) *gambe*] *slang* **:** LEG ⟨those trim ~*s* of yours —J.H.Burns⟩ ⟨most people . . . think I have nice ~*s* —Ethel Merman⟩

3gam \"\ *n* -S [perh. short for obs. *gammon* talk, chatter — more at GAMMON] **1 :** a visit or friendly conversation esp. between whalers or other seamen at sea or ashore ⟨the story . . . had been told, in ~ after ~, wherever whaleships met —A.B.C.Whipple⟩ ⟨there'd be a famous ~ up and down the sandy beach —Alan Villiers⟩ **2 :** a school of whales **:** POD

4gam \"\ *vb* **gammed; gammed; gamming; gams** *vi* **:** to engage in a gam ⟨whalers *gammed* in midocean on a hot tropical day —A.B.C.Whipple⟩ ~ *vt* **1 :** to have a gam with **:** visit with ⟨I decided to ~ some friends of mine —H.A. Chippendale⟩ **2 :** to pass in conversation **:** WHILE ⟨congregate . . . to ~ the hours away —H.A.Chippendale⟩

gam- *or* **gamo-** *comb form* [NL, fr. Gk, marriage, fr. *gamos* — more at BIGAMY] **1 :** united **:** joined ⟨*gamophyllous*⟩ ⟨*gamosepalous*⟩ **2 :** sexual **:** sexuality ⟨*gamic*⟩ ⟨*gamobium*⟩ ⟨*gamogenesis*⟩

-gam \,gam, ,gaa(ə)m\ *n comb form* -S [NL *-gamia* class of plants having a (specified) means of reproduction, fr. Gk *-gamia* -gamy] **:** plant belonging to a group having a (specified) means of reproduction ⟨*cryptogam*⟩

gam *abbr* gamut

gama \'gamə\ *or* **gama grass** *n* -S [prob. alter. of *grama, grama grass*] **:** a tall coarse American grass (*Tripsacum dactyloides*) valuable for forage

-gamae \gə,mē\ *n pl comb form* [NL, fem. pl. of *-gamus* -gamous] **:** plants having (such) sexual organs or (such) a means of reproduction — in taxonomic names in botany ⟨*Agamae*⟩

ga·ma·ri \gə'märē\ *n* -S [Beng *gāmāri*, fr. Skt *gambhārī*] **:** GUMHAR

ga·mash·es \gə'mashəz\ *n pl* [MF *gamaches*, pl. of *gamache*, modif. of OProv *garamacha, galamacha*, modif. of OSp *guadameci* colored or embossed leather, fr. *guadameci*, adj., colored or embossed (said of leather), modif. of Ar *ghadāmasīy* of Gadàmes, town in Tripoli where ornate leather was made] *archaic Scot* **:** leggings or gaiters worn by horseback riders

gamb *or* **gambe** \'gam(b), -aa(ə)m-\ *n* -S [F dial. (northern) *gambe* leg, fr. ONF, fr. LL *gamba, camba* hock (of a horse), leg — more at GAMBOL] **:** LEG, SHANK — used chiefly in heraldry

gam·ba \'gämbə, 'gam-,'gaam-,'gȧm-\ *n* -S [It *gamba* leg (in *viola da gamba*), fr. LL *gamba, camba*] **:** VIOLA DA GAMBA

gamba bass *n* **:** a labial pipe-organ stop of 16-foot pitch and string quality

gam·bade \(')gam¦bād, -bȧd\ *n* -S [F — more at GAMBOL] **:** 2GAMBADO ⟨a particularly explosive ~ that assaulted the rider after he had completely left the saddle —P.A.Rollins⟩ ⟨in his early youth . . . had himself tried musical and poetic ~*s* —Francis Hackett⟩

1gam·ba·do \gam'bā(,)dō, -bä(-\ *n, pl* **gambadoes** *also* **gambados** [perh. modif. (influenced by E *-ado* in such words as *bastinado, palisado*) of It *gambale* boot top, legging, greave, fr. *gamba* leg] **1 :** a long boot or legging attached to each side of a saddle to protect the rider's feet and legs from the wet or cold **2 :** a long gaiter or legging

2gambado \"\ *n, pl* **gambadoes** *also* **gambados** [modif. (influenced by E *1gambado*) of F *gambade*] **1 :** a spring of a horse **2 a :** a droll or fantastic movement **:** CAPER, GAMBOL ⟨pirouetted into a reckless ~ —L.C.Douglas⟩ **b :** a sudden, unexpected, or fantastic move, sally, or flourish **:** ANTIC

gam·bel oak \'gambəl-\ *n, usu cap G* [after William *Gambel* †1849 Am. ornithologist] **:** a shrub or small tree (*Quercus gambelii*) of the Rocky mountains with thin scaly gray-brown bark, thick firm leaves with 7 to 11 lobes, and acorns enclosed to half their length by the scaly pubescent cup

gambel quail *or* **gambel's quail** *n, usu cap G* **:** a largely bluish gray black-crested quail (*Lophortyx gambelii*) of the southwestern U.S.

gambel sparrow *or* **gambel's sparrow** *n, usu cap G* **:** a common sparrow (*Zonotrichia leucophrys gambelii*) of western No. America that is largely brown above with a white stripe over each eye

gam·ben bass \'gȧm|bən-, 'gam|, 'gaam|, 'gȧm|\ *n* [*gamben* prob. fr. G, pl. of *gambe* viola da gamba, fr. It *gamba* leg (in *viola da gamba*)] **:** GAMBA BASS

gam·be·son \'gambəsən, -bəzən\ *n* -S [ME *gambesoun*, fr. MF *gambeson, gambeison*, fr. OF, aug. of *gambais*, of Gmc origin; akin to OHG *wamba* belly — more at WOMB] **:** a medieval garment of stuffed and quilted cloth or leather orig. worn under the hauberk as a pad but later used alone as a defensive garment

gam·bet \'gambə̇t\ *n* -S [earlier *gambetta*, fr. NL, fr. It, dim. of *gamba* leg] **:** REDSHANK 1

gam·bette \(')gam¦bet\ *n* -S [prob. fr. *gamba* + *-ette*] **:** a 4-foot pipe-organ stop of the viola da gamba family

gam·bia \'gambēə\ *adj, usu cap* [fr. *Gambia*, country in western Africa] **:** of or from the country of Gambia **:** of the kind or style prevalent in Gambia

gam·bi·ae \'gambē,ē\ *n* -S [NL *gambiae* (specific epithet of *Anopheles gambiae*), fr. *Gambiae*, gen. of *Gambia*, country in West Africa] **:** an African mosquito (*Anopheles gambiae*) introduced into Brazil that is a very efficient vector of malaria

gambia fever *n, usu cap G* **:** a trypanosomiasis of cattle and sometimes other domestic animals in central Africa that resembles nagana but appears to be caused by a different trypanosome — called also *paranagana*

gam·bi·an \-ēən\ *n* -S *cap* [*Gambia*, Africa + E *-an*] **:** a native or inhabitant of Gambia — **gambian** *adj, usu cap*

gambia pod *n, usu cap G* **:** the pod of babul

gam·bier *also* **gam·bir** \'gam,bi(ə)r, -iə\ *n* -S [Malay *gambir*] **:** a yellowish catechu obtained from a Malayan woody vine (*Uncaria gambir*) of the family Rubiaceae, used for chewing with the betel nut, and exported for tanning and dyeing — called also *pale catechu, terra japonica, white cutch*; see DYE table I (under *Natural Brown 3*)

gam·bist \'gambə̇st, 'gäm-,'gaam-,'gȧm-\ *n* -S [*gamba* + *-ist*] **:** a performer on the viola da gamba

1gam·bit \'gambə̇t, 'gaam-, *usu* -əd-+V\ *n* -S [alter. (prob. influenced by F *gambit*, fr. Sp *gambito*, modif. of It *gambetto*) of earlier *gambet, gambett*, fr. It *gambetto* gambit, act of tripping someone, fr. *gamba* leg] **1 :** a chess opening in which a player voluntarily risks one or more pawns or a minor piece to gain an advantage in position **2 a** (1) **:** a remark or comment designed to launch a conversation or to make a telling point **:** SALLY ⟨"I decided to see you myself", was his opening ~ —*Newsweek*⟩ ⟨opened . . . with the ~ of inquiring whether present conditions were satisfactory —Jeremy Potter⟩ ⟨this was her usual opening ~ with the young —Elizabeth Goudge⟩ ⟨he could not, if he had pondered conversational ~*s* for an hour, have hit on a more successful one —C.D.Lewis⟩ (2) **:** TOPIC ⟨to smoke or not to smoke still flourishes as a useful conversational ~ —*Saturday Rev.*⟩ ⟨three other popular conversational ~*s* —Harold Strauss⟩ **b** (1) **:** a calculated move, maneuver, or device ⟨employs the classic melodramatic ~ of the innocent who walks straight into somebody else's intrigue —*Time*⟩ ⟨worked up a neat legislative ~ to further their interests —*New Republic*⟩ ⟨threw up its hands and retired to think up a new ~ —Richard Thruelsen⟩ (2) **:** a tactical maneuver in which an airplane awaiting favorable opportunity to attack keeps out of sight of a submarine periscope

2gambit \"\ *vi* -ED/-ING/-S **:** to make a gambit

1gam·ble \'gambəl\ *Midland var of* GAMBREL 2

2gam·ble \'gambəl, 'gaam-\ *vb* **gambled; gambled; gambling** \-b(ə)liŋ\ **gambles** [prob. back-formation fr. *gambler*] *vi* **1 a :** to play a game of chance for money or other stakes **b :** to wager money or other stakes on an uncertain outcome (as of a horse race or an athletic game) **2 :** to stake something of value on an uncertain event or contingency **:** take a chance **:** speculate esp. recklessly ⟨*gambled* on beating the Americans in air transport with jet airliners —Howard Marshall⟩ ⟨we cannot ~ on offending anyone —*Reporter*⟩ ⟨~ in the stock market⟩ ~ *vt* **1 :** to risk or lose by gambling **:** WAGER, BET ⟨they've all been *gambled* and lost by her husband that morning —Henri Michaux⟩ — often used with *away* ⟨*gambled* away his inheritance⟩ **2 :** to expose (something of value) to risk or hazard in the hope of advantage or gain ⟨decided to ~ my ship and our lives by going left —H.A.Chippendale⟩ ⟨*gambled* hundreds of thousands of dollars in research funds to work on the project —*Phoenix Flame*⟩

3gamble \"\ *n* -S **1 :** an act of playing a game of chance for money or other stakes ⟨the bishop . . . has not the slightest objection to a gentlemanly ~ —Norman Douglas⟩ **2 a :** an act or transaction having an element of risk or uncertainty **:** CHANCE, RISK ⟨a joint tenancy involves a ~ as to who dies first —*Deerfield (Wisc.) Independent*⟩ ⟨spent two billion dollars on the greatest scientific ~ in history —H.S.Truman⟩ ⟨companies . . . were unwilling to take the ~ and declined to go along —Freeman Lincoln⟩ **b :** something that is the object of a gamble ⟨every crop was a ~ —F.L.Paxson⟩

gam·bler \-blə(r)\ *n* -S [prob. alter. of obs. E *gamner, gamener*, fr. obs. E *gamen*, v., to play (fr. ME *gamenen*, fr. OE *gamenian*) + E *-er*; akin to ON *gamna* to amuse; denominative fr. the root of OE *gamen* game — more at GAME] **:** one that gambles: as **a :** one that habitually plays games of chance for money **:** GAMESTER **b :** one that for pay or other financial advantage provides the space and equipment needed to permit others to gamble **c :** one that takes risks ⟨if a publisher doesn't want to be a ~, he shouldn't be a publisher —*Publishers' Weekly*⟩; *specif* **:** SPECULATOR ⟨the . . . financial ~*s* who now have all our livelihoods at their mercy —G.B.Shaw⟩

gambling *n* -S [fr. gerund of *2gamble*] **1 :** the act or practice of betting **:** the act of playing a game and consciously risking money or other stakes on its outcome **2 :** the act of risking something on an uncertain event **:** WAGERING; *specif* **:** speculation in securities by uninformed persons or on thin margins

gambling device *n* **:** an instrumentality, contrivance, or apparatus reasonably designed and intended for the playing of a game for a reward of money or something of value for the player in which chance is a substantial factor

gambling house *or* **gambling hell** *n* **:** a place where gambling is carried on or allowed as a business **:** a place kept as a gambling resort

gam·bo \'gam(,)bō\ *n* -S [W] **:** a farm cart used esp. in Wales

gam·boge \(')gam¦bō|j, -aam-, -bül, |zh\ *n* -S [NL *gambogium*, alter. of *cambugium*, irreg. fr. *Cambodia*, region (now country) in southeast Indochina] **1** *or* **cam·boge** \(')kam-, (')kaam-\ **:** an orange to brown gum resin that becomes bright yellow when powdered, is obtained from various southeast Asian trees of the genus *Garcinia* (as *G. hanburyi*), and is used by artists as a yellow pigment and in medicine as a cathartic **2** *or* **gamboge yellow :** a strong yellow that is redder and less strong than yolk yellow or light chrome yellow

gam·bo hemp \'gam(,)bō-\ *n* [*gambo* fr. Bare'e (Austronesian language spoken in central Celebes) *gambu* fiber] **:** AMBARI HEMP

1gam·bol \'gambəl, 'gaam-\ *n* -S [earlier *gambolde, gambalde*, modif. of MF *gambade* spring of a horse, gambol, prob. fr. (assumed) OProv *gambada, cambada* (whence Prov *gambado, cambado*), fr. OProv *camba* leg, fr. LL *gamba, camba* hock (of a horse), leg, modif. of Gk *kampē* bend — more at CAMP] **:** a skipping or leaping about in play **:** a frolicking movement **syn** see 2PLAY

2gambol \"\ *vi* **gamboled** *or* **gambolled; gamboled** *or* **gambolled; gamboling** *or* **gambolling** \-b(ə)liŋ\ **gambols :** to bound or spring as in dancing or play **:** skip about **:** FRISK, CAVORT **syn** see PLAY

gam·brel \'gambrəl, 'gaam-\ *n* -S [ONF *gamberel* crooked stick used by butchers in suspending slaughtered animals, dim. of (assumed) ONF *gambier* crooked stick used by butchers in suspending slaughtered animals (var. of ONF *jambier*), fr. ONF *gambe* leg, fr. LL *gamba, camba*] **1 :** the hock of an animal (as a horse) **2** *or* **gambrel stick :** a stick or iron crooked like a horse's hind leg and used by butchers in suspending slaughtered animals **3 :** GAMBREL ROOF

gambrel roof *n* **:** a curb roof of the same section in all parts with a lower steeper slope and an upper flatter one — compare MANSARD

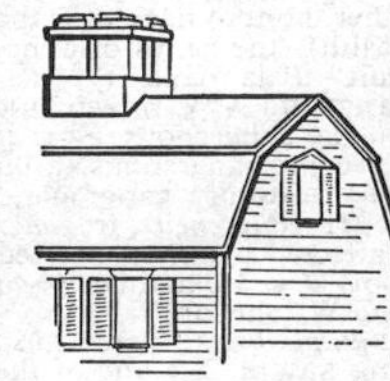
gambrel roof

gambs *pl of* GAMB

gam·bu·sia \gam'byüzh(ē)ə\ *n* [NL, modif. of AmerSp (Cuban) *gambusino* gambusia] **1** *cap* **:** a genus of topminnows (family Poeciliidae) of the warmer parts of No. America and the West Indies that feed largely on aquatic larvae and have been introduced as valuable exterminators of mosquito larvae **2** *pl* **gambusia** *or* **gambusias :** any fish of the genus *Gambusia*

¹game \'gām\ *n* -s [ME, fr. *gamen*, fr. OE; akin to OHG & ON *gaman* pleasure, amusement] **1 a** (1) **:** an amusement or pastime **:** DIVERSION, PLAY ⟨children at their ~*s*⟩ ⟨regarded his poetic activity as a ~ to while away tedious hours⟩ (2) **:** the equipment used to play a game ⟨what ~*s* will you buy the children for Christmas⟩ **b :** a practical joke **:** FOOLERY, FUN, PRANK, SPORT, LARK ⟨don't get mad, it was all a ~⟩ ⟨I'm tired of your ~*s*⟩ — often used in the phrase *to make game* ⟨the women were always making ~ of her —W.D.Steele⟩ ⟨the queer wicked grin . . . you do have the time you're making ~ with a man —J.M.Synge⟩ **2 a :** a scheme or strategy employed in the pursuit of an object or purpose **:** method of procedure **:** COURSE, PLAN, TACTIC ⟨the authorities decided to play a waiting ~ —Philip Rooney⟩ ⟨the ~ was to look frightened and then relieved —Alan Harrington⟩ ⟨the president tried another ~ —S.E.Morison & H.S.Commager⟩ ⟨the ~ is up⟩ **b** (1) **:** an illegal, fraudulent, or shady scheme or maneuver **:** RACKET, DODGE, TRICK ⟨a bad plan for that kind of ~ — our police are too good —John Buchan⟩ ⟨picked up after bilking a filling-station attendant in a short-change ~ —*Springfield (Mass.) Union*⟩ (2) **:** a particular occupation, profession, or other field of gainful activity **:** LINE ⟨the fight ~⟩ ⟨the newspaper ~⟩ ⟨a commercial traveler in the hardware ~ —Richard Bissell⟩ (3) **:** a specified type of activity or mode of behavior ⟨the ~ of sin is never worth while —F.A.Swinnerton⟩ ⟨the ~ of love⟩ ⟨the ~ of politics⟩ **3 a** (1) **:** a physical or mental competition conducted according to rules in which the participants play in direct opposition to each other, each side striving to win and to keep the other side from doing so — see GAME OF CHANCE (2) **:** a division or subdivision of a larger contest ⟨two ~*s* in a row gave them a 700-point rubber⟩ ⟨he won the first set by a score of six ~*s* to two but lost the match⟩ (3) **:** a single contest lasting until a designated limit (as a set time or a certain number of innings or points) is reached (4) **:** the number of points necessary to be scored in order to win ⟨in casino 21 points is ~⟩ ⟨in shuffleboard 50 points is ~⟩ (5) **:** points credited on the score in some card games (as seven-up) to the player whose cards count up the highest (6) **:** the ten-spot of trumps counting a point to the one securing it in play in pedro, cinch, and certain other card games (7) **:** any of the available bids or declarations that impose specific obligations on the bidder in skat and related games (8) **:** SCORE ⟨the bowler's ~*s* were 197, 189, and 200⟩ (9) **:** a statistical unit for measuring the relative competitive standing of the teams in a league ⟨three ~*s* behind⟩ (10) **:** the manner, quality, or style of playing in a contest ⟨they play a very rough ~⟩ ⟨occasionally . . . put aside domestic cares to keep up her ~ at the local country club —M.F. & Katharine Pringle⟩ ⟨he is off his ~⟩ ⟨shoots in the low 80s when he is on his ~ —*Time*⟩ (11) **:** the set of rules according to which a game is played ⟨will you teach me the ~⟩ **b games** *pl* **:** organized athletics ⟨~*s* and circuses are not as good as art, music, and literature —Walter Moberly⟩ **c :** CHARADES — used with *the* **d :** a contest, rivalry, or struggle of any kind ⟨delegates who are anxious to back a winner . . . early in the ~ —*Newsweek*⟩ **4 a** *obs* **:** sport in the hunting field **b** (1) **:** animals under pursuit or taken in hunting **:** QUARRY (2) **:** animals considered worthy of pursuit by sportsmen; *esp* **:** wild animals hunted for sport or food (3) **:** the flesh of a game animal considered as food **c** (1) **:** a kept herd or flock — now used of swans (2) **:** GAME FOWL (3) *archaic* **:** the combative spirit held to be typical of game fowl **d :** a butt, target, or object esp. of ridicule, exploitation, pursuit, or attack ⟨they are also bores — always the richest ~ for the comic instinct —V.S.Pritchett⟩ — often used in the phrase *fair game* ⟨all the customers in the speakeasies were fair ~ —George Raft⟩ **syn** see FUN

²game \"\ *vb* -ED/-ING/-S [ME *gamen* to play, fr. *game*, n. — more at ¹GAME] *vi* **:** to play for a stake (as with cards, dice, or billiards) ⟨the men became sufficiently acquainted to ~ together —Frances Trollope⟩ ~ *vt, archaic* **:** to lose or squander by gambling — used chiefly with *away*

³game \"\ *adj* -ER/-EST [¹*game*] **1 :** having a resolute unyielding spirit ⟨he was ~ to the end⟩ **2 :** of or relating to game ⟨~ laws⟩ ⟨~ warden⟩

⁴game \"\ *adj, sometimes* -ER/-EST [perh. fr. ³*game*] **:** LAME ⟨a ~ leg⟩

game animal *n* [¹*game*] **:** an animal made legitimate quarry by state or other law

game bag *n* **:** a pouch usu. equipped with straps for wearing on the back and used esp. by bird hunters for carrying their take

game ball *n* **:** the service that wins a racket game for the server if it results in his scoring a point

game bird *n* **1 :** a bird made legitimate quarry for hunters by state or other law **2** *badminton* **:** GAME BALL

game cart *n* **:** a four-wheeled dogcart

gamecock \'=,=\ *n* [¹*game*] **1 :** a male game fowl **2 :** a combative indomitable plucky person ⟨fierce little ~ of a commander —Dixon Wecter⟩ ⟨the slim and defiant little ~ of a man —Edgar Johnson⟩

game fish *n* **1 :** a fish of the family Salmonidae **2 :** SPORT FISH; *esp* **:** any of various fishes made a legal catch by specific legislation

game fowl *n* [¹*game*] **:** a bird of any of various strains of domestic fowls developed orig. chiefly for the production of fighting cocks — see MODERN GAME, OLD ENGLISH GAME

gamekeeper \'=,==\ *n* **:** one who has charge of the breeding and protection of game animals or birds on private preserves

gam·e·lan \'gamə,lan, -lən\ *also* **gam·e·lang** \-,laŋ\ *or* **gam·e·lin** \-lən\ *n* -s [Jav *gamelan* percussion instrument related to the xylophone] **1 a :** an orchestra of varying size originating in the islands of southeastern Asia and consisting chiefly of percussion instruments of both definite and indefinite pitch, flutes, and bowed instruments **b :** the music of such an orchestra **2 :** an East Asian percussion instrument that is akin to the xylophone and is used in gamelan orchestras

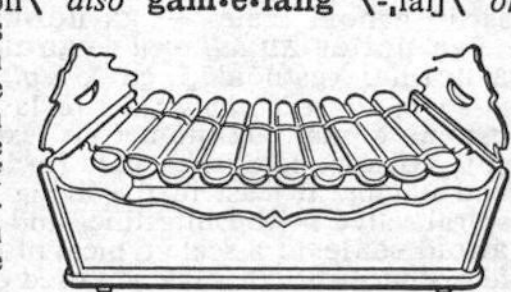
gamelan 2

ga·me·lo·te \,gamə'lōd·ē\ *n* -s [AmerSp, alter. of *gramalote*, fr. Sp *gramal* field of coarse grass, fr. *grama* coarse grass — more at GRAMA] **:** any of several grasses: as **a :** GUINEA GRASS 1 **b :** either of two foxtails of the West Indies (*Setaria porretiana* and *S. paniculifera*)

game·ly *adv* [³*game* + *-ly*] **:** in a plucky manner **:** SPIRITEDLY ⟨fought a losing battle ~ —H.L.Merillat⟩

game·ness *n* -ES [³*game* + *-ness*] **:** ENDURANCE, PLUCK

game of chance : a game (as a dice game) in which chance rather than skill determines the outcome

game of skill : a game (as chess) in which skill rather than chance determines the outcome

game point *n* **:** the point that wins a game for one side or the other

game room *n* **:** a recreation room; *esp* **:** one fitted out for the playing of table games

games *pl of* GAME, *pres 3d sing of* GAME

games-all \(')=¦=\ *n* -s [*games* pl. of ¹*game*] **:** a tie score in tennis at five games or more each

games·man \'gāmzmən\ *n, pl* **gamesmen** [¹*game* + *-s-* (as in *craftsman*) + *man*] **:** one who practices gamesmanship

games·man·ship \-,ship\ *n* -s **1 :** the art or practice of winning a sports contest by expedients of doubtful propriety (as by distracting an opponent) without actual violation of the rules of the game ⟨~ is practiced in golf more freely than in any other sport —*Time*⟩ **2 :** the use of ethically or intellectually dubious methods to achieve an objective ⟨the proposed analysis . . . is pure ~, supported neither by phonetic nor by phonemic data —H.G.Lunt⟩

games master *n, Brit* **:** a schoolteacher who organizes, directs, and leads games and play

games mistress *n, Brit* **:** a female games master

game·some \'gāmsəm\ *adj* [ME *gamsum*, fr. *game, gam* game + *-some, -som, -sum* -some] **:** exhibiting good-humored playfulness ⟨a woman that's joyous and ~ and witty —Donagh MacDonagh⟩ — **game·some·ly** *adv* — **game·some·ness** *n* -ES

gamest superlative of GAME

game·ster \-mztə(r), -mst-\ *n* -s **1 :** one who plays games (as games of chance) **2 a** *obs* **:** a competitor in a game or contest **:** ATHLETE **b** *dial Eng* **:** a player at cudgels or singlestick

gamet- *or* **gameto-** *comb form* [NL, fr. *gameta*] **:** gamete ⟨*gamet*al⟩ ⟨*gameto*cide⟩

ga·me·tal \gə'mēd·ᵊl, 'ga,m-\ *adj* [*gamet-* + *-al*] **:** GAMETIC

gam·e·tan·gial \¦gamə¦tanj(ē)əl\ *adj* [*gametangium* + *-al*] **:** of or relating to a gametangium

gam·e·tan·gi·um \,==¦=jēəm\ *n, pl* **gametan·gia** \-jēə\ [NL, fr. *gamet-* + *-angium*] **:** the cell or organ in which gametes are developed — compare SPORANGIUM

ga·mete \gə'mēt, 'ga,mēt\ *n* -s [NL *gameta*, fr. Gk *gametēs* husband & *gametē* wife, fr. *gamein* to marry, fr. *gamos* marriage — more at BIGAMY] **:** a mature germ cell (as a sperm or egg) possessing a haploid chromosome set and capable of initiating formation of a new individual by fusion with another gamete — compare FERTILIZATION, MATURATION, ZYGOTE

game theory *n* **:** THEORY OF GAMES

ga·met·ic \gə'med·ik, 'ga,m-\ *adj* [*gamet-* + *-ic*] **:** of, relating to, being, or derived from a gamete — **ga·met·i·cal·ly** \-d·ək(ə)lē, -li\ *adv*

gametic number *n* **:** the haploid number of chromosomes typical of gametes

ga·me·to·cide \gə'mēd·ə,sīd\ *n* -s [*gamet-* + *-cide*] **:** an agent that destroys the gametocytes of a malaria parasite

ga·me·to·cyte \-,sīt\ *n* -s [ISV *gamet-* + *-cyte*] **:** a cell that divides to produce gametes **:** SPERMATOCYTE **:** OOCYTE

game·to·gen·e·sis \gə,mēd·ə'jenəsəs, ,gamə(,)tō'j-\ *n* [NL, fr. *gamet-* + L *genesis*] **:** the production of gametes — compare MATURATION — **game·to·gen·ic** \gə¦mēd·ə¦jenik, ¦gamə(,)tō¦j-\ *or* **gam·e·tog·e·nous** \¦gamə¦täjənəs\ *adj* — **gam·e·tog·e·ny** \,gamə'täjənē\ *n* -ES

game·to·go·ni·um \gə,mēd·ə'gōnēəm, ,gamətō'g-\ *n, pl* **gametogo·nia** \-nēə\ [NL, fr. *gamet-* + *-gonium*] **:** GAMETOCYTE

gam·e·tog·o·ny \,gamə'tägənē\ *n* -ES [ISV *gamet-* + *-gony*] **:** gamogenesis esp. of protozoans

gam·e·toid \'gamə,tȯid\ *n* -s [*gamet-* + *-oid*] **:** a multinucleate gamete

game·to·kinetic hormone \gə¦mēd·ō, ¦gamə(,)tō+ . . . -\ *n* [*gametokinetic* fr. *gamet-* + *kinetic*] **:** FOLLICLE-STIMULATING HORMONE

ga·me·to·phore \gə'mēd·ə,fō(ə)r\ *n* -s [*gamet-* + *-phore*] **:** a modified branch bearing gametangia (as in the thalloid liverworts) — **ga·me·to·phor·ic** \gə¦mēd·ə¦fórik\ *adj*

ga·me·to·phyte \gə'mēd·ə,fīt\ *n* -s [ISV *gamet-* + *-phyte*] **:** the individual or generation of a plant exhibiting alternation of generations that bears sex organs, constitutes the major part of the plant body in most algae, fungi, and mosses, exists as an independent transitory thalloid body in ferns and related plants, and is reduced to a microscopic or rudimentary structure in seed plants — distinguished from *sporophyte* — **ga·me·to·phyt·ic** \=¦==¦fid·ik\ *adj*

gamey *var of* GAMY

gam·ic \'gamik\ *adj* [*gam-* + *-ic*] **:** requiring fertilization **:** SEXUAL ⟨a ~ egg⟩ ⟨~ reproduction⟩

-gam·ic \'gamik, -mēk\ *adj comb form* [ISV *-gam-* (fr. NL *-gamia* — as in *Cryptogamia* —, fr. Gk *-gamia* -gamy) + *-ic*] **1 :** having (such) reproductive organs ⟨cleisto*gamic*⟩ ⟨dicho*gamic*⟩ **2 :** having (such) a mode of fertilization ⟨poro*gamic*⟩

gam·ie \'gāmē\ *n* -s [*game* (in *gamekeeper*) + *-ie*] *Scot* **:** GAMEKEEPER

gamier *comparative of* GAMY

-gamies *pl of* -GAMY

gamiest *superlative of* GAMY

gam·i·ly \'gāməlē, -li\ *adv* **:** in a gamy manner **:** PLUCKILY ⟨expressing himself quite ~ about the grosser aspects of love —Winthrop Sargeant⟩

¹gam·in \'gamən\ *n* -s [F] **1 :** a boy who runs the streets **:** a roguish impudent boy **:** URCHIN ⟨won the confidence of the street ~*s* —E.S.Bates⟩ ⟨the jeers and stones of . . . ~*s* flung at outraged farmers —Harriot B. Barbour⟩ **2 :** GAMINE 2

²gamin \"\ *adj* **:** of, relating to, or having the characteristics of a gamin ⟨a snub nose and a ~ smile —*Danceland*⟩ ⟨as debonair, as ~ . . . as ever —*Time*⟩ ⟨tough fifty-year-old ~ face —Eleanor Clark⟩

¹gam·ine \(')ga¦mēn, 'gamən\ *n* -s [F, fem. of *gamin*] **1 :** a girl who runs the streets ⟨a tough little ~ —Geoffrey Household⟩ ⟨as ignorant as a ~ —T.B.Costain⟩ **2 :** a girl of ingratiating qualities, typically slight build, and a pert saucy air or a wistful elfish charm ⟨a trio of glamorous ~*s* —Lois Long⟩ ⟨a droll, touching ~ —Constance Tomkinson⟩ ⟨one of the most coquettish ~*s* I have ever watched —*New Yorker*⟩

²gamine \"\ *adj* **:** of or relating to a gamine ⟨her oddly ~ . . . face —C.A.Lejeune⟩ ⟨the girls are built along shapely . . . ~ lines —Winthrop Sargeant⟩

gam·ine·rie \'gamənrē, ga,mēn(ə)'rē\ *n* -s [F, fr. *gamin* + *-erie* -ery] **:** impudent, roguish, or wisecracking spirit ⟨there is just the same ~ and contempt of the conventional —*Times Lit. Supp.*⟩

gam·i·ness \'gāmēnəs, -min-\ *n* -ES **:** the quality or state of being gamy

gaming *n* -s [fr. gerund of ²*game*] **:** the act or practice of playing games for stakes ⟨a passion for ~⟩

gaming house *n* **:** GAMBLING HOUSE

gaming room *n* **:** a room habitually used for gambling

gaming table *n* **1 :** a table that is designed esp. for gambling and that often has depressions for counters and designs painted, inlaid, or in needlework appropriate to gaming **2 :** a table where gambling games are played

¹gam·ma \'gamə\ *n* -s [ME, fr. LL, fr. Gk, of Sem origin; akin to Heb *gīmel* gimel] **1 :** the third letter of the Greek alphabet — symbol Γ or γ; see ALPHABET table **2 a :** the degree of contrast of a developed photographic image **b :** the slope of the straight-line portion of the characteristic curve of a photographic material or process **c :** a measure of the faithfulness with which the brightness variation in a television scene is reproduced in the displayed picture **3 a :** a unit of magnetic intensity equal to 0.00001 oersted **b :** a gamma-ray quantum **c :** one millionth of a gram **:** MICROGRAM

²gamma \"\ *or* γ- \"\ *adj* **1 :** of or relating to one of three or more closely related chemical substances ⟨γ-yohimbine⟩ — used somewhat arbitrarily to specify ordinal relationship or to specify a particular physical form, esp. an allotropic modification (as in γ-iron), or an isomeric or stereoisomeric form (as in γ-benzene hexachloride) **2 :** third in position in the structure of an organic molecule from a particular group or atom or having a structure characterized by such a position ⟨γ-hydroxy acids⟩ ⟨γ-lactones⟩ **3 :** third in order of brightness — used of a star in a constellation **4** *of streptococci* **:** producing no hemolysis on blood agar plates

gamma acid *n* [¹*gamma*] **:** a crystalline acid $HOC_{10}H_5(NH_2)SO_3H$ made from G acid and used as an intermediate for azo dyes; 7-amino-1-naphthol-3-sulfonic acid

gamma benzene hexachloride *n* [²*gamma*] **:** LINDANE

gamma cellulose *n* [²*gamma*] **:** CELLULOSE d

gam·ma·cism \'gamə,sizəm\ *also* **gam·ma·cis·mus** \,==ˈsizməs\ *n, pl* **gammacisms** *also* **gammacismuses** [*gammacism* fr. NL *gammacismus*, fr. LL *gamma* + *-cismus* (as in *iotacismus* iotacism); *gammacismus* NL] **:** difficulty in pronouncing velar consonants (as \g\ and \k\)

gamma cross *n* [¹*gamma*] **:** GAMMADION

gam·ma·di·on \gə'madē,än, ga'-, -madē-, -ēən\ *also* **gam·mat·i·on** \-mad·ē-\ *n, pl* **gamma·dia** *also* **gammat·ia** \-ēə\ [modif. of ML *gammadium*, irreg. fr. LL *gamma*] **:** a cross formed of four capital gammas esp. in the figure of a swastika or in that of a voided Greek cross — called also *crux gammata, gammate cross*

1 2

gammadion: *1* swastika; *2* voided Greek cross

gamma function *n* [¹*gamma*] **:** a function of a variable γ defined by the definite integral $\Gamma(\gamma)=\int_0^\infty x^{\gamma-1}e^{-x}dx$

gamma globulin *n* [ISV ²*gamma* + *globulin*] **1 a :** a protein fraction of blood rich in antibodies **b :** a sterile solution of gamma globulin from pooled human blood administered esp. for passive immunity against measles, rubella, infectious hepatitis, or poliomyelitis **2 :** any of numerous globulins of plasma or serum that have less electrophoretic mobility at alkaline pH than serum albumins, alpha globulins, or beta globulins and that include most antibodies

gam·ma·graph \'gamə,graf, -rȧf\ *n* [¹*gamma* + *-graph*] **:** a radiograph produced by gamma rays — **gam·ma·graph·ic** \¦==¦grafik\ *adj*

gamma infinity *n* [¹*gamma*] **:** the maximum degree of contrast to which a sensitive photographic material can be developed

gamma iron *n* [²*gamma*] **:** an iron that is stable between 910°C and 1400° C and that is characterized by a face-centered cubic crystal structure — compare ALPHA IRON, DELTA IRON

gamma moth *n* [NL *gamma* (specific epithet of *Plusia gamma*), fr. LL, third letter of the Greek alphabet; fr. the likeness in shape of the marks on the forewings to small gammas] **:** a migratory European noctuid moth (*Plusia gamma*) having a bright silvery Y-shaped mark on each of the fore wings and a larva that feeds on the cabbage and other vegetables — called also *silver Y moth*

gamma nasal *n* [¹*gamma* + *nasal*, adj.] *in ancient and modern Greek* **:** gamma pronounced \ŋ\, its value before κ, χ, ξ, or another gamma

gamma ray *n* [¹*gamma*] **1 :** a photon or radiation quantum emitted spontaneously by a radioactive substance **2** *or* **gamma radiation :** a continuous stream of gamma rays

¹gammarid \"\ *adj* [NL *Gammaridae*] **:** of or relating to the family Gammaridae

²gam·ma·rid \'gamərəd, -,rid\ *n* -s [NL *Gammaridae*] **:** an amphipod crustacean of the family Gammaridae

gam·mar·i·dae \gə'marə,dē, ga'-\ *n pl, cap* [NL, fr. *Gammarus*, type genus + *-idae*] **:** a large family of swimming amphipod crustaceans of both marine and freshwater forms

gam·ma·rus \'gamərəs\ *n, cap* [NL, alter. (influenced by LL *gambarus*, alter. of L *cammarus*) of L *cammarus* sea crab, lobster — more at CAMBARUS] **:** a genus (the type of the family Gammaridae) of swimming amphipod crustaceans

gam·mate cross \'ga,māt-\ *n* [part trans. of NL *crux gammata*, fr. L *crux* cross + NL *gammata*, fem. of *gammatus* composed of gammas, fr. ML, shaped like a gamma, fr. LL *gamma* + L *-atus* -ate] **:** GAMMADION

gamme \'gam\ *n* -s [F, fr. OF *game*, fr. ML *gamma*, fr. LL, third letter of the Greek alphabet; fr. the use of the letter gamma by Guido d'Arezzo †1050? Benedictine monk and musical reformer to represent the lowest note of the gamut] **:** GAMUT ⟨produces a ~ of sounds that are beautiful —Janet Flanner⟩ ⟨a recurrent ~ of color —Helen Gardner⟩

gammed *past of* GAM

gam·mel·ost \'gamə,lȯst\ *also* **gammelost cheese** *n* -s [Norw, fr. *gammel* old (fr. ON *gamall*) + *ost* cheese, fr. ON *ostr*; akin to OE *gamol* old and perh. to L *hiems* winter — more at HIBERNATE, JUICE] **:** a Norwegian blue-mold cheese made from soured skim milk

gam·mer \'gamə(r)\ *n* -s [prob. contr. of *godmother*] **:** an old woman — compare GAFFER

Gam·mex·ane \ga'mek,sān, gə'-; 'gamik-\ *trademark* — used for lindane

gamming *pres part of* GAM

¹gam·mon \'gamən\ *n* -s [ONF *gambon* ham (of a hog), aug. of *gambe* leg — more at GAMB] **1** *dial* **a :** LEG **b :** THIGH **2 a :** a ham or flitch of cured bacon ⟨the ~ was given as a reward and encouragement to handfasting couples —Dorothy G. Spicer⟩ **b :** the lower end of a side of bacon

²gammon \"\ *n* -s [origin unknown] **:** GAMMONING

³gammon \"\ *vt* -ED/-ING/-S **:** to fasten (a bowsprit) to the stem of a ship by lashings of rope or chain or by a band of iron

⁴gammon \"\ *n* -s [perh. alter. of ME *gamen* game, sport — more at GAME] **1** *archaic* **:** BACKGAMMON **2 :** the winning of a backgammon game before the loser has borne off any men

⁵gammon \"\ *vt* -ED/-ING/-S **:** to beat by scoring a gammon

⁶gammon \"\ *n* -s [obs. E *gammon* talk, chatter, perh. fr. obs. E slang *gammon* (in the expressions *give someone gammon* to stand close to someone while another person is picking his pocket, *keep someone in gammon* to divert someone's attention while another person is robbing him), perh. fr. E *gammon* leg, thigh, flitch of cured bacon — more at ¹GAMMON] **:** talk intended to deceive **:** HUMBUG ⟨it's all ~ —G.B.Shaw⟩

⁷gammon \"\ *vb* ED/-ING/-S *vi* **1 :** to talk gammon **2 :** PRETEND, FEIGN ~ *vt* **:** to influence with gammon **:** FOOL ⟨critics were not ~*ed* by this latest prodigy —Roland Gelatt⟩

gammoning *n* -s [fr. gerund of ³*gammon*] **:** the lashing or iron band by which the bowsprit of a ship is fixed to the stem

gammon iron *n* [²*gammon*] **:** a metal hoop or band attached to the stemhead of a yacht through which the bowsprit runs

gam·my \'gamī\ *adj* -ER/-EST [prob. irreg. fr. ⁴*game* + *-y*] *dial Brit* **:** LAME, SORE ⟨a ~ foot⟩

gamo- — see GAM-

ga·mo·bi·um \gə'mōbēəm, ga'-\ *n, pl* **gamo·bia** \-ēə\ [NL, fr. *gam-* + *-bium*] **:** the sexually reproducing generation when sexual and asexual generations alternate

gam·o·deme \'gamə,dēm\ *n* [*gam-* + *deme*] **:** a more or less isolated breeding community of organisms

ga·mog·a·my \gə'mägəmē, ga'-\ *n* -ES [*gam-* + *-gamy*] **:** GAMETOGONY

gam·o·gen·e·sis \,gamə'jenəsəs\ *n* [*gam-* + *genesis*] **:** reproduction by means of gametes **:** sexual reproduction — **gam·o·ge·net·ic** \¦gaməjə¦ned·ik\ *adj* — **gam·o·ge·net·i·cal·ly** \-d·ək(ə)lē\ *adv*

gam·o·gen·ic \¦gamə¦jenik\ *adj* [*gam-* + *-genic*] **:** produced by sexual reproduction

ga·mog·e·ny \gə'mäjənē, ga'-\ *n* -ES [*gam-* + *-geny*] **:** GAMOGENESIS

ga·mog·o·ny \gə'mägənē, ga'-\ *n* -ES [ISV *gam-* + *-gony*] **1 a :** GAMOGENESIS **b :** multiple fission producing sporozoan gametes **2 :** SPOROGONY

ga·mol·e·pis \gə'mäləpəs\ *n, cap* [NL, fr. *gam-* + *-lepis*] **:** a small genus of southern African herbs or shrubs (family Compositae) with alternate pinnatisect leaves and flowers resembling marigolds and having the bracts of the involucre united for one third or one half their length

gam·one \'ga,mōn\ *n* -s [ISV *gam-* + *-one* (as in *hormone*); prob. orig. formed as G *gamon*] **:** any of various substances believed to be liberated by eggs or sperms and to affect germ cells of the opposite sex

gam·ont \'ga,mänt\ *n* -s [ISV *gam-* + *-ont*] **:** a protozoan gametocyte

gamoos *or* **gamouse** *var of* ZAMOUSE

gam·o·pet·a·lae \,gamə'ped·ᵊl,ē\ [NL, fr. *gam-* + *-petalae*] *syn of* METACHLAMYDEAE

gam·o·pet·a·lous \¦==¦=ᵊləs\ *adj* [NL *gamopetalus*, fr. *gam-* + *-petalus* -petalous] **1 :** having the corolla composed of united petals ⟨the morning glory is ~⟩ **2 :** of or relating to the Metachlamydeae

gam·o·phyl·lous \¦gamə¦filəs\ *adj* [prob. fr. (assumed) NL *gamophyllus*, fr. NL *gam-* + *-phyllus* -phyllous] **:** having united leaves or parts resembling leaves — used esp. of a floral envelope not differentiated into calyx and corolla

gam·o·sep·a·lous \¦gamō¦sepələs\ *adj* [prob. fr. (assumed) NL *gamosepalus*, fr. NL *gam-* + *-sepalus* -sepalous] **:** having the sepals united

-gamous \-gəməs\ *adj comb form* [Gk *-gamos*, fr. *gamos*

marriage — more at BIGAMY] **1 :** characterized by having or practicing (such) a marriage or (such or so many) marriages ⟨endogamous⟩ ⟨exogamous⟩ **2** [prob. fr. NL *-gamus*, prob. fr. LL, characterized by having (such) a marriage or (such or so many) marriages, fr. Gk *-gamos*] **:** -GAMIC 1

ga·mow barrier \'gä,mäv-\ *n, usu cap G* [after George *Gamow* †1968 Am. physicist] **:** the potential barrier that in wave-mechanical theory is assumed to oppose the escape of alpha particles from an atomic nucleus in radioactive disintegration

gamp \'gamp\ *n* -S [after Sarah *Gamp*, nurse with a large cotton umbrella in Charles Dickens's *Martin Chuzzlewit* (1843-44)] *Brit* **:** a large umbrella ⟨halfway to the station my ~ blew inside out —*Sydney (Australia) Bulletin*⟩; *often* **:** one that is untidily or loosely tied up ⟨if you carry an umbrella use it tightly rolled and never as a ~ —S.D.Barney⟩

gam·phrel \'gamfrəl\ *n* -S [origin unknown] *Scot* **:** a stupid person **:** BLOCKHEAD

gams *pl of* GAM, *pres 3d sing of* GAM

-gams *pl of* -GAM

gam·ut \'gamət, -əd·+V\ *n* -S [prob. modif. of (assumed) ML *gamma ut*, fr. ML *gamma* lowest note of the Guidonian scale (fr. LL, third letter of the Greek alphabet) + *ut* lowest note of each hexachord in the Guidonian scale — more at GAMMA, UT] **1 a :** the first or lowest note of each hexachord of Guido's great scale **b :** GREAT SCALE **c :** the whole series of recognized musical notes; *sometimes* **:** a recognized scale **d :** the compass of a voice or instrument **2 :** an entire range from one extreme to another **:** a graded series including all kinds ⟨an Italian running through his whole possible ~ of tone —Edward Sapir⟩ ⟨the pets . . . ranged the ~ of animal life about us —Agnes M. Cleaveland⟩ ⟨deliberate murder (with a whole ~ of possible motives) —A.L.Guérard⟩ ⟨the complete ~ of the spectrum —C.T.Elvey⟩ **syn** see RANGE

gamy *also* **gam·ey** \'gāmē, -mi\ *adj* **gamier**; **gamiest** [¹*game* + *-y*] **1 :** showing an unyielding spirit to the last **:** PLUCKY, GAME — used esp. of animals ⟨the ~ fish does most of its fighting below the surface —*Nat'l Geographic*⟩ ⟨a ~ cow pony⟩ **2 a :** having or suggesting the flavor of game ⟨begins to lose its rich ~ flavor when it has been out of the water less than an hour —*Ford Times*⟩; *esp* **:** having the flavor of game kept uncooked till near the condition of tainting **b :** MALODOROUS ⟨she had a huge brown billy goat . . . so she was usually pretty ~ herself —Crary Moore⟩ **3 a :** treating of scandalous or sensational themes or happenings **:** SPICY, RACY, SORDID, TITILLATING ⟨three other episodes are rather broad and ~ —John McCarten⟩ ⟨skips the asterisks and gives you the ~ details —V.P.Hass⟩ ⟨a ~ rape story —*Time*⟩ **b :** morally tainted **:** DISREPUTABLE ⟨as ~ an assemblage of solons as the nation then offered —Dwight Macdonald⟩

-gamy \gəmē, -mi\ *n comb form* -ES [ME *-gamie*, fr. LL *-gamia*, fr. Gk — more at BIGAMY] **1 a :** marriage ⟨exog*amy*⟩ **b :** union for propagation or reproduction ⟨allog*amy*⟩ **2** [NL *-gamia* (as in *Cryptogamia*), fr. Gk *-gamia* -gamy (marriage)] **a :** possession of (such) reproductive organs ⟨cleisto*gamy*⟩ **b :** possession of (such) a mode of fertilization ⟨poro*gamy*⟩

gan *past of* GIN

ga·nan·cial \gə'nanchəl, *Sp* gänän'thyäl *or* -'syäl\ *adj* [Sp, relating to profit, held jointly by husband and wife, fr. *ganancia* profit, fr. *ganar* to gain, earn, perh. of Gmc origin; akin to ON *gana* to gape, stare; akin to Gk *chaskein* to gape, yawn] **:** being, relating to, or held under the Spanish system of law that controls the title and disposition of the property acquired during marriage by a spouse

ganch *also* **gansh** \'ganch, -ä-\ *vt* -ED/-ING/-ES [modif. of Turk *kancalamak* to put on a hook, fr. *kanca* large hook, modif. of Gk *gampsos* curved] **:** to execute or kill by impaling on stakes or hooks ⟨field mice . . . ~*ed* upon the hooks —D.C. Peattie⟩

gan·da \'gandə, 'gän-\ *n, pl* **ganda** *or* **gandas** *usu cap* **1 a :** a Bantu-speaking people of Uganda **b :** a member of such people **2 :** the Bantu language of the Ganda people spoken also with slight differences by several neighboring peoples and used as the official language of Uganda

¹gan·der \'gandə(r), 'gaan-\ *n* -S [ME, fr. OE *gandra*; akin to D *gander*, MLG *ganre* gander, OE *gōs* goose — more at GOOSE] **1 :** the adult male goose **2 :** a stupid or foolish fellow **:** SIMPLETON ⟨a silly, immature little ~ —Elizabeth Bowen⟩

²gander \"\ *vi* -ED/-ING/-S *dial* **:** WANDER, STROLL ⟨~*ed* down to . . . the great whaling port —H.A.Chippendale⟩ ⟨a man could ~ around and have his pleasure —Conrad Richter⟩

³gander \"\ *n* -S [prob. fr. ¹*gander*; fr. the outstretched neck of a person craning to look at something] *slang* **:** LOOK, GLANCE ⟨take a ~ at that picture⟩

gander pull *or* **gander pulling** *n* **:** a pastime esp. formerly in the South and Southwest in which a person on horseback rides rapidly past a goose hanging with its neck down and greased and tries to pull off its head

gan·dha·ra \gən'därə, -gan'd-\ *or* **gan·dha·ran** \-rən\ *adj, usu cap* [*Gandhara*, ancient region in northwest Punjab and part of eastern Afghanistan] **:** of or relating to ancient Gandhara, its people, or its hybrid Greco-Buddhist art

gan·dhi·an \'gändēən, 'gan-,'gaan-,'gán-, -dion\ *adj, usu cap* [Mohandas K. *Gandhi* †1948 Indian nationalist and spiritual leader + E *-an*] **:** of or relating to Gandhi or his principle of nonviolence ⟨resigned myself with a *Gandhian* shrug —Herbert Passin⟩ ⟨*Gandhian* prejudice against violent pressures —Edmond Taylor⟩

gan·dhi cap \-dē-, -di-\ *n, usu cap G* **:** a white cap worn in India that has a wide band and narrow crown and is similar in outline to an overseas cap

gan·dhism \-,dizəm\ *or* **gan·dhi·ism** \-dē,izəm, -di,iz-\ *n* -S *usu cap* **:** SATYAGRAHA

gan·dou·ra *or* **gan·dou·rah** \gan'dùrə, gän-\ *n* -S [Ar *qandūrah*] **:** a long loose gown with or without sleeves that is worn chiefly in northern Africa

gan·dy dancer \'gandē-\ *n* [perh. fr. the now defunct *Gandy* Manufacturing Company, Chicago, Illinois, which made tools used by railroad laborers] **1 :** a laborer in a railroad section gang **2 :** an itinerant or seasonal laborer

gane *past part of* GAE

ga·nef \'gänəf\ *n* -S [Yiddish *ganef*, *gannef*, fr. Heb *gannābh* thief] *slang* **:** THIEF, RASCAL

¹gang \'gaŋ, 'gaiŋ\ *n* -S *often attrib* [ME, fr. OE; akin to OHG *gang* act of going, ON *gangr* act of going, Goth *gang* street, Gk *kochōnē* perineum, Skt *jaṅghā* shank] **1 :** the act, manner, or means of going **:** PASSAGE, COURSE, JOURNEY; *also* **:** GAIT **2 a** *dial chiefly Brit* (1) **:** PASSAGE, WAY, ROAD, LANE (2) **:** a pasturage for cattle **b** *chiefly Scot* **:** JOURNEY; *esp* **:** one undertaken to perform an errand **c** *chiefly Scot* **:** the amount (as of wood, water, or peat) that can be carried at one time or in one trip **3 a** (1) **:** a set or full complement of articles **:** OUTFIT ⟨a ~ of oars⟩ (2) **:** a combination of similar implements or other items arranged so as to act together to save time or labor ⟨a ~ of saws⟩ or to produce in one operation or as one unit ⟨a ~ of printing plates printing several jobs on a single sheet⟩ **b :** a number of individuals making up a group: as (1) **:** a group of persons working under the same direction or at the same task ⟨migrants . . . laboring in ~*s* in the woods, mines, and fields —*Amer. Guide Series: Wash.*⟩ ⟨~*s* of expert bottomers —B.H.Sprague⟩ (2) **:** a company of criminals ⟨a ~ of desperate banditti —Tobias Smollett⟩ ⟨squealed on the other members of the ~⟩ (3) **:** an elementary and close-knit social group of spontaneous origin; *esp* **:** such a unit composed of antisocial adolescents ⟨teenage ~*s*⟩ (4) **:** a group of persons acting in accord who are believed to engage in improper acts or to be influenced by self-seeking, corrupt, or unworthy motives ⟨made captive by the ~ which seized power —A.H. Sulzberger⟩ ⟨denounced the musical ~ then in power —Virgil Thomson⟩ ⟨a political ~ . . . dragged out the racial issue to divert attention from itself —Oscar Handlin⟩ (5) **:** a group of congenial persons having close and informal social relations **:** a group of persons drawn together by a community of tastes, interests, or activity ⟨one of a ~ that call one another great —O.W.Holmes †1935⟩ ⟨invite the ~ plus some pretty girls —Dorothy Bradbury⟩ ⟨where's the ~ going tonight⟩ ⟨the ~ in the office⟩ (6) **:** a flock or herd of animals ⟨a ~ of little chickens —J.H.Stuart⟩ ⟨a ~ of elk⟩

²gang \"\ *vb* -ED/-ING/-S *vt* **1 :** to attack (a person) as a gang ⟨young hoodlums . . . always ~ you —W.R.Burnett⟩ ⟨try to ~ him and take it away from him —*Springfield (Mass.) Union*⟩ **2 a :** to assemble or operate (mechanical or electronic parts) simultaneously as a group ⟨circuits ~*ed* together by gears⟩ **b :** to arrange in or produce as a gang (as type pages or printed sheets) — often used with *up* ~ *vi* **:** to form a group or gang **:** keep company **:** GO, TRAVEL ⟨empty-headed, idle-handed widows who ~ together —Henry Miller⟩ ⟨~*s* with those kids on the next block⟩ — often used with *up* ⟨the boys would ~ up around the corner drugstore⟩

³gang \"\ *vi* [ME *gangen* to go, walk, fr. OE *gangan*; akin to OHG *gangan* to go, ON *ganga*, Goth *gaggan* to go, OE *gang* act of going] *Scot* **:** GO

⁴gang *var of* GANGUE

gan·ga·mop·ter·is \,gaŋgə'mäptərəs\ *n, cap* [NL, fr. Gk *gangamon* small round oyster net + NL *-pteris*] **:** a genus of fossil plants of Permian and Lower Triassic resembling ferns

gan·gava \gan'gavə, gaŋ'-, -'gävə\ *n* -S [NGk *gangaba*, irreg. fr. Gk *gangamon*] **:** a widemouthed dredge for taking sponges from the sea bottom

gangboard \'=,=\ *n* [¹*gang* + *board*] **1 :** a narrow platform extending from the quarterdeck to the forecastle of a deep-waisted ship for use esp. as a passageway **2 :** GANGPLANK

gang days *n pl* [ME *gang dayes*, fr. OE *gangdagas*, fr. *gang* act of going + *dagas*, pl. of *dæg* day] **:** ROGATION DAYS

gange \'ganj\ *vt* -ED/-ING/-S [origin unknown] **:** to protect (the part of a line next a fishhook or the hook itself) by winding with wire

¹gang·er \'gaŋə(r)\ *n* -S [ME, fr. *gangen* to go, walk + *-er*] **1** *Scot* **:** a foot traveler **:** WALKER **2** *dial Brit* **:** a fast horse

²ganger \"\ *n* -S [¹*gang* + *-er*] *Brit* **:** a work gang foreman

gang·er·el \'gaŋ(ə)rəl\ *var of* GANGREL

gan·ges dolphin \'gan(,)jēz-, 'gaan\ *n, usu cap G* [*Ganges*, river of north and northeast India and East Pakistan] **:** SUSU

ganges shark *n, usu cap G* **:** a shark (*Carcharhinus gangeticus*) of southeastern Asia and the East Indies that commonly enters fresh water

gan·get·ic \(')=¦jed·ik\ *adj, usu cap* [L *gangeticus*, fr. Gk *gangētikos*, irreg. fr. *Ganges* Ganges] **:** of or relating to the Ganges

gang-gang \'gaŋ,gaŋ\ *also* **gan·ga** \'gaŋgə\ *or* **gan·gan** \'gaŋ,gaŋ\ *n* -S [native name in Australia] **:** a small cockatoo (*Callocephalon fimbriatum*) of Australia and Tasmania that is largely gray with the male distinguished by a scarlet crest

gang hook *n* [¹*gang* + *hook*] **:** two or three fishhooks with their shanks joined together

¹ganging *pres part of* GANG

²gang·ing \'ganjiŋ, -jən\ *n* -S [fr. gerund of *gange*] **1 :** the special or protected part of a fishline to which the hook is ganged or fastened **:** SNELL **2 :** GANGION

gan·gion \'ganjēən, -jən\ *or* **gang·in** *also* **gang·en** \-jən\ *n* -S [alter. of ²*ganging*] **:** one of the short lengths of moderate-weight line that bear hooks and are attached at regular intervals to the groundline of a setline by beckets of heavy twine

gang·land \'gaŋ,land, 'gaiŋ-, -lənd, -,laa(ə)nd\ *n, often attrib* [¹*gang* + *land*] **:** organized crime **:** the criminal element **:** UNDERWORLD ⟨~ . . . demands that he permit the opening of a gambling joint —Frederic Morton⟩ ⟨gunned down in a typical ~ execution⟩

gangli- *or* **ganglio-** *comb form* [NL, fr. Gk *ganglion*] **:** ganglion ⟨*gangli*ectomy⟩ ⟨*ganglio*plexus⟩

gan·gli·al \'gaŋglēəl, -aiŋ-\ *adj* [*gangli-* + *-al*] **:** of, relating to, or like a ganglion

gan·gli·ar \-ēə(r), -ē,är\ *adj* [*gangli-* + *-ar*] **:** GANGLIAL **:** GANGLIONIC

gan·gli·at·ed \-ē,ād·əd\ *also* **gan·gli·ate** \-,āt, -,ət\ *adj* [*gangliated* fr. *gangli-* + *-ate* + *-ed*; *gangliate* fr. *gangli-* + *-ate*] **:** GANGLIONATED

gangliated cord *n* **:** either of the two main trunks of the sympathetic nervous system, one on each side of the spinal column

gan·gli·form \-lə,fȯrm\ *adj* [ISV *gangli-* + *-form*] **:** having the form of a ganglion

gan·gling \'gaŋgliŋ, -aiŋ-, -lēŋ\ *adj* [perh. irreg. fr. *gangrel*] **:** having a spindling or awkwardly long growth **:** loosely built **:** LANKY ⟨a ~ gawky child . . . whose legs were too long for her skirts —Edna Ferber⟩

gan·gli·o·blast \'gaŋglēō,blast\ *n* [*gangli-* + *-blast*] **:** an embryonic cell that produces gangliocytes

gan·gli·o·cyte \-,sīt\ *n* -S [*gangli-* + *-cyte*] **:** a nerve cell having its body outside the central nervous system — called also *ganglion cell*

gan·gli·o·ma \,gaŋglē'ōmə\ *n, pl* **gangliomas** *or* **ganglio·ma·ta** \-məd·ə\ [NL, fr. *gangli-* + *-oma*] **:** a tumor of a ganglion

gan·gli·on \'gaŋglēən, -aiŋ-\ *n, pl* **gan·glia** \-ēə\ *also* **gan·glions** [LL & Gk; LL, cystic tumor, fr. Gk, cystic tumor, mass of nerve tissue — more at GALL (excrescence)] **1 a :** a small cystic tumor containing viscid fluid and connected either with a joint membrane or tendon sheath esp. about the wrist or ankle **b :** a mass of nerve tissue containing nerve cells: (1) **:** an aggregation of such cells forming an enlargement upon a nerve or upon two or more nerves at their point of junction or separation (2) **:** a mass of gray matter within the brain or spinal cord **:** NUCLEUS — see BASAL GANGLION **2 :** a center or focus esp. of strength or energy ⟨the central ~ of the world's largest . . . chemical empire —J.W.Bellah⟩

gan·gli·on·ary \-ēə,nerē\ *adj* [ISV *ganglion* + *-ary*] **:** GANGLIONIC

gan·gli·on·at·ed \-,nād·əd\ *also* **gan·gli·on·ate** \-,nāt\ *adj* [*ganglionated* fr. (assumed) NL *ganglionatus* (fr. NL *ganglion* — fr. LL & Gk — + L *-atus* -ate) + E *-ed*; *ganglionate* fr. (assumed) NL *ganglionatus*] **:** furnished with ganglia

ganglion cell *n* **:** GANGLIOCYTE

gan·gli·on·ec·to·my \,===='nektəmē\ *n* -ES [ISV *ganglion* + *-ectomy*] **:** surgical removal of a ganglion

gan·glio·neuroma \,gaŋglē(,)ō+\ *n* [NL, fr. *gangli-* + *neuroma*] **:** a neuroma derived from ganglion cells

gan·gli·on·ic \,gaŋglē¦änik, ¦gaiŋ-, -nēk\ *adj* [ISV *ganglion* + *-ic*] **:** of, containing, or affecting ganglia or gangliocytes

gan·gli·on·it·is \,gaŋglēə'nīd·əs\ *n* -ES [NL, fr. *ganglion* + *-itis*] **:** inflammation of a ganglion

gan·gli·o·side \'gaŋglēō,sīd\ *n* -S [ISV *gangli-* + *-oside*] **:** any of a group of glycolipides closely related to the cerebrosides and found mainly in the ganglion cells of the nervous system and in increased amounts in certain lipoidoses

gan·gly \'gaŋglē, -aiŋ-, -li\ *adj, often* -ER/-EST [alter. (influenced by *-y*) of *gangling*] **:** GANGLING, LANKY ⟨a hawk-beaked ~ man —Flora Lewis⟩

gang mill *n* [¹*gang* + *mill*] **1 :** a sawing machine used in lumbering that has a heavy frame supporting numerous saw blades **2 :** a composite milling cutter made up of several cutters set in the same arbor in such relation as to give a cut having some desired profile — **gang milling** *n*

gang net *n* [¹*gang* + *net*] **:** a series of gill nets fastened together and fished as a unit

gan·go·sa \gaŋ'gōsə\ *n* -S [Sp, fem. of *gangoso* that talks through the nose, characterized by nasal resonance, of imit. origin] **:** a destructive ulcerative condition believed to be a manifestation of yaws that usu. originates about the soft palate and spreads into the hard palate, nasal structures, and outward to the face, eroding intervening bone, cartilage, and soft tissues

gangplank \'=,=\ *n* [¹*gang* + *plank*] **:** a long narrow movable platform or bridge used in entering or leaving a ship (as from a wharf) — called also *gangboard*

gangplank

gangplow \'=,=\ *n* [¹*gang* + *plow*] **:** a plow with two or more moldboard or disc bottoms operating together to turn parallel furrows

gang press *n* [¹*gang* + *press*] **:** MULTIPLE-DIE PRESS

¹gang punch *n* [¹*gang* + *punch* (n.)] **:** a device used for gang punching

²gang punch *vt* [¹*gang punch*] **:** to punch (common information) into a number of cards

gang·rel \'gaŋ(ə)rəl\ *n* -S [ME, irreg. fr. *gangen* to go — more at GANG] **1** *chiefly Scot* **a :** VAGABOND, ROVER **b :** TRAMP, VAGRANT **2** *chiefly Scot* **a :** a child just beginning to walk **:** TODDLER **b :** a gangling lanky person

¹gan·grene \'gaŋ,grēn, 'gan,-, 'gaiŋ,-, 'gaan,-, =¦=\ *n* -S [L *gangraena*, fr. Gk *gangraina*; akin to Gk *gran* to gnaw — more at CRESS] **1 :** local death of soft tissues (as from disease, injury, or infection) resulting from loss of blood supply — see DRY GANGRENE, GAS GANGRENE, MOIST GANGRENE, SENILE GANGRENE **2 :** a pervasive, deeply rooted moral, social, or other nonphysical evil that endangers (as moral or social health) ⟨the germs of a moral ~ which will soon . . . bear its fruit —Bela Menczer⟩

²gangrene \"\ *vb* -ED/-ING/-S *vt* **:** to produce gangrene in **:** make gangrenous ~ *vi* **:** to become affected with gangrene **:** become gangrenous ⟨a bullet wound that *gangrened*⟩

gan·gre·nous \'gaŋgrənəs, 'gaiŋ-\ *adj* [prob. fr. F *gangréneux*, fr. MF *gangreneux*, fr. *gangrene* (fr. L *gangraena*) + *-eux* -ous] **:** affected by, characterized by, or likened to gangrene ⟨a ~ foot⟩ ⟨~ stomatitis⟩ ⟨~ septicemia⟩ ⟨a ~ racial problem —G.W.Johnson⟩

gangs *pl of* GANG, *pres 3d sing of* GANG

gang saw *n* **1 :** one of the thin toothed saw blades 6 to 10 inches wide used in a gang mill **2 :** GANG MILL

gang sawyer *n* **:** an operator of a gang saw

gang·ster \'gaŋztə(r), 'gaiŋ-, -ŋ(k)st-\ *n* -S [¹*gang* + *-ster*] **:** a member of a gang of criminals **:** GUNMAN, THUG; *also* **:** a person who uses violence, intimidation, or other extralegal means of coercion for business ends **:** RACKETEER ⟨a ~ . . . in some kind of syndicate that controls stores and nightclubs —Chandler Brossard⟩ ⟨named one ~ as the real boss of the city —*Current Biog.*⟩

gang·ster·ism \-tə,rizəm\ *n* -S **:** the organized use of violence, intimidation, or other extralegal means of coercion for personal or group ends **:** underworld activity ⟨criminal activities suggest ties between politics and ~ —*Americana Annual*⟩

gang switch *n* [¹*gang* + *switch*] **1 :** a set of two or more switches in as many circuits operated simultaneously by a single control **2 :** a number of independent switches side by side and having a common switch plate

gang–there–out \¦=(,)=¦=\ *adj* [³*gang* + *there* + *out*] *archaic Scot* **:** VAGRANT

gangue *also* **gang** \'gaŋ, -anj\ *n* -S [F & G; F *gangue*, fr. G *gang* vein of metal, course, act of going, fr. OHG, act of going — more at GANG] **:** the worthless rock or vein matter in which valuable metals or minerals occur

gang up *vi* [²*gang* + *up*] **1 :** to combine for a specific purpose ⟨sellers *gang up* to raise prices —*Picture Post*⟩ ⟨*ganged up* to kill the bill⟩ **:** attack or oppose someone or something as a group — often used with *on* or *against* ⟨planning to *gang up* on us and push us around —Dorothy C. Fisher⟩ ⟨*ganged up* on him one night and beat him up⟩ ⟨all *ganged up* against each power that in succession became strongest —Elmer Davis⟩ ⟨the whole world *ganged up* against Britain —H.L.Matthews⟩ **2 :** to take sides ⟨gave . . . an impression of *ganging up* with her against me —Nigel Balchin⟩

gan·gwa \'gaŋ(g)wə\ *n* -S [origin unknown] **:** BLIND-YOUR-EYES

gang war *or* **gang warfare** *n* **:** feuding between gangs; *esp* **:** feuding between groups of gangsters

gangway \'=,=\ *n* [¹*gang* + *way*] **1 :** a passage or way into, through, or out of any place **2 a** *archaic* **:** GANGBOARD 1 **b :** either of the sides of the upper deck of a ship between the deckhouse and the rail and the quarterdeck and forecastle **c :** the opening through the bulwarks of a ship by which persons enter or leave it **d :** GANGPLANK **3** *Brit* **:** a passage between rows of seats **:** AISLE ⟨we hear a disturbance at the back of the auditorium and three men in uniform dash down the ~ and leap on to the stage —R.W.Speaight⟩ **4 :** a main level or haulageway in a mine **5 :** JACK LADDER 2a **6 a :** a narrow aisle running crosswise dividing the front benches from the back benches in the British House of Commons **b :** a broad aisle in the British House of Commons and other British Parliamentary buildings that divides the chamber lengthwise with the benches on each side facing each other, those to the right of the speaker for members of the government party and those to the left for the opposition party **7 :** a temporary way of planks **8 :** a clear passage (as through a crowd) ⟨shouted out: "A ~, lads," and they made . . . room for me to go into the center —Arnold Bennett⟩

gang week *n* [¹*gang* + *week*] **:** ROGATION WEEK

gan·is·ter *also* **gan·nis·ter** \'ganəstə(r)\ *n* -S [origin unknown] **1 :** a fine-grained quartzite used in the manufacture of silica brick **2 :** a mixture of ground quartz and fireclay used for lining certain metallurgical furnaces

gan·ja *also* **gan·jah** \'gänjə, 'gan-, -(,)jä, *or* **gun·ja** *or* **gun·jah** \'gənjə, -(,)jä, (,)gən'jä\ *n* -S [Hindi *gāṅjā*, fr. Skt *gṛñja*, *gañjā*] **:** cannabis used esp. in India for smoking — compare BHANG, HASHISH, MARIJUANA

gan·ner \'ganə(r)\ *dial Brit var of* GANDER

gan·net \'ganət, *usu* -əd·+V\ *n, pl* **gannets** *also* **gannet** [ME *ganet*, fr. OE *ganot*; akin to OHG *ganazzo* gander, OE *gōs* goose — more at GOOSE] **1 :** any of several large web-footed fish-eating seabirds constituting a family (Sulidae), flying great distances and remaining at sea for long periods, and breeding in large colonies chiefly on offshore islands **2 :** WOOD IBIS

gan·net·ry \-ətrē\ *n* -ES **:** a breeding colony of gannets; *also* **:** the place of such colony whether birds are in residence or not

gan·o·ceph·a·la \,ganō'sefələ\ *n pl, cap* [NL, fr. *gano-* (fr. Gk *ganos* brightness, joy) + *-cephala*; fr. the brightness of the bony plates; akin to Gk *gēthein* to rejoice — more at JOY] *in some classifications* **:** a group of labyrinthodonts including *Archegosaurus* and related genera having the head armored with bony plates — **gan·o·ceph·a·lan** \¦=¦=¦==lən\ *adj or n* — **gan·o·ceph·a·lous** \-ləs\ *adj*

gan·o·der·ma \,ganō'dərmə\ *n, cap* [NL, fr. *gano-* + *-derma*] *in some classifications* **:** a genus of bracket fungi (family Polyporaceae) that are often included in the genus *Fomes* but when separated are distinguished on the basis of having double-walled spores with one end truncated and with a spiny brownish endospore

¹gan·o·dont \'ganə,dänt\ *adj* [NL *Ganodonta*] **:** of or relating to the Taeniodonta

²ganodont \"\ *n* -S [NL *Ganodonta*] **:** TAENIODONT

gan·o·don·ta \,ganə'däntə\ [NL, fr. *gan-* (fr. Gk *ganos*) + *-odonta*] *syn of* TAENIODONTA

gan·o·dus \'ganədəs\ *n, cap* [NL, fr. *gan-* + *-odus*] **:** a genus of Jurassic chimaeroid fishes

¹gan·oid \'ga,nȯid\ *adj* [NL *Ganoidei*] **:** of or relating to the Ganoidei **:** having ganoid scales

²ganoid \"\ *n* -S [NL *Ganoidei*] **:** a ganoid fish; *broadly* **:** a primitive-looking fish having thick, shiny, though not necessarily ganoid scales — **ga·noi·dal** \(')ga¦nȯid°l, gə'n-\ *adj* — **ga·noi·de·an** \-ēən\ *adj or n* — **ga·noi·dan** \-dēən\ *adj or n*

ga·noi·dei \ga'nȯidē,ī, gə'-\ *n pl, cap* [NL, fr. *gan-* + *-oidei*] *in some classifications* **:** a subclass or other division of Teleostomi containing numerous extinct fishes and the living sturgeons, paddlefishes, gars (order Ginglymodi), and bowfin and having at least in the living forms a conus arteriosus, a spiral valve in the intestine, and an optic chiasma

ganoid scale *n* **:** a scale typical of the Ganoidei and found in a few other fishes that is composed of an inner layer of bone and an outer layer of ganoin

gan·o·in *or* **gan·o·ine** \'ganəwən\ *n* -S [ISV *gano-* (fr. *ganoid*) + *-in*, *-ine*] **:** the covering of a ganoid scale composed of a shining material that resembles enamel

ga·nom·a·lite \gə'nämə,līt\ *n* -S [Sw *ganomalit*, fr. Gk *ganōma* brightness (fr. *ganos*) + Sw *-lit* -lite] **:** a mineral $Ca_2Pb_3Si_3O_{11}$ consisting of a colorless to gray silicate of lead and calcium in tetragonal crystals or massive

gan·o·phyl·lite \,ganə'fi,līt\ *n* -S [Sw *ganophyllit*, fr. *gano-* (fr. Gk *ganos*) + *phyll-* + *-it* -ite] **:** a mineral consisting of a brown hydrous silicate of manganese and aluminum in prismatic crystals or foliated

ga·no·sis \gə'nōsəs\ *n, pl* **gano·ses** \-ō,sēz\ [Gk *ganōsis* action of polishing, fr. *ganoun* to polish, fr. *ganos* brightness] **:** a process of toning down the glare of marble esp. on nude parts as practiced by sculptors in classical antiquity

gan·sel \'gan(t)səl\ *n* -S [ME (Sc) *gansell*, fr. ME, garlic sauce, fr. MF *ganse aillie*] *Scot* **:** a sharp remark or rebuke

gan·ser syndrome \'gänz|ə(r)-, 'ganz|, 'gan(t)s|\ *n, usu cap G* [after Sigbert *Ganser* †1931 Ger. psychiatrist] **:** a pattern of psychopathological behavior (as verbal) characterized by the giving of approximate answers (as 2x2 = about 5) and found in prisoners and in others who consciously or unconsciously seek to give misleading information regarding their mental state

gan·sey \'ganzi\ *n* -s [irreg. fr. *Guernsey*, one of the Channel islands] *dial Brit* : a knitted jacket or sweater : JERSEY

gansh *var of* GANCH

1**gant** \'gant, -á-,-ō-\ *vi* -ED/-ING/-S [ME (Sc) *ganten;* perh. akin to OE *gānian* to gape, yawn, L *hiare* — more at YAWN] *chiefly Scot* : YAWN

2**gant** \"\ *n* -s [ME (Sc) *gant*, fr. *ganten*] *chiefly Scot* : YAWN

3**gant** \'gant\ *dial var of* GAUNT

4**gant** \"\ *vt* -ED/-ING/-S *dial* : to make thin or lean by insufficient feeding ⟨I rode two nights and ~*ed* a mule looking for a place to sleep —Alan LeMay⟩ — often used with *up*

gan·te·lope \'gant³l,ōp\ *or* **gant·lope** \-t,lōp\ *n* -s [modif. of Sw *gatlopp*, fr. OSw *gatulop*, fr. *gata* road, lane + *lop* course, run, fr. MLG *lōp;* akin to ON *gata* road, lane and to ON *hlaup* leap — more at GATE, LOPE] *archaic* : GAUNTLET

1**gantlet** *var of* GAUNTLET

2**gant·let** \'gȯntlət, 'gän-,'gán-, *usu* -ȯd·+V\ *n* -s [2*gauntlet*] : a stretch of railroad track (as over a bridge or in a narrow pass) where two lines of track overlap so that one rail of each track is within the rails of the other in order to obviate switching

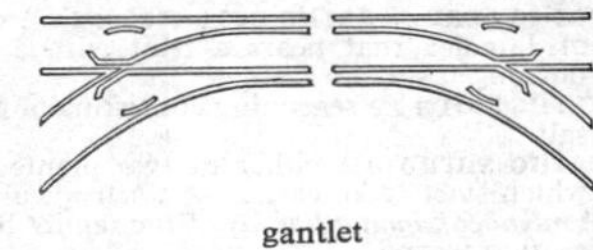
gantlet

3**gantlet** \"\ *vt* -ED/-ING/-S : to run together (railroad tracks) so as to make a gantlet

gant·line \'gant,lin\ *n* [perh. alter. of *girtline*] : a line rove through a block (as at the end of a bowsprit) for hoisting rigging or hanging clothing — called also *girtline*

Gan·tri·sin \'gan·trəsən\ *trademark* — used for sulfisoxazole

gan·try *also* **gan·tree** \'gan·trē, -ri\ *n, pl* **gantries** *also* **gantrees** *sometimes sing in constr* [perh. modif. of ONF *gantier*, fr. L *cantherius* trellis, rafter, gelding, prob. of non-IE origin; akin to the source of Gk *kanthēlios* pack ass] **1 :** a frame used for supporting barrels (as in a cellar) or for rolling barrels to a higher level **2 :** a frame structure raised on side supports so as to span over or around something and usu. of large dimensions: as **a :** a bridge or platform carrying a traveling crane or winch and supported by a pair of towers or by trestles or side frames running on parallel tracks **b :** a structure supporting a number of railroad signals for several tracks

gantry crane *n* : a bridge crane in which the beam or bridge is carried at each end by a trestle that travels on tracks on the ground

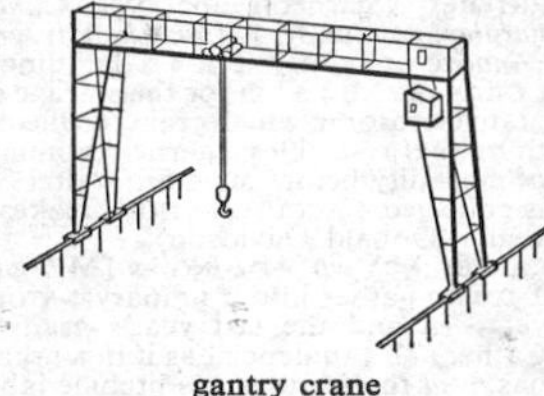
gantry crane

gan·y·mede \'ganə,mēd\ *n* -s *usu cap* [L *Ganymedes*, cupbearer of the gods, fr. Gk *Ganymēdēs*] : a youth who serves liquors : CUPBEARER

gaol \'jāl, *esp before pause or consonant* -āəl\ *chiefly Brit var of* JAIL

ga·on \'gä,ōn, ='=\ *n, pl* **ge·o·nim** \gä'ōnəm, ,gäō'nēm\ *also* **gaons** *often cap* [Heb *gā'ōn* majesty, excellence (pl. *gĕ'ōnīm*)] **1 :** a Jewish head of one of the Babylonian academies at Sura and Pumbedita from about A.D. 589–1038 and usu. an eminent religious scholar and judicial authority — used as a title of honor; compare EXILARCH **2 :** an outstanding intellectual and Talmudic scholar ⟨the celebrated 18th century ~ of Vilna⟩

ga·on·ate \-ō,nāt\ *n* -s *often cap* : the office of gaon

gaonic *often cap, var of* GEONIC

1**gap** \'gap\ *n* -s [ME *gap, gappe*, fr. ON *gap* chasm, hole; akin to ON *gapa* to gape — more at GAPE] **1 a :** a break in a barrier (as a wall or hedge); *specif* : a breach in a line of military defense ⟨a ~ appeared in the front ranks of the Macedonian army —Tom Wintringham⟩ **b :** an assailable position : VULNERABILITY ⟨a fatal ~ in our security structure —H.S.Truman⟩ **2 :** a small cleft or notch ⟨a pipe wedged between a ~ in his teeth —Judson Philips⟩ **3 a :** a notch in the crest of a ridge : mountain pass : COL ⟨US 64 enters a ~ in Crowley's Ridge and passes between the rolling slopes —*Amer. Guide Series: Ark.*⟩ **b :** a gorge cutting through a ridge : RAVINE — compare WATER GAP, WIND GAP **c** *archaic* : a hole in the ground : CHASM ⟨great holes and ~s had worn into the soil —Charles Dickens⟩ **d :** a break in a levee through which a distributary stream may flow : tidal inlet ⟨the tide . . . flows in and out through ~s —V.C.Finch & G.T.Trewartha⟩ **e :** a steep-sided furrow that cuts transversely across a ridge in the ocean bottom **4 a :** a separation in space : an intervening distance: as (1) : the shortest distance between the planes of the chords of the upper and lower wings of a biplane (2) : SPARK GAP **b :** a place from which something is missing ⟨into the ~ left by mobilized men have come women —A.R. Williams⟩ **5 :** a break in continuity : INTERVAL, HIATUS ⟨intervening ~ of over thirty years —Osbert Sitwell⟩ **6 :** a break in the vascular cylinder of a plant where a vascular trace departs from the central cylinder — see BRANCH GAP, LEAF GAP **7 a :** a wide difference in character or attitude ⟨~ between generations⟩ **b :** a wide difference in condition or quality ⟨~ between rich and poor⟩ **8 :** a lack of balance between exports and imports : DOLLAR GAP ⟨half the ~ in the trade balance represented machinery —Harry Gilroy⟩ **syn** see BREAK

2**gap** \"\ *vb* **gapped; gapped; gapping; gaps** *vt* **1 :** to make jagged : NOTCH **2 :** to make an opening in : BREACH — usu. used in past tense ⟨the magnificent row of houses was *gapped* in two places where bombs had fallen —C.D.Lewis⟩ **3 :** to adjust the space between the electrodes of (a spark plug) ~ *vi* **1 :** to become notched or jagged ⟨steel *gapped* and lost its edge —*Reader*⟩ **2 :** to become separated ⟨do not let the collar . . . ~ away from the neck —*N.Y. Herald Tribune*⟩ ⟨causing his . . . shirt to ~ open —Calvin Kentfield⟩

3**gap** \"\ *dial var of* GAPE

1**gape** \'gāp *sometimes* 'gap *or* 'gaa(ə)p\ *vb* -ED/-ING/-S [ME *gapen*, fr. ON *gapa;* akin to OE *ofergapian* to neglect, MD *gapen* to gape, MHG *gaffen* to stare with open mouth, OHG *geffida* observation, L *hiare* to gape, yawn — more at YAWN] *vi* **1 a :** to open the mouth wide esp. with intent to bite or swallow ⟨baby birds ~ until they are fed⟩ **b :** to open like a mouth : spread apart along an edge or make a cavity ⟨the shell of a clam ~*s*⟩ ⟨holes ~ in pavements after floods⟩ **2 a :** to stare openmouthed in surprise or admiration — usu. used with *at* ⟨the men *gaped* at me in utter amazement —R.H. Davis⟩ ⟨~*s* round-eyed at the astonishing world —Rose Macaulay⟩ **b :** to stare with the mouth open vacantly as if not comprehending ⟨*gaped* vaguely at the skylight —Dorothy Sayers⟩ ⟨depicts man lost and blindly *gaping* amidst the chaos —Rhys Gwyn⟩ **3** *archaic* **a :** to yearn esp. for something of questionable value — usu. used with *after* or *for* ⟨~ after new spiritual incarnations —J.C.Hare⟩ **b :** to want earnestly to do something : CRAVE — used with infinitive ⟨*gaping* with mouths wide open to have their curiosity satisfied —*Sporting Mag.*⟩ **4 :** to draw a deep involuntary breath with the mouth open esp. as a result of fatigue or boredom : YAWN ⟨a dull lecture makes the students ~⟩ **5** *archaic* : SHOUT, BELLOW ⟨you'll leave your noise anon . . . ye rude slaves leave your *gaping* — Shak.⟩ ~ *vt* : to make an opening in ⟨a fearful battlefield, the earth of it *gaped* open by shells and bombs —Ira Wolfert⟩ **syn** see GAZE

2**gape** \"\ *n* -s **1 :** an act of gaping: **a :** YAWN **b :** an openmouthed stare **c** *archaic* : an eager search after : QUEST ⟨a perpetual ~ after knowledge —Joseph Addison⟩ **2 :** an unfilled space or extent : VACUUM ⟨the huge attentive ~ of emptiness —Thomas Wolfe⟩ **3 a :** the median margin-to-margin length of the open mouth **b :** the line along which the mandibles of a bird close **c :** an opening at the edge of a mollusk shell when the valves are shut **d :** the width of an opening that resembles a mouth ⟨gyratory crushers having a ~ suitable for the coarsest crushing —A.M.Gaudin⟩ **e :** the distance between the barb and shank on a fishhook **4 gapes** *pl but sing in constr* **a :** a disease of young chickens, turkeys, and other birds in which nematode worms (*Syngamus trachea*) invade and irritate the trachea causing coughing and labored breathing often with the neck extended and the beak open ⟨~*s* is a common disease of chicks aged three to eight weeks —W.P.Blount⟩ — see GAPEWORM **b :** a fit of yawning — used with *the* ⟨as the lecture dragged on, he got the ~*s*⟩

gap·er \-pə(r)\ *n* -s **1 :** one that gapes ⟨made herself the center of a crowd of ~*s* —Arnold Bennett⟩ **2 :** any of several comparatively large sluggish burrowing clams (family Myacidae) having a shell that flares out at each end including several excellent food clams

gapeseed \'=,=\ *n* **1** *dial Brit* : something that causes gaping looks **2** *dial Brit* : a person who looks or stares gapingly

gapeworm \'=,=\ *n* : a strongyloid nematode worm (*Syngamus trachea* or *S. trachealis*) that infests the trachea and bronchi of birds and causes gapes

gap-framepress *n* : a punch press with an opening in the front of the frame at a level with the bed to permit the insertion of wide work or the feeding of strip stock across the bed from one side to the other

gaping *adj* [fr. pres. part. of 1*gape*] **1 :** wide open ⟨~ wounds⟩ ⟨a ~ gravel pit⟩ **2 :** exhibiting desire, wonder, or vacuity : AGAPE ⟨with their ~ eyes and their sweet words —J.M. Synge⟩ **3 :** of broad extent : GREAT, IMPORTANT ⟨~ omissions⟩ — **gap·ing·ly** *adv*

gapped *past of* GAP

gapped scale *n* [*gapped* past part. of 2*gap*] : an incomplete musical scale; *specif* : a scale established or patterned on the omission of certain notes or tones from a complete tonal series

gap·per \'gapə(r\ *n* -s *Brit* : a machine for thinning sugar beets or other crops by cutting gaps in the row

gapping *pres part of* GAP

gap·py \'gapē, -pi\ *adj, often* -ER/-EST [1*gap* + -*y*] : having gaps : BROKEN, UNCONNECTED ⟨a ~ hedge⟩ ⟨a ~ history⟩

gaps *pl of* GAP, *pres 3d sing of* GAP

gap-toothed \'=;=\ *adj* : having gaps between the teeth

1**gar** \'gär\ *vt* **garred; garred; garring; gars** [ME *geren, garen*, fr. ON *gera, gōra, gōrva* to prepare, make, do; akin to OE *gierwan* to prepare, OHG *garawen;* causative-denominative fr. the root of OE *gearu, gearo* ready — more at YARE] *now chiefly Scot* : to make (a person) do something : COMPEL, FORCE ⟨good manners ~*s* us keep the Sabbath inviolate — William Black⟩

2**gar** \'gär, 'gà(r\ *interj* [euphemistic alter. of *God*] — a mild oath

3**gar** \"\ *n* -s [short for *garfish*] : any of various fishes that have an elongate body resembling that of a pike and long and narrow jaws: as **a :** NEEDLEFISH **b :** any of various halfbeaks of Australia and New Zealand **c :** any of several freshwater ganoid fishes forming an order Ginglymodi and family Lepisosteidae, having hard shining rhombic scales and flesh that is rank and tough, and being destructive of other fishes — see ALLIGATOR GAR, LONGNOSE GAR, SHORTNOSE GAR

gar *abbr* garage

gar·ad pod \'garəd-\ *n* [Ar *qaraḍ*] : the pod of babul

1**ga·rage** \gə'räzh, -räj, |j, *chiefly Brit* 'ga,räzh *sometimes* 'garij\ *n* -s [F, garage, act of docking (a ship), act of sidetracking, fr. *garer* to dock, sidetrack, move out of the way (fr. MF, to dock) + -*age;* MF *garer* of Gmc origin; akin to OHG *biwarōn* to keep, protect — more at WARE] **1 :** a building or compartment of a building used for housing an automotive vehicle **2 :** a repair shop for automotive vehicles **3 :** a siding in a canal

2**garage** \"\ *vt* -ED/-ING/-S : to keep or put in a garage ⟨automobile owners are advised to ~ their cars at night to preserve the finish —*Science News Letter*⟩

ga·rage·man \-,man, -,maa(ə)n\ *n, pl* **garagemen** : a worker in a garage

garage-porch \='=;=\ *n* : CARPORT

gar·a·man·tes \,garə'man(,)tēz\ *n pl, usu cap* [L, fr. Gk] : an ancient Hamitic people of the eastern Sahara region from the time of Herodotus into the Roman period

ga·ram·bu·lla \,gäram'bü(y)ə\ *or* **ga·ram·bu·llo** \-ü(,)(y)ō\ *n* -s [MexSp *garambullo*, perh. alter. of Sp *carambolo* carambola (tree), fr. *carambola* carambola (fruit), fr. Marathi *karambal*] **1 :** an arborescent cactus (*Myrtillocactus geometrizans*) of western Mexico that bears a small oblong edible berry **2 :** the fruit of the garambulla

gar·an·cine \'garən;sēn\ *n* -s [F, fr. *garance* madder (fr. OF) + -*ine;* OF *garance*, of Gmc origin; akin to OHG *rezza* madder] : a dye or pigment made by treating ground madder with sulfuric acid

garand *or* **garand rifle** \gə'rand-, -'raa(ə)nd-, 'garənd-\ *n* -s *usu cap G* [after John C. *Garand* b1888 Am. inventor who designed it] : M-1 — see RIFLE illustration

ga·ra·pa·ta \,garə'päd·ə\ *also* **ga·ra·pa·to** \-d·(,)ō\ *n* -s [Sp *garrapata*] : TICK; *esp* : the spiny ear tick — compare CARRAPATO

gar·a·vance \'garə,van(t)s\ *also* **car·a·vance** \'ka-\ *or* **cal·a·vance** \'kalə-\ *n* -s [modif. of Sp *garbanzo*] : CHICK-PEA

gar·a·wi \'garə(,)wē\ *n, pl* **garawi** [EgyptAr *garwi* white poppy, small colocynth] : SUDAN GRASS

1**garb** \'gärb, 'gàb\ *n* -s [ONF *garbe*, of Gmc origin; akin to OHG *garba* sheaf; akin to Skt *gṛbhnāti, gṛhṇāti* he seizes — more at GRAB] *heraldry* : a sheaf of grain (as wheat)

2**garb** \"\ *n* -s [MF or OIt; MF *garbe* graceful outline, contour, grace, fr. OIt *garbo* grace, perh. modif. of Ar *qālab* mold, model] **1** *obs* : stylishness in looks or bearing : ELEGANCE ⟨ladies and gentlemen that are of any ~ —Richard Lassels⟩ **2 :** prevailing mode : STYLE ⟨could not speak English in the native ~ —Shak.⟩ **3** *obs* : manner of behavior : CONDUCT ⟨this sullen ~, this moody discontent —Nicholas Rowe⟩ **4 a :** style of apparel : COSTUME ⟨in formal ~, a tail coat with silk binding . . . gray spats and shiny patent leather shoes — W.A.White⟩ **b :** style of expression : outward form ⟨give their lie the further appearance of truth and their madness the outward ~ of sanity —Lewis Mumford⟩

3**garb** \"\ *vt* -ED/-ING/-S **1 :** to cover with clothing : DRESS ⟨~*ed* themselves in cowboy outfits —*Savings Banker*⟩ **2 :** to cover as if with clothing : INVEST ⟨~*ed* each one of them with . . . individual dignity —R.G.Swing⟩

1**gar·bage** \'gärbij, 'gàb-, -bēj\ *n* -s *often attrib* [ME] **1** *archaic* : the internal parts of an animal : VISCERA ⟨in Newfoundland they improve their ground with the ~ of fish —John Mortimer⟩ **2** *archaic* : a sheaf esp. of grain : FAGOT, BUNDLE ⟨all such horses . . . to be substantially served . . . in hay, ~, and litter — *Household Ordinances*⟩ **3 a :** refuse of any kind : WASTE ⟨an infinite variety of industrial ~ and poisons —K.S.Dixon⟩ **b :** refuse resulting from the preparation, cooking, and dispensing of food : SCRAPS ⟨scrape the plates and take out the ~⟩ **4 :** worthless or objectionable matter put into writing or speech : TRASH ⟨one publisher's idea of a fine book may be a competitor's idea of ~ —Bennett Cerf⟩ **5 :** a card game in which each player is dealt five cards which he plays in a series of different games **syn** see REFUSE

2**garbage** \"\ *vb* -ED/-ING/-S *vt, obs* : to remove the entrails from : EVISCERATE ⟨a turkey cock that when he was pulled and *garbaged* weighed thirty pounds —John Josselyn⟩ ~ *vi* : to feed on or as if on garbage : SCAVENGE ⟨the finest diet won't stop a dog from *garbaging* —B.J.Rowles⟩

garbage tankage *n* : a fertilizer material made by rendering, drying, and grinding garbage

garbage worm *n* : TRICHINA

gar·ban·zo \gär'ban(,)zō\ *also* **gar·ban·za** \-nzə\ *or* **gar·van·zo** \-'van(,)zō\ *n* -s [Sp *garbanzo*, alter. (prob. influenced by OSp *garroba* carob, fr. Ar *kharrūbah*) of OSp *arvanço*, perh. of Gmc origin; akin to OHG *araweiz* pea — more at ERS] : CHICK-PEA

garbill \'=,=\ *n* [3*gar* + *bill*] : RED-BREASTED MERGANSER

1**gar·ble** \'gärbəl, 'gàb-\ *vt* **garbled; garbled; garbling** \-b(ə)liŋ, -lēŋ\ **garbles** [ME *garbelen*, fr. OIt *garbellare* to sift, fr. Ar *gharbala* to sift, *ghirbāl* sieve, fr. LL *cribellum* small sieve — more at CRIBELLUM] **1** *archaic* : to sort or pick out : select the best parts of : CULL **2 :** to remove dross or dirt from : REFINE; *specif* : to sift impurities from (as spices) ⟨*garbled* Tellicherry pepper . . . sells for ¼¢ a pound above the ungarbled —F.P.Tucker⟩ **3 a :** to make misleading selections from : deliberately pervert : DISTORT ⟨their disputes on the merits of these arguments have not been edifying, since both sides have been apt to ~ the question —Gilbert Ryle⟩ **b :** to mix up through accident or ignorance : MUTILATE, DISARRANGE, JUMBLE ⟨statements . . . *garbled* into absurdity when copied into the newspapers —Havelock Ellis⟩; *specif* : to introduce textual error into (a message) by inaccurate enciphering, transmitting, or receiving

2**garble** \"\ *n* -s **1 :** worthless material : WASTE; *specif* : the impurities removed from spices **2** *archaic* : ALLOY **3 :** an act or instance of garbling; *specif* : an error in the encipherment, transmission, or reception of a message ⟨there is a ~ in "8" and the following telegram corrects the ~ —*N.Y.Times*⟩

gar·ble·able \-bələbəl\ *adj, archaic* : that can be or is likely to be garbled ⟨all sorts of wares or merchandise ~, as sugar, pepper, cloves —William Leybourn⟩

gar·bler \-b(ə)lə(r)\ *n* -s : one that garbles; *specif* : one that sifts spices

garb·less \-bləs\ *adj* : being without garb

garble table *n* : PERMUTATION TABLE

gar·bling \-b(ə)liŋ, -lēŋ\ *n* -s [ME *garbeling*, fr. *garbelen* + -*ing*] **1** *archaic* **a :** the act or process of sorting out the best part : CULLING; *specif* : the sifting of spices **b :** the refuse produced by culling — usu. used in pl. **2 :** an act or instance of distortion : GARBLE ⟨a wholesale ~ of titles and proper names —J.H.Buckley⟩

gar·board \'gär,bō(ə)rd\ *or* **garboard strake** *n* [obs. D *gaarboord*, fr. obs. D *gaar-* (perh. fr. D *garen* to gather, fr. MD, contr. of *gaderen*) + D *boord* board, ship's side; akin to OE *gaderian* to gather and to OE *bord* board, ship's side — more at GATHER, BOARD] : the plank or planking in a wooden ship and the plate or plating in a steel ship lying next to the keel — see SHIP illustration

gar·boil \'gär,bȯil\ *n* -s [MF *garbouil*, fr. OIt *garbuglio*] *archaic* : a state of disturbance : TURMOIL

gar·bure \(')gär¦byu̇(ə)r\ *n* -s [F, fr. Prov *garburo*] : a thick soup of bacon and cabbage or other vegetables usu. with cheese and stale bread added

gar·butt rod *also* **gar·bet rod** \'gärbət-\ *n* [perh. fr. the name *Garbet*] : a rod attached to the cage of a standing valve of an oil-well pump in such a way that the standing valve is lifted out of the well when the plunger is withdrawn

garb willow *n* : WEEPING WILLOW

gar·cin·ia \gär'sinēə\ *n* [NL, fr. Laurent *Garcin* †1751 Fr. botanist + NL -*ia*] **1** *cap* : a large genus of tropical Asiatic trees (family Guttiferae) having thick coriaceous leaves and baccate fruit with arilled seed — see GAMBOGE, KOKUM BUTTER, MANGOSTEEN **2** -s : any tree of the genus *Garcinia*

gar·çon \(')gär¦sōⁿ, *F* gȧrsōⁿ\ *n, pl* **garçons** \-ōⁿ(z)\ [F, boy, servant, fr. OF, boy, menial, knave, prob. of Gmc origin; akin to OHG *reccho, reckio* banished man — more at WRETCH] : a serving man; *esp* : a waiter in a French restaurant

gardant *var of* GUARDANT

garde·bras \,gärdə¦brä\ *n, pl* **gardebras** \-rä(z)\ [alter. (influenced by MF *garde-bras*) of MF *garbrasse*, modif. of MF *garde-bras*, fr. *garder* to guard + *bras* arm, fr. L *brachium* — more at GUARD, BRACE] : a piece of armor to protect the arm

garde-collet \,gärdə(,)kō¦lā\ *n* [F, fr. *garder* to guard + *collet* collar — more at COLLET] : a raised plate or ridge on the shoulder piece of armor to protect the neck

gar·deen \(')gär¦dēn\ *dial var of* GUARDIAN

garde-manger \,gärd(ə),mäⁿ'zhā\ *n* -s [F, fr. OF *garde-mangier* official in charge of the kitchen in a royal household, fr. *garder* to guard + *mangier* food — more at BLANCMANGE] **1 :** a cook who specializes in the preparation of cold meat dishes **2 :** a refrigerated pantry unit where cold dishes are prepared

1**gar·den** \'gärdᵊn, 'gàd-\ *n* -s [ME *gardin*, fr. ONF, fr. *gart* garden, of Gmc origin; akin to OHG *gart* enclosure — more at YARD] **1 a :** a plot of cultivated ground adjacent to a dwelling and usu. devoted in whole or in part to the growing of herbs, fruits, flowers, or vegetables for household use — compare KITCHEN GARDEN, YARD **b** (1) : a tract of land devoted to the raising of crops ⟨the date ~*s* extend for over 150 miles —*Statesman's Yr. Bk.*⟩ (2) *dial Brit* : a usu. small field in which a crop is grown ⟨potato ~⟩ (3) : a natural grove ⟨vast ~*s* of wild oranges⟩ (4) : an area devoted to the raising of animals ⟨underseas ~*s* in which the oysters are planted —*Amer. Guide Series: Conn.*⟩ **c :** something that resembles a garden ⟨coral ~*s* that delight the imagination —J.A.Michener⟩ ⟨~ of memories —Van Wyck Brooks⟩ **d :** a rich well-cultivated region ⟨a semitropical ~ of sugarcane, pineapples, and sunshine —*N.Y.Herald Tribune*⟩ **2 a :** a public recreation area or park ⟨[the] usually staid Public Garden assumes an air of gaiety as the annual Festival of Arts takes up its stand —C.M.Barss⟩; *specif* : an open-air establishment furnished with tables and chairs and serving refreshments — see BEER GARDEN, TEA GARDEN **b :** a large hall for an indoor athletic contest (as basketball, hockey, racing, boxing), a spectacular show (as of horses, motorboats, flowers), or a circus ⟨coliseums, ~*s*, and convention halls are springing up everywhere —E.M.Smith⟩ **3** *slang* : the outfield of a baseball diamond

2**garden** \"\ *vb* **gardened; gardened; gardening** \-d(ᵊ)niŋ\ **gardens** *vi* **1 :** to lay out or work in a garden : practice horticulture ⟨bought a house in the country so he could ~⟩ **2 :** to attempt to level an uneven spot on a cricket wicket by patting it with one's bat ~ *vt* **1 :** to make into a garden : bring under cultivation ⟨the long landscape . . . ~*ed* into more perfect beauty —Bayard Taylor⟩ **2 :** to ornament with gardens ⟨a ~*ed* esplanade —*Amer. Guide Series: N.C.*⟩

3**garden** \"\ *adj* **1 a :** of or relating to a garden ⟨~ gate⟩ **b :** used in or frequenting the garden ⟨~ hose⟩ ⟨~ toad⟩ **2 a :** of a kind that is grown in the garden esp. as distinguished from a more delicate hothouse variety ⟨~ chrysanthemum⟩ **b :** of a familiar kind : COMMONPLACE ⟨domestic shorthairs as the ~ variety of cat is technically known to fanciers —*Nat'l Geographic*⟩ **3 :** having a garden ⟨~ community⟩

gar·den·age \-ᵊnij\ *n* -s **1** *archaic* : HORTICULTURE **2** *archaic* : garden produce

garden apartment *n* **1 :** a ground floor apartment whose rental includes the use of a garden **2 :** an apartment building enclosing a gardened court for the use of the tenants

garden bagworm *n* : a European bagworm (*Apterona crenulella*) with a case resembling a snail shell that is now established in the western U.S. and is apparently parthenogenetic as no males are known

garden balm *n* : LEMON BALM

garden balsam *n* : a plant (*Impatiens balsamina*) having a more or less pubescent stem, lanceolate sharply serrate leaves tapering to a short petiole, and flowers borne in the axils of the leaves and varying in color from white to purple and rose — called also *balsam, balsamine*

garden bond *n* : a pattern of bricklaying in which each course usu. consists of three stretchers followed by a header

garden burnet *n* : SALAD BURNET

garden buttercup *n* : a commonly cultivated European crowfoot (*Ranunculus aconitifolius*) with white or yellow often double flowers

garden catchfly *n* : LOBEL'S CATCHFLY

garden celandine *n* : CELANDINE 1

garden centipede *n* : a minute symphilid (*Scutigerella immaculata*) that often infests the underground parts of truck and greenhouse crops — called also *garden symphilid*

garden chafer *n* : a European beetle (*Phyllopertha horticola*) that resembles a scarab and feeds on the blossoms and leaves of fruit trees and rosebushes

garden city *n, sometimes cap G&C* : a real-estate movement originating in England about 1875 and advocating the development of planned residential communities with park and planted areas

garden columbine *n* : a commonly cultivated Eurasian herb (*Aquilegia vulgaris*) with spurred blue and purple flowers

garden cress *also* **garden pepper cress** *n* : an Asiatic annual herb (*Lepidium sativum*) that is sometimes cultivated for its pungent basal leaves and that has small whitish flowers followed by round flattened pods

garden currant *n* **:** a European red currant (*Ribes sativum*) with greenish yellow flowers in drooping racemes

garden egg *n* **:** EGGPLANT

gar·den·er \'gärd(ᵊ)nər, 'gȧd(ᵊ)nə(r\ *n* -S [ME *gardiner*, prob. fr. ONF *gardinier*, fr. *gardin* garden + *-ier* (fr. L *-arius* -ary)] **1 :** one that gardens; *specif* **:** one employed to care for the gardens or grounds about a home, business concern, or other property **2** *slang* **:** a baseball outfielder

gardener bird *n* **:** any of several small plainly colored bowerbirds (genus *Amblyornis*) of New Guinea that make a garden of moss ornamented with flowers in front of the bower

gardener's–delight \'≈(≈)≈≈,≈\ *n, pl* **gardener's–delights :** MULLEIN PINK

gardener's–garters \'≈(≈)≈,≈\ *n pl but sing or pl in constr* **:** RIBBON GRASS

gar·den·esque \,gärdᵊn¦esk\ *adj* **:** of, relating to, or resembling a garden ⟨~ lily⟩ ⟨~ factory grounds⟩

garden flea *n* **:** FLEA BEETLE

garden fleahopper *n* **:** a widely distributed black fleahopper (*Halticus bracteatus*) that sometimes feeds destructively on the foliage of various cultivated plants causing white spots and when abundant the death of infested foliage

garden–fresh \¦≈≈¦≈\ *adj* **1 :** being picked or dug extremely recently ⟨*garden-fresh* fruit⟩ ⟨*garden-fresh* vegetables⟩ **2 :** consisting of garden-fresh produce ⟨a *garden-fresh* salad⟩ **:** having the desirable taste or quality of garden-fresh produce ⟨*garden-fresh* cottage cheese⟩

gar·den·ful \'gärdᵊn,fu̇l\ *n* -S **:** a quantity sufficient to fill a garden ⟨~ of roses⟩

garden–gate \¦≈≈¦≈\ *n* **1** *dial Eng* **:** HEARTSEASE 2a(1) **2** *dial Eng* **:** HERB ROBERT

garden heliotrope *n* **1 :** a tall perennial rhizomatous herb (*Valeriana officinalis*) that is native to Europe and northern Asia but widely naturalized as an escape and has very fragrant tiny white, pinkish, lavender, or sometimes red flowers in large paniculate corymbs and roots and rhizomes which yield the drug valerian — called also *valerian* **2 :** a shrubby Peruvian heliotrope (*Heliotropium arborescens*) widely cultivated in mild regions for its very fragrant usu. lilac or violet flowers — called also *common heliotrope*

garden house *n* **1 :** a small usu. open structure providing shelter in a garden **2** *chiefly South & Midland* **:** PRIVY

garden huckleberry *n* **1 :** BLACK NIGHTSHADE **2 :** the fruit of black nightshade

gar·de·nia \gär'dēnyə, gȧ'-, -nēə\ *n* [NL, fr. Alexander *Garden* †1791 Scot. naturalist + NL *-ia*] **1** *cap* **:** a large genus of Old World tropical trees and shrubs (family Rubiaceae) having showy fragrant white or yellow flowers **2** -S **:** any plant or flower of the genus *Gardenia; esp* **:** CAPE JASMINE

gardening *n* -S [fr. gerund of ²*garden*] **:** the laying out or care of gardens

gar·den·ize \'gärdᵊn,īz\ *vb* -ED/-ING/-S *vi* **:** GARDEN ~ *vt* **1 :** to transform into or supply with a garden ⟨this world shall be *gardenized* —*Voice*⟩ **2 :** to cultivate (a native or wild plant) in a garden ⟨~ arbutus⟩

gar·den·less \-ᵊnləs\ *adj* **:** lacking a garden

gar·den·ly \-ᵊnlē\ *adj* **:** resembling a garden

garden mint *n* **:** SPEARMINT

garden nasturtium *n* **:** a cultivated plant of the genus *Tropaeolum* (esp. *T. majus*)

garden nightshade *n* **:** BLACK NIGHTSHADE

garden of eden \,gärd(ᵊ)nə'vēdᵊn, ,gȧd-\ *usu cap G&E* [*Eden*, the garden where Adam and Eve resided before the fall (Gen 3) — more at EDEN] **:** PARADISE 2

garden orache *n* **:** an Asiatic herb (*Atriplex hortensis*) resembling spinach and often used as a potherb

garden orpine *n* **:** a cultivated orpine or one common in cultivation (as *Sedum triphyllum*)

garden party *n* **:** a social affair held in an outdoor setting

garden peppergrass *n* **:** GARDEN CRESS

garden pink *n* **:** any of several plants of the genus *Dianthus; esp* **:** COTTAGE PINK

garden plague *n* **:** GOUTWEED

garden plow *n* **:** HAND PLOW

garden poppy *n* **:** a cultivated plant of the genus *Papaver; esp* **:** OPIUM POPPY

garden portulaca *n* **:** a portulaca (*Portulaca grandiflora*)

garden rocket *n* **1 :** an erect much-branched European annual herb (*Eruca sativa*) sometimes grown for salad and having pinnately lobed leaves and whitish yellow flowers **2 :** DAME'S VIOLET

gardens *pl of* GARDEN, *pres 3d sing of* GARDEN

garden sage *n* **:** SAGE 1a

garden sass *n, chiefly Midland* **:** ¹SASS

garden slug *n* **:** a slug infesting cultivated areas; *esp* **:** the gray garden slug (*Deroceras agrestis* or *D. reticulatum*)

garden snail *n* **:** any of several snails (esp. *Helix aspersa* and *H. hortensis*) often destructive in gardens — compare BROWN SNAIL

garden sorrel *n* **:** a European sorrel (*Rumex acetosa*) with hastate leaves usu. much longer than broad that is grown for salad and spring greens

garden speedwell *n* **:** FIELD SPEEDWELL

garden spider *n* **:** a garden-frequenting spider esp. of the family Argiopidae: as **a :** a common European spider (*Aranea diademata*) **b :** a widely distributed No. American spider (*Argiope aurantia*) with bright yellow markings on a dark gray or black background

garden spot *n* **1 :** a space set aside for gardening ⟨window overlooking the *garden spot*⟩ **2 :** an esp. fertile region ⟨owning twenty-six thousand acres of land in one of the *garden spots* of Iowa —Bertha M. H. Shambaugh⟩

garden springtail *n* **:** a common springtail (*Bourletiella hortensis*) that is destructive to seedlings in parts of northern No. America

garden stuff *n* **:** vegetables grown in a garden

garden symphylan *n* **:** GARDEN CENTIPEDE

garden truck *n* **:** GARDEN STUFF; *specif* **:** vegetables raised for market

garden valerian *n* **:** GARDEN HELIOTROPE 1

garden–variety \¦≈≈¦≈≈≈\ *adj* **:** ³GARDEN 2b

garden verbena *n* **:** VERBENA 2

garden violet *n* **:** SWEET VIOLET

garden wall bond *n* **:** GARDEN BOND — see ENGLISH GARDEN WALL BOND, FLEMISH GARDEN WALL BOND, GARDEN WALL CROSS BOND

garden wall cross bond *n* **:** a pattern in bricklaying in which a course of stretchers alternates with a course consisting of one header followed by three stretchers

garden warbler *n* **:** a brownish gray European warbler (*Sylvia borin*) — compare BECCAFICO

garden webworm *n* **:** the web-making larva of a pyralidid moth (*Loxostege similalis*) injurious to vegetables esp. in No. and So. America

garden white *n* **:** any of several small white butterflies (as the cabbage butterfly) constituting the genus *Pieris*

gar·deny \'gärd(ᵊ)nē\ *adj* [¹*garden* + *-y*] **:** suggestive of a garden ⟨a real ~ place to shut out the gales —Sinclair Lewis⟩

garde·robe \'gär,drōb\ *n* [ME, fr. MF; akin to ONF *warderobe* wardrobe — more at WARDROBE] **1 :** a wardrobe or its contents **2 :** a private room **:** BEDROOM **3 :** PRIVY

gar·de·vin \'gärdə,vin\ *or* **gar·de·vine** \-,vēn, -,vīn\ *n* -S [F *garder* to keep, guard + *vin* wine, fr. L *vinum* — more at GUARD, WINE] **1** *Scot* **:** a large bottle or decanter for wine ⟨a tumbler and the ~ for the dominie —D.S.Meldrum⟩ **2** *Scot* **:** a wine closet

gar·dez \(')gär¦dā\ *v imper* [short for earlier *gardez la reine*, fr. F, guard the queen] — used to warn a chess opponent that his queen is in danger of immediate capture

gar·di·nol \'gärdᵊn,ōl, -ōl\ *n* -S [fr. *Gardinol*, a trademark] **:** any of various commercially produced detergents consisting essentially of salts of sulfated fatty alcohols (as sodium lauryl sulfate)

gar·dy \'gärdē\ *n* -ES [origin unknown] *Scot* **:** ARM

gar·dy·loo \,gärdi'lü\ *v imper* [perh. fr. F *garde à l'eau!* attention to the water!] — used as a warning shout in Scotland when it was customary to throw household slops from upstairs windows

¹**gare** \'gär\ *Scot var of* ²GORE

²**gare** \"\ *var of* GAIR

gare·fowl \'ga(a)(ə)r,fau̇l\ *n, pl* **garefowl** *or* **garefowls** [of Scand origin; akin to ON *geirfugl* great auk, fr. *geirr* spear + *fugl* bird — more at GORE, FOWL] **:** GREAT AUK

garfish \'≈,≈\ *n* [ME *garfysshe*, prob. fr. ME (northern) *gar*, *gare* spear (fr. OE *gār*) + ME *fysshe, fish* fish — more at GORE, FISH] **:** GAR

gar·ga·ney \'gärgənē\ *n* -S [It dial. (16th cent., region of Bellinzona, Ticino canton, southern Switzerland) *garganei*, of imit. origin] **:** a European teal (*Anas querquedula*) having the male distinguished by a broad white stripe from eye to nape

gar·gan·tuan \(')gär¦ganch(əw)ən, (')gȧ¦-, -¦gaan-\ *adj, often cap* [*Gargantua*, gigantic king who is the hero of the novel *Gargantua* (1535) by François Rabelais †1553 Fr. humorist and satirist + E *-an*] **:** of tremendous size or volume **:** GIGANTIC, COLOSSAL ⟨a ~ land of rolling prairies, grass-blanketed plains, towering mountains —R.A.Billington⟩ ⟨~ laughter like the bellow of a joyful bull —Leslie Charteris⟩ **syn** see HUGE

gar·get \'gärgət\ *n* -S [prob. fr. (assumed) obs. E *garget* throat, fr. ME *garget, gargat*, fr. MF *gargate*, fr. OF, of imit. origin] **1** *archaic* **:** a disease in swine and cattle marked by inflammation of the head or throat **2 :** mastitis of domestic animals; *esp* **:** chronic bovine mastitis with gross changes in the form and texture of the udder **3** *or* **garget plant** *or* **garget root :** POKEWEED

gar·gety \-ədˑē\ *adj* [*garget* + *-y*] **:** of, relating to, or affected with garget; *specif* **:** STRINGY, CLOTTED — used esp. of milk drawn from cows afflicted with mastitis

¹**gar·gle** \'gärgəl, 'gȧg-\ *vb* **gargled; gargled; gargling** \-g(ə)liŋ\ **gargles** [modif. of MF *gargouiller* to gurgle, bubble, of imit. origin] *vt* **1 a :** to hold (a liquid) in the mouth or throat and keep in motion by a stream of air from the lungs ⟨~ salt water⟩ **b :** to cleanse or disinfect (the inside of the mouth) in this manner ⟨~ a sore throat⟩ **2 :** to utter with a gargling sound ⟨~s his words⟩ ~ *vi* **1 :** to use a gargle ⟨~ every morning⟩ **2 :** to utter as if gargling ⟨soprano with a tendency to ~ on the high notes⟩ **3 :** to make a sound that resembles a gargle ⟨a camel . . . ~*ing* as it were with rage —Nathan Davis⟩

²**gargle** \"\ *n* -S **1 a :** a liquid (as a mouthwash) intended for use in the mouth and throat **b :** an act of gargling ⟨a ~ with a small amount of baking soda will help to clear the throat —Morris Fishbein⟩ **2 :** a sound that resembles that of a liquid being gargled ⟨heard his breath go out in a ~ —Marcia Davenport⟩

gar·gler \-g(ə)lə(r)\ *n* -S **:** one that gargles

gargling *n* -S [fr. gerund of ¹*gargle*] **:** liquid gargled by a patient and then subjected to laboratory analysis — usu. used in pl.

gar·gouil·lade \¦gär,(,)gü¦yäd\ *n* -S [F, fr. *gargouiller* to gurgle, bubble + *-ade*] *ballet* **:** a pas de chat with a double rond de jambe

gar·goyle \'gär,gȯil, 'gȧ,-\ *also* **gur·goyle** \'gər,-, 'gō,-, 'gəi,-\ *n* -S [ME *gargoyl*, fr. MF *gargouille, gargoule*, fr. OF *gargoule*, of imit. origin] **1 a :** a spout often having the form of a grotesque figure or animal and projecting from a roof gutter to throw rainwater clear of a building ⟨listening to the avid gabble of water running from a ~ at the corner of the schoolhouse —Eve Langley⟩ **b :** any grotesquely carved figure ⟨strange Ethiopian ~s carved upon the ebony footposts of his bed —Hervey Allen⟩ **2 :** a person with a face resembling that of a gargoyle ⟨what you need is a woman — older, of course . . . but not a gorgon or a ~ —Mary Fitt⟩

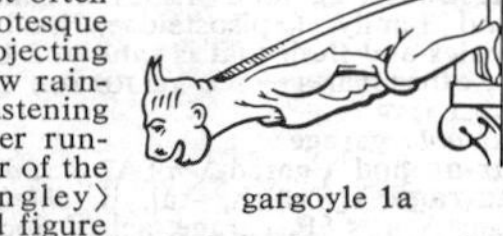
gargoyle 1a

gar·goyled \-ld\ *adj* [¹*gargoyle* + *-ed*] **:** decorated with gargoyles ⟨the ~ tops of cathedrals —*Times Lit. Supp.*⟩ ⟨the ~ and crenelated skyline —Frederic Marton⟩

gar·goyl·ism \-ȯi,lizəm\ *n* -S **:** a genetic variation in man involving extensive structural defects of the skeleton and gross mental deficiency

garh·wa·li \gər'wälē\ *n* -S *usu cap* **:** a Pahari dialect spoken in Garhwal, India

gar·i·bal·di \,garə'bȯldē, -di *also* ,ger-\ *n* -ES [after Giuseppe *Garibaldi* †1882 Ital. patriot] **1 :** a woman's blouse copied from the red shirt worn by the Italian patriot Garibaldi **2 :** a brilliant orange-red California market fish (*Hypsypops rubicundus*) of the family Pomacentridae

¹**gar·i·bal·di·an** \¦≈≈¦dēən, -diən\ *adj, usu cap* [Giuseppe *Garibaldi* †1882 + E *-an*] **:** of, relating to, or supporting Garibaldi

²**garibaldian** \"\ *or* **gar·i·bal·dist** \,≈≈'≈dəst\ *n* -S *usu cap* [Giuseppe *Garibaldi* †1882 + E *-an* or *-ist*] **:** a supporter of Garibaldi

ga·rigue *also* **gar·rigue** \gə'rēg\ *n* -S [F *garrigue*, fr. MF, fr. OProv *garriga*, fr. *garric* kermes oak, prob. of non-IE origin; akin to the source of Sp *carrasca* kermes oak] **:** a low open scrubland characterized by many evergreen shrubs, low trees, and bunchgrasses and found in poor land in the Mediterranean region

gar·ish \'ga(a)rish, 'ger-, -rēsh\ *adj* [origin unknown] **1 :** clothed in vivid colors ⟨as ~ as a gypsy —Victoria Sackville-West⟩ **2 a :** excessively vivid **:** FLASHY ⟨~ colors⟩ ⟨~ oratory⟩ **b :** offensively bright **:** GLARING ⟨~ klieg lights⟩ **c :** vulgarly obtrusive **:** BLATANT ⟨~ perfume⟩ **3 a :** tastelessly showy or overdecorated **:** FLAMBOYANT ⟨this front room is furnished with ~ theatrical magnificence —Arnold Bennett⟩ **b :** offensive to the sensibilities **:** REVOLTING ⟨its cynical and corrupt elements, its ~ violence —Orville Prescott⟩ **syn** see GAUDY

gar·ish·ly *adv* **:** in a garish manner

gar·ish·ness *n* -ES **:** the quality or state of being garish

¹**gar·land** \'gärlənd, 'gȧl-\ *n* -S [ME *gerland, garland*, fr. MF *garlande*, fr. OF, perh. of Gmc origin; akin to MHG *wieren* to adorn, OHG *wiara* fine gold — more at WIRE] **1 a :** a wreath, chaplet, or coronet worn as a mark of distinction: as (1) *obs* **:** a royal crown ⟨till Richard wear the ~ of the realm —Shak.⟩ (2) **:** a wreath awarded to a hero or to the victor in ancient games ⟨where one gaineth a ~ of bays, hundreds have had a wreath of hemp —Thomas Fuller⟩ **b :** a mark of esteem or affection **:** ACCOLADE ⟨so beloved a . . . minister that he held one charge for 40 years and was retired with ~s —A.W.Long⟩ **c** *obs* **:** a person who is highly prized **:** JEWEL ⟨call him noble that was now your hate, him vile that was your ~ —Shak.⟩ **2 :** a headband of gold, silver, precious stones, or other costly material ⟨a dazzling ~ of diamonds for the hair —A.P.Herbert⟩ **3 :** a wreath or festoon of leaves or flowers to be worn on the head or used to decorate an object ⟨crowned the May queen with a ~⟩ ⟨laid a ~ of oak leaves at the foot of the statue⟩ **4 :** something that resembles a garland: as **a :** an object that reminds one of a wreath or festoon ⟨~s of lights on the ferries —Brooks Atkinson⟩ **b** (1) **:** a grommet or ring of rope used for various purposes aboard ship (2) *archaic* **:** a band of rope, iron, or wood used on ships or in shore batteries to hold shot in place **c :** a carved wreath serving as a decorative motif ⟨an ornate fireplace carved in oak with . . . high≈relief ~s and swags —H.S.Morrison⟩ **d :** a heraldic wreath of laurel or of oak leaves and acorns **e :** a strip of cotton cloth or burlap used in military camouflaging to thicken overhead cover or to conceal edges of a net ⟨tie ~s of colored cloth onto a fishnet to make it resemble foliage —Carl Mann⟩ **5 :** a collection of extracts **:** ANTHOLOGY ⟨several of these essays make up a kind of friendship's ~ —Willard Thorp⟩; *esp* **:** a chapbook containing ballads or songs

²**garland** \"\ *vt* -ED/-ING/-S [ME *garlanden*, fr. *garland*, n.] **1 :** to form into a garland ⟨thine are these early wilding flowers though ~*ed* by me —P.B.Shelley⟩ **2 a :** to crown with or as if with a garland ⟨~*ed* his shaggy head with roses —P.B.Kyne⟩ ⟨goose stealers sat in the stocks ~*ed* with goose wings —S.P.B.Mais⟩ **b :** to confer an accolade upon ⟨~*ed* as a brilliant leader after the first Battle of Bull Run —A.W.Long⟩ **3 :** to surround or deck with or as if with a garland **:** ENGARLAND ⟨~ the crowns of profile hats —Lois Long⟩ ⟨one of the devices of the modern camoufleur is the use of nets ~*ed* with strips of burlap —*Newsweek*⟩

garland chrysanthemum *n* **:** a European herb (*Chrysanthemum coronarium*) with white or yellowish flowers

garland crab *n* **:** AMERICAN CRAB APPLE

garland dance *n* **:** a folk dance in which the dancers carry garlands

garland flower *n* **1 :** BUTTERFLY LILY **2 :** a widely cultivated low evergreen shrub (*Daphne cneorum*) with fragrant pink to rose-red flowers in dense terminal clusters **3 :** a heath (*Erica persoluta*) of southern Africa

gar·land·less \-n(d)ləs\ *adj* **:** lacking a garland

gar·lic \'gärlik, 'gȧl-, -lēk\ *n* -S *often attrib* [ME *garlek*, fr. OE *gārlēac*, fr. *gār* spear + *lēac* leek — more at GORE, LEEK] **1 :** any of several plants of the genus *Allium*; *esp* **:** a European bulbous herb (*A. sativum*) now widely naturalized elsewhere **2 :** the bulb of the garlic plant which has a strong and persistent odor and taste, is composed of a number of smaller bulbs, and is used as a condiment — see ¹CLOVE

garlic bread *n* **:** slices of French or Italian bread spread with garlic-seasoned butter and heated in the oven until crisp

garlic germander *n* **:** WATER GERMANDER

gar·licky \-ləkē, -ki\ *adj* [*garlic* + *-y*] **1 :** resembling or containing garlic ⟨~ wheat⟩ **2 :** smelling or tasting of garlic ⟨~ breath⟩ ⟨~ stew⟩

garlic mustard *n* **:** a European herb (*Alliaria officinalis*) that smells like garlic — called also *hedge garlic*

garlic oil *n* **:** a yellowish essential oil that has a strong odor of garlic and that is obtained by steam distillation of garlic and used in flavoring

garlic pear *or* **garlic pear tree** *n* **:** a tree (*Crataeva gynandra*) of Jamaica that bears a fruit with a scent of garlic and a burning taste

garlic salt *n* **:** a seasoning consisting of ground dried garlic and salt

garlic shrub *n* **:** either of two plants the bruised foliage of which smells like garlic: **a :** a tropical American woody vine (*Adenocalymna alliacea*) of the family Bignoniaceae **b :** GUINEA-HEN WEED

gar·lion \'gärlyən\ *n* -S [*garlic* + *onion*] **:** a hybrid vegetable resulting from a cross between garlic and onion

¹**gar·ment** \'gärmənt, 'gȧm-\ *n* -S *often attrib* [ME *garment, garnement*, fr. MF *garnement, garniment* article of clothing or armor, fr. OF, fr. *garnir* to equip, prepare + *-ment* — more at GARNISH] **1 a :** an article of outer clothing (as a coat or dress) usu. exclusive of accessories **b :** an article of underclothing; *specif* **:** FOUNDATION GARMENT ⟨a ~ that gives you the bust and waistline contours the new fashions demand —*McCall's*⟩ **2 :** the outward dress in which something is seen ⟨clothe his ideas in a ~ of reality —Bertrand Russell⟩ ⟨our birch in its spring ~ —Richard Semon⟩

²**garment** \"\ *vt* -ED/-ING/-S **:** to clothe with or as if with a garment — used chiefly in past participle ⟨went about oddly ~*ed* —W.J.Ghent⟩ ⟨~*ed* in high poetry —G.C.Sellery⟩

gar·ment·less \-ləs\ *adj* **:** lacking a garment

¹**garn** \'gärn\ *n* -S [ME, fr. ON — more at YARN] *dial Eng* **:** YARN

²**garn** \"\ *v imper* [alter. of *go on*] *Brit.* — used interjectionally to express disbelief or ridicule

¹**gar·ner** \'gärnər, 'gȧnə(r\ *n* -S [ME *garner, gerner*, fr. OF *gernier, grenier*, fr. L *granarium*, fr. *granum* grain + *-arium* -ary — more at CORN] **1 a :** a building in which grain is stored **:** GRANARY **b :** a bin for the storage of grain; *specif* **:** a bin in a grain elevator in which grain is collected for weighing **c :** something that resembles a garner ⟨you may be gathered into the ~ of mortality before me —Sir Walter Scott⟩ **2 :** something that is collected **:** ACCUMULATION ⟨makes an entirely fresh ~ each year —Donald Davidson⟩

²**garner** \"\ *vb* -ED/-ING/-S [ME *garneren*, fr. *garner*, n.] *vt* **1 a :** to gather into a granary **:** STORE ⟨the new crop was not yet ~*ed* and the last year's grain was getting low —Willa Cather⟩ **b :** to deposit as if in a granary ⟨volumes in which he has ~*ed* the fruits of his lifetime labors —Reinhold Niebuhr⟩ **2 a :** to acquire as the result of effort **:** EARN, REAP ⟨~ financial support from business circles —W.J.Jorden⟩ ⟨~s publicity by floating through the air from a flying trapeze beneath a helicopter —*Newsweek*⟩ **b :** to pick up **:** ACCUMULATE, COLLECT ⟨~*ed* the spoils with an all-encompassing rake —Sidney Warren⟩ ⟨~*ed* a fine array of folk songs —Julian Dana⟩ ~ *vi* **:** to become stored **:** ACCUMULATE ⟨wrath that ~s in my heart —Alfred Tennyson⟩ **syn** see REAP

garnering *n* -S [fr. gerund of ²*garner*] **:** something that has been garnered ⟨did add their ~s to their nests —E.A.Armstrong⟩

¹**gar·net** \'gärnət, 'gȧn-, *usu* -ədˑ+V\ *n* -S [ME *gernet, grenat*, fr. MF *grenat*, fr. OF, fr. *grenat*, adj., red like a pomegranate, fr. *grenate* (in *pome grenate* pomegranate) — more at POMEGRANATE] **1 :** a brittle and transparent to subtransparent silicate mineral of the general formula $R_3''R_2'''(SiO_4)_3$ in which R″ may be calcium, magnesium, ferrous iron, or manganese and R‴ aluminum or some other trivalent element having a vitreous luster and usu. red color, occurring mainly in crystals but also massive and in grains, found commonly in gneiss and mica schist, and used as a semiprecious stone and as an abrasive (hardness 6.5–7.5, sp. gr. 3.15–4.3) **2 :** a variable color averaging a dark red that is yellower and duller than cranberry, bluer and duller than pomegranate, and bluer, stronger, and very slightly darker than average wine

²**garnet** \"\ *n* -S [ME *garnett*] **:** GARNET HINGE

³**garnet** \"\ *n* -S [ME *garnett*] **1 :** a tackle usu. rigged on the mainstay of a sailing ship for hoisting cargo in or out **2 :** CLEW GARNET

garnetberry \'≈≈- — *see* BERRY\ *n* **:** a common red currant (*Ribes rubrum*) grown in gardens

garnet brown *n* **:** a dark red to moderate reddish brown that is redder than wallflower

garnet cloth *n* **:** a cloth similar to garnet paper in preparation and uses

garnet hinge *n* [²*garnet*] **:** a hinge with an upright bar and a horizontal strap

gar·net·if·er·ous \¦≈nəd·¦if(ə)rəs\ *adj* **:** containing garnets ⟨~ schist⟩

garnet lac *n* **:** lac refined by treating with a solvent and marketed in irregularly shaped pieces having a garnet color

garnet paper *n* **:** paper covered with crushed garnet on one side and used as an abrasive and polisher

garnet red *n* **:** a dark to deep red that is bluer and slightly darker than chrysanthemum

¹**gar·nett** \(')gär¦net\ *n* -S [prob. fr. the name *Garnett*] **1 a :** a machine of the breaker type used to remove foreign matter from fiber (as wool) before carding **b :** a similar machine used to reduce textile waste to fibrous form **2 :** the waste produced by the operation of a garnett machine

²**garnett** \"\ *vt* -ED/-ING/-S **:** to remove foreign substances from (fiber) or to reduce (textile waste) to fiber by passing through a machine provided with garnett wire

garnett wire *n* **:** a steel ribbon with teeth for use in the spiral groove of a cylinder on a garnett

gar·ni \gȧrnē\ *adj* [F, past part. of *garnir* to garnish, equip, prepare] **:** GARNISHED

gar·ni·er·ite \'gärnēə,rīt, gär'ni,r-\ *n* -S [Jules *Garnier* †1904 Fr. geologist + E *-ite*] **:** a soft mineral prob. $(Mg,Ni)_3Si_2O_5(OH)_4$ consisting of hydrous nickel magnesium silicate having an earthy luster and an apple-green or pale green color, having no crystal structure, and constituting an important ore of nickel (sp. gr. 2.3–2.8)

¹**gar·nish** \'gärnish, 'gȧn-, -nēsh, *esp in pres part* -nəsh\ *vt* -ED/-ING/-ES [ME *garnishen* to embellish, equip., fr. MF *garniss-*, stem of *garnir* to garnish, equip, prepare, arn, of Gmc origin; akin to OHG *wernen* to refuse, *warnōn* to take heed — more at WARN] **1 a :** to make fancy or striking **:** EMBELLISH ⟨a very handsome demi-peaked saddle . . . ~*ed* with a double row of silver-headed studs —Laurence Sterne⟩ ⟨the heroism of the men of the Alamo needs no ~*ing* —*Amer. Guide Series: Texas*⟩; *specif* **:** to add garlands to (a camouflage net) **b :** to add decorative or savory touches to (food) ⟨the chef had ~*ed* her entree with Chinese vegetable leaves —Thomas Gallagher⟩ **2 a** *obs* **:** to equip or arm (oneself) ⟨~*ed* for the chase —William Shenstone⟩ **b :** to equip for use **:** FURNISH ⟨huge stone fireplaces ~*ed* with shining copper warming pans and cooking utensils —Richard Joseph⟩ **3 :** GARNISHEE **syn** see ADORN

²**garnish** \"\ *n* -ES [ME, fr. *garnishen*, v.] **1 :** a set of flatware (as of pewter) **2 a :** something added for decoration **:** EMBELLISHMENT ⟨coat with a ~ of fur⟩ ⟨after-dinner speeches that have a ~ of humor⟩ **b :** a decorative or flavorful adjunct to a dish prepared for the table ⟨~ of parsley⟩ **3 a :** an unauthorized fee (as drink money for the other prisoners)

formerly extorted from a new inmate by the keeper of an English jail **b :** a similar payment required of a workman in celebration of his first job

gar·nish·able \-shəbəl\ *adj* **:** suitable for being garnished

garnished *adj* [ME, fr. past part. of *garnishen* to garnish] **1 :** EQUIPPED, EMBELLISHED **2** *heraldry* **:** TRIMMED, ADORNED, DECORATED — used with either specification of a tincture or name of an adornment ⟨four batons argent ~ azure⟩ ⟨a ring ~ with a sapphire⟩

¹gar·nish·ee \ˌ≠nə̇ˈshē\ *n* -S [¹*garnish* + *-ee*] **:** one who is served with a garnishment

²garnishee \"\ *vt* **garnisheed; garnisheed; garnisheeing; garnishees** **1 :** to serve with a garnishment **2 :** to attach (the wages or other property belonging to a debtor)

garnishee order *n* **:** an order served upon a person by way of garnishment

gar·nish·er \ˈ≠nishə(r), -nēsh-\ *n* -S **:** one that garnishes

gar·nish·ment \ˈ≠nishmənt, -nēsh-\ *n* -S [MF *garnissement* equipment & AF *garnissement* legal garnishment, fr. OF *garnissement* equipment, fr. *garniss-, garnisse-* (stem of *garnir*) + *-ment*] **1 :** GARNISH **2 :** a legal notice concerning the attachment of property to satisfy a debt: as **a :** a summons to a third party to appear in court and answer to the suit of the plaintiff to the extent of his liability to the defendant **b :** a warning to a person holding property belonging to a debtor not to deliver it to him pending the outcome of litigation **3 :** a legal proceeding begun by the service of a garnishment **4 :** a stoppage of a specified sum from wages to satisfy a creditor

gar·nish·ry \-nə̇shrē\ *n* -ES [*garnish* + *-ry*] **:** DECORATION ⟨saw in the stars mere ~ of heaven —Robert Browning⟩

gar·ni·ture \-nə̇chə(r), -nēch-, -ˌchu̇(ə)r, -u̇ə\ *n* -S [MF *garniture* equipment, alter. of OF *garneture, garnesture,* fr. *garnir*] **1 :** something that equips or furnishes; *specif* **:** the material in fireworks that produces stars, fiery rain, or other display after explosion **2 a :** an accessory of dress **:** TRIMMING **b :** a decorative accessory **:** ORNAMENT; *specif* **:** a usu. ceramic set of objects designed for use on a mantel or cabinet top ⟨dessert services and mantel ~*s* —*N.Y.Times*⟩ **3 :** GARNISH 2

garns *pl of* GARN

ga·ro \ˈgä(ˌ)rō\ *n, pl* **garo** *or* **garos** *usu cap* **1 a :** a Mongoloid people of the Garo hills, Assam **b :** a member of such people **2 :** the Sino-Tibetan language of the Garo people

ga·roo \ˈgä(ˌ)rü, gəˈrü\ *n* -S [Malay *gaharu*] **:** AGALLOCH

ga·roo·kuh \gəˈrükə\ *n* -S [origin unknown] **:** a short-keeled fishing boat used in the Persian gulf

garotte *var of* GARROTE

garpike \ˈ≠,≠\ *n* **:** ³GAR c

garran *var of* GARRON

gar·ra·pa·ta \ˌgarəˈpäd·ə\ *n* -S [Sp] **:** TICK; *esp* **:** CATTLE TICK

garred *past of* GAR

¹gar·ret \ˈgarət *also* ˈger-, *usu* -əd.+V\ *n* -S [ME *garette, garite* watchtower, fr. MF *garite* watchtower, place of refuge, perh. modif. of OProv *garida,* fr. *garir* to protect, of Gmc origin; akin to OHG *werien* to defend — more at WEIR] **1 a :** an unfinished part of a house immediately under or within the roof **:** LOFT — compare ATTIC 1c ⟨new college edifice . . . three stories and ~ in height —H.S.Morrison⟩ **b :** a room on the top floor of a house ⟨lives a recluse in a ~ —R.L.Stevenson⟩ **2** *slang* **:** a person's head **:** UPPER STORY

²garret \"\ *vt* -ED/-ING/-S [prob. by alter.] **:** GALLET

gar·re·teer \ˌgarəˈti(ə)r, -rəd-ˈ;i-\ *n* -S *archaic* **:** one that lives in a garret; *esp* **:** a literary hack

gar·rick \ˈgarik\ *n* -S [origin unknown] **:** LEERFISH

garrigue *var of* GARIGUE

garring *pres part of* GAR

¹gar·ri·son \ˈgarəsən *also* ˈger-\ *n* -S *often attrib* [ME *garisoun* protection, treasure, stronghold, fr. OF *garison* protection, provisions, fr. *garir* to protect, of Gmc origin; akin to OHG *werien* to defend] **1 :** a place of security **:** STRONGHOLD; *specif* **:** GARRISON HOUSE **2 a :** a place in which troops are quartered **:** a military post; *esp* **:** a permanent military installation **b :** a group of people associated with a military installation ⟨the ~ is small, consisting largely of expert workmen employed in the machine shops —*Amer. Guide Series: Texas*⟩; *specif* **:** a body of troops stationed at a military post ⟨a colony of Moors left as ~ by the old-time Turkish government —G.W.Murray⟩ **c :** something that resembles a defensive stronghold ⟨storming Conservative ~*s* with his Liberal dervishes —V.L.Albjerg⟩ **d :** a place that is used as a military stronghold ⟨Berlin . . . has become a ~ of the Allies —Eric Linklater⟩ — **in garrison :** manning a usu. permanent military post

²garrison \"\ *vt* -ED/-ING/-S **1 :** to furnish with soldiers **:** supply (a military post) with troops for defense ⟨a small stockaded Fort Sackville was built but not permanently ~*ed* —T.R.Hay⟩ **2 a :** to assign as a garrison **:** STATION ⟨did not ~ any troops in Manchuria —H.E.Abend⟩ **b :** to secure or defend by manning with troops **:** OCCUPY ⟨these three areas are the strategic heart of Europe and there can be no real peace or relaxation of tension as long as . . . troops ~ them —H.W. Baldwin⟩ **3 a :** to cause to serve in a garrison ⟨petty duties that become tragedies to ~*ed* soldiers —*Combat Forces Jour.*⟩ **b :** to furnish living quarters for (a garrison) **:** ACCOMMODATE ⟨temporary sheet-iron buildings . . . capable of ~*ing* about 1500 soldiers —*Amer. Guide Series: La.*⟩

garrison backstay *n* **:** a broad piece of leather covering the back seam of a shoe and extending forward on each side to the breast of the heel

garrison cap *n* **:** a visorless folding textile cap worn as part of a military uniform ⟨all officers wear grade insignia on the left side of *garrison caps* —*Nat'l Geographic*⟩ — compare SERVICE CAP

garrison court-martial *n* **:** a military court for the trial of other than capital offenses now superseded by the special court-martial — compare COURT-MARTIAL

gar·ri·son finish \ˈga|rəsən- *also* ˈge|\ *n, usu cap G* [prob. after Snapper *Garrison,* 19th cent. Am. jockey who came from behind to win the Suburban Handicap in 1892] **:** an unexpected last-minute victory in a contest ⟨another *Garrison finish:* . . . drop-kicked a field goal in the last 40 seconds —*Time*⟩

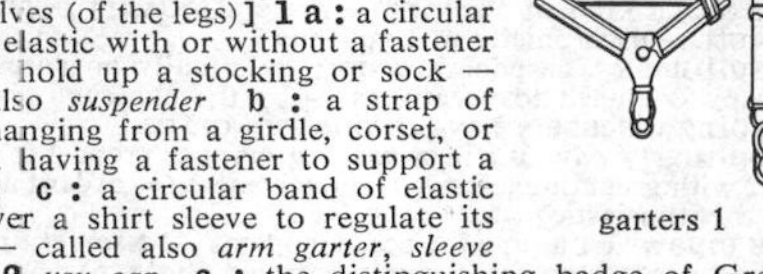

garrison cap

garrison flag *n* [¹*garrison*] **:** the largest size of national flag used by the U.S. army and flown on national holidays and special occasions — compare HOLIDAY FLAG

garrison house *n* **1 :** a fortified house with thick protective walls used by American settlers as a protection against Indian attack **2 :** BLOCKHOUSE **3 :** a house (as of colonial times) having the second story overhanging the first in the front elevation

gar·ri·so·nian \ˌgarəˈsōnēən, -ōnyən *also* ˌger-\ *or* **gar·ri·son·ite** \ˈ≠≠ˌsəˌnīt\ *n* -S *usu cap* [William Lloyd *Garrison* †1879 Am. abolitionist + E *-ian* or *-ite*] **:** an advocate of direct emancipation of slaves in America without compensation to their owners

gar·ri·son·ism \ˈ≠≠ˌsəˌnizəm\ *n* -S *usu cap* [William L. *Garrison* †1879 + E *-ism*] **:** the principles or doctrines of the Garrisonians

garrison prisoner *n* **:** a prisoner at a military post or garrison charged with an offense not entailing dismissal or dishonorable discharge — compare GENERAL PRISONER

garrison ration *n* **:** the food allowance for one soldier for one day used as the basis for calculating the money credit to be allotted a company commander to purchase food for his men

garrison state *n* **:** a centralized state dominated by military rather than by civilian personnel and policies; *esp* **:** one whose military preparations threaten to convert it into a totalitarian state — compare POLICE STATE

gar·ron *or* **gar·ran** \ˈgarən, ˈger-, gaˈrōn\ *n* -S [IrGael *gearrān* gelding, horse & ScGael *gearran* gelding, fr. MIr *gerrān* gelding, fr. *gerraim* I cut; akin to Skt *hrasva* short — more at CHRESTOMATHY] **1** *Scot & Irish* **:** a small sturdy workhorse **2** *Scot & Irish* **:** an old broken-down worn-out horse

gar·rot \ˈgarō\ *n, pl* **garrots** \-ō(z)\ [F] **:** GOLDENEYE 1

¹gar·rote *or* **gar·rotte** *also* **gar·otte** \gəˈrä|t, gaˈr-, -ˈrō|, ˈgarə| *also* ˈgerə|, *usu* |d·+V\ *n* -S [Sp *garrote* club, garrote, prob. fr. MF *garrot* heavy wooden projectile] **1 a :** a Spanish method of execution by means of an iron collar affixed to a post and tightened by a screw until the victim is strangled **b :** the instrument with which the execution is effected ⟨before each turn of the *garrotte* the Greek was ordered to tell the truth —W.S.Maugham⟩ **2 a :** strangulation as if with the garrote esp. with robbery as the motive **b :** an implement (as a length of piano wire with wooden handles) used for this purpose

²garrote *or* **garrotte** *also* **garotte** \"\ *vt* **garroted** *or* **garrotted** *also* **garotted; garroted** *or* **garrotted** *also* **garotted; garroting** *or* **garrotting** *also* **garotting; garrotes** *or* **garrottes** *also* **garottes** **1 :** to execute with or as if with a garrote ⟨the rule now is to ~ culprits within the walls of the prison —*Westminster Gazette*⟩ **2 :** to seize by the throat from behind in order to strangle and rob ⟨men . . . who would rather ~ a traveler than anything else in the world —Nicholas Monsarrat⟩

gar·rot·er *or* **gar·rot·ter** \-d·ə(r), -tə-\ *n* -S **:** one that garrotes

gar·ru·li·ty \gəˈrüləd·ē, gaˈ-,geˈ-, -ətē, -i *sometimes* gərˈyü- *or* garˈyü- *or* gerˈyü-\ *n* -ES [MF or L; MF *garrulité,* fr. L *garrulitat-, garrulitas,* fr. *garrulus* + *-itat-, -itas* -ity] **:** the quality or state of being garrulous **:** LOQUACITY, GARRULOUSNESS

gar·ru·lous \ˈgarələs *also* ˈger- *or* -ryə-\ *adj* [L *garrulus,* fr. *garrire* to babble, chatter — more at CARE] **1 a :** given to conversation **:** LOQUACIOUS, TALKATIVE ⟨~ . . . when talking of war or of his own experiences —C.S.Forester⟩ **b :** characterized by long-winded or diffuse statements **:** WORDY ⟨all day ~ speeches had echoed from the tribune —*Newsweek*⟩ **c :** full of rambling detail **:** CHATTY ⟨this delightfully ~ volume of memoirs —*Book-of-the-Month Club News*⟩ **2 :** suggestive of or having the effect of loquacity ⟨ruins . . . ~ of better days —John Ruskin⟩ **syn** see TALKATIVE

gar·ru·lous·ly *adv* **:** in a garrulous manner

gar·ru·lous·ness *n* -ES **:** the quality or state of being garrulous **:** GARRULITY

gar·ru·lus \-ləs\ *n, cap* [NL, fr. L, garrulous] **:** a large genus of Old World jays including the common jay of Britain and Europe

gar·ru·pa \gəˈrüpə\ *n* [Pg *garoupa* — more at GROUPER (fish)] **1** -S **:** a grouper esp. in Spanish America **2** -S **:** a Californian rockfish **3** *cap* [NL, fr. Pg *garoupa*] **:** a genus of Serranidae comprising the black jewfish

gar·rya \ˈgarēə\ *n, cap* [NL, fr. Nicholas *Garry,* 19th cent. official of Hudson's Bay Co.] **:** a genus of evergreen shrubs and small trees (family Cornaceae) with coriaceous opposite leaves and small dioecious flowers that are borne in silky racemes which resemble catkins and are pistillate with two stipes — see BEAR BRUSH, GARRYACEAE

gar·ry·a·ce·ae \ˌgarēˈāsēˌē\ *n pl, cap* [NL, fr. *Garrya,* type genus + *-aceae*] *in some classifications* **:** a family of dicotyledonous plants coextensive with the genus *Garrya*

gar·ry oak \ˈgarē-\ *n, usu cap G* [after Nicholas *Garry*] **:** OREGON OAK

gars *pres 3d sing of* GAR, *pl of* GAR

garse \ˈgärs\ *archaic var of* GRASS

garshuni *usu cap, var of* KARSHUNI

gar·sil \ˈgärsəl\ *n* -S [ME *garsell,* of Scand origin; akin to OSw *gærthsl* fencing material, Norw dial. *gjerdsl;* suffixal derivative fr. the verb represented by OSw *gærtha* to fence in, denominative fr. the noun represented by ON *garthr* yard — more at YARD] *dial Eng* **:** UNDERBRUSH

gar·ten \ˈgärtən\ *n* -S [by alter.] *Scot* **:** GARTER ⟨wear yellow ~*s* —P.M.Preston⟩

¹gar·ter \ˈgär|d·ər, ˈgȧ|d·ə(r, |tə-\ *n* -S [ME, fr. ONF *gartier,* fr. *garet, garret* bend of the knee, hock, of Celt origin; akin to W *gar* shank, OIr *gairri* calves (of the legs)] **1 a :** a circular band of elastic with or without a fastener worn to hold up a stocking or sock — called also *suspender* **b :** a strap of elastic hanging from a girdle, corset, or belt and having a fastener to support a stocking **c :** a circular band of elastic worn over a shirt sleeve to regulate its length — called also *arm garter, sleeve garter* **2** *usu cap* **a :** the distinguishing badge of Great Britain's Order of the Garter consisting of a strip of dark blue velvet edged with gold, having a buckle and pendant of gold, and worn below the left knee by men and on the left arm by women **b :** membership in the Order of the Garter ⟨he declined the offer of the *Garter*⟩ **c :** GARTER KING OF ARMS **d :** a circular band borne on the collar, badge, and star and about the armorial escutcheon of a member of the Order of the Garter that is inscribed with the motto of the Order and merges at its bottom into a representation of the buckle and free end as they appear when the garter is worn buckled in the prescribed manner — compare CIRCLET 1c **3 :** a wavy band that resembles a heraldic garter and is incorporated into an emblem or seal usu. to carry a motto ⟨the U.S. shield, encircled with a ~ bearing the words *E Pluribus Unum* —Elizabeth W. King⟩ **4 :** a tape or streamer held for a circus performer to leap over **5 :** GARTER SNAKE

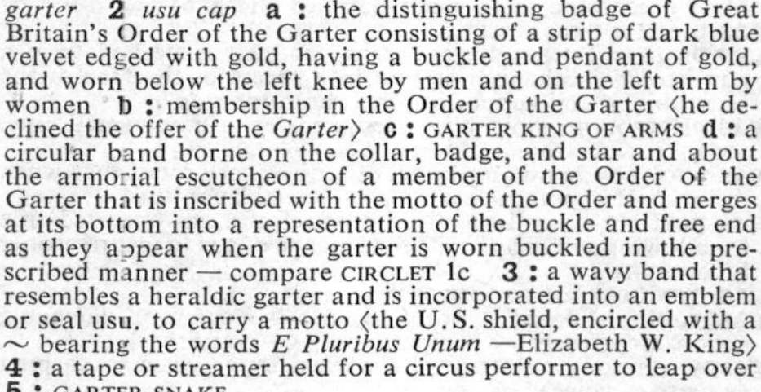

garters 1

²garter \"\ *vt* -ED/-ING/-S [ME *garteren,* fr. *garter,* n.] **:** to fasten with or as if with a garter ⟨see to ~ his hose — Shak.⟩

garter belt *n* **:** a woman's undergarment consisting of a relatively narrow band of fabric to which long garters are attached for the support of stockings — called also *suspender belt*

garter-blue \ˌ≠≠ˈ≠\ *adj* **:** of a dark blue resembling the ribbon of the Knights of the Garter

gartered *adj* [fr. past part. of ²*garter*] **1 :** having garters **2 :** invested with the badge of the Order of the Garter **3 :** surrounded or supplied with a heraldic garter

garter king of arms *usu cap G&K&A* **:** the highest-ranking king of arms in the English College of Arms who has concurrent jurisdiction with the provincial kings of arms in their respective provinces and who also is king of arms of the Order of the Garter — compare CLARENCEUX KING OF ARMS, NORROY AND ULSTER KING OF ARMS, NORROY KING OF ARMS

gar·ter·less \-ə(r)lə̇s\ *adj* **:** lacking a garter

garter mission *n, usu cap G&M* **:** a mission by a delegation headed by the Garter King of Arms to confer the Order of the Garter on a foreigner

garter snake *n* **1 :** any of numerous widely distributed active viviparous harmless American colubrid snakes constituting the genus *Thamnophis* and having more or less distinct longitudinal stripes on the back **2 :** any of several venomous African ringed elapid snakes of the genera *Elapsoidea* and *Elaps* related to the New World coral snakes

garter spring *n* **:** a spiral steel spring formed into a closed elastic ring

garter stitch *n* **:** a pattern of horizontal ridges formed by knitting both sides of a fabric instead of knitting one side and purling the other

garter stitch

¹garth \ˈgärth\ *n* -S [ME, fr. ON *garthr* yard — more at YARD] **1 a** *archaic* **:** a small yard or enclosure **:** CLOSE **b :** CLOISTER GARTH **2 a :** dam or weir for catching fish

²garth \"\ *dial Eng var of* GIRTH

gärt·ner's bacillus \ˈgertnərz-\ *n, usu cap G* [after August Gärtner †1934 Ger. bacteriologist] **:** a motile salmonella (*Salmonella enteritidis*) that causes enteritidis and is widely distributed in the intestinal tract of man and various other mammals

gartner's duct *n, usu cap G* [after Hermann T. *Gärtner* †1827 Dan. anatomist] **:** DUCT OF GARTNER

garvanzo *var of* GARBANZO

gar·vey \ˈgärvē\ *n* -S [prob. fr. the name *Garvey*] **:** a small scow of the New Jersey coast

gar·vie \ˈgärvi\ *n* -S [origin unknown] *Scot* **:** SPRAT

gary \ˈga(a)rē, ˈger-,ˈgär-, -ri\ *adj, usu cap* [fr. *Gary,* Indiana] **:** of or from the city of Gary, Indiana ⟨*Gary* steel mills⟩ **:** of the kind or style prevalent in Gary

¹gas \ˈgas, -aa(ə)s,-ais\ *n, pl* **gases** *also* **gasses** *often attrib* [NL, alter. of *chaos* air, fr. L, chaos — more at CHAOS] **1 a :** a fluid (as air) that has neither independent shape nor volume but tends to expand indefinitely **:** a substance at a temperature above its critical temperature and therefore not liquefiable by pressure alone — compare KINETIC THEORY, PERMANENT GAS, STATE OF AGGREGATION; LIQUID 1, VAPOR 2 **2 a :** a gas or gaseous mixture with the exception of atmospheric air — not used scientifically **b :** a gas or gaseous mixture (as laughing gas or ethylene) used to produce anesthesia **c :** a combustible gaseous mixture (as for fuel or illumination) ⟨heated his house with ~⟩ — see LIQUEFIED PETROLEUM GAS, MANUFACTURED GAS, NATURAL GAS **3** *slang* **:** empty boasting talk **:** BOMBAST, HUMBUG, NONSENSE **4 :** the state of having or an accumulation of gas in the digestive tract; *also* **:** distress caused by this **5 :** a substance (as a war gas or tear gas) whether gaseous, liquid, or solid under ordinary conditions that can be used to produce a poisonous, asphyxiating, or irritant atmosphere — compare SMOKE 1b **6 a :** GASOLINE **b :** the accelerator of a gasoline-powered vehicle ⟨had the ~ to the floor most of the way⟩

²gas \"\ *vb* **gassed; gassed; gassing; gasses** *vt* **1 :** to affect or treat with gas: as **a :** SINGE 1b **b :** to subject to the action of gas ⟨fruit *gassed* with ethylene⟩; *sometimes* **:** to injure or cause to deteriorate by the action of gas **c :** to poison or asphyxiate with a gas esp. in warfare **d :** to cause (as a metal) to absorb gas **2** *slang* **:** to address gas to **:** deceive or befuddle with idle boasting talk **3 :** to supply with gas or esp. gasoline — often used with *up* ⟨decided to ~ up the car the night before they were to start⟩ ~ *vi* **1 :** to give off gas (as of a storage battery during charging or a molten metal during cooling) ⟨the new well *gassed* for several days before oil appeared⟩ **2** *slang* **:** to indulge in idle, garrulous, or boastful talk **:** chat idly or casually ⟨stopped in to ~ with the boys⟩ **3 :** to fill the tank (as of a car, airplane, or motor) with gasoline — often used with *up* ⟨~ up on the way back⟩

³gas *pl of* GA

gasal *var of* GHAZEL

gas attack *n* **:** a military attack in which gas is used as a weapon

gas bacillus *n* **:** any of several bacteria that form gas in wounds infected with them (esp. *Clostridium perfringens* syn. *C. welchii*)

gasbag \ˈ≠,≠\ *n* **1 :** a bag for holding gas: as **a :** a bag inserted empty into a gas or other line and inflated to serve as a temporary plug (as during repair or alteration) **b :** one of the gas-filled bags or a single such bag making up the inflated buoyant envelope of an airship or balloon; *broadly* **:** AIRSHIP, BALLOON **2 :** a person given to idle boastful talk **:** one that gasses

gas black *n* **:** CHANNEL BLACK

gasboat \ˈ≠,≠\ *n* **:** a boat powered by a gasoline motor; *esp* **:** one using a converted automobile engine

gas bomb *n* **:** a military explosive projectile filled with noxious gas that is usu. liquefied under pressure and released when the projectile explodes — called also *gas shell*

gas buoy *n* **:** a metal buoy filled with a compressed illuminating gas and surmounted by a lantern where a light fed by the gas burns night and day

gas burner *n* **:** a nozzle or a set of openings through which combustible gas escapes and burns

gas carbon *n* **:** carbon in a dense form deposited on the interior of a gas retort

gas cell *n* **:** a cell containing a gas electrode

gas chamber *n* **:** a chamber in which prisoners are executed by poisonous gas

gascheck \ˈ≠,≠\ *n* **1 :** a device in a gun or chemical projector that prevents escape of gas **2 :** a small copper cup fitted to the base of a lead bullet for small arms to prevent the melting of the base at the temperatures and pressures created by high-velocity smokeless powder

gas checking *n* **:** a frosty wrinkled appearance of some coatings (as various tung-oil varnishes) caused by exposure to gas fumes

gas coal *n* **:** a coal used for making gas by distillation ordinarily being a caking bituminous coal

gas coke *n* **:** coke made in a gas retort as distinguished from that made in a coke oven

gas company *n* **:** a utilities company supplying gas

¹gas·con \ˈgaskən, -aas-,-ais-\ *n* -S *usu cap* [ME *Gascoun,* fr. MF *gascon*] **1 a :** a native or inhabitant of Gascony **b :** a boastful swaggering person **2 :** a Romance speech of the area between the Garonne river and the Pyrenees that is sometimes classified as a dialect of Provençal but that is in some respects more closely allied to Aragonese and Catalan **3 :** a common widely distributed saurel (*Trachurus trachurus*)

²gascon \"\ *adj* **1** *usu cap* **a :** of, relating to, or characteristic of Gascony in southwestern France **b :** of, relating to, or characteristic of the people of Gascony **2** *usu cap* **:** of, relating to, or characteristic of the Gascon language **3 :** BRAGGART, SWAGGERING

¹gas·con·ade \ˌ≠skəˈnād\ *n* -S [F *gasconnade,* fr. *gasconner* to boast (fr. *gascon* boaster, Gascon) + *-ade*] **:** BOAST, BOASTING, BRAVADO

²gasconade \"\ *vi* -ED/-ING/-S **:** to boast or bluster esp. to excess **:** show off by lauding oneself or one's accomplishments **:** BRAG **syn** see BOAST

gas·con·ad·er \-də(r)\ *n* -S **:** one that gasconades

gas·con·ism \ˈgaskəˌnizəm\ *n* -S *often cap* [ˈ*Gascon* + *-ism*] **:** a bombastic boastful way or spirit **:** BRAVADO

gas constant *n* **:** a general constant in the equation of state of gases that is equal in the case of an ideal gas to the product of the pressure and volume of one mole divided by the absolute temperature — see GAS LAW c

gas cutting *n* **:** the cutting of a preheated metal by a jet of oxygen

gas disease *n* **:** a disorder of fishes marked by formation of gas bubbles in the tissues and body fluids and occurring when the tension of gases becomes higher in the body fluids than in the surrounding water

gas edema *n* **:** any of several diseases (as blackleg or malignant edema) found in mammals and marked by crepitating gassy swelling of the tissues

gas·e·i·ty \gaˈsēəd·ē\ *n* -ES [*gaseous* + *-ity*] **:** GASEOUSNESS

gas-electric \ˌ≠≠ˈ≠\ *adj* **:** GASOLINE-ELECTRIC

gas electrode *n* **:** an electrode consisting of a conductor covered with a gas

gaselier *var of* GASOLIER

gas engine *n* **:** an internal-combustion engine similar to a gasoline engine but using natural or manufactured gas instead of gasoline vapor; *broadly* **:** INTERNAL-COMBUSTION ENGINE

gas·e·ous \ˈga|sēəs, ˈgaa|, |sh(y)əs, *Brit often* ˈgāziəs *or* ˈgāsi-\ *adj* [¹*gas* + *-eous*] **1 a :** having the form of or being gas ⟨~ matter⟩ **:** of or relating to gases ⟨~ laws⟩ ⟨~ content⟩ **b :** SUPERHEATED ⟨use of ~ steam in industrial boilers⟩ **2 :** lacking substance or solidity **:** TENUOUS ⟨unconnected, ~ information —J.F.Stephen⟩

gaseous diffusion *n* **:** diffusion of gases through a porous barrier at a rate of speed in direct proportion to the weight of the molecules, being used as the basis of a method of separating isotopes (as fissionable uranium 235 from the nonfissionable uranium 238)

gas·e·ous·ness *n* -ES **:** the quality or state of being gaseous; *often* **:** EFFERVESCENCE

gases *pl of* GAS

gas field *n* **:** a district where natural gas is produced in commercial quantities

gas-filled tube \ˈ≠,≠-\ *n* **:** GAS TUBE

gas-fired \ˈ≠ˈ≠\ *adj* **:** heated by the combustion of gaseous fuel ⟨*gas-fired* furnace⟩

gas fitter *n* **:** a workman who installs or repairs gas pipes and appliances

gas fitting *n* **1 :** the trade or occupation of a gas fitter **2 a gas fittings** *pl, archaic* **:** the equipment (as piping, valves, and meters) conveying gas from the main to the fixtures of an individual installation **b :** one of the pipe fittings of a gas≠ supply installation

gas fixture *n* **:** a device for conveying illuminating or combustible gas from the pipe to the gas burner

gas gangrene *n* **:** progressive gangrene marked by impregnation of the dead and dying tissue with gas and caused by one or more toxin-producing clostridia that enter the body through wounds and proliferate in necrotic tissue

gas generator *n* **:** an apparatus for generating gas: as **a :** a laboratory apparatus (as a Kipp generator) for the production of carbon dioxide, hydrogen, chlorine, or other gases **b :** GENERATOR 2b

gas gland *n* **:** a glandular structure that secretes gas (as the oxygen-releasing mechanism of a fish's air bladder)

gas grenade *n* **:** a grenade containing gas in liquid form which is released by the bursting of the grenade

¹gash \ˈgash, -aa(ə)sh,-aish\ *vb* -ED/-ING/-ES [alter. of ME *garsen*, fr. ONF *garser* to scarify, wound, fr. (assumed) VL *charissare*, fr. Gk *charassein* to sharpen, cut into furrows, engrave, carve — more at CHARACTER] *vt* **1 :** to make a gash in **:** cut or disrupt the surface of ⟨turpentiners who ~ the southern pines⟩ ⟨the knife slipped and ~*ed* his finger⟩ ⟨moldboard plows ~*ing* the prairie⟩ **2 :** to rough-mill or rough-hob (the teeth of a gear wheel) preparatory to finish-machining ~ *vi* **:** to make a gash **:** CUT, SLASH ⟨blades that ~ and tear⟩

²gash \ˈ"\ *n* -ES [alter. of ME *garse*, fr. *garsen*, v.] **1 a :** a deep long cut esp. in flesh ⟨came out of the wreck bruised and shaken and with a long ~ over one eye⟩ **b :** a deep narrow depression in land whether natural (as a gorge or cleft between rocks) or made by man (as in road building) **c :** the female pudenda **:** an object of male sexual desire; *also* **:** SEXUAL INTERCOURSE — usu. considered vulgar **2 :** an act or instance of gashing ⟨gave the sack a ~ with his knife so that flour ran over the ground⟩

³gash \ˈ"\ *adj* [origin unknown] *archaic Scot* **:** dismal or grim in appearance

⁴gash \ˈ"\ *adj* -ER/-EST [origin unknown] **1** *chiefly Scot* **:** KNOWING, SHREWD, WITTY, SHARP **2** *chiefly Scot* **:** having a fine appearance or air **:** well dressed **:** TRIM **3** *Scot* **:** TALKATIVE

⁵gash \ˈ"\ *vi, Scot* **:** to chatter idly **:** PALAVER

⁶gash \ˈ"\ *n* -ES *Scot* **:** empty talk **:** CHITCHAT

⁷gash \ˈ"\ *n* -ES [origin unknown] *slang* **:** extra food (as a second helping or leftovers); *often* **:** the garbage remaining after a meal ⟨all ~ should be burned or buried⟩

gas helmet *n* **:** GAS MASK

gash fracture *n* **:** a rock fracture due to tension and therefore tending to remain open — opposed to *shear fracture*

gash·ful \ˈgashfəl\ *adj* [alter. (influenced by ²*gash*) of *ghastful*] *now dial Brit* **:** GHASTLY, FRIGHTFUL

gasholder \ˈ=,==\ *n* **:** a container for gas; *esp* **:** a large gastight cylindrical or spherical tank for storing combustible gases for use as fuel

gasholder (simple type): *a,a*, steel structure to guide cylindrical gas tank, *b*, in rising or falling through contact with wheels, *c,c,c,c*; *d,d*, masonry or steel tank containing water, *e*; *f* inlet, *g* outlet, gas pipes

gashouse \ˈ=,=\ *n* **:** GASWORKS; *sometimes* **:** a building in which gas is made (as for heating or illumination)

gash vein *n* **:** a vein resulting from the filling and sometimes enlargement of a joint or crack that does not extend beyond the stratum in which it occurs

gashy \ˈgashē\ *adj* -ER/-EST **:** resembling or having a gash

gas·i·fi·ca·tion \,gasəfəˈkāshən\ *n* -S **:** an act or a process of gasifying (as of a fuel) ⟨~ of coal by burning or by reaction with oxygen and superheated steam⟩

gas·i·fi·er \ˈgasə,fī(ə)r\ *n* -S **:** an apparatus for manufacturing gas (as synthesis gas from coal)

gas·i·form \-,fȯrm\ *adj* [¹*gas* + *-iform*] **:** in the form of gas **:** GASEOUS

gas·i·fy \-,fī\ *vb* -ED/-ING/-ES [¹*gas* + *-ify*] *vt* **:** to convert (a solid or liquid) into gas (as by heat or a chemical process) ~ *vi* **:** to become gaseous ⟨liquid ammonia *gasifies* readily⟩

gas jet *n* **:** a flame of illuminating gas; *also* **:** GAS BURNER ⟨ill-kept glass box lit by a small *gas jet* —W.J.Locke⟩

¹gas·ket \ˈgaskət, -aas-,-ais-, *usu* -əd·+V\ *n* -S [prob. alter. of F *garcette*, fr. OF, girl, dim. of *garce* girl, prostitute, fr. *gars, garz, garçon* boy, servant, wretch, scoundrel — more at GARÇON] **1 :** a line or band used to lash a furled sail securely — see HARBOR GASKET, SEA GASKET **2 a :** plaited hemp or tallowed rope for packing pistons or for making pipe joints or other joints fluid-tight **b :** packing for the same purpose made of rubber, asbestos, metal, or other elastic material usu. in the form of sheets or rings — see SPARK PLUG illustration **c :** a separate or attached sealer used in making and closing hermetic or liquid containers to ensure tightness

²gasket \ˈ"\ *vt* -ED/-ING/-S **1 :** to fasten (a sail) with a gasket **2 :** to seal (as mechanical parts) fluid-tight by means of a gasket

¹gas·kin \ˈgaskən\ *n* -S [prob. short for *galligaskin*] **1** *obs* **:** HOSE, BREECHES **2 :** a part of the hind leg of a horse or other quadruped between the stifle and the hock — see HORSE illustration

²gaskin \ˈ"\ *also* **gas·king** \-kiŋ\ *n* -S [by alter.] **:** GASKET

gas lamp *n* **:** a lamp burning illuminating gas; *esp* **:** one on a public way

gas law *n* **:** any of several statements of physics and chemistry relating to the behavior of gases: as **a :** BOYLE'S LAW **b :** CHARLES'S LAW **c :** a statement that the product of the pressure and volume of one mole of a gas equals the product of the gas constant by the absolute temperature (as expressed by the equation $pv=RT$) — called also *ideal-gas law;* compare VAN DER WAALS'S EQUATION

gas·less \ˈ=ləs\ *adj* **:** having no gas **:** using or producing no gas

gas lift *n* **:** the flowing of oil from a well due to natural-gas pressure or to pressure of gas forced into the well by pumping

gaslight \ˈ=ˌ=\ *n, often attrib* **1 :** light yielded by the combustion of illuminating gas ⟨the mellow radiance of ~⟩ **2 :** a gas jet or gas burner; *also* **:** GAS LAMP — **gaslighted** \ˈ=ˌ==\ *adj*

gas–lighting \ˈ=ˌ==\ *n* **:** lighting by means of gaslight

gaslight paper *n* **:** a slow developing-out photographic paper

gas lime *n* **:** hydrated lime that has been used in purifying gas, contains other compounds (as calcium carbonate, calcium sulfide), and is used as a land dressing

gas liquor *n* **:** ammonia liquor obtained in the manufacture of coal gas or coke-oven gas

gaslit \ˈ=,=\ *adj* **:** illuminated by gaslight

gas log *n* **:** a hollow perforated imitation of a log used as a gas burner in a fireplace

gas·man \ˈ=,man, -aa(ə)n\ *n, pl* **gasmen 1 :** one connected with the distribution, installation, or sale of gas: as **a :** a producer or manufacturer of gas for heating or illumination **b :** a supervisor of the gas lamps formerly used for theatrical illumination **c :** GAS FITTER **d :** a person who tests or reads gas meters **e :** a worker who operates units that produce fuel gas **2 :** FIRE BOSS

gas mask *n* **:** a close-fitting facepiece connected to a canister through which all air breathed is drawn to protect the respiratory tract and face against irritating and poisonous gases **:** RESPIRATOR

gas mask: *1* lens, *2* outlet valve, *3* canister

gas meter *n* **:** an instrument for recording the quantity of gas passing through a particular outlet

gas·o·gene \ˈgasə,jēn\ *or* **gaz·o·gene** \-azə-\ *also* **gas·o·gen** \-asəjən, -,jen\ *n* -S [F *gazogène*, fr. *gaz* gas (fr. NL *gas*) + *-o-* + *-gène* -gen — more at GAS] **1 a :** an apparatus for attachment to a vehicle (as an automobile) that produces a combustible gas for a motor fuel by partial burning esp. of charcoal or wood **b :** the motor fuel produced by a gasogene **2 :** a portable apparatus for carbonating liquids

gas oil *n* **:** any of various hydrocarbon oils used esp. formerly for making oil gas or carbureted water gas and now used chiefly as diesel oils, fuel oils, or feedstock for cracking operations; *specif* **:** a petroleum distillate intermediate in boiling range and viscosity between kerosine and lubricating oil

gas·o·lier *also* **gas·e·lier** \ˌgasəˈli(ə)r, -iə\ *n* -S [*gasolier* alter. of *gaselier; gaselier* fr. ¹*gas* + *-elier* (as in *chandelier*)] **:** a chandelier equipped with gaslights

gas·o·line *also* **gas·o·lene** \,gasəˈlēn, ,gaa|, ,gai|, ˈ==,= *sometimes* |zə-\ *n* -S [¹*gas* + *-ol* + *-ine* or *-ene*] **:** a volatile flammable liquid hydrocarbon mixture suitable for use as a fuel esp. for internal-combustion engines and now consisting usu. of a blend of several products from natural gas and petroleum (as natural gasoline, straight-run gasoline, cracked gasoline, alkylates) or of products from other sources (as from the hydrogenation of coal gas or water gas) together with antiknock agents, antioxidants, or other additives — called also *petrol;* compare NAPHTHA — **gasolinic** *adj*

gasoline–electric \ˌ==,==ˌ=\ *adj* **:** propelled by electricity furnished from an engine generator driven by gasoline or oil

gasoline engine *n* **:** an internal-combustion engine having its piston driven by explosions of a mixture of air and vapor of gasoline or other volatile fuel ignited by an electric spark

gas·o·line·less \,==ˈ=ləs, ˈ==,=-\ *adj* **:** having no gasoline; *often* **:** characterized by restriction or prohibition of the sale or use of gasoline ⟨~ Sundays during the war⟩

gasoline pump *n* **:** a filling-station unit that meters and supplies gasoline to motor vehicles

gas·o·lin·er \,==ˈlēnə(r), ˈ==,l-\ *n* -S **:** a powerboat with a gasoline engine

gas·om·e·ter \gaˈsämәd·ə(r) *sometimes* -ˈzä-\ *n* [F *gazomètre*, fr. *gaz* gas + *-o-* + *-mètre* -meter] **1 :** a laboratory apparatus (as a graduated glass tube or bottle with inlet and outlet tubes fitted with stopcocks) for holding and measuring gases **2 :** GASHOLDER

gas·o·met·ric \ˌgasəˈme·trik *sometimes* ˌgazə-\ *adj* [¹*gas* + *-o-* + *-metric*] **:** of or relating to the measurement of gases (as in chemical analysis) — **gas·o·met·ri·cal·ly** \-rək(ə)lē\ *adv*

gas–operated \ˈ=ˌ=,==\ *adj, of an automatic or autoloading weapon* **:** utilizing part of the powder gases to operate the action

¹gasp \ˈgasp, -aa(ə)sp, -aisp, -åsp\ *vb* -ED/-ING/-S [ME *gaspen;* akin to ON *geispa* to yawn & perh. to OE *geonian* — more at YAWN] *vi* **1 :** to catch the breath convulsively and audibly often as an expression of shock, concern, or emotion ⟨he ~*ed* as he stepped into the icy water⟩ ⟨~*ing* with surprise as he saw the new house⟩ **2 :** to breathe laboriously with open mouth **:** pant strongly and audibly ⟨the exhausted runner threw himself down and ~*ed*⟩ ⟨a dying man ~*ing* for breath⟩; *broadly* **:** to become completely exhausted ⟨a handful of hypertrophied capitalists ~*ing* under the load of their growing millions —G.B.Shaw⟩ **3 :** to make a sound like that of a gasped breath ⟨cans ~*ed* under the knives —W.W.Haines⟩ ⟨the engine ~*ed*, caught, and settled into a smooth purr⟩ ~ *vt* **:** to emit or utter with gasps ⟨she ~*ed* a shocked denial⟩ — often used with *forth, out, away* ⟨he ~*ed* out a plea for mercy⟩

²gasp \ˈ"\ *n* -S **:** an act of gasping or a gasping utterance

gas packing *n* **:** packing (as of a food) in an airtight container in which the air has been replaced by an oxygen-free gas to prevent oxidative deterioration of the stored product

gasp·er \-pə(r)\ *n* -S **1 :** one that gasps **2** *slang Brit* **:** CIGARETTE

gas·per·eau \ˌgaspəˈrō\ *n* -S [CanF *gaspareau, gasparot*, fr. F *gasparot*, a kind of herring] *Canad* **:** ALEWIFE 1 a

gas·per·gou \ˈgaspə(r)ˌgü\ *n* -S [LaF *casburgot, casseburgau*, fr. F dial *casse-burgot*, a kind of fish, fr. *casser* to break + *burgau*, a kind of shellfish — more at QUASH] **:** FRESHWATER DRUM — used chiefly in Louisiana

gasp·i·ness \ˈgaspēnəs\ *n* -ES **:** the quality or state of being gaspy ⟨reduced to breathless ~ by the climb⟩

gasping disease *n* **:** INFECTIOUS BRONCHITIS 1

gasp·ing·ly *adv* **1 :** in a gasping manner ⟨read her lines ~⟩ **2 :** with great or excessive responsiveness ⟨~ ardent attention⟩ ⟨~ enthusiastic⟩

gas pipe *n* **1 :** a pipe for conveying gas **2 :** something resembling a gas pipe (as a single-barreled shotgun)

gas plant *n* **:** FRAXINELLA

gas plate *n* **1 :** a hot plate using gas **2 :** a steel plate in a gun breech mechanism resting in a recess in the face of the breechblock and supporting the obturator ring

gas pliers *n pl* **:** stout pliers designed for gripping small pipe, rods, or other round objects

gas pool *n* **:** a continuous area of sedimentary rocks that when drilled yields natural gas in commercial quantities

gas port *n* **:** a small hole in the barrel of a gas-operated rifle for allowing sufficient controlled escape of gas to insure proper functioning

gas producer *n* **:** PRODUCER 3

gasproof \ˈ=ˌ=\ *adj* **:** proof against the entry or damaging action of gases ⟨a ~ compartment⟩ ⟨~ varnishes⟩

gaspy \ˈgaspē\ *adj* -ER/-EST **:** marked by or given to gasping ⟨a tense ~ voice⟩

gas refrigeration *n* **:** refrigeration that involves the use of machinery in which the refrigerant is heated by a gas flame

gas retort *n* **:** ³RETORT 1b

gas ring *n* **1 :** an obturator ring **2 :** a ring-shaped portable gas burner with stand and sometimes a handle

gas sand *n* **:** a sandstone or other rock containing natural gas

gassed *past of* GAS

gas·ser \ˈgasə(r), ˈgaas-,ˈgais-\ *n* -S **1 :** one that gasses: as **a :** a well (as an oil well) that yields gas **b** *slang* **:** a talkative or bragging person **c :** a worker who singes cloth, yarn, or thread **2** *slang* **:** something outstanding of its kind ⟨the new show is a real ~⟩

gas·se·ri·an ganglion \(ˈ)gaˈsirēən-\ *n, sometimes cap 1st G* [Johann L. *Gasser* †1765 Austrian anatomist + E *-ian*] **:** the large flattened sensory root ganglion of the trigeminal nerve lying within the skull and behind the orbit — called also *semilunar ganglion*

gasses *pl of* GAS, *pres 3d sing of* GAS

gas shell *n* **:** GAS BOMB

gas·si·ness \ˈgasēnəs, ˈgaas-,ˈgais-, -sin-\ *n* -ES **:** the quality or state of being gassy

gassing *n* -S [fr. gerund of ²*gas*] **1 :** an act or process of causing something to interact with gas **2 a :** the deliberate or inadvertent poisoning of persons exposed to noxious gases or fumes **b :** the destruction of pests (as insects) by the use of poisonous gases (as hydrogen cyanide or methyl bromide) **:** FUMIGATION **3 :** the evolution of gas bubbles from the acid in a lead storage battery while charging

gas spurt *n* **:** one of the little heaps that occur on the surface of certain geological strata containing organic matter and that are believed to be due to the escape of gas during early formative stages of the strata

gas station *n* **:** FILLING STATION

gas storage *n* **:** storage of fruits or vegetables in an atmosphere high in carbon dioxide and low in oxygen to delay ripening

gas·sy \ˈgasē, ˈgaas-,ˈgais-, -si\ *adj* -ER/-EST [¹*gas* + *-y*] **1 a :** full of or containing gas **b** *of a vacuum tube* **:** defective by reason of accumulated gas developed in service from structural components **2 :** having the characteristics of gas ⟨a ~ odor⟩ **3 :** full of boastful or insincere talk **:** INFLATED, WINDY ⟨a ~ speaker⟩ ⟨~ oratory⟩

¹gast *vt* -ED/-ING/-S [ME *gasten*, fr. *gast, gost* soul, spirit, ghost — more at GHOST] *obs* **:** SCARE ⟨~*ed* by the noise I made, full suddenly he fled —Shak.⟩

²gast \ˈgäst\ *n* -S *Scot* **:** a state of fright or alarm

³gast \ˈ"\ *adj* [akin to OFris *gēst, gāst* high, dry, barren, MLG *gēst* high dry land near the sea, OSw *gistiun* cracked open from dryness, and perh. to OE *geonian* to yawn — more at YAWN] *dial Eng* **:** BARREN — used of a domestic animal

gas·tal·do \gəˈstäl(,)dō\ *n, pl* **gastal·di** \-(,)dē\ [It *castaldo, gastaldo*, fr. ML *castaldus, gastaldus*, fr. a Lombard word akin to OE *gesteald* abode, fr. *ge-* (perfective & collective prefix) + *-steald* (akin to OE *stealdan* to possess); akin to OHG *hagustalt* day laborer, bachelor, Goth *gastaldan* to acquire, possess, OE *steall* place, position, stall — more at STALL] **1 :** the representative of a king on his domains in medieval Italy esp. among the Lombards **2 :** a steward in a nobleman's household

gas tank *n* **1 :** a tank for the storage of natural or manufactured gas **2 :** the fuel tank supplying a gasoline engine

gas·ter \ˈgastə(r)\ *n* -S [NL, fr. Gk *gastēr* belly — more at GASTRIC] **:** the enlarged part of the abdomen behind the pedicel in ants and other hymenopterous insects

gaster- *or* **gastero-** *comb form* [NL, fr. Gk *gastero-* belly, fr. *gaster-, gastēr*] **1 :** ventral area ⟨*Gasteropoda*⟩ ⟨*gasterostome*⟩ **2 :** stomach ⟨*gasteralgia*⟩ ⟨*Gasterophilus*⟩

-gaster \ˌgastə(r), ˌgaas-, ˌgais-\ *n comb form* -S [NL, fr. Gk *gastēr*] **1 :** part having a (specified) relation to the stomach ⟨meso*gaster*⟩ ⟨meta*gaster*⟩ **2 :** organism having a (specified) type of digestive tract — esp. in generic names ⟨*Microgaster*⟩ ⟨myxo*gaster*⟩

gas·te·ria \gaˈstirēə\ *n* [NL, fr. *gaster-* + *-ia*] **1** *cap* **:** a genus of usu. stemless southern African plants (family Liliaceae) having thick succulent leaves arranged in two ranks or a rosette and long racemes of scattered largely greenish flowers, being closely related to the aloes, growing in desert regions, and including several plants that are cultivated as ornamentals in warm dry regions or in the greenhouse **2** -S **:** any plant of the genus *Gasteria*

gas·tero·lichenes \ˌgastə(,)rō+\ *n pl, cap* [NL, fr. *gaster-* + *Lichenes*] *in some classifications* **:** a group of angiocarpous lichens in which the fungus is a gasteromycete

gas·tero·my·cete \ˈ"+,mīˌsēt *or* ˌmī,s-\ *n* -S [NL *Gasteromycetes*] **:** a fungus of the class Gasteromycetes **:** a basidiomycete with basidia and spores enclosed in a peridium — **gas·tero·my·ce·tous** \-ēd·əs\ *adj*

gas·tero·my·ce·te·ae \ˈ"+,mīˌsēd·ē,ē\ [NL, fr. *gaster-* + *-mycetes* + *-eae*] *syn of* GASTEROMYCETES

gas·tero·my·ce·tes \,gastə(,)rō,mīsēd·(,)ēz\ *n pl, cap* [NL, fr. *gaster-* + *-mycetes*] *in some classifications* **:** a class or subclass of fungi including all basidiomycetes with the basidia and spores enclosed in a peridium (as the puffballs and stinkhorns)

gas·ter·o·phil·i·dae \,gastə(,)rōˈfilə,dē\ *n pl, cap* [NL, fr. *Gasterophilus*, type genus + *-idae*] **:** a family of two-winged flies comprising the horse botflies, resembling honeybees in size and proportions, and having the adult mouthparts vestigial and the antennae sunken in facial grooves

gas·ter·oph·i·lo·sis \,gastə,räfəˈlōsəs\ *n, pl* **gasterophiloses** \-ō,sēz\ [NL, fr. *Gasterophilus* + *-osis*] **:** infestation with horse botflies

gas·ter·oph·i·lus \-ˈräfələs\ *n, cap* [NL, fr. *gaster-* + *-philus*] **:** a genus of botflies containing one form (*G. intestinalis*) that commonly infests the horse

gas·ter·o·pod \ˈgast(ə)rə,päd\ *adj or n* [NL *Gasteropoda*, syn. of *Gastropoda*, fr. *gaster-* + *-poda*] **:** GASTROPOD

¹gas·ter·os·te·id \ˌgastəˈrästēəd\ *adj* [NL *Gasterosteidae*] **:** of or relating to the Gasterosteidae

²gasteroste id \ˈ"\ *n* -S **:** a fish of the family Gasterosteidae **:** STICKLEBACK

gas·ter·o·ste·idae \,gastərōˈstēə,dē\ *n pl, cap* [NL, fr. *Gasterosteus*, type genus (fr. *gaster-* + *osteus*) + *-idae*] **:** a family of small spiny-finned freshwater or salt-water fishes that consists of the sticklebacks and constitutes with related forms a suborder of Scleroparei or is placed with the cornetfishes and pipefishes in the order Solenichthyes — **gas·ter·os·te·i·form** \,gastəˈrästēə,fȯrm\ *adj* — **gas·ter·os·te·oid** \-stē,ȯid\ *adj*

gas·ter·o·sto·ma·ta \,gastərōˈstōməd·ə\ *n pl, cap* [NL, fr. *Gasterostomum* genus of trematode worms (fr. *gaster-* + *-stomum*) + *-ata*] *in some classifications* **:** an order of Digenea coextensive with the family Bucephalidae — compare PROSOSTOMATA

gas·ter·o·stome \ˈgastərə,stōm\ *n* -S [NL *Gasterostomata*] **:** a trematode of the family Bucephalidae

gast·haus \ˈgäst,haůs\ *n, pl* **gasthauses** \-haůzəz\ *or* **gast·häus·er** \-hȯizə(r)\ [G, fr. OHG *gasthūs*, fr. *gast* guest + *hūs* house — more at GUEST, HOUSE] **:** a German inn or tavern

gas thermometer *n* **:** a thermometer containing gas (as hydrogen) as the enclosed thermometric substance, variations in temperature being indicated by the change in pressure of a fixed quantity of gas required to maintain the gas at a constant volume or the change in volume of a fixed quantity of gas maintained at a constant pressure

gastight \ˈ=ˌ=\ *adj* **1 :** impervious to gas **2 :** constructed or arranged so that gas (as a noxious or flammable gas) will not enter an enclosed space under specified conditions (as of pressure) — **gas·tight·ness** *n*

gastness *n* -ES [ME *gastnesse*, fr. *gast* afraid (fr. past part. of *gasten* to frighten) + *-nesse* -ness — more at GAST] *obs* **:** FRIGHT, DREAD

gas·tor·nis \gaˈstȯrnəs\ *n, cap* [NL, fr. *Gaston* Planté †1889 Fr. physician + Gk *ornis* bird — more at ERNE] **:** a genus of large extinct birds (order Diatrymiformes) from the Eocene formations of the Paris basin that are similar and related to those of the genus *Diatryma*

gastr- *or* **gastro-** *also* **gastri-** *comb form* [Gk, belly, fr. *gastr-, gastēr* — more at GASTRIC] **1 :** ventral area ⟨*gastropod*⟩ **2 :** stomach ⟨*gastrectomy*⟩ ⟨*gastrology*⟩ **3 :** gastric and ⟨*gastroduodenal*⟩ ⟨*gastrohepatic*⟩

gas·traea *also* **gas·trea** \gaˈstrēə\ *n* -S [NL, fr. Gk *gastr-, gastēr* belly] **:** a hypothetical metazoan ancestral form corresponding in organization to a simple invaginated gastrula — **gas·trae·al** \(ˈ)gaˈstrēəl\ *adj*

gas·trae·adae \gaˈstrēə,dē\ *n pl, cap* [NL, irreg. fr. *Gastraea* + *-idae*] **:** a hypothetical group of ancestral metazoan animals structurally comparable to the gastrula

gas·tral \ˈgastrəl\ *adj* [*gastr-* + *-al*] **:** of or relating to the stomach or digestive tract ⟨the ~ cavity of a sea anemone —C.L.Prosser⟩

gas·tral·gia \gaˈstralj(ē)ə\ *n* -S [NL, fr. *gastr-* + *-algia*] **:** pain in the stomach or epigastrium esp. of a neuralgic type — **gas·tral·gic** \(ˈ)gaˈstraljik\ *adj*

gas·tra·li·um \gaˈstrālēəm\ *n, pl* **gastra·lia** \-ēə\ [NL, fr. *gastr-* + L *-alis* -al + NL *-ium*] **1 :** ABDOMINAL RIB **2 :** a spicule located immediately beneath the inner cellular wall of a sponge

gas trap *n* **1 :** a drain trap **:** sewer trap **2 :** an apparatus for separating natural gas from the petroleum in which it is dissolved

gas·trec·to·my \gaˈstrektəmē\ *n* -ES [ISV *gastr-* + *-ectomy*] **:** surgical removal of all or part of the stomach

-gastria \ˈgastrēə\ *n comb form* -S [NL, fr. *gastr-* + *-ia*] **:** condition of having (such) a stomach or (such or so many) stomachs ⟨micro*gastria*⟩ ⟨poly*gastria*⟩

gas·tric \ˈgastrik, -aas-,-ais-, -rēk\ *adj* [Gk *gastr-, gastēr* belly, paunch, womb (alter. of — assumed — Gk *grastēr*, fr. Gk *gran* to gnaw, eat) + E *-ic* — more at CRESS] **1 :** of, relating to situated near, or originating in the stomach ⟨~ disorders⟩ **2 :** resembling a stomach in form or function ⟨a ~ polyp⟩ ⟨a ~ vacuole⟩

gastric artery *n* **1 :** a branch of the coeliac artery that passes to the cardiac end of the stomach and along the lesser curvature **2 :** any of several branches of the splenic artery distributed to the greater curvature of the stomach

gastric cecum *n* **:** one of the elongated pouches projecting from the upper end of the insect stomach

gastric gland *n* **:** any of various glands in the walls of the stomach that secrete the gastric juice

gastric juice *n* **:** the digestive fluid secreted by the glands in the mucous membrane of the stomach consisting of a thin watery fluid with an acid reaction because of the presence of 0.2 to 0.4 percent of free hydrochloric acid and containing several enzymes (as pepsin and rennin)

gastric mill *n* **:** a grinding apparatus consisting of several movable calcareous or chitinous pieces in the pharynx or stomach of certain invertebrates

gastric ostium *n* **:** the opening leading into a gastric pouch in scyphozoans

gastric pouch *n* **:** any of the pouched radial divisions of the stomach in scyphozoans

gastric ulcer *n* **:** a peptic ulcer situated in the stomach

gas·tril·e·gous \(ˈ)gaˈstriləgəs\ *adj* [*gastr-* + L *legere* to gather + E *-ous* — more at LEGEND] **:** gathering pollen by means of a pollen brush on the abdomen ⟨~ bees⟩ — compare PODILEGOUS

gas·tril·o·quist \gaˈstriləkwəst\ *n* -S [*gastr-* + *-loquist* (as in *ventriloquist*)] **:** VENTRILOQUIST

gas·trin \ˈgastrən\ *n* -S [ISV *gastr-* + *-in*] **:** a hormone that is produced chiefly in the antrum of the stomach, induces secretion of gastric juice, and may be identical with histamine

gas·tri·tis \ga'strīd·əs\ *n, pl* **gastrit·i·des** \-rid·ə,dēz\ [NL, fr. *gastr-* + *-itis*] **:** inflammation of the stomach esp. of its mucous membrane

gastro- — see GASTR-

gas·tro·anastomosis \¦ga(,)strō+\ *n* [NL, fr. *gastr-* + *anastomosis*] **:** the formation by surgical means of a communication between the pyloric and cardiac ends of the stomach when the normal channel is obstructed or contracted

gas·tro·blast \'gastrə,blast\ *n* [*gastr-* + *-blast*] **:** a nutritive zooid of a tunicate colony

gas·tro·cen·tral \¦gastrō¦sen·trəl\ *or* **gas·tro·cen·trous** \-rəs\ *adj* [*gastr-* + *central* or *-centrous* (fr. NL *centrum* + E *-ous*)] **1 :** having the centrum formed of the interventral elements **2 :** having gastrocentral vertebrae ⟨~ reptiles⟩

gas·tro·chae·na \,==ˈkēnə\ *n, cap* [NL, fr. *gastr-* + *-chaena* (fr. Gk *chainein* to yawn, gape) — more at YAWN] **:** a genus of bivalve mollusks (order Eulamellibranchia) that bore in coral, soft rock, or hardened mud and have long siphons and a widely gaping shell

gas·troc·ne·mi·al \¦gastrō¦nēmēəl, -,sträk¦n-\ *adj* [NL *gastrocnemius* + E *-al*] **:** of or relating to the gastrocnemius

gas·troc·ne·mi·us \,=(,)=ˈ=mēəs\ *n, pl* **gastrocne·mii** \-mē,ī\ [NL, fr. Gk *gastroknēmē* calf of the leg, fr. *gastro-* belly + *knēmē* shin, leg — more at GASTR-] **:** the largest and most superficial muscle of the calf of the leg arising by two heads from the condyles of the femur and having its tendon of insertion united with that of the soleus to form the Achilles' tendon

gas·tro·coel *also* **gas·tro·coele** \'gastrō,sēl\ *n* -s [F *gastrocèle*, fr. *gastr-* + *-cèle* -coele] **:** ARCHENTERON

gas·tro·colic \¦gastrō+\ *adj* [ISV *gastr-* + *colic*] **:** of, relating to, or uniting the stomach and colon ⟨~ ligament⟩

gastrocolic omentum *n* **:** GREATER OMENTUM

gas·tro·dermal \"+\ *adj* [NL *gastrodermis* + E *-al*] **:** of, relating to, or consisting of gastrodermis

gas·tro·dermis \"+\ *n* [NL, fr. *gastr-* + *-dermis*] **:** the lining membrane of the alimentary tract of an invertebrate — used esp. when the germ-layer origin is obscure

gas·tro·dis·coi·des \,==də'skȯi(,)dēz\ *n, cap* [NL, fr. *gastr-* + LL *discoides* quoit-shaped — more at DISCOID] **:** a genus of amphistome trematode worms including a common intestinal parasite (*G. hominis*) of man and swine in southeastern Asia

gas·tro·duodenal \¦ga(,)strō+\ *adj* [ISV *gastr-* + *duodenal*] **:** of, relating to, or involving both the stomach and duodenum ⟨a ~ ulcer⟩

gas·tro·duodenitis \"+\ *n* [NL, fr. *gastr-* + *duodenitis*] **:** inflammation of the stomach and duodenum

gas·tro·enteric \"+\ *adj* [*gastr-* + *enteric*] **:** GASTROINTESTINAL

gas·tro·enteritis \"+\ *n* [NL, fr. *gastr-* + *enteritis*] **:** inflammation of the lining membrane of the stomach and the intestines

gas·tro·en·ter·ol·o·gist \,ga(,)strō,entə'räləjəst\ *n* -s **:** a specialist in gastroenterology; *specif* **:** a physician specializing in the diagnosis and treatment of gastrointestinal disorders

gas·tro·en·ter·ol·o·gy \-jē\ *n* -ES [ISV *gastr-* + *enter-* + *-logy*] **:** the study of the stomach and the intestines esp. in respect to their diseases and pathology

gas·tro·en·ter·os·to·my \-ästəmē\ *n* [ISV *gastr-* + *enterostomy*] **:** the surgical formation of a passage between the stomach and small intestine

gas·tro·epiploic artery \¦ga(,)strō+ . . . -\ *n* [*gastr-* + *epiploic*] **:** either of two arteries forming an anastomosis along the greater curvature of the stomach, the right being derived from the gastroduodenal artery and the left from the splenic artery

gas·tro·esophageal \"+\ *adj* [*gastr-* + *esophageal*] **:** of, relating to, or involving the stomach and esophagus

gas·tro·gen·ic \¦gastrə¦jenik\ *or* **gas·trog·e·nous** \(')ga¦sträjənəs\ *adj* [*gastr-* + *-genic*, *-genous*] **:** of gastric origin **:** being due to causes originating in the stomach ⟨~ anemia⟩

gas·tro·intestinal \¦ga(,)strō+\ *adj* [*gastr-* + *intestinal*] **1 :** of, relating to, consisting of, or involving both stomach and intestine ⟨~ inflammation⟩ **2 :** of or from the gastrointestinal tract ⟨the ~ wall⟩ ⟨~ absorption⟩

gastrointestinal tract *n* **:** the stomach and intestine as a functional unit

gas·tro·jejunal \"+\ *adj* [*gastr-* + *jejunal*] **:** of, relating to, or involving both stomach and jejunum ⟨~ lesions⟩

gas·tro·jejunostomy \"+\ *n* [ISV *gastr-* + *jejunostomy*] **:** the surgical formation of a passage between the stomach and jejunum **:** GASTROENTEROSTOMY

gas·tro·lith \'gastrə,lith\ *n* -s [ISV *gastr-* + *-lith*] **1 a :** CRAB'S-EYE 1 **b :** a stone or pebble found in the stomach of some fishes and reptiles and presumably used for grinding up their food **2 :** a gastric calculus

gas·tro·lo·bi·um \,gastrə'lōbēəm\ *n* [NL, fr. *gastr-* + *-lobium* (fr. Gk *lobion*, dim. of *lobos* lobe) — more at LOBE] **1** *cap* **:** a genus of Australian evergreen leguminous shrubs that have opposite or whorled compound leaves which are poisonous to livestock, showy yellow to deep orange flowers with a reddish purple keel, and 2-seeded pods **2** -s **:** any plant of the genus *Gastrolobium* **:** POISON BUSH

gas·trol·o·ger \ga'sträləjə(r)\ *n* -s **:** GOURMET

gas·tro·log·i·cal \¦gastrə¦läjəkəl\ *adj* **:** of, relating to, or concerned with the needs and demands of the stomach

gas·trol·o·gist \ga'sträləjəst\ *n* -s **:** a specialist in gastrology

gas·trol·o·gy \-jē\ *n* -ES [Gk *gastrologia*, title given to a poem describing a gastronomical tour of the known world, by Archestratos, 4th cent. B.C. Greek poet, fr. *gastro-* belly + *-logia* -logy — more at GASTR-] **:** the art or science of caring for the stomach either medically or gastronomically

gas·trol·y·sis \ga'sträləsəs\ *n* [NL, fr. *gastr-* + *-lysis*] **:** the surgical operation of freeing the stomach from adhesions

gas·tro·my·ce·tes \,gastrō,mī'sēd·(,)ēz\ [NL, fr. *gastr-* + *Mycetes*] *syn of* GASTEROMYCETES

gas·tro·nome \'gastrə,nōm\ *n* -s [F, back-formation fr. *gastronomie* gastronomy] **1 :** one fond of good living **:** EPICURE; *esp* **:** an enthusiast over and expert judge of excellence in food and drink **2** *or* **gas·tro·nom** \¦gastrə¦näm\ [Russ *gastronom*, lit., gastronome (sense 1), fr. F *gastronome*] **:** a delicatessen in the U.S.S.R. **syn** see EPICURE

gas·tron·o·mer \ga'stränəmə(r)\ *n* -s [fr. *gastronomy*, after such pairs as *astronomy: astronomer*] **:** GASTRONOME 1 **syn** see EPICURE

gas·tro·nom·ic \¦gastrə¦nämik, -mēk\ *also* **gas·tro·nom·i·cal** \-məkəl, -mēk-\ *adj* [F *gastronomique*, fr. *gastronomie* + *-ique* -ic, -ical] **:** of or relating to gastronomy — **gas·tro·nom·i·cal·ly** \-mək(ə)lē, -mēk-, -li\ *adv*

gas·tron·o·mist \ga'stränəməst\ *n* -s **:** a specialist in gastronomy **:** GASTRONOME

gas·tron·o·my \-mē,-mi\ *n* -ES [F *gastronomie*, fr. Gk *gastronomia*, title given to a 4th cent B.C. poem also called *Gastrologia*, fr. *gastro-* belly + *-nomia* -nomy — more at GASTROLOGY, GASTR-] **1 :** the art or science of good eating **2 :** culinary customs or style (as of a particular region) ⟨why not introduce oriental ~ to the Western menu —Norbert Mühlen⟩

gas·tro·pancreatic fold \¦ga(,)strō+ . . . -\ *or* **gastropancreatic ligament** *n* [*gastr-* + *pancreatic*] **:** a peritoneal fold extending from the pylorus to the pancreas

gas·tro·parietal \"+\ *adj* [*gastr-* + *parietal*] **:** connecting the stomach and body wall

gas·tro·pexy \'gastrə,peksē\ *n* -ES [ISV *gastr-* + *-pexy*] **:** a surgical operation in which the stomach is sutured to the abdominal wall

gas·troph·i·lus \ga'sträfələs\ [NL, fr. *gastr-* + *-philus*] *syn of* GASTEROPHILUS

gas·tro·phren·ic \¦gastrə¦frenik\ *adj* [ISV *gastr-* + *phrenic*] **:** of, relating to, or connecting the stomach and diaphragm

gas·tro·plication \¦ga(,)strō+\ *n* -s [ISV *gastr-* + *plication*] **:** a surgical operation for reducing chronic stomach dilatation by plication

¹gas·tro·pod \'gastrə,päd\ *also* **gas·trop·o·dan** \(')ga¦sträpəd°n\ *adj* [*gastropod* fr. NL *Gastropoda*; *gastropodan* fr. NL *Gastropoda* + E *-an*] **:** of, relating to, or characteristic of the class Gastropoda ⟨~ anatomy⟩

²gastropod \"\ *also* **gastropodan** \"\ *n* -s **:** a mollusk of the class Gastropoda **:** a snail, slug, or related mollusk

gas·trop·o·da \ga'sträpədə\ *n pl, cap* [NL, fr. *gastr-* + *-poda*] **:** a large and varied class of Mollusca known from the Cambrian on that includes mollusks with a univalve shell (as a periwinkle or whelk) which is not divided into chambers and is usu. spirally coiled and some (as the slugs and heteropods) with the shell greatly reduced or lacking, usu. with a definite head bearing one or two pairs of sensory tentacles, a pair of eyes sometimes at the end of the tentacles, and a mouth often at the end of a proboscis and in some instances fitted with a toothed radula, with the ventral surface modified into a flattened foot used in creeping or lobed (as in pteropods) for swimming, and with oviparous or sometimes ovoviviparous reproduction, and usu. with distinct larval trochophore and veliger stages — see EUTHYNEURA, STREPTONEURA; compare SCAPHOPODA — **gastropodous** *adj*

gas·tro·pore \'gastrə,pō(ə)r\ *n* [*gastr-* + *pore*] **:** a pore occupied by a gastrozooid in a hydrozoan coral

gas·tro·pri·val \¦gastrō¦prīvəl\ *adj* [*gastr-* + L *privare* to deprive + E *-al* — more at PRIVATE] **:** caused by or associated with lack of essential gastric factors or substances ⟨~ pellagra⟩

gas·trop·to·sis \,ga,sträp'tōsəs\ *n* [NL, fr. *gastr-* + *ptosis*] **:** abnormal sagging of the stomach into the lower abdomen

gas·tros·chi·sis \ga'sträskəsəs\ *n* -ES [NL, fr. *gastr-* + *-schisis*] **:** congenital fissure of the ventral abdominal wall

gas·tro·scope \'gastrə,skōp\ *n* [ISV *gastr-* + *-scope*] **:** a hollow tubular instrument designed to pass into the stomach by way of the mouth and esophagus and fitted with optical and lighting equipment that permits visual inspection of the stomach — **gas·tro·scop·ic** \¦gastrə¦skäpik\ *adj* — **gas·tros·co·pist** \ga'sträskəpəst\ *n* -s — **gas·tros·co·py** \-pē\ *n* -ES

gas·tro·splenic ligament \¦gastrō+ . . . -\ *n* [*gastrosplenic*, fr. *gastr-* + *splenic*] **:** a mesenteric fold passing from the greater curvature of the stomach to the spleen

gas·tros·te·gal \(')ga¦strästəgəl\ *adj* **:** of, relating to, or being a gastrostege

gas·tro·stege \'gastrə,stēj\ *n* -s [*gastr-* + *-stege*] **:** one of the large linearly ordered scales on the ventral surface of most snakes

gas·tro·ste·idae \,gastrə'stēə,dē\ [NL, alter. of *Gasterosteidae*] *syn of* GASTEROSTEIDAE

gas·tro·stome \'gastrə,stōm\ *n* -s [*gastr-* + *-stome*] **:** the orifice of a gastropore

gas·tros·to·my \ga'strästəmē\ *n* -ES [ISV *gastr-* + *-stomy*; prob. orig. formed as F *gastrostomie*] **1 :** the surgical formation of an opening through the abdominal wall into the stomach to serve for the introduction of food **2 :** the opening made by gastrostomy

gas·tro·style \'gastrə,stīl\ *n* [*gastr-* + *style*] **:** a spiculated projection at the base of a gastropore extending into the gastrozooid

gas·tro·trich \'gastrə·,trik\ *n* -s [NL *Gastrotricha*] **:** an animal of the group Gastrotricha

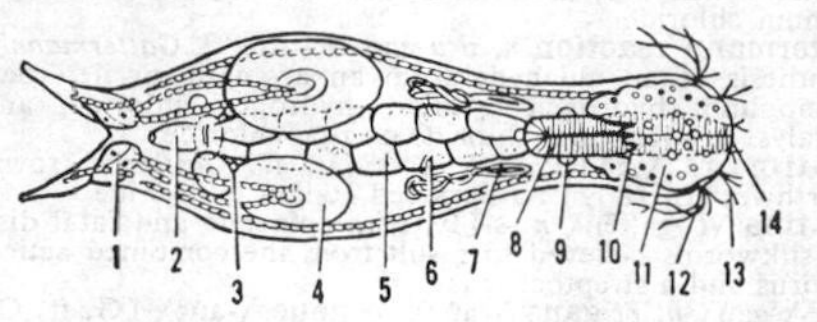

gastrotrich: dorsal view of adult female: *1* cement gland, *2* rectum, *3* ovary, *4* egg, *5* intestine, *6* excretory pore, *7* excretory canal, *8* pharynx, *9* posterior salivary gland, *10* anterior salivary gland, *11* brain, *12* posterolateral bristles, *13* anterolateral bristles, *14* mouth

gas·trot·ri·cha \ga'strä·trəkə\ *n pl, cap* [NL, fr. *gastr-* + *-tricha*] **:** a small class or other group of minute freshwater multicellular animals superficially resembling infusorians, having cilia on the ventral side, and being related to the rotifers and with these included in the phylum Aschelminthes — **gas·trot·ri·chan** \(')ga¦strä·trəkən\ *adj*

gas·tro·vascular \¦ga(,)strō+\ *adj* [ISV *gastr-* + *vascular*] **:** functioning in both digestion and circulation ⟨the coelenteron of a medusa serves as a ~ system⟩

gas·tro·zooid \¦gastrə+\ *n* [ISV *gastr-* + *zooid*] **:** a zooid provided with a mouth and digestive organs **:** TROPHOZOOID

gas·tru·la \'gastrələ\ *n, pl* **gastrulas** \-ləz\ *or* **gastru·lae** \-,lē, -,lī\ [NL, fr. *gastr* + L *-ula* (fem. dim. suffix)] **:** an early metazoan embryo consisting of a hollow 2-layered cellular cup made up of an outer epiblast and an inner hypoblast that meet along the marginal line of a blastopore and jointly enclose the archenteron, forming typically by invagination of part of the blastula wall or in many yolk-filled eggs by overgrowth of cells formed about the animal pole and epiboly, and in eggs producing discoblastulas and in mammalian eggs being greatly modified in both organization and course of formation — see DELAMINATION, INVOLUTION; compare BLASTULA, MORULA — **gas·tru·lar** \-lə(r)\ *adj*

gas·tru·late \-,lāt\ *vi* -ED/-ING/-S [NL *gastrula* + E *-ate*] **:** to become or form a gastrula ⟨*gastrulating* embryos of the frog⟩ — **gas·tru·la·tion** \,==ˈlāshən\ *n* -s

gasts *pres 3d sing of* GAST, *pl of* GAST

gas tube *n* **:** an electron tube containing gas at a low pressure sufficient to influence the electrical performance of the tube

gas turbine *n* **:** an internal-combustion engine in which air compressed in a compressor goes into a combustion chamber and is compressed further by the combustion of sprayed liquid or powdered fuel, the hot compressed gases of combustion then expanding and driving a turbine having blades similar to those of a steam turbine

gas turbine locomotive *n* **:** a locomotive powered by a gas-turbine engine

gas vent *n* **1 :** a passage or slot built into a sedimentation chamber to allow the escape of gas and prevent its passage through the settling chamber **2 :** a vent pipe leading to the outer air from a gas furnace, oven, or other gas-fired equipment for removal of products of combustion

gas warfare *n* **:** warfare in which poisonous, asphyxiating, and corrosive gases are used as weapons

gas welding *n* **:** fusion welding in which the required heat is obtained from a gas flame

gas well *n* **:** a well that produces chiefly natural gas

gasworker \'=,==\ *n* **:** a gasworks laborer

gasworks \'=,=\ *n pl but sing in constr* **:** a plant for manufacturing gas

gas zone *n* **:** a rock formation holding gas at a pressure great enough to discharge it at the surface through a well

¹gat *archaic past of* GET

²gat \'gat, *usu* -ad·+V\ *n* -s [prob. fr. D, lit., hole, opening, fr. MD; akin to OE *geat* door, opening — more at GATE] **:** a channel or passage from a shore inland (as between sandbanks or cliffs) or from one body of water to another

³gat \"\ *n* -s [short for *gatling*, fr. *Gatling* (*gun*)] *slang* **:** PISTOL

GAT *abbr* Greenwich apparent time

ga·ta \'gäd·ə\ *n* -s [AmerSp, fr. Sp, female cat, fr. LL *catta* cat — more at CAT] **:** a shark (*Ginglymostoma cirratum*) of the warmer parts of the Atlantic ocean — called also *nurse shark*

gatch \'gach, 'gäch\ *n* -ES [Per *gach*, fr. MPer] **:** a plaster used esp. in Persian architectural ornamentation

gatch bed \'gach-\ *n, usu cap G* [after Willis D. *Gatch* b1878 Am. surgeon] **:** HOSPITAL BED

gatchwork \'=,=\ *n* **:** work in which gatch is used; *also* **:** ornamentation with gatch

¹gate \'gāt, *usu* -ād·+V\ *n* -s *often attrib* [ME *gat, gate, yate*, fr. OE *geat, gæt* door, gate, opening; akin to OFris *jet* hole, opening, OS & ON *gat*, Gk *chezein* to defecate, Skt *hadati* he defecates] **1 :** an opening for passage in an enclosing wall, fence, or barrier; *esp* **:** such an opening with a movable frame or door for closing it ⟨rushed down the path and through the ~⟩ **2 :** a structure or part of a structure comprising a passageway with its collateral structures (as towers, approaches) esp. when designed for defense ⟨the ~ of a walled city⟩ ⟨a temple ~⟩ **3 a :** the frame or door that closes a gate and is legally a part of the wall, fence, or other enclosure which it interrupts **:** a swinging or sliding barrier used to fill or close a gateway esp. when made of a grating or open frame or forming a heavy or rough structure **b :** a movable barrier that can be placed (as by swinging or lowering) so as to block passage along a way (as at a railroad crossing) **4 a :** a means of entrance or sometimes egress ⟨I'll lock up all the ~s of love — Shak.⟩ ⟨determination is a ~ to success⟩ ⟨a small untended wound may become a ~ for infection⟩ **b :** a pass or defile in mountains serving as a way of entrance into a country **c** (1) **:** a usu. numbered gate from a passenger terminal or pier to an embarkation area (2) **:** such a gate together with the embarkation area (as a railroad loading platform) to which it gives access **d :** STARTING GATE **e :** an opening between two flags through which a skier must pass in a slalom race **5 :** something shaped or functioning like a gate: as **a :** a door, valve, or other device for controlling the passage of fluid or other material (as through a sluice, channel, or pipe) ⟨a penstock ~ for a waterwheel⟩ ⟨a blast ~ for a forge⟩ ⟨an oil ~⟩ **b :** GATING 1 **c :** ²SASH 2 **d** *slang* **:** a railroad track switch **e :** a signal (as a square-wave signal) that makes an electronic circuit operative for a chosen short period **f :** a device used in gating (sense 2) **g** *or* **gateleg** \'=,=\ **:** a movable supporting bracket for a drop leaf consisting of a pair of legs separated and stabilized by horizontal spreaders and arranged to fold against the frame of the piece of furniture when the leaf is dropped **6 :** a hinged iron band secured to the topmast trestletrees to hold in place the heel of the topgallant mast **7 a :** a metal part behind the cylinder in old-pattern revolvers that in loading is turned outward to expose the chambers **b :** the cover for the magazine opening in a breech-loading rifle **8 a** (1) **:** a channel in a foundry mold through which the molten metal flows into the cavity made by the pattern **:** INGATE (2) **:** the waste piece of metal cast in the opening of a gate **b :** the channel in each impression of a set of drop-forging dies that connects the flash with the sprue **9 a** *also* **gate money :** the total admission receipts esp. of a sports event **b :** the number of spectators admitted **10** *slang* **:** a state of rejection or separation (as from employment or intimate association) — used esp. in the phrase *give (one) the gate* ⟨after the quarrel she gave her boyfriend the ~⟩ ⟨got the ~ for being late too often⟩ **11 :** the part of a camera, printer, or projector that includes the picture mask or aperture and the guiding tracks and surfaces which assist in positioning the film **12 :** the slotted guide for the gearshift lever of a multiple-speed automobile transmission **13 :** an electronic circuit having an output and two or more inputs so arranged that the output is energized only under certain conditions (as when both of two input wires receive pulses) **14 :** ³GAIT

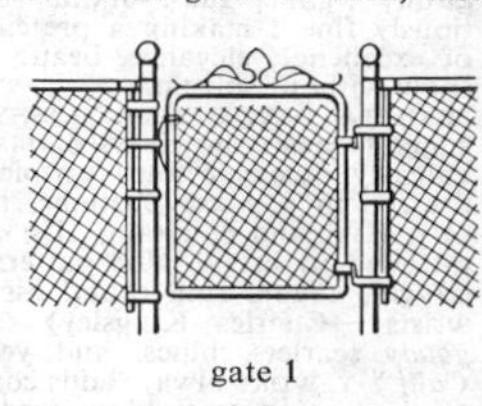

gate 1

²gate \"\ *vt* -ED/-ING/-S **1 :** to supply with a gate **2** *Brit* **:** CAMPUS **3 :** to adjust (a loom) esp. for actual weaving **4 a :** to control by means of a gate (sense 5a) **b :** to make (an electronic device) operate in accordance with a gate **5 a :** to supply (a foundry pattern) with extra parts to bring about the molding of the necessary gates **b :** to supply (a foundry mold) with gates

³gate \"\ *n* -s [ME, fr. ON *gata* road, path; akin to OHG *gazza* road, street, Goth *gatwo* street, and perh. to OE *geat* door, opening] **1** *archaic* **:** a way for travel **:** STREET, PATH ⟨gang down the ~ to Luckie Gregson's —Sir Walter Scott⟩ **2** *now dial* **a :** METHOD, WAY, TECHNIQUE **b :** customary or habitual style **3** *Scot* **:** JOURNEY, TRIP **4** *chiefly Scot* **:** route of travel **:** DIRECTION ⟨he's gone some other ~⟩ **5** *chiefly Scot* **:** DISTANCE ⟨a long ~ from Heddon Rig⟩ **6** *dial Eng* **:** pasturage esp. on common lands

ga·te·a·do \,gäd·ē'ä(,)dō, ¦gäd·ē¦aů\ *n* -s [AmerSp, fr. Sp, adj., catlike, striped like a civet cat, fr. *gato* cat, fr. LL *cattus*; fr. the streaks in the wood — more at CAT] **:** a tropical American timber tree (*Astronium graveolens*) of the family Anacardiaceae that yields a hard dense heavy black-streaked brown timber used as a cabinet wood and that has bark rich in tannin

gate·age \'gād·ij\ *n* -s [¹*gate* + *-age*] **1 a :** the use of gates (as in controlling flow of water) **b :** the gates so used **2 :** the area of gate opening (as of a turbine gate)

ga·teau \(')gä¦tō\ *n, pl* **ga·teaux** \-ō(z)\ [F *gâteau*, fr. OF *gastel*, prob. of Gmc origin; akin to OS *wist* food, OHG, sojourn, dwelling place, food, ON *vist*, Goth *wists* being, nature, OE *wesan* to be — more at WAS] **:** CAKE; *esp* **:** a fancy cake filled with custard and glacéed fruits and nuts

gate-crash \'=,=\ *vb* [back-formation fr. *gate-crasher*] *vt* **:** to enter, attend, or participate in without invitation or ticket and often by misrepresenting oneself ~ *vi* **:** to engage in gate-crashing

gate-crasher \'=,==\ *n* [fr. the phrase *crash the gate*] **:** one that engages in gate-crashing

gat·ed \¦gād·əd, -ātəd\ *adj* [¹*gate* + *-ed*] **:** having or controlled by a gate ⟨~ sluiceways⟩ ⟨a ~ microphone⟩

gatefold \'=,=\ *n* [¹*gate* + *fold*] **:** a folded insert (as a map) in a book or other publication larger in some dimension than the page

gatehouse \'=,=\ *n* [ME *gatehous*, fr. *gate* + *hous* house] **:** a house or other building connected or associated with a gate: as **a :** a part of a gate (as of a city wall or palace) with rooms often formerly used for prisoners or guards **b :** an erection (as a power station) over a dam from which the gates are controlled

gatekeeper \'=,==\ *n* **1 :** a person who tends or guards a gate **2 :** a mottled brown Old World butterfly (*Pararge megaera*)

gateleg table \'=,=-\ *also* **gate-legged table** \'gāt,leg(d)-, -gəd-\ *n* **:** a drop-leaf table with leaves supported by movable brackets consisting of paired legs linked by horizontal stretchers which fold against the frame when the leaves are dropped

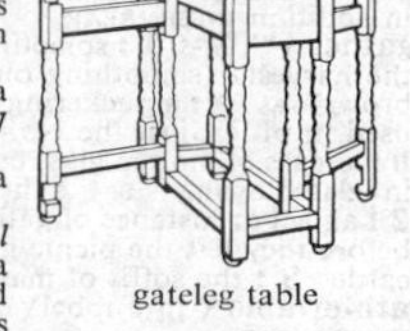

gateleg table

gate·less \'gātləs\ *adj* **:** lacking a gate ⟨a ~ valve⟩ — **gate·less·ly** *adv*

gatelike \'=,=\ *adj* **:** resembling a gate

gate·man \'=mən, -,man\ *n, pl* **gatemen 1 :** a man who tends a gate; *esp* **:** one who checks and supervises the traffic that flows through a gate **2 :** an attendant at a railroad grade crossing who bars traffic from the crossing when a train approaches

gate money *n* **:** GATE 9a

gate net *n* **:** a net used chiefly by poachers to catch hares seeking escape by a gate

gate pin *n* **:** a vertical runner used in founding to connect the pouring basin with the gates below

gatepost \'=,=\ *n* **:** either of two posts that bound and support a gate: **a :** the post to which a gate is hung — called also *hinging post, swinging post* **b :** the post against which a gate closes — called also *shutting post*

gat·er \'gād·ə(r)\ *n* -s [¹*gate* + *-er*] **:** SPRUER

gates *pl of* GATE, *pres 3d sing of* GATE

gates-ajar collar \'gātsə,jär-\ *n, slang* **:** WING COLLAR

gate saw *n* **:** SASH SAW

gates·head \'gāts,hed\ *adj, usu cap* [fr. *Gateshead*, England] **:** of or from the county borough of Gateshead, England **:** of the kind or style prevalent in Gateshead

gate valve *n* **:** a valve in a pipeline consisting essentially of a flat or wedge-shaped gate that can be lowered into a seat to seal off the line or raised into an external recess so that the full area of the line is open — compare GLOBE VALVE

gate·ward \'gāt,wȯ(ə)rd\ *n* -s [ME, fr. OE *geatweard*, fr. *geat* door, gate, opening + *weard* guard — more at GATE, WARD] *archaic* **:** GATEKEEPER

gate·wards \'gātərdz, -t·wə-\ *adv* [³*gate* + *-wards*] *archaic Scot* **:** directly toward **:** along the road to

gateway \'=,=\ *n* **1 a :** ¹GATE 1,2 **b :** a supporting frame or arch in which a gate is hung **2 a :** GATE 4a **b :** a passage for navigation or travel: as (1) **:** any one of a limited number of points by which the traffic of a defined region can enter (2) **:** a point at which freight moving from one such region to another is interchanged **c :** a basing point on or near the boundary of a rate or classification territory on which freight rates are constructed

ga·tha \'gätə, -(,)tä\ *n* -s *often cap* [Av *gāthā-;* akin to Skt *gāthā* song, verse, *gāyati* he sings — more at CHOUGH] **:** one of 17 hymns or psalms traditionally attributed to Zoroaster that form an important part of the Avesta

[1]**gath·er** \'gaṯẖə(r), 'geṯẖ- *sometimes* 'gȧṯẖ-\ *vb* **gathered; gathered; gathering** \-th(ə)riŋ\ **gathers** [ME *gaderen,* fr. OE *gadrian, gaderian;* akin to OFris *gaderia* to gather, MLG *gadderen* to gather, MHG *gatern* to unite, OFris *gadia* — more at GOOD] *vt* **1 a :** to bring together into a crowd, group, body, or mass **:** CONCENTRATE, COLLECT ⟨the balloon start had ~*ed* a little crowd of people —H.G.Wells⟩ ⟨reformers ~*ing* their forces against corrupt city administrations —*Amer. Guide Series: N. Y. City*⟩ ⟨~ a supply of firewood⟩ ⟨~*ing* the frightened children about her⟩ **b** (1) **:** to draw up or together **:** ACCUMULATE (2) **:** to gain gradually with steady increase or acceleration ⟨art will ~ social purpose —J.T.Farrell⟩ ⟨a movement ~*ing* force⟩ ⟨the car ~*ed* speed⟩ **c :** to collect (melted glass) on the end of a tube for samples or for blowing **2 a :** PICK, PLUCK, HARVEST ⟨~*ed* a bunch of flowers⟩ ⟨~*ing* walnuts⟩ **b :** to cull, take, pick up, receive, or appropriate by or as if by picking or harvesting ⟨many souvenirs . . . ~*ed* from all parts of the world —*Amer. Guide Series: Maine*⟩ ⟨the vigilantes ~*ed* up Plummer and his gang and hanged them —Seth Agnew⟩ ⟨~ meaning not from reading the Constitution but from reading life —Felix Frankfurter⟩ **c :** to accumulate and place in order or readiness for being used or carried — often used with *up* ⟨he ~*ed* up his tools⟩ **d :** to assemble in sequence (the signatures and inserts of a volume) for binding **e** (1) *chiefly Brit* **:** to scoop up (as a rolling ball) neatly off the ground (2) **:** to catch (a baseball) on the fly — usu. used with *in* ⟨the shortstop easily ~*ed* in the soft liner⟩ **3 :** to attract or serve as a center of attraction for **:** cause or facilitate a bringing together or accumulating of ⟨the past . . . ~*s* round it all the inscrutable mystery of life and death —G.M.Trevelyan⟩ ⟨Puritanism . . . ~*ed* about it . . . all the forces of unrest —V.L.Parrington⟩ ⟨an age devoted to ornate decor that ~*ed* dust and moths⟩ **4 :** to effect the collection of (as tax, tribute, dues, contributions) ⟨~ tax moneys for the king⟩ **5 a :** to summon up **:** muster together **:** ACCUMULATE **:** bring together and coordinate ⟨his poor, shattered soul had ~*ed* to itself just then a great courage —Liam O'Flaherty⟩ ⟨we must . . . get out of the tumult of the market place to ~ our thoughts —M.R.Cohen⟩ ⟨reporters ~*ing* the news of the campaign⟩ **b :** to prepare (as oneself) by mustering strength and force ⟨the victim had been ~*ing* himself to run across the court —T.B.Costain⟩ **6 a :** to bring or draw together the parts of **:** collect and compress by or as if by grasping and holding ⟨~*ed* her long full skirt in each hand and sprang across the little stream⟩ **b :** to draw (as a covering) over, about, or close to something ⟨seizing his hat and ~*ing* his cloak about him⟩ ⟨~*ed* the bedclothes up to his neck⟩ **c :** to pull (fabric) along one or two lines of stitching so as to draw into puckers **:** PLAIT ⟨~ the neckline and stitch on the binding⟩ **d** (1) **:** to haul in or take up (as slack of a rope) (2) **:** to begin or increase movement in (a way or direction specified) ⟨the ship ~*ed* headway⟩ **e :** to cause (opposite walls of masonry) to approach or come together (as in the abrupt narrowing of the upper part of a fireplace to meet the flue) **7 :** to conclude on reflection **:** draw as an inference **:** DEDUCE, INFER **:** presume to be the case ⟨I ~ that the meeting was not a success⟩ **8 :** COLLECT 5a ~ *vi* **1 a :** to come together in a body, group, crowd, cluster, heap, or mass ⟨a crowd quickly ~*ed* and shouted for a speech —*Amer. Guide Series: Md.*⟩ ⟨the swallows . . . are ~*ing* to fly farther away —Padraic Colum⟩ ⟨the way the wrinkles ~*ed* about his merry gray eyes —Ellen Glasgow⟩ **b :** to accumulate, cluster, or form around a focus of attraction ⟨a romance . . . ~*s* round the wedge-shaped or cuneiform characters —Edward Clodd⟩ ⟨the unpopularity that ~*ed* about the name of Mather —V.L.Parrington⟩ **2 a :** to enlarge in coming to a head **:** swell and fill with pus **:** HEAD ⟨the boil is ~*ing*⟩ **b :** to become concentrated or intense **:** GROW, INCREASE ⟨where the cold ~*ed* more thickly —E.H.Collis⟩ ⟨a time when the ~*ing* dangers were only too apparent —Sir Winston Churchill⟩ **3 :** to become drawn or compressed together often in folds or creases ⟨a coat that ~*s* over the shoulders⟩ **4** *of a ship* **:** to make progress **:** APPROACH ⟨the boat continued to ~ toward the southeast⟩ ⟨swiftly ~*ing* on the ship ahead⟩

syn COLLECT, ASSEMBLE, CONGREGATE: GATHER, a general term, indicates the fact of bringing or coming together and lacks much especial connotation ⟨it was customary for merchants to *gather* outside to discuss business affairs —*Amer. Guide Series: R. I.*⟩ It may suggest a picking, culling, or harvesting ⟨a trading post to collect goods already *gathered* by the native population —R.A.Billington⟩ COLLECT is often interchangeable with GATHER but may imply greater purposiveness and more careful selectivity ⟨Columbus was forced to *collect* the natives one night and threaten to darken the moon —Stringfellow Barr⟩ ⟨the mass of movable wealth *collected* in the shops and warehouses of London alone —T.B.Macaulay⟩ Used in reference to persons coming together, ASSEMBLE may stress a definite aim or purpose and may suggest greater unity or organization in the group formed; used in reference to things brought together, it suggests a logical ordering or uniting ⟨Flandrau . . . *assembled* a force of volunteers at St. Peter and hastened to the relief of the village —*Amer. Guide Series: Minn.*⟩ ⟨immediately after they shall be *assembled* in consequence of the first election —*U.S.Constitution*⟩ ⟨*assembling* and interpreting statistics on the nation's war programs —*Current Biog.*⟩ CONGREGATE may apply to a gregarious flocking together of similar types ⟨the drivers *congregated* in saloons around the square —Green Peyton⟩ ⟨the older people sat rather stiffly in the corners, the young men *congregated* uneasily in impermanent groups —Irwin Shaw⟩ **syn** see in addition INFER, REAP

[2]**gather** \"\ *n* -s **1 :** something that is gathered ⟨the final ~ of the harvest⟩ ⟨smoothing out the ~*s* of thought between her brows⟩: as **a :** a puckering in cloth made by gathering — usu. used in pl. ⟨adjust the ~*s* evenly and sew on the waistband⟩ **b :** a mass of molten glass collected on a gathering iron for use in glassblowing **c :** a lightly collected stance of a horse **2 :** an act or instance of gathering ⟨made a final ~ of the trash before they left the picnic grounds⟩; *esp, West* **:** a roundup of cattle **3 :** the soffit of masonry formed by gathering

gath·er·able \-ṯẖ(ə)rəbəl\ *adj* **:** capable of being gathered; *esp* **:** INFERABLE

gathered *past of* GATHER

gath·er·er \-ṯẖərə(r)\ *n* -s [ME *gaderer,* fr. *gaderen* to gather + *-er* — more at GATHER] **1 :** one that collects and brings together **:** COLLECTOR, COMPILER ⟨a ~ of moral anecdotes⟩ ⟨these ~*s* of dead statistics⟩ **2 a :** a collector of money (as for fees, taxes, or other fixed charges) — often used in combination ⟨a tax *gatherer*⟩ ⟨rent *gatherers*⟩ **b** *obs* **:** MISER **3 :** a worker or device that gathers something: as **a :** one that gathers molten glass on the end of a blowpipe **b :** a person or machine that gathers sheets, leaves, or signatures for binding **c :** a sewing-machine operator or attachment that gathers fabric **4 :** an incisor of a horse

gath·er·ing \-ṯẖ(ə)riŋ, -rēŋ\ *n* -s [ME *gadering, gaderung,* fr. OE *gaderung,* fr. *gadrian, gaderian* to gather + *-ung, -ing* -ing — more at GATHER] **1 a :** the action or an instance of coming together or accumulating ⟨a ~ of dust on the shelves⟩ ⟨that black ~ of clouds foretold a shower⟩ ⟨the ~ of melted snow into little streams⟩ **b :** a coming together of people in a group (as for social, religious, or political purposes) **:** ASSEMBLY, MEETING ⟨cultural and civic ~*s*⟩ ⟨the outstanding social ~ of the year⟩ **c :** a suppurating swelling **:** ABSCESS **2 a :** the act or work of a gatherer (as in contracting, accumulating, or assembling something) **b :** the collecting or gleaning of food and other raw materials from the wild ⟨peoples whose economy is based on ~ are ill-situated to attain the stability essential to any high level of civilization⟩ **3 :** something that is gathered: as **a :** a collection (as of money for charity) or compilation (as of literary fragments) **b :** PARISON **c :** a gather in cloth **d :** the leaves of a book that are folded and stitched into one signature **e :** sap collected at one time in a sugar-maple orchard ⟨the evening ~ is usually much larger than the morning one is⟩

gathering coal *n* **:** a large lump of coal left smothered in embers to hold a fire (as during the night)

gathering hoop *n* **:** a hoop used by coopers to draw together the ends of barrel staves so that the hoops can be put on

gathering iron *or* **gathering rod** *n* **:** an iron rod used for gathering molten glass for glassblowing

gathering machine *n* **:** a machine consisting of pockets or bins with devices for removing book signatures placed in each bin, dropping them on a movable chain belt, and delivering the assembled books complete

gathering pallet *n* **:** a revolving finger in striking clocks and repeating watches that moves the rack for each blow struck — compare TUMBLER 3c(1)

gathering peat *n* **1 :** a peat used as a gathering coal **2 :** a fiery peat formerly sent round by the Scottish borderers as an alarm signal — compare FIERY CROSS

gathering ring *n* **:** one of the clay rings placed on molten glass to keep surface impurities from the center area and provide space where highest quality glass can be gathered

gathering table *n* **1 :** a table or board on which book signatures are laid out to be gathered **2 :** a circular revolving table used for gathering book signatures

gathers *pres 3d sing of* GATHER, *pl of* GATHER

gather shot *n* **:** a billiards shot that brings the object balls back into favorable position for the succeeding shot

gath·er·um \-ṯẖərəm\ *n* -s [[1]*gather* + L *-um* (neut. n. ending)] **:** a collection esp. of miscellaneous items

ga·thic \'gätik\ *n* -s *usu cap* [*Gatha* + *-ic*] **:** a language of ancient Persia in which the Gathas were composed

gat·ing \'gād·iŋ\ *n* -s [[1]*gate* + *-ing*] **1 :** an opening in a lock tumbler into or through which the fence passes upon the operation of the bolt **2 :** the process of selecting those parts of an electromagnetic wave that exist during a selected time interval or that have magnitudes between selected limits

gat·ling gun \'gatliŋ-, -lēŋ-\ *also* **gatling** *n* -s *usu cap Gatling* [after Richard J. *Gatling* †1903 Am. inventor] **:** a machine gun consisting of a cluster of barrels that when revolved by a crank are loaded and fired once each during a revolution of the group

ga·to \'gä(,)tō\ *n* -s [AmerSp, lit., cat, fr. LL *cattus* — more at CAT] **:** an Argentine composition in lively ¾ time for singing and dancing

ga·tor \'gād·ə(r), -ātə-\ *n* -s [by shortening] **:** ALLIGATOR

gats *pl of* GAT

gat·ter·mann–koch reaction \'ga|d·ə(r)mən'kȯk-, 'gä|, -kȯk-,-kōk-,-käk-\ *n, usu cap G&K* [after Ludwig *Gattermann* †1920 and J.A. *Koch fl*1897 Ger. chemists] **:** a synthesis of an aldehyde from an aromatic hydrocarbon, carbon monoxide, hydrogen chloride, and a catalyst containing aluminum chloride

gattermann reaction *n, usu cap G* [after L.*Gattermann*] **:** a synthesis of an aldehyde from an aromatic or heterocyclic compound, hydrogen cyanide, hydrogen chloride, and a catalyst of aluminum chloride or zinc chloride

gat·ti·na·ra \,gäd·ē'närə\ *n* -s [It, fr. *Gattinara,* town in northwestern Italy] **:** a dark red Italian table wine

gat·tine \(')ga¦tēn\ *n* -s [F] **:** an epidemic and fatal disease of silkworms believed to result from the combined action of a virus and a streptococcus

gau \'gau̇\ *n, pl* **gaus** \-au̇z\ *or* **gaue** \-au̇ə\ [G, fr. OHG *gouw-, gewi* district, region; akin to OE *-gē* district, region (in place names), OFris *gā,* OS *-gō* (in place names), Goth *gawi;* all prob. fr. a prehistoric WGmc-EGmc compound whose components are represented respectively by OHG *gi-* (perfective and collective prefix) and *ouwa* land by water, meadow — more at YCLEPT, ISLAND] **1 :** a region or district in German tribal organization including two or more marks and inhabited by kindred tribes **2 :** one of the 20 party districts into which Germany including Austria was divided by the National Socialists

gau·by \'gȯbi\ *var of* GABY

gauche \'gōsh\ *adj, sometimes* -ER/-EST [F, lit., left, on the left, fr. MF, fr. *gauchir* to turn aside, swerve, alter. of *guenchir,* of Gmc origin; akin to OHG *wankōn* to stagger, sway — more at WINK] **1 a :** lacking in social graces or ease, tact, and familiarity with polite usage **:** likely or inclined to commit social blunders esp. from lack of experience or training **b :** lacking finish or exhibiting crudity (as of style, form, or technique) ⟨an excellent script and cast wasted by ~ direction⟩ ⟨a ~ turn of phrase⟩ **2 :** not plane **:** TWISTED, SKEW ⟨a ~ curve⟩ **3 :** being or designed for use with the left hand **:** LEFT-HAND ⟨a ~ or left-hand weapon, used mainly for guarding and reserve —Foster Harris⟩ **syn** see AWKWARD

gauche·ly *adv* **:** in a gauche manner **:** AWKWARDLY, CLUMSILY, CRUDELY

gauche·ness *n* -ES **:** the quality or state of being gauche ⟨the ~ of such a remark⟩

gau·che·rie \¦gōshə¦rē, (')gō¦shrē; 'gōsh(ə)rē, -)ri\ *n* -s [F, fr. *gauche* + *-erie* -ery] **:** a tactless or awkward action; *often* **:** a bit of social or literary crudity ⟨the claptrap and ~*s* that too often fill the daily papers⟩

gau·cher's disease \(')gō¦shāz-\ *n, usu cap G* [after Philippe C.E.*Gaucher* †1918 Fr. physician] **:** a rare chronic disorder prob. of genetic origin that is characterized by enormous enlargement of the spleen, pigmentation of the skin, and bone lesions and is marked by the presence of large amounts of kerasin in the cells of the reticuloendothelial system

gau·cho \'gau̇(,)chō\ *also* **gua·cho** \'gwä(-\ *n* -s *often attrib* [AmerSp *gaucho,* prob. fr. Quechua *wáhcha* poor person, orphan] **:** a cowboy or herdsman of the pampas usu. of mixed Spanish and Indian descent ⟨~*s* . . . wearing loose trousers with tight cuffs at the ankles, soft hats, and long wool ponchos —Natalie Raymond⟩ ⟨bright ~ shirts⟩

gau·cie *or* **gau·cy** *var of* GAWSIE

[1]**gaud** \'gȯd, 'gäd\ *n* -s [ME *gaude,* prob. fr. OF *gaudir* to enjoy, rejoice, have a good time, fr. L *gaudēre* to rejoice — more at JOY] **1** *archaic* **:** a gay trick or jape; *sometimes* **:** a deceitful trick or artifice **:** FRAUD **2 :** ORNAMENT; *esp* **:** a showy or flashy bit of jewelry or finery **3 :** showy and often empty display or ceremony — usu. used in pl. ⟨surrounded by the pointless ~*s* of a royal household⟩

[2]**gaud** \"\ *vt* -ED/-ING/-S *archaic* **:** to decorate with gauds **:** ADORN, PAINT

[3]**gaud** \"\ *n* -s [ME *gaude*] **:** a distinctive bead used to mark a division in a rosary

[4]**gaud** \'gȯd, 'gȧd\ *Scot var of* GOAD

[5]**gaud** \"\ *Scot var of* GAD

gaude lake \'gōd-\ *n* [F *gaude* weld (dyestuff), of Gmc origin; akin to MLG *wolde* weld — more at WELD] **:** MIMOSA 3

gaud·ery \'gȯdərē, 'gäd-, -ri\ *n* -ES [[1]*gaud* + *-ery*] **:** ostentatious display or items contributing to such display **:** FRIPPERIES, FINERY

gau·di·an \gau̇'dēən\ *adj, usu cap* [Antonio *Gaudí* y Cornet †1926 Catalan architect + E *-an*] **:** of, relating to, or resembling the architect Gaudí or his style marked esp. by fantastic and elaborate detail

gaud·i·fy \-də,fī\ *vt* -ED/-ING/-ES [*gaudy* + *-fy*] **:** to make showy

gaud·i·ly \-dᵊl|ē, -dəl|, |i\ *adv* **:** in a gaudy manner **:** SHOWILY, GARISHLY

gaud·i·ness \-dēnəs, -din-\ *n* -ES **:** the quality or state of being gaudy **:** SHOWINESS

gauds·man \'gȯdzmən, 'gȧdz-\ *n, pl* **gaudsmen** [by alter.] *Scot* **:** GOADMAN

[1]**gaudy** \'gȯdē, 'gäd-, -di\ *adj* -ER/-EST [[1]*gaud* + *-y*] **:** ostentatiously fine **:** making a pretentious but often hollow show of excellence, elegance, beauty, richness, or worth **:** having show without substance

syn TAWDRY, GARISH, FLASHY, MERETRICIOUS: GAUDY may suggest cheap showiness of taste, over-bright coloration, or vulgarly excessive and conspicuous ornamentation ⟨he was dressed in a *gaudy* costume, resembling on the whole that of a Highland chieftain. His knees, wrists, and throat were tattooed in bright blue patterns; and he carried sword and dagger, a gold ring round his neck, and gold rings on his wrists —Charles Kingsley⟩ ⟨swarthy Mojaves, garbed in *gaudy* scarlets, blues, and yellows —*Amer. Guide Series: Calif.*⟩ TAWDRY always adds connotations of cheap pretension to those of GAUDY ⟨decorated in *tawdry* baroque, it might have been built about thirty years ago and not repainted since. On the ceiling, an immense pink, blue and gold design of cherubim, roses, and clouds was peeled and patched with damp —Christopher Isherwood⟩ GARISH may suggest offensive or harsh unrestrained brightness ⟨the *garish* splendor of the orchis —D.G.Hoffman⟩ ⟨"a red scarf?" said John pensively. "I have noted his taste for colors more *garish* than perhaps beseems a servant. Usually it was violet, whether scarf or cloak" —J.H.Wheelwright⟩ FLASHY may apply to the facilely gay or momentarily dazzling that is speedily revealed as shallow and vulgar ⟨I liked the flaring yellow scarf bound loose about her throat, I liked her showy purple gown and *flashy* velvet coat —Ralph Hodgson⟩ MERETRICIOUS may suggest the tawdry allure of false show or promise ⟨his smile was wide and rather *meretricious,* that exaggerated photograph-smile so often seen (as if only happiness should be recorded). She could imagine how it had faded the moment the camera clicked —Elizabeth Taylor⟩ ⟨girls who deck themselves with gems, false hair, and *meretricious* ornament, to chain the fleeting fancy of a man —W.S.Gilbert⟩

[2]**gau·dy** \"\ *n* -ES [prob. fr. L *gaudium* joy — more at JOY] **:** a feast, festival, or entertainment esp. in the form of an annual college dinner in a British university

gaudy dutch *or* **gaudy welsh** *n, usu cap G&D&W* **:** earthenware with colorful bold designs made in Staffordshire, England in the first quarter of the 19th century

gaudy green \"*gaudy*" *like* [1]GAUDY\ *n* [ME *gaude grene, gaudy grene,* fr. MF *gaude* weld + ME *grene* green — more at GAUDE LAKE, GREEN] **:** SPINACH GREEN

gaudy night *n* **:** a festal night

gaudy·ware \'==,=\ *n* **:** GAUDY DUTCH

gaue *pl of* GAU

gauffer *var of* GOFFER

gauffered *or* **gauffred** *var of* GOFFERED

gauf·frage \'gȯfrij, 'gōf-; (')gȯ¦fräzh, (')gō¦-\ *n* -s [F *gaufrage,* fr. *gaufrer* to emboss, goffer + *-age* — more at GOFFER] **:** ornamentation with goffering

gauf·fre *also* **gau·fre** \(')gȯ¦frā, (')gō¦-\ *adj* [F *gaufré,* fr. past part. of *gaufrer*] **:** GOFFERED; *often* **:** ornamented with embossing ⟨~ velvet⟩

gau·fre \'gōfr(ᵊ), -f(rə); 'gōfə(r), 'gȯf-\ *n, pl* **gaufres** \-fr(ᵊ), -f(rə), -fə(r)z\ [F, fr. OF — more at GOFFER] **:** a very thin crisp wafer baked with a wafer iron

gau·frette \(')gȯ¦fret, (')gō¦-\ *n* -s [F, dim. of *gaufre*] **:** a wafer of crisply fried potato cut to resemble a small waffle

[1]**gauge** *or* **gage** \'gāj\ *n* -s [ME *gauge,* fr. ONF, prob. of Gmc origin; akin to OHG *galgo* cross, gallows — more at GALLOWS] **1 a :** measurement esp. according to some standard or system ⟨make a note of the ~ of each barrel⟩ **b :** the dimensions or extent of something ⟨cannot mark the ~ of her sufferings⟩ ⟨glanced about to take the ~ of the situation⟩ **2 a :** an instrument for or means of testing ⟨used a notched rod for a ~ to estimate the content of the barrels⟩ **b** *usu gage* **:** an instrument for checking or measuring a particular dimension of an object (as thickness, depth, or diameter) **c :** a carpenter's tool for scribing a line parallel to the edge of a piece of work — called also *marking gauge;* compare MORTISE GAUGE **d** *usu gage* **:** any of various instruments usu. provided with a graduated scale or dial for measuring or indicating quantity ⟨gasoline *gage*⟩ **e :** a bookbinders tool used to secure uniform size, spacing, or position of materials **f :** PERFORATION GAUGE; *sometimes* **:** PERFORATION NUMBER **g** *printing* (1) **:** GUIDE (2) **:** HEIGHT GAUGE 2 (3) **:** LINE GAUGE (4) **:** PAGE GAUGE **3 a :** relative position of a ship with reference to another ship and the wind — see LEE GAUGE, WEATHER GAUGE **b :** the depth to which a ship sinks in the water when fully loaded **4 a** *usu gage* **:** the distance between the heads of the rails of a railroad measured at right angles thereto at a point ⅝ inch below the top of the rail, standard gage in most countries being now 4 feet 8½ inches **b :** the distance between a pair of wheels on an axle — compare WHEELBASE **5 :** the quantity of plaster of paris used with mortar to accelerate its setting for special purposes — see GAUGE STUFF **6 :** the size of a shotgun expressed as the number in a pound of round lead balls of a size to just fit into the barrel ⟨a 12-*gauge* shotgun⟩ ⟨shotguns of different ~*s*⟩ — compare BORE, CALIBER **7 :** the thickness esp. of sheet metal or the diameter esp. of wire, a hypodermic needle, or a screw — see WIRE GAUGE 2 **8 a :** the number of needles in 1½ inches of the needlebar of a knitting machine **b :** the fineness of a knitted fabric determined by the number of loops per 1½ inch based in turn on the number of needles per 1½ inch ⟨51-*gauge* hosiery is sheerer than 45-*gauge*⟩ **c :** the number of stitches per inch in hand knitting and crocheting — used esp. in describing patterns **syn** see STANDARD

PRINCIPAL RAILROAD GAGES OF THE WORLD

WIDTH English units	WIDTH metric units	PLACE
5′6″	1.676 m	Argentina, Ceylon, Chile, India, Pakistan, Portugal, Spain
5′3″	1.600 m	Brazil, Ireland, Australia
5′	1.524 m	Finland, Panama, U.S.S.R.
4′9⅕″	1.45 m	Algeria
4′8⅘″	1.44 m	France, Tunisia
4′8½″	1.435 m	Algeria, Argentina, Australia, Canada (except Newfoundland), Chile, China, Cuba, European continent (except Spain), Finland, Great Britain, Iran, Iraq, Jamaica, Japan, Korea, Lebanon, Mauritius, Mexico, Morocco, Paraguay, Peru, Portugal, Saudi Arabia, Syria, Trinidad, Turkey, U.A.R., U.S.S.R., U.S., Uruguay
3′6″	1.067 m	Angola, Australia, Chile, Congo (Kinshasa), Costa Rica, Ecuador, China (Taiwan), Ghana, Haiti, Honduras, Indonesia, Japan, Malawi, Mozambique, Newfoundland, New Zealand, Nicaragua, Nigeria, Philippines, Republic of So. Africa, Rhodesia, Sudan, Sweden, West Africa, Western Australia, Zambia
3′5¼″	1.05 m	Algeria, Jordan, Syria
3′3⅜″	1.00 m	Algeria, Argentina, Bolivia, Brazil, Burma, Cambodia, Chile, China, Colombia, East Africa, Ecuador, Ethiopia, Greece, India, Iraq, Malaysia, Pakistan, Paraguay, Portugal, Spain, Surinam, Switzerland, Thailand, Tunisia, U.A.R., Vietnam, West Africa, Yugoslavia
3′1⅖″	0.95 m	Ethiopia, Italy
3′	0.914 m	Colombia, El Salvador, Guatemala, Ireland, Mexico, Panama, Peru, Spain
2′11″	0.891 m	Sweden
2′6″	0.762 m	Bulgaria, Ceylon, Chile, China (Taiwan), India, Nigeria, Pakistan, Sierra Leone, Yugoslavia
2′5½″	0.750 m	Argentina, Ecuador, Turkey, U.A.R.
2′	0.610 m	India, Republic of So. Africa, Venezuela
1′11⅗″	0.60 m	Algeria, Bulgaria, Chile, Indonesia

COMMON SHOTGUN GAUGES

GAUGE	INTERIOR DIAMETER OF BARREL	GAUGE	INTERIOR DIAMETER OF BARREL
10	.775 inches	20	.615 inches
12	.729 inches	28	.550 inches
16	.662 inches	.410[1]	.410 inches

[1]actually a caliber but called a gauge

[2]**gauge** *or* **gage** \"\ *vt* -ED/-ING/-S [ME *gaugen,* fr. ONF *gaugier,* fr. *gauge,* n.] **1 a :** to measure exactly **:** determine precisely the size of (as a standardized part), amount of (as rainfall), dimensions, or other measurable value of (as intensity

or velocity); *broadly* : to estimate (some quantity) by practical or logical means ⟨*gauging* his progress by the milestones he passed⟩ **b** : to determine the capacity or amount of contents of (as a cask or comparable vessel) **c** : to measure the capacity, character, or ability of : APPRAISE, JUDGE ⟨*gauging* the probable response of the electorate by sampling techniques⟩ ⟨I would not ~ the future on what I know of the past⟩ ⟨how would you ~ his conduct?⟩ **d** *usu gage* : to determine the flow of (a stream) by measurement of the cross section and the velocity **2 a** : to check or limit with or as if with a gauge ⟨he *gauged* each part of the model with calipers⟩; *broadly* : to cause to conform to a standard (as of measurement or performance) **b** : to measure off or set out (~ the line for the foundation); *sometimes* : to set bounds to **c** (1) : to determine the perforation number of (a stamp) (2) : to have (an indicated perforation number) by measurement ⟨a stamp *gauging* 10⟩ **3** : to mix (plaster) in certain definite proportions (as for quick drying) : mix plaster of paris with (mortar) for quick setting **4** : to dress (bricks or stones) to size by rubbing or chipping **5** : to set (an insert) in the right position in bookbinding **6 a** : to gather (sewing) with alternating short and long stitches **b** : to hold evenly distributed gathers with (as smocking)

gauge·able \-jəbəl\ *adj* : capable of being gauged : measurable or determinable by gauging — **gauge·ably** \-blē\ *adv*

gauge cock *n* : a vent cock used to ascertain the level of liquid in a container

gauged arch *n* : a masonry arch that has bricks or stones gauged in such a manner that the joints radiate from a common center

gauge glass *n* : the glass tube of a water gauge by which the water level in a boiler or tank is observed

gauge knife *n* : a knife with a gauge to limit the cut

gauge line *n* : a line ⅝ inch below the center of the running surface of a railroad rail along the side of the head nearer the center of track

gauge pin *n* : a pin attached to the tympan of a platen press to hold the sheet and act as a feed guide

gauge point *n* : a reference point to which a gauge is applied or from which measurements are taken in gauging

gauge pressure *n* : the pressure at a point in a fluid above that of the atmosphere — compare ABSOLUTE PRESSURE

gaug·er *or* **gag·er** \'gājə(r)\ *n* -s [ME, fr. AF *gaugeour*, fr. ONF *gaugier* + AF *-our* -or] : one that gauges: as **a** *chiefly Brit* : an exciseman or customs officer who checks, measures, and sometimes assesses the levy on dutiable bulk goods (as liquors) **b** : a worker who inspects and checks the dimensions of small parts in a machine shop **c** : one that gauges the quantity and temperature of oil in storage tanks and controls the flow of oil into pipelines

gaug·er·ship \-,ship\ *n* : the office of a gauger

gauge stuff *n* : gauged mortar used for making specialized structures (as cornices or moldings) in which speedy setting is important

gauge wheel *n* : an adjustable wheel attached to a plow or planter that regulates the depth of penetration into the soil

gauging plaster *n* : a special gypsum plaster mixed with lime putty for use in finishing plastered surfaces

gaul \'gȯl\ *n* -s *cap* [fr. *Gaul*, ancient region of Europe including most of what is now France and in earliest times also including northern Italy, fr. F *Gaule*, fr. L *Gallia*] **1** : a member of the Celtic people that inhabited ancient Gaul as well as areas in the Balkans and Asia Minor — compare GALATIAN **2** : FRENCHMAN

gaul·ding \'gȯl(d)ən, -ldiŋ\ *also* **gau·lin** \-lən\ *n* -s [origin unknown] *West Indies* : HERON

gau·lei·ter \'gau̇,līd·ə(r)\ *n* -s [G, fr. *gau* + *leiter* leader, fr. OHG *leitāri*, fr. *leiten* to lead + *-āri* -er — more at LEAD] **1 a** : a district leader of the German National Socialist party formerly serving in his territory as provincial governor **b** : a political functionary occupying a similar subordinate but important position in a totalitarian regime or hierarchy **2** : a person that in outlook and social responses may be likened to a gauleiter; *often* : an arrogant overbearing subordinate or henchman ⟨how these conductors feel their oats. They are ~s of music in their respective cities —D.S.Moore⟩ ⟨recognized ~s in penology —*Prison World*⟩

gaul·ic \'gȯlik\ *adj, usu cap* [*Gaul* (country) + E *-ic*] : GALLIC

¹gaul·ish \'gȯlish\ *adj, usu cap* [*Gaul* (country) + E *-ish*] : of or relating to the Gauls, their language, or land

²gaulish \"\ *n* -ES *cap* : the Celtic language of the ancient Gauls esp. as represented by Celtic loanwords in Latin and Old French — called also *Continental Celtic;* see INDO-EUROPEAN LANGUAGES table

gaull·ism \'gō,lizəm, 'gȯ-,-\ *n* -s *usu cap* [F *Gaullisme*, fr. Gen. Charles de *Gaulle* *b*1890 Fr. soldier and political leader + F *-isme* -ism] **1** : a political movement among Frenchmen during World War II characterized by allegiance to policies of Charles de Gaulle and by opposition to the Vichy regime **2 a** : a political movement emerging in France after World War II under the leadership of Charles de Gaulle and usu. associated with rightist policies **b** : the principles and beliefs associated with this movement

gaull·ist \-,ləst\ *n* -s *usu cap* [F *gaulliste*, fr. Gen. de *Gaulle* + F *-iste* -ist] : a follower of the French military and political leader Charles de Gaulle either during World War II or in postwar French rightist politics

gault *also* **galt** \'gȯlt\ *n* -s [prob. of Scand origin; akin to ON *galdr*, *gald* hard-packed snow, Norw dial. *gald* hard ground, mountain path, and prob. to ON *gadd* hard-packed snow, Norw dial., trampled spot of ground, Sw dial, narrow path, rabbit track] : a heavy thick clay soil

gaul·the·ria \gȯl'thirēə\ *n* [NL, irreg. fr. Jean-François *Gaultier* †1756 Fr. botanist in Canada + NL *-ia*] **1** *cap* : a widely distributed genus of evergreen shrubs (family Ericaceae) that are upright or creeping in growth, have opposite leaves and axillary white flowers, and produce small often aromatic fruits resembling berries — see CREEPING SNOWBERRY, SALAL, WINTERGREEN **2** -s : any plant of the genus *Gaultheria* (as the checkerberry)

gaultheria oil *n* : WINTERGREEN OIL

gaul·the·rin \'gȯlthərən, gȯl'thir-\ *n* -s [ISV *gaulther-* (fr. NL *Gaultheria*) + *-in*] : a crystalline glycoside $C_{19}H_{26}O_{12}$ of methyl salicylate found esp. in sweet birch and various gaultherias

¹gaum \'gȯm, 'gäm\ *n* -s [ME *gome*, fr. ON *gaum*, *gaumr;* akin to OE *gīeme* care, OHG *gouma* attention, ON *geyma* to keep, watch, heed, mind — more at FAVOR] **1** *dial Eng* : HEED, ATTENTION **2** *dial Eng* : UNDERSTANDING, PERCEPTION

²gaum \"\ *vt* -ED/-ING/-S **1** *dial Eng* : to pay attention to : HEED **2** *dial Eng* : to perceive the significance of : UNDERSTAND

³gaum \"\ *n* -s [perh. alter. of ³*gum*] *dial* : a greasy or sticky mess

⁴gaum \"\ *vt* -ED/-ING/-S [perh. alter. of ⁴*gum*] *dial* : to smudge or smear esp. with something sticky or greasy — often used with *up* ⟨the kitchen floor was all ~*ed* up with spilled molasses⟩

⁵gaum \"\ *vi* -ED/-ING/-S [origin unknown] *dial* : to behave in a stupid or awkward manner (as by staring or gaping)

⁶gaum \"\ *n* -s *dial* : an awkward lout : a stupid doltish person : CLOWN

gaum·less \-ləs\ *adj* [¹*gaum* + *-less*] *dial* : lacking comprehension or awareness : dull and stupid

gaumy \-mē\ *adj* [³*gaum* + *-y*] **1** *dial* : SMEARED, STICKY **2** *dial* : UNTIDY, SLOVENLY, DISORDERED; *broadly* : awkward and clumsy

gaun \'gȯn, 'gän\ *dial Brit pres part of* GO *or pres part of* GAE

gaung·baung \'gau̇ŋ,bau̇ŋ\ *n* -s [native name in Burma] : a Burmese headcloth usu. of bright colored silk

¹gaunt \'gȯnt, 'gänt, 'gánt\ *adj* -ER/-EST [ME, perh. of Scand origin; akin to Icel *gandur* thin stick, Norw dial. *gand* thin stick] **1** *of a person* **a** *archaic* : desirably or pleasingly slim : of slender form or build **b** : thin and angular : attenuated esp. by fasting or suffering : LANK, HAGGARD **2** : grim and forbidding : BARREN, DESOLATE ⟨the ~ leafless trees⟩ ⟨a ~ heath⟩ **syn** see LEAN

²gaunt \"\ *vt* -ED/-ING/-S : to make (an individual) gaunt ⟨~*ed* and hollow-eyed —Alan LeMay⟩; *usu* : to train fine (as for a race)

³gaunt \"\ *n* -s [prob. alter. of *gant*, obs. var. of *gannet*] : GREAT CRESTED GREBE

⁴gaunt \"\ *chiefly Scot var of* ¹GANT, ²GANT

¹gaunt·let \'gȯntlət, 'gänt-,'gȧn-, *usu* -əd·+V\ *n* -s [ME *gauntlette*, fr. MF *gantelet*, dim. of *gant* glove, of Scand origin; akin to MLG & MD *want*, *wante* mitten, ON *vöttr* gloves and perh. to ON *vöndr* wand — more at WAND] **1** : a glove designed to protect the hand from injury: as **a** : a reinforced glove used with armor during the middle ages and evolving with such armor to become in the 14th century a covering of small minutely articulated steel plates for the whole back of the hand, fingers, and thumb — see ARMOR illustration **b** : ²CESTUS **c** : any of various gloves used primarily for protection of the hands (as in industry), extending usu. well above the wrist, and being of strong and often impervious material (as rubber or asbestos) **2** : a challenge to combat — usu. used as the object of *throw down* or *take up* ⟨threw down the ~, defying the whole world⟩ ⟨a tense situation and apparently no one dared to take up the ~⟩ **3 a** *also* **gauntlet glove** : a dress glove extending above the wrist and having a deep flared, circular, or otherwise expanded cuff **b** : the cuff of any gauntlet

gauntlet 1c

²gauntlet \"\ *or* **gant·let** \"\ *n* -s [by folk etymology (influence of ¹*gauntlet*) fr. *gantelope*] **1** : two rows of men facing each other and armed with clubs or other weapons with which they strike at an individual who is made to run between them ⟨forced to run a ~ of clubs, revolver butts, and blackjacks —*Harper's*⟩ ⟨some had been beaten with gun butts, some made to run a ~ barefoot —*Newsweek*⟩ **2** : a cross fire of any kind ⟨run the ~ of cannon and machine-gun blasts from each level —Byron Kennerly⟩ ⟨walked a ~ of spitting demonstrators at the airport —*United Press*⟩ ⟨ran the candidate through a savage ~ of technical questions —Alva Johnston⟩ ⟨ran the ~ of interested glances —Hortense Calisher⟩; *broadly* : an ordeal or test ⟨American graduates must run the ~ of American life —Perry Miller⟩ ⟨the treaty has to run a formidable ~ —*New Republic*⟩

gauntlet cuff *n* : a cuff (as on women's wear) narrow at the wrist and flaring above in resemblance to the cuff of a gauntlet

gaunt·let·ed *or* **gaunt·let·ted** \-ləd·əd\ *adj* : having, wearing, or protected by a gauntlet ⟨a ~ glove⟩

gaunt·ly *adv, sometimes* -ER/-EST : in a gaunt manner : with a gaunt appearance

gaunt·ness *n* -ES : the quality or state of being gaunt

gaunty \'gȯntē, 'gän-,'gȧn-, -ti\ *adj, often* -ER/-EST [¹*gaunt* + *-y*] : somewhat gaunt : rather lean

gaup \'gȯp\ *vb* -ED/-ING/-S [alter. of ME *galpen* to yawn, gape; akin to OE *gielpan* to boast, praise — more at YELP] *vi, dial* : STARE, GAPE ~ *vt, dial* : to gulp or swallow greedily

gaur \'gau̇(ə)r\ *n, pl* **gaur** *also* **gaurs** [Hindi, fr. Skt *gaura;* akin to Skt *go* bull, cow — more at COW] : a large East Indian wild ox (*Bibos gaurus*) with a broad forehead and short thick conical horns — compare GAYAL

gau·ra \'gȯrə\ *n* [NL, fr. Gk *gaurē*, fem. of *gauros* majestic, splendid; fr. the beautiful flowers of some of the species] **1** *cap* : a genus of American herbs (family Onagraceae) having flowers in terminal spikes or racemes **2** -s : any plant of the genus *Gaura*

gaus *pl of* GAU

gau·se's principle *also* **gause's rule** \'gau̇zəz-\ *n, usu cap G* [after G. F. *Gause*, *b*1910 Am. ecologist] : a statement in ecology: two species that have identical ecological requirements cannot exist in the same area at the same time

gau·sha·la \'gau̇shəlä\ *n* -s [Skt *gośālā* cowshed, fr. *go* cow + *śālā* shed, hall — more at COW, HALL] : an Indian shelter for homeless or unwanted cattle that often also serves as a center for breed improvement and for study of bovine nutrition and welfare

gausie *var of* GAWSIE

gauss \'gau̇s\ *n, pl* **gauss** *also* **gausses** [after Karl Friedrich *Gauss* †1855 Ger. mathematician] **1** : OERSTED — used before official adoption of *oersted* in 1932 **2** : the cgs electromagnetic unit of magnetic induction equal to the magnetic flux density that will induce an electromotive force of one abvolt in each linear centimeter of a wire moving laterally with a speed of one centimeter per second at right angles to a magnetic flux

gauss·i·an curvature \-sēən-\ *or* **gauss curvature** *n, usu cap G* [K. F. *Gauss* †1855 + E *-ian*] : the reciprocal of the product of the two principal radii of curvature of a surface at any of its points

gaussian curve *n, usu cap G* : PROBABILITY CURVE

gaussian distribution *n, usu cap G* : a theoretical frequency distribution used in statistics that is bell-shaped, symmetrical, and of infinite extent

gauss meter *n* [after K. F. *Gauss*] : an instrument that indicates the strength of a magnetic field at any point directly in gauss

gauss point *n, usu cap G* [after K. F. *Gauss*] : CARDINAL POINT 2

gauss' theorem *or* **gauss's theorem** \'gau̇s(əz)-\ *n, usu cap G* [after K. F. *Gauss*] : a statement in physics: the total electric flux across any closed surface in an electric field equals 4π times the electric charge enclosed by it

gaus·ter \'gȯstə(r), 'gäs-\ *vi* -ED/-ING/-S [ME *galstern*] **1** *dial Brit* : to behave boldly or boisterously : SWAGGER, BULLY **2** *dial Brit* : to waste time conspicuously esp. by talking and gossiping

¹gauze \'gȯz\ *n* -s *often attrib* [MF *gaze*, prob. fr. *Gaza*, city in Palestine] **1 a** : a thin often transparent woven fabric: as (1) : any of various sheer textile fabrics used chiefly for clothing or draperies (2) : a loosely woven cotton fabric similar to cheesecloth that is extensively used for surgical dressings (3) : a firm woven fabric of metal or plastic filaments — usu. used with a qualifying term ⟨plastic ~s for screening windows⟩ **b** : LENO 1 **2** : HAZE, MIST

²gauze \"\ *vt* -ED/-ING/-S *chiefly Brit* : to cover with gauze or give a gauzy appearance to ⟨midges *gauzed* the air —Elizabeth Bowen⟩; *esp* : to screen (as a window) with wire gauze

gauzelike \'=,=\ *adj* : resembling gauze esp. in sheer transparent texture : GAUZY

gauz·i·ly \'gȯzəlē, -li\ *adv* : in a gauzy manner : so as to resemble gauze ⟨cobwebs floating ~ in the light air⟩

gauz·i·ness \-zēnəs, -zin-\ *n* -ES : the quality or state of being gauzy : resemblance to gauze ⟨a ~ in the air that dimmed the further hills⟩

gauzy \'gȯzē, -zi\ *adj* -ER/-EST : of, relating to, or resembling gauze : thin and slight as gauze

ga·vage \gə'väzh\ *n* -s [F, fr. *gaver* to stuff, feed forcibly (fr. F dial. — Picardy —, fr. *gave* gullet, gizzard, fr. OF) + *-age*] : introduction of material (as nutrients) into the stomach by means of a stomach tube

gave *past of* GIVE

¹gav·el \'gavəl\ *n* -s *often attrib* [ME, fr. OE *gafol*, fr. the stem of *giefan* to give — more at GIVE] **1** : periodic payment (as of rent or tribute) to a superior in ancient and medieval England whether in service or produce **2** *obs* : interest on money : USURY

²ga·vel \'gävəl\ *chiefly Scot var of* GABLE

³gav·el \'gavəl\ *n* -s [ME, fr. ONF *gavelle* sheaf, bundle of fagots, perh. fr. (assumed) VL *cavella*, dim. of LL *cavus*, fr. L, hollow — more at CAVE] **1** : a quantity of mowed grain sufficient to make a sheaf; *esp* : grain dropped in a straight pile from a cradle or reaper after cutting **2 a** : a bundle (as a sheaf or shock) of grain, hay, or straw **b** *Brit* : a bundle of straw or reeds ready for use in thatching

⁴gavel \"\ *vt* **gaveled** *or* **gavelled**; **gaveled** *or* **gavelled**; **gaveling** *or* **gavelling** \-v(ə)liŋ\ **gavels** [ME *gavelen*, fr. *gavel*, n.] : to rake or collect (grain or hay) in gavels

⁵gavel \"\ *n* -s [short for *gavelkind*] **1** : GAVELKIND 2 **2** : a body of joint tenants (as under gavelkind) that are usu. blood relatives

⁶gavel \"\ *vt* **gaveled** *or* **gavelled**; **gaveled** *or* **gavelled**; **gaveling** *or* **gavelling** \-v(ə)liŋ\ **gavels** : to subject to or distribute according to the custom of gavelkind

⁷gavel \"\ *n* -s [origin unknown] **1** : a mason's setting maul **2 a** : the mallet of a presiding officer (as in a legislative body, public assembly, court) **b** : a mallet used (as by an auctioneer) to attract or command attention or to confirm an act (as of selling)

gavel 2

⁸gavel \"\ *vt* **gaveled** *or* **gavelled**; **gaveled** *or* **gavelled**; **gaveling** *or* **gavelling** \-v(ə)liŋ\ **gavels** **1** : to demand, require, or force by use of the gavel usu. with disregard of parliamentary courtesies ⟨a sound that the presiding officer . . . ~*ed* into silence —F.G.Slaughter⟩ **2** : to declare arbitrarily without regard to parliamentary practice — compare STEAMROLLER

gav·el·age \'gav(ə)lij\ *n* -s [ME *gaffelage*, fr. *gavel*, *gaffel* (tribute) + *-age*] *archaic* : ¹GAVEL 1

gav·el·kind \'gavəl,kīnd\ *n* [ME *gavelkynde*, fr. ¹*gavel* + *kynde*, *kinde* kind — more at KIND] **1** : a common-law tenure of land abolished by 1926 but existing chiefly in Kent from Anglo-Saxon times and marked by various peculiar features among which are that (1) upon the death of the tenant in fee intestate the land is divided equally among all the sons or among brothers or other collateral heirs on failure of direct or nearer heirs, (2) a tenant in fee can make disposal of his land by feoffment at the age of 15, (3) there is no escheat upon judgment of death for felony, and (4) the right of dower or curtesy vests in the surviving spouse **2** : the custom of dividing an intestate's estate equally among the sons or other heirs

gav·el·kind·er \-də(r)\ *n* -s : a tenant by gavelkind

gav·el·ler *also* **gav·el·er** \'gav(ə)lə(r)\ *n* -s [¹*gavel* + *-er*] **1** : an officer of the British crown granting plots in the Forest of Dean to miners for mining on a royalty basis **2** : a tenant paying gavel for land in Britain

gav·el·man \-vəlmən\ *n, pl* **gavelmen** [¹*gavel* + *man*] *archaic* : a person paying gavel

gav·elock \'gavlək\ *n* -s [ME *gavelok*, fr. OE *gafeluc*, of Celt origin; akin to W *gaflach* javelin, *gafl* forked branch, fork — more at GAFFLE] **1** *archaic* : a spear or dart : JAVELIN **2** *dial Brit* : an iron crowbar or lever

ga·via \'gāvēə\ *n, cap* [NL, fr. L, a bird (prob. sea mew)] : a genus of somewhat primitive aquatic birds comprising the loons and having the legs placed far back under the body which results in a clumsy floundering gait on land — see GAVIIFORMES

ga·vi·al \'gāvēəl\ *also* **gha·ri·al** \'gərēəl\ *n* -s [F, modif. of Hindi *ghariyāl*] **1** : a large crocodilian (*Gavialis gangeticus*) of India inhabiting chiefly the basins of the Ganges, Brahmaputra, and Indus rivers and distinguished from the typical crocodiles by long slender jaws with teeth of nearly uniform size and soft, swollen, and inflatable nose tip and by completely webbed feet **2** : any of several living or extinct reptiles related to and resembling the gavial including one extinct Asiatic form (*Ramphosuchus crassidens*) of more than 50 feet in length — **ga·vi·al·oid** \-ə,lȯid\ *adj*

ga·vi·al·i·dae \,gāvē'alə,dē\ *n pl, cap* [NL, fr. *Gavialis*, type genus (fr. F *gavial*) + *-idae*] *in some classifications* : a family of crocodilians comprising the gavials and a few related extinct forms

ga·vi·ifor·mes \,gāvēə'fȯr,mēz\ *n pl, cap* [NL, fr. *Gavia* + *-i-* + *-formes*] : an order of large aquatic birds including those of the genus *Gavia* and a few related extinct birds — compare LOON

¹ga·votte *also* **ga·vot** \gə'vät, *usu* -äd·+V\ *n* -s [F *gavotte*, fr. MF, fr. OProv *gavoto*, fr. *gavot* Alpine dweller, fr. *gava* crop, goiter] **1** : a dance of French peasant origin characterized by the raising rather than sliding of the feet **2** : a French dance tune in moderately quick 4/4 time comprised of two sections each of which is repeated and always beginning on the third beat

²gavotte \"\ *vi* -ED/-ING/-S : to dance a gavotte

¹gaw \'gȯ, 'gä\ *n* -s [alter. of ²*gall*] *chiefly Scot* **1** : ²GALL 1a, 2a **2** : a small channel cut for drainage purposes : FURROW, TRENCH

²gaw \'gȯ\ *dial Brit var of* GOD

GAW *abbr* guaranteed annual wage

gaw·bli·my \gȯ'blīmi\ *var of* GORBLIMY

gawd *archaic var of* ¹GAUD

gawdy *archaic var of* ¹GAUDY

¹gawk \'gȯk, 'gäk\ *vi* -ED/-ING/-S [perh. alter. (influenced by E dial. *gawk* left-handed) of obs. E *gaw* to stare, fr. ME *gawen*, fr. ON *gā* to heed, mark — more at FAVOR] : to look without intelligent awareness : gape or stare stupidly — often used with *at* ⟨passers-by ~*ed* at the wreck⟩ — **gawker** *n* -s

²gawk \"\ *n* -s [prob. fr. E dial. *gawk* left-handed] : an ungainly clumsy stupid person : LOUT

gawk·ham·mer \'gau̇k,hamə(r), 'gäk-,'gȯk-\ *adj* [²*gawk* + E dial. *hammer* clumsy person] *dial Eng* : AWKWARD, CLUMSY

gawk·i·ly \'gȯkəlē, 'gäk-, -li\ *adv* : in a gawky manner : with gawkiness ⟨how herself ~ as though she didn't know how to cope with the length of her limbs —W.S.Maugham⟩

gawk·i·ness \-kēnəs, -kin-\ *n* -ES : the quality or state of being gawky

gawk·ish \'gȯkish, 'gäk-, -kēsh\ *adj* [²*gawk* + *-ish*] : being like a gawk : awkward, shy, and stupid — **gawk·ish·ly** *adv* — **gawk·ish·ness** *n* -ES

¹gawky \'gȯkē, 'gäk-, -ki\ *adj* -ER/-EST [²*gawk* + *-y*] : lacking grace or elegance often from being too large or awkwardly put together ⟨a tall ~ house⟩; *often* : overgrown and gangling and consequently self-conscious and awkward ⟨a ~ lad, at that uncomfortable age when . . . the great hands and ankles protrude a long way from garments which have grown too tight for them —W.M.Thackeray⟩ **syn** see AWKWARD

²gawky \"\ *n* -ES : a gawky person

gawm *var of* ⁴GAUM

gaw·ney \'gȯni\ *n* -s [origin unknown] *chiefly dial Eng* : SIMPLETON, GAWK

¹gawp *var of* GAUP

²gawp \'gȯp\ *n* -s [¹*gawp*] *dial* : a stupid awkward person : SIMPLETON

gaw·sie *or* **gaw·cie** *or* **gaw·cey** \'gȯsē\ *adj* [origin unknown] **1** *Scot, of a person* : well-fed and hearty looking : plump and cheerful **2** *Scot, of a domestic animal* : well filled out : in good condition **3** *Scot* : good-sized : presenting an imposing and ample appearance ⟨the house . . . *gawcey* and substantial —G.D.Brown⟩

¹gay \'gā\ *adj* -ER/-EST [ME, fr. MF *gai*, prob. fr. OProv, of Gmc origin; akin to OHG *gāhi* rapid, hurried, impetuous] **1** : excited and merry : manifesting or inclined to joyous exhibition of content or pleasure ⟨~ carefree children⟩ ⟨a ~ word of greeting⟩ **2 a** : bright and lively in appearance ⟨~ sunny meadows⟩ **b** : brilliant in color ⟨the dress a bit too ~ for her years⟩ **c** *chiefly Brit, of poultry* : marked with white ⟨Anconas often become *gayer* with age⟩ **3** *obs* **a** : FIRST-CLASS, FINE, EXCELLENT **b** : speciously or artfully brilliant — used of things immaterial (as reasoning or rhetoric) **4 a** : given to social pleasures **b** : inclined to the dissipations of society : LICENTIOUS, LOOSE **c** *of a woman* : leading an immoral life; *esp* : engaging in prostitution **5** *dial Eng, of health or physical condition* : GOOD ⟨not feeling so ~ today⟩ ⟨looked quite ~ after his spell⟩ **6 a** *of an animal* : ALERT, KEEN, LIVELY **b** *of a tail* : carried high, erect, or curled over the back ⟨the tail of a Persian cat should never be ~⟩ **7** : impertinent and forward : BRASH, FRESH — usu. used with *get* ⟨don't get ~ with me if you want to keep out of trouble⟩ **8 a** : HOMOSEXUAL **b** : of, relating to, or being a socially integrated group oriented toward and concerned with the welfare of the homosexual ⟨a ~ newspaper⟩ **syn** see LIVELY

²gay \"\ *n* -s [ME, fr. *gay*, adj.] **1** *obs* : a gay person or pastime **2** *dial Eng* **a** : a toy or ornament esp. for a child **b** : an illustration in a book or paper ⟨haven't got my glasses but I can still read the *gays*⟩

³gay \"\ *adv* [ME, fr. *gay*, adj.] : GAILY, BRIGHTLY, JOYOUSLY — used in combination ⟨the *gay*-colored flowers⟩

⁴gay \"\ *vb* -ED/-ING/-S [¹*gay*] *vi* : to behave gaily : become gay ⟨a bird ~*ing* on a branch before the window⟩ ~ *vt* : to make gay, bright, or cheerful — usu. used with *up* ⟨fresh paint and new curtains will ~ up a dingy kitchen⟩

⁵gay *var of* GEY

ga·ya \gə'yä\ *adj, usu cap* [fr. *Gaya*, India] **:** of or from the city of Gaya, India **:** of the kind or style prevalent in Gaya

ga·yal \gə'yäl\ *n, pl* **gayals** *also* **gayal** [Beng *gayāl*; akin to Skt *go* bull, cow — more at cow] **:** an ox (*Bibos frontalis*) domesticated in India that differs from the gaur of which it may be a domesticated variety in its longer slenderer horns and white legs

ga·ya·tri \'gäyə,trē\ *n* -s [Skt *gāyatrī*, fr. *gāyatra* song, hymn, fr. *gāyati* he sings — more at CHOUGH] **1 :** an ancient Vedic meter of 24 syllables generally arranged in a triplet **2 :** a composition in this meter (as a noted Hindu mantra used daily by the devout)

gaycat \'=,=\ *n* **1** *slang* **:** a tramp who will work if the inducement is sufficient **2** *slang* **:** a young and inexperienced tramp

gay·di·ang \'gīdē,aŋ\ *n* -s [Annamese] **:** an Annamese ship with two or three masts and lofty triangular sails

gay dog *n* **:** a man given to gay or licentious self-indulgence

gayety *var of* GAIETY

gayfeather \'=,==\ *n* **:** BUTTON SNAKEROOT 1; *esp* **:** a widely distributed purple-flowered perennial herb (*Liatris pycnostachya*) of central No. America that is sometimes cultivated as an ornamental and for cut flowers

gay lady's-slipper *n* **:** SHOWY LADY'S-SLIPPER

gaylies *var of* GEYLIES

gay-lus·sac \,gāləˌsak\ *adj, usu cap G&L* [after Joseph L. *Gay-Lussac* †1850 Fr. chemist and physicist] **:** of, relating to, or developed by the French chemist Joseph L. Gay-Lussac

gay·lus·sacia \,gālə'sāsh(ē)ə, -'sakēə\ *n, cap* [NL, fr. J. L. *Gay-Lussac* + NL *-ia*] **:** a large genus of American shrubs (family Ericaceae) comprising the true huckleberries and being distinguished by a 10-locular 10-ovuled ovary and anthers without awns

gay-lussac's law *n, usu cap G&1stL* [after J. L. *Gay-Lussac*] **1 :** a statement in chemistry and physics: when two or more gaseous substances combine to form a gaseous compound the volume of the product is either equal to the sum of the volumes of the factors or is less than and bears a simple ratio to this sum — called also *law of combining volumes;* compare AVOGADRO'S LAW **2 :** CHARLES'S LAW

gay-lussac tower *n, usu cap G&L* [after J. L. *Gay-Lussac*] **:** a large packed tower that is situated after the chambers in the chamber process of making sulfuric acid and that contains strong sulfuric acid for absorbing nitrogen oxides from the spent gases with the formation of nitrous vitriol — see GLOVER TOWER

gay·lus·site \'gālə,sīt\ *n* -s [F, fr. J. L. *Gay-Lussac* + F *-ite*] **:** a mineral $Na_2Ca(CO_3)_2.5H_2O$ consisting of a yellowish white translucent hydrous carbonate of calcium and sodium

gayly *var of* GAILY

gay·ness *n* -ES [ME *gaynesse*, fr. ¹*gay* + *-nesse* -ness] **:** the quality or state of being gay **:** GAIETY

ga·yo \'gī(,)ō, 'gä(,)yō\ *n, pl* **gayo** *or* **gayos** *usu cap* [native name in northern Sumatra] **1 :** an Indonesian people of northern Sumatra **2 :** a member of the Gayo people

gay science *n* **:** POETRY; *esp* **:** amatory poetry

gay·some \'gāsəm\ *adj* [¹*gay* + *-some*] **:** full of gaiety **:** BLITHE, CHEERY

gayway \'=,=\ *n* **:** MIDWAY 3a

gaywings \'=,=\ *n pl but sing or pl in constr* **:** a common trailing perennial milkwort (*Polygala paucifolia*) of eastern No. America having leaves suggesting those of the wintergreen and rosy purple or occasionally white flowers with winged sepals and fringed crest on the corolla — called also *flowering wintergreen, fringed polygala*

gay·you \'gā|(,)(y)ü, 'gī|\ *n* -s [Annamese *ghe hâu* fine boat] **:** an Annamese narrow flat-bottomed boat with an outrigger and two or three masts with square sails or lugsails

gaz *abbr* gazette; gazetted; gazetteer

¹**gazabo** *var of* GAZEBO

²**ga·za·bo** \gə'zā(,)bō\ *n* -s [origin unknown] *slang* **:** FELLOW, PERSON, GUY

ga·za·nia \gə'zānēə\ *n* [NL, irreg. fr. Teodoro *Gaza*, 15th cent. Greek scholar + NL *-ia*] **1** *cap* **:** a genus of southern African tomentose herbs (family Compositae) that are often cultivated for their brilliant flower heads which usu. have conspicuous ray florets variously colored in red and yellow **2** -s **:** any plant or flower of the genus *Gazania*

¹**gaze** \'gāz\ *vb* -ED/-ING/-s [ME *gasen, gazen*, prob. of Scand origin; akin to Sw dial. *gasa* to stare, Norw dial. *gase* fool, *gasa* to rush forward, and perh. to ON *gassi* reckless person, Icel, gander, Dan dial. *gåse* gander, ON *gās* goose — more at GOOSE] *vi* **:** to fix the eyes in a steady and intent look **:** look with eagerness (as in admiration, wonder) or with studious attention ⟨*gazing* delighted at the scurrying throng⟩ ⟨*gazing* after the slowly vanishing boat⟩ ~ *vt, archaic* **:** to view with attention **:** gaze on

syn GAZE, GAPE, STARE, GLARE, PEER, and GLOAT can mean in common, but with marked differences, to look at long and attentively. GAZE usu. implies fixed and prolonged attention ⟨*gaze* absently into the distance⟩ ⟨could only sigh, and *gaze* at her wonderingly —George Meredith⟩ ⟨she *gazed* into his faded blue eyes as if yearning to be understood —Joseph Conrad⟩ GAPE usu. implies an open-mouthed, often stupid, wonder ⟨*gape* at an apparition in astonishment⟩ ⟨sit *gaping* at the spring sunshine⟩ STARE implies a fixed and direct, unwavering gaze ⟨*stare* at a stranger impolitely⟩ ⟨*stare* at a TV screen⟩ GLARE adds to STARE the idea of intenseness, usu. of fierceness or anger ⟨he *stared* at her from doorways, and *glared* at her from passages as she went about with her partners; and the more he *stared*, the more taken was he —Rudyard Kipling⟩ ⟨*glare* at a disobedient child⟩ ⟨he put his paw on the prize, and *glared* across the water with a defiant growl —C.G.D. Roberts⟩ PEER suggests a looking closely or curiously, esp. with partly closed eyes or from behind something ⟨the haggard face . . . that *peered* at him out of the angle of the wall —Liam O'Flaherty⟩ ⟨we *peered* at the muddy waters through an intricate pattern of bridgework —David Fairchild⟩ ⟨she had *peered* at it keenly through her spectacles —Agnes S. Turnbull⟩ GLOAT implies prolonged or frequent gazing upon something, usu. with profound, often unholy satisfaction ⟨there were residents of Boston who couldn't take their eyes from the passing carts, but stood and *gloated* —Kenneth Roberts⟩ ⟨as a boy he used to *gloat* in the Museum of Düsseldorf over the wood-carvings —G.G.Coulton⟩ ⟨spent hours *gloating* over his money⟩

²**gaze** \"\ *n* -s **1** *archaic* **:** an object gazed on **2 a :** act of looking fixedly ⟨made a long slow ~ the length of the ridge⟩ **b :** a fixed intent look **:** a continued look of attention ⟨his ~ was steady, his mien reproachful⟩ — **at gaze 1 :** depicted with the face turned directly to the front — used of heraldic representations of beasts of chase **2 a** *of a stag or other deer* **:** assuming a position expressing sudden fear or surprise (as when first hearing hounds) **b :** standing staring (as in wonder, alarm, dismay) **:** GAZING

¹**ga·ze·bo** *also* **ga·zee·bo** \gə'zā(,)bō, -zē(-\ *or* **ga·za·bo** \-zā(-\ *n, pl* **gazebos** *or* **gazeboes** [perh. fr. ¹*gaze* + L *-ebo* (as in *videbo* I shall see)] **:** BELVEDERE

²**ga·ze·bo** \gə'zā(,)bō, -zē(-\ *var of* ²GAZABO

gazehound \'=,=\ *n* **:** a dog that hunts by sight rather than by scent; *sometimes* **:** GREYHOUND

gazel *var of* GHAZEL

gaze·less \'gāzləs\ *adj* **:** UNSEEING **:** lacking power of sight ⟨turned blind and ~ eyes⟩

ga·zel·la \gə'zelə\ *n, cap* [NL, fr. F *gazelle*] **:** a genus of antelopes comprising the typical gazelles — **ga·zel·line** \-e,līn, -elən\ *adj*

¹**ga·zelle** \gə'zel\ *n, pl* **gazelles** *also* **gazelle** [F, fr. MF, fr. Ar *ghazāl*] **1 :** any of numerous small graceful and swift African and Asiatic antelopes constituting *Gazella* and related genera and noted for the luster and soft expression of their eyes **2** *or* **gazelle brown :** a grayish brown to grayish yellowish brown that is paler than soot brown or gold bronze and slightly greener and lighter than mummy brown (sense 2b) — called also *grouse, racquet*

²**gazelle** \"\ *vi* -ED/-ING/-s **:** to move in easy leaps suggesting those of a gazelle ⟨*gazelling* over the hurdles —*Newsweek*⟩

gazelle-eyed \'=,'=\ *adj* **:** having soft lustrous expressive eyes

gazelle-faced wallaby \=',=,'=\ *n* **:** any of various naked-eared wallabies of New Guinea that constitute the genus *Dorcopsis* and resemble the pademelons

gazelle hound *n* **:** a dog (as the saluki) used for coursing gazelles

gaze·ment \'gāzmənt\ *n* -s [¹*gaze* + *-ment*] *archaic* **:** prolonged observation or a stare

gaz·er \'gāzə(r)\ *n* -s **1 :** one that gazes **2** *slang* **:** a policeman or government narcotic agent

gazes *pres 3d sing of* GAZE, *pl of* GAZE

ga·zet *or* **ga·zett** \gə(d)'zet\ *n* -s [It *gazzetta*, fr. Venetian dial. *gazeta*, perh. dim. of *gaza* magpie, fr. L *Gaja*, a name for women] **:** a small Venetian copper coin of the 16th and 17th centuries

ga·zet·tal \gə'zed·ᵊl, -etᵊl\ *n* -s *Brit* **:** an act of gazetting ⟨~ of new appointments⟩

¹**ga·zette** \gə'zet, *usu* -ed·+V\ *n* -s [F, fr. It *gazzetta*, fr. Venetian dial. *gazeta* gazet, periodical that sold for a gazet] **1 :** a news sheet published periodically **:** NEWSPAPER — used chiefly in the names of newspapers **2 :** an official journal published at regular intervals (as twice a week in London and Edinburgh) containing records of various official acts, lists of promotions and honors, names of bankrupts, and public notices **3** *Brit* **:** an announcement in an official gazette ⟨just saw the ~ of his appointment⟩

²**gazette** \"\ *vt* -ED/-ING/-s **1** *chiefly Brit* **:** to announce or publish in a gazette **:** announce (as an appointment or a case of bankruptcy) publicly ⟨an Order in Council *gazetted* in Jerusalem —*Manchester Guardian Weekly*⟩ **2** *Brit* **:** to announce the appointment or status of in an official gazette ⟨he was *gazetted* to the regiment in 1932⟩ ⟨white troops *gazetted* for permanent duty in Africa —*N.Y.Times*⟩

¹**gaz·et·teer** \,gazə'ti(ə)r, -iə\ *n* -s [prob. fr. F *gazetier* (formerly spelled *gazettier*), fr. *gazette* + *-ier* -er] **1 a** *archaic* **:** a writer for a newspaper **b** *Brit* **:** a journalist in government employment serving usu. as a public-relations officer or publicist **2** *obs* **:** NEWSPAPER, GAZETTE **3** [fr. the *Gazetteer*, shortened form of *The Gazetteer's: or, Newsman's Interpreter: Being a Geographical Index* (1693), edited by Laurence Echard †1730 Eng. historian] **:** a geographical dictionary in which names and descriptions of places are usu. given in alphabetical order; *often* **:** a book in which something (as wines or restaurants) is treated esp. in regard to geographical distribution and regional specialization

²**gazetteer** \"\ *vt* -ED/-ING/-s **:** to describe in a gazetteer

gazi *often cap, var of* GHAZI

gazing *pres part. of* GAZE

gazing ball *n* **1 :** a glass ball used in crystal gazing **2 :** GAZING GLOBE

gazing globe *n* **:** a mirrored metallic often colored globe usu. mounted on a pedestal and used as a garden ornament

gaz·ing·ly *adv* **:** in a gazing manner **:** with an intent look

gazingstock \'==,=\ *n* -s **:** a person or thing gazed at by many esp. with curiosity or contempt

gazogene *var of* GASOGENE

gazoo *var of* KAZOO

ga·zook \gə'zük, -zůk\ *n* -s [origin unknown] *slang* **:** GUY

ga·zoz \gə'zōz\ *n* -ES [Ar *gāzūzah* (dial. *gāzōza*), fr. It *gazzosa, gassosa*, fr. fem. of *gazzoso, gassoso* gassy, fr. *gas* (fr. NL) + *-oso* -ous (fr. L *-osus*) — more at GAS] **:** a carbonated nonalcoholic drink

gaz·pa·cho \gȧth'pä(,)chō, gȧ'sp-\ *n, pl* **gazpachos** \-ōz,-ōs\ [Sp] **:** a soup made of uncooked chopped tomatoes, cucumbers, peppers, onion, garlic with vinegar, oil, and condiments, often thickened with bread crumbs, and served cold

GB *abbr* **1** games behind **2** gold bond **3** guidebook **4** gunboat

gba·ri \gə'bärē\ *or* **gwa·ri** \'gwärē, gə'w-\ *n, pl* **gbari** *or* **gbaris** *or* **gwari** *or* **gwaris** *usu cap* **:** a widespread peasant people of west central Nigeria to the north of the Niger-Benue confluence who are linguistically related to the Yoruba

gbo \gə'bō\ *n, pl* **gbo** [native name in Dahomey, Africa] **:** a charm that protects its owner from evil and has the power to hurt its owner's enemies

GC *abbr* **1** general circular **2** golf club **3** grand commander **4** grand cross **5** great circle **6** group captain **7** gun control

GCA *abbr* **1** general claim agent **2** ground-controlled approach

GCD *abbr* greatest common divisor

GCF *abbr* greatest common factor

GCI *abbr* ground-controlled interception

GCL *abbr* ground-controlled landing

g clef *n, usu cap G* **:** a clef that places G above middle C, on the second line of the staff — called also *treble clef;* see CLEF illustration

GCM *abbr* general court-martial

GCT *abbr* Greenwich civil time

gd *abbr* **1** good **2** ground **3** guard

GD *abbr* **1** general delivery **2** general duty **3** good delivery **4** granddaughter **5** grand duchess; grand duchy; grand duke

Gd *symbol* gadolinium

gdansk \gə'dänzk, -dan-, -n(t)sk\ *adj, usu cap* [Pol *Gdańsk* Danzig] **:** DANZIG

gde *abbr* gourde

gdn *abbr* **1** garden **2** guardian

gds *abbr* goods

gdsm *abbr* guardsman

gdyn·ia \gə'dinēə\ *adj, usu cap* [fr. *Gdynia*, Poland] **:** of or from the city of Gdynia, Poland **:** of the kind or style prevalent in Gdynia

¹**ge** *var of* GEE

²**ge** \'zhā\ *n, pl* **ge** *or* **ges** *usu cap* [Pg *gê*, of AmerInd origin] **1 a :** a group of Indian peoples of eastern Brazil **b :** a member of any of such peoples **2 :** the language of the Ge peoples

ge- *or* **geo-** *comb form* [ME *geo-*, fr. MF & L; MF, fr. L, fr. Gk *gē-, ge-, geō-*, fr. *gē* earth, land] **1 :** earth, ground, soil ⟨*geo*biology⟩ ⟨*geo*genic⟩ ⟨*geo*phyte⟩ ⟨*geo*tropic⟩ **2** geographical **:** geography and ⟨*geo*history⟩ ⟨*geo*politics⟩

GE *abbr* gilt edges

Ge *symbol* germanium

-gea — see -GAEA

¹**geal** \'jē(ə)l\ *vi* -ED/-ING/-s [ME *gellen*, fr. MF *geler* to freeze, fr. L *gelare* to freeze, congeal — more at COLD] *now dial* **:** CONGEAL

²**geal** \"\ *n* -s *dial* **:** JELLY

³**ge·al** \'jēəl\ *adj* [*ge-* + *-al*] **:** of, relating to, or caused by the earth

gean \'gēn\ *n* -s [MF *guisne, guine*] **1 a** *chiefly Brit* **:** SWEET CHERRY 1; *esp* **:** a wild sweet cherry **b :** HEART CHERRY **2 :** the fruit of a gean

ge·anticlinal \(¦)jē+\ *adj* [*ge-* + *anticlinal*] **:** of, relating to, or having geanticlines

ge·anticline \(')jē+\ *also* **geo·anticline** \¦jē(,)ō+\ *or* **ge·anticlinal** \(¦)jē+\ *n* [*geanticline, geoanticline* fr. *ge-* + *anticline; geanticlinal* fr. *ge-* + *anticlinal*] **:** a great upward flexure of the earth's crust — opposed to *geosyncline*

¹**gear** \'gi(ə)r, -iə\ *n* -s [ME *gere*, fr. ON *gervi, gørvi*; akin to OS & OHG *garuwi* equipment, clothing, ON *gervi, gørvi*; derivatives fr. the root of E *yare*] **1 a :** CLOTHING, GARMENTS **b :** personal belongings or equipment ⟨the sheds where the cowboys kept their ~⟩ **c :** movable property **:** household stuff **:** GOODS ⟨all the ~ that goes with a summer cottage⟩ **d** *dial chiefly Brit* **:** food and liquor **:** SUSTENANCE **2 :** EQUIPMENT, PARAPHERNALIA ⟨photographic ~⟩ ⟨fishing ~⟩ ⟨military ~⟩ **3 a** (1) **:** RIGGING; *specif* **:** the equipment required for any particular sail, spar, or function (2) **:** the harness of horses or cattle **:** TRAPPINGS **b** *archaic* **:** the organs of generation **4 a** *obs* **:** a leaf of heddles **b :** a single complete setline **5** *dial chiefly Brit* **:** RUBBISH, TRASH, JUNK **6** *dial chiefly Brit* **:** CONCERN, DOINGS **7 a** (1) **:** a mechanism that performs a specific function in a complete machine ⟨a valve ~⟩ ⟨a steering ~⟩ (2) **:** a toothed wheel ⟨a bevel ~⟩ ⟨a spur ~⟩ ⟨a train of ~s⟩ (3) **:** working relation or adjustment ⟨in ~⟩ ⟨out of ~⟩ **b :** one of two to several adjustments of a motor-vehicle transmission that determine mechanical advantage, relative speed, and direction of travel — compare ¹HIGH 1c(6), ⁴LOW 3f **syn** see EQUIPMENT

²**gear** \"\ *vb* -ED/-ING/-s [ME *gearwe*, fr. *gere*, n.] *vt* **1 :** DRESS, EQUIP ⟨women ~*ed* out in the height of fashion⟩ **2 a :** to provide (as machinery) with gearing **:** connect by gearing **:** put into gear **b :** to harness (as a work animal) — often used with *up* **3 a :** to put into a desired state of thorough internal coordination for effective and usu. immediate operation ⟨soldiers ~*ed* to strike in instantaneous retaliation⟩ **b :** to bring into precise adjustment so as to satisfy, conform, or harmonize or into close working relation so as to keep pace or qualify for integration ⟨an institution ~*ed* to the needs of the blind⟩ ⟨is the program ~*ed* to a fixed salary increase schedule? —W.H. Whyte⟩ ~ *vi* **1** *of machinery* **:** to be in or come into gear **2 :** to adjust or become adjusted so as to match, blend, or harmonize ⟨industry ~*ing* with consumer needs⟩

gearbox \'=,=\ *n* **:** TRANSMISSION 2

gear change *n, Brit* **:** GEAR SHIFT

gear cluster *n* **:** CLUSTER GEAR

gear cutter *n* **1 :** a machine for milling, hobbing, planing, or shaping gear teeth — compare GEAR HOBBER, GEAR SHAPER **2 :** a milling cutter esp. contoured to cut gear teeth — see MILLING CUTTER illustration

gear down *vt* **:** to gear so that the driven part goes slower than the driving part

geared *adj* **1 :** having gears **2 :** being in gear

geared turbine *n* **:** a turbine having its drive shaft attached to a set of reduction gears

gear hobber *n* **:** a machine for milling gear teeth by means of a hob rotated at an angular velocity having a definite ratio to that of the work

gearing *n* -s **1 :** the act or process of providing or fitting with gears **2 a** *chiefly dial* **:** HARNESS **b :** the parts by which motion is transmitted from one portion of machinery to another **:** GEAR; *specif* **:** a train of gear wheels

gearing chain *n* **:** an endless chain to transmit motion from one sprocket wheel to another

ge·ark·sut·ite \jē'ärksə,tīt\ *n* -s [*ge-* + *arksutite* $Na_5Al_3F_{14}$ fr. *Arksut* (*Arsuk*) fjord, Greenland + E *-ite*] **:** a mineral $CaAl(OH)F_4.H_2O$ consisting of an earthy clayey hydrous calcium aluminum fluoride occurring with cryolite

gear·less \'gi(ə)rləs, -iəl-\ *adj* **:** having no gear **:** operating without a gear

gearless traction *n* **:** traction without reduction gears (as in a high-speed electric elevator drive in which the driving sheave is mounted directly on the armature shaft)

gear level *vt* **:** to gear so that the driven part goes at the same rate as the driving part — compare GEAR DOWN, GEAR UP

gear·man \'=mən\ *n, pl* **gearmen 1 :** one that looks after gears **2 :** a keeper of engine-room stores aboard a ship

gearmotor \'=,==\ *n* **:** an electric motor with various output speeds secured by attached combinations of gears

gear pump *n* **:** a rotary pump consisting of two meshing gear wheels in a suitable casing whose contrarotation entrains the fluid on one side and discharges it on the other

gear ratio *n* **:** the ratio of the angular speed of the initial or driving member of a gear train or equivalent mechanism to that of the final or driven member; *specif* **:** the number of engine revolutions per revolution of the rear wheels of an automobile

gears \'gi(ə)rz\ *n pl* [ME *geres*, pl. of *gere* gear — more at GEAR] *Midland* **:** HARNESS

gearset \'=,=\ *n* **:** a set of gears forming a unit group

gear shaper *n* **:** a machine in which gear teeth are shaped by a cutter in the form of a pinion; *also* **:** one that shapes gears

gearshift \'=,=\ *n* **:** a mechanism by which the transmission gears in a power-transmission system are engaged and disengaged; *also* **:** the functioning of such a mechanism

gear up *vt* **1 :** to gear so that the driven part goes faster than the driving part **2 :** to speed up ⟨*gear up* production to meet military needs⟩ **:** ACCELERATE

gear wheel *n* **:** a wheel that gears with another piece; *specif* **:** COGWHEEL

geason *adj* [ME *geson*, fr. OE *gǣsne*; akin to OHG *geisinī* barrenness, and perh. to OE *gād* lack, need, desire, Goth *gaidw* lack, OE *gān* to go — more at GO] *obs* **:** UNPRODUCTIVE, SCANT, SCARCE

A B

gear wheels, *A* and *B*, in mesh

ge·aster \(')jē¦astə(r)\ [NL, fr. *ge-* + *-aster* (star)] *syn of* GEASTRUM

ge·as·trum \jē'astrəm\ *n, cap* [NL, fr. *ge-* + *-astrum* (fr. Gk *astēr* star) — more at STAR] **:** a genus (the type of the family Geastraceae) of basidiomycetous fungi having the outer peridium when dry splitting into starlike segments — compare EARTHSTAR

geat \'ya(a)t, 'yaət\ *n, pl* **geats** \-əts\ *also* **gea·tas** \-ə,täs\ *usu cap* [OE *Gēat*] **:** a Scandinavian people of southern Sweden subjugated by the Swedes in the 6th century and believed to be ancestors of the Gotlanders — **geat·ish** *adj, usu cap*

ge·bang \gə'baŋ, -bäŋ\ *or* **gebang palm** *n* -s [Malay *gěbang*] **:** a Malayan fan palm (*Corypha gebanga*) having large leaves that are split and used for thatching or plaiting into containers

ge·ban·ga \-ŋgə\ *n* -s [NL (specific epithet of *Corypha gebanga*), fr. Malay *gěbang*] **:** the leaf fiber of the gebang palm

ge·brauchs·mu·sik \gə'braůks(,)mü,zēk\ *n, usu cap* [G, fr. *gebrauch* use + *musik* music] **:** music composed for use outside the concert field (as for amateur groups, celebrations, films)

ge·car·cin·i·dae \,jē,kär'sinə,dē\ *n pl, cap* [NL, fr. *Gecarcinus*, type genus + *-idae*] **:** a family of brachyuran crabs comprising the common land crabs — see GECARCINUS

ge·car·ci·nus \jē'kärsᵊnəs\ *n, cap* [NL, fr. *ge-* + Gk *karkinos* crab] **:** the type genus of the family Gecarcinidae comprising the black crab and other land crabs of the West Indies and tropical western Africa

gecconid *var of* GEKKONID

gec·con·i·dae \ge'känə,dē\ *syn of* GEKKONIDAE

geck \'gek\ *vi* -ED/-ING/-s [LG *gecken* to make a fool of, fr. MLG, fr. *geck* fool] **1** *chiefly Scot* **:** to be scornful or derisive **:** MOCK — usu. used with *at* ⟨~ at me because I'm poor —Robert Burns⟩ **2** *chiefly Scot* **:** to show scorn or derision by tossing the head or casting sidelong glances

¹**gecko** *also* **gec·co** \'ge(,)kō\ *n, pl* **geckos** *or* **geckoes** *also* **geccos** *or* **geccoes** [Malay *ge'kok*, of imit. origin] **:** any of numerous small chiefly tropical usu. nocturnal lizards (family Gekkonidae) that have large eyes and vertical elliptical pupils, amphicoelous vertebrae, and toes generally expanded and furnished with adhesive disks and that are completely harmless and valuable destroyers of insects though often locally reputed to be venomous

²**gecko** \"\ [NL, fr. Malay *ge'kok*] *syn of* GEKKO

geck·oid \'ge,kȯid\ *n or adj* [NL *gecko* + E *-oid*] **:** GEKKONOID

geck·o·nes \'gekə,nēz, ge'kō(,)n-\ *n syn of* GEKKONES

geck·on·i·dae \ge'känə,dē\ *syn of* GEKKONIDAE

ged *or* **gedd** \'ged\ *n* -s [ME *gedd, gedde*, fr. ON *gedda* — more at GOAD] *chiefly Scot* **:** ⁴PIKE 1a

ged·a·nite \'gedᵊn,īt, 'je-\ *n* -s [G *gedanit*, fr. *Gedanum* Danzig, city in northern Poland + G *-it* -ite] **:** a fossil resin similar to amber

ge·dank·en·experiment \gə'däŋkən+,=,==\ *n* [G, fr. *gedanke* thought + *experiment*] **:** an experiment carried out by proposing a hypothesis in thought only

ge·deckt \gə'dekt\ *or* **ge·dackt** *also* **ge·dact** \-däkt, -dakt\ *n* -s [*gedeckt* fr. G, fr. past part. of *decken* to cover, fr. OHG *deckan; gedackt, gedact* fr. G *gedackt*, fr. archaic past part. of *decken* — more at THATCH] **:** a labial pipe-organ stop of 2-foot, 4-foot, 8-foot, 16-foot, or 32-foot pitch and of flute quality

gedeckt pom·mer \-,pämə(r), -,pȯm-\ *n* [G *gedacktpommer*, *gedecktpommer*, fr. *gedackt, gedeckt* + *pommer*] **:** a gedeckt pipe-organ mixture stop that is used to produce a strong harmonic at the twelfth as well as the fundamental tone

ge·deckt·work \-k,twərk\ *n* **:** the flue stops in a pipe organ with covered pipes

ge·din·ni·an \jə'dinēən, zhə'-\ *adj, usu cap* [F *Gedinnian*, subdivision of the European Devonian, fr. F *Gédinnien*, fr. *Gédinne*, village in Belgium + F *-ien* -ian] **:** of, relating to, or constituting a subdivision of the European Devonian — see GEOLOGIC TIME table

ged·rite \'je,drīt\ *n* -s [F *gédrite*, fr. *Gèdre*, village in southern France + F *-ite*] **:** a mineral consisting of an aluminous variety of anthophyllite

ge·dunk \'gē,dəŋk\ *n* -s [origin unknown] *slang* **:** something (as a sundae) sold at a soda fountain or snack bar

¹**gee** \'jē\ *v imper* [origin unknown] — used (1) as a command to a team or draft animal to turn to the right or move ahead or (2) as a call in square dancing to progress to the right; compare

5HAW ~ *vi* **geed; geed; geeing; gees 1 :** to cry out the command *gee* to a draft animal ⟨we *geed* and hawed until we were hoarse —A.M.Bailey⟩ **2 :** to turn to the off or right side ⟨the mare *geed* when she should have hawed⟩ **3 :** to obey the command *gee* ⟨teaching a pair of young steers to ~⟩

2gee \"\ *n* -s *slang Brit* **:** HORSE

3gee *also* **ge** \"\ *n* -s **1 :** the letter *g* **2** [fr. the initial letter of *grand*] *slang* **:** a thousand dollars **3** [fr. the initial letter of *guy*] *slang* **:** MAN, INDIVIDUAL ⟨nobody is gettin' away with anything on this ~ —J.T.Farrell⟩

4gee \"\ *vi* **geed; geed; geeing; gees** [origin unknown] *chiefly dial* **:** to get along **:** AGREE, JIBE ⟨these various powerful themes do not always quite ~ —*Time*⟩

5gee \'gē\ *n* -s [origin unknown] *chiefly Scot* **:** a capricious notion **:** WHIM; *esp* **:** a perverse inclination

6gee *or* **jee** \'jē\ *interj* [euphemism for *Jesus*] — often used as an introductory expletive for emphasis and sometimes to express surprise or enthusiasm

7gee \"\ *n* -s *usu cap* [origin unknown] **:** an aeronautical navigation system similar to loran and developed in England during World War II as a bombing aid

gee·bung \'jē,bəŋ\ *n* -s [native name in Australia] **:** any of numerous chiefly Australian shrubs and small trees that constitute a genus (*Persoonia*) of the family Proteaceae, have hard narrow leaves and long-lasting yellow or white flowers, and produce small edible but insipid 1-celled or 2-celled drupes

gee·chee \'gēchē\ *n* -s *usu cap* [fr. the *Ogeechee* river, Ga.] **1 :** a dialect containing English words and words of native African origin spoken chiefly by the descendants of Negro slaves settled on the Ogeechee river in Georgia — compare GULLAH **2 :** a Geechee-speaking Negro

geegaw *var of* GEWGAW

gee-gee \'jē(,)jē\ *n* -s [redupl. of 1*gee*] *slang* **:** HORSE; *esp* **:** RACEHORSE

gee ho \(')jē¦hō\ *v imper* **:** 1GEE

geek \'gēk\ *n* -s [prob. fr. E dial. *geek, geck* fool, fr. LG *geck*, fr. MLG] **:** a carnival performer often billed as a wild man whose act usu. includes biting the head off a live chicken or snake

geel·bec *or* **geel·bek** *or* **geel·beck** \'gēl,bek\ *n* -s [Afrik *geelbek*, fr. *geel* yellow (fr. MD *ghele*) + *bek* beak, fr. MD *bec*, fr. OF; akin to OHG *gelo* yellow — more at YELLOW, BEAK] **1 :** a wild yellow-billed duck (*Anas undulata*) of Africa **2 :** a large sciaenid fish (*Atractoscion aequidens*) shaped like a mackerel and favored as a leading food and game fish in southern Africa and Australia

geel·dik·kop \gēl'di,kăp\ *n* -s [Afrik, fr. *geel* yellow + *dikkop*, a disease of sheep, fr. *dik* thick + *kop* head — more at DIKKOP] **:** a serious photodynamic disease of southern African sheep due to sensitization to light following the ingestion of certain plants and characterized by intense jaundice and a severe facial edema

geel·hout \'gēl,haůt\ *n* -s [Afrik, fr. *geel* yellow + *hout* wood; akin to OHG *holz* wood — more at HOLT] **:** any of several southern African trees of the genera *Podocarpus* and *Elaeodendron* whose wood is sometimes used for interior work

gee pole *n* [1*gee*] **:** a steering pole at the front of a dog sled

geepound \'⸗,⸗\ *n* [3*gee* (the initial letter of *gravity*) + *pound*] **:** 3SLUG 10

geese *pl of* GOOSE

geest \'gāst, 'gēst\ *n* -s [G, fr. LG, high dry land near the sea, fr. MLG *gēst* — more at GAST] **1 :** alluvial matter not of recent origin on the surface of land **2 :** loose material (as earth or soil) formed by decay of rocks in a place — compare LATERITE, SAPROLITE

gee string *var of* G-STRING

geet \(')gēt\ *Scot var of* GET

gee-throw \'⸗,⸗\ *n* [1*gee*] **:** a strong wooden lever with a curved metal point used to break out logging sleds

gee-up *also* **gee-hup** \(')jē'(h)əp\ *v imper* **:** 1GEE

gee whiz *also* **ge whizz** \(')jē'(h)wiz\ *or* **gee whil·li·kers** \-(h)wiləkə(r)z, -lēk-\ *or* **gee whil·li·kins** \-kənz\ *interj* [6*gee* + *whiz* or *whizz* or *whillikers* or *whillikins*, of unknown origin] **:** 6GEE

1geez *var of* JEEZ

2ge·ez \gē'ez, gä'-\ *n, cap* **:** ETHIOPIC 1

ge·zer \'gēzə(r)\ *n* -s [prob. alter. of *guiser*] *slang* **:** a queer, odd, or eccentric man

ge·fil·te fish *also* **ge·füll·te fish** *or* **ge·fill·te fish** \gə'filtə-\ *n* [Yiddish *gefilte fish*, lit., filled fish] **:** a Jewish dish of stewed or baked fish stuffed with a mixture of the fish flesh, bread crumbs, eggs, and seasoning or prepared as balls or oval cakes boiled in a fish stock

geg *usu cap, var of* GHEG

ge·gen·ion \'gāgən+,-\ *n* -s [G, fr. *gegen* against, counter- + *ion*] **:** COUNTERION

ge·gen·schein \'gāgən,shīn\ *n* -s *often cap* [G, fr. *gegen* against, counter- + *schein* shine] **:** a faint elliptical nebulous light about 20° across on the ecliptic and opposite the sun best seen during September and October when in the constellations Aquarius and Pisces and probably associated in origin with the zodiacal light — called also *counterglow*

ge·gen·stands·the·o·rie \'⸗⸗,shtän(t)s,tāō,rē\ *n* -s *usu cap* [G, fr. *gegenstand* object + *theorie* theory] **:** a theory of objects; *esp* **:** a theory of intentional objects

ge·heim·rat \gə'hīm,rät, *G* -räät\ *n* -s *usu cap* [G, fr. older *geheimerat*, fr. *geheime, geheimde* secrecy (fr. *geheim*, adj. secret, fr. MHG, secret, familiar, pertaining to the household, fr. *ge-*, collective prefix — fr. OHG *gi-* — + *heim* house, dwelling, fr. OHG) + *rat* counselor, counsel, fr. OHG *rāt* advice, provisions — more at CO-, HOME, READ] **:** PRIVY COUNCILOR

ge·hen·na \gə'henə\ *n* -s *usu cap* [LL *Gehenna, Geenna*, fr. Gk *Geenna*, fr. Heb *Gē' Hinnōm* lit., valley of Hinnom] **1 :** HELL 1a(2) **2 :** a place or state of misery ⟨all around you a ~ of mad industrial life —Norman Douglas⟩

geh·len·ite \'gālə,nīt\ *n* -s [G *gehlenit*, fr. A. F. *Gehlen*, 19th cent. Ger. chemist + G *-it* -ite] **:** a mineral $Ca_2Al_2SiO_7$ consisting of calcium aluminum silicate occurring in prismatic crystals isomorphous with akermanite

gei·ge \'gīgə\ *n, pl* **gei·gen** \-gən\ [G, fr. OHG *gīga* — more at JIG] **:** FIDDLE, VIOLIN

gei·gen principal \'gīgən-\ *n* [G *geigenprinzipal*, fr. *geige* + *prinzipal* open diapason] **:** VIOLIN DIAPASON

gei·ger \'gīgə(r)\ *n* -s *usu cap* [by shortening] **1 :** GEIGER COUNTER **2 :** a particle capable of detection by a Geiger counter

geiger counter \'⸗⸗¦⸗⸗\ *or* **geiger-mül·ler counter** \'⸗⸗-¦⸗⸗¦⸗⸗ -'myü̇lə(r)-, -'mil, -'mül, -'məl\ *n, usu cap G&M* [after Hans *Geiger* †1945 Ger. physicist and W. *Müller*, 20th cent. Ger. physicist, its inventors] **1 :** GEIGER-MÜLLER TUBE **2 :** an instrument consisting of a Geiger-Müller tube and the electronic equipment used in conjunction with it to record (as by a series of clicks) the momentary current pulsations in the tube gas

geiger-müller tube *or* **geiger tube** *n, usu cap G&M* [after H. *Geiger* and W. *Müller*] **:** a gas-filled counting tube with a cylindrical cathode and axial wire electrode for detecting the presence of cosmic rays or radioactive substances by means of the ionizing particles that penetrate its envelope and set up momentary current pulsations in the gas

geiger-nut·tall law *also* **geiger-nuttall relation** \'⸗⸗¦nəd-,ól-\ *n, usu cap G&N* [after H. *Geiger* and John M. *Nuttall* †1958 Brit. physicist] **:** a statement in nuclear physics: for an alpha-emitting radioactive substance the logarithm of the decay constant and the logarithm of the range in air of the emitted alpha rays are in linear relation to each other

geiger tree *n* [after John *Geiger fl ab* 1832 Am. friend of Audubon] **:** a small often shrubby tropical American evergreen tree (*Cordia sebestena*) with thick rough deep-green leaves, orange or scarlet flowers borne in large open terminal clusters, and fruit that is a small white 4-celled edible drupe

gei·kia \'gēkēə\ *n, cap* [NL, fr. Sir Archibald *Geikie* †1924 Scot. geologist + NL *-ia*] **:** a genus of rather small toothless dicynodont reptiles from the Upper Permian of Scotland

gei·kie·lite \'gēkē,līt\ *n* -s [Sir Archibald *Geikie* †1924 + E *-lite*] **:** a mineral $MgTiO_3$ consisting of magnesium titanate, being isomorphous with pyrophanite, and occurring as bluish black or brownish black rolled pebbles

geil·siek·te \'gāl,sēktə\ *n* -s [Afrik, fr. *geil* fertile, rich, rank + *siekte* disease] **:** a hydrocyanic-acid poisoning in southern African sheep and goats due to forage high in cyanogenetic glucosides

gei·sha \'gā¦shə, 'gē¦\ *n, pl* **geisha** *or* **geishas** [Jap, fr. *gei* art, performance + *-sha* person] **1 :** a Japanese girl who is trained to provide (as by playing on the samisen, dancing, serving food or drinks or by sympathetic, witty, or amusing talk) entertaining and lighthearted company (as for a man or a group of men) **2 :** COURTESAN

gei·son \'gī,sän, 'gī,-\ *n, pl* **gei·sa** \-(,)sä\ [Gk *geison, geisson*, prob. of non-IE origin] **:** CORNICE

ge·isotherm \(')jē+\ *n* -s [*ge-* + *isotherm*] **:** ISOGEOTHERM — **ge·isothermal** \(¦)jē+\ *adj*

geiss·ler bulb \'gīslə(r)-\ *n, usu cap G* [after Heinrich *Geissler* †1879 Ger. mechanic] **:** a potash bulb consisting usu. of two upper bulbs connected by three lower smaller bulbs — often used in pl.

geissler pump *n, usu cap G* [after H. *Geissler*] **:** an air pump based on the principle of the Torricellian vacuum and having its vacuum produced by the flow of mercury back and forth between a fixed and a vertically adjustable reservoir

geissler tube *n, usu cap G* [after Heinrich *Geissler*] **:** a gas-filled discharge tube having various shapes and usu. a narrowly constricted portion in which the luminosity is intensified

Geissler tubes

geisso- *comb form* [NL, fr. Gk *geisson, geison* cornice] **:** like a cornice ⟨*Geissorhiza*⟩

geist·lich \'gīstlik\ *adv* (*or adj*) [G, fr. OHG *geistlīch* (trans. of L *spiritualis*), fr. *geist* spirit + *-līch* -ly — more at GHOST] **:** with deep feeling **:** SOULFULLY — used as a direction in music

gei·to·nog·a·mous \,gīt°n¦ägəməs\ *adj* **:** of or relating to geitonogamy

gei·to·nog·a·my \,⸗⸗'⸗⸗mē\ *n* -ES [ISV *geitono-* (fr. Gk *geitōn* neighbor) + *-gamy*] **:** pollination of one flower by another growing on the same plant

gek·ko \'ge(,)kō\ *n, cap* [NL, fr. Malay *ge'kok*, of imit. origin] **:** the type genus of Gekkonidae comprising a number of typical geckos

gek·ko·nes \'gekə,nēz, ge'kō(,)n-\ *n pl, cap* [NL, fr. *Gekko*] *in some classifications* **:** a major division of Lacertilia comprising the family Gekkonidae and a few related extinct lizards

1gek·ko·nid *also* **gec·co·nid** \'gekə,nid, -nəd\ *adj* [NL *Gekkonidae*] **:** of or relating to the family Gekkonidae

2gekkonid *also* **gecconid** \"\ *n* -s **:** a lizard of the family Gekkonidae **:** GECKO

gek·kon·i·dae \ge'känə,dē\ *n pl, cap* [NL, fr. *Gekkon-, Gekko*, type genus + *-idae*] **:** a large family of Old World and New World lizards with amphicoelous vertebrae and other apparently primitive characters — see GEKKO

1gek·ko·noid \'gekə,nóid\ *adj* [NL *Gekkones* + E *-oid*] **:** of or relating to the group Gekkones or to the geckos

2gekkonoid \"\ *n* -s **:** a lizard of the group Gekkones

gek·ko·ta \ge'kōd·ə\ [NL, fr. *Gekko*] *syn of* GEKKONES

1gel \'jel\ *n* -s [-*gel* (as in *hydrogel, alcogel*), fr. *gelatin*] **:** a colloid in a more solid form than a sol: as **a :** a semisolid apparently homogeneous substance that may be elastic and jellylike (as gelatin) or more or less rigid (as silica gel) and that is formed by coagulation of a sol in various ways (as by cooling, by evaporation, or by precipitation with an electrolyte) **:** a disperse system consisting typically of a high-molecular-weight compound or an aggregate of small particles in very close association with a liquid — see AEROGEL, JELLY 2a, XEROGEL **b :** a nonhomogeneous gelatinous precipitate **:** COAGEL

2gel \"\ *vi* **gelled; gelled; gelling; gels :** to change into or take on the form of a gel **:** become more solid **:** SET — compare SOLATE — **gel·able** \-ləbəl\ *adj*

gel *abbr* gelatinous

gela·da \'jelədə, 'ge-; jə'läda, gə'-\ *n* -s [prob. fr. Ar *qilādah* collar, mane] **:** an ape (*Theropithecus gelada*) of Ethiopia remarkable for the long mane of hair on the neck and shoulders of the adult male

ge·län·de·läu·fer \gə'lendə,lóifə(r)\ *n* -s [G, fr. *gelände* open field + *läufer* runner] **:** a skier making a cross-country run **:** LANGLÄUFER

ge·län·de·sprung \-,s(h)prüŋ\ *also* **gelände jump** *n* -s [G, fr. *gelände* open field + *sprung* jump] **:** a jump in skiing made from a low crouching position with the aid of both ski poles and usu. over an obstacle

ge·la·sian \jə'lāzh(ē)ən\ *adj, usu cap* [*Gelasius* I †496 + E *-an*] **:** of or relating to Pope Gelasius

ge·las·i·mus \jə'lasəməs\ [NL, fr. Gk *gelasimos* laughable, fr. *gelan* to laugh] *syn of* UCA

ge·las·tic \jə'lastik\ *adj* [Gk *gelastikos* able to laugh, fr. *gelastos* laughable (fr. *gelan* to laugh) + *-ikos* -ic; akin to Arm *całr* laughter — more at CLEAN] **:** RISIBLE

ge·las·to·cor·i·dae \jə,lastə'kórə,dē\ *n pl, cap* [NL, fr. *Gelastocoris*, type genus (fr. Gk *gelastos* laughable + *koris* bug) + *-idae*] **:** a family of bugs (order Hemiptera) consisting of the toad bugs

gel·ate \'je,lāt\ *vi* -ED/-ING/-S [1*gel* + *-ate*] **:** 2GEL

ge·lat·i·fi·ca·tion \jə,lad·əfə'kāshən\ *n* -s [*gelatin* + *-fication*] **:** GELATINIZATION

gel·a·tig·e·nous \¦jelə¦tijənəs\ *adj* [*gelatin* + *-genous*] **:** producing or yielding gelatin

gel·a·tin *also* **gel·a·tine** \'jelət°n, -ətən,-əd·ən, *chiefly Brit* -ə,tēn *or* ,⸗⸗'tēn\ *n* -s [F *gélatine* (originally, a kind of thick broth), fr. It *gelatina*, fr. *gelato* (past part. of *gelare* to freeze, congeal, fr. L) + *-ina* (fr. L, fem. of *-inus* 1ine) — more at COLD] **1 :** animal jelly **:** glutinous material obtained from animal tissues by prolonged boiling; *esp* **:** a colorless to yellowish transparent colloidal protein that is hard and brittle when dry but swells in water, dissolving in hot water and forming a jelly on cooling, that is obtained usu. in sheets, flakes, or powder by the partial hydrolysis of collagen from animal skins, tendons, ligaments, and bones by cooking in water, and that is used chiefly as a food, in photography, and in medicine — compare GLUE 1, ISINGLASS **2 a :** any of various substances (as agar) resembling gelatin in physical properties ⟨vegetable ~*s*⟩ **b :** an edible jelly formed with gelatin **c :** any of several jellylike blasting explosives (as blasting gelatin or gelatin dynamite) **d :** a thin colored transparent sheet used over a stage light in order to color it

gel·a·tin·ase \'jelət°n,ās, -āz, jə'lat°n,ā-\ *n* -s [*gelatin* + *-ase*] **:** an enzyme causing liquefaction or hydrolysis of gelatin and occurring esp. in bacteria

ge·lat·i·nate \jə'lat°n,āt\ *vb* -ED/-ING/-S [*gelatin* + *-ate*] **:** GELATINIZE — **ge·lat·i·na·tion** \⸗,⸗⸗'āshən\ *n* -s

gelatin boot *n* **:** a dressing for varicose veins or ulcers consisting of a paste made of zinc oxide, gelatin, glycerin, and water that is applied first directly to the lower leg before it is wrapped in a spiral bandage and then again to the outside of the bandage — called also *Unna's boot*

gelatin dynamite *n* **:** a powerful water-resistant blasting explosive consisting of a jellylike mass of nitroglycerin and lower-nitrated cellulose nitrate incorporated with a base (as wood pulp mixed with sodium nitrate) — compare AMMONIA GELATIN, BLASTING GELATIN

gel·a·tined *pronunc at* GELATIN + d\ *adj* **:** coated with gelatin

gelatin film *n* **:** a pliable translucent absorbable film used in the surgical repair of defects

gel·a·tin·ig·er·ous \¦jelət°n¦ijərəs\ *adj* [*gelatin* + *-i-* + *-gerous*] **:** secreting a gelatinous covering — used of certain choanoflagellates

ge·lat·i·ni·za·tion \jə,lat°nə'zāshən, ,jelət°nə'-, -°n,ī'z-, -ə,nī'z-\ *n* -s **:** the process of gelatinizing

ge·lat·i·nize \jə'lat°n,īz, 'jelət°n,īz\ *vb* -ED/-ING/-S [*gelatin* + *-ize*] *vt* **1 :** to convert into a gelatinous form or into a jelly ⟨strong heating with water ~*s* starch⟩ — compare JELLY **2 :** to coat or treat with gelatin ~ *vi* **:** to become gelatinous or change into a jelly

ge·lat·i·niz·er \-zə(r)\ *n* -s **:** one that gelatinizes

ge·lat·i·no·bromide \jə¦lat°n(,)ō, ,jelə¦tinə +\ *n* [*gelatin* + *-o-* + *bromide*] **:** a light-sensitive preparation of gelatin and silver bromide used in photography

ge·lat·i·no·chloride \"+\ *n* [*gelatin* + *-o-* + *chloride*] **:** a light-sensitive preparation of gelatin and silver chloride used in photography

ge·lat·i·nous \jə'lat°nəs\ *adj* **1 :** resembling gelatin or jelly esp. in appearance and consistency **:** VISCOUS, FLOCCULENT ⟨~ ferric hydroxide⟩ **2 :** of, relating to, or containing gelatin — **ge·lat·i·nous·ly** *adv* — **ge·lat·i·nous·ness** *n* -ES

gelatinous fiber *n* **:** a plant fiber having a jellylike inner wall

gelatin process *n* **:** any of various processes involving the use of gelatin: as **a :** a photographic process in which gelatin is used as the dispersing vehicle for the sensitive silver salts **b :** a printing process for reproducing pictures or drawings based upon the action of light on a bichromated gelatin film — compare AQUATONE, CARBON PROCESS **c :** a method of producing facsimile copies of a written or drawn original with a pad of gelatin (as in a hectograph)

gelatin sponge *also* **gelatin foam** *n* **:** a sterile absorbable porous gelatin product that is used for the control of bleeding in surgery

1ge·la·tion \jə'lāshən, jē'-\ *n* -s [L *gelation-, gelatio*, fr. *gelatus* (past part. of *gelare* to freeze, congeal) + *-ion-, -io* -ion — more at COLD] **:** the action or process of freezing

2ge·la·tion \je'lāshən, jə'-\ *n* [1*gel* + *-ation*] **:** the formation of a gel from a sol

1geld \'gel(d)\ *adj* [ME, fr. ON *geldr*; akin to OE *gelde* barren, sterile, OHG *galt*, ON *gelda* to castrate — more at 2GELD] *dial chiefly Eng, of an animal* **:** not producing young **:** BARREN, STERILE

2geld \'geld\ *vt* **gelded** \-ldəd\ *also* **gelt** \-lt\ **gelded** *also* **gelt; gelding; gelds** [ME *gelden*, fr. ON *gelda*; akin to OE *gelte* young sow, OHG *galza, gelza* castrated swine, ON *göltr, galti* boar, MW *geleu, gelyf* knife, Gk *gallos* priest of Cybele, eunuch, Skt *hala* plow; basic meaning: cutting] **1 :** CASTRATE, EMASCULATE; *also* **:** SPAY **2 :** to remove the husks and chaff from **:** PRUNE **3 a :** DEPRIVE, EXCISE ⟨a man ~*ed* of his wages⟩ **b :** to lessen the force of ⟨~ an argument⟩ **c :** EXPURGATE ⟨~ a book⟩

3geld \"\ *also* **gelt** \-lt\ *n* -s [OE *gield, geld, gild* service, sacrifice, tax, tribute; akin to OHG *gelt* retribution, compensation, income, value, ON *gjald* tribute, payment, retribution, Goth *gild* tax, OE *gieldan* to pay, pay for — more at YIELD] **:** the crown tax paid under Anglo-Saxon and Norman kings; *also* **:** a division of people or territory paying it

4geld \'geld\ *vb* -ED/-ING/-S *vt* **:** to levy a geld on ~ *vi* **:** to pay geld

geld·ing \'geldiŋ, -dēŋ\ *n* -s [ME, fr. ON *geldingr*, fr. *gelda* to castrate + *-ingr* -ing] **1 :** a castrated animal; *specif* **:** a castrated male horse **2 :** EUNUCH

1ge·lech·i·id \jə'lekēəd\ *adj* [NL *Gelechiidae*] **:** of or relating to the Gelechiidae

2gelechiid \"\ *n* -s **:** any moth of the family Gelechiidae

gel·e·chi·idae \,jelə'kīə,dē\ *n pl, cap* [NL, fr. *Gelechia*, type genus (fr. Gk *gelechēs* sleeping on the earth + NL *-ia*) + *-idae*] **:** a large family of small moths having slender wings with the outer margin of the hind wing usu. concave and including important economic insects (as the pink bollworm, the Angoumois grain moth, and various leaf rollers)

Gel·foam \'jel,fōm\ *trademark* — used for a gelatin sponge

gel·id \'jeləd\ *adj* [L *gelidus*, fr. *gelu* cold, frost — more at COLD] **:** extremely cold **:** ICY ⟨the ~ waters of the Atlantic⟩ ⟨a man of ~ reserve —*New Yorker*⟩ — **ge·lid·i·ty** \jə'lidəd·ē, je'-\ *n* -ES — **gel·id·ly** \'jelədlē\ *adv*

ge·lid·i·a·ce·ae \jə,lidē'āsē,ē\ *n pl, cap* [NL, fr. *Gelidium*, type genus + *-aceae*] **:** a family of red algae coextensive with the order Gelidiales

ge·lid·i·a·les \jə,lidē'ā(,)lēz\ *n pl, cap* [NL, fr. *Gelidium* + *-ales*] **:** a small order of red algae (subclass Florideae) containing a single family and including *Gelidium* and a few related genera that are sometimes placed in Nemalionales

ge·lid·i·um \jə'lidēəm\ *n* [NL, fr. L *gelidus* (influenced in meaning by L *gelare* to freeze, congeal) + NL *-ium*; fr. the fact that the plants are boiled down to make a jelly] **1** *cap* **:** a genus of red algae (family Gelidiaceae) having cartilaginous terete or compressed much-branched fronds and cystocarps immersed in swollen branchlets and being important sources of agar — see GELIDIALES **2** -s **:** any alga of the genus *Gelidium*

gel·ig·nite \'jeləg,nīt\ *n* -s [*gel*atin + L *ignis* fire + E *-ite* — more at IGNITE] **:** a gelatin dynamite in which the adsorbent base is largely potassium nitrate or a similar nitrate usu. with some wood pulp

ge·li·lah \gə'lēlə\ *n* -s [Heb *gĕlīlāh*, lit., rolling, wrapping] **:** the rolling up of the scroll of the law preparatory to wrapping it in its vestments after reading from it in the synagogue

ge·li·notte \zhəlēnót\ *n, pl* **gelinottes** \-t(s)\ [F, fr. MF, dim. of *geline* hen, fr. L *gallina* — more at GALLINACEOUS] **:** HAZEL HEN

gell \'gel\ *n* -s [alter. of *gale*] **1** *Scot* **:** GALE **2** *Scot* **:** SPREE

gelled *past of* GEL

gelling *pres part of* GEL

gel mineral *n* **:** a noncrystalline mineral that originated as a gel — compare MINERALOID

gel·om·e·ter \je'lämed·ə(r)\ *n* [1*gel* + *-o-* + *-meter*] **:** an instrument for measuring jelly strength

ge·long \'gā,lòŋ\ *n* -s [Tibetan *geloṅ* (*dgesloṅ*), fr. *dgeba* (*gewa*) virtue + *sloṅ* (*loṅ*) to beg] **:** a Lamaist mendicant friar, bhikshu, or ordained priest

gel·ose \'je,lōs *also* -ōz\ *n* -s [ISV 1*gel* + *-ose*] **:** an amorphous polysaccharide obtained from agar and like gelatin in its ability to form a jelly; *broadly* **:** a polysaccharide (as agar) occurring in red algae and capable of forming a jelly

gels *pl of* GEL, *pres 3d sing of* GEL

gel·se·mic acid \(')jel¦semik-, -semik-\ *or* **gel·se·min·ic acid** \¦jelsə¦minik-\ *n* [*gelsemic*, ISV, fr. *gelsem-* (fr. NL *Gelsemium*) + *-ic*; *gelseminic*, ISV, fr. *gelsemin-* (fr. NL *Gelseminium*, alter. of *Gelsemium*) + *-ic*] **:** SCOPOLETIN

gel·se·mine \'jelsə,mēn, -mən\ *n* -s [ISV *gelsem-* (fr. NL *Gelsemium*, genus name of *Gelsemium sempervirens*) + *-ine*] **:** a crystalline alkaloid $C_{20}H_{22}N_2O_2$ from gelsemium

gel·se·mi·um \jel'sēmēəm\ *n* [NL, modif. of It *gelsomino* jasmine, fr. Ar *yāsamīn* jasmine — more at JASMINE] **1** *cap* **:** a small genus of woody vines (family Loganiaceae) of Asia and the southern U. S. — see YELLOW JESSAMINE **2** *pl* **gelsemiums** \-mēəmz\ *or* **gelsemia** \-mēə\ **:** the root of the yellow jessamine formerly used in medicine

gel·sen·kir·chen \¦gelzən¦kirkən\ *adj, usu cap* [fr. *Gelsenkirchen*, Germany] **:** of or from the city of Gelsenkirchen, Germany **:** of the kind or style prevalent in Gelsenkirchen

gel strength *n* **:** JELLY STRENGTH

1gelt \'gelt\ *var of* GELD

2gelt \"\ *past of* GELD

3gelt \"\ *n* -s [D *geld* (fr. MD *ghelt* payment, money) & G *geld* & Yiddish *gelt*, both fr. OHG *gelt* retribution, compensation, income, value — more at GELD] *slang* **:** MONEY

1gem \'jem\ *n* -s [ME *gemme*, fr. MF, fr. L *gemma* bud, gem; prob. akin to OE *camb* comb — more at COMB] **1 a :** a jewel (as a stone or pearl) having value and beauty that are intrinsic and not derived from its setting **:** a precious or sometimes semiprecious stone cut and polished for ornament **b :** a semiprecious stone (as a cameo or intaglio) of value because carved or engraved **2 a :** something (as a work of art or poem) prized esp. for great beauty or perfection **b :** a highly prized or well-beloved person **3 :** an old size of type between brilliant and diamond **4 :** MUFFIN 1a ⟨graham ~*s*⟩

2gem \"\ *vt* **gemmed; gemmed; gemming; gems 1** *archaic* **:** to put forth (as blossoms or fruit) **2 :** BEGEM ⟨millionaires on the hills with villas —Lucien Price⟩

gem- *comb form, usu ital* [1*geminate*] **:** having two like groups attached to the same atom ⟨*gem*-dimethyl-piperidine⟩ — esp. in names of organic compounds

ge·ma·ra \gə'märə, -mórə\ *n* -s *usu cap* [Aram *gĕmārā* completion] **:** a rabbinic commentary on and interpretation of the Mishnah; *broadly* **:** TALMUD

ge·ma·ric \-rik\ *adj, usu cap* **:** of or relating to the Gemara

ge·ma·rist \-rəst\ *n* -s *usu cap* **:** a specialist in the study of the Gemara

ge·ma·tria \gə'mā·trēə, ,gemə'trēə\ *n, pl* **gematri·ot** \-ē,ōt\ [LHeb *gimaṭriyā*, fr. Gk *geōmetria* — more at GEOMETRY] **1 :** a cryptograph in the form of a word whose letters have the numerical values of a word taken as the hidden meaning **2 :** the cabalistic method of explaining the Hebrew Scriptures by means of the cryptographic significance of the words

ge·ma·tri·al \-ēəl\ *or* **ge·ma·tri·cal** \gə'mā·trəkəl\ *adj* **:** of or relating to gematria

ge·mauve \gə'mōv\ *n* -s [modif. of F *guimauve,* fr. OF *widmalve, vimauve,* modif. (influenced by *vist* mistletoe and *malve, mauve* mallow) of L *hibiscus* marsh mallow] **:** a tropical mallow (*Malachra capitata*) with yellow flowers in loose axillary heads that is important in harboring the cotton stainer bug

ge·mein·de \gə'mīndə\ *n, pl* **gemein·den** \-dən\ [G, community, congregation, gemeinde, fr. OHG *gimeinida* community, congregation, fr. *gimeini* common, general — more at MEAN] **:** a unit of local government in Germany corresponding to a municipality

ge·mein·schaft \gə'mīn,shäft\ *n, pl* **gemeinschaf·ten** \-tən\ [G, community, fr. *gemein* common, general (fr. OHG *gimeini*) + *-schaft* -ship (fr. OHG *-scaf*)] **:** a spontaneously arising organismic social relationship characterized by strong reciprocal bonds of sentiment and kinship within a common code of tradition; *also* **:** a community or society characterized by such a relationship — contrasted with *gesellschaft*

¹gem·el *also* **gem·mel** \'jeməl\ *n* -s [ME, twin, fr. MF *gemel,* fr. L *gemellus,* dim. of *geminus* — more at GEMINATE] **1** *obs* **:** HINGE **2 :** a ring of two separable hoops — compare GIMBAL **3** *or* **gemel bar** *also* **ge·melle** *or* **ge·mell** \jə'mel, 'jeməl\ **:** BAR GEMEL **4 :** a pair of glass bottles blown separately and then fused usu. with the two necks pointing in different directions

gemel 4

²gemel \"\ *adj* [ME, twin] **:** PAIRED **:** TWIN ⟨a ~ arch⟩

gem·eled \'jeməld\ *or* **gemelled** \", jə'meld\ *adj* **:** PAIRED

gemel hinge *n* **:** a hinge consisting of an eye or loop and a hook

ge·mel·lion \jə'melyən\ *n* -s [ML *gemellion-, gemellio,* fr. L *gemellus* twin + *-ion-, -io* -ion] **:** one of a pair of basins formerly used to wash the hands at meals

ge·mel·lus \jə'meləs\ *n, pl* **gemel·li** \-,lī\ *also* **gemelluses** [NL, fr. L, twin] **:** either of two small muscles of the hip that insert into the tendon of the internal obturator, a superior originating chiefly from the outer surface of the ischial spine and an inferior originating chiefly from the ischial tuberosity

gemel window *n* **:** a window filling a pair of openings

gem-fruit \'=,=\ *n* **:** FALSE MITERWORT

¹gem·i·nate \'jemənə̇t, -,nāt, *usu* ǀd·+V\ *adj* [L *geminatus,* past part. of *geminare* to double, fr. *geminus* twin; akin to MIr *emon, emuin* pair of twins, Skt *yama* twin] **1 :** BINATE ⟨~ flowers⟩ **2 :** GEMINATED — **gem·i·nate·ly** *adv*

²gem·i·nate \-,nāt, *usu* -ād·+V\ *vb* -ED/-ING/-S [L *geminatus,* past part.] *vt* **:** to cause to become geminated **:** DOUBLE ~ *vi* **:** to become double or paired

³gem·i·nate \-,nə̇ǀt, -,nāt, *usu* ǀd·+V\ *n* -s [¹*geminate*] **:** a geminated consonant or vowel

geminated *adj* **1** *of a consonant or vowel letter or phonetic symbol* **:** occurring twice in succession in a transcription ⟨the ~ *-dd-* in *ladder*⟩ **2** *of a consonant or vowel sound* **a :** occurring twice in succession and receiving individual pronunciation ⟨the *-tt-* in *cattail* is ~⟩ **b :** ¹LONG 5

gem·i·na·tion \,jemə'nāshən\ *n* -s [L *gemination-, geminatio,* fr. *geminatus* (past part. of *geminare*) + *-ion-, -io* -ion] **:** a doubling, duplication, or repetition: as **a :** a formation of two teeth from a single tooth germ **b** (1) **:** a writing of a letter twice in succession in the spelling of a word (2) **:** a making, becoming, or being geminated

¹gem·i·na·tive \'jemə,nād·iv\ *adj* [L *geminatus* + E *-ive*] **:** relating to, produced by, or showing gemination

²geminative \"\ *n* -s **:** a geminated letter or sound

gem·i·ni \'jemə(,)nē, 'jemə,nī, 'gemə,nē\ *n pl* [ME, fr. L, twins, pl. of *geminus* — more at GEMINATE] **1** *usu sing in constr, usu cap* **:** the 3d sign of the zodiac — see SIGN table; ZODIAC illustration **2** *often sing in constr, obs* **:** PAIR, COUPLE ⟨a ~ of asses . . . would make just four of you —William Congreve⟩ **3** [prob. euphemism for LL *Jesu domine* Jesus lord!] *archaic* — used as an interjection **4 :** bivalent chromosomes

gem·i·ni·flo·rous \,jemənē'flōrəs\ *adj* [L *geminus* + E *-i-* + *-florous*] **:** having flowers in pairs

gem·i·nous \'jemənəs\ *adj* [L *geminus,* fr. *geminus,* n., twin — more at GEMINATE] **:** DOUBLED, PAIRED

gemlike \'=,=\ *adj* **1 :** resembling a gem **2 :** PERFECT, EXQUISITE ⟨~ beauty⟩ ⟨~ stories⟩

gem·ma \'jemə\ *n* [L, bud, gem — more at GEM] **1** *pl* **gem·mae** \-(,)mē\ **:** BUD; *broadly* **:** an asexual reproductive body that becomes detached from a parent plant and is unicellular in algae and fungi and some hepatics but multicellular in many mosses, hepatics, and some ferns — compare CHLAMYDOSPORE, GEMMATION **2** [NL, fr. L] *cap* **:** a monotypic genus of small round clams (family Veneridae) having a shining white, yellow, or pink shell marked with amethyst and being widely distributed on both coasts of No. America

gem·ma·ceous \(')je'māshəs\ *adj* **:** of or relating to gemmae

gemma cup *n* **:** the cupule of a liverwort

gem·ma·ry \'jemərē\ *n* -ES [¹*gem* + *-ary*] **:** the science of gems

¹gem·mate \'je,māt\ *adj* [L *gemmatus,* past part.] **1 :** having gemmae **2 :** reproducing by a bud

²gemmate \"\ *vi* -ED/-ING/-S [L *gemmatus,* fr. *gemmatus* past part. of *gemmare* to put forth buds, fr. *gemma* bud — more at GEM] *of coral* **:** to produce or propagate by a bud

gem·ma·tion \je'māshən\ *n* -s [L *gemmatus* + E *-ion*] **:** asexual reproduction in which a new organism originates as a localized area of growth on the surface or within the body of the parent subsequently differentiating into a new individual

gem·ma·tive \'je,mād·iv, -,məd-·\ *adj* [*gemmation* + *-ive*] **:** of or relating to gemmation

gemmed *past of* GEM

gemmel *var of* GEMEL

gem·mer \'jemə(r)\ *n* -s [¹*gem* + *-er*] **:** one that seeks or mines for gems

gem·mif·er·ous \(')je'mif(ə)rəs\ *adj* [L *gemma* + E *-i-* + *-ferous*] **1 :** producing or containing gems **2** [NL *gemma* + E *-i-* + *-ferous*] **:** bearing or reproducing by a gemma

gem·mi·fi·ca·tion \,jeməfə'kāshən\ *n* -s [NL *gemma* + E *-i-* + *-fication*] **:** production of a gemma

gem·mi·form \'jemə,fȯrm\ *adj* [ISV *gemma* + *-i-* + *-form*] **:** resembling a gemma

gem·mi·ly \'jemə̇lē\ *adv* **:** in such a manner as to resemble or suggest a gem

gemming *pres part of* GEM

gem·mip·a·ra \je'mipərə\ *or* **gem·mip·a·res** \-,rēz\ *n pl* [NL, fr. L *gemma* bud + NL *-para* or *-pares* (fr. L *parere* to bear) — more at PARE] **:** animals that reproduce by budding

gem·mip·a·rous \(')je'mipərəs\ *adj* [NL *gemmiparus,* fr. L *gemma* bud + *-parus* -parous] **:** producing, bearing, or reproducing by a bud — **gem·mip·a·rous·ly** *adv*

gem·moid \'je,mȯid\ *adj* [NL *gemma* + E *-oid*] **:** resembling a gemma

gem·mo·log·i·cal *or* **gem·o·log·i·cal** \,jemə'läjəkəl\ *adj* **:** of or relating to a gem or gemmology

gem·mol·o·gist *or* **gem·ol·o·gist** \je'mäləjə̇st\ *n* -s **:** a specialist in gems; *specif* **:** one who appraises gems

gem·mol·o·gy *or* **gem·ol·o·gy** \je'mäləjē\ *n* -ES [*gemmology* fr. L *gemma* bud, gem + E *-o-* + *-logy; gemology* alter. (influenced by ¹*gem*) of *gemmology*] **:** the science of gems

gem·mu·la \'jemyələ\ *n, pl* **gemmu·lae** \-,lē\ [NL, fr. L, little bud] **:** GEMMULE

gem·mu·la·tion \,jemyə'lāshən\ *n* -s [ISV *gemmule* + *-ation*] **:** GEMMATION

gem·mule \'je(,)myül\ *n* -s [F, fr. L *gemmula* little bud, dim. of *gemma* bud, gem — more at GEM] **1 :** a small plant bud **2 :** any of various minute self-multiplying particles considered in the theory of pangenesis to be transmitted from somatic to germ cells and to mediate the production in a new individual of cells like those in which they originated — compare BIOPHORE **3 :** a bud produced in gemmation; *esp* **:** an internal resistant asexual reproductive body of sponges (as of the genus *Spongilla*)

gem·mu·lif·er·ous \,jemyə'lif(ə)rəs\ *adj* [*gemmule* + *-i-* + *-ferous*] **:** bearing or producing a gemmule

gem·my \'jemē\ *adj* -ER/-EST [¹*gem* + *-y*] **1 :** having the characteristics (as hardness, brilliance, color) desired in a gemstone ⟨~ rock crystal⟩ **2 :** GLITTERING, BRIGHT ⟨a ~ spring day⟩

ge·mot *or* **ge·mote** \gə'mōt\ *n* -s [OE *gemōt,* fr. *ge-* (perfective and collective prefix) + *mōt* assembly, council — more at YCLEPT, MOOT] **:** a judicial or legislative assembly in England before the Norman conquest — compare FOLKMOOT, MOOT; see WITENAGEMOT

gem peg *var of* GIM PEG

gem·pyl·i·dae \jem'pilə,dē\ *n pl, cap* [NL, fr. *Gempylus,* type genus (fr. Gk *gempylos* young tunny) + *-idae*] **:** a family of elongated oily-fleshed percomorph fishes of open seas that resemble mackerels and comprise the escolars

¹gems *pl of* GEM, *pres 3d sing of* GEM

²gems \'gem(p)s\ *or* **gem·se** \-mzə\ *n, pl* **gems·es** \-m(p)səz, -mzəz\ [G, fr. OHG *gamiza,* fr. LL *camoc-, camox*] **:** CHAMOIS

gems·bok \'gemz,bäk\ *n, pl* **gemsbok** *also* **gemsboks** [Afrik, lit., male chamois, fr. G *gemsbock,* fr. *gems, gemse* chamois + *bock* male goat or antelope, fr. OHG *boc* male goat — more at BUCK] **:** a large strikingly marked oryx (*Oryx gazella*) formerly abundant in parts of southern Africa; *also* **:** any of several related oryxes

gems·buck \-,bək\ *n, pl* **gemsbuck** *also* **gemsbucks** [part trans. of Afrik *gemsbok*] **:** GEMSBOK

gem shell *n* **:** a clam of the genus *Gemma*

gems·horn \'gem(p)s, 'gemz +\ *n* [G, fr. *gems, gemse* chamois + *horn,* fr. OHG — more at HORN] **:** a labial pipe organ stop intermediate in quality between a string tone and a reed tone

gem stick *n* **:** a stick on which gems are cemented preparatory to cutting

gemstone \'=,=\ *n* [¹*gem* + *stone*] **:** a mineral or petrified material that when cut and polished can be used in jewelry

gemul *var of* GUEMAL

gen \'jen\ *n* -s [short for *general*] *slang Brit* **:** general information

¹gen- *or* **geno-** *comb form* [Gk *genos* race, descent, kin, sex, kind, fr. the stem of *gignesthai* to be born — more at KIN] **1 :** generating **:** offspring ⟨*geno*blast⟩ **2 :** race ⟨*geno*cide⟩ **3 :** sex ⟨*geno*phobia⟩ **4** [influenced in meaning by NL *genus*] **:** genus **:** kind ⟨*geno*type⟩ **5** [*generate*] **:** a substance that produces or generates — specif. in names of oxides of alkaloids in which the oxygen is attached to nitrogen ⟨*gen*alkaloids⟩ ⟨*geno*morphine⟩

²gen- *or* **geno-** *comb form* [²*gene*] **:** gene ⟨*gen*oid⟩ ⟨*geno*cline⟩

-gen \jən, ,jen\ *also* **-gene** \,jēn\ *n comb form* -s [F *-gène,* fr. Gk *-genēs* born, fr. root of *gignesthai* to be born — more at KIN] **1 :** one that generates ⟨halo*gen*⟩ ⟨melano*gen*⟩ ⟨andro*gen*⟩ **2 :** one that is produced or generated ⟨exo*gen*⟩ ⟨culti*gen*⟩ ⟨phos*gene*⟩

gen *abbr* **1** gender **2** general **3** generation **4** generator **5** generic **6** genetics **7** genitive **8** genus

ge·na \'jēnə, 'genə\ *n, pl* **ge·nae** \'jē,nē, 'ge,nī\ [L, cheek — more at CHIN] **:** the cheek or lateral part of the head: as **a :** the feathered side of the under mandible of a bird **b :** the lateral part of the cephalic shield of a trilobite **c :** the lateral part of the head capsule of an insect bounded above by the margin of the eye

¹ge·nal \'jēnᵊl, 'gen-\ *adj* [*gena* + *-al*] **:** of, relating to, or constituting the cheek or broadly the lateral part of the head ⟨the ~ combs of a flea⟩

²gen·al \'jēnᵊl\ *adj* [¹*gene* + *-al*] **:** of, relating to, or caused by a gene

¹ge·nappe \jə'nap, zhə-\ *n* -s [fr. *Genappe,* Belgium] **:** a smooth worsted yarn that has been genapped

²genappe \"\ *vt* -ED/-ING/-S **:** to subject (worsted yarns) to singeing

gen·darme \'zhän,därm, -däm *also* 'jän- *or* 'jen-\ *n* -s [F, fr. MF, back-formation fr. *gensdarmes,* pl. of *gent d'armes,* lit., armed people] **1 :** a cavalryman in the old French army **2 a** (1) **:** a rural policeman esp. in France (2) **:** a continental European policeman or a policeman elsewhere resembling a continental European policeman; *esp* **:** a French policeman **b** *slang* **:** POLICEMAN **3 :** a pinnacle of rock on a ridge **4 :** a flaw in a diamond or other precious stone **5** *or* **gendarme blue :** a moderate bluish green to greenish blue that is deeper than cyan blue and duller than parrot blue

gen·dar·mer·ie *or* **gen·dar·mery** \-'=ərē, -əri, '=,===\ *n, pl* **gendarmeries** [MF *gendarmerie,* fr. *gendarme* + *-erie* -ery] **:** a body of gendarmes

¹gen·der \'jendə(r)\ *n* -s [ME *gendre,* fr. MF *gendre, genre,* fr. L *gener-, genus* birth, race, kind, class — more at KIN] **1 a** *archaic* **:** KIND, SORT **b :** SEX ⟨black divinities of the feminine ~ —Charles Dickens⟩ **2** *linguistics* **a :** any of two or more subclasses within a grammatical class of a language (such as noun, pronoun, adjective, verb) that are partly arbitrary but also partly based on distinguishable characteristics such as shape, social rank, manner of existence (as animate or inanimate), or sex (as masculine, feminine, or neuter) and that determine agreement with and selection of other words or grammatical forms ⟨Latin has three ~*s*, masculine, feminine, and neuter⟩ ⟨French has two ~*s*, masculine and feminine⟩ **b :** membership of a word or a grammatical form in such a subclass ⟨a Latin noun has ~, number, and case⟩ ⟨an English noun has, strictly speaking, no ~⟩ **c :** an inflectional form showing membership in such a subclass ⟨a Latin adjective agrees in ~ with the noun it modifies⟩

²gender \"\ *vb* **gendered; gendered; gendering** \-d(ə)riŋ\ **genders** [ME *gendren, genderen,* fr. MF *gendrer,* fr. L *generare,* fr. *gener-, genus*] *vt* **:** BREED ~ *vi* **:** COPULATE

³gen·der \'gen,de(ə)r, '=,=, gən'd-\ *n* -s [Jav *gendèr*] **:** a Javanese percussion instrument like a xylophone

¹gene \'zhen, 'zhān, *F* zheen\ *n* -s [F *gêne,* fr. OF *gehine* torture (to make one confess), fr. *gehir, jehir* to confess, of Gmc origin; akin to OHG *jehan* to speak, say — more at JOKE] **:** EMBARRASSMENT, UNEASINESS ⟨a certain amount of ~ with relatives —Evelyn Waugh⟩

²gene \'jēn\ *n* -s [G *gen,* short for *pangen*] **:** one of the elements of the germ plasm serving as specific transmitters of hereditary characters and usu. regarded as portions of deoxyribonucleic acids linearly arranged in fixed positions and as functioning through control of the synthesis of specific polypeptide chains

-gene — see -GEN

ge·ne·a·log·i·cal \,jēnēə'läjəkəl, -ājēk- *also* ,jen-\ *also* **gene·a·log·ic** \-ājik,-äjek\ *adj* [MF *genealogique,* fr. *genealogie* + *-ique* -ical, -ic] **:** of or relating to genealogy — **gene·a·log·i·cal·ly** \-jək(ə)lē, -jēk-, -li\ *adv*

ge·ne·al·o·gist \÷,==\ǀäləjə̇st, ǀal- *sometimes* jēn'y\ *or* jen'y\ *n* -s **1 :** a specialist or expert in genealogy **2 :** a person who traces, makes studies of, or records genealogies

ge·ne·al·o·gize \-,jīz\ *vb* -ED/-ING/-S *vi* **:** to investigate or relate the history of descents ⟨the grotesque *genealogizing* that decaying aristocracies affect —H.L.Mencken⟩ ~ *vt* **:** to trace or chart the genealogy of

ge·ne·al·o·giz·er \-zə(r)\ *n* -s **:** one that genealogizes

ge·ne·al·o·gy \-jē, -ji\ *n* -ES [ME *genealogie,* fr. MF, fr. LL *genealogia,* fr. Gk, fr. *genea* race, family + *-logia* -logy — more at KIN] **1 :** an account or history of the descent of a person, family, or group from an ancestor or ancestors or from older forms **:** an enumeration of ancestors and their descendants in the natural order of succession **2 :** regular descent of a person, family, or group of organisms from a progenitor or older form **:** PEDIGREE, LINEAGE **3 :** a study of family pedigrees and the methods of investigation of them **4 :** an account of the descent of property with respect to its previous owners

gen·ecologic *or* **gen·ecological** \(,)jēn, (,)jen+\ *adj* **:** of or relating to genecology—**gen·ecologically** *adv*

gen·ecologist \,jēn, ,jen +\ *n* **:** a specialist in genecology

gen·ecology \,jēn, 'jen+\ *n* -ES [Gk *genos* race (fr. *gignesthai* to be born) + E *ecology* — more at KIN] **:** a branch of ecology concerned primarily with the species and its genetically variant subdivisions, with their position in nature and, with the controlling genetic and ecological factors

gene complex *n* [²*gene*] **:** all the genes of an individual or of a potentially interbreeding population that constitute an interacting functional unit

gene flow *n* **:** the passage and establishment of genes typical of one breeding population into the gene complex of another through hybridization and backcrossing

gene frequency *n* **:** the percentage of occurrence of a specified gene in the chromosomes of a population

gen·emo·tor \'jenə+,-\ *n* -s [*generator* + *motor*] **:** DYNAMOTOR

gene mutation *n* **:** mutation due to fundamental intramolecular reorganization of a gene

ge·ner \'ge,ne(ə)r\ *n* -s [L; akin to Gk *gambros* son-in-law, Skt *jāmātā,* Lith *žentas,* & prob. to L *gignere* to beget — more at KIN] *Roman & civil law* **:** SON-IN-LAW

genera *pl of* GENUS

gen·er·a·ble \'jen(ə)rəbəl\ *adj* [ME, fr. L *generabilis,* fr. *generare* to beget, create + *-abilis* -able — more at GENERATE] **:** capable of being created or produced (as by human intellect or imagination)

¹gen·er·al \'jen(ə)rəl\ *adj* [ME, fr. MF, fr. L *generalis,* fr. *gener-, genus* birth, race, class, kind + *-alis* -al — more at KIN] **1 :** involving or belonging to the whole of a body, group, class, or type **:** applicable or relevant to the whole rather than to a limited part, group, or section ⟨appearance of ~ decay⟩ ⟨a ~ change in temperature⟩ **2 :** involving or belonging to every member of a class, kind, or group **:** applicable to every one in the unit referred to **:** not exclusive or excluding ⟨ladies, a ~ welcome from his grace salutes ye all —Shak.⟩ ⟨those first assemblies were ~, with all freemen bound to attend —*Amer. Guide Series: Md.*⟩ **3 a :** applicable or pertinent to the majority of individuals involved **:** characteristic of the majority **:** PREVALENT, USUAL, WIDESPREAD ⟨the ~ opinion⟩ ⟨a custom ~ in these areas⟩ ⟨the conflict became ~⟩ ⟨we, the people of the United States, in order to . . . promote the ~ welfare —*U.S.Constitution*⟩ **b :** concerned or dealing with universal rather than particular aspects ⟨~ history⟩ **4 :** marked by broad overall character without being limited, modified, or checked by narrow precise considerations **:** concerned with main elements, major matters rather than limited details, or universals rather than particulars **:** approximate rather than strictly accurate ⟨a ~ outline⟩ ⟨bearing a ~ resemblance to the original⟩ ⟨the rock formations of the state have a ~ northeast-southwest trend —*Amer. Guide Series: N.H.*⟩ **5 :** not confined by specialization or careful limitation **:** not limited to a particular class, type, or field **:** inclusive and manifesting or characterized by scope, diversity, or variety **:** BROAD, CATHOLIC, COMPREHENSIVE ⟨a ~ drugstore⟩ ⟨a ~ surgeon⟩ **6 :** belonging to the common nature (as of a group of like individuals) **:** GENERIC ⟨the ~ characteristics of a species⟩ ⟨long shaggy hair is ~ among bears⟩ **7 :** holding superior rank **:** taking precedence (as over others similarly titled) ⟨~ manager⟩ **:** having wide authority or responsibility ⟨a ~ captain⟩ ⟨the ~ board⟩ — sometimes used postpositively ⟨the master ~⟩ **8 :** designed for students without special ability or vocational plans ⟨a ~ course in science⟩ — compare COLLEGE-PREPARATORY, COMMERCIAL **9 :** of or relating to a universal term or proposition or a quantified statement in logic — opposed to *singular* **10 :** involving or affecting practically the entire organism **:** not local ⟨~ nervousness⟩ **syn** see UNIVERSAL

²general \"\ *n* -s **1** *archaic* **:** WHOLE, TOTAL **2 a :** something (as a concept, fact, idea, principle, proposition, or statement) that comprehends the whole or total ⟨a description that spends too much time on the ~ and too little on the particular⟩; *specif* **:** GENERALITY **b :** GENUS, UNIVERSAL **3 a** *archaic* **:** the general public **:** PEOPLE **b** *Brit* **:** a servant for general work **4** [ML *generalis,* fr. L *generalis,* adj. (in such phrases as *abbas generalis,* lit., general abbot)] **:** the chief of a religious order of all houses or congregations under one religious rule; *specif* **:** SUPERIOR GENERAL **5** [MF, fr. OIt *generale* (also, chief of a religious order), fr. ML *generalis*] *archaic* **:** the commander in chief of an army **6 a :** a military officer of high rank — see BRIGADIER GENERAL, GENERAL OF THE AIR FORCE, GENERAL OF THE ARMY, LIEUTENANT GENERAL, MAJOR GENERAL **b :** a military officer who is junior only to a general of the army, to a general of the air force, or to a field marshal, wears 4 stars, and ranks with a four-star admiral of the navy **7 :** the supreme commander of the Salvation Army — compare SALVATIONIST — **in general** *adv* **1** *obs* **a :** without exception **:** INCLUSIVELY **b :** in all things **:** in all respects **2 :** for the most part **:** GENERALLY

general ability *n* **:** ABILITY 2

general acceptance *n* **:** an unqualified acceptance bill

general act *n* **:** GENERAL LAW

general administrator *n* **:** a legal administrator appointed at the domicile of a deceased person to settle and distribute the entire estate of the decedent or in case a will is annexed to his appointment to execute the will in accordance with law — compare PUBLIC ADMINISTRATOR

general agent *n* **1 :** one employed to transact generally all legal business of his principal entrusted to him or to do all acts connected with a particular trade, business, or employment esp. at a particular place **:** one whose authority is to conduct a series of transactions in the continuous service of his principal **2 :** a representative of an insurance company or often of several companies (as in fire insurance) who appoints and supervises selling agents and administers the company's business within a specified territory

general american *n, sometimes cap G & cap A* **:** the native speech of natives of the U. S. whose speech is not that of the South or of the *r*-dropping Northeast; *specif* **:** such speech excluding that of the Middle Atlantic states and western Pennsylvania

general anesthesia *n* **:** anesthesia affecting the entire body and accompanied by loss of consciousness

general appearance *n* **:** an appearance made in general terms giving a court full and absolute jurisdiction in the matter in issue (as by asking for any relief other than a ruling that the court has no jurisdiction over the person of the party)

general assembly *n* **1 :** the highest ecclesiastical judiciary or governing board of certain national churches (as of the Presbyterian Church) **2 :** a legislative body; *specif* **:** the legislature of some states of the U.S. (as So. Carolina) **3 :** a supreme deliberative body (as of the United Nations)

general assignment *n* **:** an assignment of all one's property not exempt by law for the benefit of all one's creditors with only such preferences as may be allowed

general assumpsit *n* **:** COMMON ASSUMPSIT

general atonement *n* **:** a theological doctrine that the reconciliation effected between God and man by the sufferings of Jesus Christ was efficacious for all men — compare LIMITED ATONEMENT

general average *n* **:** a loss that arises from the voluntary sacrifice of part of a ship or cargo to save the residue of the ship or cargo or from extraordinary expenses incurred in protecting the interests involved under pressure of a common risk and that is shared proportionally by all parties concerned — compare PARTICULAR AVERAGE

general baptist *n, usu cap G&B* **:** a member of a British Baptist body of the 17th to 19th centuries that held Arminian doctrines or a member of a similar Baptist sect in the U. S. — called also *Arminian Baptist;* compare PARTICULAR BAPTIST

general bass *n* **:** CONTINUO

general canon *n* **:** a canon enacted at a general convention of the Protestant Episcopal Church and effective within all dioceses

general cargo *n* **:** a mixed cargo (as carried by ships that take merchandise for all persons indifferently)

general certificate of education : a certificate awarded on the successful completion of an examination taken by British secondary-school students

general conference *n, usu cap G&C* **:** the highest legislative and judicial body in various religious denominations ⟨the *General Conference* of the Methodist Church⟩

general confession *n* **1 :** confession of sins made by a number of persons in common (as in public prayer) **2 :** a confession in which the penitent gives a summary of his sins

general convention *n* **:** a legislative body of a church (as of the Protestant Episcopal Church)

general counsel *n* **:** a lawyer at the head of the legal department (as of a corporation or governmental subdivision)

general course *n* **:** the pass course at British universities

general court *n, usu cap G&C* **:** the legislature of the states of Massachusetts and New Hampshire

general court-martial *n* **:** a court-martial consisting of at least five officers one of whom is a law member and having authority to impose a sentence of dishonorable discharge or death — compare SPECIAL COURT-MARTIAL, SUMMARY COURT-MARTIAL

general cover *n* **:** insurance covering fluctuating quantities of

goods at locations specified and subject to limitations as imposed by contract
general creditor *n* : a creditor not secured by a lien or other security : a creditor not having a preference
general custom *n* : a custom or usage throughout the jurisdiction that is general, uniform, and certain and of such long standing that the courts will take judicial notice of its existence as part of the common law of the jurisdiction — compare PARTICULAR CUSTOM
gen·er·al·cy \'jen(ə)rəlsē, -si\ *n* -ES : the office or term of a general
general damages *n pl* : damages awarded for injury (as from defamation) in the absence of any specific pecuniary loss
general degree *n* : PASS DEGREE
general delivery *n* : a mail-delivery service or a department of a post office that handles the delivery of mail at a post office window to persons who do not have any permanent street address or for other reasons call for it or to persons who call for their mail without waiting for or in the absence of carrier service — often used as an address
general deposit *n* : a deposit of money under common law made by a depositor in a banking institution that creates a debt of the bank to the depositor to be paid by an equivalent sum but not by return of the identical money and that resembles the irregular deposit of the civil law
general deputy *n* : a deputy authorized to exercise the whole of the powers of another official
general discharge *n* : a formal release from military service given under honorable conditions and for satisfactory service to a member of the armed forces not qualifying for an honorable discharge — compare DISCHARGE
general editor *n* : one who supervises other editors or publications issued in a series — compare EDITOR IN CHIEF, MANAGING EDITOR
general education *n* : a program of education (as in some liberal-arts colleges and secondary schools) intended to develop students as personalities rather than trained specialists and to transmit a common cultural heritage — compare LIBERAL EDUCATION
general election *n* : an election usu. held at regular intervals prescribed by law or custom in which candidates are chosen in all or most constituencies of a nation or state ⟨the promptness with which Parliament meets . . . after a *general election* —F.A.Ogg & Harold Zink⟩ ⟨as well qualified to vote at a primary as at a *general election* —E.C.Meyer⟩ — compare BY-ELECTION, PRIMARY 6b
general endorsement *n* : an endorsement (as on a check) that does not specify a payee
general equilibrium *n* : simultaneous equilibrium for all economic variables
general expense *or* **general charge** *n* : an overhead expense not directly identifiable with a particular activity or department; *specif* : a charge in railroads incurred for the benefit of the road as a whole
general failure of issue : INDEFINITE FAILURE OF ISSUE
general farmer *n* : a farmer producing several commodities none of which represents as much as 40 percent of the total value of the products of the farm
general formula *n* : a chemical formula applicable to a series of compounds (as MNO_2 for metallic nitrites, ROH for alcohols, C_nH_{2n+2} for alkanes where *n* is an integer)
general grammar *n* : the study of general principles believed to underlie the grammatical phenomena of all languages — called also *philosophical grammar, universal grammar*
general headquarters *n* : the headquarters of an officer in command of all armed forces of a unit
general hospital *n* **1** : a hospital in which patients with many different types of ailments are given care **2** : a military hospital usu. located in a communications zone that gives treatment to all kinds of cases
gen·er·a·lia \,jenə'rālēə, -lyə\ *n pl* [L, pl. of *generale* generality, fr. neut. of *generalis*] : general principles : GENERALITIES
general-in-chief \¦=(=)==¦=\ *n, pl* **generals-in-chief** : a military officer in chief command (as of the entire armed forces operating at a front or in some services of an army division)
general integral *n* : GENERAL SOLUTION
gen·er·a·lis·si·mo \,jen(ə)rə'lisə,mō, *rapid* -nər'l-\ *n* -S [It, fr. *generale* general + *-issimo* superlative suffix (fr. L *-issimus*] **1** : the chief commander of an army : COMMANDER IN CHIEF **2** : one of the officers of a commandery of Knights Templar
general issue *n* : a legal plea that traverses and denies an indictment, declaration, petition, or complaint in its entirety without admitting the truth of any allegations and without offering special matters to avoid the legal effect of the allegations set forth — compare SPECIAL ISSUE
gen·er·al·ist \'jen(ə)rələst, *rapid* -nərl-\ *n* -S [¹*general* + *-ist*] : one who devotes himself to, is conversant with, or can handle several different skills, fields, or aptitudes — opposed to *specialist*
gen·er·al·i·ty \,jenə'ralədē, -lətē, -i\ *n* -ES [ME *generalite*, fr. MF *generauté, generalité*, fr. LL *generalitat-, generalitas*, fr. *generalis* general + *-itat-, -itas* -ity — more at GENERAL] **1** : the quality or state of being general : total applicability **2 a** : a general statement, law, principle, or proposition **b** : a vague, insufficient, or inadequate statement **3** : the main body : the greatest part : BULK ⟨the complaint of the ~ of the nation's taxpayers —Raymond Moley⟩ **4** : a fiscal and civil administrative district of France under the kingdom — **for the generality** *or* **in the generality** *adv, obs* : in general
gen·er·al·iz·able \'jen(ə)rə,līzəbəl, *rapid* 'jenər,l-; ¦=(=)=¦===\ *adj* : that may be generalized
gen·er·al·iza·tion \,jen(ə)rələ'zāshən, -,lī'z-, *rapid* ,jenər(,)l-\ *n* -S **1** : the act or action of generalizing **2** : the result of the process of generalizing: as **a** : a general concept, idea, or notion **b** : a general inference or proposition : a quantified statement **3** : the act or process whereby response is made to a stimulus similar to but not identical with a reference stimulus
gen·er·al·ize \'jen(ə)rə,līz, *rapid* -nər,l-\ *vb* -ED/-ING/-S *see -ize in Explan Notes* [F *généraliser*, fr. *général* general + *-iser* -ize] *vt* **1** : to make general : reduce to general laws : give a general form to **2 a** : to derive or induce (a general conception or principle) from particulars **b** : to derive or induce a general conception, principle, or inference from **3** : to make general (as by existential or universal qualification) : render applicable to a wider class **4** : to give general applicability to ⟨~ a law⟩; *also* : to make indefinite (as by blurring particular features) **5 a** : to modify or eliminate (nonessential details on a map) for improving the legibility or for emphasizing some particular feature (as the location of mountains or the essential character of a coastline) **b** : to portray or emphasize in painting general rather than particular features and characteristics of ~ *vi* **1** : to form generalizations : make inductions or general inferences; *also* : to be prone to make vague or indefinite statements **2** : to become extended throughout the human body **3** : to generalize the details on a map
generalized *adj* : made general : extended into a generalization; *esp* : not highly differentiated biologically nor strictly adapted to a particular environment ⟨the modern hedgehog, a persistently primitive and ~ mammal —C.O.Dunbar⟩
generalized coordinate *n* : ³COORDINATE 2b
generalized edema *n* : ANASARCA
gen·er·al·iz·er \-zə(r)\ *n* -S : one that generalizes
general journal *n* : JOURNAL 1 b(2)
general law *n* : a law unrestricted as to time and applicable throughout the entire territory subject to the power of the legislature that enacted it and applying to all persons in the same class in the same situation — called also *general act, general statute*; distinguished from *local law* and *special law*; compare PUBLIC LAW
general ledger *n* : the principal and controlling ledger of a business enterprise containing individual or controlling accounts for all assets, liabilities, net worth items, revenue, and expenses
general legacy *n* : a testamentary gift of tangible or intangible personal property not amounting to a bequest of specific money or of a particular thing and not identified by a description that sets it apart from all other assets of the same kind in the testator's estate — compare SPECIFIC LEGACY
general license *n* : a license permitting exportations within certain limitations without a specific license document
general lien *n* : a lien for the satisfaction of a balance due from an owner of personal property not confined to the amount due in respect of the property itself — compare PARTICULAR LIEN
general linguistics *n* : a study of the phenomena, historical changes, and functions of language without restriction to a particular language or to a particular aspect (as phonetics, grammar, stylistics) of language
general listing *n* : MULTIPLE LISTING
gen·er·al·ly \'jen(ə)rəlē, -nərlē, -li, *-R rapid* -nᵊl-\ *adv* [ME, fr. ¹*general* + *-ly*] : in a general manner: as **a** *obs* : as a whole : COLLECTIVELY **b** *obs* : with respect to all : UNIVERSALLY **c** : in a reasonably inclusive manner : in disregard of specific instances and with regard to an overall picture ⟨~ speaking⟩ ⟨inflation ~ assumed to have been caused by war⟩ **d** : on the whole : as a rule ⟨elections are held ~ every other year⟩
general mortgage *n* : BLANKET MORTGAGE
gen·er·al·ness *n* -ES : the quality or state of being general
general officer *n* : ²GENERAL 6 a — compare FLAG OFFICER
general of the air force : an air force officer of the highest rank whose insignia is five stars
general of the armies : the highest U. S. Army rank of World War I (as conferred upon General John J. Pershing upon his retirement)
general of the army : an army officer of the highest rank whose insignia is five stars
general order *n* **1** : any one of the orders issued by an authorized military headquarters that include important permanent directive matter of general interest — usu. used in pl.; compare SPECIAL ORDER **2** : any one of the permanent guard orders that govern the duties of all sentries — usu. used in pl.
general paresis *also* **general paralysis** *n* : syphilis of the cerebral cortex and overlying membranes usu. of insidious onset with personality changes and protean manifestations that change from month to month progressing to dementia and paralysis
general partner *n* : a partner whose liability for partnership debts and obligations is unlimited — distinguished from *special partner*
general partnership *n* : a common-law partnership in which each partner has a general liability for all partnership debts and obligations in full — compare LIMITED PARTNERSHIP
general pause *n* : a nonrhythmic rest in all parts in ensemble music — abbr *G. P.*; called also *cutoff*
general physiology *n* : a branch of physiology concerned with the basic functional activities of living matter : protoplasmic physiology
general post *n* **1** : blindman's buff in which players are designated by place names and are called upon to change seats two at a time until the call "general post" when all exchange **2** *chiefly Brit* : a general exchange of positions or locations
general post office *n, usu cap G&P&O* : a main post office in a capital or a large city (as London); *also* : a postal system
general power of appointment : a power to appoint property that can be exercised entirely in favor of the donee, his nominee, or his estate — compare SPECIAL POWER
general practitioner *n* : a physician or veterinarian who does not limit his practice to a specialty
general prisoner *n* : a military prisoner who has been sentenced to confinement and to dismissal or discharge — compare GARRISON PRISONER
general property *n* : the absolute ownership usu. of personal property with the right of complete dominion over it including the incidental rights of possession, of use and enjoyment, and of disposition or alienation — distinguished from *special property*
general property tax *n* : a tax levied on the assessed value of all nonexempt property
general proposition *n* : a universal proposition; *also* : a law or principle
general-purpose \¦=(=)=¦==\ *adj* : utilized or designed to be used for two or more basic purposes, products, or functions
general-purpose bomb *n* : a bomb designed to be effective against both troops and materiel
general-purpose flour *n* : ALL-PURPOSE FLOUR
general quarters *n pl* : a condition of maximum readiness of a warship for action with all hands at battle stations
general retainer *n* : a retainer of an attorney by a client to advise and represent the client for compensation and for a fixed time in all legal matters in which he may seek legal assistance; *also* : the retaining fee itself
general revelation *n* : revelation available to all men — compare SPECIAL REVELATION
general rule *n* : a standing order governing practice and general procedure in a court — compare SPECIAL RULE
generals *pl of* GENERAL
general science *n* : a subject or course of study in school or college in which the elements of several sciences are studied
general semantics *n pl but usu sing in constr* : a doctrine and educational discipline due to Alfred Korzybski (1879–1950) intended to improve habits of response of human beings to their environment and one another esp. by training in the better and more critical uses of words and other symbols
general service car *n* : a railroad car suitable for carrying a variety of classes of freight; *esp* : a gondola car having practically the entire bottom composed of drop doors hinged at the center to dump outside of the rails
general service school *n* : a unit in the system of military education at which officers and enlisted men of all arms and services are given advanced training — compare SPECIAL SERVICE SCHOOL
general sessions *n pl* : a court of criminal jurisdiction
gen·er·al·ship \'=(=)=,ship\ *n* -S **1** : office or tenure of office of a general : exercise of the functions of a general **2** : military skill in a general officer or high commander **3** : LEADERSHIP, MANAGEMENT
general ship *n* : a ship not chartered or let to particular parties but advertised for the general receipt of goods from the public indiscriminately to be carried on a voyage
general six-principle baptist *n, usu cap G&S&P&B* : a member of an Arminian Baptist sect founded in Providence, R. I., in 1653 on the six principles of repentance, faith, baptism, laying on of hands, resurrection of the dead, and eternal judgment
general solution *n* **1** : a solution of an ordinary differential equation of order *n* that involves exactly *n* essential arbitrary constants — called also *complete solution, general integral* **2** : a solution of a partial differential equation that involves arbitrary functions — called also *general integral*
general staff *n* : a group of officers in an army division or similar or larger unit who assist their commander in planning, coordinating, and supervising operations; *also* : a similar group assisting a chief of staff — compare SPECIAL STAFF
general statement *n* : a statement in logic that contains one or more bound variables — contrasted with *singular statement*
general statute *n* : GENERAL LAW
general store *n* : a retail store located usu. in a small or rural community which carries a wide variety of consumer convenience goods including groceries but is not departmentized
general strike *n* : a simultaneous striking by all unionized workers of all trades and industries
general synod *n, often cap G&S* : the highest governing body of a church ⟨the *General Synod* of the United Church of Christ⟩
general tail *n* : a fee-tail estate not restricted to particular descendants of the first owner thereof but designed to pass to all of said owner's descendants so long as such issue is alive
gen·er·al·ty \'jen(ə)rəltē\ *n* -ES [ME *generalte*, fr. MF *generauté, generalité* — more at GENERALITY] *archaic* : GENERALITY
general will *n* : the will of a community which is the embodiment or expression of its common interest; *specif* : the social or collective will of a community resulting from the interrelations (as the exchange of opinion) between its members
¹gen·er·ate \'jenə,rāt, *usu* -ād·+V\ *vb* -ED/-ING/-S [L *generatus*, past part. of *generare* to beget, create, fr. *gener-, genus* birth, race, class, kind — more at KIN] *vt* **1** : to cause to be : bring into existence; *esp* : PROCREATE ⟨~ innumerable offspring⟩ **2** : to originate (something material) by a physical or chemical process : PRODUCE ⟨would ~ a tremendous amount of electricity —*Collier's Yr. Bk.*⟩ ⟨mountain ranges . . . should ~ more heat than low-lying plains —A.E.Benfield⟩ **3** : to define (as a mathematical or linguistic set or structure) by the application of one or more rules or operations to given quantities ⟨a mathematical group consisting of the powers of one element A is said to be *generated* by A⟩ ⟨a set of phrase structure rewriting rules that ~ underlying sentence structures —P.S.Rosenbaum⟩; *esp* : to trace out (as a curve) by a moving point or (as a surface) by a moving curve — see CYCLOID illustration **4** : to form (gear teeth or screw threads) with theoretical accuracy **5** : to be the cause of (a state of mind, an action, or something immaterial or intangible) ⟨forces *generating* interracial conflict⟩ ⟨these stories . . . ~ a good deal of psychological suspense —*Atlantic*⟩ ⟨~s mistaken opinions, wrong attitudes —H.A.Overstreet⟩ ~ *vi* **1** : to produce offspring : PROPAGATE **2** : to come into existence : ORIGINATE, ARISE
²gen·er·ate \'jen(ə)rət\ *adj* [L *generatus*] : GENERATED
generating station *n* : a plant for generating electric power
gen·er·a·tion \,jenə'rāshən\ *n* -S [ME *generacioun*, fr. MF *generation*, fr. L *generation-, generatio*, fr. *generatus* + *-ion-, -io* -ion] **1 a** : a body of men, animals, or plants having a common parent or parents and constituting a single degree or step in the line of descent from an ancestor ⟨five ~s are shown in this family portrait⟩ ⟨its surface enriched with the . . . carcasses of hundreds of ~s of buffalo —B.K.Sandwell⟩ ⟨studied a bacterial culture through 60 ~s⟩ **b** (1) : the whole number of human beings born and living contemporaneously ⟨our ~ has seen immense changes⟩ ⟨his work affected the life and thought of later ~s⟩ (2) : a particular category of individuals born and living contemporaneously ⟨inspired . . . a whole ~ of theoreticians —*Newsweek*⟩ ⟨long after that ~ of scholars had passed away —G.B.Shaw⟩ ⟨uses the vocabulary of his philosophic ~ —John Dewey⟩ ⟨the present ~ of insects appears to have developed immunity to the spray⟩ (3) : the average span of time variously computed and varying according to cultural and other conditions between the birth of parents and that of their children ⟨among primitive peoples twenty years may make a ~⟩ ⟨a ~ . . . is roughly equal to the mean age of mothers at the birth of their daughters —*Demographic Yearbook*⟩ ⟨fifty years constitutes roughly a working lifetime, a period covering two ~s —Arthur Geddes⟩ ⟨the cornerstone of the moral system . . . for ~s —Joe Alvin⟩ (4) : a group of individuals having contemporaneously a status (as that of students in a school) which each one holds only for a limited period ⟨repeated by ~ after ~ of pupils —H.G.G. Herklots⟩ (5) : a type or class of objects derived or developed from an earlier type ⟨the Air Force's new ~ of powerful supersonic fighters —Kenneth Koyen⟩ **2 a** : the act or process of producing offspring : PROCREATION ⟨the organs of ~⟩ **b** : origination by some mathematical, chemical, or other process : PRODUCTION, FORMATION ⟨the ~ of heat⟩ ⟨the ~ of sounds⟩; *specif* : the formation of a geometrical figure by the motion of some other figure ⟨the ~ of a line by a point⟩ **c** : the process of coming into being : GENESIS, DEVELOPMENT, RISE ⟨the spontaneous ~ of these churches —Oscar Handlin⟩ ⟨factors in the ~ of income —G.V.Cox⟩ **3** *obs* : RACE, KIND, BREED, STOCK, FAMILY
gen·er·a·tion·al \,jenə¦rāshənᵊl, -shnəl\ *adj* **1** : of or relating to generation ⟨~ sterility⟩ **2** : of or relating to a generation or to the relations between generations ⟨an example of a ~ . . . difference in language —Paul Schach⟩
gen·er·a·tion·ism \,jenə'rāshə,nizəm\ *n* -S : TRADUCIANISM; *also* : CREATIONISM
gen·er·a·tive \'jenə,rād·|iv, 'jen(ə)rə|, |t|, |ēv *also* |əv\ *adj* [ME, fr. MF *generatif*, fr. LL *generativus*, fr. L *generatus* (past part. of *generare* to beget, create) + *-ivus* -ive — more at GENERATE] **1** : having the power or function of generating, propagating, originating, producing, or reproducing ⟨~ organs⟩ **2** : of, relating to, or acting in generation ⟨grew out of a long ~ process —Owen & Eleanor Lattimore⟩ — **gen·er·a·tive·ly** \|əvlē, -li\ *adv*
generative cell *n* : a sexual reproductive cell : GAMETE; *esp* : a generative nucleus together with its associated cytoplasm — see BODY CELL 2
generative nucleus *n* : the one of the two nuclei resulting from the first division in the pollen grain of a seed plant that gives rise to sperm nuclei — see GENERATIVE CELL; compare TUBE NUCLEUS
gen·er·a·tor \'jenə,rād·ə(r), -ātə-\ *n* -S [L, fr. *generatus* + *-or*] **1** : one that generates, causes, or produces : ORIGINATOR ⟨the most important ~ of industrial expansion —Andrew Shonfield⟩ ⟨rival ~s or experts in foreign policy —E.S.Griffith⟩ **2 a** : an apparatus (as a steam boiler) in which vapor or gas is formed from a liquid or solid by heat or a chemical process **b** : an apparatus for the manufacture of gas (as water gas) involving the combustion of fuel; *esp* : the chamber for holding the fuel — compare PRODUCER 3 **c** : GAS GENERATOR a **3** : a machine by which mechanical energy is changed into electrical energy usu. by electromagnetic induction : DYNAMO — compare ELECTROSTATIC GENERATOR
gen·er·a·trix \,jenə¦rā·triks\ *n, pl* **generatri·ces** \,jenə'rā·trə,sēz, -rə'trī(,)sēz\ [NL, fr. L, fem. of *generator*] **1** : a point, line, or surface whose motion generates a line, surface, or solid **2** : a set of elements in a cryptological tabulation which form a line in any direction and have significance as a set
¹ge·ner·ic \jə'nerik, -rēk\ *adj* [F *générique*, fr. L *gener-, genus* birth, race, class, kind + F *-ique* -ic — more at KIN] **1 a** : relating or applied to or descriptive of all members of a genus, species, class, or group : common to or characteristic of a whole group or class : typifying or subsuming : not specific or individual : GENERAL ⟨the diseases grouped under the ~ heading of regional enteritis —W.H.Hale⟩ ⟨there is no such thing as a ~ "Asian" mind —R.A.Smith⟩ ⟨the same ~ similarity that one finds in the professional officers of any armed service —Joseph Alsop⟩ ⟨the novel has always had a ~ habit of reaching out to the extremes of literary expression —Mark Schorer⟩ **b** : available for common use : not protected by trademark registration : NONPROPRIETARY ⟨nylon and aspirin are ~ names⟩ — used esp. in trademark law **2** : relating to or having the rank of a biological genus **syn** see UNIVERSAL
²generic \"\ *n* -S : an element of a compound proper name that is general and often lowercased (as *river* in "Mississippi River" and *store* in "XYZ Store")
ge·ner·i·cal \-rəkəl, -rēk-\ *adj* [F *générique* + E *-al*] *archaic* : GENERIC
ge·ner·i·cal·ly \-k(ə)lē, -li\ *adv* : in a generic manner ⟨those pioneering tales now ~ called "Westerns" —Saxe Commins⟩ ⟨the dowdy . . . people whom you call, ~, suffragettes —G.B. Shaw⟩
generic judgment *n* : a judgment in logic in which the predicate gives generic characteristics of the subject : a universal judgment
ge·ner·ic·ness *n* -ES : the quality or state of being generic
generic wine *n* : a wine (as California burgundy or New York State sherry) named from the geographical location where the wine type to which it belongs originated — compare VARIETAL WINE
ge·ner·i·type *also* **ge·ner·o·type** \jə'nerə,tīp\ *n* [NL *gener-, genus* + E *-i-* or *-o-* + *type*] : GENOTYPE
gen·er·os·i·ty \,jenə'räsəd·ē, -s(ə)tē, -i\ *n* -ES [ME *generosite*, fr. L *generositat-, generositas*, fr. *generosus* + *-itat-, -itas* -ity] **1** *archaic* : nobility of birth or breeding : high quality **2 a** : liberality in spirit or act : MAGNANIMITY, BENEVOLENCE ⟨pleads for greater ~ in regard to immigration —S.K.Padover⟩ ⟨will make gestures of the greatest ~ to his opposition —W.S. White⟩; *esp* : liberality in giving **b** : an act or instance of magnanimity or munificence ⟨his countless *generosities*⟩ **3** : ABUNDANCE, COPIOUSNESS ⟨the extreme ~ of technical illustration —*Science*⟩ : LARGENESS, AMPLITUDE ⟨a . . . ~ of hips not sanctioned by the styles —Mary Deasy⟩
gen·er·ous \'jen(ə)rəs\ *adj* [MF or L; MF *genereus*, fr. L *generosus*, fr. *gener-, genus* birth, race, class, kind + *-osus* -ous — more at KIN] **1** *archaic* : of honorable birth or origin : of good stock : HIGHBORN **2 a** : characterized by a noble or forbearing spirit : animated by or exhibiting high ideals : MAGNANIMOUS, LOFTY, BENEVOLENT, KINDLY ⟨unusually ~ in his judgments of people —Osbert Sitwell⟩ ⟨projecting a more ~ basis for the reorganization of society —V.L.Parrington⟩ ⟨a ~ national credo which actuality often fails to live up to

—C.J.Rolo⟩ ⟨capable of ~ enthusiasms —Alfred Buchanan⟩ ⟨the dreams of all the ~ visionaries of the past —Carl Van Doren⟩ **b :** liberal or reflecting liberality in giving **:** not stingy or niggardly **:** OPENHANDED ⟨a ~ hospitality⟩ ⟨~ with the loot he has accumulated from his victims —Frederic Morton⟩ ⟨advocating a ~ system of old age pensions⟩ ⟨of a ~ disposition, he freely shared his supply —*Amer. Guide Series: N. H.*⟩ **c** (1) **:** marked by abundance or ample proportions **:** furnished without stint **:** COPIOUS, EXPANSIVE, LAVISH ⟨set himself up in ~ style —*Amer. Guide Series: Maine*⟩ ⟨the harvests . . . were ~ —Theodore Saloutos⟩ ⟨wide overhangs and ~ verandas —Lewis Mumford⟩ ⟨~ portions of food⟩ ⟨sets a ~ table⟩ ⟨a shirt with ~ cuffs⟩ (2) *of a wine* **:** full of spirit or strength **:** STIMULATING, RICH ⟨like a draught of some ~ southern wine —Norman Douglas⟩ **syn** see LIBERAL

gen·er·ous·ly *adv* **:** in a generous manner

gen·er·ous·ness *n* -ES **:** the quality or state of being generous ⟨an unusual ~ of spirit —T.O.Heggen⟩

genes *pl of* GENE

-genes *pl of* -GENE

gen·eserine \jən+\ *n* [ISV ²*gen-* (fr. L *generare* to beget, create) + *eserine* — more at GENERATE] **:** a crystalline alkaloid $C_{15}H_{21}N_3O_3$ found in the Calabar bean **:** an *N*-oxide of physostigmine

-ge·ne·sia \jə'nēzh(ē)ə\ *n comb form, pl* **-genesi·ae** \-z(h)ē,ē\ [NL, fr. Gk, fr. *genesis* + *-ia* -y] **:** genesis **:** formation ⟨para*genesia*⟩

ge·ne·sic \jə'nesik, -nēsik,-nēzik\ *adj* [*genesis* + *-ic*] **:** GENERATIVE

gen·e·sis \'jenəsəs\ *n, pl* **gene·ses** \-ə,sēz\ [L, fr. Gk, fr. the stem of *gignesthai* to be born — more at KIN] **:** the origin or coming into being of anything **:** development into being esp. by growth or evolution **:** the process or mode of origin ⟨the ~ of a book⟩ ⟨the ~ of a culture pattern⟩ ⟨the ~ of a disease⟩

gene–spread \'ₛ,ₛ\ *n* **:** GENE FLOW

gene–string \'ₛ,ₛ\ *n* **:** the linear functional gene group of a chromosome **:** a chromonema with the genes it carries

ge·nes·trole \jə'ne,strōl\ *n* -S [F, fr. Prov *genestrolo*, fr. *genesto* broom, fr. OProv *genesta*, fr. L *genista*] **:** DYER'S BROOM

¹gen·et \'jenət\ *also* **ge·nette** \jə'net\ *n* -S [ME *jonet, genete*, fr. MF *genete*, fr. Ar *jarnayt*] **:** any of several small Old World carnivorous mammals comprising the genus *Genetta* and related to the civets but having the scent glands less developed and the claws perfectly retractile

²gen·et \'jenət\ *var of* JENNET

³ge·net \zhə'nā\ *n, pl* **genets** \-āz\ [F *genêt* (also, broom), fr. L *genista, genesta* broom] **1 :** WOODWAXEN **2 :** DYER'S BROOM

¹ge·neth·li·ac \jə'nethlē,ak\ *n* -S [in sense 1, fr. LL *genethliacus*, fr. Gk *genethliakos*, fr. *genethliakos*, adj.; in sense 2, fr. LL *genethliace*, fr. (assumed) Gk *genethliakē*, fr. fem. of *genethliakos*, adj.] **1** *archaic* **:** a calculator of nativities **2** *archaic* **:** NATIVITY

²genethliac \"\ *or* **gen·eth·li·a·cal** \ˌje,neth'līəkəl, -ˌnəth-\ *adj* [*genethliac* fr. LL *genethliacus*, fr. Gk *genethliakos*, fr. *genethlē* race, stock, family, offspring, fr. the stem of *gignesthai* to be born; *genethliacal* fr. LL *genethliac*us + E *-al*] **:** relating to nativities or birthdays **:** showing position and influence of stars at one's birth — **gen·eth·li·a·cal·ly** \ˌₛ(,)ₛ'līək(ə)lē\ *adv*

ge·net·ic \jə'ned·|ik, -et|, |ēk\ *also* **ge·net·i·cal** \|ə̇kəl, |ēk-\ *adj* [fr. *genesis*, after such pairs as *antithesis: antithetic, antithetical*] **1 a :** relating to or determined by the origin, development, prior history, or causal antecedents of some phenomenon **:** CAUSAL, HISTORICAL, EVOLUTIONARY ⟨the ~ factors in juvenile delinquency⟩ ⟨the ~ features of rocks —L.V.Pirsson⟩ ⟨the ~ development of a legal doctrine⟩ ⟨traces the ~ development . . . of his neurotic conflict —Lionel Ovesey⟩ **b :** based on or determined by evolution from a common source ⟨the relationship . . . is not causal but ~ . . . both are derived from a common source, a literary convention —F.H.Ellis⟩ — used esp. of relations among languages or among words and grammatical forms of languages ⟨classes of words . . . relied upon in establishing ~ connections between languages —M.J.Andrade⟩ **c :** concerned with or seeking to explain, interpret, or understand (as a literary or psychological phenomenon) in terms of its origin and development or of its causal antecedents ⟨the general reaction against . . . historical or ~ criticism of any type —Malcolm Cowley⟩ ⟨what we call the evolutionary approach or the historical attitude is technically labeled the ~ method —John Dewey⟩ ⟨~ psychology⟩ **2 :** of or relating to genetics **:** characterized or produced by the agencies and operations of genetics **:** employed in the processes of genetics ⟨~ studies⟩ **3 :** of, relating to, produced by, or being a gene **:** GENIC ⟨~ combinations⟩ — **ge·net·i·cal·ly** \|ə̇k(ə)lē, |ēk-, -li\ *adv*

-genetic \ₛ'ₛₛₛ\ *adj comb form* **1 :** relating to generation or genesis ⟨spermato*genetic*⟩ ⟨pan*genetic*⟩ **2 :** generating **:** producing **:** yielding ⟨cyto*genetic*⟩ **3 :** generated **:** produced **:** yielded ⟨psycho*genetic*⟩

genetic aggregation *n* **:** a group of blood kindred **:** a population descended through common lines undisturbed by immigration

genetic definition *n* **:** a definition that indicates how that to which a word or expression refers comes into existence (as "a circle is a closed plane curve generated by the motion of a point at a constant distance from a fixed point")

genetic drift *n* **:** random changes in the gene complex of a population due to chance preservation or extinction of particular genes

genetic fallacy *n* **:** the fallacy of employing the genetic method under inapplicable circumstances or in inappropriate ways; *esp* **:** an invalid resolution of phenomena into their antecedents

genetic individual *n* **:** INDIVIDUAL 1c, 1d

ge·net·i·cism \jə'ned·|ə,sizəm, -et|\ *n* -S **:** a theory explaining the perceptions, attitudes, and behavior of an individual primarily in terms of his heredity and development — compare NATIVISM

ge·net·i·cist \-ˌsəst\ *n* -S **:** a specialist in genetics

ge·net·ics \|iks, |ēks\ *n pl but sing in constr* **1 a :** a branch of biology that deals with the heredity and variation of organisms and with the mechanisms by which these are effected **b :** a treatise or textbook on this subject **2 :** the genetic makeup and phenomena of an organism, type, group, or condition ⟨the ~ of drosophila⟩ **3 :** GENESIS ⟨the psychological analysis of religious experience; its ~ and causal conditions —F.P. Clarke⟩ ⟨a classification of clouds based on . . . their physical and meteorological ~ and structure —D.W.Perrie⟩

genetic spiral *n* **:** a spiral formed by passing a line through the point of insertion of each leaf on a stem from the lowest to the highest

ge·neto·troph·ic \jə'ned·ə'träfik, -rōf-\ *adj* [*genetic* + *-o-* + *-trophic*] **:** relating to or involving genetic predisposing and nutritional precipitating factors — used esp. of certain deficiency diseases

gen·e·trix \'jenə·(,)triks\ *n, pl* **genetri·ces** \ˌjenə·'trī(,)sēz\ [L, fr. the stem of *gignere* to beget — more at KIN] **:** MOTHER ⟨a ~ of aldermen and beadles —Francis Berry⟩

genets *pl of* GENET

ge·net·ta \jə'ned·ə\ *n, cap* [NL, fr. F *genette* genet, fr. MF *genete* — more at GENET] **:** a genus of Old World mammals (family Viverridae) comprising the genets

genette *var of* GENET

¹ge·ne·va \jə'nēvə\ *adj, usu cap* [fr. *Geneva*, Switzerland] **:** of or from the city of Geneva, Switzerland **:** of the kind or style prevalent in Geneva **:** GENEVAN, GENEVESE

²geneva \"\ *n* -S [modif. (influenced by *Geneva*, city in Switzerland) of obs. D *genever* (now *jenever*), lit., juniper, fr. MD *geniver, genēver*, fr. OF *geneivre, genevre*, fr. (assumed) VL *jeniperus*, fr. L *juniperus* — more at JUNIPER] **:** a strongly alcoholic liquor flavored with juniper berries and made in the Netherlands **:** HOLLANDS

Geneva bands

geneva bands *n pl, usu cap G* **:** clerical bands consisting of two narrow strips of white cloth hanging down from the front collar of the ecclesiastical dress of some Protestant clergymen and modeled after the bands worn by the Calvinist clergy of Switzerland

geneva convention *n, usu cap G* **:** one of a series of agreements concerning both the treatment of prisoners of war, the sick, wounded, and dead in battle and the status of those responsible for them first made and signed at Geneva, Switzerland, in 1864 and subsequently accepted in later revisions by the majority of nations

geneva cross *n, usu cap G* **:** RED CROSS

geneva crystal *n, usu cap G* **:** a very thin round watch glass used in closed-top pocket watches

geneva gown *n, usu cap 1st G* **:** a loose large-sleeved black academic gown adopted as a vestment for preaching by the Calvinistic clergy of Geneva and widely used by Protestants

geneva movement *n, often cap G* **1** *or* **geneva motion :** a device for obtaining intermittent motion in which a cam on a driving wheel engages slots in a driven wheel **2 :** BAR MOVEMENT

¹ge·ne·van \jə'nēvən\ *n* -S *cap* [*Geneva*, Switzerland + E *-an*] **1 :** a native or resident of Geneva, Switzerland **2 :** a supporter of Genevan doctrines **:** CALVINIST

²genevan \"\ *adj, usu cap* **1 :** of or relating to Geneva, Switzerland **2 :** of or relating to Geneva about the time of John Calvin and the beginning of the Reformation **:** PROTESTANT, CALVINISTIC ⟨*Genevan* theology⟩

geneva stop *n, usu cap G* **1 :** a device used in watches with going barrels that limits the power of the mainspring to its middle portion so that the action starts with the same even force as when it abruptly stops rather than gradually running down **2 :** MALTESE CROSS

geneva system *or* **geneva nomenclature** *n, usu cap G* **:** a system of nomenclature adopted by an international congress of organic chemists in Geneva in 1892 and later modified and added to by the International Union of *Pure and Applied* Chemistry resulting in a systematic nomenclature in which names of compounds are formed from those of parent hydrocarbons with use of prefixes and suffixes (as 2-methylₛbutane for isopentane, butanone for methyl ethyl ketone, hexanoic acid for caproic acid)

gen·e·vese \ˌjenə'vēz, -ēs\ *n or adj, usu cap* [*Geneva*, Switzerland + E *-ese*] **:** GENEVAN

¹ge·nial \'jēnyəl, -nēəl\ *adj* [L *genialis*, fr. *genius* + *-alis* -al — more at GENIUS] **1** *archaic* **:** of or relating to marriage or generation **:** NUPTIAL, GENERATIVE ⟨the ~ bed —John Milton⟩ **2 a :** favorable to growth or human comfort **:** not harsh or severe **:** pleasantly warm **:** MILD ⟨in these ~ regions . . . one's wants are naturally diminished —Herman Melville⟩ ⟨a sun as bright and ~ as we would desire —Tyrone Power †1841⟩ ⟨the climate should be ~ . . . with ample rainfall —W.C. Bennett⟩ **b :** marked by or diffusing good cheer, warmth, sympathy, or friendliness **:** KINDLY, AFFABLE, AMIABLE ⟨the handsome, ~ face with its kindliness of glance, its smiling mouth —S.H.Adams⟩ ⟨the pleasure-loving, ~, imperturbable traveler —Saxe Commins⟩ ⟨the extremely comfortable and ~ atmosphere of the upper middle class —*Amer. Guide Series: Ind.*⟩ **3** *obs* **:** belonging to one's genius or nature **:** NATIVE, INBORN **4 :** displaying or marked by genius ⟨new, ~ insights —Susanne K. Langer⟩ ⟨however ~ his intuitions may be —George Santayana⟩ ⟨we rarely read . . . to share some ~ vision —Herbert Read⟩ **syn** see GRACIOUS

²ge·ni·al \jə'nī(ə)l\ *adj* [Gk *geneion* chin, beard (fr. *genys* jaw) + E *-al* — more at CHIN] **:** of or relating to the chin

ge·ni·al·i·ty \ˌjēnē'aləd·ē, jēn'ya-, -ətē, -i\ *n* -ES [LL *genialitas*, fr. L *genialis* + *-itas* -ity] **:** the quality of being genial; *esp* **:** sympathetic cheerfulness **:** warmth of disposition and manners ⟨overflowing with joy and a noisy, hearty ~ —Vicki Baum⟩

ge·nial·ize \'jēnyə,līz, 'jēnēə,-\ *vt* -ED/-ING/-S **:** to make genial ⟨scheme for *genializing* the world —D.G.Hoffman⟩

ge·nial·ly \-əlē, -ēli\ *adv* **1** *obs* **:** by genius or nature **:** NATURALLY **2 :** in a genial manner **:** CHEERFULLY, PLEASANTLY

ge·nial·ness \-nələs\ *n* -ES **:** the quality or state of being genial

gen·ic \'jēnik, 'jen-, -nēk\ *adj* [²*gene* + *-ic*] **:** of, relating to, produced by, or being a gene **:** GENETIC — compare ACQUIRED — **gen·i·cal·ly** \-nə̇k(ə)lē, -nēk-, -li\ *adv*

-gen·ic \ˌjenik, -nēk, *in senses 3 & 4* ˌjēn- *or* ˌjen-\ *adj comb form* [ISV *-gen* & *-geny* + *-ic*] **1 :** producing **:** forming ⟨carcino*genic*⟩ ⟨acro*genic*⟩ **2 :** produced by **:** formed from ⟨nephro*genic*⟩ **3** [*genic*] **:** of or relating to a gene ⟨intra*genic*⟩ **:** having (a stipulated kind or number of) genes ⟨poly*genic*⟩ **4** [*photogenic*] **:** suitable for production or reproduction by a (given) medium ⟨tele*genic*⟩

genic balance *n* **:** the relation whereby a specific gene acts as a part of the entire gene complex in the production of a particular phenotypic character

ge·nic·u·late \jə'nikyələt, -,lāt\ *or* **ge·nic·u·lat·ed** \-,lād·əd\ *adj* [L *geniculatus*, fr. *geniculum* small knee, knot (dim. of *genu* knee, knot) + *-atus* -ate, -ated — more at KNEE] **1 :** bent abruptly at an angle like a bent knee ⟨a ~ twin crystal⟩ **2 :** relating to the geniculate ganglion ⟨~ neuralgia⟩ — **ge·nic·u·late·ly** \-lətlē, -,lāt-\ *adv*

geniculate body *n* **:** any of four oval prominences of the diencephalon functioning as centers of synapse in paths to the cerebral cortex

geniculate ganglion *n* **:** a small reddish ganglion consisting of sensory and sympathetic nerve cells located at the sharp backward bend of the facial nerve

ge·nic·u·lum \-ˌləm\ *n, pl* **genicu·la** \-lə\ [NL, fr. L, knee, knot] **:** a small knee-shaped anatomical structure or abrupt bend

ge·nie *also* **ge·nii** \'jēnē, -ni\ *n, pl* **genies** *or* **genii** \'jēnē, -nē,ī *also* -n,yī\ [F *génie*, modif. (influenced by *génie* genius, fr. L *genius*) of Ar *jinnīy* demon, spirit] **:** JINNI ⟨the invisible ~*s*, water and heat —T.M.Longstreth⟩ ⟨all the good *genii* of the universe —Joseph Tetlie⟩

-genies *pl of* -GENY

ge·nii *pl of* GENIUS *or of* GENIE

gen·in \'jenən, jə'nēn\ *n* -S [*-genin*] **:** any of numerous aglycons or similar compounds obtained by hydrolysis of compounds that are not glycosides — compare BUFAGIN, SAPOGENIN

-genin \'jenən; ˌjənən, -,nēn\ *n comb form* -S [ISV ²*-gen* + *-in*] **:** compound formed from another compound — in names of aglycons or similar compounds derived from the names of the parent compounds ⟨sali*genin* from salicin⟩ ⟨digito*genin* from digitonin⟩

genio- *comb form* [ISV, fr. Gk *geneio-*, fr. *geneion* chin, beard — more at GENIAL] **1 :** chin ⟨*genio*plasty⟩ **2 :** chin and ⟨*genio*glossal⟩

ge·nio·glossal \jə'nīō+\ *adj* [*genio-* + *glossal*] **:** of or relating to the chin and tongue

ge·nio·glos·sus \ₛ,ₛₛ'gläsəs, -lȯs-\ *n, pl* **genioglos·si** \|,sī\ [NL, fr. *genio-* + *-glossus* (fr. Gk *glōssa* tongue) — more at GLOSS] **:** either of a pair of fan-shaped muscles arising from the superior mental spine and inserting on the hyoid bone and into the tongue that serve to advance and retract and also to depress the tongue

ge·nio·hyoglossus \jə'nīō+\ *n, pl* **geniohyoglossi** [NL, fr. *genio-* + *hyoglossus*] **:** GENIOGLOSSUS

ge·nio·hyoid \"+\ *adj* [*genio-* + *hyoid*] **:** of or relating to the chin and hyoid bone — used chiefly of a pair of slender muscles arising from the inner side of the symphysis of the lower jaw and inserted on the hyoid bone

ge·nip *or* **gi·nep** \kə'nep, g|, [a'-, -'nip\ *n* -S [Sp *genipa*, fr. F *genipa, genipat*, fr. Guarani] **1 :** a plant or fruit of the genus *Genipa*; *esp* **:** GENIPAP **2 a :** a West Indian tree (*Melicocca bijuga*) **b :** the fruit of this tree

ge·ni·pa \jə'nēpə, -nīpə\ *n* [NL, fr. Sp *genipa* genip] **1** *cap* **:** a genus of tropical American trees (family Rubiaceae) bearing yellow flowers and succulent edible fruit with a thick rind — see GENIPAP **2** -S **:** any tree or fruit of the genus *Genipa*

gen·i·pap \'jenə,pap\ *also* **gen·i·pa·po** \ˌjenə'pa(,)pō, ˌzhenə'pa(,)pü\ *n* -S [Pg *genipapo*, fr. Tupi] **1 :** a tree (*Genipa americana*) of the West Indies and northern So. America **2 :** the edible orange-sized fruit of genipap

ge·ni·sa·ro *or* **ge·ni·ze·ro** *or* **ge·ni·za·ro** \he'nēsə,rō, ge-,je-\ *n* -S [AmerSp (Nicaragua) *jenisero, jenisaro*] **:** RAIN TREE

ge·nis·ta \jə'nistə\ *n* [NL, fr. L, broom] **1** *cap* **:** a large genus of Old World often spiny shrubs (family Leguminosae) with simple leaves and yellow flowers **2** -S **:** CANARY BROOM

ge·nis·te·in \jə'nistēən, -'ni,stēn\ *n* -S [ISV *Genista, genist-* (fr. NL genus name of *Genista tinctoria*) + *-ein*] **:** a colorless crystalline compound $C_{15}H_{10}O_5$ derived from isoflavone, occurring usu. combined as genistin, and dyeing pale yellow

ge·nis·tin \jə'nistən\ *n* -S [NL *Genista* + E *-in*] **:** a pale yellow glucoside $C_{21}H_{20}O_9$ obtained from woodwaxen or soybean meal and yielding genistein and glucose on hydrolysis

gen·i·tal \'jenəd·ᵊl, -nətᵊl\ *adj* [ME, fr. L *genitalis*, fr. *genitus* (past part. of *gignere* to beget) + *-alis* -al — more at KIN] **1 :** GENERATIVE **2 :** of, relating to, or being a sexual organ **3 :** of, relating to, or characterized by the stage of mature psychosexual development in which oral and anal impulses are subordinated to adaptive interpersonal mechanisms

genital bulb *n* **:** BULB 5e

genital cord *n* **:** a mesenchymal shelf in the female mammalian fetus enclosing the developing uterus and the posterior part of the wolffian ducts and giving rise to the broad ligaments of the uterus

genital crisis *n* **:** an adult sexual phenomenon (as transitory uterine bleeding) occurring in the newborn presumably as a result of transplacental passage of maternal hormones

genital gland *n* **:** a gland producing or capable of producing germ cells **:** OVOTESTIS, OVARY, TESTIS

genital glanders *n pl but sing or pl in constr* **:** DOURINE

genital horsepox *n* **:** coital exanthema of the horse

gen·i·ta·lia \ˌjenə'tālēə, -lyə\ *n pl* [L, fr. neut. pl. of *genitalis*] **:** the organs of the reproductive system; *esp* **:** the external genital organs

gen·i·ta·lic \ˌjenə'talik, -'tāl-\ *also* **gen·i·ta·li·al** \-'tālēəl\ *adj* [*genitalia* + *-ic* or *-al*] **:** of or relating to the genitalia

gen·i·tal·i·ty \ˌjenə'taləd·ē, -ətē\ *n* -ES [prob. fr. F *génitalité*, fr. *génital* (fr. L *genitalis*) + *-ité* -ity] **:** possession of full genital sensitivity and capacity to develop orgasmic potency in relation to a sexual partner of the opposite sex

genital ridge *n* **:** a ridge of embryonic mesoblast developing from the wolffian body and giving rise to the gonad on either side of the body

gen·i·tals \'jenəd·ᵊlz, -nətᵊlz\ *n pl* [ME, fr. *genital*, adj. + *-s*] **:** GENITALIA

genital wart *n* **:** CONDYLOMA

gen·i·ti·val \ˌjenə'tīvəl\ *adj* [*genitive* + *-al*] **:** possessing genitive form **:** relating to or derived from the genitive case ⟨*anyways, needs, backwards* are ~ adverbs⟩ — **gen·i·ti·val·ly** \-vəlē\ *adv*

¹gen·i·tive \'jenəd·iv, -ətiv\ *adj* [ME, fr. L *genetivus, genitivus*, lit., of birth, of generation (trans. of Gk *genikos* in *genikē ptōsis* genitive case), irreg. fr. *gener-, genus* birth, race, class, kind + *-ivus* -ive — more at KIN] **1** *of a grammatical case* **:** marking typically a relatively close, unchanging, and exclusive relationship such as that of possessor or source ⟨the words ending in *'s* in the phrases *the boy's shoes, the sun's light, the speaker's arrival*, and *a member's expulsion from the club* are in the ~ case⟩ — compare POSSESSIVE **2** *of a word or word group* **:** not characterized by case inflection but nevertheless expressing a relationship that in some inflected languages is often marked by a genitive case — used esp. of English prepositional phrases introduced by *of* ⟨the phrases *of the sun* in "the light of the sun" and *of the speaker* in "the arrival of the speaker" are ~ phrases⟩ **3 :** of or relating to the genitive case ⟨a ~ ending⟩

²genitive \"\ *n* -S [L *genitivus, genetivus* (trans. of Gk *genikē*), fr. *genitivus, genetivus*, adj.] **1 :** a genitive case **2 :** a genitive word or word group

genitive absolute *n* **:** a construction in Greek in which a noun or pronoun and its adjunct both in the genitive case form together an adverbial phrase expressing generally the time, cause, or an attendant circumstance of an action (as *Konōnos stratēgountos* in *taut' eprachthē Konōnos stratēgountos* "this was done when Conon was general")

genito- *comb form* [*genital*] **:** genital and ⟨*genito*urinary⟩

gen·i·to·crural \ˌjenə(,)tō+\ *adj* [*genito-* + *crural*] **:** GENITOFEMORAL

gen·i·to·femoral \"+\ *adj* [*genito-* + *femoral*] **:** of or relating to the genital organs and the thigh ⟨the ~ nerve⟩

gen·i·tor \'jenəd·ər, -nə,tȯ(ə)r\ *n* -S [ME *genytur*, fr. L *genitor*, fr. *genitus* (past part. of *gignere* to beget) + *-or* — more at KIN] **:** one who begets **:** FATHER, PARENT ⟨the ~ of that political hybrid, the corporate state —Avro Manhattan⟩; *specif* **:** the biological as distinguished from the legal father among certain primitive peoples — compare PATER

gen·i·to·urinary \ˌjenə(,)tō+\ *adj* [ISV *genito-* + *urinary*] **1 :** of or relating to the genital and urinary organs or functions **2 :** specializing in care of genitourinary diseases ⟨a ~ surgeon⟩ ⟨~ dispensaries⟩

gen·i·ture \'jenə,chü(ə)r, -nəchər, -,t(y)ü(ə)r\ *n* -S [L *genitura*, fr. *genitus* + *-ura* -ure] **:** NATIVITY, BIRTH ⟨a man's lineage and ~ —A.T.Quiller-Couch⟩ ⟨the ~ of a prince may involve the slaughter of vast multitudes —Lynn Thorndike⟩

ge·nius \'jēnyəs *also* -nēəs\ *n, pl* **geniuses** \-əsəz\ *or* **ge·nii** \-nē,ī *also* -n,yī\ *see numbered senses* [L, fr. *gignere* to beget — more at KIN] **1** *pl* **genii :** an attendant spirit of a person or place **:** tutelary deity ⟨every human being has a ~ . . . associated with him from the moment of conception —C.D. Forde & G.I. Jones⟩ **2 a :** a strong leaning or inclination **:** decided taste **:** BENT, PENCHANT ⟨fate did not allow him to indulge his ~ till those last few years —Norman Douglas⟩ **b** (1) **:** peculiar, distinctive, or identifying character **:** essential nature or spirit **:** prevailing taste or sentiment ⟨at odds with the ~ of the theater —*Time*⟩ ⟨a spirit hostile to the ~ of our government —John Marshall⟩ ⟨suited to the ~ of a free people —Robert Cutler⟩ ⟨the ~ of the age we have under discussion —Benjamin Farrington⟩ ⟨the ~ of Elizabethan literature⟩ (2) **:** a personification or embodiment esp. of a quality or condition **:** INCARNATION ⟨essentially the ~ of the mediocre —H.J.Laski⟩ **c :** the distinctive character or quality of a place or the body of traditions and influences associated with it ⟨under the spell of the ~ of the ancient university town⟩ ⟨the ~ of this land was in its great irregularity and variety —Donald Davidson⟩ **3** *pl usu* **genii a :** a nature spirit or an elemental spirit **:** GENIE, DEMON ⟨these malevolent *genii* of the deep —Norman Douglas⟩ **b :** a person who influences another (as in character or behavior) for good or bad ⟨he was the evil ~ of that unhappy prince⟩ **4** *pl usu* **geniuses a** (1) **:** a singular strongly marked capacity or aptitude **:** notable talent ⟨had a ~ for getting along with boys —Mary Ross⟩ ⟨a ~ at . . . carpentry —Tom Corkery⟩ ⟨has a ~ for cooking —H.E.Scudder⟩ (2) **:** a strongly marked tendency, disposition, or flair of any kind ⟨developing a ~ for making people furious —W.J.Reilly⟩ ⟨has a ~ for understatement —John Buchan⟩ ⟨has a positive ~ for saying the wrong thing⟩ **b :** extraordinary native intellectual power esp. as manifested in unusual capacity for creative activity of any kind ⟨in the contemporary novel ~ is hard to find, talent is abundant —*Brit. Book News*⟩ **c :** a person endowed with transcendent mental superiority, inventiveness, and ability ⟨the rare, fortunate ~*es* like the Curies, Darwin, or Newton —Oliver La Farge⟩; *specif* **:** a person with a very high intelligence quotient usu. in the range of 140 or above **syn** see GIFT

genius lo·ci \-'lō,sī, -,sē, -,kē\ *n* [L] **1 :** a tutelary deity or spirit of a place ⟨a priest or prophet who serves . . . the *genius loci* —*Hibbert Jour.*⟩ **2 :** the cluster of associations identified with a place **:** pervading spirit ⟨whose hurries unduly will never catch the *genius loci* of these regions —Norman Douglas⟩ ⟨its *genius loci* . . . eluded the researchers altogether —*Times Lit. Supp.*⟩

ge·ni·zah \gə,nē'zä, -'nēzə\ *n, pl* **geni·zoth** *or* **geni·zot** \-,nē-'zōt(h), -'nē,zōs\ *or* **genizahs** [Heb *gĕnīzāh*] **1 :** a storeroom or repository in a synagogue used for discarded, damaged, or defective books and papers and sacred objects ⟨valuable old manuscripts found in the ~ at Cairo⟩ **2 :** the contents of a genizah

genizero *or* **genizaro** *var of* GENISARO

genl *abbr* general

gennet *var of* JENNET

geno- — see GEN-

gen·oa \'jenəwə, *chiefly in substand speech* jə'nōə\ *adj, usu cap* [fr. *Genoa*, Italy] **:** of or from the city of Genoa, Italy **:** of the kind or style prevalent in Genoa **:** GENOESE

genoa jib *n, often cap* **:** an oversize jib which overlaps the mainsail and is controlled outside the rigging and is used chiefly in races to give a boat more speed

gen·o·blast \ˈjenə,blast\ *n* [¹*gen-* + *-blast*] **:** a matured germ cell — **gen·o·blas·tic** \ˌ==ˈblastik\ *adj*
gen·o·ci·dal \ˌjenəˈsīdᵊl\ *adj* [*genocide* + *-al*] **:** tending toward or producing genocide ⟨~ acts⟩ ⟨the degradation of anthropology to a ~ weapon by the Nazis —*Scientific Monthly*⟩
gen·o·cide \ˈjenə,sīd\ *n* -S [¹*gen-* + *-cide*] **1 :** the use of deliberate systematic measures (as killing, bodily or mental injury, unlivable conditions, prevention of births) calculated to bring about the extermination of a racial, political, or cultural group or to destroy the language, religion, or culture of a group **2 :** one who advocates or practices genocide
gen·o·cline \ˈjenə,klīn\ *n* [²*gen-* + *cline*] **:** a sequence of intergrading forms produced by hybridization between adjacent genetically distinct populations — compare ECOCLINE, GENE FLOW
¹**gen·o·ese** \ˌjenəˈwēz, -ēs\ *adj, usu cap* [*Genoa*, Italy + E *-ese*] **1 :** of, relating to, or characteristic of Genoa, Italy **2 :** of, relating to, or characteristic of the Genoese
²**genoese** \"\ *n, pl* **genoese** *cap* **:** a native or resident of Genoa, Italy
genoese jib *n, often cap* **:** GENOA JIB
ge·noid \ˈjē,nȯid\ *n* -S [ISV ²*gen-* + *-oid*] **:** a cytoplasmic body resembling a virus and functioning in the manner of a gene **:** PLASMAGENE
ge·nome \ˈjē,nōm\ *or* **ge·nom** \-,nŏm\ *n* -S [G *genom*, fr. ²*gen-* + *chromosom* chromosome] **:** one haploid set of chromosomes with the genes they contain — **ge·nomic** \(ˈ)jēˈnōmik, -ˈnäm-\ *adj*
ge·no·mere \ˈjēnə,mi(ə)r\ *n* -S [²*gen-* + *-mere*] **:** a hypothetical subsection of a gene
ge·no·ne·ma \ˌjēnəˈnēmə\ *n* -S [NL, fr. ²*gen-* + *-nema*] **:** CHROMONEMA
ge·no·some \ˈjēnə,sōm\ *n* -S [²*gen-* + chromo*some*] **:** a portion of a chromosome that is coextensive with a given gene
ge·no·species \ˌjēnō+\ *n* [¹*gen-* + *species*] **1 :** PURE LINE **2 :** the sum of the genotypes of a taxonomic species
geno·type \ˈjēnə,tīp, ˈjen-\ *n* [in sense 1, fr. ¹*gen-* + *type*; in sense 2, fr. ²*gen-* + *type*] **1 :** the type species of a genus **2 a :** the genetic constitution of an individual or group **:** the totality of genes possessed by an individual or group **b :** a class or group of individuals sharing a specified genetic makeup — compare PHENOTYPE — **geno·typ·ic** \ˌ==ˈtipik\ *also* **geno·typ·i·cal** \-pəkəl\ *adj* — **geno·typ·i·cal·ly** \-k(ə)lē\ *adv* — **geno·ty·pic·i·ty** \ˌ==tiˈpisəd·ē\ *n* -ES
-ge·nous \jənəs\ *adj comb form* [*-gen* + *-ous*] **1 :** producing **:** yielding ⟨alkali*genous*⟩ **2 :** produced by **:** arising or originating in ⟨neuro*genous*⟩ ⟨endo*genous*⟩
gen·o·vese \ˌjenəˈvēz, -ēs\ *adj or n, usu cap* [It, fr. *Genova* Genoa, Italy + *-ese*] **:** GENOESE
genre \ˈzhä(ⁿ)nrə, ˈ(ə)r, ˈnrə, ˈnə(r), ˈnə(r), ˈn, ˈnˈ\ *n* -S *often attrib* [F, fr. OF *genre, gendre* — more at GENDER] **1 :** KIND, SORT, STYLE, SPECIES, CATEGORY ⟨a singer of quite a different ~ —Thomas Heinitz⟩ ⟨infantrymen without bluster, tall and imperturbable, they share one military ~ —A.J.Liebling⟩ ⟨large flappy rag dolls, a ~ favored by two-year-olds —*New Yorker*⟩ **2 :** a category of artistic composition characterized by a particular style, form, or content ⟨a fine introduction to twelve-tone music for those who have had little experience with the ~ —Arthur Berger⟩: as **a :** paintings that depict scenes or events from everyday life usu. realistically ⟨painters of ~ who . . . paint informal subjects, typical situations in the everyday world —Dorothy Adlow⟩; *also* **:** the school or style of painting featured by the use of such subject matter ⟨examples in which romanticism begins to blend with pure ~ —R.M.Coates⟩ **b :** a distinctive type or category of literary composition ⟨such unpromising ~*s* as Indian treaties, Colonial promotional tracts, and theological works —*New Yorker*⟩ ⟨an essay in that difficult ~, contemporary history —F.C. Barghoorn⟩ ⟨the noblest of ~*s*, the epic —George Sherburn⟩ **syn** see CLASS
gen·ro \ˈgenˈrō, =ˈ=\ *n pl, often cap* [Jap *genrō*, lit., principal elders] **:** the elder statesmen of Japan
¹**gens** \ˈjenz, ˈgenz, ˈgen(t)s\ *n, pl* **gen·tes** \ˈjen·,tēz, ˈgen·,tās\ [L — more at GENTLE] **1 :** a Roman clan embracing the families of the same stock in the male line with the members having a common name and being united in worship of their common ancestor — compare CURIA 1a **2 :** CLAN; *esp* **:** the patrilineal clan **3** [NL, fr. L] **:** a distinguishable group of related organisms: **a :** a subspecific biological group isolated by its habits **b :** a temporal sequence of extinct biological forms of which the divergence between extremes approaches the generic level
²**gens** *pl of* GEN
-gens *pl of* -GEN
genseng *var of* GINSENG
¹**gent** \ˈjent\ *adj* [ME, fr. OF, fr. L *genitus*, past. part. of *gignere* to beget — more at KIN] **1** *archaic* **:** GRACEFUL, PRETTY, ELEGANT **2** *obs* **:** of gentle birth **:** NOBLE
²**gent** \"\ *n* -S [short for *gentleman*] **:** MAN, FELLOW, GUY ⟨a big shaggy ~ with broad shoulders and a lot of rampant black hair —E.C.Marston⟩ ⟨was easier to be a vagabond than a landed ~ with no land —Claud Cockburn⟩
¹**gen·teel** \(ˈ)jenˈtēl, *esp before pause or consonant* -ēəl\ *adj, sometimes* **genteeler**; *sometimes* **genteelest** [MF *gentil* — more at GENTLE] **1 a :** appropriate to the status or manners of the gentry or upper class **:** having an aristocratic quality or flavor **:** STYLISH, FASHIONABLE ⟨Latin is ~, and I have sent my eldest boy to learn it —George Borrow⟩ ⟨like ~ tailors, they rated their services very high —Herman Melville⟩ ⟨call it very ~ . . . real stylish —John Buchan⟩ ⟨say a bouquet . . . 'tis more ~ —W.M.Thackeray⟩ ⟨preferred the ~ sword cane and the pistol —Green Peyton⟩ **b :** characteristic of or relating to the gentry or upper class **:** of or relating to a class ranking above the commonalty ⟨not a ~ face to be seen —Jane Austen⟩ ⟨a patrician with a ~ background —A.S. Link⟩ ⟨by their education . . . the boys came to occupy a ~ position —G.F.Whicher⟩ **c :** elegant or graceful in manner, appearance, or shape ⟨looking at the misty autumn landscape of a ~ park —Anthony West⟩ ⟨a graceful speaker with ~ motions —Earl of Chesterfield⟩ **d :** free from vulgarity or rudeness **:** marked by delicacy of manner **:** POLITE, COURTEOUS, POLISHED ⟨impeccably ~, she said "Yes, that's exactly what I wanted" —Helen Howe⟩ ⟨her letter, couched in majestic but most ~ phrase —Margaret Deland⟩ ⟨the symbol of the privileged classes . . . on the surface, hard as nails underneath —Martin Turnell⟩ **2 a :** maintaining or striving to maintain the air, forms, or pretense of superior or middle-class social status or respectability ⟨a shabby ~ residential district —W.L.Sperry⟩ ⟨a . . . mansion of faded charm and ~ shabbiness —*Amer. Guide Series: Del.*⟩ ⟨spent most of her declining years in ~ poverty —F.H.Cramer⟩ ⟨people seem to think that an antique dealer is a ~ crook —Sam Boal⟩ **b** (1) **:** characterized by extreme or excessive regard for conventional morality or ideals **:** marked by false delicacy, prudery, or affectation **:** excessively nice or refined **:** PURITANICAL, VICTORIAN ⟨readers are tired of delicate ~ novels —David Daiches⟩ ⟨her ideas were ~ and middle-class —Charles Partridge⟩ ⟨escaping from the ~ censorship that had been a nuisance to literature —Edmund Wilson⟩ ⟨the ~ expression is "bovine attendant" —F.D.Smith & Barbara Wilcox⟩ (2) **:** conventionally or insipidly pretty **:** conforming to traditional canons **:** not bold or vigorous ⟨a thin and ~ artistic style⟩
²**genteel** \"\ *n* -S **:** a genteel person
gen·teel·ism \jenˈtē,lizəm\ *n* -S **:** a word (as *paying guest* or *perspiration*) believed by its user to be socially preferable to a common synonym (as *boarder* or *sweat*) ⟨threatened and debased on all sides by jargon, wrong constructions, solecisms, ~*s* —*Atlantic*⟩
gen·teel·ly \-ē(ə)l(l)ē, -)i\ *adv* **:** in a genteel manner ⟨frowned ~ on Asian guests and members —Peggy Durdin⟩
gen·teel·ness \-ē(ə)lnəs\ *n* -ES **:** the quality or state of being genteel
gentes *pl of* GENS
genthel·vite \ˈgen(t)thəl,vīt, (ˈ)gentˈhel,-, genˈthel,-\ *n* -S [Frederick A. *Genth* †1893 Am. mineralogist born in Germany + E *helvite*] **:** a mineral (Zn,Fe,Mn)$_8$Be$_6$Si$_6$O$_{24}$S$_2$ consisting of a silicate and sulfide of zinc and beryllium and usu. containing also iron and manganese isomorphous with danalite and helvite
genth·ite \ˈgen,thīt\ *n* -S [F.A.*Genth* + E *-ite*] **:** a mineral approximately (Ni,Mg)$_4$Si$_3$O$_{10}$.6H$_2$O, consisting of a soft amorphous pale green or yellowish nickel magnesium silicate
gen·tian \ˈjenchən\ *n* -S [ME *gencian*, fr. MF *genciane*, *gentiane*, fr. L *gentiana*, perh. after *Gentius*, 2d cent. B.C. Illyrian king said to have discovered its virtues] **1 :** a plant of the genus *Gentiana* — see CLOSED GENTIAN, FRINGED GENTIAN **2** *also* **gentian root :** the rhizome and roots of the yellow gentian (*Gentiana lutea*) used as a tonic and stomachic

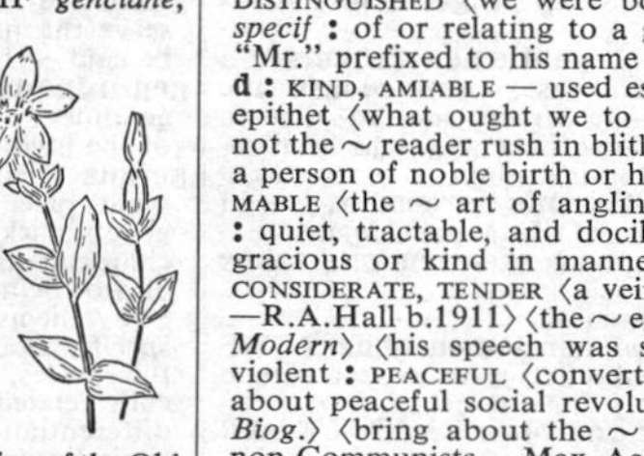
gentian of the Old World

gen·ti·ana \ˌjencheˈanə, -ˈänə,-ˈānə\ *n, cap* [NL, fr. L, gentian] **:** the type genus of Gentianaceae comprising numerous annual, biennial, or perennial herbs which have smooth opposite leaves and showy solitary or cymose flowers with 4-lobed or 5-lobed corolla and some of which contain a bitter glycoside often used as a tonic — see GENTIAN
gen·tia·na·ce·ae \ˌjench(ē)əˈnāsē,ē\ *n pl, cap* [NL, fr. *Gentiana*, type genus + *-aceae*] **:** a large nearly cosmopolitan family of chiefly herbaceous plants (order Gentianales) that usu. have showy flowers with tubular or segmented calyx and lobed corolla — see GENTIANA — **gen·tia·na·ceous** \ˌ=(=)=ˈnāshəs\ *adj*
gen·tia·na·les \-ā(,)lēz\ *n pl, cap* [NL, fr. *Gentiana* + *-ales*] **:** an order of dicotyledonous plants having gamopetalous and usu. actinomorphic flowers with two carpels and mostly opposite leaves — compare APOCYNACEAE, ASCLEPIADACEAE, GENTIANACEAE, LOGANIACEAE, OLEACEAE, SALVADORACEAE
gentian blue *n* **:** a moderate purplish blue that is redder, lighter, and stronger than marine blue, bluer and duller than average cornflower, and bluer and lighter than old glory blue
gen·tia·nel·la \ˌjench(ē)əˈnelə\ *n* -S [NL, dim. of L *gentiana*] **:** any of several gentians; *esp* **:** a low-growing perennial alpine gentian (*Gentiana acaulis*) that is often cultivated for its large showy typically blue flowers
gentian family *n* **:** GENTIANACEAE
gen·tian·in \ˈjenchənən\ *n* -S [ISV *gentian-* (fr. NL *Gentiana*) + *-in*] **1 :** GENTISIN **2 :** a bluish red anthocyanin pigment obtained in the form of the chloride C$_{30}$H$_{27}$ClO$_{14}$ from the petals of a blue gentian (*Gentiana acaulis*)
gen·tian·ose \-chə,nōs *also* -ōz\ *n* -S [ISV *gentian-* (fr. NL *Gentiana*) + *-ose*] **:** a crystalline nonreducing trisaccharide C$_{18}$H$_{32}$O$_{16}$ obtained from fresh gentian root
gentian violet *n, often cap G&V* **:** a dye consisting of one or more methyl derivatives of pararosaniline used as a biological stain, as a bactericide, fungicide, and anthelmintic, and in the treatment of burns: as **a :** CRYSTAL VIOLET **b :** METHYL VIOLET **a c :** a mixture of crystal violet and methyl violet
gentian violet lake *n, usu cap G&V&L* **:** an organic pigment — see DYE table I (under *Pigment Violet 3*)
¹**gen·tile** \ˈjen·,tīl\ *n* -S [ME *gentil, gentile*, fr. LL *gentilis* foreigner, heathen, fr. L, member of the same family or gens, fellow countryman, fr. *gentilis*, adj.] **1 a** *often cap* **:** a person of a non-Jewish nation or of non-Jewish faith; *esp* **:** a Christian as distinguished from a Jew — used esp. by Jews **b :** HEATHEN, PAGAN ⟨earnest exhortations to the ~*s* —David Daiches⟩ **c** *among the Mormons, often cap* **:** a non-Mormon **2 :** a word denoting country, race, or nationality **3** [L *gentilis*] *in Roman law* **:** a member of the same Roman gens
²**gentile** \"\ *adj* [ME *gentil, gentile*, fr. LL *gentilis* foreign, heathen, fr. L, of the same clan or family, of the same nation — more at GENTLE] **1** *often cap* **a :** belonging to the nations at large as distinguished from the Jews; *also* **:** belonging or relating to Christians as distinguished from the Jews **b :** belonging or relating to non-Mormons **2 :** PAGAN, HEATHEN **3** [L *gentilis*] **:** relating to a tribe or clan ⟨the science of ~ or tribal society —Benjamin Farrington⟩ **4 :** denoting a people or country **:** GENTILIC ⟨*Canadian* and *Irish* are ~ nouns⟩
gen·ti·lesse \ˌjentəˈles\ *n* -S [ME, fr. MF *gentilesce*, fr. *gentil* noble, pleasant, friendly + *-esce, -esse* -ess — more at GENTLE] *archaic* **:** the quality of being gentle **:** good breeding
¹**gen·til·ic** \(ˈ)jen·ˈtilik\ *adj* [L *gentilis* + E *-ic*] **1 :** TRIBAL, RACIAL, NATIONAL **2 :** of or relating to a noun or adjective that denotes ethnic or national affiliation
²**gentilic** \"\ *n* -S **:** a name with gentilic value
gentilish *adj* [²*gentile* + *-ish*] *obs* **:** HEATHENISH, GENTILE
gentilism *n* -S [¹*gentile* + *-ism*] *obs* **:** HEATHENISM, PAGANISM
gen·ti·li·tial \ˌjentəˈlishəl\ *adj* [L *gentilicius, gentilitius* (fr. *gent-, gens* clan, family, race, people) + E *-al* — more at GENTLE] **1 :** relating or peculiar to a people or family **2 :** of gentle birth **:** GENTLE
gen·ti·li·tious \-shəs\ *adj* [L *gentilicius, gentilitius*] **:** GENTILITIAL
gen·til·i·ty \jenˈtiləd·ē, -ətē, -i\ *n* -ES [ME *gentilete*, fr. MF *gentileté*, fr. L *gentilitat-, gentilitas* state or condition of belonging to the same clan or family, fr. *gentilis* of the same clan or family + *-itat-, -itas* -ity — more at GENTLE] **1 a :** the condition of belonging to the gentry or to a class ranking above the commonalty **:** gentle birth or status ⟨when her family lost its money . . . she lost her ~ and was allowed to work —Virginia Woolf⟩ **b :** the members of the upper class **:** GENTLEFOLK, GENTRY ⟨a ball given by the governor for the ~ —Esther Forbes⟩ ⟨the social strata midway between the lower ~ and the upper class of poor white —Ellen Glasgow⟩ ⟨recruit its nobility and ~ from loyal servants of . . . middle-class origin —J.W.Saunders⟩ **c :** the rank or heraldic status of a gentleman ⟨the purchase of ~ from the heralds was resented by the county gentry —F.P.Bornard⟩ **2 a** (1) **:** niceness, refinement, or decorum of conduct or manner **:** CIVILITY, POLISH, ELEGANCE, POLITENESS ⟨the ~ and sweet tolerance of liberal methods of government —S.L.A.Marshall⟩ ⟨combined . . . natural ~ and refinement of manner —G.R.Stewart⟩ ⟨a French trading post . . . with morals and manners that did not err on the side of ~ —*Amer. Guide Series: Mich.*⟩ (2) **:** extreme or excessive regard for conventional morality or ideals **:** the display of false delicacy, prudery, affectation, or excessive refinement esp. in cultural attitudes or activity ⟨instrumental in . . . the freeing of American letters from the bonds of ~ —Alexander Klein⟩ ⟨an impassioned diatribe against ~ in American literature —Mark Schorer⟩ ⟨the pervading malady of educated folk in late-nineteenth-century America — ~ —F.L.Allen⟩ **b** (1) **:** superior social status or prestige evidenced by manners, possessions, mode of life, or associations ⟨an academy . . . famous for its ~ —Nathaniel Burt⟩ ⟨the hat, like the sandals . . . were marks of ~ —Elizabeth Janeway⟩ ⟨the characteristic American attempt to maintain ~ by means of a detached house —G.R.Stewart⟩ (2) **:** the maintenance of the air, forms, or pretense of superior or middle-class social status esp. in the face of decayed elegance or prosperity ⟨a shabby ~ displayed against a . . . dreary background —David Daiches⟩ ⟨look of respectable but threadbare ~ —*N.Y.Times*⟩
gen·ti·o·bi·ose \ˌjenchēōˈbī,ōs *also* -ōz\ *n* -S [ISV, blend of *gentianose* and *bi-*] **:** a crystalline dextrorotatory disaccharide C$_{12}$H$_{22}$O$_{11}$ that is not fermented by top yeasts and that is obtained from gentianose by hydrolysis or from glucose by the action of acids; 6-β-D-glucosyl-D-glucose
gen·ti·o·pic·rin \-ˈpikrən\ *n* -S [ISV *gentio-* (fr. NL *Gentiana*) + *-picrin*] **:** a bitter crystalline glucoside C$_{16}$H$_{20}$O$_9$ obtained esp. from gentian root
gen·ti·sate \ˈjentə,sāt\ *n* -S [*gentisic* + *-ate*] **:** a salt or ester of gentisic acid
gen·tis·ic acid \(ˈ)jen·ˈti|sik-, ˈzik-\ *n* [ISV *gentisin* + *-ic*] **:** a crystalline acid C$_6$H$_3$(OH)$_2$COOH formed by fusion of gentisin with caustic and by biological oxidation of salicylic acid and used in medicine in the form of its sodium salt similarly to sodium salicylate; 2,5-dihydroxy-benzoic acid
gen·ti·sin \ˈjentəsən\ *n* -S [ISV *genti-* (fr. NL *Gentiana*, genus name of *Gentiana lutea*) + *-sin* (as in *pepsin, trypsin*)] **:** a yellow crystalline anthoxanthin pigment C$_{14}$H$_{10}$O$_5$ obtained from gentian root
¹**gen·tle** \ˈjentᵊl\ *adj* **gentler** \-t(ᵊ)lə(r)\ **gentlest** \-t(ᵊ)l-\ [ME *gentil*, fr. OF, fr. L *gentilis* of the same clan or family or race, fr. *gent-, gens* clan, family, race (fr. the stem of *gignere* to beget) + *-ilis* -ile — more at KIN] **1 a :** belonging to a family of high social station **:** of noble or aristocratic birth ⟨two distinct classes; the ~ . . . and the ungentle —E.E.Reynolds⟩; *specif* **:** having the rank or status of a gentleman (sense 1b) **b** *archaic* **:** having the qualities ascribed to a person of noble birth **:** CHIVALROUS, COURTEOUS **c :** HONORABLE, NOBLE, DISTINGUISHED ⟨we were both of ~ blood —T.B.Costain⟩; *specif* **:** of or relating to a gentleman ⟨a man of ~ birth, as "Mr." prefixed to his name . . . indicates —Eleanor Dobson⟩ **d :** KIND, AMIABLE — used esp. in address as a complimentary epithet ⟨what ought we to do, ~ sisters —W.S.Gilbert⟩ ⟨let not the ~ reader rush in blithely —D.F.Fleming⟩ **e :** suited to a person of noble birth or high social station **:** WORTHY, ESTIMABLE ⟨the ~ art of angling⟩ **2 a :** TAMED, DOMESTICATED **:** quiet, tractable, and docile ⟨a ~ horse⟩ **b** (1) **:** benignly gracious or kind in manner **:** not harsh or stern **:** MILD, CONSIDERATE, TENDER ⟨a vein of ~ irony that makes us smile —R.A.Hall b.1911⟩ ⟨the ~ eyes of my professor —*Years of the Modern*⟩ ⟨his speech was soft, his manners ~⟩ (2) **:** not violent **:** PEACEFUL ⟨convert the natives by ~ means⟩ ⟨bring about peaceful social revolution by ~ persuasion —*Current Biog.*⟩ ⟨bring about the ~ coexistence of Communists and non-Communists —Max Ascoli⟩ (3) **:** not boisterously energetic ⟨his mother came of a *gentler* and less adventurous stock — W.B.Parker⟩ **3 a** (1) **:** not rough **:** SOFT ⟨the ~ touch of her hand⟩ ⟨a ~ mind⟩ ⟨his ~ tongue —Jean Stafford⟩ (2) **:** not flowing roughly or rapidly ⟨a ~ stream⟩ **b** (1) **:** not loud or noisy **:** SOOTHING, SOFT, LOW, HUSHED ⟨a ~ voice⟩ ⟨heard a ~ knock on the door⟩ (2) **:** delicate in mood, texture, or taste **:** not harsh or blatant ⟨a ~ nocturne⟩ ⟨the most delicate and ~ pink —Geoffrey Grigson⟩ ⟨a ~ wine⟩ **4 a :** moderate in operation or degree ⟨a ~ sun shone down⟩ ⟨a ~ heat⟩ ⟨give ~ exercise every day —Emily Holt⟩ **b :** not steep ⟨a ~ hill⟩ ⟨a ~ slope⟩ **5** *dial Brit* **:** of, relating to, or frequented by fairies ⟨a ~ place⟩ ⟨~ bushes⟩ **syn** see SOFT
²**gentle** \"\ *n* -S [ME *gentil*, fr. MF, fr. *gentil*, adj.] **1 :** a person of gentle birth or status **:** GENTLEMAN ⟨a custom . . . merging the ~*s* with the burghers —G.M.Trevelyan⟩ ⟨the whole lot of them, ~*s* and simples —Virginia Woolf⟩ **2 :** MAGGOT; *esp* **:** one used as bait or as food for birds or small animals
³**gentle** \"\ *vb* -ED/-ING/-S [¹*gentle*] *vt* **1 :** to raise from the commonalty **:** ENNOBLE ⟨trading class, which having enriched itself, sought desperately to ~ itself —Sam Pollock⟩ **2 a :** to make gentle or mild in character or manner ⟨honored for *gentling* the barbarian —*New Yorker*⟩ ⟨the tough admiral *gentled* by memories of personal loss —Lee Rogow⟩ **b :** to make (an animal) tame and docile ⟨a wild pony that nobody could ~⟩ ⟨as a lion man ~*s* a cageful of cats —R.L.Taylor⟩ **c :** MOLLIFY, APPEASE, SOFTEN, PLACATE ⟨the old man is in a rage of excitement and has to be *gentled* incessantly —Clemence Dane⟩ **d** (1) **:** to make soft or smooth (as in texture, tone, or appearance) ⟨time may have *gentled* her face and hair —Kathryn Grondahl⟩ ⟨a liquid blend of herbs which ~*s* the taste of liquor —*Time*⟩ (2) **:** to make moderate (as in degree or intensity) **:** CALM ⟨play the music a little too fast . . . while others ~ it down —*New Yorker*⟩ ⟨*gentled* her nerves by reading the glad tidings again —Jean Stafford⟩ (3) **:** to stroke gently or soothingly **:** PET, FONDLE ⟨*gentled* the panther for a few minutes —Rudyard Kipling⟩ ⟨listened quietly, *gentling* a dog's ear meanwhile —James Reynolds⟩ **3 :** to make (one's way) gently ⟨a light that *gentled* its way into my parents' bedroom —Richard Church⟩ ⟨the broad-shouldered train ~*s* its way —Karl Shapiro⟩ ~ *vi* **:** to become gentle ⟨some cows never ~ —Agnes M. Cleaveland⟩ ⟨the wind *gentled* to a murmur —Kris Neville⟩ ⟨wine which . . . ~*s* with age —*Sunset*⟩
gentleboy \ˈ==,=\ *n* **:** a young gentleman ⟨accused me . . . of masquerading in the discarded cap of a ~ —F.A.Swinnerton⟩
gentle breeze *n* **:** wind having a speed of 8 to 12 miles per hour — see BEAUFORT SCALE table
gentlefolk *also* **gentlefolks** \ˈ==,=\ *n pl* **:** persons of gentle or good family and breeding ⟨~ too sure of themselves to alter their ways —S.H.Adams⟩
gentlehearted \ˈ==ˈ==\ *adj* **:** having a gentle heart
gen·tle·hood \ˈ==,hu̇d\ *n* **:** the state or position of one who is of gentle birth or nature
gentle lemur *n* **:** any of several small nocturnal lemurs (genus *Cheirogaleus* or *Mioxicebus*) living in bamboo jungles of northeastern Madagascar and feeding on shoots and roots of the bamboo
gen·tle·man \ˈjentᵊlmən, ÷-nᵊl-\ *n, pl* **gentlemen** *often attrib* [ME *gentilman*, fr. *gentil* noble, gentle + *man* — more at GENTLE] **1 a :** a man of noble or gentle birth **:** one belonging to the nobility or aristocracy **:** a man of quality ⟨the count . . . though a rogue was a ~ by birth —W.S.Maugham⟩ **b :** a man entitled to bear a coat of arms though not of noble rank **:** a member of the gentry ⟨those whose right to bear arms was not established had to sign a form of disclaimer . . . to the title of ~ —A.R.Wagner⟩ ⟨this great revolution had been brought about by the *gentlemen* of England —L.G.Pine⟩ **c** (1) **:** a man who combines gentle birth or rank with chivalrous qualities (2) **:** a man irrespective of social status having chivalrous qualities **:** a man whose conduct conforms to a certain standard of propriety or correct behavior ⟨being a ~, he rose and gave the lady his seat⟩ ⟨no girl should go out with that man; he's no ~⟩ ⟨a ~ will never let you down —Katharine F. Gerould⟩ ⟨the law of the land requires an officer of the U.S. armed forces to be a ~ —*Time*⟩ **d** (1) **:** a man of independent means who does not engage in any occupation or profession for gain **:** a man of wealth and leisure ⟨anyone in Suffolk who is not engaged in farming and appears to exist on private means is designated a ~ —Adrian Bell⟩ ⟨the curriculum was constructed for *gentlemen*; technical or vocational subjects were unknown —Benjamin Fine⟩ (2) **:** a man who does not engage in any menial occupation or in manual labor for gain ⟨ruled that he could not compete because he had once worked with his hands and was therefore not a ~ —*Time*⟩ **2 a :** VALET — often used in the phrase *gentleman's gentleman* ⟨the unctuous conversation of gentlemen's *gentlemen* —F.A.Swinnerton⟩ **b :** an attendant upon a sovereign or other person of high station who is himself of noble or gentle birth or rank **3 a :** a man whose dress, refined speech, manners, or regard for punctilio marks him as a member of the educated or upper class ⟨a ~ . . . was a man who used a butter knife even when alone —Robertson Davies⟩ ⟨a ~ don't fling stones —George Meredith⟩ **b :** a man of a lower, uneducated, or indeterminate social class or condition who is called a gentleman ⟨draymen . . . and the laborers on the canal were . . . denominated "them *gentlemen*" —Frances Trollope⟩ ⟨retired private chauffeur with 1953 car seeks another retired ~ —*N. Y. Herald Tribune*⟩ — often used in the pl. in addressing the men in an audience or group ⟨ladies and *gentlemen*⟩ ⟨these rambling talks have come to an end, *gentlemen* —Bliss Perry⟩ **c :** a man who is a member of a representative legislative body (as the U.S. House of Representatives) — used with *the* ⟨the time of the ~ from Kansas has expired —*Congressional Record*⟩ **d :** an amateur cricketer — contrasted with *player* **4 :** a formidable or dangerous opponent not to be trifled with or underrated ⟨must confess I do not like the ~, and would rather fight two Indians than one of these bears —Edmund Christopherson⟩
gentleman–at–arms \ˈ====ˈ=\ *n, pl* **gentlemen–at–arms :** one of a military corps of forty gentlemen who attend the British sovereign on state occasions — called also *gentleman pensioner*
gentleman–commoner \ˈ===ˈ===\ *n, pl* **gentlemen–commoners :** one of a privileged class of commoners formerly required to pay higher fees than ordinary commoners at the universities of Oxford and Cambridge
gentleman cow *n, pl* **gentlemen cows** *dial* **:** BULL
gentleman farmer *n, pl* **gentlemen farmers :** a man who farms for pleasure rather than for profit
gentleman friend *n, pl* **gentlemen friends :** a woman's male friend **:** BOYFRIEND ⟨a charming girl whose *gentleman friend* was said to be . . . high up in the fur business —Sinclair Lewis⟩
gentlemanlike \ˈ===,=\ *adj* **:** resembling or appropriate to a gentleman ⟨a very kind and ~ individual —W.M.Thackeray⟩ — **gen·tle·man·like·ness** *n* -ES
gen·tle·man·li·ness \ˈ===lēnəs, -lin-\ *n* -ES **:** the quality or state of being gentlemanly
¹**gen·tle·man·ly** \-lē, -li\ *adv* [ME *gentilmanly*, fr. *gentilman* + *-ly* (adv. suffix)] **:** in the manner of a gentleman ⟨he was sitting ~ up in the . . . taxi —Saul Bellow⟩
²**gentlemanly** \"\ *adj* [ME *gentilmanly*, fr. *gentilman* + *-ly* (adj. suffix)] **:** having the character of or characteristic of a gentleman in nature, behavior, or appearance ⟨~ instincts⟩

gentleman of fortune : a gentleman seeking his fortune in daring or risky enterprises : ADVENTURER
gentleman-pensioner \ˌ⸗⸗⸗ˈ⸗(⸗)⸗\ *n, pl* **gentlemen-pensioners :** GENTLEMAN-AT-ARMS
gentleman-ranker \ˌ⸗⸗⸗ˈ⸗⸗\ *n, pl* **gentlemen-rankers :** a gentleman serving in the British army as an enlisted man ⟨the *gentleman-ranker* that Kipling met from time to time in India . . . was in many cases an ex-officer who had been removed from his regiment —C.S.Jarvis⟩
gentleman's agreement *or* **gentlemen's agreement** *n* **:** an agreement secured only by the honor of the participants
gentleman's-cane \ˈ⸗⸗⸗ˌ⸗\ *n, pl* **gentleman's-canes :** PRINCE'S-FEATHER 2
gentleman's sorrel *n* **:** SHEEP SORREL 1
gentleman-usher \ˌ⸗⸗⸗ˈ⸗⸗\ *n, pl* **gentlemen-ushers** [ME *gentilman husher*] **:** a gentleman who acts as usher to a person of rank
gentleman-usher of the black rod *often cap G&U&B&R* **:** BLACK ROD
gentlemen-and-ladies \ˌ⸗⸗⸗⸗ˈ⸗⸗\ *n pl but sing or pl in constr* **:** a shooting star (*Dodecatheon meadia*)
gen·tle·ness *n* -ES [ME *gentilnesse*, fr. *gentil* gentle + *-nesse* -ness — more at GENTLE] **:** the quality or state of being gentle; *esp* **:** mildness of manners or disposition
gentlepeople \ˈ⸗⸗,⸗⸗\ *n pl* **:** GENTLEFOLK
gentler *comparative of* GENTLE
gentles *pres 3d sing of* GENTLE, *pl of* GENTLE
gentle sex *n* **:** the female sex **:** women in general — used with *the* ⟨a member of the *gentle sex*⟩
gentlest *superlative of* GENTLE
gentle thistle *n* **:** a coarse European herb (*Cirsium anglicum*) with prickly-margined leaves
gentlewoman \ˈ⸗⸗,⸗⸗\ *n, pl* **gentlewomen** [ME *gentilwoman*, fr. *gentil* + *woman*] **1 a :** a woman of noble or gentle birth **:** a woman of quality ⟨a ~ of good and honorable stock —Francis Hackett⟩ ⟨a lady, as ladies went in Colombia . . . but she wasn't a ~ —Donn Byrne⟩ **b :** a woman attendant upon a lady of rank **2 :** a woman of refined manners or good breeding **:** LADY ⟨~ seeks part-time employment as companion or social secretary —*Saturday Rev.*⟩ **3 :** a woman member of a representative legislative body (as the U.S. House of Representatives) — used with *the* ⟨the chair recognizes the ~ from Connecticut⟩
gen·tle·wo·man·ly \ˈ⸗⸗,⸗⸗,lē, -li\ *adj* **:** having the appearance, traits, or character of a gentlewoman ⟨a valiant and ~ flourish —Rose Macaulay⟩
gentling *pres part of* GENTLE
gent·ly \ˈjentlē, -li\ *adv* [ME *gentilly*, fr. *gentil* gentle + *-ly* — more at GENTLE] **:** in a gentle manner: as **a** (1) **:** NOBLY, HONORABLY ⟨hated women ~ born —John Masefield⟩ (2) **:** COURTEOUSLY, SOFTLY, ELEGANTLY ⟨~ mannered family —G.B.Shaw⟩ ⟨a ~ spoken young man (3) **:** in an atmosphere of elegance or refinement **:** with much attention to good manners or deportment ⟨~ bred people who had never been forced to face much unpleasantness in the world —J.R.Chamberlain⟩ ⟨public schools were not to be considered for a ~ bred young girl —Maude Couch⟩ **b** (1) **:** QUIETLY, GRADUALLY, SLOWLY ⟨the wind whistling ~⟩ ⟨parkland that lifts ~ toward rolling hills —Frederick Nebel⟩ ⟨sway ~ back and forth —Fred Zimmer⟩ ⟨the slide in industrial production will continue ~ —D.M.Keezer⟩ ⟨the trout is ~ boiled —Jane Nickerson⟩ (2) **:** ²EASY ⟨for the first two weeks I took things ~ —*Linguaphone Mag.*⟩ **c :** with gentleness **:** MILDLY, TENDERLY ⟨humorous and ~ satiric verses —*Encyc. Americana*⟩
gen·too \ˈjen,tü, ⸗ˈ⸗\ *n* -S [Pg *gentio*, lit., Gentile, fr. LL *gentilis* — more at GENTILE] **1** *usu cap, archaic* **:** HINDU **2** *or* **gentoo penguin :** a penguin (*Pygoscelis papua*) of the subantarctic islands with a slaty gray back and throat, white underparts, and white spots above the eyes and on the back and side of the neck
gen·trice \ˈjen·trəs\ *n* -S [ME *gentrise*, fr. OF *genterise*, alter. of *gentilise*, *gentelise*, fr. *gentil* noble, gentle — more at GENTLE] *archaic* **:** gentility of birth **:** RANK
gen·try \ˈjen·trē, -ri\ *n* -ES [ME *gentrie*, alter. of *gentrise*] **1 a** *obs* **:** the qualities ascribed or appropriate to a man of gentle birth **:** good breeding **:** GENEROSITY, COURTESY ⟨show us so much ~ and goodwill —Shak.⟩ **b :** the condition or rank of a gentleman ⟨a favorite topic of discussion was whether apprenticeship to trade annulled ~ —A.R.Wagner⟩ **2 a :** people of quality or the class to which they belong **:** upper or ruling class **:** NOBILITY, ARISTOCRACY, ELITE ⟨retains the idea of the ~ versus the lower classes —Sinclair Lewis⟩ ⟨the two chief classes of New England: the yeomanry . . . and the ~, a group of capable merchants —V.L.Parrington⟩ ⟨a ~ . . . a class of rich people able to cultivate themselves with an expensive education —G.B.Shaw⟩ **b :** a class whose members are entitled to bear a coat of arms though not of noble rank; *esp* **:** the landed proprietors having such status ⟨the English ~ have never had the permanence of the Scottish landed families —L.G.Pine⟩ **c :** a class of landed proprietors marked by an aristocratic spirit and typically wielding large economic, social, and political influence; *also* **:** the persons making up such a class ⟨rural ~ from the 169 towns of Connecticut —*Amer. Guide Series: Conn.*⟩ ⟨no love was lost between . . . ~ and hillbilly commoners —C.V.Woodward⟩ **3 a :** people of a specified class or kind **:** FOLKS ⟨redingotes in the loud, colored checks, popular with the sporting ~ —*N.Y.Times*⟩ **b :** a particular group of people of doubtful, erroneous, or improper ideas, manners, or conduct ⟨they do a lot of damage . . . these ~ with their open diplomacy, openly arrived at —Howard Spring⟩ ⟨provide a wealth of . . . data on the activities of these ~ —*Amer. Polit. Sci. Rev.*⟩ **4** *dial chiefly Brit* **:** FAIRIES ⟨the ~ who harass travelers with tricks —James Reynolds⟩
gents *pl of* GENT
gen·ty \ˈjenti\ *adj* [prob. modif. of F *gentil* — more at GENTLE] **1** *chiefly Scot* **:** dainty and graceful **2** *chiefly Scot* **:** COURTEOUS, GENTEEL ⟨~ manners⟩
genu \ˈjē(,)n(y)ü, ˈje(-; ˈge(,)nü\ *n, pl* **gen·ua** \ˈjenyəwə, ˈgenəwə\ [NL, fr. L, knee — more at KNEE] **:** KNEE 4c — **gen·u·al** \ˈjenyəwəl\ *adj*
gen·u·flect \ˈjenyə,flekt\ *vi* -ED/-ING/-S [LL *genuflectere* to genuflect, fr. L *genu* knee + *flectere* to bend] **1 a :** to bend the knee **b :** to touch the knee to the floor or ground esp. in worship ⟨~ and walk out of the chapel —Joseph Dever⟩ **2 :** to be servilely or humbly obedient or respectful **:** KOWTOW ⟨each political party has ~*ed* before it —B.M.Bowie⟩ ⟨~*ed* before the . . . bureaucrats and rewrote their poems —Harvey Breit⟩
gen·u·flec·tion *also* **gen·u·flex·ion** \ˌ⸗⸗ˈflekshən, ˈ⸗⸗,⸗⸗\ *n* [LL *genuflexion-*, *genuflexio*, fr. *genuflexus* (past part. of *genuflectere*) + *-ion-*, *-io* -ion] **1 :** the act or an instance of bending the knee and sometimes touching it to the floor or ground esp. in worship **2 :** the act or an instance of according servile or humble obedience or respect **:** a respectful gesture ⟨a ~ in the direction of Marxist orthodoxy —Alex Inkeles⟩
gen·u·flec·to·ry \ˌ⸗⸗ˈflekt(ə)rē\ *adj* **:** relating to or characterized by genuflection ⟨the tone of his mother's voice, sad, velvety, ~ —Mary McCarthy⟩
gen·u·ine \ˈjenyəwən *sometimes* ÷-,wīn\ *adj* [L *genuinus*, prob. irreg. (influence of *ingenuus* native, free-born) fr. *gen-* (stem of *gignere* to beget) + *-inus* -ine — more at INGENUOUS, KIN] **1** *obs* **:** not foreign **:** NATIVE, NATURAL **2 a :** actually having the reputed or apparent qualities or character **:** not adulterated or cheapened **:** PURE ⟨a ~ fine quality tea⟩ ⟨a ~ vintage wine⟩ **b :** actually produced by or proceeding from the reputed or alleged source or author **:** not faked or counterfeit **:** AUTHENTIC ⟨a ~ antique⟩ ⟨a ~ signature⟩ ⟨a ~ text⟩ **c :** sincerely and honestly felt or experienced **:** not forced but arising naturally **:** not feigned, factitious, or hypocritical ⟨the child of sinful but ~ love —H.O.Brogan⟩ **d :** having a real existence **:** conforming to reality **:** not abstract or frivolous ⟨the questions which are asked . . . are ~ questions —John Dewey⟩ ⟨~ confrontations of the human condition —Anthony Quinton⟩ **e :** conforming precisely to its name or description **:** properly so called **:** TRUE ⟨a ~ conservative⟩ ⟨a ~ idealist⟩ ⟨a slight sprinkling of ~ pickpockets —Joseph Conrad⟩ **3 :** of or relating to the original stock ⟨the ~ breed of mastiffs⟩ **4 :** free from hypocrisy or pretense **:** SINCERE, FRANK ⟨could be friends with anyone who was ~, not a snob, not a prig, not a pedant —H.S.Canby⟩ ⟨how much more ~ . . . their work than the pretentious efforts of our contemporaries —Henry Miller⟩ **syn** see AUTHENTIC
gen·u·ine·ly *adv* **:** in a genuine manner ⟨policies which will ~ serve the national interests —A.M.Schlesinger b.1917⟩ ⟨can be said ~ to aim at a scientific . . . treatment —M.R.Cohen⟩
gen·u·ine·ness \-n(n)əs\ *n* -ES **:** the quality or state of being genuine ⟨would hesitate on the threshold, mistrusting the ~ of the invitation —H.F.Ellis⟩
ge·nus \ˈjēnəs *sometimes* ˈjen-\ *n, pl* **gen·era** \ˈjenərə\ [L, birth, race, class, kind — more at KIN] **1 :** a class, kind, or group marked by common characteristics or by one common characteristic **:** a group capable of including subgroups and also of being subsumed in a larger group ⟨such streams are a ~ by themselves and not miniature rivers —John Buchan⟩; *specif* **:** a taxonomic category ranking between the family and the species, comprising a group of structurally or phylogenetically related species or an isolated species exhibiting unusual differentiation, and being designated by a Latin or latinized capitalized singular noun which constitutes the first word of the technical name of a species or of any of its subdivisions and which is often used usu. uncapitalized and pluralized with a regular ending or sometimes a latinate plural as a vernacular name for plants or animals of the included species ⟨the species of oak collectively form the ~ *Quercus*⟩ — compare CLASSIFICATION 1a, NOMENCLATURE 4c **2** [NL, fr. L] **:** a class of objects divided into several subordinate species **:** a class more extensive than a species **3 :** MODE; *specif* **:** one of three basic tetrachords in Greek music **syn** see CLASS
genu val·gum \-ˈvalgəm\ *n* [NL] **:** KNOCK-KNEE
genu va·rum \-ˈva(a)rəm\ *n* [NL] **:** BOWLEG
geny- *or* **genyo-** *comb form* [ISV, fr. Gk *genys* jaw, chin — more at CHIN] **:** lower jaw ⟨*genyo*plasty⟩
-ge·ny \jənē, -ni\ *n comb form* -ES [Gk *-geneia* act of being born, fr. *-genēs* born + *-ia* -y — more at -GEN] **:** generation **:** production **:** science of origin ⟨chondro*geny*⟩ ⟨morpho*geny*⟩ ⟨onto*geny*⟩
geo \ˈgyō\ *n* -S [of Scand origin; *akin to* ON *gjā* chasm, Norw dial. *gjo, jo;* akin to OE *geonian* to yawn — more at YAWN] *Scot* **:** a deep narrow rocky-sided coastal inlet — often used in place names
geo- — see GE-
geoanticline *var of* GEANTICLINE
ge·o·bi·ont \ˌjēōˈbī,änt, jēˈōbē,-\ *n* [*ge-* + *-biont*] **:** an organism inhabiting the soil
geo·botanical \ˌjē(,)ō+\ *also* **geo·botanic** \"+\ *adj* [*ge-* + *botanical, botanic*] **:** of or relating to phytogeography — **geo·botanically** \"+\ *adv*
geo·botanist \"+\ *n* [*ge-* + *botanist*] **:** PHYTOGEOGRAPHER
geo·botany \"+\ *n* [*ge-* + *botany*] **:** PHYTOGEOGRAPHY
ge·o·car·pic \ˌjēōˈkärpik\ *adj* [ISV *ge-* + *-carpic*] **:** producing or ripening the fruit beneath the surface of the ground ⟨the peanut is one of the few plants . . . which are ~ —W.P.Jacobs⟩ — **ge·o·car·py** \ˈ⸗⸗,⸗pē\ *n* -ES
ge·o·cen·tric \ˌjēōˈsen·trik, -rēk\ *adj* [*ge-* + *-centric*] **1 :** relating to, measured from, or as if observed from the earth's center **:** having or relating to the earth as center — compare HELIOCENTRIC **2 :** taking or based on the earth as the center of perspective and valuation — **ge·o·cen·tri·cal·ly** \-rək(ə)lē, -rēk-, -li\ *adv*
ge·o·cen·tri·cism \ˌ⸗⸗ˈsen·trə,sizəm\ *n* -S **:** a geocentric theory or belief
geocentric latitude *n* **1 :** the celestial latitude of a body as seen from the earth's center **2 :** the angle between the plane of the celestial equator and a line from the earth's center to a given point on the earth's surface — compare TERRESTRIAL LATITUDE
geocentric longitude *n* **1 :** celestial longitude based on or as seen from the earth's center — opposed to *heliocentric longitude* **2 :** GEOGRAPHICAL LONGITUDE
geocentric parallax *n* **:** the difference in the apparent direction or position of a celestial body as observed from the center of the earth and from a point on the surface of the earth
ge·o·ce·rite \ˌjēōˈsi,rīt\ *also* **ge·o·ce·rain** \-ˈsi,rān\ *n* -S [*geocerite* modif. (influenced by *-ite*) of G *geozerain*, fr. *geo-* ge- + L *cera* wax + G *-in*; *geocerain* fr. G *geozerain* — more at CEREOUS] **:** a mineral consisting of carbon, hydrogen, and oxygen occurring as a white waxy substance in brown coal
geo·chemical \ˌjēō+\ *adj* [*ge-* + *chemical*] **:** of, relating to, or using the methods of geochemistry — **geo·chemically** \"+\ *adv*
geochemical prospecting *n* **:** prospecting for minerals with portable chemical kits designed for rapid testing of metallic elements in surface waters
geo·chemist \ˌjēō+\ *n* [*ge-* + *chemist*] **:** a specialist in geochemistry
geo·chemistry \"+\ *n* [*ge-* + *chemistry*] **1 :** a science that deals with the chemical composition of and the actual or possible chemical changes in the crust of the earth **:** earth chemistry **2 :** the related chemical and geological properties of a substance ⟨the ~ of the rare earths⟩
geo·chronic \ˌjēō+\ *adj* [*ge-* + *chronic*] **:** of or relating to geochrony
geo·chronological *or* **geo·chronologic** \"+\ *adj* [*ge-* + *chronological, chronologic*] **:** of or relating to geochronology
geo·chronologist \"+\ *n* **:** a specialist in geochronology
geo·chronology \"+\ *n* [*ge-* + *chronology*] **:** the chronology of the past as indicated by geologic data rather than human records
geo·chronometric \"+\ *adj* [*ge-* + *chronometric*] **:** of or relating to geochronometry
geo·chronometry \"+\ *n* [*ge-* + *chronometry*] **:** the measurement of past time by geochronological methods, esp. those involving radioactive minerals or elements
ge·och·ro·ny \jēˈäkrənē\ *n* -ES [*ge-* + Gk *chronos* time + E *-y*] **:** geologic chronology **:** a system of time divisions used in geology
ge·o·cline \ˈjēō,klīn\ *n* [*ge-* + *-cline*] **:** the gradation in variation of any widespread polytypic group of organisms along geographical lines — compare ALLEN'S RULE, BERGMANN'S RULE
ge·o·coc·cyx \ˌjēōˈkäksiks\ *n, cap* [NL, fr. *ge-* + Gk *kokkyx* cuckoo — more at CUCKOO] **:** a genus of birds (family Cuculidae) comprising the roadrunners
ge·o·crat·ic \ˌjēōˈkrad·ik\ *adj* [ISV *ge-* + *-cratic* (as in *democratic*)] **:** of or relating to predominance or enlargement of land areas in relation to oceanic areas
ge·oc·ro·nite \jēˈäkrə,nīt\ *n* -S [G *geokronit*, fr. *geo-* ge- + *Kronos*, leader of the Titans in Greek mythology (fr. Gk) + G *-it* -ite] **:** a mineral $Pb_5(Sb,As)_2S_8$ consisting of a usu. massive lead-gray lead antimony arsenic sulfide
geo·cyclic \ˌjēō+\ *adj* [*ge-* + *cyclic*] **1 :** circling round the earth periodically **2 :** of, relating to, or illustrating the rotation of the earth ⟨a ~ machine⟩
ge·ode \ˈjē,ōd\ *n* -S [L *geodes*, fr. Gk *geōdēs* earthlike, fr. *gē* earth] **1 :** a nodule of stone having a cavity lined with crystals or mineral matter **2 :** the cavity in a geode
¹ge·o·des·ic \ˌjēəˈdesik, -ˈdēs-\ *adj* [F *géodésique*, fr. *géodésie* + *-ique* -ic, -ical] **1** *also* **ge·o·des·i·cal** \-səkəl\ **:** GEODETIC **2 :** constructed in the form of a geodesic dome ⟨a ~ house⟩
²geodesic \"\ *also* **geodesic line** *n* -S **:** the shortest line between two points on a mathematically derived surface (as a straight line on a plane or an arc of a great circle on a sphere)
geodesic dome *n* **:** a dome or vault made of light straight structural elements largely in tension ⟨the principle of the *geodesic dome* is an effort to reduce most structural stresses to tensions . . . and to reduce the weight of the structure to a point at which the building and the manufacture of building parts will be more economical —Peter Blake⟩
ge·od·e·sist *also* **ge·od·e·cist** \jēˈädəsəst\ *n* -S [*geodesist* fr. *geodesy* + *-ist*; *geodecist* alter. of *geodesist*] **:** a specialist in geodesy
ge·od·e·sy \-dəsē, -si\ *n* -ES [Gk *geōdaisia*, fr. *geō-* ge- + *daisia* (fr. *dais-*, stem of *daiesthai* to divide + *-ia* -y) — more at TIDE] **1 :** a branch of applied mathematics that determines by observation and measurement the exact positions of points and the figures and areas of large portions of the earth's surface, the shape and size of the earth, and the variations of terrestrial gravity and magnetism **2 :** GEODETIC SURVEYING
ge·o·det·ic \ˌjēəˈded·ik, -et|, |ēk-\ *also* **ge·o·det·i·cal** \|əkəl, |ēk-\ *adj* [fr. *geodesy*, after such pairs as E *genetic: genesis*] **1 :** of, relating to, or determined by geodesy **2 :** relating to the geometry of geodetic lines **3 :** employing metal strips built up in a basket-weave pattern in such a way that the material is distributed in proportion to the applied stresses — used of a type of airplane construction — **ge·o·det·i·cal·ly** \|ək(ə)lē, |ēk-, -li\ *adv*
geodetic latitude *n* **:** astronomical latitude corrected for station error
geodetic line *n* **:** a geodesic line on the earth
geodetic longitude *n* **:** GEOGRAPHICAL LONGITUDE
ge·o·det·ics \ˌ⸗⸗ˈded·iks\ *n pl but sing in constr* **:** GEODESY
geodetic survey *n* **:** a survey of a large land area in which corrections are made for the curvature of the earth's surface
geodetic surveying *also* **geodetic engineering** *n* **:** surveying in which account is taken of and corrections made for the curvature of the earth's surface — compare PLANE SURVEYING
ge·o·dia \jēˈōdēə\ *n, cap* [NL, fr. Gk *geōdēs* earthlike + NL *-ia* — more at GEODE] **:** a genus (the type of the family Geodiidae) of large deep-sea sponges of the class Demospongiae with anchoring structures that resemble roots — **ge·od·i·id** \-dēəd\ *adj or n*
ge·od·ic \(ˈ)jēˈädik\ *or* **ge·o·dal** \(ˈ)jēˈōdᵊl\ *adj* [*geode* + *-ic* or *-al*] **:** of, relating to, or resembling a geode
ge·o·dif·er·ous \ˌjēˌōˈdif(ə)rəs\ *adj* [*geode* + *-i-* + *-ferous*] **:** containing geodes
Ge·o·dim·e·ter \ˌjēōˈdimədə(r)\ *trademark* — used for an electronic-optical device that measures distance on the basis of the velocity of light
ge·od·ist \ˈjē,ōdəst\ *n* -S [*geode* + *-ist*] **:** a student of geodes
geo·duck *or* **go·ey·duc** *or* **goo·ey·duck** *or* **gwe·duc** \ˈgüē,dək\ *n* -S [Chinook Jargon *go-duck*, of Chinookan origin; akin to Chinook *-tgwi-* neck and *-tk* something attached to something else] **:** a very large edible clam (*Panope generosa*) that weighs over five pounds, has siphons which when fully extended measure several feet in length and cannot be withdrawn into the shell, and is found burrowing deeply in sandy mud along the Pacific coast of No. America
geo·dynamic *or* **geo·dynamical** \ˌjēˌō+\ *adj* [ISV *ge-* + *dynamic, dynamical*] **:** of or relating to dynamic forces or processes within the earth
geo·dynamics \"+\ *n pl but sing in constr* [ISV *ge-* + *dynamics*] **:** a study of dynamic forces or processes within the earth
geo-economic \"+\ *adj* [*ge-* + *economic*] **:** of, relating to, or characterized by economic conditions or policies that are influenced by geographic factors and exist or are carried out on the international level ⟨a *geo-economic* atlas⟩
ge·o·gen \ˈjēəjən, -ə,jen\ *n* -S [ISV *ge-* + *-gen*] **:** a physical, biologic, or human environmental factor occurring in a particular region and favoring the development of particular diseases — distinguished from *pathogen*
ge·og·e·nous \(ˈ)jēˈäjənəs\ *adj* [*ge-* + *-genous*] **:** growing on or in the ground
ge·o·glos·sa·ce·ae \ˌjē(,)ō,gläˈsāsē,ē\ *n pl, cap* [NL, fr. *Geoglossum*, type genus + *-aceae*] **:** a family (order Helotiales) of ascomycetous fungi having the hymenium covering the upper convex part of clavate or cap-shaped fruiting bodies
ge·o·glos·sum \ˌ⸗⸗ˈgläsəm\ *n, cap* [NL, fr. *ge-* + *-glossum* (fr. Gk *glōssa* tongue) — more at GLOSS] **:** the type genus of Geoglossaceae comprising the earthtongues
¹geo·glyphic \ˌjēō+\ *adj* [*ge-* + *glyphic*] **:** of or relating to geoglyphics
²geoglyphic \"\ *n* -S **:** a mark (as an amphibian track or worm trail) found in rock and giving evidence of past geological events
ge·og·nost \ˈjē,äg,näst, ˈjēəg-; jēˈäg,näst, -,nəst\ *also* **ge·og·no·sist** \jēˈägnəsəst\ *n* -S [*geognost* fr. F *géognoste*, fr. *géo-* ge- + Gk *gnōstēs* one that knows, fr. *gignōskein* to know; *geognosist* fr. *geognosy* + *-ist*] **:** a specialist in geognosy
ge·og·nos·tic \ˌjēˌägˈnästik, ˌjēəg-\ *or* **ge·og·nos·ti·cal** \-təkəl\ *adj* **:** of or relating to geognosy — **ge·og·nos·ti·cal·ly** \-tək(ə)lē\ *adv*
ge·og·no·sy \jēˈägnəsē\ *n* -ES [ISV *ge-* + *-gnosy*] **:** a branch of geology that deals with the materials of the earth and its general exterior and interior constitution
ge·o·gon·ic \ˌjēəˈgänik\ *or* **ge·o·gon·i·cal** \-nəkəl\ *adj* [ISV *geogony* + *-ic*, *-ical*] **:** of or relating to geogony
ge·og·o·ny \jēˈägənē\ *n* -ES [*ge-* + *-gony*] **:** a science or a theory of the formation of the earth
ge·og·ra·pher \jēˈägrəfə(r) *also* ÷ˈjäg-, *chiefly in substand speech* -gəf-\ *n* -S [LL *geographus* (fr. Gk *geōgraphos*, fr. *geō-* ge- + *-graphos*, fr. *graphein* to write) + E *-er* — more at CARVE] **:** a specialist in geography
geographer cone *n* [so called fr. the resemblance of the blotches to the appearance of land masses upon a map] **:** a somewhat barrel-shaped venomous Indo-Pacific cone (*Conus geographus*) whose shell is mottled with brown blotches
ge·o·graph·ic \ˌjēəˈgrafik, -fēk\ *or* **ge·o·graph·i·cal** \-fəkəl, -fēk-\ *adj* [LL *geographicus*, fr. Gk *geōgraphikos*, fr. *geōgraphein* to describe the surface of the earth + *-ikos* -ic, -ical — more at GEOGRAPHY] **1 :** of or relating to geography ⟨~ field techniques —P.E.James⟩ **2 :** belonging to or characteristic of a particular region ⟨the special ~ and industrial perplexities in such industries as lumber, tool and die making —S.T. Williamson & Herbert Harris⟩ — **ge·o·graph·i·cal·ly** \-fək(ə)lē, -fēk-, -li\ *adv*
geographical biology *n* **:** BIOGEOGRAPHY
geographical botany *n* **:** PHYTOGEOGRAPHY
geographical coordinate *n* **:** either of the two lines of latitude and longitude whose intersection determines the geographical point of a place
geographical distribution *n* **:** the natural arrangement and apportionment of the various forms of animals and plants in the different regions and localities of the earth
geographical latitude *n* **:** the angle between the plane of the earth's equator and the line perpendicular to the standard spheroid at a given point on the earth's surface — compare TERRESTRIAL LATITUDE
geographical longitude *n* **:** terrestrial longitude based on the meridian defined by the perpendicular to the standard spheroid at the observer's position — called also *geodetic longitude*
geographical mile *n* **:** NAUTICAL MILE
geographical point *or* **geographical position** *n* **:** the point on the earth's surface for which a given celestial body is in the astronomical zenith
geographic race *n* **:** a subdivision of a biological species coincident with a geographic region and presumably the resultant of environmental peculiarities **:** a geographic subspecies — called also *geographical variety*
ge·o·graph·ics \ˌjēəˈgrafiks, -fēks\ *n pl but sing in constr* **:** GEOGRAPHY
geographic terrapin *or* **geographic tortoise** *n* [so called fr. the resemblance of its shell to a map] **:** MAP TURTLE
geographic tongue *n* [so called fr. the resemblance of the patches to land masses on a map] **:** a condition in which the tongue exhibits smooth patches surrounded by slightly elevated grayish margins — called also *wandering rash*
geographic variation *n* **:** the differentiation of distinctive subdivisions from geographically isolated parts of a potentially interbreeding population due to restriction of interbreeding between fractions and natural selection of locally valuable mutations **:** the primary mechanism of subspeciation
ge·og·ra·phize \jēˈägrə,fīz *also* ÷ˈjäg-\ *vb* -ED/-ING/-S [*geography* + *-ize*] *vi* **:** to study geography ~ *vt* **:** to study or describe the geography of **:** treat geographically
ge·og·ra·phy \jēˈägrəfē, -fi *also* ÷ˈjäg-, *chiefly in substand speech* -gəf-\ *n* -ES *often attrib* [L *geographia*, fr. Gk *geōgraphia*, fr. *geōgraphein* to describe the surface of the earth (fr. *geō-* ge- + *graphein* to write) + *-ia* -y — more at CARVE] **1 :** a science that deals with the earth and its life; *esp* **:** the description of land, sea, air, and the distribution of plant and animal life including man and his industries with reference to the mutual relations of these diverse elements — see BIOGEOGRAPHY, COMMERCIAL GEOGRAPHY, ECONOMIC GEOGRAPHY, MATHEMATICAL GEOGRAPHY, PHYSICAL GEOGRAPHY, POLITICAL GEOGRAPHY **2 :** the geographic features of an area ⟨the ~ of Ohio⟩ **3 :** a treatise on geography **4 :** a delineation or systematic arrangement of constituent elements

: CONFIGURATION ⟨the philosophers . . . have tried to construct *geographies* of human reason —*Times Lit. Supp.*⟩

geography cone *n* : GEOGRAPHER CONE

geo·history \ˌjē(ˌ)ō+\ *n* [*ge-* + *history*] : history interpreted on the basis of geographic factors

geo·hydrologist \"+\ *n* : a specialist in geohydrology

geo·hydrology \"+\ *n* [*ge-* + *hydrology*] : a science that deals with the character, source, and mode of occurrence of underground water

ge·oid \ˈjēˌȯid\ *n* -s [G, fr. Gk *geoeidēs* earthlike, fr. *ge-* + *-oeidēs* -oid] : the surface within or around the earth that is everywhere normal to the direction of gravity, coincides with mean sea level in the oceans, and approximates to the shape of an ellipsoid of revolution — **ge·oi·dal** \(ˈ)jēˈȯidᵊl\ *adj*

geo·isotherm \ˌjē(ˌ)ō+\ *n* [ISV *ge-* + *isotherm*] : ISOGEOTHERM

ge·ol·o·ger \jēˈäləjə(r)\ *or* **ge·o·lo·gian** \ˌjēəˈlōj(ē)ən\ *n* -s [*geology* + *-er* or *-ian*] : GEOLOGIST

ge·o·log·ic \ˌjēəˈläjik, -jēk\ *or* **ge·o·log·i·cal** \-jəkəl, -jēk-\ *adj* [*geology* + *-ic, -ical*] : of, relating to, or based on geology : described or ascertained by geology ⟨~ strata⟩ ⟨a ~ lecture⟩ — **ge·o·log·i·cal·ly** \-jək(ə)lē, -jēk-, -li\ *adv*

geological age *n* : an age earlier than the postglacial and hence datable only by geology

geological survey *n* **1** : a systematic examination of an area to determine the character, relations, distribution, and origin or mode of formation of its rock masses and mineral resources **2** *usu cap G&S* : a governmental bureau charged with making geological surveys

geologic column *n* **1** : a columnar diagram that shows the rock formations of a locality or region and that is arranged to indicate their relations to the subdivisions of geologic time **2** : the sequence of rock formations in a geologic column

ge·o·lo·gi·cian \ˌjēəlōˈjishən\ *n* -s : GEOLOGIST

geologic section *n* : the sequence of rock strata or lithologic units in a locality : the local geologic column

geologic thermometer *n* : a mineral or mineral aggregate that yields information concerning the limits of temperature within which it was formed

geologic time *n* : the long period dealt with by historical geology; *esp* : the period prior to human history

ge·ol·o·gist \jēˈäləjəst\ *n* -s [*geology* + *-ist*] : a specialist in geology

ge·ol·o·gize \-ˌjīz\ *vb* -ED/-ING/-S [*geology* + *-ize*] *vi* : to study geology or make geologic investigations ~ *vt* : to study geologically

ge·ol·o·graph \-ˌgraf, -råf\ *n* [*geology* + *-graph*] : an automatic recorder of the rate of penetration of a bit during rotary drilling of wells

ge·ol·o·gy \jēˈäləjē, -ji\ *n* -ES *often attrib* [NL *geologia*, fr. *geo-* ge- + *-logia* -logy] **1** : a science that deals with the history of the earth and its life esp. as recorded in the rocks — see DYNAMIC GEOLOGY, ECONOMIC GEOLOGY, ENGINEERING GEOLOGY, GEOGNOSY, HISTORICAL GEOLOGY, PALEONTOLOGIC GEOLOGY, PHYSICAL GEOLOGY, PHYSIOGRAPHIC GEOLOGY, STRATIGRAPHY, STRUCTURAL GEOLOGY **2** : the geologic features of an area : the attributes of rocks, rock formations, or rock constituents of a district ⟨the ~ of Massachusetts⟩ **3** : a treatise on geology

geo·magnetic \ˌjē(ˌ)ō+\ *adj* [*ge-* + *magnetic*] **1** : dealing with, derived from, or relating to terrestrial magnetism **2** : of or relating to the geomagnetic field

geomagnetic equator *n* : the great circle of the earth whose plane is perpendicular to the axis of the geomagnetic field — compare MAGNETIC EQUATOR

geomagnetic field *n* : a conventionalized symmetrical approximation of the earth's magnetic field having one diameter of the earth as its axis

geo·magnetician \"+\ *n* : a geophysicist who specializes in terrestrial magnetism

geomagnetic latitude *n* : a system of latitude reckoned like geographical latitude but along the geomagnetic meridians from the geomagnetic equator

geomagnetic meridian *n* : a great circle of the earth through the geomagnetic poles — compare MAGNETIC MERIDIAN

geomagnetic pole *n* : either of two spots on the earth's surface that are at the ends of the axis of the geomagnetic field and that do not coincide with the geographical poles or the magnetic poles

geo·magnetism \ˌjē(ˌ)ō+\ *n* [*ge-* + *magnetism*] : TERRESTRIAL MAGNETISM

ge·om·a·lic \jēˈämə(ˌ)lik, ˌjēōˈmalik\ *adj* [*ge-* + Gk *homalos* level, even (fr. *homos* common, same) + E *-ic* — more at SAME] : of or relating to geomalism

ge·om·a·lism \jēˈäməˌlizəm\ *n* -s [*ge-* + Gk *homalismos* action of leveling, fr. *homalos* + *-ismos* -ism] : a tendency of an organism to be influenced in growth by gravitation so that one side or lateral organ balances with another

ge·o·man·cer \ˈjēəˌman(t)sə(r)\ *n* -s [ME, fr. *geomancie* + *-er*] : one that practices geomancy ⟨went and found a ~ and asked him for a lucky day for burials —Pearl Buck⟩

ge·o·man·cy \-sē\ *n* -ES [ME *geomancie*, fr. MF, fr. ML *geomantia*, fr. LGk *geōmanteia*, fr. Gk *geō-* ge- + *-manteia* -mancy] : divination by means of configurations of earth or by means of figures derived from even or odd numbers of dots jotted down hastily at random

ge·o·man·tic \ˌjēəˈmantik\ *also* **ge·o·man·ti·cal** \-təkəl\ *adj* [ML *geomanticus*, fr. *geomantia* + L *-icus* -ic, -ical] : of or relating to geomancy — **ge·o·man·ti·cal·ly** \-tək(ə)lē\ *adv*

ge·o·mat·ic \ˌjēəˈmad·ik\ *or* **ge·o·mat·i·cal** \-d·əkəl\ *adj* [*ge-* + *mathematic, mathematical*] : of or relating to geomatics

ge·o·mat·ics \ˌ==ˈmad·iks\ *n pl but sing in constr* [*ge-* + *mathematics*] : the mathematics of the earth

geo·medical \ˌjē(ˌ)ō+\ *adj* [*ge-* + *medical*] : relating to or concerned with geomedicine

geo·medicine \"+\ *n* [*ge-* + *medicine;* trans. of G *geomedizin*] : a branch of medicine that deals with geographic factors in disease

ge·om·e·ter \jēˈämәd·ə(r), -ətə- *also* ÷ ˈjäm-\ *n* [ME, fr. MF or L; MF *geometre*, fr. L *geometres*, *geometra*, fr. Gk *geōmetrēs*, fr. *geōmetrein* to measure or survey land — more at GEOMETRY] **1** : a specialist in geometry **2** : a moth or moth larva of the family Geometridae : LOOPER

[1]**ge·o·met·ric** \ˌjēəˈme·trik, -rēk\ *or* **ge·o·met·ri·cal** \-rəkəl, -rēk-\ *adj* [MF or L; MF *geometrique*, fr. L *geometricus*, fr. Gk *geōmetrikos*, fr. *geōmetrēs* + *-ikos* -ic, -ical] **1 a** : of, relating to, or according to the methods or principles of geometry : determined by geometry ⟨the ~ solution of a problem⟩ **b** : increasing in a geometric progression ⟨~ population growth⟩ **2** *usu cap* : of or relating to a style of Greek pottery made from the 10th century to about 700 B.C. and characterized by geometric decorative motifs (as bands, meanders, zigzags, chevrons, lozenges, or triangles) that were applied in black on a yellowish or buff surface **3** : having or utilizing rectilinear or simple curvilinear motifs or outlines that bear little resemblance to natural forms ⟨a buffalo hide painted with ~ designs in red and black —Alice Marriott⟩ — **ge·o·met·ri·cal·ly** \-rək(ə)lē, -rēk-, -li\ *adv*

[2]**geometric** \"\ *n* -s : something (as a textile or rug) characterized by geometric design or decoration

geometrical clamp *n* : a clamp that holds a rigid body immovable by keeping it in six-point contact with an immovable rigid support

geometrical construction *n* : construction employing only straightedge and compasses or effected by drawing only straight lines and circles — opposed to *mechanical construction*

geometrical optics *n pl but sing in constr* : a branch of optics that deals with those phenomena of reflection and refraction that can be mathematically deduced from simple empirical laws

geometrical pitch *n* : the distance an element of an airplane propeller would advance in one revolution if it were moving along a helix having an angle equal to that between the chord of the element and a plane perpendicular to the propeller axis

geometrical radius *n* : the pitch-circle radius of a gear

geometric design *n* : highway design in which the dimensions of the roadway are intended to promote safe, convenient, and economical movement of traffic

ge·om·e·tri·cian \(ˌ)jēˌäməˈtrishən\ *n* -s : GEOMETER 1

geometric isomerism *n* : stereoisomerism ascribed to different directional arrangements of specifically located groups in the molecule and usu. considered to be caused by prevention of free rotation in parts of the molecule (as by a double bond or a ring) — compare OPTICAL ISOMERISM

geometric lathe *n* : an instrument for engraving complicated patterns of interlacing lines (as on bank notes)

geometric mean *n* : the *n*th root of the product of *n* numbers; *specif* : a number that is the second term of three consecutive terms of a geometric progression ⟨the *geometric mean* of 9 and 4 is 6⟩

geometric plane *n* : GROUND PLANE

geometric progression *n* **1** : a sequence (as 1, ½, ¼) in which the ratio of a term to its predecessor is always the same — called also *geometric sequence* **2** : GEOMETRIC SERIES

geometric series *n* : a series (as $1+x+x^2+x^3+\ldots$) whose terms form a geometric progression

geometric spider *n* : any of numerous three-clawed eight-eyed sedentary spiders (family Epeiridae) that spin webs composed chiefly of radial and spiral threads (as the common garden spider *Miranda aurantia*)

geometric stairs *n pl* : continuous stairs that turn or wind about a central wellhole which has rounded corners or is circular or elliptical and that have the strings and rails arranged upon geometric principles and running continuously from top to bottom

geometric tortoise *n* [so called fr. the geometric patterns of the shells] **1** : a common southern African tortoise (*Testudo geometrica* or *Psammobates geometrica*) with ornately sculptured dorsal shields raised into conical eminences and alternately streaked with yellow and black **2** : any of several forms related to the geometric tortoise

geometric unit *n* : a unit of length, area, volume, or angular magnitude

GEOLOGIC TIME AND FORMATIONS

NORTH AMERICA				EUROPE				YEARS AGO (dates established by lead-uranium ratios)	EARLIEST RECORD OF	
eras	periods and systems	epochs and series	principal mountain-making episodes	eras	periods and systems	epochs series, and stages	principal mountain-making episodes		ANIMALS	PLANTS
Cenozoic	Quaternary	Holocene (Recent) Pleistocene (Glacial)	Cascadian	Cenozoic	Quaternary	Holocene (Recent) Pleistocene (Glacial)			mankind	
	Tertiary	Pliocene Miocene Oligocene Eocene Paleocene			Tertiary	Pliocene Miocene Oligocene Eocene Paleocene	Alpine	70,000,000	placental mammals	
	Cretaceous (Upper Cretaceous)	Laramie Montana Colorado Dakota	Laramide (Rocky mts.)		Cretaceous	Danian Senonian Turonian Cenomanian Albian Aptian Barremian Neocomian				
Mesozoic	Comanchean (Lower Cretaceous)	Washita Fredericksburg Trinity Arundel Patuxent		Mesozoic						grasses and cereals
	Jurassic	Upper Middle Lower	Nevadan		Jurassic	Malm Dogger Lias		160,000,000	birds mammals	flowering plants
	Triassic	Upper Middle Lower			Triassic	Keuper Muschelkalk Bunter				
	Permian	Ochoan Guadalupian Leonardian Wolfcamp	Appalachian		Permian	Zechstein Rothliegende	Hercynian *or* Armorican	230,000,000		ginkgos cycads and conifers
	Pennsylvanian	Virgilian Missourian Desmoinesian Atokan Morrowan			Upper Carboniferous ("Coal Measures")	Stephanian Westphalian Namurian			insects	lepidodendrons, calamites, cordaites, etc.
	Mississippian	Chesterian Meramec Osagian Kinderhook			Carboniferous Lower Carboniferous ("Mountain Limestone")	Dinantian *or* Culm	Culmide		reptiles	
Paleozoic	Devonian	Chautauquan Senecan Erian Ulsterian	Acadian	Paleozoic	Devonian ("Old Red Sandstone")	Fammenian Frasnian Givetian Eifelian Coblenzian Gedinnian			amphibians	seed ferns vascular plants: lycopods, horsetails, ferns, etc.
	Silurian	Cayugan Niagaran Medinan			Silurian	Downtonian Ludlovian Wenlockian Llandoverian	Caledonian	390,000,000		
	Ordovician	Cincinnatian Champlainian Canadian	Taconic		Ordovician	Bala Llandeilo Llanvirn Arenig			fishes	
	Cambrian	Croixan Albertan Waucobian			Cambrian	Tremadoc Lingulella Menevian Harlech		500,000,000		mosses
Proterozoic	not divided into periods	Keweenawan, Beltian Huronian, Grand Canyon	Killarney Algoman	Precambrian	Algonkian (not divided into periods)	Torridonian, Jotnian Dalradian		620,000,000	invertebrates	spores of uncertain relationship marine algae
Archeozoic		Timiskaming, Vishnu Keewatin	Laurentian		Archean	Gothian Moine Lewisian, Svecofennian		1,420,000,000 2,300,000,000		

[1]**ge·om·e·trid** \jē'ämə·trəd, ¦jēə¦me·t-\ *adj* [NL *Geometridae*] **:** of or relating to the family Geometridae

[2]**geometrid** \"\ *n* -s **:** a geometrid moth **:** GEOMETER

ge·o·met·ri·dae \,jēə'me·trə,dē\ *n pl, cap* [NL, fr. L *geometres, geometra* geometer + NL *-idae;* fr. the looping movement, suggestive of earth measurement — more at GEOMETER] **:** a family of mostly medium-sized and slender-bodied moths with large wings and larvae that are loopers and that often feed destructively on various trees and cultivated plants

ge·om·e·trist \jē'ämə·trəst *also* ÷ 'jäm-\ *n* -s [*geometry* + *-ist*] **:** GEOMETER

ge·om·e·tri·za·tion \(,)jē,ämə·trə'zāshən, -,trī'z-\ *n* -s **:** the act or process of geometrizing

ge·om·e·trize \jē'ämə·,trīz\ *vb* -ED/-ING/-S [*geometry* + *-ize*] *vi* **:** to work by or as if by geometric methods or laws **:** investigate and draw conclusions by using geometric constructions and principles ~ *vt* **1 :** to represent geometrically **2 :** to make conform to geometric principles and laws **:** apply geometric principles and laws to

ge·om·e·triz·er \-zə(r)\ *n* -s **:** one that geometrizes

ge·om·e·try \jē'ämə·trē, -ri *also* ÷'jäm-\ *n* -ES *often attrib* [ME *geometrie,* fr. MF, fr. L *geometria,* fr. Gk *geōmetria,* fr. *geōmetrein* to measure or survey the earth (fr. *geō-* ge- + *metrein* to measure, fr. *metron* measure) + *-ia* -y — more at MEASURE] **1 a :** a branch of mathematics that deals with the measurement, properties, and relationships of points, lines, angles, surfaces, and solids **b :** a particular type or system of geometry **c :** a treatise on geometry **2 a :** CONFIGURATION ⟨~ of an automotive steering linkage⟩ ⟨~ of an optical system⟩ **b :** surface shape (as of a mechanical part or a crystal) **3 :** an arrangement of objects or parts that suggests geometrical figures or outlines ⟨the picturesque ~ of spars, masts, ropes, pulleys, and all the busy trappings of a Vineyard fisherman —Samuel Chamberlain⟩ ⟨what is of interest to musicians in "Wozzeck" is its ~, its contrapuntal plan, its structure —Robert Craft⟩

ge·o·mor·phic \¦jēə¦mȯrfik\ *adj* [*ge-* + *-morphic*] **:** of or relating to the form of the earth or its surface features **:** resembling the earth **:** GEOMORPHOLOGIC ⟨classification of geologic structures for purposes of ~ description —*Jour. of Geol.*⟩

geomorphic cycle *n* **:** CYCLE OF EROSION

ge·o·mor·phist \-fəst\ *n* -s [*geomorphy* + *-ist*] **:** GEOMORPHOLOGIST

geo·morphogenic \¦jē(,)ō+\ *adj* **:** of or relating to geomorphogeny

ge·o·mor·phog·e·nist \,jē(,)ō,mȯr'fäjənəst\ *n* -s **:** a specialist in geomorphogeny

geo·morphogeny \¦jē(,)ō+\ *n* [ISV *ge-* + *morphogeny;* orig. formed as F *géomorphogénie*] **:** a science that deals with the genesis of earth forms

geo·morphography \"+\ *n* [*ge-* + *morphography*] **:** the descriptive phase of geomorphology

geo·morphologic *or* **geo·morphological** \"+\ *adj* **:** of or relating to geomorphology

geo·morphologist \"+\ *n* **:** a specialist in geomorphology

geo·morphology \"+\ *n* [ISV *ge-* + *morphology*] **1 :** a science that deals with the land and submarine relief features of the earth's surface and seeks a genetic interpretation of them through using the principles of physiography in its descriptive aspects and of dynamic and structural geology in its explanatory phases **2 a :** the features dealt with in geomorphology ⟨the ~ of the Black hills⟩ **b :** a treatise on geomorphology

ge·o·mor·phy \'jēə,mȯrfē\ *n* -ES [ISV *ge-* + *morph-* + *-y*] **:** GEOMORPHOLOGY

[1]**ge·o·my·id** \¦jēə¦mīəd\ *adj* [NL *Geomyidae*] **:** of or relating to the family Geomyidae

[2]**geomyid** \"\ *n* -s **:** a rodent of the family Geomyidae

ge·o·my·i·dae \,jēə'mīə,dē\ *n pl, cap* [NL, fr. *Geomys,* type genus (fr. *ge-* + Gk *mys* mouse) + *-idae* — more at MOUSE] **:** a family of No. American sciuromorph burrowing rodents comprising the pocket gophers and extinct related forms

[1]**ge·o·my·oid** \¦jēə¦mī,ȯid\ *adj* [NL *Geomyoidea*] **:** of or relating to the superfamily Geomyoidea

[2]**geomyoid** \"\ *n* -s **:** a rodent of the superfamily Geomyoidea

ge·o·my·oi·dea \,jē(,)ō,mī'ȯidēə\ *n pl, cap* [NL, fr. *Geomys* genus of rodents + *-oidea*] **:** a superfamily of rodents comprising those with external cheek pouches (as the pocket gophers and the kangaroo rat)

geo·navigation \¦jē(,)ō+\ *n* [*ge-* + *navigation*] **:** navigation by reckoning the course from other places on the earth's surface (as in piloting and dead reckoning)

geo·negative \"+\ *adj* [*ge-* + *negative*] **:** characterized by negative geotropism or geotaxis

ge·on·ic \(')gā¦ōnik, -¦än-\ *or* **ga·on·ic** \(')gā¦ōn-\ *adj, often cap* [*Geonim* or *Gaon* + *-ic*] **:** of or relating to the geonim

geonim *pl of* GAON

ge·on·o·ma \jē'änəmə\ *n* [NL, fr. Gk *geōnomos* colonist, fr. *geō-* ge- + *-nomos* (fr. *nemein* to distribute) — more at NIMBLE] **1** *cap* **:** a genus of tropical American palms with nearly entire or pinnately cleft leaves and a small fruit like a berry **2** -s **:** any palm of the genus *Geonoma*

geo·pathology \¦jē(,)ō+\ *n* [*ge-* + *pathology*] **:** a science that deals with the relation of geographic factors to peculiarities of specific diseases ⟨~ of hypertension⟩

ge·o·pha·gia \,jēō'fāj(ē)ə\ *n* -s [NL, fr. *ge-* + *-phagia*] **:** GEOPHAGY

ge·oph·a·gism \jē'äfə,jizəm\ *n* -s [ISV *ge-* + Gk *phagein* to eat + ISV *-ism* — more at BAKSHEESH] **:** GEOPHAGY

ge·oph·a·gist \-jəst\ *n* -s [*geophagy* + *-ist*] **:** one that eats earth

ge·oph·a·gous \(')jē¦äfəgəs\ *adj* [*ge-* + *-phagous*] **1 :** eating earth ⟨a ~ tribe⟩ **2 :** feeding on soil ⟨~ worms⟩

ge·oph·a·gy \jē'äfəjē\ *n* -ES [ISV *ge-* + *-phagy*] **:** the practice of eating earthy substances (as clay) that is widespread among primitive or depressed peoples and is held to represent an attempt to supply elements lacking in a scanty or unbalanced diet

ge·oph·i·la \jē'äfələ\ *n pl, cap* [NL, fr. *ge-* + *-phila*] *in some classifications* **:** a group of pulmonate gastropods including the land snails and slugs

ge·o·phil·o·morph \¦jē(,)ō¦filə,mȯrf\ *adj* [NL *Geophilomorpha*] **:** of or relating to the order Geophilomorpha

ge·o·phil·o·mor·pha \,⸗(,)⸗,⸗⸗'mȯrfə\ *n pl, cap* [NL, fr. *Geophilus* + *-o-* + *-morpha*] **:** an order of small extremely elongate centipedes living in soil and under stones and having more than 30 pairs of legs

ge·oph·i·lous \(')jē¦äfələs\ *adj* [*ge-* + *-philous*] **:** living or growing in or on the ground ⟨~ insects⟩ ⟨~ plants⟩

ge·oph·i·lus \jē'äfələs\ *n, cap* [NL, fr. *ge-* + *-philus*] **:** a cosmopolitan genus (the type of the family Geophilidae) of geophilomorph centipedes

ge·o·phone \'jēə,fōn\ *n* [Fr. *Geophone,* a trademark] **:** an instrument designed to detect vibrations passing through rocks, soil, or ice

geo·photo \¦jēō+\ *n* [*ge-* + *photo*] **:** a photograph usu. taken from an airplane for use in geologic investigations

geo·physical \"+\ *adj* [*ge-* + *physical*] **:** of, relating to, or based on geophysics ⟨financing a ~ survey of its properties —*Wall Street Jour.*⟩ — **geo·physically** \"+\ *adv*

geophysical engineering *n* **:** a branch of engineering that deals with scientific methods of locating and studying underground deposits of ores, minerals, oil, gas, or water

geo·physicist \"+\ *n* [*geophysics* + *-ist*] **:** a specialist in geophysics

geo·physics \"+\ *n pl but sing in constr* [ISV *ge-* + *physics*] **1 :** the physics of the earth including the fields of meteorology, hydrology, oceanography, seismology, volcanology, magnetism, radioactivity, and geodesy **2 :** GEOPHYSICAL ENGINEERING

ge·o·phyte \'jēə,fīt\ *n* -s [*ge-* + *-phyte*] **:** a perennial plant that bears its overwintering buds below the surface of the soil — compare CHAMAEPHYTE, PHANEROPHYTE

ge·o·plana \,jēō'plānə, -lanə,-länə\ *n, cap* [NL, fr. *ge-* + L *plana,* fem. of *planus* flat, level — more at FLOOR] **:** a large genus (the type of the family Geoplanidae) of chiefly tropical terrestrial triclad turbellarian worms having a marginal band of eyes about the body

geo·polar \¦jē(,)ō+\ *adj* [*ge-* + *polar*] **:** of or relating to a pole of the earth

geo·political \"+\ *adj* [*ge-* + *political;* trans. of G *geopolitisch*] **:** of, relating to, or based on geopolitics ⟨the weakest link . . . is his tendency to ignore the ~ relationship of Western Europe to the worldwide situation —J.S.Roucek⟩ — **geo·politically** \"+\ *adv*

geo·politician \"+\ *n* [*ge-* + *politician;* trans. of G *geopolitiker*] **:** a specialist in geopolitics

geo·politics \"+\ *n pl but sing in constr* [*ge-* + *politics;* trans. of G *geopolitik*] **1 :** a study of the influence of such physical factors as geography, economics, and demography upon the politics and esp. the foreign policy of a state ⟨the present tendency to study ~ in colleges —Thomas Woody⟩ — compare POLITICAL GEOGRAPHY **2 :** a Nazi expansionist doctrine that emphasized strategic frontiers, lebensraum, and racial, economic, and social pressures as factors demanding reallocation of the earth's surface and resources ⟨made ~ into an effective organ of propaganda —G.H.Sabine⟩ **3 :** a governmental policy guided by geopolitics ⟨the ~ of the Japanese government⟩ **4 :** the combination of political and geographic factors characterizing a particular state or region ⟨a study of the ~ of the United Kingdom and the rest of the empire —*Armed Forces Talk*⟩

geo·po·li·tik \,gāō,pōlē'tēk\ *n* -s *usu cap* [G, fr. *ge-* + *politik* politics — more at REALPOLITIK] **:** GEOPOLITICS

geo·po·li·ti·ker \,gā(,)ōpō'lētikər\ *n* -s *sometimes cap* [G, fr. *geo-* ge- + *politiker* politician, fr. *politik* + *-er*] **:** GEOPOLITICIAN

ge·o·pon·ic \¦jēə¦pänik\ *also* **ge·o·pon·i·cal** \-nəkəl\ *adj* [Gk *geōponikos,* fr. *geōponein* to till the soil (fr. *geō-* ge- + *ponein* to toil) + *-ikos* -ic, -ical] **:** of or relating to tillage **:** AGRICULTURAL

ge·o·pon·ics \,⸗⸗'päniks\ *n pl but sing in constr* [MGk *geōponika,* fr. Gk, neut. pl. of *geōponikos*] **:** an art or science of cultivating the earth **:** HUSBANDRY

geo·positive \¦jē(,)ō+\ *adj* [*ge-* + *positive*] **:** characterized by positive geotropism or geotaxis

geo·potential \"+\ *n* [*ge-* + *potential*] **:** the work that must be done at a given altitude in raising a unit mass from sea level to that altitude against the earth's gravitational field

ge·o·prum·non \,jēō'prəm,nän\ *n, cap* [NL, fr. *ge-* + Gk *proumnon* plum] **:** a small genus of herbs (family Leguminosae) bearing fleshy indehiscent pods — see EARTH PLUM, MILK VETCH

ge·o·rama \,jēə'ramə, -rämə\ *n* -s [F *géorama,* fr. *gé-* ge- + *-orama* (as in *panorama*)] **:** a hollow globe whose inner surface contains a map of the world for examination by one standing inside

geor·die \'jȯrdē\ *n* -s *usu cap* [fr. Sc *Geordie,* dim. of the name *George*] **1** [fr. the image of St. George such coins once bore] *chiefly Scot* **:** GUINEA ⟨jingling the *Geordies* in his hand —Neil Munro⟩ **2** *chiefly Scot* **a :** a coal miner esp. from the region around Tyneside **b :** a native of Scotland or northern England **3** *chiefly Scot* **:** a collier brig **4** *chiefly Scot* **:** a coal miner's safety lamp

[1]**george** \'jȯ(ə)rj, 'jȯ(ə)j\ *n* -s *usu cap* [after St. *George* †*ab* A.D. 303 Cappadocian martyr, patron saint of England] **1 :** either of two of the insignia of the British Order of the Garter: **a :** a jewel appended to the collar of the order — called also *Great George* **b :** a jewel appended to the ribbon of the order — called also *Lesser George* **2 :** a British half crown or guinea bearing the image of St. George

[2]**george** \"\ *usu cap* [fr. the name *George*] — a communications code word for the letter *g*

georg·es bank flounder \¦jȯr¦jəz-, ¦jȯ(ə)|\ *n, usu cap G&B* [fr. Georges Bank, elevation under the sea east of Cape Cod, Mass.] **:** a brownish yellow flounder (*Pseudopleuronectes americanus dignabilis*) — called also *lemon sole*

george town \'jȯrj,taůn, 'jȯ(ə)j-\ *adj, usu cap G&T* [fr. *George Town,* Federation of Malaya] **:** of or from the city of George Town, Federation of Malaya **:** of the kind or style prevalent in George Town

geor·gette \(')jȯr¦jet, (')jȯ(ə)¦-\ *also* **georgette crepe** *n* -s [fr. *Georgette,* a trademark] **:** a thin strong clothing crepe woven from hard twisted yarns to produce a dull pebbly surface

geor·gia \'jȯr|jə, 'jȯ(ə)| *sometimes* |jēə\ *adj, usu cap* [fr. *Georgia,* state in the southern U. S., fr. *George* I †1727 king of England] **:** of or from the state of Georgia **:** of the kind or style prevalent in Georgia **:** GEORGIAN

georgia bark *n, usu cap G* **:** the bitter bark of a fever tree (*Pinckneya pubens*) used as a tonic and vermifuge

geor·gia·des·ite \jȯ(r)'jädə,sīt\ *n* -s [F *georgiadésite,* fr. *Georgiades,* 20th cent. Greek mine director + F *-ite*] **:** a mineral $Pb_3(AsO_4)Cl_3$ consisting of a lead chloro-arsenate and occurring in white or brownish yellow orthorhombic crystals

georgia heart pine *n, usu cap G* **:** LONGLEAF PINE

[1]**geor·gian** \'jȯrjən, 'jȯ(ə)| *sometimes* |jēən\ *n* -s *cap* [ME *Georgyen,* fr. MF *georgien,* fr. *Georgie* Georgia, region in the southern Caucasus + MF *-en* -an] **1 :** a native or inhabitant of Georgia in the Caucasus **2 :** the South Caucasic language of the Georgian people

[2]**georgian** \"\ *adj, usu cap* **1 a :** of, relating to, or characteristic of Georgia in the Caucasus **b :** of, relating to, or characteristic of the Georgians **2 :** of, relating to, or characteristic of the Georgian language

[3]**georgian** \"\ *n* -s *cap* [*Georgia,* state + E *-an*] **:** a native or resident of the state of Georgia

[4]**georgian** \"\ *adj, usu cap* **1 :** of, relating to, or characteristic of the state of Georgia **2 :** of, relating to, or characteristic of the people of Georgia

[5]**georgian** \"\ *adj, usu cap* **1** [after *George* I †1727, *George* II †1760, *George* III †1820, and *George* IV †1830, kings of England] **:** of, relating to, or characteristic of the reigns of the first four Georges of Great Britain ⟨the *Georgian* age having been . . . the most momentous age of our history —Robert Southey⟩ ⟨gracious *Georgian* beauty of Mount Vernon —Howard Fast⟩ **2** [after *George* V †1936 king of England] **:** of, relating to, or characteristic of the reign of George V of Great Britain ⟨the *Georgian* poets . . . wrote about their own personal relationships with trivial objects —C.D. Lewis⟩

[6]**georgian** \"\ *n* -s *usu cap* **1 :** one belonging to either of the Georgian periods; *specif* **:** a poet of the second decade of the 20th century ⟨the *Georgians'* general recommendations were the discarding of archaistic diction . . . and of pomposities generally —Lawrence Durrell⟩ **2 :** Georgian taste or style esp. in architecture

georgian architecture *n, usu cap G* [[5]*Georgian*] **:** architecture of or in the style of the Georgian era, esp. the period 1714–60

georgian furniture *n, usu cap G* **:** furniture of or in the style of the Georgian era, esp. the period 1750–90 — compare ADAM, CHIPPENDALE, HEPPLEWHITE, SHERATON

georgia pine *or* **georgia pitch pine** *or* **georgia yellow pine** *n, usu cap G* **:** LONGLEAF PINE

georgia stock *n, usu cap G* **:** a plow beam with handles and a standard to which a moldboard, shovels, teeth, or sweeps are attached

[1]**geor·gic** \'jȯr|jik, 'jȯ(ə)|, |jēk\ *n* -s [after the *Georgics,* a poem dealing with agriculture by Vergil (Publius Vergilius Maro) †19 B.C. Roman poet, fr. L *Georgica,* fr. Gk *geōrgika* lands under cultivation (title of a poem about agriculture by Nicander, 2d cent. B.C. Greek poet), fr. neut. pl. of *geōrgikos* agricultural, fr. *geōrgos* farmer (fr. *geō-* ge- + *-ergos,* fr. *ergon* work) + *-ikos* -ic — more at WORK] **:** a poem dealing with agriculture and rural affairs

[2]**georgic** \"\ *also* **geor·gi·cal** \|jəkəl, -jēk-\ *adj* [L *georgicus,* fr. Gk *geōrgikos*] **:** of or relating to agriculture and rural affairs **:** RUSTIC

geor·gi·na gidgee \(')jȯ(r)¦jēnə-\ *n, usu cap 1st G* [fr. *Georgina river*] **:** a scrubby Australian acacia (*Acacia georginae*) of the Georgina river district that much resembles and is sometimes considered a hybrid of the common gidgee and that has been implicated as a causative factor of Georgina River disease in animals that feed on its seed pods

georgina river disease *also* **georgina disease** *n, usu cap G&R* [fr. *Georgina river,* Northern Territory and Queensland, Australia] **:** a severe intoxication of Australian sheep and cattle due to ingestion of poisonous plant material believed to be the seeds of Georgina gidgee

geos *pl of* GEO

geo·science \¦jē(,)ō+\ *n* [*ge-* + *science;* trans. of G *geowissenschaft*] **1 :** the sciences (as geology, physical geography, geomorphology, geophysics, geochemistry) dealing with the earth **2 :** any of the geosciences

ge·o·scop·ic \¦jēə¦skäpik\ *adj* [*geoscopy* + *-ic*] **:** of or relating to geoscopy

ge·os·co·py \jē'äskəpē\ *n* -ES [*ge-* + *-scopy*] **:** knowledge of the earth, ground, or soil gained by inspection

geo·selenic \¦jē(,)ō+\ *adj* [*ge-* + *selenic*] **:** of or relating to the earth and the moon

geo·sere \'jē(,)ō,si(ə)r\ *n* [*ge-* + *sere* (cycle)] **:** a sequence of ecological climax communities following one another through geologic time in response to repeated physical and climatic alteration of a habitat

geo·sphere \¦jē(,)ō+,-\ *n* [*ge-* + *sphere*] **1 :** the solid earth — distinguished from *atmosphere* and *hydrosphere* **2 :** one of the shells or spherical layers within the earth delimited above and below by discontinuities

ge·o·spi·za \,jēō'spīzə, jē'äspəzə\ *n, cap* [NL, fr. *ge-* + Gk *spiza,* a kind of finch] **:** a genus of finches of black or dark color confined to the Galápagos islands and commonly considered to form a distinct subfamily of Fringillidae

geo·static \¦jēō+\ *adj* [ISV *ge-* + *static*] **:** relating to pressure exerted by earth or a similar substance

geo·strategic \¦jē(,)ō+\ *adj* **:** of or relating to geostrategy

geo·strategist \"+\ *n* **:** a specialist in geostrategy

geo·strategy \"+\ *n* [*ge-* + *strategy*] **1 :** a branch of geopolitics that deals with strategy **2 :** the combination of geopolitical and strategic factors characterizing a particular geographic region ⟨after a preliminary briefing . . . on the ~ of the Pacific basin —*Jour. of Geol.*⟩ **3 :** the use by a government of strategy based upon geopolitics ⟨German ~ soon gave rise to the first clear exposition of the nature and main features of total war —Andrew Gyorgy⟩

ge·o·stroph·ic \¦jēō¦sträfik\ *adj* [*ge-* + Gk *strophikos* turned, fr. *strophē* action of turning + *-ikos* -ic — more at STROPHE] **:** of or relating to deflective force due to the rotation of the earth

geostrophic wind *n* **:** a wind whose direction and speed are determined by a balance of the pressure-gradient force and the force due to the earth's rotation

geo·synclinal \¦jē(,)ō+\ *adj* **:** of or relating to a geosyncline

geo·syncline *or* **geo·synclinal** \"+\ *n* [*ge-* + *syncline, synclinal*] **:** a great downward flexure of the earth's crust — opposed to *geanticline*

ge·o·tac·tic \¦jēō¦taktik\ *adj* [*ge-* + *-tactic*] **:** of or relating to geotaxis — **ge·o·tac·ti·cal·ly** \-tək(ə)lē\ *adv*

ge·o·tax·is \¦jēō¦taksəs\ *or* **ge·o·taxy** \'⸗⸗,⸗sē\ *n, pl* **geotax·es** \-k,sēz\ *or* **geotaxies** [*geotaxis,* NL, fr. *ge-* + *taxis; geotaxy* fr. *ge-* + *-taxy*] **:** a taxis in which the force of gravity is the directive factor

geo·technic \¦jēō+\ *adj* [*ge-* + *technic*] **:** of or relating to geotechnics

geo·technics \"+\ *n pl but sing in constr* [*ge-* + *technics*] **:** a science of making the earth more habitable

geo·technology \¦jē(,)ō+\ *n* [*ge-* + *technology*] **:** the application of scientific methods and engineering techniques to the exploitation and utilization of natural resources (as mineral resources)

ge·o·tec·tol·o·gy \,jēō,tek'täləjē\ *n* -ES [*geotectonic* + *-logy*] **:** a study of structural geology

geo·tectonic \¦jēō+\ *adj* [*ge-* + *tectonic*] **:** of or relating to the form, arrangement, and structure of rock masses of the earth's crust **:** STRUCTURAL

geotectonic geology *n* **:** STRUCTURAL GEOLOGY

geo·tectonics \"+\ *n pl but sing in constr* [*ge-* + *tectonics*] **:** STRUCTURAL GEOLOGY

ge·o·teu·this \,jēō'tüthəs, -ō·'tyü-\ *n, cap* [NL, fr. *ge-* + Gk *teuthis* squid] **:** a genus of extinct cuttlefishes abundant in the Upper Liassic formations of Europe

ge·o·therm \'jēō,thərm\ *n* -s [*ge-* + *-therm*] **:** a geothermal isopleth

geo·thermal *or* **geo·thermic** \¦jēō+\ *adj* [ISV *ge-* + *thermal, thermic*] **:** of or relating to the heat of the earth's interior ⟨economic development of ~ energy —M.P.McIntyre⟩

geothermal gradient *n* **:** the increase in the temperature of the earth from the surface downward averaging about 1°F for each 70 feet

geo·thermometer \¦jē(,)ō+\ *n* [ISV *ge-* + *thermometer*] **1 :** GEOLOGIC THERMOMETER **2 :** a thermometer designed to measure temperatures in deep-sea deposits or in bore holes deep below the surface of the earth

ge·ot·ri·cho·sis \jē,ä·trə'kōsəs\ *n* -ES [NL, fr. *Geotrichum* genus of fungi (fr. *ge-* + *-trichum,* fr. Gk *trich-, thrix* hair) + *-osis* — more at TRICHINA] **:** infection of the bronchi or lungs and sometimes the mouth and intestines by certain fungi (genus *Geotrichum*)

ge·o·trop·ic \¦jēə·¦träpik\ *adj* [*ge-* + *-tropic*] **:** characterized by, exhibiting, or relating to geotropism — **ge·o·trop·i·cal·ly** \-pək(ə)lē\ *adv*

ge·ot·ro·pism \jē'ä·trə,pizəm\ *n* [ISV *ge-* + *-tropism;* orig. formed as G *geotropismus*] **1 :** tropism in which gravitational attraction is the orienting factor (as in roots growing down, shoots growing up, and the climbing, swimming, or right-side-up orientation of certain animals) **2 :** tropism in which turning or movement is toward rather than away from the earth — compare APOGEOTROPISM

ge·ot·ro·py \jē'ä·trəpē\ *n* -ES [*ge-* + *-tropy*] **:** GEOTROPISM

ge·o·tru·pes \,jēə·'trü(,)pēz\ *n, cap* [NL, irreg. fr. *ge-* + Gk *trypē* hole] **:** a genus of bronze or black dung beetles that dig vertical tunnels in the soil and provision them with dung in which their larvae feed and grow

ge·phyr·ea \jə'firēə, jefə'rēə\ *n pl, cap* [NL, fr. Gk *gephyra* bridge; perh. akin to Arm *kamurj* bridge] **:** a prob. artificial group of marine worms variously regarded as a phylum or as a class of Annelida, including Echiuroidea, Sipunculoidea, and Priapuloidea, and comprising worms that are unsegmented as adults and have coeloms and separate sexes and typically a single pair of nephridia — **ge·phyr·e·an** \jə'firēən, ¦jefə-'rēən\ *adj or n*

geph·y·ro·cer·cal \¦jefə(,)rō¦sərkəl\ *adj* [Gk *gephyro-* (fr. *gephyra*) + E *-cercal*] **1 :** having the dorsal and anal fins confluent at the aborted end of the vertebral column of a fish's tail **2 :** having or relating to a gephyrocercal tail — **geph·y·ro·cer·cy** \'⸗⸗⸗,sərsē\ *n* -ES

gep·i·dae \'jepə,dē, 'ge-\ *or* **gep·ids** \-pədz\ *n pl, cap* [LL *Gepidae*] **:** a Germanic people akin to the Goths and eventually absorbed by the Lombards

ger \'ge(ə)r\ *n, pl* **ge·rim** \'gerəm\ [Heb *gēr*] **1 :** an alien resident in Hebrew territory protected in accordance with early Hebrew law by a native patron from oppression **2 :** PROSELYTE 2

ger *abbr* gerund; gerundial; gerundive

ge·rah *or* **ge·ra** \'girə\ *n* -s [Heb *gērāh,* lit., grain, bean] **:** an ancient Hebrew unit of weight equal to $\frac{1}{20}$ shekel

ge·ra·ni·a·ce·ae \jə,rānē'āsē,ē\ *n pl, cap* [NL, fr. *Geranium,* type genus + *-aceae*] **:** a family of mostly herbaceous plants (order Geraniales) having chiefly opposite or whorled leaves and flowers with one-seeded carpels that separate individually from a central column when ripe — **ge·ra·ni·a·ceous** \⸗¦⸗⸗¦āshəs\ *adj*

[1]**ge·ra·ni·al** \jə'rānē,al\ *n* -s [ISV *gerani-* (fr. NL *Geranium*) + *-al* (aldehyde)] **:** the trans form of citral

[2]**ge·ra·ni·al** \-nēəl\ *adj* [NL *Geraniales*] **:** of or relating to the order Geraniales

ge·ra·ni·a·les \jə,rānē'ā(,)lēz\ *n pl, cap* [NL, fr. *Geranium* + *-ales*] **:** an order of mostly herbaceous or shrubby dicotyledonous plants that have 5-parted regular flowers with stamens usu. a multiple of the number of sepals and a syncarpous ovary and that include the geraniums and cranesbills, wood sorrels, jewelweeds, flaxes, and a large but variable number of related plants — see EUPHORBIACEAE, GERANIACEAE

ge·ran·ic acid \jə'ranik-\ *n* [ISV *geraniol* + *-ic*] **:** a liquid unsaturated acid $C_9H_{15}COOH$ formed by oxidation of citral or geraniol

ge·ra·ni·ol \jə'rānē,ōl, -,ȯl\ *n* -s [ISV *gerani-* (fr. NL *Geranium*) + *-ol*] **:** a fragrant liquid unsaturated alcohol $C_{10}H_{17}OH$ that occurs both free and combined in many essential oils (as geranium and citronella oils) and is used chiefly in rose and other perfumes and in soap — compare CITRAL, NEROL

ge·ra·ni·um \jə'rānēəm, -nyəm\ *n* [NL, fr. L *geranion,* *geranium*, any of several plants of the family Geraniaceae, fr. Gk *geranion*, dim. of *geranos* crane — more at CRANE] **1 a** *cap* **:** a widely distributed genus of plants (family Geraniaceae) having regular flowers without spurs and with glands that alternate with the petals — see WILD GERANIUM **b** -s **:** the dried rhizomes of the wild geranium (*G. maculatum*) formerly used as an astringent **2** -s **a :** any plant of the genus *Geranium* **b :** PELARGONIUM 2 — see FISH GERANIUM **3** -s **a :** a strong red that is yellower and lighter than geranium red, paler than Goya, and bluer and lighter than average cherry red **b** *of textiles* **:** a vivid red that is bluer, lighter, and slightly stronger than apple red and bluer, lighter, and stronger than carmine or scarlet

geranium lake *n* **1 :** any of various brilliant red lakes made from eosin **2 :** a vivid red that is lighter and slightly yellower and stronger than apple red, yellower, lighter, and stronger than carmine, and bluer, lighter, and stronger than scarlet — called also *spark*

geranium oil *n* **1 :** a pale yellow or greenish essential oil that has an odor like that of roses, that is obtained from various plants of the genus *Pelargonium*, and that is used chiefly in perfumes and soap **2 :** PALMAROSA OIL

geranium pink *n* **1 :** a variable color averaging a moderate to strong pink that is redder than nymph pink and bluer and darker than peachblossom **2 :** a deep pink that is bluer, lighter, and stronger than average coral (sense 3b) and bluer and deeper than fiesta — called also *Bermuda*

geranium red *n* **:** a strong red that is bluer and darker than geranium (sense 3a) or average cherry red and bluer, less strong, and slightly lighter than Goya

geranium rose *n* **:** a variable color averaging a moderate red that is bluer, lighter, and stronger than cerise or claret, bluer and lighter than average cherry, and yellower, lighter, and stronger than carnation red

ge·ra·nyl \jəˈranᵊl, -ā,nil, ˈjerə,nil\ *n* -s [*geraniol* + *-yl*] **:** a univalent radical $C_{10}H_{17}$ that is derived from geraniol ⟨~ acetate⟩

ge·rar·dia \jəˈrärdēə\ *n* [NL, fr. John *Gerard* †1612 Eng. botanist + NL *-ia*] **1** *cap* **:** a genus of annual or perennial herbs (family Scrophulariaceae) that are often root-parasitic and have showy pink, purple, or yellow flowers with the corolla often distended on the lower side **2** -s **:** any plant of the genus *Gerardia* — see FALSE FOXGLOVE

geras *pl of* GERA

ger·a·sene \ˈgerə,sēn, ˈje-, ,==ˈ=\ *or* **ger·ge·sene** \ˈgərgə,-, ,==ˈ=\ *n* -s *cap* [LL *Gerasenus, Gergesenus*, fr. Gk *Gerasēnos, Gergesēnos*, fr. *Gerasa, Gergesa* ancient town in Palestine] **:** an inhabitant of the ancient Palestinian town Gerasa

ger·ate \ˈje,rāt\ *vt* -ED/-ING/-S [ME *geratten*] **:** to powder or spot (a shield) with such heraldic charges as mullets or roundels

ge·rat·ic \jəˈrad·ik\ *adj* [Gk *gērat-, gēras* old age + E *-ic* — more at CORN] **:** of or relating to old age **:** GERONTIC

ger·a·to·log·ic \ˌjeratəˈläjik\ *or* **ger·a·tol·o·gous** \ˌjerəˈtäləgəs\ *adj* **:** of or relating to geratology

ger·a·tol·o·gy \ˌjerəˈtäləjē\ *n* -ES [Gk *gērat-, gēras* + E *-logy*] **:** a scientific study of aging and its phenomena esp. as exhibited in biological groups nearing extinction

gerbe *or* **gerb** \ˈjərb\ *n* -S [F *gerbe*, lit., sheaf, fr. OF *jarbe*, of Gmc origin; akin to OHG *garba* sheaf — more at GARB] **:** a firework throwing a shower of sparks

ger·bera \ˈgərbərə, ˈjərb-, jərˈberə\ *n* [NL, after Traugott *Gerber* (*Gerberus*) †1743, Ger. naturalist] **1** *cap* **:** a genus of southern African or Asiatic herbs (family Compositae) having basal tufted leaves and solitary heads of yellow, pink, or orange flowers with prominent rays — see TRANSVAAL DAISY **2** -s **:** any plant or flower of the genus *Gerbera*

ger·ber convention \ˈgərbər-\ *n, usu cap G* [after John *Gerber*, 20th cent. Am. who devised it] **:** a bidding method in contract bridge that is based on the Blackwood convention and that uses a bid of four clubs instead of four no-trump as the asking bid, with responses of four diamonds to show no ace, four hearts one ace, four spades two aces, four no-trump three aces, and five clubs four aces

ger·bil \ˈjərbəl\ *or* **ger·bille** \", jərˈbē\ *n* -s [F *gerbille*, fr. NL *Gerbillus*] **:** any of numerous Old World burrowing desert rodents of *Gerbillus* and related genera that have long hind legs well adapted for leaping

ger·bil·lus \jərˈbiləs\ *n, cap* [NL, dim. of *gerboa, jerboa*, fr. Ar *yarbūʻ*] **:** a genus of rodents that constitutes with various related genera a subfamily of Cricetidae and comprises typical gerbils of Africa and Asia

ge·re·fa \yeˈrā(,)vä\ *n* -s [OE *gerēfa* — more at REEVE] **:** an administrative officer in Anglo-Saxon England

ge·rent \ˈjirənt\ *n* -s [L *gerent-, gerens*, pres. part. of *gerere* to bear, wage, cherish, manage — more at CAST] **:** one that rules or manages

ge·re·nuk \ˈgerə,nu̇k, gəˈrenək\ *n* -s [Somali *garanug*] **:** a long-necked antelope (*Litocranius walleri*) native to eastern Africa

gerfalcon *var of* GYRFALCON

gergesene *cap, var of* GERASENE

ger·hardt·ite \ˈger,härd·,īt\ *n* -s [Charles F. *Gerhardt* †1856 Fr. chemist + E *-ite*] **:** a mineral $Cu_2(NO_3)(OH)_3$ consisting of an emerald-green basic copper nitrate

ger·i·at·ric \ˌjerēˈa·trik, -rēk\ *adj* [Gk *gēras* old age + E *iatric* — more at CORN] **1 :** of or relating to geriatrics ⟨the ~ department of the hospital⟩ **2 :** of or relating to the aged or the process of aging ⟨significant ~ disorders⟩

ger·i·a·tri·cian \ˌjerēəˈtrishən\ *or* **geri·atrist** \ˌjerēˈa·trəst, ˈ==,== *also* jəˈrīə·t-\ *n* -s [*geriatrics* + *-ian* or *-ist*] **:** a specialist in geriatrics

ger·i·at·rics \ˌjerēˈa·triks, -rēks\ *n pl but sing in constr* [Gk *gēras* + E *-iatrics*] **:** a branch of medicine that deals with the problems and diseases of old age and aging people — compare GERONTOLOGY

gerim *pl of* GER

gerio·psychosis \ˌjirē(,)ō, ˌje\ *n* [NL, fr. *gerio-* (fr. *gēras* old age) + *psychosis*] **:** SENILE PSYCHOSIS

gerkin *var of* GHERKIN

¹germ \ˈjərm, ˈjəm, ˈjəim\ *n* -s *often attrib* [F *germe*, fr. L *germin-, germen*, alter. of (assumed) OL *genmin-, genmen*, fr. L *gen-*, stem of *gignere* to beget — more at KIN] **1 a :** a small mass of living substance capable of developing into an animal or plant or into an organ or part **:** BUD, SEED ⟨supernumerary tooth ~*s* may cause formation of supernumerary teeth —K.H. Thoma⟩ **b :** the embryo with the scutellum of a cereal grain that usu. is separated from the starchy endosperm during the milling ⟨the ~ of the wheat grain is very rich in oil content —Leslie Smith⟩ **2 a :** something from which development takes place or that serves or may serve as an origin **:** BEGINNING, RUDIMENT ⟨the Rule of St. Benedict . . . already contains the small ~ of that freedom and movement which developed in every branch of life —R.W.Southern⟩ **b :** HOMOEOMERY 1 **3 :** MICROORGANISM ⟨pathogenic bacteria are ~*s*⟩ ⟨virus ~⟩ **:** MICROBE, DISEASE GERM ⟨the cecal worm carries the ~ of blackhead in turkeys —B.F.Kaupp & R.C.Surface⟩ **syn** see MICROORGANISM

²germ \"\ *vb* -ED/-ING/-S **:** GERMINATE

¹ger·man \ˈjərmən, ˈjəm-, ˈjəim-\ *archaic var of* GERMANE

²german \"\ *n* -S [MF *germain* brother, cousin, fr. *germain*, adj., having the same parents, fr. L *germanus*, irreg. fr. *germin-, germen* + *-anus* -an] *obs* **:** a near relative ⟨you'll have coursers for cousins, and gennets for ~*s* —Shak.⟩

³german \"\ *n* -S [ML *Germanus*, fr. L, any member of the Germanic peoples that inhabited western Europe in Roman times] **1** *cap* **a :** a native or inhabitant of Germany **b :** a person of German descent **2** *cap* **a :** the West Germanic language spoken mainly in Germany, Austria, and parts of Switzerland — see HIGH GERMAN, LOW GERMAN; INDO-EUROPEAN LANGUAGES table **b :** the literary and official language of Germany — called also *High German;* see MIDDLE HIGH GERMAN, OLD HIGH GERMAN **3** *cap* **:** one who speaks the German language or its dialectal variants outside Germany (as a Swiss German) **4** *sometimes cap* **a** *or* **german cotillion :** a dance consisting of capriciously involved figures intermingled with waltzes **b** *chiefly Midland* **:** a dancing party; *specif* **:** one at which the german is danced **5** *usu cap* **:** ALBACORE 1

⁴german \"\ *adj, usu cap* [L *Germanus* of or relating to the Germanic peoples that inhabited western Europe in Roman times] **1 a :** of, relating to, or characteristic of Germany **b :** of, relating to, or characteristic of the Germans **2 :** of, relating to, or constituting the German language — **ger·man·ly** *adv, usu cap*

¹german-american \ˈ==ˈ===\ *n, usu cap G&A* **:** an American of German ancestry

²german-american \"\ *adj, usu cap G&A* **:** of, relating to, or having the characteristics of a German-American

german band *n, usu cap G* **:** a street band

german baptist brethren *n pl, usu cap G & both Bs* **:** DUNKERS — not used officially since 1908

german bee *n, usu cap G* **:** BLACK BEE

german bezoar *n, usu cap G* **:** a bezoar composed of interlaced fibers of hair with organic cementing matter

german brown *or* **german brown trout** *n, usu cap G* **:** BROWN TROUT

german carp *n, usu cap G* **:** CARP 1a

german catchfly *n, usu cap G* **:** a Eurasian perennial herb (*Lychnis viscaria*) with red or purple flowers that has viscid patches on the stem below the flower clusters and is used as an ornamental

german chamomile *n, usu cap G* **:** a wild chamomile (*Matricaria chamomilla*) with a fragrance like that of a pineapple

german chamomile oil *n, usu cap G* **:** CHAMOMILE OIL b

german coach *n, usu cap G&C* **:** a German breed of large rather coarse heavy harness horses that are bay, brown, or black in color

german cockroach *n, usu cap G* **:** CROTON BUG

ger·man·der \jərˈmandər, ˈjər,m-\ *n* -s [ME *germaunder*, fr. MF *germandree*, fr. ML *germandrea*, alter. of L *chamaedrys*, fr. Gk *chamaidrys*, fr. *chamai* on the ground + *drys* oak, tree — more at HUMBLE, TREE] **1 :** a plant of the genus *Teucrium* — see AMERICAN GERMANDER, WALL GERMANDER **2 :** any of several plants of the genus *Veronica; esp* **:** GERMANDER SPEEDWELL 1

germander sage *n* **:** WATER GERMANDER

germander speedwell *n* **1 :** an Old World speedwell (*Veronica chamaedrys*) with leaves resembling those of the wall germander **2** *also* **germander chickweed :** FIELD SPEEDWELL

¹ger·mane \jə(r)ˈmān, ˈjərˈm-, (ˈ)jəˈm-, (ˈ)jəiˈm-\ *adj* [ME *germain, germane*, lit., having the same parents, fr. MF *germain* — more at GERMAN] **1** *archaic* **:** true or complete **:** GENUINE **2** *obs* **:** closely akin **3 :** having a close relationship **:** APPROPRIATE, PERTINENT ⟨their bizarre ideas . . . were scarcely ~ to the central lines of medieval thought —H.O. Taylor⟩ **syn** see RELEVANT

²germane \"\ *n* -S [ISV, fr. NL *germanium* + ISV *methane*] **1 :** a compound of germanium and hydrogen; *specif* **:** the tetrahydride GeH_4 obtained as a colorless gas of nauseating odor by reducing other germanium compounds **2 :** a derivative (as trichloro-germane $GeHCl_3$) of a germane

ger·mane·ly *adv* **:** in a germane manner

ger·mane·ness \-ānnəs\ *n* -ES **:** the quality or state of being germane

german fingering *n, usu cap G* **:** marking on piano music that indicates the thumb by the figure 1 and the fingers by the figures 2, 3, 4, and 5 — compare AMERICAN FINGERING

german flute *n, usu cap G* **:** the modern flute

german fried potatoes *n pl, usu cap G* **:** raw or cooked potatoes sliced and fried in a skillet

german gold *n, usu cap G* **:** DUTCH METAL

¹ger·man·ic \jə(r)ˈmanik, ˈjərˈm-, (ˈ)jəˈm-, (ˈ)jəiˈm-, -nēk\ *adj, usu cap* [ML & L; ML *Germanicus* German, fr. L, of the Germanic peoples in western Europe in Roman times, fr. *Germanus* member of such people + *-icus* -ic] **1 a :** GERMAN **b :** of a more or less German nature **:** having characteristics that are somewhat German **2 :** of, relating to, or characteristic of the Teutons **:** TEUTONIC **3 :** of, relating to, or constituting Germanic

²germanic \"\ *n* -S *cap* **:** a branch of the Indo-European language family containing English, German, Dutch, Afrikaans, Flemish, Frisian, the Scandinavian languages, and Gothic — called also *Teutonic;* see INDO-EUROPEAN LANGUAGES table

³germanic \", -mān-\ *adj* [NL *germanium* + E *-ic*] **:** of, relating to, or containing germanium — used esp. of compounds in which this element is tetravalent

germanic consonant shift *n, cap G* **:** CONSONANT SHIFT 1

ger·man·ics \(,)=ˈmaniks, -nēks\ *n pl but sing in constr, usu cap* **:** a study of Germanic languages **:** Germanic philology

ger·man·i·fy \-nə,fī\ *vt* -ED/-ING/-ES *often cap* [⁴*German* + *-ify*] **:** to make German in quality or character **:** GERMANIZE 2

ger·ma·nin \-ˈmānən\ *n* -s [ISV *german-* (fr. NL *germanium*) + *-in*] **:** SURAMIN

german iris *n, usu cap G* **1 :** any of several Old World bearded irises: as **a :** a large purple-flowered to white-flowered iris (*Iris germanica*) native to central and southern Europe **b :** any of several chiefly European irises (as *I. kochii* and *I. flavescens*) usu. considered to be closely related to or sometimes varieties of the German iris (*I. germanica*) **2 :** any of numerous tall bearded horticultural irises derived from the wild German irises (esp. *Iris germanica*) by hybridization and selection

ger·man·ish \ˈjərmənish\ *adj, usu cap* **:** GERMANIC 1b

ger·man·ism \ˈjərmə,nizəm, ˈjəm-, ˈjəim-\ *n* -s *usu cap* **1 :** a characteristic feature of German occurring in another language or dialect **2 :** allegiance to or partiality for Germany or German customs and culture **3 :** the policies, practices, or objectives believed to be distinctive of Germany or the German people

ger·man·ist \-nəst\ *n* -s *usu cap* [G, fr. L *Germania* land occupied by the Germanic peoples in western Europe in Roman times + G *-ist*] **1 :** a specialist in the German language, Germanics, or German literature and culture **2 :** an historian who magnifies the influence of Germanic institutions in the development of European civilization — compare ROMANIST

ger·man·is·tic \ˌ=məˈnistik, -tēk\ *adj, usu cap* **:** of or relating to Germanistics or Germanists

ger·man·is·tics \ˌ==ˈ=stiks, -tēks\ *n pl but sing in constr, usu cap* [G *Germanistik*, fr. *Germanist* + *-ik* -ics] **:** GERMANICS

ger·man·ite \ˈ==,nīt\ *n* -s [ISV *germani-* (fr. NL *germanium*) + *-ite;* orig. formed as G *germanit*] **:** a mineral $Cu_3(Ge,Fe,etc.)(S,As)_4$ consisting of a copper iron germanium sulfide occurring in metallic reddish gray masses

¹germanity *n* -ES [*germane* + *-ity*] *obs* **:** KINSHIP

²ger·man·i·ty \jə(r)ˈmanəd·ē, ˌjərˈ-, jəˈ-, jəiˈ-, -nətē, -i\ *n* -ES *usu cap* [⁴*german* + *-ity*] **:** the quality or spirit characteristic of Germany or the Germans ⟨an Aryan God who is no more than a concept of composite *Germanity* —Theodore Maynard⟩

ger·ma·ni·um \jə(r)ˈmānēəm, ˌjərˈ-, jəˈ-, jəiˈ-\ *n* -s [NL, fr. ML *Germania* Germany (fr. L, land inhabited by the Germanic peoples in Roman times) + NL *-ium*] **:** a grayish white hard brittle metalloid element resembling silicon but with a valence of 2 as well as 4 that occurs combined esp. in rare minerals (as germanite and argyrodite), in the ash of some lignites and coals, and in zinc-refinery residues from which it is recovered by conversion to its volatile tetrachloride, and that is used as a semiconductor (as in transistors) — symbol *Ge;* see ELEMENT table

german ivy *n, usu cap G* **:** a twining or creeping southern African plant (*Senecio mikanioides*) with yellow flowers and leaves resembling those of ivy

ger·man·iza·tion \ˌjərmənəˈzāshən, ˌjəm-, ˌjəim-, -ˌnīˈz-\ *n* -s *often cap* **:** the act or process of germanizing or the state of being germanized

ger·man·ize \ˈ==,nīz\ *vb* -ED/-ING/-S *often cap* [⁴*german* + *-ize*] *vt* **1** *archaic* **:** to translate into German **2 a :** to cause to acquire German customs or attitudes; *esp* **:** to force into conformity with German cultural patterns or governmental policies ⟨cities of the Polish Corridor . . . were *germanized* when the Nazis took over —Mario Pei⟩ **b :** to give a German quality to (speech or writing) by the use of German words or grammatical constructions ~ *vi* **:** to adopt German customs and manners or become German in sympathies and predilections

german knot *n, usu cap G* **:** a figure-eight knot

german knotgrass *n, usu cap G* **:** KNAWEL

german lilac *n, usu cap G* **:** RED VALERIAN

german madwort *n, usu cap G* **:** a low hairy annual herb (*Asperugo procumbens*) of the family Boraginaceae with blue flowers and a root used as a substitute for madder

german measles *n pl but sing in constr, usu cap G* **:** RUBELLA

german millet *n, usu cap G* **:** a foxtail millet (*Setaria italica stramineofructa*) with yellow fruits in large drooping often lobed spikes — called also *golden wonder millet;* compare SIBERIAN MILLET

¹germano- *comb form, usu cap* [NL, fr. ML *Germanus* German, fr. L, any member of the Germanic peoples inhabiting western Europe in Roman times] **:** German ⟨*Germanophile*⟩ **:** German and ⟨*Germano*-Russian⟩

²germano- *comb form* [ISV, fr. NL *germanium*] **:** germanium — esp. in names of compounds containing germanium in place of carbon ⟨*germano*chloroform $GeHCl_3$⟩

¹ger·man·o·phile \jə(r)ˈmanə,fīl, ˌjərˈ-, jəˈ-, jəiˈ-\ *or* **ger·man·o·phil** \-,fil\ *adj, usu cap* [¹*Germano-* + *-phile, -phil*] **:** approving or favoring the German people and their institutions and customs

²germanophile \"\ *or* **germanophil** \"\ *n, usu cap* **:** one who is Germanophile

ger·man·o·phobe \-,fōb\ *n* -s *usu cap* [¹*Germano-* + *-phobe*] **:** one having Germanophobia

ger·mano·pho·bia \(,)=,==ˈfōbēə; ˌjərmənōˈf-, ˌjəm-, ˌjəim-\ *n, usu cap* [NL, fr. ¹*Germano-* + *-phobia*] **:** an intense dislike or fear of Germany and German characteristics, customs, and governmental activities ⟨~ . . . continues extremely strong in France —D.F.Schoenbrun⟩

ger·ma·nous \(ˈ)jərˈmānəs\ *adj* [NL *germanium* + E *-ous*] **:** of, relating to, or containing germanium in the bivalent state

german pancake *n, usu cap G* **:** a pancake oven-cooked in a skillet until brown and puffy

german process *n, usu cap G* **1 :** the process of reducing copper ore in a blast furnace after roasting **2 :** the discontinuous or batch method of cupeling lead bullion

german reformed *adj, cap G&R* **:** of or relating to the Reformed Church in the United States that derives from the Reformed Church of Germany and whose first synod was organized in 1747

german roach *n, usu cap G* **:** CROTON BUG

german rum *n, usu cap G* **:** a Jamaica rum very highly flavored esp. for export to Europe

germans *pl of* GERMAN

german script *n, usu cap G* **:** a cursive handwriting used extensively in German-speaking countries since the 15th century

german sesame oil *n, usu cap G* **:** CAMELINE OIL

german shepherd *or* **german shepherd dog** *or* **german police dog** *n, usu cap G* **:** a shepherd dog of a breed originating in northern Europe at an uncertain date that has a long well-muscled body, a long wedge-shaped head, powerful jaws, a long bushy tail, and a smooth coat varying in color from white through all the shades and mixtures to black but with wolf coloring, tans, mixed brown, brindle, and black predominating, is 22 to 26 inches in height, is intelligent and responsive and trains well, and is often used as a guard dog, in police work, and as a guide dog for the blind — called also *Alsatian*

german shorthaired pointer *n, usu cap G* **:** a liver or liver-and-white hunting dog of a breed developed in Germany by crossing the Spanish pointer with the bloodhound and mating the offspring with the common pointer

german silver *n, usu cap G* **:** NICKEL SILVER

german sixth *n, usu cap G* **:** an augmented sixth chord consisting of a musical tone with its major third, perfect fifth, and augmented sixth above the lowest tone (as A♭, C, E♭, F♯)

german tamarisk *n, usu cap G* **:** a Eurasian shrub (*Myricaria germanica*) of the family Tamaricaceae that resembles the tamarisk

ger·man·town \ˈjərmən,tau̇n, ˈjəm-,ˈjəim-\ *n* -s *usu cap* [fr. *Germantown*, Pa.] **1** *or* **germantown wagon :** a four-wheeled one-horse covered wagon **2 :** a lightly twisted yarn usu. of 4-ply worsted used esp. for knitting and crocheting

ger·ma·ny \-mənē, -ni *also* -mn-\ *adj, usu cap* [fr. *Germany*, country in central Europe] **:** of or from Germany **:** of the kind or style prevalent in Germany **:** GERMAN

ger·mar·i·um \(,)jərˈma(a)rēəm\ *n* -s [NL, fr. *germen* + *-arium*] **:** the egg-producing part of the ovary in many flatworms and rotifers; *also* **:** the corresponding part of a testis — distinguished from *vitellarium*

germ band *n* **:** the thickening of the blastoderm of an insect egg from which the embryo proper arises

germ cell *n* **:** a cell set apart from the rest of the body to develop usu. after union with another of the opposite sex into a new individual **:** an egg or sperm cell or one of their antecedent cells — distinguished from *somatic cell*

germ center *n* **:** the lightly staining central proliferative area of a lymphoid follicle

germ disc *n* **:** GERMINAL DISC

germed *past of* GERM

ger·men \ˈjərmən, -,men\ *n* -s [L — more at GERM] **1** *archaic* **a:** the rudiment of an organism **:** GERM **b :** a young branch **:** SHOOT **2** [NL, fr. L] **a :** GONAD **b :** the germ cells and their precursors

germfree \ˈ=ˌ=\ *adj* [*germ* + *free*] **:** free of microorganisms **:** AXENIC

germ gland *n* **:** GONAD

ger·mi·ci·dal \ˌjərməˈsīdᵊl, ˌjəm-, ˌjəim-\ *adj* **:** of or relating to a germicide **:** destroying germs

ger·mi·cide \ˈ==,sīd\ *n* -s [¹*germ* + *-i-* + *-cide*] **:** an agent that destroys germs (as disease germs) **:** BACTERICIDE — compare ANTISEPTIC, DISINFECTANT

germier *comparative of* GERMY

germiest *superlative of* GERMY

ger·mi·na·bil·i·ty \ˌ==nəˈbilədˌē, -ətē, -i\ *n* -ES **:** the capacity to germinate ⟨the ~ of the seed⟩

ger·mi·na·ble \ˈ==nəbəl\ *adj* [*germinate* + *-able*] **:** capable of germination

ger·mi·nal \ˈ=mənᵊl\ *adj* [F, fr. L *germin-, germen* + F *-al*] **1 a :** being in the germ or earliest stage of development **:** INCIPIENT, EMBRYONIC ⟨the ~ philosophical ideas underlying western culture —*Bull. of Bates Coll.*⟩ **b :** creative or productive of new ideas or forces ⟨a highly original and ~ critic —Malcolm Ross⟩ **2 a :** of, relating to, or having the characteristics of a germ or germ cell **b :** of, relating to, or resembling the cells or tissues characteristic of the early stage of an embryo — **ger·mi·nal·ly** \-ᵊlē, -ᵊli\ *adv*

germinal apparatus *n* **:** EGG APPARATUS

germinal area *n* **:** the part of the blastoderm that forms the embryo proper of an amniote vertebrate

germinal cell *n* **:** an embryonic cell of the early vertebrate nervous system that is the source of neuroblasts and neuroglial cells

germinal center *n* **:** GERM CENTER

germinal disc *n* **1 :** BLASTODISC **2 :** GERMINAL AREA

germinal epithelium *n* **:** the epithelial covering of the genital ridges and of the gonads derived from them — see PRIMORDIAL OVUM

germinal layer *n* **1 :** GERM LAYER **2 :** a layer of cells from which new tissue is constantly formed; *specif* **:** the innermost layer of the epidermis

germinal membrane *n* **:** BLASTODERM

germinal vesicle *n* **:** the enlarged nucleus of the primary oocyte prior to completion of the reduction divisions

ger·mi·nant \ˈjərmənənt, ˈjəm-,ˈjəim-\ *adj* [L *germinant-, germinans*, pres. part. of *germinare*] **:** germinating or having the capacity to grow or develop ⟨the tendency to proselytize . . . was ~ in Israelitish religion —Moses Buttenwieser⟩

ger·mi·nate \-mə,nāt, *usu* -ād·+V\ *vb* -ED/-ING/-S [L *germinatus*, past part. of *germinare* to sprout, put forth, fr. *germin-, germen* bud, sprout, germ — more at GERM] *vt* **1 :** to cause to sprout or grow ⟨~ a broad bean on damp flannel —John Percival⟩ **2 :** to cause to originate or develop ⟨until recently the university presses *germinated* no ideas at all —M.S.Watson⟩ ~ *vi* **1** *archaic* **:** to shoot forth like a plant **:** EFFLORESCE ⟨the stone on which the native alum . . . ~*s* is black and shining —William Brownrigg⟩ **2 :** to begin to grow **:** SPROUT — used esp. of a spore or seed ⟨the seed . . . ~*s* on access of water, air, and warmth —W.F.Ganong⟩ **3 :** to come into being **:** EVOLVE ⟨before Western civilization began to ~ —A.L.Kroeber⟩

ger·mi·na·tion \ˌ==ˈnāshən\ *n* -s [L *germination-, germinatio*, fr. *germinatus* + *-ion-, -io* -ion] **:** the beginning, process, or result of germinating: **a :** the initial development of a spore involving either production of a germ tube or internal breakup ⟨the first stage in ~ of a spore is the absorption of water —George Smith⟩ **b :** the resumption of growth by the embryo in a seed after planting that involves the development of a young plant from the embryo after a period of dormancy **:** SPROUTING ⟨~ starts when the seed coat is broken —F.S. Baker⟩ **c :** the development of a bud **d :** the production of a pollen tube by a pollen grain **2 :** the beginning of growth or development **:** EVOLUTION ⟨the ~ of newer and more tentative ideas —J.T.Edsall⟩

ger·mi·na·tive \'==,nā|d·|iv, -,nə|, |t|, |ēv *also* |əv\ *adj* **:** of or relating to germination: **a :** having the power to germinate ⟨~ and virulent spores⟩ **b :** having the power to develop **:** EVOLVING ⟨afraid of falsifying his ~ perceptions by working over his drafts —*Brit. Bk. News*⟩ — **ger·mi·na·tive·ly** \|əvlē, -li\ *adv*

germinative vesicle *n* **:** GERMINAL VESICLE

ger·mi·na·tor \-,nād·ə(r), -ātə-\ *n* -s **1 :** one that germinates seeds **2 :** a cabinet or other container in which moistened seeds are tested for their ability to germinate

germing *adj* [fr. pres. part. of 2*germ*] **:** RUDIMENTARY, UNDEVELOPED

ger·mi·par·i·ty \,jərmə'parəd·ē\ *n* -ES [*germ* + *-i-* + L *parere* to produce + E *-ity* — more at PARE] **:** reproduction by germs — **ger·mip·a·rous** \(')jər¦mipərəs\ *adj*

ger·mis·ton \'jərməstən\ *adj, usu cap* [fr. *Germiston*, Union of So. Africa] **:** of or from the city of Germiston, Union of South Africa **:** of the kind or style prevalent in Germiston

germ layer *n* **:** any of the three primary layers of cells in the embryos of triploblastic animals that are differentiated during and immediately following gastrulation and that are precursors of the various tissues and organs of the adult — see ECTODERM, ENDODERM, MESODERM

germ·less \'=ləs\ *adj* **:** free from germs

germ line *or* **germ track** *n* **:** the sequence of cells from zygote to functional germ cell **:** GERM PLASM

germ·ling \'=liŋ\ *n* -s [1*germ* + *-ling*] **:** a young gametophyte produced by the germination of a tetraspore; *also* **:** a young sporophyte

germ nucleus *n* **:** the nucleus of the egg or sperm cell

ger·mon \zhermōn\ *n, pl* **germons** \-ōn(z)\ [F] **:** ALBACORE 1

germ peg \'jərm-\ *n* [by folk etymology fr. *gem peg*] **:** GIM PEG

germ plasm *n* **1 :** germ cells and their precursors regarded as bearers of hereditary characters and as at all times fundamentally independent of other body cells **2 :** the hereditary material of the germ cells **:** GENES

germ pore *n* **:** a pore, pit, or thin area in the outer wall of a spore or pollen grain through which the germ tube or pollen tube makes its exit on germination

germproof \'=¦=\ *adj* **:** impervious to the penetration or action of germs

germs *pl of* GERM, *pres 3d sing of* GERM

germ separator *n* **:** a tank or other device for floating off the detached germs from the wet-milled grains of corn or sorghum in a starch factory

germ theory *n* **:** a theory in medicine: infections, contagious diseases, and certain other conditions (as suppurative lesions) result from the action of microorganisms

germ tube *n* **:** the slender tubular outgrowth first produced by most spores in germination

germ·ule \'jər(,)myül\ *n* -s [1*germ* + *-ule*] **:** a small germ

germ warfare *n* **:** biological warfare employing microorganisms to harass the enemy, his livestock, or his crops ⟨charges about *germ warfare* which bacteriological experts have demonstrated to be false —*Foreign Policy Bull.*⟩

germy \'jərmē\ *adj, often* -ER/-EST [1*germ* + *-y*] **:** full of germs ⟨the water in New York Harbor is oily, dirty, and ~ —Joseph Mitchell⟩

ger·o·der·ma \,jerō'dərmə\ *or* **ger·o·der·mia** \-mēə\ *n* -s [NL, irreg. fr. Gk *gerōn* old man + NL *-derma* or *-dermia*] **:** premature aging of the skin (as in Simmonds' disease)

ge·ron·i·mo \jə'ränə,mō\ *interj, usu cap* [after *Geronimo* †1900 Apache Indian chief] — used as a battle cry by paratroopers typically at the moment of jumping

geront- *or* **geronto-** *comb form* [F, *géront-*, *géronto-*, fr. Gk *geront-*, *geronto-*, fr. *geront-*, *gerōn* old man; akin to Gk *gēras* old age — more at CORN] **:** old age ⟨*geronto*logy⟩

ge·ron·tal \jə'ränt°l\ *adj* [*geront-* + *-al*] **:** GERONTIC

ge·ron·tic \-tik\ *adj* [Gk *gerontikos* of or for old men, like an old man, fr. *geront-*, *gerōn* old man + *-ikos* -ic] **:** of or relating to decadence or old age

ger·on·toc·ra·cy \,jerən·'täkrəsē, -,rän·-\ *n* -ES [F *gérontocratie*, fr. *géronto-* geront- + *-cratie* -cracy] **:** rule by elders; *specif* **:** a form of social organization in which a group of old men or a council of elders dominates or exercises control — **ge·ron·to·crat** \jə'räntə,krat\ *n* -s — **ge·ron·to·crat·ic** \=¦==¦krad·ik\ *adj*

ge·ron·to·ge·ous \jə¦räntō¦jēəs\ *adj* [*geront-* + *ge-* + *-ous*] **:** of or relating to the Old World or the eastern hemisphere

ge·ron·to·log·i·cal \jə¦räntō¦läjəkəl, ¦jeränt°l¦ä-\ *adj* **:** of or relating to gerontology ⟨~ research⟩

ger·on·tol·o·gist \,jerən·'täləjəst, -,rän·-\ *n* -s **:** a specialist in gerontology

ger·on·tol·o·gy \-jē,-ji\ *n* -ES [ISV *geront-* + *-logy*] **:** a scientific study of the phenomena of aging and of the problems of the aged — compare GERIATRICS

ge·ron·to·mor·phic \jə¦räntō¦mȯrfik\ *adj* [*geront-* + *-morphic*] **:** characterized by physical specialization most fully developed in the old male of a species ⟨~ traits⟩

ge·ron·to·mor·pho·sis \=,=='mȯrfəsəs *sometimes* -,mȯr'fōsəs\ *n* -ES [NL, fr. *geront-* + *-morphosis*] **1 :** phylogenetic change involving specialization of the characters of adult organisms and accompanied by decreased capacity for further change **2 :** tendency toward racial senescence — compare FETALIZATION, PAEDOMORPHOSIS

ge·ron·to·phil·ia \jə,räntō'filēə\ *n* -s [NL, fr. *geront-* + *-philia*] **:** sex attraction toward old persons

-gerous \j(ə)rəs\ *adj comb form* [L *-ger* (fr. *gerere* to bear, wage, cherish) or F *-gère* (fr. L *-ger*) + E *-ous* — more at CAST] **:** bearing, producing — preceded by *i* ⟨crystalli*gerous*⟩ ⟨denti*gerous*⟩

ge·rou·sia *also* **ge·ru·sia** \jə'rüzh(ē)ə\ *n* -s *usu cap* [L & Gk; L *gerusia*, fr. Gk *gerousia*, fr. *geront-*, *geron* old, old man + *-ia* -y] **1 :** a council of elders in ancient Greece; *specif* **:** the Spartan senate **2 :** SANHEDRIN

ger·res \'je(,)rēz\ *n, cap* [NL, fr. L, a sea fish of little value] **:** the type genus of the family Gerridae comprising long-bodied compressed marine fishes with protrusible mouths and large silvery scales

ger·rho·no·tine \¦jerə¦nō,tīn\ *adj* [NL *Gerrhonotus* + E *-ine*] **:** of or relating to the genus *Gerrhonotus*

ger·rho·no·tus \,=='nōd·əs\ *n, cap* [NL, fr. Gk *gerrho-* (fr. *gerrhon* hide-covered shield, anything made of wickerwork) + NL *-notus;* akin to ON *kjarr* bush, *kass* willow basket, Arm *car* tree] **:** a genus of long-tailed slow-moving chiefly terrestrial lizards (family Anguidae) that are widely distributed in western No. America — see ALLIGATOR LIZARD

ger·rho·sau·rid \,jerō'sȯrəd\ *n* -s [NL *Gerrhosauridae*] **:** a lizard of the family Gerrhosauridae

ger·rho·sau·ri·dae \-ȯrə,dē\ *n pl, cap* [NL, fr. *Gerrhosaurus*, type genus (fr. Gk *gerrho-* + NL *-saurus* + *-idae*] **:** a family of African and Malagasy lizards somewhat resembling the skinks

1**ger·ri·dae** \'jerə,dē\ *n pl, cap* [NL, fr. *Gerris*, type genus + *-idae*] **:** a family of true bugs including the water striders

2**gerridae** \"\ *n pl, cap* [NL, fr. *Gerres*, type genus + *-idae*] **:** a family of chiefly tropical marine percoid fishes comprising various locally important food fishes — see GERRES, MOJARRA

1**ger·ry·man·der** \'jerē,mandə(r), -ri,m-, -maan-, ,=='== *also* 'ge- *or* ,ge-; *the "G" in the surname "Gerry" is pronounced* g\ *n* -s [Elbridge *Gerry* †1814 Amer. statesman + sala*mander;* fr. the fancied resemblance to a salamander (made famous by caricature) of the irregularly shaped outline of an election district in northeastern Mass. that had been formed for partisan purposes in 1812 during Gerry's governorship] **1 :** the act or method of gerrymandering ⟨the district was the product of a 1950 ~ —Gladwin Hill⟩ **2 :** a district or pattern of districts varying greatly in size or population as a result of gerrymandering ⟨three new ~s in New York City —Gus Tyler⟩

2**gerrymander** \"\ *vb* **gerrymandered; gerrymandered; gerrymandering** \-d(ə)ring\ **gerrymanders** *vt* **1 :** to divide (a territorial unit) into election districts in an unnatural and unfair way with the purpose of giving one political party an electoral majority in a large number of districts while concentrating the voting strength of the opposition in as few districts as possible ⟨California's Republican legislature ~*ed* the 26th . . . to make it overwhelmingly Democratic and turn four adjoining districts into Republican strongholds —*Time*⟩ **2 :** to divide (an area) into political units in an unnatural and unfair way with the purpose of giving special advantages to one group ⟨plans to ~ school districts so that de facto segregation could be maintained —Don Pryor⟩ **~** *vi* **:** to follow the practice of creating gerrymanders ⟨the electorate may punish them if they ~ too brazenly —W.K.Hancock⟩

gers \'gers\ *dial Brit var of* GRASS

gers·dorff·ite \'gerz,dȯr,fīt, 'gers,-\ *n* -s [G *gersdorffit*, fr. the von *Gersdorff* family, 19th cent. Austrian mine owners + G *-it* -ite] **:** a mineral NiAsS consisting of a silver-white to steel-gray nickel sulfarsenide that may also contain some iron and cobalt

ger·sum \'gersəm\ *n* -s [ME, jewel, costly gift, gersum, fr. OE *gærsum*, *gærsuma* jewel, costly gift, treasure, fr. ON *gersemi*, *görsemi*, fr. *görr* ready, equipped + *-semi* (fr. *-samr* -some) — more at YARE] **:** a fine paid by a vassal in feudal England to his superior usu. on taking a holding

ger·trude \'gər·,trüd\ *n* -s [fr. the name *Gertrude*] **:** an infant's slip usu. made of cotton and buttoned at each shoulder

gertrude

ger·und \'jerənd\ *n* -s [LL *gerundium*, fr. L *gerundus*, gerundive of *gerere* to bear, act, perform — more at CAST] **1 :** a verbal noun in Latin that occurs in the genitive singular, dative singular, accusative singular, and ablative singular and that expresses the action of the verb as generalized or in continuance ⟨in Latin *ars vivendi* "the art of living" and *fratrem laudando* "in quoting your brother", *vivendi* and *laudando* are ~*s*⟩ **2 :** any of several linguistic forms in languages other than Latin that are felt to be analogous to the Latin gerund; *esp* **:** the English verbal noun in *-ing* that has the function of a substantive (as subject or object of a verb, object of a preposition, or complement of a verb) and at the same time shows the verbal features of tense and voice (as *choosing*, *having chosen*, *being chosen*), capacity to take adverbial qualifiers, and capacity to govern objects when the verb is transitive and that may have a subject in the objective or common case but often takes in place of a subject a possessive qualifier denoting the agent of its action esp. in literary use and when the agent is a pronoun or a noun denoting a person or persons ⟨in the sentences "I am surprised at his taking the matter so lightly" and "he left without anyone in the room noticing his departure", *taking* and *noticing* are ~*s*⟩ — see 3-ING

gerund–grinder \'==,==\ *n* **:** a pedantic teacher esp. of Latin grammar

gerund–grinding \'==,==\ *n* **:** pedantic instruction esp. in Latin grammar

ge·run·di·al \jə'rəndēəl, (')je¦r-\ *adj* [LL *gerundi*um + E *-al*] **:** of, relating to, or like a gerund ⟨the ~ suffix⟩ — **ge·run·di·al·ly** \-əlē\ *adv*

ger·un·di·val \¦jerən¦dīvəl *sometimes* jə'rəndəvəl *or* -'rəndēv-\ *adj* **:** of, relating to, or like a gerundive

ge·run·dive \jə'rəndiv, -dēv *also* -dəv\ *n* -s [ME, fr. LL *gerundivus*, fr. *gerundium* + *-ivus* -ive — more at GERUND] **1 :** the Latin adjective that serves as the future passive participle, expresses necessity or fitness, and has the same suffix as the gerund **2 :** a verbal adjective in a language other than Latin analogous to the gerundive

gerusia *usu cap, var of* GEROUSIA

Ger·vais \(')zher¦vā\ *trademark* — used for cheese and milk products

ge·ryg·o·ne \jə'rigə(,)nē\ *n, cap* [NL, fr. Gk *gērygonē*, fem. of *gērygonos* born of sound, fr. *gērys* sound, voice + *gonos* that which is born, child, fr. *gignesthai* to be born — more at CARE, KIN] **:** a genus of small insectivorous Australasian warblers

ger·y·o·nia \,jerē'ōnēə\ *n, cap* [NL, fr. *Geryon* (monster of Greco-Roman mythology having three bodies and powerful wings, fr. L, fr. Gk *Gēryōn*) + NL *-ia*] **:** a genus of craspedote medusae having six simple radial canals with corresponding tentacles

ger·ze·an \'gerzēən, 'gər-\ *adj, usu cap* [fr. *Gerze*h, Egypt + E *-an*] **:** of or relating to an Aeneolithic culture of Upper Egypt characterized by the increased importance of agriculture, new techniques in industry, and expansion in the amount and area of foreign trade with a resulting influx of new materials and artifacts

ges *pl of* GE

ge·san \'zhās°n\ *n* -s *usu cap* [irreg. fr. 2*ge* + *-an*] **:** a language stock in So. America including the Apinayé, Botocudo, Caingang, Cayapo, and Ge

ge·sell·schaft \gə'zel,shäft\ *n, pl* **gesellschafts** \-f(t)s\ *also* **gesellschaf·ten** \-tən\ [G, lit., company, society, fr. OHG *giselliscaft* companionship, fr. *gisellio* one that rooms with another, companion (fr. *gi-*, perfective, associative, and collective prefix + *sal* hall) + *-scaft* -ship — more at CO-, SALOON] **1 :** a rationally developed mechanistic type of social relationship characterized by impersonally contracted associations between persons — contrasted with *gemeinschaft* **2 :** a society characterized by the relationships existing in a gesellschaft

gesh·u·rite \'geshə,rīt, gə'shu̇,r-\ *n* -s *cap* [*Geshur*, region in ancient Palestine + E *-ite*] **1 :** a member of an Aramaean tribe in northeastern Palestine that was independent in David's time **2 :** a member of a tribe in southern Palestine

ge·sith \ye'sēth\ *n* -s [OE *gesīth*, lit., companion, one of a retinue of warriors; akin to OHG *gisind*, *gisindo* one of a retinue of warriors, ON *sinni*, Goth *gesinthja;* derivatives fr. the root of E *send*] **:** a wellborn companion or attendant of an Anglo-Saxon king **:** THANE — compare COMES

ge·sith·cund \-,ku̇nd\ *n* -s [OE *gesīthcund*, fr. *gesīth* + *-cund* (akin to OE *cynd* kind) — more at KIND] **:** the rank or class of the gesiths

ge·sith·cund·man \-n(d)mən\ *n, pl* **gesithcundmen :** a man of the rank of the gesiths

ges·nera \'gesnərə\ [NL, after K. *Gesner*] *syn of* GESNERIA

ges·ner·a·ce·ae \,gesnə'rāsē,ē\ [NL, fr. *Gesnera*, type genus + *-aceae*] *syn of* GESNERIACEAE

ges·ner·ad \'gesnə,rad\ *or* **ges·ne·ri·ad** \ge'snirē,ad\ *n* -s [NL *Gesnera* or *Gesneria* + E *-ad* (kind of plant)] **:** a plant of the genus *Gesneria* or of the family Gesneriaceae

ges·ne·ria \ge'snirēə\ *n* [NL, fr. Konrad *Gesner* †1565 Swiss naturalist + NL *-ia*] **1** *cap* **:** a large genus (the type of the family Gesneriaceae) of tropical American herbs having showy tubular flowers **2** -s **:** any plant of the genus *Gesneria*

ges·ne·ri·a·ce·ae \(,)ge,snirē'āsē,ē\ *n pl, cap* [NL, fr. *Gesneria* + *-aceae*] **:** a large family of tropical herbs or rarely woody plants (order Polemoniales) having chiefly opposite leaves and strongly zygomorphic flowers

ges·ne·ri·a·ceous \(¦)=¦==¦āshəs\ *or* **ges·ner·a·ceous** \¦gesnə¦rā-\ *adj* [NL *Gesneriaceae* or *Gesneraceae* + E *-ous*] **:** of or relating to the family Gesneriaceae

gesneria family *n* **:** GESNERIACEAE

gesse \'jes\ *archaic var of* JESS

1**ges·so** \'je(,)sō\ *n* -ES [It, lit., chalk, gypsum, plaster, fr. L *gypsum* — more at GYPSUM] **1 a :** plaster of paris or gypsum prepared with glue for use in painting or making bas-reliefs **b :** a paste prepared from mixing whiting with size or glue and spread upon a surface to fit it for painting or gilding **2 :** a surface prepared by spreading gesso upon it

2**gesso** \"\ *adj* **:** having gesso as a coating or constituent part ⟨some paintings are executed on ~ panels —Paul Ziff⟩ ⟨a kidney-shaped chest of ~ work —*New Yorker*⟩

3**gesso** \"\ *vt* -ED/-ING/-ES **:** to apply gesso to ⟨the article was to be ~*ed* all over —*N.Y. State Univ. Bull.*⟩

1**gest** *or* **geste** \'jest\ *n* -s [ME *gest*, *jest*, *geste*, *jeste* deed, action, story, tale — more at JEST] **1 :** a notable deed or action **:** ADVENTURE, EXPLOIT ⟨knightly ~*s* and courtly pageantries —Elizabeth B. Browning⟩ **2 :** a tale of achievements or adventures; *esp* **:** a romance in verse ⟨~*s* and historic ballads written upon the story of Wallace —P.F.Tytler⟩

2**gest** *var of* GESTE

3**gest** *n* -s [alter. of earlier *gist*, fr. ME *giste* lodging for the night, fr. OF, fr. *gesir* to lie — more at GIST] *obs* **:** a stage or route in traveling esp. in a royal progress

ges·ta·gen *also* **ges·to·gen** \'jestəjən\ *n* -s [*gest*ate + connective *-a-* or *-o-* + *-gen*] **:** a progestational substance

ge·stalt \gə's(h)tält, -tȯlt\ *n, pl* **gestalts** \-lts\ *also* **gestalt·en** \-lt°n\ *often attrib* [G, shape, form, fr. MHG, appearance, nature, back-formation fr. *ungestalt* misshapen figure, fr. *ungestalt* ugly, fr. OHG, fr. *un-* 1un- + *gestalt*, past part. of *stellen* to place, set up, shape — more at STALL] **1 :** a structure or configuration of physical, biological, or psychological phenomena so integrated as to constitute a functional unit with properties not derivable from its parts in summation **2 :** the pattern or figure assumed by a gestalt structure or system

ge·stalt·ist \-ltəst\ *n* -s *often cap* **:** GESTALT PSYCHOLOGIST

gestalt psychologist *n, sometimes cap G* **:** one who accepts or practices the principles of Gestalt psychology

gestalt psychology *n, usu cap G* **:** the study of perception and behavior from the standpoint of the organism's response to configurational wholes with stress on the identity of psychological and physiological events and rejection of atomistic or elemental analysis of stimulus, percept, and response — called also *configurationism*

ge·sta·po \gə'stä(,)pō, -tȧ(-\ *n* -s *often attrib* [G, secret-police organization in Nazi Germany, fr. *Ge*heime *Sta*ats*po*lizei, lit., secret state police] **:** a secret-police organization that operates esp. against persons suspected of treason or sedition and employs methods held to be underhanded and terrorist

ges·tate \'je,stāt, *usu* -ād·+V\ *vb* -ED/-ING/-S [back-formation fr. *gestation*] *vt* **1 :** to carry in the uterus during pregnancy ⟨enabling the mammal to ~ its young inside its body —G.B. Shaw⟩ **2 :** to conceive and gradually develop in the mind ⟨he was *gestating* quite another character, the hero of the next chapter —Florence B. Lennon⟩ **~** *vi* **:** to be in the process of gestation

ges·ta·tion \je'stāshən\ *n* -s [L *gestation-*, *gestatio*, fr. *gestatus* (past part. of *gestare* to bear, fr. *gestus*, past part. of *gerere* to bear, act) + *-ion-*, *-io* -ion — more at CAST] **1** *archaic* **:** exercise in which one is carried ⟨~ in a carriage or in a boat has . . . good effects —Thomas Watson †1882⟩ **2 a :** the carrying of young usu. in the uterus from conception to delivery **:** PREGNANCY ⟨other acute . . . illnesses occur in the early months of ~ —J.P.Greenhill⟩ **b :** the incubation of eggs **3 :** conception and development esp. in the mind ⟨this extraordinary book, thirty years in ~ —W.R.Parker⟩

ges·ta·tion·al \(')je¦stāshən°l, -shnəl\ *adj* **:** of or relating to gestation

gestation period *also* **gestation** *n* **:** the length of time during

GESTATION PERIODS OF
REPRESENTATIVE MAMMALS

ANIMAL	PERIOD OF GESTATION	
	average	limits
ass	365 days	340–385 days
bats (various)	35–50 days	uncertain
bear	208 days	180–225 days
camel	406 days	370–440 days
cat	63 days	52–69 days
chinchilla	110 days	105–115 days
cow	281 days	210–353 days
dog	63 days	53–71 days
elephant	624 days	510–720 days
goat	148 days	135–160 days
guinea pig	68 days	58–75 days
hamster (golden)	16 days	15–19 days
horse	336 days	264–420 days
kangaroo (giant)	38–40 days	uncertain
lion	108 days	105–113 days
man	267 days*	240–313 days**
mouse	19 days	18–31 days
opossum (Virginia)	12½ days	uncertain
rabbit	31 days	30–35 days
rat	21 days	21–30 days
sheep	151 days	135–160 days
swine	114 days	101–130 days
tiger	105–112 days	uncertain

*From last ovulation or 274–280 days from beginning of last menses

**The longest period of gestation in man that has ever been admitted in the law courts in Great Britain is 360 days.

which gestation takes place ⟨the *gestation period* of a mare is about eleven months —F.A.Wrensch⟩ ⟨a new line of presses that would have a *gestation period* of about five years from drawing board to introduction —Joel Dean⟩

ges·ta·tive \'jestəd·iv, -,stād·-\ *adj* **:** GESTATIONAL

1**geste** *var of* GEST

2**geste** *also* **gest** \'jest\ *n* -s [MF *geste*, fr. L *gestus*, fr. *gestus*, past part. of *gerere*] **1** *archaic* **:** BEARING, DEPORTMENT ⟨his heroic grace and honorable *gest* —Edmund Spenser⟩ **2** *archaic* **:** GESTURE, MOVEMENT ⟨in the least ~ — the dropping low of the lid, the wrinkling of the brow —Elizabeth B. Browning⟩

ges·tic \-tik\ *adj* [2*geste* + *-ic*] **:** relating to or consisting of bodily movements or gestures ⟨artists who hold the most fantastically diverse theories as to what dancing is . . . — all recognize its ~ character —Susanne K. Langer⟩

ges·tic·u·lant \(')je¦stikyələnt *also* jə's-\ *adj* [L *gesticulant-*, *gesticulans*, pres. part. of *gesticulari*] **:** GESTICULATING

ges·tic·u·lar \-lə(r)\ *adj* [LL *gesticul*us + E *-ar*] **:** characterized or accompanied by gesticulation ⟨a ~ language⟩

ges·tic·u·late \je'stikyə,lāt *also* jə'-, *usu* -ād·+V\ *vb* -ED/-ING/-S [L *gesticulatus*, past part. of *gesticulari* to gesticulate, fr. (assumed) L *gesticulus* gesture (whence LL), dim. of L *gestus* gesture, deportment] *vt* **:** to express or indicate by gesture or gesticulation ⟨my mother *gesticulated* her wrath and despair —Hugh McCrae⟩ **~** *vi* **:** to make gestures or motions of the body or limbs esp. when speaking ⟨talking excitedly and *gesticulating* with her hands —Louis Auchincloss⟩ ⟨*gesticulated* to the waiter for the bill —Rebecca West⟩

ges·tic·u·la·tion \(,)je,stikyə'lāshən *also* jə,-\ *n* -s [L *gesticulation-*, *gesticulatio*, fr. *gesticulatus* + *-ion-*, *-io* -ion] **1 :** the act of gesticulating ⟨~ . . . is not art; it is expression —Susanne K. Langer⟩ **2 :** an expressive motion of the body or limbs (as in emphasizing an argument) ⟨these people suddenly ceased muttering, but redoubled their ~*s* —*Encore*⟩ — compare GESTURE

ges·tic·u·la·tive \='=kyə,lād·iv, ,ləd·-\ *adj* **:** inclined to or marked by gesticulation — **ges·tic·u·la·tive·ly** \-d·əvlē\ *adv*

ges·tic·u·la·tor \-,lād·ə(r)\ *n* -s [L, fr. *gesticulatus* + *-or*] **:** one that gesticulates; *esp* **:** ACTOR

gestic·u·la·to·ry \-,lə,tōrē\ *adj* **:** full of or characterized by gesticulations ⟨~ action⟩

ges·tion \'jes(h)chən\ *n* -s [L *gestion-*, *gestio*, fr. *gestus* (past part. of *gerere* to bear, act, manage) + *-ion-*, *-io* -ion — more at CAST] **1 :** the act or process of carrying on **:** CONDUCT, MANAGEMENT ⟨that participation in the ~ of affairs which his office made incumbent on him —Thomas Jefferson⟩ **2** *Roman & civil law* **:** management of or interference with the business or affairs of another without authority **:** INTERMEDDLING

gestio pro hae·re·de \'gestē,ō,prō,hī'rā(,)dā\ *n* [L, behavior as heir] *Roman, civil, & Scots law* **:** conduct as an heir that makes one liable for the debts of an ancestor

gestogen *var of* GESTAGEN

gests *pl of* GEST

ges·tur·al \'jes(h)chərəl\ *adj* **:** of, relating to, or consisting of gestures ⟨the study of ~ communication⟩ ⟨acts with a ritual and ~ perfection —Walker Percy⟩

1**ges·ture** \'jes(h)chə(r)\ *n* -s [ML *gestura* mode of action, fr. L *gestus* (past part. of *gerere* to bear, act) + *-ura* -ure — more at CAST] **1** *archaic* **:** the manner of carrying the body **:** CARRIAGE, BEARING ⟨the fashion of the countenance and the ~ of the body . . . is so correspondent to this state of mind —Edmund Burke⟩ **2** *obs* **:** the position or attitude of the body esp. in prayer ⟨as for their ~ or position, the men lay down leaning on their left elbow —Sir Thomas Browne⟩ **3 :** the use of motions of the limbs or body as a means of intentional expression ⟨we deduce motion from ~ —W.E.Allen⟩ ⟨~ may be deliberate . . . or even symbolic —Susanne K. Langer⟩ **4 :** a movement usu. of the body or limbs that symbolizes or emphasizes an idea, sentiment, or attitude ⟨she gave a ~ of despair —H.G.Wells⟩ ⟨the ability to find the appropriate ~*s* to convey the dramatic content of the work —*Encounter*⟩ — compare GESTICULATION **5 :** a notable or expressive action: as **a :** something said or done by way of formality or courtesy ⟨the invitation had been a ~ of sympathy toward a keen young officer without friends or relations —R.S.Porteous⟩ **b :** something said or done to bring about a desired end (as in diplomacy) ⟨diplomatic authorities brushed aside today the . . . proposal for an all-European security meeting as an insincere ~ and a propaganda appeal —W.H.Waggoner⟩ ⟨the words were far more than a political ~ to draw popular support —V.L.Parrington⟩ **c :** something said or done as a symbol or token ⟨a ~ of royal authority⟩ ⟨many members . . . deliberately invalidated their ballots as a protest ~ —*Current Biog.*⟩

²gesture \"\ *vb* -ED/-ING/-S *vi* **:** to make gestures **:** GESTICULATE ⟨*gesturing* vaguely with her full hands —Laura Krey⟩ ~ *vt* **1 :** to indicate or express by gestures ⟨what way is there of *gesturing* the cruelly impounded thought —Donald Davidson⟩ **2 :** to direct by gestures ⟨the policeman *gestured* him into the fork on the other side —Richard Llewellyn⟩

gesture language *n* **:** communication by gestures; *esp* **:** SIGN LANGUAGE ⟨*gesture languages* have not developed far because they occupy the hands —G.R.Harrison⟩

ge·sund·heit \gəˈzu̇nt,hīt\ *interj* [G, lit., health, fr. MHG *gesuntheit*, fr. *gesunt* healthy (fr. OHG *gisunt*) + *-heit* -hood (fr. OHG) — more at SOUND] — used to wish good health esp. to one who has just sneezed

geswarp *var of* GUESS-WARP

¹get \(ˈ)get, *usu* |d·+V; (ˈ)git|, *widely regarded as substandard, is quite frequent in educated speech when the verb does not have heavy stress as when a heavily stressed syllable immediately follows*\ *vb* **got** \(ˈ)gät\ *or archaic* **gat** \(ˈ)gat\ **got** \(ˈ)gät\ *or* **got·ten** \ˈgätᵊn\ **getting** \ˈged·iŋ, -etiŋ\ **gets** \(ˈ)gets, (ˌ)gits\ [ME *geten, getten*, fr. ON *geta* to get, beget, learn, name, speak; akin to OE *bigietan* to beget, OHG *pigezzan* to obtain, Goth *bigitan* to find, L *prehendere* to seize, grasp, Gk *chandanein* to hold, contain, Alb *gjet* to find, to get back; basic meaning: grasping, seizing] *vt* **1 a :** to gain possession of through one's own efforts ⟨men are not born rich, and in *getting* wealth the man is generally sacrificed —R.W. Emerson⟩ **b :** to earn from one's business or employment ⟨what they ~ by day they spend by night —Daniel Defoe⟩ **c :** to acquire or earn by or as if by labor or service ⟨if I ~ your daughter's love, what dowry shall I have —Shak.⟩ ⟨*got* an excellent reputation as an administrator⟩ **d :** to become the recipient or possessor of ⟨~*s* a check from his uncle every Christmas⟩ **2 a** (1) **:** to obtain by way of advantage or superiority ⟨~ the better of their opponents⟩ ⟨~ the upper hand⟩ ⟨*got* a good start and won the race⟩ (2) **:** to receive by way of benefit or profit ⟨is likely to ~ little for all his political activity⟩ **b** (1) **:** to achieve as a result of military activity ⟨having *gotten* the victory, pursued it to the utmost —Laurence Clarke⟩ (2) **:** to gain possession of by military activity ⟨and when the city Troy we shall have *got* —Thomas Hobbes⟩ **3 a :** to obtain by or as if by concession or entreaty ⟨*got* his father's consent to use the car⟩ ⟨rapped vigorously on the door but could ~ no answer⟩ **b :** to come to have ⟨~ a good night's sleep⟩ ⟨always ~*s* his own way⟩ ⟨walked up the hill to ~ a view of the town⟩ ⟨*got* the idea that he could do what he wanted to⟩ **c :** to come down with (an illness) **:** CATCH ⟨*got* measles from his brother⟩ **4 a :** to cause to be provided or supplied **:** seek out and obtain ⟨the officers *got* a search warrant⟩ ⟨hoped to ~ dinner at the inn⟩ **b :** to obtain for oneself or for another ⟨in the spring the wanton lapwing ~*s* himself another crest —Alfred Tennyson⟩ ⟨~ him his hat⟩ ⟨sent the boy to ~ help from the neighbors⟩ **c** *obs* **:** to obtain in marriage ⟨I wonder why such a handsome . . . young gentleman as you do not ~ some rich widow —Jonathan Swift⟩ **d** (1) **:** to obtain by hunting or fishing ⟨went into the woods and *got* six squirrels in an hour⟩ ⟨*got* several trout before breakfast⟩ (2) **:** to obtain by harvesting **:** GATHER ⟨*got* a good crop of wheat from the lower field⟩ (3) **:** to obtain by mining ⟨in proceeding to ~ the coal, the collier . . . works upon the face of the bed —*Collieries & Coal Trade*⟩ **5 :** BEGET ⟨~ you the sons your fathers *got*, and God will save the queen —A.E.Housman⟩ **6** *obs* **:** to arrive at **:** REACH ⟨if the wind blows strong and you cannot ~ the harbor, you must anchor —Woodes Rogers⟩ **7 a :** to succeed in bringing or conveying **:** cause to come or go ⟨*got* his luggage through customs in a few minutes⟩ ⟨*got* his car to the garage before the gas ran out⟩ **b :** to cause to move or be removed ⟨~ thee out from this land and return unto the land of thy kindred —Gen 31:13 (AV)⟩ ⟨~ the ladder away from the tree⟩ ⟨~ the cat out of the house⟩ **c :** to cause to be in a certain state, position, or condition ⟨soon *got* the animal under control⟩ ⟨*got* his feet wet⟩ ⟨*got* the fender dented⟩ ⟨will ~ himself into a jam if he's not careful⟩ ⟨*getting* everything right that can by perseverance or expense be *got* right —Richard Mallett⟩ **d :** to make ready **:** PREPARE ⟨promised to ~ breakfast by eight o'clock⟩ **8 a :** to take hold of **:** SEIZE ⟨the dog *got* the thief by the leg⟩ **b :** to make a captive of ⟨have *got* your fellow tribune and hale him up and down —Shak.⟩ **c :** to obtain the mastery of **:** OVERCOME ⟨such practices will surely ~ you in the end⟩ **d :** to have an emotional effect on **:** MOVE, TOUCH ⟨you say that the music seemed to you very sad, that it *got* you —Olin Downes⟩ **e :** to be a source of bafflement to **:** PUZZLE ⟨this problem really ~*s* me⟩ **f :** to cause annoyance to **:** IRRITATE ⟨his conceit ~*s* me⟩ **g :** to bring to retribution **:** take vengeance on; *specif* **:** KILL ⟨she had not brought it along for fun; she was out to ~ her rival —Cabell Phillips⟩ **9 a :** to be subjected to **:** meet with ⟨*got* a bad fall from the horse⟩ ⟨*got* a severe wound in battle⟩ ⟨expects to ~ the worst of the bargain⟩ **b :** to receive or suffer by way of punishment ⟨~*s* a whipping at least once a week⟩ ⟨*got* six months in jail⟩ **c :** to suffer a specified injury to ⟨*got* his nose broken playing football⟩ **d :** to strike with force **:** HIT ⟨the blow *got* him in the mouth⟩ **10 a :** to acquire by study or experience ⟨~ wisdom —Prov 4:5 (RSV)⟩ ⟨*got* a good education at the university⟩ **b :** to learn as a result of concentrated study ⟨was told to ~ the poem by heart⟩ ⟨~*s* his lessons faithfully⟩ **c :** to ascertain through calculation or experiment **:** find out by arithmetical or other processes ⟨worked the problem and *got* 46 as the answer⟩ **d :** to learn by hearing ⟨sorry, but I didn't ~ your name⟩ **e :** to apprehend the meaning of **:** COMPREHEND, UNDERSTAND ⟨the audience readily *got* the speaker's point⟩ ⟨don't ~ me wrong⟩ **11 :** to prevail on **:** PERSUADE, INDUCE ⟨*got* the publisher to bring out a new deluxe edition⟩ **12 a :** to come into or be in possession of — used in the past participle with the auxiliary *have* for emphasis ⟨he has *got* ten dollars⟩ **b :** to have as an obligation or necessity — used in the past participle with the auxiliary *have* ⟨they've *got* to go to a funeral⟩ ⟨you've *got* to eat more meat⟩ **13 :** to succeed in finding ⟨wondered what he could ~ to scold her about —William Black⟩ **14 a :** to establish communication with ⟨tried all afternoon to ~ them on the telephone⟩ **b :** to receive by radio or on television ⟨can ~ five stations since his new aerial was installed⟩ **15** *chiefly Brit* **:** to hold out for **:** STAY ⟨only a wonder of a horse can ~ those four miles and a half of ditches and fences —*London Daily Chronicle*⟩ **16 :** to cause (an opposing player) to be put out **:** RETIRE ⟨the shortstop's throw *got* the runner at first base⟩ ~ *vi* **1 a :** to bring oneself **:** succeed in coming or going ⟨hopes to ~ to New York for the holidays⟩ ⟨*got* safely across the street⟩ ⟨~ into the car⟩ ⟨the car *got* through the mud⟩ **b :** to come in the course of a journey ⟨planned to ~ to the city before dark⟩ ⟨they *got* home sooner than they had expected⟩ **c :** to come in reaching a desired end or in attaining a state toward which progress has been made ⟨finally *got* to sleep after midnight⟩ **d :** to come into existence **:** APPEAR ⟨dust *got* all over the books while we were away⟩ **2 a :** to acquire wealth or property ⟨whilst he was secretary . . . he had *gotten* vastly —John Evelyn⟩ ⟨*getting* and spending we lay waste our powers —William Wordsworth⟩ **b** *obs* **:** to derive profit **:** GAIN ⟨gamesters are wont to . . . ~ by using false dice —William Penn⟩ **3 a :** to have an opportunity **:** be able **:** CONTRIVE, MANAGE — used with following infinitive ⟨he never *got* to go to college —Edmund Wilson⟩ ⟨was lucky to ~ to see the new play⟩ **b :** to come to be — used with following present participle ⟨they *got* talking about old times and sat up half the night⟩ **4 :** to succeed in becoming **:** make oneself **:** BECOME ⟨how to ~ clear of all the debts I owe —Shak.⟩ ⟨~ well soon⟩ ⟨~*s* acquainted with the best people⟩ — often used as a passive auxiliary ⟨*got* caught in the rain⟩ ⟨*got* married last week⟩ ⟨behind every story there is another story that often never ~*s* told —Regina S. Jacobsen⟩ **5 :** to go away at once **:** leave immediately ⟨he presented a cocked revolver and told them to ~ —*Graceville (Minn.) Transcript*⟩

syn OBTAIN, PROCURE, SECURE, ACQUIRE, GAIN, WIN: GET is very general in its meaning and simple and familiar in its use. OBTAIN is likewise rather general. It may suggest that the thing sought has been long desired or that it has come into possession only after the expenditure of considerable effort or the lapse of considerable time ⟨the satisfaction *obtained* by the sentiment of communion with others, of the breaking down of barriers —John Dewey⟩ ⟨in western New York where her early education was *obtained* —H.W.H.Knott⟩ PROCURE is likely to suggest planning and contriving over a period of time and the use of unspecified or questionable means ⟨the Duma laid claim to full power . . . and on March 15 *procured* the abdication of the frightened and despondent Nicholas II —F.A.Ogg & Harold Zink⟩ ⟨some gifted spirit on our side *procured* (probably by larceny) a length of mine fuse —H.G.Wells⟩ SECURE may suggest safe lasting possession or control ⟨the large income and fortune which a prospering business *secures* for him is of his own making —J.A.Hobson⟩ ⟨almost absolute safety against infection could be *secured* by the simple precaution of using safe, potable water —V.G. Heiser⟩ ACQUIRE may suggest devious acquisition ⟨the destruction of that ship by a Confederate cruiser, although it had *acquired* a British registry in order to avoid capture —H.W.H.Knott⟩ It may also indicate continued, sustained, or cumulative acquisition ⟨the habit of any virtue, moral or intellectual, cannot be assumed at once, but must be *acquired* by practice —C.H.Grandgent⟩ GAIN often implies competition in acquiring something of value ⟨if a London merchant, however, can buy at Canton for half an ounce of silver a commodity which he can afterwards sell at London for an ounce, he *gains* a hundred percent —Adam Smith⟩ ⟨few men are placed in such fortunate circumstances as to be able to *gain* office —F.S.Oliver⟩ WIN may suggest favorable qualities leading naturally to the acquisition of something desired despite competition or obstacles ⟨the errors of his time were connected with his labors to remedy them and *win* a firmer knowledge than dialectic could supply —H.O.Taylor⟩ ⟨Mrs. Woolf's fiction is too negligent of the requirements of the common reader to *win* a wide following —F.B.Millett⟩ — **get after :** to subject to exhortation, reprimand, or attack ⟨lax in *getting after* home-repair racketeers —*Wall Street Jour.*⟩ — **get ahead :** to achieve success ⟨struggles to *get ahead* as an interior decorator —J.W.Aldridge⟩ — **get anywhere :** to be successful — usu. used with preceding negative ⟨I don't think he will *get anywhere* with his plans⟩ — **get around 1 :** to get the better of **:** CIRCUMVENT ⟨a small group of aggressive citizens has managed to *get around* . . . the largest, richest, most powerful international combine in the history of the world —Fred Smith⟩ **2 :** to escape the force of **:** EVADE ⟨there is no *getting around* it: meaning implies convention —J.M.Barzun⟩ — **get at 1 :** to reach with or as if with the hand ⟨it is hard to *get at* the spark plugs without a proper wrench⟩ **2 :** to acquire knowledge or understanding of ⟨a fundamental method for *getting at* symbolism has been achieved —C.C.Walcutt⟩ ⟨can *get at* the minds of companions only imaginatively —Bernard DeVoto⟩ **3 :** to influence corruptly **:** BRIBE ⟨take care she doesn't *get at* him —John Galsworthy⟩ **4 a :** to make an attack on or do injury to ⟨he hates us, and we are where he can *get at us* —Dorothy C. Fisher⟩ **b :** to turn one's attention to **:** apply oneself to ⟨a volume . . . which I long to *get at* but which must take its turn —O.W.Holmes †1935⟩ **5 :** to try to prove or make clear ⟨what he is *getting at* is continuity of experience —L.A. White⟩ — **get behind :** to give active support or endorsement to ⟨suggests that businessmen should *get behind* bond issues for school improvements —*Nation's Business*⟩ — **get down on :** to develop dislike for ⟨had no chance of promotion once the boss *got down on* him⟩ — **get even :** to get even with someone **:** get revenge — **get even with :** to repay in kind ⟨was determined to *get even with* him as soon as he could⟩ — **get home :** to reach the final resting place or goal in a board game (as parchesi) — **get into :** to gain possession or control of **:** come over ⟨can't understand what has *got into* that child⟩ — **get it 1 :** to receive a scolding or punishment **2 :** to understand the meaning of what is seen or heard **:** COMPREHEND — **get nowhere :** to be unsuccessful ⟨is likely to *get nowhere* with such a scheme⟩ — **get on 1 :** ENTER, BOARD, MOUNT ⟨*got on* the horse and rode away⟩ **2 :** to produce an unfortunate effect on **:** DISTURB, UPSET ⟨that sort of talk *gets on* my nerves⟩ **3 :** to give attention or consideration to ⟨doesn't know when to stop talking once he *gets on* music⟩ **4 :** to subject to reprimand or punishment ⟨promised to *get on* him for his negligence⟩ — **get one's goat :** to make one angry, irritated, or annoyed ⟨*gets my goat* to hear a man always grumbling —Adrian Bell⟩ — **get one's hand in :** to regain one's skill in an activity by practice ⟨after playing no tennis for some years, it took him time to *get his hand in*⟩ — **get one's hooks on** *slang* **:** to obtain possession or control of **:** take over — **get out from under :** to escape impending danger or risk — **get over 1 a :** OVERCOME, SURMOUNT ⟨once these difficulties were *got over* the work speeded up⟩ **b :** to recover from ⟨you can *get over* a disease by lying in bed —Charlton Laird⟩ **c :** to become accustomed to **:** reconcile oneself to ⟨the town will forget and forgive . . . and the parents will somehow *get over it* —Agnes S. Turnbull⟩ **2 :** to move or travel across **:** COVER, TRAVERSE ⟨was necessary for me to *get over* ground as fast as possible —A.W.Long⟩ — **get religion :** to undergo religious conversion ⟨she *got religion* and died in the odor of sanctity —Horace Wyndham⟩ — **get somewhere :** to be successful ⟨works so hard and so devotedly that he is sure to *get somewhere*⟩ — **get the hook :** to be removed or discharged — **get there :** to be successful ⟨he'll *get there* if hard work means anything⟩ — **get through 1 :** to reach the end of **:** COMPLETE ⟨*gets through* a greater amount of work with less expenditure of energy —James Hewitt⟩ **2 :** to while away **:** succeed in passing ⟨she found that there was . . . half an hour to be *got through* on a Friday afternoon —Robertson Davies⟩ — **get to 1 :** to arrive at the point of **:** BEGIN ⟨she *gets to* worrying if I leave her too long —Winifred Bambrick⟩ **2 a :** to succeed in establishing contact with **:** REACH ⟨adjusting the hours of our discussion groups so as to *get to* mothers who cannot afford baby-sitters —B.M.Beck⟩ **b :** to have an effect on **:** INFLUENCE ⟨it *got to* me until I couldn't think or sit still —Mickey Spillane⟩ — **get together 1 :** to bring together **:** COLLECT, ACCUMULATE ⟨in a few years he *got together* a good record collection⟩ **2 :** to come together **:** ASSEMBLE ⟨all the members of the family *get together* at least once a year⟩ **3 :** to reach an agreement ⟨the committee finally *got together* on its proposals⟩ — **get up :** to cause oneself to climb, ascend, or mount ⟨was hardly strong enough to *get up* the stairs⟩ — **get wind of :** to become aware of **:** learn of through hints or rumors ⟨*got wind of* the situation and came home⟩ — **get with :** to pay attention to **:** become busy about ⟨there were signs and sounds that television was about to *get with* it —*Newsweek*⟩

²get \ˈget, *usu* -ed·+V\ *n* -s [ME, fr. *geten, getten*, v.] **1** *now dial Eng* **:** something that is gained; *esp* **:** EARNINGS **2 a :** something that is begotten: (1) **:** OFFSPRING ⟨tries to make a hash of the lives of his innumerable ~ —John McCarten⟩ (2) **:** the entire progeny of a male animal ⟨a stallion's ~⟩ — compare PRODUCE (3) *Scot* **:** CHILD; *specif* **:** BASTARD **b :** LINEAGE ⟨a colt of champion ~⟩ **3 :** a return of a shot in a game (as tennis) that usu. scores for an opponent

³get *also* **gett** \"\ *n, pl* **gittin** [Heb *gēṭ*] **1** *Jewish law* **:** a document of release from obligation; *specif* **:** BILL OF DIVORCE **2** *Jewish law* **:** a religious divorce

ge·ta \ˈge(ˌ)tä\ *also* **getas** \-äz\ *n pl* [Jap *geta*] **:** Japanese wooden clogs for outdoor wear

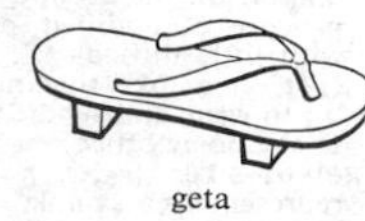

geta

getable *var of* GETTABLE

get about *vi* **1 a :** to be up and about **:** begin to walk ⟨has recovered from his injuries and is *getting about* again⟩ **b :** to come and go at will **:** be physically active ⟨the students really *get about* on weekends⟩ **2 :** to become current **:** CIRCULATE ⟨the idea has *got about* that he's dangerous —Ellen Glasgow⟩ ⟨the fear that it might *get about* among her acquaintances —Geoffrey Gorer⟩

get across *vi* **:** to become clear or convincing ⟨her thesis . . . would never *get across* if she didn't know how to make people in action both probable and interesting —H.C.Webster⟩ ~ *vt* **:** to make clear or convincing ⟨there will be cash to help *get* this point *across* —Helen Fuller⟩

ge·tae \ˈjē,tē, ˈge,tī\ *also* **ge·tai** \ˈge,tī\ *n pl, usu cap* [L & Gk; L *Getae*, fr. Gk *Getai*] **1 :** a people of ancient times that lived in the region corresponding approximately to eastern Bulgaria, the Dobruja, Walachia, Moldavia, and Bessarabia **2 :** all the northern Thracian peoples, of whom the Dacians and Getae were the two main elements

get along *vi* **1 a :** to proceed toward a destination **:** move on ⟨let's *get along* . . . and tell him about it —Marjory S. Douglas⟩ **b :** to proceed with a series of acts or measures **:** PROGRESS ⟨my mother was *getting along* with her housework —Maeve Brennan⟩ **c :** to approach an advanced stage ⟨it was *getting along* in the afternoon as we worked down this ridge —G.M. Dodge⟩; *esp* **:** to approach old age ⟨she's *getting along* and that's a big place for an old lady to handle —Ruth Moore⟩ **2 :** to meet one's needs **:** FARE, MANAGE ⟨books explaining how to *get along* in an uninhabited place —J.D.Hart⟩ ⟨those who have hardly enough money to *get along* on —A.N.Whitehead⟩ **3 :** to be or remain on congenial or harmonious terms ⟨he is hard to *get along* with if you don't agree with him —O.W.Holmes †1935⟩

¹ge·tan \ˈjētᵊn\ *adj, usu cap* [*Getae* + *-an*] **:** GETIC

²getan \"\ *n* -s *usu cap* **:** a member of the Getae

get around *vi* **1 a :** to go from place to place ⟨people . . . continued to *get around* in horse-drawn vehicles —*Amer. Guide Series: Wash.*⟩ **b :** to travel or socialize extensively and so have wide knowledge or experience ⟨is a good mixer and also *gets around* with the black-tie crowd —N.C.Stageberg⟩ **2 :** to become known or current ⟨sooner or later everybody's business *gets around* —Hamilton Basso⟩ **3 a :** to find or take the necessary time or effort — used with *to* ⟨those who never *got around* to reading the full work —R.E.Sherwood⟩ **b :** to give attention or consideration usu. after considerable delay — used with *to* ⟨knew we'd have to *get around* to the subject of seasickness sooner or later —Richard Joseph⟩

get·at·able \(ˈ)ged·ˈad·əbəl\ *adj* [*get at* (phrase) + *-able*] **:** capable of being reached, attained, got, or known **:** APPROACHABLE, ACCESSIBLE ⟨a very ~ man⟩ ⟨both oil and coal are there but not in economical quantities or ~ locations⟩

get away *vi* **1 :** to make one's escape **:** succeed in departing ⟨went on, making straight for the road beyond, thinking only about *getting away* —Robert Westerby⟩ ⟨something that's ingrained . . ., something that you can't *get away* from —Leslie Rees⟩ **2 :** to start on a course **:** set out ⟨the hikers planned to *get away* at dawn⟩ ~ *vt* **1 :** to equip and send out **:** put into action ⟨*got away* eight lifeboats and radioed a plea for more —*Time*⟩ **2 :** to get rid of after brief possession ⟨never saw anybody who could *get* the ball *away* faster —Ted Williams⟩ — **get away with 1 :** to do (as a reprehensible act) without criticism or penalty **:** perform without suffering the consequences ⟨can now *get away with* breaches of the rules and traditions which would never be allowed to others —Woodrow Wyatt⟩ **2 :** to eat or drink **:** CONSUME ⟨they *get away with* more alcohol than any other nation in the world —Emily Hahn⟩

getaway \ˈ≈,≈\ *n* -s [*get away*] **:** an act or instance of getting away: as **a :** the making of or the ability to make a start from complete rest ⟨a car with a good ~⟩ **b :** ESCAPE ⟨the thieves made their ~ in a stolen car⟩

get back *vi* **1 :** to come or go again to a person, place, or condition **:** RETURN, REVERT, RETREAT ⟨*getting back* to earth costs him all his balloons —Ellen L. Buell⟩ **2 :** to gain revenge **:** RETALIATE — used with *at* ⟨found an occasion for *getting back* at the First Consul by embroiling him with the Americans —Oscar Handlin⟩ ~ *vt* **:** to regain possession of **:** RECOVER ⟨*got back* nearly all the money he had lost⟩

get by *vi* **1 :** to make ends meet **:** MANAGE, SURVIVE ⟨*got by* for a time by hunting furs —M.C.Boatright⟩ ⟨a marvel to me how all these . . . little two-by-four stores *get by* —John McNulty⟩ **2 :** to succeed with the least possible effort or accomplishment ⟨knew that with a little brushing up I could probably *get by* on an examination —Norman Cousins⟩ **3 a :** to succeed without being discovered, criticized, or punished **:** pass unnoticed or unchallenged ⟨a group of drivers is *getting by* with known violations —D.S.Buck⟩ ⟨hold their jobs and *get by* socially . . . because they are easy to get along with —W.J.Reilly⟩ **b :** to pass for a white person ⟨all four grandparents were colored, but all could *get by* —W.L. White⟩

get down *vi* **1 :** to alight esp. from a vehicle **:** DESCEND ⟨the bus . . . was so jammed that I couldn't *get down* in time —Anna M. Ortese⟩ **2 :** to give one's attention or consideration — used with *to* ⟨having discussed the general theories . . . let's *get down* to cases —Richard Joseph⟩ ⟨*get down to* business⟩ ~ *vt* **1 :** to cause to be physically, mentally, or emotionally exhausted **:** DEPRESS ⟨it did not *get us down*, but it got us thoroughly bored —A.L.Rowse⟩ ⟨the heat was beginning to *get her down* —Mary Manning⟩ **2 :** to bring oneself to eat **:** SWALLOW ⟨one thing that he couldn't *get down* was baby octopus⟩ **3 :** to commit to writing **:** DESCRIBE, DEPICT ⟨she *gets* it all *down:* the real ruins, the fake ruins, . . . the litter in the fountains —Sean O'Faolain⟩

gete \ˈjēt\ *n* -s *usu cap* [L *Getae*, n. pl.] **:** GETAN

geth·er *dial var of* GATHER

geth·sem·a·ne \geth'semənē, -ni\ *n* -s *usu cap* [fr. the Garden of *Gethsemane* on the Mount of Olives near Jerusalem where Christ was arrested (Mt 26), fr. Gk *Gethsēmanē, Gethsēmanei*] **:** a place or occasion of great esp. mental or spiritual suffering

¹ge·tic \ˈjēd·ik, ˈjed·-\ *adj, usu cap* [*Getae* + *-ic*] **:** of or relating to the Getae or their language

²getic \"\ *n* -s *usu cap* **:** the language of the Getae prob. belonging to the Thraco-Phrygian branch of the Indo-European family

get in *vi* **1 a :** to make or effect an entrance **:** ENTER ⟨the burglar *got in* through an unlocked window⟩ **b :** to reach one's destination **:** ARRIVE ⟨the train *gets in* at noon⟩ **c :** to succeed in having sexual intercourse; *specif* **:** to make an entrance at the beginning of coitus — usu. considered vulgar **2 a :** to become friendly **:** be on congenial terms ⟨*got in* with a group of playboys and failed two freshman courses⟩ **b :** to become involved ⟨and now scamper . . . before you *get in* deeper with this bunch —Julian Maclaren-Ross⟩ **3 :** to become accepted for membership or chosen for office ⟨the mayor *got in* by the slimmest of margins⟩ **4 :** to reach the hawk as soon as the quarry has been killed ~ *vt* **1 a :** GATHER, HARVEST ⟨hopes to *get* the hay *in* before the rainy season⟩ **b :** PLANT, SOW ⟨hopes to *get* the seed *in* by the end of the month⟩ **2 a :** to include in one's schedule or routine ⟨intended to *get in* some golf during the summer⟩ **b :** to succeed in doing, making, or delivering ⟨his dogs were badly mauled before he could *get* a shot *in* to kill the leopard —*Farmer's Weekly (So. Africa)*⟩ **3 :** to cause to become involved **:** IMPLICATE ⟨he'll *get* you *in* so deep you'll be lucky if you don't get a longer stretch than he does —Hartley Howard⟩

get·ling \ˈgetliŋ\ *n* -s [²*get* + *-ling*] *Scot* **:** CHILD; *esp* **:** BASTARD

get off *vi* **1 :** to make a start **:** set out **:** DEPART ⟨intended to *get off* on his vacation early in the morning⟩ **2 :** to escape from a dangerous situation or from punishment ⟨expected to *get off* with a light prison term —S.L.A.Marshall⟩ **3 :** ALIGHT, DISMOUNT ⟨the bus broke down and all the passengers had to *get off*⟩ **4 :** to leave work with the permission or knowledge of one's superior ⟨*got off* early and went to the ball game⟩ ~ *vt* **1 :** to bring about the departure of ⟨*got* him *off* on the evening train⟩ **2 :** to secure the release of or procure a modified penalty for ⟨his lawyers *got* him *off* with little difficulty⟩ **3 a :** to give expression to : UTTER ⟨*got off* a joke that none of his friends had heard before⟩ **b :** to write and send : DISPATCH ⟨plans to *get off* a long cable to the home office⟩

get-of-sire \'ˌ=ˌ=\ *n* [²*get*] **1 :** the entire progeny or a representative sample of the progeny of a sire **2 :** a class in a livestock show for judging the progeny of different sires

get on *vt* : to dress oneself in : DON ⟨*get on* thy boots: we'll ride all night —Shak.⟩ ~ *vi* **1 a :** to continue toward a destination : move along ⟨finished his drink and said that he had to be *getting on*⟩ **b :** to continue with one's work or business : PROCEED ⟨his desire to *get on* with his studies —T.B.Costain⟩ **c :** to draw near : come close ⟨it was *getting on* to four in the morning, and he had not yet closed an eye —F.W.Crofts⟩ **d :** to become late ⟨it was *getting on* in the afternoon and we were tired —L.A.Viereck⟩ **e :** to become old : AGE ⟨I am indeed *getting on* . . . and a helpmate would cheer my declining days —W.S.Gilbert⟩ **2 a :** to achieve success : PROGRESS, PROSPER ⟨watched every opportunity because he wanted to *get on* —Robert Westerby⟩ **b :** to carry on one's affairs : FARE, MANAGE ⟨the legacy . . . came after he was well started, and he always says he could have *got on* without it —Ellen Glasgow⟩ **3 :** to maintain a friendly relationship : be on good terms ⟨will she *get on* with your father's wife —Rose Macaulay⟩ **4 :** to gain knowledge or understanding : grasp the meaning : catch on — used with *to* ⟨he soon *got on* to the racket they were working⟩ **5** *chiefly Brit* : to make contact — used with *to* ⟨I'll *get on* to the telephone people first thing in the morning —Dorothy Sayers⟩

get out *vi* **1 a :** EMERGE, ESCAPE ⟨doubted that he would *get out* alive⟩ **b :** to leave a vehicle ⟨the passengers *got out* and walked across the bridge⟩ **c :** to go away at once — often used in the imperative as an interjection to express disbelief or amazement **2 :** to dispose of one's stock ⟨switched into the stock market, made a killing, and *got out* —Erle Stanley Gardner⟩ **3 :** to become known : leak out ⟨the remarks made at the secret hearing soon *got out*⟩ **4 :** to take part in social activities ⟨advise him not to read so much and to *get out* and mix more with people —Paul Woodring⟩ ~ *vt* **1 :** to cause to emerge or escape ⟨how can I *get* myself *out* of this muddle —C.W.H.Johnson⟩ **2 :** PUBLISH, PRODUCE ⟨*got out* an anthology of war poetry⟩ **3 :** to give forth with some effort : EMIT ⟨the lark could scarce *get out* his notes for joy —Alfred Tennyson⟩ **4 :** to cause to go to the polls ⟨party leaders worked hard to *get out* the vote⟩

get-out \'ˌ=ˌ=\ *n* -S [*get out*] : an escape from an awkward or difficult situation ⟨never uses in his own behalf the old *get-out* about being misreported by the press —*Punch*⟩ — compare ALL GET-OUT

get over *vi* : to become clear ⟨only if presented in that way can the ideas of industry *get over* to the workers —E.R.Smith⟩ ~ *vt* **1 :** to bring to an end : have done with : FINISH ⟨reckon I'll be glad to *get it over* —Ellen Glasgow⟩ **2 :** to make clear ⟨efforts were made to *get over* . . . the relationship of public officials toward individual citizens —P.P.Van Riper⟩

getpenny \'ˌ=ˌ=ˌ=\ *n* [¹*get* + *penny*] *archaic* : a profitable venture or asset

get-rich-quick \(ˈ)=ˈ=ˈ=\ *adj* : characterized by or appealing to a desire for quick wealth and often lacking in financial stability or scruples ⟨*get-rich-quick* promoters⟩ ⟨the false prosperity of a *get-rich-quick* era⟩

get round *vb* : to get around

gets *pres 3d sing of* GET, *pl of* GET

get·sul \'get,sůl\ *n* -S *usu cap* [Tibetan *getshul* (*dgetshul*)] : a Lamaist priest or monk not yet fully ordained

gett *var of* GET

get·ta·ble *also* **get·able** \'ged·əbəl\ *adj* [¹*get* + *-able*] : capable of being got : ATTAINABLE, OBTAINABLE

¹get·ter \'ged·ə(r)\ *n* -S [ME *geter, getter*, fr. *geten, getten* to get + *-er* — more at GET] : one that gets: as **a :** a chemically active substance (as metallic barium) introduced into a vacuum tube or incandescent electric lamp to remove traces of gas remaining after exhaustion of the enclosed space **b :** a sire esp. when a producer of superior progeny

²getter \"\ *vb* -ED/-ING/-S *vi* : to use a getter (as in evacuating a vacuum tube) ~ *vt* : to submit to the action of a getter

get through *vi* **1 :** to reach a destination ⟨the train failed to *get through* because of the floods⟩ **2 a :** to receive approval ⟨the bill *got through* by a margin of two votes⟩ **b :** to pass an examination or course ⟨many students *get through* with little study⟩ **3 a :** to become understood : make oneself clear ⟨our feelings must have *gotten through* to him quickly —E.L.Wallant⟩ **b :** to complete a telephone connection ⟨couldn't *get through* and . . . a surprised Sussex voice asked if he didn't know that the cable was down —Clemence Dane⟩ **4** *chiefly NewEng* : to resign or lose a job ⟨he *got through* at the mill last week⟩

getting *pres part of* GET

get-together \'ˌ=ˌ=ˌ=\ *n* -S [fr. the phrase *get together*] : MEETING; *esp* : an informal social gathering

get-tough \ˌ=ˈ=\ *adj* [fr. the phrase *get tough*] : characterized by firmness and determination to act if and as necessary ⟨a *get-tough* international policy⟩

ge·tu·li·an \jēˈtülēən, jēˈtyü-\ *also* **ge·tu·lan** \-lən\ *adj, usu cap* [L *Gaetuli, Getuli* people inhabiting northwestern Africa in ancient times (fr. Gk *Gaitouli*) + E *-an*] : of or relating to the culture of any of the nomadic peoples of Libya and the eastern Sahara in Neolithic and Aeneolithic times

get up *vi* **1 a :** to arise from bed ⟨he *gets up* late on Sundays⟩ **b :** to rise to one's feet ⟨*got up* from the chair when the guests came in⟩ **c :** CLIMB, ASCEND, MOUNT ⟨*got up* on the roof to watch the eclipse⟩ **2 :** to increase in force or violence ⟨the added motion of the ship told him the sea was *getting up* —J.E.Macdonnell⟩ **3 :** to draw near : come close ⟨the batteries . . . opened on our approach and the fire was returned as our ships *got up* —Horatio Nelson⟩ **4 :** to go ahead or go faster — used in the imperative as a command to horses ~ *vt* **1 :** to cause to rise : RAISE ⟨finally *got* the anchor *up* and set sail⟩ **2 :** to make preparations for : set on foot : ORGANIZE ⟨*got up* a party for the newcomers⟩ ⟨*get up* a petition⟩ **3 :** to arrange as to external appearance : FINISH, DRESS ⟨the printed libretto . . . is handsomely and usefully *gotten up* —Herbert Weinstock⟩ ⟨he is *got up* for the artist's part — purple velvet coat, great flowing tie, black sombrero —H.J.Laski⟩ **4 :** to acquire a knowledge of : study for a special purpose ⟨was advised to *get up* German during the summer⟩ **5 :** to create in oneself : work up : GENERATE ⟨cannot *get up* an atom of sympathy for them⟩

getup \'ˌ=ˌ=\ *n* -S [*get up*] **1 a :** general composition or structure : manner in which the parts of a thing are combined : makeup and style (as of dress) : FORMAT **b :** OUTFIT, COSTUME, RIG ⟨you're never going to the party in that ~⟩ **2 :** act or time of getting up **3** *or* **get-up-and-go** *or* **get-up-and-get** \(ˌ)=ˌ=ˌ=ˈ=\ : initiative and determination : SPUNK

ge·ul·lah *also* **ge·u·lah** \gə(ˌ)üˈlä, gəˈü(ˌ)lä\ *n* -S *usu cap* [Heb *gĕʼullāh* redemption] : the recital of the prayer of thanks to God for the redemption of Israel from Egypt in the Jewish ritual in the daily liturgy

ge·um \'jēəm\ *n* [NL, fr. L *gaeum, geum* herb bennet] **1** *cap* : a genus of perennial herbs (family Rosaceae) with pinnate or lyrate leaves and flowers with long plumose persistent styles **2** -S : AVENS

-geu·sia \'gyüzh(ē)ə\ *n comb form* -S [NL, fr. Gk *geusis* sense of taste, taste (fr. *geuesthai* to taste + *-sis*) + NL *-ia* — more at CHOOSE] : a (specified) condition of the sense of taste ⟨para*geusia*⟩

geu·si·o·lep·tic \ˌgyüzēōˈleptik\ *adj* [Gk *geusis* + E *-o-* + Gk *leptos* peeled, fine, delicate (fr. *lepein* to peel) + E *-ic* — more at LEPER] : having or characterized by pleasant flavor

gew·gaw \'gyü,gȯ *also* ˈgü,gȯ *sometimes* ˈjü,jȯ *or* ˈjü,gȯ\ *also* **gee·gaw** \'jē,gȯ, ˈgē,gȯ, ˈjē,jȯ\ *n* -S *often attrib* [origin unknown] **1 :** something lacking in substantial value : a thing of no account or worth : TRIFLE ⟨in such a society these accomplishments were no more ~*s*⟩ **2 :** something showy or gaudy and usu. with little intrinsic worth ⟨decked out with all sorts of ~*s*⟩ — **gew·gawed** \-ȯd\ *adj* — **gew·gaw·ish** \-ȯish,-ōēsh\ *adj* — **gew·gawy** \-ȯi,-ōē\ *adj*

gew·gaw·ry \-ȯrē\ *n* -ES : cheap showiness

¹gey \'gaī\ *adj* [alter. of ¹*gay*] *chiefly Scot, of quantity and number* : CONSIDERABLE, FAIR ⟨waited a ~ while in the cold⟩

²gey \"\ *adv* [alter. of ³*gay*] *chiefly Scot* : VERY, QUITE, RATHER ⟨it's ~ dark and getting darker —John Buchan⟩

gey·an \'gaiən\ *adv* [¹*gey* + *an* (alter. of *and*)] *chiefly Scot* : TOLERABLY, CONSIDERABLY

gey·lies \'gailēz\ *adv* [*geyly* + *-es*] *Scot* : tolerably well : very much

gey·ly \-lē\ *Scot var of* GAILY

¹gey·ser *in sense 1* ˈgīzə(r), *Brit also* ˈgāz- *or* ˈgēz-; *in sense 2 usu* ˈgēz-\ *n* -S [Icel *Geysir* (name of a geyser in Haukadal, Iceland), lit., gusher, fr. *geysa* to rush forward, gush, fr. ON; akin to ON *gjōsa* to gush, Goth *giutan* to pour — more at FOUND] **1** *also* **gey·sir** \"\ : a spring that throws forth intermittently escaping jets of heated water and steam as a result of the contact of subterranean water with rock hot enough to generate steam under conditions which prevent free circulation — see GEYSERITE **2** *Brit* : an apparatus for heating water rapidly esp. by injected steam (as for a bath or for washing dishes) — **gey·ser·al** \-zərəl\ *adj* — **gey·ser·ic** \'ˌ=zərik, (ˈ)=ˈzerik\ *adj*

²geyser \"\ *vb* -ED/-ING/-S *vi* : to spurt like a geyser or cause spurting like that of a geyser ⟨blood ~*ed* from the cut⟩ ⟨the shells fell short and ~*ed* into the water⟩ ~ *vt* : to cause (something) to spurt like a geyser ⟨shells ~*ing* the water⟩

gey·ser·ine \'ˌ=zə,rīn, -rēn\ *adj* : of or relating to a geyser

gey·ser·ite \-rīt\ *n* -S [F *geysérite*, fr. *geyser* (fr. Icel *Geysir*) + *-ite*] : a hydrous form of silica that constitutes one variety of opal and is deposited around some hot springs and geysers in white or grayish concretionary masses which are porous, filamentous, or scaly

ge·ze·rah \gə,zaˈrä, gəzāˈ-; gəˈzā(,)rä, ˈgzā(-\ *n, pl* **geze·roth** *or* **geze·rot** \gə,zaˈrōt(h), gzāˈ-; gəˈzā(,)rōs, ˈgzā(-\ [Heb *gĕzērāh*] : a temporary rabbinical decree issued as a preventive measure to meet the needs of the time

GFA *abbr* **1** general freight agent **2** good fair average

GFE *abbr* government furnished equipment

g flat *n, usu cap G* **1 :** the keynote of G-flat major **2 :** the tone a half step below G

g-flat major \'ˌ=ˌ=ˈ=\ *n, usu cap G* : the major musical key having a signature of six flats

GG *abbr* **1** gamma globulin **2** governor general **3** great gross

GH *abbr* growth hormone

GHA *abbr* Greenwich hour angle

ghaf·fir \(ˈ)gaˈfi(ə)r\ *n* -S [Ar *ghafīr*] : a native Egyptian guard or watchman

ghaist \'gāst\ *Scot var of* GHOST

gha·na \'gänə, ˈgä- *also* ˈga-\ *adj, usu cap* [fr. *Ghana*, country in western Africa] : of or from Ghana : of the kind or style prevalent in Ghana : GHANAIAN

¹gha·na·ian \-n(ə)yən,-nēən\ *adj, usu cap* [*Ghana* + *-ian*] **1 :** of, relating to, or characteristic of Ghana **2 :** of, relating to, or characteristic of the Ghanaians

²ghanaian \"\ *or* **gha·ni·an** \"\ *n* -S *cap* : a native or inhabitant of Ghana

gha·nese \(ˈ)=ˈnēz, -ēs\ *adj, usu cap* [*Ghana* + *-ese*] : GHANAIAN

gharial *var of* GAVIAL

ghar·ry *or* **ghar·ri** \'garē, ˈgä-\ *n, pl* **gharries** *or* **gharris** [Hindi *gāṛī*] : a horse-drawn cab used esp. in India

gharry-wal·lah \ˌ=ˈ=wälə\ *n* [Hindi *gāṛīwālā*, fr. *gāṛī* + *-wālā* (agent suffix)] : a gharry driver

ghasel *var of* GHAZEL

ghash·ghai \'gäsh,gī\ *n* -S *usu cap* **1 :** a people of southern Iran **2 :** a member of the Ghashghai people

ghas·sa·nid \gəˈsänəd, gaˈ-\ *n* -S *usu cap* [*Ghassan*, a 6th cent. A.D. people of northwestern Arabia + E *-id*] : one of an Arab dynasty governing under the suzerainty of the Roman and Byzantine empires the Arab tribes of Palestine and the region about Palmyra from the 5th century A.D. to A.D. 636

ghas·su·li·an \(ˈ)gaˈsülēən\ *adj, usu cap* [Teleilat *Ghassul*, site in Jordan + E *-ian*] : of, relating to, or being an Aeneolithic culture of Palestine

ghast \'gast, -aa(ə)-,-ai-,-á-\ *adj* [by shortening] *archaic* : GHASTLY

ghast·ful \-fəl\ *adj* [ME *gastful*, fr. *gast, gost* spirit, ghost + *-ful* — more at GHOST] **1** *obs* : full of fear : FRIGHTENED ⟨the prelate saw their fall with ~ eyes —John Ozell⟩ **2** *archaic* : giving rise to fear : FRIGHTFUL ⟨this ~ dream . . . soon awoke him —John Lane *fl*1620⟩ — **ghast·ful·ly** \-fəlē\ *adv, obs*

ghast·li·ly \-tᵊlᵊlē\ *or* **ghast·i·ly** \-tᵊlē\ *adv* : in a ghastly manner

ghast·li·ness \-tlēnəs, -tlin-\ *n* -ES : the quality or state of being ghastly ⟨the ~ of the monster with its popeyes, gaping mouth, and horns —L.E.Schmeckebier⟩

¹ghast·ly \'gastlē, ˈgaas-,ˈgais-,ˈgás-, -li\ *adj, usu* -ER/-EST [ME *gastly*, fr. OE *gāstlic* spiritual — more at GHOSTLY] **1 :** giving rise to terror : FRIGHTENING, TERRIFYING ⟨along the parapet rose great pyramids of German helmets, empty, ~, like . . . heaps of skulls —Louis Bromfield⟩ **2 :** resembling or suggestive of a ghost : DEATHLIKE, PALE, WAN ⟨his face was so ~ that it could scarcely be recognized —T.B.Macaulay⟩ ⟨her eyes are lighted up with a smile so ~ that people quake as they look at her —W.M.Thackeray⟩ **3** *obs* : filled with fear : TERRIFIED ⟨in great haste and fear with ~ . . . looks —Thomas Herbert⟩ **4 :** intensely unpleasant, disagreeable, or objectionable : TERRIBLE — often used as a generalized expression of disapproval ⟨such a life seems ~ in its emptiness and sterility —Aldous Huxley⟩ ⟨engaged in the ~ job of revising the curriculum —H.J.Laski⟩ **5 :** very great — used as an intensive ⟨the whole business is a ~ mistake —D.B.Chidsey⟩ ⟨the ~ waste of time that we indulge in —J.C.Powys⟩

²ghastly \"\ *adv* : in a ghastly manner ⟨her face was ~ pale —Washington Irving⟩

ghat *also* **ghaut** \'gȯt, ˈgät\ *n* -S [Hindi *ghāṭ*, fr. Skt *ghaṭṭa*] **1** *India* **a :** MOUNTAIN RANGE **b :** a mountain pass **2** *India* **a :** a landing place or platform on the bank of a river **b :** a passage or flight of steps leading from a landing place or platform to the water's edge (as for the convenience of bathers) — compare BURNING GHAT

ghat·ti gum \'gad·ē-\ *n* [native name in India] : an Indian gum obtained from the dhawa and related trees and used as a substitute for gum arabic

gha·wa·zee *or* **gha·wa·zi** \gəˈwä(,)zē\ *n pl* [Ar *ghawāzī*, pl. of *ghāziyah*] : Egyptian dancing girls who usu. perform in the public streets

ghaz·el *or* **ghaz·al** *also* **gaz·el** *or* **gas·el** *or* **ghas·el** \'gazəl\ *n* -S [Ar *ghazal*] : an Arabic lyric poem that begins with a rhymed couplet whose rhyme is repeated in all even lines and that is esp. common in Persian literature

gha·zi *or* **ga·zi** \'gä(,)zē\ *n* -S *often cap* [Ar *ghāzī*] : a Muslim warrior; *esp* : one victorious in battle with the opponents of Islam — often used as a title of honor

ghaz·na·vid *or* **ghaz·ne·vid** \'gäznə,vid\ *n* -S *usu cap* [irreg. fr. *Ghazni*, Afghanistan + E *-id*] : one of a Muslim dynasty ruling in southwestern Asia from the 10th to the 12th centuries

ghed·da wax \'gedə-\ *n, sometimes cap G* [prob. fr. Telugu *gedda* lump] : beeswax from Indian and African bees

ghee *or* **ghi** \'gē\ *n* -S [Hindi *ghī*, fr. Skt *ghṛta*; akin to MIr *gert* milk and perh. to Skt *jigharti* he besprinkles, Per *āgārdan* to mix] **1 :** a semifluid clarified butter made in India and neighboring countries usu. from buffalo milk **2 :** a fat made from vegetable oils

gheg *or* **geg** \'geg\ *n* -S *usu cap* [Alb *geg*] **1 :** one of the northern Albanians — compare TOSK **2** *also* **gheg·ish** \-egish\ : the language of the Ghegs that constitutes the principal literary dialect of Albanian

ghent \'gent\ *adj, usu cap* [fr. *Ghent*, Belgium] : of or from the city of Ghent, Belgium : of the kind or style prevalent in Ghent

ghent azalea *n, usu cap G* : any of various rather hardy cultivated hybrid azaleas that have white to deep red flowers often marked with yellow or orange, result from interbreeding an Old World azalea (*Rhododendron flavum*) with one or more New World azaleas (as the complex hybrid *R.* × *mortieri*), and are commonly treated as forming a distinct hybrid group (*R.* × *gandavense*)

ghenting *n* -S [*Ghent*, Belgium + E *-ing*] *obs* : a linen cloth orig. made in Ghent

gher·kin *or* **ger·kin** \'gərkən, ˈgɔ̄k-,ˈgəik-\ *n* -S [D *gurken*, pl. of *gurk* cucumber, fr. *augurk*, fr. LG *augurke*, fr. MLG, fr. Pol *ogurek*, fr. MGk *agouros* watermelon, cucumber, prob. fr. MPer *angārah* watermelon] **1 a :** a small oblong prickly cucumber of West Indian origin that is used chiefly for pickling — called also *bur gherkin, West Indian gherkin* **b :** a slender annual trailing vine (*Cucumis anguria*) that bears gherkins **2 :** the immature fruit of the common cultivated cucumber esp. when used for pickling

¹ghet·to \'ged·(,)ō, ˈge(,)tō\ *n, pl* **ghettos** *also* **ghettoes** [It] **1 a :** a quarter of a city (as in Italy) in which Jews were formerly required to live **b :** a quarter of a city in which the residents are chiefly Jews ⟨the tide of immigration from the ~*s* of Europe . . . streamed into New York —*Amer. Mercury*⟩ **2 :** a quarter of a city in which members of a minority racial or cultural group live esp. because of social, legal, or economic pressure ⟨there have long been self-imposed ~*s* in our big industrial centers —Charles Abrams⟩ ⟨the racial ~*s* which now shelter and set apart from the rest of the community Negroes and Chinese . . . are invariably located in the slum —R.E. Park⟩ **3 :** an isolated or segregated group ⟨they're in an economic ~, which . . . forces them to live in some cheap section —Morley Callaghan⟩

²ghetto \"\ *vt* -ED/-ING/-S : GHETTOIZE

ghet·to·iza·tion \ˌ=(ˌ)=əˈzāshən, -ˌīˈz-\ *n* -S : segregation in or as if in a ghetto

ghet·to·ize \'=(ˌ)=ˌīz\ *vt* -ED/-ING/-S : to isolate in or as if in a ghetto

ghi *var of* GHEE

ghib·el·line \'gibə,lēn, -,līn, -,lən\ *n* -S *usu cap* [It *ghibellino*, fr. OIt, fr. MHG *Wībeling*, appellative of the Salian emperors, fr. *Wībeling*, castle in Franconia, Germany] : a member of an aristocratic political party in Italy supporting the authority of the German emperors from the 12th to the 15th centuries — compare GUELF

ghib·el·lin·ism \-,nizəm\ *n* -S *usu cap* **1 :** the policy and principles of the Ghibellines **2 :** adherence to Ghibellinism

ghillie *var of* GILLIE

ghil·zai \'gil,zī\ *n* -S *usu cap* : an Afghan people believed to be of Turkish origin

ghimel *var of* GIMEL

ghior·des \gēˈȯrdəs, ˈgō-\ *n, pl* **ghiordes** *usu cap* [fr. Gördes (*Ghiordes*), town in Manisa, Turkey] : an Anatolian rug characterized by fine knotting, mellow colors, a wool pile, and a cotton web; *esp* : a fine prayer rug of the 17th and 18th centuries

ghiordes knot *n, usu cap G* [fr. Gördes (*Ghiordes*), Turkey] : a knot used in making carpets and rugs in which the two ends of pile yarn appear together at the surface between the two adjacent warp yarns around which they are twisted — called also *Turkish knot*; compare SEHNA KNOT

Ghiordes knot

ghobar numeral *var of* GOBAR NUMERAL

ghol \'gōl, ˈgōl\ *n* -S [Hindi *ghol, gholā*] : a sciaenid fish (*Sciaena miles*) of the Indian coast whose liver is extremely rich in vitamin A

ghon tubercle \'gän-\ *also* **ghon focus** *n, usu cap G* [after Anton *Ghon* †1936 Czechoslovakian pathologist] : the primary tubercle occurring in the lung of a child as the initial lesion of tuberculous infection and appearing as a bean-shaped shadow in the roentgenogram

ghor·khar \'gȯr,kär\ *n* -S [Per] : a wild ass of northwestern India believed to be identical with the onager

¹ghost \'gōst\ *n* -S *often attrib* [ME *gost, gast*, fr. OE *gāst*; akin to OS *gēst* spirit, OHG *geist* spirit, ON *geiskafullr* full of terror, Goth *usgaisjan* to frighten, Skt *heḍa* anger] **1 a :** the life principle or vital spark : the soul regarded as the seat of life or intelligence — now used chiefly in the phrase *to give up the ghost* **b** *archaic* : the spirit of man as distinguished from the body : the conscious being ⟨knowledge of what the world ought to be to us who are body and ~ together —Nathaniel Fairfax⟩ **2 a :** a disembodied soul; *esp* : the soul of a dead person believed to be an inhabitant of the unseen world or to appear to the living in bodily likeness ⟨believe in the survival of the soul after death in the form of a ~ —Edward Sapir⟩ **b :** APPARITION, SPECTER **3 :** SPIRIT, DEMON ⟨that affable familiar ~ which nightly gulls him with intelligence —Shak.⟩; *esp* : a harmful or malevolent disembodied human spirit regarded as a power to be propitiated or averted by religious or magical rites **4** *obs* : PERSON ⟨no knight so rude . . . as to do outrage to a sleeping ~ —Edmund Spenser⟩ **5** *obs* : CORPSE ⟨a timely-parted ~ of ashy semblance, meager, pale, and bloodless —Shak.⟩ **6 :** a mark or visible sign left by something dead, lost, or no longer present : REMAINS ⟨the ~ of grandeur that lingers between the walls of abandoned haciendas —Mary Austin⟩ **7 a :** a faint shadowy outline or semblance : TRACE ⟨would search the white skies for the ~ of a cloud —Vicki Baum⟩ **b :** the least bit : IOTA, PARTICLE — usu. used with preceding negative ⟨hadn't . . . the ~ of a prospect of raising the money —Christopher Isherwood⟩ ⟨didn't have a ~ of a chance of defending himself against . . . this master killer —Frank Dufresne⟩ **8 a :** a false image : REFLECTION: **a** *or* **ghost image :** an unwanted or false image on a photographic negative caused by internal reflections in the camera lens **b :** a faint spurious line appearing in a grating spectrum as a result of a defect in the ruling of the grating **c** *or* **ghost image :** a faint double image appearing on a television screen as a result of the reflection of signals from external objects (as buildings) before they reach the receiving antenna **9 :** one who does literary or artistic work for and in the name of another ⟨it is his lot to serve as ~ for successful comic-strip artists —John McCarten⟩; *specif* : GHOST-WRITER **10 :** a tissue, cell, or other structure that does not stain normally because of degenerative changes; *specif* : a red blood cell that has lost its hemoglobin **11 :** a light band that alternates with a dark one or runs through a dark mass, appears on a tooled or polished surface of steel, and indicates a zone of material made harder by a difference in composition **12 ghosts** *pl but sing in constr* [so called fr. the fact that the eliminated person is called a ghost] : a word game in which a player names a letter of the alphabet to which each succeeding player adds a letter that makes part of but does not complete a word, a player being eliminated from the game usu. after five instances in which he has either completed a word or been guilty of adding a letter that does not contribute to making a word **13 :** PHANTOM **14 :** an outline of a former crystal shape or rock structure bounded by inclusions that make it visible and outlined by bubbles or foreign substances

²ghost \"\ *vb* -ED/-ING/-S *vt* **1 :** to haunt like a ghost ⟨ask not . . . what madness ~*s* this old man —Robert Burton⟩ **2 :** to write for and in the name of another ⟨the common report that he ~*ed* the whole document —Bruce Bliven b. 1889⟩ ~ *vi* **1 a :** to move silently like a ghost ⟨the waiter ~*ed* up to the table —Hugh MacLennan⟩ **b :** to sail quietly with or as if with no apparent wind ⟨all day the fleet ~*ed* westward in light southerly airs —S.E.Morison⟩ **2 :** to engage in writing for and in the name of another ⟨you have no qualms about ~*ing* —E.C.Marston⟩

ghost crab *n* [so called fr. its color] : a pale yellowish crab (*Ocypode albicans*) common on sandy beaches from Rhode Island to Brazil

ghost dance *n* : a group dance for communication with the spirits of the dead; *specif* : a messianic cult and circle dance of Plains and Plateau Indians during the late 19th century

ghost·dom \'gōs(t)dəm\ *n* -S : the realm of ghosts

ghost·ess \-stəs\ *n* -ES [¹*ghost* + *-ess*] : a female ghost

ghostfish \'ˌ=ˌ=\ *n* **1 :** any of several whitish or transparent fishes (as the young of the ladyfishes) **2 :** the leptocephalus stage of an eel

ghostflower \'ˌ=ˌ=\ *n* : INDIAN PIPE

ghost fly *n* : GREENHOUSE WHITEFLY

ghost·i·ly \-tᵊlē\ *adv* : in a manner resembling or suggestive of a ghost

¹ghostlike \'ˌ=ˌ=\ *adj* [¹*ghost* + *-like*] : resembling or sugges-

tive of a ghost ⟨an occasional ~ stand of dead oaks —*Amer. Guide Series: Fla.*⟩
2ghostlike \"\ *adv* **:** in a manner suggestive of a ghost ⟨gliding ~ about their subterranean apartments —W.H. Hudson †1922⟩
ghost·li·ness \'gōstlēnəs, -lin-\ *n* -ES [ME *gostlines,* fr. *gostly* + *-nes* -ness] **:** the quality or state of being ghostly
ghostlore \'≈,≈\ *n* **:** lore dealing with ghosts
1ghost·ly \'gōstlē, -li\ *adj* -ER/-EST [ME *gostly,* fr. OE *gāstlīc,* fr. *gāst* spirit, ghost + *-līc* -ly — more at GHOST, -LY] **1 :** of or relating to the soul **:** not carnal **:** SPIRITUAL ⟨many disorders, ~ and bodily, are transmitted to us by inheritance —John Tyndall⟩ **2 :** of or relating to the church **:** not secular **:** RELIGIOUS ⟨shall not be the worse for a ~ adviser —George Meredith⟩ ⟨snatching with ~ hands at scepters —Nathaniel Hawthorne⟩ **3 :** of, relating to, or having the characteristics of a ghost **:** SPECTRAL, SHADOWY ⟨a whole troupe of delightful but ~ spirits from another world —Scott Goddard⟩ ⟨startled to see the ~ silhouette of a submarine gliding under the railway bridge —Stewart Beach⟩ **4 :** of or relating to a ghost-writer ⟨a book written without ~ assistance⟩
2ghostly \"\ *adv* [ME *gostly,* fr. OE *gastlice,* fr. *gāstlīc*] **:** in a ghostly manner ⟨two strips of snow shone ~ —Clive Arden⟩
ghost moth *n* [so called fr. the white color of the male and its habit of hovering in flight] **:** a moth of the family Hepialidae most American members of which are crepuscular
ghost·ol·o·gy \gō'stäləjē\ *n* -ES [1*ghost* + *-o-* + *-logy*] **:** GHOSTLORE
ghost plant *n* **1 :** INDIAN PIPE **2 :** a tumbleweed (*Amaranthus graecizans*)
ghosts *pl of* GHOST, *pres 3d sing of* GHOST
ghost·ship \'gōs(t),ship, -ōsh,ship\ *n* [1*ghost* + *-ship*] **:** the state of being a ghost
ghost shrimp *n* **1 :** a mud-dwelling anomuran crustacean (*Callianassa californiensis*) with a long slender translucent body **2 :** any of various crustaceans similar to the ghost shrimp
ghost spot *n* **:** a disease of the tomato characterized by small whitish rings on the fruit surface
ghost story *n* **1 :** a story about ghosts **2 :** a tale based on imagination rather than fact
ghost surgery *n* **:** the practice of performing surgery on another physician's patient by arrangement with the physician but unknown to the patient
ghost town *n* **:** an abandoned town or village that is at least in part still standing
ghost word *also* **ghost name** *n* **:** an accidental word form never in established usage; *esp* **:** one arising from an editorial or typographical error or a mistaken pronunciation (as *phantomnation* or *dord*)
ghostwrite \'≈,≈\ *vb* [back-formation fr. *ghost-writer*] *vi* **:** to write as a ghost-writer ~ *vt* **:** to write (as a speech) for another who is the presumed author
ghostwriter \'≈,≈≈\ *n* **:** one that writes for and in the name of another
ghosty \'gōstē\ *adj* -ER/-EST [1*ghost* + *-y*] **:** of, relating to, or resembling a ghost
ghoul \'gül\ *n* -S [Ar *ghūl,* fr. *ghāla* to seize] **1 :** a legendary evil being held to rob graves and feed on corpses ⟨they are neither man nor woman, they are neither brute nor human; they are ~*s* —E.A.Poe⟩ **2 :** one resembling or suggestive of a ghoul ⟨that glamour ~, the lanky young witch with the chalk-white skin and the hearse-black gown and locks —John Mason Brown⟩; *specif* **:** one who preys upon the dead
ghou·lie \'gülē\ *n* -S [alter. (influenced by *ghoul*) of *goulash* (hand) + *-ie*] **:** contract bridge in which only goulash hands are played — usu. used in pl.
ghoul·ish \'gülish, -lēsh\ *adj* **:** of, resembling, or suggestive of a ghoul ⟨something ~ in the avidity with which they will pounce upon the misfortune of their friends —W.S.Maugham⟩ — **ghoul·ish·ly** *adv* — **ghoul·ish·ness** *n* -ES
GHQ *abbr* general headquarters
ghurkha *usu cap, var of* GURKHA
ghur·ry \'gərē\ *n* -ES [Hindi *gharī,* fr. Skt *ghaṭikā* water pot (used as a water clock), space of time, fr. *ghaṭa* pot, perh. of Dravidian origin; akin to Tamil *kuṭam* pot] **1** *India* **:** either of two periods of time: **a :** the 60th part of a day **:** 24 minutes **b :** HOUR **2** *India* **a :** TIMEPIECE; *specif* **:** WATER CLOCK **b :** a metal disk on which the hours are struck
ghuz *or* **ghuzz** \'güz\ *n, pl* **ghuz** *or* **ghuzz** *usu cap* **:** a descendant of certain early Turkish invaders of Persia
ghyll *var of* 5GILL
GHz *abbr* gigahertz
gi \'gē\ *n, pl* **gi** *usu cap* **:** 2DAN
gi *abbr* gill
1GI \(')jē'ī\ *adj* [fr. unofficial abbr. (used by U.S. Army quartermaster clerks in listing such articles as garbage cans) for *galvanized iron,* but taken to be abbr. for *government issue* or *general issue*] **1 :** carried or provided by an official supply department of the U.S. armed forces ⟨said the *GI* shoes hurt his feet —Jimmy Cannon⟩ **2 :** of, relating to, or characteristic of enlisted personnel of the U.S. armed forces ⟨that meal's scaled to a *GI* appetite —*Mademoiselle*⟩ **3 a :** conforming to military regulations or customs ⟨his fuzzy red-dyed hair cut in *GI* style —*Nat'l Geographic*⟩ **b :** devoted to or demanding strict military discipline ⟨he was, the men complained, too *GI* —a stickler for spit and polish —A.R.Matthews⟩ **4 :** designed for the use or benefit of military personnel ⟨more than 30 new *GI* training bills in the legislative hopper —*Time*⟩
2GI \"\ *n, pl* **GI's** *or* **GIs :** a member or former member of the U.S. armed forces; *esp* **:** an enlisted man ⟨many *GI's* showed an abysmal lack of knowledge —*Reporter*⟩
3GI \"\ *vt* **GI'd; GI'd; GI'ing; GI's** [1*GI*] **:** to prepare for or as if for military inspection ⟨the barracks . . . were in fine order — they'd been *GI'd* the night before —*New Republic*⟩
4GI \"\ *adv* [1*GI*] **:** in strict conformity with military regulations or customs ⟨men like to have everything run *GI* —R.V. Cassill⟩
GI *abbr* **1** galvanized iron **2** gastrointestinal **3** general issue; government issue
giai \'jī\ *n, pl* **giai** *usu cap* **:** a Tai affiliated people inhabiting the valley lands of the Claire, Song-Chay, and Red rivers of upper Tonkin in Vietnam — called also *Nhang*
gial·lo an·ti·co \'jä(,)lō,an·'tē(,)kō, -,än-·\ *n* [It, lit., ancient yellow] **:** an ornamental marble found among Italian ruins and believed to have come orig. from Algeria
gial·lo·li·no \,jälə'lē(,)nō\ *n* -S [It, fr. *giallo* yellow] **:** any of various yellow pigments (as Naples yellow)
1gi·ant \'jīənt\ *n* -S [ME *geaunt, giaunt,* fr. MF *geant,* fr. (assumed) VL *gagant-, gagas,* alter. of L *gigant-, gigas,* fr. Gk] **1 :** a legendary manlike being of huge stature and great strength and of more than mortal but less than godlike power and endowment **2 a** (1) **:** a person of unusual stature or size ⟨a fair-haired young ~, slim and lean-faced —Liam O'Flaherty⟩ ⟨perceived the inner worth of the gaunt frontier ~ —Charles Lee⟩ (2) **:** a person exhibiting gigantism ⟨troupe of tiny people with a seven-foot ~ —*Amer. Guide Series: Wash.*⟩ **b :** a person of extraordinary powers or endowments ⟨one of the nation's journalistic ~*s* —J.A.Morris b.1904⟩ ⟨one of the ~*s* of his times . . . he imparted to his students his own contagious enthusiasm for literature —N.M. Pusey⟩ **3 :** something unusually large or powerful ⟨too small a crew to handle the clumsy ~ he commanded —Frank Yerby⟩ ⟨the tools needed . . . were among the ~*s* of the forging industry —E.A.Mossein⟩ ⟨imposes setbacks on its architectural ~*s* to let a little light and air into the city —Flora Lewis⟩ ⟨it rolls, with irresistible power, majestic and silent; a young ~ among rivers —Tom Marvel⟩ **4 :** GIANT STAR **5 :** a large nozzle used in hydraulic mining
2giant \"\ *adj* **1 :** resembling a giant **:** characterized by unusual size, proportion, scope, strength, power, or significance **:** extremely large ⟨the ~ corporation whose activities spread over many fields —R.B.Heflebower⟩ ⟨behind the local broadcasting station is the ~ network —Stuart Chase⟩ ⟨time has not staled his ~ intellect —*Saturday Rev.*⟩ ⟨they battle through bitter cold and ~ drifts —*Newsweek*⟩ **2** *of a plant or animal* **:** extremely large as contrasted with members of related species or varieties **syn** see HUGE
giant anteater *n* **:** ANT BEAR
giant arborvitae *n* **:** CANOE CEDAR
giant armadillo *n* **:** a large armadillo (*Priodontes giganteus*) measuring about three feet in length exclusive of the tail
giant bamboo *n* **:** a plant of the genus *Dendrocalamus; esp* **:** an immense Indo-Malayan grass (*D. giganteus*) with tough hollow stems that resemble tree trunks
giant bass *or* **giant black sea bass** *n* **:** a very large serranid fish (*Stereolepis gigas*) that is dark brown or black above and lighter below and is an important food and game fish of southern and Lower California — called also *black sea bass, jewfish*
giant book *n* **:** a large cardboard dummy of a book designed for display purposes
giant cabuya *n* **:** a Brazilian plant (*Furcraea gigantea*) that is closely related to and much resembles the agaves and is cultivated in warm regions for its hard fiber — see MAURITIUS HEMP
giant cactus *n* **:** SAGUARO
giant cane *n* **:** a tall grass (*Arundinaria gigantea*) of the southern U.S. — see CANEBRAKE
giant cedar *n* **:** RED CEDAR 2a
giant cell *n* **:** an unusually large cell; *esp* **:** a large multinuclear often phagocytic cell (as those characteristic of tubercular lesions, various sarcomas, or the megakaryocytes of the red marrow)
giant chinquapin *n* **:** a chinquapin (*Castanopsis chrysophylla*)
giant clam *n* **:** a very large clam; *specif* **:** a clam (*Tridacna derasa* or *T. gigas*) found on the coral reefs of the Indian and Pacific oceans that sometimes weighs more than 500 pounds
giant clover *n* **:** SWEET CLOVER
giant cockroach *n* **:** any of several large tropical American cockroaches constituting a genus (*Blaberus*) that is considered closely related to *Blattella* or sometimes made the type of a separate family
giant crab *n* **1 :** a Japanese deep-sea edible spider crab (*Macrocheira kaempferi*) that measures about a foot across the shell and has legs many feet in length **2 :** an immense Australian edible sea crab (*Pseudocarcinus gigas*) that attains a weight of 30 pounds and has the large claw 17 inches in length
giant daisy *n* **1 :** a tall European herb (*Chrysanthemum uliginosum*) resembling an aster **2 :** any of several herbs of the genus *Wyethia* of the western U.S.
giant danio *n* **:** a blue and yellow striped cyprinid fish (*Danio malabaricus*) of southeast Asia that attains a length of four inches and is often kept in tropical aquariums
gi·ant·esque \,jīənt·'esk, -ən-,te-\ *adj* **:** having the characteristics of a giant **:** IMMENSE
gi·ant·ess \'jīəntəs\ *n* -ES [ME *geauntesse, giauntesse,* fr. *geaunt, giaunt* giant + *-esse* -ess — more at GIANT] **:** a female giant; *esp* **:** an unusually large woman
giant fennel *n* **:** a tall Eurasian garden plant (*Ferula communis*)
giant fern *n* **:** either of two ferns: **a :** GOLDEN FERN **b :** a fern (*Acrostichum excelsum*) with smooth woody unarmed petioles
giant fiber *n* **:** a very large nerve fiber; *specif* **:** one formed by the confluence of processes from numerous segmental nerve cell bodies in the ventral chain of nerve ganglia of annelids and crustaceans
giant fir *n* **:** LOWLAND FIR
giant fish killer *n* **:** GIANT WATER BUG
giant flying squirrel *n* **:** a large brightly colored Asiatic flying squirrel of the genus *Petaurista*
giant forest mole *n* **:** FOREST MOLE
giant forget-me-not *n* **:** a Chatham Island herb (*Myosotidium nobile*) of the family Boraginaceae with large basal leaves and dense clusters of brilliant blue flowers
giant foxtail *n* **:** either of two coarse annual foxtails of the genus *Setaria* that are naturalized weeds in parts of the U.S.: **a :** an Asiatic foxtail (*S. faberii*) widely established in the eastern U.S. **b :** a West Indian foxtail (*S. magna*) established chiefly in the southeastern and southern U.S.
giant fulmar *n* **:** GIANT PETREL
giant granadilla *n* **1 :** a tropical American passionflower (*Passiflora quadrangularis*) **2 :** the oblong fruit of the granadilla
giant granite *n* **:** PEGMATITE
giant grouper *n* **:** any of several large groupers
giant helleborine *n* **:** STREAM ORCHID
giant hill *n* **:** a virus disease of the potato characterized by the formation of large tops and few tubers
giant holly fern *n* **:** a fern (*Polystichum munitum*) of western No. America with stiff auricled pinnae
gi·ant·hood \'jīənt,hud\ *n* -S **:** HUGENESS, IMMENSITY
giant hornet *n* **:** a large black and orange European hornet (*Vespa crabro germana*) that is now established in the northeastern U.S. and is sometimes a pest because of its painful sting and its habit of gnawing the bark from twigs
giant hyssop *n* **:** a plant of the genus *Agastache*
gi·ant·ism \'jīənt-,izəm, -ən-,ti-\ *n* -S **1 :** the quality or state of being a giant **:** extreme or unusual largeness ⟨parallel to ~ in industry is the economic concentration of power into the hands of a relatively few corporations —R.J.Harris⟩ ⟨the new skyline . . . rose even above her, overwhelming the stars with the blatant ~ of the new New York —Booth Tarkington⟩ **2 a :** GIGANTISM 2 **b :** GIGANTISM 3
giant kangaroo *n* **:** a very large grayish brown kangaroo (*Macropus giganteus*) formerly abundant in open wooded areas in Australia but now greatly reduced in numbers
giant kelp *n* **:** any of several large Pacific kelps (esp. *Macrocystis pyrifera*)
giant kidney worm *n* **:** a blood-red nematode worm (*Dioctophyme renale*) that sometimes exceeds a yard in length and that invades the kidneys of dogs and occas. other mammals including man
giantlike \'≈,≈\ *adj* **:** resembling a giant ⟨a man ~ in strength and stature⟩
giant lily *n* **1 a :** GIANT CABUYA **b :** an Australian amaryllid (*Doryanthes excelsa*) that is cultivated in warm regions for its tall spikes of brilliant red flowers **2 :** a tall Asiatic lily (*Lilium giganteum*) that bears long racemes of large white flowers in midsummer
gi·ant·ly *adj, sometimes* -ER/-EST *archaic* **:** GIANTLIKE ⟨aspire with such a ~ presumption —Christopher Marlowe⟩
giant moss *n* **:** a large erect moss of the genus *Dawsonia* (esp. *D. superba*)
giant nettle *n* **:** AUSTRALIAN NETTLE TREE
giant newt *n* **:** a newt (*Triturus torosus*) of western No. America that is six inches or more in length and is distinguished by a uniformly yellow or orange-red ventral surface
giant panda *n* **:** PANDA 2
giant pangolin *n* **:** a large scaly anteater (*Manis gigantea*) of western Africa
giant parsley *or* **giant parsnip** *n* **:** COW PARSNIP
giant perch *n* **:** BEGTI
giant petrel *n* **:** a large dusky brownish petrel (*Macronectes giganteus*) chiefly of antarctic seas that has a heavy pale-colored beak and approximates an albatross in size though not in wingspread
giant pig *n* **:** ENTELODONT
giant powder *n* **:** a blasting powder consisting of nitroglycerin, sodium nitrate, sulfur, rosin, and sometimes kieselguhr
giant puffball *n* **:** an edible puffball (*Calvatia gigantea*) that sometimes attains a diameter of two feet and may exceed 25 pounds in weight
giant pyramidal cell *n* **:** any of the large nerve cells in the fifth layer of the cerebral cortex that give rise to the fibers of the pyramidal tract
giant ragweed *n* **:** GREAT RAGWEED
giant rat *n* **1 :** a very large dull-brown Chinese rat (*Rattus edwardsi*) **2 :** any of several large coarse-furred West African cricetid rats (genus *Cricetomys*)
giant red-wing *n* **:** a large heavy-billed redwing blackbird (*Agelaius phoeniceus arctolegus*) that breeds in northern No. America and winters chiefly in the southern U.S.
giant reed *n* **1 :** a tall European grass (*Arundo donax*) with woody stems used in making organ reeds **2 :** DITCH REED **3 :** UVA GRASS
giant ryegrass *n* **:** a grass (*Elymus condensatus*) of the western U.S. with a thick spiky inflorescence
giants *pl of* GIANT
giant salamander *n* **1 :** a large edible salamander (*Megalobatrachus or Cryptobranchus maximus*) of Japan and China that attains a length of three to five feet **2 :** HELLBENDER
giant scallop *n* **:** a very large scallop (*Pecten magellanicus*) of the Atlantic coast of No. America
giant's cauldron *or* **giant's kettle** *n* **:** a large deep pothole formed in rock by the fall of a stream into the crevasse of a glacier
giant schnauzer *n* **:** a schnauzer that attains a height of 21½ to 25½ inches
giant sequoia *n* **:** BIG TREE
gi·ant·ship \'jīənt,ship\ *n* [1*giant* + *-ship*] **:** the quality or state of being giantlike
giant silkworm *n* **:** the larva of a moth of the family Saturniidae
giant skipper *n* **:** any of various large strong-flying butterflies that constitute the family Megathymidae
giant slalom *n* **:** a long zigzag downhill run in skiing
giant sloth *n* **:** a very large recently extinct So. American sloth (genus *Megatherium*) attaining the size of an elephant
giant snail *n* **:** a snail of the genus *Achatina*
giant squid *n* **:** any of several very large squids of *Architeuthis* and related genera
giant squirrel *n* **:** any of several very large reddish or black arboreal squirrels (genus *Ratufa*) of tropical Asiatic forests
giant star *n* **:** a star (as Capella or Arcturus) of great intrinsic luminosity and therefore of large mass
giant star grass *n* **:** a perennial grass (*Cynodon plectostachyum*) that has stems attaining a height of three to four feet and that is used esp. in Africa and India for pasture and hay
giant stride *n* **:** a gymnastic apparatus consisting of an upright pole surmounted by a revolving disk to which are hooked grips that when grasped enable one to take great strides around the pole

giant stride

giant sunflower *n* **:** a tall No. American sunflower (*Helianthus giganteus*) with edible tuberous roots — called also *Indian potato*
giant swing *n* **:** a complete swing of the body at full arms' length around a horizontal bar
giant tortoise *n* **:** any of numerous large long-lived slow-moving herbivorous land tortoises of the genus *Testudo* formerly abundant on the islands of the western Indian ocean and on the Galápagos islands but now largely exterminated by man
giant urticaria *n* **:** urticaria marked by an eruption of unusually large often confluent wheals
giant water bug *n* **:** any of several very large aquatic bugs (family Belostomatidae) having the hind legs flattened and fringed for use in swimming; *esp* **:** a very large dark No. American bug (*Lethocerus americanus*) often destructive to small freshwater fishes
giant water lily *n* **:** ROYAL WATER LILY
giant whortleberry *n* **:** HIGHBUSH BLUEBERRY
giant wild pig *n* **:** a large wild hog (*Sus barbatus*) of the Malay peninsula
giant wild rye *n* **:** a stout perennial grass (*Elymus condensatus*) of western No. America with short stout rhizomes and stiff erect flower spikes
giaour \'jaù(ə)r\ *n* -S [Turk *gâvur,* fr. Per *gawr, gabr*] **:** one outside the Muslim faith **:** INFIDEL, UNBELIEVER ⟨an unadulterated Arab place of entertainment, seldom profaned by the presence of ~*s* —*Harper's*⟩
giar·dia \jē'ärdēə, 'jär-\ *n* [NL, fr. Alfred M. *Giard* †1908 Fr. biologist + NL *-ia*] **1** *cap* **:** a genus of zooflagellates inhabiting the intestines of various mammals and including a species (*Giardia lamblia* syn. *Lamblia intestinalis*) that is associated with but not demonstrably the cause of diarrhea in man **2** -S **:** any flagellate of the genus *Giardia*
giar·di·a·sis \(,)jē,är'dīəsəs, ,jēər-, ,jär-\ *also* **giar·di·o·sis** \jē,ardē'ōsəs, ,jär-\ *n, pl* **giardia·ses** \-ī·ə,sēz\ *also* **giardio·ses** \-ē'ō,sēz\ [NL, fr. *Giardia* + *-iasis*] **:** infestation with or disease caused by flagellates of the genus *Giardia*
1gib \'gib\ *n* -S [ME *Gibbe, Gib,* a common name for cats, prob. by shortening & alter. fr. the name *Gilbert*] **1** *obs* **:** an old woman **2 :** a male cat; *specif* **:** a castrated male cat
2gib \"\ *n* -S [origin unknown] **1 :** a removable plate of metal or other material that is notched, tapered, or otherwise machined to hold other mechanical parts in place, bind them together, afford a bearing surface, or provide means for taking up wear **2 a :** a hooked projection that appears on the lower jaw of adult male salmon during or after the breeding season **b** *dial Eng* **:** GIB FISH
3gib \"\ *vt* **gibbed; gibbed; gibbing; gibs :** to secure or fasten with a gib
4gib \'gib\ *var of* GIP
5gib \'jib\ *var of* JIB
gibaro *var of* JIBARO
gibbed \'gibd\ *adj* [1*gib* + *-ed*] *of a cat* **:** CASTRATED
1gib·ber \'jibə(r) *sometimes* 'gi-\ *or* **jib·ber** \'ji-\ *vi* **gibbered** *or* **jibbered; gibbered** *or* **jibbered; gibbering** *or* **jibbering** \-b(ə)riŋ\ **gibbers** *or* **jibbers** [imit.] **:** to speak rapidly, inarticulately, and often foolishly **:** CHATTER ⟨the old hag . . . howled and ~*ed* with filthy gestures, calling for the thunderstorm —Charles Kingsley⟩ ⟨children were ~*ing* in their animal innocence —R.A.W.Hughes⟩ ⟨were as near ~*ing* idiots as men can get without being locked up —R.N. Ingersoll⟩
2gibber \"\ *n* -S **:** rapid, inarticulate, and often foolish utterance **:** GIBBERING ⟨have listened to ~ about . . . our present form or methods of governments —*Nation*⟩
3gib·ber \'gibə(r)\ *n* -S [native name in Australia] *Austral* **:** PEBBLE, STONE, BOULDER; *esp* **:** a desert stone polished or sculptured by sandblast
gibber bird *n* [3*gibber*] **:** a small grayish brown Australian warbler (*Ashbyia lovensis* or *Epthianura lovensis*) that frequents dry stone-covered plains
gib·ber·el·la \,jibə'relə\ *n, cap* [NL, dim. of L *gibber* hump on the back] **:** a genus of fungi (family Nectriaceae) having bluish perithecia cespitose or scattered on or around the stroma and occurring esp. on cereal grasses often in association with various abnormalities (as kernel scabs, foot rot, or seedling blight) — see EAR ROT, POKKAH BOENG
gib·ber·el·lic acid \≈≈'≈lik-\ *n* [*gibberellin* + *-ic*] **:** a crystalline acid $C_{18}H_{21}O_4COOH$ associated with the gibberellins and having similar effects on plants
gib·ber·el·lin \,≈≈'≈lən\ *n* -S [NL *Gibberella* (genus name of *Gibberella fujikuroi*) + E *-in*] **:** any of several plant-growth regulators that are produced by a fungus (*Gibberella fujikuroi*) and that act like auxins in promoting growth of shoots when applied in low concentrations but differ from auxins in some other effects (as in stimulating bud development under some conditions)
1gib·ber·ish \'jib(ə)rish, -rēsh *also* 'gi-\ *n* -ES [prob. fr. 1*gibber* + *-ish*] **1 :** confused, unintelligible, or meaningless speech or language ⟨sounded . . . like human language but was only such ~ as children may be heard amusing themselves with —Nathaniel Hawthorne⟩ **2 a :** a strange, barbarous, or outlandish language or dialect ⟨commenced talking in a ~ of which I understood very little but which he intended for French —George Borrow⟩ **b :** a technical or esoteric language used by workers in a particular activity or field of knowledge ⟨surrounded by a trainer, a jockey, and grooms speaking an impenetrable ~ —A.J.Liebling⟩ **3 :** pretentious or needlessly obscure speech or language ⟨deliberately confecting . . . ~ on the theory that the less the yokels understand, the more they will be impressed —C.J.Rolo⟩
2gibberish \"\ *adj, archaic* **:** lacking intelligibility or meaning
gibber plain *n, Austral* **:** a desert plain strewn with gibbers
1gib·bet \'jibət, *usu* -əd·+V\ *n* -S [ME *gibet* gallows, fr. OF, forked stick, gallows] **1** *or* **gibbet tree a :** an upright post with a projecting arm for hanging the bodies of executed criminals in chains or irons **b :** GALLOWS **2 :** the projecting arm of a crane **:** JIB
2gibbet \"\ *vt* -ED/-ING/-S **1 a :** to hang on a gibbet as a warning or for exposure to public scorn ⟨soon should I . . . be mangled on a wheel, then ~*ed* to blacken for the vultures —Samuel Rogers⟩ **b :** to expose to infamy or public scorn

⟨libel suits were successfully brought by men . . . who had been incidentally ~*ed* —*Times Lit. Supp.*⟩ **2 a :** to execute by hanging on a gibbet ⟨~*ed* the Covenanters because they denied the rights of a civil sovereign to frame liturgies —J.S. Blackie⟩ **b :** to hang as if on a gibbet ⟨half a dozen great cats hung ~*ed* there and rows of stoats —David Garnett⟩

³gibbet *n* -s [perh. alter. of MF *jupet* distance to which one can shout, fr. *juper* to shout, of imit. origin] *obs* **:** a hunting signal (as to a dog or hawk)

gibbing *pres part of* GIB

gib·ble-gab·ble \ˈgibəlˌgabəl\ *n* [redupl. of ²*gabble*] **:** GABBLE

gib·bles \ˈgibəlz\ *n pl* [origin unknown] *Scot* **:** TOOLS, GADGETS

gib·bon \ˈgibən\ *n* -s [F] **:** any of several apes of southeastern Asia and the East Indies that constitute the genera *Hylobates* and *Symphalangus*, are the smallest and most perfectly arboreal anthropoid apes, and have very long arms, small but distinct ischial callosities, and no cheek pouches or tail

gib·bon·oid \-ˌnȯid\ *adj* **:** of, relating to, or resembling the gibbons

gib·bose \jəˈbōs, giˈb-, ˈgi,b-\ *adj* [LL *gibbosus*, fr. L *gibbus* hump on the back + *-osus* -ose] **:** GIBBOUS

gib·bos·i·ty \jəˈbäsəd-ē, giˈb-\ *n* -ES [ME *gibbositee*, fr. MF *gibbosité*, fr. ML *gibbositat-, gibbositas*, fr. LL *gibbosus* + L *-itat-, -itas* -ity] **1 :** PROTUBERANCE, SWELLING; *specif* **:** KYPHOSIS **2 :** the quality or state of being gibbous; *specif* **:** the condition of being humpbacked

gib·bous \ˈjibəs, ˈgi-\ *adj* [ME, fr. MF *gibbeux*, fr. LL *gibbosus*] **1 a :** marked by convexity **:** ROUNDED, PROTUBERANT **b** *of the moon or a planet* **:** seen with more than half but not all of the apparent disk illuminated — see CONFIGURATION illustration, MOON illustration **c :** swollen or protuberant on one side **2 :** having a hump **:** HUMPBACKED ⟨these ~ human shapes —Thomas Hardy⟩ — **gib·bous·ly** *adv* — **gib·bous·ness** *n* -ES

gibbs–helm·holtz equation \ˈgibzˈhelmˌhōlts-, -ˈheu̇l\ *n, usu cap G&H* [after Josiah Willard *Gibbs* †1903 Am. mathematician and physicist and Hermann L. F. von *Helmholtz* †1894 Ger. scientist] **:** an equation in thermodynamics that is applicable to reversible isobaric chemical processes: the difference between the change in free energy and the heat of reaction equals the product of the absolute temperature and the rate of change of free energy with temperature

gibbs·ite \ˈgibˌzīt\ *n* -s [George *Gibbs* †1833 Am. mineralogist + E *-ite*] **:** a mineral $Al(OH)_3$ consisting of light-colored translucent aluminum hydroxide occurring as monoclinic crystals and also in stalactitic and spheroidal forms — **gibbs·it·ic** \(ˈ)gibˈzid·ik\ *adj*

gibbs's mole \ˈgibz(əz)-\ *n, usu cap G* [George *Gibbs* †1873 Am. ethnologist] **:** a small mole (*Neurotrichus gibbsii*) of the western U.S.

gib·bus \ˈjibəs, ˈgi-\ *n* -ES [L] **:** HUMP; *specif* **:** the hump of the deformed spine in Pott's disease

gib–cat \ˈ=,=\ *n, dial Eng* **:** ¹GIB 2

¹gibe *or* **jibe** \ˈjīb\ *vb* -ED/-ING/-S [perh. fr. MF *giber* to shake, handle roughly] *vi* **:** to utter taunting sarcastic words **:** express scorn **:** SNEER — often used with *at* ⟨his friends *gibed* at him for his cowardice —B.L.K.Henderson⟩ ~ *vt* **:** to reproach with taunting sarcastic words **:** sneer at **:** MOCK ⟨you *gibed* each other . . . over the extent to which you found yourself shifted from the firm ground of reasoned conclusion —Mary Austin⟩ **syn** see SCOFF

²gibe *or* **jibe** \"\ *n* -s **:** a taunting sarcastic comment or expression **:** a scornful reproach **:** JEER ⟨was determined not to allow the young bloods' ~*s* to hurt him visibly —C.S.Forester⟩

³gibe *var of* JIBE

gi·bel \ˈgēbəl\ *n* -s [G *giebel* (formerly spelled *gibel*)] **:** CRUCIAN CARP

gib·e·on·ite \ˈgibēəˌnīt\ *n* -s *cap* [*Gibeon*, city in ancient Palestine + E *-ite*] **:** one of the people of Gibeon in ancient Palestine condemned to be hewers of wood and drawers of water because of their deception of the Israelites

gib·er *or* **jib·er** \ˈjībə(r)\ *n* -s **:** one that gibes

gib fish *n* [²*gib*] *dial Eng* **:** a male salmon

gib–head key *n* [²*gib*] **:** a key with a projecting end that resembles the end of a gib and serves as a stop

gib·ing·ly \ˈjībiŋlē\ *adv* **:** in a gibing manner

gib·leh \ˈgiblə, -lē\ *n* -s [Ar *qiblīy* south wind] **:** a hot desert wind of northern Africa esp. Libya — compare HARMATTAN, SIROCCO

gib·let \ˈjiblət *also* ÷ ˈgi-, *usu* -əd.+V\ *also* **jib·let** \ˈji-\ *n* -s [ME *gibelet* entrails, garbage, fr. MF, stew of wildfowl, fr. OF (Picardy dial.), prob. irreg. dim. of *gibier*, *gebier* flesh of birds, of Gmc origin; akin to MHG *gebeize* hunt using falcons, fr. *beizen* to hunt birds with falcons, fr. OHG *beizzen*, causative of *bīzan* to bite — more at BITE] **1 :** an edible visceral organ of a fowl — usu. used in pl. **2 giblets** *pl, archaic* **:** odds and ends **:** TRIFLES ⟨the great ladies with their grace, lace, and ~*s* —Peter Hawker⟩

gi·boia \jəˈbȯi(y)ə\ *n* -s [Pg, fr. Tupi *giboia, jibóya*] **:** BOA CONSTRICTOR

gib plate *n* [²*gib*] **:** GIB 1

¹gi·bral·tar \jəˈbrȯltə(r)\ *adj, usu cap* [fr. *Gibraltar*, Brit. fortified colony on the Rock of *Gibraltar* in the south of the Iberian peninsula] **:** of or from the British colony of Gibraltar **:** of the kind or style prevalent in Gibraltar

²gibraltar \"\ *n* -s *usu cap* [fr. *Gibraltar*, Brit. colony] **1 :** an impregnable stronghold ⟨isolationist plea for retreat to the American *Gibraltar* —*Frontier*⟩ **2** *also* **gibraltar rock :** a hard white candy flavored usu. with peppermint or lemon

gibraltar candytuft *n, usu cap G* **:** an evergreen perennial herb (*Iberis gibraltarica*) used in rock gardens that has the flower stems branched above and the leaves usu. dentate toward their apex

gibraltar fever *n, usu cap G* **:** BRUCELLOSIS a

gi·bral·tar·i·an \jəˌbrȯlˈta(a)rēən, ˌji,b-\ *n* -s *usu cap* **:** a native or inhabitant of Gibraltar

gibs *pl of* GIB, *pres 3d sing of* GIB

gib·son \ˈgibsən\ *n* -s *usu cap* [fr. the name *Gibson*] **:** a cocktail consisting of gin and dry vermouth garnished with pearl onions

¹gibson girl *n, usu cap 1st G & often cap 2d G* [after Charles Dana *Gibson* †1944 Amer. illustrator] **1 :** an American girl regarded as representative of the fashions and manners of the 1890s **2** [so called from the curved shape of the transmitter] **:** a portable crank-operated radio transmitter orig. designed for use by aviators forced down at sea

²gibson girl *adj, usu cap 1st G & often cap 2d G* **:** of or relating to a style in women's clothing characterized by high necks, full sleeves, and wasp waists

gi·bus \ˈjībəs\ *also* **gibus hat** *n* -ES [F *gibus*, fr. *Gibus*, name of its 19th cent. Fr. inventor] **:** OPERA HAT

gid \ˈgid\ *n* -s [back-formation fr. ¹*giddy*] **:** a disease principally affecting sheep that is caused by the presence in the brain of the coenurus of a tapeworm (*Multiceps multiceps*) of the dog and related carnivores and is characterized by cerebral disturbances, dilated pupils, dizziness and circling movements, emaciation, and usu. death — called also *sturdy, turn-sick, waterbrain*

GI'd *past of* GI

gid·dap \gidˈap, -əp\ *also* **gid·dy·ap** \ˌgidē-\ *or* **gid·dy·up** \-ˈəp\ *v imper* [alter. of *get up*] — a command to a horse to go ahead or go faster

gid·di·fy \ˈgidəˌfī\ *vt* -ED/-ING/-ES [¹*giddy* + *-fy*] **:** to make giddy **:** CONFUSE

gid·di·ly \ˈgidᵊlē, -dᵊli, -dəl-\ *adv* **:** in a giddy manner ⟨the lantern tossing ~ with the motion —T.B.Costain⟩ ⟨a very different crowd — mostly female, ~ hatted and all atwitter —Mollie Panter-Downes⟩

gid·di·ness \ˈgidēnəs, -din-\ *n* -ES [ME *gidinesse, gedinesse*, fr. *gidy, gedy* + *-nesse* -ness] **:** the quality or state of being giddy ⟨all the gaiety and spirits, but . . . little of the ~ of youth —Earl of Chesterfield⟩ ⟨a dimness and ~ crept over him —Charles Dickens⟩

¹gid·dy \ˈgidē, -di\ *adj* -ER/-EST [ME *gidy, gedy* mad, foolish, dizzy, fr. OE *gydig, gidig* possessed, mad, fr. the stem of *god* + *-ig* -y — more at GOD] **1 :** characterized by exuberance, impulsiveness, or thoughtlessness **:** lighthearted or harebrained ⟨he was no longer young and he had no wish to get entangled with a ~ girl —W.S.Maugham⟩ ⟨a ~, abandoned, hugely popular show —E.J.Kahn⟩ **2 a :** having a sensation of whirling or reeling about **:** affected with or as if with vertigo **:** DIZZY ⟨he was ~ . . . and the meadow swam like fishes under the high sun —Jean Stafford⟩ ⟨he paused, somewhat ~ from his quick descent of the stairs —Elinor Wylie⟩ **b :** causing a sensation of whirling or reeling about **:** tending to make dizzy ⟨staring down the coiling silvery barrel of his gun, down its circling and ~ bore —Eve Langley⟩ ⟨could almost feel . . . the lift as the car began its ~ rise into the air —*New Yorker*⟩ **c :** whirling or turning around with great rapidity **:** GYRATORY ⟨the ~ round of Fortune's wheel —Shak.⟩ ⟨swept me on before, ~ as a whirling stick —Edna S.V.Millay⟩ **3** *dial Eng* **:** crazed with anger **:** FURIOUS, WILD **4 :** suffering from gid — used esp. of sheep **5 :** extravagantly decorated or extremely ornate **:** GARISH, SHOWY ⟨a ~ organdy . . . apron festooned with ribbons and Christmas-tree balls —*New Yorker*⟩ ⟨long rococo halls, ~ with plush and whorled designs in gold —Djuna Barnes⟩

²giddy \"\ *vb* -ED/-ING/-ES *vt* **:** to make giddy ⟨the sight of so much that was growing and green *giddied* his senses —Gordon Webber⟩ ~ *vi* **:** to become giddy ⟨my head swims, my brain *giddies* —Sylvester Judd⟩

³giddy \"\ *n* -ES **:** GID

giddy gander *n* **:** MALE ORCHIS

gid·e·on \ˈgidēən\ *n* -s *usu cap* [after *Gideon*, Biblical leader of the Jews (Judg 6-8), fr. Heb *Gidh'ōn*] **:** a member of an interdenominational organization of laymen whose activities include the placing of Bibles in hotel rooms

gid·gee \ˈgijē\ *or* **gid·gea** *also* **gid·ya** *or* **gid·yea** \", -jə\ *n* -s [native name in Australia] **1 a :** a somewhat scrubby Australian acacia (*Acacia cambagei*) that grows chiefly in dry inland regions and has an extremely foul-smelling blossom **b :** GEORGINA GIDGEE **c :** YARRAN 1 **2 :** the dense hard dark wood of gidgee and various other small Australian acacias that is valued for turning and carving and used also for fencing and fuel

gie \ˈgē\ *vb* **gied** \-ēd\ **gied** \"\ *or* **gien** \-ēn\ **gieing; gies** [by alter.] *chiefly Scot* **:** GIVE

gi·em·sa stain \gēˈemzə-\ *also* **giemsa's stain** *or* **giemsa** *n, usu cap G* [after Gustav *Giemsa* †1948 Ger. chemotherapist] **:** a stain consisting of a mixture of eosin and methylene azure and used chiefly in differential staining of blood films

gier–eagle \ˈgi(ə)r, ˈgī(ə)r, ˈji(ə)r+ˌ-\ *n* [D *gier* vulture, fr. MD; akin to OHG *gīr* vulture, *giri* greedy, Norw dial. *gir* desire, passion, OE *geonian* to yawn — more at YAWN] **:** a bird pronounced unclean in ancient Jewish law ⟨and the pelican and the *gier-eagle* and the cormorant —Deut 14:17 (AV)⟩

gif \(ˌ)gif, ˌgəf\ *conj* [ME *gif, yif, if* — more at IF] *archaic* **:** IF

gif·blaar \ˈgifˌblär\ *also* **gif** *n* -s [Afrik *gifblaar*, fr. *gif* poison + *blaar* leaf] **:** a perennial shrub (*Dichapetalum cymosum*) of southern Africa that is deadly poisonous to stock

¹giff·gaff \ˈgifˌgaf\ *n* -s [prob. by alter. & redupl. fr. ¹*give*] **1** *dial Brit* **:** mutual assistance **:** fair exchange — often used in proverbs ⟨~ makes good fellowship⟩ **2** *dial Brit* **:** exchange of words **:** BANTER, REPARTEE ⟨the swift ~ that Kate and her lads were used to maintain —Neil Munro⟩

²giffgaff \"\ *vi* -ED/-ING/-S **:** to bandy words **:** BANTER

gif·o·la \ˈjifələ, ˈgi-; jəˈfōlə, gəˈ-\ *n, cap* [NL, anagram of *Filago*] *syn of* FILAGO

¹gift \ˈgift\ *n* -s *often attrib* [ME, fr. ON *gift, gipt*; akin to OE & OHG *gift*, Goth *fragifts* bestowal, betrothal; derivative fr. the root of OE *giefan* to give — more at GIVE] **1 :** a special or notable capacity, talent, or endowment either inherent, acquired, or given by a deity ⟨whatever physical ~*s* she may have are carefully cultivated —Lafcadio Hearn⟩ ⟨a sense for mathematics . . . is mainly a ~ of the gods —Bertrand Russell⟩ ⟨a ~ for pungent satire⟩ ⟨sight reading is an acquired ~⟩ **2 :** something that is voluntarily transferred by one person to another without compensation: as **a** (1) **:** a legal alienation with respect to real estate (2) **:** the conveyance of an estate tail as distinguished from a feoffment or from a demise or lease (3) **:** a voluntary transfer of real or personal property without any consideration or without a valuable consideration — distinguished from *sale* **b** *Christian relig* **:** one of the communion elements of bread and wine ⟨the Mass of the Presanctified ~*s*⟩ **c :** the point given in the game of seven-up to the eldest hand if he begs and the dealer insists upon the turnup for trump **3 :** the act, right, or power of giving or bestowing ⟨the office is not in his ~⟩ **4** *dial Eng* **:** a white speck on the fingernail which is supposed to portend a present

syn FACULTY, APTITUDE, TALENT, GENIUS, BENT, KNACK: GIFT indicates a special capacity inherent in one that facilitates doing, accomplishing, or knowing ⟨their excellent strategy and their *gift* for intrigue which brought many Indian tribes to their assistance —R.W.Murray⟩ ⟨anyone who happens to be blessed or cursed with the *gift* of humor —Sidney Alexander⟩ FACULTY in this sense simply indicates any distinct capacity or ability to do or accomplish; it lacks the connotative power of many of the others in this group ⟨there was mental *faculty* in those pliable brows to see through, and combat, an unwitting Wise Youth —George Meredith⟩ ⟨they . . . recover warmth and animation after the creative *faculty* has revived them —Ellen Glasgow⟩ APTITUDE may imply a natural liking for or an inherent potential ability at, without, however, implying anything more than promise ⟨many women . . . have no *aptitude* for domestic work —G.B.Shaw⟩ ⟨evidence is growing that the feminine mind has a special *aptitude* for detective fiction —*Times Lit. Supp.*⟩ TALENT indicates an inherent ability and may suggest an endowment which one should develop, a capacity for effective, facile execution or accomplishment, a less exalted power of accomplishment than is indicated by GENIUS ⟨he had . . . but to go forward to be supreme as soon as his *talent* could develop its full effect —Hilaire Belloc⟩ ⟨a surpassing *talent* for improvisation, an ability to call forth *genius* to flesh out his dreams —Henry Wallace⟩ ⟨what Goethe did really say was "the greatest *talent*", not "the greatest *genius*". The difference is important because, while *talent* gives the notion of power in a man's performance, *genius* gives rather the notion of felicity and perfection in it —Matthew Arnold⟩ GENIUS may indicate a strong aptitude for a particular matter, an aptitude ensuring successful execution ⟨has a *genius* for saying new and surprising things about old subjects —Aldous Huxley⟩ More generally, GENIUS is likely to designate a superior transcendent combination of intelligence, vision, and creative or interpretative power ⟨whose practical sense equaled his intuitive *genius* —Henry Adams⟩ ⟨a really great and successful writer must have a good deal of talent as well as a good deal of *genius* —J.W.Krutch⟩ BENT indicates an inherent inclination to some study or activity which militates toward successful execution ⟨he early showed a *bent* for journalism, and the year after he reached his majority . . . he became editor —W.B.Shaw⟩ KNACK may imply a ready dexterity or adroitness in execution hard to analyze, a dexterity independent of any great mental power ⟨improvisation was his *knack* and forte; he wrote rapidly and much — sometimes an entire novel in a month —Carl Van Doren⟩

²gift \"\ *vt* -ED/-ING/-S **1 :** to endow with some power, quality, or attribute **:** INVEST ⟨the Lord ~*ed* him with the power of forceful speech⟩ **2 a** *chiefly Brit* **:** to make a gift of ⟨~*ed* the money in memory of his uncle —*Brit. Agric. Bull.*⟩ ⟨I hear Her Excellency's ~*ed* the land —Kamala Markandaya⟩ **b :** to present with a gift **:** PRESENT ⟨generously ~*ed* us with a copy —*Saturday Rev.*⟩ ⟨~*ed* his parents with a television set —*Sydney (Australia) Sunday Telegraph*⟩ ⟨~*ed* her with a large heart-shaped diamond —Louella Parsons⟩

giftbook \ˈ=,=\ *n* **1 :** a book intended for giving away **2 :** an illustrated literary miscellany (as of verse, tales, and sketches) in vogue for gift purposes in the second quarter of the 19th century in the U.S. and published annually in ornamental format — called also *annual, keepsake*

gift cau·sa mor·tis \-ˌkau̇səˈmȯrd·əs, -ˌkau̇zə-, -ˌkȯzə-\ *n* [L *causa mortis* because of death] **:** a gift of personal property made by the donor in expectation of imminent death but revocable until his death

gift certificate *n* **:** a certified statement entitling the recipient to select merchandise in the amount stated thereon

gifted *adj* **1 :** endowed by nature or training with a gift: as **a :** having a special talent or other desirable quality ⟨~ with . . . spontaneous ease and charm —Dorothy Sayers⟩ ⟨~ in making coffee or chicken salad —Agnes S. Turnbull⟩ ⟨so much in love with the word and so little ~ for the deed —Lewis Galantiere⟩ ⟨a ~ linguist⟩ **b :** having superior intellectual capacity usu. with an intelligence quotient in the genius class ⟨a ~ child⟩ **2 :** reflecting or revealing a special gift or talent **:** OUTSTANDING, NOTABLE ⟨had a ~ voice —Jean Stafford⟩ ⟨two novels . . . were recognized as remarkably ~ —*Time*⟩ — **gift·ed·ly** *adv* — **gift·ed·ness** *n* -ES

gift·ie \ˈgifti\ *n* -s [¹*gift* + *-ie*] *Scot* **:** GIFT, FACULTY ⟨O wad some pow'r the ~ gie us to see oursels as others see us —Robert Burns⟩

gift of gab *or* **gift of the gab :** a talent for talking fluently

gift of tongues : ecstatic speech that is usu. unintelligible to hearers and is uttered in worship services of various contemporary religious groups laying great stress on religious excitation and emotional fervor

gift over *n* [fr. *gift over*, v.] **:** the transfer by will or other instrument of property upon the termination of the estate of one owner to the owner of the next succeeding estate therein

gifts *pl of* GIFT, *pres 3d sing of* GIFT

gift tax *n* **:** a tax that is imposed by the federal government and a number of states in the U.S. primarily as a supplement to and to prevent avoidance of death taxes through gifts of property before death inter vivos and that is assessed to the donor at graduated rates somewhat below death-tax rates and sometimes on a tax base which is cumulative during the lifetime of the donor with the tax rate on gifts in any one year being dependent upon the total amount of all prior gifts since adoption of the law

giftware \ˈ=,=\ *n* **:** wares or goods suitable for gifts

gift wrap *vt* **:** to wrap (merchandise intended as a gift) in specially attractive or fancy wrapping usu. with ribbons and bows

gi·fu \ˈgē(ˌ)fü\ *adj, usu cap* [fr. *Gifu*, Japan] **:** of or from the city of Gifu, Japan **:** of the kind or style prevalent in Gifu

¹gig \ˈgig\ *n* -s [ME *gigg, gigge* giddy girl, top; perh. of Scand origin; akin to Dan *gig* top, ON *geiga* to turn aside; akin to OE *geonian* to yawn — more at YAWN] **1 :** something that whirls: as **a** *obs* **:** TOP, WHIRLIGIG **b** *or* **gig mill :** a rotary cylinder covered with teasels or wire teeth for napping fabrics (as wool) **c :** a three-number combination selected to appear among the numbers to be drawn from a lottery wheel **2 a** *archaic* **:** JOKE, WHIM **b** *dial Eng* **:** FUN, SPORT **c :** a person of odd or grotesque appearance **:** ODDITY, FOOL ⟨we would look like a lot of ~*s* in that rig-out —*Punch*⟩ **3 a :** a long light ship's boat for oars or sail usu. clinker-built and fast and usu. appropriated for the commanding officer ⟨the captain's ~⟩; *also* **:** a boat assigned for the captain's exclusive use **b :** a rowboat designed for speed rather than for work or carrying **4 :** a light carriage that has one pair of wheels and is drawn by one horse **:** CHAISE

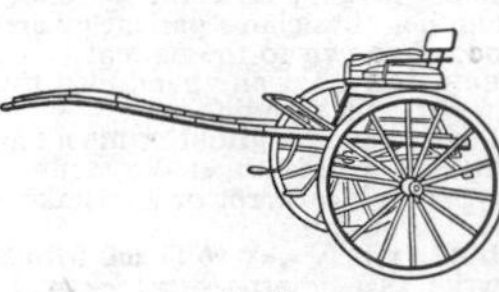
gig 4

²gig \"\ *vb* **gigged; gigged; gigging; gigs** *vt* **1 :** to nap (fabric) with the use of a gig **2 :** to move backwards and forwards ~ *vi* **:** to travel in a gig

³gig \"\ *n* -s [short for *fishgig*] **1 :** FISHGIG **2 :** an arrangement of hooks to be drawn through a school of fish when they will not bite in order to hook them in the bodies

⁴gig \"\ *vb* **gigged; gigged; gigging; gigs** *vt* **1 :** to spear with a fishgig ⟨~ a flounder⟩ **2 a** *chiefly West* **:** SPUR ⟨*gigged* him with the spurs —Ross Santee⟩ **:** PROD, JAB ⟨*gigged* him in the ribs —A.B.Guthrie⟩ **b :** HARASS, ANNOY ⟨~*s* . . . politicos with biting irony or refined ridicule —*Time*⟩ **c :** GOAD, PROVOKE, ROUSE ⟨~ his students into practice in the arts of thinking and analysis —*N.Y. Herald Tribune*⟩ ~ *vi* **:** to fish with a fishgig ⟨*gigging* for fish⟩

⁵gig \"\ *n* -s [origin unknown] *slang* **:** an official report of an infraction of military rules; *also* **:** demerits or light punishment resulting from such a report

⁶gig \"\ *vt* **gigged; gigged; gigging; gigs** *slang* **:** to report unfavorably for an infraction of military rules ⟨would be *gigged* by the first officer who saw him —*Life*⟩; *also* **:** to assign demerits or light punishment for such infraction ⟨gets *gigged* . . . for being eleven minutes late —J.G.Cozzens⟩

⁷gig \"\ *n* -s [origin unknown] **1 :** a single engagement; *esp* **:** ONE-NIGHT STAND ⟨graduate work in music, with as much sideline work, as many ~*s*, as the student can find time to develop his jazz skills —Barry Ulanov⟩ **2 :** JOB

gi·ga \ˈjēgä\ *n, pl* **gi·ghe** \-gā\ [It, fr. OIt, fiddle, of Gmc origin; akin to OHG *gīga* fiddle — more at JIG] **:** GIGUE

giga- \ˈjigə, ˈgigə\ *comb form* [ISV, fr. Gk *gigas* giant] **:** billion ⟨*gigacycle*⟩ ⟨*gigavolt*⟩

giga·hertz \ˈjigə + ,-\ *n* [ISV *giga-* + *hertz*] **:** a unit of frequency equal to one billion hertz — abbr. *GHz*

gigalira *var of* GIGELIRA

gigant- *or* **giganto-** *comb form* [Gk fr. *gigant-, gigas*] **:** giant ⟨*gigantism*⟩ ⟨*Giganto*pithecus⟩

gi·gant·an·thro·pus \ˌjīˌgant·ˈan(t)thrəpəs, jə̇ˌg-, -ˌgan·ˈtan-; -ˌgant·anˈthrōp-\ [NL, fr. *gigant-* + *-anthropus*] *syn of* GIGANTOPITHECUS

gi·gan·te·an \ˌjīˌganˈtēən, -gən-; ˌjīˌgantē-, -jəˈg-\ *adj* [L *giganteus* of the giants (fr. *gigant-, gigas* giant, fr. Gk) + E *-an*] **:** GIGANTIC ⟨a ~ granite altar —*Time*⟩ **syn** see HUGE

gi·gan·tesque \ˌjīˌganˈtesk, -ˌgan-; jīˈgan-,t-, jəˈg-\ *adj* [F, fr. It *gigantesco*, fr. *gigant-* + *-esco* -esque] **:** of enormous or grotesquely large proportions **:** GIGANTIC ⟨Greek comedy is ~ buffoonery —J.J.Chapman⟩ ⟨a ~ novel⟩

gi·gan·tic \(ˈ)jīˈgantik, -gaan-, -tēk *also* jəˈg-\ *adj* [Gk *gigantikos*, fr. *gigant-* + *-ikos* -ic] **1** *obs* **:** of or relating to a giant **2 a :** like or suggesting a giant (as in size or strength) ⟨of a ~ stature . . . about eight feet in height and proportionally large —Mary W. Shelley⟩ ⟨wind and waves . . . were hurled with ~ force —*Encore*⟩ **b :** markedly larger than others of the same class or group **:** greater in size than the usual or expected ⟨a ~ fir⟩ ⟨a ~ wave⟩ ⟨a ~ tanker⟩ **c :** of extraordinary, towering, or superhuman intellectual or moral stature or force ⟨up in my mind rose the ~ artist of Rome in all his genius and glory —Eve Langley⟩ ⟨the ~ figures of Washington⟩ ⟨his personality became ~ . . . it overrode the man to whom he talked —Sherwood Anderson⟩ **d :** extremely large or great **:** ENORMOUS ⟨suffered a ~ setback⟩ ⟨possessed of a ~ hunger —Niccolò Tucci⟩ ⟨a ~ enterprise⟩ ⟨a ~ annual folk festival —J.A. Morris b. 1904⟩ **syn** see HUGE

gigantical *obs var of* GIGANTIC

gi·gan·ti·cal·ly \-tə̇k(ə)lē, -tēk-, -li\ *adv* **:** in a gigantic manner **:** in the manner of a giant **:** ENORMOUSLY ⟨yawned ~⟩

gi·gan·tic·ness *n* -ES **:** the quality or state of being gigantic **:** extremely great size **:** HUGENESS

gigantic pine *n* **:** SUGAR PINE

gi·gan·tism \jīˈganˌtizəm, jəˈg-, -gaan-, ˈjī,g-, ˈjīgən-\ *n* -s [ISV *gigant-* + *-ism*] **1 :** GIANTISM 1 ⟨trade unions are as subject to ~ and centralization as are the industries to which they are related —Aldous Huxley⟩ ⟨the tendency toward ~ in American publishing —Howard M. Jones⟩ **2 :** development to abnormally large size from excessive growth of the long bones accompanied by muscular weakness and sexual impotence and usu. caused by overactivity of the pituitary gland before normal ossification is complete — compare ACROMEGALY **3 :** excessive vegetative growth frequently induced by the use of colchicine that results in the doubling of the number of chromosomes and is often accompanied by the inhibiting of reproduction

gi·gan·to·pi·the·cus \(ˌ)jīˌgantōpəˈthēkəs, jəˌg-, -ōˈpithə̇kəs\ *n, cap* [NL, fr. *gigant-* + *-pithecus*] **:** a genus of giant fossil primates from the Pleistocene of China intermediate in a number of characters between the great apes and primitive man and sometimes classed with the Hominidae

gi·gan·tos·tra·ca \(ˌ)jīˌganˈtästrəkə, jəˌg-\ *n pl, cap* [NL, fr. *gigant-* + *-ostraca*] **:** a group of arthropods comprising the eurypteroids and sometimes related forms including the xiphosurans — compare MEROSTOMATA — **gi·gan·tos·tra·can** \ˌjīˌganˈtästrəkən; jīˌg-, jəˌg-\ *adj or n* — **gi·gan·tos·tra·cous** \-kəs\ *adj*

gig·ar·ti·na \ˌjigə(r)ˈtīnə, -tēnə\ *n, cap* [NL, fr. Gk *gigarton* grape seed + NL *-ina*; prob. akin to Gk *gēras* old age — more at CORN] **:** the type genus of Gigartinaceae comprising red algae mainly of the Pacific ocean having fleshy or cartilaginous compressed fronds with numerous outgrowths resembling teats on which the cystocarps are born

gig·ar·ti·na·ce·ae \ˌjigə(r)təˈnāsēˌē\ *n pl, cap* [NL, fr. *Gigartina*, type genus + *-aceae*] **:** a family of red algae (order Gigartinales) having procarps and large often unbranched fronds — see CHONDRUS GIGARTINA

gig·ar·ti·na·les \-ā(ˌ)lēz\ *n pl, cap* [NL, fr. *Gigartina* + *-ales*] **:** an order of red algae (subclass Florideae) in which the auxiliary cell arises as a vegetative cell of the gametophyte prior to fertilization — see GIGARTINACEAE

gi·gas \ˈjīˌgas\ *adj* [L, n., giant, fr. Gk] *of a polyploid plant* **:** having a thicker stem, taller growth, thicker and darker leaves, and larger flowers and seeds than a corresponding diploid plant

gig back *vt* [²*gig*] **:** to move back (a sawmill carriage) on the return stroke

gigback \ˈ=ˌ=\ *n* -s [*gig back*] **:** a mechanism for gigging back a sawmill carriage

gi·ge·li·ra *also* **gi·ga·li·ra** \ˌjēgəˈlirə\ *n, pl* **gigeli·re** *also* **gigali·re** \-rē\ [It *gigalira*, fr. *giga* fiddle + *lira* lyre] **:** XYLOPHONE

gi·ge·ri·um \jəˈjirēəm\ *n, pl* **gige·ria** \-ēə\ [NL, fr. L *gigeria*, pl., entrails of fowl, perh. of Iranian origin; akin to Per *jigar* liver] **:** GIZZARD 1

gigged *past of* GIG

gig·ger \ˈgigə(r)\ *n* -s [²*gig* + *-er*] **:** one that uses a gig; *specif* **:** a textile worker who raises nap on cloth by running it through a gig — called also *teaseler*

gigging *pres part of* GIG

¹gig·gle \ˈgigəl\ *vb* **giggled; giggled; giggling** \-ig(ə)liŋ\ **giggles** [imit.] *vi* **:** to laugh with continued short convulsive catchings of the voice or breath caused usu. by efforts at restraint **:** titter nervously **:** laugh in an affected or silly manner ~ *vt* **:** to express by or utter with a giggle

²giggle \ˈ"\ *n* -s **:** the act of giggling **:** a light silly laugh ⟨whispered . . . with a shocked ~ —Ruth Park⟩

gig·gler \ˈgig(ə)lə(r)\ *n* -s **:** one that giggles

gig·gling·ly *adv* **:** in a giggling manner

gig·gly \ˈgig(ə)lē, -li\ *adj* -ER/-EST **:** prone to giggling ⟨hospitable, faintly ~, and shy —*Harper's*⟩

gighe *pl of* GIGA

gig·let *also* **gig·lot** \ˈgiglət\ *n* -s [ME *gigelot, giggelot*, prob. fr. *gigg, gigge* silly girl — more at GIG] **1** *archaic* **:** a lascivious woman **:** WANTON ⟨set upon the ~ and beat her . . . soundly —S.H.Adams⟩ **2 :** a giddy frivolous frolicsome girl ⟨that overgrown ~ —Osbert Sitwell⟩

gig mill *n* [¹*gig*] **1 :** GIG 1b **2 :** a textile mill using gigs

gig·o·lo \ˈjigəˌlō *sometimes* ˈzhig-, ˈzhēg-\ *n* -s [F, back-formation fr. *gigolette* girl who frequents public dances, prostitute, fr. *giguer* to dance, jig — more at JIG] **1 :** a man living on the earnings of or supported by a woman **2 :** a professional dancing partner or male escort

gig·ot \ˈjigət\ *n* -s [MF, dim. of *gigue* fiddle; fr. its shape — more at JIG] **1 :** a leg (as of lamb or mutton) esp. when cooked **2** *also* **gigot sleeve :** a leg-of-mutton sleeve

gigs *pl of* GIG, *pres 3d sing of* GIG

gigue \ˈzhēg\ *n* -s [F — more at JIG] **1 :** a medieval fiddle or viol **2 :** JIG 1 **3 :** a lively dance movement (as of the suite of the 17th and 18th centuries) having compound triple rhythm and consisting of two sections each of which is repeated

GI'ing *pres part of* GI

gi·jón *or* **gi·jon** \hēˈhōn, -ˈhōn\ *adj, usu cap* [fr. *Gijón*, Spain] **:** of or from the city of Gijón, Spain **:** of the kind or style prevalent in Gijón

gi·la·ki \gəˈläkē\ *n, pl* **gilaki** *or* **gilakis** *usu cap* **1 a :** a forest people of northern Persia inhabiting the southwestern shore of the Caspian sea **b :** a member of such people **2 :** the Iranian language of the Gilaki people

gi·la monster \ˈhēlə-\ *also* **gila** *n* -s *usu cap G* [fr. *Gila* river, Arizona] **:** a large stout sluggish venomous lizard (*Heloderma suspectum*) that has venom glands in the lower lip, grooved teeth in the lower jaw, a thick tail, and a rough tuberculated skin pinkish or dull orange marked with black and that is found esp. in the arid regions of Arizona and New Mexico; *also* **:** a closely related lizard (*H. horridum*) of Mexico with an entirely black head — called also *beaded lizard*

gila trout *n, usu cap G* [fr. *Gila* river] **:** BONYTAIL

gila woodpecker *n, usu cap G* [fr. *Gila* river] **:** a large red-crowned woodpecker (*Melanerpes hypopolius uropygialis*) of southwestern No. America having the back finely barred with black and white and the underparts grayish brown

gil·bert \ˈgilbə(r)t, *usu* -d·+V\ *n* -s [after William *Gilbert* †1603 Eng. physicist] **:** the cgs unit of magnetomotive force equivalent to 10÷4π ampere-turn

gil·bert·ese \ˌgilbə(r)d·ˈēz, -ēs\ *n, pl* **gilbertese** *cap* [*Gilbert* islands in the central Pacific + E *-ese*] **1 :** a Micronesian native or inhabitant of the Gilbert islands **2 :** the Melanesian language of the Gilbertese

gil·ber·ti·an \(ˈ)gilˈbərd·ēən\ *adj, usu cap* [William S. *Gilbert* †1911 Eng. playwright + E *-ian*] **:** of, relating to, or suggesting the playwright Gilbert or the comic, wildly improbable, or topsy-turvy situations found in the Gilbert and Sullivan operas ⟨a *Gilbertian* world, peopled with foundlings and changelings —T.C.Worsley⟩ ⟨by various *Gilbertian* maneuvers . . . secured for himself the key positions —K.N.Cameron⟩

gil·bert's relief grass \ˈgilbə(r)ts-\ *n, usu cap G* [fr. the name *Gilbert*] **:** SOUTHERN CANARY GRASS

gil·christ's disease \ˈgilˌkri(s)t(s)-, -ˌkrə̄\ *n, usu cap G* [after Thomas C. *Gilchrist* †1927 Amer. dermatologist] **:** NORTH AMERICAN BLASTOMYCOSIS

¹gild \ˈgild\ *vt* **gilded** \-dəd\ *or* **gilt** \-lt\ **gilded** *or* **gilt; gilding; gilds** [ME *gilden*, fr. OE *gyldan*; akin to OHG *ubargulden* to gild all over, ON *gylla* to gild; causative-denominatives fr. the root of E *gold*] **1 a :** to overlay with a thin covering of gold ⟨~ a frame⟩ **b :** to tinge with a golden or yellowish light ⟨the night was ~*ed* by the streetlights —Marguerite Steen⟩ ⟨a gleam of sun ~*ed* the Abbey Towers —L.P. Smith⟩ **2 a :** to supply with money **:** give the attraction or prestige of wealth to ⟨money ~*s* the fool⟩ **b** (1) **:** to give an attractive but deceptive outward appearance to **:** EMBELLISH ⟨~ a lie⟩ ⟨~*ing* the future with the same old rose color —Virginia D. Dawson & Betty D. Wilson⟩ (2) **:** to make attractive **:** ADORN, BRIGHTEN ⟨~*ing* hardship with a saving grace —Bergen Evans⟩ ⟨glitter . . . and embroidery ~ femininity —*Fashion Digest*⟩ **c** *archaic* **:** to make bloody **:** smear with blood **d** *obs* **:** to make flushed (as with drinking) — often used with *over* — **gild the lily :** to add excessive or unnecessary ornamentation to something beautiful in its own right **:** paint the lily

²gild *var of* GUILD

gilded *adj* **1 :** covered or tinged with gold or a golden color ⟨~ icons⟩ **2 :** displaying a fine but deceptive outward appearance **:** superficially resplendent **:** ORNATE, MERETRICIOUS, TAWDRY ⟨the ~ and perfumed but inwardly rotten nobility —R.A.Hall b.1911⟩ ⟨a conglomeration of ~ parasites —*N.Y. Times*⟩ ⟨slickly readable but ~ and thin —Nolan Miller⟩ **3 :** having a background of wealth and luxury **:** PROSPEROUS, LUXURIOUS ⟨you'll see Rome's most ~ youth dancing by —P.E.Deutschman⟩ ⟨the ~ days of the twenties⟩ ⟨~ boys and girls —Carl Van Doren⟩ ⟨eating box lunches and staying away from the ~ dining rooms —*Wall Street Jour.*⟩

gilded flicker *n* **:** a flicker (*Colaptes chrysoides*) of the southwestern U.S. resembling the common eastern flicker in having the undersurface of the wings and tail yellow but lacking the red nape

¹gil·der \ˈgil(d)ə(r)\ *n* -s [ME, of Scand origin; akin to Norw dial. *gilder* trap, ON *gildra, gildri*; akin to ON *gilja* to entice, OSw *gjælskap* lewdness and perh. to Gk *thelein* to wish, OSlav *želěti* to desire] *dial Eng* **:** SNARE; *esp* **:** one made of horsehair and used to catch birds

²gild·er \ˈgildə(r)\ *n* -s [¹*gild* + *-er*] **:** one that gilds; *esp* **:** one whose occupation is to overlay with gold or gilt

gilder's wax *n* **:** a preparation of wax, verdigris, and other substances for imparting a tint to gilding by burning off the wax so that the copper from the verdigris combines with the gold

gilder's whiting *n* **:** whiting ground to medium fineness

gildhall *var of* GUILDHALL

gilding *n* -s [ME, fr. gerund of *gilden* to gild — more at GILD] **1 a** (1) **:** the art or practice of overlaying or covering with gold (2) **:** the similar use of some other yellow metal (as brass) **b :** the surface so decorated **c :** the material used for such decoration **2 :** a superficial prettifying or embellishment ⟨his great story needs no ~ —Burke Wilkinson⟩

gilding metal *n* **1 :** a brass rich in copper from which articles to be gilded were formerly made **2 :** brass containing 95 percent copper and 5 percent zinc or a similar alloy

gil·e·ad·ite \ˈgilēəˌdīt\ *n* -s *usu cap* [*Gilead*, region in Jordan + E *-ite*] **1 :** a member of a branch of the ancient Israelite tribe of Manasseh **2 :** an inhabitant of ancient Gilead

gi·le·ño \gəˈlān(ˌ)yō\ *n, pl* **gileño** *or* **gileños** *usu cap* [Sp, fr. the *Gila* river + Sp *-eño* (suffix added to place names to form names of inhabitants)] **1 :** a group of Athapaskan peoples comprising the Chiricahua, Mimbreño, Mogollon, and Warm Spring Apaches of the Gila river headwaters in New Mexico and Arizona **2 :** a member of the Gileño peoples

gi·let \zhēˈlā\ *n* -s [F, fr. Sp *gileco, jaleco, chaleco*, fr. Ar *jalīkah*, a garment worn by slaves in Algeria, fr. Turk *yelek* waistcoat, vest] **:** WAISTCOAT; *specif* **:** a woman's dickey resembling a waistcoat or blouse

gil·gai \ˈgilˌgī\ *n* -s [native name in Australia] **:** MELON HOLE

gil·gul \ˈgilˌgül\ *n, pl* **gil·gu·lim** \gilˈgüləm\ [Heb *gilgūl* (*nephesh*) metempsychosis, lit., turning over of the soul] **:** DYBBUK

gil·guy \ˈgilˌgī\ *n* -s [origin unknown] **1 :** a rope temporarily used as a guy or lanyard **2 :** GADGET — used esp. by sailors

gil·ia \ˈjilēə\ *n* [NL, fr. Felipe *Gil* 18th cent. Sp. botanist + NL *-ia*] **1** *cap* **:** a genus of No. American herbs (family Polemoniaceae) with often dissected leaves and campanulate to infundibuliform flowers of various colors **2** -s **:** any plant of the genus *Gilia* — see STANDING CYPRESS

giliak *usu cap, var of* GILYAK

¹gill \ˈjil\ *n* -s [ME *gille*, perh. fr. MF *gille, gelle* vat, tub,fr. L *gerulus* bearer, carrier, fr. *gerere* to bear — more at CAST] **1 :** either of two units of capacity: **a :** a British unit equal to ¼ imperial pint or 8.669 cubic inches **b :** a U.S. liquid unit equal to ¼ U.S. liquid pint or 7.218 cubic inches — see MEASURE table **2** *dial Eng* **:** half a pint

²gill \ˈ"\ *vi* -ED/-ING/-S *dial Brit* **:** TIPPLE

³gill \ˈgil\ *n* -s [ME *gile, gille*, prob. of Scand origin; akin to OSw *gel, geel, gäl*, jaw, ODan *gæln* gill, ON *gjölnar* lips; akin to Gk *chelynē* lip, jawbone, *cheilos* lip, Arm *jełun* palate, ceiling] **1 :** an organ for obtaining oxygen from water: as **a :** one of the highly vascular lamellar or filamentous processes of the pharynx of fishes and many larval amphibians by which oxygen dissolved in the surrounding water is absorbed through a thin enclosing membrane and certain wastes are given up **b :** any of various functionally comparable but structurally dissimilar organs of invertebrates (as the ctenidia within the mantle cavity of a bivalve mollusk or the branching respiratory tree that arises from the cloaca of a sea urchin) **c** (1) **:** the entire respiratory apparatus of a water-breathing animal (2) **gills** *pl* **:** the gills of a fish together with supporting branchial arches, branchial clefts, gill covers, and associated structures **2 a :** the fleshy flap below the beak of a fowl **:** WATTLE **b :** the flesh under or about the chin or jaws — usu. used in pl. ⟨decidedly pink about the ~*s* —Norman Douglas⟩ **c :** one of the radiating gill-shaped plates forming the undersurface of the pileus of various basidiomycetes **d :** one of the fallers which comb and arrange fibers or filaments in parallel order prior to spinning **e :** a corrugation or series of lips or fins usu. for promoting radiation of heat from a tube or plate (as in a heating system) — **to the gills** *adv* **:** as full as possible ⟨old cars loaded *to the gills* with household furniture —Meridel Le Sueur⟩

⁴gill \ˈ"\ *vb* -ED/-ING/-S [ME *gillen*, fr. *gile, gille*, n.] *vt* **1 :** to remove the insides of (fish) **2 :** to catch (fish) by the gills in a gill net **3 :** to treat (fibers or filaments) in a gill box ~ *vi* **:** to become entangled in a gill net — used of fish

⁵gill \ˈ"\ *n* -s [ME *gille, gylle*, fr. ON *gil*; akin to MLG *gil* throat, OHG *gil* hernia, OE *gǣlan* to hinder, impede, ON *gīna* to yawn — more at YAWN] **1** *Brit* **:** a narrow steep-sided rocky valley sometimes containing a stream **:** RAVINE **2** *Brit* **:** a narrow stream or rivulet; *esp* **:** one flowing through a gill

⁶gill *or* **jill** \ˈjil\ *n* -s *often cap* [ME *gill*, short for the name *Gillian*] **1 :** GIRL, SWEETHEART — usu. used in conjunction with *Jack* ⟨every Jack must have his *Gill*⟩ **2** *dial Eng* **:** GROUND IVY

⁷gill \ˈ"\ *n* -s [origin unknown] *dial Eng* **:** a two-wheeled frame for moving timber

gil·lar \gəˈlär\ *n* -s [native name in India] **:** a disease of East Indian sheep marked by loss of appetite, weakness, and diarrhea, usu. found fatal within a few days, and caused by infestation with immature paramphistome flukes

gill arch *n* [³*gill*] **:** BRANCHIAL ARCH

gil·la·roo \ˌgiləˈrü\ *n* -s [IrGael *giolla ruadh*, fr. *giolla* boy + *ruadh* red] **:** an Irish trout (*Salmo stomachicus*) in which the distal part of the stomach has thickened walls resembling a gizzard and serving to crush the shells of freshwater mollusks

gill bailer *n* [³*gill*] **:** a flat membranaceous expansion of the second maxilla in the crayfish and other decapod crustaceans by which water is scooped out of the gill cavity — called also *gill scoop*

gill basket *n* [³*gill*] **:** BRANCHIAL BASKET

gill box *n* [³*gill*] **:** a machine containing gills for drafting and combing fibers or filaments

gill cavity *or* **gill chamber** *n* [³*gill*] **:** the space between the gill arches and the gill cover into which the gill filaments project

gill cleft *n* [³*gill*] **:** BRANCHIAL CLEFT

gill cover *n* [³*gill*] **:** the fold of skin usu. stiffened by bony plates and often covered with scales that protects externally the gill apparatus of most fishes — compare OPERCULUM

gill disease *n* [³*gill*] **:** a destructive disease of trout and other fishes (as in hatcheries) marked by swollen eroded gills and usu. anemia and severe general debility and considered due to an unidentified bacterium or to a dietary deficiency

gilled \ˈgild\ *adj* [³*gill* + *-ed*] **:** provided with gills ⟨a ~ tadpole⟩ ⟨a ~ tube⟩

gil·le·nia \jəˈlēnēə, gə-\ *n, cap* [NL, fr. Arnold Gill (*Gillenius*) 17th cent. Ger. botanist + NL *-ia*] **:** a genus of American herbs (family Rosaceae) having trifoliolate leaves and white or pale rose flowers — see FALSE IPECAC, INDIAN PHYSIC

gill·er \ˈgilə(r)\ *n* -s [⁴*gill* + *-er*] **1 :** one that guts fish; *esp* **:** a member of a fish-dressing gang who cuts out the gills and entrails of fish **2 :** one that catches fish with a gill net **3 :** one that supplies slivers to a gill box

gil·les·pite \gəˈlesˌpīt\ *n* -s [Frank *Gillespie*, 20th cent. Am. collector of mineralogical specimens + E *-ite*] **:** a mineral $BaFeSi_4O_{10}$ consisting of a micaceous silicate of barium and iron

gill filament *or* **gill leaflet** *n* [³*gill*] **:** one of the filamentous or laminar processes making up a gill

gillflirt \ˈ=ˌ=\ *n* [⁶*gill* + *flirt*] *archaic* **:** a giddy or shameless girl

gill fungus *n* [³*gill*] **:** a basidiomycete having gills

gill-go-by-the-ground \ˈ=ˌ===ˌ=\ *n* [⁶*gill*] **:** GROUND IVY

gill helix *n* [³*gill*] **:** a spiral accessory branchial organ resembling a gill in certain characinids and clupeids

gillhooter \ˈ=ˌ==\ *n* [⁶*gill* + *hooter*] *dial Eng* **:** OWL; *esp* **:** BARN OWL

¹gil·lie *or* **gil·ly** *or* **ghil·lie** \ˈgilī\ *n, pl* **gillies** *or* **ghillies** [ScGael *gille* & IrGael *giolla* boy] **1 :** a male attendant or servant to a Scottish Highland chief **2** *Scot & Irish* **:** a fishing and hunting guide **3 :** a low-cut shoe with a decorative lacing; *esp* **:** a shoe tied by means of a cord that runs through loops or slots instead of eyelets and often winds around the ankle

gillie 3

²gillie \ˈ"\ *vi* **gillied; gillied; gillying; gillies :** to serve as a gillie

³gill·ie \ˈjilī\ *n* -s [⁶*gill* + *-ie*] **1** *dial* **:** a stupid person **2** *dial* **:** a woman of easy virtue

⁴gill·ie \ˈ"\ *n* -s [¹*gill* + *-ie*] *Scot* **:** a gill of liquor

gil·lie cal·lum \ˌgiliˈkaləm\ *n, pl* **gillie callums** *usu cap G&C* [ˈ*gillie* + *callum*, of unknown origin] **:** a solo sword dance of the Scottish Highlands

gilliflower *var of* GILLYFLOWER

gilling *n* -s [fr. gerund of ⁴*gill*] **:** the process of laying fibers or filaments parallel by combing

gilling thread *n* [fr. pres. part. of ⁴*gill*] **:** a fine twisted cord used in making gill nets

gil·li·ver \ˈjiləvə(r)\ *dial Eng var of* GILLYFLOWER

gill·more needles \ˈgilˌmō(ə)r-\ *n pl, usu cap G* [fr. the name *Gillmore*] **:** two needles used in determining the rate of setting of cement paste

gill net *n* [³*gill*] **:** a flat net suspended vertically in the water with meshes that allow the head of a fish to pass but entangle its gill covers as it seeks to withdraw

gillnet \ˈ=ˌ=\ *vt* [*gill net*] **:** to catch (fish) with a gill net ⟨*gillnetted* over 5 tons of herring⟩

gill-netter \ˈ=ˌ==\ *n* **:** one that fishes with a gill net; *also* **:** a boat equipped for or engaged in such fishing

gill-over-the-ground \ˈ=ˌ===ˌ=\ *or* **gill-over-ground** \ˈ=ˌ==ˈ=\ *n* [⁶*gill*] **:** GROUND IVY

gill raker *also* **gill rake** *n* [³*gill*] **:** one of the bony processes on the inside of the branchial arches of fishes that help to prevent solid substances from being carried out through the branchial clefts

gill rod *n* [³*gill*] **:** one of the oblique supporting rods of the pharynx in lancelets

gills *pl of* GILL, *pres 3d sing of* GILL

gill scoop *n* [³*gill*] **:** GILL BAILER

gill slit *n* [³*gill*] **1 :** BRANCHIAL CLEFT **2 :** the external opening of the gill cavity when a gill cover is present

¹gilly *var of* GILLIE

²gil·ly \ˈgilē\ *n* -ES [⁷*gill* + *-y*] **:** a lumber wagon or any local wagon or truck hired for hauling circus or carnival paraphernalia

³gilly \ˈ"\ *vb* -ED/-ING/-ES *vt* **:** to transport by means of a gilly ~ *vi* **:** to be transportable on a gilly

gil·ly·flow·er *also* **gil·li·flow·er** \ˈjilē, -li + ˌ-\ *n* [by folk etymology fr. ME *gilofre, gelofer*, fr. MF *girofle, gilofre*, fr. L *caryophyllon*, fr. Gk *karyophyllon*, fr. *karyon* nut + *phyllon* leaf — more at CAREEN, BLADE] **1 a** *obs* **:** ⁴CLOVE 1a **b :** CLOVE PINK 1; *broadly* **:** any of several plants of the genus *Dianthus* **c :** STOCK 24a **d :** WALLFLOWER 1 **2** *dial Eng* **:** an aging Jezebel

gil·ly·gau·pus \ˌgiliˈgȯpəs, -ˈgäp-\ *n* -ES [¹*gillie, gilly* + *-gaupus* (fr. ²*gawp*)] *dial Brit* **:** a stupid awkward person

gil·py *or* **gil·pey** \ˈgilpī\ *n, pl* **gilpies** *or* **gilpeys** [origin unknown] *chiefly Scot* **:** a lively frolicsome boy or girl ⟨I was a *gilpey* . . . na past fifteen —Robert Burns⟩

¹gil·rav·age \gəlˈravij\ *vi* [origin unknown] **1** *chiefly Scot* **a :** to live riotously and intemperately; *esp* **:** to practice intemperate eating and drinking **b :** to be noisy and boisterous in merrymaking **2** *chiefly Scot* **:** GAD, GALLIVANT

²gilravage \ˈ"\ *n, chiefly Scot* **:** UPROAR, COMMOTION

Gil·son·ite \ˈgilsəˌnīt\ *trademark* — used for uintaite

¹gilt \ˈgilt\ *adj* [ME, fr. past part. of *gilden* to gild — more at GILD] **:** covered with gold or gilt **:** of the color of gold **:** GILDED

²gilt \ˈ"\ *n* -s **1 :** gold or something that resembles gold laid on the surface of a thing **:** GILDING **2** *slang* **:** MONEY **3 :** superficial or shoddy prettiness or brilliance **:** false glitter ⟨the ~ has worn off some of these sparkling aphorisms —M.D.Geismar⟩

³gilt \ˈ"\ *or* **yilt** \ˈyilt\ *n* -s [ME *gilte, gylte*, fr. ON *gyltr, gylta* sow; akin to OE *gelte* young sow, MLG *gelte* spayed sow — more at GELD] **:** an immature female swine; *also* **:** a young sow usu. prior to production of her first litter but sometimes until bred to produce a second litter

gilt bronze *n* **:** bronze gilded and used in decoration (as for moldings or scrollwork) esp. in 17th and 18th century France — called also *bronze-doré*

gilt-edged *or* **gilt-edge** \ˈ=ˈ=\ *adj* **1 :** having a gilt edge **2 :** of the best quality ⟨a *gilt-edged* theatrical cast⟩ — used esp. of securities (as government obligations) of the safest character

gilthead \ˈ=ˌ=\ *n* **:** any of several marine fishes: as **a :** a valuable sparid food fish (*Sparus auratus*) common in the Mediterranean **b :** a cunner (*Crenilabrus melops*) of the British coasts

gil·yak \(ˈ)gilˈyak\ *or* **gil·iak** \", ˈgilēˌak\ *n, pl* **gilyak** *or* **gilyaks** *or* **giliak** *or* **giliaks** *usu cap* **1 a :** a people of hunters and fishers of Siberia that have classical pure Mongolian traits, are related to the Tungus, Goldi, and Buryats, and are found in the lower course of the Amur river and in adjacent northern Sakhalin Island **b :** a member of such people **2 :** the language of the Gilyak people **3 :** a language family consisting only of Gilyak

gim \ˈjim\ *adj* [origin unknown] *dial Eng* **:** NEAT, TRIM

gim·bal \ˈgimbəl, ˈji-\ *or* **gimbal ring** *n* -s [alter. of *gemel*] **:** a contrivance that permits a body to incline freely in any direction or suspends something (as a barometer or a ship's compass) so that it will remain level when its support is tipped and that consists of a ring in which the body can turn on an axis through a diameter of the ring while the ring itself is so pivoted to its support that it can turn about a diameter at right angles to the first — usu. used in pl.

gimbals supporting a compass

gim·baled \-ld\ *adj* **:** provided with or supported on gimbals

gim·ber·nat's ligament \ˌhimbə(r)ˈnäts-, ˈgi-\ *n, usu cap G* [after Antonio de *Gimbernat* y Arbós †1816 Span. surgeon] **:** the portion of the aponeurosis of the external oblique muscle that is reflected from Poupart's ligament along the iliopectineal line

gim·ble \ˈgimbəl, ˈji-\ *vi* -ED/-ING/-S [origin unknown] **:** to make a face **:** GRIMACE

¹gim·crack *or* **jim·crack** \ˈjimˌkrak\ *n* -s [origin unknown] **1 a :** something usu. characterized by flimsy or tricky ingenuity rather than substance or worth **:** DOODAD, GADGET **b :** TOY, GEWGAW, KNICKKNACK, TRIFLE **2** *archaic* **:** a showily fashionable or affected person **:** FOP

²gimcrack *or* **jimcrack** \ˈ"\ *adj* **1 :** hastily or shoddily constructed **:** having an improvised air or appearance **:** FLIMSY, UNSUBSTANTIAL ⟨a mess of ~ bungalows —J.B.Priestley⟩ ⟨~ stands for the sale . . . of ice-cream cones —Jean Stafford⟩ ⟨they were terrible ~ planes we flew in —W.S.Maugham⟩ **2 :** TRIVIAL, FRIVOLOUS ⟨you expect me to pay for this ~ excursion of yours —Katherine Mansfield⟩

gim·crack·ery \-kərē, -ri\ *n* -ES **1 :** a quantity of gimcracks ⟨colored candles and ~ . . . of odd origin —Kathryn Hulme⟩ **2 :** cheap, contrived, or shoddy effects or expedients ⟨his interpretations are quite without sentimental ~ —Virgil Thomson⟩

¹gim·el *or* **gim·mel** *also* **ghim·el** \ˈgiməl *sometimes* ˈgēm-\ *n* -s [Heb *gīmel*, lit., camel] **1 :** the 3d letter of the Hebrew alphabet — symbol ג; see ALPHABET table **2 :** the letter of the Phoenician or of any of various other Semitic alphabets corresponding to Hebrew gimel

²gimel *var of* GYMEL

¹gim·let \ˈgimlət, *usu* -əd·+V\ *n* -s [ME *gimlet, gimelot*, modif. of MF *guimbelet*, prob. modif. of MD *wimmelkijn* gimlet, fr. *wimmel* auger + *-kijn* -kin — more at WIMBLE, -KIN] **:** a small woodworking tool with a screw point, grooved shank, and cross handle for boring holes

²gimlet \ˈ"\ *adj* **:** having a piercing, penetrating, or driving quality ⟨one of the ~ characters who, by diligence and memory . . . gain prizes in their school days —G.D.Brown⟩

³gimlet \ˈ"\ *vb* -ED/-ING/-S **:** to pierce or penetrate with or as if with a gimlet ⟨~*ing* through her inquisitor with her eyes —Elizabeth Bowen⟩

⁴gimlet \ˈ"\ *n* -s [¹*gimlet*; fr. the fluted structure of the stem] **:** an Australian gum tree (*Eucalyptus salubris*)

gimlet

⁵gimlet \ˈ"\ *n* -s [prob. fr. ¹*gimlet*] **:** a cooling drink esp. of the British Pacific colonies (as Hong Kong) consisting usu. of sweetened lime juice, gin, and water either carbonated or plain

gimlet bit *n* **:** a bit with a spiral flute and a sharp threaded point for boring small holes in wood

gimlet eye *n* [1*gimlet*] **:** a piercing or watchful eye ⟨a man with a *gimlet eye* for the future —*Newsweek*⟩ — **gimlet-eyed** \ˈ⸗⸗ˌ⸗\ *adj*

gim·lety \-əd·|ē, -ət|, |i\ *adj* [1*gimlet* + -*y*] **:** like a gimlet **:** PIERCING, PENETRATING ⟨~ eyes⟩

1**gim·mal** \ˈgiməl, ˈji-\ *n* -s [alter. of *gemel*] **1 gimmals** *pl* **:** joined work (as clockwork) whose parts move within each other **2** *or* **gimmal ring :** a pair or series of interlocked rings

2**gimmal** \"\ *also* **gim·maled** \-ld\ *adj* **:** made or consisting of gimmals or interlocked rings or links

1**gim·me** \ˈgimē, -mi\ [by contr.] *slang* **:** give me

2**gimme** \"\ *adj, slang* **:** expecting or requesting a money contribution, a handout, or a special privilege ⟨on the list of countless ~ organizations —*Printer's Ink Monthly*⟩ ⟨the ~ concept of government which is held by so many citizens —Harold Zink⟩

3**gimme** \"\ *n* -s *slang* **:** extreme desire for presents — usu. used in pl. ⟨a bad case of the ~*s* —Eric Soames⟩

gimmel *var of* GIMEL

1**gim·mer** \ˈgimər\ *n* -s [ME *gymbyre, gymmer*, fr. ON *gymbr* a live lamb one year old — more at CHIMERA] **1** *chiefly Scot* **:** a yearling female sheep **:** a two-tooth ewe **2** *dial Brit* **:** a woman friend **:** CRONY

2**gim·mer** *or* **gim·mor** \ˈjimə(r)\ *n* -s [prob. alter. of 1*gemel*] **1** *dial* **:** HINGE, CLASP **2** *obs* **:** GIMMAL — usu. used in pl.

1**gim·mick** \ˈgimik, -mēk\ *n* -s [origin unknown] **1 a** (1) **:** a mechanical device by which a gambling apparatus (as a roulette wheel) can be secretly and dishonestly controlled (2) **:** a mechanical device used to cheat or deceive **b :** an ingenious or novel mechanical device **:** GADGET ⟨a new ~ . . . claimed to unscrew the stickiest container —*Wall Street Jour.*⟩ ⟨no experimental ~*s* were installed —*N.Y. Herald Tribune*⟩ ⟨we have . . . radios, washing machines, bathtubs, and ~*s* of all sorts —H.F.Peters⟩ **c :** a decisive or strategic element or feature that is purposely hidden, unobtrusive, or not immediately apparent **:** CATCH, JOKER ⟨in some states ~*s* in the law make it almost impossible to successfully prosecute —*Best True Fact Detective*⟩ ⟨what's the ~ . . . what's in it for you —Maxwell Griffith⟩ ⟨you look for the ~ in innocent queries like that —*Ring*⟩ **2 :** a new and ingenious device, scheme, or idea for solving a problem or achieving an end **:** a new angle of approach **:** a novel or unconventional twist ⟨the ~ was simple . . . we would take great historical moments and place microphones on the scene as if the network had . . . commentators covering the events —Goodman Ace⟩ ⟨commercial promotional ~*s* —Dwight MacDonald⟩ ⟨any ~ or glimmer of an amusing idea is a suitable substitute for professional talent —Elsa Maxwell⟩ ⟨a new book on Hamlet must have a new ~ —Robert Halsband⟩

2**gimmick** \"\ *vt* -ED/-ING/-S **1 :** to alter or influence by means of a gimmick or similar device or method ⟨~*ing* up some difficult padlocks —W.L.Gresham⟩ **2 :** to provide with a gimmick (as with an attention-catching device, a novel twist, or a gadget) ⟨one of the stories . . . is ~*ed* up —Gilbert Millstein⟩ ⟨now the show has been ~*ed* . . . with flashing lights and bad jokes —John Crosby⟩ ⟨the mechanism was ~*ed* . . . to prove what the missile could do —*Time*⟩

gim·mick·ery *or* **gim·mick·ry** \-k(ə)rē, -ri\ *n* -ES **:** an array or profusion of gimmicks ⟨carried an incomprehensible mass of miniature coils . . . and other electronic *gimmickry* —*N.Y. Times*⟩

gim·micky \-məkē, -ki\ *adj* **:** having or being like a gimmick ⟨a ~ side to stereo — recordings deliberately souped up and distorted —Roland Gelatt⟩

1**gimp** \ˈjimp\ *var of* JIMP

2**gimp** \ˈgimp\ *n* -s [perh. fr. D] **1 a :** a flat narrow braid often with a wire or coarse cord running through it used as a trimming or decorative finish for upholstery and clothing **b :** a thread or yarn for embroidery or knitting made by twisting a heavy thread around a core thread **c :** a coarse thread for outlining a design in a piece of lace; *sometimes* **:** the pattern as opposed to the ground **2 :** a silk fishline strengthened with wire

3**gimp** \"\ *vt* -ED/-ING/-S **:** to trim or make with gimp

4**gimp** \"\ *n* -s [origin unknown] **:** SPIRIT, VIM ⟨she does get some ~ into her characters —J.R.Chamberlin⟩ ⟨if I had an ounce of ~ in me —*Atlantic*⟩

5**gimp** \"\ *n* -s [origin unknown] **:** CRIPPLE ⟨the ~ swayed to one side —Jerry McClung⟩; *also* **:** a limping walk ⟨walks with a ~ in one leg —Damon Runyon⟩

6**gimp** \"\ *vi* -ED/-ING/-S **:** LIMP, HOBBLE ⟨came ~*ing* across the floor on three legs —Nelson Algren⟩ ⟨~*ing* along to the bus station —W.C.Williams⟩

gim peg \ˈjim-\ *or* **gem peg** \ˈjem-\ *n* [*gim* alter. of *gem*] **:** a cranked iron support in a lapidary's mill for the block into which the gem stick is stuck

gimp nail *or* **gimp tack** *n* [2*gimp*] **:** a small nail with a rounded head used to fasten gimp to furniture

gimpy \ˈgimpē, -pi\ *adj* -ER/-EST [5*gimp* + -*y*] **:** CRIPPLED, LAME, LIMPING ⟨threw himself again into his burlesque ~ gait —L.A.Fiedler⟩ ⟨a grizzled old veteran with a ~ leg —I.S. Cobb⟩

1**gin** \ˈgin\ *vb* **gan** \ˈgan\ **gun·nen** \ˈgənən\ **ginning; gins** [ME *ginnen*, short for *onginnen* to begin (fr. OE *onginnan*) & *beginnen* to begin — more at BEGIN] *archaic* **:** BEGIN

2**gin** \ˈjin\ *n* -s [ME *gin*, modif. of OF *engin* skill, mechanical contrivance — more at ENGINE] **:** any of several machines, tools, or mechanical devices: as **a :** a snare or trap for game **b :** a machine for raising or moving heavy weights (as a tripod formed of poles united at the top, with a windlass, pulleys, and ropes) **c :** a cotton gin or any similar device used for separating seed or foreign matter from fiber to be used commercially; *also* **:** a building where cotton is ginned

3**gin** \"\ *vt* **ginned; ginned; ginning; gins 1 :** to catch in a gin **:** SNARE **2 :** to separate (cotton fiber) from seeds and waste material

4**gin** \(ˌ)gin\ *conj* [perh. alter. of *gif*] *dial* **:** IF ⟨~ a body meet a body —Robert Burns⟩

5**gin** \ˈjin\ *n* -s [by shortening and alter. fr. 2*geneva*] **1 a :** a strong alcoholic liquor extensively made in the Netherlands by distilling a mash of grain (as rye) in pot stills with juniper berries — called also *Hollands* **b :** a similar liquor made from plain spirit flavored with an aromatic (as juniper berries, aniseed, coriander, fennel, or turpentine) and usu. containing about 40 percent of alcohol by weight **2 a :** GIN RUMMY **b :** the act of going gin **:** the act of laying down a full hand of matched cards in gin rummy; *also* **:** the bonus of usu. 20 or 25 points for doing so

6**gin** \"\ *adj* **:** having all 10 of one's cards in gin rummy matched in sets

7**gin** \"\ *adv* **:** with all 10 of one's cards in gin rummy matched in sets

8**gin** \(ˌ)gin\ *prep* [by shortening & alter. fr. 2*again*] *dial* **:** BEFORE, BY ⟨I'll be home ~ midnight⟩

9**gin** *conj, dial* **:** by the time that **:** WHEN ⟨~ daylight came he had gone⟩

10**gin** \ˈgin\ *dial past of* GIVE

11**gin** \ˈjin\ *n* -s [native name in Australia] *Austral* **:** an aboriginal woman

gin and it \ˌjinəˈnit\ *n* [5*gin* + *and* + *it*, short for *Italian vermouth*] *chiefly Brit* **:** a drink of sweet vermouth and gin

gin and tonic *n* **:** a cooling drink consisting of dry gin and quinine water flavored and garnished with lime or lemon peel

gin block *n* [2*gin*] **:** an iron or steel tackle block containing one or more pulleys

gin buck *n* **:** a cocktail with a gin base to which are added lime or lemon juice and ginger ale served iced and garnished with lime or lemon peel

ginep *var of* GENIP

ging \ˈgiŋ\ *n* -s [ME, alter. of *genge*, fr. OE, troop, fr. *gangan* to go — more at GANG] *archaic* **:** CREW, COMPANY, TROOP, GANG

gin·gel·ly *also* **jin·ji·li** \ˈjinjəlē\ *n, pl* **gingellies** *also* **jinjilis** [Hindi & Marathi *jinjalī*, fr. Ar *juljulān*] **:** SESAME SEED

gingelly oil *n* **:** SESAME OIL

1**gin·ger** \ˈjinjə(r)\ *n* -s *often attrib* [ME *ginger, gingere*, alter. of *gingivere*, alter. (influenced by OF *gingembre, gingibre* ginger, fr. ML *gingiber*) of OE *gingifer*, modif. of ML *gingiber*, alter. of L *zingiber*, fr. Gk *zingiberi*, prob. modif. of Skt *śṛṅgavera*] **1 :** a thickened irregular rhizome that is extremely pungent and aromatic, is widely used as a spice and sometimes in medicine as a carminative, stimulant, or counterirritant, and is usu. prepared by drying and grinding to a fine brownish powder — see BLACK GINGER, CANTON GINGER, JAMAICA GINGER, LIMED GINGER, WHITE GINGER **2 :** a tropical perennial herb (*Zingiber officinale*) that is prob. native to the Pacific islands but is widely cultivated for its rhizome which constitutes most of the ginger of commerce; *broadly* **:** any plant of the genus *Zingiber* **3 :** any of various plants of which some part (as root or juice) has a pungency or flavor suggestive of ginger (as various tansies and sedums or the wild gingers) **4 :** high spirit **:** METTLE, PEP, VIGOR ⟨written . . . with the wit, bounce, and ~ that characterize the dances she has composed —*New Yorker*⟩ ⟨you've got an awful lot of ~ to you —Joseph Hergesheimer⟩ ⟨the only capital he had was the ~ to care hard and work hard —Willa Cather⟩ **5 :** a strong brown that is stronger and slightly yellower and darker than average russet, deeper and slightly yellower than rust, and very slightly darker than gypsy — called also *Kaiser brown*

2**ginger** \"\ *vt* **gingered; gingered; gingering** \-nj(ə)riŋ\ **gingers 1 :** to make lively or animated **:** stir to activity **:** pep up **:** REVIVE ⟨loyalty at home . . . is always ~*ed* by state executions —Francis Hackett⟩ — often used with *up* ⟨~ up the tourist trade —*N.Y.Times*⟩ ⟨~*ing* up the flow of revenue —Leslie Charteris⟩ **2 :** 4FIG 2

3**ginger** \"\ *adj* **:** having the color of ginger ⟨with a youthful figure and ~ hair —A.J.Liebling⟩

4**ginger** \"\ *adj, chiefly dial* [back-formation fr. *gingerly*] **:** GINGERLY

5**ginger** \"\ *adv, chiefly dial* **:** GINGERLY ⟨got up, handling myself kind of ~ —Helen Eustis⟩

gin·ger·ade \ˌjinjəˈrād\ *n, Brit* **:** a beverage flavored with ginger ⟨bought a bottle of ~ —Flora Thompson⟩

ginger ale *n* **:** a sweetened carbonated beverage flavored mainly with ginger extract — called also *ginger pop*

ginger beer *n* **:** a sweetened carbonated beverage heavily flavored with ginger or capsicum or both

1**gin·ger·bread** \ˈjinjə(r)ˌbred\ *n, often attrib* [ME *gingerbreed*, by folk etymology (influence of ME *ginger, gingere* ginger) fr. *gingebreed* gingerbread, ginger paste, by folk etymology (influence of ME *breed* bread) fr. *gingebras* ginger paste, fr. OF *gingembras, gingebraz*, fr. *gingembre, gingibre* ginger — more at GINGER] **1 :** a cake made with molasses, flavored with ginger, often cut in fancy shapes, and frosted **2 :** something showy but unsubstantial or tasteless; *esp* **:** tawdry, gaudy, or superfluous ornament or embellishment in architecture ⟨interiors from which ~ and plush were banished —Edgar Kaufmann⟩

2**gingerbread** \"\ *adj* **:** adorned with, characterized by, or being gingerbread **:** showily, tawdrily, or elaborately ornamented ⟨a ~ clubhouse⟩ ⟨a frame dwelling with ~ trim —*Amer. Guide Series: N.C.*⟩ ⟨the ~ style of the Victorian era⟩ ⟨~ scrollwork⟩

gingerbread palm *n* [so called fr. the flavor of the fruit] **:** DOOM PALM

gingerbread plum *n* **1 :** a West African tree (*Parinarium macrophyllum*) that has a strong light-brown wood and edible fruit **2 :** the fruit of the gingerbread plum having a soft mealy edible pulp, a kernel rich in oil, and a cottony protective layer around the seeds that is used locally for tinder

gin·ger·bready \-dē, -di\ *adj* [1*gingerbread* + -*y*] **:** like fancy gingerbread **:** tawdrily showy **:** overly ornamented ⟨~ architecture⟩

ginger brown T-5902 *n, usu cap G&B* **:** an organic pigment — see DYE table I (under *Pigment Brown 5*)

ginger cake *n* **:** GINGERBREAD

ginger coral *n* **:** SEA GINGER

ginger family *n* **:** ZINGIBERACEAE

ginger grass *n* **1 :** any of various East Indian grasses of the genus *Cymbopogon* (esp. *C. martinii* var. *sofia*) **2 :** a coarse grass (*Panicum glutinosum*) of the West Indies and tropical America useful as fodder

ginger-grass oil *n* **:** an essential oil that resembles palmarosa oil but has an odor like that of common ginger and that is obtained esp. from a ginger grass (*Cymbopogon martinii* var. *sofia*)

ginger group *n, chiefly Brit* **:** a group or element that serves as a driving, stimulating, or energizing force within a larger body (as a political party) ⟨a new body was formed to act as a high-level *ginger group* or steering committee —Richard Scott⟩

ginger lily *n* **:** BUTTERFLY LILY 1

gin·ger·li·ness \ˈjinjə(r)lēnəs, -lin-\ *n* -ES **:** the quality of being gingerly ⟨koala bears . . . show by their ~ how indispensable tails are to carefree tree living —Alan Devoe⟩

1**gin·ger·ly** \-lē,-li\ *adj* [perh. fr. 1*ginger* + -*ly*] **:** very cautious or tentative ⟨the issue . . . was handled only in a ~ way —W.S.White⟩ ⟨~ footwork suggested house guests trying to decide whether the lawn is too damp for croquet —*New Yorker*⟩

2**gingerly** \"\ *adv* [prob. fr. 1*gingerly*] **:** with extreme care concerning the result of a movement or act **:** very cautiously ⟨tread their way ~ over the jagged stones —Brian Murtough⟩ ⟨~ laid the packages down —John Steinbeck⟩ ⟨handles the subject ~ —H.G.Merriam⟩

ginger nut *n* **:** a cookie spiced with ginger **:** GINGERSNAP

ginger oil *n* **:** a yellowish thick aromatic essential oil obtained from ginger and used chiefly as a flavoring material

ginger pine *n* **:** PORT ORFORD CEDAR

ginger plant *n* **1 :** GINGER 2a **2 :** a tansy (*Tanacetum vulgare*)

ginger pop *n* **:** GINGER ALE

gingerroot \ˈ⸗⸗ˌ⸗\ *n* **1 :** the unpulverized ginger rootstock **2 :** COLTSFOOT a

gingers *pl of* GINGER, *pres 3d sing of* GINGER

gingersnap \ˈ⸗⸗ˌ⸗\ *n* **:** a thin brittle cookie flavored with ginger and usu. sweetened with molasses

gingerspice \ˈ⸗⸗ˌ⸗\ *n* **:** RUSTIC BROWN

ginger wine *n* **:** a ginger-flavored beverage sometimes fermented or effervescent

gin·gery \ˈjinj(ə)rē, -ri\ *adj* [1*ginger* + -*y*] **1 :** having the characteristics or color of ginger **:** flavored with ginger **:** SHARP, SPICY **2 :** full of vigor **:** HIGH-SPIRITED, PEPPY, METTLESOME ⟨the high quick ~ ways of thoroughbreds —John Masefield⟩ ⟨in ~ good health —*Newsweek*⟩

ging·ham \ˈgiŋəm\ *n* -s [modif. of Malay *genggang* checkered cloth] **:** a clothing fabric usu. of yarn-dyed cotton in plain weave made in solid colors, checks, plaids, and stripes and in various weights and qualities

gingiv- *or* **gingivo-** *comb form* [L *gingiv-*, fr. *gingiva* gum] **1 :** gum **:** gums ⟨*gingiv*ectomy⟩ ⟨*gingiv*itis⟩ **2 :** of the gums and ⟨*gingivo*stomatitis⟩ **:** gingival and ⟨*gingivo*labial⟩

gin·gi·va \jinˈjīvə\ *n, pl* **gingi·vae** \-ˌvē\ [L — more at CONGER] **:** 1GUM

gin·gi·val \(ˈ)jinˈjīvəl, ˈjinjəv-\ *adj* [L *gingiva* + E -*al*] **:** of or relating to the gums: as **a :** ALVEOLAR **b :** being between alveolar and dental

gingival crevice *n* **:** a narrow space between the free margin of the gingival epithelium and the adjacent enamel of a tooth

gin·gi·vec·to·my \ˌjinjəˈvektəmē\ *n* -ES [ISV *gingiv-* + -*ectomy*] **:** the excision of a portion of the gingiva

gin·gi·vi·tis \ˌjinjəˈvīdəs\ *n* -ES [NL, fr. *gingiv-* + -*itis*] **:** inflammation of the gingival tissue

gingivostomatitis \jinˌjīvō, ˌjinjə(ˌ)vō+\ *n* [NL, fr. *gingiv-* + *stomatitis*] **:** inflammation of the gums and of the mouth

gin·gly·form \ˈjiŋgləˌfȯrm, ˈgi-\ *adj* [ISV *gingly-* (fr. NL *ginglymus*) + -*form*] **:** GINGLYMOID

gin·glymo·arthrodia \ˌ⸗⸗(ˌ)mō+\ *n* [NL, fr. *ginglymo-* (fr. *ginglymus*) + *arthrodia*] **:** a composite anatomical joint of which one element has an axial or hinge motion and the other a simple gliding motion — **gin·glymo·arthrodial** \"+\ *adj*

gin·gly·mo·di \ˌjiŋgləˈmōˌdī, ˌgi-\ *n pl, cap* [NL, irreg. fr. Gk *ginglymos*] **:** an order of ganoid fishes coextensive with the family Lepisosteidae and comprising the gars of fresh waters of No. America — compare HOLOSTEI — **gin·gly·mo·di·an** \ˌ⸗⸗ˈmōdēən\ *adj or n*

gin·gly·moid \ˈ⸗⸗ˌmȯid\ *adj* [Gk *ginglymoeidēs* like a hinge, fr. *ginglymos* hinge + -*oeidēs* -oid] **:** of, relating to, or resembling a ginglymus

gin·gly·mos·to·ma \ˌ⸗⸗ˈmästəmə\ *n, cap* [NL, fr. *ginglymo-* (fr. *ginglymus*) + -*stoma*] **:** a genus of galeoid sharks of shallow tropical seas in which more than one series of teeth are functional at a time — **gin·gly·mos·to·moid** \ˌ⸗⸗ˈ⸗stəˌmȯid\ *adj*

gin·gly·mus \ˈjiŋgləməs, ˈgi-\ *n, pl* **gingly·mi** \-ˌmī, -ˌmē\ [NL, fr. Gk *ginglymos* hinge, joint] **:** a hinge joint (as between the humerus and ulna) admitting of motion in one plane only

ginhouse \ˈ⸗ˌ⸗\ *n* [2*gin* + *house*] **:** a building where cotton is ginned

gink \ˈgiŋk\ *n* -s [origin unknown] *slang* **:** PERSON, GUY, FELLOW ⟨a calm, responsible-looking ~ —Saul Bellow⟩ ⟨deceased was a dashed unpleasant old ~ —Dorothy Sayers⟩

gink·go \ˈgiŋ(ˌ)kō *sometimes* ˈji- *or* -ŋk(ˌ)gō *or* -ŋk(ˌ)yō\ *n* [NL, fr. Jap *ginkyo*, fr. *gin* silver (fr. Chin *yin*2) + *kyo* apricot, fr. Chin *hsing*4] **1** *cap* **:** a monotypic genus of broad-leaved gymnospermous trees (family Ginkgoaceae) that are native to eastern China, have apparently been preserved as temple trees being very rare in the wild, and are distinguished by fan-shaped deciduous leaves and yellow fruits resembling drupes **2** *or* **ging·ko** \"\ *also* **gin·ko** \"\ *pl* **ginkgos** *or* **ginkgoes** *or* **gingkos** *or* **gingkoes** *also* **ginkos** *or* **ginkoes :** a tree (*Ginkgo biloba*) that is the sole representative of the genus *Ginkgo* — called also *maidenhair tree*

gink·go·ace·ae \ˌ⸗⸗ˈāsēˌē\ *n pl, cap* [NL, fr. *Ginkgo*, type genus + -*aceae*] **:** a family of gymnospermous plants that is coextensive with the order Ginkgoales and includes the genus *Ginkgo* and certain form genera of extinct plants — **gink·go·aceous** \ˌ⸗⸗ˈāshəs\ *adj*

gink·go·ales \ˌ⸗⸗ˈā(ˌ)lēz\ *n pl, cap* [NL, fr. *Ginkgo* + -*ales*] **:** an order of gymnospermous trees that first appeared in the Permian and is represented by a single surviving species (*Ginkgo biloba*)

gink·go·ites \ˌ⸗⸗ˈīd·(ˌ)ēz\ *n, cap* [NL, fr. *Ginkgo* + L -*ites*] **:** a form genus of the family Ginkgoaceae comprising Mesozoic plants with the leaves usu. indented but not deeply divided into segments and with distinct petioles

ginkgo nut *n* **:** the fruit of the ginkgo

gin mill *n, slang* **:** a commercial establishment where alcoholic liquor is served **:** BAR, SALOON

ginned *past of* GIN

gin·ner \ˈjinə(r)\ *n* -s **:** an operator of a cotton gin or linter

gin·nery \ˈjinərē\ *n* -ES **:** an establishment where cotton is ginned

gin·ney \ˈginē, -ni\ *n* -s [alter. of *guinea*] *slang* **:** ITALIAN — usu. used disparagingly

1**gin·ning** \ˈgi-\ *pres part of* GIN

2**gin·ning** \ˈji-\ *n* -s [fr. gerund of 3*gin*] **1 :** the process or an instance of separating cotton fiber from seeds and waste plant material **2 :** cotton as it comes from the cotton gin

ginny \ˈjinē, -ni\ *adj, often* -ER/-EST [5*gin* + -*y*] **:** of, suggesting, or affected with gin ⟨a ~ smell⟩ ⟨~ hilarity⟩ ⟨reports of ~ Village parties —Joseph Mitchell⟩

gino·rite \ˈjinəˌrīt, jəˈnȯrˌīt\ *n* -s [It, fr. Piero *Ginori*-Conti †1939 Ital. scientist + It -*ite*] **:** a mineral $Ca_2B_{14}O_{23}·8H_2O$ consisting of hydrous borate of calcium

gin pole *n* **1 :** any one of the three poles of a hoisting gin **2 :** a single pole held in a nearly vertical position by guys that supports a block and tackle used for lifting loads

gin rummy *n* [5*gin* (suggested by the identity in sound of *rum* meaning an alcoholic drink and *rum* meaning a card game) + *rummy*] **:** a card game for two players who are each dealt 10 cards from a 52-card pack similar to knock rummy except that a player may knock only if his unmatched cards count 10 or less

gins *pres 3d sing of* GIN, *pl of* GIN

gin saw *n* **:** the saw used to draw fibers through a cotton gin

gin·seng \ˈjinˌsaŋ, -ˌsaiŋ, -ˌseŋ, -ˌsiŋ; -in(t)siŋ, -in(t)sēŋ\ *also* **gen·seng** \", ˈjen-\ *n* -s [Chin (Pek) *jen*2*-shen*1] **1 :** a Chinese herb (*Panax schinseng*) having 5-foliolate leaves and umbels of small greenish flowers succeeded by scarlet berries **2 :** any of several plants (genus *Panax*) related to or used as substitutes for the Chinese ginseng; *esp* **:** a No. American woodland herb (*P. quinquefolius*) with 5-foliolate leaves **3 :** the aromatic root of either Chinese or American ginseng that has a sweetish taste suggestive of licorice and is highly valued as a medicine in China though of value chiefly as a demulcent

ginseng family *n* **:** ARALIACEAE

gin·shang \ˈjinˌshaŋ, -shaiŋ\ *dial var of* GINSENG

gin trap *n* [2*gin*] *chiefly Brit* **:** a trap used esp. for catching rabbits

gin·zo \ˈgin(ˌ)zō\ *n* -ES [prob. alter. of *guinea*] **:** a person of Italian extraction — usu. taken to be offensive

gio \ˈgyō\ *var of* GEO

gio·co·so \jōˈkō(ˌ)sō\ *adj (or adv)* [It, jocose, fr. L *jocosus* — more at JOCOSE] **:** LIVELY, HUMOROUS — used chiefly as a direction in music

gio·jo·so *also* **gio·io·so** \jōˈyō(ˌ)sō\ *adj (or adv)* [It *gioioso* joyous, fr. OIt, fr. OF *joios* — more at JOYOUS] **:** JOYOUS, GAY — used as a direction in music

gior·gio·nesque \ˌjȯrjōˈnesk\ *adj, usu cap* [It *giorgionesco*, fr. *Giorgione* (Giorgio Barbarelli) †1511 Venetian painter + It -*esco* -esque] **:** characteristic of or resembling the style of the Italian painter Giorgione Barbarelli ⟨the whole sheet overflows with *Giorgionesque* motifs —*Art in America*⟩

gior·gi system \ˈjȯr(ˌ)jē-\ *n, usu cap G* [after Giovanni *Giorgi* †1950 Ital. physicist] **:** the mks system of units

giot·tesque \(ˈ)jōˈtesk, jēˌō;t-\ *adj, usu cap* [It *giottesco*, fr. *Giotto* di Bondone †1337? Florentine painter + It -*esco* -esque] **:** resembling the broad and simple style of the painter Giotto

1**gip** *interj* [origin unknown] *obs* — used to express anger, impatience, surprise, or contempt

2**gip** \ˈgip\ *also* **gib** \-ib\ *vt* **gipped** *also* **gibbed; gipped** *also* **gibbed; gipping** *also* **gibbing; gips** *also* **gibs** [prob. of Scand origin; akin to Norw dial. *gipa* to cause to gape; akin to L *hiare* to gape, yawn — more at YAWN] **:** to remove the insides of (fish) — **gip·per** \-pə(r)\ *n* -s

gipon \jiˈpän, ˈ⸗ˌ⸗\ *n* -s [ME *gipoun*, fr. MF *jupon* — more at JUPON] **:** JUPON

gipsy *var of* GYPSY

gir \ˈgi(ə)r\ *n* [fr. *Gir* Forest, near Veraval, western India] **1** *usu cap* **:** a breed of medium-sized Indian cattle of dairy type usu. having a distinctive dull red or brown speckling on a white background, widely distributed in tropical regions, and much used for crossbreeding **2** -s *often cap* **:** an animal of the Gir breed

gir *abbr* girder

gi·raf·fa \jəˈrafə\ *n, cap* [NL, fr. It, giraffe] **:** a genus of artiodactylous mammals comprising the giraffes which together with the okapis and extinct related forms constitute a family and sometimes a superfamily of Artiodactyla — **gi·raf·fid** \-fəd\ *adj or n* — **gi·raf·foid** \-ˌfȯid\ *adj*

gi·raffe \jəˈraf, -raa(ə)l, -rail, -rä\ *n, pl* **giraffes** \fs also |vz\ [It & Ar; It *giraffa*, fr. Ar *zirāfah, zarāfah*, prob. of African origin; akin to Egypt *sr* giraffe] **1 :** a large fleet African ruminant mammal (*Giraffa camelopardalis*) that is the tallest of living quadrupeds and has a very long rather stiff neck with only the usual seven vertebrae, long front legs, a pair of short skin-covered horns and a median frontal protuberance in both sexes, and a short coat of fawn or cream-colored hair marked with large reddish or brown blotches — called also *camelopard* **2 :** a wing-shaped upright piano of the 18th and early 19th centuries **3 :** a car higher at one end than at the other for use on inclines in mining

giraffe

giraffe camel *n* **:** any of several long-necked No. American fossil camels of the Miocene

gi·raff·ine \-fən, -ˌfīn\ *adj* [*giraffe* + -*ine*] **:** like a giraffe

gi·raff·ish \-fish,-fēsh\ *adj* **:** like a giraffe ⟨a roguish, ~ expression —May L. Becker⟩

gir·an·dole \ˈjirən,dōl\ *n* -s [F & It; F, fr. It *girandola*, fr. *girare* to turn, fr. LL *gyrare* — more at GYRE] **1 :** a radiating and showy or ornamental composition (as a cluster of skyrockets fired together or a fountain with rising column of water which spreads) — compare ANTHEMION **2 a :** an ornamental branched candle holder; *esp* **:** a brass figural candelabrum ornamented with glass prisms **b :** a mirror having attached candle holders **c :** an often convex circular mirror framed in a deep gilt molding and typically trimmed with gilt balls **3 :** a pendant earring usu. with three ornaments or stones hanging from a central piece

girandole 2c

girandole clock *n* **:** a clock similar to a banjo clock but having a large circular base resembling a girandole

gi·rard reagent \jəˈrärd-\ *or* **gi·rard's reagent** \-dz-\ *n, usu cap G* [after André *Girard*, 20th cent. Fr. chemist] **:** any of several hydrazides that contain a quaternary ammonium radical and are useful esp. in separating aldehydes or ketones (as some steroid hormones) from mixtures by forming soluble hydrazones: as **a :** a crystalline compound $(CH_3)_3N(Cl)CH_2CONHNH_2$ derived from trimethylamine or betaine — called also *Girard T reagent* **b :** a crystalline compound $C_5H_5N(Cl)CH_2CONHNH_2$ derived from pyridine — called also *Girard P reagent*

gir·a·sol \ˈjirə,sȯl, -sōl, -säl\ *or* **gir·a·sole** \-sōl\ *n* -s [It *girasole*, fr. *girare* to turn + *sole* sun, fr. L *sol* — more at SOLAR] **1 :** JERUSALEM ARTICHOKE **2 :** an opal of varying color which gives out fiery reflections in a bright light — called also *fire opal*

girasol thorn *n* **:** JERUSALEM THORN 2

gir·bo·tol process \ˈgərbə,tōl-, -tȯl-\ *n, usu cap G* [*girbotol* fr. *Girdler* Corporation, Louisville, Kentucky, company where the process was developed + Robert R. *Bottoms* b1890 Am. chemist that devised the process + E *-ol*] **:** a process used industrially for removing acidic impurities (as hydrogen sulfide or carbon dioxide) from gases by passing them through a solution of an ethanolamine

1**gird** \ˈgər|d, ˈgə̄|, ˈgəi|\ *vb* **girded** \|dəd\ *also* **girt** \|t, *usu* |d.+V\ **girded** *also* **girt; girding; girds** [ME *girden*, fr. OE *gyrdan*; akin to OHG *gurten* to gird, ON *gyrtha* to gird, OE *geard* yard — more at YARD] *vt* **1 a :** to encircle or bind with any flexible band (as a belt) ⟨the waist is ~*ed* by a purple . . . sash —*New Yorker*⟩ **b :** to make fast or secure (as a sword by a belt or clothing with a cord) **:** GIRDLE **c :** SURROUND, ENCIRCLE ⟨no castellated ramparts ~ Madrid —E.O.Hauser⟩ ⟨~*ed* round by an open porch —A.W.Turnbull⟩ **d** *chiefly Scot* **:** to put a rim or hoop on (a barrel or cask) **2 a :** PROVIDE, EQUIP ⟨~*ed* himself with an amulet . . . and a short stabbing spear —Charles Beadle⟩; *esp* **:** to invest with the sword of knighthood ⟨the marshal ~*ed* him, kissed him, "and so he was a knight" —R.W.Southern⟩ **b :** to invest with powers or attributes ⟨thou hast ~*ed* me with strength unto the battle —Ps 18:39 (AV)⟩ ⟨hast ~*ed* me with gladness —Ps 30:11 (AV)⟩ **3 :** to prepare (oneself) for a struggle, test of strength, or other action **:** BRACE ⟨the men ~*ed* themselves for the coming final blow⟩ ⟨the reader ~*s* himself for yet another disappointment —Charles Lee⟩ ~ *vi* **:** to prepare for a struggle, test of strength, or other action ⟨he ~*ed* for a rough fight —John Kobler⟩ ⟨~*ing* to repulse a new challenge to his powers —*N.Y. Times*⟩ **syn** see SURROUND — **gird one's loins :** to prepare for a test of strength or other trial **:** muster up one's resources **:** set to work — often used with *up* ⟨can the British *gird up their loins* and move ahead —Samuel Van Valkenburg & Ellsworth Huntington⟩

2**gird** \", *dial Brit* " *or* ˈgird\ *vb* -ED/-ING/-S [ME *girden*, *gurden* to strike, move rapidly, thrust] *vt* **1** *dial Brit* **:** STRIKE, SMITE **2 :** to sneer at **:** MOCK, GIBE ⟨the British public has never ceased ~*ing* him —Augustine Birrell⟩ ~ *vi* **1** *dial Brit* **:** to move or act quickly or energetically **:** RUSH **2 :** GIBE, JEST, RAIL — usu. used with *at* ⟨~*s* at your preoccupation . . . with bodily games —A.T.Quiller-Couch⟩ ⟨I shall not ~ at realism —W.T.Stace⟩ ⟨~*ing* at the wrongheadedness of . . . officials —*Times Lit. Supp.*⟩ **syn** see SCOFF

3**gird** \"\ *n* -s [ME (Sc), stroke, blow, fr. ME *girden*, *gurden* to strike] **:** a sarcastic remark **:** GIBE, SNEER, DIG ⟨trenchant ~*s* inspired by strong and genuine feeling against the modern changes —*Times Lit. Supp.*⟩

4**gird** \ˈgir(d)\ *n* -s [alter. of obs. *girth* hoop for a barrel or tub, fr. ME *girth* hoop for a barrel or tub, strap round the body of an animal to fasten something on its back — more at GIRTH] *Scot* **:** a hoop esp. for a barrel or tub; *also* **:** a hoop used as a child's plaything

girded *var of* GIRT

gird·er \ˈgərdər; ˈgə̄də(r, ˈgəidə(r\ *n* -s [1*gird* + *-er*] **1 a :** a horizontal main member supporting vertical concentrated loads (as from beams) **b :** BEAM; *esp* **:** an iron or steel beam either made in a single piece or built up typically of plates, flitches, latticework, or bars and often of very large proportions — compare BOWSTRING BEAM, BOX GIRDER, LATTICE GIRDER, PLATE GIRDER, TRUSS **c :** a structure built of reinforced concrete for a similar purpose **2 :** a rolled metal unit of I section or other section or a built-up unit of rolled members and plate that may be transverse or longitudinal depending on the structure to be supported

girder bridge *n* **:** a bridge in which the supporting members are girders

girder rail *n* **:** a heavy railroad rail having a deep web and used in a street where paving is laid

girding *n* -s [ME *girdinge*, *girding*, fr. *girden* to gird, encircle + *-inge*, *-ing*] **:** something with which one is girded; *specif*, *Scot* **:** a saddle girth

1**gir·dle** \ˈgərdᵊl, ˈgə̄d-,ˈgəid-\ *n* -s [ME *girdel*, fr. OE *gyrdel*; akin to OHG *gurtil* girdle, ON *gyrthill* girdle, OE *gyrdan* to gird — more at GIRD] **:** something that girds, encircles, confines, or restrains: as **a** (1) **:** a belt, sash, or article of dress encircling the body usu. at the waist to fasten or confine garments or to furnish a means of carrying things (as keys or a sword) ⟨her fingers playing . . . at the ~ of her frock —Donn Byrne⟩ (2) **:** a cord, narrow band, or belt worn as an ecclesiastical vestment around the waist to confine the alb (3) **:** a woman's close-fitting undergarment often boned and usu. partly or wholly elasticized and extending from the waist or just above to below the hips for figure control **b :** either of the two more or less complete bony rings at the anterior and at the posterior ends of the vertebrate trunk supporting the arms and legs respectively — see PECTORAL GIRDLE, PELVIC GIRDLE **c :** an architectural band **:** CINCTURE **d :** the edge of a brilliant that is grasped by the setting — see BRILLIANT illustration **e** (1) **:** either of the two bands resembling a hoop and forming the sides of the two valves of a diatom **:** CINGULUM (2) **:** the part of the shell lying between the epivalve and hypovalve in certain dinoflagellates (3) **:** the muscular and spicule-bearing peripheral part of the mantle of a chiton encircling the shell plates **f :** a belt or ring made by the removal of the bark and cambium around a tree, stem, or twig **g :** a plant disease characterized by girdling of the stem or branches

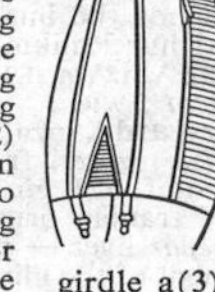
girdle a(3)

2**girdle** \"\ *vt* **girdled; girdled; girdling** \-d(ᵊ)liŋ\ **girdles** **1 :** to put a girdle on **:** encircle or bind about with a girdle or sash **2 a :** to encircle as if with a belt or mesh ⟨50,000 miles of track in operation in 1870, enough to ~ the earth twice —R.H.Brown⟩ **b :** to move or travel around **:** make the circuit of ⟨two times *girdled* the world —Horace Sutton⟩ ⟨these engines . . . *girdled* the earth —*Amer. Guide Series: Conn.*⟩ ⟨a satellite *girdling* the moon⟩ **3 a :** to make a circular cut around (as a tree) through the outer bark and cortex in order to produce death by interrupting the circulation of water and nutrients **b :** to remove a ring of bark from (as a tree) for the purpose of increasing productivity and size of fruit by preventing passage to the roots of food elaborated by the leaves **c :** to destroy a ring of bark and conducting tissues about or remove one from (a plant stem) — used of a gnawing animal (as a rodent or an insect) and of disease ⟨raspberry canes *girdled* by crown rot⟩ **syn** see SURROUND

3**gir·dle** \", ˈgird³l\ *n* -s [ME (Sc) *girdill*, *girdil*, alter. of ME *gridel* — more at GRIDDLE] *chiefly Scot* **:** GRIDDLE

girdle band *n* **:** GIRDLE e(1)

girdlecake \ˈ==,=\ *n*, *dial Brit* **:** GRIDDLE CAKE

girdle of ve·nus \,===ˈvēnəs\ *usu cap G&V* [after *Venus*, Italian goddess identified by the Romans with Aphrodite, Greek goddess of love] **:** a line that appears on the palm at the base of the fingers, that forms a semicircle beginning between the first and second fingers and ending between the third and fourth fingers, and that is held by palmists to indicate a high-strung nervous temperament and sometimes a tendency toward hysteria or despondency

gir·dler \ˈgərd(ᵊ)lər; ˈgə̄d(ᵊ)lə(r, ˈgəid-\ *n* -s [ME *girdeler*, fr. *girdel* girdle + *-er*] **1 :** a maker of girdles **2 :** one that girdles; *esp* **:** an insect that feeds on bark and gnaws grooves about stems and twigs

girdle-tailed lizard \ˈ==,=-\ *n* [so called fr. its practice of rolling its spiny tail over its soft belly as a protection when threatened] **:** a lizard of the family Cordylidae — called also *zonure*; see KLIPSALAMANDER

girds *pres 3d sing of* GIRD, *pl of* GIRD

gi·rel·la \jəˈrelə\ *n*, *cap* [NL, fr. F *girelle*] **:** the type genus of the family Girellidae

gi·rel·li·dae \-lə,dē\ *n pl*, *cap* [NL, fr. *Girella*, type genus + *-idae*] **:** a family that comprises herbivorous marine fishes with movable incisors and is closely related to Kyphosidae

gir·ga·shite \ˈgərgə,shīt\ *or* **gir·ga·site** \-,sīt\ *n* -s *usu cap* **:** a member of one of the ancient Canaanite tribes conquered by the Israelites

girl *R* ˈgərl, *chiefly before pause or consonant* ˈgər·əl; *–R* ˈgə̄l *or* ˈgəil; *Brit sometimes* ˈgeəl *or* ˈgaəl *or* ˈgiəl\ *n* -s *often attrib* [ME *girle*, *gerle*, *gurle* young person of either sex] **1 a :** a female child ⟨announced the birth of a ~⟩ ⟨a study of the performance of primary-school boys and ~*s*⟩ **b :** a young unmarried woman **:** MAIDEN ⟨a ~ of striking beauty⟩ **c :** a single or married woman of any age ⟨gossipy old ~*s* of about seventy —J.B.Clayton⟩ **2 a** (1) **:** a female servant **:** MAID ⟨the ~ brought in and cleared away the dishes —Flora Thompson⟩ (2) **:** a female employee (as a secretary) ⟨I'll get my ~ to have a look through the card index —Nevil Shute⟩ **b :** PROSTITUTE **c :** SWEETHEART ⟨took his ~ to the movies⟩ **d :** DAUGHTER ⟨entered his ~ at a fashionable school⟩

girl·een \(ˈ)gərˈlēn\ *n* -s *Irish* **:** a young girl

girl friday *n*, *often cap G & usu cap F* [*girl* + *Friday* (as in *man Friday*)] **:** a valued private secretary or other female employee or assistant who gives efficient and devoted service and is usu. entrusted with a wide range of tasks ⟨the firm's *girl friday* — the head bookkeeper, scourge of the clerks, chief worrier — *Wall Street Jour.*⟩

girl friend *n* **1 :** a female friend **2 :** a favorite female companion of a boy or man **3 :** the female partner in an intimate or esp. an illicit relationship

girl guide *n* **:** a girl member of the Girl Guides organized in Great Britain in 1910 for carrying out a program of social and educational activities among young girls and for developing good citizenship and healthy useful living — compare BOY SCOUT, GIRL SCOUT

girlhood \ˈ=,hu̇d\ *n* -s **:** the condition or time of being a girl

1**girl·ie** *pronunc at* GIRL +ē *or* i\ *n* -s [*girl* + *-ie*] **1 :** GIRL — often used to indicate affection or intimacy **2** *slang* **:** PROSTITUTE

2**girlie** *var of* GIRLY

girl·ish *pronunc at* GIRL +ish *or* ēsh\ *adj* **:** of, relating to, or having the characteristics of a girl or girlhood **:** MAIDENLY ⟨~ hesitancies . . . delays and refusals —S.H.Adams⟩ — **girl·ish·ly** *adv* — **girl·ish·ness** *n* -ES

girls-and-boys \ˈ==,=ˈ=\ *n pl but sing or pl in constr* **:** either of two plants of the genus *Dicentra*: **a :** DUTCHMAN'S-BREECHES **b :** SQUIRREL CORN

girl scout *n* **1 :** a member of the Girl Scout movement founded in the U.S. in 1912 on the plan of the British Girl Guides for developing good citizenship and healthy useful living among girls from 7 through 17 — compare BOY SCOUT, GIRL GUIDE **2 :** a girl scout approximately 10 through 17 years old as distinguished from a brownie

girly *pronunc at* GIRL + ē *or* i\ *adj* [*girl* + *-y* (adj. suffix)] **1 :** GIRLISH ⟨silly ~ sugary crudity has given way to womanly suavity —George Meredith⟩ **2** *or* **girl·ie** \"\ [1*girlie*] **:** featuring scantily clothed girls ⟨~ shows⟩ ⟨slick ~ magazines⟩

girly-girly \ˈ==ˈ==\ *adj* [redupl. of 1*girly*] **:** exaggeratedly or affectedly girlish ⟨manages to give sensible guidance without being prissy or *girly-girly* —*Newsweek*⟩

1**girn** \ˈgirn\ *vi* -ED/-ING/-S [ME *girnen*, alter. of *grinnen* — more at GRIN] **1** *chiefly Scot* **a :** to show the teeth **:** GRIMACE, SNARL **b :** to whimper and whine **:** complain peevishly **2** *chiefly Scot* **:** GRIN, SNEER

2**girn** \"\ *n* -s **1** *chiefly Scot* **a :** a snarl of rage **b :** a whining peevish tone **:** WHIMPER **2** *chiefly Scot* **:** GRIMACE, GRIN

3**girn** \"\ *n* -s [ME (Sc), alter. of ME *grin* — more at GRIN] *chiefly Scot* **:** SNARE, NOOSE, TRAP

4**girn** \"\ *vt* -ED/-ING/-S *chiefly Scot* **:** SNARE, TRAP

gir·nel *or* **gir·nal** \ˈgirnᵊl\ *n* -s [ME (Sc), prob. alter. of ME *garner*, *gerner* garner — more at GARNER] **1** *obs*, *Scot* **:** GRANARY **2** *Scot* **:** a meal chest or barrel ⟨sitting on a ~ in the stable —Ian MacLennan⟩

girn·ie \ˈgirnī\ *adj* [1*girn* + *-ie*] *chiefly Scot* **:** ILL-TEMPERED, PEEVISH

gi·ro \ˈjī(,)rō\ *n* -s **:** AUTOGIRO

giron *var of* GYRON

girr \ˈgir\ *n* -s [by alter.] *Scot* **:** GIRD

girs *pl of* GIR

1**girse** \ˈgirs, ˈgərs\ *dial Brit var of* GRASS

2**girse** \ˈgi(r)s, ˈgərs\ *dial Eng var of* GIRTH

gir·sle \ˈgirsəl\ *chiefly Scot var of* GRISTLE

1**girt** \ˈgər|t, ˈgə̄|, ˈgəi|, *usu* |d.+V\ *adj* [fr. past part. of 1*gird*] **1** *also* **gird·ed** \|dəd\ **:** bound by a cable — used of a ship moored with such short cables that it strikes against one of them **2 :** PREPARED, READY, GEARED ⟨is it ~ for a supreme test —*Christian Science Monitor*⟩ ⟨~ for speed and action —F.L.Mott⟩

2**girt** \"\ *vb* -ED/-ING/-S [partly fr. ME *girten*, alter. of *girden* to gird, encircle; partly fr. 3*girt* — more at GIRD] *vt* **1 :** GIRD: as **a :** ENCIRCLE **b :** EQUIP, INVEST **2 :** to fasten by means of a girth ⟨a farmer's saddle had been ~*ed* on him —*Country Gentleman*⟩ **3 :** to surround with a line or cord to measure the girth **:** measure the girth of ⟨~ a tree⟩ ~ *vi* **:** to measure in girth

3**girt** \"\ *n* -s [alter. of *girth*] **1 :** GIRTH; *esp* **:** a measure around or across a curved or broken surface (as a molding) ascertained by following its profile **2 :** GIRDER: as **a :** a heavy timber framed into the second-floor corner posts as a footing for the roof rafters in housebuilding **b :** a horizontal member running from column to column or from bent to bent of a building frame or a trestle to stiffen the framework and to carry siding material

4**girt** \ˈgirt, ˈgərt\ *dial Brit var of* GREAT ⟨~ white birds —Llewelyn Powys⟩

1**girth** \ˈgər|th, ˈgə̄|, ˈgəi|; |t, *usu* |d.+V\ *n* -s [ME *girth*, *gerth*, fr. ON *gjörth*, *gerth* belt; akin to MD *gerde* belt, Goth *gairda* belt, OE *gyrdan* to gird, encircle — more at GIRD] **1 :** a band or strap that encircles the body of a horse or other animal to fasten a saddle, pack, blanket, or other article upon its back — see HARNESS illustration **2 a :** a measure round the body of something **:** CIRCUMFERENCE ⟨the ~ of a tree trunk⟩ ⟨the ~ of a ship⟩; *esp* **:** the measure round a human body (as at the waist or belly) ⟨for the man of more than average ~ —Agnes M. Miall⟩ **b :** SIZE, DIMENSIONS ⟨the river was twice its usual ~⟩ ⟨when one looks at the ~ of standard works —*Times Lit. Supp.*⟩ **3 :** a horizontal longitudinal brace; *esp* **:** such a brace in square-set mine timbering **4 :** either of two thongs of leather or bands of webbing attached to the rounce of a hand printing press to move the carriage back and forth

2**girth** \"\ *vb* -ED/-ING/-S [ME *girthen* to gird, encircle, fr. *gerth*, *girth*, n.] *vt* **1 :** to extend around **:** ENCIRCLE **2 :** to bind or fasten with a girth **:** put a girth on **3 :** to measure the girth of; *specif* **:** to determine the approximate weight of (an animal) by measuring the girth with a tape that converts linear measure to normal or average weight ~ *vi* **:** to measure in girth

girthline \ˈ=,=\ *n* [prob. fr. 4*girt* + *line*] **:** GANTLINE

gis *n*, *cap* [by alter. and shortening] *obs* **:** JESUS — used in the phrase *by Gis*

GIs *pl of* GI

GI's *pl of* GI, *pres 3d sing of* GI

gi·sant \zhēzäⁿ\ *n*, *pl* **gisants** \-äⁿ(z)\ [F, fr. pres. part. of *gésir* to lie, lie flat, fr. L *jacēre* to lie] **:** a recumbent sculpture of a deceased person shown usu. with arms crossed over the chest

gi·sarme \gēˈzärm, jē-,zhē-\ *n* -s [ME, fr. OF *gisarme*, *guisarme*, of Gmc origin; akin to OHG *getīsarn* weeding tool, fr. *jetan*, *getan* to weed + *īsarn* iron — more at IRON] **:** a medieval weapon mounted on a long staff and carried by foot soldiers

gism *var of* JISM — usu. considered vulgar

gismo *var of* GIZMO

gis·mon·dite \jizˈmän,dīt, ˈjizmən-\ *or* **gis·mon·dine** \-,dēn\ *n* -s [*gismondite* fr. *gismondine* + *-ite*; *gismondine* fr. G *gismondin*, fr. C. G. *Gismondi* †1824 Ital. mineralogist + G *-in* -ine] **:** a mineral $CaAl_2Si_2O_8.4H_2O$ consisting of a light-colored hydrous calcium aluminum silicate occurring in pyramidal crystals

gist \ˈjist\ *n* -s [AF, it lies (said of a legal action), fr. MF, 3d pers. sing. pres. indic. of *gesir* to lie, fr. L *jacēre* to lie, fr. *jacere* to throw — more at JET (to spout)] **1 :** the ground or foundation of a legal action without which it would not be sustainable **2 :** the main point or material part (as of a question or debate) **:** the pith of a matter **:** ESSENCE ⟨the ~ of a question⟩ ⟨the ~ of all that can be said upon the matter —R.L. Stevenson⟩

git \(ˈ)git, *usu* -id.+V\ *dial var of* GET

gi·tal·in \jəˈtalən, ˈjid·ᵊlən; *sometimes* jəˈtāl- *or* -ˈtäl- *or* -ˈtȧl-\ *n* -s [ISV *gital-* (fr. NL *digitalis*) + *-in*] **1 :** a crystalline water-soluble glycoside $C_{35}H_{56}O_{12}$ obtained from digitalis **2 :** an amorphous water-soluble mixture of glycosides of digitalis used similarly to digitalis

gi·ta·na \hēˈtänə\ *n* -s [Sp, fem. of *gitano*] **:** a Spanish gypsy girl or woman

gi·ta·ne·muk \,jid·əˈnēmək\ *n*, *pl* **gitanemuk** *or* **gitanemuks** *usu cap* **:** SERRANO

gi·ta·no \hēˈtä(,)nō\ *n* -s [Sp, prob. modif. of (assumed) ML *aegyptanus*, fr. L *Aegyptus* Egypt, country in northeastern Africa formerly reputed to be the homeland of the gypsies (fr. Gk *Aigyptos*) + *-anus* -an] **:** a Spanish male gypsy

gite *var of* GYTE

git-fid·dle \ˈgit,==\ *n* [*git-* (by shortening & alter. fr. *guitar*) + *fiddle*] *slang* **:** GUITAR

gi·tog·e·nin \jəˈtäjənən, -,nen; ,jid·əˈjenən\ *n* [ISV *gito-* (fr. *gitonin*) + *-genin*] **:** a crystalline steroid sapogenin $C_{27}H_{44}O_4$ obtained esp. by hydrolysis of gitonin

gi·to·nin \jəˈtōnən, ˈjid·ənən\ *n* -s [ISV, fr. *digitonin*] **:** a crystalline steroid saponin $C_{51}H_{82}O_{23}$ occurring with digitonin

gi·tox·i·genin \jə,täksəˈjenən; (,)ji,täkˈsijənən, -,nen\ *n* [ISV *gitoxi-* (fr. *gitoxin*) + *-genin*] **:** a crystalline steroid lactone $C_{23}H_{34}O_5$ obtained by hydrolysis of gitoxin

gi·tox·in \jəˈtäksən\ *n* [ISV, fr. *digitoxin*; orig. formed in G] **:** a poisonous crystalline steroid glycoside $C_{41}H_{64}O_{14}$ that is obtained from digitalis and from lanatoside B by hydrolysis

git·tar \ˈgi,tär, -tä(r\ *dial var of* GUITAR

git·ter cell \ˈgid·ə(r)-\ *n* [G *gitter* lattice, grating, prob. alter. of MHG *geter*, fr. OHG *getiri*; akin to OHG *gataro* door and prob. to OE *gaderian* to gather — more at GATHER] **:** an enlarged phagocytic cell of microglial origin having the cytoplasm distended with lipid granules and being characteristic of certain organic brain lesions

git·tern *R* ˈgid·ərn *or* -itərn, *–R* -id·ən *or* -itᵊn *or* -itən\ *n* -s [ME *giterne*, fr. MF *guiterne*, fr. OF, modif. of OSp *guitarra* — more at GUITAR] **:** a medieval stringed instrument of the guitar family played with a plectrum

gittern of the early 14th century

gittin *pl of* GET

git·tite \ˈgi,tīt, ˈgid·,īt, *usu* -īd·+V\ *n* -s *usu cap* **:** an inhabitant of ancient Gath in Palestine, one of the chief cities of the Philistines

git-up \ˈgid·,əp\ *n* -s [alter. of *getup*] **:** DRIVE, ENERGY, AGGRESSIVENESS ⟨can always find something to do if he has a little *git-up* —Calder Willingham⟩

giulio *var of* JULIO

giust \ˈjüst\ *archaic var of* JOUST

giu·sta·men·te \,jüstəˈmentē\ *adv* [It, fr. *giusto* correct, just] **:** with precision **:** in strict tempo — used as a direction in music

giu·sto \ˈjü(,)stō\ *adj (or adv)* [It, correct, just, fr. L *justus* just — more at JUST] **:** in strict tempo **:** with exactness — used as a direction in music

1**give** \ˈgiv\ *vb* **gave** \ˈgāv\ *or substand* **give** \ˈgiv\ *or dial* **gin** \ˈgin\ *or* **guv** \ˈgəv\ **giv·en** \ˈgivən *also* -ivᵊm *or* -ibᵊm\ *or substand* **give** *or dial* **gin** *or* **guv; giving; gives** [ME *given*, of Scand origin; akin to OSw *giva* to give; akin to OE *giefan* to give, OHG *geban*, ON *gefa*, Goth *giban* to give, *gabei* wealth, L *habēre* to have, hold, OIr *gaibid* he takes, Lith *gabenti* to take away, Skt *gabhasti* hand] *vt* **1 a :** to confer the ownership of without receiving a return **:** make a present of ⟨*gave* him a watch on his birthday⟩ ⟨*gave* his books to the college⟩ **b :** to assign the future ownership of by will **:** BEQUEATH, DEVISE ⟨*gave* and bequeathed a larger sum to the college than any other person in its history —B.F.Wright⟩ **c :** to contribute without compensation ⟨did no more than a . . . citizen might be expected to do — bought bonds, *gave* blood, served as a civil-defense warden —H.N.Fairchild⟩ **2 a :** to grant or bestow by or as if by formal action ⟨has just been *given* two new honors —Harvey Breit⟩ ⟨responsible for the law *giving* women . . . equal pay with men —Laura M. Berrien⟩ **b :** to let have in or as if in answer to a prayer — used with *me* as indirect object ⟨as for me, ~ me liberty or ~ me death —Patrick Henry⟩ ⟨~ me the good old days⟩ **c :** to accord or yield to another ⟨had never *given* him her confidence —Ellen Glasgow⟩ **3 a :** to put into the possession of another for his use **:** HAND ⟨I'll ~ you a card to him and you go in there . . . and pick out what you want —S.H.Adams⟩ **b :** to provide or supply one with (food or drink) ⟨~ me a slab of that pie —K.M.Dodson⟩ **c** (1) **:** to administer as a sacrament ⟨*giving* extreme unction⟩ (2) **:** to administer as a medicine ⟨*gave* her spirits of ammonia and put ice on her forehead —Scott Fitzgerald⟩ **d :** to commit to the trust or keeping of another for a definite purpose ⟨*gave* him a letter to mail⟩ ⟨*gave* his suitcase to the porter⟩ ⟨~ the deck to the exec and get all the officers in the wardroom —Wirt Williams⟩ **e** (1) **:** to transfer from one's authority, custody, or responsibility ⟨*gave* the prisoner to the officials from the federal penitentiary⟩ (2) **:** to transfer from parental authority and care ⟨who *giveth* this woman to be married to this man —*Bk. of Com. Prayer*⟩ **f :** to execute and deliver ⟨all new employees must ~ bond⟩ **g :** to offer (something immaterial) for conveyance or transmittal ⟨~ my regards to your family⟩ ⟨~ our greetings to all our friends⟩ **4 a :** to offer to the action of another **:** PROFFER, EXPOSE ⟨I *gave* my back to the smiters —Isa 50:6 (RSV)⟩ ⟨he got up and *gave* his hand to the visitor⟩ ⟨~ the sails to the wind⟩ **b :** to yield (oneself) to a man in sexual intercourse ⟨a wild, harum-scarum woman who would have *given* herself to him . . . without marriage —Erle Stanley Gardner⟩ **c :** to perform the action appropriate or necessary to a public presentation or production of ⟨the orchestra ~*s* 10 concerts . . . each season —Claudia Cassidy⟩ ⟨a serious effort to ~ us a real puppet show —R.L.Shayon⟩ ⟨asked the soprano to ~ the group a song⟩ **d :** to present to view or observation ⟨the injured man *gave* a few signs of life⟩ ⟨*gave* evidence of promising intellectual gifts —C.A.Duniway⟩ ⟨*gave* them a good example⟩ **e :** to have or show as an armorial bearing or emblem, badge, or livery ⟨all his successors . . . may ~ the dozen white luces in their coat —Shak.⟩ **f :** to provide by way of entertainment **:** serve as host at ⟨*gave* a dinner in honor of his guests⟩ ⟨*gave* a ball for his nieces⟩ ⟨~ weekly teas⟩ **g :** to propose as a toast ⟨I rise to ~ . . . the memory of a man well known to all —John Wilson †1854⟩ ⟨gentlemen . . . I'll ~ you the ladies —Charles Dickens⟩ **h** *archaic* **:** to impart a tendency or propensity to **:** INCLINE **5 a :** to designate as a share or portion **:** ALLOT ⟨all the earth to thee and to thy race I ~ —John Milton⟩ ⟨immediate and infallible revelation of this kind is not *given* to man —W.R. Inge⟩ ⟨*gave* him the best room available⟩ **b :** to make assignment of (a name) ⟨the term Bushmen . . . was *given* in the 17th century by the Dutch settlers to the diminutive hunting peoples —C.D.Forde⟩ ⟨*gave* the child the name John⟩ **c :** to set forth as an actual or hypothetical datum **:** ASSUME ⟨three points of a circle are *given*⟩ **d :** to attribute in thought or speech **:** ASCRIBE ⟨*gave* all the glory to God⟩ ⟨*gave* full weight to the evidence⟩ ⟨a sound argument for *giving* the painting to Rembrandt⟩ **e** *obs* **:** to appoint a person to the office or function of ⟨and he *gave* some, apostles; and some, prophets; and some, evangelists; and some, pastors and teachers —Eph 4:11 (AV)⟩ **f** *obs* **:** to set down **:** REGARD, CONSIDER, DEEM ⟨men's reports ~ him much wronged —Shak.⟩ — usu. used with *for* ⟨*gave* him for drowned in one of the canals —Joseph Addison⟩ **6 a :** to yield or furnish as a product, consequence, or effect **:** PRODUCE, EMIT ⟨the gas *gave* its final flicker and went out —Jack McLaren⟩ ⟨the can, now quite empty and resonant, *gave* forth a hollow clatter — C.G.D.Roberts⟩ ⟨bushes . . . ~ forth a pungent aroma when the sun beats upon them —Norman Douglas⟩ ⟨cows ~ milk⟩ ⟨flints ~ sparks⟩ ⟨a compound that ~*s* a red color with iodine —Henry Tauber⟩ **b :** to yield or exhibit as a result of calculation or measurement ⟨84 divided by 12 ~*s* 7⟩ ⟨the amount of lead . . . would by simple calculation ~ the age of the material —W.E.Swinton⟩ ⟨a thermometer ~*s* the temperature of the room —James Jeans⟩ **c :** to bring forth **:** BEAR ⟨the largest ewe *gave* triplets —*Breeder's Gazette*⟩ **7 a :** to yield possession of by way of exchange **:** hand over in exchange for something or in discharge of a debt or obligation **:** PAY ⟨what shall a man ~ in return for his life —Mt 16:26 (RSV)⟩ **b :** to dispose of for a price **:** hand over for a consideration **:** SELL ⟨I can ~ you a jade necklace for five rupees —Robert Sherrod⟩ **c** *archaic* **:** to procure in exchange **:** be worth **:** FETCH ⟨the country . . . so much overstocked with timber that it would ~ no price — James Robertson⟩ **8 a :** to deliver or deal by some bodily action ⟨*gave* him a push down the stairs⟩ ⟨*gave* her a kiss⟩ **b :** to carry out (a movement of or as if of the body) **:** EXECUTE, MAKE ⟨he *gave* a cryptic smile —Hallam Tennyson⟩ ⟨could feel the ship ~ a convulsive lurch —T.B.Costain⟩ **c :** to inflict or impose as punishment ⟨*gave* the slave 20 lashes⟩ ⟨*gave* the boy a whipping⟩ **d :** to cause to be fired **:** DISCHARGE ⟨*gave* a short burst and damaged the enemy plane⟩ ⟨*gave* a salute of 21 guns⟩ **9 a :** to put forth (a sound) **:** VOICE ⟨he hesitated and *gave* a nervous laugh —Haldane Macfall⟩ ⟨*gave* a hiss to attract the attention of the others —T.B.Costain⟩ **b :** to deliver verbally **:** UTTER ⟨has never *given* me a cross word in his life —Ellen Glasgow⟩ ⟨the student raised his hand and *gave* the right answer⟩ ⟨his uncle *gave* him sound advice⟩ ⟨the sergeant *gave* the command to the troops⟩ ⟨the old man *gave* his blessing to the bride and groom⟩ **c :** to express as a wish **:** BID ⟨I *gave* him good day and he stopped and looked at me —S.H.Adams⟩ ⟨*gave* us good night and went sedately away —Eve Langley⟩ **d** (1) **:** to award by formal verdict **:** deliver by appropriate legal authority ⟨the judge *gave* him 10 years⟩ ⟨the judgment was *given* against the plaintiff⟩ (2) *cricket* **:** to rule on a fielder's appeal ⟨the umpire *gave* the batsman out⟩ **e :** to offer, suggest, or imply in the course of speaking ⟨the top kick always *gave* us that old business —Tom Shehan⟩ ⟨don't ~ me that legal double-talk —Louis Auchincloss⟩ **10 a :** to offer for the consideration, acceptance, or use of another ⟨can ~ several explanations of the passage⟩ ⟨~*s* no really good reason for his absence⟩ ⟨after several years' work he finally *gave* his novel to the world⟩ **b :** to provide a description of **:** REPRESENT, PORTRAY ⟨show me something of hers, something that seems to ~ her —H.G.Wells⟩ ⟨an artist who *gave* a scene as it must have happened —Roger Fry⟩ **c :** to make known **:** impart knowledge of or information about ⟨can ~ only a hint of the treasures to be found —Dana Burnet⟩ ⟨the results were *given* in a long paper⟩ ⟨the soldier *gave* his name, rank, and serial number⟩ ⟨will you ~ me the right time⟩ **11 a :** to suffer the loss of **:** SACRIFICE ⟨had *given* two legs in the Second World War — Marya Mannes⟩ ⟨gallantly *gave* his life for his country⟩ **b :** to offer by or as if by way of dedication or devotion **:** CONSIGN, COMMEND ⟨a resolution to ~ to God the half of his services . . . and the half of his money —M.J.Guest⟩ ⟨*gave* Mr. Dorrit to the devil with great liberality —Charles Dickens⟩ **c :** to apply freely or fully **:** DEVOTE ⟨children were *giving* themselves wholeheartedly to some raucous game —Maeve Brennan⟩ ⟨he *gave* his youth to literature, languages, and mechanics — Edward Clodd⟩ **d :** to offer as a pledge ⟨I ~ you my word of honor that it's true⟩ **12 a :** to cause to have or receive **:** OCCASION ⟨what dreams may come . . . must ~ us pause — Shak.⟩ ⟨it *gave* his views a foundation of solid fact which was impressive —H.J.Laski⟩ ⟨was buried in sight of the mountains which always *gave* him pleasure —Broadus Mitchell⟩ **b :** to cause a person to catch by or as if by contagion, infection, or exposure ⟨she *gave* him her cold⟩ ⟨the draft *gave* him a sore throat⟩ **c :** to produce (as a feeling) in a person or thing **:** bring about ⟨you do not ~ self-respect and self-reliance by censorship —Joyce Cary⟩ ⟨we ought not to ~ ourselves airs —Benjamin Jowett⟩ ⟨the stage sets ~ charm to the production⟩ **d :** to be the source or origin of ⟨this group ~*s* some of our really vicious criminals —R.L.Jenkins⟩ **e** *obs* **:** PUT, SET ⟨~ some stop to those atheistical and epicurean opinions —Matthew Hale⟩ **f :** to allow to have or take **:** PERMIT, CONCEDE ⟨~ me a day to think the problem over⟩ ⟨*gave* him 10 yards and still won the race⟩ ⟨the patients are *given* a long rest every afternoon⟩ ⟨was willing to ~ his opponent that point in the debate⟩ **g :** to be the cause of **:** be responsible for — used with an infinitive phrase as object ⟨a novelist of experience . . . ~*s* us to share his swift insight — *Nation*⟩ ⟨you *gave* me to believe that the school meant more to you than anything —Lael Tucker⟩ **13 :** to care to the extent of — usu. used with negative ⟨bewitched, bothered, and bewildered by life, he doesn't ~ a damn —Moore Raymond⟩ ⟨didn't ~ a hang —Nelson Algren⟩ **14 :** to make a telephone connection with ⟨asked central to ~ him the long-distance operator⟩ **~** *vi* **1 :** to make gifts or presents **:** CONTRIBUTE, DONATE ⟨it is more blessed to ~ than to receive —Acts 20:35 (RSV)⟩ **2** *archaic* **:** to deliver a blow or make an attack ⟨furiously *giving* upon the enemy with a great shout —Henry Holcroft⟩ **3 a :** to yield to physical force or strain **:** respond to pressure ⟨the dummy . . . has a breakable shoulder bone built to ~ when its human counterpart would —R.M.Yoder⟩ **b :** to collapse from the application of force or pressure **:** break down ⟨the rail of the fence *gave* suddenly under his weight —R.L.Stevenson⟩ **c :** to undergo or submit to a change through the modification of an inflexible attitude or the withdrawal from a rigid position **:** accept or make a concession ⟨if something does not ~ . . . the whole North Atlantic fare structure could be thrown wide open —Richard Witkin⟩ **4** *obs* **:** to become moist **:** WEEP ⟨flinty mankind whose eyes do never ~ but thorough lust and laughter —Shak.⟩ **5 a** *of weather* **:** to become mild **b** *of frozen ground* **:** THAW **6 :** to afford a view or passage **:** OPEN, LEAD ⟨a venerable lane *giving* on the cathedral close —Russell Kirk⟩ ⟨a cluster of stores and boatyards *giving* onto the harbor —Pete Barrett⟩ ⟨a cheerful compartment on the main deck with . . . a porthole *giving* out to sea —Horace Sutton⟩ ⟨flung open the door which *gave* upon the landing —Dorothy Sayers⟩ **7 a :** to enter wholeheartedly into an activity **:** get into the spirit of things ⟨if the teacher himself is . . . skillful in inspiring his pupils they will let go and ~ —F.R.Rogers⟩ **b :** to impart information **:** TALK ⟨he just won't ~; he glares straight ahead and keeps his mouth closed —Bennett Cerf⟩ **8** [trans. of G *gibt* (in the expression *was gibt's?* what is going on?), 3d pers. sing. pres. indic. of *geben* to give, fr. OHG *geban*] **:** to take place **:** HAPPEN, OCCUR — usu. used in the phrase *what gives* ⟨you poor dewy-eyed academics don't know what ~*s* in the rough-and-tumble —Frances G. Patton⟩ — **give a good account of :** to acquit (oneself) well ⟨able to *give a good account of* himself in a street brawl —W.J.Ghent⟩ — **give and take :** to engage in give-and-take ⟨faculty members will have to *give and take* in creating new courses or revising old ones — M.L.Wardell⟩ — **give battle :** to engage in a determined fight ⟨threw up log and earthwork defenses and *gave battle* —*Amer. Guide Series: La.*⟩ ⟨public opinion . . . against which Congress was not prepared to *give battle* —H.J.Laski⟩ — **give birth :** to bear a child ⟨she *gave birth* last Friday⟩ — **give birth to 1 :** to bring forth **:** BEAR ⟨*gave birth to* a son⟩ **2 :** to be the source of **:** ORIGINATE ⟨*gave birth . . . to* a smoldering feeling of discontent, an inarticulate desire for change —G.G.Coulton⟩ — **give ground :** to withdraw before or as if before superior force **:** RETREAT ⟨as the Roman legions advanced to the attack, this center *gave ground* slowly —Tom Wintringham⟩ ⟨the bond market is *giving ground* before the advance of the economy — Paul Heffernan⟩ — **give guard :** to inform a batsman if his bat is at guard — used of an umpire in cricket — **give it to :** to administer a beating or scolding to **:** attack vigorously ⟨looked at his colleagues . . . and *gave it to* them right between the eyes —*New Republic*⟩ — **give one his head :** to allow (as a horse) free rein ⟨the advanced students often are *given their heads* and allowed to launch scientific programs of their own — Karl Detzer⟩ — **give or take :** to add or subtract (a specified small unit) without material alteration ⟨a man 80 years old, *give or take* a year⟩ **:** allow a small inaccuracy of **:** accept a tolerance of — **give place 1 :** to yield precedence or superiority ⟨a house and garden of the king's *giving place* to few — Thomas Herbert⟩ **2 :** to yield by way of being succeeded or replaced ⟨fields of sugar beets . . . *give place* to wheat and grazing lands —*Amer. Guide Series: Oreg.*⟩ ⟨uneasiness *gave place* to alarm —Osgood Hardy⟩ — **give rise to :** to bring about **:** PRODUCE, OCCASION ⟨has exercised the skill of . . . scholars and *given rise to* an enormous body of literature — Edward Clodd⟩ ⟨a watershed that *gives rise to* two large river systems —*Amer. Guide Series: N.H.*⟩ — **give suck** *archaic* **:** SUCKLE — **give thanks :** to express gratitude; *specif* **:** to say grace ⟨and he took bread, and when he had *given thanks* he broke it and gave it to them —Lk 22:19 (RSV)⟩ — **give the gun 1 :** to open the throttle of ⟨the motor began to cough and die so he *gave* it *the gun*⟩ **2 :** to increase the speed of markedly ⟨on the open highway he *gave* the car *the gun*⟩ — **give the lie to 1 :** to accuse of falsehood ⟨they *gave* the queen *the lie* — Richard Bancroft⟩ **2 :** to show the falsity of ⟨the record . . . seems to have *given the lie to* ancient creeds —W.L.Sperry⟩ — **give voice 1 :** SING ⟨he emerged, pink and scrubbed, still *giving voice* —C.B.Kelland⟩ **2 :** to express strong feelings usu. of objection or displeasure — used with *to* — **give way 1 a :** to retreat before an advancing force ⟨our troops . . . *gave way* on the right —William Tennant⟩ **b** *archaic* **:** to make way **:** clear the way ⟨respect induced passengers to *give way* to the father and daughter —Sir Walter Scott⟩ **c :** to yield the right of way ⟨if it is your duty to *give way*, never leave your alteration of course until the last moment —Peter Heaton⟩ ⟨drivers *give way* to traffic coming in on the right — *Meet New Zealand*⟩ **2 a** *archaic* **:** to allow free scope, opportunity, or liberty of action ⟨they who through weakness *gave way* to the ill designs of bad men —Edmund Burke⟩ **b :** to yield oneself without check, restraint, or control **:** abandon oneself ⟨she horrified the young man by *giving way* to tears, publicly —F.A.Swinnerton⟩ **c :** to lose control of oneself ⟨courage kept her from quite *giving way* —Edna Lyall⟩ **3 a :** to yield to or as if to physical force or pressure **:** break down **:** COLLAPSE, FAIL ⟨bridges . . . can *give way* under the pounding hooves of a herd of bawling, jostling longhorns — S.E.Fletcher⟩ ⟨his fragile health *gave way* under the stress of study —H.W.Wiley⟩ **b :** to yield under entreaty or insistence **:** CONCEDE ⟨argued until, with a shrug of his shoulders, he *gave way* —Francis King⟩ **4 :** to yield place ⟨the desert landscape . . . had *given way* everywhere to abundant green vegetation —Rex Moorfoot⟩ ⟨discussion of specific issues *gave way* to very broad generalities —Walter Goodman⟩ **5 :** to begin to row or to row with increased energy ⟨the coxswain ordered the crew to *give way*⟩ **6 :** to decline in value — used of stocks

2**give** \"\ *n* -S **1 :** capacity or tendency to yield to force or strain ⟨placing their saddles a little farther back . . . they say the horse's spine has more ~ or bend at this point —S.E. Fletcher⟩ **2 :** the quality or state of being springy **:** ELASTICITY, RESILIENCE ⟨the ~ . . . of the knitted fabric makes it ideal for uses where any variables of conformation or stress exist — G.A.Urlaub⟩

give-and-go \¦==¦=\ *n* **:** a basketball maneuver in which the player in possession of the ball makes a short pass to a teammate and then cuts for the basket

1**give-and-take** \¦==¦=\ *adj* [1*give* + *and* + *take*, v.] **1** *Brit* **:** of or relating to a race in which the horses carry weights that vary according to their heights **2** [2*give-and-take*] **:** characterized by give-and-take ⟨*give-and-take* methods of adjustment —Dexter Perkins⟩

2**give-and-take** \"\ *n* [1*give* + *and* + *take*, v.] **1 :** the practice of making mutual concessions **:** COMPROMISE ⟨negotiation in the nature of things entails *give-and-take* —G.W.Johnson⟩ **2 :** good-natured exchange of ideas ⟨the *give-and-take* of conversation⟩ ⟨prefers the *give-and-take* of the committee room to the fanfare of the forum —*Today*⟩

give away *vb* [ME *given away*, fr. *given* to give + *away*] *vt* **1 :** to make a present of **:** DONATE ⟨a beautiful streamlined television set . . . is being practically *given away* —Stuart Chase⟩ **2** *obs* **:** to make a sacrifice of ⟨be merry, Cassio, for thy solicitor shall rather die than *give* thy cause *away* —Shak.⟩ **3 :** to perform the ceremony of delivering (a bride) to the bridegroom at a wedding **4 a :** to expose to detection or ridicule **:** BETRAY ⟨it would be useless to call him a cad for *giving* a woman *away* —O.S.J.Gogarty⟩ ⟨no prisoner would *give* a fellow prisoner *away* —Rex Ingamells⟩ **b :** to allow (as a secret) to be known **:** DISCLOSE, REVEAL ⟨the incident . . . also *gives away* an essential point —*Times Lit. Supp.*⟩ ⟨a chef does not *give away* all his culinary secrets —Darius Milhaud⟩ **5 :** to give an advantage by competing under a handicap of ⟨the thirty-year-old welterweight *gave away* six and a quarter pounds to his . . . middleweight arch foe —Jesse Abramson⟩ **~** *vi* **:** to yield to or as if to physical force or strain ⟨accidents are caused by the safety belt not being fastened or by the seat itself *giving away* —H.G.Armstrong⟩

giveaway \'==,=\ *n* -S *often attrib* [*give away*] **1 :** a game or a method of playing a game in which the object is to lose **2 :** an unintentional revelation or betrayal ⟨your approach to her is a ~ with respect to your theater comprehension —Stark Young⟩ **3 :** something given away free; *specif* **:** an item of merchandise presented as a gift or premium ⟨a rash of all types of gimmicks, ~*s*, and novel promotion ideas introduced . . . to bring in the customers —Dolores Plested⟩ **4 :** a radio or television program on which prizes are given away

give back *vi* **:** to withdraw from a position or place **:** RETIRE, RETREAT ⟨militiamen around the door *gave back* to let . . . the judges through —H.L.Davis⟩ **~** *vt* **:** to send in return or reply **:** RESTORE, RETURN ⟨*gave* her *back* the looks she was sending him —Mary Deasy⟩

give down *vt* **:** to let (milk) flow — used of a cow ⟨his cows didn't recognize him clean shaven and wouldn't *give down* their milk —Ross Wurm⟩

give in *vt* **1 :** to hand in **:** DELIVER, SUBMIT ⟨I desire to *give in* my notice —Henry Green⟩ **2 :** to make a formal announcement of **:** DECLARE ⟨*gave in* their adherence to the peace — Charlotte Yonge⟩ **~** *vi* **:** to yield under pressure, insistence, or entreaty **:** SURRENDER ⟨it's weakness in me to *give in*, but he broke my will when I was a child —Ellen Glasgow⟩ ⟨have *given in* to the whims of their betters —Isabelle Mallet⟩

1**given** *adj* [ME, fr. past part. of *given* to give] **1 :** presented as a gift **:** bestowed without compensation ⟨the millionaire . . . finds that ~ goods never prosper —*London Daily News*⟩ **2 :** marked by an inclination or disposition **:** PRONE — used with *to* ⟨armies everywhere and in all ages have been ~ to swearing —Burges Johnson⟩ **3** *of an official document* **:** having been executed **:** DATED ⟨~ under my hand and seal this 30th day of June⟩ **4 a :** definitely stated **:** FIXED, SPECIFIED ⟨the number of musicians to be engaged for a ~ concert — Robert Lawrence⟩ **b :** assumed as actual or hypothetical **:** set forth as or as if known **:** DETERMINED, GRANTED ⟨~ the national panickiness . . . liberals have to be very careful of the company they keep —H.J.Muller⟩ **5 :** immediately presented specif. without interpretation or elaboration ⟨the ~ element is this incorrigible presentational element; the criticizable and dubitable element is the element of interpretation —C.I. Lewis⟩ — used esp. in philosophy

2**given** *n* -S **:** something given **:** DATUM ⟨it is taken as a ~ that language is the principal mode of communication for human beings —G.L.Trager⟩; *esp* **:** the component of the knowing process that is distinguished from what is supplied by thought or inference or from the hypothetical ⟨in a sense the ~ is ineffable; it is that which remains untouched and unaltered, however it is construed by thought —C.I.Lewis⟩

given name *n* **:** CHRISTIAN NAME, FORENAME

giv·en·ness \-ən(n)ə̇s,-ᵊmnə̇s\ *n* -ES **:** the quality or state of being given ⟨the ~ of the environment dominates everything — A.N.Whitehead⟩

give off *vt* **1** *obs* **:** to put an end to **:** QUIT ⟨was persuaded to *give off* riding —Robert Peirce⟩ **2 :** to send out as a branch ⟨antlers with their . . . branches pointing forward and *giving off* short tines, like twigs —D.C.Peattie⟩ **3 :** to throw off **:** EMIT ⟨as the blood passes through the lungs it . . . *gives off* its excess nitrogen —H.G.Armstrong⟩ ⟨antique tapestries which . . . *gave off* a sickening odor of mold —L.C.Douglas⟩ **~** *vi* **1** *obs* **:** to come to an end **:** CEASE **2 :** to send out a branch **:** branch off

give on *vi* **1** *obs* **:** to make an attack ⟨the Trojans first *gave on* —George Chapman⟩ **2 :** to pay contango

give out *vb* [ME *given out*, fr. *given* to give + *out*] *vt* **1 a :** to make known to or as if to the public **:** DECLARE, PUBLISH ⟨*giving out* that the doctor was not well and required a few days of complete rest —Charles Dickens⟩ ⟨some . . . reader would *give out* at the top of his voice the war news and the racing —C.E.Montague⟩ **b** (1) **:** to read the words of (a hymn or psalm) for congregational singing (2) *archaic* **:** to play (a hymn tune) over so as to facilitate congregational singing **2 :** to send forth **:** EMIT ⟨an elaborate afternoon dress of cream-colored chiffon which *gave out* a continual rustle — Scott Fitzgerald⟩ **3 :** to make distribution of **:** ISSUE ⟨the sergeant *gave out* new uniforms to the troops⟩ **~** *vi* **1 a :** to become physically exhausted **:** COLLAPSE ⟨when one of his oxen *gave out*, he pushed it aside and stepped into the yoke himself —Meridel Le Sueur⟩ **b :** to break down **:** FAIL ⟨his voice *gave out* before he reached his most dramatic moment — *Sydney (Australia) Bull.*⟩ **c :** to come to an end **:** run short ⟨the food at last began to *give out* —O.E.Rölvaag⟩ **2 a :** to enter freely or unrestrainedly into an activity **:** let oneself go — used with following *with* ⟨his orchestra *gave out* with Latin rhythms that made staying in your seat difficult —P.T. Hartung⟩ **b :** to give expression to one's feelings or thoughts — used with following *with* ⟨*gave out* with the smile and the V-sign —*N.Y. Times*⟩ ⟨removed his false teeth in his eagerness to *give out* with a really untrammeled yell —Ben Crisler⟩

give over *vb* [ME *given over*, fr. *given* to give + *over*] *vt* **1 :** to bring to an end **:** put a stop to **:** CEASE, QUIT ⟨I resolved to *give over* all thoughts of you —Mary W. Montagu⟩ ⟨you'll have to *give over* that hammering —Rex Ingamells⟩ **2 a :** to yield (oneself) without check, restraint, or control **:** ABANDON ⟨she *gave* herself *over* to laughter before she could go on — H.D.Skidmore⟩ **b :** to set apart for or give up to a particular purpose or use **:** DEVOTE — usu. used in passive ⟨the area is now *given over* to a children's playground —*Amer. Guide Series: Oreg.*⟩ ⟨the second meeting . . . will probably be *given over* to the consideration and adoption of the constitution —A.T.Weaver⟩ **3** *archaic* **:** to pronounce incurable ⟨had been ill of a fever and *given over* by her physician —Anna Jameson⟩ **4 :** to put in charge or keeping **:** ENTRUST ⟨took him to the apartment and *gave* the old man *over* to his housekeeper —Nevil Shute⟩ **5** *archaic* **:** to despair of finding or seeing ⟨was now almost *given over*, the ponds and even the river . . . having been dragged —S.T.Coleridge⟩ **~** *vi* **:** to bring an activity or a course of action to an end **:** STOP ⟨mother told him to *give over* and let me alone —Brendan Behan⟩

giv·er \'givə(r)\ *n* -S [ME *giver*, *givere*, fr. *given* to give + *-er*, *-ere* -er] **:** one that gives **:** DONOR ⟨God loves a cheerful ~ — 2 Cor 9:7 (RSV)⟩ — often used in combination ⟨alms*giver*⟩

gives *pres 3d sing of* GIVE, *pl of* GIVE

gi·ve·tian \zhə̇'vēshən, -vāsh-\ *adj, usu cap* [F *givétien*, fr. *Givet*, commune in Ardennes, France + F *-ien* -ian] **:** of or relating to the European Devonian — see GEOLOGIC TIME table

give up *vb* [ME *given up*, fr. *given* to give + *up*] *vt* **1 :** to hand over to or as if to another **:** RELINQUISH, SURRENDER ⟨the death of his wife a few years later caused him to *give up* his . . . home —J.M.Phalen⟩ ⟨things went from bad to worse until finally he had to *give up* his position —Scott Fitzgerald⟩ **2 :** to breathe forth **:** EMIT — now used esp. in the phrase *give up the ghost* **3** *obs* **:** to deliver verbally **:** PRESENT ⟨how he may be brought to *give up* the clearest evidence —Francis Atterbury⟩ **4 :** to have done with **:** desist from **:** FORSAKE, SACRIFICE ⟨men will never *give up* seeking to influence one another —R.M.Weaver⟩ ⟨you wouldn't *give up* science or your career —Susan Ertz⟩ ⟨*gave* the idea *up* in sheer weariness —T.B.Costain⟩ **5 a :** to yield (oneself) to a particular feeling, influence, or activity **:** ABANDON ⟨*gave* himself *up* completely to despair⟩ ⟨shutting himself away from the world and *giving* himself *up* to writing his novel —Edmund Wilson⟩ **b :** to set apart or devote to a particular purpose or use — usu. used in passive ⟨Mondays and Tuesdays were often *given up* to drink, cockfights, bear-baiting —J.H.Plumb⟩ **6 :** to declare incurable or insoluble ⟨the patient was *given up* by the doctors⟩ ⟨couldn't answer the riddle and so *gave* it *up*⟩ **7 a :** to make public **:** REVEAL ⟨we do not *give up* the names of our contributors —*Lippincott's Mag.*⟩ **b :** to make known (the name of a principal) in the process of completing a transaction on a stock exchange **8 :** to despair of seeing ⟨it's so late we *gave* you *up* —Charles Dickens⟩ **~** *vi* **:** to withdraw from an activity or course of action often as an admission of failure **:** STOP ⟨had lost flies and broken leaders until he had *given up* —Alexander MacDonald⟩ ⟨doctor tried to get your father to *give up* for a while —Ellen Glasgow⟩

give-up \'=,=\ *n* -S [*give up*] **:** a transaction on an exchange in which the broker reveals the name of his principal who is under obligation to complete the transaction

giv·ey *or* **givy** \'givē\ *adj* **givier**; **giviest** [1*give* + *-y*] **:** inclined to give ⟨the ground was soft and ~ —Conrad Richter⟩

giving *n* -S [fr. gerund of 1*give*] **:** something given **:** GIFT ⟨their total ~*s* . . . have probably yielded a dividend of another $750,000,000 —Bernard Kalb⟩

giz·mo *or* **gis·mo** \'giz,mō\ *n* -S [origin unknown] **:** something whose name is unknown or forgotten **:** GADGET ⟨a ~ which blends the images of two cameras on the screen at once — Arthur Rankin⟩

gizz \'jiz\ *n* -ES [prob. by shortening & alter. fr. *jasey*] *chiefly Scot* **:** WIG

giz·zard \'gizə(r)d\ *n* -S [earlier *gysard*, alter. of *gysar*, fr. ME *giser*, *gyser*, fr. ONF *guisier* liver (esp. of a fowl), gizzard, modif. of L *gigeria* (neut. pl.) cooked entrails of poultry, perh. of Iranian origin; akin to Per *jigar* liver; akin to Gk *hēpat-*, *hēpar* liver — more at HEPATIC] **1 a :** the muscular enlargement of the alimentary canal of birds that immediately follows the crop, is best developed in seed-eating birds, typically has thick muscular walls and a tough horny lining, and serves to grind the food, its muscular action being commonly assisted by gravel swallowed by the bird **b :** a thickened part of an alimentary canal similar in function to the crop of a bird (as the proventriculus of an insect or the enlargement immediately in front of the intestine of an earthworm) **2 :** INNARDS ⟨it warms my ~ . . . and I am proud of you —O.W.Holmes †1935⟩ ⟨this notion has long stuck in my ~ —W.S.Maugham⟩

gizzard erosion *n* **:** an obscure dietary-deficiency disease of young chickens marked by local lesions or extensive sloughing of the gizzard lining

gizzard shad *n* **1 :** a forage fish (*Dorosoma cepedianum*) of eastern and central No. America — called also *hickory shad* **2 :** any of several fishes related to the gizzard shad

gizzard stone *n* **:** a fossil gastrolith

gizzard trout *n* **:** GILLAROO

gizzard worm *n* **:** any of various nematode worms parasitic in the gizzard of birds: as **a :** a spiruroid worm of the genus *Acuaria* that is a destructive parasite of chickens, turkeys, and related game birds **b :** a spiruroid worm (*Amidostomum anseris*) sometimes fatal to ducks and geese

giz·zen \'gizᵊn\ *or* **giz·zened** \-ᵊnd\ *adj* [*gizzen* of Scand origin (akin to Norw dial. *gisen* dried out, leaky); *gizzened* fr. past part. of Sc *gizzen*, v., to dry out, become leaky, of Scand origin; akin to Norw dial. *gisna* to dry out, become leaky, fr. *gisen* dried out, leaky; akin to L *hiare* to gape, yawn — more at YAWN] **1** *chiefly Scot* **:** dried out **:** leaky because of dryness — used of wood products **2** *chiefly Scot* **:** WIZENED, SHRIVELED — used of a person

giz·zern \'gizə(r)n\ *n* -s [ME *gisarn*, alter. of *giser*, *gyser* gizzard] *dial* : GIZZARD
gjet·ost *also* **gjed·ost** \'y|ād,ōst, 'j|, |ed-, -,ōst\ *n* -s [Norw *gjetost*, fr. *gjet* goat (fr. ON *geit*) + *ost* cheese, fr. ON *ostr* — more at GOAT, JUICE] : a hard dark brown cheese usu. made of goat's milk but sometimes made of a combination of cow's and goat's milk
GK *abbr* goalkeeper
gl *abbr* **1** gill **2** glass **3** glaze **4** gloria **5** gloss **6** glossary
GL *abbr* **1** Gothic letter **2** grand lodge **3** grid leak **4** ground level **5** gunlaying
gla·bel·la \glə'belə\ *n, pl* **glabel·lae** \-,lē, -,lī\ [NL, fr. L, fem. of *glabellus* hairless, smooth, fr. *glaber* bald — more at GLAD] **1** : the smooth prominence of the forehead between the eyebrows; *also* : the part of the frontal bone that lies immediately above the root of the nose or a point in the midsagittal plane of this area — see CRANIOMETRY illustration **2** : the median convex lobe of the cephalic shield of a trilobite — **gla·bel·lar** \-lə(r)\ *adj*
gla·bel·lo-occipital length \glə¦be(,)lō+ . . . -\ *n* [*glabello-occipital* fr. *glabella* + *-o-* + *occipital*] : the distance between the glabella and the opisthocranion
gla·bel·lum \glə'beləm\ *n, pl* **glabel·la** \-lə\ [NL, fr. L, neut. of *glabellus*] : GLABELLA
gla·brate \'glā,brāt, -,brət\ *adj* [L *glabratus*, past part. of *glabrare* to make bald, fr. *glabr-*, *glaber* bald] : GLABROUS, GLABRESCENT
gla·bres·cent \(')glā¦bres°nt\ *adj* [L *glabrescent-*, *glabrescens*, pres. part. of *glabrescere* to become bald, fr. *glabr-*, *glaber*] : glabrous or tending to become glabrous
gla·brous \'glābrəs\ *adj* [L *glabr-*, *glaber* bald + E *-ous*] : having a smooth even surface : free of roughness; *specif* : having an epidermal covering that is totally or relatively devoid of hairs or down ⟨the ~ leaves of some plants⟩ ⟨the ~ skin of the American Indian⟩ — **gla·brous·ness** *n* -ES
[1]**gla·cé** \(')gla¦sā\ *adj* [F, past part. of *glacer* to glaze, cover with icing, freeze, fr. L *glaciare* to freeze, fr. *glacies* ice — more at GLACIER] **1** : made or finished so as to have a smooth glossy effect : having a lustrous surface — used of leathers or fabrics ⟨~ kid gloves⟩ ⟨~ silk⟩ **2** : coated with a glaze : GLAZED, CANDIED ⟨~ fruits⟩
[2]**glacé** \"\ *n* -s **1** : a glacé material **2** : a glacé finish
[3]**glacé** \"\ *vt* **glacéed**; **glacéed**; **glacéing**; **glacés 1** : to give a glacé finish to **2** : to coat with a glaze : CANDY
[4]**glace** \'glas\ *n* -s [F, lit., ice, fr. LL *glacia* — more at GLACIER] **1** : a frozen dessert (as ice cream or sherbet) **2** : a coating of glaze (as on candied fruits)
[1]**gla·cial** \'glāshəl\ *adj* [L *glacialis*, fr. *glacies* ice + *-alis* -al] **1 a** : having the nature of ice : suggestive of ice : ICY: (1) : extremely cold : FRIGID, FREEZING, CHILLING ⟨a ~ wind⟩ ⟨the air in the cave was ~, penetrated to the very bones —Willa Cather⟩ (2) : devoid of warmth and cordiality ⟨a ~ handshake⟩ : chillingly hostile ⟨froze him in his tracks with a ~ stare —Roger Butterfield⟩ (3) : coldly immobile or imperturbable ⟨~ conservatism⟩ ⟨preserved a ~ calm⟩ **b** (1) : of, relating to, or produced by glaciers ⟨~ erosion⟩ ⟨~ deposits⟩ ⟨~ lakes⟩ : characterized by the presence of glaciers ⟨the ~ ages of the earth⟩ (2) : suggestive of the movement of glaciers : moving with extreme slowness : moving slowly and irresistibly or relentlessly ⟨the ~ pace of European integration —A.E. Stevenson †1965⟩ **c** : of or relating to a time or region of glaciation ⟨~ man⟩ : of, relating to, or produced by the Glacial epoch or one of the glacial ages ⟨~ climates⟩ **2** : tending at freezing temperature to form crystals resembling ice if pure but not if in aqueous solutions ⟨~ acrylic acid⟩ ⟨~ phosphoric acid⟩ — **gla·cial·ly** \-əlē, -əli\ *adv*
[2]**glacial** \"\ *n* -s : one of the glacial ages or stages of the Pleistocene epoch
glacial acetic acid *n* : acetic acid containing usu. less than 1 percent of water and obtained as a pungent caustic hygroscopic liquid that crystallizes readily and is a good solvent (as for oils and resins)
glacial boulder *n* : a boulder carried by glaciers to a point far beyond its original location
glacial drift *n* : DRIFT 2g(2)
glacial epoch *n* **1** : any of those parts of geologic time from Precambrian onward in both the northern and southern hemispheres during which a much larger portion of the earth was covered by glaciers than at present **2** *usu cap G & often cap E* : the Pleistocene epoch

ing loose rock and other debris and eroding land forms and having a perennial snowfield on which falling snow is converted to a granular icy mass which through the pressure of successive snowfalls and through the freezing of seasonal meltwater becomes solid ice and flows plastically downward to form the body of the glacier which grows or shrinks according to whether snowfall exceeds the rate of melting or not
glacier bear *n* : a small bluish gray bear of the glacier region of southern Alaska that is prob. a color variant of the black bear although sometimes considered a distinct species (*Ursus emmonsi* or *Euarctos emmonsi*)
glacier cataract *n* : the passage of a glacier over a declivity in its bed
gla·ciered \-ə(r)d\ *adj* : covered with glaciers : GLACIATED
gla·cier·et \,glāsh(ē)ə¦ret, -āzhə¦-\ *n* -s **1** : a miniature alpine glacier **2** : a small accumulation of névé that resembles a glacier
gla·cier·ist *pronunc at* GLACIER + əst\ *n* -s : GLACIALIST
gla·cier·iza·tion \,glāshərə'zāshən, -,rī'z- *sometimes* -lāzhə- *or* -lāshēə-\ *n* -s [*glacier* + *-ize* + *-ation*] : GLACIATION
gla·cier·ize \'=(=)=,rīz\ *vb* -ED/-ING/-S *see -ize in Explan Notes* [*glacier* + *-ize*] : GLACIATE
glacier lily *n* : a Rocky mountain dogtooth violet (*Erythronium grandiflorum*) with light yellow flowers — called also *snow lily*
glacier mill *n* [*mill* trans. of F *moulin*] : MOULIN
glacier table *n* : a block of stone supported above the surface of a glacier on a pedestal of ice
glacier theory *n* : a theory in glaciology: drift was deposited through the agency of glaciers in the Glacial epoch
glac·i·fi·ca·tion \,glasəfə'kāshən\ *n* -s [L *glacies* ice + E *-fication*] **1** : GLACIATION 1 **2** : GLACIATION 2a
glacio- *comb form* [ISV, fr. *glacier*] **1** : glacier ⟨*glacio*logy⟩ **2** : glacial and ⟨*glacio*marine⟩
gla·cio·fluvial \¦glās(h)ē(,)ō+\ *adj* : of, relating to, or coming from streams deriving much or all of their water from the melting of a glacier ⟨~ deposits⟩
gla·cio·lacustrine \"+\ *adj* : of, relating to, or coming from lakes deriving much or all of their water from the melting of a glacier ⟨~ clays and silts⟩
gla·ci·o·log·i·cal \¦glās(h)ēə¦läjəkəl\ *adj* : of or relating to glaciology
gla·ci·ol·o·gist \,glās(h)ē'äləjəst\ *n* -s [ISV *glaciology* + *-ist*] : a specialist in glaciology
gla·ci·ol·o·gy \-jē\ *n* -ES [ISV *glacio-* + *-logy*] **1** : a science concerned with the causes and modes of ice accumulation and with ice action on the earth's surface; *specif* : a branch of geology that treats of glacial epochs, glaciation, and the effects of ice in modifying the earth's surface and in affecting the life and distribution of plants and animals **2** : the glacial features of a region ⟨the ~ of Greenland⟩
gla·ci·om·e·ter \-'ämǝd·ə(r)\ *n* : an instrument that measures glacial motion
gla·cio·natant \¦glās(h)ē(,)ō+\ *adj* : of, relating to, or derived from masses of floating ice usu. glacial in origin
gla·cis \'glasē, -si, gla'sē, 'glasəs, 'glāsəs\ *n, pl* **glacis** \-sēz,-siz\ *also* **glacises** \-səsəz\ [F, fr. MF, fr. *glacer* to freeze, slide, fr. OF *glacier*, fr. L *glaciare* to freeze, fr. *glacies* ice — more at GLACIER] **1 a** : a gentle slope : INCLINE **b** : a slope used for defense against attack; *specif* : a natural or artificial slope that runs downward from the top of a counterscarp or covered way so as to expose attackers to firing from ramparts **2 a** : an area lying beyond the borders of a country and used as a buffer against an enemy : a protective barrier; *specif* : BUFFER STATE **b** : a combat area ⟨the ~ on which the future of mankind will be decided —H.W.Weigert⟩
glacis plate *n* : sloping armor plate formerly often used on the deck of naval vessels (as about hatches or turrets)
glack \'glak\ *n* -s [ScGael *glac* valley, hollow, palm of the hand, fr. MIr *glacc* hand; prob. akin to L *galla* gall on a plant — more at GALL (excrescence)] *Scot* : a narrow valley : RAVINE
gla·con \(')gla¦sōⁿ\ *n, pl* **glacons** \-ōⁿ(z)\ [F *glaçon* piece of ice, fr. OF, fr. *glace* ice — more at GLACIER] : a piece of sea ice ranging in size from a small fragment to a floe of medium dimensions
[1]**glad** \'glad, -aa(ə)-,-ai-\ *adj, usu* **gladder**; *usu* **gladdest** [ME, shining, glad, fr. OE *glæd*; akin to OHG *glat* shining, smooth, ON *glathr* glad, sunny, L *glaber* bald, smooth, Russ *gladkiĭ* smooth, and perh. to OE *geolu* yellow — more at YELLOW] **1** *archaic* : having a cheerful or happy disposition by nature **2 a** : experiencing pleasure, joy, or delight through some immediate cause : made happy : filled with joy ⟨if you are happy, I am ~⟩ ⟨~ that they succeeded⟩ ⟨~ at the announcement⟩ ⟨were ~ to meet him⟩ **b** (1) : GRATIFIED, SATISFIED, PLEASED ⟨both his high-school friends were ~ of his company —William Du Bois⟩ (2) : not at all sorry : quite without regret or remorse ⟨they got what they deserved and I'm ~ of it⟩ **c** : very willing : quite content ⟨~ to do anything you say⟩ **3 a** (1) : marked by, expressive of, or caused by happiness and joy ⟨a ~ countenance⟩ ⟨up we climb with ~ exhilaration —John Muir †1914⟩ ⟨the others gave a ~ shout —Francis Shean⟩ (2) : surrounded by or attended with happiness and joy ⟨a ~ occasion⟩ **b** : causing happiness and joy ⟨the ~ news was flashed through the encampment —F.V.W.Mason⟩ : PLEASANT, CHEERING ⟨the same ~ assurance of meeting again —W.W. Howells⟩ **4** : full of brightness and cheerfulness : having a beautiful radiance ⟨a ~ spring morning⟩
syn HAPPY, CHEERFUL, LIGHTHEARTED, JOYFUL, JOYOUS: GLAD is generally the opposite of *sad* and *gloomy;* it indicates a degree of pleasure ranging from pleased satisfaction to elation ⟨always gleeful and jocular, even as afterward his entire saintly life was *glad* with an invincible gaiety of spirit —H.O.Taylor⟩ In cursory conventional expressions it indicates gratification or lack of reservation or regret ⟨I shall be *glad* of your company —G.B.Shaw⟩ HAPPY, often interchangeable with GLAD, may imply a more positive and demonstrative sense of well-being, satisfaction, and enjoyment ⟨like most men with a *happy* family life, it was no hardship for him to be alone —H.S. Canby⟩ ⟨all the delightful signs of their *happy* intimacy —Morley Callaghan⟩ CHEERFUL suggests lively, hearty, and optimistic good spirits arising from a naturally sanguine disposition or from some particular cause of happiness ⟨they [suicidal attempts] could not enter the *cheerful*, sanguine, courageous scheme of life . . . in part natural to her —Havelock Ellis⟩ ⟨as *cheerful* as could be expected, for his broken leg was knitting nicely —Jack London⟩ LIGHTHEARTED suggests a carefree, debonair, easygoing freedom from concern giving rise to lively mirth ⟨the gayest of worried people in Europe . . . they can be *lighthearted* in the midst of misery and joke at their own expense —H.J.Forman⟩ ⟨*lighthearted* optimistic libertarianism —M.R.Cohen⟩ JOYFUL and JOYOUS are very close together in indicating joy, marked happiness, high pleasure, elation; JOYOUS may hint a more lasting or more certain elated happiness, JOYFUL a more demonstrative happiness arising from a particular cause ⟨a bright and happy Christian, a romping optimist, who laughed away sin and doubt, a *joyful* Puritan —Sinclair Lewis⟩ ⟨thou with the smile on thy face and the *joyful* eyes and clear —William Morris⟩ ⟨that *joyous* serenity we think belongs to a better world than this —Sir Winston Churchill⟩ ⟨a *joyous*, lighthearted, and hilarious mode of life which offered a strong contrast to the more sober lives of New England —C.A. & Mary Beard⟩
[2]**glad** \"\ *vb* **gladded**; **gladded**; **gladding**; **glads** [ME *gladen*, fr. OE *gladian*, fr. *glæd*] *vt, archaic* : to make glad ~ *vi, obs* : to be glad
[3]**glad** \"\ *adv* [[1]*glad*] *archaic* : GLADLY
[4]**glad** \"\ *n* -s [by shortening] : GLADIOLUS 1b
glad·den \-d°n\ *vb* **gladdened**; **gladdened**; **gladdening** \-d(°)niŋ\ **gladdens** [[1]*glad* + *-en*] *vt* : to make glad ⟨something that will ~ your eyes —S.M.Crothers⟩ ~ *vi, archaic* : to be glad **syn** see PLEASE
gladder *comparative of* GLAD
gladdest *superlative of* GLAD
glad·don \'glad°n\ *n* -s [ME *gladen*, *gladene*, fr. OE *glædene*, perh. modif. of L *gladiolus* small sword, gladiolus] **1** *dial Eng* : IRIS; *esp* : STINKING IRIS **2** *dial Eng* : CATTAIL 1
glad·dy \'gladi\ *n* -ES [origin unknown] *dial Eng* : YELLOWHAMMER 1
glade \'glād\ *n* -s [perh. fr. [1]*glad*] **1 a** (1) : an open space surrounded by woods : CLEARING (2) : a wooded or open area lying between wooded slopes (3) *archaic* : an open stretch or group of interconnected openings forming a passage through woodland **b** : GROVE; *esp* : an open grove of tall old trees **2** : a marshy and usu. low-lying area: as **a** *South* : a periodically inundated grassy marsh often running between adjacent slopes **b** : a marshy area bounding or forming the headwaters of a stream **3** *obs* : a bright streak or patch of light
glade mallow *n* : a tall American herb (*Napaea dioica*) of the family Malvaceae with palmate leaves and small white dioecious flowers
gladey *var of* GLADY
glad eye *n* : a pleasant friendly glance : a welcoming glance ⟨giving the *glad eye* to voters of every persuasion —C.L. Becker⟩; *usu* : a glance indicating sexual interest and usu. intended to encourage sexual advances ⟨girls giving sailors the *glad eye*⟩
glad·ful \'=fəl\ *adj* [ME, fr. *glad*, n., gladness (fr. *glad*, adj.) + *-ful*] *archaic* : full of happiness and joy : GLAD
glad hand *n* [[1]*glad* + *hand*] **1** : a warm friendly handshake ⟨moving among his patrons with a welcoming smile and a *glad hand* —Edwin Corle⟩ **2** : a warm welcome, greeting, or reception ⟨an affable people always ready to give strangers a *glad hand*⟩; *esp* : an effusive welcome, greeting, or reception usu. basically insincere and often marked by a display of obnoxious familiarity ⟨potential customers getting the *glad hand*⟩ ⟨master of the *glad hand* and the soft soap —H.A. Burton⟩
glad-hand \'=¦=\ *vb* [*glad hand*] *vt* : to extend a glad hand to ⟨political candidates *glad-handing* everyone they met⟩ ~ *vi* : to extend a glad hand ⟨you'll never find him *glad-handing* if he can help it⟩
glad-hander \"ə(r)\ *n* **1** : one given to glad-handing : one ready to extend a glad hand ⟨the home-loving, comfort-loving, rotund *glad-hander* —Christopher Rand⟩ ⟨this big, friendly fellow — a *glad-hander* who really seemed to mean it — R.M.Yoder⟩ **2** : one who is appointed to meet or greet others and win their goodwill ⟨a shy *glad-hander*, a public-relations man with a highly developed sense of privacy —Dwight Macdonald⟩
glad·i·ate \'gladē,āt, -ē,ət\ *adj* [NL *gladiatus*, fr. L *gladius* sword + *-atus* -ate] : shaped like a sword : ENSIFORM ⟨the ~ leaves of a gladiolus⟩
glad·i·a·tor \'gladē,ād·ə(r), -ātə-\ *n* -s [L, fr. *gladius* sword, of Celt origin; akin to W *cleddyf* sword; akin to L *clades* destruction, defeat, Gk *klados* sprout, twig, branch, OSlav *kladivo* hammer, Gk *klan* to break — more at HALT (lame)] **1 a** : one (as a professional combatant or a captive, slave, or condemned criminal) equipped with some means of attack and defense and pitted against another or against a wild animal in a fight to the death for the entertainment of the public (as in the arena of the ancient Roman amphitheater) **b** : one that opposes another in a usu. public controversy : DISPUTANT, CONTROVERSIALIST ⟨the debates of the House were substantially carried on by some score of chosen ~s — Christopher Hollis⟩ **c** : a trained fighter; *specif* : PRIZEFIGHTER ⟨whether you consider it from his worth as a ~ or from the point of view of the box office —Gene Tunney⟩ **2** *obs* : a professional swordsman
glad·i·a·to·ri·al \¦gladēə¦tōrēəl, -tór-\ *adj* **1** : of, relating to, or suggestive of gladiators or the combats of gladiators ⟨bloody ~ spectacles⟩ **2** : inclined toward controversy or contention : QUARRELSOME ⟨~ newspaper columnists⟩ ⟨those ~ contests in which the participants are encouraged to let their hostilities run riot —R.H.Wittcoff⟩
gladiatorian *adj, obs* : GLADIATORIAL
glad·i·a·tor·ship \'=,=,=,ship\ *n* : a display of gladiatorial skill
gladiatory *adj* [L *gladiatorius*, fr. *gladiator*] *obs* : GLADIATORIAL
glad·i·o·la \,gladē'ōlə\ *n* -s [back-formation fr. *gladiolus*, taken as a plural] : GLADIOLUS 1b
gladi·o·lar \¦gladē¦ōlə(r) *sometimes* glə'dīəl-\ *adj* [*gladiolus* + *-ar*] : of or relating to the gladiolus (sense 3)
glad·i·ole \'gladē,ōl\ *n* -s [ME *gladiol*, fr. L *gladiolus*] : GLADIOLUS 1b
gladi·o·lus \,gladē'ōləs *sometimes* glə'dīələs\ *n* [NL, fr. L, small sword, gladiolus, dim. of *gladius* sword] **1 a** *cap* : a genus of plants (family Iridaceae) native chiefly to Africa with a few native to Europe and Asia that have erect sword-shaped leaves and spikes of brilliantly colored irregular flowers arising from flattened corms **b** *pl* **gladiolus** \"\ *or* **gladio·li** \-ē'ō,lī, -ē'ō(,)lē; -'īə,lī\ *also* **gladioluses** : any plant of the genus *Gladiolus* **2** -ES : a strong red that is bluer and paler than Goya, bluer than average cherry red, and bluer and darker than geranium (sense 3a) **3** *pl* **gladioli** : the large middle portion of the sternum lying between the upper manubrium and the lower xiphoid process — called also *mesosternum*

gladiolus 1b

gladiolus thrips *n* : a small thrips (*Taeniothrips simplex*) lemon-yellow when a nymph and grayish black when adult that feeds on all parts of the gladiolus causing bleaching and browning of leaves and whitening and blasting of flowers
glad·ite \'gla,dīt\ *n* -s [Sw *gladit*, fr. *Gladhammar*, Sweden, its locality + Sw *-it* -ite] : a mineral $PbCuBi_5S_9$ consisting of a complex sulfide of lead, copper, and bismuth
gla·di·us \'glādēəs\ *n, pl* **gla·dii** \-ē,ī\ [NL, fr. L, sword] : [3]PEN 5
glad·less \'gladləs, -aad-, -aid-\ *adj* [obs. E *glad*, n., gladness (fr. ME, fr. *glad*, adj.) + E *-less*] : devoid of happiness and joy ⟨a ~ life⟩
[1]**glad·ly** *adj* -ER/-EST [ME, fr. OE *glædlīc* pleasant, shining] *archaic* : GLAD
[2]**glad·ly** *adv, sometimes* -ER/-EST [ME, fr. OE *glædlīce*, adv. fr. *glædlīc* pleasant, shining, fr. *glæd* shining, glad + *-līc* -ly (adj. suffix)] : in a glad manner: **a** : with happiness and joy : JOYFULLY ⟨~ welcomed him home again⟩ **b** : very willingly : CHEERFULLY ⟨your money will be ~ refunded⟩
glad·ness *n* -ES [ME *gladnesse*, fr. OE *glædnes*, fr. *glæd* glad + *-nes* -ness] : the quality or state of being glad : happiness and joy ⟨days filled with ~⟩ ⟨his voice . . . had such a warm, infectious ~ running through it —O.E.Rölvaag⟩
glad rags *n pl, slang* : dressy clothes : clothes worn at parties or on other festive social occasions : best clothes; *often* : formal dress (as evening clothes)
glads *pres 3d sing of* GLAD, *pl of* GLAD
glad·some \'=səm\ *adj, sometimes* -ER/-EST [ME *gladsom*, fr. *glad*, n., gladness (fr. *glad*, adj.) + *-som* -some] : GLAD — **glad·some·ly** *adv* — **glad·some·ness** *n* -ES

GLACIAL EPOCHS

EPOCHS	AGES AND STAGES: North America		Europe	APPROXIMATE TIME
Recent	Postglacial			
	Wisconsin: *Mankato, *Cary, *Tazewell, *Iowan		Würm: *Würm IV, " III, " II, " I	5000–15000 B.C.
				125,000 B.C.
Pleistocene	Sangamon	III Interglacial	Riss-Würm	275,000 B.C.
	Illinoian		Riss	375,000 B.C.
	Yarmouth	II Interglacial	Mindel-Riss	675,000 B.C.
	Kansan		Mindel	750,000 B.C.
	Aftonian	I Interglacial	Günz-Mindel	900,000 B.C.
	Nebraskan		Günz	1,000,000 B.C.
Pliocene	Preglacial			

*Substage

gla·cial·ism \-ə,lizəm\ *n* -s : GLACIATION
gla·cial·ist \-ələst\ *n* -s **1** : GLACIOLOGIST **2** : one that supports the glacier theory
gla·cial·ize \-ə,līz\ *vt* -ED/-ING/-S : GLACIATE
glacial meal *n* : ROCK FLOUR
glacial period *n* **1** : GLACIAL EPOCH **2** *usu cap G & often cap P* : the Pleistocene epoch
glacial theory *n* : GLACIER THEORY
gla·ci·ar·i·um \,glāshē'a(a)rēəm\ *n* -s [L *glacies* ice + E *-arium*] : a skating rink with a floor of artificial ice
gla·ci·ate \'glāshē,āt *also* -sē-\ *vb* -ED/-ING/-S [L *glaciatus*, past part. of *glaciare* to freeze, fr. *glacies* ice] *vt* **1** : to convert into ice : FREEZE **2 a** : to cover with or as if with ice or snow; *specif* : to cover with glaciers ⟨no greenery could be seen in the whole *glaciated* region⟩ **b** : to subject to or alter by the action of glaciers : produce glacial effects (as erosion or the deposition of glacial drift) in or upon — usu. used in passive ⟨a valley which has been vigorously *glaciated* —W.J.Miller⟩ ⟨striated rocks found in that widely *glaciated* area⟩ ~ *vi* **1** : to become ice : become frozen **2** : to become covered with or as if with ice or snow; *specif* : to become covered with glaciers ⟨the poles *glaciated* —Martin Gardner⟩
gla·ci·a·tion \,glās(h)ē'āshən\ *n* -s [prob. fr. (assumed) NL *glaciation-*, *glaciatio*, fr. L *glaciatus* + *-ion-*, *-io* -ion] **1 a** : the action or process of becoming ice : FREEZING ⟨the ~ of clouds⟩ **b** : the formation of ice sheets; *specif* : the formation of glaciers ⟨an age of extensive ~⟩ **2 a** : the condition of being covered by ice sheets or glaciers; *specif* : GLACIAL ⟨deposits laid down during the period of the second ~ —*Amer. Anthropologist*⟩ **b** (1) : subjection to the action of glaciers ⟨cycles of weathering and ~ —Russell Lord⟩ (2) : the effects produced by the action of glaciers ⟨~ that is clearly evident throughout the area⟩
gla·cier \'glāshə(r) *sometimes* -āzhə- *or* -āshēə-, *Brit usu* 'glasiə(r *or* -asyə-\ *n* -s [F dial. (Savoy), fr. MF dial. (Savoy, Vaud, Valais), fr. MF *glace* ice, fr. LL *glacia*, alter. of L *glacies*; akin to L *gelu* frost — more at COLD] : a large body of ice moving slowly down a slope or valley or spreading outward on a land surface and usu. carrying, pushing, or deposit-

glad·stone \'gladz,tōn, -d,st-, *chiefly Brit* -_tən\ *or* **gladstone bag** *n* -s *often cap G* [after William E. *Gladstone* †1898 Brit. statesman] **:** a traveling bag typically of leather and about two feet long with flexible sides on a rigid steel frame and opening flat into two equal compartments

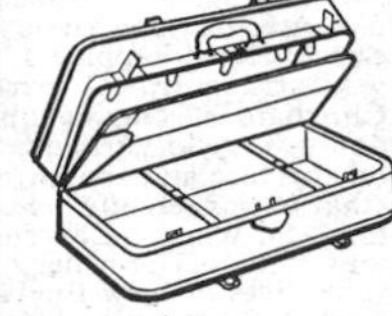
gladstone

glad·sto·ni·an \(')gladz¦tōnēən, -d¦st-\ *adj, usu cap* [William E. *Gladstone* †1898 + E *-ian*] **:** of, relating to, or characteristic of W.E.Gladstone, his political policies, or the party that supported him

glady *also* **glad·ey** \'glādē\ *adj* **gladier; gladiest** [*glade* + *-y*] **1 a :** having glades; *esp* **:** full of glades ⟨a ~ countryside⟩ **b :** resembling a glade ⟨it was a ~ place, and ferns and moss grew all around —H.E.Giles⟩ **2 :** having a shallow soil and limestone outcrops ⟨extensive ~ areas wherein well-preserved fossils are abundant —*Jour. of Geol.*⟩

gla·gah *or* **gla·ga** \'glägə\ *n* -s [Malay *gĕlagah*] **:** KANS

glag·o·lit·ic \¦glagə¦lid·ik\ *also* **glag·o·lith·ic** \-lithik\ *adj, usu cap* [irreg. fr. Serbo-Croatian *glagolica* Glagolitic alphabet + E *-ic*] **:** written in, constituting, or belonging to an alphabet of which the invention is attributed to St. Cyril in the 9th century A.D. and which was formerly used in writing various Slavic languages but is now used only in Catholic liturgical books in a limited area along the eastern coast of the Adriatic — compare CYRILLIC ALPHABET

gla·go·li·tsa \,glägə'gōlyētsə, -,sä\ *n* -s *usu cap* [Serbo-Croatian *glagolica;* akin to OSlav *glagolŭ* word, *glasŭ* voice — more at CALL] **:** the Glagolitic alphabet

glaik \'glāk\ *n* -s [origin unknown] **1 glaiks** *pl, chiefly Scot* **:** derisive deception **:** MOCKERY **2** *chiefly Scot* **:** a flash of light

glai·kit *or* **glai·ket** *or* **gla·ked** \'glākət, -əd\ *adj* [ME (Sc) *glaikit, glakit*] *chiefly Scot* **:** showing a lack of common sense and good judgment **:** FOOLISH, SILLY, GIDDY

¹glair *or* **glaire** \'gla(a)(ə)r, -le(, |ə\ *n* -s [ME *gleyre* white of an egg, fr. MF *glaire*, fr. OF, modif. of (assumed) VL *claria*, fr. L *clarus* clear — more at CLEAR] **1 :** a sizing liquid made from egg white beaten with vinegar and applied to book covers before laying on gold leaf or to book edges before gilding **2 :** a viscid or slimy substance suggestive of the white of an egg

²glair *or* **glaire** \"\ *vt* -ED/-ING/-S **:** to apply glair to ⟨~*ed* book edges⟩

glair·e·ous \|rēəs\ *adj* [¹*glair* + *-eous*] *archaic* **:** GLAIRY

glair·i·ness \|rēnəs\ *n* -ES **:** the quality or state of being glairy

glairy \|rē\ *adj* -ER/-EST [¹*glair* + *-y*] **1 :** having the characteristics of glair **:** VISCID, SLIMY ⟨~ mucus⟩ **2 :** overlaid with or as if with glair ⟨a sticky ~ surface⟩

glais·tig *or* **glas·tig** \'glashtig\ *n* -s [ScGael *glaistig*] **:** a female sprite in Celtic mythology

glaive \'glāv\ *n* -s [ME *glaive, gleyve*, fr. OF *glaive* javelin, modif. of L *gladius* sword — more at GLADIATOR] **1** *obs* **:** HALBERD **2** *archaic* **:** SWORD; *esp* **:** BROADSWORD

glaiz·ie \'glāzi\ *Scot var of* GLAZY

glam \'glam\ *var of* GLAUM

gla·mor·gan·shire \glə'mȯrgən,shi(ə)r, -_shər\ *or* **glamorgan** *adj, usu cap* [fr. *Glamorganshire, Glamorgan*, county in Wales] **:** of or from the county of Glamorgan, Wales **:** of the kind or style prevalent in Glamorgan

glam·or·iza·tion \,glamərə'zāshən, -,rī'z-\ *n* -s **:** the act of glamorizing or the process of being glamorized

glam·or·ize *also* **glam·our·ize** \'==,rīz\ *vt* -ED/-ING/-S **1 :** to make glamorous **:** add glamour to **:** make more attractive esp. in a superficial illusory way ⟨*glamorizing* a living room⟩ **2 :** to attribute glamour to **:** look upon as glamorous **:** view or treat (as in writing) romantically **:** IDEALIZE, ROMANTICIZE, GLORIFY ⟨*glamorizing* war⟩ ⟨poverty *glamorized* into something alluring —Rose Thurburn⟩ — **glam·or·iz·er** \-zə(r)\ *n* -s

glam·or·ous *also* **glam·our·ous** \'glam(ə)rəs\ *adj* **:** characterized by or full of glamour **:** FASCINATING, ENCHANTING, ALLURING ⟨~ movie stars⟩ — **glam·or·ous·ly** *adv* — **glam·or·ous·ness** *n* -ES

¹glam·our *or* **glam·or** \'glamə(r)\ *n* -s [Sc *glamour, glamer*, alter. of E *grammar;* fr. the popular association of erudition with occult practices] **1 :** a magic spell **:** BEWITCHMENT ⟨the girls appeared to be under a ~ —Llewelyn Powys⟩ ⟨casting a ~ over the affairs of merchant princes —O.S.J.Gogarty⟩ **2 :** an elusive mysteriously exciting and often illusory attractiveness that stirs the imagination and appeals to a taste for the unconventional, the unexpected, the colorful, or the exotic ⟨the ~ of the French Foreign Legion⟩ **:** a strangely alluring atmosphere of romantic enchantment ⟨a beautifully decorated room that was filled with ~⟩ **:** a bewitching intangible irresistibly magnetic charm ⟨it was simply the ~ of the unknown that she had felt in him —Ellen Glasgow⟩; *often* **:** personal charm and poise combined with unusual physical and sexual attractiveness ⟨an actress radiant with ~⟩

²glamour \"\ *vt* **glamoured; glamoured; glamouring** \-m(ə)riŋ\ **glamours** [Sc, fr. *glamour, glamer*, n.] **1 :** to cast a magic spell upon **:** BEWITCH ⟨soon created such a realm of gorgeous marvel as ~*ed* the age with fantasy —H.B.Alexander⟩ **2 :** GLAMORIZE ⟨*glamoured*-up blondes were a dime a dozen — Raymond Chandler⟩

glamour boy *n* **:** a man (as an actor or adventurer) with whom glamour is esp. associated

glamour girl *n* **:** a woman (as an actress or model) with whom glamour is esp. associated

glam·ou·rie *or* **glam·ou·ry** \-mərē\ *n, pl* **glamouries** [Sc, alter. of *glamour, glamer*, n.] *archaic* **:** GLAMOUR 1

glam·our·less \-mə(r)ləs\ *adj* **:** devoid of glamour ⟨she was handsome in her ~ way —Edmund Wilson⟩

glamour puss *n, slang* **:** one that has a glamorously attractive face ⟨some *glamour puss* with two expressions and eighteen changes of costume —Raymond Chandler⟩

¹glance \'glan(t)s, -aa(ə)-,-ai-,-à-\ *vb* -ED/-ING/-S [alter. of ME *glencen, glenchen*, perh. alter. of *glenten* to move quickly esp. in an oblique direction, strike something obliquely and so glance aside, look sideways at something, gleam — more at GLENT] *vi* **1 a** (1) **:** to strike a surface obliquely so as to be deflected and go off at an angle **:** RICOCHET — usu. used with *off* ⟨the spear *glanced* off the heavy metal shield⟩ ⟨the bullet *glanced* off the stone wall and smashed through a window⟩ (2) **:** to strike a surface obliquely and bound onward at an angle often following with one or more additional oblique impacts and forward bounds **:** SKIP ⟨threw the small flat stone so that it *glanced* lightly across the pond⟩ (3) *of a ray of light* **:** to strike a reflecting surface obliquely and dart out at an angle ⟨light from the setting sun *glanced* off the oil tanks —Malcolm Lowry⟩ **b** (1) *obs* **:** to move swiftly (as in springing or dodging) esp. in an oblique or crosswise direction (2) **:** to make a glance in cricket **c** *archaic* **:** to move swiftly (as in speaking or writing) from one subject to another **2 a** (1) **:** to flash or gleam with quick intermittent rapidly successive rays of light (as those produced by sudden quick movements of a reflecting surface) **:** SPARKLE, SCINTILLATE, CORUSCATE ⟨clear mountain brooks *glancing* brightly in the morning sun⟩ (2) **:** to make sudden quick movements that cause quick intermittent flashes of light (as from a moving reflecting surface) ⟨dragonflies *glancing* and zigzagging over the pond⟩ **b :** to shine with a steady dazzling radiance **:** BEAM ⟨the *glancing* sun⟩ **3 a :** to touch briefly or indirectly on a subject (as in speaking or writing) **:** make an incidental reference **:** make an allusion — usu. used with *at* ⟨a book on contemporary civilization that often ~*s* at the customs of ancient cultures⟩ **b :** to refer briefly to something by way of censure or satire **:** cast discredit on something in a passing reference ⟨full of sly, *glancing* allusions to life as it is lived today —Gerald Bullett⟩ **4 a** *of the eyes* (1) **:** to move swiftly from one thing to another ⟨his eyes *glanced* from the judge to the jury and back again⟩ (2) *archaic* **:** to light upon something by or as if by chance ⟨her eye *glanced* on something which made her change color —T.L.Peacock⟩ **b :** to take a quick look at something ⟨*glancing* at the morning headlines⟩ **:** look briefly, hurriedly, or cursorily ⟨*glanced* about as though fearful of being overheard —Sherwood Anderson⟩ **:** look around here and there **:** make a quick inspection ⟨the bar, where we *glanced* first, was crowded —Scott Fitzgerald⟩ ~ *vt* **1 a** *obs* **:** to turn (the eyes or gaze) quickly aside or away **b** *archaic* **:** to turn (the eyes or gaze) quickly or briefly toward something **c** *archaic* (1) **:** to take a quick look at **:** view quickly **:** survey rapidly (2) **:** to catch a glimpse of **2** *obs* **a :** to allude to **b :** to barely touch **:** GRAZE **3 :** to give an oblique path of direction to: **a :** to throw (as a spear or stone) or shoot (as a bullet) so that the object thrown or shot glances from a surface **b** *archaic* **:** to aim (as an innuendo) indirectly **:** INSINUATE **4** *archaic* **:** to cause the reflection of ⟨*glanced* back the flame of the lamp merrily —Sir Walter Scott⟩ **5 :** to play (a bowled cricket ball) with a glance

²glance \"\ *n* -s **1 a** (1) **:** a quick intermittent flash or gleam of light (as one produced by sudden quick movements of a reflecting surface) ⟨the ~ of a brightly polished sword⟩ (2) *archaic* **:** a sudden quick movement (as of a reflecting surface) that produces flashes or gleams of light **b :** a ray of light shining with a steady radiance **:** BEAM ⟨the first ~ of sunlight sends the snow slithering in soft cascades —Adrian Bell⟩ **2 a** *archaic* **:** a rapid oblique or crosswise movement **b** *archaic* **:** a deflected impact or blow **c :** a stroke in the game of cricket made with a slanted bat that deflects the ball to leg **3 a :** a swift movement of the eyes from one thing to another ⟨the suspect's shifting ~⟩ **b :** a quick, brief, hurried, or cursory look ⟨the two old ladies darting ~*s* at us and smiling secretively —William Thornton⟩ ⟨museums in which pictures of a single style or artist can be compared and enjoyed at a ~ —R.J.Goldwater⟩ ⟨it was clear at first ~ that his condition was serious —T.B.Costain⟩ **4** *archaic* **a :** a brief satirical or censorious reference to something **:** GIBE **b :** a brief incidental reference **:** ALLUSION

³glance \"\ *n* -s [G *glanz* mineral sulfide, luster, shine] **:** any of several mineral sulfides that are mostly dark colored and that have a metallic luster

⁴glance \"\ *vt* -ED/-ING/-S [prob. fr. D *glanzen* to polish, gleam, fr. MD *glansen* to gleam, fr. *glans*, n., luster, shine, fr. MHG *glanz*, fr. OHG, fr. *glanz*, adj., bright — more at GLENT] **:** to give a high luster to (as by burnishing)

glance coal \"-,\ *n* [trans. of G *glanzkohle*, fr. *glanz* luster, shine + *kohle* coal] **:** a hard lustrous coal; *esp* **:** ANTHRACITE

glance pitch *n* [²*glance*] **:** a pure asphalt — compare MANJAK

glanc·er \-sə(r)\ *n* -s [¹*glance* + *-er*] **:** FENDER SKID

glancing *adj* [fr. pres. part. of ¹*glance*] **1 :** INCIDENTAL, INDIRECT ⟨the book has a variety of ~ references to prominent personalities⟩ **2 :** CASUAL, UNSTUDIED, OFFHAND ⟨a citizen of the world who knew the Near East with the same ~ familiarity —H.V.Gregory⟩ ⟨he evoked the town and its surrounding countryside with his habitual ~ art —*Times Lit. Supp.*⟩ — **glanc·ing·ly** *adv*

glancing angle *n* [*glancing* fr. gerund of ¹*glance*] **:** the angle between an incident beam (as of X rays or electrons) and the surface upon which it is incident **:** the complement of the angle of incidence

glancing boom *n* **:** FENDER BOOM

¹gland \'gland, -aa(ə)-\ *n* -s [F *glande* gland (organ of secretion), glandular swelling esp. on the neck, fr. MF, acorn, gland (organ of secretion), glandular swelling esp. on the neck, fr. OF, acorn, glandular swelling esp. on the neck, fr. *glant, gland* acorn, fr. L *gland-, glans;* akin to Gk *balanos* acorn, Lith *gilė*] **1 a :** a cell or group of cells that selectively removes materials from the blood, concentrates or alters them, and secretes them for further use in the body or for elimination from the body and that typically consists of columnar or cuboidal epithelium resting on a basement membrane that is surrounded by a plexus of blood vessels — see ENDOCRINE, EXOCRINE, HOLOCRINE, MEROCRINE **b :** any of various animal structures suggestive of glands though not glandular in function: as (1) **:** LYMPH GLAND (2) **:** GLANS **c glands** *pl* **:** a diseased or inflamed condition of glands (as the lymph or salivary glands of the neck) **2 a :** any of various special secreting organs of plants: as (1) **:** one or more of the hairs on the leaves of sundew (2) **:** one or more of the extrafloral nectaries of many plants **b :** any of certain small protuberances of plants (as on the petiole of a peach leaf)

²gland \"\ *n* -s [origin unknown] **1 :** a device (as a series of carbon rings or of interlocking teeth) for preventing leakage of steam, water, gas, or other fluid past a joint (as in machinery); *specif* **:** the movable part of a stuffing box by which the packing is compressed **2 :** a short tube fitted to the envelope of a balloon or airship so that a rope may slide through without causing leakage

glan·dered \'glandə(r)d, -laan- *sometimes* -lån-\ *adj* **:** affected with glanders ⟨a ~ horse⟩

glan·der·ous \-d(ə)rəs\ *adj* **1 :** GLANDERED **2 :** produced by or resembling the effects of glanders ⟨a ~ condition⟩

glan·ders \-də(r)z\ *n pl but sing or pl in constr* [MF *glandres*, pl. of *glandre* glandular swelling esp. on the neck, fr. OF, fr. L *glandula*, dim. of *gland-, glans* acorn] **:** a highly contagious and very destructive disease of horses and other equines or sometimes of other animals (as dogs, guinea pigs, or man) that is caused by a bacterium (*Actinobacillus mallei* syn. *Malleomyces mallei* or *Pfeifferella mallei*) and that is characterized by caseating nodular lesions which tend to break down and form ulcers in mucous membranes, skin, and visceral organs and esp. in lymph nodes and along the course of lymphatic vessels and which may be accompanied by fever and edema and secondary symptoms referable to pulmonary, gastrointestinal, or other special organ involvement — compare FARCY

glandes *pl of* GLANS

gland·less \'glandləs, -laan-, *rapid* -nl-\ *adj* **:** devoid of glands

gland of bar·tho·lin \-,bär'tōlən\ *usu cap B* [after Kaspar *Bartholin* †1738 Dan. physician] **:** either of two oval racemose glands lying one on each side of the lower part of the vagina and secreting a lubricating mucus

gland of bow·man \-'bōmən\ *usu cap B* [after Sir William *Bowman* †1892 Eng. ophthalmic surgeon] **:** any one of the tubular and often branched glands occurring beneath the sensory epithelium of the nose

gland of brunner *usu cap B* **:** BRUNNER'S GLAND

gland of cowper *usu cap C* **:** COWPER'S GLAND

gland of external secretion : EXOCRINE GLAND

gland of internal secretion : ENDOCRINE GLAND

gland of lieberkühn *usu cap L* **:** LIEBERKÜHN'S GLAND

gland of moll \-'mōl, -ō-,-ä-\ *usu cap M* [after Jacob A. *Moll* †1914 Du. ophthalmologist] **:** any of the small glands near the free margin of each eyelid regarded as modified sweat glands

gland of ty·son \-'tīsᵊn\ *usu cap T* [after Edward *Tyson* †1708 Eng. anatomist] **:** any of the small glands at the base of the glans penis that secrete smegma

glands *pl of* GLAND

glan·du·la \'glanjələ\ *n, pl* **glandu·lae** \-,lē, -,lī\ [NL, fr. L, glandular swelling esp. on the neck] **:** ¹GLAND 1; *esp* **:** a small gland

glan·du·lar \-_lə(r)\ *adj* [F *glandulaire*, fr. *glandule* glandula, fr. L *glandula*] **1 a** (1) **:** of, relating to, or involving glands or gland cells ⟨~ cancer⟩ ⟨~ functions⟩ (2) **:** derived from glands or gland cells ⟨~ secretions⟩ **b :** having the characteristics or function of a gland ⟨~ tissue⟩ **c :** containing, bearing, or made up of glands or gland cells ⟨~ organs⟩ **2 a :** controlled or influenced by the secretions of glands; *esp* **:** resulting from abnormal functioning of glands ⟨the theory of ~ criminal behavior⟩ **b :** INNATE, INHERENT, INSTINCTIVE ⟨he had grown up with a ~ dislike for everything pretentious⟩ **c :** EARTHY, PHYSICAL; *esp* **:** SEXUAL ⟨he has adopted, as an interim substitute for love, an entirely ~ relationship with the proprietress of his café—W.M.Frohcok⟩ — **glan·du·lar·ly** *adv*

glandular epithelium *n* **:** the epithelium that forms the secreting surface of a gland

glandular fever *n* **:** INFECTIOUS MONONUCLEOSIS

glan·du·lif·er·ous \¦glanjə¦lif(ə)rəs\ *adj* [obs. E *glandule* glandula, glandular swelling esp. on the neck (fr. MF, glandula) + E *-i-* + *-ferous*] **:** bearing small glands

glan·du·los·i·ty \,glanjə'läsəd·ē\ *n* -ES [L *glandulosus* glandulous + E *-ity*] **:** the quality or state of being glandulous

glan·du·lous \'glanjələs, -laan-\ *adj* [ME *glandelous*, fr. MF *glanduleus*, fr. L *glandulosus*, fr. *glandula* + *-osus* -ose] **:** GLANDULAR — **glan·du·lous·ness** *n* -ES

gla·nen·che·li \glə'neŋkə,lī\ *n pl, cap* [NL, fr. *glan-* (fr. Gk *glanis* sheatfish) + *-encheli* (fr. Gk *enchelys* eel) — more at ANGUIS] *in some classifications* **:** a suborder of Ostariophysi comprising the electric eels

glan·i·os·to·mi \,glanē'ästə,mī\ *n pl, cap* [NL, fr. *glanio-* (fr. Gk *glanis*) + *-stomi*] *in some esp former classifications* **:** an order of fishes consisting of the sturgeons

glans \'glanz, -aa(ə)-\ *n, pl* **glan·des** \-n,dēz\ [L *gland-, glans* acorn, glans penis — more at GLAND] **1 a** *or* **glans pe·nis** \-'pēnəs\ **:** a conical vascular body forming the extremity of the penis **b** *or* **glans cli·to·ri·dis** \-klə'tōrədəs, -,klī'-\ **:** a conical vascular body forming the extremity of the clitoris **2 :** a nut enclosed by or seated in an involucre

glar \'glär\ *var of* GLAUR

¹glare \'gla(a)(ə)r, 'gle(, |ə\ *vb* -ED/-ING/-S [ME *glaren;* akin to MD & MLG *glaren* to gleam, glare, OE *glæs* glass — more at GLASS] *vi* **1 a :** to shine esp. by reflection with a harsh uncomfortably brilliant light ⟨the heat was terrific, the pavements *glared* —Aldous Huxley⟩ ⟨the town was baking and *glaring* in the somniferous New York heat —Edmund Wilson⟩ **:** shine with an intense disagreeable brightness ⟨the sun *glared* down relentlessly⟩ ⟨a single naked bulb *glared* pitilessly in the center of the room⟩ **:** shine blindingly ⟨shielding our eyes as we crossed the white sand beach that blazed and *glared*⟩ ⟨miles of frozen snow that *glared* in the morning sunlight⟩ **b** *archaic* **:** to stand out offensively **:** be unpleasantly conspicuous **:** OBTRUDE **2 :** to stare with intense hostility, annoyance, or dislike **:** stare angrily or fiercely **:** GLOWER, SCOWL ⟨where two armies ~ at each other across a geographical line —Lindesay Parrott⟩ ⟨*glared* at him as he walked in late⟩ ~ *vt* **1 :** to express (as hostility) by glowering or scowling ⟨*glaring* defiance at each other —J.B.Priestley⟩ **2** *archaic* **:** to cause to be sharply reflected **syn** see BLAZE, GAZE

²glare \"\ *n* -s **1 a** (1) **:** a harsh uncomfortably bright light or reflection of light **:** intense disagreeable brightness ⟨the unshaded bulbs threw a cheap yellow ~ over the walls —A.P. Gaskell⟩ ⟨the ~ of publicity⟩; *specif* **:** painfully bright sunlight ⟨the ~ on the meadows was as blinding as if it shone on tin —Jean Stafford⟩ (2) *archaic* **:** the quality or state of being lustrous or glistening **:** SHININESS **b :** cheap showy brilliance **:** GARISHNESS, GAUDINESS ⟨art was partly corrupted by the fondness for ~, expensiveness, and size —F.W.Farrar⟩ **2 :** a fixed glowering look **:** a look expressive of intense hostility, annoyance, or dislike **:** an angry or fierce stare **:** SCOWL ⟨the baleful ~ of their eyes⟩ ⟨gave the jury a ~⟩

³glare \"\ *n* -s [prob. fr. ²*glare*] **:** a surface, sheet, or glaze of glare ice

⁴glare \"\ *archaic var of* GLAIR

glare ice *n* [prob. fr. ²*glare*] **:** ice that has a smooth slippery glassy surface ⟨sidewalks covered with *glare ice*⟩

glare·less \'=ləs\ *adj* **:** free from glare ⟨opaque ~ paper⟩

gla·re·o·la \glə'rēələ\ *n, cap* [NL, dim. of L *glarea* gravel; prob. akin to L *granum* grain — more at CORN] **:** a genus (the type of the family Glareolidae) of Old World shorebirds that comprises the pratincoles which are closely related to the coursers

glar·e·ole \'gla(a)rē,ōl\ *n* -s [NL *Glareola*] **:** PRATINCOLE

¹glareous *var of* GLAIREOUS

²glar·e·ous \'gla(a)rēəs\ *adj* [L *glarea* gravel + E *-ous*] **:** growing in gravelly soil ⟨~ plants⟩

glar·i·ness \'gla(a)rēnəs\ *n* -ES **:** the quality or state of being glary ⟨the ~ of the dusty roads⟩

glar·ing \'gla(a)riŋ, -ler-, -reŋ\ *adj* [ME *glaringe*, fr. *glaren* to glare + *-inge, -ing* -ing] **1 :** marked by a fixed look of hostility, fierceness, or anger **:** GLOWERING, SCOWLING ⟨trembled at the sight of their ~ eyes⟩ **2 a :** shining with or reflecting a harsh uncomfortably bright light **:** blindingly bright ⟨~ spotlights⟩ ⟨the still surface of the ~ sea⟩ **b** (1) **:** showily brilliant **:** GARISH, GAUDY ⟨~ colors⟩ (2) **:** vulgarly ostentatious **:** blatantly crude ⟨the more raffish and ~ manners of the Regency —R.E. Roberts⟩ **3 :** painfully obvious **:** too apparent not to be noticed **:** FLAGRANT ⟨the gullibility with which we perpetuate ~ errors —Joseph O'Connor⟩ ⟨the self-assurance I have mentioned appears at its most ~ in a stupid man —Albert Dasnoy⟩ **:** unavoidably noticeable **:** inescapably evident **:** CONSPICUOUS ⟨the contrast between their words and their deeds today is ~ —O.M.Green⟩ **syn** see FLAGRANT

glar·ing·ly *adv* **:** in a glaring manner ⟨the need is ~ apparent⟩

glar·ing·ness *n* -ES **:** the quality or state of being glaring ⟨embarrassed by the ~ of this error⟩

glary \'gla(a)rē, -ler-, -ri\ *adj, usu* -ER/-EST [²*glare* + *-y*] **:** shining with or reflecting a harsh uncomfortably bright light **:** full of glare **:** GLARING ⟨sun-scorched, ~, waterless pieces of rock —Harry Luke⟩

glase *obs var of* GLAZE

gla·se·ri·an fissure \glə|'zirēən-, glä|\ *n, usu cap G* [*glaserian* fr. Johann Heinrich *Glaser* †1675 Swiss anatomist + E *-ian*] **:** PETROTYMPANIC FISSURE

glas·gow \'gla|(,)skō, -laa|, -lai|, -lå|, |s(,)gō *also* 'glaz(,)gō *or* -läz-\ *adj, usu cap* [fr. *Glasgow*, city in Scotland] **:** of or from the city of Glasgow, Scotland ⟨the *Glasgow* shipyards⟩ **:** of the kind or style prevalent in Glasgow

glasite *usu cap, var of* GLASSITE

¹glass \'glas, -aa(ə)-,-ai-,-à-\ *n* -ES [ME *glas*, fr. OE *glæs;* akin to OHG *glas* amber, OE *glær* amber, ON *gler* glass, OE *geolu* yellow — more at YELLOW] **1 a :** an amorphous inorganic usu. transparent or translucent substance consisting typically of a mixture of silicates or sometimes borates or phosphates formed by fusion of sand or some other form of silica or by fusion of oxides of boron or phosphorus with a flux (as soda, potash) and a stabilizer (as lime, alumina) and sometimes metallic oxides or other coloring agents so that a mass is produced that cools to a rigid condition without crystallization and that may be blown, cast, pressed, rolled, drawn, or cut into various forms — see CROWN GLASS, FIBER GLASS, FLINT GLASS; compare CULLET, FRIT **b :** any of various inorganic or organic substances resembling glass esp. in transparency, hardness, and amorphous nature ⟨sodium phosphate ~⟩ ⟨organic ~*es* made from plastics⟩ — compare ²GLAZE 2a **c :** a substance (as obsidian, pumice) produced by the quick cooling of an igneous magma **2 a :** something made wholly or almost wholly of glass: as (1) **:** a glass container; *esp* **:** a glass drinking vessel (as a tumbler or a goblet) (2) **:** a glass mirror **:** LOOKING GLASS (3) **:** a sheet of glass (as a windowpane, the plate-glass front of a display case, the glass covering of a picture) (4) **:** a shaped hollow protective glass covering (as the bell-shaped covering set over some clocks or plants, the chimney of most oil lamps) (5) **:** a slightly curved or flat piece of glass covering the dial of a watch or clock **:** CRYSTAL (6) **:** OPTICAL GLASS (7) **:** either piece of glass or other transparent material in a pair of glasses (8) **:** an hourglass or half-hour glass (9) **:** WEATHERGLASS **b** (1) **:** an optical instrument (as a telescope or microscope) or device that has one or more lenses and that is designed to aid in the viewing of objects otherwise wholly or partly incapable of being seen by the average eye ⟨the captain kept his ~ fixed on the nearby shore⟩; *specif* **:** BINOCULARS ⟨stole the captain's ~*es*⟩ (2) **glasses** *pl* **:** a device used to correct defects of vision (as nearsightedness) or to protect the eyes (as from glare, dust, flying sparks) and consisting typically of two pieces of glass designed to bend light rays or of two pieces of ordinary colored or plain glass or other transparent material that are supported by a bridge resting on the nose and by sidepieces extending over the ears ⟨she put her ~*es* on the table⟩ — often used with *pair* ⟨bought a new pair of ~*es*⟩; called also *eyeglasses, spectacles;* compare GOGGLES, PINCE-NEZ **3 a :** the quantity held by a glass container (as a drinking glass) **:** GLASSFUL ⟨drank two ~*es* of water⟩ **b :** the time required for one end of an hourglass or half-hour glass to empty ⟨the ship had been sighted two ~*es* earlier⟩ **4 :** articles made of glass **:** GLASSWARE ⟨a sparkling new set of dinner ~⟩ **:** glass products ⟨famous for the manufacture of beautiful ~⟩ **5** *obs* **:** GLOSS **6** *obs* **:** the organ of sight **:** EYE

²glass \"\ *vb* -ED/-ING/-ES *vt* **1 a** (1) **:** to fit, set, or equip (as a window frame) with glass ⟨only three windows had been ~*ed*⟩ ⟨peered in through the ~*ed* upper half of the fruitshop door —I.S.Cobb⟩ (2) **:** to fit or equip with eyeglasses ⟨had been ~*ed* at an early age⟩ **b :** to cover or protect with glass ⟨~*ed* the picture before framing it⟩ **:** enclose, case, or wall with glass ⟨sunlight streamed into the porch which had been ~*ed* in⟩ **c :** to pack and seal hermetically in glass containers for preservation or transportation ⟨~*ed* fruits⟩ ⟨~*ed* coffee⟩ — compare ³CAN 1a **2 a :** to cause to have a glassy surface or appearance **:** make glassy ⟨boredom ~*ed* his eyes⟩ **b :** to smooth or polish (leather) with a glass burnisher ⟨~*ing* the hides⟩ **3 a :** to cause to be mirrored **:** REFLECT ⟨a solitary tree that was ~*ed* by the pool's still surface⟩ **b :** to see mirrored **:** see the reflection of ⟨considered her shining nails, as if ~*ing* her indolent beauty in them —Edith Wharton⟩ **4 :** to scan (as a terrain) with an optical instrument (as a pair of binoculars) esp. in an effort to discover game ⟨went out that afternoon and ~*ed* the country from the hills —Ernest Hemingway⟩ ⟨he may not notice you at a distance; you can ~ him, watch him, study him —Paul Schubert⟩ **~** *vi* **:** to become glassy ⟨the river is ~*ing* in a breathless calm —A.N.Whitehead⟩

³glass \"\ *adj* **1 a** (1) **:** made wholly or nearly wholly of glass ⟨a ~ bottle⟩ (2) **:** having walls or sides and often top or bottom made wholly or nearly wholly of glass panes, panels, or blocks ⟨a ~ porch⟩ ⟨a ~ recording studio⟩ **b :** resembling or suggestive of glass **:** GLASSY ⟨the ~ surface of the water⟩ **2 :** set or fitted with glass ⟨the plants were kept under a ~ frame⟩

glass arm *n* **:** an arm the muscles of which too easily become stiff and sore in use ⟨he's a good fielder but he's got a *glass arm*⟩

glass bell *n* **:** a bell jar made of glass

glass bender *n* **1 :** a worker who shapes glass disks in molds or under forming presses to make lenses for clocks, speedometers, headlights **2 :** a worker who heats and bends glass tubing for neon signs and fuses the electrodes into place

glass block *n* **:** a hollow translucent block usu. with ribbed exterior made by fusing two sections of clear pressed glass at high temperature and used as a building material chiefly for wall panels

glassblower \ˈ=,==\ *n* **:** one skilled in the art of glassblowing — compare LAMPWORKER

glassblowing \ˈ=,==\ *n* **:** an art of shaping a mass of glass by inflating it through a tube after the glass has been heated to a viscid state — compare LAMPWORKING

glass catfish *n* **:** a small transparent catfish (*Kryptopterus bicirrhus*) of southeast Asia

glass cement *n* **:** a binding mixture used to affix glass to glass or to some other material (as metal)

glass cloth *n* **1 :** an absorbent lintless plain-weave cloth (as of linen) used for wiping glass and china — called also *glass toweling* **2 :** a fabric formed of woven fiber glass

glass crab *n* **:** a transparent crustacean larva (as a phyllosoma) — called also *glass shrimp*

glass curtain *n* **:** a usu. sheer translucent or transparent window curtain hung immediately over the glass of a window or over a window shade and usu. not extending much beyond the sides of the window frame

glass cutter *n* **:** one that cuts or scores glass: as **a** (1) **:** a worker who cuts sheets of glass into specific sizes (as for windowpanes, mirrors) (2) **:** a worker who decorates the surface of glass by cutting, scoring, grinding, and polishing **b :** a tool (as a metal hand tool equipped with a small wheel of hardened steel or a tool with a diamond point) used for cutting or scoring glass

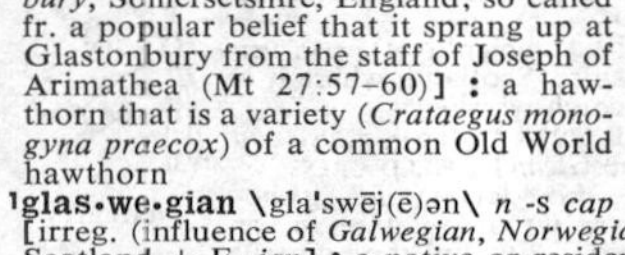

glass cutters b

glass cutting *n* **:** the art or process of cutting glass **:** the art of the glass cutter

glassed *past of* GLASS

glass eel *n* [so called fr. its transparency in its early stages] **:** ELVER

glass electrode *n* **:** an electrode that consists typically of a glass tube sealed at the bottom with a thin-walled glass bulb containing a solution of constant pH (as a chloride buffer) and a silver-silver chloride reference electrode and that is immersed in an unknown solution usu. along with a calomel electrode for determining the pH of this solution

glass·en \-sᵊn\ *adj* [ME, fr. *glas* glass + *-en*] **1** *archaic* **:** made of glass **2** *archaic* **:** resembling glass **:** GLASSY

glass·er \-sə(r)\ *n* -s **:** a machine used for glassing leather

glas·ser's disease \-sə(r)z-\ *n, usu cap G* [prob. fr. the name *Glasser*] **:** swine influenza marked by arthritis

glasses *pl of* GLASS, *pres 3d sing of* GLASS

glass eye *n* [³*glass* + *eye*] **1 a glass eyes** *pl, obs* **:** GLASSES **b :** an artificial eye made of glass **2 a** (1) **:** a condition of impaired eyesight or blindness in horses marked by a bright glassy eye and dilated pupil (2) **:** a horse affected with this condition **b** (1) **:** lymphomatosis of the eyes in chickens (2) **:** a chicken affected with this condition **3 a :** an eye having a pale, whitish, or colorless iris **b :** one that has such an eye

glasseye \ˈ=,=\ *n* [³*glass* + *eye*] **:** WALLEYED PIKE

glass-eye \ˈ=,=\ *n* [³*glass* + *eye*] **:** any of several African forest warblers constituting a genus (*Camaroptera*) of the family Sylviidae

glass-eyed \ˈ=ˈ=\ *adj* **1 :** having a glass eye **2 :** affected with the condition of glass eye

glass fiber *n* **:** a strong continuous filament or staple fiber made from molten glass; *esp* **:** a variety of such a filament or fiber that is extremely fine and pliable

glassfish \ˈ=,=\ *n* **:** any of several small Old World fishes constituting a genus *Ambassis* of the family Centropomidae, having a transparent body that allows the bones and viscera to be clearly visible, and being often kept in the tropical aquarium

glass·ful \-s,fu̇l\ *n* -s **:** the quantity held by a glass container (as a drinking glass)

glass gall *n* **:** a saline whitish scum sometimes cast up from glass in fusion

glass garden *n* **:** a small glass container (as a bowl) in which plants are grown **:** TERRARIUM — compare WARDIAN CASE

glass-glazed \ˈ=ˈ=\ *adj* **:** having a heavy glaze coating that gives a noticeably glassy appearance ⟨*glass-glazed* pottery⟩

glass green *n* **:** a light yellow green that is greener, lighter, and stronger than reed green and yellower and paler than sky green

glass-hard \ˈ=ˈ=\ *adj* **:** having a maximum degree of hardness ⟨*glass-hard* steel⟩

glass harmonica *n* **:** a musical instrument of the 18th and 19th centuries consisting of a series of hemispherical glasses turning on an axis and played by touching the edges with a dampened finger

glasshouse \ˈ=,=\ *n* [ME *glashous*, fr. *glas* glass + *hous* house] **1 a :** GLASSWORKS **b :** the part of a glassworks in which the glass is melted and shaped **2** *chiefly Brit* **:** GREENHOUSE

glass·ie *or* **glassy** \ˈglasē, -laas-,-lais-,-lȧs-, -si\ *n, pl* **glass·ies** [¹*glass* + *-ie, -y*] **1 :** a playing marble made of glass **2 :** a transparent diamond crystal

glassier *comparative of* GLASSY

glassiest *superlative of* GLASSY

glass·i·ly \-sələ̄, -li\ *adv* **:** in a glassy manner

glass·ine \(ˈ)=ˈsēn\ *n* -s [¹*glass* + *-ine*] **:** a thin dense transparent or semitransparent paper that is highly resistant to the passage of air and grease ⟨doughnuts packaged in ~ bags⟩ ⟨reading the address through the envelope's ~ window⟩

glass·i·ness \ˈ=sēnə̇s, -sin-\ *n* -ES **1 :** the quality or state of being glassy **2 :** WATER CORE 2

glassing *pres part of* GLASS

glass·ite *or* **glas·ite** \-,sīt\ *n* -s *usu cap* [John *Glass* (or *Glas*) †1773 Scot. clergyman who founded the sect + E *-ite*] **:** a member of a Christian sect founded about 1730 and holding that there is no authority in the New Testament for giving the civil magistrate as such any function in the church — called also *Sandemanian*

glass jaw *n* **:** a jaw (as of a boxer) that is highly vulnerable to punches

glass·less \-sləs\ *adj* **:** devoid of glass

glassmaker \ˈ=,==\ *n* **:** one that makes glass

glassmakers' soap *n* **:** a substance (as manganese dioxide) used by glassmakers to remove a green color produced in glass by iron salts

glassmaking \ˈ=,==\ *n* **:** the art or process of manufacturing glass

glassman \-mən, -,man\ *n, pl* **glassmen 1 :** a dealer in glass products **2 :** GLASSMAKER

glass paper *n* [¹*glass* + *paper*] **1 :** a strong paper faced with pulverized glass and used in abrading or smoothing slight irregularities in surfaces (as of wood) **2 :** a paper made from extremely fine glass fibers and marked by high resistance to moisture, heat, light, and vermin

glass-paper \ˈ=,==\ *vt* [*glass paper*] **:** to abrade or smooth with glass paper

glass pot *n* **:** a small fireclay crucible in which are fused the materials for making glass in small-scale operations—compare TANK FURNACE

glass run *n* **:** one of the grooves in which a glass window (as of an automobile) moves

glass sensation *n* **:** a consciousness of filled space evoked by transparent nonselective media (as glass) — compare BULKY COLOR

glass shot *n* **:** a motion-picture or television shot in which a part of a scene is made through a glass plate having other parts of the scene painted on its surface

glass shrimp *n* **:** GLASS CRAB

glass silk *n* **:** FIBER GLASS; *esp* **:** fiber glass in the form of continuous filaments used in textiles

glass snail *n* **:** any of numerous small transparent land snails constituting *Vitrina* and related genera and resembling slugs

glass snake *n* **1 :** a limbless lizard (*Ophisaurus ventralis*) of the southern U.S. superficially resembling a snake and having a tail capable of being broken off completely into one or more small pieces and replaced by a new tail **2 :** any of several lizards similar to the No. American glass snake that are found in the Old World

glass soap *n* **:** GLASSMAKERS' SOAP

glass sponge *n* [so called fr. the glassy spicules] **:** a siliceous sponge of the class Hyalospongiae

glass toweling *or* **glass towel** *n* **:** GLASS CLOTH 1

glassware \ˈ=,=\ *n* **:** articles made of glass; *esp* **:** tableware of glass used in serving food and drink

glass wool *n* **:** glass fibers in a mass resembling cotton batting or wool and used esp. for thermal insulation and air filters or fabricated into various products (as acoustic tile or wallboard)

glasswork \ˈ=,=\ *n* **1** *also* **glassworking** \ˈ=,==\ **a :** the making of glass or of glass articles **b :** work involving working with or on glass or glass articles: as (1) **:** the work of fitting or equipping with glass (as in fitting window frames with glass, equipping display cases with glass) (2) **:** the work of a glassblower, glass bender, or glass cutter **2 a :** articles made of glass **:** GLASSWARE **b :** sheets of glass cut into specific sizes (as for windowpanes, mirrors)

glassworker \ˈ=,==\ *n* **:** one that does glasswork; *specif* **:** GLAZIER

glassworks \ˈ=,=\ *n pl but usu sing in constr* **:** an establishment (as a factory) in which glass is made

glass worm *n* [so called fr. its transparency] **:** ARROWWORM

glasswort \ˈ=,=\ *n* [so called fr. its former use in the manufacture of glass] **1 :** a plant of the genus *Salicornia* (esp. *S. europaea*) **2 :** a saltwort (*Salsola kali*) with awl-shaped stiff leaves — called also *kelpwort*

¹glassy \ˈglasē, -laas-,-lais-,-lȧs-, -si\ *adj, usu* -ER/-EST [¹*glass* + *-y*] **1 a :** having the characteristics or appearance of glass **:** VITREOUS ⟨~ porcelain⟩ **b :** resembling or suggestive of glass (as in shininess, smoothness or slipperiness, fragility, transparency) ⟨the pavement was wet, ~ with water —Willa Cather⟩ ⟨the ~ surface of the lake⟩ **2 a :** marked by or having a dull fixedness of expression (as from boredom, shock, or stupidity) **:** LACKLUSTER, APATHETIC **:** FISHY ⟨his explanation awoke no response in their ~ eyes⟩ ⟨moonishly amused at anything that passed before their ~ eyes —Rebecca West⟩ **b :** cold and unsympathetic **:** devoid of cordiality **:** FORBIDDING ⟨gave him a disdainful ~ stare⟩ ⟨unable to penetrate their ~ reserve⟩ **c :** HARD, UNYIELDING, UNWAVERING ⟨a ~ determination to win⟩ ⟨staring at the floor with a rather ~ concentration —Louis Auchincloss⟩ **d :** lacking overtones **:** SHARP, SHRILL, STRIDENT ⟨a good recording except for the ~ quality of the strings⟩ **e :** smoothly superficial ⟨approached the problem with a ~ assurance⟩ **f :** breathlessly calm and bright ⟨a good many desert areas have this feeling of ~ stillness in the late afternoon —H.L.Davis⟩ ⟨a ~ quiver of heat —Eve Langley⟩ ⟨sun-drenched, ~ days —W.H.Hale⟩

²glassy *var of* GLASSIE

glass yarn *n* **:** yarn composed of glass fibers twisted from continuous filament strands or from staple fiber sliver

glassy-eyed \ˈ=ˈ=ˈ=\ *adj* **:** marked by or having glassy eyes ⟨a book so dull it makes anyone *glassy-eyed* in five minutes⟩

glassy feldspar *n* **:** SANIDINE

glastig *var of* GLAISTIG

glas·ton·bury chair \ˈglastən,berē- *also* -sᵊn-\ *n, usu cap G* [*Glastonbury*, Somersetshire, England; so called fr. its having been designed in imitation of the abbot of Glastonbury's chair preserved in the bishop's palace at Wells, Somersetshire] **:** a small light folding chair with sloping arms and back and two crossed straight legs at the right and left sides

Glastonbury chair

glastonbury thorn *n, usu cap G* [*Glastonbury*, Somersetshire, England; so called fr. a popular belief that it sprang up at Glastonbury from the staff of Joseph of Arimathea (Mt 27:57–60)] **:** a hawthorn that is a variety (*Crataegus monogyna praecox*) of a common Old World hawthorn

¹glas·we·gian \glaˈswēj(ē)ən\ *n* -s *cap* [irreg. (influence of *Galwegian*, *Norwegian*) fr. *Glasgow*, city in Scotland + E *-ian*] **:** a native or resident of Glasgow

²glaswegian \(ˈ)=ˈ=(=)=\ *adj, usu cap* **1 :** of, relating to, or characteristic of Glasgow **2 :** of, relating to, or characteristic of Glaswegians

glau·ber·ite \ˈglau̇bə,rīt *also* ˈglȯb-\ *n* -s [F *glaubérite*, fr. Johann R. *Glauber* †1668 Ger. chemist + F *-ite*; so called fr. its resemblance in chemical composition to Glauber's salt] **:** a light-colored brittle sodium calcium sulfate $Na_2Ca(SO_4)_2$ having a vitreous luster and saline taste

glauber's salt \-bə(r)(z)-\ *also* **glauber salt** *n, usu cap G* [after Johann R. *Glauber* †1668] **:** the crystalline decahydrate $Na_2SO_4.10H_2O$ of sodium sulfate occurring naturally as mirabilite, obtained also from salt cake, and used chiefly in dyeing and in medicine as a laxative; *sometimes* **:** anhydrous sodium sulfate — sometimes used in pl.

glauc- *or* **glauco-** *comb form* [L *glauc-* gleaming, gray, fr. Gk *glauk-, glauko-*, fr. *glaukos* — more at GLAUCOUS] **:** glaucous ⟨*glauco*chroite⟩ ⟨*glauc*ope⟩

glau·ces·cence \glȯˈsesᵊn(t)s\ *n* -s [prob. fr. (assumed) NL *glaucescentia*, fr. *glaucescent-, glaucescens* glaucescent + L *-ia* -y] **:** the quality or state of being glaucescent

glau·ces·cent \(ˈ)=ˈsesᵊnt\ *adj* [prob. fr. (assumed) NL *glaucescent-, glaucescens*, fr. L *glauc-* + *-escent-, -escens* -escent] **:** slightly glaucous **:** becoming glaucous

glau·cid·i·um \glȯˈsidēəm\ *n, cap* [NL, fr. Gk *glaukidion* small owl, dim. of *glauk-, glaux* owl] **:** a genus of small owls comprising the pygmy owls

glau·cine \ˈglȯ,sēn, -ōsᵊn\ *n* -s [ISV *glauc-* (fr. NL *Glaucium*) + *-ine*] **:** a crystalline alkaloid $C_{21}H_{25}NO_4$ found esp. in the horned poppy

glau·ci·o·net·ta \,glȯsēōˈned·ə\ [NL, fr. Gk *glaukion*, a duck, fr. *glaukos*] *syn of* BUCEPHALA

glau·ci·um \ˈglȯsēəm\ *n, cap* [NL, perh. fr. Gk *glaukion* juice of a papaveraceous plant, fr. *glaukos*] **:** a small genus of Eurasian herbs (family Papaveraceae) with yellow flowers and a yellow acrid juice

glau·co·cer·i·nite \,glȯ(,)kōˈserə,nīt\ *n* -s [G *glaucokerinit*, fr. *glauc-* + Gk *kērinos* made of wax (fr. *kēros* wax) + G *-it* -ite — more at CEREUS] **:** a mineral perhaps $Zn_3Cu_7Al_8(SO_4)_2(OH)_{60}.4H_2O$ consisting of a hydrous basic sulfate of copper, zinc, and aluminum

glau·cochro·ite \,glȯkəˈkrō,īt, glȯˈkäkrə,wīt\ *n* -s [*glauc-* + Gk *chrōs* color + E *-ite* — more at CHROMATIC] **:** a mineral $CaMnSiO_4$ that consists of calcium manganese silicate, occurs in bluish green prismatic crystals, and is related to monticellite

glau·co·dot \ˈglȯkə,dät\ *also* **glau·co·dote** \-,dōt\ *n* -s [G *glaukodot*, fr. *glauk-* glauc- + *-dot* (fr. Gk *dotēr* giver, fr. *didonai* to give) — more at DATE] **:** a mineral $(Co,Fe)AsS$ consisting of a grayish white metallic-looking cobalt iron sulfarsenide occurring in orthorhombic crystals or massive (hardness 5, sp. gr. 5.9–6.0)

glau·co·ma \glȯˈkōmə, glau̇ˈ-\ *n* -s [L, cataract (of the eye), fr. Gk *glaukōma*, fr. *glaukos* gleaming, gray] **:** a disease of the eye marked by increased pressure within the eyeball that damages the optic disk and results in gradual loss of vision and ultimate blindness

glau·coma·tous \(ˈ)=ˈkōmədəs, -ˈkäm-\ *adj* [L *glaucomat-, glaucoma* + E *-ous*] **:** of, relating to, or affected with glaucoma

glau·co·mys \ˈglȯkə,mis\ *n, cap* [NL, fr. *glauc-* + *-mys*] **:** a genus of mammals comprising the No. American flying squirrels

glau·co·nia \glȯˈkōnēə\ [NL, perh. irreg. fr. L *glaucus* gleaming, gray, fr. Gk *glaukos*] *syn of* LEPTOTYPHLOPS

glau·co·nif·er·ous \,glȯkəˈnif(ə)rəs\ *adj* [ISV *glauconite* + *-i-* + *-ferous*] **:** containing glauconite

glau·co·nite \ˈglȯkə,nīt\ *n* -s [G *glaukonit*, fr. Gk *glaukon* (neut. of *glaukos*) + G *-it* -ite] **:** a mineral approximately $K_{15}(Fe,Mg,Al)_{4-6}(Si,Al)_8O_{20}(OH)_4$ consisting of a dull green earthy and micaceous iron potassium silicate occurring abundantly in greensand

glau·co·nit·ic \ˌ==ˈnid·ik\ *adj* [ISV *glauconite* + *-ic*] **:** containing or resembling glauconite ⟨~ limestone⟩

glau·co·nit·iza·tion \,==,nīd·əˈzāshən\ *n* -s [*glauconite* + *-ize* + *-ation*] **:** formation of or conversion into glauconite

glau·cope \ˈglȯ,kōp\ *n* -s [*glauc-* + *-ope* (as in *cyanope*)] **:** a person with fair hair and blue eyes — compare CYANOPE — **glau·co·pi·an** \(ˈ)=ˈkōpēən\ *adj*

glau·co·phane \ˈglȯkə,fān\ *n* -s [G *glaukophan*, fr. *glauk-* glauc- + *-phan* -phane] **:** a mineral $Na_2(Mg,Fe)_3Al_2Si_8O_{22}(OH)_2$ consisting of a blue, bluish black, or grayish silicate of sodium, aluminum, iron, and magnesium occurring in certain crystalline schists

glau·coth·oe \glȯˈkäthə,wē\ *n* -s [NL, perh. irreg. fr. L *glaucus* or Gk *glaukos*] **:** a young hermit crab that has completed the swimming larval stages

¹glau·cous \ˈglȯkəs\ *adj* [L *glaucus* gleaming, gray, fr. Gk *glaukos*; perh. akin to OE *clǣne* pure, clear — more at CLEAN] **1 a :** of a pale yellow green color **b :** of a light bluish gray or bluish white color **2 :** having a powdery or waxy coating that gives a frosted appearance and tends to rub off ⟨~ plums⟩ ⟨~ stems⟩ ⟨~ cabbage leaves⟩ ⟨~ grapes⟩ — **glau·cous·ness** *n* -ES

²glaucous \"\ *n* -ES **:** a pale yellow green that is yellower and stronger than smoke gray, greener and deeper than oyster gray, and yellower than average Nile

glaucous blue *n* **:** a grayish blue that is greener and paler than electric or copenhagen and greener and lighter than Gobelin

glaucous gray *n* **:** a light bluish gray to light gray that is redder and darker than skimmed-milk white and very slightly greener than cinerous

glaucous green *n* **:** a very pale green that is yellower and slightly less strong than tourmaline and yellower and duller than emerald tint

glaucous gull *n* **:** a large boreal gull (*Larus hyperboreus*) that is pure white with a bluish mantle when adult — called also *burgomaster*

glaucous honeysuckle *n* **:** a No. American vine (*Lonicera dioica*) having glaucous leaves and purplish flowers

glaucous willow *n* **:** a pussy willow (*Salix discolor*)

glaucous-winged gull \ˈ==,=-\ *n* **:** a white gull (*Larus glaucescens*) having a pale gray mantle and pale gray wing tips and ranging from the Bering sea to California and Japan

glau·cus \ˈglȯkəs\ *n, cap* [NL, fr. L, gleaming, gray] **:** a genus of slender elongate pelagic nudibranchs with three pairs of lateral lobes — see SEA LIZARD

glaum \ˈglȧm, -ó-\ *vb* -ED/-ING/-S [prob. fr. ScGael *glàim* to handle awkwardly, seize voraciously] *dial chiefly Brit* **:** GRAB, CLUTCH, GROPE

glaur \ˈglȯr\ *n* -s [origin unknown] *chiefly Scot* **:** soft slimy mud **:** MIRE

glaux \ˈglȯks\ *n, cap* [NL, fr. L, a plant, fr. Gk *glaux, glax* swine cress] **:** a cosmopolitan genus of fleshy perennial herbs (family Primulaceae) having opposite leaves and small whitish flowers — see SEA MILKWORT

glave *obs var of* GLAIVE

glaver *vi* -ED/-ING/-S [ME *glaveren*] *obs* **:** to talk in a deceitfully kind or pleasant manner **:** FLATTER

gla·ver·ing \ˈglāv(ə)riŋ\ *adj* [ME *glaveringe*, fr. *glaveren* + *-inge*, *-ing* -ing] *archaic* **:** deceitfully kind, pleasant, or flattering ⟨a ~ smile⟩

¹glaze \ˈglāz\ *vb* -ED/-ING/-S [ME *glasen*, fr. *glas* glass — more at GLASS] *vt* **1 a :** ²GLASS 1a(1) **b :** ²GLASS 1b **2 a :** to cover or coat with or as if with a glaze ⟨the storm *glazed* roads and trees with ice⟩ ⟨a new process for *glazing* pottery⟩ **:** apply a glaze to ⟨*glazing* doughnuts⟩; *specif* **:** to cover (as frozen fish) with an ice coating to prevent dehydration in storage and shipping **b :** to vitrify the surface of ⟨stones that the blast had *glazed*⟩ **3 a** (1) **:** to cause to shine like glass **:** give a smooth glossy or lustrous surface or finish to (as by calendering) **:** GLOSS ⟨*glazed* paper⟩ ⟨*glazed* textiles⟩ ⟨*glazing* fur coats⟩ ⟨*glazed* leather⟩ **:** cause to shine brightly (as by rubbing) **:** POLISH, BURNISH ⟨*glazing* metal surfaces⟩ (2) **:** to make smooth and even (as the walls of a house) by filling in depressions on the surface with a hard-drying putty before painting **b :** FERROTYPE **4 :** to dull the abrasive particles of (a grinding wheel) so that they no longer cut freely **~** *vi* **1 :** to become glazed or glassy ⟨his eyes *glazed*, his body twitched spasmodically —Gerald Beaumont⟩ ⟨then put in the sweetbreads to ~ —Hannah Glasse⟩ **2 :** to form a glaze ⟨ice *glazed* over each clear wedge of grass —P.M.Swatek⟩

²glaze \"\ *n* -s **1 a :** a smooth slippery coating of thin ice; *esp* **:** an ice coating that forms when cold rain comes into contact with objects (as rocks, pavements) that are below the freezing point — called also *sleet* **b :** a stretch of smooth slippery ice ⟨hiked over the ~ that lay between them and the camp⟩ **2 a :** material usu. applied to something as a solution or suspension in order to provide a distinctive surface coating; as (1) **:** a liquid preparation (as sugar syrup, gelatine dissolved in meat stock) brushed over or otherwise applied to food (as meat, fish, pastry) on which after application it hardens or becomes firm and adds flavor and a glossy appearance (2) **:** a glassy silica-containing mixture of oxides that is applied and fused to the surface of clayware for decoration or to make it nonporous (3) **:** a usu. dark transparent or semitransparent color applied to a lighter painted surface or to another color so as to achieve a decorative, unifying, or enriching effect **b** (1) **:** a thin smooth glossy or lustrous surface or finish consisting of or resembling glass (as the coating produced by application of a glaze, the smooth glossy finish produced on paper or cloth by calendering) ⟨staring at window reflections in the ~ of the teapot —Elizabeth Bowen⟩ **:** SHEEN ⟨chintz with a beautiful ~⟩ (2) **:** a bright shininess **:** GLOW ⟨her skin had the healthy ~ that comes from sunshine —Harold Brodkey⟩ **3 :** a fine transparent or translucent glassy film ⟨the senile ~ of his eyes —Fred Majdalany⟩ ⟨the ~ that had come over the dead man's eyes⟩

³glaze \"\ *vi* -ED/-ING/-S [prob. blend of *gaze* and *glare*] *archaic* **:** STARE, GLARE

glazed *adj* [fr. past part. of ¹*glaze*] **1 a :** covered or coated with a glaze ⟨~ food products⟩ **b :** having a surface made smooth and glossy or lustrous (as by calendering) ⟨~ paper⟩ ⟨~ cloth⟩ ⟨~ leather⟩ **c :** covered with or as if with a glassy film **:** marked by glassiness ⟨the ~ vacancy of his eyes —Stephen Crane⟩ ⟨his eyes wore that ~, unseeing expression which is the outward token of vague thinking —Carl Van Vechten⟩ **d :** rigidly fixed in expression **:** lacking mobility or vitality of expression **:** grimly set ⟨the ~ faces of survivors —W.H.Hale⟩ **2 :** fitted, set, or equipped with glass (as windowpanes) ⟨four ~ walls⟩

glazed frost *n, Brit* **:** GLAZE 1a

glaze kiln *n* **:** a kiln in which glazed pottery is fired

gla·zen \ˈglāzᵊn\ *adj* [ME *glasen*, fr. OE *glæsen*, fr. *glæs* glass + *-en*] *archaic* **:** GLASSEN

glaz·er \-zə(r)\ *n* -s [ME *glaser* one whose work is cutting and setting glass (as windowpanes), fr. *glasen* to glaze + *-er*] **1 :** one that glazes: as **a :** an operator of a machine that puts a gloss on leather by rubbing it with a hard roller after it has been oiled **b :** one that coats pottery, brick, or tile by dipping the product into a glaze solution **c :** one that gives furs a glossy finish **d :** PANMAN **2 :** a tool, machine, or other device used for glazing

glazes *pres 3d sing of* GLAZE, *pl of* GLAZE

gla·zier \'glāzhə(r), -zēə-\ *n* -s [ME *glasier*, fr. *glas* glass + *-ier*] **1 :** one whose work is cutting and setting glass (as windowpanes) — called also *glassworker* **2 :** one that heats and glazes the tapered ends of glass tubes (as used in making hypodermic syringe cylinders)

glazier's point *n* **:** a small triangular or diamond-shaped piece of thin sheet metal used to hold a pane of glass in a wooden sash while the putty is hardening or in case the putty loosens

gla·ziery \-zhərē, -zēərē, -ri\ *n* -ES [*glazier* + *-y*] **:** GLASSWORK

glaz·i·ly \'glāzəlē\ *adv* **:** in a glazy manner

glaz·i·ness \-zēnəs\ *n* -ES **:** the quality or state of being glazy

glazing *n* -s [ME *glasinge, glasing*, fr. *glasen* to glaze + *-inge, -ing* -ing] **1 :** the act or process or trade of using or applying or providing with glaze **2 a :** GLASSWORK **b :** GLAZE

glazing compound *n* **:** a caulking compound used esp. for holding window glass in place because it remains soft underneath the surface

glazing jack *n* **:** a device consisting of a glass or agate roller attached to the arm of a power-driven machine and used to glaze leather

glazy \-zē\ *adj* -ER/-EST [*²glaze* + *-y*] **:** having the appearance or suggestive of a glaze **:** resembling a glaze ⟨a ~ surface⟩ **:** GLAZED, GLASSY ⟨looked at them with an uncomprehending, ~ stare⟩

gld *abbr* guilder

1glead *var of* GLEDE

2glead *obs var of* GLEED

1gleam \'glēm\ *n* -s [ME *glem, gleem*, fr. OE *glǣm*; akin to OHG *gleimo* glowworm, ON *glja* to glitter, Gk *chliein* to luxuriate, OE *geolu* yellow — more at YELLOW] **1 a** *obs* **:** a brilliantly bright radiance of light (as of the sun) **:** dazzling splendor **b :** a transient appearance or occurrence of emitted or reflected light that is subdued (as when seen through darkness or water or some other intervening medium or as when seen at a distance) ⟨through the swirling fog they glimpsed the ~ of the white sand beach⟩ ⟨the silvery ~ of trout in the brook⟩ ⟨the ~ of the far-off lanterns⟩ or that is slowly changing (as from faintness to greater intensity) ⟨the ~ of dawn in the east⟩ or that has a merely relative brightness (as by contrast with a dark background) ⟨the ~ of many lights reflected in the dark waters of the river⟩ **:** a transient brightness ⟨she read the closely written sheets by the last ~ of daylight —Ellen Glasgow⟩ or a shifting play of subdued diffused reflected light ⟨the rich ~ of the polished mahogany⟩ **c** (1) **:** a small bright light ⟨the quick ~ of a match⟩ **:** a pinpoint of light **:** GLINT ⟨the ~ of anticipation in his eye⟩ (2) **:** a small beam or flash of emitted or reflected light ⟨a ~ of sunlight fell on the page he was reading⟩ ⟨the ~ of helmets in the sun⟩ **2 :** a brief or faint appearance, occurrence, or manifestation (as of a quality) ⟨a ~ of hope⟩ ⟨the ~ of gratitude in the eyes of an old man —H.M.Lydenberg⟩ ⟨a ~ of understanding in the prisoner's face —C.S.Forester⟩ **:** a faint trace ⟨there are perhaps ~s of truth in it here and there —G.B.Shaw⟩ ⟨a ~ of resemblance between the two⟩

2gleam \"\ *vb* -ED/-ING/-S [ME *glemen*, fr. *glem, gleem*, n.] *vi* **1 :** to shine with subdued emitted or reflected light ⟨the sun ~*ed* on the water —Robert Keable⟩ ⟨the firelight is ~*ing* and flashing from the polished brass —Osbert Lancaster⟩ **:** send out gleams ⟨a light ~*ed* through the chinks in the wall —Charles Dickens⟩ **:** become lighted up with gleams ⟨his eye ~*ing* at the sight of the two women —Louis Bromfield⟩ **2 :** to appear briefly, faintly, or transiently ⟨amusement ~*ed* swiftly at her from the boy's eyes —Harriet La Barre⟩ ⟨a light ~*ed* suddenly in the night⟩ ~ *vt* **:** to cause to gleam **:** emit or reflect by gleaming ⟨his monocle ~*ed* polite hostility —Christopher Isherwood⟩

gleam·ing·ly *adv* [*gleaming* (pres. part. of *²gleam*) + *-ly*] **:** in a gleaming manner ⟨lights shining ~⟩

gleam·less \-ləs\ *adj* **:** that does not gleam **:** having no gleam **:** lacking brightness **:** DULL, LACKLUSTER ⟨~ wit⟩

gleamy \-mē\ *adj* -ER/-EST [*¹gleam* + *-y*] **:** marked by gleams **:** GLEAMING

glean \'glēn\ *vb* -ED/-ING/-S [ME *glenen*, fr. MF *glener*, fr. LL *glenare, glennare*, of Gaulish origin; akin to MIr *digliunn* I glean; akin to Russ *glyadet'* to look — more at GLENT] *vi* **1 :** to pick up or gather together the scattered remainder of grain or other produce dropped or left lying by reapers or other regular gatherers ⟨spent hours ~*ing* in the wheat fields⟩ **2 :** to pick up, gather together, or acquire information or other material bit by bit from some source **:** gradually scrape together facts or other material found here and there in some source ⟨they learned what they wanted to know by ~*ing* through the library⟩ ~ *vt* **1 a :** to pick up or gather together (scattered grain or other produce left by reapers or other regular gatherers) ⟨~*ing* stray ears of corn⟩ **b :** to strip (as a grain field) by gleaning **:** leave bare by gleaning ⟨~*ing* a vineyard⟩ **2 a :** to pick up or scrape together (information, facts, or other material) in piecemeal fashion **:** acquire bit by bit from some source ⟨many stimulating ideas can be ~*ed* from that magazine⟩ **:** manage to get ⟨later on I ~*ed* an idea of your mother's strong character —Clemence Dane⟩ ⟨~*ed* a little hope from that —H.A.Chippendale⟩ ⟨some money can be ~*ed* from the venture⟩ **b :** to go over or through carefully so as to discover and pick up bits of information or other material ⟨the writings of our bolder ancestors are ~*ed* for signs of conformity —Philip Edwards⟩ **3 :** to find out in a superficial way or gain a cursory knowledge of by piecing together bits of information or other material picked up from some source ⟨I will call again to ~ your views —H.J.Laski⟩ **:** make out **:** LEARN, ASCERTAIN ⟨I could not ~ what he really meant⟩ ⟨~*ing* their whereabouts from what they had said before leaving⟩ **syn** see REAP

glean·er \-nə(r)\ *n* -s **:** one that gleans ⟨the ~s must follow the reapers if full profit is to be realized —E.E.Pratt⟩

glean·ings \-niŋz, -nēŋz\ *n pl* [fr. *gleaning*, gerund of *glean*] **:** things acquired by gleaning ⟨the ~ of long hours of research⟩

gle·ba \'glēbə\ *n, pl* **gle·bae** \-ē,bē\ [NL, fr. L *gleba, glaeba* clod] **:** the sporogenous tissue forming the central mass of the sporophore in some basidiomycetes (as the puffballs, stinkhorns) — **gle·bal** \-bəl\ *adj*

glebe \'glēb\ *n* -s [L *gleba, glaeba* clod, land — more at CLIP] **1** *archaic* **:** EARTH, LAND, SOIL, SOD; *specif* **:** a plot of cultivated land **2** [AF or ML; AF *glebe*, fr. ML *gleba*, fr. L *gleba, glaeba*] **a** or **glebe land :** the land belonging or yielding revenue to a parish church or ecclesiastical benefice **b :** a parsonage with or without the land appurtenant

glebe house *n, archaic* **:** PARSONAGE

gleby \-bē\ *adj* -ER/-EST [*glebe* + *-y*] **1** *archaic, of soil* **:** RICH, FERTILE **2** *obs* **:** abounding in rich soil

gle·cho·ma \glē'kōmə\ *syn of* GLECOMA

gle·co·ma \"\ *n, cap* [NL, irreg. fr. Gk *glēchōn, blēchōn* pennyroyal] **:** a small genus of creeping Eurasian herbs (family Labiatae) having orbicular or reniform leaves and axillary clusters of blue flowers

1gled \'gled\ *Scot var of* GLAD

2gled \"\ *chiefly Scot var of* GLEDE

1glede *also* **glead** \'glēd\ *n* -s [ME *glede*, fr. OE *glida*; akin to ON *gletha* kite; derivative fr. the root of OE *glīdan* to glide — more at GLIDE] **:** any of several birds of prey (as the common European buzzard or the osprey); *esp* **:** the common European kite (*Milvus milvus*)

2glede *obs var of* ¹GLEED

gle·ditsch·ia \glə'dichēə\ [NL, fr. Johann G. *Gleditsch* †1786 + NL *-ia*] *syn of* GLEDITSIA

gle·dit·sia \-itsēə\ *n, cap* [NL, irreg. fr. Johann G. *Gleditsch* †1786 Ger. botanist + NL *-ia*] **:** a genus of thorny trees (family Leguminosae) with pinnate or bipinnate leaves and inconspicuous greenish spikes of flowers succeeded by large flat pods — see HONEY LOCUST

1glee \'glē\ *n* -s [ME, fr. OE *glēo* entertainment, fun, music; akin to ON *glȳ* joy, Gk *chleuē* joke, Russ *glum*] **1 :** high-spirited joy typically accompanied by exuberant outward display ⟨dancing with ~⟩ ⟨shouting with boyish ~⟩ ⟨a gasp of surprised ~ —*Newsweek*⟩ ⟨he appeared to be almost choking with ~ —Rex Ingamells⟩ and often mixed with or wholly prompted by maliciously delighted and exultant satisfaction over another's misfortune, predicament, or failure ⟨rubbing their hands in ~ over his discomfiture⟩ ⟨grinning with diabolical ~⟩ ⟨it betrayed the ~ felt by the meanspirited when they see people who do not deserve humiliation forced to suffer it —Rebecca West⟩ **:** delighted or triumphant happiness **:** REJOICING, GLADNESS, MIRTH, MERRIMENT **2 :** an unaccompanied song for three or more solo usu. male voices that was esp. popular in the 18th and 19th centuries

2glee \"\ *vi* **gleed**; **gleed**; **gleeing**; **glees** [ME *gleen, gleyen, glien*] **1** *chiefly Scot* **a :** SQUINT **b :** to take a sidelong look **2** *chiefly Scot* **:** to take a look with one eye; *specif* **:** AIM

3glee \"\ *n* -s **1** *chiefly Scot* **a :** SQUINT **b :** a sidelong look **2** *chiefly Scot* **:** a look with one eye; *specif* **:** AIM

4glee \"\ *adj, chiefly Scot* **:** SQUINT-EYED

glee club *n* **:** a group organized for singing glees, part-songs, ballads, choral pieces

1gleed \'glēd\ *n* -s [ME *gleed, glede*, fr. OE *glēd*; akin to OHG *gluot* fire, glow, ON *glōth* ember, glowing coal; derivative fr. the root of OE *glōwan* to glow — more at GLOW] **1** *dial Brit* **:** a burning or glowing coal **:** EMBER **2** *dial Brit* **:** FIRE, FLAMES

2gleed \"\ *adj* [ME (Sc) *gleid*, fr. ME *gleyen* to squint + *-ed*] **1** *chiefly Scot* **:** affected with squint in one or both eyes **:** SQUINT-EYED **2** *chiefly Scot* **:** CROOKED, ASKEW

glee·ful \'glēfəl\ *adj* **:** full of glee **:** exuberantly or exultantly joyful **:** delightedly or triumphantly happy **:** GLAD, MIRTHFUL, MERRY ⟨a ~ romp in the countryside⟩ ⟨~ over the downfall of their enemies⟩ — **glee·ful·ly** \-fəlē, -li\ *adv* — **glee·ful·ness** *n* -ES

1gleek \'glēk\ *n* -s [MF *glic*, fr. MD *gelijc* equal, alike; akin to OE *gelīc* equal, alike — more at ALIKE] **1 :** a card game popular in England throughout the 16th to 18th centuries **2** *obs* **:** a group of three **:** TRIO

2gleek \"\ *n* -s [origin unknown] **1** *archaic* **a :** GIBE, JEST **b :** a practical joke **2** *archaic* **:** a flirtatious glance

3gleek \"\ *vb* -ED/-ING/-S *vt, obs* **:** to gain an advantage over (as by trickery) ~ *vi, archaic* **:** GIBE, JEST

glee·man \'glēmən\ *n, pl* **gleemen** [ME, fr. OE *glēoman*, fr. *glēo* entertainment, music + *man*] **:** a medieval usu. itinerant professional entertainer (as in England or Scotland) who sang songs often to his own accompaniment on a stringed instrument (as a harp), chanted or recited poetry, or related stories

glee·some \'glēsəm\ *adj, archaic* **:** GLEEFUL — **glee·some·ly** *adv, archaic* — **glee·some·ness** *n* -ES *archaic*

1gleet \'glēt, *usu* -ēd·+V\ *n* -s [ME *glet, glette* slimy or mucous matter, fr. MF *glete*, fr. L *glittus* sticky, viscous; akin to L *glut-, glus* glue — more at CLAY] **:** a chronic inflammation of a bodily orifice in man or animals usu. accompanied by an abnormal discharge from the orifice ⟨nasal ~⟩; *specif* **:** the discharge itself (as the urethral mucous discharge in gonorrhea)

2gleet \"\ *vi* -ED/-ING/-S *archaic* **:** to vent an abnormal discharge **:** discharge gleet

gleety \-ēd·ē, -ētī, |i\ *adj* -ER/-EST [*¹gleet* + *-y*] **:** having the appearance or characteristics of gleet ⟨a ~ discharge⟩

gleg \'gleg\ *adj* [ME, quick in perception, fr. ON *gløggr* clear, clear-sighted; akin to OE *glēaw* wise, OHG *glou* clever, Goth *glaggwo* exactly, and prob. to OE *glōwan* to glow — more at GLOW] **1** *chiefly Scot* **:** quick in perception and action **:** alert and nimble **2** *chiefly Scot* **:** having a keen edge **:** SHARP — **gleg·ly** *adv, chiefly Scot* — **gleg·ness** *n* -ES *chiefly Scot*

glei *var of* GLEY

glei·che·nia \glī'kēnēə\ *n, cap* [NL, fr. W. F. von *Gleichen* †1783 Ger. naturalist + NL *-ia*] **:** a genus (the type of the family Gleicheniaceae) of leptosporangiate ferns having sessile sporangia that lack an indusium and dehisce by a transverse annulus

gleich·schal·tung \'glīk,shäl(,)tuŋ, -,təŋ\ *n, pl* **gleich·schaltungen** \-,tuŋən, -,təŋ-\ *usu cap* [G, coordination, fr. *gleichschalten* to coordinate, fr. *gleich* equally, alike (fr. OHG *gilicho*, adv. of *gilīh* equal, alike) + *schalten* to govern, direct, fr. OHG *scaltan* to push; akin to OS *skaldan* to shove (a boat), OHG *scalta* boathook, ON *skalda* ferryboat, Gk *skallein* to hoe — more at LIKE, SHELL] **:** the act, process, or policy of achieving rigid and total coordination and uniformity (as in politics, culture, communication) by forcibly repressing or eliminating independence and freedom of thought, action, or expression **:** forced reduction to a common level **:** forced standardization or assimilation ⟨brutal *Gleichschaltung* by police methods⟩ ⟨the political *Gleichschaltung* of a reluctant adult population —Reinhard Bendix⟩

gleid \'glēd\ *var of* ¹GLEED

glei·za·tion \glā'zāshən\ *n* -s [*gley* + *-ize* + *-ation*] **:** the development of gley **:** conversion into gley

glen \'glen\ *n* -s [ME (Sc), valley, fr. (assumed) obs. ScGael *glenn* (whence ScGael *gleann*); akin to MIr *glend, glenn* valley, W *glyn*] **:** a secluded narrow valley **:** a narrow depression between mountains or hills

glen·gar·ry \glen'garē, -ri\ *or* **glengarry bonnet** *also* **glengarry cap** \(')=¦==-\ *n* -ES *often cap G* [*Glengarry*, valley in Inverness-shire, Scotland] **:** a woolen cap of Scottish origin typically having a crease in the crown from front to back and edges bound with ribbon that ends at the back in two small streamers

glengarry

glen·liv·et *or* **glen·liv·at** \glen'livət\ *n* -s *usu cap* [*Glenlivet*, Banffshire, Scotland, where it is manufactured] **:** a Scotch whiskey

glenn pepper *or* **glenn weed** \'glen-\ *n, usu cap G* [prob. fr. the name *Glenn*] **:** FIELD CRESS

gleno·humeral \¦gle(,)nō, -lē(-+\ *adj* [*gleno-* (fr. *glenoid*) + *humeral*] **:** of, relating to, or connecting the glenoid cavity and the humerus

glenoid \'gle,nȯid, -lē,-\ *also* **glenoi·dal** \(')=¦nȯidᵊl\ *adj* [*glenoid* fr. Gk *glēnoeidēs*, fr. *glēnē* socket of a joint, eyeball + *-oeidēs* -oid; *glenoidal* fr. *glenoid* + *-al*; perh. akin to OHG *kleini* delicate, dainty — more at CLEAN] **1 :** having the form of a smooth shallow depression — used chiefly of skeletal articulatory sockets **2 :** of or relating to the glenoid cavity or glenoid fossa

glenoid cavity *n* **:** the shallow cavity of the upper part of the scapula by which the humerus articulates with the shoulder girdle

glenoid fossa *n* **:** the depression in each lateral wall of the skull with which the mammalian mandible articulates

glen plaid *also* **glen check** \'glen,-\ *n, often cap G* **:** a twill pattern of broken checks in which stripes of two dark and two light yarns alternate with stripes of four dark and four light yarns and in which the same colors and design are used crosswise and lengthwise; *also* **:** a fabric that is woven in this pattern

1glent \'glent, 'glint\ *vi* -ED/-ING/-S [ME *glenten* to move quickly esp. in an oblique direction, strike something obliquely and glance aside, look sideways at something, gleam, of Scand origin; akin to ON *glettask* to utter taunts, Norw dial. *gletta* to look, Sw dial. *glänta* to clear up; akin to OHG *glanz* bright, Russ *glyadet'* to look, OE *geolu* yellow — more at YELLOW] **1** *dial Brit* **a :** to move quickly esp. in an oblique direction **b :** to strike something obliquely and glance aside **2** *dial Brit* **a :** to look askance **:** look sideways at something **3** *dial Brit* **:** GLEAM, FLASH, SHINE

2glent \"\ *n* -s [ME, fr. *glenten*] **1** *dial Brit* **a :** a quick look **b :** a quick movement **2** *dial Brit* **:** GLEAM, FLASH

glen·ur·quhart \gle'nərkərt\ *or* **glenurquhart plaid** *also* **glenurquhart check** \(')=¦==-\ *n* -s *often cap G* [*Glen Urquhart*, valley in Inverness-shire, Scotland] **:** GLEN PLAID

gless \'gles\ *Scot var of* GLASS

gles·site \'gle,sīt\ *n* -s [G *glessit*, fr. L *glaesum, glesum, glessum* amber + G *-it* -ite; L *glaesum, glesum, glessum* of Gmc origin; akin to OHG *glas* amber — more at GLASS] **:** a fossil resin resembling amber

glew *obs var of* GLUE

1gley \'glə̄i, 'glē\ *Scot var of* GLEE

2gley *also* **glei** \'glā\ *n* -s [Russ *glei* clay; akin to Pol *glej* muddy ground, OE *clǣg* clay — more at CLAY] **:** a bluish gray or olive-gray sticky layer of clay formed under the surface of certain waterlogged soils

gleyd \'glēd, 'glād\ *var of* ²GLEED

gleyde \'glīd\ *n* -s [origin unknown] **1** *dial Brit* **:** a decrepit old horse **:** NAG **2** *dial Brit* **:** a disagreeable old man **:** CURMUDGEON

gli- *or* **glio-** *comb form* [NL, fr. MGk *glia* glue — more at CLAY] **1 :** gliomatous ⟨*glio*blastoma⟩ ⟨*glio*myoma⟩ **2 :** neuroglial ⟨*glio*some⟩ ⟨*glio*cyte⟩ ⟨*gli*osis⟩ **3 :** embedded in a gelatinous matrix ⟨*glio*bacteria⟩ **4 :** substance resembling glue ⟨*gli*ode⟩

glia \'glīə, 'glēə\ *n* -s [NL, fr. MGk, glue] **:** NEUROGLIA — **gli·al** \-əl\ *adj*

-glia \,glēə, 'glīə, 'glēə\ *n comb form* -s [NL, fr. MGk *glia* glue] **:** neuroglia made up of a (specified) kind or size of element ⟨macro*glia*⟩ ⟨micro*glia*⟩

gli·a·din \'glīədᵊn\ *n* -s [It *gliadina*, fr. *gliad-* (fr. MGk *glia* glue + *-ina* -in] **:** PROLAMIN; *usu* **:** a prolamin found esp. in wheat and rye and obtained as a soft sticky material by extracting gluten with dilute alcohol

1glib \'glib\ *n* -s [IrGael] **:** a mass of hair worn thickly matted so as to overhang the forehead and eyes and constituting a manner of hair arrangement at one time customary among the men of Ireland

2glib \"\ *adj, usu* **glibber**; *usu* **glibbest** [prob. modif. of LG *glibberig* slippery, fr. MLG *glibberich*] **1** *archaic* **:** having a smooth or slippery surface ⟨the snow lies ~ as glass —Robert Browning⟩ **2 a :** marked by lack of constraint, stiffness, or formality **:** free and easy **:** UNFORCED, CASUAL, NONCHALANT ⟨the ~ congeniality of college life⟩ ⟨~ manners⟩ **b** (1) **:** marked by little or no forethought or preparation **:** OFFHAND, UNSTUDIED, IMPROMPTU ⟨quick ~ answers⟩ ⟨an account which poured from her lips with such ~ alacrity that it might have been memorized —Erle Stanley Gardner⟩ (2) **:** marked by hastiness and lack of requisite forethought and preparation **:** UNTHINKING, UNREFLECTING ⟨jumping to ~ conclusions⟩ **c** (1) **:** lacking depth and substance **:** SUPERFICIAL, SHALLOW, EMPTY ⟨~ generalizations⟩ (2) **:** too easily arrived at and basically inadequate **:** PAT ⟨mouthing ~ solutions to the problem⟩ (3) **:** too easily made, done, or produced **:** SLICK ⟨a ~ frothy comedy⟩ ⟨turning out one ~ book after another⟩ ⟨the tale is ~, preposterous —Anthony Boucher⟩ **3 a :** characterized by a propensity for, ability to use, or production of a smooth ready flow of words **:** VOLUBLE ⟨a ~ tongue⟩ ⟨a ~ speaker⟩; *esp* **:** facile in the use of words to a degree indicative of superficiality, trickery, or deceitfulness ⟨a ~ writer on economics⟩ ⟨~ politicians⟩ **b :** spoken or written in an overly smooth easy manner ⟨~ phrases⟩ **syn** see VOCAL

3glib \"\ *vt* **glibbed**; **glibbed**; **glibbing**; **glibs** *archaic* **:** to make smooth or slippery **:** LUBRICATE; *esp* **:** to cause (as the tongue) to move freely as if by oiling

4glib *vt* **glibbed**; **glibbed**; **glibbing**; **glibs** [prob. alter. of *lib*] *obs* **:** CASTRATE

glib·bery \'glibərē\ *adj* [prob. fr. LG *glibberig*] **1** *now chiefly dial* **:** SMOOTH, SLIPPERY **2** *now chiefly dial* **:** not trustworthy **:** UNRELIABLE

glib-gab·bet \'glib,gabət\ *adj* [*²glib* + Sc *-gabbet* having (such) a mouth, -mouthed, fr. *gab* mouth + *-et* -ed (vb. suffix or adj. suffix), fr. ME (Sc) *-it, -ed*, fr. ME *-ed* — more at GAB] *Scot* **:** GLIB-TONGUED

glib·ly *also* **glib** *adv* **:** in a glib manner: **a :** EASILY, SMOOTHLY, READILY **b :** VOLUBLY

glib·ness *n* -ES **:** the quality or state of being glib

glib-tongued \'=¦=\ *adj* **:** having a glib tongue **:** VOLUBLE

1glid·der \'glidə(r)\ *vt* -ED/-ING/-S [obs. *glidder*, adj., slippery, fr. (assumed) ME *glidder*, fr. OE *glidder, glider*; akin to OE *glīdan* to glide] *dial Eng* **:** to glaze over (as with ice)

2glidder \"\ *n* -s [fr. or akin to obs. *glidder*, adj.] *dial Brit* **:** a loose stone (as on a hillside)

glid·dery \-dəri\ *adj* [*¹glidder* + *-y*] *dial Eng* **:** SLIPPERY

1glide \'glīd\ *vb* **glided** \-dəd\ *or archaic* **glid** \'glid\ *also archaic* **glode** \'glōd\ **glided** *or archaic* **glid** *also archaic* **glode**; **gliding** \'glīdiŋ\ **glides** [ME *gliden*, fr. OE *glīdan*; akin to OHG *glītan* to glide, ON *gleithr* standing with legs far apart, and prob. to OE *geolu* yellow — more at YELLOW] *vi* **1 a :** to move smoothly, continuously, and effortlessly ⟨a canoe *gliding* over the still lake⟩ ⟨silvery fish *gliding* about in the depths of the pool⟩ ⟨snowy gulls *glided* through the blue of the sky⟩ **:** move with a quiet smoothness marked by little or no perceptible or distracting extraneous motion ⟨began *gliding* about with a tray full of glasses —Willa Cather⟩ ⟨watched the skiers ~ swiftly and silently down the slope⟩ **:** move lightly and silently ⟨*glided* out of the room as noiselessly as she had entered⟩ **b :** to move stealthily **:** move cautiously and furtively **:** SLIP, STEAL, CREEP ⟨*gliding* along the wall until they were out of sight⟩ **2 a :** to elapse gradually and imperceptibly ⟨hours *gliding* tranquilly by⟩ **b :** to pass or taper off into something different gradually and imperceptibly by slight progressive changes **:** MERGE ⟨feelings of hostility . . . ~ into those of peculiar courtesy —Archibald Alison⟩ **:** slip gradually into something ⟨*glided* into telling you the secret —Charles Dickens⟩ **3** *of an airplane* **:** to descend at a normal angle of attack with little or no thrust **4** *of the tongue* **:** to change position in the articulation of a glide **5 :** GLANCE *vi* 1b (2) ~ *vt* **1 :** to cause to glide ⟨*gliding* the airplane to a safe place to land⟩ ⟨*gliding* the boat over the water⟩ **2 :** to fly over in or as if in a glider ⟨wondered whether, if I got up enough momentum, I could . . . ~ the Atlantic —Richard Joseph⟩

2glide \"\ *n* -s **1 :** the action of gliding **:** a gliding movement; *specif* **:** the flight of a gliding aircraft ⟨saw the long ~ of the airplane⟩ **2 :** a calm stretch of shallow water flowing smoothly and gently ⟨fishing in the ~s of a stream⟩ **3 a :** PORTAMENTO 1 **b :** a nonsignificant sound produced by the passing of the vocal organs to or from the articulatory position of a speech sound; *specif* **:** the less prominent vowel or sound like a vowel in the articulation of two consecutive vowel sounds unequal in prominence (as the very brief \ē\ or \i\ sound of \y\ in \'yel\ *yell*) — see OFF-GLIDE, ON-GLIDE **4 a :** a fencing attack in which the forte of the weapon is pressed against the foible of the antagonist's weapon and the point then slid along his blade **b :** GLANCE 2c **5 :** a circular typically dome-shaped usu. metal button attached to the bottom of furniture legs or supports so as to provide a low-friction surface for easy movement of the furniture

glide-bomb \'=,=\ *vt* [*¹glide* + *bomb*, v.] **:** to bomb (a target) with a bomb released from a gliding airplane

glide bomb *also* **glider bomb** *n* [*glide bomb* fr. *¹glide* + *bomb*, n.; *glider bomb* fr. *glider* + *bomb*, n.] **:** a bomb fitted with airfoils so that it glides toward its target with or without a guidance system

glide·less \'glīdləs\ *adj* **:** having no glide ⟨a ~ sound⟩

glide path *also* **glide slope** *n* **:** the path of descent of an airplane as marked out by a radio beam along which a pilot may bring an airplane to a safe landing when flying on instruments; *also* **:** the radio beam that marks out such a path

glide plane *n* **:** a crystallographic plane of symmetry that requires identity of the structure of the crystal with its original configuration following the combination of reflection of the crystal across the plane with movement of the structural configuration parallel to the plane

glid·er \'glīdə(r)\ *n* -s [ME *glydare*, fr. *glyden, gliden* to glide + *-are, -er, -ere* -er] **1 :** one that glides: as **a :** an aircraft similar to an airplane but without an engine — compare SAILPLANE **b :** a flat powerboat of shallow draft and high speed **c :** a porch seat or lounge suspended from uprights of an underframe by means of short chains or metal straps at the corners so as to permit its swinging smoothly back and forth **2 :** something that aids gliding ⟨an anterior pair of wings used as ~s⟩; *specif* **:** GLIDE 5

glider 1c

gliderport \'=,=,=\ *n* **:** a landing place for gliders

gliding *adj* [ME *glidinge, gliding*, fr. *gliden* to glide + *-inge, -ing* -ing] **:** that glides **:** marked by gliding ⟨a ~ way of walking⟩ — **glid·ing·ly** *adv*

gliding angle *n* [*gliding* fr. gerund of *¹glide*] **:** the angle between the plane of the horizon and the path of a glider or airplane; *esp* **:** the least angle at which a glider or airplane will glide to earth in still air

gliding growth *n* **:** plant growth marked by the sliding of a cell wall over the surface of a cell or cells adjacent to it (as in the formation of new initials in the cambium) — called also *sliding growth;* compare INTRUSIVE GROWTH, SYMPLASTIC GROWTH

gliding joint *n* : ARTHRODIA

1gliff \'glif\ *vt* -ED/-ING/-S [ME *gliffen* to look quickly, glance] *dial Brit* : FRIGHTEN

2gliff \"\ *n* -S [E dial. (northern) *gliff*, v., to look quickly, glance, fr. ME *gliffen*] **1** *chiefly Scot* **a** : GLIMPSE **b** : a faint trace : SUGGESTION **2** *chiefly Scot* : a sudden fright : SCARE **3** *chiefly Scot* : a brief moment : INSTANT

gliff·ing \-fiŋ\ *n* -S [fr. gerund of E dial. (northern) *gliff*, v.] *Scot* : INSTANT

1glim \'glim\ *n* -S [perh. short for 2*glimmer*] **1** : GLIMMER ⟨not a ~ of hope —P.E.Green⟩ **2** *slang* : a brief look : GLANCE **3 a** (1) : something (as a lamp, flashlight, candle) that furnishes light (2) : ILLUMINATION; *esp* : illumination from a particular source of light ⟨~*s* from a half dozen hurricane lamps spotted a path to the far door —Richard Llewellyn⟩ **b** *archaic* : EYE

2glim \"\ *vt* **glimmed; glimmed; glimming; glims** *slang* : to take a look at : glance at : WATCH

gli·ma \'glēmə\ *n* -S [Icel *glīma*, fr. OIcel] : a wrestling technique whose object is to throw an opponent to the floor on his back

1glime \'glīm\ *vi* -ED/-ING/-S [origin unknown] *dial chiefly Brit* : to look obliquely at something : steal a glance

2glime \"\ *n* -S *dial chiefly Brit* : an oblique glance

1glim·mer \'glimə(r)\ *vi* **glimmered; glimmered; glimmering** \-m(ə)riŋ\ **glimmers** [ME *glimeren, glemeren;* akin to MHG *glim* spark, *glimmen* to glow, *glimmern* to glow, ON *gljā* to glitter — more at GLEAM] **1 a** : to emit feeble or intermittent rays of light : shine faintly or unsteadily ⟨flickering candles ~*ed* in the windows of the old inn⟩ ⟨just below the intruder's pockmarked face ~*ed* the barrel of an automatic pistol —F.V.W.Mason⟩ **b** : to shimmer softly ⟨her white satin dress ~*ed* in the dusk⟩ **2** : to appear indistinctly with or as if with a faintly luminous quality ⟨the chalk cliffs ~*ed* far off in the night⟩

2glimmer \"\ *n* -S **1 a** : a feeble or intermittent light : a faint or unsteady shining ⟨the space beyond the ~ of her lantern —Ellen Glasgow⟩ ⟨the first ~ of dawn⟩ **b** : a soft shimmer ⟨the moonlit ~ of the pool⟩ **2 a** : a dim perception : a faint idea ⟨the interview gave them a ~ of what they could expect⟩ **b** : a vague manifestation or indication : INTIMATION, INKLING ⟨had given the world only a ~ of her potential as a gay slaughterer of convention —Bernard Kalb⟩ **c** : an indistinct appearance marked by or as if by a faintly luminous quality ⟨he saw the ~ of her face in the shadow —R.P.Warren⟩ **3** : a small amount or degree : a faint trace : BIT ⟨a ~ of hope showing in his eyes —T.B.Costain⟩ ⟨a ~ of intelligence⟩

3glimmer \"\ *n* -S [G, back-formation fr. *glimmern* to glow, fr. MHG] : MICA

glimmer gowk *n, dial Eng* : OWL

glimmer ice *n* : ice newly formed in cracks, holes, or surface puddles of other ice

1glimmering *adj* [ME *glimeringe, glimering*, fr. *glimeren* to glimmer + *-inge, -ing* -ing (v. suffix or adj. suffix)] : that glimmers ⟨the ~ mist of a spring rain splashed by sun and streaked by rainbow —Claudia Cassidy⟩ — **glim·mer·ing·ly** *adv*

2glimmering *n* -S [ME *glimeringe, glimering*, fr. *glimeren* to glimmer + *-inge, -ing* -ing (n. suffix)] : GLIMMER ⟨the last faint ~*s* of twilight —T.L.Peacock⟩ ⟨a ~ of happiness —W.R. Burnett⟩ ⟨~*s* of economic theory in the writings of the Greeks —Leo Fishman⟩

glim·mery \-m(ə)rē\ *adj* [1*glimmer* + *-y*] : tending to glimmer or having an effect suggestive of glimmering ⟨a peculiar ~ color⟩

1glimpse \'glim(p)s\ *vb* -ED/-ING/-S [ME *glimsen;* akin to MHG *glimsen* to glimmer, *glim* spark] *vi* **1** *archaic* : GLIMMER **2** : to take a brief look : give a passing glance ⟨he *glimpsed* at the letter, then threw it impatiently aside⟩ ~ *vt* **1** *archaic* : to furnish a brief look at **2** : to get a brief look at : see momentarily or incompletely ⟨*glimpsed* the man as he sped through the forest⟩ ⟨from the fragments of sculpture that remain we can ~ the strength and beauty of the figures that adorned the temples —W.K.Ferguson⟩ — **glimps·er** \-sə(r)\ *n* -S

2glimpse \"\ *n* -S **1** *archaic* : GLIMMER **2** : a brief fleeting look : a momentary or incomplete view ⟨an occasional ~ of her husband's face behind the morning newspaper —Grace Nagle⟩ ⟨had interesting ~*s* of them as they went in and out of the various cabins —Joseph Conrad⟩

1glint \'glint\ *vb* -ED/-ING/-S [ME *glinten*, alter. of *glenten* — more at GLENT] *vi* **1 a** *archaic* : to move rapidly and usu. obliquely; *specif* : to glance off an object struck ⟨the majority of the shells struck armor and simply ~*ed* off —W.A.M. Goode⟩ **b** *of rays of light* : to strike a reflecting surface obliquely and dart out at an angle ⟨light gleaming and sparkling on the sea . . . ~*ing* from the sand —J.L.Lowes⟩ **2 a** : to shine usu. by reflection: (1) : to shine with tiny bright flashes : SPARKLE ⟨the slightly ruffled surface of the lake was ~*ing* brilliantly in the morning sunlight⟩ ⟨little tin cups that ~ like bright money —Lillian Smith⟩ ⟨you can see the rocks and pebbles ~*ing* under the shimmering veil of water —William Goyen⟩ (2) : to shine with a hard bright metallic luster of scattered light : GLITTER ⟨eyes ~*ing* with anger⟩ ⟨sunlight ~*ed* on the vicious edges of the bottle fragments —Harriet La Barre⟩ (3) : to shine with a subdued scattered light : GLEAM ⟨moonlight ~*ed* on the brass bed —Sloane Wilson⟩ **b** : to emit scattered rays of light ⟨held a magnifying glass over my hand and let the sun ~ through —Charles Spielberger⟩ **3** : to look quickly or briefly : PEEP **4** : to appear briefly, faintly, or transiently ⟨across the river the village . . . ~*ed* through the palms —H.O.Forbes⟩ ~ *vt* : to cause to glint : reflect in tiny flashes or gleams ⟨the dark surface of the water caught the lights of the boat and ~*ed* them brightly back⟩

2glint \"\ *n* -S **1 a** (1) : a tiny bright usu. reflected flash of light : SPARKLE ⟨watched the twin ~*s* of his eyeglasses⟩ (2) : a hard bright metallic point of light ⟨the singularly venomous ~ in her eye —Ngaio Marsh⟩ (3) : a small point of subdued light : GLEAM ⟨~*s* of ruddy light playing over the polished dark mahogany⟩ **b** : a ray of scattered light ⟨the little room was dusky, save for a narrow ~ streaming through the not quite closed door of the room —Charles Dickens⟩ **c** (1) : a shining appearance produced by tiny bright scattered flashes : sparkling brightness ⟨the ~ of unshed tears blurring the clear bright blue of his eyes —Marcia Davenport⟩ ⟨the ~ of spring and autumn sunlight —Donn Byrne⟩ (2) : a glittering metallic luster ⟨his bright eyes burning with a sharp wild ~ of madness —Thomas Wolfe⟩ (3) : a subdued radiance : GLEAMING ⟨the ~ of moonlight through the leaves⟩ **2** *archaic* : GLANCE, GLIMPSE **3** : a brief, faint, or transient appearance or manifestation (as of a quality) ⟨thought I detected a ~ of recognition in her expression⟩

glint o' gold : a moderate yellow that is slightly stronger than mustard yellow and duller than colonial yellow

glio- — see GLI-

glio·blas·to·ma \,glī(,)ō,bla'stōmə\ *n, pl* **glioblastomas** \-məz\ *or* **glioblastoma·ta** \-məd·ə\ [NL, fr. *gli-* + *blast-* + *-oma*] : SPONGIOBLASTOMA

gli·o·cla·di·um \,glīō'klādēəm\ *n, cap* [NL, fr. *gli-* + *-cladium* (fr. Gk *klados* branch) — more at GLADIATOR] : a genus of molds resembling those of the genus *Penicillium* but with the conidia of a spore head becoming surrounded by a slimy deposit that binds them into a rounded mass

gli·o·cyte \'glīō,sīt\ *n* -S [*gli-* + *-cyte*] : a neuroglial cell

gli·o·ma \glī'ōmə\ *n, pl* **gliomas** \-məz\ *or* **glioma·ta** \-məd·ə\ [NL, fr. MGk *glia* glue + NL *-oma* — more at CLAY] : a tumor arising from neuroglia — **gli·o·ma·to·sis** \(,)glī-,ōmə'tōsəs\ *n, pl* **gliomato·ses** \-ō,sēz\ — **gli·oma·tous** \(')glī¦ämәd·əs, -¦ōm-\ *adj*

gli·o·sis \glī'ōsəs\ *n, pl* **glio·ses** \-ō,sēz\ [NL, fr. *gli-* + *-osis*] : excessive development of neuroglia esp. interstitially — compare GLIOMA — **gli·ot·ic** \(')glī¦äd·ik\ *adj*

glio·toxin \¦glīō+\ *n* [ISV *glio-* (fr. NL *Gliocladium*) + *toxin*] : a crystalline antibiotic $C_{13}H_{14}N_2O_4S_2$ that is toxic to higher animals as well as to animal and plant pathogens and that is produced by various fungi esp. of the genus *Gliocladium*

gli·res \'glī,rēz\ *n pl, cap* [NL, fr. L, pl. of *glir-, glis* dormouse] : a superorder or other division of Eutheria comprising the typical rodents and the lagomorph rodents and including the orders Rodentia (sense 1) and Lagomorpha

glir·i·cid·ia \,glirə'sidēə\ *n, cap* [NL, fr. *gliri-* (fr. NL *Glires*) + L *-cida* -cide + NL *-ia*] : a genus of low-branching trees (family Leguminosae) with odd-pinnate leaves having 7 to 15 large leaflets, pink flowers borne in great profusion, dark durable wood, and roots that together with the leaves are believed to be poisonous to mice and rats

1glirid \'glirəd, -līr-\ *adj* [NL *Gliridae*] : of or relating to the Gliridae

2glirid \"\ *n* -S : a rodent of the family Gliridae : DORMOUSE

glir·i·dae \'glirə,dē\ *n pl, cap* [NL, fr. *Glir-, Glis*, type genus + *-idae*] : a family of widely distributed Old World myomorph rodents including the dormice

glir·i·form \'glirə,fȯrm\ *adj* [*glir-* (fr. NL *Glires*) + *-iform*] **1** : resembling a rodent **2** *of incisor teeth* : having the form characteristic of the rodents

gli·rine \'glī,rīn\ *adj* [*glir-* (fr. NL *Glires*) + *-ine*] : of or relating to the Glires

glis \'glis\ *n, cap* [NL *Glir-, Glis*, fr. L *glir-, glis* dormouse — more at GALEA] : a genus comprising the common Old World dormice and being the type of the family Gliridae

1glisk \'glisk\ *n* -S [origin unknown] **1** *chiefly Scot* : GLIMPSE **2** *chiefly Scot* : GLEAM **3** *chiefly Scot* : a brief moment : INSTANT

2glisk \"\ *vb* -ED/-ING/-S *vt, chiefly Scot* : to glance at : look at cursorily ~ *vi, chiefly Scot* : to get a glimpse

gliss \'glis\ *n* -ES [by shortening] *slang* : GLISSANDO

1glis·sade \glə'säd, glē'-, -säd *sometimes* -sād\ *vi* -ED/-ING/-S [F *glissade*, n.] **1 a** : to slide by design or with control; *specif* : to make a controlled slide in a standing or sitting position without skis, toboggans, or other similar devices down a snow-covered slope ⟨the exhilaration of *glissading* down the side of a mountain⟩ **b** : to slide or slip haphazardly or without control ⟨rock rubble *glissading* down from the crumbling heights —C.A.Cotton⟩ **2** : to move along smoothly and effortlessly : GLIDE ⟨the boat was light and buoyant, *glissading* gracefully over each swell in the lake⟩; *specif* : to perform a ballet glissade — **glis·sad·er** \-də(r)\ *n* -S

2glissade \"\ *n* -S [F, social error, slip, action of glissading, landslide, gliding step in ballet, glissando, fr. MF, social error, fr. *glisser* to slip, slide (fr. OF *glicier*, alter. of *glier*, fr. an OFrk verb akin to OHG *glītan* to glide) + *-ade* — more at GLIDE] **1 a** : the action of glissading ⟨a long ~ to the foot of the mountain⟩ **b** : a mass of glissading material ⟨her foot sent a tiny ~ of snow slithering down the bank —Victor Canning⟩ **c** : a slope suitable for glissading ⟨at last discovered a good ~⟩ **2** : a gliding step in ballet **3** : GLISSANDO

1glis·san·do \glə'sän(,)dō, glē'-\ *n* [prob. modif. (influenced by It *-ando* as in *accelerando*) of F *glissade*, n.] **1** *pl* **glissan·di** \-dē\ *or* **glissandos** **a** : a rapid series of consecutive notes played on a piano, harp, or other similar instrument by sliding one or more fingers across adjacent keys or strings **b** (1) : a rapid series of chromatic notes played on a violin or other similar instrument by minute interruptions in sliding the finger along the string being bowed (2) : a series of notes (as on a clarinet) forming a nearly unbroken change of pitch **c** : PORTAMENTO 1 **2** -S : the technique of gradually increasing the electric current in the application of electroshock so as to minimize the shock of the total current applied

2glissando \"\ *adv* (*or adj*) : in the manner of a glissando — used as a direction in music

glis·sé \glə'sā, glē'-\ *n* -S [F, fr. past part. of *glisser* to slip, slide] : GLISSADE

glis·sile \'glisəl\ *adj* [F *glisser* to slip, slide + E *-ile*] : capable of gliding — used esp. of a dislocation or other fault in a crystal — compare SESSILE

glis·son's capsule \'glisᵊnz-\ *n, usu cap G* [after Francis *Glisson* †1677 Eng. physician] : an investment of loose connective tissue entering the liver with the portal vessels and sheathing the larger vessels in their course through the organ

1glis·ten \'glisᵊn\ *vi* **glistened; glistened; glistening** \-s(ᵊ)niŋ\ **glistens** [ME *glistnen, glisnen*, fr. OE *glisnian;* akin to OE *glisian* to glitter, Sw dial. *glīsa* to peep out, W *glwys* beautiful, OE *geolu* yellow — more at YELLOW] : to shine brightly usu. by reflection with a sparkling radiance ⟨early-morning dew ~*ing* on the grass⟩ ⟨a crust of snow ~*ing* in the sun⟩ or with the sleek shininess of or suggestive of a wet or oiled surface ⟨the drenched streets of the brightly lit city ~*ed* in the night⟩ ⟨the ~*ing* bodies of the swimmers⟩ ⟨her eyes were ~*ing* with happiness⟩ or with a glossy lustrousness ⟨brushed the dog's coat until it ~*ed*⟩

2glisten \"\ *n* -S : the quality or state of glistening ⟨the brass of the clock was polished to a mirrorlike ~ —J.C.Lincoln⟩

glis·ten·ing·ly *adv* [*glistening* (pres. part. of 1*glisten*) + *-ly*] : in a glistening manner ⟨black hair that shone ~⟩

1glis·ter \'glistə(r)\ *vi* **glistered; glistered; glistering** \-t(ə)riŋ\ **glisters** [ME *glistren;* akin to OE *glisian* to glitter] : GLISTEN

2glister \"\ *n* -S : GLISTEN

glis·ter·ing·ly *adv* [*glistering* (fr. pres. part. of 1*glister*) + *-ly*] : GLISTENINGLY

1glit·ter \'glid·ə(r), -itə-\ *vb* -ED/-ING/-S [ME *gliteren, gleteren*, fr. ON *glitra;* akin to OE *glitenian* to glitter, OHG *glīzan* to shine, ON *glita* to glitter, Goth *glitmunjan* to glisten, Gk *chlidē* luxury, effeminacy, OE *geolu* yellow — more at YELLOW] *vi* **1** : to shine resplendently usu. by reflection with many quick small flashes of brilliant light ⟨a crown of jewels ~*ed* on her head⟩ ⟨a landscape ~*ing* with sun and rain —Ambrose Bierce⟩ or with a hard bright often metallic luster made up of many small scattered rapidly appearing and disappearing points of light ⟨dragonflies darting about and ~*ing* iridescently in the bright sunlight⟩ ⟨the horses tossed their heads, their well-oiled hooves ~*ing* as they shifted their feet nervously —Dorothy C. Fisher⟩ ⟨the sun of the late summer ~*ed* on the gold cups —Edith Sitwell⟩ or with a dazzling brilliance marked by stabbing rays of light ⟨shields and swords polished like mirrors ~*ed* in the morning sun⟩ ⟨sequins ~*ing* under the spotlights⟩ and often with a showy or gaudy effect ⟨the tree was lavishly hung with tinsel that quivered and ~*ed*⟩ : sparkle with twinkling points of light ⟨myriads of stars that ~*ed* in the dark and frigid lonesomeness of the sky⟩ ⟨far off they could see the lights of the city ~*ing* in the night⟩ : shine with a hard cold glassy brilliance marked by quick intermittent rapidly successive points of intense light ⟨her little eyes ~*ed* cruelly —Haldane Macfall⟩ **2** : to be brilliantly or compellingly attractive usu. in a superficial way : make a brilliant appearance or impression ⟨the possibility of fame in the theater ~*ed* before them⟩ ~ *vt* **1** : to cause to glitter ⟨brilliant stars ~*ing* the sky⟩ **2** : to trim, sprinkle, or cover with something that glitters ⟨a belt that was ~*ed* with rhinestones⟩

2glitter \"\ *n* -S **1 a** : glittering brilliancy ⟨a great ~ of sunlight on the blue water —Ira Wolfert⟩ : glittering showiness or gaudiness ⟨the ~ of opening night at the opera⟩ ⟨the ~ of costume jewelry⟩ : glittering brightness ⟨the ~ of icicles⟩ ⟨the unnerving ~ of a glass eye —Weston La Barre⟩ **b** : glittering attractiveness ⟨the ~ of a career in the foreign service⟩ **2** : small glittering objects (as sequins, rhinestones) or tiny glittering bits (as of tinsel, glass) used for ornamentation ⟨a neckline trimmed with ~⟩ or decoration ⟨at the base of the Christmas tree was a snowy sheet sprinkled with ~⟩

glit·ter·ance \-ərən(t)s\ *n* -S [1*glitter* + *-ance*] : GLITTER

glittering *adj* [fr. pres. part. of 1*glitter*] **1** : that glitters: **a** : RESPLENDENT, BRILLIANT ⟨a ~ costume⟩ ⟨~ society⟩ **b** : SPARKLING, TWINKLING ⟨a ~ sky⟩ **c** : shining glassily with a play of shifting points of intense light ⟨feverish ~ eyes⟩ **d** : SHOWY, GAUDY ⟨~ ornaments⟩ **2 a** : brilliantly or compellingly attractive usu. in a superficial way ⟨a ~ personality⟩ **b** : superficially convincing in a smoothly misleading or deceptive way : misleadingly or deceptively appealing ⟨the ~ generalities of propaganda⟩ — **glit·ter·ing·ly** *adv*

glit·tery \-ərē,-əri\ *adj* [2*glitter* + *-y*] : GLITTERING; *esp* : having much glitter ⟨~ chandeliers⟩

gli·wi·ce \glē'vētsə\ *adj, usu cap* [fr. *Gliwice*, city in Poland] : of or from the city of Gliwice, Poland : of the kind or style prevalent in Gliwice

1gloam \'glōm\ *vi* -ED/-ING/-S [back-formation fr. *gloaming*] *chiefly Scot* : to become twilight : grow toward dark : become dusk

2gloam \"\ *n* -S *archaic* : TWILIGHT, DUSK

gloam·ing \'glōmiŋ, -mēŋ\ *n* -S [ME (Sc) *gloming*, fr. OE *glōmung*, fr. *glōm* twilight; akin to OE *glōwan* to glow — more at GLOW] : TWILIGHT, DUSK ⟨leaving the robin to sing in the ~ —C.G.Glover⟩

1gloat \'glōt, *usu* -ōd·+V\ *vi* -ED/-ING/-S [prob. of Scand origin; akin to ON *glotta* to grin scornfully, Sw *glutta* to peep; akin to MHG *glotzen* to stare wide-eyed, OE *geolu* yellow — more at YELLOW] **1** *obs* **a** : to look or gaze at something indirectly or furtively **b** : to look or gaze at something admiringly or affectionately **2** : to look at, gaze at, or think about something with great self-satisfaction or intense often passionate gratification or gleefully triumphant joy ⟨a miser ~*ing* over his gold⟩ ⟨always ready to ~ over a new victory⟩ : linger over or dwell upon something with extreme often evil delight : REVEL ⟨a vision of demons ~*ing* over the tortures of the damned⟩ ⟨~*ing* over every detail of the murder⟩ : exult over something with intense often malicious pleasure ⟨~*ed* at his discomfiture⟩ ⟨used to make wax images of the vital organs of a hated person, and hold them over a fire, ~*ing* to see them drip —Emma Hawkridge⟩ **syn** see GAZE

2gloat \"\ *n* -S **1 a** : the act of gloating ⟨the accomplishments of a great hunter, told without ~, without passion —Robert Bean⟩ **b** : an outward indication of gloating ⟨to watch the ~ in his eye —John Galsworthy⟩ **2** : a feeling of triumphant often malicious satisfaction or joy ⟨enjoying a ~ over his success⟩

gloat·ing·ly *adv* [*gloating* (pres. part. of 1*gloat*) + *-ly*] : in a gloating manner ⟨spoke ~ of the number of people he had swindled⟩

glob \'gläb\ *n* -S [perh. blend of *globe* and *blob*] **1 a** : a small drop : GLOBULE, BLOB ⟨tiny ~*s* of mercury⟩ ⟨spattered ~*s* of ink⟩ **b** : a lumpish usu. rounded mass of usu. large size ⟨threw ~*s* of mud at them⟩ ⟨a ~ of rice⟩ ⟨heaped the shortcake with great ~*s* of whipped cream⟩ **2** : a touch, smear, or splash esp. of paint ⟨warm and appetizing ~*s* of color on the otherwise bleak and functional walls —Irwin Shaw⟩

glob·al \'glōbəl\ *adj* **1** : having the shape of a globe : SPHERICAL ⟨the earth is a ~ mass⟩ **2 a** (1) : of, relating to, or involving the entire world ⟨~ economic problems⟩ ⟨~ health conditions⟩ ⟨~ warfare⟩ (2) : including or adapted to the entire world ⟨~ plans for peace⟩ ⟨a ~ point of view⟩ ⟨~ strategy⟩ : not narrow or provincial : unrestricted in outlook or application : BROAD, UNIVERSAL ⟨a philosophy which takes a ~ view —Alan Gewirth⟩ (3) : distributed over or extending throughout the entire world : WORLDWIDE ⟨~ airlines⟩ ⟨a system of ~ communication⟩ : ranging over or around the entire world ⟨~ travelers⟩ ⟨~ bombers⟩ **b** : of, relating to, or involving the globe of the eye ⟨~ anesthesia in cataract surgery⟩ **3 a** (1) : COMPREHENSIVE, ALL-INCLUSIVE, GRAND ⟨the ~ total of national income in the U. S.⟩ : OVERALL, TOTAL ⟨limiting the ~ tonnage of that country's navy⟩ ⟨the ~ output of a factory⟩ (2) : 3BLANKET 1 ⟨a ~ allocation of funds⟩ (3) : exhaustively complete ⟨a catalog noted for its ~ coverage of new recordings⟩ **b** (1) : of, relating to, or constituting an organic whole : not divided into parts : not fractionalized : UNIFIED, ORGANISMIC ⟨the newer psychiatry seeks to understand in a ~ way the dynamic structure of the patient's personality —*Psychological Abstracts*⟩ : emphasizing a totality rather than the constitutive elements of a totality ⟨the ~ method of reading that aims at immediate recognition of whole words⟩ (2) : of, relating to, or consisting of similar or identical parts : HOMOGENEOUS ⟨a country trying to perfect a ~ form of social community⟩ (3) : not admitting a choice : solidly uniform : MONOLITHIC ⟨confronted with a ~ list of political candidates⟩ **c** : marked by absence of particularizing detail : simple and highly undifferentiated : GENERALIZED ⟨~ perceptions of the world outside the self⟩ ⟨the typically ~ nature of primitive art⟩ — **glob·al·ly** \-bəlē, -li\ *adv*

glob·al·ism \-bə,lizəm\ *n* -S **1** : GLOBALIZATION **2** : a policy or system favoring or promoting globalization ⟨proponents of ~ as a means of safeguarding national security⟩

glob·al·ist \-ˌləst\ *n* -S : one that favors or advocates globalism

glo·bal·i·ty \glō'baləd·ē\ *n* -ES : the condition of being global ⟨the ~ of the war —Frank Gervasi⟩

glob·al·iza·tion \,glōbələ'zāshən, -,lī'z-\ *n* -S : the act of globalizing or condition of being globalized

glob·al·ize \'==,līz\ *vt* -ED/-ING/-S : to make global; *esp* : to make worldwide in scope or application ⟨*globalizing* democracy —O.L.Reiser & Blodwen Davies⟩

glo·bate \'glō,bāt\ *adj* [L *globatus*, past part. of *globare* to make into a ball, fr. *globus* ball] : GLOBULAR 1a

glo·bat·ed \-ād·əd\ *adj* [L *globat*us + E *-ed*] *archaic* : formed into a globe

glob·by \'gläbē\ *adj, usu* -ER/-EST [*glob* + *-y*] : full of globs ⟨the paint would not spread evenly and the finished product looked ~⟩

1globe \'glōb\ *n* -S [MF, fr. L *globus* — more at CLIP] **1** : something that is spherical or rounded : SPHERE, BALL: as **a** (1) : a round typically hollow and metal ball that has a map of the earth drawn on it and that is usu. set so as to be rotatable at an angle corresponding to the inclination of the earth's axis ⟨rotated the terrestrial ~ until the crimson triangle of India was opposite their eyes —Aldous Huxley⟩ (2) : a similar ball that shows the configurations of the heavens (as the location and arrangement of the constellations) ⟨referring to a celestial ~ during the lecture⟩ **b** : PLANET ⟨still undiscovered ~*s* in space⟩; *esp* : EARTH — usu. used with *the* or *this* ⟨journeys over much of the ~ —R.A.Cordell⟩ ⟨every habitable part of this ~⟩ ⟨airglow appears to be present at all times and is distributed over the entire ~ —C.T.Elvey⟩ **c** : a golden ball carried by sovereigns as an emblem of authority : ORB 1c(3) ⟨His the scepter, crown, and ~ —P.B.Shelley⟩ **d** : a spherical or rounded typically glass vessel (as a fishbowl) or covering (as a lampshade) or housing (as an electric light bulb) **e** : EYEBALL **2** *obs* : a closely massed group or compact body

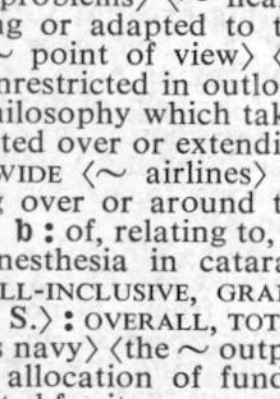

globe 1a(1)

2globe \"\ *vb* -ED/-ING/-S *vt, archaic* : to form into a globe ~ *vi, archaic* : to appear as a globe : take the form of a globe

globe amaranth *n* : an Indian herb (*Gomphrena globosa*) often cultivated for its globose flower heads that can be dried with nearly full retention of their color

globe animalcule *n* : an organism of the genus *Volvox*

globe artichoke *n* : ARTICHOKE 1, 2

globed *adj* [fr. past part. of 2*globe*] **1** : having the form of a globe ⟨the rocket burst into ~ masses of fire⟩ **2** : provided with a globe ⟨~ lamps burning with a yellow glow⟩

globe daisy *n* : a plant of the genus *Globularia*

globefish \'=,=\ *n* **1** : any of numerous chiefly tropical marine fishes forming the family Tetraodontidae of the order Plectognathi which can distend themselves to a globular form and float belly upward on the surface and most species of which are highly poisonous because of a powerful gastrointestinal irritant contained esp. in the skin and viscera — called also *balloonfish, puffer* **2** : OCEAN SUNFISH

globeflower \'=,=\ *n* : a plant with globose flowers or flower clusters: as **a** : a plant of the genus *Trollius* with globose yellow flowers **b** : GLOBE DAISY **c** : BUTTONBUSH **d** : JAPANESE ROSE 1

globe joint *n* : BALL-AND-SOCKET JOINT

globe lichen *n* : a lichen having globular fruiting bodies

globe lightning *n* : BALL LIGHTNING

globe mallow *n* : a plant of the genus *Sphaeralcea*

globe sight *n* : a front sight (as for a rifle) consisting of a small ball or a disk with a hole in it placed on the top of a pin

globe thistle *n* **1** : ARTICHOKE 1 **2** : a plant of the genus *Echinops*

1globe–trot \'=,=\ *vi* [back-formation fr. *globe-trotter*] : to do globe-trotting ⟨an economical way to *globe-trot* —*Better Homes & Gardens*⟩

2globe–trot \"\ *n* : a globe-trotting journey ⟨nearing the end of a three-month *globe-trot* —*Time*⟩

globe–trotter \'=,==\ *n* [1*globe* + *trotter*] : one that does globe-trotting esp. often or habitually ⟨a confirmed adventurer and *globe-trotter*⟩

¹globe-trotting \ˈ=,==\ *n* [¹*globe* + *trotting*, fr. gerund of *trot*, v.] **:** traveling about to many or widely separated countries esp. in a hurried or cursory manner and typically for the sake of sightseeing **:** traveling widely throughout the world ⟨travel bureaus that emphasize the joys of *globe-trotting*⟩

²globe-trotting \ˈ=,==\ *adj* **:** marked by, inclined toward, or given to globe-trotting ⟨long *globe-trotting* trips⟩ ⟨*globe-trotting* authors —Bennett Cerf⟩

globe tulip *n* **:** an herb of the genus *Calochortus*

globe valve *n* **:** a valve enclosed in a globular chamber

globical *adj* [¹*globe* + *-ical*] *obs* **:** GLOBULAR 1a

glo·bi·ceph·a·la \ˌglōbəˈsefələ\ *n, cap* [NL, fr. *globi-* (fr. L *globus* ball) + *-cephala* (fr. Gk *kephalē* head) — more at GLOBE, CEPHALIC] **:** a genus of rather small dark-colored toothed whales related to the grampus and killer whale and comprising the blackfish

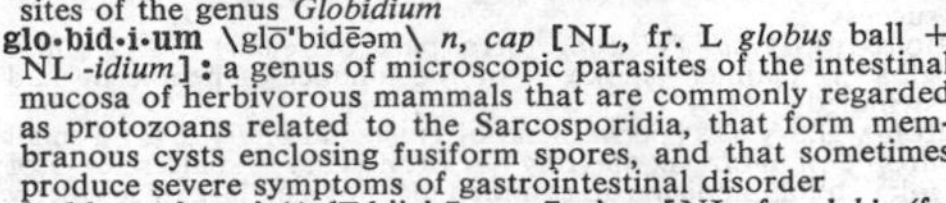

globe valve

glo·bid·i·al \(ˈ)glōˈbidēəl\ *adj* [NL *Globidium* + E *-al*] **:** of, relating to, or produced by parasites of the genus *Globidium* ⟨~ cysts⟩

glo·bid·i·o·sis \(ˌ)=,=ēˈōsəs\ *n, pl* **globidio·ses** \-ō,sēz\ [NL, fr. *Globidium* + *-osis*] **:** infection with or disease caused by parasites of the genus *Globidium*

glo·bid·i·um \glōˈbidēəm\ *n, cap* [NL, fr. L *globus* ball + NL *-idium*] **:** a genus of microscopic parasites of the intestinal mucosa of herbivorous mammals that are commonly regarded as protozoans related to the Sarcosporidia, that form membranous cysts enclosing fusiform spores, and that sometimes produce severe symptoms of gastrointestinal disorder

glo·big·e·ri·na \(ˌ)glō,bijəˈrīnə, -rēnə\ *n* [NL, fr. *globi-* (fr. L *globus* ball) + *ger-* (fr. L *gerere* to carry, bear) + *-ina* — more at CAST] **1** *cap* **:** a genus (the type of the family Globigerinidae) of foraminifers having calcareous shells and living near the surface of the sea **2** *pl* **globigeri·nae** \-ī(,)nē, -ē,nī\ *also* **globigerinas a :** a foraminifer of the genus *Globigerina* **b :** the shell of a globigerina

glo·big·er·i·nal \=ˌ==ˈrīnᵊl, -rēnᵊl\ *adj* [NL *Globigerina* + E *-al*] **:** GLOBIGERINE

globigerina ooze *n* **:** a layer of soft mud made up in large part of the shells of dead globigerinae and covering great areas of the sea bottom at depths of 1000 to 3000 feet

glo·big·er·ine \glōˈbijə,rīn, -,rən\ *adj* [NL *Globigerina*] **:** of, relating to, or derived from *Globigerina* or globigerinae ⟨~ muds⟩

glo·bin \ˈglōbən\ *n* -s [ISV *glob-* (fr. L *globus* ball) + *-in*; orig. formed in G] **:** a colorless protein obtained by removal of heme from a hemoglobin or similar conjugated protein

globing *pres 3d sing of* GLOBE

globin zinc insulin *n* **:** a preparation for treating diabetes mellitus that contains insulin modified by the addition of zinc chloride and globin obtained from beef blood and is intermediate in duration of action between regular insulin and protamine zinc insulin

glo·bi·o·ceph·a·la \ˌglōbē(ˌ)ōˈsefələ\ *or* **glo·bi·o·ceph·a·lus** \-ləs\ [NL, fr. *globi-* (fr. L *globus* ball) + *-o-* + *-cephala* (fr. Gk *kephalē* head) *or -cephalus*] *syn of* GLOBICEPHALA

globo- *comb form* [NL, fr. L *globus* ball] **1 a :** global **:** spherical ⟨globocell⟩ **:** globular ⟨*globo*sphaerite⟩ — often joined to second element with a hyphen ⟨*globo*-cumulus⟩ **b :** worldwide ⟨*globo*-historical⟩ **2 :** globe **:** sphere ⟨*globo*ferous⟩

glo·boid \ˈglō,bȯid\ *n or adj* [ISV *glob-* (fr. L *globus* ball) + *-oid*] **:** SPHEROID

glo·bose \ˈglō,bōs, =ˈ=\ *adj* [L *globosus*, fr. *globus* + *-osus* -ose] **:** GLOBULAR 1a — **glo·bose·ly** *adv*

glo·bos·i·ty \glōˈbäsəd-ē\ *n* -ES [LL *globositat-, globositas*, fr. L *globosus* globose + *-itat-, -itas* -ity] **:** the quality or state of being globose ⟨the ~ of the earth⟩

glo·bous \ˈglōbəs\ *adj* [obs. F or L; obs. F *globeux*, fr. L *globosus*] *archaic* **:** GLOBULAR 1a

globs *pl of* GLOB

glob·u·lar \ˈgläbyələ(r)\ *adj* [L *globulus* globule + E *-ar*] **1 a :** having the shape of a globe or globule **:** round like a ball **:** wholly or approximately spherical **:** GLOBOSE ⟨little ~ houses, like mud-wasp nests —Zane Grey⟩ **b :** fully rounded out **:** having nothing lacking **:** WHOLE, ENTIRE ⟨for the sake of ~ completeness —H.J.Mackinder⟩ **c :** worldwide in extent or range **:** GLOBAL ⟨~ air travel⟩ **2 :** having globules ⟨made up of globules ⟨~ masses of fish eggs⟩ — **glob·u·lar·ly** *adv* — **glob·u·lar·ness** *n* -ES

globular chart *n* **:** a chart made on the globular projection

globular cluster *n* **:** a cluster of stars, galaxies, or supergalaxies that is usu. approximately spherical with compactness apparently increasing toward the center

glob·u·lar·ia \ˌgläbyəˈla(a)rēə\ *n, cap* [NL, fr. L *globulus* + NL *-aria*] **:** a genus (the type of the family Globulariaceae) of European herbs or shrubs with blue flowers in globose heads

glob·u·lar·i·a·ce·ae \-,la(a)rēˈāsē,ē\ *n pl, cap* [NL, fr. *Globularia*, type genus + *-aceae*] **:** a family of perennial herbs or small heathlike shrubs of the order Polemoniales with obovate entire often radical leaves and flowers in dense usu. globular heads — **glob·u·lar·i·a·ceous** \ˌ=ˌ==ˌ==ˈāshəs\ *adj*

glob·u·lar·i·ty \ˌgläbyəˈlarəd-ē\ *n* -ES **:** the quality or state of being globular ⟨the ~ of the planets⟩

globular lightning *n* **:** BALL LIGHTNING

globular projection *n* **:** a perspective projection of a hemisphere upon a plane parallel to its base sometimes used in cartography

globular sailing *n* **:** SPHERICAL SAILING

glob·ule \ˈgläb(ˌ)yül\ *n* -s [F, fr. L *globulus*, dimin. of *globus* globe] **1 :** a small often minute spherical mass (as of a liquid or semiliquid substance) **:** a small globular body (as a drop of water or a bead of sweat) **:** a tiny globe or ball ⟨~*s* of mercury⟩ ⟨~*s* of fat⟩; *specif* **:** a small spherical pill of compressed sugar usu. saturated with an alcoholic tincture and used in homeopathy **2 :** the male reproductive organ of a plant of the family Characeae

glob·u·let \ˈgläbyələt\ *n* -s [*globule* + *-et*] **:** a very small globule ⟨~*s* of water shone on her taut young skin —G.A. Wagner⟩

glob·u·lif·er·ous \ˌ=ˌ=ˈlif(ə)rəs\ *adj* [*globule* + *-iferous*] **:** SPHERULITIC

glob·u·lin \ˈgläbyələn\ *n* -s [ISV *globul-* (fr. L *globulus* globule) + *-in*] **:** any of a class of simple proteins (as myosin, edestin, gamma globulin) that are characterized by their almost complete insolubility in pure water or usu. in half-saturated ammonium sulfate or sodium sulfate solutions and by their solubility in dilute salt solutions, that are coagulable by heat, and that occur widely in plant and animal tissues (as blood plasma or serum); *esp* **:** SERUM GLOBULIN — see EUGLOBULIN, PSEUDOGLOBULIN

glob·u·lite \-,līt\ *n* -s [F, fr. *globule* + *-ite*] **:** a tiny globular body of mineral crystallite — **glob·u·lit·ic** \ˌ=ˌ=ˈlid-ik\ *adj*

glob·u·lous \ˈgläbyələs\ *adj* [F *globuleux*, fr. *globule* + *-eux* -ous] **:** GLOBULAR

glo·bus hys·ter·i·cus \ˈglōbəs·həˈsterəkəs\ *n* [NL, lit., hysteric ball] **:** a choking sensation (as of a lump in the throat) commonly experienced in hysteria

globus pal·li·dus \-ˈpalədəs\ *n* [NL, lit., pale globe] **:** the median portion of the lenticular nucleus consisting chiefly of large bulliform cells

globy \ˈglōbē\ *adj* [¹*globe* + *-y*] *archaic* **:** GLOBULAR

glo·chid \ˈglōkəd\ *n* -s [NL *glochidium*] **:** GLOCHIDIUM 1

glo·chid·e·ous \glōˈkidēəs\ *adj* [NL *glochidium* + E *-eous*] **:** GLOCHIDIATE

glo·chid·i·al \-ēəl\ *adj* [NL *glochidium* + E *-al*] **:** of or relating to glochidia

glo·chid·i·ate \-ēət, -ē,āt\ *adj* [NL *glochidium* + E *-ate*] **1 :** having glochidia **2 :** having barbed tips ⟨~ leaves⟩

glo·chid·i·um \-ēəm\ *n, pl* **glochid·ia** \-ēə\ [NL, fr. Gk *glōchis* projecting point + NL *-idium* — more at GLOSS (explanation)] **1 :** a barbed hair or spine (as on the massulae of a water fern or on some cacti) **2 :** a larval freshwater mussel of the family Unionidae that hatches in the gill cavity of the parent mussel, is subsequently discharged into the water, and attaches itself as an external parasite to the gills or fins or other parts of fish

glo·chis \ˈglōkəs\ *n, pl* **glochi·nes** \glōˈkī(,)nēz\ [NL *glochin-, glochis*, fr. Gk *glōchin-, glōchis* projecting point] **:** GLOCHIDIUM 1

glock·en·spiel \ˈgläkən,s(h)pēl\ *n* -s [G, fr. *glocke* bell (fr. OHG *glocka*, of Celt origin; akin to MIr *clocc*) + *spiel* play, fr. OHG *spil* — more at CLOCK, SPIEL] **1 :** CARILLON **2 a :** a percussion musical instrument consisting of a series of graduated metal bars tuned to the chromatic scale and played with two hammers **b :** any of various similar instruments with tubes or bells instead of bars **3 :** a pipe-organ percussion stop that imitates the tone quality of the glockenspiel

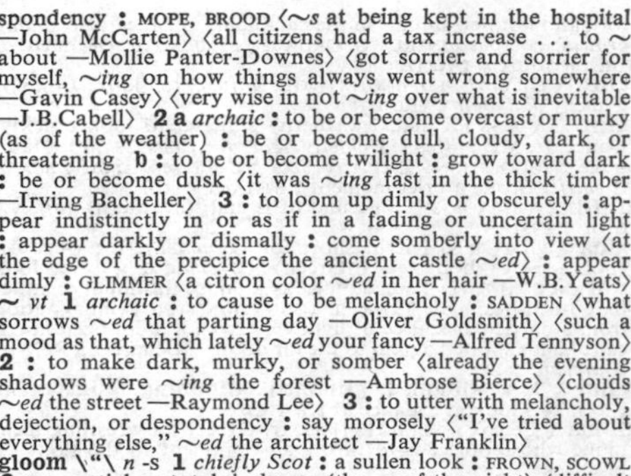

glockenspiel 2a

glode *archaic past of* GLIDE

gloea \ˈglēə\ *n* -s [NL, fr. LGk *gloia* glue; akin to L *glut-, glus* glue — more at CLAY] **:** an adhesive mucoid substance that some protozoans and other low organisms secrete about themselves — **gloe·al** \-əl\ *adj*

gloeo- *or* **gloio-** *comb form* [NL, fr. Gk *gloio-*, fr. *gloios* glutinous substance, gum; akin to L *glut-, glus* glue] **:** sticky **:** glutinous ⟨*Gloeo*capsa⟩ ⟨*Gloio*peltis⟩

gloe·o·cap·sa \ˌglēōˈkapsə\ *n, cap* [NL, fr. *gloeo-* + L *capsa* case — more at CASE (box)] **:** a genus of unicellular blue-green algae (family Chroococcaceae) inhabiting both fresh and salt water, colonies of some species forming a characteristic dull bluish green film on damp soil (as in tropical greenhouses)

gloe·o·din·i·um \-ˈdinēəm\ *n, cap* [NL, fr. *gloeo-* + *din-* (fr. Gk *dinos* rotation, whirling, whirlpool) + *-ium* — more at DINO-] **:** a genus of subspherical greenish brown freshwater algae (order Dinocapsales) that form compact colonies within homogeneous or stratified envelopes

gloe·o·spo·ri·um \-ˈspōrēəm\ *n, cap* [NL, fr. *gloeo-* + *-sporium*] **:** a form genus of several hundred imperfect fungi (family Melanconiaceae) having no setae around the acervuli and often causing anthracnoses of cultivated plants — compare COLLETOTRICHUM

gloff \ˈgläf\ *n* -s [origin unknown] *Scot* **:** a sudden fright **:** SCARE

glo·ger's rule \ˈglōgə(r)z-\ *n, usu cap G* [after C. W. L. *Gloger* †1863 Ger. zoologist] **:** a statement in zoology: within a species of warm-blooded animals the degree of melanin pigmentation tends to vary directly with the mean environmental temperature

glogg \ˈglüg, ˈgləg\ *n* -s [Sw *glögg*, fr. *glödga* to burn, mull, fr. OSw, fr. *glödhoger*, adj., glowing, fr. *glöth* ember, glowing coal; akin to OE *glēd* ember, glowing coal — more at GLEED] **:** a Swedish hot punch served usu. as a Christmas drink and made from a sweetened highly spiced mixture of wines and whiskey or brandy and containing almonds, raisins, and usu. orange peel

gloi·o·pel·tis \ˌglȯiōˈpeltəs\ *n, cap* [NL, fr. *gloeo-* + *-peltis* (prob. fr. Gk *peltē* small shield); prob. akin to L *pellis* skin — more at FELL (skin)] **:** a small genus of red algae closely related to *Gloiosiphonia* and furnishing a glue — see FUNORI, GLUE PLANT

gloi·o·si·pho·nia \-ō,sīˈfōnēə\ *n, cap* [NL, fr. *gloeo-* + L *siphon-, sipho* siphon, tube + NL *-ia* — more at SIPHON] **:** a small genus (the type of the family Gloiosiphoniaceae) of gelatinous red algae of the order Cryptonemiales — compare GLOIOPELTIS

¹glom \ˈgläm, -ȯ-\ *vt* **glommed; glommed; glomming; gloms** [prob. alter. of *glaum*] **1** *slang* **:** STEAL ⟨*glommed* a pile of money⟩ **2** *slang* **:** SEIZE, CATCH; *specif* **:** ARREST ⟨*glommed* the thugs⟩ — **glom on to 1** *slang* **:** to grab hold of **:** take possession of **:** appropriate to oneself ⟨she *glommed on to* every cent I'd saved —John McPartland⟩ **2** *slang* **:** to catch on to **:** UNDERSTAND ⟨*glomming on to* an idea⟩

²glom \"\ *vt* **glommed; glommed; glomming; gloms** [origin unknown] *slang* **:** to take a look at ⟨*glommed* her as she walked by⟩

³glom \"\ *n* -s *slang* **:** LOOK, VIEW ⟨got a good ~ at them⟩

glo·mal \ˈglōməl\ *adj* [NL *glomus* + E *-al*] **:** of or relating to a glomus

glome \ˈglōm\ *n* -s [L *glomus* ball, clew] **1** *archaic* **:** the center on which something is or is felt to be wound ⟨this is your last hour, this the butt, the ~ of all your days —Llewelyn Powys⟩ **2 :** a prominent rounded part of the frog of a horse's hoof on each side of the cleft

¹glom·er·ate \ˈglämə,rāt, *usu* -ād·+V\ *vb* -ED/-ING/-S [L *glomeratus*, past part. of *glomerare* to form into a ball, fr. *glomer-, glomus* ball — more at CLAM (clamp)] **:** AGGLOMERATE, CONGLOMERATE — **glom·er·a·tion** \ˌ=ˌ=ˈrāshən\ *n* -s

²glom·er·ate \-mərə|t, -mə,rā|, *usu* |d·+V\ *adj* [L *glomeratus*] **:** AGGLOMERATE, CONGLOMERATE

glom·er·el·la \ˌgläməˈrelə\ *n, cap* [NL, fr. L *glomer-, glomus* ball + NL *-ella*] **:** a genus of fungi closely related to *Gnomonia* and characterized by one-celled hyaline ascospores in rostrate perithecia borne in or on a stroma — see BITTER ROT, COTTON ANTHRACNOSE

glomerul- *or* **glomerulo-** *comb form* [NL, fr. *glomerulus*] **:** glomerulus of the kidney ⟨*glomerul*ar⟩ ⟨*glomerulo*nephritis⟩

glo·mer·u·lar \gläˈmer(y)ələ(r), glə-\ *adj* **:** of, relating to, or produced by a glomerulus ⟨~ nephritis⟩ ⟨~ filtration⟩

glo·mer·u·late \-lət, -,lāt\ *adj* [NL (assumed) NL *glomerulatus*, fr. *glomerulus* + L *-atus* -ate] **1 :** arranged in small compact clusters ⟨~ inflorescences⟩ ⟨~ capillaries⟩ **2 :** having glomeruli ⟨a ~ organ of the body⟩

glom·er·ule \ˈglämə,rül, -ər,yül\ *n* -s [NL *glomerulus*] **1 :** a compacted or sessile cyme (as of a boxtree) that resembles the flower head of a composite **2 :** GLOMERULUS

glo·mer·u·lo·nephritis \glä¦mer(y)ə(,)lō+, glə-\ *n* [NL, fr. *glomerul-* + *nephritis*] **:** nephritis marked by inflammation of the capillaries of the renal glomeruli caused by toxins from infectious processes elsewhere in the body and accompanied by changes in other renal structures and by edema, albuminuria, and other symptoms

glo·mer·u·lo·sa \glä,mer(y)əˈlōsə, glə-, -ōzə\ *n, pl* **glo·merulo·sae** \-,sē, -,zē, -,sī, -,zī\ [NL, fr. fem. of *glomerulosus* glomerulose] **:** a narrow outer zone of columnar cells arranged in loops and ovoids in the adrenal gland — called also *zona glomerulosa* — **glo·mer·u·lo·sal** \ˌ=ˌ==ˈsəl, -zəl\ *adj*

glo·mer·u·lo·sclerosis \glä¦mer(y)ə(,)lō+, glə-\ *n* [NL, fr. *glomerul-* + *sclerosis*] **:** nephrosclerosis involving the glomeruli

glo·mer·u·lose \=ˈ==,lōs\ *adj* [prob. fr. NL *glomerulosus*, fr. *glomerulus* + L *-osus* -ose] **:** GLOMERULATE 1

glo·mer·u·lus \-ləs\ *n, pl* **glomeru·li** \-,lī, -,lē\ [NL, glomerulus, glomerule, fr. L *glomer-, glomus* ball + NL *-ulus*] **:** a small convoluted or intertwined mass (as of organisms, nerve fibers, or capillaries): as **a :** a tuft of capillaries that is covered by epithelium, is situated at the point of origin of each vertebrate nephron, and normally passes a protein-free filtrate from the blood into the proximal convoluted tubule **b :** the convoluted secretory part of a sweat gland **c :** a dense entanglement of nerve fibers situated in the olfactory bulb and containing the primary synapses of the olfactory pathway **d :** a compact body of terminal fibers of neurons within an insect nerve center

glo·mus \ˈglōməs\ *n, pl* **glom·era** \ˈglämərə\ *also* **glo·mi** \ˈglō,mī, -,mē\ [NL, fr. L *glomer-, glomus* ball] **:** a small arteriovenous anastomosis together with its supporting structures: as **a :** a vascular tuft that suggests a renal glomerulus and that develops from the embryonic aorta in relation to the pronephros **b** *or* **glomus caroticum** \-kəˈräd·əkəm\ **:** CAROTID BODY **c :** a tuft of the choroid plexus protruding into each lateral ventricle of the brain

¹gloom \ˈglüm\ *vb* -ED/-ING/-S [ME *gloumen, gloumben*; akin to MHG *beglūmen* to make turbid, deceive, Norw dial. *glome* to stare somberly and suspiciously, OSw *glūna* to look askance, OE *geolu* yellow — more at YELLOW] *vi* **1 a :** to be, look, or act sullen, displeased, or annoyed **:** FROWN, LOWER, SCOWL, GLOWER ⟨~*ing* over his coffee at the way he had been tricked⟩ **b :** to be, look, or act low in spirits **:** feel or show dejection or cheerlessness **:** feel or show melancholy or despondency **:** MOPE, BROOD ⟨~*s* at being kept in the hospital —John McCarten⟩ ⟨all citizens had a tax increase . . . to ~ about —Mollie Panter-Downes⟩ ⟨got sorrier and sorrier for myself, ~*ing* on how things always went wrong somewhere —Gavin Casey⟩ ⟨very wise in not ~*ing* over what is inevitable —J.B.Cabell⟩ **2 a** *archaic* **:** to be or become overcast or murky (as of the weather) **:** be or become dull, cloudy, dark, or threatening **b :** to be or become twilight **:** grow toward dark **:** be or become dusk ⟨it was ~*ing* fast in the thick timber —Irving Bacheller⟩ **3 :** to loom up dimly or obscurely **:** appear indistinctly in or as if in a fading or uncertain light **:** appear darkly or dismally **:** come somberly into view ⟨at the edge of the precipice the ancient castle ~*ed*⟩ **:** appear dimly **:** GLIMMER ⟨a citron color ~*ed* in her hair —W.B.Yeats⟩ ~ *vt* **1** *archaic* **:** to cause to be melancholy **:** SADDEN ⟨what sorrows ~*ed* that parting day —Oliver Goldsmith⟩ ⟨such a mood as that, which lately ~*ed* your fancy —Alfred Tennyson⟩ **2 :** to make dark, murky, or somber ⟨already the evening shadows were ~*ing* the forest —Ambrose Bierce⟩ ⟨clouds ~*ed* the street —Raymond Lee⟩ **3 :** to utter with melancholy, dejection, or despondency **:** say morosely ⟨"I've tried about everything else," ~*ed* the architect —Jay Franklin⟩

²gloom \"\ *n* -s **1** *chiefly Scot* **:** a sullen look **:** FROWN, SCOWL **2 a :** partial or total darkness ⟨the ~ of the night⟩ ⟨difficult for the most practiced eye to pierce far into the ~ —J.L. Motley⟩ **:** glimmering obscurity **:** DIMNESS ⟨the cool ~ of the cathedral⟩ ⟨the light coming through the windows set high in the walls had darkened to the sudden ~ of the summer storm —Mary Deasy⟩ **:** deep shadowiness or shadiness ⟨resting for a moment in the quiet ~ of the forest⟩; *esp* **:** a dismally depressing darkness or murkiness ⟨a raw and detestable winter day and the ~ and noise of the huge town oppressed the soul —Leonard Bacon⟩ **b :** a partially or totally darkened place, spot, or region ⟨in this Italian glare I pine for the ~*s* of London —Aldous Huxley⟩ **:** a shadowy or shady place ⟨within the green ~*s* of the shadowy oak —J.R.Lowell⟩ **3 a :** a state of melancholy or depression **:** lowness of spirits **:** DEJECTION, DESPONDENCY ⟨the results of the Rome meeting were rather inconclusive and discouraging as the delegates departed in ~ —S.B.Fay⟩ **b :** an appearance or atmosphere of melancholy and despondency ⟨constant repinings at the dullness of everything around them threw a real ~ over their domestic circle —Jane Austen⟩ **4 :** one who is depressingly melancholy ⟨I'd have been a ~ in all that commencement gaiety —Mark Reed⟩ **:** KILLJOY ⟨a set of ~*s* called censors —H.C.Witwer⟩ **syn** see SADNESS

gloom·ful \-fəl\ *adj, archaic* **:** GLOOMY

gloom·i·ly \-məlē, -lī\ *adv* **:** in a gloomy manner ⟨~ staring at nothing —G.G.Carter⟩

gloom·i·ness \-mēnəs, -min-\ *n* -ES **:** the quality or state of being gloomy ⟨hating ~ like the plague⟩

¹glooming [fr. pres. part. of ¹*gloom*] *adj* **:** dimly glimmering **:** DARK, GLOOMY ⟨the ~ interior of an old inn⟩ — **glooming·ly** *adv*

²gloom·ing \ˈglümiŋ, -mēŋ\ *n* -s [prob. fr. gerund of ¹*gloom*] *archaic* **:** GLOAMING

gloom·less \-mləs\ *adj* **:** devoid of gloom ⟨~ joy⟩

glooms \ˈglümz\ *n pl* [pl. of ²*gloom*] **:** BLUES 1 — usu. used with *the* ⟨the sick morning ~ of debauchees —George Eliot⟩

gloomy \ˈglümē, -mi\ *adj, usu* -ER/-EST [¹*gloom* + *-y*] **1 a :** full of gloom **:** partially or totally dark ⟨the ~ night⟩ **:** SHADOWY ⟨the ~ center of the forest⟩ **:** dimly or murkily glimmering ⟨the ~ depths of the lake⟩; *esp* **:** dismally and depressingly dark ⟨~ weather⟩ ⟨oppressed by the squalor of the ~ tenements⟩ **b :** having an appearance of gloom **:** having a frowning or scowling appearance ⟨~ sullen savages⟩ **:** FORBIDDING, BLACK-BROWED ⟨tried to avoid the ~ stare of his wife⟩ **c :** low in spirits **:** MELANCHOLY, DOWNCAST, DEJECTED ⟨~ at the thought of what they had to face⟩ **2 :** causing gloom **:** DEPRESSING ⟨a sordid ~ story⟩ **:** devoid of brightness, color, and joy **:** SOMBER, DREARY ⟨a ~ landscape⟩ **:** DISHEARTENING, CHEERLESS ⟨a ~ report on the spread of crime⟩ **:** marked by little or no hopefulness **:** DESPONDENT, PESSIMISTIC ⟨contrary predictions are being made, some ~, some optimistic —J.T. Farrell⟩ **syn** see DARK, SULLEN

glop·pen \ˈgläpən\ *vt* -ED/-ING/-S [ME *glopnen*, fr. ON *glūpna* to be surprised, frightened, or downcast; akin to Sw dial. *glūpa* to gape, swallow, OFris *glūpa* to look, MLG *glūpen* to look with half-closed eyes, and perh. to OE *geolu* yellow — more at YELLOW] *now dial Eng* **:** SURPRISE, ALARM, ASTONISH

glore \ˈglō(ə)r\ *vi* -ED/-ING/-S [ME *gloren*, prob. of Scand origin; akin to ON eldsglōr glow of fire, Icel *glōra* to stare, gleam, Norw *glore* to gleam, glitter, Sw dial. *glora* to shine faintly; akin to MD *gloren* to gleam, Gk *chlōros* greenish yellow — more at YELLOW] *dial Eng* **:** to look fixedly **:** STARE

glo·ria \ˈglōrēə, -ōr-\ *n* -s [LL, fr. L, glory] **1** *often cap* **:** a Christian doxology sung or recited in liturgies and worship services **2** [prob. fr. It, lit., glory, fr. L] **a :** AUREOLE 2, NIMBUS **b :** a representation (as in a painting) of dazzling light bursting from the opened heavens **3** [prob. fr. Sp, lit., glory, fr. L] **:** a lightweight closely-woven fabric usu. in plain weave made orig. with silk warp and a worsted or cotton filling and used chiefly for umbrellas or dresses

glo·ri·a·tion \ˌ=ˌ=ˈāshən\ *n* -s [L *gloriation-, gloriatio*, fr. *gloriatus* (past part. of *gloriari* to boast, glory, fr. *gloria*, n., glory) + *-ion-, -io* -ion] *archaic* **:** the action of glorying

gloried *past of* GLORY

glories *pres 3d sing of* GLORY, *pl of* GLORY

glo·ri·fi·ca·tion \ˌglōrəfəˈkāshən, -ōr-\ *n* -s [LL *glorification-, glorificatio*, fr. *glorificatus* (past part. of *glorificare* to glorify) + L *-ion-, -io* -ion] **:** the act of glorifying or the state of being glorified

glo·ri·fi·er \ˈ==,fī(ə)r, -īə\ *n* -s **:** one that glorifies

glo·ri·fy \-,fī\ *vb* -ED/-ING/-ES [ME *glorifien*, fr. MF *glorifier*, fr. LL *glorificare*, fr. L *gloria* glory + *-ficare* -fy] *vt* **1 a** (1) **:** to make glorious **:** surround with glory **:** secure honor, praise, or admiration for ⟨~*ing* the achievements of the nation⟩ (2) **:** to exalt to a state of glory; *esp* **:** to exalt to the glory of heaven ⟨Jesus was not yet *glorified* —Jn 7:39 (RSV)⟩ **b :** to throw a resplendent light upon **:** make splendid with light **:** light up brilliantly ⟨sparkling chandeliers *glorified* the entire room⟩ **c :** to cause to have great beauty, charm, or appeal ⟨a book that *glorifies* the apparently trivial incidents of everyday life⟩; *esp* **:** to cause to be or seem to be in some way superior to what would be or is the actual condition of the thing so acted upon ⟨a recipe for ~*ing* pancakes⟩ **d :** to express hearty approval of **:** engage in praise of **:** EXTOL ⟨~*ing* everything they did without exception⟩ **2 :** to give worshipful praise, honor, and thanksgiving to ⟨~*ing* God for all their blessings⟩ **3** *archaic* **:** VAUNT ~ *vi, obs* **:** GLORY

glo·ri·ole \-rē,ōl\ *n* -s [prob. blend of *glory* and *aureole*] **:** AUREOLE 2

glo·ri·o·sa \ˌglōrēˈōsə, -ōr-, -ˈōzə\ *n* [NL, fr. L, fem. of *gloriosus* glorious] **1** *cap* **:** a genus of tropical African and Asiatic climbing tuberous herbs (family Liliaceae) with flowers that are red or yellow and that resemble typical lilies **2** -s **:** any plant of the genus *Gloriosa* — called also *climbing lily*

glo·ri·ous \ˈglōrēəs, -ōr-\ *adj* [ME, glorious, vainglorious, fr. MF & L; MF *glorieus, glorios* glorious, fr. L *gloriosus* glorious, vainglorious, fr. L *gloria* glory, vainglory + *-osus* -ose] **1 a :** possessing or deserving glory **:** ILLUSTRIOUS, PRAISEWORTHY ⟨a country that is ~ in the wealth of its literature⟩ ⟨a long and ~ career of service⟩ **b :** conferring or entitling to glory ⟨a struggle that was ~ to all that took part in it⟩ **2 :** marked by great beauty or splendor **:** RESPLENDENT, MAGNIFICENT ⟨a ~ spring morning⟩ ⟨a ~ work of art⟩ **3** *obs* **:** VAINGLORIOUS **4 :** extremely pleasant **:** WONDERFUL **:** intensely delightful **:** highly enjoyable ⟨enjoyed a ~ weekend⟩ **5** *archaic* **:** hilariously drunk **syn** see SPLENDID

glo·ri·ous·ly *adv* [ME, fr. *glorious* + *-ly*] **:** in a glorious manner

glo·ri·ous·ness *n* -ES [ME *gloriousnesse*, fr. *glorious* + *-nesse* -ness] **:** the quality or state of being glorious

¹glo·ry \ˈglōrē, -ōrē, -ri\ *n* -ES [ME *glorie*, fr. MF & L; MF *glorie, gloire* glory, fr. L *gloria* glory, vainglory] **1** *obs* **:** VAINGLORY **2 a :** lofty praise, honor, or admiration extended by common consent **:** high renown ⟨the ~ and riches they expect may never come —R.L.Stevenson⟩ **b :** worshipful praise, honor, and thanksgiving ⟨giving ~ to God⟩ **3 a :** something that merits or secures lofty praise, honor, or admiration ⟨the ~ of a brilliant career⟩ : a cause for or occasion of jubilant pride and boasting ⟨her children were a ~ to her⟩ : a source of intense joy or satisfaction ⟨pianissimos that were a ~ to hear —Winthrop Sargeant⟩ **b** : a highly distinguished, splendid, or renowned quality, attribute, possession, or action ⟨a place to visit . . . for the sake of its ancient *glories* —John Buchan⟩ : a resplendent asset or ornamentation ⟨the intellectual *glories* of the time —H.O.Taylor⟩ ⟨a ~ to the medical profession —Carson McCullers⟩ **4 a** (1) : great beauty or splendor : RESPLENDENCE, MAGNIFICENCE ⟨the grandeur of the wild wintry seas is matched only by the ~ of the summer combination of blue sea, golden-sanded bay, and purple cliffs —L.D.Stamp⟩ (2) : something marked by great beauty or resplendence ⟨a grand, red, rosy, crimson day — a perfect ~ of a day —John Muir †1914⟩ **b** : the splendor and beatific happiness of heaven : eternal life in heaven ⟨thou dost guide me with thy counsel, and afterward thou wilt receive me to ~ —Ps 73:24 (RSV)⟩; *broadly* : ETERNITY **5** : a condition of supreme exaltation or splendor ⟨an epoch of ~ for all the arts⟩ : a state of unhindered gratification, self-satisfaction, or enjoyment ⟨when he's teaching, he's in his ~⟩ : height of prosperity, power, or achievement ⟨ancient Greece in its ~⟩ **6 a** : a ring of light: as (1) : AUREOLE, NIMBUS (2) : CORONA 2a (3) : the head portion of a Brocken specter (4) : a set of concentric colored rings of light (as often surrounding the head portion of a Brocken specter) **b** : an emanation or play of light : a luminous glow : RADIANCE ⟨the dying *glories* of evening —George Meredith⟩ : a soft brightness ⟨wild flowers made a ~ on the hillside —Edith Hamilton⟩ **c** (1) : a dazzling illumination : a burst or blaze of blindingly bright light ⟨rockets rushed upward in a complete fiery encirclement and burst into ~ against the night sky —L.C.Stevens⟩; *specif* : a representation (as in a painting) of dazzling light bursting from the opened heavens (2) : SHEKINAH **syn** see FAME

²**glory** \"\ *vb* -ED/-ING/-ES [ME *glorien*, fr. L *gloriari* to boast, glory, fr. *gloria*, n.] *vi* **1 a** : to rejoice proudly : EXULT ⟨~*ing* in their strength⟩ ⟨*gloried* in their country's success⟩ **b** : to experience intense delight or self-satisfaction : REVEL ⟨~*ing* in this unaccustomed independence, she told herself that she intended . . . to have a wonderful time —Aurelia Levi⟩ **2** *obs* : BOAST **3** *archaic* : to shine radiantly or brilliantly ⟨a low sea sunset ~*ing* around her hair —Alfred Tennyson⟩ ~ *vt, archaic* : to give glory to : make glorious

³**glory** \"\ *or* **glory be** \,==ˈ=\ *interj* [*glory* fr. ¹*glory*; *glory be* fr. ¹*glory* + *be*, 3d pers. sing. pres. subj. of *be*, v.; fr. the use of the words "glory" or "glory be" at the beginning of doxologies] — used to express surprise, wonder, or delight

glory-bower \ˈ==,=\ *n* : a vine of the genus *Clerodendron*

glory-bush \ˈ==,=\ *n* : TIBOUCHINA 2; *esp* : a Brazilian spiderflower (*Tibouchina semidecandra*) that is widely grown in warm regions for its terminal clusters of large purple flowers with conspicuous yellow anthers on crooked filaments

glory-flower \ˈ==,==\ *n* : GLORY PEA

glory hole *n* **1 a** : a furnace for softening glass when it becomes stiff in offhand working and for fire-polishing glass **b** : an opening directly into the interior of such a furnace; *specif* : BOTTOMING HOLE **2** : a receptacle (as a box or cupboard) or area into which odds and ends are put haphazardly and in no particular order **3 a** : LAZARETTO 3 **b** : the quarters of stewards or stokers on board a ship **4** : an opencut or funnel-shaped excavation formed by drawing off soft or broken ore through an underground passage — called also *mill hole*

glory-lily \ˈ==ˈ==\ *n* : GLORIOSA 2

glory-of-the-snow \ˈ====\ *n, pl* **glory-of-the-snows** : any of several hardy spring-flowering Old World bulbous herbs of the genus *Chionodoxa*; *esp* : a widely cultivated plant (*C. luciliae*) with intensely blue white-centered or occas. pink or solid-white flowers

glory-of-the-sun \ˈ====\ *n, pl* **glory-of-the-suns** : a small bulbous scapose Chilean perennial herb (*Leucocoryne ixioides*) of the family Amaryllidaceae often cultivated for its lavender flowers that are borne in few-flowered umbels and have an involucre of two linear bracts

glory pea *n* : either of two clianthuses that are sometimes cultivated in warm climates for their racemes of large predominantly bright red flowers: **a** : STURT'S DESERT PEA **b** : KAKA BILL

glose \ˈglōz\ *archaic var of* GLOZE

¹**gloss** \ˈgläs, -ȯ-\ *n* -ES [prob. of Scand origin; akin to Icel *glossi* flame, spark, *glossa* to glow, flame, Norw dial. *glose* to glow; akin to MHG *glosen* to glow, OE *geolu* yellow — more at YELLOW] **1** : a superficial soft glowing luster or glistening brightness : a smooth soft surface shininess ⟨the ~ of satin⟩ ⟨the yellowish ~ of old ivory —Willard Robertson⟩ : SLEEKNESS ⟨brushed the dog's coat to a beautiful ~⟩ **2 a** [prob. influenced in meaning by ³*gloss* and ¹*gloze*] : something (as a motive alleged) designed to veil or hide what would otherwise be objected to : a plausible pretext : SHOW, PRETENSE, SEMBLANCE, DODGE, EXCUSE ⟨giving national aggrandizement the ~ of moral sanction⟩ **b** : a deceptively attractive external appearance ⟨selfishness that had a ~ of humanitarianism about it⟩

²**gloss** \"\ *vt* -ED/-ING/-ES **1 a** : to give a deceptively attractive external appearance to : WHITEWASH : make appear right or acceptable (as by minimizing or playing down obviously objectionable features) — usu. used with *over* ⟨endeavored to ~ the matter over —Dorothy Sayers⟩ ⟨no attempt is made to ~ over discreditable behavior —Philip Friedman⟩ **b** : to veil or hide (something that would otherwise be objected to or to prove a source of difficulty) by some plausible pretext, subterfuge, pretense, or excuse — usu. used with *over* ⟨not wish to ~ over the fragmentary state of our present knowledge —A.S.Eddington⟩ ⟨a tendency to ~ over inadequacies in the data with generalizations —R.M.Adams⟩ **2** : to give a soft glowing luster or glistening brightness to : make glossy ⟨the tarred road was ~*ed* by the noonday sun⟩ ⟨feathers that were ~*ed* by much preening⟩ **syn** see PALLIATE

³**gloss** \"\ *n* -ES [alter. (influenced by L *glossa*) of *gloze*, fr. ME *glose*, fr. OF, fr. ML *glosa*, alter. of L *glossa* difficult word requiring explanation, fr. Gk *glōssa* difficult word requiring explanation, language, tongue; akin to Gk *glōchin-*, *glōchis* projecting point and perh. to OSlav *glogŭ* thorn] **1 a** (1) : a brief explanation or a translation or definition (as one appearing in the margin or between the lines of a text or in a wordbook based on the text) of a textual word or expression felt to be difficult or obscure (2) : an expanded interpretation of or commentary on a textual word or expression (3) : a usu. willfully misleading or otherwise false explanation or interpretation of or commentary on a textual word or expression : an interpretation marked by usu. conscious sophistry **b** (1) : GLOSSARY (2) : a continuous interlinear translation (3) : a continuous explanation or commentary accompanying a text; *specif* : a commentary (as made at Bologna from the 12th century to the 14th century) on the texts of Roman or Civil law **2** : a poetical composition consisting of an amplification of a stanza of a poem into several stanzas so that each of the new stanzas ends with a line or couplet of the text stanza

⁴**gloss** \"\ *vb* -ED/-ING/-ES *vi* **1** : to make glosses : introduce or furnish glosses ⟨spent much time in reading and ~*ing*⟩ **2** *archaic* : to make usu. unfavorable remarks : comment adversely ~ *vt* **1** : to make glosses on : introduce glosses into : furnish glosses for ⟨medieval scholars, when they found in a Latin text a word not familiar to them, were accustomed to ~ it —J.W.Krutch⟩ **2** : to make a false or perverse interpretation of; *specif* : to dispose of or reduce to nothing (as a difficult problem) by false or perverse interpretation ⟨trying to ~ away the irrationalities of the universe —Irwin Edman⟩

gloss- *or* **glosso-** *comb form* [L, tongue, fr. Gk *glōss-*, *glōsso-*, fr. *glōssa*] **1 a** : tongue ⟨*gloss*algia⟩ : glottal and ⟨*glosso*hyal⟩ **b** : structure or organ like a tongue ⟨*Glosso*phora⟩ **2** : language ⟨*glosso*logy⟩

gloss *abbr* glossary

glos·sa \ˈgläsə, -lȯsə\ *n, pl* **glos·sae** \-,sē, -,sī\ *also* **glossas** [NL, fr. Gk *glōssa* tongue] : a tongue or lingual structure esp. in an insect: as **a** : the median distal lobe of the labium of many insects : LINGUA; *also* : either of the two segments of which this lobe is often formed **b** : the long spirally coiled tongue of many butterflies and moths

-glossa \"\ *n comb form, pl* **-glossa** [NL, fr. Gk *glōssa*] : one or ones having (such) a tongue or part like a tongue — in taxonomic names in biology ⟨*Eriglossa*⟩ ⟨*Cheiroglossa*⟩

glos·sal \-səl\ *adj* [*gloss-* + *-al*] : of or relating to the tongue ⟨~ inflammation⟩

glos·sal·gia \glä'salj(ē)ə, glȯ'-\ *n* -S [NL, fr. *gloss-* + *-algia*] : pain localized in the tongue; *esp* : neuralgic pain in the tongue

glos·sar·i·al \(ˈ)=ˈsa(a)rēəl\ *adj* : of, relating to, or having the characteristics of a glossary ⟨a ~ index⟩ ⟨~ notes⟩

glos·sa·rist \ˈ=sərəst\ *n* -S **1** : one that makes textual glosses **2** : a compiler of a glossary

glos·sa·ry \ˈgläsərē, -ri *also* ˈglȯs-\ *n* -ES [ML *glossarium*, fr. L *glossa* difficult word requiring explanation + *-arium* -ary] : a collection of textual glosses ⟨an edition of Shakespeare with a good ~⟩ or of terms limited to a special area of knowledge ⟨a ~ of technical terms⟩ or usage ⟨a ~ of dialectal words⟩

glos·sate \ˈglä,sāt, ˈglȯ,-\ *adj* [NL *glossa* + E *-ate*] **1** : having a glossa **2** : HAUSTELLATE

glos·sa·tor \ˈglä,sād·ə(r), ˈglȯ,-, =ˈ==\ *n* -S [ME *glosatour*, fr. ML *glosator*, fr. *glosatus* (past part. of *glosare* to gloss, fr. *glosa*, n., gloss) + L *-or* — more at GLOSS (explanation)] : GLOSSARIST

glossed *past of* GLOSS

glos·se·mat·ic \¦gläsə¦mad·ik, ¦glȯs-\ *adj* [ISV *glossemat-* (fr. *glosseme*) + *-ic*] : of or relating to glossematics or a glosseme ⟨~ theory⟩

glos·se·ma·ti·cian \,==mə'tishən\ *n* -S [ISV *glossematics* + *-ian*] : a specialist in glossematics

glos·se·mat·ics \-'mad·iks\ *n pl but sing in constr* [ISV *glossemat-* (fr. *glosseme*) + *-ics*] : linguistic analysis based on the distribution and interrelationship of glossemes

glos·seme \ˈglä,sēm, ˈglȯ,-\ *n* -S [ISV *gloss-* + *-eme*] : the smallest unit (as a word, a stem, a grammatical element, an intonation, or an order of words) that signals a meaning in a language — **glos·se·mic** \(ˈ)=ˈsēmik\ *adj*

glosses *pl of* GLOSS, *pres 3d sing of* GLOSS

-glos·sia \ˈgläsēə, ˈglȯs-\ *n comb form* -S [NL, fr. Gk *-glōssia*, fr. *glōssa* tongue + *-ia* -y — more at GLOSS (explanation)] : condition of having (such) a tongue or (so many) tongues ⟨di*glossia*⟩ ⟨pachy*glossia*⟩

glossier *comparative of* GLOSSY

glossies *pl of* GLOSSY

glossiest *superlative of* GLOSSY

glos·si·ly \ˈgläsəlē, ˈglȯs-, -li\ *adv* : in a glossy manner

glos·si·na \=ˈsīnə, -ˈsēnə\ *n* [NL, fr. *gloss-* + *-ina*] **1** *cap* : an African genus of two-winged flies with a long slender sharp proboscis and plumose aristae comprising the tsetse flies — compare SLEEPING SICKNESS; see GLOSSINIDAE **2** -S : any insect of the genus *Glossina* : TSETSE FLY

glos·si·ness \ˈ=sēnəs, -sin-\ *n* -ES : the quality or state of being glossy

glossing *pres part of* GLOSS

glos·sin·i·dae \glä'sinə,dē, glȯ'-\ *n pl, cap* [NL, fr. *Glossina*, type genus + *-idae*] *in some classifications* : a family of two-winged flies that is closely related to Muscidae and includes *Glossina* and a few closely related genera usu. included among the Muscidae

glos·si·pho·nia \,gläsə'fōnēə, ,glȯs-\ *n, cap* [NL, fr. *glos-* (fr. Gk *glōssa* tongue) + L *siphon-*, *sipho* siphon, tube + NL *-ia* — more at GLOSS (explanation), SIPHON] : the type genus of the family Glossiphoniidae comprising common often brightly colored freshwater leeches with one or more pairs of simple eyes

¹**glos·si·pho·ni·id** \¦==ˈ=nēəd\ *adj* [NL *Glossiphoniidae*] : of or relating to the Glossiphoniidae

²**glossiphoniid** \"\ *n* -S [NL *Glossiphoniidae*] : a leech of the family Glossiphoniidae

glos·si·pho·ni·idae \,==fə'nīə,dē\ *n pl, cap* [NL, fr. *Glossiphonia*, type genus + *-idae*] : a family of rhynchobdellid leeches having the posterior sucker sharply demarked

gloss·ist \ˈgläsəst, ˈglȯs-\ *n* -S *archaic* : GLOSSARIST

glos·si·tis \=ˈsīd·əs\ *n* -ES [NL, fr. *gloss-* + *-itis*] : inflammation of the tongue

gloss·less \ˈgläsləs, ˈglȯs-\ *adj* : devoid of gloss

gloss·me·ter \-,smēd·ə(r)\ *n* : a photometer for measuring the gloss of test surfaces

glosso- — see GLOSS-

glos·so·dyn·ia \,gläsō'dinēə, ,glȯs-\ *n* -S [NL, fr. *gloss-* + *-odynia*] : GLOSSALGIA

glos·sog·ra·pher \glä'sägrəfə(r), glȯ'-\ *n* -S [Gk *glōssographos* writer of explanations of difficult words (fr. *glōsso-* — fr. *glōssa* difficult word requiring explanation — + *-graphos* -grapher) + E *-er* — more at GLOSS (explanation), -GRAPHER] : GLOSSARIST

glos·sog·ra·phy \-fē\ *n* -ES [prob. fr. *glossographer*, after such pairs as E *geographer: geography*] : the writing or compilation of glosses

glos·so·hy·al \¦gläsō¦hīəl, ¦glȯs-\ *adj* [*gloss-* + *hy-* (fr. *hyoid*) + *-al*] : of or relating to the hyoid arch and tongue; *specif* : of or relating to the median basihyal or an anterior extension or segment of it extending into and supporting the tongue

glos·soid \ˈ=,sȯid\ *adj* [Gk *glōssoeidēs*, fr. *glōss-* gloss- + *-oeidēs* -oid] : resembling a tongue ⟨a ~ proboscis⟩

gloss oil *n* [¹*gloss*] : a spirit varnish consisting of a solution of rosin partially neutralized with lime in mineral spirits or other paint thinner

glos·so·kinesthetic \¦gläsō, ¦glȯsō+\ *adj* [*gloss-* + *kinesthetic*] : of or relating to sensations of tongue movement ⟨~ centers⟩

glos·so·la·lia \,==ˈlālēə\ *n* -S [NL, fr. *gloss-* + *-lalia*] : GIFT OF TONGUES

glos·so·log·i·cal \¦==sə¦läjəkəl\ *adj* [*glossology* + *-ical*] *archaic* : LINGUISTIC

glos·sol·o·gist \ˈ=ˈsäləjəst\ *n* -S [*glossology* + *-ist*] *archaic* : LINGUIST

glos·sol·o·gy \-jē\ *n* -ES [*gloss-* + *-logy*] **1** *archaic* : LINGUISTICS **2** *archaic* : NOMENCLATURE

glos·so·palatine arch \¦gläs|(,)sō, ¦glȯs|+. . .-\ *n* [*glossopalatine* fr. NL *glossopalatinus* of the tongue and palate, fr. *gloss-* + (assumed) NL *palatinus* of the palate — more at PALATINE] : either of the anterior pillars of the fauces; *also* : the arch formed by both

glossopalatine nerve *n* : the branch of the facial nerve that supplies the anterior tongue and parts of the palate and fauces — called also *nerve of Wrisberg*, *nervus intermedius*

glos·so·pal·a·ti·nus \,=(,)=,palə'tīnəs, -ˈtēn-\ *n, pl* **glossopalati·ni** \-tī,nī, -tē,nē\ [NL, fr. *glossopalatinus*, adj., of the tongue and palate] : a thin muscle arising from the soft palate on each side and inserted into the side and dorsum of the tongue

glos·sop·a·thy \glä'säpəthē\ *n* -ES [*gloss-* + *-pathy*] : tongue disease

glos·so·pet·ra \,==sō'pe·trə\ *n, pl* **glossopet·rae** \-,trē, -,trī\ [NL, fr. L, tongue-shaped gem, fr. *gloss-* + *petra* rock, fr. Gk] : any of certain isolated fossil shark teeth

glos·soph·a·ga \=ˈsäfəgə\ *n, cap* [NL, fr. *gloss-* + *-phaga*] : a genus of small So. American bats (family Phyllostomatidae) having a long extensile tongue apparently used to scoop out the inside of fruits

glos·soph·a·gine \-fə,jīn, -jən\ *adj* [NL *Glossophaga* + E *-ine*] : of or relating to the *Glossophaga*

glos·so·pha·ryngeal \¦gläs|(,)sō, ¦glȯ|+\ *adj* [prob. fr. NL *glossopharyngeus* glossopharyngeal (fr. *gloss-* + *pharyngeus* pharyngeal) + E *-al* — more at PHARYNGEAL] **1** : of or relating to both tongue and pharynx **2** : of or relating to the glossopharyngeal nerve ⟨~ lesions⟩

glossopharyngeal nerve *also* **glossopharyngeal** *n* : a mixed nerve that is either of the 9th pair of cranial nerves, that has sensory fibers arising from the superior and petrosal ganglia and motor fibers arising with those of the 10th nerve from the lateral wall of the medulla, and that supplies chiefly the pharynx, posterior tongue, and parotid gland with motor and sensory fibers including gustatory and autonomic secretory and vasodilator fibers

glos·soph·o·ra \=ˈsäfərə\ *n pl, cap* [NL, fr. *gloss-* + *-phora*] *in some classifications* : a division of mollusks consisting of those having a radula

glos·so·pode \ˈgläsə,pōd, ˈglȯs-\ *n* -S [NL *glossopodium*] : GLOSSOPODIUM

glos·so·po·di·um \,==ˈpōdēəm\ *n, pl* **glossopo·dia** \-ēə\ *or* **glossopodiums** [NL, fr. *gloss-* + *-podium*] : the sheathing leaf base in the quillworts

glos·sop·ter·is \=ˈsäptərəs\ *n* [NL, fr. *gloss-* + *-pteris*] **1** *cap* : a genus of chiefly Permian and Triassic fossil ferns or fernlike plants characterized by thick entire fronds with anastomosing veins **2** -ES : any plant of the genus *Glossopteris*

glos·so·py·ro·sis \,gläsō,pī'rōsəs, ,glȯs-\ *n* [NL, fr. *gloss-* + Gk *pyrōsis* burning, inflammation — more at PYROSIS] : a burning sensation in the tongue

glos·so·the·ri·um \-ō'thirēəm\ *n, cap* [NL, fr. *gloss-* + *-therium*] : a genus of large So. American Pleistocene ground sloths related to the genus *Mylodon* that have the nostrils completely enclosed by the premaxillae so that the skull has a superficial likeness to that of a turtle

gloss white *n* [¹*gloss*] : an extender pigment made by coprecipitation of blanc fixe and a hydrate of alumina and used chiefly in printing inks

¹**glossy** \ˈgläsē, ˈglȯs-, -si\ *adj, usu* -ER/-EST [¹*gloss* + *-y*] **1** : having a superficial soft glowing luster ⟨rich ~ leather⟩ or glistening brightness ⟨~ green foliage⟩ or smooth shininess ⟨the ~ pages of those magazines⟩ ⟨photographs printed on ~ paper⟩ or glowing sleekness ⟨the horse's ~ coat⟩ : LUSTROUS, SHINING, SILKY **2 a** : having a superficial largely deceptive or artificial attractiveness typically marked by apparent opulence ⟨a ~ nightclub⟩ or sophistication ⟨a ~ gathering of celebrities⟩ or smoothly captivating display ⟨a ~ musical⟩ : smoothly pretentious : SHOWY **b** : marked by urbanity and usu. only apparent conviction and sincerity : SUAVE, SMOOTH, GLIB ⟨the ~ commercials of radio and television⟩ ⟨~ salesmen⟩

²**glossy** \"\ *n* -ES **1** : SLICK 6 **2** : a photograph printed on smooth shiny paper

glossy ibis *n* : any of several ibises having dark-colored plumage with a more or less metallic luster and constituting the genus *Plegadis* of the family Threskiornithidae

glost \ˈglȯst, -ä-\ *n* -S [alter. of ¹*gloss*] : ²GLAZE 2a(2); *also* : clayware with glaze applied but not yet fired — called also *glostware*

glost fire *n* : the fire used for fusing a glaze to biscuit

glost firing *n* : a separate firing by which glaze is fused to clayware

-glot \,glät, *usu* -äd·+V\ *adj comb form* [Gk *-glōttos*, *-glōssos*, fr. *glōtta*, *glōssa* language, tongue — more at GLOSS (explanation)] : having knowledge of or using (a specified number of) languages ⟨mono*glot*⟩ ⟨tetra*glot*⟩

glott- *or* **glotto-** *comb form* [Gk *glōtt-*, *glōtto-*, *glōss-*, *glōsso-*, tongue, fr. *glōtta*, *glōssa*] : language ⟨*glotto*logy⟩

glot·tal \ˈgläd·ᵊl, -ätᵊl\ *adj* [*glottis* + *-al*] : of, relating to, or produced in or by the glottis ⟨~ constriction⟩

glot·tal·ic \(ˈ)glä¦talik\ *adj* : GLOTTALIZED

glot·tal·iza·tion \,gläd·ᵊlə'zāshən, -ätᵊl-, -ᵊl,ī'z-\ *n* -S : the act of glottalizing

glot·tal·ize \ˈ==,īz\ *vt* -ED/-ING/-S : to articulate or accompany the articulation of with whole or partial glottal closure ⟨*glottalized* consonants⟩

glottal stop *also* **glottal catch** *or* **glottal plosive** *n* : complete closure of the glottis under breath pressure recognized by the ear chiefly by the occlusion or by the explosive release ⟨in New York City the *tt* in *bottle* is sometimes pronounced as a *glottal stop*⟩

¹**glot·tic** \ˈgläd·ik\ *adj* [Gk *glōttikos* of the tongue, fr. *glōtta*, *glōssa* tongue + *-ikos* -ic] *archaic* : LINGUISTIC

²**glottic** \"\ *adj* [ISV *glott-* (fr. NL *glottis*) + *-ic*] : GLOTTAL

glot·tis \ˈgläd·|əs, -ät|\ *n, pl* **glottises** \|əsəz\ *or* **glotti·des** \|ə,dēz\ [NL, fr. Gk *glōttis*, fr. *glōtta*, *glōssa* tongue] : the space between the vocal fold and arytenoid cartilage of one side of the larynx and those of the other side; *also* : the structures that surround this space — compare EPIGLOTTIS

glot·to·chronological \¦gläd·(,)ō, -ä(,)tō +\ *adj* : of or relating to glottochronology

glot·to·chronology \"+\ *n* [*glott-* + *chronology*] **1** : the study of the time during which two or more languages have evolved separately from a common source **2** : a technique for estimating by statistical comparison of vocabulary samples the time during which two or more languages have evolved separately from a common source

glot·to·gon·ic \¦gläd·ō¦gänik, -lätō-\ *adj* [*glott-* + Gk *gonē* generation + E *-ic*; akin to Gk *gignesthai* to be born — more at KIN] : of or relating to the origin of language ⟨~ problems⟩

glot·to·log·i·cal \¦gläd·ᵊl¦äjəkəl, -ätᵊl-\ *adj* [*glottology* + *-ical*] : LINGUISTIC

glot·tol·o·gist \glä'täləjəst\ *n* -S [*glottology* + *-ist*] : LINGUIST

glot·tol·o·gy \-jē\ *n* -ES [*glott-* + *-logy*] : LINGUISTICS

¹**glouces·ter** \ˈglästə(r), ˈglȯs-\ *adj, usu cap* [fr. *Gloucester*, county and county borough in England] **1** : of or from the county borough of Gloucester, England : of the kind or style prevalent in Gloucester **2** : GLOUCESTERSHIRE

²**gloucester** \"\ *or* **gloucester cheese** *n* -S *usu cap G* [fr. *Gloucester*, county in England, where it was originally made] : a hard cheese resembling derby

gloucester old spots \-ˈōl(d)z,päts, -),sp-\ *n pl but sing or pl in constr, usu cap G&O&S* [fr. *Gloucester*, county in England, where the breed was developed] : an old British breed of hardy black-and-white-spotted swine now chiefly used for crossbreeding

glouces·ter·shire \ˈglästə(r),shi(ə)r, ˈglȯs-, -shər\ *or* **gloucester** *adj, usu cap* [fr. *Gloucestershire* or *Gloucester*, county in England] : of or from the county of Gloucester, England : of the kind or style prevalent in Gloucester

gloup \ˈglüp\ *n* -S [prob. of Scand origin; akin to Norw dial. *glūp* hole, gorge, abyss; akin to Sw dial. *glūpa* to gape, swallow, OFris *glūpa* to look, MLG *glūpen* to look with half-closed eyes, and perh. to OE *geolu* yellow — more at YELLOW] : an opening in the roof of a sea cave through which incoming waves may force air to rush upward or water to spout intermittently : BLOWHOLE 3

glout \ˈglüt, ˈglaůt\ *vi* -ED/-ING/-S [ME *glouten*, prob. of Scand origin; akin to ON *glotta* to grin scornfully, Sw *glutta* to peep — more at GLOAT] *archaic* : FROWN, SCOWL

¹**glove** \ˈgləv\ *n* -S [ME, fr. OE *glōf*; akin to ON *glōfi* glove; both prob. fr. a prehistoric NGmc-WGmc compound whose first constituent is represented by OE *ge-* (perfective, associative, and collective prefix) and whose second constituent is represented by ON *lōfi* palm of the hand, Goth *lofa*; akin to OHG *laffa* palm of the hand, Lith *lopa* claw, Russ *lapa* paw — more at CO-] **1 a** : a covering for the hand having separate sections or merely separate openings for each of the fingers and the thumb and often extending part way up the arm and made of various materials (as leather, wool, rubber) either with or without a snap or button or other fastening at the wrist and used to protect the hand against cold ⟨a bitter day and they wore wool-lined ~*s*⟩ or intense heat ⟨asbestos ~*s*⟩ or irritation ⟨wore a pair of rubber ~*s* while washing the dishes⟩ or superficial injury ⟨a falconer's ~⟩ ⟨an archer's ~⟩ or to avoid contamination ⟨surgeons wearing sterile ~*s*⟩ ⟨~*s* for handling radioactive materials⟩ or as a dress accessory ⟨a pair of silk evening ~*s*⟩ — often used with *pair*; distinguished from *mitt* and *mitten* **b** : GAUNTLET 1a ⟨a ~ of mail⟩ **c** : GAUNTLET 2 ⟨threw down the ~ to skeptical critics —C.R.Anderson⟩ **2 a** : a usu. leather covering for the hand padded and reinforced at the palm and fingers and often having sections designed to cover more than one finger instead of having separate finger sections and used by defending players in the game of baseball to protect the hand when catching a thrown or struck ball — compare MITT **b** : BOXING GLOVE ⟨getting rusty in his boxing, hasn't put the ~*s* on for six months⟩ — **with gloves** *or* **with kid gloves** *or* **with velvet gloves** *adv* : with gentleness, consideration, or tact : CAUTIOUSLY, GINGERLY ⟨they've

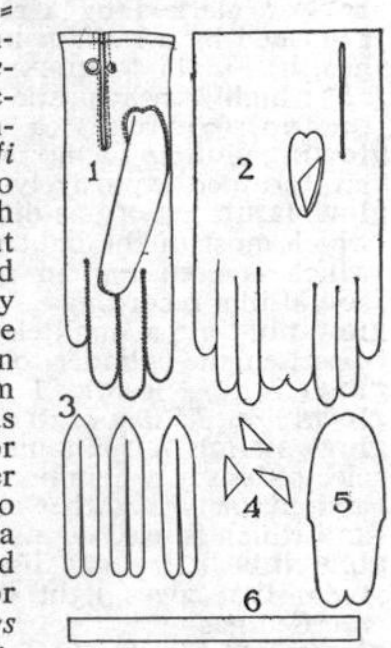

glove 1a: *1* finished glove, *2* trank, *3* fourchettes, *4* gussets, *5* thumb, *6* slit binding

got to be handled *with kid gloves*) — **with gloves off** *or* **without gloves** *adv* **1** : without restraint : UNSPARINGLY, UNMERCIFULLY **2** : without caution or ceremony : boldly and directly ⟨attacked the problem *with gloves off*⟩

²glove \"\ *vt* -ED/-ING/-S **1 a** : to cover with or as if with a glove : draw a glove over ⟨*gloving* his right hand as he spoke⟩ **b** : to furnish with gloves ⟨warmly bundled up and *gloved* for the trip⟩ **2** : to catch (a baseball) in one's gloved hand ⟨*gloved* a stinging line drive and fired it to first base⟩

glove–and–stocking anesthesia *n* : glove anesthesia accompanied by anesthesia in the foot sometimes extending farther up the leg and usu. associated with hysteric states

glove anesthesia *n* : anesthesia in the hand sometimes extending farther up the arm and usu. associated with hysteric states

glove box *n* : a sealed protectively lined compartment having ports to which are attached gloves for use in handling materials inside the compartment

glove compartment *n* : a small storage cabinet in the dashboard of an automobile

glove doll *or* **glove puppet** *n* : HAND PUPPET

glove grain *n* : GRAIN 4b(1)

glove·less \ˈgləvləs\ *adj* : devoid of gloves

glove·man \-mən\ *n, pl* **glovemen** : FIELDER a

glov·er \-və(r)\ *n* -S [ME, fr. ¹*glove* + -*er*] : one that makes or sells gloves

glov·er scale \"-\ *also* **glover's scale** *n, usu cap G* [after Townend *Glover* †1883 Am. entomologist] : a widespread tropical armored scale (*Lepidosaphes gloverii*) esp. destructive to citrus

glover tower *n, usu cap G* [after John *Glover*, 19th cent. Eng. chemist] : a large packed tower that is situated before the chambers in the chamber process of making sulfuric acid and that serves esp. to cool the hot mixture of sulfur dioxide and air on its way to the chambers, to supply water vapor, to remove the nitrogen oxides from nitrous vitriol entering at the top from the Gay-Lussac tower, and to concentrate sulfuric acid also entering at the top from the chambers

glove silk *n* : a fine knit fabric of silk or artificial fiber used esp. for women's gloves and underwear

glove sponge *n* [so called fr. its shape] : a soft inferior commercial sponge of the Bahamas and Florida

glov·ing \ˈgləviŋ\ *n* -S [¹*glove* + -*ing*] : the making of gloves

¹glow \ˈglō\ *vb* -ED/-ING/-S [ME *glowen*, fr. OE *glōwan*; akin to OHG *gluoen* to glow, ON *glōa* to glow, OE *geolu* yellow, and perh. to Gk *chloos* green, light green, light green color — more at YELLOW] *vi* **1 a** (1) : to be or become hot to the point of radiating a suffused often slowly and unevenly pulsating light and an intense flameless heat : become heated to red heat or white heat : be or become incandescent ⟨heated the metal until it ~*ed*⟩ ⟨coals still ~*ing* in the fireplace⟩ (2) : to shine with a suffused radiance as if intensely heated : emit or become lit up with an incandescent light : gleam in a suffused manner ⟨gaily lighted houses ~*ed* in the dark⟩ ⟨her eyes ~*ed* with pleasure⟩ ⟨saw the harbor lights ~*ing* in the distance⟩ **b** (1) : to have a rich warm suffused coloration typically reddish in hue or touched by reddish highlights ⟨his troubled face ~*ing* in the firelight —Guy McCrone⟩ ⟨paintings that ~*ed* with color⟩ ⟨the leaves of the maple trees ~*ed* red and yellow in the sunlight —J.P. Marquand⟩ (2) : to have a radiant warm typically ruddy coloration of the kind associated with youthfulness and physical well-being ⟨cheeks ~*ing* with health⟩ (3) : to have a markedly heightened reddish coloration (as that arising from strong emotion or embarrassment) : FLUSH, BLUSH ⟨she was filled with excitement and her face ~*ed*⟩ **2 a** (1) : to experience a sensation of tingling pervasive warmth ⟨rubbed themselves with Turkish towels until they ~*ed* all over⟩ ⟨a drink that makes the whole body ~⟩ (2) : to experience a sensation as if of intense heat : burn with emotion or passion ⟨~*ing* with rage and resentment⟩ ⟨~*ing* with fervor⟩ **b** : to be full of or show exuberance, elation, joyous good spirits ⟨~*ing* with maternal pride —Carleton Beals⟩ : be buoyant and vibrantly alive ⟨every page of the book ~*s* with good humor⟩ ~ *vt, obs* : to cause to glow ⟨fans whose wind did seem to ~ the delicate cheeks which they did cool —Shak.⟩ **syn** see BLAZE

²glow \"\ *n* -S **1** : the quality or state of having a glowing coloration ⟨the rich ~ of the mahogany table⟩ ⟨the bright ~ in her cheeks⟩ **2 a** (1) : considerable warmth of feeling or intensity of emotion or passion ⟨the ~ of new love⟩ (2) : tingling pervasive warmth or a sensation of such warmth ⟨a ~ of happiness⟩ ⟨walked away satisfied and all in a ~⟩ ⟨they started pouring the stuff down steadily, feeling the warm ~ rising inside —D.M.Davin⟩ **b** : a feeling or outward display of exuberance, elation, joyous good spirits ⟨the good news left them with a ~ in their hearts⟩ ⟨there was no mistaking the happy ~ on his face⟩ ⟨the ~ of success⟩ **3 a** : the state of glowing with heat and light ⟨the ~ of dying embers⟩ : INCANDESCENCE; *specif* : a relatively faint luminosity due to luminescence ⟨the cathode ~ in a Crookes tube⟩ — compare AFTERGLOW 2 **b** : glowing radiance : suffused gleaming ⟨happy to see the ~ in her eyes⟩ ⟨the ~ of the lighted Christmas tree⟩

glow discharge *n* : a silent luminous electrical discharge without sparks through a gas

¹glow·er \ˈglau̇(ə)r, -au̇ə, *chiefly in southern US* -au̇wə(r), *chiefly in substand speech* -lō(ə)r *or* -lōə\ *vi* -ED/-ING/-S [ME (Sc) *glowren*, perh. of Scand origin; akin to ON *glyrna* eye, Norw dial. *glyra* to look askance; akin to MLG *glûren* to watch, D *gluren* to peep, MHG *glosen* to glow — more at GLOSS (luster)] **1** *dial Brit* : to look intently; *esp* : to stare in amazement **2** : to look or stare with sullen brooding annoyance or anger : gaze blackly : SCOWL, LOWER

²glower \"\ *n* -S **1** *dial Brit* : an intent look; *esp* : an amazed stare **2** : a sullen brooding look of anger : SCOWL

³glow·er \ˈglō(ə)r, -ōə\ *n* -S [¹*glow* + -*er*] : the luminous element in a Nernst lamp

glow·er·ing·ly *adv* [*glowering* (pres. part. of ¹*glower*) + -*ly*] : in a glowering manner ⟨looked ~ at the morning headlines⟩

glowing *adj* [ME *glowinge, glowing*, fr. *glowen* to glow + -*inge*, -*ing* -ing] : that glows: **a** : burning incandescently **b** (1) : marked by a rich warm coloration ⟨~ colors⟩ (2) : marked by a healthfully ruddy coloration ⟨~ good health⟩ **c** (1) : ARDENT, FERVID, IMPASSIONED ⟨~ devotion⟩ (2) : highly enthusiastic : WARM, EXUBERANT ⟨a ~ account of the trip⟩ ⟨~ praise⟩ ⟨a ~ description⟩ — **glow·ing·ly** *adv*

glowing cloud *n* : a mixture of hot volcanic gas and particles of lava erupted explosively from a volcano

glow lamp *n* : a gas-discharge hot-cathode electric lamp in which most of the light proceeds from the cathode glow and which is used esp. in stroboscopes and in variable-density sound-film recording

glow plug *n* : a small electric heating element placed inside a diesel-engine cylinder to preheat the air and facilitate starting

glowr *var of* ²GLOWER 1

glows *pres 3d sing of* GLOW, *pl of* GLOW

glow switch *n* : an inert-gas discharge tube in which one electrode is a bimetallic strip that bends as the tube warms up and contacts the other electrode thus short-circuiting the tube and which is used as a starting switch in fluorescent lamps

glow tube *n* : a gas-discharge tube (as of the cold-cathode type) that gives light due to electric discharge through a rarefied gas

glowworm \ˈ⸗,⸗\ *n* [ME, fr. *glowen* to glow + *worm*] **1** : any of various luminous insects with wings rudimentary or lacking: as **a** : one of the wingless females or larvae of beetles of the family Lampyridae which emit light from some of the abdominal segments **b** : one of the web-making larvae of a New Zealand fungus gnat (*Bolitophila luminosa*) — compare FIREFLY **2** : SEARED GREEN

glox·in·ia \gläkˈsinēə *also* -sēn-\ *n* [NL, fr. Benjamin P. *Gloxin*, 18th cent. Ger. physician and botanist + NL -*ia*] **1** *cap* : a small genus of tropical American herbs (family Gesneriaceae) with leafy stems and axillary flowers **2** -S : a greenhouse herb of the genus *Sinningia*; *esp* : a Brazilian herb (*S. speciosa*) that is the source of many horticultural varieties

gloy \ˈglȯi\ *n* -S [ME, modif. of MF *glui*] *Scot* : STRAW

¹gloze \ˈglōz\ *n* -S [ME *glose* flattery, plausible pretext, explanation of a difficult word — more at GLOSS (explanation)] **1** *archaic* : smooth empty talk; *esp* : FLATTERY **2** *archaic* : ¹GLOSS 2 **3** *archaic* : ³GLOSS 1

²gloze \"\ *vb* -ED/-ING/-S [ME *glosen* to use flattery, flatter, make glosses, make glosses on, fr. OF *gloser* to make glosses, make glosses on, fr. *glose*, n., explanation of a difficult word — more at GLOSS (explanation)] *vi* **1** *archaic* : to use smooth empty talk : FAWN; *esp* : to use flattery **2** *archaic* : ⁴GLOSS *vi* 1 ~ *vt* **1** *archaic* : to address with smooth empty talk : fawn upon; *esp* : FLATTER **2** *archaic* : ⁴GLOSS *vt* 1 **3** : ⁴GLOSS *vt* 2

³gloze \"\ *vt* -ED/-ING/-S [²*gloze* (influenced in meaning by ²*gloss*)] : ²GLOSS 1 ⟨the past, though *glozed* beyond all semblance of truth —Joseph Furphy⟩ — often used with *over* ⟨saw everything and *glozed* over nothing —William Irvine⟩ **syn** see PALLIATE

⁴gloze \"\ *vt* -ED/-ING/-S [¹*gloss*] *archaic* : to light up : BRIGHTEN

glozing *adj* [ME *glosinge, glosing*, fr. *glosen* to flatter + -*inge*, -*ing* -ing] *archaic* : FAWNING, FLATTERING

glt *abbr* gilt

¹glub \ˈgləb\ *n* -S [imit.] : a gurgling, bubbling, or gulping sound (as of water running down a drain) — often reduplicated ⟨listened to the ~, ~, ~ of the milk bottle as it sank below the surface of the pond⟩ : an inarticulate strangled sound (as of someone attempting to speak while under water)

²glub \"\ *vi* **glubbed; glubbed; glubbing; glubs** : to make a glub — often reduplicated ⟨like cold molasses *glub-glubbing* from a barrel —James Street⟩

gluc- *or* **gluco-** *comb form* [ISV, fr. *glucose*] **1 a** : glucose ⟨*glucogenic*⟩ : related to or containing glucose ⟨*glucomannans*⟩ **b** *gluco-, usu ital* : having the stereochemical arrangement of atoms or groups found in glucose ⟨D-*gluco*⸗pentahydroxy-pentyl⟩ **2** : GLYC- 1 ⟨*glucoproteins*⟩ — not now in frequent use

glu·ca·gon \ˈglükə,gän\ *n* -S [*gluc-* + -*agon* (perh. fr. Gk *agōn*, pres. part. of *agein* to lead, drive) — more at AGENT] : a crystalline protein that is obtained from the islets of Langerhans of the pancreas, is present in some preparations of insulin, and increases the content of sugar in the blood by increasing the rate of breakdown of glycogen in the liver — called also *hyperglycemic-glycogenolytic factor*

glu·ca·mine \ˈglükə,mēn, -ˌmən\ *n* [ISV *gluc-* + *amine*] : an amine $HOCH_2(CHOH)_4CH_2NH_2$ obtained by reduction of glucosyl-amine or of glucose oxime; glucityl-amine

glu·car·ic acid \(ˈ)glüˈkarik-\ *n* [*gluc-* + -*aric* (as in *saccharic*)] : SACCHARIC ACID

glu·cide \ˈglü,sīd\ *n* -S [ISV *gluc-* + -*ide*] : any of a class of carbohydrates comprising both the glycoses and the glycosides

glu·cin·i·um \glüˈsinēəm\ *or* **glu·ci·num** \-ˈsīnəm, -ˈsēn-\ *n* -S [NL, fr. F *glucina* beryllium oxide (fr. F *glucine*, irreg. fr. Gk *glykys* sweet + F -*ine*) + -*ium* or -*um* (as in *aluminum*) — more at DULCET] : BERYLLIUM

glu·ci·tol \ˈglüsə,tȯl, -tōl\ *n* -S [*gluc-* + -*itol*] : a hexahydric alcohol $C_6H_8(OH)_6$ formed by reduction of glucose — see SORBITOL

glu·ci·tyl \-,til\ *n* -S [*glucitol* + -*yl*] : a univalent radical $HOCH_2(CHOH)_4CH_2$— derived from glucitol by removal of the hydroxyl group from the carbon atom at position one — compare GLUCOSE illustration

¹gluck \ˈglək\ *vi* -ED/-ING/-S [imit.] : GLUG — often reduplicated

²gluck \"\ *n* -S : GLUG — often reduplicated

glucke \ˈglu̇kə\ *also* **gluck** \-k\ *n* -S [G *glucke*, lit., clucking hen, of imit. origin] : a roller-canary tour suggestive of a hen's clucking

glu·co·corticoid \ˌglü(,)kō+\ *n* [*gluc-* + *corticoid*] : a corticoid (as cortisone) that affects chiefly carbohydrate metabolism

glu·co·genesis \,glükō+\ *n* [NL, fr. *gluc-* + L *genesis*] : formation of glucose within the animal body from any product of glycolysis — compare GLUCONEOGENESIS

glu·co·lipid *also* **glu·co·lipide** \ˌglükō+\ *n* [*gluc-* + *lipid, lipide*] : a glycolipid that yields glucose on hydrolysis

glu·co·nate \ˈglükə,nāt\ *n* -S [*glucon-* (fr. *gluconic acid*) + -*ate*] : a salt of gluconic acid (as calcium gluconate)

glu·co·neogenesis \ˌglükō+\ *n* [NL, fr. *gluc-* + *ne-* + L *genesis*] : formation of glucose within the animal body esp. by the liver from proteins, fats, and substances other than carbohydrates — compare GLUCOGENESIS — **glu·co·neogenetic** \"+\ *or* **glu·co·neogenic** \"+\ *adj*

glu·con·ic acid \(ˈ)glüˈkänik-\ *n* [*gluconic* ISV *gluc-* + -*onic*] : a crystalline acid $HOCH_2(CHOH)_4COOH$ that is obtained by oxidation of glucose (as by fermentation with molds), that readily dehydrates to form lactones, and that is used chiefly in cleaning metals

glu·co·protein \ˌglü(,)kō+\ *n* [*gluc-* + *protein*] : GLYCOPROTEIN

glu·co·pyranose \"+\ *n* [*gluc-* + *pyranose*] : one of the modifications of glucose characterized by a pyranose ring

glu·co·py·ran·o·side \,glü(,)kō,pīˈranə,sīd\ *n* -S [*glucopyranose* + -*ide*] : a glucoside that contains a pyranose ring in its structure

glu·co·py·ran·o·syl \-,sil\ *n* -S [*glucopyranose* + -*yl*] : a glucosyl radical that contains a pyranose ring in its structure

glu·co·sa·mine \glüˈkōsə,mēn, -ōzə-\ *n* [ISV *glucose* + *amine*] : a crystalline amino derivative $HOCH_2(CHOH)_3CH(NH_2)CHO$ of glucose occurring in the D-form as chitosamine and obtainable as the *N*-methyl derivative of the L-form by hydrolysis of streptomycin; 2-deoxy-2-amino-glucose

glu·co·san \ˈglükə,san\ *n* -S [ISV *glucose* + -*an*] **1** : any of several intramolecular anhydrides $C_6H_{10}O_5$ of glucose — compare LEVOGLUCOSAN **2** : a hexosan (as dextran or starch) that yields essentially only glucose on hydrolysis

glu·co·sa·zone \glüˈkōsə,zōn, -kōzə-\ *n* [*gluc-* + *osazone*] **1** : the osazone of glucose, mannose, or fructose **2** : GLUCOSE PHENYLOSAZONE

glu·cose \ˈglü,kōs *also* -ōz\ *n* -S [F, modif. of Gk *gleukos*

	open-chain form	cyclic forms	
1	CHO	HCOH	HOCH
2	HCOH	HCOH	HCOH
3	HOCH	HOCH	HOCH
4	HCOH	HCOH	HCOH
5	HCOH	HCO—	HCO—
6	CH₂OH	CH₂OH	CH₂OH
	D-glucose	α-D-glucose	β-D-glucose

must, sweet wine; akin to Gk *glykys* sweet — more at DULCET] **1** : an aldose sugar $HOCH_2(CHOH)_4CHO$ known in dextrorotatory, levorotatory, and racemic forms; *esp* : the sweet colorless soluble dextrorotatory D-form that is readily obtained crystalline in both the alpha and beta modifications, that occurs esp. in plant saps and fruits, normally in blood, pathologically in the urine (as in diabetes mellitus), and combined in many disaccharides, trisaccharides, polysaccharides, and glucosides in most plant and animal tissues, and that is a chief source of protoplasmic energy and in its simple state is the usual form in which carbohydrate is assimilated into the animal body — see DEXTROSE, INVERT SUGAR, SUCROSE; compare GLYCERALDEHYDE, STRUCTURAL FORMULA **2** : STARCH SYRUP — used chiefly commercially

glucose phenylosazone *n* : a yellow insoluble compound $C_6H_{10}O_4(=NNHC_6H_5)_2$ formed by reaction of glucose or mannose or fructose with phenylhydrazine and used as a derivative for identifying glucose

glucose phosphate *n* : a phosphoric derivative of glucose: as **a** : an acylal $C_6H_{11}O_5(OPO_3H_2)$ that reacts in the presence of phosphorylase with aldoses and ketoses to yield disaccharides (as with fructose yielding sucrose and phosphoric acid) or with itself in liver and muscle to yield glycogen and phosphoric acid; glucose 1-phosphate — called also *Cori ester* **b** : an ester $C_6H_{11}O_5(OPO_3H_2)$ formed from glucose and adenosine triphosphate in the presence of hexokinase and regarded as the essential first stage in the metabolism of glucose, subsequent changes being its enzymatic transformations into the corresponding fructose phosphate, glucose phosphate (sense a), and related compounds; glucose 6-phosphate — called also *Robison ester*

glu·co·si·dal \ˌglükəˈsīdᵊl\ *adj* : GLUCOSIDIC

glu·co·si·dase \glüˈkōsə,dās, -ōzə-, -āz\ *n* -S [ISV *glucoside* + -*ase*] : an enzyme (as maltase) that hydrolyzes a glucoside

glu·co·side \ˈglükə,sīd\ *n* -S [ISV *glucose* + -*ide*] : GLYCOSIDE; *usu* : a glycoside that yields glucose on hydrolysis ⟨methyl ~⟩ — **glu·co·sid·ic** \ˌglükəˈsidik\ *adj* — **glucosidically** *adv*

glu·co·sone \ˈglükə,sōn\ *n* [ISV *gluc-* + *osone*] : the osone $C_6H_{10}O_6$ of glucose

glu·co·sul·fone \ˌglü(,)kō+\ *n* [*gluc-* + *sulfone*] : a drug derived from glucose and *para*-amino-phenyl sulfone and used chiefly in treating leprosy in the form of the sodium salt $[C_6H_{12}O_5(SO_3Na)NHC_6H_4]_2SO_2$

glu·cos·uria \,glü-\ *n* -S [NL, fr. ISV *glucose* + NL -*uria*] : GLYCOSURIA

glu·co·syl \ˈglükə,sil\ *n* -S [*glucose* + -*yl*] : a glycosyl radical $C_6H_{11}O_5$ derived from glucose — compare MALTOSE

glu·cu·ron·ic acid \ˌglükyəˈränik-\ *n* [*glucuronic* fr. *gluc-* + Gk *ouron* urine + E -*ic* — more at URINE] : a crystalline aldehyde-acid $HOOC(CHOH)_4CHO$ obtainable from gum arabic by hydrolysis or from methyl glucoside by oxidation and occurring naturally esp. in the urine combined as glucuronides with toxic metabolic products (as phenols or indoxyl) or with steroid hormones

glu·cu·ron·i·dase \,glükyəˈränə,dās, -āz\ *n* -S [*glucuronide* + -*ase*] : an enzyme that hydrolyzes a glucuronide; *esp* : an enzyme that occurs widely (as in liver and spleen) and is active toward a beta-glucuronide ⟨the physiological role of beta⸗*glucuronidase*⟩

glu·cu·ro·nide \glüˈkyu̇rə,nīd\ *n* -S [*glucuron-* (fr. *glucuronic acid*) + -*ide*] : a glycosidic compound that yields glucuronic acid on hydrolysis ⟨beta-*glucuronides* of estrogenic hormones⟩

glu·cu·rono·lactone \glüˌkyu̇rə(,)nō, ˌglükyəˌränə+\ *n* [*glucuron-* (fr. *glucuronic acid*) + -*o-* + *lactone*] : a crystalline aldehydic lactone $C_6H_8O_6$ made from glucuronic acid by heating and used in medicine

glu·cu·ron·o·side \,glükyəˈränə,sīd\ *n* -S [*glucuron-* (fr. *glucuronic acid*) + -*ose* + -*ide*] : GLUCURONIDE

¹glue \ˈglü\ *n* -S [ME *glu, glew*, fr. MF *glu* birdlime, glue, fr. OF, fr. LL *glut-, glus* glue — more at CLAY] **1 a** (1) : a hard protein substance that absorbs water to form a jelly or a viscous solution with strong adhesive properties that is obtained from animal materials by cooking down materials (as hides, bones) yielding collagen and is usu. considered to contain gelatin along with other products and is used for sticking together relatively heavy materials (as wood) — see ANIMAL GLUE, FISH GLUE; compare MUCILAGE, PASTE; CEMENT 2 a (2) : a viscous solution of animal glue or fish glue — compare LIQUID GLUE **b** : any of various other strong adhesive substances (as casein glue, vegetable glue) **2** : something that binds together ⟨patriotism is the psychological ~ which helps to hold people of the same country together —R.S.Ellery⟩ or holds tightly ⟨his plunging spirit had got stuck in the ~ of convention and hypocrisy —Victoria Sackville-West⟩ in a manner suggestive of glue

²glue \"\ *vb* **glued; glued; gluing** *also* **glueing; glues** [ME *gluen, glewen*, fr. MF *gluer*, fr. OF, fr. *glu*, n.] *vt* **1** : to join or fix or cause to stick tightly with or as if with glue ⟨*gluing* the wings onto the model airplane⟩ ⟨reading attentively, his eyes *glued* to the page⟩ **2** : to daub, smear, or cover with glue ⟨got their hands all *glued* up⟩ ~ *vi* : to become glued : undergo gluing ⟨a wood that *glues* easily⟩

glue cell *n* : ADHESIVE CELL

glued–up stock \ˈ⸗,⸗-\ *n* [*glued* fr. past part. of ²*glue*] : edge⸗glued or laminated wood

glue·man \ˈglümən\ *n, pl* **gluemen 1** : GLUER **2** : one who makes glue

glue off *vt* : to apply glue to (the spine of a book) during the process of binding

glue plant *n* : an alga of the genus *Gloiopeltis* used chiefly in Japan and China for making glue or as a food

glue pot *n* [ME *glew pot*, fr. *glu, glew* glue + *pot*] **1** : a double boiler designed esp. for melting glue **2** *Austral* : a stretch of deep sticky mud on a bush road

glu·er \ˈglüə(r), -ü(ə)r, -üə\ *n* -S [ME *glewer*, fr. *glewen* to glue + -*er*] : one that glues; *specif* : a worker who glues articles — called also *cementer*

glue up *vt* : to glue off

glu·ey \ˈglüē, -üi\ *adj, usu* **gluier**; *usu* **gluiest** [ME *gluwy, glewy*, fr. *glu, glew* glue + -*y*] **1** : having the quality of glue ⟨what we call a colloid, a ~ mass —W.E.Swinton⟩ : resembling or suggestive of glue (as in stickiness or viscous consistency) ⟨he thought how much he would like a beer to wash down the last gob of ~ rice —Earle Birney⟩ : STICKY, GUMMY **2** : daubed, smeared, or covered with glue ⟨a ~ surface⟩

¹glug \ˈgləg\ *n* -S [imit.] : a gurgling sound (as of liquid issuing from a bottle with intermittent partial air blockage) : GLUB — often reduplicated

²glug \"\ *vi* **glugged; glugged; glugging; glugs** : to make a glug — often reduplicated ⟨glasses clinked . . . and the wine bottles *glugged* —Gerald Durrell⟩

glu·gea \ˈglüj(ē)ə\ *n, cap* [NL] : a large genus of intracellular parasitic microsporidians related to *Nosema* that attack various insect larvae and fishes

gluh·wein \ˈglüe,vīn\ *n* -S [G *glühwein*, fr. *glühen* to mull, glow (fr. OHG *gluoen* to glow) + *wein* wine, fr. OHG *wīn* — more at GLOW, WINE] : mulled wine

glu·i·ly \ˈglüəlē, -li\ *adv* : in a gluey manner

glu·i·ness *or* **glu·ey·ness** \ˈglüēnəs, -üin-\ *n* -ES : the quality or state of being gluey

¹glum \ˈgləm\ *vi* **glummed; glummed; glumming; glums** [ME *glomen*, prob. alter. of *gloumen* — more at GLOOM] *chiefly dial* : to look glum : FROWN

²glum \"\ *adj, usu* **glummer**; *usu* **glummest 1 a** : broodingly morose : sullenly ill-humored or displeased ⟨looked ~ when they heard the news⟩ **b** : DISMAL, DREARY, GLOOMY ⟨with a countenance as ~ as an undertaker's —W.M.Thackeray⟩ **2** *dial Eng* : OVERCAST, THREATENING ⟨the weather looks ~ today⟩ **syn** see SULLEN

glu·ma·ceous \(ˈ)glüˈmāshəs\ *adj* [prob. fr. (assumed) NL *glumaceus*, fr. NL *gluma* + L -*aceus* -aceous] : consisting or having the character of glumes ⟨~ flowers⟩

glume \ˈglüm\ *n* -S [NL *gluma*, fr. L, hull, husk; akin to L *glubere* to peel — more at CLEAVE] : a chaffy bract; *specif* : one of the two empty bracts at the base of the spikelet in grasses

glume blotch *n* : any of several fungous diseases causing diffuse dark spots on the glumes

glu·mif·er·ous \(ˈ)glüˈmif(ə)rəs\ *adj* [*glume* + -*iferous*] : bearing glumes

glu·mi·flo·rae \,glüməˈflōr,ē\ *n pl, cap* [NL, fr. *glumi-* (fr. *gluma* glume) + -*florae* (fr. L *flor-, flos* flower) — more at BLOW (to bloom)] *syn of* GRAMINALES

glum·ly *adv* : in a glum manner

glum·ness *n* -ES : the quality or state of being glum

glump \ˈgləmp\ *vi* -ED/-ING/-S [prob. alter. of ¹*glum*] *dial* : to look glum : FROWN

glump·ish \-pish\ *adj, archaic* : somewhat grumpy

glump·y \-pē\ *adj, usu* **glumpier**; *usu* **glumpiest** [*glump* + -*y*] *archaic* : GRUMPY

¹glunch \ˈglənch\ *vi* -ED/-ING/-ES [perh. alter. of ¹*glum*] *chiefly Scot* : to look sour or glum : FROWN ⟨glowered and ~*ed* at him —John Buchan⟩

²glunch \"\ *n* -ES *chiefly Scot* : a sour or glum look ⟨a ~ of sour disdain —Robert Burns⟩

glu·side \ˈglü,sīd\ *n* -S [NL *glusidum*, perh. irreg. fr. Gk *glykys* sweet + NL -*idum* -ide — more at DULCET] : SACCHARIN

¹glut \ˈglət, *usu* -əd·+V\ *vb* **glutted; glutted; glutting; gluts** [ME *glotten, glouten*, prob. fr. MF *glotir, gloutir* to swallow, fr. L *gluttire* — more at GLUTTON] *vt* **1** : to feed, fill, or gratify to the fullest possible extent : indulge to the point of satiety or revulsion : SATIATE, GORGE, SURFEIT ⟨*glutting* themselves with food and drink⟩ ⟨before he had quite *glutted* his great appetite —C.G.D.Roberts⟩ ⟨the crowd, perhaps *glutted* with blood, is ominously silent —Claudia Cassidy⟩ **2** : to flood (the business market) with goods so that supply exceeds demand ⟨selling *glutted* the market and cracked it —Lewis Nordyke⟩ ~ *vi* : to feed upon something without restraint and to the point of satiety or revulsion : become gorged ⟨sat by to ~ and laugh —J.H.Allen⟩ **syn** see SATIATE

²glut \"\ *n* -S **1** *archaic* : the act of glutting or state of being glutted : full or excessive gratification : SURFEITING **2** : an excessive quantity; *specif* : OVERSUPPLY ⟨when there is a ~ in the wheat market —M.R.Cohen⟩ ⟨the mounting ~ of indifference —Claudia Cassidy⟩

3glut \"\ *n* -s [perh. fr. 1*glut*] *archaic* : DRAFT, SWALLOW

4glut \"\ *vt* **glutted; glutted; glutting; gluts** *archaic* : to swallow greedily : gulp down : WOLF

5glut \"\ *n* -s [origin unknown] **1** : a block (as metal, wood) that is often tapered and that is used as a wedge or shim or lever fulcrum **2** : material (as a piece of canvas with a thimble or pieces of rope with a thimble or becket) which is sewed or spliced near the center of the head of a square sail and to which a bunt jigger is hooked in hauling up the bunt for furling **3** : a small brick used to fill out a course

glut·acon·ic acid \ˌglüd·əˈkänik-\ *n* [*glutaconic* prob. ISV *glut-* (fr. *gluten*) + *aconic* (in *aconic acid*)] : a crystalline unsaturated dicarboxylic acid $HOOCCH_2CH{=}CHCOOH$ isomeric with citraconic acid

glu·ta·mate \ˈglüd·əˌmāt\ *n* -s [*glutam-* (fr. *glutamic acid*) + *-ate*] : a salt or ester of glutamic acid; *esp* : MONOSODIUM GLUTAMATE

glu·tam·ic acid \(ˈ)glüˈtamik-\ *n* [*glutamic* ISV *glut-* (fr. *gluten*) + *amic* (in *amic acid*)] : a crystalline amino dicarboxylic acid $HOOCCH_2CH_2CH(NH_2)COOH$ that exists in three optically isomeric forms and occurs usu. as the dextrorotatory L-form both free and combined in glutamine and many proteins in plants and animals, that is usu. obtained by hydrolysis of gluten or from the waste waters of beet-sugar manufacture or by fermentation, and that takes part in transaminations and related metabolic reactions in the living organism; α-amino-glutaric acid

glu·ta·min·ase \ˈglüd·əməˌnās, glüˈtam-, -āz\ *n* -s [ISV *glutamine* + *-ase*] : an enzyme that hydrolyzes glutamine to glutamic acid and ammonia

glu·ta·mine \ˈglüd·əˌmēn, -ˌmən\ *n* -s [ISV *glut-* (fr. *gluten*) + *amine*] : a crystalline amino acid $H_2NOCCH_2CH_2CH(NH_2)$-COOH that occurs both free and combined in proteins in plants and animals and that yields glutamic acid and ammonia on hydrolysis; L-glutamic acid monoamide

glu·ta·min·ic acid \ˌglüd·əˈminik-\ *n* [*glutaminic* ISV *glutamine* + *-ic*] : GLUTAMIC ACID

glu·tamyl \ˈglüd·əˌmil, glüˈtaməl\ *also* **glu·tam·o·yl** \glüˈtaməˌwil\ *n* -s [ISV *glutam-* (fr. *glutamic acid*) + *-yl* or *-oyl*] : the bivalent radical $-OCCH_2CH_2CH(NH_2)CO-$ of glutamic acid

glu·tar·ic acid \(ˈ)glüˈtarik-\ *n* [*glutaric* prob. ISV *glut-* (fr. *gluten*) + *-aric* (as in *tartaric acid*)] : a crystalline dicarboxylic acid $HOOC(CH_2)_3COOH$ made usu. by oxidation of cyclopentanone — compare KETOGLUTARIC ACID

glu·ta·ryl \ˈglüd·əˌril, glüˈtarəl\ *n* -s [*glutar-* (fr. *glutaric acid*) + *-yl*] : the bivalent radical $-OC(CH_2)_3CO-$ of glutaric acid

glu·ta·thi·one \ˌglüd·əˈthīˌōn, -ˌthīˈōn\ *n* -s [ISV *gluta-* (fr. *glutamic acid*) + *thi-* + *-one*] : a crystalline tripeptide $C_{10}H_{17}N_3O_6S$ of glutamic acid, cysteine, and glycine that occurs in blood and other animal and plant tissues and that plays an important role in the activation of some enzymes and in biological oxidation-reduction processes

glu·te·al \ˈglüd·ēəl, (ˈ)glüˈtē-\ *adj* [NL *gluteus* + E *-al*] : of, relating to, or in the region of the gluteus muscles

gluteal artery *n* : one of the arteries supplying the gluteal muscles on each side of the body

gluteal nerve *n* : one of the nerves arising from the sacral plexus and supplying the gluteal muscles and adjacent parts

glu·telin \ˈglüd·ᵊlən, glüˈtel-\ *n* -s [ISV, irreg. fr. *gluten*] : any of a group of simple proteins (as glutenin) that occur esp. in the seeds of cereals and that are insoluble in neutral solvents and soluble in dilute acids or alkalies

glu·ten \ˈglütᵊn\ *n* -s [MF or L; MF *gluten*, fr. L, glue; akin to LL *glut-*, *glus* glue — more at CLAY] **1** *archaic* **a** : a sticky substance : ADHESIVE **b** : an albuminous element found in animal tissues **2 a** : a tenacious tough elastic protein substance characteristic of flour (as from wheat) that gives to bread dough cohesiveness and ability to retain gas, that is usu. obtained by washing the starch out of wheat flour, and that consists chiefly of gliadin and glutenin **b** : CORN GLUTEN — **glu·ten·ous** \-t(ᵊ)nəs\ *adj*

gluten bread *n* : bread made of wheat flour of high gluten and low starch content

gluten feed *n* : CORN GLUTEN FEED

glu·te·nin \ˈglütᵊnən\ *n* -s [*gluten* + *-in*] : a glutelin found esp. in wheat and obtained by extracting gluten with dilute alkali

gluten meal *n* : CORN GLUTEN MEAL

gluteo- *comb form* [NL *gluteus*] : gluteal and ⟨*gluteo*femoral⟩

glu·te·us \ˈglüd·ēəs, glüˈtē-\ *n, pl* **glu·tei** \-ēˌī\ [NL *glutaeus*, *gluteus*, irreg. fr. Gk *gloutos* buttock — more at CLOUD] : any one of certain muscles of the buttocks — see GLUTEUS MAXIMUS, GLUTEUS MEDIUS, GLUTEUS MINIMUS

gluteus max·i·mus \-ˈmaksəməs\ *n, pl* **glutei maxi·mi** \-səˌmī\ [NL, lit., largest gluteus] : the outermost muscle of three muscles found in each of the human buttocks that arises from the sacrum, coccyx, back part of the ilium and adjacent structures and that is inserted into the fascia lata of the thigh and the gluteal tuberosity of the femur

gluteus me·di·us \-ˈmēdēəs\ *n, pl* **glutei me·dii** \-dēˌī\ [NL, lit., middle gluteus] : the middle muscle of three muscles found in each of the human buttocks that arises from the outer surface of the ilium and that is inserted into the great trochanter of the femur

gluteus mi·ni·mus \-ˈminəməs\ *n, pl* **glutei mini·mi** \-nəˌmī\ [NL, lit., smallest gluteus] : the innermost muscle of three muscles found in each of the human buttocks that arises from the outer surface of the ilium and that is inserted into the great trochanter of the femur

glut herring *n* : an anadromous herring (*Pomolobus aestivalis*) of the coast from New England to the Carolinas that appears in great numbers esp. southward later than the alewife and shad — called also *summer herring*

glu·ti·nin \ˈglütᵊnən\ *n* -s [prob. fr. *agglutinin*] : BLOCKING ANTIBODY

glu·ti·nize \-tᵊnˌīz\ *vt* -ED/-ING/-S [*glutin*ous + *-ize*] : to make glutinous

glu·ti·nose \-tᵊnˌōs\ *adj* [L *glutinosus*] : GLUTINOUS

glu·ti·nos·i·ty \ˌglütᵊnˈäsəd·ē\ *n* -ES [ME *glutinosite*, fr. (assumed) NL *glutinositat-*, *glutinositas*, fr. L *glutinosus* + *-itat-*, *-itas* -ity] : the quality or state of being glutinous

glu·ti·nous \ˈglüt(ᵊ)nəs\ *adj* [MF or L; MF *glutineux*, fr. L *glutinosus*, fr. *glutin-*, *gluten* glue + *-osus* -ose] : having the quality of glue esp. in physical properties ⟨a ~ substance⟩ : GLUEY, STICKY, GUMMY, ROPY ⟨all had ~ chipped beef on rocklike toast —Sloan Wilson⟩; *specif* : having a sticky surface ⟨~ plant leaves⟩ — **glu·ti·nous·ly** *adv* — **glu·ti·nous·ness** *n* -ES

glu·ti·tion \glüˈtishən\ *n* -s [LL *gluttition-*, *gluttitio*, fr. L *gluttitus*, past part of *gluttire* to swallow] : DEGLUTITION

glu·toid \ˈglüˌtȯid\ *n* -s [ISV *glut-* (fr. *gluten*) + *-oid*] : gelatin hardened with formaldehyde and used in making enteric capsules and as a coating for enteric pills

glu·tose \ˈglüˌtōs *also* -ōz\ *n* -s [ISV *glu-* (fr. *glucose*) + *-tose* (fr. *fructose*)] : an unfermentable carbohydrate fraction formed by the action of alkali on glucose or fructose or found in cane molasses

gluts *pres 3d sing of* GLUT, *pl of* GLUT

glutted *past of* GLUT

glutting *pres part of* GLUT

glut·ting·ly *adv, archaic* : GLUTTONOUSLY

1glut·ton \ˈglətᵊn\ *n* -s [ME *glotoun*, fr. OF *gloton*, fr. L *glutton-*, *glutto;* akin to OE *ceole* throat, OHG *kela*, L *gula* throat, *gluttire* to swallow, Gk *delear* bait, Russ *glotat'* to swallow, gulp] **1 a** : one that eats too much : one given to excessive eating and drinking : one that gluts **b** (1) : one that greedily or excessively indulges in something as if voraciously devouring it ⟨~*s* of morning air —Christopher Morley⟩ ⟨a ~ of books⟩ ⟨a literary ~⟩ (2) : one that has a great capacity for accepting or enduring something ⟨a ~ for work⟩ ⟨a ~ for punishment⟩ **2** [trans. of G *vielfrass*] : WOLVERINE 1a; *esp* : one occurring in the Old World **syn** see EPICURE

2glutton \"\ *adj* [ME *glotoun*, fr. *glotoun*, n.] *archaic* : GLUTTONOUS

3glutton \"\ *vb* -ED/-ING/-S [1*glutton*] *archaic* : GLUT

4glutton \"\ *also* **glutton bird** *n* -s [1*glutton*] : GIANT PETREL

glut·ton·ize \ˈglətᵊnˌīz\ *vb* -ED/-ING/-S *vi, archaic* : to feast gluttonously ~ *vt, archaic* : to feast gluttonously on

glut·ton·ous \ˈglət(ᵊ)nəs\ *adj* [ME *glotonous*, fr. *gloton*, *glotoun* glutton + *-ous*] : marked by or given to gluttony **syn** see VORACIOUS

glut·ton·ous·ly *adv* [ME *glotonously*, fr. *glotonous* + *-ly*] : in a gluttonous manner

glut·ton·ous·ness *n* -ES : the quality or state of being gluttonous

glut·tony \ˈglət(ᵊ)nē, -ni\ *n* -ES [ME *glotonie*, fr. OF, fr. *gloton* glutton + *-ie* -y] **1** : excess in eating and drinking esp. when habitual **2** : greedy or excessive indulgence of any desire or faculty

glyc- *or* **glyco-** *comb form* [ISV, fr. Gk *glyk-* sweet, fr. *glykys* — more at DULCET] **1** : sugar ⟨*glyco*genic⟩ : related to or containing a sugar ⟨*glyc*emia⟩ ⟨*glyco*alkaloid⟩ ⟨*glyc*itol⟩ : sweet ⟨*glyco*gen⟩ **2 a** : glycerol ⟨*glyco*gelatin⟩ **b** : glycogen ⟨*glyco*static⟩ **c** : glycol ⟨*glyco*stat⟩ **d** : glycine ⟨*glyc*yl⟩ — used also to indicate other compounds spelled with initial *glyc-* **3** : GLUC- 1a

gly·can \ˈglīˌkan\ *n* -s [*glyc-* + *-an*] : POLYSACCHARIDE

gly·ce·mia *also* **gly·cae·mia** \glīˈsēmēə\ *n* -s [NL, fr. *glyc-* + *-emia*] : the presence of glucose in the blood — **gly·ce·mic** \(ˈ)glīˈsēmik\ *adj*

glycer- *or* **glycero-** *comb form* [ISV, fr. *glycerin*] **1** : glycerol ⟨*glycer*yl⟩ : related to glycerol or glyceric acid ⟨*glycero*phosphoric acid⟩ ⟨*glycer*aldehyde⟩ **2** *glycero-*, *usu ital* : having the stereochemical arrangement of atoms or groups found in glyceraldehyde ⟨2-(D-*glycero*-1-hydroxyethyl)-benzimidazole⟩

glyc·era \ˈglisərə\ *n, cap* [NL, fr. L *Glycera* (feminine proper name)] : a common widely distributed genus (the type of the family Glyceridae) of usu. brightly colored burrowing marine polychaete worms having simple parapodia and an extremely large introvert armed with four chitinous jaws suggestive of hooks — **glyc·er·id** \-rəd\ *adj or n*

glyc·er·aldehyde \ˌglisər+\ *n* : a sweet crystalline compound that exists in solution as the monomeric dihydroxy aldehyde $HOCH_2CHOHCHO$ in dextrorotatory, levorotatory, and racemic forms but in the anhydrous state only as the crystalline dimer $C_6H_{12}O_6$, that is formed as an intermediate in carbohydrate metabolism by the breakdown of sugars, that yields glycerol on reduction, and that may be regarded as a triose and the simplest aldose capable of existing in both D- and L-stereoisomeric forms, which serve as reference standards for differentiating the stereoisomeric forms of all other sugars and also of other stereoisomeric compounds — called also *glyceric aldehyde*, *glycerose;* compare GLUCOSE 1, STRUCTURAL FORMULA

CHO H–C–OH CH₂OH	CHO HO–C–H CH₂OH
dextrorotatory D-glyceraldehyde	levorotatory L-glyceraldehyde

glyc·er·ate \ˈglisəˌrāt\ *n* -s [ISV *glycer-* + *-ate*] : a salt or ester of glyceric acid

gly·ce·ria \gləˈsirēə, glīˈ-\ *n, cap* [NL, fr. Gk *glykeros* sweet + NL *-ia*] : a genus of chiefly No. American perennial paludal or aquatic grasses having lemmas very prominently 5- to 9-nerved

gly·cer·ic acid \gləˈserik-, (ˈ)gliˈserik-, ˈglisərik-\ *n* [*glyceric* ISV *glycer-* + *-ic*] : a syrupy hydroxy acid $HOCH_2$-CHOHCOOH obtainable by oxidation of glycerol or glyceraldehyde

glyceric aldehyde *n* : GLYCERALDEHYDE

glyc·er·ide \ˈglisəˌrīd, -ˌrəd\ *n* -s [ISV *glycer-* + *-ide*] : any of a large class of compounds that are esters of glycerol esp. with fatty acids, that occur naturally as fats and fatty oils or are made synthetically, and that are classed as monoglycerides, diglycerides, and triglycerides according to the number of hydroxyl groups of glycerol esterified or as simple glycerides or mixed glycerides depending on whether one or more than one kind of acid radical is present — **glyc·er·id·ic** \ˌglisəˈridik\ *adj*

1glyc·er·in \ˈglis(ə)rən\ *or* **glyc·er·ine** \" *sometimes* ˈglisəˌrēn *or* ˌglisəˈrēn\ *n* -s [F *glycérine*, fr. Gk *glykeros* sweet + F *-ine;* akin to Gk *glykys* sweet — more at DULCET] **1** : GLYCEROL — used esp. of the products for industrial and pharmaceutical uses **2** : GLYCERITE

2glycerin \"\ *or* **glycerine** \"\ *vt* -ED/-ING/-S : GLYCERINATE

glyc·er·in·ate \ˈglis(ə)rəˌnāt\ *vt* -ED/-ING/-S : to treat with or preserve in glycerin — **glyc·er·in·ation** \ˌglis(ə)rəˈnāshən\ *n* -s

glycerinated gelatin *n* [*glycerinated* fr. past part. of *glycerinate*] : a jellylike preparation that is made from glycerin, gelatin, and water and that is used as a base for suppositories and ointments

glyc·er·in·ize \ˈglis(ə)rəˌnīz\ *vt* -ED/-ING/-S : GLYCERINATE

glycerin jelly *n* : a mixture of gelatin and glycerin used in the mounting of microscopic material

glycerin soap *n* : transparent toilet soap having glycerin as an ingredient

glyc·er·ite \ˈglisəˌrīt\ *n* -s : a medicinal preparation made by mixing or dissolving a substance in glycerin

glyc·er·ize \-ˌrīz\ *vt* -ED/-ING/-S : GLYCERINATE

glyc·ero·gelatin \ˌglisə(ˌ)rō+\ *n* : any of several medicated dermatologic preparations made from glycerin and glycerinated gelatin

glyc·er·ol \ˈglisəˌrȯl, -rōl\ *n* -s [*glycer-* + *-ol*] : a sweet syrupy hygroscopic trihydroxy alcohol $HOCH_2CHOHCH_2$-OH that occurs combined as glycerides and is formed by alcoholic fermentation of sugars, that is usu. obtained as a by-product in the manufacture of soap or fatty acids by the saponification of fats or as a synthetic product from propylene or allyl alcohol, and that is used chiefly as a solvent and plasticizer, as a moistening agent, emollient, and lubricant, as an emulsifying agent, and as a starting material in the manufacture of many derivatives; 1,2,3-propane-triol — called also *glycerin;* see ALKYD, CHLOROHYDRIN, ESTER GUM, NITROGLYCERIN

1glyc·er·o·late \ˈglis(ə)rəˌlāt\ *n* -s [*glycerol* + 1*-ate*] : GLYCERITE

2glycerolate \"\ *vt* -ED/-ING/-S [*glycerol* + 4*-ate*] : GLYCERINATE

glyc·er·ole \ˈglisəˌrōl\ *n* -s [irreg. fr. *glycer-*] : GLYCERITE

glyc·er·o·lize \ˈglis(ə)rəˌlīz\ *vt* -ED/-ING/-S [*glycerol* + *-ize*] : GLYCERINATE

glyc·ero·phosphate \ˌglisə(ˌ)rō+\ *n* [ISV *glycer-* + *phosphate*] : a salt or ester of either of the glycerophosphoric acids

glyc·ero·phosphoric acid \ˌglisə(ˌ)rō+ . . . -\ *n* [*glycerophosphoric* ISV *glycer-* + *phosphoric*] : either of two syrupy isomeric dibasic acids $C_3H_5(OH)_2OPO_3H_2$ occurring naturally in combined form as lecithin and cephalin, obtained usu. as a mixture of the two by reaction of glycerol and phosphoric acid, and used in medicine in the form of salts: **a** : the alpha isomer existing in dextrorotatory, levorotatory, and racemic forms; glycerol 1-phosphate — called also *alpha-glycerophosphoric acid* **b** : the optically inactive beta isomer; glycerol 2-phosphate — called also *beta-glycerophosphate*

glyc·er·ose \ˈglisəˌrōs *also* -ōz\ *n* -s [ISV *glycer-* + *-ose*] : GLYCERALDEHYDE — used esp. in relation to other sugars

glyc·er·oxide \ˌglisər+\ *n* : a derivative of glycerol in which a metal (as sodium) replaces hydroxylic hydrogen

glyc·er·yl \ˈglis(ə)rəl\ *n* -s [ISV *glycer-* + *-yl*] : a trivalent radical CH_2CHCH_2 derived from glycerol by removal of all three hydroxyl groups; *sometimes* : a univalent or bivalent radical derived from glycerol by removal of hydroxyl ⟨~ mono-stearate⟩

glyceryl triacetate *n* : ACETIN c

glyceryl trinitrate *n* : NITROGLYCERIN

gly·cid·ic acid \gləˈs|idik-, (ˈ)glīˈs|\ *n* [*glycidic* ISV *glycid-* (as in E *glycidol*) + *-ic*] : a volatile mobile liquid C_2H_3-OCOOH used in the form of derivatives in perfumes; α,β-epoxy-propionic acid

glyc·i·dol \ˈglisəˌdȯl, -dōl\ *n* -s [obs. E *glycide* glycidol (fr. E *glyc-* + *-ide*) + E *-ol*] : a liquid alcohol $C_2H_3OCH_2OH$ obtained from glycerol by indirect dehydration; 2,3-epoxy-1-propanol

gly·cin \ˈglīsᵊn\ *also* **gly·cine** \", -īˌsēn\ *n* -s [prob. fr. 1*glycine*] : a poisonous compound $HOC_6H_4NHCH_2COOH$ used in photography as a fine-grain developer; *N-(para-*hydroxy-phenyl)glycine

1gly·cine \"\ *n* -s [ISV *glyc-* + *-ine*] : a sweet crystalline amino acid NH_2CH_2COOH that is formed by the hydrolysis of many proteins (as gelatin), hippuric acid, and glycocholic acid but is usu. made by reaction of chloroacetic acid and ammonia — called also *aminoacetic acid*, *glycocoll*

2glyc·i·ne \ˈglisᵊnˌē\ [NL, irreg. fr. Gk *glykys* sweet — more at DULCET] *syn of* APIOS

glyci·nin \ˈglīsᵊnən, ˈglis-\ *n* -s [NL *Glycine* + E *-in*] : a globulin found in the seeds of the soybean

glyciphagus *syn of* GLYCYPHAGUS

glyco- — see GLYC-

gly·co·chol·ate \ˌglīkōˈkäˌlāt, -ˈkōˌlāt; glīˈkäkəˌlāt\ *n* -s [ISV *glycochol-* (fr. *glycocholic acid*) + *-ate*] : a salt or ester of glycocholic acid

gly·co·cholic acid \ˌglīkōˈkōlik-, -ˈkälik-\ *n* [*glycocholic* ISV *glyc-* + *cholic* (as in *cholic acid*)] : a crystalline acid $(HO)_3C_{23}H_{36}CONHCH_2COOH$ that occurs in bile esp. of man and herbivorous animals and that yields glycine and cholic acid on hydrolysis

gly·co·coll \ˈglīkōˌkäl\ *n* -s [ISV *glyc-* sweet (fr. Gk *glyk-*, fr. *glykys*) + *-o-* + *-coll*] : GLYCINE

gly·co·cy·a·mine \ˌglīkōˈsīəˈmēn, -ˌsīˈamən\ *n* [ISV *glyc-* + *cy-* (fr. *cyan-*) + *amine*] : a crystalline amino acid NH_2-$C(=NH)NHCH_2COOH$ that is produced enzymatically in the animal body from glycine and arginine and that yields creatine on methylation — called also *guanidoacetic acid*

gly·co·gen \ˈglīkəjən, -ˌjen\ *n* -s [ISV *glyc-* + *-gen*] : a white amorphous tasteless polysaccharide $(C_6H_{10}O_5)_x$ constituting the principal form in which carbohydrate is stored in animal tissues, occurring esp. in the liver and in muscle and also in fungi and yeasts, and resembling starch in molecular structure and in the formation of only glucose on complete hydrolysis — called also *animal starch*

gly·co·gen·e·sis \ˌglīkəˈjenəsəs\ *n* [NL, fr. *glyc-* + L *genesis*] **1** : formation of sugar from glycogen (as in the liver) **2** : formation of glycogen (as from sugars or some amino acids)

gly·co·ge·net·ic \ˌglīkəjəˈned·ik\ *adj* [fr. NL *glycogenesis*, after E *genesis: genetic*] : of, relating to, or produced by glycogenesis

gly·co·gen·ic \ˌglīkəˈjenik\ *adj* [ISV *glycogen* + *-ic*] **1** : of, relating to, or involving glycogen **2** [ISV *glyc-* + *-genic*] : GLYCOGENETIC

gly·co·gen·ol·y·sis \ˌglīkəjəˈnäləsəs\ *n, pl* **glycogenoly·ses** \-ˌsēz\ [NL, fr. *glycogeno-* (fr. ISV *glycogen*) + *-lysis*] : the breakdown of glycogen esp. to glucose in the animal body

gly·co·gen·o·lyt·ic \ˌglīkəˌjenᵊlˈid·ik\ *adj* [ISV *glycogen* + *-o-* + *-lytic*] : of, relating to, or inducing glycogenolysis ⟨~ enzymes⟩ ⟨a ~ system⟩

gly·co·gen·o·tropic \-nəˈträpik, -rōp-\ *adj* [ISV *glycogen* + *-o-* + *-tropic*] : tending to induce glycogenolysis ⟨a ~ hormone⟩

gly·cog·e·nous \(ˈ)glīˈkäjənəs\ *adj* [*glyc-* + *-genous*] : GLYCOGENETIC

gly·col \ˈglīˌkȯl, -kōl\ *n* -s [ISV *glyc-* + *-ol*] **1** : ETHYLENE GLYCOL **2** : any of the large class of dihydroxy alcohols (as propylene glycol) of which ethylene glycol is the simplest member — compare DIOL

gly·col·aldehyde \ˌ==+\ *n* [ISV *glycol* + *aldehyde*] : a compound that in solution exists as the monomeric hydroxy aldehyde $HOCH_2CHO$ and as such is the simplest monosaccharide but that in the anhydrous state exists only as the crystalline dimer $C_4H_8O_4$; hydroxy-acetaldehyde — compare DIOSE

gly·co·late \ˈglīkəˌlāt\ *or* **gly·col·late** \", glīˈkälət\ *n* -s [*glycol* + *-ate*] : a salt or ester of glycolic acid

gly·col·ic acid *or* **gly·col·lic acid** \(ˈ)glīˈkälik-\ *n* [*glycolic*, *glycollic* ISV *glycol* + *-ic*] : a translucent crystalline compound $HOCH_2COOH$ found esp. in unripe grapes and in sugar beets, made usu. by hydrolysis of chloroacetic acid or as an intermediate in the manufacture of ethylene glycol, and used chiefly in processing textiles and leather and in cleaning metals

gly·co·lipid *also* **gly·co·lipide** \ˌglīkō+\ *n* [*glyc-* + *lipid*, *lipide*] : any of a class of lipids that yield on hydrolysis a sugar (as galactose or glucose), sphingosine or a related amino alcohol, fatty acids, and sometimes other acids and that include the cerebrosides and the gangliosides

gly·col·y·sis \glīˈkäləsəs\ *n, pl* **glycoly·ses** \-əˌsēz\ [NL, fr. *glyc-* + *-lysis*] : the enzymatic breakdown of glucose, glycogen, or other carbohydrate by way of phosphate derivatives with the production esp. of lactic acid in animals and of pyruvic acid in plants and with the release of energy — see ADENOSINE DIPHOSPHATE; compare FERMENTATION 1, RESPIRATION 2

gly·co·lyt·ic \ˌglīkəˈlid·ik\ *adj* [ISV *glyc-* + *-lytic*] : of, relating to, or inducing glycolysis ⟨a ~ enzyme system⟩ ⟨the ~ pathway⟩ — **gly·co·lyt·i·cal·ly** \-d·ək(ə)lē\ *adv*

gly·co·neogenesis \ˌglīkō+\ *n* [NL, fr. *glyc-* + *ne-* + L *genesis*] : GLUCONEOGENESIS

1gly·con·ic \glīˈkänik\ *n* -s *sometimes cap* [*Glycon*, Greek poet of unknown date to whom the invention of this verse was ascribed in the 2d century A.D. + E *-ic*] : a variable verse or rhythmic system typically of the form ⏓⏓–⏑⏑–⏑– that may have a choriambus or dactyl at the beginning, middle, or end

2glyconic \(ˈ)=ˈ==\ *adj, sometimes cap* : of, relating to, or consisting of glyconics

glyconic acid *n* [*glyconic* ISV *glyc-* + *-onic*] : ALDONIC ACID

gly·co·peptide \ˌglī(ˌ)kō+\ *n* [*glyc-* + *peptide*] : GLYCOPROTEIN

gly·co·protein \ˌ=(ˌ)=+\ *n* [*glyc-* + *protein*] : any of a group of complex compounds containing sugar units or polysaccharides combined usu. covalently with amino acid units or polypeptides and including many common albumins and globulins (as egg albumin, some serum albumins, and some serum globulins) — called also *glycopeptide;* compare MUCOPROTEIN

gly·cose \ˈglīˌkōs *also* -ōz\ *n* -s [F, alter. (influenced by Gk *glykys* sweet) of *glucose*] **1** *archaic* : GLUCOSE 1 **2** : a simple sugar (as arabinose, glucose, or fructose) existing structurally in either its open-chain aldehyde or ketone modification or in its cyclic hemiacetal forms that contain furanose or pyranose rings : MONOSACCHARIDE

gly·co·si·dase \glīˈkōsəˌdās, -ōzə-, -āz\ *n* -s [ISV *glycoside* + *-ase*] : an enzyme that hydrolyzes a glycoside, esp. a simple glycoside or an oligosaccharide

gly·co·side \ˈglīkəˌsīd\ *n* -s [ISV *glycose* + *-ide*] : any of a large class of natural or synthetic compounds (as anthocyanins) that are acetal derivatives of sugars and that on hydrolysis (as by the action of enzymes or dilute acids) yield one or more molecules of a sugar and often a noncarbohydrate : a mixed acetal of which a cyclic form of a glycose is the hemiacetal and which may be classified as a furanoside or pyranoside according to the size of the ring of the glycose or as an alpha glycoside or a beta glycoside according to the optical rotation ⟨methyl ~*s*⟩ — see AGLYCON; compare GLUCOSE illustration, GLUCOSIDE, OLIGOSACCHARIDE, POLYSACCHARIDE — **gly·co·sid·ic** \ˌglīkəˈsidik\ *adj* — **gly·co·sid·i·cal·ly** \-dək(ə)lē\ *adv*

gly·cos·uria \ˌglī(ˌ)kōˈs(h)u̇rēə, -ōsˈyu̇-\ *n* -s [NL, fr. ISV *glycose* + NL *-uria*] : the presence in the urine (as in diabetes mellitus) of abnormal amounts of sugar (as glucose) — compare GLYCURESIS — **gly·cos·uric** \ˌ=(ˌ)=ˈ=rik\ *adj*

gly·co·syl \ˈglīkəˌsil\ *n* -s [*glycose* + *-yl*] : a univalent radical derived from a cyclic form of glycose by removal of the hemiacetal hydroxyl group — compare GLUCOSYL

gly·co·trop·ic \ˌglīkōˈträpik\ *also* **gly·co·trophic** \-räfik, -rōf-\ *adj* [*glyc-* + *-tropic* or *-trophic*] : antagonizing the action of insulin esp. with regard to the production of hypoglycemia ⟨a ~ anterior-pituitary fraction⟩

glycu·re·sis \ˌglikyəˈrēsəs, ˌglīk-\ *n, pl* **glycure·ses** \-ēˌsēz\ [NL, fr. *glyc-* + *uresis*] : physiologic excretion of large amounts of sugar in the urine following excessive carbohydrate intake — compare GLYCOSURIA

glycu·ron·ic acid \ˌglik|yəˈränik-, ˌglīk|\ *n* [*glycuronic* ISV *glyc-* + *uron-* (fr. Gk *ouron* urine) + *-ic* — more at URINE] **1** *archaic* : GLUCURONIC ACID **2** : a uronic acid (as galacturonic acid) derived from a glycose (as galactose)

glycyl \ˈglīsəl, ˈglis-, -ˌsēl\ *n* -s [ISV *glyc-* + *-yl*] : the univalent acyl radical NH_2CH_2CO- of glycine

glyc·y·mer·i·dae \ˌglisəˈmerəˌdē\ *n pl, cap* [NL, fr. *Glycymeris*, type genus (fr. L, a shellfish, prob. modif. of Gk *glykymaris* cockle) + *-idae*] **:** a family of bivalve mollusks (suborder Myacea) comprising the dog cockles

gly·cyph·a·gus \glīˈsifəgəs, gləˈ-\ *n, cap* [NL, fr. *glycy-* (fr. Gk *glykys* sweet) + *-phagus* -phagous (fr. Gk *-phagos*) — more at DULCET] **:** a genus (the type of the family Glycyphagidae) of broad-bodied mites that are often abundant in stored organic material (as dried fruits, hides, and grain) and that sometimes cause a form of grocer's itch in persons handling infested material

glyc·yr·rhi·za \ˌglisəˈrīzə\ *n* [NL, fr. L, licorice root — more at LICORICE] **1** *cap* **:** a genus of widely distributed perennial herbs or subshrubs (family Leguminosae) with odd-pinnate leaves, racemose or spicate flowers, and leathery often prickly pods — see LICORICE **2** -s [L] **:** LICORICE 1a

glyc·yr·rhi·zic acid \ˌglisəˈrīzik-\ *n* [*glycyrrhizic* ISV *glycyrrhiz-* (fr. NL *Glycyrrhiza*) + *-ic*] **:** GLYCYRRHIZIN

glyc·yr·rhi·zin \ˌglisəˈrīzᵊn\ *n* -s [ISV *glycyrrhiz-* (fr. NL *glycyrrhiza*) + *-in*] **:** a crystalline glycosidic acid $C_{42}H_{62}O_{16}$ constituting the sweet constituent of licorice root

glyde \ˈglaid\ *var of* GLEYDE

gly·ox·al \glīˈäkˌsal, ˌ==ˈ=\ *n* -s [ISV *gly-* (fr. *glycol*) + *ox-* (oxal-) + *-al*] **:** a reactive yellow low-melting aldehyde CHOCHO made by catalytic oxidation of ethylene glycol and usu. handled in aqueous solution because of its ease of polymerization to an amorphous white solid

gly·ox·a·lase \glīˈäksəˌlās, -āz\ *n* -s [*glyoxal* + *-ase*] **:** an enzyme that accelerates reversibly the conversion in the presence of glutathione of pyruvaldehyde to lactic acid

gly·ox·al·ic acid \ˌglīˌäkˈsalik-\ *n* [*glyoxalic* ISV *glyoxal* + *-ic*] **:** GLYOXYLIC ACID

gly·ox·al·i·dine \ˌglīˌäkˈsaləˌdēn, -ələdᵊn\ *n* -s [*glyoxal* + *-idine*] **:** IMIDAZOLINE

gly·ox·a·line \glīˈäksəˌlēn, -ˌlən\ *n* -s [ISV *glyoxal* + *-ine*] **:** IMIDAZOLE

gly·ox·ime \(ˈ)glīˈäkˌsēm, -ˌsəm\ *n* [ISV *gly-* (fr. *glyoxal*) + *oxime*] **:** a white crystalline compound $(CH{=}NOH)_2$ that is the oxime of glyoxal — compare DIMETHYLGLYOXIME

gly·ox·yl·ic acid \ˌglīˌäkˈsilik-\ *n* [*glyoxylic* ISV *glyox-* (fr. *glyoxal*) + *-yl* + *-ic*] **:** a syrupy or crystalline aldehyde acid CHOCOOH or $CH(OH)_2COOH$ that occurs esp. in unripe fruits

glyph \ˈglif\ *n* -s [Gk *glyphē* carved work, fr. *glyphein* to carve — more at CLEAVE] **1 :** an ornamental vertical groove (as in a triglyph) **2 :** a symbolic figure or a character usu. incised or carved in relief; *specif* **:** the basic unit in the Maya system of writing consisting of a pictorial or conventionalized sign or of two or more such signs enclosed in a frame line having typically the form of a square with rounded corners ⟨many of the ~s represent, not Maya words or constructions, but universal ideas —A.A.Hill⟩

glyph·ic \ˈglifik\ *adj* **:** of, relating to, consisting of, or resembling glyphs ⟨a ~ system of writing⟩ ⟨~ inscriptions⟩

glypt- *or* **glypto-** *comb form* [F, fr. Gk *glypt-*, fr. *glyptos* carved, fr. *glyphein* to carve] **1 :** engraving ⟨*glyptology*⟩ **2 :** carved ⟨*Glyptodon*⟩

Glyp·tal \ˈgliptᵊl\ *trademark* — used for an alkyd

¹glyp·tic \ˈgliptik\ *n* -s [prob. fr. F *glyptique*, fr. Gk *glyptikē*, fr. *glyptos* carved] **:** the art or process of carving or engraving esp. on gems ⟨one of the most beautiful types of ~ ornamentation —Dorothy Daniel⟩

²glyptic \"\ *adj* **:** of or relating to glyptic

glyp·to·don \ˈgliptəˌdän\ *n* [NL, fr. *glypt-* + *-odon*] **1** *cap* **:** a genus of large extinct mammals (order Edentata) that are related to the armadillos, have a head shield, have the back covered by a large rigid carapace composed of small 5-sided or 6-sided bony plates covered with horny plates and the tail encircled by rings of bony plates, and are represented by numerous remains in the Pleistocene of So. America and of southern No. America **2** -s **:** GLYPTODONT

glyp·to·dont \-nt\ *n* -s [NL *Glyptodont-, Glyptodon*] **:** a mammal of the genus *Glyptodon*

glyp·to·graph \-təˌgraf, -āf\ *n* [prob. back-formation fr. *glyptography*] **:** a glyptic carving or engraving — **glyp·to·graph·ic** \ˌ==ˈgrafik\ *adj*

glyp·tog·ra·phy \glipˈtägrəfē\ *n* -ES [F *glyptographie*, fr. Gk *glypt-* + F *-graphie* -graphy] **:** GLYPTIC

glyp·to·lith \ˈgliptəˌlith\ *n* -s [*glypt-* + *-lith*] **:** VENTIFACT

glyp·tol·o·gy \glipˈtäləjē\ *n* -ES [ISV *glypt-* + *-logy*] **:** the study of glyptic

glyp·tos·tro·bus \glipˈtästrəbəs, ˌgliptəˈstrōbəs\ *n, cap* [NL, fr. *glypt-* + L *strobus* tree yielding an odoriferous gum] **:** a genus of conifers (family Taxodiaceae) having awl-shaped leaves, pear-shaped long-stalked cones with obovate scales, and small winged seeds

gm *abbr* gram

GM *abbr* **1** Geiger-Müller **2** general manager **3** general merchandise **4** general mortgage **5** gold medal **6** grand master **7** Greenwich meridian **8** guided missile **9** gunmetal

g major *n, usu cap G* **:** the major musical key having a signature of one sharp

g–man \ˈjēˌman, -maa(ə)n\ *n, pl* **g–men** *usu cap G* [prob. fr. *g* (initial letter of *government*) + *man*] **:** a special agent of the Federal Bureau of Investigation of the U.S. Department of Justice

g–m counter \(ˈ)jēˈem-\ *n, usu cap G&M* [fr. *Geiger-Müller counter*] **:** GEIGER COUNTER

GME *abbr* gilt marbled edges

gmeli·na \gəˈmelənə, -māl-\ *n, cap* [NL, fr. Johann Georg *Gmelin* †1755 Ger. botanist] **:** a small genus of Australasian trees and shrubs (family Verbenaceae) with simple leaves and panicled tubular flowers — see QUEENSLAND BEECH

gmelin·ite \-ˌnīt\ *n* -s [Christian G. *Gmelin* †1860 Ger. chemist + E *-ite*] **:** a mineral $(Na_2,Ca)Al_2Si_4O_{12}{\cdot}6H_2O$ consisting of a colorless or light-colored zeolite isomorphous with chabazite (hardness 4.5, sp. gr. 2–2.2)

gme·lin's blue \gəˈmālənz-, -ˌlēnz-\ *n, often cap G* [after Christian G. *Gmelin*] **1 :** ULTRAMARINE 1b **2 :** TURNBULL'S BLUE **3 :** FRENCH BLUE

gmelin's test *or* **gmelin's reaction** *n, usu cap G* [after Leopold *Gmelin* †1853 Ger. chemist] **:** a test for bile pigments (as in the urine) that is made by carefully mixing the solution to be tested with nitric acid containing some nitrous acid and that shows a positive result when a series of colors appears at the juncture of the solution and the acid

g minor *n, usu cap G* **:** the minor musical key having a signature of two flats

GMT *abbr* Greenwich mean time

g–m tube \(ˈ)jēˈem-\ *n, usu cap G&M* [fr. *Geiger-Müller tube*] **:** GEIGER-MÜLLER TUBE

GMV *abbr* gram-molecular volume

gn *abbr* **1** general **2** green **3** guinea **4** gun

GN *abbr* golden number

gnam·ma hole (g)əˈnamə-\ *n* [*gnamma* fr. native name in Australia] **:** a hollow or hole eroded or indented in solid rock of Australian deserts that sometimes contains water

¹gnap \ˈnap\ *vi* **gnapped; gnapped; gnapping; gnaps** [ME *gnappen*, prob. of imit. origin] *Scot* **:** BITE, SNAP

²gnap \"\ *n* -s *Scot* **:** MORSEL, BITE

gna·pha·li·oid \nəˈfālēˌȯid\ *adj* [NL *Gnaphalium* + E *-oid*] **:** of or relating to the genus *Gnaphalium*

gna·pha·li·um \-lēəm\ *n, cap* [NL, alter. of L *gnaphalion* cudweed, modif. of Gk *gnaphallion*, fr. *gnaphallon* flock of wool, fr. *gnaptein* to card, alter. of *knaptein*; akin to OE *hnæppan* to strike, ON *hnaja* to cut, Lith *knabéti* to peel, L *cinis* ashes — more at INCINERATE] **:** a large genus of hoary or woolly-tomentose widely distributed herbs (family Compositae) having whitish persistent involucres — see BALSAMWEED 1

gnaphalium green *n, often cap 1st G* **:** a pale green that is lighter and stronger than celadon gray and yellower and darker than spray green

gnar *or* **gnarr** \ˈnär, ˈnȧ(r\ *vi* **gnarred; gnarred; gnarring; gnars** *or* **gnarrs** [imit.] **:** SNARL, GROWL — used chiefly of dogs

¹gnarl \R ˈnärl, *chiefly before pause or consonant* -rəl, *–R* ˈnȧl\ *vi* -ED/-ING/-S [prob. freq. of *gnar*] **1 :** GROWL, SNARL ⟨and wolves are ~*ing* who shall gnaw thee first —Shak.⟩ **2** *dial Eng* **:** GNAW, NIBBLE

²gnarl \"\ *vt* -ED/-ING/-S [back-formation fr. *gnarled*] **:** to twist or contort into or as if into a state of deformity ⟨the wind seems to have ~*ed* the dispositions of men and women as it has ~*ed* the apple trees —Carl Van Doren⟩ **syn** see DEFORM

³gnarl \"\ *n* -s **:** a knot in wood **:** a hard protuberance with twisted grain on a tree

gnarled \-ld\ *adj* [prob. alter. of *knurled*] **1 :** warped or twisted with or as if with gnarls **:** CROSS-GRAINED, KNOTTY ⟨the hand all ~ with work —D.H.Lawrence⟩ ⟨three ~ cedars stand at the entrance —*Amer. Guide Series: La.*⟩ **2 :** crabbed in disposition, aspect, or character **:** HARD-BITTEN ⟨public life abounds in ~ and striking figures; and the literary scene presents a splendid row of great eccentrics —*Times Lit. Supp.*⟩ ⟨a prose . . . knotty and ~ —D.L.Morgan⟩ ⟨in an environment tightly ~, among unimaginative folk, dependent upon agriculture for a living —*Saturday Rev.*⟩

gnarly \-ärlē, -ȧl-, -li\ *adj* -ER/-EST [³*gnarl* + *-y*] **:** GNARLED

¹gnash \ˈnash, -aa(ə)-, -ai-\ *vb* -ED/-ING/-ES [alter. of ME *gnasten, gnaisten*, prob. of imit. origin] *vi* **1 :** to grind or strike the teeth together ⟨he ~*ed* and kept me awake for hours⟩ **2 :** to grind together — used of the teeth ⟨his teeth ~*ed* audibly⟩ ~ *vt* **1 :** to strike or grind (the teeth) together esp. in anger or pain **2 :** to grind the teeth on **:** bite with grinding teeth ⟨the tiger ~*ed* the fox, the ermine, and the sloth —W.S. Landor⟩

²gnash \"\ *n* -ES **:** GNASHING, BITE ⟨the ~ and clash of cutlery on china —James Jones⟩

gnat \ˈnat, *usu* -ad.+V\ *n* -s [ME, fr. OE *gnætt*; akin to MHG *gnaz* scurf, ON *gnōtra* to rattle, OE *gnagan* to gnaw — more at GNAW] **1 a :** any of various small two-winged flies: as **a** *Brit* **:** MOSQUITO **b :** any of certain tiny biting flies (as a midge, blackfly, or sand fly) **c :** FUNGUS GNAT **2 :** any of various artificial flies tied as fishing lures

gnatcatcher \ˈ=ˌ==\ *n* **:** any of several very small No. and So. American insectivorous warblers constituting a genus (*Polioptila*) of the family Sylviidae

gnatflower \ˈ=ˌ=\ *n* **:** BEE ORCHIS

gnath- *or* **gnatho-** *comb form* [NL, fr. Gk *gnath-*, fr. *gnathos*; akin to Gk *genys* jaw — more at CHIN] **:** jaw ⟨*gnath*itis⟩ ⟨*gnatho*plasty⟩

-gna·tha \gnəthə\ *n comb form, pl* **-gnatha** [NL, fem. sing. and neut. pl. of *-gnathus* -gnathous] **:** one or ones having (such) a jaw — in taxonomic names in zoology ⟨A*gnatha*⟩ ⟨Chaeto*gnatha*⟩

-gna·thae \gnəˌthē\ *n pl comb form* [NL, fem. pl. of *-gnathus* -gnathous] **:** ones having (such) a jaw — in taxonomic names in zoology ⟨Desmo*gnathae*⟩

gnat hawk *n* **:** the common European nightjar (*Caprimulgus europaeus*)

gnath·ic \ˈnathik\ *or* **gnathal** \ˈnathəl, ˈnath-\ *adj* [*gnath-* + *-ic* or *-al*] **:** of or relating to the jaw

gnathic index *n* **:** the anthropometric ratio of the distance from the nasion to the basion to that from the basion to the alveolar point multiplied by 100

gnathi·on \ˈnathēˌän, ˈnath-\ *n* -s [NL, irreg. fr. Gk *gnathos* jaw] **1 :** the midpoint of the lower border of the human mandible — see CRANIOMETRY illustration **2 :** the most anterior point of the premaxillae on or near the middle line in various lower mammals

gnathism \ˈnāˌthizəm, ˈnaˌth-, *in combination* gnəˌth-\ *n* -s [ISV *gnath-* + *-ism*] **:** the projection of the upper jaw beyond the general plane of the face — often used in combination ⟨meso*gnathism*⟩ ⟨ortho*gnathism*⟩ ⟨pro*gnathism*⟩; compare FACIAL ANGLE

gnathite \ˈnāˌthīt, ˈnaˌth-\ *n* -s [*gnath-* + *-ite*] **:** a mouth appendage (as a mandible, maxilla, or maxilliped) of an arthropod

gnatho·base \ˈnathəˌbās, ˈnath-\ *n* [*gnath-* + *base*] **:** a joint or process of the proximal part of the appendage of an arthropod modified to aid in carrying or masticating food — **gnatho·ba·sic** \ˌ==ˈbāsik\ *adj*

gnathob·del·lae \ˌ=ˌthäbˈde(ˌ)lē\ [NL, fr. *gnath-* + *-bdellae* (fr. Gk *bdella* leech)] *syn of* GNATHOBDELLIDA

gnathob·del·lid \ˌ=ˈ=ˈdeləd\ *adj* [NL *Gnathobdellida*] **:** of or relating to the Gnathobdellida

gnathob·del·li·da \-ˌlədə\ *n pl, cap* [NL, fr. *gnath-* + *bdell-* + *-ida*] **:** an order or other division of leeches comprising those lacking a proboscis and having 2-toothed or 3-toothed chitinous jaws (as the medicinal leech, the horseleech, and the land leeches)

gnatho·ceph·a·lon \ˌ=(ˌ)thōˈsefəˌlän, -lən\ *n* [NL, fr. *gnath-* + *cephalon*] **:** the part of the insect head that lies behind the protocephalon, consists of several fused segments, and bears the mandibles and maxillae

gnatho·chi·lar·i·um \-ˌkīˈla(a)rēəm\ *n* -s [NL, fr. *gnath-* + *chil-* + *-arium*] **:** the lower lip of certain arthropods usu. considered to consist of the fused maxillae; *sometimes* **:** LABIUM

gna·thon·ic \(ˈ)näˈthänik\ *adj* [L *gnathonicus*, fr. *Gnathon-, Gnatho* (sycophant in the comedy *Eunuchus* by Terence †*ab* 159B.C. Roman playwright) + L *-icus* -ic] **:** SYCOPHANTIC, TOADYING ⟨somewhat of a ~ and parasitic soul —Charles Kingsley⟩

¹gnatho·pod \ˈnathəˌpäd, ˈnath-\ *adj* [NL *Gnathopoda*] **:** of or relating to the Gnathopoda

²gnathopod \"\ *n* [ISV *gnath-* + *-pod*] **:** GNATHOPODITE

gna·thop·o·da \nəˈthäpədə\ *n pl, cap* [NL, fr. *gnath-* + *-poda*] *in some esp former classifications* **:** a group that comprises invertebrate animals whose jaws are modified limbs and that is coextensive with or a subdivision of Arthropoda — **gna·thop·o·dous** \-dəs\ *adj*

gna·thop·o·dite \-ˌdīt\ *n* [*gnath-* + *-podite*] **:** a segmental appendage of an arthropod when modified wholly or in part to serve as a jaw; *esp* **:** MAXILLIPED

gnatho·so·ma \ˌnathəˈsōmə, ˌnath-\ *also* **gnatho·some** \ˈ==ˌsōm\ *n* [NL *gnathosoma*, fr. *gnath-* + *-soma*] **:** CAPITULUM 2e

gna·thos·te·gite \nəˈthästəˌjīt\ *n* -s [*gnath-* + *-stegite*] **:** one of a pair of broad plates that are developed from the outer maxillipeds of some crustaceans (as crabs) and that serve to cover the other mouthparts

¹gna·thos·to·ma \nəˈthästəmə\ *n pl, cap* [NL, fr. *gnath-* + *-stoma*] *in some classifications* **:** a division of Crustacea comprising the Branchiopoda, Ostracoda, and Copepoda

²gnathostoma \"\ *n, cap* [NL, fr. *gnath-* + *-stoma*] **:** a genus (the type of the family Gnathostomatidae) of spiruroid nematodes comprising parasites living in tumors of the stomach wall of various Old World carnivorous mammals and occas. invading the subcutaneous tissues of man

gnatho·sto·ma·ta \ˌnathəˈstōmədə, ˌnath-\ *n pl, cap* [NL, fr. *gnath-* + *-stomata*] **:** a superclass or other division of Vertebrata comprising those with jaws — compare AGNATHA

gnatho·stoma·tous \ˌ==ˈstäməd·əs, -tōm-\ *or* **gna·thos·to·mous** \nəˈthästəməs\ *adj* [NL *Gnathostomata, Gnathostoma* + E *-ous*] **:** of or relating to Gnathostoma or Gnathostomata

gnatho·stome \ˈnathəˌstōm, ˈnath-\ *n* -s [NL *Gnathostomi*] **:** a vertebrate animal that possesses true jaws

gna·thos·to·mi \nəˈthästəˌmī\ [NL, fr. *gnath-* + *-stomi*] *syn of* GNATHOSTOMATA

gna·thos·to·mi·a·sis \nəˌthästəˈmīəsəs\ *n* -ES [NL, fr. ²*Gnathostoma* + *-iasis*] **:** infestation with or disease caused by worms of the genus *Gnathostoma*

gnatho·thoracic \ˌnathō, ˌnathō+\ *adj* [fr. *gnathothorax*, after E *thorax*: *thoracic*] **:** of, relating to, or constituting a gnathothorax

gnatho·thorax \"+\ *n* [*gnath-* + *thorax*] **:** the thorax and the part of the head bearing the feeding organs of an arthropod regarded as one of the primary body regions — compare PROTOCEPHALON

-gna·thous \gnəthəs\ *adj comb form* [NL *-gnathus* -gnathous, fr. Gk *gnathos* jaw; akin to Gk *genys* jaw — more at CHIN] **:** having (such) a jaw ⟨oxy*gnathous*⟩

-gna·thus \gnəthəs\ *n comb form* [NL, fr. *-gnathus* -gnathous] **:** one having (such) a jaw — in generic names of animals ⟨Desmo*gnathus*⟩

gnat·ling \ˈnatliŋ\ *n* -s [*gnat* + *-ling*] **:** a small or insignificant person or thing; *specif* **:** a small gnat

gnatsnap \ˈ=ˌ=\ *or* **gnatsnapper** \ˈ=ˌ==\ *n* **:** a small bird that feeds on insects

gnat·ter \ˈnatə(r)\ *vb* -ED/-ING/-S [prob. imit.] *vt, dial Brit* **:** NIBBLE ~ *vi* **1** *dial Brit* **:** to talk rapidly and idly **2** *dial Brit* **:** to be peevish **:** GRUMBLE

gnat·ty \ˈnad·ē\ *adj* -ER/-EST [*gnat* + *-y*] **:** infested with gnats

gnaw \ˈnȯ\ *vb* **gnawed** \-ȯd\ **gnawed** \"\ *also* **gnawn** \-ȯn\ **gnawing; gnaws** [ME *gnawen*, fr. OE *gnagan*; akin to OHG *gnagan, nagan* to gnaw, ON *gnaga* to gnaw, and perh. to Russ *gnit'* to rot] *vt* **1 a :** to bite or chew on with the teeth **:** wear away or remove a part from by persistent or repeated biting or nibbling ⟨the dog was ~*ing* a bone⟩ ⟨sheep ~ the tough grass off the range and leave it barren —Green Peyton⟩ **b :** to make by persistent or repeated biting or nibbling ⟨rats ~*ed* a hole in the floor⟩ **2 a :** to be a source of annoyance, worry, or vexation to **:** HARASS, PLAGUE ⟨the restraints of censorship . . . ~*ed* every correspondent —*Atlantic*⟩ ⟨her brain was ~*ed* by savage and distorted thoughts —James Boyd⟩ **b :** to cause (as the stomach) to feel discomfort similar to that produced by persistent biting ⟨hunger ~*ed* his vitals⟩ **3 :** to wear away by or as if by erosion or corrosion ⟨time shall ~ the proudest towers —Phineas Fletcher⟩ ~ *vi* **1 :** to bite persistently or repeatedly with the teeth ⟨the dog ~*ed* away at the bone⟩ ⟨he ~*ed* nervously at his underlip —Oscar Wilde⟩ ⟨a thousand men that fishes ~*ed* upon —Shak.⟩ **2 :** to produce an effect of or as if of gnawing **:** EAT ⟨the waves are ~*ing* away at the soft cliffs —Richard Joseph⟩ ⟨some of the roads ~ at the tires —Claudia Cassidy⟩ ⟨strange truths that have ~*ed* on her lonely heart —Lillian Smith⟩ ⟨inflation and taxation ~ increasingly at the savings of the people —*Freedom & Union*⟩

gnaw·er \ˈnȯ(ə)r, -ȯə\ *n* -s **:** one that gnaws; *esp* **:** RODENT

gnawing *n* -s **1 :** a persistent pain esp. in the stomach or bowels resembling that caused by gnawing **2 gnawings** *pl* **:** PANGS ⟨~s of hunger⟩

gnaw·ing·ly *adv* **:** in the manner of something that produces gnawing ⟨a ~ persistent sensation in the stomach⟩

gnd *abbr* ground

gneiss \ˈnīs\ *n* -ES [G *gneis*, prob. alter. of MHG *gneiste, ganeiste* spark, fr. OHG *gneisto*; akin to OE *gnāst* spark, ON *gneisti*] **:** a laminated or foliated metamorphic rock corresponding in composition to granite or some other feldspathic plutonic rock and often named for a conspicuous mineral constituent ⟨biotite ~⟩ ⟨hornblendic ~⟩ or for the plutonic or sedimentary rock of origin ⟨syenitic ~⟩ ⟨conglomerate ~⟩ — see ORTHOGNEISS, PARAGNEISS — **gneiss·ic** \-sik\ *adj* — **gneiss·ose** \-ˌsōs\ *adj*

gneiss·oid \-ˌsȯid\ *adj* **:** resembling gneiss **:** having the laminated structure of gneiss

gnesio–lutheran \ˌnēzē(ˌ)ō+\ *n, usu cap G&L* [Gk *gnēsios* genuine, born in wedlock + E *lutheran*; akin to Gk *genos* race, kin — more at KIN] **:** a Lutheran extremist opposed to the moderation of Melanchthon

gne·ta·ce·ae \nəˈtāsēˌē\ *n pl, cap* [NL, fr. *Gnetum*, type genus + *-aceae*] **:** a family of plants (order Gnetales) having small unisexual flowers and fleshy or winged fruits — see EPHEDRA, GNETUM, WELWITSCHIA — **gne·ta·ceous** \-āshəs\ *adj*

gne·ta·le·an \-ālēən\ *adj* [NL *Gnetales* + E *-an*] **:** of, relating to, or characteristic of the order Gnetales

gne·ta·les \-ā(ˌ)lēz\ *n pl, cap* [NL, fr. *Gnetum* + *-ales*] **:** an order of chiefly tropical or xerophytic woody gymnospermous plants that have two cotyledons, opposite leaves, vessels in the wood, and compound male and female strobili, consist of a single family (Gnetaceae), and are practically unknown as fossils but are sometimes considered on structural grounds to be near or on the ancestral line of the angiosperms

gne·tum \ˈnēd·əm\ *n, cap* [NL, alter. of *gnemon*, modif. of Moluccan Malay *ganemu*] **:** a genus (the type of the family Gnetaceae) of tropical shrubs or small trees usu. having climbing jointed stems and terminal spikes of flowers, the fruit being usu. drupaceous and aggregated in a rough cone

gnib \ˈnib\ *adj* [origin unknown] *Scot* **:** quick in response **:** READY, SHARP

gnoc·chi \ˈnäkē, ˈnȯkē, *It* ˈnʸȯkkē\ *n pl* [It, pl. of *gnocco*, alter. of *nocchio* knot in wood, perh. of Gmc origin; akin to MHG *knoche* bone, knot in wood; akin to OE *cnocian, cnucian* to knock — more at KNOCK] **:** dumplings of a pasta often made with cheese or riced potato and served with a sauce

¹gnome \ˈnōm, -ōˌmē\ *n, pl* **gnomes** \-ōmz, -ōˌmēz\ *or* **gno·mae** \-ōˌmē\ [Gk *gnōmē* maxim, opinion, intelligence, fr. *gignōskein* to know — more at KNOW] **:** a brief reflection or maxim **:** APHORISM, PROVERB

²gnome \ˈnōm\ *n* -s [F, fr. NL *gnomus*] **1 :** an ageless often deformed dwarf creature of folklore conceived as living in the earth and usu. guarding precious ores or treasure **2 :** a dry wizened little old man ⟨a gnarled, unshaven ~ —Truman Capote⟩

gnome owl *n* [²*gnome*] **:** PYGMY OWL

gno·mic \ˈnōmik\ *adj* [LL *gnomicus*, fr. Gk *gnōmikos*, fr. *gnōmē* maxim + *-ikos* -ic] **1 a :** characterized by or expressive of aphorism or sententious wisdom esp. concerning human condition or conduct ⟨a ~ wisdom which appealed both to the intelligence and to the emotions —John Buchan⟩ ⟨a ~ and oracular tone —J.C.Powys⟩ ⟨~ poetry⟩ **b** *of a poet* **:** given to the composition of gnomic poetry **2 :** expressive of what is true generally, universally, or always — used of certain tenses ⟨"day follows night" is an example of the ~ present⟩ ⟨~ aorist⟩

gnom·ish \ˈnōmish\ *adj* [²*gnome* + *-ish*] **:** resembling a gnome ⟨that ~ nobleman with the abbreviated legs and a great genius —John Mason Brown⟩

gno·mo·log·ic \ˌnōməˈläjik\ *also* **gno·mo·log·i·cal** \-jəkəl\ *adj* [*gnomologic* fr. Gk *gnōmologikos*, fr. *gnōmologia* + *-ikos* -ic; *gnomological* fr. *gnomologic* + *-al*] **:** characterized by or consisting of gnomes or precepts **:** GNOMIC

gno·mol·o·gy \nōˈmäləjē\ *n* -ES [Gk *gnōmologia* anthology of gnomes, sententious style, fr. *gnōmo-* (fr. *gnōmē* maxim) + *-logia* -logy] **1 :** an anthology of gnomes **2 :** gnomic writing

gno·mon \ˈnōˌmän, -ˌmən\ *n* -s [L, fr. Gk *gnōmōn* interpreter, discerner, pointer on a sundial, carpenter's square, fr. *gignōskein* to know — more at KNOW] **1 :** an object that by the position or length of its shadow serves as an indicator esp. of the hour of the day: as **a :** the style, pin, or vertical plate of an ordinary sundial usu. set parallel to the earth's axis **b :** a column or shaft erected perpendicular to the horizon and formerly used to find the sun's meridian altitude **2 :** the remainder of a parallelogram after the removal of a similar parallelogram containing one of its corners **3** *archaic* **:** NOSE **4** *obs* **:** a rule of faith or conduct **:** CANON, TENET

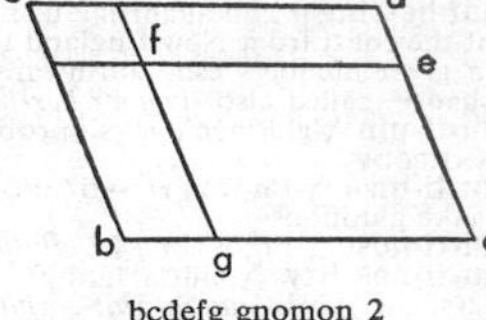

bcdefg gnomon 2

gno·mo·nia \nōˈmōnēə\ *n, cap* [NL, fr. Gk *gnōmōn* carpenter's square + NL *-ia*; fr. the shape of the ostiole] **:** a genus (the type of the family Gnomoniaceae) of ascomycetous fungi having rostrate perithecia and hyaline 2-celled to 4-celled ascospores

gno·mon·ic \(ˈ)nōˈmänik\ *also* **gno·mon·i·cal** \-ə̇nəkəl\ *adj* [*gnomonic* fr. L *gnomonicus*, fr. Gk *gnōmonikos*, fr. *gnōmon-, gnōmōn* pointer on a sundial + *-ikos* -ic; *gnomonical* fr. L *gnomonicus* + E *-al*] **1 :** of or relating to the gnomon of a sundial or its use in telling time **2 :** GNOMIC

gnomonic chart *n* **:** a chart on the gnomonic projection

gnomonic projection *n* **:** an azimuthal projection of a part of a hemisphere showing the earth's grid as projected by radials from a point at the center of the sphere onto a tangent plane so that all straight lines represent arcs of great circles thereby making this projection valuable for navigation when used in conjunction with the Mercator projection — called also *great-circle chart*

gno·mo·nics \nōˈmäniks\ *n pl but sing in constr* **:** the art of using or making dials, esp. sundials

-gno·my \gnəmē, -mi\ *n comb form* -ES [LL *-gnomia*, fr. Gk *-gnōmia*, alter. of *-gnōmonia*, fr. *gnōmon-, gnōmōn* interpreter, discerner + *-ia* -y — more at GNOMON] **:** science, art, or means of judging ⟨patho*gnomy*⟩

gno·ri·mo·sche·ma \ˌnōrəmōˈskēmə\ *n, cap* [NL, fr. *gnorimo-* (fr. Gk *gnōrimos* well known) + L *schema* shape, form; akin to Gk *gignōskein* to know — more at SCHEME] **:** a genus of small dull narrow-winged moths related to the pink bollworm and including larvae that cause galls in plants, others that are leaf miners, and still others that are borers — see POTATO TUBERWORM

gno·se·o·log·i·cal *or* **gno·si·o·log·i·cal** \¦==ə¦läjəkəl\ *adj* **:** of or relating to gnoseology — **gno·se·o·log·i·cal·ly** *or* **gno·si·o·log·i·cal·ly** \-k(ə)lē\ *adv*

gno·se·ol·o·gy *or* **gno·si·ol·o·gy** \,nōsē'äləjē, -ōzē-\ *n* -ES [NL *gnoseologia,* fr. *gnoseo-* (fr. Gk *gnōsis* knowledge) + L *-logia* -logy] **:** the philosophic theory of knowledge **:** inquiry into the basis, nature, validity, and limits of knowledge ⟨~ became coextensive with the whole of metaphysics —C.A. Hart⟩

-gno·sia \g'nōzh(ē)ə\ *n comb form* -S [NL, fr. Gk *-gnōsia,* fr. *gnōsis* knowledge] **:** -GNOSIS ⟨pharmaco*gnosia*⟩

gno·sis \'nōsəs\ *n, pl* **gno·ses** \-ō,sēz\ [Gk *gnōsis,* lit., knowledge, fr. *gignōskein* to know] **1 :** immediate knowledge of spiritual truth; *esp* **:** such knowledge as professed by the ancient Gnostics and held to be attainable through faith alone **2 :** the act or process of cognition or knowing

-gno·sis \(g)'nōsəs\ *n comb form, pl* **-gno·ses** \-ō,sēz\ [L, fr. Gk *gnōsis* knowledge] **:** knowledge **:** cognition **:** recognition ⟨baro*gnosis*⟩ ⟨psycho*gnosis*⟩

¹gnos·tic \'nästik\ *n* -S *usu cap* [LL *gnosticus,* fr. Gk *gnōstikos,* adj.] **:** an adherent of gnosticism or of a philosophy or theology influenced by gnosticism; *esp* **:** an adherent of any of several Gnostic sects of the 2d to 6th centuries adjudged heretical by the early Christian church

²gnostic \"\ *adj* [Gk *gnōstikos,* fr. *gnōstos* known (fr. *gignōskein* to know) + *-ikos* -ic — more at KNOW] **1 :** of, relating to, or characterized by knowledge or cognition **:** INTELLECTUAL, KNOWING **2** [¹*gnostic*] *usu cap* **:** of or relating to gnosticism or the Gnostics **3 :** SHREWD, CLEVER — **gnos·ti·cal·ly** \-tək(ə)lē\ *adv*

-gnos·tic \g¦nästik, -tēk\ *or* **-gnos·ti·cal** \-təkəl, -tēk-\ *adj comb form* [*-gnostic* fr. ML *-gnosticus* knowing, fr. Gk *gnōstikos,* adj.; *-gnostical* fr. ML *-gnosticus* + E *-al*] **:** knowing **:** characterized by or relating to (such) knowledge ⟨geo*gnostic*⟩ ⟨geo*gnostical*⟩

gnos·ti·cism \'nästə,sizəm\ *n* -S *often cap* [¹*gnostic* + *-ism*] **:** the thought and practice of any of various cults of late pre-Christian and early Christian centuries declared heretical by the church and distinguished chiefly by pretension to mystic and esoteric religious insights, by emphasis on knowledge rather than faith, and by the conviction that matter is evil

gnos·ti·cize \-tə,sīz\ *vb* -ED/-ING/-S [¹*gnostic* + *-ize*] *vi* **:** to embrace or propound Gnostic views ~ *vt* **:** to make Gnostic **:** give Gnostic color or quality to ⟨threatened for a time to ~ Christianity⟩

-gno·sy \gnəsē, -si\ *n comb form* -ES [NL *-gnosia,* fr. Gk *-gnōsia,* fr. *gnōsis* knowledge] **:** -GNOSIS ⟨astro*gnosy*⟩

GNP *abbr* gross national product

gnr *abbr* gunner

gnu \'n(y)ü\ *n, pl* **gnu** *or* **gnus** [modif. of Bushman *nqu*] **:** any of several rather large but compact and blocky African antelopes (genera *Connochaetes* and *Gorgon*) having a large head like that of an ox, short mane, long and flowing tail, and horns in both sexes that curve downward and outward and then up with the bases forming a frontal shield in old individuals

gnu

gnu goat *n* **:** TAKIN

¹go \(¦)gō, *when followed without pause by a stressed syllable sometimes* gə *or* +V gəw\ *vb* **went** \(¦)went\ *or dial* **goed** \(¦)gōd\ **gone** \(¦)gón *also* (¦)gän\ *or substand* **went; going** \¦gō|iŋ, (¦)gō|, |ēŋ; *"going to" followed without pause by a verb is often* ¦gōənə *or* ¦gónə\ *or dial Brit* **gaun** \(¦)gón\ **goes** \(¦)gōz\ [ME *gon, goon, gan,* fr. OE *gān;* akin to OFris & OS *gān* to go, OHG *gān, gēn,* OSw & ODan *gā,* Crimean Goth *geen* to go, Gk *kichanein* to reach, attain, Skt *jahāti* he leaves, abandons] *vi* **1 a :** to move on a course **:** pass from point to point or station to station **:** proceed by any of several means ⟨~ by train⟩ ⟨a good day to ~ for a ride⟩ ⟨*went* as fast as he could through the snow⟩ ⟨held the rail as he *went* down the stairs⟩ ⟨the wheel ~*es* round and round⟩ **b :** to be in motion — used esp. in a sentry's challenge ⟨halt! who ~*es* there?⟩ **c :** to move away from something or thitherward **:** pass from one point to or toward another that is regarded as farther away **:** LEAVE, DEPART ⟨the lobby was filled with people coming and ~*ing*⟩ ⟨had to ~ so as to catch the train⟩ ⟨*went* two by two into the dining room⟩ ⟨~ from one city to another⟩ ⟨told the dog to ~ get the ball⟩ ⟨~ and catch a falling star —John Donne⟩ ⟨the men ~ and cut bamboos in the jungle and bring them to the beach —J.G.Frazer⟩ **d :** to ride to hounds **2 a :** to take a certain course or follow a certain procedure ⟨people who want to know how . . . they can help to make the world ~ —Victor Reynolds⟩ **b :** to pass in a course determined by established procedure ⟨reports ~ through channels to the president⟩ **c :** to pass by a process felt to resemble journeying ⟨the message *went* by wire⟩ ⟨my eyes *went* into all corners of the stable —Owen Wister⟩ **d :** to proceed by or as if by a mental process or operation ⟨was determined to ~ to the bottom of the mystery⟩ **e :** to proceed without delay — used esp. to intensify a complementary verb ⟨if that infernal young fool hadn't *gone* and got killed —Dorothy Sayers⟩ ⟨told him to ~ hang himself⟩ **f** (1) **:** to extend from point to point or in a certain direction **:** RUN ⟨a new road that ~*es* from the north shore to the south shore⟩ ⟨his land ~*es* almost to the river⟩ ⟨dates back as far as our records ~ —T.B.Costain⟩ (2) **:** to give access **:** LEAD ⟨that door ~*es* to the cellar⟩ ⟨a path ~*ing* to the barn⟩ **3** *obs* **:** to move or travel on one's feet at an ordinary pace **:** WALK ⟨but when he could not ~, yet forward would he creep —Phineas Fletcher⟩ ⟨I have resolved to run when I can, to ~ when I cannot run —John Bunyan⟩ **4 a :** to be habitually in a certain state or condition ⟨children like to ~ bareheaded⟩ ⟨were advised to ~ armed after dark⟩ **b :** to be pregnant ⟨the fruit she ~*es* with I pray for heartily, that it may find good time, and live —Shak.⟩ ⟨the elephant ~*es* with young nearly two years⟩ **5 a** (1) **:** to come to be taken away, lost, or consumed ⟨a large part of the market for Welsh coal had *gone* forever —L.D.Stamp⟩ ⟨reserves to be brought up when the poet's youth is ~*ing* —Max Beerbohm⟩ (2) **:** to come to be spent ⟨the money that he inherited *went* in a few years⟩ **b** (1) **:** to come to the end of life **:** DIE ⟨the doctor says he may drag on this way for several weeks, or he may ~ suddenly at any time —Ellen Glasgow⟩ (2) **:** to pass by **:** slip away **:** ELAPSE ⟨the trip . . . *went* much more quickly than I had expected —A.N.Whitehead⟩ ⟨the evening *went* pleasantly enough⟩ **c :** to come to be given up, rejected, or abolished ⟨if a day on the links left dad too tired . . . it really looked as if the golf had better ~ —Dorothy Barclay⟩ ⟨one-room schools devoid of plumbing . . . had to ~ —*Saturday Rev.*⟩ **d :** to pass by sale ⟨many items at the auction *went* for less than their true value⟩ ⟨~*ing,* ~*ing, gone*⟩ **e** *cricket* (1) **:** FALL ⟨three wickets *went* during the afternoon⟩ (2) **:** to have one's innings ended by dismissal ⟨the batsman *went* with his score at 50⟩ **f :** to become impaired or weakened **:** lose strength or effectiveness ⟨his hearing started to ~ —George Kent⟩ **g :** to give way esp. under great force or pressure **:** BREAK ⟨the starboard boat did ~, taking with it both davits and part of the starboard rail —H. A.Chippendale⟩ **h :** to cease to have an effect or influence ⟨the pain has finally *gone*⟩ **6 a :** to take place **:** HAPPEN, OCCUR ⟨you seem to try and get me into any . . . trouble that's ~*ing* —Robert Westerby⟩ **b :** to have course or issue **:** FARE ⟨at the end of her first day on the job, he asked her how it *went* —Burnham Carter⟩ ⟨I only keep my eyes open and see how life ~*es* —Eden Phillpotts⟩ **c :** to be in general or on an average **:** furnish a usual standard or measure ⟨an old town as American towns ~ —Dana Burnet⟩ ⟨the modest price makes it quite a bargain as handsomely illustrated books ~ —*Nation*⟩ **d :** to be or become esp. as the result of a contest **:** turn out to be ⟨a second election *went* in favor of his opponent —Broadus Mitchell⟩ ⟨the size of the Democratic margin in those cities . . . determines whether these states ~ Democratic —*Newsweek*⟩ **e :** to come to be performed or executed **:** proceed in a certain manner ⟨ the play . . . had been ~*ing* none too well —S.H. Adams⟩ **f :** to accomplish what is attempted or intended **:** turn out well **:** SUCCEED ⟨successful novelists whose first plays failed to ~ —Henry Hewes⟩ ⟨when there was a party he wanted to make it ~ —W.S.Maugham⟩ **7 a :** to apply or set oneself ⟨*went* to fighting among themselves⟩ **b :** to put or subject oneself ⟨~ to a great deal of trouble⟩ ⟨*went* to unnecessary expense⟩ **c** *chiefly South & Midland* **:** to have a mind **:** INTEND — usu. used in the negative and with a following infinitive ⟨I didn't ~ to do it⟩ **8 :** to have recourse to another as a recognized authority for corroboration, vindication, or decision **:** carry an action or interest **:** RESORT ⟨decided to ~ to court to recover damages⟩ ⟨the government will ~ to the country with this issue⟩ ⟨one must ~ to the original documents for an account of the colony's early years⟩ **9 a :** to begin an action or motion ⟨here ~*es*⟩ ⟨~ when the light turns green⟩ — often used in the imperative as a signal to start a race ⟨on your mark, get set, ~⟩ **b :** to maintain or perform a certain action or motion ⟨the music ~*es* round and round⟩ ⟨all day the drums and the flutes had been ~*ing* strong —John Berry⟩ ⟨his pulse ~*es* quite rapidly⟩ **c :** to function in the proper or expected manner ⟨finally succeeded in getting the motor to ~⟩ **d :** to keep time ⟨a clock that will ~ a week without winding⟩ **e** (1) **:** to make a clear resonant sound **:** RING ⟨it was midnight when the bell *went* and I came up to his room —Ngaio Marsh⟩ (2) **:** to make a characteristic noise **:** SOUND ⟨as soon as the starting gun *went* the contestants began the race⟩ **10 a :** to pass at or as if at face value **:** have currency ⟨traveler's checks ~ everywhere⟩ ⟨a bit of gossip that once *went* for truth⟩ **b :** to pass from person to person **:** be current **:** CIRCULATE ⟨the report ~*es* that the expedition was a failure⟩ **c :** to become known ⟨herring residues . . . ~ as a manure under the name of fish guano —S.J.Watson⟩ ⟨*went* by an alias for two years⟩ **11 a :** to come to be guided, governed, or regulated **:** act in accordance or harmony ⟨a good rule to ~ by⟩ ⟨was criticized for refusing to ~ with the times⟩ **b :** to come to be allotted or determined ⟨hanging and wiving ~*es* by destiny —Shak.⟩ ⟨the crushing . . . realization that this is how things ~ —Bosley Crowther⟩ **c :** to come to be applied or appropriated ⟨a large part of the budget ~*es* for military purposes⟩ **d** (1) **:** to pass by or as if by award, assignment, or lot ⟨the prize *went* to a sophomore⟩ ⟨nearly all the estate *went* to the creditors of the deceased⟩ (2) **:** to pass by inheritance or succession ⟨the farm *went* to the eldest son⟩ ⟨the title ~*es* to the late duke's nephew⟩ **e** (1) **:** to contribute to an end **:** be among the constituents necessary for achieving a purpose or result ⟨the qualities that ~ to make a hero⟩ (2) **:** to be equivalent **:** AMOUNT ⟨100 cents ~ to a dollar⟩ **12 :** to be about, intending, or expecting something — used in a progressive tense with infinitive ⟨may be ~*ing* to have a relapse⟩ ⟨is ~*ing* to leave town⟩ ⟨is ~*ing* to be a doctor⟩ ⟨was ~*ing* to sing a solo⟩ **13 a :** to carry one's action to a certain point of progress or completeness ⟨*went* to great lengths in order to meet the deadline⟩ **b :** to reach a certain point **:** ATTAIN, EXTEND ⟨his knowledge fails to ~ very deep⟩ ⟨the differences ~ further than is commonly believed⟩ **c** (1) **:** to come or arrive at a certain state or condition — usu. used with *to* ⟨the flowers have *gone* to seed⟩ ⟨~ to sleep⟩ (2) **:** to come or arrive at a certain amount or sum — usu. used with *to* ⟨the bidding *went* to $50 before the chair was sold⟩ **14 a :** to come to be **:** BECOME ⟨*went* sound asleep⟩ ⟨the tire *went* flat⟩ ⟨he felt his hands ~ clammy as he spoke —Marcia Davenport⟩ ⟨serious matters and noble conventions get out of hand and ~ pompous —Virgil Thomson⟩ **b :** to undergo a change or transformation **:** TURN ⟨the light from the autumn afternoon was fading and the sky . . . was ~*ing* from blue to gray —C.B.Flood⟩ **15 a :** to be in phrasing or expression **:** appear esp. in writing or print **:** READ ⟨the great mass of the public or, as the phrase ~*es,* the man in the street —A.B. Walkley⟩ ⟨when he was eight years old, so the story ~*es,* he began preaching to the barnyard fowl —H.H.Reichard⟩ **b :** to flow or glide rhythmically ⟨these poems ~ with a lilt⟩ **c :** to be capable of being sung or played ⟨a merry ballad . . . ~*es* to the tune of "Two maids wooing a man" —Shak.⟩ ⟨the tune ~*es* like this⟩ **16 a :** to be compatible, suitable, or becoming **:** HARMONIZE — usu. used with *together* or *with* ⟨the colors blue and gray ~ together⟩ ⟨claret ~*es* with beef⟩ ⟨his tie doesn't ~ with his suit⟩ **b :** to be congenial **:** fit in — usu. used with *with* ⟨the sort of person who can ~ with any group⟩ **17 a :** to be capable of passing ⟨the piano will barely ~ through the door⟩ **b :** to be capable of being contained or inserted ⟨will these clothes ~ in your suitcase?⟩ ⟨the rod ~*es* into a small hole near the top⟩ **c :** to be capable of extending ⟨a belt long enough to ~ around his waist⟩ ⟨enough cotton to make a rope that would ~ from coast to coast⟩ **d :** to have a usual or proper place or position **:** BELONG ⟨these books ~ on the top shelf⟩ **18 :** to have a tendency **:** serve as a means **:** CONDUCE ⟨the incident ~*es* to show that he can be trusted⟩ **19 :** to admit of being played by all the players — used of a suit in cards ⟨led a spade and hoped that it would ~⟩ **20 a** (1) **:** to pass as accepted or authorized **:** carry authority ⟨what she said, *went;* when she summoned, prior engagements were to be broken —DeLancey Ferguson⟩ (2) **:** to be acceptable, satisfactory, or adequate **:** meet with or as if with approval ⟨you make up your own rules today and anything ~*es* —Huntington Hartford⟩ **b :** to hold true **:** be valid ⟨the old saying that it takes all kinds of people to make a world ~*es* for our train —F.J.Taylor⟩ **c :** to be of interest or concern ⟨as far as his speech ~*es,* my point about it is this —Arthur Cavanaugh⟩ **21 :** to empty the bladder or bowels ⟨don't ask for the bedpan during the night unless you really have to ~ —Betty Smith⟩ ~ *vt* **1 :** to proceed along or according to **:** FOLLOW ⟨from the outset he ~*es* his own pace —H.S. Bennett⟩ ⟨asked me if I was ~*ing* his way⟩ **2 :** to pass or travel through **:** TRAVERSE ⟨to ~ its length . . . with the old houses on one side finally giving way to modern stores . . . is to experience the meeting of old and new —R.W.Hatch⟩ **3 :** to set out on **:** UNDERTAKE ⟨I am very tired and I oughtn't to ~ another journey —Mrs. Patrick Campbell⟩ **4 a :** to make a wager of **:** BET ⟨was willing to ~ a dollar on the outcome of the game⟩ **b :** to make an offer of **:** BID ⟨was willing to ~ $50 for the clock⟩ ⟨~ four no-trump⟩ **5 a :** to serve in the capacity of **:** assume the function or obligation of ⟨promised to ~ bail for his friend⟩ **b :** to participate to the extent of ⟨decided to ~ halves if either of them found the treasure⟩ **6 a :** to indicate by sounding **:** STRIKE ⟨the clock on the mantel *went* nine⟩ **b :** to cause (a characteristic sound) to exist or occur ⟨the gun *went* bang⟩ ⟨the bell ~*es* dingdong⟩ **7 :** YIELD, PRODUCE, WEIGH ⟨*went* a considerable amount⟩ ⟨a gigantic striped bass that would ~ a hundred pounds —*Saturday Rev.*⟩ **8 a :** to put up with **:** ENDURE, TOLERATE — usu. used with a negative ⟨it's that stink of caribou about them that I can't ~ —Gontran de Poncins⟩ **b :** to bear without serious financial detriment **:** AFFORD — usu. used with a negative ⟨insisted that he couldn't ~ $20,000 for a house⟩ **9 a :** to occupy oneself with **:** engage in ⟨didn't like anybody to ~ smelling his rose —Eudora Welty⟩ ⟨don't ~ shooting at moose —S.H.Holbrock⟩ **b :** to take pleasure in or receive satisfaction from **:** ENJOY ⟨I could ~ a soda —Hal Ellson⟩

syn LEAVE, DEPART, QUIT, WITHDRAW, RETIRE: GO is a general term indicating moving out or away; it is a neutral opposite for *come.* LEAVE centers attention on the fact of separation from a person, place, or thing ⟨*leaving* his family with their relatives⟩ ⟨*leaving* his boyhood town⟩ ⟨*leaving* the company after 10 years⟩ ⟨he is *leaving* on the noon plane⟩ DEPART is a slightly formal antonym for *arrive* ⟨cheers for the ex-president *departing* for his home⟩ ⟨*departing* from the country⟩ ⟨*departed* on the adventure late in 1523 —C.L.Jones⟩ QUIT may suggest a separating and going off or away attended by disengaging, freeing, ridding, or disentangling ⟨had given him a disgust to his business, and to his residence in a small market town; and, *quitting* them both, he had removed with his family —Jane Austen⟩ ⟨hesitating to spread its wings and *quit* forever the body which had been its home —Arnold Bennett⟩ WITHDRAW may suggest a deliberate removal for good reason ⟨constrained by the strength of his convictions to *withdraw* from the Catholic Church —W.L.Sullivan⟩ ⟨the family swarmed about her, shaking hands, pecking her on the cheek, then *withdrawing* to survey her from a distance —Olive H. Prouty⟩ ⟨spent three years in Paris with scientific friends; but feeling the need of solitude, he *withdrew* to Holland —Frank Thilly⟩ RETIRE may indicate a removal attended with renunciation, relinquishment, retreat, recession, or recoil ⟨prose has had the stage pretty much to itself for the past hundred years largely because poetry has refused to compete with it, preferring instead to *retire* to a private literary world of its own —Archibald MacLeish⟩ ⟨the British *retired* from Augusta, and loyalism in Georgia and South Carolina was severely checked —H.B.Fant⟩ ⟨had been moving forward into a narrower and narrower space as the enemy's center *retired* —Tom Wintringham⟩

— **go about :** to busy oneself with **:** take upon oneself **:** set about **:** UNDERTAKE ⟨the committee *went about* its assignment in a serious manner —Harold Zink⟩ — **go after :** to set out in pursuit or quest of **:** try to get ⟨are now urging their members to *go after* increases from their employers —Harry Conn⟩ — **go against 1 :** to run counter to **:** be or act contrary to **:** OPPOSE ⟨don't want you children to *go against* your mother's wishes —Dorothy C. Fisher⟩ **2 :** to turn out unfavorably for ⟨the umpire's decision *went against* the home team⟩ — **go ahead 1 :** to move forward **:** make one's way to the front (as in a race) **2 :** to continue without delay or hesitation **:** PROCEED ⟨*go ahead* with the job without bothering me —W.F. Davis⟩ **3 :** to develop to a higher, better, or more advanced stage **:** PROGRESS ⟨dairying has *gone ahead* rapidly —*Amer. Guide Series: Ind.*⟩ — **go all the way 1 :** to enter into complete agreement **2 :** to engage in sexual intercourse — **go at 1 a :** to make an attack on ⟨picking up a chair . . . and *going at* her with smashing blows —Glenway Wescott⟩ **b :** to make an approach to ⟨not every succeeding critic has *gone at* the book in this general fashion —R. R. Von Abele⟩ **2 :** to engage in vigorously or energetically **:** UNDERTAKE ⟨curious to know for what . . . reason we have *gone at* organizing with such abandoned enthusiasm —C.W.Ferguson⟩ — **go back on 1 :** to recede or withdraw from **:** ABANDON ⟨to do so would be to *go back on* our own first principles —A.W.Griswold⟩ **2 :** to be disloyal to **:** BETRAY ⟨refused to believe that his friend had *gone back on* him⟩ **3 :** to prove inadequate for **:** FAIL ⟨in advanced years a man's mind might *go back on* him at some unpredictable moment —Elmer Davis⟩ — **go before :** to precede esp. in time ⟨was greatly indebted to those who had *gone before* him⟩ — **go begging :** to be in little demand ⟨fish *went begging* when the cannery went out of business⟩ — **go bush 1** *Austral, of an animal* **:** to go wild **:** revert to a wild state ⟨they're good horses . . . descendants of stud horses *gone bush* —*Sydney (Australia) Bull.*⟩ **2** *Austral, of a person* **:** to live in the bush ⟨has *gone bush* for long periods, dressing and living much like the aborigines he knows so well —C.P.Mountford⟩ — **go down the drain :** to come to be outmoded, discarded, or lost ⟨our opinions . . . will have either *gone down the drain* or become every man's private conviction —Virgil Thomson⟩ — **go down the line :** to give wholehearted support — usu. used with *for* ⟨*went down the line* for a civil-rights program backed by the full power of the federal government —*Springfield (Mass.) Daily News*⟩ — **go far :** to be successful ⟨told him he was a great fellow and would *go far* —H. W. Van Loon⟩ — **go for 1 :** to pass for or serve as ⟨the bits of silvered glass that *went for* mirrors in those days —Charlotte Upton⟩ **2 :** to try to secure **:** aim at ⟨in money matters he *went for* the last penny —V.S.Pritchett⟩ **3 a :** to give support or approval to **:** FAVOR, ACCEPT ⟨I can *go for* no such resolution as this —B.F. Wade⟩ **b :** to have or display an active interest in or liking for ⟨she *went for* him in a big way —Chandler Brossard⟩ **4 :** to attack or assail physically or verbally ⟨his opponent *went for* him when his back was turned⟩ — **go for broke :** to put forth all one's strength or resources ⟨would *go for broke* in organizing textile employees —*Wall Street Jour.*⟩ — **go glimmering :** to pass from or as if from existence ⟨by this time the hope of a short war had *gone glimmering* —J.P.Baxter b. 1893⟩ — **go great guns :** to achieve great success ⟨the book was *going great guns* in twelve countries —George Thomas b. 1892⟩ — **go hang :** to cease to be of interest or concern **:** pass from memory or thought ⟨those who would take care of themselves and let the rest of the world *go hang* —H.M.Wriston⟩ — **go into 1 :** to dress oneself in **:** WEAR ⟨*went into* mourning⟩ **2 :** to pass into or let oneself be given up to ⟨*went into* hysterics⟩ **3 :** to take part or a place in; *esp* **:** to enter as a profession or occupation ⟨finally decided to *go into* law⟩ **4** *obs* **:** to agree or concur with ⟨we will all *go into* your opinion —Joseph Addison⟩ **5 :** to subject to examination or discussion **:** look into ⟨insisted that the problem be *gone into* carefully⟩ **6 :** to be capable of being contained in ⟨5 *goes into* 60 12 times⟩ — **go it 1 :** to behave esp. in a reckless, excited, or improper manner **:** carry on ⟨he had been *going it* a bit too hard —Angus Mowat⟩ **2 :** to proceed esp. in a rapid or furious manner ⟨was delighted to hear a Cockney call out above the cheering crowd "*go it,* old girl" —R.T.B.Fulford⟩ **3 :** to conduct one's affairs **:** ACT ⟨had casually toyed with the idea of *going it* alone —John McNulty⟩ — **go one better :** OUTDO, SURPASS ⟨all of his tone poems demand an orchestra of at least ninety players, and in at least one . . . he *goes* Wagner *one better,* calling for an orchestra of one hundred and sixteen —Deems Taylor⟩ — **go over 1 a :** to subject to careful consideration ⟨*went over* all the arguments before making up his mind⟩ **b :** to subject to careful inspection ⟨*went over* the house and grounds before deciding to buy⟩ **2 a :** REPEAT ⟨*goes over* the same story again and again⟩ **b :** STUDY ⟨*goes over* his lessons every night⟩ **3 :** to be suitable for covering **:** be capable of being put over ⟨bought an awning to *go over* the doorway⟩ **4 :** to examine carefully and revise ⟨students were told to *go over* their essays before handing them in⟩ — **go places :** to be on the way to success or achievement ⟨it is that kind of mechanic who *goes places* —C.B.Rawson⟩ — **go steady :** to have frequent dates exclusively with one member of the opposite sex ⟨argued that all the other girls were *going steady* and that this was the only way to be in on the fun —Geraldine Roberts⟩ — **go through 1 :** to subject to thorough examination, consideration, or study ⟨*went through* the items one by one⟩ **2 :** EXPERIENCE, UNDERGO ⟨*go through* hell and high water⟩ **3 :** to carry out **:** PERFORM ⟨the children *went through* their part of the program without a hitch⟩ **4 :** to appear in published form in ⟨the book has *gone through* six editions⟩ — **go to bed 1 :** to go to press ⟨when the paper *went to bed* at midafternoon he relaxed —T.W.Duncan⟩ **2 :** to engage in sexual relations ⟨is in the habit of *going to bed* with practically anybody who asks her to —Wolcott Gibbs⟩ **3 a** *of a card* **:** to fail to win through being withheld during early play **b** *of a cardplayer* **:** to lose the opportunity to win by withholding a winning card from early play — **go to one's head 1 :** to cause one to become confused, excited, or dizzy ⟨the wine *went to his head*⟩ **2 :** to cause one to become conceited or overconfident ⟨success *went to his head*⟩ — **go to pieces :** to become shattered in or as if in nerves or health — **go to sea :** to adopt the occupation of a sailor ⟨*went to sea* as a boy of 12⟩ — **go to town 1 :** to work or act rapidly, efficiently, or enthusiastically ⟨your friends were *going to town* on me properly when you arrived —Hartley Howard⟩ **2 :** to be successful ⟨military-aircraft production . . . has really begun to *go to town* in the last few months —*Popular Science Monthly*⟩ **3 :** to indulge oneself excessively ⟨his ability to enlarge an emotional experience without *going to town* sentimentally about it —Virgil Thomson⟩ — **go with 1 a :** ACCOMPANY ⟨*went with* me to the library⟩ **b :** DATE ⟨has been *going with* her for two years⟩ **2** *chiefly dial* **:** to become of **:** happen to ⟨my folks don't know what *went with* me —Archie Binns⟩ — **go without saying :** to be self-evident — **to go 1 :** REMAINING, LEFT ⟨there was only five minutes *to go* before the organist started the first hymn —Evelyn Waugh⟩ **2 :** available for taking out or suitable to be taken out ⟨ordered two toasted limburger-cheese sandwiches *to go* —James Jones⟩

²go \'gō\ *n* -ES **1 :** the act or manner of going ⟨a great come and ~ of officials, with district commissioners arriving and departing in a flurry of uniforms and salutes —Alan Moorehead⟩ **2 :** the height of fashion **:** RAGE ⟨elegant shawls labeled . . . "quite the ~" —R.S.Surtees⟩ **3 :** a turn of affairs that is often unexpected **:** INCIDENT, OCCURRENCE ⟨funniest ~ you ever did see —Ngaio Marsh⟩ **4 a :** the quantity used or furnished at one time ⟨you can obtain a ~ of brandy for sixpence —C.B.Fairbanks⟩ **b :** the vessel containing such a quantity ⟨a pewter ~⟩ **5 a :** a situation in cribbage when a player has no card that will not carry the count over 31 **b :** the score given to the cribbage player who brings the count exactly to or nearest to 31 **6 :** ENERGY, VIGOR, SPIRIT ⟨all sapped of ~ and foresight and perseverance by a cruel providence —John Galsworthy⟩ ⟨a play abounding in freshness, vitality, essential theatrical ~ —E.J.West⟩ **7 a :** a turn esp. in a game ⟨told his opponent that it was his ~⟩ **b :** ATTEMPT, TRY ⟨poets . . . who produce perfect results at the first ~ —W.H.Auden⟩ ⟨was going to have a ~ at setting down my observations of public life —A.W.Barkley⟩ **c :** CHANCE, OPPORTUNITY ⟨was given a ~ at building up the savings department —N.M.Clark⟩ **8 a :** a spell or period of activity ⟨it makes a lot of difference in the drying if one can get a large amount into the sheds in one ~ —Eve Langley⟩ **b :** an attack of illness ⟨I shall never forget her kindness to me when I had a bad ~ of pneumonia —Richard Rhodes⟩ **9 a :** SUCCESS ⟨figure out a new type vampire or werewolf yarn and it's a sure ~ —Dallas Ross⟩ **b :** BARGAIN, DEAL ⟨we've got opium to sell and your people want to buy it and it's a ~ —W.H. Smith⟩ **10 :** MATCH, CONTEST ⟨didn't want him to have a hard ~ the first time out because he wasn't sure how well his leg would stand up —G.F.T.Ryall⟩; *specif* **:** a boxing match — **from the word go :** from the very beginning ⟨he was a drag and a brake on me *from the word go* —W.D.Howells⟩ — **no go :** to no avail **:** USELESS, HOPELESS ⟨nobody'll ever know all the things I tried before I finally decided it was *no go* —Saul Bellow⟩ — **on the go 1** *archaic* **:** in a state of decline ⟨as to poor old England, I never see a paper but I think . . . that she is *on the go* —Edward FitzGerald⟩ **2 :** in a state of constant or restless activity ⟨a typical society woman — always *on the go* —Hiram Haydn⟩

³go \"\ *n* -ES [Jap] **:** a Japanese game that is played with black and white stones on a board marked by 19 vertical lines and 19 horizontal lines to make 361 intersections and that has as its object the possession of the larger part of the board and the capturing of the opponent's stones

GO *abbr* **1** general office; general officer **2** general order **3** grand organ; great organ

¹goa \'gōə\ *adj, usu cap* [fr. *Goa*, region in India] **:** of or from Goa, India **:** of the kind or style prevalent in Goa **:** GOANESE

²goa \"\ *n* -S [Tibetan *dgoba*] **:** a common gazelle (*Gazella picticaudata*) of Tibet

³goa \"\ *n* -S [fr. *Goa*, India] **:** ²MUGGER

goa ball *n, usu cap G* [¹goa] **:** a mixture of drugs made up in the form of a ball and formerly used as a remedy for fever

goa bean *n, usu cap G* [¹goa] **1 :** a tropical Old World herbaceous annual vine (*Psophocarpus tetragonolobus*) bearing purplish or blue flowers in a close raceme and pods with four jagged wings **2 :** the edible seed of the Goa bean

go about *vi* **1 a :** to pass from one place to another **:** go here and there ⟨*went about* with a gang of people I don't care about —Dorothy Sayers⟩ **b :** to have currency **:** CIRCULATE ⟨there's not that kind of money *going about* now —George Macbean⟩ **2 :** TACK ⟨in . . . sailing there are two ways of *going about* — a right way and a wrong way —Peter Heaton⟩

go-about \'==,=\ *n* -S [*go about*] **:** VAGRANT

goa butter *n, usu cap G* [¹goa] **:** KOKUM BUTTER

goa cedar *or* **goa cypress** *n, usu cap G* [¹goa; fr. the belief that it was native to India] **:** PORTUGUESE CYPRESS

¹goad \'gōd\ *n* -S [ME *gode*, fr. OE *gād* goad, arrowhead, spear point; akin to Langobardic *gaida* spear, OHG *Gaido*, a personal name, ON *gedda* pike (fish), Skt *hinvati, hinoti* he urges on, throws] **1 :** a rod pointed at one end or fitted with a spike and used to urge on an animal — see OXGOAD **2 a :** something that wounds or pricks like a goad **:** STING, THORN ⟨French forts and . . . armies so near us will be everlasting ~*s* in our sides —Benjamin Franklin⟩ **b :** something that urges or stimulates like a goad **:** SPUR, STIMULUS ⟨insecurity, considered by some management people as the indispensable ~ for workers' efficiency —*Dun's Rev.*⟩ **syn** see MOTIVE

²goad \"\ *vt* -ED/-ING/-S **1 :** to drive with a goad or some other pointed instrument ⟨bound them to the plow and ~*ed* them onward with his lance —Charles Kingsley⟩ **2 :** to drive, incite, or rouse as if with a goad ⟨his editorials were so skillfully written that he often ~*ed* the opposition to madness —W.E.Smith⟩ ⟨knows what it is like to be ~*ed* by technical problems into achieving new insights —J.L.Stewart⟩ **syn** see URGE

goad·man \-dmən\ *or* **goads·man** \-dzm-\ *n, pl* **goadmen** *or* **goadsmen :** one who drives an animal or team by means of a goad

goad stick *n* **:** a stick used as a goad ⟨they banged the donkeys with their *goad sticks* —Mark Twain⟩

¹go-ahead \'==,=\ *adj* [fr. the phrase *go ahead*] **1 :** marked by energy and enterprise **:** PROGRESSIVE ⟨helps spread prosperity and promotes *go-ahead* communities —N.M.Clark⟩ ⟨possessors of the *go-ahead* spirit essential to men —A.E. Rodway⟩ **2 :** indicating that one may proceed ⟨the committee's vote was the *go-ahead* signal . . . to make final plans —W.M.Blair⟩

²go-ahead \"\ *n* -S [fr. the phrase *go ahead*] **1 a :** ENERGY, SPIRIT, ENTERPRISE ⟨you're a bright youngster with lots of *go-ahead* —S.V.Benét⟩ **b :** a person possessing go-ahead ⟨the child'll be a *go-ahead* —A.T.Quiller-Couch⟩ **2 :** a sign, signal, or authority to proceed **:** GREEN LIGHT ⟨planes were waiting . . . for the *go-ahead* on the hazardous 2400-mile overwater hop —R.E.Byrd⟩ ⟨the first to mass-produce automobiles after the government *go-ahead* becomes effective —*Newsweek*⟩

go-ahead·ative·ness *or* **go-ahead·itive·ness** \,gōə'hedəd-ivnəs\ *n* -ES [*go-ahead* + *-ative* or *-itive* + *-ness*] **:** PROGRESSIVENESS

go·ai \'gō,ī\ *var of* KOWHAI

go·a·ji·ro \,gōə'hi(,)rō\ *n, pl* **goajiro** *or* **goajiros** *usu cap* [Sp *guajiro, goajiro*, of AmerInd origin] **1 a :** an Arawakan people of the peninsular region northwest of Lake Maracaibo **b :** a member of such people **2 :** the Arawakan language of the Goajiro people

¹goal \'gōl, *chiefly in dial or substand speech* 'gül\ *n* -S [ME *gol* boundary, limit; perh. akin to OE *gǣlan* to hinder, impede — more at GILL (ravine)] **1 a :** the mark to which the contestants in a race run **:** the terminal point of a race ⟨runners who run well from the starting place to the ~ —Benjamin Jowett⟩ **b :** an area that is to be reached for safety or as the objective in children's games **c :** the conical column that marks each of the two turning points in a chariot race ⟨the space between the two . . . ~*s* was filled with statues and obelisks —Edward Gibbon⟩ **2 :** the end toward which effort or ambition is directed **:** AIM, PURPOSE ⟨leisure is a real commodity, a prize of life, a ~ to strive for —C.C.Furnas⟩ **:** a condition or state to be brought about through a course of action **3 a :** a station, area, cage, basket, or pair of uprights with or without a crossbar toward which the players in various games (as football, basketball, polo, lacrosse, hockey) attempt to advance the ball or puck and usu. through or into which it must go in order to score points — see FIELD HOCKEY illustration **b :** the act of causing the ball or puck to go through or into such a goal **c :** the score resulting from such an act **4 :** GOALKEEPER **5 :** the object complement of a verb **syn** see INTENTION — **in goal :** in one of the two parts of the ground immediately at the ends of the field of play in rugby and between the touchlines produced to the dead-ball lines

²goal \"\ *vi* -ED/-ING/-S **:** to seek or score a goal

go·ala \gō'ālə\ *n* -S *usu cap* [Hindi *goālā*, fr. Skt *gopālaka* cowherd, fr. *go* cow, bull + *pālaka* protector — more at COW, WALLAH] **:** a member of a Hindu caste employed chiefly in dairying

goal crease *n* **:** CREASE 3b

goal-directed *adj* **:** aimed toward a goal or toward completion of a task **:** having an object or anticipated reward **:** PURPOSEFUL, MEANINGFUL, NONRANDOM ⟨*goal-directed* behavior⟩ ⟨repetition must always be *goal-directed* —J.B.Carroll⟩

goal·ie \'gōlē, -li\ *n* -S [¹*goal* + *-ie*] **:** GOALKEEPER

goalkeeper \'=,==\ *n* **:** a player who defends the goal in various games (as hockey, lacrosse, soccer)

goal kick *n* **:** a kick-in awarded a defending soccer player when the ball is driven by a member of the opposing team over the end line but not between the goalposts

goal·less \'gōlləs\ *adj* **:** having no goal scored by either team

goal line *n* **:** a line marking each end of the field of play in various games and extending from one side of the field to the other or from one goalpost to the other — see FOOTBALL illustration

go along *vi* **1 :** to move along **:** CONTINUE, PROCEED ⟨the car *went along* at a moderate speed⟩ ⟨had to teach himself and he is . . . assistants as they *went along* —Robert Berkelman⟩ **2 :** to go or travel as a companion ⟨having no particular interest in antiques, he *went along* for the ride —R.M.Hodesh⟩ — often used with *with* ⟨invited him to *go along* with us on the trip⟩ **3 :** to act in cooperation or express agreement ⟨were unwilling to take the gamble and declined to *go along* —Freeman Lincoln⟩ — often used with *with* ⟨were glad enough to *go along with* his tentative theory —Robert Shaplen⟩

goalpost \'=,=\ *n* **:** one of two vertical posts that with a crossbar constitute the goal in various games

goal set *n* **:** a preparatory set oriented toward a goal

goaltender \'=,==\ *n* **:** GOALKEEPER

¹go·an \'gōən\ *adj, usu cap* [*Goa*, region in India + E *-an*] **:** GOANESE

²goan \"\ *n* -S *cap* **:** GOANESE

¹go·a·nese \'gōə,nēz, -ēs\ *adj, usu cap* [*Goa* + *-nese* (as in *Chinese*)] **1 :** of, relating to, or characteristic of Goa **2 :** of, relating to, or characteristic of the people of Goa

²goanese \"\ *n, pl* **goanese** *cap* **:** a native or inhabitant of Goa

go·an·na \gō'anə\ *n* -S [alter. of *iguana*] *chiefly Austral* **:** any of several large monitor lizards of the family Varanidae — compare IGUANA

goa powder *n, usu cap G* [¹goa] **:** a bitter powder found in the wood of a Brazilian tree (*Vataireopsis araroba*) and valued as the chief source of the drug chrysarobin

go around *vi* **1 a :** to pass from place to place **:** go here and there ⟨friends of your own age to *go around* with —Caroline Slade⟩ **b :** to have currency **:** CIRCULATE ⟨an amusing story is *going around* these days⟩ **2 :** to satisfy the demand **:** fill the need ⟨hardly enough food to *go around*⟩

go-around \'==,=\ *n* -S [*go around*] **1 a :** ROUND ⟨apparent agreement . . . during the first *go-around* doesn't necessarily mean they'll see eye to eye indefinitely —*Newsweek*⟩ **b :** a heated argument, dispute, or struggle ⟨tried to tell them that this was a lousy way to treat a member of the family, and after a real *go-around* he had won —Don Tracy⟩ **2 :** RUNAROUND ⟨he's been giving us the *go-around* —Del Carnes⟩ **3 :** an act or instance of going around (as in a traffic pattern) ⟨cockpit work load is highest in a *go-around* from a missed instrument approach —E.W.Norris⟩

goas *pl of* GOA

go-ashore \'gōə,shō(ə)r\ *n* -S [prob. by folk etymology fr. Maori *'kōhua* cooking pot] *NewZeal* **:** a 3-footed iron caldron

goa stone *n, usu cap G* [¹goa] **:** GOA BALL

go-as-you-please \'====\ *adj* **:** not bound by rule, law, or convention **:** EASYGOING ⟨bewildered by the old *go-as-you-please* liberty of alliterative rhythm —George Saintsbury⟩

¹goat \'gōt, *usu* -ōd.+V\ *n* -S *often attrib* [ME *gote*, *goot*, *gat*, fr. OE *gāt*; akin to OHG *geiz* goat, ON *geit*, Goth *gaits* goat, L *haedus* kid] **1 a :** any of various alert agile Old World hollow-horned ruminant mammals (genus *Capra*) closely related to the sheep and like them often domesticated but of lighter build and with backwardly arching horns that often form a closely twisted spiral, a short tail, and comparatively straight hair, the male usu. having a distinct beard — compare IBEX, MARKHOR **b :** any of several related animals of similar habits or characteristics — see GOAT ANTELOPE, MOUNTAIN GOAT **2 :** CAPRICORN **3 :** a licentious or lustful man **:** LECHER ⟨the doctor is . . . an old ~ and has ideas about spiriting his lovely client off to a little hideout —Wolcott Gibbs⟩ **4 :** GOATSKIN ⟨a book bound in ~⟩ **5 :** SCAPEGOAT ⟨dairy farmers have been made the ~ for all that's to be criticized in the government support program —Richard Lewis⟩ **6** *slang* **a :** a West Point cadet having the lowest academic rank in his class **b :** one who is being initiated into a fraternity or sorority **7 :** BROCCOLI BROWN **8 :** a yard locomotive

²goat \"\ *var of* GOTE

goat antelope *n* **:** any of several bovid mammals (as the chamois, goral, Rocky Mountain goat) related to the goats but in some respects resembling the antelopes

goatbrush \'=,=\ *n* **:** OREGON BOX

goatbush \'=,=\ *n* **:** a spiny shrub (*Castela texana*) of the family Simaroubaceae of Mexico and the southwestern U.S. having a bitter bark

goa·tee \(,)gō'tē\ *n* -S [¹*goat* + *-ee*; fr. the resemblance to the beard of a he-goat] **:** a small trim pointed or tufted beard on a man's chin

goatee

goa·teed \-ēd\ *adj* **:** having a goatee ⟨a courtly ~ scholar⟩

goat fever *n* **:** BRUCELLOSIS

goat fig *n* **:** any of several wild figs; *esp* **:** CAPRIFIG

goatfish \'=,=\ *n* **:** a fish of the family Mullidae **:** MULLET 2

goat grass *n* **:** any of various grasses of the genus *Aegilops*; *esp* **:** a European grass (*A. triuncialis*) naturalized as a weed in No. America whose sharp-pointed fruits cause injury when eaten by livestock

goat·herd \'gōt,hərd\ *n* [ME *gootherde*, fr. OE *gāthyrde*, fr. *gāt* goat + *hyrde* herder — more at GOAT, HERD] **:** one who tends goats

goatier *comparative of* GOATY

goatiest *superlative of* GOATY

goat·ish \'gōd·ish, -ōt|, |ēsh\ *adj* **1 :** of, relating to, or having the characteristics of a goat **2 :** LASCIVIOUS, LECHEROUS — **goat·ish·ness** *n* -ES

goat-kneed \'=,nēd\ *adj* **:** KNEE-SPRUNG

goatlike \'=,=\ *adj* **:** resembling that of a goat ⟨a ~ odor⟩

goat·ling \'gōtliŋ\ *n* -S *Brit* **:** a young goat; *esp* **:** a female goat between one and two years old

goat moth *n* [so called fr. the fact that its larva exhales an odor suggestive of a he-goat] **:** any of the large stout-bodied moths of the family Cossidae; *esp* **:** a European moth (*Cossus cossus*) whose larva bores in the wood of living trees

goat nut *n* **:** JOJOBA

goat pepper *also* **goat's pepper** *n* **:** any of various small-fruited hot peppers

goat-pox \'=,=\ *n* **:** a virus disease of goats that resembles cowpox and is either localized in the udder or occurs over the surface of the body

goats *pl of* GOAT

goatsbeard \'=,=\ *n* **1 :** a plant of the genus *Tragopogon* **2 :** any of several plants of the genus *Aruncus*; *esp* **:** an herb (*A. sylvester*) cultivated for its small white flowers **3 :** a fungus of the genus *Clavaria*

goat's chico·ry *n* **:** PILEWORT 3

goats·foot \'gōts,fu̇t\ *n* -S **1 :** a southern African plant (*Oxalis caprina*) with bluish yellow flowers **2 :** GOUTWEED

goatsfoot convolvulus *n* **:** a tropicopolitan vine (*Ipomoea pes-caprae*) having coarse succulent leaves and showy purple flowers

goat's hair *n* **:** a bundle of short white hairy cirrus clouds believed to portend rain

goat's horn *n* [so called fr. the shape of the pod] **:** an herb (*Astragalus aegiceras*) of southern Europe

goat·skin \'=,=\ *n* **1 :** the skin of a goat **2 :** leather made from goatskin

goat's rue *n* **1** *or* **goat rue :** a tall bushy blue-flowered European perennial plant (*Galega officinalis*) sometimes grown in flower gardens **2 :** CATGUT 3a

goat's thorn *n* **:** any of several thorny shrubs of the genus *Astragalus* (as *A. tragacanthus* and *A. poterium*) native to southern Europe and the Levant

goat·stone \'=,=\ *n* **1 :** a bezoar from a goat **2 goatstones** *pl* **:** the clustered growths of any of several Old World orchids of the genus *Orchis*

goatsucker \'=,==\ *n* [so called fr. the belief that it sucks the milk from goats] **:** any of various medium-sized long-winged crepuscular or nocturnal birds (as the whippoorwills and nighthawks) constituting the family Caprimulgidae, having a short wide bill, short legs, and soft mottled plumage, and feeding on insects which they catch on the wing — called also *nightjar*; see FROGMOUTH

goat·weed \'=,=\ *n* **1 :** GOUTWEED **2 :** either of two West Indian plants (*Capraria biflora* and *Stemodia durantifolia*) of the family Scrophulariaceae **3 :** BILLY-GOAT WEED **4 :** a plant of the genus *Croton* **5 :** KLAMATH WEED

goatweed emperor *n* **:** a common brown and orange butterfly (*Anaea andria*) of the central U.S. that has larvae which feed on plants of the genus *Croton*

goat willow *n* **:** a sallow (*Salix caprea*)

goaty \'gōd·|ē, -ōt|, |i\ *adj* -ER/-EST **:** GOATISH

goave *var of* GOVE

go·away bird \'gōə'wā-\ *also* **go·way bird** \(')gō'wā-\ *n* [imit.] **:** any of several African and Australian birds; *esp* **:** any of various African touracos

goa yam *n, usu cap G* [¹goa] **:** KAAWI YAM

¹gob \'gäb\ *n* -S [ME *gobbe*, fr. MF *gobe* large morsel of food, large mouthful, back-formation fr. *gobet* mouthful, bite, piece — more at GOBBET] **1 :** a lump or mass of indefinite or variable shape ⟨the mud was thick . . . and clung to our shoes like huge ~*s* of discolored dough —H.D.Skidmore⟩ ⟨high fat clouds like ~*s* of whipped cream —William Faulkner⟩ **2 :** a large amount — usu. used in pl. ⟨he has ~*s* of money —P.B. Kyne⟩ ⟨they will certainly find in it ~*s* . . . of unadulterated narrative —C.J.Rolo⟩ **3 a :** a large mouthful of food ⟨a beer to wash down the last ~ of gluey rice —Earle Birney⟩ **b :** a large lump of some substance that is chewed and not swallowed (as tobacco) **4 :** a mass of molten glass gathered on a blowpipe or in a feeder as the initial step in forming a glass object **5 a :** the broken waste or filling left or placed in old mine workings **b :** a space from which material (as coal) has been mined

²gob \"\ *n* -S [IrGael & ScGael, beak, protruding mouth] **:** MOUTH ⟨a short stumpy man with a pipe perpetually in his ~ —Walter Macken⟩

³gob \"\ *n* -S [origin unknown] **:** SAILOR — usu. used of an enlisted man in the U.S. Navy

go·bar numeral *or* **gho·bar numeral** \(')gō'bär-\ *or* **gu·bar numeral** \(')gü'bär-\ *n* [Ar *ghubār* dust, board with sand used for writing] **:** one of a set of ancient numerals which the Arabs developed from Hindu numerals and from which the modern arabic numerals are derived — see NUMBER table

gobbe \'gäb\ *n* -S [native name in the Caribbean] **:** BAMBARRA GROUNDNUT

¹gob·bet \'gäbət, *usu* -əd·+V\ *n* -S [ME *gobet*, fr. MF, mouthful, bite, piece, fr. *gober* to gulp down, swallow, prob. of Celt origin; akin to IrGael & ScGael *gob* beak, snout, protruding mouth] **1 a :** a piece or portion of food or raw meat **:** MORSEL ⟨smoking ~*s* of ready-cooked fish, chicken, and turkey —H.L. Davis⟩ ⟨slice them into ~*s* and fling their flesh to the dogs —Henry Taylor⟩ **b :** a mouthful of food ⟨slices of bread covered with honey which he was shoveling into himself in dripping gouts and ~*s* —Kenneth Roberts⟩ ⟨the masses of raw immigrants . . . were unwelcome ~*s* to the Brahmin stomach —V.L.Parrington⟩ **2 :** a lump or mass usu. of indefinite or variable shape **:** GOB ⟨a ~ of gold —Amy Lowell⟩ ⟨some revolting ~*s* of cotton —Jean Stafford⟩ ⟨watching the volcano throw up its ~*s* of smoke —Wallace Stegner⟩ **3 :** a fragment or extract of literature or music ⟨snippets and ~*s* of information culled from the classics —*Listener*⟩ ⟨unrelated ~*s* of quantitative knowledge —A.W.Griswold⟩ **4 :** a small quantity of liquid **:** DROP ⟨~*s* of oil —William Beebe⟩ ⟨she shipped a ~ of sea, only a thin little runnel that escaped at once through the open scuppers —Victoria Sackville-West⟩

²gobbet \"\ *vt* -ED/-ING/-S [ME *gobeten*, fr. *gobet*, n.] **1** *archaic* **:** to cut up (as a trout) **2** *obs* **:** to swallow in gobbets ⟨they ~ down his flesh —Robert Stapylton⟩

¹gob·ble \'gäbəl\ *vb* **gobbled; gobbled; gobbling** \-b(ə)liŋ\ **gobbles** [prob. fr. ¹*gob* + *-le* (freq. suffix)] *vt* **1 :** to eat greedily or swallow hastily and noisily in large mouthfuls **:** GULP ⟨they *gobbled* what was left of the breakfast —S.H. Adams⟩ ⟨turned themselves into tigers and *gobbled* up human beings —*Newsweek*⟩ **2 :** to seize or capture greedily or hastily **:** take eagerly **:** GRAB — usu. used with *up* ⟨permitting the three small countries to be *gobbled* up individually by their aggressive neighbor⟩ ⟨a bond issue was quickly *gobbled* up —E.O. Hauser⟩ **3 :** to read rapidly or greedily ⟨many bright girls can ~ up such books —Louise S. Bechtel⟩ ~ *vi* **:** to eat greedily and hastily

²gobble \"\ *vb* -ED/-ING/-S [imit.] *vi* **1 :** to make the natural guttural noise of a turkey-cock ⟨the older toms ~ and strut to attract the attention of the females⟩ **2 :** to make a sound resembling the gobble of a turkey ⟨a tiny geyser *gobbled* —Rudyard Kipling⟩ ~ *vt* **:** to utter or emit by or as if by gobbling ⟨the obscenities that poured out of him were *gobbled* so that their point was lost —Walter Macken⟩

³gobble \"\ *n* -S **:** a noise made by or as if by gobbling

gob·ble·dy·gook *or* **gob·ble·de·gook** \'gäbəldē,gu̇k, -di¦-, -,gük\ *n* [irreg. fr. ³*gobble*] **:** wordy and generally unintelligible jargon: **a :** inflated, involved, and obscure verbiage usu. associated with bureaucratic pronouncements ⟨the current law is a masterpiece of complexity and ~ —Roswell Magill⟩ **b :** the specialized language of a group or organization that is usu. wordy and complicated and often unintelligible to an outsider ⟨I don't get all this real-estate ~: twenty-seven-five, five down, exclusive development, unspoiled area, last frontier —Steve McNeil⟩ ⟨writing in a linguistic ~ unintelligible to everyone except the specialist —G.S.Lane⟩ **c :** a meaningless jumble of words ⟨only the teachers in the English department teach English; the others let their students get by with any old ~ —S.E.Morison⟩

¹gob·bler \'gäb(ə)lə(r)\ *n* -S [¹*gobble* + *-er*] **:** one that gobbles; *esp* **:** one that reads rapidly or greedily ⟨a great ~ of books⟩

²gobbler \-blə(r)\ *n* -S [²*gobble* + *-er*] **:** TURKEY-COCK

gobbo *var of* GOBO

¹gobe·lin \'gōbələn, 'gäb-\ *adj, usu cap* [fr. the *Gobelin* dyehouse and tapestry works, Paris, France, established by the *Gobelin* family, 15th cent. Fr. dyers] **:** of, relating to, or being a French tapestry noted for its handworked pictorial designs

²gobelin \"\ *n* -S *usu cap* **1 a :** a Gobelin tapestry **b :** a handmade or machine-made imitation of a Gobelin **2** *or* **gobelin blue :** a grayish blue that is greener and paler than electric or average shadow blue, greener and duller than copenhagen, and greener and less strong than old china

gobelin green *n, usu cap 1st G* **:** a moderate green that is yellower and slightly duller than sea green (sense 1a) and yellower and paler than myrtle (sense 3a)

gobelin stitch *n, usu cap G* **:** any of several small vertical or slanting stitches worked over one or more threads of canvas to form a solid ground of stitches

gobe-mouche \(,)gōb¦müsh\ *n, pl* **gobe-mouches** \-sh(əz)\ [F, fr. *gober* to gulp down, swallow + *mouche* fly, fr. L *musca* — more at GOBBET, MIDGE] **:** a credulous person; *esp* **:** one who believes everything he hears ⟨as words here cost nothing, the gulping ~ is plentifully supplied —Richard Ford⟩

go·ber·na·do·ra \,gōbə(r)nə'dōrə\ *n* -S [MexSp, fr. Sp, wife of a governor, fem. of *gobernador* governor, fr. *gobernar* to govern, fr. L *gubernare* to pilot, steer, govern — more at GOVERN] **:** CREOSOTE BUSH

go-between \'==,=\ *n* -S [fr. the phrase *go between*] **1 :** one that goes between: as **a :** one who promotes a love affair esp. by carrying messages and arranging meetings ⟨enjoying his mysterious importance as . . . *go-between* with the man she loves —Elizabeth Janeway⟩ **b :** one who negotiates a marriage **:** MARRIAGE BROKER ⟨conduct of negotiations . . . by parents through a *go-between* —G.P.Murdock⟩ **c :** an intermediate agent between two individuals or groups (as in politics) **:** EMISSARY, INTERMEDIARY ⟨the *go-between* taking messages from mother to son —Mary Webb⟩ ⟨the *go-between* who arranged the compromise between the two rival factions in the legislature⟩ **2 :** a connecting link or bridge ⟨the Crimea formerly played the part of *go-between* with the Mediterranean world —E.D.Laborde⟩ **3 :** one that belongs in part to each of two groups or classes ⟨these children of the wilds . . . could pass either as white or red and were in truth *go-betweens* —*Amer. Guide Series: Minn.*⟩

go·bi \'gōbē, -bi\ *n* -S [fr. the *Gobi* desert, Mongolia] **:** the lenticular mass of sedimentary deposits that occupies a tala or downwarp basin

gobies *pl of* GOBY

¹go·bi·e·soc·id \gō¦bīə¦säsəd, ¦gōbēə-\ *adj* [NL *Gobiesocidae*] **:** of or relating to the Gobiesocidae

²**gobiesocid** \"\ *n* -s : a gobiesocid fish

go·bi·e·soc·i·dae \(,)gō,bīə'sässə,dē, ,gōbēə-\ *n pl, cap* [NL, fr. *Gobiesoc-, Gobiesox,* type genus + *-idae*] : a family of small marine teleost fishes that have soft dorsal and anal fins and a large sucker formed in part by the pelvic fins located well forward on the throat and that form an order Xenopterygii or in some classifications a highly specialized suborder of Percomorphi — compare CLINGFISH

go·bi·e·soc·i·form \gō,bīə'sässə,fȯrm, ¦gōbēə-\ *adj* [NL *gobieosocidae* + E *-form*] : resembling the Gobiesocidae

go·bi·e·sox \'gōbīə,säks, 'gōbēə-\ *n, cap* [NL, fr. L *gobius* gudgeon + *esox* pike — more at GOBY, ESOX] : the type genus of Gobiesocidae

¹**go·bi·id** \'gōbēəd\ *adj* [NL *Gobiidae*] : of or relating to the Gobiidae

²**gobiid** \"\ *n* -s : a gobiid fish

go·bi·idae \gō'bīə,dē\ *n pl, cap* [NL, fr. *Gobius,* type genus + *-idae*] : a family of bony fishes that consists of the gobies and with a few related families constitutes a suborder Gobioidea of the order Percomorphi

go·bi·iform \'gōbēə,fȯrm\ *adj* [NL *Gobiiformes*] **1** : GOBIOID **2** : resembling a goby

go·bi·ifor·mes \,==='fȯr,mēz\ [NL, fr. *Gobius* + *-iformes*] *syn of* GOBIOIDEA

go·bi·nism \'gōbə,nizəm\ *n* -s *usu cap* [F *gobinisme,* fr. Comte Joseph A. de *Gobineau* †1882 Fr. orientalist + F *-isme* -ism] : the theory or doctrine that the white and esp. the Germanic race is the superior race among men

go·bio \'gōbē,ō\ *n, cap* [NL, fr. L gudgeon — more at GOBY] : a genus of freshwater cyprinid fishes that contains the true gudgeons

¹**go·bi·oid** \'gōbē,ȯid\ *adj* [NL *Gobioidea*] : of or relating to the Gobioidea

²**gobioid** \"\ *n* -s : a gobioid fish

go·bi·oi·dea \,=='ȯidēə\ *n pl, cap* [NL, fr. *Gobius* + *-oidea*] : a suborder of Percomorphi comprising the gobies and related fishes

go·bi·oi·dei \-dē,ī\ [NL, fr. *Gobius* + *-oidei*] *syn of* GOBIOIDEA

go·bi·us \'gōbēəs\ *n, cap* [NL, fr. L, gudgeon — more at GOBY] : the type genus of Gobiidae

¹**gob·let** \'gäblət, *usu* -əd.+V\ *n* -s [ME *gobelet, goblett,* fr. MF *gobelet,* prob. of Celt origin; akin to IrGael & ScGael *gob* beak, snout, protruding mouth] **1** *archaic* **a** : a bowl-shaped cup or drinking vessel without handles and sometimes footed and covered **b** : a wine cup **2** : a drinking glass with a foot and stem — compare TUMBLER

goblet 2

²**goblet** *n* -s [by alter.] *obs* : GOBBET

goblet cell *n* [¹*goblet;* fr. its shape] **1** : a mucus-secreting epithelial cell (as of columnar epithelium) that is distended at the free end with secretion or precursors **2** : a freshwater choanoflagellate (genus *Monosiga*) that is commonly attached to aquatic plants by a slender stalk — called also *chalice cell*

gob·lin \'gäblən\ *n* -s *often attrib* [ME *gobelin,* fr. MF, fr. ML *gobelinus,* fr. (assumed) ML *gobelus* goblin, modif. of Gk *kobalos* rogue, spirit resembling a satyr] : an ugly or grotesque sprite sometimes conceived as evil and malicious and sometimes as merely playful and mischievous ⟨~s haunt from fire or fen —William Collins †1759⟩ ⟨an amiable ~ attached to the old house from time immemorial —*Brit. Book News*⟩

gob·line \'gä,blīn\ *n* [*gob* (origin unknown) + *line*] : a backrope from the dolphin striker

gob·lin·esque \¦gäblə¦nesk\ *adj* : GOBLINISH

goblin fish *n* : a small Australian scorpion fish (*Glyptauchen panduratus*) noted for its grotesque appearance

gob·lin·ish \'gäblənish\ *adj* : resembling or suggestive of a goblin in appearance or behavior ⟨a fantastic ~ wink —J.C. Powys⟩

gob·lin·ry \-nrē\ *n* -ES : the acts or practices of goblins ⟨~ intended to deceive you —Lafcadio Hearn⟩

goblin scarlet *n* : CASTILIAN RED

goblin shark *n* : a galeoid shark (genus *Scapanorhynchus*) that has protrusible jaws and a greatly elongate snout and is found off the coasts of Japan and Portugal

¹**go·bo** \'gō(,)bō\ *n* -s [Jap *gobō*] **1** : a burdock (*Arctium lappa*) cultivated in Japan as a vegetable **2** *or* **gob·bo** \'gä(-\ : OKRA

²**gobo** \"\ *n, pl* **gobos** *also* **goboes** [origin unknown] **1** : a portable black cloth-covered screen or dark strip of wallboard used in television and motion pictures to shield the camera from unwanted light **2** : a portable screen covered with sound-absorbing material that is used to protect (as a microphone) from unwanted sound

gob·o·nat·ed \'gäbə,nād·əd\ *adj* [prob. fr. obs. *gobon* slice (fr. ME *goboun, gobin,* fr. — assumed — AF *gobon,* fr. OF *gobet* mouthful, bite, piece) + E *-ate* + *-ed*] : COMPONY

go·bo·ny \gə'bōnē\ *adj* [obs. *gobon* + *-y* (fr. F *-é* -ate, fr. L *-atus*)] : COMPONY

go·boon \(')gä¦bün, gə'b-\ *var of* ²GABOON

gobs *pl of* GOB

gobstick \'=,=\ *n* [²*gob* + *stick*] : a stick for removing the hook from the gullet of a fish

go by *vi* **1** : PASS ⟨as time *goes by*⟩ **2** : to make a brief visit : CALL ⟨all the family was at home when he *went by* yesterday⟩

go-by \'gō,bī\ *n* -s [*go by*] : intentional disregard or avoidance : RUNAROUND — usu. used in the phrase *give the go-by* ⟨I was good enough to see after they gave you the big *go-by,* wasn't I —Thomas Wolfe⟩

go·by \'gōbē, -bi\ *n, pl* **gobies** *also* **goby** [L *gobius, cobius, gobio* gudgeon, fr. Gk *kōbios,* prob. of non-IE origin] : any of numerous spiny-finned fishes constituting the family Gobiidae, usu. having a broad depressed head, large mouth, no lateral line, and the pelvic fins thoracic and often united to form a sucking disk, and occurring chiefly in shallow coastal waters — see MUDSKIPPER, MUDSUCKER

go-bye *or* **go-by** \'gō,bī\ *n* -s [*go by*] : the act of a greyhound that has gained a length's lead over an opponent after having started a length behind and passed him in a straight run

GOC *abbr* general officer commanding

go-cart \'=,=\ *n* **1** : WALKER ⟨as much a prisoner as a child in a *go-cart* —Maria Edgeworth⟩ **2** : HANDCART ⟨pushing his belongings in a *go-cart* —*Johannesburg Rand Daily Mail*⟩ **3** : a light open carriage **4** : STROLLER ⟨wheeling my brother . . . in his *go-cart* —Willard Price⟩

go·cle·ni·an sorites \gō'klēnēən-, -lā\ *n, usu cap G* [Rudolf *Goclenius* †1628 Ger. logician + E *-an*] : a sorites in which the order of the premises is reversed

¹**god** \'gäd *sometimes* 'gȯd\ *n* -s [ME, fr. OE; akin to OFris & OS *god,* OHG *got,* ON *goth, guth,* Goth *guth* god and prob. to OIr *guth* voice, Gk *kauchasthai* to boast, Skt *havate* he calls, invokes; basic meaning: to call, invoke] **1** : a being of more than human attributes and powers; *esp* : a superhuman person conceived as the ruler or sovereign embodiment of some aspect, attribute, or department of reality and to whom worship is due and acceptable ⟨ancestor worship . . . occurs where ~s are thought once to have been human beings —E.A. Hoebel⟩ ⟨the grim wrath of the ~s on high —J.B.Noss⟩ ⟨the Greek ~s of love and war⟩ — often used interjectionally esp. as a cap. oath **2** : an artificial or natural object (as a carved idol or an animal or tree) that is thought to be the seat of divine powers, the expression of a divine personality, or itself a supernatural or divine agency ⟨also he makes a ~ and worships it —Isa 44:15 (RSV)⟩ ⟨not . . . every mummified and carefully buried animal had been a ~ —S.A.B.Mercer⟩ **3** : a person or thing that is honored as a god or deified : something held to be of supreme value ⟨his father — the adored ~ who had unjustly condemned him —Douglas Hubble⟩ ⟨power for power's sake was his mastering ~ —Hodding Carter⟩ **4** : one who wields great or despotic power ⟨the ruling ~s of the circulating libraries —Frederick Pollock⟩ **5 a** : an occupant of the gallery of a theater ⟨one young ~ between the acts favored the public with a song —W.M.Thackeray⟩ **b gods** *pl* : the gallery of a theater ⟨the applause . . . came mainly from a crowd of youngsters in the ~s —Frank Clune⟩ **6** : a human being of extraordinarily attractive physical stature ⟨a ~ . . . with great broad shoulders and a magnificent chest —W.S.Maugham⟩ — **ye gods and little fishes** — used to express surprise or indignation

²**God** \"\ *n* : the supreme or ultimate reality : the Deity variously conceived in theology, philosophy, and popular religion: as **a** (1) : the holy, infinite, and eternal spiritual reality presented in the Bible as the creator, sustainer, judge, righteous sovereign, and redeemer of the universe who acts with power in history in carrying out his purpose ⟨the Hebraic thought of ~ as the living sovereign Jehovah —O.C.Quick⟩ ⟨~ in Three Persons, blessed Trinity —Reginald Heber⟩ (2) : the eternal, invisible, arbitrarily omnipotent Lord of the worlds and final judge of all men presented in the Koran as all-knowing, just, compassionate, merciful, and unchangeable ⟨Allah hath said: Choose not two gods; there is only One ~ —*Koran*⟩ **b** (1) : the unchangeably perfect Being that is the first and final cause of the universe ⟨it is necessary that there should be as the first cause of the series of motions an unmoved mover or ~ —Frank Thilly⟩ — compare DEISM (2) : the whole of the universe in its unity ⟨religion is not forced to choose . . . the pantheistic ~ of idealism —James Collins⟩ — compare PANTHEISM (3) : reality opposed to appearance : ABSOLUTE ⟨Hegel claims that . . . religion is the self-consciousness of ~ . . . how the Absolute Spirit is conscious of itself in finite spirit —John Baillie⟩ (4) : the creative, integrative, and redemptive process at work in the world that is the supremely worthful actuality of all existence and upon which all other forms of existence depend for life, meaning, freedom, purpose, value, and the realization of their highest destiny ⟨we are invited to behold a growing universe and to discern at its heart . . . a finite growing ~ —T.B.Kilpatrick⟩ (5) : the one ultimate infinite reality that is pure existence, consciousness, and bliss without distinctions (as of time and space) ⟨~ in Hinduism is not the creator of individual selves and other eternal entities — Satischandra Chatterjee⟩ (6) *Christian Science* : infinite Mind : the incorporeal divine Principle ruling over all as eternal Spirit ⟨~ . . . the all-knowing, all-seeing, all-acting, all-wise, all-loving, and eternal; Principle; Mind; Soul; Spirit; Life; Truth; Love; all substance; intelligence —Mary B. Eddy⟩ **c** (1) : the Being supreme in power, wisdom, and goodness that men worship and to whom they pray ⟨turn to ~ in time of trouble⟩ (2) : the ideal or essence of what is best in human life ⟨to them ~ became a symbol for the highest human aspirations and without reality apart from the minds of men —K.S. Latourette⟩ — **for God's sake** — used typically to express surprise, disgust, or indignation — **God forbid** — used as a mild invocation ⟨if he should fail, *God forbid,* all will be lost⟩ — **with God** : in heaven — used of one who has died

³**god** \"\ *vt* **godded; godded; godding; gods** : to treat as a god : WORSHIP, IDOLIZE, DEIFY ⟨how the good priest ~s himself —Alfred Tennyson⟩ ⟨this last old man . . . loved me above the measure of a father; nay, *godded* me indeed —Shak.⟩

god-a-mercy \,=ə'mərsē\ *interj, usu cap G* [ME *God a mercy* God have mercy] *archaic* — used to express gratitude or thanks ⟨*God-a-mercy* . . . what a happy thing —*Bystander*⟩

god-awful \(')=¦==\ *adj, often cap G* : extremely unpleasant, disagreeable, or objectionable : ABOMINABLE ⟨the *god-awful* mess I'm in —Dorothy Baker⟩

godchild \'=,=\ *n* [ME, fr. *god* + *child*] **1** : one for whom a person becomes sponsor at baptism and whom he promises to see brought up as a Christian : GODSON, GODDAUGHTER ⟨both the bride and bridegroom were *godchildren* of the king and queen —*N.Y. Times*⟩ **2** : a child of another religious or cultural group having a relationship to a man or woman similar to that of a Christian godchild to his sponsor

¹**god·damn** *or* **god·dam** \'gäd¦dam, -daa(ə)m\ *n* -s *often cap* : DAMN ⟨they were in no mood to give a good ~ about anything —Robert Lowry⟩

²**goddamn** *or* **goddam** \(')=¦=\ *vb, sometimes cap, vt* : DAMN *vt* 5 ⟨I'll be ~*ed* —T.H.Martin⟩ ⟨he ~*ed* himself because he was getting soft —J.T.Farrell⟩ ~ *vi* : DAMN *vi* ⟨you feel like swearing and ~*ing* worse and worse —Ernest Hemingway⟩

god·damned \'=,dam(d), -,daa(ə)m(d), *before* "*-est*" (')=¦=\ *or* **god·damn** *or* **god·dam** \-m\ *adj* : ¹DAMNED ⟨put that in your ~ notebook —Martha Gellhorn⟩

²**goddamned** \"\ *or* **goddamn** *or* **goddam** \"\ *adv* : ²DAMNED ⟨you're ~ right I want to go —John Steinbeck⟩

goddaughter \'=,==\ *n* [ME *goddoughter,* fr. OE *goddohtor,* fr. *god* — *dohtor* daughter — more at DAUGHTER] : a girl or woman whom one sponsors at baptism ⟨his responsibility for the religious education of his ~⟩

god·dess \'gädəs\ *n* -ES [ME *godesse, goddesse,* fr. *god* + *-esse* -ess] **1** : a female god : a divinity or deity of the female sex ⟨the Hindu assassins used hashish as devotees of the ~ — Thuggee —Weston La Barre⟩ ⟨the ~ of mercy⟩ **2 a** : a woman who is the object of adoration ⟨like the lover whose imagination makes a ~ of some commonplace young woman —C.E.Montague⟩ **b** : something personified as a woman that is honored as a goddess, deified, or held to be of supreme value ⟨that characteristic middle-class ~ . . . — the English Common Law —Roy Lewis & Angus Maude⟩ **3** : a woman of great charms; *esp* : a woman of extraordinary physical beauty **4** : a female occupant of the gallery of a theater

god·dess·hood \-s,hu̇d\ *n* -s : the quality or state of being a goddess

god·dess-ship \-də(sh),ship, -dəs,sh-\ *n, often cap* [*goddess* + *-ship*] *archaic* : GODDESSHOOD — used with preceding possessive pronoun ⟨in all thy perfect *goddess-ship* —Lord Byron⟩ ⟨her *Goddess-ship* approves the air —Thomas Moore⟩

go·det \gō'det\ *n* -s *often attrib* [F, lit., drinking cup, mug, prob. of Gmc origin; akin to MLG *kodde* cylindrical piece of wood, MD *codde* chunk of wood, club] **1** : a triangular inset of cloth placed in a seam or slash to give fullness at the bottom edge of a skirt or sleeve **2** : a usu. glass or plastic roller around which synthetic filaments are passed under tension for stretching

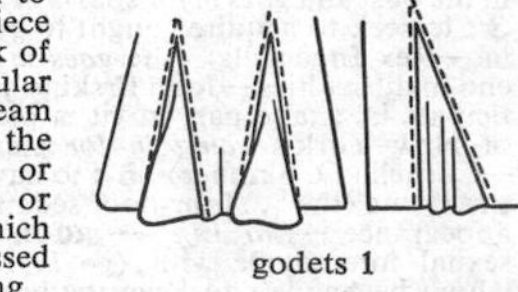

godets 1

go·de·tia \gō'dēsh(ē)ə\ *n* [NL, fr. C. H. *Godet* †1879 Swiss botanist + NL *-ia*] **1** *cap* : a small genus of western American plants (family Onagraceae) having flowers in leafy racemes or spikes, the calyx often colored, and lilac or white petals that are often spotted with crimson or purple — see FAREWELL-TO-SPRING **2** -s : any plant of the genus *Godetia*

go-devil \'=,==\ *n* : any of various machines or devices: **a** : a weight formerly dropped into a borehole (as of an oil well) to explode a cartridge previously lowered; *also* : a small torpedo dropped in for the same purpose **b** : a cleaning scraper that is rotated and propelled through a pipeline by the force of the flowing oil **c** : ALLIGATOR 6b **d** : BUCK RAKE **e** : a cultivator having wooden sled runners equipped on each side with curved knives or discs that is designed to follow listed furrows and is used esp. for the first two cultivations of corn — called also *sled cultivator* **f** : a handcar or small gasoline-powered car used by railroad section gangs for transporting laborers and supplies

¹**godfather** \'=,==\ *n* [ME *godfader,* fr. OE *godfæder,* fr. *god* + *fæder* father — more at FATHER] **1** : a man who sponsors a person at baptism ⟨there shall be for every male child to be baptized . . . two ~s and one godmother —*Bk. of Com. Prayer*⟩ **2** : a man who assists in the Jewish rite of circumcision by holding the child upon his knees and may thereafter take an interest in the child's upbringing and welfare **3** : one having a relation to someone or something analogous to that of a male sponsor to his godchild: **a** *archaic* : a person who gives a name to someone or something ⟨these earthly ~s of heaven's lights that give a name to every fixed star —Shak.⟩ **b** : one primarily responsible for the care and development of someone or something ⟨the editor had been ~ to many an unknown young writer⟩ ⟨these two museums have long been benevolent ~s to contemporary painting⟩ **c** : one held to be the principal creator or original exponent of a school of thought or mode of behavior ⟨the spiritual ~ of the . . . demagogue in his addiction to reckless attacks for political purposes —*New Republic*⟩

²**godfather** \"\ *vt* : to act as godfather to; *esp* : to assume responsibility for the care or development of ⟨a novice writer is sometimes ~*ed* by a prominent editor⟩ ⟨proud that their company helped ~ this new industry —*Service*⟩

god-fear·er \'=,firə(r)\ *n, cap G* : a devoutly religious person

god-fearing \'=,==\ *adj, usu cap G* : having a reverential and loving feeling toward God : devoutly religious : PIOUS ⟨a *God-fearing* and law-abiding people —H.L.Mencken⟩

god·for·sak·en \¦gädfə(r)¦sākən\ *adj, sometimes cap* **1** : situated in a remote or desolate place ⟨another winter . . . in that ~ wilderness crossroads —H.L.Davis⟩ **2** : neglected in appearance : WRETCHED, DISMAL — used chiefly of places or objects ⟨the toughest, dreariest, most ~ looking country —Richard Bissell⟩ **3** : pitiable in circumstances : MISERABLE, UNFORTUNATE — used chiefly of persons ⟨for teaching poor ~ school children to write before they can read —H.L.Mencken⟩

god·ful \-fəl\ *adj, usu cap* : DIVINE, AWE-INSPIRING ⟨endless inspiring *Godful* beauty —John Muir †1914⟩

god-given \'=,==\ *adj, usu cap 1st G* **1** : given directly by God ⟨a *God-given* victory⟩ **2** : ordained by God in the nature of something : NATURAL ⟨we are so accustomed to our own slowly altering division of powers between the nation and the states that it seems to us . . . *God-given* —*Yale Rev.*⟩

god·head \-,hed\ *n* [ME *godhed,* fr. *god* + *-hed, -hede* -hood (akin to ME *-hod, -had* -hood)] **1** : the quality or state of being divine : DEITY 1a, DIVINITY ⟨a denial of our Lord's equality with the Father in ~ —B.J.Kidd⟩ ⟨life has not measured the success of its attempts at ~ by the beauty . . . of the result —G.B.Shaw⟩ **2** *cap* **a** : ²GOD, DEITY 1b — usu. used with *the* ⟨the devil and anathema of our forefathers hides the *Godhead* which we seek —D.H.Lawrence⟩ ⟨the Hindu, with Rama as the *Godhead,* accepts a pantheon of divinities —Andrew Mellor⟩ **b** : the nature of God esp. when regarded as triune : TRINITY ⟨the eternal relations within the *Godhead* itself —O.C.Quick⟩ ⟨the beginning and the end is the hidden darkness of the eternal *Godhead* —Frank Thilly⟩ **3** *sometimes cap* : ¹GOD 1 ⟨he was deliberately deified; . . . made the ~ of a creed —Frank Gorrell⟩ ⟨the nymphs and native ~s yet unknown —John Dryden⟩

god·hood \-,hu̇d\ *n* -s *sometimes cap* [ME *godhod,* fr. *god* + *-hod* -hood] **1** : GODHEAD 1 ⟨millions venerate the cow as a symbol of life and ~ —*N.Y. Times*⟩ **2** : the state or position of being God or a god ⟨bred to believe that ~ comes . . . to those killed in battle —*Time*⟩ ⟨implies for God that absolute ~ which makes worship imperative —O.J.Baab⟩

god·kin \-dkən\ *n* [*god* + *-kin*] : GODLING

god-king \'=¦=\ *n* : a human ruler believed to be a god or to possess godlike powers or qualities ⟨the absolutist *god-kings* of Asia Minor and Egypt —Weston La Barre⟩

god·less \-ləs\ *adj* **1** : refusing to acknowledge God : lacking reverence for God ⟨the center of ~ world communism —*Newsweek*⟩ **2** : refusing to obey God's laws : UNGODLY, IMPIOUS, WICKED ⟨the Romans were ~, full of the grossest thoughts, and void of natural affection —Leslie Stephen⟩ ⟨she is a ~ woman of the world —W.M.Thackeray⟩ — **god·less·ness** *n* -ES

god·let \-lət\ *n* -s : GODLING ⟨scores of lesser ~s who haunt the streams and forests —Kenneth Roberts⟩

godlike \'=,=\ *adj, sometimes cap* **1** : resembling or having the qualities of God or a god : DIVINE ⟨venerated by them as a ~ man —*Times Lit. Supp.*⟩ **2** : appropriate to or befitting God or a god ⟨man must play God, for he has acquired certain ~ powers —R.H.Rovere⟩ ⟨a man of ~ sagacity —V.L.Parrington⟩ — **god·like·ness** *n* -ES

god·li·ly \-dlə¦lē, ¦li\ *adv, sometimes cap, archaic* : in a godly fashion ⟨we should live soberly, righteously and ~ —John Norris †1711⟩

god·li·ness \-dlēnəs, -lin-\ *n* -ES : the conforming of one's life to the revealed character and purpose of God : RIGHTEOUSNESS

god·ling \-liŋ,-lēŋ\ *n* -s [ME, fr. *god* + *-ling*] **1** : an inferior or purely local deity : a supernatural being midway between a god and a fetish ⟨the friendly little ~s who presided over the routine of daily life —John Buchan⟩ ⟨as futile as the petty ~s . . . which they worship —James Muilenburg⟩ **2** : the image of a godling ⟨the magic that he carries in his calabash is a ~ —Padraic Colum⟩

¹**god·ly** \-lē,-li\ *adj* -ER/-EST [ME, fr. *god* + *-ly*] **1** : of, relating to, or emanating from God : DIVINE ⟨everything is black or white, evil or good, satanic or ~ —*Saturday Rev.*⟩ **2** : reverencing God : obedient to the will of God from love and reverence for his character : PIOUS, RIGHTEOUS, DEVOUT ⟨that we may hereafter lead a ~, righteous, and sober life —*Bk. of Com. Prayer*⟩ ⟨gifted and ~ men —F.S.Mead⟩

²**godly** *adv, archaic* : in a godly fashion : PIOUSLY, DEVOUTLY, RIGHTEOUSLY ⟨all that will live ~ in Christ Jesus shall suffer persecution —2 Tim 3:12 (AV)⟩

godmamma *pronunc at* GOD + *pronunc at* MAMMA\ *n* : GODMOTHER

god-man \'=¦man\ *n* **1** *usu cap* : one who is both God and man : CHRIST 1 ⟨when man prays, the sacred image of the *God-man* is with him —H.O.Taylor⟩ **2** *pl* **god-men** : one who is both a god and a man or who has the qualities of both : DEMIGOD, SUPERMAN ⟨their safety . . . is bound up with the life of one of these *god-men* —J.G.Frazer⟩

god-manhood \(')=¦=,hu̇d\ *n, usu cap* [*god-man* + *-hood*] : the quality or state of being both God and man ⟨through men the whole of the material universe is elevated to a certain participation in *God-manhood* —G.A.Ellard⟩

godmother \'=,==\ *n* [ME *godmoder,* fr. OE *godmōdor,* fr. *god* + *mōdor* mother — more at MOTHER] : a woman who sponsors a person at baptism ⟨for each male child to be baptized the rubric . . . requires two godfathers and one ~ —R.P.Crum⟩

go down *vi* **1 a** : to proceed or move to or as if to a lower place ⟨some *went down* to the sea in ships —Ps 107:23 (RSV)⟩ ⟨*went down* to the cellar to check the furnace⟩ **b** : to lead to or as if to a lower place ⟨a path *goes down* to the village⟩ **c** : to fall to or as if to the ground ⟨the plane *went down* in flames⟩ ⟨the boxer *went down* for a count of eight⟩ **d** *of a heavenly body* : to go below the horizon : SET **e** : to become submerged : SINK ⟨the ship *went down* with all hands aboard⟩ ⟨saved as he *went down* for the third time⟩ **f** *of mumps* : to descend into the testes **2** : to admit of being swallowed ⟨the medicine *went down* smoothly enough⟩ **3** : to undergo defeat or overthrow ⟨if America *goes down* we take the entire free world down with us —Sidney Hyman⟩ **4 a** : to find acceptance ⟨had an instinct . . . of knowing what answers *went down* well —Elizabeth Taylor⟩ **b** : to come to be considered or remembered esp. in posterity ⟨that story will *go down* as the best fairy tale I ever wrote —T.E.N.Driberg⟩ ⟨would *go down* in history as a nice try —R.M.Yoder⟩ **5 a** : to undergo a decline or decrease ⟨his temperature *went down* this morning⟩ ⟨the stock market is *going down*⟩ ⟨the number of members has *gone down*⟩ **b** : to become less violent : SUBSIDE ⟨the wind *went down* during the night⟩ **6** *Brit* **a** : to leave a college or university **b** : to graduate from a college or university **7** : to extend in time ⟨the first volume *goes down* to the end of the war⟩ **8** : to become sick ⟨are always *going down* . . . with that malaria —Eve Langley⟩ **9 a** : to fail to make one's contract in a card game **b** : to lie legally exposed on the table — used of the dummy hand in contract bridge **c** : to meld some or all of one's cards in rummy

go-down \'gō,daun\ *n* -s [*go down*] *archaic* : a swallow or draft esp. of water or liquor ⟨a bottle of wine apiece, kept down by large *go-downs* of brandy —*Sporting Mag.*⟩

go·down \"\ *n* -s [Malay *gudang*] : a warehouse or storeroom in an oriental country ⟨traders whose ~s were crammed with U.S. goods . . . have no way of replenishing their stocks —*Time*⟩ ⟨the ~s in which were stored the families' food supplies —Christine Weston⟩

godpapa *pronunc at* GOD + *pronunc at* PAPA\ *n* : GODFATHER

godparent \'=,==\ *n* : GODFATHER, GODMOTHER, SPONSOR ⟨in case the parents die, the ~s will see to the welfare of the child —R.P.Crum⟩

god·par·ent·hood \'=,==,hu̇d\ *n* -s [*godparent* + *-hood*] : the state or condition of being a godparent ⟨~ inaugurates a set of enduring mutual obligations —Sol Tax⟩

gods *pl of* GOD, *pres 3d sing of* GOD

god's acre *n, cap G* [trans. of G *gottesacker*] : CHURCHYARD, BURYING GROUND, CEMETERY ⟨*God's acre* let out to the dead for so much per square foot —Sean O'Casey⟩

god's country *n, usu cap G* : a place conceived of as esp.

favored by God: as **a :** an area of civilization (as a city) away from the frontier ⟨music heard long before . . . in *God's country* in the East —*Springfield* (*Mass.*) *Republican*⟩ **b :** a place away from a city; *esp* **:** the open country ⟨out of the slums into *God's country*⟩ **c :** one's native or home state or region ⟨boosters go so much to the other extreme, talking about *God's country* —Sinclair Lewis⟩

god·send \'gäd,send\ *n* -s [back-formation fr. *god-sent*] **1 :** some desirable or needed thing that comes unexpectedly as if sent by God ⟨what a ~ your inexpensive books have been —R.J.Crohn⟩ ⟨the rain after the long drought was a ~⟩ **2 :** a happy or welcome event ⟨the experience was a ~ to a mind that was growing torpid —V.L.Parrington⟩

god·sent \-nt\ *adj* **:** sent by or as if by God

god's-eye \'ˌ=,=\ *n, pl* **god's-eyes** *usu cap G* **:** GERMANDER SPEEDWELL

god·ship \'=,ship\ *n* [*god* + *-ship*] **:** the rank, character, or personality of a god **:** DEITY, DIVINITY ⟨your name and mine were used with less reverence than became our ~s —John Dryden⟩

god-smith \'=,=\ *n, archaic* **:** one that creates gods or idols usu. from metal ⟨gods . . . of every shape and size that *god-smiths* could produce —John Dryden⟩

godson \'=,=\ *n* [ME *godsone*, fr. OE *godsunu*, fr. *god* god + *sunu* son — more at SON] **:** a boy or man whom one has sponsored at baptism

god's peace *n, cap G* **:** PEACE OF GOD

god·speed \'gädz'pēd, -d;sp-\ *n, usu cap* [ME *god speid*, fr. the phrase *God spede* (*the*, etc.) may God prosper (you, etc.)] **1 :** a prosperous journey **:** SUCCESS ⟨wished him *Godspeed* and a safe return —Bruce Marshall⟩ ⟨bid the fliers *Godspeed* —A. R.Griffin⟩ **2** *archaic* **:** the nick of time **:** CONCLUSION — usu. used in the phrase *in the Godspeed* ⟨a devil came in just in the *Godspeed* —Roger L' Estrange⟩ **3 :** a wish for success given at parting ⟨the captain also received a hearty *Godspeed* —Mary S. Watts⟩

god's penny *n, often cap G* [ME *godes peny*] **:** a penny or small sum paid as earnest money esp. on concluding a purchase or hiring a servant ⟨among merchants the *god's penny* binds the contract of sale —Frederick Pollock & F.W.Maitland⟩ — called also *argentum dei, denarius dei, denier à dieu*

god's plenty *n, usu cap G* **1 :** a quantity larger than human need or desire **:** SUPERABUNDANCE ⟨since critics were . . . praising the use of symbols novelists determined to furnish the symbols, and in *God's plenty* —Malcolm Cowley⟩ **2 :** a very large number or amount ⟨the book was issued in *God's plenty* —J.D.Hart⟩

god's truce *n, cap G & usu cap T* **:** TRUCE OF GOD

god's word *n, cap G & usu cap W* **:** BIBLE 1a

god tree *n, usu cap G* **1 :** CEIBA 2a **2 :** DEODAR

[1]**god·ward** \'gädwə(r)d\ *or* **god·wards** \-)dz\ *adv, usu cap* [ME *godward*, fr. *god* + *-ward*] **1 :** with reference to God ⟨you are the most temperate man *Godward* and the most intemperate yourselfward —Jonathan Swift⟩ **2 :** toward God ⟨as if, being in the world, their tendency was *Godward* —Elizabeth B. Browning⟩ ⟨any heart, turned *Godwards*, feels more joy in one short hour of prayer —P.J.Bailey⟩

[2]**godward** \"\ *adj, usu cap* **:** directed or tending toward God ⟨the student of theological questions is actually living either a *Godward* or a godless life —Walter Moberly⟩

god·win·i·an \(')gäd'winēən\ *adj, usu cap* [William *Godwin* †1836 Eng. philosopher + E *-ian*] **:** of, relating to, or having the characteristics of William Godwin or his writings

god·wit \'gäd,wit\ *n* -s [origin unknown] **:** any of several long-billed wading birds that constitute a genus (*Limosa*) of the family Scolopacidae and that are much like the curlews but have the bill slightly curved upward — see BAR-TAILED GODWIT, BLACK-TAILED GODWIT, HUDSONIAN GODWIT, MARBLED GODWIT, PACIFIC GODWIT

goed *dial past of* GO

goeduck *or* **goeyduc** *var of* GEODUCK

go·el \'gō,el, -ˌāl\ *n* -s *often cap* [Heb *gō'ēl*] **:** REDEEMER, RECLAIMANT; *esp* **:** a next of kin upon whom according to ancient Hebrew custom devolved certain family rights and duties including the avenging of a murdered kinsman's blood and the redemption of the person or property of a kinsman in debt or helpless circumstances

go·er \'gō(ə)r, -ōə\ *n* -s [ME, fr. *gon* to go + *-er* — more at GO] **:** one that goes: **a :** something that moves (as a horse or vehicle) considered in reference to its gait or speed ⟨the mare was a pretty good ~ —F.M.Ford⟩ **b :** a departing traveler or guest — used chiefly in the phrase *comers and goers* ⟨all these comers and ~s lodge at the inn⟩ **c :** one that attends regularly or frequents — used chiefly in combination ⟨a strange and rich tonal world . . . alien to contemporary concert*goers* —R.D.Darrell⟩ ⟨less than one fifth of the agricultural population are weekly film*goers* —*Irish Digest*⟩

goes *pres 3d sing of* GO, *pl of* GO

goe·the·an *also* **goe·thi·an** \'gər|d·ēən, 'gə|, |tē- *also* -gā| *sometimes* 'gœ\ *adj, usu cap* [Johann Wolfgang von *Goethe* †1832 Ger. poet + E *-an* or *-ian*] **:** of, relating to, or having the characteristics of Goethe or his works ⟨the *Goethean* insistence on the inseparability of mind and matter —H.W. Pfund⟩

goe·thite *or* **gö·thite** \|d·īt, |,tīt\ *n* -s [G *göthit*, fr. J. W. von *Goethe* + G *-it* -ite] **:** a mineral $HFeO_2$ consisting of an iron hydrogen oxide that occurs massive and in prismatic crystals with a fibrous, reniform, or stalactic structure and that is the commonest constituent of many forms of natural rust or limonite esp. in the gossans of sulfide-bearing ore deposits — compare LEPIDOCROCITE

go·et·ic \(')gō;ed·ik\ *adj* [Gk *goētikos*, fr. *goēt-, goēs* wizard, juggler (fr. *goan* to groan, weep, lament) + *-ikos* -ic — more at KITE] *archaic* **:** of or relating to goety

go·ety \'gōəd·ē\ *n* -ES [Gk *goēteia*, fr. *goēt-, goēs* + *-eia* -y] *archaic* **:** black magic or witchcraft in which the assistance of evil spirits is invoked **:** NECROMANCY

go·fer \'gōfə(r)\ *n* -s [F *gaufre* — more at GOFFER] *dial* **:** WAFFLE

[1]**goff** \'gäf\ *n* -s [MF *goffe* clumsy, awkward] *now dial Eng* **:** a stupid fool **:** DOPE, SIMPLETON

[2]**goff** \"\ *archaic var of* GOLF

[1]**gof·fer** *also* **gauf·fer** \'gäfə(r), 'gōf-, 'gȯf-\ *vt* -ED/-ING/-S [F *gaufrer*, fr. *gaufre* honeycomb, waffle, of Gmc origin; akin to MD *wafel* honeycomb, waffle — more at WAFFLE] **1 :** to crimp, plait, or flute (as linen or lace) esp. by means of a heated iron ⟨took pleasure in perfectly ~*ing* the frill on her father's shirts⟩ **2** *usu gauffer* **:** to indent or emboss (the gilt edges of a book) for decorative effect — compare [3]CHASE 1a

[2]**goffer** *also* **gauffer** \"\ *n* -s **1 :** a tool or device (as a heated iron or a press) used in goffering **2 :** GOFFERER

gof·fered *also* **gauf·fered** *or* **gauf·fred** \-fə(r)d\ *adj* **1 :** dressed or finished with crimps or frills **:** CURLED, CRIMPED ⟨a stiff ~ ruff⟩ **2** *usu gauffered, of a book or its margin* **:** ornamented by gauffering **:** patterned (as by tooling or stenciling) over gilt

gof·fer·er *also* **gauf·fer·er** \-fərə(r)\ *n* -s **:** one that goffers (as linens or books) — usu. *gaufferer* in book-trade use

gof·fer·ing *also* **gauf·fer·ing** \-f(ə)riŋ\ *n* -s **1 :** the practice of one that goffers **2 :** a product of goffering **:** an embossed design CRIMP, FRILL; *broadly* **:** something ornamented or finished with goffering

gof·fle \'gäfəl\ *vt* -ED/-ING/-S [by alter.] *dial Eng* **:** [1]GOBBLE 1 ⟨as long as the fish ~s the bait —H.G.Tapply⟩

[1]**gog** *n* -s [back-formation fr. *agog*] *obs* **:** STIR, EXCITEMENT, EAGERNESS

[2]**gog** \'gäg\ *n* -s [origin unknown] *now dial Eng* **:** BOG, QUAGMIRE

go gage *n* **:** a limit gage that will just go in or on the part being tested — compare NO-GO GAGE

go-getter \'=;==\ *n, often attrib* **:** an enterprising pushing often aggressive person who goes after and gets what he wants **:** HUSTLER ⟨a nation of doers and *go-getters* —Telford Taylor⟩ ⟨live wires and *go-getters* are . . . heroes to the bulk of the people —*School & Society*⟩

[1]**go-getting** \'=;==\ *adj* **:** ENTERPRISING, AGGRESSIVE ⟨the *go-getting* materialism of the American environment —M.J. Adler⟩ ⟨a red-blooded, *go-getting*, two-fisted American he-man —Weston La Barre⟩

[2]**go-getting** \"\ *n* -s **:** AGGRESSIVENESS, ENTERPRISE ⟨admired as an example of successful *go-getting* —*Harper's*⟩ ⟨the current American psychology emphasizes *go-getting* —*Amer. Rev. of Reviews*⟩

[1]**gog·gle** \'gägəl\ *vb* **goggled; goggled; goggling** \-g(ə)liŋ\ **goggles** [ME *gogelen*] *vi* **1 a** *archaic* **:** to turn the eyes to one side or the other **:** look obliquely **:** SQUINT ⟨wink and ~ like an owl —Samuel Butler †1680⟩ **b :** to stare with wide or protuberant eyes usu. as a result of amazement, fright, or surprise ⟨the lieutenant *goggled* . . . like a fish in a glass jar —Kenneth Roberts⟩ ⟨sold . . . for sums that make one ~ in retrospect —J.T.Soby⟩ **2** *of the eyes* **a** *archaic* **:** to turn to one side or the other **:** take an oblique position ⟨mark on which side . . . the eyes do ~ —Thomas Raynalde⟩ **b :** to become wide or protuberant usu. as a result of amazement, fright, or surprise ⟨the frog's hideous large eyes were *goggling* out of his head —W.M.Thackeray⟩ **3 :** to fish underwater with a spear **:** SPEARFISH **~** *vt* **:** to turn (the eyes) to one side or from side to side **:** ROLL ⟨the stranger *goggled* about his eyes in an attempt to fix them steadily —T.L.Peacock⟩

[2]**goggle** \"\ *adj, of the eyes* **:** full and rolling **:** PROTUBERANT, STARING ⟨a rather moony, fair brat . . . with those ~ eyes gazing bluely at you —F.M.Ford⟩

[3]**goggle** \"\ *n* -s **1 :** a rolling or protuberance of the eyes **:** a wide-eyed stare ⟨the child's ~ at the room full of toys⟩ **2 goggles** *pl* **a :** eye coverings resembling spectacles but with shields at the sides and short projecting eye tubes with the glass fixed in the front end used to protect the eyes (as from water, light, dust, or cold) — often used with *pair* ⟨a pair of ~s⟩; see EYECUP 1b **b :** colored spectacles for relief from intense light ⟨got their sun ~s from the rucksacks —J.R.Ullman⟩ **3 :** a single framed protective device usu. of glass or plastic that is worn in front of the eyes and held in place by a headband

goggles 2a

goggled *adj* **1** *archaic* **:** GOGGLE ⟨one eye . . . was bigger and more ~ than the other —G.W.Dasent⟩ **2 :** wearing goggles ⟨the ~ men . . . turning iron rivets into so many showers of sparks —J.B.Priestley⟩

goggle-eye \'==,=\ *n* [ME *gogeleye*, fr *gogelen* + *eye*] **:** a fish having relatively large and prominent eyes: as **a :** WHITE CRAPPIE **b :** ROCK BASS 1 **c** *or* **goggle-eye jack :** BIG-EYED SCAD **d :** BLACK CRAPPIE **e :** WARMOUTH

goggle-eyed \'==;=\ *adj* [ME *gogeleyed*, fr. *gogelen* + *eyed*] **:** having or marked by bulging or rolling eyes often as a result of amazement or wonder ⟨the visitors seem to loiter with particularly *goggle-eyed* wonder in front of . . . the fabulous objects of lapis and rock crystal —Mollie Panter-Downes⟩

goggle-eyed perch *n* **:** CRAPPIE

goggle fish *vi* **:** GOGGLE 3, SPEARFISH

goggle-nose \'==,=\ *n* [so called fr. the dark spots on its bill] **:** SURF SCOTER

gog·gler \'gäg(ə)lə(r)\ *n* -s **1 :** one that goggles; *esp* **:** one that spearfishes ⟨most experienced ~s have their own favorite fishing holes —*Nat'l Geographic*⟩ **2 :** BIG-EYED SCAD

gog·gly \-lē\ *adj* -ER/-EST **:** GOGGLING ⟨she seemed in . . . the same excited ~ state —J.B.Priestley⟩ ⟨sorrows with ~ eyes —*Dial*⟩

gog·let \'gäglət\ *also* **gug·let** \'gəg-\ *n* -s [Pg *gorgoleta*, dim. of *gorja* throat, fr. LL *gurga* — more at GORGE] **:** a long-necked water vessel usu. of porous earthenware that is used esp. in India for cooling water by evaporation ⟨~s cooling among walls —James Merrill⟩

[1]**go-go** \gō'gō\ *n* -s [Tag *gugò*] **:** a vine (*Entada scandens*) found in the Philippines the bark of which is macerated to produce a substitute for soap

[2]**go-go** \'gō(,)gō\ *n, pl* **gogo** *or* **gogos** *usu cap* **1 :** a Bantu people of the Unyamwezi highlands in Tanganyika who are similar to the Masai in manners and customs **2 :** a member of the Gogo people

gogs *pl of* GOG

go·han·na \gō'hanə\ *var of* GOANNA

goi *var of* GOY

goi·del \'gȯid·ᵊl\ *n* -s *cap* [MIr *Gōidel*] **1 :** a member of the Gaelic branch of Celts **:** GAEL **2 :** a speaker of one of the Goidelic languages — compare BRYTHON

[1]**goi·del·ic** \(')gȯi¦delik\ *adj, usu cap* [*Goidel* + *-ic*] **1 :** of, relating to, or characteristic of the Goidels **2 :** of, relating to, or characteristic of the division of the Celtic languages that includes Irish, Gaelic, and Manx — compare BRYTHONIC

[2]**goidelic** \"\ *n* -s *cap* **:** the Goidelic branch of the Celtic languages — see INDO-EUROPEAN LANGUAGES table

go in *vi* **1 a :** to make or effect an entrance **:** ENTER ⟨asked him to *go in* and wait⟩ **b :** to move forward **:** ADVANCE ⟨the officer was not long in *going in* on the whale —H.A. Chippendale⟩ **2 a :** to take part in a game or contest **b :** to go to bat in cricket **c :** to call the opening bet in poker **:** STAY **3** *of a heavenly body* **:** to become obscured by a cloud **4 :** to form a union or alliance **:** JOIN — often used with *with* ⟨they outlined the plan and asked the rest of us to *go in* with them⟩ — **go in for 1 :** to give support to or express approval of **:** ADVOCATE ⟨an overwhelming majority of the . . . candidates have *gone in for* disestablishment —*Manchester Examiner*⟩ **2 a :** to make one's particular interest or specialty ⟨so you think you'd like to *go in for* farming —Adrian Bell⟩ ⟨these big uniform people . . . *go in for* policemen's and firemen's uniforms and regalia for lodges —*Amer. Fabrics*⟩ **b :** to have or show an interest in or liking for ⟨lives more in the present than in the past and *goes in for* sports in a big way —Richard Joseph⟩ **3 :** to seek to acquire ⟨ought to *go in for* a better place to live in —Rex Ingamells⟩ ⟨she *goes in for* freedom and they both end in difficulties —John Erskine †1951⟩ **4 :** to engage or participate in **:** take part in ⟨it is pleasant to toy with the idea of New York's *going in for* similar salutes to its heritage —Cornelia O. Skinner⟩ **5 :** to have as a striking characteristic **:** FEATURE ⟨the . . . four-door sedan *goes in for* the longer, lower appearance —*Car Life*⟩ — **go in to** *or* **go in unto :** to have sexual intercourse with ⟨*go in to* your father's concubines whom he has left to keep the house —2 Sam 16:21 (RSV)⟩

[1]**going** *n* -s [ME, fr. gerund of *gon, goon* to go — more at GO] **1 a :** the act or action of going ⟨had to restrict myself to a careful routine of one hour's ~ and ten minutes' halt —D.L.Bush⟩ — often used in combination ⟨play*going*⟩ ⟨sea*going*⟩ **b :** DEPARTURE ⟨stand not upon the order of your ~, but go at once —Shak.⟩ **c :** the manner or style of going ⟨erect his port and firm his ~ —William Wordsworth⟩ **2 a :** a way (as a path or road) that leads from one place to another ⟨the . . . rail, which keeps horses from the inner ~, altered the layout of the course —*Sydney* (*Austral.*) *Sun and Guardian*⟩ **b :** a run of stairs **3 goings** *pl* **:** course of life **:** BEHAVIOR **:** ACTIONS ⟨for his eyes are upon the ways of man, and he seeth all his ~s —Job 34:21 (AV)⟩ **4 :** the condition of the ground (as for walking or racing) ⟨the surface of the cotton patch was baked hard, and climbing the fence we found the ~ better —Joseph Nelson⟩ **5 :** advance toward or as if toward an objective **:** PROGRESS ⟨wanted to build up enough capital to start farming . . . but the ~ was slow —John Bird⟩ ⟨in the new world he found it rough ~ —W.L.Gresham⟩

[2]**going** *adj* [ME, fr. pres. part. of *gon, goon*] **1 a :** that goes — often used in combination ⟨easy*going*⟩ ⟨out*going*⟩ **b :** MOVING, OPERATING, WORKING ⟨the interior of the shop was in ~ order —Arnold Bennett⟩ **2 a :** EXISTING, LIVING ⟨the finest crime novelist ~ —Anthony Boucher⟩ **b :** available for use or enjoyment ⟨watched his movements with the eyes of a hungry dog who believes that there is provender ~ —John Buchan⟩ **3 :** commonly or widely current or accepted **:** PREVAILING ⟨when you marketed your crops abroad, you sold in free markets for the ~ price —A.E.Stevenson b. 1900⟩ ⟨his fee was about five times larger than the ~ rate of our native talent —E.A. Weeks⟩ **4 :** conducting business, operations, or activities with the likelihood of indefinite continuance **:** actively carried on ⟨were not going to throw away their interest in a ~ concern for a hazardous new venture —Elmer Davis⟩ — **going and coming :** lacking a way out **:** having no escape ⟨they've got you now *going and coming* —Meridel Le Sueur⟩ — **going on :** drawing near to **:** APPROACHING ⟨it's *going on* eight —J.B.Clayton⟩ ⟨my son is six *going on* seven⟩

going-away \'===;=\ *adj* [fr. pres. part. of *go away*] **:** designed for wear when leaving on a honeymoon ⟨had just decided how to have my *going-away* dress made —*Lippincott's Mag.*⟩

going barrel *n* **:** a mainspring barrel in a watch or clock that has teeth on its periphery for driving the train and that is mounted on an arbor which is stationary except during winding

going-concern value *n* **:** the value of the assets of an enterprise considered as an operating business and therefore based on its earning power and prospects rather than on the value of the same assets in the event of liquidation

going forth *n* [fr. the phrase *go forth*] **1** *archaic* **:** a way or place of exit ⟨mark well the entering in of the house, with every *going forth* of the sanctuary —Ezek 44:5 (AV)⟩ **2** *archaic* **:** BOUNDARY ⟨and the *going forth* thereof shall be from the south to Kadesh-barnea —Num 34:4 (AV)⟩

going light *n* [fr. the phrase *go light*] **:** any of various diseases of poultry marked by loss of weight; *specif* **:** AVIAN TUBERCULOSIS

going-over \'==;==\ *n, pl* **goings-over** [fr. the phrase *go over*] **1 :** a careful or thorough inspection, examination, or investigation ⟨price control has weathered six thorough congressional *goings-over* —Bruce Bliven b. 1889⟩ **2 a :** a severe scolding **:** DRESSING DOWN ⟨got a good *going-over* in the morning . . . on account of my clothes —Mark Twain⟩ **b :** BEATING ⟨someone sure gave her a mean *going-over* —A.C.Tudor⟩

goings-on \'==;=\ *n pl* [fr. pres. part. of *go on*] **:** ACTIONS, EVENTS, HAPPENINGS ⟨there's some of the awfullest *goings-on* at her house —Sinclair Lewis⟩ ⟨gives her main attention to studying the *goings-on* in the . . . world around her —Jean C. Jones⟩ ⟨the present cry for change is a revulsion from the *goings-on* between wars —C.H.Grattan⟩

going to Jerusalem *usu cap J* **:** MUSICAL CHAIRS

going train *n* **:** the gearing in a striking or chiming timepiece that drives the hands

goit \'gȯit\ *var of* GOTE

goi·tcho \'gȯi(,)chō\ *n* -s [native name in northern Queensland, Australia] **:** a low weedy tropical herb (*Boerhavia diffusa*) used in Australia as forage

goi·ter *also* **goi·tre** \'gȯid·ə(r), -ȯitə-\ *n* -s [F *goitre*, fr. MF, back-formation fr. *goitron* throat, fr. (assumed) VL *guttrion-, guttrio*, fr. L *guttur* throat, crop of a bird + *-ion*, *-io* -ion — more at COT] **:** an enlargement of the thyroid gland that is commonly visible as a swelling of the anterior part of the neck, that often results from insufficient intake of iodine and then is usu. accompanied by hypothyroidism, and that in other cases is associated with hyperthyroidism usu. together with toxic symptoms and exophthalmos — called also *struma*

goi·tered *also* **goi·tred** \-ə(r)d\ *adj* **:** affected with goiter

goiter stick *n* **:** the stalk of any of several brown algae (as of the genera *Sargassum* and *Laminaria*) used in So. America as a remedy for goiter

goi·tro·gen \'gȯi·trəjən, -,jen\ *n* -s [*goitro-* (fr. *goiter*) + *-gen*] **:** a substance (as thiourea or thiouracil) that induces goiter formation

goi·tro·genesis \¦gȯi·trə+\ *n* [NL, fr. *goitro-* + *genesis*] **:** the action or process of inducing goiter formation

goi·tro·gen·ic \¦gȯi·trə¦jenik\ *also* **goi·ter·o·gen·ic** \", ¦gȯid·ərō¦-\ *adj* [*goitre* or *goiter* + *-o-* + *-genic*] **:** producing or tending to produce goiter

goi·tro·ge·nic·i·ty \,gȯi·trəjə'nisəd·ē\ *n* -ES **:** the property of inducing goiter formation **:** the state of being a goitrogen

goi·trous *also* **goi·ter·ous** \'gȯi·trəs; -ȯid·ər,--ȯitər-\ *adj* [F *goitreux*, fr. MF *goitre* + *-eux* -ous] **:** relating to, affected with, or resembling goiter

gol \'gäl\ *interj* [euphemism for *God*] — a mild oath ⟨"~," said the peddler, "I believe it" —*Atlantic*⟩

[1]**go·la** \'gōlə\ *n* -s [It, lit., throat, fr. L *gula* — more at GLUTTON] **:** CYMA

[2]**go·la** *or* **go·lah** \'gōlə, -(,)lä\ *n* -s [Hindi *golā*] **:** a warehouse for grain in India **:** STOREROOM, GRANARY

[3]**go·la** \'gōlə\ *n, pl* **gola** *or* **golas** *usu cap* **1 a :** an African people of Liberia and Sierra Leone **b :** a member of such people **2 :** the West-Atlantic language of the Gola people

gol·ach \'gäläk, -ək\ *n* -s [ScGael *gaillseach*] *Scot* **:** any of various small arthropods (as a beetle or centipede)

go·lah \gō'lä, 'gōlə\ *n* -s *sometimes cap* [Heb *gōlāh* exile] **:** DIASPORA, GALUTH

gol·con·da \gäl'kändə\ *n* -s *usu cap* [fr. *Golconda*, city in Hyderabad, India, formerly the center of the diamond trade] **:** a source of great wealth ⟨this means a *Golconda* for makers and sellers of accessories —*Newsweek*⟩; *esp* **:** a rich mine

[1]**gold** \'gōld\ *n* -s [ME, fr. OE; akin to OFris, OS, & OHG *gold*, ON *gull*, Goth *gulth* gold, OE *geolu* yellow — more at YELLOW] **1 a :** a very malleable, ductile, yellow trivalent and univalent metallic element that occurs chiefly in the free state but also in a few minerals as sylvanite or nagyagite, is indifferent to most chemicals but attacked by chlorine and aqua regia, and is hardened or changed in color for commercial use (as in coins, jewelry, dentures) by alloying with copper, silver, zinc, cadmium, and other metals — symbol *Au*; see ELEMENT table **b :** the heraldic metal or **2 a** (1) **:** gold coins (2) **:** a gold piece **b :** MONEY, RICHES **c :** a monetary standard linked directly to the value of the metal gold ⟨England went off ~ —A.M.Young⟩ **3 a :** thread or fabric made wholly or partly of gold **b :** decoration in gold leaf or gold color **:** GILDING **4 a :** a variable color averaging deep yellow **b :** a light olive brown **5 :** something resembling gold; *esp* **:** something treasured as the essence or finest exemplification of its kind ⟨taking bits of this and that and transmuting them into culinary ~ —Harold Sinclair⟩ ⟨a heart of ~⟩ **6 a :** the gilded or golden bull's-eye of an archery target **b :** a hit on such a bull's-eye ⟨you've made a ~⟩

[2]**gold** \"\ *adj* -ER/-EST [ME, fr. *gold*, n.] **1 a :** made or consisting of gold ⟨the gleaming ~ band ring —Carson McCullers⟩ **b :** of the heraldic metal or **2 :** having the color of gold **:** GOLDEN ⟨russet and ~ chrysanthemums —Louis Bromfield⟩ **3 a :** of, relating to, or payable in gold coin — see GOLD BOND **b :** of or relating to a monetary gold standard **4 :** of outstanding value, quality, or excellence ⟨the ~ tones of an alpine horn —Willa Cather⟩ **5** [so called fr. the practice during the construction of the Panama canal of paying skilled white labor in gold and unskilled colored labor in silver] **:** of or for the white population in the Panama Canal Zone

[3]**gold** \"\ *n* -s [ME *golde*, fr. OE, fr. [1]*gold*] **1** *dial Brit* **:** POT MARIGOLD **2 :** CORN MARIGOLD

[4]**gold** *usu cap, var of* GOLDI

gold-and-silver flower \,==;==-\ *n* **:** the flower of the European honeysuckle

gold-and-silver plant *n* **:** HONESTY

gold apple *n* **:** TOMATO

[1]**gol·darn** \(')gäl¦därn, -dän, *or* **gol·durn** \-dərn, -dən, -dəin\ *vb* [euphemism for *goddamn*] *vt* **:** DAMN *vt* 5 **~** *vi* **:** DAMN *vi*

[2]**goldarn** \'=;=\ *or* **goldurn** \"\ *adj* [euphemism for *goddamned*] **:** [1]DAMNED 2a, 2b

[3]**goldarn** \"\ *or* **goldurn** \"\ *adv* [euphemism for *goddamned*] **:** [2]DAMNED

[4]**goldarn** \'=;=\ *or* **goldurn** \"\ *n* [euphemism for *goddamn*] **:** [2]DAMN ⟨I don't give a ~ what your terms are —Erskine Caldwell⟩

goldarned *or* **goldurned** \'=;=, *before* "-est" (')=;=\ *adj* **:** [1]DAMNED 2a, 2b

[2]**goldarned** *or* **goldurned** \"\ *adv* **:** [2]DAMNED

goldback *var of* GOLDENBACK

gold-ball \'=,=\ *n* **:** GOLDCUP

goldband lily \'=,=-\ *n* **:** a highly scented lily (*Lilium auratum*) having wide trumpet-shaped white flowers with strongly recurved segments each of which has a median yellow band — called also *golden-banded lily*

gold bar *n* **:** a bar of gold; *specif* **:** ASSAY BAR

gold basis *n* **:** a financial basis with prices adjusted to the gold standard

gold bass *n* **1 :** SMALLMOUTH BLACK BASS **2 :** YELLOW BASS

goldbeater \'=,==\ *n* [ME *goldbeter*, fr. *gold* + *beter* beater] **:** one that beats gold into gold leaf

goldbeater's skin *n* **:** the prepared outside membrane of the large intestine of cattle used for separating the leaves of metal in goldbeating and sometimes as the moisture-sensitive element in hygrometers

goldbeating \'=,==\ *n* **:** an act, art, or process of hammering gold into thin leaves

gold·berg·ian \(ˈ)gōl(d)¦bərgēən\ *adj, usu cap* [Rube *Goldberg* †1970 Am. cartoonist + E *-ian*] **:** grotesquely complex **:** contrived with inept and excessive intricacy ⟨a strange *Goldbergian* contraption resembling a birdcage —*Newsweek*⟩
gold beryl *n* **:** CHRYSOBERYL
gold bloc *n* **:** a group of countries basing their currencies on a gold standard
gold blocking *n* **:** gold stamping (as of book covers) with an engraved block
gold–bloom \ˈ=,=\ *n, dial Eng* **:** a marsh marigold (*Caltha palustris*)
gold bond *n* **:** a bond payable in gold coin of a specified weight and fineness — compare CURRENCY BOND
gold book *n* **:** a paper book usu. 3¾ inches by 3½ inches containing 25 sheets of gold leaf between the chalked leaves
gold braid *n* **1 :** any of various gold-colored braids used esp. on uniforms **2 :** ²BRAID 3
¹gold·brick \ˈgōl(d),brik\ *n* **1 a :** a worthless brick that appears to be made of gold **b :** something that appears to be valuable but is actually worthless **2** *also* **gold·brick·er** \-kə(r)\ -s [*goldbrick* fr. ²*goldbrick; goldbricker* fr. ²*goldbrick* + *-er*] **a :** a soldier free from regular military routine because of assignment to special duty **b :** a soldier who evades or halfheartedly performs assigned work ⟨would have a ~ court-martialed —R.O.Bowen⟩ **3** *also* **goldbricker** -s [*goldbrick* fr. ²*goldbrick; goldbricker* fr. ²*goldbrick* + *-er*] **:** one who evades work for which he is responsible **:** LOAFER, SHIRKER ⟨~*s* are turning up in offices and factories —*Tomorrow*⟩
²goldbrick \"\ *vb* [¹*goldbrick;* fr. a form of swindle in which worthless goldbricks are passed off as being actually made of gold] *vt* **:** SWINDLE ~ *vi* **:** to evade or halfheartedly perform assigned work **:** shirk duty or responsibility **:** goof off ⟨a man who ~*s* on work details and lets the others carry the load —Gregor Felsen⟩
gold bronze *n* **1 :** a powdered copper alloy used in printing to simulate gold and in the manufacture of gold paint **2 :** a grayish brown to yellowish brown that is very slightly deeper than soot brown and stronger and slightly darker than mummy brown (sense 2b) — called also *Vienna brown*
gold brown *n* **:** a strong brown that is yellower and paler than rust or average russet and yellower and paler than average copper brown — compare GOLDEN BROWN
goldbug \ˈ=,=\ *n* **:** an advocate or supporter of the gold standard
gold bullion standard *n* **:** a gold standard under which the coinage and circulation of gold is usu. prohibited but the shipment of gold in international transactions is permitted and a gold bullion reserve is maintained as a support for the currency
gold cake *n* **:** a butter cake in which the yolks but not the whites of eggs are used
gold carp *n* **:** GOLDFISH
gold certificate *n* **:** a paper certificate issued by a public treasury against deposited gold; *specif* **:** a certificate first issued in 1934 by the U.S. Treasury to be held only by Federal Reserve banks and exchanged under treasury license for gold at the rate prevailing at the time of exchange — compare GOLD BULLION STANDARD, GOLD STANDARD, MANAGED CURRENCY; SILVER CERTIFICATE
gold–chain \ˈ=,=\ *n* **1 :** a stonecrop (*Sedum acre*) **2 :** LABURNUM 2
gold chloride *n* **1 :** a chloride of gold; *esp* **:** the trichloride $AuCl_3$ or Au_2Cl_6 obtained as a dark red crystalline mass by the action of chlorine on heated gold and used chiefly in photography and in gilding and coloring ceramic ware and glass **2 :** CHLOROAURIC ACID — used chiefly commercially
gold clause *n* **:** a provision in a contract requiring payment to be made in gold coin or its equivalent
gold cloth *n* **1 :** CLOTH OF GOLD **2 :** LAMÉ
¹gold coast *adj, usu cap G&C* [fr. the *Gold Coast* (now *Ghana*), region in western Africa] **1 :** of, relating to, or characteristic of the Gold Coast, now Ghana, western Africa **2 :** of, relating to, or characteristic of the people of the Gold Coast
²gold coast *n, often cap G&C* [fr. *Gold Coast,* nickname for an exclusive residential section in Chicago] **:** an exclusive residential district
goldcrest \ˈ=,=\ *n* **:** GOLDEN-CRESTED KINGLET; *specif* **:** a tiny European kinglet (*Regulus regulus*) having a bright yellow crown patch bordered with black
goldcup \ˈ=,=\ *n* **1 :** BUTTERCUP 1 **2 :** a marsh marigold (*Caltha palustris*)
gold cure *n* **:** CHRYSOTHERAPY
gold cushion *n* **:** a wooden frame with a padded top surface on which gold leaf is laid out for cutting
gold democrat *n, usu cap G&D* **:** a member of the Democratic party favoring the gold standard; *esp* **:** one of a group of dissident Democrats supporting an independent ticket in the presidential election of 1896 — compare NATIONAL SILVER
gold–dig \ˈ=,=\ *vb* [back-formation fr. *gold digger*] *vt* **:** to extract money or gifts from by coaxing or flattery ⟨why did you coax him, tease him, *gold-dig* him —Sinclair Lewis⟩ ~ *vi* **:** to extract money or gifts from men by coaxing or flattery ⟨she went with him wherever he wanted to go, and she never tried to maneuver him or *gold-dig* —Ann Chidester⟩
gold digger *n* **1 :** one that digs gold esp. in alluvial deposits **2 :** an avaricious woman; *esp* **:** one who uses her feminine charms to extract money or gifts from men ⟨found out the truth . . . called her a *gold digger* and walked out —Erle Stanley Gardner⟩
gold digging *n* **1 :** a gold placer mine **2 gold diggings** *pl* **:** a district containing gold placer mines
gold dust *n* **1 :** particles and sometimes flakes and pellets of gold obtained in placer mining **2 a :** BASKET-OF-GOLD **b :** a common stonecrop (*Sedum acre*)
gold–dust tree *or* **gold dust** *n* **:** an aucuba (*Aucuba japonica variegata*) with yellow-spotted leaves
gold dust twins *n pl* [so called fr. the twin Negro boys depicted on the box of *Gold Dust,* a trademarked soap powder] **:** a pair of inseparable and indefatigable workers
¹gold·en \ˈgōldən\ *adj, usu* -ER/-EST [ME, fr. ¹*gold* + *-en*] **1 a :** consisting of or relating to gold **:** made of gold ⟨a purse with a ~ frame —F.M.Stenton⟩ **b :** containing, bearing, or abounding in gold **:** AURIFEROUS **2 a :** having the color of gold ⟨~ grain⟩ **b :** BLOND — used of the color of hair **3 :** having the luster or sheen of gold **:** SHINING, AUREATE ⟨there is a ~ brightness in the air —Amy Lowell⟩ **4 :** characterized by a high degree of excellence **:** approaching a standard of perfection **:** SUPERB ⟨there was a quality of ~ goodness about him —Willa Cather⟩ **5 :** characterized by great prosperity, happiness, and achievement **:** FLOURISHING, SPACIOUS ⟨the world's great age begins anew, the ~ years return —P.B. Shelley⟩ ⟨the ~ days of river steamboats —*Amer. Guide Series: Ark.*⟩ **6 a :** radiant, youthful, or vigorous in person or manner ⟨~ lads and girls all must, as chimney sweepers, come to dust —Shak.⟩ **b :** colorful and successful esp. in athletics **:** possessed of a variety of talents that promise worldly success **:** popular and charming **:** WHITE-HEADED — often used with *boy* ⟨the ~ boys of the airlines⟩ ⟨a ~ boy who comes to dust —*New Republic*⟩ **7 :** constituting or yielding wealth **:** PROFITABLE ⟨Pakistan's ~ fiber, jute —William Costello⟩ **8 :** highly favorable **:** opportunely advantageous ⟨the first affirmative speaker in a debate has a ~ opportunity to influence the audience —A.T.Weaver⟩ ⟨if management fails to step in to fill their needs it passes up a ~ opportunity —Bruce Payne⟩ ⟨had the ~ opportunity to utilize a famous squelch —Bennett Cerf⟩ ⟨~ opportunities for anyone with some originality —W.H.Dowdeswell⟩ **9 :** of, relating to, or marking a 50th anniversary **10 :** rich and mellow in timbre or resonance ⟨the song of the wood thrush is more ~ and leisurely —John Burroughs⟩ ⟨had a smooth ~ tenor —*Current Biog.*⟩ — **gold·en·ly** *adv*
²golden \"\ *vb* -ED/-ING/-S *vt* **:** to make golden in color ⟨a full moon . . . ~*ed* the road —Edward Kimbrough⟩ ~ *vi* **:** to take on a golden color ⟨the pumpkin ripened and ~*ed* —J.M.Neale⟩
golden age *n, often cap G&A* **:** a period of great happiness, prosperity, and achievement: **a :** an idyllic state of nature held to have existed in the past and regarded as man's original condition ⟨believes that mankind in their development down from the *golden age* are destined to degenerate —K.R.Popper⟩ **b :** a time of ideal perfection regarded as attainable in the future ⟨a *golden age* of the human community is a distinct promise —*Saturday Rev.*⟩ **c :** the most flourishing period in the history of something **:** the time of highest achievement or greatest development ⟨the *golden age* of the novel⟩ ⟨the *golden age* of Spain⟩ — compare SILVER AGE
golden agouti *n* **:** a common tropical American rodent (*Dasyprocta aguti*) — compare AGOUTI
golden alexanders *n pl but sing or pl in constr, often cap A* **:** a showy No. American yellow-flowered perennial herb (*Zizia aurea*) of the carrot family that occurs in moist woods and meadows; *also* **:** any of several related herbs
golden anniversary *n* **:** a 50th anniversary
golden apple *n* **1 :** BEL **2 :** TOMATO **3 :** HOG PLUM 1
golden aster *n* **:** an American plant of the genus *Chrysopsis* (esp. *C. mariana*)
goldenback \ˈ==,=\ *or* **goldback** \ˈ=,=\ *n* **:** a gold fern (*Pityrogramma triangularis*) of the Pacific coastal region of No. America that has erect fronds with dark brown shining stipes and broad coriaceous blades with the segments broadly rounded
golden balls *n pl* **:** three gilt balls used as a pawnbroker's sign
golden bamboo *n* **:** a grass (*Bambusa vulgaris aureo-variegata*) with yellow-striped leaves
golden–banded lily \ˈ==,==-\ *n* **:** GOLDBAND LILY
golden barb *n* **:** a small golden-yellow Indian fish (*Barbus gelius*) sometimes kept in the tropical aquarium
golden bat *n* **:** SUCKER-FOOTED BAT
golden bell *n* **:** a shrub of the genus *Forsythia* — often used in pl.
golden bough *n* **:** MISTLETOE 1a
golden brown *n* **:** a variable color averaging a strong brown that is yellower and slightly darker than gold brown, yellower and paler than average russet, and yellower and less strong than rust
golden buck *n* **:** welsh rabbit topped with poached egg
goldenbush \ˈ==,=\ *n* **1 :** a heathlike New Zealand shrub (*Cassinia fulvida*) of the family Compositae with evergreen yellowish foliage and white flowers **2 :** RABBIT BRUSH **3 :** a plant of the genus *Haplopappus*
golden calf *n* [so called fr. the golden calf made by Aaron for the Israelites to worship (Exod 32)] **:** an object of materialistic or unworthy worship; *esp* **:** MONEY ⟨this . . . material age when everything goes down before the *golden calf* —Eliot Gregory⟩
golden calla *n* **:** any of several callas of the genus *Zantedeschia* having yellow spathes
golden cat *n* **:** either of two small reddish or yellowish wildcats: **a :** a rather pale solid-colored cat (*Felis aurata*) of northwestern Africa **b :** a variably marked cat (*F. temminckii*) of southeastern Asia
golden chain *also* **golden chain tree** *n* **:** LABURNUM 2
golden chestnut *n* **:** a moderate brown that is redder, lighter, and stronger than chestnut brown and yellower, lighter, and stronger than bay — called also *pecan brown*
golden chinquapin *n* **:** a Pacific coast tree (*Castanopsis chrysophylla*) having evergreen tapering leathery leaves with golden yellow scales on the lower surface
golden clematis *n* **:** a clematis (*Clematis tangutica*) with serrate leaves and large yellow flowers
golden club *n* **:** an American aquatic plant (*Orontium aquaticum*) of the family Araceae with a spadix of minute yellow flowers
golden corydalis *n* **:** a diffusely branched herbaceous annual or biennial (*Corydalis aurea*) with golden-yellow flowers
golden cottonwood *n* **:** GOLDENBUSH 1
golden cress *n* **:** GOLDEN PEPPERGRASS
golden crest *n* **:** a woolly bog herb (*Lophiola americana*) of eastern No. America with loose panicles of yellowish flowers
golden–crested kinglet *also* **golden–crested wren** \ˈ==,==-\ *n* **:** any of several kinglets having the crown patch golden yellow — see GOLDCREST
golden crown *n* **1 :** GOLDFLOWER 1b **2 :** a low perennial spreading grass (*Paspalum dilatatum*) of So. America
golden crownbeard *n* **:** a coarse annual yellow-flowered herb (*Ximenesia encelioides*) of the family Compositae
golden–crowned \¦==¦=\ *adj* **:** having the top of the head yellow — used of birds
golden–crowned accentor *n* **:** OVENBIRD 2
golden–crowned kinglet *n* **:** the American golden-crested kinglet (*Regulus satrapa*)
golden–crowned sparrow *n* **:** a rather large sparrow (*Zonotrichia atricapilla*) of the Pacific coast of No. America having a plain yellow crown bordered on each side by black
golden cudweed *n* **:** either of two composite plants (*Helichrysum orientale* and *Pterocaulon virgatum*) having golden-yellow flower heads that are sometimes used as everlastings
golden cup *n* **1 :** GOLDCUP 1 **2 :** a poppy (*Hunnemannia fumariaefolia*) having yellow flowers with separate sepals — called also *Mexican tulip poppy*
golden–cup oak *n* **:** CANYON LIVE OAK
golden currant *n* **1 :** a fragrant yellow-flowered ornamental shrub (*Ribes aureum*) of the western U.S. **2 :** BUFFALO CURRANT 1
golden cypress *n* **:** any of several ornamental trees or shrubs of the genus *Cupressus* having yellowish foliage
golden dewdrop *n* **:** a tropical American shrub (*Duranta repens*) sometimes planted for hedges in the southern and central U.S.
golden dock *n* **:** an American dock (*Rumex maritimus*)
golden eagle *n* **:** a large and powerful eagle (*Aquila chrysaetos*) of the northern hemisphere that has brownish yellow tips on head and neck feathers
golden eardrops *n pl but usu sing in constr* **:** a stout California herb (*Dicentra chrysantha*) with glaucous bipinnate leaves and yellow irregular flowers
goldened *past of* GOLDEN
golden eggs *n pl but usu sing in constr* **:** SUNCUP
golden elder *n* **:** a common European elder (*Sambucus nigra aurea*) with yellow foliage and white flowers
goldener *comparative of* GOLDEN
goldenest *superlative of* GOLDEN
goldeneye \ˈ==,=\ *n* **1 a :** a large-headed swift-flying diving duck (*Bucephala clangula* or *Glaucionetta clangula*) of Eurasia and No. America having the male strikingly marked in black and white and the female mottled gray with brown head, white collar, and white wing patches **b :** BARROW'S GOLDENEYE **2** *also* **golden–eyed fly** \ˈ==,=-\ **:** a lacewing of the family Chrysopidae **3 :** a golden aster (*Chrysopsis villosa*) of central No. America with hairy foliage and golden-yellow flower heads
golden–eyed \¦==¦=\ *adj* **:** having the eye or iris yellow or golden
golden–eyed duck *n* **:** GOLDENEYE 1
golden–eyed grass *n* **:** a yellow-flowered California herb (*Sisyrinchium californicum*) with leaves that resemble blades of grass
golden feather *n* **:** an ornamental feverfew with yellow foliage
golden–feather yellow *n* **:** PYRETHRUM YELLOW
golden fern *n* **:** a stout tropical American fern (*Acrostichum aureum*) with large fronds that are golden yellow beneath
golden fig *n* **:** STRANGLER FIG b
golden fir *n* **:** CALIFORNIA RED FIR
golden fizz *n* **:** a fizz made from lemon juice, gin, egg yolk, and sugar
golden flax *n* **:** a European flax (*Linum flavum*) commonly cultivated for its bright yellow flowers
goldenfleece \ˈ==,=\ *n* **:** a rayless goldenrod (*Chrysothamnus arborescens*)
golden flower *n* **1 :** any of several plants of the genus *Chrysanthemum; esp* **:** CORN MARIGOLD **2 :** a moss of the genus *Polytrichum* **3 :** GOLDENROD
golden glow *n* **1 :** a tall branching herb (*Rudbeckia laciniata hortensia*) with showy yellow much-doubled flower heads **2 :** a moderate orange yellow to strong yellow
golden gram *n* **:** MUNG BEAN
golden green *n* **:** a grayish to dark grayish yellow that is very slightly greener than light stone — called also *cloudy amber*
golden grouper *n* **:** either of two Pacific groupers that have both a dark and a yellow color phase: **a :** a grouper (*Mycteroperca pardalis*) of the Gulf of California that is greenish gray to brown with brown spots or golden yellow more or less splashed with black **b :** a closely related fish of the Galápagos islands that is greenish brown with purple to brown spots or a solid brilliant orange-yellow and that is placed in a separate species (*M. olfax*) or considered a geographical variety of the more northerly fish
goldenhair \ˈ==,=\ *n* **:** a southern African shrub (*Chrysocoma coma-aurea*) of the family Compositae with golden-yellow flowers
golden hamster *n* **:** a small tawny hamster (*Mesocricetus auratus*) native to Asia Minor but kept as a pet in many places
golden hardhack *n* **:** SHRUBBY CINQUEFOIL
golden hawkweed *n* **1 :** KING DEVIL **2 :** ORANGE HAWKWEED 1
golden hedge hyssop *n* **:** GOLDENPERT
golden hop *n* **:** a pistillate hop (*Humulus lupulus*) with yellow foliage
golden horde *n, usu cap G&H* [trans. of Tatar *altūn ordū;* fr. the golden tent of Batu Khan †1255 Mongol ruler] **:** a body of Mongol Tatars overrunning eastern Europe in the 13th century, establishing the Kipchak khanate, and keeping Russia in subjection until 1486
golden horse *n* **:** PALOMINO
golden horseshoe bat *n* **:** a small Australian leaf-nosed bat (*Rhinonycteris aurantia*) with fur of a delicate tawny hue
goldening *pres part of* GOLDEN
golden ironweed *or* **golden honey plant** *n* **:** a perennial composite herb (*Actinomeris alternifolia*) of the eastern U.S. with showy yellow flowers
golden jerusalem *n, usu cap J* **:** CONEFLOWER a
golden jubilee *n* **:** GOLDEN ANNIVERSARY
golden larch *n* **:** a Chinese coniferous tree (*Pseudolarix amabilis*) with golden-yellow deciduous leaves
golden leaf *n* **:** a golden-leaved tree of the genus *Chrysophyllum*
golden lip *var of* GOLD LIP
goldenlocks \ˈ==,=\ *n pl but sing or pl in constr* **:** WALL FERN
golden loosestrife *n* **:** LOOSESTRIFE 1
golden lungwort *n* **:** WALL HAWKWEED
golden maidenhair *n* **1 :** WALL FERN **2 :** HAIRCAP MOSS
golden marguerite *n* **:** YELLOW CHAMOMILE
golden meadow parsnip *n* **:** an American herb (*Zizia aurea*) with serrate leaflets
golden mean *n* **:** the way of wisdom and reasonableness between extremes **:** the happy medium between excess and defect
golden millet *n* **:** FOXTAIL MILLET
golden mole *n* **:** any of several fossorial insectivores of southern Africa constituting *Chrysochloris* and related genera and having iridescent guard hairs mingled with the underfur
golden monkey *n* **:** a monkey (*Rhinopithecus roxellanae*) of the high uplands of Tibet and China having a brilliant blue face and a dark coat overlaid with long silvery hairs
golden moss *n* **:** a stonecrop (*Sedum acre*)
golden mouse *n* **:** a tawny arboreal cricetid mouse (*Ochrotomys nuttalli*) of the southeastern U.S.
goldenmouthed \¦==¦=\ *adj* **:** distinguished for lofty or persuasive utterance **:** ELOQUENT
golden nematode *n* **:** a small yellowish Old World nematode worm (*Heterodera rostochiensis*) established locally as a serious pest of potatoes in eastern No. America
gold·en·ness \ˈgōldən(n)əs\ *n* -ES **:** the quality or state of being golden
golden net *n* **:** a virus disease of peaches, plums, and apricots that causes marginal yellowing of the leaf veins
golden number *n* **:** the number of a particular calendar year in the Metonic cycle used to fix the date of Easter — compare DOMINICAL LETTER, EPACT; see EASTER table
golden oak *n* **1 :** DOWNY FALSE FOXGLOVE **2 :** oak (as in furniture or cabinetwork) finished in a light golden brown; *also* **:** a finish resembling that of golden oak
golden ocher *n* **:** OCHER BROWN
golden olive *n* **:** a variable color averaging a light olive that is greener and deeper than citrine, redder and deeper than grape green, and redder and stronger than old moss green
golden orange *n* **:** a strong orange that is deeper and slightly yellower than pumpkin and redder and duller than cadmium orange
golden oriole *n* **:** an Old World oriole (*Oriolus oriolus*) having the male brilliant yellow with black tail and wings and the female largely greenish yellow, breeding in central and southern Europe and western Asia, and wintering chiefly in Africa and southern Asia
golden osier *n* **1 :** GOLDEN WILLOW **2 :** SWEET GALE
golden palm civet *n* **:** a Ceylonese paradoxure (*Paradoxurus aureus*)
golden pea *n* **:** FALSE LUPINE
golden peppergrass *n* **:** an annual European herb (*Lepidium sativum*) naturalized in No. America and cultivated for its pungent foliage
golden perch *n* **:** CALLOP
gold·en·pert \ˈ==,pərt\ *n* -S **:** a small yellow-flowered No. American herb (*Gratiola aurea*)
golden pheasant *n* **:** a brilliantly colored pheasant (*Chrysolophus pictus*) of China and Tibet often raised in captivity as an ornamental bird
golden pileolated warbler *n* **:** a Pacific coast warbler (*Wilsonia pusilla chryseola*) similar to but brighter in color than the pileolated warbler
golden pine *n* **:** GOLDEN LARCH
golden plover *n* **:** either of two gregarious plovers of the genus *Pluvialis* having dark upperparts spotted with gold in all plumages and a dark black belly in breeding birds: **a :** one (*P. apricaria*) that breeds in northern Europe and northwestern Asia and winters from northern Africa to eastern India **b :** one (*P. dominica*) that breeds in the Arctic tundra and on Arctic beaches of America and Siberia and winters in Hawaii and the southern hemisphere
golden polypody *n* **1 :** WALL FERN **2 :** SERPENT FERN
golden poppy *n* **1 :** any of several yellow or orange poppies (as a California poppy) **2 :** a vivid reddish orange that is yellower and much lighter than international orange and stronger and slightly redder and lighter than chrome orange
golden ragwort *n* **:** a ragwort (*Senecio aureus*) of the U.S. having basal cordate leaves, lyrate or clasping stem leaves, and an open cluster of yellow-rayed flowers
golden rain *n* **:** LABURNUM 2
goldenrain tree \¦==¦=-\ *also* **goldenrain** \ˈ==,=\ *n* **:** a round-headed tree (*Koelreuteria paniculata*) having very long showy clusters of yellow flowers — called also *varnish tree*
golden rectangle *n* **:** a rectangle whose width is to its length as the length is to the sum of the width and length — compare GOLDEN SECTION
golden red *n* **:** a yellowish red
golden retriever *n* **:** a medium-sized golden-coated retriever developed chiefly in England by interbreeding Russian shepherd dogs with bloodhounds
golden robin *n* **:** BALTIMORE ORIOLE
goldenrod \ˈ==,=\ *n* **1 :** any of numerous chiefly No. American composite plants mostly of the genus *Solidago* that are summer-blooming and fall-blooming perennials or biennials with stems resembling wands, variously shaped leaves, and heads of small yellow or sometimes white flowers often clustered in panicles — compare RAYLESS GOLDENROD **2 a :** a vivid yellow **b :** a strong yellow
goldenrod tree *n* **:** a Canary island shrub (*Bosea yervamora*) of the family Amaranthaceae with greenish yellow flowers
golden rule *n* **1** *usu cap G&R* **:** a rule stating that one should do to others as he would have others do to him — with reference to Mt 7:12 and Lk 6:31 **2 :** a first consideration or guiding principle ⟨the *golden rule* for eating and drinking is moderation —K.A.Henderson⟩
golden rust *n* **:** a rust fungus (*Puccinia glumarum*) that bears its urediospores in bright yellow sori
goldens *pres 3d sing of* GOLDEN
golden samphire *n* **:** a European maritime plant (*Inula crithmoides*) with bright yellow flowers
golden saxifrage *also* **golden spleen** *n* **:** any of several low aquatic herbs of the genus *Chrysosplenium; specif* **:** a plant (*C. americanum*) with yellowish flowers
goldenseal \ˈ==,=\ *n* **1 :** a perennial American herb (*Hydrastis canadensis*) with a thick knotted yellow rootstock and large rounded leaves **2 :** the dried rhizome and roots of goldenseal used as an alterative and tonic

golden section *n* **:** the division of a line or the proportion of a geometrical figure in which the smaller dimension is to the greater as the greater is to the whole ⟨the *golden section* has for centuries been regarded as . . . a key to the mysteries of art —Herbert Read⟩ — called also *extreme and mean ratio*
golden shad *n* **1 :** ALEWIFE 1a **2 :** a skipjack (*Pomolobus chrysochloris*)
golden shiner *n* **:** a common cyprinid fish (*Notemigonus crysoleucas*) of eastern No. America having silvery sides with bright golden reflections
golden shower *n* **:** any of several leguminous shrubs or trees having drooping racemes of bright yellow flowers; *esp* **:** DRUMSTICK TREE
golden slipper *n* **:** any of several lady's slippers having yellow flowers (esp. *Cypripedium calceolus pubescens* and *C. calceolus parviflorum*)
golden spider lily *n* **:** a Chinese bulbous plant (*Lycoris aurea*) cultivated for its yellow flowers
golden spoon *n* **:** a usu. shrubby tropical American tree (*Byrsonima crassifolia*) that is sometimes cultivated for its sweet edible yellow fruits; *broadly* **:** ¹NANCE
golden star *n* **1 :** GOLDEN ASTER **2 :** GOLD JOINT **3 :** a plant of the genus *Bloomeria* (esp. *B. crocea*) **4 :** a tunicate of the genus *Botryllus* having zooids grouped like stars in the greenish yellow tunic
golden stool *n* **:** a wooden stool partly covered with gold that serves as the symbol of authority of Ashanti kings
golden syrup *n, chiefly Brit* **:** TREACLE 2b
golden text *n* **:** a brief passage of Scripture chosen as embodying the thought of a Sunday-school lesson
golden thistle *n* **:** any of several erect somewhat spiny composite herbs of the Mediterranean region that constitute the genus *Scolymus* and have sessile yellow flower heads of ligulate flowers — see SPANISH OYSTER PLANT
golden thread *n* **1 :** LOVE-IN-A-MIST 1. **2 :** GOLDTHREAD 1
golden–tongued \ˈ≈¦≈¦≈\ *adj* **:** gifted with superior powers of utterance or persuasion **:** ELOQUENT
goldentop \ˈ≈≈,≈\ *n* **:** a European grass (*Lamarckia aurea*) with showy one-sided yellow panicles
golden trout *n* **1 :** a variable and brilliantly colored trout (*Salmo agua-bonito*) native to the high Sierras but introduced in other upland waters of western No. America — see ROOSEVELT TROUT, STEWART WHITE TROUT **2 :** SUNAPEE TROUT
golden tuft *n* **1 :** BASKET-OF-GOLD **2 :** GOLDEN CUDWEED
goldentwig \ˈ≈≈,≈\ *also* **goldentwig dogwood** *n* **:** a red osier dogwood (*Cornus stolonifera flaviramea*) with yellow branchlets
golden warbler *n* **:** YELLOW WARBLER 1a
golden wasp *n* **:** CUCKOO WASP
golden wattle *n, Austral* **:** any of several yellow-flowered acacias; *esp* **:** a medium-sized tree (*Acacia pycnantha*) with very fragrant intensely yellow flowers in globular heads that is widely distributed in New South Wales and So. Australia, has a bark used in tanning, and is cultivated as an ornamental in mild climates
golden wave *n* **:** a Texas annual herb (*Coreopsis drummondii*) with a profusion of yellowish purple flowers
golden wedding *n* **:** a golden anniversary of a wedding
golden willow *n* **:** a European willow (*Salix vitellina*) whose yellow twigs are used in basketmaking
golden willow herb *n* **:** LOOSESTRIFE 1
goldenwing \ˈ≈≈,≈\ *also* **golden–winged woodpecker** \ˈ≈≈,≈-\ *n* **:** a flicker (*Colaptes auratus*)
golden–winged warbler *also* **goldenwing** *n* **:** a small No. American warbler (*Vermivora chrysoptera*) with a patch of bright yellow on the wing
golden wolf *n* **:** CHANCO
golden wonder millet *n* **:** GERMAN MILLET
golden yellow *n* **1 :** a variable color averaging a vivid yellow that is redder and duller than average buttercup or goldenrod (sense 2a) **2 :** a moderate to strong orange yellow that is very slightly yellower and stronger than Indian yellow and very slightly yellower and paler than Dutch orange
¹**golder** *comparative of* GOLD
²**gol·der** \ˈgäl(d)ə(r)\ *var of* GOLLAR
goldest *superlative of* GOLD
gold–exchange standard *n* **:** a monetary standard under which gold does not circulate domestically and international debts are settled primarily in currency of nations that maintain a gold and esp. a gold bullion standard
gold export point *n* **:** the point of variation in the price of foreign exchange at which the export of gold becomes preferable to the use of exchange in settlement of international obligations — called also *gold point;* compare GOLD IMPORT POINT
goldeye \ˈ≈,≈\ *n* **1 :** YELLOW STAR GRASS **2 :** a small isospondylous edible fish (*Amphiodon alosoides*) widely distributed in lakes and streams of northern and western No. America
gold fern *n* **:** any of several ferns (as members of the genera *Notholaena* and *Pityrogramma*) having the lower surfaces of the fronds covered with a golden yellow spore mass or group of sori
gold fever *n* **:** the contagious excitement of a gold rush
goldfield \ˈ≈,≈\ *n* **:** a gold-mining district
gold fields *n pl but sing or pl in constr* **:** any of several yellow-flowered composite herbs constituting the genus *Baeria* and occurring along the western coast of No. America
gold–filled \ˈ≈¦≈\ *adj* **:** covered with a layer of gold so as to constitute filled gold — used esp. of jewelry
goldfinch \ˈ≈,≈\ *n* [ME, fr. OE *goldfinc*, fr. *gold* + *finc* finch — more at FINCH] **1 :** a small brightly colored European finch (*Carduelis carduelis*) that has the front of the head and throat bright red, the nape with part of the wings and tail black, and the wings marked in bright yellow and that is often kept as a cage bird **2 :** YELLOWHAMMER 1 **3 :** any of several small American finches of the genus *Spinus* typically having the male in summer plumage variably yellow with black wings, tail, and crown
goldfinny \ˈ≈,≈≈\ *n* -ES [prob. alter. of *goldsinny*] **1 :** a small brightly colored European wrasse (*Ctenolabrus rupestris*) **2 :** any of several European wrasses related to the goldfinny
¹**goldfish** \ˈ≈,≈\ *n* [¹*gold* + *fish*] **1 a :** a small usu. golden yellow or orange cyprinid fish (*Carassius auratus*) that is native to China, closely related to the common carp, and much used as an aquarium and pond fish **b :** GARIBALDI **2** *slang* **:** canned salmon
²**goldfish** \"\ *adj* **:** resembling that of a goldfish; *specif* **:** exposed to public view ⟨patiently endured this ~ life —*Time*⟩
goldfish bowl *n* **1 :** a transparent glass bowl used as an aquarium for goldfish **2 :** a place or situation offering no privacy or secrecy ⟨the *goldfish bowls* in which an actor and his wife dwell —James Cagney⟩
goldflower \ˈ≈,≈\ *n* **1 :** any of several yellow-flowered or predominantly yellow-flowered composite plants: as **a :** either of two European everlastings (*Helichrysum stoechas* and *H. orientale*) **b :** any of various bristly leaved annual herbs of southern Africa that constitute the genus *Gorteria* and have solitary or corymbose flower heads with ligulate orange-yellow ray flowers marked with brown **c :** a biennial herb (*Hymenoxys biennis*) of dry uplands of the southwestern U.S. that has yellow flower heads with fertile ray flowers **2 :** a shrubby hybrid St.-John's-wort (*Hypericum* × *moserianum*) with large golden yellow flowers
gold flux *n* **:** gold aventurine
gold foil *n* **:** gold beaten or rolled out very thin; *specif* **:** gold in sheets thicker than gold leaf
gold glass *n* **:** glassware ornamented with designs engraved on gold foil that is attached to the glass and then covered with a thin film of glass
gold–green \ˈ≈¦≈\ *adj* **:** dark green
gold heather *n* **:** BEACH HEATHER
gol·di \ˈgōldē, ˈgōl-\ *or* **gold** \-ld\ *n, pl* **goldi** *or* **goldis** *or* **golds** *usu cap* **1 a :** a group of Tungus peoples living along the Amur river **b :** a member of any of such peoples **2 :** the Tungusic language of the Goldi peoples
goldier *comparative of* GOLDY
gol·die's fern \ˈgōldēz-\ *or* **goldie–fern** *or* **goldie's shield fern** *or* **goldie's wood fern** *n, usu cap G* [after John *Goldie* †1886 Scot. traveler in the U.S., its discoverer] **:** a No. American fern (*Dryopteris goldiana*) with a blackish lustrous stipe
goldiest *superlative of* GOLDY
gold·i·locks *or* **goldy·locks** \ˈgōldē,läks, -di,-\ *n pl but sing or pl in constr* [*goldy* + *locks*, pl. of *lock* (curl)] **1 :** a European herb (*Linosyris vulgaris*) of the family Compositae with heads of flowers resembling those of goldenrod **2 :** any of several shrubby southern African composite plants (genus *Chrysocoma*) that have bright yellow flower heads **3 :** a European buttercup (*Ranunculus auricomus*)
gold import point *n* **:** the point of variation in the price of foreign exchange at which the import of gold becomes preferable to the use of exchange in settlement of international obligations — called also *gold point;* compare GOLD EXPORT POINT
gold·ish \ˈgōldish\ *adj* [ME, fr. ¹*gold* + *-ish*] **:** somewhat golden **:** having a tinge of gold
gold·ite \ˈgōl,dīt\ *n* -S [¹*gold* + *-ite*] **:** an advocate of a gold monetary standard ⟨they were ~s to the last coin in the sock —John Gunther⟩
gold joint *n* **:** a perennial herb (*Chrysogonum virginianum*) of the family Compositae of the southeastern U.S. that has long-stalked leaves and radiate yellow flowers
gold knife \ˈ≈,≈\ *n* **:** a long-bladed roundnosed knife for cutting gold leaf
gold lace *n* **:** lace or braid formerly made of gold wire but now usu. of gold silk or gold silk and cotton and used on uniforms or official robes to denote rank
gold–laced \ˈ≈¦≈\ *adj* **:** adorned with gold lace
gold leaf *n* **:** a sheet of gold ordinarily varying from four to five millionths of an inch in thickness that is used esp. for gilding and lettering on glass
gold·less \ˈgōldləs\ *adj* **:** lacking gold ⟨the ~ age, where gold disturbs no dreams —Lord Byron⟩
gold lip *or* **golden lip** *n* **:** a very large pearl oyster (*Pinctada maxima*) having the inner shell margin yellowish — see SILVER LIP
gold mine *n* [ME] **1 :** a place where gold is obtained by mining operations **2 :** a rich source of something desired or sought for ⟨that fantastic *gold mine* of early Americana —A.O. Vietor⟩ ⟨the Haydn piano sonatas . . . represent a *gold mine* of melody and of instrumental imagination —Virgil Thomson⟩
goldmist \ˈ≈¦≈\ *n* **:** a grayish yellow that is greener and very slightly lighter than chamois and greener, lighter, and stronger than old ivory or crash
gold mohur tree *n* [by folk etymology fr. *gulmohur*] **:** ROYAL POINCIANA
gold moss *also* **goldmoss stonecrop** *n* **:** a stonecrop (*Sedum acre*)
gold number *n* **:** a measure of the protective power of a lyophilic colloid expressed as the amount of the dry material that just protects a red gold sol under specified conditions — compare PROTECTIVE COLLOID
gold of pleasure **:** an annual European false flax (*Camelina sativa*) that was formerly cultivated for its oil-rich seeds and is widely naturalized in No. America
gold pheasant *n* **1 :** GOLDEN PHEASANT **2 :** a brownish orange that is redder and duller than leather and slightly yellower and lighter than prairie brown, Windsor tan, Titian, or amber brown — called also *platina yellow, Prussian brown*
gold plate *n* **1 :** vessels or tableware of gold **2 :** gold electroplate — compare ROLLED GOLD
gold–plate \ˈ≈¦≈\ *vt* **:** to electroplate with gold
gold point *n* **1 :** GOLD EXPORT POINT **2 :** GOLD IMPORT POINT
gold premium *n* **:** the excess of purchasing power or exchange value of gold currency over another form of money (as paper dollars) of nominally equal value
gold reserve *n* **:** a fund of gold coin or bullion: as **a :** the fund of gold held by the U. S. Treasury **b :** the gold held by the central bank and the stabilization fund of a country
gold rocker *n* **:** CRADLE 3a
gold room *n* **:** a room in the N. Y. Stock Exchange formerly used for trading in gold
gold ruby glass *or* **gold ruby** *n* **:** RUBY GLASS
gold rush *n* **1 :** a rush to newly discovered goldfields in pursuit of riches ⟨the *gold rush* to Alaska⟩ **2 :** the headlong pursuit of sudden wealth in some new or lucrative field ⟨led the *gold rush* of the comic artists, whose output is minted daily —*N.Y. Herald Tribune*⟩ ⟨that *gold rush* of frightened businessmen toward higher prices —T.W.Arnold⟩
golds *pl of* GOLD
gold·schmidt·ine \ˈgōl(d),shmid·,ēn\ *n* -S [Victor *Goldschmidt* †1933 Ger. crystallographer + E *-ine*] **:** a mineral Ag_2Sb consisting of a silver antimonide that occurs in thin gray-white orthorhombic crystals
gold·schmidt·ite \-d·,īt\ *n* -S [V. *Goldschmidt* + E *-ite*] **:** SYLVANITE
gold·schmidt's process \ˈgōl(d),shmits-\ *n, usu cap G* [after Hans *Goldschmidt* †1923 Ger. chemist] **:** ALUMINOTHERMY
gold shell *n* **:** a jingle shell (esp. *Anomia simplex*) of the Atlantic coast of No. America with a shell sulphur yellow to coppery red or sometimes silver gray or black
gold·sin·ny \ˈgōl(d),sinē\ *n* -ES [origin unknown] **:** GOLDFINNY
gold size *n* **:** any of several adhesive compositions used for attaching gold leaf to surfaces
gold·smith \ˈgōl(d),smith\ *n* [ME, fr. OE, fr. ¹*gold* + *smith*] **1 :** an artisan who makes vessels, jewelry, or other articles of gold **2 :** a manufacturer of and dealer in articles of gold
goldsmith beetle *n* **:** any of several large bright yellow scarabaeid beetles with adults that feed on foliage and larvae that live in the soil and feed on roots: as **a :** a widely distributed European beetle (*Cetonia aurata*) **b :** a No. American beetle (*Cotalpa lanigera*) that is sometimes a locally important defoliator of deciduous trees
gold·smith·ery \-thərē\ *or* **gold·smith·ry** \-thrē\ *n* -ES [ME *goldsmithrie*, fr. *goldsmith* + *-rie* -ry] **1 :** the work, art, or trade of a goldsmith **2 :** articles manufactured by goldsmiths
gold·smith·ing \-thiŋ\ *n* **:** GOLDSMITHERY 1
gold sodium thiosulfate *n* **:** a soluble compound of gold $Na_3Au(S_2O_3)_2.2H_2O$ administered by intravenous injection in the treatment of rheumatoid arthritis and lupus erythematosus — called also *sodium aurothiosulfate*
gold solder *n* **:** a solder containing about 60 percent gold, 20 percent silver, and 20 percent copper
gold sol test *n* **:** a test of the ability of the globulins of an individual's cerebrospinal fluid to precipitate gold from colloidal solution, a positive result usu. being indicative of neurosyphilis
gold·spink \ˈ≈,≈\ *n* **1** *chiefly Scot* **:** the European goldfinch **2** *chiefly Scot* **:** the European yellowhammer
gold spring *n* **:** a thin spring of gold that is attached to a chronometer detent and serves to unlock the escape wheel — called also *passing spring*
gold stamp *or* **gold stamping** *n* **:** genuine gold lettering or ornamentation on book covers
gold standard *n* **:** a monetary standard under which the basic unit of currency is defined by a stated quantity of gold and that is usu. characterized by the coinage and circulation of gold, unrestricted convertibility of other money into gold, and the free export and import of gold for the settlement of international obligations — compare GOLD BULLION STANDARD, GOLD-EXCHANGE STANDARD, MANAGED CURRENCY, STANDARD OF VALUE
gold star *adj* **:** entitled to display a gold star on a service flag as a symbol of a soldier killed in war ⟨a *gold star* mother⟩
gold stick *n* **1 :** the gold-headed staff presented by the British sovereign to the colonel of a regiment of Life Guardsmen or to the captain of the gentlemen-at-arms **2** *usu cap G&S* **:** one entitled to carry the gold stick on state occasions ⟨*Gold Sticks* and Silver Sticks have waited closely upon the persons of their sovereign —Elizabeth II⟩
goldstone \ˈ≈,≈\ *n* **:** aventurine spangled close and fine with particles of gold-colored material
gold–tail \ˈ≈,≈\ *or* **gold–tail moth** *n* **:** either of two white moths of the family Lymantriidae having yellow abdominal tufts: **a :** a European moth (*Euproctis similis*) that is closely related to the brown-tail moth **b :** an Australian moth (*Acyphas chionitis*)
gold therapy *also* **gold treatment** *n* **:** CHRYSOTHERAPY
goldthread \ˈ≈,≈\ *n* **1 :** a plant of the genus *Coptis; esp* **:** a low smooth perennial No. American herb (*C. groenlandica*) with alternately divided leaves and a bright yellow rootstock **2 :** DODDER
goldtit \ˈ≈,≈\ *n* **:** VERDIN
goldurn *var of* GOLDARN
gold washer *n* **:** one that recovers gold by washing (as in a cradle); *also* **:** an apparatus for this purpose
gold washing *n* **1 :** the act or process of washing auriferous soil for gold **2 gold washings** *pl* **:** a place where gold washing is done
goldwasser *n* -S *often cap* [G, fr. *gold* (fr. OHG) + *wasser* water, fr. OHG *wazzer* — more at GOLD, WATER] **:** DANZIGER GOLDWASSER
gold watch *n* **:** SPATTERDOCK 1
goldwater \ˈ≈,≈≈\ *n* [trans. of G *goldwasser*] **:** DANZIGER GOLDWASSER
goldweed \ˈ≈,≈\ *n* **:** any of several plants of the genus *Ranunculus; esp* **:** CORN CROWFOOT
gold weight *n, obs* **:** the accuracy required in weighing gold
gold–winged woodpecker \ˈ≈,≈-\ *n* **:** a flicker (*Colaptes auratus*)
goldwork \ˈ≈,≈\ *n* **1 :** the act or art of working in gold **2 :** work done in gold (as by a smith)
goldworker \ˈ≈,≈≈\ *n* **:** a person whose occupation is the obtaining or working of gold
goldworkings \ˈ≈,≈≈\ *n pl* **:** a place where mining or washing for gold is done
gold·wyn·ism \ˈgōldwə̇,nizəm\ *n* -S *usu cap* [Samuel *Goldwyn* *b*1882 Am. motion-picture producer + *-ism*] **:** a phrase or expression (as "include me out") involving a grotesque use of a word — compare IRISH BULL, MALAPROPISM
goldy \ˈgōldē\ *adj* -ER/-EST [ME, fr. ¹*gold* + *-y*] **:** GOLDEN
gold yellow *n* **:** GOLDEN YELLOW
goldylocks *var of* GOLDILOCKS
go·lem \ˈgōləm, ˈgāl-, ˈgōil-\ *n* -S [Yiddish *goylem*, fr. Heb *gōlem* something shapeless] **1** *Jewish folklore* **:** an artificial figure constructed to represent a human being and endowed with life; *specif* **:** such a figure created by the cabalist Rabbi Löw of Prague in the 16th century **2 :** a senseless mechanical creature **:** AUTOMATON, ROBOT ⟨a total machine civilization is at best but a ~ —*Jewish Weekly News*⟩ **3 :** BLOCKHEAD 2
goles \ˈgōlz\ *n, cap* [euphemism] *dial Eng* **:** ²GOD — used in oaths
¹**golf** \ˈgälf, ˈgȯlf *also* ˈgäf *or* ˈgȯf *sometimes* ˈgəlf\ *n* -S *often attrib* [ME (Sc), prob. modif. of MD *colf, colve* club, stick used in a game resembling golf or field hockey; akin to OHG *kolbo* club, ON *kōlfr* clapper of a bell, bulb, arrow, L *galla* gallnut — more at GALL] **1 :** a game whose object is to sink a golf ball into each of the 9 or 18 successive holes on a golf course by using as few strokes of a golf club as possible and avoiding various natural or artificial hazards or obstacles — compare APPROACH, DRIVE, FAIRWAY, MATCH PLAY, MEDAL PLAY, PUTT, PUTTING GREEN, ROUGH, TEE **2** *or* **golf red :** BLOOD RED

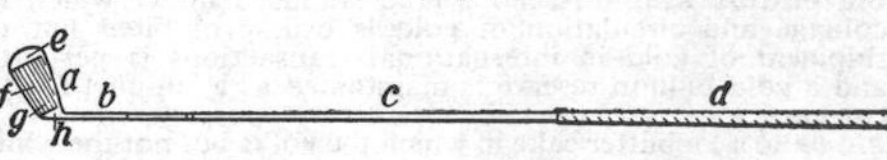

golf club (iron): *a* head, *b* hosel, *c* shaft, *d* grip, *e* toe or nose, *f* face, *g* heel, *h* neck

²**golf** \"\ *vb* -ED/-ING/-S *vi* **:** to play golf ~ *vt* **:** to hit as if with a golf club **:** LOFT ⟨the batter ~*ed* a pop fly⟩
³**golf** \"\ *usu cap* — a communications code word for the letter *g*
golf bag *n* **:** a bag for carrying golf clubs and golf balls
golf ball *n* **:** a tough-covered ball used in golf and made of rubber thread wound about a center
golf club *n* **:** a long-shafted club with a head of wood or iron used to hit the ball in golf — see BRASSIE, DRIVER, NIBLICK, PUTTER, SPOON
golf course *n* **:** an area of land laid out for the game of golf with a series of 9 or 18 holes each including tee, fairway, and green and often one or more natural or artificial hazards — called also *golf links*
golf·er \-fə(r)\ *n* -S **:** one that golfs
golf green *n* **:** a dark yellowish green that is yellower and paler than holly green (sense 1), greener, lighter, and stronger than deep chrome green, and yellower, lighter, and stronger than average hunter green
golf hose *n* **:** knee-length woolen socks worn with knickers or shorts for sports

golf bag

golf links *n pl* **:** GOLF COURSE
golf shoe *n* **:** an oxford shoe of waterproof leather with sole spikes or hobnails that is worn esp. for golfing
golf widow *n* **:** a woman whose husband spends much time on the golf course
gol·gi \ˈgȯl(,)jē\ *adj, usu cap* [after Camillo *Golgi* †1926 Ital. physician] **:** of, relating to, or constituting the Golgi apparatus ⟨the *Golgi* net of a nerve cell⟩
golgi apparatus *n, usu cap G* [after C. *Golgi*] **:** a cytoplasmic component esp. of functionally active cells that prob. plays a part in elaboration and secretion of cell products and when differentiated by special staining appears either as a net or as discrete particles although both appearances are prob. more or less artifactual — see CELL illustration
golgi body *n, usu cap G* [after C. *Golgi*] **:** a discrete mass of Golgi material as observed in certain stained preparations — called also *dictyosome*
golgi cell *n, usu cap G* [after C. *Golgi*] **:** a neuron with short dendrites and with either a long axon or an axon that breaks into processes soon after leaving the nerve-cell body
golgi material *or* **golgi substance** *n, usu cap G* [after C. *Golgi*] **:** specialized cytoplasm that constitutes the Golgi apparatus
golgi method *n, usu cap G* [after C. *Golgi*] **:** a method of preparing tissues for the study of nerves by using potassium bichromate and silver nitrate
golgi's organ *n, usu cap G* [after C. *Golgi*] **:** a spindle-shaped sensory end organ within a tendon
gol·go·tha \ˈgälgəthə, ˈgȯl- *also* ≈ˈgäthə *or* ≈ˈgȯthə\ *n* -S [fr. *Golgotha*, the hill near Jerusalem where Christ was crucified, fr. LL, fr. Gk, fr. Aram *gulgulthā*, fr. Heb *gulgōleth*, lit., skull] **1 :** a place of burial **:** CEMETERY, CHARNEL **2 :** a place of torment or martyrdom
gol·iard \ˈgōlyərd, -,yärd\ *n* -S *often cap* [F, fr. OF *goliart, goliard* glutton, drunkard, trickster, prob. fr. *gole* throat, gullet (fr. L *gula*) + *-art, -ard* — more at GLUTTON] **:** a wandering student of the 12th or 13th century given to the writing of goliardic verse and to convivial living and minstrelsy
gol·iar·dic \(ˈ)gōl¦yärdik\ *adj, often cap* **1 :** of, relating to, or being a type of medieval satirical poetry written in Latin **2 :** written in a manner suggestive of goliardic verse
go·li·ath \gəˈlīəth\ *n* -S *often cap* [after *Goliath*, biblical giant of the Philistines slain by David (1 Sam 17)] **:** GIANT ⟨slug it out with business ~s or that multitentacled giant squid, the U.S. government —Warner Olivier⟩
goliath beetle *n, sometimes cap G* **:** any of several very large African beetles of the family Cetoniidae commonly reddish brown marked with white and attaining a length of four inches
goliath crane *also* **goliath** *n* -S **:** a powerful traveling crane mounted on a movable gantry of large span
goliath frog *n* **:** a frog (*Rana goliath*) of the Cameroons and Gabon that attains a length of 1 foot and a weight sometimes exceeding 10 pounds
goliath heron *also* **goliath** *n* **:** a very large chiefly African heron (*Ardea goliath*) having the head, neck, and underparts brown and the back slaty gray
go·li·lla \gəˈlē(y)ə, -ēlyə\ *n* -S [Sp, dim. of *gola* throat, fr. L *gula* — more at GLUTTON] **:** a starched white collar worn by some Spanish magistrates

golilla

goll *n* -S [origin unknown] *obs* **:** HAND
¹**gol·lar** *or* **gol·ler** \ˈgälə(r)\ *vi* -ED/-ING/-S [imit.] **1** *dial Brit*

: to call out in a loud voice : SHOUT, ROAR **2** *dial Brit* : to make a gurgling sound

²**gollar** *or* **goller** \"\ *n* -s **1** *chiefly Scot* : YELL, ROAR **2** *chiefly Scot* : an outburst of hasty words

gol·li·wog *or* **gol·li·wogg** \'gälē,wäg, -li,-\ *n* -s [after *Golliwogg*, an animated doll in books for children written by Bertha Upton †1912 Am. writer and illustrated by Florence Upton †1922 Am. portrait painter and illustrator] **1** : a grotesque black doll ⟨among the dappled rocking horses and ~*s* —Osbert Sitwell⟩ **2** : a grotesque person ⟨she gave one the impression of some blonde ~ —Ion Braby⟩

gol·lop \'gäləp\ *dial var of* GULP

gol·ly \'gälē, -li\ *interj* [euphemism for *God*] — a mild oath

goloch *var of* GOLACH

go·los *or* **go·lus** \'gōləs\ *n* -ES *usu cap* [Yiddish *goles*, fr. Heb *gālūth* exile] : GALUTH

go·losh \gə'läsh\ *chiefly Brit var of* GALOSH

golpe *or* **golp** \'gälp\ *n* -s [prob. fr. Sp *golpe* blow, bruise, fr. LL *colpus* — more at COPE] : a heraldic roundel purpure

gom \'gäm\ *var of* ⁶GAUM

go·ma·ri·an \gō'marēən, -ma(a)r-\ *also* **go·ma·rist** \-'märəst\ *or* **go·ma·rite** \-'mä,rīt\ *n* -s *usu cap* [Franciscus *Gomarus* (Gommer) †1641 Dutch Calvinistic theologian + E *-ian* or *-ist* or *-ite*] : a follower of the Calvinist Gomarus

gom·been \gäm'bēn\ *n* -s [IrGael *gaimbīn*] *Irish* : USURY

gombeen–man \-,man\ *n, pl* **gombeen–men** *Irish* : USURER

¹**gombo** *var of* GUMBO

²**gom·bo** \'gäm(,)bō\ *also* **gombo hemp** *n* -s [Pg *gombó*] : KENAF

gom·broon ware *also* **gom·brun ware** \(')gäm¦brün\ *n* -s *usu cap G* [fr. *Gombroon* (Bandar Abbas), Iran] **1** : a medieval Persian porcellaneous ware with pierced decoration filled by flowing glaze **2** *archaic* : LOWESTOFT WARE **2**

go·mel \'gōməl, 'gȯm-\ *adj, usu cap* [fr. *Gomel*, U.S.S.R.] : of or from the city of Gomel, U.S.S.R. : of the kind or style prevalent in Gomel

gom·er·al *or* **gom·er·el** *or* **gom·er·il** \'gäm(ə)rəl\ *n* -s [origin unknown] *dial chiefly Brit* : SIMPLETON, FOOL ⟨he's a liar and you're a ~ to hearken till him —Sir Walter Scott⟩

gom–gom *var of* GUM-GUM

gom·mi·er \'gämē,ā, 'gəm-, -mə,yā\ *n* -s [F, fr. *gomme* gum — more at GUM] : a Caribbean tree (*Pachylobus excelsa*) of the family Burseraceae that exudes a gum resembling incense

go·mon·tia \gō'mänch(ē)ə\ *n, cap* [NL, fr. Maurice *Gomont*, 19th cent. Fr. botanist + NL *-ia*] : a genus of branching green algae (family Trentepohliaceae) including an alga (*G. polyrhiza*) that bores into marine mussel shells or dead algae and one (*G. lignicola*) that penetrates wood

gom·paauw *also* **gom paw** *or* **gom·pow** \'gäm,paù, -,pō\ *n* -s [Afrik *gompaauw*, *gompou*, fr. *gom* gum (fr. MD, fr. OF *gomme*) + *paauw*, *pou* peafowl, fr. MD *pau*; akin to OE *pēa* peafowl — more at GUM, PEACOCK] : a large bustard (*Choriotis kori*) of southern Africa that feeds chiefly on acacia gum — called also *kori bustard*

gom·pho·car·pus \,gäm(p)fō'kärpəs\ *n, cap* [NL, fr. Gk *gomphos* tooth, peg, bolt, bond + NL *-carpus* — more at COMB] : a large genus of herbs and shrubs (family Asclepiadaceae) of southern Africa having showy flowers with corolla hoods that lack appendages

gom·pho·dont \'gäm(p)fə,dänt\ *adj* [Gk *gomphos* + E *-odont*] : having the teeth implanted in sockets

gom·pho·lo·bi·um \,gäm(p)fə'lōbēəm\ *n, cap* [NL, fr. Gk *gomphos* + *lobos* pod, capsule, lobe + NL *-ium* — more at LOBE] : a genus of Australian shrubs (family Leguminosae) having alternate simple trifoliate leaves and showy flowers with the stamens all free — see POISON BUSH

gom·pho·sis \gäm'fōsəs\ *n* -ES [NL, fr. Gk *gomphōsis*, lit., a bolting together, fr. *gomphoun* to fasten with bolts (fr. *gomphos*) + *-sis*] : a union or immovable articulation in which a hard part is received into a bone cavity (as the teeth into the jaws)

gom·pho·the·ri·idae \,gäm(p)fōthə'rīə,dē\ *n pl, cap* [NL, fr. *Gomphotherium*, type genus + *-idae*] : a family of widely distributed fossil elephants extinct since the Pleistocene

gom·pho·the·ri·um \,gäm(p)fō'thirēəm\ *n, cap* [NL, fr. Gk *gomphos* + NL *-therium*] : a large genus (the type of the family Gomphotheriidae) of extinct elephants widely distributed in the Miocene and Pliocene and distinguished by a greatly elongated lower jaw bearing broad flat terminal tusks shaped like shovels

gom·phre·na \gäm'frēnə\ *n, cap* [NL, alter. of L *gromphaena*, a kind of amaranth] : a genus of tropical herbs or low shrubs (family Amaranthaceae) having opposite leaves and flowers in close heads — see GLOBE AMARANTH

go·mu·ti \gō'müd·ē\ *n* -s [Malay (*pohon*) *gĕmuti*] **1** *also* **gomuti palm** : a Malayan feather palm (*Arenga pinnata*) that has large leaves with the bases densely clothed with fibers, yields a sweet sap from which jaggery and palm wine are made, and has a pith that furnishes a sago **2** : the black wiry fiber obtained from gomuti used esp. for marine cordage and cable

gon \'gän\ *n* -s [short for *gondola*] : a railroad gondola

gon– *or* **gono–** *comb form* [LL *gono*-, fr. Gk *gon*-, *gono*-, fr. *gonos* offspring, procreation, seed, genitals, fr. the stem of *gignesthai* to be born — more at KIN] : sexual : generative : semen : seed ⟨*gon*angium⟩ ⟨*gono*duct⟩

–gon \,gän *sometimes* gən\ *n comb form* -s [NL *-gonum*, fr. Gk *-gōnon*, fr. *gōnia* angle; akin to Gk *gony* knee — more at KNEE] : figure having (so many) angles ⟨nona*gon*⟩

go·nad \'gō,nad *sometimes* 'gä,-\ *n* -s [NL *gonad-*, *gonas*, fr. Gk *gonos*] : a primary sex gland : OVARY, TESTIS — **go·nad·al** \(')gō¦nadᵊl, (')gä¦-\ *adj*

go·nad·ec·to·mize \,gō,nadˈektə,mīz, ¦,nə'd- *sometimes* ,gä¦\ *vt* -ED/-ING/-S : to remove the gonads from

go·nad·ec·to·my \-təmē\ *n* -ES [*gonad* + *-ectomy*] : surgical removal of ovary or testis

gonado·trop·ic \(¦)gō¦nadə¦träpik, -rōp-, (¦)gä¦-, ¦gänədō-¦-\ *or* **gonado·tro·phic** \-¦träfik\ *adj* [ISV *gonad* + *-o-* + *-tropic* or *-trophic*] : acting on or stimulating the gonads ⟨the ~ hormone of the anterior lobe of the pituitary gland⟩

go·nad·o·tro·pin \(,)gō,nadə'trōpən, (,)gä,-, ,gänədō-'-\ *or* **go·nad·o·tro·phin** \-rōfən\ *n* -s [ISV *gonadotropic*, *gonadotrophic* + *-in*] : a gonadotrophic substance (chorionic ~)

gon·a·duct \'gänə,dəkt\ *var of* GONODUCT

gon·a·kie *or* **gon·a·ke** \'gänəkē\ *n* -s [native name in western Africa] : BABUL; *esp* : the pods of babul

go·nan·gi·al \(')gō¦nanjēəl\ *adj* [NL *gonangium* + E *-al*] : of or relating to a gonangium

go·nan·gi·um \-ēəm\ *n, pl* **gonan·gia** \-ēə\ *or* **gonangiums** [NL, fr. *gon-* + *-angium*] **1** : a reproductive member of a hydrozoan colony producing gonophores or medusa buds **2** : GONOTHECA

gon·apophysal \¦gan+\ *or* **gon·apophysial** \(¦)gän+\ *adj* [NL *gonapophysis* + E *-al*] : of, relating to, or constituting a gonapophysis

gon·apophysis \¦gän+\ *n, pl* **gonapophyses** [NL, fr. *gon-* + *apophysis*] : an organ or process of the anal region of an insect that serves in copulation, oviposition, or stinging — used chiefly of such structures when paired and regarded as modified appendages

gon·ca·lo al·ves \gən,salō'alvəs\ *n* [Pg *gonçalo-alves*] **1** : a tall tropical American timber tree (*Astronium fraxinifolium*) of the family Anacardiaceae that is esp. abundant in eastern Brazil **2** : the hard strong durable heavy wood of the goncalo alves that has a straight grain and dark stripes on a yellowish to pinkish ground and is widely used for veneer, fine furniture, and heavy construction where its durability is important — called also *kingwood*, *zebrawood*

gond \'gänd\ *n* -s *usu cap* **1** : a member of a Dravidian or pre-Dravidian people of central India **2** : GONDI

gon·dang \'gän,dan\ *n* -s [Jav *gondang*] : a Javanese fig tree (*Ficus subracemosa*) the latex of which yields a wax

gondang wax *n* : the hard cream-colored wax obtained from the gondang — called also *fig wax*

gondi \'gändē\ *n* -s *usu cap* : the language of the Gonds

gon·do·la \'gändələ, ÷ gän'dōlə, ÷ gən'dō-; *some speakers who use* '≈≈ *for sense 1 use* ≈'≈≈ *for some of the other senses*\ *n* -s [It, fr. MGk *kondoura* small vessel] **1** : a long narrow flat-bottomed boat with a high prow and stern used on the canals of Venice and usu. propelled by a gondolier who stands at the stern facing the prow and usu. sculls with a single long oar **2** *or* **gun·da·low** *or* **gun·de·low** \'gəndə,lō, -n(d),lō\ : a heavy flat-bottomed boat used on New England rivers as a gunboat in the Revolutionary War and subsequently in the barge traffic there and on the Ohio and Mississippi rivers **3** *or* **gondola car** : a railroad car with no top, flat bottom, fixed sides, and sometimes demountable ends that is used chiefly for hauling steel, rock, or heavy bulk commodities **4 a** : an elongated car attached to the underside of an airship **b** : a metallic often spherical airtight enclosure suspended from a balloon for carrying passengers or meteorological or other instruments **5** *or* **gondola chair** : an upholstered chair whose back curves forward at both sides to form the arms **6** : an island fixture used in self-service retail stores to display merchandise **7** : a motor truck or trailer having a large hopper-shaped container for transporting mixed concrete

gondola 1

gon·do·let \¦gändə¦let\ *n* -s [It *gondoletta*, dim. of *gondola*] : a small gondola

gon·do·lier \¦gändə¦li(ə)r, -iə\ *n* -s [F, fr. It *gondoliere*, fr. *gondola* + *-iere* -er] : one who propels a gondola

¹**gone** \'gȯn *also* 'gän\ *adj* [fr. past part. of *go*] **1 a** : PAST ⟨sweet memories of ~ summers —John Cheever⟩ **b** *of an arrow* : having passed above the mark **2 a** : ADVANCED, INVOLVED, ABSORBED ⟨had expected to find her . . . far ~ in hysteria —Frank Yerby⟩ **b** : INFATUATED ⟨in love! she is so far ~ she does not know which way to sail —Edna S. V. Millay⟩ — often used with *on* ⟨was real ~ on that man —Pete Martin⟩ **c** : PREGNANT ⟨a woman seven months ~⟩ **3 a** : DEAD ⟨the stupid inanimate limbs of the ~ wretch —George Meredith⟩ **b** : done for : LOST, RUINED ⟨if he loses the steam and blacks out the ship we're ~ ducks —R.F.Mirvish⟩ **c** *obs* : DRUNK **d** : EXHAUSTED, FATIGUED ⟨nothing like cold spring water to put life back into a poor ~ body —Rebecca Caudill⟩ **e** : SINKING ⟨the empty or ~ feeling in the abdomen so common in elevators —H.G.Armstrong⟩ **4** *slang* : GREAT — used as a generalized expression of approval ⟨the duke qualifies as a real ~ fashion reporter —Inez Robb⟩

²**gone** \'gōn\ *n* -s [Gk *gonē* seed, offspring, fr. the stem of Gk *gignesthai* to be born — more at KIN] : GERM CELL

gone–by \'≈,≈\ *adj* : long past or gone : BYGONE ⟨her gown of a *gone-by* century —Winston Churchill⟩

gonecium *var of* GONOECIUM

gon·ef \'gänəf\ *var of* GANEF

gone feeling *or* **gone sensation** *n* : a feeling of faintness or weakness

gone goose *also* **gone gosling** *n* : a person who is doomed : one in a hopeless predicament ⟨they got me now, boy . . . I'm a *gone goose* —Nathaniel Burt⟩ ⟨when she goes after a man he's a *gone goose* —W.H.Rudkin⟩

gone·ness \'gȯnnəs *also* 'gänn-\ *n* -ES : a state of exhaustion : FAINTNESS

gon·er \'gȯnə(r) *also* 'gän-\ *n* -s [*gone* + *-er*] : one that is irrevocably lost or ruined : one whose fate is sealed : a hopeless case ⟨this ship's a ~ —E.L.Beach⟩ ⟨if you fall behind . . . you're ~*s* —Kenneth Roberts⟩ ⟨felt is the surprise fabric of the season. Just when everybody thought it was a ~ it resurges in new strength —*Women's Wear Daily*⟩

goney *var of* GONY

gon·fa·lon \'gänfə,län, -,lən\ *n* -s [It *gonfalone*, fr. OIt, fr. OF *gonfanon*, *gonfalon* — more at GONFANON] **1** : the ensign or standard in use by certain princes or states (as the medieval republics of Italy) **2** : a flag that hangs from a crosspiece or frame ⟨the state flower was used by the candidate on his guidons and ~*s*⟩

gon·fa·lon·ier \¦gänfə,lä¦ni(ə)r, -,lə¦n-\ *n* -s [It *gonfaloniere*, fr. OIt, fr. OF *gonfanonier*, *gonfalonier*, fr. *gonfanon*, *gonfalon* + *-ier* -er] **1** : one who bears the gonfalon : STANDARD-BEARER; *specif* : a papal official at Rome who bears the standard of the church **2** : the chief magistrate or other official of any of several republics in medieval Italy

gon·fa·lo·nie·re \,≈≈,län'yerē, -,lən-, -e(,)rā\ *n, pl* **gonfa·lonie·ri** \-,rē\ [It] : GONFALONIER

gon·fa·non \'gänfə,nän, -,nən\ *n* -s [ME *gonfanoun*, fr. MF *gonfanon* gonfalon, of Gmc origin; akin to OHG *gundfano* war flag, fr. *gund*- battle, war + *fano* cloth — more at DEFEND, VANE] : GONFALON; *esp* : one beneath the head of a knight's lance

¹**gong** \'gäŋ, 'gȯŋ\ *n* -s [Malay & Jav, of imit. origin] **1** : a bronze plate with upturned rim that gives a subdued but very resonant penetrating sound when struck with a usu. padded hammer — called also *Chinese gong*, *tam-tam* **2 a** *or* **gong bell** : a flat bell resembling a saucer rung by striking it with a small hammer operated by some commonly electric mechanism **b** : a hardened wire rod wound in a flat spiral that is used in clocks and repeating watches to sound the time or chime or alarm

²**gong** \"\ *vi* -ED-ING/-S : to make the sound of a gong ⟨the cemetery bells . . . ~*ed* in the air —Owen Dodson⟩

gong 2a

gong buoy *n* : a buoy equipped with a set of three or four gongs each having a different tone

gon·go·resque \¦gäŋgə¦resk, ¦gȯŋ\ *adj, usu cap* [Luis de *Góngora* y Argote †1627 Span. poet + E *-esque*] : of or relating to the poet Góngora or to Gongorism ⟨putting into verses of *Gongoresque* lineage . . . the authentic qualities of an entirely contemporary emotion —Pedro Salinas⟩

gon·go·rism \'≈≈,rizəm\ *n* -s [Sp *gongorismo*, fr. Luis de *Góngora* y Argote + Sp *-ismo* -ism] **1** *usu cap* : a Spanish literary style esp. associated with the poet Góngora and his imitators characterized by a studied obscurity of meaning and expression and by extensive use of metaphorical imagery, exaggerated conceits, paradoxes, neologisms, and other ornate devices — compare EUPHUISM **2 a** : an excessively involved, ornate, and artificial style of writing ⟨her sheer virtuosity as a creator of images seems on the verge of ~ —*Saturday Rev.*⟩ **b** : an instance of such a style ⟨a swaggering rhetorician who . . . has to stop and search for the appropriate ~ —Malcolm Cowley⟩ — **gon·go·ris·tic** \¦≈≈¦ristik\ *adj*

gon·gy·lo·ne·ma \,gänjəlō'nēmə\ *n, cap* [NL, fr. Gk *gongylos* round + NL *-nema*] : a genus of spiruroid nematodes (family Thelaziidae) infesting the tissues of the digestive tract of various mammals and birds including man

goni– *or* **gonio–** *comb form* [Gk *gōnia* — more at -GON] **1** : corner : angle ⟨*gonio*meter⟩ **2** : gonion

gonia *pl of* GONION *or of* GONIUM

go·ni·al \'gōnēəl\ *also* **go·ni·ac** \-ē,ak\ *adj* [*goni-* + *-al* or *-ac* (as in *maniac*)] **1** : of or relating to the gonion **2** : of or relating to gones or gonia

go·ni·as·ter \¦gōnē¦astə(r)\ *n, cap* [NL, fr. *goni-* + *-aster*] : a common genus (the type of the family Goniasteridae) of cushion stars consisting of nearly pentagonal, rigid, and often brightly colored starfishes

go·ni·a·tite \'gōnēə,tīt\ *n* -s [NL *Goniatites*] : an ammonoid of the genus *Goniatites* or family Goniatitidae

go·ni·a·ti·tes \,≈≈≈'tīd·(,)ēz\ *n, cap* [NL, irreg. fr. Gk *gōnia* angle] : a genus (the type of the family Goniatitidae) of ammonoids widespread in the Devonian and the Carboniferous and having a discoidal coiled shell with angular-lobed sutures — **go·ni·a·tit·ic** \¦≈≈≈'tid·ik\ *adj* — **go·ni·ati·tid** \¦≈≈≈'tid·əd\ *n* -s — **gon·i·a·ti·toid** \¦≈≈≈'tīd·,ȯid\ *adj or n*

go·ni·au·lax \,gōnē'ō,laks\ *syn of* GONYAULAX

gon·i·dan·gi·um \,gänə'danjēəm\ *n, pl* **gonidan·gia** \-ēə\ [NL, fr. *gonidium* + *-angium*] : a sporangium that contains or produces gonidia

gonidi– *or* **gonidio–** *comb form* [NL *gonidium*] : gonidium ⟨*gonidio*genous⟩

gonidia *pl of* GONIDIUM

go·nid·i·al \gō'nidēəl\ *also* **go·nid·ic** \-dik\ *adj* [*gonidi-* + *-al* or *-ic*] : relating to, consisting of, or containing a gonidium

gonidial layer *n* : a layer of green chlorophyll-bearing cells found within the thallus of a lichen

go·nid·i·oid \-dē,ȯid\ *adj* [*gonidi-* + *-oid*] : resembling or having the nature of gonidia

go·nid·i·um \gō'nidēəm\ *n, pl* **gonid·ia** \-ēə\ [NL, fr. *gon-* + *-idium*] **1 a** : an asexual reproductive cell or group of cells arising in or on the gametophyte usu. in special organs — see GONIDANGIUM **b** : one of the green chlorophyll-bearing cells that are found within the thallus of a lichen and that sometimes constitute a definite layer but are often scattered — called also *brood cell* **2** : one of the supposed reproductive granules formed internally in certain bacteria (as of the genus *Azotobacter*)

–gonies *pl of* -GONY

gon·if *or* **gon·iff** \'gänəf\ *var of* GANEF

gon·i·mo·blast \'gänəmō,blast\ *n* [Gk *gonimos* productive (fr. stem of *gignesthai* to be born) + E *-blast* — more at KIN] : one of the sporogenous filaments which arise from the fertilized carpogonium in most red algae; *also* : the aggregation of such filaments

gon·i·mo·lobe \-,lōb\ *n* [*gonimo*blast + *lobe*] : the terminal cell of a gonimoblast that produces a carpospore

go·ni·o·co·tes \,gōnēə'kōd·(,)ēz\ *n, cap* [NL, fr. *goni-* + *-cotes* (fr. Gk *kotis*, *kottis* occiput)] : a genus of bird lice attacking various wild and domestic birds — see FLUFF LOUSE

go·ni·o·des \,gōnē'ō(,)dēz\ *n, cap* [NL, fr. *goni-* + *-odes*] : a genus of biting lice attacking various wild and domestic birds

go·ni·om·e·ter \,gōnē'ämәd·ə(r)\ *n* [*goni-* + *-meter*] **1** : an instrument for measuring angles (as in surveying, anthropometry, or mineralogy) **2 a** : a mutual inductor with a rotatable secondary coil connected to one or more antennas **b** : DIRECTION FINDER **3** : an instrument with which the range of motion in a joint is measured

go·ni·o·met·ric \¦gōnēə¦me·trik\ *also* **go·ni·o·met·ri·cal** \-rəkəl\ *adj* : of or relating to goniometry : relating to or determined with a goniometer — **go·ni·o·met·ri·cal·ly** \-rək(ə)lē\ *adv*

go·ni·om·e·try \,gōnē'ämə·trē\ *n* -ES [F *goniométrie*, fr. *gonio-* goni- + *-métrie* -metry] : measurement of angles

go·ni·on \'gōnē,än\ *n, pl* **go·nia** \-ēə\ [NL, fr. Gk *gōnia* angle — more at -GON] : the point at the angle of the human lower jaw on each side — see CRANIOMETRY illustration

go·ni·o·ne·mus \,gōnēə'nēməs\ *n, cap* [NL, fr. *goni-* + *-nemus* (fr. *nēma* thread)] : a genus of small cosmopolitan hydrozoan jellyfishes (order Trachomedusae)

go·ni·oph·o·lis \,gōnē'äfələs\ *n, cap* [NL, fr. *goni-* + Gk *pholis* horny scale — more at PHOLID-] : a genus of extinct crocodiles with amphicoelous vertebrae known from remains found in the Upper Jurassic of Europe and No. America

go·nio·photometer \¦gōnē(,)ō+\ *n* [*goni-* + *photometer*] : a photometer for measuring the intensity of light specularly or diffusely reflected at different angles from a surface — **go·nio·photometric** \"+\ *adj*

go·ni·o·scope \'gōnēə,skōp\ *n* [*goni-* + *-scope*] : an instrument consisting of a contact lens to be fitted over the cornea and an optical system with which the interior of the eye can be viewed — **go·ni·o·scop·ic** \¦≈≈≈¦skäpik\ *adj* — **go·ni·os·co·py** \,gōnē'äskəpē\ *n* -ES

go·ni·o·stat \'gōnēə,stat\ *n* -s [*goni-* + *-stat*] : a device used in cutting gem facets

go·ni·tis \gō'nīd·əs\ *n* -ES [NL, fr. Gk *gony* knee + NL *-itis* — more at KNEE] : inflammation of the knee

¹**go·ni·um** \'gōnēəm\ *n, cap* [NL, fr. Gk *gōnia* angle, corner — more at -GON] : a genus of colonial plantlike flagellates related to *Volvox* and forming small flat colonies of biflagellate cells

²**gonium** \"\ *n, pl* **go·nia** \-ēə\ *also* **goniums** [NL, fr. *gon-* + *-ium*] : an undifferentiated primitive germ cell : OOGONIUM, SPERMATOGONIUM — often used in combination ⟨arche*gonium*⟩ ⟨spermato*gonium*⟩

gon·nard·ite \'gänə(r),dīt\ *n* -s [F *gonnardite*, fr. Ferdinand *Gonnard*, 19th cent. Fr. mineralogist + F *-ite*] : a mineral approximately $Na_2CaAl_4Si_6O_{20}.7H_2O$ consisting of a zeolite and occurring in radiating spherules (sp. gr. 2.3)

gono– — see GON-

gon·o·blas·tid·i·al \¦gänō¦bla¦stidēəl\ *adj* [NL *gonoblastidium* + E *-al*] : of or relating to a gonoblastidium

gon·o·blas·tid·i·um \,≈≈¦≈'≈≈əm\ *also* **gon·o·blas·tid** \¦gänō'blastəd\ *n, pl* **gonoblastid·ia** \-ēə\ *also* **gonoblastids** [NL *gonoblastidium*, fr. *gon-* + Gk *blastos* sprout + NL *-idium*] : BLASTOSTYLE

gon·o·cho·ric \¦gänə¦kōrik\ *adj* : having the sexes separate : not hermaphroditic : DIOECIOUS

gon·o·cho·rism \¦gänə¦kōr,izəm\ *n* -s [ISV *gon-* + *-chorism* (fr. Gk *chōrismos* separation, fr. *chōrizein* to separate); orig. formed as G *gonochorismus* — more at CHORISIS] **1** : DIOECISM **2** : the development or evolution of sex — **gon·o·cho·ris·mal** \¦gänəkō¦rizməl\ *adj*

gon·o·cho·rist \¦gänə¦kōrəst\ *n* -s [ISV *gon-* + *-chorist* (fr. Gk *chōristos* separable, fr. *chōrizein* to separate) orig. formed in G] : a dioecious individual or race; *esp* : one in which sex is determined by developmental rather than hereditary mechanisms — **gon·o·cho·ris·tic** \¦gänəkō¦ristik\ *adj*

gon·o·coc·cal \¦gänə¦käkəl\ *or* **gon·o·coc·cic** \-'käk(s)ik\ *adj* [NL *gonococcus* + E *-al* or *-ic*] : of, relating to, or caused by gonococci

gon·o·coc·cus \,≈≈'käkəs\ *n, pl* **gonococ·ci** \-ä,kī, -ä(,)kē, -äk,sī, -äk(,)sē\ *sometimes cap* [NL, fr. *gon-* + *-coccus*] : a pus-producing bacterium (*Neisseria gonorrhoeae*) that causes gonorrhea

gon·o·coel *or* **gon·o·coele** \'gänə,sēl\ *n* -s [*gon-* + *-coel*, *-coele*] : the body cavity that contains the gonads and that is sometimes considered the evolutionary precursor of the entire coelom of higher animals

gon·o·cox·ite \,gänə'käk,sīt\ *n* -s [*gon-* + L *coxa* hip + E *-ite*] : the inner segment of a gonapophysis

gon·o·cyte \'gänə,sīt\ *n* -s [ISV *gon-* + *-cyte*] : a cell that produces gametes : GAMETOCYTE

gon·o·duct *also* **gon·a·duct** \'gänə,dəkt\ *n* [*gonoduct* fr. *gon-* + *duct*; *gonaduct* blend of *gonad* and *duct*] : the duct of a gonad being often coextensive in whole or in part with the excretory duct of a nephron

go·noe·ci·um *also* **go·ne·ci·um** \gə'nēs(h)ēəm, gä'-,gō'-\ *n, pl* **gonoe·cia** \-ēə\ [NL, fr. *gon-* + Gk *oikia* house + NL *-ium* — more at VICINITY] : one of the modified reproductive zooecia of a bryozoan

gon·of *or* **gon·oph** \'gänəf\ *var of* GANEF

gono·genesis \¦gänō+\ *n* [NL, fr. *gon-* + *genesis*] : the maturation of germ cells : OOGENESIS, SPERMATOGENESIS

go no–go gage *or* **go not–go gage** \'≈'≈,≈-\ *n* : a set of two complementary limit gages consisting of a go gage and a no-go gage

go·nol·o·bus \gō'näləbəs\ *n, cap* [NL, fr. *gon-* + *-lobus*] : a genus of American herbaceous vines (family Asclepiadaceae) with opposite cordate leaves, small whitish flowers in axillary clusters, and erect follicles

gon·o·mere \'gänə,mi(ə)r\ *n* -s [ISV *gon-* + *-mere*] : a pronucleus retaining its identity for a time during cleavage — **gon·o·mer·ic** \¦gänə¦merik\ *adj*

gon·om·ery \gō'nämərē\ *n* -ES [ISV *gon-* + *-mery*] : the state or condition in which gonomeres are present

gon·o·phore \'gänə,fō(ə)r\ *n* -s [ISV *gon-* + *-phore*] **1** : a sporophyll-bearing prolongation of the axis **2** : a reproductive zooid of a hydroid colony representing the free-swimming medusa stage but differing from a medusa in remaining attached to the hydroid stock — see SPOROSAC — **gon·o·phor·ic** \¦≈≈'fōrik\ *adj* — **go·noph·o·rous** \gō'näf(ə)rəs\ *adj*

gon·o·plasm \'gänə,plazəm\ *n* [*gon-* + *-plasm*] : the part of the protoplasm of the antheridium that enters into zygote formation in fungi of the family Peronosporaceae — compare PERIPLASM

gon·o·pod \-,päd\ *n* -s [*gon-* + *-pod*] : an appendage in many arthropods modified to serve as a copulatory organ

gon·o·po·di·al \¦gänə¦pōdēəl\ *also* **gon·o·po·dal** \-dᵊl, gə'näpədᵊl\ *adj* [NL *gonopodium* + E *-al*] : of, relating to, or being a gonopodium

gon·o·po·di·um \,gänə'pōdēəm\ *n* [NL, fr. *gon-* + *podium*] : the anal fin of a male fish when modified to serve as a copulatory organ

gono·poietic \¦gänə+\ *adj* [*gon-* + *-poietic*] : productive of germ cells

gon·o·pore \'gänə,pō(ə)r\ *n* [*gon-* + *pore*] : a genital pore

gon·o·rhyn·chus \\,gänə'riŋkəs\\ *n, cap* [NL, irreg. fr. *goni-* + *-rhynchus*] **:** a genus of slender cylindrical marine fishes without adipose fin, air bladder, or teeth that constitutes a family (Gonorhynchidae) and is the sole surviving representative of a distinct suborder of the order Isospondyli

gon·or·rhea *also* **gon·or·rhoea** \\,gänə'rēə\\ *n* -s [NL, fr. LL, spermatorrhea, blennorrhea, fr. Gk *gonorrhoia*, fr. *gon-* + *-rrhoia* -rrhea] **:** a contagious inflammation of the genital mucous membrane caused by the gonococcus — called also *clap* — **gon·or·rhe·al** *also* **gon·or·rhoe·al** \\¦==¦=əl\\ *adj*

gon·o·some \\'gänə,sōm\\ *n* -s [*gon-* + *-some*] **:** the totality of reproductive zooids of a hydroid — compare TROPHOSOME

gon·o·sto·mat·i·dae \\,gänəstō'mad·ə,dē\\ *n pl, cap* [NL, fr. *Gonostomat-*, *Gonostoma*, type genus (fr. *gon-* + *stomat-*, *stoma* mouth) + *-idae* — more at STOMACH] **:** a small family of slender elongate deep-sea isospondylous fishes of the Pacific and Indian oceans — compare VIPERFISH

gon·o·the·ca \\,gänə'thēkə\\ *n, pl* **gonothe·cae** \\-ē(,)sē\\ [NL, fr. *gon-* + *-theca*] **:** the protective covering of a gonangium — **gon·o·the·cal** \\¦==¦=,kəl\\ *adj*

go·not·o·kont *or* **go·not·o·cont** \\gō'näd·ə,känt\\ *n* -s [*gon-* + Gk *tokōnt-*, *tokōn*, pres. part. of *tokan* to be near delivery; akin to Gk *teknon* child — more at THANE] **1 :** GONOCYTE **2 :** a cell or organ in which meiosis occurs

gon·o·tome \\'gänə,tōm\\ *n* -s [ISV *gon-* + *-tome*] **:** the portion of a somite that participates in gonad formation

gon·o·tyl \\'gänə,til\\ *n* -s [*gon-* + Gk *tylos* knob, penis — more at THOLE] **:** a sucker surrounding the genital opening and often intimately associated with the acetabulum of certain trematode worms

gono·zooid \\¦gänə+\\ *n* [*gon-* + *zooid*] **1 a :** a sexual zooid or medusa bud of a hydroid **:** GONOPHORE **b :** a sexual zooid of a tunicate **2 :** OVICELL

gons *pl of* GON

-gons *pl of* -GON

go·ny *or* **go·ney** \\'gōni, 'gȯ-\\ *n, pl* **gonies** *or* **goneys** [origin unknown] **1** *dial chiefly Brit* **:** BOOBY, DUNCE **2 :** GOONEY

-go·ny \\gənē, -ni\\ *n comb form* -ES [L *-gonia*, fr. Gk *goneia*, fr. *gonos* offspring, procreation, seed + *-eia* -y — more at GON-] **:** generation, reproduction, or manner of coming into being of a (specified) thing ⟨cosmo*gony*⟩ ⟨sporo*gony*⟩ ⟨theo*gony*⟩

go·ny·au·lax \\,gōnē'ȯ,laks\\ *n* [NL, fr. Gk *gony* knee + *aulax* furrow — more at KNEE] **1** *cap* **:** a large genus of phosphorescent marine dinoflagellates that when unusually abundant cause red tide and a serious mussel poisoning of man — see MUSSEL POISONING **2** -ES **:** any member of the genus *Gonyaulax*

go·nys \\'gōnəs\\ *n* -ES [NL, prob. modif. of Gk *genys* jaw, cheek — more at CHIN] **:** the prominent ridge along the line of union of the two halves of the lower mandible of certain birds (as the gulls)

go·ny·sty·lus \\,gōnə'stīləs\\ *n, cap* [NL, fr. Gk *gony* knee + *stylos* pillar; fr. the geniculate styles — more at KNEE, STEER] **:** a small genus of East Indian trees (order Malvales) constituting a monotypic family, having alternate leathery leaves, regular paniculate flowers and woody fruits, and yielding fragrant timber resembling agalloch

1**goo** \\'gü\\ *n* -s [F *goût* — more at GOÛT] **1** *chiefly Scot* **a :** a strong taste **b :** a disagreeable smell **2** *chiefly Scot* **:** LIKING, PREFERENCE, TASTE

2**goo** \\"\\ *n* -s [by shortening & alter. fr. *gaspergou*] **:** FRESHWATER DRUM

3**goo** \\"\\ *n* -s [perh. alter. of 1*glue*] **1 :** a viscid or sticky substance ⟨wash that ~ off your hair —Nancy Rutledge⟩ ⟨whisks away dirt and ~ in seconds —*advt*⟩ **2 :** sickly or cloying sentimentality ⟨of all the silly ~ —J.U.Newman⟩ ⟨the mental and aesthetic ~ . . . remains a bad taste in the mouth —Jay Leyda⟩

goober \\'gübə(r), 'gu̇b-\\ *or* **goober pea** *n* -s [of African origin; akin to Kimbundu *nguba* peanut, Kongo, kidney, peanut] *South & Midland* **:** PEANUT

gooch crucible *or* **gooch filter** \\'güch-\\ *n, usu cap G* [after Frank A. *Gooch* †1929 Am. chemist] **:** a small crucible with perforated bottom in which precipitates can be collected (as by the use of fine asbestos), dried, and weighed

1**good** \\'gu̇d, *in formulas of meeting & parting often* ,gəd\\ *adj* **bet·ter** \\'bed·ə(r), -etə-\\ **best** \\'best\\ [ME, fr. OE *gōd;* akin to OHG *guot* good, ON *gōthr*, Goth *goths* good, OFris *gadia* to unite, OHG bi*gatōn* to fit together, gi*gat* fitting, Skt *gadh* to hold fast; basic meaning: uniting, fitting] **1 a** (1) **:** having a favorable or auspicious character **:** PROSPEROUS, BENEFICIAL ⟨sailed for France with a ~ wind⟩ ⟨when the moon is ~ . . . they often pursue the chase far into the night —James Stevenson-Hamilton⟩ ⟨the country is enjoying ~ times⟩ ⟨the company has had a ~ year⟩ (2) **:** conveying or reporting what is favorable or fortunate **:** WELCOME ⟨have you heard the ~ news⟩ (3) **:** producing, marked by, or favorable to a bountiful yield or a yield of high quality **:** FERTILE ⟨the land around here is not very ~⟩ ⟨wine of a ~ recent year⟩ (4) **:** favorably affecting one's interests **:** leading to or attended by a favorable or prosperous outcome ⟨as his ~ fortune would have it⟩ ⟨wished him ~ luck⟩ (5) **:** marked by or conveying approval or commendation ⟨sought to win my ~ opinion⟩ ⟨had a ~ report on his work⟩ ⟨had not one ~ word to say about him⟩ (6) **:** making a favorable impression with respect to moral character **:** inspiring trust ⟨he had a ~ face; I instinctively liked him⟩ (7) **:** making a favorable impression with respect to appearance or other physical traits **:** COMELY, ATTRACTIVE, BEAUTIFUL ⟨had a ~ face and figure⟩ ⟨she's certainly ~ to look at⟩ ⟨had lost her ~ looks⟩ ⟨an early Georgian manor of distinguished ~ looks —H.H.Johnston⟩ (8) **:** BECOMING, APPROPRIATE ⟨don't like that dress . . . it isn't ~ for you —Elizabeth Hardwick⟩ (9) **:** reserved for special occasions **:** not shabby or worn **:** BEST ⟨he's got one ~ suit —James Sheldrake⟩ ⟨she wore her ~ dress⟩ **b** (1) **:** adapted to the end designed or proposed **:** satisfactory in performance **:** free from flaws or defects **:** USEFUL, SUITABLE, FIT ⟨this light is ~ for reading⟩ ⟨a ~ car⟩ ⟨this liquor . . . will keep ~ for a long time —*Encyc. Americana*⟩ ⟨is this fruit ~ to eat⟩ (2) **:** not impaired **:** SOUND ⟨this missing eye had more expression than the . . . ~ one —Vicki Baum⟩ ⟨had to do everything with his one ~ arm⟩ ⟨your hearing is ~⟩ ⟨enjoying ~ health⟩ (3) **:** not downcast or dejected **:** amiably cheerful **:** SUNNY, SMILING ⟨found him in a ~ mood⟩ ⟨his ~ humor is infectious⟩ ⟨trying to put a ~ face on your wretchedness —William Black⟩ (4) **:** not counterfeit **:** GENUINE ⟨insisted the new car was financed with ~ money —*Springfield* (*Mass.*) *Union*⟩ **:** not depreciated ⟨bad money drives ~ money out of circulation⟩ (5) **:** commercially sound or reliable ⟨a ~ debt⟩ ⟨a ~ risk⟩ ⟨a ~ check⟩ (6) **:** having a useful life of a specified duration **:** certain to last or live for a specified term — used with *for* ⟨most swords . . . were ~ only for half a dozen hard blows —Tom Wintringham⟩ ⟨the old fellow is ~ for another 30 years⟩ ⟨from the feel of it, the storm would be ~ for three days —Robert Murphy⟩ (7) **:** having the assured capacity or willingness to pay or contribute a specified amount — used with *for* ⟨is ~ for a cool million⟩ ⟨confident his friend would be ~ for a few hundred —Henry Miller⟩ (8) **:** certain to elicit or produce a specified result — used with *for* ⟨the very sound of the word was always ~ for a laugh —Alfred Kazin⟩ ⟨that is ~ for a three months' debate by itself —*New Republic*⟩ (9) **:** PROFITABLE, LUCRATIVE, ADVANTAGEOUS ⟨made a very ~ deal⟩ — often used in the phrase *good thing* ⟨knew they were onto a ~ thing —Bryan Morgan⟩ and esp. in the phrase *make a good thing of* ⟨was supposed to be making a ~ thing out of it —Hamilton Basso⟩ ⟨British authors . . . made a ~ thing of coming over here —Richard Joseph⟩ **c** (1) **:** suited to give or giving pleasure **:** AGREEABLE, PLEASANT ⟨all had a ~ time⟩ ⟨a ~ dinner⟩ ⟨we enjoyed your ~ company⟩ (2) **:** tending to promote well-being or health **:** SALUTARY, WHOLESOME — used chiefly with *for* ⟨sunshine and fresh air are ~ for one⟩ ⟨this is ~ medicine for a cold⟩ (3) **:** entertaining by its wit or sparkle **:** AMUSING, CLEVER, FUNNY ⟨a ~ joke⟩ ⟨he got off some ~ cracks⟩ ⟨that's a ~ one⟩ **d** (1) **:** not small or insignificant **:** comfortably large **:** CONSIDERABLE ⟨quite a ~ crowd down here today —Greville Texidor⟩ ⟨outpointed the three-time national champion . . . by a ~ margin —*Current Biog.*⟩ ⟨made a ~ profit⟩ (2) **:** allowing enough time and usu. to spare **:** sufficiently early **:** AMPLE ⟨hoped to be . . . home in ~ time for 7:30 supper —Dorothy Sayers⟩ ⟨help came in ~ season⟩ (3) **:** FULL — used as a qualifier to indicate a quantity not less and generally greater than the stated figure ⟨the earrings are a ~ inch long —Lois Long⟩ ⟨she was making a ~ twenty-five knots —Wirt Williams⟩ ⟨weighs a ~ 200 pounds —*Current Biog.*⟩ ⟨a ~ four hours nightly —Eleanor S. Lowman⟩ (4) — used as an intensive ⟨took to reading in ~ earnest⟩ ⟨I have known him for a ~ many years⟩ ⟨dealt him a ~ stiff blow⟩ ⟨I didn't give a ~ continental —Eudora Welty⟩ (5) **:** half resolved or fixed upon ⟨I got a ~ mind not to tell you —J.G. Cozzens⟩ ⟨she had a ~ notion to thrash the boy⟩ **e** (1) **:** having a basis in fact or logic **:** WELL-FOUNDED, COGENT ⟨had ~ reason to distrust him⟩ ⟨offered some ~ arguments in debate⟩ ⟨gave a ~ excuse for his lateness⟩ (2) **:** not disproved or refuted — often used in the phrase *hold good* ⟨it will hold ~ when hundreds of cleverer . . . systems have vanished —J.C. Powys⟩ ⟨the same thing holds ~ for society at large —J.J. Chapman⟩ (3) **:** not potential or possible but actual **:** existing in fact **:** REAL ⟨the much-boosted prospect of oil . . . has not come ~ —*Sydney (Australia) Bull.*⟩ — often used in the phrase *make good* ⟨has made his promises ~⟩ (4) **:** having binding effect or force **:** RECOGNIZED, HONORED ⟨this offer is ~ only on orders sent direct to the publisher —*Current History*⟩ ⟨coupons ~ . . . at the local photographers —*Current Biog.*⟩ ⟨a refreshment coupon ~ for either a drink or a cigar —C.F. Wittke⟩ ⟨a union member in ~ standing⟩ (5) **:** valid or effectual for the transfer of title or the creation or vesting of rights ⟨a ~ deed⟩ ⟨a ~ tender⟩ ⟨a ~ delivery⟩ (6) **:** TRUE 3b(1); *also* **:** VALID 5 (7) **:** landing within the proper part of the court esp. in racket and net games and therefore in play — used esp. of a ball **f** (1) **:** conforming to the needs or requirements of the case **:** ADEQUATE, SUFFICIENT, SATISFACTORY ⟨took ~ care of his men⟩ ⟨gave a ~ account of himself in battle⟩ ⟨fetched him a ~ blow⟩ ⟨made ~ speed on the homeward journey⟩ ⟨sentimental history . . . revels in a ~ cry —Albert Guerard⟩ ⟨made ~ use of his time⟩ ⟨let me have a ~ look at you —T.B.Costain⟩ (2) **:** conforming to or attaining a certain standard of correctness, competence, skill, or excellence ⟨speaks ~ English⟩ ⟨plays a ~ game of tennis⟩ ⟨~ but not brilliant verse⟩ ⟨~ manners⟩ ⟨~ form⟩ (3) **:** DISCRIMINATING, CHOICE ⟨he shows unerring ~ taste⟩ (4) **:** better than average but short of excellent — used of scholastic work (5) **:** containing more lean muscle and less fat than higher grades — used of meat, esp. beef **2 a** (1) **:** conforming to a certain ideal or standard of morality or virtue **:** wholly commendable **:** VIRTUOUS, PURE ⟨~ works⟩ ⟨a truly ~ man⟩ ⟨a ~ conscience⟩ ⟨would only date ~ girls⟩ ⟨~ conduct is its own reward⟩; *specif* **:** possessing either absolute or intrinsic value (2) **:** conforming to some abstract standard or ideal (as of prudent conduct or proper condition) **:** RIGHT, DESIRABLE, WISE ⟨do what you think ~⟩ ⟨it is not ~ to fritter away one's time⟩ ⟨it is ~ to love and be loved⟩ (3) **:** directed or tending toward the welfare of another **:** BENEVOLENT, FRIENDLY, AMIABLE ⟨be ~ enough to answer this letter promptly⟩ ⟨did me a ~ turn⟩ ⟨~ intentions⟩ ⟨you have my ~ wishes⟩ ⟨sought to restore ~ feeling between England and her colonies⟩ (4) **:** well-regarded **:** being without stain **:** FAIR, HONORABLE ⟨a ~ name⟩ (5) **:** well-behaved **:** DECOROUS ⟨now, be a ~ boy⟩ (6) **:** not sulky **:** not rancorous nor given to complaint **:** not troublesome **:** GRACIOUS ⟨a ~ loser⟩ ⟨a ~ patient⟩ **b** (1) **:** belonging to the aristocracy or socially distinguished class **:** NOBLE, RESPECTABLE ⟨sardonic jabs at smug ~ families —Margaret Willis⟩ ⟨~ blood flowed in his veins —Frank Yerby⟩ **:** conferring or enhancing social prestige or respectability ⟨a comparatively new family . . . but had made ~ marriages —A.I.Macnaghten⟩ ⟨would need an apartment with a ~ address —Morley Callaghan⟩ (2) *archaic* **:** WORSHIPFUL, WORTHY — used as a conventional epithet in addressing persons of high rank (3) **:** DEAR, KIND, EXCELLENT — used as a conventional epithet in courteous address or respectful reference ⟨my ~ sir⟩ (4) — used of a ship or town as a conventional epithet ⟨the ~ town of Edinburgh⟩ ⟨sailed on the ~ ship *Enterprise*⟩ (5) *chiefly Scot* **:** standing in the relationship of an in-law of a specified kind ⟨~ brother⟩ ⟨~ sister⟩ **c** (1) **:** having or demonstrating the qualities or skills requisite or appropriate in a specified capacity or occupation ⟨a ~ doctor⟩ ⟨a ~ soldier⟩ ⟨a ~ housewife⟩ (2) **:** COMPETENT, SKILLFUL, ADROIT ⟨very ~ with children⟩ ⟨~ at tennis⟩ ⟨very ~ at dancing⟩ (3) **:** sound or faithful in doctrine or belief **:** ORTHODOX ⟨a ~ Catholic⟩ — **as good as** *prep* **:** faithful to ⟨a man *as good as* his word⟩ ⟨*as good as* his promise⟩ — **as good as gold 1 :** of the highest worth or reliability ⟨his promise is *as good as gold*⟩ **2 :** exemplary in deportment **:** well-behaved ⟨the child was *as good as gold*⟩ — **good and** *adv* **:** VERY, ENTIRELY, THOROUGHLY — used as an intensive ⟨was *good and* mad⟩ ⟨went up on deck when he was *good and* ready —William Irish⟩

2**good** \\"\\ *n* -s [ME, fr. OE *gōd*, fr. *gōd*, adj.] **1 a :** something that possesses desirable qualities, promotes success, welfare, or happiness, or is otherwise beneficial ⟨teach a child to know ~ from evil⟩ **b :** something that satisfies or commends itself to the ethical consciousness or is conceived as fitting in the moral order of the universe: (1) **:** something that is either an end in itself or a means to such an end ⟨among the concrete ~*s* traditionally nominated for the position of highest ~ of all . . . are happiness and self-realization —Lucius Garvin⟩ (2) **:** the character of human beings or of their attitudes, motives, and actions that is morally praiseworthy — compare ETHICS **c :** the good element or portion of anything ⟨cherished the ~ in him, overlooking the bad⟩ **2 :** advancement of interest or happiness **:** WELFARE, PROSPERITY, ADVANTAGE, BENEFIT ⟨worked for the ~ of the whole community⟩ ⟨what is the ~ of idle debate⟩ **3 a :** a particular advantage or benefit **:** an object of desire or endeavor **:** something beneficial; *specif* **:** something that has economic utility or satisfies an economic want **b goods** *pl* **:** tangible movable personal property having intrinsic value usu. excluding money and other choses in action but sometimes including all personal property and occas. including vessels and even industrial crops or emblements, buildings, or other things affixed to real estate but agreed to be severed **:** chattels, wares, merchandise, food products, chemical compounds, and agricultural products ⟨household ~*s*⟩ ⟨baked ~*s*⟩ **c goods** *pl but sometimes sing in constr* **:** CLOTH — compare DRESS GOODS, DRY GOODS **d goods** *pl, Brit* **:** FREIGHT ⟨heavier classes of ~*s* vehicles⟩ ⟨a ~*s* train⟩ **e goods** *pl* **:** the contents of the mash tub when the mashing process in brewing has been completed **f :** official grade for meat of medium quality **4 a :** good persons — used with *the* ⟨the ~ die young⟩ **b :** one that is good ⟨if it's any ~ you'll pay a lot for it⟩ ⟨she was no particular ~ —Ethel Wilson⟩ ⟨that's no ~; it won't work⟩ ⟨I have no use for him; he's no ~⟩ **5 goods** *pl but sometimes sing in constr* **a :** something that comes up to expectations or requirements **:** the genuine article ⟨a youthful work . . . but it is the ~*s* —Arnold Bennett⟩ **b :** the qualities required of one or necessary to accomplish a desired end ⟨that boy has the ~*s*⟩ **c :** evidence or proof of wrongdoing ⟨didn't have the ~*s* on him —T.G.Cooke⟩ — **for good** *also* **for good and all** *adv* **:** completely and finally **:** FOREVER, FULLY ⟨fearful of losing their jobs *for good* —Meridel Le Sueur⟩ — **in good with** *prep* **:** in a favored or preferred position with ⟨another effort . . . to get *in good with* their new masters —A.M.Schlesinger b.1917⟩ — **to the good 1 :** for the best **:** BENEFICIAL ⟨the government's efforts to restrict credit were all *to the good* —*Time*⟩ ⟨all this is *to the good* —Sir Winston Churchill⟩ **2 :** in a position of net gain or profit ⟨he wound up the game $10 *to the good*⟩ ⟨two wins in the home-and-home series put the team 4 points *to the good*⟩

3**good** \\"\\ *adv* **better** \\"\\ **best** \\"\\ [ME, fr. *good*, adj.] **1 a :** in a satisfactory, competent, or adequate manner **:** WELL ⟨he showed me how ~ I was doing —Herbert Gold⟩ ⟨worked here once and did real ~⟩ ⟨don't you hear so ~, teacher —W.B.Marsh⟩ — not often in formal use **b :** PROSPEROUSLY, NICELY ⟨hope you . . . are well and getting along ~ —Walt Whitman⟩ **2** *chiefly dial* **:** TOTALLY, THOROUGHLY, COMPLETELY ⟨when it got ~ dark —F.B.Gipson⟩ — **as good :** equally well ⟨*as good* almost kill a man as . . . a good book —John Milton⟩ — **as good as** *adv* **:** in effect **:** APPROXIMATELY, PRACTICALLY, VIRTUALLY ⟨he is *as good as* dead⟩

good afternoon *interj* — used conventionally as an utterance on meeting or parting in the afternoon

good-afternoon \\(,)=,=='=\\ *n* [*good afternoon*] **:** a remark on meeting or parting in the afternoon

good and lawful *adj, of a member of a grand jury* **:** having every statutory as well as common-law qualification required

good behavior *n* **:** proper or correct conduct or deportment ⟨his sentence was reduced for *good behavior* —*N.Y. Times*⟩ ⟨shall hold their offices during *good behavior* —*U.S. Constitution*⟩ — **on one's good behavior** *or* **upon one's good behavior 1 :** in a state of trial with the final disposition dependent upon proper conduct **2 :** well-behaved

1**good-bye** *or* **good-by** \\gu̇d'bī, gəd'bī, gə'bī, 'bī\\ *interj* [contr. of *God be with you*] — used conventionally as a concluding utterance at parting or often at closing a telephone conversation

2**good-bye** *or* **good-by** \\gu̇d'bī, gəd-, *attrib* " *or* 'gu̇d,bī\\ *n, pl* **good-byes** *or* **good-bys** *often attrib* **1 a :** a concluding remark at parting ⟨said *good-bye*⟩ ⟨the chorus of *good-byes* —David Wagoner⟩ **b :** a farewell gesture ⟨tearfully waving *good-bye* to a knot of friends —Winston Churchill⟩ ⟨nodding a casual *good-bye* —J.D.Beresford⟩ ⟨a *good-bye* kiss⟩ **2 a :** a taking of leave ⟨in wartime one can't afford emotional *good-byes* —Edita Morris⟩ ⟨kissed her grandmother in *good-bye* —Betty Smith⟩ **b :** a riddance to something left behind or finished with ⟨*good-bye* to all that⟩ ⟨*good-bye* to noisy blasts —*Boy Scout Handbook*⟩ ⟨the year to which we have just said *good-bye* —Harrison Smith⟩

good cause *n* **:** a cause or reason sufficient in law **:** one that is based on equity or justice or that would motivate a reasonable man under all the circumstances

good consideration *n* **1 :** a consideration of blood or of natural love and affection **2 :** a valuable consideration **:** a moral obligation founded on an antecedent legal obligation now unenforceable **:** a consideration that will sustain a contract

good dame *n* [ME *gudame*, fr. *gud*, *good* + *dame*] *archaic* **:** GRANDMOTHER

good day *interj* [ME] — used conventionally as an utterance on meeting or parting during the day

good-day \\gu̇(d)'dā, gə'dā\\ *n* [ME *good day*, fr. *good day*, interj.] **:** a remark on meeting or parting during the day

good deal \\(')gu̇¦dēl, *chiefly before pause or consonant* -ēəl\\ *n* **:** GREAT DEAL — **a good deal** *adv* **:** a great deal ⟨*a good deal* worse than expected⟩

good doer *n* **:** an animal that with normal care produces or develops especially well

goo·de·nia \\gu̇'dēnyə\\ *n, cap* [NL, fr. Samuel *Gooden*ough †1827 Eng. bishop and botanical writer + NL *-ia*] **:** the type genus of Goodeniaceae

goo·de·ni·a·ce·ae \\(,)gu̇,dēnē'āsē,ē\\ *n pl, cap* [NL, fr. *Goodenia*, type genus + *-aceae*] **:** a family of chiefly Australian herbs or shrubs (order Campanulales)

good evening *interj* — used conventionally as an utterance on meeting or parting in the evening

good-evening \\gu̇'dēv-, gə'dēv-\\ *n* [*good evening*] **:** a remark on meeting or parting in the evening

good faith *n* **:** a state of mind indicating honesty and lawfulness of purpose **:** belief in one's legal title or right **:** belief that one's conduct is not unconscionable or that known circumstances do not require further investigation **:** absence of fraud, deceit, collusion, or gross negligence — usu. used with *in* ⟨the board need have no fear of being in contempt of court if it acted in *good faith* —J.B.Martin⟩

good father \\'=,==\\ *n, chiefly Scot* **:** FATHER-IN-LAW; *sometimes* **:** STEPFATHER

good fellow *n* **1 a** *archaic* **:** a drinking companion **:** ROISTERER, REVELER **b :** a jovial agreeable person typically radiating good humor and heartiness ⟨seeking to be *good fellows* at all costs —C.W.Ferguson⟩ **2** *obs* **:** THIEF, ROBBER

good-fellowship \\(')='==,=\\ *n* **:** a spirit existing among good fellows; *esp* **:** a spirit of friendship and goodwill

good folk *n pl* **:** FAIRIES — used with *the*

good-for-naught \\'==,=\\ *n* **:** GOOD-FOR-NOTHING

1**good-for-nothing** \\'==,==, ,=='==\\ *adj* **:** of no value **:** USELESS, WORTHLESS ⟨could hear their two *good-for-nothing* canaries —Eudora Welty⟩

2**good-for-nothing** \\"\\ *n* -s **:** an idle worthless person ⟨the meeting place of all the armed *good-for-nothings* of the district —*Atlantic*⟩

good-for-nothingness \\,=='===, '==,===\\ *n* -ES **:** the quality or state of being good-for-nothing

good friday *n, usu cap G&F* [ME] **:** the Friday before Easter celebrated in churches as the anniversary of the Crucifixion of Christ and observed as a legal holiday in some states of the U.S. and in many Christian countries

good-friday grass *n, cap 1st G&F* **:** a wood rush (*Luzula campestris*) with short stolons connecting small decumbent crowns

good god \\='=\\ *n, usu cap 2d G* **:** PILEATED WOODPECKER

good-hearted \\'=¦==\\ *adj* **:** having a kindly beneficent nature or disposition ⟨a *good-hearted* man when he was sober —A. Conan Doyle⟩ **:** WELL-MEANING ⟨*good-hearted* but inept efforts —Douglass Cater⟩ — **good-heart·ed·ly** *adv* — **good-heart·ed·ness** *n* -ES

good-hen·ry \\gu̇d'henrē\\ *n, usu cap G&H* [fr. the name *Henry*] **:** GOOD-KING-HENRY

good-humored \\'=¦==\\ *adj* **:** characterized by or indicating good humor **:** GOOD-NATURED — **good-hu·mored·ly** *adv* — **good-hu·mored·ness** *n* -ES

goodies *pl of* GOODY

good·ing \\'gu̇dᵊn, -diŋ\\ *n* -s [2*good* + *-ing*] **:** an asking of alms and wishing good to the donors in rural areas of England

good·ish \\'gu̇dish, -dēsh\\ *adj* **1 :** moderately good **:** rather good ⟨a ~ local white wine —G.A.Wagner⟩ **2 :** rather considerable (as in number or extent) ⟨a ~ walk —Mary Webb⟩

good joe \\gu̇(d)'jō, 'gu̇d'jō\\ *n, often cap J* **:** a kindly obliging good-hearted person ⟨my failure to answer his letter promptly . . . furnished proof that I was not, as he'd thought, a *good Joe* —Philip Wylie⟩ ⟨you can see he's a *good joe* —James Jones⟩

good-king-hen·ry \\¦gu̇d,kiŋ'henrē\\ *n, usu cap G&K&H* [alter. (influenced by the name of *Henry* VII †1509 king of England) of *Good-Henry*] **:** a European plant (*Chenopodium bonus-henricus*) naturalized in No. America and formerly cultivated and often collected from the wild as a potherb

good lack *interj, archaic* — used to express surprise or objection

good life *n* **1 a :** a life lived in accordance with certain moral laws **:** a life of virtue ⟨most men will not attain the *good life*, and . . . for them it is necessary to institute the laws —Walter Lippmann⟩ ⟨felt most sincerely that they were trying to lead the *good life* —A.A.Cohen⟩ **b :** a life characterized by or tending toward the harmonious rounded many-sided cultural and material development of the individual **:** a life promoting individual self-realization ⟨editing a magazine is a form of the *good life;* it is creating when the world is destroying —*Time*⟩ ⟨preparing for . . . the *good life*, through one or two years of liberal studies at the graduate level —*Science*⟩ ⟨never . . . confused the *good life* with an efficient economy —Sidney Hook⟩ **2 :** a life marked by a high standard of living **:** a life of material well-being ⟨a tidy home, a new car, a television set . . . these are the measures of the *good life* for millions —A.H.Raskin⟩

goodlike \\'=,=\\ *adj* **1** *now dial Eng* **:** appearing to be good ⟨a ~ farmer⟩ **2** *now dial Eng* **:** GOOD-LOOKING, HANDSOME

good·li·ness \\'gu̇dlēnəs, -lin-\\ *n* -ES **:** the quality or state of being goodly

good liver *n* **:** a person who lives well or luxuriously **:** BON VIVANT

good-looker \\(')='==\\ *n* **:** a good-looking person ⟨didn't I tell you she was a *good-looker* —Christopher Isherwood⟩

good-looking \\'=¦==\\ *adj* **1 :** having a pleasing or attractive appearance ⟨a *good-looking* car⟩ **:** HANDSOME, COMELY **:** not plain **:** not homely **:** not ugly ⟨not *good-looking* and yet not ugly, for his features were rather good —W.S.Maugham⟩ **2 :** serving to enhance one's appearance **:** BECOMING ⟨a *good-looking* coat⟩ ⟨her hairdo is *good-looking*⟩ **syn** see BEAUTIFUL

good-look·ing·ness *n* -ES **:** the quality or state of being good-looking

good·ly \\'gu̇dlē, -li\\ *adj* -ER/-EST [ME, fr. OE *gōdlīc*, fr. *gōd* good + *-līc* -ly — more at GOOD] **1 :** of pleasing appearance, character, or quality **:** COMELY, HANDSOME, EXCELLENT ⟨a ~ person⟩ ⟨~ houses⟩ **2 :** LARGE, CONSIDERABLE ⟨a ~ crowd was assembled —Sherwood Anderson⟩

good·man \'gu̇dmən\ *n, pl* **goodmen** [ME, fr. *good* + *man*] **1 a** *chiefly archaic & dial* **:** the head of a family or household **:** HUSBAND **b** *chiefly dial* **:** INNKEEPER, LANDLORD **2** *often cap, archaic* **:** MISTER — usu. used with a surname ⟨the roof on *Goodman* Hodge's barn —John Gay⟩ **3** *archaic Scot* **:** a well-to-do yeoman **:** a man of property

good morning *interj* — used conventionally as an utterance on meeting or parting in the morning

good–morning \ˌ=ˈ==\ *n* [*good morning*] **:** a remark on meeting or parting in the morning

good–morning–spring \ˌ=ˈ==ˌ=\ *n* **:** SPRING BEAUTY 1

good morrow *interj* [ME *good morwe*] *archaic* **:** GOOD MORNING

good–morrow *n* [*good morrow*] *archaic* **:** GOOD-MORNING ⟨then to come, in spite of sorrow, and at my window bid *good-morrow* —John Milton⟩

good nature *n* **:** pleasant cheerful disposition to please and be pleased, to accede to others' wishes, and to overlook slights, impositions, or causes for offense

good–natured \ˈ=ˈ==\ *adj* **1 :** showing or reflecting good nature (as pleasantness, affability, geniality, and kindliness) **:** marked by a disposition to please ⟨you've got such a nice *good-natured* face and way with you that I'm sure we'll agree —W.M.Thackeray⟩ ⟨a *good-natured* jest⟩ **2 :** possessed or indicative of a strong inclination to please or to accede to others' wishes to the extent of submitting to slights or impositions ⟨horseplay and practical jokes . . . require *good-natured* toleration —W.G.Sumner⟩ **3** *of glass* **:** retaining temperatures high enough to permit easy working or shaping — contrasted with *short-natured* **syn** see AMIABLE

good·na·tured·ly *adv* **:** in a good-natured manner

good·na·tured·ness *n* -ES **:** the quality or state of being good-natured

good–neighbor \(ˈ)=ˈ==\ *adj* **1 :** marked by the principles of friendship, cooperation, and noninterference in the internal affairs of another country ⟨the *good-neighbor* policy⟩ **2 :** of, relating to, or involving the Latin-American countries ⟨to avoid *good-neighbor* complications the nationality of the sailors . . . will be changed from Brazilian to Portuguese in the screen version —*Newsweek*⟩

good–neighborliness \(ˈ)=ˈ====\ *n* **:** friendship and cooperation with and noninterference in the internal affairs of another country

good–neighborly \(ˈ)=ˈ===\ *adj* **:** marked by good-neighborliness ⟨a wish for *good-neighborly* relations —Werner Levi⟩

good·ness \ˈgu̇dnəs, *in exclamatory phrases also* ˈgu̇nəs\ *n* -ES [ME *goodnesse*, fr. OE *gōdnes*, fr. *gōd* good + *-nes* -ness — more at GOOD] **1 :** the quality or state of being good: as **a :** moral excellence **:** VIRTUE, BENEVOLENCE, GENEROSITY ⟨extolled the ~ of God⟩ — often used interjectionally or in such phrases as *for goodness' sake, goodness gracious,* or *goodness knows* ⟨a smuggler and forger and ~ knows what else —C.L.Boltz⟩ **b :** excellence in respect to material quality ⟨the ~ of soil⟩ **2 :** the nutritious, flavorful, or beneficial portion or element of something ⟨boil all the ~ out of the coffee⟩

good night *in sense 1 with varying stress & intonation, in sense 2 with heavy or emphatic stress on each syllable*\ *interj* [ME] **1** — used conventionally as a concluding utterance on parting at night **2** — used esp. to express surprise

good–night \gu̇dˈnīt, gə(d)ˈn-, *usu* -īd.+V\ *n* [*good night*] **1 a :** a concluding remark on parting at night ⟨left him at the church . . . with conventional *good-nights* —Harry Sylvester⟩ **b :** a farewell gesture at night ⟨back-porch *good-night* kisses —Jan Struther⟩ **2 :** a ballad telling the story of an executed criminal

good now *interj, archaic* — used to express entreaty or surprise ⟨*good now,* say so but seldom —Shak.⟩

good offices *n pl* **:** services as a mediator esp. between belligerent or disputing states ⟨Soviet *good offices* for the repatriation of British civilian internees in North Korea —*N.Y. Times*⟩

good people *n pl* **:** FAIRIES — used with *the* ⟨you shouldn't speak like that of the *good people,* it will draw them on you —Robert Gibbings⟩

goods *pl of* GOOD

good samaritan *n, usu cap G&S* [after the *good Samaritan* in the Biblical parable (Lk 10:30–37)] **:** one who compassionately renders personal assistance to the unfortunate

goods and chattels *n pl* **:** animate or inanimate personal property that is visible, tangible, and movable and has intrinsic value in itself as distinguished from real estate or freehold property or from personal property of the class of choses in action; *sometimes* **:** all personal property esp. in wills sometimes including choses in action

goods and effects *n pl* **:** all movable personal property including usu. choses in action

good sense *n* **:** sound judgment often instinctive or unlearned ⟨had the *good sense* to save his money⟩ **syn** see SENSE

goodsire *var of* GUDESIRE

goods yard *n, Brit* **:** a yard where goods wagons are received, classified, and dispatched in trains

good–tempered \ˈ=ˈ==\ *adj* **:** having or reflecting a good temper **:** not wrathful, harsh, or bitter **:** not easily vexed ⟨*good-tempered* discussions of other work in this field —D.L. Olmsted⟩ ⟨very *good-tempered* people⟩ — **good–tem·pered·ly** *adv* — **good–tem·pered·ness** *n* -ES

good templar *n, usu cap G&T* **:** a member of a secret society organized in the 19th century for the promotion of total abstinence from the use of alcoholic beverages

good time *n* **:** a deduction for good behavior made from a convict's term of imprisonment

good–time char·lie *also* **good–time char·ley** \ˌ=ˌ=ˈchär\|lē, -ˈchȧl, \|li\ *n, usu cap C* [fr. the name *Charlie, Charley,* dim. of *Charles*] **:** a happy-go-lucky convivial man given to fun making, hilarity, and the general pursuit of amusement ⟨just a *good-time Charlie,* borrowing two bucks here and five bucks there —Walter Karig⟩ ⟨I couldn't be a *good-time Charlie* . . . when I was a kid I was taught not to talk or joke or laugh at the table —A.J.Liebling⟩

good·wife \(ˈ)gu̇\|dwīf; (ˈ)gə̇\|dwəf, (ˈ)gŭ\|-, (ˈ)gi\|d-\ *n, pl* **goodwives** [ME, fr. *good* + *wife*] **1** *chiefly Scot* **a :** the lady of the house **b :** the mistress of an inn **:** LANDLADY **2** *often cap, archaic* **:** MRS., MADAM 1 — usu. used with a surname ⟨~ Brown⟩

goodwill \(ˈ)=ˈ=\ *n, often attrib* [ME *good will*] **1 a :** kindly feeling **:** WELL-WISHING, BENEVOLENCE, FRIENDLINESS ⟨none of us have anything but ~ toward you personally —Ralph Ellison⟩ ⟨a happy man . . . is a radiating focus of ~ —R.L. Stevenson⟩ ⟨a ~ tour of seven European capitals —C.B. Palmer b.1910⟩ **b :** the custom of a trade or business **:** the favor or advantage in the way of custom that a business has acquired beyond the mere value of what it sells whether due to the personality of those conducting it, the nature of its location, its reputation for skill or promptitude, or any other circumstance incidental to the business and tending to make it permanent **c :** the capitalized value of the excess of estimated future profits of a business over the rate of return on capital considered normal in the related industry **d :** the excess of the purchase price of a business over and above the value assigned to its net assets exclusive of goodwill **2 a :** cheerful consent ⟨they accepted their new burdens with surprising ~⟩ **b :** HEARTINESS, ZEAL **:** willing effort ⟨the need is for mind to be applied . . . with the particular joy and ~ of creativeness —Lionel Trilling⟩ ⟨with a little ~, two other major philosophic strategies can be derived —K.D.Burke⟩ **3** *usu* **good will :** a will acting freely from pure disinterested motives ⟨the concept of the *good will* is ultimately the concept of the formal will —R.D. Mack⟩

good·will·it \gu̇ˈdwilət, gə̇ˈ-,gŭˈ-,gi-\ *adj* [fr. earlier *gudewillit,* fr. *gudewill* (var. of *goodwill*) + *-it* (var. of *-ed*)] **:** GUIDWILLIE

¹goody \ˈgu̇dē, -di\ *n* -ES [alter. of *goodwife*] **1** *archaic* **:** a usu married woman of lowly station — often used as a title preceding a surname **2** *archaic* **:** a woman who takes care of students' rooms (as at Harvard university)

²goody \"\ *n* -ES [¹*good* + *-y* (n. suffix)] **1 a :** something (as a piece of candy) that is particularly good to eat — usu. used in pl. **b :** something that is peculiarly attractive, pleasurable, or good — usu. used in pl. ⟨other *goodies* include . . . a dance or beach dress —Lois Long⟩ ⟨such *goodies* as model trains, cameras, microscopes, and college educations —*Time*⟩ **2 :** SPOT 7 **3** *Midland* **:** the kernel of a nut

³goody \"\ *adj* [¹*good* + *-y* (adj. suffix)] **:** GOODY-GOODY

⁴goody \"\ *interj* [¹*good* + *-y* (adj. suffix)] — used esp. by children to express delight

goodyear *n, obs* — used esp. in the phrase *what the goodyear* as a mild expletive or expression of surprise, vexation, or emphasis ⟨what the ~, my lord! why are you thus out of measure sad —Shak.⟩

good·year welt \ˈgu̇dˌyi(ə)r- *also* ˈgu̇ˌji(ə)r-\ *n* [fr. *Goodyear Welt,* a trademark] **:** a method of shoe construction in which the insole, upper, and welt are sewed together and the welt is then stitched to the outsole so as to leave the upper surface of the insole free of tacks and stitches

good·yera \ˈgu̇dyərə, gu̇dˈyirə, ˈgu̇jə-, gu̇ˈji-\ *n, cap* [NL, after John *Goodyer* †1664 Eng. botanist] **:** a genus of small orchids of the northern hemisphere with creeping rhizomes, stalked ovate leaves, and small flowers in a twisted raceme — see RATTLESNAKE PLANTAIN

¹goody–goody \ˌ==ˈ==\ *adj* [redupl. of ³*goody*] **:** sentimentally, affectedly, or unctuously good ⟨a *goody-goody* boy —Havelock Ellis⟩

²goody–goody \"\ *n* **:** a person who is goody-goody ⟨her . . . generous nature had nothing in it of the *goody-goody* —Van Wyck Brooks⟩

goo·ey \ˈgüē, ˈgüi\ *adj* **goo·i·er; goo·i·est** [³*goo* + *-ey*] **1 :** VISCID, STICKY ⟨a geyser of coal-black, thick, ~ oil —H.A.Chippendale⟩ ⟨a ~ mess of grated cheese —Green Peyton⟩ **2 :** excessively effusive or sentimental **:** CLOYING ⟨gave me a big, ~ hello —Ethel Merman⟩ ⟨~ sentimentality⟩ ⟨~ romance and tear-jerking melodrama —*Time*⟩

gooey duck *var of* GEODUCK

¹goof \ˈgüf\ *n* -S [prob. alter. of ¹*goff*] **1 :** a ridiculous stupid person ⟨plays her as a simple country ~ —Harold Hobson⟩ **2 :** a blunder or mistake ⟨made a ~ —D.D.Eisenhower⟩

²goof \"\ *vb* -ED/-ING/-S *vi* **1 :** to make a mistake or blunder ⟨often misfired and ~*ed* —G.P.Crist⟩ ⟨somebody had ~*ed* —Ethel Merman⟩ **2** *slang* **a :** to spend time idly or foolishly **:** shirk work **:** kill time ⟨~*ed* on their way home from school —J.T.Farrell⟩ ⟨get into . . . jams because you were ~*ing* around —*Infantry Jour.*⟩ — often used with *off* ⟨somebody is ~*ing* off on the job —*Springfield (Mass.) Daily News*⟩ **b :** to have one's mind or attention wander **:** become abstracted — often used with *off* ⟨could see he wasn't drunk, he was ~*ing* off —Paul Monash⟩ **3** *slang* **:** to be in a state of euphoria induced by a narcotic substance ⟨bought some more stuff and ~*ed* around until night —Wenzell Brown⟩ ~ *vt* **1 :** to make a mess of (as a performance or operation) esp. through a stupid blunder **:** BUNGLE ⟨just ~*ed* it —C.B.Palmer b.1910⟩ — often used with *up* ⟨if I don't ~ up the situation —Calder Willingham⟩ ⟨you'd ~ things up good —Tom Walters⟩ **2** *slang* **:** to intoxicate or stupefy esp. with a narcotic substance — often used in the past participle with *up* ⟨pretty ~*ed* up that night —V.L.Preston⟩

goofa *or* **goofah** *var of* GUFA

goofball \ˈ=ˌ=\ *n* **1** *slang* **:** a barbiturate sleeping pill used esp. in alcoholic beverages to induce a transient euphoria **2** *slang* **:** a demented or abnormal person ⟨plenty ~*s* in this here town —Richard Bissell⟩

¹goof·er \ˈgüfə(r)\ *n* -S [¹*goof* + *-er*] **:** GOOF ⟨had a considerable understanding of ~*s* because . . . he was a little goofy himself —Esther Forbes⟩

²goo·fer \"\ *also* **guf·fer** \ˈgəfə(r)\ *n* -S [of African origin; akin to Mende *ngafa* spirit, ghost, Ewe *ga³fe³* shrine of a god, Fon *kafo* iron fetish] **1 :** a witch doctor among Negroes of the southern U.S.; *esp* **:** a voodoo doctor **2 :** a curse or spell ⟨put the ~ on us —J.S.Redding⟩

goofer dust *n* [²*goofer*] **:** a powder or dust used in conjuration; *esp* **:** earth from a grave used for such purpose

go off *vi* **1 :** to undergo removal **:** come to be taken off ⟨protesting that if he had him, his head should *go off* —John Davies †1693⟩ **2 a :** to undergo discharge or explosion **:** come to be discharged or exploded ⟨asking what happened when the hydrogen bomb *went off* must have surprised and astonished the scientists —A.P.Ryan⟩ **b :** to burst forth or break out in a sudden and often noisy manner ⟨*went off* into a . . . fit of laughter —M.V.Reidy⟩ **3 a :** to go forth or away **:** DEPART ⟨had to sit down and wait for her because I could not just *go off* like that without explaining —Francis Stuart⟩ **b :** to leave the stage ⟨the directions called for the heroine to *go off* left⟩ **4 a :** to pass into or as if into unconsciousness ⟨*went off* at the first whiff of ether —O.S.J.Gogarty⟩ **b :** DIE ⟨the doctors told me that he might *go off* any day —H.R.Haggard⟩ **5 :** to find a purchaser **:** SELL ⟨trade flourishes and his commodities *go off* well —John Locke⟩ **6 :** to undergo decline or deterioration ⟨those clarkias have *gone off* very quickly —F.A.Swinnerton⟩ ⟨a small quantity of water . . . *goes off* quickly and loses its freshness —Henry Wynmalen⟩ **7 :** to follow the expected or desired course **:** PROCEED ⟨I had the assignment of it, but it seemed to *go off* pretty well —O.W.Holmes †1935⟩ **8 :** to make a characteristic noise **:** SOUND ⟨around one in the morning the sirens had *gone off* —Irwin Shaw⟩ **:** RING — **go off the deep end 1 :** to enter recklessly upon a course **:** go off half-cocked **:** become rapidly involved (as in difficulties) **2 :** to lose self-control **:** become very much excited

go–off \ˈ=ˌ=\ *n* -S [*go off*] **:** the act or time of going off **:** BEGINNING, START ⟨awaiting the *go-off* of a bomb —Speed Lamkin⟩ ⟨we were correct at the first *go-off* —*Amer. Antiquity*⟩

goof·i·ly \ˈgüfəlē, -li\ *adv* **:** in a goofy manner

goof·i·ness \-fēnəs, -fin-\ *n* -ES **:** the quality or state of being goofy ⟨seems to detect in my remarks a slight ~ —P.G. Wodehouse⟩

goofy \ˈgüfē, -fi\ *adj* -ER/-EST [¹*goof* + *-y*] **:** CRAZY, SILLY ⟨it sounds ~, but I'll do it —Erle Stanley Gardner⟩ ⟨this guy's ~ —Earle Birney⟩

goog \ˈgüg, ˈgu̇g\ *n* -S [origin unknown] *Austral* **:** EGG

¹goo·gly \ˈgüglē, -li\ *n* -ES [origin unknown] **:** an offbreak in cricket with a leg-break action — called also *bosey, wrong 'un*

²googly \"\ *adj* [alter. of *goggly*] **:** BULGING, STARING ⟨a large scarecrow with ~ eyes —Evelyn Woodforde⟩

googly–eyed \ˌ=ˈ=ˌ=\ *adj* **:** GOGGLE-EYED

goo·gol \ˈgüˌgȯl\ *n* -S [coined by Milton Sirotta, nine-year-old nephew of Dr. Edward Kasner †1955 Am. mathematician] **:** the figure 1 followed by 100 zeroes equal to 10^{100}

goo·gol·plex \-ˌpleks\ *n* -ES [*googol* + *-plex* (as in *duplex*)] **:** the figure 1 followed by a googol of zeroes equal to $10^{10^{100}}$

¹goo–goo \ˈgü(ˌ)gü\ *adj* [prob. alter. of ¹*goggle*] **:** LOVING, ENTICING, AMOROUS — used chiefly in the phrase *goo-goo eyes* ⟨make *goo-goo* eyes at each other —*New Republic*⟩

²goo–goo \"\ *n* -S [fr. the initials of *good government*] **:** a member or advocate of a reform movement in politics esp. in the era of Theodore Roosevelt — usu. used disparagingly ⟨this group was contemptuously dismissed by machine politicians as *goo-goos* —*Fortune*⟩

³goo–goo *var of* GUGU

gooier *comparative of* GOOEY

gooiest *superlative of* GOOEY

¹gook \ˈgu̇k, ˈgük\ *n* -S [origin unknown] **:** a native belonging usu. to a brown or yellow race — usu. used disparagingly ⟨a little South Korean boy whom his father calls by a ~ and ends by loving as a son —Robert Hatch⟩

²gook \"\ *n* -S [perh. alter. of ³*goo*] **1 :** sticky or gooey stuff ⟨painted the resulting ~ on the backs of black mice —*Time*⟩ **2 :** TRASH, JUNK, NONSENSE ⟨that's a lot of ~⟩

¹gool \ˈgül\ *n* -S [MF *gole, goule* throat, narrow passage, fr. L *gula* throat — more at GLUTTON] *now dial Eng* **:** a ditch or channel for water **:** SLUICE

²gool \"\ *n* -S [by alter.] *dial* **:** GOAL ⟨use the big cedar tree for ~⟩

goold \ˈgüld\ *Scot var of* GOLD

goo·ly \ˈgülē\ *n* -ES [origin unknown] *Austral* **:** STONE ⟨someone's been bunging *goolies* through her window —Ruth Park⟩

goom \ˈgüm, ˈgu̇m\ *dial var of* GUM

goo·ma \ˈgümə\ *n* -S [native name in Australia] **:** an Australian shrub (*Bertya cunninghami*) of the family Euphorbiaceae used in arid regions as fodder

goom·bay \ˈgümˌbā, ˈgu̇m-, =ˈ=\ *n* -S [of Bantu origin; akin to Kongo *nkumbi* ceremonial drum, Tshiluba *nkumbi* drum] **:** calypso music as developed in the Bahamas

go on *vi* **1 a :** to continue with or as if with a journey ⟨*went on* by train after the plane was grounded⟩ **b :** to continue in or as if in a course of action ⟨despite the heat he *went on* with his work⟩ **2** *obs* **:** to engage in a military attack ⟨the sergeant in *going on* was shot through the body —Fynes Moryson⟩ **3 a :** to proceed by or as if by a logical step ⟨after discoursing at some length on pronunciation, the professor *goes on* to vocabulary —Nancy Mitford⟩ **b** *of time* **:** PASS ⟨new art forms developed as the century *went on*⟩ **4 :** to take place **:** HAPPEN, OCCUR ⟨learn what is *going on* elsewhere —Bernard DeVoto⟩ **5 a :** to get along **:** FARE, MANAGE ⟨wondered if he could *go on* alone after his partner's death⟩ **b :** to deport oneself **:** ACT, BEHAVE ⟨we plagued and *went on* with him shamefully —Emily Brontë⟩ **6 :** to be capable of being put on ⟨washed her gloves and found that they wouldn't *go on*⟩ **7 a :** to talk esp. in an effusive manner ⟨the way people *go on* about their ancestors —Hamilton Basso⟩ **b :** RAIL, STORM ⟨didn't you hear the canon *going on* at her this morning? —Margaret Kennedy⟩ **8 a :** to come into operation, action, or production ⟨the lights *went on* an hour after the storm had ended⟩ **b :** to appear on the stage ⟨the callboy knocked five minutes before the actor was to *go on*⟩ **c :** to begin bowling in cricket ⟨a good time for a slow left-hander to *go on*⟩ — **go on for :** APPROACH, NEAR ⟨it must be *going on for* nine —Archibald MacLeish⟩

goon \ˈgün\ *n* -S [partly short for E dial. *gooney* simpleton, var. of *gony, gawney;* partly after Alice the *Goon,* a subhuman creature appearing in the comic strip *Thimble Theatre* by E. C. Segar †1938 Am. cartoonist] **1 :** a man hired (as by a racketeer) to terrorize or eliminate opponents **:** THUG, HATCHET MAN **2** *slang* **a :** a dull or unattractive person lacking conversational ability, esprit, or other social graces ⟨I'm mad about my Fine Arts prof . . . I know he's a ~, but I can't help it —Herman Wouk⟩ **b :** DOPE, SAP, BOOB ⟨don't be a ~ . . . don't be positively medieval —Catherine Hutter⟩

goonch \ˈgünch\ *n, pl* **goonch** *or* **goonches** [Hindi *gūc*] **:** a large voracious Indian freshwater catfish (*Bagarius bagarius*) believed to attain a weight of 250 pounds and a length of 6 feet

goon·da \ˈgündə\ *n* -S [Hindi *guṇḍā* rascal, crook] *India* **:** professional terrorist **:** HOOLIGAN, GOON, THUG

goon·die \ˈgündē\ *n* -S [native name in Australia] **:** an Australian aboriginal hut

goo·ney *also* **goo·ny** *or* **goo·nie** \ˈgünē\ *n, pl* **gooneys** *also* **goonies** [prob. fr. E dial. *gooney* simpleton, var. of *gony, gawney*] **:** ALBATROSS; *esp* **:** BLACK-FOOTED ALBATROSS

goon·gar·rite \günˈgaˌrīt, ˈgüngəˌr-\ *n* -S [Lake *Goongarrie,* Western Australia + E *-ite*] **:** a mineral $Pb_4Bi_2S_7$ that consists of a sulfide of lead and bismuth and is found at Lake Goongarrie, Western Australia

¹goop \ˈgüp\ *n* -S [coined *ab*1900 by Gelett Burgess †1951 Am. humorist and illustrator] **1 :** a bad-mannered child ⟨don't act like a ~⟩ **2** *slang* **:** a dull, graceless, or simple-minded person **:** BOOB, DOPE ⟨such a big nerveless ~ —G.R. Stewart⟩ ⟨he was a ~, anyway —J.T.Farrell⟩

²goop \"\ *n* -S [prob. alter. of ³*goo*] **:** a viscid or sticky substance **:** GOO ⟨the ~ that comes from the tube —Alfred Frankenstein⟩ ⟨glanced at the brownish ~ congealed around the can —Maxwell Griffith⟩

³goop \"\ *vi* -ED/-ING/-S [prob. blend of ³*goo* and *drip*] *of a pen* **:** to drop blobs of ink on paper

goor *var of* GUR

gooral *var of* GORAL

goora·nut \ˈgu̇rəˌ=\ *n* [*goora-* of West African origin; akin to Hausa *go³ro¹* kola nut, Bambara & Malinke *goro, guro*] **:** KOLA NUT

goos *pl of* GOO

goo·san·der \güˈsandə(r), ˈ=ˌ==\ *n* -S [alter. of earlier *gossander,* prob. fr. *gos-* (as in *gosling*) + *bergander*] **:** the common merganser (*Mergus merganser*) of the northern hemisphere

¹goose \ˈgüs\ *n, pl* **geese** \ˈgēs\ *see senses 4 and 5* [ME *goos, gos,* fr. OE *gōs;* akin to OHG *gans* goose, ON *gās,* L *anser,* Gk *chēn,* Skt *haṁsa*] **1 a :** any of numerous birds constituting a distinct subfamily of Anatidae, being in many respects intermediate between the swans and ducks, having a high somewhat compressed bill, legs of moderate length, completely feathered lores, and reticulate tarsi, and being usu. larger and longer-necked than ducks; *esp* **:** a member of any of the several breeds developed in domestication for their flesh and feathers — see BARNACLE GOOSE, BRANT, SNOW GOOSE **b :** a female goose as distinguished from a gander **c :** the flesh of a goose used for food **2 :** a silly person **:** SIMPLETON ⟨such a ~ I have seldom seen —Rachel Henning⟩ **3 a :** an obsolete game played with counters on a board **b :** KENO GOOSE **4** *pl* **gooses :** a tailor's smoothing iron with a gooseneck handle **5** *pl* **gooses :** an instance of goosing; *specif* **:** a poke between buttocks

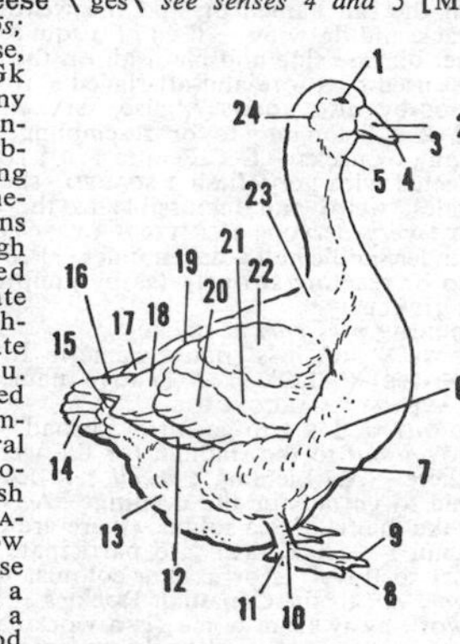

diagram of the goose: *1* eye, *2* nostril, *3* bill, *4* bean, *5* dewlap, *6* breast, *7* keel, *8* web, *9* toes, *10* shank, *11* foot, *12* pinion coverts, *13* fluff, *14* tail feathers, *15* tail coverts, *16* wing flight feathers, *17* rump, *18* wing secondaries, *19* saddle, *20* wing coverts, *21* wing bow, *22* shoulder, *23* cape, *24* ear

²goose \"\ *vt* -ED/-ING/-S [prob. so called fr. the fancied resemblance of an upturned thumb to the outstretched neck of a goose] **1 :** to poke or dig (a person) in some sensitive spot; *esp* **:** to poke (a person) between buttocks with an upward thrust of a finger or hand from the rear **2 :** to feed gasoline to (an engine) in spurts

goose barnacle *n* **:** a barnacle of the family Lepadidae attached by a leathery stalk to rocks of the intertidal zone or to floating logs or the bottom of ships where they are sometimes important fouling organisms

goose·ber·ry \ˈgüs-, ˈgüz-, *chiefly Brit* ˈgu̇z-— see BERRY\ *n* **1 a :** the acid usu. bristly or spiny fruit of any of several shrubs of the genus *Ribes* **b :** a shrub bearing gooseberries **c :** CURRANT 2 **d :** any of numerous shrubs resembling the gooseberry — usu. used with an attributive ⟨American ~⟩ ⟨Barbados ~⟩ **2 :** a dark purplish red that is bluer and duller than pansy purple, bluer and less strong than raisin, and bluer and paler than Bokhara

gooseberry gourd *n* **:** GHERKIN

gooseberry mildew *n* **1 :** a mildew affecting gooseberries; *esp* **:** a mildew caused by a powdery mildew (*Sphaerotheca mors-uvae* or *Microsphaera grossulariae*) **2 :** a fungus that causes gooseberry mildew

gooseberry rust *n* **:** any of several diseases of gooseberries caused by true rust fungi (as *Cronartium ribicola*)

gooseberry tree *n* **:** OTAHEITE GOOSEBERRY

goose bumps *n pl* **:** GOOSEFLESH

goosecap \ˈ=ˌ=\ *n, chiefly dial* **:** a silly person; *esp* **:** a flighty young girl

goose–drown·der \ˈ=ˌdrau̇ndər\ *n, chiefly Midland* **:** a heavy fall of rain **:** DOWNPOUR

goose egg *n* [so called fr. the egg-shaped numeral 0] **:** ZERO, NOTHING, FAILURE; *esp* **:** a score of zero in a game or contest

goosefish \ˈ=ˌ=\ *n, pl* **goosefish** *or* **goosefishes :** ANGLER 2

gooseflesh \ˈ=ˌ=\ *n* **:** a roughness of the skin produced by erection of its papillae and usu. caused by cold or fear — called also *goose bumps, goose pimples*

gooseflower \ˈ=ˌ=\ *n* **:** PELICAN FLOWER

goosefoot \ˈ=ˌ=\ *n, pl* **goosefoots 1 :** a plant of the family Chenopodiaceae and esp. of the genus *Chenopodium* **2 :** a southern African velvety shrub (*Aspalathus chenopoda*)

goosefoot family *n* **:** CHENOPODIACEAE

goosefoot maple *n* **:** STRIPED MAPLE

goosegirl \ˈ=ˌ=\ *n* [trans. of G *gänsemädchen*] **:** a girl goose-herd

goose·gog \ˈgüz,gäg\ *n* -s [¹goose + -gog (origin unknown)] *dial Brit* : GOOSEBERRY
goose grass *n* **1 a** : CLEAVERS **b** : KNOTGRASS 1 **c** : SILVERWEED a(1) **d** : ARROW GRASS 1 **2 a** : YARD GRASS **b** : TEXAS MILLET **c** : SOFT CHEAT **d** : HORSETAIL 2
goose gray *n* : LAMA 2
goose gull *n* : GREAT BLACK-BACKED GULL
gooseherd \ˈ=,=, *chiefly dial* ˈgäzə(r)d\ *n* : one who tends geese
goose influenza *or* **goose septicemia** *n* : a usu. fatal disease of young geese marked by pulmonary inflammation, loss of appetite, and staggering gait and believed caused by a bacterium (*Shigella septicaemiae*)
gooseneck \ˈ=,=\ *n, often attrib* : something (as a faucet or pipe) curved like the neck of a goose or U-shaped: as **a** : a connecting pipe in a distilling apparatus **b** : the bar used to couple two logging trucks or sleds; *also* : the curved iron driven into the bottom of a slide to check descending logs **c** : an iron hook connecting a spar with a mast — **goose-necked** \ˈ=,=\ *adj*
gooseneck lamp *n* : an electric table lamp or desk lamp with a flexible shaft that permits control of the direction of the light
gooseneck pediment *n* : a pediment formed of two balancing double-curved molded members ending in a scroll or rosette
gooseneck slicker *n* : an implement consisting of a long flat blade that is attached to the rear of sled runners with gooseneck arms and that runs under the soil surface to cut off weeds on fallow land
gooseneck trailer *n* : a truck trailer whose forward part is arched like a goose's neck and swiveled to the motor unit
goose pen *n* **1** : a pen for geese **2** : a hole burned in a standing tree

goose-neck lamp

goose pimples *n pl* : GOOSEFLESH — **goose-pimply** \ˈ=,=(=)=\ *adj*
goose plant *n* : PELICAN FLOWER
goose plum *n* : an American wild plum (*Prunus americana*)
goose quill *n* : a quill of a goose; *also* : a quill pen
goose rump *n* : a rump (as of a horse) having considerable slope so that the tail is set down low
goose-rumped \ˈ=,=\ *adj* : having a goose rump
gooses *pl of* GOOSE, *pres 3d sing of* GOOSE
gooseskin \ˈ=,=\ *n* **1** : the skin of a goose **2** : GOOSEFLESH **3** : a pitted surface exhibited by some fossil copal
goose step *n* [trans. of G *gänseschritt*] : a straight-legged stiff-kneed step used by foot troops of some armies when passing in review
goose-step \ˈ=,=\ *vi* [*goose step*] **1** : to march in a goose step ⟨soldiers *goose-stepped* into the ancient capital⟩ **2** : to practice an unthinking conformity in thought or action : conform esp. under social pressure or from fear of reprisal ⟨a society *goose-stepping* to a set of taboos —W.W.Howells⟩ — **goose-stepper** \ˈ=,==\ *n*
goose tansy *n* : SILVERWEED a(1)
goosetongue \ˈ=,=\ *n* **1** *dial Eng* **a** : SNEEZEWORT 2 **b** : CLEAVERS **c** : BALM 3a **2** *dial Eng* : any of certain plantains (as *Plantago maritima* and *P. juncoides decipiens*)
¹goosewing \ˈ=,=\ *n* [¹goose + wing] : the weather lower corner of a course or topsail when the middle and lee parts of the sail are hauled up
²goosewing \"\ *vt* : to make goosewinged ~ *vi* : to sail with the wind aft, the jib out on one side, and the mainsail out on the other
goosewinged \ˈ=,wiŋd\ *adj* **1** : having the lee clew and middle of the sail hauled up and the weather part extended by the tack and drawing — used of a square sail **2** : having foresail set on one side and mainsail on the other : WING AND WING — used of a fore-and-aft-rigged ship
goos·ey *also* **goosy** \ˈgüsē, -sī\ *adj* **goos·i·er**; **goos·i·est** **1 a** : belonging to or resembling a goose ⟨stretching out long ~ necks —D.C.Peattie⟩ **b** : FOOLISH, STUPID **2 a** : affected with gooseflesh : SCARED ⟨she had me quite ~ by her tales, weird and impossible as they were —Harry Lauder⟩ **b** : very nervous : SKITTISH ⟨a ~ horse . . . he hadn't been under saddle half a dozen times —F.B.Gipson⟩ **c** : susceptible to or reacting strongly (as by jumping in the air) to goosing : TICKLISH
goosing *pres part of* GOOSE
goote \ˈgüt\ *n* -s [native name in India] *India* : MARCOT
goo·tee \ˈgü,tē\ *n* -s [native name in India] *India* : AIR LAYERING, MARCOTTAGE
go out *vi* **1 a** : to go forth, abroad, or out of doors ⟨decided to *go out* to the stadium for the weigh-in and buy my ticket there —A.J.Liebling⟩; *specif* : to leave one's house ⟨induced me to *go out* for the evening —A.N.Whitehead⟩ **b** (1) : to take the field as a soldier ⟨there are other men fitter to *go out* than I —Shak.⟩ (2) : to participate as a principal in a duel **c** : to travel as or as if a colonist or immigrant ⟨a lad who *goes out* to the Canadian Rockies —*Brit. Book News*⟩ **d** : to work away from home ⟨is a workman's wife and has herself *gone out* as a char when things were difficult —*Saturday Rev.*⟩ **e** : to play the first nine holes of an 18-hole golf match ⟨*went out* in 38 and finished with 35 for a score of 73⟩ **2 a** : to come to an end ⟨March came in like a lion and *went out* like a lamb⟩ **b** : to become extinguished ⟨after a moment the hall light *went out* and she could hear . . . footsteps —Margaret A. Barnes⟩ **c** : to give up office : RESIGN ⟨an absolute certainty that the government will *go out* —Rachel M. Praed⟩ **d** : to become obsolete or unfashionable ⟨the sort of caricature that *went out* with twenty-three skiddoo —Charles Lee⟩ **e** *of the tide* : EBB, RECEDE **f** : to cease to operate or function : FAIL ⟨the men were ordered to jump when two of the plane's four engines *went out* —*Springfield (Mass.) Union*⟩ **g** : to end one's turn at bat (as in baseball) : make an out ⟨the batter *went out* on a fly to right field⟩ **h** (1) : to play the last card of one's hand (2) : to reach or exceed the total number of points required for game in cards **i** : DIE ⟨the patient caught pneumonia and *went out* shortly before midnight⟩ **3** : to take part in social activities ⟨the high-school set *went out* constantly during the holidays⟩ **4** : to take a B.A. degree at Cambridge University ⟨had *gone out* in honors, having been a second-class man —Anthony Trollope⟩ **5** : to become emotionally drawn or impelled : issue forth : flow out ⟨his sympathy *went out* to whoever suffered . . . from the injustice of society —V.L.Parrington⟩ **6** : to go on strike ⟨ready to *go out* also were 6000 textile workers —*Time*⟩ **7** : to become spread abroad : come to be issued or published ⟨an interoffice memo *goes out* in sixteen copies —J.M.Barzun⟩ **8** : to give way to pressure : BREAK, COLLAPSE ⟨a dam that might *go out* and drown many thousand people —F.D.Roosevelt⟩ **9** : to become a candidate : try out ⟨*went out* for the . . . team as a sixteen-year-old in his junior year —Stanley Frank⟩
go over *vi* **1** : to make one's way : go on or as if on a journey ⟨has *gone over* to the coast for a few days⟩ **2** : to become converted; *esp* : to turn from a religious or political belief ⟨a priest who *went over* to the Revolution and had much influence in those times —H.J.Laski⟩ **3** : to undergo postponement ⟨asked that the matter *go over* until tomorrow — and there it stands —A.H.Vandenberg⟩ **4** : to receive approval : SUCCEED ⟨the humor is rudimentary, but it *goes over* big in the wards —Hartzell Spence⟩ **5** : to make a touchdown in football ⟨the fullback *went over* from the 12-yard line⟩ — **go over the hill** **1** : to leave one's military unit without authorization ⟨the boys would *go over the hill* their first shore leave —Frederic Wakeman⟩ **2** : to disappear without warning or explanation ⟨has *gone over the hill* with the ministry's payroll —*Time*⟩
goo·zle \ˈgüzəl\ *n* -s [by alter.] *dial* : GUZZLE 2
go·pak \ˈgō,pak\ *n* -s [Russ, fr. Ukrainian *hopak*, fr. *hop*, interj. used in lively dances, fr. G *hopp*; akin to MHG *hüpfen*, *hopfen* to hop — more at HOP] : a Ukrainian folk dance with heel beats
¹go·pher \ˈgōfə(r)\ *n* -s [short for earlier *megopher*, of unknown origin] **1 a** : a burrowing land tortoise (*Gopherus polyphemus*) of the coastal region of the southern U.S. whose shell attains the length of a foot or more and whose eggs and flesh are used as food **b** : any of several related land tortoises **2 a** : any of several burrowing rodents (family Geomyidae) of western No. America, Central America, and the southern U.S. east to Georgia that are the size of a large rat and have small eyes, short ears, strong claws on the forelimbs, and large cheek pouches opening beside the mouth — called also *pocket gopher* **b** (1) : any of numerous small ground squirrels of the prairie region of No. America that belong to the genus *Citellus* and are closely related to the chipmunks (2) : any of numerous related animals (as chipmunks, marmots, prairie dogs) **3** : GOPHER SNAKE **4** *also* **gopher rock cod** : any of various rockfishes of the genus *Sebastodes* **5** *usu cap* : MINNESOTAN — used as a nickname **6** : GOPHERMAN 2
²gopher \"\ *vi* -ED/-ING/-S : to mine haphazardly in irregular holes
gopher ball *n* : a pitched ball hit for extra bases; *specif* : one hit for a home run
go·pher·ber·ry \ˈgōfə(r)- — *see* BERRY\ *n* : BUSH HUCKLEBERRY
gopher frog *n* : a frog (*Rana aesopus*) of the southeastern U.S. often found in the burrows of the gopher tortoise
gopher hole *n* **1** : the hole of a gopher **2** : COYOTE HOLE
go·pher·man \-mən, -,man\ *n, pl* **gophermen** **1** : a mine worker who extracts ore from pockets that are inaccessible to drilling machines **2** : a logger who digs earth from beneath logs at the point where the skidding chain is to be placed — called also *gopher, swamper*
gopher plant *n* : CAPER SPURGE
gopher plum *n* **1** : OGEECHEE LIME **2** *or* **gopher apple** : either of two plants of the genus *Chrysobalanus*: **a** : COCO PLUM **b** : a low spreading shrub (*C. oblongifolius*) of sandy soil of the southeastern U.S., Mexico, and the West Indies having a fruit that is important in the diet of many small animals (as the land tortoise)
gopher snake *n* **1** : INDIGO SNAKE **2** : BULL SNAKE
gopher tortoise *or* **gopher turtle** *n* : GOPHER 1
gopher wood \ˈgōfə(r),=\ *n* [Heb *gōpher*] : an unidentified wood used in the construction of Noah's ark ⟨make yourself an ark of *gopher wood* —Gen 6:14 (RSV)⟩
gopherwood \"\ *n* [¹gopher + wood] : YELLOWWOOD 1a
go·pu·ra \ˈgōpərə\ *also* **go·pu·ram** \-rəm\ *n* -s [Skt *gopura*, fr. *go* cow, bull + *pura* city, abode — more at COW, POLICE] : the gateway of a temple in southern India; *often* : the massive tower resembling a pyramid above the gateway
go-quick \ˈ=,=\ *n* : FLOWERING SPURGE
gor \ˈgȯ(ə)r, -ȯ(ə)\ *interj* [euphemism] *dial Brit* : GOD — usu. used as a mild oath ⟨by ~, he determined to improve his luck —Samuel Lover⟩
go·ra *or* **go·rah** \ˈgōrə\ *also* **gou·ra** \ˈgùrə\ *n* -s [Hottentot] : a Hottentot musical bow having its string attached to a quill or reed fixed at one end of the stick and made to vibrate by the breath of the player and combining the qualities of a stringed and a wind instrument
go·rac·co \gəˈrä(,)kō, -ra(-\ *n* -s [Hindi *gurākū*, fr. *gur* molasses — more at GUR] : a tobacco paste smoked in hookahs
go·ral \ˈgōrəl\ *or* **goo·ral** \ˈgùr-\ *n, pl* **gorals** *or* **goral** *or* **goorals** *or* **gooral** [perh. fr. a modern Indic word derived fr. Skt *gaura* gaur — more at GAUR] : any of several goat antelopes (genus *Naemorhedus*) occurring from the southern Himalayas to northern parts of China and being closely related to the Rocky Mountain goat
go·ran \gəˈrän\ *n* -s [Bengali *garān*] : either of two Indian mangroves (*Ceriops roxburghiana* and *C. candolleana*) of the family Rhizophoraceae valued for a tanning extract derived from the bark
gor·ble \ˈgȯrbəl\ *vi* [prob. by alter.] *chiefly Scot* : GOBBLE
gor·bli·mey \gȯ(r)ˈblīmī\ *interj, usu cap* [euphemism for *God blind me*] *Brit* — used to express amazement, surprise, or perplexity ⟨*Gorblimey* . . . it's fourteen feet long! —Guy Gilpatric⟩
gor·ceix·ite \ˈgȯ(r)sək,sīt\ *n* -s [G *gorceixit*, fr. Henrique *Gorceix* †1919 Brazilian mineralogist + G *-it* -ite] : a mineral $BaAl_3(PO_4)_2(OH)_5.H_2O$(?) consisting of a hydrous basic phosphate of barium and aluminum
gor·cock \ˈgȯr,käk\ *n* [*gor-* (origin unknown) + *cock*] *dial chiefly Brit* : a male red grouse
gor·crow \-,krō\ *n* [¹gore (filth) + crow] : CARRION CROW
gor·di·a·cea \,gȯ(r)dēˈāsh(ē)ə\ [NL, fr. *Gordius* genus of roundworms (after *Gordius* of Phrygia) + *-acea*] *syn of* NEMATOMORPHA
gor·di·a·cean \,=;=ˈāsh(ē)ən\ *adj or n* [NL *Gordiacea* + E *-an*] : NEMATOMORPHAN
gordiaceous *adj* [NL *Gordiacea* + E *-ous*] : of, relating to, or being a member of the Nematomorpha
¹gor·di·an \ˈgȯ(r)dēən\ *n* -s [*Gordius* of Phrygia + E *-an* (n. suffix)] **1** *usu cap, archaic* : GORDIAN KNOT **2** [NL *Gordius* genus of roundworms + E *-an*] : a member of the Gordioidea
²gordian \"\ *adj* [*Gordius* of Phrygia + E *-an* (adj. suffix)] **1** *sometimes cap* : INTRICATE, COMPLICATED **2** [NL *Gordius* + E *-an*] : of or relating to the Gordioidea
gordian knot *n, often cap G* [*Gordius*, mythological founder of Phrygia, who tied an intricate knot in a chariot thong the untying of which was pronounced by oracle to be possible only to one destined to be master of Asia (fr. L, fr. Gk *Gordios*) + E *-an*] **1** : a problem most difficult of solution : an extreme difficulty ⟨this problem of slavery was to me a *gordian knot* —C.W.Garrison⟩ — usu. used in the phrase *cut the gordian knot* ⟨the temptation to cut the *gordian knots* of meaning by essentialist definitions —H.D.Aiken⟩; compare *cut the knot* at ¹CUT **2** : a knot so involved as not to be easily unraveled : an extremely intricate knot
¹gor·di·id \ˈgȯ(r)dēəd\ *adj* [NL *Gordiidae*] : of or relating to the Gordiidae or to the hairworms
²gordiid \"\ *n* -s : a member of the family Gordiidae : HAIRWORM
gor·di·idae \gȯ(r)ˈdīə,dē\ *n pl, cap* [NL, fr. *Gordius*, type genus (after *Gordius* of Phrygia) + *-idae*; fr. the knots into which such worms twist] : the chief family of Gordioidea coextensive with its type genus (*Gordius*) and including a number of long slender smooth-bodied worms (as hairworms or horsehair snakes)
¹gor·di·oid \ˈgȯ(r)dē,ȯid\ *adj* [NL *Gordioidea*] : of or relating to the Gordioidea; *also* : resembling a member of this group
²gordioid \"\ *n* -s : one of the Gordioidea : HAIRWORM
gor·di·oi·dea \,gȯ(r)dēˈȯidēə\ *n pl, cap* [NL, fr. *Gordius* + *-oidea*] : an order of Nematomorpha comprising freshwater forms parasitic as larvae in terrestrial or aquatic arthropods, lacking natatory bristles, and having the body cavity largely obscured by mesenchyme
gor·do·nia \gȯ(r)ˈdōnēə\ *n, cap* [NL, fr. G. *Gordon*, 19th cent. Scot. naturalist + NL *-ia*] : a genus of extinct reptiles from the New Red Sandstone of Scotland related to but smaller than those of *Dicynodon*
²gordonia \"\ *n* [NL, fr. James *Gordon* †1781 Eng. gardener + NL *-ia*] **1** *cap* : a genus of Asiatic and No. American shrubs or small trees (family Theaceae) with evergreen foliage and large white flowers — see LOBLOLLY BAY **2** -s : any tree of the genus *Gordonia* — called also *franklinia*
gor·don·ite \ˈgȯ(r)dᵊn,īt\ *n* -s [Samuel G. *Gordon* b1897 Am. mineralogist + E *-ite*] : a mineral $MgAl_2(PO_4)_2(OH)_2.8H_2O$ consisting of a hydrous basic phosphate of magnesium and aluminum found near Fairfield, Utah
gor·don setter \ˈgȯ(r)dᵊn-\ *n* [after Alexander, 4th Duke of *Gordon* †1827 Scot. nobleman and sportsman who was prominent in the development of the breed] **1** *usu cap G&S* : a breed of large long-haired showy bird dogs originating in Scotland about 1820 and distinguished from other setters only by their deep black color with tan, chestnut, or mahogany markings **2** *usu cap G, often cap S* : a dog of the Gordon Setter breed
gor·du·ra grass \gȯ(r)ˈdùrə-\ *n* [Pg *gordura* fat, fatness, fr. *gordo* fat (fr. L *gurdus* dull, stupid) + *-ura* -ure] : MOLASSES GRASS
¹gore \ˈgō(ə)r, -ȯ(ə)r, -ōə, -ȯ(ə)\ *n* -s [ME, fr. OE *gor*; akin to OHG *gor* dung, ON *gor* cud, OE *gearu* ready — more at YARE] **1** *now dial Brit* : a caked mass of filth or dirt of any kind **2 a** : BLOOD; *esp* : thick or clotted blood ⟨sacrificial altars stained with ~⟩ **b** *archaic* : a pool or mass of blood
²gore \"\ *n* -s [ME, fr. OE *gāra*; akin to OE *gār* spear, OHG *gēr* spear, *gēro* wedge-shaped object, ON *geirr* spear, *geiri* gore, OIr *gae* spear, Gk *chaios* shepherd's staff, Skt *heṣas* missile] **1 a** : a small usu. triangular piece of land ⟨the narrow lots, the ~*s* and dead ends that invite congestion —A.L.Guérard⟩ **b** : a relatively small unassigned or disputed tract of land lying between larger political divisions (as townships) **c** : a minor unorganized and usu. sparsely settled or uninhabited part of a county (as in Maine and Vermont) **2 a** (1) : a tapering or triangular piece of cloth (2) : one of several flared lengthwise sections of a garment (as a skirt) **b** : GUSSET 1c (1) **3 a** : one of the triangular pieces of the covering of a dome, umbrella, balloon, or similar object **b** : one of the series of related sections of a map that is applied to the surface of a sphere in the making of a terrestrial globe **4** : a heraldic bearing imagined as two curved lines drawn respectively from the sinister or dexter chief and from the lowest point of the shield to meeting in the fess point

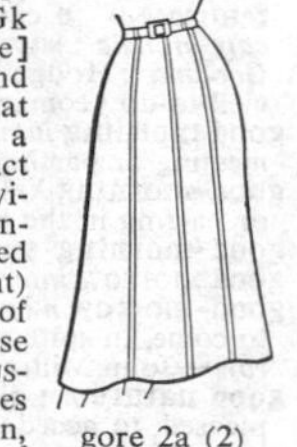
gore 2a (2)

³gore \"\ *vt* -ED/-ING/-S : to cut into a tapering triangular form : provide (a skirt) with a gore
⁴gore \"\ *vt* -ED/-ING/-S [ME *goren*, prob. fr. *gore, gare* spear, fr. OE *gār* — more at ²GORE] **1** : to pierce or penetrate with a pointed instrument ⟨~ herself with a kitchen knife —Henry Jordan⟩ **2** : to pierce or wound with the horns or tusk ⟨before the bull can ~ the man on the ground —Barnaby Conrad⟩
gore·fish \ˈgō(ə)r,fish\ *n* [alter. of *garfish*] : NEEDLEFISH
gor·e·van \ˌgȯrəˈvän\ *n* -s [fr. *Gorevan*, town in northern Iran] **1** *usu cap* : a Persian rug of carpet size made with cotton warp and characterized by a medallion field covered with large angular designs and usu. bordered by three to five stripes, the prevailing colors being shades of terracotta, apricot, and blue **2** : AUBURN
¹gorge \ˈgȯrj, -ȯ(ə)j\ *n* -s [ME, fr. MF, fr. LL *gurga*, alter. of L *gurges* whirlpool, throat; akin to OHG *querka* throat, ON *kverk* throat, Skt *gargara* whirlpool, L *vorare* to devour — more at VORACIOUS] **1** : THROAT ⟨the strong, dark golden color of her hair, her shoulder bones and ~ —John Cheever⟩ ⟨full to the ~ with misery —Djuna Barnes⟩ — often used to indicate a strong feeling of repugnance or revulsion sometimes accompanied by a physical sensation of blockage or constriction, esp. with the verb *rise* ⟨when he tried to eat the flesh of his ox his ~ rose —Pearl Buck⟩ ⟨my very ~ rises at the thought —Agnes S. Turnbull⟩ **2 a** : a hawk's crop **b** : STOMACH, MAW, BELLY, GULLET ⟨thy ~ ever cramming —P.B.Shelley⟩ **c** : a full meal : a large amount of food ⟨~*s* o' wild plums . . . clean up to his elbows —J.W.Riley⟩ ⟨if it fails to get a real ~, it . . . cannot grow or mature —H.B. Glass⟩ **3** : the entrance into a bastion or other outwork of a fort — see BASTION illustration **4 a** : a band or fillet round the shaft just under the capital at the top in some orders of columnar architecture **b** : a concave molding : CAVETTO **c** : a small groove under a coping for carrying the drip **5** : a primitive device used instead of a fishhook consisting of an object (as a piece of bone attached in the middle to a line) easy to swallow but difficult to eject **6** : a narrow passage or entrance: as **a** : a defile between mountains **b** : a ravine with steep rocky walls **c** : a narrow steep-walled canyon or a particularly narrow steep-walled part of a canyon **7** : the groove in a pulley sheave **8** : an aggregation of matter that fills or chokes up a passage or channel : MASS ⟨an ice ~ in a river⟩ **9** : the line on the front of a coat or jacket formed by the crease of the lapel and collar
²gorge \"\ *vb* -ED/-ING/-S [ME *gorgen*, fr. MF *gorger*, fr. *gorge*, n.] *vi* : to eat greedily : eat to repletion ⟨~ throughout the day on delicacies —Jean Stafford⟩ ~ *vt* **1** : to stuff to capacity (as with food) : GLUT, SATIATE, CRAM ⟨people *gorging* themselves under the eyes of others who are starving —Hans Kohn⟩ **2** : FILL : choke up ⟨a vein *gorged* with blood⟩ **3** : to swallow greedily : DEVOUR ⟨~ the bait⟩ ⟨~ one's fill⟩ **syn** see SATIATE
³gorge \"\ *n* -s : the act or an instance of gorging ⟨lions alternate heavy ~*s* with . . . periods of fasting —James Stevenson-Hamilton⟩
¹gorged \-jd\ *adj* [fr. past part. of ²*gorge*] : GLUTTED — **gorgedly** \-j(ə)dlē\ *adv*
²gorged \"\ *adj* [¹gorge + -ed] *heraldry* : having the neck encircled (as with a coronet or ring) ⟨a lion ~ with a collar⟩
gorge hook *n* **1** : GORGE 5 **2** : a hook having two barbs : two hooks with shanks joined together
gor·geous \ˈgȯrjəs, -ȯ(ə)j-\ *adj* [alter. (influenced by *-ous*) of ME *gorgayse*, fr. MF *gorgias* elegant, fond of dress, fr. *gorgias* neckerchief, wimple, fr. *gorge* throat — more at GORGE] **1 a** : dressed in splendid or vivid colors : resplendently beautiful : MAGNIFICENT, SHOWY ⟨~ in the robes of worldwide academic distinction —R.M.Lovett⟩ ⟨the costumes were ~ enough to be put into museums —Mollie Panter-Downes⟩ **b** : characterized by brilliance or magnificence of any kind : DAZZLING, FLAMBOYANT, RESPLENDENT, COLORFUL ⟨related several stories of the ~ past —Elinor Wylie⟩ ⟨poetry . . . of weighted phrase and ~ adjective —Edith Hamilton⟩ ⟨often they believed their own ~ lies —Russell Lord⟩ **2** : supremely good or delightful : TERRIFIC, SPLENDID, SUPERB ⟨really ~ — a great human book —H.J.Laski⟩ ⟨a ~ meal⟩ ⟨had a ~ time⟩ **syn** see SPLENDID
gor·geous·ly *adv* : in a gorgeous manner
gor·geous·ness *n* -ES : the quality or state of being gorgeous
gor·ger·in \ˈgȯ(r)jərən\ *n* -s [F, fr. *gorge* throat] : the part of the capital in some columns between the termination of the shaft and the annulet of the echinus; *also* : the space between two neck moldings — called also *hypotrachelium, necking*
gor·get \ˈgȯrjət\ *n* -s [ME, fr. MF, dim. of *gorge* throat] **1** : a piece of armor defending the throat — see ARMOR illustration **2** : a covering for the throat: as **a** : an ornamental collar **b** : a part of the medieval wimple covering the throat and shoulders **c** : a usu. perforated primitive artifact of bone, stone, or shell prob. used as a neck or breast ornament or as an insignia **3** : a small ornamental plate worn on a chain about the neck by officers in full uniform in some armies **4** : a specially colored patch on the throat
gor·gia \ˈgȯrjə\ *n* -s [It *gorgia*, lit., throat, fr. OIt, fr. MF *gorge* — more at GORGE] : the improvised coloratura used in 16th century singing
gor·gio \ˈgȯr(,)jō\ *n* -s [Romany *gorjo*] : one who is not a gypsy ⟨it isn't like a gypsy to take unnecessary chances or do anything foolish in entertaining the ~*s* —W.L.Gresham⟩
gor·gon \ˈgȯrgən, -ȯ(ə)g-\ *n* -s [L *Gorgon-, Gorgo*, fr. Gk *Gorgon-, Gorgō*] **1** *usu cap* : one of three sisters in Greek mythology having snake-entwined hair and glaring eyes capable of turning the beholder to stone **2** : one resembling a gorgon; *esp* : an ugly, repulsive, or terrifying woman
gor·go·na·cea \,gȯ(r)gəˈnāshēə\ *n pl, cap* [NL, fr. *Gorgonia* + *-acea*] : an order of Alcyonaria distinguished from Alcyonacea chiefly by an axial skeleton covered and secreted by a cellular coenenchyme extending between the zooids or polyps that is usu. rather horny and commonly of branching form — **gor·go·na·cean** \,=;=ˈnāshən\ *adj or n* — **gor·go·na·ceous** \-shəs\ *adj*
gor·go·nei·on \,gȯ(r)gəˈnī,än, -nē, -əˈnē,än\ *or* **gor·go·ne·um** \-ˈnēəm\ *n, pl* **gorgo·neia** \|ə\ *or* **gorgo·nea** \-ēə\ [*gorgoneion* fr. Gk, fr. neut. of *gorgoneios* of a Gorgon, fr. *Gorgon-, Gorgō*; *gorgoneum* fr. NL, fr. Gk *gorgoneion*] : a representation of the face of a Gorgon frequent as an apotropaic symbol in Greek art
gor·go·nia \gȯ(r)ˈgōnēə\ *n, cap* [NL, fr. L, coral, fr. *Gorgon-, Gorgo* + *-ia* -y] : a genus of gorgonians (the type of the family Gorgoniidae) comprising the common sea fans with flexible horny axes — **gor·go·nid** \ˈgȯ(r)gənəd\ *adj or n*
gor·go·ni·a·cea \(,)gȯ(r),gōnēˈāshēə\ [NL, fr. *Gorgonia* + *-acea*] *syn of* GORGONACEA
¹gor·go·ni·an \(ˈ)gȯ(r)ˈgōnēən, -ōnyən\ *adj* [*gorgon* + *-ian*] **1** *often cap* : of, relating to, or resembling a Gorgon : TERRIFYING **2** [NL *Gorgonia* + E *-an*] : of or relating to the Gorgonacea
²gorgonian \"\ *n* -s : a member of the Gorgonacea

gor·go·nin \'gȯ(r)gənən\ *n* -s [NL *Gorgonia* + E *-in*] **:** a complex protein frequently containing appreciable quantities of iodine and bromine that makes up the horny skeleton of typical gorgonians

gor·gon·ize \'gȯ(r)gə,nīz\ *vt* -ED/-ING/-s *see -ize in Explan Notes* [*gorgon* + *-ize*] **:** to have a paralyzing or mesmerizing effect upon **:** STUPEFY, PETRIFY ⟨could with a look ~ or melt an audience —J.E.Agate⟩ ⟨*gorgonizing* him with her opaque yellow eyes —O.Henry⟩

gor·gon·zo·la \,gȯ(r)gən'zōlə, *attrib* ¦≈≈¦≈≈\ *or* **gorgonzola cheese** *n, usu cap G* [It *gorgonzola*, fr. *Gorgonzola*, town near Milan, Italy] **:** a blue cheese usu. made of cow's milk and having blue-green marbling after curing

gor·go·sau·rus \,gȯ(r)gə'sȯrəs\ *n, cap* [NL, fr. L *Gorgo* Gorgon + *-saurus*] **:** a genus of large carnivorous dinosaurs from the Upper Cretaceous strata of Alberta

gorier *comparative of* GORY

goriest *superlative of* GORY

go·ril·la \gə'rilə\ *n* -s [NL (specific epithet of *Troglodytes gorilla*, former binomial designation for the gorilla), fr. Gk *Gorillai*, an African tribe of hairy women] **1 :** an anthropoid ape (*Gorilla gorilla* syn. *G. savagei*) that inhabits a small part of the forest region of equatorial West Africa, is closely related to the chimpanzee but less arboreal, less erect, and much larger, sometimes exceeding five and one half feet in height and 500 pounds in weight, and has massive bones, broad shoulders, very long arms, strong jaws with prominent canine teeth, a nose with a low median ridge, small ears, and a face covered with black skin **2 a :** an ugly brute of a man **b** *slang* **:** a strong-arm man **:** THUG, GOON ⟨the employment of ~*s* for purposes of intimidation —C.A.Madison⟩

go·ril·li·an \gə'rilēən\ *or* **go·ril·line** \-,līn, -,lən\ *adj* **:** of, relating to, or resembling a gorilla

go·ril·loid \-,lȯid\ *adj* **:** like a gorilla

gor·i·ly \'gōrəlē, 'gȯr-, -li\ *adv* **:** in a gory manner

¹goring *n* -s [fr. gerund of ⁴*gore*] **:** the act of goring **:** an instance of goring or of being gored ⟨his terrible ~*s* . . . had no effect on his valor at all —Ernest Hemingway⟩

²goring *n* -s [fr. gerund of ³*gore*] **1 :** the act of cutting (as cloth) into a triangular piece; *also* **:** a piece so cut **2 a :** ²GORE 3 **b :** an ugly pleat or insert esp. in slip-on shoes

gor·ki \'gȯrkē, 'gȯ(ə)k-, -ki\ *adj, usu cap* [fr. *Gorki*, U.S.S.R.] **:** of or from the city of Gorki, U.S.S.R. **:** of the kind or style prevalent in Gorki

gor·lic acid \'gȯrlik-\ *n* [ISV *gorli* (*oil*) + *-ic*; orig. formed as F *gorlique*] **:** a liquid unsaturated acid $C_5H_7(C_{12}H_{22})COOH$ occurring as the glyceride esp. in gorli oil and chaulmoogra oil

gor·lin \'gȯrlən\ *n* -s [E dial. *gor* unfledged bird + *-lin* (alter. of *-ling*)] **1** *dial Brit* **:** an unfledged bird **2** *dial Brit* **:** a callow immature person

gor·li oil \-li-\ *n* [*gorli* fr. native name in Africa] **:** a fatty oil obtained from the seeds of African trees of a genus (*Caloncoba*) of the family Flacourtiaceae and similar in composition to chaulmoogra oil

gör·litz *or* **gor·litz** *or* **goer·litz** \'gerləts, 'gər-, 'gȯr-\ *adj, usu cap* [fr. *Görlitz*, Germany] **:** of or from the city of Görlitz, Germany **:** of the kind or style prevalent in Görlitz

gor·lov·ka \gȯ(r)'lȯfkə\ *adj, usu cap* [fr. *Gorlovka*, U.S.S.R.] **:** of or from the city of Gorlovka, U.S.S.R. **:** of the kind or style prevalent in Gorlovka

gorm \'gȯ(ə)m\ *var of* ⁴GAUM

gormand *var of* GOURMAND

¹gormandize *var of* GOURMANDISE

²gor·man·dize \'gȯ(r)mən,dīz\ *vb* -ED/-ING/-s *see -ize in Explan Notes vi* **:** to eat gluttonously or ravenously ~ *vt* **1 :** to eat greedily **:** DEVOUR **2** *archaic* **:** GLUT, SATIATE

gor·man·diz·er \-zə(r)\ *n* -s **:** GOURMAND, GLUTTON

gor·maw \'gȯ(ə)r,mȯ\ *n* -s [¹*gore* + *maw* (gull)] *dial Brit* **:** CORMORANT

gorm·ing \'gȯ(ə)mən\ *or* **gormy** \'gȯ(ə)mi\ *var of* GAUMY

gorm·less \'gȯ(ə)mləs\ *var of* GAUMLESS

go round *vi* **:** to go around

go–round \'gō,≈\ *n* [*go round*] **:** GO-AROUND

gorse \'gȯ(ə)rs\ *n* -s [ME *gorst*, fr. OE — more at HORROR] **1 :** FURZE **2 :** JUNIPER

gorsechat \'≈,≈\ *n, dial Eng* **:** WHINCHAT

gor·sedd \'gȯr,seth\ *n* -s *usu cap* [W, lit., mound, court, throne] **:** a mock druidical institution established in the late 18th century that assembles twice a year for the granting of bardic degrees and the conferring of bardic titles

gorse weevil *or* **gorse seed weevil** *n* **:** a small black European weevil (*Apion ulicis*) that feeds on gorse seed and has been introduced into New Zealand for use in biological control of this plant

gor·soon \(')gȯr'sün\ *var of* GOSSOON

gorst \'gȯ(ə)rst\ *dial Brit var of* GORSE

gorsy *also* **gorsey** \'gȯrsē\ *adj* **gorsier; gorsiest** [*gorse* + *-y*] **:** of, relating to, characteristic of, or abounding in gorse ⟨windswept ~ earth —William Sansom⟩

gor·to·ni·an \gȯ(r)'tōnēən\ *n* -s *usu cap* [Samuel *Gorton* †1677 Am. religious leader + E *-ian*] **:** one of a short-lived sect composed of followers of Samuel Gorton orig. of Massachusetts and later of Rhode Island who rejected all outward forms and clergy and held that Christ was both human and divine and that heaven and hell exist only in the mind

gor·ton·ist \'gȯ(r)tᵊnəst\ *n* -s *usu cap* [S. *Gorton* + *-ist*] **:** GORTONIAN

gory \'gōrē, 'gȯr-, -ri\ *adj* -ER/-EST [ME, fr. ¹*gore* + *-y*] **1 a :** covered with gore **:** BLOODSTAINED ⟨never shake thy ~ locks at me —Shak.⟩ **b :** attended by much effusion of blood **:** MURDEROUS, SANGUINARY ⟨a lively and rather ~ prizefight —Wolcott Gibbs⟩ **2 :** of or relating to crimes, killings, or acts attended by much effusion of blood **:** BLOODCURDLING, SENSATIONAL ⟨ceremonials at which — according to a ~ legend — they made human sacrifices —*Amer. Guide Series: Calif.*⟩ ⟨~ exploitation of crime and mystery —V.L.Parrington⟩ ⟨a ~ narrative⟩

gory dew *n* **:** a gelatinous blood-red patch often seen on stones, soil, or walls and caused chiefly by a red alga (*Porphyridium cruentum*)

gos \'gäs\ *n* [by shortening] *Scot* **:** GOSHAWK

gosh \'gäsh *also* 'gärsh *or* 'gȯsh *or* 'gȯ(ə)rsh\ *interj* [euphemism for *God*] — used as a mild oath ⟨~, I was hungry —W.S. Maugham⟩

gosh–awful \'≈¦≈≈\ *adj* [euphemism] **:** GOD-AWFUL

gos·hawk *also* **gosshawk** \'gäs,hȯk\ *n* [ME *goshawke*, *goshauk*, fr. OE *gōshafoc*, fr. *gōs* goose + *hafoc* hawk — more at GOOSE, HAWK] **:** any of several long-tailed short-winged accipitrine hawks having powerful bills, long legs, and strong feet and being noted for their powerful flight, activity, and vigor — see ACCIPITER

go·shen·ite \'gōshə,nīt\ *n* -s [*Goshen*, Mass. + E *-ite*] **:** a colorless beryl

go·siute *also* **go·shute** \'gō,shüt\ *n, pl* **gosiute** *or* **gosiutes** *also* **goshute** *or* **goshutes** *usu cap* **1 :** a people of the Western Shoshoni living in northern Utah and eastern Nevada **2 :** a member of the Gosiute people

gos·lar·ite \'gäslə,rīt, -ȧzl-\ *n* -s [G *goslarit*, fr. *Goslar*, city in the Harz mts., Ger. + G *-it* ite] **:** a mineral $ZnSO_4.7H_2O$ that consists of white zinc sulfate formed by oxidation of sphalerite and that usu. occurs massive

gos·ling \'gäzliŋ, -lēŋ *sometimes* 'gȯz-\ *n* -s [ME, fr. *gos*, *goos* goose + *-ling* — more at GOOSE] **1 :** a young goose **2 a :** a foolish or callow person **3** *dial Eng* **:** CATKIN

gosling grass *or* **gosling weed** *n* **:** CLEAVERS

gosling green *n* **:** a pale yellowish green

go–slow \(')≈¦≈\ *n* -s [fr. the phrase *go slow*] *Brit* **:** SLOWDOWN ⟨a serious threat to productivity from industrial strikes and *go-slows* —*Sydney* (*Australia*) *Bull.*⟩

gos·more \'gäs,mō(ə)r, -ȧz,m-\ *n* -s [perh. alter. of *gossamer*] **:** CAT'S-EAR 1

¹gos·pel \'gäspəl *sometimes* 'gȯs-\ *n* -s [ME, fr. OE *godspel*, *gōdspel* (trans. of LL *evangelium*), fr. *gōd* good + *spell* tale — more at GOOD, SPELL, EVANGEL] **1** *sometimes cap* **a :** glad tidings; *esp* **:** the good news concerning Christ, the Kingdom of God, and salvation **b :** the teachings of Jesus and the apostles as a body or system **:** the Christian faith, revelation, or dispensation ⟨Jesus went about all Galilee . . . preaching the ~ of the kingdom —Mt 4:23 (AV)⟩ **c :** an interpretation of the gospel of Jesus Christ ⟨St. Paul's ~⟩ ⟨the social ~⟩ ⟨a highly revivalistic ~⟩ **2 a :** the story or record of Christ's life and teachings contained in the first four books of the New Testament **b** *usu cap* **:** one of the four New Testament books containing narratives of the life and death of Jesus Christ ascribed respectively to Matthew, Mark, Luke, and John; *also* **:** any of certain similar noncanonical ancient books — compare APOCRYPHA **c :** a book containing the four New Testament Gospels ⟨tracts and ~*s* were distributed by religious workers⟩ **3** *or* **gospel for the day** *usu cap G&D* **:** a lection taken from one of the New Testament gospels and forming part of a Christian liturgical service — called also *Holy Gospel* **4** *sometimes cap* **:** the message or teachings of a religious teacher **:** a doctrinal system of religious teachings ⟨the ~ of an Indian ascetic⟩ ⟨the first to bring the Buddhist ~ to China⟩ **5 a :** a message, teaching, doctrine, or course of action having certain efficacy or validity and held to or propounded with zeal **:** FAITH ⟨interested in spreading the ~ of conservation —R.M. Hodesh⟩ ⟨the ~ of progress⟩ ⟨the ~ of hard work⟩ ⟨the new proletarian ~ —J.C.Ransom⟩ **b :** something (as an assertion) of such an authoritative, infallible, or unimpeachable character or source as not to be questioned **:** absolute truth ⟨newspaper writers . . . are prone to regard it as ~ —C.J.Lovell⟩ ⟨you speak the ~ —Carl Van Vechten⟩ — often used in the phrase *gospel truth* ⟨stories like these were related as ~ truths —Herman Melville⟩

²gospel \"\ *vb* **gospeled** *or* **gospelled; gospeled** *or* **gospelled; gospeling** *or* **gospelling; gospels** [ME *gospellen*, fr. OE *godspellian*, fr. *godspel*, n.] *vt* **:** to instruct in or convert to the gospel **:** EVANGELIZE ~ *vi* **:** to preach the gospel

³gospel \"\ *adj, sometimes cap* [¹*gospel*] **:** according with or relating to the gospel **:** filled with fervor **:** EVANGELICAL ⟨~ preaching⟩ ⟨~ song⟩

gos·pel·er *also* **gos·pel·ler** \-pələ(r)\ *n* -s [ME, fr. OE *godspellere*, fr. *godspellian* + *-ere* -er] **1** *obs* **:** one of the four Evangelists **2 :** one who preaches the gospel **:** EVANGELIST **3 :** one who reads or sings the liturgical Gospel at the communion service **4 :** one who propounds a gospel of any kind ⟨the ideal ~ of American success —*Saturday Rev.*⟩

gospel hall *n* **:** a building used for the worship services of a Christian sect ⟨the larger assemblies of Plymouth Brethren own *gospel halls*⟩

gos·pel·ize \-pə,līz\ *vb* -ED/-ING/-s *vt* **:** to instruct in the gospel **:** EVANGELIZE ~ *vi* **:** to preach the gospel **:** EVANGELIZE ⟨entertaining while he *gospelized* —T.M.Pearce⟩

gospel side *n, often cap G* **:** the left side of an altar or chancel as one faces it **:** north side — used esp. in churches in which the Epistle and the Gospel are read or sung from different sides

gospel team *n* **:** a group of evangelists who work together as a unit in conducting mass meetings, in leading the singing of gospel hymns, and in preaching the gospel for the purpose of converting their hearers

gospel tree *n, often cap G* **:** a tree set to distinguish a British parish or township boundary

gospel truth *n* **:** something infallibly or absolutely true

gos·po·din \,gäspə'dēn, -əd'yēn\ *n, pl* **gospo·da** \-ə'dä\ [Russ; akin to OSlav *gospodĭ*, *gospodinŭ* lord, master, and prob. to L *hospit-*, *hospes* host — more at HOST] — used as a courtesy title in some Slavic countries

gos·port \'gä,spō(ə)rt\ *n* [fr. *Gosport*, England] **:** a flexible one-way speaking tube for communication between separate cockpits of an airplane usu. from flight instructor to student

¹gos·sa·mer \'gäsəmə(r) *sometimes* -äz(ə)m-\ *n* -s [ME *gossomer* (prob. also "Indian summer", the period when geese were eaten extensively), fr. *gos*, *goos* goose + *somer* summer; fr. its prevalence at this season of the year — more at GOOSE, SUMMER] **1 a :** a fine filmy substance consisting of fragments or strands of cobweb often seen floating in air in calm clear weather or caught on grass or bushes **b :** a fragment or strand of gossamer **2 a :** a thin sheer fabric; *esp* **:** a delicate silk veiling resembling gauze **b** *Brit* **:** HAT **c :** a thin waterproof coat or cloak **3 :** something that is infinitely or exquisitely light, delicate, or tenuous ⟨a true gift for recapturing the ~ of youth's dreams —Andrea Parke⟩

²gossamer \"\ *adj* **:** infinitely or exquisitely light, delicate, or tenuous ⟨contrives a ~ delicacy wonderful to hear —*Atlantic*⟩ ⟨try to find justifications, however ~, for their behavior —Ben Karpman⟩

gossamer fern *n* **:** HAY-SCENTED FERN

gossamer spider *n* **:** a ballooning spider

gos·sa·mery \-marē\ *adj* **:** like gossamer **:** FLIMSY

gos·san \'gäsᵊn\ *also* **goz·zan** \-äzᵊn\ *n* -s [Corn *gossen*, fr. *gōs* blood, fr. OCorn *guit*; akin to W *gwaed* blood, Bret *goad*] **:** decomposed rock or vein material of reddish or rusty color resulting from oxidized pyrites — called also *iron hat*

gosshawk *var of* GOSHAWK

¹gos·sip \'gäsəp\ *n* -s [ME *godsib*, *gossib*, fr. OE *godsibb*, fr. *god* + *sibb* kinsman, fr. *sibb*, adj., related — more at GOD, SIB] **1** *now dial chiefly Brit* **:** a person spiritually related to another through being his sponsor at baptism **2 :** a friend or comrade **:** COMPANION, CRONY ⟨a ~ of his laughed when I refused the halfpenny —W.B.Yeats⟩ ⟨taking presents of . . . strawberries to the Queen and the Princess's other ~*s* —Edith Sitwell⟩ **3 :** a person who habitually retails facts, rumors, or behind-the-scenes information of an intimate, personal, or sensational nature **:** RUMORMONGER ⟨the worst ~ in town⟩ ⟨the syndicated movie ~*s* —*Newsweek*⟩ **4 a :** rumor, report, tattle, or behind-the-scenes information esp. of an intimate or personal nature ⟨common rumor or ~ profoundly influences the conclusions of many people —Edward Jenks⟩ ⟨~ columns . . . gleefully speculate upon prospective divorces among the well-known —D.L.Cohn⟩ **b (1) :** a conversation in which gossip is exchanged ⟨settled down for what she hoped would be a ~, but thought of as a nice chat —Monica Stirling⟩ ⟨a woman standing in her doorway for a ~ —Winefride Nolan⟩ **(2) :** light familiar chatty talk or writing ⟨these reminiscences of a once brilliant court are excellent ~⟩ ⟨certain recent ~ in intellectual circles —Eleanor M. Sickels⟩ ⟨I went back . . . in high hopes of hearing good hunting ~ —S.P.B.Mais⟩ **c :** the subject matter of gossip ⟨the power, ambition, and immense personal prestige of individuals like these . . . were common ~ —H.S.Bennett⟩ **5 :** a humorous party pastime in which a sentence or anecdote is whispered from one person to the next around the group and the final version compared with the original statement

²gossip \"\ *vb* **gossiped** *also* **gossipped; gossiped** *also* **gossipped; gossiping** *also* **gossipping; gossips** *vi* **:** to converse idly ⟨don't intend to ~ about my sickness —Lillian Hellman⟩ ⟨a group of students ~*ing* —John Berger⟩; *esp* **:** to retail facts, rumors, or behind-the-scenes information about other persons ⟨must have ~*ed* about the beauty of the Queen's daughter —J.E.M.White⟩ ⟨~*s* about the doings of the town —Cornelius Weygandt⟩ ~ *vt* **:** to tell or transmit by way of gossip ⟨~*ed* from one village to the next —Ernest Beaglehole⟩

gos·sip·er \-pə(r)\ *n* -s **:** a person given to gossip **:** GOSSIP

gos·sip·i·ness \-pēnəs, -pin-\ *n* -ES **:** the quality of being gossipy

gossiping *n* -s **1** *now dial Eng* **a :** a christening feast **:** CHRISTENING **b :** a meeting of gossips or friends (as at a lying-in) **2** *now dial Eng* **:** MERRYMAKING, CAROUSAL

gos·sip·ing·ly *adv* **:** in a gossiping manner

gossipmonger \'≈≈,≈≈\ *n* **:** one who retails gossip

gos·sip·red \'gäsə,pred, -,prəd\ *n* -s [ME *gossibrede*, fr. *gossib* + *-rede* state or condition — more at KINDRED] **:** the relationship between a person and his sponsors **:** spiritual affinity **:** SPONSORSHIP

gos·sip·ry \'gäsəprē, -ri\ *n* -ES **:** CHITCHAT, GOSSIP

gos·sipy \-pē,-pi\ *adj* **:** full of or given to gossip ⟨discuss the crops with some ~ farmer —V.L.Parrington⟩ ⟨a ~ chronicle⟩

gos·soon \(')gä¦sün\ *n* -s [modif. of F *garçon* — more at GARÇON] *chiefly Irish* **:** BOY, YOUTH; *esp* **:** a serving boy

gos·syp·e·tin \gä'sipətᵊn\ *n* -s [ISV *gossypin* + *-etin* (as in *quercetin*)] **:** a yellow crystalline flavone pigment $C_{15}H_{10}O_8$ occurring in cotton flowers and obtained by hydrolysis of gossypin and gossypitrin; 8-hydroxy-quercetin

gos·sy·pin \'gäsəpən\ *n* -s [ISV *gossyp-* (fr. NL *Gossypium*) + *-in*] **:** a glucoside $C_{21}H_{20}O_{13}$ occurring in cotton flowers and hibiscus flowers

gos·syp·i·trin \gä'sipə·trən\ *n* -s [ISV *gossyp-* (fr. NL *Gossypium*) + *-itrin* (as in *quercitrin*)] **:** a yellow crystalline glucoside $C_{21}H_{20}O_{13}$ occurring in cotton flowers and hibiscus flowers

gos·syp·i·um \gä'sipēəm\ *n, cap* [NL, fr. L *gossypion* cotton] **:** a genus of herbs or shrubs of the family Malvaceae yielding the cotton of commerce and having mostly palmately lobed leaves, showy flowers, and capsular fruits containing long-tailed seeds

gos·sy·pol \'gäsə,pȯl, -pōl\ *n* -s [ISV *gossyp-* (fr. NL *Gossypium*) + *-ol*] **:** a phenolic pigment $C_{30}H_{30}O_8$ in cottonseed that crystallizes in both yellow and red forms and is toxic to some animals but is rendered harmless by processing of the seed for recovery of the oil

gos·ter \'gästə(r), 'gȯs-\ *var of* GAUSTER

gos·ther \'gästə(r), 'gȯs-\ *chiefly Irish var of* GAUSTER

got *past of* GET

¹gotch \'gäch\ *n* -ES [origin unknown] *dial Eng* **:** a potbellied jug or pitcher usu. made of earthenware

²gotch \"\ *or* **gotched** \-cht\ *adj* [*gotch* fr. Sp *gacho* having horns that project downward, having floppy ears, back-formation fr. *agachar* to bow, lower, fr. L *coactare* to constrain, force, fr. *coactus*, past part. of *cogere* to collect, compel; *gotched* fr. Sp *gacho* + E *-ed* — more at COGENT] *West* **:** DROOPING, CROPPED ⟨the sorrel with a ~ ear —Agnes M. Cleaveland⟩

gote \'gōt\ *n* -s [ME; akin to MLG & MD *gote* channel or pipe for water, OE *gēotan* to pour — more at FOUND] *now dial Brit* **:** a channel for water **:** WATERCOURSE

gö·te·borg *or* **go·te·borg** \,yād-ə¦bȯr, *Swedish* ,yœtə'bȯry\ *adj, usu cap* [fr. *Göteborg*, Sweden] **:** GOTHENBURG

goth \'gäth, 'gȯth\ *n* -s [LL *Gothi*, pl., of Gmc origin; akin to Goth *Gutthiudai* (dat.) Gothic people, OE *Gotan* (pl.) Goths, ON *Gotar*] **1** *cap* **:** a member of a Germanic people that in ancient times dwelt between the Elbe and the Vistula and in the early centuries of the Christian era overran the Roman Empire — see OSTROGOTH, VISIGOTH **2** *cap* **:** a native of the Swedish provinces of Gotland and Vestergotland **3 :** a person totally lacking in culture or refinement **:** BARBARIAN

goth·am \'gäthəm *sometimes* 'gōth-\ *adj, usu cap* [fr. *Gotham*, nickname of the city of New York, fr. *Gotham*, a proverbial town in England noted for the folly of its inhabitants, fr. ME] *slang* **:** of or relating to the city of New York ⟨a *Gotham* hotel⟩

goth·am·ite \-thə,mīt\ *n* -s *usu cap* [*Gotham* (New York) + E *-ite*] **:** an inhabitant or resident of New York City

goth·en·burg \'gäthən,bərg *sometimes* -ätᵊn-\ *adj, usu cap* [fr. *Gothenburg* (Göteborg), Sweden] **:** of or from the city of Gothenburg, Sweden **:** of the kind or style prevalent in Gothenburg

gothi·an \'gäthēən, 'gōth-\ *adj, usu cap* [F *Gothie*, Gotaland, Sweden + E *-an*] **:** of, relating to, or constituting a division of the Precambrian — see GEOLOGIC TIME table

¹goth·ic \'gäthik, -thēk *sometimes* 'gōth-\ *adj* [LL *Gothicus*, fr. *Gothi* + L *-icus* -ic] **1** *usu cap* **a :** of, relating to, or resembling the Goths, their civilization, or their language **b :** TEUTONIC, GERMANIC ⟨in German they have a kind of *Gothic* eloquence that does not survive translation —Winthrop Sargeant⟩ ⟨the eclectic idiosyncrasy and studied barbarism of Carlyle's *Gothic* style —W.H.Gardner⟩ **c (1) :** of or relating to the middle ages **:** MEDIEVAL ⟨his face was calm and beautiful . . . above the *Gothic* splendor of his raiment —Elinor Wylie⟩ ⟨the monkish or *Gothic* ages . . . were therefore despised by the scholar and the philosopher —L.G.Pine⟩ ⟨a whole *Gothic* world had come to grief . . . there was now no armor glittering in the forest glades —Evelyn Waugh⟩ **(2) :** UNCOUTH, PRIMITIVE, BARBAROUS, UNCIVILIZED ⟨the *Gothic* obscurities and barbarities of the past —Ernest Barker⟩ ⟨the *Gothic* and barbarous self-complacency of his contemporaries —P.E. More⟩ **(3) :** SAVAGE, FEROCIOUS ⟨tetanus is a disease of *Gothic* ferocity —Berton Roueché⟩ **2** *usu cap* **a (1) :** of, relating to, or having the characteristics of a style of architecture developed in northern France and spreading through western Europe from the middle of the 12th century to the early 16th century that is characterized by the converging of weights and strains at isolated points upon slender vertical piers and counterbalancing buttresses with the building becoming essentially a stone skeleton of pillars, props, and ribs upon which rest shells of vaulting, with the enclosing walls made thin or sometimes almost wholly replaced by large windows of colored glass stiffened with metalwork and stone tracery, and with pointed arches and vaulting replacing the round of the Romanesque **(2) :** of or relating to an architectural style or an example of such style patterned upon or reflecting the strong influence of the medieval Gothic esp. in outward form ⟨a *Gothic* Presbyterian church⟩ ⟨*Gothic* buildings on an American campus⟩ ⟨the eye singles out the *Gothic* Woolworth Tower —*Ford Times*⟩ **b :** of or relating to an art style flourishing esp. in northern Europe from the 12th through the 19th centuries and distinguished by an austere verticality and a tendency toward naturalism **c (1) :** of or relating to a late 18th and early 19th century style of fiction characterized by the use of medieval settings, a murky atmosphere of horror and gloom, and macabre, mysterious, and violent incidents **(2) :** of or relating to a literary style or an example of such style characterized by grotesque, macabre, or fantastic incidents or by an atmosphere of irrational violence, desolation, and decay ⟨the foremost current . . . practitioner of the gruesomely *Gothic* weird tale —*Fantasy & Science Fiction*⟩ ⟨compounded of fantasy surrealism, allegory, and *Gothic* sensationalism —William Peden⟩ **(3) :** romantic in style or content as opposed to classical **3** *usu cap* **a** *of handwriting* **:** characterized by angularity and lateral compression — used specif. of a minuscule type of handwriting which developed in the 12th century in France from the Caroline minuscule and which in turn was the prototype of the modern black letter **b :** of or relating to this type of handwriting ⟨the characteristic *Gothic* features⟩ **4 :** FANTASTIC, UNREAL, EXTRAVAGANT, BAROQUE ⟨a world of spooks and goblins . . . a ~ world —Herbert Read⟩ ⟨allowing them lunch hours of ~ proportions —*New Yorker*⟩

²gothic \"\ *n* **1** *cap* **:** the East Germanic language of the Goths esp. as represented by the surviving fragments of a 4th century biblical translation made by Bishop Wulfila (*ab* A.D. 311–381) — see CRIMEAN GOTHIC, EAST GERMANIC; INDO-EUROPEAN LANGUAGES table **2** *usu cap* **:** Gothic art style or decoration; *specif* **:** the Gothic architectural style **3** *usu cap* **:** Gothic writing or lettering **4** *often cap* **a :** BLACK LETTER **b :** SANS SERIF

Gothic

Gothic 3

goth·i·cal·ly \-thək(ə)lē, -thēk-, -li\ *adv, sometimes cap* **:** in a Gothic manner ⟨~ elaborate —James Binder⟩

gothic alphabet *n, usu cap G* **:** an alphabet based principally on the Greek uncials and devised for the Gothic language by Bishop Wulfila in the 4th century A.D.

gothic arch *n, often cap G* **:** a pointed arch; *esp* **:** one with a joint instead of a keystone at its apex

gothic chasuble *n, usu cap G* **:** a chasuble of elbow length at the sides with the front and back shaped to a downward point — see CHASUBLE illustration

gothic chippendale *n, usu cap G&C* **:** 18th century furniture with pointed arches, clustered columns, and other medieval details

goth·i·cism \-thə,sizəm\ *n* -s *usu cap* **1** *archaic* **:** lack of taste or elegance **:** barbarous spirit or quality **2 :** Gothic spirit or principles **:** conformity to or practice of Gothic style

goth·i·cist \-thəsəst\ *n* -s *usu cap* **:** a practitioner of Gothic style (as in literature)

goth·i·cize \-thə,sīz\ *vt* -ED/-ING/-s *often cap* **:** to make Gothic **:** transform to the Gothic style

goth·ic·ness *n* -ES *usu cap* **:** the quality or state of being Gothic

gothic revival *n, usu cap G&R* **:** an artistic style or movement of the 18th and 19th centuries inspired by and imitative of the Gothic style esp. in architecture

goth·ish \-thish\ *adj, usu cap* [*Goth* + *-ish*] *archaic* **:** GOTHIC

göthite *var of* GOETHITE

go·thon·ic \(')gä¦thänik, (')gȯ¦-, (')gō¦-\ *adj, usu cap* [L *Gothones*, *Gotones* Goths (of Gmc origin; akin to OE *Gotan* Goths) + E *-ic* — more at GOTH] **:** GERMANIC, TEUTONIC

go through *vi* **1 :** to continue firmly or obstinately to the end **:** PERSIST, PERSEVERE — used with *with* ⟨I was *going through* with it if it killed me —A.W.Long⟩ **2 a :** to receive approval or sanction **:** PASS ⟨the proposed amendment failed to *go through*⟩

b : to come to be agreed on ⟨the deal *went through* and the house was sold⟩
goths *pl of* GOTH
got·land·er \ˈgätˌlandə(r), - lən-\ *n* -s *cap* [*Gotland*, island in the Baltic sea belonging to Sweden + E *-er*] **:** a native or inhabitant of the island of Gotland
go to *vi* **1** *archaic* — used interjectionally as an exhortation ⟨and they said one to another, *go to*, let us make brick —Gen 11:3 (AV)⟩ **2** *archaic* — used interjectionally to express disapproval or disbelief ⟨*go to*, you are a wag —Lord Byron⟩
go–to–meeting \ˌ=ˈ=ˌ=\ *adj* **:** suitable for churchgoing or other special occasions — used esp. of clothes ⟨dressed in *go-to-meeting* attire⟩
gotten *past part of* GET
göt·ter·däm·me·rung \ˌgə(r)\|d-ə(r)ˈdamərəŋ, ˌgə̄\|, ˌge\|, ˌgä\|, \|tə-, -dem-, -məˌrůŋ\ *n, pl* **götterdämmerun·gen** \-ˌrůŋən\ *usu cap* [G, twilight of the gods, fr. *götter* (pl. of *gott* god) + *dämmerung* twilight] **:** the stage or process of collapse and dissolution (as of a political or social order) typically attended by catastrophic violence and disorder ⟨two grandiose . . . novels describing the *Götterdämmerung* of the Nazi armies in Russia —*New Yorker*⟩
gou \ˈgü\ *n* -s [by shortening] **:** GASPERGOU
gouache \ˈgwäsh, gü'ä-,gəˈwä-\ *n* -s [F, fr. It *guazzo*, lit., puddle, fr. a southern It. dial. word derived fr. L *aquatio* action of fetching water, watering, watering place, fr. *aquatus* (past part of *aquari* to fetch water, fr. *aqua* water) + *-io* -ion — more at ISLAND] **1 :** a method of painting with opaque colors that have been ground in water and mingled with a preparation of gum **2 a :** a picture painted by gouache **b :** the pigment used in gouache
gouber \ˈgübə(r), ˈgůb-\ *var of* GOOBER
goud \ˈgaůd\ *chiefly Scot var of* GOLD
gou·da \ˈgaůdə, ˈgüdə, ˈhaůdə\ *or* **gouda cheese** *n* -s *usu cap G* [fr. *Gouda*, Netherlands, where it was orig. made] **:** a whole-milk cheese of close texture and mild flavor shaped in flattened spheres and usu. covered with a red protective coating
¹gouge \ˈgaůj, *Brit sometimes* ˈgüj\ *n* -s [ME *goodg, gowge*, fr. MF *gouge*, fr. LL *gubia*, *gulbia* hollow chisel, of Celt origin; akin to OIr *gulban* sting, MW *gwlf* notch, *gylf* beak, and prob. to Gaulish *galba* fat man — more at CALF] **1 a :** a chisel with a concavo-convex cross section used in its various forms esp. for scooping or cutting holes, channels, or grooves (as in wood or stone), for doing the roughing cuts in wood turning, or for removing portions of bone in surgery **b :** an incising tool that cuts forms or blanks (as for gloves or envelopes) from leather, paper, or other material **c :** a bookbinder's blind-tooling or gilding tool having a face that forms a curve; *also* **:** the impression made by it **2** [²*gouge*] **a :** the act of gouging with or as if with a gouge **b :** a groove or cavity scooped out (as with a gouge) **3 :** an excessive or improper exaction **:** EXTORTION, SWINDLE, OVERCHARGE ⟨the only protection we have against a rubber-price ~ —*Newsweek*⟩; *also* **:** the amount extorted or overcharged ⟨the yearly ~ is closer to $200,000,000 —Lester David⟩ **4 :** soft clayey material often present between a vein and a wall or along a fault — called also *selvage*

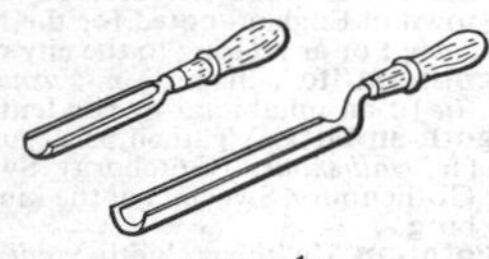
gouges 1a

²gouge \"\ *vb* -ED/-ING/-S *vt* **1 :** to cut grooves, channels, or holes in with or as if with a gouge **:** scoop out with or as if with a gouge **2 a :** to force out (an opponent's eye) with the thumb **b :** to thrust the thumb or finger into (an opponent's eye) **:** thrust the thumb or finger into the eye of ⟨*gouged* one of his eyes so thoroughly that it bulged —John Lardner⟩ ⟨kick and ~ him into insensibility —*Time*⟩ **3 :** to subject to extortion or undue exaction **:** OVERCHARGE, SWINDLE, EXPLOIT ⟨protect . . . the public against being *gouged* by ticket scalpers —M.R.Cohen⟩ ⟨unions and employers get together to ~ the consumer —C.R.Daugherty⟩ ⟨*gouged* for thousands . . . of dollars —*Newsweek*⟩ ~ *vi* **1 :** to cut grooves, channels, or holes with or as if with a gouge ⟨such moving ice . . scrapes, plucks, ~*s*, and scours —G.T.Renner & C.L.White⟩ **:** PIERCE, BORE ⟨his eyes *gouging* into mine —R.P.Warren⟩ **2 :** to thrust the thumb or finger into the eye of an opponent ⟨still kicked and punched and *gouged* —Edwin Corle⟩ **3 :** to practice extortion **:** OVERCHARGE ⟨doctors who were . . . *gouging* on patients —Milton Silverman⟩ ⟨began *gouging* on the price —Wenzell Brown⟩
gouge carving *n* **:** NICKING
gougelhof *var of* GUGELHUPF
goug·er \-jə(r)\ *n* -s **:** one that gouges: as **a :** a person who uses a gouge in shaping heels or toes of shoes **b :** a person who overcharges or takes unfair advantage of another ⟨rent ~s who objected to urban renewal programs⟩
gou·jon \ˈgüjən\ *n* -s [LaF, fr. F, gudgeon — more at GUDGEON] **:** FLATHEAD CATFISH
gouk *var of* ²GOWK
goul *chiefly Scot var of* GOWL
gou·lard's extract \(ˈ)güˌlärdz-\ *n, usu cap G* [after Thomas *Goulard* †1784 Fr. surgeon] **:** an aqueous solution of lead subacetate applied to bruises and sprains
gou·lash *also* **gu·lash** \ˈgüˌläsh, -lash,-laa(ə)sh,-laish,-lash\ *n* -ES [Hung *gulyás* herdsman, herdsman's stew] **1 a :** a beef stew with onion, paprika, and caraway — called also *Hungarian goulash* **b :** a stew of mixed ingredients **2 a :** a method of dealing in bridge in which each player arranges his 13-card hand into suits, the hands are stacked to reconstitute the pack, and this pack unshuffled is then dealt to the four players in lots of 5, 5, and 3 cards at a time, the object being to produce unusually long suits in the players' hands — called also *hollandaise, mayonnaise* **b :** a deal of the cards in this manner **c goulashes** *pl but sing in constr* **:** a bridge game in which a goulash is dealt whenever the bidding of a regular deal stops short of a game contract **d :** two-handed pinochle played with a 64-card pack **3 :** a mixture of heterogeneous elements **:** MISHMASH, MEDLEY, JUMBLE ⟨a sort of linguistic ~ . . . made of many ingredients —Charlton Laird⟩
gould \ˈgaů(l)d\ *Scot var of* GOLD
gould·ian finch \ˈgüldēən-\ *also* **gouldian** *n* -s *often cap G* [John *Gould* †1881 Eng. naturalist + E *-ian*] **:** a small brilliantly colored Australian finch (*Poephila gouldiae*) often kept as a cage or aviary bird
goum \ˈgüm\ *n* -s [F, fr. Ar dial. *gūm*, var. of Ar *qum* band, troop] **1 :** a unit of native soldiers under French officers in No. Africa **2 :** a member of a goum
gou·mi *or* **gu·mi** \ˈgümē\ *n* -s [Jap *gumi*] **:** a shrub (*Elaeagnus multiflora*) of Japan and China cultivated for its fragrant flowers and orange or reddish fruit
gou·mier \(ˈ)gümˌyā\ *n* -s [F, fr. *goum* + *-ier* -er] **:** GOUM 2
gound \ˈgaůnd\ *dial var of* GOWN
go under *vi* **:** to come to be overwhelmed, destroyed, or defeated **:** FAIL ⟨take the steps now to keep that country from *going under* —Norman Cousins⟩
goun·dou \ˈgün(ˌ)dü\ *n* -s [F, fr. a native name in western Africa] **:** a tumorous swelling of the root of the nose involving the nasal bones, occurring in certain tropical areas, and often considered a late lesion of yaws — compare GANGOSA
go up *vi* **1 a :** to proceed or move to or as if to a higher place ⟨the elevator *went up* to the fourth floor⟩ ⟨*go up* in a plane for the first time⟩ **b :** to lead to or as if to a higher place ⟨a road *goes up* to the mountain lodge⟩ **2 :** to become audible **:** come to be heard ⟨the roar that *went up*: I thought we'd burst the ribs of the roof —Gerard Perry⟩ **3** — used interjectionally esp. to express derision ⟨some small boys came out of the city and jeered at him, saying, "*Go up*, you baldhead" —2 Kings 2:23 (RSV)⟩ **4 a :** to come to ruin; *specif* **:** to become bankrupt **b :** to become destroyed ⟨caused his mansion to *go up* in flames —F.W.Saunders⟩ **5** *Brit* **a :** to enter a university **b :** to become a candidate **6 a :** to undergo construction ⟨new schools *go up* all the time —John Blofeld⟩ **b :** to come to be posted or put up ⟨placards declaring martial law were *going up* —J.P.O'Donnell⟩ **7 :** to undergo an increase (as in price or number) **:** RISE ⟨medical costs have *gone up* —Vannevar Bush⟩ ⟨world population is *going up* —Ruth Douglass⟩ **8 :** to become confused esp. with temporary loss of memory ⟨she *went up* in her lines in the third act and merely giggled —Irving Kolodin⟩
goup *var of* GAUP
¹goura *var of* GORA
²gou·ra \ˈgůrə, ˈgaůrə\ *n, cap* [NL, fr. a native name in New Guinea] **:** a genus of birds (family Columbidae) including only the crowned pigeons
gou·ra·mi \gůˈrämē\ *n, pl* **gourami** *or* **gouramis** *or* **gouramies** [Malay *gurami*] **1 a :** a large freshwater anabantid fish (*Osphronemus goramy*) that is an important food fish in southeastern Asia and the Malay archipelago **b :** any of several small brightly colored fishes of the same family that are often kept in the tropical aquarium — see CROAKING GOURAMI, THREE-SPOT GOURAMI **2 :** YELLOW GROUPER 1
gourd \ˈgō(ə)rd, ˈgȯ(-, ˈgů(-; -ōəd, -ȯ(ə)d, -ůəd\ *n* -s [ME *gourde*, fr. MF, fr. L *cucurbita*, prob. of non-IE origin like L *cucumer-, cucumis* cucumber — more at CUCUMBER] **1 a** *chiefly Brit* **:** a cucurbitaceous fruit (as a cucumber, watermelon, or squash) **:** PEPO **b** (1) **:** any of numerous hard-rinded inedible usu. large fruits (as a bottle gourd) of vines of the genus *Lagenaria* extensively used for vessels and utensils — called also *calabash* (2) **:** any of numerous hard-rinded inedible small fruits derived from a natural variety of the pumpkin (*Cucurbita pepo*) — called also *ornamental gourd* (3) **:** DISHCLOTH GOURD **c** *Brit* **:** PUMPKIN 1 a (3) **2 :** a cucurbitaceous plant whose fruits are gourds **3 :** any of various hard-rinded fruits (as of the calabash tree) resembling or used like gourds **4 :** a cleaned dried shell of a gourd used as a dipper or water bottle
gourde \ˈgů(ə)rd\ *n* -s [AmerF, fr. F, fem. of *gourd* numb, dull, heavy, fr. L *gurdus* dull, stupid] **1 a :** the basic monetary unit of Haiti — see MONEY table **b :** a coin representing this unit **2 :** DOLLAR — formerly used in Louisiana, Cuba, and Haiti
gourd family *n* **:** CUCURBITACEAE
gourdhead \ˈ=ˌ=\ *also* **gourdhead buffalo** *n* **1 :** BIGMOUTH BUFFALO **2 :** WOOD IBIS
¹gour·mand \ˈgů(ə)rˌmänd, ˈgō(ə)rˌm-, ˈgȯ(ə)rˌm-, -ůəˌm-, -ōəˌm-, -ȯ(ə)ˌm-, -ˌmənd, =ˈmänd, (ˈ)=ˈmäⁿ\ *also* **gor·mand** \ˈgȯ(ə)rmənd, -ȯ(ə)m-, -ˌmänd\ *n* -s [MF *gourmant*, adj. & n.] **1 :** a greedy or ravenous eater **:** GLUTTON ⟨can a ~ ever appreciate rare and fragile flavors —E.J.Banfield⟩ **2 :** a luxurious eater **:** EPICURE, GOURMET ⟨the French love good eating — they are all ~*s* —Laurence Sterne⟩ **syn** see EPICURE
²gourmand \"\ *also* **gormand** \"\ *adj* [MF *gourmant*] **:** fond of eating **:** GLUTTONOUS; *esp* **:** fond of dainty or luxurious food
gour·man·dise \ˈgůrmənˌdēz, ˈgōrm-, ˈgȯ(ə)rm-, -ůəm-, -ōəm-, ˌ==ˈ=\ *also* **gor·man·dize** \ˈgȯ(ə)rmənˌdīz, -dēz, ˌ==ˈdēz\ *n, pl* **gourman·dises** \-ēz(əz)\ *also* **gorman·diz·es** \-īzəz,-ēzəz\ [ME *gromandise*, fr. MF *gourmandise*, fr. *gourmant* + *-ise* -ice] **:** luxurious epicurean discrimination in eating and drinking
gour·man·diz·er \ˈ==ˌdīzə(r)\ *n* -s **:** GOURMAND 1
gour·met \ˈgů(ə)rˌmā, ˈgō(ə)rˌm-, ˈgȯ(ə)ˌm-, -ůəˌm-, -ōəˌm-, =ˈ=\ *n* -s [F, fr. MF, alter. (perh. influenced by *gourmant* gourmand) of OF *gromet*, *grommes* boy servant, wine merchant's assistant] **:** a connoisseur in eating and drinking **:** EPICURE **syn** see EPICURE
gous *pl of* GOU
gousle *var of* GUSLA
gous·ty *or* **gous·tie** \ˈgaůstī, ˈgəůs-\ *adj* [origin unknown] **1** *dial Brit* **:** desolate and dismal **2** *dial Brit* **:** EERIE, GHOSTLY
¹gout \ˈgaůt, *usu* -aůd.+V\ *n* -s [ME *goute*, fr. OF, drop, gout (considered as caused by drops of diseased humors), fr. L *gutta* drop; perh. akin to Arm *kat'*, *kat'n* drop, *kit'*, *kt'an* milk] **1 a :** a metabolic disease occurring in paroxysms and marked by a painful inflammation of the fibrous and ligamentous parts of the joints, deposits of urates in and around the joints, and at times an excessive amount of uric acid in the blood **b :** a disease esp. of wheat characterized by swellings at the nodes — see GOUT FLY **2 :** a mass or aggregate of something fluid, sticky, gaseous, or composed of fine particles **:** CLOT, BLOB, SPLASH, SPURT ⟨attacking snowy canvases with ~*s* of oil paint —*Times Lit. Supp.*⟩ ⟨the light ~ of sand the child's shovel . . . flung —William Faulkner⟩ ⟨hurled ~*s* of brown dust and gray smoke into the air —G.H.Johnston⟩ ⟨a great ~ of oil shot out of it —Ira Wolfert⟩ ⟨~ of water gushed forth —R.A.W. Hughes⟩ ⟨~*s* of blood⟩ **3 a :** waste fiber caught in yarn during spinning or accidentally woven into cloth **b :** a defect in cloth caused by gout
²gout \", ˈgōt\ *n* -s [ME *goute*, alter. of *gote*] *now dial Eng* **:** an artificial water channel; *esp* **:** CULVERT
³goût \ˈgü\ *n* -s [F, fr. L *gustus*; akin to L *gustare* to taste, enjoy — more at CHOOSE] **1 a :** taste or flavor esp. of food **b :** RELISH, LIKING — used with *for* ⟨has no ~ for that sort of adventure⟩ **2 :** artistic or literary good taste **:** DISCERNMENT ⟨the sting of having my ~ as a reader under attack —Peter De Vries⟩ ⟨has a very nice ~ in such matters⟩
goû·ter \(ˈ)güˌtā\ *n* -s [F, fr. *goûter* to taste, enjoy, eat a snack, fr. L *gustare* to taste, enjoy — more at CHOOSE] **:** an afternoon snack ⟨sat on the sands to eat a childish ~ of bread and butter —Anne Green⟩
gout fly *n* [¹*gout*] **:** any of various chloropid flies (genus *Chlorops*) whose larvae feed in wheat, barley, and other grasses causing gout in infested plants
gout·i·ly \ˈgaůd·ᵊl·ē, -aůt\, \|ᵊli, \|əl-\ *adv* **:** in a gouty manner
gout·i·ness \\|ēnəs, \|in-\ *n* -ES **:** the quality or state of being gouty
gout·ish \\|ish, \|ēsh\ *adj* [ME *goutissh*, fr. *goute* + *-issh* -ish] **:** predisposed to gout **:** GOUTY
gout stool *n* **:** a stool with an adjustable top
¹goutte \ˈgüt\ *n* -s [F, lit., drop, fr. OF *goute* — more at GOUT] **:** DROP 1c(5)
²goutté *or* **gouttée** *or* **goutty** *var of* GUTTÉE
gout tree *n* **1 :** CLAMMY CHERRY **2 :** a tree (*Varronia globosa*) of tropical America
goutweed \ˈ=ˌ=\ *n* **:** a coarse European plant (*Aegopodium podagraria*) with umbellate white flowers
gouty \ˈgaůd·ē, -aůt\, \|ī\ *adj, sometimes* -ER/-EST [ME *gowty*, fr. *goute* gout + *-y* — more at GOUT] **1 a :** diseased with gout ⟨a ~ person⟩ **b :** of or characteristic of gout ⟨a ~ paroxysm⟩ ⟨~ concretions⟩ **c :** causing or tending to induce gout ⟨some wines are distinctly ~⟩ **d :** used or for use during an attack of gout ⟨~ shoes⟩ **2 :** SWOLLEN, BULGING, OVERLARGE ⟨chairs with ~ legs —F.G.Roe⟩ **3** *archaic* **:** KNOBBY, KNOTTY
gouty stem *or* **gouty tree** *n* **:** BOTTLE TREE
gov *abbr* **1** government, governmental **2** governor
gove \ˈgōv\ *vi* -ED/-ING/-S [ME (Sc dial.) *goven*] *Scot* **:** to stare idly **:** GAPE ⟨~ away or sleep and loiter out the day —Allan Ramsay †1758⟩
gov·ern \ˈgəvə(r)n *sometimes* ˈgəvᵊm *or* ˈgəbᵊm\ *vb* **governed; governed; governing** \-və(r)niŋ, *-R sometimes* -vniŋ\ **governs** \-və(r)nz, -vᵊmz, -bᵊmz\ [ME *governen*, fr. OF *governer*, fr. L *gubernare* to steer, pilot, govern, fr. Gk *kybernan*, prob. of non-IE origin] *vt* **1 a :** to exercise arbitrarily or by established rules continuous sovereign authority over; *esp* **:** to control and direct the making and administration of policy in ⟨a cabinet which . . . is to ~ the land —C.J.Friedrich⟩ ⟨Europe was ~*ed* almost entirely by kings —Stringfellow Barr⟩ **b :** to rule without sovereign power **:** implement and carry into effect policy decisions over without having the power to determine basic policy **:** ADMINISTER ⟨the country is ruled but not ~*ed* —Frederick Puckle⟩ ⟨New York City is ~*ed* by its budget director . . . supported by department engineers, administrators —A.A.Berle⟩ **2 a** *archaic* **:** to control the workings or operation of **:** MANIPULATE ⟨~ these ventages with your fingers and thumbs . . . and it will discourse most eloquent music —Shak.⟩ **b :** to control the speed or power of (as a machine) esp. by automatic means — compare GOVERNOR 4 **3 a :** to control, direct, or strongly influence the actions and conduct of (as a person or a group) ⟨men are ~*ed* by memory rather than thought —John Dewey⟩ ⟨special students . . . are ~*ed* by the same scholastic regulations —*Bull. of Meharry Med. Coll.*⟩ **b :** DETERMINE, GUIDE, REGULATE ⟨a commission to ~ the union's business affairs⟩ ⟨deadlock and compromise largely ~*ed* the choice —B.K.Sandwell⟩ ⟨its agreements ~ working conditions in many ports —E.P.Hohman⟩ **c :** to hold in check **:** RESTRAIN ⟨this consuming passion for law made him ~ himself —H.E.Scudder⟩ ⟨I appeal to you to ~ your temper —Charles Dickens⟩ **4 a** *obs* **:** to require (a verb) to be in a certain person and number — used of the subject of a verb; compare AGREE *vi* 5 **b :** to require (a word) to be in a certain case or mood ⟨in English a transitive verb ~*s* a noun in the common case or a pronoun in the accusative case⟩ **c :** to call for (a certain case or mood) **:** REQUIRE ⟨the German preposition *mit* ~*s* the dative case⟩ ⟨the Greek conjunction *ean* ~*s* the subjunctive mood⟩ **5 :** to constitute a rule or law for **:** serve as a precedent or deciding principle for ⟨policies . . . which should ~ the services of all libraries —Helen T. Geer⟩ ⟨the principles which should ~ the creation of proletarian literature —C.I.Glicksberg⟩ ~ *vi* **1 :** to prevail or have decisive influence **:** CONTROL ⟨in all causes of passion admit reason to ~ —George Washington⟩ **2 :** to exercise authority **:** perform the functions of government esp. in the making and execution of policy **:** RULE ⟨at the beginning of the seventeenth century our kings still ~*ed* as well as reigned —Ernest Barker⟩ — compare REIGN
gov·ern·able \-ə(r)nəbəl, -ᵊməb-\ *adj* **:** capable of being governed ⟨likely to be ~ by prudent counsel —George Meredith⟩ — **gov·ern·able·ness** *n* -ES
gov·ern·ance \ˈgəvə(r)nən(t)s\ *n* -s [ME *governaunce*, fr. MF *governance*, fr. *governer*, *gouverner* to govern + *-ance* — more at GOVERN] **1 :** the act or process of governing **:** GOVERNMENT 2 ⟨the internal stresses and strains in the ~ of a nation —V.O.Key⟩ ⟨intelligence . . . in the ~ of men —Lewis Mumford⟩ **2 a :** the office, power, or function of governing ⟨invested with the ~ of the kingdom⟩ **b :** controlling or directing influence **:** AUTHORITY ⟨she disliked whatever did not yield to her ~ —Thomas Wolfe⟩ **3 :** the state of being governed ⟨the colonies . . . passed through analogous stages from ~ to self-government —Alexander Brady⟩ **4 a :** the manner or method of governing **:** conduct of office ⟨her iron-fisted ~ of her office is one of arbitrary whim and prejudice —H.L.Ickes⟩ ⟨inferred the nature of the governor from the observed mode of his ~ —I.R.Maxwell⟩ **b** *obs* **:** personal conduct, behavior, or manner of life ⟨he likest is to fall into mischiefe . . . regardless of his ~ —Edmund Spenser⟩ **5 :** a system of governing **:** GOVERNMENT 7a ⟨the ancient ~ was sapped in its foundations —John Buchan⟩ ⟨a new world ~ enforced through power —*Yale Rev.*⟩
gov·er·nante \ˈgəvə(r)nənt, ˌ==ˈnänt\ *or* **gou·ver·nante** \ˈgüv-, ˌgüv-\ *n* -s [F *gouvernante*, fr. fem. of *gouvernant*, pres. part. of *gouverner* to govern, administer, bring up, fr. OF *governer* — more at GOVERN] **1** *archaic* **:** a woman having charge of a young person **:** CHAPERON 2, GOVERNESS 2 ⟨attended by . . . an old gentlewoman for her ~ —Jedidiah Morse⟩ **2** *archaic* **:** the mistress of a household **:** HOUSEKEEPER **3** *obs* **:** GOVERNESS 1 ⟨the government devolved upon the princess, as ~ during her son's minority —Tobias Smollett⟩
¹gov·er·ness \ˈgəvə(r)nəs\ *n* -ES [ME *gouvernesse*, fr. MF *governeresse*, fr. *governeor* governor + *-esse* -ess — more at GOVERNOR] **1 :** a woman that governs **:** a female governor ⟨his mother was named by the states *Governess* of the United Provinces —Charles Butler †1832⟩ ⟨a shining example to ~*es* of religious houses —Ann Radcliffe⟩ ⟨the moon, the ~ of floods —Shak.⟩ **2 :** a woman entrusted with the care and supervision of a child or young person; *esp* **:** a female teacher employed in a private household ⟨my education and that of my brothers had been generally superintended . . . by a succession of ~*es* —Caroline Gilman⟩ **3** *archaic* **:** the wife of a governor ⟨introduced by the . . . *Governess* at Madras —Benjamin Heyne⟩
²governess \"\ *vb* -ED/-ING/-ES *vi* **:** to act or serve as a governess ⟨she's going to ~ in Winnipeg —Agnes Macdonald⟩ ~ *vt* **1 :** to act as governess to **:** INSTRUCT ⟨and ~*es* her brother's rising family —*Tait's Mag.*⟩ **2 :** to subject to or as if to the authority and instruction of a governess ⟨if you persist in ~*ing* people —G.B.Shaw⟩
governess cart *or* **governess car** *n* **:** a light two-wheeled cart entered from the rear with body partly or wholly of wickerwork and with a seat for two persons along each side — called also *tub-cart*

governess cart

gov·er·nessy \-sē\ *adj* **:** having the characteristics of or suggesting a governess; *esp* **:** PRIM ⟨a big nunlike college girl with a ~ air —Frank O'Connor⟩
governless *adj, obs* **:** lacking a government **:** UNGOVERNED
gov·ern·ment \ˈgə\|və(r)mənt, \|və(r)nm-, \|v(ᵊ)m-, \|b(ᵊ)m-\ *n* -s *often attrib* [MF *governement*, fr. *governer* to govern + *-ment*] **1** *obs* **a :** management of the limbs or the whole body ⟨shot many a dart at me . . . but I them warded all with wary ~ —Edmund Spenser⟩ **b :** moral conduct or behavior **:** DISCRETION ⟨harsh rage, defect of manners, want of ~ —Shak.⟩ **2 :** the act or process of governing **:** authoritative direction or control ⟨to make rules for the ~ and regulation of the land and naval forces —*U.S. Constitution*⟩ ⟨unusual talent for the instruction and ~ of the young —S.P.Chase & J.K.Snyder⟩ **3 a :** the office, authority, or function of governing ⟨the ~ I cast upon my brother and to my state grew stranger —Shak.⟩ ⟨persuaded . . . to accept the ~ of Dover Castle —James Tyrrell⟩ **b** *obs* **:** the term during which a governing official holds office ⟨his fact, till now in the ~ of Lord Angelo, came not to an undoubtful proof —Shak.⟩ **4** *archaic* **:** an area organized as a political unit; *esp* **:** a territorial division ruled by a governor ⟨I pass'd through most of the Protestant ~*s* in Europe —Joseph Addison⟩ ⟨the czar . . . divided the empire into eight ~*s* —Charles Whitworth⟩ **5 a :** the influence of one word on another word that is required to be in a certain case or mood when it occurs in the same construction — called also *regimen* **b :** the effect of this influence **6 a :** the continuous exercise of authority over and the performance of functions for a political unit **:** RULE ⟨the end of ~ is the good of mankind —John Locke⟩ ⟨constitutional ~ does not exist unless procedural restraints are established —C.J.Friedrich⟩ ⟨before the fourteenth century . . . ~ had meant very largely the administration of justice —Christopher Morris⟩ ⟨he was active in school ~ —*Current Biog.*⟩ **b :** the political function of policy making as distinguished from the administration of policy decisions **7 a :** the organization, machinery, or agency through which a political unit exercises authority and performs functions and which is usu. classified according to the distribution of power within it ⟨the distinction between constitutional and absolute ~*s* —G.H.Sabine⟩ ⟨framing a ~ which is to be administered by men over men —James Madison⟩ ⟨the great growth of the national ~ —W.S.Sayre⟩ ⟨advanced through the ranks of his church's ~ —*Current Biog.*⟩ ⟨industrial capitalism . . . created clusters of private ~ —R.J. Harris⟩ — see ARISTOCRACY 2a, DEMOCRACY 1b, DICTATORSHIP 3, MONARCHY, OLIGARCHY, REPUBLIC, TYRANNY **b :** the complex of political institutions, laws, and customs through which the function of governing is carried out in a specific political unit ⟨the shifting of functions . . . which has characterized American ~ —C.F.Snider⟩ ⟨students of French ~⟩ ⟨an attempt to derive information about trade-union ~ —*Times Lit. Supp.*⟩ **8 :** the body of persons that constitutes the governing authority of a political unit or organization: as **a :** the officials collectively comprising the governing body of a political unit and constituting the organization as an active agency ⟨a world in which ~*s* . . . are highly and effectively resolved to work together —F.D.Roosevelt⟩ ⟨the ~ had succeeded in transporting . . . tons of equipment inland —Wendell Willkie⟩ ⟨correspondence . . . that passed between the American ~ and the German ~ —*Chicago Daily News*⟩ **b** *usu cap* **:** the executive branch of the U.S. federal government including the political officials and usu. the permanent civil service employees **:** ADMINISTRATION 6a ⟨the senator's treatment of *Government* witnesses before the committee⟩ ⟨the *Government's* case was argued before the Supreme Court⟩ **c** *usu cap* **:** a small group of persons holding simultaneously the principal political executive offices of a nation or other political unit and responsible for the direction and supervision of public affairs: (1) **:** such a group in a parliamentary system constituted by the cabinet or by the ministry ⟨His Majesty's *Government* feel they have the right to know where they stand with the House of Commons —Sir Winston Churchill⟩ ⟨the typical opposition maneuver designed to embarrass the *Government*

—H.L.Bretton⟩ ⟨apart from providing a *Government,* the main functions of the New Zealand Parliament are firstly to legislate —Walter Nash⟩ (2) **:** ADMINISTRATION 6b **9 :** POLITICAL SCIENCE ⟨the other social sciences including economics and ~ —Weston La Barre⟩ **10 :** a security (as a bond) issued by or on behalf of the U.S. government — usu. used in pl. ⟨reserves in the form of cash or ~s —G.A.Mooney⟩

gov·ern·men·tal \ˌgəv|ə(r)n|ment³l, |və(r)n|me-, |vᵊm|e-, |bᵊm|e-\ *adj* **:** of or relating to government or to the government of a particular political unit ⟨the core of a ~ system —C.J. Friedrich⟩ ⟨serious damage done . . . to public confidence and to ~ morale —G.F.Kennan⟩

governmental atonement *n* **:** the Grotian theory of atonement that Christ's death enables God as moral governor of the world to forgive sinners freely without encouraging disorder by signally revealing that suffering often of the innocent inevitably follows when sinners violate the divine world order

gov·ern·men·tal·ism \ˌ=='==ˌizəm\ *n* -s **1 :** a theory advocating extension of the sphere and degree of government activity ⟨the keystone of ~ is the reduction of private enterprise⟩ — compare STATISM **2 :** the tendency toward extension of the role of government ⟨the growing ~ . . . of Switzerland was sanctioned —C.J.Friedrich⟩

gov·ern·men·tal·ist \-ˌəst\ *n* -s **:** one that advocates or implements governmentalism ⟨helps to perpetuate the ~s in office —*Fortune*⟩

gov·ern·men·tal·iza·tion \ˌ==ˌ===ə'zāshən, -ˌī'z-\ *n* -s **:** the action or result of governmentalizing ⟨prevent the ~ of all international economic life —William Hard⟩

gov·ern·men·tal·ize \ˌ=='==ˌīz\ *vt* -ED/-ING/-S **:** to subject to the regulation or control of a government ⟨the Federal government's effort to ~ medicine —Raymond Moley⟩

gov·ern·men·tal·ly \ˌ==|==ē, -i\ *adv* **:** by or in terms of government or the government of a political unit ⟨not sufficiently popularly or ~ controlled —*World's Work*⟩

government bill *n, sometimes cap G* **:** a public or private bill prepared, introduced, and sponsored in the legislature by a member of the government ⟨in Great Britain a *government bill* . . . is in direct charge of a minister —F.A.Ogg & Harold Zink⟩ ⟨in France . . . *government bills* are drawn up in the departments —D.W.S.Lidderdale⟩ — compare PRIVATE MEMBER'S BILL

government bream *n* [so called fr. the fact that its markings suggest the broad arrow placed on government materials by the British Board of Ordnance] **:** a highly esteemed food fish (*Lutjanus sebae*) dwelling on the bottom of tropical Australian seas and marked when young by an arrangement of scarlet bands resembling a broad arrow

government corporation *n* **:** PUBLIC CORPORATION 2 ⟨the TVA is set up as a *government corporation* outside the executive departments —W.S.Sayre⟩

government depository *n, often cap G* **:** a bank that by law may receive deposits of government funds ⟨all member banks of the Federal Reserve system may . . . be designated as *government depositories* —G.G.Munn⟩

gov·ern·ment·ese \ˌgəvə(r)mənt·ēz, |və(r)nm-, |v(ᵊ)m-, |b(ᵊ)m-, -mən·|tēz\ *n* -s [*government* + *-ese*] **:** GOBBLEDYGOOK ⟨a tongue-in-cheek definition . . . given him in ~ —A.L. Hench⟩

government–general \ˌ=(=)=|=(=)=\ *n, pl* **governments–general** *usu cap both Gs* **1 :** a territory over which a governor-general has jurisdiction ⟨Frenchmen have moved into the *Government-General* in large numbers —*N. Y. Herald Tribune*⟩ **2 :** a government headed by a governor-general ⟨administrative authority was vested in a *Government-General* —A.L. Grey⟩

government house *n* **1 :** a building containing the principal government offices esp. in a British colony or Commonwealth country **2 :** the official residence of a governor esp. of a British colony

government–in–exile \ˌ=(=)==ˌ=ˌ=\ *n, pl* **governments–in–exile :** a government temporarily established on foreign soil following the occupation of its own territory by another authority ⟨breaking off relations with the Polish *government-in-exile* —W.H.Chamberlin⟩

government issue *adj, often cap G&I* **:** issued or provided by a government or a government agency ⟨standard *government-issue* equipment —A.Q.Maisel⟩

government man *n* **1 :** a government official; *esp* **:** G-MAN **2 :** a consistent supporter of the Government in power **3 :** a convict in 19th century Australia

government note *n* **:** a currency note issued by a government — compare BANK NOTE 1

government paper *n* **:** evidences of debt (as bonds or notes) issued by a government ⟨borrowings on *government paper* were as large as on commercial bills and notes —H.G. Moulton⟩

government security *n* **:** a security (as a bond or certificate) issued by or on behalf of a government — usu. used in pl. ⟨Federal Reserve Bank holdings of *government securities*⟩

gov·er·nor *R* 'gəv(ə)nər *also* -vərnər, *-R* -v(ə)nə(r\ *n* -s [ME *governour,* fr. MF *governeor,* fr. L *gubernator* steersman, fr. *gubernatus* (past part. of *gubernare* to steer) + *-or* — more at GOVERN] **1 :** one that governs: as **a :** one that exercises authority esp. over an area or group ⟨the kings, princes and ~s of the world —*Times Lit. Supp.*⟩ ⟨the American people . . . ~s of us all —H.S.Truman⟩ ⟨the sun . . . was the ~ of the heavens —S.F.Mason⟩ **b** *often cap, archaic* **:** GOD ⟨the Deity . . . which is the supreme *governor* of all things —Ralph Cudworth⟩ **c :** an official elected or appointed to act as ruler, chief executive, or nominal head of a political unit (as a colony, state, or province) ⟨each colony has its own government headed by the ~ who represents the crown —W.E.Simnett⟩ ⟨the office of ~ in the American states —W.S.Sayre⟩ ⟨Australian . . . state ~s act on the advice of their ministers —Geoffrey Sawer⟩ **d :** COMMANDANT ⟨the ~ of the besieged fortress⟩ **e :** the managing director and usu. the principal officer of an institution or organization ⟨is ~ of the Bank of France —Harrison Smith⟩ ⟨past ~ of the local lodge —*Springfield (Mass.) Union*⟩ ⟨assistant ~ of a large English prison⟩ ⟨the ~ of an Edinburgh hospital —H.A.Albert⟩ **f :** a member of a group of persons that directs or controls an institution or society **:** DIRECTOR ⟨the board of ~s of the Federal Reserve System . . . consists of seven members —E.W.Kemmerer⟩ ⟨the board of ~s of the National Press Club —*Newsweek*⟩ ⟨a ~ of the University of British Columbia —*Current Biog.*⟩ **g :** the chief of an Indian tribe or pueblo ⟨the party executing the order of the . . . ~s of the pueblos —*Weekly New Mexican*⟩ **2** *archaic* **:** one that has charge of the education of a young man usu. of royal or noble birth ⟨at the age of seven he was . . . handed over to a ~ —Nancy Mitford⟩ **3 a** *slang* **:** one looked upon as governing (as a father, guardian, or employer) ⟨my old ~ sent me to Eton —Angela Thirkell⟩ **b :** MISTER, SIR — usu. used in informal address ⟨come and look at 'em, ~ —Henry Mayhew⟩ **4 a :** an attachment to a machine (as a gasoline or steam engine) designed to afford automatic control or limitation of speed or power; *esp* **:** such an attachment actuated by the centrifugal force of whirling weights opposed by gravity or by springs **b :** a contrivance giving automatic control (as of pressure or temperature) — called also *regulator*

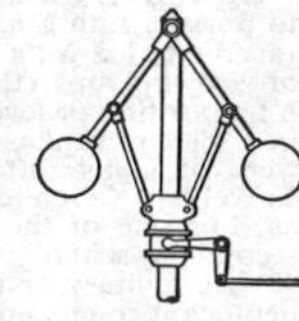
governor 4a

gov·er·nor·ate \-nərət, -ˌrāt\ *n* -s **:** an administrative division ruled by a governor ⟨Egypt is divided into . . . five ~s —*Egypt Almanac*⟩

governor–general \ˌ=(=)=|=(=)=\ *n, pl* **governors–general** *or* **governor–generals :** a governor of high rank; *esp* **:** one who governs a large territory (as a country) or has lieutenant or deputy governors under him ⟨the *governor-general* is . . . appointed by the queen on the advice of the prime minister of Canada —*Canadian Citizenship Series*⟩ ⟨as early as 1548 a royal decree created the office of *governor general* . . . of Brazil —A.N.Christensen⟩

governor–general–in–council \ˌ=(=)=|=(=)==ˌ=='==\ *n, pl* **governors–general–in–council** *or* **governor–generals–in–council :** the governor-general in a member nation of the British Commonwealth acting with the advice and consent of the nation's Privy Council usu. as a formal means of giving legal effect to cabinet decisions ⟨in South Africa . . . all provincial ordinances must be assented to by the *governor-general-in-council* —Alexander Brady⟩

governor–generalship \ˌ=(=)='=(=)=ˌ=\ *n* **1 :** the office of governor-general ⟨the *governor-generalship* of India . . . at which he aimed —T.E.Hook⟩ **2 :** the period of incumbency of a governor-general ⟨the two years of his *governor-generalship* —*Athenaeum*⟩

governor–in–council \ˌ=(=)==ˌ=='==\ *n, pl* **governors–in–council 1 :** the governor of a British colony acting with the advice and usu. in the presence of the executive council but not always with its consent ⟨referred to and decided by the *governor in council* —*Nigeria Order in Council, 1946*⟩ **2 :** GOVERNOR-GENERAL-IN-COUNCIL ⟨Canadian statutes . . . confer many and varied powers directly upon the *governor-in-council* —Alexander Brady⟩

governor's council *n* **:** an executive or legislative council elected (as in some states of the U.S.) or appointed (as in some former British colonies) to advise a governor or share in the functions of the office of governor ⟨only Maine, New Hampshire, and Massachusetts still have a *governor's council* —*Amer. Guide Series: Mass.*⟩

gov·er·nor·ship \'=(=)=ˌship\ *n* **1 a :** the office of governor ⟨the ~ was held for long periods by one man —*Amer. Guide Series: Conn.*⟩ ⟨the only man in Indiana's history to have held its ~ twice —*Current Biog.*⟩ **b :** the conduct of the office of governor ⟨his ~ of Bristol was the foundation of the impeachment —William Prynne & Clement Walker⟩ **2 :** the period of incumbency of a governor ⟨during his ~ many new laws were enacted⟩

governor's plum *or* **governor plum** *n* [so called fr. the fact that the genus *Flacourtia* was named after Etienne de Flacourt †1660 governor and historian of Madagascar] **:** a small often shrubby dioecious tree (*Flacourtia indica*) native to Madagascar and southern Asia and cultivated in tropical regions as a hedge plant and for its deep red somewhat acid fruits that resemble small plums — called also *ramontchi*

governor win·throp desk \-'win(t)thrəp-\ *n, usu cap G&W* [after *Governor* John *Winthrop* †1649 governor of Mass. Colony] **:** a desk with an oxbow front and usu. claw-and-ball feet

Governor Winthrop desk

governs *pres 3d sing of* GOVERN

goves *pres 3d sing of* GOVE

goving *pres part of* GOVE

govt *abbr* government

gow·an \'gaüən\ *n* -s [prob. alter. of ME *gollan*] **1** *chiefly Scot* **:** DAISY 1 ⟨as fresh as ~s —Jane W. Carlyle⟩ **2** *chiefly Scot* **:** a white or yellow field flower — used chiefly in combination ⟨horse ~⟩

gow·any \-ni\ *adj, Scot* **:** abounding in gowans ⟨sweeter than ~ glens —Allan Ramsay †1758⟩

goway bird *var of* GOAWAY BIRD

gowd \'gaüd\ *chiefly Scot var of* GOLD

gowd·en \'gaüdᵊn\ *chiefly Scot var of* GOLDEN

gow·en cypress \'gaüən-\ *n* [after James R. *Gowen,* 19th cent. Brit. horticulturist] **:** a small tree or shrub (*Cupressus goveniana*) with erect or stiff branches, spherical cones, and light green to yellowish green leaves that is native to California and used as an ornamental

gow·ers's tract \'gaü(ə)rz(əz)-\ *n, usu cap G* [after Sir William R. *Gowers* †1915 Eng. neurologist] **:** a crescent-shaped tract of fibers in the anterior lateral part of the spinal cord

¹gowf \'gaüf\ *Scot var of* GOLF

²gowf \"\ *n* -s [perh. fr. ¹*gowf* (also, "golf club")] *Scot* **:** a dull blow **:** CUFF, BUFFET

³gowf \"\ *vt* -ED/-ING/-S *Scot* **:** STRIKE, CUFF

go·wid·die \gō'widē\ *n* -s [origin unknown] **:** LABRADOR TEA a

go without *vi* **:** to deprive oneself ⟨those who *go without* to pay their doctor —S.B.Pettengill⟩

¹gowk \'gaük, 'gäk, 'gōk\ *n* -s [ME *goke, gowke* fr. ON *gaukr* cuckoo; akin to OE *gēac* cuckoo, OHG *gouh*] **1** *dial Brit* **:** CUCKOO **2** *dial Brit* **:** SIMPLETON, FOOL, GAWK ⟨sat there all evening like a great ~ —Flora Thompson⟩

²gowk \'gaük\ *vi* -ED/-ING/-S [ME (Sc dial.) *gowken,* perh. fr. *gowk,* n.] *chiefly Scot* **:** to gaze or stare vacantly

gowk·ed \'gaükəd, -ət\ *or* **gowk·it** \-kət\ *adj* [¹*gowk* + *-ed* or *-it* (Sc var of *-ed*)] *chiefly Scot* **:** FOOLISH, GIDDY

gowk storm *n* [so called fr. the typical occurrence of short storms in the spring at the time of the cuckoo's return] *Scot & Irish* **:** a brief storm or period of adversity

¹gowl \'gaü(ə)l, 'gül\ *vi* -ED/-ING/-S [ME *goulen, gowlen,* fr. ON *gaula;* akin to ON *geyja* to bark and perh. to Gk *chaos* abyss — more at GUM] *dial Brit* **:** HOWL, YELL ⟨the hound dog ~*ed* ~s in the chimney —R.L.Stevenson⟩

²gowl \"\ *n* -s *dial Brit* **:** a loud cry **:** HOWL, YELL ⟨burst out in kind o' ~ o' anger —S.R.Crockett⟩

¹gown \'gaün\ *n* -s [ME *goun,* fr. MF *gone, goune,* fr. LL *gunna,* a fur or leather garment] **1 :** an outer garment: **a** *archaic* **:** a usu. loose and flowing outer garment worn by men ⟨the men wore ~s in the middle ages —F.W.Fairholt⟩ **b :** the official or distinctive robe worn by men and women in certain professions (as law, education, the church, and medicine); *esp* **:** a long loose usu. black garment worn by students, graduates, and officers of colleges and universities and varying in material, cut, and trimming with the academic degree of the wearer ⟨one of the barristers . . . hitched his ~ up on his shoulder —F.W.Crofts⟩ ⟨the medieval context surviving in these ~s and hoods —A.W.Griswold⟩ — see ACADEMIC COSTUME, GENEVA GOWN **c :** a loose garment draped in soft folds worn by the ancients (as the Roman toga) ⟨the dress of peace ⟨he Mars deposed and arms to ~s made yield —John Dryden⟩ **d :** a woman's dress; *esp* **:** one suitable for afternoon or evening wear ⟨her faded calico ~ —Hamlin Garland⟩ ⟨the bride's . . . ~ and veil —*Mademoiselle*⟩ **e :** a loose informal garment esp. for lounging or resting (as a nightgown or a dressing gown) ⟨at first the baby will wear a ~ both day and night⟩ **f :** the cotton coverall worn by a surgeon in the operating room ⟨dressed in hospital ~s and masks —Grace Reiten⟩ **2 a :** the office or profession indicated by the wearing of distinctive robes ⟨men of the ~ and men of the sword⟩ **b :** the students and faculty of a college or university considered as a group distinct from the nonacademic world ⟨powerful rivalry in . . . society between town and ~ —Robertson Davies⟩

²gown \"\ *vt* -ED/-ING/-S [ME *gounen,* fr. *goun,* n.] **:** to dress in or invest with a gown ⟨to ~ herself in the latest Paris fashions —Margaret W. Hungerford⟩ ⟨capped and ~*ed* dignitaries in the commencement procession⟩

gown boy *n* **:** a boy of a foundation school ⟨the artless *gown boy* from Grey Friars —W.M.Thackeray⟩

gownd \-nd\ *dial var of* GOWN

gowns·man \-nzmən\ *n, pl* **gownsmen :** one that wears a gown: **a** *archaic* **:** one that wears the dress of peace **:** CIVILIAN ⟨military men are seldom disposed to take counsel with *gownsmen* on military matters —T.B.Macaulay⟩ **b :** one that wears a professional, official, or scholastic habit (as a lawyer, clergyman, or member of a university) ⟨the distance between the *gownsmen* and the townsmen —Charles Lamb⟩ **c** *Scot* **:** BEADSMAN 2b

gowp \'gaüp\ *var of* GAUP

gow·pen \'gaüpən\ *n* -s [ME *goupyne,* fr. ON *gaupn* (in plural only) cupped hand; akin to OHG *coufana* hand, OE *gēap* open, wide, *gōma* palate — more at GUM] **1** *chiefly Scot* **a :** the hollow of two hands held together as if forming a bowl **b** *also* **gow·pen·ful** \-ˌfü(l)\ *pl* **gowpenfuls :** a double handful ⟨gathered a *gowpenful* of flinty arrowheads —John Service⟩ **2** *Scots law* **:** the perquisite of meal from tenants by thirlage that is allowed to a miller's servant

goy *also* **goi** \'gȯi\ *n, pl* **goy·im** \-ȯi(y)əm\ *or* **goys** [Yiddish *goy,* fr. Heb *gōy* people, nation] **1 :** GENTILE 1a — often used disparagingly ⟨sure that any Jew is . . . superior to any ~ —Charles Angoff⟩ ⟨our children won't fall into the hands of the *goyim* —Isaac Metzker⟩ **2 :** a Jew who does not observe Jewish precepts — used esp. by Jews ⟨time enough for you to eat pork and be a ~ —Charles Angoff⟩

goya \'gȯi(y)ə\ *or* **goya red** *n* -s *often cap G* [after Francisco de *Goya* y Lucientes †1828 Span. painter] **:** a strong red that is deeper than geranium (sense 3a), yellower and deeper than geranium red, and bluer and deeper than average cherry red — called also *cadmium carmine, currant, English red, English vermilion, minium, oriental red, orient red, red currant, vermilion*

goy·a·zite \'gȯi(y)əˌzīt\ *n* -s [F *goyazite,* fr. *Goyaz* (Goiaz), state in Brazil + F *-ite*] **:** a mineral $SrAl_3(PO_4)_2(OH)_5.H_2O$ consisting of a granular yellowish white hydrous strontium aluminum phosphate

goy·ish \'gȯi-ish\ *adj* [*goy* + *-ish*] **:** of, relating to, or having the characteristics of a goy **:** GENTILE 1a ⟨in your ordinary ~ delicatessen —Ruth Glazer⟩ ⟨the general atmosphere was ~ —Charles Angoff⟩

goyle \'gȯi(ə)l\ *n* -s [origin unknown] *dial Eng* **:** a steep narrow valley **:** RAVINE, GULLY

gozzan *var of* GOSSAN

goz·zard \'gäzə(r)d\ *n* -s [alter. of ME *gosherde,* fr. *gos, goos* goose + *herde* herdsman — more at GOOSE, HERD] **:** GOOSEHERD

gp *abbr* group

GP *abbr* **1** general paresis **2** general pause **3** general practitioner **4** general purpose **5** geographic position **6** glide path **7** [L *Gloria Patri*] Glory be to the Father **8** great primer

GPA *abbr* general passenger agent

GPD *abbr, often not cap* gallons per day

GPH *abbr, often not cap* gallons per hour

GPI *abbr* **1** general paralysis of the insane **2** ground position indicator

GPM *abbr* **1** *often not cap* gallons per minute **2** geopotential meter

GPO *abbr* **1** general post office **2** government printing office

GPS *abbr, often not cap* gallons per second

GQ *abbr* general quarters

gr *abbr* **1** grade **2** grain **3** gram **4** grammar; grammatical **5** grand **6** graphite **7** gravity **8** gray **9** great **10** grind **11** groschen **12** gross **13** grosz **14** group

GR *abbr* **1** general reconnaissance **2** general reserve

gra \'grȯ\ *n* -s [IrGael *grādh* love, fr. L *gratus* pleasing, beloved, dear — more at GRACE] *now dial Brit* **:** DEAR

graaf·ian follicle \'gräfēən-, 'graf\ *n, sometimes cap G* [Regnier de *Graaf* †1673 Dutch anatomist + E *-ian*] **:** a vesicle in the ovary of a mammal enclosing a developing egg and consisting in the typical form of an outer fibrous sheath and an inner cellular and vascular sheath derived from the ovarian stroma and separated by a hyaline basement membrane from an epithelial zone derived from the germinal epithelium and made up of several layers of small usu. polyhedral cells that are heaped at one point into a mound which projects into the fluid-filled cavity of the vesicle and encloses the growing egg

¹grab \'grab, -aa(ə)b\ *vb* **grabbed; grabbed; grabbing; grabs** [obs. D or LG *grabben,* fr. MD & MLG, respectively; akin to OE *græppian* to seize, ME *graspen* to grasp, G *grapsen* to seize, grasp, Sw *grabba,* ON *grāpa* to snatch, Skt *grbhnāti, gṛhṇāti* he seizes] *vt* **1 a :** to take or take hold of by a sudden motion or grasp **:** SEIZE, CLUTCH **b :** CAPTURE, RESTRAIN, ARREST **2 :** to get or appropriate to oneself unscrupulously ⟨~ public lands⟩ ⟨managed to ~ three or four millions of money selling bad whiskey or forestalling the wheat harvest and selling it at three times its cost —G.B.Shaw⟩ or with a complete unconcern for another's rights or desires ⟨spend all its energy *grabbing* world markets —*Time*⟩ **3 :** to get hold of, take, or avail oneself of with dispatch or haste ⟨*grabbed* a driver and cleanly smacked a drive 225 yards —*Time*⟩ ⟨drove home, *grabbed* a bath, a shave, clean linen and city clothes —H.A.Callahan⟩ ⟨after *grabbing* a bite of food he will have to leave —Philip Hamburger⟩ **~** *vi* **1 :** to make a grab **:** SNATCH — usu. used with *at* **2** *of a horse* **:** OVERREACH **3** *of an automobile clutch or brake* **:** to engage with abnormal abruptness causing a jolt **4 :** to impede or otherwise affect as if grabbing or momentarily holding ⟨concussions were *grabbing* at his plane steadily —Ira Wolfert⟩ **syn** see TAKE — **grab hold of :** to seize or grasp firmly and usu. suddenly ⟨*grabbed hold of* the door handle and yanked the door open⟩

²grab \"\ *n* -s **1 a :** the act of grabbing: as (1) **:** a sudden grasp or attempt to grasp ⟨the child made a ~ for the candy bar⟩ (2) **:** an appropriating of something or an attempt to appropriate by unscrupulous methods ⟨a ~ for power —*Frontier*⟩ ⟨the ~ for offshore oil rights⟩ **b :** something grabbed **2 :** a device for clutching an object (as for hauling or hoisting): as **a :** any of various implements for gripping and withdrawing (as a drill or broken cable) from a borehole or well **b :** CLAMSHELL 2a **c :** SKIDDING HOOKS — **up for grabs** *slang* **:** available for anyone who takes or is able to take ⟨the prize was *up for grabs* to anyone under 16 years of age⟩

³grab \"\ *adj* **1 :** intended to be grabbed or taken hold of (as for steadying oneself) ⟨a ~ rail by the door of the bus to assist passengers in getting on or alighting⟩ **2 :** taken or to be taken at random ⟨a ~ sample⟩

⁴grab \"\ *n* -s [Ar *ghurāb,* lit., raven] **:** an oriental coasting ship of light draft and broad beam and square raking stern, sharp bow with long overhang, lateen sails, and usu. two masts

grab–all \'=ˌ=\ *n, Austral* **:** a setnet used for marine fishing near the shore

grab bag *n* **1 :** a bag or other receptacle holding small articles which are to be drawn (as at a party or fair) without being seen often on payment of a small sum **2 :** something resembling a grab bag: as **a :** something providing a miscellany of often choice items ⟨a *grab bag* of miscellaneous specimens, some of which may catch the reader's fancy —Dwight MacDonald⟩ ⟨the revue . . . is a cornucopia, a *grab bag,* a hash —Wolcott Gibbs⟩ ⟨the *grab bag* of good and bad that goes into the making of a happy and lasting marriage —Mollie Panter-Downes⟩ **b :** an assemblage or collection of often valuable things from which one may take or appropriate whatever he can grab ⟨reversing the public purse into a private *grab bag* —J.R.Aswell & E.J.Michelson⟩

grab bar *n* **:** a graspable bar attached to the wall in a shower or near a bathtub as an assistance to a bather in steadying himself

grab·ber \-bə(r)\ *n* -s **:** one that grabs esp. unscrupulously or inconsiderately ⟨horrified at the greed of the pension ~s —W.H.Upson⟩ ⟨unscrupulous land ~s —L.S.B.Leakey⟩

grab·ble \'grabəl\ *vb* **grabbled; grabbled; grabbling** \-b(ə)liŋ\ **grabbles** [D *grabbelen,* fr. MD, freq. of *grabben* to grab — more at GRAB] *vi* **1 a :** to move the hand (as in searching) in a groping fashion **:** GROPE ⟨*grabbled* about in her bag —Angela Thirkell⟩ **b** *South* **:** to remove full grown potatoes without disturbing the plant, the soil being replaced to allow other tubers to develop **c** *South* **:** to catch fish by hand by groping (as along a riverbank) **2 :** to lie or fall prone **:** SPRAWL, GROVEL **~** *vt* **1** *South* **:** to harvest by grabbling **2** *South* **:** to catch (fish) by hand — **grab·bler** \-b(ə)lə(r)\ *n* -s

grab·bots \'grabəts\ *n pl* [origin unknown] **:** refuse cotton separated from the seed in cottonseed oil mills

grab bucket *n* **:** CLAMSHELL 2a

grab·by \'grabē, -aab-, -bi\ *adj* -ER/-EST **:** tending to grab all one can get **:** GRASPING, GREEDY

grab crane *n* **:** a hoisting machine fitted with a clamshell

grab dredge *or* **grab dredger** *n* **:** a dredger that operates with a clamshell

gra·ben \'gräbən\ *n* -s [G, ditch, fr. OHG *grabo,* fr. *graban* to dig — more at GRAVE] **:** a depressed segment of the earth's crust bounded on at least two sides by faults and generally of considerable length as compared with its width — compare HORST

grab game *n* **:** a scheme, ruse, or action marked by an unscrupulous usu. sudden appropriating of money or property

grabhook \'=ˌ=\ *n* **:** a hook (as a grapnel) for grabbing (as the links of a chain)

grab iron *n* **:** a metal bar attached to the sides of railroad cars and locomotives for use as a handhold

grab link *n* **:** SLIP GRAB

grabman \'=ˌman, -mən\ *n, pl* **grabmen :** a clipper in a coal mine

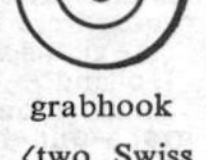
grabhook

grab off *vt* **1 :** to take or appropriate forcefully or with haste or forthrightness ⟨dash in and *grab off* choice pieces of land —F.P.Gipson⟩ ⟨two Swiss mountaineers . . . had *grabbed off* the honors for the first ascent —*Time*⟩ **2 :** to choose for a partner (as in marriage) ⟨why is it that such a beauty . . . has not long ago been *grabbed off* —Walter O'Meara⟩

grab rope *n* **:** GUEST ROPE 2

grabs *pres 3d sing of* GRAB, *pl of* GRAB

grab skipper *n* **:** a short iron pry or hammer used in logging for removing the skidding hooks from a log

¹grace \ˈgrās\ *n* -s [ME, fr. OF, fr. L *gratia* charm, favor, thanks, fr. *gratus* pleasing, beloved, grateful + *-ia* -y; akin to OHG *queran* to sigh, Skt *gṛṇāti* he praises] **1 a :** beneficence or generosity shown by God to man ⟨the very earthy problems that must be dealt with makes one rely heavily upon God for ~ and wisdom —*Guatemala News*⟩ ⟨a God who . . . works to bring his purposes to fruition through the willing response of men to his ~ —Norman Goodall⟩; *esp* **:** divine favor unmerited by man **:** the mercy of God as distinguished from his justice ⟨a man repentant and asking God's ~⟩ **b :** a free gift of God to man for his regeneration or sanctification **:** an influence emanating from God and acting for the spiritual well-being of the recipient ⟨the Methodists, following the Baptists, appealed to the people for they preached free will and universal ~ —Van Wyck Brooks⟩ ⟨it may be that they have no one praying for them, and they have squandered all the ordinary and extraordinary ~*s* allotted to them by God —D.J.Corrigan⟩ **c :** a state of acceptance with or of being pleasing to God **:** enjoyment of divine favor ⟨be in a state of ~⟩ ⟨outward and visible signs of an inward and spiritual ~⟩ **d :** a virtue or moral excellence regarded as coming from God **:** a Christian virtue ⟨the ~*s* of self-denial, humility, and love⟩ **e** *cap* **:** God as the source of grace **2 :** a short prayer either asking a blessing before or giving thanks after a meal **3 a :** disposition to kindness, favor, clemency, or compassion **:** benign goodwill ⟨the victor's ~ in treating the vanquished⟩ **b :** the display of kindly treatment usu. on the part of a superior **:** ready granting or forgiving **:** clement judging or treating ⟨thankful for this ~ on her brother's part —Margaret Deland⟩ **c** *archaic* **:** MERCY, CLEMENCY; *also* **:** FORGIVENESS **d** (1) **:** an act of kindness, favor, or goodwill ⟨do me this ~, my child —Alfred Tennyson⟩ ⟨had been some years in prison . . . where she was kept without books till at last by some special ~ a friend was allowed to send her some —Gilbert Murray⟩ (2) **:** a special favor from a person in power **:** PRIVILEGE, DISPENSATION ⟨each in his place, by right, not ~, shall rule his heritage —Rudyard Kipling⟩ ⟨woman gains entrance into such societies only through a kind of ~ bestowed upon her, not legitimately like the male —H.M.Parshley⟩ (3) **:** the prerogative of mercy exercised by an executive of the law (as by granting pardon) (4) **:** the same prerogative when exercised in the form of equitable relief through chancery (5) **:** favor shown by permitting an action to be postponed or by granting a reprieve or a temporary exemption from a penalty ⟨granted the condemned man a day of ~ to wind up his worldly affairs⟩ ⟨she didn't like to be rushed so he gave her an extra half hour's ~ before he called for her⟩ **e :** favor and approval — often used in pl. ⟨tried to stay in his employer's good ~*s*⟩ ⟨after he had fallen from ~ —*Amer. Guide Series: Pa.*⟩ ⟨worm your way into my ~*s* —Hamilton Basso⟩ **4 :** the favor shown or the portion allotted by fortune or Providence **:** LOT, FATE, LUCK **5** *obs* **:** beneficent efficacy or power **6 a** (1) **:** a charming or attractive endowment, characteristic, quality, or feature ⟨among disagreeable qualities he possessed the saving ~ of humor⟩ ⟨the little ~*s* of speech —George Sampson⟩ ⟨that quiet but unabashed hospitality which is a common ~ in Mexican households —Willa Cather⟩ (2) **:** an activity or accomplishment that lends such grace ⟨a young girl trained early in the ~*s* of singing, dancing, and playing the harp⟩ ⟨more distinguished for his learning than for his conversational ~*s* —Charles Gordon⟩ ⟨rising to receive him, with every refinement of manner known to the time, and with all the engaging ~*s* and courtesies of life —Charles Dickens⟩ **b** (1) **:** a manner of acting or of appearance adopted or affected with the intention of charming or pleasing (2) **:** AFFECTATION ⟨laughing at the woman's airs and ~*s*⟩ **c :** ATTRACTIVENESS, CHARM ⟨all the ~ of youth —John Buchan⟩ ⟨old civilizations do breed corruption as well as ~ —Sean O'Faolain⟩ ⟨the ~ of her loose falling tresses —George Meredith⟩ ⟨given an old story a new lucidity and ~ —Sara H. Hay⟩; *esp* **:** the pleasing quality associated with a special and refined fitness of proportion combined with an ease and beauty of movement, action, line, or expression ⟨a curved . . . staircase of unusual ~, with marble steps and wrought-iron railings —*Amer. Guide Series: N.Y. City*⟩ ⟨the stables had dignity and ~ in a degree one rarely sees in a modern edifice —H.J.Laski⟩ ⟨have been able to convey through the coarser medium of English prose something of this aesthetic ~, this deftness of touch —P.E.More⟩ **d :** PROPRIETY, SEEMLINESS, COMELINESS ⟨performed the necessary task without fanfare and with a quiet ~⟩ **e** *obs* **:** a thing or part characterized by beauty **:** ORNAMENT **f :** a musical decoration consisting of notes not belonging to the basic melody or harmony (as the trill, turn, appoggiatura) indicated by special symbols or small notes **7** — used with *your* in addressing a duke, a duchess, or an archbishop and formerly the king or queen of England or with *his* or *her* as a periphrastic designation for one of these **8** *at an English university* **a :** permission of a congregation to take a degree **b :** a proposal, decree, act, or vote of the governing body of an institution **c :** permission to take a degree obtained from a candidate's college or hall **9 a :** sense of propriety or right **:** GRACIOUSNESS, DECENCY ⟨had the ~ to apologize for the insulting remark⟩ **b :** VIRTUE ⟨will have to make a ~ of necessity —H.L.Ickes⟩ **c :** CONSIDERATENESS, THOUGHTFULNESS ⟨geographers in their maps have the ~ to indicate the bed of the Paroo river —C.E.W. Bean⟩ **10 a** *usu cap* **:** one of three sister goddesses in Greek mythology represented as beautiful and graceful, as associates of the Muses, and as attendants usu. on Eros, Aphrodite, and Dionysus and regarded as the givers of charm and beauty — usu. used in pl. **b :** one that resembles or represents such a goddess ⟨from every ceiling nymphs, cherubs, and ~*s* gaze down —*Amer. Guide Series: Vt.*⟩ **11 graces** *pl but sing in constr* **:** a game in which players throw and catch a small hoop by means of two sticks — used with *the;* see GRACE HOOP **syn** see MERCY — **by grace of** *or* **by the grace of :** by virtue of **:** with the help of **:** by reason of ⟨the camp existed *by grace of* the few white miners who explored the district —*Amer. Guide Series: Oreg.*⟩ ⟨survived only *by the grace of* money an uncle had left him⟩ — **do grace** *obs* **:** do credit or honor to **:** ADORN — **of grace :** reckoned from the birth of Christ ⟨born in the year *of grace* 1729⟩ — **with a bad grace** *or* **with an ill grace** *or* **with bad grace** *or* **with ill grace :** with unconcealed reluctance and usu. rudeness **:** with marked lack of grace ⟨accepted his defeat *with bad grace* and became almost insulting⟩ ⟨needed help but accepted it only *with an ill grace*⟩ — **with good grace** *adv* **:** GRACIOUSLY ⟨the Protestants of Northern Ireland have accepted *with good grace* the modern trend toward public education —Paul Blanshard⟩ ⟨*with* as *good grace* as I could summon I capitulated —George Copeland⟩

²grace \"\ *vt* -ED/-ING/-S [ME *gracen* to thank, show favor to, fr. OF *gracier*, fr. *grace*] **1** *obs* **a :** to be gracious to **:** FAVOR, COUNTENANCE **b :** GRATIFY, DELIGHT **2 :** to dignify or honor by an act of favor **:** do credit to ⟨discoveries are made every year which, in the past, would have *graced* a century —Albert Guérard⟩ **3 a :** to endow with grace **:** ADORN, EMBELLISH, ORNAMENT ⟨the fine broad meadowlands that ~ the tranquil valley floor —*Amer. Guide Series: Vt.*⟩ ⟨a banquet *graced* by a speaker —*Pleasures of Publishing*⟩ ⟨want to think of their forebears as polished courtiers who would ~ a modern drawing room —L.B.Wright⟩ ⟨the fabulous one-horned animal which ~*s* the British royal coat of arms —R.W.Murray⟩ **b :** to constitute a notable addition to or part of ⟨switches, buttons, wheels, knobs, and gadgets that may ~ the interior of any modern aircraft cockpit —H.G.Armstrong⟩ ⟨*gracing* the living room were five small aquariums and a large one —P.A.Zahl⟩ ⟨the giants among the scores of others who *graced* 17th century Holland —William Petersen⟩; *specif* **:** to embellish (a musical composition) with ornaments

grace-and-favor \ˌ⸗⸗ˈ⸗⸗\ *adj* **:** constituting a habitation granted rent-free (as to a retainer) by the English royal household ⟨her *grace-and-favor* cottage at Kensington Palace —*Newsweek*⟩

grace cup *n* **:** a cup used in drinking a final health after the grace at the end of a meal; *also* **:** a health drunk from such a cup

grace·ful \ˈ⸗fəl\ *adj, sometimes* **gracefuller**; *sometimes* **gracefullest** [ME, fr. *grace* + *-ful*] **1** *obs* **:** specially marked by divine grace **2 :** displaying grace in form or action **:** pleasing or attractive or marked by a comeliness, propriety, or fitness in line, proportion, or esp. movement ⟨a stairway rises in a ~ curve at the rear of the hall —*Amer. Guide Series: Oreg.*⟩ ⟨a ~ bend of road and river —S.H.Holbrook⟩ ⟨the most ~ tree in Europe is the silver birch —C.E.W.Bean⟩ ⟨the swifts are extraordinarily ~ in flight —*Amer. Guide Series: Wash.*⟩ ⟨the author is a ~ and disciplined writer —*New Yorker*⟩ ⟨a ~ and delicate lyricism —Joseph Frank⟩ — **grace·ful·ly** \-fəlē, -li\ *adv* — **grace·ful·ness** *n* -ES

graceful kelp crab *n* **:** a common variably colored but usu. greenish brown kelp crab (*Pugettia gracilis*) found from the Aleutians to California

grace hoop *n* **:** a hoop used in the graces

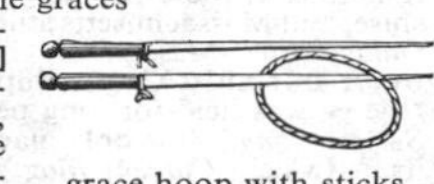
grace hoop with sticks

grace·less \-ləs\ *adj* [ME *graceles*, fr. *grace* + *-les* -less] **1 :** lacking grace: as **a :** UNREGENERATE, DEPRAVED, WICKED, IMPIOUS **b :** devoid of a sense of propriety or seemliness or befitting one devoid of such a sense ⟨a ~ and pushing person⟩ ⟨a ~ and rude remark⟩ **c :** devoid of qualities or endowments that give charm or attractiveness ⟨a lonely ~ factory girl —*Current Biog.*⟩ ⟨her body was thick and lumpish, as ~ as a bathtub —Ruth Park⟩ **:** UGLY ⟨a ~ statue⟩ **:** lacking graciousness ⟨a totally ~ hostess⟩ **d :** devoid of the special artistic quality of fitness or proportion combined with ease and beauty of movement or expression ⟨a ~ prose⟩ **2** *obs* **:** MERCILESS, CRUEL — **grace·less·ly** *adv* — **grace·less·ness** *n* -ES

grace note *n* **1 :** a musical note constituting or being part of an ornament; *esp* **:** APPOGGIATURA, ACCIACCATURA **2 :** something resembling or suggesting a grace note in forming a very small decorative unessential part of or addition to some large whole ⟨the literary contributions made by the President's collaborators . . . merely added *grace notes* to compositions that were the President's own —*New Yorker*⟩ ⟨the chanted songs . . . seem to have no real organic connection with the central theme but to be merely arbitrary and distracting *grace notes* —Wolcott Gibbs⟩

grace period *n* **:** a period of 30 days or one month during which premiums on insurance policies may be paid without penalty

graces *pl of* GRACE, *pres 3d sing of* GRACE

grace's warbler \ˈgrāsə̇z-\ *also* **grace warbler** *n, usu cap G* [after *Grace* D. Coues †1925, sister of Dr. Elliott Coues †1899 Am. ornithologist who discovered it] **:** a gray-and-white warbler (*Dendroica graciae*) black-streaked above with a yellow throat and chest and common in the southwestern U.S. and adjacent Mexico

grac·i·lar·i·a \ˌgrasəˈla(a)rēə\ *n, cap* [NL, fr. L *gracilis* slender + NL *-aria*] **:** a genus of gelatinous red algae (family Sphaerococcaceae) several species of which are important sources of agar-agar

grac·i·lar·i·id \¦⸗⸗¦⸗rēəd\ *adj* [NL *Gracilariidae*] **:** of or relating to the Gracilariidae

grac·i·la·ri·idae \ˌ⸗⸗ləˈrīəˌdē\ *n pl, cap* [NL, fr. *Gracilaria*, type genus + *-idae*] **:** a family of small dull or metallic-colored tineoid moths having larvae that mine in the leaves of various plants

grac·ile \ˈgrasəl *also* -(ˌ)sil *or* -ˌsīl\ *adj* [L *gracilis*; perh. akin to ON *horr* emaciation, L *cracent-, cracens* slender, Skt *kṛśa* emaciated, *kṛśyati* to become emaciated] **1 a :** SLENDER, THIN, SLIGHT ⟨the ~ hermit's lunch —James Merrill⟩ ⟨the human remains . . . indicate a ~ people with small teeth —D.A.Hooijer⟩ **b :** gracefully slender or slight ⟨her ~ and candid girlhood —Joseph Hergesheimer⟩ ⟨three ~, rosy-fleshed women —*Time*⟩ ⟨her red coarse little hands which did not seem to belong to those ~ arms —Arnold Bennett⟩ **2 :** GRACEFUL ⟨lifted her head high for an instant, with the ~ motion a seal has —R.P.Warren⟩ ⟨a ~ writer, thinker, and teacher —Lincoln Kirstein⟩ — **grac·ile·ness** *n* -ES

grac·i·lis \ˈgrasələ̇s\ *n* -ES [NL, fr. L, slender] **:** the most superficial muscle of the inside of the thigh arising from the lower part of the symphysis and the anterior half of the pubic arch and having its tendon inserted into the inner surface of the shaft of the tibia below the tuberosity

gra·cil·i·ty \grəˈsiləd·ē, grəˈ-\ *n* -ES [L *gracilitas*, fr. *gracilis* + *-itas* -ity] **:** GRACEFULNESS ⟨the ~ and speed of winged beauty —Clement Wood⟩; *esp* **:** graceful slenderness or slightness

gra·ci·os·i·ty \ˌgrās(h)ēˈäsəd·ē\ *n* -ES [MF *gracieuseté*, fr. LL *gratiositat-, gratiositas*, fr. L *gratiosus* + L *-itat-, -itas* -ity] **:** GRACIOUSNESS

gra·ci·o·so \ˌgräsēˈō(ˌ)sō\ *n* -s [Sp, fr. *gracioso*, adj., agreeable, amusing, fr. L *gratiosus*] **:** a buffoon or a sportive and comic character in Spanish comedy

gra·cious \ˈgrāshəs\ *adj* [ME, fr. MF *gracieus*, fr. L *gratiosus* enjoying favor, beloved, agreeable, fr. *gratia* favor, grace + *-osus* -ous — more at GRACE] **1 a** *obs* **:** marked by or having divine grace **:** PIOUS, GODLY **b** *archaic* **:** finding grace or favor **:** ACCEPTABLE ⟨but is he ~ in the people's eye —*Shak.*⟩ **2 :** marked by an attractive or pleasing character or appearance **:** characterized by grace in quality, traits, or nature: as **a :** marked by kindness and courtesy **:** markedly considerate of another's feelings or predilections ⟨a ~ and complimentary letter, encouraging him to continue his correspondence —W.M.Thackeray⟩ **b :** GRACEFUL ⟨the ~ sweep of fields shaded by stately elms —*Amer. Guide Series: Vt.*⟩ ⟨the ~ and comely form he had so skillfully mirrored in his art —Oscar Wilde⟩ **c :** marked by tact and delicacy in performance or execution **:** URBANE ⟨no more ~ yet telling caricature of the faults of a society —G.F.Kennan⟩ ⟨for austere and ~ allegory . . . the world is indebted to Spain —Helen Waddell⟩ **d** (1) **:** characterized by ease, good taste, and generosity of spirit and belonging to or suggesting the peace and tasteful leisure of wealth and good breeding ⟨a ~ and beautiful life for all who love peace and reflection, strength and youth —A.C.Benson⟩ (2) **:** befitting or associated with a life characterized in this way ⟨hansom cabs, ~ relics of a more leisurely epoch —*Amer. Guide Series: N.Y. City*⟩ ⟨a ~ plantation home⟩ (3) **:** artistically and esp. architecturally attractive in a way associated with a life or culture characterized in this way ⟨~ with carved interior cornices, mantelpieces, and dadoes —Bernard DeVoto⟩ **3 :** abounding in grace or mercy **:** characterized by marked beneficence **:** MERCIFUL, COMPASSIONATE ⟨after the insults and bad treatment of his former employer he was glad to find so ~ a master⟩ — often and esp. formerly used as a customary and courteous epithet ⟨asked if the ~ gentleman felt well —Guy McCrone⟩ esp. to royalty or those high in the scale of nobility ⟨His Most *Gracious* Majesty, the King⟩ ⟨my ~ lord, the Duke of Windsor⟩ **4** *obs* **:** LUCKY, FORTUNATE, HAPPY

syn CORDIAL, AFFABLE, GENIAL, SOCIABLE: GRACIOUS may apply to a pleasing, benign, or endearing kindliness and courtesy, esp. to inferiors ⟨seemed gratified by their excessive admiration, and gave most *gracious* smiles —Jane Austen⟩ ⟨*gracious* to everyone, but known to a very few —Willa Cather⟩ CORDIAL applies to hearty and sincere friendliness or, occas., to other deeply felt emotions ⟨the director was as *cordial* to the insignificant Martin Arrowsmith as though Martin were a visiting senator. He shook his hand warmly; he unbent in a smile —Sinclair Lewis⟩ ⟨we were friends in public, and saluted each other in the most *cordial* and charming manner —W.M.Thackeray⟩ AFFABLE applies to a smooth, benign approachability and ready friendliness and responsiveness ⟨don't find . . . that his wealth has made him arrogant and inaccessible; on the contrary he takes great pains to appear *affable* and gracious —Tobias Smollett⟩ ⟨easy of approach and *affable* in conversation. They seldom put on airs —W.S.Maugham⟩ GENIAL applies to blended cheer, warmth, and friendliness or other characteristics making one a good companion ⟨*genial* clergy of ample girth, stuffed with the buttered toast of a rectory tea —S.B. Leacock⟩ ⟨that atmosphere of peace and leisure which made his companionship so *genial* —L.P.Smith⟩ ⟨his face softened visibly, he became more and more *genial* and loquacious —W.H.Hudson †1922⟩ SOCIABLE applies to pleasure in social relationships and implies friendliness and readiness at pleasant conversation ⟨was genial and *sociable*, approachable at all times, and fond of social intercourse —J.S.Reeves⟩ ⟨a very *sociable* fellow, prone to talk as long as he can find a listener —Jack London⟩

gra·cious·ly *adv* [ME, fr. *gracious* + *-ly*] **:** in a gracious manner ⟨believed that God . . . had ~ bound himself in his covenant —J.G.Brauer⟩ ⟨writes ~, but does not cut deep —J.T.Flexner⟩ ⟨a philosopher who knows not how gracefully to leave the house in which he has lived so ~ all his life —F.J. Hoffman⟩

gra·cious·ness *n* -ES [ME *graciousnesse*, fr. *gracious* + *-nesse* -ness] **:** the quality or state of being gracious ⟨moved by the slim ~ of her figure —C.B.Kelland⟩ ⟨the courtly ~ of an old and gentle culture⟩

grack·le \ˈgrakəl\ *n* -s [alter. of earlier *gracule*, fr. NL *Gracula*, genus of birds now limited to the hill mynas, alter. of L *graculus* jackdaw; perh. akin to OHG *krogil* gossipy, OE *crāwan* to crow — more at CROW] **1 :** any of various Old World birds of the family Sturnidae (as the hill mynas) **2 :** any of several rather large American blackbirds (family Icteridae) having black plumage that is glossy and iridescent or reflects metallic shades (as green, bronze, or purple) — see BRONZED GRACKLE, PURPLE GRACKLE

¹grad \ˈgrad, -aa(ə)d\ *also* **grade** \ˈgrād\ *n* -s [F *grade* degree, fr. L *gradus*] **:** the hundredth of a right angle in the centesimal system

²grad \"\ *n* -s [short for *graduate*] *slang* **:** GRADUATE, ALUMNUS, ALUMNA

grad *abbr* **1** gradient **2** graduate; graduated

grad·able \ˈgrādəbəl\ *adj* **:** capable of being graded ⟨~ seed⟩

gradacol membrane *var of* GRADOCOL MEMBRANE

¹gra·date \ˈgrāˌdāt, ⸗ˈ⸗, ˈgrəˈd-\ *vb* -ED/-ING/-S [back-formation fr. *gradation*] *vi* **:** to shade insensibly into another (as of a color) or each other (as of colors) **:** shade off **:** BLEND ~ *vt* **1 :** to cause (a color or colors) to gradate ⟨many layers of sheer material in *gradated* colors —Lois Long⟩ **2 :** to dispose or arrange in or into steps, grades, or ranks

²gradate \"\ *adj* [L *gradatus* furnished with steps, fr. *gradus* step, degree + *-atus* -ate] **:** occurring in or characterized by a serial arrangement with nearly equal variation between adjacent members **:** having a gradient or exhibiting gradation ⟨a ~ shell with regularly increasing whorls⟩ ⟨~ maturation of fern sori⟩ ⟨a ~ butterfly wing shading from deepest blue to pale yellow⟩

gra·da·tion \grāˈdāshən *also* grəˈ-\ *n* -s [L *gradation-, gradatio*, fr. *gradus* step, degree + *-ation-, -atio* -ation — more at GRADE] **1** *obs* **:** CLIMAX 1 **2 a :** a series of things (as events or conditions) forming successive stages or steps (as in a course or action) **b :** a degree or relative position in an order or series **:** one of a series of intermediate varieties differing consecutively in form, character, or composition ⟨endless ~*s* in the balance between the denotation of words and their connotation —J.L.Lowes⟩ ⟨he grew into the scheme of things by insensible ~*s* —H.G. Wells⟩ ⟨through every ~ of increasing tenderness —Jane Austen⟩ **c** *obs* **:** RANK, POSITION **d :** the act or process of arranging in ranks, degrees, stages, or steps or the state of being so arranged **e :** a differing consecutively and often by minute differences in a way to form ranks, degrees, stages, or steps ⟨the wide range of ~ in these qualities —R.W.Murray⟩ **3 :** the act or process of progressing evenly or by regular steps **:** gradual advance ⟨the idea of progress or ~ from mineral to plant, from plant to animal, and from animal to man —*Times Lit. Supp.*⟩ **4 a :** a gradual passing from one tint or shade to another (as in painting or drawing) or a sequence or range of tints or shades that passes in this way ⟨a sequence of grays from black to white would be a ~ —S.C.Pepper⟩ **b :** the range of tones between the darkest and the lightest parts of a photographic image **c :** the rate at which the tones of a photographic image change with exposure **5 a :** change from one vowel to another accompanying a change in the degree of stress (as from the vowel of *ford* to the second vowel in *Oxford*) **b :** ABLAUT **6 :** a bringing of an area of land to a uniform or nearly uniform low grade or slope (as in the formation of plains by streams) — compare AGGRADATION, DEGRADATION **7 :** the frequency distribution of various sized grains in a soil, sediment, sedimentary rock, or other particulate material — **gra·da·tion·al** \(ˈ)grā¦dāshənᵊl, grəˈd-, -shnəl\ *adj* — **gra·da·tion·al·ly** \-nᵊlē, -nəlē, -li\ *adv*

¹gra·da·to·ry \ˈgrādəˌtōrē, ˈgrad-\ *n* -ES [prob. modif. of ML *gradatarium* stairway, fr. *gradatus* + *-arium* -ary] **:** a series of steps esp. from a cloister into a church

²gradatory \"\ *adj* [*gradation* + *-ory*] **:** progressing or advancing by gradations **:** arranged in a gradational series

grad·dan *or* **grad·den** \ˈgradᵊn\ *n* -s [ScGael *gradan*, *greadan* & IrGael *greadān*] *Scot & Irish* **:** parched grain

¹grade \ˈgrād\ *n* -s [partly fr. L *gradus* step, degree; partly fr. F *grade*, fr. L *gradus*; akin to L *gradi* to step, go, OIr *in-grenn-* to pursue, Lith *gridyti* to go, wander, and perh. to Goth *grid* (acc.) step] **1 a :** a stage in a process ⟨passing through the ~*s* of growing up⟩ ⟨the highest ~ of development of the brain⟩ **b :** a position or level in a course of advancement or decline or in a scale of ranks, qualities, or orders ⟨the country gentlemen were of many different ~*s* of wealth and culture —G.M. Trevelyan⟩ ⟨a school of collegiate ~ —*Seton Hall Univ. Bull.*⟩: as (1) **:** one of the successive levels of a usu. elementary or secondary school course that usu. represents a year's work (2) **:** a military or naval rank ⟨a naval officer with the ~ of lieutenant commander⟩ **c :** a degree esp. of force or value ⟨the varying ~*s* of success with which a poem attains its end —Samuel Alexander⟩: as (1) **:** a degree of strength of an abrasive bond (2) **:** a relative value or content of an ore or mineral ⟨high-*grade* and low-*grade* ore⟩ (3) **:** a degree of severity in illness ⟨the patient had a carcinoma of ~ III⟩ (4) **:** a degree of plant food content in fertilizer expressed in percentages of nitrogen, phosphoric acid, and potash (5) **:** a degree of purity or concentration (as of a chemical) **2 a :** a class constituted by things that are at the same stage or have the same relative position, level, rank, or degree ⟨the nobles were a higher ~ of agriculturalists —John MacNeill⟩ ⟨guilty of a very low ~ of crime⟩; *esp* **:** a body of elementary school pupils at any one established level of advancement ⟨the fourth ~ was allowed to leave school early⟩ **b :** a mark indicating a particular grade (as of a student's accomplishment in general or of a particular piece of work) ⟨always got high ~*s* in school⟩ ⟨merited a ~ of B on his composition⟩ **c :** a standard of quality applied to foods ⟨prime-*grade* beef⟩ ⟨first-*grade* potatoes⟩ **d :** a standard of quality established as acceptable ⟨threw out all lumber that was below ~⟩ **3 a :** a rate of ascent or descent (as of a railroad, highway, conduit, or ground surface) **:** GRADIENT ⟨a heavy ~⟩ **:** deviation from a level surface to an inclined plane stated as so many feet per mile ⟨a ~ of 20 feet per mile⟩ or as one foot rise or fall in so many feet of horizontal distance ⟨a ~ of 1 in 264⟩ or as so much in a hundred feet or as a percentage of horizontal distance ⟨a 10 percent ~ is one of 10 feet to 100⟩ **b :** a graded ascending, descending, or level portion (as of a road, a railroad, or an embankment) **c :** level or elevation esp. of a land or water surface: as (1) **:** a datum or reference level (2) **:** the contemplated level of the ground when the work of erecting a building is completed **:** ground level ⟨the underpinning of the tower was above ~⟩ (3) **:** ELEVATION 1c **4** [trans. of G *stufe*] **:** any one of the phases of a root or of an affix that appear in an ablaut series and that are characterized by having different vowels **:** the characteristic vowel of such a phase **5 :** a domestic animal one of whose parents is purebred and the other either a scrub or an animal containing a considerable proportion of the blood of the same breed as the purebred parent **6 : grades** *pl* **:** elementary school — used with *the* ⟨taught in the ~*s* for 10 years⟩ **7 :** one of a series of patterns for clothing **8 :** one of the three forms of braille ranging from the fully spelled to the highly contracted — **at grade** *adv* **1 :** on the same level — used of highways, railroad tracks, pedestrian walks, or combinations of these at the point where they intersect **2 :** at such a level with relation to a slope that no perceptible erosion or deposition is effected — used of a stream bed that has been so established — **make the grade** : SUCCEED ⟨tried to pass the exam twice but didn't *make the grade*⟩ ⟨yearning to *make the grade* as a social leader⟩ — **over grade** *adv* : at a higher level — used of one highway, railroad track, or pedestrian walk where it crosses another — **under grade** *adv* : at a lower level — used of one highway, railroad track, or pedestrian walk where it crosses another

²grade \"\ *vb* -ED/-ING/-S *vt* **1** : to arrange in grades : divide into classes : CLASS, SORT: as **a** : to assign to a grade or assign a grade to ⟨~ pupils according to their reading ability⟩ ⟨~ lumber by its resistance to rot⟩ ⟨spent an evening *grading* papers the class had turned in⟩ **b** : to classify (a food) according to quality, size, purity, or other appropriate standard **c** : to arrange in an increasing or decreasing graduated and usu. proportional order (as of value, weight, intensity, difficulty) : GRADUATE ⟨purchased only *graded* reading material for use in the elementary grades⟩ ⟨necessary to ~ the weight of the hammers to correspond with the thickness of the strings —A.E.Wier⟩ ⟨a *graded* inheritance tax⟩ ⟨good works to be done in satisfaction for sins and *graded* according to the seriousness of the offense —K.S.Latourette⟩ **2** : to unite by evenly modulated or slight gradations : blend one shade of (as light or color) into another **3** : to reduce (as the line of a canal or roadbed) to an even grade whether on the level or in a progressive ascent or descent ⟨offered to ~ the remaining 26 miles of unfinished roadbed —*Amer. Guide Series: Texas*⟩ **4** : to alter (a vowel) by ablaut or vowel gradation — used chiefly in the passive **5** : to improve (as native stock) by breeding the females to purebred males — often used with *up* **6** : to make (a working pattern) from a standard pattern for clothing : make (a standard pattern) into a working pattern for clothing — compare GRADER 3 ~ *vi* **1 a** : to form a gradation or a series having only slight differences ⟨the colors *graded* gradually from red to orange to yellow⟩ ⟨anthracite ~*s* by imperceptible stages into bituminous coal —*Encyc. Americana*⟩ ⟨interrelated plant communities which *graded* from one to another through orderly transitions —R.W.Finley⟩ **b** : BLEND ⟨the colors *graded* into one another at the edges⟩ ⟨any further attempt here to segregate the two would serve no purpose, for . . . the one inevitably ~*s* into the other —W.H.Dowdeswell⟩ **2** : to proceed on an incline ⟨*grading* slowly downward —R.L.Stevenson⟩ **3** : to be of or merit a particular grade ⟨lambs *grading* choice to prime — *Chicago Daily Drovers Jour.*⟩ ⟨a story which ~*s* too low in reader interest —Richard Match⟩

³grade \"\ *adj* **1** : comprising the elementary grades : belonging to an elementary grade ⟨a ~ room⟩ : teaching the elementary grades ⟨a ~ teacher⟩ **2** *of a domestic animal* : of improved but not pure stock — distinguished from *crossbred* and *purebred*; compare SCRUB

-grade \ˌgrād\ *adj comb form* [F, fr. L *-gradus* going (fr. *gradi* to step, go) — more at GRADE] : walking ⟨digiti*grade*⟩ ⟨planti*grade*⟩ — chiefly in zoological terms

grade a \(ˈ)grāˈdā\ *adj, usu cap G&A* : of the highest grade : extremely good : FIRST-CLASS ⟨a *Grade A* movie⟩ ⟨a truly *Grade A* pie is now almost a museum piece —S.W.Dean⟩

grade·abil·i·ty \ˌgrādəˈbiləd·ē\ *n* : the steepness of grade that a motor vehicle is capable of climbing at efficient speed

grade beam *n* : a sill of structural steel or reinforced concrete atop the foundation of a building and supporting a wall at or near ground level

grade crossing *n* : an intersection or crossing of highways, railroad tracks, or pedestrian walks or combinations of these at grade

graded area *n* : a region that shows characteristic speech features reflecting different degrees of influence from one or more focal areas — called also *transition area;* compare FOCAL AREA, RELIC AREA

grade down *vt* : to decrease proportionally ⟨the wage earner postpones purchases or *grades down* his buying when uncertain about his future —*Biddle Survey*⟩

grade line *n* : a longitudinal reference line or slope to which a highway or railway is built

¹grade·ly \ˈgrādli\ *adj* [ME *greithly, graithly* ready, prompt, excellent, fr. ON *greithligr* ready, prompt, fr. *greithr* ready, free + *-ligr* -ly — more at READY] **1** *dial Eng* : fine, good, and desirable: **a** : upstanding and worthy ⟨how proud I am of Rochdale and of its ~ folks —Gracie Fields⟩ **b** : promising and likely ⟨a ~ lad⟩ **c** : physically well : being in good health ⟨Mama and Papa are . . . ~ —Charlotte Brontë⟩ **d** : physically attractive : GOOD-LOOKING **2** *dial Eng* : fitting and proper : APPROPRIATE

²gradely \"\ *adv* [ME *greithly, graithly* promptly, suitably, fr. ON *greithligr* promptly, fr. *greithligr*, adj.] **1** *dial Eng* : properly and suitably **2** *dial Eng* : WELL

grad·er \ˈgrādə(r)\ *n* -S **1** : one that grades: as **a** : a worker or machine that grades and sorts materials or products according to certain specifications (as of size, color, weight, condition, quality) **b** : a clerk who assists with the correction of students' test papers and the computation of grades **c** : a machine for grading and shallow excavating usu. having an adjustable blade for pushing material **d** : a worker who grades surfaces (as of roadbeds or excavation slopes) by means of hand tools or a grading machine **2** : a pupil in an elementary or secondary school grade — used with an ordinal numeral designating the grade ⟨a fifth ~⟩ ⟨a ninth ~⟩ **3** : a clothing worker who from a standard pattern size figures out and cuts out patterns for other sizes

grader man *n* **1** : a bulldozer operator **2** : an operator of a battery of machines for cleaning and grading seed corn

grades *pl of* GRADE, *pres 3d sing of* GRADE

grade school *also* **graded school** *n* **1** : ELEMENTARY SCHOOL : an elementary school system **2** : the elementary grades ⟨a young boy still in *grade school*⟩

grade separation *n* : a crossing of two highways or of a highway and pedestrian path or railroad utilizing an underpass or overpass

grade stake *n* : a stake driven in the ground so that the top has a predetermined elevation and used to establish the grade of an engineering work

grade up *vt* : to improve the quality or grade of by gradual degrees ⟨spent much money *grading up* his herd of cattle⟩ : IMPROVE, RAISE ⟨important that we *grade up* the standard of scholarship⟩

grad·grind \ˈgradˌgrīnd\ *n* -S *usu cap* [after Thomas *Gradgrind*, a materialistic hardware merchant in the novel *Hard Times* (1854) by Charles Dickens †1870 Eng. novelist] : one that is patently and usu. as a matter of outspoken policy marked by a materialistic and philistine outlook : an uninspired and assiduous seeker after facts — **grad·grind·ian** \-dēən\ *adj, usu cap* — **grad·grind·ish** \-dish\ *adj, usu cap*

¹gra·di·ent \ˈgrādēənt\ *n* -S [L *gradient-, gradiens* (influenced in meaning by E ¹*grade*), pres. part. of *gradi* to step, go — more at GRADE] **1 a** : the inclination or the rate of regular or graded ascent or descent (as of a slope, roadway, or pipeline) **b** : a part (as of a road or pipeline) that slopes upward or downward : a portion of a way that is not level : SLOPE, GRADE, RAMP **2** : change in the value of a quantity (as temperature, pressure, or intensity of sound) per unit distance in a specified direction ⟨vertical temperature ~⟩ ⟨electric potential ~ along a wire⟩ **3** : the vector sum of the partial derivatives with respect to the three coordinate variables *x, y, z* of a scalar quantity whose value varies from point to point **4 a** : a graded difference in reactive capacity and metabolic activity along an embryonic axis or the radius of an embryonic field that constitutes a major effective agent in the organization of embryonic tissues and in the localization and differentiation of definitive structures and organs **b** : a graded difference in physiological activity esp. along the primary axis of the body

²gradient \"\ *adj* : being a gradient ⟨a ~ section of the road⟩ : constituting a gradient ⟨show definite ~ tendency — a tendency for the rate of delinquency and crime to decrease from the center outward —W.C.Reckless⟩

gradient concept *or* **gradient theory** *n* : a theory in embryology: embryonic differentiation is the result of gradation in the potentialities for development of various parts of the embryo of such nature that successful differentiation of a part inhibits the potentiality for similar change elsewhere in the system

gra·di·ent·er \-ēˌentə(r)\ *n* -S : an attachment to an engineer's transit for measuring an angle of inclination in terms of the tangent of the angle and for measuring horizontal distances

gra·di·en·tia \ˌgrādēˈench(ē)ə\ *n pl, cap* [NL, fr. neut. pl. of L *gradient-, gradiens*] **1** *in former classifications* : the lizards and the caudate amphibians regarded as a natural group **2** *in former classifications* : CAUDATA

gradient velocity *or* **gradient wind** *n* : the velocity of the air that would cause it to move parallel to the current isobar if without friction

¹gra·dine \ˈgrāˌdēn, grəˈdēn\ *or* **gra·din** \ˈgrādᵊn\ *n* -S [F *gradin*, fr. It *gradino*, dim. of *grado* step, degree, fr. L *gradus* — more at GRADE] **1** : one of a series of low steps or seats raised one above another **2** : a shelf at the back of an altar on which candlesticks and flowers are placed in a Christian church

²gra·dine \grəˈdēn\ *n* -S [F, fr. It *gradina*, fr. *grado* step] : a toothed chisel used by sculptors

grading *n* -S [fr. gerund of ²*grade*] : GRADE ⟨used several ~*s* of aggregate in making cement⟩

gra·di·no \grəˈdē(ˌ)nō\ *n, pl* **gradi·ni** \-nē\ [It] **1** : GRADINE **2** : a painting or sculpture for ornamenting an altar gradine

gra·di·om·e·ter \ˌgrādēˈämәd·ə(r)\ *n* [¹*gradi*ent + -o- + -*meter*] : an instrument for measuring the gradient of a physical quantity (as of temperature, the earth's magnetic field, a slope)

grad·o·col membrane *also* **grad·a·col membrane** \ˈgradəˌkōl-, -ˌkäl-\ *n* [G *gradokol*, fr. *grado-* (fr. ISV *grade*) + *kollodium* collodion] : a collodion membrane prepared from a solution of collodion in alcohol and ether in such a way as to have a predetermined average pore diameter and used esp. in ultrafiltration (as of a virus suspension)

grads *pl of* GRAD

¹grad·u·al \ˈgraj(ə)wəl, -jəl\ *also* **gradu·ale** \ˌgrädəˈwä(ˌ)lā; ˈgraj(ə)wəl, -jəl\ *n* -S *often cap* [ML *graduale*, alter. of LL *gradale*, fr. L *gradus* step + *-ale* (neut. of *-alis* -al); fr. its being sung on the steps of the altar — more at GRADE] **1** : an antiphon or responsory sung or recited with the alleluia or the tract between the Epistle and Gospel originally from the steps of the altar in a Christian church **2** : a service book containing the musical portion of the mass sung by the choir

²gradual \"\ *adj* [ML *gradualis*, fr. L *gradus* step, degree + *-alis* -al] **1** : arranged in grades or degrees; *also* : admitting of such an arrangement **2 a** : proceeding by steps or degrees : advancing step by step (as in ascent or from one state to another) **b** (1) : moving, changing, or developing by fine, slight, or often imperceptible gradations or modulations ⟨a ~ change for the better in the patient's condition⟩ (2) *of an incline* : not steep or abrupt ⟨a ~ slope⟩ ⟨a ~ drop down to the town⟩

³gradual \"\ *adv, chiefly dial* : GRADUALLY

grad·u·al·ism \-j(ə)wəˌlizəm, -jəˌl-\ *n* -S **1** : the policy or practice of proceeding toward a desired end by gradual stages ⟨rejected pure Marxianism and developed a doctrine of gradualism —Alys Russell⟩ — compare IMMEDIATISM **2 a** : a theory in philosophy: between two apparently opposed notions (as analytic and synthetic truths) there is no sharp distinction or definite line of demarcation but a gradually altering continuity — compare DUALISM

¹grad·u·al·ist \-ləst\ *n* -S [²*gradual* + *-ist*] : an advocate of a policy, practice, or theory of gradualism

²gradualist \"\ *or* **grad·u·al·is·tic** \ˌ=(=)=ˈlistik\ *adj* : advocating, practicing, or based on gradualism

grad·u·al·i·ty \ˌgrajəˈwaləd·ē\ *n* -ES : the quality or state of being gradual or of coming about by gradual stages ⟨the ~ of significant reforms⟩

grad·u·al·ly \ˈgraj(ə)lē, -li, -j(ə)wəl-\ *adv* : in a gradual manner ⟨then the din ~ dies down, the music stops —Lafcadio Hearn⟩ ⟨~ aware of their intense significance —Matthew Arnold⟩

grad·u·al·ness \-lnəs\ *n* -ES : GRADUALITY

gradual psalm *n, usu cap G&P* : SONG OF ASCENTS

grad·u·and \ˈgrajəˌwand\ *n* -S [ML *graduandus*, gerundive of *graduare*] *chiefly Brit* : one about to graduate : a candidate for a degree

¹grad·u·ate \ˈgraj(ə)wə̇t, -jəˌwāt, *usu* |d·+V\ *n* -S [ME *graduat*, fr. ML *graduatus*, fr. past part. of *graduare*] **1 a** : one that has received an academic degree, a diploma, or a certificate ⟨a college ~⟩ ⟨a high school ~⟩; *also* : a graduate student ⟨in all courses open to ~*s* only —*Univ. of Minn. Bull.*⟩ **b** : one who has qualified in a particular field or for a particular position ⟨the expert planner, often an economist or a ~ of some branch of social service —M.B.Smith⟩ **c** : one who has passed through a significant or unusual and esp. powerful experience often associated with an institution ⟨a ~ of the Warsaw ghetto⟩ ⟨a reformatory ~⟩ **2** : a graduated cup, cylinder, or flask

graduates 2

²graduate \"\ *adj* [ME *graduat*, fr. ML *graduatus*, past part. of *graduare*] **1 a** : holding an academic or professional degree, diploma, or certificate ⟨a ~ physician⟩ ⟨a ~ economist⟩ ⟨a ~ pilot⟩ **b** : of, relating to, or engaged in studies that go beyond the first or bachelor's degree and are usu. specialized or professional ⟨~ student⟩ ⟨~ course⟩ **2** : arranged by degrees : GRADUATED

³grad·u·ate \-jəˌwāt, *usu* -ād·+V\ *vb* -ED/-ING/-S [ML *graduatus*, past part. of *graduare*, fr. L *gradus* step, degree — more at GRADE] *vt* **1 a** : to grant an academic or professional degree, diploma, or certificate to ⟨expect to ~ approximately 380,000 this year —A.W.Griswold⟩ : dismiss with such a degree, diploma, or certificate ⟨*graduated* from the university with honors⟩ **b** : to grant the right to go or concede the completion of the qualifications for going (as from an elementary school) at the end of the course or last grade ⟨many citizens were never *graduated* from high school⟩ **c** : to move up to the next school grade ⟨~ the boy from the third to the fourth grade⟩ **2** : to qualify as proficient or learned (as in a vice or other practice) **3 a** : to mark with degrees (as the scale of a thermometer) **b** : to divide into or arrange in regular or proportional steps, grades, gradations, or intervals (as punishments in relation to crimes) **4** *obs* : TEMPER, MODIFY : improve the grade of **5** : to concentrate (a liquid) by graduation ~ *vi* **1 a** : to receive from a university, college, or school an academic degree, a diploma, or a certificate denoting fulfillment of requirements leading to it : become a graduate ⟨~ from the university⟩ ⟨~ from divinity school⟩ ⟨~ with honors⟩ **b** : to qualify in a particular field or for a particular position (as after special training or experience) ⟨*graduated* as a seaman⟩ ⟨*graduated* as a chef⟩ **c** : to pass from one stage of experience, proficiency, or prestige to or into another usu. higher ⟨began as a boy to gather stamps, coins and butterflies, then *graduated* into a connoisseur of books in general —G.F.Whicher⟩ ⟨from the comics they soon ~ to *Treasure Island* and *Robinson Crusoe* —Eamon Ryan⟩ **2** : to pass by degrees : change gradually : shade off — **grad·u·a·tor** \-ād·ə(r), -ātə-\ *n* -S

graduated *adj* **1** : being a graduate **2 a** : marked with or divided into degrees : divided into or arranged in grades, steps, or successive levels usu. proportionally ⟨a ~ series of honors⟩ **b** *of a tax* : increasing in rate with increase in taxable base (as income or inheritance) : PROGRESSIVE **3** *of a bird's tail* : made up of feathers which become successively longer from the outer layer to innermost : TAPERED

graduate nurse *n* : a person who has completed the regular course of study and practical hospital training in nurses' training school — called also *trained nurse*

graduate school *n* : a school or division of a university or college devoted entirely to graduate studies, usu. having a dean and faculty of its own, and authorized to grant advanced degrees

grad·u·ate·ship *pronunc at* ¹GRADUATE +ˌship\ *n, archaic* : the state of being a graduate or the period of one's life after graduation

grad·u·a·tion \ˌgrajəˈwāshən\ *n* -S [ML *graduation-, graduatio*, fr. *graduatus* + L *-ion-, -io* -ion] **1 a** : a division into degrees or quantity on a graduated scale ⟨faulty ~ of a thermometer⟩ **b** : a mark on an instrument or vessel indicating degrees or quantity; *collectively* : these marks **2 a** : the act of completing a phase of one's formal education; *esp* : the act of receiving a diploma, certificate, or degree from a school, college, or university ⟨went to extension classes after ~ from high school⟩ **b** : the act or ceremony of conferring academic diplomas, certificates, or degrees : COMMENCEMENT ⟨many visitors were on the campus for ~⟩ **3 a** : arrangement in or as if in degrees or gradations ⟨the abolition of the ~ of rank —Mark Pattison⟩ **b** : elevation to a higher stage of accomplishment, maturity, or prestige ⟨his ~ from . . . one of the most brilliant and lengthy childhoods on record —H.W.Wind⟩ **4** : the exposure of a liquid in large surfaces to the air so as to hasten its evaporation **5** : the smoothing of statistical data

gra·dus \ˈgrādəs\ *n* -ES [fr. *Gradus ad Parnassum* (L, lit., a step to Parnassus), a 17th cent. prosody dictionary long used in Brit. schools] **1** : a dictionary of Greek or Latin prosody and poetical phrases used as an aid in the writing of verse in Greek or Latin **2** : a handbook (as of law phrases or forms) or exercise book to assist in the mastering or performance of a difficult art or practice

graeco- — see GRECO-

¹graff \ˈgraf, -áf\ *vb* -ED/-ING/-S [ME *graffen*, fr. MF *grafier*, fr. *grafe*, n.] *archaic* : ¹GRAFT

²graff \"\ *n* -S [ME *graffe*, fr. MF *grafe*, fr. ML *graphium*, fr. L, stylus, fr. Gk *grapheion*, fr. *graphein* to write; fr. the resemblance of the scion inserted at an angle in the tree to a stylus poised for writing — more at CARVE] *archaic* : ²GRAFT

³graff \"\ *dial Brit var of* GRAVE

⁴graff \"\ *n* -S [D *graaf*, fr. MD *grave*, fr. *graven* to dig; akin to OHG *graban* to dig — more at GRAVE] : a trench, ditch, fosse, or canal used in fortification esp. as a moat

graf·fi·to \grəˈfēd·(ˌ)ō\ *n, pl* **graffi·ti** \-d·(ˌ)ē\ [It, dim. of *graffio* scratch, fr. *graffiare* to scratch, prob. fr. *grafio* stylus, fr. L *graphium* — more at GRAFF] : an inscription, figure, or design scratched on rocks or walls or on artifacts made of plaster, stone, or clay — compare SGRAFFITO

¹graft \ˈgraft, -aa(ə)-, -ai-, -á-\ *vb* -ED/-ING/-S [ME *graften*, alter. of *graffen* — more at GRAFF] *vt* **1 a** : to unite (plants or scion and stock) to form a graft ⟨impossible to ~ unrelated trees successfully⟩ : cause (a scion) to unite with a stock in a graft ⟨~*ed* a branch of white roses on his red rose tree⟩ **b** : to insert scions in (a plant) ⟨possible to cut back an old apple and ~ it with scions of a better variety⟩ **c** : to propagate (a plant) by grafting ⟨apples and most other fruits are ~*ed* to retain desirable qualities that do not come true from seed⟩ **d** : to perform the operation of preparing grafts on or of ⟨~ all our own replacement trees⟩ **2 a** : to join or fasten as if by grafting so as to bring about a close union ⟨the jute industry was also ~*ed* on to a local textile trade⟩ ⟨a hopeful ending ~*ed* on to the story —David Sylvester⟩ ⟨the level of industrial civilization ~*ed* on to a world of feudal manners —Frank Gibney⟩ ⟨the rail that was especially ~*ed* on to the grand staircase —Emily Hahn⟩ ⟨turn him adrift, ~*ing* upon him a sense of failure —Dixon Wecter⟩ **b** : to implant (living tissue) so as to form an organic union (as in a lesion) ⟨were able to ~ new skin over the badly burned area of the arm⟩ ⟨~*ed* a new piece of artery into the ruptured portion of the old artery⟩ **c** : to join or mend invisibly; *esp* : to weave together with a needle (two unfinished or broken edges of knitted fabric) **3** : to cover (as a rope, ringbolt, or stanchion on a boat) with a weaving of small cord ~ *vi* **1** : to become grafted ⟨many pears ~ well on quince rootstocks⟩ **2** : to perform grafting (as of a fruit tree or shrub) ⟨~*ing* is used especially to increase the numbers of a clonal plant or to improve the vigor of a plant of a weak-rooted variety⟩ **3** : to engage in graft

²graft \"\ *n* -S [ME *grafte*, alter. of *graffe* — more at GRAFF]

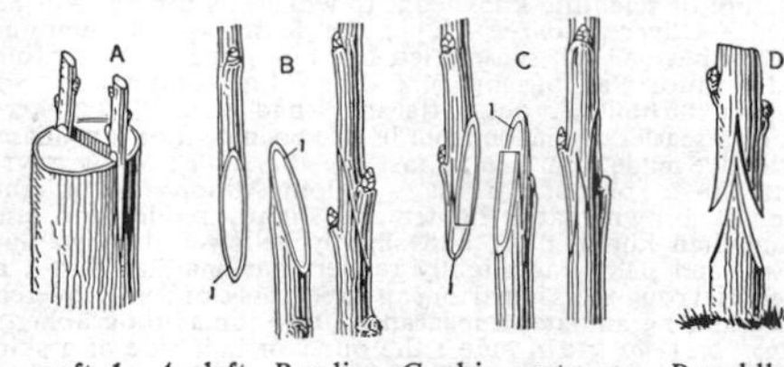

graft 1: *A* cleft, *B* splice, *C* whip or tongue, *D* saddle; *1* cambium

1 a : the growth or an individual resulting from the union of scion and stock : a grafted plant (as a rosebush) ⟨some excellent two-year-old ~*s* on dwarf rootstocks⟩ ⟨an expert can turn out a surprising number of ~*s* in a day⟩ **b** : SCION 1 **c** : the point of insertion of a scion upon a stock ⟨the ~ should be high enough to prevent the formation of scion roots⟩; *also* : the area of joining of scion and stock in grafting ⟨a poor ~ may break after several years satisfactory growth⟩ **2 a** : the act of grafting or of joining one thing to another as if by grafting ⟨a strange partial ~ of Nordic traits on broad-faced and broad-headed Mongolian physique —A.L.Kroeber⟩ **b** : something grafted in this way; *specif* : a piece of living tissue used in grafting — see AUTOGRAFT, HETEROGRAFT, HOMOGRAFT **3 a** : the acquisition of money, position, or other profit by dishonest or questionable means (as by actual theft or by taking advantage of a public office or a position of trust or employment to obtain fees, perquisites, profits on contracts, or pay for work not done or service not performed) : illegal or unfair practice for profit or personal gain ⟨tried to clear the ~, waste, and inefficiency out of government⟩ ⟨claimed that any large and complex business organization tended to breed ~ because of the inevitable towering hierarchy of command⟩ **b** : something gained in this way ⟨no matter how much ~ his subordinates may have garnered —Green Peyton⟩ **c** : something given as payment to one engaged in such a practice ⟨forced to pay out ~ to local politicians to avoid being annoyed by the police⟩ **d** : a means or method of making such gain or advantage ⟨systematic appropriation of public funds by lawless political groups . . . and the more honest ~ of special favors to real-estate or public-service interests —H.E.Davis⟩

³graft \"\ *n* -S [D *graft, gracht* ditch, canal, fr. MD; derivative fr. the stem of MD *graven* to dig, OHG *graban* — more at GRAVE] *now dial Eng* : DITCH, TRENCH

⁴graft \"\ *vi* -ED/-ING/-S [alter. of ¹*grave*] **1** *dial Eng* : DIG **2** *dial Eng* : WORK

⁵graft \"\ *n* -S *dial chiefly Brit* : WORK, LABOR; *also* : TRADE, OCCUPATION

graft·age \-tij, tēj\ *n* -S : the act or the principles and practice of grafting in horticulture : GRAFTING

¹graft·er \-tə(r)\ *n* -S [¹*graft* + *-er*] : one that grafts

²grafter \"\ *n* -S [⁴*graft* + *-er*] *chiefly Brit* : an industrious hardworking person

graft hybrid *n* : a chimeral hybrid produced by grafting in which tissue from scion and stock are intimately mingled in the new growth; *esp* : a shoot of a grafted plant exhibiting such mingling — compare CHIMERA 3

grafting *n* -S [ME, action of grafting, fr. gerund of *graften* to graft — more at GRAFT] : something grafted; *esp* : GRAFT 1, 2b

grafting tool *or* **grafting iron** *n* : an implement designed esp. for use in grafting that combines a handle, a blade for making the cut for a cleft graft and a wedge for holding it open while the scions are being inserted

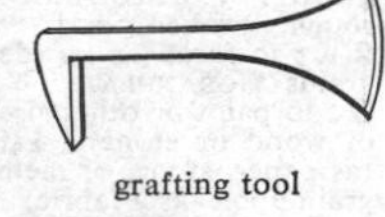

grafting tool

grafting wax *n* : a composition of rosin, beeswax, and tallow used to protect the wounds and scions of newly grafted trees or to cover the wounds on pruned trees

graf·ton·ite \ˈgraftəˌnīt\ *n* -S [*Grafton*, N.H. + E *-ite*] : a mineral $(Fe,Mn,Ca)_3(PO_4)_2$ consisting of an iron manganese calcium phosphate occurring in salmon-pink laminated intergrowths with triphylite (hardness 5, sp. gr. 3.7)

gra·ger \ˈgrägə(r)\ *or* **greg·er** *or* **greg·ger** \-reg-\ *also* **grog·ger** \-räg-\ *n* -s [Yiddish *grager, greger*, fr. Pol *grzegarz* rattle] **:** a rattle or noisemaker traditionally used by children during the Purim festival at every mention of Haman's name during the reading in the synagogue of the scroll of the Book of Esther

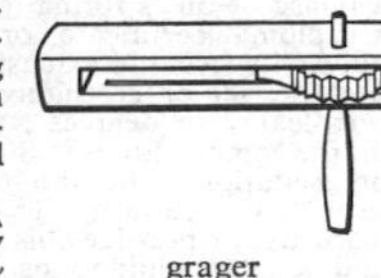
grager

gra·ham \ˈgrāəm, ˈgram, ˈgraa(ə)m\ *adj* [*graham (flour)*] **:** made wholly or largely of graham flour ⟨~ bread⟩ ⟨~ rolls⟩

graham cracker *n* [*graham (flour)*] **:** a dry slightly sweet square or rectangular cracker made mainly of whole wheat flour

graham flour *n* [after Sylvester *Graham* †1851 Am. advocate of dietary reform] **:** WHOLE WHEAT FLOUR

gra·ham·ism \-ˌmizəm\ *n* -s *usu cap* [S. *Graham* + E *-ism*] **:** a vegetarian dietary system advocated in the 19th century

¹gra·ham·ite \-ˌmīt\ *n* -s *usu cap* [S. *Graham* + E *-ite*] **:** an advocate of Grahamism

²grahamite \"\ *n* -s [J.A. and J.L. *Graham*, 19th cent. Am. mineowners + E *-ite*] **:** a lustrous pitch-black complex bituminous asphalt

graham's law *n*, *usu cap G* [after Thomas *Graham* †1869 Scot. chemist] **:** a statement in physics: under constant pressure and temperature two gases diffuse into each other at rates inversely proportional to the square roots of their respective molecular weights or densities

graham's salt *n*, *usu cap G* [after T. *Graham*] **:** sodium metaphosphate glass

¹grail \ˈgrāl, *chiefly before pause or consonant* -āəl\ *n* -s [ME *graiel*, fr. MF *grael*, fr. ML *gradale* — more at GRADUAL] *archaic* **:** GRADUAL

²grail \"\ *n* -s [ME *graal, greal*, fr. MF, bowl, grail, fr. ML *gradalis*, perh. fr. L *gradus* step + *-alis* -al; perh. fr. its having consisted originally of a series of bowls or plates arranged one above the other — more at GRADE] **1** *usu cap* **:** the cup or platter which according to medieval legend was used by Christ at the Last Supper, was brought to Britain, and thereafter became the object of knightly quests that could be achieved only by those persons who were chaste in thought, word, and deed — called also *Holy Grail* **2** *sometimes cap* **:** an eminently desirable and ultimate object of an extended effort or quest ⟨the road we travel is long, but at the end lies the ~ of peace —A.E.Stevenson †1965⟩

³grail \"\ *n* -s [perh. contr. of *gravel*] **:** GRAVEL ⟨silver globules and gold-sparkling ~ —Robert Browning⟩

¹grain \ˈgrān\ *n* -s [ME *grain, grein*, partly fr. MF *grain* cereal plant, kernel, grain, fr. L *granum*; partly fr. MF *graine* seed, kermes, dye made from kermes, fr. L *grana*, pl. of *granum* — more at CORN] **1 a** (1) *obs* **:** a single small hard seed (2) **:** the seed or fruit resembling seed of any cereal grass (as wheat, oats, rice, millet) — compare CARYOPSIS **b** (1) **:** the unhusked or the threshed seeds or fruits of various food plants including the cereal grasses and in commercial and statutory usage (as in an insurance policy or trade list) other plants (as flax, peas, sugarcane) — compare CORN 3 (2) **:** the plants producing such seed or fruit **c :** one of the drupelets of a multiple fruit (as the raspberry) **d :** a rounded prominence on the back of a sepal (as in the common dock) **2 a** (1) **:** a small hard particle (as of sand, sugar, salt, gunpowder) (2) **:** one of the individual light-sensitive crystals of a photographic material or a particle resulting from the development of such a material; *collectively* **:** such crystals or particles (3) **:** an individual crystal in a metal; *collectively* **:** such crystals **b** (1) **:** a minute portion or particle ⟨a ~ of pollen⟩ ⟨the great structure of scientific knowledge to which his little ~ will be added —Oliver LaFarge⟩ (2) **:** the least possible amount ⟨did not have a ~ of sense⟩ ⟨left him no ~ of possible hope⟩ **c :** fine crystallization (as of sugar) ⟨boiling the solution to ~⟩ ⟨stopped the boiling process after the ~ had formed⟩ **3 a :** kermes or a scarlet dye made from it **b :** cochineal or a brilliant scarlet dye made from it **c :** a fast dye **d** *archaic* **:** COLOR, TINT, SHADE ⟨in a robe of darkest ~ —John Milton⟩ **e :** a light yellowish brown that is lighter and slightly redder and less strong than khaki, paler and slightly yellower than walnut brown, and paler and slightly redder than manila **4 a :** a superficial roughness imparting an appearance of being covered with grains **:** granulated appearance ⟨the ~ on a lithographer's plate⟩ **b** (1) *or* **grain side :** the outer or hair side of a skin or hide — compare FLESH 7 (2) **:** the markings on such a grain (3) **:** a surface artificially treated to resemble such a grain **c :** small pimply projections on the upper or outer surface of fully cured and fermented cigar leaf **5 a :** a unit of weight based on the weight of a grain of wheat taken as an average of the weight of grains from the middle of the ear and equal to .0648 gram — see CARAT GRAIN, MEASURE table **b :** a degree of hardness of water calculated by analysis of the number of such units of calcium carbonate per gallon of tested water — usu. used with a preceding number designating the number of units ⟨reduce the original 22-*grain* hardness —L.C.Huffman⟩ **c** *in Malta* **:** GRANO **6 a :** the appearance and texture of wood esp. as determined by the manner in which it is cut in relation to the cells, their size, shape, and orientation and their proportions and arrangement in annual rings **:** the appearance of the wood fibers in a piece of wood esp. as to their arrangement and direction of stratification; *also* **:** the direction of stratification of wood fibers **b** (1) **:** an appearance or texture that is due to the arrangement and esp. stratification of constituent particles or fibers and that is similar to or suggests the texture of wood ⟨the ~ of a rock⟩ ⟨the ~ of a metallic surface⟩ ⟨the ~ of a piece of meat⟩ (2) **:** a linear arrangement of roughly parallel ridges and valleys commonly displayed in regions of tilted sedimentary rocks; *also* **:** the direction of such linear features ⟨the ~ of the relief runs east and west⟩ **c :** a direction of cleavage of rock at right angles to and less conspicuous than the rift **d :** a direction of threads esp. in the warp of a fabric **e :** the fiber or yarn of a woven material that is dyed or is to be dyed ⟨dyed in the ~⟩ **f :** MACHINE DIRECTION **g :** the direction in which the blades of grass on a putting green tend to bend ⟨the average player never knows or cares whether he is putting with or against the ~ of a green —Paul Gallico⟩ **7 grains** *pl* **:** the remains of grain left in a mash tun after the completion of the mashing process **8 a** (1) **:** the arrangement of the particles of a body or of matter that determines its tactile quality esp. as to roughness or hardness ⟨the ~ of the freshly split piece of marble⟩ ⟨the fine ~ of her skin —Edna Ferber⟩ (2) **:** the roughness or hardness determined by this arrangement ⟨a soft-*grain* soap⟩ (3) **:** the coarseness or fineness of an abrasive expressed by a preceding number indicating the mesh of the finest screen through which the particles will pass ⟨a 24-*grain* grinding wheel⟩ **b** (1) **:** natural disposition **:** TEMPER, INCLINATION ⟨brothers similar in ~⟩ ⟨it went against the boy's ~ to tell lies⟩ (2) **:** basic quality or kind ⟨other poets of a tougher ~ —Van Wyck Brooks⟩ ⟨his work is . . . clearly in the American ~ —*Time*⟩ **c :** prevailing direction ⟨running against the ~ of the American polity —*Times Lit. Supp.*⟩ **9 :** a piece of powder charge used in a rocket — **in grain** [ME, fr. MF *en graine* in kermes dye] **1** *of a dye* **:** RED, SCARLET **2 :** COLORFAST **3 :** DEEP-SEATED, INGRAINED ⟨anguish *in grain* —George Herbert⟩ ⟨a rogue *in grain* —Alfred Tennyson⟩ — **with a grain of salt** [trans. of L *cum grano salis*] **:** with some reservation or allowance **:** with caution ⟨take some of his more optimistic predictions *with a grain of salt*⟩

²grain \"\ *vb* -ED/-ING/-S *vt* **1 :** INGRAIN 2 ⟨her hands were rough, broken, and ~*ed* with dirt —Rearden Conner⟩ **2 a :** to form (as powder) into grains **:** cause to separate in grains **:** GRANULATE **b :** to salt out — used esp. of soap **3 :** to paint or otherwise decorate in imitation of a grain (as of wood or stone) **4 :** to impart a granulated surface to (as paper, stone, or metal for lithographic work) **:** impress a grain upon (as a fabric) **5 :** to feed with grain ~ *vi* **:** to form into grains **:** become granular **:** GRANULATE

³grain \"\ *n* -s [ME *grein, grain*, fr. ON *grein* branch, arm of the sea; akin to ON *grīna* to grin — more at GROAN] **1** *now dial Brit* **a :** an arm of the sea **b :** BRANCH, FORK ⟨a ~ of a river⟩ **c :** a branching fork in a tree **2 grains** *pl but sing in constr* **:** an iron fish spear or harpoon having two or more barbed points

⁴grain \"\ *vt* -ED/-ING/-S **:** to spear (fish) with a grains

⁵grain \"\ *vt* -ED/-ING/-S [fr. obs. *grane* trap, snare, noose, fr. ME — more at GRIN] *dial Eng* **:** STRANGLE, CHOKE

grain alcohol *n* **:** ETHYL ALCOHOL — used esp. in distinction from *wood alcohol*; see ALCOHOL 3

grain amaranth *n* **:** any of various amaranths grown esp. in So. America for their seed

grain beetle *n* **:** any of several small beetles whose larvae feed on and destroy stored grain

grain board *n* **:** plaster or gypsum wallboard bearing an imitation wood grain

grain borer *n* **:** an adult or larval insect that bores in grain

grain–burnt \ˈ=,=\ *adj, of a horse* **:** having a digestive disturbance attributed to overfeeding with grain

grain–cut \ˈ=,=\ *adj, of wood* **:** cut transversely to the grain

grain direction *n* **:** MACHINE DIRECTION

grain door *n* **:** a close-fitting removable device or partition used in boxcars hauling grain to seal openings around the lower part of permanent car doors and prevent leakage

grain drill *n* **:** a drill for sowing small grains (as of wheat) or fine seeds (as clover seed) — see CUP DRILL, SHOE DRILL

grained \ˈgrānd\ *adj* [partly fr. ¹*grain* + *-ed;* partly fr. past part. of ²*grain*] **1 a :** having, consisting of, or producing grains — usu. used with a modifier specifying kind or quantity ⟨small-*grained* wheat⟩ ⟨a fine-*grained* gunpowder⟩ ⟨a many-*grained* grass⟩ **b :** GRANULAR ⟨boiled the sugar solution down to a ~ consistency⟩ **2 a :** having a grain — usu. used with a modifier specifying the kind ⟨a straight-*grained* wood⟩ ⟨an open-*grained* fibrous material⟩ ⟨a tough-*grained* writer⟩ **b :** treated (as by painting or staining) to exhibit a grain ⟨a painted and ~ commode⟩ **3 a :** having or treated so as to have a surface marked by a roughness or by distributed or stratified prominences or ridges ⟨~ leather⟩ **b** *of the edge of a coin* **:** MILLED — **grain·ed·ness** \ˈgrānədnəs\ *n* -ES

grain elevator *n* **:** ELEVATOR 1c

¹grain·er \ˈgrānə(r)\ *n* -s [²*grain* + *-er*] **1 :** a worker that grains: as **a :** an operator of a machine for graining lithographic printing plates **b** (1) **:** a worker who uses a graining comb, roller, sponge, or brush to decorate a metal or wooden surface with a simulated wood grain (2) **:** an operator of a machine for printing lines upon furniture parts to simulate the grain of wood **c :** a worker who softens and grains hides and skins by rubbing grain sides together with a graining board or by operating a graining machine — called also *boarder, dicer* **d :** a worker who melts TNT and drains it into graining kettles where it is crystallized by agitation and cooling **2 :** a machine or device used in graining: as **a :** a machine that impresses a grain on boards **b :** a brush or tool used in graining wood or metal **c :** an instrument for graining skins **d :** an evaporating vat in which salt grains from brine

²grainer \"\ *n* -s [⁴*grain* + *-er*] **:** one that uses a grains

grain·ery \ˈgrān(ə)rē, -ri\ *n* -ES [by alter.] **:** GRANARY

grainfield \ˈ=,=\ *n* **:** a field where grain is grown

grain hay *n* **:** plants of any of the grain crops cut and cured for hay

grainier *comparative of* GRAINY

grainiest *superlative of* GRAINY

grain·i·ness \ˈgrānēnəs, -nin-\ *n* -ES **:** the quality or state of being grainy

¹grain·ing \ˈgrāniŋ, -nēŋ\ *n* -s [fr. gerund of ²*grain*] **1 a** *obs* **:** a ring of dots on a coin near the rim **b :** REEDING **2 a :** grain (as of wood, marble, or leather) or appearance of such a grain (as one achieved by painting, printing, or stamping) **b :** a process for producing an artificial grain (as in leather)

²grai·ning \"\ *n* -s [origin unknown] **:** a European freshwater cyprinoid fish (*Leuciscus leuciscus*)

³grain·ing \"\ *n* -s [fr. gerund of ⁴*grain*] **:** the action of fishing with a grains

graining board *n* **:** a cork-covered board that is strapped to the forearm and used in softening and graining hides or skins

grain itch *n* **:** an itching rash caused by the bite of the tarsonemid mite (*Pyemotes ventricosus*) that occurs chiefly on grain, straw, or straw products — compare GROCER'S ITCH

grainland \ˈ=,=\ *n* **:** land on which grain grows or is grown

grain leather *n* **:** leather usu. heavier than buffing made from the grain side of a skin and in the case of cowhide often split from a hide already tanned and dried

grain·less \ˈgrānləs\ *adj* **:** having no grain ⟨a ~ wood finish⟩ ⟨~ ear of corn⟩

grain mark *n* **:** a line on a gem facet resulting from imperfect polishing

grain mite *n* **:** any of several mites that frequent stored grain; *esp* **:** a small whitish hairy form (*Acarus siro*) sometimes causing unpleasant odors in imperfectly dry flour or grain

grain moth *n* **:** any of several small tineoid moths (as the Angoumois grain moth) whose larvae feed on stored grain

grain of paradise [ME, trans. of MF *graine de paradis*] **1 :** one of the pungent seeds of a West African plant (*Aframomum melegueta*) of the family Zingiberaceae used as a spice — usu. used in pl. **2 :** one of the dried fruits of an East Indian woody vine (*Anamirta cocculus*) — usu. used in pl.

grain raising *n* **:** irregularity in wood surfaces resulting from exposure to moisture or weathering

grain rust *n* **:** a rust that attacks a cereal grass; *esp* **:** a wheat stem rust (*Puccinia graminis*)

grains *pl of* GRAIN, *pres 3d sing of* GRAIN

grain screen *n* **:** an etched screen with an irregular stipple finish used in making mezzographs

¹grainsick \ˈ=,=\ *n* -s **:** a sickness of cattle in which the rumen is excessively distended with food

²grainsick \"\ *adj* **:** suffering from grainsick — **grain·sick·ness** *n*

grain side *n* **:** GRAIN 4b(1)

grain smut *n* **:** a smut that attacks a cereal grass; *esp* **:** a kernel smut as distinguished from one invading the entire inflorescence

grain sorghum *n* **:** any of several sorghums that are cultivated primarily for grain — see DURRA, FETERITA, HEGARI, KAFFIR, KAOLIANG, MILO, SHALLU; compare SORGO

grain thief *n* **:** a device consisting chiefly of a long tube used for taking grain samples from various depths in a load of grain — compare THIEF 3

grain thrips *n* **:** any of several thrips feeding in cereal grains; *esp* **:** a cosmopolitan insect (*Limothrips cerealium*) common in developing flower stalks of oats and wild oats

grain weevil *n* **:** any of various small insects destructive of stored grain; *specif* **:** GRANARY WEEVIL

grainy \ˈgrānē, -ni\ *adj* -ER/-EST [¹*grain* + *-y*] **1 :** consisting of or resembling grains **:** GRANULAR ⟨soil of a ~ consistency⟩ ⟨a stone that is ~ in appearance⟩ **2 a :** having a usu. marked natural or artificial grain ⟨a ~ wood⟩ ⟨a floor of ~ plastic tile⟩ **b** *of paper* **:** showing on the surface the imprint of the felt used in its manufacture (as when the felt is coarse or worn) **3** *of a developed photographic image* **:** having a mottled appearance produced by the individual particles of silver of which it is composed

¹graip \ˈgrāp\ *dial Brit var of* GROPE

²graip \"\ *n* -s [ME *grape*, of Scand origin; akin to Norw *greip* forked tool, ON *greip* hand spread out, grip; akin to OE *grāp* grasp, grip, OHG *greifa* fork, ON *grīpa* to grip, grasp — more at GRIPE] *dial Brit* **:** a usu. 3-tined garden fork or manure fork

graisse \ˈgrās\ *or* **graisse disease** *n* -s [F *graisse*, lit., grease — more at GREASE] **:** a disease of white wines and cider caused by deficiency of tannin and the action of certain anaerobic bacteria

¹graith \ˈgrāth, ˈgreth\ *vt* -ED/-ING/-S [ME *greithen, graithen*, fr. ON *greitha*, fr. *greithr* ready, prepared — more at READY] **1** *chiefly Scot* **:** to make ready and put in order **2** *chiefly Scot* **:** FURNISH, ARRAY

²graith \"\ *n* -s [ME, readiness, equipment, fr. ON *greithi*, fr. *greithr* ready, prepared] **1** *chiefly Scot* **:** equipment or apparel **:** accouterments for work, traveling, or war **:** GEAR **2 :** POSSESSIONS, WEALTH

gral·lae \ˈgraˌlē\ *n pl, cap* [NL, fr. L, stilts, fr. *gradi* to step, go — more at GRADE] **1** *in former classifications* **:** an order of birds including all the wading birds **2** *in former classifications* **:** a group of birds variously limited: as **a :** CHARADRII **b :** GRUIFORMES **c :** Charadrii and Gruiformes

gral·la·to·res \ˌgraləˈtōr(ˌ)ēz\ [NL, pl. of L *grallator* one who goes on stilts, fr. *grallae* stilts + *-ator*] *syn of* GRALLAE 1

gral·la·to·ri·al \ˌ==ˈtōrēəl\ *adj* [NL *Grallatores* + E *-ial*] **:** of or belonging to the wading birds

gral·li·na \graˈlīnə, -lēnə\ *n* [NL, fr. L *grallae* stilts + NL *-ina*] **1** *cap* **:** a genus of passerine birds including the black-and-white magpie lark of Australia **2** -s **:** any bird of the genus *Grallina* **:** MAGPIE LARK

gral·line \ˈgraˌlīn\ *adj* [NL *Grallina*] **:** GRALLATORIAL

¹gral·loch \ˈgralək, -ək\ *n* -s [ScGael *greallach*] **1** *Brit* **:** the entrails of an animal (as a deer) **2** *Brit* **:** the act of gralloching

²gralloch \"\ *vt* -ED/-ING/-S *Brit* **:** to remove the entrails from (as a deer) **:** GUT

¹gram \ˈgram, -aa(ə)m\ *n* -s [Pg *grão* (formerly also spelled *gram*) grain, seed, chick-pea, fr. L *granum* grain — more at CORN] **:** any of several leguminous plants grown esp. for their seed: as **a :** CHICK-PEA **b :** HORSE GRAM **c :** MUNG BEAN

²gram *or* **gramme** \"\ *n* -s [F *gramme*, fr. LL *gramma*, a small weight, fr. Gk, letter, a small weight, fr. *graphein* to write — more at CARVE] **1 :** a metric unit of mass and weight equal to $\frac{1}{1000}$ kilogram and nearly equal to one cubic centimeter of water at its maximum density — see METRIC SYSTEM table **2 :** the weight of the gram mass under standard gravity

³gram \"\ *n* -s [by shortening & alter.] **:** GRANDMOTHER

-gram \ˌgram, -aa(ə)m; *in "program" and in the southern US in "telegram" the preceding or* ˌgrəm\ *n comb form* -s [L *-gramma*, fr. Gk, fr. *gramma* letter, piece of writing] **:** drawing **:** writing **:** record ⟨chronogram⟩ ⟨telegram⟩ ⟨thermogram⟩ ⟨spectrogram⟩

gram *abbr* grammar; grammatical

grama *or* **grama grass** *or* **gram·ma** *or* **gramma grass** \ˈgramə(-)\ *n* -s [Sp *grama* coarse grass, fr. L *gramina*, pl. of *gramen* grass — more at GRASS] **:** a pasture grass of the western U.S. belonging to the genus *Bouteloua* (as blue grama and black grama)

gram·a·rye *or* **gram·a·ry** \ˈgramərē\ *n, pl* **gramaryes** *or* **gramaries** [ME *gramarye, gramarie*, modif. of MF *gramaire* grammar, grammar book, book of sorcery — more at GRAMMAR] **:** NECROMANCY, MAGIC, ENCHANTMENT

gram atom \ˈ=;=\ *or* **gram–atomic weight** \ˈ=;=;==-\ *n* **:** the mass of one mole of an element equal in grams to the atomic weight of the element ⟨a *gram atom* of oxygen is 16 grams⟩ — compare AVOGADRO NUMBER

gram calorie *n* **:** CALORIE a

gram–centimeter \ˈ=;==,==\ *n* **1 :** a unit of torque equal to that of a gram weight acting on a lever arm one centimeter long **2 :** a unit of work in the cgs system equal to the work done in raising a weight of one gram against the force of gravity to a height of one centimeter

gram complex \ˈgram-\ *n, usu cap G* [after Hans Christian Joachim *Gram* †1938 Dan. physician] **:** the part of a gram-positive bacterial cell responsible for the characteristic staining by Gram's method and usu. considered to be a layer of ribonucleate in complex association with polysaccharides and protein immediately underlying the cell wall

grame \ˈgrām\ *n* -s [ME, fr. OE *grama*, fr. *gram* angry, fierce, hostile; akin to OHG *gram* angry, hostile, ON *gramr* angry, hostile, OE *grimm* fierce, wild — more at GRIM] **1** *archaic* **:** ANGER **2** *archaic* **:** SORROW, HARM, MISERY

gram equivalent *n* **:** the quantity of a chemical element, radical, or compound which has a mass in grams equal to the equivalent

¹gra·mer·cy \grəˈmərsē\ *interj* [ME *grand mercy, graunt mercy, gramercye*, fr. MF *grand merci* great thanks] *archaic* — used to express gratitude, surprise, or sudden strong feeling ⟨~! they for joy did grin —S.T.Coleridge⟩

²gramercy *n, obs* **:** THANKS ⟨works of compulsion are not worth ~ —Richard Montagu⟩

gram–fast \ˈ=,=\ *adj, sometimes cap G* [after Hans C. J. *Gram* †1938 Dan. physician] **:** GRAM-POSITIVE

gram·i·ci·din \ˌgraməˈsīdᵊn\ *n* -s [*gram*-positive + *-i-* + *-cide* + *-in*] **:** a crystalline antibiotic of a polypeptide nature produced by a soil bacterium (*Bacillus brevis*) that is active against most gram-positive disease-producing bacteria in local infections but when introduced into the blood stream is destructive of red blood cells — see TYROTHRICIN

gramied *past of* GRAMY

gramies *pres 3d sing of* GRAMY

gramin- *or* **gramini-** *comb form* [L *gramin-, gramen* — more at GRASS] **:** grass ⟨*gramini*vorous⟩ ⟨*gramini*ferous⟩

gram·i·na·ce·ae \ˌgraməˈnāsēˌē\ [NL, fr. *gramin-* + *-aceae*] *syn of* GRAMINEAE

gram·i·na·ceous \ˌ==ˈnāshəs\ *adj* [*gramin-* + *-aceous*] **:** GRAMINEOUS

gram·i·na·les \ˌ==ˈnā(ˌ)lēz\ *n pl, cap* [NL, fr. L *gramin-, gramen* grass + NL *-ales*] **:** an order of monocotyledonous plants including the grasses and sedges that is characterized by small flowers usu. arranged in spikelets with the perianth absent or reduced or represented by bristles or scales and with usu. ribbon-shaped leaves

gram·ine \ˈgraˌmēn, -mən\ *n* -s [ISV *gram-* (fr. L *gramen* grass) + *-ine*] **:** a crystalline base $(C_8H_6N)CH_2N(CH_3)_2$ occurring esp. in the germ of Swedish barley and made from indole by reaction with formaldehyde and dimethylamine; 3-(dimethylamino-methyl)-indole

gra·min·e·ae \grəˈminēˌē\ *n pl, cap* [NL, L, fr. fem. pl. of *gramineus*] **:** a large family of monocotyledonous plants (order Graminales) with culms hollow, leaves generally 2-ranked, and fruit a caryopsis — see GRASS; compare BAMBOO, CEREAL

gra·min·e·al \-nēəl\ *adj* [L *gramineus* + E *-al*] **:** GRAMINEOUS

gra·min·e·ous \-nēəs\ *adj* [L *gramineus*, fr. *gramin-, gramen* grass + *-eus* -eous — more at GRASS] **1 :** resembling or relating to a grass **2 :** belonging to the family Gramineae — **gra·min·e·ous·ness** *n* -ES

gram·i·nic·o·lous \ˌgraməˈnikələs\ *adj* [*gramin-* + *-colous*] **:** living upon grass ⟨a ~ parasite⟩ ⟨a ~ fungus⟩

gram·i·niv·o·rous \-ˈniv(ə)rəs\ *adj* [*gramin-* + *-vorous*] **:** feeding on grass

¹gram·i·noid \ˈgraməˌnȯid\ *adj* [*gramin-* + *-oid*] **:** of or relating to grasses

²graminoid \"\ *n* -s **:** a graminoid plant

gram·i·nous \-nəs\ *adj* [L *graminosus*, fr. *gramin-, gramen* + *-osus* -ous] *archaic* **:** GRAMINEOUS

gramma *var of* GRAMA

gram·ma·log *or* **gram·ma·logue** \ˈgraməˌlȯg *also* -läg\ *n* -s [Gk *gramma* letter + E *-log, -logue* — more at GRAM] **1 :** a word represented in shorthand by a single stroke **2 :** the stroke that represents a grammalog **:** LOGOGRAM 1

gram·mar \ˈgramə(r)\ *n* -s [ME *gramere, gramer, grammer*, fr. MF *gramaire*, modif. of L *grammatica*, fr. Gk *grammatikē*, fr. fem. of *grammatikos* skilled in grammar, fr. *grammat-, gramma* letter, piece of writing + *-ikos* -ic — more at GRAM] **1 a :** a branch of linguistic study that deals with the classes of words, their inflections or other means of indicating relation to each other, and their functions and relations in the sentence as employed according to established usage and that is sometimes extended to include related matter such as phonology, prosody, language history, orthography, orthoepy, etymology, or semantics — see ACCIDENCE, MORPHOLOGY, SYNTAX **b :** LINGUISTICS **c :** a study of what is to be preferred and what avoided in the inflections and syntax of a language **2 :** that which is studied in grammar **:** those phenomena of language with which grammar deals **:** the characteristic system or the preferred system of inflections and syntax of a language **3 a :** a book in which grammar is methodically treated **b :** an elementary textbook for foreign language study **c :** a manner of speaking or writing that conforms to grammatical rules **:** speech or writing that is preferred to what should be avoided ⟨appalled at the bad ~ of college students⟩ **4 a :** the basic elements or principles of a science, art, discipline, practice ⟨the ~ of politics in Latin America is unfamiliar to the Anglo-Saxon mind —R.A.Humphreys⟩ ⟨the ~ of heraldry⟩ **b :** a treatise or book dealing with such elements or principles **c :** a set of such elements or principles ⟨music has universal appeal because it has a universal ~⟩ ⟨created a ~ of cinematography⟩

gram·mar·i·an \grəˈmerēən, -ma(a)r-, -mär-\ *n* -s [ME *gramarien, gramarian*, fr. MF *gramarien*, fr. *gramaire* grammar +

-*ien* -ian] **1 a :** a specialist in grammar or linguistics **:** PHILOLOGIST **b :** one who writes about or teaches grammar **2 :** one who writes on the basic elements or principles of any science, art, discipline, or practice

gram·mar·less \'gramə(r)ləs\ *adj* **1 :** lacking any marked analyzable grammatical forms and relationships ⟨a relatively ~ language⟩ **2 :** showing or marked by an ignorance of the approved forms or syntax of a language ⟨a man with a notably ~ speech and crudeness of manner⟩

grammar school *n* **1 a :** a secondary school providing instruction chiefly in Latin and often Greek usu. in preparation for college — called also *Latin grammar school* **b :** a chiefly British school providing a college preparatory course **2 a :** a school teaching the grades between the primary grades and high school **b :** the grades between the primary grades and high school **3 :** ELEMENTARY SCHOOL

gram·mat·i·cal \grə'mad·ə̇kəl, -at|, ¦ēk-\ *also* **gram·mat·ic** \ik, ¦ēk\ *adj* [*grammatical* fr. LL *grammaticalis*, fr. L *grammaticus* grammatical (fr. Gk *grammatikos* skilled in grammar) + *-alis* -al; *grammatic* fr. L *grammaticus* — more at GRAMMAR] **1 a :** of or relating to grammar ⟨a ~ rule⟩ **b :** according to or following the words taken strictly in accordance with the rules of grammar **:** LITERAL ⟨~ sense⟩ ⟨a ~ interpretation⟩ **2 a :** according to the rules of grammar **:** correct as regards grammar ⟨strictly ~ use of the words⟩ **b :** of, relating to, or being in strict accordance with the grammar or methodic principles of an art or science, discipline, or practice ⟨the foremost ~ difference in the heraldry of the continent —D.L.Galbreath⟩ — **gram·mat·i·cal·ly** \¦ə̇k(ə)lē, ¦ēk-, -li\ *adv* — **gram·mat·i·cal·ness** \¦ə̇kəlnəs, ¦ēk-\ *n* -ES

grammatical change *n* [trans. of G *grammatischer wechsel*] **1 :** the system of consonant contrasts in the Germanic strong verb according to Verner's law (OE *cēosan*, choose; *coren*, chosen) **2 :** VERNER'S LAW

grammatical gender *n* **:** GENDER 2 — distinguished from *natural gender*

grammatical meaning *n* **1 :** the meaning expressed by a grammatical ending, word order, or intonation **:** a grammatical category (as plural, interrogative, subject, superlative) **2 :** the part of meaning which varies from one form of a paradigm to another (as from *plays* to *played* to *playing*) — compare LEXICAL MEANING

grammatical subject *n* **:** a term (as a pronoun) in a sentence that occupies the position of the subject in normal English word order and anticipates a subsequent word or phrase that specifies the actual substantive content (as *it* in the sentence "it is sometimes hard to do right") — called also *formal subject;* distinguished from *logical subject*

gram·mat·i·cism \grə'mad·ə,sizəm, -atə-\ *n* -S **:** a point or principle of grammar

gram·mat·i·cize \-,sīz\ *vb* -ED/-ING/-S *vt* **:** to make grammatical **:** reduce to rules of grammar ~ *vi* **:** to discuss points of grammar

gram·ma·tist \'gramədə̇st\ *n* -S [L *grammatista* schoolmaster, fr. Gk *grammatistēs*, fr. *grammatizein* to teach reading and writing, fr. *grammat-*, *gramma* letter, piece of writing + *-izein* -ize — more at GRAM] **:** a usu. pedantic grammarian — **gram·ma·tis·ti·cal** \,gramə¦tistə̇kəl\ *adj*

gram·ma·tol·a·try \,gramə'tälə·trē\ *n* -ES [Gk *grammato-* (fr. *grammat-*, *gramma*) + E *-latry*] **:** the worship of letters or words **:** devotion to the letter (as of Scripture)

gram·ma·to·phyl·lum \,gramədə'filəm\ *n, cap* [NL, fr. Gk *grammato-* + NL *-phyllum*] **:** a small genus of epiphytic Malayan orchids with long narrow leaves and drooping flower clusters often six feet long

gramme *var of* GRAM

gram–molecular \¦=¦==¦==\ *or* **gram–molar** \'=¦==\ *adj* **:** of, relating to, or containing a gram molecule

gram molecule *or* **gram–molecular weight** *n* **:** the mass of one mole of a compound equal in grams to the molecular weight — compare AVOGADRO NUMBER

gram·my \'gramē, -mi\ *n* -ES [by shortening & alter.] **:** GRANDMOTHER

gram–negative \'=¦==\ *adj, sometimes cap G* [after Hans C. J. *Gram* †1938 Dan. physician] **:** not holding the purple dye when stained by Gram's method — used chiefly of bacteria

gram·o·phile \'gramə,fīl\ *n* -S [*gramophone* + *-phile*] **:** a lover and collector of phonograph records

gram·o·phone \-,fōn\ *n* [fr. *Gramophone*, a trademark] **:** PHONOGRAPH

gramp \'gramp, -aa(ə)mp, -aimp\ *or* **gramps** \-ps\ *n, pl* **gramps** [by shortening and alter. fr. *grandpa*] **:** GRANDFATHER

gram–positive \'=¦==\ *adj, sometimes cap G* [after Hans C. J. *Gram*] **:** holding the purple dye when stained by Gram's method — used chiefly of bacteria

gram·pus \'grampəs, -aam-, -aim-\ *n* -ES [alter. of earlier *graundepose*, *grampoys*, alter. of ME *grapay*, *graspey*, fr. MF *craspois*, *graspois*, *graspeis*, fr. *cras*, *gras* fat (fr. L *crassus*) + *pois*, *peis* fish, fr. L *piscis* — more at HURDLE, FISH] **1 a :** a cetacean (*Grampus griseus*) that is widely distributed in the seas of the northern hemisphere and that is related to the blackfish but has teeth in the lower jaw only **b :** any of various other cetaceans of similar size (as the blackfish or the killer whale) **2 :** the giant whip scorpion (*Mastigoproctus giganteus*) of the southern U.S. that is popularly but unjustifiably reputed to be exceedingly venomous

grams *pl of* GRAM

-grams *pl of* -GRAM

gram's method \'gramz-, -aa(ə)mz-\ *or* **gram method** *n, cap G* [after Hans C. J. *Gram*] **:** a method for the differential staining of bacteria by which they are treated with Gram's solution after being stained with gentian violet and are then treated with alcohol and washed in water with the result that certain species retain the dye while others are decolorized — see GRAM-NEGATIVE, GRAM-POSITIVE

gram's solution *n, usu cap G* [after H. C. J. *Gram*] **:** a solution of one part iodine, two parts potassium iodide, and 300 parts water used in staining bacteria by gram's method

gram's stain *or* **gram stain** *n, usu cap G* [after H. C. J. *Gram*] **:** GRAM'S METHOD; *also* **:** an instance of staining by this method (did a *gram's stain* on each specimen)

gram–variable \'=¦===\ *adj, sometimes cap G* [*Gram's* (*method*)] **:** staining irregularly or inconsistently by Gram's method

gra·my \'grāmē\ *vt* -ED/-ING/-ES [*grame* + *-y* (as in *worry*)] *now dial* **:** to make angry **:** ANNOY

gran \'gran, -aa(ə)n\ *n* -S [by shortening] **:** GRANDMOTHER

¹gra·na \'gränə\ *or* **grana cheese** *n* -S [It (*formaggio di*) *grana* granular cheese, fr. *grana* grain, fr. L, pl. of *granum* — more at CORN] **:** PARMESAN

²grana *pl of* GRANUM

gra·na·da \grə'nädə, -nā-\ *adj, usu cap* [fr. *Granada*, Spain] **:** of or from the city of Granada, Spain **:** of the kind or style prevalent in Granada

gran·a·dilla \,granə'dilə, -dē(y)ə\ *or* **gren·a·dilla** \,gren-\ *n* -S [Sp *granadilla*, dim. of *granada* pomegranate, fr. LL *granata* — more at GRENADE] **1 a :** GRANADILLA TREE **b :** GRANADILLA WOOD **2 a :** the oblong fruit of various passionflowers (esp. *Passiflora quadrangularis* of tropical America) widely used as a dessert and for flavoring **b :** a passionflower that produces granadillas

granadilla tree *n* **:** a West Indian tree (*Brya ebenus*) of the family Leguminosae that furnishes a fine grade of green ebony

granadilla wood *n* **1 :** the wood of the granadilla tree — called also *cocuswood* **2 :** a dark red hardwood derived from a cocobolo (*Dalbergia retusa*) of northern So. America and used in making musical instruments (as clarinets) **3** *in Puerto Rico* **:** the yellow satiny wood of a tropical American tree (*Buchenavia capitata*) of the family Combretaceae **4 :** the chocolate-brown hardwood of a tropical American tree (*Caesalpinia granadillo*)

gran·a·dillo \-di(,)lō, -dē(,)(y)ō\ *n* -S [Sp, fr. *granadilla*] **1 :** GRANADILLA TREE **2 :** any tropical American passionflower yielding the fruit called granadilla **3 :** GRANADILLA WOOD 2

gra·na·ry \'grān(ə)rē, 'gran-, -ri\ *n* -ES [L *granarium*, fr. *granum* grain + *-arium* -ary — more at CORN] **1 :** a storehouse or repository for grain esp. after it is threshed or husked; *also* **:** a region producing grain in abundance **2 :** the chief source or storehouse esp. of grain ⟨Egypt as the ~ of the ancient world —Agnes Repplier⟩ ⟨became known as the ~ of the caravans that were moving up and down the country —L.S.B. Leakey⟩ ⟨the people remain the great ~ of vital spontaneity —Jacques Maritain⟩

granary weevil *n* **:** a small brown weevil (*Sitophilus granarius*) which feeds on and lays its eggs in the kernels of stored grain (as wheat, barley, maize) in which the larva develops and within the hull of which it pupates

gran·at \'granət\ *n* -S [modif. of F *grenat* garnet — more at GARNET] **:** PONCEAU

gra·na·tum \grə'nād·əm, -näd·-\ *n* -S [NL, fr. L, pomegranate — more at GRENADE] **:** the bark or fruit rind of pomegranate which is high in tannin content

¹grand \'grand, -aa(ə)nd\ *adj* -ER/-EST [MF, fr. L *grandis* large, full-grown, old, great, grand; perh. akin to Gk *brenthos* pride, *brenthyesthai* to act proudly, swell up with pride, OSlav *grǫdi* breast; basic meaning: swelling] **1 a** *obs* **:** eminent or memorable in position or scale of operation **:** FAMOUS **b :** having more importance than others **:** PREEMINENT, FOREMOST, CHIEF ⟨remarking that death was the ~ mystery of all time⟩ **c :** having higher rank or more official dignity than others bearing the same general designation — used with titles indicating office, rank, or standing ⟨a ~ master⟩ ⟨a ~ champion⟩ ⟨a ~ duke⟩; *also* **:** having the highest or supreme rank of all the nation — used in the titles of sovereigns **2 a :** INCLUSIVE, COMPREHENSIVE ⟨the ~ total of all money paid out over the period⟩ ⟨three independent services, coordinated only to the extent necessary to have uniformity in ~ policy —T.K. Finletter⟩ **b :** DEFINITIVE, INCONTROVERTIBLE ⟨the Bible is the ~ proof in English that in the greatest writing literary beauty is not a main object but a by-product —Douglas Bush⟩ **3 :** MAIN, PRINCIPAL ⟨the ~ staircase leading up from the large front hallway⟩ ⟨the ~ ballroom⟩ ⟨to make expressive of the form within, of its volume and movement, this was the painter's ~ preoccupation —Laurence Binyon⟩ **4 a :** of large size, extent, value, or consequence **:** GREAT ⟨a ~ mistake⟩ ⟨a ~ imposture⟩ **b :** large in scope, grasp, or interest ⟨some ~ but impractical ideas about how to make money⟩ ⟨a ~ bringing together of a thousand details to make a clear and interesting lecture⟩ ⟨a ~ adventure among pirates and desperadoes⟩ **c :** being of a size or grade that confers distinction ⟨the ~ structure of the hippodrome⟩ ⟨a ~ chorus⟩ **5 a :** marked by great magnificence, display, ceremoniousness, or formality **:** SUMPTUOUS, GORGEOUS ⟨a ~ celebration in honor of the king's birthday⟩ ⟨a ~ exhibition of fireworks⟩; *also* **:** marked by a regal form and dignity ⟨the ~ manner of royalty descending from a coach —*Amer. Guide Series: Calif.*⟩ **b :** fine or imposing in appearance or impression **:** impressive because of physical, moral, or intellectual greatness **:** ILLUSTRIOUS, STATELY, NOBLE ⟨the ~ figure of the duchess at the head of the table⟩ ⟨the ~ totality of the author's literary output⟩ **:** MAJESTIC, SPLENDID, MAGNIFICENT ⟨a ~ regal ceremony⟩ ⟨made a ~ appearance in silk dress and jeweled tiara⟩ ⟨the worn, homely face, ~ in its utter simplicity —L.M.Angus-Butterworth⟩ **:** LOFTY, SUBLIME ⟨writing in the ~ style⟩ ⟨an epic poem around a ~ conception of heaven and hell⟩ **c :** pretending to or claiming social superiority **:** SUPERCILIOUS ⟨you were much too ~ to speak to us —Archibald Marshall⟩ **d :** designed to impress — used of actions ⟨a man given to ~ gestures and pretentious statements⟩ **6 :** very good **:** FINE, WONDERFUL ⟨got up in the morning feeling ~⟩ ⟨had a ~ time at the picnic⟩ **:** ADMIRABLE ⟨a ~ old man⟩ **7 :** of or relating to a grand lodge

syn MAGNIFICENT, IMPOSING, STATELY, MAJESTIC, AUGUST, NOBLE, GRANDIOSE: GRAND may apply to any sort of impressive greatness, ampleness, handsomeness, rank, dignity, or preeminence ⟨*grand* amid the hall floor was the Goth king in his gear —William Morris⟩ ⟨the *grandest* passages in the Bible —A.L.Guérard⟩ ⟨at the piano her mood exalted patriotism, uplifted in spirit by that *grand* song —Winston Churchill⟩ ⟨the great cathedral seemed so *grand* when one was all alone there with the music rolling away down the nave —J.R.Green⟩ MAGNIFICENT may apply to a most extreme and impressive scope, sumptuousness, splendor, stateliness, munificence, or handsomeness without loss of dignity or taste ⟨how *magnificent* was the sight of the royal escort, the brilliant uniforms of the troops, the marching bands —Edith Sitwell⟩ ⟨the *magnificent* marble town house, celebrated as a world's wonder, even in that age and country, in which so much splendor was lavished on municipal palaces —J.L.Motley⟩ ⟨perhaps the most *magnificent* manifestation of poetic mysticism is the last canto —G.G.Coulton⟩ IMPOSING may describe what is impressive through commanding size, dignity, or magnificence ⟨she came in, like a ship in full sail, an *imposing* creature, tall and stout, with an ample bust and an obesity girthed in —W.S.Maugham⟩ ⟨an *imposing* neoclassic structure in the form of a Greek cross with a Corinthian entrance portico —*Amer. Guide Series: Md.*⟩ ⟨an *imposing* appearance, with vast blocks or boulders of granite, sparkling with mica —*Amer. Guide Series: Texas*⟩ STATELY may suggest blended poised dignity and handsomeness, impressiveness, size and strength, or loftiness ⟨the picture of a regal and *stately* lady in court dress, with a high diamond tiara upon her noble head —A. Conan Doyle⟩ ⟨the long and *stately* flight of steps descending from the Capitoline Hill to the level of lower Rome —Nathaniel Hawthorne⟩ MAJESTIC, which blends the connotations of IMPOSING and STATELY, may also connote a lofty solemn thought-provoking or awe-inspiring grandeur ⟨calm and *majestic*, the very picture of courtly self-possession in his coat of gold brocade and black velvet breeches, with a jeweled order tangled in the rich laces upon his breast —Elinor Wylie⟩ ⟨the *majestic* movement of cosmic time —Aldous Huxley⟩ ⟨the *majestic* tradition of classic study gives to the old humanities a dignity that newer branches of learning can never attain —C.H.Grandgent⟩ AUGUST applies to an exalted impressiveness inspiring awe, wonder, reverence, or abashment ⟨a sight of the old heathen emperor is enough to create an evanescent sentiment of loyalty even in a democratic bosom, so *august* does he look, so fit to rule, so worthy of man's profoundest homage and obedience —Nathaniel Hawthorne⟩ ⟨for in the eternal city . . . a Power *august*, benignant and supreme shall then absolve thee of all farther duties —E.A. Poe⟩ NOBLE may imply illustrious, dignified excellence, stateliness, or loftiness ⟨the disinterested search for truth is certainly one of the highest and *noblest* careers that a man can choose —W.R.Inge⟩ ⟨the old artists, who attained their grand results by penetrating themselves with some *noble* and significant action —Matthew Arnold⟩ ⟨a *noble* building of rose-colored sandstone inlaid with white marble —Elinor Wylie⟩ GRANDIOSE may describe unusual largeness or scope or even majesty, but it commonly suggests an inflated pompous or preposterous pretension ⟨the *grandiose* complexities of the universe —J.W.Krutch⟩ ⟨a *grandiose* conception worthy of a feudal baron of commerce —V.L.Parrington⟩ All of these words lend themselves readily to hyperbole in application to trivial, mundane, or insignificant things being highly praised

²grand \"\ *n* -S **1** *usu cap* **a :** an officer of a fraternal society or other organization whose title contains the word *grand* ⟨a past ~⟩ **b :** the presiding officer of a club **2 :** GRAND PIANO **3** *slang* **:** a thousand dollars ⟨made about three ~ on a swindle⟩ **4 a :** one of the available bids or rounds in a card game: as (1) **:** a round in skat in which the four jacks are the only trumps (2) **:** a round in frog in which hearts are trumps — compare ¹CHICO **b :** GRAND SLAM

grand allemande *n* **:** a swing in square dancing once and a half around first grasping right forearms and then the left as each person is met in a grand right and left

gran·dam \'gran,dam, -dəm\ *n* -S [ME *graundam*, fr. OF *grant dame*, fr. *grant* grand + *dame* lady, mother] **1** *or* **gran·dame** \-,dām, -dəm\ **a :** GRANDMOTHER **b :** old woman **2** *also* **grand·dam** \-n,dam, -ndəm\ **:** a dam's or sire's dam — used of an animal

grandaunt \'=¦=\ *n* **:** the aunt of one's father or mother — called also *great-aunt*

grand·baby \'gran(d),==, -aan-\ *n* **:** an infant granddaughter or grandson ⟨have to put up with sons-in-law and two *grandbabies* —May L. Becker⟩

grand battement *n* [F, lit., great battement] **:** a battement in ballet executed with the free leg lifted high from the floor

grand canyon \'=¦=¦==\ *adj, usu cap G&C* [fr. the *Grand Canyon*, Ariz.] **:** of, relating to, or constituting a division of the Proterozoic — see GEOLOGIC TIME table

grand ca·pe \-'kā(,)pē, -'kā(,)pā\ *n* [AF *graunt cape* (part trans. of ML *cape magnum*), fr. *graunt*, *grand* large + *cape* any of several writs including the grand cape and the petit cape, fr. ML, fr. L *cape* (the first word in these writs), 2d pers. sing. imper. of *capere* to take — more at HEAVE] *Eng law* **:** a writ issued in the now obsolete real actions for the recovery of land on the failure of the defendant tenant in possession to make an appearance

grand chain *n* **:** GRAND RIGHT AND LEFT

grand·child \'gran(d),=, -aan-\ *n* **1 :** a son's or daughter's child **:** a child in the second degree of descent **2 :** something in a relationship analogous to or suggesting that of a grandchild

grand choeur \grä^n^kœr\ *adv (or adj)* [F *grand chœur*, lit., great chorus] **:** full organ — used as a direction in organ music

grand chop *n* **:** a customs clearance or receipt for dues and duties in the India and China trade

grand climacteric *n* **:** the sixty-third or the eighty-first year of a person's life

grand commander *n* **1 :** a member of one of the divisions of the highest grade in an order of knighthood **2 :** the chief fiscal officer in an order of knighthood (as the Knights Hospitalers) — **grand commandery** *n*

grand conjunction *n* **:** the occasional astrological configuration of the greater planets in a particular sign

grand cordon *n* **:** a cordon consisting of a broad ribbon usu. worn in the manner of a baldric and constituting a mark of high rank in an honorary order

grand council *n* **:** an executive council in a high or supreme position esp. as assistant to a governor or chief executive

grand council fire *n* **:** a ceremonial meeting of three or more groups of camp fire girls usu. including all the groups in a community

grand coup *n* **:** a coup in bridge or whist in which a player trumps a trick that his partner's card would otherwise have won

grand cross *n* **1 :** a decoration consisting of a cross that indicates the highest rank in many orders of knighthood **2 :** a person wearing a grand cross **:** KNIGHT GRAND CROSS

grand·dad *or* **gran·dad** \'gran,=, -raan-\ *n* [¹*grand* + *dad*] **:** GRANDFATHER

grand·dad·dy *also* **gran·dad·dy** \'gran,==, -raan-\ *n* [¹*grand* + *daddy*] **1 a :** GRANDFATHER **b :** one that is very old and venerable ⟨a cottonwood tree that was a real ~ —Richard Bissell⟩ **2 :** one that is the first, earliest, most ancient, or most venerable **:** one that has been in existence the longest ⟨the ~ of all the manufacturers of ready-built dwellings —*New Yorker*⟩ ⟨the ~ of midget-racing-car drivers⟩ ⟨the ~ of all reptiles —R.E.R.Hall⟩; *also* **:** something impressive (as in size, extent, or force) ⟨hadn't ranch winters been kind enough prior to this ~ of winters —A.B.Guthrie⟩

granddaddy graybeard *n* **:** FRINGE TREE

granddaddy longlegs *n pl but sing or pl in constr* **:** DADDY LONGLEGS

granddam *var of* GRANDAM

grand·daugh·ter \'gran,==, -raan-\ *n* **:** the daughter of one's son or daughter — **grand·daugh·ter·ly** *adj*

granddaughter–in–law \'=,===,=\ *n, pl* **granddaughters–in–law :** the wife of one's grandson

grand day *n* **:** any of the four days Candlemas, Ascension, St. John the Baptist's, and All Saints' observed as holidays in the Inns of Court and Chancery and under English law as dies non juridici

grand dragon *n* **:** an officer of superior rank in the Ku-Klux Klan hierarchy

grand drape *n* **:** a decorative narrow curtain hung along the top of a proscenium arch on the side toward the audience

grand–ducal \'gran¦==, -raan-\ *adj* **:** of, relating to, or befitting a grand duke or grand duchess

grand duchess *n* **1 :** the wife or widow of a grand duke **2 :** a woman who rules a grand duchy in her own right

grand duchy *n, often cap G&D* **:** the territory or dominion of a grand duke or grand duchess

grand duke *n* **:** the sovereign duke of a European state or country ranking immediately below a king and entitled to be called royal highness

grande cham·pagne \¦gran(d),sham¦pān, -raan(d),shaam-, grä^n^dshä^n^pän^y^\ *n* [fr. *Grande Champagne*, vineyard area of Cognac, France] **:** FINE CHAMPAGNE

grande dame \'grän'däm, grä^n^dȧm\ *n, pl* **grandes dames** *or* **grande dames** \-m(z)\ [F, lit., great lady] **:** a lady usu. elderly and of great social or professional prestige, of high rank, or of extremely dignified or imposing manner

gran·dee \(')gran¦dē, -raan-\ *n* -S [Sp *grande*, fr. *grande*, adj., large, great, grand, fr. L *grandis* — more at GRAND] **:** a man of high rank or eminence; *esp* **:** a Spanish or Portuguese nobleman of the first rank

grande écaille \,grändā'kī\ *also* **grand–ecoy** \,grändā'kȯi\ *or* **grande és·caille** \-ā'kī\ *n, pl* **grande écailles** \-ī(z)\ *also* **grand–ecoys** \-ȯi(z)\ *or* **grande éscailles** \-ī(z)\ [LaF *grande écaille*, lit., large or great scale] **:** TARPON

gran·dee·ship \=¦=,ship\ *n* **:** the position or title of a grandee

grande passion *var of* GRAND PASSION

grander *comparative of* GRAND

grandest *superlative of* GRAND

gran·deur \'granjə(r), -raan- *also* -n,dyù(ə)r *or* -n,jù- *or* -ùə *sometimes* -ndyə(r) *or* -ndə(r) *or* -n,dùə *or* -n,dər(·) *or* -n,dǝ(r\ *n* -S [ME, fr. MF, fr. *grand* great + *-eur* —or — more at GRAND] **1** *archaic* **:** greatness of power or position ⟨exalted to such a prodigious ~, Alexander was at the time of his death little more than thirty-two years old —George Grote⟩ **2 a :** personal greatness characterized chiefly by dignity of character, largeness of spirit, or significant scope of accomplishment ⟨in those rural epics . . . the descendants lose the ~ of those who first settled on the land —Sidney Alexander⟩ ⟨the moral ~ of the pioneer —C.I.Glicksberg⟩ **b :** dignity and sublimity (as of style) ⟨that lofty ~ of the diction of the English Bible —J.L.Lowes⟩ ⟨the sweetness or the ~ expected of religious music —*Time*⟩ ⟨the inability of men to sustain the ~ of their own ideal conceptions —*Times Lit. Supp.*⟩ **3 a :** the quality of being majestic, magnificent, splendid, stately, or imposing in an awe-inspiring way esp. to the view ⟨a scenic ~ in the wide view of mountains and valleys⟩ ⟨the ~ of the wild wintry seas —L.D.Stamp⟩ ⟨the former ~ of the queer castle-like homes of the Victorian era —*Amer. Guide Series: Tenn.*⟩ **b :** an instance of such a quality ⟨the most delightful of southern towns was almost certain to mix a little squalor with its ~s —Donald Davidson⟩

grandevity *n* -ES [L *grandaevitas*, fr. *grandaevus* aged (fr. *grandis* great + *aevum* time, eternity, age) + *-itas* -ity — more at GRAND, AGE] *obs* **:** great age

gran·dez·za \gran'detsə\ *or* **gran·de·za** \gran'dāsə\ *n* -S [It *grandezza* & Sp *grandeza*, fr. It & Sp *grande* large, great, grand (fr. L *grandis*) + It *-ezza* or Sp *-eza* (fr. L *-issa* -ess) — more at GRAND] *archaic* **:** grandeur or greatness esp. of manner or appearance

grand·fa·ther \'gran(d),==, -raan-\ *n* [ME *graund fader* (trans. of MF *grant pere*), fr. MF *grant* grand + ME *fader* father — more at GRAND, FATHER] **1 :** a father's or mother's father **:** an ancestor in the next degree above the father or mother in lineal ascent; *also* **:** FOREFATHER **2 :** one suggesting a grandfather in being a precursor in a line of similar things showing successive development, in being old and venerable, or in being the first or earliest in a line ⟨the church supper is the ~ of the country club —*Saturday Rev.*⟩ ⟨an old ~ of a tree⟩; *also* **:** something sizable or impressive in a way suggesting a long period of growth or development ⟨the ~ of all buttons —Ben Riker⟩

grandfather chair *or* **grandfather's chair** *n* **:** EASY CHAIR; *esp* **:** WING CHAIR

grandfather clause *n* **1 :** a clause exempting a class of persons (as from a regulatory law) because of circumstances applying before the clause takes effect; *specif* **:** a provision inserted in the constitutions of some southern states after the Civil War requiring high standards of literacy and substantial property qualifications of voters except for descendants of men voting before 1867 **2 :** one of numerous limitations on certain government regulations; *specif* **:** a provision by which an interstate carrier in bona fide operation prior to the effective date of regulation need not prove public convenience and necessity before it can be certified

grandfather clock *or* **grandfather's clock** *n* [fr. the song *My Grandfather's Clock* (1878) by Henry C. Work †1884 Am. songwriter] **:** a large pendulum clock having a long upright case usu. taller than 6½ feet

grandfather clock

grandfather graybeard *n* **1 :** FRINGE TREE **2 :** DADDY LONGLEGS

grandfather-in-law \ˈ≈,≈≈≈,≈\ *n, pl* **grandfathers-in-law :** the grandfather of one's spouse

grand·fa·ther·ly \ˈ≈,≈≈≈\ *adj* **:** of, relating to, or befitting a grandfather ⟨an eminently human person of ~ years —Lewis Nichols⟩ **:** BENIGNANT ⟨looked on the child with ~ indulgence⟩ **:** old and venerable ⟨a ~ oak tree⟩

grandfather rights *n pl* **:** rights deriving from a grandfather clause

grandfather's-beard \ˈ≈,≈≈ˈ≈\ *n, pl* **grandfather's-beards :** OLD-MAN'S-BEARD 1,4

grand·fer \ˈgranfə(r)\ *n* -s [by alter.] *dial Eng* **:** GRANDFATHER

grand finale *n* **:** a climactic finale (as of an opera or sports meet) marked by an imposing usu. colorful display or performance involving a large number of participants

grand fir *n* **:** LOWLAND FIR

grand·folks \ˈgran(d),≈, -raan-\ *n pl* **:** GRANDPARENTS

grand guard *n* **1 :** a piece of plate armor of the 15th and 16th centuries used in tournaments as extra protection for left shoulder and breast **2 :** a former outpost of a military encampment

¹grand gui·gnol \ˌgrä^nɡēnˈyȯl, -yōl\ *n, usu cap both Gs* [fr. *Le Grand Guignol,* a small theater in Montmartre, Paris, specializing in short plays full of sensationalism and horror] **:** a dramatic entertainment featuring the gruesome or horrible ⟨saw the play as a glorified *Grand Guignol* where story was the vital thing —*Theatre Arts*⟩

²grand guignol \"\ *adj, usu cap both Gs* **:** of, relating to, or having the characteristics of Grand Guignol ⟨a *Grand Guignol* program⟩ ⟨a *Grand Guignol* thriller⟩

grand hotel *n, often cap G&H* **:** a large well-equipped or imposing hotel usu. having an international clientele ⟨at Calvi . . . they would come to rest in their *grand hotel* of balconies and bathrooms —William Sansom⟩ ⟨New Delhi has become a sort of *Grand Hotel* for touring statesmen —Christopher Rand⟩

gran·di·flo·ra *or* **grandiflora rose** \ˌgrandəˈflōrə(-)\ *n* -s [NL, fr. L *grandis* great + NL *-flora* (fr. L *flor-, flos* flower) — more at GRAND, FLOWER] **:** a bush rose derived from crosses of floribunda and hybrid tea roses and characterized by production of blooms both singly and in clusters on the same plant

gran·dil·o·quence \granˈdiləkwən(t)s\ *n* -s [prob. fr. MF, fr. L *grandiloquus* (fr. *grandis* great, grand + *-loquus,* fr. *loqui* to speak) + MF *-ence* (as in *eloquence*) — more at GRAND] **:** the quality of being grandiloquent **:** the use of lofty words or phrases **:** BOMBAST

gran·dil·o·quent \(ˈ)≈ˈ≈≈kwənt\ *adj* [prob. back-formation fr. *grandiloquence*] **:** marked by a lofty, extravagantly colorful, pompous, or bombastic style, manner, or quality esp. in language ⟨a ~ and boastful speech about his great accomplishments⟩ ⟨danced to a rarely heard, ~ . . . score —Janet Flanner⟩ ⟨the latter's *Self Portrait* . . . was done in a more ~ manner —Wolfgang Stechow⟩ ⟨with a ~ gesture —Willard Robertson⟩ ⟨the ~ hero of a drama —Mary Webb⟩ ⟨~ summer estates —Bernard DeVoto⟩ — **gran·dil·o·quent·ly** *adv*

gran·dil·o·quous \-kwəs\ *adj* [L *grandiloquus*] *archaic* **:** GRANDILOQUENT

grand inquest *n* **:** GRAND JURY

grand inquisitor *n, often cap G&I* **:** the chief of a court of inquisition

gran·di·ose \ˈgrandē,ōs, ˌ≈≈ˈ≈ *sometimes* -ōz\ *adj* [F, fr. It *grandioso,* fr. *grande* great (fr. L *grandis*) + *-oso* -ose — more at GRAND] **1 :** impressive because of uncommon largeness, scope, effect, grandeur, or majesty ⟨forget what more ~, noble, or beautiful character properly belongs to religious constructions —Matthew Arnold⟩ ⟨the ~ general scheme, unifying landscape, architecture, mural painting, and sculpture, was a revelation to the public —*Amer. Guide Series: Mich.*⟩ **2 :** characterized by affectation of grandeur, by pretense and pomp or overweeningness, or by absurd exaggeration ⟨have always been partial to ~ ideas about themselves —Irving Howe⟩ **syn** see GRAND

gran·di·ose·ly *adv* **:** in a grandiose manner ⟨the pompous absurdity so marked in many of our ~ ugly public monuments —D.L.Cohn⟩

gran·di·ose·ness *n* -ES **:** GRANDIOSITY

gran·di·os·i·ty \ˌ≈≈ˈäsəd-ē, -ətē, -i\ *n* -ES [F *grandiosité,* fr. It *grandiosità,* fr. *grandioso* + *-ità* -ity (fr. L *-itat-, -itas*)] **:** the quality or state of being grandiose ⟨forgot his connubial incompetence in the *grandiosities* of his research projects —J.L.Davis⟩ ⟨feeling takes the place of comprehending, ~ the place of grandeur, pathos the place of understanding —R.H.Pearce⟩

gran·di·o·so \ˌgrändēˈō(,)sō, -ran-, -)zō\ *adv (or adj)* [It — more at GRANDIOSE] **:** in a broad and noble style — used as a direction in music

gran·dis·o·nant \(ˈ)granˈdisᵊnənt\ *or* **gran·dis·o·nous** \-ᵊnəs\ *adj* [*grandisonant* fr. LL *grandisonus* (fr. L *grandis* great + *-sonus,* fr. *sonare* to sound) + E *-ant; grandisonous* fr. LL *grandisonus* — more at GRAND, SOUND] *archaic* **:** giving the impression of grandeur

gran·di·so·ni·an \ˌgrandəˈsōnēən\ *adj, usu cap* [Sir Charles *Grandison,* a model gentleman portrayed in the novel of the same name (1753) by Samuel Richardson †1761 Eng. novelist + E *-ian*] **:** of, relating to, or befitting a model gentleman of the 18th century

gran·di·ty \ˈgrandəd-ē\ *n* -ES [L *granditas,* fr. *grandis* great, grand + *-itas* -ity — more at GRAND] *archaic* **:** grandness or an attribute or sign of it

grand je·té \ˌgrä^nzhəˈtā\ *n* [F] **:** a jeté in ballet with high kick or battement

grand jeu \grä^n ˈzhē, -ˈzhə, -ˈzhər, *F* grä^nzhœ\ *adv (or adj)* [F, lit., grand play] **:** FULL ORGAN

grand juror \ˈ≈ˈ≈≈\ *or* **grand juryman** \ˈ≈ˈ≈≈≈\ *n* [*grand juror* fr. *grand jury,* after E *jury: juror; grand juryman* fr. *grand jury,* after E *jury: juryman*] **:** a member of a grand jury

grand jury \ˈ≈ˈ≈≈\ *n* [ME *graunde jurie,* lit., large jury, fr. AF *graund jurre*] **1 :** a body of from 12 to 23 good and lawful persons of a county who are returned in England by the sheriff to every session of the peace and of the assizes and in federal courts in the U.S. and in some state courts are impaneled usu. at intervals of a month or more to serve continuously until the next impanelment and whose duty it is to examine in private sessions accusations against persons charged with crime, to find bills of indictment against them to be presented to the court if they see just cause, and to act on such other public matters as may be brought before them — compare PETIT JURY **2 :** one that investigates crime in the manner of a grand jury ⟨appointed himself a one-man *grand jury* to bring the criminals to justice⟩

grand lama *n, often cap G&L* **:** DALAI LAMA

grand larceny *n* **1 :** larceny of property of a value greater than that fixed (as by a state) as constituting petit larceny **2 :** aggravated larceny of any amount

grand lecturer *n* **:** an officer appointed by a Masonic grand lodge to supervise an exemplification

grand lodge *n* **:** the chief lodge in a major division of lodges of Freemasons and some other fraternal orders

grand·ly \-ndlē, -li, *rapid* -nl-\ *adv* **:** in a grand manner ⟨singing more ~ than anyone else —Douglas Watt⟩ ⟨occupied a house which today would seem ~ large —F.L.Allen⟩

grand·ma \ˈgran(d)|(,)mä, -raam-, -ra(m)|, -raam|, |(,)mȯ, |,mə, |(,)mȧ\ *also* **grand·ma·ma** *or* **grand·mam·ma** \ˈ|≈,≈ˈ≈\ *n* **:** GRANDMOTHER

grand mal \ˈgranˈmäl, -raam-,-rän-, -mal,-mȧl, *F* grä^nmȧl\ *n* [F, lit., *great illness*] **:** epilepsy due to an inborn usu. inherited dysrhythmia of the electrical pulsations of the brain as demonstrated by the electroencephalogram and characterized by attacks of violent convulsions, coma, constitutional disturbances, and usu. amnesia — compare PETIT MAL

grand·mam·my \ˈgran(d),≈≈, -raan-\ *n* [¹*grand* + *mammy*] *dial* **:** GRANDMOTHER

grand manner *n* [trans. of F *grande manière*] **:** a dignified formal ceremonious manner, bearing, or mode of expression; *esp* **:** an elevated or grand style (as in music or literature)

grand march *n* **:** the opening ceremony at a large ball that consists of a march characterized by simple changes of pattern and is participated in by all the guests

grand master *n* **1 a :** the head of one of the former military orders of knighthood (as the Templars, Hospitalers) **b :** the chief officer of a Masonic grand lodge or of similar lodges in some other fraternal orders **2 :** an expert player (as of chess, checkers, bridge) whose superiority has been proved by frequent tournament victories

grandmaster key \ˈ≈ˈ≈≈-\ *n* **:** a master key designed to fit a number of different master-keyed systems of locks

grandmaternal \ˌ≈ˈ≈ˈ≈\ *adj* **:** GRANDMOTHERLY

grand mi·sère \ˌgrä^nmēˈze(ə)r\ *n* **:** a bid to lose all the tricks usu. at no-trump in a card game (as Boston)

grand·moth·er \ˈgran(d),≈≈, -raan-\ *n* [ME *graundmoder* (trans. of MF *grant mere*), fr. MF *grant* grand + ME *moder* mother — more at GRAND, MOTHER] **1 a :** the mother of one's father or mother; *also* **:** FOREMOTHER **b :** an old or elderly and venerable woman **2 :** a woman or something thought of as female that is the earliest or oldest in a line of similar and usu. successively developing things ⟨the ~ of writers of modern verse⟩ ⟨the ~ of all suffragettes⟩ ⟨London . . . is the ~ of capitals —T.H.Fielding⟩

grandmother clock *n* **:** a clock that is about two thirds the size of a grandfather clock and sometimes has a repeat mechanism

grandmother-in-law \ˈ≈,≈≈≈,≈\ *n, pl* **grandmothers-in-law :** the grandmother of one's spouse

grandmotherliness \ˈ≈,≈≈≈≈\ *n* **:** a grandmotherly quality **:** grandmotherly qualities

grand·moth·er·ly \ˈ≈,≈≈≈\ *adj* **:** of or belonging to a grandmother **:** like or befitting a grandmother (as in kindness or indulgence); *specif* **:** marked by great concern for trivial details of regulation **:** FUSSY

grand mufti *n* **:** ¹MUFTI

grand national assembly *n* **:** a unicameral parliament in a government (as the Turkish republic)

grand·neph·ew \ˈgran(d)ˈ≈(,)≈, -raan-\ *n* **:** a grandson of one's brother or sister

grand·ness \ˈgran(d)nəs, -raan-\ *n* -ES **:** the quality or state of being grand

grand·niece \ˈgran(d)ˈ≈, -raan-\ *n* **:** a granddaughter of one's brother or sister

grand old man *n* **:** an elderly venerated practitioner or former practitioner of an art, profession, or sport ⟨the *grand old man* of twentieth century poetry —Babette Deutsch⟩ ⟨the *grand old man* of Italian conservative politics —Percy Winner⟩ ⟨the *grand old man* of cricket and the best batsman of his times —*Springfield (Mass.) Union*⟩

gran·do·ma·nia \ˌgrandōˈmānēə\ *n* [¹*grand* + *-o-* + *mania*] **:** a mania for elaborate, imposing, and showy buildings or furnishings

grand opera *n* **:** opera in which the plot is elaborated as in serious drama and the entire text set to music

grand organ *adv (or adj)* **:** FULL ORGAN

grand orgue \(ˈ)granˈdȯ(ə)rg, *F* grä^ndȯrg\ *adv (or adj)* [F] **:** FULL ORGAN

grand·pa \ˈgran(d)|(,)pä, -raan-, -ram|, -raam|, |(,)pȯ, |,pə, |(,)pȧ\ *also* **grand·pa·pa** \ˌ|≈,≈ˈ|≈,≈\ *n* **:** GRANDFATHER

grand·pap·py \ˌ|≈≈,≈\ *n, dial* **:** GRANDFATHER

grand·par·ent \ˈgran(d),≈≈, -raan-\ *n* **:** a parent's parent **:** a grandmother or grandfather — **grandparental** \ˌ≈≈ˈ≈\ *adj*

grand·par·ent·hood \ˈ≈,≈≈,hu̇d\ *n* -s **:** the state of being a grandparent

grand pas·sion *as grand + passion, or* grä^ndpȧsyō^n\ *also* **grande pas·sion** \"\ *n* [F *grande passion,* lit., great passion] **1 :** an overwhelming or vehement love **2 :** the object of a grand passion

grandpaternal \ˌ≈ˈ≈≈\ *adj* [*grand* + *paternal*] **:** GRANDFATHERLY ⟨taught, in deference to ~ feelings, to address his grandfather as "Mr. Wendell" —M.A.D.Howe⟩

grand pause *n* **:** GENERAL PAUSE

grand pawnee *n, usu cap G&P* **1 :** an Indian people of the Pawnee group **2 :** a member of the Grand Pawnee people

grand period of growth : the time during which a cell, organ, or organism is developing; *esp* **:** that period of development characterized by rapid increase in size

grand piano *n* **:** a wing-shaped piano in which the frame and strings are horizontal — contrasted with *upright piano*

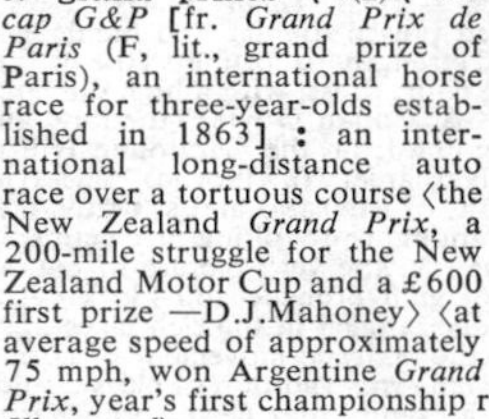

grand piano

grand prix \grä^n ˈprē\ *n, pl* **grand prix** *or* **grands prix** *or* **grand prixes** \-ē(z)\ *usu cap G&P* [fr. *Grand Prix de Paris* (F, lit., grand prize of Paris), an international horse race for three-year-olds established in 1863] **:** an international long-distance auto race over a tortuous course ⟨the New Zealand *Grand Prix,* a 200-mile struggle for the New Zealand Motor Cup and a £600 first prize —D.J.Mahoney⟩ ⟨at average speed of approximately 75 mph, won Argentine *Grand Prix,* year's first championship race, at Buenos Aires —*Sports Illustrated*⟩

grand quarter *n* **:** one of the four primary divisions of a heraldic shield which is divided quarterly; *esp* **:** a heraldic quarter that is itself quartered

grand quartering *n* **:** a quartering of a quartered coat with others in heraldic marshaling

grand rap·ids \ˈgranˈ(d)rapə̇dz, ˈgraan-\ *adj, usu cap G&R* [fr. *Grand Rapids,* Mich.] **:** of or from the city of Grand Rapids, Mich. ⟨*Grand Rapids* furniture⟩ **:** of the kind or style prevalent in Grand Rapids

grand rapids disease *n* **:** TOMATO CANKER

gran·drelle \(ˈ)granˈdrel\ *n* -s *sometimes cap* [origin unknown] **:** a yarn usu. having two plies of different colors

grand right and left *n* **:** a circular weaving in and out in a square dance in which the men go in one direction and the women in the opposite, all dancers joining first their right hands and then left

grands *pl of* GRAND

grand-scale \ˈ≈ˈ≈\ *adj* **:** being or occurring on a large scale ⟨the *grand-scale* violence of a race determined to risk extinction —Anthony Boucher⟩ ⟨low water defeated hopes of *grand-scale* river navigation —*Amer. Guide Series: Minn.*⟩

grand sei·gneur \ˌgrä^nˌsānˈyər(·)\ *n, pl* **grand seigneurs** *or* **grands seigneurs** \-ä^n,sānˈyərz,-ər(·)\ [F] **1 :** a great lord or nobleman ⟨the *grand seigneur* La Salle and his men glided through the . . . land —H.T.Kane⟩ **2 :** a man of dignity and aristocratic bearing ⟨described as a cultured country squire, a *grand seigneur* influential among his own people and a patron of the arts —A.D.Rees⟩

grand sei·gnior *or* **grand si·gnor** \ˈgran(d)ˈsēnyə(r), -raan-\ *n* **:** a former sultan of Turkey

grand sergeanty *or* **grand serjeanty** *n* [ME *graunte sergeaunte,* lit., large sergeanty, fr. AF *grand serjeanty*] **:** sergeanty requiring some special personal service to the king (as the carrying of his banner or his sword at coronation)

¹grand·sire \ˈgran(d),≈, -raan-\ *n* [ME *grauntsire,* fr. OF *grant sire,* fr. *grant* grand + *sire*] **1 a** *or* **grand·sir** \-n(t)-sə(r)\ *now dial* **:** GRANDFATHER **b** *or* **grandsir** *Scot* **:** a great grandfather **c** *archaic* **:** ANCESTOR, FOREFATHER **d** *archaic* **:** an aged man **2 :** a dam's or sire's sire — used of an animal **3 :** a method of ringing changes on a set of church bells ⟨~ maximus⟩ — see CHANGE RINGING illustration

²grandsire \"\ *vt* **:** to be grandsire to ⟨*grandsired* the modern cult by preaching sanctification —*Amer. Mercury*⟩

grand slam *n* **1 a :** the winning of all the tricks of one hand in a card game (as bridge) **b :** the winning of all or specified tournaments in a sport at one time or in one season **2 :** a home run made with the bases loaded

grand·son \ˈgran(d),sən, -raan- *sometimes* -n(t)_sən\ *n* **:** a son's or daughter's son

grandson-in-law \ˈ≈(,)≈≈,≈\ *n, pl* **grandsons-in-law :** the husband of one's granddaughter

¹grand·stand \ˈgran(d),stand, -raan(d),staa(ə)nd\ *n* [¹*grand* + *stand*] **1 :** a usu. roofed structure serving as the principal spectator stand at a racecourse, stadium, or other place designed for spectator sports **2 :** the spectators (as at a sports event) or the audience (as at a festival)

grandstand

²grandstand \"\ *vi* -ED/-ING/-S **:** to play to spectators or to an audience **:** act or conduct oneself with a view to impressing onlookers ⟨chose to ~ in court —Erle Stanley Gardner⟩ ⟨the crazy *~ing* of a glory-hungry major —Van Van Praag⟩ — **grand·stand·er** \-ə(r)\ *n*

³grandstand \"\ *adj* **1 a :** being in or as if in a grandstand ⟨join their neighbors on top of their houses where they had ~ seats for watching the next assault —F.B.Gipson⟩ **b :** resembling that provided by a grandstand ⟨a ~ view of the fight⟩ **2 :** designed or likely to impress or draw the applause of spectators ⟨behind-the-back dribbling and passing are strictly ~ stunts —Stanley Frank⟩

grand style *n* **1 :** a literary style marked by a sustained and lofty dignity, sublimity, and eloquence (as often attributed to epic poets) **2 :** an artistic style associated generally with 17th and early 18th century European works and characterized chiefly by the idealized representation of the human figure as noble and heroic in emulation of classical and Renaissance artistic prototypes

grand theft *n* **:** GRAND LARCENY

grand tier *n* **:** the tier immediately above the parterre

grand tour *n* **1 :** an extended European tour esp. through France, Germany, Italy, and Switzerland formerly commonly taken by youth of the British aristocracy as a part of their education **2 :** a tour resembling a grand tour: **a :** a tour through European capitals and places of significant historical or cultural interest **b :** a tour through a series of places of special interest ⟨a *grand tour* of the nightclubs of New York⟩ ⟨making the *grand tour* of the markets, quais, and parks —E.G. Robinson b. 1933⟩

grand trav·erse \ˈ≈ˈtravə(r)s\ *or* **grand traverse disease** \ˈ≈ˈ≈-\ *n, usu cap G&T* [fr. *Grand Traverse* county, Mich.] *North* **:** pine of cattle

granduncle \ˈ≈ˈ≈≈\ *n* **:** a father's or mother's uncle — called also *great-uncle*

grand vicar *n* **:** a vicar-general of a diocese in France

grand vizier *n* **:** the chief officer of state of a Muslim country esp. formerly of the Ottoman Empire

grange \ˈgrānj\ *n* -s [ME *grange, graunge,* fr. MF *grange, granche,* fr. ML *granica,* fr. L *granum* grain + *-ica* (fem. of *-icus* -ic) — more at CORN] **1** *archaic* **:** GRANARY, BARN **2 a :** FARM; *esp* **:** a farmhouse or country house with barns or other buildings for farming **b :** an outlying farmhouse with its barns and other buildings belonging to a monastery or to a feudal lord **c** *obs* **:** a country house **3 a :** one of the lodges of an association of farmers joined with some secret rites to further their interests and particularly to bring producers and consumers, farmers and manufacturers, into direct commercial relations **b** *usu cap* **:** the association itself

grang·er \-jə(r)\ *n* -s [ME *granger* tenant farmer, fr. MF *grangier,* fr. *grange* + *-ier* -er] **1** *archaic* **:** a farm steward **2 :** a member of a grange **3 :** FARMER — used esp. in the Northwest **4 a :** a grain-carrying railroad **b :** a stock or share in such a railroad

¹gran·ger·ism \ˈgrānjə,rizəm\ *n* -s [James *Granger* †1776 Eng. clergyman and biographer + E *-ism*] **:** the practice of grangerizing

²grang·er·ism \"\ *n* -s [*granger* + *-ism*] **:** the policy or methods of the grangers

gran·ger·ite \-jə,rīt\ *n* -s [J. *Granger* + E *-ite*] **:** one that grangerizes

gran·ger·iza·tion \ˌ≈≈ rəˈzāshən, -ˌrīˈz-\ *n* -s **:** an act or the result of grangerizing

gran·ger·ize \ˈgrānjə,rīz\ *vt* -ED/-ING/-S [James *Granger* + E *-ize*] **1 :** EXTRA-ILLUSTRATE **2 :** to mutilate (as a book or periodical) to obtain material for extra-illustration — **gran·ger·iz·er** \-zə(r)\ *n* -s

granger law *n* **:** one of the laws passed in various states of the middle west between 1869 and 1876 under influence of the Grange

grani *pl of* GRANO

grani- *comb form* [L, fr. *granum* — more at CORN] **:** grain ⟨*graniform*⟩ **:** grain or seeds ⟨*granivorous*⟩

gra·ni·ta \grəˈnēd-ə\ *n* -s [It, fr. fem. of *granito,* past part. of *granire* to grain, granulate] **:** a coarse-grained sherbet

gran·ite \ˈgranət, *usu* -ə̇d·+V\ *n* -s *often attrib* [It *granito,* fr. past part. of *granire* to grain, granulate, fr. *grano* grain, fr. L *granum* — more at CORN] **1 :** a natural igneous rock formation of visibly crystalline texture; *specif* **:** a usu. flesh-red whitish or gray very hard and durable holocrystalline-granular plutonic igneous rock consisting essentially of quartz, orthoclase or microcline, a smaller amount of acid plagioclase, usu. one or more members of the mica, amphibole, and less commonly pyroxene groups, and usu. accessories (as apatite, zircon, magnetite, and occas. topaz, tourmaline, garnet), the rock varying in texture from fine to very coarse and taking a fine polish — see APLITE, GRAPHIC GRANITE, PEGMATITE **2 :** unyielding firmness or endurance ⟨a man of ~, strong, able, and of inflexible integrity —H.S.Canby⟩ ⟨the cold ~ of Puritan formalism —V.L.Parrington⟩ **3** [It *granita*] **:** GRANITA **4** *or* **granite gray :** a purplish gray that is redder and slightly stronger than crane, darker than dove gray or cinder gray, and redder and deeper than zinc — called also *metallic gray*

granite blue *n* **:** PEARL 6 b

granite cloth *n* **:** a lightweight clothing fabric usu. of wool or worsted in various weaves and characterized by an irregular, pebbled, hard-finished surface

granite-gneiss \ˈ≈≈ˈ≈\ *n* **:** a rock consisting of an orthogneiss or paragneiss having the composition of a granite

granite paper *n* **:** a paper containing a small proportion of deeply colored fibers to produce a mottled appearance something like that of granite

graniteware \ˈ≈≈,≈\ *n* **1 a :** pottery with a speckled surface imitating that of granite **b :** a very hard pottery resembling ironstone china **2 :** ironware coated with an enamel suggestive of granite in appearance

gra·nit·ic \(ˈ)graˈnid-|ik, grəˈn-, -it|, |ēk\ *adj* **1 :** of or belonging to granite; *specif* **:** having a holocrystalline-allotriomorphic texture **2 :** resembling granite in hardness ⟨a ~ fist⟩ or in austere inflexibility ⟨a ~ and Puritanic personality⟩ ⟨a ~ morality⟩

gra·nit·i·cal \|ə̇kəl, |ēk-\ *adj, archaic* **:** GRANITIC

gran·it·iza·tion \ˌgranə̇d-ə̇ˈzāshən, -d-,ˌīˈz-\ *n* -s **1 :** the development of granite from other rocks rich in alkalies, silica, and alumina by selective fusion or metasomatism **2 :** the condition of having developed by granitization

gran·it·ize \ˈgranə̇d-,īz\ *vt* -ED/-ING/-S [*granite* + *-ize*] **:** to cause to undergo granitization

gran·it·oid \ˈ≈ə̇d-,ȯid\ *also* **gran·it·oi·dal** \ˌ≈≈ˈ≈ȯidᵊl\ *adj* **:** resembling granite **:** GRANITIC

grani·vore \ˈgrānə,vō(ə)r, -ran-\ *n* -s [back-formation fr. *granivorous*] **:** a granivorous animal or bird

gra·niv·o·rous \grəˈniv(ə)rəs, (ˈ)graˈn-, (ˈ)graˈn-\ *adj* [*grani-* + *-vorous*] **:** feeding on seeds or grain

gran·je·no \grənˈhā(,)nō\ *n* -s [MexSp] **:** a densely spiny shrub (*Celtis pallida*) occurring in Mexico and the adjacent U.S. and having edible berries

gran·nam \ˈgranəm\ *n* -s [alter. of *grandam*] *archaic* **:** GRANDMOTHER

¹gran·ny *or* **gran·nie** \ˈgranē, -ni\ *n, pl* **grannies** [by shortening & alter. fr. *grandmother*] **1 a :** GRANDMOTHER **b :** one that is markedly fussy or overly concerned about trivial details **2** *also* **granny woman** *South & Midland* **:** MIDWIFE **3 :** GRANNY KNOT

²granny \"\ *vb* -ED/-ING/-ES *vi, South & Midland* **:** to act or practice as a midwife ⟨*grannied* for over 50 years⟩ ~ *vt, South & Midland* **:** to act as a midwife for ⟨*grannied* all the babies⟩

granny knot *or* **granny's bend** *or* **granny's knot** *n* **:** an insecure knot often made instead of a square knot

granny knot

gra·no \ˈgrä(ˌ)nō\ *n, pl* **gra·ni** \-(ˌ)nē\ [It, lit., grain — more at GRANITE] **:** an old unit of monetary value of Naples and Malta equal to ⅓ of a farthing; *also* **:** a copper coin representing this value

grano- *comb form* [G, fr. *granit* granite, fr. It *granito* — more at GRANITE] **1 :** granite or a granitic substance ⟨*grano*blastic⟩ ⟨*grano*lith⟩ **2 :** granitic ⟨*grano*gabbro⟩

gran·o·blas·tic \ˌgranōˈblastik\ *adj* [ISV *grano-* + *blastic*; orig. formed as G *granoblastisch*] *of a rock* **:** having a texture in which the fragments are irregular and angular and appear like a mosaic under the microscope

grano·diorite \ˈgra(ˌ)nō+\ *n* [ISV *grano-* + *diorite*] **:** a granular intrusive quartzose igneous rock intermediate between granite and quartz diorite with plagioclase predominant over orthoclase

grano·gabbro \"+\ *n* [*grano-* + *gabbro*] **:** a plutonic rock intermediate between a granite and a gabbro and consisting of quartz, basic plagioclase, potash-feldspar, and one or more ferromagnesian minerals

gran·o·lith \ˈgranəˌlith\ *n* -s [*grano-* + *-lith*] **:** an artificial stone of crushed granite and cement — **gran·o·lith·ic** \ˌ≈≈ˈlithik\ *adj*

gran·o·phyre \ˈgranəˌfī(ə)r\ *n* -s [ISV *grano-* + *-phyre*; orig. formed as G *granophyr*] **:** a porphyritic igneous rock chiefly composed of alkalic feldspar and quartz and having a granular groundmass; *also* **:** a similar rock with the quartz and feldspar of the groundmass in micropegmatite intergrowths

gran·o·phyr·ic \ˌ≈≈ˈfirik\ *adj* **:** of, belonging to, or like granophyre

grans *pl of* GRAN

¹**grant** \ˈgrant, -aa(ə)-,-ai-,-ȧ-\ *vb* -ED/-ING/-S [ME *graunten*, *granten*, fr. OF *creanter*, *greanter*, *graanter*, fr. (assumed) VL *credentare*, fr. L *credent-*, *credens*, pres. part. of *credere* to believe — more at CREED] *vt* **1 a :** to consent to carry out for a person **:** ALLOW, ACCORD ⟨after a conference the judge ~*ed* counsel his request⟩ ⟨~ a child his wish⟩ **b** *obs* **:** AGREE, ASSENT — used with a following infinitive with *to* **c :** to permit as a right, privilege, indulgence, or favor ⟨~ himself a quick view of the treasured letter⟩ ⟨~ a few moments' conversation to his admirers⟩ ⟨the sixty-six-pound free luggage allowance ~*ed* by the transatlantic airlines —Richard Joseph⟩ ⟨seek the seclusion that a cabin ~*s* —W.S.Gilbert⟩ **2 :** GIVE, BESTOW, CONFER ⟨~*ed* a sum of $2000 to the student to help him continue his education⟩ ⟨~*ed* a large acreage to deserving settlers⟩ ⟨~ a doctor's degree to a graduate student⟩ ⟨save every drop of rain the heavens ~ —Russell Lord⟩ ⟨~ a loan to an applicant⟩ ⟨the government ~*ed* full diplomatic recognition to the new nation⟩; *specif* **:** to make a conveyance of **:** give the possession or title of esp. by a deed or formal writing **3 a** *obs* **:** ACKNOWLEDGE, CONFESS **b :** be willing to concede **:** ADMIT, CONCEDE ⟨~ a proposition is true⟩ ⟨~ that the man was lying⟩ ⟨I ~ I was wrong⟩ ⟨the government is ~*ing* no preference as between types of small business in applying for financial assistance —W.B.Barnes⟩ **c :** to assume to be true **:** deem unquestionable ⟨~*ed* that the novelist has talent, he can nevertheless sometimes expect a hard time finding a publisher⟩ **~** *vi*, *obs* **:** ASSENT, CONSENT

syn AWARD, CONCEDE, ACCORD, VOUCHSAFE: GRANT may apply to giving to a petitioner or claimant, often a subordinate, something that has been sought and that could be withheld ⟨*granted* leave of absence for a year, he went abroad —Allen Johnson⟩ ⟨at the close of the Civil War a bounty of $100 was *granted* to those who had served three years —J. W.Oliver⟩ ⟨was *granted* the triumphal insignia and the right to be consul before the legal age —John Buchan⟩ AWARD, often interchangeable with GRANT, may apply to giving something adjudged merited or condign ⟨*awarded* him a medal as champion⟩ ⟨his land, *awarded* him by the Indians in 1835 in acknowledgment of his long service in their behalf —*Amer. Guide Series: La.*⟩ ⟨a certain difficulty arises in writing about a book to which one *awards* an unreserved enthusiasm —Carl Van Vechten⟩ CONCEDE indicates a giving, giving in, or yielding to some rightful request or compelling claim ⟨because physics, history, and religion have their different valuations of experience, we are obliged to *concede* a large measure of autonomy to the different studies —W.R.Inge⟩ ⟨even his harshest critics *concede* him a rocklike integrity, boundless courage, and an immobile sort of dignity —*Time*⟩ ACCORD may indicate a granting, sometimes reluctant, of what is due ⟨treated bishops with the superficial deference that a sergeant-major *accords* to a junior subaltern —Compton Mackenzie⟩ ⟨children easily appreciate justice, and will readily accord to others what others *accord* to them —Bertrand Russell⟩ ⟨the central fact to which . . . prevailing creeds refuse to *accord* sufficiently serious attention is the obvious impossibility of attaining omniscience —M.R.Cohen⟩ VOUCHSAFE may indicate a grant, esp. in response to a petition or request, explicit or implicit, by a person in power ⟨the occasional answers that Stalin used to *vouchsafe* to inquiries from American correspondents —Elmer Davis⟩ ⟨a kindly Being, who, in return for due rites and offerings, will *vouchsafe* nourishing rains and golden harvests —L.P.Smith⟩

— **take for granted 1 :** to assume as true, accurate, real, unquestionable, or to be expected ⟨*took* it *for granted* that he would not get into trouble with the licensing authorities⟩ ⟨*taken for granted* that words have definite meanings —T.S. Eliot⟩ **2 :** to pay inadequate attention to or value too lightly (as a possession, right, or privilege) ⟨inclined to *take* one's liberties *for granted* if they are never challenged⟩ ⟨began to *take* her husband *for granted* until he threatened to leave her⟩

²**grant** \"\ *n* -s [ME *graunt*, *grant*, fr. OF *creant*, *greant*, *graant*, fr. *creanter*, *greanter*, *graanter*] **1 :** the act of granting: as **a** *obs* (1) **:** CONSENT, PERMISSION (2) **:** ACKNOWLEDGMENT, CONFESSION **b :** CONCEDING ⟨his ~ of the election to his opponent⟩ **:** ALLOWING ⟨opposed the ~ of absentee voting⟩ **:** a bestowing or conferring ⟨the ~ of exclusive privileges in a railroad station —O.W.Holmes †1935⟩ **2 :** something granted; *esp* **:** a gift (as of land or a sum of money) usu. for a particular purpose ⟨subsidized by a ~ of two million pounds yearly from the British government⟩ ⟨a ~ of land to any member who could establish a specific number of settlers —*Amer. Guide Series: N. J.*⟩ ⟨obtained a ~ to study abroad for a year⟩ ⟨the university gave the scholar a ~ of the sum of $2000 to continue his research⟩ **3 a :** a transfer of real or personal property by deed or writing — compare ASSIGNMENT 3a, GIFT 2a **b :** the instrument by which such a transfer is made; *also* **:** the property so transferred **c** *Eng law* **:** a former conveyance of an incorporeal hereditament that could pass only by deed **4 :** a minor territorial division of Maine, New Hampshire, or Vermont orig. granted by the state to an individual or institution **5** *in livestock judging* **:** a specified point in which an animal judged inferior surpasses the class winner — **lie in grant :** to be transferable legally only by grant

grant·able \-təbəl\ *adj* **:** capable of being granted ⟨a right only ~ with the consent of a court⟩

grant-aid·ed school \ˈ≈,≈≈-\ *n* **:** AIDED SCHOOL

grant caribou \ˈgra|nt-, -aa(ə)|,-ai|,-ȧ|\ *or* **grant's caribou** *n, usu cap G* [after Madison *Grant* †1937 Amer. lawyer, explorer, writer on zoology] **:** a small light-colored caribou (*Rangifer arcticus granti*) of the Alaska peninsula

granted *past of* GRANT

grant·ed·ly *adv* **:** beyond question **:** not to be doubted **:** ADMITTEDLY ⟨this ~ ancient predicament —Dudley Fitts⟩ ⟨a ~ silly thing to do⟩

grant·ee \(ˈ)granˈtē, -aan-,-ain-,-ȧn-, -nˈtē\ *n* -s [ME *graunte*, fr. *graunten*, *granten* to grant + *-e* -ee] **:** one to whom a grant is made ⟨in awarding scholarships the college picked its ~*s* carefully⟩

grant·er \ˈgrantə(r), -aan-,-ain-,-ȧn-\ *n* -s [ME *graunter*, fr. *graunten* to grant + *-er*] **:** one that grants

gran·tha alphabet \ˈgräntə-, -ran-\ *n, usu cap G* [Skt *grantha* knot, act of tying together, book — more at CRADLE] **:** a south Indian alphabet of which there are numerous varieties used in Sanskrit inscriptions in the Tamil country as early as the 5th century A.D. and still used by Tamil Brahmans for writing Sanskrit books

gran·ther \ˈgran(t)thə(r)\ *n* -s [by contr.] *chiefly NewEng* **:** GRANDFATHER

gran·thi \ˈgräntē, -ran-\ *n* -s [Hindi *granthī*, fr. *Granth*, the sacred scripture of the Sikhs] **:** a reader of the sacred scriptures of the Sikhs whose function is to lead worship services in Sikh temples and gurdwaras

gran·tia \ˈgranch(ē)ə, -ntēə\ *n, cap* [NL, fr. Robert E. *Grant* †1874 Scot. comparative anatomist + NL *-ia*] **:** a genus (the type of the family Grantiidae) of small cylindrical calcareous sycon sponges with triradiate spicules projecting into the cloacal cavity

grant-in-aid \ˌ≈≈ˈ≈\ *n, pl* **grants-in-aid 1 :** a grant or subsidy from public funds paid by a central to a local government in aid of some public undertaking (as education or highway construction) usu. conditional upon the maintenance of a specified standard or upon similar or proportional appropriations by the grantee **2 :** a grant or subsidy resembling a government grant-in-aid; *esp* **:** financial support given by a public agency or private institution to an educational institution for particular projects or to a person for educational purposes (as to further the person's education or to help complete a research project)

granting *pres part of* GRANT

grant·or \ˈgrantə(r), (ˈ)grantˈō(ə)r, -nˈtō-, -ō(ə), -raan-, -rain-,-rȧn-\ *n* -s **:** one that grants: **a :** the person by whom a grant, conveyance, or lease is made **b :** one that extends credit **:** GUARANTOR

grants *pres 3d sing of* GRANT, *pl of* GRANT

grant's gazelle *n, usu cap 1st G* [after James A. *Grant* †1892 Brit. explorer] **:** a large antelope (*Gazella granti*) of the East African plains distinguished by graceful diverging annulated horns

grant's zebra *n, usu cap G* [after James A. *Grant*] **:** a zebra that is a variety (*Equus burchelli granti*) of Burchell's zebra distinguished by complete lack of shadow striping and is widely distributed from Sudan and Ethiopia to Uganda and Kenya — compare CHAPMAN'S ZEBRA

granul- *or* **granuli-** *or* **granulo-** *comb form* [LL *granulum* — more at GRANULE] **:** granule ⟨*granuli*form⟩ ⟨*granulo*metric⟩ **:** granulation ⟨*granul*oma⟩

gran·u·lar \ˈgranyələ(r)\ *adj* [LL *granul*um + E *-ar*] **1 a :** consisting of or appearing to consist of granules ⟨boil until the syrup becomes ~⟩ **:** having a structure or texture consisting of or appearing to consist of granules ⟨a ~ stone⟩ ⟨a very ~ sugar⟩ ⟨a ~ leather surface⟩ **b :** being a granule ⟨a ~ lump in an otherwise liquid-smooth salve⟩ **2 :** having or marked by granulations ⟨~ tissue⟩ **3** *of a sound or voice* **:** giving the impression of roughness or impurity ⟨a veiled ~ tone which sounds as though emanating from a mouthful of marbles —J.W.Freeman⟩ ⟨the famous ~ twang —*Newsweek*⟩ — **gran·u·lar·ly** *adv*

granular conjunctivitis *n* **:** TRACHOMA

granular hypothesis *n* **:** a statement in cytology: the visible and submicroscopic granular content of protoplasm constitutes the essential living matter — not much used by modern cytologists; compare BIOPHORE

gran·u·lar·i·ty \ˌ≈≈ˈlarəd·ē, -ətē, -i\ *n* -ES **1 :** the quality or state of being granular ⟨a rock with medium to coarse ~⟩ **2 :** nonuniformity in light-transmitting or reflecting properties of a developed photographic image produced by its individual particles

granular layer *n* **:** the deeper layer of the cortex of the cerebellum containing numerous small closely packed cells

granular leukocyte *n* **:** a blood granulocyte; *esp* **:** a polymorphonuclear leukocyte

granular snow *n* **:** small pellets or grains of precipitation resembling snow

gran·u·lary \ˈgranyəˌlerē\ *adj* [LL *granul*um + E *-ary*] *archaic* **:** GRANULAR

¹**gran·u·late** \ˈgranyəˌlāt, *usu* -ād·+V\ *vb* -ED/-ING/-S [LL *granulum* granule + E *-ate* (v. suffix) — more at GRANULE] *vt* **:** to form or crystallize (as sugar) into grains, granules, or small masses **:** make granular **~** *vi* **1 :** to collect or become formed into grains or granules **2 :** to undergo granulation

²**gran·u·late** \-ˌlət, *usu* -əd·+V\ *adj* [NL *granulatus*, fr. LL *granulum* + L *-atus* -ate] **:** GRANULATED

granulated sugar *n* **:** a pure sugar that has been crystallized and centrifuged and then sent through a granulator where the crystals are dried, separated, and screened

gran·u·lat·er \-ˌlād·ə(r), -ātə-\ *n* -s **:** GRANULATOR

gran·u·la·tion \ˌ≈≈ˈlāshən\ *n* -s [LL *granulum* + E *-ation*] **1 a :** the act or process of granulating ⟨the ~ of sugar⟩ **b :** the condition of being granulated ⟨the ~ of the leather was rough to the touch⟩ **2 a :** one of the small elevations of a granulated surface: (1) **:** a minute mass of tissue projecting from the surface of an organ (as on the eyelids in trachoma) (2) **:** one of the minute red granules made up of loops of newly formed capillaries that form on a raw surface (as of a wound) and that with fibroblasts are the active agents in the process of healing — see GRANULATION TISSUE **b :** the act or process of forming such elevations or granules **3 a :** GRANULE 2 **b :** the appearance of the sun's surface caused by the presence of granules **4 a :** an abnormal condition of a citrus fruit usu. left on the tree late in the season in which the juice sacs are hard and firm and the fruit tasteless **b :** the process by which this condition comes about

granulation tissue *n* **:** tissue made up of granulations that temporarily replaces lost tissue in a wound or lesion and forms a vascular protective framework during the healing process

gran·u·la·tor \ˈ≈≈ˌlād·ə(r), -ātə-\ *n* -s **:** one that granulates; *specif* **:** a large revolving cylinder in which sugar is dried and granulated

gran·ule \ˈgran(ˌ)yül\ *n* -s [LL *granulum*, dim. of L *granum* grain — more at CORN] **1 a :** a little grain (as of sugar) **:** a small particle (as of pollen); *esp* **:** one of a number of particles forming a larger unit ⟨the ~*s* of the rock⟩ ⟨the carbon ~*s* in the dry-cell battery⟩ **b :** a small sugar-coated pill **2 :** one of the small, short-lived, brilliant spots on the sun's seething photosphere that are of irregular shape and several hundred miles in diameter **3 :** a clump of actinomycetes in a lesion

granule cell *n* **:** a connective tissue cell containing cytoplasmic granules that stain intensely with aniline dyes

granuli- — see GRANUL-

gran·u·lif·er·ous \ˌgranyəˈlif(ə)rəs\ *adj* [*granul-* + *-ferous*] **:** bearing, producing, or full of granules

gran·u·lite \ˈ≈≈ˌlīt\ *n* -s [ISV *granul-* + *-ite*] **:** a banded or laminated whitish granular rock consisting of alkalic feldspar, quartz, and small red garnets and occurring with crystalline schists — **gran·u·lit·ic** \ˌ≈≈ˈlid·ik\ *adj*

granulo- — see GRANUL-

gran·u·lo·blast \ˈgranyəlōˌblast\ *n* [*granul-* + *-blast*] **:** a cellular precursor of a granulocyte **:** MYELOBLAST, MYELOCYTE — **gran·u·lo·blas·tic** \ˌ≈≈≈ˈblastik\ *adj*

gran·u·lo·blas·to·sis \ˌ≈≈≈ˌblaˈstōsəs\ *n, pl* **granuloblastoses** \-ōˌsēz\ [NL, fr. ISV *granuloblast* + NL *-osis*] **:** a disorder of the avian leukosis complex characterized by the presence of excessive numbers of immature blood granulocytes in affected birds

gran·u·lo·cyte \ˈgranyəlōˌsīt\ *n* -s [ISV *granul-* + *-cyte*] **:** a cell with granule-containing cytoplasm; *specif* **:** a polymorphonuclear leukocyte — **gran·u·lo·cyt·ic** \ˌ≈≈≈ˈsid·ik\ *adj*

gran·u·lo·cy·to·pe·nia \ˌ≈≈≈ˌsīd·əˈpēnēə\ *n* -s [NL, fr. ISV *granulocyte* + NL *-o-* + *-penia*] **:** deficiency of blood granulocytes; *specif* **:** an acute febrile condition marked by severe depression of the granulocyte-producing bone marrow and by prostration, chills, swollen neck, and sore throat sometimes with local ulceration and believed to be basically a response to the side effects of certain drugs of the coal-tar series (as amidopyrine) — called also *agranulocytic angina*, *agranulocytosis* — **gran·u·lo·cy·to·pe·nic** \ˌ≈≈≈ˌ≈≈ˈ≈nik\ *adj*

gran·u·lo·cy·to·poi·e·sis \ˌ≈≈≈ˌ≈≈pȯiˈēsəs\ *n, pl* **granulocytopoie·ses** \-ēˌsēz\ [NL, fr. ISV *granulocyte* + NL *-o-* + *-poiesis*] **:** the formation of blood granulocytes typically in the bone marrow

gran·u·lo·cy·to·sis \ˌ≈≈≈ˌsīˈtōsəs\ *n, pl* **granulocyto·ses** \-ōˌsēz\ [NL, fr. ISV *granulocyte* + NL *-osis*] **:** an increase in the number of blood granulocytes — compare LYMPHOCYTOSIS, MONOCYTOSIS

gran·u·lo·ma \ˌgranyəˈlōmə\ *n, pl* **granulomas** \-ōməz\ *or* **granuloma·ta** \-ōməd·ə\ [NL, fr. *granul-* + *-oma*] **:** a mass or nodule composed of chronically inflamed tissue marked by the formation of granulations and usu. associated with an infective process — **gran·u·lom·a·tous** \ˌ≈≈ˈlämədəs, -ˈlōm-\ *adj*

granuloma in·gui·na·le \-ˌiŋgwəˈna(ˌ)lē, -ˈal(ˌ)ē, -ˈä(ˌ)lā\ *or* **granuloma ve·ne·re·um** \-vəˈnirēəm\ *n* [*granuloma inguinale*, NL, lit., inguinal granuloma; *granuloma venereum*, NL, lit., venereal granuloma] **:** a chronic condition characterized by ulceration and formation of granulations beginning in the groin and spreading to the buttocks and genitals and caused by infection with a Donovan body (*Calymmatobacterium granulomatis*)

granuloma py·o·gen·i·cum \-ˌpīōˈjenəkəm\ *n* [NL, lit., pus-forming granuloma] **:** a granuloma that develops usu. at the site of an injury and is believed to result from infection

gran·u·lo·ma·to·sis \ˌgranyəˌlōməˈtōsəs\ *n, pl* **granulomatoses** \-ōˌsēz\ [NL, fr. *granulomat-*, *granuloma* + *-osis*] **:** a chronic condition marked by the formation of numerous granulomas

gran·u·lo·pe·nia \ˌgranyəlōˈpēnēə\ *n* -s [NL, fr. *granul-* + *-penia*] **:** GRANULOCYTOPENIA

gran·u·lo·poi·e·sis \-(ˌ)lōˌpȯiˈēsəs\ *n, pl* **granulopoie·ses** \-ēˌsēz\ [NL, fr. *granul-* + *-poiesis*] **:** GRANULOCYTOPOIESIS

gran·u·lo·sa cell \ˌgranyəˈlōsə-, -ōzə-\ *n* [NL *granulosa*, fr. *granul-* + L *-osa* (fem. of *-osus* -ous)] **:** one of the cells of the epithelial lining of a graafian follicle

gran·u·lose \ˈgranyəˌlōs\ *adj* [*granul-* + *-ose*] **:** GRANULAR; *esp* **:** having the surface roughened with granules

gran·u·lo·sis \ˌ≈≈ˈlōsəs\ *n, pl* **granulo·ses** \-ōˌsēz\ [NL, fr. *granul-* + *-osis*] **:** a virus disease of larval insects distinguished by the presence of minute granular inclusions in infected cells and marked by sluggishness, loss of appetite, and whitish discoloration of the body

gran·u·lous \ˈ≈≈ləs\ *adj* [LL *granul*um granule + E *-ous* — more at GRANULE] **:** GRANULAR

gra·num \ˈgrānəm, -ran-, -rän-\ *n, pl* **gra·na** \-nə\ [L, grain, seed — more at CORN] **1 :** GRANULE **2 :** one of the laminated stacks of chlorophyll-containing material in plant chloroplasts

gran·ville wilt \ˈgranˌvil-, *chiefly in southern US* -vəl-\ *n, usu cap G* [fr. *Granville* co., N.C.] **:** a wilt of tobacco caused by a bacterium (*Pseudomonas solanacearum*)

grape \ˈgrāp\ *n* -s [ME, fr. OF *crape*, *grape* hook, grape stalk, bunch of grapes, grape, of Gmc origin; akin to MD *crappe* hook, OHG *krapfo*, *krāpfo* — more at CRAVE] **1 a :** a smooth-skinned juicy berry ranging in color from green or white to deep red, purple, or black and in shape from globose to narrowly oblong that since ancient times has been eaten both dried and fresh as a fruit and has been fermented to produce wine — see RAISIN **b :** the fermented juice of the grape **:** WINE ⟨their hearts were expanding under the ~ —L.D.Lewis⟩ **2 :** any of numerous woody plants that constitute the genus *Vitis*, usu. climb by means of tendrils, produce clustered fruits that are grapes, are nearly cosmopolitan in cultivation, and include many cultivated hybrids and horticultural varieties derived from New and Old World species (as *V. vinifera*, *V. rotundifolia*, and *V. labrusca*) — called also *grapevine*; see FOX GRAPE, MUSCADINE, WINE GRAPE **3 a grapes** *pl* **:** a cluster of raw red nodules of granulation tissue in the hollow of the fetlock of horses that is characteristic of advanced or chronic grease heels **b grapes** *pl but usu sing in constr*, *also* **grape disease :** tuberculous disease of the pleura in cattle **4 :** GRAPESHOT **5 :** PLUM PURPLE 2

grapes 1a

grape anthracnose *n* **:** BIRD'S-EYE ROT

grape-berry moth \ˈ≈,≈≈-\ *n* **:** a small slate-colored moth (*Paralobesia viteana*) whose larvae feed in grape flowers and fruit

grape co·las·pis \-kəˈlaspəs\ *n* [NL *Colaspis*, genus of leaf beetles, fr. ²*col-* + *-aspis*] **:** a small pale brown elliptical leaf beetle (*Colaspis flavida* or a closely related form) whose larva is a short-legged grub that feeds on the roots of many cultivated plants and is sometimes esp. destructive to soybeans and corn planted after clover — called also *clover rootworm*

grape cure *n* **:** treatment of disease (as tuberculosis) by the free use of grapes as food

graped \ˈgrāpt\ *adj* **:** having the grapes — used of horses or cattle

grape family *n* **:** VITACEAE

grape fern *n* **:** a fern of the genus *Botrychium*

grapefruit \ˈ≈,≈\ *n* [so called fr. its growing in clusters] **1 :** a large typically globose citrus fruit with a bitter yellow rind and inner skin and a highly flavored somewhat acid juicy pulp varying in color from pale yellow to deep reddish pink — called also *pomelo* **2** *also* **grapefruit tree :** a small round-headed tree (*Citrus paradisi*) that produces grapefruit, is probably derived from the shaddock from which it differs chiefly in fruit characters, glabrous leaves and twigs, clustered growth of flowers and fruits, and solidity of the plant axis, and is widely cultivated in subtropical areas

grapefruit knife *n* **:** a small knife with serrated blade curved at the end

grapefruit league *n* [so called fr. the games' being played in warm regions where citrus fruits are grown] **:** major-league baseball teams playing exhibition games during spring training ⟨the championship of the *grapefruit league*⟩

grapefruit spoon *n* **:** ORANGE SPOON

grape green *n* **:** a light olive color that is greener and paler than citrine, paler than old moss green, and redder, less strong, and slightly lighter than average willow green

grape house *n* **:** a greenhouse devoted to the culture of grapes

grape hyacinth *n* **:** any of several small bulbous spring-flowering perennial herbs of the genus *Muscari* that have narrow linear leaves and blue, pink, or white drooping urn-shaped flowers closely set in a terminal raceme and that are native to the Mediterranean area but cosmopolitan in cultivation

grape ivy *n* **:** an evergreen tendril-climbing vine (*Cissus rhombifolia*) that is native to northern So. America, has trifoliate leaves with reddish hairy lower surfaces, and is used widely as a house plant

grape juice *n* **:** the usu. sterilized and often diluted juice of grapes used as a beverage

grape leaf folder *n* **:** a black moth (*Desmia funeralis*) with a white border and white spots on the wings whose grass-green caterpillar rolls up and feeds in the leaf of the grapevine

grape leafhopper *n* **:** any of several small yellowish leafhoppers that constitute the genus *Erythroneura*, are marked with red or brown bands, and suck the juices of the leaves of the grapevine thereby often causing them to wither and fall off

grape·less \ˈgrāpləs\ *adj* **:** lacking grapes or the flavor of grapes **:** made without grapes ⟨~ wine⟩

grape·let \-lət\ *n* -s **:** a small grape

grape mealybug *n* **:** a widely distributed mealybug (*Pseudococcus maritimus*) that feeds on many economic plants

grape mildew *n* **1 :** a powdery mildew caused by an ascomycetous fungus (*Uncinula necator*) **2 :** a downy mildew caused by a phycomycetous fungus (*Plasmopara viticola*)

grape phylloxera *or* **grape louse** *n* **:** a small yellowish green No. American phylloxera (*Phylloxera vitifoliae*) that lives and forms galls on the leaves and roots of various grapes being relatively harmless to native forms but extremely destructive to European vinifera grapes

grape plume moth *n* **:** a common slender tan moth (*Pterophorus periscelidactylus*) whose larva makes a nest on grape leaves

graperoot \ˈ≈,≈\ *n* **1 :** the bitter tonic root of any plant of the genus *Mahonia* (as Oregon grape) **2 :** a plant that yields graperoot

grape rootworm *n* **:** a grub that is the larva of a small yellowish brown chrysomelid beetle (*Fidia viticida*) of the eastern U.S. and that attacks the roots of the grapevine — see WESTERN GRAPE ROOTWORM

grape rot *n* **:** any of several fungous diseases of the grape; *esp* **:** a black rot caused by an ascomycetous fungus (*Guignardia bidwellii*)

grape rust *n* **:** a foliage rust of grapes caused by a rust fungus (*Phakopsora vitis*)

grap·ery \ˈgrāp(ə)rē, -ri\ *n* -ES : an area or building in which grapes are grown

grape scale *n* : either of two scales (*Aspidiotus uvae* and *Eulecanium persicae*) that attack the grapevine and various fruit trees

grape-seed oil *n* : a pale to yellow usu. semidrying fatty oil obtained from grape seeds and used in foods, soap, and paint

grapeshot \ˈ=,=\ *n* [so called fr. the resemblance to a bunch of grapes] : a cluster consisting usu. of nine small iron balls put together by means of cast-iron circular plates at top and bottom with two rings and a central connecting rod and used as a charge for a cannon

grapes of wrath [fr. *The Grapes of Wrath* (1939), novel by John Steinbeck *b*1902, Am. novelist, fr. the line "He is trampling out the vintage where the *grapes of wrath* are stored", fr. *The Battle Hymn of the Republic* by Julia W. Howe †1910 Am. writer and reformer] : an unjust or oppressive situation, action, or policy that may inflame desire for vengeance : an explosive condition ⟨will the *grapes of wrath* come to another harvest —Stuart Chase⟩

grape stake *n* : a post used for supporting wires to which grapevines are tied in vineyards

grapestone \ˈ=,=\ *n* : a grape seed

grape sugar *n* : DEXTROSE

grape tree *n* **1** : GRAPE 2 **2** : SEA GRAPE 1b

grapevine \ˈ=,=\ *n* **1** : GRAPE 2 **2** [prob. so called fr. the grapevine's being thought of as a humble substitute for a telegraph line] **a** : RUMOR, REPORT; *esp* : one without foundation in fact ⟨it's all a nightmare, all a humbug and a bore; just another foolish ~ —*Atlantic*⟩ **b** *or* **grapevine telegraph** (1) : an informal means of circulating information, news, rumor, or gossip ⟨was logical to suppose that the neighborhood ~ would have had the story —Harold Sinclair⟩ ⟨the ~ had carried the news of their victory into every shop and home —Russell Whelan⟩ (2) : a means of spreading information obtained secretly or from private sources ⟨the workers hear by ~ a lot of the secrets of management —*Kiplinger Washington Letter*⟩ **3** : a figure-skating pattern traced by both skates **4** : a wrestling hold in which one or both arms or legs are twined about those of an opponent **5** : a sidewise waltz step in which one foot keeps crossing first before and then behind the other

grapevine knot *n* : BARREL KNOT b

grapevine moth *n* : an Australian moth (*Phalaenoides glycine*) having a greenish yellow black-marked caterpillar that feeds on grape leaves and fruits

grapevine knot

grapevine phylloxera *n* : PHYLLOXERA

grapevine twist *n* : a square dance in which the dancers move between successive couples of a set and then circle the woman and the man of each set in turn

grape wine *n* : a variable color averaging a dark reddish purple that is less strong than royal purple (sense 1), redder, lighter, and stronger than average plum (sense 6a), and redder and less strong than imperial or violet carmine

grapey *var of* GRAPY

¹graph \ˈgraf, -aa(ə)f, -aif, -áf\ *n* -S [short for *graphic formula*] **1** : a diagram (as a series of points, a line, a curve, an area) that represents the variation of a variable in comparison with that of one or more other variables ⟨a ~ showing the increase of population during the last 100 years⟩ **2** *of a mathematical function* : the collection of all points whose coordinates satisfy the given functional relation

²graph \"\ *vt* -ED/-ING/-S **1** : to represent or record by a graph **2** : to plot (as a curve from its equation) on a graph

³graph \"\ *n* -S [prob. fr. *-graph*] **1** : a spelling of a word **2** : a single occurrence of a letter of an alphabet in any of its various shapes (as D, d, *D*, *d*) **3** : a letter or combination of letters taken as a minimum unit in determining the phonemes of a language from written records — compare ALLOGRAPH 2, GRAPHEME

-graph \,graf, -aa(ə)f, -aif, -áf\ *n comb form* -S [MF *-graphe*, fr. L *-graphum*, fr. Gk *-graphon*, fr. neut. of *-graphos* written, writing (fr. *graphein* to write) — more at CARVE] **1** : something written ⟨crypto*graph*⟩ ⟨holo*graph*⟩ **2** : instrument for making or transmitting records ⟨chrono*graph*⟩ ⟨phono*graph*⟩ tele*graph*⟩

graph·eme \ˈgra,fēm\ *n* -S [³*graph* + *-eme*] **1** : a letter of an alphabet — compare ALLOGRAPH 2a, ³GRAPH 2 **2** : the sum of all written letters and letter combinations that represent one phoneme ⟨the *p* of *pin*, the *pp* of *hopping*, and the *gh* of *hiccough* are members of one ~⟩ — compare ALLOGRAPH 2b, ³GRAPH 3 — **gra·phe·mic** \(ˈ)graˈfēmik\ *adj* — **gra·phe·mi·cal·ly** \-mək(ə)lē\ *adv* — **gra·phe·mics** \-miks\ *n pl but usu sing in constr*

-grapher \grəfə(r), *sometimes* ,graf- *when there is a corresponding verb form in "-graph"*\ *n comb form* -S [LL *-graphus* one that writes (such) material or in (such) a way (fr. Gk *-graphos*, fr. *-graphos* written, writing) + E *-er*] : one that writes about (specified) material or in a (specified) way ⟨cranio*grapher*⟩

-graph·ia \ˈgrafēə\ *n comb form* -S [L — more at -GRAPHY] **1** : writing on a (specified) topic : representation of a (specified) object ⟨blasto*graphia*⟩ ⟨stomato*graphia*⟩ **2** : writing characterized by a (specified) psychological abnormality ⟨dys*graphia*⟩ ⟨pseud*agraphia*⟩

¹graph·ic \ˈgrafik, -fēk\ *also* **graph·i·cal** \-fəkəl, -fēk-\ *adj* [*graphic* fr. L *graphicus*, fr. Gk *graphikos*, fr. *graphein* to write + *-ikos* -ic; *graphical* fr. L *graphicus* + E *-al*] **1** : written, drawn, or engraved ⟨reproduction of the letters in ~ form —F.W.Goudy⟩ ⟨did not multiply with ~ symbols as we do —E.O.Winzerling⟩ **2 a** (1) : marked by clear and lively description or striking imaginative power ⟨its most ~ and beautiful stanzas —J.L.Lowes⟩ (2) : having the gift of clear and lively description ⟨a ~ writer⟩ **b** : sharply outlined or delineated ⟨plush buildings . . . which I saw as a ~ contrast to the slums —Ben Burns⟩ **3 a** : of or relating to the pictorial arts : pictorial or symbolic rather than verbal ⟨the natural distinction between literary and ~ art —Bliss Perry⟩ **b** : of, relating to, or involving such reproductive methods as those of engraving, etching, lithography, photography, serigraphy, and woodcut ⟨the etchings, drypoints, lithographs and engravings which together form his ~ work —*Brit. Book News*⟩ **c** : of or relating to the art of printing or the techniques associated with book production and communication by the printed word ⟨books considered as ~ rather than literary products —*Publishers' Weekly*⟩ **4** : of, relating to, or used for writing ⟨the ~ system of the Maya⟩ **5** : having mineral crystals resembling written or printed characters : exhibiting on the surface or in transverse section the appearance of such characters : having or displaying a rock fabric in which two minerals enclose each other by mutual intercrystallization **6** : of, relating to, or represented by graphs, diagrams, lines, or similar means : DIAGRAMMATIC ⟨chart a trend in ~ fashion —L.W. Hall⟩ **7** : of or relating to the written or printed word or the symbols or devices used in writing or printing to represent sound or convey meaning — **graph·i·cal·ly** \-fək(ə)lē, -fēk-, -li\ *adv* — **graph·ic·ness** \-fiknəs, -fēk-\ *n* -ES

²graphic \"\ *n* -S **1 a** : a product of graphic art (as a painting, watercolor, print) ⟨the ~*s* . . . include Chagall's graphic illustrations —Howard Devree⟩ **b graphics** *pl* : the graphic media ⟨~*s* and photography, the multiple arts; film, stage, and dance, the theatrical arts —*Museum of Modern Art Bull.*⟩ **2 a** : a picture, map, or graph used for illustration or demonstration ⟨these ~*s* embody widely accepted principles of visual education⟩ ⟨today, more and more, ~*s* are being used in company reports —*Jour. of Accountancy*⟩ **b graphics** *pl but sing in constr* : the art or science of representing a three-dimensional object on a two-dimensional surface according to mathematical rules of projection

-graph·ic \ˈ==\ *or* **-graph·i·cal** \ˈ===\ *adj comb form* [*-graphic* fr. LL *-graphicus*, fr. Gk *-graphikos*, fr. *graphikos* written; *-graphical* fr. LL *-graphicus* + E *-al*] **1** : written or transmitted in a (specified) way ⟨steno*graphic*⟩ ⟨tele*graphic*⟩ **2** : of or relating to writing in a (specified) field or on a (specified) subject ⟨bio*graphical*⟩ ⟨hagio*graphic*⟩

graphic accent *n* : ACCENT 5a

graphic arts *n pl* : the fine and applied arts of representation, decoration, and writing or printing on flat surfaces together with the techniques and crafts associated with each: as **a** : painting and drawing **b** : engraving, etching, lithography, photography, serigraphy, and woodcut **c** : writing and printing and the arts connected with bookmaking and other forms of publication

graphic formula *n* : STRUCTURAL FORMULA

graphic granite *n* : a light-colored intrusive rock having the quartz crystals so arranged in the feldspar as to appear in a transverse section like written characters — called also *Hebraic granite*, *pegmatite*, *runite*

graphic tellurium *n* : SYLVANITE

graphies *pl of* GRAPHY

-graphies *pl of* -GRAPHY

graphing *pres part of* GRAPH

graphis \ˈgrafəs, -rāf-\ *n*, *cap* [NL, fr. L, drawing, design, fr. LGk, painting, embroidery, fr. Gk, stylus, fr. *graphein* to write; fr. the appearance of the apothecia] : a genus (the type of the family Graphidaceae) of grayish white crustaceous lichens that occur on bark

¹graph·ite \ˈgra,fīt, *usu* -īd.+V\ *n* -S [G *graphit*, fr. Gk *graphein* to write + G *-it* -ite] **1** : a mineral consisting of soft black lustrous carbon that occurs both in hexagonal crystals and as foliated or granular massive, conducts electricity, and is used in lead pencils, crucibles, electrolytic anodes, as a lubricant, and as a moderator in atomic-energy plants (hardness 1–2, sp. gr. 2.09–2.23) — called also *black lead*, *plumbago*; see ELECTROGRAPHITE **2** : a dark grayish blue to dark bluish gray

²graphite \"\ *vt* -ED/-ING/-S : to coat or impregnate with graphite : GRAPHITIZE 2

graphite blue *n* : a blackish blue that is stronger than midnight and greener than Romany

gra·phit·ic \(ˈ)graˈfid·|ik, -fit|, |ēk\ *adj* : relating to, containing, derived from, or resembling graphite

graphitic carbon *n* : the portion of the carbon in iron or steel that is present as graphite — distinguished from *combined carbon*

graph·itiza·tion \,gra,fīd·əˈzāshən, -,fəd-\ *n* -S : the process of graphitizing

graph·itize \ˈ=fə,tīz, -,fīd-,īz\ *vb* -ED/-ING/-S *vt* **1** : to convert into graphite; *specif* : to anneal (cast iron or steel) so that some or all of the combined carbon is transformed into free carbon as graphite **2** : to impregnate or coat with graphite **3** : to cause graphite to form in; *specif* : to corrode and weaken (structural steel or cast-iron pipe) in service by heat so that combined carbon becomes graphite with resultant risk of metal failure ~ *vi* **1** : to become converted into graphite **2** : to cause graphite to form in a substance

graphitized carbon *n* : ELECTROGRAPHITE

graph·itoid \ˈgra,fīd-,ȯid, -,fə,tȯid\ *also* **graph·itoi·dal** \;gra-,fīd-ˈȯidᵊl, -fəˈtȯi-\ *adj* : resembling graphite

graph·i·um \ˈgrafēəm\ *n*, *cap* [NL, fr. L, stylus, fr. Gk *grapheion* pencil, paintbrush, fr. *graphein* to write — more at CARVE] : a form genus of imperfect fungi (family Stilbellaceae) with dark-colored coremia many of which (as the parasite of Dutch elm disease) have been determined to be conidial stages of members of the genus *Ceratostomella*

grapho- *comb form* [F, fr. MF, fr. Gk, fr. *graphē* writing, fr. *graphein* to write] : writing ⟨*grapho*logy⟩

graph·o·litha \,grafəˈlithə\ *n*, *cap* [NL, fr. *grapho-* + *-litha* (fr. Gk *lithos* stone)] : a genus of rather small moths (family Olethreutidae) having larvae that feed in various fruits or flower heads — see ORIENTAL PEACH MOTH

graph·o·log·i·cal \;==ˈläjəkəl\ *adj* : of or relating to graphology

gra·phol·o·gist \graˈfäləjəst\ *n* -S : a specialist in graphology

gra·phol·o·gy \-jē\ *n* -ES [F *graphologie*, fr. *grapho-* + *-logie* -logy] : the study of handwriting esp. for the purpose of character analysis ⟨if taken away from fortunetellers . . . ~ may yet become a useful handmaiden of psychology —*Time*⟩

graph·o·met·ric \;grafə;meˈtrik\ *or* **graph·o·met·ri·cal** \-rəkəl\ *adj* : of or relating to graphometry

gra·phom·e·try \graˈfämə·trē\ *n* -ES [F *graphométrie*, fr. *grapho-* + *-métrie* -metry] : the science of determining constants in handwritings

Graph·o·phone \ˈgrafə,fōn\ *trademark* — used for a phonograph using wax records

graph·or·rhea \,grafəˈrēə\ *n* -S [NL, fr. *grapho-* + *-rrhea*] : a symptom of motor excitement consisting in continual and incoherent writing

grapho·spasm \ˈgrafə + ,-\ *n* [ISV *grapho-* + *spasm*] : WRITER'S CRAMP

grapho·type \"+,-\ *n* [*grapho-* + *type*] : a form of chalk engraving — **grapho·typ·ic** \;==ˈtipik\ *adj*

graph paper *n* : paper ruled into small squares or otherwise for drawing graphs, plotting curves, or making diagrams

graphs *pl of* GRAPH, *pres 3d sing of* GRAPH

-graphs *pl of* -GRAPH

graphy \ˈgrafē, -fi\ *n* -ES [F *graphie* system of writing, fr. Gk *graphein* to write + F *-ie* -y] **1** : MATER LECTIONIS **2** : a variant spelling

-gra·phy \grəfē, -fi\ *n comb form* -ES [L *-graphia*, fr. Gk, fr. *graphein* to write + *-ia* -y — more at CARVE] **1** : writing or representation in a (specified) manner or by a (specified) means or of a (specified) object ⟨calli*graphy*⟩ ⟨carto*graphy*⟩ ⟨photo*graphy*⟩ ⟨steno*graphy*⟩ **2** : writing on a (specified) subject or in a (specified) field ⟨bio*graphy*⟩ ⟨geo*graphy*⟩ ⟨metallo*graphy*⟩

grap·nel \ˈgrapnəl\ *n* -S [ME *grapenel*, fr. (assumed) MF *grapinel*, dim. of MF *grapin*, dim. of *grape*, crape hook — more at GRAPE] **1** : GRAPPLE 1a **2** : a small anchor with four or five flukes or claws used in dragging or grappling operations and for anchoring a dory or skiff

grapnel 2

grap·pa \ˈgrä(,)pä\ *n* -S [It, fr. It dial. (Tuscany) *grappa* grape stalk, of Gmc origin; akin to MD *crappe* hook, OHG *krapfo*, *krāpfo* — more at CRAVE] : a dry usu. colorless Italian brandy made from the distilled residue of a wine press — compare MARC

grap·pi·er cement \ˈgrapē,ā-\ *n* [F *grappier*, fr. *grappe* cluster, bunch of grapes (fr. OF *grape* hook, grape stalk, bunch of grapes, grape) + *-ier* -er — more at GRAPE] : a cement made by grinding fine the lumps of underburned and overburned material left when a hydraulic lime is slaked

¹grap·ple \ˈgrapəl\ *n* -S [MF *grappelle*, dim. of *grappe*, *grape* hook — more at GRAPE] **1 a** : an instrument with iron claws designed to be thrown by a rope and formerly used esp. to fasten an enemy ship alongside before boarding **b** : GRAPNEL 2 **2** [²*grapple*] **a** : the act of grappling or the state of being grappled ⟨such scathful ~ did he make with the most noble bottom of our fleet —Shak.⟩ **b** : a hand-to-hand struggle ⟨rose . . . fresh from his fall and fiercer ~ joined —John Milton⟩ **c** : a contest for superiority or victory ⟨a final ~ with ecclesiastical tyranny —Edward Miall⟩ **3** : a bucket similar to a clamshell but having three or more jaws

²grapple \"\ *vb* **grappled**; **grappled**; **grappling** \-p(ə)liŋ\ **grapples** *vt* **1** : to seize, hold, or drag with or as if with a grapple ⟨wished to ~ this vessel and take it —Charlotte M. Yonge⟩ ⟨*grappled* the river bottom for broken chains —James Dugan⟩ **2** : to come to grips with : grasp with the hands : take hold of ⟨Junior, aged four, *grappling* the family mutt with a wrestler's stranglehold —*Springfield (Mass.) Daily News*⟩ ⟨*grappled* me to him with both arms . . . and hugged me —R.P.Warren⟩ **3** : to fasten, join, or bind with a close bond ⟨those friends thou hast, and their adoption tried, ~ them to thy soul with hoops of steel —Shak.⟩ ~ *vi* **1 a** : to fasten oneself firmly with or as if with a grapple ⟨the piece of ice we *grappled* to —Francis Smith⟩ **b** : to make fast one's ship by means of a grapple — used with *with* ⟨~ with the enemy's ships and board them —Edward Edwards⟩ **2** : to come to grips : engage in hand-to-hand encounter : contend in close combat ⟨*grappled* and commenced wrestling —John Doran⟩ ⟨*grappling* wildly with a big tough —Robert Westerby⟩ **3** : to move the hands in or as if in grasping : GROPE ⟨*grappled* about the floor among the dead bodies —Thomas Lodge⟩ **4** : to attempt to deal : COPE — used with *with* ⟨didn't ~ with any national problem until it was forced upon his attention —F.L. Allen⟩ ⟨many poets, playwrights and novelists have *grappled* with the subject —Howard Taubman⟩ **5** : to use a grapple (as in searching) ⟨*grappled* in deep water for the missing safe⟩ **syn** see WRESTLE

grapple dredge *n* : a dredger that operates with a clamshell, orange-peel, or other bucket

grapple fork *n* : HAYFORK

grapple plant *n* : an herb (*Harpagophytum procumbens*) of southern Africa having woody fruits with hooked or barbed thorns

grap·pler \ˈgrap(ə)lə(r)\ *n* -S : one that grapples: as **a** : GRAPPLE 1 **b** : WRESTLER

grapple shot *n* : a projectile used in lifesaving that has hinged claws designed to catch in a ship's rigging or to hold in the ground — called also *anchor shot*

grappling *n* -S **1 a** : GRAPPLE 1a **b** : GRAPNEL 2 **2** *archaic* : ANCHORAGE 3c

grappling iron *or* **grappling hook** *n* : a hooked iron for anchoring a boat, grappling ships to each other, or recovering sunken objects

grap·sid \ˈgrapsəd\ *adj* [NL *Grapsidae*] : of or relating to the family Grapsidae

grap·si·dae \-sə,dē\ *n pl*, *cap* [NL, fr. *Grapsus*, type genus + *-idae*] : a cosmopolitan family of crabs including pelagic and littoral and shore crabs as well as a few that have adapted to a strictly terrestrial or to a freshwater mode of life — see GRAPSUS

¹grap·soid \-,sȯid\ *adj* [NL *Grapsus* + E *-oid*] : resembling or related to the family Grapsidae

²grapsoid \"\ *n* -S : a grapsoid crab

grap·sus \-səs\ *n*, *cap* [NL, modif. of Gk *grapsaios* crab] : a genus (the type of the family Grapsidae) of crabs having a somewhat quadrilateral carapace, wide postabdomen, and short eyestalks

grap·to·lite \ˈgraptə,līt\ *n* -S [Gk *graptos* painted, written (fr. *graphein* to write) + E *-lite*] : any of numerous extinct colonial animals (group Graptolitoidea) that are known only as carbonized fossils from Upper Cambrian through Devonian rocks and that have zooids housed in small cups spaced along a chitinous support — compare GRAPTOLITOIDEA

grap·to·lith·i·da \,graptəˈlithədə\ [NL, fr. *Graptolithus* + *-ida*] *syn of* GRAPTOLITOIDEA

grap·to·li·thi·na \-p(,)tōləˈthīnə, -thēnə\ [NL, fr. *Graptolithus* + *-ina*] *syn of* GRAPTOLITOIDEA

grap·to·li·toi·dea \-ləˈtȯidēə\ *n*, *cap* [NL, fr. *Graptolitus*, genus of Graptolitoidea (alter. of *Graptolithus*, fr. Gk *graptos* painted, written + *lithos* stone) + *-oidea*] : a group of extinct animals of uncertain systematic rank and position formerly regarded as a division of Hydrozoa but now often placed in the Bryozoa or even associated with the pterobranchs in Hemichordata — see GRAPTOLITE

grap·to·zoa \,graptəˈzōə\ [NL, fr. Gk *graptos* written, painted + NL *-zoa*] *syn of* GRAPTOLITOIDEA

grapy *or* **grap·ey** \ˈgrāpē\ *adj* **grapier**; **grapiest** **1 a** : of or relating to grapes or the vine ⟨~ clusters⟩ **b** *usu grapey* : having a grape taste as well as a wine taste — used esp. of some wines made from native American grapes; compare FOXY **2** : affected with grapes

¹grasp \ˈgrasp, -aa(ə)-,-ai-,-á-\ *vb* -ED/-ING/-S [ME *graspen* — more at GRAB] *vi* **1** : to make the motion of seizing or trying to seize : CLUTCH — usu. used with *at* or *for* ⟨~*ing* for any support⟩ ⟨ready to ~ at straws⟩ **2** *obs* : EMBRACE, GRAPPLE — used with *with* or *about* ~ *vt* **1** : to clutch at : take or seize eagerly **2** : to seize and hold by clasping or embracing with or as if with the fingers or arms : take possession of ⟨thy hand is made to ~ a palmer's staff —Shak.⟩ ⟨~*ed* this moment to say —Edward Bok⟩ **3** : to lay hold of with the mind : COMPREHEND, UNDERSTAND ⟨failed to ~ the importance of the undertaking⟩ **syn** see TAKE

²grasp \"\ *n* -S **1 a** : something intended for grasping or to be grasped (as a handle or a fluke of an anchor) ⟨a sturdy shaft with the ~ roughened to keep the hand from slipping⟩ **b** : the handle of an oar **2** : an act or instance of grasping: as **a** : a hand grip **b** : EMBRACE **3** : forcible holding : POSSESSION, HOLD, CONTROL ⟨the whole space that's in the tyrant's ~ —Shak.⟩ **4 a** : the reach of the arms **b** : the power of seizing and holding ⟨success was almost within his ~⟩ **5** : mental hold or comprehension esp. when broad ⟨had a remarkable ~ of this complex subject⟩

grasp·able \-pəbəl\ *adj* : capable of being grasped : COMPREHENSIBLE, UNDERSTANDABLE ⟨a smooth ~ analysis of the situation⟩ — **grasp·able·ness** \-nəs\ *n* -ES — **grasp·ably** \-pəblē\ *adv*

grasp·er \-pə(r)\ *n* -S : one that grasps; *esp* : a grasping person

grasping *adj* **1** : being accustomed or used to grasp ⟨~ tongs⟩; *broadly* : tending to hold firmly : TENACIOUS ⟨~ roots that bind the soil⟩ **2** : desiring material possessions excessively or to such a degree as to overshadow propriety and fairness in dealings : urgently seeking wealth : AVARICIOUS **syn** see COVETOUS

grasp·ing·ly *adv* : in a grasping manner

grasp·ing·ness *n* -ES : the quality or state of being grasping

grasp·less \-pləs\ *adj* **1** : lacking the power of grasping : unable to seize and hold : relaxed as from weakness or fear ⟨the message slipped from her ~ hand⟩ — compare NERVELESS **2** : INCOMPREHENSIBLE

¹grass \ˈgras, -aa(ə)-,-ai-,-á-\ *n* -ES *often attrib* [ME *gras*, fr. OE *græs*; akin to OHG, ON, & Goth *gras* grass, OE *grōwan* to grow, and perh. to L *gramen* grass — more at GROW] **1 a** : green herbage that affords food for grazing animals and that usu. consists predominantly of narrow-leaved monocotyledonous plants of the families Gramineae, Cyperaceae, and Juncaceae often intermixed with various dicotyledonous herbs ⟨the moist spring has brought on a good growth of ~⟩ **b** *now chiefly dial* : a small herb; *esp* : one used medicinally **c** : a plant of the family Gramineae ⟨the bamboos include the largest ~*es* some of which attain a height of 120 feet⟩ **d** : any of various herbaceous plants with narrow linear foliage — used in combination; see BLUE-EYED GRASS **e** (1) : ASPARAGUS (2) *slang* : a leafy vegetable; *esp* : LETTUCE **2 a** : GRAZING ⟨~ enough to keep a cow⟩ : land set apart or available for grazing **b** : land on which grass is grown for hay or pasture : PASTURE, MEADOW, LEA **3** *obs* : the vegetative condition of a cereal before the ear of grain is developed **4** : a leaf or plant of grass — now used only in pl. ⟨hair tangled with ~*es* and twigs⟩ **5** : ground covered with growing grass ⟨keep off the ~⟩ ⟨dropped his bundles on the ~⟩ **6** *now dial* : the season at which grass springs into growth : SPRING **7** : a state or place of retirement (as from cares, responsibilities, or privileges) ⟨would like to go to ~ for a month or so⟩ ⟨has been at ~ for several years⟩ **8** : GRASS SPONGE **9** : electronic noise on a radarscope that takes the form of vertical lines resembling lawn grass

²grass \"\ *vb* -ED/-ING/-ES *vt* **1 a** : to provide (as cattle) with grass for food : furnish with pasture : GRAZE ⟨pasture to ~ 30 head⟩ **b** : to feed (livestock) on grass without grain or other concentrates **2 a** : to cover with grass ⟨it is easier but more expensive to ~ a lawn with turfs⟩; *esp* : to seed to grass ⟨decided to ~ the north 40 that year⟩ — often used with *down* ⟨~*ed* down the newly cleared land with rye grass and white clover⟩ **b** : to lay with turfs **3** : to spread (as linen for bleaching) on the grass **4** : to bring or knock to the ground : FELL ⟨~*ed* his opponent with a well-placed blow⟩; *esp* : to shoot (a game bird) down or land (a fish) on the bank of a stream ~ *vi* **1** : to produce grass — often used with *up* ⟨the new lawns are ~*ing* up well⟩ **2** *Brit, of a compositor* : to do temporary or casual work : SUB

grassation *n* -S [L *grassation-*, *grassatio*, fr. *grassatus* (past part. of *grassari* to go about, attack, rage against) + *-ion-*, *-io* -ion; akin to L *gradi* to step, go — more at GRADE] *obs* : an act of attacking violently; *also* : a lying in wait to attack

grass bass *n* : LARGEMOUTH BLACK BASS

grass beef *n* : beef from grass-fed animals

grass-bird \ˈ=,=\ *n* : any of numerous birds associated with open grassy country: as **a** : SANDPIPER; *esp* : PECTORAL SANDPIPER **b** (1) : FERNBIRD (2) : a closely related Australian bird (*Megalurus gramineus*) **c** : a small warbler (*Sphenoeacus afer*) of southern Africa

grass-blade \ˈ≈,≈\ *n* **:** one of the elongated linear leaves of a typical grass
grass bug *n* **:** any of numerous true bugs (as members of the family Miridae) that feed chiefly on grasses
grass bur *n* **:** BUR GRASS
grass captain *n, dial* **:** an aboveground supervisory employee of a mine
grass cattle *n* **:** cattle for beef that are finished on grass
grass character *n* [trans. of Chin (Pek) *ts'ao*^{3} *tzŭ*^{4}] **:** one of the irregular cursive characters of a style of Chinese and Japanese writing for business and private use
grasschat \ˈ≈,≈\ *n* [^{1}*grass* + *chat* (bird)] **:** WHINCHAT
grass cloth *n* [trans. of Chin (Pek) *hsia*^{4} *pu*^{4}] **:** a lustrous, plain, and usu. loosely woven textile made chiefly in the Orient from various grass or other vegetable fibers and used chiefly for garments and table linens; *esp* **:** such a cloth woven from ramie fibers
grass court *n* **:** a lawn-tennis court with a playing surface of turf — compare HARD COURT
grass crab *n* **:** a shallow-water spider crab (*Macrocoeloma trispinosum*) brownish in color, covered with short velvety hairs, and common alongshore from No. Carolina to Brazil — called also *sponge crab*
grasscut \ˈ≈,≈\ *n* [trans. of Hindi *ghāskhodā, ghāskātā*] **:** a servant attached to a party traveling in India who is responsible for cutting fodder for the animals of the party
grass cut *vb, slang* **:** HEDGEHOP
grass cutter *n* **1 :** one that cuts grass: as **a :** GRASSCUT **b :** a machine or device for cutting grass (as a lawn mower or a scythe) **2** *slang* **a :** a hard-hit baseball that skims the ground ⟨sent a *grass cutter* to the shortstop who fumbled it⟩ **b :** a low-flying airplane
grass cutting *n, slang* **:** HEDGEHOPPING
grass dance *n* **:** a strenuous male Indian show dance in which the dancers sometimes wear a bunch of grass at their belts
grass drake *n* **:** CORNCRAKE
grass egg *n* **:** an egg with a dark or greenish yolk that results when a hen feeds too freely on grasses or other green foods
grass·er \-sə(r)\ *n* -s **1 :** a beef animal marketed direct from the pasture or range without supplementary feeding **2 :** a calfskin or kip taken from an underfed animal and characterized by coarseness of grain
gras·se·rie \ˌgras(ə)ˈrē, ˌgräs-, ˈ≈sərē\ *n* -s [F, fr. *gras* fat (fr. L *crassus*) + *-erie* -ery — more at HURDLE] **:** a destructive polyhedrosis disease of silkworms that is related to wilt and is marked by spotty yellowing of the skin and internal liquefaction — called also *jaundice*
grasses *pl of* GRASS, *pres 3d sing of* GRASS
gras·set \graˈsā\ *n, pl* **grassets** \-ā(z)\ [LaF, fr. F, chubby, plump, fr. *gras* fat] *Louisiana* **:** any of several small plump songbirds formerly used for food; *esp* **:** CHEWINK
gras·se·yé \ˌgrasəˌyā, -sēˌā\ *adj* [F, fr. past part. of *grasseyer* to use a uvular *r*, fr. MF, fr. *gras* fat] *of r* **:** pronounced as a uvular fricative; *broadly* **:** pronounced as either a uvular fricative or trill — **gras·seye·ment** \ˌgra,sāˌmäⁿ\ *n* -s
grass family *n* **:** GRAMINEAE
grass-fat \ˈ≈,≈\ *adj, of livestock* **:** fattened only on pasture **:** not finished in a drylot or with supplementary feeding
grass-feed \ˈ≈,≈\ *vi* **:** to feed on herbage **:** use or require a diet primarily made up of grasses ~ *vt* **:** to feed (as cattle) on grass; *esp* **:** to finish (beef cattle) for market on pasture
grass fern *n* **:** an epiphytic tropical American fern (*Vittaria lineata*) with narrow linear fronds in pendent tufts; *broadly* **:** any of several other ferns of the genus *Vittaria*
grass finch *n* **1 :** VESPER SPARROW **2 :** any of various weaverbirds; *esp* **:** an Australian member of the genus *Poephila*
grassflower \ˈ≈,≈\ *n* **1 :** SPRING BEAUTY **2 :** BLUE-EYED GRASS
grass frog *n* **:** any of several frogs of semiterrestrial habits: as **a :** a common European frog (*Rana temporaria*) **b :** PICKEREL FROG
grass green *n* **1 :** a variable color averaging a strong yellowish green that is yellower and duller than shamrock green or Cyprus green **2 :** a moderate yellow green that is greener, lighter, and stronger than average moss green, yellower and deeper than average pea green, and yellower and darker than apple green (sense 1)
grass-grown \ˈ≈,≈\ *adj* **:** overgrown with grass
grass-grub \ˈ≈,≈\ *n* **1 :** a small shiny brown New Zealand cockchafer (*Odontria zealandica*) that feeds on grass; *specif* **:** its root-eating larva that is a very destructive pest of turf **2 :** CORBIE
grass gum *n* **:** GRASS TREE 1
grass hand *n* **1** *Brit* **:** a compositor on casual or job work **:** SUB **2** [trans. of Chin (Pek) *ts'ao*^{3} *shon*^{3}] **:** the style of Chinese and Japanese writing that uses grass characters
grass hare *n* **:** an African steppe hare (*Poelagus marjorita* or *Lepus marjorita*) of the uplands of Uganda
grass hook *n* **:** a sickle with a smooth blade
grass·hop \ˈ≈,häp\ *vi* [back-formation fr. *grasshopper*] **:** to move erratically from place to place
^{1}**grasshopper** \ˈ≈,≈≈\ *n* [ME *grasshoppere*, fr. *gras* grass + *hopper*] **1 :** any of numerous plant-eating orthopterous insects (suborder Saltatoria) having the hind legs adapted for leaping, biting and chewing mouthparts, stridulating organs in the males and rarely in the females, incomplete metamorphosis, and usu. wings as adults and being serious pests of plant life both because of their relatively large size and great numbers and in some areas because of their habit of engaging in migratory flights in which whole regions may be stripped of vegetation — see ACRIDIDAE, TETTIGONIIDAE; KATYDID, LONG-HORNED GRASSHOPPER, SHORT-HORNED GRASSHOPPER **2 :** a small firework that jumps about **3 :** an early locomotive with a vertical boiler and cylinders **4 :** a light unarmed scouting and liaison airplane used esp. for helping to direct field-artillery fire
^{2}**grasshopper** \"\ *vi* -ED/-ING/-S **1 :** to fish with a natural or artificial grasshopper for bait **2 :** to move a riverboat over shallows or sandbars by means of poles suggesting stilts
^{3}**grasshopper** \"\ *adj* **1 :** suggesting the grasshopper in appearance or action ⟨a ~ plow⟩ ⟨a ~ type of counterbalance⟩ **2 :** light and frivolous **:** untouched by care for the future ⟨a ~ brain⟩
grasshopper hawk *n* [so called fr. the fact that it feeds on grasshoppers] **:** SPARROW HAWK
grasshopper indian *n, usu cap G&I* **:** UTE
grasshopper lark *n* **:** a grasshopper warbler (*Locustella naevia*)
grasshopper mouse *n* **:** a mouse of a genus (*Onychomys*) of stoutly built short-tailed insectivorous mice of western No. America that are closely related to the white-footed mice
grasshopper plow *n* **:** a shallow-set plow formerly used for breaking sod in the prairie regions of No. America
grasshopper sparrow *n* **:** any of several small American sparrows constituting the genus *Ammodramus; esp* **:** a common sparrow (*A. savannarum pratensis*) of eastern No. America having a yellow patch on the front edge of the wing and a song that resembles the stridulation of grasshoppers
grasshopper warbler *n* **:** any of several Old World warblers constituting the genus *Locustella; esp* **:** a common European warbler (*L. naevia*)
grasshouse \ˈ≈,≈\ *n* **1** *obs* **:** a grassman's cottage **2** *or* **grass hut :** a habitation constructed mainly or largely of grass
grass·ie \ˈgrasē, -raas-,-rais-,-räs-\ *n* -s [^{1}*grass* + *-ie*] *Austral* **:** RED-BACKED PARROT
grassier *comparative of* GRASSY
grassiest *superlative of* GRASSY
grass ill *n* **:** a digestive disorder of young lambs caused by too suddenly starting full feeding on grass
grass·i·ness \-sēnəs, -sin-\ *n* -ES **:** grassy quality; *also* **:** an expanse of grass or turf ⟨the shady ~ beneath the old hickories⟩
grassing *pres part of* GRASS
grass itch mite *n* **:** an Australian trombiculid mite (*Acomatacarus australiensis*) that lives on grasses and bites man and domestic animals and that sometimes becomes a serious pest in suburban areas
grassland \ˈ≈,≈\ *n, often attrib* **1 :** farmland occupied chiefly by grasses and other forage plants (as clovers), used chiefly for grazing and hay, and often made a part of the regular cultural rotation — compare LEA **2 a :** land on which the natural dominant plant forms are grasses and forbs — often used in pl. ⟨the ~s of the West⟩; compare PRAIRIE, SAVANNA, TUNDRA **b :** an ecological community in which the prevailing or characteristic plants are grasses and similar plants
grassland buttercup *n* **:** a New Zealand crowfoot (*Ranunculus multiscapus*) with one-flowered scapes
grassland daisy *n* **:** a New Zealand herb (*Brachycome sinclairii*) with purplish or whitish flowers — compare SWAN RIVER DAISY
grassland farming *n* **:** a system of farming in which grass is the basic crop taken from the land whether as a direct cash crop or as a source of income through further processing (as by feeding cattle)
grass-leaved \ˈ≈ˌ≈\ *also* **grassy-leaved** \ˌ≈≈ˈ≈\ *adj* **:** having long narrow leaves that resemble blades of grass ⟨a *grass-leaved* orchid⟩
grass·less \ˈ-ləs\ *adj* **:** lacking grass and usu. bare and barren ⟨shabby ~ yards⟩
grasslike \ˈ≈,≈\ *adj* **:** resembling a grass esp. in having long slender leaves
grass lily *n* **:** an Australian herb (*Dichopogon strictus*) of the family Liliaceae with grasslike leaves and blue flowers
grass line *n* **:** a coir rope
grass linen *n* **:** grass cloth woven of ramie
grass·man \ˈ≈mən, -ˌman\ *n, pl* **grass·men** [ME *grasman*, fr. *gras* grass + *man*] **1** *obs Scot* **:** COTTER **2 :** an officer formerly in charge of grassland in the north of England
grass·mann's law \ˈgra|smənz, -raa|, -rai|, -rä|, -rä|\ *n, usu cap G* [after Hermann G. *Grassmann* †1877 Ger. mathematician & Sanskritist] **:** a statement of certain regular changes exhibited by Indo-European voiced aspirates in Sanskrit and Greek: when the aspirates occur at the beginning of successive syllables one of them, usu. the first, loses its aspiration and becomes in Greek a voiceless stop and in Sanskrit a voiced stop — compare GRIMM'S LAW
grass mat *n* **:** a woven mat simulating trimmed grass and used esp. to form backgrounds for displays or theatrical scenery
grass mildew *n* **:** a powdery mildew (*Erysiphe graminis*) that frequently attacks cereals and other grasses
grass moth *n* **:** any of numerous moths of the family *Pyralididae* including several whose larvae are destructive pests on lawn grasses — see GRASS WEBWORM
grass mouse *n* **1 :** a meadow mouse (*Microtus agrestis*) **2 :** a striped mouse (*Lemniscomys striatus*) of the African veldt
grassnut \ˈ≈,≈\ *n* **1 :** PEANUT **2 :** a California brodiaea (*Brodiaea laxa*) with purplish blue or rarely white funnel-shaped flowers borne in clusters on a tall scape, linear leaves, and a deep-seated edible corm
grass-of-par·nas·sus \-ˌpärˈnasəs,-(ˌ)päˈ-\ *n, often cap P* [fr. *Parnassus*, mountain in Greece] **:** a plant of the genus *Parnassia*
grass onion *n, dial* **:** CHIVE 1 — usu. used in pl.
grass owl *n* **:** a rather large long-legged owl (*Tyto longimembris*) that lives in tall grass and is widely distributed from India and southern China to northern Australia and Fiji
grass parrakeet *n* **:** any of numerous small Australian parrots; *esp* **:** BUDGERIGAR
grass parrot *n* **:** GRASS PARRAKEET; *esp* **:** any of several small brightly marked parrots (genera *Psephotus* and *Neophema*) — compare RED-BACKED PARROT
grass pea *n* **1 :** an Old World pea (*Lathyrus sativus*) grown in some warm areas chiefly for forage **2 :** the white wedge-shaped seed of the grass pea used as food for man in India and for stock elsewhere
grass pickerel *n* **1 :** a small dark-banded pickerel (*Esox vermiculatus*) of quiet weedy waters esp. of central No. America — called also *little pickerel, mud pickerel* **2 :** CHAIN PICKEREL
grass pike *n* **1 :** ^{4}PIKE 1a **2 :** CHAIN PICKEREL
grass pink *n* **1 :** a European pink (*Dianthus plumarius*) that is often cultivated for its very fragrant usu. pink or rosy flowers **2 :** DEPTFORD PINK **3 :** an orchid of the genus *Calopogon* (esp. *C. pulchellus*)
grassplot *also* **grassplat** \ˈ≈,≈\ *n* **:** a plot of ground covered with grass
grass plover *n* **:** UPLAND PLOVER
grass poly *n* **:** a glabrous annual loosestrife (*Lythrum hyssopifolia*) with small solitary pink flowers that is prob. native to Europe but is widely naturalized in moist areas — called also *hyssop loosestrife*
grass pondweed *n* **:** a No. American submerged aquatic plant (*Potamogeton foliosus*) with slender grasslike leaves
grass porgy *n* [so called fr. its living in eelgrass] **:** a small sparid fish (*Calamus arctifrons*) of the Florida coast
grassquit \ˈ≈,≈\ *n* [^{1}*grass* + *quit* (bird)] **:** any of several very small tropical American and West Indian finches of *Tiaris* and certain closely related genera
grass rooter \ˈ≈ˈrüd·ə(r), -ˈrü|, |tə-\ *n* **:** one that belongs to or is concerned with the grass roots
grass roots \ˈ≈ˈ≈\ *n pl but sing or pl in constr* [^{1}*grass* + *roots*] **1 :** soil at or near the surface ⟨ore was found at the *grass roots*⟩ **2 a :** the farming and rural districts of a country as distinguished from the industrial and urban **b :** the people of these districts when constituting or acting as a fundamental politico-economic group and a source of independent popular opinion **3 :** the very foundation or source ⟨attack a problem at the *grass roots*⟩ **:** the fundamental part **:** BASIS ⟨the *grass roots* of political organization⟩
grass rope *n* **:** a rope made of any vegetable fiber other than cotton — compare GRASS LINE
grass rug *n* **:** a floor covering woven from strands of a tough slender marsh grass with a cotton warp and usu. decorated with stenciled patterns
grass sack *n, Midland* **:** a burlap bag **:** GUNNYSACK
grass sandwort *n* **:** a Rocky mountain sandwort (*Arenaria formosa*) with narrow grasslike leaves
grass shears *n pl* **:** shears designed primarily for clipping grass neatly in difficult spots (as along the edges of walks, flower beds, borders)

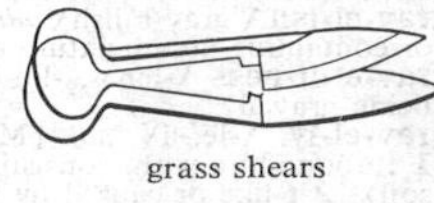
grass shears

grass shrimp *n* **1 :** any of several slender shrimps (genus *Hippolyte*) common among eelgrass along the Pacific coast of No. America **2 :** a small transparent freshwater shrimp (genus *Palaemonetes*) of the southeastern U.S. that is often used as bait by fishermen
grass sickness *also* **grass disease** *n* **:** a frequently fatal disease of grazing horses that is characterized by more or less complete interruption of normal gastrointestinal functioning with difficulty in swallowing, interruption of peristalsis, and fecal impaction and that is held to be caused by a poisonous plant or insect consumed with the forage or by an atypical form of botulism
grass silage *n* **:** silage made from young grasses or legumes and rich in protein but commonly requiring addition of acid or of a supplementary source of carbohydrate to ensure proper fermentation
grass skirt *n* **:** a skirt worn by women of some Pacific islands and made of native grasses or split leaves that hang loosely from a band; *also* **:** an imitation of this skirt
grass snake *n* **1 :** a common European ringed snake (*Natrix natrix*) **2 :** SMOOTH GREEN SNAKE **3 :** GARTER SNAKE; *esp* **:** one with indistinct or no stripes **4 :** BROWN SNAKE
grass snipe *n* **:** PECTORAL SANDPIPER
grass sorghum *n* **:** a leafy sorghum (as Sudan grass) cultivated esp. for hay or green feed
grass spider *n* **:** any of various spiders that spin concave webs on grass which are conspicuous when covered with dew; *esp* **:** a common No. American spider (*Agalena naevia*)
grass sponge *n* **:** a brittle usu. dark brown often very large inferior commercial sponge (*Spongia graminea*) occurring in the Gulf of Mexico, in the West Indies, and off the Florida coast
grass tetany *or* **grass staggers** *n* **:** a disease of cattle (as milch cows) marked by tetanic staggering, convulsions, coma, and frequently death and caused by reduction of blood calcium and magnesium when overeating on lush pasture — compare MILK FEVER
grass thrips *n* **:** a cosmopolitan thrips (*Anaphothrips obscurus*) esp. destructive to the developing inflorescence of grasses
grass tree *n* **1 :** any of several Australian arborescent plants (genus *Xanthorrhoea*) that yield acaroid resins; *esp* **:** a plant (*X. hastilis*) with a short woody stem crowned by a crowded tuft of long leaves **2 :** AUSTRALIAN GRASS TREE 2 **3 :** any of several Australasian trees with grasslike foliage: as **a :** a ti (*Cordyline australis*) **b :** LANCEWOOD **c :** a Tasmanian evergreen tree (*Richea pandanifolia*) with tapering slender leaves 3 to 5 feet long
grass-tree gum *n* **:** ACAROID RESIN; *esp* **:** the red variety of it
grassveld \ˈ≈,≈\ *n* [Afrik *grasveld*, fr. *gras* grass + *veld* field] **:** natural grassland of southern Africa
grass vetch *or* **grass vetchling** *n* **:** an annual European vetch (*Lathyrus nissolia*) with minute stipules and crimson flowers
grass warbler *n* **:** any of various small brownish Old World warblers esp. of the genera *Cisticola* and *Locustella*
grass webworm *n* **:** any of numerous small grubs that are the larvae of grass moths and that spin webs around the base and roots of the grasses on which they feed
grassweed \ˈ≈,≈\ *n* **:** EELGRASS 1
grass whip *n* **:** a long-handled grass cutter usu. having a straight blade at right angles to the handle and being used instead of a sickle to avoid stooping
grass widow *n* **1** *chiefly dial* **a :** a discarded mistress or common-law wife **b :** a woman who has had an illegitimate child **2 a :** a woman divorced or separated from her husband **b :** a woman whose husband is temporarily away from her — **grass·wid·ow·hood** \(ˈ)≈ˈ≈≈,≈\ *n*
grass widower *n* **1 :** a man divorced or separated from his wife **2 :** a man whose wife is temporarily away from him
grasswork \ˈ≈,≈\ *n* **1** *obs* **:** LAWN **2** *dial Eng* **:** mine work done at the surface **3 :** craftwork (as mats or basketry) made of grass
grassworm \ˈ≈,≈\ *n* **:** any of various moth larvae that are destructive to grass; *specif* **:** FALL ARMYWORM
grasswort \ˈ≈,≈\ *n* **:** a perennial mouse-ear chickweed (*Cerastium arvense*) widespread in Europe, Asia, and No. America and often cultivated for its large white flowers — called also *starry grasswort*
grass wrack *n* **:** EELGRASS 1
grass-wren \ˈ≈,≈\ *n* **:** any of several small Australian warblers
grassy \ˈgrasē, -raas-,-rais-,-räs-, -si\ *adj* -ER/-EST **1 a :** covered or abounding with grass ⟨a ~ lawn⟩ **b :** consisting of, relating to, or having a flavor or odor of grass ⟨~ fare⟩ ⟨~ butter⟩ **2 :** fed on grass ⟨~ sheep⟩ **3 :** resembling grass in color
grassy death camas *n* **:** a death camas with narrow leaves like blades of grass and racemes of greenish yellow flowers that is a source of livestock poisoning in parts of the northwestern U.S. and is considered a variety of the common death camas (*Zigadenus venenosus*) or made a separate species (*Z. gramineus*)
grassy-leaved *var of* GRASS-LEAVED
grat *past of* GREET
^{1}**grate** \ˈgrāt, *usu* -ād.+V\ *n* -s [ME, fr. ML *grata, crata*, modif. of L *cratis* latticework, hurdle — more at HURDLE] **1 a** *archaic* **:** an enclosing railing often of ornately wrought iron **b** *obs* **:** CAGE, PRISON **2 :** a frame containing parallel or crossed bars forming an open latticework, permitting the passage of light, air, liquid, or sound, and commonly used to prevent unwanted ingress or egress (as of persons to or from a building) or passage (as of solids into a conduit for liquids) ⟨beautifully wrought ~s over the lower windows⟩ ⟨dislodging a heavy sewer ~⟩ **3 a :** a frame, bed, or basket of iron bars for holding fuel while it is burning **b :** FIREPLACE **c :** an open latticed or barred frame for cooking over a fire **4 :** a screen or sieve for use with stamp mortars for grading ore

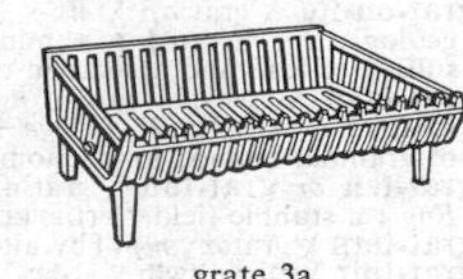
grate 3a

^{2}**grate** \"\ *vt* -ED/-ING/-S **1** *obs* **:** IMPRISON **2 :** to furnish with a grate ⟨~ a furnace⟩ **:** protect with a grating or bars ⟨~ an opening⟩
^{3}**grate** \"\ *vb* -ED/-ING/-S [ME *graten*, fr. MF *grater* to scratch, scrape, of Gmc origin; akin to OHG *krazzōn* to scratch — more at SCRATCH] *vt* **1** *archaic* **:** to scrape or rub roughly or harshly **:** ABRADE — sometimes used with *down* or *away* **2 :** to reduce to small particles by rubbing with something rough or indented ⟨~ a nutmeg⟩ **3 a :** FRET, IRRITATE, OFFEND ⟨news, my good lord, from Rome . . . ~s me —Shak.⟩ **b** *obs* **:** to get by importunity or by extortion **4 a :** to gnash or grind (one's teeth) so as to produce a harsh discordant sound **b :** to cause to make such a sound ⟨*grated* the car into gear⟩ **c :** to utter (as speech) in a harsh voice ⟨*grating* an angry reply as he turned aside⟩ ~ *vi* **1 :** to rub roughly against something so as to produce harsh discordant sound ⟨the gears *grated* into place⟩ ⟨footsteps *grating* on the gravel⟩ **:** CREPITATE, RASP, GRIND **2 a** *obs* **:** to make unreasonable or burdensome demands **:** give offense by oppressive demands or importunity — usu. used with *upon* **b** *obs* **:** to dwell irritatingly — used with *upon* **c :** to produce an irritating effect **:** PERTURB, DISTRESS, ANNOY — used with *on* or *upon* ⟨such language ~s upon me⟩ ⟨his harsh voice *grated* on our ears⟩
^{4}**grate** *n* -s [ME, fr. *graten*, v.] *obs* **:** a device for grating something **:** GRATER
grate·ful \ˈgrātfəl\ *adj, sometimes* **gratefuller;** *sometimes* **gratefullest** [obs. E *grate* pleasing, thankful (fr. L *gratus* pleasing, beloved, worthy of thanks, grateful) + *-ful* — more at GRACE] **1 a :** appreciative of benefits received **:** willing or anxious to acknowledge and repay or give thanks for benefits ⟨a ~ heart⟩ **b :** expressing or induced by gratitude ⟨a ~ word of thanks⟩ ⟨a ~ acknowledgment⟩ **2 a :** affording pleasure or contentment **:** PLEASING ⟨such doctrines are only ~ to the abstruse scholar⟩ **b :** pleasing by reason of comfort supplied or discomfort alleviated ⟨glad to rest under the ~ shade of the elms⟩ ⟨the fire threw a ~ warmth into the room⟩ **syn** see PLEASANT
grate·ful·ly \-fəlē, -li\ *adv* **:** in a grateful manner
grate·ful·ness *n* -ES **:** the quality or state of being grateful ⟨~ for such a favor⟩
grate·less \-ləs\ *adj* [^{1}*grate* + *-less*] **:** having no grate ⟨a ~ heater⟩
grat·er \ˈgrād·ə(r), -ātə-\ *n* -s [ME *gratere*, fr. *graten* to grate + *-ere* -er — more at GRATE] **:** one that grates; *esp* **:** a machine or device used for reducing material (as a nutmeg or a turnip) to small bits by rubbing or abrading
grate room *n* [^{1}*grate*] **:** a fire chamber below a glass-manufacturing furnace
gratewise \ˈ≈,≈\ *adv* [^{1}*grate* + *-wise*] **:** in the manner or form of a grate ⟨bars piled ~⟩
gra·tic·u·la·tion \grəˌtikyəˈlāshən\ *n* -s [F *graticuler* to make graticules (fr. *graticule*) + E *-ation*] **:** the division of a design or draft into squares to facilitate enlargement or reduction
grat·i·cule \ˈgrad·ə̇ˌkyül\ *n* -s [F, fr. L *craticula* fine latticework, dim. of *cratis* latticework, hurdle — more at HURDLE] **1 :** a design or draft prepared by graticulation **2 a :** a scale on glass or other transparent material in the focal plane of a telescope or other optical instrument for the location and measurement of objects **b :** the network of lines of latitude and longitude upon which a map is drawn

grater

grat·i·fi·able \ˈgrad·əˌfīəbəl, -atə-, ˌ≈≈ˈ≈≈≈\ *adj* **:** capable of being gratified **:** suitable for gratification ⟨such a wish is perfectly reasonable and ~⟩
grat·i·fi·ca·tion \ˌgrad·əfəˈkāshən, -atə-\ *n* -s [MF or L; MF, fr. L *gratification-, gratificatio*, fr. *gratificatus* (past part. of *gratificari* to gratify) + *-ion-, -io* -ion] **1 a :** an act or instance of gratifying **b :** the state of being gratified **2** *archaic* **:** REWARD, RECOMPENSE; *esp* **:** GRATUITY **3 :** a source of gratification **:** something that pleases ⟨his success is a great ~ to me⟩ **4** *obs* **:** expression of gratification (as by prayer or worship)

grat·i·fied·ly \ˈ==,fīədlē, -li, ,==ˈ===, ˈ==,fīd-\ *adv* **:** in a gratified manner **:** with gratification

grat·i·fi·er \ˈ==,fī(ə)r, -īə\ *n* -s **:** one that gratifies

grat·i·fy \ˈgrad·ə,fī, -atə-\ *vt* -ED/-ING/-ES [MF *gratifier*, fr. L *gratificari*, fr. *gratus* pleasing, grateful + *-ificari* -ify — more at GRACE] **1 a** *obs* **:** to show gratitude to (a person) or for (as a service) **:** REQUITE **b** *archaic* **:** REMUNERATE, FEE **2 :** to give or be a source of pleasure or satisfaction to ⟨beauty *gratifies* the eye⟩: as **a :** to confer a favor on **:** OBLIGE ⟨the rulers *gratified* the people with subsidies and circuses⟩ **b :** to give rein to **:** INDULGE ⟨determined to ~ his whim⟩ **3** *obs* **a :** to receive or greet with pleasure **:** WELCOME **b :** GRACE, ADORN **syn** see PLEASE

gratifying *adj* **:** tending or able to gratify **:** PLEASING, SATISFYING ⟨received a very ~ reception⟩ ⟨found their praise ~⟩ **syn** see PLEASANT

grat·i·fy·ing·ly \ˈ==,===, ,==ˈ===\ *adv* **:** in a gratifying manner ⟨~, such cases have been the exception —Gerda Luft⟩

gra·til·li·ty *also* **gra·til·i·ty** \graˈtiləd·ē\ *n* -ES [by alter.] *archaic* **:** GRATUITY

grat·in \ˈgratᵊn, -ät-\ *n* -s [F, fr. MF, fr. *grater* to scratch, scrape — more at GRATE] **:** a brown crust formed upon a gratinated dish; *also* **:** a dish with such a crust

grat·i·nate \ˈgratᵊn,āt\ *vt* -ED/-ING/-S [F *gratiner* (fr. *gratin*) + E *-ate*] **:** to cook with a covering of buttered crumbs or grated cheese until a crust or crisp surface forms

gra·ti·né \ˌgratᵊnˌā, -ät-\ *adj* [F, fr. past part. of *gratiner*] *of a food* **:** having a covering or crust (as of buttered crumbs or grated cheese)

grat·ing \ˈgrād·|iŋ, -āt|, |ēŋ\ *n* -s [¹*grate* + *-ing*] **1 :** a partition, covering, or frame of parallel bars or crossbars **:** a latticework resembling a window grate **:** GRATE 2 **2 a :** a strong usu. wooden lattice used on shipboard in fair weather to cover a hatch and still admit light and air **b :** a movable lattice used for flooring (as of a boat) **c gratings** *pl* **:** the openwork metal floors and platforms of an engine room and boiler room in a ship **3 :** a system of close equidistant and parallel lines or bars (as ruled on a polished surface) used for producing spectra by diffraction

grat·ing·ly *adv* [fr. pres. part. of ³*grate* + *-ly*] **:** with a grating sound or effect **:** so as to grate ⟨his voice fell ~ on our ears⟩

gra·ti·o·la \grəˈtīələ, -tēə-\ *n*, *cap* [NL, dim. of L *gratia* grace; fr. its alleged healing qualities — more at GRACE] **:** a genus of small widely distributed herbs (family Scrophulariaceae) with opposite sessile leaves and usu. two bracts at the base of the calyx — see HEDGE HYSSOP

gratis \ˈgra|d·əs, -rā|, |təs\ *adv* (*or adj*) [ME, fr. L *gratis*, *gratiis*, ablative pl. of *gratia* favor, kindness — more at GRACE] **:** without charge or recompense **:** FREE — often used in combination as an intensive ⟨got it free ~⟩ ⟨free ~ for nothing⟩

grat·i·tude \ˈgrad·|ə,tüd, -at|, |ə,tyüd\ *n* -s [ME (Sc dial.), fr. MF or ML; MF, fr. ML *gratitudo*, fr. L *gratus* pleasing, thankful + *-i-* + *-tudo* -tude — more at GRACE] **1** *obs* **:** FAVOR, GIFT, GRATUITY **2 :** the state of being grateful **:** warm and friendly feeling toward a benefactor prompting one to repay a favor **:** THANKFULNESS ⟨let us express our ~ positively⟩

grat·on·ite \ˈgratᵊn,īt\ *n* -s [Louis C. *Graton* b1880 Am. geologist + E *-ite*] **:** a mineral $Pb_9As_4S_{15}$ consisting of sulfide of lead and arsenic in rhombohedral crystals

grat·tage \graˈtäzh, grəˈ-\ *n* -s [F, fr. *gratter* to scratch, scrape (fr. MF *grater*) + *-age* — more at GRATE] **:** the removal of granulations (as in trachoma) by scraping or by friction

grat·ten *or* **grat·ton** \ˈgratᵊn\ *n* -s [origin unknown] *dial Eng* **:** a stubble field **:** STUBBLE

grat·ters \ˈgratəz\ *n pl* [by alter.] *Brit* **:** CONGRATULATIONS

grat·toir \(ˈ)graˌtwär, -at-ˌw-\ *n* -s [F, fr. *gratter* to scratch, scrape, fr. MF *grater* — more at GRATE] **:** THUMB FLINT

gratuital *adj* [L *gratuitus* + E *-al*] *obs* **:** GRATUITOUS

gra·tu·i·tous \grəˈtüəd·|əs, grəˈtyü-, -üət|\ *adj* [L *gratuitus*, fr. *gratus* pleasing, grateful — more at GRACE] **1 a :** given freely or without recompense **:** granted without pay or without claim or merit ⟨the ~ blessings of Heaven —Roger L'Estrange⟩ **b :** costing the recipient or participant nothing **:** FREE ⟨homemade fun is ~ —Aldous Huxley⟩ **c :** not involving a return benefit, compensation, or consideration — opposed to *onerous*; see GRATUITOUS BAILMENT, GRATUITOUS CONTRACT **2 :** not called for by the circumstances ⟨a ~ insult⟩ **:** adopted or asserted without good ground ⟨a ~ assumption⟩ — **gra·tu·i·tous·ly** *adv* — **gra·tu·i·tous·ness** *n* -ES

gratuitous bailment *n* **:** a bailment for the sole benefit of the bailor

gratuitous contract *n* **:** a contract for the sole benefit of one of the parties

gra·tu·i·ty \|ē, |i\ *n* -ES [MF *gratuité*, fr. L *gratuitus* + MF *-té* -ty] **1 a :** graciousness esp. of manner or conduct **:** courteous consideration ⟨her manner completely lacking in ~⟩ **b :** an act of graciousness **:** a graceful courtesy ⟨all sorts of little *gratuities* of behavior —Elizabeth Bowen⟩ **2 :** something given voluntarily or over and above what is due usu. in return for or in anticipation of some service: as **a** *chiefly Brit* (1) **:** a cash sum given a soldier when he reenlists, retires, or is honorably discharged (2) **:** a lump sum paid in addition to pension to a retiring employee esp. under civil service **b :** ⁸TIP **c :** a payment intended to influence a person in the payer's behalf usu. improperly **:** BRIBE **d :** a payment made to a released convict in order to help him reestablish himself in society and sometimes in lieu of wages for labor performed in prison **e :** DEATH BENEFIT **3** *obs* **:** payment made or due for services **:** WAGES **4 :** the quality or state of being gratuitous

grat·u·lant \ˈgrachələnt\ *adj* [L *gratulant-*, *gratulans*, pres. part. of *gratulari*] **:** showing gratification **:** CONGRATULATORY

¹**grat·u·late** \-,lāt\ *vb* -ED/-ING/-S [L *gratulatus*, past part. of *gratulari*, fr. *gratus* pleasing, thankful — more at GRACE] *vt* **1** *archaic* **:** to salute with declarations of joy **:** CONGRATULATE **2** *obs* **:** to show thankfulness for or to **:** GRATIFY, REPAY, RECOMPENSE **~** *vi*, *archaic* **:** to express sympathetic pleasure or satisfaction

²**gratulate** *adj* [L *gratulatus*, past part.] *obs* **:** GRATIFYING, PLEASING

grat·u·la·tion \ˌgrachəˈlāshən\ *n* -s [ME *gratulacyon*, fr. L *gratulation-*, *gratulatio*, fr. *gratulatus* + *-ion-*, *-io* -ion] **1 a :** GRATIFICATION, SATISFACTION, PLEASURE **b :** expression of gratification (as by ceremonial rejoicings) — usu. used in pl. **2 a :** CONGRATULATION **b :** words of congratulation **:** a congratulatory address **3** *obs* **a :** expression of gratitude **:** THANKS **b :** REWARD

grat·u·la·to·ri·ly \ˌgrachələˌtōrəlē\ *adv* **:** in a gratulatory manner **:** with gratulation

grat·u·la·to·ry \ˈ===,tōrē\ *adj* [LL *gratulatorius*, fr. L *gratulatus* + *-orius* -ory] **:** expressing or characterized by gratulation; *esp* **:** CONGRATULATORY

grau·pel \ˈgraüpəl\ *n* -s [G, dim. of *graupe* peeled grain, groat, prob. of Slavic origin; akin to Pol, Slovak, Serbo-Croatian, Russ, & Ukr *krupa* peeled grain, groat; akin to OE *hrēof* rough, scabby, leprous — more at DANDRUFF] **:** granular snow pellets — called also *soft hail*

grau·stark \ˈgraü,stärk, ˈgrò,s-\ *n* -s *usu cap* [fr. *Graustark*, an imaginary country in the romantic novel *Graustark* (1901) by George B. McCutcheon †1928 Am. novelist] **1 :** an imaginary place of high romance ⟨a *Graustark* located on the old Spanish invasion route where the Christians and Moslems fought it out in the Dark and Middle Ages —Alva Johnston⟩ **2** [fr. the novel *Graustark*] **:** a highly romantic piece of writing ⟨his trip through the West had a coloration of *Graustark* —Bernard DeVoto⟩ ⟨pure *Graustark* —Wolcott Gibbs⟩ — **grau·stark·ian** \(ˈ)=ˌstärkēən\ *adj*, *usu cap*

gra·va·men \grəˈvāmən, -ˈväm-; ˈgrävəm-, ˈgravəm-\ *n*, *pl* **gravamens** \-nz\ *or* **gra·vam·i·na** \-ˈvamənə, -ˈvām-, -ˈväm-\ [LL, fr. L *gravare* to burden, fr. *gravis* heavy — more at GRIEVE] **:** GRIEVANCE: as **a** *obs* **:** a formal complaint **b :** a grievance laid in convocation by the lower house before the upper house; *also* **:** the writing embodying it **c :** the material part or basis (as of a grievance or charge)

gravaminous *adj* [LL *gravamin-*, *gravamen* + E *-ous*] *obs* **:** OPPRESSIVE, GRIEVOUS

gra·vat \ˈgravət\ *chiefly Scot var of* CRAVAT

grav·a·ta \ˌgravəˌtä\ *n* -s [Pg *gravatá*, *caravatá*, fr. Tupi *caravatá*, *curuwatá*] **:** a tough resistant cordage fiber obtained from the leaves of a So. American bromeliad (*Ananas sagenaria*) that is closely related to the cultivated pineapple

¹**grave** \ˈgrāv\ *vb* **graved** \-vd\ **grav·en** \-vən\ *or* **graved**; **graving**; **graves** [ME *graven*, fr. OE *grafan*; akin to OHG & Goth *graban* to dig, ON *grafa*, OSlav *pogreti* to bury] *vt* **1** *archaic* **:** DIG, EXCAVATE **2 a :** to carve out or give shape to by cutting with a chisel **:** SCULPTURE ⟨they *graved* the figure of a calf⟩ **b :** to carve or cut (as letters or figures) on some hard substance **:** ENGRAVE ⟨*graved* the date of his death on the blank space on the stone⟩ **c :** to remove (some portion of a printing surface) by cutting (as with a burin) — used with *out* ⟨~ out the redundant comma⟩ **3 :** to impress (as a thought) deeply **:** fix indelibly ⟨you could do worse than ~ his noble words in your mind⟩ **~** *vi* **1** *archaic* **:** EXCAVATE, DIG **2 a :** CARVE 2 **b :** to practice engraving

²**grave** \ˈ"\ *n* -s [ME, fr. OE *græf*; akin to OHG *grab* grave, ON *gröf*; derivatives fr. the root of OE *grafan* to dig] **1 a :** an excavation in the earth for use as a place of burial; *broadly* **:** a place of interment **:** TOMB, SEPULCHER **b :** a final ending (as by death or destruction) ⟨the ~ comes to all men⟩ ⟨the ~ of all our hopes⟩ **2 a** *obs* **:** an excavated pit, ditch, or trench **b** *now dial Eng* **:** a storage clamp; *esp* **:** one dug partly into the ground

³**grave** \ˈ"\ *n* -s [ME, fr. MD *grāve*, *grēve* — more at BURGRAVE] **1** *obs* **:** STEWARD, OVERSEER **2 :** a former elective township officer in Yorkshire and Lincolnshire, England

⁴**grave** \ˈ"\ *vt* -ED/-ING/-S [ME *graven*] **:** to clean (the bottom of a wooden ship) of encrusting growths and treat with pitch — see GRAVING DOCK

⁵**grave** \ˈ", *in sense 6* " *or* ˈgräv *or* ˈgrav\ *adj* -ER/-EST [MF, fr. L *gravis* heavy — more at GRIEVE] **1 a** *obs*, *of a person* **:** occupying a position of consequence and dignity **b** *obs* **:** based on knowledge and understanding **:** AUTHORITATIVE **c :** deserving serious consideration or thought **:** IMPORTANT, WEIGHTY ⟨a ~ issue⟩ **d** (1) **:** involving or resulting in serious consequences **:** likely to produce real harm or damage ⟨a ~ wrong⟩ ⟨ran a very ~ risk⟩ (2) **:** very serious **:** dangerous to life — used of an illness or its prospects ⟨a ~ disease⟩ ⟨a ~ prognosis⟩ **2 :** having a serious, sedate, and dignified appearance or demeanor ⟨watching his ~ face⟩ ⟨a ~ man little given to anger⟩ **3** *archaic* **:** of great weight **:** HEAVY **4 :** dull in color **:** SOMBER, SOBER, DRAB ⟨the ~ plain dress of the countryfolk⟩ **5** *of a sound* **:** low in pitch — contrasted with *acute* **6 a** *of an accent mark* **:** having the form ` **b :** marked with a grave accent ⟨a ~ *e* in caffè⟩ **c :** of the variety indicated by a grave accent ⟨a ~ intonation⟩ **syn** see SERIOUS

⁶**grave** \ˈgräv, -ä-,-á-\ *n* -s **:** a grave accent used to show that a vowel is pronounced with a fall of pitch (as in ancient Greek), that a vowel has a certain quality (as over *e* in French), that a final *e* is stressed and close and that a final *o* is stressed and open (as in Italian), that a syllable has a degree of stress between maximum and minimum (as in phonetic transcription), or that the *e* of the English ending *-ed* is in a line of poetry not silent but is to be pronounced \ə\ for the sake of the meter (as in "this cursèd day")

⁷**gra·ve** \ˈgrä(,)vā, -rá(-\ *adv* (*or adj*) [It, heavy, grave, fr. L *gravis*] **:** slowly and solemnly — used as a direction in music

grave blanket *n* [²*grave*] **:** a grave covering that consists of evergreen plant material on a flexible wire frame and that is used chiefly in winter

grave box *n*, *dial* **:** COFFIN 2

gravecloth \ˈ=,=\ *n* **:** SUDARIUM

graveclothes \ˈ=,=\ *n pl* **:** the clothes in which a dead person is buried

graved *past of* GRAVE

gravedigger \ˈ=,==\ *n* **1 a :** one that digs graves esp. as a means of livelihood **b :** one that is responsible for the end of something ⟨~*s* of modern civilization⟩ **2 a :** BURYING BEETLE **b** an Asiatic ratel (*Mellivora indica*)

gra·ve·do \grəˈvē(,)dō\ *n* [L, fr. *gravis* heavy — more at GRIEVE] *archaic* **:** cold in the head

grave goods *n pl* **:** objects (as weapons, ornaments, tools) that are found buried with the dead in prehistoric graves

¹**grav·el** \ˈgravəl\ *n* -s *often attrib* [ME, fr. MF *gravele*, fr. OF, dim. of *grave*, *greve* pebbly ground, pebbly shore, perh. of Celt origin; akin to MBret *grouanenn* sand, W *gro* — more at GRIT] **1** *obs* **:** SAND **2 a :** loose or unconsolidated material consisting wholly or chiefly of rounded fragments of rock ranging in size from 2 millimeters to a meter or more in diameter — compare CONGLOMERATE, SAND **b :** a stratum of such material or a surface (as of a walk) covered with such material **3 :** a light grayish yellowish brown that is yellower and paler than almond brown and stronger than Cuban sand — called also *meerschaum* **4 a :** a deposit of small calculous concretions in the kidneys and urinary bladder **b :** the condition of having such a deposit

²**gravel** \ˈ"\ *vb* **graveled** *or* **gravelled**; **graveled** *or* **gravelled**; **graveling** *or* **gravelling** \-v(ə)liŋ\ **gravels** *vt* **1 :** to cover or spread with gravel **2 a :** to put at a loss **:** PERPLEX, CONFUSE, NONPLUS ⟨completely ~*ed* by his sister's reasoning⟩ **b :** IRRITATE, ANNOY, EMBARRASS, BOTHER ⟨those recurrent minor frictions that ~ the soul⟩ ⟨used to ~ her by saying that no great poet ever had such a loyal friend —Christopher Morley⟩ **3 :** to lame (a horse) by gravel lodged between the shoe and foot **~** *vi* **1** *dial* **:** to dig in gravel ⟨a dog ~*ing* for a bone⟩ **2** *of a bird* **:** to replenish the crop with gravel **3** *of rock* **:** to wear down to gravel

³**gravel** \ˈ"\ *adj* **:** harsh and usu. irritating — used chiefly of the human voice

gravel-bind \ˈ==,=\ *n* **:** FIELD BINDWEED

gravel-blind \ˈ==,=\ *adj* **:** having very weak vision **:** being almost blind — compare SAND-BLIND

gravel chickweed *n* **:** KNAWEL

gravel culture *n* **:** the growing of plants in an artificial medium using fine gravel to support the roots and supplying mineral nutrients in an aqueous solution

grave·less \ˈgrāvləs\ *adj* [²*grave* + *-less*] **:** lacking a grave: **a :** lacking usual interment **:** UNBURIED ⟨these ~ bones⟩ **b :** not requiring graves **:** DEATHLESS ⟨the ~ home of the blessed⟩

gravel-grass \ˈ==,=\ *n* **:** CLEAVERS

grav·el·ish \ˈgrav(ə)lish\ *adj* **:** somewhat gravelly **:** resembling or containing an admixture of gravel ⟨a barren ~ soil⟩

grav·el·li·ness \-lēnəs, -lin-\ *n* -ES **:** the quality or state of being gravelly

grav·el·ly \-lē, -li\ *adj* [ME *gravely*, fr. ¹*gravel* + *-ly*] **1 :** abounding with, consisting of, or containing gravel ⟨a ~ soil⟩ **2 :** like or caused by gravel (sense 4) ⟨a ~ paroxysm⟩ **3 :** harsh and usu. irritating or unpleasant **:** GRAVEL — used esp. of the human voice

gravel plant *n* **:** ARBUTUS 3

gravelrash \ˈ==,=\ *n* **:** abrasion of the skin by gravel or other rough surface

gravel roofing *n* **:** built-up roofing covered with gravel embedded in a bituminous surface

gravelroot \ˈ==,=\ *n* **1 :** MARSH MILKWEED **2 :** HORSE BALM 1

gravel stop *n* **:** a metal flashing shape attached to roof structure to protect the roof edge against water penetration and to contain a built-up roof and prevent its gravel surface from falling over the roof edge

gravelweed \ˈ==,=\ *n* **1 :** an American herb (*Verbesina helianthoides*) **2 :** BUSH HONEYSUCKLE 1 **3 :** CLEAVERS **4 :** a false gromwell (*Onosmodium virginicum*)

grave·ly \ˈgrāvlē, -li\ *adv* [⁵*grave* + *-ly*] **1 :** in a grave manner **:** with sober serious mien ⟨thanked him ~⟩ ⟨quietly and ~ reviewing our situation⟩ **2 :** to a grave degree **:** so as to cause distress, harassment, suffering **:** SERIOUSLY ⟨a ~ impaired heart⟩ ⟨in the midst of plenty millions of people remain ~ underfed⟩

grave marker *n* **:** a marker (as of metal or stone) placed on a grave to identify the person buried there

gra·ve·men·te \ˌgrävəˈmen·(,)tā\ *adv* [It, adv. of *grave* heavy, grave — more at GRAVE] **:** GRAVE — used as a direction in music

grave mixture *n* [⁵*grave*] **:** a compound pipe-organ stop sounding the lower harmonics and somber in effect

graven *past part of* GRAVE

grave·ness \ˈgrāvnəs\ *n* -ES [⁵*grave* + *-ness*] **:** the quality or state of being grave **:** SOBERNESS, SEDATENESS, SERIOUSNESS

graven image *n* [ME] **:** an object of worship carved usu. from wood or stone **:** IDOL

graveolence *also* **graveolency** *n*, *pl* **graveolences** *also* **graveolencies** [L *graveolentia*, fr. *graveolent-*, *graveolens* + *-ia* -y] *obs* **:** a strong and offensive smell

gra·ve·o·lent \grəˈvēələnt\ *adj* [L *graveolent-*, *graveolens*, fr. *gravis* heavy + *olent-*, *olens*, pres. part. of *olēre* to smell — more at GRIEVE, ODOR] **:** having a rank smell

grave plant *n* [²*grave*] **:** THORN APPLE 2

grave-post \ˈ=,=\ *n* **:** a post set up at a grave in memory and honor of the dead esp. among primitive peoples — compare GRAVESTONE

¹**grav·er** \ˈgrāvə(r)\ *n* -s [ME, fr. *graven* to dig, carve, engrave + *-er* — more at GRAVE] **:** one that graves: as **a :** ENGRAVER, SCULPTOR **b :** any of various cutting or shaving tools (as an engraver's burin) used in graving or in hand metal turning **c :** a small prehistoric tool of stone or bone used for working or marking stone, bone, ivory, horn, or pottery

²**graver** *comparative of* GRAVE

grave robber *n* **:** one that breaks open a grave to obtain interred valuables or to remove the body (as for illicit dissection) **:** a body snatcher **:** GHOUL

¹**graves** *pres 3d sing of* GRAVE, *pl of* GRAVE

²**graves** \ˈgrāvz\ *archaic var of* GREAVES

³**graves** \ˈgräv\ *n*, *pl* **graves** \-vz\ *usu cap* [fr. *Graves*, district in Gironde dept., France] **:** a red or white table wine produced in Graves, France

graves' disease \ˈgrāvz(əz)-\ *n*, *usu cap G* [after Robert J. *Graves* †1853 Ir. physician] **:** HYPERTHYROIDISM; *specif* **:** EXOPHTHALMIC GOITER

graveside \ˈ=,=\ *n* **:** the space beside a grave; *esp* **:** the point at which mourners gather by the grave at the time of a burial ⟨only ~ services were held⟩

gravest *superlative of* GRAVE

gravestone \ˈ=,=\ *n* [ME, fr. *grave* + *stone*] **:** a stone laid over or erected near a grave and usu. bearing an inscription to identify and preserve the memory of the dead **:** TOMBSTONE

gra·vette \grəˈvet\ *or* **gravette point** *n* -s [fr. La *Gravette*, France, where it was found] **:** a small sharp prehistoric flint tool consisting of a blade like that of a knife with a very sharp point, a straight back, and a groove following one entire margin

gra·vett·ian \grəˈved·ēən\ *adj*, *usu cap* [La *Gravette*, rock shelter in the Couze valley of the Dordogne, France + E *-ian*] **:** of or relating to an Upper Paleolithic culture widespread in Europe and typified by a narrow pointed-blade tool with a straight blunted back edge

grave·ward \ˈgrāvwə(r)d\ *or* **grave·wards** \-dz\ *adv* (*or adj*) [²*grave* + *-ward*, *-wards*] **:** toward or directed toward the grave

grave wax *n*, *archaic* **:** ADIPOCERE

graveyard \ˈ=,=\ *n*, *often attrib* [²*grave* + *yard*] **1 :** a yard or enclosure for the interment of the dead **:** CEMETERY **2 a :** an organization or situation that brings something to an end ⟨the Ministry of Agriculture (that ~ of English political reputations) —Roy Lewis & Angus Maude⟩ ⟨a bill lost in one of the ~ committees of the legislature⟩ **b :** a place where disused, obsolete, or worn-out equipment is stored or held in reserve for emergency use; *esp* **:** a yard where old automobiles are stored or broken up for parts and scrap **3 a :** a melancholy and romantically gloomy place ⟨a ~ school of poetry⟩ **b :** a dull or unpleasing place

graveyard shift *n* **:** a work shift beginning late at night (as 12 o'clock) and being usu. the third and last of a business day; *also* **:** the workers on such a shift

graveyard stew *n*, *slang* **:** toast and milk

graveyard vote *n* **:** a vote improperly cast in the name of a person who has died or who is ineligible (as by having moved away) to vote

graveyard watch *n* **1 :** MIDWATCH **2 :** GRAVEYARD SHIFT

graveyard weed *also* **graveyard spurge** *n* **:** CYPRESS SPURGE

gravi- *comb form* [MF, fr. L, fr. *gravis* — more at GRIEVE] **:** heavy ⟨*gravigrade*⟩ ⟨*gravi*portal⟩

gravi·cembalo \ˌgravə+\ *n*, *pl* **gravicembali** [It, alter. (influenced by *grave* heavy, grave) of *clavicembalo* — more at CLAVICEMBALO] **:** HARPSICHORD

grav·id \ˈgravəd\ *adj* [L *gravidus*, fr. *gravis* heavy — more at GRAVE] **1 a :** PREGNANT ⟨a ~ woman⟩; *esp* **:** distended by pregnancy ⟨the ~ uterus⟩ **b :** full of eggs ⟨a ~ tapeworm proglottid⟩ **:** having the body distended with ripe eggs ⟨stripping the eggs from ~ salmon⟩ **2 :** FILLED, DISTENDED — usu. followed by *with* ⟨physics is ~ with metaphysics —V.C. Aldrich⟩ ⟨~ with middle-class proprieties⟩ **3 :** awaiting or indicating the approach of something (as an ominous or distressing event) **:** PORTENTOUS ⟨clouds . . . going from white at the blue-sky edge to a ~ indigo —T.H.White b.1906⟩ — **grav·id·ly** *adv* — **grav·id·ness** *n* -ES

grav·i·da \ˈgravədə\ *n*, *pl* **gravidas** \-dəz\ *also* **gravi·dae** \-,dē\ [L, fr. fem. of *gravidus*] **:** a pregnant woman — often used in combination with a term or figure to indicate the number of pregnancies a woman has had ⟨a 4-*gravida*⟩ ⟨a ~ four⟩ ⟨a quadri*gravida*⟩; compare PARA — **gra·vid·ic** \(ˈ)graˌvidik, grəˈv-\ *adj*

gravidation *n* -s [ME *gravidacioun*, fr. LL *gravidatus* (past part. of *gravidare*, to impregnate, fr. L *gravidus*) + ME *-ioun* -ion] *obs* **:** PREGNANCY

gra·vid·i·ty \grəˈvidəd·ē, grəˈv-\ *n* -ES [L *graviditas*, fr. *gravidus* pregnant + *-itas* -ity] **:** PREGNANCY, PARITY

gra·vied \ˈgrāvēd, -vid\ *adj* **:** covered or dressed with gravy ⟨~ beef and onions⟩ ⟨helped himself to another mound of well-*gravied* potatoes⟩

gravies *pl of* GRAVY

gra·vif·ic \(ˈ)graˌvifik, grəˈv-\ *adj* [*gravi-* + *-fic*] **:** able or tending to produce weight — used of a hypothetical ethereal fluid formerly postulated to explain gravitation

gra·vig·ra·da \grəˈvigrədə, ˌgravəˈgrādə\ *n pl*, *cap* [NL, fr. *gravi-* + *-grada* (fr. *gradi* to step, go) — more at GRADE] *in some classifications* **:** a division of the Edentata consisting of the ground sloths

grav·i·grade \ˈgravə,grād\ *n* [*gravi-* + *-grade*] **:** any of several large heavy-footed mammals (as an elephant); *esp* **:** GROUND SLOTH

gravilea *var of* GREVILLEA

gra·vim·e·ter \grəˈvimәd·ə(r), graˈv-, ˈgravə,mēd-\ *n* [F *gravimètre*, fr. *gravi-* + *-mètre* -meter] **1 :** a device similar to a hydrometer for determining the specific gravity of liquid or solid substances **2 :** a sensitive weighing instrument that measures the variation in the gravitational field by detecting small differences in the weight of a constant mass at different points (as on the earth or sea)

grav·i·met·ric \ˌgravəˌme·trik\ *also* **grav·i·met·ri·cal** \-rəkəl\ *adj* [*gravi-* + *-metric*, *-metrical*] **1 :** of, involving, or relating to measurement by weight **:** measured by weight ⟨a ~ assay of a drug⟩ **2 :** of or relating to variations in the gravitational field determined by means of a gravimeter — **grav·i·met·ri·cal·ly** \-rək(ə)lē\ *adv*

gravimetric analysis *n* **:** chemical analysis in which the amounts of the constituents are determined by weighing

gravimetric density *n* **:** the mean density of the total contents including the air in the interstitial spaces of any volume filled with a granular substance (as gunpowder)

gra·vim·e·try \grəˈvimə·trē, graˈv-\ *n* -ES [*gravi-* + *-metry*] **:** the measurement of weight or density

grav·ing \ˈgrāviŋ\ *n* -s [ME, fr. gerund of *graven* to dig, to grave — more at GRAVE] **1** *archaic* **:** the act of one that graves **2 :** something graved; *esp* **:** ENGRAVING

graving dock *n* [fr. gerund of ⁴*grave*] **:** a dry dock consisting of an enclosure openly adjoining a waterway from which it may be separated by a watertight barrier which is capable of being pumped dry when so separated and which is used esp. for cleaning the underwater parts of a ship; *broadly* **:** DRY DOCK

graving piece *n* [fr. gerund of ⁴*grave*] **:** a piece of wood for insertion in a plank of a ship to replace a defective part

graving tool *n* [fr. gerund of ¹*grave*] **:** GRAVER b

gravi·portal \ˌgravə+\ *adj* [*gravi-* + *-portal* (fr. L *portare* to carry + E *-al*) — more at FARE] **:** having the body supports adapted to the bearing of great weights ⟨the elephant is a ~ mammal⟩

gravis \ˈgravəs, -äv-,-áv-\ *adj* [L, heavy, grave, severe — more at GRIEVE] **:** tending to be more than averagely virulent — used esp. of strains of diphtheria bacilli; compare INTERMEDIUS, MITIS

gravit- or **gravito-** *comb form* [ISV, fr. *gravity*] **:** gravity ⟨*gravito*chemical⟩

grav·i·tate \'gravə,tāt, *usu* -ād·+V\ *vb* -ED/-ING/-S [NL *gravitatus*, past part. of *gravitare*, fr. L *gravitas* weight — more at GRAVITY] *vi* **1 :** to obey the law of gravitation **:** exert a force or pressure or tend to move under the influence of gravitation **2 a :** to tend in a direction or toward an object ⟨the conversation *gravitated* toward politics⟩ **b :** to move casually but inexorably as though under an external force ⟨the boys *gravitated* together while the girls sat waiting⟩ **:** become attracted ⟨as children ~ toward home at dusk⟩ ~ *vt* **:** to move by gravitation: as **a :** to agitate (as gravel in diamond mining) so that the weighty parts settle to the bottom **b :** to cause or allow to flow by gravity ⟨the oil is *gravitated* through a pipeline⟩

grav·i·tat·er \-ād·ə(r)\ *n* -S **:** one that gravitates

grav·i·ta·tion \,gravə'tāshən\ *n* -S [NL *gravitation-, gravitatio*, fr. *gravitatus* + L *-ion-, -io* -ion] **1 :** an action or a process of gravitating ⟨delivery of irrigation water under ~⟩ **2 :** a tendency toward or state of being drawn to something ⟨universal ~ to quantitative, statistical, numerical description —Hugh Miller b. 1891⟩ **3 :** a force manifested by acceleration toward each other of two free material particles or bodies or of radiant-energy quanta as if they were particles (as in the bending of rays of starlight passing close to the sun), these effects being attributed in relativity theory to the physical property of space according to which moving bodies follow minimum space-time tracks that are sensibly concave toward nearby massive bodies and that apparently constrain the motions of smaller bodies encompassed by them **:** an attraction between two bodies that is proportional to the product of their masses, inversely proportional to the square of the distance between them, and independent of their chemical nature or physical state and of intervening matter

grav·i·ta·tion·al \¦==¦tashənᵊl, -shnəl\ *adj* **:** of, relating to, or caused by gravitation ⟨sufficient energy to escape from the sun's ~ field —J.G.Davies⟩ — **grav·i·ta·tion·al·ly** \-ᵊlē, -əlē, |i\ *adv*

gravitational astronomy *n* **:** CELESTIAL MECHANICS

gravitational constant *n* **:** CONSTANT OF GRAVITATION

gravitational field *n* **:** a region associated with any distribution of mass in which gravitational forces due to that mass may be detected

gravitational intensity *n* **:** a vector quantity related to the condition at any point under gravitational influence the measure of which is the gravitational force exerted upon a unit mass placed at the point in question — compare GRAVITATIONAL POTENTIAL

gravitational potential *n* **:** the scalar quantity characteristic of a point in a gravitational field whose gradient equals the intensity of the field and equal to the work required to move a body of unit mass from given point to a point infinitely remote

gravitational system *n* **:** a system of physical units based upon a unit of force that is the weight of a unit mass under a specified standard of gravity

gravitational water *n* **:** FREE WATER c

grav·i·ta·tive \'gravə,tād·|iv, -,təl, |t|, |ēv\ *adj* **:** of, caused by, or relating to gravity or gravitation ⟨high mountains on the borders of the present continents, through their local ~ attraction, raise the sea level on their borders —P.G. Worcester⟩

grav·i·tom·e·ter \,gravə'tämədə(r)\ *n* [*gravit-* + *-meter*] **:** a direct-reading instrument for the measurement of specific gravities of solids, liquids, or gases

¹grav·i·ty \'gravəd·ē, -ətē, -i\ *n* -ES [MF or L; MF *gravité*, fr. L *gravitat-, gravitas*, fr. *gravis* heavy, grave + *-tat-, -tas* -ty — more at GRIEVE] **1 :** the quality or state of being grave: as **a :** sobriety or seriousness of character or demeanor ⟨men of ~ and learning —Shak.⟩ **b :** IMPORTANCE, SIGNIFICANCE, DIGNITY; *esp* **:** SERIOUSNESS ⟨the ~ of an offense⟩ **c** *obs* **:** INFLUENCE, AUTHORITATIVENESS **d** *obs* — used as a title of respect or honor **e :** SOLEMNITY ⟨the ~ of the ceremony⟩ **2** *archaic* **:** something serious **:** a matter of importance **3 :** PONDERABILITY **4 :** WEIGHT, HEAVINESS — now used chiefly in the phrase *center of gravity* **5** [NL *gravitas*, fr. L] **a :** terrestrial gravitation **:** the gravitational attraction of the earth's mass for bodies at or near its surface as modified by the centrifugal force due to the earth's rotation; *broadly* **:** GRAVITATION **b :** ACCELERATION OF GRAVITY **c :** SPECIFIC GRAVITY

²gravity \"\ *adj* **1 :** using gravity **:** working or operated by gravity ⟨~ irrigation⟩ **2 :** utilizing thermal convection currents instead of a fluid circulated by mechanical means ⟨a ~ hot-air heating system⟩ ⟨~ ventilation⟩

gravity anomaly *n* **:** a difference between the locally observed and the theoretically calculated value of gravity that reflects local variations in density of underlying rocks and is often helpful in geophysical prospecting

gravity band *n* **:** BALANCING BAND

gravity cell *n* **:** a voltaic cell with a zinc electrode in zinc sulfate solution at the top and a copper electrode in copper sulfate solution at the bottom, the two liquids being kept from mixing by difference in specific gravity

gravity dam *n* **:** a dam so proportioned that it will resist overturning and sliding forces by its own weight

gravity fault *n* **:** NORMAL FAULT

gravity feed *n* **:** the supplying of a material (as oil to a bearing or gasoline to a carburetor) by gravity alone; *also* **:** a device or system for such supplying ⟨a carburetor with a *gravity feed*⟩

gravity hinge *n* **:** a hinge used esp. with shutters or blinds that because of gravity locks in the open position

gravity knife *n* **:** a switchblade knife in which the blade is sprung by a downward snap of the wrist

gravity meter *n* **:** GRAVIMETER 2

gravity railroad *or* **gravity railway** *n* **:** a railroad on which the cars run by gravity down slopes after being hauled up shorter but steeper inclines by stationary engines

gravity spring *n* **:** a spring in which the water issues solely in response to the direct action of gravity

gravity wave *n* **:** a wave propagated in the surface layers of water or other liquid because of the tendency of gravity to maintain a uniform level; *also* **:** a wave in a fluid (as the atmosphere) in which gravity is the restoring force

gravity wind *n* **:** a katabatic wind

gravity yard *n* **:** HUMP YARD

gra·vure \grə'vyů(ə)r, grā'v-, -ůə\ *n* -S [F, fr. *graver* to engrave (fr. MF, of Gmc origin; akin to OHG *graban* to dig, engrave) + *-ure* — more at GRAVE] **1 a :** a process for producing an intaglio printing plate on wood, copper, or other material (as by means of a burin) ⟨the process of ~, including in that generic term all forms of art which get their effect from the incision of a groove on some resistant material . . . thus includes drypoint and mezzotint, burin engraving and all forms of etching —Herbert Read⟩ — often used in combination **b :** a plate made by such a process or a print from it **2** [by shortening] **:** PHOTOGRAVURE

gra·vy \'grāvē, -vi\ *n* -ES *often attrib* [ME *gravey, grave*, fr. MF *grave*] **1 a** *obs* **:** a dressing for fish or other seafood or for vegetables usu. consisting of the liquid (as beer or wine) in which the food is cooked together with pulverized almonds and spices **b :** the juices that exude from meat during or after cooking esp. when thickened (as with flour) and seasoned for use as a sauce ⟨a helping of potatoes and ~⟩ ⟨a rich turkey ~⟩ **c :** any of several thickened sauces (as milk gravy) served esp. with meat or potatoes **d** *dial* **:** a savory juice (as from a berry pie) esp. when suitable for sopping **2 a :** something pleasing or valuable that occurs or is acquired over and above what would ordinarily be expected ⟨such a job is pure ~⟩ **b :** unforeseen profits or income **:** profits from special or unexpected sources **:** WINDFALL **c** *slang* **:** improper profits or a source of such profits (as political patronage or graft) **3** — used in the phrases *by gravy* and *good gravy* as a mild oath

gravy boat *n* **:** a low boat-shaped pitcher usu. with a long lip at one end and a handle at the other and often with a footed base or a separate or attached tray that is used chiefly for serving gravies and sauces — called also *sauceboat*

gravy train *also* **gravy boat** *n, slang* **:** a situation providing abnormal or excessive profits, advantages, or benefits for those occupying it usu. at the expense of some larger group

¹gray *or* **grey** \'grā\ *adj* -ER/-EST [ME, fr. OE *grǣg*; akin to OHG *grāo* gray, ON *grār*, OSlav *zīrěti* to see, look] **1 a :** of the color gray **:** of a color formed by a blending of white and black **b :** tending toward gray ⟨a *gray*-red⟩ **c :** dull in color **:** lacking brightness ⟨a ~ cloudy day⟩ **d** *of textiles* **:** being in an unbleached undyed state as taken from the loom **:** UNFINISHED ⟨finisher of ~ goods⟩ **2 a :** having the hair gray **:** HOARY ⟨a ~ old man⟩ **b :** ELDERLY, MATURE **:** characteristic of age ⟨~ wisdom⟩ **3 a :** clothed in gray **:** wearing a gray costume **b** *of an animal* **:** having a coat of mingled black and white hairs **4 :** lacking cheer or brightness ⟨a dim ~ report⟩ **:** dull in mood or outlook ⟨the ~ office routine⟩ **:** DISMAL, MISERABLE ⟨~ prospects of success⟩ **5 :** intermediate in position, condition, or character; *esp, of a marketing method* **:** evading the spirit of legal controls without being overtly illegal — **gray·ly** *or* **grey·ly** *adv*

²gray *or* **grey** \"\ *n* -S [ME, fr. *gray, grey*, adj.] **1 :** an animal or thing of gray color (as a horse, garment, cloth, spot) **2 a** *obs* **:** gray fur prob. of the badger **b** *archaic* **:** BADGER **3 a :** a color formed by blending black and white **b :** one of the series of neutral or achromatic object colors ranging between black and white and characteristically perceived to belong to objects that reflect diffusely to the same degree all parts of the spectrum **c :** an object color of low saturation **4** *slang Brit* **:** a halfpenny with both sides the same used by sharpers

³gray *or* **grey** \"\ *vb* -ED/-ING/-S [¹*gray, grey*] *vt* **:** to make or cause to become or appear gray or grayish ⟨~ the paint with a little lampblack⟩ ⟨~*ed* her mother's hair with worry⟩ ⟨clouds ~*ing* the sky⟩ ~ *vi* **:** to become gray

gray alder *n* **:** an alder (*Alnus incana*) that is native to Europe but introduced into and often an escape in No. America and that has whitish gray bark and doubly toothed leaves with the undersurface whitish and often heavily pubescent

gray antimony *n* **:** STIBNITE

grayback \'=,=\ *n* **1 :** a Confederate soldier **2 :** any of various animals: as **a :** GRAY WHALE **b :** ³KNOT **c :** DOWITCHER **d :** SCAUP DUCK **e :** BODY LOUSE **f :** LAKE HERRING **3** *dial* **a :** a very large wave **b :** a large boulder

grayback beetle *n* **:** a large Australian scarab beetle (*Lepidoderma albohirtum*) having larvae that destroy sugarcane roots

graybeard \'=,=\ *n* **1 :** one whose beard is gray; *specif* **:** an old man ⟨~*s* sunning themselves on marble steps —*Atlantic*⟩ **2 :** BELLARMINE **3** [so called fr. the feathery seed vessels that suggest gray hair or beard] *dial Eng* **:** VIRGIN'S BOWER

graybeard tree *n* **:** FRINGE TREE

gray birch *n* **1 :** AMERICAN GRAY BIRCH **2 :** WESTERN PAPER BIRCH **3 :** YELLOW BIRCH

gray bird *n* **:** any of numerous birds with more or less gray plumage as **a :** any of several American finches; *esp* **:** JUNCO **b :** an immature swan in gray plumage **c :** any of several cuckoo shrikes of the southwest Pacific

gray blight *n* **:** a very common disease of the tea plant esp. in India and Ceylon that is caused by a fungus (*Pestalozzia theae*) which produces black dots on the leaves

gray body *n* **:** a body that emits radiant energy and has the same relative spectral energy distribution as a blackbody at the same temperature but in smaller amount

gray box *n* **:** any of several gray-barked Australian eucalypts (as *Eucalyptus hemiphloia* and *E. bicolor*)

gray brant *n* **:** WHITE-FRONTED GOOSE

gray-brown podzolic soil *n* **:** any of a group of zonal soils developed under deciduous forest in a temperate moist climate and characterized by a comparatively thin organic covering and an organic-mineral layer above a grayish brown leached layer which in turn rests upon an illuvial brown horizon

gray cast iron *n* **:** GRAY IRON

gray-cheeked thrush \'=,chēk(t)-\ *n* **:** a thrush (*Hylocichla minima*) of No. America

graycoat \'=,=\ *n* **:** one that wears a gray coat (as a Confederate soldier in the American Civil War)

gray cobalt *n* **:** SMALTITE

gray column *n* **:** COLUMN 6c(3)

gray copper *or* **gray copper ore** *n* **:** TETRAHEDRITE

gray crane *n* **:** the common crane (*Grus grus*) of Europe and Asia

gray crow *n* **:** HOODED CROW 1

gray-crowned babbler \'=,=-\ *n* **:** an Australian babbler (*Pomatostomus temporalis*) largely dark to sooty brown with chestnut breast, white throat and tail tip, and a grayish white streak over each eye

gray cutting *n* **:** the decoration of glass with incised designs that are left unpolished to give a frosted or grayish effect

gray dawn *n* **:** ZINC 2

gray dipper *n* **:** the American water ouzel (*Cinclus mexicanus*)

gray dogwood *n* **:** an erect white fruited gray-twigged dogwood (*Cornus racemosa*) of northeastern No. America

gray drab *n* **:** QUAKER GRAY

gray drum *n* **:** BLACK DRUM

gray duck *n* **:** any of various ducks having more or less gray plumage: as **a :** GADWALL **b :** the female mallard **c :** PINTAIL 1 **d :** the black duck (*Anas superciliosa*) of Australia and New Zealand

grayed \'grād\ *adj* **:** DULLED, DIMMED, DIMINISHED — used chiefly of colors

gray eminence *n* [trans. of F *éminence grise* — more at ÉMINENCE GRISE] **:** a person that exercises power behind the scenes

grayer *comparative of* GRAY

grayest *superlative of* GRAY

gray eye *n* **:** ocular lymphomatosis of the chicken

gray-faced \'=;=\ *adj* **1 :** having the face gray ⟨*gray-faced* ewes⟩ **2 :** having the face dull, drawn, and worn (as from grief or fatigue)

gray falcon *n* **1 :** PEREGRINE FALCON **2 :** HEN HARRIER

grayfish \'=,=\ *n* **1 :** POLLACK; *esp* **:** a young pollack **2 :** DOGFISH — used esp. as a market name

gray fox *n* **:** a No. American fox (*Urocyon cinereoargenteus*) with a coarse grizzled or yellowish gray outer coat, a long full tail, furry soles of the feet, and elliptical pupils in the eyes that is most common in the southeastern U.S.

gray friar *often cap G&F, var of* GREY FRIAR

gray goldenrod *n* **:** a dyer's-weed (*Solidago nemoralis*)

gray goose *n* **:** any of various gray or grayish geese: as **a :** GREYLAG **b :** CANADA GOOSE

gray grunt *n* **:** a silvery dark-striped grunt (*Haemulon macrostomum*) of the tropical western Atlantic

gray gum *n* **:** any of several Australian eucalypts (as *Eucalyptus propinqua, E. tereticornis*, and *E. punctata*)

gray gurnard *n* **:** a small European gurnard (*Trigla gurnardus*)

grayhead \'=,=\ *n* **:** an elderly person

gray-headed woodpecker \'=,=-\ *n* **:** a common European woodpecker (*Picus canus*) with the front of the head red, the remainder of the head and throat gray, and the upper parts of the body green

gray hen *n* [ME] **:** the female black grouse

gray horn *n* **:** COLUMN 6c(3)

grayhound *var of* GREYHOUND

graying *pres part of* GRAY

gray iron *n* **:** pig or cast iron containing much graphitic carbon which causes its fracture to be dark gray

gray ironbark *n* **:** a large eucalyptus (*Eucalyptus paniculata*) with heavy dark gray furrowed bark and very hard strong durable wood that varies in color from pale gray to chocolaty brown and is much used for heavy framing

gray·ish \'grāish, -āesh\ *adj* **1 :** somewhat or moderately gray ⟨the friars wear ~ robes⟩ **2** *of a color* **:** low in saturation **:** approaching the gray scale in the object-color solid ⟨eyes of ~ blue⟩

gray jay *n* **:** a Canada jay (*Perisoreus canadensis griseus*) of western No. America resembling but larger and grayer than the typical Canada jay; *broadly* **:** CANADA JAY

gray jumper *n* **:** APOSTLE BIRD b

gray kangaroo *n* **:** GIANT KANGAROO

gray kingbird *n* **:** a kingbird (*Tyrannus dominicensis dominicensis*) that breeds in the southeastern U.S. and winters in Mexico and Central America and is similar to but larger than the eastern kingbird

gray lady *n, usu cap G&L* [so called fr. the gray uniform worn on duty] **:** a volunteer worker of the American Red Cross who provides nonprofessional care and services for the sick and convalescent usu. in hospitals

graylag *var of* GREYLAG

gray leaf *n* **:** GRAY SPECK

gray-leaf pine *n* **1 :** DIGGER PINE **2 :** TORREY PINE

gray leaf spot *n* **:** a disease of tomatoes caused by the fungus (*Stemphylium solani*) and characterized by regular water-soaked brown leaf spots that become gray with age

gray lemming *n* **:** a member of a genus (*Myopus*) of short-footed Old World lemmings — called also *red-backed lemming*

gray·ling \'grāliŋ, -lēŋ\ *n, pl* **grayling** *also* **graylings** [ME, fr. *gray* + *-ling*] **1 :** any of several salmonoid fishes (genus *Thymallus*) related to the trouts but having a broad high dorsal fin, inhabiting cold swift streams, and valued as food and sport fishes; *esp* **:** a common European fish (*T. thymallus*) found chiefly in northern Europe and the Alps and locally in England and Scotland — see ARCTIC GRAYLING **2 :** either of two salmonoid fishes (genus *Prototroctes*) of the southern hemisphere that in many respects resemble those of the genus *Thymallus:* **a :** a fish (*P. muraena*) of Australia and Tasmania **b :** a New Zealand fish (*P. oxyrhynchus*) **3 :** any of numerous grayish or brownish butterflies of the family Satyridae

graymalkin *var of* GRIMALKIN

gray mallard *n* **:** MALLARD 1

gray manganese ore *n* **:** MANGANITE 1

gray market *n* **:** a market using irregular channels of trade or undercover methods not actually or explicitly illegal and chiefly in scarce materials at excessive prices — **gray marketeer** *n* — **gray-marketing** \'=¦===\ *n*

gray matter *n* **1 :** neural tissue esp. of the brain and spinal cord that contains nerve-cell bodies as well as nerve fibers, has a brownish gray color, and forms most of the cortex and nuclei of the brain, the columns of the spinal cord, and the bodies of ganglia — distinguished from *white matter* **2 :** BRAINS, INTELLECT

gray minyan ware *n, usu cap M* **:** GRAYWARE

gray mold *also* **gray mold rot** *n* **1 a :** any of various fungous diseases of fruits, vegetables, or herbaceous plants characterized by a grayish color of the affected surfaces **b :** a fungus causing such a disease (as members of the genera *Botrytis* and *Cercospora*) **2 :** downy mildew of the grape

gray moss *n* **:** SPANISH MOSS

gray mullet *n* **:** a mullet of the family Mugilidae — distinguished from *red mullet*

gray nerve fiber *n* **:** a nonmedullated nerve fiber

gray·ness *or* **grey·ness** *n* -ES [ME *graynes*, fr. ¹*gray* + *-nes* -ness] **1 :** the quality or state of being gray **2 :** the impression of unrelieved gray color given to the eye by a newspaper page or a large portion of one consisting largely of body type without relief (as by headlines, boxes)

gray nun *often cap G&N, var of* GREY NUN

gray nurse *or* **gray nurse shark** *n* **:** an Australian sand shark (*Carcharias arenarius*) attaining a length of 15 feet and reputed to be a man-eater; *also* **:** a closely related Indo-Pacific shark

gray oak *n* **1 :** SCARLET OAK **2 :** RED OAK 1a **3 :** a low scrubby live oak (*Quercus grisea*) of the southwestern U.S. having dark gray furrowed bark and entire dusty gray-blue leaves

grayout \'=,=\ *n* -S **:** a transient dimming or haziness of vision resulting from temporary impairment of cerebral circulation

gray out *vi* **:** to experience a grayout

gray parrot *n* **:** AFRICAN GRAY

graypate \'=,=\ *n* **:** a young goldfinch (sense 1) before development of crimson head feathers

gray perch *n* **:** FRESHWATER DRUM

gray pike *n* **1 :** SAUGER **2 :** WALLEYE 4

gray pine *n* **:** any of several American pines with grayish green foliage: as **a :** DIGGER PINE **b :** a piñon (*Pinus monophylla*) **c :** JACK PINE 1

gray plover *n* **1 :** BLACK-BELLIED PLOVER **2 :** ³KNOT

gray polypody *n* **:** a No. American fern (*Polypodium polypodioides*) growing on rocks or tree trunks and having the fronds grayish and scurfy below

gray poplar *n* **:** a rapidly growing tree (*Populus canescens*) that is native to Europe but introduced and naturalized elsewhere and that has faintly lobed dentate leaves which are gray on their lower surface

gray powder *n* **:** a moist gray powder consisting essentially of finely divided mercury and chalk occas. used as a mild cathartic for children

gray rabbit *n* **:** COTTONTAIL

gray rot *n* **:** a rot caused by a gray mold (*Botrytis cinerea*)

grays *pl of* GRAY, *pres 3d sing of* GRAY

gray sage *n* **:** SILVER SAGEBRUSH

gray sassafras *n* **:** an Australian timber tree (*Cryptocarya australis*) with bright scarlet fruits

grays·by \'grāzbē\ *n* -ES [origin unknown] **:** a serranid fish (*Petrometopon cruentatus*) of the tropical western Atlantic typically reddish gray with vermilion spots but sometimes darker with brown spots or pale and banded

gray scab *n* **:** a disease of willow caused by the fungus (*Sphaceloma murrayae*) and characterized by irregular somewhat raised leaf spots with grayish white centers and narrow dark brown margins often merging to form large patches

gray scale *n* **:** a series of regularly spaced tones ranging from white to black through intermediate shades of gray used as a reference scale for control purposes in both color and black-and-white photography

gray seal *n* **:** a large grayish seal (*Halichoerus gryphus*) of the north Atlantic

gray shark *n* **:** any of several grayish sharks: as **a :** SAND SHARK a **b :** REQUIN SHARK **c :** COW SHARK

gray shrew *n* **:** a common and widely distributed shrew (*Crocidura attenuata*) of southeastern Asia

gray snapper *n* **:** a long-bodied typically grayish snapper (*Lutjanus griseus*) that is a valuable food fish and widely distributed in the tropical western Atlantic

gray·son lily \'grāsᵊn-\ *n, usu cap G* [fr. *Grayson* co., Ky.] **:** a bulbous herb (*Hymenocallis occidentalis*) of the southeastern U.S. with lanceolate leaves and showy white flowers

gray sour *n* **1 :** treatment (as of cotton) with dilute hydrochloric or sulfuric acid after scouring and before bleaching **2 :** the bath or solution used in the gray sour

gray speck *n* **:** a disease of oats caused by manganese deficiency and characterized by light green to grayish spots on the leaves and esp. the blades that later turn buff or light brown

gray spot *n* **1 :** GRAY SPECK **2 :** GRAY LEAF SPOT

gray squeteague *n* **:** GRAY TROUT 1

gray squirrel *n* **:** a common rather large squirrel (*Sciurus carolinensis*) that is usu. light gray but may be very dark or even black in parts of its range which includes most of eastern No. America and by introduction England where it is largely replacing the native squirrel

gray stone *n* **:** PIPING ROCK

gray trout *n* **1 :** a common weakfish (*Cynoscion regalis*) of the Atlantic coast of the U.S. **2 :** LAKE TROUT

gray ultramarine ash *n* **:** a light bluish gray

gray vervet *n* **:** GRIVET

gray·wacke \'grā+,-\ *n* -S [trans. of G *grauwacke*] **:** a coarse sandstone or fine-grained conglomerate that is usu. dark gray and is composed of subangular to rounded fragments of quartz, feldspars, and bits of other dark-colored minerals or rocks firmly cemented

gray wagtail *n* **:** a common wagtail (*Motacilla cinerea*) of Europe and northern and central Asia having a gray back

graywall \'=,=\ *n* [so called fr. the discoloration of the skin] **:** a disease of tomatoes prob. caused by excess sunlight and characterized by translucent grayish brown streaks or blotches on the outer surface of the fruit and browning of the vascular strands

gray walnut *n* **:** BUTTERNUT 1

gray warbler *n* **:** a small rather plainly colored warbler (*Gerygone igata*) of New Zealand

grayware \'=,=\ *n* **1 :** ancient gray pottery; *esp* **:** a usu. undecorated ware of fine gray body and good technique found in Greece — called also *gray Minyan ware* **2 :** one-coat

enameled metalware : GRANITEWARE 2
gray wedge *n* : a nonselective light-absorbing screen having transmittance progressively decreasing in one direction transverse to the light rays
gray whale *n* : a rather large whalebone whale (*Rhachianectes glaucus*) of the northern Pacific formerly much hunted though of fierce active disposition and difficult to capture
gray widgeon *n* **1** : GADWALL **2** : PINTAIL 1
gray wildcat *n* : KAFFIR CAT
gray willow *n* **1** : SILKY WILLOW 2 **2** : a Eurasian shrubby willow (*Salix cinerea*) with whitish tomentose twigs
gray wolf *n* : a timber wolf of northern and western No. America
graz \'gräts\ *adj, usu cap* [fr. *Graz*, Austria] : of or from the city of Graz, Austria : of the kind or style prevalent in Graz
graz *abbr* [It *grazioso*] graceful
[1]**graze** \'grāz\ *vb* -ED/-ING/-S [ME *grasen*, fr. OE *grasian*, fr. *græs* grass — more at GRASS] *vi* **1 a** : to feed on growing herbage : crop and eat grass ⟨cattle *grazing* on the slopes⟩; *often* : to feed while moving along a more or less definite course ⟨the heifer slowly *grazed* out of sight⟩ ⟨antelopes *grazing* toward the water hole⟩ **b** : to feed in the manner of a grazing animal esp. by nibbling at a surface growth ⟨parrot fishes *grazed* among the coral trees⟩ **2** *dial Eng* : to yield herbage for grazing **3** : to put cattle to graze ⟨we used to ~ on the upland flush in late spring⟩ ~ *vt* **1** : to crop and eat (growing herbage) : feed on the herbage of (as a pasture) — compare BROWSE **2 a** : to cause or put (as cattle) to graze ⟨*grazed* his stock on the water meadow⟩ **b** : to cause or put cattle to graze on (as herbage or a pasture) ⟨*grazed* the upper field after taking an early crop of hay⟩ — often used with *down* ⟨planned to ~ down the aftermath⟩ **c** *obs* : to have charge of (grazing cattle) **3** : to supply herbage for the grazing of ⟨count on that pasture to ~ 30 head during August⟩ **syn** see FEED
[2]**graze** \"\ *n* -S **1** : an act of grazing ⟨nothing better for a horse than a good ~ on fresh young grass⟩ **2** : herbage for or suitable for grazing **3** : grazing land
[3]**graze** \"\ *vb* [perh. fr. [1]*graze*] *vt* **1** : to rub or touch lightly in passing : touch and glance off : barely touch ⟨the falling tree just *grazed* his chair⟩ **2** : to scratch or abrade by or as if by rubbing on a rough surface ⟨we got through, though we *grazed* both fenders slightly⟩ ⟨fell and *grazed* her knee⟩ ~ *vi* : to touch or rub against something in passing or so as to produce a scratch or abrasion ⟨our fenders just *grazed*⟩
[4]**graze** \"\ *n* : a scraping along a surface or an abrasion made by such scraping: as **a** : [2]GLIDE 4a **b** : a burst of an artillery projectile on impact with the ground or other material object **c** : a superficial abrasion of the skin
graze·able *or* **graz·able** \-zəbəl\ *adj* [[1]*graze* + *-able*] : fit or suitable for grazing ⟨~ pastures⟩
graz·er \-zə(r)\ *n* -S [[1]*graze* + *-er*] : one that grazes; *esp* : an animal that feeds by grazing — compare BROWSER
gra·zier \'grāzhə(r), *chiefly Brit* -ziə(r\ *n* -S [ME *grasyer*, fr. *gras* grass + *-ier* — more at GRASS] **1** : a person who grazes cattle; *broadly* : an owner or rancher of cattle **2** *Austral* : a sheep raiser; *esp* : one occupying government-owned land
gra·ziery \-ərē\ *n* -ES : the business of grazing cattle
[1]**grazing** *n* -S [ME *grasing*, fr. gerund of *grasen* to graze] **1** : the feeding or the method of feeding of animals that graze ⟨heavy ~ may kill out the better grasses⟩ ⟨the ~ of snails left clear tracks among the algae on the aquarium wall⟩ **2** : herbage or land for grazing ⟨nomads seeking ~ for their herds⟩ ⟨an excellent property to be leased with all ~s and cropland⟩
[2]**grazing** *adj* [fr. pres. part. of [1]*graze*] **1** : feeding by grazing ⟨~ animals⟩ **2** : of, for, or relating to grazing ⟨~ land⟩ ⟨a ~ permit⟩ — **graz·ing·ly** *adv*
grazing angle *n* [fr. pres. part. of [3]*graze*] : the glancing angle occurring in grazing incidence
grazing capacity *n* : the carrying capacity of a pasture or area of range usu. expressed as the number of animals (as cattle or deer) that it will support for a specified length of time or indefinitely
grazing fire *n* [fr. pres. part. of [3]*graze*] : artillery fire approximately parallel to the ground
grazing incidence *n* [fr. pres. part. of [3]*graze*] : incidence (as of X rays) at a very small glancing angle — see GRAZING ANGLE
gra·zi·o·so \'grätsē'ō(,)sō, -)zō\ *adj (or adv)* [It, fr. L *gratiosus* enjoying favor, beloved, agreeable — more at GRACIOUS] : graceful, smooth, or elegant in style — used as a direction in music
grd *abbr* **1** grind **2** ground **3** guaranteed
[1]**grease** \'grēs\ *n* -S [ME *grese, grece*, fr. OF *craisse, graisse, cresse, gresse*, fr. (assumed) VL *crassia*, fr. L *crassus* fat + *-ia* -y — more at HURDLE] **1 a** : rendered animal fat esp. when softer than tallow, inedible, and obtained from waste products **b** : fatty tissue : FATNESS ⟨put some ~ on those thin bones of yours —S.H.Adams⟩ **c** : oily matter or a thick oily or buttery preparation esp. when not fine or pure **d** : a thick lubricant (as a petroleum oil thickened with a metallic soap) ⟨axle ~⟩ ⟨silicone ~s⟩ **2 a** : GREASE HEEL **b** : cutaneous horsepox of the pasterns **3** *or* **grease wool** : wool as it comes from the sheep retaining the natural oils or fats — **in grease** *or* **in the grease 1** *of a game animal* : fat and fit for food **2** *of wool or fur* : in the natural condition with grease and other impurities not removed
[2]**grease** \-ēs,-ēz — *for -s/-z regional differences see* GREASY\ *vb* -ED/-ING/-S [ME *gresen*, fr. *grese, grees*, n.] *vt* **1 a** : to smear or daub with grease ⟨~ a cake pan⟩ **b** : to lubricate with grease **c** : to soil with grease **2** : to influence or persuade by gifts or bribes ⟨long-striking soft-coal miners would return to the pits in a two-week truce, *greased* by retroactive pay —*Newsweek*⟩ **3** : to smooth or make easy of passage ⟨bribes *greased* their path⟩ : FACILITATE, EXPEDITE ⟨this ~s the decline in department store sales —*Wall Street Jour.*⟩ **4** *slang* : to land (a plane) smoothly ⟨*greased* the plane down the rain-slick runway —B.M.Bowie⟩ ~ *vi, slang* : to make a smooth landing with a plane ⟨he *greased* in on the first hundred feet of runway —Hugh Fosburgh⟩ — **grease the hand** *or* **grease the palm** : BRIBE, TIP — **grease the wheels** : to expedite matters : cause matters to go more smoothly to a desired end
greaseball \'=,=\ *n* : LATIN AMERICAN; *esp* : MEXICAN — usu. taken to be offensive
grease band *n* : a band of sticky material placed around a tree trunk to prevent insects from climbing up the tree
greasebush \'=,=\ *n* : GREASEWOOD
grease cup *n* : a cylindrical receptacle communicating with a bearing and having a deep screw top which may be packed full of lubricating grease and which when screwed on forces the grease into the bearing
greased \-ēst,-ēzd\ *adj, of a horse* : affected with grease heel
greased line fishing *n* : angling in which a fly line made buoyant with grease dressing is floated on the surface of the water
greased pig *n* : a small pig smeared with grease and set free for contestants to catch
greased pole *or* **greasy pole** *n* : a pole smeared with grease and erected vertically for a climbing contest or horizontally for a walking contest
grease gun *n* **1** : a small hand pump for forcing grease under pressure into bearings **2** : a submachine gun that resembles a grease gun

grease gun 1

grease heel *or* **greasy heel** *n* : a chronic inflammation of the skin of the fetlocks and pasterns of horses marked by an excess of oily secretion, ulcerations, and in severe cases general swelling of the legs, nodular excrescences, and a foul-smelling discharge and usu. affecting horses with thick coarse legs kept or worked under unsanitary conditions — compare GRAPE 3
greasehorn \'=,=\ *n, dial Eng* : FLATTERER, SYCOPHANT ⟨smooth-faced, sniveling ~ —Charlotte Brontë⟩
grease·less \'grēsləs\ *adj* : having no grease ⟨a medicated ~ cream — won't stain clothes⟩
grease monkey *n* **1** : a greaser of machinery; *specif* : an automobile serviceman who lubricates working parts of the engine and the chassis **2** : an airplane mechanic
grease-nut \'=,=\ *n* **1** : the oily nut of an Australian tree (*Hernandia bivalvis*) **2** : the tree that bears grease-nuts and furnishes soft gray timber
greasepaint \'=,=\ *n* **1** : a melted tallow or grease used in theater makeup **2** : theater makeup
grease pencil *n* : a drawing pencil in which the marking substance is pigment and grease and the casing is paper to be unraveled as needed; *also* : a lithographic pencil
greaseproof \'=,=\ *adj* : resistant to penetration by grease, oil, or wax ⟨~ wrapping paper⟩
greas·er \'grēsə(r), -ēzə-, *in sense 2 usu* -z-\ *n* -S **1** : one that greases: as **a** : a worker who lubricates the working parts of a machine or a vehicle **b** : a worker who greases unpainted metal surfaces of firearms to prevent corrosion in transit or storage **c** : DOPER a **2** : LATIN AMERICAN; *esp* : MEXICAN — usu. taken to be offensive **3 a** : RUDDY DUCK **b** : CACKLING GOOSE **4** : BULL COOK
greaser blackfish *n* : BLACKFISH 1b
greases *pl of* GREASE, *pres 3d sing of* GREASE
grease spot *n* : a disease of turf grasses caused by a fungus (*Pythium aphanidermatum*) and characterized by spots usu. under two inches in diameter but often coalesced into patches or streaks having a distinctive greasy border of blackened leaves and intermingled cottony mycelium — called also *spot blight*; compare DOLLAR SPOT
grease-spot photometer *n* : a photometer in which a grease spot on a piece of paper becomes invisible when a light on each side of the paper illuminates the spot equally
grease trap *n* : a trap in a drain or waste pipe to prevent grease from passing into a sewer system
greasewood \'=,=\ *n* **1 a** : a plant of the genus *Sarcobatus*; *esp* : a low stiff shrub (*S. vermiculatus*) common in alkaline soils in the western U.S. — called also *black greasewood* **b** : any of several other shrubs of the family Chenopodiaceae that resemble greasewood: as (1) : ORACHE (2) : HOPSAGE (3) : IODINE BUSH **2** : either of two California shrubs: **a** : CHAMISO 1 **b** : WHITE SAGE e
grease wool *n* : GREASE 3
greas·i·ly \'grēs|əlē, -ēz|, -li\ *adv* : in a greasy manner
greas·i·ness \|ēnəs, |in-\ *n* -ES : the quality or state of being greasy
greasing *pres part of* GREASE
greasy \'grēs|ē, -ēz|, |i; *chiefly* -s- *Northwest, Southwest, central North, eastern New Eng; chiefly* -z- *South (including mountain areas) & Brit; both* -s- & -z- *Midland, western Pa, Middle Atlantic, NYC; sometimes* -s- *for literal sense and neutral connotation,* -z- *to convey an unpleasant connotation*\ *adj* -ER/-EST **1 a** : smeared or soiled with grease **b** : physically or morally repulsive: as (1) : distastefully unctuous or oily in manner ⟨his . . . insinuating tones, his ~ smile —Jack London⟩ (2) : SHIFTY, UNRELIABLE ⟨with his low backstairs cunning, with his ~ good nature —A.L.Guérard⟩ (3) *obs* : GROSS, INDECENT — often used of language **2** : being grease ⟨a ~ ointment⟩ : containing an unusual amount of grease ⟨~ wool⟩ ⟨~ food⟩ **3** *of a horse* : affected with grease heel **4 a** : having or giving the appearance or feel of greasiness : seemingly unctuous to the touch or view ⟨the ~ texture of a stone⟩ ⟨the quartz had a ~ luster⟩ ⟨~, gagging fogs —Berton Roueché⟩ **b** : SLIPPERY ⟨the rain made the road ~⟩ ⟨the bank was steep and ~ with sea moss —Irwin Shaw⟩ **c** *of paper stock* : that drains with great slowness — opposed to *free* **5** : THREATENING, DIRTY — used of the weather, the day, or the sky
greasy cutworm *n* : BLACK CUTWORM
greasy grind *n, slang* : a student who studies extremely hard usu. to the exclusion of extracurricular activities
greasy spoon *n, slang* : a small esp. cheap and usu. more or less unsanitary restaurant or diner
greasy spot *n* : a disease of citrus trees of unknown cause producing dark oily spots on the leaves esp. of grapefruit
greasy wool *n, Brit* : GREASE 3
[1]**great** \'grā|t, *South often* -re(ə)| *or* -rāə|; *usu* |d.+V\ *adj* -ER/-EST [ME *grete*, fr. OE *grēat* coarse-grained, large, tall; akin to OFris *grāt* large, OS *grōt*, OHG *grōz* and prob. to OE *grēot* sand, grit — more at GRIT] **1 a** : large in spatial dimension : of notable size : BIG ⟨a boy of nine, ~ and heavy for his years —Arnold Bennett⟩ ⟨had eaten ~ juicy steaks —Bruce Marshall⟩ ⟨the ~ size of these figures — the largest man is 167 feet long and has an arm spread of 164 feet —*Amer. Guide Series: Calif.*⟩ ⟨the best forests had been reduced to ~ stretches of stump land —*Amer. Guide Series: Minn.*⟩ **b** *now dial* : PREGNANT **c** : of a kind characterized by relative largeness — used in plant and animal names **d** *archaic* : CAPITAL ⟨~ A⟩ **e** *chiefly Scot, of a stream or body of water* : HIGH, SWOLLEN **f** : ELABORATE, AMPLE ⟨a plan worked out in ~ detail⟩ **2 a** : large in number : NUMEROUS ⟨a ~ multitude of warriors⟩ ⟨a ~ company of men⟩ ⟨the respect due his ~*er* years⟩ **b** : PREDOMINANT, OVERRULING — used in such phrases as *the great majority, the great body* ⟨the ~ bulk of the populace favors peace⟩ ⟨written nearly a thousand letters about goats, the ~ majority in reply to people who have asked questions —Joan & Harry Shields⟩ **3** : considerable or remarkable in magnitude, power, intensity, degree, or effectiveness ⟨~ bloodshed⟩ ⟨a ~ weariness⟩ ⟨with ~ difficulty⟩ ⟨the year of the ~ inflation —H.H.Martin⟩ : LOUD ⟨a ~ voice⟩ ⟨a ~ uproar⟩ : HEAVY, FORCEFUL ⟨a ~ blow with the fist⟩ : INTENSE ⟨a ~ pain shooting through the arm⟩ : FAR-REACHING : big in scope ⟨when once the ~ plans for power transmission have been realized —Samuel Van Valkenburg & Ellsworth Huntington⟩ : EXTREME, MARKED ⟨showed ~ good taste⟩ : very close ⟨a ~ friend of mine⟩ : markedly accomplished ⟨a ~ lover⟩ **4 a** : full or charged esp. with an emotion ⟨~ with anger⟩ ⟨~ with pride⟩ ⟨others who returned from overseas ~ with message —E.P.Snow⟩ ⟨when kings are reduced to thumb size and beasts are ~ with wisdom —*Time*⟩ **b** *archaic* : PROUD, ARROGANT **5 a** : PROMINENT, RENOWNED ⟨a ~ politician⟩ ⟨a ~ dictator⟩ ⟨a ~ creator of confusion in the political scene⟩ : EMINENT, DISTINGUISHED ⟨a ~ poet⟩ ⟨the ~ and aging father of modern electronics⟩ : IMPORTANT, SIGNIFICANT ⟨one of the ~ theories in Christian ethics⟩ : WEIGHTY, EFFECTIVE ⟨a ~ argument in criminal-law practice⟩ ⟨a ~ truth⟩ **b** : chief or preeminent over others ⟨the ~ work of his old age was the decoration of the chapel —*Encyc. Americana*⟩ ⟨defines the scope of some of the ~ questions that call for answers —W.H. Bucher⟩ ⟨the ~ novelist of the war years⟩ — often used in titles ⟨Lord *Great* Chamberlain⟩ **c** (1) : belonging to the aristocracy ⟨most people thought it quite natural that ~ folk should have great privileges —G.B.Shaw⟩ (2) : marked by an aristocratic, dignified, lofty bearing : GRAND ⟨~ ladies descending from their chauffeured cars⟩ **d** : being to a notable degree ⟨a ~ beauty⟩ ⟨a ~ indignity⟩ **e** : being on a large scale ⟨appealed to the ~ manufacturers for help⟩ **f** : having large holdings ⟨the ~ farmers of the area⟩ **6** : long continued : lengthened in duration ⟨a ~ while⟩ ⟨a ~ interval⟩ **7** : FAVORITE ⟨a ~ trick of his⟩ ⟨a ~ word among the members of the club⟩ **8** *chiefly dial* : FRIENDLY, CHUMMY, THICK — often used with overtones of disapproval ⟨they've been mighty ~ lately, I expect it'll all blow up some day —Anna Doleshaw⟩ **9** : MAIN, PRINCIPAL ⟨held the conference in the ~ hall of the abbey⟩ ⟨came down the ~ staircase⟩ **10** : older or younger or more remote in a family relationship by a single generation than (a specified relative) ⟨a *great*-grandfather⟩ **11** : markedly superior in character or quality to others of the same class ⟨a book that could be called good but not ~⟩ : of high purpose or nature : LOFTY, NOBLE, MAGNANIMOUS ⟨a big man who needed only a little feeling to be a ~ man —H.J.Laski⟩ ⟨a person committed to ~ ends⟩ ⟨~ of soul and generous in actions⟩ **12 a** : remarkably or unusually informed or skilled — used with *at, on* ⟨a man ~ at tennis⟩ ⟨a speaker ~ on international relations⟩ **b** : unusually addicted to or enthusiastic about — used with *at, for,* or *on* ⟨a person ~ at talking by the hour⟩ ⟨a person ~ for gallivanting all over town⟩ ⟨mother was always ~ on fantasy —Catherine Hubbell⟩ ⟨a ~ church worker and well-known for his philanthropies —*Amer. Guide Series: Ind.*⟩ **c** : ASSIDUOUS, PERSISTENT ⟨a ~ talker⟩ ⟨a ~ skier although he is not very good at skiing⟩ ⟨a ~ collector of books⟩ **13** : WONDERFUL, ADMIRABLE — used as a generalized term of enthusiastic approval ⟨had a ~ time⟩ ⟨the attitude of all concerned was just ~⟩ **14** *Eastern Church* : of or relating to Holy Week ⟨~ Monday⟩
[2]**great** \"\ *adv* [ME *grete*, fr. *grete*, adj.] : in a great manner : SUCCESSFULLY, WELL ⟨things are going ~⟩
[3]**great** \"\ *n, pl* **great** *or* **greats** [ME *grete*, fr. *grete*, adj.] **1** : one that is great : one that is particularly noted or notable for superiority of accomplishment esp. in a particular field of activity ⟨the music of Mozart and Beethoven and all the other ~s —Deems Taylor⟩ ⟨his playing is less monumental . . . than that of any of the other pianistic ~ —Virgil Thomson⟩ ⟨the golfing ~s of last season⟩ ⟨some of the scientific ~s —*Science Illustrated*⟩ ⟨the ~ of London society came to their receptions —*Fashion Digest*⟩ ⟨the galaxy of football ~s —S.M.Spencer⟩ **2** [by shortening] : GREAT ORGAN **3** *greats pl, usu cap* **a** : the final examination for the B.A. in classics esp. with honors at Oxford University **b** : the course taken in preparation for this examination — compare GREAT GO
great albacore *n* : BLUEFIN 2
great angelica *n* : a large coarse American angelica (*Angelica atropurpurea*) with a usu. purplish stem
great anteater *n* : ANT BEAR 1
great antiphon *n, usu cap G&A* : one of the seven anthems beginning with an invocation (as *O Adonai*) that are sung at vespers one each day from December 17 to Christmas — called also *O Antiphon;* usu. used in pl.
great ape *n* : any of the recent anthropoid apes : GIBBON, ORANGUTAN, CHIMPANZEE, GORILLA
great assize *n* : LAST JUDGMENT
great auk *n* : a large flightless auk (*Pinguinus impennis*) two or two and a half feet long but with very small wings and formerly abundant on the coasts of the northern parts of the No. Atlantic but now extinct
great-aunt \'=,=\ *n* : GRANDAUNT
great barracuda *n* : a grayish brown barracuda (*Sphyraena barracuda*) that often attains a length of over six feet, may be dangerous to swimmers, and is highly regarded as a food and sport fish though the flesh is reputed poisonous in some areas
great beams *n pl, chiefly NewEng* : the loft or haymow of a barn
great bellflower *n* : CANTERBURY BELL
great bilberry *n* : BOG BILBERRY
great bindweed *n* : HEDGE BINDWEED 1
great black-backed gull *n* : a very large black-backed gull (*Larus marinus*) that is becoming increasingly abundant along northern coasts on both the European and American sides of the Atlantic
great black cockatoo *n* : a very large black cockatoo (*Probosciger aterrima*) of New Guinea and northern Australia that has a tall erectile crest, patches of bright red naked skin on the cheeks, and an extremely large powerful bill with which it cracks the palm nuts on which it chiefly feeds — called also *palm cockatoo*
great blue cat *n* : BLUE CAT
great blue heron *n* : a large slaty-blue American heron (*Ardea herodias*) about 50 inches long and with crested head
great blue shark *n* : a blue shark (*Carcharhinus glaucus*)
great books *adj* : of, relating to, or centered in certain classics of literature, philosophy, history, and science that are believed to contain the basic ideas of western culture ⟨an experimental *great books* program for 50 selected students —*Time*⟩
great bowerbird *n* : a large Australian bowerbird (*Chlamydera nuchalis*) common about settled areas in northern Australia and noted for the skill with which it builds its bower
great bulrush *n* : any of several large plants of the genus *Scirpus*: as **a** : a tall Eurasian sedge (*S. lacustris*) with naked terete stems and a compound umbel of numerous capitate spikes **b** : a bulrush (*S. validus*) of tropical America and southern U.S. with a stout scaly reddish rhizome, thick pliable culm, and spikelets in close fascicles or glomerules; *also* : a bulrush chiefly of northern No. America that is a variety (*S. validus creber*) of the above distinguished esp. by lax panicles
great bur *or* **great burdock** *n* : a European burdock (*Arctium lappa*) naturalized in No. America
great burnet *n* : a perennial burnet (*Sanguisorba officinalis*) with ellipsoid to short cylindric flower heads native to Eurasia but cultivated and escaped elsewhere
great bustard *n* : a bustard (*Otis tarda*) that is the largest of European land birds, attaining a weight of over 30 pounds and a wingspread of 8 feet and occurring in southern and eastern Europe and in much of Asia but formerly also in England and other parts of western Europe where it is now extinct
great carpenter bee *n* : a large carpenter bee (*Xylocopa virginica*) of eastern and southern No. America about the size of a bumblebee but distinguished by a smooth shining abdomen
great cattle *n* : all types of cattle except sheep and yearlings
great celandine *n* : CELANDINE 1
great cerebral vein *n* : a broad unpaired vein formed by the junction of Galen's veins and uniting with the inferior sagittal sinus to form the straight sinus
great chair *n* : ARMCHAIR
great chickweed *n* : a large-flowered chickweed (*Stellaria pubera*) chiefly of the southeastern U.S. — called also *star chickweed*
great circle *n* : a circle formed on the surface of a sphere by the intersection of a plane that passes through the center of the sphere; *specif* : such a circle on the surface of the earth of which an arc constitutes the shortest distance between any two terrestrial points — compare SMALL CIRCLE
great-circle chart *n* : GNOMONIC PROJECTION
great-circle sailing *n* : the navigation or conducting of a ship on a great-circle track or on a course determined in relation to a great-circle track — compare SAILING
great-circle track *n* : the track of a ship following or navigating on or in relation to a great circle
great climacteric *n, obs* : GRAND CLIMACTERIC
greatcoat \'=,=\ *n* **1** : a heavy overcoat **2** : a warm jacket
great council *n* [ME *grete counseil*] : a preeminent political council: as **a** : the principal council or assembly of England under the Norman kings composed of the sovereign's tenants in capite **b** : a municipal legislative body of former times in some Italian towns and cities **c** : a major council of No. American Indian chiefs
great crested grebe *n* : a large Old World grebe (*Podiceps cristatus*) with black projecting ear tufts
great dane *n* **1** *usu cap G&D* : a breed of smooth-coated dogs that is believed to have originated in Germany several centuries ago, that is of massive size, great strength, and 28 inches at minimum height, that ranges in color from fawn through brindle, blue, and harlequin, that was formerly used chiefly for hunting wild boar, and that has been much used for draft purposes **2** *often cap G & usu cap D* : a dog of the Great Dane breed
great deal \(')grā(t)¦dēl, *chiefly before pause or consonant* -ēəl\ *n* : a large quantity : LOT ⟨received a *great deal* of sympathy at his bereavement⟩ ⟨asked for little but received a *great deal*⟩ — **a great deal** *adv* **1** : to a considerable degree or extent : by a considerable amount ⟨a *great deal* better⟩ **2** : OFTEN, FREQUENTLY ⟨he runs a *great deal*⟩ — used with intransitive verbs **3** : HIGHLY ⟨think a *great deal* of that book⟩
great dionysia *n, usu cap G&D* : DIONYSIA b
great divide *n* [fr. the *Great Divide* (*Continental Divide*), watershed of the No. American continent] **1** : a watershed between major drainage systems **2** : a sharp or significant point of division between two strongly opposed or markedly different juxtaposed things — **cross the great divide** : DIE ⟨men who *crossed the great divide* by the alcoholic route in middle life —A.W.Long⟩
great dog *n* : a dog large enough by English forestry law to kill or maim deer or other large game
great duckweed *n* : a plant of the genus *Spirodela* (esp. *S. polyrhiza*)
great·en \'grāt³n, -ret-\ *vb* -ED/-ING/-S [[1]*great* + *-en*] *vt* : to make greater : ENLARGE, MAGNIFY, INCREASE; *also* : to make more distinguished : EXALT, ENNOBLE ~ *vi* : to become greater : increase in size or significance
great entrance *n, usu cap G&E* [trans. of MGk *megalē eisodos*] : an Entrance in the liturgy of the Eastern Church during which the eucharistic elements are brought in
greater *adj* [fr. comp. of [1]*great*] **1** *music, obs* : MAJOR **2** *usu cap, of a political or geographic unit* : consisting of an original unit together with adjacent or other areas that are naturally or administratively connected with it ⟨*Greater* London⟩
greater celandine *n* : CELANDINE 1

greater curvature *n* **:** the long border of the stomach that is primitively dorsal but in man turned to the left

greater feria *n* **1 :** a feria of the Roman Catholic church calendar (as a weekday of Advent or Lent) which must at least be commemorated in the office of a feast falling on the same day and the office of which has precedence over that of simple feasts or if privileged (as Ash Wednesday and the first three days of Holy Week) over any feast — called also *major feria* **2 :** a feria of the Anglican church calendar with a service that takes precedence over feasts of low rank falling on the same day

greater omentum *n* **:** a fatty omentum attached to the stomach and colon and hanging down over the small intestine — called also *caul, gastrocolic omentum*

greater scaup *or* **greater scaup duck** *n* **:** a No. American diving duck (*Aythya marila nearctica*) resembling the lesser scaup duck but being slightly larger and having a greenish iridescence on the head of the adult male, breeding in arctic northwestern America, and wintering on both coasts of No. America

greater shearwater *n* **:** a rather large chiefly sooty brown and white shearwater (*Puffinus gravis* or *Procellaria gravis*) of the eastern coast of No. and So. America

greater stitchwort *n* **:** a Eurasian annual herb (*Stellaria holostea*) with small white flowers

greater wax moth *n* **:** BEE MOTH

greater yellowlegs *n pl but sing or pl in constr* **:** a common No. American marsh and shore bird (*Tringa melanoleuca*) of the family Scolopacidae largely gray above and white below with black or dark gray flecking and yellow legs — compare LESSER YELLOWLEGS

greatest *superlative of* GREAT

greatest common divisor *n* **:** the largest integer or polynomial of highest degree that is an exact divisor of each of two or more integers or polynomials respectively

greatest common factor *n* **:** HIGHEST COMMON FACTOR

greatest elongation *n* **:** the configuration in which one celestial body reaches its greatest apparent distance from another ⟨the *greatest* eastern *elongation* of Venus with respect to the sun⟩ — see CONFIGURATION illustration

greatest happiness principle *n* **:** a principle in Benthamism: right and wrong are to be judged by the degree to which the action judged achieves the greatest happiness of the greatest number — called also *utility principle;* compare UNIVERSALISTIC HEDONISM

great fan palm *n* **:** PALMYRA

great fast *n, usu cap G&F* [trans. of MGk *megalē nēsteia*] *Eastern Church* **:** LENT 1

great father *n, usu cap G&F* **:** GREAT WHITE FATHER

great fee *n, in feudal law* **:** a fee held in capite

great flounder *n* **:** STARRY FLOUNDER

great friday *n, usu cap G&F* [trans. of LGk *megalē paraskeuē*] *Eastern Church* **:** GOOD FRIDAY

great go *n, archaic* **:** the final examination for the bachelor's degree in classics and mathematics at Oxford University

great goose grass *n* **:** GERMAN MADWORT

great gray kangaroo *n* **:** GIANT KANGAROO

great gray owl *n* **:** a large round-headed owl (*Strix nebulosa*) having very full fluffy plumage that is gray mottled and barred with darker gray and white and living in northern circumpolar in northern forests

great gray shrike *n* **:** a large shrike (*Lanius excubitor*) chiefly gray above with black-and-white wings and tail

great green orchis *n* **:** a greenish-flowered No. American terrestrial orchid (*Platanthera orbiculata*)

great gross *n* **:** a unit of quantity equal to 12 gross

great gun *n* **:** BIG GUN

great guns *adv* **:** with unremitting vigor or energy ⟨reaching the age of 78 . . . and still going *great guns* —*N.Y. Times*⟩; *also* **:** eminently successfully ⟨an enterprise that began slowly but after a while began to go *great guns*⟩ — often used interjectionally to express astonishment

greathead \ˈ=,=\ *n* **:** AMERICAN GOLDENEYE

greatheart \ˈ=,=\ *n* **:** a greathearted person

great·hearted \ˈ=¦==\ *adj* [ME *grete herted*] **1 :** having or characterized by bravery **:** COURAGEOUS, FEARLESS **2 :** having or characterized by largeness or generosity of spirit **:** MAGNANIMOUS

great·heart·ed·ly *adv* **:** in a greathearted manner

great·heart·ed·ness *n* -ES **:** MAGNANIMITY

great hedge bedstraw *n* **:** WILD MADDER 2a

great horde *n, usu cap G&H* [trans. of Kirghiz *ulu-juz*] **:** a subdivision of the Kirghiz living south of Lake Balkhash in Soviet Central Asia the chief divisions of which are the Kangli and the Dulat

great horned owl *n* **1 :** a large No. American owl (*Bubo virginianus*) with conspicuous ear tufts **2 :** an eagle owl (*Bubo bubo*)

great house *n, chiefly Brit & South* **:** the main house of an estate or plantation

great indian plantain : a tall perennial herb (*Cacalia reniformis*) of the southeastern U.S.

great kelp *n* **:** GIANT KELP

great lake trout *or* **great lakes trout** \ˈ;=ˈ=\ *n, usu cap G&L* [fr. *Great Lakes,* chain of lakes in central No. America] **:** LAKE TROUT

great land crab *n* **:** a large swift-moving dull-grayish land crab (*Cardisoma guanhumi*) of the family Gecarcinidae that is widely distributed from southern Florida and the West Indies to Brazil, is chiefly nocturnal, and lives in deep burrows or the open fields or woods and returns to the sea only to breed — called also *guanhumi, juey, tourlourou, white land crab*

great laurel *n* **:** BIG LAUREL

great lent *n, usu cap G&L* [trans. of MGk *megalē tessarkostē*] **:** LENT 1

great-line \ˈ=;=\ *adj, Brit* **:** using a long line in fishing **:** DEEP-WATER ⟨trawl and *great-line* catches . . . by steam vessels —*Report on the Fisheries of Scotland*⟩

great lobelia *n* **:** a tall herb (*Lobelia siphilitica*) of the eastern U.S. with showy irregular blue flowers

great·ly *adv* [ME *gretely,* fr. *grete* great + *-ly* — more at GREAT] **1 :** to a great extent or high degree ⟨contributed ~ to the improvement of international relations⟩ **:** VERY ⟨not ~ bothered by the rude remarks⟩ **:** very much ⟨said he liked her ~ —Arnold Bennett⟩ ⟨a ~ intensified sound⟩ ⟨~ in want of a friend —G.B.Shaw⟩ **2 :** in a great manner **:** NOBLY, MAGNANIMOUSLY ⟨a man may live ~ in the law —O.W.Holmes †1935⟩

great maple *n* **:** SYCAMORE 2

great mariscal *n* **:** a marshal of medieval Scotland before the bestowal of the title Earl Mariscal — compare MARISCHAL, MARSHAL 1

great master *n* **1 :** GRAND MASTER 1 **2 a :** one held to be among the greatest or most skilled in one of the arts **b :** a work of such a one esp. in painting

great mean *n, obs* **:** the third string of a bass viol or of a violin **:** the D string of a violin

great millet *n* **:** DURRA

great mogul *n, usu cap G&M* **:** the sovereign of the empire founded in India by the Moguls under Baber in the 16th century

great mullein *n* **:** a tall-stalked very woolly mullein (*Verbascum thapsus*) with yellow or occas. white flowers

great-nephew \ˈ=;=(,)=\ *n* **:** GRANDNEPHEW

great·ness *n* -ES [ME *gretenes,* fr. *grete* great + *-nes* -ness] **:** the quality or state of being great

great nettle *n* **:** STINGING NETTLE

great-niece \ˈ=;=\ *n* **:** GRANDNIECE

great northern diver *n* **:** COMMON LOON

great northern pike *n* **:** ⁴PIKE 1a

great octave *n* **:** the musical octave that begins on the second C below middle C — see PITCH illustration

great officer of state : one of the nine officers in England that were orig. officers of the royal household and include the lord high steward, lord high chancellor, lord high treasurer, lord president of the council, lord privy seal, lord great chamberlain, lord high constable, earl marshal, and lord high admiral

great one *n* **:** one esp. enthusiastic or clearly of a particular habit of mind or action — used with *for* ⟨a *great one* for skiing⟩ ⟨a *great one* for leaving things as they are —Louis Auchincloss⟩ ⟨a *great one* for the ladies —Jack Iams⟩

great organ *n* **1 :** a division of a pipe organ having the pipes of largest scale and loudest tone **2 :** the manual controlling the great organ

great panda *n* **:** PANDA 2

great park lily *n* **:** LILY OF THE VALLEY

great pastern bone *n* **:** the first phalanx of the functional digit of the foot of an equine

great pike *n* **:** MUSKELLUNGE

great plains cottonwood *n* [fr. the *Great Plains,* the continental slope of central No. America] **:** a poplar (*Populus sargentii*) of central No. America with coriaceous coarsely serrate leaves commonly broader than they are long

great pompano *n* **:** ³PERMIT 1

great power *n, usu cap G&P* **:** one of the nations that carry the greatest political influence, resources, and military strength and figure most decisively in international relations

great-power \ˈ=;=\ *adj* [*Great Power*] **:** of or relating to the Great Powers ⟨the diplomatic test of a new *great-power* conference —W.H.Chamberlin⟩

great pox *n* **:** SYPHILIS

great prim·er \-rim-\ *n* **:** a size of type approximately 18 point

great pueblo *adj, usu cap G&P* **:** of or relating to the climax of the development of the Pueblo culture in the southwestern U.S. characterized by many-storied stone buildings set in recesses in the cliffs or in the open and by an advanced development of pottery, murals, and dryland agriculture

great pyr·e·nees \-ˈpirə(,)nēz *sometimes* -,==ˈ=\ *n* [¹*great* (as in *Great Dane*) + *Pyrenees,* mountain range on the Spanish-French border] **1** *usu cap G&P* **:** a breed of very large heavy-coated white dogs that resemble the Newfoundland in conformation and are valued as herd dogs and guard dogs **2** *pl* **great pyrenees** *often cap G&P* **:** an animal of the Great Pyrenees breed

great ragweed *n* **:** a coarse annual (*Ambrosia trifida*) with some or all of the leaves usu. deeply and palmately 3-cleft or 5-cleft

great reed warbler *n* **:** a rather large olivaceous to bright brown reed warbler (*Acrocephalus arundinaceus*) that is widely distributed in warmer parts of the Old World from western Europe to southern Africa and Australia

great rhododendron *n* **:** BIG LAUREL

great russian *n, cap G&R* **1 :** a member of the Russian-speaking people largely of the central and northeastern areas of the U.S.S.R. constituting the country's largest ethnic group — compare BELORUSSIAN, LITTLE RUSSIAN **2 :** ²RUSSIAN 2a

greats *pl of* GREAT

great st.-john's-wort *n, usu cap S&J* **:** a large-flowered St.-John's-wort (*Hypericum pyramidatum*)

great sallow *n* **:** a sallow (*Salix caprea*)

great sanicle *n* **:** LADY'S-MANTLE

great scale *n* **:** the scale ascribed to Guido d'Arezzo that includes the seven hexachords and all notes recognized in medieval church music, its notes being named by letters combined with the syllables of the successive hexachords (as Gamma ut, A re, B mi, C fa ut) — compare SOLMIZATION

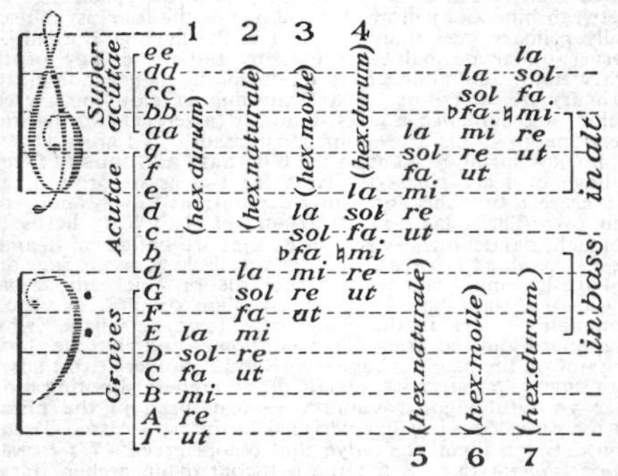

great scale

great scott \ˈ=ˈskät\ *interj, usu cap S* [fr. the name *Scott;* euphemism for *great God*] — a mild oath

great seal *n* [ME *grete seel*] **1 :** the personal seal of a monarch **2 :** the principal seal of a kingdom or state or of a bishop or of a corporation

great silver fir *n* **:** LOWLAND FIR

great skua *n* **:** a large stocky skua (*Catharacta skua*) having dusky plumage and broad rounded wings, breeding chiefly along arctic and antarctic shores, and foraging over most cold and temperate seas

great snipe *n* **:** an Old World snipe (*Capella media*) somewhat larger, darker, and more barred than the whole snipe

great soil group *n* **:** a group of soils having common characteristics usu. developed under the influence of environmental factors (as vegetation and climate) active over a considerable geographic range and comprising one or more families of soil

great solomon's-seal *n, usu cap 1st S* **:** a No. American perennial herb (*Polygonatum commutatum*) with smooth foliage and drooping axillary tubular greenish flowers

great spirit *n, usu cap G&S* **:** the chief deity in the indigenous religion of many No. American Indian tribes

great spotted woodpecker *n* **:** a common European and Asiatic woodpecker (*Dendrocopos major*) having a black back, white shoulder patches, crimson under tail coverts, and in the male a crimson patch on the nape

great spurred violet *n* **:** SELKIRK'S VIOLET

great sugar pine *n* **:** SUGAR PINE

great sunday *n, usu cap G&S* [trans. of LGk *megalē hēmera*] *Eastern Church* **:** EASTER SUNDAY

great-tailed grackle \ˈ=,=-\ *n* **:** BOAT-TAILED GRACKLE

great tit *n* **:** the largest common European tit (*Parus major*) distinguished by a glossy blue-black head and yellow underparts with a black stripe down the breast

great toe *n* **:** BIG TOE

great triangle *n, usu cap G&T* **:** a triangle formed on the palm by the lines of Life, Head, and Mercury that when well-developed is usu. held by palmists to indicate breadth of views, liberality, and generosity of spirit — called also *Triangle of Mars*

great tuna *or* **great tunny** *n* **:** BLUEFIN 2

great-uncle \ˈ=;==\ *n* **:** GRANDUNCLE

great vehicle *n, usu cap G&V* [trans. of Skt *mahāyāna*] **:** MAHAYANA

great water dock *n* **:** any of various plants of the genus *Rumex* (esp. *R. orbiculatus*)

great water parsnip *n* **:** a poisonous European herb (*Sium latifolium*) with divided leaves and tiny flowers

great week *n, usu cap G&W* [trans. of LGk *megalē hebdomas*] **:** HOLY WEEK — used in the early church and now esp. in the Eastern Church

great wheel *n* **:** the first wheel of a watch or clock train

great white father *also* **great father** *n, usu cap G&W&F* **1 :** the president of the U.S. **2 :** a person in a position of authority

great white heron *n* **1 :** a large white chiefly tropical egret (*Casmerodius albus*) that occurs in a number of varieties in both Old and New Worlds — compare AMERICAN EGRET **2 :** a large white heron (*Ardea occidentalis*) of Florida and Mexico

great white shark *n* **:** a large mackerel shark (*Carcharodon carcharias*) that is bluish gray when young but becomes dun or whitish in large specimens, that is widespread in warm and tropical seas, and that is a man-eater

great white trillium *n* **:** a perennial herb (*Trillium grandiflorum*) of eastern No. America with showy white petals

great white way *n, usu cap G&both Ws* [fr. the *Great White Way,* nickname for the theatrical section of Broadway in New York City] **:** a street brilliantly lighted at night and devoted chiefly to public amusements (as theaters) ⟨their *Great White Ways* flooded with pleasure-seekers —*Yale Rev.*⟩ ⟨theaters flanking a dozen *Great White Ways* —*Landscape*⟩

great willow herb *n* **:** FIREWEED b

great year *n* [ME *grete yere,* trans. of L *annus magnus,* trans. of Gk *megas eniautos*] **:** the period of about 25,800 years required for a complete cycle of precession of the equinoxes during which time the celestial pole describes a complete circle around the ecliptic pole

¹**greave** *n* -S [ME *greve,* fr. OE *grǣfa* — more at GROVE] *obs* **:** GROVE, THICKET

²**greave** \ˈgrēv\ *n* -S [ME *greve,* fr. MF, perh. fr. *greve* part in the hair, fr. *graver* to part the hair, of Gmc origin; akin to OHG *graban* to dig; fr. a comparison of the edge of the shinbone to a part in the hair — more at GRAVE] **:** armor for the leg below the knee — usu. used in pl.

³**greave** \ˈ"\ *vt* -ED/-ING/-S [by alter.] **:** ⁴GRAVE

greaved tortoise \ˈgrēv(d)-\ *n* [²*greave* + *-ed;* fr. the large plates on its front legs] **:** the largest of African tortoises (*Testudo calcarata*)

greaves \ˈgrēvz\ *n pl* [LG *greve* (pl. *greven*), fr. MLG *grēve;* akin to OHG *griobo* crackling, OE *grēot* sand, grit — more at GRIT] **:** CRACKLING 2a

grebe \ˈgrēb\ *n, pl* **grebe** *or* **grebes** [F *grèbe*] **1 :** any of various aquatic birds that constitute the family Colymbidae and order Colymbiformes, are closely related to the loons but with the toes lobate instead of webbed, have a rudimentary tail and narrow tarsi shaped like a blade, and are very expert divers and able to swim long distances under water — see GREAT CRESTED GREBE, RED-NECKED GREBE **2 :** a nearly neutral slightly reddish dark gray that is darker and slightly redder than lead

gre·bo \ˈgrā(,)bō\ *n, pl* **grebo** *or* **greboes** *usu cap* **1 :** a member of a Negro people of the Liberian coast **2 :** a Kwa language of the Grebo people

grecanic *adj, usu cap* [L *Graecanicus,* fr. *Graecus* — more at GREEK] *obs* **:** GRECIAN, GREEK

grece *or* **grice** \ˈgrēs\ *n* -S [ME *grece,* fr. OF *grez, greiz* steps, pl. (taken as sing.) of *gré, greit* step — more at GREE] **1** *now dial Eng* **:** a flight of steps; *also* **:** one of the steps in a flight **2** *or* **griece** \ˈ"\ **:** DEGREE 1b

¹**gre·cian** \ˈgrēshən\ *n* -S *cap* [L *Graecia* Greece (fr. *Graecus* + *-ia* -y) + E *-an*] **1 a :** a native of Greece **:** GREEK **b :** a hellenized Jew of the Diaspora **2 a** *archaic* **:** a specialist in the Greek language and Greek literature **b :** one skilled in Greek **3 :** a student in the sixth form of a school (as Christ's Hospital, London)

²**grecian** \ˈ"\ *adj, usu cap* **1 a :** of, relating to, or characteristic of Greece **b :** of, relating to, or characteristic of the Greeks **2** *of a woman's gown* **:** having flowing lines, layers of pleats, and many soft folds

grecian fire *n, usu cap G* **:** GREEK FIRE

gre·cian·ize \-shə,nīz\ *vt* -ED/-ING/-S *often cap* **:** GRECIZE

grecian rose *n, often cap G* **:** a dark yellowish pink

grecian sandal *n, usu cap G* **:** an open sandal consisting of a sole attached to the foot by an arrangement of interlaced straps crossing the toes and instep and fastening around the ankle

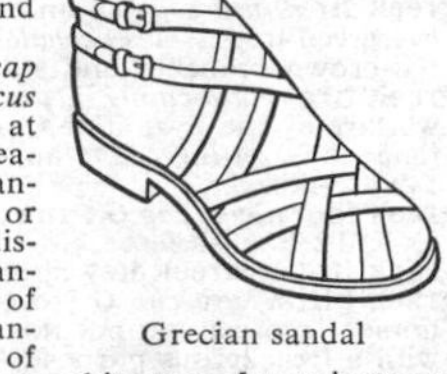
Grecian sandal

gre·cism \ˈgrē,sizəm\ *n* -S *usu cap* [ML *Graecismus,* fr. L *Graecus* Greek + *-ismus* -ism — more at GREEK] **1 :** a characteristic feature of Greek occurring in another language **2 a :** a quality or mode of thought or action distinctive of the Greeks esp. of ancient Greece **b :** the spirit of Greek art or culture esp. in ancient times **3 a :** imitation of Greek art, literature, sculpture, or architecture **b :** an instance of such imitation

gre·cize \-,sīz\ *vt* -ED/-ING/-S *often cap* [F *gréciser,* fr. LL *graecizare,* alter. of L *graecissare,* fr. Gk *graikizein* to speak Greek, fr. *graikos* Greek + *-izein* -ize] **1 :** to make Greek or Hellenistic in quality, traits, or cultural characteristics ⟨the *grecized* eastern capital of the Roman Empire⟩ ⟨steps toward *grecizing* the Jews of Asia Minor⟩ **2 :** to modify (as a word, phrase, language) to accord with characteristically Greek language forms esp. in spelling

greco- *or* **graeco-** *comb form, usu cap* [L *Graeco-,* fr. *Graecus* Greek — more at GREEK] **1 :** Greece or Greeks ⟨*Grecophile*⟩ ⟨*Grecomania*⟩ **2 :** Greek and ⟨*Greco*-Latin⟩ ⟨*Greco*-Persian⟩ ⟨*Graeco*-Roman⟩

greco-roman \¦grē(,)kō, -re(- *sometimes* -rā(-+\ *adj, usu cap G&R* [*Greco-* + *Roman*] **:** having characteristics that are partly Greek and partly Roman; *specif* **:** having the characteristics of Roman art done under strong Greek influence

greco-roman wrestling *n, usu cap G&R* **:** wrestling in which the use of the legs for attack or defense is forbidden and a fall is gained by the contestant who pins both his opponent's shoulders to the ground

¹**gree** \ˈgrē\ *n* -S [ME, fr. MF *gré,* fr. LL *gratum,* fr. neut. of L *gratus* pleasing, thankful — more at GRACE] *archaic* **:** GOODWILL, FAVOR, PLEASURE, SATISFACTION — **make gree** *archaic* **:** to give satisfaction (as for an injury)

²**gree** \ˈ"\ *n* -S [ME, fr. MF *gré* step, degree, fr. L *gradus* — more at GRADE] **1** *obs* **:** rank or position esp. in a social scale **2** *chiefly Scot* **:** MASTERY, SUPERIORITY; *also* **:** the reward for these qualities — **bear the gree** *chiefly Scot* **:** to carry off the prize

³**gree** \ˈ"\ *vb* -ED/-ING/-S [ME *green,* short for *agreen* — more at AGREE] *now dial* **:** AGREE

greece \ˈgrēs\ *adj, usu cap* [fr. *Greece,* country in southeastern Europe] **:** of or from Greece **:** of the kind or style prevalent in Greece **:** GREEK

greed \ˈgrēd\ *n* -S [back-formation fr. *greedy*] **1 :** inordinate or all-consuming and usu. reprehensible acquisitiveness esp. for wealth or gain **:** COVETOUSNESS, AVARICE ⟨a passionate ~ for other people's money⟩ **2 :** extreme or voracious desire esp. for food or drink; *also* **:** behavior motivated by such desire **syn** see CUPIDITY

greed·i·ly \-dᵊlē, -dəl|, |i\ *adv* [ME *grediliche, gredily,* fr. OE *grǣdilīce,* fr. *grǣdig* + *-līce* -ly] **:** in a greedy manner **:** in a way that shows great desire or marked acquisitiveness; *esp* **:** in a way showing great hunger or thirst ⟨ate ~⟩ ⟨weakened by thirst, the party drank ~ —*Amer. Guide Series: Calif.*⟩

greed·i·ness \-dēnəs, -din-\ *n* -ES [ME *gredinesse,* fr. OE *grǣdignæsse,* fr. *grǣdig* + *-næsse, -ness* -ness] **:** the quality or state of being greedy: **a :** extreme or excessive desire for food or drink; *also* **:** behavior giving evidence of this **:** VORACITY **b :** extreme or excessive desire for wealth or gain **:** COVETOUSNESS **c :** strong desire or longing **:** EAGERNESS ⟨moved by a ~ for a more exciting existence⟩

greedy \-dē,-di\ *adj* -ER/-EST [ME *gredy,* fr. OE *grǣdig;* akin to OHG *grātag* greedy, ON *grāthr* greed, hunger, *grāthugr* greedy, Goth *gredus* hungry, *gredags* hungry, and perh. to OE *giernan* to long for — more at YEARN] **1 :** having or showing a very strong desire for food or drink **:** RAVENOUS, VORACIOUS — often used with *of* ⟨a lion ~ of his prey⟩ **2 :** having or marked by an intense usu. reprehensibly excessive or selfish desire esp. for possessions ⟨~ for money and power⟩ ⟨~ of her love⟩ ⟨so thoroughly mercenary, so frankly ~ —Dashiell Hammett⟩ ⟨the powerful depiction of the ~, obsessed, invalid love of the heroine —Anthony Quinton⟩ ⟨all who engaged in politics were ~ of office —G.M.Trevelyan⟩ **3 :** EAGER, KEEN ⟨went at the task with ~ interest⟩ ⟨elated and ~ for the future —Frances G. Patton⟩ **syn** see COVETOUS

greedy scale *n* **:** a scale (*Hemiberlesia rapax*) that is native to Europe but has been introduced into America and Australia and attacks many woody plants

greegree *var of* GRIS-GRIS

¹**greek** \ˈgrēk\ *n* -S [ME *Greke,* fr. OE *Grēcas,* pl., fr. L *Graecus,* fr. Gk *Graikos*] **1** *cap* **a :** a native or inhabitant of Greece **:** one of the Greek people; *specif* **:** a member of one of the races of ancient Greece — compare ACHAEAN, AEOLIAN, DORIAN, HELLADIC, HELLENE, HELLENISTIC 1, IONIAN, MYCENAEAN, PELASGIAN **b :** one that is of Greek descent **c :** one that is Grecian in physical form or beauty of face **:** one suggesting a figure of classical Greek sculpture ⟨the best athlete in our village, a young *Greek* in his movements —C.H.Towne⟩ **2** *cap* **a :** the language that has been used by the Greeks in its various stages of development from prehistoric times to the

present and that constitutes by itself a branch of the Indo-European language family — see AEOLIC, ARCADIAN, ATTIC, CYPRIOT, DORIC, IONIC, KOINE, LATE GREEK, MIDDLE GREEK, NEW GREEK; INDO-EUROPEAN LANGUAGES table **b** : ancient Greek as used from the time of the earliest records to the end of the 2d century A.D. **c** [trans. of L *Graecum* (in the medieval proverb *Graecum est; non potest legi* It is Greek; it cannot be read)] : something unintelligible; *esp* : GIBBERISH ⟨the theory of relativity is *Greek* to most people⟩ **3** *cap* : a member of an Eastern Orthodox church : ORTHODOX **4** *often cap* **a** *archaic* : SWINDLER, SHARPER; *esp* : CARDSHARPER **b** *obs* : a hail-fellow-well-met and reveler **5** *usu cap* : a member of a Greek-letter fraternity or sorority

[2]**greek** \"\ *adj, usu cap* [ME *greke*, fr. *Greke*, n.] **1 a** : of, relating to, or characteristic of Greece **b** : of, relating to, or characteristic of the Greeks **c** : of, relating to, or characteristic of the language of the Greeks **2** *of architecture* : of, relating to, or imitating the architecture of classical Greece : marked by pedimented structures that employ the Greek architectural orders **3 a** : Eastern Orthodox **b** : of, relating to, or being an Eastern church using the Byzantine rite in Greek **c** : of, relating to, or being the established Orthodox church of Greece autocephalous under a holy synod since 1833

greek alphabet *n, usu cap G* : an alphabet that has been used from ancient times for writing the Greek language, that is of Semitic origin but differs from Semitic alphabets in having characters for the vowels, and that has given rise directly or indirectly to various other alphabets (as the Latin, the Coptic, the Cyrillic)

greek calends *or* **greek kalends** *n pl, usu cap G* [trans. of L *kalendas graecas* (in *ad kalendas graecas solvere* to go without paying, lit., to pay at the Greek calends); fr. the fact that the Greeks did not reckon time by calends] : a time that will never arrive ⟨a bill he planned to pay at the *Greek calends*⟩

[1]**greek catholic** *adj, usu cap G&C* **1** : Eastern Orthodox **2** : of, relating to, or being a Uniate church using the Byzantine rite

[2]**greek catholic** *n, usu cap G&C* **1** : a member of an Eastern church **2** : a member of a Greek Catholic Uniate church

greek chorus *n, usu cap G* **1** : a chorus in a classical Greek play typically serving to formulate, express, and comment on the moral issue that is raised by the dramatic action or to express an emotion appropriate to each stage of the dramatic conflict **2** : a group of people who with persistence express esp. similar views or feelings about a particular action or series of actions

greek cross *n, usu cap G* : a cross having an upright and a transverse shaft equal in length and intersecting at their middles so that all four arms are equal in length

greek-cross plan *n, usu cap G* : a plan of a building having a square central mass and four equal arms

Greek cross

greek fir *n, usu cap G* : an ornamental Grecian evergreen tree (*Abies cephalonica*) with lustrous red-brown branches and stiff pointed leaves

greek fire *n, usu cap G* **1** : an incendiary composition used in warfare by the Byzantine Greeks and said to have burst into flame on wetting **2** : any of several flammable mixtures : WILDFIRE

greek foot *n, usu cap G* : an ancient Greek unit of length equal to 1.012 English feet

greek fret *or* **greek key** *n, usu cap G* : [4]FRET 2

greek gift *n, usu cap G* [so called fr. the story of the Trojan horse — more at TROJAN HORSE] : a gift given or a favor done with a treacherous purpose

greek·ish \'grēkish\ *adj, usu cap* [ME *grekkish*, fr. OE *grēcisc*, fr. *Grēcas*, pl., Greeks + *-isc* -ish — more at GREEK] **1** *archaic* : GREEK **2** [[2]*greek* + *-ish*] : Greek or somewhat Greek in quality or characteristics

greek·ish·ness *n* -ES *usu cap* : the quality or state of being somewhat Greek in characteristics

greek·ist \-kəst\ *n* -S *usu cap* : a specialist in Greek

greek·ize \'grē,kīz\ *vt* -ED/-ING/-S *often cap* : GRECIZE

greek juniper *n, usu cap G* : an ornamental Eurasian tree (*Juniperus excelsa*) having a pyramidal shape, scaly leaves, and bluish black berrylike fruits

greek·less \'grēkləs\ *adj, usu cap* : being without an ability to translate Greek : having no training in the Greek language ⟨writes for a *Greekless* reader —G.M.Messing⟩ — **greek·less·ness** *n* -ES *usu cap*

greek-letter fraternity *n, usu cap G* : a fraternity designated by usu. three Greek letters

greek-letter society *n, usu cap G* : a Greek-letter fraternity or sorority

greek-letter sorority *n, usu cap G* : a sorority designated by usu. three Greek letters

greek·ling \'grēkliŋ\ *n* -S *cap, archaic* : a small, insignificant, or contemptible Greek

greek mode *n, usu cap G* : a descending musical scale based upon the tetrachord in which the octave species consists of two disjunct tetrachords

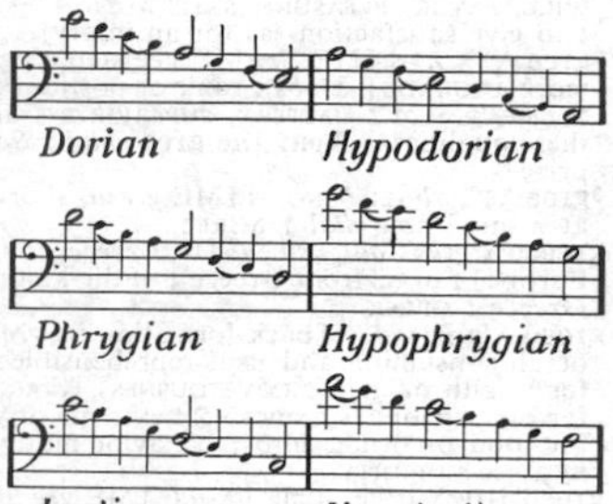

greek·ness *n* -ES *usu cap* : the quality or state of being Greek

greek orthodox *adj, usu cap G&O* : Eastern Orthodox; *specif* : GREEK 3c

greek partridge *n, usu cap G* : ROCK PARTRIDGE; *esp* : one of the variety (*Alectoris graeca graeca*) of mountainous southern Europe with gray, black, and chestnut plumage

Dorian · Hypodorian · Phrygian · Hypophrygian · Lydian · Hypolydian · Mixolydian · [Hypomixolydian would be equivalent to Dorian.]

Greek modes

greek revival *n, cap G & usu cap R* **1** : a style of architecture in the first half of the 19th century marked by the use or imitation of Greek orders **2** : a style of decoration (as of furniture) using or imitating the decorative motifs of ancient Greece

greeks *pl of* GREEK

greek tea *n, usu cap G* : FRENCH TEA

greek tortoise *n, usu cap G* : EUROPEAN TORTOISE

greek valerian *n, usu cap G* : any of several plants of the genus *Polemonium*; *esp* : JACOB'S LADDER 1a

greek wave *n, usu cap G* : a curvilinear variant of the Greek fret

[1]**green** \'grēn\ *adj* -ER/-EST [ME *grene*, fr. OE *grēne*; akin to OHG *gruoni* green, ON *grœnn* green, OE *grōwan* to grow — more at GROW] **1 a** : of the color green ⟨a ~ jade⟩ **b** : having the color of growing fresh grass or of the emerald ⟨~ lawns⟩ **2 a** : having abundant verdure : covered by green growth or foliage : VERDANT ⟨the hills are low and very beautiful because they are ~ —John Welman⟩ **b** : pleasant and alluring : exceedingly broad and fair ⟨an original scientist turns his feet ruinously into the wide ~ descent to popular science —Carl Van Doren⟩ **c** *of a season of the year* : characterized by mildness : TEMPERATE ⟨a ~ yule⟩ **d** : consisting of green plants, herbs, or vegetables ⟨a ~ salad⟩ ⟨gathered their ~ cargoes and returned to their rewarding trade —Anne Dorrance⟩ **3 a** : full of life and vigor : YOUTHFUL ⟨the Fates had ruled that he should reach a ~ old age —Robert Graves⟩ ⟨with his white head and his loneliness he remained young and ~ at heart —John Galsworthy⟩ **b** : strikingly alive : vivid despite the passage of time ⟨my memory of all of them is still ~ —J.J.Mallon⟩ ⟨hard to bring events into sharp and stable focus . . . while one's emotions about them are still ~ —Cabell Phillips⟩ **4 a** *of a plant* : YOUNG, FRESH, TENDER ⟨the burro . . . can subsist equally well on succulent ~ grasses or dry bark —*Amer. Guide Series: Ariz.*⟩ **b** *of a fruit or vegetable* : not ripened or matured : IMMATURE ⟨~ apples⟩ **5** *of a wound* : recently incurred : FRESH, UNHEALED ⟨like a ~ wound at first I felt it not —John Home⟩ **6** : marked by a pale or sickly appearance ⟨is ~ with envy⟩ ⟨was scared ~⟩ ⟨wakes it now to look so ~ and pale —Shak.⟩ **7 a** : not fully processed or treated: as (1) *of coffee* : partly raw : RAW : not roasted (2) *of meat* : freshly killed : not dried or salted (3) *of market fish* : as taken from the water : not cleaned (4) *of liquor* : not aged (5) *of a bone* : not seasoned or dried and often containing marrow (6) *of a hide or pelt* : not dressed or tanned (7) *of lumber* : freshly sawed : UNSEASONED (8) *of ceramics* : not yet baked in an oven or kiln : not fired (9) *of metal powder* : not sintered **b** : not in condition for a particular use: as (1) *of concrete or mortar* : not sufficiently hardened (2) *of paper* : incompletely seasoned (3) *of an inking roller* : freshly cast (4) *of printer's proof* : not corrected **c** (1) *of a female fish* : not ready to spawn — compare RIPE, SPENT (2) *of a crab* : not quite ready to shed **8 a** : marked by inexperience or immaturity : lacking training, knowledge, or experience ⟨we are beginners and the humblest and ~*est* of the tribe —John Mason Brown⟩ ⟨shipped as a ~ hand on a vessel —W.J.Ghent⟩ **b** : lacking sophistication : unfamiliar with worldly ways : GULLIBLE, NAÏVE ⟨wasn't so ~ as to expect suspicious characters to look suspicious —G.K. Chesterton⟩ **c** *of a horse* : not fully qualified for or experienced in a particular function: (1) *of a workhorse* : broken but not trained (2) *of a Thoroughbred* : not yet raced for premiums or money or speeded against time (3) *of a hunter* : not previously exhibited or hunted **9** *obs* : recently buried ⟨where bloody Tybalt, yet but ~ in earth, lies festering in his shroud —Shak.⟩ **10** *of hemolytic streptococci* : tending to produce green pigment when cultured on blood media **syn** see RUDE

[2]**green** \"\ *vb* -ED/-ING/-S [ME *grenen*, fr. OE *grēnian*; akin to OHG *gruonēn* to become green, ON *grœnast*; inchoatives fr. the root of E [1]*green*] *vi* : to become or grow green ⟨my pea jacket had ~*ed* with wear —James Still⟩ ⟨in the soft moist air the grass was ~*ing* —Dorothy C. Fisher⟩ ~ *vt* **1** : to make green : cause to acquire a green color ⟨the colors pouring down the balustrade and ~*ing* the floor —Richard Llewellyn⟩ ⟨white frock . . . which she had so carelessly ~*ed* about the skirt on the damping grass —Thomas Hardy⟩ **2** : to make fun of by or as if by a hoax ⟨some witchcraft material which came to my attention seemed so extraordinary that I suspected my friends were ~*ing* me —Vance Randolph⟩

[3]**green** \"\ *n* -S [ME *grene*, fr. *grene*, adj.] **1 a** : a color whose hue is somewhat less yellow than that of growing fresh grass or of the emerald or is that of the part of the spectrum lying between blue and yellow **b** : the one of the four psychologically primary hues that is evoked in the average normal observer under normal conditions by radiant energy of the wavelength 530 millimicrons **c** : one of the six psychologically primary object colors **2 a** : clothing or cloth of a green color **b greens** *pl* : a green uniform ⟨a sergeant of marines, very snappy in his ~*s* —John Dos Passos⟩ **3** : green vegetation ⟨new spring ~ mantled the hills⟩: as **a greens** *pl* : fresh foliage or leafy parts of plants for use as decoration; *esp* : evergreen branches for winter decorations ⟨always collected our own Christmas ~*s*⟩ **b greens** *pl* (1) : leafy herbs (as spinach, dandelions, Swiss chard) that are boiled or steamed as a vegetable : POTHERB 1 (2) : a vegetable whose foliage and foliage-bearing branches are the sole or chief edible part : GREEN VEGETABLE **4** : a grassy plain or plot: as **a** : a common or park in the center of a town or village ⟨white clapboard and red brick Georgian homes and churches looking out on the placid village ~ —Budd Schulberg⟩ **b** : BOWLING GREEN **c** : PUTTING GREEN **d** : an archery shooting range **5** : youthful vigor : VIRILITY — usu. used in the phrase *in the green* ⟨thy leaf has perished in the ~ —Alfred Tennyson⟩ **6** : a pigment or dye that colors green **7** : MONEY; *esp* : GREENBACKS **8 a** : the petticoat of an archery target **b** : a shot that hits in the petticoat **c** : an arrow that misses the target and hits the grass **9** : a card belonging to one of the four suits in the German pack of playing cards and having a leaf as its symbol

[4]**green** \"\ *vi* -ED/-ING/-S [ME *grenen*, prob. modif. of ON *girna* — more at YEARN] *Scot* : YEARN, LONG

green·able \-nəbəl\ *adj* : capable of being made green

green acid *n* : any of various mixtures of water-soluble sulfonic acid derivatives of petroleum obtained as by-products in treating white oils with sulfuric acid

green adder's mouth *n* : a low No. American herb (*Malaxis unifolia*) having a solitary leaf and flowers with reflexed petals that resemble threads

green alder *n* : any of several alders: **a** : an alder (*Alnus crispa*) of northern No. America distinguished by the light green undersurfaces of the leaves and by the winged nuts **b** : a European alder (*A. viridis*) **c** : SPECKLED ALDER

green alga *n* : an alga in which the chlorophyll is not masked or characteristically obscured by other pigments; *specif* : any alga of the division Chlorophyta

green·a·lite \-nᵊl,īt\ *n* -S [[1]*green* + connective *-a-* + *-lite*] : a mineral consisting of hydrous ferrous silicate of an earthy green color occurring as small granules in a cherty rock associated with the iron ores of the Mesabi range

green almond *n* : PISTACHIO 1a(2)

green aloe *n* : GIANT CABUYA

green amaranth *n* : PIGWEED a

green aphis *n, NewZeal* : GREEN PEACH APHID

green apple aphid *n* : APPLE APHID

green arrow arum *n* : an arrow arum (*Peltandra virginica*)

green ash *n* : a red ash (*Fraxinus pennsylvanica subintegerrima*) with branchlets, petioles, and lower leaf surfaces glabrous

greenback \'=,=\ *n* **1** : any of numerous animals variably greenish about the upper parts (as a green frog or various fishes) **2 a** : a legal-tender note issued by the U.S. government **b greenbacks** *pl* : MONEY

green-backed goldfinch \'=,=-\ *n* : a goldfinch (*Spinus psaltria hesperophilus*) of western No. America having the upper parts olive green

green·back·er \'grēn,bakə(r)\ *n* [*greenback* (money) + *-er*] **1** *usu cap* : a member of a post-Civil War American political party opposing any reduction in the amount of paper money in circulation **2** : one who advocates a paper currency backed only by the U.S. government ⟨the silverites, the ~*s*, the price stabilizers, and others . . . are pledged to a central-bank scheme —*Harper's*⟩

green·back·ism \-a,kizəm\ *n* -S *usu cap* : the principles of the greenbackers

greenback mackerel *n* : PACIFIC MACKEREL

greenback shower *n* : a shower at which gifts of money are presented to the prospective bride

greenbark \'=,=\ *or* **greenbark acacia** *n* : PALOVERDE

green bass *n* : LARGEMOUTH BLACK BASS

green bean *n* : any of numerous kidney beans that have the pods green when suitably matured for use as snap beans — compare WAX BEAN

greenbelt \'=,=\ *n* : a belt of parkways, parks, or farmlands that encircles a town or community and is designed to prevent undesirable encroachments

green-blind \'=,=\ *adj* : exhibiting or affected with deuteranopia

greenboard \'=,=\ *n* : a chalkboard with a green surface : green blackboard

greenbone \'=,=\ *n* : any of several fishes having the bones green esp. when cooked: as **a** : NEEDLEFISH **b** : EELPOUT 1a

green book *n, often cap G&B* : an official report of government affairs bound in green — used esp. of Italian, British, and British Indian reports

greenbottle fly \'=,==-\ *also* **greenbottle** *n* : any of several brilliant coppery green-bodied flies of the family Calliphoridae; *esp* : a fly of the genus *Lucilia*

greenbrier \'=,=\ *n* : a plant of the genus *Smilax*; *esp* : a prickly vine (*Smilax rotundifolia*) of the eastern U.S. with a yellowish green stem, thick leaves, and umbels of small greenish flowers

green bristle *or* **green bristlegrass** *n* : GREEN FOXTAIL

green broke *adj, of a horse* : incompletely broken or trained

green broom *n* **1** : WOODWAXEN **2** : SCOTCH BROOM

greenbug \'=,=\ *n* : a green aphid (*Schizaphis graminum*) that is very destructive to wheat, oats, and other grains

green·bul \'grēn,bu̇l\ *n* -S [short for *green bulbul*] : any of numerous variably greenish African bulbuls — called also *green bulbul*

green bulbul *n* **1** : any of numerous predominantly green bulbuls of southeast Asia and the southwest Pacific that have rich silky plumage often varied with blue, black, or yellow and that feed chiefly on fruits and nectar — called also *fruitsucker, leafbird;* see CHLOROPSIS **2** : GREENBUL

green charge *n* : a mixture of ingredients for gunpowder before the intimate mixing in the incorporating mill

green cheese *n* **1** : cheese that is not ripened : new cheese **2** : cheese (as sapsago) having a green color **3** : cheese made of whey or skim milk

green cinnabar *n* **1** : a green pigment consisting of fired oxides of cobalt and zinc **2** : a pigment consisting of chrome yellow and Prussian blue

green citrus aphid *n* : a small green aphid (*Aphis spiraecola*) esp. abundant on citrus where it causes distorting and rosetting of the leaves — called also *spirea aphid*

green cloth *n* **1** *usu cap G&C* [so called fr. the green-covered table at which the board orig. carried on its business] : a board or court of justice of the British sovereign's household that is composed of the lord steward and his officers and has cognizance of matters of justice in the household with power to correct offenders and keep the peace within the palace **2 a** : a layout for gambling **b** : BILLIARD TABLE

green cloverworm \'=',==,=\ *n* : a small slender green larva of a noctuid moth (*Plathypena scabra*) destructive to clover and other legumes

green cod *n* **1** : POLLACK **2** : LINGCOD

green cormorant *n* : a shag (*Phalacrocorax aristotelis*)

green corn *n* : the young tender ears of Indian corn suitable for cooking as a vegetable — compare SWEET CORN

green crab *n* : a nearly cosmopolitan edible crab (*Carcinus maenas*) found along shores chiefly in the intertidal zone

green dragon *n* **1** : a European arum (*Dracunculus vulgaris*) resembling the cuckoopint **2** : an American arum (*Arisaema dracontium*) differing from the related common jack-in-the-pulpit by its digitate leaves, slender greenish yellow spathe, and elongated spadix

green drake *n* **1** : any of various British mayflies **2** : a fisherman's lure resembling a green drake

green duck *n* : a young duck; *esp* : a well-fattened young duck ready for market when 9 to 13 weeks old

green-ear disease *n* : a disease of pearl millet and other grasses in which part or all of the head becomes leafy from attacks of a downy mildew (*Sclerospora graminicola*)

green earth *n* [trans. of F *terre verte* or It *terra verde*] **1** : TERRE VERTE 2 **2** : any of various naturally occurring silicates esp. of iron used chiefly as bases for green basic dyes — called also *terre verte*

green ebony *n* **1 a** : an ebony of a greenish color **b** : a tree of the genus *Diospyros* (as *D. melanoxylon*) yielding such ebony **2** : COCUSWOOD

greened *past of* GREEN

[1]**greener** *comparative of* GREEN

[2]**green·er** \'grēnə(r)\ *n* -S [[1]*green* + *-er*] : an unskilled or inexperienced workman; *esp* : one who is a recently arrived alien ⟨a ~ of the greenest order, having landed at the docks only a few hours ago —Israel Zangwill⟩

green·ery \'grēn(ə)rē, -ri\ *n* -ES [[1]*green* + *-ery*] **1** : green foliage or plants : VERDURE ⟨the lake . . . reflects the ~ of hilly shores —*Amer. Guide Series: Oreg.*⟩ **2** : decorations of green leaves and branches — compare [3]GREEN 3a ⟨an awning-covered pavilion festooned for the occasion with ~ —Harriot B. Barbour⟩ **3** : GREENHOUSE

greenest *superlative of* GREEN

green-eyed \'=',=\ *adj* : characterized by envy or distrust : JEALOUS ⟨beware, my lord, of jealousy; it is the *green-eyed* monster —Shak.⟩ ⟨the *green-eyed* locals who had spied on him —E.O.Schlunke⟩

green fee *also* **greens fee** *n* : a fee paid for the privilege of playing on a golf course

greenfeed \'=,=\ *n, Austral* : succulent forage fed to livestock without ensiling

green felt *n* **1** : an alga of the genus *Vaucheria* (esp. *V. terrestris*) **2** : a dense green growth produced by green felt

greenfinch \'=,=\ *n* **1** : a very common European finch (*Chloris chloris*) having olive-green and yellow plumage **2** : TEXAS SPARROW

green fingers *n pl* : GREEN THUMB

green fire *n* : a composition that burns with a bright green light produced usu. by barium nitrate

greenfish \'=,=\ *n* : any of several variably greenish or bluish fishes: as **a** : POLLACK **b** : BLUEFISH 1 **c** : an opaleye (*Girella nigricans*)

green flash *n* : a momentary green appearance of the uppermost part of the sun's disk that results from atmospheric refraction when the sun sinks below or rises above the horizon

greenfly \'=,=\ *n, Brit* : APHID; *esp* : GREEN PEACH APHID

green foxtail *n* : a European grass (*Setaria viridis*) naturalized in No. America where it is often a troublesome weed

green fringed orchis *n* : RAGGED ORCHIS

green frog *n* : a common frog (*Rana clamitans*) of the eastern and central U.S. and parts of Canada

green fruitworm *n* : the larva of any of several noctuid moths; *esp* : an orchard pest (*Lithophane antennata*) that feeds on leaves and fruits

green·gage \'grēn,gāj, '=',=\ *n* -S [*green* + Sir William *Gage* †1820 Eng. botanist who imported it from France] : any of several rather small rounded greenish or greenish yellow cultivated plums of European origin grown chiefly for their superior dessert quality

green gall *n* : an oak apple collected before the escape of the enclosed wasp larva while very dark in color and rich in tannin

green gentian *n* : any of several plants of the genus *Swertia* found chiefly in the Rocky mountain region

greengill \'=,=\ *n* : an oyster with gills or other parts tinged with a green pigment that results from its feeding on green vegetable organisms and that does not injure it as food — compare GREENING

green ginger *n* : undried ginger

green gland *n* : one of a pair of large green glands in crayfishes and related crustaceans that are believed to act as kidneys and that have outlets at the bases of the larger antennae

green glass *n* **1** : a low-grade soda-lime glass whose natural green color is due to impurities in the raw materials **2** : glass of any quality that has been colored green by the addition of coloring agents to the batch

green gold *n* : an alloy of 14 to 18 karat gold that is greenish in color and employs either silver or silver plus cadmium or zinc as the alloying metal

green goods *n pl* **1** : counterfeit greenbacks **2** : fresh vegetables

green goose *n* : a young goose; *esp* : a well-fattened young goose ready for market when 10 to 12 weeks old

green gown *n* [so called fr. the grass stains traditionally acquired when illicit love is made] *archaic* : a gown symbolically acquired at illicit loss of virginity ⟨many a *green gown* has been given, many a kiss, both odd and even —Robert Herrick †1674⟩

green gram *n* : MUNG BEAN

green grasshopper *n* : any of numerous green slender-bodied long-horned grasshoppers

greengrocer \'=,==\ *n, chiefly Brit* : a retailer of fresh vegetables and fruit

greengrocery \'=,=(=)=\ *n* **1** *chiefly Brit* : the wares of a greengrocer **2** *chiefly Brit* : a greengrocer's shop

green grosbeak *n* : GREENFINCH 1

green guenon *n* : GREEN MONKEY

green hand *n, dial* : GREEN THUMB

greenhead \'=,=\ *n* **1** *archaic* : GREENHORN **2 a** : MALLARD **b** : GREATER SCAUP **3** *also* **greenhead fly** : any of several green-eyed biting flies of the family Tabanidae; *esp* : a large fly (*Tabanus nigrovittatus*) common near salt marshes **4** : STRIPED BASS

green–headed *adj, obs* : marked by or based on inexperience ⟨the advice of his *green-headed* counselors —Francis Roberts⟩
greenheart \ˈ⸗,⸗\ *n* **1** : any of several tropical American trees furnishing somewhat greenish usu. hard valuable wood: as **a** : BEBEERU **b** *West Indies* : a tree (*Colubrina ferruginosa*) used in general construction work **c** *Jamaica* : a tree (*Zizyphus chloroxylon*) with very hard durable wood **d** *in northeastern So. America* : BETHABARA **2** : the wood of a greenheart
green hellebore *n* **1** : AMERICAN HELLEBORE **2** : a hellebore (*Helleborus viridis*) with large pedate leaves and solitary nodding flowers
green heron *n* : any of various small herons (genus *Butorides*); *esp* : a small American heron (*B. virescens*) with mostly greenish back and chestnut neck
greenhew \ˈ⸗,⸗\ *n* [³*green* + *hew*] : the right to cut vert
greenhide \ˈ⸗,⸗\ *n, Austral* : RAWHIDE ⟨a long-lashed stockwhip and lariat of plaited ~ —I.L.Idriess⟩
greenhorn \ˈ⸗,⸗\ *n* [obs. *greenhorn* animal with green or young horns, fr. ME *grenehorn*, fr. *grene* green + *horn*] **1** : an inexperienced or unsophisticated person ⟨an intellectual ~ from the provinces —Nigel Dennis⟩; *esp* : one easily duped or imposed upon **2** : a newcomer (as to a country) unacquainted with local manners and customs; *esp* : a recently arrived immigrant ⟨~*s* . . . looking half-starved after their long trip from the old country —Mary Deasy⟩
greenhouse \ˈ⸗,⸗\ *n* **1** : a structure enclosed by glass and devoted to the cultivation or protection of tender plants or the production of plants out of season — compare CONSERVATORY, COOLHOUSE, HOTHOUSE **2** *chiefly Brit* : a place for drying ceramic ware before firing **3** : a plastic shell covering the cockpit, cabin, turret, or nose of an airplane
greenhouse leaf tier *n* : CELERY LEAF TIER
greenhouse thrips *n* : a thrips (*Heliothrips haemorrhoidalis*) that feeds on foliage and blossoms in greenhouses or in warm regions on citrus and other cultivated plants
greenhouse whitefly *n* : a tiny white 4-winged fly (*Trialeurodes vaporariorum*) that is related to the aphids and scale insects and has minute pale green larvae which together with the adults suck the juices from plants and thereby cause them to yellow and wilt
green hydra *n* : a cosmopolitan hydra (*Chlorohydra viridissima*) made green by the presence in its cells of chlorophyll-bearing plastids
greenie *var of* GREENY
greenier *comparative of* GREENY
greenies *pl of* GREENY
greeniest *superlative of* GREENY
green·ing \ˈgrēniŋ, -nēŋ\ *n* -s [¹*green* + *-ing*] **1** : any of several green-skinned apples **2** : a green appearance of oysters caused by their feeding on green marine algae — compare GREENGILL **3** : SUNBURN 2a
green·ish \-nish,-nēsh\ *adj* [ME *grenissh*, fr. *grene* green + *-issh* -ish] : somewhat green : having a tinge of green ⟨~ yellow⟩ ⟨~ fishes⟩ — **green·ish·ness** *n* -ES
green jack *n* : a West Indian cavalla (*Caranx ruber*)
green jay *n* : a jay (*Cyanocorax yucas*) that ranges from So. America to the Rio Grande and is brilliantly marked in green, blue, black, white, and yellow
green june beetle *n, usu cap J* : a large metallic green and brown scarabaeid beetle (*Cotinis nitida*) of the eastern U.S. whose grubs are turf pests
green·keep·er \ˈgrēn,kēpə(r)\ *also* **greens·keep·er** \-nz,k-\ *n* : a person responsible for the upkeep of a golf course
green kurrajong *n* : a tall prickly Australian shrub (*Hibiscus heterophyllus*) that is sometimes cultivated for its large white purple-centered or crimson-centered flowers
green·land \ˈgrēnlənd, -,land, -,laa(ə)nd\ *adj, usu cap* [fr. *Greenland*, largest island in the world, northeast of No. America, fr. Dan *Grønland*, fr. ON *Grænland*] : of or from Greenland : of the kind or style prevalent in Greenland : GREENLANDIC
greenland caribou *n, usu cap G* : BARREN GROUND CARIBOU
green·land·er \-də(r)\ *n* -s *cap* : a native or inhabitant of Greenland
greenland halibut *n, usu cap G* : a flatfish (*Reinhardtius hippoglossoides*) of the cold parts of the Atlantic that weighs 10 to 25 pounds and is colored on both sides
¹**green·land·ic** \(ˈ)grēnˈlandik, -laan-, -dēk\ *adj, usu cap* [*Greenland* (the island) + E *-ic*] **1 a** : of, relating to, or characteristic of Greenland **b** : of, relating to, or characteristic of the Greenlanders **2** : of, relating to, or characteristic of the language of the Greenlanders
²**greenlandic** \"\ *n* -s *cap* : an Eskimo-Aleut dialect of Greenland often considered a language — compare YUPIK
green·land·ite \ˈgrēnlən,dīt, -,lan-, -,laan-\ *n* -s [*Greenland* + E *-ite*] : COLUMBITE
greenland seal *n, usu cap G* : HARP SEAL
greenland shark *n, usu cap G* : a large shark (*Somniosus microcephalus*) of arctic seas having a small head, weak jaws, small teeth, very small fins, and skin covered uniformly with minute tubercles — called also *sleeper shark*
greenland spar *n, usu cap G* : CRYOLITE
greenland whale *n, usu cap G* : the whalebone whale of the Arctic (*Balaena mysticetus*) — called also *bowhead*
green laver *n* : SEA LETTUCE
green lead ore *n* : PYROMORPHITE
green leek *n* : an Australian parrakeet (*Polytelis swainsonii*) that is chiefly green with yellow on face and throat and the breast scarlet
green·less \ˈgrēnləs\ *adj* : lacking verdure
green·let \-lət\ *n* -s : VIREO
green light *n* [so called fr. the color of traffic lights when traffic is allowed to proceed] : authority or permission to go ahead with a definite project ⟨got a message to leave town and stay lost until I got the *green light* to return —Polly Adler⟩ ⟨a city that has just given the *green light* to a program of progress —*Wall Street Jour.*⟩
green·ling \ˈgrēnliŋ\ *n* -s [¹*green* + *-ling*] **1 a** (1) : any of several moderate-sized to large scorpaenoid food fishes (family Hexagrammidae) of the rocky coasts of the northern Pacific (2) : a common food and sport fish (*Hexagrammos decagrammus*) of the west coast of No. America — called also *kelp greenling* **b** : LINGCOD **2** : POLLACK
green linnet *n* : GREENFINCH 1
green lizard *n* : a common Eurasian lizard (*Lacerta viridis*) that becomes a foot long
green louse *n* : PLANT LOUSE
green·ly *adv, usu* -ER/-EST **1 a** : with a green color ⟨the . . . stream rushing between white crusts of frozen foam and washing ~ against ice-crowned boulders —Stephen Graham⟩ **b** : with green vegetation : VERDANTLY ⟨the earth broke ~ into spring —Millen Brand⟩ **2** : in an inexperienced manner : CLUMSILY ⟨we have done but ~ in hugger-mugger to inter him —Shak.⟩
green malt *n* : grain softened by steeping in water and allowed to germinate but not yet subjected to drying — compare MALT
green man *n* : JACK-IN-THE-GREEN 1
green mangle *n* : MARSH ELDER 2
green manure *or* **green–manure crop** *n* : an herbaceous crop (as clover) plowed under while green to enrich the soil
green–manure \ˈ⸗⸗,⸗\ *vt* : to fertilize with green manure
green mealie *n, Africa* : CORN ON THE COB
green meat *n, Brit* : fresh green herbage for feeding animals
green milkweed *n* : a green-flowered herb (*Asclepias viridiflora*) of the eastern U.S. resembling the common milkweeds
green mold *n* **1** : a green or green-spored mold; *esp* : one belonging to the genus *Penicillium* or the genus *Aspergillus* — compare BLUE MOLD **2** : a disease caused by green mold
green monkey *n* : a West African long-tailed monkey (*Cercopithecus sabaeus*) that has greenish-appearing hair and is often tamed and trained
green mountain boy *n, usu cap G&M* [fr. *Green Mountain Boys*, a militia organized in Vermont during the Am. Revolution, fr. the *Green Mountains*, Vt.] : a male Vermonter — used as a nickname
green mud *n* : a deep-sea sediment consisting largely of the remains of Foraminifera and of glauconite
green muscardine *n* : a disease of silkworms and other caterpillars caused by a fungus (*Metarrhizium anisopliae*)

green·ness \ˈgrēnnəs\ *n* -ES [ME *grennes, grennesse*, fr. OE *grēnnes*, fr. *grēne* green + *-nes* -ness — more at GREEN] : the quality or state of being green: as **a** : VERDANCY ⟨carried us past banks of soft ~ shaded by tall trees —Thomas Horgan⟩ **b** : green color ⟨~ of the sea⟩ ⟨~ of shutters against the white clapboards of the house⟩ **c** (1) : youth and immaturity ⟨the ~ of his years secured him from any suspicion —Tobias Smollett⟩ (2) : lack of training or knowledge : INEXPERIENCE ⟨soldiers without battle experience had shown ~ —A.J.Liebling⟩ (3) : GULLIBILITY, NAÏVETÉ ⟨betraying his ~ to the Yankees by his questions —H.D.Thoreau⟩ **d** : VITALITY, VIGOR ⟨the affection of a child gives a ~ to old age —Peter Parley⟩
green ocher *n* **1** : TERRE VERTE 2 **2** : a green pigment prepared from yellow ocher treated with potassium ferrocyanide
gree·nock·ite \ˈgrēnə,kīt\ *n* -s [Charles M. Cathcart, Lord *Greenock* †1859 Eng. soldier + E *-ite*] : a mineral CdS consisting of native cadmium sulfide occurring in yellow translucent hexagonal crystals and as an earthy incrustation
green oil *n* : any of various oils that are green in color or that have not been refined: as **a** : ANTHRACENE OIL **b** : a fraction obtained from shale oil in the first distillation and chemical treatment
green onion *n* : a young onion pulled before the bulb has enlarged for its blanched base and lower stalk which are usu. eaten raw (as in salad)
green osier *n* : either of two dogwoods: **a** : BLUE DOGWOOD **b** : a coarse shrub (*Cornus rugosa*) with greenish branches, broadly ovate leaves, and bluish fruit — called also *round-leaved dogwood*
green out *vi* : to put forth green shoots ⟨after July's plentiful rainfall most of the state's cattle ranges were *greening out* —*Time*⟩ ~ *vt, Midland* : SWINDLE, CHEAT : make a fool of
gree·no·vite \ˈgrēnə,vīt\ *n* -s [F *grenovite*, irreg. fr. George B. *Greenough* †1855 Eng. geologist + F *-ite*] : a sphene colored red or rose by manganese
green oyster *n* : GREENGILL
green paint *n* : the dirty blue-green deposit on wave-dashed rocks at the water's edge caused by certain blue-green algae (esp. of the genera *Coelosphaerium* and *Microcystis*)
green peach aphid *n* : a yellowish green aphid (*Myzus persicae*) native to Europe but now nearly cosmopolitan in distribution that feeds on numerous cultivated plants, is frequently a vector of virus diseases, and is esp. destructive to peaches, potatoes, and spinach — called also *greenfly, spinach aphid*
green peak *n, dial Eng* : GREEN WOODPECKER
green pepper *n* : SWEET PEPPER
green pigeon *n* : any of numerous chiefly tropical Old World fruit doves with green plumage and feathered tarsi — called also *fruit pigeon*
green pike *n* **1** : CHAIN PICKEREL **2** : WALLEYED PIKE **3** : SAUGER
green plover *n* **1** : LAPWING **2** : GOLDEN PLOVER
green poppy *n* : FOXGLOVE 1
green rein orchis *n* : a No. American terrestrial orchid (*Perularic flava*) with greenish yellow flowers
green river *n, usu cap G&R* [fr. *Green river*, a stream that flows through the region in Kentucky where it is produced] : a dark air-cured tobacco used chiefly for chewing tobacco
greenroom \ˈ⸗,⸗\ *n* [prob. so called fr. its orig. being painted green] : a room in a theater or concert hall where actors or musicians relax esp. before going on stage and where they meet friends during intermissions or after performances
green rose *n* : a very large China rose (*Rosa chinensis viridiflora*) whose petals are represented by narrow green leaves
green rot *n* : a decay of fallen beech, oak, birch, or other deciduous trees in which the wood is colored a malachite green by a cup fungus (*Peziza aeruginosa*)
green rouge *n* : chromic oxide used as a polishing material esp. for platinum and stainless steel
greens *pres 3d sing of* GREEN, *pl of* GREEN
green salt *n* : coarse salt with about five percent impurities
green–salted \ˈ⸗ˈ⸗⸗\ *adj* : salted while green — used esp. of hides
greensand \ˈ⸗,⸗\ *n* **1** : a sedimentary deposit that consists largely of dark greenish grains of glauconite often mingled with clay or sand, occurs abundantly in the Cretaceous often little or not at all cemented, and is used as a water softener and as a source of potash **2** : highly siliceous sand that contains a little magnesia and alumina mixed with about one twelfth of its bulk of powdered coal or charcoal and is used when dampened for making foundry molds
green sandpiper *n* : a common Old World sandpiper (*Tringa ochropus*) related to the solitary sandpiper of America
greensauce \ˈ⸗,⸗\ *n* **1** : SHEEP SORREL 1 **2** : a wood sorrel (*Oxalis montana*)
greenschist \ˈ⸗,⸗\ *n* [¹*green* + *schist*] : a laminated metamorphic rock characterized by muscovite, quartz, and chlorite
green sea *n* : a solid wave of water coming aboard a ship ⟨rolling 30 degrees and taking *green seas* aboard —*Scientific American*⟩ — called also *green water*
green sea centipede *n* : a sea centipede (*Crabyzos longicaudatus*)
greens fee *var of* GREEN FEE
greenshank \ˈ⸗,⸗\ *n* : an Old World sandpiper (*Tringa nebularia*) related to the yellowlegs of America
green–shaving \ˈ⸗ˈ⸗⸗\ *n* : the process of scraping the flesh side of hides or skins
green shoulder *n* : a dominant genetic abnormality in the tomato characterized by lack of uniform coloration at maturity esp. about the shoulder of the fruit
green shrimp *n* **1** : a common edible shrimp (*Peneus setiferus*) of the south Atlantic coast of No. America that is whitish in color with dark antennae and with the telson edged with green **2** : an uncooked shrimp
greensick \ˈ⸗,⸗\ *adj* [back-formation fr. *greensickness*] : affected with chlorosis
green·sick·ness *n* : CHLOROSIS
greenside \ˈ⸗,⸗\ *n, dial Eng* : GRASSLAND, PASTURE
green silk *n* : any of various filamentous aquatic green algae esp. of the genus *Spirogyra* that have a silky touch when rubbed between the fingers
green singing finch *n* : a tropical African finch (*Serinus mozambicus*) that is largely green and black above and clear yellow below and is often kept as a cage bird
greenskeeper *var of* GREENKEEPER
green slate *n* : a grayish green that is yellower, less strong, and slightly lighter than slate green and yellower and duller than average bayberry or average blue spruce (sense 2a)
green sloke *n* : SEA LETTUCE
greens·man \ˈgrēnzmən\ *n, pl* **greensmen** : one who decorates motion-picture sets with grass, flowers, shrubs, and other greenery
green smelt *n* : an unfrozen smelt
green smut *n* : a disease of rice characterized by enlarged grains covered by a green powder consisting of conidia and caused by a fungus (*Ustilaginoidea virens*) — called also *false smut*
green snail *n* **1** *also* **green shell** : a large turban shell (*Turbo marmoratus*) that is common in the Indian ocean and has a bright green shell with a nacreous lining **2** : a common greenish garden snail (*Helix aperta*) that is a pest in parts of southern California
green snake *n* **1** : either of two bright green harmless largely insectivorous No. American colubrid snakes: **a** : SMOOTH GREEN SNAKE **b** : ROUGH GREEN SNAKE **2** : any of numerous African colubrid snakes of *Chlorophis* and related genera
green snow *n* : snow colored by a growth of green algae
green soap *n* : a transparent to translucent soft soap that is yellowish white to brownish to greenish yellow and that is made from vegetable oils and used esp. in skin diseases — called also *medicinal soft soap*
green sorrel *n* : GARDEN SORREL
green spleenwort *n* : a small often many-crowned fern (*Asplenium viride*) with slender linear to lanceolate fronds and slim green stipes that is widely distributed in cool parts of the northern hemisphere
green spot *also* **greenspotting** *n* : a spotting of plant parts characterized by greenish color: as **a** : OLEOCELLOSIS **b** : a leaf spot of cured tobacco caused by a fungus (*Cercospora nicotianae*)
greenstick fracture *n* : a bone fracture in a young individual in which the bone is partly broken and partly bent

green stone *n* : a grayish yellow green that is yellower and paler than average sage green, yellower, lighter, and stronger than mermaid, and yellower, lighter, and slightly stronger than palmetto
greenstone \ˈ⸗,⸗\ *n* **1** : any of numerous usu. altered dark green compact rocks (as diorite or diabase) **2** : NEPHRITE
green–striped mapleworm \ˈgrēnz,t|rīpt-, -n,st|\ *n* : a green caterpillar with black spines that is the larva of a cream and pink saturniid moth (*Anisota rubicunda*) and that occas. is a pest of maple trees
greenstuff \ˈ⸗,⸗\ *n* : green vegetation used as foodstuff
green sturgeon *n* : a rather small sturgeon (*Acipenser acutirostris*) of the Pacific coast
green sulfur bacterium *n* : a member of the family Chlorobacteriaceae — see CHLOROBACTERIUM
green sunfish *n* : a sunfish (*Lepomis cyanellus*) of the Great Lakes region and southwestward to the Rio Grande that is largely greenish above with a blue spot on each scale
green·sward \ˈgrēn,swȯ(ə)rd, -ō(ə)d\ *n* : turf that is green with growing grass ⟨went through the front door out onto a ~ hedged by boxwoods —J.M.Brinnin⟩
green table *n* [fr. *Green Tables*, nickname of the Committee of the Covenanting Government that ruled Scotland 1638–41; fr. the green cloth that covered the table where they transacted business] : COUNCIL BOARD
greentail \ˈ⸗,⸗\ *n* : MENHADEN
green–tailed towhee \ˈ⸗,⸗-\ *n* : a towhee (*Chlorura chlorura*) of the Rocky mountain region that is greenish above with chestnut crown and ashy underparts
green tea *n* : tea that is light in color from incomplete fermentation of the leaf before firing — compare BLACK TEA
greenth \ˈgrēn(t)th\ *n* -s [¹*green* + *-th* (as in *warmth*)] : green growth : VERDURE ⟨the lovely ~ and blossoms of the horse chestnuts —George Eliot⟩
green thumb *n* : an unusual ability to make plants grow ⟨had the proverbial *green thumb* and the windows were full of plants and seed boxes —*Parents' Mag.*⟩
green thursday *n, cap G&T* [trans. of G *grüner donnerstag*] : MAUNDY THURSDAY
green–tip spray *n* : PREPINK SPRAY
green toad *n* : a Eurasian toad (*Bufo viridis*) with variable chiefly green coloring
green tody *n* : a tody (*Todus todus*) of Jamaica that is largely green with a crimson throat and whitish underparts
green tree–ant \ˈ⸗ˈ⸗,⸗\ *n* : a fiercely biting Old World tropical arboreal ant (*Oecophylla virescens*) that builds a nest of leaves sewn together with silk produced by the larval ants
green trout *n* : LARGEMOUTH BLACK BASS
green turtle *n* : a large sea turtle (*Chelonia mydas*) widely distributed in warm seas that has a smooth greenish or olive-colored shell and lays highly nutritious eggs and whose flesh is much used for food
gree·nuk \ˈgrēnək\ *n* -s [by alter.] : GERENUK
green valley grass *n* : JOHNSON GRASS
green vegetable *n* : a vegetable having the edible parts rich in chlorophyll and forming an important source of vitamins and micronutrients
green vegetable bug *n* : a common and destructive cosmopolitan pentatomid bug (*Nezara viridula*) that is orange as a young nymph and bright green as an adult and that attacks many cultivated plants
green veratrum *n* : AMERICAN HELLEBORE
green verditer *n* **1** : a basic copper carbonate used as a green pigment — compare BREMEN GREEN 2 **2** : MALACHITE GREEN 3
green violet *n* : a leafy-stemmed herb (*Hybanthus concolor*) of the family Violaceae of eastern No. America having greenish white axillary flowers with petals of equal length
green vitriol *n* : ferrous sulfate heptahydrate
greenware \ˈ⸗,⸗\ *n* : unfired pottery
green water *n* **1** : the water in shore on soundings — compare BLUE WATER **2** : GREEN SEA **3** : an opaque greenish condition of the water in an aquarium that is caused by excessive growth of algae and that is harmless and usu. healthful to fishes
green wattle *n* : any of several Australian wattles (esp. *Acacia decurrens*)
green wax *n* [ME *grenewax*; trans. of ML *viridis cera*] **1** : a seal of green wax attesting a document formerly issued from the exchequer to a sheriff **2 a** : a document attested by green wax **b** : the fines or amercements collected by virtue of such a document
greenweed \ˈ⸗,⸗\ *n* : WOODWAXEN
green weight *n* : the weight of green lumber
green·wich hour angle *usu* ˈgrinij *in Greenwich, Eng, & in Great Britain as a whole, usu* ˈgrenich *or* ˈgrenēch *in Greenwich Village & in NYC as a whole, often in certain other places named Greenwich & usu by speakers unfamiliar with the local pronunc of any place named Greenwich* ˈgrēn,wich; *sometimes* ˈgrenij *or* ˈgrenēj *or* ˈgrinich *or* ˈgrinēch *or* ˈgrinēj *or* ˈgren,wich *or* ˈgrin,wich\ *n, usu cap G* [fr. *Greenwich*, England] : the hour angle of a celestial body at the meridian of Greenwich
greenwich meridian *n, usu cap G* [fr. *Greenwich*, England] : the prime meridian that passes through Greenwich
greenwich time *or* **greenwich civil time** *or* **greenwich mean time** *n, usu cap G* [fr. *Greenwich*, England] : the mean solar time of the meridian of Greenwich used as the prime basis of standard time throughout the world
greenwich village *n, usu cap G&V* [fr. *Greenwich Village*, bohemian section of New York City] : the bohemian quarter of a city
greenwing \ˈ⸗,⸗\ *or* **green–winged teal** \ˈ⸗,⸗-\ *n* : a small river duck (*Anas carolinensis*) the male of which has a chestnut head with a green eye patch and a metallic green area on the wing speculum
greenwithe \ˈ⸗,⸗\ *n* **1** : a West Indian climbing orchid (*Vanilla claviculata*) **2** : a West Indian shrub (*Forsteronia floribunda*) of the family Apocynaceae having a milky juice that yields a rubber
¹**greenwood** \ˈ⸗,⸗\ *n* [ME *grenewode*, fr. *grene* green + *wode* wood] **1** : a wood or forest green with foliage ⟨a yeoman in the ~ —Francis Hackett⟩ **2** : WOODWAXEN **3** : MOUNTAIN HOLLY 1 **4** : GREENHEART 1c
²**greenwood** \ˈ⸗,⸗\ *adj* [¹*green* + *wood*] : SOFTWOOD 2
green woodpecker *n* : a common large European woodpecker (*Picus viridis*) that is chiefly green with a yellow rump and red on the head
greenwrap \ˈ⸗,⸗\ *adj, of a tomato* : picked when immature and wrapped before packing
green wrasse *n* : a greenish Mediterranean wrasse (*Labrus viridis*) usu. with a silvery line along each side and unspotted fins
¹**greeny** \ˈgrēnē\ *adj* -ER/-EST [¹*green* + *-y*] : having a tinge of green : GREENISH
²**greeny** \"\ *also* **green·ie** \"\ *n, pl* **greenies** : GREENHORN ⟨promised his daughter to . . . a ~, just come over, but rich —S.V.Benét⟩
greenyard \ˈ⸗,⸗\ *n* **1** : a yard covered with turf **2** *Brit* : a pound for stray animals
grees *pl of* GREE, *pres 3d sing of* GREE
¹**greet** \ˈgrēt, *usu* -ēd·+V\ *vb* -ED/-ING/-S [ME *greten*, fr. OE *grētan*; akin to OHG *gruozen* to address, attack, ON *grœta* to cause to weep; causative fr. the root of E ³*greet*] *vt* **1** : to address with salutations or expressions of kind wishes : salute or accost in a friendly or courteous manner : pay respects or compliments to personally, through another, or by writing or token : HAIL, WELCOME ⟨my lord, the mayor of London comes to ~ you —Shak.⟩ **2** *obs* : to offer felicitations on **3** : to meet or receive with a salutation, demonstration, or other evidence of approbation or occas. of reproach ⟨the candidate was ~*ed* with cheers⟩ ⟨~*ing* their former hero with catcalls and boos⟩ **4** : to appear or present itself to : be perceived by ⟨offensive odors ~ the nose⟩ ⟨a surprising sight ~*ed* her eyes⟩ ~ *vi* **1** *obs* : to meet and give salutations **2** *obs* : MEET, ENCOUNTER
²**greet** *n* -s *obs* : GREETING
³**greet** \ˈgrēt\ *vi* **grat** \ˈgrat\ **grut·ten** \ˈgrətᵊn\ **greeting**; **greets** [ME *greten*, fr. OE *grǣtan*; akin to ON *grāta* to weep, Goth *gretan*, and perh. to L *hirrire* to whimper, Skt *gharghara* crackling, rattling] **1** *chiefly Scot* : WEEP, CRY, LAMENT **2** *obs* : to call in entreaty or anger

4**greet** \"\ *n* [ME *gret, grete,* fr. *greten,* v., to weep] *now chiefly Scot* : WEEPING, SOBBING

5**greet** \"\ *n* [ME *gret, grete* — more at GRIT] *dial Eng* : finely crushed earth or rock

greet·er \'grēd·ə(r), -ētə-\ *n* -s [1*greet* + *-er*] : one that greets: as **a** : a person who welcomes esp. on behalf of another **b** : one that weeps

1**greeting** *n* -s [ME *greting,* fr. OE *grēting,* fr. *grētan* to greet + *-ing* — more at GREET] **1** : an expression of kindness or joy : a salutation at meeting or a compliment from one absent ⟨write to him . . . gentle adieus and ~*s* —Shak.⟩ **2** : a formal gesture of welcome often traditional ⟨pressed his palms together in the ancient Asian ~⟩

2**greeting** *adj* [ME *greting,* fr. *greting,* n.] : of, relating to, or used for greeting — **greet·ing·ly** *adv*

greeting card *n* : 3CARD 6b

greet·ing·less \'₌₌ləs\ *adj* : having or receiving no greeting

gref·fi·er \'grefē,ā\ *n* -s [MF, fr. *grefe, grafe* stylus (fr. ML *graphium*) + *-ier* -er — more at GRAFF] : REGISTRAR, RECORDER ⟨among the town officials is a ~⟩

gregal \'grēgəl, -reg-\ *adj* [L *gregalis,* fr. *greg-, grex* herd + *-alis* -al — more at GREGARIOUS] **1** *archaic* : belonging to or characteristic of a company or multitude **2** *obs* : GREGARIOUS

gre·ga·le \grā'gä(,)lā\ *n* -s [It *grecale, gregale,* fr. *grecale, gregale* Greek, fr. LL *Graecalis,* fr. L *Graecus* + *-alis* -al — more at GREEK] : a strong cold northeast wind of the central Mediterranean — called also *Euroclydon*

greg·a·loid \'gregə,lȯid\ *adj* [*gregal* + *-oid*] : resulting from union of previously independent individuals — used of a protozoan colony

gre·gar·ia \grə'ga(a)rēə\ *n* -s [NL, fr. L, fem. of *gregarius*] : an irregularly recurrent phase in the life cycle of migratory or plague grasshoppers induced by crowded breeding conditions and marked by structural and color changes and the development of strongly gregarious behavior — compare SOLITARIA

greg·a·ri·na \,gregə'rīnə, -rēnə\ *n, cap* [NL, fr. L *gregarius* + NL *-ina*] : a genus of gregarines that are parasites in the alimentary canal of an arthropod

greg·a·ri·nae \,gregə'rī(,)nē\ *or* **greg·a·ri·nar·ia** \-,rə-'na(a)rēə\ [*Gregarinae* fr. NL, fr. L *gregarius* + *-inae,* fem. pl. of *-inus* -ine; *Gregarinaria* fr. NL, fr. *Gregarina* + *-aria*] *syn of* GREGARINIDA

1**greg·a·rine** \'gregə,rīn, -,rēn, -rən\ *adj* [NL *Gregarina*] : of or relating to the Gregarinida

2**gregarine** \"\ *n* -s [NL *Gregarina*] : a protozoan of the order Gregarinida — see MONOCYSTIS

greg·a·rin·i·an \,₌₌'rinēən\ *adj* : resembling a gregarine : GREGARINE

greg·a·rin·i·da \,₌₌'rinədə\ *n, pl, cap* [NL, fr. *Gregarina* + *-ida*] : a large order of parasitic vermiform telosporidian protozoans that usu. occur in insects and other invertebrates

greg·a·ri·ni·na \-,rə'nīnə, -nēnə\ [NL, fr. *Gregarina* + *-ina*] *syn of* GREGARINIDA

greg·a·ri·noi·dea \-'nȯidēə\ [NL, fr. *Gregarina* + *-oidea*] *syn of* GREGARINIDA

greg·a·ri·no·sis \-'nōsəs\ *n, pl* **gregarino·ses** \-ō,sēz\ [NL, fr. *Gregarina* + *-osis*] : a disease caused by the gregarines esp. in insects

gre·gar·i·ous \grə'ga(a)rēəs, grē'-, -'ger-, -'gār-\ *adj* [L *gregarius* of or relating to a herd or flock, fr. *greg-, grex* herd, flock + *-arius* -ary; akin to OIr *graig* herd of horses, Gk *ageirein* to collect, *agora* assembly, Lith *gurgulỹs* thickening] **1 a** : marked by an inclination to associate with others of one's kind : tending to live in a flock, herd, or community rather than alone ⟨fowl are ~⟩ ⟨man is a ~ animal, living in flocks with his kind, in order to face the common foe —Emil Brunner⟩ **b** : characteristic of or common throughout a group, flock, or community ⟨~ alarm at the intrusion⟩ **2** : marked by an instinctive or temperamental preference for a social rather than a solitary existence : wanting to be with others and disliking much solitude ⟨the American is sociable and ~: he does not like solitariness or the solitudes —W.L.Sperry⟩ **3 a** *of a plant* : growing in a cluster or a colony **b** : living in a community or in contiguous nests but not forming a true colony — used esp. of solitary wasps and bees **syn** see SOCIAL

gre·gar·i·ous·ly *adv* : in a gregarious manner

gre·gar·i·ous·ness *n* -ES : the quality or state of being gregarious

gregarious wave *n* : one of a constant series of waves formed by the regular movement of the sea at all times

grege *or* **greige** \'grāzh\ *n* -s [F *grège,* adj., raw (used of silk), fr. It *greggio*] **1** : RAW SILK **2 a** : BEIGE 2 **b** : NUTRIA 2

greger *or* **gregger** *var of* GRAGER

greg·gle \'gregəl\ *n* -s [origin unknown] *dial Eng* : WOOD HYACINTH

gre·go \'grē(,)gō, 'grā(-\ *n* -s [Catal, lit., Greek, fr. L *Graecus* — more at GREEK] : a coarse warm jacket or coat with a hood formerly worn by seamen

1**gre·go·ri·an** \grə'gōrēən, gre'-,grā'-, -'gȯr-\ *adj, usu cap* [Pope *Gregory* XIII (Ugo Buoncompagni) †1585 + E *-an*] : of or relating to Pope Gregory XIII or to the Gregorian calendar

2**gregorian** \"\ *adj, usu cap* [Pope *Gregory* I †604 + E *-an*] : of or relating to Pope Gregory I : of, relating to, or having the characteristics of Gregorian chant

3**gregorian** \"\ *n, usu cap* **1** *obs* : one versed in the Gregorian chant **2** : GREGORIAN CHANT

4**gregorian** \"\ *n* -s [fr. the name *Gregory* + E *-an*] **1** *sometimes cap* : a 16th and 17th century wig **2** *usu cap* : a member of an 18th century English society similar to that of the Freemasons

5**gregorian** \"\ *adj, usu cap* [St. *Gregory* the Illuminator †332 + E *-an*] : of, relating to, or being the Armenian Church

gregorian calendar *n, usu cap G* [1*Gregorian*] : a revision of the Julian calendar introduced in 1582 and adopted in Great Britain and the English colonies in America in 1752 involving the suppression of the 10 days, or after 1700 11 days, by which the vernal equinox had become displaced and providing that only those centesimal years divisible by 400 should be leap years — see MONTH table

gregorian chant *n, usu cap G* [2*Gregorian*] : one of the monodic and rhythmically free ritual melodies in one of the eight ecclesiastical modes comprising the liturgical chant of the Roman Catholic Church : PLAINSONG

gre·go·ri·an·ist \-nəst\ *n* -s *usu cap* [2*Gregorian* + *-ist*] : one who advocates using the Gregorian chants

gregorian mode *n, usu cap G* [2*Gregorian*] : ECCLESIASTICAL MODE

gregorian staff *n, usu cap G* [2*Gregorian*] : a 4-line staff with a C clef used for Gregorian music

or

Gregorian staffs

gregorian telescope *n, usu cap G* [James *Gregory* †1675 Scot. mathematician and inventor + E *-an*] : a reflecting telescope that has a paraboloidal primary mirror with a perforation through which light is reflected to the eyepiece and an ellipsoidal secondary mirror set beyond the focus and that produces an erect image but a small field of view

gregorian tone *n, usu cap G* [2*Gregorian*] **1** : one of the nine tunes with variants to which the psalms are sung in Gregorian music, eight of them being written in the eight most common ecclesiastical modes **2** : ECCLESIASTICAL MODE

gregorian year *n, usu cap G* [1*Gregorian*] : a year in the Gregorian calendar

greg·o·ry's powder \'greg|ərēz-, -rāg|, -riz-\ *n, usu cap G* [after James *Gregory* †1821 Scot. professor of medicine] : a laxative powder containing rhubarb, magnesia, and ginger

1**greige** *var of* GRÈGE

2**greige** \'grā(zh)\ *adj* [F *grège* raw (used of silk) — more at GRÈGE] : GRAY 1d

3**greige** \"\ *n* -s : a textile in the gray state of preparation

grei·sen \'grīzᵊn\ *n* -s [G] : a crystalline rock consisting of quartz and mica that is common in the tin regions of Cornwall and Saxony and that is prob. a granite altered by magmatic exhalation

gre·king \'grēkən, -kiŋ\ *n* -s [ME *griking, greking;* akin to MD *grakinge* dawn, ON *grȳjandi* dawn, OE *grǣg* gray — more at GRAY] *now dial Brit* : DAWN

1**gre·mi·al** \'grēmēəl *sometimes* 'grāmē,äl\ *n* -s [L *gremium* lap, bosom + E *-al* — more at CRAM] **1** *archaic* : a full or resident member (as of a society or university) **2** *or* **gremial veil** : a lap cloth laid across the knees of a bishop seated at mass or other services

2**gre·mi·al** \'grēmēəl\ *adj* [L *gremium* + E *-al*] **1** : of or relating to the lap or bosom **2** *archaic* : having active or resident membership (as in a society or university)

gre·mio \'grāmē,ō\ *n* -s [Sp, lit., lap, fr. L *gremium*] : GUILD, UNION; *esp* : an employers' association in some European and Latin American countries

grem·lin \'gremlən\ *n* -s [prob. fr. *grem-* (of unknown origin) + *-lin* (as in *goblin*)] : an impish little gnome reported by airmen as interfering with and disordering equipment (as motors, instruments, machine guns); *broadly* : an unaccountable disruptive influence

1**gre·nade** \grə'nād\ *n* -s [MF *granade, grenade,* fr. LL *granata* pomegranate, fr. pl. of L *granatum,* fr. neut. of *granatus* seedy, fr. *granum* grain, seed + *-atus* -ate — more at CORN] **1** *obs* : POMEGRANATE **2** : a missile consisting of a container fitted with a priming charge and a bursting charge and filled with a destructive agent (as gas, high explosive, incendiary chemicals) — see HAND GRENADE, RIFLE GRENADE **3** : a device that ejects poison gas or tear gas and is used esp. by police in dispersing mobs **4** : a glass bottle or globe that contains volatile chemicals and can be burst by throwing (as for extinguishing a fire)

2**grenade** \"\ *vt* -ED/-ING/-S : to use grenades against

grenade launcher *n* : a device attached to a rifle or carbine to permit the firing of a grenade

1**gre·na·di·an** \grə'nādēən\ *adj, usu cap* [*Grenada,* island in the West Indies + E *-ian*] : of or relating to Grenada, West Indies : of the style or kind typical of Grenada

2**grenadian** \"\ *n* -s *cap* : a native or resident of Grenada, West Indies

gren·a·dier \,grenə¦di(ə)r, -iə\ *n* -s [F, fr. *grenade* + *-ier* -er] **1 a** : a soldier who carries and throws grenades **b** : one of a company attached to each regiment or battalion taking post on the right of the line and wearing a special uniform **c** : a member of a special regiment or corps ⟨a ~ of the guard of Napoleon I⟩ **2** : any of various deep-sea fishes that are related to the cods, that constitute a family Macruridae of the order Anacanthini, and that have an elongate tapering body and compressed pointed tail — called also *rattail*

gren·a·dier·ial \-irēəl\ *adj* : of, relating to, or characteristic of a grenadier

gren·a·dier·ly \¦₌₌¦di(ə)rlē, -iəl-, -li\ *adv* : like a grenadier

grenadilla *or* **grenadillo** *var of* GRANADILLA

1**gren·a·din** \'grenədən\ *also* **gren·a·dine** \¦grenə¦dēn\ *n* -s [F *grenadin,* fr. *grenade* pomegranate + *-in* -ine — more at GRENADE] : a small fricandeau ⟨seventeen ~*s* of prime beef . . . exquisitely interlarded with pork insertions —Joel Sayre⟩

2**grenadin** \"\ *or* **grenadine** \"\ *n* -s [F *grenadine,* fr. *grenade* pomegranate + *-ine*] : CLOVE PINK; *esp* : a strongly perfumed medium-sized carnation

gren·a·dine \¦grenə¦dēn\ *n* -s [F, fr. *grenade* pomegranate + *-ine*] **1 a** : a silk yarn of two or more threads that are twisted singly and again in the ply **b** : a plain or figured fabric of various fibers often in an open weave like that of gauze **2** *or* **grenadine red** : a moderate reddish orange that is yellower and paler than flamingo or crab apple **3** : a red sweet syrup of little or no alcoholic content flavored with pomegranates and used as a sweetening, flavoring, or coloring agent with carbonated water or cocktails

grenadine pink *n* : a strong yellowish pink that is redder and stronger than average salmon, yellower and deeper than melon, and yellower and stronger than peach red

gre·na·do \grə'nā(,)dō, -nä(-\ *n* -ES [modif. of Sp *granada,* lit., pomegranate, fr. LL *granata* — more at GRENADE] *archaic* : GRENADE

gren·a·tite \'grenə,tīt\ *n* -s [F, fr. *grenat* garnet + *-ite*] : STAUROLITE

gre·no·ble \grə'nōbəl, grə'nȯbl(ᵊ), -ōb(lə)\ *adj, usu cap* [fr. *Grenoble,* France] : of or from the city of Grenoble, France : of the kind or style prevalent in Grenoble

gren·ville series \'gren,vil-, *chiefly South* -,vəl-\ *n, usu cap G* [fr. *Grenville* co., Ontario, Canada] : a series of rocks consisting mainly of highly metamorphosed limestones and other sediments occurring in eastern Canada

grenz ray \'gren(t)s-\ *n, often cap G* [part trans. of G *grenzstrahl,* fr. *grenze* border (fr. MHG *grenize,* fr. Pol *granica*) + *strahl* ray] : a soft X ray with wavelength near the limit of extreme ultraviolet used esp. in treating skin lesions — called also *infraroentgen ray*

grès \'grā\ *n, pl* **grèses** \-āz\ [F, sandstone, stoneware, of Gmc origin; akin to OE *grēot* sand, grit — more at GRIT] : ceramic stoneware esp. when decorative in quality

grès de flan·dres \grādəflääⁿ|dr(ᵊ), |d(rə)\ *n, usu cap F* [F, lit., stoneware from Flanders] : COLOGNE WARE

gresh·am's law \'greshəmz-\ *n, usu cap G* [after Sir Thomas *Gresham* †1579 Eng. financier] : an observation in economics: when two coins are equal in debt-paying value but unequal in intrinsic value, the one having the lesser intrinsic value tends to remain in circulation and the other to be hoarded or exported as bullion

gres·so·ri·al \(')gre¦sōrēəl\ *adj* [L *gressus* (past part. of *gradi* to step, go) + E *-orial* (as in *cursorial*) — more at GRADE] : adapted for walking ⟨the ~ feet of some birds⟩

1**gret·na green** \¦gretnə¦₌\ *n, often cap 1st G* [fr. *Gretna* parish, Scotland] : a moderate yellowish green to green that is less strong than Killarney green

2**gretna green** *n, usu cap both Gs* [fr. *Gretna Green,* Scottish village on the English border, famous for the runaway marriages performed there] : a place where many eloping couples are married

gre·vil·lea \grə'vilēə\ *n* [NL, after Charles F. *Greville* †1809 Scot. botanist] **1** *cap* : a large genus of Australian shrubs and trees (family Proteaceae) having usu. showy orange or red flowers with elongated curved style and woody follicles — see SILK OAK **2** *also* **gra·vil·ea** \"\ -s : a plant of the genus *Grevillea*

gré·vy's zebra \(')grā¦vēz-\ *n, usu cap G* [after François P. J. *Grévy* †1891 president of France] : a zebra (*Equus grevyi*) with narrow and discontinuous stripes on the belly and the inner surface of the thighs

1**grew** *past of* GROW

2**grew** \'grü\ *n* -s [short for *grewhound*] *now dial Brit* : GREYHOUND

grew·hound \-üənd, -ü,haůnd\ *n* [ME, alter. of *grehound* — more at GREYHOUND] *dial Brit* : GREYHOUND

grew·ia \'grüyə, -üēə\ *n, cap* [NL, fr. Nehemiah *Grew* †1712 Eng. plant physiologist + NL *-ia*] : a large genus of chiefly tropical Old World shrubs and trees (family Tiliaceae) having alternate simple leaves, cymose flowers with colored sepals, and drupaceous sometimes edible fruits

grewsome *var of* GRUESOME

1**grex** \'greks\ *vi* -ED/-ING/-ES [PaG *greckse* & G dial. *greckse, grecksen* to groan, grumble, complain, fr. early G *krachitzen* to cry hoarsely, freq. of *krachen* to crack, crash, roar, fr. OHG *krahhōn* — more at CRACK] *dial* : to grumble or complain often shrilly or scoldingly

2**grex** \"\ *n* -ES [gram per X (ten) kilometers] : a measuring unit for fibers, filaments, and yarns based on the weight in grams of 10,000 meters of fiber or yarn

grey \'grā\ *var of* GRAY

grey·cing \'grāsiŋ\ *n* -s [by contr.] *Brit* : greyhound racing

grey drake *n, Brit* : an adult female mayfly

grey friar *also* **gray friar** *n, often cap G&F* [ME *grey frere, gray frere*] : a Franciscan friar

1**grey·hound** *also* **gray·hound** \'grā,haůnd\ *n* [ME *grehound,* fr. OE *grīghund,* fr. *grīg-* (akin to ON *grey* bitch) + *hund* hound; perh. akin to OE *grǣg* gray — more at GRAY, HOUND] **1 a** : a tall slender graceful smooth-coated dog of a breed originating in the Near East that is characterized by swiftness and keen sight and has been used for coursing game for many centuries — see ITALIAN GREYHOUND **b** : any of several dogs (as a whippet or a saluki) related to or similar to the greyhound **2** : a swift steamer; *esp* : OCEAN LINER

greyhound

2**greyhound** \"\ *vi, of a hooked fish* : to alternate leaps and shallow dives at high speed

grey·lag \'grā,lag\ *or* **greylag goose** *also* **gray·lag** *n* [prob. fr. *gray* + *lag* (last)] : the common gray wild goose (*Anser anser* syn. *A. cinereus*) of Europe believed to be the chief wild ancestor of the common domestic goose

grey nun *also* **gray nun** *n, often cap G&N* : SISTER OF CHARITY OF MONTREAL

greyskin \'₌,₌\ *n, Africa* : a small percoid food fish (*Plectorhynchus griseus* or *Gaterin schotaf*) of the tropical Indo-Pacific from eastern Africa to Australia

grey wavey *n* : WHITE-FRONTED GOOSE

greywether \'₌,₌₌\ *n, dial Brit* : SARSEN

GRI *abbr* guaranteed retirement income

1**grib·ble** \'gribəl\ *n* -s [origin unknown] *dial Eng* : a young crab tree or blackthorn; *sometimes* : a cutting from one

2**gribble** \"\ *n* -s [prob. dim. of 2*grub*] : a small marine isopod crustacean (*Limnoria lignorum* or *L. terebrans*) that burrows into and rapidly destroys submerged timber (as the piles of wharves) both in Europe and America

1**grice** \'grīs\ *n* -s [ME *grys, grise,* fr. ON *gríss* — more at GRIZZLE] *now chiefly Scot* : a young pig

2**grice** \'grēs\ *var of* GRECE

1**grid** \'grid\ *n* -s *often attrib* [back-formation fr. *gridiron*] **1** : GRATING, GRIDIRON **2** : something resembling or likened to a grating: as **a** (1) : a perforated or ridged metal plate used as a conductor and as a support for the active material of a storage-battery electrode (2) : an electrode consisting of a mesh or a spiral of fine wire interposed between two other elements of an electron tube (3) : NETWORK 4 (4) : a network of pipes (as for distributing gas or water) **b** : a network of uniformly spaced horizontal and perpendicular lines; *specif* : one used for locating points (as on a map, chart, or aerial photograph) by means of a system of coordinates **c** : a wooden framework into which a boat may be floated at high tide in order that repairs may be made when the tide falls **d** : a postal cancellation with a gridiron pattern (as on an early U.S. stamp) **e** : GRIDIRON 3c **f** : GRIDIRON 3d; *broadly* : FOOTBALL 1 ⟨forgotten ~ heroes⟩

2**grid** \"\ *vt* **gridded; gridded; gridding; grids 1** : to equip or cover with a grid ⟨a map *gridded* with red lines⟩ **2** : to connect (as electric or gas lines) into a grid : distribute (as electricity or gas) by means of a grid

grid bias *n* : a small constant component of the grid potential in a vacuum tube that is usu. negative for ordinary triode control grids

grid cap *n* : a grid terminal (as on some amplifier tubes) that resembles a cap and is connected to the grid circuit by means of a spring clip

grid ceiling *n* : a perforated ceiling that allows light to shine through

grid circuit *n* : the electric circuit including the grid and cathode of an electron tube

grid condenser *n* : a capacitor connected in the grid circuit of an electron tube

grid current *n* : current flowing between the grid and cathode in an electron tube

grid·der \'gridə(r)\ *n* -s [1*grid* (gridiron) + *-er*] **1** : a football player **2** : a football fan

grid–dip meter *n* : a device for testing radio frequencies that consists of a vacuum-tube oscillator having in its grid circuit a current-indicating meter which indicates a decrease in current when the oscillator and the circuit to which it is coupled resonate at the same frequency

1**grid·dle** \'gridᵊl\ *n* -s *often attrib* [ME *gredil, gridel,* fr. ONF *gredil,* fr. LL *craticulum* fine wickerwork — more at 2GRILL] **1 a** *now dial* : GRIDIRON 1, 2 **b** : any of various grids ⟨a ~ of sheep trails over the hill⟩ **2** : a flat surface (as of soapstone or metal) on which food (as batter or bacon) is placed to be cooked by dry heat (as from a fire or an electric element); *broadly* : a cooking device consisting of or incorporating a griddle ⟨got an electric ~ for her birthday⟩ — **on the griddle** : being subjected to examination or questioning ⟨we were *on the griddle* for several hours before we convinced the officials that we were not guilty⟩

griddle 2

2**griddle** \"\ *vt* **griddled; griddled; griddling** \-d(ᵊ)liŋ\ **griddles** : to cook on a griddle

3**griddle** \"\ *vi* **griddled; griddled; griddling** \-d(ᵊ)liŋ\ **griddles** [origin unknown] *slang Brit* : to sing as a beggar — **grid·dler** \-d(ᵊ)lə(r)\ *n* -s

griddle cake *n* : a flat cake made of thin batter consisting basically of flour (as of wheat or buckwheat), liquid, and leavening and cooked on both sides on a griddle — called also *pancake*

griddle man *n* : a short-order cook

1**gride** \'grīd\ *vb* -ED/-ING/-S [ME *griden,* alter. of *girden* — more at GIRD] *vt* **1** *archaic* : to pierce or gash with a weapon **2** : to scrape or graze so as to produce a harsh rasping sound ~ *vi* : to scrape, graze, or rub against something so as to produce a harsh rasping sound

2**gride** \"\ *n* -s : a harsh scraping or cutting or the sound of it ⟨the ~ of leafless boughs in the blast of the wind⟩

grid·e·lin \'gridᵊlən\ *n* -s [modif. of F *gris-de-lin,* lit., flax gray] : a dark purplish red that is bluer and paler than pansy purple, redder, lighter, and stronger than raisin, and bluer, lighter, and stronger than Bokhara — called also *gris-de-lin*

grid–glow tube *n* : a cold-cathode gas-filled electron tube in which glow discharge is started by a grid

1**grid·iron** \'gri,dī(ə)rn, -īən\ *n* [ME *gredire,* prob. by folk etymology (influence of *ire, iren* iron) fr. *gredil, gridil* — more at GRIDDLE] **1** : an iron grating formerly used for torture by fire **2** : a grated metal frame for broiling food over coals — compare GRIDDLE, GRILL **3** : something resembling a gridiron, grating, or lattice in structure or appearance: as **a** : a network of sections (as of pipes, railroad tracks, or roads) **b** : GRID 2c **c** : the arrangement of beams over a theater stage supporting the machinery for flying scenery **d** : a football field

2**gridiron** \"\ *vt* : to cover or mark with bars or lines suggestive of those of a gridiron

gridiron pendulum *n* : a compensation pendulum in which the unequal expansion of two different metals is utilized to maintain constant effective pendulum length

gridiron–tailed lizard \'₌,₌(₌),₌-\ *n* : a lizard of the genus *Callisaurus*

grid leak *n* : a resistor used in parallel with a capacitor in the grid circuit of a vacuum tube to limit grid bias by drawing off excess electrons that accumulate on the tube grid

grid line *n* : any of a series of numbered horizontal and perpendicular lines that divide a map into squares to form a grid by means of which any point may be located by a system of rectangular coordinates

grid man *n* : OVERHEAD MAN

grid metal *n* : ANTIMONIAL LEAD; *specif* : a lead containing about 9 percent antimony and sometimes a fraction of a percent of tin and used for storage-battery grids — compare HARD LEAD

grid modulation *n* : a system of modulation in which the modulating voltage is introduced into the grid circuit of the electron tube that provides the carrier

grids *pl of* GRID, *pres 3d sing of* GRID

grid voltage *n* : the instantaneous potential difference between the grid and the cathode of a vacuum tube

grie·ben \'grēbən\ *n pl* [G, pl. of *griebe* crackling, fr. OHG *griobo* — more at GREAVES] : cracklings from goose fat usu. salted

griece *var of* GRECE

grieced \'grēst\ *adj* : 2DEGRADED

grief \'grēf\ *n* -s [ME *gref, grefe,* fr. OF *grief, gref,* adj., heavy, grave, difficult, troubled, fr. (assumed) VL *grevis,* alter. of L *gravis* — more at GRIEVE] **1** *obs* **a** (1) : SUFFERING, PAIN, DISTRESS; *also* : a cause of these (as a hurt, hardship, or wound) (2) : a bodily injury : MALADY, DISEASE **b** : an aggrieved or angered state of mind : OFFENSE **c** : GRIEVANCE 3; *also* : a document setting forth a grievance **2 a** : emotional suffering (as caused by bereavement, affliction, remorse, panic, despair) ⟨his deep ~ at his son's death⟩ ⟨a leaden ~ swept over her at thought of the past⟩ ⟨the ~ his loss in me had wrought —Alfred Tennyson⟩ **b** : a cause of such suffering ⟨such a child is a ~ to his parents⟩ **3 a** : MISHAP, MISADVENTURE, ACCIDENT, BREAKAGE ⟨the day was marred by dozens of little ~*s*⟩ **b** : difficulty and vexation esp. from mishaps and accidents ⟨the ~*s* of a repairman's life⟩ **c** : hard usage : TROUBLE, ANNOYANCE ⟨enough ~ for one day⟩ **d** : an unpleasant end or condition : FAILURE, DISASTER — used chiefly in the phrase *come to grief* ⟨the expedition came to ~ when the supplies were accidentally lost⟩ **syn** see SORROW

grief·ful \'grēffəl\ *adj* [ME *grefful*, fr. *gref, grefe* + *-ful*] : SORROWFUL, ANGUISHED — **grief·ful·ly** \-əlē\ *adv*

grief·less \'grēfləs\ *adj* : free from grief — **grief·less·ness** *n* -ES

grief stem *n* : a tube or rod of square cross section fitted into a square hole in the rotary-drill table and forming the top section of the rotary-drill shaft in an oil well

griege \'grāzh\ *n* -S [alter. of *grège*] : a variable color averaging a grayish yellow green that is yellower and paler than average sage green, mermaid, or palmetto and yellower and less strong than celadon

grien *var of* ⁴GREEN

grie·shoch \'grēshək, -əχ\ *n* -S [ScGael *grīosach*] *Scot* : a bed of hot embers

gries·ly \'grēzlē\ *archaic var of* GRISLY

griev·ance \'grēvən(t)s\ *n* -S *often attrib* [ME *grevaunce*, fr. OF *grevance*, fr. *grever* to afflict, grieve + *-ance* — more at GRIEVE] **1 a** : SUFFERING, GRIEF, DISTRESS ⟨~*s* illegally inflicted upon men by the king's ministers —J.G.Edwards⟩ **b** *archaic* : the infliction of a grievance **2** : aggrieved state : ANGER, ANNOYANCE, DISPLEASURE ⟨went their own way blithely, to the ~ of their leaders⟩ ⟨have long cherished a ~ against whistlers in public places⟩ **3 a** : a cause of uneasiness or distress felt to afford rightful reason for reproach, complaint, or resistance ⟨the ~ of taxation without representation⟩ ⟨they had many ~*s*⟩ **b** : a working condition considered unsatisfactory and objected to by labor ⟨failure to respect seniority rights was a major ~⟩; *esp* : one involving violation of a collective agreement **4** : a complaint by an employee or a body of employees of unfair treatment by the employer ⟨a joint labor-management committee to act on ~*s*⟩

grievance committee *n* : a committee formed by a labor union or by employer and employees jointly to discuss and where possible eliminate grievances

grievance procedure *n* : the several stages or steps in which a labor grievance may be settled or to which it may be appealed

griev·ant \-nt\ *n* -S [*grieve* + *-ant*] : one who submits a grievance for arbitration ⟨order the ~ reinstated with back pay —*Labor Relations Reporter*⟩

¹**grieve** \'grēv\ *n* -S [ME *greif, greff*, fr. OE (Northumbrian) *grǣfa*; akin to OE *gerēfa* reeve — more at REEVE] **1 a** *archaic* : GOVERNOR, SHERIFF **b** *dial Eng* : ³GRAVE **2** *chiefly Scot* : a farm manager, steward, or overseer

²**grieve** \"\ *vb* -ED/-ING/-S [ME *greven*, fr. OF *grever*, fr. L *gravare* to burden, oppress, fr. *gravis* heavy, grave; akin to Goth *kaurjos* (nom. pl.) heavy, *kaurjan* to weigh upon, Gk *barys* heavy, *baros* weight, Skt *guru* heavy, important] *vt* **1** *archaic* : to injure, harm, or hurt esp. with disease **2** : to occasion grief to : cause to suffer : TRY, DISTRESS ⟨the children's conduct *grieved* their grandmother⟩ **3** : to feel or show grief over **4** *obs* **a** : PROVOKE, ANGER, ENRAGE **b** : to weigh or press heavily upon ~ *vi* **1** : to feel grief : be in pain of mind on account of an evil : SORROW, MOURN — often used with *at, for*, or *over* ⟨*grieving* over their mother's death⟩ ⟨must not ~ at such trifles⟩ **2** : to enter a grievance

syn MOURN, SORROW: GRIEVE may suggest lasting mental suffering, manifested or not, often with a tendency to concentrate on one's loss or distress ⟨he *grieved*, like an honest lad, to see his comrade left to face calamity alone —George Meredith⟩ ⟨last winter she died also, and my days are passed in work, lest I should *grieve* for her —Amy Lowell⟩ MOURN may more strongly imply demonstration of grief, often a deep grief, as at a bereavement ⟨national *mourning* for a dead sovereign⟩ ⟨his widow . . . *mourned* him —C.B.Flood⟩ SORROW may indicate deep distress tinged with regret and sadness ⟨I feel it when I *sorrow* most: 'tis better to have loved and lost —Alfred Tennyson⟩

grieved \'grēvd\ *adj* [ME *greved* vexed, fr. past part. of *greven*] : afflicted esp. with grief : vexed in mind — **grieved·ly** \-v(ə)dlē\ *adv*

griev·er \-və(r)\ *n* -S **1** : one that grieves **2** : a representative of labor on a grievance committee

grieves *pres 3d sing of* GRIEVE, *pl of* GRIEVE *or obs pl of* GRIEF

grieve·ship \'grēv,ship\ *n* [¹*grieve* + *-ship*] *Brit* : the territory under a grieve

griev·ing·ly *adv* : with grief

griev·ous \'grēvəs, *chiefly in substand speech* -vēəs\ *adj* [ME *grevous*, fr. OF *greveus*, fr. *gref* grief + *-eus* -ous — more at GRIEF] **1** : weighing or falling heavily : BURDENSOME, OPPRESSIVE, ONEROUS ⟨the ~ cost of war⟩ **2** : causing, characterized by, or indicative of severe physical pain or suffering : HURTFUL, DISTRESSING, INJURIOUS ⟨a ~ wound⟩ ⟨~ lamentation⟩; *often* : INTENSE, SEVERE ⟨~ pain⟩ **3** : causing, characterized by, or indicative of great sorrow or severe emotional suffering ⟨a ~ loss⟩; *broadly* : extremely distressing or irritating ⟨a ~ insult⟩ **4 a** : SERIOUS, DEPLORABLE ⟨his most ~ fault⟩ **b** *archaic* : outrageously bad : ATROCIOUS, HEINOUS **5** : expressing or full of grief, sorrow, or anguish ⟨a ~ cry⟩ **syn** see BITTER

griev·ous·ly *adv* [ME *grevously*, fr. *grevous* + *-ly*] : in a grievous manner or to a grievous degree : FLAGRANTLY, SERIOUSLY ⟨the prison population has ~ increased in the last fifteen years —*Times Lit. Supp.*⟩

griev·ous·ness *n* -ES [ME *grevousnesse*, fr. *grevous* + *-nesse* -ness] : the quality or state of being grievous

¹**griff** \'grif\ *n* -S [origin unknown] *dial Eng* : a deep narrow glen or ravine

²**griff** \"\ *also* **grif·fin** \-fən\ *n* -S [origin unknown] *slang Brit* : an accurate account : a factually correct piece of information; *esp* : a bit of inside information : TIP

¹**griffe** \'grif\ *n* -S [F, fr. AmerSp *grifo*, fr. Sp, adj., kinky-haired, fr. *grifo*, n., griffin, fr. L *gryphus* — more at GRIFFIN] **1** : the offspring of a Negro and a mulatto : a person of three-quarter Negro and one-quarter white blood **2** : a person of mixed Negro and American Indian blood

²**griffe** *or* **griff** \"\ *n* -S [F *griffe*, lit., claw, fr. MF, of Gmc origin; akin to OHG *grīfan* to grasp, seize — more at GRIPE] **1** : an ornament resembling a claw that projects from the round base of an architectural column upon the angle formed by a corner of the plinth — called also *spur* **2** : an arrangement of parallel bars on a loom for lifting the hooked wires that raise the warp threads in weaving jacquard or dobby fabrics

¹**grif·fin** \'grifən\ *also* **grif·fon** *or* **gryph·on** \-fən, -,fän\ *n* -S [ME *griffon, griffoun*, fr. MF *grifon*, fr. *grif*, fr. L *gryphus*, fr. Gk *gryp-, grypos*, fr. *grypos* curved, having a hooked nose; akin to OE *cradol* cradle — more at CRADLE] **1 a** : a fabulous animal typically having head, forepart, and wings like those of an eagle but with visible usu. erect ears, forelegs like the legs of an eagle, and body, hind legs, and tail like those of a lion **b** : any of various fantastic animals in art that resemble the griffin or are considered to be ancestral or related to the typical griffin — see MALE GRIFFIN **2** : GRIFFON VULTURE

griffin 1b

²**griffin** \"\ *n* -S [origin unknown] **1** : a white person new to the East : one recently come from the Occident **2 a** : an untried Chinese racing pony **b** : a tough hardy Mongolian pony used esp. for polo

³**griffin** \"\ *n* -S [by alter.] : ¹GRIFFE 1

grif·fin·age \-nij\ *n* -S [²*griffin* + *-age*] : the state of being a white person recently come to the East

grif·fith·ite \'grifə,thīt\ *n* -S [*Griffith* Park, Los Angeles, Calif. + E *-ite*] : a chloritic mineral containing basic magnesium, iron, calcium, and aluminosilicate

¹**grif·fon** \'grifən, -,fän\ *n* -S *usu cap* [ME *Griffoun*, fr. MF *Grifon*] *archaic* : GREEK

²**griffon** \"\ *n* [F, lit., griffin] **1** *usu cap* : a breed of small short-faced compact dogs of Belgian origin that occur in several varieties differing chiefly in length, color, or texture of coat **2** -S *sometimes cap* : a sporting dog of a breed originating in Holland but largely developed in France and comprising medium-sized long-headed dogs with downy undercoat and harsh wiry outer coat of gray or grayish white often with chestnut markings — called also *wire-haired pointing griffon*

grif·fo·nage \,grifə'näzh\ *n* -S [F, fr. MF *grifouner* to scribble (fr. *griffon* stylus, fr. *griffe* claw) + *-age* — more at GRIFFE] : careless handwriting : a crude or illegible scrawl

grif·fonne \(')gri¦fän\ *n* -S [F, fr. *griffe* — more at GRIFFE] : a woman of three-quarter Negro and one-quarter white blood

griffon vulture *n* : any of numerous large Old World vultures constituting a genus (*Gyps*); *esp* : a large squat light-colored vulture (*G. fulvus*) of mountainous parts in southern Europe, northern Africa, and eastward to India

griffs *pl of* GRIFF

¹**grift** \'grift\ *n* -S [perh. alter. of ²*graft*] *slang* : methods or techniques of obtaining money illicitly (as in a confidence game or a crooked gamble) that depend primarily on adroitness and do not usu. involve the employment of physical force or violence — usu. used with *the*

²**grift** \"\ *vb* -ED/-ING/-S *vi, slang* : to practice the grift : live by one's wits ~ *vt, slang* : to obtain (as money) by the grift — **grift·er** \-tə(r)\ *n* -S

¹**grig** \'grig\ *n* -S [ME *grege*] **1** : a small person or creature : DWARF: as **a** : CRICKET, GRASSHOPPER **b** : a small short-legged domestic fowl (as a bantam or a creeper fowl) **c** : a small or immature eel **2** : a gay lively light-hearted and usu. small or young person ⟨a ~ of a girl⟩ — often used as the typification of light-hearted easy happiness, gaiety, or content ⟨gathered about the table merry as so many ~*s*⟩ **3** *archaic* : FARTHING

²**grig** \"\ *vi* **grigged; grigged; grigging; grigs** : to fish for grigs

³**grig** \"\ *vt* [prob. fr. IrGael *griogaim* (I) tantalize, urge, incite] *dial* : TANTALIZE, IRRITATE, ANNOY

⁴**grig** \"\ *n* -S [W *grug* or Corn *grig*] *dial Eng* : HEATHER

grig·gles \'grigəlz\ *n pl* [prob. fr. ¹*grig* + *-le*, dim. suffix] *dial Eng* : small or inferior apples left on a tree after picking

gri·gnard reaction \(')grēn¦yär(d)-\ *n, usu cap G* [after Victor *Grignard* †1934 Fr. chemist] : the reaction of a Grignard reagent with any of several types of compounds (as an aldehyde, ketone, or ester) to yield any of a variety of compounds (as an alcohol)

grignard reagent *n, usu cap G* [after Victor *Grignard*] : any of various compounds of magnesium with an organic radical and a halogen (as ethyl-magnesium iodide C_2H_5MgI) that react readily (as with water, alcohols, amines, acids) in the Grignard reaction

grigri *var of* GRIS-GRIS

gri–gri *var of* GRUGRU

gri·has·tha \gər'həstə\ *n* -S [Skt *gṛhastha*] : the second stage in the Brahmanic ashrama in which a man assumes the duties and responsibilities of a householder

grike \'grīk\ *n* -S [alter. of ME *crike*, fr. ON *kriki* crack, bend, concavity — more at CREEK] : CREVICE, CRACK; *esp* : an opening in rock widened by natural forces (as weathering or solution)

¹**grill** \'gril\ *vb* -ED/-ING/-S [F *griller*, fr. MF, fr. *gril*] *vt* **1 a** : to broil on an open grill or a griddle ⟨wait to the last minute to ~ the steaks⟩ **b** *obs* : to cook by scalloping **2 a** : to torment by or as if by broiling ⟨the sun beat down and ~*ed* them⟩ **b** : to distress with continued questioning in or as if in cross-examination : press with questions ⟨the police ~*ed* the suspect⟩ **c** : to afflict with difficulties, vexations, burdens, or onerous demands ~ *vi* **1** : to become grilled : BROIL ⟨lamb chops for ~*ing*⟩ **2** : to afflict a person with difficulties **syn** see AFFLICT

²**grill** \"\ *n* -S [F *gril* grill, gridiron, fr. MF, alter. of *gredil, gradil*, fr. LL *craticulum* fine wickerwork, alter. of L *craticula*, dim. of *cratis* wickerwork, hurdle — more at HURDLE] **1** *also* **grille** \"\ **a** : a cooking utensil on which food is exposed to red heat (as from charcoal or electricity) between bars **b** : GRIDDLE 2 **c** *Brit* : HOT PLATE **2** : food or a dish that is broiled usu. on a grill ⟨a piping hot ~ of oysters and bacon⟩ — see MIXED GRILL **3** : a grillroom or other usu. informal restaurant **4** [¹*grill*] : an act or instance of grilling

grill 1a

³**grill** \"\ *var of* GRILLE

⁴**grill** \"\ *vt* -ED/-ING/-S [³*grill*] : to impress (a stamp) with a grill

¹**gril·lade** \grē'läd, grē¦yäd\ *n* -S [F, fr. *griller* to grill + *-ade* — more at GRILL] **1** : something that is grilled: as **a** : meat broiled to order (as in a hotel) **b** *Louisiana* : a dish of veal cooked and served in a savory brown gravy **2** : an act of grilling

²**grillade** *vt* -ED/-ING/-S *obs* : to cook (food) by grilling

gril·lage \'grilij, grə'läzh, grē'yäzh\ *n* -S [F, fr. *griller* to supply with grillwork (fr. *grille*) + *-age*] **1 a** : a framework of sleepers and crossbeams of timber or steel forming a foundation in marshy or treacherous soil **b** : a similar framework of stringers and crossbeams used for supporting a load (as precast concrete floor slabs) **2 a** : an arrangement of grillwork ⟨glimpses of native women behind their ~⟩ **b** : an arrangement resembling a grille ⟨a ~ of soapboxes filled one window⟩

grill car *n* : a railroad car equipped for preparing and serving food and drinks less elaborately than a dining car and usu. for passengers on short runs

¹**grille** *also* **grill** \'gril\ *n* -S [F *grille*, fr. MF, alter. of OF *greille, graille* grille, gridiron, griddle, fr. L *craticula* fine wickerwork — more at ²GRILL] **1 a** : a grating (as of wrought iron, bronze, or wood) forming an often elaborate openwork barrier, screen, or cover (as to a door, window, or other opening): as (1) : an openwork barrier or grating in a heating or ventilating system : REGISTER (2) : an ornamental metal screen at the front of an automobile hiding the core of the radiator (3) : a mask with irregular perforations so arranged that when it is superimposed on a sheet of paper the words or other elements of a cryptographic message may be written through the perforations — see FLEISSNER GRILLE, TRELLIS CIPHER (4) : a grilled screen covering the outlet of a radio speaker or other amplifier **b** : an opening covered with a grille: as (1) : a window for the sale of tickets (2) : an air outlet (as of a ventilation system) covered with a protective or ornamental grille **2** : a square opening in the corner at the farther end of a court-tennis court on the hazard side **3** *usu* **grill** : a square or rectangular uninked pattern on a postage stamp (as on a U.S. 1867–71 issue) composed of rows of raised or sunken pyramidal bosses where the paper has been cut by corresponding bosses on a roller as a protection against illegal removal of cancellation marks

²**grille** *also* **grill** \"\ *adj, of table cutlery* : of a style characterized by unusual length of handle and shortness of blade or tine

³**grille** *var of* GRILL

grill·er \'grilə(r)\ *n* -S [¹*grill* + *-er*] : one that grills; *usu* : a device for broiling : ²GRILL

grilling *pres part of* GRILL

grillroom \'⸗,⸗\ *n* [²*grill* + *room*] : an informal dining room esp. in a hotel or club

grills *pres 3d sing of* GRILL, *pl of* GRILL

grillwork \'⸗,⸗\ *n* [³*grill* + *work*] : work so constructed as to constitute or resemble a grille

grilse \'gri̇ls *also* -lts\ *n, pl* **grilse** *also* **grilses** [ME *grills, grilles*] : a young mature Atlantic salmon returning from the sea to spawn for the first time when between 3 and 3½ years of age, being chiefly a small male of 4 to 12 pounds, and being very vigorous and active when compared with older fish; *also* : any of various other salmon at a stage of development comparable to that of the Atlantic salmon grilse

¹**grim** \'grim\ *adj* **grimmer; grimmest** [ME, fr. OE *grimm*; akin to OHG *grimm* savage, fierce, ON *grimmr* fierce, cruel, enraged, Gk *chromados* action of gnashing, Av *gram-* to get angry] **1 a** : fierce in disposition or action : savage and merciless : cruel and pitiless ⟨gaunt ~ wolves descending into the valleys⟩ **b** : stern, fierce, and resolute : UNCOMPROMISING ⟨ready to do ~ battle for their rights⟩ **2 a** : of harsh and forbidding aspect : stern or forbidding in action or appearance ⟨a ~ man loving duty more than humanity⟩ **b** : distressing or shocking to see : GRISLY, HORRIBLE ⟨the ~ row of traitors' heads over the gate⟩ **3** : unyielding and relentless : sternly determined ⟨~ purpose⟩ **4** : ghastly, repellent, or sinister in character or dealing with what is so ⟨a ~ task⟩ ⟨a ~ tale⟩ ⟨lectures seem to me a rather ~ treat —Willa Cather⟩ — **grim·ly** *adv*

²**grim** \"\ *vt* **grimmed; grimmed; grimming; grims** : to make grim and forbidding ⟨lurid clouds that ~ the silence⟩

¹**grimace** \'griməs, grə'mās\ *n* -S [F, fr. MF, alter. of *grimache*, of Gmc origin; akin to OE *grīma* mask, helmet — more at GRIME] **1** : a deliberate or involuntary distortion of the countenance expressive of some feeling (as contempt, disapprobation, complacency) : a wry face ⟨gave a little ~ of disgust⟩ **2 a** : artful show : AFFECTATION; *broadly* : SHAM, PRETENSE **b** *archaic* : an affected expression or attitude esp. of formal good manners or exaggerated gentility

²**grimace** \"\ *vi* -ED/-ING/-S [F *grimacer*, fr. *grimace*, n.] : to make grimaces : distort one's face : make faces — **grimac·er** \-sə(r)\ *n* -S

grimac·ing·ly *adv* : with grimaces

gri·mal·di·an \grə'mäldēən, -mȯl-\ *adj, usu cap G* [*Grimaldi* (*race*) + *-an*] : of or relating to the Grimaldi race

gri·mal·di race *or* **grimaldi man** \-dē-\ *n, usu cap G* [fr. *Grimaldi* caves, Liguria, Italy, where remains were found] : an early Upper Paleolithic man somewhat resembling the Cro-Magnons but also showing some negroid characteristics and being known from buried skeletons of a woman and a boy

gri·mal·kin \grə'malkən, -mȯ(l)k-\ *also* **gray·mal·kin** \grā'-\ *n* [*grimalkin* alter. of *graymalkin*; *graymalkin* fr. *gray* + *malkin*] **1** : CAT 1a; *esp* : an elderly queen **2** : an old and usu. cantankerous or otherwise unpleasant woman

¹**grime** \'grīm\ *vt* -ED/-ING/-S [ME *grimen*, fr. MD, fr. *grime* mask, soot] : to sully or soil deeply : BESMEAR, BEGRIME

²**grime** \"\ *n* -S [Flem *grijm*, fr. MD *grime* soot, mask; akin to OE *grīma* mask, helmet, OS & ON, mask, OHG *grīmo* mask, Gk *chriein* to anoint, Lith *grieti* to skim off cream — more at CHRISM] : soil (as soot or dirt) usu. firmly adhering to or deeply embedded in a surface ⟨windows coated with ~⟩ ⟨the ~ of toil that no scrubbing could wholly remove from his hands⟩; *broadly* : accumulated dirtiness and disorder ⟨the ~ of the slums⟩

grime·less \-ləs\ *adj* : free from grime : CLEAN, IMMACULATE

grime's ditch *or* **grime's dyke** *usu cap G, var of* GRIM'S DITCH

grimes' grave \'grīmz(əz)-\ *n, usu cap both Gs* [origin unknown] : one of the pits sunk near Brandon, Suffolk, England, in Neolithic times for the mining of flint

grim·ful \'grim(p)fəl\ *adj* [ME, fr. *grim* + *-ful*] *archaic* : cruel and fierce : DREADFUL

grimgribber *n* -S [fr. *Grimgribber*, an imaginary estate subject of a legal discussion in the play *Conscious Lovers* (1722) by Sir Richard Steele †1729 Brit. essayist and dramatist] *obs* : technical jargon (as of legal matters)

grimier *comparative of* GRIMY

grimiest *superlative of* GRIMY

grim·i·ly \'grīmələ̄, -li\ *adv* : in a grimy condition or manner

grim·i·ness \-mēnəs, -min-\ *n* -ES : the quality or state of being grimy

grim·ly *adj* [ME, fr. OE *grimlīc*, fr. *grimm* grim + *-līc* -ly — more at GRIM] *archaic* : GRIM, HIDEOUS, STERN

grimme \'grim\ *n* -S [F, fr. NL *grimmia* (specific epithet of the Linnaean designation *Capra grimmia*), fr. Hermann N. *Grimm* †1711 Ger. scientist + NL *-ia*] : a small West African antelope (*Cephalophus rufilotus*) of a deep bay color

grimmer *comparative of* GRIM

grimmest *superlative of* GRIM

grim·mia \'grimēə\ *n, cap* [NL, fr. Johann F. K. *Grimm* †1821 Ger. botanist + NL *-ia*] : a widely distributed genus of tufted rock mosses that is the type of the family Grimmiaceae

grim·mi·a·ce·ae \,grimē'āsē,ē\ *n pl, cap* [NL, fr. *Grimmia*, type genus + *-aceae*] : a family of acrocarpous mosses that have the capsule on a short stalk and with a single peristome the teeth of which are often split or perforated and that form dark mats or cushions lacking chlorophyll except at the tips of stems and branches — **grim·mi·a·ceous** \¦grimē¦āshəs\ *adj*

grim·mi·a·les \,grimē'ā(,)lēz\ *n pl, cap* [NL, fr. *Grimmia* + *-ales*] : an order of Musci comprising acrocarpous mosses that are usu. blackish green with branching stems and densely crowded leaves and that grow chiefly on rocks

grimming *pres part of* GRIM

grim·mish \'grimish\ *adj* : rather grim

grimm's law \'grimz-\ *n, usu cap G & often cap L* [after Jacob *Grimm* †1863 Ger. philologist] **1 a** : a statement in historical linguistics: Proto-Indo-European voiceless stops became Proto-Germanic voiceless fricatives (as in Greek *pyr, treis, kardia* compared with English *fire, three, heart*), Proto-Indo-European voiced stops became Proto-Germanic voiceless stops (as in Old Slavic *jablŭko*, Greek *dyo, genos* compared with English *apple, two, kin*), and Proto-Indo-European voiced aspirated stops became Proto-Germanic voiced fricatives (as in Sanskrit *nābhi, madhya* "mid", Latin *helvus* compared with English *navel*, Old Norse *mithr* "mid", English *yellow*), and then Proto-Germanic voiceless stops became High German affricates or voiceless fricatives (as in English *pound, open, ten, eat, corn, make* compared with German *pfund, offen, zehn, essen*, Upper German *kchorn*, German *machen*), and Proto-Germanic voiced stops (coming from Proto-Germanic voiced fricatives) became High German voiceless stops (as in English *rib, middle*, Dutch *egge* "edge" compared with German *rippe, mittel* "means", *ecke* "corner") **b** : a statement in historical linguistics: Proto-Indo-European voiceless stops became Proto-Germanic voiceless fricatives (as in Greek *pyr, treis, kardia* compared with English *fire, three, heart*), Proto-Indo-European voiced stops became Proto-Germanic voiceless stops (as in Old Slavic *jablŭko*, Greek *dyo, genos* compared with English *apple, two, kin*), and Proto-Indo-European voiced aspirated stops became Proto-Germanic voiced fricatives (as in Sanskrit *nābhi, madhya* "mid", Latin *helvus* compared with English *navel*, Old Norse *mithr* "mid", English *yellow*) **2 a** : CONSONANT SHIFT 3 **b** : CONSONANT SHIFT 1

grim·ness *n* -ES [ME *grimnesse*, fr. OE, fr. *grimm* + *-nesse* -ness] : the quality or state of being grim

gri·moire \grəm'wär\ *n* -S [F, fr. OF, alter. of *gramaire* grammar, grammar book, learned work, book of witchcraft — more at GRAMMAR] : a magician's manual for invoking demons and the spirits of the dead

grimp \'grimp\ *vi* -ED/-ING/-S [F *grimper*, fr. MF, alter. (prob. influenced by *ramper* to crawl) of *gripper* to climb, to seize with the claws or nails, of Gmc origin; akin to OS *grīpan* to grasp, seize — more at GRIPE] **1** : CLIMB **2** : to draw up ⟨the line ~*ed* into a hard knot⟩

grim reaper *n, often cap G&R* : death esp. when personified as a man or skeleton with a scythe

grims *pres 3d sing of* GRIM

grim's ditch *or* **grim's dyke** \'grimz-\ *also* **grime's ditch** *or* **grime's dyke** \'grīmz-\ *n, usu cap G* [origin unknown] : any of several ancient entrenchments found in the British Isles some of which are prehistoric

grim–the–collier \,grim-\ *n* -S [after *Grim the Collier*, character in the anonymous play *Grim the Collier of Croydon* (1662); fr. its black smutty involucre] : ORANGE HAWKWEED

grim·thorpe \'grim(p),thȯ(ə)rp\ *vt* -ED/-ING/-S [after Sir Edmund Beckett, first Baron *Grimthorpe* †1905 Eng. lawyer and architect whose restoration of St. Albans cathedral in England was severely criticized] : to remodel (an ancient building) without proper knowledge or care to retain its original quality and character

grimy \'grīmē, -mi\ *adj* **grimier; grimiest** [2*grime* + -*y*] **1 :** full of or covered with grime : BEGRIMED, DIRTY, FOUL; *also* : DUSKY, SWARTHY **2 :** mean and unpleasant : common and petty ⟨a ~ rascal⟩ ⟨told the whole story in all its ~ spite⟩

1grin \'grin\ *n* -s [ME *grin, grine, grene,* fr. OE *grin;* akin to ME *grane* snare, noose] *chiefly Scot* : SNARE, NOOSE, TRAP

2grin \"\ *vt* **grinned; grinned; grinning; grins** [ME *grenen,* fr. *grin, grine, grene,* n.] : TRAP

3grin \"\ *vb* **grinned; grinned; grinning; grins** [ME *grennen, grinnen,* fr. OE *grennian;* akin to OHG *grennen* to snarl, ON *grenja* to howl, and prob. to OE *grānian* to groan — more at GROAN] *vi* **1 :** to draw back the lips from the teeth (as of a dog in snarling or a person in laughter or pain) so as to show them; *esp* : to do this in merriment or good humor (as in a broad smile) **2 a :** to gape open : PART **b :** to appear through interstices of a covering ⟨sometimes the paint checks and lets the undercoat ~ through⟩ ~ *vt* **1 :** to show (the teeth) usu. in a grin or snarl **2 :** to form or express by grinning ⟨*grinned* reassurance to the frightened children⟩ ⟨*grinning* a foolish grin⟩ — **grin like a cheshire cat** *usu cap 1st C* : to grin broadly — **grin on the other side of one's face :** to regret one's previous behavior in some matter that at the time seemed trivial or amusing ⟨you'll *grin on the other side of your face* if you have to pay for the damage you did⟩

4grin \"\ *n* -s **1 :** a facial expression produced by grinning ⟨a ~ of pain⟩; *esp* : a broad toothy smile **2 :** something exposed like the teeth in a grin: as **a :** an unfinished portion of baseboard exposed when a building settles **b :** a portion of the basic fabric of a rug exposed when the pile parts — compare GRIN *vi* 2b

1grind \'grīnd\ *vb* **ground** \'graủnd\ *also archaic* **grinded; ground** *also archaic* **grinded** *or* **ground·en** \'graủndən\ **grinding; grinds** [ME *grinden,* fr. OE *grindan;* akin to OHG *grint* scurf, ON *grandi* sandbar, Goth *grinda*frathjis faint-hearted, L *frendere* to crush, gnash, grind, Gk *chondros* grain, Lith *grendu* I rub, scrub, OE *grēot* sand, grit — more at GRIT] *vt* **1 a :** to reduce to powder by friction (as in a mill) or with the teeth : crush into small fragments **b :** to produce by or as if by the action of millstones **2 :** to wear down, polish, or sharpen by friction : make smooth, sharp, or pointed : WHET ⟨spent the morning ~*ing* axes and scythes⟩ **3 a :** to rub or press harshly ⟨~ the snake's head under his heel⟩ **b :** to rub together with a grating noise : GRATE, GRIT ⟨~ the teeth⟩ **4 :** to oppress by severe exactions : HARASS ⟨~ the subject or defraud the prince —John Dryden⟩ **5 :** to operate or produce by turning a crank ⟨~ a hand organ⟩ ⟨~ out a tune⟩ ~ *vi* **1 :** to perform the operation of grinding **2 :** to become ground or pulverized by friction ⟨corn ~*ing* slowly⟩ **3 :** to become polished or sharpened by friction ⟨glass ~*s* smooth⟩ ⟨steel ~*s* to a sharp edge⟩ ⟨pebbles ~*ing* on the beach⟩ **4 :** to move with difficulty or friction : GRATE ⟨the gears *ground* as he shifted into high⟩ ⟨frantically *ground* on the starter —Frank Schreider⟩ **5 :** to perform hard and distasteful service : DRUDGE; *esp* : to study hard ⟨~ for an examination⟩ **6 :** to rotate the hips in a suggestive manner in or as if in a burlesque striptease

2grind \"\ *n* -s [ME, fr. *grinden,* v.] **1 a :** an act of grinding (as of reducing to powder or sharpening by friction) **b :** a sound of grinding **2 a :** steady monotonous taxing labor, occupation, or routine ⟨sometimes life seems just a dull ~ without hope or future⟩ **b :** intensive and drudging study; *also* : a task or an assignment given by an instructor **3 :** a student who studies to the exclusion of all other activities often with more diligence than delight **4 :** the result of grinding; *esp* : the size of particle obtained by grinding ⟨there are several different ~*s* of coffee⟩ ⟨a fine ~ of meal is better for bread⟩ **5 :** an action of rotating the hips with a suggestive motion (as in a dance or in a burlesque striptease) — compare 2BUMP 5 **syn** see WORK

3grind \"\ *adj, of a motion-picture theater or other show* : exhibiting continuously or continuously between certain hours

4grind \'grind\ *n* -s [of Scand origin; akin to ON *grind* gate, lattice door; akin to OE *grindel* bar, bolt, OHG *grintil* bar, bolt, L *grunda* truss of a roof, Lith *grindis* floorboard; basic meaning: beam] *Scot* : a horizontal bar gate

5grind \"\ *n, pl* **grind** [Faroese *grindkval*] : BLACKFISH 2 — used chiefly in the Faroe islands ⟨the boats will be ready when the ~ come in⟩

grind·abil·i·ty \,grīndə'bilәd·ē\ *n* : capacity for or resistance to being ground ⟨prepared an index of the ~ of various southern coals⟩

grind·able \'grīndəbəl\ *adj* : capable of being ground

grind down *vt* : to repress harshly : keep rigidly under control or in a state of submission ⟨the nobility *ground down* the peasants with an infinite variety of petty exactions⟩

grin·de·lia \grin'dēlyə, -lēə\ *n* [NL, fr. David Hieronymus *Grindel* †1836 Russ. botanist + NL *-ia*] **1** *a cap* : a large genus of coarse gummy or resinous herbs (family Compositae) chiefly of western No. America that have flower heads with involucres consisting of phyllaries with spreading tips **b** -s : a plant of the genus *Grindelia* : GUMWEED **2** -s : the dried leaves and stems of various gumweeds (as *Grindelia camporum, G. cuneifolia,* and *G. squarrosa*) used internally as a remedy in bronchitis and as a local application in ivy poisoning

grind·er \'grīndә(r)\ *n* -s [ME, fr. *grinden* to grind + *-er* — more at GRIND] **1 a :** MOLAR 1 — distinguished from *cutter* **b grinders** *pl* : TEETH **2 :** a person that grinds: as **a :** a worker who crushes or pulverizes materials (as grain, stone, clay, scrap rubber) usu. by machine **b :** a worker who shapes, smooths, or cleans roughly finished articles by means of abrasives or grinding wheels; *esp* : one that sharpens tools by grinding (as on a grinding wheel) **c** *slang Brit* : a private tutor **d** *slang* : a carnival or sideshow barker who talks up a new crowd while one show is going on **e** *slang* : a burlesque performer specializing in grinds **3 :** a machine or device for grinding: as **a :** a machine for grinding with abrasives that typically takes the form of a grinding wheel and is used to cut hardened or tempered metals and to develop a smooth finish (as on metal, wood, stone) **b :** a pulverizing machine (as a ball mill or a wood-pulp grinding machine) **4** [so called fr. its whining call] : RESTLESS FLYCATCHER **5 :** an atmospheric disturbance that is heard by a radio listener as a rumbling and is caused by distant lightning **6 :** a large sandwich made of two slabs of bread cut lengthwise from the loaf or a whole small crusty loaf cut lengthwise and containing meat (as ham, salami, or meatballs), usu. cheese, tomato and lettuce, pickles or other appetizers, and sometimes (as with meatballs) a thick spicy sauce

grind·er·man \-mәn, -,man\ *n, pl* **grindermen 1 :** one who tends an edge runner in papermaking **2 :** one who tends the grinders in preparing groundwood

grinder's green *n* : a chrome green containing usu. about 75 percent of extending pigments and commonly used for preparing green paints and pastes for tinting

grind in *vt* : to lap in (as a valve and valve seat) so that each surface serves as a lap for the other

1grinding *n* -s [ME, fr. *grinden* to grind + *-ing* — more at GRIND] : the act or the sound of one that grinds

2grinding *adj* [fr. pres. part. of 1*grind*] **1 :** used in or suitable for grinding ⟨the ~ teeth⟩ ⟨a good grade of white ~ corn⟩ **2** *of pain* **a :** extremely severe and wearing : EXCRUCIATING, AGONIZING **b :** of the type characteristic of the early stages of labor **3 :** burdensome and oppressive ⟨~ poverty⟩ ⟨a ~ suspicion⟩; *esp* : EXTORTIONATE ⟨~ levies and excessive taxes⟩ **4 a** *of sound* : harsh and strident ⟨a gritty ~ voice⟩ ⟨a bird with a peculiar ~ call⟩ **b :** characterized or accompanied by a grinding sound ⟨worn ~ gears⟩ — **grindingly** *adv*

grinding aid *n* : a material added in small amount to cement clinker to aid in the pulverizing of the clinker into powder

grinding mill *n* **1 :** any of various machines for grinding (as of grain or sugarcane) or for dressing by grinding (as of metal parts) **2 :** a lapidary's lathe

grinding wheel *n* : an abrasive wheel or disk used for cutting or smoothing hard materials

1grin·dle \'grind²l\ *n* -s [ME *grendyll*] *dial Eng* : a small stream or ditch

2grin·dle *also* **grin·dal** *or* **grin·del** \'grind²l\ *or* **grin·nel** *or* **grin·nell** \-n²l\ *n* -s [G *gründel,* fr. *grund* bottom, ground, fr. OHG *grunt* — more at GROUND] : BOWFIN

grin·dle·stone \'grin(d)²lztən, -²lst-\ *n* [ME *grindelston,* fr. *grindel-* (fr. *grinden* to grind) + *ston* stone — more at GRIND, STONE] *dial* : GRINDSTONE

grin·dle·to·ni·an \,grind²l'tōnēən\ *n* -s *usu cap* [*Grindleton,* parish in Yorkshire, Eng. + E *-ian*] : a member of an English familist sect of the 17th century

grind out *vt* : to produce in a steady stream esp. more or less mechanically as though by turning a crank ⟨*ground out* his three novels a year for over 30 years⟩

grinds *pres 3d sing of* GRIND, *pl of* GRIND

grind·stone \'grīn(d)z,tōn, -),stōn, *archaic or dial* 'grinztən *or* -in(t)st-\ *n* [ME *grindston,* fr. *grinden* to grind + *ston* stone — more at GRIND, STONE] **1 a :** MILLSTONE 1 **b :** a flat circular stone of natural sandstone that revolves on an axle and is used for grinding tools or shaping or smoothing objects **2 :** stone suitable for grindstones

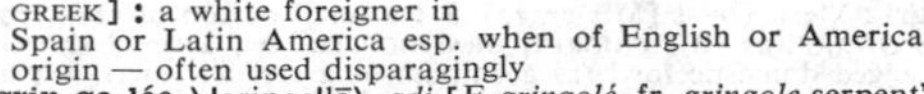
grindstone 1b

grind whale *n* [5*grind*] : BLACKFISH 2

grin·ga \'griŋgə, -ŋ(,)gä\ *n* -s [Sp, fem. of *gringo*] : a female gringo — sometimes used disparagingly

grin·go \-ŋ(,)gō\ *n* -s [Sp, alter. of *griego* Greek, unknown language, stranger, fr. L *Graecus* Greek — more at GREEK] : a white foreigner in Spain or Latin America esp. when of English or American origin — often used disparagingly

grin·go·lée \,griŋgə'lā\ *adj* [F *gringolé,* fr. *gringole* serpent's head] *of a cross* : having at the end of each arm a pair of serpent heads with each head turned outward ⟨a cross ~ in his heraldic escutcheon⟩

grinned *past of* GRIN

grin·nel·lia \grə'nelēə, -lyə\ *n, cap* [NL, fr. Henry *Grinnell* †1874 Am. merchant + NL *-ia*] : a genus related to *Delesseria* and comprising red algae with lanceolate fronds often 18 inches or more in length

grin·ner \'grinə(r)\ *n* -s [ME *grennare,* fr. *grennen, grinnen* to grin + *-are, -er* -er — more at GRIN] : one that grins

grin·nie *or* **grin·ny** \'grinē\ *n, pl* **grinnies** [origin unknown] *dial* : CHIPMUNK, GROUND SQUIRREL

grinning *pres part of* GRIN

grin·ning·ly *adv* : in a grinning manner : with a grin

grin·ny \'grinē, -ni\ *adj, usu* -ER/-EST : given to grinning

grins *pl of* GRIN, *pres 3d sing of* GRIN

grin·stone \'grinztən, -n(t)st-\ *obs or dial var of* GRINDSTONE

1grip \'grip\ *vb* **gripped** *or* **gript; gripped** *or* **gript; gripping; grips** [ME *grippen,* fr. OE *grippan;* akin to OHG *gripfen* to grip, OE *grīpan* to seize, attack — more at GRIPE] *vt* **1 :** to seize or lay hold on tightly and tenaciously : grasp firmly **2** *archaic* : to take or get possession of : SEIZE, APPROPRIATE **3 :** to give a handclasp to **4 :** to fasten or attach by a grip or clutch **5 a :** to make a tenacious impression upon ⟨the pathos of the play *gripped* the beholders⟩ **b :** GRASP *vt* 3 ~ *vi* : to take firm hold ⟨the anchor ~*s*⟩ : close tightly ⟨his jaws *gripped*⟩ : rivet attention ⟨the story ~*s*⟩

2grip \"\ *n* -s [ME, partly fr. OE *gripe* grasp, seizure; partly fr. OE *gripa* handful, sheaf; akin to OE *grīpan* to seize, attack — more at GRIPE] **1 a :** an energetic or tenacious grasp : a seizing or clutching of something tightly (as with the hand) ⟨got a good ~ on his collar⟩ **b :** strength in gripping **c :** manner or style of gripping: as (1) : a peculiar mode of clasping the hand by which members of a group (as a secret order) recognize or greet one another (2) : arrangement of and muscular force applied through the hands in grasping something ⟨notice the balanced ~ of an expert golfer⟩ **2** *dial Eng* : as much as can be gripped : HANDFUL **3 :** a spasm of pain **4 a :** power or force of hold or domination : CONTROL, MASTERY ⟨unable to escape the ~ of his bad habits⟩ **b :** power of apprehension : GRASP ⟨he has a thorough ~ of his duty now⟩ ⟨no real intellectual ~ of the subject⟩ **5 :** a part or device for gripping; *esp* : an apparatus attached to a car for clutching a traction cable **6 :** a part or device by which something is grasped (as a handle): **a** (1) : the portion of a firearm gripped by the trigger hand when firing (2) : either of the pieces (as of wood, plastic, mother-of-pearl) that are fitted one on either side to the portion of the frame of a handgun which forms the grip **b :** the plaited woolen covering on a bell rope — called also *sally* **7 :** a piece of hand luggage (as a suitcase) ⟨the bellboy carried the ~*s*⟩ **8 :** the total thickness of metal held between the two heads of a rivet in a riveted joint **9 :** SCENESHIFTER **10** [short for *gripgrass*] : CLEAVERS — **at grips** *adv* : in a relation resembling or involving a hand-to-hand struggle

3grip \"\ *also* **gripe** \'grīp\ *n* -s [ME *grippe, grip,* fr. OE *grȳpe;* akin to OE & MLG *grope* pot, MD *groepe, grope* ditch, *grope, groppe* pot, ON *greypa* to groove] *dial chiefly Eng* : a small ditch or furrow : GUTTER

4grip \"\ *vt, dial Eng* : TRENCH, DRAIN

5grip \"\ *n* -s [by alter.] : GRIPPE

grip car *n* : a car equipped with a device for gripping a traction cable by which the car is moved : CABLE CAR

1gripe \'grīp\ *vb* **griped; griped; griping; gripes** [ME *gripen,* fr. OE *grīpan;* akin to OHG *grīfan* to seize, grasp, ON *grīpa,* Goth *greipan* to seize, grasp, Lith *griebti* to reach for, grasp] *vt* **1 a** *archaic* : to take, seize, or come forcibly into possession or control of **b :** to come to have and to hold tightly or penuriously ⟨*griping* his ill-gotten gains⟩ **c :** to grasp, clutch, or hold onto tightly ⟨*griping* his sword fast⟩ **d** *obs* : to enclose tightly **2 :** AFFLICT: as **a :** to distress, hurt, or grieve by or as if by grasping or seizing tightly ⟨may the fiend ~ his entrails —O.W.Holmes †1935⟩ **b :** to oppress by want, penury, or callous grasping exaction ⟨the poverty that ~*s* the very poor⟩ ⟨in the clutches of a *griping* sweatshop operator⟩ **c :** IRRITATE, ANGER, VEX ⟨a rookie *griped* by army regulations⟩ ⟨*griped* by the new income-tax provisions⟩ **3 :** to cause pinching and spasmodic pain in the bowels of ~ *vi* **1** *archaic* : to try to clutch : start to lay hold **2 :** to experience griping pains **3** *of a ship* : to tend to come up into the wind abnormally esp. so as to require the helm to be continually put up when sailing close-hauled **4 :** to complain usu. forcefully : object and criticize with sustained grumbling ⟨*griping* about food in the mess hall⟩ ⟨~ at the new regulations⟩ **syn** see COMPLAIN

2gripe \"\ *n* -s [ME, fr. *gripen,* v.] **1 :** the act of griping, clutching, or taking fast hold : firm seizure or grasp; *broadly* : CONTROL, MASTERY ⟨a barren scepter in my ~ —Shak.⟩ **2 a :** cruel exaction : OPPRESSION : pinching distress : AFFLICTION **b :** COMPLAINT, GRUMBLING **3 :** a pinching spasmodic intestinal pain — usu. used in pl. **4 :** something adapted to be grasped : HANDLE, GRIP **5 a :** something that can be grasped in the hand : HANDFUL **b** *obs* : the hand as a gripping instrument **6 :** a device (as a brake) for grasping or holding **7 a :** a timber sometimes scarfed into the forefoot and stem of a wooden ship for additional strength; *broadly* : FOREFOOT 2 **b :** the forward end of the dished keel of a steel ship to which the stem is attached **c gripes** *pl* : canvas bands and fastenings securing a lifeboat in its cradle

3gripe \"\ *n* -s [ME, fr. L *grypus, gryphus* — more at GRIFFIN] **1** *obs* : GRIFFIN 1a **2** *archaic* : VULTURE 1

grip·er \'grīpə(r)\ *n* -s : one that gripes

gripe's egg *n* [3*gripe*] *obs* : a vessel in size and shape like a very large egg used by alchemists

gripe water *n* [2*gripe*] : DILL WATER

gripey *var of* GRIPY

gripgrass \'ₛ,ₛ\ *n* : CLEAVERS

griph *or* **griphus** *n, pl* **griphs** *or* **griphuses** [L *griphus,* fr. Gk *griphos,* lit., fishing basket, creel] *obs* : PUZZLE, RIDDLE, ENIGMA

griph·ite \'gri,fīt\ *n* -s [Gk *griphos* enigma + E *-ite;* fr. its unusual composition] : a mineral $(Na,Al,Ca,Fe)_6Mn_4(PO_4)_5(OH)_4$ consisting of basic phosphate of sodium, calcium, iron, aluminum, and manganese with a crystal structure related to that of garnet

griping *adj* **1 :** causing or characteristic of gripe ⟨~ pains⟩ ⟨some foods are ~ when eaten to excess⟩ : PAINFUL, DISTRESSING **2 :** CLUTCHING, GRASPING; *broadly* : AVARICIOUS ⟨married a selfish, ~, spoiled woman⟩ — **grip·ing·ly** *adv*

grip·less \'gripləs\ *adj* : having no grip; *also* : lacking vigor : WEAK, LIFELESS

grip·man \-mən\ *n, pl* **gripmen :** a cable-car operator who makes the car's grip clutch or unclutch a moving cable to move or stop the car as desired

gripp·al \'gripəl\ *adj* [*grippe* + *-al*] : of, relating to, or associated with grippe ⟨~ pneumonia⟩

grippe \'grip\ *n* -s [F, lit., seizure, prob. fr. *gripper* to seize — more at GRIMP] : an acute febrile contagious virus disease identical with or resembling influenza

gripped *past of* GRIP

grip·per \'gripə(r)\ *n* -s **1 :** a device that holds something firmly: as **a :** a bookbinder's mechanism that grips and impels a book or other matter into a machine **b :** a device for holding a sheet being printed **2 a :** a worker who fashions or attaches grips (as on a handgun) **b :** a clipper in a coal mine

1grip·pi·ness \'gripēnəs, -pin-\ *n* -ES [1*grippy* + *-ness*] *chiefly Scot* : MISERLINESS, STINGINESS

2grip·pi·ness \"\ *n* -ES [2*grippy* + *-ness*] : the quality or state of being affected by or feeling as if one had the grippe

gripping *adj* : having the ability to grip; *esp* : taking a powerful hold upon one's interest or feelings — used esp. of a book or play ⟨a ~ tale of suspense⟩ — **grip·ping·ly** *adv* — **grip·ping·ness** *n* -ES

grip·pit \'gripət\ *adj* [fr. Sc var. of *gripped,* past part. of 1*grip*] *Scot* : GRIPPED, CLUTCHED, APPREHENDED ⟨it will be high treason if I'm *grippit* —John Buchan⟩

1grip·ple \'gripəl\ *adj* [ME *gripel,* fr. OE *gripul,* fr. the stem of *grīpan* to seize, attack — more at GRIPE] *dial Brit* : greedy and grasping : AVARICIOUS

2gripple *vb* [prob. blend of 1*grip* and 1*grapple*] *obs* : GRAPPLE, GRASP

1grip·py \'gripē, -pi\ *adj* -ER/-EST [1*grip* + -*y*] *chiefly Scot* : MISERLY, STINGY ⟨the wife is dreadful ~⟩

2grippy \'gripē, -pi\ *adj* -ER/-EST [*grippe* + -*y*] : affected with or like the grippe ⟨the *grippiest* time of the year —*Newsweek*⟩

grips *pres 3d sing of* GRIP, *pl of* GRIP

gripsack \'ₛ,ₛ\ *n* [2*grip* + *sack*] : TRAVELING BAG

grip safety *n* : a safety device on a firearm that prevents firing until it has been depressed by the firer's hand upon the grip

gript *past of* GRIP

gripy *or* **grip·ey** \'grīpē, -pi\ *adj* **gripier; gripiest** [2*gripe* + -*y*] : resembling or tending to cause gripes ⟨~ pains⟩

griqua \'grēkwə, -rik-\ *n* -s *cap* [Afrik *Griekwa*] **1 :** one of a mixed people in Griqualand of Bushman and Hottentot descent **2 :** the mixed offspring of European, Bushman, and Hottentot ancestry esp. in Griqualand being mostly tall with dark curly hair and resembling Europeans — called also *Bastaard* **3 :** any person of mixed Caucasoid-Negroid descent — used chiefly in southwestern Africa

griqua·land·er \-,landə(r)\ *n* -s *cap* [Afrik *Griekwalander,* fr. *Griekwaland* Griqualand, region in southern Africa + *-er*] : a native or inhabitant of Griqualand

gris \'grē(s)\ *also* **grise** \-ēs\ *n, pl* **grises** \-rēsəz,-rēz\ [ME *gris,* fr. OF, fr. *gris,* adj., gray — more at GRIZZLE] : a costly gray fur used decoratively on medieval costumes

gri·saille \grə'zī, grē'-, -zäl,-zīl\ *n* -s [F, fr. *gris* gray, fr. OF] **1 a :** painting in monochrome usu. in shades of gray often as decoration to simulate sculptured relief or as underpainting for a glaze finish **b :** a covering of a dark base in porcelain and enamelwork with varying thicknesses of white so as to produce a cameo effect with the dark color showing through **c :** a coating of glasswork with white to produce an opalescent effect or as backing for a decorative pattern of colored glass **2 :** a fancy dress fabric orig. of silk with a fine crosswise rib and a grayish color resulting from interweaving black-and-white threads

grisamber *n* [by alter.] *obs* : AMBERGRIS

gris·ard \'grizə(r)d\ *n* -s [F, fr. *gris* gray + *-ard*] : a gray-headed person

gris·bet \'grizbət\ *var of* GRISTBITE

gris–de–lin \,grēd²l'an, 'grid²lən\ *n* -s [F, lit., flax gray] : GRIDELIN

grise \'grīs\ *var of* GRICE

gris·el·dy \'grizəldē\ *dial var of* GRISLY

gris·e·lin·ia \,grizə'linēə\ *n, cap* [NL, fr. Francesco *Griselini* †1783, Ital. botanist + NL *-ia*] : a small genus of New Zealand and So. American trees (family Cornaceae) that are occas. epiphytic in habit — see KAPUKA, PUKA

gris·eo·ful·vin \,grizēō'fulvən, -'fəl-\ *n* -s [NL *griseofulvum* (specific epithet of *Penicillium griseofulvum*) + E *-in*] : a fungicidal antibiotic $C_{17}H_{17}ClO_6$ produced by molds of the genus *Penicillium*

gris·e·ous \'grizēəs\ *adj* [ML *griseus,* of Gmc origin; akin to OHG *grīs* gray — more at GRIZZLE] : of a light color or white mottled with black or brown : GRIZZLED

gri·sette \grə'zet, grē'-\ *n* -s [F, fr. *grisette* inexpensive gray woolen cloth often used for dresses, fr. *gris* gray (fr. OF) + *-ette* — more at GRIZZLE] **1 :** a French girl of the working class **2 :** a young woman combining part-time prostitution with some other occupation ⟨the dusky ~*s* who sold love as well as flowers —H.S.Canby⟩ — **gri·set·tish** \-ed·ish\ *adj*

gris–gris *or* **gri·gri** *also* **gree·gree** \'grē(,)grē\ *n, pl* **gris–gris** *or* **grigris** *also* **greegrees** [F *gris-gris,* of African origin; akin to Balante *grigri* charm, amulet] : a talisman, amulet, voodoo charm, spell, or incantation believed chiefly by people of African Negro origin or ancestry capable of warding off evil and bringing good luck to oneself or of bringing misfortune to another

gris·kin \'griskən\ *n* -s [*grice* + *-kin*] **1** *Brit* : a pork loin; *esp* : the lean part **2** *Brit* : a pork chop or other broiled meat : STEAK

gri·sle \'grizəl\ *archaic var of* GRIZZLE

gris·li·ness \'grizlēnəs, -lin-\ *n* -ES [ME *grislines,* fr. *grisly* + *-nes* -ness] : the quality or state of being grisly

1gris·ly *also* **griz·zly** \'grizlē, -li\ *adj* -ER/-EST [ME, fr. OE *grislic,* fr. *gris-* (akin to OE *āgrisan* to shudder, fear) + *-lic* -ly; akin to OHG *grīsenlīh* terrible, MD & MLG *grīsen* to shudder, and prob. to OE *grēot* sand, grit — more at GRIT] **1 a :** inspiring horror or intense fear : grim and ghastly ⟨these strange and ~ events⟩; *broadly* : harsh and forbidding ⟨a grim ~ winter's night⟩ **b :** being such as to inspire distaste or disgust ⟨a ~ account of the fire⟩ **2 :** caused by what is grim or horrible or marked by a sense of grim horror ⟨reason could not rid her of that ~ fear⟩

2gris·ly \"\ *adv, often* -ER/-EST [ME, fr. *grisly,* adj.] : DREADFULLY, TERRIBLY

3grisly *obs var of* GRISTLY

4grisly *var of* GRIZZLY

gris·on \'grīz²n\ *n* [F, fr. *grison* gray, fr. MF, fr. *gris* — more at GRIZZLE] **1** -s : any of various So. American nearly plantigrade carnivorous mammals of the genus *Grison* (esp. *G. vittatus*) that resemble large weasels, are blackish below and gray above, and are often domesticated by the natives though very destructive to poultry **2** [NL, fr. F *grison*] *cap* : a genus of Mustelidae comprising the grisons

gris·sen \'gris²n\ *n* -s [ME *grecing,* fr. *grece* + *-ing* — more at GRECE] *now dial* : GRECE

gris·si·no \grə'sē(,)nō\ *n, pl* **gris·si·ni** \-)nē\ [It, fr. It dial. (Piedmont) *grissin, ghersin,* fr. *ghersa* strip] : a long slender crusty breadstick usu. of Italian style or origin

1grist \'grist\ *n* -s [ME, fr. OE *grist;* akin to OE *grindan* to grind — more at GRIND] **1** *obs* : the act of grinding **2 a :** grain for grinding ⟨some wheats make better ~ than others⟩ **b :** a batch of grain taken to a mill for custom grinding ⟨farmers bringing their ~*s* of rye, buckwheat, and wheat to the mill⟩ **c :** the product obtained from a grist of grain including the flour or meal and the grain offals (as bran) **3 :** crushed or ground malt ready for use in brewing **4 a :** a large quantity : LOT, NUMBER ⟨got a ~ of lazy kinfolk out that way⟩ ⟨you never saw such a ~ of washing for three people⟩ **b :** a required or usual amount : STINT, OUTPUT ⟨the daily ~ of copy⟩ **5 a :** matter of interest or value forming the basis of a story, analysis, or other presentation or that can be assembled into such a basis ⟨consular records and trade-association reports form much of the ~ of the foreign market analyst⟩ ⟨local news ~ collected in police courts and schools⟩ **b :** something turned to one's own advantage esp. contrary to ordinary expectation by one receiving or having to do with it — used esp. in the phrase *grist to one's mill*

[2]grist \"\ *vt* -ED/-ING/-S **:** to grind (grain) esp. as a custom operation

[3]grist \"\ *n* -S [origin unknown] **1 :** the count of a textile fiber or yarn **2** *chiefly Scot* **:** a size of rope ⟨a rope of common ~ is 3 inches in circumference with 20 yarns in each of the 3 strands⟩

grist·bite \'grizbət\ *vi* [ME *grisbiten*, fr. OE *gristbitian*, fr. *grist-bite* act of gnashing, fr. *grist* act of grinding + *bite* biting, fr. *bītan* to bite — more at GRIST, BITE] *dial chiefly Brit* **:** to grind or gnash the teeth

gris·thor·pia \gris'thȯ(r)pēə\ *n, cap* [NL, fr. *Gristhorpe*, Yorkshire, England + NL *-ia*] **:** a genus of fossil plants of the Jurassic formations of England that are usu. considered to be angiosperms and have pyriform carpels or carpellary fruits enclosing ovule or seed

gris·tle \'gris|əl *sometimes* -iz|\ *n* -S [ME *gristil*, fr. OE *gristle*; akin to OE *grost* gristle, OFris & MLG *gristel*, and prob. to OE *grindan* to grind — more at GRIND] **1 :** CARTILAGE; *broadly* **:** tough cartilaginous, tendinous, or fibrous matter esp. in table meats **2** *obs* **:** a young or delicate person visualized as having the bones soft and cartilaginous and not yet hardened into bone **3 :** strength of character **:** BACKBONE ⟨a hard-working man with some ~ —Erskine Caldwell⟩

gris·tli·ness \|(ə)lēnəs, -lin-\ *n* -ES **:** the quality or state of being gristly

gris·tly \|(ə)lē, -li\ *adj* -ER/-EST [ME *gristly*, fr. *gristil* gristle + *-y*] **:** consisting of or containing gristle ⟨tough ~ steak⟩

gristmill \'ₛ,ₛ\ *n* **:** a mill for grinding grain; *esp* **:** a custom mill that grinds for different customers — **gristmiller** \'ₛ,ₛₛ\ *n* — **gristmilling** \'ₛ,ₛₛ\ *n*

grisy *adj* [ME *gris* gray (fr. MF) + E *-y* — more at GRIS] *obs* **:** GRIZZLED

[1]grit \'grit, *usu* -id.+V\ *n* -S [ME *gryt* bran, chaff, fr. OE *grytt*; akin to OHG *gruzzi* bran, OE *grēot* sand, grit — more at [2]GRIT] **1** *obs* **:** milling offals **:** the coarse parts of meal **:** CHAFF **2 grits** *pl but sing or pl in constr* **a :** coarsely ground hulled grain (as maize, wheat, or rice) ⟨had boiled ~s fried with side meat for supper⟩ — compare HOMINY **b :** coarsely ground soybean oil cake used as a protein-rich supplement in animal rations and some commercial food products

[2]grit \"\ *n* -S *see sense 4b* [alter. (influenced by [1]*grit*) of ME *grete*, *greet*, fr. OE *grēot*; akin to OHG *grioz* gravel, sand, ON *grjōt* gravel, stone, L *furfur* bran, Gk *kenchros* millet, grain, Gk *chrōs* skin, Latvian *graûds* grain, Lith *graužas* gravel; basic meaning: rubbing] **1 a** *obs* **:** SAND, GRAVEL **b :** a hard sharp granule (as of sand); *also* **:** material (as many abrasives) composed of such granules **2 a :** a sandstone with grains of very unequal sizes **b :** a hard coarse-grained siliceous sandstone ⟨millstone ~⟩ — called also *gritrock* **c :** a finer sharp-grained sandstone ⟨grindstone ~⟩ **3** *now dial* **:** EARTH, SOIL **4 a :** the structure of a stone that adapts it to grind or sharpen ⟨quarried stones of excellent ~⟩ **:** hold of a grinding substance ⟨a hone of good ~⟩ **b** *pl* **grit :** the size of abrasive particles usu. expressed as their mesh ⟨diamond dust of 80 ~⟩ **5 :** firmness of mind or spirit **:** unyielding courage **6** *usu cap* **:** a Liberal in Canadian politics **syn** see FORTITUDE

[3]grit \"\ *vb* **gritted; gritted; gritting; grits** *vi* **:** to give forth a grating sound ⟨the dry snow *gritting* beneath our feet⟩ ~ *vt* **1 :** to cover or spread with grit; *esp* **:** to smooth (as marble) by means of a coarse abrasive preparatory to polishing **2 :** to cause (as one's teeth) to grind or grate ⟨*gritted* his gears when shifting into high⟩ **3 :** to utter harshly through or as if through gritted teeth

grit cell *n* **:** a stone cell esp. in leaves or fleshy fruits (as pears and quinces)

grith \'grith\ *n* -S [ME, fr. OE, fr. ON] **1 a** *obs* **:** assured security or protection (as by safe conduct) **b :** peace or security imposed or guaranteed in Anglo-Saxon and early medieval England by conditions arising out of associations of time and place: as (1) **:** the sanctuary or asylum afforded by the precincts of a church (2) **:** KING'S PEACE **2** *archaic* **:** a place of security **:** REFUGE, ASYLUM, SANCTUARY **3** *obs* **:** quarter in battle

grith·man \-mən\ *n, pl* **grithmen** [ME, fr. *grith* + *man*] *archaic* **:** a man who has taken sanctuary (as through church grith)

grit·less \'gritləs\ *adj* **:** free from grit; *esp* **:** lacking firmness and stability of character

gritrock \'ₛ,ₛ\ *or* **gritstone** \'ₛ,ₛ\ *n* **:** GRIT 2b

grit·ti·ly \'grid-|ᵊl|ē, -it|, |əl|, |i\ *adv* **:** in a gritty manner ⟨our feet sounded ~ on the shale⟩ ⟨behaved very ~ for a youngster⟩

grit·ti·ness \'grid-|ēnəs, -it|, |in-\ *n* -ES **:** the quality or state of being gritty

grit·tle \'gritᵊl\ *vt* -ED/-ING/-S [[1]*grit* + *-le*] *dial Brit* **:** to grind (grain) coarsely

grit·ty \'grid-|ē, -it|, |i\ *adj* -ER/-EST **1 a :** containing or resembling sand or grit **:** consisting of grit ⟨~ slopes⟩ **b :** suggestive of the presence of grit ⟨~ footsteps on the walk⟩ **2 :** courageously persistent **:** having grit **:** RESOLUTE, PLUCKY

gri·va·tion \grə'vāshən, grī'v-\ *n* -S [*grid variation*] **:** the angle between north as indicated by a grid on a map and magnetic north at any point — used esp. in aerial navigation

griv·et \'grivət, grə'vā\ *n* -S [F] **:** a monkey (*Cercopithecus aethiops*) of the upper Nile and Abyssinia having the back dull olive green and the lower parts white

gri·vois \grēvwä\ *adj* [F, fr. *grivois*, n., alert soldier, fr. *grive* thrush, war (in soldier slang)] **:** free and bold **:** BROAD, INDECENT

gri·voi·se·rie \grēvwäzrē\ *n, pl* **grivoiseries** \-rē(z)\ [F, fr. *grivois* + *-erie* -ery] **:** bold licentious behavior **:** IMPROPRIETY; *often* **:** an act of impropriety

[1]griz·zle \'grizəl\ *adj* [ME *grisel*, fr. MF, fr. OF, fr. *gris* gray, of Gmc origin; akin to OFris, OS, & OHG *gris* gray, ON *grīss* pig, and perh. to OE *grǣg* gray — more at GRAY] **:** GRAY, ROAN

[2]grizzle \"\ *n* -S **1** *archaic* **a :** gray hair **b :** a gray wig **2 a** (1) **:** GRAY 3a (2) **:** a roan coat pattern or color **b :** a gray or roan animal **3 :** a second-rate brick that is underburned, gray in color, and deficient in strength

[3]grizzle \"\ *vb* **grizzled; grizzled; grizzling** \-z(ə)liŋ\ **grizzles** *vt* **:** to make grayish ~ *vi* **:** to become grayish

[4]grizzle \"\ *vi* -ED/-ING/-S [origin unknown] **1** *Brit* **:** to complain vociferously ⟨always *grizzling* about the work being too much for him —Vance Palmer⟩ **:** GRIPE, GRUMBLE **2** *Brit* **:** FRET, WHIMPER ⟨children ~ a lot, get finicky over their food, and look pale and thin —*Auckland (New Zealand) Weekly News*⟩ **3** *Brit* **:** MOURN, LAMENT, GRIEVE ⟨*grizzling* over a corpse —Margery Allingham⟩

[5]grizzle \"\ *n* -S *Brit* **:** an irritable or lugubrious mood

griz·zled \-zəld\ *adj* [ME *griseled*, fr. MF *grisel* + ME *-ed*] **:** sprinkled, streaked, or mixed with gray ⟨~ hair hanging about her face⟩ ⟨~ chickens huddled in the rain⟩

griz·zler \-z(ə)lə(r)\ *n* -S [[4]*grizzle* + *-er*] *Brit* **:** a peevish person **:** a chronic griper

[1]griz·zly *or* **gris·ly** \'grizlē, -li\ *adj* -ER/-EST [[1]*grizzle* + *-ly*] **:** somewhat gray **:** GRIZZLED

[2]grizzly *or* **grisly** \"\ *n* -ES **1 :** GRIZZLY BEAR **2 a :** a coarse screening device used for ore, coal, gravel, or soil; *specif* **:** a heavy steel-bar screen for ore having moving chains **b :** a similar coarse grating (as for catching trash or large stones at a water inlet)

[3]grizzly *var of* GRISLY

grizzly bear *n* [[1]*grizzly*] **1 :** a very large powerful typically brownish yellow bear (*Ursus horribilis*) of the uplands of western No. America that is closely related to the brown bear of Europe but much larger and heavier and that is very dangerous when brought to bay esp. because of its great strength and fierceness — compare SILVERTIP **2 :** a ragtime dance popular about the period of World War I

grizzly-bear cactus *also* **grizzly bear** *n* **:** a prickly pear (*Opuntia erinacea*) of the southwestern U.S. with very long flexible ashy gray spines

griz·zly·man \-mən\ *n, pl* **grizzlymen** [[2]*grizzly* + *man*] **:** a worker that screens ore in a grizzly

grm *abbr* **1** germination **2** gram

grn *abbr* green

gro *abbr* **1** gross **2** group

[1]groan \'grōn\ *vb* -ED/-ING/-S [ME *gronen*, fr. OE *grānian*; akin to OHG *grīnan* to distort the mouth, mutter, grumble, growl, ON *grīna* to bare the teeth, sneer] *vi* **1 a :** to make a deep usu. inarticulate and involuntary often strangled sound typically abruptly begun and ended and usu. indicative of pain or grief or tension or desire or sometimes disapproval or annoyance ⟨the dying man ~*ed* with every jolt of the ambulance⟩ ⟨men ~*ing* under the weight of the loads they were carrying⟩ ⟨~*ed* with rage and frustration⟩ **b :** to make a harsh sound (as of heavy creaking, grating, rasping) upon subjection to sudden or prolonged strain (as of a heavy load) ⟨let himself fall into an armchair which ~*ed* under him —H. M.Ledig-Rowohlt⟩ ⟨wagons that swayed and ~*ed* up the hill⟩ **2 a :** to experience pain or grief enough to make one groan ⟨~*ed* when he read the telegram⟩ **b :** to undergo strain or oppression or overburdening enough to make one groan ⟨men who were once free now ~ in slavery⟩ ⟨tables which ~*ed* under the weight of good things —Norman Douglas⟩ **c :** to desire something intensely enough to make one groan ⟨~*ing* to be with her again⟩ ⟨death ~*ing* for fresh victims⟩ **d :** to disapprove of something or become annoyed with something enough to make one groan ⟨~*ing* over their stupidity⟩ ⟨one ~*s* at the absence of an index —Sean O'Faolain⟩ ~ *vt* **1 :** to utter or express with groaning **:** breathe out with groaning ⟨will ~ out some prayer —William Barrett⟩ ⟨~*ing* their despair⟩ **2 :** to express disapproval of or annoyance with by groaning ⟨~*ing* them through the streets —Broadus Mitchell⟩ ⟨the consuls were ~*ed* down —J.A.Froude⟩

[2]groan \"\ *n* -S [ME *gron*, *grone*, fr. *gronen*, v.] **1 :** a deep usu. inarticulate and involuntary often strangled sound typically abruptly begun and ended and usu. indicative of pain or grief or tension or desire or sometimes disapproval or annoyance **2 :** a harsh sound (as of heavy creaking, grating, rasping) produced by subjection to a sudden or prolonged strain (as of a heavy load)

groan·ful \-fəl\ *adj, archaic* **:** marked by groaning; *specif* **:** dismal and sad

groaning *n* -S [fr. gerund of [1]*groan*] *now chiefly dial* **:** LYING-IN; *specif* **:** LABOR 1b

groan·ing·ly *adv* **:** in a groaning manner

[1]groat \'grōt, *usu* -ōd.+V\ *n* -S [ME *grotes*, pl., fr. OE *grotan*; akin to OE *grot* particle, *grēot* sand, grit — more at GRIT] **1** *usu* **groats** *pl but sing or pl in constr* **:** hulled grain broken into fragments larger than grits **2 a :** the part of a grain of oats or barley or buckwheat exclusive of the hull **b :** the hulled kernel of one of these grains

[2]groat \"\ *n* -S [ME *grote*, *groot*, fr. MD *groot*, *grot*, modif. (by false analogy of such pairs as MD *groot* large: MHG *grōz* large) of MHG *gros*, fr. ML (*denarius*) *grossus* — more at GROSCHEN] **1 :** one of several onetime European coins of varying chiefly small value; *esp* **:** a British coin worth fourpence **2 :** the bit of British Guiana

gro·bi·an \'grōbēən\ *n* -S [G, after *Grobian*, a fictional patron saint of vulgar people, fr. ML (*Sanctus*) *Grobianus*, fr. MHG *grob-*, *grop* coarse, vulgar (fr. OHG *gerob*, *grob* thick, coarse) + L *-ianus* -ian — more at GRUFF] **:** a slovenly crude often buffoonish individual **:** BOOR, LOUT

gro·bi·an·ism \-ə,nizəm\ *n* -S **:** behavior typical of a grobian **:** BOORISHNESS

gro·cer \'grōsə(r)\ *n* -S [ME *grocer*, *grosser* wholesale merchant, grocer, fr. MF *grossier* wholesale merchant, fr. *gros* thick, coarse, wholesale + *-ier* -er — more at GROSS] **:** a dealer in staple foodstuffs (as coffee, sugar, flour) and usu. meats and other foods (as fruits, vegetables, dairy products) and many household supplies (as soap, matches, paper napkins)

grocer's itch *n* **:** an itching dermatitis prob. allergic in nature that results from prolonged or repeated contacts with certain mites esp. of the family Acaridae, their products, or materials (as feeds, flour, or copra) infested by them — compare GRAIN ITCH

gro·cery \'grōs(ə)rē, -ri\ *n* -ES [ME *grocerie*, fr. *grocer* + *-ie* -y] **1 groceries** *pl* **a :** articles of food and other goods sold by a grocer ⟨went out to buy some *groceries*⟩ ⟨a bag of *groceries*⟩ — usu. sing. in Brit. usage ⟨had been sent with a parcel of ~ to the cottage —Sabine Baring-Gould⟩ **b** *dial* **:** intoxicating drink **:** LIQUOR **2** *or* **grocery store a :** the place of business of a retail grocer **:** a grocer's store **b** *dial* **:** BARROOM

gro·cery·man \-mən, -,man, -,maa(ə)n\ *n, pl* **grocerymen** **:** GROCER

gro·ce·te·ria \,grōsə'tirēə\ *n* -S [*grocery* + *-teria*] **:** a self-service grocery store

groe·nen·dael \'grünən,däl, -rōn-,-rän-,-ren-\ *n* -S *usu cap* [fr. *Groenendael*, village in Belgium where it was developed] **:** a black-coated Belgian sheepdog with a heavily plumed tail — compare MALINOIS

groff \'gräf\ *Scot var of* GRUFF

[1]grog \'gräg *also* 'grȯ|\ *n* -S [fr. *Old Grog*, nickname of Edward Vernon †1757 Eng. admiral who ordered the sailors' rum to be diluted; *Grog* short for *grogram*; fr. his habit of wearing a grogram cloak in bad weather] **1 :** spirituous liquor; *specif* **:** liquor (as rum) cut with water and now often served hot with lemon juice and sugar sometimes added **2 :** fired refractory material (as crushed pottery, firebricks) used in the manufacture of products (as crucibles) designed to resist extreme heat

[2]grog \"\ *vb* **grogged; grogged; grogging; grogs** *vi* **:** to drink grog ⟨had been *grogging* with the steward —Lyndall Hadow⟩ ~ *vt* **:** to soak (a liquor cask) with hot water so as to draw out the spirits from the wood

grog blossom *n* **:** RHINOPHYMA

grogger *var of* GRAGER

grog·gery \'gräg(ə)rē\ *n* -ES [[1]*grog* + *-ery*] **1 :** a usu. low-class barroom **2 :** a liquor store **:** PACKAGE STORE

grog·gi·ly \|gəlē, -li\ *adv* **:** in a groggy manner **:** DAZEDLY ⟨~ opened his eyes⟩ **:** UNSTEADILY ⟨groped his way ~ across the room⟩

grog·gi·ness \|gēnəs, |gin-\ *n* -ES **:** the quality or state of being groggy

grog·gy \|gē, |gi\ *adj, usu* -ER/-EST [[1]*grog* + *-y*] **1** *archaic* **:** INTOXICATED, DRUNK **2 a** *of a horse* **:** weakened (as from age, overwork, or disease) in the fetlock joints and entire forelegs so as to have a hobbling gait marked by the knuckling over of the fetlock joints **b** *of a boxer* **:** weakened from fighting and esp. from blows on the head so as to be unsteady on the feet or to stagger and to have an impaired consciousness **3 :** weak, sleepy, exhausted, ill, or otherwise physically affected in such a way as to be sluggish in one's reactions, torpid mentally, and usu. unsteady on the feet **:** LOGY, FOGGY, DAZED, MUDDLED **4 :** tending to wear away ⟨pumice and other soft ~ materials⟩ or crumble ⟨a ~ tooth⟩ or collapse ⟨a ~ old wooden tower⟩

gro·gnard \(,)grōⁿ;nyär\ *n* -S [F, fr. *grogner* to grunt, grumble (fr. OF *gronir*, *grogner*, fr. L *grunnire* to grunt) + *-ard*] **1 :** an old soldier **2** *often cap* **:** a soldier of the original imperial guard that was created by Napoleon I in 1804 and that made the final French charge at Waterloo

grog·ram \'grägrəm, -rōg-\ *n* -S [modif. of MF *gros grain* large grain, coarse texture] **1 :** a coarse loosely woven fabric of silk or of silk and mohair or orig. of silk and wool and often stiffened with gum **2 :** a garment (as a coat) made of grogram

grogshop \'ₛ,ₛ\ *n, chiefly Brit* **:** a usu. low-class barroom **:** GROGGERY

[1]groin \'grȯin\ *n* -S [ME, fr. MF, fr. LL *grunium*, fr. L *grunnire* to grunt — more at GRUNT] *dial Brit* **:** the nose and sometimes the upper lip of an animal (as a swine)

[2]groin \"\ *n* -S [alter. (influenced by [1]*groin*) of ME *grynde*, fr. OE, abyss; akin to OE *grund* ground — more at GROUND] **1 :** the fold or depression marking the line between the lower part of the abdomen and the thigh; *also* **:** the region of this line — called also *inguen* **2 a** (1) **:** the projecting edge forming the curved line along which two intersecting vaults meet (2) **:** a rib (as of wood, stone) designed to cover this edge **b** (1) **:** the curved surface of a vault — not often in technical use (2) **:** the spandrel of a vault — not often in technical use **3** *also* **groyne** \"\ **:** a rigid structure built out at an angle from a shore to protect the shore from erosion by currents, tides, and waves or to trap sand (as for making a beach)

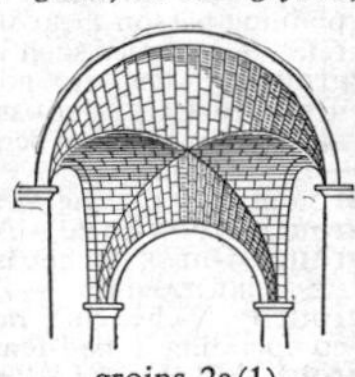

groins 2a(1)

[3]groin \"\ *vt* -ED/-ING/-S **:** to build or equip with groins ⟨a high corridor with a ~*ed* ceiling⟩ ⟨~*ed* vaults⟩

groining *n* -S [fr. gerund of [3]*groin*] **:** a set or series of groins **:** groined work ⟨lofty halls with beautiful ~⟩

gromet *var of* GRUMMET

gro·mia \'grōmēə\ *n, cap* [NL] **:** a genus (the type of the family Gromiidae) of testacean rhizopods widely distributed in fresh and salt water and in soil

[1]grom·met \'grämət, 'grəm-, *usu* -əd.+V\ *also* **grum·met** \'grəm-\ *n* -S [perh. fr. obs. F *gormette* curb of a bridle] **1 :** a ring or loop of metal, rope, fabric, or other material that is passed through something (as the eyelet of a sail) to hold it in place or that fits around something (as an oar) to support or control it or that is built into something (as a machine belt) to reinforce it **2 a :** an eyelet of metal, plastic, or other material set into a perforation (as at the edge of a mailbag) so as to strengthen and protect the inner circumference of the perforation and the immediately surrounding area **b :** a device like a ring that is designed to protect or insulate something passed through it: as (1) **:** a bushing designed to protect from abrasion a cord or wire passing through a hole (2) **:** a washer designed to insulate an electric wire passing through a hole **3 :** a gasket or packing used to prevent leakage (as of steam) or entry (as of dust)

[2]grommet \"\ *vt* -ED/-ING/-S **1 :** to equip with grommets ⟨mailbags that have been properly ~*ed*⟩ **2 :** to fasten, support, or reinforce with grommets ⟨the sail is ~*ed* to its stay⟩

grommet nut *n* **:** a screw-thread nut with a blind hole and rounded head as used in connection with a machine screw for fastening a hinge to a door leaf

grom·well \'gräm,wel, -,wəl\ *n* -S [alter. of ME *gromil*, fr. MF *gromil*, *gremil*, fr. OF, fr. *gres* sandstone + *mil* millet — more at GRÈS, MILLET] **:** a plant of the genus *Lithospermum* (esp. *L. officinale*)

gro·ning·en \'grōniŋən\ *adj, usu cap* [fr. *Groningen*, Netherlands] **:** of or from the city of Groningen, Netherlands **:** of the kind or style prevalent in Groningen

[1]groom \'grüm, -ü-\ *n* -S [ME *grom*, *grome*; perh. akin to OE *grōwan* to grow — more at GROW] **1 a** *obs* **:** a young male **:** BOY **b** *archaic* **:** an adult male **:** MAN, FELLOW **2 a** (1) *archaic* **:** a male attendant **:** MANSERVANT (2) **:** one of several officers of the English royal household — used with a specifying phrase ⟨served as ~ of the chamber⟩ **b :** a man or boy in charge of the feeding, conditioning, and stabling of horses **3** [by shortening] **:** BRIDEGROOM

[2]groom \"\ *vb* -ED/-ING/-S *vt* **:** to make presentable, acceptable, or attractive: as **a :** to attend to the cleaning of (as an animal); *esp* **:** to maintain the health and condition of the coat of (as a horse) by brushing, combing, currying, or similar attention ⟨~*ed* the horses until their coats shone sleekly⟩ **b :** to bring about or increase the acceptability or attractiveness of (as one's physical appearance) esp. by carefully attending to details of cleanliness and neatness **:** freshen up **:** spruce up ⟨spent a long time ~*ing* himself before he ventured out⟩ make neat **:** make tidy ⟨a carefully ~*ed* lawn⟩ **c :** to remove crudity or other objectionable features from **:** make smooth or elegant **:** POLISH, REFINE ⟨was master of the epigram which Wilde was later to ~ for the drawing room —Maurice Edelman⟩ **d :** to get into readiness for some specific objective **:** READY, PREPARE ⟨was being ~*ed* as a presidential candidate⟩ ⟨~*ing* players for the Olympics⟩ ~ *vi* **:** to groom oneself ⟨is said to be ~*ing* for the top position⟩ ⟨~*ing* for dinner⟩

[3]groom \"\ *n* -S [origin unknown] *dial Eng* **:** a forked stick used by thatchers

groom's cake *n* **:** a light fruitcake served at a wedding

grooms·man \-mzmən\ *n, pl* **groomsmen** **:** a male friend who attends a bridegroom at his wedding

groop \'grüp, -ü-\ *n* -S [ME *grope*, *groupe*, fr. MD *grope*, *groepe* — more at GRIP] *dial Eng* **:** DITCH, DRAIN

[1]groove \'grüv\ *n* -S [ME *grofe*, *groof*; akin to OHG *gruoba* pit, cave, ON *grōf*, Goth *groba* pit, cave, OE *grafan* to dig — more at GRAVE] **1** *dial Eng* **:** a mining shaft **:** MINE **2 a :** a long narrow hollow or channel made artificially in a surface: as (1) **:** the rectangular rabbet in the edge of a board designed to receive the tongue of another board in matching (2) **:** one of the spiral cuts of rifling (3) **:** the indentation on the bottom of a piece of printing type between the feet — compare NICK (4) **:** one of the cuts made across the back of an unbound hand-sewn book designed to receive the cords that secure the covers of the book — called also *kerf* (5) **:** the track on a phonograph record along which the stylus travels **b :** a long narrow depression occurring naturally on the surface of an organism or an anatomical part **c :** a long narrow furrow produced along a surface by a continuing erosive or otherwise wearing force (as of flowing water) **3 a** (1) **:** a fixed routine **:** settled course ⟨had hoped that the daily life on the farm would slip back into orderly ~*s* —Ellen Glasgow⟩ **:** HABIT, CUSTOM, PRACTICE ⟨will get you into the writing ~ —Cy Lance⟩ (2) **:** an undeviating tiresomely predictable and often mechanical way of living or acting or thinking **:** RUT ⟨walled in by authority which saw to it that he moved in a prescribed ~ —W.P.Webb⟩ ⟨far too many of us feel safer in ~*s* —F.A.Swinnerton⟩ ⟨fail to realize how often their thoughts revolve in ancient ~*s* and circles —Thomas Munro⟩ **b :** a situation (as a profession, a way of living or acting) best suited to one's abilities or interests **:** NICHE ⟨found his ~ in advertising —*Newsweek*⟩ **4 :** an imaginary line from the pitcher to the catcher representing the course of a pitched ball in the game of baseball; *esp* **:** such a line passing over the center of the plate about waist high — usu. used with *the* ⟨hurled the ball right down the ~⟩ **5 a :** top form ⟨after a couple of measures the jazz trio really got into the ~⟩ ⟨a hot bath and a drink will put you back in the ~⟩ ⟨it made no difference, when he was in the ~, what he chose to talk about —Henry Miller⟩ **b :** currently favored style — usu. used in the phrase *in the groove* ⟨a new song that's right in the ~⟩

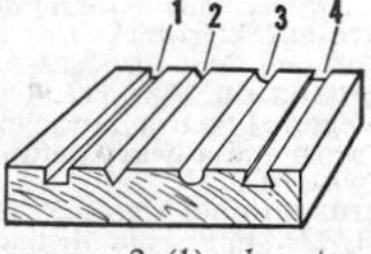

grooves 2a(1): *1* rectangular; *2* vee; *3* semicircular; *4* dovetail

[2]groove \"\ *vb* -ED/-ING/-S *vt* **1 a** (1) **:** to make a groove in **:** provide with a groove ⟨a set of scenery that is *grooved* and quickly movable⟩ (2) **:** to make a disc recording of ⟨*grooving* a popular song as soon as it is written⟩ **b** (1) **:** to join by a groove ⟨wide boards that had been *grooved* together⟩ (2) **:** to cause to be fixed into a groove **:** cause to be ingrained ⟨a deeply *grooved* habit of honesty⟩ **c :** to hollow out in the form of a groove **:** FURROW ⟨the experience that has been *grooved* into a person⟩ ⟨the years had *grooved* her mind that way —Bob Hope⟩ **2 :** to execute (as the delivery of a ball, the swing of a golf club) with maximum control and effect ⟨*grooved* the ball down the bowling alley⟩ ⟨developing a *grooved* swing⟩; *esp* **:** to pitch down the center of the groove ⟨*grooved* a fast ball past the batter⟩ ~ *vi* **1 :** to become settled into a groove **:** move in a groove ⟨*grooving* along in the routine of the job⟩ **2 :** to become joined or fitted by a groove ⟨elements of this rather intricate artistic pattern seem to ~ into each other —Scott Fitzgerald⟩ **3 :** to form a groove ⟨eyes with faint white wrinkles at the corners that *grooved* merrily when he smiled —Ernest Hemingway⟩

[3]groove \"\ *adj* **:** produced through a narrow deep opening formed at the free end of the tongue ⟨a ~ fricative such as \s\⟩ — compare SLIT

groove-billed ani \'ₛ,ₛ-\ *n* **:** a rather small ani (*Crotophaga sulcirostris*) having the upper mandible marked by several curved grooves and ridges

grooved ax *n* **:** a prehistoric stone ax typical of the woodland pattern in No. America with a groove in which the handle fits

groove diameter *n* **:** the width of the bore of a rifled arm that is measured between diametrically opposite grooves

grooved shrimp *n* **:** a shrimp with lateral grooves along the carapace; *esp* **:** BRAZILIAN SHRIMP

groove·less \-vləs\ *adj* **:** having no grooves

groov·er \-və(r)\ *n* -S [in sense 1, fr. [1]*groove* + *-er*; in other senses, fr. [2]*groove* + *-er*] **1** *dial Eng* **:** MINER **2 a :** a device that makes grooves (as by cutting, punching) **b :** a worker who makes grooves (as the operator of a machine that cuts tongues and grooves in box boards)

groov·i·ness \-vēnə̇s, -vin-\ *n* -ES **:** the quality or state of being groovy ⟨in the graduate . . . ~ is a grave defect, but it is also a common one —Walter Moberly⟩

grooving *n* -s **1 a :** a set of grooves **:** GROOVE **b :** the formation of grooves **2 :** a design made up of grooves

grooving saw *n* **:** a coarse-toothed circular saw used for cutting grooves in timber

groovy \-vē,-vi\ *adj, usu* -ER/-EST **1 :** settled into a fixed often tiresomely undeviating way of living or acting or thinking ⟨so-called leaders who have become ~ dolts⟩ **2 :** that is in the groove ⟨~ jazz⟩ ⟨a ~ recording⟩ — often a generalized expression of approval ⟨bought a ~ new convertible⟩

¹grope \'grōp\ *vb* -ED/-ING/-S [ME *gropen*, fr. OE *grāpian;* akin to OE *grīpan* to seize, attack — more at GRIPE] *vi* **1 a :** to feel about (as with the hands) blindly or uncertainly or hesitantly in an attempt to find something or touch something ⟨*groping* around in the shadowy room for a switch to turn on the light⟩ ⟨*groping* for her arm⟩ **:** reach out blindly ⟨tottered at the edge of the cliff, *groping* at the air⟩ **b :** to look for something blindly or uncertainly or hesitantly **:** search about blindly ⟨*groping* for the simplest ground rules of conduct —Gilbert Seldes⟩ ⟨*groped* confusedly for words —E.A. McCourt⟩ ⟨it was as though she *groped* after something which was vanishing —Victoria Sackville-West⟩ **2 :** to move or act blindly or uncertainly or hesitantly **:** feel one's way ⟨*groping* along through the darkness until they arrived at the door⟩ ⟨when her mind is *groping* about in this new attitude it will be easy for me to influence her —Liam O'Flaherty⟩ ⟨*groping* toward a solution to the problem⟩ **~** *vt* **1 a** (1) *obs* **:** TOUCH, HANDLE; *specif* **:** GRASP (2) **:** to pass the hands over (the person of another) for the sake of sexual pleasure **b** *now dial Brit* **:** to subject (as a criminal) to a manual search **2 :** to come upon, ascertain, or find (as one's way) by feeling about blindly or uncertainly or hesitantly **:** search out blindly ⟨the effort which it has cost our predecessors to ~ their way through the mists of ignorance and superstition —J.G.Frazer⟩ ⟨*groped* his way from the balcony to the bedroom door —Geoffrey Household⟩

²grope \"\ *n* -s **:** the action of groping

¹grop·er \-pə(r)\ *n* -s [¹*grope* + *-er*] **:** one that gropes

²gro·per \"\ *n* -s [modif. of Pg *garoupa* — more at GROUPER] **1 :** one of several groupers: as **a :** a very large voracious and dangerous fish (*Promicrops lanceolatus*) of tropical Indo-Pacific waters **b :** a food fish (*Polyprion oxygeneios*) of southern seas **2 :** a large Australian and Tasmanian labrid food fish (*Achoerodus gouldii*) having two well-marked color phases of purplish blue and red

groping *adj* [ME, fr. pres. part. of *gropen* to grope — more at GROPE] **:** blindly searching ⟨gazing up at her with a strange, ~ expression —Ellen Glasgow⟩ **:** moving or acting uncertainly **:** HESITANT ⟨a ~ uncertainty concerning the future forms of American life —Oscar Handlin⟩ — **grop·ing·ly** *adv*

gros \'grō\ *n, pl* **gros** \-ōz\ [F, fr. *gros*, adj., heavy, thick, coarse — more at GROSS] **:** a heavy durable fabric; *esp* **:** a cross-ribbed fabric

gros·beak *also* **gross·beak** \'grōs,bēk\ *n* [part. trans. of F *grosbec*, fr. *gros* thick, coarse + *bec* beak] **:** one of several finches of Europe or America having large stout conical bills: as **a :** HAWFINCH **b :** EVENING GROSBEAK

gro·schen \'grōshən *also* -rȯsh- *or* -rāsh-\ *n, pl* **groschen** [G, fr. MHG dial. (Bohemia) *grosch, grosche*, fr. Czech *groš*, fr. ML (*denarius*) *grossus* thick (denarius) — more at GROSS] **1 :** a German coin worth a varying fraction of a taler and issued from the 13th century to the latter part of the 19th century **2 :** an Austrian coin worth ¹⁄₁₀₀ schilling — see MONEY table

gros de lon·dres \,grōdə'lōⁿdr(ᵊ), -d(rə)\ *n, usu cap L* [F, lit., London gros] **:** a lightweight silk or rayon dress fabric with alternating wide and narrow crosswise ribs often of two different colors and often with a glossy finish

gro·ser \'grōzə(r)\ *n* -s [modif. of MF *groselle*, of Gmc origin; akin to MD *croesel*besie gooseberry, G *kräusel*beere, G dial. (Switzerland) *chrusel*] *dial Eng* **:** GOOSEBERRY

gro·set \'grōzə̇t\ *also* **gros·sart** \-ōzə(r)t\ *n* -s [alter. of *groser*] *Scot* **:** GOOSEBERRY

gros·grain \'grō,grān\ *n* -s [F *gros grain* large grain, coarse texture] **:** a firm fabric in plain weave usu. with a silk or rayon warp and a heavy cotton filling that forms pronounced crosswise ribs

gros mi·chel \,grōmə̇'shel\ *n, pl* **gros michels** \-l(z)\ *usu cap G&M* [F, lit., big Michael] **:** JAMAICA BANANA

gros point \'grō,pȯint\ *n, pl* **gros points** [F, lit., large point] **1 :** RAISED POINT **2 a :** canvas work made with large tent stitches each of which crosses two vertical and two horizontal threads **b :** a stitch used in making such canvas work — compare PETIT POINT

¹gross \'grōs *sometimes* -ȯ-\ *adj, usu* -ER/-EST [ME, fr. MF *gros*, thick, coarse, fr. L *grossus;* perh. akin to MIr, W, Corn & Bret *bras* thick, large] **1 a** *archaic* **:** immediately obvious **:** PLAIN, EVIDENT ⟨'tis ~ you love my son —Shak.⟩ **b** (1) **:** glaringly noticeable **:** FLAGRANT ⟨one ~ error after another⟩ (2) **:** OUT-AND-OUT, COMPLETE, UTTER, UNMITIGATED, RANK ⟨a ~ traitor⟩ ⟨a ~ fool⟩ ⟨~ injustice⟩ **c :** visible without the aid of a microscope **:** large enough to be seen with the naked eye **:** MACROSCOPIC, MANIFEST ⟨~ lesions⟩ — compare OCCULT **2 a** (1) *archaic* **:** physically large **:** BIG, BULKY, MASSIVE ⟨the piers being extremely ~ —George Semple⟩ (2) **:** strongly and heavily built **:** STOCKY, BURLY ⟨a ~ giant of a man⟩ (3) **:** excessively fat or dumpy **:** excessively corpulent or lumpish ⟨a great, ~ girl with a fleshy face and small eyes —Margaret Long⟩ **b :** growing or spreading with excessive or abnormal luxuriance ⟨a ~ riot of vegetation⟩ **3 a** (1) **:** of, relating to, or dealing with general aspects or broad distinctions **:** not specific or closely detailed ⟨acquainted him with the ~ outlines of the matter⟩ **:** GENERAL, GENERALIZED, OVERALL ⟨important to understand the ~ behavior of the sexually responding animal —A.C.Kinsey⟩ (2) *archaic* **:** lacking clarity and precision **:** VAGUE, FOGGY **b :** consisting of an overall total exclusive of deductions ⟨~ earnings⟩ ⟨~ production⟩ ⟨~ annual profit⟩ — opposed to *net* **4 a :** made up of many closely compacted particles ⟨~ clouds of dust⟩ or drops ⟨a ~ fog⟩ ⟨~ vapors⟩ **:** DENSE, THICK **b :** made up of elements that are material or perceptible to the senses **:** EARTHY, CARNAL, ANIMAL ⟨both the intellectual and the ~*er* part of human nature⟩ **c** *archaic* **:** made up of or yielding relatively large or coarse parts or particles ⟨tarras or other ~ matter —John Smeaton⟩ **5** *archaic* **a :** undistinguished or poor in quality **:** COMMON, CHEAP, INFERIOR ⟨fish and oil and such ~ commodities —Daniel Defoe⟩ **b :** not fastidious in taste **:** UNDISCRIMINATING ⟨their diet is extremely ~ —E.W.Lane⟩ **c :** lacking delicacy of perception **:** slow to respond **:** DULL, STUPID, OAFISH **6 :** lacking knowledge or culture **:** IGNORANT, UNREFINED, RUDE, CLODDISH, PRIMITIVE, BARBARIC ⟨the ~ herd of the people⟩ **7 a :** coarse in nature, manner, or expression ⟨~ interests⟩ ⟨~ pleasures⟩ ⟨a ~ way of behaving⟩ **b :** lacking civility or decency **:** LOW, VULGAR, CRUDE, OFFENSIVE, OBSCENE ⟨a revoltingly ~ expletive⟩ ⟨habitually used ~ language⟩ **syn** see COARSE, FLAGRANT, WHOLE

²gross \"\ *n* -ES [ME, fr. *gross*, adj.] **1 a** *obs* **:** AMOUNT ⟨I cannot instantly raise up the ~ of full three thousand ducats —Shak.⟩ **b :** an overall total exclusive of deductions (as taxes, expenses) **:** sum total ⟨the company's ~ doubled in five years⟩ **2** *archaic* **:** the main body **:** principal part **:** BULK, MASS ⟨the ~ of the army —Thomas Carlyle⟩ — **by the gross** *adv* **:** in large quantities and usu. at lower than retail prices **:** WHOLESALE ⟨bought bottle openers *by the gross*⟩ — **in gross 1** *obs* **:** in a general way **:** without going into details ⟨the unlettered Christian who believes *in gross* —John Dryden⟩ **2** *archaic* **:** by the gross **3** *of a right* **:** independently existing, belonging to a person, and not attached to land ⟨an advowson *in gross*⟩ — **in the gross** *archaic* **:** in totality **:** in entirety **:** as an undivided whole ⟨not to accept the past *in the gross* —R.C. Trench⟩

³gross \"\ *vt* -ED/-ING/-ES [¹*gross*] **:** to make, earn, or bring in (an overall total) exclusive of deductions (as taxes, expenses) ⟨a musical comedy that ~*ed* a million dollars⟩

⁴gross \"\ *n, pl* **gross** [ME *grosse, groce*, fr. MF *grosse*, fr. fem. of *gros* thick, coarse — more at ¹GROSS] **:** an aggregate of 12 dozen things **:** an aggregate of 144 things; *specif* **:** a lot made up of 12 dozen usu. relatively small and substantially identical commercial objects ⟨ordered a ~ of pencils⟩ ⟨3 *gross* of can openers⟩

gross adventure *n* **:** the loan of money upon bottomry

gross anatomy *n* **:** a branch of anatomy that deals with the macroscopic structure of tissues and organs — compare HISTOLOGY

gross area *n* **:** the total area across a masonry unit including the hollow spaces

gross average *n* **:** GENERAL AVERAGE

grossbeak *var of* GROSBEAK

gross·en \'grōsᵊn *sometimes* -rȯs-\ *vt* **grossened; grossened; grossening** \-s(ᵊ)niŋ\ **grossens** ['gross + *-en*] **:** to make gross ⟨~*ed* faces . . . and thickened waists —J.G.Cozzens⟩

gross·er \-sə(r)\ *n* -s [²*gross* + *-er*] **1 :** PANMAN **3 2 :** a product or production yielding a large volume of business ⟨top box-office ~⟩

gross·flö·te \'grōs,flœtə\ *n, pl* **grossflö·ten** \-tᵊn\ *often cap* [G, fr. *gross* large + *flöte* flute] **:** a labial pipe-organ stop of 8-foot pitch and powerful flute quality

gross income *n* **1 :** the total of all revenue or receipts usu. for a given period except receipts or returns of capital **2 :** all income derived from any source except for items specif. excluded by law and deductions of certain outlays (as cost of goods sold or expenses in connection with rental income)

gross·ly *adv* **:** in a gross manner

gross national product *n* **:** the total value of the goods and services produced in a nation during a specific period (as a year) and also comprising the total of expenditures by consumers and government plus gross private investment

gross negligence *n* **:** negligence marked by total or nearly total disregard for the rights of others and by total or nearly total indifference to the consequences of an act — compare ORDINARY NEGLIGENCE, SLIGHT NEGLIGENCE

gross·ness *n* -ES **:** the quality or state of being gross

gross premium *n* **:** the sum of the net premium in insurance and the load

gross ton *n* **:** TON 1a

gross tonnage *n* **:** TONNAGE 4a

¹gros·su·lar \'gräs(y)ələ(r)\ *n* -s [NL *Grossularia*] **:** GROSSULARITE

²grossular \"\ *adj* [NL *Grossularia*] **:** of, relating to, or resembling a gooseberry

gros·su·lar·ia \,==¦la(a)rēə\ *n* [NL, irreg. fr. F *groseille* gooseberry (fr. OF *groselle*) + NL *-aria* — more at GROSER] **1** *cap, in some classifications* **:** a genus of shrubs (family Saxifragaceae) now usu. included in the genus *Ribes* and characterized by spines at the nodes and by fruit that does not disarticulate from the stalk **2** -s **:** GROSSULARITE

gros·su·la·ri·a·ce·ae \,==,larē'āsē,ē\ *n pl, cap* [NL, fr. *Grossularia*, type genus + *-aceae*] *in some classifications* **:** a family of shrubs comprising those members of the family Saxifragaceae whose fruit is a berry and being usu. coextensive with the genus *Ribes* — **gros·su·lar·i·a·ceous** \¦==,==¦āshəs\ *adj*

gros·su·lar·ite \'gräs(y)ələ,rīt\ *n* -s [G *grossularit*, fr. NL *Grossularia* + G *-it* -ite; fr. the color of some varieties that is reminiscent of the gooseberry] **:** a colorless or green, yellow, brown, or red garnet $Ca_3Al_2(SiO_4)_3$

gros ventre \'grō,väⁿt\ *n, pl* **gros ventre** \"\ *or* **gros ventres** \-ts\ *usu cap G&V* [F, lit., big belly] **1 :** ATSINA **2 :** HIDATSA

grosz \'grȯsh\ *n, pl* **gro·szy** \-shē\ [Pol, fr. Czech *groš* — more at GROSCHEN] **:** a Polish monetary unit equal to ¹⁄₁₀₀ zloty; *also* **:** a coin representing this unit — see MONEY table

grot \'grät\ *n* -s [MF *grotte*, fr. It *grotta* — more at GROTTO] **:** GROTTO

¹gro·tesque \(')grō¦tesk\ *n* -s [MF & OIt; MF *grotesque, crotesque*, fr. OIt *grottesca*, fr. (*pittura*) *grottesca*, lit., cave painting, ancient painting found in the ruins of Rome; *grottesca*, fem. of *grottesco*, adj.] **1 a :** decorative art (as in sculpture, painting, architecture) characterized by fanciful or fantastic representations of human and animal forms often combined with each other and interwoven with representations of foliage, flowers, fruit, wreaths, or other similar figures into a bizarre hybrid composite that is typically aesthetically satisfying but that may use distortion or exaggeration of the natural or the expected to the point of comic absurdity, ridiculous ugliness, or ludicrous caricature **b** (1) **:** a piece of decorative art done in this style (2) **:** one of the figures or designs in such a piece of decorative art (3) **:** something suggestive of or resembling such art or the figures or designs of such art ⟨his life was a ~, a mixture of sober realities and absurd incongruities⟩ **2 :** SANS SERIF

²grotesque \"\ *adj, sometimes* -ER/ -EST [F & It; F, fr. It *grottesco*, lit., of a cave, fr. *grotta* cave + *-esco* -esque — more at GROTTO] **:** of, relating to, having the characteristics of, or suggestive of the style of decorative art called grotesque: as **a :** FANCIFUL, FANTASTIC, BIZARRE ⟨a ~ Halloween costume⟩ **b :** comically incongruous or absurd **:** ridiculously ugly ⟨a wizened and ~ little old man⟩ **c :** having a quality of ludicrous caricature ⟨a ~ display of what was meant to be politeness⟩ **d :** departing markedly from the natural, the expected, or the typical (as by distortion, exaggeration) **:** ATYPICAL, ECCENTRIC ⟨a ~ form of animal life⟩ **syn** see FANTASTIC

gro·tesque·ly *adv* **:** in a grotesque manner

gro·tesque·ness *n* -ES **:** the quality or state of being grotesque

gro·tes·que·rie \grō'teskərē, -ri, (,)grō,teskə'rē\ *also* **gro·tes·que·ry** \=¦===\ *n, pl* **grotesqueries** [²*grotesque* + F *-erie* -ery or E *-ery*] **1 a** (1) **:** a grotesque figure or design (2) **:** a group of such figures or designs (3) **:** a piece of grotesque decorative art **b :** something suggestive of or resembling grotesque decorative art or the figures or designs of such art **:** something grotesque **2 :** GROTESQUENESS

groth·ite \'grōd-,īt, -ō,thīt\ *n* -s [Paul von *Groth* †1927 Ger. mineralogist + E *-ite*] **:** SPHENE

gro·tian \'grōsh(ē)ən\ *adj, usu cap* [Hugo *Grotius* †1645 Dutch statesman + E *-an*] **:** of or relating to Grotius or his legal and theological theories ⟨the *Grotian* conception of Christ's death —Williston Walker⟩ — **gro·tian·ism** \-,nizəm\ *n* -s *usu cap*

grott·huss-dra·per law \'grōt¦,hu̇s'drāpə(r)-, 'grät¦, ¦,hüs¦\ *n, usu cap G&D* [after Theodor von *Grotthuss* †1822 Ger. physicist and John W. *Draper* †1882 Am. chemist] **:** a statement in physical chemistry: radiation produces photochemical action only through absorption of its energy by the substance affected

grot·to \'gräd·(,)ō, -ä(,)tō\ *n, pl* **grottoes** *also* **grottos** [It *grotta, grotto*, fr. L *crypta* vault, cavern — more at CRYPT] **1 a :** a natural covered opening in the earth: (1) **:** a cave typically picturesque and rocky and of limited size (2) **:** a recess in a cave (3) **:** a usu. arched recess or hollow place (as in the side of a hill) making a natural shelter and formed by or resembling the mouth of a cave **b :** an artificial recess or structure typically arched and rocky and made to resemble a natural grotto **2** *or* **grotto blue :** a strong greenish blue that is greener and paler than cobalt blue and greener, lighter, and stronger than average cerulean blue (sense 1a) or indigo carmine

grot·toed \-ōd\ *adj* **:** enclosed in or made into a grotto ⟨a shady ~ spot in the mountains⟩

grot·zen \'grȯtsən\ *n* -s [G, lit., core of a fruit] **:** the center back strip of a fur pelt

¹grouch \'grau̇ch\ *n* -ES [prob. alter. of ²*grutch*] **1 a :** a fit of bad temper or irritability ⟨don't go near him, he has a ~ on this morning⟩ **b :** GRUDGE, COMPLAINT ⟨never nursed a ~ five minutes —W.A.White⟩ ⟨his chronic ~ at the press —*Newsweek*⟩ **2 :** an habitually irritable or bad-tempered or complaining person **:** GRUMBLER ⟨the irritable ~, the eternal quarreler — becomes such a nuisance —H.A.Overstreet⟩

²grouch \"\ *vi* -ED/-ING/-ES [prob. alter. of ¹*grutch*] **:** GRUMBLE, COMPLAIN, GROUSE ⟨finds every political and social situation a problem to be solved . . . instead of a cause for ~*ing* —E.K.Lindley⟩

grouch bag *n, slang* **:** PURSE

grouch·i·ly \-chəlē, -li\ *adv* **:** in a grouchy manner

grouch·i·ness \-chēnə̇s, -chin-\ *n* -ES **:** bad temper **:** SULKINESS, IRRITABILITY

grouchy \-chē,-chi\ *adj* -ER/-EST **:** given to grumbling and complaining **:** bad-tempered **:** PEEVISH, TOUCHY

grouf \'grüf\ *n* -s [ME (*one*) *gruff*, (*one the*) *groffe* on the face, prone, fr. ON *á grūfu* — more at GROVELING (adv.)] *Scot* **:** the ventral surface of the body; *specif* **:** STOMACH

¹ground \'grau̇nd\ *n* -s *often attrib* [ME *ground, grund*, fr. OE *grund;* akin to OHG *grunt* ground, bottom, ON *grunnr* bottom, Goth *grundu*waddjus foundation wall, Gk *chrainein* to graze, touch slightly, and perh. to OE *grindan* to grind — more at GRIND] **1 a** *obs* **:** the lowest part **:** the surface that limits the downward extent of something **:** BOTTOM, FOUNDATION **b :** the bottom of the sea or a body of water **:** solid bottom — now used chiefly in nautical phrases ⟨had to anchor about a mile off shore and the holding ~ was not good —A.F.Ellis⟩ ⟨the boat struck ~⟩; compare AGROUND **c grounds** *pl* (1) **:** sediment at the bottom of a liquor or liquid (2) **:** ground coffee beans after brewing **d** *obs* **:** the pit of a theater **2 a :** the foundation or basis on which knowledge, belief, or conviction rests **:** a premise, reason, or collection of data upon which something (as a legal action or an argument) is made to rely for cogency or validity ⟨the reference to natural law as a ~ for the authority of civil law —Glenn Negley⟩ ⟨opposing divorce on religious ~*s*⟩ **b :** a sufficient and determining condition **:** a logical condition, physical cause, or metaphysical basis — used esp. of what is regarded as more fundamental than a merely natural cause ⟨the first principle or ~ of the universe —Frank Thilly⟩ **3 a :** the area surrounding and delimiting a figure or design **:** BACKGROUND **b :** the basic surface for figures in relief **c :** the surface upon which a picture or decoration is painted (as a preliminary coating laid on a canvas) **d :** the surface appearance of a fabric distinguished by a weave, color, texture; *specif* **:** the plain or background portion of a patterned fabric **e :** a stiff yet yielding substance (as wood or a pitch bed) on which a design is beaten into relief in repoussé work **f :** the pieces of net or the brides that support or hold together the patterns in lace; *also* **:** the net that serves as a foundation (as for appliqué) **g :** an acid-resistant liquid or paste that is made from varying proportions of wax, gum, and resin and that is used in etching to carry the design and to protect areas of the plate where no biting action is intended — see HARD GROUND, LIFT GROUND, SOFT GROUND **h :** a plain tinted coat which is applied to a wallpaper and over which a pattern is then printed **i :** wood or metal strips placed around all openings and along the top of the wall base to serve as guides in finishing the plaster **4 a :** a plainsong or other traditional tune used as the bass of a polyphonic musical composition **b :** GROUND BASS **c :** a composition making use of a ground **5 :** the surface on which man stands, moves, and dwells and on which objects naturally rest: as **a :** the surface of the earth ⟨deep under the ~⟩ ⟨a branch 60 feet above the ~⟩ ⟨uneven ~⟩ ⟨high ~⟩ **:** the earth as contrasted with the air ⟨~ troops⟩ ⟨~ attack⟩ or the water ⟨glad to feel firm ~ again after the rough voyage⟩ **b** *obs* **:** COUNTRY, LAND **c** *now dial* **:** a parcel of land enclosed for tillage or pasture **:** FIELD **d :** an area appropriated to or used for a particular purpose ⟨picnic ~⟩ ⟨parade ~⟩ ⟨camping ~⟩ **e grounds** *pl* **:** the gardens, lawn, and planted areas immediately surrounding and belonging to a house or other building ⟨hospital ~*s*⟩ **f :** an area to be won or defended in or as if in battle ⟨yielding ~ step by step⟩ ⟨shifting the ~ of his attack⟩ **g :** a topic or field of study or discourse **:** SUBJECT ⟨touch on forbidden ~⟩ ⟨cover a great deal of ~ in an hour's lecture⟩ **h** (1) **:** a cricket field (2) **:** the part of the field beginning at the popping crease and extending backward past the stumps ⟨a batsman may be stumped or run out only when he is out of his ~⟩ (3) *or* **ground staff :** the professional players employed by a cricket club **i** *chiefly Brit* **:** FLOOR ⟨kneeling on the ~ beside the couch he leaned over her —Aldous Huxley⟩ ⟨her gown swept the ~⟩ **6 a :** SOIL, EARTH ⟨till the ~ —Gen 2:5(AV)⟩ **b :** a special soil ⟨produce of each ~⟩ **c :** rock or formation through which mine workings are driven ⟨soft, wet, or loose ~⟩ **7 a :** a metal object buried in the earth to make electrical connection with it (as in a telephone or radio circuit) **b :** a large conducting body (as the chassis of a car or radio, the fuselage of a plane, or the earth itself) used as a common return for an electric circuit and as an arbitrary zero of potential **c :** electric connection with the earth or other ground **syn** see REASON — **from the ground up 1 :** entirely anew or afresh ⟨if one could begin *from the ground up* in each generation —Thomas Munro⟩ **2 :** from top to bottom **:** THOROUGHLY ⟨learning the business *from the ground up*⟩ — **into the ground** *adv* **:** beyond what is necessary or tolerable **:** to exhaustion **:** to death ⟨patiently labored an issue *into the ground* —*Newsweek*⟩ ⟨caution is no doubt a virtue but don't run it *into the ground*⟩ ⟨ran the other horses *into the ground* in the first half mile⟩ — **off the ground** *adv* **:** in or as if in flight ⟨the story . . . dramatically never gets *off the ground* —*New Republic*⟩ **:** off to a good start **:** under way ⟨difficult for his second-party movement to get *off the ground* —*Time*⟩ — **on the ground** *adv* **:** at the scene of action **:** on the spot ⟨already *on the ground*, energetically organizing —S.H.Adams⟩ — **take the ground :** to run aground ⟨choose a boat that is able to *take the ground* easily —Peter Heaton⟩ — **to ground** *adv* **:** into a burrow **:** into hiding ⟨the fox went *to ground* under a rocky escarpment —James Reynolds⟩ ⟨gone *to ground* in his country estate to avoid awkward questions⟩ ⟨till I have run the author *to ground* and exposed the whole shameful affair —John Buchan⟩ — **to the ground** *adv* **:** ENTIRELY, COMPLETELY, UTTERLY ⟨this life here suits me *to the ground* —Rose Macaulay⟩

²ground \"\ *vb* -ED/-ING/-S [ME *grounden, grunden*, fr. *ground, grund*, n.] *vt* **1 :** to bring to the ground **:** force down on the ground **:** FLOOR **2 a** *obs* **:** to set (a building) on a foundation **b :** to furnish a ground for **:** set on a basis (as of reason or principle or belief) ⟨sought to ~ the social good on the good of individuals —K.J.Arrow⟩ ⟨~*ed* their philosophy of life on logic as well as on metaphysics —Frank Thilly⟩ **c :** to instruct in elements or first principles **:** furnish (oneself or others) with a foundation of knowledge ⟨the study helped to ~ them in the mechanics of research⟩ ⟨must have every American citizen well ~*ed* in the classical ideals —Calvin Coolidge⟩ **3 :** to cover (a painting surface) with a ground **4 :** to place on or cause to touch the ground ⟨~ a rifle⟩ ⟨~ a ship on a sandbar⟩ **5 :** to prepare the surface of (leather) by scraping the flesh side with a moon knife **6 :** to connect electrically with a ground **7 a :** to restrict (a pilot, passenger, or airplane) to the ground to avoid accident (as from mechanical failure, ill health, or unfavorable flying weather) or to enforce a regulation (as of licensing or discipline) **b :** to bar (a jockey) from racing **c :** to bar (a licensed driver) from operating a vehicle **~** *vi* **1 :** to have a ground or basis **:** RELY — usu. used with *on* or *upon* ⟨the institutions . . . ~ on . . . four socializing forces —S.H.Chapman⟩ **2 :** to run aground **:** strike bottom ⟨the ship ~*ed* gently on a mud bank⟩ ⟨masses of ice had ~*ed* on the shore⟩ **3** *archaic* **:** to come to the ground **:** fall or light on the ground **4 :** to hit a grounder ⟨~*ed* into a double play⟩ ⟨~*ed* out to the shortstop⟩ **syn** see BASE — **ground arms :** to lay weapons on the ground in front of one esp. in token of surrender

³ground *past of* GRIND

ground·age \'grau̇ndij\ *n* -s *Brit* **:** a fee or charge for a ship to anchor in a port

ground almond *n* **:** CHUFA

ground angle *n* **:** the angle that an airplane's wing chord makes with the horizontal when the airplane is standing at rest

ground angling *n* **:** fishing with a floatless weighted line

ground annual \'grau̇nd-, 'grau̇n(d)-\ *n* [ME *ground annuall*, fr. *grund* ground + *annuall, annual* annual — more at ANNUAL] *Scots law* **:** an annual duty or payment laid as a real burden upon land

ground an·nu·al·er \-'anyə(wə)lər\ *n, pl* **ground annualers** *Scots law* **:** one that pays a ground annual

ground ash *n* **1 a :** an ash sapling **b :** a walking stick made from ground ash **2 :** GOUTWEED **3 :** WILD ANGELICA **4 :** EUROPEAN ASH **5 :** WHITE ASH 1a

ground bait *n* **:** bait scattered on the water so as to attract fish

ground ball *n* **:** a batted ball in baseball that touches the ground before a fielder can field it; *esp* **:** GROUNDER

ground bass *n* **:** a bass passage usu. of four or eight measures continually repeated below constantly changing melody and harmony — called also *basso ostinato*

ground beam *n* **1 :** SLEEPER 2a **2 :** GROUND PLATE 1

ground beetle *n* **:** a beetle of the family Carabidae

ground·ber·ry \'grau̇n(d)- — see BERRY\ *n* **1 :** CHECKERBERRY 1a; *also* **:** the plant producing this berry **2** *Austral* **:** NATIVE CRANBERRY **3 :** a thick trailing evergreen shrub

(*Rubus hespidus*) of eastern No. America that is used as a ground cover esp. on banks and in rock gardens and that has hispid canes and glossy foliolate leaves
ground birch *n* **:** DWARF BIRCH
groundbird \'=,=\ *n* **1 :** any of several Australian passerine birds constituting a genus (*Cinclosoma*) of the family Timaliidae and resembling thrushes **2 :** any of various small ground-nesting birds (as the field and vesper sparrows)
ground boss *n* **:** the captain of a mine
ground box *n* **:** DWARF BOX 3
groundbreaker \'=,==\ *n* **:** PIONEER, INNOVATOR
ground burnut *n* **:** PUNCTURE VINE
ground cable *n* **:** a mooring cable or chain that runs from a mooring anchor to a buoy
ground casing *n* **:** an unfinished casing for a window that serves as a plaster ground
ground cedar *n* **1 :** GROUND PINE 2 **2 :** a common highly variable juniper (*Juniperus communis*) that is cultivated in many varieties as an ornamental and esp. for foundation plantings
ground centaury *n* **1 :** AMERICAN COLUMBO **2 :** an annual herb (*Polygala nuttallii*) of the eastern U.S. with slender erect stems and greenish purple flowers
ground chain *n* **1 :** a length of chain attached along the first length of an anchor cable by which the anchor when weighed may be swung free of the ship — compare CAT CHAIN **2 :** GROUND CABLE
ground-cherry *n* **1 :** any of several shrubby European dwarf cherries (esp. *Prunus fruticosa*) **2 a :** a plant of the genus *Physalis* — called also *husk-tomato;* see CAPE GOOSEBERRY, CHINESE LANTERN PLANT, STRAWBERRY TOMATO **b :** the fruit of such a plant
ground circuit *n* **:** a telegraph or telephone circuit partly through the ground
ground clamp *n* **:** a metal strip for making electrical connection with a ground (as a water pipe)
ground cloth *n* **1 :** a canvas covering for the floor of a stage **2 :** GROUNDSHEET
ground coat *n* **1 :** the undercoat of paint in graining or scumbling **2 a :** PRIMING **b :** the first coat of enamel on a metal usu. with blue cobalt oxide added to promote adherence
ground-controlled approach *also* **ground-control approach** \'==,=-\ *n* **:** a blind landing in which the airplane is observed from the ground by means of radar and directed along a suitable glide path by radioed instructions to the pilot — abbr. *GCA*
ground-controlled interception *n* **:** an interception in air defense in which the fighter pilot is directed to his target by signals from a ground radar station — abbr. *GCI*
ground course *n* **:** the horizontal course of masonry next to the ground
ground cover *n* **1 :** all small plants (as mosses, ferns, grasses and other herbaceous plants and shrubs) in a forest except young trees **2 a :** a planting of prostrate or low plants (as ivy, pachysandra, myrtle) that covers the ground in place of turf **b :** a plant adapted for such use
ground crew *n* **:** a crew of mechanics and technicians who maintain and service aircraft
ground cuckoo *n* **:** ROADRUNNER
ground current *n* **:** EARTH CURRENT
ground detector *n* **:** a device for determining whether a circuit is well insulated from the ground
ground dove *n* **:** any of numerous very small chiefly tropical doves; *esp* **:** any of various tiny very tame American doves (genus *Columbigallina*) that nest on the ground or in low trees or bushes
grounded *past of* GROUND
ground·ed·ly *adv, archaic* **:** in a well-founded manner **:** FIRMLY, THOROUGHLY
ground effect *n* **:** the apparent increase in aerodynamic lift experienced by an aircraft when flying near the ground and observed up to a distance above the ground approximately equal to the wing span
ground elder *n, Brit* **:** GOUTWEED
grounden *archaic past part of* GRIND
ground·er \'graůndə(r)\ *n* -S **:** one that grounds: as **a :** a ball (as in baseball, cricket, or soccer) that bounds or rolls along the ground; *esp* **:** a batted ball that strikes the ground almost immediately **b :** a worker who prepares a ground of surface or color (as on leather or paper)
ground fern *n* **:** MARSH FERN 1
ground fielding *n* **:** the fielding of grounders in cricket
ground finch *n* **1 :** TOWHEE **2 :** any of several dull-colored large-billed finches constituting a genus (*Geospiza*) that is restricted to the Galápagos islands
ground fir *n* **:** any of several club mosses (as *Lycopodium selago* and *L. obscurum*) having a stiff erect habit
ground fire *n* **1 :** a forest fire that burns the humus and usu. does not appear at the surface **2 :** SURFACE FIRE
groundfish \'=,=\ *n* **:** a bottom fish; *esp* **:** any of the commercially important fishes (as cod, haddock, pollack, flounder) that live on the sea bottom
ground flax *n* **:** GOLD-OF-PLEASURE
ground flea *n* **1 :** FLEA BEETLE **2 :** SPRINGTAIL
ground floor *n* **1 :** the floor of a house most nearly on a level with the ground — compare FIRST FLOOR **2 :** a favorable position or privileged opportunity (as in making a speculative investment) usu. on terms obtained by the original or early participants — used chiefly in the phrase *in on the ground floor* ⟨he's heard of the boom along this coast, and wants to get in on the *ground floor* —O.Henry⟩
ground fog *n* **:** fog extending only a few feet from the ground; *specif* **:** one not exceeding the height of a man
ground form *n* [trans. of G *grundform*] **:** a root, stem, or word viewed as the common base from which various forms or words have developed **:** THEME
ground frost *n* **1 :** frozen ground **2 :** a temperature dropping below freezing at or near ground level and causing damage to vegetation
ground game *n, Brit* **:** game (as hares and rabbits) living on the ground — distinguished from *wing game*
ground gas *n* **:** gas including air held in openings or pores within the earth
ground gecko *n* **:** any of various small weak-limbed geckos of the southwestern U.S. and northern Mexico that constitute the genus *Coleonyx*, are strictly terrestrial in habits, and are variously barred and blotched with reddish or dark brown on a creamy or yellow ground
ground glass *n* **1 :** glass whose surface has been made light-diffusing by etching with hydrofluoric acid, sandblasting, or grinding with an abrasive; *specif* **:** a sheet of such glass used as a focusing screen in photography **2 :** glass reduced to powder by grinding or crushing for use as an abrasive
ground-glass \'=¦=\ *adj* [*ground glass*] **:** relating to or characterized by ground glass: as **a :** having a surface polished **b :** having a surface ground or etched to a semi-transparency **c :** having a surface ground to fit ⟨*ground-glass* joint⟩
ground goldenrod *n* **:** a low velvety prairie goldenrod (*Solidago mollis*) of central No. America
ground goldflower *n* **:** a golden aster (*Chrysopsis falcata*) of the eastern U.S. with velvety foliage
ground hemlock *n* **:** any of several prostrate evergreen shrubs of the genus *Taxus* (esp. *T. canadensis* of eastern No. America) with low straggling stems, abruptly pointed leaves, and bright red fruits
groundhog \'=,=\ *n* **1 :** WOODCHUCK **2 :** SANDHOG
groundhog case *n, South* **:** a desperate or critical situation **:** a situation with no alternative ⟨his was a *groundhog case;* it was take to the water or the dogs will get you —F.B. Gipson⟩
groundhog day *n, usu cap G&D* [so called fr. the belief that on that day the groundhog comes out of his burrow and if he casts a shadow returns for an additional period of winter weather] **:** February 2 in most parts of the U.S. or February 14 in some parts (as Missouri) which is popularly considered to indicate if sunny the continuance of wintry weather or if cloudy the early coming of spring
ground hold *n, obs* **:** GROUND TACKLE
ground holly *n* **1 :** PIPSISSEWA **2 :** WINTERGREEN 2a
ground honeysuckle *n* **:** BIRD'S-FOOT TREFOIL 1a
ground hornbill *n* **:** a hornbill of the African genus *Bucorvus* partly terrestrial in habits
ground ice *n* **1 :** ANCHOR ICE **2 :** clear ice in permanently frozen ground
groundier *comparative of* GROUNDY
groundiest *superlative of* GROUNDY
grounding *n* -S [fr. gerund of ²*ground*] **:** training or instruction esp. in the fundamentals of an art, science, or other field of knowledge **:** FOUNDATION ⟨a good ~ in chemistry⟩
ground itch *n* **:** an itching inflammation of the skin marking the entrance into the body of larval hookworms
ground ivy *n* [ME] **1 :** a trailing Eurasian mint (*Nepeta hederacea*) that is common as a weed in No. America and has rounded leaves and rather showy blue-purple flowers — called also *gill-over-the-ground* **2 :** any of several low-growing or trailing plants
ground jasmine *n* **:** an evergreen southern African shrub (*Passerina stelleri*) of the family Thymelaeaceae with white flowers
ground joint *n* **:** a joint (as between glass parts) of which the contacting surfaces are ground together to a close fit
ground joist *n* **:** SLEEPER 2a
ground juniper *n* **:** DWARF JUNIPER
groundkeeper \'=,==\ *n* **1 :** one that tends the grounds (as of a sports field, cemetery, park) **2 :** an undesired plant arising from self-sown seed or from roots in a planting of a desired species or variety
ground lag *n* **:** the horizontal distance by which the actual trajectory of a bomb in air lags behind the theoretical path in a vacuum
ground landlord *n* **:** the owner of a ground rent
ground lark *n* **:** PIPIT
ground laurel *n* **:** ARBUTUS 3
ground lead \-,lēd\ *n* **1 :** a contrivance for guiding a cable that hauls logs along the ground **2 :** GROUND WIRE
ground lease *n* **:** BUILDING LEASE
ground lemon *n* **:** MAYAPPLE
ground·less \'graůndləs *rapid* -nl-\ *adj* [ME *groundeles* bottomless unfathomable, fr. OE *grundlēas*, fr. *grund* ground + *-lēas* -less — more at GROUND, -LESS] **:** having no ground or foundation **:** lacking cause or reason for support ⟨~ fears⟩ ⟨a ~ charge of treason⟩ — **ground·less·ly** *adv* — **ground·less·ness** *n* -ES
ground level *n* **:** GROUND STATE
ground lily *n* **:** any of several plants of the genus *Trillium* (esp. *T. cernuum*)
groundline \'=,=\ *n* **1 a :** strong hard-laid line that is used to form the main line of a setline and is usu. provided in bundles of 300 fathoms weighing 48, 40, or sometimes 32 pounds **b :** the main line of a setline consisting of one or more bundles of groundline **2 a :** the base line which represents a ground plane in pictures having no indication of spatial depth and upon which all figures and objects are placed irrespective of their real spatial relationship **b :** the bottom line of the picture plane of a drawing in linear perspective **c :** the bottom line of a photograph **d :** the line representing ground level in an architectural plan or drawing **3 :** FOUNDATION, BASIS
ground·ling \'graůndliŋ, -lēŋ, *rapid* -nl-\ *n* -S [¹*ground* + *-ling*] **1 :** one that keeps close to the ground; *specif* **:** a fish (as the loach) that keeps at the bottom of the water **2 a :** a spectator in the cheaper part of a theater **b :** one of ordinary or unsophisticated taste or critical judgment **3 :** one that lives, works, or fights on the ground as distinct from in the air or on the sea
ground liverwort *n* **1 :** a common liverwort (*Marchantia polymorpha*) **2 :** a lichen (*Peltigera canina*) somewhat similar to the liverwort in appearance
ground lizard *n* **:** any of various small lizards of terrestrial habits; *esp* **:** a lizard (*Leiolopisma laterale*) of the southern U.S.
ground log *n* **:** a ship's log for use in shallow water and strong currents in which the chip is replaced by a sinker that rests on the bottom and measures speed over the ground rather than through the water
ground loop *n* **:** a sharp uncontrollable turn made by an airplane on the ground in landing, taking off, or taxiing
ground-loop \'=¦=\ *vb* [*ground loop*] *vi, of an airplane or pilot* **:** to make a ground loop ~ *vt* **:** to cause (an airplane) to ground-loop
ground mahogany *n* **:** a Mexican mahogany tree (*Swietenia humilis*) that has harder, heavier, and darker-colored wood than the West Indian mahogany
ground mail *n, Scot* **:** the fee for interment in a graveyard
ground mallow *n* **:** DWARF MALLOW
ground·man \'graůn(d),man, -,mən\ *n, pl* **groundmen 1 a :** a strip-mine worker who moves dirt and coal within reach of power shovels **b :** a mine worker who deepens haulageways by digging out the bottom and lowering tracks **2 :** a member of a work crew who performs the tasks that can be done on or from the ground: as **a :** one who digs holes and raises poles for electric power or telephone lines and lifts equipment and tools to linemen **b :** one who assists with the erection of oil-well drilling rigs or power lines, the driving of piles, or the construction or wrecking of buildings **3 :** GROUNDKEEPER 1 **4 :** an electrician who attends to grounding connections
ground maple *n* **:** ALUMROOT
groundmass \'=,=\ *n* **:** the fine-grained or glassy base of a porphyry in which the larger distinct crystals are embedded
ground meristem *n* **:** the part of the primary apical meristem of a plant that remains after the protoderm and procambium have been differentiated
ground mist *n* **:** GROUND FOG
ground moraine *n* **:** a moraine deposited beneath a glacier and back from its edge or end
groundneedle \'=¦==\ *n* **:** a storksbill (*Erodium moschatum*) with short-stalked leaves
ground noise *n* **:** noise in reproduced or amplified sound caused by a source (as needle scratch, tube noise) other than the signal
ground note *n* **:** FUNDAMENTAL 2
ground·nut \'graůn(d),nət, -aů,nət\ *n* **1 :** CHUFA **2 :** any of several plants having edible tuberous roots: as **a :** a No. American vine (*Apios tuberosa*) with pinnate leaves and clusters of brownish purple fragrant flowers **b :** DWARF GINSENG **c :** HARBINGER-OF-SPRING **d** *chiefly Brit* **:** PEANUT **3 :** the root of a groundnut
groundnut oil *n, chiefly Brit* **:** PEANUT OIL
ground oak *n* **1 :** DWARF OAK **2 :** GOPHER PLUM 2b
ground observer *n* **:** one that observes, tracks, and reports the movement of aircraft from an observation post
ground out *vi* **:** STRAND ⟨a small vessel could lie snug behind it, though she *grounded out* at low water —G.W.Brace⟩
ground owl *n* **:** BURROWING OWL
ground parrot *n* **1 :** KAKAPO **2 :** a formerly common ground-frequenting Australian parrot (*Pezoporus wallicus*) having green plumage barred with black and yellow and a scarlet patch on the forehead
ground pea *n* **1 :** PEANUT **2 :** GROUNDNUT 2a
ground pearl *n* **:** an encysted form of the female of various coccid insects of *Margarodes* and closely related genera in which a shelly covering is formed that in some regions is collected and strung into necklaces; *also* **:** a coccid having such an encysted form and sometimes being a serious pest of turf
ground pig *n* **:** CANE RAT 1
ground pigeon *n* **:** any of numerous pigeons that live largely on the ground (as the tooth-billed pigeon and the crowned pigeons)
ground pine *n* **1 :** a European bugle (*Ajuga chamaepitys*) with a resinous odor **2 :** any of several club mosses (esp. *Lycopodium clevatum* and *L. complanatum*) with long creeping stems and erect branches **:** GROUND FIR
ground pink *n* **:** MOSS PINK
ground pistachio *n* **:** PEANUT
ground plan *n* **1 :** a plan of the ground floor or of any floor of a building as distinguished from an elevation or perpendicular section **2 :** a first or basic plan **3 :** the pattern described on the ground by dancers
ground plane *n* **:** the horizontal plane of projection in perspective drawing
ground plate *n* **1** *archaic* **:** a timber laid horizontally on or near the ground to support the uprights of a building **:** SILL **2 :** a metallic plate buried in the ground to connect a circuit to earth
groundplot \'=,=\ *n* **:** the determining of an aircraft's position by multiplying ground speed by time on course and measuring off the resultant distance from a previously known position
ground plum *n* **1 :** any of several milk vetches (esp. *Astragalus caryocarpus*) of the western U.S. **2 :** the fruit of a ground plum
ground-position indicator *n* **:** an instrument that indicates to the pilot of an aircraft his position relative to the ground
ground puppy *n* **1 :** CHANGA **2 :** HELLBENDER
ground quiver *n* **:** a device for holding arrows upright on the ground consisting of a metal rod with a horizontal ring at the top

ground quiver

ground raspberry *n* **:** GOLDENSEAL
ground rat *n* **:** CANE RAT 1
ground rattler *or* **ground rattlesnake** *n* **:** MASSASAUGA b
ground rent *n* **1 :** a price per year or term of years paid for the right to occupy and improve a piece of land; *also* **:** money or compensation so paid — compare ECONOMIC RENT **2 :** a rent charge reserved to himself and his heirs by the grantor of land in fee simple or on perpetual lease or lease for a term of years renewable forever and found chiefly in Pennsylvania and Maryland
ground robin *n* **:** TOWHEE
ground roller *n* **:** any of certain Madagascan birds (family Coraciidae) of terrestrial and crepuscular habits frequenting forests and feeding on insects, worms, or other small invertebrates
ground rope *n* **:** a weighted rope that keeps a trawlnet on the bottom
ground rose *n* **:** a low-growing prickly and often bristly shrub (*Rosa spithamaea*) of southern Oregon and California with creeping rootstocks and usu. corymbose flowers
groundrow \'=¦=\ *n* [¹*ground* + *row*] **:** a low flat piece of scenery often representing a distant horizon and used to mask the lower part of a cyclorama or backdrop
ground rule *n* **1 :** a sports rule adopted to modify play on a particular field, court, or course (as because of space limitations or the encroachment of spectators on a playing field) ⟨if the backstop is less than 60 feet from home plate a *ground rule* will be necessary —Clement Wood & Gloria Goddard⟩ **2 :** a rule of procedure or a principle of action specified for or intended to apply to a particular event or situation ⟨having developed the primary purpose and general objectives of the company, a firm set of *ground rules* is therefore provided for the necessary detailed planning —C.F.Robinson⟩ ⟨the first fundamental change in labor-relations *ground rules* in nearly twelve years —*Time*⟩
grounds *pl of* GROUND, *pres 3d sing of* GROUND
ground school *n* **:** a school giving courses in aerodynamics, map making, photography, and other pertinent subjects for aviators
ground sea *n* **:** GROUND SWELL
ground seal *n* **:** BEARDED SEAL
¹**ground·sel** \'graůn(d)səl\ *n* -S [ME *grundeswele*, fr. OE *grundeswelge*, fr. *grunde, grund* ground + *-swelge* (fr. *swelgan* to swallow, absorb), prob. by folk etymology fr. earlier *gundæswelge*, fr. *gund* pus + *-swelge;* akin to OHG *gund, gunt* pus, Norw dial. *gund* scab, Goth *gund* cancerous abscess, Gk *kanthylē* tumor, swelling — more at GROUND, SWALLOW] **:** an herb of the genus *Senecio* (esp. *S. vulgaris* in England and *S. aureus intercursus* in America) that is used sometimes as an emmenagogue
²**groundsel** \"\ *n* -S [ME *gronsell, ground sille*, fr. *ground* + *sille* sill — more at SILL] **1** *archaic* **:** a bed piece or foundation timber supporting a timber superstructure (as a wooden house or a set of mine timbers) **2** *archaic* **:** the lowest piece or the foundation of a structure **:** a fundamental principle **:** BASIS
groundsel bush *or* **groundsel tree** *n* **:** a No. American maritime shrub or small tree (*Baccharis halimifolia*) with leaves resembling those of groundsel; *broadly* **:** a plant of the genus *Baccharis*
ground shark *n* **1 :** any of numerous active voracious sharks (genus *Carcharhinus*) found in shallow water along all warm coasts: as **a :** CUB SHARK **b :** BROWN SHARK 2 **2 :** GREENLAND SHARK
groundsheet \'=,=\ *n* **:** a waterproof sheet placed on the ground for protection from moisture ⟨slipped the newspaper . . . into my haversack thinking to use it as a ~ against the damp —Paul Roche⟩ — called also *ground cloth*
ground·sill \'graůn(d)səl, -,sil\ *n* [ME *ground sille*] *archaic* **:** ²GROUNDSEL
grounds keeper *n* **1 :** GARDENER; *esp* **:** one that cares for the grounds of a large property (as an estate) **2 :** GROUNDKEEPER 1
ground skidder *n* **:** a device that transports logs without lifting them clear of the ground
ground sloth *n* **:** any of various large and often very large extinct American edentate mammals related to the recent sloths and anteaters — compare MEGATHERIUM, MYLODON
ground sluice *n* **:** a channel or trough in the ground through which auriferous earth is sluiced for placer mining
grounds·man \'graůn(d)zmən\ *n, pl* **groundsmen 1 :** GROUNDKEEPER 1 **2** *chiefly Brit* **:** GROUNDMAN 2 **3 :** CRANE-FOLLOWER
ground snake *n* **:** any of numerous small terrestrial colubrid snakes: as **a :** any of a No. American genus (*Sonora*) of shy brightly ringed snakes **b :** a small reddish gray snake (*Haldea striatula* syn. *Potamophis striatula*) of the eastern U.S.
ground sparrow *n* **:** any of various small ground-nesting sparrows (as the song sparrow, vesper sparrow, or Savannah sparrow)
ground speed *n* **:** the velocity of an airplane with relation to the ground — compare AIRSPEED
ground squirrel *n* **1 :** any of various burrowing rodents (family Sciuridae): as **a :** *chiefly South & Midland* **:** CHIPMUNK **b :** a member of the African genus *Xerus* **c :** any of numerous often striped rodents of western No. America that constitute *Citellus* and sometimes related genera, are often destructive pests of cultivated land, and in some areas serve as vectors of plague **2** *also* **ground-squirrel pea :** TWINLEAF
ground staff *n* **:** GROUND 5h (3)
ground state *n* **:** the energy level of an atomic electron system, atomic nucleus, or other systems of interacting elementary particles having the least energy of all its possible states — called also *ground level*
ground story *n* **:** GROUND FLOOR
ground-strafe \'=,=\ *vt* **:** STRAFE
ground strake *n* **:** GARBOARD STRAKE
ground stroke *n* **:** a stroke made on a ball in tennis after it has rebounded from the ground — compare VOLLEY
ground substance *n* **:** a more or less completely homogeneous or apparently homogeneous matrix that forms the background in which the specific formed or differentiated elements of a system are suspended or enclosed: as **a :** the intercellular substance of tissues **b :** HYALOPLASM
ground sweet *n* **:** ARBUTUS 3
ground swell *n* **1 :** a broad deep swell or undulation of the ocean caused by a long-continued gale or seismic disturbance and felt even at a remote distance **2 :** a movement (as of political sentiment or political opinion) that is unmistakably evident but often lacking in visible leadership or overt expression ⟨by next year the *ground swell* of interest among veteran and labor groups may well push cooperative housing through Congress —Catherine Bauer⟩
ground table *n* **:** EARTH TABLE
ground tackle *or* **ground tackling** *n* **:** the anchors, cables, and other tackle used to secure a ship at anchor
ground thistle *n* **1 :** a stemless European thistle (*Carlina acaulis*) with crimson flower heads **2 :** CARDOON
ground thrush *n* **1 :** PITTA 2 **2 :** any of numerous Old World thrushes chiefly of a genus (*Geocichla*) of the family Turdidae

ground tier *n* **1 :** the lowest tier of articles stowed in a ship's hold **2 :** the lowest row of boxes in a theater or amphitheater
ground tissue *n* : PARENCHYMA 1
ground tone *n* : FUNDAMENTAL 2
ground vine *n* : TWINFLOWER
ground warbler *n* : any of various American warblers living or nesting chiefly on the ground
ground·ward \ˈgrau̇ndwə(r)d, *rapid* -nw-\ *also* **ground·wards** \-dz\ *adv* : toward the ground : DOWN
groundwater \ˈ=,==\ *n* : water within the earth that supplies wells and springs; *specif* : water in the zone of saturation where all openings in rocks and soil are filled, the upper surface of which forms the water table
groundwater level *n* **1 :** WATER TABLE **2 :** the depth or elevation above or below sea level at which the surface of groundwater stands
ground wave *n* : a radio wave that is propagated along the surface of the earth
ground ways *n pl* : heavy timbers laid on the ground on each side of the keel of a ship under construction that form a track for launching and support the sliding ways that carry the ship into the water — called also *standing ways*
ground wire *n* **1 :** a wire making a ground connection **2 :** the part of a circuit formed by the earth
groundwood \ˈ=,=\ *n* : wood ground into small particles by revolving grindstones and used in paper pulp ⟨~ pulp⟩ ⟨~ paper⟩; *also* : the pulp made from such wood
groundwork \ˈ=,=\ *n* : something that forms a foundation or support : BASIS, GROUND
ground worm *n* **1 :** EARTHWORM **2 :** WORM SNAKE
ground wren *n* **1 :** WREN-TIT **2 :** HEATH-WREN
groundy \ˈgrau̇ndē\ *adj* -ER/-EST *of coffee* : having an earthy taste or aroma
ground yew *n* **1 :** CROWBERRY 1a **2 :** a ground hemlock (*Taxus canadensis*)
ground zero *n* : the point on the surface of the ground or water directly below which, above which, or at which the explosion of an atom bomb occurs
¹group \ˈgrüp\ *n* -s [F *groupe*, fr. It *gruppo* group, knot, of Gmc origin; akin to OHG *kropf* craw — more at CROP] **1 :** two or more figures (as in sculpture or painting) forming a distinctive unit complete in itself or forming part of a larger composition ⟨the bronze ~ represents a mortally wounded southern soldier supported by Fame —*Amer. Guide Series: N.C.*⟩ ⟨a foreground ~ of satyrs and nymphs⟩ **2 a :** a relatively small number of individuals assembled or standing together ⟨a ~ of indifferent bystanders looked on⟩ ⟨~s of prisoners marching to their destination⟩ — compare CROWD **b :** an assemblage of objects regarded as a unit because of their comparative segregation from others ⟨a ~ of buildings⟩ ⟨a ~ of towns . . . were able to develop increasing commerce with the Near East —Stringfellow Barr⟩ ⟨a ~ of . . . highly finished, memorable stories —Paul Pickrel⟩: as (1) : a cluster of islands ⟨the ~ consists of four tiny islands⟩ ⟨contemplated the investigation of the South Sandwich ~ —R.N.Rudmose-Brown⟩ (2) : a cluster of hits on a target fired with the same sight setting and the same point of aim **3 :** a number of individuals bound together by a community of interest, purpose, or function: as **a** (1) : a social unit comprising individuals in continuous contact through intercommunication and shared participation in activities toward some commonly accepted end — see PRIMARY GROUP, SECONDARY GROUP (2) : CLASS 1a ⟨a government representative of all the great social ~s⟩ ⟨a small ~ of wealthy families virtually governed the province⟩ (3) : a relatively small number of persons associated formally or informally for a common end or drawn together through an affinity of views or interests : CIRCLE ⟨a dance ~⟩ ⟨a study ~⟩ ⟨a stamp ~⟩ ⟨a vanguard ~ of artists⟩ ⟨there grew up in the universities a ~ called the "New Critics" —F.O.Baker⟩ **b :** a number of students taking part in the same educational or extracurricular activities : CLASS 2b **c :** a combination of persons who are usu. employees of a single employer and are covered by a blanket or single insurance policy **d :** a combination of elected parliamentary representatives bound together by a common program or by a general identity of political views — used esp. of a grouping in the French National Assembly **e :** a combination of companies or other enterprises having interlocking interests or a single owner or management : SYNDICATE, TRUST, CHAIN ⟨vary in size from two-paper ~s to one which includes 20 papers —F.L.Mott⟩ ⟨the powerful hydroelectric ~⟩ **f** (1) : an administrative and tactical military unit consisting of a headquarters and two or more battalions not a permanent organic part of the group (2) : a unit of an echelon of the U. S. Air Force higher than a squadron and lower than a wing and composed of a headquarters and two or more squadrons **g :** the basic program unit of Camp Fire Girls consisting of no more than 20 Blue Bird members or camp fire girls and no more than 30 members in a Horizon Club plus a leader and often an assistant leader **4 a :** an assemblage of related organisms ⟨the A ~ of beta hemolytic streptococci⟩ — often used to avoid taxonomic connotations when the kind or degree of relationship is not clearly defined **b** (1) : an assemblage of atoms forming part of a molecule : RADICAL ⟨a methyl ~ (CH_3)⟩ ⟨the alcohol ~ (OH)⟩ — compare LIGAND (2) : an assemblage of elements forming one of the vertical columns of the periodic table **c** (1) : a stratigraphic division of the first order comprising the rocks deposited during an era — used in the system of nomenclature adopted by the International Geological Congress (2) : a stratigraphic division composed of two or more named formations — used in the system of nomenclature of the U. S. Geological Survey (3) : a consecutive series of beds or assemblage of related igneous rocks (4) : GREAT SOIL GROUP **d :** a syllable or series of syllables uttered with a single primary or quasi-primary stress : STRESS-GROUP **e :** a set of three or more cards of the same rank in the game of rummy **5 :** a mathematical aggregate in which the product of two elements is an element of the aggregate
²group \"\ *vb* -ED/-ING/-S [F *grouper* to group, fr. *groupe*, n.] *vt* **1 :** to form a group of : CLUSTER ⟨nine tennis courts are ~*ed* at one end of the field —*Bull. of Bates Coll.*⟩ ⟨with the other . . . pilots ~*ed* around him —Ed Cunningham⟩ **2 a :** to combine in a group or in groups : assign to a group : CLASSIFY ⟨the large class of barbaric ideas ~*ed* under sympathetic magic —Edward Clodd⟩ ⟨her mind was busily assorting and ~*ing* the faces before her —Ellen Glasgow⟩ ⟨~*ing* liberty of the press with trial by jury —Zechariah Chafee⟩; *specif* : to determine the blood group of ⟨after the patient and donor have been ~*ed* —R.L.Haden⟩ **b :** to arrange (as figures) in an artistic composition with regard to the aesthetic effect ⟨an oil painting . . . over the fire: horsemen ~*ed* apprehensively at midnight —Elizabeth Bowen⟩ ~ *vi* **1 :** to form a group : become a member of a group : BELONG, HARMONIZE ⟨he ~s with Tennyson and Spenser in contrast to Shakespeare and Donne —F.R.Leavis⟩ **2 :** to make well-defined groups of hits on a target
³group \"\ *adj* **1 :** of or relating to a group : belonging to or shared by the members of a group as a whole : COLLECTIVE ⟨an individual is not responsible for ~ acts⟩ ⟨a sad absence of ~ awareness —Julian Huxley⟩ ⟨~ discussion⟩ **2 :** constituting a unit of syntax composed of a word group ⟨*to be in need of* meaning "to need" is a ~ verb⟩ ⟨*impossible-to-be-realized* in "an impossible-to-be-realized wish" is a ~ adjunct⟩ ⟨*man of honor's* in "a man of honor's word" is a ~ genitive⟩
group agglutination *n* : CROSS AGGLUTINATION
group analysis *n* : the application of psychoanalysis to group psychotherapy
group annuity *n* : a pension plan providing annuities at retirement for all eligible persons under a single master contract usu. issued to an employer for the benefit of employees
group banking *n* : a system of control over two or more commercial banks by a holding company
group bonus *n* : an incentive wage divided among a number of workers cooperating on a task in proportion to time worked and rank held by each
group captain *n* : an officer (as in the British Royal Air Force) equivalent in rank to a colonel in the army
group dynamics *n pl but often sing in constr* **1 :** the forces and processes of interaction operating within a relatively small human group **2 :** the study of the forces and processes operating within a relatively small human group esp. within the theoretical framework of the view that the group is a sociological whole with dynamic properties of its own (as organization, stability, and goals) which can be objectively analyzed and accurately measured
grouped columns *n pl* : three or more columns placed upon the same pedestal or otherwise closely associated
¹grou·per \ˈgrüpə(r)\ *n, pl* **groupers** *also* **grouper** [Pg *garoupa*, prob. of AmerInd origin; akin to Galibi *croupy*, a species of fish] **1 :** any of numerous fishes of the family Serranidae esp. of the genera *Epinephelus* and *Mycteroperca* that are typically solitary bottom fishes of warm seas and sometimes attain immense size — compare CABRILLA, HIND **2 :** TRIPLETAIL **3 :** any of several rockfishes (family Scorpaenidae)
²group·er \"\ *n* -s *usu cap* [Oxford *Group* + E *-er*] : a member of the Oxford Group : BUCHMANITE
group house *n* : ROW HOUSE
grouping *n* -s **1 :** the act, manner, or an instance of placing in groups ⟨~ should be considered by teachers . . . and administrators as primarily an instructional problem —Helen Heffernan⟩ ⟨achieve with ~ and composition . . . the impression of a great painting —*Ency. Britannica*⟩ ⟨the ~s of fact and argument and illustration so as to produce a cumulative and mass effect —B.N.Cardozo⟩ **2 a :** an assemblage of individuals grouped in a certain manner (as for utility or artistic effect) or naturally forming a distinct pattern or configuration ⟨jewelry designed to grow in size from a single diamond to a magnificent ~ of diamonds —*Jewelers' Circular-Keystone*⟩ ⟨a new type of population ~ . . . seen wherever a constellation of towns is clustered around a dominating metropolitan center —F.A.Ogg & P.O.Ray⟩ ⟨word ~s peculiar to advertising —W.H.Whyte⟩ ⟨the almost inevitable Vermont ~ of Civil War monument, cannon, and bandstand —*Amer. Guide Series: Vt.*⟩ **b :** pattern of organization or relationship : ALIGNMENT ⟨strict party lines were being replaced by sectional ~s —C.H. Lincoln⟩ ⟨clannish in their internal ~s, they are divided into many organizations —*Amer. Guide Series: Mich.*⟩ **c :** an assemblage of like individuals : GROUP ⟨the writings . . . fall into five well-defined ~s —E.M.Hinton⟩
group insurance *n* : insurance issued upon a group of persons under a single or blanket policy — compare GROUP LIFE INSURANCE
group·ism \ˈgrü,pizəm\ *n* -s : the tendency to think and act as members of a group : the tendency to conform to the cultural pattern of a group at the expense of individualism and cultural diversity ⟨~ . . . rests not on obvious group emergencies but on the vague disquietude of lonely individuals —David Riesman⟩
group·let \ˈgrüplət\ *n* -s : a small group
group life insurance *n* : insurance upon the lives of a number of persons under a blanket policy without medical examination and at low cost
group marriage *n* **1 :** COMMUNAL MARRIAGE **2 :** a system wherein common marital relations exist between a definite group of men and a definite group of women — compare PIRRAURA, PUNALUA
group·ment \ˈgrüpmənt\ *n* -s [F *groupement*, fr. *grouper* to group + *-ment* — more at GROUP] : GROUP; *esp* : a group of military units
group mind *n* **1 :** the beliefs and desires common to a social group as a whole **2 :** a hypothetical psychic unity or collective consciousness of a group of individuals
group practice *also* **group medicine** *n* : medicine practiced by a group of associated physicians (as specialists in different fields) working as partners or as partners and employees
group psychotherapy *n* : psychotherapy in which directive, inspirational, didactic, or analytic means are employed to bring about favorable personality changes in a group of patients; *esp* : psychotherapy in which a therapist leads or guides a group of emotionally ill patients in a discussion and sharing of their personal problems designed to promote relief from emotional conflict and tension and further social adjustment
group rate *n* : a uniform rate charged to or from any one of a group or block of points within a given territory — called also *blanket rate, block rate*
groups *pl of* GROUP, *pres 3d sing of* GROUP
group-specific \ˈ;==ˈ==\ *adj* : having a specific relation to a particular blood group — used of polysaccharides found in red blood cells, tissues, and body fluids and usu. also in bodily discharges; compare ISOHEMAGGLUTINOGEN, NONSECRETOR, SECRETOR
group test *n* : a mental or achievement test (as the Army General Classification Test) designed to be administered to many individuals at once
group therapist *n* : a person who conducts group psychotherapy
group therapy *n* **1 :** therapy in which patients with the same diagnosis (as obesity) are brought together to share their difficulties in group discussions designed to build morale and stimulate interest **2 :** GROUP PSYCHOTHERAPY
group velocity *n* : the velocity with which some definite peculiarity of a composite wave train (as an interference maximum) advances through a medium — compare PHASE VELOCITY
group·wise \ˈgrüp,wīz\ *adv* : with reference to the group : as a group ⟨the problem . . . is to help people see themselves and others ~ —Martin Chworowsky⟩
group work *n* : a technique within the field of social work wherein various groups (as educational and recreational) are guided by an agency leader to more effective personal adjustment and community participation
¹grouse \ˈgrau̇s\ *n, pl* **grouse** *or* **grous·es** [origin unknown] **1 a :** any of numerous birds that constitute the family Tetraonidae, are mostly of medium to rather large size, have a plump body, strong feathered legs, and plumage less brilliant than that of pheasants and generally with reddish brown or other protective color, and include numerous important game birds (as the capercaillie, black grouse, and hazel hen of Europe and Asia or the ruffed grouse, prairie chicken, sage grouse, and others of America) **b** *Brit* : RED GROUSE **2 :** GAZELLE 2
²grouse \"\ *vi* -ED/-ING/-S : to seek or shoot grouse
³grouse \"\ *vi* -ED/-ING/-S [origin unknown] : to complain typically with sustained grumbling ⟨people ~ about excessive taxation, rationing —*Atlantic*⟩ **syn** see COMPLAIN
⁴grouse \"\ *n* -s : COMPLAINT, GROUCH ⟨a temporary outlet for ~s against the party in power —Mollie Panter-Downes⟩
grouse·ber·ry \ˈgrau̇s- —*see* BERRY\ *n* **1 :** CHECKERBERRY 1a **2** *also* **grouse whortleberry** : a blueberry (*Vaccinium scoparium*)
grouse disease *n* : an infectious disease of grouse characterized by hoarseness, cyanosis of the conjunctiva, emaciation, and quick tiring on flying
grouse·less \ˈgrau̇sləs\ *adj* [¹*grouse* + *-less*] : having no grouse
grouse locust *n* : a grasshopper of the family Tetrigidae
¹grou·ser \ˈgrau̇zə(r)\ *n* -s [origin unknown] **1 :** a heavy pointed timber thrust down to serve as an anchor for a floating dredge or similar machine **2 :** one of a set of cleats on a tractor wheel or track for increasing traction
²grous·er \ˈgrau̇sə(r)\ *n* -s [³*grouse* + *-er*] : a person who grouses; *specif* : one who habitually complains or grumbles
¹grout \ˈgrau̇t, *usu* -au̇d·+V\ *n* -s [ME, fr. OE *grūt*; akin to MD *grūte* malt, dregs, MHG *grūz* grain, sand, OE *grytt* grit — more at GRIT (coarse meal)] **1** *archaic* **a :** coarse meal : hulled grain **b grouts** *pl* : OATS **2** *now dial Eng* **a :** a malt infusion before or during fermentation **b :** SMALL BEER **3** *archaic* : porridge of grout or groats **4 :** LEES, DREGS, GROUNDS **5 a** (1) : thin mortar fluid enough to be poured and used for filling in spaces (as the joints of masonry, brickwork, brick or stone block pavements, forced under pressure as into prepacked graded stone to form concrete, into fissures in foundation rock, into railroad ballast or the subgrade, or into the space between tunnel lining and the surrounding earth) (2) : material used for a similar purpose; *specif* : a mixture of portland cement and water applied under pressure during oil-well drilling to prevent contamination of the oil by sealing off undesirable fluids and also to provide a protective wall around the metal casing **b** (1) : a coarse plaster or cement used for coating the wall of a building and usu. studded with small stones after application (2) : a fine plaster or cement used for finishing ceilings **c :** CONCRETE **d :** MORTAR
²grout \"\ *vt* -ED/-ING/-S : to fill up or finish with or as if with grout ⟨the material used in sealing or ~*ing* them —*U. S. War Dept. Technical Manual*⟩
³grout \"\ *vi* -ED/-ING/-S [perh. alter. of obs. E *grewt, grut* dry earth, soil, fr. ME *grut* mud, earth; akin to OE *grūt* grout, *grēot* grit, sand, earth — more at GRIT (sand)] *Brit* : ROOT, GRUB ⟨~*ing* in the grass —Virginia Woolf⟩
grout·er \ˈgrau̇d·ə(r), -au̇tə-\ *n* -s [²*grout* + *-er*] **1 :** a machine for grouting joints **2 :** a worker who operates a grouter
grouting *n* -s **1 :** the process of applying or using grout by flowing it into place by gravity or under pressure **2 :** GROUT 5
grout·ite \ˈgrau̇d·,īt\ *n* -s [Frank F. *Grout* †1958 Am. geologist and mineralogist + E *-ite*] : a mineral $HMnO_2$ consisting of manganese, hydrogen, and oxygen, polymorphous with manganite, and belonging to the diaspore group
grout·man \ˈgrau̇tmən, -,man\ *n, pl* **groutmen** : a worker who mixes grout and fills the joints between pavement blocks or bricks
grouty \ˈgrau̇d·ē\ *adj* -ER/-EST [perh. fr. ¹*grout* + *-y*] : CROSS, SULKY, SULLEN ⟨those old warrior-priests were but gruff and ~ at the best —Herman Melville⟩ ⟨~, bad-tempered, and rude —Al Newman⟩
grouze \ˈgrau̇z\ *vt* -ED/-ING/-S [perh. of imit. origin] *dial Eng* : to chew or crunch noisily
¹grove \ˈgrōv\ *n* -s [ME, fr. OE *grāf*; akin to OE *grǣfa* grove, thicket, and perh. to Norw *greivla* to branch out] **1 a :** a smaller group of trees than a forest often without underwood and planted or growing naturally as if arranged by art : a wood of small extent ⟨a picnic ~⟩ **b** (1) : a planting of fruit or nut trees : ORCHARD ⟨a pecan ~⟩ ⟨a coffee ~⟩; *specif* : a planting of citrus trees ⟨an orange ~⟩ (2) : BED ⟨a ~ of kelp⟩ **2 :** a group resembling a grove ⟨had already set up a ~ of little shelter tents —John Buchan⟩
²grove \"\ *dial Eng var of* GRAVE
³grove \"\ *dial Brit var of* GROOVE
grov·el \ˈgrävəl, ˈgrəv-\ *vi* **groveled** *or* **grovelled**; **groveled** *or* **grovelled**; **groveling** *or* **grovelling** \-v(ə)liŋ\ **grovels** [back-formation fr. ²*groveling*] **1 :** to creep on the earth or with the face to the ground as one's natural gait or manner of locomotion : CRAWL ⟨vampires can walk, rather than ~ like other bats —R.L.Ditmars & A.M.Greenhall⟩ **2 a :** to lie prone, go down on one's knees with the head bent, or drag oneself along with the body prostrate esp. in token of complete subservience or abasement or as an act of humiliation ⟨~*ed* across the floor to kiss the feet of the sultan —*Time*⟩ **b :** to abase or humble oneself : display oneself to be abject : CRINGE ⟨he ~s and is polite to me —O.W.Holmes †1935⟩ ⟨~s in proud self-abasement —V.L.Parrington⟩ **3 :** to take delight in or give oneself over to what is base or unworthy : WALLOW ⟨here is the petty official ~*ing* in sentimentality —James Stern⟩ **syn** see WALLOW
grov·el·er *or* **grov·el·ler** \-v(ə)lə(r)\ *n* -s : a person who grovels
grove·less \ˈgrōvləs\ *adj* : devoid of groves
¹grov·el·ing *or* **grov·el·ling** \ˈgräv(ə)liŋ, ˈgrəv-\ *or* **grov·el·ings** *or* **grov·el·lings** \-ŋz\ *adv* [ME *groveling, grufelinge, grovelings, gruflinges*, fr. *gruf, groffe*, adv., on the face, prone (fr. ON *ā grūfu*) + *-ling, -lings*; akin to ON *grūfa* to grovel, *krjūpa* to creep — more at ON, CREEP] *archaic* : in prostrate position
²groveling *or* **grovelling** \"\ *adj* **1 a :** having the face or body on or toward the ground : not upright : PRONE ⟨the ~ creatures of the woods and fields⟩ **b :** having a creeping or crawling gait or locomotion ⟨the dominant creatures of the Cambrian seas were the . . . ~ arthropods —C.O.Dunbar⟩ **2 a :** ABJECT, SERVILE, CRINGING ⟨at once ~ and arrogant in the most peculiar fashion —Louis Bromfield⟩ ⟨without any ~ appeal for sympathy —Anthony West⟩ **b :** LOW, BASE ⟨who ever entertained so ~ a thought —Henry Fielding⟩
grov·el·ing·ly *or* **grov·el·ling·ly** *adv* : in a groveling manner
grovy \ˈgrōvē\ *adj* -ER/-EST : relating to or resembling a grove : situated in or frequenting groves
grow \ˈgrō\ *vb* **grew** \ˈgrü\ *also dial* **growed** \ˈgrōd\ **grown** \ˈgrōn\ *also dial* **growed**; **growing**; **grows** [ME *growen*, fr. OE *grōwan*; akin to OHG *gruoen, gruowan* to grow, ON *grōa*] *vi* **1 a :** to spring up and come to maturity : have vegetal or animal life : exist as a living organism or one of its parts in a specified place : exist as native : THRIVE ⟨some plants will not ~ in sandy soils⟩ ⟨the mosquitoes . . . ~ in the swamps and marshy areas —Morris Fishbein⟩ ⟨unsightly hair ~s on his face⟩ ⟨immense beds of oysters ~ in the harbor —Joseph Mitchell⟩ ⟨rice ~s in warm countries⟩ **b :** to issue or become attached by or as if by a process of natural growth ⟨depicted with wings ~*ing* from his shoulders⟩ ⟨a plant ~*ing* out of a rock⟩ ⟨the vines *grew* together, concealing the naked stone⟩ **2 a :** to develop by natural processes: as (1) : to increase in size or substance by assimilation of new matter into the living organism ⟨the tree *grew* to an immense size⟩ ⟨the child stopped ~*ing* at an early age⟩ (2) : to increase in size by a natural inorganic process whereby material is added to the surface in such a way as to continue the established regular or periodic structure ⟨crystals, as well as plants, ~ —E.S.Dana⟩ **b :** to increase in any way : EXPAND, GAIN ⟨the wealth and power of the republic *grew*⟩ ⟨the city *grew* by leaps and bounds⟩ ⟨the saw making the woodpile ~ —Meridel Le Sueur⟩ ⟨~s in wisdom⟩; *specif* : to advance intellectually or morally ⟨at 90 he is still ~*ing* and helping others to ~ —H.A.Larrabee⟩ ⟨the subject should enable . . . the college student to ~ on several levels —Marion F. Stewart⟩ **3 a :** RESULT, ORIGINATE ⟨a lot of important business connections have *grown* from friendships between our wives and wives of executives of other companies —W.H.Whyte⟩ — usu. used with *out* ⟨a smile of polite incredulity which *grew* out of . . . ignorance —H.J.Laski⟩ **b :** to come into existence : become established : ARISE ⟨the original settlement . . . had *grown* on the Canberra site —H.W.H. King⟩ — often used with *up* ⟨a wicked practice had *grown* up⟩ ⟨a troublesome situation has *grown* up⟩ **4 a :** to pass by degrees into a state or condition : come to be : develop by degrees : BECOME ⟨*grew* pale at the sight⟩ ⟨have *grown* to like her⟩ ⟨*grew* bald⟩ ⟨the amount of land per person is ~*ing* constantly less —W.P.Webb⟩ ⟨his cold *grew* into pneumonia⟩ **b** *obs* : to come gradually or by degrees ⟨~ this to what adverse issue it can, I will put it in practice —Shak.⟩ **c** (1) : to obtain an increasing influence or command — used with *on* or *upon* ⟨a bad habit ~s on a man⟩ (2) *obs* : PRESUME (3) : to gain steadily in interest or attraction or in one's affection or estimation ⟨this seemingly artless music . . . ~s and ~s the more we listen —Roland Gelatt⟩ ⟨his poetry ~s in one's mind —Delmore Schwartz⟩ — usu. used with *on* or *upon* ⟨her looks were the kind that ~ on a man —Fred Majdalany⟩ **5** *of a ship's cable* : to stretch out : TEND, LEAD ~ *vt* **1 a :** to cause to grow : CULTIVATE, PRODUCE ⟨~ a crop⟩ ⟨~ wheat⟩ ⟨~ calves⟩ ⟨this cheese was *grown* . . . in Nottinghamshire —Joyce Warren⟩ ⟨Algeria ~s good wines —A.J.Liebling⟩ **b :** to let grow on the body : develop on the body ⟨decided to ~ a beard⟩ ⟨this prehistoric animal *grew* a thick protective covering⟩ **2 :** to cover or surround with vegetation of a specified kind ⟨all *grown* up to . . . bushes and grass —Dorothy C. Fisher⟩ ⟨*grown* up with cottonwood and birch —Corey Ford⟩ ⟨the house that was . . . *grown* about with weeds —Donn Byrne⟩ **3 :** DEVELOP 7 ⟨~s a craving to tell the world what he thinks of it —*Spectator*⟩ — **grow on trees** : to be so plentiful as to be easily acquired ⟨I was at Tours, where the girls *grew on trees* —K.S.Alling⟩ ⟨good jobs don't *grow on trees* —James Jones⟩
grow·able \ˈgrōəbəl\ *adj* : capable of being grown
grow·er \-ō(ə)r, -ōə\ *n* -s **1 :** one that grows esp. in a specified way ⟨those trees are fast ~s⟩ **2 :** a person who grows a specified fruit or other product ⟨a trading center for apple ~s⟩ ⟨a supply point for livestock ~s⟩
growing *adj* **1 :** characterized by or displaying vegetal or animal life ⟨a broad window framed in ~ philodendron —*Monsanto Mag.*⟩ **2 :** increasing esp. in number, size, or degree ⟨~ evidence of a world depression —D.M.Fisher⟩ ⟨his ~ reputation for persuasive oratory⟩ ⟨made no attempt to cover the whole of a ~ subject —Harvey Graham⟩ **3 :** relating to or suitable for growth ⟨the ~ season for corn⟩ ⟨good ~ weather⟩ — **grow·ing·ly** *adv*

growing pains *n pl* **1 :** pains in the legs of children caused by fatigue, postural defects, emotional disturbances, or other factors having no demonstrable relation to growth **2 :** the stresses and strains attending the formative period (as of an industry) or any process of rapid or dynamic change or growth ⟨merely natural *growing pains* of a new economy —*Atlantic*⟩ ⟨the country's social and economic *growing pains* —J.H. Huizinga⟩ ⟨our fruit-canning industry . . . is still suffering from its *growing pains* —*Farmer's Weekly (So. Africa)*⟩

growing point *n* **1 :** the undifferentiated end of a plant shoot that is made up of a single apical cell or a group of cells and that produces primary meristematic tissue from which the tissues of the shoot differentiate **2 :** a point at which growth of any kind is generated or has its beginning ⟨the *growing points* of the economy must be invigorated —*Harper's*⟩ ⟨may be the *growing point* of philosophy in our time —C.W. Hendel⟩

growing zone *n* **1 :** a zone in front of the anus in certain annelid worms from which new segments are proliferated **2 :** a region behind the scolex in tapeworms similar in function to the growing zone in annelid worms

¹growl \'grau̇l, *esp before pause or consonant* -au̇əl\ *vb* -ED/-ING/-S [prob. of imit. origin] *vi* **1 a :** RUMBLE ⟨it sounds like your guts are ~*ing* —Joseph Mitchell⟩ ⟨thunder faintly ~*ing* in the distance⟩ ⟨artillery ~*ed* and belched on the horizon —Earle Birney⟩ **b :** to utter a deep guttural threatening sound ⟨the dog ~*ed* at the stranger⟩ **c :** to make or move with a sound resembling or suggestive of the growl of an animal ⟨a truck . . . ~*ed* out onto the road —H.D.Skidmore⟩ ⟨listening to the water ~*ing* past —H.A.Calahan⟩ **2 :** to express oneself in an angry or surly manner : complain angrily : GRUMBLE ⟨hobnobbing together . . . and ~*ing* about the war —Zechariah Chafee⟩ ⟨~*ed* because the place . . . where they always parked, was taken —Greville Texidor⟩ ~ *vt* **:** to express with or by a growl : utter in a harsh, angry, or rasping tone or manner ⟨~*ing* out . . . lyrics in a hoarse contralto —J.S.Wilson b.1913⟩ ⟨~*ing* a deep and hollow roar —J.F.Dobie⟩ ⟨~*ed* out a stern warning⟩

²growl \"\ *n* -S **1 a :** a deep guttural inarticulate sound ⟨backed away as he heard the dog's warning ~⟩ ⟨broken now and then by . . . little bass ~*s* of laughter⟩ ⟨gave a ~ of amusement⟩ ⟨the full-throated ~ of an enraged lion⟩ **b :** a growling or rumbling sound resembling or suggestive of the growl of an animal ⟨the distant ~ of cannon⟩ ⟨the noisy, angry ~ of an aircraft engine —J.N.Bell⟩ **2 :** an utterance made in a harsh, rasping, or angry tone : a muttering complaint ⟨again the ~*s* began in the ranks —F.V.W.Mason⟩ ⟨~ that businessmen have replaced the clergy on governing boards —Perry Miller⟩ ⟨my letter of 31st December was a ~ against you —*Indian Information*⟩ **3 :** FLUTTER-TONGUING

growl·er \-au̇lə(r)\ *n* -S **1 :** one that growls ⟨the man was a notorious ~⟩ **2** *Brit* **:** CLARENCE **3 :** a container (as a can or pitcher) for beer bought by the measure **4 :** a small iceberg or mass of floe ice large enough to be a menace to ships **5 :** an electromagnetic device with two adjustable pole pieces used for finding short-circuited coils and for magnetizing and demagnetizing

growling *adj* **:** marked by a growl ⟨a low ~ voice⟩ ⟨listened to the ~ thunder⟩ — **growl·ing·ly** *adv*

growly \'grau̇lē\ *adj* -ER/-EST **:** resembling a growl ⟨uttered a ~ sound⟩; *also* **:** IRRITABLE

grown \'grōn\ *adj* **1 :** arrived at maturity : FULL-GROWN, MATURED, GROWN-UP ⟨children may do . . . that which would be ridiculous in a ~ maiden —Fred Whishaw⟩ ⟨a ~ man⟩ **2** *of grain* **:** having sprouted before reaping **3 :** roughly conforming to the required curvature in its natural shape — used of a shipbuilding timber of curved pattern **4 a :** cultivated or produced in a specified way or locality — used in combinations ⟨a home*grown* wine⟩ ⟨shade-*grown* tobacco⟩ **b :** overgrown with — used in combinations ⟨a cress-*grown* stream —*Amer. Guide Series: Ark.*⟩ ⟨the terrace . . . had been weed-*grown* for many years —Kathleen Freeman⟩

¹grown-up \'≈¦≈\ *adj* [fr. past part. of *grow up*] **1 :** ADULT ⟨a *grown-up* woman —Hugh Walpole⟩ **2 :** of, for, or characteristic of adults ⟨the only *grown-up* way to keep peace in the world —Leverett Saltonstall⟩ ⟨began reading *grown-up* books at an early age⟩ ⟨insisted on wearing *grown-up* clothes⟩

²grown-up \"\ *n* -S **:** ADULT ⟨the attitude of *grown-ups* has changed —Pamela L. Travers⟩

grown-up·ness \(')≈¦≈nəs\ *n* -ES **:** the quality or state of being grown-up

grow out *vt* **:** to cause to grow toward or arrive at maturity ⟨*grow out* a steer⟩ — **grow out of :** OUTGROW ⟨the boy *grew out of* his clothes⟩ ⟨before Britain *grew out of* tyranny —P.L. Ritzema⟩

grows *pres 3d sing of* GROW

growth \'grōth\ *n* -S [ME (Sc dial.) *grouth*, fr. ON *grōthr*, *grōthi*, fr. *grōa* to grow — more at GROW] **1 a (1) :** stage in the process of growing : SIZE ⟨the river reaches its greatest ~ a few miles above St. Louis⟩ ⟨the tree hasn't got its full ~⟩ : STATURE ⟨give added ~ and dimension to a book —Norman Cousins⟩ **(2) :** full growth ⟨by the looks of him he would be every inch of six feet when he attained his ~ —Archie Binns⟩ **b :** the process of growing: as **(1) :** an increase in the size of an organism or part esp. when involving increase in the amount of protoplasm — compare DEVELOPMENT, DIFFERENTIATION **(2) :** increase in size by a natural inorganic process whereby material is added to the surface in such a way as to continue the established regular or periodic structure ⟨~ or regrowth of mica under the influence of late solutions —*Economic Geology*⟩ **(3) :** a progressive development from lower or simpler to higher or more complex forms of organization ⟨this history . . . history of the ~ of writing —A.N. Whitehead⟩ ⟨the ~ and decay of languages —G.R.Harrison⟩ **(4) :** progressive intellectual or moral advance or development : cultural or spiritual self-enrichment ⟨a lifetime of learning and continuous ~ is required of us —R.H.Wittcoff⟩ ⟨novels provide the basis for ~, experiences which can be rich and full —*Irish Digest*⟩ ⟨learning and ~ are always a result of what the individual brings to the learning situation —H.R.Douglass⟩ ⟨the theory that our native writers suffered from arrested ~ —C.I.Glicksberg⟩ **(5) :** RISE, EMERGENCE ⟨his lifetime encompassed the . . . ~ of the solidly Democratic South —*Current History*⟩ ⟨the first ~ and development of Macedonia . . . into the first of all known powers —George Grote⟩ **(6) :** qualitative or quantitative increase : EXPANSION ⟨the ~ of the oil industry⟩ ⟨the rapid ~ in luxury and sophistication —Carl Van Doren⟩ ⟨the ~ of urban population⟩ ⟨the ~ of illiteracy⟩ **2 a :** something that grows or has grown: as **(1) :** a stand of forest ⟨the road is bordered with close ~*s* of willow —*Amer. Guide Series: La.*⟩ ⟨a young ~ dedicated in 1926 —*Amer. Guide Series: Pa.*⟩ — see OLD GROWTH, SECOND GROWTH **(2) :** a cover of vegetation : VEGETATION ⟨a dense . . . ~ of European grasses which formed a thick sod —P.E.James⟩ ⟨the only other ~ here showing is a very little salt grass —G.R.Stewart⟩ **(3) :** PLANT ⟨this weed is a very noxious ~⟩ **(4) :** a lateral shoot or branch on the main stem of a plant **b :** abnormal proliferation of tissue (as a tumor) **c :** OUTGROWTH, OFFSHOOT ⟨a lovely phrase . . . which is really a ~ from the main tune —Herbert Wiseman⟩ **d :** the result of growth : PRODUCT, EFFECT, DEVELOPMENT ⟨Protestantism was a relatively recent ~⟩ ⟨this was the ~ of habit —Ellen Glasgow⟩ ⟨Virginia City and other Nevada towns were mushroom ~*s* from silver ore —*Dict. of Amer. History*⟩ **3 :** PRODUCTION, CULTIVATION, ORIGIN ⟨goods of foreign ~⟩ ⟨all his fruit and vegetables were of his own ~⟩

growth curve *n* **:** a graphic representation of the relative growth of an organism or population during a sequence of similar-length periods

growth factor *n* **:** a substance (as a vitamin, hormone, antibiotic, or metallic ion) exclusive of those used as sources of energy that when present in minute amounts promotes the growth of an organism — compare GROWTH REGULATOR

growth form *n* **1 a :** a structural category consisting of individuals or species of the same general habit of growth but not necessarily related **b :** a category of plants in Raunkiaer's system based on the degree of protection of their winter buds **2 :** the form assumed by an organism (as a plant) in immediate response to the interaction of a particular environment on its genetic potentialities

growth hormone *n* **1 :** a vertebrate polypeptide hormone that is secreted by the anterior lobe of the pituitary gland and regulates growth **2 :** any of various plant substances (as an auxin or gibberellin) that regulate growth

growth·less \'grōthləs\ *adj* **:** having no growth

growth regulator *or* **growth substance** *n* **:** a substance that affects growth; *esp* **:** a synthetic substance (as naphthaleneacetic acid or dichlorophenoxyacetic acid) that resembles a naturally occurring hormone in producing a specific effect — compare AUXIN, GROWTH FACTOR

growth ring *n* **:** a layer of wood developed during any one continuous growth period; *usu* **:** ANNUAL RING

growth·some \-thsəm\ *adj* **:** conducive to growth : FERTILE ⟨life is greener, more ~ here —Frederic Morton⟩

growth stock *n* **:** investment shares of a company having a steady growth in business and profits over a long period of years

growthy \-thē\ *adj* -ER/-EST **1 :** favorable to growth ⟨the weather is unusually ~ —*Auckland (New Zealand) Weekly News*⟩ **2 :** capable of growth esp. to large size ⟨these bulls are ~ and rugged —*Pacific Stockman*⟩

grow up *vi* **:** to grow toward or arrive at full stature or physical or mental maturity ⟨just before she *grows up*, her mother tells her all about the . . . changes that are coming to her —Valeria H. Parker⟩ ⟨middle-aged children who had refused to *grow up* —Cyril Connolly⟩ ⟨*grew up* . . . in Brooklyn, getting good grades in school —Barbara B. Jamison⟩

growze \'grau̇z\ *var of* GROUZE

groyne *var of* GROIN

gro·zart \'grōzə(r)t\ *var of* GROSET

gro·zer *var of* GROSER

gro·zing iron \'grōziŋ-\ *n* [part trans. of D *gruisijzer*, fr. *gruizen* (dial. *groezen*) to crush, trim glass (fr. *gruis* gravel, fragments, fr. MD *gruus*) + *yzer* iron; akin to MLG *grūs*, *grōs* crushed stone, gravel, OE *grēot* grit — more at GRIT (sand)] *archaic* **:** a steel tool for cutting glass

groz·ny \'grȯznē\ *adj, usu cap* [fr. *Grozny*, U.S.S.R.] **:** of or from the city of Grozny, U.S.S.R. **:** of the kind or style prevalent in Grozny

GR-S \¦jē¦är¦es\ *also* **GR-S rubber** *n* [government rubber + styrene] **:** any of a class of general-purpose synthetic rubbers that are made by copolymerizing emulsions of butadiene and styrene commonly at a temperature of either 122°F or 41°F and that are used esp. in tires — see COLD RUBBER

gru *var of* ³GRUE

¹grub \'grəb\ *vb* **grubbed; grubbed; grubbing; grubs** [ME *grobben, grubben*; akin to MD *grobben* to scramble, scrape, OHG *grubilōn* to dig, search, ON *gryfja* hole, pit, ditch, OE *grafan* to dig, grave — more at GRAVE (dig)] *vt* **1 :** to remove roots or stumps from : clear or break up the surface of by digging ⟨loggers cut off the virgin timber and farmers *grubbed* out their clearings —R.A.Billington⟩ ⟨women and children helped to ~ the land —E.H.Collis⟩ **2 a :** to dig up by the roots : root out by digging ⟨a palmetto was *grubbed* from the site —*Amer. Guide Series: Fla.*⟩ ⟨*grubbing* up bulbs and edible roots —E.J.Sawyer⟩ ⟨*grubbing* out stumps might be a long and costly business —*Amer. Guide Series: Minn.*⟩ **b :** to extract esp. by digging ⟨followed by sappers who *grubbed* up the mines —J.F.C.Fuller⟩ ⟨*grubbed* the mote as well as I could by the deficient light —Joseph Furphy⟩ **c :** to bring to light, assemble, or acquire by plodding, painful, or tedious effort ⟨barely *grubbing* a subsistence —Daniel Friedenberg⟩ ⟨the task of *grubbing* out new data —J.D.Hicks⟩ ⟨seems to have *grubbed* his materials together —A.S.Stein⟩ **3 :** to provide with food : FEED ⟨five children to ~⟩ ~ *vi* **1 a :** to dig in or under the ground esp. for an object that is difficult to reach or extricate ⟨*grubbing* in the earth for potatoes⟩ ⟨*grubbed* for clams on the mud flats⟩ ⟨scholars will ~ in the ruins for . . . records and fragments —W.P.Webb⟩ **b :** to search about esp. laboriously as if by digging : RUMMAGE ⟨*grubbed* hopelessly about the cupboard shelves —Arthur Morrison⟩ ⟨love to ~ through junk shops —Leo Lerman⟩ ⟨*grubbed* in the countryside for food and fuel —*Lamp*⟩ ⟨to ~ for origins is none of my business —Clive Bell⟩ **2 :** to lead a laborious or a drearily plodding life : TOIL, DRUDGE ⟨*grubbing* along from day to day⟩ ⟨have to begin *grubbing* all over again —Ellen Glasgow⟩ ⟨folks who ~ for money —James Street⟩ **3 :** to take food : EAT ⟨time to ~⟩ **syn** see DIG

²grub \"\ *n* -S [ME *grobbe, grubbe*, fr. *grobben, grubben*, v.] **1 :** a soft thick wormlike larva of an insect (as a beetle) **2 a :** a dull unattractive person : DRUDGE **b :** a person of grubby or slovenly appearance or of unpleasant or ill-bred manners **3 :** FOOD, VICTUALS ⟨a pot of coffee on the fire and warm ~ —F.B.Gipson⟩ **4 :** a root or stump in the ground

grub ax *n* **:** a mattock used in grubbing

grub·ber \'grəbə(r)\ *n* -S [ME, fr. *grubben* to grub + *-er*] **1 :** one that grubs: as **a :** one that digs in the ground ⟨controlling her spinning maids and the ~*s* digging in the walled garden —Sinclair Lewis⟩ **b :** a laborious or plodding worker : DRUDGE ⟨the private browsing grounds of historical ~*s*⟩ **c :** MONEY-GRUBBER ⟨the ~*s* . . . almost unceasingly preoccupied with money —*New Republic*⟩ **d (1) :** a hand tool (as a grub ax) for use in grubbing **(2)** *Brit* **:** a cultivator that breaks up the surface of land by digging : ²CHISEL 2 **e (1) :** a person who grubs up trees, stumps, or brush **(2) :** an implement (as a grub hook) for grubbing up trees, stumps, or brush **2 :** BONEFISH 1

grub·bi·ly \-bəlē, -li\ *adv* **:** in a grubby manner ⟨~ dirty and poorly dressed —Cabell Phillips⟩

grub·bi·ness \-bēnəs, -bin-\ *n* -ES **:** the state of being grubby: as **a :** the condition of being dirty, grimy, or slovenly : grubby look ⟨her occasional appearances in bare feet and her general look of ~ —*Life*⟩ **b :** SORDIDNESS, MEANNESS ⟨the ~ of being poor —Willa Cather⟩

grub·ble \'grəbəl\ *vb* -ED/-ING/-S [prob. alter. (influenced by ¹*grub*) of *grabble*] *archaic* **:** GROPE

grub·by \'grəbē, -bi\ *adj* -ER/-EST [²*grub* + *-y*] **1** *chiefly dial* **a :** small and incompletely formed **b :** DWARFISH, STUNTED **2 :** infested with fly maggots **3 :** dirty, shabby, or slovenly in condition or appearance : GRIMY, MEAN ⟨their ~ little fingers —Roderick Finlayson⟩ ⟨colorless face, hair in curlers, clothes as ~ as the fog —Edith C. Rivett⟩ ⟨streets that looked as parched and ~ as I was —Thomas Wood †1950⟩ ⟨felt particularly ~ and unshaven —Robert Keable⟩ **4 :** low, sordid, or ignoble in character : BASE, CONTEMPTIBLE ⟨the pamphleteer's ~ motives —Albert Lynd⟩ ⟨a ~ lot of tax collectors, mortgage makers, moneylenders —J.R.Newman⟩ ⟨a ~ man of pleasure —C.J.Rolo⟩

grub hoe *or* **grubbing hoe** *n* **1 :** a heavy hoe for grubbing **2 :** GRUB AX

grub hook *n* **:** an implement resembling a plow for uprooting stumps

grub·less \-bləs\ *adj* **:** lacking food

grubroot \'≈,≈\ *n* **:** a blazing star (*Chamaelirium luteum*) with small white star-shaped flowers in a narrow raceme

grubs *pres 3d sing of* GRUB, *pl of* GRUB

grub screw *n* **:** a small headless screw that is slotted at one end to receive a screwdriver and when placed in a continuous threaded hole between two adjacent pieces prevents lateral movement

¹grubstake \'≈,≈\ *n* [²*grub* (*food*) + *stake*; fr. the lender's staking or risking the provisions so furnished] **1 :** supplies or funds furnished to a mining prospector on promise of a share in his discoveries **2 :** material assistance (as a gift, loan, advance) provided for a person in difficult circumstances or for the launching of an enterprise or project ⟨the ex-governor promised a . . . ~ for the unemployed —*Current Biog.*⟩ ⟨needed a ~ or he wouldn't have taken the job —Ross Santee⟩ ⟨meant to leave Cincinnati as soon as he could get a ~ —Arthur Krock⟩

²grubstake \"\ *vt* **:** to provide with a grubstake ⟨it is the public which pays . . . for the handsome profit to those who have *grubstaked* the candidates —P.H.Douglas⟩

grub·stak·er \"ə(r)\ *n* **1 :** one that gives a grubstake **2 :** one that receives a grubstake

grub street \'grəb-\ *n, usu cap G&S* [after *Grub Street* (now Milton Street), London, formerly inhabited by literary hacks] **:** the world or category of usu. mediocre, needy, and disdained writers who write for hire : the world of literary hacks ⟨*Grub Street* compilers —H.R.Warfel⟩ ⟨the translator . . . knows he'll always live on *Grub Street* —Richard Winston⟩

grubworm \'≈,≈\ *n* **:** GRUB

¹grudge \'grəj\ *vb* -ED/-ING/-S [ME *gruggen, grudgen*, alter. of *grucchen, grutchen*, fr. OF *grucier, groucier*, of Gmc origin; akin to MHG *grogezen* to howl, lament] *vi* **:** COMPLAIN, GRUMBLE ⟨let us have parties and our friends in, and never *grudged* —Rose Macaulay⟩ ~ *vt* **:** to be unwilling to give or allow or to give or allow with reluctance or with resentment : BEGRUDGE ⟨~*s* you every morsel of food you eat —William Thornton⟩ ⟨surely you do not ~ him his superiority —G.B. Shaw⟩ ⟨you come to ~ even the sun for shining —Virginia Woolf⟩

²grudge \"\ *n* -S *often attrib* [ME *grugge*, fr. *gruggen*, v.] **:** a feeling of deep-seated resentment or ill will ⟨personal enemies against whom one has a ~ —R.F.Barton⟩ ⟨held no ~ against any . . . who had misused him —Willa Cather⟩ ⟨a ~ fence⟩ ⟨as we had never liked each other our collision would have elements of a ~ match —A.W.Turnbull⟩ ⟨fiction's ~ fights and revenges —Bernard De Voto⟩ **syn** see MALICE

grudge·ful \-fəl\ *adj* **:** harboring a grudge : full of resentment

grudge·less \-ləs\ *adj* **:** free of grudges or resentment

grudging *adj* **1 :** that grudges : UNWILLING, RELUCTANT : ILLIBERAL, UNGENEROUS ⟨conceived in a surly and ~ spirit —A.L.Guérard⟩ ⟨merit a larger recognition than has been accorded by a ~ posterity —V.L.Parrington⟩ **2 :** that is grudged : given, accorded, or permitted reluctantly, unwillingly, or stintingly : PARSIMONIOUS ⟨the basic biological sciences are given ~ governmental support —L.E.Hoyme⟩ ⟨his slow and ~ return to favor of a sort —*Encounter*⟩ ⟨lived on a ~ allowance from her father-in-law —G.F.Whicher⟩ — **grudg·ing·ly** *adv*

grudg·ing·ness *n* -ES **:** the quality or state of being grudging

¹grue \'grü\ *vi* -ED/-ING/-S [fr. earlier *grow*, fr. ME *gruen, growen*, prob. fr. MD *grūwen*; akin to OHG *ingrūēn* to shiver, shudder, and prob. to OE *grēot* sand — more at GRIT] *now chiefly dial* **:** to shiver or shudder esp. with fear or cold ⟨exposed to the gruesome so extensively . . . we simply don't ~ any more —John Crosby⟩

²grue \"\ *n* -S **1 :** a fit of shivering : SHIVER ⟨the sound of wind in the rigging . . . gave him the chills and the ~*s* —R.B. Robertson⟩ ⟨impossible to read without a certain cold ~ —S.V.Benét⟩ **2 :** gruesome quality or effect ⟨a mystery novel . . . resolved with true ~ —Anthony Boucher⟩ ⟨serves the chilliest ~ with perfect elegance —J.S.Sandoe⟩

³grue \"\ *n* -S [ME] *now chiefly Scot* **:** PARTICLE, BIT ⟨hasn't a ~ of sense⟩

⁴grue \"\ *n* -S [origin unknown] *chiefly Scot* **:** thin floating ice : SNOW

gru·el \'grüəl, -ü̇əl *also* -ü̇l, *chiefly Brit* ¦(,)il\ *n* -S [ME *grewel*, fr. MF *gruel*, fr. OF, of Gmc origin; akin to OE *grūt* grout — more at GROUT] **1 :** a liquid food made by boiling a cereal (as cornmeal, oatmeal, flour) in water or milk : thin porridge **2** *chiefly Brit* **:** PUNISHMENT, MEDICINE; *sometimes* **:** DEATH ⟨the Labor rank and file took their ~ wonderfully well —*Spectator*⟩

¹gru·el·ing *or* **gru·el·ling** *pronunc at* GRUEL + iŋ *or* ēŋ\ *n* -S [fr. gerund of obs. E *gruel* to punish, fr. *gruel*, n.] *Brit* **:** a severe beating or punishment : LICKING ⟨improved pastures . . . took a ~ from an adverse season —*Sydney (Australia) Bull.*⟩

²grueling *or* **gruelling** \"\ *adj* [fr. pres. part. of obs. E *gruel*, v.] **:** trying or taxing to the point of exhaustion : making severe demands : PUNISHING ⟨a ~ race⟩ ⟨delivering them to the . . . laboratories for ~ tests —*Monsanto Mag.*⟩ ⟨the labor that goes into building these terraces . . . is ~ —M.J.Herskovits⟩

gru·el·ly *pronunc at* GRUEL + ē *or* i\ *adj* **:** having the consistency of gruel : like gruel

gruen·ling·ite \'grünliŋ,īt, -rēn-\ *n* -S [G *grünlingit*, fr. Friedrich *Grünling* †1919 Ger. mineralogist + G *-it* -ite] **:** a mineral Bi_4TeS_3 consisting of sulfide and telluride of bismuth

gru·es \'grü(,)ēz\ *n pl, cap* [NL, pl. of *Grus*] **:** a suborder of Gruiformes consisting of the cranes, limpkins, trumpeters, rails, and a few chiefly extinct related forms

grue·some *also* **grew·some** \'grüsəm\ *adj, sometimes* -ER/-EST [*gruesome* alter. (influenced by ¹*grue*) of earlier *grewsome*, *growsome*; *grewsome* alter. of obs. E *growsome*, fr. *grow* (later, *grue*) + E *-some*] **:** inspiring horror or repulsion : FEARFUL, GRISLY, HIDEOUS ⟨~ scenes of battle and death —E.J.Fitzgerald⟩ ⟨a ~ little laugh⟩ ⟨the ~ details of a murder⟩

grue·some·ly *adv* **:** in a gruesome manner

grue·some·ness *n* -ES **:** the quality or state of being gruesome

¹gruff \'grəf\ *adj* -ER/-EST [fr. earlier *grof, groiff*, fr. D *grof*, fr. MD; akin to OHG *grob, gerob* thick, coarse, *hruf* pock, scurf — more at DANDRUFF] **1** *now chiefly Scot* **:** having a coarse texture : COARSE-GRAINED **2 :** rough or stern in manner, speech, or aspect : SEVERE, HARSH, UNGRACIOUS ⟨a ~ burly man⟩ ⟨~ of manner and slow of speech —Ross Annett⟩ ⟨gave a ~, uneasy laugh —W.H.Wright⟩ ⟨covered his . . . friendly nature with a ~ exterior —Bruce Bliven b. 1889⟩ **3 :** deep and harsh : low-pitched and rough or hoarse ⟨spoke in a series of ~ barks —Dorothy Sayers⟩ ⟨heard the ~ voice of her father raised in anger —Christopher Bloom⟩ **syn** see BLUFF

²gruff \"\ *vt* -ED/-ING/-S **:** to utter in a gruff voice or manner ⟨"hurry it up," he ~*ed* at the hose tender —Wirt Williams⟩ ⟨~*ed*: "This is the first time I've ever been called a handmaiden" —*Time*⟩

gruff·ly *adv* **:** in a gruff manner

gruff·ness *n* -ES **:** the quality or state of being gruff

gruffs \'grəfs\ *n pl* [pl. of obs. E *gruff*, fr. ¹*gruff*] **:** the tough parts not easily reducible to powder that remain in the process of powdering drugs — called also *tailings*

gru·gru \'grü(,)grü\ *n* -S [AmerSp (Puerto Rico) *grugrú*, of Cariban origin; akin to Yao *grugru*, lit., basket made of grugru] **1** *also* **grugru palm** *or* **gri-gri** \'grē(,)grē\ **:** any of several tropical American spiny palms (as the West Indian *Acrocomia aculeata* and the Brazilian *A. sclerocarpa*) **2** *or* **grugru grub** *also* **grugru worm :** a large edible grub that is the larva of certain tropical American weevils (genus *Rhynchophorus*) and that develops in and feeds on the pith of coconut and other palm trees and sometimes sugarcane

gru·idae \'grüə,dē\ *n pl, cap* [NL, fr. *Grus*, type genus + *-idae*] **:** a family (order Gruiformes) of long-legged wading birds comprising the cranes

gru·iform \-ə,fȯrm\ *adj* [in sense 1, fr. L *grus* crane + E *-iform*; in sense 2, fr. NL *Gruiformes* — more at GRUS] **1 :** resembling a crane **2 :** of or relating to the Gruiformes

gru·ifor·mes \,≈≈'fȯr,mēz\ *n pl, cap* [NL, fr. *Grus* + *-iformes*] **:** a nearly cosmopolitan order of birds that are typically marsh-dwelling and wading birds with long legs, neck, and bill and rather heavy flight and that include the cranes, rails and coots, bustards, and a number of related tropical birds — see CARIAMA

gru·ine \'grü,īn, -üən\ *adj* [L *grus* crane + E *-ine*] **:** belonging to or resembling the cranes

gruing *pres part of* GRUE

gru·lla \'grüyə\ *also* **gru·llo** \-ü(,)yō\ *n* -S [MexSp, fr. Sp *grulla* crane, prob. alter. of OSp *gruya, grúa*, fr. L *grus*; fr. its crane color] *Southwest* **:** a mouse-dun horse

grum \'grəm\ *adj* **grummer; grummest** [prob. blend of *grim* and *glum*] **:** MOROSE, GLUM, SOUR, SURLY ⟨a very ~ countenance —Mary S. Watts⟩ — **grum·ly** *adv* — **grum·ness** *n* -ES

¹grum·ble \'grəmbəl\ *vb* **grumbled; grumbled; grumbling** \-b(ə)liŋ\ **grumbles** [prob. modif. of MF *grommeler*, fr. OF *grumeler*, fr. *gromer*, fr. MD *grommen*; akin to MLG *grummen* to grumble, OHG umbe*grummōn* to gnaw, *grimm* savage — more at GRIM] *vi* **1 :** to mutter in discontent : express dissatisfaction esp. in a low harsh voice and surly manner : COMPLAIN ⟨*grumbling* about no jobs, and no grub —Richard Llewellyn⟩ ⟨*grumbled* at her, continually muttering complaints —Kenneth Roberts⟩ **2 a :** to make low indistinct noises : GROWL **b :** to make a low heavy rumbling sound ⟨thunder *grumbled* in the distance⟩ ⟨heavy traffic *grumbling* along⟩ ⟨the anchor chain . . . began to ~ aboard —Victor Canning⟩ ~ *vt* **:** to express or utter with grumbling ⟨consumers *grumbled* their endless . . . complaints —B.F.Fairless⟩ ⟨*grumbled* his annoyance⟩ **syn** see COMPLAIN

²grumble \"\ *n* -S **1 a :** the act of expressing discontent esp. by muttering : COMPLAINT ⟨a final ~ . . . that the best part of this book has long been available at a much cheaper rate —*Times Lit. Supp.*) **b :** a cause or reason for grumbling ⟨the high cost of living was his daily ~⟩ **2 :** GROWL, RUMBLE ⟨creak and ~ of heavy trucks —Virginia A. Oakes⟩

grum·bler \-b(ə)lə(r)\ *n* -s **:** one that grumbles

grumbling *n* -s [fr. gerund of ¹*grumble*] **1 :** a mutter of discontent **:** COMPLAINT ⟨the subject of general ~ —*Collier's Yr. Bk.*⟩ **2 :** a growling or rumbling noise ⟨these whooshings and ~s . . . were apt to punctuate any time of the day —J.M. Brinnin⟩

grum·bling·ly *adv* [fr. pres. part. of ¹*grumble* + *-ly*] **:** in a grumbling manner

grume \'grüm\ *n* -s [F *grume, grumeau,* fr. MF *grumeau,* fr. OF, fr. L *grumus* hillock, pile of dirt — more at CRUMB] **:** a thick viscid fluid; *esp* **:** a clot of blood

gru·mi·cha·ma *also* **gru·mi·xa·ma** \,grümə'shämə\ *n* -s [modif. of Pg *grumixama, grumuchama*] **:** a Brazilian plant of the genus *Eugenia*; *esp* **:** a low-growing tree (*E. dombeyi* or *E. brasiliensis*) with glossy leaves and white flowers that is sometimes cultivated in mild climates for its dark red thin-skinned fruit which resembles the sweet cherry in appearance and flavor

grum·ly \'grəmli\ *adj* -ER/-EST [prob. fr. obs. E *grummel* sediment, dregs (prob. of Scand origin) + E *-y*; akin to Sw *grummel* sediment, dregs] *now chiefly Scot* **:** turbid and troubled ⟨cold and watery grew the wind and ~ grew the sea —*Sir Patrick Spens*⟩

¹**grum·met** \'grəmət\ *n* -s [MF *gromet* cabin boy, servant — more at GOURMAND] **1** *also* **grom·et** \",'gräm-\ **:** a cabin boy on a ship **2** *now dial Brit* **:** an awkward lad

²**grummet** *var of* GROMMET

gru·mose \'grü,mōs\ *adj* [*grumous* + *-ose*] **:** formed of clustered grains or granules

gru·mous \-məs\ *adj* [*grume* + *-ous*] **1 :** resembling or containing grume **:** THICK, CLOTTED ⟨~ blood⟩ **2 :** GRUMOSE

¹**grump** \'grəmp\ *n* -s [fr. obs. E *grumps* snubs, prob. of imit. origin] **1 grumps** *pl* **:** a fit of ill humor or sulkiness ⟨get out of one's seclusive ~s —H.A.Overstreet⟩ **2 :** a person given to complaining **:** a sulky, ill-humored, or querulous person ⟨she's such a ~ lately —Mary Manning⟩

²**grump** \"\ *vb* -ED/-ING/-S *vi* **1 :** SULK ⟨just ~ed around the house —Robie Macauley⟩ **2 :** GRUMBLE, COMPLAIN ⟨~ed about the weather⟩ ⟨swore and stamped and ~ed —G.W. Brace⟩ ~ *vt* **:** to utter in a grumpy manner

¹**grumph** \'grəm(p)f\ *n* -s [imit.] *chiefly Scot* **:** GRUNT

²**grumph** \"\ *vb* -ED/-ING/-S *chiefly Scot* **:** GRUMP

grumph·ie \-m(p)fi, -mpi\ *n* -s [¹*grumph* + *-ie*] *chiefly Scot* **:** PIG; *specif* **:** SOW

grump·i·ly \'grəmpəlē, -li\ *adv* **:** in a grumpy manner

grump·i·ness \-pēnəs, -pin-\ *n* -ES **:** the quality or state of being grumpy

grump·ish \'grəmpish, -pēsh\ *adj* [¹*grump* + *-ish*] **:** GRUMPY

¹**grumpy** \'grəmpē, -pi\ *adj* -ER/-EST [¹*grump* + *-y*] **:** moodily cross **:** SURLY, ILL-HUMORED ⟨don't be surprised if the driver is ~ and rude —T.H.Fielding⟩

²**grumpy** \"\ *n* -ES **:** a grumpy person

¹**grun** \'grün, 'grən\ *vb* **grun; grun; grunning; gruns** [by alter.] *dial Brit* **:** ¹GRIND

²**grun** \"\ *dial Brit var of* GROUND

grund·riss \'grünt,ris\ *n, pl* **grundris·se** \-sə\ *usu cap* [G, fr. *grund* basis, foundation (fr. OHG *grunt* ground, bottom) + *riss* drawing, fr. OHG *riz* letter of the alphabet; akin to OHG *rīzan* to tear, write — more at GROUND, WRITE] **:** a comprehensive and systematic outline esp. of a science ⟨a severely technical *grundriss* of the many interrelated fields —L.M. Hollander⟩

¹**grundt·vig·ian** \(')grünt¦vigēən\ *adj, usu cap* [Nikolai F.S. *Grundtvig* †1872 Dan. theologian and poet + E *-ian*] **:** of or relating to Grundtvigians or Grundtvigianism

²**grundtvigian** \"\ *n* -s *usu cap* **:** an adherent or advocate of Grundtvigianism

grundt·vig·ian·ism \-ə,nizəm\ *n, usu cap* **:** a religious movement among Danish Lutherans that arose out of the activities of Nikolai Grundtvig in behalf of the principles of greater religious freedom for both laity and clergy and of the authority of the living Christ as opposed to formal creeds

grun·dy \'grəndē, -di\ *n* -ES *usu cap* [by shortening] **:** MRS. GRUNDY ⟨prudes in gumshoes and *Grundies* with head colds —D.C.Peattie⟩

grun·dy·ism \-dē,izəm, -di,iz-\ *n* -s *usu cap* **:** a narrow prudish intolerant conventionality esp. as to the proprieties

grun·dy–swal·low \'grəndē,==, -di-\ *n* [by folk etymology] **:** ¹GROUNDSEL

grü·ner·ite *or* **gru·ner·ite** \'grünə,rīt\ *n* -s [G *grünerit,* fr. E.L.*Grüner* 19th cent. German, who analyzed it + G *-it* -ite] **:** a variety of amphibole $Fe_7Si_8O_{22}(OH)_2$

grun·ion \'grənyən\ *n* -s [prob. fr. Sp *gruñón* grunter, fr. *gruñir* to grunt, fr. L *grunnire*] **:** a silversides (*Leuresthes tenuis*) of the California coast notable for the regularity with which it comes inshore to spawn at the time of a nearly full moon

grun·stane \'grənz,tān, -n,st-\ *chiefly Scot var of* GRINDSTONE

¹**grunt** \'grənt\ *vb* -ED/-ING/-S [ME *grunten, gronten,* fr. OE *grunnettan,* freq. of *grunian, grunnian*; of imit. origin like OHG *grunnizōn* to grunt, *grunzen* to grunt, ON *krytja* to murmur, L *grunnire* (OL *grundire*) to grunt, Gk *gry* grunt, *gryzein* to grunt, grumble] *vi* **1 a :** to make the natural throat noise of a hog **b :** to make a similar sound ⟨ferries ~*ing* . . . on the river —Robert Henderson⟩ ⟨only ~*ed* in answer —Kenneth Roberts⟩ **2** *dial* **:** to groan and complain **:** GRUMBLE ~ *vt* **1 :** to express with a grunt ⟨~*ed* what might have been assent —S.E.White⟩ ⟨~*ed* his approval —Hugh Walpole⟩ **2 :** to utter in a short, sharp, or surly manner ⟨~*ed* a few ungracious words in reply⟩

²**grunt** \"\ *n* -s **1 a :** the deep short sound characteristic of a hog **b :** a similar sound ⟨a ~ of satisfaction —Sherwood Anderson⟩ ⟨gave an offended ~ —Carolyn Hannay⟩ **2** [so called fr. the noise it makes when taken from the water] **:** any of numerous chiefly tropical marine percoid fishes of the family Pomadasidae related to the snappers — see FRENCH GRUNT, GRAY GRUNT, WHITE GRUNT, YELLOW GRUNT **3** [so called fr. the noise it makes when steaming] *chiefly New Eng* **:** a dessert made by dropping biscuit dough on top of boiling berries and covering and steaming ⟨blackberry ~⟩ **4** [prob. so called fr. the noise the helper emits under the load] **:** a groundman who assists in the erection of power lines

grunt·er \-tə(r)\ *n* -s [ME *gruntare,* fr. *grunten* + *-are, -er* -er] **1 :** one that grunts; *specif* **:** HOG **2 :** any of various fishes which make a grunting noise: as **a :** GRUNT **b :** DRUM; *esp* **:** FRESHWATER DRUM **c :** either of two sea breams of southern Africa **3 :** a horse subject to grunting

¹**grunting** *n* -s [ME, fr. gerund of *grunten*] **1 :** the act or an instance of grunting ⟨groanings and ~s on all sides⟩ ⟨a lot of ~ from the guys on crutches —R.O.Bowen⟩ **2 :** abnormal respiration in a horse marked by a laryngeal sound emitted when it is struck or moved suddenly — compare ROARING

²**grunting** *adj* [fr. pres. part. of ¹*grunt*] **:** sounding like a grunt **:** resembling a grunt ⟨the breathing is shallow and ~ —Morris Fishbein⟩ ⟨a ~ mirthless laugh —Barnaby Conrad⟩ — **grunting·ly** *adv*

¹**grun·tle** \'grəntᵊl, *dial Brit* " *or* 'grün-\ *vb* -ED/-ING/-S [ME *gruntlen,* freq. of *grunten* to grunt — more at GRUNT] *vi, now dial Brit* **:** GRUNT, GRUMBLE ~ *vt* [back-formation fr. *disgruntle*] **:** to put in good humor **:** SATISFY, SOOTHE, PLACATE ⟨were *gruntled* with a good meal and good conversation —W.P.Webb⟩ ⟨the warden was far from *gruntled* to find that the villagers had . . . pinched all the timber —Emrys Hughes⟩ ⟨was *gruntling* the cats —Christopher Morley⟩ — compare DISGRUNTLE

²**grun·tle** \'grəntᵊl\ *n* -s **1** *chiefly Scot* **:** the snout of a pig **2** *chiefly Scot* **:** FACE

grunt·ling \'grəntliŋ\ *n* -s [¹*grunt* + *-ling*] **:** a young pig

grup·pet·to \grü'ped·(,)ō\ *n, pl* **gruppet·ti** \-(,)ē\ [It, lit., small group, dim. of *gruppo*] **:** a 16th century musical ornamentation having the character of a trill

grup·po \'grü(,)pō\ *n, pl* **grup·pi** \-pē\ [It, group — more at GROUP] **:** GRUPPETTO

grus \'grüs, 'grəs\ *n, cap* [NL, fr. L, crane; akin to Lith *gervė* crane — more at CRANE] **:** the type genus of Gruidae consisting of the typical cranes

grush·ie \'grəshi\ *adj* [alter. of ¹*gross* + *-ie*] *Scot* **:** THRIVING

gruss \'grüs\ *n* -ES [G *grus,* fr. LG, fr. MLG *grūs, grōs*; akin to OE *grēot* grit — more at GRIT] **:** a rock that is finely granulated but not decomposed by weathering

¹**grutch** \'grəch, -ü-\ *vb* -ED/-ING/-ES [ME *grucchen, grutchen* — more at GRUDGE] *now chiefly dial* **:** MURMUR, COMPLAIN

²**grutch** \"\ *n* -ES [ME *gruch, grucche,* fr. *grucchen,* v.] *now dial* **:** GRUDGE

grutten *past part of* GREET

gru·yère cheese \(')grü¦yə(ə)r-, (')grē¦(y)|, |eə-\ *also* **gruyère** *n* -s *usu cap G* [fr. *Gruyère* district, Fribourg canton, Switzerland, where it was orig. made] **1 :** a pressed whole-milk cheese of a pale yellow color and nutty flavor and usu. with small holes **2 :** a process cheese made in small forms and wrapped in foil

gryl·lid \'grilad\ *n* -s [NL *Gryllidae*] **:** a member of the Gryllidae **:** CRICKET

gryl·li·dae \-lə,dē\ *n pl, cap* [NL, fr. *Gryllus,* type genus + *-idae*] **:** a family of insects (order Orthoptera) consisting of the crickets

gryl·lo·blat·to·dea \,grilō(,)bla'tōdēə\ *n pl, cap* [NL, fr. *Grylloblatta,* a genus of insects (fr. *gryllo-* — fr. L *gryllus* cricket — + L *blatta* cockroach) + *-odea*] **:** a small extremely primitive suborder of Orthoptera often considered a separate order and comprising a few soft-bodied unpigmented wingless insects with long cerci and antennae and commonly no eyes or ocelli that occur near snow in mountains of western No. America and Japan and constitute a single family

gryl·lo·tal·pa \-lə'talpə\ *n, cap* [NL, fr. *gryllo-* (fr. L *gryllus* cricket) + L *talpa* mole] **:** a genus (the type of the family Gryllotalpidae) of large burrowing insects comprising the mole crickets that are related to the true crickets but have the forelimbs modified for digging

gryl·lus \'griləs\ *n* [NL, fr. L, cricket, grasshopper, a kind of comic figure, fr. Gk *gryllos* Egyptian dance, performer of an Egyptian dance, comic figure, caricature] **1** *cap* **:** a genus (the type of the family Gryllidae) of crickets once construed as including all known crickets but now restricted to certain typical Old World forms — compare ACHETA **2** *pl* **gryl·li** \-i,lī\ [L] **:** a comic combination of animals or of animal and human forms in Greco-Roman glyptic art esp. in intaglios

gryllus 2

gry·phaea \grə'fēə, grī'-\ *n, cap* [NL, fr. L *gryphus* or *gryph-, gryps* griffin — more at GRIFFIN] **1 :** a genus of fossil mollusks related to the oyster but having the left valve arched with an incurved beak and the right valve flat **2** *in some classifications* **:** CRASSOSTREA — **gryph·ae·oid** \'grifē,ȯid\ *adj*

gryphon *var of* GRIFFIN

gry·po·sis \grə'pōsəs, grī'-\ *n, pl* **grypo·ses** \ō,sēz\ [LL, fr. LGk *grypōsis,* fr. Gk *grypousthai* to become hooked (fr. *grypos* hooked, curved) + *-sis* — more at GRIFFIN] **:** abnormal curvature esp. of the fingernail

grys·bok \'grās,bäk, -rīs-\ *also* **grys·buck** \-,bək\ *n, pl* **grysbok** *also* **grysboks** [Afrik *grysbok,* fr. *grys* gray (fr. MD *grîs*) + *bok* male antelope] **:** a small reddish antelope (*Raphicerus melanotis*) of southern Africa

gs *abbr* gauss

GS *abbr* **1** general schedule **2** general secretary **3** general semantics **4** general service **5** general sessions **6** general staff **7** general superintendent **8** general support **9** gold standard **10** grammar school **11** grandson **12** ground speed

g's *or* **gs** *pl of* G

g salt *n, cap G* **:** a salt of G acid; *esp* **:** the dipotassium salt $HOC_{10}H_5(SO_3K)_2$

g sharp \'=,=\ *n, usu cap G* **1 :** the keynote of G-sharp minor **2 :** the tone a half step above G

g–sharp minor \'=,=¦==\ *n, usu cap G* **:** the minor musical key having a signature of five sharps

GSO *abbr* general staff officer

GST *abbr* Greenwich sidereal time

g star *n, usu cap G* **:** a star of spectral type G — see SPECTRAL TYPE table

g–string \'=,=\ *n, usu cap G* **1** *usu* **g string :** a string (as the lowest string of the violin) tuned to G **2** *also* **gee string a :** a breechcloth consisting usu. of a strip of cloth passed between the legs and supported by a waist cord **b :** a fancy theatrical and burlesque costume of similar design **3** [fr. the initials of *Georg Goubou b*1906 Amer. physicist born in Germany, its inventor] **:** a high-frequency transmission line consisting of a wire covered by dielectric of such proportions and material that a large percentage of the propagated wave lies close to the wire

g suit *n, usu cap G* [gravity *suit*] **:** an aviator's suit having a built-in system of air bladders that become inflated in rapid aerial maneuvers and exert pressure on the body and legs of the wearer to counteract the physiological effects of acceleration greater than unity and prevent blackout

gt *abbr* **1** gilt **2** great **3** [L *gutta*] drop

GT *abbr* **1** *often not cap* gilt top **2** gross ton

GTC *abbr* good till canceled; good till countermanded

gtd *abbr* guaranteed

GTE *abbr* gilt top edge

GTM *abbr* **1** general traffic manager **2** good this month

gtt *abbr* [L *guttae*] drops

GTW *abbr* good this week

gu *abbr* **1** guarantee; guaranteed **2** guinea **3** gules

GU *abbr* genitourinary

guaca *var of* HUACA

gua·ca·coa \,gwäkə'kōə\ *n* -s [AmerSp, fr. Taino] **:** a Cuban tree (*Daphnopsis guacacoa*) of the family Thymelaeaceae that yields a strong white bast fiber

gua·ca·mo·le *also* **gua·cha·mo·le** \,gwäkə'mōlē\ *n* -s [AmerSp *guacamole,* fr. Nahuatl *ahuacamolli,* fr. *ahuacatl* avocado + *molli* sauce, stew] **:** a mixture of mashed avocado, tomato, and onion seasoned with condiments

gua·cha·ro \'gwächə,rō\ *n* -s [Sp *guácharo*] **:** OILBIRD

gua·chi·pi·lin \¦gwächəpə¦lēn\ *n* -s [AmerSp *guachipilin, guachipelin,* fr. (assumed) Nahuatl *cuauhchipilin,* fr. *cuahuitl* tree + *chipilin,* a species of Crotalaria] **:** a Central American timber tree (*Diphysa robinioides*) of the family Leguminosae that yields a fine-grained hard yellow wood and a yellow dye

guacho *var of* GAUCHO

gua·ci·mo \'gwäsə,mō\ *or* **gua·ci·ma** *or* **gua·si·ma** \-səmə\ *or* **hua·si·ma** \'wä-\ *n* -s [AmerSp *guácimo, guácima, guásima, guázuma,* fr. Taino *guácima, guaçúm*] **:** any of several tropical American timber trees esp. of the genus *Guazuma* (as *G. ulmifolia*) having inner bark that yields a mucilaginous substance used in medicine and a tough bast from which cordage is made

gua·co \'gwä(,)kō\ *n* -s [AmerSp] **1 :** either of two plants believed to provide an antidote for snake bites: **a :** a tropical American vine (*Mikania guaco*) **b :** a birthwort (*Aristolochia maxima*) **2 :** BEE PLANT a

gua·da·gni·ni \,gwädə'nēnē *also* -dən'yē-\ *n* -s *usu cap* [fr. *Guadagnini,* name of a noted family of 18th cent. Ital. violin makers] **:** a violin made by one of the Italian Guadagnini family in the 18th century

gua·da·la·ja·ra \,gwädələ'härə, -ᵊlth-\ *adj, usu cap* [fr. *Guadalajara,* city in Mexico] **:** of or from the city of Guadalajara, Mexico **:** of the kind or style prevalent in Guadalajara

gua·dal·caz·a·rite \,gwädᵊl'kazə,rīt\ *n* -s [G *guadalcazarit,* fr. *Guadalcázar,* San Luis Potosí state, Mex., its locality + G *-it* -ite] **:** a mineral (Hg,Zn)S consisting of a zincky metacinnabarite

gua·da·lupe caracara \'gwädᵊl,üp-, ,==¦=-, ¦==¦üpē-\ *n, usu cap G* [fr. *Guadalupe,* a Mexican island off the western coast of Lower Calif.] **:** a caracara (*Polyborus lutosus*) formerly endemic on Guadalupe Island but now extinct

guadalupe cypress *n, usu cap G* **:** a low widely spreading evergreen tree (*Cupressus guadalupensis*) that is endemic on Guadalupe Island and is cultivated for its bluish foliage

guadalupe fur seal *n, usu cap G* **:** a fur seal (*Arctocephalus townsendi*) formerly common along the coast of California and Mexico but now limited to a small area where it is protected by the Mexican government

guadalupe palm *n, usu cap G* **:** a stout palm (*Erythea edulis*) of Guadalupe Island with edible buds and sweet pulpy fruit

guadalupe plum *n, usu cap G* **:** the fruit of the Guadalupe palm

gua·da·lu·pi·an \¦==¦üpēən\ *adj, usu cap* [*Guadalupe Basin,* west Texas and New Mexico + E *-ian*] **:** of, relating to, or constituting a subdivision of the American Permian — see GEOLOGIC TIME table

gua·de·loupe \'gwädᵊl,üp, ,=='=\ *adj, usu cap* [fr. *Guadeloupe,* island in the West Indies] **:** of or relating to the island of Guadeloupe **:** of the kind or style prevalent in Guadeloupe

gua·dua \'gwädəwə\ *n* -s [AmerSp] **:** a tropical American bamboo (*Guadua latifolia*) of the family Gramineae used esp. for construction and in paper manufacture

gua·guan·che \(g)wə'(g)wänchē\ *or* **gua·guan·cho** \-(,)chō\ *n* -s [AmerSp] **:** a barracuda (*Sphyraena guachancho*) of the Caribbean area and adjacent Atlantic coasts that is typically yellowish to olive above, silvery below, and spotted with black or dark brown

gua·ha·ri·bo \,gwä(h)ə'rē(,)bō, gwä'r-\ *n, pl* **guaharibo** *or* **guaharibos** *usu cap* [Sp, of AmerInd origin] **1 a :** a Shirianá people of the upper Orinoco valley, Venezuela **b :** a member of such people **2 :** the language of the Guaharibo people

gua·hi·ban \gwä'(h)ēbən\ *adj, usu cap* **:** of or relating to the Guahibo people or their language

gua·hi·bo \-ē(,)bō\ *also* **gua·hi·vo** \-ē(,)vō\ *n, pl* **guahibo** *or* **guahibos** *usu cap* [Sp, of AmerInd origin] **1 a :** a group of peoples of eastern Colombia and southwestern Venezuela **b :** a member of any of such peoples **2 :** the language of the Guahibo people

guai·ac \'g(w)ī,ak, -īək\ *also* **gai·ac** \'gī-\ *n* -s [NL *Guaiacum*] **1 :** GUAIACUM 1b, 1c **2** *in French Guiana* **:** TONKA BEAN **3 :** a tree bearing the tonka bean

guai·a·col \'g(w)īə,kȯl, -kōl\ *n* -s [*guaiacum* + E *-ol*] **:** a liquid or a crystalline solid $CH_3OC_6H_4OH$ with an aromatic odor ranging from colorless to yellowish in appearance and obtained by distilling guaiacum or from wood-tar creosote or synthetically and used chiefly as an expectorant and as a local anesthetic; *ortho*-methoxy-phenol

guaiac resin *n* **:** GUAIACUM 1c

guai·a·cum \'g(w)īəkəm\ *n* [NL, fr. Sp *guayaco, guayacán,* fr. Taino *guayacan*] **1 a** *cap* **:** a genus of tropical American trees and shrubs (family Zygophyllaceae) having pinnate leaves, mostly blue flowers, and capsular fruit **b** -s **:** the hard greenish brown wood yielded by trees of this genus (esp. *G. officinale*) — see LIGNUM VITAE **c** -s **:** a resin with a faint balsamic odor obtained as tears or masses from the trunk of either of two trees (*G. officinale* or *G. sanctum*) of this genus used formerly in medicine as a remedy for gout or rheumatism and now in various tests (as for peroxidases or blood stains) because of the formation of a blue color on oxidation **2** -s **a :** a tree (*Porlieria angustifolia*) of Texas and Mexico closely related to trees of the genus *Guaiacum* **b :** the wood of this tree **c :** the resinous exudate from this wood

guaiac wood *also* **guaiacum wood** *n* **1 :** the heartwood of a palo santo (*Bulnesia sarmienti*) that yields an oil having an odor of tea or violets and used esp. as a fixative in perfumery **2 :** the palo santo that yields guaiac wood

guai·can \(')gwī¦kän\ *n* -s [Sp *guaicán,* fr. Taino *guaican*] **:** REMORA

guai·cu·ru *or* **guay·cu·rú** \¦gwīkə¦rü\ *n, pl* **guaicuru** *or* **guaicurus** *or* **guaycurú** *or* **guaycurús** *usu cap* [Sp *guaicurú, guaycurú,* of AmerInd origin] **1 a :** an Indian people living in southern Mato Grosso, Brazil **b :** a member of such people **2 :** the language of the Guaicuru people

guai·cu·ru·an *or* **guay·cu·ru·an** \,==¦=ən\ *n* -s *usu cap* **:** a language family of the Chaco region in So. America

guaimi *usu cap, var of* GUAYMI

guai·ol \'g(w)ī,ōl, -,ōl\ *n* -s [ISV *guai-* (fr. NL *Guaiacum*) + *-ol*] **:** a crystalline sesquiterpenoid alcohol $C_{15}H_{25}OH$ found esp. in the oil of guaiacum wood

guai·ta·ca \,gwīd·ə¦kä\ *n, pl* **guaitaca** *or* **guaitacas** *usu cap* [prob. fr. Pg *guaitacá,* of AmerInd origin] **1 a :** an extinct people of eastern Brazil **b :** a member of such people **2 :** the language of the Guaitaca people

guaj·a·cum \'g(w)īəkəm\ [NL *Guaiacum*] *syn of* GUAIACUM

gua·ji·llo \¦gwä'hē(,)(y)ō\ *also* **gua·ji·lla** \-ē(y)ə\ *n* -s [MexSp] **:** a deep-rooted usu. spiny shrub (*Acacia berlandieri*) of the southwestern U.S. that has leaves with numerous leaflets and flowers in globose heads and that is an important honey plant when abundant

gua·ji·ra \gwä'hirə\ *n* -s [AmerSp (Cuba), lit., peasant woman] **:** a Cuban peasant dance tune or song whose rhythm shifts from 6/8 to 3/4 time while the eighth note retains the same time value

gua·ma \gwə'mä\ *n* -s [AmerSp *guamá,* fr. Taino *guama*] **:** any of several plants of the genus *Inga*; *esp* **:** a tropical American tree (*I. laurina*) used as a shade for coffee plantations

gua·ma·ni·an \gwä'mānēən, gwə'män-\ *n* -s *cap* [*Guam,* island in the Pacific ocean + E *-anian* (as in *Panamanian*)] **:** a native or inhabitant of Guam; *specif* **:** a Chamorro of Guam

gua·mo \'gwä(,)mō\ *n, pl* **guamo** *or* **guamos** *usu cap* [Sp, of AmerInd origin] **1 a :** a people of southwestern Venezuela **b :** a member of such people **2 :** the language of the Guamo people

guamuchil *var of* HUAMUCHIL

guan \'gwän\ *n* -s [AmerSp] **:** any of various large tropical American birds (family Cracidae) that are highly regarded for sport and food, somewhat resemble turkeys in proportions and size, and are widely distributed in dense lowland forests

¹**guana** *var of* IGUANA

²**gua·ná** \gwə'nä\ *n, pl* **guaná** *or* **guanás** *usu cap* [Sp, of AmerInd origin] **1 a :** an Arawakan people or group of peoples of Mato Grosso, Brazil, and the Chaco region of Paraguay **b :** a member of any of such peoples **2 :** the language of the Guaná people

³**gua·na** \'gwänə\ *n* -s [AmerSp (Cuba)] **:** MAJAGUA

gua·na·ba·na \gwə'näbənə\ *n* -s [Sp *guanábana* fruit of the soursop, fr. Taino, soursop] **:** SOURSOP

gua·na·cas·te \,gwänə'kastē\ *n* -s [Sp — more at CONACASTE] **:** CONACASTE

gua·na·co \gwə'nä(,)kō\ *or* **hua·na·co** \wə-\ *n, pl* **guanacos** *also* **guanaco** *or* **huanacos** *also* **huanaco** [Sp *guanaco, huanaco,* fr. Quechua *huanacu*] **:** a South American mammal (*Lama guanicoe*) that is related to the camel, lacks a dorsal hump, resembles a deer in appearance, and has a soft thick fawn-colored coat — compare ALPACA, LLAMA

gua·na·jua·tite \,gwänə'(h)wä,tīt\ *n* -s [*Guanajuato,* Mex., its locality + E *-ite*] **:** a mineral Bi_2Se_3 consisting of bismuth selenide occurring in bluish gray crystals or masses

gua·namine \'gwänə,mēn, ,==¦=, '==mən, gwə'namən\ *n* [*guanidine* + *amine*] **:** any of a series of bases formed by heating guanidine salts of the fatty acids and used to produce crystalline derivatives of fatty acids and in the manufacture of resins; a 2,4-diamino-6-alkyl-triazine

gua·na·qui·to \,gwänə'kē(,)tō\ *n* -s [Sp, lit., small guanaco, dim. of *guanaco*] **:** the pelt of a young guanaco

gua·nase \'gwä,nās, -āz\ *n* -s [*guanine* + *-ase*] **:** an enzyme present in most animal tissues that hydrolyzes guanine to xanthine and ammonia

gua·nay \gwə'nī\ *also* **guanay cormorant** *n, pl* **guanay·es** \-ī,āz\ *or* **guanays** \-īz\ [*guanay* fr. AmerSp (Peru), prob. fr. Quechua] **:** a white-breasted Peruvian cormorant (*Phalacrocorax bougainvillii*) that is a source of guano

guan·che \'gwän(,)chā\ *n, pl* **guanches** *also* **guanche** *usu cap* [Sp] **:** one of a native people who formerly inhabited the Canary islands and who bore a superficial skeletal resemblance to the Cro-Magnon type — see HAMITE

guan·go \'gwäŋ(,)gō\ *n* -s [AmerSp] *West Indies* **:** RAIN TREE

gua·ni·dine \'gwänə,dēn, -dən\ *n* -s [ISV *guan-* (fr. *guanine*) + *-idine*] **:** a strong deliquescent crystalline base NH=C-$(NH_2)_2$ found esp. in beet juice, vetch seedlings, or the embryo chick, formed by the oxidation of guanine but usu. made commercially by the reaction of dicyandiamide with ammonium nitrate, and used in the form of salts in organic synthesis and in medicine and in the form of organic derivatives as rubber accelerators

gua·ni·di·no \¦gwänə¦dē(,)nō\ *also* **gua·ni·do** \'gwänə,dō\ *adj* [*guanidino-, guanido-*] **:** relating to or containing the group $H_2NC(=NH)NH—$ of guanidine

guanidino- *also* **guanido-** *comb form* [*guanidino-,* ISV, fr. *guanidine* + *-o-*; *guanido-* fr. *guanidine* + *-o-*] **:** containing the univalent group $H_2NC(=NH)NH-$ derived from guanidine by removal of one hydrogen atom

gua·ni·do·acetic acid \ˌgwänədō+. . .-\ *n* [*guanido-* + *acetic*] **:** GLYCOCYAMINE

gua·nif·er·ous \(ˈ)gwäˈnif(ə)rəs\ *adj* [*guano* + *-i-* + *-ferous*] **:** yielding guano

gua·nine \ˈgwäˌnēn, -änən\ *n* -s [*guano* + *-ine*] **:** a crystalline purine base $C_5H_5N_5O$ found esp. in guano and other animal excrements and in many leguminous plants and obtained by hydrolysis of nucleic acids; 2-amino-6-hydroxy-purine

¹gua·no \ˈgwä(ˌ)nō *sometimes* gyüˈanə\ *n* -s [Sp, fr. Quechua *huanu* dung] **1 :** a substance that is found on some coasts or islands frequented by sea fowl, is composed chiefly of their partially decomposed excrement, is rich in phosphates, nitrogenous matter, and other material for plant growth, and has been used extensively as a fertilizer **2 :** a product comparable to bird guano esp. as a fertilizer ⟨a ~ of fish-cannery refuse⟩

²guano \"\ *vt* -ED/-ING/-s **:** to enrich with or as if with guano

³guano *var of* IGUANA

⁴gua·no \ˈgwä(ˌ)nō\ *n* -s [AmerSp, fr. Taino] *West Indies* **:** BALSA 1

gua·no·phore \ˈgwänə,fō(ə)r\ *n* -s [*guano-* (fr. *guanine*) + *-phore*] **:** a chromatophore that is characterized by pale granules or iridescent crystals of guanine and occurs notably in the skin of fishes and reptiles **:** LEUCOPHORE, IRIDOPHORE

guano sack *n* [¹*guano*] *chiefly Midland* **:** GUNNYSACK

gua·no·sine \ˈgwänəˌsēn, -sən\ *n* -s [ISV, blend of *guanine* and *ribose*] **:** a crystalline nucleoside $C_{10}H_{13}N_5O_5$ that is isolated esp. from vetch seedlings or coffee leaves and berries, that is obtained by partial hydrolysis of ribonucleic acid, and that yields on hydrolysis guanine and ribose

guans *pl of* GUAN

gua·nyl \ˈgwänᵊl\ *n* -s [*guanidine* + *-yl*] **:** the amidino group

gua·nyl·ic acid \(ˈ)gwäˈnilik-\ *n* [*guanine* + *-yl* + *-ic*] **:** an amorphous nucleotide $C_{10}H_{14}N_5O_8P$ formed by partial hydrolysis of ribonucleic acid; an ester of guanosine and orthophosphoric acid

guao \ˈgwau̇\ *n* -s [AmerSp (Cuba), fr. Taino] **:** any of certain small tropical American trees constituting a genus *Comocladia* of the family Anacardiaceae, having odd-pinnate often spiny leaves, hard heavy reddish wood, and a caustic sap that poisons on contact, and yielding tannins and a dye extract — see MAIDEN PLUM

gua·pe·na \gwəˈpēnə\ *n* -s [AmerSp *guabina*, a kind of river fish, fr. Taino] **:** a West Indian ribbon fish (*Eques lanceolatus*)

gua·pi·lla \gwəˈpē(y)ə\ *n* -s [MexSp, istle (plant)] *Mexico* **:** ISTLE

gua·pi·nol \ˈgwäpəˌnōl, -nōl\ *n* -s [AmerSp, fr. Nahuatl *cuauh-pinolli*, lit., tree flour, fr. *cuahuitl* tree + *pinolli* flour, dust] **:** COURBARIL

guar \ˈgwär\ *n* -s [Hindi *guār*] **:** a drought-tolerant legume (*Cyanopsis psoralioides*) grown for forage and for its seeds which produce a gum used as a thickening agent and as a sizing material for paper and textiles

guar *abbr* guarantee; guaranteed; guarantor; guaranty

¹gua·ra \gwəˈrä\ *n* -s [Pg *guará*, fr. Tupi] **:** SCARLET IBIS

²guara \ˈgwä(ə)rə\ [NL, fr. Pg *guará* scarlet ibis] *syn of* EUDOCIMUS

³gua·ra \gwəˈrä\ *n* -s [Pg *guará*, *aguara* — more at AGOUARA] **:** AGOUARA

⁴gua·ra \ˈgwärə\ *n* -s [AmerSp] **:** a tropical American tree of the genus *Cupania*

gua·ra·bu \ˌgwärəˈbü\ *n* -s [Pg *guarabú*, fr. Tupi] **:** any of several Brazilian timber trees of the genus *Astronium* (family Anacardiaceae) having heavy hard wood with close grain

gua·ra·cha \gwəˈrächə\ *n* -s [Sp, fr. OSp *guar* place, spot, site + *hacha* a dance performed with legs and feet only] **1 a :** a lively stamping Spanish solo dance **b :** music for this dance **2 a :** a lively Cuban dance tune in 6/8 time **b :** a ballroom dance with a box step developed in Cuba from the Spanish model

guarache *var of* HUARACHE

gua·ra·guao \ˌgwärəˈgwau̇\ *n* -s [AmerSp, fr. Taino] **:** any of several West Indian timber trees of the family Meliaceae; *esp* **:** a Puerto Rican timber tree (*Guarea guara*) that yields a wood resembling the related mahogany

gua·ra·na \ˌgwärəˈnä\ *n* -s [Sp & Pg *guaraná*, fr. Tupi] **1 :** a dried paste made from the seeds of a Brazilian climbing shrub (*Paullinia cupana*) containing tannin and caffeine and used in making an astringent drink **2 :** a drink flavored with guarana

gua·ra·ni \ˌgwärəˈnē\ *n, pl* **guarani** *or* **guaranis** *or* **guaranies** [Sp *guaraní*, of AmerInd origin] **1** *or* **guaraní** *usu cap* **a :** a Tupi-Guaranian people of Bolivia, Paraguay, and southern Brazil **b :** a member of such people **2** *or* **guaraní** *usu cap* **:** the language of the Guarani people **3 a :** the basic monetary unit of Paraguay — see MONEY table **b :** a note representing one guarani

gua·ra·ni·an \gwəˈränēən\ *adj, usu cap* **:** of or relating to the Guarani people

gua·ra·ño·ca \ˌgwärənˈyōkə\ *n, pl* **guarañoca** *or* **guarañocas** *usu cap* [Sp *Guarañoca*, of AmerInd origin] **1 a :** a Zamuco people of the Department of Santa Cruz, Bolivia **b :** a member of such people **2 :** the language of the Guarañoca people

¹guar·an·tee \ˌgarənˈtē *also* ÷ˈgär- *or* ˈger- *or* ÷ˈgär-\ *n* -s [prob. alter. (influenced by such words as *assignee*, *lessee*) of ¹*guaranty*] **1 :** one who makes a guaranty **:** one who acts as a surety or gives security (as for a debt) **2 :** the act of one who makes a guaranty or acts as a surety **:** GUARANTY 1 **3 a :** an agreement by which one person undertakes to secure another in the possession or enjoyment of something **b :** an expressed or implied assurance of the quality of goods offered for sale or the length of satisfactory use to be expected from a product **c :** an expressed assurance of satisfaction with a definite promise of purchase money to be returned or goods to be replaced or other specified assurance **4 :** something given by way of security **:** something made or held as a security **:** GUARANTY 3

²guarantee \"\ *vt* **guaranteed; guaranteed; guaranteeing; guarantees 1 :** to be a guarantee, warranty, or surety for **:** undertake to answer for the debt, default, or miscarriage of (another) **:** become responsible for the fulfillment of (the agreement of another) **:** assume a suretyship for **2 :** to engage for the existence, permanence, or nature of (something) **:** undertake to do or secure (something) ⟨~ the winning of three tricks in a suit by losing the first trick⟩ **3 :** to give a guaranty to (another) **:** give or furnish security to **:** SECURE **4 :** to state or declare with conviction or an air of certainty ⟨he *guaranteed* that I had had appendicitis several times without knowing it —Arnold Bennett⟩

guaranteed annual wage *n* **:** an arrangement whereby an employer guarantees his employees a minimum amount of wages or employment during a year

guaranteed bond *n* **:** a bond on which payment of interest or principal or both are guaranteed by a corporation other than the issuer

guaranteed rate *n* **:** a minimum rate of pay assured to an incentive worker regardless of his output

guaranteed stock *n* **:** stock the dividends on which are guaranteed by a corporation other than the issuing corporation

guaranteed value *n* **:** NONFORFEITURE BENEFIT

guaranteed wage *n* **:** an assurance by an employer to qualified workers of continuing wage payments for a specified period of time

guar·an·tor \ˌgarənˈtȯ(ə)r, -ō(ə), ˈgarəntə(r)\ *n* -s [*guaranty* + *-or*] **1 :** one that guarantees ⟨our Strategic Air Command is the ~ of our security —Carl Spaatz⟩ **2 :** one that makes or gives a guaranty or guarantee **:** one that enters in a guaranty

¹guar·an·ty \ˈgarəntē, -ti\ *n* -ES [MF *garantie*, *guarantie*, fr. OF, fr. (influenced by *garir*, *guarir* to protect, preserve, from a Gmc verb represented by OHG *werien* to defend) *garant*, *guarant* warrant, defender, protection, of Gmc origin; akin to OHG *werēnto* guarantor — more at WEIR, WARRANT] **1 :** an undertaking to answer for the payment of some debt or the performance of some duty of another in case of the failure of such other to pay or perform **:** a promise to answer for the debt, default, or miscarriage of another **2 :** GUARANTEE 3a **3 :** something given or possessed as security for the existence or continuance of something **:** something given or had as a means of securing the existence, performance, or fulfillment of something **:** SECURITY **4 :** a person who accepts or gives assurance of responsibility for something **:** GUARANTOR **5 :** the protection of a right afforded by legal provision (as in a constitution) ⟨the individual *guaranties* of personal liberty⟩

²guaranty \"\ *vt* -ED/-ING/-ES **:** GUARANTEE

guaras *pl of* GUARA

gua·rau·no \gwəˈrau̇(ˌ)nō\ *n* -s *usu cap* [Sp, of AmerInd origin] **:** WARRAU

gua·ra·yo \gwəˈrī(ˌ)ō\ *n, pl* **guarayo** *or* **guarayos** *usu cap* [Sp, of AmerInd origin] **1 a :** a Tacanan people of northwestern Bolivia **b :** a member of such people **2 :** the language of the Guarayo people

gua·ra·yú \ˌgwärəˈyü\ *n, pl* **guarayú** *or* **guarayús** *usu cap* [Sp, of AmerInd origin] **1 a :** a Guaranian people of Bolivia **b :** a member of such people **2 :** the language of the Guarayú people

¹guard \ˈgärd, ˈgȧd\ *n* -s [ME *garde*, fr. MF, fr. OF *garde*, *guarde*, fr. *garder*, *guarder*, v.] **1 :** one that defends against injury, danger, or attack ⟨his greatness was no ~ to bar heaven's shaft —Shak.⟩: as **a :** a bowl or stone played to a position where it protects another from attack in bowls or curling **b :** a low card held with a valuable higher card in the same suit **c** (1) **:** one of two players on either side of the center in the line in football (2) **:** either of two players stationed at the rear of the court in basketball whose play is primarily defensive **2 :** a man or body of men stationed to protect or control a person or position: as **a :** a soldier, sailor, marine, or airman or a number of them on guard duty ⟨~*s* were posted about the army camp⟩ ⟨slipped past the palace ~*s*⟩ **b guards** *pl* **:** troops attached to the person of a ruler (as a sovereign or governor) ⟨Royal Horse *Guards*⟩ ⟨Governor's Foot *Guards*⟩ ⟨Grenadier *Guards*⟩ ⟨Dragoon *Guards*⟩ **c :** a group loyal to a defeated person or to an outmoded principle ⟨an Old *Guard* Republican⟩ **d** (1) *Brit* **:** a railroad conductor (2) **:** a brakeman or gateman (as on a train of an elevated railroad or subway) **e :** one who is responsible for the safety and discipline of inmates of a prison, reformatory, or other place of detention while they are within the institution, in transit to or from the institution, or on work detail **f :** an officer of a society (as a secret order) whose duty it is to prevent intrusion by nonmembers **g :** a gateman or watchman of a building or plant **3** *obs* **:** an ornamental trimming of lace or embroidery on the edge of a garment **4 a :** a state of watchfulness and readiness against danger **:** state of standing in defense of a person or thing against possible injury, attack, or theft ⟨standing ~ over the treasure⟩ **b :** the service or duties of one who keeps military watch ⟨assigned to ~ duty on the border⟩ **5 a :** a posture of defense (as in fencing or boxing) **:** the position of the body or the arms in defense ⟨got a blow in under his ~⟩ ⟨caught him off ~⟩ ⟨kept his ~ up to protect his face⟩ **b :** the position of a cricketer's bat held perpendicularly at a point where it will stop a straight bowled ball that would otherwise hit the wicket **6 :** a fixture or attachment designed to protect or secure against injury, soiling, defacement, theft, or loss: as **a :** the part of a sword hilt that protects the hand **b :** a chain or band for holding in place or safeguarding from loss ⟨belt ~⟩ ⟨watch ~⟩ **c :** GUARD RING 1 **d :** TRIGGER GUARD **e :** FENDER 1 *Brit* **:** PILOT 4a **7 a :** a piece of protective body armor ⟨nose ~⟩ **b :** any of various devices worn by contestants as a protection against injury to some part ⟨shin ~⟩ **c :** the hard calcareous fusiform or subcylindrical piece which ensheathes the phragmacone and forms the rear end of the shell of belemnites — called also *rostrum* **8 a :** a fence or rail to prevent falling from the deck of a ship **b guards** *pl* **:** an extension of the deck of a ship beyond the hull; *esp* **:** the framework of timber in a side-wheel steamship protecting the paddle wheel and shaft **9 a :** a projecting paper or cloth strip bound with book leaves onto which an insert (as a map or folding plate) is fastened — called also *stub* **b :** a narrow leaf usu. ½ to ¾ inches wide that compensates for an object mounted to a full page (as in a scrapbook or album) — called also *stub* **c :** the supporting paper applied in rebinding to the broken folds of the leaves of a book before sewing **d :** a paper or cloth strip added to the fold of the first and last section of a book for additional strength

²guard \"\ *vb* -ED/-ING/-S [MF *garder*, fr. OF *garder*, *guarder* to ward, guard, of Gmc origin; akin to OHG *wartēn* to watch, take care — more at WARD] *vt* **1 :** to finish and protect an edge of with an ornamental border or lace edging **2 a :** to protect from danger **:** DEFEND, SHIELD **b :** to stand on the border or at the entrance of as if on guard ⟨lawns ~*ed* by stately elms⟩ or as a barrier ⟨rapids ~*ing* the lower reaches of the river⟩ **c :** to protect (a card or a man) in a game by safeguards or support ⟨forced to discard diamonds in order to ~ the king of clubs⟩ ⟨the separated pawns could not both be ~*ed*⟩ **3** *archaic* **:** to accompany for protection **:** ESCORT **4 a :** to watch over so as to prevent escape ⟨a closely ~*ed* secret⟩ ⟨~ a prisoner⟩ or restrain from violence or indiscretion ⟨warned her to ~ her tongue in the presence of these people —L.C. Douglas⟩ **b** *of a player in a goal game* **:** to maintain a position so as to prevent (an opponent) from playing effectively **5 :** to furnish with proper checks or corrections **:** SAFEGUARD ⟨~ an experiment⟩ **6 :** to equip (as a book, a machine, a window) with a guard ~ *vi* **:** to watch by way of caution or defense **:** be in a state or position of defense ⟨hitting with his right, ~*ing* with his left⟩ **:** stand guard **:** take precautions ⟨~ against mistakes by double-checking⟩ **syn** see DEFEND

guardage *n* -s *obs* **:** GUARDIANSHIP

¹guar·dant \ˈgärdᵊnt\ *adj* [MF *gardant*, pres. part. of *garder*] **1** *also* **gar·dant** \"\ *heraldry* **:** having the head turned toward the spectator — used of a beast whose body is seen from the side ⟨a lion passant ~⟩ **2** *obs* **:** acting as a guard or guardian

²guardant *n* -s *obs* **:** GUARDIAN, KEEPER

guard boat *n* **:** a boat that is detailed on guard duty (as in a harbor)

guard book *n, Brit* **:** SCRAPBOOK, ALBUM, FOLDER

guard brush *n* **:** a metallic brush for picking up the current from the live rail of an electric railroad

guard cartridge *n* **:** a cartridge for guard purposes having a reduced powder charge and giving a low muzzle velocity to the bullet

guard cell *n* **:** one of the two crescent-shaped epidermal cells united at their ends whose changes in turgidity determine opening and closing of a stoma

guard chamber *n* **:** GUARDROOM

guard circle *n* **:** a final groove on a disc record that returns upon itself in order to protect the pickup from damage by being thrown toward the center of the record

guarded *adj* **1 :** PROTECTED, DEFENDED **2 :** CAUTIOUS, WARY, CIRCUMSPECT ⟨he was ~ in his expressions⟩ **:** framed or uttered with caution ⟨a ~ statement⟩ — **guard·ed·ly** *adv* — **guard·ed·ness** *n* -ES

guard·ee \ˈgärdē, ˈgȧd-, -di\ *n* -s [¹*guard* + *-ee*] *Brit* **:** GUARDSMAN

guard·er \ˈgärdər, ˈgȧdə(r\ *n* -s **:** one that guards **:** WATCHMAN, WARDER, GUARD

guard flag *n* **:** a flag flown at anchor by a warship having the day's guard duty

guard hair *n* **:** any of the long coarse hairs forming a protective coating over the underfur of a furred mammal; *also* **:** the coat formed by these hairs

guardhouse \ˈ=,=\ *n* [¹*guard* + *house*] **:** a building that serves as headquarters for the guard and as a lockup for military offenders

guardhouse lawyer *n* **:** a person in the military service who pretends to wide knowledge of regulations, military law, and his rights; *esp* **:** one who so pretends while in confinement

¹guard·i·an \ˈgärdēən, ˈgȧd-\ *n* -s [ME *gardein*, fr. AF, fr. OF *guardenc*, fr. *garder*, *guarder* to ward, watch] **1 :** one that guards or secures **:** one to whom a person or thing is committed for protection, security, or preservation **2** [ME *gardian*, fr. MF *gardien*, fr. OF, fr. *garder* to guard + *-ien* -an — more at GUARD] **:** a superior of a Franciscan monastery **3 :** one who has or is entitled or legally appointed to the care and management of the person or property of another (as a minor or a person incapable of managing his own affairs) — compare COMMITTEE, CURATOR, TUTOR; see GUARDIAN AD LITEM, GUARDIAN BY CUSTOM, GUARDIAN BY ELECTION, GUARDIAN BY STATUTE, GUARDIAN FOR NURTURE, GUARDIAN IN SOCAGE, NATURAL GUARDIAN, TESTAMENTARY GUARDIAN; WARD **4** *often cap* **:** the spiritual leader of the Bahais **5 :** an adult leader of a group of intermediate camp fire girls — compare ADVISER, LEADER

²guardian \"\ *adj* **:** performing or appropriate to the office of a protector ⟨the ~ lions by the entrance are strikingly rendered —*Amer. Guide Series: Vt.*⟩

guardian ad litem *n* **:** a guardian appointed by a court to represent in a particular lawsuit the interests of a party who is minor or an incompetent person or of a person unborn or unascertained who may become interested in property involved in the litigation

guardian angel *n* **:** an angel believed to have special care for a particular individual

guardian by custom 1 : a guardian according to a custom concerning lands of copyhold tenure where the right of guardianship falls to the next of blood incapable of inheriting the estate or may be claimed by special custom by the lord of the manor or his nominee **2 :** a guardian according to a now disused custom of London

guardian by election : a guardian elected by an infant himself having lands in socage upon attaining his 14th year

guardian by nature : NATURAL GUARDIAN

guardian by statute : a guardian appointed by a father by deed or will for his minor child under authority of a statute and sometimes having custody of both the person and the estate of the minor until he attains the age of 21

guardiance *n* -s [*guardian* + *-ance*] *obs* **:** GUARDIANSHIP

guard·i·an·ess \ˈgärdēənəs, ˈgȧd-\ *n* -ES [¹*guardian* + *-ess*] **:** a female guardian

guardian for nurture *or* **guardian by nurture** *Eng common law* **:** a father and upon his decease prob. the mother of children under 14 years of age having custody of their persons and not of their estates — compare NATURAL GUARDIAN

guardian in socage : the guardian of an infant who inherited lands held in socage under feudal tenure

guard·i·an·less \-ləs\ *adj* **:** lacking a guardian

guard·i·an·ly \-lē, -li\ *adj* **:** relating to a guardian

guardian of the poor : a member of a board appointed or elected to care for the relief of the poor or administer the poor laws within a township, parish, or district in England

guard·i·an·ship \-ˌship\ *n* **:** PROTECTION, CARE; *specif* **:** the relationship existing between guardian and ward

guardian spirit *n* **:** a tutelary being **:** GENIUS

guarding *n* -s [fr. gerund of ²*guard*] **:** involuntary reaction to protect an area of pain (as by spasm of muscle on palpation of the abdomen over a painful lesion)

guard·ing·ly *adv* [fr. pres. part. of ²*guard* + *-ly*] **:** in a protective or defensive manner

guard iron *n, Brit* **:** PILOT 4a

guard·less \ˈgärdləs, ˈgȧd-\ *adj* **1 a :** DEFENSELESS, UNPROTECTED **b :** UNWARY **2 :** lacking a guard ⟨~ swords⟩

guard line *n* **1 :** BEARER 5b (3) **2 :** a line constituting the inner side of the flangeway of a railroad crossing or switch and comprised of guardrails and wing rails — compare GAGE LINE

guard lock *n* **1 :** a tide lock at the mouth of a dock or basin or a lock for preventing flooding of a canal **2 :** a lock guarding the keyhole or bolt of another lock and having to be unlocked before the key of the main lock can be operated

guard mail *n* **:** mail delivered locally (as to a naval vessel) by messenger

guard mount *also* **guard mounting** *n* **1 :** the military ceremony of installing the new guard and relieving the old one **2 :** guard duty

guard of honor : a guard turned out to greet or accompany a distinguished person or to accompany the casket at a military funeral — compare COLOR GUARD

guard of the standard : the color guard of a cavalry regiment

guard pin *n* **:** a pin in a lever-escapement watch set into the pallet fork for preventing accidental unlocking of the escapement

guardrail \ˈ=,=\ *n* **1 :** a railing for guarding against danger or trespass **2 :** a timber bolted outside a ship along the planksheer to act as a fender **3 :** a rail placed on the inside of a main rail (as on a bridge or a curve or at a switch) as a safeguard against derailment

guard report *n* **:** a formal report submitted by the commander of a guard to higher authority at the close of each period of guard duty

guard ring *n* **:** a close-fitting finger ring worn outside another to keep the latter from slipping off

guardroom \ˈ=,=\ *n* **:** the room occupied by the guard during its term of duty

guards *pl of* GUARD, *pres 3d sing of* GUARD

guard·ship \-ˌship\ *n* [¹*guard* + *-ship*] **:** GUARDIANSHIP

guard ship \"\ *n* **:** a warship under way or at anchor assigned to a special administrative duty or required to maintain temporarily a higher degree of readiness than others of the squadron

guards·man \ˈgärdzmən, ˈgȧd-\ *n, pl* **guardsmen** [in sense 1, fr. *guard's* (gen. of ¹*guard*) + *man*; in sense 2, fr. *guards* (pl. of ¹*guard*) + *man*] **1** *archaic* **:** one who guards **:** GUARD, WARDER, WATCHMAN **2 :** a member of any military body called *guard* or *guards*

guard's van *n, Brit* **:** CABOOSE

guard tent *n* **:** a tent occupied by a military guard

guard timber *n* **:** a piece of timber used to maintain the spacing of ties in a railroad track

gua·rea \ˈgwärēə\ *n, cap* [NL, fr. AmerSp *guara*] **:** a genus of chiefly tropical American trees or shrubs (family Meliaceae) with pinnate leaves, small clustered flowers, and capsular fruits

guar gum *n* **:** a gum consisting of the ground endosperm of guar seeds that swells and disperses in water and is used chiefly as a thickening agent, in papermaking, and in ore dressing

gua·ri·ba \gwəˈrēbə\ *n* -s [Pg, fr. Tupi] **:** HOWLER MONKEY; *esp* **:** a monkey (*Alouatta caraya*) of Brazil

guar·ne·ri·us \gwärˈnirēəs, -wä|, |ˈner-, |ˈnēr-, |ˈnär-\ *or* **guar·ne·ri** \-ˈre,rī\ *also* **guar·nie·ri** \|nˈyer-, |nyär-\ *n, pl* **guarneriuses** *or* **guarneris** *also* **guarnieris** *usu cap* [NL *Guarnerius*, fr. It *Guarneri*, *Guarneri*, name of a noted family of 17th & 18th cent. Ital. violin makers] **:** a violin made by one of the Italian Guarneri family in the 17th and 18th centuries

guar·nie·ri body \|nˈyere-, -yäre-, -ri-\ *or* **guarnieri's body** *n, usu cap G* [after Giuseppe *Guarnieri* †1918 Ital. pathologist] **:** a minute inclusion body characteristic of variola and vaccinia

guar·ri \ˈgwärē\ *n* -s [native name in southern Africa] **:** the fruit of any of several African trees or shrubs of the genus *Euclea* (as *E. pseudebenus*) — compare CAPE EBONY

guars *pl of* GUAR

gua·sa \ˈgwäsə\ *n* -s [Sp] **:** a grouper (*Epinephelus guaza*) of Europe and the south Atlantic; *broadly* **:** any of various related fishes (as the spotted jewfish)

gua·sa·par \ˌgwäsəˈpär\ *n, pl* **guasapar** *or* **guasapars** *usu cap* [Sp *guazapar*, *guaziper*, of AmerInd origin] **1 :** a Varohio people of Chihuahua, Mexico **2 :** a member of the Guasapar people

gua·sa·ve \gwəˈsävē\ *n, pl* **guasave** *or* **guasaves** *usu cap* [Sp *guazave*, *guayave*, of AmerInd origin] **1 :** a Cahita people of Sinaloa, Mexico **2 :** a member of the Guasave people

guasima *var of* GUACIMO

gua·so \ˈgwä(ˌ)sō\ *n* -s [Sp, fr. Quechua *huasu*] **:** a Chilean agricultural laborer

guas·tal·line \ˈgwästəˌlēn, gwäˈstälən\ *n* -s *usu cap* [after Countess of *Guastalla* †ab 1569, who founded the sisterhood] **:** a member of a Roman Catholic sisterhood established in Milan about 1535 to manage an institute for the orphans of noble families — called also *Daughter of Mary*

gua·tam·bu \ˌgwädəmˈbü\ *n* -s [Pg *guatambú*, fr. Tupi] **1 :** a Brazilian timber tree (*Aspidosperma tomentosa*) **2 :** the bright yellow rather soft wood of the guatambu

gua·te·ma·la \ˌgwädəˈmälə, -wätə-, -mälə\ *adj, usu cap* [fr. *Guatemala*, country in Central America] **1 :** of or from Guatemala **:** of the kind or style prevalent in Guatemala **:** GUATEMALAN **2** *or* **guatemala city** *usu cap G&C* [fr. *Guatemala* or *Guatemala City*, capital of Guatemala] **:** of or from Guatemala City, the capital of Guatemala **:** of the kind or style prevalent in Guatemala City **:** GUATEMALAN

guatemala grass *n, usu cap 1st G* **1 :** TEOSINTE **2 :** a perennial grass (*Tripsacum laxum*) of the Caribbean area that is widely grown in warm regions for fodder and hay

1gua·te·ma·lan \-lən\ *adj, usu cap* [*Guatemala* + E *-an*] **1 a :** of, relating to, or characteristic of Guatemala **b :** of, relating to, or characteristic of the people of Guatemala **2 a :** of, relating to, or characteristic of Guatemala City **b :** of, relating to, or characteristic of the people of Guatemala City

2guatemalan \"\ *n* -s *cap* **:** a native or inhabitant of Guatemala

1gua·te·mal·tec·an \ˌ==ˌmälˈtekən, -ˌmäl-\ *adj, usu cap* [Sp *guatemalteco* + E *-an*] **:** GUATEMALA

2guatemaltecan \"\ *n* -s *cap* **:** GUATEMALAN

gua·te·mal·te·co \ˌ==ˌ=ˈte(ˌ)kō, -ˈtä(-\ *n* -s *cap* [Sp, fr. *Guatemala*] **:** GUATEMALAN

gua·ti·be·ro \gwäˈtēbəˌrō\ *or* **gua·ti·ve·re** \-ēvəˌrā\ *n* -s [AmerSp (Cuba) *guatibere*] **:** any of several groupers; *esp* **:** CONEY 5a

gua·tó \gwäˈtō\ *n, pl* **guató** *or* **guatós** *usu cap* [Sp & Pg, of AmerInd origin] **1 a :** a people of southwestern Mato Grosso, Brazil **b :** a member of such people **2 :** the language of the Guató people constituting the Guatoan language family

gua·to·an \-ōən\ *adj, usu cap* **:** of, relating to, or being the So. American Indian language family comprising Guató

gua·tu·san \gwäˈtüsᵊn\ *adj, usu cap* **:** of or relating to the Guatuso people or their language

gua·tu·so \gwäˈtü(ˌ)sō\ *n, pl* **guatuso** *or* **guatusos** *usu cap* [Sp *guatuso, guatuzo, huatuso*, of AmerInd origin] **1 a :** a Chibchan people of Costa Rica **b :** a member of such people **2 :** a language of the Guatuso people

gua·va \ˈgwävə *also* -wȯvə\ *n, pl* **guavas** *also* **guava** [Sp, alter. of *guayaba*, of Arawakan origin; akin to Galibi *goyaba* guava, Tupi *guaiába, guayava*] **1 a :** a small shrubby tropical American tree (*Psidium guajava*) that is widely cultivated in warm regions for its sweet or somewhat acid usu. globular yellow fruit **b :** any of several other plants of the genus *Psidium* that bear edible fruit (as the strawberry guava or the Brazilian guava) **2 :** the fruit of a guava **3 :** INGA 2; *esp* **:** a West Indian tree (*Inga vera*) resembling the common guava and similarly used

gua·vi·na \gwäˈvēnə\ *n* -s [AmerSp *guabina*, fr. Taino] **1 :** a fish of the family Eleotridae **2 :** any of several gobies of the warmer parts of America

gua·xi·ma \gwäˈshēmə\ *n* -s [Pg *guaxima, guaxuma* caesar weed, fr. Tupi *aguaixima*] **:** a strong soft lustrous cordage fiber produced in parts of Africa and Brazil from Caesar weed

gua·ya·ba \gwəˈyäbə\ *n* -s [Sp — more at GUAVA] **:** GUAVA

gua·ya·bi \ˌgwīəˈbē\ *n* -s [AmerSp *guayabi, guayaibi*, fr. Guarani *guayavi*] **1 :** a large So. American timber tree (*Patagonula americana*) of the family Boraginaceae **2 :** the highly valued hard tough heavy wood of the guayabi: **a :** a thick whitish or pale brown sapwood that is used esp. for parts or articles (as tool handles and oars) subject to rough usage and recurrent strain **b :** a heartwood usu. variegated in shades of brown or blackish purple and capable of taking a high polish that is used for fine furniture, turning, and cabinetwork

gua·ya·bo \gwəˈyä(ˌ)bō\ *n* -s [Sp, guava (tree), fr. *guayaba* — more at GUAVA] **:** GUAVA

gua·ya·can \ˌgwīəˈkän\ *n* -s [Sp *guayacán* — more at GUAIACUM] **1 :** any of several So. and Central American timber trees typically with strong dense hard wood: as **a :** any of certain lignum vitae of the genus *Guaiacum* (esp. *G. sanctum*) **b :** any of certain trees of the genus *Tabebuia* **c :** an Argentine tree (*Caesalpinia melanocarpa*) yielding a timber used for railway ties, paving, and heavy construction **d :** GUAIACUM WOOD **2 :** GUAIACUM 2

gua·ya·ki \ˌgwīəˈkē\ *n, pl* **guayakí** *or* **guayakís** *usu cap* [Sp *guayaquí*, of AmerInd origin] **1 a :** a Guaranian people of Paraguay **b :** a member of such people **2 :** a language of the Guayaki people

gua·ya·quil \ˌgwīəˈkēl, -kil, ˌ==ˈ=\ *adj, usu cap* [fr. *Guayaquil*, city in Ecuador] **:** of or from the city of Guayaquil, Ecuador **:** of the kind or style prevalent in Guayaquil

guaycurú *usu cap, var of* GUAICURU

guay·mi *also* **guai·mi** \(ˈ)gwīˈmē\ *n, pl* **guaymi** *or* **guaymis** *usu cap* [Sp *guaymí, guaimí*, of AmerInd origin] **1 a :** a Chibchan people or group of peoples of Panama and Costa Rica **b :** a member of such people or group of peoples **2 :** a language of the Guaymi people

gua·yu·le \(g)wīˈüˌlē\ *or* **hua·yu·le** \wī-\ *n* -s [AmerSp, fr. Nahuatl *cuauhuli*, lit., tree gum, fr. *cuahuitl* tree + *uli* gum] **1 :** a much-branched subshrub (*Parthenium argentatum*) with slender silvery leaves and small white flowers that is native to dry parts of Mexico and the adjacent southwestern U. S. and has been cultivated as a source of rubber **2** *or* **guayule rubber :** rubber obtained from guayule

gua·zu·ma \gwäˈzümə\ *n, cap* [NL, fr. AmerSp *guázuma* — more at GUACIMO] **:** a small genus of chiefly tropical American trees (family Sterculiaceae) with alternate toothed leaves, cymose flowers, and a woody capsule — see BASTARD CEDAR *e*

gua·zu·ti \ˌgwäzəˈtē\ *n* -s [AmerSp *guazutí*, fr. Guarani, lit., white deer, fr. *guazú* deer + *ti* white] **:** PAMPAS DEER

gubar numeral *var of* GOBAR NUMERAL

gub·ber·tushed \ˈgübə(r)ˌtüsht, ˈgəbə(r)ˌtəsht\ *adj* [*gubber*, of unknown origin + *tushed*, alter. of *toothed*] *now dial Eng* **:** having large projecting teeth **:** BUCK-TOOTHED

gub·bins \ˈgəbənz\ *also* **gub·bings** \", -biŋz\ *n pl but sing or pl in constr* [*gubbins*, pl. of *gubbin* fragment, paring, alter. of obs. E *gobone* gobbet, portion, fr. ME *gobyn, goboun; gubbings*, alter. of *gubbins*] **1** *dial Brit* **:** fish parings or refuse; *broadly* **:** any bits and pieces **:** SCRAPS **2** *Brit* **:** GADGETS, GADGETRY ⟨the ~ for changing a tire⟩ ⟨all the navigational ~ —J.L.Rhys⟩ **3** *Brit* **:** a foolish or futile person **:** SIMPLETON ⟨you silly ~⟩

guber *var of* GOOBER

gu·ber·nac·u·lar \ˌg(y)übə(r)ˈnakyələ(r), ˌgüb-\ *adj* **:** of, relating to, or constituting a gubernaculum

gu·ber·nac·u·lum \ˌ==ˈ==ləm\ *n, pl* **gubernacu·la** \-lə\ [NL, fr. L, rudder, fr. *gubernare* to steer + *-culum* -cle — more at GOVERN] **:** a part or structure that serves as a guide: as **a :** a fibrous cord that connects the fetal testis with the bottom of the scrotum and by failing to elongate commensurately with the rest of the fetus causes the descent of the testis **b :** a posterior flagellum of certain protozoans **c :** a sclerotized accessory structure associated with the copulatory spicules of various nematode worms

gu·ber·na·tion \ˌ==ˈnāshən\ *n* -s [ME *gubernacioun*, fr. L *gubernation-, gubernatio*, fr. *gubernatus* (past part. of *gubernare* to govern, steer) + *-ion-, -io* -ion] *archaic* **:** GOVERNMENT

gu·ber·na·tive \ˈ==ˌnād·iv, -ˌnəd-\ *adj* [ME, fr. MF or LL; MF *gubernatif*, fr. LL *gubernativus* governing, fr. L *gubernatus* (past part.) + *-ivus* -ive] **:** concerned with or devoted to government or governing — **gu·ber·na·tive·ly** \-d·əvlē\ *adv*

gu·ber·na·tor \-ˌnād·ə(r)\ *n* -s [L, fr. *gubernatus* (past part.) + *-or*] **:** RULER, GOVERNOR

gu·ber·na·to·ri·al *R & -R* ˌgübənəˈtōrēəl, -tȯr- *also* ˌgyüb- *or* ˌgüb- *sometimes* ˌgəb-, *R also* -bərn-\ *adj* [LL *gubernatorius* controlling, governing (fr. L *gubernator* governor) + E *-al*] **:** of or relating to a governor or to government

gubernatrix *n* -ES [L, fem. of *gubernator*] *obs* **:** a female ruler

gu·ber·ni·ya *or* **gu·ber·nia** \güˈbernē(y)ə\ *n* -s [Russ *guberniya* government, guberniya, prob. fr. Pol *gubernja*, fr. L *gubernare* to govern] **1 :** a territorial subdivision of prerevolutionary Russia **2 :** a former provincial soviet — compare OBLAST

guck \ˈgək\ *n* -s [perh. blend of *goo* and *muck*] *slang* **:** something unpleasant or offensive ⟨an unbroken diet of custards and such ~⟩; *usu* **:** oozy sloppy dirt or debris ⟨beds of ~ from the cleaned sewers —Saul Bellow⟩

gu·dame \(ˈ)gœˈdām, (ˈ)gï-, (ˈ)gi-, ˈ=ˌdəm\ *n* -s [ME (northern dial.) *gudame, guddame*, fr. *gud, gude* (var. of *good*) + *dame*] *Scot* **:** GRANDMOTHER

guddee *var of* 1GADDI

gud·dle \ˈgədᵊl\ *vb* -ED/-ING/-S [prob. of imit. origin] *vt* **:** to catch (fish) with the hands by groping (as under banks or stones) ~ *vi* **1 :** to grope for fish in their lurking places **2** *chiefly Scot* **:** to feel one's way with or as if with the hands **:** GROPE

1gude \ˈgœd, ˈgïd, ˈgid\ *Scot var of* GOOD

2gude \ˈgüd\ *Scot var of* GOD

gude·sire \(ˈ)gœdˌsī(ə)r, (ˈ)gïd-, (ˈ)gid-, ˈ=ˌs(h)ər, ˈgəchər\ *n* [ME (Scot. dial.) *gudsire*, fr. *gud* (var. of *good*) + *sire*] *Scot* **:** GRANDFATHER

gude·wife \(ˈ)gœˈdwəif, (ˈ)gïˈ-, (ˈ)giˈ-\ *var of* GOODWIFE

1gud·geon \ˈgəjən\ *n* -s [ME *gudyon, gogoyne, goione*, fr. MF *gougon, goujon*, fr. OF *gogon, gojon*, perh. fr. LL *gubia, gulbia* hollow chisel — more at GOUGE] **1 :** PIVOT, JOURNAL: as **a :** an iron or steel pivot fixed in the end of a wooden shaft **b :** a crosshead pin on which a connecting rod turns **2 a :** a ring at the base of a hinge that encloses and turns on the pintle of the hinge **b :** a metal socket attached to the sternpost of a boat to receive the rudder pintle **c :** a notch in carrick bitts to receive a spindle bush **3 :** an iron pin for fastening together blocks of stone

2gudgeon \"\ *n* -s [ME *gojune, gojon, gogyn*, fr. MF *gougon, gouvion*, fr. OF, fr. L *gobion-, gobio, cobion-, cobio* — more at GOBY] **1 a :** a small easily caught European freshwater fish (*Gobio gobio*) that is related to the carps and is often used for food and for bait **b** (1) **:** any of various gobies (2) **:** any of several Australian fishes of the family Eleotridae **c :** any of various killifishes **d :** BURBOT **2 a :** a person easily duped or cheated **b :** BAIT, ALLUREMENT

3gudgeon \"\ *vt* -ED/-ING/-S *archaic* **:** to deprive fraudulently **:** CHEAT, DUPE

gudgeon pin *n* **:** WRIST PIN

gud·mun·dite \ˈgüdmənˌdīt\ *n* -s [G *gudmundit*, fr. *Gudmundstorp*, Sweden, its locality + G *-it* -ite] **:** a mineral FeSbS that is a sulfide and antimonide of iron

gu·dok \(ˈ)güˈdȯk\ *n* -s [Russ, fr. *gudet'* to sound, drone, hum — more at GUSLA] **:** a primitive 3-stringed Russian viol instrument

gue \ˈgyü\ *n* -s [modif. of Norw (dial.) *gjija*, fr. ON *gīgja* fiddle — more at JIG] **:** a 2-stringed viol instrument formerly used in Shetland

guel·der rose \ˈgeldə(r)-\ *n* [fr. *Guelders* or *Guelderland* (D *Gelderland*), province, Netherlands] **:** CRANBERRY BUSH 2; *esp* **:** a cultivated form of the cranberry bush with large globose heads of sterile flowers — see SNOWBALL

guelf *or* **guelph** \ˈgwelf, -eůf\ *n* -s *usu cap* [It *Guelfo*, fr. ML *Guelphus*, fr. MHG *Welf*, name of a German princely family, fr. OHG *welf, hwelf* whelp — more at WHELP] **:** a member of a political faction in Italy from the 12th to the 15th centuries that opposed the authority of the German emperors in Italy and was made up of a church party asserting the papacy to be independent of the emperors and a party of principalities and city republics contending for their own rights and liberties — compare GHIBELLINE — **guelf·ic** *or* **guelph·ic** \-fik\ *adj, usu cap*

guelph keg \"-\ *n, usu cap G* [fr. the name *Guelph*] **:** a cylindrical wooden vessel made of two or three layers of veneer

gue·mal \ˈg(w)āməl\ *or* **gue·mul** \gwäˈmül\ *or* **ge·mul** \gäˈmül\ *or* **hue·mul** \wäˈmül\ *n* -s [AmerSp *güemul, guamul, huemul*, fr. Araucan *huemul*] **:** either of two small So. American deer (*Hippocamelus bisulcus* and *H. antisiensis*) having simple forked antlers

gue·non \gəˈnōⁿ, -nän\ *n* -s [F, fr. MF] **:** any of various long-tailed chiefly arboreal African monkeys of *Cercopithecus* and related genera (as the green monkey and grivet)

1guer·don \ˈgərdᵊn\ *n* -s [ME, fr. MF *guerdon, guerredon*, fr. OF, modif. (influenced by L *donum* gift) of OHG *widarlōn*, fr. *widar* again, against + *lōn* reward — more at WITH, LUCRE] **:** something that one has earned or gained **:** REWARD, RECOMPENSE, REQUITAL

2guerdon \"\ *vt* -ED/-ING/-S [ME *gerdonen*, fr. MF *guerredoner*, fr. OF, fr. *guerredon*, n.] **1 :** to give guerdon to **:** REWARD ⟨richly ~*ed* for his aid⟩ **2 :** to be a recompense for ⟨a gem to ~ faithful service⟩

guer·don·less \-ləs\ *adj* [ME *gwerdounles*, fr. *guerdoun, guerdon* + *-les* -less] **:** receiving no guerdon

gue·reza \gəˈrezə\ *n* -s [native name in Ethiopia] **:** any of several African monkeys of the genus *Colobus* (esp. *C. guereza*) that have along the sides of the body and on the tail long white fringes of silky hair contrasting with the black or occas. reddish ground color of the coat

gue·ri·don \gärēdōⁿ\ *n, pl* **gueridons** \-ōⁿ(z)\ [F *guéridon*, fr. the name *Guéridon*] **:** a small stand or table (as for a lamp or vase) usu. ornately carved and embellished

gue·rite \(ˈ)gāˈrēt\ *n* -s [F *guérite*, fr. MF, prob. alter. of OF *garite, guarite* watchtower — more at GARRET] **:** a turret or shelter for a sentry on an old fort

1guern·sey \ˈgərnzē, ˈgōn-, ˈgəin-, -zi\ *adj, usu cap* [fr. *Guernsey*, Channel islands] **:** of or from the island of Guernsey, Channel islands **:** of the kind or style prevalent in Guernsey

2guernsey \"\ *n* **1** -s **:** a heavy knitted garment usu. in the form of a shirt and worn esp. by sailors — compare JERSEY 2 **2 a** *usu cap* **:** a breed of fawn and white dairy cattle larger than Jerseys and producing rich yellowish milk that was developed on the island of Guernsey from stock of French origin **b** -s *often cap* **:** an animal of this breed

guernsey elm *n, usu cap G* **:** JERSEY ELM

guernsey lily *n, usu cap G* **:** a southern African bulbous plant (*Nerine sarniensis*) with bright red umbellate flowers that is naturalized on the island of Guernsey and widely cultivated as an ornamental

guernsey partridge *n, usu cap G* **:** RED-LEGGED PARTRIDGE

guer·ril·la *also* **gue·ril·la** \gəˈrilə\ *n* -s *often attrib* [Sp *guerrilla*, lit., small war, dim. of *guerra* war, fr. OHG *werra* discord, strife, quarrel — more at WAR] **1** *archaic* **:** irregular war carried on by independent bands **2 a :** one who carries on or assists in an irregular war or engages in irregular warfare in connection with a regular war; *esp* **:** a member of an independent band engaged in predatory excursions in wartime **b :** a member of a military detachment functioning in the rear of enemy lines esp. in guerrilla warfare

guer·ril·la·ism \-ləˌizəm\ *n* -s **:** the activities of guerrillas **:** GUERRILLA WARFARE

guerrilla warfare *n* **:** military actions carried out by small forces in the rear of an enemy with the object of harassing the enemy, interrupting his lines of communication, and destroying his supplies

guer·ri·lle·ro \ˌgerə(l)ˈye(ˌ)rō\ *n* -s [Sp, fr. *guerrilla*] **:** GUERRILLA 2a

gues *pl of* GUE

guesd·ism \ˈgeˌdizəm\ *n* -s *usu cap* [Jules B. *Guesde* †1922 Fr. political leader + E *-ism*] **:** Marxian socialism as advocated by Jules Guesde

guesd·ist \-dəst\ *n* -s *usu cap* [J. *Guesde* + E *-ist*] **:** an advocate of or adherent to Guesdism

1guess \ˈges\ *vb* -ED/-ING/-ES [ME *gessen*, prob. of Scand origin; akin to Icel *gizka* to guess, Norw & Sw *gissa*; akin to MD *gissen, gessen* to guess, MLG *gissen* to guess, ON *geta* to get, guess — more at GET] *vt* **1 :** to form a judgment or opinion of without knowledge or often without means of knowledge: **a :** to form an opinion of from insufficient, uncertain, or ambiguous evidence or on grounds of probability alone **:** CONJECTURE, ESTIMATE, SURMISE ⟨could only ~ what the final result of this study would be⟩ ⟨~*ed* his age and missed by five years⟩ ⟨correctly ~*ed* the height of the building⟩ ⟨looked at the sky and ~*ed* that there would be rain before morning⟩ **:** ASSUME, DEDUCE, INFER ⟨the theory has first to be ~*ed*, and its consequences drawn out and tested afterwards —Maurice Cranston & J.W.N.Watkins⟩ ⟨what can be deduced and ~*ed* from these quaint and curious volumes of forgotten lore —A.M.Young⟩ **b :** to form an opinion of without evidence **:** make a random judgment or supposition concerning ⟨amused themselves by ~*ing* the identity of their fellow passengers⟩ ⟨a prize for ~*ing* correctly the number of beans in a beanbag⟩ ⟨~ which hand holds a coin⟩ **2 :** to conjecture correctly: **a :** to hit upon or solve by a conjecture **:** arrive at (a correct answer or solution) partly or solely by chance or intuition ⟨~*ed* my age the first time⟩ ⟨an amazing ability at ~*ing* riddles⟩ ⟨an attempt to ~ the acrostic with more than half the lines unsolved —J.E.S. Thompson⟩ ⟨new words can be ~*ed*, shades of meaning deduced from a second reading —J.M.Barzun⟩ **b :** to form a true or proper opinion of esp. without pertinent knowledge of one's own **:** CONCEIVE, DIVINE, GATHER ⟨an objective the full nature of which may not have been ~*ed* —Mary Austin⟩ ⟨enough is said for the reader to ~ something of what it must have meant to stand at last on the summit of the world —E.F.Norton⟩ **3 :** BELIEVE, IMAGINE, SUPPOSE, THINK — usu. used with an objective clause or with *so* ⟨~ I'll go to bed⟩ ⟨said he ~*ed* he knew as much as the next man⟩ ⟨thought for a moment and then answered that he ~*ed so*⟩ ⟨what saved him, I ~, was his unfaltering sense of the ridiculous —Giles Romilly⟩ ~ *vi* **:** to make a guess **:** form a random judgment **:** CONJECTURE ⟨if you don't know the answers, ~⟩ ⟨a matter we can only ~ about⟩ ⟨~*ed* wrong⟩ ⟨~*ed* at the probable outcome of the discussions⟩ **syn** see CONJECTURE

2guess \"\ *n* -ES [ME *gesse*, fr. *gessen*, v.] **:** an opinion formed without sufficient or decisive evidence or grounds **:** CONJECTURE, SURMISE ⟨when he had made his scientific ~, his hypothesis, he computed what ought to happen, if it were true, in certain definite cases —Josiah Royce⟩ — **by guess and by god** *also* **by guess and by gosh** *or* **by guess and by golly :** without employment of an ordinary degree of technical accuracy or knowledge (as in measuring or in formulating materials) ⟨some of these surveys were done completely *by guess and by god*⟩

3guess \"\ *adj* [prob. fr. D *gust*, fr. MD; akin to LG *güste* barren, EFris *güst, geste* barren, OHG *geisini* barrenness — more at GEASON] *dial Eng, of a cow or ewe* **:** BARREN, DRY

guess·able \-səbəl\ *adj* **:** being such as may be guessed

guess·er \-sə(r)\ *n* -s [ME *gessare*, fr. *gessen*, v. + *-are, -er*] **:** one that guesses

guessing game *n* **:** a game in which the participants compete individually or in teams in the identification of something indicated obscurely (as in riddles or charades); *broadly* **:** a situation (as in politics or international relations) in which opposing factions attempt to gain advantages by each keeping its own intentions dark

guess·ing·ly *adv* [fr. pres. part. of 1*guess* + *-ly*] **:** by means of guessing **:** by guesswork

guess-rope \ˈgesˌrōp\ *n* [alter. (influenced by *guess-warp*) of earlier *guest rope*] **1 :** GUESS-WARP **2 :** GUEST ROPE

guess stick *n* **1** *slang* **:** SLIDE RULE **2** *slang* **:** SCALE RULE

1guess·ti·mate *or* **gues·ti·mate** \ˈgestəˌmāt\ *vt* -ED/-ING/-S [blend of 1*guess* and *estimate*, v.] *slang* **:** to form an estimate of (as future population, costs, employment) without adequate factual or statistical information

2guess·ti·mate *or* **gues·ti·mate** \-ˌmət\ *n* -s *slang* **:** an estimate arrived at solely or chiefly by guesswork

guess-warp *or* **ges·warp** \ˈgeˌswȯrp\ *n* [ME *gyes warp*, fr. *gyes* (origin and meaning unknown) + *warp*] **1 :** a line carried in a small boat from a ship to a buoy, an anchor, or the shore **2 :** GUEST ROPE **3 :** a line led from a ship through a fairlead on a boat boom for small boats to make fast to

guesswork \ˈ=ˌ=\ *n* [2*guess* + *work*] **:** work performed or results obtained by guess **:** CONJECTURE

1guest \ˈgest\ *n* -s *often attrib* [ME *gest, gist*, fr. ON *gestr*; akin to OE *gæst, giest* guest, stranger, OHG *gast*, Goth *gasts* guest, stranger, L *hostis* stranger, enemy] **1** *obs* **:** STRANGER **2 a :** a person entertained in one's house or at one's table ⟨had unexpected ~s for supper⟩ ⟨~ towels⟩ ⟨invited ~s for Christmas⟩ **b :** a person to whom hospitality (as of a home or club) is extended; *esp* **:** one invited to participate in some activity (as an excursion) at the expense of another ⟨played golf at the country club as the ~ of one of the members⟩ ⟨a theater party of six, the host and five ~s⟩ ⟨enjoyed ~ privileges at several clubs⟩ **c :** a person who lodges, boards, or receives refreshment for pay (as at a hotel, boardinghouse, restaurant) whether permanently or transiently **:** PATRON **d :** a traveler who in return for compensation receives from an innkeeper or hotelkeeper for an indefinite time board, lodging, and entertainment and for whose safety and comfort and the safeguarding of whose property the innkeeper or hotelkeeper is responsible under law — compare LODGER **e :** one who visits or travels in an area (as a state or province) beyond the boundaries of his established residence or work **f :** one who visits, travels or resides abroad by permission of a foreign country ⟨~ of Canada⟩ **g :** a person who accepts transportation (as in a motor vehicle) for which he makes no financial recompense **3 :** an organism sharing the dwelling of another; *usu* **:** an insect inhabiting or breeding in a nest or gall of another insect often without causing much inconvenience to the original owner except by consuming the supply of food **:** INQUILINE — compare MYRMECOPHILE **4 :** a mineral introduced into and usu. displacing a preexistent mineral or rock **5 a** *or* **guest artist** *or* **guest star :** a person usu. of prominence in the entertainment world who appears temporarily on a program (as a radio or television show) or with an organization (as an orchestra or theatrical stock company) ⟨a ~ announcer⟩ ⟨doubled his income by making ~ appearances⟩ **b :** a person not a regular member of a cast or company (as a member of a studio audience) who participates in a show

2guest \"\ *vb* -ED/-ING/-S [ME *gesten*, fr. *gest*, n.] *vt* **:** to receive or entertain as a guest ⟨local members ~*ed* most of the delegates⟩ ~ *vi* **1** *archaic* **:** to be or act the part of a guest **2 :** to appear as a guest (as on radio or television or in a theatrical performance)

guestchamber \ˈ=ˌ=ˌ=\ *n* **:** GUEST ROOM

guest-conduct \ˌ==ˈ=\ *vt* **:** to lead or direct (a musical organization) as a guest — **guest conductor** *n*

guest·en \ˈgestən\ *adj* [ME *geston*, prob. fr. pl. of *gest*] *archaic* **:** for guests

guest·er \ˈgestə(r)\ *n* -s **:** one that guests

guest flag *n* **:** a blue rectangular flag with a diagonal white stripe flown on a yacht to indicate that the craft is being used by a guest of the owner in the owner's absence

guesthouse \ˈ=ˌ=\ *n* [ME *gest house*, fr. *gest* guest + *house*] **:** a building for guests: as **a :** a separate building in a monastic establishment provided esp. formerly for the reception of travelers **b :** a separate establishment on a private estate for the accommodation of guests **c :** a superior boardinghouse usu. providing for its guests recreational and social amenities as well as food and lodging

guest·ing \ˈgestiŋ\ *n* -s [ME *gesting*, fr. gerund of *gesten*] *archaic* **:** the action of lodging or entertaining a guest

guest·less \ˈgestləs\ *adj* **:** having no guests; *sometimes* **:** INHOSPITABLE

guest·ly \-lē\ *adj* **:** like a guest **:** suitable for guests

guestmaster \ˈ=ˌ==\ *n* **:** one whose duty it is to receive and entertain guests in a religious house **:** HOSTELER

guest of honor 1 : one in whose honor a social function or ceremony is held **2 :** an eminent person invited to a social function or ceremony

guest ranch *n* **:** DUDE RANCH

guest right *n* **:** a claim to a privilege (as entertainment or protection) to which a guest is entitled usu. for a brief period by custom or law; *also* **:** the right esp. among primitive peoples to make such a claim on the basis of blood or other relationship

guest room *n* **:** a room for the use of guests: as **a :** a bedroom in a home not regularly occupied by a member of the household and kept primarily for guests **:** a spare room **b :** a room in a hotel or lodging house for occupation by guests

guest rope \ˈgeˌstrōp\ *n* [prob. alter. of *guess* (as in *guess-warp*)] **1 :** a line that is supplementary to a towline and is used esp. to keep the tow steady **2 :** a line run along a ship's side or out to the end of a boom for small boats to hold to — called also *boat line, grab rope*

guestwise *adv, obs* **:** like a guest **:** in the manner proper to a guest

guet·a·pens \ˌged·əˈpäⁿ\ *n, pl* **guetapens** \-äⁿ(z)\ [F *guet-apens*, fr. MF, fr. *de guet apens* with premeditation, alter. of *de guet apensé*] **:** AMBUSH, SNARE, TRAP ⟨a trick to lure him into some new ~ —Rafael Sabatini⟩

gue·tar *or* **gue·tare** \gwäˈtär\ *n, pl* **guetar** *or* **guetars** *or* **guetare** *or* **guetares** *usu cap* [Sp *Güetar*, of AmerInd origin] **1 a :** a Chibchan people of central Costa Rica **b :** a member of such people **2 :** the language of the Guetar people

gue·tre \ˈgäd·ə(r)\ *archaic var of* GAITER

guet·tar·da \gəˈtärdə\ *n* [NL, after Jacques Étienne *Guettard* †1786 Fr. naturalist] **1** *cap* **:** a genus of tropical American shrubs or trees (family Rubiaceae) with hard fine-grained yellowish brown to gray wood **2** -s **:** any plant of the genus *Guettarda*

gu·fa *or* **guf·fa** *also* **goo·fa** *or* **goo·fah** \'güfə\ *or* **ku·fa** *or* **koo·fah** \'kü-\ *n* -s [Ar *quffah* basket] **:** a round boat made of wickerwork used in Mesopotamia from ancient times

gufa

guff \'gəf\ *n* -s [prob. of imit. origin] **:** utterances that are foolish, intended to mislead or deceive, and often truculent **:** HUMBUG, BALDERDASH; *broadly* **:** idle chitchat

[1]**guf·faw** \(,)gə'fȯ, '≈,≈\ *n* -s [imit.] **:** a loud or boisterous burst of laughter

[2]**guffaw** \"\ *vi* -ED/-ING/-s **:** to laugh noisily or coarsely

guf·fer \'gəfər\ *n* -s [origin unknown] *Scot* **:** EELPOUT 1a

gu·gel·hupf \'gügəl,hü(p)f\ *or* **gu·gel·hof** *also* **gou·gel·hof** \-hōf\ *n* -s [G *gugelhupf, gugelhopf,* fr. *gugel* cowl, monk's hood (fr. MHG *gugel, gugele,* fr. OHG *cucula, cugela,* fr. LL *cuculla*) + *hupf, hopf,* var. of dial. (Bavaria) *hepfen* yeast (fr. OHG *heffan* to raise, heave) — more at COWL (hood), HEAVE] **:** a semisweet cake usu. of yeast-leavened dough containing raisins, citron, and nuts and baked in a fluted tube pan

gug·gen·heim \'gügən,hīm, 'gùg- *sometimes* 'gəg-\ *n* -s *usu cap* [fr. the name *Guggenheim*] **:** CATEGORY 3

[1]**gug·gle** \'gəgəl\ *vb* **guggled; guggled; guggling** \-g(ə)liŋ\ **guggles** [imit.] *vi* **1 :** to make a sound like that of liquid poured from a flask **2 a :** to flow with a guggling sound **:** GURGLE ⟨water *guggling* over the stones⟩ **b :** to drink (as from a jug) with such a sound ~ *vt* **:** to pour or drink (as liquor) with a guggling sound

[2]**guggle** \"\ *n* -s **:** a sound of guggling **:** GURGLE

guglet *var of* GOGLET

gu·glia \'gülyə\ *or* **gu·glio** \-l(,)yō\ *n* -s [It *guglia,* alter. (resulting from incorrect division of *l'aguglia*) of obs. It *aguglia* (also, needle), fr. OProv *agulha,* fr. LL *acucula* ornamental pin — more at AGLET] **:** OBELISK

gu·gu *or* **goo–goo** \'gü(,)gü\ *n* -s [origin unknown] **:** a native of the Philippine islands — used chiefly in Hawaii and often disparagingly

guhr \'gù(ə)r\ *n* -s [G *guhr, gur;* akin to MHG *gern* to ferment, OHG *jesan* — more at YEAST] **1 :** a loose earthy deposit from water occurring in the cavities of rocks, being mostly white but sometimes red or yellow, and consisting of a varying mixture of clay or ocher **2** [by shortening] **:** KIESELGUHR

gui·ana \gē'anə *also* -'änə *or* -'ànə, *chiefly in British Guiana* gī'anə\ *adj, usu cap* [fr. *Guiana,* region in northern So. America] **:** of or from Guiana, a region of northern So. America **:** of a kind or style prevalent in Guiana **:** GUIANESE

guiana chestnut *n, usu cap G* **:** the seed of the provision tree

gui·anan \-nən\ *adj or n, usu cap* [*Guiana,* the region + E *-an*] **:** GUIANESE

guiana plum *n, usu cap G* **1 :** any of several tropical American shrubs or small trees of the genus *Drypetes* (family Euphorbiaceae); *esp* **:** a shrubby tree (*D. lateriflora*) whose range extends northward into southern Florida — called also *Florida plum* **2 :** the usu. reddish rather dry drupaceous fruit of a Guiana plum

guiana tree *n, usu cap G* **:** a timber tree (*Helicostylis poeppigiana*) of the family Moraceae that has reddish brown hard heavy wood and is widely distributed in northern So. America

[1]**gui·a·nese** \,gēə'nēz, ,gīə-, -nēs\ *adj, usu cap* [*Guiana,* the region + E *-ese*] **1 :** of, relating to, or characteristic of the region of Guiana **2 :** of, relating to, or characteristic of the people of Guiana

[2]**guianese** \"\ *n* -s *usu cap* **:** a native or inhabitant of the region of Guiana

gui·ano–brazilian \gē¦a(,)nō, -¦ä(-, -¦à(-, ¦gēə,nō, ¦gīə,nō +\ *adj, usu cap G&B* [*Guiana,* the region + E *-o-* + [1]*Brazilian*] **:** of or relating to Guiana and Brazil; *broadly* **:** BRAZILIAN 3

guib \'gib\ *n* -s [native name in Africa] **:** a small harnessed antelope (*Tragelaphus scriptus*) of western Africa

gui·chet \gē'shā\ *n* -s [F, fr. OF, of Gmc origin; akin to MD *wiket, winket* wicket — more at WICKET] **:** a grill opening (as a hatch or wicket); *esp* **:** a ticket window

guid \'gæd, 'gïed, 'gid\ *Scot var of* GOOD

gui·da \'gwēdə\ *n* -s [It, guide, fr. OIt *guidare* to guide, direct, fr. OProv *guidar*] **1 :** the subject of a fugue or the antecedent of a canon **2 :** DIRECT 1 **3 :** a sign indicating the points of entry in a round or canon

guid·able \'gīdəbəl\ *adj* [[2]*guide* + *-able*] **:** capable of being guided **:** TRACTABLE

guid·ance \'gīdən(t)s\ *n* -s *often attrib* **1 a :** an act of guiding **:** the superintendence or assistance rendered by a guide **:** DIRECTION, LEADING ⟨the blind boy depended on the ~ of his dog⟩ ⟨a manual for the ~ of home handymen⟩ **b :** advice in choosing courses, preparing for a vocation or further education, or coping with personal problems given to students by a teacher or a professional counselor ⟨a ~ specialist⟩ **2 :** a program or service functioning to promote the adjustment of special groups (as disturbed or delinquent children or prisoners) chiefly through psychological counseling and appraisal **3 :** the process of controlling the course of a projectile (as a missile or bomb) by a built-in mechanism ⟨~ system⟩ — compare GUIDED MISSILE

[1]**guide** \'gīd\ *n* -s [ME *gide,* fr. MF *guide,* fr. OProv *guida,* fr. *guidar* to guide, direct, of Gmc origin; akin to OE *witan* to look after, depart, *witan* to know — more at WIT] **1 a :** a person who leads or directs another in his way or course (as in a strange country or through difficult terrain) **b :** a person who exhibits and usu. discusses or explains points of interest (as of a city, a museum collection, or a building) to sightseers **c :** something (as a guidebook, signpost, or instruction manual) that provides a person with guiding information **d :** one (as a teacher) who directs a person in his conduct or course of life **:** DIRECTOR, SUPERVISOR ⟨no boy ever had a better ~ than I in the fundamental decencies of life⟩ **2 a :** a contrivance for directing the motion of something; *esp* **:** such a contrivance (as in a tool) having a directing edge, surface, or channel **b :** a device (as a ring or loop) made usu. of metal or agate and attached to a fishing rod to hold the line in position **c :** the groove in which the plow used in bookbinding moves **d :** a small device for guiding threads or strands of fiber on a spinning, winding, quilling, or other textile machine **e :** a device in a printing press or folding machine for holding and releasing a sheet **f :** a grooved director for a surgical probe or knife **g :** a sheet of metal or other material or a card with projecting edge or tab for labeling that is inserted in a card catalog, index, or other file to facilitate reference **3 a :** a person or vehicle upon whom the movements or alignments of a military command are regulated — used esp. in commands ⟨~ right⟩ ⟨~ center⟩ **b :** a warship on which others in a formation regulate their positions **4 a :** GIRL GUIDE **b :** an 11-year-old to 16-year-old girl guide — distinguished from *brownie*

[2]**guide** \"\ *vb* -ED/-ING/-s [ME *giden, guiden,* fr. MF *guider,* alter. (influenced by *guide,* n.) of OF *guier,* of Gmc origin; akin to OE *witan* to look after, depart, *witan* to know — more at WIT] *vt* **1 :** to act as a guide to **:** direct in a way **:** CONDUCT, PILOT ⟨*guided* us through the city⟩ **2 a :** to regulate and manage **:** direct or supervise esp. toward some desirable end, course, way, or development **b :** to superintend the training or education of **:** INSTRUCT, ADVISE, COUNSEL ⟨his studies were *guided* by one of the great educators of the day⟩ **3** *Scot* **:** to treat or handle esp. another person or an animal ⟨*guided* her ill⟩ ~ *vi* **:** to act or work as a guide

syn LEAD, STEER, PILOT, ENGINEER: GUIDE may apply to the act of conducting or directing along a course as performed by one with certain, specific, or intimate knowledge or by something equally trustworthy ⟨*guided* by a native on their expedition through the mountains⟩ ⟨*guide* patrons to their proper seats⟩ ⟨inspired and galvanized by the personality of a great man who was *guiding* them in their art —Stephen Williams⟩ ⟨be *guided* by good judgment —C.S.Kilby⟩ LEAD suggests preceding to show the way; sometimes, in addition, it indicates keeping those following in order; it may refer to taking initiative, determining procedure, or assuming a director's role ⟨*led* his men to safety⟩ ⟨*led* the caravan west⟩ ⟨*leading* the supporters of the amendment⟩ ⟨the man *leading* the research project⟩ STEER suggests the action of one planning or adhering to a course with concomitant controlling, governing, or maneuvering ⟨*steering* the ship past the sandbars into the harbor⟩ ⟨deftly *steered* the Council of the International Congress through its problems concerned with the place of the next session —A.L.Kroeber⟩ ⟨secure in the faith that his reasoned intelligence will *steer* him correctly at all times —H. N.Maclean⟩ PILOT suggests guiding or steering over a dangerous, intricate, or complicated course or route ⟨*pilot* the ship through the channel⟩ ⟨wagon trains *piloted* by bearded scouts⟩ ⟨took his sister's arm and *piloted* her to a safer corner⟩ ⟨*piloting* important bills through the senate —*Current Biog.*⟩ ENGINEER may refer to planning and supervising construction; it often indicates carrying through, executing, or effectuating with contriving, maneuvering, manipulating, and calculating ⟨the influential Americans in Hawaii, with the connivance of U. S. Minister Stevens and the "moral" support of American marines, *engineered* a revolution, deposed the Queen —J.W. Ellison b.1891⟩ ⟨spokesman for the party when graceful adjustments were to be made or delicate compromises *engineered* —S.H.Adams⟩ ⟨behind it all was the Soviet leviathan skilfully, though at times crudely, pulling strings, *engineering,* manipulating, staging, and, if need be, intimidating and compelling —Alexander Dallin⟩

guideboard \'≈,≈\ *n* **:** a board (as upon a guidepost) having upon it directions or information about the way

guide·book \'gīd,bùk\ *n* **:** HANDBOOK 1; *esp* **:** a book for tourists containing information about routes, accommodations, and places of historical or cultural interest — **guide·book·ish** \-kish\ *adj* — **guide·booky** \-kē\ *adj*

guide card *n* **:** GUIDE 2g

guided *adj* [fr. past part. of [2]*guide*] **1 :** accompanied or supervised by a guide ⟨a ~ tour⟩ ⟨~ groups⟩ **2 :** controllable as to direction of motion in the same way as a guided missile ⟨~ bomb⟩ ⟨~ plane⟩

guided missile *n* **:** a missile whose course toward a target may be altered during passage (as by means of a preset control, a built-in mechanism remotely controlled by radio, a target-seeking radar device, or a self-reacting device)

guide dog *n* **:** a dog trained to lead the blind

guide flag *or* **guide pennant** *n* **:** a flag or pennant flown on the ship that is to act as guide during a fleet maneuver

guide fossil *n* **:** INDEX FOSSIL

guide key *n* **:** HOME KEY

guide·less \'gīdləs\ *adj* **:** having no guide **:** lacking leadership or control — **guide·less·ness** *n* -ES

guideline \'≈,≈\ *n* **:** a line by which one is guided: as **a :** a cord or rope to aid a passer over a difficult point (as on a trail) or to permit retracing a course (as in a cave) **b** (1) **:** an identifying number, letter, or word written on copy or set in a single line of type and placed above type matter for the guidance of copyreader and printer (2) **:** a line drawn from a typographical change to a mark in the margin **c :** an indication or outline of future policy or conduct (as of a government)

guide meridian *n* **:** a line that is marked by monuments, that runs north and south between other more carefully established meridians, and that is used for reference in surveying

guide mill *n* **:** a small roll train with guides on each side used in metalworking to prevent rolled bars from jamming

guide pin *n* **:** a pin or peg for aligning a tool or die properly with the work **:** PILOT — called also *leader pin*

guidepost \'≈,≈\ *n* **1 :** a post (as at the fork of a road) with guideboards on it to direct travelers **2 :** GUIDE PIN **3 :** INDICATION, SIGN

guidepost 1

guid·er \'gīdə(r)\ *n* -s [ME *gidour, gider,* fr. MF *guideor, guideur,* alter. (influenced by *guide*) of OF *guieor, guieur,* fr. *guier* to guide + *-eor, -eur* -or — more at GUIDE (v.)] **:** one that guides: as **a :** a device that functions as a guide (as in some production operation) **b :** an adult volunteer leader of a girl guide company in Britain, Canada, and various other countries

guide rail *n* **:** a track or rail that serves as a guide; *specif* **:** one designed to guide a sliding door

guide rope *n* **:** a rope hung from a balloon or dirigible so as to trail along the ground for about half its length and used esp. to preserve altitude by variation of the length dragging without loss of ballast or gas

guides *pl of* GUIDE, *pres 3d sing of* GUIDE

guide·ship \'gīd,ship\ *n* -s [[1]*guide* + *-ship*] *Scot* **:** TREATMENT

guideway \'≈,≈\ *n* **:** a channel, slot, or track in which something is fitted so that its line of motion is controlled

guide wheel *n* **:** either wheel of a pair of small wheels used to stabilize the rear of a bicycle for learners and young children

guide word *n* **:** CATCHWORD 1b

guiding *pres part of* GUIDE

guiding telescope *n* **:** a visual telescope mounted rigidly parallel to a photographic telescope and used by an observer to supplement the clock motion in maintaining immovable the image of a heavenly body on the photographic plate

guid·man \(')gæd¦man, (')gïed-, (')gid-\ *Scot var of* GOODMAN

gui·don \'gīdən, -īd°n\ *n* -s [MF, fr. OProv *guidoo,* fr. *guida* guide — more at GUIDE (n.)] **1 :** a flag resembling but smaller than a standard, cleft or rounded at the outward end, bearing a badge, arms, or other distinctive emblem, and borne as a personal cognizance of some person of rank orig. for military use but later chiefly for display at his funeral **2 a :** a small flag or streamer carried by mounted troops to indicate the side toward the guide when marching and to mark the line on which to make a formation **b :** a usu. swallow-tailed flag borne by a military unit (as of the U. S. armed forces) usu. as a unit marker **c :** a flag rounded and cleft at the outward end and borne as a unit marker (as by a British regiment of dragoons) **3 :** one who carries a guidon

gui·do·ni·an \gwē'dōnēən\ *adj, usu cap* [*Guido* d'Arezzo (also called Fra Guittone) †*ab*1050 Benedictine monk and musical reformer — E *-ian*] **:** relating to the 11th century musician Guido d'Arezzo or his theory of movable hexachords

guidonian hand *n, usu cap G* **:** a figure representing the tones of the gamut on the joints of the left hand to which a singing master could point in teaching solmization

guidonian syllable *n, usu cap G* **:** one of the six syllables *ut* or *do, re, mi, fa, sol, la* used for the tones of the hexachord — compare SOLMIZATION

guid·sire *var of* GUDESIRE

guid·wife \(')gæ¦dwaif, (')gïe¦-, (')gi¦-\ *var of* GOODWIFE

guid·willie \gæ'dwili, gïe'-, gi'-\ *adj* [*guidwill* (var. of *goodwill*) + *-ie*] **1** *Scot* **:** LIBERAL, GENEROUS **2** *Scot* **:** CORDIAL, CHEERING ⟨we'll tak a right *guidwillie* waught for auld lang syne —Robert Burns⟩

guige \'gēj, 'gēzh\ *n* -s [ME *gige,* fr. MF *guige, guiche,* fr. OF] **:** an extra leather strap by which the shield of a knight was slung

guignar·dia \gēn'yärdēə, g(w)ig'nä-\ *n, cap* [NL, fr. Léon *Guignard* †1928 Fr. botanist + NL *-ia*] **:** a genus of fungi (family Sphaeriaceae) having single-celled or unequally 2-celled spindle-shaped hyaline ascospores — see BLACK ROT

guigne \'gēnʸ, -nyə\ *n, pl* **guignes** \-nʸ, -nyəz\ [F, fr. MF *guigne, guine*] **:** GEAN

gui·gnet's green \(')gēn¦yāz-\ *n, usu cap 1st G* [after C.E. *Guignet,* 19th cent. Fr. chemist who discovered the process] **1 :** a bluish green pigment of good brilliance and permanence consisting of a hydrated chromic oxide made by fusion of sodium dichromate and boric acid and hydrolysis of the product **2 :** a dark bluish green that is greener and stronger than average teal green and greener, lighter, and stronger than invisible green (sense 2) — called also *Mittler's green*

gui·gnol \gēn'yōl, -yōl\ *n* -s *sometimes cap* [F, prob. after *Guignol,* reputed name of a silkworker of Lyons and character of the puppet theater which Laurent Mourquet installed there for the earliest performance (in 1795) of French puppet shows] **1 :** PUPPET; *esp* **:** HAND PUPPET — compare MARIONETTE **2 :** PUPPET SHOW **3 :** a theatrical production featuring melodramatic tension, horror, and shock

gui·gno·let \,gēnyə¦lā\ *n* -s [F, fr. dim. of *guigne*] **:** a French liqueur made from black sweet cherries

gui·jo \(')gē¦hō\ *n* -s [PhilSp, fr. Tag *gihò*] **1 :** a large Philippine timber tree (*Shorea guiso*) of the family Dipterocarpaceae having strong heavy hard wood with a striking figure and moderately fine texture **2 :** the wood of the guijo

guil·an·di·na \,gwilən'dīnə, -dēnə\ *n, cap* [NL, after *Gulandini* (Melchior Wieland) †1589 Prussian botanist in Italy] *in some classifications* **:** a genus that comprises tropical American woody vines, scrambling shrubs, and trees having seeds enclosed in large prickly pods and that is usu. included in the genus *Caesalpinia*

guild *also* **gild** \'gild\ *n* -s [ME *gilde,* fr. ON *gildi* guild, payment, tribute; akin to OE *gild, gield* service, tribute — more at GELD (tax)] **1 :** an association of men belonging to the same class, engaged in kindred pursuits, or having common interests or aims: as **a :** any of various medieval associations having both social and semireligious features **b :** a medieval association of merchants controlling local trade in some parts of Britain and sometimes constituting the local governing body **c :** a medieval association of members of a craft or trade established to promote the welfare of that craft and its members and sometimes replacing the merchants' guild as a governing body **d :** any of various modern associations, societies, or brotherhoods resembling the medieval guilds in their aims ⟨a ~ for charitable work⟩ ⟨the hospital ~ of our church⟩; *broadly* **:** FELLOWSHIP, SOCIETY **2** *obs* **:** the headquarters or meeting place of a guild **:** GUILDHALL **3 :** an ecological group of plants distinguished from ordinary herbs, shrubs, and trees by a special mode of life (as the saprophytic, parasitic, epiphytic, or twining) usu. involving some degree of dependence on other plants

guild church *n* **:** an English metropolitan church that has been freed from parish responsibilities in order to minister full time to nonresident city workers during their hours in the city

[1]**guil·der** \'gildə(r)\ *n* -s [modif. (influenced by E *-er*) of D *gulden* — more at GULDEN] **:** GULDEN, *esp* **:** a Dutch gulden — see MONEY table

[2]**guild·er** \"\ *n* -s [*guild* + *-er*] **:** a member of a modern guild

guild·hall \'gild¦hȯl\ *n* [ME *gildhal, gildehalle,* fr. *gilde* guild + *hal, halle* hall — more at HALL] **:** the hall where a guild or corporation usu. assembles **:** TOWN HALL

guild·ite \'gil,dīt\ *n* -s [Frank N. *Guild* †1939 Am. mineralogist + E *-ite*] **:** a dark chestnut brown mineral $(Cu,Fe)_3(Fe,Al)_4(SO_4)_7(OH)_4 \cdot 15H_2O$ that is a basic hydrated sulfate of copper and iron

guild merchant *n* [*guild* + *merchant* (adj.)] **:** GUILD 1b

guild·ry \'gildri\ *n* -ES **1** *Scot* **:** guild membership **2** *often cap, Scot* **:** the municipal corporation of a royal Scottish burgh ⟨the ~ of Stirling⟩

guild·ship \'gild,ship\ *n* [*guild* + *-ship*] **1 :** GUILD 1a, 1b, 1c **2 :** the status of a guild member

guilds·man \'gil(d)zmən\ *n, pl* **guildsmen** [*guild's* (gen. of *guild*) + *man*] **1 :** a guild member **2 :** an advocate of guild socialism

guild socialism *n* **:** a socialistic theory advocating state ownership of all industries with monopolistic control and management in each by a guild composed of all its handworkers and brainworkers and restricted only by regulations safeguarding the consumers' interests; *esp* **:** such a theory developed in England early in the 20th century

guild tree \'gil(d)-\ *n* [obs. Sc. *guild,* alter. of [3]*gold*] **:** COMMON BARBERRY

[1]**guile** \'gīl, *esp before pause or consonant* -īəl\ *n* -s [ME *gile,* fr. OF *guile,* prob. of Gmc origin; akin to OE *wīgle* divination — more at WILE] **1 :** crafty or deceitful cunning **:** DUPLICITY, DECEIT, TREACHERY **2** *archaic* **:** STRATAGEM, DEVICE, TRICK **syn** see DECEIT

[2]**guile** \"\ *vt* -ED/-ING/-s [ME *gilen, guilen,* fr. OF *guiler,* fr. *guile,* n.] *archaic* **:** BEGUILE, DECEIVE

guile·ful \-fəl\ *adj* [ME *gileful,* fr. *gile* guile + *-ful*] **:** full of guile **:** characterized by cunning, deceit, or treachery **syn** see SLY

guile·ful·ly \-fəlē, -li\ *adv* [ME *gilefully,* fr. *gileful* + *-ly*] **:** in a guileful manner **:** with guile

guile·ful·ness *n* -ES [ME *gilefulnesse,* fr. *gileful* guileful + *-nesse* -ness] **:** guileful quality or state

guile·less \'gī(ə)lləs\ *adj* **:** free from guile; *broadly* **:** innocent, naïve, and unsophisticated ⟨children raising their ~ eyes from play⟩ — **guile·less·ly** *adv* — **guile·less·ness** *n* -ES

guil·ery \'gīləri\ *n* -ES [ME *gilerie, gilrie,* fr. MF *gilerie,* fr. *giler, guiler* to guile + *-erie* -ery] *now dial Eng* **:** a trick or beguilement

guil·lain–bar·re syndrome \,gē,yanʸbə'rā-\ *n, usu cap G&B* [after Georges *Guillain* *b*1876 Fr. physician and neurologist and Jean A. *Barré* 20th cent. Fr. neurologist] **:** a neurologic disorder of unknown cause characterized by sensory disturbances in the extremities and slight to severe locomotor impairment

guil·le·met \,gē(y)ə¦mā, ,gilə¦met\ *n* -s [F, irreg. dim. of *Guillaume* William, reputed name of its inventor] **:** either of the marks ⟨⟨or⟩⟩ used as quotation marks in French writing

guil·le·mot \'gilə,mät\ *n* -s [F, fr. MF, irreg. dim. of *Guillaume* William] **:** any of several narrow-billed auks of northern seas constituting two genera (*Uria* and *Cepphus*) of the family Alcidae and having skins, feathers, and eggs that are highly valued by natives of regions where they breed — see BLACK GUILLEMOT, MURRE

guil·loche \gə'lōsh, gē'(y)ō-\ *n* -s [F *guillochis,* fr. MF, perh. fr. the name *Guilloche,* fr. *Guillot,* familiar form of *Guillaume* William] **1 :** an architectural ornament in the form of two or more bands twisted over each other in a series leaving circular openings which are filled with round devices **2 :** a pattern (as on metalwork) made by interlacing curved lines

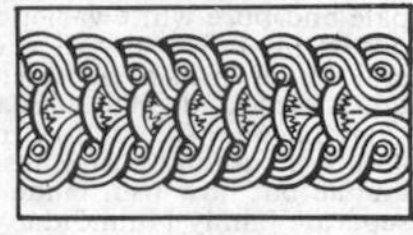
guilloche 1

[1]**guil·lo·tine** \'gilə,tēn, ,≈≈'≈; 'gē(y)ə'tēn, '≈≈,≈\ *n* -s [F, after Joseph Ignace *Guillotin* †1814 Fr. physician who in 1789 proposed its use] **1 :** a machine for beheading by means of a heavy ax or blade that slides down in vertical guides **2 :** a shearing machine or instrument (as a paper cutter or metal cutter) that in action resembles a guillotine **3 :** a surgical instrument that consists of a ring bearing a sliding knife blade and is used for cutting out a tonsil or other protruding structure capable of being engaged by the ring **4 :** closure by the imposition of a predetermined time limit on the consideration of specific sections of a bill or portions of other legislative business ⟨announced that the Transport Bill was to pass — under a ~ — by 10 p.m. on Monday —*Punch*⟩ ⟨the New Zealand House has not had to adopt the ~ —Walter Nash⟩ **5 :** a window with a vertically sliding sash and without counterbalanced sash weights **6 :** something likened to a guillotine esp. in bringing about an abrupt termination (as of a former occupation) ⟨that ~ of joys, bedtime —Nadine Gordimer⟩ — compare AXE 3 **7 :** a wrestling fall in which from a cross-body ride the aggressor shifts his own arms and head under the opponent's locked arm and grasps the opponent's head in a reverse half nelson while retaining a scissors grip on his near leg

[2]**guillotine** \"\ *vb* -ED/-ING/-s [F *guillotiner,* fr. *guillotine*] *vt* **1 a :** to behead with a guillotine **b :** to trim with a guillotine **2 :** to cut off or cut short as if with a guillotine ⟨*guillotining* needless waste⟩ **3 :** to subject (as a bill) to the guillotine ⟨the power to ~ bills in standing committee —Herbert Morrison⟩ ~ *vi* **:** to impose the guillotine ⟨the power to ~⟩

guillotine amputation *n* **:** a surgical amputation (as of a leg) in which the skin is incised circumferentially and allowed to retract, successive layers of muscle are then circularly divided, and finally the bone is divided and which is used esp. as an emergency procedure

guil·lo·tin·er \-nə(r)\ *n* -s **:** the operator of a guillotine

guillotine shears *n* **:** power shears in which the upper knife slides between vertical guides

[1]**guilt** \'gilt\ *n* -s [ME *gilt, gult,* fr. OE *gylt*] **1** *obs* **a :** delinquency or failure in respect to one's duty **:** OFFENSE, TRESPASS **b :** responsibility for an offense **:** FAULT **c :** state of deserving punishment **:** DESERTS **2 :** the fact of having com-

mitted a breach of conduct esp. violating law and involving a penalty; *broadly* **:** guilty conduct ⟨a life of ~ and shame⟩ **3 a :** the state of one who has committed an offense esp. consciously **:** CULPABILITY ⟨his ~ was written in his face⟩ **b :** feelings of culpability esp. for imagined offenses or from a sense of inadequacy **:** morbid self-reproach often manifest in marked preoccupation with the moral correctness of one's behavior **:** SELF-ACCUSATION ⟨aggressive responses originating in inner ~ and uncertainty⟩ **4 :** the state of being liable to penalty for offense against law — used in respect to persons and sometimes property that by reason of illegal usage has become liable to forfeiture or other burden

²guilt \"\ *archaic var of* GILT

guilt by association : moral guilt or unfitness presumed to exist on the basis of one's known associations ⟨the doctrine of *guilt by association* has on occasion been used to brand as currently disloyal persons who at some past time had been members of an organization not known to be or considered subversive at the time they were members⟩

guilt·i·ly \-tᵊlē, -li\ *adv* **:** in a guilty manner **:** with guilt

guilt·i·ness \-tēnəs, -tin-\ *n* -ES [ME *giltines*, fr. *gilty* guilty + *-nes*, *-ness* -ness] **:** the quality or state of being guilty

guilt·less \-tləs\ *adj* [ME *giltlesse*, fr. *gilt* guilt + *-lesse* -less] **1 :** free from guilt or evil **:** INNOCENT ⟨a ~ man⟩ ⟨~ of any evil intent⟩ **2 :** lacking experience, familiarity, or dealings — used postpositively and with *of* ⟨a bowed old house long ~ of paint⟩

guilt·less·ly *adv* **:** in a guiltless manner

guilt·less·ness *n* -ES **:** the quality or state of being guiltless

guilt offering *n* [so called fr. allusion to Num 5] **:** an animal sacrifice made in ancient Israel in atonement for trespass against the property of God or man following full restitution of property plus one fifth — called also *trespass offering*

guiltsick \'=,=\ *adj* [¹*guilt* + *sick*] **:** REMORSEFUL

guilty \'giltē, -ti\ *adj* -ER/-EST [ME *gilty*, fr. OE *gyltig*, fr. *gylt* guilt + *-ig* -y] **1 a :** having committed a breach of conduct **:** justly chargeable with or responsible for a delinquency, crime, or sin ⟨~ in the eyes of his fellowmen⟩ **b :** justly chargeable with or culpably responsible for a specified fault or crime ⟨~ of bad taste⟩ ⟨~ of larceny⟩ **2** *obs* **:** justly liable to or deserving of a penalty ⟨they answered and said, He is ~ of death Mt 26:66 (AV)⟩ **3 a :** suggesting, showing, or involving guilt ⟨~ looks⟩ ⟨~ acts⟩ **b :** filled with or suffering from guilt ⟨a ~ conscience⟩ ⟨~ minds⟩ **c :** resulting from a sense of guilt ⟨~ fears⟩ **4** *obs* **:** CONSCIOUS, COGNIZANT **syn** see BLAMEWORTHY

guim·bard \'gim,bärd, 'gam-\ *n* -S [F *guimbarde* jew's harp (formerly, a kind of dance), perh. fr. Prov *guimbardo*, a kind of dance, fr. *guimba* to leap, gambol, fr. OProv *guimbar*, *cembar* to leap, gambol, fr. *camba* leg — more at GAMBOL] **:** JEW'S HARP

gui·met's blue \(')gē¦māz-\ *n*, *often cap G* [after Jean Baptiste *Guimet* †1871 Fr. chemist] **1 :** ULTRAMARINE **2 :** FRENCH BLUE

guimpe \'gamp, 'gimp\ *n* -S [F, fr. OF *guimple*, *wimple* veil, pennant, wimple, of Gmc origin; akin to OE *wimpel* wimple, cloak — more at WIMPLE] **1 :** CHEMISETTE; *also* **:** a blouse worn under a jumper or pinafore **2 :** a wide usu. stiffly starched cloth used to cover the neck and shoulders by nuns of some orders **3** [by alter.] **:** GIMP 1

gui·nau \gē'naü\ *n*, *pl* **guinau** *or* **guinaus** *usu cap* [Sp *guinao*, of AmerInd origin] **1 a :** an extinct Arawakan people of Venezuela **b :** a member of such people **2 :** the language of the Guinau people

¹guin·ea \'ginē, -ni\ *adj*, *usu cap* **1** [fr. *Guinea*, region in West Africa] **a :** of or from the region of Guinea, West Africa **:** of the kind or style prevalent in the region of Guinea **b :** trading with Guinea ⟨a *Guinea* merchant⟩ ⟨*Guinea* ships⟩ **2** [fr. *Guinea*, republic in West Africa] **:** of or from the Republic of Guinea **:** of the kind or style prevalent in the Republic of Guinea

²guinea \"\ *n* -S [after *Guinea*, region in West Africa] **1 a** [so called fr. the fact that it was supposedly first made out of gold from Guinea] **:** an English gold coin issued from 1663 to 1813 and fixed in 1717 as the equivalent of 21 shillings **b :** a unit of value equivalent to one guinea coin ⟨a five-*guinea* coin⟩ **c :** a unit of value equal to 21 shillings ⟨accounts are sometimes kept in and prices are sometimes quoted in *guineas*⟩ **d :** the Saudi Arabian sovereign first issued in 1951 **2 a :** a slave newly imported into the U. S. from Africa **b :** a person noticeably foreign **c** *slang* **:** ITALIAN — usu. used disparagingly **d** *usu cap* **:** one of a group of people of mixed white, Indian, and Negro ancestry who live chiefly in West Virginia and Maryland — often used disparagingly **3** [by shortening] **:** GUINEA FOWL **4 :** one who works in or about a stable; *specif* **:** a horse groom

guinea carmine B *n*, *usu cap G&C* [¹*Guinea*] **:** an acid dye — see DYE table I (under *Acid Violet 12*)

guinea corn *n*, *usu cap G* **1 :** any of several grain sorghums; *esp* **:** DURRA **2 :** a variegated Indian corn

guinea duck *n*, *sometimes cap G* **:** MUSCOVY DUCK

guinea fast red *n*, *usu cap G&F&R* [¹*Guinea*] **:** either of two acid dyes — see DYE table I (under *Acid Red 34* and *37*)

guinea fowl *n* **:** a West African bird (*Numida meleagris*) that is raised usu. on a small scale for food in most parts of the world and that has typically a bare neck and head, the latter surmounted by a bony casque, and slaty plumage speckled with white though pale and pure white varieties occur; *broadly* **:** any of several similar birds of continental Africa and Madagascar sometimes considered to constitute a subfamily of Phasianidae but now usu. made a separate family Numididae

guinea fowl

guinea gold *n* **1 :** gold of 22 karats from which guineas were coined **2 :** an alloy containing 88 percent of copper and 12 percent of zinc that is used esp. for cheap jewelry — called also *red brass*

guinea gold vine *or* **guinea flower** *n* **:** any of several Australian evergreen vines constituting a genus (*Hibbertia*) closely related to *Dillenia* and widely cultivated for their large bright yellow single flowers

guinea grain *n* **:** GRAIN OF PARADISE 1 — usu. used in pl.

guinea grass *n* **1 :** a tall African forage grass (*Panicum maximum*) introduced into tropical America and the southern U. S. where it is used for hay **2 :** JOHNSON GRASS

guinea green *n*, *often cap 1st G* **:** a strong bluish green that is bluer and deeper than average emerald (sense 2c) and greener and deeper than average bright turquoise

guinea green B *n*, *usu cap both Gs* **:** an acid green triphenylmethane dye used chiefly in coloring foods — called also *Acid Green B*; see DYE table I (under *Acid Green 3*)

guinea hen *n* **:** a female guinea fowl; *broadly* **:** GUINEA FOWL

guinea-hen flower *n* **:** a Eurasian checkered lily (*Fritillaria meleagris*) that has in early spring pendent bell-shaped flowers usu. veined and checkered with purple or maroon on a paler ground and that is widely cultivated as an ornamental

guinea-hen weed *n* **:** a tropical American herb (*Petiveria alliacea*) having a strong odor suggesting the onion

guin·ea·man \-mən\ *n*, *pl* **guineamen** *usu cap* [¹*Guinea* + *man*] **1** *archaic* **:** a merchant or a ship trading with Guinea **2 :** ¹GUINEAN

¹guin·e·an \'ginēən\ *n*, *cap* **1** [*Guinea*, region in West Africa + E *-an*] **:** a native or inhabitant of the region of Guinea, West Africa **2** [*Guinea*, republic in West Africa + E *-an*] **:** a native or inhabitant of the Republic of Guinea

²guinean \"\ *adj*, *usu cap* **1 a :** of, relating to, or characteristic of the region of Guinea, West Africa **b :** of, relating to, or characteristic of the people of the region of Guinea **2 a :** of, relating to, or characteristic of the Republic of Guinea **b :** of, relating to, or characteristic of the people of the Republic of Guinea

guinea negro *n*, *usu cap G&N* **:** a Negro from the Guinea coast of Africa; *broadly* **:** any newly arrived Negro slave in the southern U.S.

guinea peach *n*, *usu cap G* **1 :** COUNTRY FIG 1 **2 :** the fruit of the country fig somewhat resembling a large firm seedy strawberry and said to be emetic if eaten to excess

guinea pepper *n*, *usu cap G* **1 :** the pungent aromatic fruit of a tropical African tree (*Xylopia aethiopica*) that is used as a condiment and in folk medicine **2 :** any of various peppers usu. of moderate pungency that are cultivated or naturalized in Africa **3 :** GRAIN OF PARADISE 1 **4 :** a plant bearing Guinea peppers

guinea pig *n* **1** [prob. so called fr. the fact that *Guinea* represented the name of a distant country] **a :** a small stout-bodied short-eared nearly tailless domesticated hystricomorph rodent (genus *Cavia*) often kept as a pet and widely used in biological research, occurring in many combinations of black, white, and tawny red, having short or long hair, and being commonly considered a distinct species (*C. cobaya*) although probably a domesticated variety of some So. American species (as *C. porcellanus* or *C. cutleri*) — called also *cavy*; see APEREA **b :** an animal of *Cavia* or of related genera — often used with a qualifying term ⟨mountain *guinea pigs* of the genus *Microcavia*⟩ **2** *Brit* **a** [so called fr. the payment of guineas as fee to the vessel's captain] **:** MIDSHIPMAN **b :** a person receiving a guinea as a fee — often used of a doctor or clergyman substituting for another **3** [so called fr. the wide use made of guinea pigs in experimentation and research] **:** a subject of experimentation or testing designed to yield data for drawing scientific conclusions or large-scale calculations

guinea pig

guinea plum *n* **:** a large West African tree (*Parinarium excelsum*) with a rough-skinned reddish brown fruit that resembles a plum and is a locally important emergency food and a hard heavy durable wood that varies from yellowish white to reddish brown

guinea rush *n* **:** a widely distributed tropical sedge (*Cyperus articulatus*) with a rootstock that is used in folk medicine as a carminative or tonic and to check vomiting

guineas *pl of* GUINEA

guinea squash *n* **:** EGGPLANT

guinea worm *n*, *often cap G* **:** a slender nematode worm (*Dracunculus medinensis*) attaining a length of several feet, occurring as an adult in the subcutaneous tissues of man and various mammals in parts of Africa and other warm countries, and having a larva that develops in small freshwater crustaceans (as cyclops) and when ingested with drinking water passes through the intestinal wall and tissues to lodge beneath the skin of a mammalian host and there mature

gui·pure \gē'p(y)ü(ə)r\ *n* -S [F, fr. MF, a kind of lace, fr. *guiper* to cover with silk or wool (of Gmc origin) + *-ure*; akin to MD *wippen* to swing, vibrate, OHG *wīfan* to reel, wind, Goth *weipan* to crown — more at VIBRATE] **:** any of various handmade or machine-made laces that lack a mesh background, consist of heavy or large pattern sections joined by brides or cutouts of cloth joined by bars, and are used esp. for women's dresses, trimmings, appliqués

gui·puz·co·an \gē·püthkəwən, -üsk-\ *n* -S *usu cap* [Sp *guipuzcoano*, fr. *guipuzcoano*, adj., of Guipúzcoa, fr. *Guipúzcoa*, province in northern Spain + Sp *-ano* (fr. L *-anus* -an)] **:** a dialect of the Basque language spoken largely in the province of Guipúzcoa in northern Spain

gui·ro \'(g)wē(,)rō\ *n*, *pl* **guiro** [AmerSp *güiro*, lit., bottle gourd, calabash, prob. fr. Taino] **:** a percussion instrument of Latin American origin made of a serrated gourd and played by scraping a stick along its surface

¹gui·sard \(')gē¦zärd\ *n* -S *usu cap* [F, fr. *Guise*, name of a powerful 16th cent. ducal family of Lorraine + F *-ard*] **:** a partisan of the Guises in France in the 16th century

²gui·sard \'gīzərd\ *n* -S [fr. earlier *gysart*, *gyzard*, fr. obs. Sc *gys*, *gyse* to disguise (fr. ME *gysen* to dress, attire) + Sc *-art*, *-ard*] *Scot* **:** a masker or mummer

¹guise \'gīz\ *n* -S [ME *gise*, *guise*, fr. OF *guise*, of Gmc origin; akin to OHG *wīsa* manner, style — more at WISE (manner)] **1 :** form or style of dress **:** COSTUME ⟨wondered if she should appear in such disordered ~⟩; *esp* **:** dress that is unexpected on or foreign to the wearer ⟨the lady clad in peasant ~⟩ **2** *archaic* **a :** MANNER, STYLE, FASHION, WAY ⟨it never was our ~ to slight the poor —Alexander Pope⟩ **b :** customary course or way (as of speaking or behaving) **3 a :** external appearance ⟨concerned more with the ~ than the inner worth of his product⟩; *broadly* **:** SHAPE, SEMBLANCE, ASPECT ⟨a fiend in frightful ~⟩ **b :** a superficial seeming **:** an artful or simulated appearance (as of propriety or worth) ⟨that such misconduct should take the ~ of religious ritual is shameful⟩ ⟨tricked the widow in the ~ of a friend of her late husband⟩ **4** *obs Scot* **:** a masked play or masquerade party

²guise \"\ *vb* -ED/-ING/-S [ME *gysen*, fr. *gyse*, *gise* (n.)] *vt* **:** DRESS, ARRANGE; *usu* **:** to provide with a foreign guise **:** DISGUISE ⟨the three younger children *guised* as angels⟩ ~ *vi*, *now dial Brit* **:** to appear in disguise esp. as a mummer **:** go mumming

guis·er \'gīzər\ *n* -S [ME (northern dial.) *gysar*, fr. *gysen*, v. + *-ar*, *-er* -er] *chiefly Scot* **:** a person in disguise **:** MUMMER; *esp* **:** a Christmas mummer

guis·quil \'gwē,skēl\ *var of* HUISQUIL

¹gui·tar \gə'tär, -tä(r, *chiefly substand* 'gi,t- *also* 'gē,t-\ *n* -S [F *guitare*, fr. MF, fr. OSp *guitarra*, fr. Ar *qītār*, fr. Gk *kithara* cithara] **:** a flat-bodied stringed instrument that has a long fretted neck and usu. six strings, is played with a plectrum or plucked with the fingers, sounds an octave lower than written, and has a compass of over three octaves up from E in the great octave — called also *Spanish guitar*; compare ELECTRIC GUITAR, HAWAIIAN GUITAR

²guitar \"\ *vi* **guitarred; guitarred; guitarring; guitars :** to play the guitar

guitar fiddle *n* **:** VIELLE

gui·tar·fish \-tär,fish, -tä,f-\ *n* **:** any of several viviparous rays of the family Rhinobatidae somewhat resembling a guitar in outline when viewed from above

gui·tar·ist \-tärəst, -tär-\ *n* -S **:** one who performs on the guitar

guitar mandolin *n* **:** a guitar-shaped instrument strung, tuned, and played like a mandolin

guitar

guitar plant *n* **:** an Australian shrub (*Lomatia tinctoria*) of the family Proteaceae that furnishes a pink dye from the mealy dust of its seed coat

gui·tar-shaped \-tär,shāpt, -tä,sh-\ *adj* **:** having a strongly rounded lower portion separated from a comparable but often smaller upper portion by a smooth and gradual intermediate constriction so as to suggest the outline of the body of a guitar ⟨the hourglass figure was really more nearly *guitar-shaped*⟩

guit·er·man·ite \'gid·ə(r)mə,nīt\ *n* -S [Frank *Guiterman* 19th cent. Am. metallurgist + E *-ite*] **:** a bluish gray mineral $Pb_{10}As_6S_{19}$ occurring in compact masses that is a compound of lead, arsenic, and sulfur (sp. gr., 5.94)

guit·guit \'gwit,gwit\ *n* -S [imit.] **:** any of several small tropical American honeycreepers

guit·to·ni·an \gwə'tōnēən\ *adj*, *usu cap* [*Guittone* d'Arezzo †1294 It. poet + E *-ian*] **:** of or relating to Guittone d'Arezzo, an Italian poet who is said to have devised the sonnet

gui·zard *var of* ²GUISARD

gu·jar \'güjə(r), 'güj-, -jär\ *n*, *pl* **gujar** *or* **gujars** *usu cap* [Hindi *Gūjar*, fr. Skt *Gurjara* Gujar, Gujarat] **1 :** a people of Kashmir that is divided into many subgroups, characterized by rather fair skin, and of uncertain relationship to other peoples of the area **2 :** a member of the Gujar people

gu·ja·ra·ti \,güjə'räd·ē, ,gùj-\ *n*, *pl* **gujarati** *usu cap* [Hindi *gujarātī*, fr. *Gujarāt* Gujarat, region in western India, fr. Skt *Gurjara*, *Gūrjara*] **1 :** the language of Gujarat, Baroda, and neighboring regions in northwestern India **2 :** an alphabet that is essentially a more carefully formed less cursive type of the Kaithi script and is now the principal alphabet used in writing the Gujarati language **3** *or* **guj·ra·ti** \'güj'r-, güj-\ [Hindi *Gujarātī*, *Gujrātī*, fr. *Gujarāt*, *Gujrāt* Gujarat] **:** one of a people chiefly of Gujarat speaking the Gujarati language and specializing in mercantile pursuits

gu·je·rat \'güjə'rät, 'güj-\ *n* -S *usu cap* [alter. of *Gujarati*] **1 :** GUJARATI 3 **2 :** a heavy wooden cart of India usu. drawn by oxen

guj·ran·wa·la \'güjrən'wälə, 'güj-\ *adj*, *usu cap* [fr. *Gujranwala*, city in Pakistan] **:** of or from the city of Gujranwala, Pakistan **:** of the kind or style prevalent in Gujranwala

gul \'gül, 'gùl\ *n* -S [Per — more at ROSE] **:** ROSE

gu·la \'g(y)ülə\ *n*, *pl* **gu·lae** \'g(y)ü,lē, 'gü,lī\ *or* **gulas** [ME, fr. L, throat, gullet — more at GLUTTON] **1 a :** the upper front of the neck next to the chin **:** the upper throat **b :** a plate in many insects including most beetles that forms the central part of the lower surface of the head and supports the submentum **2 a :** a molding or group of moldings having a large hollow **b :** OGEE

gu·la·man \gü'lämən\ *n* -S [Tag] **:** CEYLON MOSS

gu·lan·cha \gü'länchə\ *n* -S [Hindi *gulāca*, fr. Skt *guḍacī*] **:** an East Indian woody vine (*Tinospora cordifolia*) of the family Menispermaceae with a bitter root believed to have tonic properties

¹gu·lar \'g(y)ülə(r)\ *adj* [*gula* + *-ar*] **:** of, relating to, or situated on the gula

²gular \"\ *n* -S **:** a gular plate or scale (as on the throat of a fish)

gu·laris \g(y)ü'la(a)rəs, gü'lär-\ *n* -ES [NL, perh. fr. L *gula* gullet, throat + *-aris* -ar] **:** either of two West African top minnows: **a :** a topminnow (*Fundulopanchax gularis*) — called also *yellow gularis* **b :** a top minnow (*F. coeruleus*) — called also *blue gularis*

gulash *var of* GOULASH

¹gulch \'gəlsh, -gəl-, -lch\ *vb* -ED/-ING/-ES [ME *gulchen*; akin to Norw *gulka* to gulp, Sw dial. *gulka* to sob, Sw *gylka* to vomit, and prob. to Norw *gylpa* to gulp — more at GULP] *vt*, *now dial Eng* **:** to gulp or swallow greedily ~ *vi*, *now dial Eng* **:** to eat or drink with considerable noise and unbecoming haste

²gulch \"\ *n* -ES *now dial Eng* **:** a self-indulgent person (as a drunkard or glutton)

³gulch \"\ *n* -ES [perh. fr. ¹*gulch*] *now dial Eng* **:** a heavy fall

⁴gulch \"\ *vi* -ED/-ING/-ES *now dial Eng* **:** to fall heavily

⁵gulch \'gəlch\ *n* -ES [perh. fr. ¹*gulch*] **:** a deep or precipitous cleft in a hillside **:** a ravine or gully; *esp* **:** one that is short, steep-sided, and occas. occupied by a torrent

gul·den \'güldən *also* 'gùl- *or* 'gəl-\ *n*, *pl* **guldens** *or* **gulden** [ME (Sc dial.), Dutch gulden, fr. MD *gulden (florijn)*, fr. *gulden* golden + *florijn* florin; akin to OE *gylden* golden, OHG *guldīn*; derivatives fr. the stem of E *gold*] **1 :** a German, Austrian, or Dutch gold coin patterned after the Florentine florin; *esp* **:** an old German coin issued from the 15th to the 17th centuries **2 :** any of various silver coins: as **a :** GULDENGROSCHEN **b :** an old Austrian silver coin worth 60 kreuzers before 1859 and 100 kreuzers from 1859 until its issue ceased in 1892 **3 :** any of various units of monetary value: as **a :** a unit of value equal to one gold or silver gulden **b** (1) **:** the basic monetary unit of the Netherlands — see MONEY table (2) **:** a coin or note representing this unit **c** (1) **:** the basic unit of value in Danzig 1920–39 (2) **:** a coin representing this value

guldengroschen \'==,==\ *n*, *pl* **guldengroschens** *or* **guldengroschen** [G, fr. *gulden* (fr. D) + *groschen*] **:** an old German silver coin that preceded the taler in the 15th century, was at first worth one gold gulden, and in the 17th century had the value of ⅔ of a taler — called also *guldentaler*

guldentaler \'==,==\ *n* -S [G, fr. *gulden* + *taler*] **:** GULDENGROSCHEN

gule of august \'gyül-\ *usu cap G&A* [part trans. of AF *goul de Aust*, *gule de Aust* (fr. *goul*, *gule* beginning, opening, lit., throat — fr. L *gula* — + *de* of + *Aust* August), trans. of ML *gula Augusti* — more at GLUTTON] **:** LAMMAS 1

¹gules \'gyülz\ *n*, *pl* **gules** [ME *goules*, fr. MF *goules*, *gueules*, fr. OF, fr. *goles*, *goules*, *gueules* fur neckpiece frequently dyed red, pl. of *gole*, lit., throat — more at GULLET] **1 :** the heraldic color red **2 a :** a red color **b :** something red

²gules \"\ *adj* **:** of the color gules — abbr. *gu*

¹gulf \'gəlf, 'gəüf\ *n* -S *often attrib* [ME *goulf*, *golf*, fr. MF *golfe*, fr. OF, fr. OIt *golfo*, fr. LL *colpus*, *colfus*, fr. Gk *kolpos* bosom, bay, gulf; akin to OE *hwealf* vault, arch, OHG *walbo* vault, arch, *hwelben* to vault, arch, ON *hvalf* vault, Goth *hwilftrjom*, dat. pl., coffin] **1 :** a part of an ocean or sea extending into the land **:** a partially landlocked sea that is usu. larger than a bay ⟨the *Gulf* of Mexico⟩ **2 a :** a hollow place in the earth **:** a deep chasm or basin **:** ABYSS ⟨a ~ opened between the little town . . . and its suburbs —Charles Lyell⟩ **b :** a deep narrow pass ⟨the state's three central north-south ~s . . . are the natural gateways through mountains otherwise impassable by road —*N.Y.Times*⟩ **3 a :** a sucking eddy **:** WHIRLPOOL ⟨and whirl round the ~ before they sink —Samuel Johnson⟩ **b :** something that swallows up or devours ⟨the ~s . . . in which the population of the country is lost —Jeremy Bentham⟩ **4 :** an impassable or unbridgeable gap that serves as a means of separation **:** a wide interval ⟨the broad and deep ~ which . . . divides the living from the dead, the organic from the inorganic —W.R.Inge⟩ ⟨theory and reality, principles and practice — how many have fallen in the ~ between them —Theodore Draper⟩ **5** *archaic* **:** DRAFT 2

²gulf \"\ *vt* -ED/-ING/-S **1 :** to swallow up **:** ENGULF **2 :** to pass (a British university student) without honors

gulf coast tick *n*, *usu cap G & often cap C* [*Gulf Coast*, coastal area along the Gulf of Mexico] **:** a tick (*Amblyomma maculatum*) of the southern U. S. that is related to the lone star tick and that is often destructive to young game birds and also to the cattle of some regions

gulf flounder *or* **gulf fluke** *n*, *usu cap G* [*Gulf* of Mexico] **:** a flounder (*Paralichthys albiguttus*) of the southern Atlantic and Gulf coasts of the U. S.

gulf menhaden *n*, *usu cap G* [*Gulf* of Mexico] **:** a marine fish (*Brevoortia patronus*) of the Gulf of Mexico

gulf stream weed *n*, *usu cap G&S* [*Gulf Stream*, warm ocean current in the North Atlantic Ocean that flows out of the Gulf of Mexico] **:** GULFWEED

gulfweed \'=,=\ *n* [*Gulf* of Mexico + *weed*] **:** any of several seaweeds of the genus *Sargassum*; *esp* **:** a branching olive-brown seaweed (*S. bacciferum*) having numerous berrylike air vesicles and occurring in tropical American seas

gulf-weed crab *n* **:** a cosmopolitan pelagic crab (*Planes minutus*) common on gulfweed in the Sargasso sea and occas. found along the No. American shore

gulfy \-fē\ *adj*, *usu* -ER/-EST **:** full of whirlpools or hollows

gu·li hin·nai \,gülēhi¦nī\ *or* **gu·li hen·na** \,=='henə\ *n* [Per *guli ḥinnā'*, fr. Per *gul* flower, rose + Ar *ḥinnā'* henna] **:** a Persian rug design consisting of a plant with central stem and attached star flowers

¹gull \'gùl, 'gəl\ *n* -S [ME *goll*, prob. fr. *gull*, *goule* yellow, fr. ON *gulr* — more at YELLOW] *now dial Eng* **:** an unfledged bird; *specif* **:** GOSLING

²gull \'gəl\ *n* -S [ME, of Celt origin; akin to W *gwylan* gull, OCorn *guilan*, Bret *gouelan*] **1 :** any of numerous long-winged web-footed aquatic birds that constitute the family Laridae; *esp* **:** any member of *Larus* or closely related genera all of which differ from the terns in their usu. larger size, stouter build, thicker bill somewhat hooked at the tip, less pointed wings, and short unforked tail, are largely white birds as adults with the back and upper surface of the wings mantled with some shade of gray, and usu. remain near shore or about inland waters where they feed largely on offal and are important harbor scavengers — see BLACK-BACKED GULL, HERRING GULL, KITTIWAKE, MEW **2 a :** a nearly neutral slightly yellowish medium gray that is darker than agate gray and lighter than flint gray or old silver **b** *of textiles* **:** a pinkish gray that is yellower and duller than pussywillow gray

³gull \"\ *n* -S [ME *golle* throat, gullet, fr. MF *gole*, *goule* throat, mouth — more at GULLET] **1** *now dial* **a :** a deep gully made by and containing a running stream **b :** RAVINE **2 :** a fissure filled with fragments of rock

⁴gull \"\ *vt* -ED/-ING/-S [fr. obs. E *gull* throat, gullet, fr. ME *golle*] **1** *obs* **:** to guzzle or gulp greedily **2 :** to make a dupe of : DECEIVE, CHEAT ⟨a subtle trick intended to ~ the unwary and naive —R.C.Bone⟩ **3** [³gull] *now dial Eng* : to wash away : ERODE **syn** see DUPE

⁵**gull** \"\ *n* -s **1** : a person who is easily deceived or cheated : DUPE, SUCKER ⟨had been brought down to be the ~ of this intriguer —R.L.Stevenson⟩ **2** *obs* : TRICK, DECEPTION, FRAUD ⟨I should think this a ~ but that the white-bearded fellow speaks it —Shak.⟩

gull·able \ˈgələbəl\ *adj* [⁴gull + -able] : GULLIBLE

gul·lah \ˈgələ *sometimes* ˈgülə\ *n* -s *usu cap* **1** : one of a group of Negroes inhabiting the sea islands and coastal districts of So. Carolina, Georgia, and a small part of northeastern Florida **2** : the language of the Gullahs

gull-billed tern \ˈ=,=-\ *n* : a large tern (*Gelochelidon nilotica*) having a stout short bill like that of a typical gull

gull chaser *n* : POMARINE JAEGER

gul·ler \ˈgələr\ *Scot var of* GOLLAR

¹**gull·ery** \ˈgələrē\ *n* -ES [⁴gull + -ery] *archaic* : TRICKERY, DECEPTION ⟨you think . . . that you may put any ~ you will on me —Sir Walter Scott⟩

²**gullery** \"\ *n* -ES [²gull + -ery] : a breeding place of gulls

¹**gul·let** \ˈgələt, *usu* -əd·+V\ *n* -s [ME *golet*, fr. MF *goulet*, dim. of OF *gole*, *goule* throat, fr. L *gula* — more at GLUTTON] **1** : the tube by which food passes from the pharynx to the stomach : ESOPHAGUS; *broadly* : THROAT **2** : something that resembles a gullet in shape or function: as **a** : a variably tubular invagination of the cytoplasm of various protozoans that sometimes functions in the intake of food **b** : a channel for water **c** : DEFILE, RAVINE, GULLY **d** : the space between the tips of adjacent saw teeth **e** : a preparatory cut in excavations that is wide enough to allow the passage of earth in conveyors **3** : the dewlap of a goose or other bird

²**gullet** \"\ *vt* -ED/-ING/-S **1** : to make gullets in **2** : to excavate by means of gullets

gulleting file *n* : a blunt round file for deepening the gullets of large-toothed saws

gullet plate *n* : the iron arch under the pommel of a saddle

gullet worm *n* : a nematode worm infesting the gullet; *esp* : any of various worms (as *Gongylonema pulchrum* or *Syngamus laryngeus*) that invade the epithelial lining of the esophagus of ruminants

gull gray *n* : a purplish gray that is bluer, lighter, and slightly stronger than crane, bluer and lighter than granite, and bluer and slightly lighter than cinder gray

gull·ibil·i·ty \,gələˈbiləd·ē, -ətē, -i\ *n* -ES : the quality or state of being gullible ⟨monstrous was the ~ of the people —Arnold Bennett⟩

gull·ible \ˈgələbəl\ *adj* [⁴gull + -ible] : easily deceived or cheated : readily duped ⟨the innocents of those days were certainly naive; they were ~ —Bruce Bliven b. 1889⟩ — **gul·li·bly** \-blē, -li\ *adv*

gulling *pres part of* GULL

gul·li·on \ˈgülyən, ˈgəl-\ *n* -s [prob. alter. of *cullion*] **1** *dial Eng* : a vile worthless person **2** *dial Eng* : STOMACHACHE

gull·ish \ˈgəlish\ *adj* [⁵gull + -ish] : FOOLISH, STUPID

gulls *pl of* GULL, *pres 3d sing of* GULL

gull wing *n* : an airplane wing slanting upward from the fuselage for a short distance and then leveling out

¹**gul·ly** \ˈgüli, ˈgəli\ *or* **gully knife** *n* -ES [*gully* short for *gully knife*, fr. *gully* (fr. obs. Sc. dial. *guly*, prob. alter. of ME *golet* gullet) + *knife*] **1** *dial Brit* : a large knife (as a butcher knife or carving knife) **2** *dial Brit* : SWORD

²**gul·ly** *or* **gul·ley** \ˈgəlē, -li\ *n, pl* **gullies** *or* **gulleys** [fr. obs. E *gully*, *gullye* gullet, prob. alter. of ME *golet* gullet — more at GULLET] **1 a** : a miniature valley or gorge worn in the earth orig. by running water through which water usu. runs only after rains **b** : a small ravine in the face of a precipice **2** *now dial* : a deep gutter : DRAIN **3** : a diminutive valley or gulch; *esp* : a wooded hollow with steep sides **4 a** : the part of a cricket field lying between point and third man **b** : a fielder placed in the gulley

³**gully** \"\ *vb* -ED/-ING/-ES *vt* : to make gullies in : erode so as to produce gullies in ~ *vi* : to undergo erosion : become gullied

⁴**gully** \ˈgüli, ˈgəli\ *n* -ES [¹gull + -y] *dial Eng* : ¹GULL

gully erosion *n* : soil erosion produced by running water esp. after heavy rains

gullygut *n* [*gully*- (prob. fr. ⁴gull) + *gut*] *obs* : GLUTTON

gully-raker \ˈ=,=,==\ *n* [²gully] **1** *Austral* : a thief who steals stray or unbranded cattle **2** *Austral* : a large stockwhip

gully root *n, West Indies* : the root of the guinea-hen weed

gully washer *n, dial* : an extremely heavy fall of rain usu. of short duration : CLOUDBURST

gul·mo·har \ˈgülmə,här\ *also* **gul·mo·hur** \-hů(ə)r\ *n* -s [Hindi *gulmohur*, fr. Per *gul* rose, flower + *muhr* seal, gold coin] : ROYAL POINCIANA

gu·lo \ˈgyü(,)lō\ *n, cap* [NL, fr. L, glutton, epicure, fr. *gula* gullet, throat — more at GLUTTON] : the genus containing the glutton and wolverine

gulo- *comb form* [gulose] *usu ital* : having the stereochemical arrangement of atoms or groups found in gulose ⟨*gulo*=saccharic acid⟩

gu·lose \ˈg(y)ü,lōs *also* -ōz\ *n* -s [ISV, irreg. fr. *glucose*] : a sugar $C_6H_{12}O_6$ stereoisomeric with glucose and obtainable by synthesis from xylose

gu·los·i·ty \gyüˈläsəd·ē\ *n* -ES [ME (Sc. dial.) *gulosite*, fr. LL *gulositas*, fr. L *gulosus* gluttonous (fr. *gula* throat, gullet + *-osus* -ose) + *-itas* -ity — more at GLUTTON] : excessive appetite : GREEDINESS

¹**gulp** \ˈgəlp\ *vb* -ED/-ING/-S [ME *gulpen*, fr. a MD or MLG word; akin to D & Fris *gulpen* to bubble forth, drink in large drafts, Norw *gylpa* to gulp, OE *gielpan* to boast — more at YELP] *vt* **1 a** : to swallow in large drafts or pieces hurriedly or greedily ⟨corrected me for ~*ing* my food —Rex Ingamells⟩ — often used with *down* ⟨~*ed* down the whiskey and put on our coats —Nevil Shute⟩ **b** : to consume in one swallow — often used with *down* ⟨raw meat is usually not chewed but ~*ed* down like an oyster —H.B.Collins⟩ **2 a** : to take in or absorb in any manner : DEVOUR — usu. used with *down* ⟨their attempts to ~ down knowledge and to regulate their lives by received ideas —*Atlantic*⟩ **b** : to accept without investigation or question : swallow whole — usu. used with *down* ⟨the old man . . . ~*ed* down the whole narrative —Henry Fielding⟩ **3** : to keep back as if by swallowing : SUPPRESS — often used with *down* ⟨~*ed* down her sobs and was resolved to be firm —Anthony Trollope⟩ ~ *vi* **1** : to catch the breath as if in taking a long drink ⟨the white settler ~*s* hard and smiles wanly —*Time*⟩ **2** : to swallow food or drink hurriedly or greedily ⟨should learn to taste rather than to ~ —*Current Biog.*⟩

²**gulp** \"\ *n* -s **1 a** : the act or an instance of gulping ⟨swallowed the medicine at one ~⟩ **b** : the amount taken in a single large swallow ⟨had time only for a ~ of hot coffee⟩ **2 a** : a spasmodic action of the throat made in or as if in swallowing **b** : the sound of such action ⟨eyes wide and luminous, cheeks flushed . . . she spoke in ~*s* —Murray Schumach⟩

gulp·er \-pə(r)\ *n* -s **1** : one that gulps **2** *also* **gulper eel** : any of several usu. small deep-sea fishes that resemble degenerate eels with greatly enlarged mouths, have a leptocephalus stage, and constitute the family Saccopharyngidae now usu. placed in the order Lyomeri

gulph *archaic var of* GULF

gul·pin \ˈgülpən, ˈgəl-\ *n* -s [perh. alter. of *galopin*] *dial Eng* : a gullible person : SIMPLETON

gulp·ing·ly *adv* : with a gulp

gulpy \ˈgəlpē\ *adj* -ER/-EST : marked by gulping

guls *pl of* GUL

gul·sach \ˈgəls(h)ə(k)\ *n* -s [ME *gowel sowght* (part trans. of ON *gulusótt*), fr. *gowel* yellow (fr. ON *gulr*) + *sowght*, *sought* sickness, fr. OE *suht*; akin to OHG *suht* sickness, ON *sótt*, Goth *sauhts* sickness, *siuks* ill — more at YELLOW, SICK] *now Scot* : JAUNDICE

guly *adj* [¹gules + -y] *obs* : of the color gules : RED

¹**gum** \ˈgəm, *dial* ˈgüm\ *n* -s *often attrib* [ME *gome*, fr. OE *gōma* palate; akin to OHG *guomo* palate, ON *gómr* gum, Gk *chaunos* loose, porous, *chaos* abyss] : the tissue that surrounds the necks of teeth and covers the alveolar parts of the jaws : the portion of it in either jaw or attached to a single tooth ⟨a ~ canker on the upper jaw⟩; *broadly* : the alveolar portion of a jaw with its enveloping soft tissues — usu. used in pl. ⟨a year later he could chew practically anything with his ~*s*⟩ — see TOOTH illustration

²**gum** \"\ *vb* **gummed**; **gummed**; **gumming**; **gums** *vt* **1** : to enlarge or deepen the spaces between the teeth of (a worn saw) — often used with *out* ⟨if you ~ out that saw it will probably go another year⟩ **2** *chiefly dial* : to chew (as food) with the gums ⟨can't find his store teeth half the time so he ~*s* his food⟩ ⟨*gummed* off a fresh portion of the fragment of plug tobacco —Noel Barker⟩ ~ *vi, dial* : to chew food or any other substance with the gums instead of teeth ⟨been *gumming* since he had his teeth drawn last month⟩

³**gum** \ˈgəm\ *n* -s *often attrib* [ME *gomme*, *gumme*, fr. OF *gomme*, fr. L *gummi*, *cummi*, fr. Gk *kommi*, fr. Egypt *qmy.t*] **1 a** : any of numerous colloidal polysaccharide substances that are gelatinous when moist but harden on drying, that are exuded by plants or extracted from them by solvents and either soluble in or swelling up with water, and that are salts of complex organic acids yielding hexuronic acids and aldoses on hydrolysis — compare MUCILAGE 1 **b** : any of various plant exudates (as a mucilage, oleoresin, or gum resin) **2** : a natural gum prepared for industrial or other use (as in pharmacy or cloth finishing or for adhesives or emollients) **3** : a substance in some respect resembling a natural plant gum: as **a** : a dextrin adhesive **b** : a gummy coating chiefly of sericin on the outside of a raw silk fiber **c** : thickened secretion (as at the corner of the eyes) **d** : a tarry deposit (as in a cylinder, bearing, or storage tank) left by an unsaturated hydrocarbon fuel (as gasoline) or lubricant **e** : a rubber composition containing only the ingredients essential for vulcanization — called also *high gum*, *pure gum* **4** *also* **gum tree a** : any of several trees that yield gums: as (1) : BLACK GUM (2) : SWEET GUM (3) : any of several West Indian laticiferous trees (as *Metopium toxiferum* and *Sapium laurifolium* (4) : SAPODILLA **b** *Austral* : a tree of the genus *Eucalyptus*; *esp* : any of various smooth-barked eucalyptus trees — compare ¹BOX 2a **5 a** *also* **gumwood** \ˈ=,=\ : the wood or lumber of any gum; *esp* : that of the sweet gum **b** *chiefly Midland* : a vessel or container made of a hollow log — compare BEE GUM **6** : a rubber boot or overshoe **7** : CHEWING GUM — **in the gum** *of silk* : in a stage of manufacture before the gum has been removed by boiling

⁴**gum** \"\ *vb* **gummed**; **gummed**; **gumming**; **gums** [ME *gommen*, *gummen*, fr. *gomme*, *gumme*, n.] *vt* **1** : to smear or treat with gum : close or seal with gum : unite or stiffen by gum or a gummy substance **2** : to impede or clog with or as if with gum — often used with *up* ⟨*gummed* up the whole program⟩ ⟨the motor is all *gummed up*⟩ **3** [prob. fr. ³gum (tree); prob. fr. the observation that opossums and raccoons often hide in a sweet-gum tree when hunted] : HUMBUG, TRICK, CHEAT **4** : to fill the spaces between the cutting particles of (as a file or an abrasive wheel) with the material being cut ~ *vi* **1 a** : to exude or form gum **b** : to become gummy (as by softening or thickening) ⟨some oils ~ readily⟩ **2** : to have the spaces between the cutting particles filled with the material being cut — used of an abrasive

⁵**gum** \"\ *interj, often cap* [alter. of *God*] — used as a mild oath

gum acacia *n* : GUM ARABIC; *esp* : gum arabic used in pharmacy

gum accroides *n* : ACAROID RESIN

gum aloes *n pl but sing or pl in constr* : ALOE 4

gum ammoniac *n* : AMMONIAC

gum arabic *n* [ME *gumme arabik*, part trans. of MF *gomme arabic*, fr. *gomme* gum + *arabic* Arabic, fr. L *Arabicus* — more at ARABIC] : a water-soluble gum obtained from several acacias (esp. *Acacia senegal* and *A. arabica*) used particularly in the manufacture of adhesives, inks, confectionery, in textile finishing, and in pharmacy — called also *gum acacia*

gum arabic tree *n* : a tree that yields gum arabic; *esp* : BABUL 1a

gum benjamin *or* **gum benzoin** *n* : BENZOIN 1

gum-bichromate *adj* : GUM-DICHROMATE

¹**gum·bo** *also* **gom·bo** \ˈgəm(,)bō\ *n* -s [AmerF (Louisiana) *gombo*, of Bantu origin; akin to Umbundu *ochinggômbo* okra, Tshiluba *chinggômbô*] **1** : the okra plant or its edible pods **2 a** : a soup thickened with okra pods or with filé and usu. containing a variety of vegetables with meat (as chicken) or seafoods **b** : a thick conserve of one or more fruits **3 a** : any of various fine-grained silty soils common in the central U. S. that when saturated with water become impervious and soapy or waxy and very sticky **b** : a heavy sticky mud ⟨the track was sheer ~ after the rains⟩ **c** : something notably sticky or gummy ⟨brushes coated with a ~ of old oil and paint⟩ **4** *often cap* [AmerF *gombo*, perh. fr. Kongo *nkômbô* goat, runaway slave] : a patois used by Negroes and Creoles esp. in Louisiana **5** : MIXTURE, MÉLANGE ⟨New Orleans is a ~ — a composition of many peoples, many viewpoints, many riches —H.T.Kane⟩

²**gumbo** \"\ *adj* : of, relating to, or like gumbo

gumbo filé *n* [AmerF (Louisiana) *gombo filé*, fr. *gombo* gumbo + *filé*, n.] **1** : gumbo prepared with filé **2** : FILÉ

gumboil \ˈ=,=\ *n* : an abscess in the gum : PARULIS

gumbo lily *n* : PRAIRIE LILY 2

gumbo-lim·bo \ˌ=,=ˈlim(,)bō\ *n* [perh. fr. ¹gumbo + *limbo*, of Bantu origin; akin to Kongo *edimbu* birdlime] **1** : a tropical American tree (*Bursera simaruba*) with smooth coppery bark that peels like that of some birches and a reddish resin used locally in cements and varnishes — called also *gum elemi* **2** : PARADISE TREE 1a

gum boot *n* : RUBBER BOOT

gum·boot·ed \ˈ=,büd·əd, -ütəd\ *adj* : wearing gum boots

gum·bo·til \ˈgəmbō,til\ *n* -s [¹gumbo + *till* (glacial drift)] : a dark leached nonlaminated very sticky clay that results from the weathering of glacial till

gum·by \ˈgumbē, ˈgüm-\ *also* **gum·bé** \-,bā, =ˈ=\ *n, pl* **gumbies** *also* **gumbés** [of Bantu origin; akin to Kongo *nkumbi* ceremonial drum, Tshiluba *nkumbi* drum] : a drum made by stretching a skin over a piece of a hollowed tree and used esp. by West Indian Negroes

gum camphor *n* : dextrorotatory camphor

gumchewer \ˈ=,==\ *n* : a person that chews gum esp. habitually

gum copal *n* : COPAL

gum dammar *or* **gum damar** *n* : DAMMAR

gum-dichromate *adj* : relating to or constituting a photographic printing process that employs paper coated with a solution of gum or glue containing a pigment in suspension and sensitized with a dichromate, the print being developed and fixed by washing in water

gumdigger \ˈ=,==\ *n, NewZeal* : one that digs fossil kauri resin

gum disease *n* : GUMMING DISEASE

gum drag·on \ˌgəmˈdragən, -raig-\ *n* [by folk etymology (influence of *dragon*) fr. earlier *gum dragant*, part modif., part trans. of F *gomme adragante*, *gomme adragant*, fr. MF *gomme adragant*, fr. *gomme* gum + *adragant* tragacanth, alter. of *tragacanthe*, *tragacanth* — more at TRAGACANTH] : TRAGACANTH

gumdrop \ˈ=,=\ *n, often attrib* : a candy made usu. from corn syrup with cornstarch, gelatin, or gum arabic according to the consistency desired, cast in molds that are typically nearly hemispherical, and coated with sugar crystals

gum·drop·py \-,dräpē\ *adj* [*gumdrop* + -y] : resembling a gumdrop esp. in texture

gum duct *or* **gum canal** *n* : an intercellular canal in a plant for the secretion or passage of gum

gum elastic *n* [prob. trans. of F *gomme élastique*] **1** : RUBBER 2a **2** : BUCKTHORN 2; *esp* : FALSE BUCKTHORN

gum elemi *n* [alter. of earlier *gumme elimi*, part trans. of NL *gumi elimi*, fr. *gumi* gum (fr. L *gummi*, *cummi*) + *elimi* elemi, prob. fr. Ar *al-lāmī* the elemi] **1** : ELEMI **2** : GUMBO-LIMBO 1

gum eraser *n* : a small gummy rubber block used esp. to remove smudges from paper

gumfield \ˈ=,=\ *n* : an area where kauri resin occurs

gumflower \ˈ=,==\ *n, Scot* : an artificial flower

gum flux *n* : GUMMOSIS

gum game *n* [prob. fr. ³gum (tree) + *game*; prob. fr. the observation that opossums and raccoons often hide in a sweet=gum tree when hunted] *slang* : a trick intended to cheat or swindle a victim

gum ghat·ti *or* **gum gat·tie** \ˌgəmˈgad·ē\ *n* [*ghatti*, *gattie* native name in India] : GHATTI GUM

gum guaiac *or* **gum guaiacum** *n* : GUAIACUM 1c

gum-gum \ˈgəm,gəm\ *also* **gom-gom** \ˈgäm,gäm\ *n* [perh. native name in the Moluccas] : an iron bowl played as a musical instrument by striking with a stick; *also* : a graded set of such bowls

gum·har \ˈgəm,här\ *n* -s [prob. modif. of Beng *gāmāri*, fr. Skt *gambhārī*] : an Indian timber tree (*Gmelina arborea*) of the family Verbenaceae yielding a light brown lustrous wood that is highly resistant to moisture, easily worked, and used esp. for cabinetwork, carving, interior finishes, and boats and having roots, leaves, and fruits that are locally used in medicine — called also *gamari*

gumi *var of* GOUMI

gum juniper *n* : SANDARAC 3

gum ka·raya \ˌgəmkəˈrīə\ *n* : STERCULIA GUM

gum kino *n* : KINO 1

gum·lah \ˈgəmˈlä\ *n* -s [Hindi *gamlā*] : a large pottery jar used in India for water

gum·less \ˈgəmləs\ *adj* : free from or lacking gum ⟨a ~ oil⟩ ⟨old ~ stamps⟩

gum·lie *or* **gum·ly** \ˈgəmli\ *adj* [alter. of *grumly*] **1** *Scot* : MUDDY, TURBID **2** *Scot* : GLOOMY

gumlike \ˈ=,=\ *adj* : resembling gum : GUMMY

gum·ma \ˈgəmə\ *n, pl* **gum·mas** \-məz\ *also* **gum·ma·ta** \-məd·ə\ [NL, fr. LL, gum, fr. L *gummi*, *cummi* — more at GUM] : a tumor of gummy or rubbery consistency that resembles granulomatous tissue and is characteristic of the tertiary stage of syphilis — **gum·ma·tous** \-məd·əs\ *adj*

gum mastic *n* [ME *gumme mastyck*, fr. *gomme*, *gumme* gum + *mastyck*, *mastik* mastic] : MASTIC 1

gummed \ˈgəmd\ *adj* [ME *gommed*, fr. past part. of *gommen*, *gummen* to gum] : coated, smeared, stiffened, or mixed with gum ⟨~ labels⟩ ⟨hands all ~ with tar⟩

¹**gum·mer** \ˈgəmə(r), *dial* ˈgüm-\ *n* -s **1** : a tool or machine for gumming a worn saw **2** : an old sheep that has lost all its teeth

²**gum·mer** \ˈgəmə(r)\ *n* -s [⁴gum + -er] **1** : one that applies gum or glue (as to envelopes, labels, or tape) **2** : a person that gathers gum from the trees that produce it

gum·mif·er·ous \ˌgəˈmif(ə)rəs\ *adj* [ISV *gummi-* (fr. L *gummi* gum) + *-ferous*] : producing or bearing gum

gum·mi·ly \ˈgəməlē, -li\ *adv* : in a gummy manner

gum·mi·ness \-mēnəs, -min-\ *n* -ES : the quality or state of being gummy

gumming *n* -s [fr. gerund of ⁴gum] **1** : an act of discharging gum or becoming gummy ⟨there was severe ~ of the cylinder walls with the new fuel⟩; *esp* : GUMMOSIS **2** : the application of a gummy preparation (as gum arabic) to a lithographic printing surface **3** : the gathering of gum (as spruce gum)

gumming disease *n* : any of various plant diseases characterized by gummosis (as mal di gomma of citrus trees or Cobb's disease of sugarcane)

gum·mite \ˈgə,mīt\ *n* -s [G *gummit*, fr. *gummi* gum (fr. MHG, fr. L *gummi*, *cummi*) + *-it* -ite; fr. the gummy appearance of some specimens — more at GUM] : a yellow to reddish brown mixture of hydrous oxides of uranium, thorium, and lead consisting perhaps largely of curite — called also *uranium=ocher*

gum·mo·sis \ˌgəˈmōsəs\ *n, pl* **gummo·ses** \-ō,sēz\ [NL, fr. L *gummi* gum + NL *-osis*] : the pathological production of gummy exudates in plants (as various citrus and stone-fruit trees) as a result of cell degeneration usu. forming clear to amber hardened crusts or masses — see EXANTHEM; *broadly* : a plant disease marked by gummosis

gummosity *n* -ES [ME *gummosite* gummy substance, prob. fr. (assumed) ML *gummositat-*, *gummositas*, fr. L *gummosus* + *-itat-*, *-itas* -ity] **1** *obs* : a gummy substance **2** *obs* : the quality or state of being gummy

gum·mous \ˈgəməs\ *adj* [L *gummosus*, fr. *gummi*, *cummi* gum + *-osus* -ose] : resembling or composed of gum : GUMMY ⟨~ changes in tissue⟩

¹**gum·my** \ˈgəmē, -mi\ *adj* -ER/-EST [ME, fr. *gomme*, *gumme* gum + -y] **1 a** : consisting of, containing, or producing gum ⟨a ~ mass⟩ **b** : covered with gum or a gumlike substance ⟨how did you get your hands so ~⟩ **c** : viscous and sticky ⟨the road had become a wallow of ~ mud⟩; *esp* : viscous and sticky but without lubricating value ⟨~ residues in motor oil⟩ **2 a** : having lumps as if of gum ⟨a ~ tumor⟩ ⟨a ~ ankle⟩ **b** *of a horse's leg* : lacking clear-cut lines : PUFFY **3** : lacking ease and smoothness : UNPLEASANT ⟨a very ~ state of affairs⟩ ⟨this ~ little essay⟩

²**gum·my** \", *dial* ˈgüm-\ *adj* -ER/-EST [¹gum + -y] : showing the gums ⟨a ~ smile⟩; *esp* : TOOTHLESS ⟨a ~ old woman⟩

³**gum·my** \ˈgəmē, -mi\ *n* -ES **1** : GUMMY SHARK **2** *Austral* : ¹GUMMER 2

gummy shark *n* : any of several small sluggish Indo-Pacific sharks esp. of the genus *Mustelus* sometimes used for food

gum olibanum *n* : FRANKINCENSE 1

¹**gump** \ˈgəmp\ *n* -s [origin unknown] *chiefly dial* : a foolish or dull-witted person

²**gump** \"\ *vb* -ED/-ING/-S [origin unknown] *chiefly Scot* : GUDDLE

gumphion *or* **gumpheon** *n* -s [ME (Sc) *gumfioun*, *gunfioun* gonfanon, alter. of ME *gonfanoun* — more at GONFANON] *obs Scot* : a funeral banner

gum plant *n* : GUMWEED

gum pocket *n* : a gum-filled cavity in the woody tissue of various plants

gump·tion \ˈgəm(p)shən\ *n* -s [origin unknown] **1** : shrewd common sense ⟨the business ~ that comes from experience⟩ **2** : courageous or ambitious enterprise : blended initiative, resolution, and effort ⟨the ~ to defend the position against odds⟩ **3 a** : the art of preparing painters' colors **b** : MEGILP **syn** see SENSE

gump·tious \-shəs\ *adj* [fr. *gumption*, after such pairs as E *ambition*: *ambitious*] : having gumption : ALERT, EAGER, VIGOROUS ⟨a ~ little helper⟩ — **gump·tious·ly** *adv*

gum resin *n* : a product consisting essentially of a mixture of gum and resin usu. obtained by making an incision in a plant and allowing the juice which exudes to solidify — **gum-resinous** \ˈ=ˈ===\ *adj*

gum rosin *n* : rosin obtained from the oleoresin of living pine trees (as slash pine) by distilling off the volatile turpentine

gums *pl of* GUM, *pres 3d sing of* GUM

gum senegal *n, usu cap S* : SENEGAL GUM

gum shiraz *n* [*Shiraz*, city in southwest central Iran] : a gum similar to ghatti gum but insoluble in water

¹**gumshoe** \ˈ=,=\ *n* [³gum + *shoe*] **1 a** : a rubber overshoe **b** : a sneaker with a rubber sole **2** *also* **gumshoer** \ˈ=,==\ : DETECTIVE, POLICEMAN, INVESTIGATOR

²**gumshoe** \"\ *adj* : carried on or behaving surreptitiously ⟨a ~ campaign⟩ ⟨a ~ man⟩

³**gumshoe** \"\ *vi* : to go stealthily; *broadly* : SNOOP, PRY

gum spirits *n pl but sing or pl in constr* : TURPENTINE 2a

gum spot *n* : a gummy streak or spot in lumber

gum succory *n* : a European biennial weed (*Chondrilla juncea*) with large pinnatifid basal leaves and branching wiry stems bearing yellow-rayed flowers; *broadly* : a plant of the genus *Chondrilla*

gumsucker \ˈ=,==\ *n* [³gum + *sucker*; prob. fr. the children's habit of sucking gum exuded by eucalyptus trees] : an Australian esp. from Victoria — used as a nickname

gum thus *n* **1** : FRANKINCENSE 1 **2** : TURPENTINE 1b; *esp* : the oleoresin that hardens on the tree and is scraped off

gum tragacanth *n* : TRAGACANTH

gum tree *n* : ³GUM 4

gum turpentine *n* : TURPENTINE 1, 2a

gumweed \ˈ=,=\ *n* : a plant of the genus *Grindelia* (esp. *G. squarrosa* and *G. robusta*)

gumwood \ˈ=,=\ *n* **1** : ³GUM 5a **2** : a shrub (*Commidendron rugosum*) of the family Compositae that is endemic but rare on the island of St. Helena

¹**gun** \ˈgən\ *n* -s [ME *gonne*, *gunne*, prob. irreg. fr. *Gonnilda*, *Gunnilda*, *Gunilda*, fem. proper name (sometimes applied to an engine of war), fr. ON *Gunnhildr*, fem. proper name] **1 a** : a piece of ordnance on a carriage or other mounting for throwing projectiles by the force of some explosive (as gunpowder) usu. with high muzzle velocity and with comparatively flat trajectory and consisting of a tube or barrel closed at one end where the projectile is placed in front of the explosive charge to be ignited : a piece of ordnance — distinguished from *howitzer* and *mortar* **b** : a portable firearm

(as a rifle, shotgun, carbine, pistol) — compare SMALL ARM **c** : a device (as an air rifle or a set gun) resembling such a piece of ordnance or such a firearm in that it throws or drives a projectile **2 a** : a discharge of a gun in a salute or as a signal ⟨a salute of 21 ~s⟩ ⟨the evening ~⟩ **b** : something serving as a signal of this kind esp. marking a beginning or ending of an enterprise ⟨his speech was the opening ~ of the campaign⟩ **3** [prob. by folk etymology fr. *ganef*] *slang* : THIEF **4 a** : one who shoots a gun : HUNTER **b** : a professional killer ⟨two loose ~s . . . who turn buffalo hunters in the last days of the burning West —Whitney Balliett⟩ **5** : something suggesting a gun in shape or function: as **a** : a small hand pump for projecting oil, grease, or other lubricating material : GREASE GUN **b** : an apparatus for forcibly spraying (as paint or caulking) or throwing on cement, concrete mixtures, or similar material **c** (1) : AIR HAMMER (2) : ELECTRIC HAMMER **d** : DUST GUN **e** : FLASHGUN **f** : TACKER 1f **g** : a stapling device **h** : an electric soldering tool with pistol grip **i** : ELECTRON GUN **6** : a throttle or throttle lever esp. of an airplane engine **7** *Austral* : an expert sheepshearer — **jump the gun** *or* **beat the gun 1** : to start in a race before the starting signal ⟨disqualified for *jumping the gun*⟩ **2** : to act, move, or begin something before the approved, appropriate, or proper time ⟨were scheduled to be married in June but they *jumped the gun*⟩ — **under the gun** *or* **under the guns 1** : under the surveillance of an armed guard **2** : called upon in a game of poker to bet or drop when several players not yet heard from may raise — used of the first and second players in turn after the deal

²**gun** \"\ *vb* **gunned; gunned; gunning; guns** *vi* **1** : to hunt with a gun : go hunting **2** : to move or progress usu. rapidly in a vehicle by gunning the motor ⟨*gunned* into the road, following the fresh tracks —Nard Jones⟩ ~ *vt* **1** : to equip with a gun **2 a** : to fire upon **b** : SHOOT ⟨he was . . . *gunned* down on the streets —*Time*⟩ ⟨famous anarchist, was *gunned* to death —Alexander Dallin⟩ **c** : to hunt in ⟨nonresidents who have *gunned* the Dakotas —Nash Buckingham⟩ **3** : to direct the fall of (a tree) in forestry **4 a** : to open up the throttle of (an engine) usu. rapidly so as to increase speed **b** : to increase the speed of (a motor-driven vehicle) markedly by opening the throttle or to drive by doing this ⟨*gunned* the car up the steep grade⟩ ⟨~ a motorboat⟩ — **gun for 1** : to seek with determination the opportunity to catch (as a burglar) or bring to ruin or defeat (as an enemy) ⟨a malcontent *gunning for* his superior officer⟩ **2** : to turn all one's energy or efforts to acquire (as a position)

gu·na \'gunə, 'gü-\ *n* -s [Skt *guṇa* thread, quality] **1** : one of three primal qualities or elements of matter according to Sankhya philosophy — see RAJAS, SATTVA, TAMAS **2** : a Sanskrit ablaut grade that strengthens the simple vowels by prefixing an *a* element to each so that *i* or *ī* becomes *e* (for earlier *ai*), *u* or *ū* becomes *o* (for earlier *au*), *r* becomes *ar*, and *l* becomes *al*, but *a* and *ā* remain unchanged

gu·nate \'=,nāt\ *vb* -ED/-ING/-S [*guna* + *-ate*] *vt* : to subject to or change by guna (sense 2) ~ *vi* : to be subject to guna — **gu·na·tion** \=ˈnāshən\ *n* -s

gunboat \'=,=\ *n* **1** : an armed ship of shallow draft **2** : a small wheeled car for hauling coal or ore up an incline in a mine — called also *skip* **3** : CATAMARAN 4 **4** *slang* : one of a pair of markedly large shoes — usu. used in pl.

gun breech *n* : a mass of metal at the rear end of a cannon that extends from the rear face to the rifling

gun brig *n* : an armed 2-masted square-rigged sailing ship

gunbright \'=,=\ *n* -s [¹*gun* + *bright*, adj., fr. its use in scouring gun barrels] : a scouring rush (*Equisetum hyemale*)

gun burner *n* : a burner for oil-burning furnaces that atomizes the fuel as it escapes under pressure

gun camera *n* **1** : an aerial camera connected to and operated by the fire control mechanism of an airplane to photograph the effect of the fire on the target **2** : a camera mounted on a gun stock to be held and aimed like a gun

gun captain *n* : a petty officer in command of the crew of a gun on a ship

gun carriage *n* : a mechanism upon which a gun is mounted for maneuvering, firing, and sometimes being transported — see BARBETTE CARRIAGE; compare CASEMATE 2, TURRET 4b

gun chamber *n* : the part of a gun that receives the charge esp. in one using fixed ammunition

guncotton \'=,==\ *n* : any of various cellulose nitrates; *esp* : an explosive consisting of a higher-nitrated product (as one containing at least 13.2% nitrogen) used chiefly in smokeless powder — compare PYROCELLULOSE, PYROXYLIN

gun crew *n* : the petty officers and men assigned to the service of a gun on a naval vessel

gun·da·low *or* **gun·de·low** \'gəndə,lō\ *var of* GONDOLA

gun deck *n* [¹*gun* + *deck*] : a deck (as the first deck below the weather deck) on old-time warships carrying the ship's guns

gundeck \'=,=\ *vt* [*gun deck*] *slang* : to fake or falsify esp. by writing up (as a series of official reports) as if meeting requirements but actually without having carried out the required procedures

gun·di \'gəndē\ *n* -s [Maghrebi Ar *gundī*, perh. modif. of Berber *gerdi, gerda* rat] : a short-tailed northern African rodent (*Ctenodactylus gundi*) about eight inches long that with a few related African forms comprises the family Ctenodactylidae — see COMB RAT

gundog \'=,=\ *n* : a dog (as a pointer, setter, or retriever) that has been trained to accompany sportsmen when they hunt with guns

gun·dy \'gəndi\ *n* -ES [prob. alter. of *candy*] *Scot* : candy made with treacle

¹**gunfight** \'=,=\ *n* : a fight between two persons using guns

²**gunfight** \"\ *vi* : to engage in a gunfight

gunfighter \'=,==\ *n* : one noted for taking part in gunfights or for his skill in gunfighting

gunfire \'=,=\ *n* **1 a** : the firing of guns **b** : the time of the firing of a gun **2** : the use of guns as weapons of war as distinguished from the use of other weapons or methods (as swords or shock tactics)

gunflint \'=,=\ *n* **1** : a small sharp flint for use in a flintlock to produce a spark of fire to ignite the priming **2** *usu cap* [so called fr. the use of old gunflints during Dorr's Rebellion in 1842] : RHODE ISLANDER — a nickname

gunge *or* **gunj** \'gənj\ *n, pl* **gunges** *or* **gunjes** [Hindi *gāj*, of Iranian origin; akin to Per *ganj* treasure] *India* : GRANARY, MARKET

gung ho \'gəŋ'hō\ *adj* [*Gung Ho*, slogan of certain U.S. forces in Asia in World War II, fr. Chin(Pek) *kung¹-ho²* (short for *ch'ing¹-kung¹-yeh² ho²-tso⁴ shê⁴* Light Industries Cooperative Society), taken to mean "work together"] : extremely or overly zealous or enthusiastic

gun glaze *n* : a surfacing glaze applied with a spray gun to a vehicle body as a preliminary to painting

gunhand \'=,=\ *n* : one hired by an individual to carry or handle a gun for the protection of the individual's property, workers, or enterprise or for the carrying on of his private warfare with other persons

gunhouse \'=,=\ *n* : a ship's gun enclosure made of relatively light armor for protection against weather and splinters

gunite \'gə,nīt\ *vb* -ED/-ING/-S *vi* : to apply a Gunite mixture ~ *vt* : to apply a Gunite mixture to

Gun·ite \"\ *trademark* — used for a mixture of cement, sand, and water applied by pneumatic pressure through a specially adapted hose

gun·it·er \-īd·ə(r)\ *n* -s **1** : one that applies a Gunite mixture with a cement gun **2** : GROUTER 2

gun·ja *or* **gun·jah** \'gənjə\ *var of* GANJA

gunk \'gəŋk\ *n* -s [prob. imit.] : filthy, sticky, or greasy matter usu. objectionably messy or smelly; *specif* : undesirable sludge or residue ⟨all fouled up with bananas, sweat, blood, and the ~ from the street —Vincent McHugh⟩ ⟨a sticky ~ to settle dusty cattle feed —*This Week Mag.*⟩

gunkhole \'=,=\ *n* : a shallow cove or channel nearly unnavigable because of mud, rocks, or vegetation

gunlayer \'=,==\ *n, Brit* : a sailor who aims a ship's guns

gunlaying \'=,==\ *n* [*laying*, fr. gerund of *lay*] : the process of aiming (as by determining range, azimuth, and elevation) a large gun at a target ⟨~ by radar⟩

gun·less \'gənləs\ *adj* : having or requiring no gun

gunline \'=,=\ *n* : a line or cable (as a towrope) one end of which can be shot (as from one ship to another) by a gun device

gunlock \'=,=\ *n* : a mechanism attached to or usu. integral with a firearm by which the charge is ignited — compare FLINTLOCK, MATCHLOCK, PERCUSSION LOCK, WHEEL LOCK

gunmaker \'=,==\ *n* [ME *gonmaker*, fr. *gonne, gunne* gun + *maker*] : a maker or manufacturer of guns

gun·man \'gənmən, -,man, -,maa(ə)n\ *n, pl* **gunmen 1 a** : a man who is armed with or fires a gun; *also* : a guard armed with a gun **b** : a man noted for his speed or skill in handling a gun in gunplay or gunfights **2** : a criminal whose crimes involve the use of a gun : KILLER; *esp* : one hired to kill another with a gun

gunmetal \'=,==\ *n* **1 a** (1) : a bronze ordinarily composed of nine parts of copper and one of tin and formerly much used as a material for cannon (2) : a metal or alloy used as a material for guns **b** : any of various alloys or metals treated so as to imitate nearly black tarnished copper-alloy gunmetal and used for the manufacture of metal novelties **2** *or* **gunmetal gray** : a nearly neutral slightly purplish dark gray that is darker and slightly redder than steel gray

gun moll *n* [¹*gun* (thief) + *moll*] **1** *slang* : a female thief **2** [influenced in meaning by ¹*gun* (firearm)] *slang* : the girl friend of a gangster; *also* : a female criminal noted for her carrying or use of a gun

gun money *n* : debased coins issued by James II in Ireland in 1689 and made partly of metal from old cannon

gun motor carriage *n* : a vehicle on which a gun is mounted

gun mount *n* : a structure that supports a gun

gunned *past of* GUN

¹**gun·nel** \'gən³l\ *n* -s [origin unknown] **1** : a small slimy elongate marine blenny (*Pholis gunnellus*) found on both sides of the North Atlantic — called also *butterfish* **2** : any of several blennies closely related to or resembling the gunnel

²**gunnel** *var of* GUNWALE

gunnen *past part of* GIN

gun·ner \'gənə(r)\ *n* -s [ME *gonner, gunner*, fr. *gonne, gunne* gun + *-er*] **1** : one who handles or works a gun: as **a** : a member of an artillery unit (as the Royal Artillery) **b** : an artillery corporal (as in the U.S. Army) whose specialty is the aiming of a gun **c** : one who shoots game **d** : one who shoots whales with a harpoon gun **2** : a warrant officer (as in the U.S. Navy) whose specialty is supervision of ordnance and ordnance stores

gun·nera \(,)gə'nirə, -nerə\ *n* [NL, fr. Johan Ernst *Gunnerus* †1773 Norw. botanist] **1** *cap* : a genus of widely distributed herbs (family Haloragaceae) several of which are used as garden ornamentals with large orbicular basal leaves and a thick spike of small flowers **2** -s : any plant of the genus *Gunnera*

gun·ne·ra·ce·ae \,gənə'rāsē,ē\ *n pl, cap* [NL, fr. *Gunnera*, type genus + *-aceae*] *in some classifications* : a family coextensive with Haloragaceae

gunner's mate *n* : a petty officer (as in the U.S. Navy) responsible for the care and maintenance of a ship's weapons and ammunition

gunner's quadrant *n* : an instrument consisting of a graduated limb with a spirit level, and an arm by which it is applied to a cannon or mortar in adjusting the piece to the elevation for the desired range

gun·nery \'gən(ə)rē, -ri\ *n* -ES [¹*gun* + *-ery*] **1** : the use of or instruction in the use of guns; *specif* : a part of military science that deals with the flight of projectiles and with the manner of using guns so as to achieve the desired effect **2** *archaic* : the firing of guns

gunnery officer *n* : an officer (as in the U.S. Navy) who has general charge of the care and maintenance of the battery, ordnance material, and ammunition of a warship, superintends gun drills, and directs the gunnery training of the crew

gunnery sergeant *n* : a noncommissioned marine officer rating just below a first sergeant and above a staff sergeant

gunning *n* -s [fr. gerund of ²*gun*] : the shooting of a gun: **a** : hunting or shooting at game **b** : the criminal shooting or killing of a person

gunning stick \'==,=\ *also* **gunstick** \'=,=\ *n* : a device made of wood strips several feet long crossed like a pair of scissors that is placed against an undercut in felling a tree to determine the direction of fall

gun·ny \'gənē, -ni\ *or* **gunny cloth** *n* -ES [Hindi *ganī, goṇī*, fr. Skt *goṇī* sack, prob. of Dravidian origin; akin to Kanarese *gōni* sack] **1** : a strong coarse loosely woven material made from jute for bagging and sacking **2** : BURLAP

gunnysack *or* **gunny-bag** \'==,=\ *n* : a sack made of gunny or burlap

gun·ny·sack·ing \-iŋ\ *n* : GUNNY

gun pendulum *n* : an apparatus used to determine ballistics data (as the initial velocity of a projectile or conditions existing in the bore of a gun during passage of the projectile) by means of measurement of the recoil caused by the discharge of a gun suspended as a pendulum — compare BALLISTIC PENDULUM

gun pit *n* : an excavation often with a parapet in front to protect a fieldpiece and its men from direct fire

gunplay \'=,=\ *n* : the shooting of small arms with intent to kill or scare : the action of men gunfighting

gunpoint \'=,=\ *n* : the point of a gun — **at gunpoint** *adv* : under a threat of death by being shot ⟨forced the bank president *at gunpoint* to open the safe —George Courson⟩

gunpointer \'=,==\ *n* [¹*gun* + *pointer*] : a sailor who elevates, depresses, and fires a manually controlled gun aboard ship

gunport \'=,=\ *n* : an opening (as in a ship's side, a gun turret, a pillbox, or the nose, fuselage, or wing of an airplane) through which a gun can be fired

gunpowder \'=,==\ *n* [ME *gonnepoudre*, fr. *gonne, gunne* gun + *poudre* powder] **1 a** : a black or brown explosive consisting of an intimate mechanical mixture of potassium nitrate, charcoal, and sulfur manufactured orig. as a powder and later usu. in grains of various sizes for different uses and used as the first and only military propellant until the introduction of smokeless powder — see BLACK POWDER, BROWN POWDER **b** : any of various powders used in guns as propelling charges ⟨smokeless ~⟩ — compare SMOKELESS POWDER **2** : GUNPOWDER TEA

gunpowder hammer *n* : a hammer or impact tool driven by the explosion of gunpowder

gunpowder tea *n* : a green tea each leaf of which is rolled into a small ball or pellet

gun·pow·dery \-,paud(ə)rē, -ri\ *adj* [*gunpowder* + *-y*] **1** *archaic* : VIOLENT, EXPLOSIVE **2** : smelling of gunpowder

gunpower \'=,==\ *n* : the total weight of metal that can be thrown by the major battery of a battleship in one broadside

gun-rivet \'=,==\ *vt* : to rivet with a pneumatic hammer

gun room *n* : an apartment on a British warship usu. aft of the berth deck orig. used by the gunner and his mates but now by the midshipmen and junior officers

gunrunner \'=,==\ *n* : one engaged in gunrunning

gunrunning \'=,==\ *n* : contraband traffic in arms and ammunition esp. when involving international relations or violation of customs laws

guns *pl of* GUN, *pres 3d sing of* GUN

gun·sel \'gən(t)səl\ *n* -s [prob. fr. Yiddish *genzel* gosling, fr. MHG *gensel*, dim. of *gans* goose, fr. OHG — more at GOOSE] **1** *slang* : a young, naïve, or stupid person **2** *slang* : a treacherous person **3** *slang* : CATAMITE **4** [influenced in meaning by ¹*gun*] *slang* : GUNMAN

gunshot \'=,=\ *n* [ME *gonneshot*, fr. *gonne, gunne* gun + *shot*] **1** : shot or a shot fired from a gun **2** : the distance to which shot can be thrown from a gun so as to be effective : the range of a gun

gun-shy \'=,=\ *adj* **1** : afraid of the sound of a gun or of other similar loud noises — used esp. of a dog **2** : afraid or markedly distrustful ⟨if you are a big-league player, you cannot very well afford to be *gun-shy* and duck away in panic from a ball —Paul Gallico⟩ ⟨was *gun-shy* of newspaper reporters —Charles Michelson⟩ ⟨the son of a bewildered age, *gun-shy* of propaganda —Dixon Wecter⟩

gunsight \'=,=\ *n* : ¹SIGHT 11a

gunsight lamp *n* : an optical sight permitting a gunner to aim at an airplane approaching directly down the glare from the sun's face

gunslick \'=,=\ *n, slang* : one who is noted for his fast handling of a gun esp. in gunfights

gun slide *n* : a fixed part of a gun mount on the upper surface of which the recoiling part travels

gunsling \'=,=\ *n* : SLING 3a (1)

gunslinger \'=,==\ *n* [¹*gun* + *slinger*] : GUNMAN ⟨the three ~s who committed the crimes —Allan Bruce⟩ ⟨backed up his reputation as a ~ —Hoffman Birney⟩

gunslinging \'=,==\ *n* [*slinging* fr. gerund of *sling*] : the shooting of a gun esp. in a gunfight ⟨irresponsible ~⟩

guns·man \'gənzmən\ *n, pl* **gunsmen** [*gun's* (gen. of ¹*gun*) + *man*] *archaic* : GUNMAN 1

gunsmith \'=,=\ *n* : one whose occupation is to design, make, or repair small firearms

gunsmithing \'=,==\ *n* [¹*gun* + *smithing*] : the work of a gunsmith

gunsmithy \'=,==\ *n* [¹*gun* + *smithy*] : the workshop of a gunsmith

gunstick *var of* GUNNING STICK

gunstock \'=,=\ *n* [ME *gonnestok*, fr. *gonne, gunne* gun + *stok* stock] : the stock to which the barrel and mechanism of a firearm are secured

gunstone \'=,=\ *n* [ME *gunneston*, fr. *gonne, gunne* gun + *stoon, ston* stone] **1** *obs* : CANNONBALL 1 **2** *heraldry* : a roundel sable : OGRESS, PELLET

gun tackle *n* : a block-and-tackle arrangement formerly used for running a gun carriage to and from a gun part or raising or lowering a gun — see GUNTACKLE PURCHASE; TACKLE illustration

guntackle purchase \'=,==-\ *n* [*gun tackle* + *purchase*, n.] : a pulley tackle using two single blocks

gun·ter iron \'gəntə(r)-\ *n* : a fitting on a gunter rig consisting of two double eyes united by side bars so that one eye in each pair slides freely over a lower mast and the other serves as a step for a topmast

gunter rig *also* **gunter** *n* -s [after Edmund *Gunter* †1626 Eng. mathematician; fr. its resemblance to an instrument used in making mathematical calculations according to a system devised by Gunter] : a rig used on a small sailing boat consisting of an upper mast stepped in a gunter iron and moved up or down on a lower mast and supporting a yard to which is laced a triangular sail — called also *sliding gunter*

gunter's chain *n, usu cap G* [after Edmund *Gunter* †1626] : a chain 66 feet long consisting of 100 links of 7.92 inches that is the unit of length for surveys of U.S. public lands

gun-toting \'=,==\ *adj* [*toting* fr. pres. part. of *tote*] : carrying and using a gun usu. for criminal purposes ⟨the *gun-toting* brothers wanted here for armed assault —*Springfield (Mass.) Union*⟩

gun toting *n* -s [*toting* fr. gerund of *tote*] : the carrying and use of a gun usu. for criminal purposes ⟨stiffer punishment for *gun toting* —W.T.Brannon⟩

gunter rig: *1* lower mast, *2* upper mast, *3* gunter irons, *4* halyard

guntub \'=,=\ *n* : the circular steel shield around a ship's gun

gun·wale *or* **gun·nel** *also* **gun·whale** \'gən³l\ *n* -s [*gunwale* & *gunnel* fr. ME *gonnewale*, fr. *gonne, gunne* gun + *wale*; *gunwhale* by folk etymology fr. *gunwale*; fr. its former use as a support for guns — more at WALE] **1 a** : the part of a vessel where topsides and deck meet **b** : the upper edge of the side or the rail of a small boat (as a canoe) **2** : a fore-and-aft member lying on or against the heads of the frames and inside the upper strake in boatbuilding — see INWALE — **gunwale down** *or* **gunwale to** : tipping or sinking until the gunwale is on a level with the water

gun·yah \'gənyə\ *n* -s [native name in Australia] **1** *Austral* : an aboriginal hut **2** *Austral* : a small hut or crude shelter built for use in the bush ⟨the camp consisted of dome-shaped bough ~s, roofed with sacks —Francis Ratcliffe⟩

gun·yang \'gən,yaŋ\ *n* -s [native name in Australia] : the kangaroo apple of Australia

günz \'gin(t)s, -ɯ-\ *n* -ES *usu cap* [*Günz* river, Bavaria, Germany] : the earliest of four geologic stages marked by an advance of the ice during the Pleistocene glaciation of Europe — **günz·ian** \-sēən\ *adj, usu cap*

günz-min·del \-ˈmind³l\ *n, usu cap G&M* : the first geologic interglacial stage of the European Pleistocene between the Günz and Mindel stages of ice advance

¹**gup** *interj* [perh. contr. of *go up*] *obs* — used to express reproof, derision, or remonstrance

²**gup** \'gəp\ *n* -s [Hindi *gap*] *slang* : foolish talk : NONSENSE ⟨see what sort of ~ he's handed out —Ngaio Marsh⟩

¹**gup·py** \'gəpē, -pi\ *n* -ES [after R.J. Lechmere *Guppy* of Trinidad, who first presented specimens to the British Museum] : a small topminnow (*Lebistes reticulatus*) of the Barbados, Trinidad, and Venezuela frequently kept as an aquarium fish, the females reaching a length of about two inches and being plainly colored, the males being much smaller and having black, blue, and red markings

²**guppy** \"\ *n* -ES *sometimes cap* [greater underwater propulsive *power* + *-y*] : a submarine that has been streamlined (as by the removal of guns and the recessing of deck fittings) and equipped with snorkel

gup·ta \'güptə, 'gup-\ *adj, usu cap* [*Gupta*, dynasty of kings of northern India] : of or relating to a dynasty of Brahman kings of northern India of the 4th to the 7th centuries and esp. to the art forms (as in religious sculpture or temple architecture) that characterized the period of that dynasty and spread from India into other eastern countries (as Ceylon and China)

¹**gur** *or* **goor** \'gu̇(ə)r\ *n* -s [Hindi *gur* coarse sugar, molasses, fr. Skt *guḍa*] : JAGGERY

²**gur** \"\ *n* -s *usu cap* : a branch of the Niger-Congo language family including Mossi, Dagomba, Senufo, Bariba, Gurma, and Gurunsi centered in the upper Volta river valley in Ghana and the Upper Volta territory, West Africa — called also *Mossi-Gurunsi, Voltaic*

gu·ra·ge \gü'rä(,)gā\ *n* -s *cap* : a Semitic language or group of closely related languages spoken in southern Ethiopia

gur·dwa·ra \gu̇r'dwärə\ *n* -s [Panjabi *gurduārā*, fr. Skt *guru* teacher + *dvāra* door; akin to Skt *dvār* door — more at GURU, DOOR] : a Sikh shrine or place of worship

gur·dy \'gərdē\ *n* -ES [short for *hurdy-gurdy*] : a revolving drum or large spool used in hauling nets and lines aboard commercial fishing boats

gurdy man *n* : a worker who coils fishing lines as they are pulled in and the fish removed

¹**gurge** \'gərj\ *vi* -ED/-ING/-S [L *gurges*, n.] : SURGE, SWIRL

²**gurge** \"\ *n* -s [L *gurges* whirlpool — more at GORGE] : a turbulent fountain : SURGE, EDDY

gur·geons \'gərjənz\ *n pl* [ME *gurgeones*] *now dial Eng* : coarse meal

gur·geon stopper \'gərjən-\ *n* [*gurgeon* perh. alter. of *gurjun*] : a small tree (*Eugenia buxifolia*) of southern Florida and the West Indies with hard wood — called also *Spanish stopper*

gur·ges \'gər,jēz\ *n* -ES [L, whirlpool] : a heraldic charge consisting of a spiral made up of two narrow bands argent and azure and conventionally representing a whirlpool

gurges

gur·gi·ta·tion \,gərjə'tāshən\ *n* -s [LL *gurgitatus* (past part. of *gurgitare* to engulf, fr. L *gurgit-, gurges* whirlpool) + E *-ion*] : a boiling or surging of a liquid : usu. violent ebullition

¹**gur·gle** \'gərgəl, 'gēg-,'gəig-\ *vb* **gurgled; gurgled; gurgling** \-g(ə)liŋ\ **gurgles** [prob. imit.] *vi* **1** : to run or flow in a broken irregular chuckling current ⟨the brook *gurgled* over the rocks⟩ ⟨the water *gurgled* out of the narrow mouth of the bottle⟩ **2** : to make a sound like that of a gurgling liquid ⟨the baby *gurgling* in its crib⟩ ~ *vt* : to utter with a gurgling sound ⟨the woman *gurgled* her greetings to the children⟩

²**gurgle** \"\ *n* -s **1** : the act of gurgling ⟨the ~ of a brook over rocks⟩ **2** : the sound of gurgling or a single throaty chuckling sound made in gurgling ⟨the ~s of the contented baby⟩

gurgling *n* -s [fr. gerund of ¹*gurgle*] : the sound of one that gurgles ⟨makes uncalled-for ~s of a bestial nature —Norman Douglas⟩

gur·gling·ly *adv* [*gurgling* (pres. part. of ¹*gurgle*) + *-ly*] : in the manner of one that gurgles ⟨the hostess approached them ~ and with a fatuous smile of joy⟩

gurgoyle *var of* GARGOYLE

gu·ri·an \'gu̇rēən\ *n* -s *cap* **:** a member of a Caucasian people closely related to the Georgians

gur·jun *also* **gur·jan** \'gərjən\ *n* -s [Bengali *garjan*] **1 :** GURJUN BALSAM **2 a :** a tree yielding gurjun balsam **b :** the wood of such a tree

gurjun balsam *n* **:** a thin oleoresin derived from several East Indian trees of the genus *Dipterocarpus* and resembling copaiba — called also *wood oil*

gurk \'gərk\ *n* -s [perh. fr. ScGael *garrach*] *Scot* **:** a stout well-built person

¹gur·kha *or* **ghur·kha** \'gu̇(ə)rkə, 'gər-\ *n, pl* **gurkha** *or* **gurkhas** *or* **ghurkha** *or* **ghurkhas** *usu cap* **1 :** a member of a Rajput race that is Hindu in religion and Indo-European in speech and that settled in the province of Gurkha, Nepal, in the latter half of the 18th century and made themselves supreme **2 :** a soldier from Nepal in the British and Indian armies

²gurkha \"\ *adj, usu cap* **:** of, relating to, or consisting of Gurkhas

gurl \'gərl\ *vi* -ED/-ING/-S [ME *gurlen*, of imit. origin] *Scot* **:** HOWL, GROWL, SNARL

gurly \-li\ *adj* -ER/-EST [*gurl* + -*y*] **1** *Scot* **:** rough and boisterous: **a** *of weather* **:** STORMY **b** *of a person* **:** uncouth and inclined to be surly ⟨the ~ brute —G.D.Brown⟩ **2** *Scot* **:** GURGLING ⟨the sounds of ~ burns⟩

gur·ma \'gu̇(ə)rmə\ *n, pl* **gurma** *or* **gurmas** *usu cap* **1 :** a Negro people inhabiting the region adjacent to the White Volta river in West Africa **2 :** a Gur language of the Gurma people

gur·mu·khi \'gu̇rmə(,)kē\ *n* -s *usu cap* [Panjabi *gurmukhī*, lit., from the mouth of the teacher, fr. Skt *guru* teacher + *mukha* mouth (prob. of Dravidian origin & akin to Tamil *mukam*); fr. the tradition that it was invented by the guru Angad in the 16th century — more at GURU] **:** the alphabet that the sacred texts of the Sikhs in whatever language are written in and that is also used by the Sikhs in secular writing in Panjabi

gur·nard \'gərnərd\ *n, pl* **gurnard** *or* **gurnards** [ME, fr. MF *gornart*, irreg. fr. *grogner*, *grognier* to grunt, grumble (fr. L *grunnire* to grunt) + -*ard*, -*art* -ard — more at GRUNT] **1 :** any of various marine scorpaenid fishes constituting the family Triglidae, having the head armored and spined and three pairs of fingerlike processes which are modified ventral rays of the pectoral fins and are used as feelers and in crawling on the sea bottom, and including a few European forms that are used as food — see FLYING GURNARD, SEA ROBIN **2 :** a dragonet (*Callionymus draco*)

gur·ney \'gərnē\ *n* -s [prob. fr. the name *Gurney*] *West* **:** a wheeled cot or stretcher

gur·ney·ite \-,īt\ *n* -s *usu cap* [Joseph J. *Gurney* †1847 Eng. Quaker minister + E -*ite*] **:** a follower of an English Friend who toured America preaching an evangelical Christianity that stressed biblical authority, the atonement, justification, and sanctification — compare WILBURITE

gu·ro \'gü(,)rō\ *n, pl* **guro** *or* **guros** *usu cap* **:** a people of the interior of the Ivory Coast now known chiefly for their wood carvings (as dancing masks) — called also *Kweni*

gurr \'gər\ *vi* -ED/-ING/-S [imit.] *chiefly Scot* **:** GROWL, SNARL

gur·ry \'gərē\ *n* -ES [origin unknown] **:** fishing offal: as **a :** the refuse from cutting up a whale and trying out the oil **b :** a slimy gummy substance (as that scraped off the back of a right whale or removed from a sponge in commercial processing) **c :** FISH OIL

gurs *pl of* GUR

gurt \'gərt\ *dial Eng var of* GREAT

gu·ru \gə'rü, 'gu̇(,)rü, 'gü(-\ *n* -s [Hindi *gurū*, fr. Skt *guru*, lit., heavy, weighty, venerable — more at GRIEVE] **1 a :** a personal religious teacher and spiritual guide in Hinduism **b** *often cap* **:** one of a line of ten chief spiritual leaders in Sikhism recognized within the Sikh community as personal exemplars and temporal leaders as well beginning with Guru Nanak (1469–1538) and ending in 1708 with the death of Guru Govind Singh **2 :** a person who acts as one's teacher and guide in matters of fundamental intellectual concern ⟨seeking the clique or the ~ essential to his soul —John Masefield⟩

gu·run·si \gə'rün(t)sē\ *n, pl* **gurunsi** *or* **gurunsies** *usu cap* **1 :** a Negro people of the Ivory Coast of West Africa **2 :** a Gur language of the Gurunsi people

gu·ru·ship *pronunc at* GURU + ,ship\ *n* **:** the office or function of a guru

gur·witsch ray \'gu̇rvich-, -rwich-\ *n, usu cap G* [after Aleksandr G. *Gurvich* b1874 Russ. biologist] **:** MITOGENETIC RAY

¹gush \'gəsh\ *vb* -ED/-ING/-ES [ME *guschen*, *gosshen*, perh. of imit. origin] *vi* **1 :** to pour, issue, flow, or spout copiously or violently ⟨the blood ~*ed* from the wound⟩ ⟨the spectacular fountains of lava that ~ for hundreds of feet into the air —Howel Williams⟩ — often used with *forth* or *out* ⟨the water ~*ed* forth from the hole in the tank⟩ ⟨words and yet more words ~*ed* out of him in an endless meaningless stream⟩ **2 :** to give free rein to a sudden copious flow or issuing forth (as of blood or tears) — often used with *forth* or *out* ⟨the cut ~*ed* forth with blood⟩ ⟨always ~*ing* out in tears⟩ ⟨~ forth with a wondrous flow of eloquence⟩ **3 :** to make an unrestrained and excessively sentimental usu. prolonged and often habitual display of affection or enthusiasm ⟨a woman who tended to ~ at the very mention of babies⟩ ⟨she would rush to him with all the girlish excitement . . . and ~ about everybody having a good time —E.A.Peeples⟩ ~ *vt* **1 :** to emit or pour in a copious free flow ⟨the broken main ~*ed* a stream of water over the road⟩ — often used with *forth* or *out* ⟨the old man's eyes ~*ed* sudden tears —L.C.Douglas⟩ **2 :** to say or utter in gushing ⟨"I'm dying to get to Europe," he ~*ed*. "It's positively the only, only place for those who wish to live the cultured life" —Rex Ingamells⟩ ⟨the woman ~*ed* maudlin greetings to everybody at the party⟩ **syn** see POUR

²gush \"\ *n* -ES **1 a :** a gushing forth (as of a liquid) ⟨a sudden ~ of water from the hose nozzle⟩ **b :** the fluid emitted in such a gushing forth ⟨the ~ of oil spread out in a thin slippery film over the road⟩ **c :** a free usu. sudden outpouring **:** GUST, BURST ⟨a ~ of sound from the horns⟩ ⟨a ~ of feeling from the heart⟩ ⟨a ~ of flame⟩ ⟨a ~ of cheerful light —Charles Dickens⟩ ⟨a mighty ~ of energy —*Science Yr. Bk.*⟩ **2 :** an unrestrained often prolonged display of sentiment ⟨a poem marked chiefly by ~⟩ ⟨a city which provides unusual opportunities for ~, for it has abundant superficial charm —Robertson Davies⟩ ⟨the insight of a cultivated mind and the ~ of the immature enthusiast —John Dewey⟩

gush·er \'gəshə(r)\ *n* -s **1 :** one that gushes; *specif* **:** an oil well with a copious natural flow usu. sudden and violent in its initial uncontrolled stage **2 :** something suggesting a gusher oil well in its flowing or spouting ⟨~*s* of critical applause⟩

gush·et \'gəshət\ *n* -s [ME (Sc) *guschet* piece of armor protecting the armpit, fr. MF *gouchet*, *gousset* piece of armor protecting the armpit, armpit — more at GUSSET] **1** *Scot* **:** the clock of a stocking **2** *Scot* **:** ¹GUSSET 2a

gush·i·ly \'gəshəlē, -li\ *adv* **:** in a gushy manner ⟨a rather ~ pleasant hostess⟩

gush·i·ness \-shēnəs, -shin-\ *n* -ES **:** the quality or state of a person that gushes or the quality of his expression ⟨a man of inexcusable ~ that poured sentiment like syrup over everyone⟩ ⟨the ~ of his prose writings⟩

gush·ing·ly *adv* [*gushing* (pres. part. of ¹*gush*) + -*ly*] **:** in the manner of one that gushes ⟨a ~ prolific writer of saccharine verse⟩ ⟨~ idealistic ladies —G.B.Shaw⟩

gushy \'gəshē, -shi\ *adj* -ER/-EST [²*gush* + -*y*] **:** marked by gushiness ⟨a laudation marked more by ~ sentiment than sincere admiration⟩ ⟨wrote particularly unrestrained and ~ poetry⟩

gus·la *or* **gus·le** *or* **gous·le** *also* **guz·la** \'gü|slə, 'gu̇|, |zlə\ *n* -s [Serbo-Croatian *gusle*; akin to Bulg *gŭsla* gusla, Russ *gusli* gusli, OSlav *gǫsli* psaltery, Russ *gudet'* to sound, drone, Lith *gausti* — more at KITE] **:** a rudimentary musical instrument of the Balkans made with a round concave body, parchment sounding board, and one horsehair string and held between the knees and played with a curved bow

gus·li *also* **gus·lee** \-lē\ *n* -s [Russ] **:** a Russian musical instrument of the zither class having approximately 28 gut strings and played with a keyboard

¹gus·set \'gəsət, *usu* -əd.+V\ *n* -s [ME, fr. MF *gouchet*, *gousset* piece of armor protecting the armpit, armpit, fr. *gousse* pod + -*et*] **1 a :** a piece of chain mail or plate at the openings of the joints in a suit of armor **b :** a usu. triangular or diamond-shaped insert (as of cloth or leather) placed in a seam (as of a sleeve, pocketbook, glove) to give ease or expansibility; *also* **:** a similar piece made by adding stitches at the heel of hose **c :** any V-shaped or triangular insert (as in a sail or skirt): as (1) **:** an elastic insert in a shoe upper (as for providing a snug fit) (2) *or* **gusset tongue :** BELLOWS TONGUE **d :** a pleat or fold esp. in bookbinding **2 :** something resembling a gusset: as **a :** a gore of land **b** (1) *or* **gusset plate :** a connecting or reinforcing plate that joins the truss members in a truss joint or fits at a joint of a frame structure or set of braces (2) *or* **gusset stay :** a bracket or angular piece of iron for strengthening angles of a structure (as an airplane or a bridge) **3 :** a pretended abatement in heraldry consisting of either side of a pall without the top opening

1, 1 gussets 1b

²gusset \"\ *vt* -ED/-ING/-S **:** to provide with, connect, or reinforce with a gusset

¹gust \'gəst\ *n* -s [ME *guste*, fr. L *gustus* taste; akin to L *gustare* to taste — more at CHOOSE] **1** *obs* **a :** the sensation of taste **b :** INCLINATION, LIKING **2 a** *archaic* **:** special flavor or taste (as of food or drink) **b** *obs* **:** FORETASTE **3** [prob. fr. Sp *gusto* delight, pleasure, taste, fr. L *gustus* taste] **a** *obs* **:** GRATIFICATION, ENJOYMENT **b :** great or keen delight — often used formerly with *of*, *in*, or *to* but now usu. with *for* ⟨~ of the things of the world —Jeremy Taylor⟩ ⟨a ~ for London —Samuel Johnson⟩ ⟨her father's early ~ for color and for amusement —E.K.Chambers⟩

²gust \'güst, 'gəst\ *vt* -ED/-ING/-S [ME *gusten*, fr. L *gustare*] *now Scot* **:** TASTE, RELISH

³gust \'gəst\ *n* -s [prob. fr. ON *gustr*; akin to OHG *gussa* flood, ON *gjōsa* to gush, MIr *guss* violence, anger, Goth *giutan* to pour — more at FOUND] **1 a :** a sudden brief rushing or driving of wind **b :** a sudden change with respect to the earth in the speed or the direction or both of the wind of sufficient magnitude to produce a significant load upon the structure of an airplane encountering it **2 a :** a burst, puff, outrush, or brief emission (as of rain, fire, smoke) suggesting a gust of wind ⟨a ~ of rain came down —Frank Taubes⟩ **b :** an outburst or quick venting esp. of temper or feeling ⟨unruly ~*s* of passion —William Black⟩ ⟨a ~ of laughter —John Wain⟩ ⟨his ~*s* of honest jocularity —Francis Hackett⟩ **c :** something that appears or comes into being or is experienced suddenly and usu. transiently **:** WAVE, SURGE ⟨a ~ of pain —Fred Majdalany⟩ ⟨a sudden ~ of frustration —Alan Moorehead⟩ ⟨a ~ of loneliness —Jean Stafford⟩ ⟨a ~ of personal concern —Janet Flanner⟩ **syn** see WIND

⁴gust \"\ *vi* -ED/-ING/-S **:** to blow or move in gusts ⟨the winds, now ~*ing* in the reverse direction —David Beaty⟩ ⟨the wind . . . ~*ed* in through the holes —Irwin Shaw⟩

gus·ta·ble \'gəstəbəl\ *adj* [LL *gustabilis*, fr. L *gustare* to taste + -*abilis* -able] **1** *archaic* **:** APPETIZING, SAVORY, TASTY **2** *archaic* **:** perceptible or distinguishable by taste ⟨an increased number of ~ differences —Herbert Spencer⟩

gus·ta·tion \,gə'stāshən\ *n* -s [L *gustation-*, *gustatio*, fr. *gustatus* (past part. of *gustare*) + -*ion-*, -*io* -ion] **:** the act or sensation of tasting

gus·ta·tive \'gəstəd·iv\ *adj* [ML *gustativus*, fr. L *gustatus* + -*ivus* -ive] **:** GUSTATORY — **gus·ta·tive·ness** *n* -ES

gus·ta·to·ri·al \,gəstə'tōrēəl, -tȯr-\ *adj* [*gustatory* + -*al*] **:** GUSTATORY

gus·ta·to·ri·ly \-rəlē, -li\ *adv* **:** in a gustatory manner

gus·ta·to·ry \'==,=rē, -ri\ *adj* [L *gustatus* + E -*ory*] **:** of, relating to, affecting, associated with, or being the sense of taste ⟨~ nerves⟩ ⟨~ stimulation⟩

gustatory cell *n* **:** one of the sensory epithelial cells of a taste bud **:** TASTE CELL

gus·ta·vi·an \(,)gə'stāvēən, gu̇'s-, -täv-\ *adj, usu cap* [*Gustavus* (any of several kings of Sweden) + E -*ian*] **:** of or relating to the reign of the Swedish kings or any one of the Swedish kings named Gustavus (as III and IV)

¹gust·ful \'gəstfəl\ *adj* [¹*gust* + -*ful*] *archaic* **:** APPETIZING, SAVORY — **gust·ful·ly** \-fəlē\ *adv*

²gustful \"\ *adj* [³*gust* + -*ful*] **:** GUSTY, WINDY

¹gust·i·ly \'gəstəlē, -li, *Scot* " *or* 'güs-\ *adv* [²*gusty* + -*ly*] **:** with great relish ⟨picked up a long wrinkled-looking sausage . . . then crunched on it ~ —P.E.Deutschman⟩

²gust·i·ly \'gəs-\ *adv* [¹*gusty* + -*ly*] **:** in gusts ⟨the wind blew ~⟩ **:** in a manner suggesting a gust ⟨she sighed ~⟩

gust·i·ness \-tēnəs, -tin-\ *n* -ES [¹*gusty* + -*ness*] **:** the quality or state of being gusty; *specif* **:** the ratio of the maximum difference of wind velocity to its mean velocity in a given interval of time

gus·to \'gə(,)stō\ *n* -ES [Sp, delight, pleasure, taste, fr. L *gustus* taste; akin to L *gustare* to taste — more at CHOOSE] **1 a :** TASTE, LIKING, APPRECIATION **b :** keen or intense appreciation **:** great usu. enthusiastic and vigorous enjoyment or delight ⟨describes the adventure . . . with enormous ~ —Robert Payne⟩ **c :** vitality marked by an overabundance of healthy positive and often unrefined vigor and enthusiasm ⟨the good animal ~ of a child of nature —Aldous Huxley⟩ ⟨its pioneering ~ and its tremendous physical energy —Green Peyton⟩ ⟨his gigantic ~, his delight in toil and struggle, his superb aliveness —H.L.Mencken⟩ **2** *archaic* **:** artistic style esp. marked by lofty spirit or taste

gus·to·so \gü'stō(,)sō,)zō\ *adj* (*or adv*) [It, adj., tasteful, fr. *gusto* taste, fr. L *gustus*] **:** with taste — used as a direction in music

gusts *pl of* GUST, *pres 3d sing of* GUST

gust tunnel *n* **:** an enclosed space within which a jet of air is made to impinge upon an airplane model in free flight for investigating the effects of atmospheric gusts upon the flight of airplanes

¹gusty \'gəstē, -ti\ *adj* -ER/-EST [³*gust* + -*y*] **1 a :** blowing in gusts ⟨a ~ wind⟩ **:** marked by gusts ⟨a characteristic of hurricane winds is their irregular ~ nature —*Amer. Guide Series: La.*⟩ ⟨~ weather⟩ **:** giving forth gusts ⟨a series of ~ explosions⟩ **:** coming forth in a gust ⟨a ~ sigh⟩ ⟨~ squalls of rage —Edith Sitwell⟩ **b :** marked by outbursts of empty bombastic talk ⟨~ oratory —C.G.Bowers⟩ **2 :** marked by gusto **:** exhibiting an overabundance of healthy positive often unrefined vigor and enthusiasm ⟨a ~, warmhearted woman —*Time*⟩ ⟨a lusty, ~ humor —*N.Y.Times*⟩ ⟨a ~ love of life —W.D.Edmonds⟩

²gusty \'güs-,'gəs-\ *adj* -ER/-EST [¹*gust* + -*y*] *chiefly Scot* **:** SAVORY, APPETIZING

¹gut \'gət, *usu* -əd.+V\ *n* -s [ME, fr. OE *guttas* (pl.); akin to OE *gyte* action of pouring, MD *gote* gutter, OHG *guz* action of pouring, OE *gēotan* to pour — more at FOUND] **1 a** (1) **:** BOWELS, ENTRAILS — usu. used in pl. ⟨chicken ~*s* rank high among good catfish baits —J.R.Harlan & E.B.Speaker⟩ ⟨felt their ~*s* contract with fear —Barnaby Conrad⟩ (2) **:** INTESTINE ⟨see whether an amebicide acts directly on the amoeba or on commensal organisms in the ~ —*Lancet*⟩ (3) **:** the alimentary canal or cavity or the portion from the stomach down — usu. used in pl. ⟨would feel hunger nudging my ribs, twisting my empty ~*s* until they ached —Richard Wright⟩ (4) **:** STOMACH, BELLY — usu. used in pl.; not often in formal use ⟨his huge ~ hung far below his belt —L.M.Uris⟩ ⟨gave the man a poke in the ~*s*⟩ ⟨my stupidity in keeping that hustler's ~ filled with beer, T-bone steaks and whiskey —Frederic Wakeman⟩ **b :** CAT GUT 1 **c :** the inner usu. essential parts — usu. used in pl. ⟨working somewhere in the ~*s* of the machinery⟩ ⟨tear the word from the ~*s* of the dictionary —O.W.Holmes †1935⟩ ⟨land which has had its ~*s* mined out of it —A.J. Bruwer⟩ ⟨have you ever seen the ~*s* of a poem laid bare —F.J.Jennings⟩ **d :** a basic concept or consideration **:** ESSENCE — usu. used in pl. ⟨gets down to the very ~*s* of the matter⟩ ⟨getting . . . into the real ~*s* of the subject —H.J. Laski⟩ **2 a :** a narrow sea passage (as a strait) **:** a small creek or narrow waterway (as in a marsh or on a tidal flat) ⟨inlets and ~*s* scoured by the rushing tides —R.W.Miner⟩ **b :** GULLY, RAVINE, VALLEY ⟨the deep ~ of the hills —Ian Hamilton⟩ **3 :** the sac of fluid silk that is taken from a silkworm ready to spin its cocoon from which a coarse strong thread suitable for forming the leader of a fishline is produced **4 guts** *pl* **:** strength or force of character **:** moral stamina **:** COURAGE, FORTITUDE **:** determined persistence ⟨he alone . . . has the ~*s* to grapple with the enemy on every political front —*New Republic*⟩ ⟨was a tower of strength, holding everything together by sheer unrelenting ~*s* —Nicholas Monsarrat⟩ **syn** see FORTITUDE — **hate one's guts** *slang* **:** to hate with extreme intensity ⟨I don't dislike him, I *hate his guts* —Erle Stanley Gardner⟩

²gut \"\ *vt* **gutted; gutted; gutting; guts** [ME *gutten*, fr. gut, n.] **1 a :** to take out the bowels of **:** EVISCERATE ⟨his body opened and *gutted*, and the entrails burnt in the fire —J.H.Wheelwright⟩ ⟨found a dead rabbit, *gutted* it —*Time*⟩ **b :** to plunder of contents **:** remove the contents of ⟨a mob *gutted* the house⟩ **c :** to extract all the essential portions or passages from (as a book) **2 a :** to destroy totally the inside of ⟨fire *gutted* the building⟩ **b :** to burn out ⟨a warehouse whose roof had been burned away and whose floors had been *gutted* —*Time*⟩ **c :** to destroy in essence ⟨the isolationist effort to ~ foreign aid —*Atlantic*⟩ ⟨inflation has already *gutted* the economy of country after country —*U.S.Code*⟩ **3 :** to cause (as by wear) to develop ruts and holes ⟨a *gutted* road⟩

³gut \'güt, 'gət\ *dial var of* GOUT

gutbucket \'=,==\ *n* **:** hot jazz music played in a brash style with much improvisation and with a strong 2-beat rhythm **:** BARRELHOUSE

gut-hammer \'=,==\ *n* **:** the gong in a logging camp usu. consisting of a triangle of steel that is struck to summon lumberjacks to meals

gu·ti \'güd·ē\ *n, pl* **guti** *or* **gutis** *usu cap* **1 :** a mountain people ruling Sumer and Akkad in the 24th century B.C. **2 :** a member of the Guti people

gu·ti·an \-ēən\ *n* -s *usu cap* [*Guti* + -*an*] **:** GUTI 2

gu·ti·er·re·zia \,güd·ēə'rēzh(ē)ə\ *n, cap* [NL, fr. *Gutiérrez*, noble Span. family + NL -*ia*] **:** a genus of American herbs or low shrubs (family Compositae) with alternate linear entire leaves and yellow flower heads in corymbose clusters — see MATCHWEED

gut·less \'gətləs\ *adj* **1 :** lacking courage, pluck, manliness, determination **:** being a moral weakling **:** COWARDLY ⟨the ~ captain wobbles, crosses up his men, plots to run out on the job —*Time*⟩ **2 a :** lacking in vital physical qualities **:** lacking a substantial or human character ⟨~ spirit⟩ **b :** having no substance that is significant or worthy of respect ⟨a ~ profession⟩ ⟨a ~ enterprise⟩ — **gut·less·ness** *n* -ES

gut·nish \'gütnish\ *or* **gut·nic** \-nik\ *n, pl* **gutnishes** *also* **gutnics** *usu cap* [G *gutnisch*, fr. ON *gotneskr*, adj., of Gotland] **:** a Swedish dialect spoken on the island of Gotland

¹gut out *vt* [²*gut* + *out*] **:** to remove in the process of gutting ⟨the forests were *gutted out* and mined in the same fashion as the minerals —Lewis Mumford⟩

²gut out *vb* [prob. alter. (influenced by ¹*gut out*) of *gutter out*] *vt* **:** to snuff out ⟨burned so feebly and was so quickly *gutted out* —Van Wyck Brooks⟩ ~ *vi* **:** to gutter and go out

guts *pl of* GUT, *pres 3d sing of* GUT

gutshoot \'=,=\ *vt* [¹*gut* + *shoot*] *slang* **:** to shoot or wound in the stomach or abdomen

gutshot \'=,=\ *n* [¹*gut* + *shot*] *slang* **:** a wound in the stomach or abdomen from rifle fire or gunfire

gutstring \'=,=\ *n* **:** string made of sheep gut used esp. for surgical sutures

gutsy \'gətsē\ *adj, usu* -ER/-EST [*guts* (pl. of ¹*gut*) + -*y*] **1** *slang* **:** having guts **:** COURAGEOUS ⟨kids thought they were ~ to chuck a few stones through her windows —Ruth Park⟩ **2** *slang* **:** forceful, passionate, or lusty in quality **:** forthright and provocative in its effect upon the physical esp. sexual passions ⟨a ~ singer⟩

gutt *abbr* **1** [L *gutta*; *guttae*] drop; drops **2** guttural

¹gut·ta \'gəd·ə, 'gu̇d·ə\ *n, pl* **gut·tae** \-d·,ē, -üd·,ī\ *also* **guttas** [L, lit., drop — more at GOUT] **:** one of a series of ornaments in the Doric entablature that is usu. in the form of a frustum of a cone but is sometimes cylindrical — called also *campana*, *drop*, *treenail*

²gutta \'gəd·ə, -ətə\ *n* -s [Malay *gĕtah* sap, latex] **1 a :** GUTTA-PERCHA **b :** the coagulated latex of any of various trees (esp. of the genera *Palaquium* and *Payena*) and vines that is used to adulterate gutta-percha and to mix with chicle in the making of chewing gum **2 :** a white crystalline polymeric hydrocarbon $(C_5H_8)_x$ stereoisomeric with rubber hydrocarbon and constituting the principal ingredient of gutta-percha and balata

gutta balata *n* [²*gutta*] **:** BALATA 1

gutta gam·ba \'==,gambə\ *n* [perh. fr. Malay *gĕtah* sap, latex + E *gamba* (irreg. fr. *Cambodia*, region or country in southeast Indochina)] **:** GAMBOGE

gutta–gum tree *n* [*gutta-gum* prob. fr. ²*gutta* + *gum*] **:** a tropical American tree (*Vismia guianensis*) of the family Hypericaceae having red sap which yields American gamboge

gut·ta–per·cha \,==ˈpərchə, -pəch-,-pəich-\ *n* -s [Malay, fr. *gĕtah* sap, latex + *pĕrcha* tree producing gutta-percha] **:** a gray to brown tough plastic substance consisting essentially of gutta hydrocarbon with some resin that is obtained from the latex of several Malaysian sapotaceous trees of the genera *Payena* and *Palaquium* and is used esp. as electric insulation for submarine cables and in dentistry — compare BALATA

gutta ro·sa·cea \,==rō'zās(h)ēə\ *or* **gutta ro·sea** \-'rōzēə\ *n* [ML, lit., rosy drop] **:** ACNE ROSACEA

gutta se·re·na \,==sə'rēnə\ *n* [NL, lit., clear drop] **:** AMAUROSIS

¹gut·tate \'gəd·,āt\ *adj* [L *guttatus* speckled, fr. *gutta* drop, spot — more at GOUT] **:** resembling a drop or having spots that resemble drops

²guttate \"\ *vi* -ED/-ING/-S [prob. back-formation fr. *guttation*] **1 :** to lose moisture by guttation **2 :** to exude in the process of guttation

gut·tat·ed \-ād·əd\ *adj* [L *guttatus* + E -*ed*] **:** GUTTATE

gut·ta·tim \,gə'tād·əm, gu̇'täd·-\ *adv* [L, fr. *gutta* drop] **:** drop by drop — used in prescriptions

gut·ta·tion \,gə'tāshən\ *n* -s [ISV *gutt-* (fr. L *gutta* drop) + -*ation*; orig. formed in G] **:** the exudation of moisture from an uninjured surface of a plant (as from a hydathode)

gutted *past of* GUT

guttée *also* **gut·té** *or* **gut·tée** *or* **gout·té** \(')gə|tā, (')gə|-\ *or* **gut·ty** *or* **gout·ty** \'güd·ē, 'gəd·ē\ *adj* [MF *gouttë* spotted, speckled, fr. L *guttatus* speckled] *heraldry* **:** semé of drops

guttée d'eau \-'dō\ *adj* [*guttée* + F *d'eau* of water] *heraldry* **:** semé of drops argent

guttée de larmes \-,də'lärm\ *adj* [*guttée* + F *de larmes* of tears] *heraldry* **:** semé of drops azure

guttée de poix \-də'pwä\ *adj* [*guttée* + F *de poix* of pitch] *heraldry* **:** semé of drops sable

guttée de sang \-də'säⁿ\ *adj* [*guttée* + F *de sang* of blood] *heraldry* **:** semé of drops gules

guttée d'huile \-'dwēl\ *adj* [*guttée* + F *d'huile* of oil] *heraldry* **:** semé of drops vert

guttée d'olive \-,də'lēv\ *adj* [*guttée* + F *d'olive* of olive (color)] *heraldry* **:** GUTTÉE D'HUILE

guttée d'or \-'dȯ(ə)r\ *adj* [*guttée* + F *d'or* of gold] *heraldry* **:** semé of drops or

¹gut·ter \'gəd·ə(r), 'gətə-\ *n* -s [ME *goter*, *guter*, *gotere*, fr. OF *gotiere*, *goutiere* eaves, eaves trough, fr. *gote*, *goute* drop — more at GOUT] **1 a** *archaic* **:** WATERCOURSE, BROOK **b :** a channel or gully worn by running water **2 :** something forming or intended to form a channel: as **a :** a groove at an eaves or a usu. metal trough under an eaves to catch rainwater and carry it off (as to a downspout) **b :** a low area, course, ditch, or furrow (as at a roadside) to carry off surface water (as to a sewer) **c :** a V-shaped trough used in turpentining for guiding the turpentine into a cup **d :** a trough-shaped course behind the animals in a cattle barn into which dung and other wastes drop **e :** a grooved piece extending over the windows and doors of an automobile to catch and carry off water **f :** a depression or narrow trough on each side of a bowling alley to catch balls that roll off **g :** a depressed furrow between body parts (as on the surface between a pair of adjacent ribs or in the dorsal wall of the body cavity on either side of the vertebral column) **h :** FIRELINE 2c **3 a :** GUTTER STICK **b :** a space between adjoining long sides at right angles to the foot of 4-page sections in a printing form **c :** the space in a form that produces the inside margins of a printed page; *also* **:** the white space formed by the adjoining inside margins of two facing pages (as of a book or magazine) **d :** RIVER 4 **4 :** the lowest most vulgar level or condition of usu. urban civilization ⟨raised in the ~ and condemned to a life of crime⟩ ⟨slang right out of the ~⟩ **5** *Austral* **:** the dry bed of a river of Tertiary age containing alluvial gold — called also *bottom* **6 :** the space between the barriers and sides of a cabinet in which electric wiring is concealed **7 :** BACKFLASH 3 **8 :** the wide space between the panes of an uncut sheet of stamps

²gutter \"\ *vb* -ED/-ING/-S [ME *guteren*, fr. *guter, gutere*, n.] *vt* **1 :** to cut or wear furrows or channels in ⟨a heavy rain ~*ing* the plowed field⟩ **2 :** to provide with a gutter ~ *vi* **1 a :** to flow in rivulets ⟨tears ~*ed* down her cheeks⟩ **b** *of a candle* **:** to melt away by reason of a channel forming on the side of the cup hollowed out by the burning wick so that the melted wax runs off rapidly **2 a :** to incline downward in a draft of wind — used of a candle or lamp flame **b :** to burn feebly ⟨torch of . . . liberty ~*ed* low —F.V.W.Mason⟩

³gutter \"\ *adj* [¹*gutter*] **:** of, relating to, or befitting the gutter ⟨a ~ urchin⟩; *esp* **:** marked by extreme vulgarity, cheapness, or indecency ⟨~ profanity⟩ ⟨~ journalism⟩

⁴gutter \"\ *n* -S [²*gut* + *-er*] **:** a worker who cuts or pulls the guts from animals or fish or one who operates a machine that removes heads, tails, and guts from fish

gutter away *vi* **:** to disappear by degrees but usu. rapidly ⟨a brilliant orange flash split the darkness . . . and then *guttered away* to nothing —Nicholas Monsarrat⟩

guttering *n* -S [¹*gutter* + *-ing*] **1 :** the material for or of gutters **2 a :** a length or section of a gutter **:** ¹GUTTER 2a ⟨saw a sparrow repeatedly slide down inside a short bent pipe from the ~ at the top —Alice E. Millard⟩ **b :** GUTTERS **3** [fr. gerund of ²*gutter*] **:** the melted wax that runs down a candle

gutter ledge *n* [¹*gutter*] **:** a bar fitting across a hatchway on a ship as a support for the hatch

gut·ter·man \-mən\ *n, pl* **guttermen** [¹*gutter* + *man*] **:** SWAMPER 2a

gutter out *vi* **1 :** to become reduced to a small flame or glow and then become extinguished ⟨the candle *guttered out*⟩ **2 :** to come to an end or die feebly or undramatically ⟨another day of our life *gutters out* in . . . sleep —Ernest Beaglehole⟩ ⟨rebellion *guttered out* in the rain —*Time*⟩

gutters *pl of* GUTTER, *pres 3d sing of* GUTTER

guttersnipe \'==,=\ *n* -S **1 :** one belonging to or suited to the lowest moral or economic condition of usu. urban civilization **:** a street urchin **:** HOODLUM ⟨a pint-sized ~ whom he forces to pose as his son —*Time*⟩ ⟨now this bloodthirsty ~ must launch his mechanized armies upon new fields of slaughter —Sir Winston Churchill⟩ **2 :** a small poster; *also* **:** HANDBILL **3 a :** WILSON'S SNIPE **b :** SPOTTED SANDPIPER — **gut·ter·snip·ish** \-pish\ *adj*

gutter stick *n* **1 :** a length of wood furniture with a gutter running lengthwise used to separate adjoining pages imposed side by side in a chase **2 :** furniture used as a gutter stick

gut·tide \'gət,tīd, 'gət,-\ *n* -S [alter. (influenced by ¹*gut*) of earlier *good tide* Shrove Tuesday, fr. ¹*good* + *tide*] *now dial Eng* **:** a time of feasting; *specif* **:** SHROVE TUESDAY

gut·tie \'gət,tī\ *n* -S [¹*gut* + *tie*, n.] **:** colic in young cattle due to strangulation of a loop of intestine

gut·tif·er·ae \,gə'tifə,rē\ *n pl, cap* [NL, fr. fem. pl. of *guttifer* guttiferous] **:** a family of widely distributed chiefly tropical trees and shrubs (order Parietales) usu. having opposite or whorled leaves, unisexual flowers, resinous sap, and oil glands and including plants producing valuable fruits, oils, and resins, and some usable timber

gut·tif·er·a·les \,=,=='rā(,)lēz\ *n pl, cap* [NL, fr. *Guttiferae* + *-ales*] *in some classifications* **:** an order of plants coextensive with Parietales

¹gut·tif·er·ous \,gə'tif(ə)rəs\ *adj* [NL *guttifer* guttiferous (fr. *gutti-* — fr. L *gutta* drop — + L *-fer* -ferous) + E *-ous* — more at GOUT] **:** yielding gum or resinous substances

²guttiferous \"\ *adj* [NL *Guttiferae* + E *-ous*] **:** relating to the Guttiferae

gut·ti·form \'gəd·ə,fȯrm\ *adj* [prob. fr. (assumed) NL *gutti-formis*, fr. NL *gutti-* (fr. L *gutta* drop) + L *-formis* -form] **:** having the shape of a drop (as a spot of color)

gut·ti·ness \'gəd·ēnəs\ *n* -ES *slang* **:** the quality or state of being gutty

gutting *pres part of* GUT

gut·tle \'gəd·ᵊl, -ət·ᵊl\ *vb* **guttled; guttled; guttling** \-d·ᵊliŋ, -t(ᵊ)l-\ **guttles** [irreg. fr. ¹*gut*] **:** to eat or drink greedily and noisily — **gut·tler** \-d·ᵊlə(r), -t(ᵊ)l-\ *n* -S

gut·tu·la \'gəchələ\ *n, pl* **guttu·lae** \-,lē\ [LL, dim. of L *gutta* drop] *biol* **:** a small spot shaped like a drop — **gut·tu·lar** \-lə(r)\ *adj* — **gut·tu·late** \-lət, -,lāt\ *adj*

gut·tule \'gə(,)chül\ *n* -S [LL *guttula*] **:** GUTTULA

¹gut·tur·al \'gəd·ərəl, -ətər- *also* -ə·trə-\ *adj* [MF, prob. fr. ML *gutturalis*, fr. L *guttur* throat + *-alis* -al — more at COT] **1 :** of or relating to the throat **2 a :** being or belonging to a speech sound or a language or speaker having sounds that do not occur in standard English and that are articulated in the throat ⟨the glottal stop, uvular *r*, the sound of *ch* in German *Buch*, and the sound of *g* in *Wagen*, in some German speech are ~⟩ **b :** being or belonging to a sound or utterance or a language or speaker having sounds that are strange, unpleasant, or disagreeable **c :** VELAR, PALATAL — not often used technically **3 :** marked by or producing guttural sounds ⟨a ~ voice⟩ ⟨laughed in his quiet, ~ way —Julian Dana⟩ ⟨acres of ~ frogs —Marjory S. Douglas⟩ — **gut·tur·al·ism** \-rə-,lizəm\ *n* -S — **gut·tur·al·i·ty** \,gəd·ə'raləd·ē, ,gətə-, -ətē, -i\ *n* -ES — **gut·tur·al·ly** \'gəd·ərəlē, -ətər-, -li *also* 'gə·tr-\ *adv* — **gut·tur·al·ness** *n* -ES

²guttural \"\ *n* -S **:** a guttural sound or symbol or guttural speech or utterance

gut·tur·al·iza·tion \,gəd·ərələ'zāshən, ,gətər-, -,lī'z- *also* ,gə·tr-\ *n* -S **:** the act or process of gutturalizing or the state of being gutturalized

gut·tur·al·ize \'gəd·ərə,līz, 'gətər- *also* 'gə·tr-\ *vb* -ED/-ING/-S [¹*guttural* + *-ize*] *vt* **1 :** to pronounce or utter in a guttural manner **2 :** VELARIZE ~ *vi* **:** to speak in a guttural manner

¹gut·turo·nasal \,gəd·ə(,)rō, -ətə-+\ *adj* [*gutturo-* (fr. ¹*guttural*) + *nasal*] **:** both velar and nasal — used of the sound \ŋ\

²gutturonasal \"\ *n* -S **:** a gutturonasal sound **:** the sound \ŋ\

¹gutty *var of* GUTTÉE

²gut·ty \'gəd·ē\ *adj* -ER/-EST [¹*gut* + *-y*] **1** *Scot* **:** fat-bellied and gross **2 :** having guts: as **a :** marked by vital and bold realism esp. in its physical detail ⟨a ~, scalp-raising account of the war . . . in southeast Asia —*Time*⟩ **b :** marked by or having courage or fortitude ⟨a ~ little kid —Oakley Hall⟩ ⟨the *guttiest* thing I ever saw a man do, in a life that has produced some fairly rugged moments —Philip Wylie⟩ **c :** having a significant or challenging substance or quality ⟨a ~ role in a play⟩ ⟨the ~, exciting pursuit of big or small game —Edison Marshall⟩ **d :** forthright and provocative in its effect upon the physical esp. sexual passions

gutweed \'=,=\ *n* [¹*gut*] **:** a perennial sow thistle (*Sonchus arvensis*)

gut·zeit test \'güt,sīt-\ *n, usu cap G* [after Max Adolf *Gutzeit* †1915 Ger. chemist] **:** a test for arsenic used esp. in toxicology that is based on the formation of arsine (as in the Marsh test) and the production by the arsine of a brown stain on filter paper moistened with mercuric chloride solution

guv *dial past of* GIVE

¹guy \'gī\ *vt* -ED/-ING/-S [ME *gyen*, fr. MF *guier* — more at GUIDE] *archaic* **:** GUIDE

²guy \"\ *n* -S [prob. fr. D *gei* brail] **:** a rope, chain, or rod attached to something (as an object being hoisted or lowered) to brace, steady, or guide it **:** a cable connecting a suspension bridge with the land on either side to prevent lateral swaying

³guy \"\ *vt* -ED/-ING/-S **:** to steady or reinforce (as a vertical structure) or guide (as an object being hoisted) with a guy

⁴guy \"\ *n* -S [after *Guy* Fawkes †1606 Eng. conspirator] **1 a** *often cap* **:** a ragged and grotesque effigy of the English conspirator Guy Fawkes customarily paraded and burned in England on Guy Fawkes day ⟨dresses like a *Guy* —W.S. Gilbert⟩ **b :** an effigy of any person similarly treated **2 a** *chiefly Brit* **:** a person of grotesque appearance or dress **b :** LAUGHINGSTOCK ⟨they'd make a ~ of you in Latin, Greek and Hebrew —S.H.Adams⟩ **3 :** MAN, BOY, FELLOW ⟨a well-fed ~, wearing a gray sports jacket —Eli Waldron⟩ ⟨the greatest ~ he had ever known —T.O.Heggen⟩ **4** *Brit* **:** a hasty or secret departure **:** hurried decamping

⁵guy \"\ *vt* -ED/-ING/-S **:** to make fun of **:** ridicule often lightly or good-humoredly ⟨allows himself in one chapter to ~ the Court of King Arthur in a way of which few children will approve —*Times Lit. Supp.*⟩ ⟨the ~*ing* of authority is inherent in the English spirit —Kenneth Young⟩ ⟨. . . liked to ~ me and make me the subject of practical jokes —W.A.White⟩

guy·ana \(')gī'(y)anə, -ān-, -ȧn-\ *adj, usu cap* [fr. *Guyana*, country in northeastern So. America] **:** of or from the country of Guyana **:** of the kind or style prevalent in Guyana

¹guy·a·nese \,gīə'nēz, -ēs\ *adj, usu cap* [*Guyana*, the country + E *-ese*] **1 :** of, relating to, or characteristic of Guyana **2 :** of, relating to, or characteristic of the people of Guyana

²guyanese *n, cap* **:** a native or inhabitant of Guyana

guy derrick *n* **:** a derrick whose mast is held upright by guy cables attached at the top

guy fawkes day \'gī'fȯks-\ *n, usu cap G&F&D* [after *Guy Fawkes* †1606 Eng. conspirator] **:** the anniversary of Nov. 5, 1605, when Guy Fawkes was seized for an attempt to blow up the House of Lords that is celebrated by bonfires

guy·ot \(')gē;ō\ *n* -S [after Arnold H. *Guyot* †1884 Am. geographer and geologist born in Switzerland] **:** a flat-topped submarine mountain or seamount, commonly found in the Pacific ocean where the flat summits are at depths below the surface of the water as great as 5000 feet

guy·trash \'gī·trash\ *n* -ES [origin unknown] *dial Eng* **:** a specter or ghost esp. in the form of an animal

guy·ver \'gīvə(r)\ *n* -S [origin unknown] *Austral* **:** fantastic talk or explanations

guze \'gyüz\ *n* -S [origin unknown] *heraldry* **:** a roundel sanguine

gu·ze·rat \,güzə'rät\ *n* [*Gujarat*, *Guzerat*, region of northwestern Bombay state, India] **1** *usu cap* **:** a breed of large heavy-boned Indian cattle widely used in crossbreeding to produce heat-resistant beef cattle **2** -S *often cap* **:** an animal of the Guzerat breed

guzla *var of* GUSLA

guz·man·ia \güz'manēə\ *n* [NL, fr. A. *Guzmán fl* 1800? Span. naturalist + NL *-ia*] **1** *cap* **:** a large genus of tropical American chiefly epiphytic herbs (family Bromeliaceae) resembling *Tillandsia* but having the perianth segments connate basally or closely connivent and the anthers on the perianth throat **2** -S **:** any plant of the genus *Guzmania*

¹guz·zle \'gəzəl\ *vb* **guzzled; guzzled; guzzling** \-z(ə)liŋ\ **guzzles** [origin unknown] *vi* **:** to drink esp. liquor, beer, or wine greedily **:** drink habitually or frequently ⟨spent a weekend *guzzling* and playing cards⟩ ~ *vt* **1 :** to drink greedily, continually, or habitually ⟨~ beer⟩; *sometimes* **:** to eat greedily ⟨coming in here to ~ your muffins —Richard Blaker⟩ ⟨the monster *guzzled* its meal —C.G.D.Roberts⟩ **2 :** to use up (as money) in guzzling ⟨*guzzled* away the family fortune⟩

²guzzle \"\ *n* -S **1** *now dial* **:** a small stream often flowing through a marsh **2** *dial* **:** THROAT; *often* **:** ADAM'S APPLE

guz·zler \'gəz(ə)lə(r)\ *n* -S [¹*guzzle* + *-er*] **1 :** one that guzzles **2 :** a device for preserving water for the use of game birds in arid regions

gvl *abbr* gravel

gwa·li·or \'gwälē,ó(ə)r\ *adj, usu cap* [fr. *Gwalior*, city in north central India] **:** of or from the city of Gwalior, India **:** of the kind or style prevalent in Gwalior

gwari *usu cap, var of* GBARI

gweduc *var of* GEODUCK

gwine \(;)gwīn, 'gwīən\ *dial pres part of* GO

gwyn·i·ad \'gwinē,ad\ *also* **gwyn·i·ard** \-ē,ärd\ *n* -S [W *gwyniad*, fr. *gwyn* white — more at FINNOCK] **:** a fish (*Coregonus pennantii*) of Bala Lake in North Wales related to the lake whitefish

gy *abbr* **1** gray **2** gunnery **3** gyro

gy·a·ni \gē'änē\ *n* -S [Panjabi *gyānī*, fr. Skt *jñānin* one who has knowledge, fr. *jñāna* knowledge — more at JNANA] **:** a Sikh religious official who expounds religious lore and participates in gurdwara services

gya·rung \gē'äruŋ\ *n* -S *usu cap* **:** a member of a people living on the eastern boundary of Tibet

gy·as·cu·tus \,gīə'sk(y)üd·əs, -'skəd-\ *n* -ES [origin unknown] **:** an imaginary large four-legged beast with legs on one side longer than on the other for walking on hillsides

gy·as·sa \gī'asə\ *n* -S [Ar *qay(y)āsah*] **:** a flat-bottomed lateen-rigged seagoing barge used in the local coasting trade of the Gulf of Suez, the Red sea, and the eastern Mediterranean esp. for transporting cargoes of coal or rice

gybe *var of* JIBE

gy·gis \'jījəs, 'gī-\ *n, cap* [NL, fr. Gk *gygēs*, a water bird; perh. akin to Lith *gužūtys* stork] **:** a genus of tropical terns with pure white plumage

gyle \'gī(ə)l\ *or* **gail** \'gā(ə)l\ *n* -S [ME *gyle*, fr. MD *gijl*, fr. *gilen* to boil, ferment] **1 :** wort in the process of fermentation added to a stout or ale **2 :** the beer produced at one brewing **:** BREWING 3

gym \'jim\ *n* -S *often attrib* [short for *gymnasium*] **1 :** GYMNASIUM ⟨played handball in the ~ twice a week⟩ **2 :** PHYSICAL EDUCATION ⟨~ is a required course for all freshmen⟩ **3 :** a metal frame supporting an assortment of outdoor play equipment (as a swing, seesaw, rings)

gym 3

gym·el *or* **gim·el** \'jiməl\ *n* -S [modif. of MF *gemel* twin — more at GEMEL] **1 :** vocal part writing in medieval music in which the voices usu. progress in parallel thirds **2 :** a direction for divisi singing used in 16th century choral music

gy·min·da \jə'mində\ *n, cap* [NL, anagram of *Myginda*, genus of trees or shrubs fr. Francis von *Mygind* 18th cent. Ger. botanist] **:** a small genus of tropical American shrubs and trees (family Celastraceae) with opposite leathery leaves and unisexual flowers in axillary cymes followed by small blue or black drupaceous fruits

gym·khana \jim'kānə, -kanə, -kȧnə\ *n* -S [prob. modif. (influenced by E *gymnasium*) of Hindi *gend-khānā* racket court, fr. Per *khāna* house] **:** a meet or festival featuring sports contests or athletic skills: as **a :** a horseback-riding meet featuring games and novelty contests (as musical chairs, potato spearing, bareback jumping) **b :** a festival featuring gymnastics and athletic showmanship and often including pageantry **c :** an obstacle run for automobiles or a series of events designed to test driving skill

gymn- *or* **gymno-** *comb form* [NL, fr. Gk, fr. *gymnos* — more at NAKED] **:** naked **:** bare **:** uncovered ⟨*gymn*anthous⟩ ⟨*gymno*-branchiate⟩

gym·na·de·nia \,jimnə'dēnēə\ *n, cap* [NL, fr. *gymn-* + Gk *adēn* gland + NL *-ia* — more at ADEN-] **:** a genus of European terrestrial orchids having greenish flowers with the lip of the corolla entire

gym·na·de·ni·op·sis \,=,=nē'äpsəs\ *n, cap* [NL, fr. *Gymnadenia* + *-opsis*] *in some classifications* **:** a genus of No. American terrestrial orchids that have appendages on the beak of the stigma and are now usu. included in the genus *Habenaria*

gym·nan·thes \jim'nan(,)thēz\ *n, cap* [NL, fr. *gymn-* + *-anthes*] **:** a small genus of tropical American shrubs or trees (family Euphorbiaceae) with alternate evergreen leaves, a milky juice, and a 3-lobed capsular fruit

gym·nan·thous \(')jim;nan(t)thəs\ *adj* [*gymn-* + *-anthous*] **:** ACHLAMYDEOUS

gym·nar·chus \jim'närkəs\ *n, cap* [NL, fr. *gymn-* + Gk *archos* anus; fr. the absence of anal fins] **:** a monotypic genus (the type of the family Gymnarchidae) that contains a soft-finned African river fish having a sense organ in the tail that functions like radar

gym·na·sial \jim'nāzēəl, -āzh(ē)əl\ *adj* **:** of or relating to a gymnasium

gym·na·si·arch \-zē,ärk\ *n* -S [L *gymnasiarchus*, fr. Gk *gymnasiarchos*, fr. *gymnasion* gymnasium + *archos* chief, ruler — more at ARCHI-] **1 :** one responsible for the training of athletes in ancient Greece **2 :** the head or head tutor of a school or college

gym·na·si·ast \-zē,ast, -ēəst, -ē,aa(ə)st\ *n* -S [G, fr. NL *gymnasiasta*, fr. G *gymnasium* + NL *-asta* (fr. Gk *-astēs* -ast)] **1 :** a student in or graduate of a gymnasium **2** [*gymnasium* + *-ast*] **:** GYMNAST

gym·na·si·um \jim'nāzēəm *sometimes* -zhəm, *in sense 2* gim-'näzēəm *or* -nȧz- *or* -ē,ủm\ *n, pl* **gymnasiums** \-mz\ *or* **gymna·sia** \-zēə,-zhə\ [L, gymnastic school, school, fr. Gk *gymnasion*, fr. *gymnazein* to train naked, exercise, fr. *gymnos* naked — more at NAKED] **1 a :** a large room used for various indoor sports (as basketball, boxing, volleyball) and equipped with gymnastic apparatus **b :** a building (as on a college campus) containing appropriate space and equipment for various indoor sports activities associated with a program of physical education and typically including spectator accommodations, locker and shower rooms, a swimming pool, offices, and classrooms **2** [G, fr. L] **:** a secondary school designed to prepare students for the university; *esp* **:** a German secondary school whose curriculum stresses the classics, history, mathematics, and modern languages

gym·nast \'jim,nast, -,nəst, -,naa(ə)st\ *n* -S [MF *gymnaste*, fr. Gk *gymnastēs* trainer of athletes, fr. *gymnazein*, v.] **:** one who is expert in gymnastics

¹gym·nas·tic \jim'nastik, -aas-, -tēk\ *also* **gym·nas·ti·cal** \-tәkəl, -tēk-\ *adj* [MF or L; MF *gymnastique*, fr. L *gymnasticus*, fr. Gk *gymnastikos*, fr. (assumed) *gymnastos* (verbal of *gymnazein* to train naked) + *-ikos* -ic] **:** of or relating to gymnastics **:** ATHLETIC — **gym·nas·ti·cal·ly** \-tək(ə)lē, -tēk-, -li\ *adv*

²gymnastic \"\ *n* -S [MF *gymnastique*, fr. Gk *gymnastikē*, fr. fem. of *gymnastikos*] **1 a :** physical exercise ⟨good ~ which will give health to the body —Benjamin Jowett⟩; *esp* **:** exercise that consists of calisthenics and performance on apparatus (as rings, bars) and is designed to promote strength, flexibility, agility, coordination, and body control — now usu. used in pl. ⟨~s have become one of the institutions of the country —James Grant⟩ **b gymnastics** *pl but sing in constr* **:** the art or practice of such exercise ⟨modern apparatus ~s was founded in the early 19th century —*Time*⟩ **2 :** something resembling gymnastics; *esp* **:** an exercise in intellectual or artistic dexterity ⟨my earlier philosophic study had been an intellectual ~ —John Dewey⟩ ⟨the pleasure that is derived from sheer mental ~s —Carlos Lynes⟩ **3 :** a physical feat, exercise, or contortion ⟨like a . . . wrestler about to embark upon some inexplicable ~ —Gordon Sager⟩ ⟨the ~s necessary for the killer to have swung from the fire escape —E.D.Radin⟩

gym·nic \'jimnik\ *adj* [L *gymnicus*, fr. Gk *gymnikos*, fr. *gymnos* naked + *-ikos* -ic] *archaic* **:** GYMNASTIC

gym·nics \-ks\ *n pl, archaic* **:** GYMNASTICS

gymno- — see GYMN-

gym·no·blast \'jimnə,blast\ *adj or n* [NL *Gymnoblastea*] **:** ANTHOMEDUSAN

gym·no·blas·tea \,jimnə'blastēə\ [NL, fr. *gymn-* + *-blastea* (fr. *-blastus* -blast)] *syn of* ANTHOMEDUSAE

gym·no·blas·tic \,jimnə'blastik\ *adj* [*gymn-* + *-blastic*] **:** having naked medusa buds — used of anthomedusan hydroids

gym·no·ca·lyci·um \,jim(,)nōkə'lis(h)ēəm\ *n, cap* [NL, fr. *gymn-* + *calyc-* + *-ium*] **:** a genus of low globular So. American cacti with strongly tuberculate spiny ribs

gym·no·car·pe·ae \-'kärpē,ē\ *n pl, cap* [NL, fr. *gymn-* + *-carpeae* (fr. *-carpus* -carpous)] *in some classifications* **:** a group comprising those lichens whose fruiting body is open

gym·no·car·pous \,jimnə'kärpəs\ *also* **gym·no·car·pic** \-pik\ *adj* [*gymnocarpous* fr. Gk *gymnokarpos*, fr. *gymn-* + *-karpos* -carpous; *gymnocarpic* fr. *gymn-* + *carp-* + *-ic*] **:** having the hymenium open or exposed on the surface of the thallus or fruiting body — used of lichens and fungi; compare ANGIOCARPOUS 2 — **gym·no·car·py** \'==,=pē\ *n* -ES

gym·no·cer·a·ta \,jim(,)nō'serəd·ə\ *n pl, cap* [NL, fr. *gymn-* + *-cerata* (fr. Gk *kerat-*, *keras* horn) — more at HORN] **:** a division of Heteroptera comprising true bugs with the antennae as long as or longer than the head and including most terrestrial bugs and the water striders — compare CRYPTOCERATA — **gym·no·cer·a·tous** \;=,='serəd·əs\ *adj*

gym·no·cid·i·um \,jimnə'sidēəm\ *n, pl* **gymnocid·ia** \-ēə\ [NL, fr. *gymn-* + *-ocidium* (prob. fr. Gk *oikidion* small house, dim. of *oikos* house) — more at VICINITY] **:** APOPHYSIS 2

gym·no·cla·dus \jim'näkladəs\ *n, cap* [NL, fr. *gymn-* + Gk *klados* sprout, branch — more at GLADIATOR] **:** a genus of trees (family Leguminosae) with twice-pinnate leaves, paniculate flowers, and thick pulpy pods — see KENTUCKY COFFEE TREE

gym·no·co·nia \,jimnə'kōnēə\ *n, cap* [NL, fr. *gymn-* + Gk *konis* dust + NL *-ia* — more at INCINERATE] **:** a genus of rusts (order Uredinales) having naked aecial sori and 2-celled teliospores and including a rust (*G. interstitialis*) of the raspberry and blackberry

gym·no·din·i·a·ce·ae \-,dinē'āsē,ē\ *n pl, cap* [NL, fr. *Gymnodinium*, type genus + *-aceae*] **:** a family of typically brownish algae (class Dinophyceae) that includes *Gymnodinium* and related genera when these are considered to be algae

gym·no·din·i·a·les \-ā(,)lēz\ *n pl, cap* [NL, fr. *Gymnodinium* + *-ales*] **:** an order of greenish brown algae (class Dinophyceae) having no cell wall but often a firm periplast that is longitudinally striated and comprising the naked dinoflagellates — compare PERIDINIALES

gym·no·din·i·um \-'dinēəm\ *n, cap* [NL, fr. *gymn-* + Gk *dinein* to whirl + NL *-ium*] **:** a large genus (the type of the family Gymnodiniidae) of marine and freshwater naked dinoflagellates that includes forms which are colorless or tinted yellowish to reddish brown, blue, or green by chromatophores and a few forms which cause red tide

gym·no·dont \'jimnə,dänt\ *adj or n* [NL *Gymnodontes*] **:** TETRAODONT

gym·no·don·tes \,jimnə'dän(,)tēz\ [NL, fr. *gymn-* + *-odontes*] *syn of* TETRAODONTOIDEA

gym·no·glos·sa \-'gläsə, -lósə\ *n pl, cap* [NL, fr. *gymn-* + *-glossa*] *in some classifications* **:** a division of Pectinibranchia comprising gastropods lacking jaws or radula — **gym·no·glos·sate** \;=(,)=;glä,sāt, -ós-, -,sāt\ *adj*

gym·nog·y·nous \(')jim;näjənəs\ *adj* [*gymn-* + *-gynous*] *bot* **:** having a naked ovary

gym·no·gyps \'jimnə,jips\ *n, cap* [NL, fr. *gymn-* + Gk *gyps* vulture] **:** a genus of very large dark carrion-eating birds (family Cathartidae) containing solely the California condor

gym·no·lae·ma \,jimnə'lēmə\ [NL, prob. alter. of *Gymnolaemata*] *syn of* GYMNOLAEMATA

gym·no·lae·ma·ta \-məd·ə\ *n pl, cap* [NL, fr. *gymn-* + *laem-* (fr. Gk *laimos* throat, gullet) + *-ata*; prob. akin to Gk *laimos* greedy — more at LURE] **:** a class or other division of Bryozoa comprising chiefly marine bryozoans with a circular lophophore about the mouth and including most recent and extinct forms — compare PHYLACTOLAEMATA — **gym·no·lae·ma·tous** \;=;=;məd·əs\ *adj*

gym·no·no·ti \,jimnə'nōd·,ī\ *n pl, cap* [NL, fr. *gymn-* + *-noti* (pl. of *-notus*); fr. the absence of a dorsal fin] *in some classifications* **:** a group of fishes including the electric eel and related forms

gym·no·pae·dia *or* **gym·no·pe·dia** \-'pēdēə\ *n* -S [NL, fr. Gk *gymnopaidia*, fr. *gymno-* gymn- + *paidia* childish play, amusement, game (fr. *paizein* to play, sport, fr. *paid-*, *pais* child) — more at FOAL] **:** a choral dance of religious origin performed by naked youths at ancient Greek festivals — **gym·no·pae·dic** \;=;=;pēdik\ *adj*

gym·no·phi·o·na \-'fīənə\ *n pl, cap* [NL, fr. *gymn-* + *-ophiona* (fr. Gk *ophioneos* of a snake, serpentlike, fr. *ophis* serpent, snake) — more at ANGUIS] **:** an order of Amphibia that is coextensive with the family Caeciliidae and is distinguished by the limbless small-headed short-tailed form of its nearly eyeless members which are widely distributed in moist soil in tropical parts of the New and Old Worlds

gym·no·plast \'jimnə,plast\ *n* -S [*gymn-* + *-plast*] **:** a cell or mass of protoplasm devoid of a distinct cell wall

gym·no·rhi·na \\ˌjimnəˈrīnə\\ *n, cap* [NL, fr. *gymn-* + *-rhina*] **:** a genus of oscine birds that are included in Laniidae or placed in a distinct family and that include the piping crows of Australia

gym·no·so·ma·ta \\ˌjimnəˈsōməd·ə\\ *n pl, cap* [NL, fr. *gymn-* + *-somata*] *in some classifications* **:** a division of Pteropoda comprising forms that lack shells — compare THECOSOMATA

gym·no·soph·i·cal \\ˌjimnəˈsäfəkəl\\ *adj* **:** NUDIST ⟨a ~ society⟩

gym·nos·o·phist \\jimˈnäsəfəst\\ *n* -S [L *gymnosophista*, fr. Gk *gymnosophistēs*, fr. *gymno-* gymn- + *sophistēs* wise man, philosopher (fr. *sophos* wise) — more at NAKED] **1 :** one of a sect of ancient Hindu philosophers who went naked, lived ascetically, and practiced meditation **2 :** one resembling a gymnosophist

gym·nos·o·phy \\-fē\\ *n* -ES **:** the doctrine of the gymnosophists; *esp* **:** NUDISM

gym·no·sperm \\ˈjimnəˌspərm\\ *n* [NL *Gymnospermae*] **:** a plant of the class Gymnospermae

gym·no·sper·mae \\ˌ==ˈspər(ˌ)mē\\ *n pl, cap* [NL, fr. *gymn-* + *-spermae*] **:** a class of Pteropsida or in some classifications a subdivision of Spermatophyta comprising seed plants (as cycads and conifers) that produce naked seeds not enclosed in an ovary and in some instances have motile spermatozoids and including the subclasses Cycadophytae and Coniferophytae — compare ANGIOSPERMAE, FILICINEAE

gym·no·sper·mal \\ˈ==ˈ=məl\\ *also* **gym·no·sper·mic** \\-mik\\ *adj* [NL *gymnospermus* + *-al* or *-ic*] **:** GYMNOSPERMOUS

gym·no·sper·mous \\ˈ==ˈ=məs\\ *adj* [NL *gymnospermus* having naked seeds, fr. Gk *gymnospermos*, fr. *gymno-* gymn- + *-spermos* -spermous] **:** of, relating to, or characteristic of the class Gymnospermae; *esp* **:** having ovules and seeds naked and without an enclosing ovary — contrasted with *angiospermous* — **gym·no·sper·my** \\ˈ==ˌ=mē\\ *n* -ES

gym·no·sporangium \\ˈjim(ˌ)nō+\\ *n, cap* [NL, fr. *gymn-* + *sporangium*] **:** a genus of heteroecious rusts (family Pucciniaceae) that have mostly 2-celled teliospores whose pedicels and walls form a gelatinous mass when wet, that in the telial stage produce galls on cedars and other conifers of the genera *Juniperus* and *Libocedrus*, and that in the aecial stage cause rust spots on the leaves and fruit of apples, pears, and other plants of the family Rosaceae — see APPLE RUST

gym·no·spore \\ˈjimnəˌspō(ə)r\\ *n* [ISV *gymn-* + *spore*] **:** a spore not developing in a sporangium **:** a naked spore — **gym·nospo·rous** \\ˈjimnəˈspōrəs, (ˈ)jimˈnäspərəs\\ *adj*

gym·no·sto·ma·ta \\ˌjimnəˈstōməd·ə\\ *n pl, cap* [NL, fr. *gymn-* + *-stomata*] **:** a suborder of holotrichous ciliates comprising holozoic forms with cytostome but without peristome or specialized oral cilia

gym·no·stoma·tous \\ˈ==ˈstäməd·əs, -tōm-\\ *or* **gym·nos·to·mous** \\(ˈ)jimˈnästəməs\\ *adj* [*gymn-* + *-stomatous* or *-stomous*] **:** having no peristome

gym·no·thorax \\ˈjimnə+\\ *n, cap* [NL, fr. *gymn-* + *thorax*] **:** a large genus of morays that have only the anterior nostrils provided with barbels and that may be poisonous when eaten

1**gym·no·tid** \\jimˈnōtəd\\ *adj* [NL *Gymnotidae*] **:** of or relating to the Gymnotidae

2**gymnotid** \\"\\ *n* -S **:** a fish of the family Gymnotidae

gym·noti·dae \\jimˈnäd·əˌdē, -nōd·-\\ *n pl, cap* [NL, fr. *Gymnotus*, type genus + *-idae*] **:** a family of So. American cyprinoid fishes that sometimes includes the electric eel but is usu. restricted to elongated forms lacking electric organs

gym·no·tus \\-ˈnōd·əs\\ *n, cap* [NL, fr. *gymn-* + *-notus*] **:** the type genus of the family Gymnotidae

1**gym·nu·ra** \\-ˈ(y)u̇rə\\ *n, cap* [NL, fr. *gymn-* + *-ura*] **:** a small genus of widely distributed stingrays that is usu. placed in the family Dasyatidae but sometimes in a separate family (Gynuridae) and includes the butterfly rays

2**gymnura** \\"\\ [NL, fr. *gymn-* + *-ura*] *syn of* ECHINO-SOREX

gym·nure \\ˈjimˌn(y)u̇(ə)r\\ *n* -S [NL *Gymnura*] **:** MOONRAT

1**gym·nu·rine** \\ˈjimn(y)əˌrīn, -ˌrən\\ *adj* [NL *Gymnura* + E *-ine*] **:** of or relating to the genus *Echino-sorex*

2**gymnurine** \\"\\ *n* -S **:** a mammal of the genus *Echino-sorex*

gym·pie \\ˈgimpē\\ *or* **gympie nettle** *n* -S [fr. *Gympie*, Queensland, Australia] **:** an Australian nettle tree (*Laportea moroides*) having foliage and twigs covered with stinging hairs

gyms *pl of* GYM

gym shoe *n* **:** SNEAKER

gyn *abbr* gynecologic; gynecologist; gynecology

gyn- *or* **gyno-** *in words which contain this or a related comb form & in which the pronunc of "gy" is indicated by the symbol* =, *pronounce* ji (*when unstressed* jə), gī *sometimes* jī *or* gi (*or when unstressed* gə)\\ *comb form* [Gk *gyn-*, fr. *gynē* — more at QUEEN] **1 a :** woman **:** of or relating to a woman ⟨*gyn*iatrics⟩ ⟨*gyno*cracy⟩ **b :** female **:** female and ⟨*gyn*androus⟩ **:** womanish **2 :** female reproductive organ **:** ovary ⟨*gyno*phore⟩ **:** pistil ⟨*gyno*dioecious⟩

-gyn \\jən, ˌjin\\ *n comb form* -S [NL *-gynia*] **:** plant having (so many) pistils ⟨hexa*gyn*⟩

gynaec- *or* **gynaeco-** — see GYNEC-

gynae·can·drous \\ˈ=nəˈkandrəs — *see* GYN-\\ *adj* [*gynec-* + *-androus*] **:** bearing both staminate and pistillate flowers in the same cluster with the female flowers uppermost — compare ANDROGYNOUS 3a

gynae·ce·um \\ˌ=nəˈsēəm — *see* GYN-\\ *n* -S [L, fr. LGk *gynaikeion*, fr. neut. of Gk *gynaikeios* of women, feminine, fr. *gynaik-*, *gynē* woman, wife] **1 :** the women's apartments in an ancient Greek or Roman house **2** [NL, fr. L, women's apartments] **:** GYNOECIUM

gy·nae·co·morph \\=ˈnēkəˌmȯrf — *see* GYN-\\ *n* -S [*gynec-* + *-morph*] **:** a male resembling a female in appearance

gynae·co·ni·tis \\ˌ=nəkōˈnīd·əs — *see* GYN-\\ *n* -ES [L *gynaeconitis*, fr. Gk *gynaikōnitis*, fr. *gynaik-*, *gynē* woman] **1 :** GYNAECEUM 1 **2 :** the part of an Eastern Orthodox church reserved for women; *esp* **:** one side of the nave

gynae·co·phor·ic \\ˈ===ˈfȯrik — *see* GYN-\\ *also* **gyne·coph·o·ral** \\ˈ==ˈkäfərəl — *see* GYN-\\ *adj* [*gynecophore* + *-ic* or *-al*] **:** constituting the ventral groove in which a male schistosome clasps the female

gynaeo- — see GYNEO-

gy·nan·der \\=ˈnandə(r) — *see* GYN-\\ *n* -S [*gyn-* + *-ander* (fr. Gk *andr-*, *anēr*) — more at ANDR-] **:** a mosaic individual made up of diploid female portions of biparental origin and haploid male portions originating from an extra egg or sperm nucleus

gy·nan·drae \\jəˈnan(ˌ)drē\\ [NL, fr. *gyn-* + *-andrae*, pl. of *-andra*] *syn of* ORCHIDALES

gynan·drar·chy \\=ˈnandrärkē, ˈ=ˌnən- — *see* GYN-\\ *n* -ES [*gyn-* + *andr-* + *-archy*] **:** social organization among insects differing from gynarchy in that the male takes part in establishing the colony

1**gy·nan·dria** \\=ˈnandrēə — *see* GYN-\\ *n pl, cap* [NL, fr. Gk *gynandros* of doubtful sex, womanish (fr. *gyn-* + *andr-*, *anēr* man) + NL *-ia*] *in former classifications* **:** a class comprising plants with gynandrous flowers

2**gynandria** \\"\\ *n* -S [NL, fr. Gk *gynandros* + NL *-ia*] **:** GYNANDRY

gy·nan·drism \\-ˌdrizəm\\ *n* -S [*gyn-* + *andr-* + *-ism*] **:** GYNANDRY

gy·nan·dri·um \\-ˌdrēəm\\ *n, pl* **gynan·dria** \\-ēə\\ *also* **gynandriums** [NL, fr. *gyn-* + *andr-* + *-ium*] **:** COLUMN 5b

1**gy·nan·droid** \\-ˌdrȯid\\ *adj* [ISV *gynandr-* (fr. *gynandry*) + *-oid*] **:** exhibiting gynandry

2**gynandroid** \\"\\ *n* -S **:** a gynandroid person

gy·nan·dro·morph \\-ˌdrəˌmȯrf\\ *n* -S [ISV *gyn-* + *andr-* + *-morph*] **:** an abnormal individual exhibiting characters of both sexes in various parts of the body **:** a sexual mosaic — compare HERMAPHRODITE, INTERSEX — **gy·nan·dro·mor·phic** \\=ˈ==ˈmȯrfik\\ *adj* — **gy·nan·dro·mor·phism** \\=ˌ==ˈ=ˌfizəm\\ *n* -S — **gy·nan·dro·mor·phous** \\=ˈ==ˈ=ˌfəs\\ *adj* — **gy·nan·dro·mor·phy** \\=ˈ==ˌ=fē\\ *n* -ES

gynan·dro·spor·ous \\=ˈnandrəˈspōrəs, ˈ=ˌnənˈdräspərəs — *see* GYN-\\ *adj* [*gyn-* + *andr-* + *-sporous*] **:** bearing androspores on the same filament as the oogonia and usu. near them — compare IDIOANDROSPOROUS

gynan·drous \\(ˈ)=ˈnandrəs — *see* GYN-\\ *adj* [Gk *gynandros* of doubtful sex, fr. *gynē* woman + *andr-*, *anēr* man] **1 :** having the androecium and gynoecium united in a column **2 :** characterized by gynandry

gynan·dry \\-drē\\ *n* -ES [2*gynandria*] **:** HERMAPHRODITISM, INTERSEXUALITY; *specif* **:** the condition of the pseudohermaphroditic female in which the external genitalia simulate those of the male

gynan·ther·ous \\(ˈ)=ˌnan(t)thərəs — *see* GYN-\\ *adj* [*gyn-* + *-antherous*] **:** having stamens abnormally converted into pistils

gynar·chy \\ˈ=ˌnärkē — *see* GYN-\\ *n* -ES [*gyn-* + *-archy*] **1 :** government by women **2 :** a form of social organization among insects (as ants, bees, wasps) in which only the female parent takes part in establishing the colony

gyne \\ˈjīn, ˈgīn\\ *n* -S [Gk *gynē* woman — more at QUEEN] **:** FEMALE; *esp* **:** a functional female of one of the social insects

gyne- *comb form* [Gk *gynē* woman] **:** GYN- ⟨*gyne*cytology⟩

-gyne \\ˌjīn\\ *n comb form* -S [Gk *gynē* woman] **1 :** woman **:** female ⟨pseudo*gyne*⟩ **2 :** female reproductive organ ⟨tricho*gyne*⟩

gynec- *or* **gyneco-** *also* **gynaec-** *or* **gynaeco-** *comb form* [Gk *gynaiko-*, fr. *gynaik-*, *gynē* woman] **:** GYN- ⟨*gyneco*cracy⟩ ⟨*gyneco*logy⟩ ⟨*gynec*oid⟩

gynecium *var of* GYNOECIUM

gyne·co·cen·tric \\ˈ=nəkō + — *see* GYN-\\ *adj* [*gynec-* + *-centric*] **:** centering or centered on or in the female **:** dominated by or emphasizing feminine interests or point of view ⟨a ~ society⟩ — contrasted with *androcentric*

gyne·coc·ra·cy \\ˌ=nəˈkäkrəsē — *see* GYN-\\ *n* -ES [Gk *gynaikokratia*, fr. *gynaiko-* gynec- + *-kratia* -cracy] **1 :** political and social supremacy of women — contrasted with *androcracy;* compare MATRIARCHY **2 :** petticoat rule — usu. used disparagingly — **gyne·co·crat** \\=ˈnēkəˌkrat, ˈ=nəkōˌ-\\ *n* -S — **gyne·co·crat·ic** \\=ˈnēkəˈkrad·ik, ˈ=ˌnəkōˈ-\\ *also* **gyne·co·crat·i·cal** \\-d·əkəl\\ *adj*

gyne·co·gen·ic \\ˈ=nəkōˈjenik — *see* GYN-\\ *adj* [*gynec-* + *-genic*] **:** tending to induce female characteristics ⟨a ~ hormone⟩

1**gyne·coid** \\ˈ=nəˌkȯid — *see* GYN-\\ *adj* [*gynec-* + *-oid*] **1 a :** having female characteristics **:** typical of a woman ⟨a ~ distribution of fat⟩ ⟨the ~ form of certain castrates⟩ **b** *of the pelvis* **:** having the rounded form typical of the human female — compare ANDROID **2 :** of, relating to, or exhibiting the characteristics of a gynecoid

2**gynecoid** \\"\\ *n* -S **:** an individual (as an egg-laying worker ant) that functions as a fully developed female although structurally incomplete

gyne·co·log·ic \\ˈ=nəkəˈläjik, -nēk-, -jēk — *see* GYN-\\ *also* **gyne·co·log·i·cal** \\-jəkəl, -jēk-\\ *adj* **:** of, relating to, or falling in the province of gynecology ⟨~ surgery⟩ ⟨~ patient⟩ ⟨~ tuberculosis⟩

gyne·col·o·gist \\ˌ==ˈkäləjəst\\ *n* -S **:** a physician who specializes in gynecology

gyne·col·o·gy \\-jē,-ji\\ *n* -ES [ISV *gynec-* + *-logy*] **:** a branch of medicine that deals with women, their diseases, hygiene, and medical care

gyne·co·mast \\=ˈnēkəˌmast, ˈ=nəkō- — *see* GYN-\\ *n* -S [NL *gynecomastia*] **:** a male having a female degree of mammary development

gyne·co·mas·tia \\ˌ=nəkōˈmastēə, =ˌnēkəˈ-\\ *n* -S [NL, fr. *gynec-* + *-mastia*] **:** excessive development of the breast in the male

gyne·co·mor·phous \\ˈ=nəkōˈmȯrfəs, -ˈnēkəˈ- — *see* GYN-\\ *adj* [GK *gynaikomorphos*, fr. *gynaiko-* gynec- + *-morphos* -morphous] **:** having the form or morphological characters of a female

gynecophoral *var of* GYNAECOPHORIC

gy·ne·co·phore \\=ˈnēkəˌfō(ə)r — *see* GYN-\\ *n* -S [ISV *gynec-* + *-phore*] **:** gynaecophoric canal

gyneo- *or* **gynaeo-** *comb form* [Gk *gynaios* of women, fr. *gynē* woman — more at QUEEN] **:** GYN- ⟨*gyneo*cracy⟩

Gyner·gen \\ˈ=nə(r)jən, -ˌjen — see GYN-\\ *trademark* — used for ergotamine tartrate

gynes *pl of* GYNE

-gynes *pl of* -GYNE

gyne·type \\ˈ=nəˌtīp — *see* GYN-\\ *n* [*gyne-* + *type*] **:** a designated female type specimen

-gyn·ia \\ˈjinēə, ˈgi-\\ *n pl comb form* [NL, fr. *-gynus* -gynous + *-ia*] **:** plants having (such or so many) pistils — in Linnaean botanical orders ⟨di*gynia*⟩ — **-gyn·i·an** \\ˈ=nēən\\ *adj or n comb form* — **-gyn·i·ous** \\-ēəs\\ *adj comb form*

gynic \\ˈ=nik — *see* GYN-\\ *adj* [*gyn-* + *-ic*] **:** of or relating to a female person — contrasted with *andric*

-gynies *pl of* -GYNY

gyno- — see GYN-

gyno·base \\ˈ=nō+ — *see* GYN-\\ *n* [*gyn-* + *-base*] **:** a prolongation of or from the receptacle bearing the gynoecium (as in the members of the Boraginaceae) — **gyno·ba·se·ous** \\ˈ==-ˈbāsēəs\\ *adj* — **gyno·bas·ic** \\-ās|ik, |ēk *sometimes* -āz|\\ *adj*

gyno·car·dia oil \\ˈ=nəˈkärdēə- — *see* GYN-\\ *n* [NL *Gynocardia*, genus of plants fr. which it is obtained, fr. *gyn-* + Gk *kardia* heart — more at HEART] **1 :** a pale yellow drying oil obtained from the seeds of an East Indian tree (*Gynocardia odorata*) of the family Flacourtiaceae **2 :** CHAULMOOGRA OIL

gy·noc·ra·cy \\=ˈnäkrəsē — *see* GYN-\\ *n* -ES [*gyn-* + *-cracy*] **:** GYNECOCRACY

gyno·dioecious \\ˈ=nō+ — *see* GYN-\\ *adj* [*gyn-* + *dioecious*] **:** dioecious but having some hermaphrodite or perfect flowers on an individual plant that bears mostly pistillate flowers — **gyno·dioeciously** \\"+\\ *adv* — **gyno·dioecism** \\"+\\ *n* -S — **gyno·dioecy** \\"+\\ *n* -ES

gy·noe·ci·um *also* **gy·ne·ci·um** \\=ˈnēs(h)ēəm — *see* GYN-\\ *n, pl* **gynoe·cia** *also* **gyne·cia** \\-ēə\\ [NL, alter. (influenced by Gk *oikion* house) of *gynaeceum*] **1 :** the aggregate of carpels or megasporophylls in the flower of a seed plant **:** PISTILS **2 :** the female inflorescence in liverworts

gyno·gamone \\ˈ=nō+ — *see* GYN-\\ *n* [ISV *gyn-* + *gamone*] **:** a gamone that occurs in an egg

gyno·genesis \\"+\\ *n* [NL, fr. *gyn-* + *-genesis*] **:** development in which the embryo contains only maternal chromosomes due to activation of an egg by a sperm that degenerates without fusing with the egg nucleus — compare ANDROGENESIS — **gyno·genetic** \\"+\\ *adj* — **gyno·genetically** \\"+\\ *adv* — **gyno·gen·e·tism** \\ˌ==ˈjenəˌtizəm\\ *n* -S

gyno·gonidium \\ˈ=nō+ — *see* GYN-\\ *n, pl* **gynogonidia** [NL, fr. *gyn-* + *gonidium*] **:** a female germ cell of various colonial plantlike flagellates (as members of the genus *Volvox*)

gyno·monoecious \\ˈ==(ˈ)=ˈ==\\ *adj* [*gyn-* + *monoecious*] **:** having monoclinous and pistillate flowers on the same plant but no staminate flowers — **gyno·monoeciously** \\"+\\ *adv* — **gyno·monoecism** \\"+\\ *n* -S — **gyno·monoe·cy** \\ˈ==ˈmäˌnēsē, -ˈmōˌ-\\ *n* -ES

gy·nop·a·ra \\=ˈnäpərə — *see* GYN-\\ *n, pl* **gynopa·rae** \\-əˌrē\\ [NL, fr. *gyn-* + *-para*] **:** a winged or wingless parthenogenetic viviparous aphid that produces the sexual generation of various aphids having a complex life cycle and host relations — **gy·nop·a·rous** \\(ˈ)=ˈ===\\ *adj*

gyno·phore \\ˈ=nəˌfō(ə)r — *see* GYN-\\ *n* -S [*gyn-* + *-phore*] **1 a :** a prolongation of the receptacle that functions as a stalk and bears the gynoecium at its apex (as in the flowers of members of the Capparidaceae) — compare ANTHOPHORE, CARPOPHORE **b :** the developing multinucleate female reproductive structure in fungi (as those of the genus *Pyronema*) **2 :** one of the branches bearing the female gonophores in siphonophores — **gyno·phor·ic** \\ˈ==ˈfȯrik\\ *adj*

gyno·sporangium \\ˈ=nō+ — *see* GYN-\\ *n* [NL, fr. *gyn-* + *sporangium*] **:** MEGASPORANGIUM

gyno·spore \\"+ˌ-\\ *n* [*gyn-* + *spore*] **:** EMBRYO SAC

gyno·ste·gi·um \\ˌ=nōˈstējēəm — *see* GYN-\\ *n, pl* **gynostegia** \\-jēə\\ [NL, fr. *gyn-* + *steg-* + *-ium*] **1 :** a covering of the gynoecium **2 :** the staminal crown in plants of the genus *Asclepias*

gyno·ste·mi·um \\-ˈstēmēəm\\ *n, pl* **gynoste·mia** \\-mēə\\ [NL, fr. *gyn-* + Gk *stēmōn* warp, thread + NL *-ium* — more at STAMEN] **:** the column formed by the union of androecium and gynoecium (as in an orchid)

gyno·termone \\ˈ=nō+ — *see* GYN-\\ *n* [ISV *gyn-* + *termone*] **:** a female termone

-gy·nous \\ˌjənəs, ˈjīn-, ˈgīn-\\ *adj comb form* [NL *-gynus*, fr. Gk *-gynos*, fr. *gynē* woman — more at QUEEN] **1 :** of, relating to, or having (such or so many) females ⟨poly*gynous*⟩ or female characteristics ⟨andro*gynous*⟩ **:** female ⟨ergato*gynous*⟩ **:** woman **2 :** of, relating to, or having (such or so many) female organs, esp. pistils (in such a way or at such a time) ⟨hexa*gynous*⟩ ⟨proto*gynous*⟩

-gyns *pl of* -GYN

gy·nu·ra \\=ˈn(y)u̇rə — *see* GYN-\\ *n, cap* [NL, fr. *gyn-* + *-ura*] **:** a genus of tropical Asiatic and African herbs (family Compositae) having inconspicuous discoid heads of yellow flowers in loose terminal clusters — see VELVET PLANT

-gy·ny \\jənē, -ni\\ *n comb form* -ES [Gk *gynē* woman + E *-y*] **1 :** existence of or condition of having (such or so many) females ⟨mono*gyny*⟩ **2** [*-gynous* + *-y*] **:** existence of or condition of having (such or so many) female organs, esp. pistils (in such a way or at such a time) ⟨epi*gyny*⟩

gyo·ku·ro \\ˈgyōkəˌrō, ˌ==ˈ=\\ *n* -S [Jap, lit., dew, pearly dew, fr. *gyoku* precious stone, gem + *ro* dew] **:** a high-grade tea made in Japan from the leaves of shaded bushes and used for domestic consumption

1**gyp** \\ˈjip\\ *n* -S [prob. short for 1*gypsy*] **1 :** a male college servant (as at Cambridge University) ⟨the old ~ comes tapping at the door to learn my intentions for the evening —A.C.Benson⟩ — compare SCOUT 4 **2 a :** one who cheats **:** SWINDLER ⟨if any ~ does try to shake them down —A.H. Raskin⟩ **b :** an act or instance of cheating **:** FRAUD, SWINDLE ⟨have worked every tin-pot ~ you could think up to get a few dollars —*N.Y. Herald Tribune*⟩ **3** *chiefly South & Midland* **:** a female dog **:** BITCH ⟨as pretty a ~ as he'd ever laid eye on . . . a Walker hound with a brown streak running back from her ears —F.B.Gipson⟩ **4 :** a small-scale racehorse owner who trains and often rides his own horses

2**gyp** \\"\\ *vb* **gypped; gypped; gypping; gyps :** CHEAT

3**gyp** \\"\\ *n* -S [origin unknown] **:** a hard time — used in the phrase *to give* (a person) *gyp* ⟨apart from weariness, hunger, and a fair mental strain, my leg was giving me ~ —*Yale Rev.*⟩

4**gyp** \\"\\ *n* -S [by shortening] **:** GYPSUM ⟨~ is very common in hard waters —W.F.Cloud⟩

5**gyp** \\"\\ *n* -S [by shortening] **:** GYPSOPHILA

gy·pa·etus \\jəˈpād·əs\\ *n, cap* [NL, fr. Gk *gyp-*, *gyps* vulture + *aetos* eagle — more at AETO-] **:** a genus of Old World vultures consisting of the lammergeiers

gyp corn \\ˈjip-\\ *n* [short for *Egyptian corn*] **:** SORGHUM; *esp* **:** DURRA

1**gype** \\ˈgīp\\ *n* -S [of Scand origin; akin to ON *geip* nonsense, *geipa* to talk nonsense, *gīpr* mouth, throat, Norw dial. *geipa* to talk nonsense; akin to MD *gīpen* to gasp, OE *gīpian*, *geonian* to yawn — more at YAWN] *Scot* **:** FOOL

2**gype** \\"\\ *vi* -ED/-ING/-S *Scot* **:** to stare like a fool

gyp joint *n* [2*gyp*] **1 :** a crooked gambling establishment **2 :** an establishment (as a store, restaurant, or bar) that cheats customers by charging excessive prices for shoddy goods or inferior service

gyp·per \\ˈjipə(r)\\ *n* -S [2*gyp* + *-er*] **:** one that gyps

gyp·pery \\ˈjip(ə)rē, -ri\\ *n* -ES [2*gyp* + *-ery*] **:** the act or practice of gypping **:** SWINDLING

gyp·po *also* **gypo** \\ˈji(ˌ)pō\\ *n* -S [by shortening & alter. fr. 1*gypsy*] **1 :** a small logging operator who usu. works on a contract basis **2 :** contract work done by a gyppo

gyps \\ˈjips\\ *n, cap* [NL, fr. Gk, vulture; akin to Gk *gypē* cave — more at COVE] **:** a genus of Old World vultures including the griffon vulture and related African and Asiatic vultures

gyp·se·ian *or* **gip·se·ian** \\ˈjipsēən, =ˈ==\\ *adj* **:** of or relating to gypsies

gyp·se·ous \\ˈjipsēəs\\ *adj* [LL *gypseus*, fr. L *gypsum*] **:** resembling, containing, or consisting of gypsum

gyp·sif·er·ous \\(ˌ)jipˈsif(ə)rəs\\ *adj* [*gypsi-* (fr. *gypsum*) + *-ferous*] **:** bearing gypsum

gyp·site \\ˈjipˌsīt\\ *n* -S [*gyps*um + *-ite*] **:** earthy gypsum

gyp·sog·ra·phy \\jipˈsägrəfē\\ *n* -ES [*gyps*um + *-o-* + *-graphy*] **:** the art or practice of engraving on gypsum

gyp·soph·i·la \\jipˈsäfələ\\ *n* [NL, fr. *gypso-* (fr. L *gypsum*) + *-phila*] **1** *cap* **:** a large genus of Old World herbs (family Caryophyllaceae) having small delicate paniculate flowers with naked gamosepalous calyx and 5-clawed petals **2** -S **:** any plant of the genus *Gypsophila* — called also *baby's breath*

gyp·soph·i·lous \\(ˈ)=ˈ==ləs\\ *adj* [*gypso-* (fr. *gypsum*) + *-philous*] *of a plant* **:** flourishing in or on a substratum rich in gypsum — **gyp·soph·i·ly** \\=ˈ==lē\\ *n* -ES

gyp·so·plast \\ˈjipsəˌplast\\ *n* -S [*gypso-* (fr. *gypsum*) + *-plast*] **:** a cast in plaster of paris or in white lime

1**gyp·sum** \\ˈjipsəm\\ *n* -S *often attrib* [L *gypsum*, *gypsus*, fr. Gk *gypsos* chalk, gypsum, cement, of Sem origin; akin to Ar *jibs* plaster, mortar] **1 :** a widely distributed mineral $CaSO_4.2H_2O$ consisting of hydrous calcium sulfate that is colorless when pure, occurs massive or in the form of monoclinic crystals that easily split into folia, and is used chiefly as a soil amendment, as a retarder in portland cement, and in making plaster of Paris (hardness 2, sp. gr. 2.31-2.32) **2 :** PLASTERBOARD ⟨~ lath⟩ ⟨~ sheathing⟩ ⟨~ wallboard⟩

2**gypsum** \\"\\ *vt* -ED/-ING/-S **:** to treat (as soil or water) with gypsum

gypsum block *n* **:** a gypsum building tile or block for use in nonbearing walls in the interior of a building

gypsum pink *n* **:** BABY'S BREATH 1a

gypsum plaster *or* **gypsum cement** *n* **:** a plaster produced from the basic material gypsum — compare CEMENT PLASTER, PLASTER OF PARIS

1**gyp·sy** *or* **gip·sy** \\ˈjipsē, -si\\ *n* -ES *often attrib* [by shortening & alter. fr. 2*Egyptian*] **1** *cap* **:** one of a dark Caucasoid people coming orig. from India and entering Europe in the 14th or 15th century that are now found chiefly in Turkey, Russia, Hungary, Spain, England, and the U.S., still maintain somewhat their itinerant life and tribal organization, and are noted as fortune-tellers, horse traders, metalworkers, and musicians **2 :** one resembling a Gypsy esp. in appearance, manners, or mode of life ⟨dark of eye, tawny of skin, black as to her tangled hair, . . . a veritable ~ of a child —Richard Free⟩ ⟨oilmen . . . have been *gypsies* of the prairies, seeking, drilling, and never finding—*Lamp*⟩ **3** *cap* **:** ROMANY 2 **4 :** a strong brown that is stronger and slightly yellower than average russet, deeper and slightly yellower than rust, and very slightly lighter than ginger — called also *Caledonian brown* **5 :** an independent truck operator who has no regular route but hires his vehicle to others or follows seasonal or irregular sources of traffic **6 :** GYP 4 **7** [by shortening] **a :** GYPSYHEAD **b :** GYPSY WINCH

2**gypsy** *or* **gipsy** \\"\\ *vi* -ED/-ING/-ES **:** to live or roam like a Gypsy

gyp·sy·dom *or* **gip·sy·dom** \\-dəm\\ *n* -S **:** the realm of Gypsies **:** Gypsies and their life

gyp·sy·fy *or* **gip·sy·fy** \\-səˌfī, -sēˌ-\\ *vt* -ED/-ING/-ES **:** to make gypsylike esp. in appearance

gypsy hat *also* **gypsy bonnet** *n* **:** a simple broad-brimmed hat worn by women and children

gyp·sy·head \\-sēˌhed, -siˌ-\\ *n* **:** a small auxiliary drum on the end of a winch or windlass

gyp·sy·ish *or* **gip·sy·ish** \\-sēish, -si·ish\\ *adj* **:** GYPSYLIKE

gyp·sy·ism *or* **gip·sy·ism** \\-sēˌizəm, -siˌi-\\ *n* -S **:** the life and ways of Gypsies

gyp·sy·like *or* **gip·sy·like** \\ˈ==ˌ=\\ *adj* **:** resembling or suggestive of a Gypsy

gypsy moth *n* **:** an Old World tussock moth (*Porthetria dispar*) introduced about 1869 into the U.S. that has a brown male and a larger whitish female with wings marked by dark lines and that develops as a grayish brown mottled hairy caterpillar which is a very destructive defoliator of many trees

gypsy scale *n* **:** HUNGARIAN GYPSY SCALE

gypsyweed *or* **gipsyweed** \\ˈ==ˌ=\\ *n* **1 :** a water horehound (*Lycopus virginicus*) **2 :** SPEEDWELL

gypsy winch *n* **1 :** a small winch that may be operated by a crank **2 :** a winch with a gypsyhead

gyr- *or* **gyro-** *comb form* [prob. fr. MF, fr. L, fr. Gk, fr. *gyros* — more at GYRE] **1 :** ring **:** circle ⟨*gyro*mancy⟩ **:** spiral ⟨*Gyro*ceras⟩ **2 :** gyral ⟨*gyro*scope⟩ ⟨*gyr*encephalate⟩ **3 :** gyroscope ⟨*gyro*compass⟩

gyr·acan·thus \\ˈjir, ˈjīr +\\ *n, cap* [NL, fr. *gyr-* + *-acanthus*] **:** a genus of acanthodian fishes of the Carboniferous known solely from large round sculptured spines

1**gy·ral** \\ˈjīrəl\\ *adj* [2*gyre* + *-al*] **1 :** GYRATORY **2 :** of or involving a convolution of the brain — **gy·ral·ly** \\-rəlē, -li\\ *adv*

2**gyral** \\"\\ *n* -S **:** 2GYRE

1**gy·rate** \\ˈjīˌrā|t, -ˌrə|, *usu* |d·+V\\ *adj* [L *gyratus* circular, rounded, fr. *gyrus* circle, ring + *-atus* -ate] **:** winding or coiled round **:** CURVED, RINGED, CONVOLUTED ⟨a ~ branch⟩

[2]**gy·rate** \ˈjī,rāt, ·ˈ·, *usu* -ād·+V\ *vi* -ED/-ING/-S [LL *gyratus*, past part. of *gyrare* to gyrate, turn] **1 :** to revolve around a central point **:** move spirally about an axis ⟨the dory *gyrated* slowly and without direction near the marvelously stiff body of the plane —Kay Boyle⟩ **2 :** to turn or swing back and forth often rapidly with or as if with a circular or spiral motion ⟨seems to ~ wildly between the poles of sentimentalism and cold-blooded commercialism —Fredson Bowers⟩ ⟨the rain eddied and *gyrated* past them like a horizontal cataract —J. C.Powys⟩ **syn** see TURN

gy·ra·tion \jīˈrāshən\ *n* -S [MF or LL; MF *gyration, giration*, fr. LL *gyration-, gyratio*, fr. *gyratus* (past part.) + L *-ion-, -io* -ion] **1 :** the act or an instance of rotation in a circle or spiral **:** TURNING, WHIRLING, REVOLUTION **2 :** something that resembles gyration ⟨the first ~*s* of wishful thinking about the crash —Leo Gurko⟩ **3 :** the pattern of convolutions of a spiral shell — **gy·ra·tion·al** \-shənᵊl,-shnəl\ *adj*

gy·ra·tor \ˈjī,rād·ə(r), -ātə-, ·ˈ··\ *n* -S **:** one that gyrates

gy·ra·to·ry \ˈjīrə,tōrē, -tȯr-, -ri\ *adj* [*gyration* + *-ory*] **1 :** moving in a circle or spiral **:** REVOLVING **2** *Brit* **:** ROTARY — used of a system of traffic control

gyratory crusher *n* **:** a mill for crushing ore or rock or other materials that consists of a cone-shaped burr rotating in the throat of a broad stationary funnel

gy·rau·lus \jīˈrȯləs\ *n, cap* [NL, fr. *gyr-* + Gk *aulos* tube, groove, reed instrument like an oboe — more at ALVEOLUS] **:** a genus of freshwater snails (family Planorbidae) important in eastern Asia as intermediate hosts of the human intestinal fluke

[1]**gyre** \ˈjī(ə)r\ *vb* -ED/-ING/-S [ME *giren*, fr. LL *gyrare*, fr. L *gyrus*, n.] *vt* **:** to cause to turn around **:** REVOLVE, SPIN, WHIRL ~ *vi* **:** to move in a circle or spiral ⟨the bomber was *gyring* and diving —Stephen Spender⟩

[2]**gyre** \"\ *n* -S [L *gyrus*, fr. Gk *gyros*; akin to Gk *gyros* round, curved — more at COWER] **1 :** a circular motion or a circle described by a moving body **:** REVOLUTION **2 :** a circular or spiral form **:** RING, VORTEX

[3]**gyre** \ˈgī(ə)r\ *n* -S [ON *gȳgr* witch, giantess; perh. akin to Skt *gūhati* he conceals, Lith *gužė* goddess of travel] *Scot* **:** a malignant spirit or spook

gyre carline *n, Scot* **:** WITCH, HAG

gy·rec·to·my \jīˈrektəmē\ *n* -ES [*gyrus* + E *-ectomy*] **:** excision of a cerebral gyrus

gyr·en·ceph·a·late \ˌjī,renˈsefələt, -,rən-\ *also* **gyr·en·ce·phal·ic** \ˌjī,rensəˈfalik\ *or* **gyr·en·ceph·a·lous** \ˌjī,renˈsefələs, -,rən-\ *adj* [NL *Gyrencephala*, group of higher mammals (fr. *gyr-* + *encephala*) + E *-ate* or *-ic* or *-ous*] *of higher mammals* **:** having the surface of the brain convoluted

gy·rene \ˈjī,rēn, ·ˈ·\ *n* -S [prob. by alter.] *slang* **:** MARINE ⟨a young fellow in a ~ uniform —MacKinlay Kantor⟩

gyr·falcon *or* **ger·falcon** *also* **jer·falcon** \ˈjər+,-\ *n* [ME *gerfaucun*, fr. MF *girfaucon, gerfaut*, fr. OF, prob. fr. ON *geirfalki*, fr. *geirr* spear + *falki* falcon (prob. fr. MD *valke, valc*); akin to OHG *falcho* falcon — more at GORE (piece of land), FALCON] **:** any of various large falcons of the arctic regions of Europe, Asia, and America that commonly constitute a subgenus (*Hierofalco*) of the genus *Falco* and are about two feet long and more powerful though less active than the peregrine falcon — see BLACK GYRFALCON, WHITE GYRFALCON

gyri *pl of* GYRUS

gy·rin·i·dae \jəˈrinə,dē, jī-\ *n pl, cap* [NL, fr. *Gyrinus*, type genus (fr. Gk *gyrinos* tadpole, fr. *gyros* round) + *-idae*] **:** a family of aquatic beetles comprising the whirligig beetles

[1]**gy·ro** \ˈjī(,)rō\ *n* -S **1** [by shortening] **:** GYROSCOPE **2 :** any of various devices whose operation depends on a gyroscope: as **a** [by shortening] **:** GYROCOMPASS **b** [by shortening] **:** GYROHORIZON

[2]**gyro** \"\ *adj* **:** GYROSCOPIC

gyro- — see GYR-

gy·ro·car \ˈjīrō+,-\ *n* [*gyr-* + *car*] **:** a monorail car

gy·roc·era·cone \jīˈrasərə+,-\ *n* [NL *Gyroceras* + E *cone*] **:** a nautiloid shell coiling like that of members of the genus *Gyroceras* — **gy·roc·era·conic** \·ˌ···+\ *adj*

gy·roc·er·an \jīˈräsərən\ *adj* [NL *Gyroceras* + E *-an*] **:** of or relating to the genus *Gyroceras*

gy·roc·er·as \-əs\ *n, cap* [NL, fr. *gyr-* + *-ceras*] **:** a genus of fossil nautiloid cephalopods having the shell in the form of a loosely coiled discoidal spiral

gy·ro·compass \ˌjīrō+\ *n* [*gyr-* + *compass*] **:** a compass consisting of a continuously driven gyroscope whose supporting ring confines the spinning axis to a horizontal plane so that the earth's rotation causes it to assume a position parallel to the earth's axis and thus point to the true north

gy·ro·cot·y·le \ˌjīrōˈkäd·ᵊl(,)ē\ *n, cap* [NL, fr. *gyr-* + Gk *kotylē* cup, small vessel — more at KETTLE] **:** a genus (the type of the family Gyrocotylidae) comprising cestodarian worms with a flattened body, an anterior sucker, and a posterior organ in the form of a frilled rosette and sometimes also including worms in which the rosette is replaced by a contractile cylindrical structure that ends in a strong sphincter — compare AMPHILINA

[1]**gy·ro·cot·y·lid** \ˌ··ˈ··ˌəd\ *adj* [NL *Gyrocotylidae*, family of worms, fr. *Gyrocotyle*, type genus + *-idae*] **:** of or relating to the genus *Gyrocotyle* or the family Gyrocotylidae

[2]**gyrocotylid** \"\ *n* -S **:** a gyrocotylid worm

[1]**gy·ro·dac·ty·loid** \ˌjīrōˈdaktə,lȯid\ *adj* [NL *Gyrodactylus* + E *-oid*] **:** of or relating to the genus *Gyrodactylus* or to worms of this or related genera

[2]**gyrodactyloid** \"\ *n* -S **:** a gyrodactyloid worm

gy·ro·dac·ty·lus \ˌ··ˈ··ˌləs\ *n, cap* [NL, fr. *gyr-* + *dactylus*] **:** a genus (the type of the family Gyrodactylidae) of small monogenetic trematodes parasitic on fishes

gy·ro·dyne \ˈjīrō,dīn\ *n* -S [*gyr-* + *-dyne* (as in *aerodyne*)] **:** an aircraft intermediate between the helicopter and the autogiro in that the total available engine power is divided in varying proportions between a lifting rotor and a propeller

Gyro Flux Gate *trademark* — used for an airplane compass that is horizontally stabilized by a gyroscope and that determines directions by means of a flux gate which responds to the earth's magnetic field

gy·ro·frequency \ˈjīrō+\ *n* [*gyr-* + *frequency*] **:** the frequency with which an electron or other charged particle executes spiral gyrations in moving obliquely across a magnetic field

gy·rog·o·nite \jīˈrägə,nīt\ *n* -S [NL *Gyrogonites*] **:** a minute ovoid spiral-marked body that is the residue of the calcareous incrustation about the female sex organs of a fossil stonewort

gy·rogo·ni·tes \(,)·,··ˈnīd·(,)ēz, ,gīrōgəˈ-\ *n, cap* [NL, fr. *gyr-* + *gon-* + L *-ites* -ite] **:** a form genus of stoneworts based on gyrogonites

gyro horizon *n* **:** ARTIFICIAL HORIZON 2

gy·roi·dal \(ˈ)jīˌrȯidᵊl\ *adj* [*gyr-* + *-oidal*] **:** spiral or gyratory in arrangement — used esp. of the planes of crystals — **gy·roi·dal·ly** \-dᵊlē\ *adv*

gy·ro·lite \ˈjīrə,līt\ *n* -S [*gyr-* + *-lite*] **:** a mineral $Ca_2Si_3O_7(OH)_2.H_2O$ consisting of hydrous calcium silicate in white concretions

gy·ro·lith \-,lith\ *n* -S [*gyr-* + *-lith*] **:** the fossil nutlet of a stonewort

gy·ro·ma \jīˈrōmə\ *n* -S [NL, fr. Gk *gyroun* to round, bend, fr. *gyros* ring, circle — more at GYRE] **:** CONVOLUTION: as **a :** the annulus of a fern **b :** a shield somewhat resembling a button in lichens of the genus *Gyrophora*

gy·ro·magnetic \ˌjīrō+\ *adj* [*gyr-* + *magnetic*] **:** of or relating to the magnetic properties of a rotating electrical particle

gyromagnetic ratio *n* **:** the ratio of the magnetic moment of a spinning electrical particle (as an electron) to its mechanical angular momentum

gy·ro·man·cy \ˈjīrə,man(t)sē\ *n* -ES [prob. fr. MF *gyromancie*, fr. *gyro-* gyr- + *-mancie* -mancy] **:** divination in which one walking in or around a circle falls from dizziness and prognosticates from the place of the fall

gy·ro·mi·tra \ˌjīrōˈmī·trə\ *n, cap* [NL, fr. *gyr-* + *mitra*] **:** a genus of fungi (family Helvellaceae) forming large stipitate ascomata with folded ascus-bearing caps and including a form (*G. esculenta*) that produces edible fruiting bodies which may be poisonous if eaten raw

gy·ron *or* **gi·ron** \ˈjīrən, -,rän\ *n* -S [MF *giron* wedge-shaped piece of material, fr. OF, fr. Gmc origin; akin to OHG *gēro* wedge-shaped object — more at GORE] **:** a heraldic charge of triangular form having one side at the edge of the field and the opposite angle usu. at the fess point

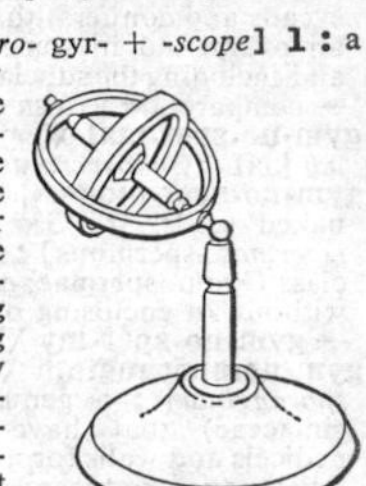
gyrons

gy·ron·ny \ˈjīrənē, ˈjīrənē\ *adj* [ME *jerownde, gerundi*, fr. MF *gironné, geronné*, fr. OF, fr. *giron, geron*, n.] **:** divided so as to form a number of gyrons — used of a heraldic coat of arms

gy·roph·o·ra \jīˈräfərə\ *n, cap* [NL, fr. *gyr-* + *-phora*] **:** a genus (the type of the family Gyrophoraceae) of foliose rock-inhabiting lichens that includes the edible manna lichen (*G. esculenta*) of Japan — compare UMBILICARIA — **gy·roph·o·ra·ceous** \(ˌ)·ˌ···ˈrāshəs\ *adj*

Gy·ro·pilot \ˈjīrō+,-\ *trademark* — used for an automatic pilot

gy·ro·plane \ˈjīrō,plān\ *n* [ISV *gyro-* (fr. *gyroscope*) + *-plane* (fr. *airplane*)] **:** an airplane balanced and supported by the aerodynamic forces acting on rapidly rotating horizontal or slightly inclined planes

gy·ro·scope \ˈjīrə,skōp\ *n* [F, fr. *gyro-* gyr- + *-scope*] **1 :** a wheel or disk mounted to spin rapidly about an axis and also free to rotate about one or both of two axes perpendicular to each other and to the axis of spin so that a rotation of one of the two mutually perpendicular axes results from application of torque to the other when the wheel is spinning, the entire apparatus offering considerable opposition depending on the angular momentum to any torque that would change the direction of the axis of spin **2 :** something resembling a gyroscope **:** BALANCE WHEEL 2 ⟨systematic retirement programs can thus serve as a sort of economic ~ —*New Republic*⟩

gyroscope 1

gy·ro·scop·ic \ˌ··ˈskäpik, -pēk\ *adj* **:** of, relating to, or having the characteristics of a gyroscope — **gy·ro·scop·i·cal·ly** \-pək(ə)lē, -pēk-, -li\ *adv*

gyroscopic compass *n* **:** GYROCOMPASS

gy·ro·scop·ics \ˌ··ˈ·piks, -pēks\ *n pl but sing in constr* **:** a branch of mechanics that deals with gyroscopes and their use in control and stabilization

gy·rose \ˈjī,rōs\ *adj* [[2]*gyre* + *-ose*] **:** marked with wavy lines **:** UNDULATE, SINUATE

gy·ro·stabilization \ˌjīrō+\ *n* **:** the process of stabilizing or the condition of being stabilized by means of a gyrostabilizer

gy·ro·stabilized \"+\ *adj* **:** stabilized by means of a gyrostabilizer

gy·ro·stabilizer \"+\ *n* [*gyro* + *stabilizer*] **:** a stabilizing device (as for a ship or airplane) consisting of a continuously driven gyro spinning about a vertical axis and pivoted in trunnions so that its axis of spin may be tipped fore-and-aft in the vertical plane and serving to oppose sideways motion

gy·ro·stat \ˈjīrə,stat\ *n* -S [ISV *gyr-* + *-stat*] **:** GYROSTABILIZER

gy·ro·stat·ic \ˌ··ˈstad·ik\ *adj* **:** of or relating to a gyrostat or to its stabilizing effect — **gy·ro·stat·i·cal·ly** \-d·ək(ə)lē\ *adv*

gyrostatic compass *n* **:** GYROCOMPASS

gy·ro·vague \ˈjīrō,väg\ *n* [F *gyrovague*, fr. LL *gyrovagus*, fr. L *gyro-* gyr- + *vagus* wandering — more at VAGARY] **:** a wandering and usu. dissolute monk of the early church

gy·rus \ˈjīrəs\ *n, pl* **gy·ri** \-,rī\ [NL, fr. L, circle — more at GYRE] **:** a convoluted ridge between grooves; *esp* **:** one of the characteristic ridges of superficial gray matter of the cerebral hemispheres

gyte \ˈgīt\ *adj, chiefly Scot* **:** DERANGED, MAD

gy·trash \ˈgī·,trash\ *var of* GUYTRASH

gyt·tja \ˈyi(,)chä\ *n* -S [Sw, fr. *gjuta* to pour, fr. OSw *giūta*; akin to ON *gjōta* to bear young, drop one's young — more at FOUND (pour)] **:** a lacustrine mud containing abundant organic material

[1]**gyve** \ˈjīv\ *n* -S [ME] **:** FETTER, BOND, CHAIN — usu. used in pl.

[2]**gyve** \"\ *vt* -ED/-ING/-S [ME *gyven*, fr. *gyve*, n.] **:** to bind or restrain with fetters **:** SHACKLE, CHAIN

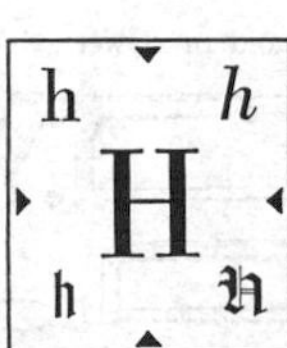

1h \ˈāch\ *n, pl* **h's** *or* **hs** \ˈāchəz\ *often cap, often attrib* **1 a :** the eighth letter of the English alphabet **b :** an instance of this letter printed, written, or otherwise represented **c :** a speech counterpart of orthographic *h* (as *h* in *hoe, ahead,* or German *hügel*) **2 :** a printer's type, a stamp, or some other instrument for reproducing the letter *h* **3 :** someone or something arbitrarily or conveniently designated *h* esp. as the eighth in order or class **4 :** something having the shape of the letter H ⟨grooved and slotted to receive H bronze members —Kenneth Cheesman⟩

2h *abbr, often cap* **1** hail **2** haler **3** half **4** hall **5** handily **6** harbor **7** hard; hardness **8** [Ger *hauch*] film **9** haze **10** headquarters **11** heat **12** hecto- **13** height **14** helicopter **15** heller **16** hence **17** henry **18** [L *heres*] heir **19** heroin **20** high **21** hit **22** holy **23** home **24** honor **25** horizon; horizontal **26** horn **27** horse **28** hot **29** hour **30** house **31** humidity **32** hundred **33** husband **34** hydrant

3h *symbol* **1** *cap* hydrogen **2** *cap* enthalpy **3** *cap* intensity of magnetic field **4** Planck constant

H3 *or* **3H** \(ˈ)āchˌthrē\ *symbol* tritium

H2 *or* **2H** \(ˈ)āchˌtü\ *symbol* deuterium

1ha *or* **hah** \ˈhä, ˈhȧ\ *interj* [ME *ha*] — used to express surprise, joy, or grief or sometimes doubt or hesitation or to request repetition or clarification of something just said

2ha \"\ *vi* -ED/-ING/-S **:** to utter the exclamation *ha*

3ha *or* **hah** \"\ *n* -S **:** an utterance of the exclamation *ha*

4ha *or* **ha'** \hə, (ˌ)ha\ *var of* A

5ha *dial Brit pres 1st & 2d sing & pres pl of* HAVE

ha *abbr* hectare

HA *abbr* **1** heavy artillery **2** high-angle **3** *often not cap* [L *hoc anno*] in this year; [L *huius anni*] of this year **4** horse artillery **5** hot air **6** hour angle

ha' \ˈhȯ, ˈhȧ\ *Scot var of* HALL

HAA *abbr* heavy antiaircraft

haab \ˈhäb\ *n* -S [Maya] **1 :** TUN **2 :** the 365-day year of the Maya calendar — often distinguished from *tun*

haak–en–steek \ˈhäkən,stēk\ *n* -S [Afrik, lit., hook and sting; fr. the fact that it has some curved and some straight thorns] **:** UMBRELLA THORN

haar \ˈ(h)är\ *n* -S [prob. fr. a LG or D dial. word akin to D dial. *harig* damp, misty, MD *hare* sharp wind, piercing cold, Fris *harig* misty, ON *hārr* gray, hoary — more at HOAR] *dial Brit* **:** a cold wet sea fog

haar·der *var of* 2HARDER

haar·lem \ˈhärləm, ˈhäl-\ *adj, usu cap* [fr. *Haarlem,* Netherlands] **:** of or from the city of Haarlem, Netherlands **:** of the kind or style prevalent in Haarlem

haas·tia \ˈhästēə\ *n* -S [NL, fr. Sir John F. J. von *Haast* †1887 German-born geologist and explorer in New Zealand + NL *-ia*] **:** RAOULIA 2

hab *abbr* habitat

HAB *abbr* high-altitude bombing

ha·ba \ˈ(h)äbə\ *n* -S [Sp, fr. L *faba* bean — more at BEAN] **:** BROAD BEAN

ha·bab \həˈbäb, ˈhä,bäb\ *n, pl* **habab** *usu cap* **1 a :** a nomadic people of the Red sea region in Africa **b :** a member of such people **2 :** the Semitic language of the Habab

ha·ba·ne·ra \ˌ(h)äbəˈnerə, *often* ÷ -bənˈye- *although the fifth letter in Spanish is not ñ*\ *n* -S [Sp (*danza*) *habanera,* lit., Havanan dance, fr. *danza* dance + *habanera,* fem. of *habanero* Havanan, fr. La *Habana,* Cuba + *-ero* -er] **1 :** a Cuban dance of voluptuous character in slow duple time **2 :** a slow Cuban dance tune in duple time with the distinctive rhythm of a dotted eighth note, a sixteenth note, and two eighth notes throughout

ha·ba·ne·ro \-e(ˌ)rō\ *n* -S *cap* [Sp, fr. La *Habana* (Havana), Cuba + *-ero* -er] **:** a native or inhabitant of Havana, Cuba

hab·ble \ˈhäbəl\ *Scot var of* HOBBLE

hab·da·lah *or* **hav·da·lah** \ˌhävdəˈlä, häv'dōlə\ *n* -S [Heb *habhdālāh* separation, division] **:** a Jewish religious ceremony marking the close of a Sabbath or of holidays and consisting of the recital by the head of a household of appropriate benedictions over a cup esp. of wine, a spice box, and a newly lighted special candle

ha·be·as cor·pus \ˈhābēəˈskȯrpəs, -bia'-, -kō(ə)p-\ *n* [ME, fr. ML, lit., you should have the body (the opening words of the writ)] **1 :** any of several common-law writs that have for their object the bringing of a party before a court or judge and that are issued out of court or awarded by a judge in vacation; *esp* **:** HABEAS CORPUS AD SUBJICIENDUM ⟨the privilege of the writ of *habeas corpus* shall not be suspended, unless when in cases of rebellion or invasion the public safety may require it —*U.S. Constitution*⟩ **2 :** the right of a citizen to obtain a writ of habeas corpus as a protection against illegal imprisonment

habeas corpus ad fa·ci·en·dum et re·cip·i·en·dum \-ad-ˌfāshēˈendəm·etrə,sipēˈendəm\ *n* [NL, lit., you should have the body for doing and receiving] **:** a writ issued from a superior court to an inferior court requiring that a defendant be produced with the cause of his being taken and held

habeas corpus ad pro·se·quen·dum \-ˌpräsəˈkwendəm\ *n* [NL, lit., you should have the body for prosecuting] **:** a writ for removing a prisoner for trial to the jurisdiction in which the offense was committed

habeas corpus ad sub·ji·ci·en·dum \-(ˌ)səb,jisēˈendəm\ *n* [NL, lit., you should have the body for submitting] **:** a writ for inquiring into the lawfulness of the restraint of a person who is imprisoned or detained in another's custody

habeas corpus ad tes·ti·fi·can·dum \-ˌtestəfəˈkandəm\ *n* [NL, lit., you should have the body for testifying] **:** a writ for bringing a person in custody into court as a witness

habeas corpus cum cau·sa \-(ˌ)kəmˈkȯzə\ *n* [NL, lit., you should have the body with the cause] **:** HABEAS CORPUS AD FACIENDUM ET RECIPIENDUM

hab·e·nar·ia \ˌhabəˈna(a)rēə\ *n* [NL, fr. L *habena* strap, thong (fr. *habēre* to have, hold) + NL *-aria;* fr. the shape of parts of the flowers — more at GIVE] **1** *cap* **:** a very large genus of somewhat glabrous orchids chiefly of the northern hemisphere with usu. small flowers having the lip lobed, entire, or fringed and borne in racemes or spikes — see FRINGED ORCHIS, REIN ORCHIS **2** -S **:** any plant of the genus *Habenaria* or its flower

ha·ben·dum \həˈbendəm\ *n* -S [NL, fr. L, to be had, neut. of *habendus,* gerundive of *habēre* to have, to hold (the first word of this part of the deed)] **:** the part of a deed that formerly limited and defined an estate and the extent of ownership granted and sometimes the type of tenancy by which the grantees would hold an estate but that is now rarely encountered or is merely formal in deeds in which a fee simple absolute is presumed granted

ha·ben·u·la \həˈbenyələ\ *n, pl* **habenu·lae** \-yə(ˌ)lē\ [L, dim. of *habena* strap, thong] **1** *also* **ha·ben·u·lar trigone** \-lə(r)-\ **:** an anatomic structure in the form of a band; *esp* **:** a small triangular area of the surface of the epithalamus on either side of the base of the pineal body **2** *also* **habenular nucleus :** a nucleus underlying each habenula and connected by commissural fibers that forms a correlation center for olfactory stimuli — called also *nucleus habenulae*

haber *var of* HAVER

haberah *var of* HAVERAH

hab·er·dash·er \ˈhabə(r),dashə(r)\ *n* -S [ME *haberdassher,* fr. modif. of AF *hapertas* petty merchandise + ME *-er*] **1** *Brit* **:** a dealer in small wares or notions (as needles, thread, buttons) **2 :** a dealer in men's furnishings (as shirts, ties, hats)

hab·er·dash·ery \-sh(ə)rē, -ri\ *n* -ES [ME *haberdassherie,* fr. *haberdassher* + *-ie* -y] **1 :** the goods sold by a haberdasher **2 :** a haberdasher's shop

haberdine *n* -S [ME, fr. MF *habordean,* by false division (the *l* being taken as the definite article) fr. *labordean,* fr. *Labourd,* Basque district in France] *obs* **:** a cod salted and dried

ha·be·re fa·ci·as pos·ses·si·o·nem \həˈbirēˈfāshēəspə,zesēˈō,nem\ *n* [ML, you should cause to have possession (the opening words of the writ)] **:** a writ of execution in ejectment orig. in England in cases of chattels real

habere facias sei·si·nam \-ˈsēzə,nam\ *n* [ML, you should cause to have seisin] **:** a common-law writ formerly used in real actions to recover seisin

hab·er·geon \ˈhabərjən, həˈbərj(ē)ən\ *or* **hau·ber·geon** \ˈhōb-, hōˈ-\ *n* -S [ME *haubergeon,* fr. MF *haubergeon,* dim. of *hauberc* — more at HAUBERK] **1 :** a medieval jacket of mail shorter than a hauberk **2 :** HAUBERK

ha·ber process \ˈhäbə(r)-\ *n, usu cap H* [after Fritz *Haber* †1934 Ger. chemist] **:** a catalytic process for synthesizing ammonia from nitrogen and hydrogen at elevated temperature and pressure

hab·ile \ˈhabəl\ *adj* [F, fr. L *habilis* — more at ABLE] **1** *obs* **:** FIT, SUITABLE **2 :** ABLE, ADROIT, SKILLFUL ⟨that astonishing ~ use of his lean little hands —J.G.Cozzens⟩

ha·bil·i·ment \həˈbiləmənt\ *n* -S [MF *habillement,* fr. *abillier, habiller* to prepare a log for working, prepare, dress (fr. *bille* log, trunk) + *-ment* — more at BILLET] **1 habiliments** *pl* **:** TRAPPINGS, EQUIPMENT, GEAR ⟨the disintegrative process of the frontier . . . stripping them of the ~s of civilization —W.P. Webb⟩ ⟨all the psychological trappings and ~s of a crusade —W.A.White⟩ **2 habiliments** *pl, archaic* **:** necessary equipment and material (as for war) **:** OUTFITTING **3 a :** the dress suited to or characteristic of a calling, occupation, or occasion **:** GARB, COSTUME, VESTMENT — usu. used in pl. ⟨dressed in shabby gaucho ~s —W.H.Hudson †1922⟩ ⟨~s of a priest⟩ ⟨the antique forms and ~s which their Roman ancestors had found congenial —G.C.Sellery⟩ **b :** CLOTHES, GARMENT, DRESS — usu. used in pl. ⟨pointed in silence to my torn and muddied ~s —Hugh McCrae⟩ ⟨seize a buttonhole, or any little bit of the ~s, of the man she was addressing —George Meredith⟩

ha·bil·i·men·ta·tion \hə,biləˌ)men'tāshən\ *n* -S **:** the arts and industries connected with the manufacture and use of clothes

ha·bil·i·ment·ed \həˈbilə,mentəd\ *adj* **:** CLOTHED

ha·bil·i·tate \həˈbilə,tāt, *usu* -ād+V\ *vb* -ED/-ING/-S [LL *habilitatus,* past part. of *habilitare,* fr. L *habilitas* aptness, ability — more at ABILITY] *vt* **1** *archaic* **:** QUALIFY, ENTITLE **2 :** to fit out (as a mine) **:** equip for working **3 :** CLOTHE, DRESS ~ *vi* **:** to qualify oneself (as for teaching in a university) ⟨had just *habilitated* as a privatdocent in the theological faculty —Jack Finegan⟩

ha·bil·i·ta·tion \hə,biləˈtāshən\ *n* -S [ML *habilitation-, habilitatio,* fr. LL *habilitatus* + L *-ion-, -io* -ion] **:** the act of habilitating **:** QUALIFICATION ⟨thesis for ~ as docent⟩ **:** CAPACITATION ⟨~ of cerebral palsy patients⟩

ha·bil·i·ty \həˈbilədē\ *n* -ES **:** the quality of being habile **:** EXPERTNESS

ha·bi·ru \ˈhäbē,rü, həˈbē(ˌ)rü\ *also* **ha·bi·ri** \-ē(ˌ)rē\ *n pl, usu cap* [Bab *khabiru*] **:** a nomadic people mentioned in Assyro-Babylonian literature from 2000 B.C. on and often identified as the Hebrews of the Bible

1hab·it \ˈhabət, *usu* -əd-+V\ *n* -S [ME *habit, abit,* fr. OF, fr. L *habitus* condition, appearance, attire, character, disposition, habit, fr. *habēre* to have, hold — more at GIVE] **1** *archaic* **a :** CLOTHING, APPAREL ⟨costly thy ~ as thy purse can buy —Shak.⟩ **:** mode of dress ⟨in the vile ~ of a village slave —Alexander Pope⟩ **b :** a garment or a suit of clothes **:** OUTFIT **2 a :** a costume indicative or characteristic of a calling, rank, or function ⟨monk's ~⟩ **b :** RIDING HABIT **3 :** BEARING, CONDUCT, BEHAVIOR — used esp. in Scots law in the phrase *habit and repute* ⟨marriage by ~ and repute⟩ **4 a :** bodily appearance or makeup **:** physical type **:** PHYSIQUE ⟨his corpulent ~ of body, natural both to the vigor of his type and to a sedentary way of life —Osbert Sitwell⟩ **b** *obs* **:** the body as a physiological organism **:** the system of bodily processes **c** *obs* **:** the body's surface **5 :** the prevailing disposition or character of a person's thoughts and feelings **:** mental makeup ⟨where he has gone to indulge a contemplative ~ —L.J.Halle⟩ ⟨a whole ~ of sensibility —F.R.Leavis⟩ **6 a** *of a person* **:** a settled tendency of behavior or normal manner of procedure **:** CUSTOM, PRACTICE, WAY ⟨contributed letters to the newspapers — a ~ that became a lifelong one —B.J.Hendrick⟩ ⟨the local ~ of building in perishable materials —Bernard Newman⟩ **b** *of a thing* **:** a usual manner of occurrence or behavior **:** TENDENCY ⟨black clouds there have a ~ of sitting right on the water —Ira Wolfert⟩ ⟨paste has a ~ of going hard and lumpy once opened⟩ **7 a :** a behavior pattern acquired by frequent repetition or developed as a physiologic function and showing itself in regularity ⟨the daily bowel ~⟩ or increased facility of performance or in a decreased power of resistance ⟨a drug ~⟩ **b :** an acquired or developed mode of behavior or function that has become nearly or completely involuntary ⟨put the keys back in his pocket through force of ~⟩ **8** *of an organism* **:** characteristic mode of growth or occurrence ⟨elms have a spreading ~⟩ ⟨a grass ubiquitous in its ~⟩ **9 :** the characteristic crystalline size and form of a substance **10** *archaic* **:** close acquaintance **:** FAMILIARITY ⟨he inclines to a sort of disgust . . . with the system and he has few . . . ~s with any of its professors —Edmund Burke⟩ **11 :** a generic entity occurring as an external or supernatural reality or force constitutive of or acting on an individual **12 :** ADDICTION 2a ⟨was forced to steal to feed his drug ~⟩

syn HABITUDE, PRACTICE, USAGE, CUSTOM, USE, WONT: these all have in common the sense of a way of behaving that has become more or less fixed; in most cases they have the sense of such a way considered collectively or in the abstract. HABIT, usu. applying to individuals, signifies a way of acting or thinking done frequently enough to have become unconscious or unpremeditated in each repetition or to have become compulsive ⟨the *habit* of dawdling on the way to school⟩ ⟨a persistent *habit* of coughing⟩ ⟨*habits* of mind⟩ ⟨speech *habits*⟩ HABITUDE usu. suggests habitual or usual state of mind or attitude ⟨you who are so sincere with me are never quite sincere with others. You have contracted this bad *habitude* from your custom of addressing the people —W.S.Landor⟩ ⟨a confusion of assertions, viewpoints, personal motives and prejudices, and local *habitudes* can serve only to darken counsel —*Yale Rev.*⟩ PRACTICE suggests an act, often habitual, repeated with regularity and usu. by choice ⟨the team made a *practice* of leaving their scenarios unfinished until actual production —*Current Biog.*⟩ ⟨promised the people that he would establish democratic *practices* —*Collier's Yr. Bk.*⟩ ⟨the *practice* of supplementing poultry and hog feeds with antibiotics —*Americana Annual*⟩ ⟨the *practice* of self-examination —Anne Fremantle⟩ USAGE suggests more a customary action, a practice followed so generally that it has become a social norm ⟨an unwritten constitution comprising ancient British conventions and *usage* —*Americana Annual*⟩ ⟨earn a living in a business community without yielding to its *usages* —W.H.Hamilton⟩ ⟨better versed in diplomatic *usage* than any of his colleagues —F.A.Ogg & Harold Zink⟩ CUSTOM can apply to habit, practice, or usage that has become public and associated with an individual or group because of its long continuance, its uniformity, and often, its morally compulsive quality ⟨it is the Arabian *custom* to date, if possible, the birth of sons by unusual events —*Current Biog.*⟩ ⟨in contemporary society it is not a fashion that men wear trousers; it is the *custom* —Edward Sapir⟩ ⟨the *custom* — and this is all that it can be properly called — according to which Congress and the President tacitly agree to abide by the interpretation of the Court —M.R.Cohen⟩ USE, rare in current speech, signifies a customary act or practice more or less distinctive of an individual or particular group ⟨the polite *uses* of society⟩ ⟨the religious *use* and wont of the country people⟩ WONT applies to a habitual or customary manner, method, or practice distinguishing an individual or group; it differs from USE only in extending to manner ⟨intended to come oftener to church than had been his *wont* of late —William Black⟩ ⟨this nice balance between sovereignty and liberty is maintained by use and *wont* —V.L.Parrington⟩ ⟨a people living by *wont* in a natural atmosphere of suspicion and mistrust, and consumed by fantasies —V.S.Pritchett⟩ **syn**

2habit \"\ *vt* -ED/-ING/-S **:** CLOTHE, DRESS ⟨the nature of such pedantry to ~ itself in a harsh and crabbed style —R.M. Weaver⟩

3habit \"\ *vb* -ED/-ING/-S [ME *habiten* to dwell, reside, fr. MF *habiter,* fr. L *habitare* to have possession of, inhabit, dwell, abide, fr. *habitus,* past part. of *habēre* to have, hold — more at GIVE] *vi, obs* **:** LIVE, ABIDE ~ *vt* **1** *archaic* **:** INHABIT **2** *archaic* **:** ACCUSTOM, HABITUATE

hab·it·abil·i·ty \ˌhabədəˈbilədē\ *n* **:** the state of being habitable

hab·it·able \ˈhabədəbəl, -bətəb-\ *adj* [ME *abitable,* fr. OF *habitable, abitable,* fr. L *habitabilis,* fr. *habitare* + *-abilis* -able] **:** capable of being inhabited **:** that may be inhabited or dwelt in ⟨the ~ world⟩; *specif, of a dwelling* **:** reasonably fit for occupation by a tenant of the class for which it was let or of the class ordinarily occupying such a dwelling — **hab·it·able·ness** *n* -ES — **hab·it·ably** \-blē, -li\ *adv*

habitacle *n* -S [ME, fr. OF, fr. L *habitaculum* — more at BINNACLE] **1** *obs* **:** a dwelling place **2** *obs* **:** a niche in a wall (as for a statue)

hab·it·al·ly \ˈhabədᵊlē\ *adv* [irreg. fr. *habitat* + *-ly*] **:** with respect to habitat

hab·it·ancy \ˈhabədənsē\ *n* -ES **1 :** the fact of residence **:** INHABITANCY **2 :** the whole number of inhabitants **:** POPULATION

1hab·i·tant \ˈhabədənt\ *n* -S [MF, fr. pres. part. of *habiter* to dwell, inhabit — more at HABIT] **1 :** INHABITANT, RESIDENT **2** *or* **ha·bi·tan** \ˌ(h)abēˌtäⁿ\ [CanF *habitant,* fr. F, inhabitant] **:** a settler or descendant of a settler of French origin belonging to the farming class in Canada

2ha·bi·tant \ˌ(h)abēˌtäⁿ\ *adj* **:** relating to, characteristic of, or produced by the French farmers of Canada ⟨~ furniture⟩ ⟨~ homespun⟩

hab·i·tat \ˈhabə,tat, *usu* -ad-+V\ *n* -S [L, it inhabits, 3d pers. sing. pres. indic. of *habitare* to inhabit (the initial word in Latin descriptions of species of fauna and flora in old natural histories) — more at HABIT] **1 a :** the place where a plant or animal species naturally lives and grows ⟨found as weeds throughout the tropics, but their original ~ has not been determined —Walter Bally⟩ **b :** the kind of site or region with respect to physical features (as soil, weather, elevation) naturally or normally preferred by a biological species ⟨provides three main kinds of ~, namely rocks, sand, and mud —W.H.Dowdeswell⟩ ⟨shell opaque and dull, varying in solidity according to the ~⟩ **c :** the purely physical environment of a locality occupied by a human group ⟨unable to maintain themselves as rulers in the steppe ~ of the nomads —Owen & Eleanor Lattimore⟩ **2 :** the place where something is commonly found ⟨has its natural ~ in university, in government, or in industrial laboratories —B.B.Watson⟩

habitat form *n* **:** ECAD

habitat group *n* **:** a museum exhibit showing plant and animal specimens in such attitudes and with their natural surroundings so reproduced as to picture their habits and habitat

hab·i·ta·tion \ˌhabəˈtāshən\ *n* -S [ME *habitacioun,* fr. MF *habitation,* fr. L *habitation-, habitatio,* fr. *habitatus* (past part. of *habitare* to inhabit, dwell) + *-ion-, -io* -ion — more at HABIT] **1 a :** the act of inhabiting **:** state of inhabiting or dwelling or of being inhabited **:** OCCUPANCY **b :** the right of one with his family to occupy the residential property of another as a home **2 :** a dwelling place **:** HOUSE, HOME, RESIDENCE ⟨a map showing towns, villages, and scattered ~s⟩ ⟨his notebooks . . . gave his ideas a local ~ —Van Wyck Brooks⟩ **3 :** SETTLEMENT, COLONY ⟨their ~s were usually spoken of as camps, sometimes composed of 200 tents —Clark Wissler⟩ — **hab·i·ta·tion·al** \ˌ==ˈtāshənᵊl, -shnəl\ *adj*

habit clinic *n* **:** a clinic dealing with the prevention and treatment of behavior problems in young children

habited *adj* **1** *obs* **:** fixed by habit **:** ACCUSTOMED **2** *archaic* **:** INHABITED **3 :** CLOTHED; *esp* **:** dressed in a habit ⟨the monasteries were gone, the ~ men and women were but memories —Sigmund Beale⟩

habit–forming \ˈ==,==\ *adj* **:** inducing the formation of a habit or an addiction ⟨a *habit-forming* drug⟩

habiting *pres part of* HABIT

habits *pl of* HABIT, *pres 3d sing of* HABIT

habit spasm *n* **:** TIC 1

1ha·bit·u·al \həˈbich(ə)wəl, -chəl\ *adj* [ML *habitualis,* fr. L *habitus* condition, habit + *-alis* -al — more at HABIT] **1 :** of the nature of a habit **:** according to habit **:** established by or repeated by force of habit **:** CUSTOMARY ⟨~ smoking⟩ ⟨~ courtesy⟩ ⟨~ morning walk⟩ **2 :** doing, practicing, or acting in some manner by force of habit **:** customarily doing a certain thing ⟨an ~ drunkard⟩ ⟨~ playgoer⟩ ⟨his ~ position by the door⟩ **3 :** used or involved in the practice of a habit **:** USUAL ⟨~ topic⟩ **4 :** existing as a part of the inward constitution or habit **:** inherent in an individual ⟨~ faith⟩ ⟨~ grace⟩; *also* **:** NATIVE, INBORN ⟨~ tact⟩ **syn** see USUAL

2habitual \"\ *n* -S **:** an habitual offender; *esp* **:** an habitual drunkard, criminal, or user of drugs **:** ADDICT

habitual abortion *n* **:** recurrent abortion in successive pregnancies

habitual criminal *n* **:** one convicted of a crime who has a certain number of prior convictions for offenses of a character specified by statute (as felonies) and is thereby under some statutes subject to an increased penalty (as life imprisonment)

ha·bit·u·al·i·ty \hə,bichəˈwalədē\ *n* -ES **:** the state of being controlled (as in thinking) by old habits

ha·bit·u·al·ly \-lē, -li\ *adv* **1 :** by habit **:** CUSTOMARILY, UNTHINKINGLY **2 :** CONSISTENTLY, PERSISTENTLY, REPEATEDLY, USUALLY

ha·bit·u·al·ness *n* -ES **:** the quality or state of being habitual

1habituate *adj* [LL *habituatus*] *obs* **:** formed by habit **:** HABITUAL

2ha·bit·u·ate \həˈbichə,wāt, *usu* -ād-+V\ *vb* -ED/-ING/-S [LL *habituatus,* past part. of *habituare,* fr. L *habitus* condition, appearance, habit — more at HABIT] *vt* **1 a :** to make familiar to through use or experience **:** ACCUSTOM, FAMILIARIZE **b :** to make acceptable or desirable to through use or experience **:** ADDICT, DEVOTE **2** *obs* **:** to make (an action) habitual **3** *archaic* **:** to go to or be in frequently **:** FREQUENT ~ *vi* **:** to cause habituation ⟨marijuana may be *habituating*⟩

ha·bit·u·a·tion \=,==ˈwāshən\ *n* -S [ME *habituacioun,* fr. ML *habituation-, habituatio,* fr. LL *habituatus* + L *-ion-, -io* -ion] **1 :** the act or process of making habitual or accustomed ⟨the essence of the tragedy of Macbeth — the ~ to crime —T.S. Eliot⟩ **2 a :** tolerance to the effects of a drug acquired through continued use and manifested by decreasing effectiveness of the same amount of drug administered in successive doses ⟨cathartic ~⟩ ⟨narcotic ~⟩ **b :** the psychic or emotional counterpart of acquired tolerance that is manifested by psychologic dependence upon a drug after a period of use — often distinguished from *addiction*

1ha·bit·u·a·tive \=ˈ==,wād·iv\ *adj* [*2habituate* + *-ive*] *of a grammatical form* **:** expressing habitual action or condition — compare INCIPIATIVE

2habituative \"\ *n* -S **:** an habituative form

hab·i·tude \ˈhabə,tüd, -ə,tyüd\ *n* -S [ME *abitude,* fr. MF *habitude,* fr. L *habitudo,* fr. *habitus,* past part. of *habēre* to have, hold — more at GIVE] **1 a** *archaic* **:** native or essential character **:** normal constitution **b** *obs* **:** RELATION, RESPECT **2** *obs* **:** habitual association **:** FAMILIARITY **3 a :** habitual disposition or mode of behavior or procedure ⟨the sense of fitness and proportion that comes with years of ~ in the practice of an art —B.N.Cardozo⟩ **b :** HABIT, CUSTOM ⟨congressional investigation . . . has acquired the sanction of ~ —R.H.Rovere⟩ **syn** see HABIT

hab·i·tu·di·nal \ˌhabəˈtüd(ᵊ)nəl, -əˈtyü-\ *adj* [L *habitudin-, habitudo* + E *-al*] **:** relating to or associated with a habitude ⟨occupational and ~ diseases, such as . . . lead poisoning and extreme obesity —*Quarterly Rev.*⟩

ha·bit·ué \həˈbichə,wā, =,==ˈ=\ *n* -S [F, fr. past part. of *habituer* to frequent, fr. LL *habituare* — more at HABITUATE] **1 :** one who frequents a place ⟨Paris ~s⟩ or class of places ⟨an ~ of the theater⟩ **2 :** ADDICT

hab·i·tus \ˈhabədəs\ *n, pl* **habitus** [NL, fr. L, condition, appearance, character — more at HABIT] **1 a :** the body build and constitution esp. as related to predisposition to disease ⟨ulcer ~⟩ **:** HABIT 4a — see CONSTITUTIONAL TYPE **b :** HABIT 8 **2 a :** a mental power or faculty **b :** HABIT 6a

hab·nab \ˈ(h)ab,nab\ *also* **hab or nab** \ˈ(h)abə(r)ˈnab\ *adv* [fr. (assumed) ME dial. *habbe nabbe, habbe or nabbe* whether he (she, I) has (have) or does (do) not have, fr. ME dial, *habbe,* 1st & 3d pers. sing. pres. subj. of *habben* to have (fr. OE *habban*) + ME *or* + ME dial. *nabbe,* 1st & 3d pers. sing. pres. subj. of *nabben* not to have, fr. OE *nabban,* fr. *ne* not + *habban* to have — more at HAVE, OR, NO] *dial Brit* **:** in one way or another **:** by hook or crook

ha·boob \həˈbüb\ *n* -S [Ar *habūb* violent wind] **:** a violent dust storm or sandstorm of northern Africa or India

habro- *comb form* [NL, fr. L, fr. Gk, fr. *habros*] : graceful — in generic names in zoology ⟨*Habronema*⟩

hab·ro·brac·on \ˌhabrōˈbrakən\ *n* [NL, fr. *habro-* + *Bracon* genus of ichneumon flies — more at BRACONIDAE] **1** *cap* : a genus of very small wasps (family Braconidae) that are parasitic on caterpillars and that are valuable for laboratory studies of genetics **2** -s *often cap* : any insect of the genus *Habrobracon*

hab·ro·ne·ma \-ˈnēmə\ *n, cap* [NL, fr. *habro-* + *-nema*] : a genus of parasitic nematode worms (family Spiruridae) having developmental stages in flies of the genera *Musca* and *Stomoxys* and adult stages in the stomach of the horse or the proventriculus of various birds — see HABRONEMIASIS, SUMMER SORES

hab·ro·ne·mi·a·sis \ˌhabrōnēˈmīəsəs\ *also* **hab·ro·ne·mo·sis** \-ˈmōsəs\ *n* -ES [NL, fr. *Habronema* + *-iasis* or *-osis*] : infestation with or disease caused by roundworms of the genus *Habronema* and characterized in the horse by gastric tumors and inflammation or by summer sores

hab·ro·ne·mic \ˌhabrōˈnēmik\ *adj* [NL *Habronema* + E *-ic*] : relating to or caused by worms of the genus *Habronema*

ha·bu \ˈhä(ˌ)bü\ *n* -s [native name in the Ryukyu islands] : a dangerously venomous pit viper (*Trimeresurus flavoviridis*) common in the Ryukyu islands

ha·bu·ka \ˈhäˌbükə\ *var of* HAPUKU

ha·bu·tai *or* **ha·bu·tae** \ˈhäbəˌtī\ *n* -s [Jap *habutae*, lit., glossy silk] : a soft lightweight Japanese silk in plain weave

ha·ček \ˈhaˌchek\ *n* -s [Czech] : a diacritic ˇ placed over a letter (as in *č, ě, ğ, š*) to modify it : an inverted circumflex — called also *wedge*

ha·cen·da·do \ˌ(h)äsenˈdä(ˌ)dō\ *also* **ha·ci·en·da·do** \-sēe-\ *n* -s [Sp, fr. *hacienda*] : the owner or proprietor of a hacienda : rural landlord : LANDOWNER

ha·cen·de·ro \ˌ(h)äsenˈde(ˌ)rō\ *also* **ha·ci·en·de·ro** \-sēen-\ *n* -s [Sp, fr. *hacienda* + *-ero* -er] : HACENDADO

ha·ché \(h)äˈshā\ *adj* [F, fr. past part. of *hacher* to chop up, mince, hash, hatch (a map) — more at HASH] : MINCED, HASHED

¹ha·chure \haˈshü(ə)r, ˈhashər\ *also* **hatch·ure** \ˈhachə(r)\ *n* -s [F, *hachure*, fr. *hacher* + *-ure*] : a short line used for shading and denoting surfaces in relief (as in map drawing) and drawn in the direction of slope, being short, broad, and close together for a steep slope and long, narrow, and far apart for a gentle slope — compare CONTOUR LINE

²hachure \ˈ"\ *also* **hatchure** \ˈ"\ *vt* -ED/-ING/-S : to shade with or show by hachures — compare CROSSHATCH

h acid *n, usu cap H* : a crystalline acid $H_2NC_{10}H_4(OH)(SO_3H)_2$ made from naphthalene and used as a dye intermediate; 8-amino-1-naphthol-3,6-disulfonic acid

ha·ci·en·da \ˌ(h)äsēˈendə, ˌ(h)as-\ *n* -s [Sp, fr. L *facienda*, things to be done, neut. pl. of *faciendus*, fut. passive part. of *facere* to do, make — more at DO] **1 a** : a large estate (as a ranch or farm) in present or formerly Spanish-speaking countries : PLANTATION **b** : the main building of a farm or ranch **c** : the buildings of a mining or manufacturing establishment **2** *chiefly Southwest* : a ranch dwelling typically with low rambling lines and wide porches **3** : the state revenue or its administration in a Spanish-speaking country ⟨was appointed minister of ~⟩

¹hack \ˈhak\ *vb* -ED/-ING/-S [ME *hakken*, fr. OE *-haccian* (attested in *tōhaccian* to chop to pieces); akin to MLG *hacken* to hack, OHG *hacchōn*, OE *haca* door fastener, ON *haka* chin — more at HOOK] *vt* **1 a** : to cut with repeated irregular or unskillful blows ⟨was ~*ed* to pieces with swords⟩ ⟨plaster had been ~*ed* out of the wall⟩ **b** : to sever with repeated blows ⟨~*ed* off a bough with his hunting knife⟩ **c** : to mangle or mutilate with or as if with cutting blows ⟨we ~*ed* reputations to pieces —H.J.Laski⟩ ⟨the original story had been ~*ed* almost beyond recognition⟩ **d** : to trim or shape by or as if by crude or ruthless strokes ⟨lyrical expressions ~*ed* out with broad strokes of a brush charged with pure color —F.J.Mather⟩ ⟨huge sums were ~*ed* off the original appropriation⟩ **2** : to clear (a path or area) by cutting away vegetation ⟨~*ed* their way through the jungle⟩ ⟨farms ~*ed* out of the wilderness⟩ **3 a** : to break up the surface of (land) **b** : to break up the soil and sow (seed) at the same operation — used with *in* ⟨~ in wheat⟩ **c** : to cut, trim, or uproot with a hack, hook, or sickle **4** : CHIP *vt* 4 **5 a** : to roughen or dress (stone or concrete) with a hack hammer **b** : to tilt (a face brick) slightly in a wall so that the bottom is set in to prevent shadows **c** : to interrupt (a course of stones) by the use of two smaller courses in walling **6** : to kick the shins of (an opposing player) in rugby **7** *chiefly Midland* **a** : ACHIEVE, MANAGE ⟨I can't quite ~ it⟩ **b** : to put up with : TOLERATE ⟨I can't ~ something like stealing —B.J.Friedman⟩ **8** : to call out or give directions to (a bird dog) **9** : to enter (a gamecock) in a single match **10** *chiefly Midland* : to disconcert and embarrass esp. by teasing : HECKLE ⟨he was so ~*ed* he could hardly talk⟩ ~ *vi* **1** : to make cutting blows or rough cuts : CHOP ⟨~*ing* away at the vines and shrubs⟩ **2** *now dial Eng* : to speak haltingly : STAMMER **3** : to cough in a short dry manner : cause short dry coughing ⟨a ~*ing* asthma⟩ **4 a** : to kick or kick at a rugby opponent's shins deliberately **b** : to strike or hold the arm of a basketball opponent with the hand **5** *slang* : LOAF, IDLE, KNOCK — used with *around* ⟨~*ing* around at the corner drugstore —Ruth McKenney⟩

²hack \ˈ"\ *n* -s [ME *hak*; akin to MHG & MD *hacke* mattock, hoe, pickax; derivatives fr. the root of E ¹*hack*] **1** : a tool or implement for hacking (as a pick, mattock, or hoe) **2** : CUT, NICK, NOTCH; *esp* : a blaze cut in a tree **3** *now dial Eng* : a stumbling or stammering in speech **4** : a short dry cough **5 a** : a hacking blow ⟨a vicious ~ across the neck stunned him⟩ **b** : TRY, ATTEMPT, TURN, WHACK ⟨let me take a ~ at it⟩ **c** : an individual match of gamecocks **6** : a kick on the shins in rugby **7** : a foothold cut in the ice four yards behind the tee in curling **8 a** *chiefly Midland* : a state of embarrassed confusion — often used with *under* ⟨he put Joe under ~ teasing him about his girl⟩ **b** : restriction to quarters as punishment for naval officers — usu. used with *under* ⟨he had some of the officers under ~ and some of the crew grumbling —Fletcher Pratt⟩

³hack \ˈ"\ *n* -s [blend of ¹*hatch* and ¹*heck*] **1 a** : the board on which a falcon's meat is served **b** : the state of partial liberty in which a falcon is kept before training — used chiefly with *at* ⟨kept at ~⟩ ⟨flying at ~⟩ **2** : FRAME, GRATING: as **a** : a frame for drying fish or cheese **b** : a rack for feeding cattle **c** : a grating in a millrace or above a dam **3** : a long low pile into which bricks are built for drying after being molded

⁴hack \ˈ"\ *vt* -ED/-ING/-S **1** : to keep (a hawk) in a state of partial liberty **2** : to put (fish or cheese) on a frame for drying

⁵hack \ˈ"\ *n* -s [short for *hackney*] **1 a** (1) : a horse let out for common hire (2) : a horse used in all kinds of work **b** : a horse worn out in service : JADE **c** : a light easy saddle horse; *esp* : a three-gaited saddle horse **2 a** : a coach or carriage let for hire : HACKNEY ⟨on horse, on foot, in ~*s* and gilded chariots —Alexander Pope⟩ **b** *slang* : HEARSE **c** (1) : TAXICAB (2) : CABDRIVER **d** *slang* : CABOOSE **3 a** : one who hires out his professional service : one who forfeits individual freedom of action or initiative or professional integrity in exchange for wages or other assured reward : HIRELING, MERCENARY ⟨party ~*s* have replaced earnest New Dealers —*New Republic*⟩; *esp* : a writer who works on order from publishers **b** : a writer whose writings aim mainly at commercial success rather than literary quality **c** *slang* : a prison guard or custodian **4** : a watch or inferior chronometer for use in place of the standard chronometer in marking time when taking observations at sea

⁶hack \ˈ"\ *adj* **1** : working for hire ⟨~ attorney⟩ ⟨~ critic⟩ **2** : performed by, suited to, or characteristic of a hack : MEDIOCRE, UNINSPIRED ⟨~ writing⟩ ⟨the staging and lighting were mostly on a ~ level —*New Republic*⟩ **3** : HACKNEYED, TRITE ⟨~ dramatic scenes⟩

⁷hack \ˈ"\ *vb* -ED/-ING/-S *vt* **1** : to make trite and commonplace by frequent and indiscriminate use ⟨the word "remarkable" has been so ~*ed* —J.H.Newman⟩ **2** *archaic* : to employ as a hack writer **3** : to use as a hack : let out (as a horse) for hire ~ *vi* **1** : to ride or drive at an ordinary pace or over the roads as distinguished from racing or riding across country **2** : to become exposed or offered to common use for hire ⟨was then ~*ed* in the park for a year before going to stud —Dennis Craig⟩ **3** : to live the life of a literary drudge or hack : do hack writing **4** : to ride in a hackney coach or in a taxicab **5** : to operate a taxicab

hackamatak *var of* HACKMATACK

hack·a·more \ˈhakəˌmō(ə)r, -ō(ə)r, -ōə, -ō(ə)\ *n* -s [by folk etymology fr. Sp *jáquima*, fr. OSp *xaquima*, fr. Ar *shakīmah*] **1** : a bridle that consists of a halter often of soft rope or braided horsehair, has a loop capable of being tightened about the nose in place of a bit, and is used esp. in breaking and training horses **2** : a primitive or emergency bridle consisting of a continuous length of rope or rawhide with a slip noose at one end that is passed over the lower jaw, the free end being looped over the head behind the ears and slipped through the noose on the opposite side so as to serve as a single rein

hackamore knot *n* : a knot that consists of a loop formed by concentric hitches and is used as a sling for a jug or bottle or as a rope bridle for a horse

hackbarrow \ˈ=ˌ=(ˌ)=\ *n* [³*hack* + *barrow*] : a barrow for taking bricks from the molders to the hacks

hackberry \ˈhak- — *see* BERRY\ *n* [alter. of *hagberry*] **1** : any of several No. American trees or shrubs of the genus *Celtis*; *esp* : a large round-headed tree (*C. occidentalis*) of eastern and central U.S. that has dark purple edible berries and is sometimes planted for shade or in shelterbelts — called also *sugarberry* **2** : the pale to grayish or greenish yellow moderately hard tough wood of hackberry (esp. *C. occidentalis*)

hackamore knot

hack·but \ˈhakˌbət\ *or* **hag·but** \-ag,-\ *n* -s [MF *haguebute*, *hacquebute*, modif. of MD *hakebusse* — more at HARQUEBUS] : HARQUEBUS

hack·but·eer \ˌhakbəˈti(ə)r\ *or* **hack·but·ter** \ˈhakˌbəd·ə(r)\ *n* -s [MF *haquebutier*, *hacquebutier*, fr. *haquebute*, *hacquebute* + *-ier* -er] : a soldier armed with a hackbut

hacked *past of* HACK

hacked bolt *n* [fr. past part. of ¹*hack*] : JAG BOLT

hack·ee \ˈhakē\ *n* -s [prob. of imit. origin] : CHIPMUNK

¹hack·er \ˈhakə(r)\ *n* -s [¹*hack* + *-er* (n. suffix)] **1** : one that hacks: as **a** *dial Eng* : a hand implement or hooked fork for grubbing out roots **b** : one that handles green brick in ceramics manufacturing **c** : CHIPPER d **2** : one who is inexperienced or unskilled in a sport ⟨an insouciance and grace in the man's movements which mean the difference between a willing courageous ~ . . . and a great artist —Barnaby Conrad⟩

²hacker \ˈ"\ *vi* -ED/-ING/-S [¹*hack* + *-er* (v. suffix)] *dial Eng* : to hesitate in speaking : STAMMER

³hacker \ˈ"\ *n* -s [⁵*hack* + *-er*] : CABDRIVER

hack·ery \ˈhakərē\ *n* -ES [perh. fr. Bengali *hākārī* shouting (of drivers), fr. *hākā* shout] *India* : a bullock cart

hack hammer *n* [²*hack*] : a hammer that resembles an adz and is used in dressing stone and roughening

hack·ia \ˈhakēə\ *n* -s [fr. a native name in Brit. Guiana] : any of several tropical American trees (as of the genus *Tabebuia*) that yield notably hard heavy durable timber

hack·ie \ˈhakē, -ki\ *n* -s [⁵*hack* + *-ie*] : CABDRIVER

hacking *n* -s [fr. gerund of ¹*hack*] : the system of low cuts or scratches and grooves in a lap to hold diamond powder for cutting and polishing gems

hacking coat *or* **hacking jacket** *n* [fr. pres. part. of ⁷*hack*] : a riding jacket with slits at the side or at the back and slanted flap pockets

hacking knife *n* [fr. pres. part. of ¹*hack*] : a knife with a short blade and stout handle used for rough work (as removing old putty)

hack·ing·ly *adv* : in a hacking manner

¹hack·le \ˈ(h)akəl\ *n* -s [ME *hakel*, fr. OE *hacele* cloak; akin to OHG *hachul* mantle, ON *hökull*, Goth *hakuls*, and prob. to OE *hēcen* kid, MLG *hōken* kid, OSlav *koza* goat] *now dial Eng* : any of various coverings: as **a** : the natural coat of an animal **b** : a bird's plumage **c** : a straw covering for a bee skep

²hackle \ˈ"\ *vt* -ED/-ING/-S *dial Eng* : to cover with a hackle

³hack·le \ˈhakəl\ *n* -s [ME *hakell*, *hekele* — more at HATCHEL] **1** : a comb or board with long metal teeth for dressing flax, hemp, or jute **2 a** : one of the long narrow feathers on the neck or saddle of a bird (as the domestic fowl) **b** : the neck plumage of the male domestic fowl — see COCK illustration **3 hackles** *pl* **a** : erectile hairs along the neck and back of a dog or other animal **b** : TEMPER, DANDER ⟨don't get your ~*s* up about nothing⟩ **4 a** *or* **hackle fly** : an artificial fishing fly made chiefly of the filaments of a cock's neck feathers **b** : filaments of cock feather projecting downward from the head of an artificial fly — see FLY illustration

⁴hackle \ˈ"\ *vt* **hackled**; **hackled**; **hackling** \-k(ə)liŋ\ **hackles** **1** : to separate the long fibers of (flax, hemp, or jute) from waste material and from each other by combing with a hackle **2** : to furnish (a fishing fly) with a hackle

⁵hackle \ˈ"\ *vt* -ED/-ING/-S [freq. of ¹*hack*] : to chop up or chop off roughly : HACK

⁶hackle \ˈ"\ *n* -s *often attrib* : fracture (as of glass) that results in hackly edges ⟨the coarser the ~ the more violent and sudden was the parting of the glass —C.J.Phillips⟩ ⟨~ marks⟩ ⟨~ structure⟩

hackleback \ˈ==ˌ=\ *n* -s [³*hackle* + *back*] **1** *also* **hackleback sturgeon** [so called fr. the projecting scales on its back] : SHOVELNOSE STURGEON **2** : an untrimmed barrel stave

hack·ler \ˈhak(ə)lə(r)\ *n* -s [⁴*hackle* + *-er*] : one that hackles; *esp* : a worker who hackles hemp, flax, or broomcorn

hacklog \ˈ=ˌ=\ *n* [¹*hack* + *log*] : CHOPPING BLOCK

hack·ly \ˈhak(ə)lē, -li\ *adj, sometimes* -ER/-EST [⁵*hackle* + *-y*] : looking as if hacked : ROUGH, JAGGED, BROKEN ⟨~ fracture surface of a mineral⟩

hack·man \ˈhakmən\ *n, pl* **hackmen** [⁵*hack* + *man*] : CABDRIVER

hack·man·ite \ˈhakməˌnīt\ *n* -s [Victor *Hackman*, 19th cent. Finnish scientist + E *-ite*] : a sodalite containing a little sulfur and usu. fluorescing orange or red under ultraviolet light

¹hack·ma·tack \ˈhakməˌtak\ *n* -s [of Algonquian origin; akin to Abnaki *akemantak* snowshoe wood] **1** : any of several coniferous trees: as **a** : a tamarack (*Larix laricina*) **b** : COMMON JUNIPER **2** : the wood of hackmatack **3** : BALSAM POPLAR

²hackmatack \ˈ"\ *also* **hack·a·ma·tak** \-kəm-\ *n* -s [alter. of *tacamahac*] : a tree (*Calophyllum tacamahaca*) that produces tacamahac

¹hack·ney \ˈhaknē, -ni\ *n* [ME *hakeney*, *hakenai*, prob. fr. *Hakeneye* Hackney, formerly a town, now a metropolitan borough of London, England] **1** -s **a** : a horse suitable for ordinary riding or driving : NAG **b** : a trotting horse used chiefly for driving **2 a** *usu cap* : a breed of rather compact usu. chestnut, bay, or brown horses with a conspicuously high knee and hock flexion in stepping that originated in and about Norfolk, England as a result of interbreeding local trotting mares with Thoroughbred and Arabian sires **b** -s *often cap* : a horse of this breed **3** -s **a** *obs* : a horse or pony kept for hire **b** *obs* : one that works for hire : DRUDGE, SLAVE **c** *obs* : PROSTITUTE **4** -s : a carriage or automobile kept for hire : HACK, CAB

²hackney \ˈ"\ *adj* **1** : kept for public hire ⟨~ cab⟩ ⟨~ carriage⟩ **2** : HACKNEYED **3** *archaic* : done or suitable for doing by a drudge

³hackney \ˈ"\ *vt* -ED/-ING/-S **1 a** : to make common or frequent use of (as a horse) : wear out in common service **b** : to make trite, vulgar, or commonplace **2** *obs* : to ride hard : wear out by driving **3** *archaic* **a** : to make coarse (the sensibilities) **b** : to make sophisticated or jaded (as through worldly experience) ⟨~*ed* as he was in the ways of life —Tobias Smollett⟩

hackney coach *n* : a coach used as a hackney carriage; *esp* : a four-wheeled carriage drawn by two horses and having seats for six persons

hackneyed *adj* [fr. past part. of ³*hackney*] : COMMONPLACE ⟨~ phrase⟩ ⟨~ metaphor⟩ ⟨histrionic rhetoric and ~ gesture —H.V.Gregory⟩ **syn** see TRITE

hack·ney·man \ˈhaknēmən, -nim-\ *n, pl* **hackneymen** [ME *hakeneyman*, fr. *hakeney* + *man*] : a man who hires out horses and carriages

hackney pony *n, often cap H* : a Hackney horse less than 14.2 hands high

hacks *pres 3d sing of* HACK, *pl of* HACK

hacksaw \ˈ=ˌ=\ *n* [¹*hack* + *saw*] : a hand or power-driven fine-tooth saw with blade under tension in a bow-shaped frame for cutting metal or other hard materials

hacksaws

hackster *n* -s [¹*hack* + *-ster*] **1** *obs* : RUFFIAN, ASSASSIN **2** *obs* : PROSTITUTE

hack·thorn \ˈhakˌthȯrn\ *n* [part modif., part trans. of Afrik *haakdoring*, fr. *haak* hook + *doring* thorn] : a southern African wattle (*Acacia detinens*)

hacktree \ˈ=ˌ=\ *n* [*hackberry* + *tree*] : HACKBERRY 1

hack watch *n* [⁵*hack*] : a watch having a device for stopping the balance so that the hour, minute, and sweep-second hands may be reset at a desired instant — compare ⁵HACK 4

hackwork \ˈ=ˌ=\ *n* [⁶*hack* + *work*] : literary, artistic, or other professional work done on order or according to formula or conformity with commercial standards of quality; *esp* : work done by a hack writer ⟨the evil effect of ~ and two wars upon an outstanding talent —V.S.Pritchett⟩

hacky \ˈhakē\ *adj* -ER/-EST [¹*hack* + *-y*] : HACKING ⟨a ~ cough⟩

hacqueton *var of* HAQUETON

had *past of* HAVE — see PAST PERFECT

ha·da·da \ˈhadədə\ *n* -s [Afrik *hadida*, of imit. origin] : HADEDAH IBIS

hadarim *pl of* HEDER

had·bot *or* **had·bote** \ˈhädˌbōt\ *n* s [OE *hādbōt*, fr. *hād* person, degree + *bōt* remedy, recompense — more at -HOOD, BOOT] : recompense demanded under old English law for violence or insult to a person in holy orders

hadden *Scot past part of* HOLD

had·der \ˈhädər\ *chiefly Scot var of* HEATHER

haddest *archaic past 2d sing of* HAVE

had·die \ˈhädi\ *n* -s [by alter.] *Scot* : HADDOCK

had·ding·ton·shire \ˈhadiŋtənˌshi(ə)r, -ˌshər\ *or* **haddington** *adj, usu cap* [fr. *Haddingtonshire* or *Haddington* county (now usu. called *East Lothian*), Scotland] : EAST LOTHIAN

had·do \ˈha(ˌ)dō\ *n* -s [Nisqualli *huddoh*] : HUMPBACK SALMON

had·dock \ˈhadək\ *n, pl* **haddock** *also* **haddocks** [ME *haddok*] **1** : an important food fish (*Melanogrammus aeglefinus*) of the family Gadidae that is usu. smaller than the common cod, has a black lateral line and a dark spot just behind the gills, and occurs on both sides of the Atlantic from Iceland south to the Mediterranean and Cape Hatteras **2 a** : HAKE **b** : ROSEFISH

had·dock·er \-kə(r)\ *n* -s : one that fishes for haddock

¹hade \ˈ(h)ād\ *n* -s [origin unknown] *now dial Eng* : an unplowed strip left between plowed parts of a field

²hade \ˈhād\ *vi* -ED/-ING/-S [origin unknown] : to deviate from the vertical (as of a vein, fault, or lode)

³hade \ˈ"\ *n* -s : the angle made by a rock fault plane or a vein with the vertical

ha·de·an \(ˈ)hāˈdēən\ *adj, usu cap* : of, relating to, or characteristic of Hades

ha·de·dah ibis \ˈhadədə-\ *n* [Afrik *hadida*, of imit. origin] : a largely grayish brown African ibis (*Hagedashia hagedash*) having the wing coverts tinged with iridescent green

ha·den·doa *or* **ha·den·do·wa** \həˈdendəwə\ *n, pl* **hadendoa** *or* **hadendoas** *or* **hadendowa** *or* **hadendowas** *usu cap* **1** : a chiefly nomadic Beja-speaking people of Nubia between the Nile and the Red sea related to the Beni Amer and Bisharin **2** : a member of the Hadendoa people

ha·des \ˈhāˌdēz\ *n, pl* **hades** *usu cap* [fr. *Hades*, god of the underworld, abode of the dead in Greek mythology, fr. Gk *Haidēs*, *Aidēs*] **1** : the abode or state of the dead : the place of departed spirits — compare NETHERWORLD, SHEOL **2** : HELL ⟨go to ~⟩ ⟨hotter than ~ out on the firing range⟩ ⟨what in ~ are you doing here⟩

hadfield manganese steel \ˈhadˌfēl(d)-\ *n, usu cap H* [after Sir Robert *Hadfield* †1940 Eng. metallurgist] : a wear-resistant austenitic steel containing about 12 percent manganese and 1.2 percent carbon

¹ha·dhra·mau·tian *or* **ha·dra·mau·tian** \ˌhädrəˈmȯshən\ *adj, usu cap* [*Hadhramaut*, *Hadramaut*, region of southeastern Arabia + E *-ian*] : of, relating to, or characteristic of the land, people, or dialect of Hadhramaut in southeastern Arabia

²hadhramautian *or* **hadramautian** \ˈ"\ *n* -s *usu cap* : HADHRAMI

ha·dhra·mau·tic \-ȯd·ik\ *n* -s *usu cap* [*Hadhramaut* + E *-ic*] : the Arabic dialect of Hadhramaut

ha·dhra·mi *or* **ha·dra·mi** \ˈhädrəmē\ *n, pl* **hadhrami** *also* **hadhramis** *or* **hadrami** *also* **hadramis** *usu cap* **1** : an Arabian theocratic people living in the region between Aden and Oman in southern Arabia **2** : a member of the Hadhrami people

hading *n* -s [fr. gerund of ²*hade*] : ³HADE

ha·dith \həˈdēth\ *also* **ha·dit** \-ēt\ *n, pl* **hadith** *or* **hadiths** *also* **hadit** *or* **hadits** *often cap* [Ar *hadīth*] **1** : a narrative record of the sayings or customs of Muhammad and his companions **2** : the collective body of traditions relating to Muhammad and his companions

hadj *var of* HAJJ

hadj·e·mi *or* **haj·e·mi** \ˈhajəmē\ *n* -s *cap* [Per] : a Persian of mixed Iranian and Turkish or Turkic stock

hadji *var of* HAJI

had·land \ˈ(h)adlənd\ *dial Eng var of* HEADLAND

had·ley chest \ˈhadlē-\ *n, usu cap H* [fr. *Hadley*, Mass.] : an Early American chest that has three panels in the front, a well, and one, two, or rarely three drawers and that is ornamented over the entire front with flat carving usu. involving a tulip motif and sometimes including the initials of the owner

had·na \ˈhadnə\ [by alter.] *Scot* : had not

hadn't \ˈhadᵊn(t)\ [by contr.] : had not

hadn't ought *chiefly dial* : ought not — usu. used with *to* ⟨you really *hadn't ought* to do that⟩

had ought *chiefly dial* : OUGHT — usu. used with *to* ⟨I *had ought* to go but I don't want to⟩

hadr- *or* **hadro-** *comb form* [NL, fr. L, fr. Gk, fr. *hadros* thick, bulky; akin to Gk *hadēn* enough — more at SAD] : thick ⟨*hadrome*⟩ : heavy ⟨*Hadrosaurus*⟩

had·rome \ˈhaˌdrōm\ *also* **had·rom** \ˈhadrəm\ *n* -s [G *hadrom*, fr. *hadr-* + *-om* -ome] **1** : the part of the mestome that conducts water **2** : the somewhat rudimentary xylem in cryptogams

had·ro·me·ri·na \ˌhadrōməˈrīnə\ *n pl, cap* [NL, fr. *hadr-* + *mer-* (part) + *-ina*] : an order of Demospongiae including the boring sponges

had·ro·mycosis \ˌhadrō+\ *n* [NL, fr. *hadr-* + *mycosis*] : infestation of the xylem of a plant by a fungus; *also* : a plant disease due to such a cause

had·ro·my·cot·ic \ˌhadrō(ˌ)mīˈkäd·ik\ *adj* [fr. NL *hadromycosis*, after such pairs as NL *psychosis*: E *psychotic*] : relating to or caused by hadromycosis

had·ro·saur \ˈhadrəˌsȯ(ə)r, -ȯ(ə)\ *n* -s [NL *Hadrosaurus*] : a dinosaur of the genus *Hadrosaurus* or family Hadrosauridae : DUCK-BILLED DINOSAUR

had·ro·sau·rus \ˌ==ˈsȯrəs\ *n, cap* [NL, fr. *hadr-* + *-saurus*] : a genus (the type of a family Hadrosauridae) of heavy herbivorous dinosaurs found in the Cretaceous of No. America that attained a length of over thirty feet and had a large head with a broad bill like that of a duck and numerous small teeth

hadst *archaic past 2d sing of* HAVE

hae *chiefly Scot var of* HAVE & *chiefly Scot pres 1st sing & pres pl & Scot pres 2d sing of* HAVE

haec·ce·i·tas \hekˈsēəˌtas, hēk-\ *n* -ES [ML] : HAECCEITY

haec·ce·i·ty *or* **hec·ce·i·ty** \-əd·ē\ *n* -ES [ML *haecceitas*, fr. L *haec*, *haecce*, fem. of *hic*, *hicce* this + *-itas* -ity] : the status of being an individual or a particular nature : INDIVIDUALITY, SPECIFICITY, THISNESS; *specif* : what makes something to be an ultimate reality different from any other — compare QUIDDITY 2

¹haeck·e·li·an \(ˈ)heˌkēlēən\ *adj, usu cap* [Ernst H. *Haeckel* †1919, Ger. biologist + E *-ian*] : relating to Haeckel or his theories — compare RECAPITULATION THEORY

²haeckelian \ˈ"\ *n* -s *usu cap* : a believer in Haeckel's theories

haeck·el·ism \'hekə,lizəm\ *n* -s *usu cap* [Ernst H. *Haeckel* + E *-ism*] **:** Haeckel's theories and speculations
haed *past of* HA, *Scot past of* HAVE
haeing *Scot pres part of* HAVE
haeltzuk *usu cap, var of* HEILTSUK
haem *var of* HEME
haem- *or* **haemo-** — see HEM-
haema- — see HEMA-
hae·ma·dip·sa \,hēmə'dipsə, ,hem-\ *n, cap* [NL, fr. *hem-* + Gk *dipsa* thirst] **:** a genus of small tropical land leeches that are troublesome to men and animals esp. because their bites result in prolonged bleeding
hae·ma·go·gus \-'gōgəs\ *n, cap* [NL, fr. LL, adj., drawing off blood, fr. Gk *haimagōgos*, fr. *haim-* hem- + *-agōgos* (fr. *agein* to lead, drive) — more at AGENT] **:** a genus of strong-flying diurnal Neotropical mosquitoes including several vectors of jungle yellow fever
hae·ma·moe·ba \-'mēbə\ [NL, fr. *hem-* + *amoeba*] *syn of* PLASMODIUM
hae·man·thus \hē'man(t)thəs\ *n, cap* [NL, fr. *hem-* + *-anthus;* fr. the color of some of the flowers] **:** a genus of African bulbous herbs (family Amaryllidaceae) comprising the blood lilies and having flowers in a dense head with a whorl of colored spathes
hae·ma·phy·sa·lis \,hēmə'fīsələs, ,hem-\ *n, cap* [NL, fr. *hem-* + Gk *physallis* bladder] **:** a cosmopolitan genus of small eyeless ticks (family Ixodidae) some of which are disease carriers
haemat- *or* **haemato-** — see HEMAT-
hae·mat·i·num \hē'madənəm\ *also* **hae·mat·i·non** \-d·ə-,nän\ *n* -s [NL, fr. neut. of L *haematinus* blood-colored, fr. Gk *haimatinos* bloody, fr. *haimat-* hemat- + *-inos* -ine] **:** a hard opaque red glass made by the ancients; *also* **:** a modern imitation of this
hae·ma·to·bran·chia \,hēməd·ō'braŋkēə, ,hem-\ *n pl, cap* [NL, fr. *hemat-* + *-branchia*] *in some classifications* **:** a division of arthropods consisting of the trilobites, eurypterids, and king crabs — **haem·a·to·branch·i·ate** \¦==¦braŋkēət, -ē,āt\ *adj*
hae·ma·to·do·cha \,hēməd·ō'dōkə, ,hem-, hē,mad·ə'-\ *n* -s [NL, fr. *hemat-* + Gk *dochē* receptacle] **:** a fibrous elastic sac in the palpus of male spiders that is distended with hemolymph during pairing
hae·ma·to·pi·nus \-'pīnəs\ *n, cap* [NL, fr. *hemat-* + *-pinus* (fr. Gk *pinein* to drink)] **:** a genus of sucking lice including various serious pests of domestic animals
hae·mat·o·pus \hē'mad·əpəs\ *n, cap* [NL, fr. *hemat-* + *-pus*] **:** a genus (the type of the family Haematopodidae) of shorebirds consisting of the oyster catchers
hae·ma·tox·y·lon \,hēmə'täksə,län, ,hem-\ *n* [NL, fr. *hemat-* + *-xylon;* fr. its red color] **1** *cap* **:** a genus of tropical American bushy and usu. thorny trees (family Leguminosae) having pinnate leaves and small yellow flowers borne in showy axillary racemes — see LOGWOOD **2** -s **:** the wood or dye of logwood
-hae·mia \'hēmēə\ — see -EMIA
haemin *var of* HEMIN
hae·mo·bartonella \¦hēmō, ¦hemō+\ *n* [NL, fr. *hemat-* + *Bartonella*] **1** *cap* **:** a genus of rickettsiae (family Anaplasmataceae) that are blood parasites in various mammals **2** *pl* **haemobartonellae :** any rickettsia of the genus *Haemobartonella*
hae·mo·do·ra·ce·ae \,hēmōdə'rāsē,ē, ,hem-\ *n pl, cap* [NL, fr. *Haemodorum*, type genus (fr. *hem-* + Gk *dōron* gift) + *-aceae*] **:** a family of chiefly tropical plants (order Liliales) having flowers with three stamens and an inferior ovary arranged in a complex paniculate inflorescence — **hae·mo·do·ra·ceous** \¦===¦rāshəs\ *adj*
haemoglobin *var of* HEMOGLOBIN
hae·mo·gregarina \¦hēmō, ¦hemō+\ *n, cap* [NL, fr. *hem-* + *Gregarina*] **:** a genus (the type of the family Haemogregarinidae) of coccidia that are parasites at different stages of their life cycle of the circulatory system of vertebrates and of the digestive tract of invertebrates — **hae·mo·gregarine** *or* **he·mo·gregarine** \"+\ *adj or n*
hae·mon·cho·sis \,hē,mäŋ'kōsəs\ *or* **hae·mon·chi·a·sis** \,hē,mäŋ'kīəsəs\ *n* -ES [NL, fr. *Haemonchus* + *-osis* or *-iasis*] **:** infestation with or disease caused by worms of the genus *Haemonchus* (esp. *H. contortus*), being typically characterized by anemia, digestive disturbances, and emaciation resulting from the bloodsucking habits of the worms
hae·mon·chus \hē'mäŋkəs\ *n, cap* [NL, fr. *hem-* + *-onchus* (irreg. fr. Gk *onkos* barb of an arrow)] **:** a widely distributed genus of nematode worms (family Trichostrongylidae) comprising chiefly a parasite (*H. contortus*) of the abomasum of sheep and other ruminants and rarely in man — see HAEMONCHOSIS
haem·op·is \hē'mäpəs\ *n, cap* [NL, fr. *hem-* + *-opis*] **:** a genus of large aquatic leeches (family Hirudinidae) that have few teeth or none and feed chiefly on small aquatic invertebrates
hae·mo·pro·te·id \,hēmō'prōd·ēəd, ,hem-\ *adj* [NL *Haemoproteidae*] **:** of or relating to the Haemoproteidae or to protozoans of this family
hae·mo·pro·te·i·dae \,hēmō(,)prō'tēə,dē, ,hem-\ *n pl, cap* [NL, fr. *Haemoproteus*, type genus + *-idae*] **:** a family of Haemosporidia related to the malarial parasites but having the schizogenous phases typically in visceral endothelium of various birds and including the two genera *Haemoproteus* and *Leucocytozoon*
hae·mo·proteus \¦hēmō, ¦hemō+\ *n, cap* [NL, fr. *hem-* + *Proteus*] **:** a genus of protozoan parasites occurring in the blood of certain birds (as pigeons)
haem·or·rha·gia \,hemə'rājēə\ *n* -s [L — more at HEMORRHAGE] **:** HEMORRHAGE
hae·mo·spo·rid·ia \,hēmōspə'ridēə, ,hem-\ *n pl, cap* [NL, fr. *hem-* + *-sporidia*] **:** an order of minute telosporidian protozoans parasitic at some stage of the life cycle in the blood cells of vertebrates that includes the malaria parasites (family Plasmodiidae), numerous bird parasites (family Haemoproteidae), and the piroplasms and related pathogens of cattle (family Babesiidae) — **hae·mo·spo·rid·ian** \¦===¦ridēən\ *adj or n*
hae·mu·li·dae \hē'mjülə,dē\ [NL, fr. *Haemulon*, type genus (fr. *hem-* + Gk *oulon* gum) + *-idae*] *syn of* POMADASIDAE
haen *chiefly Scot past part of* HAVE
haereditas *var of* HEREDITAS
ha·e·re·mai \'hīä,rä'mī(,)ē, 'hīərə,mī\ *interj* [Maori, lit., come here] *Austral & NewZeal* — used to express welcome
haeres *var of* HERES
haes *Scot pres 3d sing of* HAVE
haet \'hāt\ *n* -s [contr. of *hae it* (in such phrases as *Deil hae it!* Devil take it!)] *chiefly Scot* **:** a small quantity **:** PARTICLE **:** WHIT
haff \'häf\ *n* -s [G, fr. LG, fr. MLG *haf* sea — more at HAVEN] **:** a long shallow lagoon separated from the open sea by a narrow sandbar or barrier beach (as on the Baltic coast of Germany)
haf·fet *or* **haf·fit** \'hafət\ *n* -s [ME (Sc dial.) *halfheid*, fr. *half* + *heid*, Sc var. of *hed* head — more at HEAD] *Scot* **:** CHEEK, TEMPLE; *esp* **:** the hair growing at the temple
haff·lins \'häflənz\ *var of* HALFLINGS
ha·fiz \'häfəz\ *n, pl* **hafiz** *or* **hafis** \-əs\ [Ar *ḥāfiẓ*, lit., one who remembers] **:** a Muslim who knows the Koran by heart — used as a title of respect
haf·ner ware \'häfnə(r)-\ *n, usu cap H* [G *hafnerware* pottery fr. *hafner* potter + *ware*] **:** mid-16th century German earthenware often in the form of stove tiles and heavy vessels
haf·ni·um \'hafnēəm\ *n* -s [NL, fr. *Hafnia* (Copenhagen), Denmark] **:** a high-melting gray tetravalent metallic element closely resembling zirconium chemically, occurring in most zirconium minerals, and useful because of its ready emission of electrons (as in filaments for incandescent lamps) — symbol *Hf;* see ELEMENT table
¹haft \'haft, 'hȧft\ *n* -s [ME, fr. OE *hæft;* akin to OE *hæft* bond, fetter, captive, OHG *haft* fetter, captivity, *hefti* handle, ON *hapt* fetter, *hepti* handle, Goth *-hafts* burdened, *-hafjan* to carry — more at HEAVE] **:** the handle of a weapon (as a sword or dagger) or tool (as a sickle, awl, file)
²haft \"\ *vt* -ED/-ING/-S [ME *haften*, fr. *haft*, n.] **:** to set in or furnish with a haft ⟨~ a dagger⟩
³haft \'(h)aft\ *vt* -ED/-ING/-S [prob. of Scand origin; akin to ON *hefthka* to gain (land) by right of occupation, *hefth* possession, act of gaining by occupation, ON *hafa* to have — more at HAVE] **1** *dial Brit* **:** to accustom (sheep) to a different pasture **2** *dial Brit* **:** to settle or establish esp. in a place of residence ⟨we are now nicely ~*ed* here⟩
⁴haft \"\ *n* -s **1** *dial Brit* **:** an established pasture **2** *dial Brit* **:** a dwelling place
haf·ta·rah *or* **haph·ta·rah** *or* **haf·to·rah** *or* **haph·to·rah** \,häftə'rä, häf'tōrə\ *n, pl* **hafta·roth** \,häftə'rōth\ *or* **hafta·rot** \-ōt\ *or* **haftarahs** *or* **haphtaroth** *or* **haphtarot** *or* **haphtarahs** *or* **haftoroth** *or* **haftorot** *or* **haftorahs** *or* **haphtoroth** *or* **haphtorot** *or* **haphtorahs** [Heb *haphṭārāh* conclusion] **:** one of the biblical selections esp. from the Books of the Prophets bearing on and read immediately after the parashah in the Jewish synagogue service on sabbaths, festivals, and fast days
¹hag \'hag, -aa(ə)g, -aig\ *n* -s [ME *hagge, hegge*, prob. fr. a shortened form of OE *hægtesse* harpy, witch; akin to MD *haghetisse* witch, OHG *hagzissa, hagazussa* harpy, witch; all fr. a prehistoric WGmc compound whose components are akin respectively to OE *haga* hedge and to G dial. (Westphalia) *dǖs* devil; akin to Norw *tysja* elf, crippled woman, Gaulish *dusius* demon, incubus, Corn *dus, diz* devil, OE *dūst* dust — more at HEDGE, DUST] **1** *archaic* **a :** a female demon **:** FURY, HARPY **b :** an evil or frightening spirit **:** ELF, BOGEY, HOBGOBLIN ⟨blue meager ~, or stubborn unlaid ghost —John Milton⟩ **c :** NIGHTMARE **2 :** a woman who has compacted with the devil **:** WITCH ⟨you secret, black and midnight ~s —Shak.⟩ **3 a :** an ugly or evil-looking old woman **b :** a woman of haggard or slatternly appearance **c** *obs* **:** an old man **4 :** HAGFISH **5** [by shortening] **:** HAGDON
²hag \'(h)ag\ *vt* **hagged; hagged; hagging; hags 1** *dial Brit* **:** HARASS, HARRY **2** *dial Brit* **:** to urge on **:** GOAD **3** *dial Brit* **:** to tire out **:** FATIGUE
³hag \"\ *n* -s [ME, prob. fr. ON *hagi* enclosed pasture; akin to OE *haga* hedge] *dial Eng* **:** an enclosed wooded area **:** WOODS
⁴hag \"\ *vt* **hagged; hagged; hagging; hags** [ME *haggen*, of Scand origin; akin to ON *höggva* to chop — more at HEW] *dial Brit* **:** HACK, CHOP, HEW
⁵hag \"\ *n* -s [of Scand origin; akin to ON *högg* stroke (as of an ax or sword), blow, ravine, *höggva* to chop] **1** *dial Brit* **:** NOTCH, HACK **2** *dial Brit* **a :** a section of timber marked off for felling **b :** felled timber or brushwood **3** *dial Brit* **:** QUAGMIRE, MARSH, BOG **4** *dial Brit* **:** a firm spot in a bog **5** *dial Brit* **a :** the projection of peat where cutting has stopped **b :** the overhanging edge of a stream
hag·berry \'(h)agbəri\ *n* [*hag-* (of Scand origin; akin to ON *heggr* bird cherry, Sw *hägg*, Dan *hæg*) + *berry* — more at HEDGE] *dial Brit* **:** EUROPEAN BIRD CHERRY
hagborn \'=,=\ *adj* [¹*hag* + *born*] **:** born of a witch
hagbut *var of* HACKBUT
hag·don \'hagdən\ *n* -s [origin unknown] **:** any of several seabirds chiefly of the No. Atlantic: as **a :** SHEARWATER **b :** FULMAR
ha·gen \'hägən\ *adj, usu cap* [fr. *Hagen*, Germany] **:** of or from the city of Hagen, Germany **:** of the kind or style prevalent in Hagen
ha·ge·nia \hə'jēnēə\ *n, cap* [NL, fr. Karl Gottfried *Hagen* †1829 Ger. botanist + NL *-ia*] **:** a genus of pinnate-leaved Ethiopian trees (family Rosaceae) having large panicles of flowers — see BRAYERA
hagfish \'=,=\ *n* [¹*hag* + *fish*] **:** any of several marine cyclostomes (order Hyperotreta) that are related to the lampreys and in general resemble eels but have a round mouth surrounded by eight tentacles, a single nostril opening behind the pharynx, a tongue with horny teeth, and rudimentary eyes and labyrinthine apparatus and that feed upon fishes by boring into their bodies and consuming their viscera and flesh
hagg \'(h)ag\ *var of* ⁵HAG
hag·ga·da *or* **hag·ga·dah** \hə'gä|də, -gȯ|\ *n, pl* **hagga·doth** *or* **hagga·dot** \-|,dōt(h), -ōs\ *usu cap* [Heb *haggādhāh*, fr. *higgīdh* to tell] **1** *or* **ag·ga·da** \ə'g-\ **:** explanatory matter occurring in rabbinical literature, often taking the form of story, anecdote, legend, or parable, and treating such varied subjects as astronomy, astrology, magic, medicine, mysticism **2 :** explanatory matter in the Talmud interpreting the Scriptures as distinguished from that regulating religious practice — compare HALAKAH, MIDRASH — **hag·gadic** \-'gadik, -'gäd-\ *also* **hag·gadi·cal** \-dəkəl\ *adj, often cap*
hag·ga·dist \hə'gädəst\ *n* -s *often cap* **:** a haggadic writer **:** a student of the Haggada — **hag·ga·dis·tic** \¦hagə¦distik\ *adj, often cap*
¹hag·gard \'hagə(r)d, 'haig- *sometimes* 'haag-\ *adj* [MF *hagard*] **1 a** *of a hawk* **:** caught after acquiring adult plumage **:** UNTAMED **b** *obs* **:** INTRACTABLE, WILLFUL **c** *obs* **:** WANTON, UNCHASTE ⟨if I do prove her ~ . . . I'll whistle her off —Shak.⟩ **2 :** wild in appearance: as **a** *of the eyes* **:** wild and staring **b** *of a person* **:** WILD-EYED ⟨staring his eyes, and ~ was his look —John Dryden⟩ **c :** having a worn or emaciated appearance caused by privation, suffering, anxiety, or age **:** HARROWED, GAUNT ⟨thin and worn, ~ from sleeplessness —Adria Langley⟩ — **hag·gard·ly** *adv* — **hag·gard·ness** *n* -ES
²haggard \"\ *n* -s **1 :** an adult hawk caught wild — compare EYAS **2** *obs* **:** an intractable person; *esp* **:** a woman reluctant to yield to wooing ⟨I have loved this proud disdainful ~ —Shak.⟩
³hag·gard \'(h)agəd\ *n* -s [of Scand origin; akin to ON *heygarthr* stockyard, fr. *hey* hay + *garthr* yard — more at HAY, YARD] *dial Brit* **:** a small plot of farm land; *esp* **:** an open area between the house and barn for keeping cattle or storing grain
hagged \'(h)agd\ *adj* [¹*hag* + *-ed*] **1** *dial Brit* **a :** BEWITCHED **:** ENCHANTED **b :** resembling a witch or a hag **2** *dial Brit* **:** HAGGARD, GAUNT
hagging *pres part of* HAG
hag·gis \'hagəs\ *n* -ES [ME *hagese, hagws, hagas*, prob. fr. *haggen* to hack, chop — more at HAG] **:** a pudding esp. popular in Scotland made of the heart, liver, and lungs of a sheep or a calf minced with suet, onions, oatmeal, and seasonings and boiled in the stomach of the animal
hag·gish \'hagish\ *adj* [¹*hag* + *-ish*] **:** resembling or characteristic of a hag — **hag·gish·ly** *adv* — **hag·gish·ness** *n* -ES
¹hag·gle \'hagəl, -aig-\ *vb* **haggled; haggled; haggling** \-g(ə)liŋ\ **haggles** [freq. of ⁴*hag*] *vt* **1 :** to cut roughly or clumsily **:** HACK ⟨~ a branch off⟩ **2** *archaic* **:** to annoy or exhaust with wrangling or heckling **:** NAG ~ *vi* **1 :** to cut roughly or clumsily **:** HACK ⟨~ at a branch of the tree⟩ **2 :** to bargain or make difficulties in reaching a bargain **:** WRANGLE ⟨when it comes to making peace, we must not ~ over trifles —H.J.Laski⟩ **3** *now chiefly dial* **:** to go wearily or haltingly
²haggle \"\ *n* -s **:** an act or instance of haggling
³hag·gle \'h)agəl\ *n* -s [ME *hagel* — more at HAIL] *dial Eng* **:** HAIL
hag·gler \'hag(ə)lə(r), -aig-\ *n* -s **1 :** one that haggles **2** *dial chiefly Brit* **:** HUCKSTER 1
hag·gy \'hagi\ *adj* -ER/-EST [⁵*hag* + *-y*] *chiefly Scot* **:** boggy and uneven
ha·gi \'hägē\ *n* -s [Jap] **:** BICOLOR LESPEDEZA
hagi- *or* **hagio-** *comb form* [LL, fr. Gk, fr. *hagios*] **1 :** holy ⟨*hagio*grapha⟩ ⟨*hagio*scope⟩ **2 :** saints ⟨*hagio*graphy⟩
ha·gia \'hājēə\ *n pl* [LGk, fr. neut. pl. of Gk *hagios*] **:** consecrated eucharistic elements in the Eastern Church
ha·gi·gah \hə'gēgə\ *or* **cha·gi·gah** \kə'-\ *n pl* [Heb *hăghīghāh*] **:** the voluntary sacrifices offered with the paschal lamb at the Passover and on other festivals by Jews on their pilgrimages to the temple at Jerusalem
hag·i·oc·ra·cy \,hagē'äkrəsē, ,hājē-\ *n* -ES [*hagi-* + *-cracy*] **:** government by a body of persons regarded as holy; *also* **:** a state so governed
hag·i·og·ra·pher \-grəfə(r)\ *n* -s [ML *hagiographus* theological writer (fr. LL *hagi-* + *-graphus* one that writes) + E *-er* — more at -GRAPHER] **1 :** one of the writers of the 13 books forming the third division of the Jewish Old Testament Scriptures **2 :** a writer of hagiography
hag·i·o·graph·ic \¦hagēə¦grafik, ¦hājē-\ *or* **hag·i·o·graph·i·cal** \-fəkəl\ *adj* **:** of or relating to the 13 books forming the third division of the Jewish Old Testament Scriptures **:** of or relating to hagiography
hag·i·og·ra·phist \,hagē'ägrəfəst, ,hājē-\ *n* -s [ML *hagiographus* + E *-ist*] **:** HAGIOGRAPHER
hag·i·og·ra·phy \-fē, -fi\ *n* -ES [*hagi-* + *-graphy*] **1 a :** biography of saints **:** saints' lives **b :** HAGIOLOGY a **2 :** biography of an idealizing or idolizing character ⟨the tone is one of personal affection rather than of ~ or impartial assessment —*Times Lit. Supp.*⟩
hag·i·ol·a·ter \,hagē'äləd·ə(r), ,hājē-\ *n* -s [*hagi-* + *-later*] **:** one that invokes or worships saints
hag·i·ol·a·trous \,==¦älətrəs\ *adj* **:** of or relating to the invocation or worship of saints
hag·i·ol·a·try \,==¦älətrē\ *n* -ES [*hagi-* + *-latry*] **:** the invocation or worship of saints
hag·i·o·lith \'hagēə,lith, 'hājē-\ *n* -s [*hagi-* + *-lith*] **:** a stone monument or edifice (as a dolmen, a menhir, or an obelisk) erected for religious or ceremonial purposes — **hag·i·o·lith·ic** \¦===¦lithik\ *adj*
hag·i·o·log·ic \¦hagēə¦läjik, ¦hājē-\ *or* **hag·i·o·log·i·cal** \-jəkəl\ *adj* **:** of or relating to hagiology
hag·i·ol·o·gist \,hagē'äləjəst, ,hājē-\ *n* -s **:** one skilled in hagiology
hag·i·ol·o·gy \-jē\ *n* -ES [*hagi-* + *-logy*] **:** the history or description of sacred writings or of sacred persons: as **a :** a narrative of the lives of saints **b :** a catalog of saints
hag·i·o·scope \'hagēə,skōp, 'hājē-\ *n* -s [*hagi-* + *-scope*] **:** an opening in the interior walls of a cruciform church so placed as to afford a view of the altar to those in the transept — called also *squint* — **hag·i·o·scop·ic** \¦===¦skäpik\ *adj*
hag·let \'haglət\ *n* -s [origin unknown] **:** SHEARWATER
hag·me·na \,hägmə'nā\ *sometimes cap, var of* HOGMANAY
hag moth *n* [¹*hag*] **:** a No. American eucleid moth (*Phobetron pithecium*) whose larva feeds on trees and shrubs
hagride \'=,=\ *vt* [¹*hag* + *ride*] **1** *archaic, of a witch or female demon* **a :** RIDE 1a **b :** TORMENT **2 :** to afflict with or as if with a nightmare **:** oppress with dread or anxiety **:** HARASS, TORMENT ⟨the great martian panic which showed how *hagridden* the American public had become —D.W.Brogan⟩ **3 :** to burden unduly ⟨families *hagridden* by poverty would find . . . a better life —Dixon Wecter⟩ **:** OBSESS ⟨*hagridden* by social prejudice and suspicion —J.E.P.Grigg⟩
hags *pl of* HAG, *pres 3d sing of* HAG
hagseed \'=,=\ *n* [¹*hag* + *seed*] **:** the offspring of a witch
hag's taper \'hagz-\ *also* **hagtaper** \'=,==\ *n, pl* **hag's tapers** *also* **hagtapers** [alter. of earlier *higgis taper, hickis taper, higtaper*, fr. *higgis, hickis, hig* (origin unknown) + *taper* (candle)] **:** MULLEIN **:** GREAT MULLEIN
hagstone \'=,=\ *n* **:** a naturally perforated stone used as an amulet against witchcraft
hague \'hāg\ *adj, usu cap* [fr. *(The) Hague*, Netherlands] **:** of or from The Hague, capital of the Netherlands **:** of the kind or style prevalent in the Hague
hag·worm \'(h)ag,wərm, -,wə̄m\ *n* [ME, prob. fr. *hagge* hag + *worm*] **1** *dial Eng* **:** a common snake (as an adder or viper) **2** *dial Eng* **:** BLINDWORM
hah *var of* HA
¹ha-ha \(')hä'hä\ *interj* [ME, fr. OE *ha ha*, of imit. origin] — used to express amusement or derision
²ha-ha \'hä,hä, =¦=\ *also* **haw-haw** \'hȯ,hȯ, =¦=\ *n* -s [F *haha*, prob. fr. *haha*, interj. used to express surprise] **:** SUNK FENCE
haham *var of* HAKAM
hahn·e·mann·ism \'hänəmə,nizəm\ *n* -s *usu cap* [Samuel *Hahnemann* †1843 Ger. physician + E *-ism*] **:** HOMEOPATHY
hai·a·ri \hī'ärē\ *n* -s [native name in British Guiana] **1 :** FISH POISON **2 :** a plant of the genus *Lonchocarpus* that contains rotenone
hai·a·tha·lah \,hīə'tälə\ *n, pl* **haiathalah** *usu cap* **:** EPHTHALITE
hai·da \'hīdə\ *n, pl* **haida** *or* **haidas** *usu cap* **1 a :** a Skittagetan people of the Queen Charlotte islands, British Columbia, and Prince of Wales Island, Alaska **b :** a member of such people **2 :** the language of the Haida people **3 :** a language stock of the Na-dene phylum comprising Haida only — called also *Skittagetan* — **hai·dan** \-dᵊn\ *adj, usu cap*
hai·ding·er·ite \'hīdiŋə,rīt\ *n* -s [Wilhelm Karl von *Haidinger* †1871 Austrian mineralogist + E *-ite*] **:** a mineral $HCaAsO_4 \cdot H_2O$ consisting of white hydrous calcium arsenate
hai·duk \'hī,dük\ *n* -s [G *heiduck, haiduck*, fr. Hung *hajdúk*, pl. of *hajdú* robber] **1 :** a Balkan outlaw opposed to Turkish rule **2 :** a Hungarian mercenary foot soldier of a class eventually elevated to noble rank **3 :** a male attendant or servant in various European countries dressed in livery resembling the costume of Hungarian haiduks
hai·fa \'hīfə\ *adj, usu cap* [fr. *Haifa*, Israel] **:** of or from the city of Haifa, Israel **:** of the kind or style prevalent in Haifa
hai·gle \'hāgəl\ *var of* HAGGLE *vi* 3
¹haik *also* **haick** \'hīk, 'hāk\ *n, pl* **haiks** *or* **haika** *also* **haicks** [Ar *ḥā'ik, hayk*] **:** a voluminous piece of usu. white cloth worn as an outer garment by men and women in northern Africa
²haik *var of* HAKE
hai·kai \'hī,kī\ *n, pl* **haikai** [Jap] **:** an often playful type of Japanese verse or prose cultivated in the later feudal ages — compare HAIKU, HOKKU
hai·kal \'hī,käl, 'hä,-\ *n* -s [Syriac *haykal* & Heb *hēkhāl*, fr. Assyr-Bab *ēkallu*, fr. Sumerian *e gal* temple, palace, fr. *e* house + *gal* great] **1 :** a sanctuary of a Coptic church cut off from the nave by a screen and containing three altars **2 :** the main altar
hai·ku \'hī(,)kü\ *n, pl* **haiku** [Jap] **:** an unrhymed Japanese poem of three lines containing 5, 7, and 5 syllables respectively, referring in some way to one of the seasons of the year, and constituting a late 19th century development of the hokku; *also* **:** a poem written in the haiku form or a modification of it but in a language other than Japanese
hai·kwan tael \'hī'kwän-\ *n* [*haikwan* fr. Chin (Pek) *hai³*= *kuan¹* maritime customs, lit., gate of the sea] **:** a unit of value used in China for reckoning customs duties **:** customs tael
¹hail \'hāl\, *esp before pause or consonant* -āəl\ *n* -s [ME *hail, hagel, hawel*, fr. OE *hægl, hagol;* akin to OHG *hagal* hail, ON *hagl*, Runic Goth *haal* (name of a rune), Gk *kachlēx* pebble] **1 a :** precipitation in the form of small balls or lumps usu. consisting of concentric layers of clear ice and compact snow produced by the oscillation of raindrops within cumulonimbus clouds or by the freezing of raindrops from nimbus clouds **b** *archaic* **:** a shower of hail **:** HAILSTORM ⟨a very considerable portion of this country has been desolated by a ~ —Thomas Jefferson⟩ **2 :** something that gives the effect of falling hail ⟨a ~ of shot kicked up river sand —F.B.Gipson⟩
²hail \"\ *vi* -ED/-ING/-S [ME *haylen, hawelen*, fr. OE *hagalian*, fr. *hagol*, n.] **1 :** to precipitate hail ⟨it rained and ~*ed*⟩ **2 :** to pour down like hail **:** strike in the manner of hail ⟨flak ~s upon the plane —*Science Yr. Bk.*⟩
³hail \"\ *interj* [ME *hail, heil*, fr. ON *heill*, fr. *heill*, adj., healthy — more at WHOLE] **1 —** used to express acclamation ⟨~ to the chief —Sir Walter Scott⟩ ⟨~, King of the Jews —Mk 15:18 (RSV)⟩ **2** *archaic* — used as a salutation ⟨all ~, sweet madam, and fair time of day —Shak.⟩ ⟨good morrow to you both. *Hail* to your grace —Shak.⟩ **3 :** HURRAH — used to express good feeling or enthusiasm ⟨*hail, hail*, the gang's all here⟩
⁴hail \"\ *vb* -ED/-ING/-S [ME *hailen, heilen*, fr. *hail, heil*, interj.] *vt* **1 a :** SALUTE, GREET, ACCOST ⟨~*ed* the report with undisguised satisfaction —J.B.Matthews⟩ ⟨~*ed* him and gave him her hand —P.B.Kyne⟩ **b :** to greet with enthusiastic approval **:** ACCLAIM ⟨~ him as a hero⟩ ⟨~ the advances audio has made —R.D.Darrell⟩ **2 :** to greet or summon by calling to ⟨~ a passing ship⟩ ⟨~ a taxi⟩ **3** *chiefly Scot* **:** to reach (the goal) esp. in a game of shinny ~ *vi* **1 :** to call out; *esp* **:** to call a greeting to a passing ship ⟨the ship ~*ed* as we passed⟩ — **hail from :** to have origin or home base in **:** come from ⟨he *hails from* the hill country⟩
⁵hail \"\ *n* -s **1 :** an exclamation of greeting **:** SALUTATION ⟨he heard a ~ and his own name called —George Meredith⟩; *specif* **:** a shout of acclamation ⟨greeted the emperor with a ~⟩ **2 :** a calling to attract attention **:** act of hailing ⟨after such ~, the windward yacht shall at once allow the leeward yacht room to tack —Guy Pennant⟩ **3** *chiefly Scot* **a :** the cry uttered when a goal is struck in a game (as shinny) **b :** GOAL ⟨defeated by four ~s⟩ — **within hail :** within hearing distance ⟨*within hail* of the telephone —Nevil Shute⟩

[6]**hail** \"\ *var of* HALE

hail columbia *n, usu cap H&C* [euphemism; fr. *Hail Columbia* (1798), patriotic song by Joseph Hopkinson †1842 Am. jurist] **:** HELL ⟨give them *Hail Columbia*⟩

hail·er \ˈhālə(r)\ *n* -s **:** one that hails

[1]**hail-fellow** \ˈ=,(=)=\ *or* **hail-fellow-well-met** \ˈ=,=(,)=ˈ=ˈ=\ *adj* [fr. the archaic salutations *hail, fellow!* & *hail, fellow! well met!*] **:** heartily informal **:** COMRADELY ⟨extended a *hail-fellow* hand —Edith Wharton⟩ ⟨a giant of a man — rough, hearty, violent, *hail-fellow-well-met* —Kenneth Roberts⟩

[2]**hail-fellow** \"\ *or* **hail-fellow-well-met** \"\ *n, pl* **hail-fellows** *or* **hail-fellows-well-met 1 :** a boon companion **:** PAL ⟨all were *hail-fellows-well-met* by the time the convention opened —*Typewriter Topics*⟩ **2 :** the quality or state of comradeship ⟨there was a *hail-fellow-well-met*, a camaraderie, a gregariousness about it —*N.Y. Times*⟩

hailing distance *n* [fr. gerund of [4]*hail*] **1 :** the limit to which a human voice is heard ⟨when a patron lives within *hailing distance* —*U.S. Post Office Manual*⟩ **2 :** a close proximity **:** short reach ⟨within *hailing distance* of knowledge —H.J. Muller⟩

hail insurance *n* [[1]*hail*] **:** insurance against loss resulting from damage by hail esp. to growing crops

hail mary *n, usu cap H&M* [ME *hail Marie, heil Marie;* trans. of ML *Ave Maria*] **:** AVE MARIA 1, 3

hailproof \ˈ=,=\ *adj* **:** impervious to hail ⟨~ netting over tobacco plants⟩

hails *pl of* HAIL, *pres 3d sing of* HAIL

hailshot \ˈ=,=\ *n, pl* **hailshot** [ME *hayle shotte*] *archaic* **:** small shot that scatters like hail

hailstone \ˈ=,=\ *n* [ME, fr. OE *hagolstān* (akin to ON *haglsteinn* hailstone), fr. *hagol* hail + *stān* stone — more at HAIL, STONE] **:** a single ball or lump of ice falling from a cloud **:** a pellet of hail

hailstorm \ˈ=,=\ *n* -s **1 :** a storm accompanied by hail **:** a shower of hail ⟨the rain changed to a violent ~ —*McClure's*⟩ **2 :** something that resembles a hailstorm in concentrated violence ⟨a ~ of contempt —William James⟩

haily \ˈhālē\ *adj* **:** made of or accompanied by hail

haim \ˈhām\ *chiefly dial var of* HAME

haim·suck·en \ˈhām,səkən\ *var of* HAMESUCKEN

[1]**hain** \ˈ(h)ān\ *vt* -ED/-ING/-S [ME *hanen, haynen,* fr. ON *hegna* to enclose; akin to MLG *hegenen* to enclose, MHG *heinen* to enclose, OHG *hagan* thornbush, ON *hagi* enclosed pasture — more at HAG] *dial Brit* **1 :** to fence or enclose (a tract of land) for grass **2 :** to put aside **:** SAVE, SPARE

[2]**hain** \"\ *vt* -ED/-ING/-S [ME *heyen, heynen* to raise, fr. OE *hēan,* fr. *hēah* high — more at HIGH] *dial Eng* **:** to cause (a price or fee) to be increased **:** RAISE

hai·nai \ˈ(h)ī,nī\ *n, pl* **hainai** *or* **hainais** *usu cap* **1 :** a Caddo people of the Texas panhandle **2 :** a member of such people — compare HASINAI

hai·nan·ese \ˌhīnəˈnēz, -ēs\ *n, pl* **hainanese** *cap* [*Hainan,* island in the So. China Sea + E *-ese*] **:** a native or inhabitant of the Chinese island of Hainan

hainch \ˈ(h)änsh\ *dial Brit var of* HAUNCH

haing *pres part of* HA

hain't \(ˈ)(h)ānt\ [partly contr. of *have not, has not;* partly alter. of *ain't*] **:** AIN'T

hai·phong \ˈhīˈfŏŋ\ *adj, usu cap* [fr. *Haiphong,* northern Vietnam] **:** of or from the city of Haiphong, northern Vietnam **:** of the kind or style prevalent in Haiphong

[1]**hair** \ˈha(a)(ə)r, ˈhe|, |ə\ *n* -s *often attrib* [ME *her, heer, hare, heir, hair,* fr. OE *hǣr;* akin to OFris *hēr* hair, OHG & ON *hār,* and perh. to MIr *carrach* scurfy, mangy, Lith *šerys* bristle, Skt *kapucchala* hair on the back of the head] **1 :** a slender threadlike outgrowth of the epidermis of an animal; *esp* **:** one of the usu. pigmented filaments that form the characteristic coat of a mammal, contain neither blood vessels nor nerves, and are composed chiefly of elongated and modified epidermal cells covered by a cuticle of flat imbricated cells that produce a rough surface — compare BRISTLE, HAIR FOLLICLE, ROOT, SPINE **2 a :** the hairy covering of an animal or of some particular part of him; *specif* **:** the coating of fairly coarse and relatively straight individual hairs on a human head — distinguished from *fur* and *wool* **b :** HAIRCLOTH **3 a** (1) **:** a minute distance or amount **:** TRIFLE ⟨won by a ~⟩ (2) **:** a precise degree **:** NICETY ⟨aligned to a ~⟩ **b :** something likened to hair ⟨~s of fire came up through the busted plates —Saul Bellow⟩ ⟨eucalyptus . . . tossed their purple-black ~ of leaves in the air —Eve Langley⟩ **4** *obs* **:** KIND, NATURE, CHARACTER ⟨the quality and ~ of our attempt brooks no division —Shak.⟩ **5 a :** a filamentous structure that resembles hair ⟨leaf ~⟩ **b :** BOW HAIR — **against the hair** *archaic* **:** contrary to the normal tendency **:** against the grain ⟨if you should fight, you go *against the hair* of your professions —Shak.⟩ — **hair of the dog :** a small amount of the cause of an ill used as a remedy for it; *specif* **:** a drink of liquor the morning after a drinking bout ⟨I'd fetched a bottle — a little of the *hair of the dog* would do me good —Ross Santee⟩ — **in one's hair :** persistently annoying ⟨people could be friendly without getting *in each other's hair* —J.R.Chamberlain⟩ — **in the hair 1** *of raw furs* **:** with the fur outward **2** *of hides* **:** with the hair on — **one's hair down :** one's normal reserve in abeyance ⟨management with *its hair down* —*Time*⟩ **:** one's guard down ⟨that doesn't mean you have to let *your hair down* and tell him all the innermost secrets of your business —Franklin Spier⟩ ⟨they took *their hair down* and we felt that we made progress . . . in getting the type of information we are after —J.P.Richards⟩ — **out of one's hair :** eliminated as an annoying factor ⟨keep the children of the guests occupied and *out of their mothers' hair* —Marvin Schwartz⟩

[2]**hair** \"\ *vb* -ED/-ING/-S *vt* **1 :** to remove hair from ⟨~ a hide⟩ **2 :** to apply hair to ⟨~ a doll⟩ ⟨~ a fiddlestick⟩ **:** cover with or as if with hair ⟨a thick, white hand . . . ~*ed* over with fine reddish fuzz —William Faulkner⟩ ~ *vi* **:** to produce hair or something resembling hair ⟨these woods would not ~ up —*Scientific American*⟩

hair ball \ˈ=,=\ *n* **1 :** a compact mass of hair in the stomach occurring esp. during shedding in an animal (as a cat) that cleanses its coat by licking **2 :** PHYTOBEZOAR

hairbeard \ˈ=,=\ *n* **:** a wood rush (*Luzula campestris*)

hairbell *n* **:** HAREBELL

hairbird \ˈ=,=\ *n* [so called fr. its use of horsehair in its nest] **:** CHIPPING SPARROW

[1]**hairbrain** \ˈ=,=\ *n* -s [by folk etymology] **:** HAREBRAIN

[2]**hairbrain** \"\ *adj* **:** HAREBRAINED

hairbrained \ˈ=ˈ=\ *adj* [by folk etymology] **:** HAREBRAINED

hair-branch tree *n* **:** an African shrub (*Trichocladus crinitus*) of the family Hamamelidaceae

hair brand *n* **:** a temporary cattle brand made by scorching or picking out the hair without scarring the skin and used esp. by rustlers

[1]**hairbreadth** *or* **hairsbreadth** \ˈ=,=\ *n* **1 :** a narrow margin ⟨lost the governorship by a ~ —W.V.Shannon⟩ **2 :** HAIR 3a

[2]**hairbreadth** \"\ *adj* **:** having the breadth of a hair **:** very narrow ⟨~ escape⟩

hair brown *n* **:** a dark gray to brownish gray that is lighter and slightly redder than beaver gray — called also *argali, limestone, quail*

hairbrush \ˈ=,=\ *n* **1 :** a brush for the hair **2 :** a brush made of hair

hair calf *n* **:** SLINK 1

haircap moss *n* **:** a moss of the genus *Polytrichum* (esp. *P. juniperinum*)

hair cell *n* **:** a cell with hairlike processes; *esp* **:** one of the sensory cells in the auditory epithelium of the organ of Corti

[1]**hair-check** \ˈ=,=\ *n* **:** a fine crack resulting from shrinkage on the surface of concrete or paint — **hair-checking** \ˈ=,==\ *n*

[2]**hair-check** \"\ *vi* **:** [1]CRAZE *vi* 3

haircloth \ˈ=,=\ *n* -s **1 :** any of various stiff wiry fabrics having a hair weft esp. of horsehair or camel's hair and a cotton, linen, or wool warp and being used for upholstery or stiffening in garments **2 :** an article of haircloth; *esp* **:** HAIR SHIRT

haircomb \ˈ=,=\ *n* **:** a way of combing the hair ⟨this form of ~ was almost a tradition among old-time bartenders —Herman Goodman⟩

hair compass *n* **:** a compass that permits of minute adjustment

haircut \ˈ=,=\ *n* **1 :** the act or process of cutting and shaping the hair **2 :** a hairstyle achieved by cutting and shaping

haircutter \ˈ=,==\ *n* **:** one that cuts hair

haircutting \ˈ=,==\ *n* **:** the art or occupation of a barber

hair dividers *n pl* **:** HAIR COMPASS

hairdo \ˈ=,=\ *n* -s **:** a way of dressing the hair ⟨go in for elaborate ~s —Agnes M. Miall⟩; *esp* **:** a modish coiffure for women ⟨season's favorite ~ —*N.Y. Times*⟩

hair-drawn \ˈ=ˈ=\ *adj* **:** HAIRSPLITTING ⟨impatient of such *hair-drawn* distinctions —S.H.Adams⟩

hairdress \ˈ=,=\ *n* **:** COIFFURE

hairdresser \ˈ=,==\ *n* **1 :** one whose business or occupation is hairdressing and giving beauty treatments **:** COSMETOLOGIST **2** *Brit* **:** BARBER ⟨having a shave at the *hairdresser's* —A.J. Liebling⟩

hairdressing \ˈ=,==\ *n* **1 a :** the action or process of washing, cutting, curling, or arranging the hair **b :** the occupation of a hairdresser **c :** HAIRDO **2 :** a dressing (as a pomade) for the hair

haired \ˈha(a)(ə)rd, ˈhe|, |əd\ *adj* [ME *hered,* fr. *her, heer* + *-ed*] **:** having hair — usu. preceded by a descriptive term ⟨corn ~⟩ ⟨fair-*haired*⟩ ⟨wavy ~⟩ ⟨sparsely ~ leaves⟩

hair·en \ˈharən\ *adj* [ME *heren,* fr. OE *hǣren,* fr. *hǣr* hair + *-en* — more at HAIR] *chiefly dial* **:** made of hair

hair fern *n* [short for *maidenhair fern*] **:** MAIDENHAIR

hair-fibered \ˈ=ˈ==\ *adj, of plaster* **:** containing fiber as a binder

hair follicle *n* **:** the tubular epithelial sheath surrounding the lower part of a hair shaft and enclosing at the bottom a vascular papilla that supplies the growing basal part of the hair with nourishment — compare ROOT

hair grass *n* **1 :** any of several grasses having slender wiry stems or leaves: as **a :** ROUGH BENT **b :** any of several grasses of the genera *Deschampsia, Muhlenbergia,* and *Aira* **2 :** any of several fine-leaved strictly aquatic spike rushes including some that are popular as aerators for the balanced aquarium

hair grip *n, chiefly Brit* **:** BOBBY PIN

hairhound \ˈ=,=\ *n* [by folk etymology] **:** HOREHOUND

hair hygrometer *n* **:** an absorption hygrometer with a sensitive element of human hair

hairier *comparative of* HAIRY

hairies *pl of* HAIRY

hairiest *superlative of* HAIRY

hair·i·ness \ˈha(a)rēnəs, ˈher-, -rin-\ *n* -ES [ME *heryness,* fr. *hery, heeri* hairy + *-ness*] **:** the quality or state of being hairy

hairing *pres part of* HAIR

hair kiln *n* **:** a kiln floor which consists of open-woven horsehair cloth supported on laths of wood and on which hops are placed to dry

hairlace *n* [ME *harlas,* fr. *har, heer* hair + *las* lace] *obs* **:** a fillet (as of net) for the hair

hair·less \ˈha(a)(ə)rləs, ˈhe|, |əl-\ *adj* **:** lacking hair — **hair·less·ness** *n* -ES

hairlike \ˈ=,=\ *adj* **:** resembling a hair **:** elongated, slender, and filamentous ⟨~ appendages of a crustacean⟩

[1]**hairline** \ˈ=,=\ *n* **1** *archaic* **:** a cord (as a fishline) made of hair **2 a :** a very slender line ⟨faint ~ of light around the edges of the windows —Shirley A. Grau⟩; *specif* **:** a tiny line or crack on a surface (as of paint) **b :** a very small difference **:** narrow margin ⟨the ~ that divides the comic from the grotesque —Wolcott Gibbs⟩ **c** (1) **:** a fine line connecting thicker strokes in a printed letter — called also *thin stroke* (2) **:** a fine line on a printer's rule or ornament (3) **:** a fine line drawn or etched for reproduction (as on a steel engraving) (4) **:** a fine strand of surplus metal on the face of newly cast type or slugs **:** WHISKER **d** (1) **:** a printed or woven textile design consisting of lengthwise or crosswise lines usu. one thread wide (2) **:** a fabric with such a design **3 a :** the line at which the hair meets the scalp ⟨receding ~⟩ **b :** the way the hair frames the face ⟨has a nice ~⟩ — **to a hairline** *adv* **:** to a nicety **:** with exactitude ⟨matched *to a hairline*⟩

[2]**hairline** \"\ *adj* **1 :** of or relating to a very slender line **:** THIN ⟨~ mustache⟩ ⟨~ shading⟩ **2 a :** hinging on very small differences **:** CLOSE ⟨~ victory⟩ **b :** marked by exactitude **:** PRECISE ⟨~ accuracy⟩

hair man *n* **:** an operator of a machine in which cattle hair is washed, dried, and baled

hair moss *n* [by shortening] **:** HAIRCAP MOSS

hair moth *n* **:** a moth that destroys goods made of hair or fur; *esp* **:** WEBBING CLOTHES MOTH

hairn \ˈhärn\ *var of* HARN

hairnet \ˈ=,=\ *n* **:** an open-meshed net made usu. of human hair or silk and worn over the hair to keep it in place

hair orchid *n* **:** a Himalayan orchid (*Trichosma suavis*) with yellowish purple-streaked flowers

hair pencil *n* **1 :** a brush or pencil made of fine hair (as of a camel) and used in painting **2 :** a close tuft of hairs occurring on parts of the body of certain caterpillars

hairpiece \ˈ=,=\ *n* **:** TOUPEE 2

[1]**hairpin** \ˈ=,=\ *n* **1 :** a pin to hold the hair in place; *specif* **:** a two-pronged U-shaped pin made of wire, plastic, or bone **2 a :** something shaped like a hairpin; *specif* **:** a sharp turn in a road having relatively parallel approaches ⟨at the top of a long swinging ~ he looked back and saw the moving lights of a car —Wallace Stegner⟩ **b :** two closed slalom gates placed one immediately below the other on a ski slope

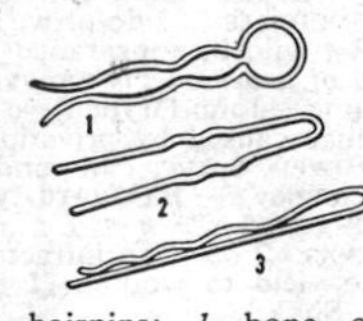

hairpins: *1* bone or plastic, *2* wire, *3* bobby pin

[2]**hairpin** \"\ *adj* **:** having the shape of a hairpin ⟨~ curve⟩

[3]**hairpin** \"\ *vb* [[1]*hairpin*] *vt, West* **:** to get up on (as a horse) **:** MOUNT ⟨*hairpinning* . . . at sight anything on four hoofs —P.A.Rollins⟩ ~ *vi* **:** to make a hairpin turn ⟨the road ~s up the mountainside —Tom Marvel⟩

hairpin lace *n* **:** a lace with looped edges made by crocheting around the prongs of a U-shaped needle

hair pyrites *n* [so called fr. its interwoven capillary crystals that suggest a wad of hair] **:** MILLERITE

hair-raiser \ˈ=,==\ *n* **:** one that is hair-raising **:** CHILLER ⟨the ingredients for an old-fashioned *hair-raiser* —*Theatre Arts*⟩

hair-raising \ˈ=,==\ *adj* **:** making the hair stand on end: **a :** causing fear or shock **:** TERRIFYING ⟨have listened to some *hair-raising* confessions in my time —Mary R. Rinehart⟩ **b :** causing surprise or excitement **:** THRILLING ⟨no vivid or brilliant or *hair-raising* item of song or dance —*Dance News*⟩ — **hair-rais·ing·ly** *adv*

hairs *pl of* HAIR, *pres 3d sing of* HAIR

hair salt *n* [trans. of G *haarsalz*] **1 :** ALUNOGEN **2 :** epsomite when in silky fibers

hairsbreadth *var of* HAIRBREADTH

hair seal *n* **1 :** a seal whose coat lacks underfur **2 a :** the fur of the hair seal **b :** an article made of this fur

hairsheep \ˈ=,=\ *n* [so called fr. the fact that the hide comes fr. a sheep that grows hair instead of wool] **:** a leather used in bookbinding — compare CABRETTA

hair shirt *n* **1 :** a shirt made of coarse rough animal hair worn next to the skin as a penance ⟨led him . . . to give himself to fasting, a *hair shirt,* and prayer —K.S.Latourette⟩ **2 :** one that flagellates **:** SCOURGE ⟨the *hair shirt* of duty —L.D.Lewis⟩ ⟨uncomfortable to live with — a regular *hair shirt* of a man —E.B.White⟩ — **hairshirted** *adj*

hair sieve *n* [ME *herseve,* fr. *her, heer* hair + *seve* sieve] **:** a strainer with a haircloth bottom

hairslip \ˈ=,=\ *n* **:** loosening of the hair from a hide due to improper or inadequate curing

hair snake *n* **:** HORSEHAIR SNAKE

hair sofa *n* **:** a sofa upholstered in haircloth

hair space *n* **:** a very thin space used in printing (as the ½-point copper space or the 1-point brass space)

hairspace \ˈ=,=\ *vt* [*hair space*] **:** to set with hair spaces

hairsplitter \ˈ=,==\ *n* **:** one that indulges in hairsplitting **:** QUIBBLER

[1]**hairsplitting** \ˈ=,==\ *adj* **:** making excessively fine or trivial distinctions in reasoning ⟨ancient ~ technicalities of special pleading —Charles Sumner⟩ ⟨tricky ~ statesmen —Weston La Barre⟩

[2]**hairsplitting** \"\ *n* **:** hairsplitting reasoning or argument ⟨an excessive penchant for intellectual and verbal ~ —J.W. Beach⟩

hairspring \ˈ=,=\ *n* **:** a slender spiraled recoil spring that regulates the motion of the balance wheel of a timepiece — called also *balance spring*

hairst \ˈhārst\ *chiefly Scot var of* HARVEST

hair·stane \ˈhār,stān\ *Scot var of* HOARSTONE

hairstone \ˈ=,=\ *n* [prob. trans. of G *haarstein*] **:** quartz thickly penetrated with hairlike crystals of rutile, actinolite, or other mineral

hair straightener *n* **:** an agent (as heat or a chemical preparation) used for straightening kinky hair

hairstreak \ˈ=,=\ *n* **:** any of various small butterflies of *Strymon* and related genera usu. having striped markings under the wings and thin filamentous projections from the hind wings

hair stroke *n* **1 :** a delicate stroke in writing **2 :** SERIF

hairstyle \ˈ=,=\ *n* **:** a way of wearing the hair **:** COIFFURE

hairstyling \ˈ=,==\ *n* **:** the art or practice of a hair stylist

hair stylist *n* **:** one who designs individualized hairdos esp. for women and often dresses the hair in the suggested style

hairtail \ˈ=,=\ *n* [so called fr. the fact that the tail ends in a hairlike filament] **:** CUTLASS FISH

hair trigger *n* **:** a gun trigger so delicately adjusted that it releases the cock at the slightest touch

hair-trigger \ˈ=ˈ==\ *or* **hair-triggered** \ˈ=ˈ==\ *adj* [*hair trigger*] **1 a :** disposed to react quickly ⟨*hair-trigger* children who needed only a leader . . . to break into happy riot —John Steinbeck⟩ **b :** immediately responsive to the slightest stimulus ⟨*hair-trigger* nerves⟩ ⟨there is a *hair-trigger* ferocity about leopards —Alan Moorehead⟩ **c :** marked by promptness **:** INSTANTANEOUS ⟨*hair-trigger* service on inquiries —J.J. Canavan⟩ **2 :** delicately adjusted or easily disrupted ⟨*hair-trigger* schedule⟩ ⟨*hair-trigger* balance⟩

hair-trigger flower *n* **:** an Australian plant of the genus *Stylidium* (esp. *S. graminifolium*) whose column of stamens reacts sensitively to the touch

hair trunk *n* **:** a trunk covered with hide from which the hair has not been removed

hairweed \ˈ=,=\ *n* **1 :** a filamentous green alga **2 :** any of several plants of the genus *Cuscuta; esp* **:** CLOVER DODDER

hairwood \ˈ=,=\ *n* [by alter.] **:** HAREWOOD 2

hairwork \ˈ=,=\ *n* **1 :** the making of wigs, switches, and other articles from hair **2 :** articles made of hair

hair worker *n* **:** one that combs, sorts, and washes hair for use in hairwork

hairworm \ˈ=,=\ *n* **:** any of various very slender elongated worms: as **a :** a worm of the nematode genus *Capillaria* **b :** a worm of the order Gordioidea **:** HORSEHAIR SNAKE

[1]**hairy** \ˈha(a)rē, ˈher-, -ri\ *adj* -ER/-EST [ME *heery,* fr. *heer* hair + *-y*] **1 :** covered with or as if with hair ⟨~ ape⟩ ⟨~ overcoat⟩; *specif* **:** having a downy fuzz on the stems and leaves ⟨~ lotus⟩ **2 :** made of or resembling hair ⟨~ gown and mossy cell —John Milton⟩ **3 a :** rough and broken **:** RUGGED ⟨we are getting into some ~ country —Adrian Bell⟩ **b :** CRUDE, FRIGHTENING, UNPLEASANT ⟨~ bodyguard⟩ ⟨had some pretty ~ moments —L.A.Viereck⟩

[2]**hairy** \"\ *n* -ES **:** one that is hairy; *specif* **:** a draft horse with heavy feathering on the legs

hairy armadillo *n* **:** a peludo (*Euphractus villosus*)

hairy arum *n* **:** a foul-smelling aroid (*Helicodiceros muscivorus*) of southern Europe having a hairy purple spadix

hairy-bait \ˈ==,=\ *n* **:** LUGWORM

hairy-chested \ˈ==ˈ==\ *adj* **:** full of strength or vigor **:** ROBUST ⟨*hairy-chested* mining history —Phil Spelman⟩

hairy china cardamom *n, usu cap 1st C* **:** an aromatic seed of a Chinese herb (*Amomum villosum*) used as a substitute for true cardamom

hairy chinch bug *n* **:** a bug closely related to and possibly a short-winged variety of the chinch bug that is sometimes destructive to turf in the northeastern U.S.

hairy crab *n* **:** a subglobose crab of the group Dromiacea having the body partially covered with bits of algae and debris

hairy crabgrass *n* **:** CRABGRASS 1a

hairy-foot \ˈ==,=\ *n, pl* **hairy-foots** [so called fr. the hairy down at the base of the stem] **:** an inedible mushroom (*Marasmius personatus*) related to the fairy-ring mushroom

hairy frog *n* **:** any of three large western African frogs of the genus *Astylosternus* (family Ranidae) having hairlike outgrowths of skin on the sides of the trunk and thighs

hairy grama *n* **:** a grama (*Bouteloua hirsuta*) having the rachis prolonged beyond the spikelets as a naked point and the leaf blades sparsely hairy — called also *black grama*

hairy greenweed *n* **:** a southern European shrub (*Genista pilosa*) cultivated as forage for sheep

hairy head *also* **hairy crown** *n* **1 :** HOODED MERGANSER **2 :** RED-BREASTED MERGANSER

hairy honeysuckle *n* **:** a twining shrub (*Lonicera hirsuta*) of moist woodlands of the northern and eastern U.S. and adjacent Canada with dull dark green leaves that are sessile or short-petioled and pubescent on both surfaces and with crowded terminal spikes of orange or yellow flowers

hairy indigo *n* **:** a shrubby perennial (*Indigofera hirsuta*) with hirsute stems and foliage, flowers in dense clusters, and the calyx lobes often nearly as long as the petal that is native to Asia, Africa, and Australia and has been introduced into the southern U.S. as a forage and soil-improvement crop

hairy lip fern *n* **:** WOOLLY LIP FERN

hairy-nosed wombat \ˈ==,=-\ *n* **:** a southern Australian wombat (*Lasiorhinus latifrons*) distinguished by an extremely hairy rhinarium

hairy pipewort *n* **:** a low herb (*Lachnocaulon anceps*) of the family Eriocaulaceae of the southeastern U.S. having a 3-angled hairy scape

hairy rat *n* **:** a long-tailed Australian rat (*Mesembryomys hirsutus*)

hairy root *n* **:** a phase of the crown-gall disease esp. in apples characterized by abnormal development of fine fibrous roots

hairy saki *n* **:** a tropical American monkey (*Pithecia monacha*) with a purplish brown face covered with short white hair and a body coat that varies from black to brown and yellowish white

hairy shore crab *n* **:** YELLOW SHORE CRAB

hairy solomon's seal *n, usu cap 1st S* **:** a pubescent alternate-leaved perennial herb (*Polygonatum pubescens*) of eastern No. America

hairy spurge *n* **:** a much-branched hirsute weed (*Euphorbia hirsuta*) that has decumbent or prostrate stems in a dense mat and is native to northeastern No. America

hairy sumac *n* **:** STAGHORN SUMAC

hairy-tailed mole \ˈ==,=-\ *n* **:** BREWERS' MOLE

hairy vetch *or* **hairy tare** *n* **:** a European vetch (*Vicia villosa*) extensively cultivated as a cover and early forage crop

hairy willow herb *n* **:** a European willow herb (*Epilobium hirsutum*) with a stout hairy stem and rose-purple flowers

hairy woodpecker *n* **:** a common No. American woodpecker (*Dendrocopos villosus*) closely resembling but larger than the downy woodpecker

hais·la \ˈhīslə\ *n, pl* **haisla** *or* **haislas** *usu cap* **1 :** a Kwakiutl people of British Columbia — compare WAKASHAN **2 :** a member of the Kwakiutl people

hait \ˈhāt\ *interj* [ME] *chiefly Scot* — used to urge on an animal

haith \ˈhāth\ *interj* [prob. euphemism for *faith*] *chiefly Scot* — used as a mild oath

hai·thal \ˈhī,täl\ *n, usu cap* **:** EPHTHALITE

hai·ti \ˈhād·|ē, -ät|, |i\ *adj, usu cap* [fr. *Haiti,* country in the West Indies] **:** of or from Haiti **:** of the kind or style prevalent in Haiti **:** HAITIAN

[1]**hai·tian** \ˈhāshən, ˈhād·|ēən, -ät|, |iən\ *adj, usu cap* [*Haiti* + E *-an*] **1 :** of, relating to, or characteristic of the island of Haiti **2 :** of, relating to, or characteristic of the people of Haiti

[2]**haitian** \"\ *n* -s **1** *cap* **:** a native or inhabitant of Haiti — compare TAINO **2** *or* **haitian creole** *usu cap H&C* **:** CREOLE 4b

hai·tsai \ˈhīˈtsī\ *n* -s [Chin (Pek) *hai³-ts'ai⁴,* fr. *hai³* sea + *ts'ai⁴* herb, green vegetable] **1 :** a transparent gelatinous substance prepared from a red alga (*Gloiopeltis tenax*) and used by the Chinese for lanterns and windows and for stiffening cloth **2 :** the alga that yields haitsai

hai·ver \ˈhāvə(r)\ *var of* HAVER

ha·je \ˈhäjē\ *n* -s [Ar *ḥayyah* snake] **:** an Egyptian cobra (*Naja haje*)

hajemi *cap, var of* HADJEMI

haji *or* **hadji** *or* **hajji** \'hajē\ *n* -s [Ar *ḥajjī*, fr. *ḥajj*] **:** one who has made a pilgrimage to Mecca — often used as a title

ha·jib \'hä,jib\ *n* -s [Ar *ḥājib*, lit., one who prevents from entering] **:** a Muslim court official often corresponding to a chamberlain or a prime minister

hajj *or* **hadj** *or* **haj** \'haj\ *n* -ES [Ar *ḥajj*] **:** the pilgrimage to Mecca prescribed as a religious duty for Muslims

ha·ka \'hä,kä\ *n* -s [Maori] **:** a Maori posture dance accompanied by rhythmic chanting

ha·ka·foth *or* **ha·ka·fot** *or* **hak·ka·fot** \'häkə,fōth, -ōs, -ōt\ *n pl* [Heb *haqqāphōth*, pl. of *haqqāphāh* circuit] **:** a ceremony in the Jewish synagogue typically on Simhath Torah in which members of the congregation carrying the scrolls of the Torah make seven processional circuits around the bimah to the accompaniment of traditional hymns and songs

ha·kam *or* **ha·ham** \kä'kām\ *also* **cho·chem** \'kōkəm\ *n, pl* **haka·mim** *or* **haha·mim** \,käkä'mēm\ [Heb *ḥākhām* wise, wise man; *chochem* fr. Yiddish *khokhem*, fr. Heb *ḥākhām*] **1 :** one learned in Jewish law **:** WISE MAN; *specif, pl* **:** the rabbinical interpreters of biblical law of the first two Christian centuries whose interpretations are recorded in the Mishnah and contemporary works **2 :** a title given to a rabbi by the Sephardic Jews

¹**hake** \'hāk\ *n, pl* **hake** *also* **hakes** [ME] **1 :** any of several fishes (the genus *Merluccius*) that are related to the cods but often regarded as forming a separate family and several of which are of importance as food fishes **2 :** any of various marine fishes of *Urophycis* and related genera (family Gadidae) resembling the cod and having narrow filamentous pelvic fins placed under the throat — called also *codling;* compare SILVER HAKE, SQUIRREL HAKE, STOCKFISH, WHITE HAKE **3 :** NORTHERN WHITING

²**hake** \"\ *vi* -ED/-ING/-S **:** to fish for hake

³**hake** \"\ *vi* -ED/-ING/-S [ME *haken*] **1** *chiefly Scot* **:** to wander around idly **:** LOAF **2** *chiefly Scot* **:** to trudge or tramp — often used with *about* or *around*

⁴**hake** \"\ *n* -s **:** a person in the habit of haking

⁵**hake** \'(h)āk\ *n* -s [prob. of Scand origin; akin to Icel *haki* hook — more at HOOK] **1** *dial Eng* **:** HOOK; *esp* **:** POTHOOK 1 **2** *dial Eng* **:** a clevis of a plow

⁶**hake** *or* **haik** \'hāk\ *n* -s [prob. by alter.] **:** ³HACK 2

ha·kea \'häkēə, 'hāk-\ *n, cap* [NL, after C. L. von *Hake* †1818 Ger. horticulturist] **:** a genus of Australian shrubs and small trees (family Proteaceae) having evergreen often spiny leaves and showy flowers in dense clusters — see CUSHION-FLOWER

ha·ken·kreuz \'häkən,krȯits\ *n, pl* **hakenkreu·ze** \-tsə\ *or* **hakenkreuzes** *often cap* [G, fr. *haken* hook (fr. OHG *hācko, hāko*) + *kreuz* cross, fr. OHG *krūzi*, fr. L *cruc-, crux* — more at HOOK, CROSS] **:** the swastika used as a symbol of German anti-Semitism or of German Nazism

ha·ken·kreuz·ler \-tslə(r)\ *n, pl* **hakenkreuzler** *or* **hakenkreuzlers** *usu cap* [G, fr. *hakenkreuz*] **:** a member of any German-speaking organization in Europe after World War I using the swastika as an emblem of anti-Semitism or of extreme nationalist sentiment

¹**ha·kim** \hə'kēm\ *n, pl* **hakims** \-mz\ *also* **hu·ka·ma** \,hakə'mä\ [Ar *ḥakīm*, lit., wise one] **:** a Muslim physician

²**ha·kim** \'hä,kēm\ *n, pl* **hakim** *or* **hakims** [Ar *ḥākim*] **:** a Muslim ruler, governor, or judge

hak·ka \'häk'kä, 'hakə\ *n, pl* **hakka** *or* **hakkas** *usu cap* **1 a :** a people of the Yellow River plain that migrated into the hilly areas of southeastern China possibly during the T'ang dynasty **b :** a member of such people **2 :** a dialect of Chinese spoken in part of Kwangtung province

hakkafot *or* **hakkafoth** *var of* HAKAFOTH

ha·ko \'hä(,)kō\ *n* -s [Pawnee] **:** a Pawnee Indian ceremony representing the union of Heaven and Earth and the birth of life performed with prayers, invocation by pipe, and eagle dances to ensure long life and posterity to the participants

ha·ko·da·te \,häkə'däd·ä\ *adj, usu cap* [fr. *Hakodate*, Japan] **:** of or from the city of Hakodate, Japan **:** of the kind or style prevalent in Hakodate

hal- *or* **halo-** *comb form* [F, fr. Gk, fr. *hals* salt — more at SALT] **1 :** of or relating to a salt ‹*halochromism*› **2** [ISV, fr. *halogen*] **a :** halogen ‹*halide*› **b** *now usu* **halo- :** containing halogen ‹*haloalkyl groups*› — compare CHLOR- 3

ha·la \'hälə\ *n* -s [Hawaiian] **:** a screw pine (*Pandanus odoratissimus* syn. *P. tectorius*) native from southern Asia west to Hawaii having a trunk supported by a clump of slanting aerial roots, branches ending in spiral tufts of long narrow leaves which are used for plaiting mats, baskets, and hats, and fruits resembling pineapples but falling apart on ripening into many wedge-shaped yellow to red sections which are used as food in Micronesia and for leis in Polynesia

hal·a·car·i·dae \,halə'karə,dē\ *n pl, cap* [NL, fr. *Halacarus*, type genus (fr. *hal-* + *Acarus*) + *-idae*] **:** a small family of leathery-bodied free-living mites (group Hydrachnellae) that frequent marine algae

ha·laf·ian \hə'läfēən\ *also* **ha·laf** \hə'läf\ *adj, usu cap* [fr. Tell *Halaf*, site in northeastern Syria on the Turkish border near the village of Ras el 'Ain] **:** of or belonging to an early Aeneolithic culture of Syria and north Mesopotamia characterized by the use of stone as well as copper, adobe buildings, and a fine polychrome pottery

ha·la·kah *or* **ha·la·chah** *or* **ha·la·cha** \hä'läkä, ,hälä'kä, hə'läkə\ *n, pl* **ha·la·kahs** \-käz, -kəz\ *or* **ha·la·koth** *or* **ha·la·choth** \hä'lä,kōth, ,hälä'kōth, -ōt, -ōs\ *often cap* [Heb *hălākhāh*, lit., way] **:** the body of Jewish oral laws supplementing written law or both oral and written law together or any particular law or custom prescribed by the legal codices

ha·lak·ic *or* **ha·lach·ic** \hə'lakik\ *adj, often cap* **:** of or relating to the halakah

ha·lal \hə'läl\ *vt* **halalled; halalled; halalling; halals** [Ar *ḥalāl* that which is lawful] **:** to slaughter for food according to Moslem law

hal·al·cor \-,kō(ə)r\ *n* -s [Hindi *halālkhor*, fr. Per, fr. Ar *ḥalāl* + Per *khor* eating] **:** a person in Iran and India to whom any food is lawful

ha·la·pe·pe \,hälə'pāpē\ *n* -s [Hawaiian] **:** a tree (*Dracaena aurea*) of the Pacific islands having flowers resembling lilies and yielding a wood used for carving

hal·ate \'ha,lāt\ *n* -s [*hal-* + *-ate*] **:** a salt of chloric, bromic, or iodic acid

ha·la·tion \hā'lāshən, hə-, ha-\ *n* -s [*halo* + *-ation*] **1 :** the spreading of light beyond its proper boundaries in a developed photographic image (as around a window facing the sky in an interior view or around other bright objects) caused principally by reflection from the back of the film or plate **2 :** a bright ring that sometimes encompasses the point at which a bright light shows on a television screen

halavah *var of* HALVAH

hal·a·zone \'halə,zōn\ *n* -s [*hal-* + *az-* + *-one*] **:** a white crystalline powdery acid $C_6H_4(SO_2NCl_2)COOH$ used as a disinfectant for drinking water; *para-(N,N'-dichloro-sulfamyl)-benzoic acid*

hal·berd \'halbərd, 'hȯlb-, 'häl-\ *or* **hal·bert** \-rt\ *n* -s [ME *haubert, halberd*, fr. MF *hallebarde*, fr. MHG *helmbarte*, fr. *helm* handle + *barte* ax, fr. OHG *barta*, fr. *bart* beard; akin to OHG *halb* handle — more at HELVE, BEARD] **:** a weapon used esp. in the 15th and 16th centuries that consists typically of a battle-ax and pike mounted on a handle about six feet long

hal·berd·ier \,==ˈdi(ə)r\ *n* -s [MF *hallebardier*, fr. *hallebarde* + *-ier* -er] **:** a person armed with a halberd; *esp* **:** a guard who carries a halberd as a symbol of his duty

hal·chid·ho·ma \,halchə'dōmə\ *n, pl* **halchidhoma** *or* **halchidhomas** *usu cap* **1 :** an Indian people in the Colorado River valley near the mouth of the Gila allied with the Maricopa **2 :** a member of the Halchidhoma

heads of halberds

¹**hal·cy·on** \'halsēən\ *n* [ME *alceon, alicion*, fr. L *halcyon, alcyon*, fr. Gk *halkyōn, alkyōn*] **1** -s **a :** a bird identified with the kingfisher that was fabled by the ancients to nest at sea in a floating nest about the time of the winter solstice and to calm the waves during incubation **b :** KINGFISHER **2** [NL, fr. L *halcyon, alcyon*] *cap* **:** a genus of large kingfishers widely distributed in warmer parts of the Old World

²**halcyon** \"\ *adj* **1 :** belonging to or suggestive of the period commonly reckoned as 14 days assumed by the ancients to occur at the time of the winter solstice during the nesting period of the halcyon ‹~ calm› **2 a :** pleasingly or idyllically calm or peaceful **:** SERENE ‹a ~ atmosphere› **b :** HAPPY, GOLDEN ‹a ~ era› ‹the ~ days of youth› **c :** PROSPEROUS, AFFLUENT ‹the ~ days of the clipper-ship trade› **syn** see CALM

hal·dane's law *or* **haldane's rule** \'hȯl,dānz-\ *n, usu cap H* [after John B. S. *Haldane* b1892 Scottish geneticist] **:** a principle in genetics: when in an interspecific cross one sex is absent, rare, or sterile in the offspring, that sex is heterogametic

hal·dan·ite \'hȯl(,)dā,nīt, -,də-,-\ *n* -s *usu cap* [James Alexander *Haldane* †1851 and Robert *Haldane* †1842, his brother, Scot. clergymen and evangelists + E *-ite*] **:** a follower of an evangelical movement in Scotland led by the Haldane brothers

hal·du \'häl(,)dü\ *n* -s [Hindi *haldū*] **1 :** a timber tree (*Adina cordifolia*) of the family Rubiaceae with light-yellow even-grained wood **2 :** the wood of haldu

¹**hale** *also* **hail** \'hāl, *esp before pause or consonant* -āəl\ *adj* -ER/-EST [partly fr. ME (northern dial.) *hal, hale*, fr. OE *hāl;* partly fr. ME *hail, heil*, fr. ON *heill* — more at WHOLE] **1 :** free from defect, disease, or infirmity **:** SOUND, HEALTHY, ROBUST ‹a ~ body› ‹~ in youth› **2** *chiefly Scot* **:** WHOLE **syn** see HEALTHY

²**hale** \"\ *adv* [partly fr. ME *hal, hale*, fr. *hal, hale*, adj.; partly fr. ME *hail, heil*, fr. *hail, heil*, adj.] *now dial Brit* **:** WHOLLY

³**hale** \"\ *vb* -ED/-ING/-S [ME *halen*, fr. MF *haler* — more at HAUL] *vt* **1 :** HAUL, PULL, DRAW **2 :** to compel (a person) to go ‹~ a vagrant into court› **3** *obs* **:** VEX, ANNOY ~ *vi* **1** *obs* **:** to move briskly (as of a ship) **2** *now dial Brit* **:** to pour or flow copiously ‹the sweat was *haling* off him› **3 :** to pull or tug ‹*haling* at the plow› **syn** see PULL

⁴**ha·le** \'hä(,)lā\ *n* -s [Hawaiian] *in Hawaii* **:** HOUSE

hal·e·co·mor·phi \,haləkō'mȯr,fī\ [NL, fr. L *Halec*, genus of fish (fr. L *halec, hallec, alec, allec* fish brine) + NL *-o-* + *-morphi*] *syn of* CYCLOGANOIDEI

hal·e·cos·to·mi \,halə'kästə,mī\ *n pl, cap* [NL, fr. *Halec* + NL *-o-* + *-stomi*] **:** an order of extinct ganoid fishes resembling herrings

hale·ness *n* -ES **:** the quality or state of being hale ‹the ~ of the old man at 90 was surprising›

ha·le·nia \hə'lēnēə\ *n, cap* [NL, fr. Johann *Halen*, 19th cent. Ger. botanist + NL *-ia*] **:** a genus of herbs (family Gentianaceae) with opposite leaves and spurred flowers — see SPURRED GENTIAN

¹**hal·er** \'hā(ə)lə(r)\ *n* -s [³*hale* + *-er*] **:** one that hales

²**ha·ler** \'hälər, -,le(ə)r\ *n, pl* **halers** \-rz\ *or* **hale·ru** \-,lə,rü\ [Czech, fr. MHG *hallære, haller, heller* — more at HELLER] **:** a monetary unit of Czechoslovakia equal to ¹⁄₁₀₀ of the koruna — see MONEY table

hales \'ālz\ *n pl* [prob. of Scand origin; akin to ON *hali* tail, pointed end; akin to Gk *kēlon* arrow, MIr *cail* spear, Skt *śala* stick, porcupine quill] *dial Eng* **:** handles on an implement (as a plow or a wheelbarrow)

ha·le·sia \hə'lēzh(ē)ə, ha'-\ *n* [NL, fr. Stephen *Hales* †1761 Eng. physiologist + NL *-ia*] **1** *cap* **:** a genus of small trees (family Styracaceae) of southeastern No. America having alternate leaves and white bell-shaped flowers borne in great profusion before the leaves — see SILVER BELL **2** -s **:** any plant of the genus *Halesia*

hale·some \'hālsəm\ *adj* [ME (northern dial.) *halsum*, fr. *hal, hale* healthy + *-sum* -some — more at HALE] *chiefly Scot* **:** WHOLESOME

hale water *n, chiefly Scot* **:** a heavy rainfall

ha·ley-over \'hālē'==\ *n* [origin unknown] **:** ANTONY OVER

¹**half** \'haf, haa(ə)f, haif, hȧf, häf; *in sense 2b the f is often lost when "past" follows*\ *n, pl* **halves** \|vz\ [ME, fr. OE *healf;* akin to OHG & Goth *halba* side, half, ON *halfa*, L *scalpere* to cut, scratch, Gk *skalops* mole (animal), OE *sciell* shell — more at SHELL] **1** *obs* **:** PART, SIDE **2 a :** one of two equal parts into which a thing is divisible ‹~ of it› ‹~ of the profits›; *also* **:** a part of a thing approximately equal to the remainder ‹the larger ~ of the fortune› **:** a sizable portion ‹the bottom ~ of the social pyramid —N.E.Eliason› — often used without *of* esp. when a quantitative word follows ‹~ the money› **b :** half an hour — used in designation of time ‹~ past ten› ‹~ after five› **3 :** one of a pair: as **a :** PARTNER **b :** SEMESTER, TERM **c** (1) **:** one of the two playing periods usu. separated by an interval that together make up the playing time of certain games (as football) — see QUARTER 21b (2) **:** the turn of one team to bat in baseball ‹first ~ of the eighth inning› **4 a :** HALF CROWN **b :** HALF-DOLLAR **5 :** significant part **:** CRUX, WHOLE — used with a negative ‹that's not the ~ of it› **6** (by shortening) **:** HALFBACK **7 :** HALF TIME — **and a half** *slang* **:** of great size, importance, difficulty, or perplexity ‹a job and a half› — **by half** *adv* **:** by a great deal **:** far and away ‹too stupid *by half*› — **by halves** *adv* **:** inadequately or incompletely **:** HALFHEARTEDLY ‹let's not do things *by halves*› — **half a mind :** more or less of an intention ‹have *half a mind* to go swimming› **:** more or less intending ‹am *half a mind* to go swimming› — **in half** *adv* **:** into two equal or nearly equal parts ‹cut an apple *in half*›

²**half** \"\ *adj* [ME, fr. OE *healf;* akin to OHG *halb* half, ON *halfr*, Goth *halbs*, OE *healf*, n.] **1 a :** being one of two equal parts ‹a ~ share› ‹a ~ sheet of paper› **b** (1) **:** amounting to nearly half **:** approximately a half (2) **:** PARTIAL, IMPERFECT ‹~ knowledge of a subject› **2 a :** reaching only half the normal distance ‹a ~ gunshot away› **b :** extending or covering only half (as of the regular or normal area) ‹a ~ window› ‹a ~ mask› **c :** covering the backbone and one quarter of the boards away from the backbone and sometimes the corners ‹a book bound in ~ leather› ‹a *half*-vellum binding› — compare FULL 12c **d :** PART-TIME ‹working only ~ days› ‹~ shift› **3** *chiefly dial Brit* **:** of a species of small size — used of birds and sometimes of fish

³**half** \"\ *adv* [ME, fr. *half*, adj.] **1 a :** in an equal part or degree **b :** only partially **:** not completely **:** IMPERFECTLY ‹~ digested› ‹~ persuaded› **2 a :** at all **:** REALLY — used with a negative ‹a performance that wasn't ~ bad› **b** — used with a negative and before a verb to imply the opposite of what is expressed ‹didn't ~ beat up the policeman› **3 a :** by half an hour less ‹~ ten o'clock› — used chiefly in Scotland and Ireland **b** — used before a numeral in designating soundings to add one half to the numeral ‹~ six fathoms› **c** — used in the nomenclature of points of the compass between the names of two points to designate a position or direction half a point from the first compass point in the direction of the second

hal·fa \'halfə\ *var of* ALFA

half-a-crown \'===\ *n* **1 :** HALF CROWN **2 :** the sum of two shillings and sixpence

half a dollar *n* **:** HALF-DOLLAR

¹**half-and-half** \'===\ *n* **:** something that is half one thing and half another: as **a :** a mixture of two malt beverages (as porter and ale or beer and stout) **b :** solder made of equal parts of lead and tin

²**half-and-half** \"\ *adj* **1 :** half one thing and half another ‹a *half-and-half* mixture› **2 a :** EQUAL ‹a job demanding *half-and-half* cooperation› **b :** demanding equal participation on the part of two persons ‹a *half-and-half* proposition› **3 :** PARTIAL ‹*half-and-half* enthusiasm›

³**half-and-half** \"\ *adv* **1 :** into two equal parts ‹divided *half-and-half*› **2 :** EQUALLY ‹a duty shared *half-and-half* by husband and wife›

half an eye *n* **:** partial vision; *esp* **:** a casual or careless glance

half-ape \'==\ *n* **:** one of the lower primates (as a lemur or tarsier)

half-armor \'===\ *n* **:** armor protecting only a part of the body

half-assed \'==\ *adj* **1** *slang* **:** lacking significance, adequacy, or completeness **:** DEFICIENT ‹wasn't going to do a *half-assed* job —R.O.Bowen› **2** *slang* **:** lacking intelligence, ability, or experience **:** STUPID ‹those *half-assed* women on Quality Hill want to kick it out of town —Conrad Richter›

half aunt *n* **:** the half sister of a parent

halfback \'==\ *n* **1 :** one of the backs stationed near either flank in football **2 :** a player stationed immediately behind the forward line (as in field hockey or soccer or rugby)

half-baked \'==\ *adj* **1 :** only imperfectly baked **:** UNDERDONE **2 a :** not well planned **:** poorly contrived ‹a *half-baked* plan› **b :** lacking judgment, intelligence, or common sense ‹a *half-baked* individual› ‹dramatic ideas that are often trivial or *half-baked* —Winthrop Sargeant›

half-ball stroke *n* **:** a stroke in billiards in which the center of the striker's ball is made to hit the extreme edge of an object ball

half bat *n* **:** one half of a brick

halfbeak \'==\ *n* **:** any of a family (Hemiramphidae) of small elongate fishes resembling the gar, closely allied to the flying fishes and like these often moving some distance through the air above the water, having on the lower jaw an extension like a beak, and inhabiting chiefly warm seas

half-beam \'==\ *n* **:** a beam in a ship extending from one of the sides to a deck opening (as a hatchway)

half-bent \'==\ *n* **:** the first notch in the tumbler of a gunlock for the sear point to enter to half-cock the piece

half binding *n* **:** a book binding in which one kind of material (as leather, cloth, or vellum) covers the backbone, one quarter of the boards away from the backbone, and sometimes the corners while another kind of material covers the rest — compare FULL BINDING, QUARTER BINDING, THREE-QUARTER BINDING

half bishop *n* **:** an artist's canvas measuring 45 by 56 inches — compare BISHOP'S LENGTH

half blood *n* **1 a :** the relation between persons having one parent but not both in common — compare BLOOD 2, CONSANGUINEOUS, DEMISANG, UTERINE, WHOLE BLOOD **b :** a person so related to another **2 :** HALF-BREED 1 **3 :** a grade of wool next below fine in a descending scale of fineness — compare BLOOD 7, BRAID 2, QUARTER BLOOD **4 a :** an animal tracing from a pure breed or strain through one parent only **:** GRADE 5 **b :** an individual heterozygous for a specified character

half-blooded \'===\ *also* **half-blood** \'==\ *adj* **1 :** having half blood or being a half-breed **2 :** having one parent of good and one of inferior stock ‹a *half-blooded* sheep›

half board *n* **:** a maneuver of luffing a boat sailing close-hauled so that it shoots into the wind but before it has quite lost headway of putting the helm up again and letting the boat fill away on the same tack

half bog soil *n* **:** an interzonal group of soils developed under swamp-forest types of vegetation, having mucky or peaty surface soil underlain by gray mineral soil, and appearing mostly in humid or subhumid climates

half boot *n* **:** a boot with a top reaching somewhat above the ankle

half-bound \'==\ *adj* **:** having a half binding ‹a *half-bound* book›

half-box \'==\ *n* **:** a section of a page of a newspaper or periodical being usu. rectangular and marked off at the top and bottom by rules or an ornamental border — see BOX 9a

half-breadth plan *n* **:** a plan of one side of a ship showing by horizontal longitudinal sections the forms of the various waterlines, rail and deck lines at the side, the frame stations, and the buttock lines

¹**half-bred** \'==\ *adj* **:** HALF-BLOODED

²**half-bred** \'==\ *n* -s **:** a half-blooded animal

¹**half-breed** \'==\ *n* -s **1 :** the offspring of parents of different races; *esp* **:** the offspring of an American Indian and a white person **2 a** *usu cap* **:** a member of the faction of the Republican party that supported President Garfield in his controversy in 1881 with Senators Conkling and Platt of New York State over a civil-service appointment **b :** an insurgent faction in a political party **3 :** an animal or plant produced by crossing two distinct forms — often used to distinguish the product of such a cross within a species; compare HYBRID

²**half-breed** \'==\ *adj* **:** HALF-BLOODED

half brother *n* [ME] **:** a brother by one parent only

half-bull \'==\ *n* **:** a male fur seal not fully adult

half cadence *or* **half close** \'=,klōz\ *n* **:** a musical chord sequence giving a sense of partial harmonic completion (as tonic to dominant) — see CADENCE illustration

¹**half-caste** \'==\ *n* **:** a person of mixed racial or cultural descent **:** HALF-BREED

²**half-caste** \"\ *adj* **:** of the rank of or relating to a half-caste

half-castrate \'===, ==\ *vt* **:** to remove the descended testis of (a unilateral ridgeling) to prevent breeding

half-cell \'==\ *n* **:** a device consisting of a single electrode immersed in an electrolytic solution and thus developing a definite potential difference

half cent *n* **:** a coin representing one half a cent (as the copper half cent coined by the U. S. 1793–1857)

half chronometer *n* **:** a watch having an escapement compounded of the lever and chronometer escapements; *also* **:** a fine lever-escapement watch adjusted for temperature

half-close \'=,klōs\ *adj* **:** MID 3

half cock *n* **1 :** the position of the hammer of a firearm when about half retracted and held by the sear so that it cannot be operated by a pull on the trigger **2 :** a state of inadequate preparation or mental confusion — used with *at* ‹the whole project went off at *half cock*›

half-cock \'==\ *vt* **:** to place the hammer of (a firearm) at half cock

half-cocked \'==\ *adj* **1 :** being at half cock **2 :** lacking clear or rational preparation, knowledge, or intention ‹go off *half-cocked*›; *also* **:** STUPID, FOOLISH ‹*half-cocked* public officials›

half column *n* **:** an engaged column which projects from a wall by approximately half its diameter

half cone *n* **:** the part of a cone formed by half lines from the vertex — opposed to *double cone*

half-course \'==\ *n* **:** a course at a school, college, or university having fewer weekly meetings than the regular course and carrying correspondingly fewer credits

half cousin *n* **:** the child of a half uncle or half aunt

half-cracked \'==\ *adj* **:** HALF-WITTED

half crown *n* **:** a British coin worth 2*s* 6*d* being in the 16th cent. of gold, from 1601–1946 of silver, and then of cupronickel; *sometimes* **:** the sum of 2*s* 6*d*

half deck *n* **1 :** an incomplete deck; *specif* **:** a portion of the deck of a sailing ship next below the spar deck between mainmast and cabin **2 :** a slipper limpet of the genus *Crepidula*

half-decked \'==\ *adj* **:** partly decked and partly open ‹*half-decked* craft . . . used by the later Vikings —C.I.Elton›

half-deck·er \'='dekə(r)\ *n* **:** a half-decked ship

half-diamond indention *n* **:** a style of display typesetting in which succeeding lines are indented at each end, each line being shorter than the preceding line — called also *inverted-pyramid indention*

half dime *n* **:** a silver five-cent coin struck by the U. S. mint in 1792 and from 1794 to 1873

half disme *n* **:** a half dime struck in 1792

half-dollar \'==\ *n* **1 :** a coin representing one half of a dollar ‹a U. S. or Canadian *half-dollar*› **2 :** the sum of fifty cents or one half of a dollar

half door *n* **1 :** either part of a Dutch door **2 :** a swing door that fills only a part of the doorway

half eagle *n* **:** the five-dollar gold piece issued by the U. S. 1795–1916 and in 1929 — compare EAGLE

half-evergreen \'===\ *adj, of a plant* **:** incompletely evergreen: as **a :** having foliage that is functional and persistent during part of the winter or dry season **b :** tending to be evergreen in the milder but deciduous in the more rigorous part of the range

half-faced \'==\ *adj* **1 :** showing a profile **2 :** closed or protecting on three sides but open on the front ‹a *half-faced* tent› ‹a *half-faced* cabin›

half fare *n* **:** a reduced fare (as on railroads or buses) available to underage children, to employees, or to passengers who ride at a particular time or under certain circumstances

half gainer *n* **:** a gainer in which the diver executes a half-backward somersault and enters the water headfirst and facing the board

half gerund *n* **:** the gerund in *-ing* when taking certain constructions suggestive of the participle (as *coming* in "I don't like him coming here" and *climbing* in "he tears his shirt climbing trees")

half-hardy \'===\ *adj, of a plant* **:** able to withstand a moder-

ately low temperature but injured by severe freezing and surviving the winter in cold climates only if carefully protected
half-hardy annual *n* **:** a plant that may endure a few degrees of frost but is killed at lower temperatures (as China aster or zinnia)
half hatchet *n* **:** a hatchet with a straight edge broader than the edge of a lathing hatchet and with a flat hammer face on the end opposite the cutting edge — see HATCHET illustration
halfhead bedstead \'=,=-\ *n* **:** a bedstead with posts lower than the headboard
half header *n* **:** half a brick used to close a course
halfhearted \'=¦==\ *adj* **:** lacking heart, spirit, or interest ⟨a ~ try⟩ — **half·heart·ed·ly** *adv* — **half·heart·ed·ness** *n* -ES
half hitch *n* **:** a knot usu. tied double and used for temporarily securing a rope to an object by making a turn around the object, around the standing part, under the turn, and when double, around the standing part again and through the last bight

half hitch

half-holiday \'=¦==,=\ *n* **:** a holiday limited to half a day
half hose *n* **:** men's socks reaching halfway to the knee
half hour *n* [ME] **1 :** thirty minutes **2 :** the midpoint of an hour — **half-hourly** \'=¦==\ *adv (or adj)*
half-hour glass \'=¦=,=\ *n* **:** an instrument for measuring time in half-hour intervals
half hunter *n* **:** a watch having the outer half of the crystal protected by a metal casing
halfies *pl of* HALFY
half-inferior \¦=====\ *adj* **:** borne below the androecium in a concave receptacle but free from the axis — used of the ovary (as in perigynous flowers)
half island *or* **half isle** *n* **:** PENINSULA
half joe \'=¦jō\ *n, pl* **half joes** [*half* + *joe*, short for *johannes*] **:** JOHANNES
half-knot \'=¦=\ *n* **:** a knot joining the ends of two cords and used in tying other knots (as the square knot); *also* **:** OVERHAND KNOT
half lap *n* **:** END LAP
half-length \'=¦=\ *n* **:** something that is or represents only half the complete length (as a portrait showing only the upper half of a person)
half-life \'=¦=\ *also* **half-life period** *n* **1 :** the time required for half of the atoms of a radioactive substance present at the beginning to become disintegrated ⟨rays from uranium have a *half-life* of millions of years —F.B.Colton⟩ ⟨this isotope has *half-life* of twenty-three minutes —L.J.Levert⟩ ⟨there will still be one quarter of the element left at the end of two *half-life periods* —G.E.Owen⟩ **2 :** the time required for half the amount of a substance (as a drug or radioactive tracer) in or introduced into a living system to be eliminated whether by excretion, metabolic decomposition, or other natural process
half-light \'=,=\ *n* **:** grayish light (as of dim interiors, evening, or mist); *also* **:** the portion of a work of art showing such light
half line *n* **:** a straight line in mathematics beginning at a given point and extending indefinitely in one direction only — called also *half ray*
¹half·ling *pronunc at* HALF + lən *or* liŋ\ *or* **half·lin** \-lən\ *n* -S [*half* + *-ling*] **1** *chiefly Scot* **:** a half-grown person **2** *chiefly Scot* **:** half of a silver penny
²halfling \"\ *or* **halflin** \"\ *adj, chiefly Scot* **:** not fully grown **:** IMMATURE
half·lings \-nz,-ŋz\ *adv* [ME *halfling, halflings*, fr. *half* + *-ling, -lings*] *Scot* **:** half or approximately half **:** PARTIALLY ⟨while Jennie ~ is afraid to speak —Robert Burns⟩
half-long \'=¦=\ *adj, of a speech sound* **:** intermediate in duration between long and short
half-loop \'=¦=\ *n* **:** a flight maneuver in which an aircraft pulls up in an inside loop but continues upside down in level flight in the direction from which it came
half·ly *adv* [ME, fr. *half* + *-ly*] **:** ³HALF
half-marrow \'=¦=(,)=\ *n, now dial Brit* **:** a partner or mate; *specif* **:** SPOUSE
¹half-mast \'=¦=\ *n* **:** a point some distance but not necessarily halfway down below the top of a mast or staff or the peak of a gaff ⟨a flag flown at *half-mast* as a token of mourning⟩
²half-mast \'=¦=\ *adj* **:** located below the top of the mast ⟨a *half-mast* position⟩
³half-mast \"\ *vt* [¹*half-mast*] **:** to cause to hang at half-mast ⟨*half-mast* a flag⟩
half measure *n* **:** a partial, halfhearted, or weak line of action ⟨victory is seldom won by *half measures*⟩
half·mens \'hälf,men(t)s\ *n, pl* **halfmens** \"\ *or* **half·men·se** \-n(t)sə\ [Afrik, fr. *half* + *mens* human being, person] **:** a southern African plant (*Pachypodium namaquam*) of the family Apocynaceae having an upright naked stem surmounted by a crown of leaves and suggesting in outline the figure of a human
half-minded \'=¦==\ *adj* **:** being of an undecided or partial intent, desire, or will ⟨*half-minded* to do something desperate⟩
half-monitor \'=¦===\ *n* **:** a roof for hog or poultry houses shaped like a saw tooth
half-moon \'=¦=\ *also* '=¦=\ *n* **1 :** the moon at the quarters when half its disk appears illuminated — see MOON illustration **2 :** a figure or object that is pointed at both ends, is about a fourth as wide as it is long, and in plane outline is half of a circle with the straight section curved in so that one side is concave while the other is convex ⟨an island *half-moon*⟩ **3 :** the lunule of a fingernail **4 a :** a bluish black California marine food fish (*Medialuna californiensis*) of the family Scorpididae — called also *blue perch* **b :** SCALARE
half-mooned \'=¦müind\ *adj* **:** shaped like a half-moon ⟨in his *half-mooned* chair —Thomas Coryat⟩
half mourning *n* **1 :** a period of mourning succeeding that of deep mourning **2 :** mourning dress lightened by the use of white, gray, or lavender
half nelson *n* **:** a wrestling hold in which one arm is thrust under the corresponding arm of the opponent generally from behind and the hand placed upon the back of his neck — compare FULL NELSON, QUARTER NELSON, THREE-QUARTER NELSON
half nephew *n* **:** the son of a half brother or half sister
half·ness *n* -ES **:** the quality or state of being half
half niece *n* **:** the daughter of a half brother or half sister
half note *n* **:** a musical note of half the value of a whole note — called also *minim*
half nut *n* **:** a screw nut split lengthwise so that either one part may be arranged to ride on a screw or the two parts may be arranged to clamp about a screw

half notes

half-one \'=¦=, *in sense 2* '=¦=\ *n* **1 :** a golf handicap of one stroke subtracted on alternate holes **2** *Irish* **:** a half a glass of whiskey
half-open \'=¦==\ *adj* **:** MID 3
half-orphan \'=¦==\ *n* **:** a child with only one parent living
half·pace *pronunc at* HALF + ,pās\ *n* [by folk etymology fr. MF *haut pas*, lit., high step] **1 :** a raised floor or dais or a platform or footpace at the top of steps (as for a throne or an altar) **2 :** a landing of a staircase like a broad step between two half flights — compare QUARTERPACE
half·pen·ny \'hāp(ə)nī\ *n, pl* **half·pence** \-pən(t)s\ *or* **halfpennies** \-p(ə)nīz\ [ME *halfpeny, halfpeni*, fr. *half* + *peny, peni* penny] **1 :** a coin or token representing one half of a penny (as a British coin issued from the time of Edward I) **2 :** the sum of half a penny **3 :** a small amount ⟨not a ~ less⟩
halfpenny post *n, Brit* **:** second-class mail
half·pen·ny·worth \-ī,wərth, 'hāpəth\ *n* **:** something that is worth or costs a halfpenny ⟨a ~ of fish⟩
half-pike \'=,=\ *n* **:** a pike with a short shaft — compare BOARDING PIKE, SPONTOON
half-pint \'=¦=\ *n* **1 :** half a pint **2** *slang* **:** a short, small, or inconsequential person
half-pitch \'=¦=\ *adj* **:** having a gradient of one to two ⟨a *half-pitch* slope⟩
half plane *n, math* **:** the part of a plane on one side of an indefinitely extended straight line drawn in it
half principal *n* **:** a principal roof rafter that does not extend to the ridge
half-rat·er \'=¦==\ *n* **:** a small sailing yacht of about 15-ft. waterline built under the rating rule in use in Great Britain about the end of the 19th century
half ray *n* **:** HALF LINE
half rest *n* **:** a rest in music corresponding in value with a half note
half rhyme *n* **:** a terminal consonance other than rhyme in two or more words (as in the unstressed final syllables of *hollow* and *shallow* or the matching terminal consonant clusters of *stopped* and *wept*)
half ring *n* **:** one of the incomplete cartilaginous rings that support the upper part of the bronchial tubes of most birds and in singing birds form a part of the syrinx
half-ripe \'=¦=\ *or* **half-ripened** \'=¦==\ *adj* **:** of, relating to, or consisting of the current growth of a tree, shrub, or woody plant that has not yet reached the mature wood stage ⟨*half-ripe* part⟩
¹half-roll \'=¦=\ *n* **:** a flight maneuver in which an airplane rolls halfway over and then flies upside down along its original line of flight
²half-roll \"\ *vi, of an airplane* **:** to perform a half-roll
half-round \'=¦=\ *adj* **1 :** semicircular or approximately so; *also* **:** flat on one side and round on the other **2** *of veneer* **:** cut from a log placed off center in a lathe so that it comes into contact with the blade on rotation only when the projecting portion reaches the blade
half round \"\ *n* **:** something half-round (as a chisel or molding)
half-round file *n* **:** a file made flat on one side and convex on the other
half run *n* **:** a contract purchased from an advertising agency whereby a card of a type suitable for bus, subway, or train advertising is required to be placed in half of the cars in a specified district
half-saved \'=¦=\ *adj, now dial Eng* **:** HALF-WITTED
half-seas over \'=,=¦==\ *adj, slang* **:** DRUNK
half sheet *n* **:** a sheet imposed and printed by the work-and-turn method
half shell *n* **:** either of the valves of a bivalve — **on the half shell :** in either of the halves of a shell ⟨oysters *on the half shell*⟩
half shirt *n* **:** a man's shirtfront or a woman's chemisette worn in the late 17th century; *also* **:** STOMACHER
half-shot \'=¦=\ *adj, slang* **:** partially drunk
half-shrub \'=,=\ *n* **:** a perennial plant in which the stems are more or less woody esp. at the base — **half-shrubby** \'=¦==\ *adj*
half-sib \'=¦=\ *also* **half-sibling** \'=¦==\ *n* **:** a half brother or half sister — compare SIB
half-silvered \'=¦==\ *adj, of a mirror or glass block* **:** having a metallic film backing of such thinness that only half the incident light is reflected with the remainder being transmitted through the backing
half sister *n* [ME] **:** a sister by one parent only
half size *n* **:** a size in suits, coats, or dresses for short or short-waisted women with full figures
half sleeve *n* **:** any of various sleeves that reach to a little above the elbow or to a little below the elbow
¹half-slip \'=,=\ *n* **:** PETTICOAT 1c
²half-slip \'=¦=\ *adj* **:** of or relating to the degree of ripeness of a melon when the peduncle is separated from the fruit by pulling or pressure
half-snap \'=¦=\ *n* **:** a quick movement of a shotgun to the shoulder followed by a rapid check on the alignment of the piece before it is fired
half snipe *n* **:** JACKSNIPE
half sole *n* **:** a shoe sole extending from the shank forward **:** TAP
half-sole \'=¦=\ *vt* [*half sole*] **:** to attach a half sole to esp. in repairing (a shoe)
half sovereign *n* **:** a British gold coin worth ten shillings or ½ pound sterling regularly issued up to 1916 and since then only occasionally (as in 1937)
half space *n* **:** a halfpace in a stair
half-staff \'=¦=\ *n* **:** HALF-MAST — used of a flag on a flagpole
half step *n* **1 :** a walking step of 15 inches or in double time of 18 inches **2 :** the pitch interval in music between two adjacent keys on a keyboard instrument — called also *semitone*
half-stopped \'=¦=\ *adj* **:** partly covered at the top — used of an organ pipe
half story *n* **:** an uppermost story which is usu. lighted by dormer windows and in which a sloping roof replaces the upper part of the front wall
half-stripe \'=,=\ *n* **:** the narrow ¼-inch stripe which together with the full ½-inch stripe makes up the sleeve and shoulder-board rank insignia of naval officers below flag rank
half stuff *or* **half stock** *n* **:** paper pulp; *esp* **:** paper pulp from rags partly processed (as by washing, bleaching, and draining) and ready for the beater
half sweep *n* **:** a sweep with a blade on only one side for use in cultivating close to a crop row
half-sword *n* **1** *obs* **:** a sword of small size **2** *obs* **:** half the length of a sword — **at half-sword** *adv, obs* **:** at close quarters
half tester bed *n* **:** a bed with a low foot and a canopy projecting from the posts at the head
half tide *n* **:** the time or state halfway between flood and ebb
half timber \'=¦==\ *or* **half-timbered** \'=¦==\ *adj* **:** being of the Tudor or Elizabethan construction employing wood framing with spaces filled with masonry — **half-timbering** \'=¦=(=)=\ *n*
half time *n* **:** time marking the completion of half of a game or contest; *also* **:** the intermission between the second and third quarters of a game (as football and basketball)
half-timer \'=¦==\ *n* **1 :** one that spends only half the usual time at anything **2** *Brit* **:** a child who is permitted to work half his time at some employment
half tint *n* **:** DEMITINT
half title *n* **1 :** the title of a book usu. standing alone on a right-hand page directly preceding the title page — called also *bastard title* **2 :** the title of a book standing alone on a usu. right-hand page immediately preceding the first page of text or at the head of the first page of text
half-toe \'=,=\ *n* **:** the ball of the foot as the base of support in a dance step
halftone \'=,=\ *n, often attrib* **1 :** HALF STEP 2 **2 a :** any of the shades of gray between the darkest and the lightest parts of a photographic image — called also *middletone* **b** [so called fr. the fact that this process was the first that was successful in reproducing the halftones of a photo] **:** a photoengraving made from an image photographed through a screen having a lattice of horizontal and vertical lines and then etched so that the details of the image are reproduced in fine dots with the darker areas appearing as heavy and concentrated dots and the lighter areas as fine and diffused dots; *also* **:** a print made from a halftone — compare DROPOUT
half-tongue \'=,=\ *n* [ME *half tong*; intended as trans. of ML *medietas linguae*] **:** a jury de medietate linguae in English law
¹half-track \'=,=\ *n* -S **1 :** a chain-track drive system serving to propel a vehicle supported in front by a pair of wheels and consisting of an endless metal belt on each side of the vehicle driven by one of two inside sprockets, running on bogie wheels mounted on the frame, and laying down on the ground as it revolves a flexible track of cleated steel or hard-rubber plates **2 :** a motor vehicle equipped with half-tracks in the rear and wheels in the front; *specif* **:** such a vehicle lightly armored for military use
²half-track \'=,=\ *also* **half-tracked** \'=,=\ *adj* **:** equipped with half-tracks
half-truth \'=¦=\ *n* **:** a partially true or partially fabricated statement made to deceive or to escape censure ⟨a public led astray by the *half-truths* of a dictator⟩
half-turn \'=¦=\ *n* **:** reversal of direction (as in a staircase) either by one 180-degree turn or two right-angle turns
half twist *n* **1 :** a dive done in either pike or layout position from a springboard or platform in which the diver executes a half turn of the body on a longitudinal axis before entering the water — compare FULL TWIST **2 :** a half turn of the body in the air on a longitudinal axis executed alone or in conjunction with other maneuvers (as on a trampoline, from a springboard, or in vaulting)
half uncial *n* **:** a book hand formed by combining uncial characters with carefully written cursive forms and used as the typical book hand from the earliest times in Ireland and from the 7th century to the Norman Conquest in England

half uncials

half uncle *n* **:** the half brother of a parent
half-value layer *n* **:** the thickness of an absorbing substance necessary to reduce by one half the initial intensity of the radiation traversing it
half volley *n* **:** a ball that is stroked or batted at the instant it rebounds from the ground: as **a :** a kick in soccer taken on the run as a ball rebounds from the ground **b :** a dropkick in rugby **c :** a bowled cricket ball that lands near enough to the blockhole to be readily hit as soon as it leaves the ground
half-volley \'=¦==\ *vb* [*half volley*] *vt* **:** to drive (a tennis ball) as a half volley ~ *vi* **:** to play a half volley in tennis
half-wave plate *n* **:** a crystal plate that reduces by ½ cycle the phase difference between the two components of polarized light traversing it — compare QUARTER-WAVE PLATE
half-wave rectifier *n* **:** a rectifier that utilizes one half cycle of alternating current and suppresses the other
¹halfway \'=¦=\ *adv* [ME, fr. *half* + *way*] **1 :** at a point at or near the middle **:** MIDWAY ⟨two ships passing ~ across the ocean⟩ **2 :** with concessions **:** in a state of readiness to negotiate **:** AMENABLY ⟨the revolutionists met the national government ~⟩ **3 a :** PARTIALLY, ALMOST **:** very nearly ⟨the fighter ~ yielded⟩ **b :** MORE OR LESS ⟨a ~ kind remark⟩
²halfway \"\ *adj* **1 :** equally distant from the extremes of a space or course **:** midway between two points ⟨a ~ point⟩ **2 :** PARTIAL ⟨~ measures⟩
halfway covenant *n, cap H&C* **:** a form of church membership among the Congregational churches of New England allowed by decisions in 1657 and 1662 and permitting baptized persons of moral life and orthodox faith to enjoy privileges of full membership except the partaking of the Lord's Supper
halfway house *n* **:** an inn or place of call midway on a journey; *also* **:** any halfway place in a progress
half wellington *n, usu cap W* **:** a loose-topped leather boot similar to the Wellington but shorter and usu. worn under trousers
half-wit \'=,=\ *n* **:** a foolish person **:** DOLT, BLOCKHEAD
half-witted \'=¦==\ *adj* **1 :** SILLY, SENSELESS **2 :** mentally deficient **:** FOOLISH, IMBECILE — **half-wit·ted·ly** *adv* — **half-wit·ted·ness** *n* -ES
half-world \'=,=\ *n* **1 :** HEMISPHERE ⟨will prevent economic development of our *half-world* —Hamish Hamilton⟩ **2 :** DEMIMONDE ⟨the painted hussies of the *half-world* . . . in pinchbeck finery —Donn Byrne⟩ **3 :** UNDERWORLD ⟨a criminal not previously connected with the *half-world* —Frank Mullady⟩

half Wellington

halfy *pronunc at* HALF + ē *or* i\ *n* -ES *slang* **:** a beggar who has had both legs amputated
half year *n* [ME] **1 :** one half of a year (as January to June or July to December) **2 :** one of two academic terms **:** SEMESTER — **half-yearly** \'=¦==\ *adv (or adj)*
hali- *comb form* [NL, fr. Gk, fr. *hals* salt, sea — more at SALT] **1 :** sea ⟨*hali*plankton⟩ **2 :** salt **:** a salt ⟨*hali*steresis⟩
hal·i·ae·e·tus \,halē'ēəd·əs\ *n, cap* [NL, fr. Gk *haliaetos, haliaietos*, a bird (prob. the osprey), fr. *hali-* + *aetos, aietos* eagle] **:** a genus of eagles including the bald eagle and many sea eagles
hal·i·but \'haləbət *also* 'häl-; *usu* -bəd·+V\ *n, pl* **halibut** *also* **halibuts** [ME *halybutte*, fr. *haly, holy* holy + *butte* flatfish, fr. its being eaten on holy days — more at HOLY, BUTT] **:** the largest of the flatfishes formerly regarded as forming a single species but now usu. divided into an Atlantic species (*Hippoglossus hippoglossus*) and a Pacific (*H. stenolepis*), being an inhabitant of all northern seas, and constituting one of the largest of teleost fishes, the female sometimes weighing several hundred pounds though the male rarely weighs over 50 pounds — see ARROW-TOOTHED HALIBUT, CALIFORNIA HALIBUT
hal·i·but·er \-(,)bəd·ə(r), -ətə-\ *n* -S **:** one that fishes for halibut; *also* **:** a boat used in such fishing
halibut-liver oil *n* **:** a yellowish to brownish fatty oil from the liver of the halibut used chiefly as a source of vitamin A
hal·i·car·nas·si·an *also* **hal·i·car·nas·se·an** \¦halə(,)kär¦nasēən\ *adj, cap* [*Halicarnassus*, ancient city in Asia Minor + E *-ian* or *-ean*] **:** of or belonging to ancient Halicarnassus
hal·i·choe·rus \,halə'kirəs, -kēr-\ *n, cap* [NL, fr. *hali-* + Gk *choiros* young pig] **:** the genus comprising the gray seal
hal·i·clys·tus \-'klistəs\ *n, cap* [NL, fr. *hali-* + *-clystus* (prob. fr. Gk *klystēr* syringe)] **:** a widely distributed genus of stauromedusan jellyfishes (class Scyphozoa)
ha·lic·o·re \hə'likə(,)rē\ [NL, fr. *hali-* + Gk *korē* girl] *syn of* DUGONG
ha·lic·ti·dae \hə'liktə,dē\ *n pl, cap* [NL, fr. *Halictus*, type genus + *-idae*] **:** a cosmopolitan family of small black or brightly metallic solitary bees including many pollinators valuable to agriculture — **ha·lic·tine** \-,tīn, -,tən\ *adj*
ha·lic·tus \hə'liktəs\ *n, cap* [NL, irreg. fr. Gk *halizein* to gather, assemble, fr. *halēs* assembled, pressed together] **:** a cosmopolitan genus of gregarious but not social burrowing bees that provision the larval cells with pollen and nectar and include important pollinators of economic plants — see SWEAT BEE
halide \'ha,līd,'hā,-,-ləd\ *n* -S [*hal-* + *-ide*] **:** a binary compound of a halogen with a more electropositive element or radical
hal·i·dom \'halədəm\ *or* **hal·i·dome** \-,dōm\ *n* -S [ME, fr. OE *hāligdōm*, fr. *hālig* holy + *-dōm* -dom — more at HOLY] *archaic* **:** a holy place or relic — often used in the phrase *by my halidom*
hal·i·eu·tic \,halē'(y)üd·ik\ *also* **hal·i·eu·ti·cal** \-d·əkəl\ *adj* [LL *halieuticus*, fr. Gk *halieutikos*, fr. (assumed) *halieutos* verbal of *halieuein* to fish, fr. *hals* salt, sea) + *-ikos* -ic — more at SALT] **:** of or relating to fishing — **hal·i·eu·ti·cal·ly** \-d·ək(ə)lē\ *adv*
hal·i·eu·tics \-d·iks\ *n pl but sing in constr* **:** the art or practice of fishing; *also* **:** a treatise on fishes or fishing
hal·i·fax \'halə,faks\ *adj, usu cap* **1** [fr. *Halifax*, county borough in England] **:** of or from the county borough of Halifax, England **:** of the kind or style prevalent in Halifax **2** [fr. *Halifax*, N. S.] **:** of or from Halifax, the capital of Nova Scotia **:** of the kind or style prevalent in Halifax
¹hal·i·go·ni·an \,halə'gōnēən\ *n* -S *cap* [ML *Haligonia* Halifax + E *-an*] **:** a native or inhabitant of Halifax, Nova Scotia or Halifax, England
²haligonian \¦==¦===\ *adj, usu cap* **:** of or belonging to Haligonians
hal·i·me·da \,halə'mēdə\ *n, cap* [NL, after *Halimede*, a nereid, fr. Gk *Halimēdē*] **:** a genus (family Codiaceae) of calcareous marine green algae remarkable for the jointed coenocytic thallus which in most of the species (as *H. tuna*) resembles a prickly-pear cactus in miniature
haling *pres part of* HALE
hal·ing hands \'haliŋ,-\ *n pl* [*haling* fr. gerund of ³*hale*] **:** heavy woolen gloves or mittens worn esp. by sailors
hal·i·o·tis \,halē'ōd·əs\ *n* [NL, fr. *hali-* + Gk *ōt-, ous* ear] **1** *cap* **:** a genus (the type of the family Haliotidae) of gastropod mollusks comprising the abalones **2** *pl* **haliotis :** any mollusk of the genus *Haliotis* **:** ABALONE — **hal·i·o·toid** \¦==¦ōd,ȯid\ *adj*
hali·plankton \,halə+\ *n* [ISV *hali-* + *plankton*] **:** oceanic plankton
hal·i·se·ri·tes \,haləsə'rīd·(,)ēz, hə,lis-\ *n, cap* [NL, fr. *hali-* + Gk *seris* endive + NL *-ites*] **:** a genus of Old World cretaceous fossil plants of uncertain relationship possibly related to the dicotyledonous genus *Fontainea* but by some considered thallophytes because of the dichotomous flat leaves
ha·lis·i·do·ta \hə,lisə'dōd·ə\ *n, cap* [NL] **:** a genus of arctiid moths several of which have larvae that feed on the foliage of trees
hal·i·ste·re·sis \,haləstə'rēsəs, hə,lis-\ *n, pl* **halistere·ses**

\-ē(,)sēz\ [NL, fr. *hali-* + Gk *-steresis* loss] : loss of salts esp. of lime from bone (as in osteomalacia)

hal·i·ste·ret·ic \¦haləstə¦red·ik, hə¦lis-\ *adj* : affected with or constituting halisteresis

halite \'haˌlīt, 'hā-\ *n* -s [NL *halites*, fr. *hal-* + *-ites* -ite] : a mineral NaCl consisting of sodium chloride : native salt : ROCK SALT

hal·i·the·ri·um \ˌhalə'thirēəm\ *n, cap* [NL, fr. *hali-* + *-therium*] : a genus of sirenians that is known from remains found in the Oligocene and Miocene of southern Europe and the Oligocene of Madagascar and is made type of a separate family or included in Dugongidae

hal·i·to·sis \ˌhalə'tōsə̇s\ *n, pl* **halito·ses** \-ō,sēz\ [NL, fr. L *halitus* breath (fr. *halare* to breathe) + NL *-osis* — more at EXHALE] : a condition of having fetid breath

hall \'hȯl\ *n* -s *often attrib* [ME *halle, hal*, fr. OE *heall;* akin to OHG *halla* hall, ON *hǫll*, L *cella* small room, Gk *kalia* hut, nest, Skt *śālā* hut, OE *helan* to conceal — more at HELL] **1 a** : the castle or house of a medieval king or noble **b** : the chief living room in such a structure used for eating, sleeping, and entertaining **c** *chiefly dial* : the living room or parlor of a house **2** : the manor house or residence of a landed proprietor — often used in proper names ⟨Locksley *Hall*⟩ ⟨Headlong *Hall*⟩ **3** *sometimes cap* : a large usu. imposing building used for public or semipublic purposes; *specif* : TOWN HALL — now used chiefly in proper names ⟨Westminster *Hall*⟩ ⟨Faneuil *Hall*⟩ **4 a** (1) : a building used by a college or university for teaching or research ⟨~*s* of learning⟩ — often used in proper names ⟨Goodheart *Hall*⟩ (2) : DORMITORY **b** : a college or a division of a college at some universities **c** (1) : the common dining room of an English college (2) : a meal served there **5 a** *archaic* : a cleared passageway through a crowd — used in the exclamation *a hall, a hall* **b** (1) : the entrance room or passageway of a residence or other building : FOYER, LOBBY ⟨the front ~ of the house⟩ ⟨left his rubbers in the back ~⟩ (2) : a corridor or passage in a building **6** : a large room for assembly usu. equipped with seats (as for lectures or concerts) : AUDITORIUM ⟨a lecture ~⟩ ⟨a concert ~⟩ **7** : a place used for public entertainment: as **a** : a building or room used for a particular kind of amusement or play ⟨a pool ~⟩ ⟨a gambling ~⟩ **b** : a building with an auditorium used for public musical entertainments; *specif* : MUSIC HALL **8** : a building belonging to or used as the place of assembly, social center, or headquarters of a fraternal society or trade union ⟨his office was the union ~ —R.F.Mirvish⟩ — often used in proper names ⟨Hungarian *Hall*⟩

hal·lah *or* **chal·lah** \'kälə, kä'lä\ *n, pl* **hal·loth** *or* **hal·lot** \'käˌlōt(h), -ōs, ˌ=ˈ=\ *or* **hal·lahs** \'käləz\ [Heb *ḥallāh*] : a loaf of white bread often baked in braided or twisted form and used among Jews esp. at a Friday evening meal inaugurating the Sabbath and on holidays

hal·la·li \¦halə¦lē\ *n* -s [imit.] : a huntsman's bugle call ⟨his ~ rang high —George Meredith⟩

hal·lan \'halən, 'häl-\ *n* -s [origin unknown] *dial Brit* : a partition in a cottage esp. between the door and the fireplace

hal·lan·shak·er \-ˌshākər, -ˌshak-\ *n* **1** *chiefly Scot* : a wandering beggar **2** *chiefly Scot* : RASCAL, SCOUNDREL

hall bedroom *n* : a small narrow bedroom formed by a partition at one end of a hall

hallboy \'=ˌ=\ *n* **1** : CALLBOY **2** : a boy employed to clean the halls of a hotel

hall church *n* [trans. of G *hallenkirche*] : a Gothic church esp. in Germany in which in place of the clerestory the aisles are carried up to nearly the height of the nave

hallcist \'=ˌ=\ *n* -s [*hall* + *cist* (grave)] : a large rectangular earth-covered corridor made of rock slabs and used in ancient times as a tomb

hall clock *n* : GRANDFATHER CLOCK

hall coefficient \'hȯl-\ *or* **hall constant** *n, usu cap H* [after Edwin H. *Hall* †1938 Am. physicist] : the quotient of the potential difference per unit width of metal strip in the Hall effect divided by the product of the magnetic intensity and the longitudinal current density

hal·le \'hälə\ *adj, usu cap* [fr. *Halle*, Germany] : of or from the city of Halle, Germany : of the kind or style prevalent in Halle

hall effect *n, usu cap H* [after Edwin H. *Hall*] : a potential difference observed between the edges of a strip of metal carrying a longitudinal current when placed in a magnetic field perpendicular to the plane of the strip

häl·le·flin·ta \¦helə¦flintə\ *n* -s [Sw, fr. *hälle-* slab, rock (fr. OSw *hælło-, hælla*) + *flinta* flint, fr. OSw; akin to ON *hella* cliff, mountain, Goth *hallus* cliff, and to OE *flint* — more at HILL, FLINT] : a very compact banded rock resembling felsite and consisting of minute particles of feldspar and quartz with fine scales of mica and chlorite — **häl·le·flin·toid** \-nt,ȯid\ *adj*

hal·lel \hä'läl, 'häˌläl, 'haˌlel\ *n, usu cap* [Heb *hallēl* praise] : a selection of psalms of praise chanted on Passover, Shabuoth, Sukkoth, Hanukkah, and Rosh Hodesh

¹hal·le·lu·jah \ˌhalə'lüyə\ *interj, sometimes cap* [Heb *halălūyāh* praise (ye) the Lord] — used to express praise, joy, or thanks ⟨the mighty voice of a great multitude in heaven, crying, "*Hallelujah!*" —Rev 19:1 (RSV)⟩

²hallelujah \"\ *n* -s : a shout or song of praise or thanksgiving ⟨jubilant ~*s* for . . . the Minister of Housing —Mollie Panter-Downes⟩

³hallelujah \"\ *adj* [²*hallelujah*] : of or belonging to the Salvation Army ⟨~ lass⟩ ⟨~ bonnet⟩ ⟨~ meeting⟩

hal·len *var of* HALLAN

hal·len·kir·che \'hälənˌkirkə\ *n, pl* **hallenkir·chen** \-rkən\ *usu cap* [G, fr. *halle* hall + *kirche* church] : HALL CHURCH

hal·ley's method \'ha\|lēz- *also* ÷'hā\|\ *n, cap H* [after Edmund *Halley* †1742 Eng. astronomer] : a method of finding the parallax of Venus and hence the sun's distance by observing the duration of a transit of Venus from stations widely separated in latitude

hallgirl \'=ˌ=\ *n* : a girl employed to clean the halls of a hotel

hall house *n, chiefly Scot* : MANOR HOUSE

halliard *var of* HALYARD

hal·ling \'häliŋ, 'hal-\ *n* -s [Norw, fr. *Hallingdal* a valley in southern Norway] **1** : an acrobatic Norwegian dance in duple measure for one to three single dancers **2** : a lively dance tune written in a major key usu. in ²⁄₄ time and usu. played on the Hardanger fiddle

hal·lion \'halyən\ *n* -s [origin unknown] *chiefly Scot* : SCAMP, SCOUNDREL

¹hall·mark \'hȯlˌmärk, -mȧk\ *n* [Goldsmiths' *Hall*, London, England, where gold and silver articles were assayed and stamped + E *mark*] **1 a** *in England* : an official mark stamped on gold and silver articles to attest their purity and comprised of the king's or queen's mark, the maker's mark, the assayer's mark, and a letter of the alphabet for the year, a new style being used when the alphabet in one style is exhausted **b** : a mark stamped on gold and silver articles consisting of the word "sterling" accompanied by the name or mark of the manufacturer **c** : a mark or device placed or stamped upon an article of trade to indicate origin, purity, or genuineness ⟨the ~ of a potter of the Ming dynasty⟩ **d** : the identifying mark or device (as of a company) ⟨the new ~ will be a small, bright spot on company letterheads —*Bull. Standard Oil of Calif.*⟩ **2** : a distinguishing or identifying characteristic, trait, or feature ⟨avoidance of such constructions . . . has become a ~ of social respectability —Thomas Pyles⟩ ⟨the ~ of the adult human being is responsibility —Weston La Barre⟩ ⟨his solicitude for the poor . . . is the ~ of his best stories —Hakon Stangerup⟩

²hallmark \"\ *vt* **1** : to stamp with a hallmark **2 a** : to constitute a distinguishing or identifying feature or trait of ⟨two great faults and two great virtues ~*ed* the work of the late . . . associate justice —Fred Rodell⟩ **b** : to have or display the distinguishing, validating, or identifying traits or features of ⟨a host of inconspicuous but ~*ed* spinsters —*Times Lit. Supp.*⟩ ⟨my one genuine ~*ed* ghost story —Rudyard Kipling⟩

hall·moot \'hȯlˌmüt\ *n* [ME *halimot*, fr. *hal* hall + *-imot* (fr. OE *gemōt* assembly) — more at HALL, GEMOT] : a private court for the lord of a manor : COURT BARON

¹hal·lo *or* **hal·loa** \hə'lō, ha'-, 'ha(ˌ)lō\ *or* **hal·loo** \-lü\ *or* **hul·loo** \(ˌ)hə'lü, 'hə(ˌ)lü\ *interj* [origin unknown] **1** — used to attract attention **2** — used as a call of encouragement or jubilation

²hallo *or* **halloa** *or* **halloo** *or* **hulloo** \"\ *vb* -ED/-ING/-S *vi* : to cry *hallo* : call out : HOLLER ~ *vt* **1 a** : to call or cry *hallo* to : attract the attention of **b** : to call encouragement to **2** : to utter loudly : HOLLER

³hallo *or* **halloa** *or* **halloo** *or* **hulloo** \"\ *n, pl* **hallos** *or* **halloes** *or* **halloas** *or* **halloos** *or* **hulloos** : an exclamation or call of *hallo* : a halloing or shouting

⁴hal·lo \"\ *chiefly Brit var of* HELLO

hal·lock \'halək\ *n* -s [after *Hallock*, 19th cent. Am. box manufacturer] : a rectangular wood veneer berry box with straight sides and a raised bottom

hall of fame *usu cap H&F* **1** : a hall, building, room, or other structure housing statues, busts, tablets, or other memorials commemorating famous or illustrious persons usu. selected for inclusion by a qualified group of electors ⟨a *Hall of Fame* honoring great merchants of America was inaugurated tonight —*Springfield (Mass.) Union*⟩ ⟨ground-breaking ceremonies were held today for the national cowboy *Hall of Fame* here —*N.Y. Times*⟩ **2** : a group of individuals in some particular category formally selected by a group of qualified electors or informally adjudged by popular opinion as most illustrious or meriting immortal fame ⟨earned herself a permanent place in the trotters' *Hall of Fame* —R.E.Meyer⟩

halloth *or* **hallot** *pl of* HALLAH

¹hal·low \'hal\|(ˌ)ō, \|ə, *often* -ləw + V *sometimes* 'hä\|\ *vt* **hal·lowed** \\|(ˌ)ōd, \|əd\ **hal·lowed** \", *in the Lord's Prayer* " *or* \|ləwə̇d *or* \|ōə̇d\ **hallowing; hallows** [ME *halowen*, fr. OE *hālgian*, fr. *hālig* holy — more at HOLY] **1** : to make holy : set apart for holy or religious use : treat or keep as sacred : CONSECRATE ⟨~ed be thy name —Mt 6:9 (RSV)⟩ **2** : to respect greatly : VENERATE, REVERE ⟨institutions ~*ed* for their classical learning —*Loyola Univ. Bull.*⟩ ⟨the most ~*ed* of all law-enforcement agencies —Dwight MacDonald⟩

²hal·low \"\ *vb* -ED/-ING/-S [ME *halowen*, fr. MF *halloer*, fr. *hallo*, interj.] : HALLO ⟨~*ed* at several to explain himself —A.E.Fife⟩

³hal·low \'halə, +V " *or* -ləw\ *dial var of* HOLLOW

hal·low·day \'haləˌdā, -lō,-\ *n* [short for *All Hallow Day*, fr. ME *all halowen day*, lit., all the saints' day] **1** *dial Eng, usu cap* : ALL SAINTS' DAY **2** *dial Eng* : a saint's day : HOLIDAY

hallowed *see* ¹HALLOW\ *adj* [ME *halowed*, fr. past part. of *halowen* to hallow — more at HALLOW] **1** : CONSECRATED, BLESSED **2** : REVERED, VENERATED, SACRED ⟨the ~ heroes of the past —Oscar Fraley⟩ ⟨the ~ customs of our group —M.R. Cohen⟩

hal·lowed·ly *adv* : in a hallowed manner

hal·lowed·ness *n* -ES : the quality or state of being hallowed : HOLINESS

hal·low·een *also* **hal·low·e'en** \¦halə¦wēn, ÷¦häl-\ *n* -s *usu cap* [short for *All Hallow E'en*] : the evening preceding All Saints' Day : the evening of October 31 which is often devoted by young people to merrymaking (as with jack-o'-lanterns) and playing pranks sometimes involving petty damage to property

hal·low·mas \'halō\|mas, -lə\|, \|maa(ə)s, \|ˌmais, \|məs *sometimes* \|ˌmas\ *n* -ES *cap* [short for *Allhallowmass*] : the feast of All Saints

hal·loy·site \hə'lȯiˌsīt, ha'-, -ˌzīt\ *n* -s [F, fr. Omalius d'*Halloy* †1875 Belg. geologist + F *-ite*] : a clay mineral $Al_2Si_2O_5(OH)_4.nH_2O$ occurring in soft white or light-colored masses and in at least two states of hydration $n=2$, $n=4$

hall porter *n, chiefly Brit* : a porter or attendant who carries the luggage of patrons and performs other chores at a hotel

hall process \'hȯl-\ *n, usu cap H* [after Charles M. *Hall* †1914 Am. chemist] : the process by which aluminum is produced consisting of electrolysis of a molten solution of purified alumina in cryolite at a temperature of about 950°C

halls *pl of* HALL

hall scale *n, usu cap H* [after Maurice C. *Hall* *b*1886 Amer. zoologist] : an Asiatic scale (*Nilotaspis halli*) that has been introduced into California where it is a serious pest of stone fruit trees

hall's honeysuckle *n, usu cap 1st H* [after G. R. *Hall*, 20th cent. Am. physician who introduced the plant from China] : a honeysuckle (*Lonicera japonica halliana*) that is a vining variety of Japanese honeysuckle with flowers initially pure white but yellowing with age, is often used as an ornamental climber or ground cover, and has established itself as an aggressive escape in much of the southeastern U. S.

hallstand \'=ˌ=\ *n* : a tall piece of furniture with a mirror, several pegs or arms for hats and other articles of clothing, a rack for umbrellas, and a compartment for storage

hallstand

hall·statt *or* **hall·stadt** \'hȯlˌstat, 'hälˌshtät\ *adj, usu cap* [fr. *Hallstatt*, village in Austria] **1** : of or belonging to Hallstatt, Austria or the archaeological remains there **2** : of or relating to the earlier period of the Iron Age in Europe characterized by transition from the use of bronze to iron, possession of domestic animals, agriculture, and skill in the making of pottery and ornaments — compare LA TÈNE

hall·statt·an *also* **hall·stadt·an** \(')hȯl¦stad·ēən, (')häl¦shtäd·-\ *adj, usu cap* [*Hallstatt*, Austria + E *-an*] : HALLSTATT

hall tree *n* : CLOTHES TREE

hal·lu·ci·nate \hə'lüsᵊnˌāt *also* həl'yü-\ *vb* -ED/-ING/-S [L *hallucinatus, alucinatus*, past part. of *hallucinari, alucinari* to talk idly, prate, dream, prob. fr. Gk *halyein, alyein* to be distraught, to wander] *vt* : to affect with visions or imaginary perceptions ⟨they are not *hallucinated*, they know that the object is not really there —R.S.Woodworth⟩ ⟨a poor *hallucinated* invalid —Marguerite Young⟩ ~ *vi* : to have hallucinations ⟨most normal persons have occasionally *hallucinated* —William McDougall⟩

hal·lu·ci·na·tion \=ˌ==ˈāshən\ *n* -s [L *hallucination-, hallucinatio, alucination-, alucinatio*, fr. *hallucinatus, alucinatus* + *-ion-, -io* -ion] **1 a** : perception of objects with no reality : experience of sensations with no external cause usu. arising from disorder of the nervous system (as in delirium tremens or in functional psychosis without known neurological disease) **b** : the object of a hallucinatory perception **2** : a completely unfounded or mistaken impression or notion : DELUSION ⟨that popular ~ from which not even great scientists are . . . free —Lewis Mumford⟩ — **hal·lu·ci·na·tion·al** \=¦==¦āshənᵊl, -āshnəl\ *adj* — **hal·lu·ci·na·tive** \=ˈ==ˌād·iv, =ˈ== əd·iv\ *adj*

hal·lu·ci·na·to·ry \=ˈ== əˌtōrē\ *adj* : partaking of or tending to produce hallucination : not objectively perceived : IMAGINED, UNREAL ⟨fleeing in terror from a ~ wolf —Mark Kanzer⟩ ⟨succumbed to ~ rhetoric —Irving Howe⟩ ⟨the bizarre, ~ dreams of fever —Jean Stafford⟩

hal·lu·cino·gen \=ˈ==ᵊˌjen, -jən, ˌhalyə'sinə-\ *n* -s [*hallucination* + *-o-* + *-gen*] : a substance that induces hallucinations; *esp* : one taken orally ⟨mescaline is a ~⟩ — **hal·lu·ci·no·gen·ic** \hə¦lüsᵊnə¦jenik *also* həl¦yü-\ *adj*

hal·lu·ci·no·sis \həˌlüsᵊn'ōsə̇s *also* həlˌyü-\ *n, pl* **hallucino·ses** \-ōˌsēz\ [NL, fr. L *hallucinatio* + NL *-osis*] : a pathological mental state occurring esp. as a manifestation of alcoholism in which awareness consists largely or exclusively of hallucinations

hal·lux \'haləks\ *n, pl* **hallu·ces** \-l(y)əˌsēz -ləˌs-\ [NL, fr. L *hallus, hallux* big toe] : the first or preaxial digit of the hind limb : BIG TOE

hallux val·gus \-'valgəs\ *n* [NL, lit., wry big toe] : an abnormal deviation of the big toe toward the outside of the foot associated esp. with the wearing of ill-fitting shoes — compare BUNION

hall·wachs effect \'hälˌväks-\ *n, usu cap H* [after Wilhelm *Hallwachs* †1922 Ger. physicist] : a photoelectric effect in which a negatively charged body in a vacuum is discharged upon exposure to ultraviolet radiation

hallway \'=ˌ=\ *n* : HALL; *esp* : an entrance hall

halm *var of* HAULM

Hal·ma \'halmə\ *trademark* — used for a game played by two or four players on a board having 256 squares with the object being for each player to move or jump his men from their home corner to a corresponding position in the opposite corner

¹ha·lo \'hā(ˌ)lō\ *n, pl* **halos** *or* **haloes** [L *halos* halo of the sun, fr. Gk *halōs* threshing floor, disk of the sun or the moon, halo around the sun or moon; akin to Gk *halōn* threshing floor, and perh. to *lyein* to loosen — more at LOSE] **1** : a circle, arc, or splotch of light either white or prismatically colored and definitely situated with reference to a luminous body and resulting from the reflection or refraction or both of its light; *specif* : circles round the sun or moon caused by the presence of ice particles in the atmosphere and differing from coronas in being of definite size usu. of about 22° or 46° radius and if colored in showing red on the side nearest to the luminary **2** : something resembling a halo: as **a** : NIMBUS **b** : a differentiated zone surrounding a central object ⟨the ~ around a boil⟩ ⟨the presence of a ~ of alteration has been used as a guide to ore finding —A.M.Bateman⟩; *specif* : a zone usu. of lighter colored tissue characteristically surrounding the lesions in certain plant diseases esp. of bacterial origin **c** : a circlet of flowers, a ribbon, or a small hat worn off the face and back on the head by women **3** : the aura of glory, veneration, prestige, or sentiment surrounding an idealized person or thing ⟨a . . . positive ~ surrounds scientific endeavors —John Dewey⟩ ⟨put a romantic ~ about the old plantation life —Oscar Handlin⟩ ⟨the exclusiveness of the institute . . . gave it a ~ —Romola Nijinsky⟩

²halo \"\ *vt* -ED/-ING/-ES : to form or surround with a halo : encircle as if with a halo ⟨red-gold hair . . . ~*ing* a slim face —Frank Yerby⟩ ⟨the ~*ed* lights burned her eyes —John Dos Passos⟩ ⟨~*ed* by publicity —F.L.Allen⟩

³halo \'ha(ˌ)lō\ *adj* [*hal-*] : containing halogen — used esp. of organic compounds ⟨~ aldehydes⟩

halo- — see HAL-

ha·lob·a·tes \hə'läbəˌtēz\ *n, cap* [NL, fr. *hal-* + *-bates*] : a genus of small wingless marine water striders having the thorax large and the abdomen very small

hal·o·bi·ont \¦halō¦bīˌänt\ *n* -s *often attrib* [*hal-* + *-biont*] : an organism (as a plant) that flourishes in a saline habitat

halo blight *n* **1** *also* **halo spot** : a blight of beans and occas. other legumes that is caused by a bacterium (*Pseudomonas phaseolicola*) and typically produces on the leaves, stems, and pods round water-soaked lesions surrounded by a yellowish zonation, the lesions finally turning brick red **2** : blight affecting the leaves of oats and other grasses caused by a bacterium (*Pseudomonas coronafaciens*) characterized by oval water-soaked lesions turning gray to brownish and surrounded by a pale zonation

hal·o·chro·mism \ˌhalə'krōˌmizəm\ *n* -s [*hal-* + *chrom-* + *-ism*] : the phenomenon or property of the formation of strongly colored salts by addition of acids to colorless or faintly colored compounds

halo effect *n* : a tendency for a general opinion or attitude derived from rating an individual as high or low on one item of a test to exert an influence upon the rating of other and separate items, traits, or responses; *esp* : generalization from the perception of one outstanding personality trait to an overevaluation of the whole personality

hal·o·form \'haləˌfȯrm\ *n* [*hal-* + *-form* (as in *chloroform*)] : a compound CHX_3 (as chloroform) derived from methane by replacement of three atoms of hydrogen by halogen

hal·o·gen \-jən, -ˌjen\ *n* -s [Sw, fr. *halo-* hal- + *-gen*] : any of the five elements fluorine, chlorine, bromine, iodine, and astatine forming part of group VII A of the periodic table and existing in the free state normally as diatomic molecules — compare PSEUDOHALOGEN — **ha·log·e·nous** \(')ha¦läjənəs\ *adj*

hal·o·gen·ate \'haləjəˌnāt, ha'läj-\ *vt* -ED/-ING/-S : to treat or cause to combine with a halogen : introduce a halogen into (as an organic compound) — **hal·o·gen·a·tion** \ˌhaləjə'nāshən, haˌläj-\ *n* -s

hal·o·gen·ide \'haləjəˌnīd, ha'läj-\ *n* -s [ISV *halogen* + *-ide*] : HALIDE — used in the nomenclature adopted by the International Union of Pure and Applied Chemistry

hal·o·gen·oid \-ˌnȯid\ *n* -s : PSEUDOHALOGEN

hal·o·ge·ton \ˌhalə'jētᵊn\ *n* [NL, fr. *hal-* + Gk *geitōn* neighbor] **1** *cap* : a small genus of Mediterranean and central Asian herbs and shrubs (family Chenopodiaceae) with fleshy semicylindrical leaves and axillary clusters of flowers — see BARILLA 1b **2** -s : any plant of the genus *Halogeton; esp* : a coarse annual herb (*H. glomeratus*) introduced into No. America from Siberia and now a noxious weed in western American rangelands dangerous to sheep and cattle because of its high oxalate content

hal·o·hy·drin \-'hīdrən\ *n* -s [ISV *hal-* + *-hydrin*] : any of a class of organic compounds derived from glycols or polyhydroxy alcohols (as glycerol) by substitution of halogen for part of the hydroxyl groups — compare CHLOROHYDRIN

halolike \'=(ˌ)=ˌ=\ *adj* : resembling a halo

hal·o·lim·nic \¦halō¦limnik\ *adj* [ISV *hal-* + *limn-* + *-ic*] *of a marine organism* : capable of living in fresh water

ha·lom·e·ter \ha'läməd·ə(r)\ *n* [ISV *hal-* + *-meter*] : an instrument for measuring the forms of crystals of salts

hal·o·mor·phic \¦halə¦mȯrfik\ *adj* [*hal-* + *-morphic*] : of or relating to intrazonal soils characterized by the presence of either neutral or alkali salts or both — compare CALOMORPHIC, HYDROMORPHIC — **hal·o·mor·phism** \ˌ==ˈ=ˌfizəm\ *n* -s

hal·o·phile \'haləˌfīl\ *n* -s [ISV *hal-* + *-phile;* prob. orig. formed as Sw *halofil*] : a halophilic organism

hal·o·phil·ic \¦==¦filik\ *or* **ha·loph·i·lous** \(')ha¦läfələs\ *also* **hal·o·phile** \'haləˌ\ *or* **hal·o·phil** \-ˌfil\ *adj* [*hal-* + *-philic* or *-philous* or *-phile, -phil*] *of an organism* : flourishing in a salty environment

hal·o·phyte \'haləˌfīt\ *n* -s [ISV *hal-* + *-phyte*] : a plant that grows naturally in soils having a high content of various salts, that usu. resembles a true xerophyte and that occurs in many families (as Chenopodiaceae, Compositae, Plumbaginaceae) — compare MESOPHYTE — **hal·o·phyt·ic** \¦==¦fid·ik\ *adj*

hal·o·ra·ga·ce·ae \ˌhalərə'gāsēˌē, həˌlȯr-\ *n pl, cap* [NL, fr. *Haloragis*, type genus + *-aceae*] : a family (order Myrtales) of usu. monoecious plants having predominantly unisexual flowers with 4 or 8 stamens and an inferior ovary

hal·o·rag·i·da·ce·ae *or* **hal·or·rhag·i·da·ce·ae** \ˌhaləˌrajə'dāsēˌē\ [NL, fr. *Haloragid-, Haloragis* + *-aceae*] *syn of* HALORAGACEAE

hal·o·ra·gis \ˌhalə'rājə̇s\ *n, cap* [NL, irreg. fr. *hal-* + Gk *rhag-, rhax* berry] : the type genus of Haloragaceae — see SEABERRY

halos *pl of* HALO

hal·o·saur \'haləˌsȯ(ə)r\ *n* -s [NL *Halosaurus*] : a member of the Halosauridae

hal·o·sau·rid \¦==¦sȯrə̇d\ *adj* [NL *Halosauridae*] : of or relating to the Halosauridae

hal·o·sau·ri·dae \ˌ=='sȯrəˌdē\ *n pl, cap* [NL, fr. *Halosaurus*, type genus + *-idae*] : a family (order Heteromi) of mostly extinct deep-sea fishes having cycloid scales

hal·o·sau·rus \-rəs\ *n, cap* [NL, fr. *hal-* + *-saurus*] : the type genus of the Halosauridae

hal·o·sere \'haləˌsi(ə)r\ *n* [*hal-* + *sere*] : an ecological sere originating in a saline habitat

halo spot *n* : HALO BLIGHT 1

halo·tolerant \¦halō+\ *adj* [*hal-* + *tolerant*] : HALOXENE

ha·lot·ri·chite \hə'lätrəˌkīt\ *n* -s [G *halotrichit*, fr. *hal-* + *trich-* + *-it* -ite] **1** : a mineral $FeAl_2(SO_4)_4.22H_2O$ consisting of a hydrous iron aluminum sulfate **2** : any of several sulfates similar to halotrichite in construction and habit

halo·tyd·e·us \¦halō¦tidēəs, -tid-, tīˌd(y)üs\ *n, cap* [NL, fr. *hal-* + *Tydeus*, genus of mites, after *Tydeus*, Greek mythological hero] : a genus of soft-bodied phytophagous mites that have the front pair of legs modified as sensory organs and that are destructive to legumes and certain other crops in southern Africa and Australia — see SANDMITE

hal·oxene \(')ha¦läkˌsēn, 'haləˌzēn\ *adj* [*hal-* + Gk *xenos* foreign — more at XEN-] *of an organism* **:** tolerating but not preferring a saline habitat — compare HALOPHILIC

hals *or* **halse** \ˈhȯs, -ä-,-a-\ *n, pl* **halses** [ME *hals,* fr. OE *heals* — more at COLLAR] **1** *now dial Brit* **:** NECK **2** *now dial Brit* **a :** THROAT, WINDPIPE **b :** PASS, DEFILE, COL

halse \"\ *vt* -ED/-ING/-S [ME *halsen,* fr. *hals,* n.] *now dial Brit* **:** EMBRACE, HUG

hal·sen \ˈälzən, ˈȯzᵊn\ *vt* -ED/-ING/-S [ME *halsnen* to adjure, conjure, fr. *halsen* to adjure, conjure, entreat, greet (fr. OE *hālsian*) + *-nen* -en; akin to OHG *heilisōn* to predict, adjure, conjure, ON *heilsa* to greet; derivatives fr. the root of OE *hāl* healthy, whole — more at WHOLE] *now dial Eng* **:** DIVINE, PREDICT

halsh \ˈ(h)alsh\ *vt* -ED/-ING/-ES [ME *halchen* to embrace, tie, knot, prob. alter. of *halsen*] *dial Eng* **:** KNOT

¹**halt** \ˈhȯlt\ *adj* [ME, fr. OE *healt;* akin to OHG *halz* lame, ON *haltr,* Goth *halts* lame, L *clades* destruction, disaster, Gk *klan* to break, *kolos* docked, hornless, *kolobos* docked, curtailed, Lith *kalti* to beat, forge; basic meaning: beating, hewing] **:** having a halting walk **:** LAME ⟨gave alms to the ~ and . . . the poor —Jean Stafford⟩ ⟨a place for everyone . . . old and young, hale and ~ —Sir Winston Churchill⟩

²**halt** \"\ *vi* -ED/-ING/-S [ME *halten,* fr. OE *healtian;* akin to OHG *halzēn* to be lame, limp; derivatives fr. the root of E ¹*halt*] **1 :** to walk or proceed lamely **:** LIMP ⟨so lamely . . . that dogs bark at me as I ~ by them —Shak.⟩ **2 :** to stand in perplexity or doubt between alternate courses **:** WAVER **3 :** to display weakness or imperfection (as in argument, development, or meter) **:** proceed raggedly or falteringly **:** FALTER, LAPSE ⟨the translation ~*s* now and then —*Brit. Book News*⟩ ⟨the verse that ~*s* in places⟩ ⟨the argument often ~*s* and sometimes breaks down completely⟩

³**halt** \"\ *n* -S [G, fr. MHG, fr. *halt!,* imp. of *halten* to hold, stop, fr. OHG *haltan* — more at HOLD] **1 :** a temporary or definitive stop in marching or walking or in any action or process **:** arrest of progress ⟨the car came to a sudden ~⟩ ⟨economic progress was brought to a ~⟩ ⟨a ~, rather than a complete stoppage, in the flow of talent —*Irish Digest*⟩ ⟨time to call a ~ in a useless struggle⟩ **2** *chiefly Brit* **:** a stopping place for public transport; *esp* **:** a railway flag stop ⟨a slow train stopping at every station including ~*s* —*Punch*⟩

⁴**halt** \"\ *vb* -ED/-ING/-S [G *halten* to hold, stop, fr. OHG *haltan*] *vi* **1 :** to cease marching or journeying **:** stop for a longer or shorter period **:** stand still ⟨ordered his troops to ~⟩ ⟨made two or three . . . paces about the room, and suddenly ~*ed* —W.J.Locke⟩ ⟨many families ~*ed* and took up land in the mountain valleys —*Amer. Guide Series: Tenn.*⟩ **2 :** to discontinue temporarily or permanently **:** TERMINATE, END, SUSPEND ⟨hostilities ~*ed* while the generals conferred⟩ ⟨the project ~*ed* because of inadequate financial support⟩ ~ *vt* **1 :** to cause to cease marching or journeying **:** bring to a stop ⟨~*ed* the wagon train at a small settlement⟩ ⟨~*ed* the advance of his troops⟩ ⟨slid the bowl back down the bar and ~*ed* it before the soldier —Kay Boyle⟩ ⟨marshes that would have ~*ed* any vehicle —*Amer Guide Series: N.C.*⟩ **2 :** to cause the discontinuance of **:** terminate the existence or progress of **:** STOP, DISCONTINUE ⟨did the best he could to ~ the erosion —D.L.Graham⟩ ⟨consumer spending . . . rose and ~*ed* the decline —*Dun's Rev.*⟩ ⟨~ hostilities⟩ ⟨sought to ~ corruption and increase efficiency⟩

¹**hal·ter** \ˈhȯltə(r)\ *n* -S *often attrib* [ME, fr. OE *hælftre;* akin to OHG *halftra* halter, MLG *halchter,* MD *halfter, halchter;* derivatives fr. the root of E *helve*] **1 a :** a rope or strap with or without a headstall for leading or tying a horse or other animal **b :** a headstall of rope or leather and usu. with noseband and throatlatch to which a lead may be attached **2 :** a rope for hanging criminals **:** NOOSE; *also* **:** death by hanging **3 a :** a woman's or girl's waist typically held in place by bands or straps around the neck and across the back and leaving the back, arms, and midriff bare **b :** an adaptation of this style for the necklines of other garments (as blouses, dresses, bathing suits) **c** *or* **halter strap :** SLING 3a(3)

halter 1b

²**halter** \"\ *vt* **haltered; haltered; haltering** \-t(ə)riŋ, -ltriŋ\ **halters 1 a :** to catch with or as if with a halter **:** put a halter on (as a horse) **b :** to put a hangman's halter on **:** HANG **2 :** to put restraint upon **:** BRIDLE, FETTER, HAMPER, RESTRAIN ⟨~ his conscience⟩ ⟨measures that had the effect of ~*ing* the daily press⟩

³**hal·ter** \", ˈhal- *or* **hal·tere** \-ˌti(ə)r, -iə\ *n, pl* **hal·teres** \ˌ=ˈti(ˌ)rēz; ˈ=ˌti(ə)rz, -iəz\ [NL, fr. L, jumping weight, fr. Gk *haltēr,* fr. *hallesthai* to jump — more at SALLY] **:** one of the modified second pair of wings in Diptera and the first pair in Strepsiptera that are reduced to club-shaped organs and that function as flight instruments — called also *balancer, poiser*

halterbreak \ˈ==ˌ=\ *vt* **:** to break (as a colt) to a halter

hal·te·rid·i·um \ˌhaltəˈridēəm\ [NL, fr. L *halter* + NL *-idium*] *syn of* HAEMOPROTEUS

hal·ti·ca \ˈhaltikə\ [NL, prob. fr. Gk *haltikos* good at leaping — more at ALTICA] *syn of* ALTICA

halting *adj* [ME, fr. pres. part. of *halten* to limp — more at HALT] **1 a :** marked by a limp **:** LAME, LIMPING ⟨recognized the cripple's ~ walk⟩ **b :** slow and hesitant or reluctant **:** DRAGGING, UNCERTAIN ⟨walked home with heavy heart and ~ steps⟩ **c :** lacking smoothness, facility, verve, or display of easy command in delivery **:** marked by abrupt halts and starts **:** FALTERING, AWKWARD, UNGRACEFUL ⟨his speaking voice . . . is thin and ~ —*Current Biog.*⟩ ⟨too wise to let his ~ utterance weaken the impression of his facile pen —John Buchan⟩ ⟨his ~ delivery of the play's longest speech —Henry Hewes⟩ **2 a :** displaying weakness or imperfection (as in argument, development, or meter) **:** marked by lapses (as of grammar, interest, continuity) **:** proceeding raggedly or falteringly ⟨a very ~ argument⟩ ⟨the poem's weak and ~ rhymes⟩ ⟨the ~ development of this thin plot⟩ **b :** lacking in sureness (as of purpose, drive, or continuity) **:** proceeding by fits and starts **:** FUMBLING, INDECISIVE, VACILLATING, INEFFECTIVE ⟨development of the military intelligence service . . . was slow and ~ —G.F.Ashworth⟩ ⟨the season got off to a ~ start⟩ ⟨made ~ advance toward solving their difficulties —C.L.Jones⟩ — **halt·ing·ly** *adv*

halt·ing·ness *n* -ES **:** DEFECTIVENESS, FAULTINESS

halts *pres 3d sing of* HALT, *pl of* HALT

hal·uck·et \ˈhaləkət\ *adj* [fr. past part. of Sc *hallock, haluck* to behave in a giddy or foolish manner, fr. *hallock, haluck* giddy, foolish girl] *Scot* **:** wild and giddy **:** HALF-WITTED

ha·luk·kah *or* **cha·luk·kah** *also* **ha·lu·ka** *or* **cha·lu·ka** \ˌkälüˈkä, kəˈlükə\ *n* -S [Heb *ḥălūqqāh* portion, division] **:** a fund collected from Jews throughout the world for support of the needy in Palestine

ha·lutz *or* **cha·lutz** \käˈlüts\ *n, pl* **ha·lutz·im** *or* **cha·lutz·im** \ˌkä,lüˈtsēm, käˈlütsim\ [NHeb *ḥālūṣ,* fr. Heb, warrior, vanguard] **:** a Jewish immigrant to Palestine working in the Jewish settlements at tasks that contribute to the development of the country as a Jewish homeland

ha·lutza *or* **cha·lutza** \ˌkäˌlütˈsä\ *n, pl* **halutz·oth** *or* **halutz·ot** *or* **chalutz·oth** *or* **chalutz·ot** \ˌkäˌlütˈsōt(h), -ōs, =ˈ=ˌ=\ [NHeb *ḥălūṣāh,* fem. of *ḥālūṣ*] **:** a female halutz

ha·lutz·i·ut *or* **cha·lutz·i·ut** \ˌkäˌlütsēˈüt\ *n* -S [NHeb *ḥălūṣiut,* fr. *ḥālūṣ*] **:** PIONEERING; *specif* **:** the pioneer movement of the halutzim in Palestine

hal·vah *or* **hal·va** *or* **halavah** \h|äl'vä, k|, |äl'vä; ˈhäl(ˌ)vä, ˈhäl(ˌ)vä, -l(ə)və, -lə,v-; ˈhalvə\ *n* -S [Yiddish *halva,* fr. Romanian, fr. Turk *helva,* fr. Ar *ḥalwā* sweetmeat] **:** a flaky confection of crushed sesame seeds in a base of honey or other syrup

¹**halve** \ˈhav, -aa(ə)-,-ai-,-ȧ-,-ä-\ *vt* -ED/-ING/-S [ME *halven, halfen,* fr. *half,* n. — more at HALF] **1 a :** to divide into two equal parts **:** separate into halves ⟨~ an apple⟩ ⟨ripe walnuts, *halved* and picked from the shell —Nora Waln⟩ **b :** to reduce to one half ⟨*halving* the purchase tax on cotton goods —*New Republic*⟩ ⟨doubling the profit by *halving* the cost⟩ **c :** to share equally ⟨was it the double of my dream . . . or did we ~ a dream? —W.B.Yeats⟩ ⟨it didn't much matter that he was here to ~ my triumph —Max Beerbohm⟩ **2 :** to join two pieces of (timber) by cutting away each for half its thickness at the joining place and fitting together **3 :** to play (as a hole, round, match) in the same number of strokes as one's opponent at golf

²**halve** \"\ *n* -S **:** a tie score on a hole or a round of golf ⟨salvaged a ~ on the 147-yard third —*N.Y. Herald Tribune*⟩

halved *adj* **1 :** reduced to one half ⟨had to get along with a ~ income⟩ **2 :** appearing as if one side or one half were cut away **:** DIMIDIATE

halv·ers \-və(r)z\ *n pl* **:** half shares **:** HALVES ⟨went ~ on the price⟩

halves *pl of* HALF *or pres 3d sing of* HALVE

hal·yard *or* **hal·liard** \ˈhalyə(r)d\ *also* **haul·yard** \ˈhȯl-\ *n* -S [alter. of ME *halier,* fr. *halen* to pull — more at HALE] **:** a rope or tackle for hoisting and lowering (as a yard, spar, sail, flag) — see SHIP illustration

hal·yik·wa·mai \halˈyikwəˌmī\ *n, pl* **halyikwamai** *or* **halyikwamais** *usu cap* **1 :** an Indian people in the Colorado river valley below the mouth of the Gila allied with the Cocopa **2 :** a member of the Halyikwamai people

hal·y·si·tes \ˌhaləˈsīd·(ˌ)ēz\ *n, cap* [NL, fr. Gk *halysis* chain + NL *-ites*] **:** a genus consisting of the chain corals

hal·zoun \(ˈ)halˈzün\ *n* -S [prob. fr. Ar *ḥalzūn* snail] **:** infestation of the larynx and pharynx by worms esp. of the genus *Fasciola* consumed in raw liver

¹**ham** \ˈam\ *n* -S [ME (attested only in place names), fr. OE *hamm;* akin to MLG *ham* enclosed land, OE *hemm* border — more at HEM] *now dial Eng* **:** a piece of grassland

²**ham** \ˈham, -aa(ə)-\ *n* -S [ME *hamme,* fr. OE *hamm;* akin to OHG *hamma* popliteal space, thigh, haunch, ON *hǫm* haunch, Gk *knēmē* shinbone, OIr *cnāim* bone, leg] **1 a :** the part of the leg behind the knee **:** the hollow of the knee **:** POPLITEAL SPACE ⟨such a case as yours constrains a man to bow in the ~*s* —Shak.⟩ **b :** a buttock with its associated thigh or with the hinder part of a thigh — usu. used in pl. ⟨squatted submissively on his ~*s* —Joseph Conrad⟩ **c :** a hock or the hinder part of a hock **2 a :** the thigh of an animal prepared for food ⟨deer or elk ~*s* —R.R.Camp⟩; *esp* **:** the thigh of a hog either fresh or cured by salting and smoking ⟨~*s* . . . from . . . peanut-fed hogs —*U.S. Code*⟩ — see PORK illustration **b :** something that resembles such a ham in shape; *specif* **:** a cushion used esp. by tailors for pressing curved areas of garments **3** [short for *hamfatter*] **a :** an unskillful but flamboyant performer **:** EXHIBITIONIST, STRUTTER ⟨a wrestling match between a couple of ~*s*⟩ ⟨an oratorical ~⟩ ⟨the basset is a natural ~ —Charlotte Paul⟩; *esp* **:** an inept or ineffective actor esp. in an overtheatrical style ⟨a typical down-and-out vaudeville ~ —Bennett Cerf⟩ **b :** an inexperienced or incompetent telegraph operator **c :** a government-licensed operator of an amateur radio station ⟨once on the air, he got in touch with ~*s* on the mainland and they in turn warned ships away from the dangerous coast —R.B. Gehman⟩ **4 a :** melodrama or mawkish sentimentality **:** overdone theatricality ⟨a film scenario full of tears and ~ —V.S.Pritchett⟩ **b :** a tendency to histrionics **:** theatrical streak ⟨dignity may suffer as the ~ emerges in response to the camera's grinding —Walter Goodman⟩

³**ham** \"\ *adj* **1 :** HAMMY ⟨~ actor⟩ ⟨less ~ than its rivals —William Empson⟩ ⟨in all his life he had never been in any situation so corny, so ~ —Charles Jackson⟩ **2 :** of or relating to amateur radio ⟨~ operator⟩ ⟨~ radio band⟩ ⟨~ shack⟩

⁴**ham** \"\ *vb* **hammed; hammed; hamming; hams** *vt* **1 :** to execute with exaggerated speech or gestures **:** OVERACT ⟨spoofed the story and *hammed* the action —Paul Jaretzki⟩ — often used with *up* ⟨~ it up in beer-hall fashion —*Metronome*⟩ **2 :** to infuse with melodrama or mawkish sentimentality ⟨the narration was overly *hammed* in the writing —*Billboard*⟩ ~ *vi* **:** to overplay a part ⟨~*s* and mugs and . . . misses most of his best effects by underestimating his own simple power —Virgil Thomson⟩

hamada *var of* HAMMADA

¹**ha·ma·dan** \ˈhaməˌdan, ¦hamə¦dan\ *n* -S *usu cap* [fr. *Hamadan,* Iran] **1 :** a Persian rug made in and around Hamadan usu. of wool mixed with camels' hair, tied with the Ghiordes knot, and characterized by muted colors and small angular all-over patterns **2 :** a Kurdish rug marketed in Hamadan

²**hamadan** \"\ *adj, usu cap* [fr. *Hamadan,* Iran] **:** of or from the city of Hamadan, Iran **:** of the kind or style prevalent in Hamadan

ham·a·dry·ad \ˌhaməˈdrīəd, -ī,ad\ *n* -S [L *Hamadryad-, Hamadryas,* fr. Gk, fr. *hama* together with + *Dryad-, Dryas* Dryad — more at DRYAD] **1 :** a nymph of trees and woods; *esp* **:** a nymph whose life begins and ends with that of a particular tree **2 a** [trans. of NL *hamadryas* (specific epithet of *Naja hamadryas*), fr. L *Hamadryas*] **:** KING COBRA **b** [trans. of NL *hamadryas* (specific epithet of *Papio hamadryas*), fr. L *Hamadryas*] **:** SACRED BABOON

ham·a·dry·as baboon \ˌ==¦drīəs-\ *n* [NL *hamadryas,* specific epithet of *Papio hamadryas*] **:** SACRED BABOON

ha·mal *also* **ham·mal** \həˈmäl, -mȯl\ *n* -S [Ar *ḥammāl* porter] **:** a burden bearer in Turkey and other countries of the eastern Mediterranean **:** PORTER

ha·ma·ma·tsu \ˌhäməˌmäˈt(ˌ)sü\ *adj, usu cap* [fr. *Hamamatsu,* Japan] **:** of or from the city of Hamamatsu, Japan **:** of the kind or style prevalent in Hamamatsu

ham·a·mel·i·da·ce·ae \ˌhaməˌmeləˈdāsēˌē\ *n pl, cap* [NL, fr. *Hamamelid-, Hamamelis,* type genus + *-aceae*] **:** a family of shrubs and trees (order Rosales) having small often clustered flowers and a bicarpellate bilocular ovary and comprising the witch hazels and related plants — see FOTHERGILLA, HAMAMELIS — **ham·a·mel·i·da·ceous** \ˌ==¦==¦dāshəs\ *adj*

ham·a·mel·i·dan·the·mum \ˌ====ˈdan(t)thəməm\ *n, cap* [NL, fr. *Hamamelid-, Hamamelis* + *-anthemum*] **:** a genus of fossil plants having flowers resembling those of the witch hazel and found in amber of Oligocene age in the region of the Baltic sea

ham·a·mel·i·dox·y·lon \-ˈdäksəˌlän\ *n, cap* [NL, fr. *Hamamelid-, Hamamelis* + *-o-* + *-xylon*] **:** a genus of fossil plants having wood identical with or similar to that of the witch hazel

ham·a·me·lis \-ˈmēləs\ *n, cap* [NL, fr. Gk *hamamēlis* medlar, fr. *hama* together with + *mēlon* apple, fruit — more at MELON] **:** a genus of shrubs or small trees (family Hamamelidaceae) having pinnately veined leaves and clustered flowers with elongated ribbon-shaped petals — see WITCH HAZEL

ham·a·mel·i·tes \ˌhaməˈmeləˌtēz, -ˌməˈlīd·(ˌ)ēz\ *n, cap* [NL, fr. *Hamamelis* + *-ites*] **:** a genus of fossil plants having leaves similar to those of the witch hazel

ha·man·tasch *also* **ha·man·tash** \ˈhämənˌtäsh, ˈhəm-\ *n, pl* **hamantasch·en** \-shən\ [Yiddish *homentash,* fr. *Homen,* biblical chief minister of Ahasuerus and enemy of the Jews (Esth 3–7) + *tash* pocket, bag, fr. OHG *tasca,* fr. (assumed) VL *tasca* task, compensation, purse — more at TASK] **:** a three-cornered cake with a poppy-seed or prune filling traditionally eaten in Jewish households at Purim

ha·mar·tia \ˌhäˌmärˈtēə, həˈmärd·ēə\ *n* -S [Gk, fr. *hamartanein* to err] **1 :** a defect of character **:** error, guilt, or sin esp. of the tragic hero in a literary work **2 :** HAMARTOMA — **ha·mar·ti·al** \ˌhäˌmärˈtēəl, həˈmärd·ēəl\ *adj*

ha·mar·ti·ol·o·gy \həˌmärd·ēˈäləjē\ *n* -ES [Gk *hamartia* sin + E *-o-* + *-logy*] **:** a part of theology treating the doctrine of sin — compare PONEROLOGY

ham·ar·to·ma \ˌhamə(r)ˈtōmə\ *n, pl* **hamartomas** *or* **hamartomata** [NL, fr. Gk *hamartia* + NL *-oma*] **:** a mass resembling a tumor assumed to represent anomalous development of tissue natural to a part or organ rather than a true tumor — **ham·ar·to·ma·tous** \ˌhamə(r)¦tämədəs, -tōm-\ *adj*

ha·mate \ˈhāˌmāt\ *adj* [L *hamatus,* fr. *hamus* hook + *-atus* -ate; perh. akin to Gk *chamos* bent] **:** bent at the end into a hook **:** HOOKED

ha·mat·ed \-mād·əd\ *adj* [L *hamatus* + E *-ed*] **:** HAMATE

¹**ha·math·ite** \ˈhāməˌthīt, -ˌma,-\ *n* -S *usu cap* [*Hamath* (Hama), Syria + E *-ite*] **:** a native or inhabitant of the ancient city of Hamath in western Syria

²**hamathite** \"\ *adj, usu cap* **1 :** of, relating to, or characteristic of Hamath **2 :** of, relating to, or characteristic of the people of Hamath

ha·ma·tum \həˈmād·əm, -hāˈ-\ *n, pl* **hama·ta** \-d·ə\ *or* **hamatums** [NL, fr. neut. of L *hamatus* hooked] **:** a bone on the inner side of the second row of the carpus in mammals that apparently represents a fusion of the fourth and fifth carpal bones — called also *unciform*

ham beetle *n* **:** any of several small beetles that feed in cured or dried food products; *esp* **:** RED-LEGGED HAM BEETLE

ham·berg·ite \ˈham(ˌ)bərˌgīt\ *n* -S [Sw *hambergit,* fr. Axel *Hamberg* †1933 Swed. mineralogist + Sw *-it* -ite] **:** a mineral $Be_2(OH)BO_3$ consisting of beryllium borate and occurring as grayish white prismatic crystals (hardness 7.5, sp. gr. 2.35)

ham·ble \ˈam(b)əl\ *vi* -ED/-ING/-S [perh. akin to LG *humpeln* to limp, OIr *camm* crooked — more at CHANGE] *dial Eng* **:** to limp or stumble in walking

ham·ble·to·nian \ˌhambəlˈtōnēən, -ōnyən\ *adj, usu cap* [after *Hambletonian,* 19th cent. Am. stallion fr. which this strain has descended] **:** a strain of American trotting horses

ham·bo \ˈhäm(ˌ)bü\ *n* -S [Sw, fr. *Hambo,* parish in Hälsingland, Sweden] **:** a Swedish round danced to various melodies in triple time

hambone \ˈ=ˌ=\ *n* [²*ham* + *bone*] *slang* **:** a performer doing an imitation of Negro dialect

ham·bro·line \ˈhambrəˌlīn, -ˌlən\ *also* **ham·ber·line** \-bə(r),-\ *or* **ham·ber** \-bə(r)\ *n* -S [*hambroline, hamberline* fr. E *hambro-, hamber-* (irreg. fr. *Hamburg,* Germany) + E *line; hamber* short for *hamberline*] **:** right-handed 3-strand usu. tarred hemp or jute marine cordage used for small seizings — compare ROUNDLINE

¹**ham·burg** \ˈhamˌbərg, ˈhäm-, -bə̄g,-bəig\ *n* -S [fr. *Hamburg,* Germany] **1** *sometimes cap* **:** a machine-embroidered usu. fine cotton edging for trimming women's clothes **2** *usu cap* **:** a European breed of rather small domestic fowls with plumage usu. spangled or penciled with white, rose combs, and lead-blue legs **3** [short for *hamburg steak*] **:** HAMBURGER

²**hamburg** \", ˈhäm,bu̇r|g, ˈhäm-, -üə|, |k\ *adj, usu cap* [fr. *Hamburg,* Germany] **:** of or from the city of Hamburg, Germany **:** of the kind or style prevalent in Hamburg

hamburg brandy *n, usu cap H* **:** an imitation grape brandy made by adding flavoring to potato or beet spirit

ham·burg·er \ˈhamˌbərgər, ˈhaam-, -bə̄gə(r, -bəigə(r\ *n* -S *often attrib* [short for *hamburger steak*] **1 a :** ground beef **b :** a cooked patty of ground beef — compare SALISBURY STEAK **2 :** a sandwich made of a hamburger patty in a split round bun

hamburg parsley *n, usu cap H* **:** a parsley (*Petroselinum crispum* var. *tuberosum*) having smooth uncurled foliage and being cultivated primarily for its enlarged edible taproot which resembles a small very savory parsnip

hamburg steak *pronunc at* ¹HAMBURG +\ *or* **hamburger steak** *n, sometimes cap H* [²*Hamburg* or G *Hamburger* of Hamburg, fr. *Hamburg,* Germany] **:** HAMBURGER

¹**hame** \ˈhām\ *n* -S [ME, prob. fr. MD; akin to OE *ham* undergarment, *hama* covering, OHG *hamo,* ON *hamr* covering, shape, Skt *śāmulya* woolen shirt] **:** one of the two curved wooden or metal supports that go along the sides of the collar of a draft horse and often terminate in essentially nonfunctional projections

²**hame** \"\ *Scot var of* HOME

ha·meil \ˈhāməl\ *adj* [of Scand origin; akin to ON *heimill, heimall* domestic, at one's disposal, fr. *heimr* home, homeland — more at HOME] *Scot* **:** domestic and homelike

¹**hamel** *or* **hamil** \ˈaməl, ˈ(h)äm-\ *n* -S [MF *hamel* — more at HAMLET] *now dial Eng* **:** HAMLET

²**ham·el** \ˈhaməl\ *n* -S [Afrik, fr. MD; akin to OE *hamola* man with cropped hair, OHG *hamal* wether, *hamal* castrated, ON *hamla* to castrate, *skammr* short, Skt *śamala* error, damage; basic meaning: castrated] *Africa* **:** WETHER

ha·me·lia \həˈmēlyə\ *n* [NL, fr. Henri L. Du*hamel*-Dumonceau †1782 Fr. agriculturist + NL *-ia*] **1** *cap* **:** a genus (family Rubiaceae) of tropical American shrubs having flowers in scorpioid cymes with the corolla distinctly 5-ribbed **2** -S **:** any plant of the genus *Hamelia*

hame·suck·en *also* **haim·suck·en** \ˈhāmˌsəkən\ *n* -S [ME *hamsoken,* fr. OE *hāmsōcn,* fr. *hām* home + *sōcn* attack; akin to ON *sōkn* attack, OE *sēcan* to attack, seek — more at HOME, SEEK] **1** *Scots law* **:** the assaulting of a person in his own house or dwelling place **2** *Anglo-Saxon law* **a** (1) **:** a franchise of trying persons charged with assaulting a person in his own home and receiving the fines or damages imposed (2) **:** such fines or damages **b :** BURGLARY, HOUSEBREAKING

ha·metz *or* **cha·metz** *or* **cho·metz** \kōˈmāts, ˈkōˌmets\ *n* -ES [Heb *ḥāmēṣ*] **:** leaven or leavened food banned during Passover

hame·with \ˈhāmwōth\ *adv (or adj)* [alter. of earlier *hameward,* fr. ²*hame* + *-ward*] *Scot* **:** HOMEWARD

ham·fare \ˈhamˌfa(a)|(ə)r, -fe|\ *n* [ME *hamfare,* fr. *ham* home + *fare* journey, expedition — more at FARE] **:** HAMESUCKEN

ham·fat·ter \ˈhamˌfad·ə(r)\ *n* -S [fr. "The Ham-fat Man," Negro minstrel song + E *-er*] *slang* **:** ²HAM 3a

ham-fisted \ˈ=¦==\ *adj, chiefly Brit* **:** HAM-HANDED 2

ham-handed \ˈ=¦==\ *adj* **1 :** having especially large hands ⟨a *ham-handed* companion who looked like a heavyweight wrestler —W.M.Swann⟩ **2 :** HEAVY-HANDED, CLUMSY ⟨*ham-handed* dramatist —J.C.Trewin⟩ ⟨tms made up of ponderous or *ham-handed* players —H.N.Maclean⟩

hami *pl of* HAMUS

ha·mi·form \ˈhāməˌfȯrm\ *adj* [L *hamus* hook + E *-iform* — more at HAMATE] **:** HOOKED 1

ha·milt \ˈhāməlt, -ld\ *var of* HAMEIL

ham·il·ton \ˈhaməltᵊn, -tən\ *adj, usu cap* [fr. *Hamilton,* Ontario] **:** of or from the city of Hamilton, Ontario **:** of the kind or style prevalent in Hamilton

¹**ham·il·to·ni·an** \ˌ==¦tōnēən, -ōnyən\ *adj, usu cap* **1** [Alexander *Hamilton* †1804 Am. statesman + E *-ian*] **1 :** of or relating to the statesman Hamilton or to his political and social doctrines or program characterized by advocacy of a strong central government of a unitary type, protection of industrial and commercial interests, and a general distrust of the political capacity or wisdom of the common man ⟨the *Hamiltonian* creed of selective suffrage —S.H.Adams⟩ ⟨the *Hamiltonian* tradition in the U.S. —Alexander Brady⟩ ⟨the clash of Jeffersonian and *Hamiltonian* America —R.M.Weaver⟩ ⟨the *Hamiltonian* realistic concern with . . . the protection of American industries —T.I.Cook & Malcolm Moos⟩ **2** [James *Hamilton* †1829 Brit. language teacher + E *-ian*] **:** of or relating to the scholar Hamilton or his system of language teaching **3** [Sir William *Hamilton* †1856 Scottish philosopher + E *-ian*] **:** of or relating to the philosopher Hamilton or his theories — compare HAMILTONISM **4** [Sir William R. *Hamilton* †1865 Irish mathematician + E *-ian*] **:** of or relating to the mathematician Hamilton or his system of dynamics

²**hamiltonian** \"\ *n* -S *usu cap* **:** a follower or exponent of Hamiltonian doctrines or theories; *esp* **:** a follower or advocate of the social or political doctrines of Alexander Hamilton

ham·il·to·ni·an·ism \ˌhaməlˈtōnēəˌnizəm, -ōnyə,-\ *n* -S *usu cap* [¹*Hamiltonian* + E *-ism*] **:** the body of social and political doctrines held by or associated with the statesman Hamilton **:** the Hamiltonian program or ideology

ham·il·ton·ism \ˈhaməltᵊnˌizəm, -ltəˌni-\ *n* -S *usu cap* [Sir William *Hamilton* + E *-ism*] **:** the philosophical and logical teachings of Sir William Hamilton esp. concerning the doctrine of natural realism and the quantification of the predicate

ham·i·noea \ˌhaməˈnēə\ *n, cap* [NL] **:** a common genus of bubble shells (family Akeridae) of the Pacific coast of No. America with a shell so thin that the pulsation of the heart of the translucent yellowish brown animal within is commonly visible through it

ham·ite \ˈhaˌmīt, *usu* -īd·+V\ *n* -S *usu cap* [*Ham,* son of Noah, eponymous ancestor of the Hamites (Gen 10:6–20) + E *-ite*] **1 :** a descendant of Ham, one of the sons of Noah **2 a :** a member of a group of African peoples including the Berber peoples north of the Sahara, the Tuaregs and Tibbu in the Sudan, possibly the extinct Guanches of the Canaries, the ancient Egyptians and their descendants, and the Galla of east Africa that are mostly Muslims, are highly variable in appearance but mainly Caucasoid, and are believed by many to be late-Paleolithic or post-Paleolithic colonists of western Europe **b :** a native speaker of a Hamitic language — compare COPT, ETHIOPIAN

ha·mi·tes \həˈmīd·(ˌ)ēz\ *n, cap* [NL, fr. L *hamus* hook + NL *-ites* — more at HAMATE] **:** a genus of extinct Cretaceous ammonoids with a shell forming repeated V-shaped loops in one plane

¹ham·it·ic \(ˈ)haˈmid·ik, həˈm-, -mitik\ *adj, usu cap* [*Hamite* + *-ic*] **1 :** of, relating to, or characteristic of the Hamites **2 :** of, relating to, or characteristic of one of the Hamitic languages

²hamitic \ˮ\ *n* -s *usu cap* **:** HAMITIC LANGUAGES ⟨an authority on *Hamitic*⟩

ham·it·i·cized \haˈmid·ə,sīzd, həˈm-\ *adj, usu cap* **:** conjectured or presumed to have acquired through interbreeding certain traits hypothetically characteristic of the ancient ancestors of the Hamitic-speaking peoples

hamitic languages *n pl, usu cap H* **:** the Berber, Cushitic, and sometimes Egyptian branches of the Afro-Asiatic or Hamito-Semitic languages formerly regarded as constituting an independent language family or as constituting one of two coordinate subfamilies of the Hamito-Semitic languages

ham·i·tism \ˈhamə,tizəm\ *n* -s *usu cap* **:** the quality or state of being Hamitic

hamito- *comb form, usu cap* [*Hamitic*] **:** Hamitic and ⟨*Hamito*-Bantu⟩ ⟨*Hamito*-Semitic⟩ — usu. with hyphen

¹hamito-semitic \ˌhamə,tō+\ *adj, usu cap H&S* [*Hamito-* + *Semitic*] **:** of, relating to, or characteristic of the Hamito-Semitic languages

²hamito-semitic \ˮ\ *n, usu cap H&S* **:** HAMITO-SEMITIC LANGUAGES

hamito-semitic languages *n pl, usu cap H&S* **:** AFRO-ASIATIC LANGUAGES

¹ham·let \ˈhamlə̇t, *usu* -əd·+V\ *n* -s [ME, fr. MF *hamelet*, dim. of *hamel*, dim. of *ham*, of Gmc origin; akin to OE *hām* homeland, village, house — more at HOME] **1 :** a settlement that is smaller than a village ⟨performances are being contemplated in cities, in towns, and even in ~s —Joseph Wechsberg⟩ **2 :** the smallest incorporated unit of municipal government ⟨incorporation into a ~, the bottom rung of the municipal ladder —*N.Y.Times*⟩

²hamlet \ˮ\ *n* -s [origin unknown] **1 a :** a large grouper (*Epinephelus striatus*) common from Florida to Brazil and in the Caribbean and important as a food fish — called also *Nassau grouper* **b** *Bahamas* **:** any young grouper **2 :** a yellow and black thickly spotted moray (*Gymnothorax moringa*) used for food in the West Indies

³hamlet \ˮ\ *n* -s *usu cap* [after *Hamlet*, chief character of the tragedy *Hamlet* (1600–1601) by William Shakespeare †1616 English dramatist] **:** a brooding indecisive person ⟨the very *Hamlet* of our age . . . a philosopher thrust into power at a time of violence —Michael Amrine⟩ ⟨tortured by indecision, a *Hamlet* in politics —*Newsweek*⟩

hamlike \ˈ=,=\ *adj* **:** resembling a ham ⟨swung a ~ fist toward the west window of the kitchen —Kenneth Roberts⟩

ham·ma·da *or* **ha·ma·da** \həˈmädə\ *n* -s [Ar *hammādah*] **:** a rock-floored or rock-strewn desert region esp. in the Sahara

hammal *var of* HAMAL

ham·mar·ite \ˈhamə,rīt\ *n* -s [Sw *hammarit*, fr. Gladhammar, Sweden, its locality + Sw *-it* -ite] **:** a mineral prob. $Pb_2Cu_2Bi_4S_9$ consisting of lead, copper, and bismuth sulfide

hammed *past of* HAM

¹ham·mer \ˈhamə(r)\ *n* -s *often attrib* [ME *hamer*, fr. OE *hamor*; akin to OHG *hamar* hammer, ON *hamarr* hammer, crag, Gk *akmōn* anvil, Skt *áśma* stone, Gk *akmē* edge — more at EDGE] **1 a :** a hand tool consisting of a solid head set crosswise on a handle and used for pounding (as in driving nails, breaking stone, beating metal surfaces) — see BALL PEEN HAMMER, CLAW HAMMER, SLEDGEHAMMER; compare MALLET **b :** a power tool that often substitutes a metal block or a drill for the hammerhead (as in driving posts, stamping or forging metal, or breaking up rock surfaces) — see AIR HAMMER, DROP HAMMER, JACKHAMMER; compare PILE DRIVER **2 :** one that strikes like a hammer ⟨we need a concerted, vigorous voice; we need a ~ —Harvey Breit⟩ ⟨wielding this problem as the ~ with which they must smash the last vestiges of Christian thought —L.J. Shehan⟩ ⟨the ~ thrust of radio and television —*Saturday Rev.*⟩ **3 :** something that resembles a hammer in form or action: as **a :** a lever with a striking head for ringing a bell or striking a gong (as in a clock or an electric bell) **b** *obs* **:** a door knocker **c** (1) **:** a steel cover for the powder pan of a flintlock gun against which the flint strikes to ignite the powder; *also* **:** an arm that holds the flint for striking **:** ¹COCK 4 (2) **:** an arm that strikes the cap in a percussion lock to ignite the propelling charge (3) **:** a part of the action of a modern gun that strikes the primer of the cartridge in firing or that strikes the firing pin to ignite the cartridge **d :** MALLEUS 1a **e :** GAVEL; *specif* **:** a gavel with which an auctioneer indicates that an article is sold to the last bidder **f** (1) **:** a padded mallet in a piano action for striking a string (2) **:** a hand mallet for playing on a percussion instrument of fixed pitch (as a dulcimer or a xylophone) **4 :** a metal sphere hurled in the hammer throw that usu. weighs 16 pounds and together with its flexible wire handle measures not more than four feet in length — **under the hammer** *adv* **:** for sale at auction ⟨priceless heirlooms went *under the hammer*⟩

²hammer \ˮ\ *vb* **hammered; hammered; hammering** \-m(ə)riŋ\ **hammers** [ME *hameren*, fr. *hamer*, n.] *vi* **1 a :** to strike blows esp. repeatedly with or as if with a hammer **:** POUND ⟨the impounded water ~s at the weak spots —Russell Lord⟩ ⟨his pulses ~*ing* in his head —Clive Arden⟩ **b :** WATER-HAMMER **2 :** to become insistent or urgent **:** be in or keep up a state of agitation ⟨these thoughts . . . ~*ed* in her indignant consciousness —J.C.Powys⟩ **3 :** to make repeated efforts as if shaping with a hammer: **a :** to reiterate an opinion or attitude repeatedly and emphatically **:** to place emphasis by constant repetition or discussion ⟨continually ~s on the danger of intrigue —O.M.Green⟩ — often used with *away* ⟨letters and pamphlets all ~*ed* away at the same point —Nathan Kelne⟩ **b :** to work persistently or tirelessly **:** TOIL, LABOR ⟨Beethoven thought of an air, ~*ed* at it, altered it again and again —C.W.H.Johnson⟩ **4** *now dial Eng* **:** to speak haltingly **:** STAMMER ~ *vt* **1 a :** to strike with a hammer **:** beat, drive, or shape with repeated blows ⟨~ a nail⟩ ⟨~ a horseshoe⟩ ⟨~ out a tray⟩ **b :** to fasten with a hammer (as by nailing) ⟨~ down a lid⟩ **c :** to build with hammer and nails — usu. used with *together* ⟨~ together a cold frame⟩ **2 :** to strike as if with a hammer: **a :** to hit or drive with the force of a hammer ⟨~*ed* three home runs in one game —Bob Broeg⟩ ⟨the incoming train ~*ed* the rear of the shorter train —*Springfield (Mass.) Union*⟩ **b :** to strike with repeated blows **:** POUND, THUMP ⟨~ a typewriter⟩ ⟨~*ing* a rather hard pillow into a more comfortable shape —Dorothy Sayers⟩ **c :** to bring or keep under attack **:** BELABOR ⟨the State Department is being badly ~*ed* on this issue —*New Republic*⟩ **3 :** to produce or bring about as if by means of repeated blows: **a :** to shape or put together by persevering effort ⟨~ our words to fit a song —Charles Fox⟩ ⟨~*ed* together an alliance —*Newsweek*⟩ — often used with *out* ⟨~ out a policy⟩ ⟨~ out an empire⟩ ⟨sat at the piano for hours . . . trying to ~ out an original tune —Noel Coward⟩ **b :** to force or drive into the consciousness by reiteration ⟨~*ing* in day after day the same few and relatively simple beliefs —John Dewey⟩ — often used with *home* ⟨~s home the theme of freedom to think —Brooks Atkinson⟩ **c :** to level off **:** make smooth **:** ADJUST — usu. used with *out* ⟨differences are ~*ed* out in discussion —Walter Moberly⟩ **d** (1) **:** to force down the price of (a stock) by selling short ⟨told the broker whom I had been using to ~ down the stock to continue his operations —B.M.Baruch⟩ (2) **:** to declare (a member of the London stock exchange) to be a defaulter ⟨broke away to the stock exchange and at twenty-four was insolvent and ~*ed* —*Times Lit. Supp.*⟩

ham·mer-ai·toff projection \ˌhämə(r)ī,tôf-\ *n, usu cap H&A* [after Ernst von *Hammer* †1925 Ger. geographer and David *Aitoff* †1933 Russ. geographer] **:** AITOFF PROJECTION

hammer and sickle *n, sometimes cap H&S* [fr. its adoption (1923) by the U.S.S.R. on its national flag] **1 :** an emblem consisting of a crossed sickle and hammer used as a symbol of peasant and worker **2 :** a flag bearing the insignia of the hammer and sickle

hammer and tongs *adv (or adj)* **:** with the force and violence of a blacksmith pounding iron **:** with all one's strength **:** in a rough-and-tumble manner ⟨the wedding party going it *hammer and tongs* down the road —Richard Llewellyn⟩ ⟨go after a witness in the old *hammer-and-tongs* style —Mitchell Dawson⟩ ⟨has gone at his job in a *hammer-and-tongs* way that has annoyed — and offended — a good many businessmen —*Newsweek*⟩

hammer beam *n* **:** either of the short horizontal beams or cantilevers projecting from the top of a pair of opposite walls to support a roof principal for a Gothic roof and thus dispense with the necessity for a tie beam

1 hammer beams

hammerbird \ˈ=,=\ *n* **:** HAMMERKOP

hammerblow \ˈ=,=\ *n* **:** a stroke of or as if of a hammer; *specif* **:** a pounding of the rails by the driving wheels of a locomotive caused by the inertia of unbalanced parts

hammer brace *n* **:** a bracket under a hammer beam

hammer butt *n* **:** a block into which the base of a hammer shank in a piano action is fitted

hammercloth \ˈ=,=\ *n* [ME *hamerclothe*] **:** an ornamented often fringed cloth hung over the coachman's seat esp. of a ceremonial coach

hammerdress \ˈ=,=\ *vt* **:** to dress or face (stone) with a hammer

hammer drill *n* **:** a percussion rock drill in which a plunger or hammer strikes rapid blows on the shank of a loosely held drill — compare PISTON DRILL

hammered *adj* **:** having surface indentations produced or appearing to have been produced by hammering ⟨she wore a knit dress . . . and a necklace and matching bracelet of dark ~ metal —Douglass Wallop⟩

hammered glass *n* **:** rolled glass made nontransparent by embossing it on one side to resemble beaten metal

ham·mer·er \ˈhamərə(r)\ *n* -s **:** one that hammers

hammerhead \ˈ=,=\ *n* **1 :** the striking part of a hammer *specif* **:** a part of a hammer in a piano action that strikes the strings **2 :** one that is dense or stupid **:** BLOCKHEAD, NUMSKULL ⟨a big ~ but even if he had had a smart head, a no-good horse —Richard Wormser⟩ **3 :** something that resembles the striking part of a hammer: as **a :** any of various medium-sized sharks of the family Sphyrnidae that have the eyes at the ends of lateral extensions of the flattened head, are active voracious fishes sometimes considered man-eaters, are widely distributed in warm seas, and include some (as *Sphyrna zygaena* and *S. tudes*) which are fished for their hides and vitamin-rich livers **b** (1) **:** HOG SUCKER (2) **:** HAMMERHEADED BAT (3) *or* **hammerheaded stork** \ˈ=,=,=-\ **:** HAMMERKOP

hammerhead crane *n* **:** a heavy-duty crane with a horizontal counterbalanced jib

hammerheaded \ˌ=ˈ=\ *adj* **1 :** having a head shaped like that of a hammer **2 :** DENSE, STUPID, THICKHEADED

hammerheaded bat *n* **:** a West African fruit bat (*Hypsignathus monstrosus*) in which the male has a large truncate head with a hammer-shaped muzzle and well developed voice organs

hammerhead shark *also* **hammerheaded shark** *n* **:** HAMMERHEAD 3a

hammerhead stall *n* **:** a maneuver in which an airplane pulls up in a vertical climb until it almost stalls and then drops the nose in a wingover so that direction of flight is reversed

hammering *n* -s **1 :** the act or process of beating or pounding with or as if with a hammer ⟨the art of silver ~⟩ ⟨slow ~ of heavy guns —Kenneth Roberts⟩ ⟨under ~s from me . . . the legislature passed a bill —F.D.Roosevelt⟩ **2 :** a pattern of shallow indentations produced with a hammer

ham·mer·ing·ly *adv* **:** in a hammering manner

ham·mer·kop \ˈhamə(r),käp\ *also* **hammerkop bird** *or* **hammerkop stork** *n* -s [Afrik *hamerkop*, fr. *hamer* hammer + *kop* head] **:** a chiefly dusky brown African wading bird (*Scopus umbretta*) intermediate in some respects between storks and herons but distinguished by its large head with heavy bill and thick dorsal crest and by its huge domed nest

ham·mer·less \-,ləs\ *adj* **1 :** lacking a hammer **2 :** having the hammer concealed — used of a gun having the hammer enclosed within the receiver

hammerlock \ˈ=,=\ *n* **:** a wrestling hold in which an opponent's arm is held bent behind his back

ham·mer·man \-mən, -,man\ *n, pl* **hammermen** [ME, fr. *hamer* hammer + *man*] **:** one that works with a hammer; *esp* **:** an operator of a power-driven hammer (as a jackhammer)

hammer mill *n* **1 :** a grinder in which feed and other products are pulverized by several rows of thin steel hammers revolving at high speed **2 :** a crusher in which minerals (as ores, rock, coal) are broken up by the impact of swinging hammer bars hinged to a rapidly rotating shaft

hammer oyster *n* **:** any of several bivalve mollusks of *Malleus* and related genera of Chinese and Australian waters having elongated handle-shaped shells that resemble an oyster on the interior and that are prolonged in both directions at the dorsal margin to suggest the head of a hammer

hammer post *n* **:** a pendant in the shape of a pilaster that serves as impost to a hammer brace

hammer price *n* **:** the price at which a defaulter's contract is settled on the London stock exchange

hammer rail *n* **:** a padded strip of wood supporting the hammers in a piano action when at rest

hammers *pl of* HAMMER, *pres 3d sing of* HAMMER

hammer scale *n* **:** a scale that forms on heated metal when it is hammered

hammer shank *n* **:** a wooden dowel onto which a hammer in a piano action is fitted

hammer shell *n* **:** HAMMER OYSTER; *also* **:** its shell

hammersmith \ˈ=,=\ *n* **1 :** a smith who works with a hammer **2 :** one who supervises work done with drop hammers or power presses

hammer spring *n* **:** a spring that actuates a hammer (as in a gun or a piano action)

hammer spur *n* **:** a projection on the hammer of a gun by which it is cocked

hammerstone \ˈ=,=\ *n* **:** a prehistoric hammering implement consisting of a rounded stone

hammer throw *n* **:** a field event in which a metal sphere attached to a flexible handle is hurled for distance from inside a circle with a 7-foot diameter

hammertoe \ˌ=ˈ=\ *n* **:** a deformed claw-shaped toe and esp. the second that results from permanent angular flexion between one or both phalangeal joints — called also *claw toe*

hammer tongs *n* **:** blacksmith's tongs having projecting lugs for engaging holes of hammerheads during forging

hammer-weld \ˈ=,=\ *vt* **:** to weld by blows with a hammer

hammer welding *n* **:** forge welding by mechanical hammering

hammerwort \ˈ=,=\ *n* **:** PELLITORY 1

hammer-wrought \ˌ=ˈ=\ *adj* **:** shaped with a hammer

hamming *pres part of* HAM

¹ham·mock \ˈhamək *also* -mik *or* -mēk\ *n* -s *often attrib* [Sp *hamaca*, fr Taino] **1 :** a swinging couch or bed usu. made of netting or canvas and slung by cords from supports at each end ⟨two trees just wide enough apart to swing a ~⟩ **2 :** something that resembles a hammock (as the suspended nest of an oriole); *specif* **:** a length of light twine netting hung along or across a sleeping-car berth to hold wearing apparel and other personal belongings

hammock 1

²hammock \ˮ\ *vt* -ED/-ING/-s **:** to suspend in or as if in a hammock ⟨~*ed* him in her shawl in a loop that placed him close to her breast —John Steinbeck⟩ ⟨content to ~ himself passively in the amplitude of enveloping time —Victoria Sackville-West⟩

³hammock \ˮ\ *n* -s *often attrib* [origin unknown] **1 :** HUMMOCK **2 :** a fertile area in the southern U.S. (as Florida) that is often somewhat higher than its surroundings and is characterized by hardwood vegetation and soil of greater depth and containing more humus than that of the flatwoods or pinelands; *specif* **:** an island of dense tropical undergrowth in the Everglades

hammock batten *n* **1 :** one of the battens on a ship's beam from which a hammock is slung **2 :** a bar used for spreading hammock clews

hammock clew *n* [¹*hammock*] **:** CLEW 3b

hammock cloth *n* **:** a tarpaulin or piece of canvas used on a ship to cover stowed hammocks or to place over the openings in hammock nettings — called also *top cloth*

hammock hickory *n* [³*hammock*] **:** a Florida tree (*Carya floridana* or *C. magnifloridana*) having gray bark, reddish brown to gray twigs, leaves with 5 to 7 leaflets, and fruit that is broadly ellipsoid to pyriform

hammock netting *also* **hammock berthing** *n* **:** a net or a box trough to hold sailors' hammocks when not in use

ham·my \ˈhamē, ˈhaam-, -mi\ *adj* -ER/-EST **1 a :** flavored with or tasting of ham **b :** resembling ham in flavor or appearance **2 :** like or characteristic of a ham actor **:** exaggeratedly and usu. self-consciously theatrical **:** OVERACTED ⟨children are not dismayed by ~ acting provided the story is good —Rose M. Daly⟩

ha·mo·tzi \häˈmōtsē\ *n* -s [Heb *hammōṣī*, lit., the one who brings forth; fr. the concluding words of the benediction] **:** the recital of the Hebrew benediction over bread before meals

¹ham·per \ˈhampə(r), ˈhaam-, ˈhaim-\ *vt* **hampered; hampered; hampering** \-p(ə)riŋ\ **hampers** [ME *hamperen*; perh. akin to Flem *hampern* to stutter, MD *hāperen*] **1 a :** to restrict the movement of by bonds or obstacles **:** FETTER, IMPEDE ⟨elaborate ~*ing* clothes —James Laver⟩ ⟨icebergs ~*ed* the progress of the ship⟩ ⟨pitching . . . violently in the seaway, ~*ed* by her heavy tow —R.S.Porteous⟩ **b :** to interfere with the operation of **:** DISRUPT ⟨radio communications ~*ed* by static —*Globe & Mail*⟩ **2 a :** CURB, RESTRAIN, LIMIT ⟨the view . . . that rhyme and meter ~ the poet's free expression —J.L. Lowes⟩ ⟨did nothing to ~ the boisterousness of the occasion —Silas Spitzer⟩ **b :** to interfere with **:** ENCUMBER, HANDICAP, OBSTRUCT ⟨an obsolete ideology can ~ an economy —V.G. Childe⟩ ⟨~*ed* by lack of money as often as by lack of initiative —H.J.Hanham⟩

syn CLOG, TRAMMEL, FETTER, SHACKLE, MANACLE, HOG-TIE: HAMPER, the most general of these terms, can imply any impediment or restraining agent that encumbers, delays, or interferes with an action ⟨like other branches of science, history is now encumbered and *hampered* by its own mass —Henry Adams⟩ ⟨his principle was to choose competent lieutenants, and then to leave them to work without *hampering* interference —*Irish Digest*⟩ ⟨*hampered* in his progress by the weight of a large bundle on his back⟩ CLOG usu. implies a foreign useless impediment that clings, gums up, or obstructs ⟨all common ambitions, rank, possessions, power, the things which *clog* man's feet —John Buchan⟩ ⟨his mind is *clogged* with the strangest miscellany of truth and marvel —V.L. Parrington⟩ ⟨waved the traffic away from the *clogged* thoroughfare —Ralph Gustafson⟩ TRAMMEL suggests entanglement by or confinement within a net ⟨had now become *trammeled* in events —Ethel Wilson⟩ ⟨a landscape of increasing strangeness, replete with things shocking to a culture-*trammeled* understanding —B.L.Whorf⟩ FETTER suggests the total or almost total crippling restraint of chains or manacles ⟨a tendency toward introversion . . . had slowly mastered him, *fettering* his actions and segregating him in an unhappy little world —I.V.Morris⟩ ⟨watched a world prepare for war while he was *fettered* by the nation's propensity for isolationism —Estes Kefauver⟩ SHACKLE and MANACLE are very similar to although stronger than FETTER, usu. suggesting a total impeding of action ⟨if the power of the courts stereotypes legislation within the forms and limits . . . expedient in the 19th or perhaps the 18th century, it *shackles* progress and breeds distrust and suspicion of the courts —B.N.Cardozo⟩ ⟨keep Rome *manacled* hand and foot: no fear of unruliness —Robert Browning⟩ HOG-TIE implies a making completely helpless or a total thwarting ⟨as soon as the senator can get us *hog-tied* to that extent, he will . . . ram these unconstitutional measures down our throats —*Congressional Record*⟩ ⟨accuse Americans of being *hog-tied* to business —*advt*⟩

²hamper \ˮ\ *n* -s **1** *archaic* **:** something that impedes **:** OBSTRUCTION, SHACKLE ⟨if the Fourteenth Amendment is not to be a greater ~ . . . than I think was intended —O.W.Holmes †1935⟩ **2 :** TOP-HAMPER

³hamper \ˮ\ *n* -s [ME *hampere*, alter. of *hanaper* — more at HANAPER] **:** a basket or box usu. with a cover for packing, storing, or transporting food and other articles: as **a :** a basket often of wickerwork for carrying food or drink ⟨a picnic ~⟩ ⟨helped . . . the yardman to pack the game in ~s —Adrian Bell⟩ **b :** a container of standardized capacity for shipping fruits and vegetables that is of splint, stave, or fiberboard construction and is circular, elliptical, or polygonal in shape with a top diameter usu. greater than the bottom, with slatted sides, and with a bottom that may be loose, stapled, or nailed in place or formed by a continuation of the sides — compare BASKET 1 **c :** a small ventilated receptacle for laundry made of wood, plastic, or metal and usu. having a flat side to fit against a wall **d :** a large canvas container on casters used for sorting and moving mail in a post office

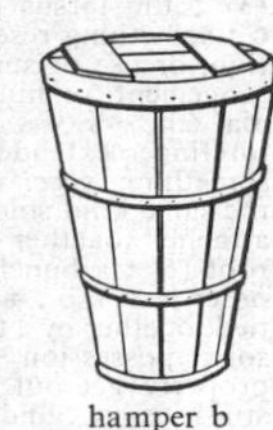

hamper b

⁴hamper \ˮ\ *vt* **hampered; hampered; hampering** \-p(ə)riŋ\ **hampers** *chiefly Brit* **1 :** to pack in a hamper ⟨trifles . . . ~*ed* up together —T.A.Browne⟩ **2 :** to present with a hamper of food or wine ⟨something particularly charming about being ~*ed* at Christmas time —*Westminster Gazette*⟩

hamp·race \ˈham,prās\ *n, usu cap* [¹*Hampshire* + Land*race*] **:** MONTANA 2a

¹hamp·shire \ˈham(p),shi(ə)r, ˈhaam-, -,shə(r), -,shə(r)\ *n* [fr. *Hampshire*, England] **1** *usu cap* **:** an American breed of black, white-belted swine with white forelegs, rather long head, and straight face **2** -s *often cap* **:** an animal of the Hampshire breed

²hampshire \ˮ\ *adj, usu cap* [fr. *Hampshire*, England] **:** of or from Hampshire, England **:** of the kind or style prevalent in Hampshire

³hampshire \ˮ\ *also* **hampshire down** \ˈ=(,)=ˈdaůn\ *n* [²*Hampshire*] **1** *usu cap H&D* **:** a British breed of medium-wooled mutton-type sheep that are large, thick-fleshed, and hornless and have dark faces and legs **2** -s *usu cap H often cap D* **:** a sheep of the Hampshire breed

hams *pl of* HAM, *pres 3d sing of* HAM

ham·socn \ˈhäm,sōkən\ *n* -s [OE *hāmsōcn* — more at HAMESUCKEN] **:** HAMESUCKEN

ham·ster \ˈhamztə(r), ˈhaam-, -m(p)st-\ *n* -s [G, fr. OHG *hamustro* (akin to OS *hamustra* hamster), of Slavic origin; akin to OSlav *chomĕstorŭ* hamster] **:** any of numerous Old World rodents of *Cricetus* and related genera having very large cheek pouches and somewhat resembling the American white-footed mouse but short-tailed and commonly larger and of burrowing habits — see GOLDEN HAMSTER

ham·stery \-tərē\ *n* -ES **:** an establishment for breeding and raising hamsters

¹hamstring \ˈ=,=\ *n* [²*ham* (popliteal space) + *string*] **1 a :** either of two groups of tendons bounding the upper part of the popliteal space at the back of the knee and forming the tendons of insertion of certain muscles of the back of the thigh **b :** the large tendon above and behind the hock of a quadruped **:** ACHILLES' TENDON **2 :** a restrictive power **:** regulatory control ⟨fend for itself . . . among myriad regulations, restrictions, and government ~s —*Atlantic*⟩

²hamstring \ˮ\ *vt* **hamstring; hamstrung; hamstringing; hamstrings 1 a :** to deprive of the power of locomotion by cutting the leg tendons **:** CRIPPLE, DISABLE ⟨wolf packs ~ and destroy many moose —Frank Dufresne⟩ **b :** to cut the muscle or tendons in the small of a whale ⟨it is sometimes the custom when fast to a whale more than commonly powerful and alert, to seek to ~ him —Herman Melville⟩ **2 :** to make ineffective or powerless **:** limit or destroy the effectiveness of **:** HINDER, IMPAIR ⟨supporting rather than ~*ing* our negotiators —F.L. Allen⟩ ⟨talents *hamstrung* by respectability —Cyril Connolly⟩ ⟨~ . . . arms production by wresting away raw-material sources —Virginia Prewett⟩

ham·u·lar \ˈhamyələ(r)\ *adj* [L *hamulus* + E *-ar*] **:** HAMATE

ham·u·lus \-ləs\ *n, pl* **hamu·li** \-,lī\ [NL, fr. L, little hook, dim. of *hamus*] **:** a hook or hooklike process; *esp* **:** a little hook terminating the barbicel of a feather

ha·mus \ˈhāməs\ *n, pl* **ha·mi** \-,mī\ [NL, fr. L, hook — more at HAMATE] *biol* **:** a hook or curved process

ham·za or **ham·zah** \'hamzə\ n -s [Ar hamzah, lit., compression (as of the larynx)] **1** : the sign for a glottal stop in Arabic orthography — usu. represented in English by an apostrophe **2** : the sound for which the hamza stands

ham·zat·ed \-,zād·əd\ adj : bearing a hamza — used of a letter of the Arabic alphabet or of a word written in the Arabic alphabet ⟨a ~ alif⟩

1**han** dial Brit pres pl of HAVE

2**han** \'hän, -a-\ adj, usu cap [Han, Chin. dynasty (206 B.C.–A.D. 220)] **1** : of, relating to, or having the characteristics of the period of the Han dynasty ⟨Han pottery⟩ **2** : of, relating to, or being a nationality group in China descended from the original Chinese and constituting an overwhelming majority of the population and the dominant cultural group : belonging to the Chinese proper as distinguished from other nationality groups (as the Manchu or Mongols) ⟨the Han race⟩

3**han** \"\ n, pl han or hans usu cap **1** : an Athapaskan people of the Yukon river district in east central Alaska and the Yukon Territory of Canada **2** : a member of the Han people

han' \'(h)an, 'hón\ Scot var of HAND

han·a·fi \'hanə(,)fē\ n -s usu cap [Ar ḥanafīy, after abu-Hanifah †767 Muslim jurist] **1** : an orthodox school of Muslim jurisprudence predominating in Turkey and India — compare HANBALI, MALIKI, SHAFI'I **2** or **han·a·fite** \-,fīt\ : a follower of the Hanafi school

han·a·hill or **han·na·hill** \'hanə,hil\ n -s [origin unknown] : a sea bass (Centropristes striatus) of the Atlantic coast

han·ap \'ha,nap, -nəp\ n -s [ME, fr. MF hanap, henap, of Gmc origin; akin to OE hnæpp bowl, drinking vessel, OS hnapp, MD & MLG nap, OHG hnapf, ON hnappr] : an elaborate medieval goblet or standing cup usu. having a cover

han·a·per \'hanəpə(r)\ n -s [ME (also, case to hold hanaps), fr. MF hanapier case to hold hanaps, fr. hanap + -ier -er] Brit : a small wicker case used as a repository for legal documents

han·a·ster \'hanəstə(r)\ n -s [ME hanster, fr. hans hansa + -ster — more at HANSA] : a person admitted to the merchant guild in Oxford, England

han·ba·li \'hanbə(,)lē\ n -s usu cap [Ar ḥanbalīy, after ibn-Hanbal †855 Arab jurist] **1** : an orthodox school of Muslim jurisprudence predominating in Saudi Arabia — compare HANAFI, MALIKI, SHAFI'I **2** or **han·ba·lite** \-ə,līt\ : a follower of the Hanbali school

hance \'han(t)s\ n -s [obs. E hance, haunce lintel, fr. hance, haunce to raise, fr. ME hauncen, prob. short for enhauncen — more at ENHANCE] **1** : a curved contour on a ship (as the fall of the fife rail to the deck) **2** **a** (1) : the arc of minimum radius at the springing of an elliptical or similar arch (2) : the haunch of an arch **b** : a small arch joining a straight lintel to a jamb

hance arch n : an arch having greater curvature at its springings than at the crown

hanch \'hanch\ vb [ME hanchen, fr. MF hancher] vt, now dial Eng : to snap at noisily or greedily ~ vi, now dial Eng : to snap noisily and greedily

han·cock·ite \'han,kä,kīt\ n -s [E. P. Hancock, 19th cent. Am. mineralogist + E -ite] : a complex silicate that contains lead, calcium, strontium, and other metals and is isomorphous with epidote

1**hand** \'hand, -aa(ə)-\ n -s often attrib [ME, fr. OE hand, hond; akin to OHG hant hand, ON hönd, Goth handus] **1** **a** (1) : the terminal part of the vertebrate forelimb when modified (as in man) as a grasping organ being made up of wrist, metacarpus, terminal fingers, and opposable thumb or of these parts excluding the wrist and exhibiting unusual mobility and flexibility both of the digits and the whole organ (2) : the segment of the forelimb of a vertebrate above the fishes that corresponds to the hand (as the pinion of a bird) irrespective of its form or functional specialization ⟨a kangaroo's forearms seem undeveloped, but the powerful five-fingered ~s are skilled at feinting and clouting —Springfield (Mass.) Union⟩ **b** : a part serving the function of or resembling a hand: as (1) : the hind foot of an ape (2) : the chela of a crustacean (3) : the tarsus of either forelimb of an insect (as a fly) **c** : something resembling a hand in appearance, shape, function, or use or suggesting the fingers of a hand in shape, arrangement, or number: as (1) : an indicator or pointer on a dial ⟨the ~s of a clock⟩ (2) : a stylized figure of a hand with forefinger extended to point a direction or call attention to something; specif : INDEX 9 (3) : five articles (as oranges) of the same kind sold together (4) : a bunch of 8 to 20 bananas attached together on their stem (5) : a palmate form of gingerroot (6) : a bunch of large leaves tied together usu. with another leaf; esp : a bunch of 5 to 20 uniform leaves of tobacco tied together by a tie leaf at the butt end of the leaves **2** **a** : personal possession — usu. used in pl. ⟨anxious not to let the property get out of his ~s⟩ **b** (1) : CONTROL, DIRECTION, SUPERVISION ⟨guided the proceedings from the front row with a very helpful ~ —Sydney (Australia) Bull.⟩ — usu. used in pl. ⟨kept the management of the firm in his own ~s⟩ ⟨the reception was already in the ~s of the florists and caterers⟩ (2) : right or privilege in controlling or directioning ⟨allowed the teacher a free ~ in her treatment of the children⟩ **3** **a** : SIDE, DIRECTION ⟨armed men were running and fighting on either ~⟩ **b** : one of two sides of an issue or argument : one of two or more aspects of a subject or matter of consideration ⟨on the one ~ we can appeal for peace, or on the other declare war⟩ ⟨on the one ~ I should like to give the child a great deal of freedom but on the other ~ I don't want him totally out of my control⟩ **c** (1) : the manner of twisting or going round whether right-handed or left-handed ⟨the ~ of a spiral⟩ ⟨a right-hand screw⟩ (2) : the characteristic of a door determining whether it opens to the right or to the left as viewed from the outside (as of a cupboard or closet) or from the inside (as of a room) with door opening away — compare LEFT-HAND, LEFT-HAND REVERSE BEVEL, RIGHT-HAND, RIGHT-HAND REVERSE BEVEL (3) : the characteristic of a hinge determining whether it is to be fitted to a right-handed or left-handed door — compare LEFT-HAND, RIGHT-HAND (4) : the characteristic of a lock determining whether it throws to the right or left — compare LEFT-HAND, RIGHT-HAND **4** **a** : a pledge or indication of agreement or of satisfaction with terms (as of a contract) ⟨without further talk he gave me his ~ on the deal and we closed it⟩ **b** : a pledge of betrothal or bestowal in marriage ⟨asked the man for his daughter's ~⟩ **5** **hands** pl : skill in handling the reins in horsemanship ⟨he didn't ride well, he hadn't good ~s —H.G.Wells⟩ **6** **a** : style of penmanship : HANDWRITING ⟨a handsome ~⟩ ⟨a crabbed ~⟩ ⟨left behind her twenty-six volumes written in her own ~ —Elizabeth Bowen⟩ ⟨in the cuneiform ~ —J.H.Breasted⟩ **b** : SIGNATURE ⟨some writs require a judge's ~⟩ **7** **a** : SKILL, ABILITY ⟨wished to try his ~ at painting⟩ ⟨the comedienne tries her ~ at singing and dancing . . . for the first time —Theatre Arts⟩ **b** : an instrumental part ⟨several men had a ~ in the crime⟩ ⟨letting private industry have a bigger ~ in developing nuclear energy —Wall Street Jour.⟩ **8** : a unit of measure equal to 4 inches used esp. for the height of horses — compare HANDBREADTH **9** **a** : assistance or aid esp. involving physical effort ⟨gave the old man a ~ with his heavy bundles⟩ **b** : PARTICIPATION, INTEREST, CONCERN ⟨a project in which several people had a ~⟩ ⟨took a ~ in planning the new curriculum⟩ **c** : a round of applause ⟨won a good ~ for his acting⟩ ⟨gave the singer quite a ~⟩ **10** **a** (1) : a player in a card game or board game (2) : the cards or pieces held by a player after a deal or distribution (3) : a set of cards or pieces in a player's possession at any point during a game (4) : the period of a game during which all cards are played or pieces distributed at one time are played (5) : a portion of undealt cards available for play in solitaire **b** : the force or solidity of one's position usu. as a negotiator against an opposing force ⟨these developments greatly strengthened the ~ of union policymakers —Collier's Yr. Bk.⟩ — often used in pl. **11** **a** : one who performs or executes a particular work ⟨two portraits by the same ~⟩ ⟨essays by various ~s in praise of her work —Collier's Yr. Bk.⟩ **b** (1) : one employed at manual labor or general tasks ⟨a ranch ~⟩ (2) : WORKER, EMPLOYEE ⟨business was so successful the company soon was employing over a hundred ~s⟩ **c** : a member of a ship's crew ⟨all ~s on deck⟩ **d** : one relatively skilled in or disposed to perform a particular action or engage in a particular pursuit ⟨quite a ~ at figures⟩ ⟨a great ~ at carpentry⟩ **e** : a specialist in a usu. designated activity or region ⟨a Latin America ~⟩ — compare OLD HAND **12** archaic : one that is a source of information **13** **a** archaic : a touch or stroke esp. of a brush on a painting **b** : HANDIWORK ⟨the destruction showed the ~ of vandals⟩ **c** : style of execution : WORKMANSHIP ⟨the very brushstrokes showed the ~ of a master⟩ : manner of handling : TOUCH ⟨in all the masques and pageants . . . his ~ was heavy and his invention flat —Francis Hackett⟩ ⟨treated the child with a light ~⟩ **14** : the pawl that rotates the cylinder of a revolver **15** dial : the near horse **16** dial Brit : a locality or neighborhood ⟨he comes from over near Kendal ~⟩ **17** or **hand game** : a gambling game played by American Indians consisting of guessing the whereabouts of pieces of bone or other small objects which are passed rapidly from hand to hand **18** [trans. of L manus] : MANUS 2 **19** : a turn of play in which there is an opportunity to score in a game : INNING **20** : the feel of cloth or leather or tactile reaction to its textural qualities of smoothness, flexibility, softness ⟨the warm, dry, luxurious ~ of silk —Collier's Yr. Bk.⟩ **21** also **hand cheese** : any of several cheeses of a kind orig. molded by hand — **at close hand** adv : in close proximity : NEARBY ⟨as a personal friend he saw the great man at close hand on many occasions⟩ — **at first hand** adv : FIRSTHAND ⟨got the facts at first hand by going in person to the scene of the accident⟩ — **at hand** : near in time or place ⟨rather than buy more wood we used what was at hand⟩ ⟨the day of reckoning was at hand⟩ — **at second hand** adv : through an intermediary : INDIRECTLY ⟨got all his information at second hand rather than from original sources⟩ — **at the hands of** or **at the hand of** : by the act or instrumentality of ⟨the old way of life became totally outdated at the hand of the new technology and psychology⟩ : from the hands of ⟨received bad treatment at the hands of his master⟩ — **at third hand** adv : from a thirdhand source : in thirdhand condition : through more than one intermediary ⟨an account that was as unreliable as most information got at third hand⟩ — **by hand** adv **1** : with the hands : by manual labor ⟨tilled the garden by hand⟩ **2** : in handwriting ⟨a typewritten letter with a note added by hand⟩ **3** : with personal care and attention ⟨bring a child up by hand⟩ **4** : without the use of a machine that is usu. used for the purpose ⟨became disgusted with the adding machine so added the figures by hand⟩ — **for one's own hand** : for one's own advantage ⟨the group refused to work cooperatively, each member rather playing for his own hand⟩ — **from hand to hand** : from possession by one person to that of another : through successive possession by a number of people ⟨a bauble of little worth that went from hand to hand⟩ — **from hand to mouth** : with provision sufficient only for present needs : PRECARIOUSLY ⟨always poor and living from hand to mouth⟩ ⟨vagrants who live happily from hand to mouth —Brooks Atkinson⟩ — **in hand** adv **1** **a** : in one's possession ⟨when he had enough money in hand he bought a car⟩ **b** : in control ⟨kept the children in hand by a system of rewards and punishments⟩ **c** : at one's disposal ⟨for a poor man he had a large amount of property in hand because of his position⟩ : to spare ⟨a race won with plenty of time in hand⟩ **2** obs : with one or accompanying one often on a leash **3** **a** : in preparation ⟨a new play in hand⟩ : under consideration ⟨took the matter in hand at a board meeting⟩ : in course of transaction ⟨a business deal in hand⟩ **b** : under effective control or management ⟨got the business in hand before planning new sales campaigns⟩ **4** : HAND IN HAND **5** of a ball : not yet in play or put out of play by the rules of the game — opposed to in play — **into hand** adv : into control or supervision ⟨the most troublesome children were taken into hand by special counselors⟩ — **lift a hand** or **raise a hand** : to make an effort : WORK — **of all hands** obs : on all sides : on every side — **off one's hands** : out of one's care or charge ⟨relieved to get so great a responsibility off his hands⟩ — **of one's hands** obs : of valor, skill, or ability esp. in fighting — **on all hands** adv : on every hand ⟨in the dark of the woods he could hear twittering and scurrying on all hands⟩ — **on every hand** adv : in or from every direction : EVERYWHERE ⟨as I . . . went into business, I found on every hand that quantity counted for more than quality —Edward Bok⟩ — **on hand** adv **1** : in present possession and easily available ⟨a large stock of goods on hand⟩ **2** : about to appear : PENDING, AFOOT ⟨reported there was trouble on hand⟩ **3** : in attendance : PRESENT ⟨I will be on hand when you call⟩ — **on one's hands** : in one's possession, care, or management, often as a responsibility or a burden ⟨a lot of worthless property on his hands⟩ ⟨a problem child on her hands for a week⟩ ⟨a whole afternoon on his hands to do with as he wished⟩ — **out of hand** adv **1** : without delay, hesitation, or preparation : FORTHWITH, PROMPTLY ⟨hanged the man out of hand without waiting for trial⟩ ⟨dismissed the traditional logic out of hand —J.A.Passmore⟩ **2** : done with ⟨the business was finally out of hand⟩ **3** : out of control ⟨let his temper get out of hand⟩ ⟨the children got out of hand and had to be spanked⟩ — **put one's hand on** or **lay one's hand on** : FIND, LOCATE ⟨arranged the files so he could put his hand on any fact he wanted in a moment⟩ — **put one's hand to** or **set one's hand to** **1** : to take hold of ⟨put his hand to the plow⟩ **2** : to engage in : UNDERTAKE ⟨knew he would succeed in whatever he put his hand to⟩ — **to hand** adv **1** : into possession ⟨used whatever came to hand and didn't cost anything⟩ **2** : within reach : easily available ⟨weapons ready to hand⟩ ⟨convenient local ammunition lying to hand —Mollie Panter-Downes⟩ **3** : into control or subjection ⟨the insurgents were brought quickly to hand⟩ — **to one's hand** : already prepared to appeal to one's taste or special talents ⟨a subject matter for a playwright just made to his hand⟩ — **under the hand of** : authenticated by the handwriting or signature of ⟨a deed executed under the hand of the owner⟩ — **with a heavy hand** **1** : with little mercy : STERNLY, RIGOROUSLY ⟨put down a revolt with a heavy hand⟩ **2** : without grace, delicacy, or sensitivity : CLUMSILY ⟨went at the task with a heavy hand neglecting essential distinctions⟩ — **with clean hands** : UNCORRUPTED, INNOCENT ⟨although the opportunity to profit by dishonesty was always near he came out with clean hands⟩

2**hand** \"\ vb -ED/-ING/-S vt **1** **a** obs : to manage with the hands : MANIPULATE; also : to lay hands on **b** : FURL ⟨~ed the mainsail —Thomas Horgan⟩ **2** : to lead, guide, or assist with the hand : CONDUCT ⟨~ a lady into a bus⟩ ⟨~ed herself along the life line and followed her shipmates to the poop —Roland Barker⟩ **3** : to give, pass, or transmit with the hand ⟨~ a person a letter⟩ **4** : to make (one's way) by means of or by swinging with the hands ⟨an animal that ~s its way through the trees —Weston La Barre⟩ **5** : to compel a person to submit to : administer forcefully to a person ⟨the smaller boy ~ed the bully a terrible beating⟩ ~ vi : to hand a sail — **hand it to** : to give credit to : concede the excellence of ⟨had to hand it to the committee for doing such a good job in getting out the vote⟩

hand–adz \'=,=\ n : a prehistoric celt-shaped tool usu. of stone having one flat and one curved surface and an adz type of cutting edge

hand alphabet n : MANUAL ALPHABET

hand and foot adv [ME, fr. OE hand and fōt] **1** : in a way to prevent escape or totally impede action ⟨bound the prisoner hand and foot⟩ **2** : TOTALLY, COMPLETELY, ASSIDUOUSLY ⟨a woman who waited on her husband hand and foot⟩

hand apple n : an apple suitable for eating without cooking

handarm \'=,=\ n : HANDGUN

hand ax n : a prehistoric stone implement consisting of a biface core having one end pointed for cutting and the other end rounded for holding in the hand

handbag \'=,=\ n **1** : TRAVELING BAG **2** : a woman's bag made in various shapes of fabric, leather, or plastic, held in the hand or looped by handles over the shoulder, and used for carrying usu. small personal articles and accessories

handball \'=,=\ n **1** : a small hollow black rubber ball used in the game of handball **2** : a game similar to squash played in a walled court or against a single wall or board by two or four players who use their hands to strike the ball

handbank \'=,=\ vt : to haul (logs) to be banked for further transportation — **hand·bank·er** \'=,=ə(r)\ n

handbarrow \'=,(,)=\ n [ME handberwe, fr. hand + berwe, barew, barowe barrow — more at BARROW] : a flat rectangular frame with handles at both ends that is carried by two persons — compare WHEELBARROW

handbasin \'=,==\ n : WASHBOWL

handbell \'=,=\ n : a small bell with a handle; esp : one of a set tuned in a scale for musical performance

handbill \'=,=\ n : a small printed sheet to be distributed (as for advertising) by hand and often doubling as a poster

handbook \'=,=\ n [trans. of G handbuch] **1** **a** : a book capable of being conveniently carried as a ready reference : MANUAL **b** : a concise reference book covering a particular subject or field of knowledge ⟨a ~ of geology⟩ ⟨a ~ of fungi⟩ ⟨a ~ of scouting⟩ ⟨a Milton ~⟩ **c** : a book of directions and information for travelers ⟨a ~ of France⟩ **2** **a** : a bookmaker's book of bets **b** : a place where bookmaking is carried on

handbell

hand·book·ing \'=,=iŋ\ n : BOOKMAKING 2

handbow \'=,=\ n : a bow drawn by hand as distinguished from a crossbow

hand brake n : a brake (as on an automobile) operated by hand

hand·breadth \'han(d),=\ or **hands·breadth** \-n(d)z,=\ n : the breadth of a hand; also : any of various units of length based on the breadth of a hand varying from about 2½ to 4 inches — compare HAND 8

hand·bred \'han,brēd, 'hón-\ n [ME handbrede, fr. OE handbred, fr. hand, hond hand + bred surface, board; akin to OE bord piece of sawed lumber — more at HAND, BOARD] chiefly Scot : HANDBREADTH

hand breeding n : controlled mating in which both the time and the mating individuals are selected by the breeder — called also hand mating; opposed to pasture breeding

H and C abbr, often not cap hot and cold running water

handcar \'=,=\ n : a small four-wheeled car propelled by a hand-operated mechanism or by a small motor or fastened as a trailer to a motor-propelled car and used on railroad tracks for transporting men and materials in railroad-track construction and maintenance work

handcart \'=,=\ n : a cart drawn or pushed by hand

hand cheese n : HAND 21

handclap \'=,=\ n : a clap of the hands in indication of approval or praise ⟨a flurry of ~s greeted his appearance as the featured pianist⟩

handclasp \'=,=\ n : a clasping of hands usu. by two people during an introduction of one to the other done as a formality upon meeting or parting or as a sign of friendship, affection, unanimity, or good wishes : HANDSHAKE

handcart

hand composition n : the work of a hand compositor

hand compositor n : one that sets type by hand esp. as contrasted with a typesetting-machine keyboard operator

1**handcraft** \'=,=\ n [ME, fr. OE handcræft, fr. hand + cræft craft] : HANDICRAFT

2**handcraft** \"\ vt : to fashion by handicraft ⟨a distinguished weathervane ~ed of heavy aluminum —House Beautiful⟩ ⟨~ed dress materials —New Yorker⟩ ⟨a ~ed chassis that uses no production shortcuts —advt⟩

hand·craft·man \-f(t)mən\ or **hand·crafts·man** \-f(t)sm-\ n, pl **handcraftmen** or **handcraftsmen** : one who is skilled in handicraft

1**handcuff** \'=,=\ vt **1** : to apply handcuffs to : MANACLE **2** : to restrain esp. completely or so as to prevent action by or as if by means of handcuffs ⟨the wording of the present charter would ~ the present parliament by preventing any revisions —Current History⟩

2**handcuff** \"\ n : a metal fastening that can be locked around a wrist and that is usu. connected by a chain or bar with another such fastening which can be locked about the other wrist of the same person or the wrist of another person : MANACLE — usu. used in pl. and often with pair

hand cultivator n : WHEEL CULTIVATOR 2

h and d curve \,āchən'dē-\ n, usu cap H&D [after Ferdinand Hurter and Charles Driffield fl 1890 Brit. photographers] : CHARACTERISTIC CURVE a

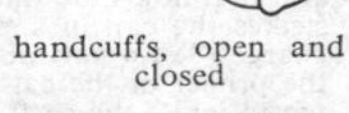
handcuffs, open and closed

hand down vt **1** : to transmit in succession (as from father to son or from predecessor to successor) ⟨the family property was handed down from generation to generation⟩ **2** **a** : to deliver to the proper office of an inferior court (the decision or opinion of an appellate court) **b** : to make official formulation of and express (the opinion of any court) **c** : to promulgate (as a policy) with authoritative force brooking no opposition ⟨the dictator handed down his decision⟩

hand–down n -s [by shortening] : HAND-ME-DOWN

hand drill n **1** : a small portable drilling machine resembling a breast drill but designed to be held and operated by hand **2** : a primitive drill consisting of a shaft carrying a point of stone, bone, shell, or metal and revolved usu. by the palms of the hands

hand drill: 1 chuck, 2 change gear, 3 crank, 4 frame, 5 handle, 6 idler pinion, 7 detachable side handle, 8 pinion

h and d speed \,āchən'dē-\ n, usu cap H&D [after Ferdinand Hurter and Charles Driffield fl 1890] : a number indicating the sensitivity of a photographic emulsion determined by the method of Hurter and Driffield

h and d system n, usu cap H&D [after Ferdinand Hurter and Charles Driffield fl 1890] : a system for determining the speed of photographic materials that is based on the characteristic curve and related to the inertia of the material

hand·ed \'handəd, 'haan-\ adj **1** : having hands ⟨a ~, vertical, tree-living animal —Weston La Barre⟩ **2** : being either right-hand, left-hand, right-hand reverse bevel, or left-hand reverse bevel — used of doors, hinges, locks, screws

hand·ed·ness n -ES **1** : the quality or state of being handed **2** : a tendency to use one hand rather than the other ⟨a test for ~⟩

han·de·lian \(')han'dēlyən, -lēən\ adj, usu cap [George F. Handel, (Händel) †1759 Ger. composer + E -ian] : of or relating to the German composer Handel or belonging to, befitting, or suggesting his music

hand·er \'handə(r), 'haan-\ n -s **1** dial Brit : a blow on the hand **2** : one that drops tobacco hands to the prizer for packing in hogsheads

hander–in \'=,=\ n, pl **handers–in** : a textile worker who assists in the drawing-in of the warp

1**handfast** \'=,=\ vt [ME handfesten, handfasten, fr. ON handfesta, fr. hand-, hönd hand + festa to fasten, fr. fastr fast — more at HAND, FAST] archaic : to bind in contract by joining hands; esp : BETROTH

2**handfast** \"\ n, archaic : a contract or covenant esp. of betrothal or marriage

3**handfast** \"\ adj [1hand + fast] archaic : having a firm or close grasp : CLOSEFISTED

handfasting n -s **1** archaic : BETROTHAL **2** : an irregular or probationary marriage contracted by joining hands and agreeing to live together as man and wife; also : the living together under such an agreement

hand–feed \'=,=\ vt : to provide and apportion rations to (animals) at regular intervals in quantities sufficient for a single feeding — compare SELF-FEED

hand file n : a file of rectangular section with parallel sides and slightly thicker than a mill file

1**handfish** \'=,=\ n [1hand + fish (n.); fr. the pectoral fins that resemble hands] : a fish of the family Brachionichthyidae

2**handfish** \'=,=\ vi [1hand + fish (v.)] : to catch fish with the hands sometimes with bait as a lure : GUDDLE

hand–fives \'=,=\ n pl but sing in constr : FIVES

handflag \'=,=\ n : one of usu. two flags used in transmitting messages by semaphore

handflower tree \'⸗,⸗-\ *n* : HAND TREE

hand fly *n* [so called fr. its being nearest the angler's hand] : DROPPER 1a

hand frame *n* : a textile machine (as a knitting frame) worked by hand or foot power

hand·ful *also* **hand·full** \'han(d),fu̇l, 'haan-\ *n, pl* **hand·fuls** \-n(d),fu̇lz\ *or* **hands·ful** \-n(d)z,fu̇l\ [ME, fr. OE *handfull,* fr. *hand* hand + *full* full — more at HAND, FULL] **1** : as much or as many as the hand will grasp or contain ⟨the child grabbed a ~ of jelly beans⟩ **2** : a small quantity or number ⟨only a ~ of people have ever seen that great high region —*London Calling*⟩ ⟨bought for liquor and a ~ of pin money the huge tracts near the present Twin Cities —*Amer. Guide Series: Minn.*⟩ ⟨this figure had shrunk to only a ~ —Walter Sullivan⟩ ⟨only a few of our people are killers; only a ~ would take a man's life so greedily —Lillian Smith⟩ **3** : as much as one can control or manage using all one's effort ⟨the rearing of the children and the keeping of the house proved to be a ~ for one of her frail constitution⟩ ⟨a snake as savage as this one would be a ~ —W.L.Gresham⟩

hand gallop *n* [so called fr. the fact that the horse is kept well in hand to control his speed] : a fast pace in horseback riding between a canter and a gallop : a very fast easy canter : a moderate gallop

hand game *n* : HAND 17

hand glass *n* **1** : a small mirror with a handle **2** : a 14-second or 28-second sandglass used in timing the running out of a nautical log line

handgrab \'⸗,⸗\ *n* : a bar or handle (as on a ship) used for steadying or supporting oneself

handgrasp \'⸗,⸗\ *n* : HANDLE

handgravure \'⸗⸗,⸗\ *n* : copperplate printing in which the inked plate is wiped by hand before each impression

hand grenade *n* : a grenade designed to be thrown by hand

handgrip \'⸗,⸗\ *n* [ME *hand grip,* fr. OE *handgripe,* fr. *hand* hand + *gripe* grip — more at HAND, GRIP] **1** : a grasping with the hand : HANDCLASP **2** : something that is attached to or forms part of an object and is designed to be grasped by the hand in lifting the object: as **a** : HANDLE ⟨the ~ of the revolver⟩ ⟨a pot with two small projecting ~*s*, one on each side⟩ **b** : HILT ⟨the ~ of a sword⟩ **c** : the outer usu. projecting end of the arm of an armchair ⟨it has nearly flat scrolled arms that . . . terminate in down-scrolled ~*s* —T.H.Ormsbee⟩ **3 handgrips** *pl* : close and usu. critical or desperate struggle : hand-to-hand combat — usu. used in the phrases *at handgrips* or *come to handgrips* ⟨before they lost the town the soldiers were at ~*s* with the enemy⟩ ⟨the struggle was so evenly matched the soldiers came to ~*s* before the issue was decided⟩

handguard \'⸗,⸗\ *n* **1 a** : a guard on a sword — compare CROSS GUARD **b** : a guard on a knife or dagger similar to that on a sword **2** : a wooden piece above the barrel of a rifle

handgun \'⸗,⸗\ *n* [ME *handgunne,* fr. *hand* + *gunne* gun — more at GUN] : a firearm held and fired with one hand

¹hand·hab·end \'⸗,habənd\ *or* **handhaving** \'⸗,⸗⸗\ *adj* [*handhabend* fr. ME, fr. OE *handhabbend,* fr. *hand, hond* hand + *habbend,* pres. part. of *habben* to have — more at HAND, HAVE] : having possession of stolen goods — used in Old English law of a thief caught with the loot

²handhabend \"\ *or* **handhaving** \"\ *n* -s : the jurisdiction to try a handhabend thief

handhold \'⸗,⸗\ *n* **1** : HOLD, GRIP ⟨got a ~ on the edge of the dock and pulled himself out of the water⟩ ⟨has a ~ on a rich chunk of the empire and he will not let go —*Time*⟩ **2** : something to hold on to (as in mountain climbing) ⟨swinging from one ~ to the next in a line⟩; *specif* : the part of an implement fashioned for grasping with the hand

handhole \'⸗,⸗\ *n* **1** : a hole large enough only for insertion of a hand (as for lifting) or of a hand and arm (as for cleaning out otherwise inaccessible places or giving access to enclosed parts) **2** : a shallow form of manhole giving access to a top row of ducts in an underground electrical system

hand·hol·er \'⸗,⸗ə(r)\ *n* : an operator of a machine for cutting handholes in the ends of wooden boxes

hand horn *n* : a natural French horn whose pitch a player can modify or alter by inserting his hand in the bell

hand horse *n, dial* : the near horse

¹hand·i·cap \'handē,kap, 'haan-, -də,-\ *n* -s *often attrib* [fr. obs. E, a game of forfeits and exchanges in which the players held forfeit money in a cap, alter. of *hand in cap*] **1** : a race or any contest of agility, strength, or skill in which in order to equalize chances of winning an artificial disadvantage is imposed on a supposedly superior contestant or an artificial advantage is given to one supposedly inferior **2 a** : an advantage given a weaker contestant or a disadvantage imposed upon a stronger contestant in the form of points, strokes, weight to be carried, or distance from the target or goal in order to equalize chances of winning **b** : a disadvantage that makes achievement unusually difficult; *esp* : a physical disability that limits the capacity to work

²handicap \"\ *vb* **handicapped; handicapped; handicapping; handicaps** *vt* **1 a** : to give a handicap to **b** : to assign handicaps to in order to equalize chances of success ⟨the horses were admirably *handicapped* in the race⟩ **2** : to put at a disadvantage ⟨*handicapped* in his job by worries over debts⟩ ~ *vi* : to engage in handicapping

hand·i·cap·per \-pə(r)\ *n* -s : one that handicaps in racing: **a** : the official (as of a jockey club) who assigns the weights to be carried by the horses in a handicap **b** : one whose job is handicapping ⟨earned some money as a ~ for a local newspaper⟩

handicapping *n* -s : the occupation of predicting winners in horse races usu. for publication

hand·i·craft \-,kraft, -aa(ə)-,-ai-,-à-\ *n* [ME *handie-crafte,* alter. (influenced by *handiwerk* handiwork) of *handcraft,* fr. *hand* + *craft*] **1 a** : an occupation in which articles are fashioned totally or chiefly by hand esp. with manual and often artistic skill usu. as either a trade or a hobby **b** : the articles fashioned by those engaged in such an occupation **2** *archaic* : one living by handicraft : HANDICRAFTSMAN

hand·i·craft·er \-tə(r)\ *n* -s : one that engages in a handicraft usu. as a hobby or avocation

hand·i·crafts·man \-f(t)smən\ *n, pl* **handicraftsmen** : one that engages in a handicraft : ARTISAN

hand·i·cuff \'⸗⸗,kəf\ *n* -s [¹*hand* + -*icuff,* as in *fisticuff*] *archaic* : a blow with the hand : FISTICUFF

handier *comparative of* HANDY

handiest *superlative of* HANDY

Handie–Talkie \'handē,tòkē\ *trademark* — used for a small portable radio transmitter-receiver

hand·i·grips \'handē,grips\ *archaic var of* HANDGRIPS

hand·i·ly \'handəlē, 'haan-, -li\ *adv* [*handy* + -*ly*] **1** : in a handy manner: as **a** : DEXTEROUSLY ⟨applied the brush ~ and finished the painting in a few minutes⟩ **b** : EASILY ⟨despite the handicap the horse won the race ~⟩ **c** : CONVENIENTLY ⟨kept the eraser ~ beside him as he wrote⟩ **2** *Midland* : JUSTLY, FAIRLY, RIGHTLY ⟨you can't ~ tell him to go home⟩

hand in *vt* : SUBMIT ⟨his thoughts were concentrated on *handing in* reports that would injure nobody —Alfred Burmeister⟩

hand–in \'⸗,⸗\ *n* -s [*hand in*] *in squash or badminton* : the player who serves the ball or his period of service

hand·i·ness \'handēnəs, 'haan-, -din-\ *n* -ES [*handy* + -*ness*] : the quality or state of being handy

handing *pres part of* HAND

hand in glove *or* **hand and glove** *adv* : in extremely close relationship or agreement esp. for nefarious purposes ⟨mass production is the outgrowth of the so-called industrial revolution and has had a part *hand in glove* with it —A.H.Compton⟩ ⟨the police were found to be working *hand in glove* with the racketeers⟩

hand in hand *adv* **1** *of two people* : with hands clasped usu. in affection or intimacy **2** : in the manner of things that are inseparably interrelated : in union : CONJOINTLY ⟨freedom of speech and true democratic government go *hand in hand*⟩ ⟨more and more architecture and landscape architecture go *hand in hand* —*Collier's Yr. Bk.*⟩ ⟨illness and bad housing go *hand in hand* —*Times Lit. Supp.*⟩

hand–in–hand \'⸗⸗'⸗\ *adj* [*hand in hand*] **1** *of two people* : having the hands clasped usu. in affection or intimacy **2** : being close or intimate : going side by side or in close relationship

handiron \'⸗,⸗\ *n* [by folk etymology] *dial* : ANDIRON

hand·i·work \'handē,⸗, 'haan-, -di,-\ *n* [ME *handiwerk,* fr. OE *handgeweorc,* fr. *hand* hand + *geweorc,* fr. *ge-* (collective and perfective prefix) + *weorc* work — more at HAND, CO-, WORK] **1 a** : work done by the hands ⟨occupied his time around the house with ~ of various kinds⟩ **b** : work done personally : personal or individual achievement ⟨his fortune is his own ~ —S.N.Behrman⟩ ⟨showed the ~ of a master criminal⟩ **2** : the product of handiwork ⟨the fiddle was . . . the ~ of the great Italian master violin maker —*Fortnight*⟩ ⟨selling baskets, ~, and curios to tourists —*Amer. Guide Series: Maine*⟩

handjar *var of* KHANJAR

hand·ker·cher \'haŋkə(r)chə(r), 'haiŋ-\ *dial var of* HANDKERCHIEF

hand·ker·chief \'haŋkə(r)chə̇f, 'haiŋ-, -(,)chif, -,chēf\ *n, pl* **handkerchiefs** *also* **handkerchieves** \|fs, |vz; *many whose pl is* -ēvz *have* ə *or* i *as a last-syllable vowel in the sing*\ [*hand* + *kerchief*] **1** : a piece of cloth usu. square and often printed, edged, or embroidered that is used for various usu. personal purposes (as the wiping of the nose or eyes) or as a costume accessory **2** : KERCHIEF 1

handkerchief dance *n* : a dance in which kerchiefs are waved or in which dancers are linked by the kerchiefs they hold in their hands

handkerchief table *n* : a folding triangular table that becomes square when the drop leaf supported by a swinging leg is raised

hand–kissing \'⸗,⸗⸗\ *n* -s : the custom in some countries (as France) of a gentleman's pressing his lips to the back of a woman's hand as a gesture of courtesy (as in an introduction) or of affection

hand labor *n* : manual labor as distinct from machine work

handlaid \'⸗'⸗\ *adj* **1** *of paper* : HANDMADE **2** *of a rope or line* : laid by hand

hand language *n* : communication by means of a manual alphabet : DACTYLOLOGY

¹han·dle \'handᵊl, 'haan-, *rapid* -nᵊl\ *n* -s [ME *handel,* fr. OE *handle;* akin to MLG *hantel* handle; derivatives fr. the root of E ¹*hand*] **1** : a part that is designed esp. to be grasped by the hand or that may be grasped by the hand (as for lifting or steering) **2 a** : something that resembles a handle in appearance, use, or function **b** : something (as a pretext or opportunity) that may be figuratively seized as a means of dealing with some larger abstract unit ⟨the only ~ he has for laying hold of the future —Dixon Wecter⟩ ⟨the ~ by which the writer grasps reality —Max Lerner & Edwin Mims⟩ **3 a** *slang* : NAME ⟨bore an odd ~⟩ ⟨with the heavenly ~ of St. Thomas —*Newsweek*⟩ : TITLE ⟨an Englishman with a ~ to his name—Baron or something⟩ **b** *dial* : a given name that is somewhat unusual ⟨what did they go and give the poor kid a ~ like that for —Edna Reynolds⟩ **4** : HAND 20 ⟨a well-scoured acetate fabric will have a soft springy ~ —*Dyestuffs*⟩ **5** [²*handle*] : the total amount of money bet on a race, game, or event or over a period of time (as a season) **6** *chiefly NewZeal* : a measure of beer approximately one pint — **off the handle** *adv* : into a state marked esp. by sudden and violent anger ⟨her nerves were so bad that she flew *off the handle* at the least provocation⟩

²handle \"\ *vb* **handled; handled; handling** \-(ᵊ)liŋ\ **handles** [ME *handelen,* fr. OE *handlian;* akin to OHG *hantalōn* to take with the hands, ON *höndla* to handle, seize; derivatives fr. the root of E ¹*hand*] *vt* **1 a** : to touch, feel, hold, take up, move, or otherwise affect with the hand : use the hands upon ⟨~ a material to find out how rough it is⟩ ⟨please do not ~ the merchandise⟩ **b** : to manage in using with the hands (as a spade or a weapon) : PLY, MANIPULATE, WIELD ⟨~ a scythe⟩ ⟨~ a gun with precision⟩ ⟨excellent at *handling* a horse⟩ **c** *of a batsman in cricket* : to pick up or touch with the hand (a ball in play) except at the request of the fielding side — used esp. in the phrase *out, handled the ball* **2 a** : to deal with or treat of in writing or speaking or in the plastic arts (as a theme, subject, argument, or objection) ⟨the writer ~*s* the matter briefly and concisely⟩ ⟨told him how to ~ color in using oil paints⟩ **b** : to conduct oneself in relation to : assume an attitude to **c** (1) : MANAGE, CONTROL, DIRECT ⟨was asked to ~ the staff of researchers in the absence of the director⟩ ⟨a lawyer who ~*s* the affairs of several corporations⟩ (2) : to have immediate physical charge in the care and training of (an animal) ⟨a good man to ~ his stable of horses⟩; *also* : to hold and incite (a sporting animal or bird) in a match (3) : to train (a pugilist) and act as the second during a fight (4) : to engage professionally in showing or exhibiting (an animal) in a show-ring **d** : to supervise, oversee, or control (as a worker) in such a way as to encourage a maximum of work output or persuade to a particular course of action or conduct ⟨a boss whose special gift was an ability to ~ men⟩ **e** : to deal with : act upon : dispose of : perform some function with regard to ⟨a period in which to ~ the day's mail and clear up back business⟩ ⟨told how much freight was *handled* at the port of New York⟩ ⟨a disposal unit that could ~ the city's garbage⟩ **f** : to trade in : engage in the buying, selling, or distributing of (a commodity) ⟨will be *handling* new and used cars⟩ : have or cause to pass through one's hands in commercial transactions **g** (1) : to perform or do to the point of completeness or success ⟨a man who would really ~ the job⟩ (2) : to drink (intoxicating drinks) without losing the normal control of one's faculties or actions or acting in foolish ways ⟨could not ~ liquor and always began to giggle and get maudlin after two drinks⟩ **3** *in hunting* : KILL **4** : to move up and down or draw out and replace (hides) in the pit in the process of tanning — see HANDLER 3 **5** : to be competent enough or fit to act upon, perform, manage, direct, solve, or deal with successfully in some other way ⟨a singer unable to ~ the difficult passages of the score⟩ ⟨equal to *handling* any amount of business that came along⟩ ⟨unable to ~ the boys⟩ ⟨his inability to ~ so difficult a problem —Sherwood Anderson⟩ ⟨a faucet that ~*s* hot and cold water simultaneously⟩ ⟨a typewriter that can ~ almost any number of carbons⟩ **6** : to have within its jurisdiction ⟨a court that ~*s* only probate matters⟩ ~ *vi* : to act, behave, or feel in a certain way when handled or directed ⟨bought a car that ~*s* well⟩ ⟨the schooner . . . ~*s* easily —Kenneth Roberts⟩ ⟨the dog ~*s* well in field trials⟩; *specif* : to submit obediently to direction or control ⟨the dog *handled* well in the trials⟩

syn HANDLE, MANIPULATE, WIELD, SWING, and PLY can mean in common to deal with as with the hands, esp. in an easy or dexterous manner. HANDLE implies at the least enough skill, and usu. a specified degree more, to accomplish one's end ⟨knew better than most men how to *handle* a blade —L.C. Douglas⟩ ⟨able to *handle* a foreign language with proficiency⟩ ⟨doubted that their economy could ever *handle* more than the natural population increase —*Time*⟩ MANIPULATE implies dexterity and adroitness in handling, esp. a mechanical or technical skill, and extends to suggest, in figurative use, a dealing with something in a crafty, artful, often fraudulent way ⟨the kind of courage required for mountaineering, for *manipulating* an aeroplane, or for managing a small ship in a gale —Bertrand Russell⟩ ⟨was able to *manipulate* sequences of words in blank verse in a manner which is quite his own — T.S.Eliot⟩ ⟨agencies by which some human beings *manipulate* other human beings for their own advantage —John Dewey⟩ ⟨a genius of legal dishonesty in *manipulating* stocks⟩ WIELD implies mastery and vigor in the handling of a tool, weapon, or other implement ⟨the longbow, which was so tall that the man *wielding* it had to pull the string back to his eye or ear —Tom Wintringham⟩ ⟨a past master in *wielding* a golf club⟩ ⟨*wield* the scalpel —G.B.Shaw⟩ ⟨*wield* tremendous political power —Green Peyton⟩ ⟨he *wields* . . . a very capable scholarship that gives backbone to his work —N.L.Rothman⟩ SWING in literal use implies a wide sweep of action ⟨*swing* a ball bat⟩ ⟨being able to *swing* an oar —H.A.Chippendale⟩ but in an extended figurative use it can imply the successful handling of something large or difficult in relation to one's capacities ⟨a task too hard for him to *swing*⟩ ⟨*swing* a big deal in high finance⟩ PLY is interchangeable with HANDLE or WIELD when great diligence or industry is implied ⟨tell them where it will best repay them to *ply* their pickaxes and spades —F.R. Leavis⟩ ⟨the experts *plied* their pens —R.F.Harrod⟩ **syn** see in addition TREAT

—**handle with gloves on** *or* **handle with kid gloves** : to treat with extreme care

han·dle·able \-ᵊləbəl\ *adj* : capable of being handled ⟨bucket feeding . . . makes the heifers gentle and ~ —*Australian Home Beautiful*⟩ ⟨a set of ~ . . . and inexpensive volumes —Margaret Marshall⟩

hand lead \-,led\ *n* : a small lead for sounding in shallow water

handlebar \'⸗⸗,⸗\ *n* **1** : a straight or bent bar with a handle or serving as a handle **2 a** (1) *or* **handlebars** *pl* : the shaped bar that forms part of a cycle's steering mechanism and that is grasped by the hands — see BICYCLE illustration (2) : one end of such a bar usu. grasped by one hand while riding (3) : a part of a steering mechanism suggesting or shaped like such a bar or one end of such a bar **b handlebars** *pl* : HANDLEBAR MOUSTACHE

handlebar moustache *n* : a man's heavy moustache with long slightly curved sections at each end

handle blank *n* : a piece of dimension lumber often of hickory and suitable for making handles

han·dled \'handᵊld, 'haan-, *rapid* -nᵊld\ *adj* : having a usu. specified type of handle ⟨a pearl-*handled* penknife⟩ ⟨a long-*handled* knife⟩

handled cross *n* : ANKH

han·dle·less \'han(d)ᵊl(l)ə̇s, 'haan-\ *adj* : having no handle

hand lens *n* : a magnifying glass designed to be held in the hand

han·dler \'hand(ᵊ)lə(r), 'haan-, *rapid* -n(ᵊ)l-\ *n* -s [ME, fr. *handelen* to handle + -*er*] **1** : one that handles ⟨all ~*s* of food in restaurants require a health certificate⟩ ⟨the railroad was one of the largest ~*s* of coal in the world⟩: as **a** : a worker whose task it is to move, carry, stow, or arrange materials or objects by hand or chiefly by hand **b** : one in immediate physical charge of an animal **c** : one that holds and incites a dog, gamecock, or other sporting animal in a match or hunt **d** : one that helps to train a pugilist or acts as his second during a match **e** : one professionally engaged in exhibiting animals in the show ring **f** : one that guides, directs, and acts as publicity man and general agent for another (as for a political candidate during a campaign) **2** : a worker who affixes handles (as to pottery or baskets) **3** : a pit containing tanning liquor in which hides are worked over or handled in the tanning process

handles *pl of* HANDLE, *pres 3d sing of* HANDLE

hand·less \'handlə̇s, 'haan-, *rapid* -nl-\ *adj* [ME, fr. ¹*hand* + -*less*] **1** : having no hands ⟨a ~ war veteran⟩ **2** : inefficient, clumsy, or incompetent in manual tasks ⟨could hardly empty a scuttle of ashes, so ~ was the poor creature —Mary H. Vorse⟩

hand letter *n* : a single letter usu. cut in brass that is applied by hand to the binding of a book

hand–letter \'⸗,⸗⸗\ *vb* [*hand letter*] *vt* **1** : to print by hand ⟨a *hand-lettered* notice in chalk on the wall⟩ **2** : to apply hand letters to (a book or its binding) ~ *vi* : PRINT

hand level *n* : a surveyor's level designed to be held in the hand and consisting of a telescope with a bubble tube so attached that the position of the bubble can be seen when looking through the telescope

h and l hinge *n, cap 1st H&L* : a door hinge resembling a ligature of a capital H and L

handlike \'⸗,⸗\ *adj* : shaped like a hand or grasping in the manner of a hand

¹handline \'⸗,⸗\ *n* **1** : a line managed chiefly by direct contact with the hands: as **a** : any of several comparatively simple arrangements of hooks and line designed for use in the hands of or under the immediate and continuous supervision of a fisherman — opposed to *setline* **b** : the line on a hand lead **c** : a line used without rod or reel for fishing **2** : a fire hose of small diameter

H and L hinge

²handline \'⸗,⸗\ *vi* : to fish with a handline — **hand·lin·er** \'⸗,⸗ə(r)\ *n*

handling *n* -s [ME, fr. OE *handlung,* fr. *handlian* to handle + -*ung* -ing — more at HANDLE] **1 a** : the action of one that handles something ⟨a child who needed a good deal of ~⟩ ⟨the horses seemed to thrive under his ~⟩ **b** : a process by which something is handled esp. in a commercial transaction ⟨the problem was not the sales but the ~ of the merchandise⟩; *esp* : the packaging and shipping of an object or a material (as to a consumer) ⟨made a small ~ charge for all deliveries of goods outside the city limits⟩ **2** : the manner in which something is handled ⟨the coach liked his ball ~ and made him captain of the team⟩ ⟨improved in his ~ of language⟩; *esp* : the mode or style of treatment or presentation (as of a theme) in a musical, literary, or art work ⟨the dramatist's ~ of the climax of the action was ineffective⟩ **3** : the manner in which something acts when handled ⟨the ~ of the automobile was smooth and effortless⟩

handling room *n* : a compartment opening into magazines and shell rooms in which ammunition is arranged and placed on hoists to be sent directly to the guns of a naval vessel

hand–lining \'⸗,⸗⸗\ *n* : fishing with a handline

handlist \'⸗,⸗\ *n* : a handy orig. fairly brief list (as of newspapers or manuscripts) for purposes of reference or check ⟨a ~ of 100 books on warfare⟩ ⟨a ~ of plays produced between 1850 and 1900⟩

¹handload \'⸗'⸗\ *vt* : to load (ammunition) by hand ~ *vi* : to handload ammunition — **handloading** \'⸗'⸗⸗\ *adj*

²handload \"\ *n* : a cartridge that has been loaded by hand

handloader \'⸗'⸗⸗\ *n* : one that loads his own cartridges

handlock \'⸗,⸗\ *vt* [fr. obs. E *handlock* handcuff (n.)] *archaic* : HANDCUFF, MANACLE

handloom \'⸗'⸗\ *n* : any of several looms or weaving devices operated wholly or partly by hand or foot power

handloomed \'⸗'⸗\ *adj* : woven on a handloom

¹handmade \'⸗'⸗\ *adj* **1** : made by hand or a hand process esp. as distinguished from a machine or mechanical process ⟨~ paper⟩ ⟨~ furniture⟩ **2** : simulating something that is handmade ⟨paper with a ~ finish⟩; *also* : used in the fabrication of such simulation ⟨~ felt⟩

²handmade \"\ *n* -s : something that is handmade; *esp* : a handmade fabric or paper

handmaid \'⸗,⸗\ *n* [ME, fr. *hand* + *maid*] **1** : a personal maid or female servant or attendant **2** : something whose essential function is to serve and assist ⟨holds that the state . . . must become the servant or ~ of the church —*Times Lit. Supp.*⟩ ⟨even philosophy and logic . . . were in his eyes the mere ~*s* of the critical spirit —Richard Wollheim⟩

handmaiden \'⸗,⸗⸗\ *n* [ME, fr. *hand* + *maiden*] : HANDMAID ⟨good sense which . . . is the indispensable ~ of the critical art —Carlos Baker⟩ ⟨literature must never become the ~ of the history program or the science program —A.S.Artley⟩ ⟨ethics is not the ~ of theology —Brand Blanshard⟩ — **handmaid·en·ly** \-lē\ *adj*

handmaid moth *n* : a moth of the genus *Datana* (esp. *D. ministra*)

hand mast *n* : a mast made from one timber : POLE MAST

hand mating *n* : HAND BREEDING

¹hand–me–down \'⸗⸗,⸗\ *adj* **1** *of clothing* : ready-made and usu. cheap and shoddy ⟨cheap store clothes of the *hand-me-down* variety for export to the Southwest —Dixon Wecter⟩ **2 a** : put in use by one person or group after being already used and discarded by another : SECOND-HAND ⟨not just any old *hand-me-down* philosophy of education —*Atlantic*⟩ **b** : already having been worn or used and discarded by another (as an older brother) ⟨wearing their older sisters' *hand-me-down* evening dresses —Peter Taylor⟩

²hand–me–down \"\ *n* -s : something that is hand-me-down ⟨the terms . . . are *hand-me-downs* from former generations of businessmen —W.H.Whyte⟩ ⟨are our diet beliefs more *hand-me-downs* from the previous generation —C.R.Stackhouse⟩; *esp* : a hand-me-down garment or suit ⟨uniforms . . . had the unmistakable fit of *hand-me-downs* —Hamilton Basso⟩ ⟨wore *hand-me-downs* until he was 16 and then was allowed to buy himself a new suit⟩

hand–minded \'⸗'⸗⸗\ *adj* : naturally disposed primarily to manual activities ⟨those who are so exclusively *hand-minded* as to suggest the wisdom of drawing them off into manual or technical schools —B.P.Fowler⟩ — **hand-mind·ed·ness** *n* -ES

hand money *n* : EARNEST MONEY

hand mower *n* : a lawn mower designed to be pushed by hand — distinguished from *power mower*

hand nut *n* : WING NUT, THUMB NUT

hand off *vt* **1** : to hand (the ball) to a nearby teammate during a football play **2** : to force (a tackler) away with the open palm of the hand while carrying the ball esp. in rugby

hand-off \'=,=\ *n* -S [*hand off*] **1** : a football play in which the ball is handed by one player to another nearby ⟨scored on a ~⟩; *also* : a ball that is transferred in this manner ⟨take a ~⟩ **2** : an act of handing off an opponent esp. in rugby

hand of pork *dial Eng* : a shoulder of pork without the blade bone

hand of write *Scot* : HANDWRITING

hand on *vt* : HAND DOWN 1 ⟨the father *handed on* his good reputation to his son⟩ ⟨*handed on* the tradition of French classical painting to the generation who followed him —Robert Richman⟩

hand orchis *n* [so called fr. the fingerlike tubers] : SPOTTED ORCHIS 1

hand organ *n* : a barrel organ operated by a hand crank

hand out *vt* **1** : to give free ⟨*handing out* free samples of a new breakfast food⟩ ⟨*handing out* passes to a movie⟩ or as a master or proprietor to an inferior or one he may patronize ⟨make a bow and accept anything the king wanted to *hand out* —Dorothy C. Fisher⟩ **2** : to give freely ⟨a politician *handing out* compliments to his constituents⟩ ⟨*handing out* advice to all prospective buyers⟩ **3** : ADMINISTER ⟨reconciled to any punishment *handed out* to him⟩

hand organ

handout \'=,=\ *n* -S [*hand out*] **1** : something handed out or designed to be handed out: as **a** : a portion of food, clothing, or money given to or as if to a beggar **b** : a folder or circular of information for free distribution (as an advertising throwaway) **c** (1) : a mimeographed or printed press release by a news service (2) : a prepared statement released to the press by advertisers, government agencies or officials, or publicity agencies **2** : [5]DOWN 2c

hand over *vt* **1** : to yield control of : deliver up ⟨the thief *handed over* the stolen watch to the policeman⟩ **2** : hand on to another ⟨*handed over* the perquisites of office to his successor⟩ ⟨such privileges may be *handed over* as a dowry —Edward Sapir⟩

hand over fist *adv* : quickly and in large amounts ⟨began to make money *hand over fist*⟩

hand over hand *adv* : by grasping with the hands moving alternately one before or above the other ⟨climb a rope *hand over hand*⟩ ⟨haul in a line *hand over hand*⟩

hand over head *adv* [ME *hand ovyr hedd*] *archaic* : without heed of what one is really doing : RASHLY, RECKLESSLY

hand phone *n* : HANDSET

handpick \'=;=\ *vt* **1** : to pick by hand as opposed to a machine process ⟨machines supplanted the workers who ~*ed* the cotton⟩ ⟨~*ing* the insects from the plants⟩ **2 a** : to select with personal care for quality ⟨~ the man because of his education and training —T.M.Landy⟩ **b** : to select personally or to ensure the achievement of personal ends ⟨a party leader so strong he could ~ the political candidates⟩ ⟨a ~*ed* jury⟩

handpiece \'=,=\ *n* : the part of a mechanized device designed to be held or manipulated by hand; *esp* : the part of a mechanical shearer for sheep that is manipulated by the operator and that contains the shearing blades

hand-plant \'=,=\ *n* : the tobacco plant set in the starting hill at the beginning of a row in a tobacco field

hand plate *n* : a plate placed on a door to prevent its being soiled by the hands — called also *push plate;* compare FINGER PLATE

handplay \'=,=\ *n* **1** : an exchange of blows in hand-to-hand fighting **2** : the act of playing as high bidder in a game of skat with the cards dealt without using the skat

hand plow *n* : a light plow propelled by hand for use in gardens — called also *garden plow*

hand-pollinate \'=;==,=\ *vt* : to pollinate by hand usu. with a camel's-hair brush — **hand-pollination** \;=,==;==\ *n*

handpress \'=,=\ *n* : a hand-operated printing or proving press

hand prop *n* : a small and movable property used by an actor during the performance of a play or a small property (as a cushion or drinking glass) capable of being carried on and off a set easily

hand pump *n* : a pump operated by hand; *esp* : one for emergency use when a power-operated pump fails

hand puppet *n* : a puppet constructed with a hollow head and arms attached to a costume fitting over the puppeteer's hand and activated by movements of the fingers and thumb inserted in the head and arms — called also *glove doll*

handrail \'=,=\ *n* : a narrow rail for grasping with the hand as a support

handrailing \'=,==\ *n* : HANDRAILS; *also* : material designed for a handrail

handreader \'=,==\ *n* : PALMIST

handreading \'=,==\ *n* : PALMISTRY

handrest \'=,=\ *n* : a rest or support for the hand or for a hand tool (as on a lathe)

hand puppet

hand ride *n* : an act of hand-riding; *also* : the ride in a race in which the jockey hand-rides

hand-ride \'=;=\ *vb* [*hand ride*] *vt* : to ride (a horse) without using a whip or spurs during a race ~ *vi* : to hand-ride a racehorse

hand rope *n* **1** : GUEST ROPE 2 **2** : a very flexible wire rope made up of usu. six strands about a hemp center and used for signal pulls, steering lines, elevator-controlling devices

hand-run \'=;=\ *adj, of lace* : machine-made but finished by hand

hand running *adv* : in unbroken succession : CONSECUTIVELY ⟨won three games *hand running*⟩ ⟨could chin a pole twenty times *hand running* —W.A.White⟩

hands *pl of* HAND, *pres 3d sing of* HAND

handsale \'=,=\ *n* **1** : a form of sale made binding by a handshake and customary among the early Teutonic races **2** : money paid as earnest money to bind a sale

hands around *n pl* : a movement in square dancing in which the dancers join hands and circle left

handsaw \'=,=\ *n* : a saw used with one hand and operated by a backward and forward drive of the arm; *esp* : the common saw consisting of a wide blade with a handle at one end — compare CROSSCUT SAW, HACKSAW, RIPSAW

handsaw fish *n* [so called fr. the finely serrated edge of the dorsal ray] : a fish of the genus *Alepisaurus*

handsbreadth *var of* HANDBREADTH

hand-schül·ler-chris·tian disease \;han(d),shülə(r)'kris(h)chən-\ *n, usu cap H&S&C* [after Alfred J. *Hand* b1868 Am. physician + Artur *Schüller* b1874 Austrian neurologist + Henry *Christian* b1876 Am. physician] : an inflammatory histiocytosis associated with disturbances in cholesterol metabolism that occurs chiefly in young children and is marked by cystic defects of the skull, exophthalmos, and diabetes insipidus

[1]**hand-screen** \'=,=\ *n* : a small usu. ornamented screen designed to be held in the hand and used formerly as a shade against heat or light

[2]**hand-screen** \'=;=\ *vt* : to print by the silk-screen process

hand screw *n* : a screw or screw device turned by hand — compare THUMBSCREW

hand-screw clamp *n* : a woodworker's clamp with two hardwood jaws joined by a pair of right-hand and left-hand threaded screws that maintain parallel adjustment of the jaws when their handles are turned in the same direction

hands down *adv* **1** : without much effort : EASILY ⟨won the race *hands down*⟩ **2** : without question or the possibility of dispute ⟨is *hands down* the most competent craftsman in his field⟩

hands-down \'=;=\ *adj* [*hands down*] **1** : achieved without great effort : EASY ⟨won a *hands-down* victory⟩ **2** : UNQUESTIONABLE, UNDISPUTED ⟨was the *hands-down* popular choice for the presidency⟩ ⟨books that were *hands-down* favorites of the editors and critics —Raymond Walters b.1912⟩

[1]**hand·sel** *also* **han·sel** \'han(t)səl\ *n* -S [ME *hansell,* prob. fr. ON *handsal* obligation confirmed by a handshake, handshake, promise, fr. *hand-, hond* hand + *sal* payment, payday; akin to ON *selja* to give, sell — more at HAND, SELL] **1** *obs* **a** : a token of luck : LUCK **b** : AUGURY **2** : a gift made as a token of good wishes or luck esp. at the beginning of a new course of action or upon someone's entering upon a new condition: as **a** : a bridegroom's present to the bride on her wedding day **b** : money given at the new year **3** : something received first (as in a day of trading or at a shop newly opened) and taken to be a token of good luck **4 a** : a first installment or earnest money **b** : EARNEST, FORETASTE ⟨our present tears . . . are but the ~s of our joys hereafter —Robert Herrick †1674⟩

[2]**handsel** \"\ *also* **hansel** \"\ *vt* **handseled** *or* **handselled; handseled** *or* **handselled; handseling** *or* **handselling** \-s(ə)liŋ\ **handsels** [ME *handsellen,* fr. *handsel,* n.] **1** *chiefly Brit* : to give a handsel to **2** *chiefly Brit* : to celebrate the beginning of the existence or use of : inaugurate with a token or gesture of luck or pleasure ⟨~ a new house with a banquet⟩ **3** *chiefly Brit* : to use or do for the first time : be the first to try or experience

handsel monday *n, usu cap H&M* : the first Monday of the new year when handsels are given (as to servants, children) esp. in Scotland

handservant \'=,==\ *n* : HANDMAID

handset \'=,=\ *n* : a telephone mouthpiece and earpiece and the respective microphone and speaker mounted on a single handle — called also *French telephone*

hand-set \'=;=\ *adj* : consisting of or printed or cast from individual pieces of type assembled by hand

hand-setting \'=;==\ *n* : the setting or casting of hand-set printed matter

handshake \'=,=\ *n* : a grasping with the right hand of another's right hand or a grasping of right hands by two people often with a slight up and down shake of the hands usu. upon meeting or taking leave as a sign of friendship, affection, or good wishes or as a mere polite formality : HANDCLASP

handshaker \'=,==\ *n* **1** : one that makes capital of shaking hands or showing extreme politic friendliness ⟨money raisers, speechmakers, ~s, and official greeters —H.S.Commager⟩ **2** : one that is usu. naively fond of meeting people ⟨a natural ~ in the good sense of that abused word —S.H.Adams⟩

handsheet \'=,=\ *n* : a single sheet of paper made by a hand process for testing purposes (as to determine qualities of paper to be made from a given batch of pulp)

handshield \'=,=\ *n* : a welder's protective mask designed to be held up before the face by hand

handsled \'=,=\ *or* **handsleigh** \'=,=\ *n* : a sled that can be pulled by hand and that is usu. suitable for only one to ride : a small sled : a child's sled

hands-off \'=;=\ *adj* [*hands off*] : practicing noninterference ⟨preserved their *hands-off* policy toward the internal affairs of other countries⟩ : advocating or insisting upon noninterference ⟨showed a rather belligerent *hands-off* attitude when people came near his possessions⟩

hands off *v imper* : refrain from touching : refrain from interference : leave (one) alone

[1]**hand·some** \'han(t)səm, 'haan-,'hain-\ *adj, usu* -ER/-EST [ME *handsom, handsum* easy to manipulate, perh. fr. (assumed) MD *handsaem* (whence D *handzaam*), fr. *hand* + *-saem* -some (akin to OHG *-sam*)] **1** *now dial* **a** : HANDY **b** : easy to handle or maneuver : suitable for handling **c** : conveniently near : ready and at hand **2** *chiefly dial* **a** : APPROPRIATE, SUITABLE **b** : of good quality ⟨~ vegetables⟩ **3 a** : of considerable value or of scope large enough to gratify highly : SIZABLE, AMPLE ⟨a very considerable, I may say a very ~, inheritance —Ngaio Marsh⟩ ⟨the soil, everywhere of ~ depth and finest quality —Thomas Carlyle⟩ ⟨winning the election by a ~ margin⟩ **b** : marked by or calling for skillful execution : ADROIT, ACCOMPLISHED, APT ⟨combining scholarship, imagination, literary flair, practical aptitude and personal gusto in the *handsomest* proportions —Richard Watts⟩ **4 a** : marked by or given with becoming graciousness, generosity, largess, magnanimity : not sparing : not merely equable or proper ⟨~ contributions to charities⟩ ⟨assuredly, the archbishop . . . leaves something ~ for the servants —George Borrow⟩ **b** : given to graceful commendation or laudation ⟨passed a ~ resolution in my favor —R.M.Lovett⟩ **5** : having an impressive and pleasing appearance: **a** : attractive, well-proportioned, and good-looking usu. in a way suggesting poise, dignity, and strength ⟨with reddish brown hair, bright brown eyes, fine forehead, and firm mouth and chin, he was exceptionally ~ —Allan Nevins & H.S.Commager⟩ ⟨though she had lost long ago her virginal loveliness, she had ripened . . . into a ~ and fruitful-looking woman —Ellen Glasgow⟩ **b** : imposing or noticeable through some combination of symmetry, proportion, size, or color ⟨a very ~ house with white marble steps . . . and a delicate silver knocker —Frances Trollope⟩ ⟨a very ~ . . . saddle, quilted on the seat with green plush, garnished with a double row of silver-headed studs —Laurence Sterne⟩ ⟨the red lizard, a ~ . . . form of the common olive-brown newt —*Amer. Guide Series: N.H.*⟩ **syn** see BEAUTIFUL, LIBERAL

[2]**handsome** \"\ *adv* -ER/-EST [ME *handsom,* fr. *handsom, handsum,* adj.] *now dial* : HANDSOMELY ⟨handsome is as ~ does⟩

handsome har·ry \,==ˈharē\ *n, pl* **handsome harrys** *usu cap 2d H* : a deer grass (*Rhexia virginica*) having stems with pubescent internodes

hand·some·ly *adv* **1** : in a handsome manner ⟨a ~ bound book⟩ ⟨a ~ large donation to charity⟩ **2** *naut* **a** : slowly and carefully ⟨ease off a line ~⟩ **b** : in a shipshape manner ⟨the yacht hove alongside ~⟩

hand·some·ness *n* -ES : the quality or state of being handsome ⟨the man's ~ excused a slight slowness of wit⟩

hand·span \'=,=\ *n* : a distance equal to or an area equivalent in its circumference to a span ⟨a ~ waist⟩

hand·speak \'hanz,pēk, -n,sp-, -pik\ *dial var of* HANDSPIKE

hand specimen *n* **1** : a fragment of rock trimmed and shaped to dimensions of about 4x3x1 inches **2** : a fragment of rock with at least one freshly broken surface and small enough to be easily handled for megascopic study

[1]**hand·spike** \'han(d)z,pīk, -),sp-, 'haan-\ *n* [by folk etymology fr. D *handspaak,* fr. *hand* + *spaak* pole] : a wooden bar or pole used as a lever (as in turning a windlass) or as a support (as for carrying timber)

[2]**handspike** \'=,=\ *vt* **1** : to use a handspike on **2** : to move with a handspike

handspoke \'=,=\ *n, now dial Brit* : either of two bars used to carry a coffin at a funeral

handspring \'=,=\ *n* : an act or a feat esp. in tumbling in which the body turns forward or backward in a full circle from a standing position and lands first on the hands and then on the feet

hand stack *n, chiefly Midland* : a small pile of hay : HAYCOCK

[1]**handstamp** \'=;=\ *n* **1** : a stamp (as of rubber) that is operated by hand **2** : a stamping (as a postal marking) that has been made by hand

[2]**handstamp** \'=,=\ *vt* **1** : to stamp by hand **2** : to impress (a marking) by means of a handstamp

handstamper \'=;==\ *n* : HANDSTAMP 1

handstand \'=,=\ *n* : an act of supporting the body on the hands with the trunk and legs balanced in air

handstick \'=,=\ *n, Midland* : HANDSPIKE

handstone \'=,=\ *n* **1** : COUP DE POING **2** : a stone held in the hand and applied to a milling stone for the grinding of seeds or grain

handstroke \'=,=\ *n* **1** : a blow with the hand **2** : a bell ringer's pull on the rope that swings a church bell to its mouth-up position : the sounding stroke — compare BACKSTROKE 2

handstruck \'=,=\ *adj, Brit* : HANDSTAMPED ⟨a ~ postage stamp or overprint⟩

hand's turn *n* : an act of manual labor; *esp* : a single usu. small expenditure of effort ⟨would not do a *hand's turn* to save himself from starvation⟩

hands up *v imper* : put (one's) hands up in the air and hold them up : SURRENDER

hand-tailor \'=;=\ *vt* **1** : to make chiefly by individual workmanship or by a specified number of hand operations to individual specifications ⟨a *hand-tailored* suit⟩ **2** : to make to order ⟨a truck or trailer *hand-tailored* to his own specifications —*Steelways*⟩

hand tap *n* : a tap for forming screw threads that is turned by hand

hand-tight \'=;=\ *adj* : being as tight as can be made by the hand alone : moderately tight

hand to hand *adv* [ME — more at HAND] : at very close quarters ⟨fought the bear *hand to hand* to the death —*Amer. Guide Series: Oreg.*⟩

hand-to-hand \;==;=\ *adj* [*hand to hand*] **1** : being at very close quarters ⟨*hand-to-hand* combat⟩ **2** : passed from person to person ⟨*hand-to-hand* delivery . . . of registered mail —*U.S. Post Office Manual*⟩

hand-to-mouth \;==;=\ *adj* : having or providing nothing to spare or having or providing barely enough esp. of money or the necessities of existence : PRECARIOUS ⟨leading a *hand-to-mouth* existence⟩ ⟨found employment in shoveling sidewalks, sawing wood, and other *hand-to-mouth* jobs —Dixon Wecter⟩ ⟨steel users . . . report that they are operating on a *hand-to-mouth* basis with less than a week's supply —*Newsweek*⟩

hand-tool \'=;=\ *vt* : TOOL *vt* 1

hand tooling *n* : the operation or product of hand-tooling

hand torch *n, Brit* : FLASHLIGHT

hand towel *n* : a small towel for the hands and usu. the face

handtrap \'=,=\ *n* : a mechanical device held in the hand and used to hurl clay targets into the air for shooting practice

hand-traverse \'=,==, '=;=,=, ;==;=\ *n* : a method used in mountaineering to cross a ledge that lacks standing room in which a climber grasps the ledge and moves along using his hands and allowing his body and legs to hang free

hand tree *n* : a tree (*Chiranthodendron pentadactylon*) of the family Sterculiaceae that is cultivated for its showy flowers whose spreading stamens suggest an open hand

hand truck *n* **1** : a small hand-propelled truck or wheelbarrow; *esp* : one consisting of a rectangular frame having at one end a pair of handles and at the other end a pair of small heavy wheels and a projecting edge or nose plate to slide under a load (as a trunk or box) and hold it in place **2** : a small truck having a motor for propulsion or lifting the load and controlled by a walking or riding operator

hand tub *n* : a fire-fighting apparatus consisting of an often tub-shaped reservoir of water pumped out through a hose by means of a pump with brakes that are rocked up and down by a number of men on each side of the apparatus; *also* : such an apparatus together with the wagon it is mounted on

hand truck 1

hand vise *n* : a small clamp or vise on a handle designed for holding small objects while they are being worked usu. by hand

hand vote *n* : a vote taken by counting the raised right hands of voters

hand wagon *n* : HANDCART

handwaled \'=;=\ *adj* [[1]*hand* + *waled* past part. of *wale* (to choose)] *chiefly Scot* : individually selected : HANDPICKED

handweave \'=;=\ *vt* : to produce (fabric) on a handloom; *often* : to produce (fabric) on a loom on which the shuttle is actually thrown by hand — **handweaver** \'=;==\ *n*

handweaving \'=;==\ *n* : the occupation of one that hand weaves or the product of hand weaving

handwheel \'=,=\ *n* : a wheel worked by hand; *esp* : one whose rim serves as the handle by which a valve, lathe feed, or other part is operated

handwhile \'=,=\ *n* [ME, fr. OE *handhwīl,* fr. *hand, hond* hand + *hwīl* while — more at HAND, WHILE] *now Scot* : MOMENT, INSTANT

handwork \'=,=\ *n* [ME *handwerk,* fr. OE *hand-weorc*] : work done with the hands as distinguished from work done by a machine : HANDIWORK

handworked \'=;=\ *adj* : formed by hand or chiefly by hand processes ⟨~ lace⟩ ⟨a ~ iron railing⟩

handworker *or* **handworkman** \'=,==\ *n, pl* **handworkers** *or* **handworkmen** [[1]*hand* + *worker* or *workman*] : one who is skilled at working with the hands

handwoven \'=;==\ *adj* : produced on a handloom on which the shuttle is often actually thrown by hand ⟨a ~ fabric⟩

handwrist \'=,=\ *n* [ME, fr. OE *hand-wyrst,* fr. *hand* + *wyrst* wrist — more at WRIST] *now dial Brit* : WRIST

handwrit \'=,=\ *n* [ME, fr. *hand* + *writ*] *now dial* : HANDWRITING

[1]**handwrite** \'=,=\ *vt* [back-formation fr. *handwriting*] : to write by hand ⟨words in a written contract may be *handwritten* —E.M.Robinson⟩ ⟨these *handwritten* missives —Amy Lowell⟩

[2]**handwrite** \'=,=\ *n* -S **1** *now dial* : HANDWRITING **2** *now dial* : a person's signature

handwriting \'=,==\ *n* [[1]*hand* + *writing*] **1** : writing in which the hand forms the letters with a pen, pencil, stylus, or similar writing implement; *also* : the cast or form of such writing peculiar to a particular person **2** : something written by hand : MANUSCRIPT — **the handwriting on the wall** [so called fr. the mysterious handwriting in the Bible that appeared on the wall of Belshazzar's palace to foretell his doom (Dan 5)] : a doom foreshadowed : an omen of one's fate usu. unpleasant

handwriting analysis *n* : GRAPHOLOGY

handwrought \'=;=\ *adj* : fashioned by hand or chiefly by hand processes ⟨~ nails⟩ ⟨~ silver⟩ ⟨~ details⟩

[1]**handy** \'handē, 'haan-, -di\ *adj* -ER/-EST [[1]*hand* + *-y*] **1** *obs* : performed by hand ⟨~ strokes —John Milton⟩ **2 a** : ready to the hand : conveniently near and accessible ⟨a ~ restaurant just around the corner⟩ ⟨kept his gun ~ as long as danger was near⟩ **b** : convenient for handling, for use, or for reference ⟨a ~ volume⟩; *also* : convenient for or adaptable to a variety of uses ⟨a ~ tool in the kitchen⟩ **c** *of a ship* : easily handled : obedient to the helm **3** : clever in using the hands esp. in a variety of convenient ways ⟨a man who is ~ around the house⟩ : ADROIT, DEXTEROUS ⟨~ with a paintbrush⟩ **syn** see DEXTEROUS

[2]**handy** \"\ *adv, dial* : HANDILY

handy-an·dy \,==ˈandē, -'aan-, -di\ *n* -ES [after *Handy Andy* Rooney, hero of the novel *Handy Andy* by Samuel Lover †1868 Irish novelist] : HANDYMAN 1, 2

handy-bil·ly \,==ˈbilē, -li\ *n* -ES **1** : WATCH TACKLE **2** : a small portable pump used chiefly aboard ship

handy boy *n* : a boy whose work is the doing of general tasks (as around a farm)

handycuff *var of* HANDICUFF

[1]**handy-dan·dy** \,==ˈdandē, -'daan-, -ndi\ *n* [ME, something held in a clasped hand, by redupl. fr. *hand*] *now dial Eng* : a child's game in which one child guesses in which closed hand another holds some small object

[2]**handy-dandy** \"\ *adv, dial Brit* : with quick alternation of place, circumstance, or condition

handy·man \-,man, -aa(ə)-\ *n, pl* **handymen** **1** : one whose work is the doing of general miscellaneous tasks; *esp* : one who performs miscellaneous or routine tasks (as about a home, public building, factory, laboratory) **2** : one that is competent in a variety of small skills or inventive or ingenious in repair or maintenance work (as around a house) or in the construction of handy devices **3** : one who has sufficient training to take responsibility for one or more phases of a trade (as in the shipbuilding industry) but who is not proficient enough to perform all its work phases **4** : JUMPER 1f

handy-pan·dy \,handi'pandi\ *or* **handy-span·dy** \-'sp-\ *dial Brit var of* HANDY-DANDY

handy·weight \'==,=\ *adj, of a market animal* : intermediate in weight

handywoman \'==,==\ *n, pl* **handywomen** : a female handyman

handywork *archaic var of* HANDIWORK

1hang \'haŋ, 'haiŋ *sometimes* 'heŋ\ *vb* **hung** \'həŋ\ *also* **hanged; hung** *also* **hanged; hanging; hangs** [partly fr. ME *hon* (past, *heng, hing, hang, hong;* past part. *hangen, hongen*), fr. OE *hōn* (vt); partly fr. ME *hangen, hongen,* fr. OE *hangian* (vi & vt); partly fr. ME *hengen, hingen,* fr. ON *hengja* (vt), causative fr. the root of ON *hanga* to hang; all akin to OHG *hāhan* to hang (vt), *hangēn* (vi), Goth *hāhan* to hang, and prob. to L *cunctari* to hesitate, Skt *śaṅkate* he wavers, doubts, fears, Hitt *ganki* he hangs] *vt* **1 a :** to fasten to some elevated point without support from below **:** SUSPEND ⟨~ a coat on a hook⟩ ⟨~ a pan from a beam over a stove⟩ ⟨~ meat to ripen⟩ ⟨a picture *hung* on the wall⟩ **b** (1) **:** to put to death by suspending from a cross, gibbet, or gallows — sometimes *hanged* in the past ⟨condemned to be ~*ed* by the neck until dead⟩ (2) **:** to bring to justice or doom **:** expose in evil actions or objectionable ways in such a manner as to bring to punishment or an appropriate fate ⟨the criminal's very brazenness will ~ him sooner or later⟩ ⟨the chef's arrogant manner finally *hung* him and he lost his job⟩ — often used interjectionally as a mild imprecation ⟨I'll be ~*ed*⟩ ⟨~ it all⟩ **c :** to fasten so as to allow free motion within given limits upon a point of suspension ⟨~ a pendulum⟩; *also* **:** to install by fastening in such a way ⟨can fit and ~ 20 doors in less than two hours —*Amer. Builder*⟩ **d :** to fit or fix in position or at a proper angle (a part of an implement that is swung in use) ⟨~ an ax to its helve⟩ **e :** to adjust the hem of (a skirt) so as to hang evenly and at a proper height when worn ⟨spent an hour ~*ing* a skirt⟩ **2 :** to cover, decorate, or furnish by hanging pictures, trophies, drapery, or other decorations ⟨*hung* the room with evergreen boughs⟩ ⟨able to ~ themselves . . . with a variety of ostentatious ornaments —Jacquetta & Christopher Hawkes⟩ **3 :** to hold or bear in a suspended or inclined manner ⟨~ her head in embarrassment⟩ **4 a :** to fasten (as with glue or paste) to a wall ⟨~ wallpaper⟩ ⟨~ tile in the bathroom⟩ **b :** to cause (a name) to stick ⟨*hung* several nasty nicknames on him during the campaign⟩ **5 a :** to style or set (as a paragraph) in printing with a hanging indention ⟨~ each boldface entry word one em⟩ **b :** to place below the foot of a type page (overset type matter) **6 a :** to append or attach (as a rider) additionally to a legislative bill **b :** to impose (as an idea) upon a convenient form or medium for artistic expedience ⟨*hung* his sardonic and sometimes savage satire on romantic opera —*Time*⟩ **7 :** to prevent (as a jury) from reaching a decision (as by one member's refusal to join in a verdict which must be unanimous) **8 a :** to display (an exhibition of pictures) in a gallery or hall **b :** to display the works of (an artist) in a gallery **9 :** to catch (a fish) with a hook **10 :** to strike a blow with ⟨*hung* that left on the Dutchman's jaw —Ring Lardner⟩ **11 :** to give no further consideration to **:** neglect totally ⟨would ~ the responsibility and go fishing⟩ **~ vi 1 a :** to become suspended or fastened to some point above without support from below **:** DANGLE ⟨a purse ~*ing* from a strap⟩ ⟨a sign ~*ing* from a nail⟩ ⟨meat ~*ing* to ripen⟩ ⟨a picture ~*ing* on the wall⟩ **b** (1) **:** to die or become dead by hanging —sometimes *hanged* in the past ⟨he ~*ed* for his crimes⟩ (2) **:** to come to justice **:** become subjected to an appropriate unpleasant doom **c** (1) **:** to remain poised or stationary in midair round about or overhead as if suspended ⟨a dim, oblong patch of light ~*ing* slantwise in the darkness —Liam O'Flaherty⟩ ⟨clouds ~*ing* low overhead⟩ ⟨the bird *hung* in the air a moment and then swooped⟩ ⟨musty air *hung* in the alleyway⟩ ⟨foggy weather had been ~*ing* over the prairie —O.E.Rölvaag⟩ **:** HOVER ⟨around each *hung* a spirit, an emanation —Anton Vogt⟩ (2) **:** to have only a precarious hold ⟨meadows ~*ing* on ridge and mountain slopes —John Muir †1914⟩ (3) **:** to stay with persistence ⟨the notion *hung* in his mind for days⟩ (4) **:** to await as if exposed ⟨that Indian property . . . ~*s* as a rich prize for the taking —D'Arcy McNickle⟩ **d** (1) **:** to become fastened so as to allow free motion on the point of suspension ⟨the door ~*s* on its hinges⟩ (2) **:** to be in a specified position on a point of suspension ⟨the casement window *hung* open over the street⟩ **e :** to be imminent **:** IMPEND ⟨evils ~ over the nation⟩ **f :** to be circumstantially relevant ⟨thereby ~*s* a tale —Shak.⟩ **g :** to fall or droop from a usu. tense or taut position ⟨his lower lip *hung* open —J.D.Wall⟩ ⟨the reins *hung* loose on the horse's back⟩ **2 :** to rest or depend for authority or resolution ⟨an election often ~*s* on one vote⟩ ⟨the question of unity ~*s* on what the writer deems the veritable topic of his work —H.O. Taylor⟩ **3 :** to support things that are suspended or attached or that incline over or downward ⟨trees ~*ing* with festoons of moss⟩ **4 a** (1) **:** to take hold for support **:** CLING, CLEAVE, ADHERE ⟨the woman seemed faint and *hung* on his arm⟩ ⟨*hung* to the trolley-car strap⟩ (2) **:** to keep persistent contact ⟨the dogs *hung* to the trail of the fox⟩ **b :** to be burdensome **:** act as an oppressive weight or care ⟨the worry *hung* on his mind until he was frantic⟩ ⟨time ~*s* on his hands and he is unutterably bored⟩ **c :** LEAN ⟨~*ing* on the rail of the ship watching the sea⟩ **5 a :** to be indecisive or uncertain **:** be in suspense **:** suffer delay ⟨the decision is still ~*ing*⟩ **b :** to occupy an uncertain mid-position ⟨his career *hung* for several years between law and medicine⟩ **6 :** to lean, incline, or jut over or downward ⟨high above it ~*s* the rocky pinnacle —*Hot-Metal Magic*⟩ **7 :** to be in a state of rapt attention — usu. used with *on* ⟨*hung* on his every word⟩ **8 :** IDLE, LOITER ⟨found the boys ~*ing* around poolrooms⟩ ⟨making the acquaintance of quiet gentlemen ~*ing* about the fringes of tourist parties —Louis Bromfield⟩ — compare HANG AROUND **9 :** to have the charge stuck or arched in one part while the part underneath falls away so as to leave a gap — used esp. of a blast furnace for iron **10 :** to fit or fall from the figure in easy lines ⟨the coat ~*s* loosely⟩ **11 a** *of a ball* **:** to rebound unexpectedly or unusually slowly (as in a game of cricket or tennis) **b** *of a racehorse* **:** to run at less than top speed **syn** see DEPEND — **hang fire 1 :** to be slow in the explosion of a charge after its primer has been discharged **2 :** to delay or be delayed usu. momentarily or temporarily ⟨the love of a young man who *hung fire* about carrying out his pledges —William de Morgan⟩ ⟨the plans had to *hang fire* until the city council approved them⟩ — **hang in the air :** to be uncompleted, unverified, or inadequately authorized ⟨something to be done, tested, made accurate, not left *hanging in the air* —A.N.Whitehead⟩ — **hang in the balance :** to be doubtful or uncertain ⟨the prisoner's fate *hangs in the balance*⟩ — **hang one on 1** *slang* **:** to inflict a heavy blow upon ⟨*hung one on* him and he was taken off in an ambulance⟩ **2** *slang* **:** to get very drunk — **hang over one's head :** to be an imminent threat or danger to one ⟨a charge of treason *hung over his head* for some time⟩ ⟨depression and insecurity *hanging over the head* of the entire nation⟩

2hang \"\ *n* -s **1 a :** the manner in which a thing hangs ⟨the ~ of the ax on its helve⟩ ⟨the ~ of the gown⟩ **b :** a position taken on any piece of gymnastics apparatus in which the center of gravity of a gymnast is below the point of support **2 :** DECLIVITY, SLOPE; *also* **:** DROOP ⟨the ~ of his lower lip⟩ **3 a :** the peculiar and significant order or meaning ⟨can't get the ~ of the discourse⟩ ⟨get the ~ of harmony singing —Dinah Shore⟩ **b :** the special method of doing, using, or dealing with something **:** KNACK ⟨took some time to get the ~ of driving the tractor⟩ **4 :** a hesitation, pause, or slackening in motion or in a course ⟨a marked ~ of the car in the air before it dipped⟩ **5 :** the action of a furnace that hangs — called also *hanging* — **give a hang** *or* **care a hang :** to be concerned or worried ⟨does not *give a hang* whether he wins or not⟩

hang·able \-ŋəbəl\ *adj* **1 :** capable of being hanged esp. legally ⟨a person not ~ according to the law until he is of a certain age⟩ **2 :** punishable by hanging ⟨a ~ offense⟩

1hangar \'haŋə(r), 'haiŋ-, -ŋgə- *sometimes* 'heŋ- *or* -ŋ,gär *or* ŋ,gä(r)\ *n* -s [F, fr. MF, prob. fr. ML *angarium* shed for shoeing horses, perh. fr. *angaria* carriage, wagon, fr. LL, compulsory service — more at ANGARIA] **:** SHELTER, SHED; *esp* **:** a covered and usu. enclosed area or a large shed for housing and repairing aircraft (as airplanes)

2hangar \"\ *vt* -ED/-ING/-S **:** to place or store in a hangar

hangar deck *n* **:** a deck on an aircraft carrier that is below the flight deck and that is used as a hangar

hang around *vi* **1 a :** to pass time or stay around a particular place aimlessly **:** loiter idly ⟨found nothing to do so spent his time just *hanging around* in the house⟩ ⟨*hanging around* in poolrooms⟩ **b :** to wait or occupy oneself in some adventitious way because of delay ⟨my ship was not ready to sail so that I was forced to *hang around* for several hours impatiently⟩ **2 :** to spend one's time in company esp. idly ⟨if you want to *hang around* with a bunch of football players that's your business —R.H.Newman⟩

hang back *vi* **1 a :** to drag behind others ⟨a small child following the older children but *hanging back* a little⟩ **b :** to delay purposely in advancing to a particular point ⟨we came almost alongside the ship but *hung back* until the captain's signal to come close⟩ **2 :** to be reluctant **:** HESITATE, FALTER

hang behind *vi* **:** to hang back

hangbird \'=,=\ *n* [so called fr. its habit of suspending its nest from a branch] **:** BALTIMORE ORIOLE

hang·by \'=,bī\ *n* [fr. *hang by,* v.] *now dial Eng* **:** a flattering hanger-on **:** SYCOPHANT

hang·chow \'haŋ¦chaů, 'häŋ¦jō\ *adj, usu cap* [fr. *Hangchow,* China] **:** of or from the city of Hangchow, China **:** of the kind or style prevalent in Hangchow

1hangdog \'=,=\ *adj* [1*hang* + *dog*] **1 :** befitting a hangdog ⟨your manners have been of that silent and sullen and ~ kind —Charles Dickens⟩ **2 a :** ASHAMED, GUILTY ⟨had a ~ air about him even though he didn't get caught in the theft⟩ **b :** DEJECTED, COWED, PITIFUL ⟨the child's ~ look when told to go in the house⟩

2hangdog \"\ *n* [1*hang* + *dog*] **:** a despicable or miserable fellow

hange \'hanj\ *n* -s [ME *henge, hinge,* fr. *hengen, hingen* to hang — more at HANG] *dial Eng* **:** 2PLUCK 2a

hanged *past of* HANG

hang·er \'haŋə(r), 'haiŋ- *sometimes* 'heŋ-\ *n* -s [ME, fr. *hangen* to hang + *-er* — more at HANG] **1 :** one that hangs: as **a :** HANGMAN **b :** a workman who hangs up articles to make them easily accessible or to position them for inspection or processing (as smoking, drying) **c :** a member of a hanging committee at an art exhibit **2 :** something that hangs, overhangs, or is suspended: as **a :** a decorative strip of cloth (as on a costume or a wall) **b :** a steep wooded declivity **c :** a depending part containing a bearing for a revolving piece; *esp* **:** a metal frame secured to the ceiling and carrying a bearing for overhead shafting **d :** a layer of tobacco leaves or stalks hung on sticks in a curing barn **3 :** a device or contrivance by which or to which something is hung or hangs: as **a :** a strap or loop on a sword belt by which a sword or dagger can be suspended **b :** a loop or chain (as on a collar) by which a garment is hung up **c :** a chain or S-shaped rod on which a pot is hung by a pothook **d :** a usu. metal or wooden device that fits inside a garment (as a suit) from shoulder to shoulder for hanging from a hook or rod (as in a closet) **e :** a metal strap used to hold an eaves in place **f :** a dangling leather loop or wooden handle that standing passengers in a moving trolley car, bus, or subway train may hold on to for keeping balance **g :** one of the devices upon which a sliding door is sometimes suspended **4 :** the written character ʃ resembling a pothanger and used as an exercise in teaching beginners to write — used chiefly in the phrase *pothooks and hangers* **5 :** a bobbin in bobbin lace holding a thread in one position **6 :** a vertical tension member receiving its stress only from the part of a structure directly attached to it **7 :** an iron box secured to and projecting from a wall or beam to carry one end of a joist or girder **8 :** 3TANGLE **9 :** a metal frame for holding photographic film in tank development

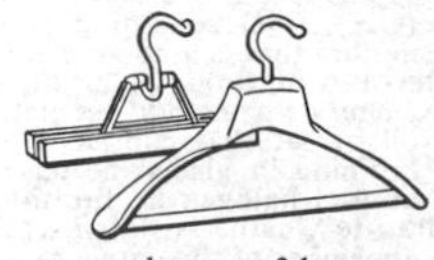
hangers 3d

hanger bolt *n* **:** a bolt made with a tapered lag-screw thread on one end and a machine-bolt thread on the other and used in timber construction

hanger bolt

hanger case *n* **:** a traveling bag with hangers and space for one or two suits

hang·er·man \-,man, -mən\ *n, pl* **hangermen :** one who installs hangers and brackets for supporting pipelines on ships — called also *bracketman*

hanger-off \'==¦=\ *n, pl* **hangers-off** *or* **hanger-offs** [*hang off,* v. + *-er*] **:** a slaughterhouse worker who suspends finished sheep carcasses from an overhead trolley and puts inspection stamps on them

hanger-on \'==¦=\ *n, pl* **hangers-on** *or* **hanger-ons** [*hang on* + *-er*] **:** one that hangs around a person, place, or institution in hope of personal gain (as patronage or preferment) ⟨soldiers became *hangers-on* of saloons and free-lunch bars —Dixon Wecter⟩ ⟨czars, princes and aristocracy, and their *hanger-ons* —F.D.Roosevelt⟩; *often* **:** one that hangs around in this manner with annoying persistence **syn** see PARASITE

hangersmith \'==,=\ *n* **:** one who makes hangers and brackets for supporting pipelines on ships

hanger wood *n* **:** drooping branches on a fruit tree (as peach)

hang-fair \'=,=\ *n, now dial Eng* **:** a public execution ⟨come to attend the *hang-fair* next day —Thomas Hardy⟩

hangfire \'=,=\ *n* [fr. the phrase *hang fire*] **:** a delay in the explosion of the charge of a gun after the primer has been fired **:** the temporary failure of a primer or igniter

hangi \'häŋē\ *n* -s [Maori] **:** an underground oven used by the Maoris that consists of a pit in which stones are heated, wrapped food is placed on stones, and branches, wet sacks, and earth are used to cover the stones and food

hang·ie \'haŋi\ *n* -s [1*hang* + *-ie*] *dial Brit* **:** HANGMAN

1hanging *n* -s [ME, fr. *hangen* to hang + *-ing* — more at HANG] **1 a :** the act of suspending something ⟨requested that the entire exhibition committee be at the ~ to assist in positioning the pictures⟩ **b :** a killing or execution in which a noose at the end of a suspended rope is placed around a person's neck and then the support under him quickly removed so that he drops or swings free and dies from a broken neck or from asphyxiation ⟨sentenced to ~⟩ — see GALLOWS; compare GIBBET 1 **2 :** something hung: as **a :** CURTAIN — usu. used in pl. **b :** a covering (as a tapestry or wallpaper) for a wall — usu. used in pl. **3 :** a downward slope or inclination **:** DECLIVITY ⟨the ~ of a ship's deck⟩ **4 :** HANG 5

2hanging *adj* **1 :** situated or lying on steeply sloping ground ⟨a ~ meadow on the mountainside⟩ or on top of some high place (as a wall or roof) ⟨a fine ~ garden aloft on breezy inaccessible heights —John Muir †1914⟩ **2 a :** leaning over or downward **:** drooping or jutting out and downward **:** OVERHANGING ⟨a ~ rock⟩ ⟨~ wood⟩ **b :** SUSPENDED, PENDENT **c :** supported only by the wall on one side ⟨a ~ staircase⟩ ⟨a ~ balcony⟩ **d :** situated at or having a discordant junction ⟨a ~ cirque⟩ **3** *obs* **:** being in suspense or abeyance **4** *archaic* **:** downcast or dejected in appearance **5 :** adapted for sustaining a hanging object **6 a :** deserving, likely to cause, or prone to inflict death by hanging ⟨a ~ crime⟩ ⟨a ~ judge⟩ **b :** being of great moment or significance ⟨not disposed to make a ~ matter of it —*Manchester Guardian Weekly*⟩ **7** *of a chess pawn* **:** connected and abreast

hanging barrel *n* **:** the going barrel in a watch whose arbor is supported by attachment to the upper plate only allowing the movement to be made very thin

hanging basket *n* **:** a container made (as of wood or wire) to resemble a basket to hold a plant hung up for decoration or for greenhouse cultivation (as of orchids)

hanging block *n* **:** a preparation like a hanging drop but with agar replacing the liquid medium

hanging bog *n* **:** QUAKING BOG

hanging buttress *n* **:** a buttress usu. supported on a corbel

hanging clamp *n* **:** a clamp that can be fixed to various parts of a ship to serve as a fixed iron for attachments (as for a tackle block or a stage)

hanging committee *n* **:** a committee having charge of the hanging of pictures in an exhibition

hanging drop *n* **:** a drop of liquid suspended from a cover glass usu. placed over the cavity of a depression slide and containing microorganisms or cells for microscopic study (as in an agglutination test)

hanging fly *n* **:** a mecopterous insect of the family Bittacidae

hanging glacier *n* **:** a body of ice or névé that breaks off abruptly at the edge of a precipice or steep slope

hanging indention *n* **:** indention in which the first word of the first line of a passage is set flush with the left-hand margin and the first words of the second and subsequent lines are set to the right of the left-hand margin

hanging keel *n* **:** BAR KEEL

hanging lie *n* **:** the position of a golf ball which comes to rest on ground sloping downward in the direction it is to be played

hanging moss *n* **1 :** a lichen of the genus *Usnea* **2 :** SPANISH MOSS

hanging paper *n* **:** partly processed paper that is to be converted (as by coating and printing) into wallpaper

hanging participle *n* **:** a participle that dangles syntactically

hanging rail *n* **:** the rail of a door or casement to which hinges are attached

hanging side *n* **:** the hanging-wall side of a geologic vein, fault, or bed

hanging sleeve *n* **1 :** an ornamental straight-hanging oversleeve of the 15th century usu. set in or tied on at the armhole **2 :** a loose open sleeve on a child's garment

hanging stairs *n pl* **:** stairs that are or appear to be supported along one side only (as by brackets projecting from an adjacent wall or by having one end of each step built into a wall, the front edge of each step being supported along the back edge of the step below)

hanging stile *n* **1** *also* **hanging head** *or* **hanging post :** the stile of a door to which hinges are secured **2 :** the upright of a window frame to which casements are hinged or in which the pulleys for sash windows are fastened

hanging valley *n* **:** a valley whose lower end is notably higher than the level of the valley or the shore to which it leads

hanging wall *n* **:** the upper or overhanging wall of an inclined vein, fault, or other geologic structure — opposed to *footwall*

hang·le \'haŋəl\ *n* -s [1*hang* + *-le* (suffix denoting an instrument)] *dial Eng* **:** an iron pothook

hang·man \'haŋmən, 'haiŋ-, -,man, -,maa(ə)n *sometimes* 'heŋ-\ *n, pl* **hangmen** [ME *hangeman,* fr. *hangen* to hang + *man*] **1 :** one who hangs another; *esp* **:** a public executioner **2 :** a game in which one player chooses a word and the others try to guess it one letter at a time, a part of a picture of a hanged man being drawn for each wrong guess

hangman's halter *or* **hangman's knot** *n* **:** a slip noose usu. made with eight or nine turns for hanging a condemned person

hang·man·ship \'==,ship\ *n* **:** the office or the occupation of a hangman

hang·ment \'haŋ,ment\ *n* -s [ME *hangement,* fr. *hangen* to hang + *-ment*] *now dial chiefly Eng* **:** HANGING

hang·nail \'haŋ,nāl, 'haiŋ- *sometimes* 'heŋ-\ *n* [by folk etymology fr. *agnail, angnail* — more at AGNAIL] **:** a piece of skin from the nail fold hanging loose at the side or root of a fingernail

hangman's halter

hangnest \'=,=\ *n* [so called fr. its habit of suspending its nest from a branch] **:** BALTIMORE ORIOLE

hang off *vi* **:** to hang back

hang on *vi* **1 a :** to keep hold **:** hold onto something usu. tightly ⟨the truck was bouncing so much we had to *hang on* to save ourselves from being thrown against the sides⟩ **b :** to persist tenaciously in an enterprise **:** refuse to give up ⟨even at the end of his life he was still *hanging on,* still seeking justice⟩ **2 :** to continue to cause suffering **:** resist getting better in health ⟨a winter cold that seemed to *hang on* all spring⟩ **3 a** *of a sound* **:** to continue to sound ⟨the strains of music *hung on* for a long time⟩ **b :** to continue listening on a telephone **:** keep a telephone connection open ⟨*hang on* a minute while I look it up⟩ — **hang on to :** to hold, grip, or keep tenaciously ⟨the child **hung on to** the lollipop for dear life⟩ ⟨swore he would *hang on to* the job until they fired him⟩

hang out *vi* **1** *obs* **:** to protrude in a downward direction **2 a** *slang* **:** LIVE, RESIDE ⟨*hung out* at a boardinghouse in town⟩ **b :** to spend one's time idly or in loitering around or in a particular place ⟨did a lot of *hanging out* in barrooms⟩ **~** *vt* **:** to suspend from something outside in order to display usu. to the public ⟨*hung out* a sign advertising his products⟩ ⟨*hung* Christmas decorations *out* around the windows⟩

hangout \'=,=\ *n* -s [*hang out*] **1 :** a place where one resides, stays, or tends to frequent or lounge around ⟨adopts the corner drugstore as his ~ —C.C.Scott⟩ **2 a :** an often low-class place of entertainment ⟨got a beer at the ~ in the next block⟩

hang over *vi* **:** to remain to be handled or completed (as of unfinished business at the end of a meeting) ⟨the meeting adjourned and left the plans *hanging over*⟩ ⟨let the case *hang over* for the new administration —*Time*⟩

hangover \'=,==\ *n* -s [*hang over*] **1 :** something that remains from what is past (as a surviving trait or custom) ⟨manners that were really a ~ from an earlier day⟩ **2 a :** disagreeable physical effects (as headache, stupor, or nausea) following heavy consumption of alcohol **b :** disagreeable aftereffects from the use of drugs **c :** a letdown or deflation following great excitement or excess ⟨an exhausted silence seemed to come down over the capitol, a colossal election ~ —Mollie Panter-Downes⟩ **3 :** undue prolongation and indistinct articulation of bass notes from a loudspeaker because of poor design or inadequate damping

hangrod \'=,=\ *n* **:** a horizontal rod on which clothing is hung by means of coat hangers

hangs *pres 3d sing of* HANG, *pl of* HANG

hangtag \'=,=\ *n* **:** a tag attached to an article of merchandise giving information about the quality of its material and about its proper care

hang together *vi* **1 :** to remain united **:** stand by one another ⟨the boys felt a strong loyalty and *hung together* when in strange company⟩ ⟨the immigrant races had tended to *hang together,* united by language, a foreign-language press —F.L. Paxson⟩ **2 :** to form a consistent or coherent whole ⟨a set of facts that seem to *hang* well *together* —Edward Clodd⟩ **:** have unity (as of artistic construction) ⟨the story *hangs together* pretty well⟩

1han·gul \'häŋgəl\ *n* -s [Kashmiri *hāṅgul*] **:** a deer (*Cervus cashmiriensis*) of Kashmir closely related to the red deer of Europe

2hangul *usu cap, var of* HANKUL

hang up *vt* **1 a :** to place on a hook or hanger designed for the purpose ⟨told the child to *hang up* his coat⟩ **b :** to place (a telephone receiver or earpiece) back on the hook or cradle so that the connection is broken **c** *Austral* **:** to tie (a horse) to a ring or post **d :** to cause (a tree) to catch in another tree in falling **2 :** to keep delayed, suspended, or held up ⟨the negotiations were *hung up* for a week by the illness of the prime minister⟩ **3 :** to cause (a record) to be set **:** ACHIEVE ⟨has *hung up* a record for the hundred-yard dash⟩ **4 :** to cause to stick or snag immovably ⟨the ship was *hung up* on a sandbar for two hours⟩ **~** *vi* **1 :** to hang up a telephone receiver or earpiece ⟨the speaker said goodbye and *hung up* abruptly⟩ **2 :** to become stuck or snagged so as to be immovable ⟨if the ship *hangs up* on a sandbar, we remove the passengers in lifeboats⟩ **3 :** to break a trip (as by automobile) for a night's rest

hang-up \'=,=\ *n* -s [*hang up*] **1 :** a tree caught in another tree in felling **2 :** an immovable obstacle (as a tree stump) in a skid road

ha·nif \ha'nēf, hä'-\ *n* -s [Ar *ḥanīf,* prob. fr. Aram *ḥănēf* hypocrite, heretic] **:** a pre-Islamic hermit of Arabia that lived a wandering ascetic life and professed a vague form of monotheism

hani·fite \'hanə,fīt, ha'nē,f-\ *n* -s *usu cap* [Abū-*Ḥanīfah* †767 Muslim jurist + E *-ite*] **:** HANAFI 2

ha·nis \'hänəs\ *n, pl* **hanis** *or* **hanises** *usu cap* **1 :** a Kusan people on the shores of the Coos river and Coos Bay, Oregon **2 :** a member of the Hanis people

1hank \'haŋk, 'haiŋk\ *vt* -ED/-ING/-S [ME *hanken,* of Scand origin; akin to ON *hanka* to coil, fasten, fr. *hank-, hönk,* n.] **1 :** to fasten with a hank **2 :** to fold, loop, or coil into a hank

2hank \"\ *n* -s [ME, of Scand origin; akin to ON *hönk* hank, coil, skein, clasp, *hanki* clasp; fr. or akin to MLG *hank* handle, fr. the stem of OHG *hengen, henken* to hang, causative fr. the root of *hāhan* to hang — more at HANG] **1 :** a coil, loop, or ring esp. of rope: as **a** *dial Eng* **:** a loop used to fasten or suspend something (as a strap on a door) **b :** a coiled or looped bundle (as of yarn, rope, wire) usu. containing a definite yardage ⟨a ~ of cotton yarn contains 840 yards⟩ —

see COUNT 8a; compare SKEIN 1 **c** : a ring (as of wood, iron, or rope) attached to the edge of a jib or staysail and running on a stay **2** *now chiefly dial* : ADVANTAGE, POWER, HOLD ⟨shouldn't let them get such a ~ over you⟩

¹han·ker \ˈhaŋkə(r), ˈhaiŋ-\ *vb* **hankered; hankered; hankering** \-k(ə)riŋ\ **hankers** [prob. fr. Flem. *hankeren* (akin to D *hunkeren*), freq. of *hangen* to hang; akin to OHG *hāhan* to hang — more at HANG] *vi* **1** *now chiefly dial* : to linger or hang around esp. in anticipation or desire ⟨used to ~ around the stillroom —Thomas Hughes⟩ **2 a** : to desire strongly and yearn in distress ⟨a thirsty man *~ing* for water⟩ **b** : to experience a controlled but persistent desire — usu. used with *for* or *after* ⟨~ to spend an evening in general conversation —Clifton Fadiman⟩ ⟨has always *~ed* to do a bit of acting —Bennett Cerf⟩ ⟨spend a lot of time *~ing* after forbidden pleasures⟩ ⟨*~ed* for a good cup of coffee⟩ **3** *chiefly Scot* : to hesitate or pause esp. in speaking ⟨he hums and he *~s* —Robert Burns⟩ *~ vt* : to yearn for : want badly ⟨it supplies what we have long *~ed* —*Saturday Rev.*⟩ **syn** see LONG

²hanker \"\ *n* -s : HANKERING

han·ker·er \-kərə(r)\ *n* -s : one that hankers ⟨*~s* after pleasure⟩

hankering *n* -s : the experience of one that hankers: **a** : strong desire : great yearning ⟨the same ~ for swift success, the same hasty greed —*Times Lit. Supp.*⟩ **b** : a controlled but persistent desire ⟨push out of his consciousness the ~ to spend an evening alone⟩

han·ker·ing·ly *adv* : in the manner of one that hankers ⟨kept thinking ~ about seeing his family again⟩

hank for hank *adv, of boats* : on the same tack together and making equal speed ⟨sailing *hank for hank*⟩

han·kie or **han·ky** *also* **han·key** \ˈhaŋkē, ˈhaiŋ-, -ki\ *n, pl* **hankies** [by shortening & alter.] : HANDKERCHIEF

han·kle \ˈhaŋkəl\ *vt* -ED/-ING/-S [freq. of ¹*hank*] *now dial Eng* **1** : TWIST, ENTANGLE **2** : to involve (a person) in something by luring or enticing — usu. used with *in* or *on* ⟨didn't want to join but they *hankled* him on⟩

han·kow \ˈhaŋ¦kau̇, ˈhan¦kau̇, -kō; ˈhän¦kō\ *adj, usu cap* [fr. *Hankow*, China] : of or from the city of Hankow, China : of the kind or style prevalent in Hankow

hanks·ite \ˈhaŋk,sīt\ *n* -s [Henry G. *Hanks* †1907 Am. mineralogist + E *-ite*] : a mineral $Na_{22}K(SO_4)_9(CO_3)_2Cl$ consisting of white or yellow sulfate-carbonate-chloride of sodium and potassium occurring in hexagonal crystals

han·kul \ˈhän,kül\ *also* **han·gul** \-ŋ,gül\ *n* -s *usu cap* [Korean] : the alphabet of 24, formerly 25, characters invented in the 15th century in which Korean is usu. written — called also *onmun*

han·ky-pank \ˌhaŋkē¦paŋk\ *adj* [short for *hanky-panky*] : marked by or derived from hanky-panky ⟨*hanky-pank* joints —*Life*⟩ ⟨their pockets full of *hanky-pank* money —Herbert Gold⟩

han·ky-pan·ky \-¦paŋkē\ *also* **hankey-pankey** *n, pl* **hanky-pankies** *also* **hankey-pankeys** [alter. (perh. influenced by *handkerchief*) of *hocus-pocus*] **1** : questionable, deceitful, or fraudulent activity : TRICKERY : MISCHIEF ⟨there's been some *hanky-panky* going on, and we haven't got to the bottom of it —F.W.Crofts⟩ ⟨wanted things to be completely above board and no *hanky-panky*⟩ ⟨while the philandering physician was playing *hanky-panky* with his patients—Alan Hynd⟩ **2** : meaningless or foolish activity or talk ⟨people went in for too much hullabaloo and *hanky-panky* —John Steinbeck⟩ ⟨had a thorough grasp of the political and social *hanky-panky* of his period —*Time*⟩

han·na \ˈhanə\ *dial Brit* : have not

hannahill *var of* HANAHILL

han·nay·ite \ˈhanē,īt\ *n* -s [G *hannayit*, fr. J. B. *Hannay*, 19th cent. Scot. chemist + G *-it* -ite] : a mineral $Mg_3(NH_4)_2H_4(PO_4)_4.8H_2O$ consisting of a hydrous acid ammonium magnesium phosphate occurring in guano

han·ni·bal·ic \ˌhanə¦balik\ *also* **han·ni·ba·lian** \-¦bālyən, -lēən\ *adj, usu cap* [*Hannibal* †183 B.C. Carthaginian general who made war against Rome + E *-ic* or *-ian*] : of or relating to the Carthaginian general Hannibal

ha·no \ˈhä,nō, ˈha,-\ *n, pl* **hano** or **hanos** *usu cap* [Sp, of AmerInd origin] **1** : a Tanoan people occupying a pueblo in Arizona **2** : a member of the Hano people

ha·noi \(ˈ)ha¦nȯi *also* haˈn-\ *adj, usu cap* [fr. *Hanoi*, North Vietnam] : of or from Hanoi, the capital of North Vietnam : of the kind or style prevalent in Hanoi

han·o·ver or **han·no·ver** \ˈha(,)nōvə(r), -anəv-, *G* häˈnōvər or häˈnōfər\ *adj, usu cap* [fr. *Hanover* (Hannover), Germany] : of or from the city of Hanover, Germany : of the kind or style prevalent in Hanover

¹han·o·ve·ri·an \ˌhanō¦virēən, -anə¦- *also* -ver-\ *adj, usu cap* [*Hanover*, province of Prussia, Germany (fr. G *Hannover*) + E *-ian*] **1 a** : of, relating to, or subject to the Prussian province of Hanover **b** : of, relating to, or supporting the former ducal house of Hanover **c** : of, relating to, or supporting the British House of Hanover **2** : of, relating to, or being a period of architectural development in western Europe usu. held to be equivalent to the 18th century

²hanoverian \"\ *n* **1** *-s cap* **a** : a native or inhabitant of Hanover, Germany **b** : a member of the former ducal house of Hanover **c** : a member or supporter of the British House of Hanover **2 a** *usu cap* : a breed of horses developed by crossing heavy cold-blooded German horses with Thoroughbreds **b** *-s often cap* : any animal of this breed

hans *pl of* HAN

han·sa \ˈhan(t)sə, ˈhän(,)zä\ or **hanse** \ˈhan(t)s, ˈhänzə\ *n* -s *usu cap* [*hansa*, fr. ML, fr. MLG *hanse*; *hanse* fr. ME *hans*, *hanze*, fr. MF & MLG; MF *hanse* fr. MLG; akin to OE *hōs* company, OHG *hansa* troop of warriors, Goth, company, multitude] **1 a** : a merchant guild in a medieval town **b** : an association for trading in foreign countries; *esp* : the league first constituted of merchants of various free German cities dealing abroad in the medieval period and later of the cities themselves and organized to secure greater safety and privileges in trading and mutual defense against foreign aggression either by law or arms **2 a** : the entrance fee to a merchant guild **b** : the tax levied upon traders not belonging to a guild

¹han·sard \ˈhan(t)sərd, -n,särd, -nzərd, -n,zärd\ *n* -s *usu cap* [*hansa* + *-ard*] : a merchant of one of the Hansa towns

²han·sard \ˈhan(t)sərd, -n,särd\ *n* -s *usu cap* [after Luke *Hansard* †1828 Eng. printer who printed the journals of the House of Commons] : the official published report of proceedings in the British parliament

¹han·se·at·ic \ˌhan(t)sē¦ad·|ik, ¦haan-, -at|, |ēk *also* -nzē-\ *adj, usu cap* [ML *Hanseaticus*, fr. *hansa* — more at HANSA] : of or relating to the Hansa (sense 1b)

²hanseatic \"\ *n -s usu cap* : a member of the Hansa (sense 1b)

hansel *var of* HANDSEL

han·sen·osis \ˌhan(t)səˈnōsə̇s\ *n* -ES [NL, fr. A. G. H. *Hansen* + NL *-osis*] : LEPROSY

han·sen·ot·ic \¦==¦näd·ik\ *adj* [fr. NL *hansenosis*, after such pairs as NL *neurosis*: E *neurotic*] : LEPROUS 1

han·sen's bacillus \ˈhan(t)sənz-\ *n, usu cap H* [after Armauer G. H. *Hansen* †1912 Norw. physician who discovered the bacillus] : the bacterium (*Mycobacterium leprae*) that causes leprosy

hansen's disease *n, usu cap H* [after A. G. H. *Hansen*] : LEPROSY

hansh *var of* HANCH

han·som \ˈhan(t)səm, ˈhaan-, ˈhain-\ or **hansom cab** *n* -s [after Joseph Aloysius *Hansom* †1882 Eng. architect who designed such a vehicle] : a light two-wheeled covered carriage with the driver's seat elevated behind and with the reins passed over the top

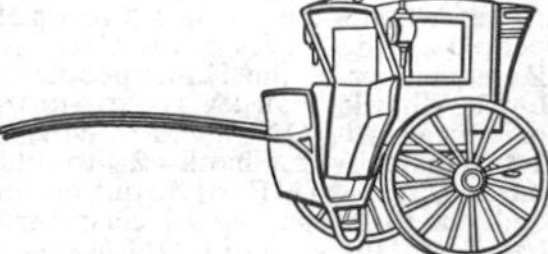

hansom

hans·wurst \(ˈ)hän(t)s¦vu̇(ə)rst\ *n -s usu cap* [G, fr. LG *Hanswurst*, lit., Jack sausage] : a broadly farcical or burlesque stock character common in German comedy in the 16th to the 18th centuries

han't \(ˈ)(h)ānt, *chiefly Brit* (ˈ)(h)ȧnt\ [by contraction] *dial* : have not : has not

hant \ˈhant, -aa(ə)-,-ai-,-á-,-ā-\ *var of* HAUNT

h antigen *n, usu cap H* [G, fr. *hauchantigen*, fr. *hauch* breath + *antigen*] : FLAGELLAR ANTIGEN

han·tik \ˈhän·,tēk\ *n, pl* **hantik** or **hantiks** *usu cap* [native name on Panay] **1 a** : a Bisayan people inhabiting western Panay, Philippines **b** : a member of such people **2** : an Austronesian language of the Hantik people that is sometimes considered a dialect of Bisayan

han·tle \ˈhantᵊl\ *n* -s [prob. alter. of *handful*] *chiefly Scot* **1** : HANDFUL **2** : QUANTITY, AMOUNT; *esp* : a sizable or considerable amount ⟨a ~ of money⟩ ⟨a good ~ of people⟩

ha·nuk·kah or **ha·nu·kah** or **cha·nu·kah** *also* **cha·nuk·kah** \ˈk̟länəkə, ˈh|, |än-, -nük-, -,kä, -,kȧ, -nikə,-nēkə\ *n* -s *usu cap* [Heb *ḥănukkāh* dedication] : the eight-day Jewish festival of lights beginning on the 25th of Kislev and commemorating the victory of the Maccabees over Antiochus of Syria and their rededication of the defiled Temple of Jerusalem

hanum *var of* KHANUM

hanu·man \ˈhənu̇,män, ˈhän-, ˌ==ˈ=\ *n* -s [Hindi *Hanumān*, a monkey god, hanuman, fr. nom. of Skt *hanumant*, lit., possessing (large) jaws, fr. *hanu* jaw — more at CHIN] : a common Indian monkey (*Presbytis entellus*) protected in its homeland as a protégé of a monkey god

ha·nu·nóo \ˌhänə¦nō\ *n, pl* **hanunóo** or **hanunóos** *usu cap* **1 a** : a predominantly pagan people inhabiting southern Mindoro, Philippines **b** : a member of such people **2** : an Austronesian language of the Hanunóo people

ha·nus·ite \ˈhänə,s(h)īt\ *n* -s [Czech *hanušit*, fr. Josef *Hanuš* †1956 Czech chemist + Czech *-it* -ite] : a mineral $Mg_2Si_3O_7(OH)_2.H_2O$ consisting of a hydrous basic silicate of magnesium that is a component of pectolite

ha·nus method \ˈhänəs(h)-, -,nüsh-\ *n, usu cap H* [after J. *Hanuš*] : a method for determining the iodine number of an oil or fat that consists in adding a mixture of iodine and bromine in glacial acetic acid and estimating the excess of unused halogen by titration with sodium thiosulfate

hao·le \ˈhau̇lē, -(,)lā\ *n* -s [Hawaiian] *Hawaii* : one who is not a member of the native race of Hawaii; *esp* : a member of the white race

hao·ma \ˈhau̇mə\ *n* -s [Av — more at SOMA (intoxicant)] : a sacred drink used ritually in Zoroastrianism and sometimes personified as a deified being — compare SOMA

hao·ri \ˈhau̇rē\ *n* -s [Jap] : a loose outer garment resembling a coat and extending to the knee and worn in Japan

¹hap \ˈhap\ *n* -s [ME *hap*, *happe*, fr. ON *happ* good luck; akin to OE *gehæp* suitable, Sw dial. *happa* (*sig*) to take place, Norw *heppa* to take place, OIr *cob* victory, OSlav *kobĭ* augury] **1** : something that happens or befalls without plan, apparent cause, or predictability ⟨odd little *~s* and mishaps of domestic life⟩ **2** : a force which shapes events unpredictably : CHANCE, LUCK, FORTUNE ⟨by some bad tide or ~ . . . the ill-made catamaran was overset —Herman Melville⟩ ⟨the fish of evil ~ . . . had been caught and frozen fast —Llewelyn Powys⟩ **syn** see CHANCE

²hap \"\ *vi* **happed; happed; happing; haps** [ME *happen*, fr. *hap*, *happe*, n.] **1** : to have the fortune : HAPPEN, CHANCE ⟨what's to be done, if a man *~s* to go wrong⟩ ⟨if ~ it must, that I must see thee lie —Robert Herrick †1674⟩ **2** : to come by chance : LIGHT — used with *on* or *upon* ⟨*happed* upon the very book he was looking for⟩

³hap \"\ *vt* **happed; happed; happing; haps** [ME *happen*] *dial* : to wrap up for warmth : CLOTHE, COVER ⟨at the kitchen fire, *happed* in an old overcoat —Michael Murphy⟩

⁴hap \"\ *n* -s *dial* : something that serves as a covering or wrap (as a bed quilt or cloak)

ha·pa haole \ˈhäpə¦hau̇lē, -(,)lā\ *adj* [Hawaiian, fr. *hapa* half (fr. E *half*) + *haole* white person] *Hawaii* : of part-white ancestry or origin; *esp* : Hawaiian-Caucasian

hap·a·lo·nych·ia \ˌhapəlōˈnikēə\ *n* -s [NL, fr. Gk *hapalos* soft + NL *-onychia*] : abnormal softness of the fingernails or toenails

hapax *n* -ES [by shortening] : HAPAX LEGOMENON

ha·pax le·go·me·non \ˌha,paksləˈgämə,nän, ¦hā,pak-, ¦hä-,päk-, -nən\ *n, pl* **hapax legome·na** \-,nə, -,nä\ [Gk, something said only once] : a word or form evidenced by a single citation : a word or form occurring once and only once in a document or corpus

hapchance \ˈ=,=\ *n* [¹*hap* + *chance*] : a fortuitous or chance event or circumstance ⟨the ~ of a sounding word —Richard Llewellyn⟩ ⟨this ~ . . . enterprise is nothing to sneeze at —Dave Roberts⟩

ha'·pen·ny \ˈhāp(ə)ni\ *n* [by contr.] : HALFPENNY

hap-harlot \ˈ=,==\ *n* [³*hap* + *harlot* (knave)] *now dial Eng* : a coarse coverlet

¹haphazard \(ˈ)=¦==\ *n* [¹*hap* + *hazard*] CHANCE, ACCIDENT, RANDOM ⟨this little remnant preserved by the ~ of chance —Edith Hamilton⟩ ⟨take our principles at ~ —John Locke⟩

²haphazard \"\ *adj* : marked by lack of plan, regularity, order, guidance, or direction : made, performed, or selected according to chance, whim, or speculation rather than on the basis of considered judgment or firm knowledge : AIMLESS, RANDOM ⟨his ~ untidy ways —Virginia Woolf⟩ ⟨not . . . a collection of ~ schemes, but rather the orderly component parts of a connected and logical whole —F.D.Roosevelt⟩ ⟨there must be some guidance unless selection is to be ~ —Muna Lee⟩ ⟨the room was . . . filled with ~ furniture —Howard Griffin⟩ ⟨~ ascriptions have been made —A.M.Young⟩ **syn** see RANDOM

³haphazard \"\ *adv* [²*haphazard*] : HAPHAZARDLY ⟨were built . . . without any regard to their situation, placed ~, wherever it was convenient —Edith Hamilton⟩

hap·haz·ard·ly *adv* : in a haphazard manner ⟨a little cluster of islands grouped ~ about a bigger green island —Louis Bromfield⟩

hap·haz·ard·ness *n* -ES : the quality or state of being haphazard

hap·haz·ard·ry \-rē\ *n* -ES : haphazard character or order : CHANCINESS, FORTUITY ⟨the good things in his work always have an air of ~ —*Manchester Guardian Weekly*⟩ ⟨whose forebears had known only the ~ of idol and fetish worship —Galbraith Welch⟩

haphtarah or **haphtorah** *var of* HAFTARAH

hapl- or **haplo-** *also* **apl-** or **aplo-** *comb form* [NL, fr. Gk *hapl-*, *haplo-*, fr. *haploos*, *haplous*, *haplos*, fr. *ha-* one (akin to Gk *homos* same) + *-ploos*, *-plous*, *-plos* multiplied by; akin to L *-plus* multiplied by — more at SAME, DOUBLE] **1** : single : simple ⟨*haploscope*⟩ **2** [*haploid*] : of or relating to the haploid generation or condition

hap·less \ˈhapləs\ *adj* [¹*hap* + *-less*] : marked by the absence of good luck : UNFORTUNATE ⟨~ beings caught in the grip of forces we can do little about —W.H.Whyte⟩ **syn** see UNLUCKY

hap·less·ly *adv* : in a hapless manner

hap·less·ness *n* -ES : the quality or state of being hapless

haplite *var of* APLITE

hap·lo·bi·ont \¦haplō¦bī,änt, haˈplōbē,änt\ *n* -s [*hapl-* + *-biont*] : a plant producing only sexual haploid individuals — compare DIPLOBIONT, HAPLONT — **hap·lo·bi·on·tic** \¦hap(,)lō,bī¦äntik, haˌplōbē¦äntik\ *adj*

hap·lo·caulescent \¦ha(,)plō+\ *adj* [*hapl-* + *caulescent*] : having a simple axis — used of a plant (as the poppy) capable of developing reproductive organs on the primary axis; compare DIPLOCAULESCENT, TRIPLOCAULESCENT

hap·lo·chlamydeous \"+\ *adj* [*hapl-* + *chlamydeous*] : having rudimentary perianth leaves protecting the sporophylls (as in pistillate flowers of a walnut tree) — compare HOMOCHLAMYDEOUS

¹hap·lo·diploid \"+\ *adj* [*hapl-* + *diploid*] : of, relating to, or characterized by haplodiploidy

²haplodiploid \"\ *n* : an individual produced by haplodiploidy

hap·lo·diploidy \"+\ *n* [*hapl-* + *diploidy*] : sex differentiation in which haploid males are produced from unfertilized eggs and diploid females from fertilized eggs (as in certain insects)

hap·lo·diplont \"+\ *n* [*hapl-* + *diplont*] : a haploid plant reproducing by spores

hap·lod·o·ci \haˈpläd·ə,sī\ *n pl, cap* [NL, fr. *hapl-* + *-doci* (fr. Gk *dokos* beam, bar)] : an order of spiny-finned fishes comprising the toadfishes

hap·lo·dont \ˈhaplə,dänt\ *adj* [*hapl-* + *-odont*] : having or constituting molar teeth with simple crowns without tubercles — **hap·lo·don·ty** \-ntē\ *n* -ES

hap·lo·dri·li \ˌhapləˈdrī,lī\ [NL, fr. *hapl-* + *-drili* (fr. Gk *drilos* worm)] *syn of* ARCHIANNELIDA

hap·log·ra·phy \haˈplägrəfē\ *n* -ES [*hapl-* + *-graphy*] : the omission in writing or copying of one of two or more adjacent and similar letters, syllables, words, or lines

¹hap·loid \ˈha,plȯid\ *adj* [ISV, fr. Gk *haploeidēs* single, fr. *hapl-* + *-oeidēs* -oid] **1** : having the gametic number of chromosomes or half the number characteristic of the somatic cells **2** : MONOPLOID

²haploid \"\ *n* -s : a haploid individual

hap·loi·dy \ˈha,plȯidē\ *n* -ES : the condition of being haploid

¹hap·lo·lep·id \ˌhapləˈlepə̇d, haˈpläləp-\ *adj* [NL *Haplolepidae*] : of or relating to the family Haplolepidae

²haplolepid \"\ *n* -s : a fish of the family Haplolepidae

hap·lo·lep·i·dae \ˌhapləˈlepə̇,dē\ *n pl, cap* [NL, fr. *Haplolepis*, type genus + *-idae*] : a family of small primitive Upper Carboniferous bony fishes with large scales

hap·lo·le·pis \ˌhapləˈlēpə̇s, haˈpläləp-\ *n, cap* [NL, fr. *hapl-* + Gk *lepis* scales of a fish] : the type genus of the family Haplolepidae

hap·lol·o·gy \haˈpläləjē\ *n* -ES [ISV *hapl-* + *-logy*] : contraction of a word by the omission of one or more similar sounds or syllables in pronunciation (as in \ˈlībrē\ for *library* or \ˈprȧblē\ for *probably*)

hap·lo·mi \haˈplō,mī\ *n pl, cap* [NL, fr. *hapl-* + *-omi* (fr. Gk *ōmos* shoulder)] : a small order of teleost fishes having cycloid scales, abdominal pelvic fins, a persistent air duct, and typically no mesocoracoid arch that is now usu. restricted to the pikes, the Alaska blackfish, and a few related forms but formerly included also the Microcyprini and some other fishes — **hap·lo·mous** \-məs\ *adj*

¹hap·lo·mid \-mə̇d\ *adj* [NL *Haplomi* + E *-id*] : of or relating to the order Haplomi

²haplomid \"\ *n* -s : a fish of the order Haplomi

hap·lo·mitosis \ˌha(,)plō+\ *n* [NL, fr. *hapl-* + *mitosis*] : a primitive mitosis occurring in certain flagellates in which chromosomes are imperfectly differentiated and the endosome functions as a division center — compare MESOMITOSIS, PROMITOSIS

hap·lont \ˈha,plänt\ *n* -s [ISV *hapl-* + *-ont*] : an organism having somatic cells with the haploid chromosome number and only the zygote diploid — compare DIPLONT, GAMETOPHYTE — **hap·lon·tic** \(ˈ)ha¦pläntik\ *adj*

hap·lo·pap·pus \ˌhaplōˈpapəs\ *n, cap* [NL, fr. *hapl-* + *pappus*] : a genus of perennial herbs (family Compositae) of the western U. S. with mostly alternate rigid leaves and yellow flowers

hap·lo·peristomic *also* **hap·lo·peristomous** \¦ha(,)plō+\ *adj* [*hapl-* + *peristome* + *-ic* or *-ous*] : APLOPERISTOMATOUS

hap·lo·phase \ˈhaplō,fāz\ *n* [ISV *hapl-* + *phase*] : the haploid phase (as the gametophyte) in the life cycle of certain plants

¹hap·lo-polyploid \¦ha(,)plō+\ *adj* [*hapl-* + *polyploid*] *of a polyploid* : having the gametic number of chromosomes

²haplo-polyploid \"\ *n* : a haplo-polyploid individual

hap·lor·chis \haˈplȯrkə̇s\ *n, cap* [NL, fr. *hapl-* + Gk *orchis* testicle — more at ORCHIS] : a genus of minute digenetic trematodes (family Heterophyidae) infesting the intestines of flesh-eating birds and mammals and occas. man in tropical areas

hap·lo·scope \ˈhaplə,skōp\ *n* [ISV *hapl-* + *-scope*] : a simple stereoscope used in the study of depth perception — **hap·lo·scop·ic** \¦==¦skäpik\ *adj*

hap·lo·sis \haˈplōsə̇s\ *n, pl* **haplo·ses** \-ō,sēz\ [NL, fr. *hapl-* + *-osis*] : the halving of the somatic chromosome number by meiosis — compare DIPLOSIS

hap·lo·spo·rid·ia \ˌhap(,)lōspəˈridēə\ *n pl, cap* [NL, fr. pl. of *Haplosporidium* genus of Acnidosporidia, fr. *hapl-* + *sporidium*] : a small order of Acnidosporidia comprising parasites in invertebrates and lower vertebrates and being of no known economic importance

¹hap·lo·spo·rid·i·an \¦=(,)==¦ridēən\ *adj* [NL *Haplosporidia* + E *-an*] : of or relating to the order Haplosporidia

²haplosporidian \"\ *n* -s : a member of the order Haplosporidia

hap·lo·stemo·nous \¦haplō¦stēmənəs, -tem-\ *adj* [ISV *hapl-* + *-stemonous*] : ISOSTEMONOUS

hap·lo·thrips \ˈhaplō,thrips\ *n, cap* [NL, fr. *hapl-* + L *thrips* — more at THRIPS] : a widespread genus of thrips including forms extremely destructive to cultivated plants

hap·lo·type \-,tīp\ *n* [*hapl-* + *type*] : the sole species included in the original description of a genus : ORTHOTYPE — **hap·lo·typ·ic** \¦==¦tipik\ *adj*

hap·ly \ˈhaplē, -li\ *adv* [ME, fr. *hap*, *happe* hap + *-ly* — more at HAP] : by chance, luck, or accident ⟨the sound of many a word in mocking echoes ~ overheard —George Santayana⟩

hap'orth or **ha'porth** *n* -s [by contr.] : HALFPENNYWORTH

happed *past of* HAP

¹hap·pen \ˈhapən, -pᵊm\ *vb* **happened** \-pənd,-pᵊnd\ **happened** \"\ **happening** \-p(ə)niŋ\ **happens** \-pənz,-pᵊmz\ [ME *happenen*, *hapnen*, fr. *hap*, *happe*, n., hap + *-enen* — more at HAP] *vi* **1 a** : to occur fortuitously, casually, or coincidentally : come about without previous design — often used with impersonal *it* ⟨it *~s* the 500-mile auto race is in progress —Bruce Westley⟩ ⟨as it *~s*, I have the book right here⟩ **b** : to come into existence spontaneously or as if spontaneously without causal necessity, effort, or other process ⟨no success in life merely *~s* —Katharine F. Gerould⟩ ⟨we were together and love *~ed* —Galway Kinnell⟩ **2 a** : to present itself as an event or process : become a reality : come into being : take place : OCCUR ⟨a study of what *~s* when we sleep⟩ ⟨accidents are continually *~ing*⟩ ⟨cloudbursts do not ~ . . . often —G. W.Murray⟩ ⟨hurried to the scene . . . where the shooting *~ed* —*Current Biog.*⟩ **b** (1) : to present itself as an experience or effect — used with *to* ⟨creep is what *~s* to a hot metal when you pull it —R.P.Lister⟩ ⟨all sorts of pleasant things *~ed* to him⟩ (2) : to present itself by way of injury or harm — used with *to* ⟨the tickbirds . . . make sure that nothing *~s* to their rhino —Jule Mannix⟩ ⟨I'd have something ~ to me if I did —Rose Macaulay⟩ **3** : to have the luck or fortune ⟨he *~s* to be a very rich man⟩ ⟨efforts of the ~ to be adjusted to their environment —W.R.Inge⟩ ⟨I *~ed* to hear it⟩ **4** : to chance to come : FALL, LIGHT ⟨while leafing through a journal . . . I *~ed* across this passage —R.A.Hall b.1911⟩ ⟨*~ed* on a cottage almost hidden in elm tree boughs —*Times Lit. Supp.*⟩ ⟨*~ed* upon a remarkable and neglected volume —Charlton Laird⟩ **5** : to come or go casually : make an appearance : turn up : drop in ⟨he *~ed* into the typists' room to borrow a stamp —Dorothy Sayers⟩ ⟨hoping that no wayfarer would ~ along the lane —Joseph Conrad⟩ ⟨any person who might ~ by was expected to . . . visit —*Amer. Guide Series: Texas*⟩ *~ vt, dial* : to become of : occur to : BEFALL ⟨little I mind what *~s* me —Augusta Gregory⟩ ⟨what would ~ my little business if I . . . married her —Frank O'Connor⟩

syn CHANCE, OCCUR, TRANSPIRE, BEFALL, BETIDE: HAPPEN is a general term without special connotation and signifies to take place either with or without plan, motivation, or apparent or assignable cause. CHANCE, perhaps somewhat archaic or literary in suggestion, stresses lack of plan or causation ⟨a novel that *chanced* to be local and concrete and true —Sinclair Lewis⟩ ⟨he *chanced* to sit banqueting with the mariners about the hour of tierce —G.G.Coulton⟩ OCCUR, often interchangeable with HAPPEN, has the additional meaning of be found, be met with, exist, may more strongly suggest an event which commands attention or consideration, and is more frequent than HAPPEN with negatives ⟨a sluggish, smoke-colored animal, *occurring* in shallow swamp waters —L.P.Schultz⟩ ⟨a bismuth bearing vein *occurs* on Charley Creek —*Encyc. Americana*⟩ ⟨when once a certain detachment from possessive vice and objective ambition has *occurred* in the mind —J.C. Powys⟩ ⟨this is possible in theory, but, actually, never seemed to *occur* —V.G.Heiser⟩ TRANSPIRE means to leak out and become known; by semantic change it has come to mean simply OCCUR, although it is likely to be used of events of some importance ⟨all memorable events . . . *transpire* in morning time and in a morning atmosphere —H.D.Thoreau⟩ ⟨no clear-cut issue developed and no real contest *transpired* —E.E.Robinson⟩ BEFALL and BETIDE, both rather literary, may suggest occurring because of destiny or fate and may be used esp. with reference to unpleasant matters ⟨a . . . piece of ill fortune, which about this time *befell* me —Charles Lamb⟩ ⟨the fate which Beria meted out to so many should now have *befallen* him —Malcolm Muggeridge⟩ ⟨woe *betide* a known traitor⟩

²**happen** \"\ *adv, now dial* : MAYBE, PERHAPS ⟨and ~ they'll tell him so too —Angus Wilson⟩

happenchance \'==,=\ *n* [¹*happen* + *chance*] : HAPPENSTANCE

happening *n* -s : OCCURRENCE ⟨~*s* of major significance⟩

happen-so \'==,=\ *n, dial* : chance occurrence : HAPPENSTANCE

hap·pen·stance \'hapənz(,)-, -pᵊmz(,)-, -ən(,)s-, -ᵊm(,)s- — *last syllable as at* CIRCUMSTANCE\ *n* -s [*happen* + *circumstance*] : a circumstance regarded as due to chance

hap·per \'hapər\ *Scot var of* HOPPER

happied *past of* HAPPY

happier *comparative of* HAPPY

happies *pres 3d sing of* HAPPY

happiest *superlative of* HAPPY

hap·pi·fy \'hapə,fī, -pē,f-\ *vt* -ED/-ING/-ES [*happy* + *-fy*] : to make happy ⟨~ existence by constant intercourse with those adapted to elevate it —Mary B. Eddy⟩

hap·pi·ly \-pəlē, -li\ *adv* [ME, fr. *happy* + *-ly*] **1** : by good fortune : FORTUNATELY, LUCKILY ⟨the date . . . has been ~ preserved for posterity —Sydney Race⟩ **2** *archaic* : by chance : HAPLY **3** : in a happy manner or state : with feelings of contentment ⟨I was driving ~ along —Richard Joseph⟩ **4** : in an adequate or fitting manner : APTLY, SUCCESSFULLY, APPROPRIATELY, FELICITOUSLY ⟨poetry writing and breadwinning do not go ~ together —Kenneth Mackenzie⟩ ⟨chances are he will mix the two very ~ —Leslie Check⟩ ⟨a matured poetic intelligence . . . ~ fused with the creative heat of poetic imagination —H.V.Gregory⟩

hap·pi·ness \-pēnəs, -pən-\ *n* -ES [*happy* + *-ness*] **1** *archaic* : good fortune : good luck : PROSPERITY ⟨all ~ bechance to thee —Shak.⟩ **2 a** (1) : a state of well-being characterized by relative permanence, by dominantly agreeable emotion ranging in value from mere contentment to deep and intense joy in living, and by a natural desire for its continuation (2) : a pleasurable or enjoyable experience ⟨I had the ~ of seeing you —W.S.Gilbert⟩ **b** *Aristotelianism* : EUDAEMONIA **3** : APTNESS, FELICITY ⟨his examples lack ~⟩ ⟨a striking ~ of expression⟩

syn FELICITY, BEATITUDE, BLESSEDNESS, BLISS: HAPPINESS is the general term denoting enjoyment of or pleasurable satisfaction in well-being, security, or fulfillment of wishes ⟨pleasures may come about through chance contact and stimulation; such pleasures are not to be despised in a world full of pain. But *happiness* and delight are a different sort of thing. They come to be through a fulfillment that reaches to the depths of our being — one that is an adjustment of our whole being with the conditions of existence —John Dewey⟩ FELICITY, a more bookish or elevated word, may denote a higher, more lasting, or more perfect happiness ⟨all the *felicity* which a marriage of true affection could bestow —Jane Austen⟩ ⟨*felicity* or continued happiness consists not in having prospered, but in the process of prospering —Frank Thilly⟩ BEATITUDE refers in this sense to the highest happiness, the felicity of the blessed ⟨the years of loving sacrifice in scraping that boxful without letting Patty go short were amply crowned for John by this one moment. He sat down again in the corner wrapped in *beatitude* —Mary Webb⟩ ⟨a sense of deep *beatitude* — a strange sweet foretaste of Nirvana —Max Beerbohm⟩ BLESSEDNESS suggests the deep joy of pure affection or of acceptance by a god ⟨the *blessedness* of the saints⟩ BLISS may apply to a complete and assured felicity ⟨all my life's *bliss* from thy dear life was given —Emily Brontë⟩ ⟨now safely lodged in perfect *bliss;* and with spirits elated to rapture —Jane Austen⟩

happing *pres part of* HAP

¹**hap·py** \'hapē, -pi\ *adj, usu* -ER/-EST [ME, fr. *hap, happe* hap + *-y* — more at HAP] **1** : favored by luck or fortune : FORTUNATE, PROSPEROUS, PROPITIOUS, FAVORABLE ⟨perennially ~ dice should be inspected to discover whether they are loaded —J.R.Newman⟩ ⟨scientific discoveries . . . seem to drop out of the blue, the gift of ~ chance —*Lamp*⟩ ⟨they experiment in color . . . with results sometimes ~, sometimes disastrous —Roger Fry⟩ **2** : notably well adapted or fitting : markedly effective : APT, FELICITOUS, APPROPRIATE, JUST ⟨he will seek to establish by law the ~ mean —G.L.Dickinson⟩ ⟨the ~ diction, and the graceful phrase —E.G.Bulwer-Lytton⟩ ⟨the passage in the finale was particularly ~ —Virgil Thomson⟩ ⟨television is an especially ~ medium —Irving Kolodin⟩ ⟨the attendants had a ~ thought —Jeremiah Dowling⟩ **3 a** : having the feeling arising from the consciousness of well-being ⟨would forbid any novelist to represent a good man as ever miserable or a wicked man as ever ~ —Havelock Ellis⟩ **b** : characterized or attended by happiness : expressing, reflecting, or suggestive of happiness : not tragic : PLEASANT, JOYOUS ⟨the ~ years of childhood⟩ ⟨a ~ family life⟩ ⟨a book with a ~ ending⟩ ⟨it had been a merciful passing, even a ~ one —S.H.Adams⟩ ⟨the ~ noises of prolonged mastication —C.H. Rickword⟩ ⟨paints a ~ picture of rural life⟩ ⟨past ~ brooks flashing to the sun —G.D.Brown⟩ **c** : GLAD, PLEASED ⟨I am ~ to meet you⟩ ⟨I would be ~ for the president to declare his policy —*Time*⟩ **d** : having or marked by an atmosphere of good fellowship or camaraderie : HARMONIOUS, CONGENIAL, FRIENDLY ⟨sailormen prefer a ~ to a taut ship, where strict discipline is the only diet —A.R.Griffin⟩ ⟨I know that they will find . . . a ~ welcome on the Canadian shore —F.D. Roosevelt⟩ ⟨its ~ industrial relations and the loyal spirit of its workers —Sam Pollock⟩ **4** *obs* : BLESSED **5** : having a feeling of well-being as a result of drink ⟨came home a bit ~⟩ **6 a** : characterized by a dazed irresponsible state — used as a terminal element in combination with the cause of the condition indicated ⟨a punch-*happy* prizefighter⟩ ⟨the gold-*happy* miners decided to have a horse race —J.A.Michener⟩ **b** : impulsively, nervously, or obsessively quick to use something — used as a terminal element in combinations with the object indicated ⟨they'll be gun-*happy* and . . . let go at anything that moves —William Wright⟩ ⟨trigger-*happy* soldiers⟩ **c** : enthusiastic to the point of obsession : OBSESSED — used as a terminal element in combinations with the object of the feeling indicated ⟨I know your type . . . publicity-*happy* —Ellery Queen⟩ ⟨that guy is stripe-*happy* —Norman Mailer⟩ ⟨sailor-*happy* girls who move around after the fleet —Katharine T. Kinkead⟩ **syn** see FIT, GLAD, LUCKY

²**happy** \"\ *vt* -ED/-ING/-ES *now dial* : to make happy ⟨it don't ~ me up any —Howard Troyer⟩

happy dust *n, slang* : COCAINE; *also* : HEROIN

happy family *n, Austral* : an Australian babbler (genus *Pomatostomus*) of sociable habits; *esp* : GRAY-CROWNED BABBLER

happy-go-lucky \'==,=,'==\ *adj* : marked by blithe lack of concern, care, plan, or serious forethought : disposed to accept cheerfully whatever happens : CAREFREE, EASYGOING ⟨on carefully prepared lines rather than as a *happy-go-lucky* venture —*Country Life*⟩ ⟨his amiable but *happy-go-lucky* household —*Amer. Guide Series: Fla.*⟩ **syn** see RANDOM

happy hunting ground *n* **1** : the No. American Indian paradise conceived as a region to which the souls of warriors and hunters pass after death for the purpose of spending a happy hereafter in hunting and feasting **2** : a choice or profitable area of operation or exploitation ⟨the reef limestones . . . have been the *happy hunting ground* for fossil collectors —*Jour. of Geol.*⟩ ⟨a *happy hunting ground* for crooks of all nationalities —David Masters⟩ ⟨junkyards . . . have become *happy hunting grounds* for the man in search of spare parts —G.H.Waltz⟩

happy jack *n, Austral* : HAPPY FAMILY

happy warrior *n* [so called fr. the use of the term in *Character of the Happy Warrior* (1807), poem by William Wordsworth †1850 Eng. poet] : one who is undaunted by difficulties : CRUSADER ⟨the *happy warrior* who . . . was to fight for all the revolution had stood for —Van Wyck Brooks⟩

¹**haps** *pl of* HAP, *pres 3d sing of* HAP

²**haps** \'haps\ *dial Eng var of* HASP

hapt- *or* **hapto-** *comb form* [ISV, fr. Gk *haptein* to fasten — more at APSIS] : contact : combination ⟨*hapto*phore⟩

hap·ten \'hap,ten\ *also* **hap·tene** \-tēn\ *n* -s [G *hapten*, fr. *hapt-* + *-en* -ene] **1** : a nonantigenic or very weakly antigenic substance that reacts in vitro with an antibody **2** : a substance not antigenic in itself that in combination with a carrier antigen confers specificity or antigenicity or both — **hap·ten·ic** \(')hap¦tenik\ *adj*

hap·tere \'hap,ti(ə)r\ *n* -s [NL *hapteron*] : HAPTERON

hap·ter·on \'haptə,rän\ *n, pl* **hap·tera** \-tərə\ [NL, fr. Gk *haptein* to fasten] : a discoid outgrowth or swelling of the stem by which a plant is fixed to its substratum (as in many rock-inhabiting seaweeds) : HOLDFAST

hap·tic \'haptik\ *or* **hap·ti·cal** \-tə̇kəl\ *adj* [ISV *hapt-* + *-ic, -ical*] **1** : relating to or based on the sense of touch ⟨~ impressions⟩ **2** : characterized by a predilection for the sense of touch ⟨a ~ person⟩

hap·to·phore \'haptə,fō(ə)r\ *adj* [ISV *hapt-* + *-phore* (fr. Gk *-phoros* -phorous)] *immunol* : having an ability to enter into combination

hap·to·po·da \hap'täpədə\ *n pl, cap* [NL, fr. *hapt-* + *-poda*] : an order of extinct arachnids not closely related to any living group

hap·tor \'haptər *also* -,tō(ə)r\ *n* -s [NL, fr. *hapt-* + *-or*] : an organ of attachment in a parasitic worm; *esp* : a complex organ usu. with multiple suckers and strong hooks on the posterior end of many monogenetic trematodes — **hap·to·ral** \-,tərəl\ *adj*

hap·to·trop·ic \¦haptə¦träpik\ *adj* [ISV *hapt-* + *-tropic*] : exhibiting haptotropism — **hap·to·trop·i·cal·ly** \-pə̇k(ə)lē\ *adv*

hap·tot·ro·pism \hap'tä·trə,pizəm\ *n* [ISV *hapt-* + *-tropism*] : positive stereotropism esp. of plants

ha·pu \'hä(,)pü\ *n* -s [Maori] : a Maori clan or tribal subdivision

ha·pu·ku *or* **ha·pu·ka** \'hä,pükə\ *n, pl* **hapuku** *or* **hapuka** [Maori *hapuku*] *NewZeal* : GROPER 1b

haque·ton \'haktən\ *n* -s [ME *hacton*, alter. of *aketoun* — more at ACTON] *archaic* : ACTON

har *var of* HAAR

har *abbr* harbor

ha·ra·ke·ke \'härə,kākē\ *n* -s [Maori] : NEW ZEALAND FLAX

hara-kiri *also* **hari-kari** \,harē'kirē, ,hari'kari, -arə'k-, -'kar- *also* ,her- *or* -'ker-\ *n* -s [Jap *harakiri*, fr. *hara* belly + *kiri* ending, cutting] **1** : suicide by disembowelment formerly practiced by the Japanese samurai or decreed to one of its members by the feudal court in consideration of his social status in lieu of the ordinary death penalty **2** : suicide by any means

haram *var of* HAREM

¹**ha·rangue** \hə'raŋ, -raiŋ\ *n* -s [ME *arang*, fr. MF *arenge, harengue, harangue*, fr. OIt *aringa, arenga* public address, fr. *aringare* to make a speech, fr. *aringo* public square, prob. fr. an (assumed) Gmc compound whose components are akin respectively to Goth *harjis* host and to OHG *hring* ring — more at HARRY, RING] **1 a** : a speech addressed to a public assembly : ORATION, DECLAMATION ⟨listening to his capacious ~ and its immaculate delivery —Sir Winston Churchill⟩ **b** : a bombastic ranting speech or writing ⟨found it a subject for rabble-rousing ~*s* —W.F.Jenkins⟩ ⟨embark on emotional and frequently violent ~*s* —K.E.Read⟩ ⟨the long, tiresome ~ so characteristic of . . . books on the subject —J.H.Donnelly⟩ **c** : a didactic, scolding, or hortatory talk or discussion : LECTURE ⟨launch into a brilliant ~ on the habits of trout —Honor Tracy⟩ ⟨gave me a ~ on the subject of my poor grades⟩ **2** : an animated discussion or conversation ⟨neglected to call up in the evening for our nightly ~ —Vli Beigel⟩ ⟨the morning ~*s* of husband-and-wife teams —M.G.Faught⟩

²**harangue** \"\ *vb* -ED/-ING/-S [F *haranguer*, fr. MF, fr. *harangue*] *vi* : to make a harangue : DECLAIM ⟨poets . . . and philosophers recited their works, and *harangued* for diversion —Tobias Smollett⟩ ~ *vt* : to address in a harangue ⟨that lady was still *haranguing* the girl —F.M.Ford⟩

ha·rangu·er \-ŋə(r)\ *n* -s : one that harangues

ha·rap·pa \hə'rapə\ *also* **ha·rap·pan** \-pən\ *adj, usu cap* [*Harappa* fr. *Harappa*, locality in West Punjab, Pakistan; *Harappan* fr. *Harappa* + E *-an*] : of or relating to a city culture of the Indus valley in the third and second millenniums B.C. characterized by a complex social and economic structure and an art largely concerned with the reproduction of animal forms

ha·ra·ri \hə'rärē\ *n, pl* **harari** *or* **hararis** *usu cap* [fr. *Harar*, region of Ethiopia] **1 a** : a people of eastern Ethiopia now mixed with the Somali but orig. Himyaritic Semites **b** : a member of such people **2** : a Semitic language of the Harari people

ha·ras \a'rä, ä'rä\ *n, pl* **haras** \-rä(z)\ [ME *harace, haras*, fr. OF *haraz*] **1** *archaic* : a horse-breeding establishment : stud farm **2** : HARRAS

¹**harass** \hə'ras, 'harəs, -'raa(ə)s,-'rais *also* 'herəs *or* ha'r-\ *vt* -ED/-ING/-ES [F *harasser*, fr. MF, fr. *harer* to set a dog on, fr. OF *hare*, interj. used to incite dogs, of Gmc origin; akin to OHG *hara, hera* hither; akin to OHG *hiar* here — more at HERE] **1 a** : to lay waste (as an enemy's country) : RAID, HARRY ⟨hostile Indians ~*ed* the frontier⟩ **b** : to worry and impede by repeated attacks ⟨his guerrilla forces cooperated with United States parachute troops in ~*ing* the Japanese —*Current Biog.*⟩ ⟨~*ed* the enemy retreat⟩ **2 a** : to tire out (as with physical or mental effort) : EXHAUST, FATIGUE ⟨I have been ~*ed* with the toil of verse —William Wordsworth⟩ **b** : to vex, trouble, or annoy continually or chronically (as with anxieties, burdens, or misfortune) : PLAGUE, BEDEVIL, BADGER ⟨sciatica occasionally ~*ed* her —Arnold Bennett⟩ ⟨~ the pilot and thus keep him in a constant state of . . . upset —H.G.Armstrong⟩ ⟨~*ed* . . . by lack of funds —Henry Miller⟩ **syn** see WORRY

²**harass** \"\ *n* -ES *archaic* : WORRY, HARASSMENT

harassed \-st\ *adj* **1** : WORN-OUT, EXHAUSTED, FATIGUED ⟨breathless and ~ at the end of the climb —Wyn Roberts⟩ **2 a** : sorely troubled, vexed, or burdened (as with cares, importunities, misfortune) : BADGERED ⟨looked like a ~ draper's clerk⟩ ⟨one of the . . . busiest and most ~ men in the country —S.H.Adams⟩ ⟨led a ~ life⟩ **b** : expressing or reflecting harassment ⟨wrote a series of ~ letters⟩ ⟨wore a ~ look on his face⟩

harassed·ly \-sədlē, -stlē, -li\ *adv* : in a harassed manner

harass·ing *adj* : causing or tending to cause harassment ⟨a series of ~ lawsuits —T.W.Arnold⟩ ⟨I've had many a ~ disappointment —E.B.Barrett⟩

harassing fire *n* : fire designed to disturb the rest, curtail the movement, or lower the morale of enemy troops; *esp* : artillery fire having these objects

harass·ing·ly *adv* : in a harassing manner

harass·ment \-smənt\ *n* -s **1** : the act or an instance of harassing : VEXATION, ANNOYANCE ⟨the ~ of unions . . . will become more difficult —T.W.Arnold⟩ ⟨chafed by the ~*s* of travel —R.L.Taylor⟩ ⟨the weather, taxes, . . . and various ~*s* of a more personal nature —*New Yorker*⟩ ⟨border incidents . . . no longer have the character of mere ~ —*Atlantic Monthly*⟩ **2** : the condition of being harassed ⟨showed signs of ~ —E.M.Lustgarten⟩ ⟨his continuing ~ may have been due in great part to his own . . . contentious personality —Stuart MacClintock⟩

harateen *var of* HARRATEEN

har·a·tin *also* **har·ra·tin** \¦harə¦tēn\ *n, pl* **haratin** *or* **haratins** *usu cap* **1 a** : a negroid Berber people of the southern slope of the Atlas mountains **b** : a member of such people **2** : a half-breed of Berber and Sudanese Negro parentage

har·bin \'härbən, (')här¦bin\ *adj, usu cap* [fr. *Harbin*, Manchuria] : of or from the city of Harbin, Manchuria : of the kind or style prevalent in Harbin

¹**har·bin·ger** \'härbənjər, 'härbənjə(r\ *n* -s [ME *herbergere, herbergeour, herbengar* (also, one who provides lodging, host), fr. OF *herbergere, herbergeor* one that makes camp, one that provides lodgings, host, fr. *herberge* army encampment, hostelry, of Gmc origin; akin to OHG *heriberga* army encampment, hostelry — more at HARBOR] **1** : a person sent before to provide lodgings; *esp* : an officer of the English royal household formerly sent ahead to prepare lodgings (as on a royal progress) **2 a** *archaic* : a person sent before to announce the coming of someone : HERALD ⟨be myself the ~ and make joyful the hearing of my wife —Shak.⟩ **b** : one who pioneers in or initiates a major change (as in art, science, or doctrine) : PRECURSOR, FORERUNNER, TRAILBLAZER, APOSTLE ⟨the ~*s* of organized religion in Oregon were four . . . Indians —*Amer. Guide Series: Oregon*⟩ ⟨the great legal ~ of the New Deal revolution —*Time*⟩ ⟨the ~*s* of peace to a hitherto distracted . . . people —David Livingstone⟩ **c** : something that presages or foreshadows what is to come : PORTENT, OMEN, SIGN, INDICATION, SYMBOL ⟨robins are revered . . . as ~*s* of spring —E.A.Bauer⟩ ⟨the sinister white owl . . . the ~ of destruction —Alan Moorehead⟩ ⟨a proper wife is the surest ~ of success for the soldier —H.H. Arnold & I.C.Eaker⟩ ⟨winter's sad ~*s*, the yellow leaves —J.G.Frazer⟩

²**harbinger** \"\ *vt* -ED/-ING/-S : to be a harbinger of : PRESAGE

harbinger-of-spring \¦====¦=\ *n, pl* **harbingers-of-spring** : a small tuberous early-blooming No. American herb (*Erigenia bulbosa*) of the family Umbelliferae with ternate leaves and umbellate white flowers

¹**har·bor** \'härbər, 'hȧbə(r\ *n* -s *see -or in Explan Notes, often attrib* [ME *herberge, herberwe, herber, harborowe;* akin to OHG & OS *heriberga* army encampment, hostelry, MLG *herberge* hostelry, ON *herbergi;* all fr. a prehistoric WGmc-NGmc compound whose components are akin respectively to OHG *heri* army and to OHG *bergan* to shelter, hide — more at HARRY, BURY] **1 a** : a place of security and comfort : HAVEN, ASYLUM, REFUGE, SHELTER ⟨the . . . Loyalists found ~ in the same areas —W.G.Hardy⟩ ⟨a very ~ from the raging streets —Charles Dickens⟩ ⟨the beauty and the ~ of a snug house —Meridel Le Sueur⟩ **b** : the resting place or lair of a wild animal (as a deer) **2 a** : a small bay or other sheltered part of a considerable body of water usu. well protected either naturally or artificially (as by jetties) against high waves and strong currents and deep enough to furnish anchorage for ships or other craft; *esp* : such a place in which port facilities are provided ⟨Halifax ~⟩ ⟨a yacht ~⟩ **b** : INLET ⟨Pearl *Harbor*, Hawaii⟩ ⟨Otago *Harbor*, N. Z.⟩ ⟨Grays *Harbor*, Wash.⟩ ⟨Charlotte *Harbor*, Fla.⟩ ⟨Little Egg *Harbor*, N.J.⟩

syn HAVEN, PORT: HARBOR applies to a part of a body of water (as a sea or lake) partially or almost totally enclosed so that ships or boats entering it may be protected when they are moored, and by extension applies to any place of protection ⟨the boat arrived safely in the *harbor* by nightfall⟩ ⟨two promontories of land forming a natural *harbor*⟩ ⟨find a *harbor* until the financial panic had passed⟩ HAVEN, now chiefly literary except in names, adds to HARBOR the idea of refuge or place of peace ⟨a blessed *haven* into which convoys could slip from the submarine-infested Atlantic —Stewart Beach⟩ ⟨the colony acquired an unsavory reputation for providing a friendly *haven* for pirates —*Amer. Guide Series: R.I.*⟩ ⟨leave for a while their own crowded homes and find a calm cozy *haven* where they can talk without interruption —Ernest & Pearl Beaglehole⟩ ⟨an excellent *haven* for game birds and deer —*Amer. Guide Series: Minn.*⟩ PORT signifies a place, usu. both harbor and adjacent town or city, suitable for landing men or goods, and by extension applies to a destination or goal ⟨transatlantic steamers docked in the *port* of New York⟩ ⟨the home *port* of steamers formerly navigating the waters of the lake —*Amer. Guide Series: N.H.*⟩ ⟨unsteamboat *ports* on the Columbia —Dayton Kohler⟩ ⟨unload a damaged ship at the first available *port*⟩

²**harbor** \"\ *vb* **harbored; harbored; harboring** \-b(ə)riŋ\ **harbors** *see -or in Explan Notes* [ME *herbergen, herberwen, herberen, harborowen*, fr. *herberge, herberwe, herber, harborowe*, n.] *vt* **1 a** (1) : to give shelter or refuge to : take in ⟨benefited by ~*ing* and absorbing displaced European psychiatrists —Lauretta Bender⟩ ⟨~*ed* white renegades and strays from hostile tribes —*Amer. Guide Series: Tenn.*⟩ ⟨return of Greek children ~*ed* in other countries —*Americana Annual*⟩ (2) : to receive clandestinely and conceal (a fugitive from justice) (3) : to have (an animal) in one's keeping ⟨may not ~ a dog without a permit⟩ **b** (1) : to be the home or habitat of : CONTAIN ⟨the pool normally ~*s* several large trout —Alexander MacDonald⟩ ⟨her home . . . had ~*ed* her family for four generations —*Current Biog.*⟩ ⟨this structure ~*s* a mirror and bookrest —*New Yorker*⟩ ⟨the . . . buildings ~ a maze of ducts and pipes —Lewis Mumford⟩ ⟨caves which . . . certainly ~ bats —Thomas Barbour⟩ ⟨the same county that ~*s* the depressing cotton towns —L.D.Stamp⟩ (2) : to be the host of (a parasite) ⟨one of the pigs ~*ed* . . . kidney worms —J.E.Alicata⟩ **c** : to track (an animal) to lair or hiding place **2** : CHERISH, ENTERTAIN ⟨~ thoughts⟩ ⟨~ feelings⟩ ⟨~ a deep resentment against the U. S. —Winifred Raushenbush⟩ ⟨any power which might ~ aggressive designs —C.A.Fisher⟩ ⟨~*ed* a mistrust of expressed emotion —Stewart Cockburn⟩ **3** : to place (a ship) for shelter ~ *vi* **1 a** : to find or take shelter : be present ⟨it was quite thinkable that dreadful heresies might ~ there —G.W.Johnson⟩ **b** (1) *of an animal* : to rest or hide away esp. habitually ⟨fierce boars ~*ed* in the dense wood⟩ (2) : LIVE ⟨parasites that ~ in the blood⟩ **2** : to take shelter or come to anchor in a harbor **3** : to conceal a fugitive from justice ⟨you can be shot for ~*ing*, she thought —Ion Braby⟩

har·bor·age \-b(ə)rij\ *n* -s **1 a** : SHELTER, REFUGE ⟨talking as if he had a right to ~, attention, and affection —Clemence Dane⟩ ⟨for this ~ . . . hostility seemed to her a little price to pay —Katherine Freeman⟩ **b** : a place of shelter or refuge : RESTING-PLACE ⟨the island was a ~ for privateersmen and runaway slaves⟩ **c** : a place offering favorable environmental conditions for growth and life ⟨to reduce a rat population, competition must be increased by reducing food or ~ —*Wildlife Rev.*⟩ ⟨weedy hedgerows . . . are thus a ~ for many troublesome pests —F.D.Smith & Barbara Wilcox⟩ **2 a** : shelter for ships : harbor facilities ⟨the long indented coast offers excellent ~⟩ **b** : HARBOR ⟨the ship . . . was lifted over the sandbars into the safe ~ of Matanzas —J.B.Cabell & A.J. Hanna⟩

har·bor·er \-bərə(r)\ *n* -s **1** : one that harbors ⟨the ~ of suspicion does not inspire faith in himself —L.P.Stryker⟩ **2** : a person who tracks a deer to its harbor and keeps watch on it there

harbor gasket *n* : a canvas or sennit band used to secure a sail

harbor line *n* : a line defining the limits of a harbor

harbor master *n* **1** : an officer charged with the duty of executing the regulations respecting the use of a harbor esp. as to berthing and mooring **2** : an officer who directs the policing of a harbor area by members of a municipal police force

harbor porpoise *n* : a common porpoise (*Phocaena phocaena*) of the north Atlantic and Pacific

harbor seal *n* : a small seal (*Phoca vitulina*) about four feet long living along the north Atlantic coasts, occas. occurring as far south as the Mediterranean and New Jersey, usu. keeping near land, and often ascending rivers; *also* : a similar seal (*P. richardii*) of the north Pacific coasts

¹**har·bor·ward** \-bə(r)wə(r)d\ *adv* [¹*harbor* + *-ward*] : toward the harbor ⟨a pleasant little frame house . . . looking ~ —*New Yorker*⟩

²**harborward** \"\ *adj* : facing the harbor ⟨lined on both the ~ and landward sides by residences —Lewis Mumford⟩

harbour *Brit var of* HARBOR

¹**hard** \'härd, 'hȧd\ *adj* -ER/-EST [ME, fr. OE *heard;* akin to OHG *hart* hard, ON *harthr* hard, Goth *hardus* severe, Gk *kratos* strength, *kratys* strong, and prob. to Skt *karkara* hard] **1 a** (1) : not easily penetrated, cut, or separated into parts : not easily yielding to pressure : FIRM, SOLID, COMPACT ⟨an extremely ~ stone⟩ ⟨wriggled uncomfortably in his ~ chair⟩ ⟨these apples are very ~⟩ (2) : having rigid boards on the sides covered in cloth or paper ⟨a ~ binding⟩ ⟨selling methods . . . to fit the ~ books —Henry Garfinkle⟩ (3) : HARDWOOD 2 **b** *of liquor* (1) : having a harsh, sharp, or acid taste ⟨a ~ wine⟩ (2) : STRONG, SPIRITUOUS, INTOXICATING; *specif* : having an alcoholic content of more than 22.5 percent **c** (1) : characterized by the presence of dissolved substances (as salts of magnesium and calcium) that prevent the formation of lather with soap — used of water and water solutions (2) *of oil* : too thick to pour at ordinary temperatures (3) : characterized by radiation of relatively high penetrating power ⟨~ X rays⟩; *also* : relating to or constituting a high-vacuum tube that produces such radiation ⟨~ tube⟩ (4) : having or producing relatively great photographic contrast ⟨a ~ negative⟩ ⟨~ paper⟩ (5) : difficult to fuse or soften ⟨a ~ glass⟩ ⟨a ~ enamel⟩ **d** (1) *of money* : metallic as distinct from paper ⟨the colonies suffered from a shortage of ~ money⟩ ⟨ranchers . . . who were known to keep their wealth in the form of ~ money —W.H.Breen⟩ (2) *of currency* : convertible into gold or heavily backed by a gold reserve and typically stable, high, or

appreciating in value ⟨the period of the eighteen-nineties witnessed a bitter struggle between the *hard*-money and the cheap⸗money groups —C.B.Swisher⟩; *also* **:** available to borrowers in limited supply and at high interest rates ⟨a *hard*-money policy⟩ (3) *of a currency* **:** soundly backed and usu. readily convertible into foreign currencies without restrictions or large discounts ⟨they require payment in dollars, pounds, or other ~ . . . currency —Joseph Wechsberg⟩ (4) **:** constituting currency as distinct from promissory notes or other documents of contingent value — often used as an intensive in the phrase *hard cash* ⟨he has to be paid in *hard* cash⟩ ⟨pay the writing schools ~ cash to liberate their muse —Edward Uhlan⟩ (5) *of prices* **:** high and firm **e** (1) **:** TIGHT — used esp. of yarns with many twists per inch (2) **:** NAPLESS — used esp. of woolen and worsted fabrics with a smooth clear finish (3) *of plumage* **:** close-fitting and firm in texture (4) *of individual feathers* **:** uniformly colored **2 a** (1) **:** capable of great physical exertion or endurance **:** not flabby or soft **:** physically fit ⟨nice animals in good ~ condition —R.M.Daw⟩ ⟨all likely lads in ~ condition —John Buchan⟩ (2) **:** resistant esp. to stress or disease **:** HARDY ⟨children of ~*er* stock —Ernest Beaglehole⟩ **b :** free of weakness or other flaw **:** STRONG, UNYIELDING, TEMPERED ⟨brought out of the war a character austere and not a little ~ —Edmund Wilson⟩ ⟨a man of ~ unbending will⟩ **c** (1) **:** not tentative or contingent **:** FIXED, DEFINITE, BINDING, CONCRETE ⟨failure . . . to make ~, firm decisions at high levels —*Science*⟩ ⟨the continuing lack of a ~ agreement with the U.S. —Benjamin Welles⟩ (2) **:** not speculative or conjectural **:** based on fact **:** objectively existent **:** FACTUAL, ACTUAL, RELIABLE ⟨backed by evidence which he considers ~ —*American Anthropologist*⟩ ⟨a comprehensive set of ~ figures emerged for the first time —*Time*⟩ ⟨most facts are independent of our volitions; that is why they are called ~ —Bertrand Russell⟩ ⟨~ evidence that the government's optimism is not unfounded —Sydney Gruson⟩ (3) **:** HARD-AND-FAST ⟨there can be no ~ line of division between these two groups of changes —Edward Sapir⟩ (4) **:** CLOSE, SEARCHING, CONCENTRATED ⟨took a last ~ look at the old homestead⟩ ⟨at a later date I will take a ~ look at my political future —*N.Y.Times*⟩ (5) *of news* **:** not trivial, diverting, or sensational **:** important in its economic, political, or other large bearing ⟨~ news refers to the less exciting and more analytical stories of public affairs, economics, social problems —F.L.Mott⟩ — compare SOFT **d :** free from sentimentality or illusions **:** viewing objectively or coolly **:** REALISTIC, PRACTICAL ⟨the ~ modern mind —*College English*⟩ ⟨the later version is ~*er*, less "poetic" in the Romantic sense, less sentimental —Louis MacNeice⟩ ⟨the most practical place to teach ~ practical thinking is in . . . sociology —*Nat'l Catholic Educational Assoc. Bull.*⟩ ⟨a Scotsman's ~, keen sense of the practical —R.W. Chapman⟩ ⟨notable for his ~ sense, frugality, and industry⟩ **3 a** (1) **:** difficult to bear or endure **:** not easy to put up with or consent to **:** GRIEVOUS, UNPLEASANT, DISTRESSING, BAD ⟨you've had very ~ luck⟩ ⟨the dory was . . . in ~ shape —G.W.Brace⟩ ⟨the ~ years dragged by⟩ ⟨too much reading is ~ on the eyes⟩ ⟨that traffic cop gave me a ~ time⟩; *specif* **:** economically depressed ⟨~ times followed, and domestic creditors suffered equally with the foreign —S.E.Morison & H.S.Commager⟩ ⟨the Alaska gold rush . . . put an end to ~ times —*Amer. Guide Series: Wash.*⟩ (2) **:** OPPRESSIVE, INEQUITABLE, UNJUST ⟨musicians also find it ~ that they must pay heavy duty . . . on orchestral instruments —*Report: (Canadian) Royal Commission on Nat'l Development*⟩ ⟨the ~ system of apprenticeship, virtual peonage, was failing rapidly —*Amer. Guide Series: Tenn.*⟩ **b** (1) **:** harsh or severe in one's dealings **:** lacking compassion or gentleness **:** UNFEELING, CALLOUS ⟨he was a stern, ~, cruel man —Anthony Trollope⟩ ⟨people who are ~, grasping, selfish —G.B.Shaw⟩ ⟨don't be too ~ on the boy⟩ (2) **:** INTRACTABLE, HARDENED, INCORRIGIBLE, TOUGH ⟨my first real assignment was as a sort of scoutmaster to a ~ gang of boys —R.M.Lovett⟩ ⟨a prison warden of long standing and accustomed to dealing with ~ cases⟩ (3) **:** devoid of fine or refined feelings **:** impudently bold **:** BRAZEN, SHAMELESS ⟨a ~, cheap, frightened floozy —Arthur Knight⟩ **c** (1) **:** harsh, severe, or offensive in tendency or effect **:** UNPALATABLE, CRUEL ⟨this is a ~ saying to people who have worked so much —Clement Attlee⟩ ⟨said some very ~ things to me⟩ **:** HOSTILE, RESENTFUL ⟨no ~ feelings, I'm sure⟩ **:** ROUGH, COARSE ⟨~ and frugal fare, yet we throve upon it⟩ **:** making no concession **:** STRICT, UNRELENTING ⟨he drives a very ~ bargain⟩ ⟨a credit to the ~ religious system under which they were bred —G.M. Trevelyan⟩ (2) **:** tending to put in a bad or sinister light **:** UNFAVORABLE, FORBIDDING ⟨~ stories too were told about him; something . . . concerning an hereditary propensity to eat men —Herman Melville⟩ (3) **:** RIGOROUS, INCLEMENT, VIOLENT ⟨one of the ~*est* winters in men's memories⟩ ⟨a ~, driving rain⟩ ⟨in ~ weather he stayed in his . . . house —Mary Webb⟩ **d** (1) **:** intense in force, manner, or degree **:** SHARP, PROFOUND, DEEP ⟨a ~ spell of coughing —Ellen Glasgow⟩ ⟨dealt him a ~ blow⟩ ⟨fell into a ~ sleep⟩ ⟨going at a ~ trot down that steep hill —Rachel Henning⟩ (2) **:** carried on, performed, or waged with great intensity, exertion, or energy **:** ARDUOUS, STRENUOUS, UNREMITTING ⟨got where he is by ~ work⟩ ⟨this question requires ~ thinking —W.H.Whyte⟩ ⟨with some the sell is ~, with big advertising budgets . . . and platoons of agents on the road —Blake Ehrlich⟩ (3) **:** performing or carrying on an activity or one's work with great energy, intensity, or persistence ⟨a ~ drinker⟩ ⟨one of the ~*est* workers on the floor⟩ ⟨a very ~ smoker —Tadhg Murphy⟩ (4) **:** subjecting to a severe strain **:** INTENSIVE, PUNISHING ⟨was nearing a century of ~ wear when it lost a cover —R.W.Chapman⟩ ⟨this garment will stand ~ use⟩ (5) **:** useful for a long time **:** DURABLE ⟨~ merchandise⟩ **e :** giving the impression of or suggesting hardness: as (1) **:** lacking in shading, delicacy, or subtlety **:** HARSH, STRIDENT ⟨this is for ~ big tone —Warwick Braithwaite⟩ ⟨it has a ~ but brilliant note —Robert Donington⟩ (2) **:** characterized by sharp or harsh outline, rigid execution, and stiff drawing ⟨exaggerated shadows to intensify crisp outlines and ~ forms —Katharine Kuh⟩ ⟨a portrait in the ~ but sincere and living fashion of the period —G.K.Chesterton⟩ (3) **:** sharply defined **:** STARK, CRISP, PRECISE ⟨looking . . . at the ~ shadows we cast on the ground —John Skölle⟩ ⟨in the early twilight the outlines of the castle loomed ~ and clear⟩ (4) **:** not softened or shaded in any way **:** GLARING, VIVID ⟨~ bright sunlight at the water's edge —Oscar Handlin⟩ ⟨the light is so ~ and brilliant that . . . you have to screw up your eyes —Thomas Wood †1950⟩ ⟨had the ~ dull flush of the steady heavy drinker —Thomas Wolfe⟩ ⟨staring at the ceiling in the ~ light of the one unshaded lamp —Nevil Shute⟩ (5) **:** sounding as in *arcing* and *geese* respectively — used of *c* and *g* or their sound (6) *of a consonant* **:** VOICELESS (7) **:** constituting a vowel before which there is no \y\ sound and no \y\-like modification of a consonant or constituting a consonant in whose articulation there is no \y\-like modification and which is not followed by a \y\ sound (as in Russian) — compare PALATALIZE (8) **:** indicative or suggestive of severity, firmness, toughness, or insensitivity of temperament or character ⟨the same faint, ~ smile around the edges of her mouth —Thomas Wolfe⟩ ⟨with a rather ~ mouth and a supercilious manner —Scott Fitzgerald⟩ ⟨a fund of English openness and good nature legible in his ~ features —William Heath⟩ ⟨a ~ pair of eyes that belied his unmanly, almost effeminate face —Barnaby Conrad⟩ — often used in combination ⟨a *hard*-faced businessman who knows all the latest salacious limericks —Harold Wincott⟩ ⟨a *hard*-eyed little man⟩ **4 :** presenting difficulties, obstacles, or perplexities: as **a** (1) **:** difficult to accomplish, master, resolve, or acquire **:** not easy **:** TROUBLESOME, PERPLEXING ⟨this ailment is ~ to cure⟩ ⟨the American habit of tipping . . . is a ~ one to break —Richard Joseph⟩ ⟨of course all languages are ~ —Bernard Bloch⟩ ⟨a ~ decision⟩ ⟨she's playing ~ to get⟩ ⟨a distinctly ~ problem⟩ (2) **:** difficult to comprehend or explain **:** OBSCURE, DARK, THORNY ⟨a ~ saying, no doubt, . . . but it has its meaning —Havelock Ellis⟩ ⟨this is at first sight a very ~ saying, but a little consideration will show that it is only natural —J.A.Todd⟩ ⟨a book full of long, ~ words⟩ (3) **:** difficult to untie or unravel ⟨he tied his shoelaces in ~ knots —Erskine Caldwell⟩ **b** *archaic* **:** having difficulty in doing something **c :** attended or marked by drudgery, hardship, or other painful experience ⟨many perished on the long ~ march to safety⟩ ⟨fishing and lumbering . . . are ~ trades —Upton Sinclair⟩ ⟨the birth was ~ —Farley Mowat⟩

syn DIFFICULT, ARDUOUS: HARD is a general antonym for *easy* and is applicable to any activity requiring great exertion ⟨a *hard* task⟩ ⟨the *hard* work of digging the shaft⟩ ⟨a subject *hard* to teach⟩ ⟨inspirations such as these do not necessarily eliminate all the *hard* work that goes into developing them and putting them down on paper —J.D.Cook⟩ DIFFICULT may imply obstacles to be surmounted, problems to be solved, complications to be removed, simplifications to be made, or trials to be faced by skill, ingenuity, or resolution ⟨to climb a mountain which, as all who have climbed it testify, is long, steep, and *difficult* —W.R.Inge⟩ ⟨business of a delicate and *difficult* nature, which might get people into trouble —Charles Dickens⟩ ⟨trying to write things that have not been written before, and that were very *difficult* to write —Havelock Ellis⟩ ⟨the more *difficult* task of changing the ways of thinking, the habits, and the practices of the Japanese people —*Collier's Yr. Bk.*⟩ ARDUOUS may suggest need for perseverance and resolute exertion ⟨the local railways . . . worked their *arduous* ways up the mining valleys —O.S.Nock⟩ ⟨the *arduous* task of formulating legislation necessary to the country's welfare —F.D. Roosevelt⟩ ⟨the scientific spirit, like the spirit of sanctity, can be acquired only by the *arduous* methodical discipline —M.R. Cohen⟩ **syn** see in addition FIRM

— **hard up 1 :** short of money **:** economically distressed ⟨he managed to pay his way although awfully *hard up* at the time⟩ ⟨the region was perennially *hard up*⟩ **2 :** experiencing an acute want or deprivation of any kind ⟨far past the age when any woman, however *hard up*, would look at him twice —Ruth Park⟩ ⟨he's very *hard up* for friends⟩ — **the hard way** *adv* **1 :** in a manner difficult to bear or accomplish **:** RIGOROUSLY, LABORIOUSLY ⟨had come up *the hard way*, through modeling, the chorus line, dramatic school, little theaters and bit parts in screen and TV shows —Fergus McGill⟩ **2 :** by throwing a doublet in craps (as when the point is 4, 6, 8, or 10 and is made respectively by 2-2, 3-3, 4-4, or 5-5) ⟨to make 8 *the hard way* —C.B.Davis⟩

[2]hard \"\ *adv* -ER/-EST [ME *harde*, fr. OE *hearde;* akin to OHG *harto* extremely, ON *hartha;* derivative fr. the root of E [1]*hard*] **1 a :** with great or utmost effort or energy **:** VIGOROUSLY, STRENUOUSLY, EARNESTLY ⟨the men were ~ at work⟩ ⟨the lumbermen lived and played ~⟩ ⟨you've been going too ~ the last six months⟩ ⟨it forces one to think ~⟩ **b :** VIOLENTLY, FIERCELY ⟨drove the muzzle ~ into the gangster's face⟩ ⟨the rain came down ~⟩ ⟨the wind is blowing ~⟩ **c** (1) **:** to the full extent or the extreme limit — used in nautical directions esp. to the helmsman ⟨~ right⟩ ⟨~ alee⟩ ⟨~ aport⟩ (2) **:** to a considerable extent **:** MASSIVELY, LARGELY ⟨if . . . you wish to persevere with the present tree, cut it back ~ —*Sydney (Australia) Bull.*⟩ ⟨the strike cut production back ~⟩ **d :** in an immoderate manner **:** to an extreme degree **:** INTENSIVELY, UNREMITTINGLY ⟨he is hitting the bottle ~⟩ **e :** in a searching, close, or concentrated manner **:** INTENTLY ⟨looked ~ at him⟩ ⟨listen ~ to what I have to say⟩ **f :** in a sharp or emphatic manner **:** POINTEDLY ⟨the incident brought home to him ~ his inadequate grasp of the subject⟩ **2 a :** in such a manner as to cause hardship, difficulty, or pain **:** HARSHLY, SEVERELY, CRUELLY, BADLY ⟨the Stamp Act and other laws which bore ~ on colonial prosperity —H.E.Scudder⟩ ⟨such levies hit the poor ~*er* than the rich —*Collier's Yr. Bk.*⟩ ⟨things have gone very ~ with us⟩ **b :** with extreme rancor, bitterness, or grief **:** with animus or resentment of — often used with *take* ⟨this expansion of Russia's . . . was taken very ~ in the liberal Western world —*New Republic*⟩ ⟨it was his first taste of defeat . . . he took it ~ —S.H.Adams⟩ **c :** AUSTERELY, FRUGALLY ⟨they deserved to live ~ even if it deprived them of . . . leisure in which to think high —F.M.Ford⟩ **3 :** TIGHTLY, FIRMLY, FAST ⟨hold on ~⟩ **4 :** to the point of hardness ⟨like my eggs boiled ~⟩ ⟨the river froze ~⟩ **5 :** with difficulty **:** LABORIOUSLY ⟨breathing ~ after that long run⟩ **6 :** in close or immediate proximity in time or space ⟨caught the fish ~ in to the shore⟩ ⟨the house stood ~ by the river⟩ ⟨~ on the heels of the Supreme Court decision⟩ ⟨darkness was ~ at hand⟩ ⟨steamships berth ~ up against the main streets —William Sansom⟩

[3]hard \"\ *n* -s [ME, something that is hard, fr. *hard*, adj.] **1** *chiefly Brit* **:** a firm foreshore or landing place **2** *slang chiefly Brit* **:** HARD LABOR ⟨ten years ~ . . . for clouting some bloke —Richard Llewellyn⟩ **3 :** ERECTION 2 — used in the phrase *hard on;* usu. considered vulgar

hard-and-fast \¦⸗⸗¦⸗\ *adj* **:** not subject to deviation, revision, or modification **:** rigidly binding **:** FIXED, CATEGORICAL, ABSOLUTE ⟨*hard-and-fast* rules⟩ ⟨*hard-and-fast* distinctions⟩ ⟨a *hard-and-fast* line⟩

har·dang·er \här'däŋər\ *n* -s [*Hardanger*, district in Norway] **:** embroidery of Norwegian origin worked over counted threads in a geometrical design

hardanger fiddle *n, usu cap H* [trans. of Norw *hardangerfele*, fr. *Hardanger* + Norw *fele* fiddle] **:** a fiddle of Norwegian origin with four stopped and four sympathetic strings used to accompany the halling and other Scandinavian dances

[1]hardback \'⸗,⸗\ *adj* **:** HARD 1a (2)

[2]hardback \"\ *n* **:** a book bound in hard covers

hardbake \'⸗,⸗\ *n, Brit* **:** a sweetmeat of sugar or molasses and almonds

hardball \'⸗,⸗\ *n* **:** BASEBALL

hard-bark hickory *n* **:** MOCKERNUT

hard beech *n* **:** a tall beech (*Nothofagus truncata*) with very hard wood found in south temperate regions esp. in New Zealand

hard-bill \'⸗,⸗\ *n* **:** any of numerous birds with a hard strong bill adapted to cracking seeds and nuts — compare SOFT-BILL

hard-bitten \'⸗¦⸗⸗\ *adj* [[1]*hard* + *-bitten* having (such) a bite (fr. *bitten*, past part. of *bite*)] **1 :** having a hard bite **:** inclined to bite hard ⟨so *hard-bitten* an animal that all the torture you can use will not make him leave his hold —Martin Hunter⟩ **2 a :** seasoned or steeled in battle **:** tough in fighting ⟨*hard⸗bitten* tribesmen, their . . . faces flecked with the blood of the fighting —T.E.Lawrence⟩ ⟨the rangers . . . were a *hard-bitten* lot, and they went after outlaws in a businesslike way —W.M. Raine⟩ **b** (1) **:** seasoned or steeled in struggle or experience of any kind **:** having the qualities appropriate to a veteran ⟨this genial but *hard-bitten* career diplomat —*Newsweek*⟩ (2) **:** CONFIRMED, INVETERATE ⟨*hard-bitten* amateur high-fidelity operators —R.S.Lanier⟩ ⟨*hard-bitten* bachelors complained that they were too shy to approach women —*Atlantic*⟩ **3 a** (1) **:** marked by severity or austerity of character **:** of tough moral fiber **:** UNYIELDING, INDOMITABLE, RUGGED ⟨a *hard-bitten*, granite⸗faced, Scotch-Irish Presbyterian —*Newsweek*⟩ ⟨his *hard⸗bitten* New England independence —Edwin Clark⟩ ⟨one of those *hard-bitten* ruggedly individualistic men —Pamela Taylor⟩ (2) **:** full of difficulties or hardships **:** HARSH ⟨the life of the farmer was all too often a lonely *hard-bitten* existence —*Amer. Guide Series: Ind.*⟩ **b :** lacking polish or refinement **:** rough or coarse in manner or appearance **:** TOUGH, HARD⸗BOILED ⟨patronized by roistering, *hard-bitten* seafarers —*Amer. Guide Series: Fla.*⟩ **c :** lacking sensitivity or compassion **:** CALLOUS, RUTHLESS, HARD ⟨the typical story of the *hard-bitten* man who clawed his way to the top —V.P.Hass⟩ **d :** free of sentimentality or illusions **:** not credulous or naïve **:** TOUGH-MINDED, REALISTIC, PRACTICAL ⟨this *hard-bitten* gentleman has an aesthetic and romantic side —Stanley Walker⟩ ⟨a somewhat more *hard-bitten* scholarly segment . . . squared off for wordy battles with the faithful —M.W.Fishwick⟩ ⟨realistic, *hard-bitten*, and unrhetorical —*Saturday Rev.*⟩

hardboard \'⸗,⸗\ *n* **:** a composition board made by shredding wood chips by sudden release of high steam pressure and then compressing them with or without added binders or other materials at high temperatures

hard-boil \'⸗,⸗\ *vt* [back-formation fr. *hard-boiled*] **:** to cook (an egg) until hard-boiled

hard-boiled \'⸗¦⸗\ *adj* [[2]*hard* + *boiled*] **1 :** boiled until both white and yolk have solidified — used of an egg **2 :** heavily starched **:** STIFF ⟨wore a double-breasted, dark suit and a collar . . .; it was one of those *hard-boiled* old-timers —F.C. Othman⟩ — compare BOILED SHIRT **3 a :** devoid of sentimentality or weakness **:** CALLOUS, TOUGH ⟨I, a *hard-boiled* South Sea trader, was genuinely shocked —*Atlantic*⟩ ⟨*hard⸗boiled* politicians⟩ ⟨a *hard-boiled* outfit under a *hard-boiled* leader —E.J.Fitzgerald⟩ **b :** of or relating to a literary form or production characterized by impersonal matter-of-fact presentation of naturalistic or violent themes or incidents, by a generally unemotional or stoic tone, and often by a total absence of explicit or implied moral judgments ⟨the *hard-boiled* tradition of detective fiction —John Paterson⟩ ⟨the novels of the *hard-boiled* school —George Stevens⟩ **c :** DOWN-TO-EARTH, PRACTICAL, HARDHEADED, REALISTIC ⟨from the *hardest-boiled* examination of the American system, this is a blueprint for disaster —A.A.Berle⟩ ⟨handle aid programs on a friendly but *hard-boiled* business basis —*N.Y. Times*⟩ ⟨a fundamentally *hard-boiled* permanently businesslike people —*Times Lit. Supp.*⟩

hard-boiled·ness *n* -ES **:** the quality or state of being hard⸗boiled

hardboot \'⸗,⸗\ *n* **:** a person devoted to horse racing ⟨the local ~*s* tramped or rode trolleys —*Newsweek*⟩ — used esp. of Kentuckians

hardbought \'⸗¦⸗\ *adj* **:** gained or won by hard or intensive effort ⟨the ~ battle for political control —Allan Nevins⟩ ⟨lest the silent ~ knowledge show in his eyes —Ross Lockridge⟩

hardbound \'⸗¦⸗\ *adj* **:** HARD 1a (2)

hard brick *or* **hard-burned brick** \'⸗,⸗-\ *n* **:** brick that has received the proper amount of burning in the kiln

hard candy *n* **:** candy made of sugar and corn syrup boiled without crystallizing and usu. fruit-flavored

hardcase \'⸗,⸗\ *n, often attrib* **1 :** a person by nature incorrigible or intractable **:** a tough customer; *esp* **:** a hardened criminal ⟨small-time ~ —Mickey Spillane⟩ ⟨ran with a ~ crowd —Luke Short⟩ ⟨remained at peace with local ~*s* by giving demonstrations of his . . . gunnery —W.L.Gresham⟩ **2 :** a person in a pitiful plight **:** a case of hardship ⟨my ~*s* were all of the literary sort —F.M.Ford⟩

hard cherry *n* **:** BIGARREAU CHERRY

hard cider *n* **:** fermented apple juice containing usu. less than 10 percent alcohol

hard clam *n* **:** a clam with a thick hard shell; *specif* **:** QUAHOG

hard coal *n* **:** ANTHRACITE

hard-coated \'⸗¦⸗⸗\ *adj, of a dog* **:** having a crisp harsh⸗textured coat

hard core *n* **1** *usu* **hardcore** \'⸗,⸗\ *chiefly Brit* **:** brick rubbish, clinker, broken stone, or other hard material in pieces used as a bottom (as in making roads and in foundations) **2 :** an esp. resistant or enduring structural and usu. basic or central part of a larger entity: as **a :** the most militant, die-hard, or loyal element or nucleus of a group, organization, or movement ⟨this group, whose *hard core* . . . is the trade unions —C.J. Friedrich⟩ ⟨the party's *hard core* of stubborn ultraconservatives —*N.Y. Times*⟩ **b :** a group of refugees or displaced persons not readily sponsored or resettled because of physical or other incapacities; *specif* **:** a group of refugees requiring institutional care wherever they go ⟨*hard-core* cases — incurably sick people, bedridden old people, inevitable charges of the state —John Hersey⟩

hard court *n* **:** a lawn-tennis court with a paved surface (as of asphalt or concrete) — distinguished from *clay court* and *grass court*

hard-cover \'⸗,⸗⸗\ *adj* **:** HARD 1a (2)

hard crab *n* **:** HARD-SHELL CRAB

hard-drawn \'⸗¦⸗\ *adj* **:** drawn so as to produce great hardness and strength — used esp. of copper wire and tubing

[1]hard·en \'härdᵊn, 'hȧdᵊn\ *vb* **hardened**; **hardened**; **hard·ening** \-d(ᵊ)niŋ\ **hardens** [ME *hardnen*, fr. [1]*hard* + *-nen* -en] *vt* **1 :** to make hard or harder **:** make firm, tight, or compact: as **a :** to convert into solid or stiffer solid form ⟨~ an unsaturated oil by catalytic hydrogenation⟩ **b :** to make hard (as steel) by heat treatment, esp. heating and quenching in water, brine, or oil **c :** to compact (felt) by applying moisture, heat, friction, and pressure **d :** to decrease the swelling and raise the melting point of (the emulsion layer of a photographic material) by chemical treatment **2** *dial Eng* **a :** to make bold **:** urge on **:** ENCOURAGE **b :** to strengthen or confirm esp. in disposition, feelings, or a course of action **:** REINFORCE ⟨~*ed* him in his determination to leave at once⟩ ⟨a development that only ~*ed* his conviction that he was right⟩ **3 :** to make callous or unfeeling ⟨~*ed* his heart against me⟩ ⟨its influence did not ~ him; he has always risen above cynicism —L.A. Triebel⟩ **4 :** to make hardy or robust **:** INURE, TOUGHEN ⟨~ troops by long marches⟩ ⟨coarse foods . . . help to ~ the gums —Morris Fishbein⟩; *specif* **:** to inure to cold or other unfavorable environmental conditions (as by gradual exposure to lower temperatures or by decreasing the water supply) — often used with *off* **5 :** to signify that the pronunciation of (a consonant letter) is plosive rather than fricative ~ *vi* **1 :** to become hard or harder **:** acquire solidity, compactness, or rigidity ⟨mortar ~*s* by drying⟩ ⟨deviations ~ into modes of action —John Dewey⟩ **2 a :** to become confirmed or strengthened (as in feeling, disposition, or course of action) ⟨opposition began to ~ —L.S.B.Leakey⟩ **b :** to become hard in temper or disposition ⟨it was enough . . . to set up resistance in her: she ~*ed* —Elizabeth Bowen⟩ **c :** to assume an appearance or give an impression of harshness or severity ⟨her face ~*ed* instantly —Margaret Deland⟩ ⟨his face ~*ed* into anger —Liam O'Flaherty⟩ **3 :** to become higher or less subject to fluctuations downward **:** FIRM, STRENGTHEN, STIFFEN ⟨prices . . . ~*ed* quickly and drastically —R.F.Yates⟩ ⟨~*ing* commodity markets⟩

syn INURE, SEASON, ACCLIMATIZE, ACCLIMATE: HARDEN, in the sense pertinent here, is to habituate or toughen, usu. by degrees, to what generally causes pain or discomfort, or to make slowly callous to what usu. affects the feelings ⟨frontier life *hardened* most men quickly to rough conditions, often to extreme privations⟩ ⟨not yet *hardened* to the wicked world of international politics —Dexter Perkins⟩ To INURE one is to cause one to submit unwillingly, to harden one to patient endurance of the objectionable ⟨they were *inured* to hardship and unafraid of the wilderness —*Amer. Guide Series: Tenn.*⟩ ⟨an experienced judge is more or less *inured* to criticism —W.F. Brown b.1903⟩ SEASON suggests a gradual bettering of condition or increase in ability brought about by time or experience, a maturing (of a thing) to a sound, reliable condition, or a maturing (of a person or a talent) to a greater efficiency or perfection in a particular activity or calling ⟨old wood, *seasoned* by the sea wind for many decades —*Amer. Guide Series: N.Y. City*⟩ ⟨a soldier, *seasoned* by many campaigns⟩ ⟨the chapters which follow have all been tried out and *seasoned* with discussion —H.A.Overstreet⟩ To ACCLIMATIZE or to ACCLIMATE is to adapt or to accustom to new and hitherto alien conditions, ACCLIMATIZE more frequently suggesting a human agency ⟨to help *acclimatize* the new arrivals to conditions on the continent —Hanama Tasaki⟩ ⟨sheep . . . *acclimatized* to the hills —F.D.Smith & Barbara Wilcox⟩ ⟨they were *acclimatized* now to the cool atmosphere of professional life —Mary Lavin⟩ ⟨I became so well *acclimated* to German customs —David Fairchild⟩ ⟨*acclimating* the disabled veteran to the job and adjusting the job to the veteran —*Current Biog.*⟩

[2]harden \'(h)a(r)dən\ *n* -s *often attrib* [ME *herdyng*, *herden*, *harden*, irreg. fr. *herdes*, *hardes* hurds — more at HURDS] *dial Brit* **:** a fabric made of the coarser parts of flax or hemp

hard·en·abil·i·ty \,härdᵊnə'bilәd·ē\ *n* -ES **:** the property determining the depth to which a ferrous alloy can be hardened by quenching

har·den·ber·gia \,härdᵊn'bərjēə\ *n, cap* [NL, fr. Franziska von *Hardenberg*, 19th cent. Austrian noblewoman + NL *-ia*] **:** a small genus of Australian woody climbers (family Leguminosae) with small violet-blue flowers

hardened *adj* [ME *hardned*, fr. past part. of *hardnen* to harden] **1 :** made hard or harder ⟨~ brass⟩ ⟨~ roads⟩ **2 a :** grown unfeeling or callous ⟨~ as I am, I felt a thrill of horror —Allen Upward⟩ **b :** CONFIRMED, INVETERATE, VETERAN ⟨many of the findings will hardly appeal except to ~ Johnsonians —*Times Lit. Supp.*⟩ ⟨~ fishermen protested —L.F. Ranlett⟩ ⟨a commercial or otherwise ~ traveler —W.C. Brownell⟩; *specif* **:** confirmed in error or vice ⟨a ~ little reprobate —W.M.Thackeray⟩ ⟨a ~ heretic⟩ ⟨~ criminals⟩ **c :** grown or become inured or steeled ⟨the duty was easy for a ~ horseman —S.H.Adams⟩ ⟨~ fighting men⟩

hard·en·er \'härd(ᵊ)nər, 'hȧd(ᵊ)nə(r\ *n* -s **:** one that hardens: as **a** (1) **:** a worker who hardens steel objects by heating and quick cooling (2) **:** a preliminary alloy added to a melt in order to introduce alloying elements **b** (1) **:** a worker who hardens felt (2) **:** a machine for hardening felt **c :** a substance added (as to a paint or varnish) to impart greater hardness to the film **d :** a substance (as alum or formaldehyde) used in a gelatin film, emulsion, or processing bath to prevent swelling and softening during processing

hardening *n* -s [fr. gerund of ¹*harden*] **1 :** something (as a material used for converting the surface of iron into steel) that hardens **2 :** INDURATION 1d ⟨~ of the arteries⟩

hardens *pres 3d sing of* HARDEN

¹**harder** *comparative of* HARD

²**har·der** \ˈhärdə(r)\ *n* -s [Afrik, fr. D] *Africa* **:** GRAY MULLET

har·de·ri·an gland \(ˈ)här¦dirēən-\ *also* **harder's gland** *n, sometimes cap H* [after Johann J. *Harder* †1711 Swiss anatomist] **:** an accessory lacrimal gland on the inner side of the orbit in reptiles and birds but usu. degenerate in mammals

hardest *superlative of* HARD

hard–face \ˈ=,=\ *vt* **:** to weld a wear-resistant metal onto the surface of (a metal part)

hard–favored \ˈ=¦=\ *adj* **:** HARD-FEATURED — **hard–fa·vored·ness** *n* -ES

hard–featured \ˈ=¦=\ *adj* **:** having coarse, unattractive, or stern features

hard fern *n* **:** DEER FERN; *broadly* **:** any of several ferns of the genus *Blechnum*

hard fescue *n* **:** a European fescue (*Festuca ovina duriuscula*) that is a variety of sheep fescue and is sometimes used in permanent pasture and lawn mixtures

hard–fiber \ˈ=¦==\ *adj* [¹*hard* + *fiber*, n.] **:** vulcanized with zinc chloride — used of paper or boards

hard fiber *n* [¹*hard* + *fiber*, n.] **:** leaf fiber with heavily lignified walls that is hard and stiff in texture and is used in making cordage, twine, and textiles

hard finish *n* **:** a smooth finishing coat of hard fine plaster applied to the surface of rough plastering

hardfisted \ˈ=¦==\ *adj* **1 a :** having hard or strong hands esp. from labor **:** capable of hard physical labor **:** hardened to or by labor **:** STRONG ⟨had a ~ hired girl to help with the work —Floyd Dell⟩ ⟨~ sons of toil —Robert Grant †1940⟩ **b :** hard of will or temper **:** free of weakness **:** TOUGH, TOUGH-MINDED, RUTHLESS ⟨a ~ ruler and a demanding father —Diana Chang⟩ ⟨~ men of affairs⟩ **2 :** CLOSEFISTED, STINGY, MEAN ⟨as ~ . . . as any Boston landlord —G.W.Johnson⟩ — **hard·fist·ed·ness** *n* -ES

hard goods *n pl* **:** DURABLES

hard–grained \ˈ=¦=\ *adj* **1 :** having a close firm grain **2 :** of a hard nature **:** UNATTRACTIVE

hard grass *n* **:** any of several different grasses (as orchard grass and members of the genera *Sclerochloa* and *Glyceria*)

hard ground *n* **:** etching ground melted from a ball or cake onto a heated plate and spread while soft by means of a roller or dabber

hardhack \ˈ=,=\ *n* [¹ *hard* + *hack*, v.] **1 :** an American shrub (*Spiraea tomentosa*) with rusty tomentose leaves and dense terminal panicles of pink or occas. white flowers **2 :** HOP HORNBEAM **3 :** SHRUBBY CINQUEFOIL

hardhanded \ˈ=¦==\ *adj* **:** HARDFISTED — **hard·hand·ed·ness** *n* -ES

hard hat *n* **1** *Brit* **:** DERBY **2 :** a protective hat usu. with a metal crown worn esp. by construction workers

hardhead \ˈ=,=\ *n* **1 a :** a shrewd practical hardheaded person ⟨a prospect that moves ~*s* as well as visionaries⟩ **b :** BLOCKHEAD **2 a :** any of several fishes: as (1) *also* **hardhead trout :** STEELHEAD TROUT (2) **:** ATLANTIC CROAKER (3) **:** a small cyprinid fish (*Mylopharodon conocephalus*) of California streams; *also* **:** the related greaser blackfish **b :** GRAY WHALE **3 a :** RUDDY DUCK **b** *or* **hardheaded duck** \ˈ=¦==-\ **:** WHITE-EYED DUCK **4 a :** KNAPWEED — usu. used in pl. **b :** RIBGRASS **c :** SNEEZEWORT 2 **d :** CORN COCKLE **5 :** HARDHEAD SPONGE **6 a :** a hard brittle white residue obtained in refining tin by liquation and containing tin, iron, arsenic, and copper **b :** a refractory lump of ore only partly smelted

hardheaded \ˈ=¦==\ *adj* [¹*hard* + *headed*] **1 :** STUBBORN, WILLFUL ⟨always was ~ about what she wanted —Erskine Caldwell⟩ **2 :** not moved by sentiment or impulse **:** having no illusions **:** PRACTICAL, SOBER, REALISTIC ⟨a ~ appraisal of our position in Asia today —*N. Y. Times*⟩ ⟨~ realists⟩ — **hard·head·ed·ly** *adv* — **hard·head·ed·ness** *n* -ES

hardhead sponge *n* **:** any of several commercial sponges having a harsh but elastic and fairly durable fiber that occur off the West Indies and Central America

hardhearted \ˈ=¦==\ *adj* [ME *hardherted*, fr. ¹*hard* + *herted* hearted] **:** UNSYMPATHETIC, UNFEELING, CALLOUS, CRUEL, PITILESS — **hard·heart·ed·ly** *adv* — **hard·heart·ed·ness** *n* -ES

hard–hitting \ˈ=,==\ *adj* **:** ENERGETIC, VIGOROUS, AGGRESSIVE, EFFECTIVE, INTENSIVE ⟨a *hard-hitting* advertising campaign⟩ ⟨writes a fast, *hard-hitting* prose —E.J.Fitzgerald⟩

har·die *or* **har·dy** \ˈhärdē\ *n, pl* **hardies** [prob. fr. ¹*hard* + *-ie* or *-y*] **:** a blacksmith's fuller or chisel having a square shank for insertion into a hole in the anvil

hardie hole *or* **hardy hole** *n* **:** a square hole in a blacksmith's anvil for insertion of the shank of a hardie

hardier *comparative of* HARDY

hardiest *superlative of* HARDY

har·di·head \ˈhärdē,hed\ *var of* HARDYHEAD

har·di·hood \ˈhärdē,hu̇d, ˈhȧd-, -di,-\ *n* [¹*hardy* + *-hood*] **1 a :** resolute courage and fortitude **:** strong will to prevail, withstand, or survive ⟨~ is the fisherman's talent by which he wins his living from the sea —Richard Jefferies⟩ **b :** self-assured resolute audacity or disdainful insolence ⟨no historian will have the ~ to maintain that he commands this . . . view —A.J.Toynbee⟩ **2 :** VIGOR, ROBUSTNESS ⟨a man of action . . . who greatly prized and honored physical ~ —J.D.Adams⟩ **syn** see TEMERITY

har·di·ly \-dᵊlē, -li\ *adv* [ME, fr. ¹*hardy* + *-ly*] **:** in a hardy manner **:** BOLDLY, STOUTLY ⟨stared back ~ —Clemence Dane⟩

har·dim \ˈhär,dim\ *n* -s [modif. of Ar *ḥirdhawn*] **:** STARRED LIZARD

har·di·ment \ˈhärdēmənt\ *n* -s [ME, fr. MF, fr. OF *hardiment*, *hardement*, fr. *hardi* bold + *-ment* — more at HARDY] **1** *archaic* **:** HARDIHOOD, BOLDNESS, COURAGE **2** *obs* **:** a bold deed

har·di·ness \ˈhärdēnəs, ˈhȧd-, -din-\ *n* -ES [ME *hardinesse*, fr. ¹*hardy* + *-nesse* -ness] **:** the quality or state of being hardy: as **a :** the condition of being inured to fatigue or hardship **:** capability of endurance or resistance ⟨a race of great ~⟩; *specif* **:** the ability of a plant to survive under adverse conditions esp. of low temperatures **b :** BOLDNESS, AUDACITY, TEMERITY ⟨somewhere ~ failed her —Elizabeth Bowen⟩

har·ding·grass \ˈhärdiŋ,gras\ *n, often cap* [prob. fr. the name *Harding*] **:** a perennial canary grass (*Phalaris tuberosa stenoptera*) of Australia and southern Africa introduced into No. America as a forage grass

hard·ish \ˈhärdish\ *adj* **:** rather hard ⟨the seats, though cushioned, were ~ —Lucien Price⟩

har·di·shrew \ˈhȧdi,shrü\ *n* [¹*hardy* + *shrew*] *Brit* **:** a common shrew (*Sorex araneus*)

hard labor *n* **:** compulsory labor imposed upon imprisoned criminals as a part of the prison discipline but not necessarily more severe nor greater in amount than that customarily performed by ordinary laborers

hard–laid \ˈ=¦=\ *adj, of rope* **:** twisted tightly so that the angle of the strands is about 45 degrees

hard lay *n* **:** a lay in which the strands of a rope are hard-laid for greater firmness and resistance to abrasive wear

hard lead *n* **1 :** unrefined lead made hard by impurities esp. of copper, antimony, and arsenic **2 :** ANTIMONIAL LEAD; *specif* **:** an alloy containing about 5 percent antimony — compare GRID METAL

hard lines *n pl, chiefly Brit* **:** hard luck ⟨it's damned *hard lines* to have a lot of planning . . . go for nothing —F.V.W.Mason⟩ — often used with *on* ⟨*hard lines* on the kid, I say —G.A. Wagner⟩

hard liquor *n* **:** DISTILLED LIQUOR

hard liver *or* **hard liver disease** *n* **:** a toxic hepatic cirrhosis of swine and cattle due to ingestion of the seeds of a tarweed (*Amsinckia intermedia*) in the northwestern U. S.

hard·ly *adv* [ME *hardely*, *hardly*, fr. OE *heardlīce*, adv. of *heardlīc* severe, bold, fr. *heard* hard + *-līc* -ly (adj. suffix)] **1 :** with force or energy **:** VIOLENTLY, VIGOROUSLY ⟨turquoise . . . earrings jangling down ~ on diminutive gold chains —Osbert Sitwell⟩ **2 a :** in a severe or harsh manner **:** ROUGHLY, UNFAIRLY, UNPLEASANTLY, BADLY ⟨things may go ~ with us . . . before the war is over —Nevil Shute⟩ **b :** with great or excessive grief or resentment ⟨had not believed that he would take it so ~⟩ **3 :** in a difficult manner **:** by hard work or struggle **:** with trouble **:** PAINFULLY ⟨the right to play croquet had been a ~ won concession —Osbert Lancaster⟩ ⟨wondering why the lesson had to be learned so ~ —Kamala Markandaya⟩ ⟨means of existence wrung so ~ from the soil —Sir Winston Churchill⟩ **4 :** only just **:** not quite **:** not altogether **:** BARELY, SCARCELY ⟨men who were ~ literate⟩ ⟨why, I ~ know him⟩ ⟨~ knew what to say⟩ ⟨this is ~ the time to discuss such matters⟩ — sometimes used in nonstandard construction with a superfluous negative ⟨horse thieves was so bad that a man couldn't ~ keep a . . . horse —J.F.Dobie⟩

hardly ever *adv* **:** almost never **:** very seldom ⟨we *hardly ever* see them anymore⟩

hard maple *n* **1 :** a maple with notably hard wood; *esp* **:** SUGAR MAPLE **2 :** the wood of a hard maple

hardmouthed \ˈ=,=\ *adj* **1 a** *of a horse* **:** not sensitive to the bit **b :** OBSTINATE, STUBBORN ⟨~ women who laid down the law —John Galsworthy⟩ **2** *of a dog* **:** given to biting down hard on a retrieved bird

hard·ness *n* -ES [ME *hardnesse*, fr. OE *heardnes*, fr. *heard* hard + *-nes* -ness] **1 :** the quality or state of being hard: as **a** (1) **:** a property of solids, plastics, and very viscous liquids that is indicated by their solidity and firmness (2) **:** resistance of metal to indentation by an indenter of fixed shape and size under a static load or to scratching (as by a file or diamond cutting point) (3) **:** ability of a metal to cause rebound of a small standard object dropped from a fixed height (4) **:** the cohesion of the particles on the surface of a mineral as determined by its capacity to scratch another or be itself scratched — compare MOHS' SCALE **b :** a quality exhibited by water containing various dissolved salts (as of calcium and magnesium) that prevent soap from lathering by giving rise to an insoluble curdy precipitate and that cause incrustations in boilers or kettles — see PERMANENT HARDNESS, TEMPORARY HARDNESS; compare SOFTNESS **c :** a quality of radiation (as of X rays) that determines its penetrating power **d :** excessive contrast in a photographic negative or print **e** (1) **:** HARSHNESS, SEVERITY, CALLOUSNESS ⟨a ~ toward shop assistants by customers —Lucien Price⟩ ⟨free from all resentment, ~, and scorn —Oscar Wilde⟩ (2) **:** RIGOR, INCLEMENCY, DIFFICULTY ⟨the poverty of the country, the ~ of life —Felix Gilbert⟩ ⟨happier than the townsman . . . in spite of the ~ of his lot —G.E.Fussell⟩ (3) **:** freedom from sentimentality, weakness, or slackness ⟨it was Yeats's dryness and ~ that excited us —Louis MacNeice⟩ ⟨that doctrine of ~ which distinguishes the work of the best imagist poets —Jacob Isaacs⟩ **2 :** something hard to do or bear **:** HARDSHIP

hard–nosed \ˈ=¦=\ *adj* **:** HARD-BITTEN, STUBBORN ⟨a *hard-nosed* scrapping breed —Breck Porter⟩

hardock \ˈhär,däk\ *n* -s [origin unknown] **:** BURDOCK

hard–of–hearing *adj* **:** of, relating to, or characterized by a defective but functional sense of hearing

hard oil *n* **:** an interior varnish that dries with a relatively hard surface

hard pad *or* **hard pad disease** *n* **:** a serious and frequently fatal virus disease of dogs related to and sometimes indistinguishable from common distemper but typically involving bronchopneumonia, severe diarrhea, and a peculiar thickening and hardening of the skin of the pads and nose which commonly peels away as the acute stage of the disease subsides

hard palate *n* **:** a part of the human palate supported by the maxillary and palatine bones

hardpan \ˈ=,=\ *n* **1 :** a cemented or compacted and often clayey layer in soil that hampers root penetration and results from accumulation of cementing material or may be caused by repeated plowing to the same depth — compare PLOW SOLE **2 :** a firm substantial fundamental part or quality of something **:** BEDROCK ⟨gets down to the ~ of the question⟩

hard paste *n* **1 :** a ceramic body consisting of kaolin together with china stone or with feldspar and flint **2** *or* **hard–paste porcelain :** true high-fired porcelain made with a hard-paste body — compare SOFT PASTE

hard patch *n* **:** a plate riveted or welded over another to cover a break

hard pear *n* **1 :** a southern African shrub (*Olinia cymosa*) having square stems, cymose white flowers, red drupaceous fruit, and hard wood that is used for making musical instruments **2 :** a southern African tree (*Strychnos henningsii*) with elliptical leaves and spherical one-seeded fruit about ¾ inch in diameter

hard pine *n* **:** a pine (as longleaf pine or a pitch pine) having hard wood and leaves usu. in groups of two or three; *also* **:** the wood of a hard pine

hard put *adj* [*put* fr. past part. of *put*, v.] **:** faced with difficulty or perplexity **:** being in a quandary **:** barely or hardly able ⟨was *hard put* to find a satisfactory answer⟩ ⟨were *hard put* to meet mortgage payments —*Current Biog.*⟩ — often used in the phrase *hard put to it* ⟨*hard put* to it to account for the differences between the ancient Chinese and the ancient Egyptians —Bertrand Russell⟩

hard road *n* **:** a road that has been paved or otherwise hard-surfaced

hard–rock \ˈ=,=\ *adj, of a miner* **:** experienced in underground work in hard massive formations

hard rot *n* **:** any of several plant diseases characterized by lesions with hard surfaces and rotted tissue; *esp* **:** a disease of the gladiolus caused by a fungus (*Septoria gladioli*) that produces lesions on both leaves and corms

hard rubber *n* **:** a firm relatively inextensible rubber or rubber product: as **a :** a normally black substance having the texture of horn and made by vulcanizing natural rubber with high percentages (as about 30 to 50 percent) of sulfur and with or without other compounding ingredients **b :** a similar substance made from certain synthetic rubbers (as GR-S and nitrile rubber) and sulfur **c :** a similar substance made from natural or certain synthetic rubbers by the use of organic vulcanizing agents without elemental sulfur

hard rush *n* **:** a common rush (*Juncus effusus*)

¹**hards** \ˈhärdz\ *n pl* [ME *hardes*, *herdes* — more at HURDS] **:** HURDS

²**hards** *pl of* HARD

hard sauce *n* **:** a creamed mixture of butter and powdered sugar often with added cream and flavoring

¹**hardscrabble** \ˈ=,==\ *adj* [¹*hard* + *scrabble*, n.] **:** yielding or gaining a bare or meager living with greatest difficulty or hardest labor **:** BARREN, IMPOVERISHED, MARGINAL ⟨ranges from ~ farms in the hilly portions . . . to productive farms on prairie land —*Social Forces*⟩ ⟨a rather ~ life . . . among people who had few comforts and amenities —Henry Beston⟩ ⟨a ~ farmer⟩ ⟨till their ~ acres . . . intensively —*Pa. Game News*⟩

²**hardscrabble** \"\ *n* **:** hardscrabble land ⟨homestead of field, stream, hayfield, and ~ —S.T.Williamson⟩

hard seed *n* **:** seed in which the testa is unusually hard and impervious to moisture and which is therefore slow in germinating unless treated mechanically or chemically

hard sell *n* **:** aggressive high-pressure selling or salesmanship — often used with *the* ⟨everyone had keyed himself up to the *hard sell* —*Business Week*⟩; compare SOFT SELL

hard–set \ˈ=¦=\ *adj* [ME *harde sette*, fr. *harde* hard (adv.) + *sette*, *set*, past part. of *setten* to set — more at SET] **1 :** hard pressed **:** HARD PUT ⟨it's *hard set* I am to walk —J.M.Synge⟩ **2 a :** fixed in rigidity **:** HARD, FIRM ⟨there is a *hard-set* line about his mouth —*Nation*⟩ **b :** subjected to the process of incubation by setting ⟨frightened a . . . gull from her *hard-set* eggs —E.A.Armstrong⟩

¹**hard–shell** \ˈ=,=\ *adj* **1 a :** having a hard shell **b :** UNYIELDING, CONFIRMED, UNCOMPROMISING ⟨a *hard-shell* conservative⟩ **2** *often cap H&S* **:** of, relating to, or characteristic of the Hard-Shell Baptists

²**hard–shell** \ˈ=,=\ *n* **1 :** HARD-SHELL CRAB **2** *often cap H&S* **:** a Hard-Shell Baptist

hard–shell baptist *n, usu cap H&S&B* **1 :** PRIMITIVE BAPTIST **2 :** a strict and uncompromising Baptist

hard–shell clam *also* **hard–shelled clam** *n* **:** QUAHOG

hard–shell crab *or* **hard–shelled crab** *n* **:** a crab that has not recently shed its shell and hence has the shell rigid — used chiefly of edible crabs (as the blue crab)

hard–shelled \ˈ=¦=\ *adj* [¹*hard* + *shelled*, adj.] **:** HARD-SHELL

hard·ship \ˈhärd,ship, ˈhȧd-\ *n* [ME *hardshipe*, fr. ¹*hard* + *-shipe* -ship] **1 a :** SUFFERING, PRIVATION ⟨years of danger and ~⟩ ⟨inflation was a cause of ~⟩ ⟨a life of ~⟩ **b :** a particular instance or type of suffering or privation ⟨the losses and ~*s* . . . entailed by war —Bertrand Russell⟩ ⟨enduring cold, hunger, and other ~*s*⟩ **2 :** something that causes or entails suffering or privation ⟨cannot help thinking it a ~ that more indulgence is allowed to men than to women —James Boswell⟩ ⟨one of the ~*s* of town life . . . is the absence of spring water —*Amer. Guide Series: N. C.*⟩ ⟨all the ~*s* of the northern passage — head winds, fog —L.B.Schmidt⟩ **syn** see DIFFICULTY

hard–sized \ˈ=¦=\ *adj, of paper* **:** sufficiently sized to be relatively impermeable by water — compare SLACK-SIZED

hard smut *n* **:** a disease of wheat caused by nematodes of the genus *Tylenchus* that transform the kernels into galls resembling the smut balls of bunt

hard soap *n* **:** soap made by using sodium hydroxide or sodium carbonate — compare CASTILE SOAP

hard solder *n* [¹*hard* + *solder*, n.] **:** a solder that contains copper, requires a red heat to melt, and is used for brazing

hard–solder \ˈ=¦==\ *vb* [*hard solder*] **:** to solder with hard solder **:** BRAZE

hard sponge *n* **:** ZIMOCCA

hardstand \ˈ=,=\ *also* **hardstanding** \ˈ=,==\ *n* **:** a hard-surfaced area (as at an airfield) for parking an airplane

hardstem bulrush *or* **hard–stemmed bulrush** \ˈ=,=-\ *n* **:** a widely distributed No. American bulrush (*Scirpus acutus*) that has hard rigid olive green culms and a rather stiff panicle; *also* **:** any of several closely related bulrushes

hard–surface \ˈ=¦==\ *vt* [¹*hard* + *surface*, v.] **1 :** to treat (as by paving or macadamizing) the surface of (as a road) to prevent muddiness **2 :** HARD-FACE

hardtack \ˈ=,=\ *n* **1 :** a hard biscuit or loaf bread made of flour and water without salt and baked in large or small forms — called also *pilot bread, ship biscuit* **2 :** any of several mountain mahoganies; *esp* **:** a spreading shrub or small tree (*Cercocarpus betuloides*) that has obovate distally serrate leaves dark green above and whitish below

hardtail \ˈ=,=\ *n* **1 a :** BLUE RUNNER **b :** a fish related to the blue runner **2 :** MULE

hard tick *n* **:** a tick of the family Ixodidae — compare SOFT TICK

hard–times token *n* **:** one of the tokens issued during the controversy between the Jacksonian administration and the Bank of the U. S. — called also *Jackson cent*

hardtop \ˈ=,=\ *n* [¹*hard* + *top*, n.] **1 :** an automobile with a metal roof **2** *also* **hardtop convertible :** an automobile similar to a convertible in lacking vertical posts between windows but differing in having a rigid top of metal or plastic that in some models is fixed and in others is either lowerable into the rear deck or demountable

¹**hard–top** \ˈ=¦=\ *n* [¹*hard* + *top*, n.] **:** a hard-surfaced area or road

²**hard–top** \ˈ=¦=\ *vt* **:** HARD-SURFACE

hard tussock *n* **:** a fescue (*Festuca novae-zealandiae*) common in New Zealand as a forage grass

hard wall plaster *n* **:** CEMENT PLASTER

hardware \ˈ=,=\ *n* **1 :** ware (as fittings, trimmings, cutlery, tools, parts of machines and appliances, metal building equipment, utensils) made of metal **2 a :** FIREARMS ⟨while the men spoke politely . . . most of them wore ~ —*Amer. Guide Series: Ariz.*⟩ ⟨riding up with plenty of ~ in sight —F.B.Gipson⟩ **b :** metal items of military equipment for combat use (as ships, guns, tanks, airplanes, and their parts) and major support items (as trucks, jeeps, radar)

hardware cloth *n* **:** galvanized screening of steel wire woven with a close mesh commonly ⅛ inch to ¼ inch

hardware disease *n* **:** traumatic damage to the viscera of cattle due to ingestion of a foreign body (as a nail or barbed wire)

hardwareman \ˈ=,=mən\ *n, pl* **hardwaremen :** a person who makes or deals in hardware

hard waste *n* **:** textile waste rejected during manufacturing processes after spinning and consisting usu. of twisted yarns

hard wheat *n* **:** a wheat with hard flinty kernels high in gluten and yielding a strong flour esp. suitable for bread and macaroni — compare DURUM WHEAT, SOFT WHEAT

hard·wick·ia \här'dwikēə\ *n, cap* [NL, fr. Thomas *Hardwicke* †1835 Eng. artillery officer in India + NL *-ia*] **:** a small genus of Indian trees (family Leguminosae) having pinnate leaves and flowers in panicled racemes

¹**hardwood** \ˈ=,=\ *n* [¹*hard* + *wood*] **1 :** the wood of an angiospermous tree as distinguished from that of a coniferous tree, known orig. from hard European woods (as beech and oak) but including both the softest and the hardest of woods **2 :** a tree that yields hardwood **:** an arborescent angiosperm

²**hardwood** \"\ *adj* **1 :** having hardwood or made of hardwood **2 :** consisting of mature woody tissue ⟨~ cuttings⟩

hard–wooded \ˈ=¦==\ *adj* [¹*hard* + *wood* + *-ed*] **1 :** having hard wood that is difficult to work or finish **2 :** HARDWOOD 1

hardworking \ˈ=¦==\ *adj* **:** INDUSTRIOUS, LABORIOUS ⟨learned and ~ men —G.H.Turnbull⟩

¹**har·dy** \ˈhärdē, ˈhȧd-, -di\ *adj* -ER/-EST [ME *hardy*, *hardi*, fr. OF *hardi*, fr. past part. of (assumed) OF *hardir* to make hard, of Gmc origin; akin to OE *hierdan* to make hard, MD *harden*, *herden*, OHG *herten*, ON *hertha*, Goth *gahardjan*; causative-denominative fr. the root of E ¹*hard*] **1 :** BOLD, DARING, BRAVE, RESOLUTE ⟨displayed a ~ intrepid spirit⟩ **2 :** full of assurance or presumption **:** AUDACIOUS, BRAZEN **3 a :** inured to fatigue or hardships **:** capable of endurance **:** STRONG, ROBUST ⟨the boys were ~, robust . . . little fellows —Samuel Butler †1902⟩ ⟨small and ~ ponies —*Amer. Guide Series: La.*⟩ **b :** capable of living outdoors over winter without artificial protection or of withstanding other adverse conditions (as insufficient or excessive light, excessive moisture, drought, lack of nourishing food) ⟨~ plants⟩ ⟨a ~ breed of cattle⟩ — compare HALF-HARDY, TENDER

²**hardy** *var of* HARDIE

hardy annual *n* **:** an annual (as radish or spinach) capable of resisting frosts or light freezing — compare TENDER ANNUAL

hardy border *n* **:** an ornamental or decorative planting of hardy herbaceous perennials (as peony, iris, phlox)

hardy catalpa *n* **:** WESTERN CATALPA

hardyhead \ˈ=,=\ *n* [prob. fr. ¹*hardy* + *head*, n.] *Austral* **:** SILVERSIDES

hardy orange *n* **:** TRIFOLIATE ORANGE

hardy perennial *n* **:** something that lasts from year to year or appears afresh from time to time ⟨the Borgias have been among the *hardy perennials* of historical literature —C.M.L. Beuf⟩ ⟨the climatic theory . . . one of those *hardy perennials* that the frosts of scholarship do not much discourage —Charlton Laird⟩

har·dy·ston·ite \ˈhärdēstə,nīt\ *n* -s [*Hardyston*, Sussex County, northern New Jersey + E *-ite*] **:** a mineral $Ca_2ZnSi_2O_7$ consisting of a zinc calcium silicate

¹**hare** \ˈha(a)(ə)r, ˈhe|, |ə\ *n, pl* **hares** *also* **hare** [ME, fr. OE *hara*; akin to OHG *haso* hare, ON *heri*, W *ceinach*, Skt *śaśa* hare, OE *hasu* gray, OHG *hasan*, ON *höss* gray, L *canus* gray, white, hoary] **1 a :** any of various timid long-eared gnawing mammals (order Lagomorpha) with a divided upper lip, long strong hind legs adapted to leaping, and a short cocked tail that have soft usu. gray or brown fur turning white in some northern species in winter, usu. live in the open, feed chiefly on vegetation and bark, bear furred young with eyes open at birth, and are native to most parts of the world except Central and So. America, Australia, and Madagascar — compare COTTONTAIL, JACKRABBIT, RABBIT **b :** the fur or pelt of a hare often sheared and dyed to imitate more valuable furs **c :** a member of the family Leporidae — often used with a qualifying term ⟨African rock ~⟩ ⟨Asiatic harsh-furred ~⟩ **d :** an animal resembling a true hare in appearance or behavior **2 a :** one that is likened

European hare

to a hare: as (1) **:** a ridiculous person **:** FOOL ⟨made a ~ of him one time in my column —Sean O'Faolain⟩ (2) **:** the object of pursuit in a game of hare and hounds ⟨a flushed little ~ bounds past us, distributing the paper scent in his course —W.H.Rideine⟩ (3) *slang Brit* **:** a passenger traveling without a ticket ⟨the conductor came round and searched under the seats for ~*s* —Stephen Graham⟩ **b :** a topic for discussion or pursuit ⟨first raised this ~ about the decline of the novel —Harold Nicolson⟩ **3** *usu cap* **a :** an Athapaskan people west and northwest of Great Bear Lake, Canada **b :** a member of such people **c :** the language of the Hare people

²hare \"\ *vi* -ED/-ING/-S **:** to move swiftly **:** RUN ⟨scrambled down the wall and *hared* along the lane, my heart in my mouth —James Edwards⟩ — often used with *off* ⟨whichever team is called turns about and ~*s* off for base —J.B.Pick⟩

³hare \"\ *vt* -ED/-ING/-S [prob. alter. of ¹*harry*] *archaic* **:** to tease or harass esp. by frightening

hare and hounds *n* **:** a game in which two or more of the players start out first, scatter bits of paper for a trail, and try to keep ahead of the others who try to catch them before they reach a designated place

harebell \ˈ=,=\ *n* [ME *harebelle*, fr. ¹*hare* + *belle* bell] **1 :** a slender herb (*Campanula rotundifolia*) having blue flowers, cordate or ovate basal leaves, and linear stem leaves — called also *bluebell* **2 :** WOOD HYACINTH

¹harebrain \ˈ=,=\ *n* [¹*hare* + *brain*] **:** one who is flighty or foolish **:** CRACKPOT

²harebrain \"\ *adj* **:** HAREBRAINED

harebrained \ˈ=ˌ=\ *adj* [¹*hare* + *brained*] **:** FLIGHTY, FOOLISH, CRACKBRAINED — **hare·brained·ness** \ˈ=ˌbrānnəs *also* -ndnəs\ *n* -ES

hared up *adj* [perh. alter. (influenced by ¹*hair*) of *het up;* fr. the tendency of the hair on a person's head or an animal's back to stand on end as a result of extreme excitement] *dial* **:** being in a state of angry excitement **:** IRATE

hare-finder \ˈ=,=\ *n*, *Brit* **:** one that goes ahead of a coursing party in order to start the hare ⟨you stare about like a *hare-finder* —Thomas Shadwell⟩

harefoot \ˈ=,=\ *n* **:** a long narrow close-toed foot characteristic of some dogs, esp. the American foxhound

harefooted \ˈ=ˌ=\ *adj* [¹*hare* + *footed*] **1 :** moving swiftly **:** FLEET **2 :** having a harefoot

harehearted \ˈ=ˌ=\ *adj* **:** easily frightened **:** TIMID

hare kangaroo *n* **:** HARE WALLABY

harelip \ˈ=ˌ=\ *n* **1 :** a lip congenitally cleft usu. in the center of the upper one but sometimes cleft both sides of center **2 :** the deformity that a harelip exhibits

harelipped \ˈ=ˌ=\ *adj* **:** having a harelip

harelipped bat *n* **:** a large tropical American fish-eating bat (genus *Noctilio*) exhibiting marked sexual dichromatism with the males orange-rufous and the females dark brown to drab

¹ha·rem *or* **ha·ram** *also* **ha·rim** \ˈharəm, ˈher- *sometimes* ˈhär-, ˈhär-, həˈrēm\ *n* -S [Ar *ḥarīm* harem, anything forbidden or sacred & Ar *ḥaram* harem, sanctuary] **1 a :** a house or part of a house allotted to women in a Muslim household and usu. designed for maximum seclusion — called also *seraglio, zenana* **b :** the family of wives, concubines, female relatives, and servants occupying a harem **2 :** a group usu. of women associated with one man ⟨a literary lion with his ~⟩ **3 :** a Muslim sacred place (as a mosque) forbidden to non-Muslims **4 :** a group of females controlled by one male — used of polygamous animals (as the fur seal, pheasant, wild horse)

²harem \"\ *adj* **:** of a style or design resembling that associated with a Turkish harem — used esp. of a woman's dress having a full skirt with the lower edge gathered on a narrow band and then turned under

ha·rem·lik \ˈhärem,lik\ *n* -S [Turk *haremlik*, fr. *harem* (fr. Ar *ḥarīm* & Ar *ḥaram*) + *-lik* place] **:** HAREM 1a

harem slipper *n* **:** BABOUCHE

ha·ren·gi·form \həˈrenjə,fȯrm\ *adj* [*harengi-* (fr. NL *harengus* — specific epithet of the herring *Clupea harengus* —, fr. ML *harengus* herring, of Gmc origin and akin to MD *harinc, hareng* herring) + *-form* — more at HERRING] **:** having the shape of a herring

ha·ren·gu·la \həˈreŋgyələ\ *n, cap* [NL, fr. ML *harengus* herring + NL *-ula*] **:** a nearly cosmopolitan genus of small herrings (family Clupeidae)

hares *pl of* HARE, *pres 3d sing of* HARE

hare's apparatus \ˈha(a)(ə)rz-\ *n, usu cap H* [after Robert *Hare* †1858 Am. chemist] **:** an apparatus for comparing the densities of liquids in two separate vessels by means of their rise in two graduated vertical tubes immersed at their lower ends in the liquids and connected at the top by a third tube to which suction is applied

hare's-beard \ˈ=ˌ=\ *n, pl* **hare's-beards :** MULLEIN

hare's-ear \ˈ=ˌ=\ *n, pl* **hare's-ears 1 :** a European annual herb (*Bupleurum rotundifolium*) with perfoliate leaves that resemble rabbit ears and small yellowish flowers **2** *also* **hare's-ear mustard :** a glabrous annual herb (*Conringia orientalis*) having sessile entire leaves with prominent basal lobes

hare's eye *n* **:** LAGOPHTHALMOS

hare's-foot \ˈ=ˌ=\ *or* **hare's-foot clover** *n, pl* **hare's-foots** *or* **hare's-foot clovers :** RABBIT-FOOT CLOVER

hare's-foot fern *n, pl* **hare's-foot ferns 1 :** a fern (*Davallia canariensis*) of the Canary islands and Madeira having a soft gray hairy rootstock **2 :** an Australian fern (*Davallia pyxidata*) **3 :** a bristle fern (*Trichomanes boschianum*) **4 :** SERPENT FERN

hare's-foot trefoil *n, pl* **hare's-foot trefoils :** RABBIT-FOOT CLOVER

hare's-lettuce \ˈ=ˌ=\ *n, pl* **hare's-lettuces :** an annual sow thistle (*Sonchus oleraceus*)

hare's-tail \ˈ=ˌ=\ *n, pl* **hare's-tails 1 :** HARE'S-TAIL GRASS **2 :** COTTON GRASS

hare's-tail grass *n, pl* **hare's-tail grasses :** a European grass (*Lagurus ovatus*) with florets in a spike that resembles a hare's tail naturalized in California and New Zealand and used for dry bouquets

hare's-tail rush *n, pl* **hare's-tail rushes :** COTTON GRASS

hare system \ˈha(a)(ə)r- ˈhe|, |ə-\ *n* [after Thomas *Hare* †1891 Eng. political reformer] **:** a system of proportional representation that aims to achieve party representation in the closest proportion to actual voting strength by transferring votes beyond those needed to elect a candidate from him to the next indicated choice — compare LIST SYSTEM, PREFERENTIAL VOTING, SINGLE TRANSFERABLE VOTE

hare wallaby *n* **:** any of several small Australian wallabies (genus *Lagorchestes*) that resemble hares and have hairy noses

harewood \ˈ=,=\ *n* [alter. of earlier *aire-wood*, fr. obs. E *ayre*, *ayer* harewood (perh. fr. Friulian *ayar* maple tree, fr. L *acer*) + E *wood* — more at ACER] **1 :** a greenish gray figured cabinet wood obtained by chemical treatment and dyeing of sycamore maple and sometimes other maples — called also *gray harewood* **2 :** a strongly figured tropical American wood initially yellow but seasoning to silvery gray with greenish markings, obtained from a tree of the genus *Xanthoxylum*, and much used by 18th century cabinetmakers but now rarely available

har·fang \ˈhär,faŋ\ *n* -S [Sw *harfång*, lit., hare catcher, fr. *hare* (fr. OSw *hari*) + *fånga* to catch, fr. OSw *fanga*, fr. MLG *vangen;* akin to OE *hara* hare and to OHG *fāhan* to catch — more at HARE, PACT] **:** SNOWY OWL

har·grave kite \ˈhär,grāv-\ *n, usu cap H* [after Lawrence *Hargrave* †1915 Australian pioneer in aviation] **:** BOX KITE

ha·ri·a·li grass \,härēˈälē-\ *also* **ha·ri·a·la grass** \-lə-\ *n* [Hindi *hariyālī*, fr. Skt *haritālikā*] *India* **:** BERMUDA GRASS

ha·ri·a·na \,härēˈänə\ *n* [fr. *Hariana*, town in northwest India] **1** *usu cap* **:** an Indian breed of large rugged milk and draft cattle included among the Brahmans in American studbooks **2** *often cap* **:** an animal of the Hariana breed

¹har·i·cot \ˈharə,kō, -,kät, *usu* -ōd·+V\ *or* **haricot bean** *n* -S [F, perh. fr. *haricot* stew] **:** the ripe seed or the unripe pod of any of several beans of the genus *Phaseolus* (esp. *P. vulgaris*) used as a vegetable

²haricot \"\ *n* -S [F, fr. MF, prob. irreg. fr. *harigoter* to cut in pieces, fr. OF, perh. of Gmc origin; akin to OHG *heriōn* to lay waste — more at HARRY] **:** a stew esp. of mutton or lamb and vegetables

har·i·jan \ˈharə,jan\ *n* -S *often cap* [Skt *harijana* person belonging to the god Vishnu, fr. *Hari* Vishnu + *jana* person — more at KIN] **:** a member of the outcaste group in India **:** UNTOUCHABLE — used esp. by followers of Gandhi

hari-kari *var of* HARA-KIRI

harim *var of* HAREM

haring *pres part of* HARE

har·i·o·la·tion \,harēōˈlāshən\ *n* -S [L *hariolation-, hariolatio* action of prophesying, fr. *hariolatus* (past part of *hariolari* to prophesy, divine) + *-ion-, -io* -ion; prob. akin to L *haru*spex soothsayer, diviner — more at YARN] **:** the act or process of deduction **:** GUESSWORK ⟨facts as distinguished from what classical scholars call ~*s* —George Saintsbury⟩

har·i·son's yellow rose \ˈharəsənz-\ *n, usu cap H* [after Mr. *Harison*, 19th cent. Am. horticulturist] **:** a hybrid rose (*Rosa harisonii*) with yellow flowers originating as a cross between the Scotch rose and the Austrian brier

¹hark \ˈhärk, ˈhȧk\ *vb* -ED/-ING/-S [ME *herken;* akin to OFris *herkia, harkia* to listen, MD *horken, hoorken*, OHG *hōrechen*, and perh. to OHG *hōren* to hear — more at HEAR] *vt* **1** *archaic* **:** to give ear to **:** listen to ⟨~ what he himself here saith —William Beveridge⟩ **2** *Brit* **:** to urge to go ahead or to return — used with directional adverb ⟨~*ed* forward his pack of hounds —G.W.Dasent⟩ ⟨there is but one that ~*s* me back —Henry Taylor⟩ ~ *vi* **1 :** to pay close attention **:** LISTEN ⟨when . . . some far cry came faintly through the wooded hills I have seen him lift his hand and bid us ~ —Irving Bacheller⟩ — often used with *to* ⟨only natural for them to ~ to him —G.G. Black⟩ **2** *chiefly Scot* **:** WHISPER

²hark \"\ *n* -S **:** a shout of encouragement or guidance to hounds

hark back *vi* **1** *of a hunting dog* **:** to retrace a course until a scent is regained **2 a :** to turn back to an earlier topic or circumstance ⟨*hark back* . . . to a passage already quoted — Susanne K. Langer⟩ ⟨don't *hark back* to the old days unless you can be amusing about them —Agnes Rogers⟩ **b :** to go back to something as an origin or source ⟨archaisms that *hark back* to the early days of colonialism —C.J.Crowley⟩ ⟨this proposition *harks back* to Locke and Smith —*Quarterly Jour. of Economics*⟩

hark-back \ˈ=,=\ *n* -S [*hark back*] **:** a reversion or reference to something past ⟨this *hark-back* to the caveman code —Philip Gibbs⟩ ⟨*hark-backs* to the yesteryear lore of the theater —Abel Green⟩

harken *var of* HEARKEN

¹harl *or* **harle** \ˈ(h)ärl, ˈ(h)ȧl\ *vb* -ED/-ING/-S [ME *harlen* to drag] *vt* **1** *dial Brit* **:** to drag, scrape, or pull (an object) usu. along the ground **2** *chiefly Scot* **:** to plaster (a surface) with roughcast ⟨the ~*ed* walls with which for many generations the Scots had finished their houses —Ian Finlay⟩ ~ *vi, chiefly Brit* **:** to troll for fish ⟨~*ing* for spring salmon —*Atlantic*⟩

²harl *or* **harle** \ˈhȧl\ *n* -S *Brit* **:** roughcast wall facing

³harl \ˈ(h)ärl, ˈ(h)ȧl\ *vt* -ED/-ING/-S [ME *harlen* to entangle] *dial Eng* **1 :** to snarl up **:** ENTANGLE **2** *or* **harle :** to thread one leg of (a dead rabbit) through the other for ease in carrying

⁴harl \"\ *n* -S *dial Eng* **:** a tangled mass **:** SNARL

⁵harl \ˈhärl\ *n* -S [ME *herle*, prob. fr. MLG *herle, harle*] **1** *or* **harle :** a fiber in a stalk of flax or hemp **2 :** HERL

har·lan's hawk \ˈhärlənz-\ *n, usu cap 1st H* [after Richard *Harlan* †1843 Am. physician and naturalist] **:** a hawk (*Buteo harlani*) of the southern U.S. that is similar to but darker than the red-tailed hawk

har·lech \ˈhär,lek\ *adj, usu cap* [fr. *Harlech*, Wales] **:** of, relating to, or constituting a subdivision of the European Cambrian — see GEOLOGIC TIME table

har·lem blue \ˈhärləm-\ *n, usu cap H* [*Haarlem*, city in the Netherlands] **:** ANTWERP BLUE

har·lem·ite \ˈhärlə,mīt\ *n* -S *usu cap* [*Harlem*, a district of Manhattan borough, New York City + E *-ite*] **:** a native or resident of the district of Manhattan borough, New York City, north of Central Park between 8th Avenue and the East and Harlem rivers

¹har·le·quin \ˈhärlək(w)ən, ˈhäl-\ *n* -S [alter. (influenced by obs. F *harlequin*, fr. MF, fr. OIt *arlecchino*) of earlier *harlicken*, modif. of OIt *arlecchino*, fr. MF *Helquin, Hannequin, Hennequin*, leader of a troop of malevolent spirits popularly believed to fly through the air at night, fr. OF *Hellequin, Hielekin, Hierlekin*, prob. fr. (assumed) ME *Herle king* (whence ML *Herla rex*) King Herle, mythical figure who may orig. have been identical with Woden, chief god of the Germanic peoples] **1 a** *usu cap* **:** a quick-witted zany servant who is a stock character in commedia dell'arte, appears variously in European and American pantomime and ballet as a clown, a foppish simpleton, a magician, and the languishing lover of Columbine, and usu. wears a mask and parti-colored tights and carries a lath sword **b :** BUFFOON **2 :** HARLEQUIN DUCK **3 a :** a variegated pattern (as of a textile) **b :** a combination of colors in patches on a solid ground (as in the coats of some dogs) ⟨a Great Dane's handsome ~⟩

harlequin 1a

²harlequin \"\ *vt* -ED/-ING/-S **:** to make a patchwork of **:** MOTTLE ⟨his face was ~*ed* with patches of some white cream he used for his complexion —Frederick Buechner⟩

³harlequin \"\ *adj* **1 :** of a type or style inspired by or characteristic of Harlequin ⟨~ hat⟩ ⟨a ~ day, a strayed reveler from April, in glittering lozenges of blue and silver —Elinor Wylie⟩ **2 :** of variegated usu. brilliant color and pattern ⟨~ fish⟩

har·le·quin·ade \,härlək(w)əˈnād, ,häl-\ *n* -S [modif. (influenced by *harlequin*) of F *arlequinade*, fr. *arlequin* harlequin (fr. MF, fr. OIt *arlecchino*) + *-ade*] **1 a :** a play or pantomime in which the harlequin has a leading role; *esp* **:** an introductory burlesque scene dominated by a clown and a harlequin **b :** an extravaganza ballet that features a dancing clown and other figures of fantasy **2 :** a plotless comedy **:** FARCE ⟨incomparably at his best in the audacious ~ —*Atlantic*⟩ ⟨life is . . . a ~ written by a madman —H.J.Laski⟩

harlequin beetle *n* **:** a very large tropical American longicorn beetle (*Acrocinus longimanus*) having very long legs and antennae and intricately patterned red, black, and gray wing covers

harlequin bug *also* **harlequin cabbage bug** *n* **:** a black stinkbug (*Murgantia histrionica*) brilliantly marked with red, orange, and yellow that is destructive to cabbage and related plants in tropical America and the warmer parts of the U.S.

harlequin duck *n* **:** a small variegated sea duck (*Histrionicus histrionicus*) chiefly of northern No. America, Iceland, and Siberia with the male being chiefly blue with many white markings and red-brown sides

har·le·quin·ism \ˈhärlək(w)ə,nizəm\ *n* -S **:** an action or expression characteristic of a harlequin

harlequin opal *n* **:** an opal with small angular patches of brilliant color on a reddish ground

harlequin pigeon *n* **:** FLOCK PIGEON

harlequin quail *n* **1 :** a small African quail (*Coturnix delegorguei*) that frequents low-lying grassy tropical areas and is a highly regarded game and table bird **2 :** any of various chiefly tropical American quails (genus *Cyrtonyx*) having the sides of the head conspicuously patterned in black and white

harlequin snake *n* **:** CORAL SNAKE; *esp* **:** BEAD SNAKE

harlequin table *n* [prob. so called fr. a resemblance between the movable set of drawers and some of the stage machinery of the commedia dell'arte] **:** a little 18th century English table convertible into a writing desk by means of a set of drawers pulled up from the level top

harling *n* -S [fr. gerund of ¹*harl*] *Brit* **:** a method of angling for salmon in a large river by trailing a fly behind a boat while it is rowed back and forth from bank to bank

¹har·lot \ˈhärlət, ˈhäl-, *usu* -əd·+V\ *n* -S [ME *harlot, herlot*, fr. OF *herlot*] **1** *obs* **:** one of the riffraff **:** ROGUE, VAGABOND, KNAVE ⟨called him openly "beggarly ~ and cutthroat" —*Durham Depositions*⟩; *specif* **:** FORNICATOR ⟨the ~ king is quite beyond my arm —Shak.⟩ **2 :** a disreputable woman; *specif* **:** PROSTITUTE

²harlot \"\ *adj* **1 :** of or relating to a harlot ⟨~ house⟩ **2 :** not subject to control **:** FICKLE ⟨pursuing the ~ goddess Fame —W.A.White⟩

³harlot \"\ *vi* -ED/-ING/-S **:** PROSTITUTE

har·lot·ry \-lətrē, -ri\ *n* -ES [ME *harlotrie*, fr. ¹*harlot* + *-rie* -ry] **1** *obs* **:** coarse or ribald speech or action **:** OBSCENITY **2 :** PROSTITUTION **3 :** an unprincipled or immoral woman **:** BAGGAGE 4 ⟨he sups tonight with a ~ —Shak.⟩ **4 :** tawdry attractiveness **:** VULGARITY ⟨brightly rouged and painted — but without ~, with a careful art —William Sansom⟩

harls *pres 3d sing of* HARL, *pl of* HARL

¹harm \ˈhärm, ˈhȧm\ *n* -S [ME, fr. OE *hearm;* akin to OHG *harm* disgrace, injury, ON *harmr* grief, OSlav *sramŭ* shame] **1 a :** physical or mental damage **:** INJURY ⟨safety glass protects passengers from ~⟩ ⟨where the dune belt and the beach are both wide the sea did little ~ —J.A.Steers⟩ **b :** MISCHIEF, HURT, DISSERVICE ⟨his preelection declaration of independence had done him no ~ —Virginia Prewett⟩ **2 :** an act or instance of injury ⟨guess at intents and assume ~*s* —Burges Johnson⟩; *specif* **:** a material and tangible detriment or loss to a person, whether or not the law grants a remedy — distinguished from *injury* **syn** see INJURY — **out of harm's way :** in a safe place **:** remote from sources of injury ⟨a loudspeaker set high *out of harm's way* —Evelyn Waugh⟩

²harm \"\ *vt* -ED/-ING/-S [ME *harmen*, fr. OE *hearmian*, fr. *hearm*, n.] **:** to cause hurt or damage to **:** INJURE ⟨the national interest . . . was gravely ~*ed* by this attack —Elmer Davis⟩ **syn** see INJURE

³harm \"\ *adj* [¹*harm*] *South* **:** DISRESPECTFUL, UNKIND, HARMFUL ⟨never said a ~ word against your daddy —T.H.Phillips⟩

har·mal \ˈhärməl\ *or* **har·ma·la** \-lə\ *or* **har·mel** \-məl\ *n* -S [NL *harmala*, fr. Gk, perh. of Sem origin; akin to Ar *ḥarmalah* harmal] **:** an herb (*Peganum harmala*) of India and the Levant with strong-scented seeds that yield several alkaloids and are used as a vermifuge and stimulant

har·ma·line \ˈhärmə,lēn, -lən\ *n* -S [ISV *harmal* + *-ine*] **:** a crystalline alkaloid $C_{13}H_{14}N_2O$ found in harmal seeds; dihydro-harmine

har·ma·lol \-,lōl, -,lȯl\ *n* -S [ISV *harmal* + *-ol*] **:** a brown crystalline phenolic alkaloid $C_{12}H_{12}N_2O$ found in harmal seeds

har·man \ˈhärmən\ *also* **harman beck** *n* -S [origin unknown] *archaic* **:** CONSTABLE, BEADLE ⟨not the lad to betray anyone to the *harman beck* —Sir Walter Scott⟩

har·mat·tan \,härməˈtan, härˈmad·ᵊn\ *n* -S [Twi *haramata*, perh. fr. Ar *ḥarām* forbidden or evil thing; akin to Ar *ḥaram* harem] **:** a dry dust-laden wind blowing from the interior on the Atlantic coast of Africa in some seasons

harm·er \ˈhärmər\ *n* -S **:** one that harms

harm·ful \ˈhärmfəl, ˈhȧm-\ *adj* [ME, fr. ¹*harm* + *-ful*] **:** DAMAGING, TROUBLESOME, INJURIOUS ⟨~ drug⟩ ⟨~ influence⟩

harm·ful·ly \-f(ə)lē, -li\ *adv* **:** in a harmful manner

harm·ful·ness *n* -ES **:** the quality or state of being harmful

har·mine \ˈhär,mēn, -mən\ *n* -S [ISV *harmal* + *-ine*] **:** a white crystalline alkaloid $C_{13}H_{12}N_2O$ found in harmal seeds; harmalol methyl ether

harm·less \ˈhärmləs, ˈhȧm-\ *adj* [ME *harmles*, fr. ¹*harm* + *-les, -lees* -less] **1 :** free from harm **:** UNHURT **2 :** free of guilt **:** INNOCENT ⟨any child or ~ thing —W.H.Davies⟩ **3 :** free from liability or loss — often used in the phrase *to save harmless* or *to hold harmless* ⟨the company shall indemnify and save ~ each member of the committee against any and all expenses —C.M.Winslow⟩ **4 :** free of or lacking capacity or intent to injure **:** INNOCUOUS ⟨the first ball was ~ —Dorothy Sayers⟩ ⟨~ craze for the small lions of literary society —W.S.Maugham⟩ ⟨~ joke⟩

harmless error *n* **:** a trivial technical error of law not requiring in the interests of justice a reversal of a judgment or the setting aside of a verdict or a new trial

harm·less·ly *adv* **:** in a harmless manner

harm·less·ness *n* -ES **:** the quality or state of being harmless

har·mol·i·ta \härˈmäləd·ə\ *n, cap* [NL] **:** a genus of chalcid flies (family Eurytomidae) including numerous forms with larvae that feed in the stems of cereal grasses and weaken and distort them — see WHEAT JOINTWORM

har·mo·nia \härˈmōnēə, -nyə\ *n* -S [NL, fr. Gk, harmonic suture, joint — more at HARMONY] **:** HARMONIC SUTURE

harmoniacal *adj* [LL *harmoniacus* musical (fr. L *harmonia* harmony) + E *-al*] *obs* **:** HARMONIOUS

har·mo·ni·al \härˈmōnēəl\ *adj* [L *harmonia* + E *-al*] *archaic* **:** HARMONIOUS

¹har·mon·ic \(ˈ)härˈmänik, (ˈ)hȧˈ-, -nēk\ *or* **har·mon·i·cal** \-nəkəl\ *adj* [*harmonic* fr. L *harmonicus*, fr. Gk *harmonikos*, fr. *harmonia* harmony + *-ikos* -ic; *harmonical* fr. L *harmonicus* + E *-al*] **1** *archaic* **:** of or relating to music **:** MUSICAL ⟨where the ~ meetings take place —Charles Dickens⟩; *specif* **:** relating to the melody of ancient music as distinct from its rhythm **2 :** of or relating to harmony as distinguished from melody or rhythm ⟨subtleties of ~ change and tonality —Ralph Hill⟩ **3 a :** of agreeable musical consonance **:** HARMONIOUS ⟨~ chant⟩ **b :** pleasing to the ear **:** HARMONIZED ⟨great ~ orchestral effects of the older verse —J.L.Lowes⟩ **4 :** expressible in terms of sine or cosine functions — see HARMONIC PROGRESSION **5 :** of an integrated nature **:** CONGRUOUS ⟨a creative, ~, loving human being —M.F.A.Montagu⟩; *specif* **:** having the general proportions of the body in harmony with each other (as elongated face with elongated skull) **6 :** of or relating to harmonics ⟨size of the resonating cavity cannot be the only determinant of the ~ response —Robert Donington⟩; *specif* **:** sounding an octave or more higher than another organ stop of similar length ⟨~ flute⟩

²harmonic \=ˈ==\ *n* -S **1 a :** one of a series of overtones or upper partials; *esp* **:** one produced by a vibration frequency which is an integral multiple of the vibration rate producing the fundamental ⟨the ear possesses the very odd characteristic of imagining the existence of the fundamental even when it is not present, if the ~*s* are strong —Oliver Read⟩ — compare NODE 5 **b :** a flutelike tone produced on a stringed instrument (as violin or harp) by touching a vibrating string at a nodal point causing one of the vibrating sections to determine the higher pitch in the harmonic series in direct proportion to the vibration frequency of the vibrating segment — called also *flageolet tone* **2 :** a component frequency of a harmonic motion (as of an electromagnetic wave) that is an integral multiple of the fundamental frequency ⟨the second ~ has a frequency that is two times that of the fundamental⟩ ⟨if the current wave is analyzed mathematically, it is found to have a third ~ about one-third the amplitude of the fundamental 60-cycle wave —B.F.Bailey & J.S.Gault⟩ ⟨at the frequencies used for television signals, more so than on the broadcast bands, the second, third, and fourth ~*s* of the local oscillator in a superheterodyne receiver are liable to interfere with other sections of the receiver —*Television & Radar Encyc.*⟩

har·mon·i·ca \härˈmänəkə, hȧˈ-, -nēkə\ *n* -S [alter. (influenced by ¹*harmonic*) of *armonica*] **1 :** GLASS HARMONICA **2 :** an instrument of graduated strips of glass or metal struck with hammers **3 :** a small rectangular wind instrument with free metallic reeds recessed in adjacent air slots along its length from which alternate tones of the scale are sounded by exhaling and inhaling and chords or single notes are produced depending on the number of slots covered by the mouth — called also *mouth organ*

harmonica 3

har·mon·i·cal·ly \-nək(ə)lē, -nēk-, -li\ *adv* **1** *obs* **:** HARMONIOUSLY ⟨the same spirit ~ works in all believers through the world —John Flavel⟩ **2 :** in respect to relations or properties bearing some resemblance to those of musical consonances **3 :** in respect to harmony as distinguished from melody ⟨feels music melodically before he feels it ~ —Neville Cardus⟩ **4 :** in harmonic progression or division

har·mon·i·cal·ness *n* -ES **:** the quality or state of being harmonic

harmonic analysis *n* **:** the approximate expression of a periodic function known only for some values of the independent variable in a finite series of sines and cosines

harmonic analyzer *n* **:** a machine for the automatic resolution of periodic curves into the component sine curves of which they may be regarded as the resultants

harmonic close *n* **:** CADENCE 2b

harmonic conjugates *n pl* **:** the two points that divide a line segment internally and externally in the same ratio

harmonic distortion *n* **:** distortion in which harmonics of an input signal are produced in an amplifier and appear in the output along with the amplified input signal

harmonic division *n* **:** the division of a line segment at two points internally and externally in the same ratio — compare HARMONIC CONJUGATES

har·mon·i·chord \här'mänə,kȯrd\ *n* -s [F *harmonicorde,* fr. *harmonie* harmony (fr. OF *armonie*) + *-corde* -chord — more at HARMONY] **:** a keyboard instrument in which a sustained string tone is produced by the action of a rotating wooden cylinder on the strings — compare SOSTINENTE PIANOFORTE

harmonic interval *n* **:** the pitch relation between simultaneous musical tones

har·mon·i·cism \här'mänə,sizəm\ *n* -s **:** the quality or state of being harmonic

harmonic law *n* **:** the third of Kepler's laws of planetary motion

harmonic mean *n* **1 :** the reciprocal of the arithmetic mean of the reciprocals of two or more quantities **2 :** one of the terms between the first and last terms of a harmonic progression

harmonic minor scale *n* **:** a minor scale like the natural form except that the 7th tone is raised by a half step (as A-B-C-D-E-F-G♯-A)

harmonic motion *n* **:** a vibratory motion that has one frequency or amplitude (as that of a sounding violin string or swinging pendulum) or a vibratory motion that is composed of two or more such simple vibratory motions— see SIMPLE HARMONIC MOTION

har·mon·i·con \här'mänəkən, hä'-, -nēk-\ *n, pl* **harmoni·ca** \-kə\ [Gk *harmonikon,* neut. of *harmonikos* musical — more at HARMONIC] **1 :** HARMONICA **2 :** ORCHESTRION

harmonic progression *n* **:** a progression the reciprocals of whose terms form an arithmetic progression

harmonic row *or* **harmonic range** *n* **:** a set of four collinear points — compare HARMONIC CONJUGATES

har·mon·ics \här'mäniks, hä'-, -nēks\ *n pl but usu sing in constr* **:** the doctrine or science of musical sounds

harmonic sequence of vowels : VOWEL HARMONY

harmonic series *n* **1 :** the divergent series $1+\frac{1}{2}+\frac{1}{3}+\frac{1}{4}+\frac{1}{5}+\ldots$ **2 :** a series of partial tones consisting of a fundamental tone or first harmonic and all the overtones whose frequency ratio to it can be expressed in whole numbers, these harmonics usu. being consecutively numbered

C c g c′ e′ g′ ♭b′ c″d″e″f″g″
1 2 3 4 5 6 7 8 9 10 11 12

harmonic series with C as the fundamental

harmonic sign *or* **harmonic mark** *n* **:** a small circle ○ placed over a note in stringed-instrument music to indicate that it is to be played as a harmonic

harmonic stop *n* **:** a pipe-organ stop composed of pipes so constructed as to sound an octave or more higher than regular pipes of similar length

harmonic suture *n* **:** an immovable body joint formed by the contact of relatively smooth surfaces (as bones of the skull)

harmonic synthesizer *n* **:** a mechanical device (as a tide-predicting machine) that combines differing harmonics and graphs the result

harmonic theory *n* **:** a postulate in phonetics: the reinforcing vibrations produced in the superglottic cavities in vowel articulation are harmonics of the fundamental vocal-cord note — compare FORMANT, INHARMONIC THEORY

harmonies *pl of* HARMONY

har·mo·ni·ous \(ˈ)här¦mōnēəs, (ˈ)hä¦-, -nyəs\ *adj* [MF *armonieux, harmonieux,* fr. *armonie, harmonie* harmony — more at HARMONY] **1 :** musically concordant **:** agreeably consonant **2 :** having the component parts agreeably related to each other **:** CONGRUOUS ⟨~ medley of small vaulted chambers —Norman Douglas⟩ **3 :** marked by accord in sentiment or action **:** COMPATIBLE ⟨~ relationship between church and state —H.D.Hazeltine⟩ — **har·mo·ni·ous·ness** *n* -ES

har·mo·ni·ous·ly *adv* **:** in a harmonious manner **:** COMPATIBLY ⟨for such a large group of relatives to coexist ~ . . is an accomplishment —Freeman Lincoln⟩

har·mon·i·phon \här'mänə,fän\ *also* **har·mon·i·phone** \-,fōn\ *n* -s [prob. fr. F *harmoniphon,* fr. *harmonie* harmony (fr. OF *armonie*) + *-phon* (fr. Gk *phōnē* sound) — more at HARMONY, BAN] **:** an obsolete wind instrument consisting of a series of reed pipes blown with a single mouthpiece and controlled by means of a keyboard, the tone resembling that of the oboe

har·mo·nist \'härmənəst, 'hām-\ *n* -s [*harmony* + *-ist*] **1 a :** a member of a school of theorists in ancient Greece basing the principles of music on the subjective effects of tones rather than on their mathematical relations **b :** one who composes or performs music **c :** one skilled in harmony **2 :** one who shows the agreement or harmony of corresponding passages of different literary works (as the Gospels) ⟨editorial ~*s* of the Pentateuch —*Interpreter's Bible*⟩ **3 :** HARMONIZER **4** *usu cap* [*Harmony,* community in Pennsylvania + E *-ist*] **:** HARMONITE

har·mo·nis·tic \¦==¦nistik, -tēk\ *adj* **:** of, relating to, or characteristic of a harmony or harmonist ⟨~ methods⟩ — **har·mo·nis·ti·cal·ly** \-tək(ə)lē\ *adv*

har·mo·nite \'härmə,nīt\ *n* -s *usu cap* [*Harmony,* community in Pennsylvania founded in 1803 by the Harmonites + E *-ite*] **:** a member of an 18th century German communal religious sect that settled in Pennsylvania in 1803 — called also *Rappist*

har·mo·ni·um \här'mōnēəm, hä'-, -nyəm\ *n* -s [F, fr. *harmonie* harmony, fr. OF *armonie*] **:** REED ORGAN; *specif* **:** a keyboard instrument in which the tones are produced by forcing air through free metallic reeds by means of a bellows — contrasted with *American organ*

har·mo·niz·able \'härmə,nīzəbəl\ *adj* **:** capable of being brought into harmony

har·mo·ni·za·tion \,härmənə'zāshən, ,hām-, -nī-\ *n* -s **1 :** the quality or state of being in harmony ⟨style of ~⟩ **2 :** an act or instance of producing harmony ⟨has developed a wonderful faculty for ~ —Herbert Read⟩; *specif* **:** a piece of harmonized music ⟨~ for string quartet⟩

har·mo·nize \'härmə,nīz, 'hām-\ *vb* -ED/-ING/-S *see -ize in Explan Notes* [MF *harmoniser* to bring into harmony, fr. *armonie, harmonie* + *-iser* -ize] *vi* **1 :** to play or sing in harmony ⟨four small children who have been *harmonizing* in the next compartment since 6:00 a.m. —Bennett Cerf⟩ **2 a :** to be in accord **:** CORRELATE ⟨designed to ~ with normal feeding operations —W.F.Brown b.1903⟩ **b :** to become pleasingly related **:** BLEND ⟨furnishings and architecture ~ —Edgar Kaufmann⟩; *specif* **:** to unite in harmony ⟨the tenor and alto parts ~⟩ ~ *vt* **1 :** to bring into consonance **:** relate harmoniously ⟨~ the interests of his various properties —J.B. Hedges⟩ **2 :** to bring into accord **:** RECONCILE ⟨~ its practices . . . with its professed ideals —Vera M. Dean⟩ **3 :** to provide or accompany with harmony (as a melody) **syn** see AGREE

har·mo·niz·er \-zə(r)\ *n* -s **:** one that harmonizes

har·mon·o·graph \här'mänə,graf\ *n* [ISV *harmono-* (fr. Gk *harmonia* concord, harmony) + *-graph*] **:** an instrument for combining two or more vibrations usu. of two pendulums at right angles to each other and recording them in a single curve — compare LISSAJOUS FIGURE

har·mo·ny \'härmənē, 'hām-, -ni\ *n* -ES [ME *armonye,* fr. MF *armonie,* fr. OF, fr. L *harmonia,* fr. Gk, joint, concord, harmony, fr. *harmos* joint, fastening — more at ARM] **1 a** *archaic* **:** tuneful sound **:** MELODY ⟨ten thousand harps that tuned angelic *harmonies* —John Milton⟩ **b :** musicality of language ⟨tonal ~ of the poem —C.S.Kilby⟩ **2 a :** the combination of simultaneous musical notes into a chord (as a triad) **b :** the structure of a piece of music according to the composition and progression of its chords — compare MELODY, RHYTHM **c :** the science of the structure, relation, and progression of chords in homophonic composition **3 :** combination into a consistent whole **:** INTEGRATION ⟨~ of man and the machine in modern war —George Barrett⟩ **4 a :** CORRESPONDENCE, AGREEMENT, ACCORD ⟨the fullest freedom . . . comes when our desires are in ~ with those of our neighbors —A.H.Compton⟩ **b :** internal calm **:** TRANQUILLITY ⟨the moral task for man, if he is to achieve ~, is to . . . assure the supremacy of the good —Norman Kelman⟩ **5 :** a systematic arrangement of parallel literary passages (as of the Gospels) for the purpose of showing agreement or harmony **6 :** HARMONIC SUTURE **7 :** the arrangement of parts in pleasing relation to each other ⟨~ of his face —Alvin Redman⟩; *specif* **:** the orderly combination of colors resulting in an aesthetically pleasing general effect ⟨relations of contrast and ~ —John Dewey⟩ — compare COLOR BALANCE

harmony of the spheres : a doctrine promulgated by the Pythagoreans that the celestial spheres are separated by intervals corresponding to the relative lengths of strings that produce harmonious tones — compare MUSIC OF THE SPHERES

harmony of vowels : VOWEL HARMONY

har·most \'här,mäst\ *n* -s [Gk *harmostēs,* fr. *harmozein* to join together, govern; akin to Gk *harmos* joint, fastening — more at ARM] **:** a governor appointed by the Spartans over subject towns and people

har·mo·tome \'härmə,tōm\ *n* [F, fr. Gk *harmos* joint + *tomē* section, fr. *temnein* to cut; fr. its occurrence in crystalline form with an octahedron dividing parallel to the plane that passes through the terminal edges — more at TOME] **:** a mineral $(Ba,K)(Al,Si)_2Si_6O_{16}.6H_2O$ consisting of a hydrous silicate of aluminum, barium, and potassium

harms *pl of* HARM, *pres 3d sing of* HARM

¹harn \'härn\ *n* -s [ME *hernes, harnes* (pl.), of Scand origin; akin to ON *hjarni* brain; akin to OHG *hirni* brain, MD *hersene* brain, ON *hjarsi* crown of the head — more at CEREBRAL] *chiefly Scot* **:** BRAIN **:** BRAINS — usu. used in pl.

²harn \"\ *n* -s [by contr.] **:** ²HARDEN

¹har·ness \'härnəs, 'hán-\ *n* -ES *often attrib* [ME *herneis, harneis* baggage of an army or of a group of travelers, gear of a riding horse, armor, furniture, equipment, fr. OF, prob. fr. (assumed) ON *hernest* provisions for an army, fr. ON *herr* army + *nest* provisions; akin to OE *nest* food, provisions, OHG *-nest* food, *ginesan* to survive — more at HARRY, NOSTALGIA] **1 a** (1) **:** the gear or tackle other than a yoke of a draft animal (as a horse, dog, or goat) (2) **:** TACKLE, GEAR, EQUIPMENT **:** the mounting or finishing parts (as of the mechanism and gear by which a large bell is suspended and rung) **b** (1) **:** occupational surroundings **:** work routine ⟨get back into ~ after a vacation⟩ ⟨many girls . . . take on the formidable task of running in double ~, embracing both marriage and a career —Robert Reid⟩ (2) **:** close association ⟨ability to work in ~ with others —R.P.Brooks⟩ **c :** something that resembles a harness ⟨knee ~⟩ ⟨parachute ~⟩ ⟨window-washer's ~⟩ ⟨toddler on a ~⟩; *specif* **:** a prefabricated system of wiring with the necessary insulation and terminals ready to be attached (as in an ignition or lighting system) **2 :** defensive military equipment for horse or man; *specif* **:** ARMOR ⟨smote the king of Israel between the joints of the ~ —1 Kings 22:34 (AV)⟩ **3 :** clothing esp. of a specialized type ⟨a policeman's ~⟩ ⟨haven't seen her in anything but hospital ~ for a long time —L.C.Douglas⟩ **4 :** a part of the loom which holds the heddles and controls their motion and by which the warp threads are raised or depressed to form a shed — called also *leaf* — **in harness** *adv* **:** on duty ⟨constantly on call even when not *in harness*⟩ — compare *die in harness* at ¹DIE

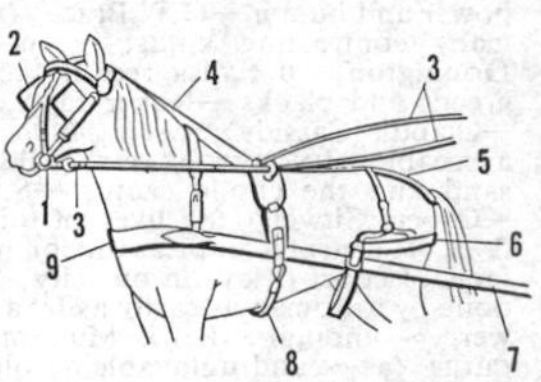

harness: *1* bit, *2* blinder, *3, 3* reins, *4* checkrein, *5* crupper, *6* breeching, *7* trace, *8* bellyband or girth, *9* breast collar

²harness \"\ *vt* -ED/-ING/-ES [ME *herneisen, harneisen,* fr. *herneis, harneis,* n.] **1** *archaic* **:** to dress or equip for battle **:** ARM ⟨~ yourselves for the war —John Bunyan⟩ **2 a :** to put a harness on ⟨~ a horse⟩ **b :** to attach by means of a harness ⟨the yellow wagon ~*ed* to . . . two stout grays —Ellen Glasgow⟩ **c :** to tie together **:** YOKE ⟨must ~ his mechanical apparatus to his creative mind —Andrew Buchanan⟩ **3 :** to put to work **:** UTILIZE ⟨~ the atom for constructive purposes —*Mech. Engineering*⟩ ⟨~ words to convey ideas —*advt*⟩ ⟨they who have ~*ed* contemporary social forces —W.H.Whyte⟩ ⟨*harnessing* the limitless power of the sun —*advt*⟩

harness bull *or* **harness cop** *n, slang* **:** a uniformed policeman ⟨the *harness bulls* just stood at attention —Mickey Spillane⟩

harness cask *n* **:** a tub on shipboard for storing or soaking salt meat preparatory to use

harnessed antelope *n* [*harnessed* fr. past part. of ²*harness*] **:** any of several antelopes of the genus *Tragelaphus* having striped markings that resemble a harness — see BUSHBUCK, GUIB

har·ness·er \-sə(r)\ *n* -s **:** one that harnesses

harness hitch *n* **:** MAN-HARNESS KNOT

harness horse *n* **1 :** a horse for racing in harness — compare PACER, TROTTER **2 :** DRAFT HORSE — distinguished from *saddle horse*

harness leather *n* **:** a strong pliable oil-finished leather made from cattle hides

harness plate *n* **:** electroplated hardware used on harness

harness race *n* **:** a trotting or pacing race between Standard-bred horses harnessed to 2-wheeled sulkies

harn·pan \'härn,pan\ *n* [ME *hernepanne, harnepanne,* fr. *herne-, harne-* (fr. *hernes, harnes* brains) + *panne* pan — more at HARN, PAN] *chiefly Scot* **:** casing for the brain **:** SKULL

harns *pl of* HARN

haro *var of* HARROW

ha·ro·seth *or* **ha·ro·set** *or* **ha·ro·ses** \hə'rōs(h)əth, -ət, -əs\ *or* **cha·ro·sety** *or* **cha·ro·set** *or* **cha·ro·ses** \kə'-\ *n pl but usu sing in constr* [Heb *ḥaroseth, ḥaroset,* fr. *ḥarsith, ḥarsit* clay or earthen pot] **:** a pastelike mixture of apples, nuts, cinnamon, and wine used during the seder meal on the Passover and symbolic of the clay from which the Israelites made bricks during their Egyptian slavery

¹harp \'härp, 'háp\ *n* -s [ME *harpe,* fr. OE *hearpe;* akin to OHG *harpha* harp, ON *harpa* harp, Gk *karphos* dry stalk, stick, Russ *korobit'* to bend, warp, and prob. to L *curvus* curved — more at CROWN] **1 a :** a musical instrument (as the clarsach, lyre) of ancient origin with strings set usu. in an open frame and plucked with the fingers **b :** an orchestral instrument with a triangular frame consisting of a large, hollow, and tapering back which is the sounding board, a vertical pillar, a curved neck to which the strings are attached by wrest pins, a base or pedestal equipped with seven pedals each of which when depressed one notch raises all strings of the same letter names one half step and when depressed two notches raises them a whole step, having usu. 46 strings tuned diatonically in C-flat major with a compass of 6½ octaves above C flat and with all C and F strings colored for ease of recognition **c :** JEW'S HARP **1 d :** HARMONICA **e :** a percussion pipe-organ stop of metal or wooden bars with resonators sounded by electric hammer action **2 :** HARPER 2 **3 :** something that resembles a harp: as **a :** a forked fitting for holding a trolley wheel or shoe in contact with a power-supplying wire or cable **b :** a many-stringed implement used in cutting the curd of Swiss cheese **c :** a metal hoop or arch that supports a lampshade **4 :** HARP SEAL **5** *often cap* **:** a person of Irish birth or descent — often taken to be offensive

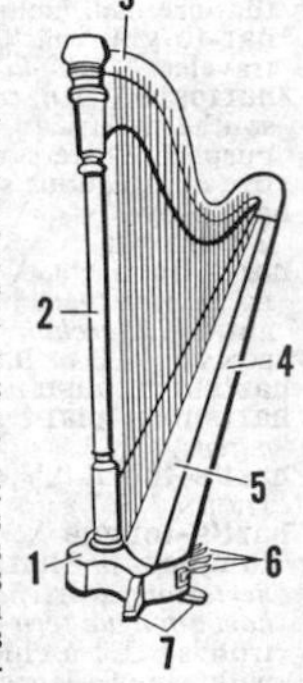

modern harp 1b: *1* base, *2* pillar, *3* neck, *4* body, *5* sound board, *6* pedals, *7* feet

²harp \"\ *vb* -ED/-ING/-S [ME *harpen,* fr. OE *hearpian,* fr. *hearpe,* n.] *vi* **1 :** to play on a harp **2 :** to dwell on a subject **:** repeat a theme with tiresome frequency ⟨continues to ~ on higher wages and shorter hours —G.W.Johnson⟩ ⟨if I seem to be ~*ing* away at the value of variety —Alistair Cooke⟩ **3** *obs* **:** to form an opinion on insufficient evidence **:** GUESS ⟨only to ~ at the matter —John Cotgrave⟩ **4 :** to make a sound like a harp ⟨hear the wind ~ —E.J.Schoettle⟩ ~ *vt* **1** *obs* **:** to play on or recite to the accompaniment of a harp ⟨a tale . . . ~*ed* in hall and bower —Thomas Warton⟩ **2** *archaic* **:** to attract or compel by playing sweetly on the harp ⟨could ~ his wife up out of hell —Alfred Tennyson⟩ **3** *archaic* **:** to discuss or refer to repeatedly and tediously **4** *archaic* **:** to guess at or give expression to ⟨thou hast ~*ed* my fear aright —Shak.⟩ **5 :** to cut and mix curd of (Swiss cheese) with a harp

har·pa \'härpə\ *n, cap* [NL, fr. LL, harp, of Gmc origin; akin to OE *hearpe* harp] **:** the sole genus of the Harpidae

har·pac·toph·a·gous \,här(,)pak¦täfəgəs\ *adj* [*harpacto-* (fr. Gk *harpaktos* stolen, got by plundering, fr. *harpazein* to snatch, seize) + *-phagous;* akin to Gk *harpagē* hook, rake — more at ASSART] **:** PREDATORY — used esp. of insects

har·pa·go \'härpə,gō\ *n, pl* **harpago·nes** \,härpə'gō,nēz\ [NL *harpagon-, harpago,* fr. L, grappling iron, irreg. fr. Gk *harpagē* hook, rake] **:** an element of the male copulatory apparatus of many insects that forms part of a clasper; *esp* **:** a modified stylus of the ninth segment forming one lateral half of a clasper — usu. used in pl.

har·pa·goph·y·tum \,härpə'gäfəd·əm\ *n, cap* [NL, fr. L *harpago* grappling hook + Gk *phyton* plant — more at PHYT-] **:** a small genus of southern African herbs (family Pedaliaceae) including the grapple plant

har·pa·gor·nis \,härpə'gȯrnəs\ *n, cap* [NL, fr. Gk *harpag-, harpax* rapacious + NL *-ornis;* akin to Gk *harpagē* hook, rake] **:** a genus of extinct birds (family Accipitridae) much larger than any existing eagle and found in the Pleistocene of New Zealand

harp·er \'härpər, 'hápə(r\ *n* -s [ME, fr. OE *hearpere,* fr. *hearpe* harp + *-ere* -er] **1 :** one that plays on a harp **2 :** any of several Irish coins of the 16th and 17th centuries having a harp on one side; *esp* **:** a silver shilling piece worth nine English pence — called also *harp shilling* **3 :** TOAD CRAB

har·pes \'här,pēz\ *n pl* [NL *harpe* (sing.), fr. Gk *harpē* sickle; akin to Gk *harpagē* hook, rake] **:** the claspers of a male moth or butterfly

harp guitar *or* **harp lute** *n* **:** a large guitar with triangular body and two extra bass strings — compare DITAL HARP

har·pi·dae \'härpə,dē\ *n pl, cap* [NL, fr. *Harpa* + *-idae*] **:** a family of tropical marine gastropod mollusks (suborder Stenoglossa) comprising the harp shells — see HARPA

harpies *pl of* HARPY

harp·in \'härpən\ *also* **harp·ing** \-piŋ\ *n* -s [prob. fr. ¹*harp* + *-ing*] **1** *archaic* **:** a wale around a ship's bow stouter than the rest of the strakes **2 :** one of the timbers used during construction of a ship to regulate and hold in place the cant frames

harping iron *or* **harping spear** *n* [*harping* prob. fr. MF *harper* to grapple, grasp + E *-ing*] *archaic* **:** HARPOON

harping johnny *n, usu cap J* [*harping* prob. fr. pres. part. of ²*harp*] **:** ORPINE

harp·ist \'härpəst, 'háp-\ *n* -s **:** a harp player

harp·less \-pləs\ *adj* **:** lacking a harp

¹har·poon \här'pün, hä'-\ *n* -s [prob. fr. D *harpoen,* fr. MD, fr. OF *harpon* brooch, fr. *harper* to grapple, grasp, prob. of Scand origin; akin to Icel *harpa* to pinch, squeeze together; prob. akin to ON *harpa* harp, OE *hearpe* — more at HARP] **1 :** a throwing weapon used in hunting large fish and sea animals; *specif* **:** a barbed whaling spear thrown by hand or shot from a gun that has a flat triangular head usu. detachable and sharpened at both edges, a long shaft, and a strong line for making the whale fast to the pursuing boat — compare TOGGLE IRON **2 :** a medical instrument with a barbed head used for removing bits of living tissue for examination

²harpoon \"\ *vt* -ED/-ING/-S **:** to strike or capture with or as if with a harpoon ⟨~ a whale⟩ ⟨~ an olive⟩

har·poon·er \-nə(r)\ *also* **har·poon·eer** \,här(,)pü¦ni(ə)r\ *n* -s [¹*harpoon* + *-er* or *-eer*] **:** one that throws or fires a harpoon **:** BOATSTEERER

harpoon fork *n* **:** a fork for loading and unloading hay **:** HAYFORK

harpoon gun *n* **:** a machine for hurling a harpoon

harpoon line *n* **:** a light strong manila rope with a flexible lay now used principally for purse lines

harpoon log *n* **:** a log consisting of a rotator and a distance-registering device combined in a cylindrical case and towed astern — compare TAFFRAIL LOG

harpoon oar *n* **:** a forward oar pulled by the harpooner as a whaling ship approaches a whale

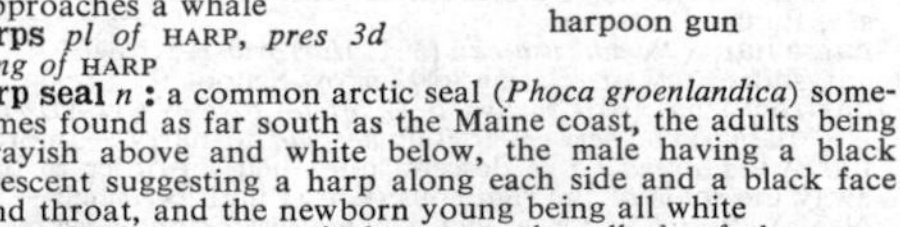
harpoon gun

harps *pl of* HARP, *pres 3d sing of* HARP

harp seal *n* **:** a common arctic seal (*Phoca groenlandica*) sometimes found as far south as the Maine coast, the adults being grayish above and white below, the male having a black crescent suggesting a harp along each side and a black face and throat, and the newborn young being all white

harp shell *n* **:** a tropical gastropod mollusk of the genus *Harpa* having a large variegated shell with prominent ribs

harp shilling *n* **:** HARPER

harpsical *also* **harpsicall** *n* -s [by alter.] *n, obs* **:** HARPSICHORD

harpsichon *also* **harpsicon** *n* -s [by alter.] *n, obs* **:** HARPSICHORD

harp·si·chord \'härpsə,kȯrd, 'hápsə,kō(ə)d\ *n* -s [modif. of It *arpicordo,* fr. *arpi-* (fr. *arpa* harp, fr. LL *harpa*) + *-cordo* (fr. *corda* cord, string, fr. L *chorda* cord) — more at HARPA, CORD] **:** a wire-stringed musical instrument resembling in shape the grand piano, usu. having two keyboards with one to four strings for each key and seven stops or pedals, and producing its tones by the plucking of its strings with quills or leather points set in jacks operated from the keyboards and capable of gradation of tone only by alternating the stops or keyboards

harpsichord

harp·si·chord·ist \-dəst\ *n* -s **:** one who plays the harpsichord

harp turtle *n* **:** LEATHERBACK

har·pu·la \'härpyələ\ *n* -s [native name in Bengal] **:** a fast-growing tree (*Harpullia cupanioides*) of India and the East Indies that yields a wood used esp. for building

har·pul·lia \här'pəlēə\ *n* [NL, fr. native name in Bengal] **1** *cap* **:** a genus of tropical Asiatic and African trees (family Sapindaceae) having pinnate leaves, panicles of greenish flowers and red or orange fruit **2** -s **:** any tree of the genus *Harpullia*

harpway tuning \'=,=-\ *n* [*harpway* fr. ¹*harp* + *way*] **:** a tuning of a viol (as in fifths and fourths: A-E-A-E-A-D) to facilitate arpeggio playing

har·py \'härpē, 'háp-, -pi\ *n* -ES [L *Harpyia,* fr. Gk] **1 :** a predatory monster in chiefly classical mythology represented as having a woman's head and the body and claws of a vulture and as being an instrument of divine vengeance **2 a :** a predatory person **:** LEECH, SWINDLER ⟨homesteaders had managed to escape other *harpies* — such as land agents offering to hurry claims through —Dixon Wecter⟩ **b :** a shrewish or depraved woman ⟨gin shops . . . crowded by day as well as by night with screaming *harpies* —Kenneth Roberts⟩

harpy bat *also* **harpy** *n* -ES **1 :** any of various East Indian fruit bats having prominent tubular nostrils and constituting the genus *Nyctimene* **2 :** an East Indian insectivorous bat (*Harpiocephalus harpia*)

harpy eagle *also* **harpy** *n* -ES **:** either of two large eagles: **a :** a largely black-and-white eagle (*Harpia harpyja*) having a double crest on the head and remarkably strong bill and claws, found in northern So. and Central America where it is believed to prey on large forest birds and various mammals **b :** a rare eagle (*Pithecophaga jefferyi*) of the Philippines held to live chiefly on monkeys

har·que·bus *or* **ar·que·bus** \'(h)ärk(w)əbəs, '(h)åk-\ *n* -ES [MF *harquebuse, arquebuse*, modif. of MD *hakebusse*, fr. *hake* hook + *busse* box, tube, gun, fr. LL *buxis* box; akin to MD *hoec* corner — more at HOOK, BOX] **1 :** a portable but heavy matchlock gun invented about the middle of the 15th century and fired from a support to which it was attached by a fixed hook, later wheel-lock or flintlock modifications being lightened and provided with a bent stock and a longer butt so that they could be fired from the shoulder **2 harquebuses** *pl, obs* **:** soldiers armed with the harquebus

har·que·bus·ade \,==bə'sād\ *n* -S [MF, fr. *harquebuse* + *-ade*] **1** *obs* **:** a shot from a harquebus **2** *archaic* **:** a volley from harquebuses

har·que·bus·ier *or* **ar·que·bus·ier** \-'si(ə)r, -'siə\ *n* -S [MF, fr. *harquebuse, arquebuse* + *-ier* -er] **:** a soldier armed with a harquebus or sometimes with a musket or other gun ⟨at the head of a company of ~*s* —Frank Yerby⟩

harr \'(h)är\ *n* -S [ME *herre, harre*, fr. OE *heorra;* akin to ON *hjarri* hinge and perh. to L *cardin-, cardo* hinge — more at CARDINAL] **1** *obs* **:** a gate or door hinge **2** *now dial Eng* **:** an upright to which hinges are fastened and from which a door or gate swings

har·ras \'harəs\ *n* -ES [ME *haras* herd of stud horses, enclosure for a herd of stud horses, fr. OF *haras, haraz*] **:** a herd of stud horses

har·ra·teen *or* **har·a·teen** \'harə,tēn\ *n* -S [origin unknown] **:** an English fabric of linen or wool used chiefly for curtains and bed hangings in the 18th and early 19th centuries

harratin *usu cap, var of* HARATIN

harri *usu cap, var of* HURRI

har·ri·cane \'harə,kān\ *dial var of* HURRICANE

har·ri·dan \'harədən *also* 'her-, -dᵊn\ *n* -S [perh. modif. of F *haridelle* worn-out horse, tall lean ugly woman] **:** a haggard old woman **:** HAG; *esp* **:** a worn-out strumpet

harried *adj* [fr. past part. of 1*harry*] **:** beset by disturbing problems or anxieties **:** HARASSED ⟨as ~ as innkeepers coping with a full house —Mary McGrory⟩ ⟨a rather ~ journalist trying to produce a maximum of copy —Edmund Wilson⟩

1har·ri·er \'harēə(r), -riə- *also* 'her-\ *n* -S [irreg. fr. 1*hare* + *-ier*] **1 :** a hunting dog from 19 to 21 inches high resembling a small foxhound and used for hunting rabbits and other small game **2 :** a runner on a cross-country team

2harrier \"\ *n* -S [1*harry* + *-er*] **1 :** one that harries **2** [alter. (influenced by 1*harry*) of earlier *harrower*, fr. 1*harrow* + *-er*] **:** any of various slender hawks with long angled wings and long legs that constitute a genus (*Circus*), feed chiefly on small mammals, reptiles, and insects which they hunt by flying low over open ground, and usu. nest on the ground — see HEN HARRIER, MARSH HARRIER, MARSH HAWK

harrier eagle *n* **:** any of numerous rather large Old World hawks constituting a genus (*Circaetus*) and intermediate in some respects between typical hawks and typical eagles — called also *short-toed eagle*

harries *pres 3d sing of* HARRY, *pl of* HARRY

har·ring·ton \'hariŋtən\ *n* -S *usu cap* [after John, 1st Baron *Harington* of Exton †1613 Eng. nobleman who coined such tokens under a patent granted by James I] **:** a copper token worth a farthing in 17th century England

har·ris buck \'harəs-\ *n, usu cap H* [after Sir William C. *Harris* †1848 Eng. traveler] **:** SABLE ANTELOPE

har·ris·burg \'harəs,bərg, -,bəg *also* 'her-\ *adj, usu cap* [fr. *Harrisburg*, capital of Pennsylvania] **:** of or from Harrisburg, the capital of Pennsylvania ⟨*Harrisburg* residents⟩ **:** of the kind or style prevalent in Harrisburg

har·ris·ia \hə'risēə\ *n, cap* [NL, fr. William *Harris*, Jamaican botanist + NL *-ia*] **:** a genus of slender spiny tropical American cacti with solitary showy white or pink flowers

har·ri·son red \'harəsᵊn-\ *n, often cap H* [perh. after Birge *Harrison* †1929 Am. landscape painter] **:** CHINESE VERMILION

harris's hawk *or* **harris hawk** *n, usu cap 1st H* [after Edward *Harris* †1863 Am. naturalist] **:** a common hawk (*Parabuteo unicinctus harrisi*) of the deserts and prairies of southwestern U.S., Mexico, and Central America chiefly dark brown with conspicuous white markings on the tail

harris's sparrow *n, usu cap H* **:** a widely distributed No. American sparrow (*Zonotrichia querula*) largely dusky brown above and white below with a black cap and black bib prolonged into a median streak on the breast

harris's woodpecker *n, usu cap H* **:** a hairy woodpecker (*Dendrocopos villosus harrisi*) occurring along the Pacific coast from British Columbia to northern California

Harris Tweed *trademark* — used for a tweed made of Scottish wool spun, dyed, and handwoven in the Outer Hebrides

1har·ro·vi·an \hə'rōvēən\ *n* -S *usu cap* [NL *Harrovia* Harrow + E *-an*, n. suffix] **:** a student of Harrow School in Middlesex, England

2harrovian \"\ *adj, usu cap* [NL *Harrovia* Harrow + E *-an*, adj. suffix] **:** of or relating to Harrow School

1har·row \'ha(,)rō, -,rə *also* 'he(-, *often* -,rəw+V\ *vt* -ED/-ING/-S [ME *harwen, herwen*, fr. OE *hergian* to harry — more at HARRY] **1** *archaic* **:** to descend into (hell) in order to bring away the souls of the righteous ⟨Christ hath ~*ed* hell —J.M. Neale⟩ **2** *archaic* **:** ROB, PILLAGE, PLUNDER ⟨long ~*ed* by oppressor's hand —Sir Walter Scott⟩

2harrow \"\ *n* -S *often attrib* [ME *harwe;* perh. akin to OSw *harf* harrow, Gk *keirein* to cut — more at SHEAR] **1 :** a cultivating implement used primarily for pulverizing or smoothing the soil and sometimes for mulching, covering seed, or removing weeds — compare BOG HARROW, BRUSH HARROW, DISC HARROW, DRAG 1d **2 a :** an implement that resembles a harrow; *specif:* a toothed framework drawn over an oyster bed to clear it of seaweed **b :** a formation that resembles a harrow — **under the harrow** *adv* **:** under constant threat of penalty or suffering ⟨every manifestation of initiative in the educated public was kept *under the harrow* —Bernard Pares⟩

3harrow \"\ *vt* -ED/-ING/-S [ME *harwen, harowen*, fr. *harwe*, n.] **1 a :** to cultivate with a harrow ⟨plowed and ~*ed* and laid his rows —Russell Lord⟩ **b :** to cultivate as if with a harrow ⟨~*ed* the ground for literature —Van Wyck Brooks⟩ **2 a :** to cut into as if with a harrow ⟨the whole thing looked ~*ed* in the pigment, rather than painted —F.J.Mather⟩ **b** *archaic* **:** to wound or tear physically **:** LACERATE ⟨~*ing* his cheeks with a few scratches —William Beckford⟩ **3 :** to cause distress or suffering to **:** AGONIZE ⟨has not set out to appall the reader with horrors nor to ~ him with miseries —Douglas Stewart⟩

4har·row *or* **haro** \'ha(,)rō, hə'rō\ *interj* [ME *harrow, harow*, fr. MF *haro, harou*, fr. OF, prob. of Gmc origin; akin to OHG *hara* hither; akin to OE *hēr* here, OHG *hier* — more at HERE] — used to express alarm or distress

5har·row \'ha(,)rō\ *adj, usu cap* [fr. *Harrow* on the Hill, urban district, Middlesex, England] **:** of or from the urban district of Harrow on the Hill, England **:** of the kind or style prevalent in Harrow on the Hill

har·row·er \'harəwə(r), *also* 'her-\ *n* -S [ME *haroer, harower*, fr. *harwen, harowen* to cultivate with a harrow + *-er*] **:** one that harrows

harrowing *adj* [fr. pres. part. of 3*harrow*] **:** acutely distressing or painful **:** AGONIZING ⟨~ tales of unfortunates who had lost limbs or had been frozen to death —V.G.Heiser⟩ — **har·row·ing·ly** *adv*

harrow-plow \'=(,)=,=\ *n* [2*harrow*] **:** ONE-WAY DISC PLOW

harrs *pl of* HARR

har·rumph \hə'rəm(p)f\ *vi* -ED/-ING/-S [imit.] **1 :** to make a pompous throat-clearing sound ⟨several students chuckled and one or two professorial alumni good-naturedly ~*ed* —W.H.Nelson⟩ **2 :** to comment disapprovingly **:** PROTEST ⟨the state department ~*ed* and . . . oil companies stood on their legal, unenforceable rights —*Time*⟩

1har·ry \'harē, -ri *also* 'her-\ *vb* -ED/-ING/-ES [ME *harien, herien*, fr. OE *hergian;* akin to OHG *heriōn* to lay waste, ON *herja;* denominative fr. the noun represented by OE *here* army, OHG *heri*, ON *herr* army, Goth *harjis* host; akin to Gk *koiranos* commander, OPer *kāra* army] *vi* **:** to attack and loot **:** RAID ⟨had *harried* widely and laid siege to Paris —Charlton Laird⟩ ~ *vt* **1 a :** ASSAULT, DEVASTATE, RAVAGE ⟨ordered his troops to ~ the town⟩ ⟨shabby trees *harried* by fire —G.R. Stewart⟩ **b** *chiefly Scot* **:** to engage in robbing or plundering ⟨shame lassie for ~*ing* birds' nests —J.M.Barrie⟩ **2 a :** ATTACK ⟨~ a person⟩ ⟨the cat reached out a big fat paw and *harried* the boy —Erskine Caldwell⟩ **b :** to force (a person) to move along ⟨saga of migratory laborers *harried* across the continent —J.D.Hart⟩ **3** *now dial Brit* **:** to drag off as plunder — usu. used with *off* or *out* ⟨the devil came and *harried* off his soul —Emily Brontë⟩ **4 a :** to keep under constant attack or threat of attack **:** HARASS ⟨*harried* by guerrillas and occasionally invaded by organized forces —T.M.Spaulding⟩ **b :** to goad by constant demands or annoyances **:** TORMENT ⟨three renegade boys who came to ~ a couple of farm women —James Kelly⟩ ⟨*harries* the doctor by telephone —Mary B. Spahr⟩ **syn** see WORRY

2harry \"\ *n* -ES **1 :** harrying action ⟨teased and broken by the ~ of the following gale —J.D.Beresford⟩ **2 :** VEXATION ⟨cut off from the hurries and *harries* of the daily world —Roger Angell⟩

1harsh \'härsh, 'håsh\ *adj* -ER/-EST [alter. of earlier *harsk*, fr. ME, of Scand origin; akin to Norw *harsk* rancid, harsh, Sw *härsk* rancid; akin to MLG *harsch* rough, and prob. to L *carrere* to card — more at CHARD] **1 :** having a coarse or uneven surface **:** rough to the touch **:** SHAGGY ⟨a small terrier with a ~ dense coat —*Dict. of Sports*⟩ ⟨granite stones ~ with lichen —Nancy Hale⟩; *specif* **:** difficult to manipulate and finish because of too many large particles of aggregate in proportion to the amount of fine particles ⟨~ mortar⟩ ⟨~ concrete⟩ **2 a :** disagreeable to taste or smell **:** RAW, ACRID, IRRITATING ⟨the cognac was ~ —Winifred Bambrick⟩ ⟨a very irritating, pungent, ~ smoke —W.W.Garver⟩ **b :** disagreeable to the ear **:** GRATING, STRIDENT, JARRING ⟨her ~ voice was full of power and humor —G.W.Brace⟩ ⟨music . . . requires sounds of many contrasting kinds: ~ as well as mellow —Robert Donington⟩ **c :** disagreeable to the eye **:** STARK ⟨~ dull greens and blacks —Roger Fry⟩ ⟨a ~, almost a violent, face —Claudia Cassidy⟩; *specif, photog* **:** HARD **d :** physically disagreeable **:** UNCOMFORTABLE ⟨wild and ~ country, full of hot sand and the cholla cactus —S.H.Adams⟩ ⟨~ north wind —Osbert Sitwell⟩ ⟨~ lives of toil in sweatshops and mines⟩ **3 a :** sharply unpleasant or rigorous **:** STERN ⟨the ~ facts of court delays in our city —S.H.Hofstadter⟩ ⟨could be done by a woman as easily as by a man . . . provided discipline were ~ enough —Lewis Mumford⟩ **b :** SEVERE, EXACTING, CRUEL ⟨as ~ and unlovable an old tyrant as one could well imagine —*Sat. Eve. Post*⟩ **4 :** lacking in aesthetic grace or refinement **:** CRUDE ⟨a ~ and sometimes unpleasant book, barren of pretty touches —Brendan Gill⟩ **syn** see ROUGH

2harsh \"\ *adv* **:** HARSHLY ⟨with *harsh*-resounding trumpets' dreadful bray —Shak.⟩

harsh·en \-shən\ *vb* -ED/-ING/-S *vt* **:** to make harsh ⟨a great gravity that ~*ed* his soft voice —*Scribner's*⟩ ~ *vi* **:** to become harsh ⟨saw the grain of his skin ~*ing* over face bones —Elizabeth Bowen⟩

harsh-furred hare \'=,=-\ *n* **:** a small hare (*Caprolagus hispidus* or *Lepus hispidus*) of the eastern Himalayan foothills with a massive skull, short ears, and a dull dark coat in which whitish bristly hairs are mingled

harsh·ly *adv* **:** in a harsh manner: **a :** coarsely to the touch **:** ROUGHLY ⟨rubbed herself ~ with a towel —I.V.Morris⟩ **b :** offensively to the senses **:** DISAGREEABLY ⟨houses on the far side, ~ white in this straight hard glare —Thomas Wood †1950⟩ **c :** unfeelingly to the sensibilities **:** RIGOROUSLY, CRUELLY ⟨~ limits the freedom of the creative imagination —Philip Toynbee⟩ ⟨he was made prisoner and ~ treated —E.M.Coulter⟩ **d :** ungracefully by aesthetic standards **:** CRUDELY ⟨a number of his canvases are slightly repellent — notably one of a ~ drawn, bedraggled mother and child —R.M.Coates⟩

harsh·ness *n* -ES [alter. of earlier *harsknes*, fr. ME, fr. *harsk* harsh + *-nes* -ness] **:** the quality or state of being harsh

hars·let \'härslət\ *dial var of* HASLET

hars·tig·ite \'härstə,gīt\ *n* -S [Sw *harstigit*, fr. *Harstig* mine, Sweden + Sw *-it* -ite] **:** a mineral $Be_2Ca_3Si_3O_{11}$ consisting of a silicate of beryllium and calcium (hardness 5.5, sp. gr. 3.05)

hart \'härt, 'håt, *usu* -d·+V\ *n, pl* **harts** *also* **hart** [ME *hert*, fr. OE *heort, heorot;* akin to OHG *hiruz* hart, ON *hjörtr*, L *cervus* hart, stag, Gk *keras* horn — more at HORN] *chiefly Brit* **:** the male of the red deer esp. over five years old **:** STAG — compare HIND

har·tal \här'täl\ *n* -S [Hindi *haṛtāl*, fr. *hāṭ* shop + *tālā* lock] **:** concerted cessation of work and business esp. as a protest against a political situation or an act of government — compare NONCOOPERATION

har·te·beest \'här|d·ə,bēst, 'hå|, |tə,-, |t,-\ *n, pl* **hartebeests** *also* **hartebeest** [obs. Afrik (now *hartbees*), fr. D *hartebeest*, *hertebeest* deer, fr. *hart, hert* deer, stag (fr. MD *hert*) + *beest* beast, fr. MD *beeste, beest*, fr. OF *beste;* akin to OE *heort*, *heorot* hart — more at HART, BEAST] **1 :** a large nearly exterminated African antelope (*Alcelaphus caama*) that is grayish brown in color with a yellow patch on the buttocks, black markings on the face, and ringed divergent horns bent back at the tips — compare SASSABY **2 :** any of several other African antelopes of the genus *Alcelaphus* — compare NORTHERN HARTEBEEST

hart·ford \'härtfərd, 'håtfəd\ *adj, usu cap* [fr. *Hartford*, capital of Connecticut] **:** of or from Hartford, the capital of Connecticut ⟨*Hartford* insurance companies⟩ **:** of the kind or style prevalent in Hartford

hartford fern *n, usu cap H* **:** CLIMBING FERN

hart·ford·ite \-,dīt\ *n* -S *cap* **:** a native or resident of Hartford, Connecticut

hart·ite \'härd·,īt\ *n* -S [G *hartit*, fr. *Oberhart*, Austria + G *-it* -ite] **:** a white fossil resin perhaps $C_{19}H_{32}$ occurring in peat beds

hart·le·ian *also* **hart·ley·an** \'härtlēən, ='==\ *adj, usu cap* [David *Hartley* †1757 Eng. philosopher, founder of the doctrine of associationism + E *-an*] **:** of or relating to the doctrine of associationism or its founder

hart·man·nia \härt'manēə\ *n, cap* [NL, fr. Emanuel *Hartmann*, 19th cent. Am. botanist + NL *-ia*] *in some classifications* **:** a small genus of American herbs (family Onagraceae) with alternate leaves and showy flowers in spikes or racemes that are usu. included in the genus *Oenothera*

1har·to·gia \här'tōjēə\ [NL, fr. J. *Hartog*, 18th cent. Du. traveler + NL *-ia*] *syn of* AGATHOSMA

2hartogia \"\ *n, cap* [NL, fr. J. *Hartog* + NL *-ia*] **:** a genus of southern African plants (family Rutaceae) having white or purplish flowers with long-clawed petals, five stamens, and five conspicuous staminodia

hart's-eye \'=,=\ *n, pl* **hart's-eyes** **1 :** CRETAN DITTANY **2 :** PARSNIP

harts·horn \'=,=\ *n* -S [ME *hertes horn*, fr. OE *heortes horn*, fr. *heortes* (gen. of *heort* hart) + *horn*] **1 :** a hart's horn or antler **2** *archaic* **a :** AMMONIA WATER **b :** AMMONIUM CARBONATE c **3** *or* **hartshorn plantain :** BUCKHORN 3b(1)

hartshorn bush *n* **:** ROYAL FERN

hartshorn plant *n* **:** an American pasqueflower (*Anemone patens*)

hart's-thorn \'=,=\ *n, pl* **hart's-thorns :** COMMON BUCKTHORN

hart's-tongue \'=,=\ *or* **hart's-tongue fern** *n, pl* **hart's-tongues** *or* **hart's-tongue ferns** [*hart's-tongue* fr. ME *hertestonge*, fr. *hertes* (gen. of *hert* hart) + *tonge* tongue; *hart's-tongue fern* fr. *hart's-tongue* + *fern;* fr. the shape of the fronds] **1 :** a chiefly Eurasian fern (*Phyllitis scolopendrium*) with simple lanceolate fronds often auriculate at the base **2 :** a tropical American fern (*Polybotria cervina*) of the family Polypodiaceae **3 :** STRAP FERN

hart's truffle *n* **:** an ascomycetous fungus of the genus *Elaphomyces* that resembles a puffball — compare LYCOPERDON NUT

1har·um-scar·um \|harəm|skarəm, *also* |herəm|skerəm\ *adv* (*or adj*) [perh. alter. (perh. influenced by 1*hare*) of 1*helter-skelter*] **:** in a rash or heedless way **:** RECKLESSLY ⟨trucks whizzing *harum-scarum* along clay streets —Allan Ashbolt⟩ ⟨dashing *harum-scarum* from one rooftop to another⟩

2harum-scarum \"\ *n* -S **:** one that is rash or heedless **:** SCATTERBRAIN ⟨do you really expect those wild young *harum-scarums* to live up to their oath —S.H.Adams⟩ — **har·um-scar·um·ness** *n* -ES

ha·rus·pex *or* **arus·pex** \(h)ə'rə,speks, '(h)ar-\ *n, pl* **ha·ruspi·ces** *or* **aruspi·ces** \-'rəspə,sēz\ [L *haruspic-, haruspex*, fr. *haru-* (akin to Gk *chordē* gut, cord) + *-spic-, -spex* (fr. *spicere, specere* to look) — more at YARN, SPY] **1 :** one that foretells events by interpreting natural phenomena (as lightning) **:** SOOTHSAYER; *esp* **:** a diviner in ancient Rome basing his predictions on inspection of the entrails of sacrificial animals — compare AUGUR **2 :** one that prophesies **:** PROGNOSTICATOR ⟨our forecast has proven far more accurate than the divinations of the Democrat ~ —O.D.Heck⟩

ha·rus·pi·cal \-'rəspəkəl\ *adj* **:** of, relating to, or having the characteristics of an haruspex

ha·rus·pi·ca·tion \(h)ə,rəspə'kāshən\ *n* -S [L *haruspic-, haruspex* + E *-ation*] **1 :** HARUSPICY **2 :** an act or instance of foretelling events **:** PROPHECY ⟨it's the best job of social ~ that's been done in years —Christopher Morley⟩

ha·rus·pi·cy *or* **arus·pi·cy** \-'rəspəsē\ *n* -ES [L *haruspicium*, fr. *haruspic-, haruspex*] **:** the art or practice of divination — compare HARUSPEX

harvard beets *n pl, usu cap H* [*Harvard* University, Cambridge, Massachusetts] **:** diced or sliced cooked beets served in a vinegar sauce thickened with cornstarch

harvard crimson *n, often cap H* **1 :** a moderate red that is slightly darker than cerise, darker than claret, darker, very slightly bluer, and less strong than average strawberry (sense 2a), and bluer and very slightly darker than Turkey red — called also *jockey* **2** *of textiles* **:** a deep purplish red that is redder and paler than hollyhock or magenta (sense 2a) and stronger and slightly bluer and lighter than American beauty

har·ve·ian \'härvēən, ='==\ *adj, usu cap* [William *Harvey* †1657 Eng. physician and anatomist + E *-an*] **:** of, relating to, or commemorating William Harvey

1har·vest \'härvəst, 'håv-\ *n* -S *often attrib* [ME *hervest* autumn, fr. OE *hærfest;* akin to OHG *herbist* autumn, ON *haust* autumn, L *carpere* to gather, pluck, Gk *karpos* fruit, Skt *kṛpāṇa* sword, Gk *keirein* to cut — more at SHEAR] **1 :** the season for gathering in agricultural crops ⟨he who has seen ten winters or ~*s* is ten years old —M.P.Nilsson⟩ ⟨considerable variation in the Territory as regards the date of the ~ —*Tanganyika Territory*⟩ **2 a :** the act or process of gathering in a crop ⟨the hay ~⟩ ⟨reduce the numbers of fish . . . through more intensive and efficient ~ by anglers —L.S. Marceau⟩ **b :** the gathering in of something other than a crop ⟨more to these poems than just the . . . ~ of a trained eye —*Times Lit. Supp.*⟩ **3 a :** a mature crop of grain or fruit **:** YIELD ⟨bountiful ~*s* of corn —John Bird⟩ **b :** the quantity of any natural product gathered usu. from a single area within a single season ⟨~ of elk⟩ ⟨~ of beaver skins⟩ ⟨salt ~⟩ ⟨ice ~⟩ **4 :** an accumulated store or productive result **:** ACHIEVEMENT, INGATHERING ⟨one's total ~ of thinking, feeling, living, and observing —T.S.Eliot⟩ ⟨the final ~ of the theocracy —V.L. Parrington⟩ ⟨~ of the guillotine —Alfred Cobban⟩ ⟨~ of half crowns —W.J.MacQueen-Pope⟩ **5** *or* **harvest brown :** a brownish orange to light brown that is lighter than sorrel or tawny, redder and lighter than raw sienna, and slightly yellower and lighter than caramel

2harvest \"\ *vb* -ED/-ING/-S [ME *hervesten*, fr. *hervest*, n.] *vt* **1 a :** to gather in (a crop) **:** REAP ⟨when all the beets are ~*ed* a steam shovel loads them on trucks —*Amer. Guide Series: Minn.*⟩ **b :** to gather (a natural product) as if by harvesting ⟨~ honey⟩ ⟨~ timber⟩ ⟨~ whales⟩ **2 a :** to accumulate a store of ⟨~ news leads and witticisms —Bennett Cerf⟩ **b :** to win as a result of achievements ⟨~*ed* rewards in fame and wealth . . . simply undreamed of —*N. Y. Herald Tribune*⟩ ~ *vi* **:** to gather in a food crop ⟨sold it standing in the field to save himself the trouble of ~*ing* —Pearl Buck⟩ ⟨the husky black bear ~*s* upon both soil and water —George Heinold⟩ **syn** see REAP

har·vest·able \-təbəl\ *adj* **:** capable of or subject to being harvested

harvest bug *n* **:** CHIGGER 2

harvest doll *or* **harvest mother** *or* **harvest queen** *n* **:** a doll decorated with grain and flowers or an image made from the last sheaf cut in the harvest and used in European celebrations of the harvest home — called also *kirn baby, mell-doll*

har·vest·er \-tə(r)\ *n* -S **:** one that harvests: as **a :** HARVESTMAN **b :** a machine for harvesting field crops — compare COMBINE 3, CORN BINDER, COTTON PICKER **c :** a gatherer of something other than crops ⟨semimonthly ~ of noteworthy pronouncements —*Official Catholic Yearbook*⟩

harvester ant *n* **:** an ant that gathers and stores up seeds for food: as **a :** a member of an Old World genus (*Messor*) common around the Mediterranean **b :** any of several western No. American ants; *esp* **:** a common ant (*Pogonomyrmex barbatus*) of southwestern U.S. — called also *agricultural ant*

harvester-thresher \'==='==\ *n* **:** COMBINE 3

harvest fish *n* **:** any of various butterfishes of the family Stromateidae: as **a :** a small marine fish (*Peprilus paru*) having a narrow deep body and being found along the Atlantic coast of America from Brazil to Cape Cod **b :** DOLLARFISH 1

harvest fly *n* **:** CICADA; *specif* **:** DOG-DAY CICADA

harvest home *n* **1 :** the gathering and bringing home of the harvest; *also* **:** the time of harvest — see HARVEST DOLL **2 :** a feast made at the close of the harvest — called also *hockey, kirn, mell, mell supper* **3 :** the song sung by the reapers at the close of the harvest

harvesting *n* -S [fr. gerund of 2*harvest*] **:** an act or instance of gathering in a crop or store ⟨what crops survived the drought are rotted in the ~ —Oliver La Farge⟩ ⟨deer . . . are controlled by heavy ~ —Robert Crichton⟩

har·vest·less \'härvəstləs\ *adj* **:** lacking a harvest **:** UNPRODUCTIVE

harvest-lice \'==,=\ *n pl but sing or pl in constr* **1 :** a hooked or barbed fruit that readily adheres to things (as clothing or the fur of an animal) which come in contact with it **2 :** a plant (as cleavers, agrimonia, or beggar-ticks of the genus *Bidens*) bearing fruits that are harvest-lice

har·vest·man \'==mən\ *n, pl* **harvestmen** **1 :** one who harvests agricultural crops **:** harvest hand **2 :** an arachnid of the order Phalangida that superficially resembles a true spider but has a small rounded body composed of an indistinctly segmented cephalothorax to which the short broad abdomen showing nine dorsal plates is broadly joined, very long slender legs, chelate chelicerae, and rather short leglike pedipalpi — called also *daddy longlegs*

harvest mite *n* **:** CHIGGER 2

harvest moon *n* **:** the full moon nearest the time of the September equinox when for mid-northern latitudes its daily delay in rising is much shorter than usual by reason of the relatively small angle the moon's orbit makes with the eastern horizon

harvest mouse *n* **1 :** a small European field mouse (*Micromys minutus*) that builds a globular nest on the stems of wheat or other plants **2 :** any of several small field mice (genus *Reithrodontomys*) of the southern U.S.

harvests *pl of* HARVEST, *pres 3d sing of* HARVEST

harvest spider *n* **:** HARVESTMAN 2

harvesttime \'==,=\ *n* [ME *hervest-time*, fr. *hervest* harvest, autumn + *time*] **:** the time during which an annual crop (as wheat) is harvested

harz·burg·ite \'härts,bər,gīt\ *n* -S [G *harzburgit*, fr *Harzburg*, Germany + G *-it* -ite] **:** a rock of the peridotite group consisting essentially of olivine and orthopyroxene

1has *pres 3d sing of* HAVE

2has *pres 3d sing of* HA, *pl of* HA

has-been \'haz,bin\ *n* -S [fr. *has been*, 3d pers. sing. perf. indic. of *be*] **1 :** one that has passed the peak of effectiveness or popularity ⟨a seedy *has-been* of an actor traveling a comeback trail —Gordon Allison⟩ ⟨that little, dried-up *has-been* of a town —J.B.Benefield⟩ ⟨obsolete, a *has-been* as a warplane —*Springfield* (*Mass.*) *Daily News*⟩ **2 has-beens** *pl* **:** old times or past events ⟨just for *has-beens* I took him to lunch —W.H.Smith⟩

haschisch *var of* HASHISH

ha·sen·pfef·fer \'häzᵊn,(p)fefə(r)\ *or* **has·sen·pfef·fer** \'häs-\ *n* -S [G *hasenpfeffer*, fr. *hase* hare (fr. OHG *haso*) + *pfeffer* pepper, fr. OHG *pfeffar* — more at HARE, PEPPER] **1 :** a stew made of rabbit meat which has been soaked for two days in vinegar and pickling spices and to which sour cream is added before serving **2 :** a card game similar to euchre

1hash \'hash, -aa(ə)sh, -aish\ *vb* -ED/-ING/-ES [F *hacher*, fr. OF *hachier*, fr. *hache* battle-ax, of Gmc origin; akin to OHG *hāppa* sickle, pruning knife; akin to Gk *koptein* to smite, cut off — more at CAPON] *vt* **1 a :** to chop to pieces; *specif* **:** to prepare for use in a meat and vegetable dish by cutting into small pieces ⟨~ the leftover pot roast⟩ **b :** to make a confused muddle of **:** JUMBLE ⟨in both dates and geography he pretty well ~*es* the history of the . . . company —Bernard De Voto⟩ **2 :** to cut with long strokes **:** SLASH ⟨they are . . . ~*ing* them down, and their blood is running down like water —Patrick Walker⟩ **3 :** to talk about **:** REVIEW ⟨~ and rehash the evidence —D.W.Peck⟩ ~ *vi* **1** *slang* **:** to serve food in a restaurant **:** wait table ⟨got my job back ~*ing* —R.P.Warren⟩ **2 :** to marshal facts **:** CONSIDER ⟨we've ~*ed* and rehashed enough —Hamilton Basso⟩

²hash \"\ *n* -ES **1 a :** chopped food; *specif* **:** a dish usu. consisting of leftover meat chopped into small pieces, mixed with potatoes, and browned by baking or frying **b** *slang* **:** a meal esp. in a cafeteria or at a lunch counter **:** FOOD ⟨called last week and took ~ with us —*Gringo & Greaser*⟩ ⟨waiter in a ~ joint —Scott Fitzgerald⟩ **2 :** a restatement of something that is already known ⟨this much is old ~, but the . . . tabulation goes on to supply some curious verification —*N.Y. Herald Tribune*⟩ **3 :** MIXTURE, JUMBLE, HODGEPODGE: as **a :** a confused muddle **:** MESS ⟨made rather a ~ of her life —Clive Arden⟩ ⟨one basic style of architecture with a ~ of every other style slapped on by successive owners —Sam Boal⟩ **b :** an undesired signal or combination of signals in a radio, radar, or television receiver due to set noise, radio noise, interference, or other cause **c :** a medley of miscellaneous steps and figures in square dancing **4** *chiefly Scot* **:** a careless or stupid person of slovenly speech or habits **:** worthless fellow

³hash \'(h)ash\ *dial var of* HARSH

hash·ab \'ha,shab\ *n* -S [Ar *khashab*] **:** a gray-barked acacia tree (*Acacia senegal*) found in the Sudan that is the source of a white or light-colored variety of gum arabic

hashed brown potatoes \'=,=-\ *also* **hash-browns** \'hash-,braünz\ *or* **hashed-browns** \-sht,-\ *n pl* **:** chopped cooked potatoes packed into a skillet and fried brown on both sides

hash·er \'hashə(r), -aash-, -aish-\ *n* -S **1** *slang* **:** WAITER, WAITRESS ⟨a ~ in the Shanghai Café —*N.Y. Times*⟩ **2 a :** COOKEE **b :** a worker who feeds into a hashing machine unmarketable meat that may be used for by-products

hash·ery \-shərē\ *n* -ES [²*hash* + *-ery*] *slang* **:** HASH HOUSE

hash house *n, slang* **:** an inexpensive eating place **:** BEANERY ⟨at an all-night *hash house* . . . he nurses a cup of coffee and a doughnut —Norman Mailer⟩

¹hash·im·ite *or* **hash·em·ite** \'hashə,mīt\ *n* -S *usu cap* [*Hashim*, great-grandfather of Muhammad (founder of the Muslim religion) + E *-ite*] **:** a member of an Arab family having common ancestry with Muhammad and founding dynasties in countries of the eastern Mediterranean

²hashimite *or* **hashemite** \"\ *adj, usu cap* **:** of, relating to, or ruled by the Hashimites

hash·ish *also* **hash·eesh** *or* **hasch·isch** \'ha\|(,)shēsh, 'haa\|, 'hai\|, \|,shish *sometimes* ='shēsh *or* ha'shēsh\ *n* -ES [Ar *ḥashīsh* dry herbage, hashish] **1 :** a narcotic drug derived from the hemp (*Cannabis sativa*) that is smoked, chewed, or drunk for its intoxicating effect ⟨inhaled the ~ of his words with which he puffed dreamlike clouds about her head —Helen Howe⟩ — compare BHANG, CANNABIS, CHARAS, GANJA, MARIJUANA **2 :** an intoxicating liquor prepared from cannabis

hash·ka·bah \häsh'käbə\ *n* -S *sometimes cap* [MHeb *hashkābhāh*, lit., lying down, fr. Heb *hashkibh* to lie down, die] **:** a recital of the memorial prayer for the dead esp. among Sephardic Jews

hash mark *n* **:** a military service stripe ⟨it takes a soldier or airman three years, and a sailor or marine four, to get a *hash mark* —*Armed Forces Talk*⟩

hash out *vt* **:** to thrash out ⟨invited by a faculty committee . . . to *hash out* their views on education theory —*Saturday Rev.*⟩

hash over *vt* **:** to talk over **:** DISCUSS ⟨*hash over* old times⟩ ⟨*hash over* a ball game⟩ ⟨plunged into the subject under discussion and *hashed* it *over* —E.J.Kahn⟩

hashslinger \'=,==\ *n* **:** WAITER, WAITRESS

hash up *vt* **1 :** to make a mess of **:** mutilate almost beyond recognition ⟨*hashed up* the account of the accident⟩ ⟨a concept that has *hashed up* remedial legislation⟩ **2 :** to warm up **:** give fresh existence to **:** REANIMATE ⟨*hashing up* ancient quarrels —*Times Lit. Supp.*⟩ ⟨*hash up* novel interpretations of men and events based on little more than the findings of their predecessors —*Listener*⟩

ha·sid *or* **cha·sid** *or* **has·sid** *or* **chas·sid** \'hasəd, 'käs-\ *n, pl* **ha·sid·im** *or* **has·sid·im** \'hasədəm, kə'sēd-\ *usu cap* [Heb *ḥāsīdh* pious, one who is pious (pl. *ḥăsīdhīm*)] **1 :** a member of a pious Jewish sect founded about the 3d century B.C. by opponents of Hellenistic innovations and devoted to the strict observance of the ritual of purification and separation — called also *assidean* **2 :** a member of a Jewish sect devoted to mysticism and opposed to secular studies and Jewish rationalism that was founded in Poland about 1750 by Rabbi Israel ben Eliezer to revive the strict practices of the earlier Hasidim — **ha·sid·ic** *or* **cha·sid·ic** *or* **has·sid·ic** *or* **chas·sid·ic** \hə'sidik, kə'-\ *adj, usu cap*

hasidean *or* **hasidaean** *usu cap, var of* ASSIDEAN

ha·si·dism *or* **chas·i·dism** *or* **has·si·dism** *or* **chass·i·dism** \'hasə,dizəm, 'käs-\ *n* -S *usu cap* **:** the practices and beliefs of the Hasidim

ha·si·nai \'häsə,nī\ *n, pl* **hasinai** *usu cap* **1 :** one of the three principal confederations of the Caddo Indians inhabiting northeastern Texas **2 :** a member of the Hasinai Confederacy

hask \'h)ask\ *adj* [ME, harsh, alter. of *harsk* — more at HARSH] **1** *now dial Eng, of weather* **:** cold and dry **2** *now dial Eng* **a :** rough and harsh to the touch **b :** harsh to the taste **3** *now dial Eng* **:** coarse and dry in texture

has·ka·lah \,haskə'lä, häs'kōlə\ *n* -S *usu cap, often attrib* [NHeb *haśkālāh*, lit., intellect, enlightenment] **:** an intellectual enlightenment movement among Jews of eastern Europe in the 18th and 19th centuries that attempted to acquaint the masses with European and Hebrew languages and secular education and culture to supplement talmudic studies — see MASKIL

has·let *or* **has·slet** \'haslət, 'häs-, -äzl-\ *n* -S [ME *hastlet*, *hastelet*, fr. MF *hastelet* piece of meat roasted on a spit, dim. of *haste* piece of meat roasted on a spit, fr. OF, modif. (influenced by OF *haste* shaft of a spear, fr. L *hasta* spear) of a Gmc word represented by OHG *harsta* frying pan; akin to OE *hierstan*, *hyrstan* to fry, roast, MHG *harst* gridiron, OE *heorth* hearth — more at HEARTH, YARD] **1 :** the edible viscera (as the heart or liver) of a butchered animal (as a hog) **2 :** a braised dish made of edible viscera

has·mo·nae·an *or* **has·mo·ne·an** \,hazmə'nēən\ *or* **as·mo·nae·an** *or* **as·mo·ne·an** \,az-\ *n* -S *usu cap* [LL *Asmonaeus* Hasmon, ancestor of the Maccabees (fr. Gk *Asamōnaios*) + E *-an*] **:** a member of a dynasty or family of Jewish patriots to which the Maccabees belonged

has·na \'haznə\ [by contr.] *dial Brit* **:** has not

hasn't \'haz'n(t)\ [by contr.] **:** has not

¹hasp \'hasp, 'haa(ə)sp, 'haisp, 'häsp\ *n* -S [ME *hasp*, *haspe*, fr. OE *hæsp*, *hæpse*; akin to MHG *haspe* hasp, ON *hespa*, and perh. to L *capsa* chest, case — more at CASE] **1 a :** a fastener esp. for a door or lid consisting of a hinged metal strap that fits over a staple and is secured by a pin or padlock **b :** a similar strap having a projecting knob that snaps into a lock and that is much used on luggage **c :** any of several other devices (as a latch) for fastening a door or window ⟨the spring of the window ~ —G.M.Fenn⟩ **2 :** a clasp for a book or an article of clothing ⟨a ledger bound with metal ~*s* —William Fifield⟩ ⟨cape with a ~ at the throat⟩ **3** *now dial Eng* **a :** a skein or hank of yarn, thread, or silk **b :** a fourth part of a spindle of such material

hasps 1

²hasp \"\ *vt* -ED/-ING/-S [ME *haspen*, fr. OE *hæpsian*, fr. *hæpse*, n.] **1 :** to fasten with or as if with a hasp ⟨~ the door⟩ **2** *obs* **:** to confine in a small space — often used with *up* ⟨~*ed* up with thee in this small vehicle —*Spectator*⟩

hasp lock *n* **1 :** a prison lock attached permanently to the hasp of a door and adapted to secure the door **2 :** a detachable lock (as a padlock) to secure a hasp

has·sall's corpuscle *also* **has·sal's corpuscle** \'hasəlz-\ *n, usu cap H* **:** CORPUSCLE OF HASSALL

has·sar \'hasə(r)\ *n* -S [Arawak *asa*] **:** any of several nest-building armored catfishes of the family Callichthyidae that occur in the Orinoco and its tributaries and are able to leave the water and travel some distance on land

hassenpfeffer *var of* HASENPFEFFER

hassid *usu cap, var of* HASID

hassidean *or* **hassidaean** *usu cap, var of* ASSIDEAN

¹has·sle *also* **has·sel** \'hasəl, 'haas-, 'hais-, 'häs-\ *n* -S [perh. blend of ²*haggle* and ²*tussle*] **1 a :** a heated argument **:** WRANGLE ⟨embroiling myself in a long, exasperating ~ with masons —S.J.Perelman⟩ **b :** a violent skirmish **:** FIGHT ⟨small units and small patrols, but for those in each ~ . . . it is still a tense, blood-curdling exchange of bullets —*N.Y. Times*⟩ **2 :** a protracted debate **:** CONTROVERSY ⟨an extremely esoteric ~ over . . . ideas and concepts —Philip Hamburger⟩ **3 a :** a state of confusion or commotion **:** TURMOIL ⟨all ~ and hurly-burly —Ellery Queen⟩ **b :** a strenuous effort **:** STRUGGLE ⟨it's been a real ~ digging up new talent —Benny Goodman⟩

²hassle \"\ *vi* **hassled; hassled; hassling** \-s(ə)liŋ\ **hassles :** ARGUE, FIGHT, DISPUTE ⟨*hassled* with the umpires a time or two too many —Leo Durocher⟩ ⟨a lot of *hassling* back and forth over the telephone —*Sports Illustrated*⟩

hasslet *var of* HASLET

has·sock \'hasək, -aas-\ *n* -S [ME, fr. OE *hassuc*] **1 :** a rank tuft of bog grass or sedge **:** TUSSOCK **2 a :** a small kneeling cushion or footstool ⟨an old-fashioned church ~ with flaps at the ends —Anna Kavan⟩ **b :** a bulky upholstered cushion used as an article of household furniture: as (1) **:** a large stuffed cushion that serves as a seat or leg rest — compare OTTOMAN, POUF (2) **:** a similar cushion or backless padded seat mounted on legs or having a hollow center for storage

hassocks 2b(1)

hassock fan *n* **:** an electric fan operating in a cylindrical hassock-shaped frame and propelling air upward from the floor

hassock grass *n* **:** TUFTED HAIR GRASS 2

has·socky \-kē\ *adj* **:** full of hassocks

has·su·na \hə'sünə\ *or* **has·su·nan** \-nən\ *adj, usu cap* [*hassuna* fr. *Hassuna*, archaeological site in northern Iraq; *hassunan* fr. *Hassuna* + E *-an*] **:** of or relating to an Aeneolithic culture of Mesopotamia earlier than the Halafian and characterized by the use of sometimes painted pottery, the manufacture of small clay figurines of women, and urn burial

hast *archaic pres 2d sing of* HAVE

has·ta \'hastə\ [contr. of *hast thou*] *dial Brit* **:** have you

has·tate \'ha,stāt\ *adj* [NL *hastatus*, fr. L *hasta* spear — more at YARD] **1 :** shaped like a spear or the head of a spear ⟨a ~ weapon like a pike or poleax⟩ **2** *of a leaf* **:** triangular with sharp basal lobes spreading away from the petiole — see LEAF illustration — **has·tate·ly** *adv*

hastato- *comb form* [NL, fr. *hastatus*] **:** hastately **:** hastate and ⟨*hastato*lanceolate⟩ ⟨*hastato*sagittate⟩

¹haste \'hāst\ *n* -S [ME, fr. OF, of Gmc origin; akin to OE *hǣst* violence, OHG *heisti* violent, *heiftig* impetuous, ON *heipt*, *heifst* feud, war, hatred, Goth *haifsts* strife, conflict, fight; perh. akin to Skt *śībham* quickly] **1 :** rapidity of motion **:** SPEED ⟨out of breath from ~ —Jane Austen⟩ **2 :** rash or headlong action **:** PRECIPITATENESS ⟨~ makes waste⟩ ⟨the beauty of speed uncontaminated by ~ —*Harper's*⟩ **3 :** overeagerness to act **:** HURRY ⟨I feel no ~ and no reluctance to depart —Edna S. V. Millay⟩

syn HURRY, SPEED, EXPEDITION, DISPATCH: HASTE indicates quickness or swiftness, often careless, on the part of persons impelled by urgency, pressure, eagerness ⟨"Why this mad *haste*?" I asked. "Bandits," he shouted. —W.O.Douglas⟩ HURRY may imply haste with confusion, agitation, and hustle ⟨there was a great *hurry* in the streets, of people speeding away to get shelter before the storm broke —Charles Dickens⟩ ⟨for whom all these women worked with such a sense of frantic *hurry* —Winifred Bambrick⟩ SPEED may focus attention on the fact of quickness, with very occasional implications of success ⟨such developments are bound to increase the *speed* of the social and economic revolution —R.W.Steel⟩ ⟨accused of slowness and undue deliberation, yet he built an adequate navy from nothing with surprising *speed* —H.K.Beale⟩ EXPEDITION and DISPATCH both designate efficient speed, the former with a suggestion of smooth efficiency, the latter of brisk promptness ⟨to move with reasonable *expedition* along the narrow pavements of Rotting Hill is impossible —Wyndham Lewis⟩ ⟨proceed with great *dispatch* and arrest the people involved —Dean Acheson⟩

²haste \"\ *vb* -ED/-ING/-S [ME *hasten*, fr. OF *haster*, fr. *haste*, n.] *vt, archaic* **:** to urge on **:** HASTEN ⟨with our fair entreaties ~ them on —Shak.⟩ ⟨~ thee, nymph, and bring with thee jest and youthful jollity —John Milton⟩ ~ *vi* **:** to move or act swiftly **:** HURRY ⟨~ to correct a seeming impression —O.W. Holmes †1935⟩ ⟨these minutes even now *hasting* into eternity —Winston Churchill⟩

haste·ful \-tfəl\ *adj* **:** full of haste **:** HASTY — **haste·ful·ly** \-fəlē\ *adv*

haste·less \-tləs\ *adj* **:** being without haste **:** UNHURRIED

has·ten \'hās°n\ *vb* **hastened; hastened; hastening** \-s(°)niŋ\ **hastens** [alter. of ²*haste*] *vt* **1 a :** to urge on **:** HURRY ⟨~*ed* her to the door —A.J.Cronin⟩ **b :** to speed up **:** ACCELERATE ⟨~ the coming of a new order —D.W.Brogan⟩ **2** *obs* **:** to send or bring quickly ⟨I pray . . . the king . . . to ~ his effectual letters —Edward Nicholas⟩ ~ *vi* **:** to move or act quickly **:** make haste **:** HURRY ⟨must ~ on to the bull ring —Mary Webb⟩ ⟨let me ~ to add that I do not mean absolute values —Kemp Malone⟩ **syn** see SPEED

has·ten·er \-s(°)nə(r)\ *n* -S **:** one that hastens

hast·er \'hāstə(r)\ *n* -S [²*haste* + *-er*] **:** HASTENER

has·ti·lude \'hastə,lüd\ *n, pl* **hastiludes** \-dz\ *or* **hastilu·dia** \,==\'lüdēə\ [ML *hastiludium*, fr. LL *hasti-* (fr. L *hasta* spear) + *-ludium* (fr. L *ludus* play, sport) — more at YARD, LUDICROUS] **:** a medieval joust **:** spear play ⟨one sport called ~*s* was no less dangerous than war itself —W.H.Dixon⟩

hast·i·ly \'hāstəlē, -li\ *adv* [ME, fr. *hasty* + *-ly*] **1 :** rapidly and often with little attention to detail **:** HURRIEDLY ⟨read it ~⟩ ⟨wartime factories were ~ built⟩ **2 :** without thorough consideration **:** RASHLY ⟨sold ~ and at a sacrifice —Raymond Weaver⟩

hast·i·ness \-tēnəs\ *n* -ES [ME *hastinesse*, fr. *hasty* + *-nesse* -ness] **:** the quality or state of being hasty

hast·ings \'(h)āstənz\ *n pl* [pl. of obs. E *hasting* early fruit or vegetable, fr. *hasting*, adj., ripening early, fr. pres. part. of E ²*haste*] *now dial Eng* **:** early fruit or vegetables; *esp* **:** early peas

has·tings·ite \'hāstiŋ,zīt\ *n* -S [*Hastings* county, Ontario, Canada, its locality + E *-ite*] **:** a sodium-calcium-iron amphibole ideally $NaCa_2Fe_5Al_2Si_6O_{22}(OH)_2$ but generally containing a little potassium and magnesium

has·tu·la \'haschələ\ *n* -S [NL, fr. L, small spear, dim. of *hasta* spear] **:** a flat often triangular expansion at the upper surface of the petiole of a palm leaf where it joins the blade

hasty \'hāstē, -ti\ *adj* -ER/-EST [ME, fr. OF *hasti*, *hastif*, fr. *haste*, n. + *-if* -ive] **1 a** *archaic* **:** rapid in action or movement **:** SPEEDY **b :** made or done in haste **:** showing signs of haste **:** HURRIED ⟨~ city-street snapshots —R.B.Heilman⟩ ⟨a ~ reading of the letter misled him⟩ **2 :** being in a hurry **:** EAGER, IMPATIENT ⟨too passionate and ~ to keep pace with the deliberate steps of his leader —Philip Marsh⟩ **3 :** ill-considered **:** PRECIPITATE, RASH ⟨warning against ~ enterprises and partial solutions —M.R.Cohen⟩ **4 :** prone to anger **:** IRRITABLE ⟨a man of ~ temper —G.B.Shaw⟩ **syn** see FAST, PRECIPITATE

hasty pudding *n* **1** *Brit* **:** a porridge or pudding made of oatmeal or flour boiled in water **2** *NewEng* **:** cornmeal mush usu. served hot with milk and maple sugar or molasses — compare INDIAN PUDDING

¹hat \'hat, *usu* -ad·+V\ *n* -S *often attrib* [ME, fr. OE *hæt*; akin to ON *höttr* head covering — more at HOOD] **1 :** a covering for the head: as **a :** a head covering typically having a shaped crown and brim and made of felt, straw, or silk and worn by men — distinguished from *cap*; compare DERBY, FELT, STETSON, STRAW HAT **b :** a decorative accessory in a wide variety of shapes and materials worn by women — compare BONNET, CARTWHEEL, CLOCHE, PILLBOX, SAILOR, TOQUE **2 a :** a head covering of distinctive color or shape worn as a symbol of office ⟨cardinal's ~⟩ **b :** an office symbolized by or as if by the wearing of a special hat ⟨the two principal ~*s* a president wears are those of ceremonial head of state and chief executive —Cabell Phillips⟩ **3 :** a layer of bark spread on the hides in a tanning pit **4 :** a container used for taking up a collection of voluntary contributions (as of money) ⟨go round with the ~⟩ ⟨pass the ~⟩ — **have one's hat in the ring** *or* **throw one's hat in the ring** *or* **toss one's hat in the ring :** to announce one's entry or readiness to enter into a fight or contest (as for elective office) — **take one's hat off to :** to acknowledge the achievement or superiority of **:** COMPLIMENT ⟨he was colossal and I *take my hat off to* him —H.J.Laski⟩

²hat \"\ *vb* **hatted; hatted; hatting; hats** *vt* **1 :** to furnish or provide with a hat ⟨smartly gowned, *hatted*, and gloved for the journey —A.N.Whitehead⟩ **2 :** to bestow a cardinal's hat on ~ *vi* **:** to make or supply hats

³hat *dial past of* HIT

⁴hat *dial Eng var of* HIT

hatable *var of* HATEABLE

hat ball *n* **:** a game of roly-poly in which the ball is rolled into hats placed on the ground

hatband \'=,=\ *n* [ME, fr. ¹*hat* + *band*, n.] **:** a band of fabric, leather, or cord around the crown of a hat just above the brim

hatbox \'=,=\ *n* **1 :** a box for holding hats **2 :** a piece of hand luggage that is usu. round and deep, has a handle, and is designed esp. for carrying hats though it is often used as a traveling bag by women

¹hatch \'hach\ *n* -ES [ME *hache*, *hacche*, fr. OE *hæc*; akin to MD *hecke* trapdoor, grating, MLG *heck* fence] **1 a** *obs* **:** the lower half of a divided door ⟨in at the window or else o'er the ~ —Shak.⟩ **b :** a small door, wicket, or serving counter ⟨equipped with an escape ~ for use in case of fire —W.H. Goodenough⟩ ⟨shop through a ~ in the wall —*Time*⟩ ⟨snatched up two plates of cold tongue . . . from the serving-room ~ —Margaret Kennedy⟩ **2 a** *obs* **(1) :** movable planking over the cargo hold of a ship — usu. used in pl. **(2) :** DECK — usu. used in pl. ⟨upon the giddy footing of the ~*es* —Shak.⟩ **b :** a door or grated cover giving vertical access down into a compartment ⟨smoke rose through the same ~ where . . . men could climb to the cannon deck —J.H.Cutler⟩ ⟨the inspector lifts the ~ in the top of the oil storage tank⟩; *specif* **:** the cover of a tank turret ⟨one of the .50-caliber guns can be . . . fired from inside without opening the turret ~ —*Military Rev.*⟩ **c :** HATCHWAY **d :** an enclosed space **:** COMPARTMENT ⟨her ~*es* were enlarged and her lumber-carrying career . . . resumed —H.G.Peterson⟩ ⟨device . . . the airman is placing in its release ~ —*N. Y. Times Mag.*⟩ **3 :** something that resembles a hatch: as **a :** FLOODGATE, SLUICE GATE **b :** an opening or door in the deck or fuselage of an airplane (as for a means of escape in an emergency or for loading cargo) **c :** a frame or weir in a river for catching fish

²hatch \'(h)ach\ *vt* -ED/-ING/-ES *now dial Eng* **:** to close (a door) with a hatch

³hatch \'hach\ *vb* -ED/-ING/-ES [ME *hacchen*; akin to MHG *hecken* to mate (said of birds)] *vi* **1 :** to produce young from an egg by incubation ⟨the hen ~*ed* today⟩ **2 a :** to emerge from an egg, pupa, or chrysalis ⟨watched the chickens ~⟩ ⟨begins to ~ from the chrysalis in early July —E.B.Ford⟩ — often used with *off* or *out* **b :** to give forth young or imagoes ⟨the eggs ~*ed* today⟩ **3 :** to incubate eggs **:** BROOD ⟨the old hen is ~*ing*⟩ ~ *vt* **1** *archaic* **:** BREED, PROPAGATE ⟨what monsters now doth nature ~ —*Miour for Magistrates*⟩ ⟨serving as a nursery bed to ~ . . . the infant plant —William Bartram⟩ **2 a :** to cause the development and hatching of (young) from eggs by providing natural or artificial heat ⟨a duck . . . which ~*ed* chickens —Margaret Deland⟩ **b :** to cause the development and hatching of young from (eggs) by providing natural or artificial heat ⟨an incubator can ~ more eggs at a time than a hen⟩ ⟨turtle eggs are ~*ed* by the sun⟩ **3 :** to bring into being **:** ORIGINATE, PRODUCE ⟨~*ing* a program of economic aid —E.K.Lindley⟩ ⟨they repair to the little summer place to garden and smoke pipes, they ~ books, they go fishing —George Spelvin⟩; *esp* **:** to concoct in secret ⟨~ a conspiracy⟩ — often used with *up* ⟨when was all this ~*ed up* —Ann Bridge⟩

⁴hatch \"\ *n* -ES **1 a :** an act of hatching ⟨congregate in family groups soon after the ~ —W.W.Haines⟩ **b :** the transformation of a swarm of insects from a water-dwelling to a winged phase ⟨trout were rising freely to a ~ of small gray flies —F.C. Craighead b.1916 & J.J.Craighead⟩ **2 :** a product of hatching **:** brood of young ⟨the entire ~ in an incubator —J.E.Shillinger & L.C.Morley⟩

⁵hatch \"\ *vt* -ED/-ING/-ES [ME *hachen*, fr. MF *hacher*, fr. OF *hachier* to chop up — more at HASH] **1 :** to inlay in fine lines **:** apply narrow bands of a different color or material to **2 :** to mark with fine closely spaced parallel or crisscrossed lines in drawing or engraving chiefly to represent shading — see ³HATCHING

⁶hatch \"\ *n* -ES **:** STROKE, LINE; *esp* **:** one used in engraving or drawing to give the effect of shading

hatch·abil·i·ty \,hachə'biləd·ē\ *n* **1 :** the quality or state of being hatchable ⟨low ~ generally means low vitality in the chicks that do hatch —*Reliable Poultry Jour.*⟩ **2 :** the ability to produce hatchable eggs ⟨turkey hens which become broody during the laying season show higher . . . ~ than nonbroody hens —*Agric. Research in S. Dak.*⟩

hatch·able \'hachəbəl\ *adj* [³*hatch* + *-able*] *of an egg* **:** capable of being hatched

hatch bar *n* **:** a bar across a hatch to batten it down

hatch beam *n* **:** a heavy portable beam across a large hatch to support the cover

hatch deck *n* **:** a temporary deck of removable planking or covers over the hold

hatcheck \'=,=\ *adj* **1 :** that checks hats and other articles of clothing ⟨~ girl⟩ **2 :** used in the checking of hats and other articles of clothing ⟨~ stand⟩

¹hatch·el \'hachəl\ *also* **hetch·el** \'hech-\ *n* -S [*hatchel* alter. of *hetchel*, fr. ME *hechele*, *hekele*, *hakell*; akin to MD *hekele* hackle, MHG *hechel*, *hachel* hackle, OHG *hāko* hook — more at HOOK] **:** ³HACKLE 1

²hatchel \"\ *vt* **hatcheled** *or* **hatchelled; hatcheled** *or* **hatchelled; hatcheling** *or* **hatchelling; hatchels** [alter. of earlier *hetchel*, fr. ME *hechelen*, fr. *hechele*, n.] **1 :** ⁴HACKLE 1 **2 :** HECKLE 2

hatch·er \'hachə(r)\ *n* -S **1 :** one that hatches; *specif* **:** a device to which eggs are transferred from the incubator shortly before they are due to hatch **2 :** one that produces or originates

hatch·ery \-ch(ə)rē, -ri\ *n* -ES **1 :** a place for hatching eggs (as of poultry or fish) **2 :** a place for the large-scale production of weanling feeder pigs

hatch·ery·man \'=(=)=,=\ *n, pl* **hatcherymen :** one who operates a hatchery

hatches *pl of* HATCH, *pres 3d sing of* HATCH

¹hatch·et \'hachət, *usu* -əd·+V\ *n* -S *often attrib* [ME *hachet*, *hacchet* small ax, fr. MF *hachette*, fr. *hache* battle-ax + *-ette* — more at HASH] **1 a :** a short-handled ax with a hammerhead to be used with one hand either for cutting or hammering **b :** TOMAHAWK **2 :** a dental excavator

²hatchet \"\ *vt* -ED/-ING/-S **1 :** to cut or kill with a hatchet ⟨~ a tree⟩ ⟨~ an enemy⟩ **2 :** to dispatch as if with a hatchet ⟨~ a proposal⟩

hatchet cactus *n* **:** a small Mexican cactus (*Pelecyphora aselliformis*) with white flowers and hatchet-shaped tubercles

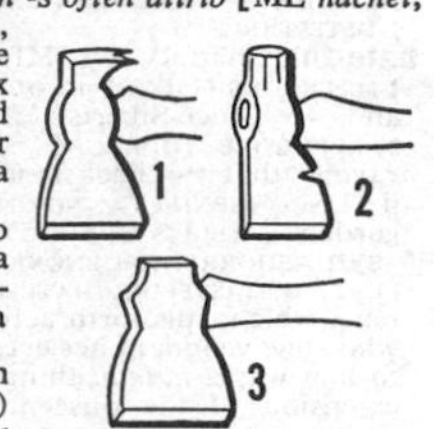

hatchets 1a: *1* claw, *2* half, *3* broad

hatchet face *n* **1 :** a long narrow face with sharp features **2 :** a person having a thin sharp face — **hatchet-faced** \'==,=\ *adj*

hatchetfish \'==,=\ *n* **:** any of several small So. American characin fishes with enlarged pectoral fins and thin wedge-shaped bodies that are often seen in tropical aquariums

hatchet job *n* **:** an act of defamation **:** malicious attack ⟨turned traitor to his class and performed a *hatchet job* on the commuting world —*Time*⟩

hatchet man *n* **1 :** a professional killer **:** TRIGGERMAN, HIGHBINDER ⟨the hooded cult retaliated and four . . . *hatchet men* were found dead in a ditch —W.M.Swann⟩ **2 a :** one who transmits orders or maintains discipline for a superior **:** HENCHMAN ⟨needed a competent and senior foreign service *hatchet man* to keep the . . . career boys under control —*Harper's*⟩; *specif* **:** an ideological watchdog or party disciplinarian ⟨served his party as chief *hatchet man* —Robert Bendiner⟩ **b** (1) **:** a writer who specializes in denunciation and invective often on orders from an employer and without regard to personal scruples ⟨our present journalistic *hatchet men* —B.R.Redman⟩ (2) **:** CRITIC ⟨a literary *hatchet man* —S.E.Hyman⟩

hatchet stake *n* **:** a sharp-edged stake on which to bend sheet metal — see STAKE illustration

hatch·ett·ine \'hachəd,ēn, -d·ən\ *or* **hatch·ett·ite** \-d·,īt\ *n* -S [Charles *Hatchett* †1847 Eng. chemist + E *-ine* or *-ite*] **:** a mineral paraffin wax $C_{38}H_{78}$ melting at 55° to 65° C in the natural state and at 79° C when pure — called also *mineral tallow*

hatch·et·to·lite \-d·ō,līt\ *n* -S [Charles *Hatchett* †1847 + E *-o-* + *-lite*] **:** a uranium-bearing pyrochlore

hatchet work *n* **:** the work of a hatchet man

hatchgate \'=,=\ *n* **1 :** WICKET **2 :** ¹HATCH 3a

¹**hatching** *n* -S [ME *hacchynge*, fr. gerund of ME *hacchen* to produce young from an egg by incubation — more at HATCH (verb)] **:** ⁴HATCH

²**hatching** *n* -S [fr. gerund of ⁵*hatch*] **1 a :** the engraving or drawing of fine lines in close proximity to each other chiefly to give an effect of shading **b :** the pattern so created **2 :** the process or result of weaving threads of one color into an adjoining area of another color in a tapestry so as to produce an effect of shading or highlights **3 :** a fine concentric line of pores in the tangential section of some woods

hatching spine *n* **:** a spine on the unhatched young of various insects used to break the embryonic envelope

hatch·ite \'ha,chīt\ *n* -S [Frederick H. *Hatch* †1932 Eng. mining engineer and geologist + E *-ite*] **:** a mineral consisting of a sulfide of lead and arsenic that occurs in triclinic crystals but whose exact composition is unknown

hatch·ling \'hachliŋ\ *n* -S **:** a recently hatched animal

hatch·man \'=mən\ *also* **hatch·mind·er** \'=,==\ *or* **hatch·way·man** \'=,=mən\ *n, pl* **hatchmen** *also* **hatchminders** *or* **hatchwaymen :** one who stands by a ship's hatch to assist with the loading and unloading

hatch·ment \'hachmənt\ *n* -S [perh. alter. of *achievement*] **:** a panel having the shape of a square placed cornerwise or of a lozenge, bearing the coat of arms of a deceased person, and displayed temporarily usu. on the outside wall of his dwelling

hatchure *var of* HACHURE

hatchway \'=,=\ *n* **:** an opening equipped with a hatch and giving access to a compartment, room, or cellar; *specif* **:** a passageway between the decks of a ship

hatch whip *n* **:** a block and tackle for hoisting cargo through a hatchway

hat dance *n* **:** a national courtship folk dance of Mexico performed by two people in which the man throws a sombrero on the ground and the girl signifies acceptance of him as her lover by dancing on its brim and then putting it on her head — compare JARABE

¹**hate** \'hāt, *usu* -ād·+V\ *n* -S *often attrib* [ME, alter. (prob. influenced by *haten*, v.) of *hete*, fr. OE; akin to OHG *haz* hate, ON *hatr* hate, Goth *hatis* wrath, Gk *kēdos* grief, mourning, Av *sādra* sorrow] **1 a :** intense hostility toward an object (as an individual) that has frustrated the release of an inner tension (as of a biological nature) ⟨quick dislike had ripened into ~ —I.V.Morris⟩ ⟨rid your mind of any hidden ~*s* or grudges —W.J.Reilly⟩; *specif* **:** a systematic esp. politically exploited expression of hate ⟨the forces of darkness, bigotry, and ~⟩ ⟨~ list⟩ ⟨~ bombings⟩ ⟨~ mail⟩ **b :** an habitual emotional attitude in which distaste is coupled with sustained ill will ⟨his life became increasingly dominated by ~⟩ **c :** a strong dislike or antipathy **:** DISTASTE ⟨developed a ~ for string quartets⟩ **2 :** an object of hatred ⟨a generation whose finest ~ had been big business —F.L.Paxson⟩

²**hate** \"\ *vb* -ED/-ING/-S [ME *haten*, fr. OE *hatian*; akin to OS *haton* to hate, OHG *hazzōn*, ON *hata*; denominative fr. the root of ¹*hate*] *vt* **1 :** to feel extreme enmity toward **:** regard with active hostility ⟨sit there *hating* one another and end up by cutting one another's throats —John Wain⟩ **2 a :** to have a strong aversion to **:** DETEST, RESENT ⟨~ what is evil, hold fast to what is good —Rom 12: 9 (RSV)⟩ ⟨they ~ being moved from one box to another —Henry Wynmalen⟩ **b :** to find distasteful **:** DISLIKE ⟨*hated* the cold and the snow —Harold Griffin⟩ ⟨so pretty she *hated* to get glasses when she needed them —John Steinbeck⟩ ⟨*hated* that young men should raise their hats to him out of respect for his superior age —Arnold Bennett⟩ ~ *vi* **:** to express or feel extreme enmity or active hostility ⟨harsh faces and *hating* eyes —Katherine A. Porter⟩

syn DETEST, LOATHE, ABHOR, ABOMINATE: HATE, the antonym of love, indicates an extreme of dislike, aversion, and enmity experienced often toward an equal with a possible accompanying feeling of grudging respect ⟨if there had been one atom of genuine passion in his duplicity, she might have despised him less even while she *hated* him more —Ellen Glasgow⟩ ⟨he *hates* Lucy Wales. I don't mean dislike, or find distasteful, or have an aversion for; I mean hate —Hamilton Basso⟩ Applied to things and qualities it indicates extreme dislike ⟨between the cruelty that we *hate* and the humor that we prize —Agnes Repplier⟩ DETEST indicates very strong aversion but may lack the actively hostile malevolence associated with HATE ⟨the boy glimpsed something of the system of slavery, and early came to *detest* it —C.E.Carter⟩ LOATHE may suggest disgust and revulsion rather than aversion and active antipathy ⟨except when I am listening to their music I *loathe* the whole race: great, stupid, brutal, immoral, sentimental savages —Rose Macaulay⟩ ⟨he is not hated, for in hate there is something of fear and something of respect, neither of which is present here. And you could not say *loathed*, for loathing is passive and this is an active feeling. Best say detested; vigorously disliked —T.O. Heggen⟩ ABHOR may suggest a revulsion or repugnance accompanied by a tendency to flinch from as though in fear or horror ⟨Rome had made herself *abhorred* throughout the world by the violence and avarice of her generals —J.A. Froude⟩ ⟨this temptation to *abhor* the flesh, which reached such a pitch that he was filled with a horror of all created life —Compton Mackenzie⟩ ⟨rats, who *abhor* light and crave privacy —V.G.Heiser⟩ ABOMINATE may indicate strong lasting hatred and loathing as of something foully unnatural ⟨the accused . . . protest, disclaim, *abominate* the honor —Robert Browning⟩ These words all weaken in hyperbolic usages.

— **hate one's guts :** to feel a particularly strong animosity or contempt for someone ⟨I don't dislike him, I *hate his guts* —E.S.Gardner⟩

³**hate** \"\ *var of* HAET

hate·able *or* **hat·able** \'hād·əbəl\ *adj* **:** subject to being hated **:** DETESTABLE

hate·ful \'hātfəl\ *adj* [ME, fr. ¹*hate* + *-ful*] **1 :** full of hate **:** MALICIOUS ⟨talk of an outbreak of the Sioux who were surly and ~ —Bruce Siberts⟩ **2 a :** exciting or deserving of hatred **:** REPULSIVE ⟨opinions ~ to the majority —M.R.Cohen⟩ ⟨avoid that ~ backslapping heartiness —R.B.McKerrow⟩ **b :** UNCONGENIAL, ANNOYING, DISTASTEFUL ⟨~ to be without a garden —Gladys B. Stern⟩

syn ABHORRENT, OBNOXIOUS, INVIDIOUS, REPUGNANT, REPELLENT, DISTASTEFUL: HATEFUL applies to that which arouses hate, which calls forth active hostility ⟨the *hateful* old cat . . . who spits venom in her every sentence —C.B.Tinker⟩ ⟨the war to him was a *hateful* thing, stupid and unjust, waged for the extension of the obscene system of negro slavery —V.L. Parrington⟩ ABHORRENT may characterize that which arouses hatred blended with feelings of horror or outrage ⟨to Greek thought the indefinite or limitless was as the monstrous and unformed, and therefore *abhorrent* to the classic ideals of perfection —H.O.Taylor⟩ ⟨they themselves consider sorcery as an *abhorrent* crime —W.J.Wallace & Edith S. Taylor⟩ OBNOXIOUS describes what is objectionable or extremely repulsive ⟨when mosquitoes grew *obnoxious* we packed up our dishes and went to the house —Della Lutes⟩ ⟨an opportunity to hang around the house and smoke too many cigars and aggravate his poor, patient wife, and exasperate his children, and make himself generally *obnoxious* to all —Simeon Ford⟩ ⟨resentment against the Stamp Act reached a climax . . . His Majesty's Ship Diligence was prevented from landing the *obnoxious* stamps —*Amer. Guide Series: N. C.*⟩ INVIDIOUS describes that which excites ill will, resentment, or hatred, and is likely to rankle ⟨bowed with an *invidious* curtness and insolently walked off the stage —Edmund Wilson⟩ ⟨the *invidious* task of improving other people's utterance —J.M.Barzun⟩ ⟨rogues, by which perhaps rather *invidious* name I designate persons who will do nothing unless they get something out of it for themselves —G.B.Shaw⟩ REPUGNANT applies to what is resisted, disliked, and shunned as incompatible with one's principles or tastes ⟨soon the pressures of male eyes, eyes expressing sex, the curious lamplike luminosity, became *repugnant* to her —Peggy Bennett⟩ ⟨the internationalism of the socialists found any barriers of race or nationality *repugnant* —Oscar Handlin⟩ ⟨the nonlegal methods of the magistrates in dispensing judgment, so *repugnant* to the spirit of the common law —V.L. Parrington⟩ REPELLENT, close to REPUGNANT, may apply to what is shunned as offensive to personal tastes and inclinations ⟨as *repellent* in form and abstract in substance as many of the German writers on aesthetics of the nineteenth century —Irving Babbitt⟩ ⟨as a cardinal's nephew he was accustomed to many and *repellent* smiles upon inimical lips —Elinor Wylie⟩ DISTASTEFUL, a somewhat less forceful term, applies to what one dislikes, usu. for strongly personal reasons ⟨don't like my letters shown about as curiosities: it is most *distasteful* to me —Oscar Wilde⟩ ⟨developed a keen interest in the purely scientific aspects of medicine, the more practical phases of a practitioner's routine being *distasteful* to him —J.F.Fulton⟩ ⟨plans to refurnish the bedrooms with her own personal belongings, since she finds it *distasteful* to think of using the personal belongings of its previous occupants —Kenneth Roberts⟩

hate·ful·ly \-fəlē, -li\ *adv* [ME, fr. *hateful* + *-ly*] **:** in a hateful manner

hate·ful·ness *n* -ES **:** the quality or state of being hateful

hate·less \'hātləs\ *adj* **:** being without hate — **hate·less·ness** *n* -ES

hatemonger \'=,==\ *n* **:** one who enjoys or makes a practice of stirring up enmity **:** AGITATOR ⟨local ~*s* were probably financed and directed from outside the state —*Associated Press*⟩

hatemongering \'=,=(=)=\ *n* **:** the act or practice of stirring up hatred or enmity

hate out *vt* **:** to drive out by hostility ⟨a common way of dealing with offenders was to *hate* them *out* of the community —C.M.Babcock⟩

hat·er \'hād·ə(r), -ātə-\ *n* -S [ME *hatere*, fr. *haten* to hate + *-ere* -er] **:** one that hates

hates *pl of* HATE, *pres 3d sing of* HATE

hate sheet *n* **:** a newspaper or periodical characterized by strong feelings against a race or a national or religious group ⟨the worst inflammatory *hate sheet* published —Walter Winchell⟩

hat·field yew \'hat,fēld-\ *n, sometimes cap H* [after T. D. *Hatfield fl*1900 Am. horticulturist] **:** an ornamental yew that is a variety (*Taxus cuspidata hatfieldii*) of Japanese yew with ascending branches and wide spreading leaves

hat·ful \'hat,fu̇l\ *n, pl* **hatfuls** *also* **hatsful** \-t,fu̇lz, ts,fu̇l\ **1 :** as much or as many as a hat will hold ⟨gathered a ~ of eggs⟩ **2 :** a considerable amount or number **:** PECK ⟨these dives can cost you a ~ of money —T.H.Fielding⟩ ⟨turned down a ~ of princes —Helen B. Woodward⟩

hath *archaic pres 3d sing of* HAVE

hatha–yoga \'həd·ə'yōgə\ *n* [Skt *haṭha* force, persistence + *yoga* disciplined activity — more at YOGA] **:** a system of physical exercises for the control and perfection of the body that constitutes one of the four chief Hindu disciplines — see YOGA

ha·thi gray \'häd·ē-\ *n* [Hindi *hāthī* elephant, fr. Skt *hastin*, fr. *hasta* hand, elephant's trunk; prob. akin to Lith *pažastė* armpit] **:** a greenish gray that is yellower, lighter, and slightly less strong than cabbage green

hath·or column \'hathə(r)-\ *n, usu cap H* [*Hathor*, ancient Egyptian goddess of love] **:** a type of Egyptian column usu. having a 4-faced capital carved with heads of the goddess Hathor

hathor–headed \'=='==\ *adj, usu cap H* **:** carved with masks of Hathor

ha·thor·ic \hə'thȯrik, -'thär-\ *adj, usu cap* [*Hathor* + E *-ic*] **:** of or relating to Hathor or to a column surmounted by her image

ha·ti \'häd·ē\ *n* -S [Egypt *ḥati*] *often cap, Egyptian relig* **:** the physical heart — compare ²AB

hating *pres part of* HATE

hat in hand *adv* **:** in an attitude of respectful humility ⟨have to apologize *hat in hand*⟩

hat leather *n* **:** leather (as sheepskin or calf) for making hat or cap sweatbands

hat·less \'hatləs\ *adj* [ME *hatles*, fr. ¹*hat* + *-les* -less] **:** being without a hat — **hat·less·ness** *n* -ES

hat money *n* **1 :** PRIMAGE 1a **2 :** money in the form of truncated tin obelisks used in Pahang, Malay Peninsula in the 19th century

hat off *n, pl* **hats off :** ADMIRATION, CONGRATULATIONS ⟨end these memories with my *hat off* to the leaders —J.J.Mallon⟩ ⟨if you can do that and come up smiling — well, then, it's *hats off* all round —Myrtle R. White⟩

hat palm *n* **:** any of various palms or plants resembling palms whose leaves are used for making hats: as **a :** JIPIJAPA **b :** a palm (*Coccothrinax argentea*) of Panama **c :** CARNAUBA **d :** any of several West Indian fan palms of the genus *Thrinax*; *esp* **:** CHIP HAT PALM **e** *Philippines* **:** any of various palms of the genera *Areca*, *Corypha*, *Livistona*, and *Pandanus*

hat piece *n, obs* **:** a protective metal skullcap worn under a hat

hatpin \'=,=\ *n* **1 :** a long straight pin with an ornamented head that is used to keep a hat in place **2 :** a plant of the genus *Eriocaulon* (esp. *E. decangulare*)

hat rack *n* **1 a** (1) **:** a wooden framework with several projecting pegs that hangs against a wall and is used to hold hats and other articles of clothing (2) **:** CLOTHES TREE (3) **:** HALLSTAND **b :** a loop (as of wire) into which to slip the brim of a hat under a theater seat or shelf or against a wall **2 :** a thin low-quality meat animal

hat rack 1a(1)

ha·tred \'hā·trəd\ *n* -S [ME *hatred*, *hatered*, *hatereden*, fr. ¹*hate* + *-reden* (fr. OE *rǣden* condition) — more at KINDRED] **1 :** HATE **2 :** a general attitude of prejudiced hostility **:** group animosity ⟨the human race lives in a welter of organized ~*s* and threats of mutual extermination —Bertrand Russell⟩

hats *pl of* HAT, *pres 3d sing of* HAT

hat·sa \'hatsə\ *n, pl* **hatsa** *or* **hatsas** *usu cap* **1 a :** a Negro African people of northern Tanganyika **b :** a member of such people **2 :** the language spoken by the Hatsa people and related to Khoisan

hatsful *pl of* HATFUL

hatstand \'=,=\ *n* **1 a :** CLOTHES TREE **b :** HALLSTAND **2 :** an accessory for a closet shelf that consists of a short rod set in a base topped with a knob or disk and used to support a hat so that it will keep its shape while not in use

hatted *adj* [fr. past part. of ²*hat*] **:** wearing a hat ⟨two neatly ~ and gloved old ladies —Claudia Cassidy⟩ ⟨a bearskin-*hatted* sentry⟩

¹**hat·ter** \'had·ə(r), -atə-\ *n* -S [ME, fr. ¹*hat* + *-er*] **1 :** one that makes, sells, or cleans and repairs hats **2** [prob. so called fr. the presumed applicability of the proverbial expression "mad as a hatter"] *Austral* **a :** a solitary bush dweller **b :** a lone miner or prospector — often used of a person who has become eccentric from too much solitude **3 :** fur esp. of rabbits for making felt hats — usu. used in pl.

²**hatter** *vt* -ED/-ING/-S [ME (Sc) *hatteren*] **1** *now dial* **:** BATTER, BRUISE **2** *archaic* **:** to wear out **:** worry and harass — sometimes used with *out*

¹**hat·te·ria** \hə'tirēə\ [NL] *syn of* SPHENODON

²**hatteria** \"\ *n* -S **:** TUATARA

hat·ti \'had·ē\ *or* **khat·ti** \'k̲a-\ *n, pl* **hatti** *or* **hattis** *or* **khatti** *or* **khattis** *usu cap* [Akkadian *ḫatti, khatti*] **1 :** a pre-Hittite people of central Anatolia **2 :** a member of such people — **hat·ti·an** \'had·ēən\ *adj, usu cap*

¹**hat·tic** \'had·ik\ *adj, usu cap* [*Hatti* + *-ic*] **:** of or relating to the Hatti people

²**hattic** \"\ *n* -S *usu cap* **:** a language known from quotations in Hittite documents and assumed to be that of the Hatti

hatting *n* -S [fr. gerund of ²*hat*] **1 a :** the making of hats **b :** the material from which hats are made **2 :** HAT 3

hat·tock \'(h)ad·ək\ *n* -S [¹*hat* + *-ock*] **1** *obs* **:** a small hat **2** *dial Eng* **a :** a grain shock with the top protected by sheaves leaned slantingly against it heads down **b :** one of the two protecting sheaves

hat tree *n* **1 a :** CLOTHES TREE **b :** HALLSTAND **2 :** either of two Australian trees (*Sterculia discolor* and *S. lurida*) that produce strong bast fibers

hat trick *n* **1 a :** a sleight-of-hand trick performed with a hat **b :** a skillful maneuver ⟨a remarkable political *hat trick* —Mollie Panter-Downes⟩ **2 a** [prob. so called fr. a former practice of rewarding this feat with a present of a new hat] **:** the dismissal by a bowler of three batsmen with three consecutive balls in cricket **b :** a similar outstanding feat in another sport: as (1) **:** the winning of three consecutive horse races (2) **:** the scoring of three goals in one game by a hockey player (3) **:** the hitting by one player of a single, double, triple, and home run in a game of baseball

hau \'hau̇\ *n* -S [Hawaiian & Marquesan] **:** MAJAGUA a

haubergeon *var of* HABERGEON

hau·ber·get \'hōbə(r)jet\ *n* -S [ML *haubergettum*] **:** an early English woolen cloth

hau·berk \'hȯ,bərk\ *n* -S [ME, fr. OF *hauberc*, of Gmc origin; akin to OE *healsbeorg* neck armor, OHG *halsberg*, ON *halsbjörg*; all fr. a prehistoric WGmc-NGmc compound whose constituents are represented respectively by OE *heals* neck and OE *beorg* protection; akin to OE *beorgan* to preserve, defend — more at COLLAR, BURY] **1 :** a long tunic of ring or chain mail that with a close-fitting helmet and a shield constituted the main defensive armor of the 12th to 14th centuries **2 :** HABERGEON

hauberk

haud \'hȯd\ *chiefly Scot var of* HOLD

hau·er·ite \'hau̇ə,rīt\ *n* -S [G *hauerit*, fr. Franz von *Hauer* †1899 Austrian geologist + G *-it* -ite] **:** a mineral MnS_2 consisting of native manganese sulfide and occurring as reddish brown or brownish black octahedral or pyritohedral crystals or massive (sp. gr. 3.46)

hauf \'häf, 'hȯf\ *dial Brit var of* HALF

haugh \'hȯ(k̲), 'hä(k̲)\ *n* -S [ME (Sc dial.) *holch*, *hawch*, fr. OE *healh* corner of land; akin to OE *holh* cave, *hol* hollow — more at HOLE] *chiefly Scot* **:** a low-lying meadow by the side of a river **:** an alluvial plain

haught *adj* [alter. (influenced by such words as *caught*, *taught*) of ME *haute*, fr. MF *haut*, lit., high, fr. L *altus* — more at OLD] **1** *obs* **:** HAUGHTY ⟨thou ~ insulting man —Shak.⟩ **2** *obs* **:** NOBLE, HIGH-MINDED, LOFTY

haugh·ti·ly \'hȯd·ᵊlē, |t|, |ᵊli, |əl- *also* 'hä|\ *adv* **:** in a haughty manner

haugh·ti·ness \|ēnəs, |in-\ *n* -ES **:** the quality or state of being haughty **:** ARROGANCE

haugh·ty \|ē, |i\ *adj* -ER/-EST [*haught* + *-y*] **1 :** disdainfully proud or overbearing **:** ARROGANT ⟨~ young beauty . . . never deigned to notice us —Herman Melville⟩ **2** *obs* **:** exalted in nature **:** NOBLE ⟨works . . . equal unto this ~ enterprise —Edmund Spenser⟩ **3 :** imposing in aspect **:** LOFTY ⟨~ cathedral⟩

syn see PROUD

¹**haul** \'hȯl\ *vb* -ED/-ING/-S [ME *halen* to pull, draw, fr. OF *haler*, of Gmc origin; akin to MD *halen* to pull; akin to OE *geholian* to obtain, OHG *halōn*, *holōn*, *holēn* to call, fetch, OS *halōn*, and perh. to OE *hlōwan* to low — more at LOW] *vt* **1 a :** to change the course of (a ship) esp. so as to sail closer to the wind — often used with directional adverb ⟨told the chief officer to ~ her off four points —*Mercantile Marine Mag.*⟩ **b :** to sail or hold on a course ⟨~*ed* his skiff all the way north —A.B.Mayse⟩ **2 a** (1) **:** to exert traction on **:** PULL ⟨~ a net⟩ ⟨~ a wagon⟩ — often followed by directional adverb ⟨~ out a stump⟩ ⟨~ up a lobster pot⟩ ⟨~ in an anchor⟩ ⟨~ down a flag⟩ (2) **:** to take by drawing in or up (as with a net) ⟨~ herring⟩ **b :** to exert influence on so as to achieve a desired end **:** DRAG ⟨his wife . . . will ~ him to a highbrow play —Francis Fergusson⟩ **c :** to transport from one place to another in a vehicle **:** CART ⟨~ passengers⟩ ⟨~ coal from the mines⟩ ⟨cattle are ~*ed* by rail⟩ **3 :** to bring before (an authority) for interrogation or punishment **:** HALE ⟨~ traffic violators into court⟩ — often used with *up* ⟨~ up a . . . president of the United States to explain his conduct in office to a congressional committee —Elmer Davis⟩ ~ *vi* **1 a :** to change course so as to sail closer to the wind — often used with *up* ⟨she ~*ed up* 'til the sails began to shiver⟩ **b :** to sail on a course ⟨decided to ~ south⟩ **2 a** (1) **:** to exert traction **:** PULL ⟨~ on a rope⟩ — often followed by directional adverb ⟨~ back on the reins⟩ ⟨~*ed* over to put a pilot aboard —H.A.Chippendale⟩ (2) **:** to take or seek a catch esp. of fish by hauling a net ⟨go ~*ing* for herring⟩ **b :** to propel oneself **:** COME, GO ⟨about three o'clock we ~*ed* into Moonridge —Kenneth Clark⟩ ⟨the bull ~*ed* back for another lunge —F.B.Gipson⟩ **c :** to carry from one place to another **:** furnish transportation ⟨nominal charge for ~*ing*⟩ **3** *of the wind* **:** to change direction **:** SHIFT ⟨the wind has ~*ed* more to the south —William Willis⟩ — often used with *around* ⟨~*ed* around to the starboard quarter⟩ **syn** see PULL — **haul down one's colors :** SURRENDER ⟨saw she was beaten and *hauled down her colors*⟩ — **haul in one's horns :** retreat from an arrogant or aggressive position ⟨admitted his error and *hauled in his horns*⟩ — **haul one over the coals :** to criticize or reprimand **:** take to task **:** CENSURE ⟨*hauled him over the coals* for loafing on the job⟩ — **haul one's wind :** head the bow of a ship closer into the wind **:** LUFF ⟨*hauled his wind* until the sail was trimmed in flat —Vincent McHugh⟩ — often used with *on, upon,* or *to*

²**haul** \"\ *n* -S **1 a :** an act of dragging **:** strong pull ⟨the rope stood up under the strain of the ~⟩ **b :** a mechanical device for pulling **:** CONVEYOR BELT ⟨mine cars on a car ~⟩ **2 :** the result of an effort to collect either legitimately or by theft **:** TAKE ⟨rich ~*s* of plankton —N.B.Marshall⟩ ⟨a mink coat ~ —Rose Thurburn⟩; *specif* **:** the fish taken in a single draft of a net **3** *ropemaking* **:** a bundle of yarns to be tarred **4 a :** an act of transporting ⟨a rail ~ meant that several hundred expensive . . . cars would have to be bought —N.M.Clark⟩ **b :** the distance or route over which a load is transported ⟨sand is normally taken from deposits within a reasonable ~ of the site of building —G.S.Brady⟩ ⟨ride first-class only on the short ~*s* —T.H.Fielding⟩ ⟨the long ~ round the Cape —Sir Winston Churchill⟩ **c :** the quantity of material transported **:** LOAD ⟨~*s* of unsifted ore —*Times Lit. Supp.*⟩

haulabout \'==,=\ *n* -S [fr. *haul about*, v.] **:** a steel barge with large hatchways and coal transporters used for coaling ships

haul·age \'hȯlij\ *n* -S *often attrib* **1 :** the act or process of hauling **2 :** a charge made for hauling

haulage rope *n* **:** TRANSMISSION ROPE

haulageway \'==,=\ *n* **:** a passage in a coal mine along which coal is transported **:** GANGWAY 4

haulaway \'==,=\ *n* -S [fr. *haul away*, v.] **:** a motor truck designed for the transportation of new automobiles

haulback \'=,=\ *n* -S [fr. *haul back*, v.] **1 :** a small wire rope used to pull the main cable back to the timber after each haulage in logging **2 :** COMEBACK 4

haulaway

hauled *past of* HAUL

haul·er \'hȯlə(r)\ *n* -S **:** one that hauls; *specif* **:** a commercial establishment whose business is hauling

haul·ier \'hȯlyə(r), -liə-\ *Brit var of* HAULER

hauling *n* -S [fr. gerund of *haul*] **1 :** an act or instance of applying physical traction to move something **2 :** the act or occupation of transporting goods in a vehicle ⟨hired a trucker to do the ~⟩

hauling ground *n* **:** an area where young male seals congregate during the breeding season

[1]**haulm** *also* **halm** \'hȯm, 'hälm\ *n* -s [ME *halm*, fr. OE *healm*; akin to OHG *halm* straw, stem, ON *halmr* straw, stem, L *culmus* stalk, Gk *kalamos* reed, OSlav *slama* straw] **1 :** the stems or tops of cultivated plants (as peas, beans, potatoes, and cereals) esp. after the crop has been gathered **:** STRAW, LITTER **2 :** an individual plant stem (as the culm of a grass)

[2]**haulm** \"\ *vt* -ED/-ING/-S *Brit* **:** to arrange (straw) for thatching

haulmy \-mi\ *adj* -ER/-EST *Brit* **:** having haulms

haul off *vi* **:** to get ready often on the spur of the moment ⟨*haul off* and hit him⟩ ⟨what makes you think you can *haul off* and leave here without paying me? —Erskine Caldwell⟩

haulover \'ₛ,ₛₛ\ *n* -s [fr. *haul over*, v.] **:** PORTAGE 4

hauls *pres 3d sing of* HAUL, *pl of* HAUL

haul seine *n* **:** a long net for commercial fishing one end of which is usu. attached to the land and the other run around a school of fish which are then drawn ashore

haul seiner *n* **:** one that fishes with a haul seine

haul up *vi* **:** to come to a stop ⟨the child circled the room and *hauled up* in front of the visitor⟩

haul–up \'ₛ,ₛ\ *n* -s [fr. *haul up*, v.] **:** a jack ladder having a V-shaped trough up which logs are drawn by a jack chain

haulyard *var of* HALYARD

haunch \'hȯnch, -ä-, -á-\ *n* -ES [ME *haunche*, fr. OF *hanche*, of Gmc origin; akin to MD *hanke* hip, haunch] **1 a :** HIP 1a(1) **b :** HINDQUARTER 2 — usu. used in pl. **2 :** HINDQUARTER 1 **3 :** either side of an arch between the springing and the crown **:** the part of an arch between the vertical lines drawn through the crown and the outer extremity of the extrados and by horizontal lines drawn through the crown and the spring point **4 :** the tapered end of a tenon **5 :** the shoulder of a highway — usu. used in pl.

haunch bone *n* **:** INNOMINATE BONE; *specif* **:** ILIUM

haunched \-cht\ *adj* **:** having haunches

haunch·less \-chləs\ *adj* **:** lacking haunches

haunchy \-chē\ *adj* -ER/-EST **:** having large haunches ⟨in her early twenties she was bulbous, and in her late twenties she was merely sort of ~ —Richard Boeth⟩

[1]**haunt** \'hȯnt, -ä-, -á-\ *vb* -ED/-ING/-S [ME *haunten*, fr. OF *hanter*, prob. of Gmc origin; akin to OE *hāmettan* to domicile, ON *heimta* to bring home, fetch, pull, claim; derivatives fr. the root of E *home*] *vt* **1 a :** to visit often **:** linger in the vicinity of (a place) **:** FREQUENT ⟨loved and ~*ed* the theater —Carlos Baker⟩ ⟨knew . . . what coverts the pheasants ~*ed* —Adrian Bell⟩ **b :** to continually seek the company of (a person) **:** hang around ⟨impostors that ~ the official in foreign ports —Van Wyck Brooks⟩ **2 a :** to have a disquieting or harmful effect on **:** TROUBLE, MOLEST ⟨the gnawing question . . . ~*ed* the uneasy royal heart —Francis Hackett⟩ ⟨crisis was to ~ her days —Charles Lee⟩ ⟨mysterious illness that . . . would not go until the being it ~*ed* lay dead —Edith Sitwell⟩ ⟨icebergs . . . which drift out to sea to ~ mariners —Glen Jacobsen⟩ **b** (1) **:** to linger in the consciousness of **:** recur constantly to ⟨the possibility of the dairy farm ~*ed* her mind —Ellen Glasgow⟩ ⟨single lines of poetry often ~ people who cannot trace them to their source —Bennett Cerf⟩ (2) **:** to reappear continually in **:** recur constantly in ⟨he returns to a certain type of beautiful uncontemplative woman who has already ~*ed* his poetry —Edmund Wilson⟩ **3 :** to visit or inhabit as a disembodied spirit ⟨spirits are supposed to ~ the places where their bodies most resorted —Charles Dickens⟩ ⟨the river is ~*ed* by certain malevolent water spirits —J.G.Frazer⟩ **~** *vi* **1 :** to stay around or persist **:** LINGER ⟨likes to ~ around the firehouse⟩ ⟨scent that can ~ for a lifetime —Flora Thompson⟩ **2 :** to appear habitually as a disembodied spirit ⟨not far from . . . where she ~*ed* appeared for a short time a much more remarkable spirit —W.B. Yeats⟩

[2]**haunt** \"\ *n* -s [ME, fr. *haunten*, v.] **1** *now dial Brit* **:** PRACTICE, CUSTOM, HABIT **2** *obs* **:** an act of frequenting in numbers **:** CONCOURSE ⟨our life, exempt from public ~, finds tongues in trees —Shak.⟩ **3 a :** a place habitually frequented **:** favorite resort **:** HOME ⟨sages in their sequestered ~*s* —Laurence Binyon⟩ ⟨own their own ships and fly them to weekend ~*s* —Phil Gustafson⟩ ⟨quiet ~*s* of beauty —S.P.B. Mais⟩ **b** (1) **:** the lair or feeding ground of an animal **:** area where an animal is usu. to be found ⟨~ of the tiger⟩ ⟨herring are most plentiful when the water in their favorite ~*s* is a degree or two warmer than average —J.P.Tully⟩ (2) **:** the favorite environment of a plant ⟨~ of the cardinal flower⟩ **4** *or* **hant** \'hant, -aa(ə)-,-ai-,-á-,-ä-\ *chiefly dial* **:** a disembodied spirit **:** GHOST

haunted *adj* **1 :** FILLED, INFESTED — now usu. used in combination ⟨a sad, kindly, God-*haunted* man —S.N.Behrman⟩ ⟨seal-*haunted* isle —A.A.MacGregor⟩ ⟨moved . . . from one dust-*haunted* base to another —Martin Quigley⟩ **2 :** inhabited by or as if by apparitions **:** frequented by ghosts ⟨a ~ house⟩ ⟨as dusk comes on Kipling's study is the most ~ place I know —Christopher Morley⟩ **3 :** HARASSED, AFFLICTED, TROUBLED ⟨the deep ~ eyes of a man whose convictions have burned him hollow —T.H.White b. 1915⟩ — **haunt·ed·ness** *n* -ES

haunt·er \-tə(r)\ *n* -s [ME *hawntare*, fr. *hawnten*, *haunten* to haunt + *-are* -er] **:** one that haunts

[1]**haunting** *n* -s [ME, fr. *haunten* + *-ing*] **:** an act of frequenting esp. by a disembodied spirit ⟨simply not the case that all incumbents vouched for ~*s* —A.G.N.Flew⟩ ⟨the beech forests harbor silence and strange ~*s* —*Times Lit. Supp.*⟩

[2]**haunting** *adj* [ME, fr. pres. part. of *haunten* to haunt — more at HAUNT] **:** that haunts: as **a :** lingering in the consciousness **:** not readily forgotten ⟨the cathedral organ and the distant voices have a ~ beauty —Claudia Cassidy⟩ **b :** having a disquieting effect **:** DISTURBING ⟨from two handsome and talented young men to two ~ horrors of disintegration —Charles Lee⟩ — **haunt·ing·ly** *adv*

haun·ty \'hȯnti, 'hän-,'han-\ *adj* -ER/-EST [origin unknown] *dial Eng* **:** UNRULY, RESTLESS

hau·pia \hau'pēə\ *n* -s [Hawaiian] **:** a Hawaiian pudding made of cornstarch and coconut cream

hau·ra·nit·ic \¦hȯrə¦nid·ik\ *adj, usu cap* [*Hauran*, region in southern Syria + E *-ite* + *-ic*] **:** of or relating to the region of Hauran

hau·ri·ant *also* **hau·ri·ent** \'hȯrēənt, 'haủr-\ *adj* [L *haurient-, hauriens*, pres. part. of *haurire* to draw (as water), drain, devour — more at EXHAUST] *heraldry, of a fish or water animal* **:** being in pale with the head up as if rising for air — compare URINANT

haus *pl of* HAU

hau·sa *also* **haus·sa** \'haủsə, |zə\ *n, pl* **hausa** *or* **hausas** *usu cap* **1 a :** a highly variable negroid people of the Sudan between Lake Chad and the Niger numbering in the millions and united primarily by language **b :** a member of such people **2 :** the Chad language of the Hausa people that is widely used in west Africa as a trade language

hause \'hȯs, 'häs\ *chiefly Scot var of* HALS

hau·sen \'haủzᵊn\ *n* -s [G, fr. MHG *hūse, hūsen*, fr. OHG *hūso* — more at HUSO] **:** BELUGA 1

haus·frau \'haủs,fraủ\ *n, pl* **hausfraus** \-aủz\ *also* **haus·frau·en** \-aủən\ [G, fr. *haus* house (fr. OHG *hūs*) + *frau* wife, woman, fr. OHG *frouwa* lady, mistress — more at HOUSE, FRAU] **:** the mistress of a household **:** HOUSEWIFE ⟨the women were dumpy, overworked ~*s*, regarded only for their ability to work harder than any hired man —Joanna Spencer⟩

haus·mann·ite \'haủsmə,nīt\ *n* -s [J. F. L. *Hausmann* †1859 Ger. mineralogist + E *-ite*] **:** an opaque mineral Mn_3O_4 consisting of manganese tetroxide found commonly in brownish black tetragonal crystals

hausse–col \(')(h)ōs¦käl\ *n* -s [F, by folk etymology (influence of F *hausser* to raise) fr. MF *housecol, hochecol, hauscol*] **:** GORGET 1

haust *abbr* [L *haustus*] draft — used in pharmacy

haus·tel·late \(')hȯ¦stelət, 'hȯstə,lāt\ *adj* [NL *haustellum* + E *-ate*] **:** having a haustellum **:** SUCTORIAL

haus·tel·lum \hȯ'steləm\ *n, pl* **haustel·la** \-lə\ [NL, fr. L *haustus* (past part. of *haurire* to draw, drawn up) + *-ellum* (dim. suffix) — more at EXHAUST] **:** a proboscis adapted for sucking blood or the juices of plants

haus·to·ri·al \(')hȯ¦stōrēəl\ *adj* [NL *haustorium* + E *-al*] **:** HAUSTELLATE

haus·to·ri·um \ₛ'ₛrēəm\ *n, pl* **hausto·ria** \-rēə\ [NL, fr. L *haustus* + *-orium*] **:** a food-absorbing outgrowth of a hypha, stem, or other plant organ: as **a :** a projection from various fungous hyphae **b :** a cell of the embryo sac or embryo in some seed plants **c :** an outgrowth of the stem or root in a parasitic seed plant (as dodder)

haus·tral \'hȯstrəl\ *also* **haus·trat·ed** \-,strād·əd\ *adj* [NL *haustrum* + E *-al* or *-ated* (fr. *-ate* + *-ed*)] **:** of, relating to, or exhibiting haustra

haus·tra·tion \hȯ'strāshən\ *n* -s [NL *haustrum* + E *-ation*] **:** the quality or state of having haustra

haus·trum \'hȯstrəm\ *n, pl* **haus·tra** \-rə\ [NL, fr. L, machine for drawing water, fr. *haustus*, past part. of *haurire* to draw (as water) — more at EXHAUST] **:** a recess in the colon

haus·tus \'hȯstəs\ *n, pl* **haustus** [L, lit., action of drawing, fr. *haustus*, past part.] *Roman & civil law* **:** a right to draw water from a well or spring on another's land and a right of passage to and from the well or spring — compare SERVITUDE

haut·bois *also* **haut·boy** \'(h)ō,bȯi\ *n, pl* **hautbois** \-ȯiz\ *also* **hautboys** \"\ [MF *hautbois*, fr. *haut* high + *bois* wood, woods, of Gmc origin; akin to OHG *busc* bush, forest — more at HAUGHT, BUSH] **1 a :** OBOE **b :** a pipe-organ stop of 16, 8, and sometimes 4-foot pitch similar to an organ oboe **2 :** a strawberry (*Fragaria moschata*) native to Europe and early brought into cultivation having the calyx strongly recurved in fruit

haut·boist \-ōiəst\ *also* **haut·boy·ist** \"\ *n* -s [F *hautboïste*, fr. *hautbois* + *-iste*] **:** OBOIST

haute cou·ture \,(h)ōt,kü'tü(ə)r\ *n* [F, lit., high sewing] **1 :** the leading dressmaking establishments for the creation of exclusive often trend-setting fashions for women **2 a :** the art of creating high fashions for women **b :** the fashions created

haute école \,(h)ōd·(,)ā'kȯl, -'kəl\ *n* [F, lit., high school] **:** a highly stylized form of classical riding **:** advanced dressage

haute–lisse \(')ōt¦lēs\ *adj* [F] **:** HIGH-WARP

hau·teur \(')hȯ¦tər, (')(h)ō¦-\ *n* -s [F, fr. *haut* high, proud + *-eur* -or — more at HAUGHT] **:** an assumption of superiority **:** arrogant or condescending manner **:** HAUGHTINESS ⟨a cold ~ and disdain which infuriated his colleagues and made him almost impossible to work with —J.H.Plumb⟩

haut monde \ō'mōⁿd, -mänd\ *n* [F, lit., high world] **:** the socially elect **:** high society

haut pas \ō'pä\ *n* [ME *hautepase*, fr. MF *haut pas*, lit., high step] **:** a raised part of a floor **:** DAIS — compare HALFPACE

haut–relief \¦ō, ¦ō+ₛ'ₛ\ *n* [F] **:** HIGH RELIEF

ha·uy·nite \ä'wē,nīt\ *or* **ha·uyne** \ä'wēn\ *n* -s [*hauynite* fr. *hauyne* + *-ite*; *hauyne* fr. F *haüyne*, fr. Abbé René Just *Haüy* †1822 Fr. mineralogist + F *-ine*] **:** an isometric silicate mineral $(Na,Ca)_{4-8}Al_6Si_6O_{24}(SO_4)_{1-2}$ consisting of sulfate of aluminum, calcium, and sodium and occurring commonly as rounded grains in various igneous rocks (hardness 5.5–6, sp. gr. 2.4–2.5)

hav *abbr* haversine

hav·age \'(h)avij\ *n* -s [[1]*have* + *-age*] *dial Eng* **:** familial descent **:** LINEAGE

ha·vai·ki \hə'vīkē\ *n, cap* [Marquesan & Tuamotuan] **:** a fabled original homeland from which the Polynesians believe themselves to have come and to which their spirits return after death

[1]**ha·va·na** \hə'vanə\ *adj, usu cap* [fr. *Havana*, Cuba] **1 :** of or from Havana, the capital of Cuba **:** of the kind or style prevalent in Havana **:** HAVANAN **2 a** *of tobacco* **:** grown in Cuba **b** *of a cigar* **:** made in Cuba or from Cuban tobacco

[2]**havana** \"\ *n* **1** -s *usu cap* [prob. fr. Sp *habano*, fr. *habano*, adj., cf Havana, fr. La *Habana* (Havana), Cuba] **a :** a cigar made partly or wholly from Cuban tobacco ⟨a box of *Havanas*⟩ **b :** tobacco raised in Cuba ⟨*Havana* leaf⟩ **2** *or* **havana brown** -s *often cap H* **:** BISMARCK BROWN **3 a** *usu cap* **:** a breed of rather small brown rabbits originating in Holland **b** -s *often cap* **:** a rabbit of this breed

[1]**ha·van·an** \-nən\ *adj, usu cap* [*Havana*, Cuba + E *-an*] **1 :** of, relating to, or characteristic of Havana, the capital of Cuba **2 :** of, relating to, or characteristic of the people of Havana

[2]**havanan** \"\ *n* -s *cap* **:** a native or resident of Havana

havana seed *n, usu cap H* **:** any of several U. S. cigar tobaccos derived from seed orig. imported from Cuba

ha·va·su·pai \,hävə'sü,pī\ *n, pl* **havasupai** *or* **havasupais** *usu cap* **1 a :** an Indian people of Cataract Canyon, a tributary of Grand Canyon, Arizona **b :** a member of such people **2 :** a Yuman language of the Havasupai people

havdalah *var of* HABDALAH

[1]**have** \(')hav, (')hev; *as an auxiliary* " *or* ,(h)əv *or after a vowel* v; *before* "to" *usu* ¦haf *or* ¦hef\ *vb, past* **had** \(')had, (')hed *as an auxiliary* " *or* ,(h)əd *or after a vowel* d\ *also archaic 2d sing* **hadst** \(')ha¦dzt, (')he¦, ,(h)ə¦, ¦dst, ¦tst\ *or* **had·dest** (with *thou*) \¦hadəst, ¦hed-\ *past part* **had** *also chiefly Scot* **haen** \(')hān\ *pres part* **hav·ing** \¦haviŋ, ¦hev-\ *pres 1st sing* **have** *also dial Brit* **ha** \(')ha, ,(h)ə\ *or chiefly Scot* **hae** \(')hā\ *2d sing* **have** *also archaic* **hast** (with *thou*) \(')hast, (')hest, ,(h)əst\ *or dial Brit* **ha**; *3d sing* **has** \(')haz, (')hez; *as an auxiliary* " *or* ,(h)əz *or after a vowel* z; *before* "to" *usu* ¦has *or* ¦hes\ *also archaic* **hath** \(')hath, (')heth, ,(h)əth\ *or dial Brit* **have**; *pl* **have** *also dial Brit* **ha** *or* **han** \(')han, ,(h)ən\ *or chiefly Scot* **hae** \(')hā\ [ME *haven, habben*, fr. OE *habban*; akin to OHG *habēn* to have, ON *hafa*, Goth *haban*, OE *hebban* to lift, raise — more at HEAVE] *vt* **1 a :** to hold in possession as property **:** OWN ⟨~ a cow⟩ ⟨~ a car⟩ ⟨~ a lot of money⟩ **b :** to hold, keep, or retain esp. in one's use, service, regard, or affection or at one's disposal ⟨can't ~ your cake and eat it too⟩ ⟨the chairman *has* all the tickets needed⟩ ⟨*has* some rare coins saved up⟩ ⟨~ him in fond remembrance⟩ ⟨~ no time to lose⟩ **c :** to consist of (as all one's elements or constituent parts) **:** CONTAIN, INCLUDE ⟨~ a subordinate part⟩ ⟨the car *has* a self-starter⟩ ⟨the lake *has* some large pickerel⟩ ⟨April *has* 30 days⟩ **d :** CARRY, BEAR, SUPPORT ⟨~ an essential part⟩ ⟨~ an attachment⟩ ⟨the house *has* a roof⟩ ⟨the dress *has* a label⟩ **:** WEAR ⟨*has* a blue suit⟩ ⟨*has* a tweed coat⟩ **e :** to be possessed by ⟨declaring she *had* a devil —Max Peacock⟩ **2 :** to feel compulsion, obligation, or necessity in regard to — used with a noun object followed by *to* and the infinitive ⟨~ a letter to write⟩ ⟨~ a task to perform⟩ ⟨~ nothing to do⟩ ⟨~ a deadline to meet⟩ **3 a :** to stand in any of several personal relationships to (as father to son, host to guest, friend to friend) ⟨the man *had* four daughters⟩ ⟨it is unpleasant to ~ enemies⟩ **b :** to be attended by or associated with often as an essential concomitant ⟨the king *has* many courtiers⟩ ⟨certain foods present special difficulties and so ~ rules of their own to make eating them easier —Agnes M. Miall⟩ ⟨the wine *had* no effect on me⟩ ⟨his proposal *had* many objections⟩ **c :** to stand or remain in any of several implicit physical, logical, or emotional relationships to ⟨as we sailed north we *had* Africa on our right⟩ ⟨*had* only six feet of water under the keel⟩ ⟨the word *has* no exact equivalent⟩ ⟨~ the voters on the right side⟩ **4 a** (1) **:** to acquire or get possession of **:** OBTAIN ⟨nothing to be *had* from the empty larder⟩ ⟨good meat could not be *had* at all during the food shortage⟩ (2) **:** GAIN ⟨*had* a lot from the trip⟩ ⟨*had* nothing from the experience⟩ (3) **:** to be able to avail oneself of or utilize (something already done or completed) ⟨in this field a student *has* many helpful monographs and handbooks⟩ (4) **:** WIN ⟨*had* the hole by two strokes⟩ ⟨ought to ~ the fight by the third round⟩ **b :** RECEIVE ⟨*had* news of the lost ship⟩ ⟨asked if the police *had* any information that might lead to an arrest⟩ ⟨*had* a letter from him⟩ **c :** ACCEPT ⟨so burnt no one would ~ a piece⟩; *specif* **:** to accept in marriage ⟨wished to marry but could find no one who would ~ him⟩ **d :** ACHIEVE ⟨believes a satisfactory peace can be *had* between the belligerent powers⟩ **e :** to copulate with ⟨rumor claimed he had never *had* a woman in his life —Norman Mailer⟩ **5 a :** to be marked, distinguished, or characterized by (as an attribute, quality, position, or a distinctive biographical fact) ⟨the cloth *has* a silky texture⟩ ⟨*had* a taste for exotic foods⟩ ⟨*has* a habit of nail biting⟩ ⟨the threat *had* the desired effect⟩ ⟨*had* a height of four feet⟩ ⟨the goods *had* a value of $1000⟩ ⟨the common law *had* its origin in a body of writs drawn from various uses —Curtis Bok⟩ **b :** EXHIBIT, SHOW, MANIFEST ⟨*had* the goodness to get a chair⟩ ⟨*had* the gall to refuse⟩ **c :** USE, EXERCISE ⟨~ a care what you say to him⟩ ⟨~ mercy on us⟩ **6 a :** to experience esp. by submitting to, undergoing, being affected by, enjoying, or suffering ⟨~ a rest⟩ ⟨~ a medical examination⟩ ⟨~ a cold⟩ ⟨the worst government they ever *had*⟩ ⟨~ an operation⟩ ⟨a book that will ~ a wide circulation⟩ **:** PASS ⟨~ a life full of suffering⟩ **b :** to carry on or engage in **:** PERFORM ⟨~ a standing feud with a political opponent⟩ ⟨~ a fight⟩ ⟨~ a talk with a friend⟩ ⟨~ a part in a play⟩; *also* **:** EXECUTE, TAKE ⟨*had* a punch at the assailant before he escaped⟩ ⟨*had* a look at the body⟩ **c :** to entertain in the mind or feelings **:** CHERISH ⟨*had* a great deal of affection for the children⟩ ⟨~ no doubt of success⟩ ⟨~ an opinion⟩ **7 a :** to cause to go **:** LEAD, CONVEY ⟨did not ~ the child anywhere where he could be exposed to measles⟩ ⟨the aunt *had* the child to live with her⟩ **b :** to cause to by persuasive or forceful means (as by inviting, ordering, compelling) — used with the infinitive without *to* ⟨*had* the chauffeur drive to town⟩ ⟨*had* the children go to bed early⟩ ⟨the court *had* him pay the man what he owed him⟩ ⟨you are going to pay for the damage and I'll ~ you know it⟩ **c :** to cause to be ⟨*has* people around at all times⟩ ⟨likes to ~ people in the office who are efficient⟩ ⟨*had* him sick with the details of the accident⟩ ⟨anxious to ~ you a satisfied customer —Richard Joseph⟩ ⟨nearly *had* the table over with her pushing and shoving⟩ ⟨*had* the tent poles down in a minute⟩ **d :** to cause to become ⟨I'll ~ him a good soldier before long⟩ **e** (1) **:** to cause to come by inviting ⟨~ friends over for an evening of bridge⟩ (2) **:** to receive as a guest ⟨I'll be over whenever you can ~ me⟩ **f :** to represent to be ⟨the author always *has* his characters doing foolish things⟩ **8 a :** to allow or to suffer to — used with the infinitive without *to* ⟨would not ~ him treat the dog so⟩ **b :** to allow to be or suffer to be ⟨will not ~ him chosen president⟩ ⟨~ women in the men's part of the building only once a month on visitors' day⟩ ⟨a strange man to ~ around⟩ **9 a** (1) **:** to be marked by an intellectual grasp of **:** KNOW, UNDERSTAND ⟨a student who *has* only a little French and no mathematics⟩ ⟨*having* no foreign language he was handicapped and ineffectual —Carl Van Doren⟩ (2) **:** to understand the character of ⟨you do not need to associate with him long before you ~ him⟩ (3) **:** to be able to handle adequately ⟨the job is so easy that in only a few days you ~ it⟩ **b :** to place in a scale of distinctions **:** CATEGORIZE ⟨sees with so many sense and other organs that you never know where to ~ him artistically —*Times Lit. Supp.*⟩ **10 a :** to maneuver into a position of disadvantage or cause to be at a disadvantage ⟨*had* his opponent at the point of defeat⟩ ⟨the criminal *had* the police nonplussed⟩ ⟨the team *had* their opponents beaten before the half⟩ **b :** to place or maneuver into a vulnerable or defenseless position or a position bringing certain defeat ⟨when he brought the charge before the court he *had* me since the evidence against me was in my own handwriting⟩ **c :** OUTWIT, OUTPLAY, OUTMANEUVER ⟨*had* his opponent in only three more moves of the chessmen⟩ **:** DEFEAT ⟨would like to play on but you ~ me steadily⟩ **:** to get the better of or triumph over by finding, achieving, getting ⟨*had* the laugh on me⟩ ⟨*had* the goods on me⟩ ⟨*had* the jump on me⟩ **d :** TRICK, CHEAT, FOOL, BAMBOOZLE ⟨in this enterprise the partners *had* him and left him without a penny⟩ ⟨the size of this bill convinces me I've been *had*⟩ **11 a :** to be in a position to exercise (as a right or privilege) ⟨as a friend he *has* the freedom of my house⟩ ⟨*has* no right to go⟩ **b :** to be in control of **:** to be responsible for ⟨was put in charge and he *has* overall direction of the program —C.E.Black & E.C.Helmreich⟩ ⟨*has* the job of directing traffic⟩ **12 :** BEAR, BEGET ⟨she is going to ~ a baby⟩ ⟨the man *had* a son last week⟩ **13 :** to partake of **:** EAT, DRINK ⟨~ dinner at 7 o'clock⟩ ⟨~ coffee every morning⟩ **:** SMOKE ⟨~ a cigarette after breakfast⟩ **14 :** to give a job to **:** HIRE ⟨no shipowner will hire him, no captain will ~ him —P.J.Scharper⟩ **15 :** to associate oneself with **:** participate in ⟨won't ~ any part of the dirty business⟩ **16 a :** to cause to do one's bidding **:** CONTROL, DOMINATE ⟨the man with the money was always able to ~ him⟩ **b :** BUY 4, BRIBE, SUBORN ⟨as long as juries, judges and law enforcement officers can be *had* for a price —D.W. Maurer⟩ **17 :** to engage and hold (as the attention) ⟨the salesman *had* the interest of the buyer⟩ ⟨the political candidate *has* the ear of the farmers⟩ **~** *verbal auxiliary* **1 :** to be in a position or state marked by an action or state completed or ended or virtually completed or ended — used with the past participle to form the present perfect, past perfect, or future perfect ⟨*has* gone home⟩ ⟨~ been here already⟩ ⟨the army *had* already taken the town when we arrived⟩ ⟨will ~ finished dinner by the time the guests arrive⟩ **2 :** to be compelled or under obligation or necessity — used with the infinitive with *to* ⟨~ to see a doctor⟩ ⟨~ to pay taxes⟩ ⟨*had* to be home by six⟩ — compare [1]GET 12b

syn HOLD, OWN, POSSESS, ENJOY: HAVE is a very general term indicating any condition or action of control, retaining, keeping, regarding, or experiencing as one's own. HOLD suggests stronger control, grasp, or retention: *to hold to an opinion* suggests greater tenacity and resolution than *to have an opinion; to hold control* implies firm retention in contrast to *to have control*, which may imply the accidental or temporary; *to hold a job* suggests continuation, *to have one* occupation at the moment. OWN may suggest holding with power to use and dispose as a legal or natural right ⟨*own* one's own house⟩ ⟨the stockholders *own* the corporation, and the corporation *owns* the assets of the incorporated business —Harold Koontz & Cyril O'Donnell⟩ ⟨when a child is old enough, he should . . . be allowed to *own* books —Bertrand Russell⟩ POSSESS may be interchangeable with HAVE; similar to OWN, it may apply more widely to intangibles ⟨he *possesses*, through his experience, knowledge not possessed by those whose experience has been different —Bertrand Russell⟩ ⟨it must be a delightful city, and *possess* all the attractions of the next world —Oscar Wilde⟩ ENJOY implies having as one's own with all benefits and advantages, usu. pleasurable, or with other concomitants, perhaps unpleasant ⟨*enjoys* worldwide fame⟩ ⟨*enjoy* unlimited opportunities⟩ ⟨shorn of the remarkable privileges which he formerly *enjoyed* —J.G.Frazer⟩ **syn** see in addition OUGHT

— **had as good** *or* **had as well :** would benefit as much to **:** might as well — used with the infinitive without *to* ⟨*had as good* throw his money away as spend it foolishly⟩ — **had as lief** *or* **had as soon :** would just as gladly — used with the infinitive without *to* ⟨*had as lief* stay home as go gadding about⟩ — **had better** *or* **had best 1 :** would be wise to — used with the infinitive without *to* ⟨*had better* try slow walks to start building up his strength⟩ **2 :** should for one's own welfare ⟨*had better* pay what the court tells him to⟩ — **had liefer** *or* **had sooner** *or* **had rather :** would rather —used with the infinitive without *to* ⟨*had liefer* sit at home than go to the dance⟩ ⟨*had sooner* drink than sleep⟩ — **had liefest** *or* **had soonest :** would like best to — used with the infinitive without *to* ⟨*had liefest* have the least seasoned dishes⟩ — **have a go :** to hit a bowled cricket ball vigorously with intent to score — **have a hand in :** to exercise some control over ⟨*have a hand in* the management of the business⟩ **:** significantly influence or direct ⟨*having a hand in* the control of American domestic corporations —T.W.Arnold⟩ — **have at :** to go at or deal with usu. hostilely ⟨flops the morning bale of poetry manuscripts upon my desk and I pull up my chair to *have at* them —H.L. Mencken⟩ ⟨the two men *had at* each other with fists and feet⟩ ⟨have seen four . . . characters *have at* each other for two very powerful concluding acts —*Theatre Arts*⟩ — **have done :** STOP, CEASE, DESIST ⟨wish you would *have done* before I go mad⟩ — used chiefly in the imperative — **have done with :** to finish doing, using, dealing with, working on, or handling ⟨when he *had done with* the pen he laid it down⟩ ⟨will he never *have done with* his persistent speechmaking⟩ — **have had it 1 :** to have had or have done all one is going to be allowed to ⟨he's been cheating me badly for years but now he's *had it*⟩ **2 :** to have experienced, endured, or suffered all that one can or as much as one can ever expect to usu. of a particular kind of experience ⟨he felt he was capable of enduring pain but after that experience he'*d had it*⟩ ⟨if that's what it takes to make him happy, he *has had it* —*Nashville Tennessean*⟩ — **have it 1 a :** ASSERT, MAINTAIN, CLAIM ⟨rumor *has it* that there will be a marked change in women's fashions⟩ ⟨all their friends *have it* that they are secretly married⟩ — often used with *will* ⟨the enemy will *have it* that we are already defeated⟩ **b :** to conceive of and act in relation to a point under consideration ⟨which way do you want to *have it*⟩ ⟨*have it* your own way⟩ **2 :** to express or phrase it ⟨he was drunk as a lord, as his friends *have it*⟩ **3 :** to endure or suffer it — used with *will not* or *would not* ⟨tried to exploit him but he would not *have it*⟩ ⟨after his insult if he tries to explain I will not *have it*⟩ **4 :** to bring about **:** ARRANGE ⟨good fortune *had it* that we arrived early⟩ **5 a :** to gain or hold an advantage **:** WIN **b :** to gain the victory in a viva-voce vote ⟨the ayes *have it*⟩ **6 :** to receive or suffer a blow, punishment, or disaster ⟨the fighter let his opponent *have it* in the face⟩ **7 :** to have or have hit on a solution or a practicable or appropriate plan or method **8 :** to be so dealt with by fortune or circumstance that one's affairs or welfare are of a (particular favorable or unfavorable) character ⟨*had it* good in times of prosperity⟩ ⟨*has it* pretty tough since his wife died⟩ — **have it coming :** to deserve or merit what one gets, benefits by, or suffers ⟨so vicious a man that whatever evil things happen to him he will *have it coming*⟩ — **have it in for :** to intend to do harm to **:** wish evil to **:** plan to harm in some way ⟨*had it in for* all foreigners⟩ — **have it in one :** to have the capability or courage ⟨*has it in him* to do better than he did⟩ — **have it out :** to settle or clear up a matter of contention by free discussion or a fight — **have it over** *or* **have it all over :** to be in a more advantageous position than ⟨*has it over* one ignorant of the language⟩ — **have kittens :** to be in an agitated mood **:** become perturbed or upset ⟨company's coming and Ma's been *having kittens*⟩ — **have none of :** to refuse to allow, tolerate, or have anything to do with ⟨will *have none of* your sloppy ways around this house⟩ ⟨as soon as he found the business was dishonest he would *have none of* it⟩ — **have nothing on :** to have no advantage or superiority over ⟨the man was a crook but *had nothing on* the men he cheated who would have cheated him far more⟩; *esp* **:** to possess no incriminating or embarrassing information about ⟨felt at ease because he knew his opponents *had nothing on* him that they could use for blackmail⟩ — **have no use for :** to hold in contempt **:** DESPISE ⟨*has no use for* dishonest politicians⟩ **:** be unwilling to tolerate or deal with in any way — **have oneself :** to indulge in or go out of one's way to have (as a good time) **:** GET ⟨the boys *had themselves* a time while the parents were away⟩ — **have one's eye on :** to have marked intentions of acquiring or possessing ⟨*had his eye on* a little cottage up in the mountains⟩ ⟨*had his eye on* his neighbor's daughter⟩ — **have one's hands full :** to have in hand as much as or more than one can conveniently handle **:** be pressed with work, engagements, difficulties — **have one's head** *of a horse* **:** to move freely without restraint from the reins ⟨on the last stretch the trainer let the mare *have her head*⟩ — **have one's head** *or* **have one's hide :** to be extremely angry at or inflict severe punishment upon (as by beheading) ⟨he said that if I didn't stop bothering him he'd *have my hide*⟩ ⟨swore he'd *have the heads* of the outlaws⟩ — **have one's own back :** to get even — **have something on :** to possess incriminating or embarrassing information about ⟨*had something on* the police chief so that he felt safe from arrest⟩ — **have to do with 1 :** to deal with ⟨the story *has to do with* real people —*Current Biog.*⟩ **2 :** to have a specified relationship with or effect on ⟨refused to *have* anything *to do with* his own relatives —Roald Dahl⟩ ⟨the size of the brain *has* nothing *to do with* intelligence —Ruth Benedict⟩ —**to have and to hold :** to possess by virtue of a lawful title (as under the habendum clause in a deed) — formerly used in deeds in English to introduce the tenendum

2have \'hav\ *n* -s **:** one that has material wealth as distinguished from one that is poor ⟨conceived of war as a battle between the ~s and the have-nots for control of the world's wealth⟩ ⟨rich and poor, employer and employee, ~s and have-nots alike —*Engineering and Mining Jour.*⟩

have·lock \'hav,läk, -vlək\ *n* -s [after Sir Henry *Havelock* †1857 Eng. general in India] **:** a covering for a cap or hat with an extended back or back and sides to protect the neck from the sun or bad weather

1**ha·ven** \'hāvən\ *n* -s [ME, fr. OE *hæfen, hæfene;* akin to OE *hæf* sea, MLG *haf* sea, *havene* harbor, MHG *hap, habe, habene* sea, harbor, ON *haf* sea, *höfn* harbor, OE *hebban* to raise, lift — more at HEAVE] **1 :** a bay, recess, or inlet of the sea or the mouth of a river that affords anchorage and shelter for shipping **:** HARBOR, PORT **2 :** a place of safety **:** SHELTER, ASYLUM **syn** see HARBOR

2**haven** \"\ *vb* -ED/-ING/-S *vi, obs* **:** to take refuge in a haven ~ *vt* **:** to shelter in a haven

ha·ven·less \-nləs\ *adj* [ME *havenlesse,* fr. *haven* + *-lesse* -less] **:** having no harbor or haven ⟨a ~ sea⟩ ⟨a ~ life⟩

have–not \'hav,nät\ *n* -s **:** one that is poor in material wealth as distinguished from one that is rich ⟨ownership of the natural resources of the earth by individuals, groups or nations, causing a struggle between the haves and *have-nots* which is the major cause of war and destruction —*Science News Letter*⟩

haven't \'havənt, 'habᵊmt\ [by contr.] **:** have not

have on *vt* **1 :** WEAR ⟨the child *had* his best clothes *on* for the party⟩ ⟨*had on* a new suit⟩ **2 :** *chiefly Brit* **:** to deceive playfully **:** FOOL ⟨you're *having* me *on* again —Alan Sillitoe⟩ **3 :** to plan to take part in **:** have (something) planned ⟨*have* a dance *on* for that night⟩ ⟨will see what he *has on* now⟩

1**hav·er** \'havə(r)\ *n* -s [ME, fr. ON *hafri;* akin to OHG *habaro,* OS *haboro;* prob. derivatives fr. the root of ON *hafr* male goat; fr. oats being used as food for goats — more at CAPRIOLE] **1** *chiefly Brit* **a :** OAT; *esp* **:** volunteer or uncultivated oats **b :** WILD OAT 1a **2** *chiefly Brit* **:** TALL OAT GRASS

2**hav·er** \'hävər\ *n* -s [ME, owner, fr. *haven* to have + *-er*] *Scots law* **:** the holder of a deed or other legal document

3**ha·ver** \'hāvə(r)\ *vi* -ED/-ING/-S [origin unknown] *chiefly Brit* **:** to hem and haw **:** stall for time (as by useless talk) ⟨waste no more time ~*ing* over a few missing guns —Marguerite Steen⟩

4**ha·ver** *or* **ha·ber** *or* **cha·ver** *or* **cha·ber** \'kävər, kä'ver\ *n, pl* **have·rim** *or* **habe·rim** \kä'värim, ,käve'rēm\ [Heb *ḥābhēr*] **:** COMRADE, ASSOCIATE

ha·ve·rah *or* **ha·be·rah** \'kävərə\ *n, pl* **have·roth** *or* **habe·roth** *or* **have·rot** *or* **habe·rot** \,kävə'rōth, -ōt\ [Heb *ḥăbhērāh,* fem. of *ḥābhēr*] **:** a female haver

havercake \'=,=\ *n* [1haver + *cake*] *Scot* **:** OATCAKE

ha·ver·el \'hāv(ə)rəl\ *n* -s [3haver + *-el*] *chiefly Scot* **:** a garrulous half-wit

havergrass \'=,=\ *n* [1haver + *grass*] **:** any of several chiefly European wild oats

ha·ver·hill fever \'hāv(ə)rəl-\ *n, usu cap H* [fr. *Haverhill,* Mass., where the disease appeared in epidemic proportions in 1926] **:** rat-bite fever not always contracted from the bite of a rat but sometimes from contaminated food

ha·ver·ing \'hāv(ə)riŋ\ *adj* [fr. pres. part. of 3haver] *dial Brit* **:** equivocal and devious ⟨some ~ jargon that might mean anything —J.C.Powys⟩

ha·ver·ings \-ŋz\ *n pl* [fr. pl. of *havering,* gerund of 3haver] *Brit* **:** absurd, pointless, or maundering talk **:** BABBLINGS ⟨a tone of fatherly impatience with my moony ~ —H.H.Richardson⟩

havermeal \'=,=\ *n* [1haver + *meal*] *Scot* **:** OATMEAL

ha·vers \'hāvərz\ *n pl* [3haver + *-s*] *chiefly Scot* **:** stuff and nonsense **:** POPPYCOCK ⟨you're talking ~ —John Buchan⟩

hav·er·sack \'havə(r),sak\ *n* [F *havresac* (formerly, bag for oats), fr. G *habersack* bag for oats, fr. *haber* oat, oats (fr. OHG *habaro*) + *sack* bag, fr. OHG *sac* — more at HAVER, SACK] **:** a bag or case similar to a knapsack but usu. worn over one shoulder

ha·ver·sian canal \hə'vərzhən-, (')hā¦v\ *sometimes* -rshən\ *n, sometimes cap H* [Clopton *Havers* †1702 Eng. physician and anatomist + E *-ian*] **:** any of the small canals through which the blood vessels ramify in bone

haversian system *n, sometimes cap H* **:** a haversian canal with the concentrically arranged laminae of bone that surround it

hav·er·sine \'havə(r),sīn\ *n* [*half versed sine*] **:** half of the versed sine — abbr. *hav*

haversack

haves *pl of* HAVE

have up *vt, chiefly Brit* **:** to bring before an authority (as a court) to answer a charge ⟨the room where new boys were examined and old ones *had up* for rebuke or chastisement —Samuel Butler †1902⟩ ⟨the man swore he would *have* them *up* for defamation of character⟩

1**ha·vey–ca·vey** \'(h)āvi'kāvi\ *adj* [origin unknown] *dial Eng* **:** precariously balanced **:** UNSTEADY

2**havey–cavey** \"\ *adv, dial Eng* **:** HELTER-SKELTER

hav·i·land \'havələnd\ *n* -s *usu cap, often attrib* [after David *Haviland,* 19th cent. Am. manufacturer in France, its originator] **:** porcelain tableware designed for the American trade and made by a factory founded in 1839 at Limoges, France

hav·il·dar \'havəl,där\ *n* -s [Hindi *ḥawāldār,* fr. Ar *ḥawāla* charge + Per *dār* having] **:** a noncommissioned officer in the Indian army corresponding to a sergeant

havildar major *n* **:** a sergeant major in the Indian army

1**having** *n* -s [ME, fr. gerund of *haven* to have] **:** something one possesses or which belongs to one **:** PROPERTY — usu. used in pl.

2**having** *adj* [fr. pres. part. of 1have] **:** GRASPING, AVARICIOUS ⟨she's got rather a ~ nature —John Galsworthy⟩

ha·vings \'hāvinz\ *n pl but sing in constr* [ME, fr. pl. of *having,* gerund of *haven* to have] *Scot* **:** DEPORTMENT, BEHAVIOR, MANNERS; *specif* **:** good manners ⟨a lady of gentle ~⟩

hav·ior \'hāvyə(r)\ *n* -s [ME *haviour* possession, alter. of *havour,* alter. (influenced by ME *haven* to have) of *aver, avoir,* fr. MF *aveir, avoir,* fr. OF, fr. *aveir, avoir,* v., to have, fr. L *habēre* — more at GIVE] *chiefly dial* **:** BEHAVIOR

hav·la·gah \,hävlə'gä\ *n* -s [Heb *habhlāghāh*] **:** SELF-RESTRAINT

hav·na \'havnə\ *dial Brit* **:** have not

1**hav·oc** \'havək, -vik\ *n* -s [ME *havok,* fr. AF, modif. of OF *havot,* n., pillage & interj. used to signal start of pillage, perh. of Gmc origin; akin to Goth *hafjan* to lift — more at HEAVE] **1 :** wide and general damage or destruction **:** DEVASTATION, WASTE ⟨appalled by the ~ and loss of life caused by the earthquake —F.J.Crowley⟩ — see *cry havoc* at 1CRY **2 :** great confusion and disorder ⟨several small children can create ~ in a house⟩ — **play havoc with** *or* **raise havoc with :** to do great damage to **:** render ineffectual **:** throw into disorder and confusion

2**havoc** \"\ *vb* **havocked; havocked; havocking; havocs :** to lay waste **:** DEVASTATE, DESTROY

havre *usu cap, var of* LE HAVRE

1**haw** \'hȯ\ *n* -s [ME *hawe,* fr. OE *haga* hedge, hawthorn — more at HEDGE] **1 :** a piece of enclosed ground **:** YARD **2 a :** a hawthorn berry **b :** HAWTHORN **3 a :** the fruit of any of several shrubs or trees of the genus *Viburnum* **b :** a shrub or tree bearing such fruit

2**haw** \"\ *n* -s [origin unknown] **:** NICTITATING MEMBRANE; *esp* **:** an inflamed nictitating membrane of a domesticated mammal

3**haw** \"\ *vi* -ED/-ING/-S [imit.] **:** to inject a haw or a sound like it into one's speech during a hesitation or pause — usu. used with *hem* ⟨did a lot of hemming and ~*ing* during his talk⟩

4**haw** \"\ *n* -s **:** a sound often made by speakers during a pause while they are collecting their thoughts

5**haw** \"\ *v imper* [origin unknown] — used (1) as a command to a team or draft animal to turn to the left; (2) as a call in square dancing to progress to the left; compare 1GEE ~ *vi* -ED/-ING/-S **1 :** to cry out the command *haw* to a draft animal ⟨we geed and ~*ed* until we were hoarse —A.M.Bailey⟩ **2 :** to turn to the near or left side ⟨the mare geed when she should have ~*ed*⟩ **3 :** to obey the command *haw*

ha·waii \hə'wä(,)(y)ē, -wī(,)(y)ē, -wȯ(,)(y)ē, -wä(,)(y)ē, -wäyə, -wȯyə, -wī(y)ə *also* hä'- *or* hȧ'- *or* -'vä(,)(y)ē *or* -vī-(,)(y)ē *or* -vä(,)(y)ē *sometimes* -'və(,)(y)ē *or* -'wə(,)(y)ē; *a glottal stop often follows the 2d-syllable vowel when no y follows & when the last vowel is* ē\ *adj, usu cap* [*Hawaii,* state of the U. S., fr. Hawaiian *Hawai'i;* akin to Marquesan *Havaiki,* fabled original homeland of the Polynesians] **:** of or from Hawaii **:** of the kind or style prevalent in Hawaii **:** HAWAIIAN

1**ha·wai·ian** \hə'wäyən, -wȯyən, -wī(y)ən\ *adj, usu cap* [*Hawaii* + E *-an*] **1 :** of or relating to the island, state, or Territory of Hawaii, the Hawaiian islands, or the inhabitants of Hawaii **2 :** of or relating to a system of kinship terminology in which the terms for cross-cousins and parallel cousins are the same as those for sisters

2**hawaiian** \"\ *n* -s *cap* **1a :** a native or resident of the Hawaiian islands, of the Territory of Hawaii, or of the state of Hawaii; *esp* **:** a Hawaiian native of Polynesian ancestry **b :** a native or resident of the island of Hawaii **2 :** the Polynesian language of the Hawaiian people

ha·waii·ana *pronunc at* HAWAII *stressed* =,== + 'anə *or* 'änə *or* 'ānə *also* 'änə\ *n pl, usu cap* [*Hawaii* + E *-ana*] **:** objects relating characteristically to Hawaii or of Hawaiian origin

hawaiian beet webworm *n, usu cap H* **:** a grub that is the larva of a pyralidid moth (*Hymenia recurvalis*) and is destructive to beets and other green crops in much of the U.S.

hawaiian crab *n, usu cap H* **:** a large Pacific swimming crab (*Portunus sanguinolentus*) that is related to the Atlantic blue crab and is an important market crab in Hawaii

hawaiian duck *n, usu cap H* **:** a small drab mallard (*Anas platyrhynchos wyvilliana*) formerly common in the Hawaiian islands but now largely restricted to the coastal wetlands and streams of Kauai up to about 3500 feet

hawaiian goose *n, usu cap H* **:** NENE

hawaiian guitar *n, usu cap H* **:** a flat-bodied stringed musical instrument that has a long fretted neck and usu. 6 to 8 strings, that is held in a horizontal position either on the knees of the player or on an adjustable stand, and that is played by plucking the strings with picks, the desired pitch being obtained by sliding a small metal bar across the raised strings **2 :** UKULELE

hawaiian mahogany *n, usu cap H* **:** KOA

hawaii–aleutian time *n, cap H & A* **:** the time of the 11th time zone west of Greenwich that includes the Hawaiian islands and the Aleutians west of the Fox group and is six hours slower than eastern time

haw·er \'hȯ(ə)r, -ȯə\ *n* -s [3haw + *-er*] **:** one that haws in speech ⟨one of your hemmers and ~s⟩

Hawaiian guitar 1

hawfinch \'=,=\ *n* [1haw + *finch*] **:** a common finch (*Coccothraustes coccothraustes*) of Europe and Asia having a large heavy bill and short thick neck, and a male that is marked with black, white, and shades of brown

1**haw–haw** *var of* HA-HA

2**haw–haw** \(')hȯ¦hȯ\ *n* -s [imit.] **:** a deep or esp. loud boisterous laugh **:** GUFFAW

3**haw–haw** \"\ *vi* -ED/-ING/-S **:** to laugh in haw-haws **:** GUFFAW

4**haw–haw** \'hȯ¦hȯ\ *adj* [redupl. of 4haw] **:** marked by or given to the use of frequent haws as a habit or affectation of speech often associated with a southern British upper-class speech ⟨that famous *haw-haw* English accent —J.B.Priestley⟩ ⟨a kind of *haw-haw* way of talking —Clements Ripley⟩

1**hawk** \'hȯk\ *n* -s [ME *hauk,* fr. OE *hafoc, heafoc;* akin to OHG *habuh* hawk, ON *haukr* hawk, Russ *kobets* falcon] **1 a :** any of numerous diurnal birds of prey belonging to the suborder Falcones of the order Falconiformes: (1) **:** any of the smaller members of this group (as falcons, buzzards, harriers, kites, caracaras, and ospreys) as distinguished from the notably large eagles and Old World vultures (2) **:** any of various typical members of the family Accipitridae (as the New World Cooper's and sharp-shinned hawks and the Old World sparrow hawks) **:** ACCIPITER — see GOSHAWK; BILL illustration; compare OWL **b :** any of various birds that suggest hawks in appearance or behavior — used chiefly in combination; see NIGHTHAWK **2 :** one (as a swindler) who preys on his fellowmen **3 :** a small board or metal sheet with a handle on the underside used to hold mortar

hawk 3

2**hawk** \"\ *vb* -ED/-ING/-S [ME *hauken,* fr. *hauk,* n.] *vi* **1 :** to hunt birds by means of trained hawks **:** practice falconry **2 :** to soar and strike like a hawk ⟨birds ~*ing* after insects⟩ ~ *vt* **:** to hunt on the wing like a hawk ⟨the small bats ~ insects in midair —J.A.Thomson⟩

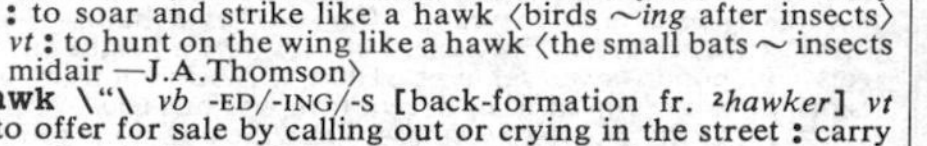

3**hawk** \"\ *vb* -ED/-ING/-S [back-formation fr. 2hawker] *vt* **:** to offer for sale by calling out or crying in the street **:** carry (merchandise) about from place to place for sale **:** PEDDLE **:** offer to various people for sale ⟨his works were ~*ed* in every street —Jonathan Swift⟩ ⟨small boys ~ large, luscious figs along the street —*Amer. Guide Series: N.C.*⟩ ⟨a dozen or so scripts which were currently being ~*ed* about town by various play agents —George Noble⟩ ~ *vi* **:** to peddle goods **:** hawk merchandise ⟨balloon-and-pennant man, ~*ing* by the grandstand gate —W.V.T.Clark⟩

4**hawk** \"\ *vb* -ED/-ING/-S [imit.] *vi* **:** to utter a harsh palatal or guttural sound in or as if in trying to clear the throat ~ *vt* **:** to raise (as phlegm) by hawking — often used with *up*

5**hawk** \"\ *n* -s **:** an audible effort to force up phlegm from the throat

hawkbell \'=,=\ *n* [ME *haukes bell, hauk bell*] **:** a small hollow spherical bell containing a free pellet and often attached to a hawk's leg

1**hawkbill** \'=,=\ *or* **hawkbill turtle** *n* [1hawk + *bill*] **:** HAWKSBILL TURTLE

2**hawkbill** \"\ *adj* [1hawk + *bill*] **:** HAWK-BILLED

hawk–billed \'=¦=\ *adj* **1 :** having a bill or jaws like a hawk's beak **2 :** shaped like a hawk's bill

hawkbit \'=,=\ *n* [*hawkweed* + (*devil's*) *bit*] **:** any of various plants of the genus *Leontodon; esp* **:** FALL DANDELION

hawk cuckoo *n* **:** any of several Asiatic cuckoos of the genus *Cuculus* that outwardly resemble hawks — see BRAIN-FEVER BIRD

hawk eagle *n* **:** any of numerous eagles (as the African crowned eagle) exhibiting rather hawklike characters

1**hawk·er** \'hȯkə(r)\ *n* -s [ME *hauker,* fr. OE *hafocere,* fr. *hafoc* hawk + *-ere* -er — more at HAWK] **1 :** FALCONER **2 :** an animal that captures its prey on the wing; *esp* **:** an insect that does this

2**hawker** \"\ *n* -s [by folk etymology fr. LG *hoker, höker* peddler, fr. MLG *hōker,* fr. *hōken, hūken* to peddle, bear on the back, squat + *-er;* akin to MD *hoken* to peddle, ON *hūka* to squat, OE *hēah* high — more at HIGH] **1 :** one that hawks wares esp. in the streets **:** PEDDLER **2 :** one that hawks wares assisted by a beast of burden or private vehicle (as a carriage)

3**hawker** \"\ *n* -s [4hawk + *-er*] **:** one that hawks as if clearing his throat esp. constantly or habitually

hawk·ery \-kərē\ *n* -ES **:** a place where hawks are kept

hawke's bay \'hȯks-\ *adj, usu cap H&B* [fr. *Hawke's Bay,* provincial district in New Zealand] **:** of or from the provincial district of Hawke's Bay, New Zealand **:** of the kind or style prevalent in Hawke's Bay provincial district

hawkeye \'=,=\ *n* **1 :** an unceasing minute scrutiny ⟨keeping . . . a ~ on all strangers riding in and out of the little village —Howard Troyer⟩ **2 :** one whose vision is markedly keen or who is esp. good in the perception of details (as errors) ⟨the ~s who trap printed mistakes before they get out to a critical public — *Trip through Brown and Bigelow*⟩ **3** *usu cap* **:** IOWAN 1 — a nickname

hawk–eyed \'=¦=\ *adj* **:** having a keen eye **:** SHARP-SIGHTED

haw·kie *also* **haw·key** \'hȯki, 'hȧki\ *n, pl* **hawkies** *also* **hawkeys** [Sc dial. *hawkit, hawked* having white spots or streaks + *-ie, -ey*] *Scot* **:** a white-faced cow — often used as a pet name for any cow

hawking *n* -s [ME *hauking,* fr. gerund of *hauken* to hawk — more at HAWK] **:** FALCONRY

hawk·ish \'hȯkish, -kēsh\ *adj* **:** resembling or suggesting a hawk or the beak of a hawk in appearance ⟨a ~ face⟩ ⟨fishing boats with ~ prows —A.H.Leighton⟩

hawklike \'=,=\ *adj* **:** resembling or suggesting a hawk in appearance or character ⟨a ~ nose —Louis Bromfield⟩ ⟨~ eagerness —*Wall Street Jour.*⟩ ⟨~ vision⟩

hawkmoth \'=,=\ *n* **:** any of numerous rather large stout-bodied moths constituting the family Sphingidae, having a long proboscis which at rest is kept coiled, long strong narrow fore wings more or less pointed at the ends, small hind wings, and stout antennae often hooked at the tip, and being usu. quiet in coloration but often handsomely patterned and graceful and hovering in flight — called also *sphinx moth;* see HORNWORM

hawk nose *n* **:** a nose curved like a hawk's beak

hawk–nosed \'=¦=\ *adj* **:** having a markedly curved and more or less pointed nose suggesting a hawk's beak ⟨the strength of the *hawk-nosed* face —Louis Bromfield⟩

hawk owl *n* **1 :** a largely diurnal owl (*Surnia ulula*) of northern forests that somewhat resembles a hawk in appearance, having a long rounded tail and rather short pointed wings **2 :** a widespread owl (*Ninox scutulata*) of eastern Asia and the Pacific islands having the facial disk little differentiated; *also* **:** any of several congeners (as the boobook owls)

hawk parrot *n* **:** a So. American parrot (*Deroptyus accipitrinus*) with a large erectile nuchal crest

hawks *pl of* HAWK, *pres 3d sing of* HAWK

hawk's–beard \'=,=\ *n, pl* **hawk's–beards** [so called fr. the large bristly pappus] **:** a plant of the genus *Crepis*

hawksbill turtle \'=,=-\ *or* **hawksbill** *n* **:** a carnivorous sea turtle (*Eretmochelys imbricata*) of tropical and subtropical seas, having a shell that rarely exceeds two feet in length and is covered with large overlapping horny plates of a brown color marbled with yellow that furnish the best tortoiseshell of commerce

hawk's–eye \'=,=\ *n, pl* **hawk's–eyes 1 :** a blue variety of tigereye **2 :** GOLDEN PLOVER

hawk·shaw \'hȯk,shȯ\ *n* -s *usu cap* [after *Hawkshaw,* a detective in the play *The Ticket of Leave Man* (1863), by Tom Taylor †1880 Eng. dramatist and in the comic strip *Hawkshaw the Detective,* by Gus Mager †1956 Am. artist] **:** DETECTIVE

hawk swallow *n* **:** a common European swift of the genus *Apus* (*A. apus*)

hawkweed \'=,=\ *n* **:** any of several composite plants esp. of the genera *Hieracium, Picris,* and *Erechtites*

hawky \'hȯkē\ *adj* -ER/-EST **:** HAWKLIKE

ha·wok \'hä,wäk\ *n, pl* **hawok** [Maidu *howok*] **:** Indian money of California consisting of shell disks or buttons

ha·wor·thia \hō'(w)ərthēə, -thēə\ *n* [NL, fr. Adrian H. *Haworth* †1833 Eng. botanist + NL *-ia*] **1** *cap* **:** a genus of xerophytic So. African succulent plants of the family Liliaceae that have thick fleshy leaves mostly crowded in a basal rosette and white or greenish flowers in a terminal spike **2** -s **:** any plant of the genus *Haworthia*

haws *pl of* HAW, *pres 3d sing of* HAW

hawse \'hȯz *also* -ȯs\ *n* -s [ME *halse,* fr. ON *hals* neck, part of the bow of a ship — more at COLLAR] **1 a :** HAWSEHOLE **b :** the part of a ship's bow that contains the hawseholes **2 :** the position or arrangement of the anchor cables of a ship when both a port and starboard anchor are used — see FOUL HAWSE, OPEN HAWSE **3 :** the distance or the space between a ship's bows and her anchor **:** the space spanned by the anchor cables ⟨the small boat anchored in the large ship's ~⟩

hawse bag *n* **:** a bag stuffed with sawdust, shavings, or oakum and used for closing a hawsehole — called also *jackass*

hawse bolster *n* **:** a wooden or iron guard at the end of or around a hawsepipe as protection against the chafing of the cable and to facilitate its movement

hawse–full \'=¦=\ *also* **hawse–fallen** \'=¦=\ *adj* **:** having the hawseholes under water **:** having the sea breaking through the hawseholes ⟨a ship riding *hawse-full* at anchor⟩

hawsehole \'=,=\ *n* **:** one of the usu. metal-lined holes in the bow of a ship through which cables pass

hawse hook *n* **:** a breasthook above the hawseholes

hawsepiece \'=,=\ *n* **:** one of the timbers in the bow of a wooden ship through which a hawsehole is cut

hawsepipe \'=,=\ *n* **:** a cast-iron or steel pipe placed in the bows of a ship on each side of the stem for the anchor chains to pass through

haw·ser \'hȯzə(r) *also* -ȯsə-\ *n* -s [ME *haucer, hauser, hawser,* fr. AF *hauceour,* fr. MF *haucier* to raise, hoist (fr. — assumed — VL *altiare,* fr. L *altus* high) + *-our* -or — more at OLD] **:** a large rope for towing or mooring a ship or securing it at a dock

hawser bend *n* **:** a method of joining the ends of two heavy ropes by means of seizings

hawser clamp *n* **:** a device for gripping a hawser as it is paid out

hawser–laid \'=¦=\ *adj* **:** CABLE-LAID

hawse timber *n* **:** HAWSEPIECE

hawsing iron *n* **:** CAULKING IRON

haw·thorn \'hȯ,thȯrn, -thȯ(ə)n\ *n* [ME *hawethorn,* fr. OE *hagathorn, haguthorn* fr. *haga* hedge, hawthorn + *thorn* thorn, thornbush — more at HEDGE, THORN] **:** a spring-flowering shrub or tree of the genus *Crataegus* (esp. the European *C.*

oxyacantha and the American *C. coccinea*) having usu. thorny branches, shining often lobed leaves, white or pink fragrant flowers, and small red fruits — see HAW, RED HAW
hawthorn china *n* **:** an oriental porcelain with a decoration of flowering plum-tree branches in white on a dark blue or black ground
hawthorn pattern *n* **:** the pattern on hawthorn china
hawthorn rust *n* **:** a rust fungus (*Gymnosporangium globosum*) in its aecial and pycnial stage
haw tree *n* **1** *obs* **:** HAWTHORN **2 :** WHITEBEAM **3 :** SERVICE TREE 1b
[1]**hay** \ˈhā\ *n* -s [ME *haie, heie,* fr. OE *hege;* akin to OE *haga* hedge, hawthorn — more at HEDGE] **1** *archaic* **:** an enclosing fence **:** HEDGE **2** *archaic* **:** a place enclosed with a hay **:** PARK
[2]**hay** \"\ *n* -s [ME *hey, hei,* fr. OE *hīeg, hīg, hēg;* akin to OHG *hewi* hay, ON *hey,* Goth *hawi* hay, OE *hēawan* to hew — more at HEW] **1 :** grass ready for mowing or esp. cut and cured for fodder; *specif* **:** the entire herbage sometimes including the seeds of grasses and other forage plants (as legumes) harvested and dried esp. for feed **2 :** a grayish greenish yellow that is slightly less strong and very slightly lighter than absinthe yellow, greener and duller than dusty yellow, and slightly deeper than yellow stone **3 :** a rewarding result of careful effort, industriousness, or cultivation (as of friendships) ⟨got some political ~ out of his association with underworld characters⟩ **4** *slang* **:** BED — used with *the* ⟨drag out of the ~ at six-thirty to dress and serve breakfast —Margaret Long⟩ ⟨caught him in the ~ with one of her maids —H.A.Smith⟩ **5 :** a trifling sum of money ⟨sells over $250,000 worth of them a year — and in the book trade that is anything but ~ —J.C.Furnas⟩
[3]**hay** \"\ *vb* -ED/-ING/-S *vi* **:** to cut and cure grass for hay and usu. haul it from the field and store it ~ *vt* **1 :** to dry (a cut grass) so as to make hay **2 :** to grow grass on for making hay ⟨~ the lower meadow⟩ **3 :** to give hay to ⟨~ the horses⟩
[4]**hay** \"\ *n* -s [ME *haye,* fr. AF *haie*] *archaic* **:** a net used for catching a wild animal (as a rabbit)
[5]**hay** *or* **hey** \"\ *n* -s [MF *haye*] **1 :** a rustic dance with much interweaving of couples **2 :** a right and left performed in a figure eight, straight line, or circular pattern in a dance
hay bacillus *n* [so called fr. the fact that isolations were formerly made from boiled hay infusions] **:** a rod-shaped spore-forming chiefly aerobic bacterium (*Bacillus subtilis*) widely distributed in soil and decaying organic matter
hay barrack *n* **:** BARRACK 4
haybird \ˈ=,=\ *n* **1 :** any of various small European birds (as the blackcap or the garden warbler) that build nests largely of grass **2 :** PECTORAL SANDPIPER
haybote \ˈ=,=\ *n* -s [ME *haybote, heybote,* fr. *haie, heie* hedge + *bote* profit, advantage, repair — more at [1]HAY, BOOT] **1 :** the wood or thorns allowed to a tenant or commoner in English law for repairing his hedges or fences — called also *hedgebote* **2 :** the right to take haybote
haybox \ˈ=,=\ *n* **:** a box packed with hay as insulation and used as a fireless cooker
hayburner \ˈ=,==\ *n, slang* **:** HORSE; *esp* **:** a second-rate racehorse
haycap \ˈ=,=\ *n* **:** a covering for a haycock
haycock \ˈ=,=\ *n* [ME *hay kock,* fr. *hay, hey* hay + *kock, cok* cock (pile) — more at HAY, COCK] **:** a small rounded somewhat conical pile of hay
hay cutter *n* **:** a machine for cutting or chopping hay into short lengths
hay·doo·dle \ˈhā,düdᵊl\ *n* [euphemism, *doodle* (as in *cock-a-doodle-do*) being substituted for [6]*cock,* associated with [1]*cock* (penis)] *chiefly Midland* **:** HAYCOCK
hay down *vt* **:** to dry (tobacco) too rapidly during curing
haye \ˈhā, ˈhī\ *n* -s [D *haai,* fr. MD *haey, haeye,* fr. ON *hār* thole, dogfish, shark; akin to OHG *huohili* small plow, Goth *hoha* plow, W *cainc* branch, OIr *cēcht* plow, Skt *śākhā* branch; basic meaning: branch] *archaic* **:** SHARK
hay·er \ˈhāə(r), ˈhe(ə)r, ˈheə\ *n* -s **:** one that hays
hay fern *n* **:** HAY-SCENTED FERN
hay fever *n* **:** an acute allergic nasal catarrh and conjunctivitis that is sometimes accompanied by asthmatic symptoms; *specif* **:** POLLINOSIS
hay fe·ver·ite \hāˈfēvə,rīt\ *n* -s **:** one who is suffering from hay fever
hay-fever weed *n* **:** RAGWEED 2
hayfield \ˈ=,=\ *n* **:** a field where grasses or legumes for hay are grown
hayfork \ˈ=,=\ *n* **1 a :** a hand fork for pitching hay **b :** a mechanically operated fork for loading or unloading hay **2 :** an attachment to a hay tedder that stirs mowed hay
hay hook *n* **:** a steel hook held in the hand for dragging a bale of hay
haying *n* -s **:** the process or season of harvesting hay
hay jack *n* **:** HAYBIRD 1
hay knife *n* **:** a long-bladed knife with large rounded serrations on the edge for sawing off sections at the end of a stack or compact pile of hay
haylift \ˈ=,=\ *n* **:** an airlift engaged in dropping emergency food to farm animals isolated esp. by deep snow
hay-loader \ˈ=,==\ *n* **:** an implement for gathering hay from a windrow or swath and loading it into a wagon or trailer

hay-loader

hayloft \ˈ=,=\ *n* **:** a loft or scaffold for hay **:** HAYMOW
haymaker \ˈ=,==\ *n* **1 a :** a worker who cuts and cures hay **b :** a machine for curing hay **2 a :** a powerful blow with the fist often resulting in a knockout **b :** an action or statement that is a stunning setback **:** an attack that overthrows or puts in a dangerous or extremely unpleasant position ⟨a leading coffee user today prepared a ~ for its coffee suppliers and announced that it plans to begin dispensing free tea with meals to discourage the use of coffee —*Springfield (Mass.) Daily News*⟩ ⟨traded ~s of innuendo and insult across the courtroom —*Time*⟩
haymaking \ˈ=,==\ *n* **1 :** the operation or work of cutting grass and curing it for hay **2 :** the act of taking full advantage of an easy opportunity ⟨the ~ of the profiteer after the war —W.R.Inge⟩
haymow \ˈ=,=\ *n* [ME *hay moghte* haystack, fr. *hay, hey* hay + *moghte, mowe* mow — more at HAY, MOW] **:** a part of a barn where hay is stored
hay plant *n* **:** WOODRUFF
hay press *n* **:** a baler for hay
hayrack \ˈ=,=\ *n* **1 :** a frame mounted on the running gear of a wagon and used in hauling hay or straw — called also *hayrig* **2 :** a feeding rack that holds hay for cattle or horses
hayrick \ˈ=,=\ *n* [ME *heyrek,* fr. *hey* hay + *rek, reke* rick — more at HAY, RICK] **:** a relatively large sometimes thatched outdoor pile of hay **:** HAYSTACK
hayride \ˈ=,=\ *n* **:** a pleasure ride usu. at night by a group in a wagon, sleigh, or open truck partly filled with straw or hay
hayrig \ˈ=,=\ *or* **hayrigging** \ˈ=,==\ *n* **:** HAYRACK
hays *pl of* HAY, *pres 3d sing of* HAY
hayscales \ˈ=,=\ *n pl* **:** large often public scales utilizing a platform for the weighing of hay on wagons or trucks
hay-scented fern \ˈ=,==-\ *n* **:** a No. American fern (*Dennstaedtia punctilobula*) with fragrant pale green fronds and an aroma like hay
hayseed \ˈ=,=\ *n* **1 a :** seed shattered from hay **b :** the bits of straw or chaff from hay that cling to clothes **2 :** a person who is markedly rustic and unsophisticated **:** YOKEL **3 :** any of various minute crustaceans (as the red feed) which live at the surface of the sea and upon which herrings and many other fishes feed
hay·sel \ˈhāsəl\ *n* -s [[2]*hay* + *sele*] *dial Eng* **:** the haying season
hayshaker \ˈ=,==\ *n, slang* **:** HAYSEED 2
hayshock \ˈ=,=\ *n, chiefly South & Midland* **:** HAYCOCK
haystack \ˈ=,=\ *n* [ME *haystak,* fr. *hay, hey* hay + *stak* stack — more at HAY, STACK] **:** a stack of hay **:** HAYRICK
hay sweep *n* **:** BUCK RAKE
hay-tal·let *or* **hay-tal·lat** \ˈhā,talət\ *n, dial Eng* **:** HAYLOFT
hay-time \ˈ=,=\ *n* **:** the period in which haying is usu. done
hayward \ˈ=,=\ *n* [ME *hayward, heyward,* fr. *haie, heie* enclosure, hedge + *ward* — more at HAY, WARD] **1 a :** an officer appointed to keep cattle from breaking through from a town common or roadway into enclosed fields and to impound strays **b :** the keeper of a town's common herd of cattle **2 :** FIELD DRIVER
[1]**haywire** \ˈ=,=\ *n* [[2]*hay* + *wire*] **:** wire used to bind bales (as of hay or straw)
[2]**haywire** \"\ *adj* [so called fr. the frequent use of baling wire to make makeshift repairs] **1 a :** inadequately equipped ⟨a ~ outfit⟩ **:** FLIMSY **b :** put together inexpensively or patched up tentatively from available odds and ends **:** JURY-RIGGED ⟨a ~ plant hurriedly built of secondhand tank cars and salvaged equipment —*Monsanto Mag.*⟩ **2 a :** being out of order **:** BROKEN-DOWN ⟨luckily for us, their range-finding and director gear must have been ~ . . . so her fire wasn't very accurate —*Outspan*⟩ **b :** tangled up **:** mixed up **:** not running or working normally **:** acting in an odd way ⟨a ~ train that came and went at the worst possible hours —*N.Y. Herald Tribune Bk. Rev.*⟩ ⟨~ development of western industrial culture —Marston Bates⟩ — often used in the predicate with *go* ⟨magnetic compasses won't work, radios go ~, and ordinary engine oil freezes —*All Hands*⟩ ⟨psychologists have gone so ~ with this new freedom that many interpretations are wild and bizarre —P.M. Symonds⟩ **3 :** emotionally excited **:** gone to pieces **:** UPSET ⟨she's pretty much ~ just now, but she'll have settled down by the time you get here —Mary R. Rinehart⟩ — often used with *go* ⟨went completely ~ and in one mad, exotic moment she bought the red pocketbook —Mary D. Gillies⟩ ⟨many boxing champions have gone ~ after winning a title —D.M. Daniel⟩ ⟨the danger that men in responsible executive positions might go ~ —Elmer Davis⟩
[3]**haywire** \"\ *n* [[1]*haywire;* fr. the appearance of the leaves] **:** a sporadic disease of potatoes that is of unknown cause but considered by some to be due to a virus or viruses but by others to be due to unfavorable conditions during tuber development and that is characterized by the production of dwarfed plants with elongated stiff sometimes rolled leaves which finally turn yellow with purplish discoloration esp. at the tips and margins
haz *abbr* hazard
ha·zan *or* **haz·zan** *or* **cha·zan** *or* **chaz·zan** \kəˈzän, ˈkäzᵊn\ *n, pl* **haza·nim** *or* **hazza·nim** \kəˈzänim\ [LHeb *ḥazzān*] **1 :** a synagogue official of the talmudic period **2 :** CANTOR 2
ha·zan·ic *or* **haz·zan·ic** *or* **cha·zan·ic** *or* **chaz·zan·ic** \-nik, -ᵊnik\ *adj* **1 :** belonging to or characteristic of a hazan **:** CANTORIAL **2 :** connected with or relating to hazanuth
ha·za·nuth *or* **ha·za·nut** *or* **haz·za·nuth** *or* **haz·za·nut** *or* **cha·za·nuth** *or* **cha·za·nut** *or* **chaz·za·nuth** *or* **chaz·za·nut** \kəˈzänət(h), -nəs\ *n* -s [LHeb *ḥazzānūth,* fr. *ḥazzān*] **1 :** cantorial singing or chanting **:** synagogal melodies **2 :** cantors of the synagogue; *collectively* **:** CANTORATE
ha·za·ra \həˈzärə\ *n, pl* **hazara** *or* **hazaras** *usu cap* **:** a Mongoloid people of Afghanistan
[1]**haz·ard** \ˈhazə(r)d\ *n* -s [ME *hasard, hazard,* fr. MF *hasard,* fr. Ar *az-zahr* the die] **1 a :** a game of chance like craps played with two dice **b :** CHUCK-A-LUCK **2 a :** an adverse chance (as of being lost, injured, or defeated) **:** DANGER, PERIL ⟨the discovery of atomic fission brought into ~ the industrial potential of any state which could not destroy its enemy before it was itself destroyed —H.J.Laski⟩ **b :** a thing or condition that might operate against success or safety **:** a possible source of peril, danger, duress, or difficulty ⟨a coast visited by frequent dense fogs and mountains subject to violent storms constitute ~s to air travel —*Amer. Guide Series: Calif.*⟩ **c :** a condition that tends to create or increase the possibility of loss **3 a :** the effect of unpredictable, unplanned, and unanalyzable forces in determining events **:** CHANCE ⟨men and women danced together, women danced together, men danced together, as ~ had brought them together —Charles Dickens⟩ **b :** an event occurring without design, forethought, or direction **:** ACCIDENT ⟨looked like a fugitive, who had escaped from something in clothes caught up at ~ —Willa Cather⟩ **4 :** something risked (as stakes in gaming) **5 :** one of the winning openings in a court-tennis court — compare DEDANS, GRILLE, WINNING GALLERY **6 :** a stroke by which a pool ball is holed after contact with another ball — compare LOSING HAZARD, WINNING HAZARD **7 :** a golf-course obstacle restricting the player's stroke (as a bunker, sand trap, watercourse) **syn** see CHANCE, DANGER — **at hazard :** at stake
[2]**hazard** \"\ *vt* -ED/-ING/-S [ME *hasarden,* fr. *hasard*] **1 a :** to lay open to the risk of being lost, captured, or taken in or as if in a game of chance **:** GAMBLE, BET, VENTURE ⟨~ed a week's salary on a single turn of the cards⟩ ⟨asked him to ~ a small sum in a business venture⟩ **b :** to expose to possible risk of loss or damage ⟨so as not to ~ other buildings —*N.Y. City Fire Dept. Manual*⟩ **2 :** to take the risk of: **a :** to accept the chances and dangers of, venturing and daring to proceed or undertake despite them ⟨decided to ~ an open battle⟩ **b :** to have the courage to put forward or offer and expose to possible rebuff or censure (as a guess or suggestion) ⟨dares not ~ a prophecy —W.R.Sharp⟩ **syn** see VENTURE
haz·ard·er \-də(r)\ *n* -s [ME *hasardour, hasarder,* fr. MF *hasardeur,* fr. *hasarder* + *-eur* -or] **1 :** one that hazards **2** *archaic* **:** a player at hazard **:** GAMESTER
haz·ard·less \-dləs\ *adj* **:** not hazardous **:** marked by no hazard **:** involving no risk or danger
haz·ard·ous \-dəs\ *adj* [MF *hasardeux,* fr. *hasard* + *-eux* -ous] **1 :** depending on hazard or on chance; *specif* **:** ALEATORY **2 :** exposed or exposing one to hazard **:** involving risk of loss **:** RISKY **syn** see DANGEROUS
haz·ard·ous·ly *adv* **:** in a hazardous manner
haz·ard·ous·ness *n* -ES **:** the quality or state of being hazardous ⟨deterred by the ~ of the enterprise⟩
hazardry *n* -ES [ME *hasarderie, hasardrie,* fr. MF, fr. *hasarder* + *-erie* -ery] *obs* **:** GAMBLING
hazard side *n* **:** the side of a court-tennis court in which service is received — compare SERVICE SIDE
[1]**haze** \ˈhāz\ *vb* -ED/-ING/-S [prob. back-formation fr. *hazy*] *vi* **1** *archaic* **:** to drizzle and fog **2 :** to become hazy or cloudy ⟨above the hotel the purple mountains *hazed* in the heat —William Sansom⟩ ~ *vt* **:** to make hazy **:** fog up **:** make dull or cloudy ⟨the purple night smoking up from the western water and *hazing* the world —Marjory S. Douglas⟩
[2]**haze** \"\ *n* -s [prob. back-formation fr. *hazy*] **1 a :** fine dust, salt particles, smoke, or particles of water finer and more scattered than those of fog causing lack of transparency of the air and making distant objects indistinct or invisible ⟨the fine ~ hanging lightly over the city and blurring its further outlines —Isolde Farrell⟩ ⟨a fog is likely soon to disappear by evaporation, while a ~ hangs on until washed out by rain, thinned by convection, or blown away by clear air —W.J.Humphreys⟩ **b :** a cloudy appearance in a transparent liquid or solid **c :** a dullness or cloudiness of finish (as on furniture) **:** BLOOM **2 :** something suggesting atmospheric haze: **a :** something giving the impression of clouds or cloudiness in the air or to the view ⟨the soft ~ of thickets of oaks —*Amer. Guide Series: Texas*⟩ ⟨a ~ of gnats danced under the bitten leaves —Elizabeth Taylor⟩ ⟨a ~ of greenery⟩ **b :** a state of mental dimness or obtuseness **:** haziness of mind or of mental perception **c :** a state in which many things tend to merge and lose their separate identity ⟨looking back through the ~ of years —Allen Johnson⟩ **d :** a frame of mind vague or uncertain in its exact character but marked by strong generalized feeling dominating the reason ⟨a ~ of disbelief⟩ ⟨in a ~ of love⟩ or a set of conditions producing such a frame of mind ⟨its ~ of wine and waltz —Frederic Morton⟩
[3]**haze** \"\ *vt* -ED/-ING/-S [origin unknown] **1** *dial Eng* **:** to intimidate by physical punishment **2 a :** to harass (as a ship's crew) by exacting unnecessary, disagreeable, or difficult work **b** (1) **:** to harass or try to embarrass or disconcert by banter, ridicule, or criticism ⟨began to brood under the roughhouse play and built up a sullen resentment against the men who were *hazing* him —D.P.Mannix⟩ (2) **:** to subject (as a freshman or a fraternity pledge) to treatment intended to put in ridiculous or disconcerting positions **3** *West* **a :** to drive (animals) from horseback ⟨cowboys *hazed* herds slowly up north along an old Indian trail —S.E.Fletcher⟩ **b :** to separate (animals from a group) from horseback ⟨~ calves from a herd⟩ — often used with *out* ⟨~ out the dogies⟩
[4]**haze** \"\ *vt* -ED/-ING/-S [origin unknown] *dial Brit* **:** to season or mellow by drying in the sun
haze blue *n* **:** a pale purplish blue that is redder and paler than hydrangea blue, redder and slightly less strong than moonstone blue, and redder than starlight blue
haze gray *n* **:** a light gray similar to smoke gray
[1]**ha·zel** \ˈhāzəl\ *n* -s [ME *hasel,* fr. OE *hæsel;* akin to OHG *hasal* hazel, ON *hasl,* OIr & OW *coll,* L *corulus*] **1 a :** a shrub or small tree of the genus *Corylus* (esp. *C. americana* and *C. cornuta* or in Europe *C. avellana*) — see FILBERT **b :** an Australian tree (*Pomaderris apetala*) grown for ornament and for its fine-grained wood **c :** the wood of either of these trees **d :** the wood of the sweet gum **2 a :** HAZELNUT 1 **b :** the fruit of the hawthorn **3 :** ASARABACCA **4** *also* **hazelnut :** a light brown to strong yellowish brown — called also *filbert, muffin, noisette*
[2]**hazel** \"\ *adj* [ME *hasel,* fr. *hasel,* n.] **1 :** consisting of hazels or of the wood of the hazel **:** relating to or derived from the hazel ⟨a ~ wand⟩ **2 :** of the color hazel **:** AVELLANEOUS
hazel alder *n* **:** SMOOTH ALDER
hazel hen *also* **hazel grouse** *n* **:** a European woodland grouse (*Tetrastes bonasia*) related to the American ruffed grouse
hazel hoe *n* **:** a large heavy grub hoe used in forests for trenching and clearing in fire fighting and for trimming small branches from tree trunks
ha·zel·ly \-zəlē\ *adj* **1 :** covered with or abounding in hazels **2 :** of the color hazel
hazel mouse *n* **:** a dormouse of the genus *Muscardinus*
hazelnut \ˈ==,=\ *n* [ME *haselnutte,* fr. OE *hæselhnutu,* fr. *hæsel* hazel + *hnutu* nut — more at HAZEL, NUT] **1 :** any of several nuts that are produced by the hazel and that have a husk little or no longer than the nut **2 :** HAZEL 4
hazel pine *n* **1 :** the wood of the sweet gum **2 :** SWEET GUM
hazelwood \ˈ==,=\ *n* **:** the wood of the sweet gum
hazelwort \ˈ==,=\ *n* **:** an asarabacca (*Asarum europaeum*)
haz·er \ˈhāzə(r)\ *n* -s **:** one that hazes: as **a :** one of two cowboys who ride beside a bucking horse to protect both horse and broncobuster **b :** a rider who assists a cowboy bulldogging steers by riding on the opposite side of the steer to keep it from veering away
hazes *pres 3d sing of* HAZE, *pl of* HAZE
ha·zi·ly \ˈhāzəlē, -li\ *adv* **:** in a hazy manner ⟨saw the distant hills ~ through the field glasses⟩ ⟨remembered only ~ where he was going⟩
ha·zi·ness \-zēnəs, -zin-\ *n* -ES **:** the quality or state of being hazy ⟨the ~ of the smoky atmosphere⟩ ⟨a ~ in his mental processes⟩
hazing *n* -s **:** the action of one that hazes: **a :** the infliction of unnecessary or excessive work esp. on sailors in order to harass **b** (1) **:** an attempt to embarrass or disconcert by ridicule or persistent criticism (2) **:** the subjecting (as of a freshman or fraternity pledge) to treatment intended to put in ridiculous or disconcerting position
ha·zle \ˈhāzəl\ *vt* -ED/-ING/-S [freq. of [4]*haze*] **:** HAZE
ha·zy \ˈhāzē, -zi\ *adj* -ER/-EST [fr. earlier *hawsey, heysey,* of unknown origin] **:** marked by haze: as **a :** obscured or made dim or cloudy by haze ⟨~ weather⟩ ⟨a ~ view of the mountains⟩ **b :** OBSCURE, VAGUE, INDEFINITE ⟨a ~ idea that he'd like to get married⟩ ⟨a somewhat ~ account of what he did⟩ ⟨~ logic⟩ **c :** CLOUDED ⟨a mirror ~ with steam⟩ ⟨some gasolines containing sulfur, when exposed to sunlight, become ~ —A.N.Sachanen⟩
hazy blue *n* **:** CAMEO GREEN
hazzan *var of* HAZAN
hazzanuth *or* **hazzanut** *var of* HAZANUTH
HB *abbr* **1** halfback **2** hard black **3** heavy bomber **4** His Beatitude; His Blessedness
Hb *symbol* hemoglobin
h bar *n, cap H* **:** a bar like an I bar but with wider flanges
h beam *n, cap H* **:** a beam like an I beam but with wider flanges
h-bomb \ˈ=,=\ *n, usu cap H* **:** HYDROGEN BOMB
h bone *n, cap H* **:** AITCHBONE
hbr *abbr* harbor
h-budding \ˈ=,==\ *n, cap H* **:** plate budding in which cuts in the bark of the stock are made in the form of an H
HC *abbr* **1** half calf **2** half chest **3** hand control **4** held covered; hold covered **5** high capacity **6** high church **7** high commissioner **8** high-compression **9** hockey club **10** Holy Communion **11** *often not cap* honoris causa **12** hot and cold **13** House of Commons **14** house of correction
hcap *abbr* handicap
HCF *abbr* highest common factor
HCL *abbr* high cost of living
hcp *abbr* handicap
hd *abbr* **1** hand **2** head **3** hogshead
HD *abbr* **1** harbor defense **2** heavy-duty **3** high density **4** home defense **5** horse-drawn
hdbk *abbr* handbook
hdg *abbr* heading
hdkf *abbr* handkerchief
hdl *abbr* **1** handle **2** headline
hdlg *abbr* handling
hdqrs *abbr* headquarters
hdw *abbr* hardware
hdwd *abbr* hardwood
hdwe *abbr* hardware
[1]**he** \(ˈ)hē, ē, (h)i\ *pron* [ME, fr. OE *hē;* akin to OE *hēo, hīo* she, *hit* it, *hīe* they, OS *hē, hie* he, OHG *hē,* ON *hann* he, Goth *himma* (dat.) this, L *cis, citra* on this side, Gk *keinos, ekeinos* that (adj.) that person, Arm *sa* this, Hitt *ki;* basic meaning: this] **1 :** that male one ⟨I'll have no father, if you be not ~ —Shak.⟩ ⟨I spoke to the boy and ~ spoke to me⟩ **:** that one regarded as masculine (as by personification) ⟨last came Anarchy: ~ rode on a white horse —P.B.Shelley⟩ — used as nominative masculine pronoun of the third person singular usu. in reference to a previously specified subject or to someone indicated by some means (as pointing) ⟨~ heard me say it and so did ~⟩ ⟨~ with the beard is the one I mean⟩; sometimes in poetry and in substandard speech used pleonastically together with a noun as subject of a verb ⟨the Senator ~ said he'd have to have you —John Dos Passos⟩ ⟨Sir Oluf ~ rideth over the plain —H.W.Longfellow⟩ — see [1]HIM, [1]HIS; compare [3]HIS, IT, SHE, THEY **2 :** that one whose sex is unknown or immaterial ⟨find out who is ringing the doorbell and what ~ wants⟩ ⟨~ that hath ears to hear, let him hear —Mt 11:15 (AV)⟩ — used as a nominative case form in general statements (as in statutes) to include females, fictitious persons (as corporations), and several persons collectively ⟨if a customer is dissatisfied ~ may return the goods⟩ ⟨one manufacturer is advertising . . . that ~ will sell cars freight-free —*Motor Trend*⟩ **3** *archaic* **:** the one **:** the other — used as a nominative masculine demonstrative pronoun in the expressions *he . . . he* and *he and he* **4 :** YOU — used as a nominative case form in speaking to or as if to a baby ⟨did ~ bump his little head⟩ and in some English dialects in addressing a boy or in addressing a person of higher or lower social status than the speaker **5 a** *substand* **:** HIM — used in a compound object ⟨between his wife and ~⟩ **b** *dial Eng* **:** HIM, IT — used emphatically as object of a verb or preposition ⟨don't give it to ~⟩
[2]**he** \ˈhē\ *n* -s *often attrib* [ME, fr. *he,* pron.] **1 :** a male person or animal ⟨the ~s would quarrel and fight with the females —Jonathan Swift⟩ — often used in combination ⟨a routine *he-she* plot⟩ ⟨*he*-goat⟩ **2 a :** one that is strongly masculine or virile — used chiefly in combination ⟨a real *he*-man⟩ ⟨that's what I call *he*-literature —Sinclair Lewis⟩ **b** *dial* **:** a large or powerful one of its kind — used chiefly in combination ⟨a regular old *he*-blizzard —Wallace Stegner⟩ **3** *Brit* **:** [3]TAG 1; *also* **:** the player who is it
[3]**he** *also* **heh** \ˈhā\ *n* -s [Heb *hē'*, perh. lit., window] **1 :** the fifth letter of the Hebrew alphabet — symbol ה; see ALPHABET table **2 :** the letter of the Phoenician alphabet or of any of various other Semitic alphabets corresponding to Hebrew he
HE *abbr* **1** high efficiency **2** high explosive **3** His Eminence **4** His Excellency; Her Excellency
He *symbol* helium
[1]**head** \ˈhed\ *n* -s *see sense 6b* [ME *heved, hed,* fr. OE *hēafod;* akin to OHG *houbit* head, ON *hǫfuth,* Goth *haubith,* L

caput head, Skt *kapucchala* hair at the back of the head] **1 :** the division of the human body that contains the brain, the eyes, the ears, the nose, and the mouth; *also* **:** the corresponding anterior division of the body of various animals including all vertebrates, most arthropods, and many mollusks and worms **2 a :** the seat of the intellect **:** the place where thought and inspiration originate **:** UNDERSTANDING, MIND ⟨two ~*s* are better than one⟩ ⟨he has some queer notions in his ~⟩ **b :** a person with respect to certain mental qualities ⟨let wiser ~*s* prevail⟩ **c :** natural aptitude or talent ⟨a good ~ for figures⟩ **d :** mental or emotional control **:** POISE ⟨can keep his ~ in a crisis⟩ ⟨level ~⟩ ⟨a situation calling for a cool ~⟩ **e :** HEADACHE ⟨it didn't give you a ~ like beer —R.O.Bowen⟩ **f :** the mouth as the organ of speech ⟨he'd better keep his ~ shut about this⟩ **3 a :** the hair on a head **b :** the hair as a head covering **:** COIFFURE, HEADDRESS **4 a :** a sculptured representation of a head ⟨a bronze ~ of Lincoln⟩ **b :** the obverse of a coin — compare HEAD OR TAIL **5 :** the antlers of a deer **6 a :** each one among a number **:** INDIVIDUAL ⟨count ~*s*⟩ ⟨a cost of $5 per ~⟩ **b** *pl* **head :** a unit of number (as of domestic animals) ⟨a thousand ~ of cattle⟩ **c** *Brit* **:** a herd or aggregation of game animals **7 a :** an end of something regarded as the upper or higher end ⟨~ of a valley⟩ ⟨~ of a slope⟩ ⟨~ of a staircase⟩ or as being the part most distant from an entrance ⟨~ of a bay⟩ or as being opposite the foot ⟨~ of a bed⟩ ⟨~ of a grave⟩ ⟨seated at the ~ of the table⟩ **b :** the source or beginning esp. of a stream ⟨the ~ of the Nile⟩ ⟨the ~ of navigation⟩ — compare FOUNTAINHEAD **c :** either end of something (as a bridge, cask, or drum) whose two ends may not or need not be distinguished **d :** an underground passage or level in a coal mine **e :** a position or direction of the set of parallel planes in a massive crystalline rock along which fracture is most difficult, being normal to the direction of strongest cohesion **f :** a round or inning played from one end of a course to the other in certain games (as bowls and curling) **8 :** one who stands in relation to others somewhat as the head does to the other members of the body **:** DIRECTOR, CHIEF: as **a :** HEADMASTER **b :** one in charge of a division or department in an office or institution; *esp* **:** one in charge of a department in a school, college, or university **c :** an officer in charge of a hall or college (as at Oxford or Cambridge) **9 a :** CAPITULUM 3b **b :** the top or foliaged part of a plant consisting of a compacted mass of leaves ⟨~ of lettuce⟩ ⟨~ of a tree⟩ or close fructification ⟨~ of grain⟩ **c :** a bunch or hank of flax, hemp, or jute packed for marketing **10 :** HEADLAND, PROMONTORY, CAPE — now used chiefly in place names **11 a :** the leading element of a military column or a procession **b :** the leader or the leading position in dancing **c :** the hottest and most active portion of an advancing forest fire or grass fire **d :** freedom to proceed on one's course or to have one's way — used chiefly in the phrases *give one his head* and *let one have his head* **e :** HEADWAY ⟨often she had to fight for her ~ as the press of sail buried her bow —C.V.Reilly⟩ **12 :** the uppermost extremity or projecting part of an object **:** TOP ⟨~ of a cane⟩ ⟨~ of a bolt⟩ ⟨~ of a mast⟩ ⟨~ of a doorway⟩: as **a :** the striking part of a weapon (as an arrow, spear, ax) or tool (as a hammer, hatchet, ram) **b :** the striking end of a racket, club, stick, or paddle — see GOLF illustration **c :** the point of a violin bow — see BOW illustration **d** *of a bowed instrument* **:** the pegbox and scroll **e :** HEAD JOINT 1 **f :** the rounded proximal end of a long bone (as the humerus) **g :** the end of a muscle nearest the origin **h :** the anterior end of an invertebrate **:** SCOLEX **i :** the end of a cigar that is placed in the mouth **j :** a protective covering for the ends of roll paper **k :** the oval part of a printed musical note **13 a :** a body of water kept in reserve at a height (as for a mill or in a reservoir); *also* **:** the containing bank, dam, or wall **b :** a mass of water in motion (as in a rip current) **c :** a sudden rush of liquid (as water through an irrigation ditch or oil from a well) **d :** the flow of water used in irrigating a field **e :** unconsolidated earth material moved by solifluction — compare CONGELITURBATE **14 a :** the difference in elevation between two points in a body or column of fluid (as between the surface and a submerged orifice at which the fluid flows outward or when pumping into an elevated tank flows inward) **b :** the resulting pressure of the fluid at the lower point expressible as this height; *broadly* **:** pressure of a fluid ⟨an engine with a full ~ of steam⟩ **15 :** the front or foremost part of something: as **a :** the bow and adjacent parts of a ship ⟨brought her ~ into the wind⟩ **b :** a ship's toilet — compare BEAKHEAD 1b **c :** a portion of a hide in front of the flare of the shoulder — see HIDE illustration **d :** the approximate length of the head of a horse ⟨won the race by a ~⟩ **16 :** the place of leadership or of honor or command **:** the most important or foremost position ⟨at the ~ of his class⟩ **17 a** (1) **:** a word or words often in larger letters placed above or at the beginning of a passage of written or printed matter in order to introduce or categorize — called also *heading, headline;* compare RUNNING HEAD, SHOULDER HEAD, SIDEHEAD (2) **:** a separate part or topic of a discourse or writing **:** POINT ⟨~*s* of a sermon⟩ ⟨you may rest easy on that ~⟩ **b :** a portion of a page or sheet that is above the first line of printing; *also* **:** the corresponding blank part of an imposed form — compare PAGE 1d **18 a :** the topmost edge of a book standing upright — compare FOOT, TAIL; BINDING EDGE, FORE EDGE **b :** the upper edge of a sail — see SAIL illustration **19 a :** the foam or scum rising on a fermenting or effervescing liquid **b :** the cream that rises on standing milk **c heads** *pl* **:** the first runnings **d heads** *pl* **:** crude ore fed to a concentrating plant — compare CONCENTRATE, MIDDLING, TAILING **20 a :** the part of a boil, pimple, or abscess at which it is likely to break **b :** culminating point of action or of tension **:** CRISIS, CLIMAX, ISSUE **c** *archaic* **:** a gathered force (as in rebellion) ⟨to save our heads by raising of a ~ —Shak.⟩ **21 a :** a cover for an alembic or other distilling apparatus — see ALEMBIC illustration **b :** the hood of a carriage **c** *Brit* **:** the top of an automobile **22 a** *or* **head metal :** an extra piece of metal on a foundry casting made by filling up a riser after the mold is full in order to supply loss from shrinkage and to permit slag or dross and unsound metal to rise clear of the casting **b :** a riser filled in in this manner **c :** a part of a railroad rail supported by a web and base that guides and provides a running surface for the flanged wheels of cars and locomotives — see T RAIL illustration **23 :** a part or attachment of an apparatus, machine, or machine tool containing a device (as a cutter, grinder, polisher, drill) for acting mechanically on something ⟨turret ~ of a lathe⟩ ⟨milling ~⟩ ⟨sheep-shearing ~⟩ ⟨safety-*head* centrifuge⟩; *also* **:** the part of an apparatus that performs the chief function ⟨the ~ of a photographic enlarging camera⟩ ⟨a shower ~⟩ ⟨a sprinkler ~⟩ ⟨welding ~⟩ **24 a :** CYLINDER HEAD **b :** a movable mount for attaching a camera to a tripod or other support **c :** a device used in recording sound for converting electrical signals into the recorded form, for converting the recorded form into electrical signals, or for removing recorded material from a record — see ERASE HEAD, MAGNETIC HEAD, RECORDING HEAD, REPRODUCING HEAD **25 :** an immediate constituent of an endocentric compound or construction having the same grammatical function as the whole (as the terms *polite old man, old man,* and *man* in "a polite old man") — **by the head :** drawing the greater depth of water forward — **off one's head :** CRAZY, DISTRACTED — **out of one's head :** unable to command one's mental powers **:** DELIRIOUS — **over one's head 1 :** beyond one's comprehension ⟨he liked pictures but art criticism was *over his head*⟩ ⟨the speech went *over the heads* of the audience⟩ **2 :** so as to pass over or ignore one's superior standing or authority ⟨quit when his juniors were promoted *over his head*⟩ ⟨went *over the head* of his boss to complain⟩ **3** *obs* **:** PAST, GONE-BY

²**head** \"\ *adj* [ME *heved, hed,* fr. *heved, hed,* n.] **1 :** of, relating to, or for a head or the head **2 :** PRINCIPAL, CHIEF, LEADING, FIRST ⟨~ chorister⟩ ⟨~ cook⟩ **3 :** situated at the head ⟨~ wall⟩ ⟨~ sails⟩ **4 :** coming from in front **:** meeting the head as it is moved forward ⟨~ sea⟩ ⟨~ tide⟩

³**head** \"\ *vb* -ED/-ING/-S [ME *hedden,* fr. *hed,* n.] *vt* **1 :** BEHEAD **2 a :** to lop off the top branches of **:** POLL ⟨~ a tree⟩ **b :** to cut back (the shoots of plants) to induce branching or check growth — often used with *in* or *back* **c :** to harvest (a crop) by cutting off the heads **3 a :** to put a head on **:** fit a head to ⟨~ an arrow⟩ ⟨~ a bolt⟩ ⟨~ a cask⟩ **b :** to form the head or top of ⟨the church tower was ~*ed* by a spire⟩ **4 :** to put oneself at the head of **:** act as leader to ⟨~ an expedition⟩ ⟨~ a revolt⟩ **5 a :** to face or oppose head on ⟨~ the waves⟩ ⟨~*ing* the driving rain⟩ **b :** to get in front of so as to hinder, stop, or turn back ⟨~ a herd of cattle⟩ **c :** to take a lead over (as in a race) **:** SURPASS **d :** to pass (a stream) by going round above the source **6 a :** to put something at the head of (as a list) **:** furnish with a heading ⟨each page was ~*ed* with the writer's name and the date⟩ **b :** to stand as the first or leading member of ⟨~*s* the list of local war heroes⟩ ⟨~*ed* his class all through school⟩ **7 :** to set the course or direct the progress of ⟨~ a ship northward⟩ ⟨~ a horse toward home⟩ **8 :** to drive or direct (as a soccer ball) by hitting with the head ~ *vi* **1 :** to form a head ⟨this cabbage ~*s* early⟩ ⟨the pimple ~*ed*⟩ **2 :** to point or proceed in a certain direction ⟨how does she ~, helmsman⟩ ⟨the fleet was ~*ing* out⟩ ⟨the dog ~*ed* for the woods⟩ ⟨the business seemed to be ~*ing* for trouble⟩ **3 a :** to have a source **:** ORIGINATE, RISE ⟨the more important rivers . . . ~ in the Rocky mountains or their foothills —*Scientific Monthly*⟩ **b :** to flow intermittently (as oil from a well)

head·ache \ˈheˌdāk *sometimes* -ˌdik *or* -ˌdēk\ *n* [ME *hedache,* fr. OE *hēafodece,* fr. *hēafod* head + *ece, æce* ache — more at HEAD, ACHE] **1 :** pain inside the head **:** CEPHALALGIA **2** [so called fr. the effect of their odor] **:** any of several poppies **3 :** a vexatious situation **:** a baffling problem **:** a source of trouble or worry ⟨the lack of funds for financing the educational needs of our communities sooner or later proves to be the principal ~ —C.A.Herter⟩

headache plant *n* [so called fr. its use as a remedy for headache] **:** AMERICAN PASQUEFLOWER

headache post *n* **:** a post placed on an oil-well derrick floor in order to prevent the walking beam from accidentally striking a workman

headache weed *n* **:** a West Indian plant of the genus *Hedyosmum* (family Chloranthaceae) held to be a remedy for headache

head–aching \-ˌdākiŋ, -kēŋ\ *adj* **:** causing headache

head·achy \ˈheˌdākē, -ki *sometimes* -ˌdik- *or* -ˌdēk-\ *adj* -ER/-EST **1 :** having headache **2 :** causing headache or attended by headache

head and front *n, archaic* **:** the foremost or essential feature or part ⟨the very *head and front* of my offending —Shak.⟩

head and shoulders *adv* **1** *archaic* **:** without good reason or excuse **:** by force **:** VIOLENTLY **2 :** beyond comparison **:** by far **:** OUTSTANDINGLY ⟨stood *head and shoulders* above the rest in character and ability⟩

head–and–tail–light \ˌ=ˈ=ˈ=ˌ=\ *also* **head–and–tail–light fish** *n* **:** a small So. American characin fish (*Hemigrammus ocellifer*) that is translucent green with orange-tinged black-tipped fins and shimmering red eyes and tail spots and is often kept in the tropical aquarium

¹**headband** \ˈ=ˌ=\ *n* [¹*head* + *band*] **1 :** a band worn on or around the head: as **a :** an ornamental band (as of cloth, flowers, jewels) **b :** a band connecting two earphones **2 :** ARCHIVOLT 1 **3 :** a plain or decorative band printed or engraved at the head of a page or a chapter **4 :** a narrow strip of cloth sewn or glued by hand to a book at the extreme ends of the backbone — compare FOOTBAND

²**headband** \"\ *vt* **:** to fasten headbands on (a book)

head betony *n* **:** WOOD BETONY 2

head blight *or* **head blighting** *n* **:** a blighting of the heads of a cereal; *esp* **:** such a blighting caused by a fungus (*Gibberella zeae*) — compare WHEAT SCAB

headblock \ˈ=ˌ=\ *n* **:** a block supporting the head of something: as **a :** a part of a sawmill carriage that supports the log **b :** a block of wood between the fifth wheel and the forward spring of a carriage or wagon **c :** one of a set of extra-long railroad ties used for supporting the operating mechanism of a point rail

headboard \ˈ=ˌ=\ *n* **1 a** (1) **:** a board stretching between the headposts of a bed (2) **:** an upright structure forming a head for a bed **b :** a light partition that separates one berth in a sleeping car from that next to it **2 :** a wooden board at the upper corner of a Bermudian mainsail to which the halyard is shackled

headborough \ˈ=ˌ=(ˌ)=\ *n* [ME *hed borwe,* fr. *hed* head + *borwe* pledge, tithing — more at BORROW] **1 :** a chief of a frankpledge or tithing — compare TITHINGMAN **2 :** BORSHOLDER

headbox \ˈ=ˌ=\ *n* **1 :** a receptacle in a papermaking machine that holds the stuff and regulates its flow onto the wire **2 :** a case covering the operating mechanism of a venetian blind

head boy *n* **:** a head prefect in a British school

head cabbage *or* **heading cabbage** *n* **:** CABBAGE 1

headcap \ˈ=ˌ=\ *n* **:** the covering leather at the head and foot of the backbone of a hand-covered book shaped over the headbands

head capsule *n* **:** an exoskeleton of the head of an insect made up of fused chitinous plates in which the primitive segmentation is obscured

head–cavity \ˈ=ˌ===\ *n* **:** one of the transitory somites of the head of an early vertebrate embryo

head cell *n* **:** CAPITULUM 3a

headcheese \ˈ=ˌ=\ *n* **:** the meat of the head, feet, and sometimes the tongue and heart esp. of a pig cut up fine, seasoned and boiled, and either made into a large sausage or pressed into a firm jellied mass

headchute \ˈ=ˌ=\ *n* **:** a pipe for ejecting refuse from a ship's head

headcloth \ˈ=ˌ=\ *n* **1 :** a cloth forming a covering or screen for the head of a bed **2 :** any of various cloth coverings for the head (as a kerchief, a kaffiyeh, a turban) **3 headcloths** *pl, obs* **:** the pieces of a woman's headdress

head cold *n* **:** a common cold in which the symptoms are primarily centered in the nasal passages and adjacent mucous tissues

head–collar \ˈ=ˌ==\ *n, Brit* **:** HALTER 1b

head couple *n* **:** a couple in a square dance set whose backs are to the music or the caller; *also* **:** the couple opposite — compare FOOT COUPLE, SIDE COUPLE

head court *n* [ME *hed court*] **:** an obsolete Scottish county freeholders' court having charge for some time prior to 1832 of the registration of voters

head ditch *n* **:** an irrigation ditch across an upper slope from which water is drawn into basins or furrows

head·dress \ˈhe(d)ˌdres\ *n* **1 :** an often elaborate covering for the head (as for ceremonial or social occasions) **2 :** a manner of dressing the hair; *esp* **:** a fanciful arrangement of a woman's hair often with accessories (as flowers, veils, ribbons, combs)

head dropper *n* **:** a slaughterhouse worker who severs heads from carcasses and removes edible portions for processing

head·ed \ˈhedəd\ *adj* [ME *hedded,* fr. past part. of *hedden* to head — more at HEAD] **1 :** having a head or a heading ⟨a ~ bolt⟩ ⟨~ paragraphs⟩ **2 :** formed into a head **:** MATURED ⟨~ cabbage⟩ **3 :** having (such) a head or (so many) heads — often used in compounds ⟨curly-*headed* boy⟩ ⟨a cool-*headed* businessman⟩ ⟨a gold-*headed* cane⟩ **4** *of lumber* **:** tongued and grooved at the ends — usu. used in the phrase *dressed and headed*

head end *n* **1 :** the first few inches of fabric that are woven in a loom after new warp is started and that are often used for notations (as various marks of identification) **2 :** the cars of a passenger train that are immediately behind the locomotive and are commonly used for handling mail, express, and baggage

head·end·er \(ˈ)heˈdendə(r)\ *n* -S [*head end* + *-er*] **:** a head-on collision

head–end revenue *n* **:** revenue from railroad traffic (as mail, express, milk) carried at the head end

head–end system *n* **:** an arrangement whereby electricity for a complete railroad train is furnished by a single generating plant located on the locomotive or tender or on a separate car

head·er \ˈhedə(r)\ *n* -S [ME *heder,* fr. *hed* head + *-er*] **1** *obs* **:** HEADSMAN **2 :** a worker or machine that removes heads; *esp* **:** a grain-harvesting machine that cuts off the grain heads and elevates them to a wagon **3 a :** a brick or stone laid in a wall with its end toward the face of the wall — opposed to *stretcher* **b :** a beam fitted between trimmers and across the ends of tail beams in a building frame **c :** a conduit or chamber (as the exhaust manifold of a multicylinder engine) into which a number of smaller conduits open **d :** a wall or barrier at either end of a motor truck or trailer body to prevent shifting of cargo on stopping or starting **4 a :** a worker or a machine that upsets rivets **b :** a cooper who puts heads on barrels by hand or by machine — called also *headerman* **5 :** an officer in charge of a whaleboat **6 :** a fall or dive head foremost ⟨tripped and took a ~ into a rosebush⟩ ⟨try a ~ off the high diving board⟩ **7 :** a dog trained to head cattle or sheep **8 :** a main shoot (as of a fruit tree) that tends to elongate with few side branches **9 :** SADDLE 12

header and thresher *n* **:** COMBINE 3

header bond *n* **:** a masonry bond in which all courses are header courses

header–box \ˈ=ˌ=ˌ=\ *or* **header barge** *n* **:** a large wagon box with one side higher than the other into which cut grain is elevated by header

header bond

header course *n* **:** a masonry course in which all the bricks are laid as headers

header fork *n* **:** a fork with three or four tines for pitching grain heads with attached straw harvested with a header

head·er·man \-mən, -ˌman\ *n, pl* **headermen 1 :** HEADER 4b **2 :** an operator of a machine for making steel bends, offsets, bolt blanks, bolt heads, and rivet heads **3 :** one who forges hot or cold metal on a bulldozer **4 :** a worker who rivets together the fitted-up metal plates of oil-storage tanks

header–up \ˌ=ˈ=ˌ=\ *n* -S [*head up,* v. + *-er*] **1 :** HEADERMAN 2 **2 :** HEADER 4b

head fast *n* **:** a mooring hawser or chain at the head of a ship

headfirst \ˈ=ˈ=\ *adv* **:** with the head foremost **:** HEADLONG, ABRUPTLY, RECKLESSLY ⟨had plunged ~ into the statehood fight —Edna Ferber⟩

headfish \ˈ=ˌ=\ *n* **:** OCEAN SUNFISH

head–flattening \ˈ=ˌ=(=)=\ *n* **:** a practice dating from prehistoric times and formerly engaged in by various peoples of No. America and So. America whereby the skull is caused to develop with a flattened top by the application of pressure during infancy

head fold *n* **:** an anterior thickening of the blastoderm immediately anterior to the neural plate of an amniotic embryo from which the anterior part of the body develops

headforemost \(ˈ)=ˈ=(ˌ)=\ *adv* **:** HEADFIRST, HEADLONG

head form *n* **:** the shape of a human head esp. with reference to the cephalic index

headframe \ˈ=ˌ=\ *n* **:** a frame structure over a mine shaft to support the hoisting sheaves — called also *gallows*

head·ful \ˈ=ˌfu̇l\ *n* -S **:** a quantity (as of information) that fills the head

head gate *n* **1 :** a gate at the upper end of a canal lock **2 :** a gate for controlling the water flowing into a race, sluice, or irrigation ditch

headgear \ˈ=ˌ=\ *n* **1 a :** a covering for the head (as a hat, cap, bonnet) **b :** a protective device for the head (as a soldier's helmet or a welder's helmet) **c :** HEAD HARNESS **2 :** hoisting or drilling gear at the top of a mine shaft or oil well

head harness *n* **:** a part of a horse's harness worn on or depending from the head and including bridle, checkrein, reins, bit, and blinders

headhouse *n* **1 :** a structure in which the headframe of a mine is housed **2 :** a part of a railroad passenger terminal providing accommodations for persons waiting for trains **3 :** a service area or building attached to a greenhouse usu. for housing the central temperature-control equipment and providing working and storage room

¹**headhunt** \ˈ=ˌ=\ *n* **:** an expedition for securing heads as trophies

²**headhunt** \"\ *vi* **1 :** to kill and decapitate enemies and preserve their heads as trophies **2 :** to seek to deprive political enemies of position or influence ⟨an opportunity for local sniping and ~*ing* in individual states and districts —*N.Y. Times*⟩

headhunter \ˈ=ˌ==\ *n* **:** one that practices headhunting

headier *comparative of* HEADY

headiest *superlative of* HEADY

head·i·ly \ˈhedᵊlē, -ᵊli, -dəl-\ *adv* [ME *hedylyche,* fr. *hedy* heady + *-lyche, -liche* -ly] **1 :** RASHLY, HEADLONG **2 :** so as to cause exhilaration or dizziness

head in *vi* **:** to take a side track in order to give way to an approaching train

head·i·ness \-dēnəs, -din-\ *n* -ES [ME *hedinesse,* fr. *hedy* heady + *-nesse* -ness] **1 :** RASHNESS, HEADSTRONGNESS ⟨~ of youth⟩ **2 :** intoxicating quality ⟨the ~ of a spring morning⟩ ⟨a perfume with a ~ impossible to describe⟩

head·ing \ˈhediŋ, -dēŋ\ *n* -S [ME *hedding,* fr. gerund of *hedden* to head] **1** *archaic* **:** DECAPITATION **2 :** the compass direction in which the longitudinal axis of a ship or airplane points **3 :** something that forms or serves as a head: as **a :** HEAD 17a(1) **b :** a plain, colored, or patterned band woven at the beginning and end of a fabric **c** (1) **:** an edge of a ruffle above the line of gathering (2) **:** an edge of a curtain rising above a curtain rod (3) **:** FOOTING 8a **4 :** material for heads of casks or barrels **5 :** DRIFT 6a, 6b **6 :** an end of a stone or brick presented outward; *also* **:** HEADING COURSE **7** *South & Midland* **:** PILLOW, BOLSTER

heading bond *n* **:** a masonry bond that is formed by courses of headers

heading broccoli *n* **:** BROCCOLI 1

heading course *n* **:** a masonry course of headers only

heading joint *n* **1 :** a joint (as between two boards) at right angles to the grain **2 :** a masonry joint between two voussoirs in the same course

heading stone *n* **:** HEADER 3a

head joint *n* **1 :** the final joint of a flute containing the embouchure **2 :** a vertical masonry joint between the ends of stretchers

head·ker·chief \ˈ=ˌ== (*with last two syllables like* KERCHIEF) *or* ˈ==(ˌ)= (*with last two syllables as in* HANDKERCHIEF)\ *n* **:** KERCHIEF

head kidney *n* **1 :** PRONEPHROS **2 :** a nephridium often early developed in the cephalic segment of larval annelids and other invertebrates

head knee *n* **:** a timber in the frame of a ship fayed edgeways to the cutwater and stem

head lamp *n* **:** HEADLIGHT

head·land \ˈhedlənd, -ˌland, -ˌlaa(ə)nd\ *n* [ME *hedeland,* fr. OE *hēafodlond,* fr. *hēafod* head + *lond* land — more at HEAD, LAND] **1 :** a ridge or strip of unplowed land at the ends of furrows or near a fence **2 :** a point or portion usu. of high land jutting out into the sea, a lake, or other body of water

hea·dle \ˈhedᵊl\ *var of* HEDDLE

headledge \ˈ=ˌ=\ *n* **1 :** either of the athwartship coamings of a hatchway or other deck opening **2 :** either of the upright end posts of a centerboard box

head·less \ˈhedləs\ *adj* [ME *hevedles, hedles,* fr. OE *hēafodlēas,* fr. *hēafod* head + *-lēas* -less — more at HEAD] **1 a :** having no head **b :** BEHEADED ⟨~ corpse⟩ **c** *of a line of verse* **:** lacking the normal first syllable **2 :** having no chief or leader **3 :** lacking good sense or prudence **:** FOOLISH, STUPID — **head·less·ness** *n* -ES

headletter \ˈ=ˌ==\ *n* **:** type or lettering suitable for use in heads or display

head lettuce *n* **:** any of various cultivated lettuces that constitute a distinct variety (*Lactuca sativa capitata*) and are distinguished by leaves arranged in a dense rosette which ultimately develops into a compact head suggesting that of cabbage — compare LEAF LETTUCE

headlight \ˈ=ˌ=\ *n* **:** a light usu. having a reflector and special lens and mounted on the front of a locomotive, streetcar, or motor vehicle for illuminating the road ahead

headlighting \ˈ=ˌ==\ *n* **:** the illumination in front of a vehicle supplied by the headlights

head·like \ˈ=ˌ=\ *adj* **:** resembling or suggesting a head in shape or function

head line *n, usu cap H* **:** LINE OF HEAD

¹**headline** \ˈ=ˌ=\ *n* [¹*head* + *line*] **1 :** HEADROPE 2, 3 **2 :** HEAD FAST **3 a :** HEAD 17a(1) **b :** a head of a newspaper story or article usu. printed in large type and devised to summarize, give essential information about, or interest readers in reading the story or article that follows **c :** BANNER 4

²headline \ˈ"\ *vt* **1 :** to provide (as a news story) with a headline ⟨the editor *headlined* the story quickly⟩ — often followed by a specified headline as a complementary object ⟨*headlined* the story *Man Bites Dog*⟩ **2 :** to publicize highly in or as if in headlines ⟨a *headlined* hero of World War II⟩ **3 :** to be engaged as a leading performer in (a show) ⟨a blues singer *headlined* the floor show⟩

head·lin·er \ˈ=,līnə(r)\ *n* -s **:** a performer whose name is printed in a headline in the bill **:** STAR

headline schedule *n* **:** HEAD SCHEDULE

headlining \ˈ=,==\ *n* [¹*head* + *lining*] **:** material that covers the ceiling of an automobile interior

headload \ˈ=,=\ *n* **:** a load carried on the head ⟨women stagger under ~*s* that would shatter the spines of pack mules —*Time*⟩ ⟨the primitive method of ~*s* is still used to convey the cacao to road or rail —A.W.Knapp⟩

headlock \ˈ=,=\ *n* **:** a wrestling hold in which one encircles his opponent's head with one arm and secures the grip by interlocking his fingers

head log *n* **:** a front bottom log on a skidway

¹head·long \ˈ=ˈlȯŋ *also* -ˈläŋ\ *adv* [ME *hedlong*, alter. of *hedling*, fr. *hed* head + *-ling*] **1 :** with the head foremost **:** HEADFIRST **2 :** without deliberation **:** RASHLY, RECKLESSLY, HEEDLESSLY **3 :** without delay or pause **:** in a rush **:** UNSWERVINGLY

²headlong \ˈ=,=\ *adj* **1 :** IMPETUOUS, RASH, PRECIPITATE, RECKLESS ⟨her childlikeness, her ~ sympathies, the impulsive traits that endeared —W.R.Benét⟩ ⟨such personal possessions as they had been able to carry with them in their ~ flight —E.J. Phelan⟩ **2 :** plunging headforemost ⟨a ~ dive into the pool⟩ **3** *archaic* **:** STEEP, PRECIPITOUS ⟨like a tower upon a ~ rock —Lord Byron⟩ **syn** see PRECIPITATE

head·long·ness \ˈ=ˈ=nəs\ *n* -ES **:** the quality or state of being headlong

head louse *n* **:** a sucking louse frequenting the head of its host; *esp* **:** a louse that is a variety (*Pediculus humanus capitis*) of the common louse of man, lives on the scalp, and attaches its eggs to hairs

head maggot *n* **:** the larva of the sheep botfly (*Oestrus ovis*)

head·man *in sense 1* ˈhed,man *or* -maa(ə)n, *in sense 2* -,mən\ *n, pl* **headmen** [ME *hevedman, hedman*, fr. OE *hēafodman*, fr. *hēafod* head + *man* — more at HEAD, MAN] **1 a :** OVERSEER, FOREMAN, CHIEF **b :** a lesser chief or subleader of a primitive community (as a clan, tribe, or village) **2 :** HEADSMAN

headmark \ˈ=,=\ *n* **1** *chiefly Scot* **:** the distinguishing characteristics esp. of the head that make one individual recognizable from another **2** *Midland* **:** a credit (as toward a prize to be awarded) given to a pupil for reaching the head position in an examination conducted with the pupils lined up and each pupil advancing toward the head of the line according to the proportionate number of his correct answers ⟨wanted to get the prize for the most ~*s* —J.H.Stuart⟩

headmaster \ˈ=ˈ==\ *n* **1 :** a man at the head of the staff of a private school usu. having some teaching duties but mainly concerned with administration, discipline, and counseling **2 :** the principal of a British secondary or elementary school

head·mas·ter·ly \-lē,-li\ *adj* **:** belonging to or characteristic of a headmaster

head·mas·ter·ship \-,ship\ *n* **:** the post of a headmaster

head matter *n* [so called fr. its being obtained fr. the head of the whale] **:** the contents of the case of the sperm whale that yield spermaceti and clear oil

head metal *n* **:** HEAD 22a

head meter *n* **:** a flowmeter whose operation is dependent upon change of pressure head

headmistress \ˈ=ˈ==\ *n* **:** a woman at the head of the staff of a private school — compare HEADMASTER

head money *n* **1 :** HEAD TAX **2 :** money paid for killing or capturing a person (as an outlaw) **:** BOUNTY

head·most \ˈ=,mōst *also chiefly Brit* -,məst\ *adj* [¹*head* + *-most*] **:** most advanced **:** most forward **:** LEADING ⟨the ~ ship in the line⟩

headnote \ˈ=,=\ *n* **1 :** a note of comment or explanation at the beginning (as of a page or chapter) **2 :** a summary prefixed to the report of a decided legal case stating the principles or rulings of the decision and usu. the main facts

head note *n* **:** HEAD TONE

head off *vt* **:** to turn back or turn aside **:** BLOCK, DIVERT, PREVENT ⟨a prime example of the way . . . troubleshooters *head off* strikes —*Time*⟩ ⟨police seemed to *head* me *off* in every direction —Adrian Bell⟩

head of horns : HEAD 5

head on \(ˈ)=ˈ=\ *adv* **1 :** with the head or front pointing directly toward an object ⟨the ship struck the rocks *head on*⟩ ⟨the cars collided *head on*⟩ **2 :** in direct opposition or contradiction ⟨to let his wife settle this question without his meeting it *head on* —Herbert Gold⟩ ⟨what happens to the savage when he meets civilization *head on* —J.F.McComas⟩

head–on \ˈ=ˈ=\ *adj* [*head on*] **1 :** having the front facing in the direction of motion ⟨swerved to avoid a *head-on* crash⟩ or line of sight ⟨a *head-on* view of a building⟩ **2 :** directly opposite or opposing **:** FRONTAL ⟨a *head-on* attack on the committee's policy⟩

head or tail *n* **1 :** this side or that side — often used in pl. in tossing a coin to decide a choice, question, or stake — compare HEADS OR TAILS **2 :** beginning or end **:** one thing or another **:** something definite ⟨could not make *head or tail* of what he said⟩

head over ears *adv* **:** up to the ears **:** DEEPLY ⟨fell *head over ears* into English literature and history —Angela Thirkell⟩ ⟨*head over ears* in debt⟩

head over heels *adv* [alter. of *heels over head*] **1 a :** in or as if in a somersault ⟨fell *head over heels* down the hill⟩ ⟨a blow sent him *head over heels* into the pond⟩ **b :** upside down ⟨swung *head over heels* from the branch⟩ **2 :** HOPELESSLY, DEEPLY ⟨fell *head over heels* in love⟩ ⟨was *head over heels* in debt⟩

headpenny \ˈ=,==\ *n* [ME *hed penny*, fr. *hed* head + *penny*] **1 :** HEAD TAX **2** *obs* **:** an individual or personal assessment or payment to church funds

headphone \ˈ=,=\ *n* **:** an earphone held over the ear by a band worn on the head

headpiece \ˈ=,=\ *n* **1 a :** a protective or defensive covering for the head; *esp* **:** any of the various helmets worn formerly by knights in armor and now by members of the armed forces, participants in some sports, and construction workers **b :** HAT, CAP **c :** HEADSTALL, HALTER **2 a :** HEAD **b :** UNDERSTANDING, BRAINS **3 a :** an ornament placed above the text matter of a page or at the beginning of a chapter — compare TAILPIECE **b :** HEADNOTE **4 :** a top part: as **a :** a headboard of a bed **b :** a lintel of a door or window

headphones

headpin \ˈ=,=\ *n* **1 :** a bowling pin that stands foremost in the arrangement of pins — called also *kingpin* **2 :** KINGPIN 2

headpin bowling *n* **:** bowling in which a bowler aims directly at the 1-3 pocket when attempting to make a strike — compare SPOT BOWLING

headplate \ˈ=,=\ *n* **:** a key plate for printing a design featuring a person's head

headpost \ˈ=,=\ *n* **1 :** one of the posts at the head of a bed **2 :** the post nearest the manger in a stall

head post *n* **:** a movable post supporting an imitation head of leather used as an object for saber exercise in a cavalry riding school

head process *n* **:** an axial strand of cells that extends forward from the primitive knot in the early vertebrate embryo and is the precursor of the notochord

headquarter \ˈ=,==, (ˈ)=ˈ==\ *vb* [back-formation fr. *headquarters*] *vi* **:** to make one's headquarters **~** *vt* **:** to place in headquarters

headquarters \ˈ=,==, (ˈ)=ˈ==\ *n pl but often sing in constr* **1 a :** a place from which a military commander issues orders and performs the functions of command **b :** the personnel associated with and assisting the commander in performing his function **2 :** a chief or usual place of business **:** the administrative center of an enterprise or activity ⟨turned the archbishop's palace into a busy ~, organizing the duties of the clergy of all ranks —J.A.Gade⟩

headquarters company *n* **:** an administrative and tactical unit furnishing the necessary specialist personnel for headquarters of a battalion or higher unit

headrace \ˈ=,=\ *n* **:** a race for conveying water to a point of industrial application (as a waterwheel or turbine)

¹head·rail \ˈhe,drāl\ *n* **1 :** one of the elliptical rails at a wooden ship's head extending from the place of the figurehead to the bow **2 a :** the upper horizontal piece of a door **b :** a solid piece at the top of the back of a chair **c :** a crosspiece at the head of a bed

²headrail \ˈ"\ *n* [trans. of OE *hēafodhrægl*, fr. *hēafod* head + *hrægl* garment — more at HEAD, RAIL] **:** a medieval head covering for women consisting usu. of a cloth draped loosely over the head and hanging down in back

¹headreach \ˈ=,=\ *vi* [¹*head* + *reach*] **:** to move ahead into the wind by momentum (as in tacking)

²headreach \ˈ"\ *n* **:** the distance covered by headreaching

head register *n* **:** the upper division in the pitch range of the human voice beginning at the point where the vocal cords readjust to produce the higher musical tone and characterized by a lighter tone quality

headrest \ˈ=,=\ *n* **:** a shaped part or attachment (as on a barber's chair) for supporting the head

head rhyme *n* **:** BEGINNING RHYME

head rice *n* **:** unbroken grains of milled rice with the hull, bran, and germ removed

headrig \ˈ=,=\ *n* **:** the main saw in a mill with or without other saws or associated equipment

headright \ˈ=,=\ *n* **1 :** a grant (as of money or land) formerly given one who fulfilled certain conditions relating esp. to settling and developing land (as in Virginia in 1619 and in Texas in 1839) **2 :** a right belonging to an Indian member of a tribe to receive a per-capita share in the distribution of income earned by the tribal trust fund (as from the sale or lease of mineral rights) or a share of the fund on its termination; *also* **:** the right of a member to a share of tribal property

headring \ˈ=,=\ *n* **1 :** an often decorated ring formed on the head by building up the hair with vegetable or animal fibers and worn by married warriors of some Kaffir tribes **2 :** a pad (as of vegetable fiber) worn to facilitate carrying a load on the head

head rod *n* **:** the switch rod nearest the point of a railroad switch

headroom \ˈ=,=\ *n* **1 :** vertical space in which to stand or move **:** HEADWAY 2 **2 :** HEADSPACE 3

headrope \ˈ=,=\ *n* [ME *hedrope*, fr. *hed* head + *rope*] **1** *obs* **:** a rope leading from a masthead as a stay **2 a :** a part of a boltrope that is sewed along the upper edge of a sail **b :** a rope along the upper edge of a fishnet **3 a :** a rope at the head of an animal (as for tying or leading it) **b :** HEADFAST **4 :** AGAL

heads *pl of* HEAD, *pres 3d sing of* HEAD

head·sail \ˈhedsəl (*usual nautical pronunc*), -,sāl\ *n* **:** a sail (as a jib or fore staysail) set forward of the foremast

headsaw \ˈ=,=\ *n* **:** a saw in a sawmill that cuts logs into planks, boards, and cants — compare RESAW

head scab *n* **:** sarcoptic mange of the head of sheep caused by a mite (*Sarcoptes scabiei* var. *ovis*)

head schedule *n* **:** a list of the type faces, type sizes, and headline forms approved for use in the headlines of a newspaper

head sea *n* **:** waves coming from directly ahead — compare FOLLOWING SEA, QUARTERING SEA

headset \ˈ=,=\ *n* **1 :** an attachment for holding an earphone and transmitter in place at one's head **2 :** a pair of headphones

headshake \ˈ=,=\ *n* **:** a shake of the head usu. signifying denial or distrust

headshaker \ˈ=,==\ *n* **:** SKEPTIC, PESSIMIST ⟨adventurers . . . knowing before they began that the mockers and ~*s* would have the laugh of them —Clemence Dane⟩

headshaking \ˈ=,==\ *n* **:** an act of shaking the head (as in disbelief or distrust)

head·ship \ˈhed,ship\ *n* **:** the position, office, or dignity of a head or chief **:** LEADERSHIP, PRIMACY

headshrinker \ˈ=,==\ *n* **1 :** a headhunter who shrinks the heads of his victims **2** *slang* **:** PSYCHIATRIST

headsill \ˈ=,=\ *n* **1 :** a horizontal member at the top of a doorframe or window frame **2 :** either of the pieces supporting the log at its ends in a saw pit

headskin \ˈ=,=\ *n* **:** a tough elastic fatty mass covering the head of a sperm whale beneath the skin

heads·man \ˈhedzmən\ *n, pl* **headsmen 1 :** an executioner who cuts off heads **2 :** HEADER 5 **3 :** PUSHER 1e

head smut *n* **1 :** a covered smut of corn and sorghum caused by a fungus (*Sphacelotheca reiliana*) **2 :** any smut affecting the heads of grains or grasses

heads or tails *n pl but sing in constr* **:** a simple gambling game in which a coin is tossed and won by the player who successfully calls the side that lands upward — compare HEAD OR TAIL

head·space \ˈ=,=\ *n* **1 :** a space between the breech and bolt face of a firearm using rimless ammunition **2 :** the space taken up by the cartridge rim in a firearm using rimmed ammunition **3 :** a space left between the contents and the ends or closure of a drum, barrel, can, or bottle in order to allow for variations in fill or expansion of contents — called also *outage*

headspring \ˈ=,=\ *n* [ME *hedspring*, fr. *hed* head + *spring*] **1 :** FOUNTAINHEAD, SOURCE **2 :** a tumbling skill similar to a handspring except that the spring is made from the head and hands instead of from the hands alone

headstall \ˈ=,=\ *n* [ME *hedstall*, fr. *hed* head + *stall*] **:** a part of a bridle or halter that encircles the head — see BRIDLE illustration

headstamp \ˈ=,=\ *n* **:** numbers or letters stamped into the base of a cartridge case by the manufacturer in order to identify the cartridge and its original loading

headstand \ˈ=,=\ *n* **:** an acrobatic feat of standing on one's head usu. with support from the hands

head start *n* [²*head*] **1 :** an advantage granted or achieved at the beginning of a race, a chase, or a competition **:** START ⟨a *head start* of 15 paces⟩ ⟨10-minute *head start*⟩ **2 :** a favorable or promising beginning **:** a good start

head stay *n* **:** FORESTAY

headstick \ˈ=,=\ *n* **:** a short stick fitted to the headrope of a jib-headed sail or an ensign to prevent twisting

headstock \ˈ=,=\ *n* **1 :** a bearing or pedestal for a revolving or moving part: as **a :** a part of a lathe that holds the revolving spindle and its attachments **b :** a part of a cylindrical grinding machine that rotates the work **c :** a part of a planing machine supporting the cutter **d :** a movable head in a measuring machine **e :** a framework containing a runway for the carriage in a spinning mule **f :** a headframe over a mine shaft **2 :** a pivoted crossbeam that supports a church bell

headstone \ˈ=,=\ *n* **1 :** the principal stone in a foundation **:** chief stone **:** CORNERSTONE **2 :** the stone at the head of a grave

headstream \ˈ=,=\ *n* **:** a stream that is the source or one of the sources of a river

head string *n* **:** a line connecting the second diamonds of the side rails at the head end of a billiard table that marks a limit on or within which the cue ball is placed in lagging for the break or beginning the game

headstrong \ˈ=,=\ *adj* [ME *hedstrong*, fr. *hed* head + *strong*] **1 :** not easily restrained **:** UNGOVERNABLE, OBSTINATE ⟨~ youth⟩ **2 :** directed by ungovernable will **:** proceeding from obstinacy ⟨violent ~ actions⟩ **syn** see UNRULY

head·strong·ly *adv* **:** in a headstrong manner

head·strong·ness *n* -ES **:** the quality of being headstrong

heads up *interj* — used as a warning to look out for danger overhead or to clear a passageway

heads–up \ˈ=,=\ *adj* [*heads up*] **:** ALERT, WIDE-AWAKE, RESOURCEFUL ⟨fast, aggressive, *heads-up* football⟩

head tax *n* **:** a tax usu. identical on every individual in a class or group: as **a :** POLL TAX **b :** a per-capita tax imposed on one (as a steamship company) bringing immigrants into the U.S.

head tie *n* **:** a kerchief for the head

headtire *n* [¹*head* + *tire* (headdress)] *obs* **:** HEADDRESS

head tone *n* **:** a vocal tone produced in the head register

head tree *n* **:** the spar tree nearest the donkey engine in a skyline logging system

head up *vt* **1 :** to close (as a barrel) at the head or with a head **2 :** HEAD *vt* 4 **~** *vi* **1 :** HEAD *vi* 3a **2 :** to come to an apex **:** find a head ⟨a bureaucracy that *headed up* in the king —W.P. Webb⟩

head voice *n* **:** the vocal tones of the head register

headwaiter \ˈ=ˈ==\ *n* **:** the head of the dining-room staff of a restaurant or hotel

headwall \ˈ=,=\ *n* **1 a :** a precipice rising above the floor of a glacial cirque **b :** a steep slope forming the head of a valley **2 :** a wall of masonry or concrete built at the outlet of a drainpipe or culvert with the end of the conduit flush with the outer surface of the wall

¹head·ward \ˈhedw(ə)rd\ *also* **head·wards** \-dz\ *adv* [¹*head* + *-ward, -wards*] **:** toward the head **:** in the direction of the head ⟨a stream lengthens its course by eroding ~⟩

²headward \ˈ"\ *adj* **:** proceeding toward the head **:** occurring at or near the head ⟨~ erosion of a valley⟩ ⟨loss of consciousness caused by ~ acceleration of the body⟩

³head·ward \-,wȯrd, -ö(ə)d\ *n* -s [trans. of OE *hēafodweard*] **:** feudal service consisting in acting as a guard to the lord

head·wark \ˈ=,wärk\ *n* -s [ME *hedewerk*, fr. OE *hēafodwærc*, fr. *hēafod* head + *wærc* pain; akin to OE *weorc* work — more at HEAD, WARK] *chiefly dial Brit* **:** HEADACHE

headwater \ˈ=,==\ *n* **:** the source and upper part of a stream — usu. used in pl.

headway \ˈ=,=\ *n* **1 a :** motion or rate of motion in a forward direction (as of a ship) **b :** ADVANCE, PROGRESS ⟨make ~ in a profession⟩ ⟨a life in which the claims of spirit and emotion will make some ~ against the necessities of physical existence —Clive Bell⟩ **2 :** clear space (as under an arch or girder) sufficient to allow of easy passing underneath **:** HEADROOM **3 :** the time interval between two vehicles traveling in the same direction on the same route

headwear \ˈ=,=\ *n* **:** apparel for the head **:** HEADGEAR 1a

head wind *n* **:** a wind blowing in a direction opposite to a course esp. of a ship or airplane ⟨delayed by strong *head winds*⟩

headword \ˈ=,=\ *n* **1 :** a word or term often in distinctive type placed at the beginning of a chapter, paragraph, or entry (as in a dictionary or a catalog) **2 :** a word qualified by a modifier ⟨it is not always easy to state the precise kind of relation that exists between the modifier and its ~ —C.C.Fries⟩

headwork \ˈ=,=\ *n* **1 :** mental labor; *esp* **:** clever thinking **2 :** ornamentation for an arch keystone **3 :** a structure for controlling the quantity of water entering a channel **4 headworks** *pl* **:** a platform or raft with tackle for warping or kedging a log raft through still water

headworker \ˈ=ˈ==\ *n* [²*head* + *worker*] **:** a director of a social agency or settlement

heady \ˈhedē, -di\ *adj* -ER/-EST [ME *hevedy, hedy*, fr. *heved, hed* head + *-y* — more at HEAD] **1 a :** WILLFUL, RASH ⟨the flow of the story is interrupted by . . . the giving of ~ opinions —S.L.A.Marshall⟩ **b :** VIOLENT, IMPETUOUS ⟨~ waters of the swollen river⟩ ⟨~ tempest⟩ **2 a :** tending to make giddy or light-headed **:** INTOXICATING ⟨~ perfume⟩ ⟨~ triumphs⟩ ⟨the ~ air of spring⟩ **b :** GIDDY, INTOXICATED, EXHILARATED ⟨students showing themselves ~ with ideas —*Time*⟩ **3 :** having or showing good judgment **:** SHREWD, CLEVER, SMART ⟨ran a ~ race⟩ ⟨one of the nimblest and *headiest* . . . quarterbacks —*Time*⟩

head yard *n* **:** a yard on a foremast

heaf \ˈhēf\ *n* -s [alter. of ⁴*haft, heft*] *dial Eng* **:** a piece of ground used as a sheep pasture

¹heal \ˈhēl, *esp before pause or consonant* -ēəl\ *vb* -ED/-ING/-s [ME *helen*, fr. OE *hǣlan*; akin to OHG *heilen* to heal, ON *heila*, Goth *hailjan*; causative denominatives fr. the root of OE *hāl* healthy, whole — more at WHOLE] *vt* **1 a :** to make sound or whole **:** restore to health **b :** to cure of disease or affliction ⟨a society to ~ convulsions or cramps —Ruth F. Kirk⟩ ⟨~ injured tissues⟩ **2 a :** to cause (an undesirable condition) to be overcome or eliminated **:** MEND ⟨the troubles . . . had not been forgotten, but they had been ~*ed* —William Power⟩ ⟨~ marital rifts and to ward off hasty divorce actions —*N.Y. Times*⟩; *specif* **:** to patch up (a rift or division) **:** CEMENT ⟨the conflicts between capital and labor . . . might temporarily be ~*ed* —J.A.Hobson⟩ ⟨~*ed* a breach between the two branches of the family —*Current Biog.*⟩ **b :** to restore to original purity or integrity **:** to make (a person) spiritually whole **:** to restore from evil ⟨~*ed* of his sins⟩ ⟨thus saith the Lord, I have ~*ed* these waters —2 Kings 2:21 (AV)⟩ **~** *vi* **1 :** to grow sound **:** return to a sound state ⟨the limb ~*s*⟩ ⟨the wound ~*s*⟩ **2 :** to effect a cure **syn** see CURE

²heal \ˈ"\ *vt* -ED/-ING/-s [ME *helen* to hide, conceal, cover, fr. OE *helan* — more at HELL] **1** *dial chiefly Eng* **:** to cover (as seeds) with earth **2** *dial chiefly Eng* **:** to cover with slates or tiles ⟨a leaky-roofed, tile-*healed* . . . cottage —F.M.Ford⟩

heal·able \ˈhēləbəl\ *adj* **:** capable of being healed

heal–all \ˈhē,lȯl\ *n, pl* **heal–alls** \-,ȯlz\ *also* **heals–alls** \-lz,ȯlz\ **1 :** SELF-HEAL **2 :** a plant of the genus *Scrophularia* **3 :** GREAT GREEN ORCHIS **4 :** YELLOW CLINTONIA

heald \ˈhēld\ *n* -s [ME *helde*, fr. OE *hefeld*; akin to MLG *hevelte* heddle, ON *hafald*; derivatives fr. the root of OE *hebban* to raise, lift — more at HEAVE] *chiefly Brit* **:** HEDDLE

heald·er \ˈhēldə(r)\ *n* -s *Brit* **:** DRAWER-IN

heal·er \ˈhēlə(r)\ *n* -s [ME *helere*, fr. *helen* to heal + *-ere* -er — more at HEAL] **1 :** one that heals ⟨time is a great ~⟩; *specif* **:** a person who engages in healing through means not requiring medical training or licensing **2 :** a Christian Science practitioner

¹healing *n* -s [ME *heling*, fr. OE *hǣling*, fr. *hǣlan* to heal + *-ing* — more at HEAL] **:** the act or process of curing or of restoring to health **:** the process of getting well

²healing *adj* [ME *heling*, fr. pres. part. of *helen* to heal] **:** tending to heal or cure **:** CURATIVE ⟨a ~ art⟩ — **heal·ing·ly** *adv*

healing blade *n* **:** BROAD-LEAVED PLANTAIN 1

healing herb *n* **1 :** COMFREY **2 :** HOARY PLANTAIN 1

heal·some \ˈhēlsəm\ *Scot var of* WHOLESOME

¹health \ˈhelth *also* -ltth\ *n* -s [ME *helthe*, fr. OE *hǣlth*, fr. *hāl* whole, healthy — more at WHOLE] **1 a :** the condition of an organism or one of its parts in which it performs its vital functions normally or properly **:** the state of being sound in body or mind ⟨nursed him back to ~⟩ ⟨he is the picture of ~⟩ ⟨dental ~⟩ ⟨mental ~⟩ — compare DISEASE **b :** the condition of an organism with respect to the performance of its vital functions esp. as evaluated subjectively or nonprofessionally ⟨how is your ~ today⟩ ⟨never in better ~⟩ ⟨her ~ is very delicate⟩ ⟨broken in ~⟩ ⟨went traveling for his ~⟩ **2 :** flourishing condition **:** WELL-BEING, VITALITY, PROSPERITY ⟨one more indication of the ~ of this pulsating . . . art form —Harriet Johnson⟩ ⟨expected the capitalist system to retain some degree of ~ —F.C.Barghoorn⟩ ⟨a serious menace to our economic ~ —F.L.Allen⟩ **3 :** a toast to someone's health, well-being, or prosperity ⟨"to her Majesty!" he said . . . and drank a long ~ —Theodore Bonnet⟩ ⟨proposed the ~ of the ladies —B.A.Botkin & A.F.Harlow⟩

²health \ˈ"\ *adj* **1 :** of, relating to, or engaged in welfare work directed to the cure and prevention of disease ⟨a ~ center⟩ ⟨~ agencies⟩ **2 :** of, relating to, or conducive to health ⟨~ foods⟩ ⟨~ drinks⟩ ⟨~ education⟩

health department *n* **:** a division of a local or larger government responsible for the oversight and care of matters relating to public health

health·ful \-thfəl\ *adj* [ME *helthful*, fr. *helthe* health + *-ful*] **1 :** beneficial to health of body or mind **:** conducive to health **:** SALUTARY ⟨a ~ climate⟩ **2 :** HEALTHY ⟨a weird translation of Dickens' relatively ~ exuberance into a morbid . . . mysticism —*Writer*⟩ ⟨physical organization . . . which was at once ~ and exquisitely delicate —Nathaniel Hawthorne⟩

syn HEALTHY, WHOLESOME, SALUBRIOUS, SALUTARY, HYGIENIC, SANITARY: HEALTHFUL and HEALTHY are both used to mean conducive to or indicative of health or soundness, the former word being preferred in some quarters ⟨a *healthful* climate⟩ ⟨better nutrition, more *healthful* housing, sounder forms of recreation —Lewis Mumford⟩ ⟨one of the *healthiest* climates in England —Arnold Bennett⟩ ⟨extolled the *healthy* air of the hills as the best way to recover from fever —Hervey Allen⟩ ⟨*healthy* and normal outlets for youthful energies —Allan Nevins & H.S.Commager⟩ WHOLESOME may more strongly suggest beneficial, upbuilding, or sustaining capacities, physically, intellectually, or spiritually ⟨*wholesome* meats⟩ ⟨the warm rays of the sun, too, were *wholesome* for him in body and soul —Nathaniel Hawthorne〉 〈one trade is healthier or cleanlier than another, that it is carried on in a more *wholesome* or pleasant locality —Alfred Marshall〉 〈*wholesome*, fast-reading adaptations for teenagers of the adult best sellers they want to read —*N.Y. Times Bk. Rev.*〉 SALUBRIOUS may suggest the pleasantly invigorating or bracing 〈these uplands are likewise often the most *salubrious* seat of living, with their fine scenery, their bracing ionized air, their range of recreation, from mountain-climbing and fishing to swimming and ice-skating —Lewis Mumford〉 SALUTARY may describe something corrective, tonic, or otherwise beneficially effective although the thing in question may in itself be unpleasant 〈in the open air, which is the most *salutary* of all things for both body and mind —R.L.Stevenson〉 〈*salutary* was the tartness with which she protested, "You're the most conceited man that ever lived!" —Sinclair Lewis〉 〈idle ladies and gentlemen are treated with *salutary* contempt, whilst the worker's blouse is duly honored —G.B.Shaw〉 HYGIENIC is likely to suggest conformity with various health principles and laws 〈anyone . . . who took the proper amount of balanced food, or consumed his excess heat units in regular exercise, and lived a reasonably *hygienic* life —V.G.Heiser〉 SANITARY implies cleanly precaution against contamination, infection, or other unhealthful developments 〈the *sanitary* appearance of the hospital kitchen〉

health·ful·ly \-fəlē, -li\ *adv* [ME *helthfully*, fr. *helthful* + *-ly*] **:** in a healthful manner

health·ful·ness *n* -ES **:** the quality or state of being healthful

health·i·ly \-thəlē, -li\ *adv* **:** in a healthy manner

health·i·ness \-thēnəs, -thin-\ *n* -ES **:** the quality or state of being healthy

health insurance *n* **:** insurance against loss through illness of the insured

health·less \-thləs\ *adj* **1 :** lacking health of body or mind **:** INFIRM **2 :** not conducive to health **:** UNWHOLESOME

health line *n, usu cap H* **:** LINE OF MERCURY

health officer *n* **:** an officer charged with the enforcement of laws relating to health and sanitation **:** an executive officer under the direction of a health department or similar public body

health physicist *n* **:** a specialist in health physics

health physics *n pl but usu sing in constr* **:** physics dealing with the medical and hygienic aspects of and precautions against exposure to radioactive radiations

health·some \-thsəm\ *adj* **:** WHOLESOME, HEALTHFUL 〈lent the street an air of good ~ quiet —William Sansom〉

healthy \-thē, -thi\ *adj* -ER/-EST **1 a :** enjoying good health **:** free from disease **:** functioning properly or normally in its vital functions 〈the examination revealed him to be a perfectly ~ man〉 〈a ~ body〉 〈~ eyes are a precious possession〉 〈a ~ tree〉 **b :** conducive to health **:** SALUTARY 〈walk three miles every day . . . a beastly bore, but ~ —G.S.Patton〉 〈his life recently had not been a ~ one —A. Conan Doyle〉 〈the *healthiest* damned island in the Pacific —John Dos Passos〉 **c :** indicating, reflecting, or suggestive of health 〈a ~ color in his cheeks —Charles Dickens〉 〈the ~ smell of grain —T.B. Costain〉 〈stretched her arms over her head with a gesture of ~ fatigue —Ellen Glasgow〉 **2 a :** morally or spiritually wholesome **:** not sickly, morbid, or sentimental **:** tending toward or indicating moral health 〈their principal purpose of giving our children ~ entertainment —Coulton Waugh〉 〈that's a good ~, cynical approach —James Street〉 〈~ vulgarity inseparable from all vital human works —Albert Dasnoy〉 〈in ~ reaction to the romantic fustian of the . . . nineteenth century —Christopher Fry〉 **b :** free from malfunctioning of any kind **:** VIABLE, PROSPEROUS, FLOURISHING, DESIRABLE 〈the restoration of a ~ economy〉 〈not a ~ state of affairs〉 〈the negative plates are probably defective . . . requiring an extended period of charging and discharging to put them back in a ~ condition —A.L.Dyke〉 〈a ~ book-publishing business —Harry Botsford〉 **c :** productive of good of any kind **:** POSITIVE, BENEFICIAL 〈showed his formidable ships of war . . . making a very ~ impression —C.S.Forester〉 〈the creation of a ~ rivalry between the services —H.B.Hinton〉 **d :** large in quantity or degree **:** CONSIDERABLE, MASSIVE 〈repairs . . . account for a ~ bit of income —Bill Wolf〉 〈the product carries a ~ price tag —*Printers' Ink*〉 **e :** VIGOROUS, HEARTY 〈a ~ appetite〉 〈gives the boat a ~ shove . . . into deeper water —*All Hands*〉 **3 :** SAFE — usu. used in negative construction 〈not so ~ to be around . . . they might take a pop at us —Giorgio De Santillana〉 〈not a ~ spot to be in at that time —H.A.Chippendale〉

syn SOUND, WHOLESOME, ROBUST, HALE, WELL: HEALTHY can imply (1) the possession of full vigor of mind or body or (2) merely freedom from any sign of disease or morbidity 〈a family with four *healthy*, active boys〉 〈keep a child *healthy* during the winter〉 〈a *healthy* outlook on life〉 SOUND implies more strongly the absence of all defects of mind or body 〈develop vigorous children, *sound* in mind and body〉 〈*sound* of limb and healthy of mind〉 WHOLESOME implies a healthiness that impresses others favorably, esp. as indicating physical, moral, or mental soundness or balance 〈her hair carelessly pinned back, her eyes shining, her face aglow, looking oddly *wholesome* in a smeared white painter's smock —Herman Wouk〉 〈a short, strongly made woman, *wholesome* and still youthful —C.B.Nordhoff & J.N.Hall〉 ROBUST is the opposite of *delicate*, implying a vigor manifest in muscularity, solidity, strength of voice, power of endurance, and so on 〈was looking *robust* and full of health and vigor —Samuel Butler †1902〉 〈*robust* and tough in fiber —I.A.Gordon〉 〈the giant zinnias are so *robust* here that you can transplant them in full bloom —Barrett McGurn〉 HALE applies chiefly to elderly persons who still retain physical qualities of men in their prime 〈this particular black panther was not old and sore, like many man-eaters. It was an exceedingly *hale* animal —David Walker〉 〈his father, though an old man, was still *hale* —Sheila Kaye-Smith〉 〈now in his 80th year but still alert, *hale* and hearty —*Wesfarmers News*〉 WELL merely implies freedom from disease 〈stay *well* amidst disease and poverty〉 〈seemingly doomed to constant illness, only once in a while did he feel really *well*〉

syn see in addition HEALTHFUL

healthy potato disease *n* **:** LATENT VIRUS DISEASE

¹heap \ˈhēp\ *n* -S [ME *heep, hepe*, fr. OE *hēap*; akin to OHG *houf, hūfo* heap, OS *hōp*, MLG *hūpe* heap, OE *hēah* high — more at HIGH] **1 :** a collection of things laid or thrown one on another **:** PILE 〈small ~s of stones at which . . . sacrifices are offered —J.G.Frazer〉 **2 :** a great number or large quantity **:** LOT 〈there would be a ~ of noise and excitement —S.H. Holbrook〉 〈it took a ~ of work —Meridel Le Sueur〉 〈made a ~ of money〉 〈there must be ~s of young poets who adore you —G.B.Shaw〉 **3 :** the totality of rivals or competitors — used in the phrase *the top of the heap* 〈it's getting to the top of the ~ that saves a man —Louis Auchincloss〉 〈remain at the top of the concert ~ indefinitely —*Time*〉 **4** *slang* **:** AUTOMOBILE; *esp* **:** an old beat-up automobile 〈that ~ wasn't worth more than thirty dollars —C.L.Lamson〉 〈my old tin ~ wouldn't start —Christopher Morley〉 — **heap sight** *dial* **:** a great deal 〈I'd a *heap sight* rather stay〉 — **of a heap** *or* **all of a heap 1 :** so as to be stupefied, amazed, or overcome 〈a lot of people were also struck *all of a heap* because . . . the favorite could do no better than finish third —G.F.T.Ryall〉 〈struck him so completely *of a heap* that he was almost a broken man —H.L.Davis〉 **2 :** all of a sudden 〈*all of a heap* they had given her perplexity, immobility, and a dreadful thought —F.M.Ford〉

²heap \"\ *vb* -ED/-ING/-S [ME *hepen*, fr. OE *hēapian*; akin to OHG *houfōn* to heap; denominatives fr. the root of E ¹*heap*] *vt* **1 a :** to throw or lay in a heap **:** pile or collect in great quantity **:** lay up **:** AMASS, ACCUMULATE 〈stacks of firewood were ~*ed* all about the store —F.V.W.Mason〉 **b :** to fill, load, or cover with a heap or heaps 〈dishes ~*ed* high with food〉 〈fields ~*ed* high with stacks of grain〉 **2 a :** to accord, assign, or bestow lavishly or in large quantities 〈~*ed* scorn and reproaches upon him〉 〈~*ing* work upon his shoulders〉 **b :** to bestow lavishly or in large quantities upon 〈~*ed* him with stewardships and sinecures —Francis Hackett〉 **3 :** to form or round into a heap (as in measuring) **:** fill (a measure) more than even full ~ *vi* **:** to form in a heap 〈the drift ~*ed* denser and denser about his legs —C.G.D.Roberts〉

heaped measure *or* **heaping measure** *n* **:** dry measure obtained by filling the container heaping full

heap roasting *or* **heap roast** *n* **:** a process in which high-sulfur ore piled in the open is roasted without fuel other than for ignition, the heat being furnished by the combustion of the sulfur in the ore

heaps \ˈhēps\ *adv* [fr. pl. of ¹*heap*] **:** very much **:** EXTREMELY 〈thanks just ~〉 — not often in formal use

hear \ˈhi(ə)r, -iə\ *vb* **heard** \ˈhərd, ˈhə̄d\ *also dial* **heared** *or* **heerd** *or* **heered** \ˈhi(ə)rd, -i(ə)d\ *or* **hearn** *or* **heern** \ˈhi(ə)rn, -i(ə)n\ **heard** *also dial* **heared** *or* **heerd** *or* **heered** *or* **hearn** *or* **heern; hearing; hears** [ME *heren*, fr. OE *hieran, hȳran, hēran*; akin to OHG *hōren* to hear, ON *heyra*, Goth *hausjan* to hear, L *cavēre* to be on one's guard, Gk *akouein* to hear, *koein* to notice, hear, Skt *kavi* clever, wise] *vt* **1 :** to be made aware of by the ear **:** apprehend by the ear 〈so great was the din that I could not ~ him〉 〈he could ~ the distant rumble of the native drums〉 **2 :** to be informed or gain knowledge of by hearing 〈~ that business is picking up〉 〈*heard* that you were ill〉 〈*heard* nothing more about the affair〉 — often used in the phrase *hear say* 〈I've *heard* say that he has been married before〉 and *heard tell* 〈ain't *heard* tell of them since I don't know when —Hamilton Basso〉 〈you may have *heard* tell of the wonder chemical, fluorine —*Amer. Girl*〉 **3 a :** to listen to with favor or compliance **:** GRANT 〈the Lord has *heard* my prayers〉 **b :** to listen to with care or attention **:** give audience to 〈won't you ~ my side of the story〉 〈would not ~ the envoy, and angrily dismissed him〉 〈would not ~ me through〉 〈they *heard* him out, hiding their skepticism —F.D.Downey〉 **c :** to attend and listen to 〈~ a concert〉 〈~ mass〉 **d :** to listen to the recitation of 〈he wants me to ~ him his part —Christopher Isherwood〉 **4 a :** to give a legal hearing to 〈~ a case〉 〈the judge refused to ~ their claims〉 **b** (1) **:** to take testimony from 〈the committee *heard* 345 witnesses〉 (2) **:** to take (testimony) usu. at a hearing 〈the committee's decision to ~ testimony . . . on the condition of natives —*Current Biog.*〉 ~ *vi* **1 :** to have the capacity of apprehending sound 〈he can't ~ at all, poor fellow〉 **2 a :** to gain information through oral communication **:** have a report **:** LEARN 〈have *heard* about your doings〉 〈who ever *heard* of such a thing〉 **b :** to receive a message or letter 〈haven't *heard* from him in two months〉 **3 :** to entertain the idea **:** CONSENT, YIELD — used in negative construction with *of* 〈will not ~ of my going〉 or *to* 〈would not ~ to it —Clyde Eagleton〉 **4 :** to receive a scolding or tongue-lashing or punishment 〈another complaint and you'll ~ from me〉 **5 —** often used in the expression *Hear! Hear!* during a speech to call attention to the words of the speaker or in applause

hear·able \ˈhirəbəl\ *adj* [ME *herable*, fr. *heren* to hear + *-able*] **:** capable of being heard

hear·er \-rə(r)\ *n* -S [ME *herere*, fr. *heren* to hear + *-ere* -er] **1 :** one that hears **:** AUDITOR **2 :** AUDIENT 2

hear·ing \ˈhiriŋ, -rēŋ\ *n* -S [ME *heringe*, fr. *heren* + *-inge* -ing] **1 a** (1) **:** the act or power of apprehending sound; *specif* **:** one of the special senses of vertebrates that is concerned with the perception of sound, is mediated through the organ of Corti of the ear in mammals or through corresponding sensory receptors of the lagena in lower vertebrates, is normally sensitive in man to sound vibrations between 16 and 27,000 cycles per second but most receptive to those between 2000 and 5000 cycles per second, is conducted centrally by the cochlear branch of the auditory nerve, and is coordinated esp. in the medial geniculate body (2) **:** an analogous perception of vibration in other animals 〈the katydid . . . whose ~ is in slits on the front legs —C.D. & Mary Michener〉 **b :** the extent within which sound may be heard **:** EARSHOT 〈within ~ —Shak.〉 **2 a** (1) **:** the act or an instance of actively or carefully listening (as to a speaker or performer) **:** AUDITION, AUDIENCE 〈a powerful version . . . and you should give it a ~ —*Jazz Jour.*〉 〈a man knows by instinct whether he'll get a tender ~ —Eden Phillpotts〉 〈the orchestra did not impress me in one ~ as being quite up to Eastern . . . standards —Virgil Thomson〉 (2) *dial Eng* **:** a church service **:** PREACHING (3) **:** opportunity to be heard or to present one's side of a case 〈at least give me a ~〉 〈the worst of men is entitled to a ~〉 (4) **:** opportunity (as for a book or doctrine) to be generally known, evaluated, or appreciated **:** public attention or patronage 〈no other book of equal seriousness ever had so quick a ~ —J.D.Hart〉 〈a new trend which is struggling for a ~ —Edward Sapir〉 〈numerous and fantastic theories of sleep continue to find a ~ —Webb Garrison〉 **b** (1) **:** a trial in equity practice (2) **:** a listening to arguments or proofs and arguments in interlocutory proceedings (3) **:** a preliminary examination in criminal procedure (4) **:** a trial before an administrative tribunal **c :** a session (as of a congressional committee) in which witnesses are heard and testimony is taken 〈the committee will hold ~s in a number of major cities〉 **3** *chiefly dial* **:** a piece of news **:** RUMOR; *esp* **:** a choice bit of gossip **4** *Scot* **:** SCOLDING, LECTURE

hearing aid *n* **:** a device that amplifies the sound reaching an auditor's receptor organs; *specif* **:** an instrument for this purpose that consists of microphone, amplifier, and reproducer and is fundamentally comparable to a miniature telephone

hearing examiner *also* **hearing officer** *n* **:** a referee appointed by an agency of government to conduct an investigation or a public or private hearing and to report his findings of fact and sometimes his recommendations so that the agency may exercise its statutory powers (as by establishing rules and regulations or deciding controversies)

heark·en *also* **hark·en** \ˈhärkən, ˈhäk-\ *vb* -ED/-ING/-S [ME *herkenen*, fr. OE *heorcnian, hyrcnian*; akin to OFris *herkia, harkia* to listen — more at HARK] *vi* **1 :** to give ear **:** LISTEN 〈~*ed* without much mental comment —Theodore Dreiser〉 〈~*ed* to all they said night after night —Glenway Wescott〉 〈stopped to ~ to the distant sound of another dog barking —Winnie Fitch〉 **2 :** to listen with attention, sympathy, or acceptance of what is said **:** give respectful attention 〈the boy was ~*ing* to another —Fanny Butcher〉 〈how was it possible . . . that nobody ~*ed* to Goethe's voice —J.P.Hodin〉 〈the humble folk who ~*ed* to these evangelists —G.M.Stephenson〉 ~ *vt, archaic* **:** to give heed to **:** HEAR

hearken back *vi* **:** to hark back 〈*hearken back* to the good old days of a century ago —Bernard Berelson〉

hearn *dial past of* HEAR

hearsay \ˈ=,=\ *n* -S *often attrib* [fr. the phrase *hear say*] **1 :** something heard from another **:** REPORT, RUMOR 〈like the ~s bandied about by the medievalists —S.N.Behrman〉 〈the qualifications and doubts that distinguish critical science from ~ knowledge —M.R.Cohen〉 〈places off the route, but known from ~ —G.F.Hudson〉 **2 :** HEARSAY EVIDENCE

hearsay evidence *n* **:** legal testimony that consists in a narration by one person of matters told him by another; *broadly* **:** evidence that does not derive its value solely from the credit given to the witness himself as such but that rests in part on the veracity and competency of some other person or sometimes of the witness at another time

hearsay rule *n* **:** a rule barring the admission of hearsay evidence as testimony by reason of the unavailability of the sanctions of cross-examination to test the accuracy of the statement

¹hearse \ˈhərs, ˈhə̄s\ *n* -S [ME *herse* harrow, fr. MF *herce* harrow, frame for holding candles, fr. L *hirpic-, hirpex* harrow, prob. of Oscan origin; akin to Oscan *hirpus* wolf, L *hircus* he-goat] **1 a :** a usu. triangular frame of wood or metal designed to hold usu. 15 candles and used esp. in the Tenebrae service in Holy Week **b :** an elaborate temporary or permanent framework erected over a coffin or tomb of a royal, noble, or distinguished person and often decorated with lighted candles, banners, heraldic devices, and hangings and with memorial verses or epitaphs attached to it **2 a** *archaic* **:** COFFIN, GRAVE, TOMB, MONUMENT **b** *obs* **:** BIER 2 **3 :** a vehicle for conveying the dead (as to the grave)

hearse 1a

²hearse \"\ *vt* -ED/-ING/-S **1 a** *archaic* **:** to place on a bier or in a coffin **b :** to convey in a hearse **2 :** BURY, ENTOMB **3 :** to carry as if with a hearse

hears·ti·an \ˈhərstēən\ *adj, usu cap* [William Randolph *Hearst* †1951 Am. newspaper publisher + E *-ian*] **:** of, relating to, or resembling the journalistic style or methods or the intense nationalism associated with the publisher William R. Hearst and his publications 〈as chauvinistic, or *Hearstian*, as ever —Ted Oster〉 〈the comic strip and other variegated features of the *Hearstian* type —*Vanity Fair*〉

hearst·ling \ˈhərstliŋ\ *n* -S *usu cap* [W. R. *Hearst* + E *-ling*] **:** a journalist employed by or sharing the views of W. R. Hearst **:** a reactionary journalist 〈how the *Hearstlings* will howl at the call for the repeal of the ban —K.N.Stewart〉

¹heart \ˈhärt, ˈhȧt, *usu* -d.+V\ *n* -S [ME *hert*, fr. OE *heorte*;

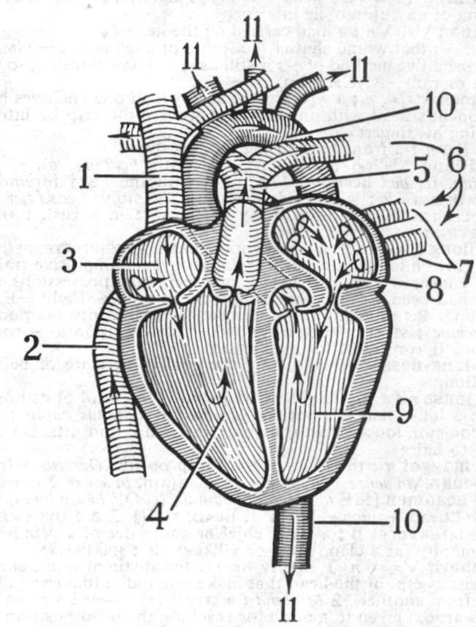

heart 1a, showing course of the blood coming from the body and entering from *1* superior vena cava and from *2* inferior vena cava; to *3* right atrium; to *4* right ventricle; to *5* pulmonary artery; to *6* lungs (not shown); to *7* pulmonary veins; to *8* left atrium; to *9* left ventricle; to *10* aorta; leaving by *11* to the head, neck, and upper extremities (not shown)

akin to OHG *herza* heart, ON *hjarta*, Goth *hairto*, L *cord-, cor*, OIr *cride*, Gk *kardia*, Arm *sirt*, Hitt *karts*] **1 a :** a hollow muscular organ of vertebrate animals that by its rhythmic contraction acts as a force pump maintaining the circulation of the blood, is in the human adult about five inches long and three and one half broad, of conical form, is placed obliquely in the chest with the broad end upward and to the right and the apex opposite the interval between the cartilages of the fifth and sixth ribs on the left side, is enclosed in a serous pericardium, and consists as in other mammals and in birds of four chambers divided into an upper pair of rather thin-walled auricles which receive blood from the veins and a lower pair of thick-walled ventricles into which the blood is forced and which in turn pump it into the arteries, back flow being prevented by valves, or in lower forms is less perfectly differentiated, having usu. two auricles and one ventricle in reptiles and amphibians and but a single auricle and ventricle in most fishes **b :** a structure in an invertebrate animal functionally analogous to the vertebrate heart: as (1) **:** a contractile ventricle with one to four thin-walled auricles that circulates the body fluid of most mollusks (2) **:** a contractile tube in most arthropods that receives blood from an investing pericardial sinus through openings provided with valves and circulates it forward and peripherally in the body (3) **:** any of a series of paired pulsating anterior blood vessels connecting the main dorsal and ventral blood vessels of certain annelids **c :** BREAST, BOSOM 〈could have hugged him to my ~ —W.M.Thackeray〉 **d :** something resembling a heart in shape: (1) **:** a conventionalized representation of a heart (as a decorative figure or a trinket) (2) **:** a red conventionalized figure of a heart stamped on a playing card (3) **:** a heart-shaped block through which a lanyard is reeved to extend stays (4) **:** the heart-shaped part of a pound net placed at the end of the leader to direct fish into the pot (5) **:** a foundry molder's heart-shaped trowel (6) **hearts** *pl but sing in constr* **:** a wood sorrel (*Oxalis montana*) **2 a :** a playing card marked with a conventionalized figure of a heart **b hearts** *pl* **:** the suit comprising cards so marked **c :** an odd bridge trick won or contracted for when hearts are trumps **d hearts** *pl but sing in constr* **:** a game resembling whist in which the object is to avoid taking tricks containing hearts and often other specified cards **3 a** (1) **:** the whole personality including intellectual as well as emotional functions or traits 〈come from the ~ that is gay, warm, friendly, and enthusiastic —Constance Foster〉 〈I say what is in my ~〉 〈deep in your own ~, you share my prejudice —Walter de la Mare〉 〈each man knew in his ~ that it was a lie —L.B.Salomon〉 (2) *obs* **:** INTELLECT, UNDERSTANDING (3) **:** MEMORY, ROTE — used in the phrase *by heart* 〈got the whole poem by ~〉 〈knew the town's 500 telephone numbers by ~ —Peg Bracken〉 (4) **:** OPINION, ATTITUDE, POSTURE — used chiefly in the phrase *change of heart* 〈two aspects to the Soviet change of ~ on the Austrian treaty —T.P.Whitney〉 **b** (1) **:** the emotional or moral as distinguished from the intellectual nature **:** CONSCIENCE, CHARACTER, SPIRIT 〈has a good ~ but a weak head〉 〈who can look into the ~ of a man〉 〈his ~ dictated one course, his reason another〉 (2) **:** generous disposition **:** SENSIBILITY, COMPASSION, FEELINGS 〈have you no ~〉 〈Oh, have a ~, lend me a dollar〉 (3) **:** hardness or flintiness of character or temper **:** unfeeling disposition — usu. used with *have* in negative construction 〈he loved his wife; he had not the ~ to deny her anything —Clara Morris〉 〈hadn't the ~ . . . to refuse to come —Ellen Glasgow〉 (4) **:** TEMPERAMENT, DISPOSITION, MOOD 〈went home with a heavy ~〉 〈are not inclined to regard free-trade agitation with a light ~ —*Dun's Rev.*〉 (5) **:** GOODWILL, WILLINGNESS, SINCERITY, ZEAL — used chiefly in the phrase *with all my heart* 〈will do it for you with all my ~〉 **c :** LOVE, AFFECTIONS 〈he lost his ~ to her at once〉 〈laid his ~ at her feet〉 〈a free public-school system . . . was one thing that lay near his ~ —A.W.Long〉 〈his speeches won him ~s from coast to coast —William Clark〉 **d :** COURAGE, ARDOR, ENTHUSIASM 〈don't lose ~; all will turn out well〉 〈felt some sinking of the ~〉 〈an unsatisfactory . . . student, for my ~ was not in it —W.S.Maugham〉 〈put ~ into me by what you say —O.W.Holmes †1935〉 〈at the sight of reinforcements, the dispirited soldiers took ~〉 〈lost all ~ for my silly chase —Arthur Grimble〉 〈many a people has kept itself in ~ when its statesmen have despaired —W.B.Adams〉 **e** (1) **:** TASTE, LIKING 〈likes music but has no ~ for grand opera〉 — used chiefly in the phrase *after one's own heart* 〈a man after his own ~〉 (2) **:** fixed purpose or desire **:** ardent wish — now used chiefly in the phrase *set one's heart on* 〈set his ~ on getting a new car〉 (3) **:** intense concern, solicitude, or preoccupation — used chiefly in the phrase *at heart* 〈people who are unaware of the issue which he has at ~ —J.H.Robinson〉 〈with victory secured, there was one other thing that he had at ~〉 **f :** one's innermost being **:** one's innermost or actual character, disposition, or feelings — used chiefly in the phrases *at heart* 〈at ~ a

heart 1d(1)

sensitive high-strung man⟩ and *heart of hearts* ⟨assisting those who in their ~ of hearts are . . . implacably anti-American —Perry Miller⟩ ⟨in his ~ of hearts I do not think he ever really surrenders faith —Edward Wagenknecht⟩ **4 :** PERSON ⟨two young ~*s* had been freed . . . from the burden of guilt and suspicion —Agnes S. Turnbull⟩ — usu. used with a qualifier ⟨poor ~! who would relieve her wants now⟩ ⟨farewell, dear ~⟩ **5 :** the central or decisive part of something **:** CENTER: as **a :** an inner central area or region ⟨a system of waterways extending into the ~ of No. America⟩ **b :** an essential part **:** the part that determines the real nature of something or gives significance to the other parts **:** the determining aspect ⟨the discernment and understanding with which he penetrates to the ~ and essence of the problem —B.N.Cardozo⟩ ⟨those words of Jesus show us the ~ of Easter's meaning —W.F.Hambly⟩ **c :** the center of activity **:** a vital part on which continuing activity or existence depends ⟨Rome was the ~ and pulse of the empire —John Buchan⟩ **d :** HEARTWOOD **e :** CORE 1h **f :** the younger central compact part of a leafy rosette (as a stalk of celery or a head of lettuce) **6** *chiefly Brit* **:** condition for bearing crops **:** FERTILITY — used chiefly in the phrase *in good heart* ⟨the land has never been in better ~ —S.P.B.Mais⟩ **syn** see CENTER — **to heart** *adv* **:** under serious consideration **:** with deep concern **:** with hurt feelings ⟨took it *to heart*⟩ ⟨Sterne . . . laid the criticism *to heart* —Virginia Woolf⟩ — **to one's heart's content :** to the point of complete satisfaction or satiety **:** to the limits of one's will or pleasure ⟨eat *to your heart's content*⟩ ⟨printers imported any foreign books they thought would be popular . . . and reprinted them *to their heart's content* —Margaret Nicholson⟩

[2]**heart** \"\ *vb* -ED/-ING/-S [ME *herten*, fr. OE *hiertan*, fr. *heorte*, n.] *vt* **1** *archaic* **:** to give heart to **:** HEARTEN, ENCOURAGE, INSPIRIT **2 :** to fix or seat in the heart **3 :** to fill in (as a wall) with rubble or similar material ~ *vi* **:** to form a compact center or heart; *specif* **:** to develop a head (as of lettuce and cabbage)

[3]**heart** \"\ *dial var of* HEARTH

heartache \'=,=\ *n* **:** anguish of mind **syn** see SORROW

heart and soul *adv* **:** without reservations **:** COMPLETELY, WHOLLY ⟨count on me to help *heart and soul*⟩

heart attack *n* **:** an acute episode of heart disease (as myocardial infarction) due to insufficient blood supply to the heart muscle itself esp. when caused by a coronary thrombosis or a coronary occlusion

heart balm *n* **:** compensation for breach of promise to marry or alienation of affections ⟨two days after the marriage . . . was sued by another woman for two hundred thousand dollars' *heart balm* —Carey McWilliams⟩

heartbeat \'=,=\ *n* **1 :** one complete pulsation of the heart **2 :** the vital center or driving impulse ⟨the dining car is the real ~ and life of a train —Richard Barnitz⟩ ⟨the school is the ~ of our organic society —Agnes Meyer⟩

heart block *n* **:** incoordination of the heartbeat in which the auricles and ventricles beat independently due to defective transmission through the atrioventricular bundle and which is marked by decreased cardiac output often with cerebral ischemia

heart bond *n* **:** a masonry bond in which no header stone stretches across the wall but two headers meet in the middle and their joint is covered by another stone

[1]**heartbreak** \'=,=\ *n* **1 :** crushing grief ⟨the sorrow and the ~ which . . . abide in the homes of so many of our neighbors —H.S.Truman⟩ **2 :** something that causes heartbreak ⟨proved a . . . ~ to the authors of his being —C.G.Glover⟩

[2]**heartbreak** \"\ *vt* [back-formation fr. *heartbroken*] **:** to break the heart of

heartbreaker \'=,==\ *n* **:** something that causes heartbreak ⟨arming merchant ships . . . has been another ~ —*Fortune*⟩

heartbreaking \'=,==\ *adj* **:** causing overpowering or intense sorrow, anguish, or distress ⟨made progress only with the most ~ efforts —Farley Mowat⟩ ⟨it is ~ to see new schools going up without proper . . . planning —Cecile Starr⟩ — **heart·break·ing·ly** *adv*

heartbroken \'=¦==\ *adj* [[1]*heart* + *broken*] **:** overcome by sorrow — **heart·bro·ken·ly** *adv* — **heart·bro·ken·ness** \'härt¦brōkən(n)əs\ *n* -ES

heartburn \'=,=\ *n* **1 :** a burning discomfort behind the lower part of the sternum usu. related to spasm of the lower end of the esophagus or of the cardia of the stomach — called also *cardialgia, pyrosis* **2 :** HEARTBURNING

heartburning \'=,==\ *n* **:** intense or rancorous jealousy or resentment ⟨his promotion to ministerial rank is bound to cause much ~ —J.A.Stevenson⟩ ⟨the seniority rule . . . prevents bitter personal rivalries, factional sniping, and ~ —S.D. Bailey⟩

heart cherry *n* **:** any of several cultivated sweet cherries with rather soft-fleshed heart-shaped fruits — compare BIGARREAU CHERRY, DUKE 5

heart cockle *n* **:** [2]COCKLE 1a; *esp* **:** a widely distributed burrowing cockle (*Isocardia cor*) with the umbones well separated giving the shell a heart-shaped appearance

heart disease *n* **:** an abnormal organic condition of the heart or of the heart and circulation

heart·ed \¦här|d·əd, ¦hȧ|, |təd\ *adj* [ME *herted*, fr. *hert* heart + *-ed* — more at HEART] **1 :** having a heart — often used in combination ⟨gave pleasure to lighter-*hearted* members of the staff —J.G.Cozzens⟩ **2 :** seated or laid up in the heart

heart·ed·ness *n* -ES **:** the condition of having a heart esp. of a specified kind — often used in combination ⟨hard*heartedness*⟩ ⟨cold*heartedness*⟩

heart·en \'härtᵊn, 'hȧt-\ *vb* **heartened; heartened; heartening** \-t(ᵊ)niŋ\ **heartens** [[1]*heart-* + *-en*] *vt* **1 :** to give heart to **:** inspire with fresh zeal, hope, or courage **:** rouse from indifference or discouragement ⟨people . . . whose presence either ~*ed* the spirit or kindled the mind —Jan Struther⟩ ⟨their supporters are enormously ~*ed* —Mollie Panter-Downes⟩ **2** *archaic* **:** to restore fertility or strength to (as land) ~ *vi* **:** to take courage **:** become imbued with fresh spirit and energy ⟨then the engine would ~ up and show off its paces —William Baucke⟩ **syn** see ENCOURAGE

heartening *adj* **:** tending or serving to hearten, inspire, or give fresh courage ⟨a ~ development⟩ — **heart·en·ing·ly** *adv*

heart failure *n* **1 :** a condition in which the heart is unable to pump blood at an adequate rate or in adequate volume — see CONGESTIVE HEART FAILURE, CORONARY FAILURE **2 :** cessation of the heartbeat **:** DEATH **3 :** a sudden feeling of faintness (as at a surprise or sudden shock)

heartfelt \'=¦=\ *adj* **:** profoundly felt **:** EARNEST ⟨~ sympathy⟩ ⟨~ thanks⟩ **syn** see SINCERE

heart-free \'=¦=\ *adj* **:** not committed or engaged in one's affections ⟨quite *heart-free* —George Meredith⟩

heart·ful \'härtfəl\ *adj* [ME *hertful*, fr. *hert* heart + *-ful* — more at HEART] **:** full of heartfelt emotion **:** HEARTY ⟨~ prayers⟩ — **heart·ful·ly** \-fəlē\ *adv*

hearth \'härth, 'hȧth *sometimes* 'harth, 'hōth\ *n* -S [ME *herth*, fr. OE *heorth;* akin to OHG *herd* hearth, ON *hyrr* fire, Goth *hauri* coal, Skt *kūḍayāti* he singes, and perh. to L *carbo* ember, charcoal, *cremare* to burn up] **1 a :** a brick, stone, or cement area of floor in front of a fireplace; *also* **:** a corresponding projection resembling a shelf on a stove **b :** the floor of a fireplace or of a brick oven on which a fire may be built **c** (1) **:** the lowest section of a blast furnace at and below the tuyeres where the molten metal and slag are collected (2) **:** the bottom of a refinery, reverberatory, or open-hearth furnace on which the ore or metal is exposed to the flame (3) **:** BLOOMERY (4) **:** the inside bottom of a cupola (5) **:** the fuel floor of a smith's forge (6) **:** the bottom of a heat-treating furnace that usu. supports the work **d :** the bed of a furnace on which pots rest in glass manufacturing **e :** a fire-hardened earth floor upon which primitive man built fires (as in an ancient rock shelter or campsite) **f :** a piece of wood against which a hardwood stick is rubbed or into which it is twirled to make fire by friction — compare FIRE DRILL **2 :** HOUSE, HOME, FIRESIDE ⟨not rest . . . until every family has a ~ of its own —James Griffiths⟩ **3 :** a nuclear area (as of high culture) **:** a vital or creative center **:** ECUMENE ⟨the small group of . . . nations that constitute the central ~ of occidental civilization —A.L. Kroeber⟩ ⟨the south and southwest of Mexico constitute one of the great culture ~*s* of the world —C.O.Sauer⟩

hearth·less \-thləs\ *adj* **:** not having a hearth

hearth money *n* **1 :** PETER'S PENCE **2 :** a 17th century English tax of two shillings on hearths in all houses paying the church and poor rates — called also *chimney money*

hearth-penny \'=,==\ *n* [ME *herthpeny*, fr. OE *heorthpenig;* fr. *heorth* hearth + *penig* penny — more at HEARTH, PENNY] **:** PETER PENNY

hearthrug \'=,=\ *n* **:** a rug for the front of the hearth

hearthside \'=,=\ *n* **:** FIRESIDE

hearthstone \'=,=\ *n* [ME *herthstone*, fr. *herth* hearth + *stone*] **1 a :** stone forming a hearth **b :** FIRESIDE, HOME **2 :** a soft stone or composition of powdered stone and pipe clay used to whiten or scour hearths and doorsteps

heartier *comparative of* HEARTY

heartiest *superlative of* HEARTY

heart·i·ly \'här|d·əlē, 'hȧ|, |tə-, -li\ *adv* [ME *hertily*, fr. *herty* hearty + *-ly*] **1 :** in a hearty manner **2 a :** with all sincerity or goodwill **:** without reservations **:** WHOLEHEARTEDLY ⟨~ in sympathy with the essence of the liberal faith —M.R.Cohen⟩ **b :** with zest or gusto **:** VIGOROUSLY ⟨threw himself ~ into his work⟩ ⟨ate and drank ~⟩ **3 :** COMPLETELY, THOROUGHLY, EXCEEDINGLY ⟨~ sick of this idle debate⟩

heart·i·ness \|d·ēnəs, |d·in-\ *n* -ES **1 :** cordiality or geniality of manner **:** CHEERINESS, FRIENDLINESS ⟨detested his back-slapping ~⟩ **2 :** ZEAL, ENTHUSIASM ⟨the music was sung with uninhibited ~ by the mountain folk —Herman Wouk⟩ ⟨enjoy themselves . . . with a ~ that makes the Londoner feel extremely envious —S.P.B.Mais⟩ **3 :** VIGOR, STRENGTH ⟨an air of rugged outdoor ~ —J.J.Godwin⟩

hearting *n* -S [fr. gerund of [2]*heart*] **1 :** CORE 11 **2 :** PUDDLE WALL **3 :** BACKING 1a

heart·land \'härt,land, 'hȧt- -,laa(ə)nd, -ˌlənd\ *n* **:** an area of decisive importance **:** a pivotal or nuclear area ⟨the entire ~ of the country, the Mississippi Basin —A.W.Baum⟩ ⟨the German industrial ~ in the Ruhr valley —Henry Wallace⟩ ⟨the temperate highlands which are the ~ of the republic —A.P.Whitaker⟩ ⟨the ~ of Eastern duck and goose shooting —*Newsweek*⟩; *specif* **:** a central land area (as northern Eurasia from the Elbe to the Amur) conceived by geopoliticians to be capable of self-sufficiency as an economic and military unit, invulnerable to sea power, and therefore having strategic advantages for mastery of the world

heartleaf \'=,=\ *n* **:** any of several wild gingers that have distinctly cordate leaves and are usu. included in the genus *Asarum* but are sometimes segregated in a separate genus

heart-leaved aster \'=,=-\ *n* **:** a common blue aster (*Aster cordifolius*) of eastern No. America

heart-leaved willow *also* **heart-leafed willow** \'=,=-\ *n* **:** a common broad-leaved American willow (*Salix cordata*) with cordate leaves

heart·less \'härtləs, 'hȧt-\ *adj* [ME *hertles*, fr. *hert* heart + *-les* -less] **1 :** devoid of heart **2 a** *archaic* **:** lacking courage or zeal **:** SPIRITLESS, DESPONDENT **b :** lacking feeling or affection **:** UNSYMPATHETIC, CRUEL ⟨it seems so ~ to leave her —G.B. Shaw⟩ ⟨a ~ mother, a false wife —W.M.Thackeray⟩ — **heart·less·ly** *adv* — **heart·less·ness** *n* -ES

heart line *n, usu cap H* **:** LINE OF HEART

heart liverleaf *or* **heart liverwort** *n* **:** a hepatica (*Hepatica triloba*)

heart-lung machine *n* **:** a mechanical pump that maintains circulation during heart surgery by shunting blood away from the heart, oxygenating it, and returning it to the body

heart murmur *n* **:** MURMUR 4

heartnut \'=,=\ *n* **:** JAPANESE WALNUT

heart of palm : the edible young terminal bud of various palms (as a cabbage palmetto) usu. served raw and dressed as a salad

heartpea \'=,=\ *n* [so called fr. the shape of the seed] **:** BALLOON VINE

heart pine *n* **:** LONGLEAF PINE

heart rate *n* **:** a measure of cardiac activity usu. expressed as number of beats per minute

heartrending \'=,==\ *adj* **:** causing intense grief, anguish, or pain ⟨gives a ~ description of his own days under a private tutor — G.G.Coveton⟩ ⟨his untimely death was . . . ~ —*Nation*⟩

heart·rend·ing·ly *adv* **:** in a heartrending manner

heartrot \'=,=\ *n* **:** any of several rots involving the central part of a plant or plant organ: as **a :** disintegration of the heartwood of a tree (as by fungi of the genus *Fomes*) **b :** a disease of beets and rutabagas caused by a fungus (*Mycosphaerella tabifica*) that brings about decay of the heart and blighting of the leaves **c :** a rot of sugar beets caused by boron deficiency

hearts *pl of* HEART, *pres 3d sing of* HEART

heart sac *n* **:** PERICARDIUM

hearts-and-flowers *n pl but sing or pl in constr* **:** show of sentiment or sentimentality **:** cloying expressions of endearment ⟨cut out the *hearts-and-flowers* —Maritta Wolff⟩ ⟨I can't stand *hearts-and-flowers* stuff —Mary Miller⟩

heart-scalded \'härt¦skȯdəd\ *adj, dial Brit* **:** tormented by sorrow or remorse **:** TROUBLED

heart-searching \'=,==\ *n* **:** introspective analysis or self-examination ⟨the decision was reached only after prolonged *heart-searching* —*Times Lit. Supp.*⟩ ⟨of course these choices will not have been made without *heart-searchings* and reservations —A.J.Toynbee⟩

hearts·ease \'härt,sēz, 'hȧt-\ *n* [ME *herts ese*, fr. *herts* (gen. of *hert* heart) + *ese* ease] **1 :** peace of mind **:** TRANQUILLITY ⟨religion failed to bring him ~ —R.H.Bainton⟩ **2 a :** any of various violas: as (1) **:** WILD PANSY (2) **:** a common Old World viola (*Viola arvensis*) with creamy often violet-tinged flowers (3) **:** a violet (*V. ocellata*) of the Pacific coast of No. America with white petals tinged or marked with yellow and deep violet **b :** any of several smartweeds **3 :** a strong violet that is redder and paler than pansy or clematis and redder and lighter than royal purple (sense 2)

heartseed \'=,=\ *n* [so called fr. the heart-shaped white spot on the black seed] **:** a plant of the genus *Cardiospermum; esp* **:** BALLOON VINE

heart shake *n* **:** a defect in timber consisting of shrinkage and separation of tissues across the annual rings usu. along the rays — compare RING SHAKE

heart shell *n* **1 :** any of numerous bivalve mollusks esp. of the families Cardiidae and Carditidae with shells that are heart-shaped in outline when viewed from the end **2 :** the shell of a heart-shell mollusk

heartsick \'=,=\ *adj* **:** very despondent **:** DEPRESSED ⟨was too ~ to rise and fight —W.A.White⟩ **:** reflecting or marked by a feeling of sickness ⟨longed with a ~ yearning for the first few days to be over —W.M.Thackeray⟩

heartsickening *adj* **:** causing depression or despondency

heartsickness \'=,==\ *n* **:** the quality or state of being heartsick ⟨died of . . . ~ after moving here and waiting for years for the man who never came —*Nat'l Geographic*⟩ ⟨the wild ~ of the desert —Lawrence Durrell⟩

heart snakeroot *n* [so called fr. the shape of the leaf] **:** WILD GINGER 2a

heart·some \'hertsəm\ *adj* [[1]*heart* + *-some*] *chiefly Scot* **:** animating and enlivening **:** giving cheer ⟨a ~ thing, the smell of frying ham on a frosty morning —G.D.Brown⟩ — **heart·some·ly** *adv*

heartsore \'=,=\ *adj* **:** HEARTSICK ⟨a ~ lover⟩

heartstring \'=,=\ *n* [ME *hertstring*, fr. *hert* heart + *string*] **1** *obs* **:** a nerve or tendon supposed to support or sustain the heart **2 :** the deepest emotions or affections — usu. used in pl. ⟨tore at the ~*s* of memory —William Beebe⟩ ⟨could touch the ~*s* of the audience —E.H.Collis⟩

heart-struck \'=¦=\ *adj* **1 :** struck to the heart **2** *archaic* **:** driven to the heart **:** infixed in the mind

heartthrob \'=,=\ *n* **1 :** the throb of a heart **2 a :** sentimental emotion **:** PASSION ⟨diary of ~*s* and rebuffs —*New Republic*⟩ **b :** SWEETHEART ⟨a girl on the . . . verge of giving her ~ the raspberry —P.G.Wodehouse⟩

heart tie *n* **:** a railroad crosstie with sapwood one fourth or less the width of the tie at the top measured at a point 20 inches to 40 inches from the middle of the tie

heart-to-heart \'==¦=\ *adj* **:** SINCERE, FRANK ⟨a *heart-to-heart* talk⟩

heart trefoil *n* [so called fr. the shape of the leaves] **:** SPOTTED MEDIC

heart urchin *n* **:** a heart-shaped sea urchin

heart wall *n* **:** CORE 11

heartwarming \'=,==\ *adj* **:** inspiring a glow of sympathetic feeling **:** pleasantly moving or stirring **:** CHEERING ⟨her story of their experiences is entertaining and ~ —*Huntting's Monthly List*⟩ ⟨most ~ literary event of the year —*New Internat'l Yr. Bk.*⟩

heartwater \'=,==\ *n* [so called fr. the accumulation of fluid in the pericardium] **:** a serious febrile disease of sheep, goats, and cattle in southern Africa caused by a rickettsial microorganism (*Cowdria ruminantium*) transmitted by a tick (*Amblyomma hebraeum*)

heartweed \'=,=\ *n* **:** LADY'S THUMB

heart-whole \'=¦=\ *adj* **1 :** not broken or depressed in spirit **:** UNDISMAYED ⟨so many clowns have been small . . . pathetic; here is one large and *heart-whole* —G.W.Stonier⟩ **2 :** having the affections free **:** not in love **3 :** free from deceit or hypocrisy **:** SINCERE, GENUINE ⟨a *heart-whole* friendship —George Meredith⟩

heartwise \'härt,wīz\ *adv* [[1]*heart* + *-wise*] **:** in the shape or manner of a heart ⟨her face . . . tapered ~ —T.B.Costain⟩

heartwood \'=,=\ *n* **:** the older harder nonliving central portion of wood usu. being darker in color, denser, less permeable, and more durable than the surrounding sapwood but in some woods (as white spruce) lacking distinctive color and then being difficult to distinguish — called also *duramen*

heartworm \'=,=\ *n* **1 :** a filarial worm (*Dirofilaria immitis*) that is esp. common in warm regions, lives as an adult in the right heart of dogs and some other carnivores, and discharges active larvae into the circulating blood whence they may be picked up by mosquitoes and transmitted to other hosts **2 :** infestation with or disease caused by the heartworm resulting typically in gasping, coughing, and nervous disorder and when severe commonly leading to death

[1]**hearty** \'här|d·ē, 'hȧ|, |tē, -i\ *adj* -ER/-EST [ME *herty*, fr. *hert* heart + *-y*] **1 a :** giving unqualified support **:** unreservedly loyal **:** THOROUGHGOING, ENTHUSIASTIC ⟨a ~ Federalist —F.J. Klingberg⟩ ⟨a ~ assumer of its full share of . . . responsibilities —F.S.C.Northrop⟩ ⟨my ~ concurrence in everything you've done —T.B.Costain⟩ **b** (1) **:** exuberantly or unreservedly cordial or genial **:** not reserved or ceremonious in manner **:** JOVIAL ⟨had a bluff and ~ bearing, but he was a rogue —Ross Annett⟩ ⟨being a shade too ~ about it —Angus Mowat⟩ ⟨a wonderful ~ manner with a boy —G.D.Brown⟩ (2) **:** giving exuberant or unrestrained expression to one's feelings ⟨a ~ burst of laughter greeted his arrival⟩ ⟨a string of ~ curses⟩ (3) **:** APPROVING ⟨no one but a Chancery lawyer had a ~ word for the Chancery —F.W.Maitland⟩ ⟨some colleagues are distinctly less ~ about the General —Hal Lehrman⟩ **2 a :** exhibiting vigorous good health ⟨the mate was as ~ as a young lion —Herman Melville⟩ ⟨is my friend ~, now I am thin and pine —A.E.Housman⟩ **b** (1) **:** having a good appetite **:** consuming abundantly or with gusto ⟨a ~ eater⟩ ⟨a ~ drinker⟩ (2) **:** ABUNDANT, AMPLE ⟨ate a ~ meal⟩ ⟨took a ~ swig⟩ **c** (1) **:** richly nutritious ⟨almost a meal in itself, with 15 tender vegetables in ~ beef stock —*Better Homes & Gardens*⟩ (2) **:** FLAVORFUL, FULL-BODIED ⟨has a ~ flavor that is much livelier than our refined . . . variety —Silas Spitzer⟩ ⟨a ~ wine with a full bouquet⟩ **3 :** vigorous or violent in manner or degree **:** VEHEMENT ⟨the breeze . . . was *heartier* . . . than before —Llewellyn Howland⟩ ⟨hooked a root and gave a ~ pull —C.S.Forester⟩ ⟨then came the rain in a ~ flood —John Muir †1914⟩ ⟨the wind had combed up some quite ~ waves —R.A.W.Hughes⟩ ⟨without any provocation at all give him a ~ kick —H.A.Chippendale⟩ **4** *chiefly Brit* **:** capable of bearing crops **:** FERTILE ⟨thistles so growing . . . signifieth the land to be ~ —Thomas Tusser⟩ **syn** see SINCERE

[2]**hearty** \"\ *n* -ES **1 a :** a bold brave fellow **:** COMRADE — used esp. in addressing sailors ⟨heave-ho, my *hearties*⟩ **b :** SAILOR ⟨the albatross mocked by the *hearties* —Stephen Spender⟩ **2** *chiefly Brit* **:** an individual of exuberant outgoing disposition or of athletic nonaesthetic tastes ⟨a Matisse reproduction could cause one's rooms to be wrecked . . . by rugger *hearties* —Jocelyn Brooke⟩

heart yarn *n* **:** yarn in the center of a rope

[1]**heat** \'hēt, *usu* -ēd·+V\ *vb* **heated** \'hēd·əd, -ētəd\ *also dial* **het** \'het, *usu* -ed·+V\ **heated** *also dial* **het; heating; heats** [ME *heten*, fr. OE *hǣtan;* akin to OHG *heizen* to heat, MD *heten*, ON *heita;* causative-denominatives fr. the root of E *hot*] *vi* **1 a :** to become warm or hot **:** rise in temperature ⟨water ~*ing* in a large kettle⟩ ⟨the room slowly ~*ed*⟩ **b :** to become hot and spoil due to excessive or abnormal respiratory or fermentative activity ⟨grain containing excessive moisture may ~ seriously in the bin⟩ **2 :** to become excited, moved, or inflamed in mind or spirit ⟨cannot see injustice without ~*ing*⟩ ~ *vt* **1 :** to make warm or hot **:** raise the temperature of ⟨~ the oven to 350 degrees⟩ ⟨water ~*ed* by the sun⟩ **2 :** to arouse the emotion or spirit of **:** excite, move, or inflame usu. intensely or to a course of action ⟨his arrogance ~*s* me beyond enduring⟩ ⟨these stirring words ~*ed* us all⟩ **3 :** to make (as the human body) feverish or excessively hot ⟨wine ~*s* the blood⟩ ⟨he was ~*ed* by the long dry climb⟩ **4** *obs* **:** to run over (ground) **:** cover (ground) in or as if in a race

[2]**heat** \"\ *n* -S [ME *hete*, fr. OE *hǣte*, *hǣtu;* akin to OFris *hēte* heat, OHG *heizi;* derivatives fr. the root of E *hot*] **1 a :** the state of a body or of matter that is perceived as opposed to cold and is characterized by elevation of temperature **:** a condition of being hot **:** WARMTH, HOTNESS ⟨the iron lost its ~ in contact with the cold ground⟩; *usu* **:** a marked or notable degree of this state **:** high temperature ⟨the ~ was intense⟩ ⟨you'll need a good ~ to burn that damp rubbish⟩ ⟨midsummer ~⟩ ⟨a ~ of 500 degrees⟩ **b** (1) **:** a feverish state of the body **:** pathological excessive bodily temperature (as from inflammation) ⟨knew the throbbing ~ of an abscess⟩ ⟨sponged him with alcohol to relieve the ~ of the fever⟩ (2) **:** a warm flushed condition of the body (as after exercise) **:** a sensation produced by or like that produced by contact with or approach to heated matter ⟨felt the ~ rise in her face as she returned his look⟩ **c :** a hot place or situation (as a fire) ⟨the legendary salamander dallying at the heart of the ~⟩ ⟨out in the ~ all afternoon long⟩ ⟨dormant flies coming out into the ~⟩ **d** (1) **:** a period of heat or of exposure to heat ⟨requires a ~ of several hours to get out all the moisture⟩ ⟨had an unbroken ~ since the first of June⟩ (2) **:** a single complete operation of heating (as at a forge or in a furnace); *also* **:** the quantity of material so heated **e** (1) **:** a form of energy the addition of which causes substances to rise in temperature, fuse, evaporate, expand, or undergo any of various other related changes, which flows to a body by contact with or radiation from bodies at higher temperatures, and which can be produced in a body (as by compression) (2) **:** the energy associated with the random motions of the molecules, atoms, or smaller structural units of which matter is composed **f :** an indication of temperature attained as manifested by the condition, appearance, or color of a body ⟨when the rod is at the proper welding ~⟩ — compare RED HEAT **g :** one of a series of discrete rates or intensities of heating ⟨an electric iron may have three ~*s*⟩ **2 a :** intensity of feeling or reaction (as in fury, vehemence, or agitation of mind) ⟨answered with considerable ~⟩ ⟨such a ~ of eloquence flowed forth⟩ **b :** the height or stress of an action or condition ⟨in the ~ of battle⟩ ⟨during the first ~ of the epidemic⟩ **c** (1) **:** sexual excitement esp. in a female mammal **:** ESTRUS **:** a state in which a female will accept service by a male — usu. used with *in* or *into* or, esp. Brit., with *on* ⟨ewes come on ~ soon after flushing⟩ ⟨like a bitch in ~⟩ (2) **:** the time or duration of heat **:** an episode of heat ⟨a mare is most likely to settle during the foal ~ that occurs two or three weeks after parturition⟩ **3 :** one of the fundamental qualities of bodies, elements, or humors recognized in medieval physiology **4 :** pungency of flavor ⟨cherry peppers have greater ~ than most⟩ ⟨the tangy ~ of crystallized ginger⟩ **5 :** a vigorous or violent unintermitted action **:** a single continuous effort ⟨set down the outline of his paper at a single ~⟩: as **a** (1) **:** a single course in a race or other contest that consists of two or more courses for all contestants ⟨won two ~*s* out of three⟩ (2) **:** one of several preliminary races held to eliminate less competent contenders from the final race when contestants are too numerous to compete at once ⟨swam in the second ~ and won, but lost out in the final race⟩ **b :** a field trial event in which two dogs compete directly with each other and usu.

by comparison with other braces competing in the field trial **c** (1) *slang* **:** the intensification of law-enforcement activity or investigational pressure usu. with special concern for a particular kind of crime or criminal ⟨the bookies are out of business till the ~ is off⟩ (2) **:** pressure or coercion intended to influence a course of action or events ⟨taxpayers got relief by turning the ~ on their congressmen⟩ (3) **:** strain, tension, or difficulty resulting from the pressure of events ⟨weaken when the ~ is on⟩ **6 a :** a charge of metal made in a Bessemer converter or the steel scrap, pig, or molten iron, limestone, and fluxes in the open-hearth or electric furnace **b :** the resulting molten steel **c :** the ingots charged into the soaking pits or the blooms charged into the reheating furnace

heat·able \ˈhēd·əbəl, -ētəb-\ *adj* **:** capable of being heated **:** suitable for heating ⟨a compact ~ apartment⟩

heat balance *n* **:** the distribution of the heat energy supplied to a thermomechanical system (as a steam power plant) among the various drains upon it including both useful output and losses; *also* **:** an evaluation or record of such distribution

heat barrier *n* **:** THERMAL BARRIER

heat-body \ˈ=,==\ *vt* **:** to increase the viscosity of (an oil) by heating — compare BODIED OIL

heat budget *n* **:** the amount of heat required to raise the waters of a lake to their maximum summer temperature calculated from their minimum winter temperature of 0° C or 4° C and usu. expressed as gram calories of heat per square centimeter of lake surface

heat canker *n* **:** a canker of plant stems caused by high temperatures esp. of the surface soil ⟨flax is subject to *heat canker*⟩

heat capacity *n* **:** the quantity of heat required to raise the temperature of a body one degree — called also *thermal capacity*

heat center *n* **:** any of various areas in the central nervous system concerned with the regulation of the body temperature

heat content *n* **:** ENTHALPY

heat cramps *n pl* **:** a condition marked by the sudden development of cramps in skeletal muscles resulting from prolonged work in high temperatures accompanied by profuse perspiration with loss of sodium chloride from the body

heat death *n* **:** an ultimate state of thermal equilibrium implying conditions of maximum entropy and zero available energy that according to the laws of thermodynamics the material universe is apparently approaching

heat devil *n* **:** a shimmering appearance in the air above a heated surface

heated *adj* **1 :** made or become hot ⟨wiped his ~ face with a large bandanna⟩ **2 :** marked by emotional heat ⟨a ~ session of the conclave⟩ **:** IRATE, ANGRY ⟨an exchange of ~ words⟩

heat·ed·ly *adv* **:** in a heated manner **:** with heat ⟨denied the charges ~⟩

heated term *n* **:** the season of hot weather

heat engine *n* **:** a mechanism (as an external-combustion engine or an internal-combustion engine) for converting heat energy into mechanical energy

heat equator *n* **:** THERMAL EQUATOR

heat·er \ˈhēd·ə(r), -ētə-\ *n* -s [ME *heter*, fr. *heten* to heat + *-er* — more at HEAT] **1 :** something that heats **:** a contrivance that imparts heat or holds something to be heated: as **a :** a stove, furnace, radiator, or other device for giving off heat **b :** an iron core for heating box irons **c :** a wire or filament in an electron tube that heats the cathode indirectly **2 a :** one whose work is to heat something — often used in combination ⟨rivet ~⟩ ⟨tire ~⟩ **b :** one that heats metal billets to make them workable **c :** one that tends the burners that heat a petroleum-products still **3** *slang* **:** PISTOL

heater car *n* **:** a freight car with heating apparatus and insulation for transporting perishables in cold or freezing weather

heater piece *n* [*heater* (core for a box iron); fr. the shape] *NewEng* **:** a triangular plot of land

heater-shaped \ˈ=,=\ *also* **heater** *adj* [*heater* (core for a box iron)] **:** triangular or ogival in outline — used chiefly of a medieval shield

heat exchanger *n* **:** a device (as an automobile radiator, a regenerator, or an intercooler) for transferring heat from one fluid to another without allowing them to mix

heat exhaustion *n* **:** a condition characterized by faintness or fainting, palpitation, nausea, vomiting, headache, and profuse sweating and resulting from physical exertion in a hot environment — called also *heat prostration;* compare HEATSTROKE

heat·ful \ˈhētfəl\ *adj* **:** full of or producing heat; *esp* **:** capable of releasing abundant heat in combustion

heath \ˈhēth, *in Maine & adjacent Canada* ˈhath\ *n* -s [ME *heth, heeth*, fr. OE *hǣth*; akin to OHG *heida* heather, MHG *heide* heath (field), heather, ON *heithr* field, plateau, Goth *haithi* field, OW *coit* forest] **1 a** *obs* **:** any of various low-growing shrubby plants of open wastelands **b :** a plant of the family Ericaceae esp. of the genera *Erica* and *Calluna* typically growing on open barren rather acid and frequently ill-drained soil **c :** any of various heathlike plants: as (1) **:** POVERTY GRASS (2) **:** a tamarisk (*Tamarix gallica*) that is native to Western Europe but established as an escape in parts of No. America (3) **:** CROWBERRY 1a (4) **:** a desert plant that was probably the savin juniper — referring to Jer 17:6 (AV) (5) **:** AUSTRALIAN HEATH **2 a :** a tract of wasteland **b :** an extensive area of rather level open uncultivated land that usu. has poor coarse soil, inferior drainage, and a surface rich in peat or peaty humus and that characteristically has plants of the family Ericaceae as the dominant floral element **c :** a plant community typically occurring on heath in cool climates and being characterized by paucity or absence of trees and dominance of plants of the family Ericaceae — **one's native heath :** the region where one was born or brought up

heath aster *n* **:** either of two common much-branched pubescent perennial No. American asters (*Aster ericoides* and *A. arenosus*) with heathlike foliage and small white crowded flower heads

heat haze *n* **:** air rising above a hot surface (as of sand or rock) with a shimmering effect that tends to obscure details of the landscape

heath bell *n* **:** BELL HEATHER

heathbird \ˈ=,=\ *n* **:** BLACK GROUSE

heath-clad \ˈ=,=\ *adj* **:** covered with heath ⟨a *heath-clad* slope⟩

heath cock *n* **:** the male black grouse **:** BLACKCOCK

heath cypress *n* **:** any of various mosses; *esp* **:** a ground fir (*Lycopodium alpinum*) that resembles a miniature cypress tree

¹hea·then \ˈhēthən\ *adj* [ME *hethen*, fr. OE *hǣthen*, adj. & n.; akin to OHG *heidan*, adj., heathen, *heidano*, n., ON *heithinn*, adj., heathen, Goth *haithno* heathen woman, prob. derivatives fr. the root of E *heath* (land)] **1 :** of or relating to the heathen, their religions, or their customs **:** PAGAN, UNENLIGHTENED **2 :** STRANGE, UNFAMILIAR, FOREIGN

²heathen \"\ *n, pl* **heathens** *or* **heathen** [ME *hethen*, fr. OE *hǣthen*] **1 a :** an unconverted member of a people or nation that does not acknowledge the God of the Bible **:** PAGAN ⟨I shall give thee the ~ for thine inheritance —Ps 2:8 (AV)⟩ **b** *biblical* **:** IDOLATER, GENTILE **2 a :** a person whose culture or enlightenment is of an inferior grade; *esp* **:** an irreligious person **b :** a person felt to resemble a heathen (as in nonconformity or ignorance) ⟨a grand old ~ who made his own place in life⟩

hea·then·dom \-dəm\ *n* -s **1 :** the part of the world where heathenism prevails; *collectively* **:** HEATHEN **2 :** HEATHENISM

hea·then·esse \ˌhēthəˈnes\ *n* -s [ME *hethenesse*, fr. OE *hǣthennes*, fr. *hǣthen* heathen + *-nes*, -ness] **:** HEATHENDOM

hea·then·ish \ˈ==nish\ *adj* **1 :** of or relating to the heathen **:** resembling or thought to be characteristic of heathens ⟨worse than ~ crimes — John Milton⟩ **2** *obs* **:** of heathen race or belief **:** HEATHEN **3 :** tending to be or somewhat heathen ⟨this ~ rhythm⟩ — **hea·then·ish·ly** *adv* — **hea·then·ish·ness** *n* -ES

hea·then·ism \-ˌnizəm\ *n* -s **:** the religious system or rites of heathens **:** IDOLATRY, PAGANISM; *also* **:** manners or morals like those of the heathen

hea·then·ize \-ˌnīz\ *vb* -ED/-ING/-S *vt* **:** to make heathen or heathenish ~ *vi* **:** to become heathen or heathenish

hea·then·ly *adj* [ME *hethenly*, fr. *hethen* heathen + *-ly*] **:** in a heathen manner **:** HEATHENISHLY

hea·then·ness \-ən(n)əs\ *n* -ES **:** the state or quality of being heathen

hea·then·ry \-ənrē, -ri\ *n* -ES **1 :** the state, quality, or character of the heathen **:** HEATHENISM **2 :** heathen nations or people **:** HEATHENDOM

¹heath·er \ˈhethə(r)\ *n* -s [ME (northern dial.) *hather, hadder*, prob. modif. of *heth, heeth* heath, heather — more at HEATH] **1 a :** HEATH 1b; *esp* **:** a common erect to almost prostrate evergreen heath (*Calluna vulgaris*) of northern and alpine regions that has small crowded sessile leaves and racemes of tiny usu. purplish pink flowers **b :** BEACH HEATHER **c :** CROWBERRY 1a **2 a** *also* **heather purple :** a grayish reddish purple that is bluer, stronger, and slightly lighter than campanula violet and bluer, lighter, and stronger than livid purple **b :** a grayish to moderate purplish red that is redder and darker than daphne red

²heather \"\ *adj* **1 :** of, relating to, prepared from, or like heather **2 :** having flecks or a mingling of various colors — used chiefly of woolen yarns and fabrics ⟨a soft ~ tweed⟩ **3 :** of the color heather

heather ale *n* **:** a Scottish traditional beverage brewed from an extract of heather blossoms with honey, spice, hops, and yeast

heather bell *n* **:** BELL HEATHER

heather-bleat \ˈ==,=\ *also* **heatherbleater** \ˈ==,==\ *or* **heather-blutter** \-ˌbləd·ər\ *n* -s *chiefly Scot* **:** a common Old World snipe (*Capella gallinago*)

heather cat *n, Scot* **:** VAGABOND, ROVER ⟨here today and gone tomorrow — a fair *heather cat* —R.L.Stevenson⟩

heather cow *n, chiefly Scot* **:** a tuft or twig of heath

heath·ered \ˈhethə(r)d\ *adj* **:** full of or covered with heather ⟨~ slopes⟩

heather grass *n* **:** HEATH GRASS

heath·ery \ˈheth(ə)rē, -ri\ *adj* **1 :** abounding in or covered with heather ⟨~ hillsides⟩ **2 :** suggesting or resembling heather ⟨a delicate ~ fragrance⟩; *esp* **:** HEATHER 2

heath family *n* **:** ERICACEAE

heath-fowl *or* **heath-game** \ˈ=,=\ *n* **1** *Brit* **:** BLACK GROUSE **2** *Brit* **:** RED GROUSE

heath grass *n* **:** a chiefly European perennial grass (*Sieglingia decumbens*) that grows commonly on heaths and moors and is indigenous in Newfoundland and in southwestern Nova Scotia

heath grouse *n* **:** BLACK GROUSE

heath hen *n* **1 :** the female black grouse **:** GRAY HEN **2 :** a grouse that was formerly abundant in the northeastern U.S. but is now completely extinct and that is usu. considered an eastern variety (*Tympanuchus cupido cupido*) of the prairie chicken

heath·land \ˈ=ˌland, -lənd\ *n* **:** HEATH 2a, MOOR 1

heath·less \ˈ=ləs\ *adj* **:** free from heath ⟨a ~ moor⟩

heathlike \ˈ=,=\ *adj* **:** resembling a heath; *usu* **:** similar to a plant of the genera *Erica* or *Calluna* in habits of growth or in having fine crowded leaves suggesting needles

heath pea *n* **:** a European leguminous herb (*Lathyrus tuberosus*) bearing small tubers used for food and in Scotland to flavor whiskey

heath peat *n* **:** peat formed chiefly from roots and stems of plants of the genera *Erica* and *Calluna*

heath poult *n* **:** the young of the black grouse

heaths *pl of* HEATH

heathwort \ˈ=,=\ *n* **:** HEATH 1b

heath-wren \ˈ=,=\ *n* **:** either of two warblers (*Hylacola pyrrhopygia* and *H. cauta*) that are shy ground-nesting birds of open rangelands of southern Australia and noted as songsters and mimics — called also *ground wren*

heathy \ˈhēthē, ˈhāth-\ *adj* -ER/-EST [ME *hethy*, fr. *heth, heeth* heath + *-y* — more at HEATH] **:** of, relating to, or resembling heath **:** abounding with heath

heat hyperpyrexia *n* **:** HEATSTROKE

heating *pres part of* HEAT

heating element *n* **:** the part of an electric heating appliance in which the electrical energy is transformed into heat

heating furnace *n* **:** REHEATING FURNACE

heating load *n* **:** the quantity of heat per unit time that must be supplied to maintain the temperature in a building or portion of a building at a given level

heat·ing·ly *adv* **:** in a heating manner **:** so as to make hot

heating mantle *n* **:** an apparatus consisting of resistance wire stitched into glass cloth or asbestos cloth and tailored to surround a vessel to which it supplies heat

heating pad *n* **:** a flexible pad for applying heat (as to the body) consisting of electric heating elements embedded in insulating material

heating plant *n* **:** the whole system (as of boiler, pipes, and radiators or of furnace, ducts, and registers) used for heating an enclosed space (as a building or group of buildings)

heat lamp *n* **:** INFRARED LAMP

heat·less \ˈ=ləs\ *adj* **:** lacking heat; *esp* **:** having no artificial heat provided ⟨a ~ apartment⟩ ⟨observing ~ days to conserve fuel⟩

heat lightning *n* **:** vivid and extensive flashes of electric light without thunder that are seen near the horizon esp. at the close of a hot day and are ascribed to far-off lightning reflected by high clouds

heat of adsorption : the heat evolved when a given amount of a substance is adsorbed

heat of combustion : the heat of reaction resulting from the complete burning of a substance and expressed variously (as in calories per gram or per mole or esp. for fuels in British thermal units per pound or per cubic foot)

heat of condensation : heat evolved when a vapor changes to a liquid; *specif* **:** the quantity of heat that is evolved when unit mass of a vapor is changed at a specified temperature to a liquid and that equals the heat of vaporization

heat of decomposition : the heat of reaction resulting from the decomposition of a compound into its elements or into other neutral compounds; *esp* **:** the quantity involved in the decomposition of a mole

heat of dilution : the heat evolved per mole of solute when a solution is greatly diluted

heat of dissociation : the heat of reaction resulting from dissociation of molecules of a compound into smaller molecules, fragments, or atoms

heat of formation : the heat of reaction resulting from the formation of a compound by direct union of its elements, usu. expressed in calories per mole of the compound

heat of fusion : heat required to melt a solid; *specif* **:** the amount required to melt unit mass of a substance at standard pressure

heat of hydration : the heat evolved or absorbed when hydration occurs; *esp* **:** the amount involved when one mole is hydrated

heat of ionization : the heat required to ionize a substance; *esp* **:** the amount required to ionize one mole

heat of neutralization : the heat of reaction resulting from the neutralization of an acid or base; *esp* **:** the quantity produced when a gram equivalent of a base or acid is neutralized with a gram equivalent of an acid or base in dilute solution

heat of reaction : the heat evolved or absorbed during a chemical reaction taking place under conditions of constant temperature and of either constant volume or more often constant pressure; *esp* **:** the quantity involved when gram equivalents of the substances enter into the reaction

heat of solution : the heat evolved or absorbed when a substance dissolves; *specif* **:** the amount involved when one mole or sometimes one gram dissolves in a large excess of solvent

heat of sublimation : the heat absorbed when a solid sublimes; *specif* **:** the heat required to sublime unit mass at a specified temperature

heat of transition : the heat evolved or absorbed when a substance changes from one physical form to another

heat of vaporization : heat absorbed when a liquid vaporizes; *specif* **:** the quantity of heat required at a specified temperature to convert unit mass of liquid into vapor

heat of wetting : the heat evolved when an insoluble solid is wetted by a liquid (as water)

heat prostration *n* **:** HEAT EXHAUSTION

heat pump *n* **:** a device for transferring heat energy from a low-temperature locality to a high-temperature locality by mechanical means involving the compression and expansion of a fluid (as in mechanical refrigeration); *specif* **:** an apparatus for heating or cooling a building by transferring heat from or to a reservoir outside the building (as the ground, water, or air)

heat rash *n* **:** PRICKLY HEAT

heat ray *n* **:** a ray producing thermal effects; *specif* **:** an infrared ray

heat rigor *n* **:** rigor of living tissue caused by exposure to excessive but not immediately lethal temperatures

heat·ron·ic \(ˈ)hēˈtränik, -ēt-ˈr-\ *adj* [blend of ²*heat* and *electronic*] **:** utilizing dielectric heating

heats *pres 3d sing of* HEAT, *pl of* HEAT

heat-seal \ˈ=,=\ *vt* **:** to unite (two or more thermoplastic surfaces) by heat and pressure to make a seam, closure, or attachment

heat seal *n* **:** a seal made by or a method of union involving heat-sealing

heat-set \ˈ=,=\ *vt* **:** to fix (as a plastic or pleats in fabric) in a permanent form through the action of heat

heatstroke \ˈ=,=\ *n* **:** a condition characterized by cessation of sweating with inadequate elimination of body heat, extremely high temperature, rapid pulse, hot dry skin, flaccid muscles, delirium, collapse, and coma and resulting from prolonged exposure to high environmental temperature which causes a breakdown of the temperature-regulating mechanism of the body — compare HEAT EXHAUSTION

heat-treat \ˈ=,=\ *vt* **:** to treat (as metals) by heating and cooling in a way that will produce desired properties (as hardness or ductility) — compare ANNEAL, HARDEN, NORMALIZE, PATENT, SPHEROIDIZE, TEMPER; MALLEABLEIZE; GRAPHITIZE

heat-treater \ˈ=,==\ *n* **:** one that heat-treats metals

heat treatment *n* **:** a process or an instance of heat-treating

heat unit *n* **1 :** BRITISH THERMAL UNIT **2 :** CALORIE

heat up *vt* **:** to cause to heat ~ *vi* **:** to become hot **:** HEAT

heat wave *n* **1 :** a wave of thermal radiation **2 :** HOT WAVE

heaume \ˈhōm\ *n* -s [MF, fr. OF *helme* — more at HELMET] **:** a large helmet chiefly of the 13th century worn over a hood of mail or close-fitting steel cap and supported by the shoulders rather than the head

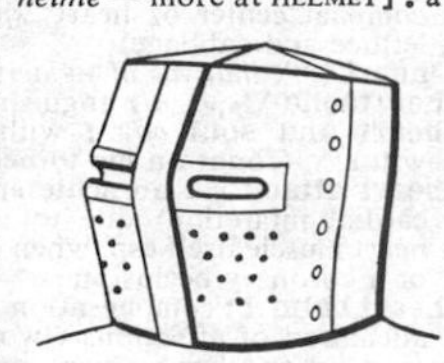

heaume

heaum·er \-mə(r)\ *n* -s **:** a maker of medieval helmets

heau·ta·rit \hōˈtärət, hyüˈt-\ *n* -s [Ar *ˈuṭārid*] *in alchemy* **:** MERCURY 1c

he·au·toph·a·ny \ˌhēˌōˈtäfənē\ *n* -ES [Gk *heautou* of oneself (fr. *he* oneself + *autos* self) + E *-phany*] **:** manifestation of self

¹heave \ˈhēv\ *vb* **heaved** \-vd\ *or* **hove** \ˈhōv\ *or dial* **hoved** \ˈhōvd\ **heaved** *or* **hove** *or archaic & dial* **ho·ven** \ˈhōvən\ **heaving; heaves** [ME *hebben, heven*, fr. OE *hebban*; akin to OHG *heffen, hevan* to lift, raise, ON *hefja* to lift, raise, Goth *hafjan* to carry, L *capere* to take, seize, Gk *kaptein* to gulp down, *kōpē* handle, Alb *kap* I grasp, Skt *kapatī* two handfuls; basic meaning: grasping] *vt* **1** *obs* **a :** to raise or exalt in state or feeling **b :** BAPTIZE; *also* **:** to stand as sponsor for **c :** to offer or consecrate (a portion of a sacrifice) by symbolically lifting up or separating for special holy use — used of the action of an ancient Israelite priest **2 :** to cause to move upward or onward by a lifting effort **:** LIFT, RAISE; *usu* **:** to lift with exertion ⟨the wave *heaved* the boat on land⟩ **3** *obs* **:** to take up and remove **:** carry off **:** take away **4 :** THROW, CAST, TOSS, HURL ⟨he *hove* the lead⟩ ⟨*heaving* down the hay⟩ ⟨just ~ your books on the bed⟩ **5 a :** to utter with obvious effort or with a deep breath that causes the chest to heave visibly ⟨pulled off her shoes and *heaved* a sigh of relief⟩ **b :** VOMIT ⟨got carsick and *heaved* his lunch⟩ **6 a :** to cause to swell or rise ⟨the wind *heaved* the sea into mountainous waves⟩ ⟨a spent horse gasping and *heaving* his chest⟩ **b** *dial Brit* **:** to cause bloat in (a ruminant) ⟨sheep are often *hoven* by a sudden change to lush pasture⟩ **c :** to displace (as a mineral vein or a rock stratum) esp. by a fault; *usu* **:** to displace laterally or horizontally **7 a :** to draw, pull, or to haul on (as a rope) ⟨~ in the cable⟩ ⟨~ a line⟩ **b :** to cause (as a ship or sail) to move or to come into some position by or as if by hauling on a rope either as a means of propulsion or as a means of arranging for a particular kind of action ⟨~ a ship ahead, aback, or in stays⟩ ~ *vi* **1 a :** to rise or become thrown or raised up usu. as a result of the action of some external force (as pressure, wind, heat, or frost) ⟨the pavement *heaved* and buckled in the heat⟩ **b** *archaic* **:** to rise upward **:** TOWER, MOUNT **c** *of plants or roots* **:** to rise or become lifted out of the ground usu. by alternate freezing and thawing **2 :** to make an effort to raise, throw, or move something **:** strain to do something difficult **:** LABOR, STRUGGLE **3 a :** to rise and fall rhythmically or with alternate motions (as of waves, a ship at sea, or the chest in heavy breathing) ⟨waves *heaving* on a storm-tossed sea⟩ **b :** to pant for breath ⟨lay *heaving* from the strain of his effort⟩ **4 a :** GAG, RETCH ⟨could ~ from sheer disgust⟩ ⟨his stomach *heaved* at sight of the mess⟩ **b :** VOMIT — sometimes considered vulgar **5 a :** to haul or pull (as on a line) or push (as at a capstan); *specif* **:** to move a line or chain by the application of force through the interposition of a mechanical device (as a capstan) — compare HAUL **b :** to cause a ship to move in a specified direction or manner **c** *of a ship* **:** to move in an indicated way or direction ⟨the schooner *hove* alongside⟩ **6** *chiefly dial Brit, of livestock* **:** to become bloated **syn** see LIFT — **heave in stays** *of a sailing ship* **:** TACK — **heave one's gorge :** NAUSEATE **:** become nauseated — **heave the lead :** to make a sounding from a ship by means of a manual sounding line — **heave the log :** to cast the log over the stern to determine the speed of a ship

²heave \"\ *n* -s **1 a :** an effort to raise something (as a weight or oneself) or to move something heavy or resistant ⟨each ~ on the rope loosened the stump a bit more⟩ **b :** an act or instance of throwing **:** HURL, CAST ⟨skimmed the notice and gave it a ~ toward the wastebasket⟩ **2 :** an upward motion **:** RISING; *esp* **:** a rhythmical rising (as of the chest wall in difficult breathing or of the waves) **3 a :** the horizontal displacement by the faulting of a rock measured in a plane at right angles to the fault strike **b :** FROST HEAVE **4 heaves** *pl but usu sing in constr* **:** chronic pulmonary emphysema of the horse usu. associated with asthma, improper diet, or severe overexertion and marked by loss of elasticity of the lungs and distention of the air vesicles resulting in difficult expiration with heaving of the flanks and a persistent cough — called also *broken wind*

heave-and-haul \ˌ=ˈ=\ *vi* **heave-and-hauled; heave-and-hauled; heave-and-hauling; heave-and-hauls :** to fish with a handline by repeatedly throwing a hook out and drawing it back again

heave down *vt* **:** to careen (a ship) usu. for repairs or cleaning ~ *vi* **:** to careen a ship

heave ho \ˈ=ˈ=\ *interj* [¹*heave* + *ho*] — used esp. by sailors when heaving on a rope

heave-ho \ˈ=ˈ=\ *n* -s [*heave ho*] **:** DISMISSAL, REJECTION — used with *the* and often with *old* ⟨the voters finally got sick of the old guard and gave the mayor the old *heave-ho* at the polls⟩

heave·less \ˈ=ləs\ *adj* **:** free from heaves or heaving **:** QUIET ⟨a glassy ~ sea⟩

¹heav·en \ˈhevən *also* -evᵊm *or* -ebᵊm\ *n* -s [ME *heven, hevene*, fr. OE *heofon*; akin to OHG *himil*, OS *heban* sky, heaven, ON *himinn*, Goth *himins* sky, heaven, OE *hama* covering — more at HAME] **1 a :** the expanse of space surrounding the earth; *esp* **:** the expanse that seems to be over the earth like a great arch or dome **:** FIRMAMENT, CELESTIAL SPHERE — usu. used in pl. **b :** the part of the atmosphere in which clouds and winds occur and birds fly and from which rain and snow fall **:** the part of the atmosphere that is relatively dense and close to solid earth and that forms part of the biosphere ⟨a flock of geese crossing the bright ~⟩ **c** *archaic* **:** CLIMATE **d :** one of a series of realms represented (as in ancient and medieval cosmographies) as extending up or out from the earth **2** *often cap* **:** the dwelling place of the Deity **:** a celestial abode of bliss **:** the place or state of the blessed dead — compare ELYSIUM, HAPPY HUNTING GROUNDS, NIRVANA, PARADISE **3** *usu cap* **:** the sovereign of heaven **:** GOD; *also* **:** heavenly beings **:** the assembly of the blessed ⟨her prayers, whom *Heaven* delights to hear —Shak.⟩ **4 a :** a place or condition or period of utmost happiness, comfort, or delight **:** perfect felicity or contentment ⟨our week at the lake was ~ after the city's heat⟩ ⟨the mountain ~ to which we hope to retire one day⟩ ⟨this shabby proletarian ~⟩ **b :** a sublime or exalted condition ⟨the ~s of the imagination⟩ **c :** a transcendent cosmos or domain; *specif* **:** a realm of subsistent or eternal forms or entities ⟨a Platonic ~ of ideas⟩ **5 heavens** *pl but sing in constr* **:** a canopy or covering used over the stage in some Elizabethan theaters **6 :** a divine state and condition of immortality in the doctrine of Christian Science in which sin is absent and all manifestations of Mind are harmoniously ordered under the divine Principle **7** *in Chinese religion* **a :** universal law **b :** NATURE **c :** cosmic ethical principle **d :** inexorable fate **e :** a supreme personal power — **heaven knows :** CERTAINLY, UNDOUBTEDLY — used as an intensive ⟨*heaven knows* we need advice⟩ ⟨our efforts, *heaven knows,* have accomplished little enough⟩ — **in heaven** *or* **under heaven** *adv* **:** among innumerable possibilities **:** EVER — used as an intensive ⟨where *in heaven* were you⟩ ⟨what *in heaven* happened⟩ ⟨what *under heaven* possessed you to do such a thing⟩ ⟨who *under heaven* would have done such a thing⟩ — **to heaven** *or* **to heavens** *or* **to high heaven** *or* **to high heavens** *adv* **:** to an unusual and often an exaggerated or excessive level or degree ⟨the muddy tide flat smelled *to high heavens*⟩ ⟨complained *to heaven* about the tax burden⟩

²heaven \"\ *vt* **heavened; heavened; heavening** \-v(ə)niŋ, -vᵊmiŋ,-bᵊmiŋ\ **heavens 1** *obs* **:** to place in happiness or bliss **:** BEATIFY **2 :** to make heavenly or utterly happy in character

heaven-born \ˈ≠≠ˌ≠\ *adj* **:** of heavenly birth or origin **:** CELESTIAL, DIVINE ⟨*heaven-born* compassion⟩

heaven-dust \ˈ≠≠ˌ≠\ *n, slang* **:** COCAINE

heav·en·less \ˈ≠≠lə̇s\ *adj* **:** having no heaven **:** having no part or place in the heaven of the Deity ⟨heathens worshiping their ~ gods⟩

heavenlike \ˈ≠≠ˌ≠\ *adv (or adj)* **:** HEAVENLY

heav·en·li·ness \-_lēnə̇s, -lin-\ *n* -ES **:** the quality or state of being heavenly

¹heav·en·ly \ˈhevənlē, -li *also* -evᵊml- *or* -ebᵊml-\ *adj, sometimes* -ER/-EST [ME *hevenly,* fr. OE *heofonlīc,* fr. *heofon* heaven + *-līc* -ly — more at HEAVEN] **1 :** of or relating to the spatial heavens surrounding the earth **2 :** of, relating to, or dwelling in the heaven of God or of a god **:** CELESTIAL ⟨~ spirits⟩ **3 a :** fit for or characteristic of the divine heaven **:** appropriate to heaven **:** SACRED, BLESSED, DIVINE ⟨the ~ music of an angel choir⟩ ⟨turn your thoughts to ~ matters⟩ **b :** eminently pleasing **:** DELIGHTFUL, ENCHANTING **:** remarkably pleasant ⟨a ~ day for a picnic⟩ ⟨had a ~ time⟩ ⟨what a ~ necklace⟩

²heavenly \"\ *adv* [ME *hevenly,* fr. OE *heofonlīce,* fr. *heofonlīc*] **1 :** in a manner or to a degree resembling that of heaven **:** to the utmost **:** EXCEEDINGLY ⟨a maid most ~ pure⟩ ⟨were ~ happy there⟩ **2 :** by the influence or agency of heaven ⟨our ~ guided soul shall climb —John Milton⟩

heavenly body *n* **:** CELESTIAL BODY

heavenly-minded \ˌ≠≠ˈ≠≠\ *adj* **:** DEVOUT, GODLY, PIOUS — **heavenly-mindedness** *n*

heavenly preceptor *n, usu cap H&P* [trans. of Chin (Pek) *tʻien¹ shih¹*] **:** a descendant of Chang Tao-ling chosen as the head of the Taoist organization — called also *celestial teacher;* used as a title

heaven-sent \ˈ≠≠ˌ≠\ *adj* **:** sent from heaven **:** PROVIDENTIAL **:** peculiarly apt or appropriate ⟨a *heaven-sent* opportunity⟩

heaven tree *n* **:** TREE OF HEAVEN

heav·en·ward \ˈ≠≠wə(r)d\ *adv (or adj)* [ME *hevenward,* fr. *heven* heaven + *-ward*] **:** toward or directed or tending toward heaven — **heav·en·ward·ly** *adv* — **heav·en·ward·ness** *n* -ES

heav·en·wards \-dz\ *adv* **:** HEAVENWARD

heave offering *n* **:** a separated portion of an ancient Israelite religious offering that was ceremonially raised and lowered in dedication to God and that afterward was reserved for the officiating priest's use

heav·er \ˈhēvə(r)\ *n* -S **:** one that heaves: as **a :** a laborer employed in handling freight or bulk goods ⟨a coal ~⟩ **b :** a bar used as a lever (as in twisting rope)

heaves *pres 3d sing of* HEAVE, *pl of* HEAVE

heave to \ˈ≠ˈtü\ *vt* **:** to bring (a ship) by the wind with after sheets in and headsails aback so as to make no headway but to lie motionless except for drift **~** *vi* **:** to heave a ship to ⟨decided to *heave to* until daylight before attempting to pass the reef⟩

heavied *past of* HEAVY

heavier-than-air \ˌ≠≠≠≠ˈ≠\ *adj, of an aircraft* **:** having greater weight than displacement

heavies *pl of* HEAVY, *pres 3d sing of* HEAVY

heav·i·ly \ˈhevə̇lē, -li\ *adv* [ME *hevily,* fr. OE *hefiglīce,* fr. *hefig* heavy + *-līce* -ly] **1 :** in a heavy manner **:** with great weight ⟨the weight bore ~ on the beams⟩ **2 :** as if burdened with a great weight **:** slowly and laboriously **:** DULLY ⟨read the lesson ~⟩ **3** *archaic* **:** SORROWFULLY, DEJECTEDLY, GRIEVOUSLY ⟨why looks your grace so ~ today? —Shak.⟩ **4 :** to a great degree **:** INJURIOUSLY, SEVERELY ⟨~ punished for his fault⟩ ⟨crops ~ damaged by frost⟩

heav·i·ness \-vēnə̇s, -vin-\ *n* -ES [ME *hevynesse,* fr. OE *hefignes,* fr. *hefig* heavy + *-nes* -ness] **:** the quality or state of being heavy ⟨a metal of surprising ~⟩ ⟨the produce markets exhibited a seasonal ~⟩

heaving *pres part of* HEAVE

heaving line *n* [fr. gerund of ¹*heave*] **:** a light line that has a weight on the free end and the other end attached to a heavier line (as a hawser) and that can be thrown across intervening space and used to draw the heavier line to a desired position (as for mooring a ship at a wharf)

heaving pile *n* **:** a heavy pile on a wharf to which are led tackles from the mastheads of a ship to be hove down

heav·i·side layer \ˈhevēˌsīd-\ *n, usu cap H* [after Oliver *Heaviside* †1925 Eng. physicist] **:** IONOSPHERE

¹heavy \ˈhevē, -vi\ *adj* -ER/-EST [ME *hevy,* fr. OE *hefig,* OS *hēbig;* akin to OHG *hebīc* heavy, ON *höfugr* heavy, OE *hebban* to lift, raise — more at HEAVE] **1 a :** having great weight **:** being such as may be lifted or moved only with effort **:** WEIGHTY, PONDEROUS ⟨a ~ load⟩ **b :** having a high specific gravity and great weight in proportion to bulk — opposed to *light* ⟨gold is one of the *heavier* metals⟩ **c** (1) *of an isotope* **:** having or being atoms of greater than normal mass ⟨carbon 13 and carbon 14 are both ~ carbons⟩ (2) *of a compound* **:** characterized by heavy isotopes ⟨~ ammonia⟩ ⟨~ ice⟩ **2 a** *obs* **:** HARSH, OPPRESSIVE **b :** hard to bear, endure, accomplish, or fulfill **:** BURDENSOME ⟨suffering under the ~ exactions of this tyrant⟩; *often* **:** GRIEVOUS, AFFLICTIVE ⟨a ~ sorrow⟩ **3 :** of weighty import **:** SERIOUS, GRAVE, CONSEQUENTIAL ⟨~ news⟩ ⟨words ~ with meaning⟩ **4 :** DEEP, PROFOUND, INTENSE ⟨a ~ silence⟩ ⟨~ late frosts destroyed the crop⟩ **5 a :** laden or borne down by something weighty or oppressive **:** ENCUMBERED, BURDENED ⟨returned with ~ spirit from the conference⟩ ⟨today's world is ~ with so-called celebrities —J.P.Jones⟩ **:** bowed down (as with care, grief, sorrow) ⟨a light wife doth make a ~ husband —Shak.⟩ **b :** PREGNANT, GRAVID; *esp* **:** approaching parturition — used chiefly in the phrase *heavy with young* **6 a :** slow or dull from or as if from loss of vitality or resiliency **:** SLUGGISH, INACTIVE ⟨a tired ~ step⟩ ⟨a ~ countenance⟩ **b :** lacking sparkle or vivacity **:** DRAB, STUPID, INERT ⟨a dull ~ style lacking liveliness and appeal⟩ ⟨a ~ writer⟩ **c :** lacking mirth or gaiety **:** DOLEFUL, LEADEN ⟨~ cheer⟩ ⟨made ~ work of the conversation⟩ **d :** characterized by declining prices ⟨the market was slow and ~⟩ ⟨government bonds have been ~ for some time⟩ **7 a :** overcome or dulled with weariness **:** DROWSY, SLEEPY ⟨eyes ~ from prolonged study⟩ **b :** dull and confused due to interruption of sleep **:** having a feeling of disorientation due to the relaxation of sleep ⟨the children were ~ with sleep⟩ **8 :** greater in quantity or quality than the average of its kind or class: as **a :** unusually or exceptionally large ⟨a ~ fall of snow⟩ ⟨~ crops⟩ ⟨~ traffic⟩ **b :** of great force or momentum ⟨a ~ storm⟩ ⟨the *heaviest* sea in the last three seasons⟩ **c :** threatening to rain or snow **:** OVERCAST, LOWERING ⟨a ~ sky⟩ ⟨~ clouds⟩ **d :** impeding motion **:** CLOGGY, CLAYEY ⟨a ~ road⟩ ⟨cold ~ soils⟩ **e :** coming as if from a depth **:** LOUD, DEEP ⟨the ~ roll of thunder⟩ ⟨a ~ bass voice⟩ **f :** MASSIVE, COARSE ⟨a ~ scar⟩ ⟨a ~ growth of timber⟩ **g :** tending to produce dullness or sleepiness **:** OPPRESSIVE ⟨the ~ odor of tuberoses⟩ **h :** STEEP, ACUTE ⟨a ~ grade⟩ **i :** LABORIOUS, DIFFICULT ⟨a ~ task⟩ ⟨likely to be ~ sledding for a while⟩ **j :** being something specified to an exceptional degree ⟨a ~ drinker⟩ ⟨~ losers⟩ ⟨industry is a ~ user of electric power⟩; *broadly* **:** operating or dealing in large quantities ⟨~ buying of steel⟩ ⟨a ~ buyer⟩ **k :** having a high alcohol content **:** rich in malt and hop constituents and usu. dark in color ⟨~ ale⟩ **l :** of large capacity or output ⟨a ~ pump⟩ **m :** having a high boiling point — used esp. of distillates (as of petroleum) ⟨~ hydrocarbons⟩ ⟨~ ends present in gasoline⟩ **n** (1) **:** set or printed in boldface (2) **:** made with too much pressure of the sheet against the printing surface ⟨a ~ impression⟩ (3) **:** 11 points thick — used of the metal of an unmounted printing surface (as a copper engraving, stereotype, or electrotype) **o** *of a domino* **:** having a comparatively large number of pips ⟨the 6-6 is *heavier* than the 6-3⟩ **9 a :** digested slowly or with difficulty usu. because of excessive richness or seasoning ⟨a ~ fruitcake⟩ **b :** not properly raised or leavened ⟨~ bread⟩ **:** lacking in lightness ⟨rich dark cakes often tend to be ~⟩ **10 a :** belonging to or concerned with a class above a certain usual weight ⟨~ woolens⟩ ⟨~ trunk lines⟩ ⟨~ breeds⟩ **b :** producing metal, mineral, oil, or other basic substances and products derived from them ⟨~ industries⟩; *specif* **:** producing products on which other industries function **11 a :** heavily armed with guns of large caliber ⟨~ dragoons⟩ **b :** having maximally concentrated firepower often from a battery of medium-caliber guns ⟨~ antiaircraft emplacements⟩ **c :** heavily armored **12 a :** having stress or conspicuous sonority ⟨~ rhythm⟩ — used esp. of syllables in accentual verse; contrasted with *light* **b :** being the strongest of three degrees of stress in speech ⟨the ~ stress on the first syllable of *basketball*⟩ **c** *of a consonant* **:** VOICED — used esp. in connection with shorthand symbolization **13 :** relating or assigned to theatrical parts or scenes of a grave or somber nature ⟨played ~ roles for years⟩

syn WEIGHTY, PONDEROUS, CUMBROUS, CUMBERSOME, HEFTY: HEAVY implies literally of greater weight than the average of its kind or class and figuratively more or less depressing, effort-taking, or unendurable to the mind or spirits, or depressed or dispirited ⟨a *heavy* bag⟩ ⟨a *heavy* child⟩ ⟨a *heavy* volume of literary criticism⟩ ⟨a *heavy* scent of lilacs⟩ ⟨a *heavy* heart⟩ WEIGHTY implies actually and not relatively heavy; figuratively it implies of serious import ⟨a boy carrying *weighty* packages⟩ ⟨a *weighty* series of international decisions⟩ ⟨*weighty* questions about our future domestic policy⟩ PONDEROUS implies literally a weighty massiveness, usu. difficult to maneuver, or figuratively something complicatedly labored, usu. suggesting a certain slow and dull deliberateness of mental effort ⟨a *ponderous* elephant⟩ ⟨heavy concentrations of troops and weapons for *ponderous* operations overland —H.H.Martin⟩ ⟨a sober and somewhat *ponderous* analysis of the police work —Anthony Boucher⟩ ⟨a book dealing with the necessity for world organization and the fundamentals of world law might be dull or at least *ponderous* reading —A.E. Stevenson †1965⟩ CUMBROUS and CUMBERSOME imply literally a heaviness and bulkiness difficult to move, carry, or otherwise deal with; figuratively, they apply to what is ponderous and unwieldy ⟨*cumbrous* old-fashioned wagons —Eddie Doherty⟩ ⟨one long and *cumbrous* sentence after another —M.W.Straight⟩ ⟨the camel . . . that lumbering and *cumbersome* beast —*Story of Camel Hair*⟩ ⟨the *cumbersome* amendment procedure of the outworn constitution —F.L.Paxson⟩ HEFTY implies, literally, heaviness or solid weightiness usu. as estimated by picking up in one's arms, holding in one's hand, or measuring by the eye against an imagined norm or, figuratively, weighty ⟨a *hefty* rock⟩ ⟨a *hefty* burden —A.J.Bruwer⟩ ⟨*hefty* peasants —*Time*⟩ ⟨*hefty* but handsome in her wedding dress —W.S.Maugham⟩ ⟨embodying so *hefty* a theme in a book —*Time*⟩

²heavy \"\ *vb* -ED/-ING/-ES [ME *hevyen,* fr. OE *hefigian,* fr. *hefig,* adj.] *vt, obs* **:** to make burdensome **:** weigh down **:** OPPRESS, BURDEN **~** *vi* **:** to play the role of a heavy

³heavy \"\ *adv* -ER/-EST [ME *hevy,* fr. OE *hefige,* fr. *hefig,* adj.] **:** in a heavy manner **:** HEAVILY ⟨time hung ~ on their hands⟩ ⟨a *heavy*-laden wagon⟩

⁴heavy \"\ *n* -ES [¹*heavy*] **1 heavies** *pl* **a :** heavy cavalry **b :** HEAVY ARTILLERY **c :** heavy tanks of an army or other military force **d :** HEAVY BOMBERS **2 a :** HEAVYWEIGHT 1a **b :** a theatrical role or an actor representing a dignified or imposing person **c :** VILLAIN 4 **3 :** something (as underwear or cloth) heavy in comparison with typical members of its kind

⁵heavy \ˈhēvē, -vi\ *adj* -ER/-EST [¹*heave* + *-y*] *of a horse* **:** affected with heaves

heavy-armed \ˌ≠≠ˈ≠\ *adj* **:** having or carrying heavy arms

heavy artillery *n* **1 a :** cannon of large caliber and great weight **b** *or* **heavy field artillery :** guns of 155 mm. or guns or howitzers of larger caliber **2 :** troops that serve heavy guns

heavy bomber *n* **:** a large long-range bomber designed primarily to carry large and heavy bomb loads to distant strategic targets — compare LIGHT BOMBER, MEDIUM BOMBER

heavy chemical *n* **:** a chemical produced and handled in large lots (as a ton or more a day) and often in a more or less crude state — used esp. of acids (as sulfuric acid), alkalies, and salts (as aluminum sulfate) — compare FINE CHEMICAL

heavy concrete *n* **:** concrete in which the usu. rock aggregates are partially or wholly replaced by aggregates of metal (as steel) and which is used esp. for counterweights or in shielding nuclear reactors

heavy cream *n* **:** cream that is markedly thick; *esp* **:** cream that by law contains not less than 36 percent butterfat

heavy cruiser *n* **:** a large naval cruiser whose principal armament usu. consists of 8-inch guns — compare LIGHT CRUISER

heavy dactyl *n* **:** a spondee resulting from substitution of a long syllable for the two short syllables in the thesis of a dactyl

heavy-duty \ˌ≠≠ˈ≠≠\ *adj* **:** able or designed to withstand unusual strain (as from heat, exposure, or wear) ⟨*heavy-duty* equipment⟩ ⟨a sturdy *heavy-duty* glove⟩

heavy-footed \ˌ≠≠ˈ≠≠\ *adj* **1 :** ponderous in or as if in movement ⟨a tired *heavy-footed* walk⟩ ⟨a *heavy-footed* literary style⟩ ⟨the conductor's rendering of the concerts was very *heavy-footed*⟩ **2** *dial* **:** PREGNANT **3 :** inclined to drive an automobile at excessive speeds ⟨issuing a few tickets to *heavy-footed* drivers —Robert Latimer⟩

heavy going *n* **:** difficult travel or progress

heavy-handed \ˌ≠≠ˈ≠≠\ *adj* **1 :** awkward or clumsy in or as if in the use of the hands: as **a :** having the hands seem heavy esp. from fatigue **b** *dial, of a cook or server* **:** inclined to be overgenerous ⟨*heavy-handed* with the potatoes⟩ ⟨much too *heavy-handed* with salt⟩ **c :** lacking or deficient in lightness, grace, or sparkle ⟨a *heavy-handed* didactic style⟩ **2 :** inclined to punish severely ⟨grandfather was *heavy-handed* with his own children but very indulgent with us grandchildren⟩; *broadly* **:** harshly oppressive ⟨*heavy-handed* tyranny⟩ — **heavy-handedly** *adv* — **heavy-handedness** *n* -ES

heavy-headed \ˌ≠≠ˈ≠≠\ *adj* **1 :** having a large or heavy head ⟨*heavy-headed* wheat⟩ **2 a :** DULL, STUPID **b :** DROWSY

heavyhearted \ˌ≠≠ˈ≠≠\ *adj* [ME *hevy herted*] **:** SADDENED, DISPIRITED, MELANCHOLY — **heavy·heart·ed·ly** *adv* — **heavy·heart·ed·ness** *n* -ES

heavy hydrogen *n* **:** an isotope of hydrogen having a mass number greater than 1; *esp* **:** DEUTERIUM

heavy-laden \ˌ≠≠ˈ≠≠\ *adj* **:** weighted down with or as if with a heavy burden **:** OPPRESSED, BURDENED ⟨a *heavy-laden* donkey⟩ ⟨*heavy-laden* with family cares⟩

heavy liquid *n* **:** a suspension of very fine particles of high specific gravity in water that forms a slurry with a specific gravity greater than that of water

heavy man *n, slang* **:** a professional criminal engaged in activities (as robbery) that involve or may involve violence

heavy metal *n* **:** a metal of high specific gravity; *esp* **:** a metal having a specific gravity of 5.0 or over

heavy mineral *n* **:** a mineral of specific gravity higher than a standard (as 2.8 or 3.0) that commonly forms a minor component of a rock

heavy nitrogen *n* **:** an isotope of nitrogen having a mass member greater than 14; *esp* **:** nitrogen of mass 15

heavy oil *n* **:** an oil of high specific gravity; *specif* **:** a high-boiling distillate from tar

heavy oil of wine : a heavy yellow oily liquid obtained in the distillation of alcohol and sulfuric acid in making ether

heavy oxygen *n* **:** an isotope of oxygen having a mass number greater than 16; *esp* **:** oxygen of mass 18

heavy pine *or* **heavy-wooded pine** *n* **:** PONDEROSA PINE

heavy racket *n, slang* **:** a branch of crime that involves or may involve personal violence — compare HEAVY MAN

heavyset \ˌ≠≠ˈ≠\ *adj* **:** stocky and compact and sometimes tending to stoutness in build ⟨a ~ man⟩

heavy solution *n* **:** a liquid of high density (as a solution of mercury iodide in potassium iodide or of the cadmium salt of a borotungstic acid) used esp. in determining the specific gravities of minerals and in separating them when mechanically mixed

heavy spar *n* **:** BARITE

heavy water *n* **:** water containing more than the usual proportion of heavy hydrogen, heavy oxygen, or both; *esp* **:** water that is enriched in deuterium so that it consists either wholly or in larger than normal proportion of deuterium oxide and that is used in tracer studies and as a moderator in nuclear reactors

heavy weapons company *n* **:** an infantry company usu. equipped with mortars, heavy machine guns, and recoilless rifles in addition to lighter weapons

heavyweight \ˈ≠≠ˌ≠\ *n, often attrib* **1 :** one that is above average in weight: as **a :** a participant (as a boxer or wrestler) in a sport or athletic contest who belongs to the heaviest of the classes into which contestants are divided; *esp* **:** a boxer weighing not less than 175 pounds — compare FEATHERWEIGHT **b :** an exceptionally massive or heavy object (as a truck or naval vessel) **2 :** one that carries unusual weight (as an outstanding writer or philosopher or a political leader) ⟨the ~s of the party gathered in New York⟩

hea·zle·wood·ite \ˈhēzəlˌwu̇ˌdīt\ *n* -S *usu cap* [*Heazlewood,* Tasmania, its locality + E *-ite*] **:** a mineral Ni_3S_2 consisting of sulfide of nickel

heb *abbr, usu cap* Hebrew

he-balsam \ˈ≠ˌ≠≠\ *n* **1 :** BLACK SPRUCE 1 **2 :** RED SPRUCE

heb·do·mad \ˈhebdəˌmad\ *n* -S [L *hebdomad-, hebdomas,* fr. Gk *hebdomad-, hebdomas,* fr. *hebdomos* seventh (fr. *hepta* seven) + *-ad-, -as* fem. suffix denoting connection with or descent from — more at SEVEN] **1 :** a group of seven ⟨a ~ of heavenly bodies⟩ **2 :** a period of seven days **:** WEEK **3** *gnosticism* **:** a group of seven aeons derived from the seven planetary deities who in most systems were half-hostile powers that created the world

¹heb·dom·a·dal \(ˈ)hebˈdäməd³l\ *adj* [LL *hebdomadalis,* fr. L *hebdomad-, hebdomas* + *-alis* -al] **1** *obs* **:** consisting of seven days **:** lasting seven days **2 :** meeting or appearing once a week **:** WEEKLY

²hebdomadal \"\ *n* -S **:** a weekly newspaper or magazine

heb·dom·a·dal·ly \-d³lē\ *adv* **:** every week ⟨contributes ~ to the magazine⟩

¹heb·dom·a·dary \hebˈdäməˌderē\ *n* -ES [ME *ebdomadary,* fr. LL *hebdomadarius,* fr. L *hebdomad-, hebdomas* + *-arius* -ary (n. suffix)] **:** a member of a Roman Catholic chapter or convent appointed for the week to sing the chapter mass and lead the recitation of the canonical hours

²hebdomadary \"\ *adj* [ML *hebdomadarius,* fr. L *hebdomad-, hebdomas* + *-arius* -ary (adj. suffix)] **:** occurring every seven days

heb·dom·a·der \-_də(r)\ *n* -S [alter. of ¹*hebdomadary*] **:** a member of a Scottish university formerly appointed for the week to superintend student discipline

¹he·be \ˈhē(ˌ)bē\ *n* [NL, after *Hebe,* goddess of youth, fr. Gk *Hēbē,* fr. *hēbē* youth; akin to Lith *pajėgà* power, ability] **1** *cap, in some classifications* **:** a genus comprising the shrubby evergreen veronicas of the southern hemisphere **2** -S **:** any veronica that can be placed in the genus *Hebe* including several of considerable horticultural interest

²hebe \ˈhēb\ *n* -S *often cap* [short for ²*Hebrew*] **:** JEW — often taken to be offensive

hebe- *comb form* [Gk *hēbē* youth, pubes] **:** puberty ⟨*hebephrenia*⟩ **:** downy **:** hairy **:** pubescent ⟨*hebeanthous*⟩

he·be·phre·nia \ˌhēbəˈfrēnēə, -hē-\ *n* -S [NL, fr. *hebe-* + *-phrenia*] **:** a schizophrenic reaction that is characterized by silliness, delusions, hallucinations, and regression and that has an early insidious onset and a usu. unfavorable prognosis — **he·be·phre·nic** \ˌ≠≠ˈfrenik *also* -rēn-\ *adj or n*

he·ber·den's node \ˈhebə(r)dᵊnz-\ *n, usu cap H* [after William *Heberden* †1801 Eng. physician] **:** any of the bony knots at joint margins (as at the terminal joints of the fingers) commonly associated with degenerative arthritis

heb·e·tate \ˈhebəˌtāt\ *vb* -ED/-ING/-S [L *hebetatus,* past part. of *hebetare* to make dull (lit. & fig.), fr. *hebet-, hebes* dull] *vt* **:** to blunt the sensitivity or keenness of **:** make dull or obtuse ⟨desultory reading . . . ~s the brain —J.R.Lowell⟩ **~** *vi* **:** to become dull or obtuse — **heb·e·ta·tion** \ˌ≠≠ˈtāshən\ *n* -S

heb·e·tude \-əˌtüd, -əˌtyüd\ *n* -S [LL *hebetudo,* fr. L *hebēre* to be dull + *-tudo* -tude; akin to L *hebes* dull] **:** the absence of mental alertness or physical sensitivity **:** DULLNESS, LETHARGY ⟨her natural ~ must disgust him and eventually destroy all affection —Hugh McCrae⟩ — **heb·e·tu·di·nous** \ˌ≠≠ˈ≠(ᵊ)nəs\ *adj*

hebona *n* [origin unknown] *obs* **:** a plant having a poisonous juice ⟨with juice of cursed ~ in a vial —Shak.⟩

he·brae·an \(ˈ)hēˈbrēən, hiˈb-, (ˈ)heˈb-, həˈb-\ *n* -S *usu cap* [L *Hebraeus* Hebrew + E *-an* — more at HEBREW] *archaic* **:** a Hebrew scholar

he·bra·ic \-ˈrāik,-ˈrāēk\ *adj, usu cap* [ME *Ebrayke,* fr. LL *Hebraicus,* fr. Gk *Hebraikos,* fr. *Hebraios,* adj., Hebrew + *-ikos* -ic — more at HEBREW] **1 :** of, relating to, or characteristic of the Hebrews or of their language, literature, or religion ⟨those early Christians who were of *Hebraic* blood instead of Greek or Roman —C.J.Bulliet⟩ ⟨a Jewish house of worship ought to be . . . *Hebraic* —A.R.Katz⟩ **2 :** characterized by preoccupation with conscience and conduct ⟨was ardently *Hebraic,* exalting righteousness above love —V.L. Parrington⟩ ⟨the Hellenic and the *Hebraic* ways of looking at God, man, and the universe —Will Herberg⟩ — **he·bra·i·cal·ly** \-ə̇k(ə)lē, -ēk-, -li\ *adv*

he·bra·i·ca \ˌ≠ˈrāəkə, -ēkə\ *n pl, usu cap* [NL, fr. LL, neut. pl. of *Hebraicus*] **:** things Hebraic; *esp* **:** Hebraic literary or historical materials ⟨a collection of *Hebraica*⟩

hebraic granite *n, usu cap H* [so called fr. its supposed resemblance to letters of the Hebrew alphabet] **:** GRAPHIC GRANITE

he·bra·ism \ˈhē(ˌ)brāˌizəm, -ˌbrē|, -ˌbrə|\ *n* -S *usu cap* [*Hebraic* + *-ism*] **1 :** a characteristic feature of Hebrew occurring in another language or dialect ⟨the first half of the book of Acts . . . is replete with *Hebraisms* —S.M.Gilmour⟩ **2 a :** the thought, spirit, or practice characteristic of the Hebrews ⟨*Hebraism* related itself to centuries of literary and philosophical creativity —J.L.Teller⟩ — compare HELLENISM 4 **b :** the moral theory of life held to be characteristic of the Hebrews ⟨the governing idea of Hellenism is spontaneity of consciousness; that of *Hebraism,* strictness of conscience —Matthew Arnold⟩

he·bra·ist \|ˌə̇st\ *n* -S *usu cap* [*Hebraic* + *-ist*] **:** a specialist in Hebrew and Hebraic studies

he·bra·is·tic \ˌ≠(ˌ)≠ˈistik, -tēk\ *adj, usu cap* **1 :** HEBRAIC 1 ⟨*Hebraistic* culture⟩ **2 :** characterized by or given to the use of Hebraisms ⟨the least *Hebraistic* writer in the New Testament —B.M.Metzger⟩

he·bra·iza·tion \ˌhēˌbrāəˈzāshən\ *n* -S *usu cap* **:** an act of hebraizing

he·bra·ize \ˈ≠(ˌ)≠ˌīz\ *vb* -ED/-ING/-S *often cap* [*Hebraic* + *-ize*] *vi* **1 :** to use Hebraisms ⟨must impeach him not only for atticizing but for *hebraizing* too —Richard Bentley †1742⟩ **2 :** to follow Hebraism ⟨here he is *hebraizing* and introducing an element . . . foreign to the law of our race —Frederick Pollock & F.W.Maitland⟩ **~** *vt* **:** to make Hebraic: **a :** to cause to become adapted to Hebraism ⟨~ this fact, erect a cosmology upon it, and we have the vital principle of Calvinism —V.L.Parrington⟩ **b :** to adapt (a foreign word) to Hebrew usage; *specif* **:** to change (a name) to a Hebrew equivalent ⟨*hebraized* his name when Israel was reborn —*Hadassah Newsletter*⟩

¹he·brew \ˈhē(ˌ)brü\ *adj, usu cap* [ME *Ebreu, Hebru, Hebrewe,* fr. OF *ebreu, ebrieu, hebreu, hebrieu,* fr. L *Hebraeus,* fr. Gk *Hebraios,* fr. Aram *ʿEbrai*] **1 :** of, relating to, or characteristic of Hebrew **2 :** of, relating to, or characteristic of the Hebrews

²hebrew \"\ *n* -S *cap* [ME *Ebreu, Hebru, Hebrewe,* fr. OF *ebreu, ebrieu, hebreu, hebrieu,* fr. LL *Hebraeus,* fr. L, adj.] **1 :** a member of or descendant from one of a group of tribes of the northern branch of the Semites that included the Israelites, Ammonites, Moabites, and Edomites; *esp* **:** ISRAELITE — compare JEW **2 a :** the Semitic language of the ancient Hebrews in which most of the Old Testament was written — called also *Biblical Hebrew* **b :** any of various later forms of this language (as Mishnaic Hebrew, rabbinical Hebrew, or modern Hebrew)

hebrew alphabet *n, usu cap H* **1 :** a Semitic alphabet used since about the 5th century B.C. for writing Hebrew and in medieval and modern times used also for Yiddish and on occasion other languages — called also *Aramaic alphabet;* see ALPHABET table **2 :** the Semitic alphabet used in writing Hebrew until about the 5th century B.C. and on occasion as late as the 2d century A.D. — called also *ancient Hebrew alphabet, early Hebrew alphabet, old Hebrew alphabet*

he·brew·ism \'hē(,)brü,izəm\ *n* -s *usu cap* : HEBRAISM

he·bri·cian \hē'brishən\ *n* -s *usu cap* [*Hebrew* + *-ician*] *archaic* : HEBRAIST

¹heb·ri·de·an \,hebrə'dēən, hē'brid-\ *or* **he·brid·i·an** \hē'bridēən\ *adj, usu cap* [*Hebrides,* islands off the western coast of Scotland + E *-an, -ian*] **1 :** of, relating to, or characteristic of the Hebrides **2 :** of, relating to, or characteristic of the Hebrideans

²hebridean \"\ *or* **hebridian** \"\ *n* -s *cap* : a native or inhabitant of the Hebrides

he·bron·ite \'hēbrə,nīt\ *n* -s [*Hebron,* Maine, its locality + E *-ite*] : AMBLYGONITE

hec·ate \'hekə,tē, -kəd-ē, -kət\ *n* -s *usu cap* [after *Hecate,* Greek goddess of witchcraft, fr. L, fr. Gk *Hekatē*] *obs* : WITCH, HAG ⟨I speak not to that railing *Hecate* —Shak.⟩

hecato- *or* **hecaton-** *comb form* [Gk *hekato-,* fr. *hekaton* hundred — more at HUNDRED] : consisting of a hundred ⟨having a hundred ⟨*hecatophyllous*⟩

hec·a·tomb \'hekə,tōm *sometimes* -tüm *or* -täm\ *n* -s [L *hecatombe,* fr. Gk *hekatombē,* fr. *hekaton* hundred + *-bē* (fr. stem of *bous* head of cattle, cow) — more at HUNDRED, COW] **1 :** an ancient Greek and Roman sacrifice consisting typically of 100 oxen or cattle **2 :** the sacrifice or slaughter of many victims ⟨make ourselves unhappy over the yearly ~ that follows the wake of the motor —Agnes Repplier⟩ **3 :** a large number or quantity ⟨the end of the war saw no ~*s* of officers slain by enfranchised privates —Dixon Wecter⟩

hec·a·ton·tar·chy \,hekə'tän,tärkē, '≈≈,≈≈\ *n* -ES [Gk *hekatont-* hundred (fr. *hekaton*) + E *-archy*] : government by 100 persons

hecceity *var of* HAECCEITY

hech \'hek\ *interj* [imit.] — used esp. in Scots to express surprise, contempt, sorrow, or pain

hechi·ma \he'chēmə, 'hechəmə\ *n* -s [Jap] : DISHCLOTH GOURD

hech·sher \'hekshər\ *n, pl* **hech·she·rim** \hek'shārəm, -,rem\ *or* **hech·shers** \'hekshərz\ [LHeb *hekhshēr,* lit., fitting] : a rabbinical endorsement or certification esp. of food products that conform with traditional Jewish dietary laws — compare KASHRUTH

hecht \'hekt\ *Scot var of* ¹HIGHT

hech·tia \'hektēə, -kshēə\ *n, cap* [NL, fr. J. G. H. *Hecht* †1837 Prussian counselor + NL *-ia*] : a genus of Mexican desert herbs (family Bromeliaceae) with rosettes of spiny leaves and ornamental floral bracts

¹heck \'hek\ *n* -s [ME *hek,* fr. OE *hæc, -hec* — more at HATCH] **1** *dial Eng* **a :** the lower half of a divided door **b :** an inner door **2** *chiefly Scot* : a wooden rack for holding fodder **3 a :** a wooden grating set across a stream to obstruct the passage of fish **b** *chiefly Scot* : a grating in a millrace **4 a :** a device on a vertical frame for controlling warp threads in textile manufacturing **b :** any of various attachments on spinning wheels or warping mills for guiding thread in textile manufacturing

²heck \"\ *n* -s [euphemism] : ¹HELL 2 ⟨that's the ~ of it⟩ ⟨~ — he can't do that⟩ ⟨a ~ of a good fighter⟩

heck·el·phone \'hekəl,fōn\ *n* [G *heckelphon,* fr. Wilhelm *Heckel,* 20th cent. Ger. instrument maker, its inventor + G *-phon* -phone] : a woodwind instrument of the oboe family pitched an octave below the normal oboe

heck·er·ism \'hekə,rizəm\ *n* -s *usu cap* [Isaac Thomas *Hecker* †1888 Am. Roman Catholic clergyman + E *-ism*] : certain religious teachings (as the adaptation of traditional beliefs to the exigencies of modern culture, the exaltation of natural above supernatural virtues, the preference for active rather than passive virtue, the revision of traditional missionary technique) held to be erroneous by Pope Leo XIII — called also *Americanism*

heck-how \'hek,haů, -e,kaů\ *n* -s [origin unknown] : POISON HEMLOCK

¹heck·le \'hekəl\ *chiefly dial var of* HACKLE

²heckle \"\ *vt* **heckled; heckled; heckling** \-k(ə)liŋ\ **heckles** [ME *hekelen,* fr. *hakell, heckele* hackle — more at HATCHEL] **1 :** ⁴HACKLE 1 **2 a :** to harass with questions, challenges, gibes, or objections designed to embarrass and disconcert : BADGER ⟨would gather in front-row seats and ~ the performers with shouts —E.J.Kahn⟩ **b :** to interfere with unjustifiably or with hostile intent : meddle with so as to annoy, disturb, or injure : MOLEST ⟨*heckled* even by photographers who . . . set off flash bulbs as he was about to start —Claudia Cassidy⟩ ⟨seemed too harried and *heckled* by her life to spare love for the other children —John Dollard⟩ **syn** see BAIT

³heckle \"\ *var of* HICKWALL

heck·ler \-k(ə)lə(r)\ *n* -s : one that heckles ⟨spoke forcefully with a ready wit that took easy care of ~*s* —J.D.Hicks⟩

hec·o·gen·in \,hekō'jenən\ *n* [*heconin* saponin found in the juice of agaves (fr. *hec-* — fr. NL *Hectia,* genus name of *Hectia texensis* — + *-onin* — as in *saponin*) + *-genin*] : a crystalline steroid sapogenin $C_{27}H_{42}O_4$ obtained from a desert herb (*Hechtia texensis*) and many agaves and used in a synthesis of cortisone

hect- *or* **hecto-** *comb form* [F, irreg. fr. Gk *hekaton* — more at HUNDRED] : hundred ⟨*hectare*⟩ ⟨*hectograph*⟩

hect·ar·age \'hek,ta(a)rij, -tär-\ *n* -s [*hectare* + *-age*] : area in hectares

hect·are \'hek,ta(a)(ə)r, -tär\ *n* -s [F, fr. *hect-* + *are*] : a metric unit of area equal to 100 ares or 10,000 square meters — see METRIC SYSTEM table

hec·ta·style \'hektə,stīl\ *n* [by alter.] : HEXASTYLE

hec·te \'hek(,)tē\ *n* -s [Gk *hektē,* fr. fem. of *hektos* sixth, fr. *hex* six — more at SIX] : an ancient Greek coin worth ⅙ stater; *esp* : an electrum coin of Phocaea and Lesbos

¹hec·tic \'hektik, -tēk\ *adj* [alter. (influenced by LL *hecticus*) of ME *etyk* (as in *fever etyk* hectic fever), fr. MF *etique,* fr. LL *hecticus,* fr. Gk *hektikos* habitual, habit-forming, consumptive, fr. *hekt-* (akin to *echein* to have) + *-ikos* -ic — more at SCHEME] **1 a :** HABITUAL, CONSTITUTIONAL, PERSISTENT; *specif, of a fever* : fluctuating but persistently recurrent ⟨~ fevers are characteristic of tuberculosis and septicemia⟩ **b :** characteristic of or habitually accompanying a hectic fever ⟨the ~ flush of tuberculosis⟩ **2 :** marked by a hectic condition : having a hectic fever : CONSUMPTIVE ⟨a ~ patient⟩ **3 :** having a glowing quality : FLUSHED, RED ⟨the ~ color had brightened in the boy's impatient face —Harriet La Barre⟩ **4 :** characterized by excitement, bustle, or feverish activity : RESTLESS ⟨the ~ years after oil was discovered —Harold Griffin⟩ ⟨~ travel through thirty different countries —Carveth Wells⟩ ⟨things were so ~ we couldn't even keep track of the people, let alone the material —N.O.Wahlstrom⟩ — **hec·ti·cal·ly** \-tək(ə)lē, -tēk-, -li\ *adv*

²hectic \"\ *n* -s [ME *etyk,* short for *fever etyk*] **1 :** a hectic fever **2 :** one affected by a hectic fever; *esp* : CONSUMPTIVE **3 :** hectic flush

hec·ti·cal \-təkəl, -tēk-\ *archaic var of* ¹HECTIC

hec·tic·ness *n* -ES : the quality or state of being hectic

hective *adj* [by alter.] *obs* : HECTIC

hec·to·cot·y·lif·er·ous \,hektə,käd-ᵊl'if(ə)rəs\ *adj* [NL *hectocotylus* + E *-i-* + *-ferous*] : bearing hectocotyli

hec·to·cot·y·li·za·tion \,≈≈,≈≈.ᵊzāshən\ *n* -s **1 :** transformation into a hectocotylus **2 :** impregnation with a hectocotylus

hec·to·cot·y·lize \-'kädᵊl,īz\ *vt* -ED/-ING/-S [NL *hectocotylus* + E *-ize*] **1 :** to change into a hectocotylus **2 :** to impregnate with a hectocotylus

hec·to·cot·y·lus \-ᵊləs\ *n, pl* **hectocoty·li** \-ᵊl,ī\ [NL, fr. *hect-* + *-cotylus* (fr. Gk *kotylē* cup, anything hollow) — more at KETTLE] : a modified arm of a male cephalopod that is specially and variously adapted to effect the fertilization of the eggs; *esp* : an arm that in argonauts and some octopods receives the spermatophores, is inserted into the female mantle cavity, and then is broken free from the body of the male

hec·to·cot·y·ly \-ᵊlē\ *n* -ES : the quality or state of having or being converted into a hectocotylus

hec·to·gram *or* **hec·to·gramme** \'hektə,gram, -raa(ə)m\ *n* [F *hectogramme,* fr. *hecto-* hect- + *gramme* gram — more at GRAM] : a metric unit of mass and weight equal to 100 grams — see METRIC SYSTEM table

¹hec·to·graph *also* **hek·to·graph** \-,graf, -raa(ə)f, -raif, -räf\ *n* [G *hektograph,* fr. *hekto-* hect- + *-graph*] : a machine for making copies of a writing or drawing by transferring it to a slab of gelatin treated with glycerin and then taking impressions from the gelatin — **hec·to·graph·ic** \¦≈≈¦grafik, -fēk\ *adj*

²hectograph \"\ *vt* : to copy with a hectograph

hec·to·liter \'hektə + ,-\ *n* [F *hectolitre,* fr. *hecto-* hect- + *litre* liter — more at LITER] : a metric unit of capacity equal to 100 liters — see METRIC SYSTEM table

hec·to·meter \'hektə,med-ə(r), hek'tämәd-\ *n* [F *hectomètre,* fr. *hecto-* hect- + *mètre* meter — more at METER] : a metric unit of length equal to 100 meters — see METRIC SYSTEM table

¹hec·tor \'hektə(r)\ *n* -s [after *Hector,* a Trojan warrior in Homer's *Iliad,* fr. L, fr. Gk *Hektōr*] : one that hectors : BULLY, BRAGGART

²hector \"\ *vb* **hectored; hectored; hectoring** \-t(ə)riŋ\ **hectors** *vi* : to play the bully : SWAGGER ~ *vt* : to harass, intimidate, bully, or domineer over by bluster, scolding, or personal pressure ⟨domineering wives who ~ their husbands and in-laws to near distraction —Harrison Forman⟩ **syn** see BAIT

hec·tor·ing·ly *adv* : in a hectoring manner

hec·tor·ite \'hektə,rīt\ *n* -s [*Hector,* Calif., its locality + E *-ite*] : a mineral $(Mg,Li)_3Si_4O_{10}(OH)_2$ consisting of a hydrous silicate of magnesium and lithium — compare MONTMORILLONITE

hed \(¦)hed, ,(h)əd\ *chiefly Scot past of* HAVE

hed·dle *also* **hea·dle** \'hedᵊl\ *n* -s [prob. alter. of ME *helde* — more at HEALD] **1 :** one of the sets of parallel cords or wires that with their mounting compose the harness used to guide warp threads and raise and lower them in weaving **2 :** a metal blade or twisted wire with an eyelet in the center through which warp threads pass in weaving

hed·dler \-d(ᵊ)lə(r)\ *n* -s : DRAWER-IN

hed·e·bo \'hedə,bō\ *n* -s [Dan. *hedebobroderi,* fr. *hedebo* dwelling on the heath (fr. *hede* heath + *bo* dwelling) + *broderi* embroidery] : an embroidery characterized by drawnwork and decorative stitching

hed·en·berg·ite \'hedᵊn,bər,gīt\ *n* -s [Sw *hedenbergit,* fr. Ludwig *Hedenberg* 19th cent. Swed. mineralogist + Sw *-it* -ite] : a mineral $CaFeSi_2O_6$ consisting of a calcium-iron pyroxene

hede·o·ma \,hedē'ōmə, ,hēd-\ *n* [NL, prob. irreg. fr. Gk *hēdys* sweet + *osmē* smell; fr. the fragrant blossoms — more at SWEET, ODOR] **1** *cap* : a small genus of American herbs (family Labiatae) having small flowers in axillary clusters and with bilabiate corolla and two stamens — see PENNYROYAL 2 **2** -s : any plant of the genus *Hedeoma*

hedeoma oil *n* : PENNYROYAL OIL

¹he·der \'hēdə(r)\ *n* -s [prob. fr. ²*he* + *deer* (animal)] *dial Eng* : a male sheep; *esp* : one past eight or nine months old that has not been sheared

²he·der *or* **che·der** *also* **che·dar** \'kādər, 'ked-\ *n, pl* **ha·da·rim** \kə'därəm, -dōr-, -,rem\ *or* **he·ders** \'kādərz, 'ked-\ [Yiddish *kheyder,* fr. Heb *ḥedher* room] : an elementary Jewish school in which children from about 7 to 13 years of age are taught to read the Pentateuch, the Prayer Book, and other books in Hebrew — compare TALMUD TORAH

hed·era \'hedərə\ *n, cap* [NL, fr. L, ivy; perh. akin to L *prehendere* to seize — more at GET] : a genus of Old World woody vines (family Araliaceae) usu. having palmate leaves but in adult form often becoming shrubby with unlobed leaves — see IVY

hed·er·a·gen·in \,hedərə'jenən; ,hedə'rajənən, -,nēn\ *n* -s [ISV *hedera-* (fr. NL *Hedera*) + *-gen* + *-in*] : a crystalline triterpenoid saponin $C_{30}H_{48}O_4$ obtained by hydrolysis of hederin and other saponins (as from soap nuts)

hed·er·in \'hedərən\ *n* -s [ISV *heder-* (fr. NL *Hedera,* genus name of *Hedera helix*) + *-in*] : a crystalline antibiotic glycoside $C_{41}H_{64}O_{11}$ active against fungi and bacteria that is found esp. in ivy — called also *alpha-hederin, helixin*

¹hedge \'hej\ *n* -s [ME *hegge,* fr. OE *hecg;* akin to OE *haga* hedge, hawthorn, OHG *hag* hedge, hedged-in enclosure, *heckis* hedge, ON *heggr* bird cherry (tree), L *caulae* sheepfold, *colum* sieve, W *cae* field, Corn *kē* hedge, fence] **1 a :** a fence or boundary formed by a row of shrubs or low trees planted close together ⟨white farmhouses with faded red barns and fields bordered with ~*s* of green —Gordon Webber⟩ **b :** any fence or wall marking a boundary or forming a barrier ⟨the high stone ~ . . . encircled the enclosure —A.L.Rowse⟩ **2 a :** a line or array forming a barrier or marking a boundary ⟨pikemen . . . present a ~ of metal points from which any cavalry would flinch —Tom Wintringham⟩ **b :** a protective or defensive barrier ⟨regarded it as the main function of their existence to raise a ~ around the law —F.W.Farrar⟩ **3 a :** a means of protection or defense — usu. used with *against* ⟨proponents of using fluorides as a ~ against tooth decay —*N.Y.Times*⟩ **b :** any of several means of protection against financial loss: as (1) **:** a bet made against the side or chance already bet on (2) **:** a purchase or sale made not primarily for income or profit but as protection against a known risk ⟨realization that common stocks are the best ~ against inflation —C.E.Merrill⟩ (3) **:** a purchase or sale of commodity futures made to offset the risk of loss from market fluctuations **4 :** a statement so qualified or calculated as to be noncommittal or ambiguous ⟨bureaucratic literature . . . festooned with ~*s* and qualifications —*Fortune*⟩ **5 :** OSAGE ORANGE

²hedge \"\ *vb* -ED/-ING/-S [ME *heggen,* fr. *hegge,* n.] *vt* **1 :** to enclose with or separate by a hedge : fence with a row of shrubs or low trees planted close together ⟨its modest lot is *hedged* by . . . hibiscus —Frederick Simpich⟩ **2 a :** to enclose as if with a hedge : ENCIRCLE ⟨meandering through an immense meadow *hedged* by forest —S.H.Holbrook⟩ ⟨a small dance floor crowded with couples and *hedged* with waiting men —Edmund Wilson⟩ **b :** to surround so as to form a protective barrier : GUARD, PROTECT ⟨remembered that no great divinity ~*s* this sovereign —Graham Greene⟩ **c :** to surround so as to prevent freedom of movement or action : FENCE, HEM, RESTRICT ⟨the bulk and pressure of the rules that ~ him on every side —B.N.Cardozo⟩ — often used with *about* or *in* ⟨are *hedged* about with many special conditions, limitations, and restrictions —F.L.Mott⟩ ⟨*hedged* themselves in with a thousand dos and don'ts —A.L.Kroeber⟩ **3 :** to obstruct with or as if with a hedge or barrier : HINDER ⟨the difficulties which *hedged* all approach —D.G.Mitchell⟩ **4** *obs* : to introduce and include within something larger or more important — used with *in* or *into* ⟨when you are sent on an errand, be sure to ~ in some business of your own —Jonathan Swift⟩ **5 a :** to reduce or eliminate the risk of (a bet) by making a bet against the side or chance already bet on ⟨is *hedging* its bets in the all-important diplomatic poker game —*Newsweek*⟩ **b :** to protect oneself against financial loss from ⟨were advising clients to ~ the imminent inflation by buying farmland —*Forum*⟩ **6 :** to form into a hedge or barrier ⟨ye are *hedged* on the borders of my path —Adah I. Menken⟩ **7 :** to qualify or modify so as to allow for contingencies or avoid rigid commitment ⟨when he states a position, he is apt to ~ it round with careful qualifications —Colm Brogan⟩ ~ *vi* **1 :** to plant or trim hedges **2 a :** to evade risk or responsibility by avoiding an open or decisive course : TRIM ⟨having found . . . every incentive to cower and cringe and ~ and no incentive whatever to stand upright as a man —Van Wyck Brooks⟩ **b :** to qualify or modify a statement or position so as to allow for contingencies or avoid rigid commitment ⟨the paper for which he was responsible never *hedged* on public questions —H.K.Rowe⟩ ⟨no mathematician is infallible; he may make mistakes; but he must not ~ —A.S.Eddington⟩ **3 a :** to protect oneself financially — usu. used with *against* ⟨in order to ~ against inflation and save . . . a part of one's possessions —George Katona⟩ **b :** to reduce or eliminate the risk of a bet by making a bet against the side or chance already bet on **c :** to buy or sell commodity futures as a protection against loss due to price fluctuations **d :** to buy or sell forward exchange as a protection against loss due to foreign-exchange fluctuations **4 :** to form a hedge or barrier ⟨invested with the sanctity that once *hedged* about a king —Dumas Malone⟩

³hedge \"\ *adj* [¹*hedge*] **1 :** of, for, or relating to a hedge ⟨a ~ corner⟩ ⟨a ~ plant⟩ ⟨~ selling on the commodity exchanges⟩ **2 :** born, living, or made near or as if near hedges : ROADSIDE ⟨a ~ parson⟩ ⟨a ~ marriage⟩ **3 :** belonging to an inferior grade or class : THIRD-RATE ⟨a ~ tavern⟩

hedge accentor *n* : HEDGE SPARROW

hedge apple *or* **hedge ball** *n* : OSAGE ORANGE

hedge·bet·ty \'≈,bed-ē\ *n* [¹*hedge* + *Betty,* the name] *dial Eng* : HEDGE SPARROW

hedge bindweed *n* **1 :** a common Eurasian and American wild convolvulus (*Convolvulus sepium*) — called also *wild morning glory* **2** *also* **hedge buckwheat :** CLIMBING FALSE BUCKWHEAT

hedge bird *n* : VAGRANT, VAGABOND

hedge·bote \'≈,bōt\ *n* -s [¹*hedge* + *bote,* obs. var. of ¹*boot*] : HAYBOTE

hedge cactus *n* : a So. American white-flowered cactus (*Cereus peruvianus*) widely grown for hedges in the tropics

hedge creeper *n, obs* : HEDGE BIRD

hedged *past of* HEDGE

hedge fence *n* : a hedge that serves as a fence

hedge fumitory *n* : FUMITORY

hedge garlic *n* : GARLIC MUSTARD

hedge·hog \'≈,≈\ *n, often attrib* [ME *heggehogge,* fr. *hegge* hedge + *hogge* hog — more at HEDGE, HOG] **1 a :** any of several nocturnal Old World insectivorous mammals that constitute the genus *Erinaceus* (esp. *E. europaeus*), have the hair on the upper part of the body mixed with prickles or spines, and are able to roll themselves up so as to present the spines outwardly in every direction **b :** any of various other spine-bearing animals (as the tenrecs or the porcupines) **2 a :** any of various prickly fruits or seed pods (as those of *Ranunculus arvensis* and *Medicago echinus*) **b :** a plant bearing such a fruit **3 :** any of various coarse variably spinose West Indian sponges **4 a** (1) **:** a military defensive obstacle made of barbed wire bound around three poles, logs, or lengths of metal (2) **:** a military defensive obstacle that is made of three 6-foot angle irons bolted together, sometimes wound with barbed wire, and usu. embedded in concrete and that is designed to damage tanks and boats in beach landings **b :** a military defensive stronghold securely entrenched or fortified with minefields and pillboxes and equipped with supplies for sustained resistance to encirclement **c :** a multiple rocket-propelled weapon used against submarines

hedgehog cactus *n* : any of several cacti with stout sharp spines: as **a :** a cactus of the genus *Echinocactus* **b** *or* **hedgehog cereus :** a cactus of the genus *Echinocereus*

hedgehog caterpillar *n* : the hairy larva of certain moths — compare WOOLLY BEAR

hedgehog fish *n* : PORCUPINE FISH

hedgehog fruit *n* : the prickly fruit of a maiden's-blush (*Echinocarpus australis*)

hedgehog fungus *also* **hedgehog mushroom** *n* [so called fr. the prickly hymenial surface] : a fungus of the genus *Hydnum* (esp. *H. erinaceum*)

hedgehog gourd *n* : an ornamental gourd (*Cucumis dipsaceus*) having a hairy fruit — called also *teasel gourd*

hedgehog grass *n* : BUR GRASS

hedge·hog·gy \'≈,≈ē, -i\ *adj* [*hedgehog* + *-y*] : tending to arouse aversion : FORBIDDING

hedgehog medic *n* : any of several plants of the genus *Medicago* (as *M. echinus*) having pods that resemble burs

hedgehog parsley *n* : a European herb (*Caucalis daucoides*) of the family Umbelliferae having fruit with prickly ribs

hedgehog rat *n* : SPINY RAT 1

hedgehog shell *n* : a spinose marine gastropod shell of *Murex* or related genera (as *M. tenuispina*)

hedgehog skate *n* : LITTLE SKATE

hedgehog tenrec *n* : a tenrec (*Setifer setosus*)

hedge·hop \'≈,≈\ *vb* [back-formation fr. *hedgehopper*] *vi* : to fly an airplane at a low altitude; *specif* : to fly an airplane close to the ground and rise over obstacles as they appear ⟨went *hedgehopping* across Holland, dodging trees, telegraph poles and houses —*Life*⟩ ⟨~ over 12,000 miles of pipeline —*advt*⟩ ~ *vt* **1 a :** to transport by flying at a low altitude ⟨*hedgehopped* his passenger to the other end of the line —*Current Biog.*⟩ **b :** to fly an airplane close to the ground and rise so as to miss (an obstacle) ⟨was accused of *hedgehopping* three planes and a hangar and buzzing the control tower —*Newsweek*⟩ **2 :** to evade or elude as if by hedgehopping ⟨*hedgehopped* Soviet censors to carry a . . . message through the Iron Curtain —*N.Y. Times*⟩

hedgehopper \'≈,≈≈\ *n* : one that hedgehops: **a :** an airplane flying at a low altitude **b :** a pilot flying an airplane dangerously close to the ground

hedge hyssop *n* **1 :** an herb of the genus *Gratiola* (as the European *G. officinalis* or the American *G. aurea*) **2 :** any of several British plants resembling hedge hyssop (as *Scutellaria minor* and *Lythrum hyssopifolium*)

hedge·less \'hejləs\ *adj* : having no hedges

hedge maple *n* : a common low-growing Asiatic tree (*Acer campestre*) sometimes used as a hedge

hedge mushroom *n* **1 :** HORSE MUSHROOM **2 :** MEADOW MUSHROOM

hedge mustard *n* : a plant of the genus *Sisymbrium; esp* : a stiffly branching Old World annual herb (*S. officinale*) with pale yellow flowers that is widely naturalized in No. America and was formerly used in medicine as a diuretic and expectorant

hedge nettle *n* : a plant of the genus *Stachys:* as **a :** a perennial shade-loving Eurasiatic herb (*S. sylvatica*) with a green creeping rhizome having a foul odor when crushed **b :** a similar plant (*S. palustris*) with an odorless rhizome that is widespread in moist places in most of the northern hemisphere

hedge parsley *n* : any of several weedy plants of the family Umbelliferae with finely cut foliage resembling that of parsley; *esp* : an erect annual Eurasian weed (*Torilis japonica*) that has dense heads of white flowers, bristly fruits, and bipinnate leaves and is widely naturalized in eastern No. America

hedgepig \'≈,≈\ *n* : HEDGEHOG

hedge pink *n* : SOAPWORT 1

hedge-priest \'≈,≈\ *n* : an itinerant usu. uneducated priest

hedg·er \'hejə(r)\ *n* -s [in sense 1, fr. ²*hedge* + *-er;* in sense 2, fr. ²*hedge* + *-er*] **1 :** one that plants or trims hedges **2 :** one that hedges (as in betting)

hedge rose *n* : any of various wild roses that tend to invade and thrive in hedgerows: as **a :** DOG ROSE **b :** SWEETBRIER **c :** MACARTNEY ROSE

hedgerow \'≈,≈\ *n* : a row of shrubs or trees enclosing or separating fields ⟨could see the white bursts of dogwood in the ~*s* —William Faulkner⟩

hedges *pl of* HEDGE, *pres 3d sing of* HEDGE

hedge school *n* [so called fr. the fact that in 17th and 18th cent. Ireland schools were held outside in out-of-the-way places to evade the law on Catholic education] : a school held out of doors esp. in Ireland

hedge sparrow *n* : a common European bird (*Prunella modularis* syn. *Accentor modularis*) that resembles a thrush, frequents hedges, and is reddish brown and ashen gray with the wing coverts tipped with white — called also *dunnock, hedge accentor*

hedge-sparrow egg *n* : a pale green to light yellowish green that is yellower and slightly lighter than cameo green

hedge violet *n* : a common European blue-flowered violet (*Viola sylvatica*) that grows in woods and hedgerows

hedge willow *n* : GREAT SALLOW

hedging *pres part of* HEDGE

hedg·ing·ly *adv* : in a hedging manner

hedgy \'hejē, -ji\ *adj* -ER/-EST : resembling or abounding in hedges ⟨~ country⟩ ⟨~ growths⟩

he·di·on·di·lla \,hedēən'dē(y)ə\ *n* -s [MexSp, fr. Sp *hediondo* stinking (fr. *heder* to stink, fr. L *foetēre, fetēre*) + *-illa* (dim. suffix) — more at FETID] : CREOSOTE BUSH

hed·ley·ite \'hedlē,īt\ *n* -s [*Hedley,* British Columbia, its locality + E *-ite*] : a mineral approximately Bi_7Te_3 consisting of an alloy of bismuth and tellurium

he·don·ic \(')hē¦dänik, -nēk\ *also* **he·don·i·cal** \-nəkəl, -nēk-\ *adj* [*hedonic* fr. Gk *hēdonikos,* fr. *hēdonē* pleasure +

-*ikos* -ic; *hedonical* fr. *hedonic* + *-al;* akin to Gk *hēdys* sweet — more at SWEET] **1 a :** of, relating to, or characterized by pleasure ⟨might have shocked them, had they been in a less ~ state —Herman Wouk⟩ **b :** involving the psychological range of feelings from pleasant to unpleasant ⟨any particular color may undergo an alteration of ~ . . . effect —Hunter Mead⟩ **2 :** HEDONISTIC **3 :** of or relating to hedonics or to the states of consciousness that it deals with ⟨the relative pleasurableness of an intent as a whole can be determined with the help of some ~ calculus —F.E.Oppenheim⟩ **4 :** concerned with the production of pleasure or pleasurable sensation — **he·don·i·cal·ly** \-nȧk(ə)lē, -nēk-, -li\ *adv*

hedonic gland *n* **:** any of several glands of various salamanders and reptiles that produce a secretion believed to function in sexual attraction and stimulation

he·don·ics \hē'däniks, -nēks\ *n pl but usu sing in constr* **1 :** a theory of ethics dealing with or based on the relation of duty to pleasure **2 :** a branch of psychology that deals with pleasant and unpleasant states of consciousness and their relation to organic life

he·do·nism \'hēdᵊn,izəm, -də,ni-\ *n* -s [Gk *hēdonē* pleasure + E *-ism*] **1 :** an ethical doctrine taught by the ancient Epicureans and Cyrenaics and by the modern utilitarians that asserts that pleasure or happiness is the sole or chief good in life — called also *ethical hedonism;* distinguished from *psychological hedonism;* compare EGOISTIC HEDONISM, EPICUREANISM, EUDAEMONISM, UNIVERSALISTIC HEDONISM **2 :** a way of life based on or suggesting the principles of hedonism ⟨she was a perfect specimen of selfish ~ —Donald Armstrong⟩

he·do·nist \-dᵊnəst, -dənə-\ *n* -s [Gk *hēdonē* + E *-ist*] **1 :** an adherent of ethical or psychological hedonism **2 :** one who practices hedonism

he·do·nis·tic \¦hēdᵊn¦istik, -də¦ni-, -tēk\ *also* **he·do·nis·ti·cal** \-tȯkəl, -tēk-\ *adj* **1 :** of, relating to, or characterized by hedonism **2 :** of, relating to, or typical of hedonists — **he·do·nis·ti·cal·ly** \-tȯk(ə)lē, -tēk-, -li\ *adv*

he·do·nom·e·ter \,hēdᵊn'ämədə(r), -də'nä-\ *n* [Gk *hēdonē* + E *-o-* + *-meter*] **:** a device for measuring pleasure

-he·dral \¦hēdrəl *sometimes chiefly Brit* ¦hed-\ *adj comb form* [NL *-hedron* + E *-al*] **:** having a (specified) number of surfaces ⟨*di*hedral⟩; having a (specified) kind of surface ⟨*eu*hedral⟩

hed·ri·oph·thal·ma \,hedrē,äf'thalmə\ [NL, irreg. fr. Gk *hedraios* sedentary, stationary (fr. *hedra* seat) + NL *-ophthalma*] *syn of* EDRIOPHTHALMA

-he·dron \¦hēdrən *sometimes* |,drän *or chiefly Brit* ¦he|\ *n comb form, pl* **-hedrons** \-nz\ *or* **-he·dra** \|drə\ [NL, fr. Gk *-edron,* fr. *hedra* seat — more at SIT] **:** geometrical figure or crystal having a (specified) form or number of surfaces ⟨holo*hedron*⟩ ⟨trapezo*hedron*⟩

hedy- *comb form* [NL, fr. Gk *hēdy-,* fr. *hēdys* — more at SWEET] **:** pleasant ⟨*hedy*phane⟩

he·dych·i·um \hē'dikēəm\ *n* [NL, fr. *hedy-* + Gk *chiōn* snow; fr. the white fragrant flowers — more at CHION-] **1** *cap* **:** a genus of tropical Asiatic herbs (family Zingiberaceae) having showy labiate flowers in a spike or spiky cluster — see BUTTERFLY LILY 1 **2** -s **:** any plant of the genus *Hedychium*

hed·y·phane \'hedə,fān\ *n* -s [G *hedyphan,* fr. *hedy-* sweet + G *-phan* -phane] **:** a mineral $(Ca,Pb)_5Cl(AsO_4)_3$ consisting of a yellowish white monoclinic lead and calcium arsenate and chloride — compare APATITE

he·dys·a·rum \hē'disərəm\ *n* [NL, fr. Gk *hēdysaron* goutweed, fr. *hēdy-* + *saron* broom] **1** *cap* **:** a genus of herbs (family Leguminosae) of the north temperate zone and northern Africa with racemose flowers and flat pods that separate into nearly orbicular joints **2** -s **:** any plant of the genus *Hedysarum*

hee·bie-jee·bies *also* **hee·by-jee·bies** \'hēbē'jēbēz\ *n pl* [coined *ab* 1925 by Billy DeBeck †1942 Am. cartoonist] **:** a tense nervous jumpy condition produced by various causes (as strain, irritation, fear, worry) and sometimes marked by hallucinations **:** jangled nerves **:** JITTERS — used with *the* ⟨the unrelenting hollow beat of the jungle drums gave them the *heebie-jeebies*⟩

¹heed \'hēd\ *vb* -ED/-ING/-s [ME *heden, heeden,* fr. OE *hēdan;* akin to OHG *huoten* to protect, guard; causative-denominatives fr. the root of OHG *huota* guard, protection — more at HOOD] *vi* **:** to concern oneself with or take notice of something **:** have regard or pay attention ⟨no sound save for the anxious telegraph machine, which was saying something important, although no one would ~ —Jean Stafford⟩ ~ *vt* **:** to concern oneself with or take notice of **:** have regard to **:** pay attention to **:** MIND ⟨had ~*ed* the call of a poor farmer —H.F.Wilkins⟩ ⟨unless the lessons of the experience are ~*ed* —Carl Spaatz⟩ ⟨will ~ only force —Rupert Emerson⟩

²heed \"\ *n* -s [ME *hede,* fr. *heden,* v.] **:** ATTENTION, NOTICE, REGARD, CARE ⟨no one paid any ~ to him —Upton Sinclair⟩ ⟨take ~ of what you do⟩ ⟨while he gives ~ to public opinion he is not unduly swayed by it —Victor Lewis⟩

heed·ful \'hēdfəl\ *adj* **:** taking heed **:** ATTENTIVE, MINDFUL, CAREFUL, OBSERVANT ⟨~ of what they were doing⟩ ⟨so ~ a writer —W.S.Maugham⟩ — **heed·ful·ly** \-fəlē, -li\ *adv* — **heed·ful·ness** *n* -ES

heed·less \'hēdləs\ *adj* **:** not taking heed **:** INATTENTIVE, UNMINDFUL, CARELESS, UNOBSERVANT, OBLIVIOUS ⟨~ of the younger lad's howling —Pearl Buck⟩ ⟨the ~ generosity and the spasmodic extravagance of persons used to large fortunes —Edith Wharton⟩ — **heed·less·ly** *adv* — **heed·less·ness** *n* -ES

¹hee-haw \'hē,hȯ\ *n, pl* **hee-haws** [imit.] **1 :** the bray of a donkey **2 :** a loud rude laugh **:** GUFFAW

²hee-haw \"\ *vi* **1** *of a donkey* **:** BRAY **2 :** to laugh loudly and rudely **:** GUFFAW

hee-hee *var of* HE-HE

¹heel \'hēl, *esp before pause or consonant* -ēəl\ *n* -s [ME *hele, heel,* fr. OE *hēla;* akin to OFris *hēl* heel, ON *hæl;* diminutives fr. the stem of OE *hōh* heel, hock — more at HOCK] **1 a :** the hind part of the foot of a human being below the ankle and behind the arch — opposed to *toe* **b :** the part of the hind limb of other vertebrates that is homologous with the human heel either occupying a similar situation (as in raccoons, bears, and other plantigrade animals) or relatively much raised above the ground (as in cows, horses, and other digitigrade animals) **:** HOCK **2 :** an anatomical structure suggestive of or associated with the hind part of the foot of a human being: as **a :** the hind part of a hoof **b :** the hind toe of a bird **c :** the spur of a cock **d :** either of the projections of a coffin bone **e :** the part of the palm of the hand nearest the wrist ⟨rubbed his eyes with the ~*s* of his hands —Warren Eyster⟩ **3 :** the foot as a symbol or instrument of violence or oppression ⟨even my bosom friend . . . has lifted his ~ against me —Ps 41:9 (RSV)⟩ ⟨under the ~ of a dictator⟩ **4 a :** one of the crusty ends of a loaf of bread **b :** one of the rind ends of a cheese **5 a :** the part of a shoe, boot, or slipper or of a sock or stocking that covers the heel of the human foot **b :** a solid part of a shoe or boot projecting downward and attached to or forming the back part of the sole under the heel of the foot — see SHOE illustration **6 a :** a latter or concluding part (as of a period of time) ⟨in the dismal ~ of . . . winter —Hamilton Basso⟩ **b :** REMAINDER, RESIDUE ⟨went to the nearest bottle of scotch and drained the ~ of it into his glass —Harry Sylvester⟩; *specif* **:** unburned and partially burned tobacco caked in the bowl of a pipe ⟨he knocked the ~ of his pipe of tobacco out on the palm of his hand —Seumas O'Kelly⟩ **7 :** a rear, low, or bottom part: as **a :** the after end of a ship's keel or the lower end of a mast **b :** the rear part of a plowshare **c :** the nut end of the bow of a musical instrument **d :** the part of a tool next to the tang or handle **e :** the crook of the head of a golf club where it joins the shaft — see GOLF illustration **f :** the base of a tuber or cutting or other part of a plant used for propagation of the plant **g :** the part of the rear extremity of a gun butt that is uppermost when the gun is held in firing position against the shoulder **h :** the rear end of a railroad frog **i :** a V-shaped piece of beef from the lower part of the round — called also *heel-of-round;* see BEEF illustration **j :** the base part of a ladder **k :** the lower end of a timber in a frame (as a post) **l :** the obtuse angle of the lower end of a rafter set sloping **8 :** a contemptible self-centered untrustworthy person **:** an altogether despicable individual; *esp* **:** a cheap double crosser ⟨a few ~*s* who appear to get away with it, but time eventually catches up with them —Frank Case⟩ **9** [²*heel*] **:** the act of heeling a ball in the game of rugby — **at heel** *adv* **:** close after **:** directly behind **:** in close pursuit ⟨the dog followed *at heel*⟩ — **by the heels :** in a tight grip **:** tightly constricted **:** securely confined ⟨the war, in which I'd hoped not to be caught, had me *by the heels* —Kenneth Roberts⟩ — **down at heel** *or* **down at the heel :** in or into a run-down, shabby, or slovenly condition ⟨old shoes which were *down at heel* —O.S.J.Gogarty⟩ ⟨they ran *down at the heel* somewhat as people will do anywhere when cut off from contact with a larger world —A.W.Long⟩ ⟨very *down at the heel* in appearance —Albert Hubbell⟩ — **on one's heels** *or* **upon one's heels :** following at heel — **on the heels of** *or* **upon the heels of :** close to the heels of **:** close after **:** immediately following ⟨*on the heels of* the news of what had happened —C.S.Forester⟩ **:** in close pursuit of ⟨stayed *on the heels of* the runaways⟩ — **to heel** *adv* **1 :** close to the heels **:** close behind ⟨at a word from his owner the dog moved *to heel*⟩ **2 :** into agreement, control, or subjection **:** into line ⟨the Commons, realizing that he was master still, came *to heel* —J.H.Plumb⟩ ⟨his disciplined mind, rejecting excuses, came heavily *to heel* —J.G.Cozzens⟩ ⟨it is hard to bring the eye *to heel* —D.L. Morgan⟩ — **under heel** *adv* **:** under control or subjection ⟨most of the continent was for a time brought *under heel* —A.L.Rowse⟩

²heel \"\ *vb* -ED/-ING/-s *vt* **1 a :** to furnish (as a shoe) with a heel **b** (1) **:** to fit (a gamecock) with a metal spur (2) **:** to arm (oneself) usu. with a gun ⟨wouldn't go through that territory without first ~*ing* himself⟩ **c** (1) **:** to supply or provide esp. with money or information ⟨a well-*heeled* customer⟩ ⟨better ~*ed* but still not flush⟩ ⟨I want to be ~*ed* when they book him —R.P.Warren⟩ (2) **:** to work for (a school newspaper or magazine) esp. as a reporter ⟨~*ed* the college paper —*Time*⟩ **2 :** to rope (as a steer) by the hind feet **3 a :** to follow closely after **:** follow at the heels of ⟨~*ed* them all the way up the ramp⟩ **b** *of a dog* **:** to urge (a lagging animal) onward by running after and nipping at the heels ⟨dogs ~*ed* the cattle and kept them on the move⟩ **4 a :** to exert pressure on with the heel: as (1) **:** to prod with the heel ⟨~*ed* his horse —A.B.Guthrie⟩ (2) **:** to crush with the heel ⟨~*ed* his cigarette out carefully —W.V.T.Clark⟩ **b :** to kick with the heel; *specif* **:** to pass (the ball) backward with the heel (as out of a scrum) in the game of rugby **5 :** to strike (a golf ball) with the heel of the club ~ *vi* **1 :** to move the heels rhythmically (as in dancing) **2 :** to move along at the heels of someone; *specif, of a dog* **:** to keep to heel ⟨a dog that ~*s* well⟩ **3 :** to move along rapidly **:** RUN ⟨~*ed* out of there as quick as he could⟩ **4 :** to heel a ball (as in the game of rugby) **5 :** to work for a school newspaper or magazine esp. as a reporter

³heel \"\ *vb* -ED/-ING/-s [alter. (prob. influenced by ¹*heel* and ²*heel*) of earlier *heeld, hield,* fr. ME *helden, heelden, hielden,* fr. OE *hieldan, heldan, hyldan;* akin to OE *heald* inclined, OHG *hald* inclined, *helden* to bow, ON *hallr* inclined, *hella* to pour out, Goth *hulths* inclination, favor, grace, Lith *šalis* side, region] *vi* **:** to tilt to one side **:** TIP, LEAN, CANT, LIST ⟨the sleigh was on one runner, ~*ing* like a yacht in a gale —Hamlin Garland⟩ — used esp. of a boat ⟨in such a strong wind the sailboat kept ~*ing* to the left⟩ and sometimes with *over* ⟨the subchaser ~*ed* over —C.F.Mitchell⟩ ~ *vt* **:** to cause (as a boat) to tilt **:** cause to list ⟨~*ing* the sloop well over and skimming her along to windward —K.M.Dodson⟩

⁴heel \"\ *n* -s **1 :** a tilt (as of a boat) to one side **:** LIST **2 :** the extent of a tilt (as of a boat) ⟨a ~ of six degrees to starboard⟩

heelaman *var of* HIELEMAN

¹heel-and-toe \¦=¦=¦=\ *adj* **:** marked by the alternating use of the heel and toe ⟨a *heel-and-toe* dance routine⟩; *specif* **:** marked by the use of a stride in which the heel of one foot touches the ground before the toe of the other foot leaves it and in which the leg is straight and the knee locked as each foot touches or leaves the ground ⟨a *heel-and-toe* walking race⟩

²heel-and-toe \"\ *n* -s **:** a heel-and-toe stride or dance step

heel-and-toe watch *n* **:** a deck watch alternating with an equal period of rest

heelball \'=,=\ *n* **1 :** the underpart of the heel of the foot **2 :** a composition of wax and lampblack used by shoemakers for polishing and by antiquaries in copying inscriptions on stone

heel block *n* **1 :** a block or last to support a shoe which is being heeled or from which heel lifts are being driven out **2 :** a filler block at the heel end of a railroad frog between the frog rails that reinforces the frog and that also serves as a foot guard

heel bone *n* **:** CALCANEUS

heel boom *or* **heeling boom** *n* **:** a log-loading boom against which the end of a log being loaded bears and is steadied as it is lifted and swung into position

heeld *var of* HIELD

heel·er \'hēlə(r)\ *n* -s [²*heel* + *-er*] **1 :** one that heels **2 :** a worker that puts heels on shoes **3 :** a dog that heels animals **4 :** a local worker for a political boss — called also *ward heeler*

heel fly *n* **:** a warble fly that attacks cattle; *esp* **:** a common warble fly (*Hypoderma lineata*) of warm parts of America

heel in *vt* [²*heel*] **:** to cover temporarily (the roots of a plant or often of several plants in one hole) with soil before setting permanently

heeling error *n* [fr. pres. part. of ³*heel*] **:** a deviation of a compass due to a ship's heeling which causes vertical magnetic forces to have a horizontal component and transverse horizontal magnetic forces to have a vertical component

heel·less \'hēlləs\ *adj* **:** having no heel

heel-of-round \'==¦=\ *n* **:** ¹HEEL 7i

heel pad *n* **:** a pad (as of leather) fixed over an insole to provide a comfortable support for the heel of the foot

heelpath \'=,=\ *n* [¹*heel* + *path;* fr. its being contrasted to *towpath,* the homophones *tow* and *toe* being punningly equated] **:** BERM d

heelpiece \'=,=\ *n* **:** a piece designed for, situated at, or forming the heel of something; *specif* **:** a piece of leather or other material used in making or repairing the heel of a shoe

heel plate *n* **1 :** BUTT PLATE **2 :** a metal plate (as one designed to protect against wear) for the heel of a shoe

heel plates 2: *1* surface type, *2* insert type

heelpost \'=,=\ *n* **1 :** a post to which a gate or door is hinged **2 :** the outer post of a stall partition in a stable

heel rope *n* **1 :** a rope fastened to the heel of a spar to control it **2 :** a rope used for hobbling a horse

heels *pl of* HEEL, *pres 3d sing of* HEEL

heel seat *n* **:** the part of a shoe to which the heel is attached

heels over head *adv, archaic* **:** head over heels

heel spur *n* **:** the calcar of a bat's foot spreading the tail membrane

heel stay *n* **:** a piece of fabric or rough-surfaced leather cemented on the inside of the shoe at the back seam to prevent slipping at the heel

heel string *n, dial* **:** ACHILLES' TENDON

heeltap \'=,=\ *n* [¹*heel* + *tap*] **1 :** a lift for the heel of a shoe **2 a** (1) **:** a small quantity of liquor remaining in a drinking glass (2) **:** a small quantity of liquor remaining in a bottle, cask, or other storage vessel **b :** DREGS **3 :** an imperfection in the glass bottom of a bottle marked by inequalities of thickness

heeltree \'=,=\ *n* [¹*heel* + *tree*] **:** the whiffletree of a harrow

heelwork \'=,=\ *n* **:** dance technique emphasizing accents with the heels

heem·raad \'hām,räd, 'hēm-\ *n, pl* **heemra·den** \-dᵊn\ *often cap* [Afrik, fr. *heem* farm, village, home + *raad* council, councilman] **1 :** a council assisting a local Boer magistrate in the government of rural districts in So. Africa prior to the establishment of British administration **2 :** a member of a heemraad

heer \'hi(ə)r\ *n* -s [ME (Sc dial.) *heir, hair,* lit., hair — more at HAIR] **:** an old unit of yarn measure of about 600 yards or ¹⁄₂₄ of a spindle

heerabol myrrh *var of* HERABOL MYRRH

heerd *or* **heered** *or* **heern** *dial past of* HEAR

heer·mann's gull \'her,mänz-\ *also* **heermann gull** *n, usu cap H* [after A. L. Heermann †1865 Am. naturalist] **:** a white-headed bluish gray gull (*Larus heermanni*) of the Pacific coast of No. America

heeze \'hēz\ *vt* -ED/-ING/-s [alter. of earlier *heise* — more at HOISE] **1** *dial Brit* **:** HOIST **2** *dial Brit* **:** EXALT

hef·ner candle \'hefnə(r)-\ *n, usu cap H* [after Friedrich von *Hefner*-Alteneck †1904 Ger. electrical engineer] **:** a German standard unit of luminous intensity equal to about 0.92 of the candela

¹heft \'heft\ *dial Brit var of* ³HAFT, ⁴HAFT

²heft \"\ *n* -s [fr. *heave,* after such pairs as E *weave: weft*] **1 :** WEIGHT, HEAVINESS ⟨his height and ~ varied a bit —A.J. Liebling⟩ ⟨plow horses of enormous ~ —Fannie Hurst⟩ **2** *archaic* **:** the greater part of something **:** BULK, MASS ⟨it's the ~ of their business —Mark Twain⟩

³heft \"\ *vb* -ED/-ING/-s *vt* **1 :** to heave up **:** HOIST, LIFT, RAISE ⟨~*ed* his pack higher on his broad shoulders —Norman Mailer⟩ **2 :** to test or ascertain the weight of by lifting or balancing ⟨picking the stone up and ~*ing* it —Emily Hahn⟩ ~ *vi* **:** to be heavy to a more or less clearly specified extent **:** WEIGH ⟨a box ~*ing* 15 pounds⟩ ⟨got an inch taller and ~*ed* heavier —C.T.Jackson⟩

heft·er \-tə(r)\ *n* -s **:** a worker who sorts and grades hides or leather

heft·i·ly \-tə̇lē\ *adv* **:** in a hefty manner **:** STRONGLY, MIGHTILY ⟨~ attacked the suggestion⟩

heft·i·ness \-tēnə̇s\ *n* -ES **:** the quality or state of being hefty

hefty \-tē, -ti\ *adj, usu* -ER/-EST [²*heft* + *-y*] **1 :** having considerable weight **:** quite heavy ⟨a couple of big ~ books⟩ **2 a** (1) **:** large or bulky and usu. strong **:** BIG, RUGGED ⟨a ~ six-footer —*Time*⟩ ⟨a ~ fellow, in the habit of standing no nonsense from his customers —W.S.Maugham⟩ (2) **:** exhibiting considerable strength or force **:** POWERFUL, MIGHTY ⟨struck a ~ blow⟩ **b :** having a size or extent that is by no means small or negligible **:** not insignificant in size ⟨had a ~ hill to climb over⟩ ⟨a ~ extent⟩ ⟨took a ~ hike⟩ **:** impressively large **:** good-sized ⟨a ~ majority —W.H.Whyte⟩ ⟨~ wage increases —*Time*⟩ ⟨paying up a pretty ~ sum for the settlement of certain debts —Claud Cockburn⟩ **:** IMPOSING ⟨tipped the scales at a ~ 224 pounds —Elizabeth Coatsworth⟩ **c :** quite rigorous or demanding by reason of size or extent ⟨received a ~ assignment that will take nearly all their time⟩ ⟨a ~ really tough job to do⟩ **3 :** generous in quantity **:** ABUNDANT, PLENTIFUL ⟨a ~ supply of ammunition —Clay Blair⟩ ⟨served up a ~ meal⟩ **syn** see HEAVY

he·gari \hə'garē, -'ger-, 'hegərē\ *n* -s [Ar (Sudan) *hegiri,* fr. Ar *hajari, hijāri* stony, stonelike] **:** any of several grain sorghums native to the Sudan region of Africa that resemble kafir and have chalky white seeds and of which one variety is grown in the southwestern U.S.

¹he·ge·li·an \hā'gālēən, hə'-, hā'jēl-, -'gēl-\ *adj, usu cap* [Georg W.F.*Hegel* †1831 Ger. philosopher + E *-ian*] **:** of or relating to Hegel or his objective idealism or dialectic

²hegelian \"\ *n* -s *usu cap* **:** a follower of Hegel or adherent of Hegelianism

he·ge·li·an·ism \-ə,nizəm\ *n* -s *usu cap* **1 :** Hegel's objective idealism according to which the rational and the real are equatable so that reason can arrive through dialectic at a comprehension of an absolute idea of which all phenomena are held to be partial representations **2 :** a philosophical system marked by the acceptance of Hegel's objective idealism and the revision of his dialectic or by rejection of his objective idealism and acceptance of his dialectic

he·ge·li·an·ize \-,nīz\ *vt* -ED/-ING/-s *often cap* **:** to bring into conformity with Hegel's objective idealism or dialectic

hegelian triad *n, usu cap H* **:** the three dialectical stages of thesis, antithesis, and synthesis often held to be Hegel's characterization of the progress of history or of logical thought

he·gel·ism \'hāgə,lizəm\ *n* -s *usu cap* [G.W.F.*Hegel* + E *-ism*] **:** HEGELIANISM

heg·e·mon \'hejə,män, 'hēj-\ *n* -s [Gk *hēgemōn* guide, leader] **:** one (as a political state) possessing hegemony

heg·e·mon·ic \¦=='mänik\ *also* **heg·e·mon·i·cal** \-nə̇kəl\ *adj* [Gk *hēgemonikos,* fr. *hēgemon-, hēgemōn* + *-ikos* -ic, -ical] **:** of, relating to, or possessing hegemony ⟨~ policies⟩ ⟨~ states⟩

he·gem·o·nis·tic \hə̇¦jemə¦nistik\ *adj* [*hegemony* + *-istic*] **:** HEGEMONIC

he·gem·o·ny \hə̇'jemənē, -ni *also* 'hejə,mōnē, -ni *sometimes* 'hegə,-\ *n* -ES [Gk *hēgemonia,* fr. *hēgemōn* guide, leader (fr. *hēgeisthai* to guide, lead) + *-ia* — more at SEEK] **1 :** preponderant influence or authority (as of a government or state) **:** LEADERSHIP, DOMINANCE ⟨aiming at world ~⟩ **2 :** a government or state possessing hegemony

he·gi·ra *also* **he·ji·ra** \hə̇'jīrə, 'hej(ə)rə\ *n* -s [fr. the *Hegira, Hejira,* the flight of Muhammad from Mecca in A.D. 622, fr. ML *hegira,* fr. Ar *hijrah,* lit., flight] **1** *usu cap* **:** the Muslim era **2 :** a journey or trip esp. when undertaken as a means of escaping from an undesirable or dangerous environment or as a means of arriving at a highly desirable destination ⟨the people wandered away on long ~*s* seeking new homesites near water —Frank Waters⟩; *specif* **:** a departure or flight made under such circumstances ⟨planning a ~ from the city to the cool peace of the mountains⟩ **3 :** EMIGRATION ⟨the ~ of many of the literati to Europe —C.I.Glicksberg⟩; *esp* **:** a mass exodus ⟨the ~ of farmers looking for new, cheap, fertile land —R.E.Riegel & G.D.Harmon⟩

he·gu·men \hə̇'gyümən\ *n* -s [LL *hegumenus,* fr. LGk *hēgoumenos,* fr. Gk *hēgoumenos* leader, president, fr. pres. part. of *hēgeisthai* to lead — more at SEEK] **:** the head of a religious community (as a small monastery) in the Eastern Church — used also as a title of honor for certain monks who are priests; compare ARCHIMANDRITE

¹heh *like* EH\ *interj* [imit.] — used typically to indicate interrogation and often to express scorn, amusement, or surprise

²heh *var of* HE

HEH *abbr* Her Exalted Highness; His Exalted Highness

he·he \'hā(,)hā\ *n, pl* **hehe** *or* **hehes** *usu cap* **1 a :** a Bantu-speaking people of Tanganyika Territory **b :** a member of such people **2 :** a Bantu language of the Hehe people

he-he *or* **hee-hee** \'hē'hē\ *interj* [imit.] — used to express or as an imitation of derisive laughter or a senile or foolish giggle

he-huckleberry \'='==- — *see* BERRY\ *n* **1 :** an ironwood (*Cyrilla racemiflora*) of the southern U.S. **2 :** PRIVET ANDROMEDA

HEI *abbr* high explosive incendiary

hei·au \'hā,aú\ *n* -s [Hawaiian] **:** a pre-Christian Hawaiian temple or other place of worship (as a stone platform or an earthen terrace)

heid \'hēd\ *dial var of* HEAD

¹hei·deg·ge·ri·an \¦hī,de¦girēən\ *adj, usu cap* [Martin *Heidegger* b1889 Ger. philosopher + E *-ian*] **:** of or relating to Heidegger or his existentialist philosophy

²heideggerian \"\ *n* -s *usu cap* **:** a follower of Heidegger or adherent of his existentialist philosophy

hei·del·berg \'hīdᵊl,bərg, -,bėg\ *adj, usu cap* [fr. *Heidelberg,* Germany] **:** of or from the city of Heidelberg, Germany **:** of the kind or style prevalent in Heidelberg

heidelberg man *or* **heidelberg race** *n, usu cap H* **:** an early Pleistocene man that is known from a massive chinless fossilized jaw with distinctly human dentition, that is the earliest hominoid generally assigned to the genus *Homo,* that is usu. placed in a distinct species (*H. heidelbergensis*), and that is considered to be closely related to Neanderthal man

heif·er \'hefə(r)\ *n* -s [ME *hayfare, hayfre, heyfre, heffre,* fr. OE *hēahfore,* perh. fr. *hēah* high + *-fore* (akin to OE *fearr* bull) — more at HIGH, PARE] **1 :** a young cow: **a :** one that is less than three years old and has freshened only once **b :** one that has never borne young or developed the proportions of a mature cow — used esp. in the meat trade **2 :** WOMAN; *esp* **:** a young woman

heif·er·ette \¦hefə¦ret\ *n* -s **:** a large heavy heifer having nearly the size and development of a mature cow

heigh \'hī, 'hā\ *interj* [origin unknown] — used to express cheeriness or exultation or to indicate interrogation or attract attention

[1]**heigh-ho** \'ˌ'ˌ\ *interj* [*heigh* + *ho*] — used typically to express boredom, weariness, or sadness and sometimes to serve as a cry of encouragement

[2]**heigh-ho** \"ˌ"\ *n* -s : [3]FLICKER

[1]**height** *also* **hight** \'hīt, *usu* -īd·+V *also* -ītth *sometimes* -īth\ *n* -s [ME *heighthe, heighte, heghte, heyeth,* fr. OE *hīehthu, hēhthu;* akin to OHG *hōhida* height, ON *hæth,* Goth *hauhitha;* derivatives fr. the root of E [1]*high*] **1 a :** the highest part of something material ⟨finally reached the ~ of the mountain⟩ : uppermost section or area or region : top part : SUMMIT, APEX, PINNACLE ⟨plunged down from the ~ of the tower⟩ **b :** the highest point of something not material ⟨at the ~ of fame⟩ : most advanced point : ZENITH ⟨the ~ of culture⟩ : most extreme degree ⟨the ~ of stupidity⟩ : fullest possible degree ⟨at the ~ of success⟩ : CULMINATION ⟨the ~ of all their desires⟩ ⟨the ~ of passion⟩ : most active or intense part : CLIMAX ⟨the ~ of an argument⟩ ⟨at the very ~ of the storm⟩ **2 a** (1) : the distance extending from the bottom to the top of something standing upright ⟨measured the ~ of the building⟩ or from the bottom to an arbitrarily chosen upper point ⟨the tree has a ~ of five feet at its first branch⟩ (2) : the distance extending from the lowest point to the highest point of an animal body esp. of a human being in a natural standing position ⟨a man who is six feet in ~⟩ or from the lowest point to an arbitrarily chosen upper point ⟨a dog two feet in ~ at the shoulder⟩ : STATURE **b** (1) : the extent of elevation above a level ⟨the land reaches a ~ of 600 feet above sea level⟩ : distance extending upwards : ALTITUDE ⟨impossible to know the exact ~ reached by the rocket⟩ (2) : the degree of approximation of the tongue to the palate in pronouncing a vowel **3 :** the quality of possessing sufficient or considerable or relatively great highness or stature or altitude ⟨a triumphal arch that would have been more impressive if it had had more ~⟩ **4 a :** an extent of land (as a hill, mountain, or plateau) rising to a considerable degree above the surrounding country : a lofty eminence **b :** a high place or point or position ⟨the ~s and depths of love⟩ **5 a** *obs* : an advanced degree of distinction (as in rank) : notable excellence : SUPERIORITY ⟨exceeded by the ~ of happier men —Shak.⟩ **b** (1) *obs* : HAUGHTINESS (2) *archaic* : loftiness of mind or spirit ⟨with something of the old Roman ~ about him —Charles Lamb⟩ **6** *obs* **a :** degree of geographical latitude **b :** position (as of a ship) off a coast

[2]**height** *also* **hight** \'hīt, 'hīkt\ *vt* -ED/-ING/-S *dial* : HEIGHTEN

height·en \'hīt[ə]n\ *vb* **heightened; heightened; heightening** \-t(ə)niŋ\ **heightens** [[1]*height* + *-en*] *vt* **1 a** (1) : to increase the amount or degree or detail or extent of : AUGMENT, AMPLIFY ⟨~*ing* his speed —Edith Sitwell⟩ ⟨conflict has ~*ed* citizens' awareness of what they want —Constance Green⟩ ⟨this only ~*s* our admiration —Edmund Wilson⟩ ⟨~*ed* their campaign against news censorship—*Americana Annual*⟩ (2) : to make (as a color, an emotional experience) brighter or more glowing or more intense : DEEPEN, INTENSIFY ⟨happiness ~*ed* the natural ruddiness of her cheeks⟩ (3) : to delineate more sharply : make more evident : bring out more strongly : point up : HIGHLIGHT ⟨shade ~*s* the brightness of light —Havelock Ellis⟩ ⟨the benevolent expression of his face was ~*ed* in later years by his white hair and beard —F.H.Dewey & E.S.Bates⟩ (4) : to make more acute : SHARPEN ⟨which had ~*ed* his appreciation of the more austere pleasures of the afternoon —Archibald Marshall⟩ (5) : to make more poignant ⟨their sorrow was ~*ed* by their forced absence from home⟩ (6) : to increase the impact of : STRENGTHEN ⟨rapid action ~*s* the effect of the drama⟩ **b** (1) : to give physical height to or increase the physical height of : raise high or higher : ELEVATE ⟨the building had been ~*ed* by the addition of a second story⟩ (2) : to raise above the ordinary or trite : make better by adding stature or distinction to ⟨how can we use this fact to ~ our civilization —C.A.Lindbergh b. 1902⟩ **2** *obs* : to cause to be elated or excited : EXALT ⟨being ~*ed* with this victory —James Ussher⟩ ~ *vi* **1** *archaic* : to become great or greater in physical height : GROW, RISE ⟨as we rode up the carriageway, the rock seemed to ~ marvelously —J.H. Newman⟩ **2 a :** to become great or greater in amount, degree, detail, or extent ⟨his youthful impatience ~*ed* —A.J.Cronin⟩ **b :** to become brighter (as of a color) or more glowing or more intense ⟨though the color had ~*ed* in his cheek, he did not flinch from his friend's gaze —James Joyce⟩ **syn** see INTENSIFY

height finder *n* : a device used to determine the height of an airborne object

height gauge *n* **1 :** a gauge having a micrometer or a vernier scale for measuring heights **2 :** a C-shaped metal device for measuring the foot-to-face height of printing type or mounted plates

heighth \'hī(t)th\ *chiefly dial var of* HEIGHT

height measure *n* : HYPSOMETER

height of burst : the vertical angle between the base of a target and the point of burst of artillery fire usu. as viewed from the firing point

height of land : [2]DIVIDE 2a

heights *pl of* HEIGHT, *pres 3d sing of* HEIGHT

heights to paper : the height of printing type measured from foot to face and standardized at 0.9186 inch in English-speaking countries — called also *type height*

heil \'hī(ə)l\ *vb* -ED/-ING/-S [G, interj., hail (used by the Nazis in such phrases as *Heil Hitler!* Hail Hitler! and *Sieg heil!* Hail victory!), fr. MHG, fr. *heil*, adj., healthy, fr. OHG — more at WHOLE] : to salute with the German exclamation *heil*

heilaman *var of* HIELAMAN

hei·li·gen·schein \'hīləgən,shīn\ *n* -s [G, lit., halo, fr. *heiliger* saint (fr. *heilig* holy, fr. OHG *heilag*) + *schein* shine, light, fr. OHG *scīn;* akin to OHG *skīnan* to shine — more at HOLY, SHINE] : a bright light around the shadow of a person's head (as on a field or lawn) caused by diffraction and reflection of sunlight by dewdrops

heils·ge·schich·te \'hīlzgə,shiktə\ *n* -s *usu cap* [G, fr. *heil* salvation + *geschichte* history] : an interpretation of history emphasizing God's saving acts and viewing Jesus Christ as central in redemption

heilt·suk *or* **haelt·zuk** \'hā(ə)lt,sük, -,zük\ *n, pl* **heiltsuk** *or* **heiltsuks** *or* **haeltzuk** *or* **haeltzuks** *usu cap* **1 :** a group of peoples including the Bellabella, China Hat, and Wikeno **2 :** a member of the Heiltsuk group

hei-mi·ao \'hā'mē'au̇\ *n, pl* **hei-miao** *or* **hei-miaos** *usu cap* *H&M* [Chin (Pek) *hei*[1] *miao*[2], fr. *hei*[1] black + *miao*[2] sprouts, shoots, descendants] **1 :** the principal division of the Miao peoples inhabiting the southeastern part of Kweichow province in southern China **2 :** a member of the Hei-Miao

hei·min \'hāmən\ *n, pl* **heimin** [Jap, fr. *hei* common + *min* people] : the class of commoners consisting of peasants and laborers and traders in the Japanese social scale — compare KWAZOKU, SHIZOKU

hei·nesque \(')hī;nesk\ *adj, usu cap* [Heinrich *Heine* †1856 Ger. poet and writer + E *-esque*] : of, relating to, or resembling the style of Heine

[1]**hei·nie** *also* **hei·ne** *or* **hei·ney** \'hīnē, -ni\ *n* -s [G *Heinrich* Henry (a common German name) + E *-ie*] : GERMAN; *esp* : a German soldier — usu. used disparagingly

[2]**heinie** \"\ *n* -s [alter. of [4]*hinder*] *slang* : BUTTOCKS

hei·nous \'hānəs *sometimes* 'hēn- *or* 'hīn-\ *adj* [ME *heynous,* fr. MF *haineus* hateful, fr. *haine* hate (fr. *hair* to hate, of Gmc origin; akin to OS *haton* to hate) + *-eus* -ous — more at HATE] : hatefully or shockingly evil : grossly bad : enormously and flagrantly criminal : ABOMINABLE, EXECRABLE ⟨~ offenses⟩ ⟨a ~ act of treason⟩ ⟨a ~ accusation⟩ ⟨proposals of the most ~ nature —Elinor Wylie⟩ **syn** see OUTRAGEOUS

hei·nous·ly *adv* [ME *heynously,* fr. *heynous* + *-ly*] : in a heinous manner

hei·nous·ness *n* -ES : the quality or state of being heinous

[1]**heir** \'e(ə)r, 'a(ə)l, |ə\ *n* -s [ME *eir, heir,* fr. OF, fr. L *hered-, heres;* akin to Gk *chēros* left, bereaved, OE *gān* to go — more at GO] **1 a :** one who inherits or is entitled to succeed to the possession of property after the death of its owner: as (1) : HEIR AT LAW (2) : [2]HERES (3) : one who in modern civil codes based upon the civil law (as in Europe) succeeds to the entire estate of a person by operation of law or by testament and has a right of renunciation and usu. a right of entry with the benefit of inventory (4) *Scots law* : one taking heritable property by destination : one who succeeds only to movable estate (5) : one who receives some of the property of a deceased person by operation of law, by virtue of a will, or in any of various other ways **b :** one who receives or is entitled to receive property during the lifetime of a former owner ⟨made his friend ~ of the farm after deciding to live elsewhere⟩ **2 :** one who inherits or is entitled to succeed to a hereditary rank, title, or office upon the death or removal from office by other cause (as abdication) of the holder ⟨~ to the principality of Monaco⟩ ⟨succession to the throne by the king's ~ following his abdication⟩ **3 :** one to whom something other than property (as a position of leadership, participation in a tradition or culture, a natural talent, a quality of character) is transmitted or seems to be transmitted in accordance with or apart from the wish of a predecessor and with or without the necessity of direct succession ⟨looked upon himself as the logical ~ of the slain dictator⟩ ⟨was the ~ of the two chief traditions of scholarship in Europe —R.W.Southern⟩

[2]**heir** \"\ *vt* -ED/-ING/-S *now chiefly dial* : INHERIT

heir apparency *n, pl* **heir apparencies** : APPARENCY 3

heir apparent *n, pl* **heirs apparent** [ME] **1 :** an heir whose right to an inheritance is indefeasible in law if he survives the legal ancestor ⟨became *heir apparent* to the throne when his grandfather . . . was killed —*Current Biog.*⟩ **2 :** HEIR PRESUMPTIVE — not used technically **3 :** one whose succession (as to a position or role) appears certain under existing circumstances ⟨*heir apparent* to Mr. Churchill as prime minister —*U.S. News & World Report*⟩ ⟨the Council of Europe, the parliamentary *heir apparent* of a federated Europe —J.R. Wike & A.Z.Rubinstein⟩

heir at law *n, pl* **heirs at law** **1** *Eng common law* : an heir in whom an intestate's real property as distinguished from his personal estate is vested by operation of law and not by will or by curtesy or by right of dower — called also *legal heir;* compare DEVISEE, LEGATEE **2** *usu* **heir-at-law** *Scots law* : an heir in whom by operation of the law of intestate succession the heritable estate and part or all of the movables of a decedent are vested — called also *heir of line, heir whatsoever, legal heir*

heir·dom \-rdəm\ *n* -s **1** *archaic* : HERITAGE **2** *archaic* : HEIRSHIP

heir·ess \'erəs, 'ar-\ *n* -ES : a female heir; *esp* : a female heir to great wealth

heiress apparent *n, pl* **heiresses apparent** **1 :** a female heir apparent **2 :** HEIRESS PRESUMPTIVE — not used technically

heiress presumptive *n, pl* **heiresses presumptive** : a female heir presumptive ⟨*heiress presumptive* to the British throne —*N.Y. Herald Tribune*⟩

heir general *n, pl* **heirs general** [ME *heire generall*] : HEIR AT LAW

heir in tail *n, pl* **heirs in tail** : one who expects to become or becomes a tenant in possession of a fee-tail estate in land upon the death of a tenant of the estate under special rules of common law or statute governing succession to such an estate as contrasted with the rules of inheritance under a statute of descent

heir·less \'ᵊləs\ *adj* : having no heir

heir·loom \'ˌ,lüm\ *n* [ME *heirlome,* fr. *heir* + *lome* implement, tool — more at LOOM] **1 :** a piece of property (as a deed or charter) that is viewed by law or special custom or will or settlement as an inseparable part of an inheritance and is so inherited with the inheritance **2 :** something having special monetary or sentimental value or significance that is handed on either by or apart from formal inheritance from one generation to another ⟨the pin is a family ~⟩ ⟨a spiritual ~ that must, at all cost, be preserved intact —Edward Sapir⟩

heirmos *var of* HIRMOS

heir of entail *n, pl* **heirs of entail** **1 :** HEIR IN TAIL **2** *Scots law* : an heir called to the succession by a destination : an heir of tailzie

heir of inventory *n, pl* **heirs of inventory** *Scots law* : BENEFICIARY HEIR

heir of line *n, pl* **heirs of line** *Scots law* : HEIR AT LAW 2

heir of provision *n, pl* **heirs of provision** *Scots law* : one who may or may not be an heir-at-law and who is called to succeed to property by the provisions of a deed or a contract or a bond : an heir by destination

heir of the body *n, pl* **heirs of the body** : a lineal heir esp. as contrasted with a collateral heir

heir portioner *n, pl* **heirs portioners** **1** *Scots law* : one of two or more female heirs coming in the absence of male issue into a succession to an estate and sharing equally according to degree of consanguinity, the share of any deceased female in the same degree going by representation to her heirs-at-law in the order of the eldest male, then other males, and finally the females **2** *Scots law* : one of two or more usu. female heirs in the same degree taking equal shares per capita

heir presumptive *n, pl* **heirs presumptive** **1 :** an heir whose legal right to an inheritance may be defeated by the birth of a nearer relative ⟨the *heir presumptive* had been the king's brother —*Springfield (Mass.) Union*⟩ — compare HEIR APPARENT **2 :** one whose succession (as to a position or role) appears likely but not certain ⟨*heir presumptive* at the foreign office —*New Statesman & Nation*⟩

heirs *pl of* HEIR, *pres 3d sing of* HEIR

heir·ship \'ˌ,ship\ *n* [ME *areschip,* fr. *are, eir* heir + *-schip, -ship* -ship] **1 a :** the condition of being an heir **b :** the right of inheritance **2** *archaic* : HERITAGE

heir whatsoever *n, pl* **heirs whatsoever** *Scots law* : HEIR AT LAW 2

hei·sen·berg's principle \'hīz[ə]n,bərgz-\ *n, usu cap H* [after Werner K. *Heisenberg* b1901 Ger. physicist] : UNCERTAINTY PRINCIPLE

[1]**heist** \'hīst\ *vb* -ED/-ING/-S [alter. of [2]*hoist*] *vt* **1** *chiefly dial* : HOIST **2** *slang* : to appropriate unlawfully and usu. with violence : make off with : STEAL **3** *slang* : to commit armed robbery on : hold up; *specif* : to break into and rob ~ *vi, chiefly dial* : HOIST

[2]**heist** \"\ *n* -s **1** *slang* **a :** armed robbery : HOLDUP; *specif* : the act of breaking into and robbing an establishment (as a bank) **b :** THEFT **2** *slang* : something (as money, jewels) acquired by robbery or theft

heist·er \-tə(r)\ *n* -s **1** *chiefly dial* : one that hoists **2** *slang* : ROBBER, THIEF

heit \'hīt\ *var of* HAIT

hei-ti·ki \'hā'tēkē\ *n, pl* **hei-tiki** *or* **hei-tikis** [Maori, fr. *hei* to hang + *Tiki,* the first man in Maori legend] : a greenstone charm in the shape of a human figure worn as a neck pendant by the Maoris

hei-tiki

[1]**he·ja·zi** \'hejəzē\ *n* -s *cap* [Ar *ḥijāzīy,* fr. *Ḥijāz* Hejaz, kingdom of western Arabia] : a native or inhabitant of the Hejaz

[2]**hejazi** \"\ *adj, usu cap* **1 :** of, relating to, or characteristic of the Hejaz **2 :** of, relating to, or characteristic of the people of the Hejaz

hejira *var of* HEGIRA

hektograph *var of* HECTOGRAPH

hel·arc·tos \he'lärktəs, -,täs\ *n, cap* [NL, irreg. fr. *heli-* + Gk *arktos* bear — more at ARCTIC] : a genus of mammals (family Ursidae)

hel·beh \'helbə\ *n* -s [Ar *ḥulbah*] : fenugreek seed that is mixed with durra in a flour commonly used in Egypt

held *past of* HOLD

held ball *n* : a situation in basketball in which two opponents have their hands on the ball at the same time so that neither can gain control without undue roughness and which results in a jump ball

hel·den·tenor \'heldənˈtä,nȯ(ə)r, -tä,nō(ə)r, -;tenər\ *n, pl* **helden·te·no·re** \-,tä'nȯrə, -'nȯrə\ *or* **heldentenors** [G, fr. *held* hero + *tenor*] : a tenor voice suited to heroic (as Wagnerian) roles : DRAMATIC TENOR

hele *var of* [2]HEAL

he·le·idae \hə'lēə,dē\ [NL, fr. *Helea,* genus of flies (fr. Gk *heleia,* fem. of *heleios* of a marsh, marsh-dwelling, fr. *helos* marsh) + *-idae* — more at HELODES] *syn of* CERATOPOGONIDAE

hel·e·na \'helənə\ *adj, usu cap* [fr. *Helena,* Mont.] : of or from Helena, the capital of Montana ⟨*Helena* businessmen⟩ : of the kind or style prevalent in Helena

hel·e·nalin \,helə'nalən, -nāl-\ *n* -s [*helen-* (fr. NL *Helenium,* genus name of the sneezeweed *Helenium autumnale*) + *-al-* (fr. NL *autumnale,* specific epithet of the sneezeweed *Helenium autumnale*) + *-in*] : a poisonous bitter crystalline compound $C_{15}H_{18}O_4$ that is the active principle of sneezeweed

hel·en flower \'helən-\ *also* **hel·en's flower** \-nz-\ *n, usu cap H* [NL *Helenium*] : a plant of the genus *Helenium*

hele·nin \'helənən, hə'lēnən\ *n* -s [NL *Helenium* + E *-in*] **1 :** alantolactone or a mixture from elecampane root containing it **2 :** HELENALIN

he·le·ni·um \hə'lēnēəm\ *n* [NL, fr. L, a plant, elecampane, fr. Gk *helenion,* perh. fr. *helenē* wicker basket; akin to Gk *helix* (adj.) twisted, (n.) spiral, anything of spiral shape, *helissein* to turn, wind, *eilein* to wind, roll, *eilyein* to enfold, enwrap — more at VOLUBLE] **1** *cap* : a genus of American herbs (family Compositae) with heads of yellow-rayed flowers and truncate-style branches — see SNEEZEWEED 1 **2** -s : any plant of the genus *Helenium*

hel·e·och·a·ris \,helē'äkərəs\ *syn of* ELEOCHARIS

hel·eo·plankton \'helē(,)ō+\ *n* [ISV *heleo-* (fr. Gk *heleos,* gen. of *helos* marsh) + *plankton* — more at HELODES] : plankton typical of small bodies of still fresh water

hel·e·pole \'helə,pōl\ *also* **he·lep·o·lis** \hə'lepələs\ *n, pl* **helepoles** \'helə,pōlz\ *also* **helepolises** \hə'lepələsəz\ [F & L; F *hélépole,* fr. L *helepolis,* fr. Gk *helepolis,* fr. *helein* to take + *polis* city — more at SELL, POLICE] : an ancient siege engine composed of a movable tower covering a battering ram

helgramite *or* **helgrammite** *var of* HELLGRAMMITE

[1]**heli-** *or* **helio-** *comb form* [L, fr. Gk *hēli-, hēlio-,* fr. *hēlios* — more at SOLAR] : sun ⟨*Heli*ornis⟩ : the sun ⟨*helio*centric⟩ ⟨*helio*scope⟩ : sunlight : solar energy ⟨*helio*gravure⟩ : sun and ⟨*helio*lithic⟩

[2]**heli-** *comb form* [by shortening] : helicopter ⟨*heli*port⟩ ⟨*heli*mail⟩

he·li·a·cal \hə'līəkəl, hē'-,he'-\ *adj* [LL *heliacus, heliacus* (fr. Gk *hēliakos,* fr. *hēlios* sun) + E *-al*] : relating to or near the sun — used esp. of the last setting of a star before and its first rising after invisibility due to conjunction with the sun — **he·li·a·cal·ly** \-ək(ə)lē\ *adv*

heliacal cycle *n* : SOLAR CYCLE

heliacal year *n* : a Sothic year

he·li·am·pho·ra \,helē'am(p)fərə\ *n, cap* [NL, fr. *heli-* (fr. Gk *helissein* to roll, wind) + L *amphora*] : a genus of So. American pitcher plants (family Sarraceniaceae) native to the mountains of British Guiana and having scapes of nodding pink or white flowers

he·li·an·tha·ceous \,helē,an;thāshəs\ *adj* [NL *Helianthus* + E *-aceous*] : resembling, belonging to, or related to the genus *Helianthus*

he·li·an·thate \,helē'an,thāt\ *n* -s [*helianthin* + *-ate*] : a salt of helianthin ⟨the ~ of streptomycin⟩

he·li·an·the·mum \,helē'an(t)thəməm\ *n* [NL, fr. [1]*heli-* + *-anthemum*] **1** *cap* : a genus of Eurasian herbs or undershrubs (family Cistaceae) having showy variously colored flowers with fugacious petals **2** -s : any plant of the genus *Helianthemum* — called also *rockrose, sunrose*

he·li·an·thin \,helē'an(t)thən\ *also* **he·li·an·thine** \",-an-,thēn\ *n* -s [ISV *helianth-* (fr. NL *Helianthus;* fr. its color) + *-in, -ine*] **1 :** a red compound $(CH_3)_2N^+{=}C_6H_4{=}NNH{-}C_6H_4SO_3^-$ of quinone structure obtained by acidifying methyl orange **2 :** METHYL ORANGE

he·li·an·thus \-an(t)thəs\ *n* [NL, fr. [1]*heli-* + *-anthus*] **1** *cap* : a genus of tall erect or sometimes much-branched American annual or perennial herbs (family Compositae) comprising the sunflowers and having flower heads with purple or yellow disk flowers and showy yellow sterile rays — see JERUSALEM ARTICHOKE **2** -ES : any plant of the genus *Helianthus*

he·li·ast \'hēlē,ast\ *n* -s [Gk *hēliastēs* member of the Heliaea, fr. *hēliazesthai* to be a member of the Heliaea, fr. *Hēliaia* Heliaea, supreme court at Athens, public place in which the court was held] : DICAST — **he·li·as·tic** \;hēlē;astik\ *adj*

he·li·az·o·phyte \,hēlē'azə,fīt\ *n* -s [Gk *hēliazein* to bask in the sun (fr. *hēlios* sun) + E *-o-* + *-phyte* — more at SOLAR] : HELIOPHYTE

helic- *or* **helico-** *comb form* [Gk *helik-, heliko-,* fr. *helik-, helix* spiral — more at HELENIUM] : helix : spiral ⟨*helic*ine⟩ ⟨*helico*graph⟩

[1]**hel·i·cal** \'heləkəl, -lēk- *also* 'hēl-\ *adj* [*helic-* + *-al*] **1 :** of, relating to, or having the form of a helix; *broadly* : SPIRAL 1a ⟨the ~ thread of a bolt⟩ ⟨metal tubing with annular or ~ fins⟩ **2 :** having the angle of a helix formed about the pitch cylinder rather than being straight and parallel to the axis (as of a gear or milling cutter) ⟨~ teeth⟩ ⟨gears cut in a ~ rather than a spur shape for smoother operation⟩

[2]**helical** \"\ *n* -s : something helical in form (as a coil extension spring)

helical gear *also* **helical** *n* -s : a gear wheel having teeth set obliquely to the axis of rotation : SCREW WHEEL

hel·i·cal·ly \-k(ə)lē, -li\ *adv* **1 :** in a helical manner ⟨thread is wound ~ on the spool⟩ ⟨~ cut gear wheels⟩ **2 :** by use of a helical ⟨an iron cot with a link spring ~ attached to the angle-steel frame⟩

helical milling *n* : milling in which the work (as a helical gear) is given simultaneously a rotary motion and an endways motion — called also *spiral milling*

helical gears

hel·iced \'heləst, 'hel-\ *adj* **1 :** decorated with or having helices **2 :** having the form of a low conical spiral (as the shell of a snail of the genus *Helix*)

hel·i·cel·la \,helə'selə, ,hēl-\ *n, cap* [NL, fr. *helic-* + *-ella*] : a genus of land snails (family Helicidae) including several snails of veterinary importance as intermediate hosts of flukes and of some nematode lungworms of sheep and other ruminants

helices *pl of* HELIX

hel·i·chryse \'helə,krīs\ *n* -s [NL *Helichrysum*] : HELICHRYSUM 2

hel·i·chry·sum \,helə'krīsəm\ *n* [NL, fr. Gk *helichrysos,* fr. *helik-* helic- + *chrysos* gold — more at CHRYSALIS] **1** *cap* : a large genus of mostly African and Australian plants (family Compositae) with flower heads having shining involucres which retain their color when dried — see STRAWFLOWER **2** -s : any plant of the genus *Helichrysum*

he·lic·i·dae \hə'lisə,dē\ *n pl, cap* [NL, fr. *Helic-, Helix,* type genus + *-idae*] : a family of pulmonate land snails (suborder Stylommatophora) including the common edible snail and a number of pests — see [2]HELIX

he·lic·i·form \-sə,fȯrm\ *adj* [ISV *helic-* + *-iform*] : SPIRAL

hel·i·ci·na \,helə'sīnə\ *n* [NL, fr. *helic-* + *-ina*] **1** *cap* : a genus of operculate land snails (suborder Rhipidoglossa) that occur chiefly in warm regions and are distinguished by a short-spired shell, a single auricle, and a pulmonary chamber replacing the gill **2** -s : any mollusk shell of the genus *Helicina*

heli·cit·ic \;helə;sid·ik, ;hel-\ *adj* [*helic-* + *-itic*] *of metamorphic rock* : marked by bands of inclusions showing the original bedding or schistosity of the rock and in many places cutting through the later formation

hel·i·cline \'helə,klīn\ *n* -s [*heli-* (fr. Gk *helix* spiral) + *-cline*] : a gradually ascending and curving ramp

helico- — see HELIC-

[1]**hel·i·coid** \'helə,kȯid\ *or* **hel·i·coi·dal** \,helə'kȯid[ə]l\ *adj* [*helicoid* fr. Gk *helikoeidēs* of spiral form, fr. *helik-* helic- + *-oeidēs* -oid; *helicoidal* fr. *helicoid* + *-al*] **1 :** having the properties of a helicoid **2 :** forming or arranged in a spiral ⟨~ inflorescence⟩; *specif, of a gastropod shell* : having the form of a flat coil or flattened spiral ⟨*Planorbis* is characterized by a ~ shell⟩

[2]**helicoid** \"\ *n* -s : a surface resembling that of a screw thread that is generated by a curve which rotates about a straight line and moves in the direction of the line with a velocity whose ratio to the velocity of rotation is constant

helicoidal saw *n* : a stonecutter's saw consisting of an endless cable made of three steel wires twisted together, supplied with sand and water, and drawn along marble or other stone to cut it — called also *wire saw*

helicoid cyme *n* : BOSTRYX

hel·i·con \ˈheləˌkän, -ləkən\ *n* -s [prob. fr. Gk *helik-, helix* spiral + E *-on* (as in *bombardon*)] **:** a very large bass tuba used in military bands that is made circular for carrying over the shoulder and around the body when marching

helicon

hel·i·co·nia \ˌheləˈkōnēə, -nyə\ *n* [NL, fr. L, fem. of *Heliconius* of Helicon, fr. Gk *Helikōnios,* fr. *Helikōn* Helicon, mountain in Greece] **1** *cap* **:** a genus of tropical American perennial herbs (family Musaceae) that have inconspicuous flowers in terminal spikes often subtended by brightly colored bracts and large leaves often showily veined or mottled with red or yellow — see WILD PLANTAIN **2** -s **:** any plant of the genus *Heliconia*

¹hel·i·co·nian \ˌheləˈkōnēən, -nyən\ *adj, usu cap* [L *Heliconius* + E *-an*] **:** of or relating to the Boeotian mountain Helicon supposed by the ancient Greeks to be the residence of Apollo and the Muses

²heliconian \"\ *n* -s [NL *Heliconius* + E *-an*] **:** a butterfly of *Heliconius* or a related genus

hel·i·co·ni·idae \ˌheləkəˈnīəˌdē\ *n pl, cap* [NL, fr. *Heliconius,* type genus + *-idae*] *in some classifications* **:** a family of chiefly tropical American butterflies with long fore wings and small rounded hind wings that is commonly included in the family Nymphalidae

hel·i·co·ni·us \ˌheləˈkōnēəs\ *n* [NL, fr. L, of Helicon] **1** *cap* **:** a large Neotropical genus of long-winged butterflies that are often brilliantly colored or mimetic and that with related American butterflies constitute a subfamily of Nymphalidae or in some classifications the separate family Heliconiidae **2** *pl* **heliconii** \-ēˌī\ **:** any butterfly of the genus *Heliconius*

¹heli·cop·ter \ˈheləˌkäptə(r), -lēˌk- *also* ˈhēl- *or sometimes substand* ˈhēlēəˌk- *or* ˈhēlyəˌk- *sometimes* ˌ==(=)ˈ==\ *n* -s *often attrib* [F *hélicoptère,* fr. *hélico-* (fr. Gk *heliko-* helic-) + *ptère* (fr. Gk *pteron* wing) — more at FEATHER] **:** an aircraft whose support in the air is derived chiefly from the aerodynamic forces acting on one or more rotors turning about substantially vertical axes

²helicopter \"\ *or* **heli·copt** \-pt\ *vb* -ED/-ING/-S *vi* **:** to travel by or as if by helicopter ⟨can ~ from the station to the airfield⟩ ⟨winged seeds that . . . come ~*ing* down —Richard Church⟩ ~ *vt* **:** to transport by helicopter ⟨~*ed* the officials aboard the ship⟩

hel·i·co·ru·bin \ˌheləkōˈrübən\ *n* -s [*helico-* (fr. NL *Helic-, Helix,* genus name of *Helix pomatia*) + L *ruber* red + E *-in*] **:** a hemoprotein occurring in the intestine and hepatopancreas of pulmonate gastropods and in the hepatopancreas of the crayfish

hel·i·co·trema \-kōˈtrēmə\ *n* -s [NL, fr. *helic-* + *-trema*] **:** the minute opening by which the two scalae communicate at the top of the cochlea of the ear

helic·te·res \ˌheləkˈtirēz, hə'liktəˌr-\ *n, cap* [NL, fr. Gk *heliktēres,* pl. of *heliktēr* anything twisted, fr. *helik-, helix* spiral — more at HELENIUM] **:** a large genus of tropical trees and shrubs (family Sterculiaceae) with axillary flowers and fruits consisting of five twisted carpels — see SCREW TREE

he·lic·tis \həˈliktəs\ *n, cap* [NL, fr. *hel-* (prob. fr. Gk *helos* marsh) + Gk *iktis* yellow-breasted marten] **:** a genus of mammals (family Mustelidae) comprising the ferret-badgers

he·lic·tite \həˈlikˌtīt, ˈheləkˌt-\ *n* -s [*helict-* (fr. Gk *heliktos* twisted, rolled, fr. *helik-, helix* spiral) + *-ite*] **:** an irregular stalactite with branching convolutions or spines

hel·i·go·land trap \ˈheləgōˌland-\ *n, usu cap H* [fr. *Heligoland* (Helgoland), island in the North sea; fr. its original use there] **:** a large funnel-shaped structure of wire mesh opening into a smaller enclosure used for trapping birds (as for banding)

heling *pres part of* HELE

¹he·lio \ˈhēlēˌō\ *n* -s [by shortening] **:** HELIOGRAPH

²helio \"\ *n* -s [by shortening] **:** HELIOTROPE

helio- — see HELI-

he·lio·centric \ˌhēlēō+\ *adj* [¹*heli-* + *-centric*] **:** referred to or measured from the sun's center or appearing as if seen from it **:** having or relating to the sun as the center (as of the planetary system) ⟨the ~ theory of Copernicus⟩ — compare GEOCENTRIC

heliocentric latitude *n* **:** the celestial latitude of a celestial body as if seen from the center of the sun

heliocentric longitude *n* **:** the celestial longitude of a celestial body as if seen from the center of the sun — opposed to *geocentric longitude*

heliocentric parallax *n* **:** the parallax of a celestial body measured with the earth's orbit around the sun as a baseline **:** the angle subtended at the celestial body by the radius of the earth's orbit — called also *annual parallax, stellar parallax*

he·lio·chrome \ˈhēlēəˌkrōm\ *n* -s [¹*heli-* + *-chrome*] **:** a photograph in natural colors made orig. by use of a photohalide form of silver chloride

he·lio·chromy \-mē\ *n* -ES [F *héliochromie,* fr. *hélio-* ¹heli- + *-chromie* -chromy] **:** COLOR PHOTOGRAPHY

he·li·o·don \ˈhēlēəˌdän\ *n* -s [NL, fr. ¹*heli-* + *-odon* (fr. Gk *hodos* way, path) — more at CEDE] **:** a device consisting of a pivoted platform and a spotlight on a vertical track used to simulate sun and shadow orientation for any latitude and day of year for a proposed building

he·li·o·dor \ˈhēlēəˌdȯ(ə)r\ *n* -s [G] **:** a golden-yellow beryl found in southern Africa

he·lio·gram \-ˌgram\ *n* [¹*heli-* + *-gram*] **:** a message transmitted by a heliograph

¹he·lio·graph \-raf, -räf\ *n* [ISV ¹*heli-* + *-graph*] **1 a :** PHOTOENGRAVING 2b **b :** PHOTOGRAPH **c :** PHOTOHELIOGRAPH **2 :** an apparatus for telegraphing by means of the sun's rays thrown from a mirror — compare HELIOTROPE 3

²heliograph \"\ *vb* **:** to signal by means of a heliograph

he·lio·graph·ic \ˌhēlēəˈgrafik\ *adj* **1** [F *héliographique,* fr. *hélio-* ¹heli- + *-graphique* -graphic] **:** of, relating to, or by means of heliography or a heliograph ⟨~ communication⟩ **2** [¹*heli-* + *-graphic*] **:** SOLAR 1 ⟨~ latitude⟩

he·li·og·ra·phy \ˌhēlēˈägrəfē\ *n* -ES **1** [F *héliographie,* fr. *hélio-* ¹heli- + *-graphie* -graphy] **:** an early photographic process producing a photoengraving on a metal plate coated with an asphalt preparation; *broadly* **:** PHOTOGRAPHY **2** [¹*heli-* + *-graphy*] **:** the system, art, or practice of signaling with a heliograph

he·lio·gra·vure \ˌhēlēōgrəˈvyü(ə)r\ *n* [F *héliogravure,* fr. *hélio-* ¹heli- + *gravure*] **:** PHOTOGRAVURE

he·li·ol·a·try \ˌhēlēˈälə·trē\ *n* -ES [¹*heli-* + *-latry*] **:** sun worship

¹he·li·o·lite \ˈhēlēəˌlīt\ *n* -s [NL *Heliolites,* genus of corals, fr. ¹*heli-* + *-lites* (prob. fr. F *-lithe* -lite)] **:** a fossil coral of the family Heliolitidae

²heliolite \"\ *n* -s [F *héliolite,* fr. *hélio-* ¹heli- + *-lite*] **:** aventurine feldspar

he·li·o·lith·ic \ˌhēlēōˈlithik\ *adj* [¹*heli-* + *-lithic*] **1 :** marked by, observing, or associated with practices (as sun worship and the erection of megaliths) held by some diffusionists to constitute a single widespread neolithic culture originating in Egypt ⟨~ culture⟩ ⟨~ peoples⟩ ⟨~ monuments⟩ **2 :** postulating an Egyptian origin for heliolithic traits found as the basis of higher culture in many parts of the world ⟨the ~ theory⟩

he·li·o·lit·i·dae \ˌhēlēōˈlidəˌdē\ *n pl, cap* [NL, fr. *Heliolites,* type genus + *-idae*] **:** a family of Paleozoic tabulate corals prob. related to the Helioporidae but having 12 radial septa in the large zooecia

he·li·om·e·ter \ˌhēlēˈämədə(r)\ *n* [F *héliomètre,* fr. *hélio-* ¹heli- + *-mètre* -meter] **:** a visual telescope that has a divided objective with two movable parts which give a double image and that was orig. designed for measuring the apparent diameter of the sun and later used for measuring angles between stars but is now largely replaced by photographic methods

he·lio·met·ric \ˌhēlēōˈme·trik\ *adj* [F *héliométrique,* fr. *hélio-* ¹heli- + *-métrique* -metric] **:** of, employing, or obtained by use of a heliometer ⟨~ observations⟩ ⟨~ results⟩ — **he·lio·met·ri·cal·ly** \-rək(ə)lē\ *adv*

he·li·om·e·try \ˌhēlēˈämə·trē\ *n* -ES **:** the art or practice of measuring with the heliometer

he·lio·micrometer \ˌhēlē(ˌ)ō+\ *n* [¹*heli-* + *micrometer*] **:** an instrument for determining heliographic positions of spots and flocculi shown on direct photographs of the sun or on spectroheliograph plates

he·li·oph·i·la \ˌhēlēˈäfələ\ *n, cap* [NL, fr. ¹*heli* + *-phila*] **:** a genus of southern African annual or partly woody perennial herbs (family Cruciferae) sometimes cultivated for their long showy racemes of bright blue flowers with white eyes

he·lio·phile \ˈhēlēəˌfīl\ *n* -s [¹*heli-* + *-phile*] **:** one attracted or adapted to sunlight ⟨~s flocking to the beach⟩; *specif* **:** an aquatic alga adapted to attain maximum exposure to sunlight

he·li·oph·i·lous \ˌhēlēˈäfələs\ *also* **he·lio·phil·ic** \ˌhēlēəˈfilik\ *adj* [¹*heli-* + *-philous* or *-philic*] **:** attracted by or adapted to sunlight

he·lio·phobe \ˈhēlēəˌfōb\ *n* -s [¹*heli-* + *-phobe*] **:** one that is abnormally sensitive to the effect of sunlight

he·li·oph·o·bous \ˌhēlēˈäfəbəs\ *also* **he·lio·pho·bic** \ˌhēlēəˈfōbik *also* -ˈfäb-\ *adj* [¹*heli-* + *-phobous* or *-phobic*] **:** avoiding the sun **:** shade loving ⟨~ plants⟩

he·li·o·phyl·lite \ˌhēlēōˈfiˌlīt\ *n* -s [Sw *heliophyllit,* fr. ¹*heli-* + *-phyll* + *-it* -ite] **:** a mineral approximately $Pb_6As_2O_7Cl_4$ consisting of oxychloride of lead and arsenic that is apparently dimorphous with ecdemite

he·li·o·phyte \ˈhēlēəˌfīt\ *n* -s [¹*heli-* + *-phyte*] **:** a plant thriving in or tolerating full sunlight

¹he·li·o·pol·i·tan \ˌhēlēəˈpälət°n\ *adj, usu cap* [LL *Heliopolitanus,* fr. L *Heliopolites* Heliopolitan (fr. Gk *Hēliopolitēs,* fr. *Hēliopolis* Heliopolis, ancient city in Lower Egypt) + *-anus* -an] **:** of or relating to ancient Heliopolis, esp. Heliopolis, Egypt

²heliopolitan \"\ *n* -s *cap* [L *Heliopolitanus,* fr. *Heliopolites* + *-anus* -an] **:** a native or inhabitant of the ancient city of Heliopolis

he·li·o·por·i·dae \ˌhēlēəˈpȯrəˌdē\ *n pl, cap* [NL, fr. *Heliopora,* type genus (fr. ¹*heli-* + *-pora*) + *-idae*] **:** a family of tabulate corals (order Coenothecalia) comprising the blue coral and extinct related forms and having the corallum composed of large zooecia interspersed with more numerous smaller tubes occupied by simple polyps without tentacles or reproductive organs

he·li·op·sis \ˌhēlēˈäpsəs\ *n, cap* [NL, fr. ¹*heli-* + *-opsis*] **:** a small genus of American herbs (family Compositae) resembling a sunflower with fertile ray flowers and a conical receptacle

he·li·or·nis \-ˈȯrnəs\ *n, cap* [NL, fr. *heli-* + *-ornis*] **:** the type genus of Heliornithidae including a single tropical American sun-grebe (*H. fulica*)

he·li·or·nith·i·dae \-ˌȯrˈnithəˌdē\ *n pl, cap* [NL, fr. *Heliornith-, Heliornis,* type genus + *-idae*] **:** a family of tropical aquatic birds (order Gruiformes) comprising the sun-grebes and having a head and bill like those of a rail, a long body and tail, short legs, and lobed feet

¹helios *pl of* HELIO

²he·li·os \ˈhēlēˌäs, -ēəs\ *n* -ES [NL, fr. Gk *hēlios* sun — more at SOLAR]**:** LUMINANCE 2

he·li·o·sis \ˌhēlēˈōsəs\ *n, pl* **helio·ses** \-ōˌsēz\ [NL, fr. LL, exposure to the sun, fr. Gk *hēliōsis,* fr. *hēliousthai* to be exposed to the sun, to be sunburned (fr. *hēlios* sun) + *-sis*] **:** SUNSTROKE

he·li·o·stat \ˈhēlēəˌstat\ *n* -s [NL *heliostata,* fr. ¹*heli-* + *-stata* (fr. Gk *-statēs* -stat)] **1 :** an instrument consisting of a mirror mounted on an axis moved by clockwork by which a sunbeam is steadily reflected in one direction — compare COELOSTAT **2 :** a geodetic heliotrope — **he·li·o·stat·ic** \ˌhēlēəˈstad·ik\ *adj*

he·lio·tactic \ˌhēlēōˈtaktik\ *adj* [¹*heli-* + *-tactic*] **:** of or relating to heliotaxis

he·lio·tax·is \ˌhēlēōˈtaksəs\ *n* [NL, fr. ¹*heli-* + *-taxis*] **:** phototaxis in which sunlight is the stimulus

he·lio·therapy \ˈhēlēō+ˌ-\ *n* [¹*heli-* + *therapy*] **:** the use of sunlight or of an artificial source of ultraviolet, visible, or infrared radiation for therapeutic purposes

he·li·o·this \ˌhēlēˈōthəs\ *n, cap* [NL, irreg. fr. Gk *hēliōtis* (n.) dawn, (adj.) of the sun, fr. *hēlios* sun] **:** a genus of medium-sized noctuid moths including several forms having larvae that are destructive pests of cultivated crops — see CORN EARWORM

heliothis moth *n, Austral* **:** CORN EARWORM

he·lio·trope \ˈhēlēəˌtrōp, -lyə-, *Brit usu* ˈhel-\ *n* -s [L *heliotropium,* fr. Gk *hēliotropion,* fr. *hēlios* sun + *-tropion* (fr. *tropos* turn) — more at SOLAR, TROPE] **1 a** *obs* **:** a plant of which the flower or stem turns toward the sun **b** [NL *Heliotropium*] **:** a plant of the genus *Heliotropium; esp* **:** GARDEN HELIOTROPE **2 c :** GARDEN HELIOTROPE 1 **2 :** BLOODSTONE 1 **3 :** an instrument used in geodetic surveying for making long-distance observations by means of the sun's rays thrown from a mirror **4 a :** a variable color averaging a moderate purple that is bluer, lighter, and stronger than cobalt violet, manganese violet, or average amethyst, bluer and deeper than average lilac (sense 3a), and redder, stronger, and slightly lighter than mignon **b :** a moderate reddish purple that is redder and duller than bishop's violet **c :** any of various dyes imparting this color **5 :** a perfume imitating the scent of the garden heliotrope (sense 1)

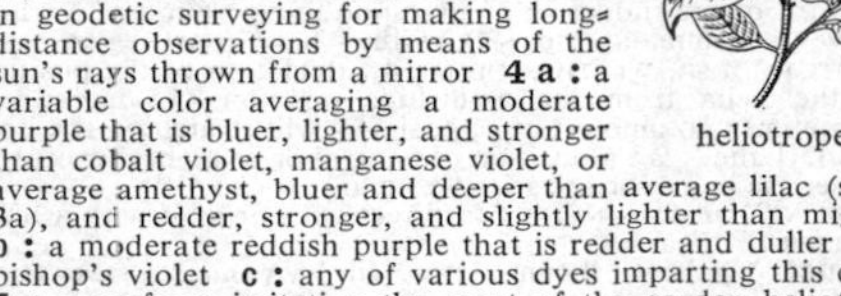

heliotrope

heliotrope gray *n* **:** a pale purple to purplish gray that is redder than plumbago gray

heliotropian *n* -s [modif. of Gk *hēliotropion*] *obs* **:** HELIOTROPE

he·lio·tropic \ˌ=(=)=ˈtrōpik, -räp-\ *adj* [ISV ¹*heli-* + *-tropic*] **:** characterized by heliotropism ⟨spiders are negatively ~⟩ — **he·lio·tropi·cal·ly** \-pək(ə)lē\ *adv*

he·lio·tro·pin \ˌhēlēəˈtrōpən, ˌhēlēˈä·trəp-\ *n* -s [ISV *heliotrop-* (fr. NL *Heliotropium*) + *-in*] **:** PIPERONAL

he·lio·tro·pism \ˌhēlēˈä·trəˌpizəm, ˈhēlēəˌtrōˌp-\ *n* [ISV ¹*heli-* + *-tropism*] **:** phototropism in which sunlight is the orienting stimulus (as in sunflower heads turning with the sun) — compare APHELIOTROPISM

he·li·o·tro·pi·um \ˌhēlēəˈtrōpēəm\ *n, cap* [NL, fr. Gk *hēliotropion* heliotrope — more at HELIOTROPE] **:** a genus of herbs and shrubs (family Boraginaceae) having small white or purple fragrant salver-shaped flowers in spikes — see HELIOTROPE 1b

he·lio·type \ˈhēlēəˌtīp\ *n* [¹*heli-* + *type*] **:** COLLOTYPE

he·lio·typography \ˌhēlē(ˌ)ō+\ *or* **he·lio·typy** \ˈhēlēəˌtīpē\ *n* -ES [*heliotypography* fr. ¹*heli-* + *typography; heliotypy* ISV ¹*heli-* + *-typy*] **:** the collotype process

he·lio·zoa \ˌhēlēəˈzōə\ *n pl, cap* [NL, fr. ¹*heli-* + *-zoa*] **:** an order of Actinopoda consisting of free-living holozoic usu. freshwater protozoans that reproduce by binary fission or budding and comprise the sun animalcules — see ACTINOPHRYS, ACTINOPODA, ACTINOSPHAERIUM — **he·lio·zo·an** \ˌhēlēəˈzōən\ *adj or n* — **he·lio·zo·ic** \-ōik\ *adj*

heli·port \ˈhelə *also* ˈhēlə+ˌ-\ *n, often attrib* [²*heli-* + *port* (harbor)] **:** a landing and takeoff place for a helicopter (as on the roof of a building in the central area of a city)

he·lip·ter·um \həˈliptərəm\ *n, cap* [NL, fr. ¹*heli-* + Gk *pteron* wing — more at FEATHER] **:** a genus of African and Australian herbs (family Compositae) having a plumose pappus and densely silky hairy achenes and grown as an everlasting

heli·so·ma \ˌheləˈsōmə, ˌhel-\ *n, cap* [NL, fr. *heli-* (prob. fr. Gk *helix* spiral) + *-soma* — more at HELENIUM] **:** a genus of freshwater snails (family Planorbidae) including intermediate hosts of echinostomes and possibly other flukes of medical or veterinary importance

he·li·um \ˈhēlēəm\ *n* -s *often attrib* [NL, fr. Gk *hēlios* sun + NL *-ium* — more at SOLAR] **:** a very light colorless inert gaseous element that is the most difficult of all gases to liquefy, that occurs throughout the universe but in economically extractable amounts only in certain natural gases (as in the Texas panhandle and Kansas), and that is used chiefly in inflating airships and balloons, in arc welding and other metallurgical and chemical processes as an inert gaseous shield, and in diluting oxygen for breathing (as by patients with respiratory ailments and by divers) — symbol *He;* see ALPHA PARTICLE; ELEMENT table

helium group *n* **:** the group of elements forming group zero of the periodic table **:** the group of inert gases

helium I \ˌ===ˈwən\ *n* **:** normal liquid helium boiling at 4.2°K under a pressure of 1 atmosphere and capable of existing between the critical point of 5.2°K and 2.26 atmosphere and the lambda point of 2.19°K

helium II \ˌ===ˈtü\ *n* **:** superfluid helium formed from helium I by cooling below the lambda point and characterized by a very low viscosity and very high thermal conductivity

¹helix \ˈhēliks, ˈhel-\ *n, pl* **heli·ces** \ˈheləˌsēz, ˈhēl-\ *also* **helix·es** \ˈhēliksəz, ˈhel-\ [L, fr. Gk — more at HELENIUM] **1 :** something spiral in form: as **a :** an ornamental volute (as in an Ionic or Corinthian capital) **b :** a coil formed by winding wire around a uniform tube **2 :** the incurved rim of the external ear **3 :** a curve traced on a cylinder by the rotation of a point crossing its right sections at a constant oblique angle **:** a space curve with turns of constant slope from the base and constant distance from the axis **:** the curve described by the thread of a bolt or by a tubular coil spring; *broadly* **:** a three-dimensional curve with one or more turns around an axis (as the space curve described by a conical coil spring)

²helix \"\ *n, cap* [NL, fr. L, something spiral in form, volute] **:** a genus (the type of the family Helicidae) of orig. chiefly Eurasian and African pulmonate land snails having a coiled shell with a low conical spire and a wide reflexed lip and including the chief edible snails (as *H. pomatia*) as well as a number of pests of cultivated plants (as the brown snail)

helix angle *n* **:** the constant angle between the tangent to a helix and a generator of the cylinder upon which the helix lies

helix·in \ˈhēliksən, ˈhel-\ *n* -s [NL *helix* (specific epithet of *Hedera helix*) (fr. L *helix* ivy, volute) + E *-in*] **:** HEDERIN

helix·om·e·ter \ˌ==ˈsäməd·ə(r)\ *n* [*helix* + *-o-* + *-meter*] **:** a tubular instrument in which an electric light and a prism and lens system enable visual examination of a small-arms bore (as in criminal investigation)

¹hell \ˈhel\ *n* -s *often attrib* [ME, fr. OE; akin to OE *helan* to conceal, OHG *hella* hell, *helan* to conceal, ON *hel* heathen realm of the dead, Goth *halja* hell, L *celare* to hide, conceal, Gk *kalyptein* to cover, conceal, Skt *śaraṇa* screening, protecting; basic meaning: concealing] **1 a :** a place or state of the dead or of the damned: as **(1) :** a place usu. under the ground in which the dead continue to exist **:** NETHERWORLD, HADES, SHEOL ⟨I will slay the last of them with the sword . . . though they dig into ~ —Amos 9:1-2 (AV)⟩ ⟨spake of the resurrection of Christ that his soul was not left in ~ —Acts 2:31 (AV)⟩ — compare LIMBO **(2) :** a netherworld in which the damned must suffer everlasting punishment (as by fire) and malevolent beings live under the rule of the devil — called also *Gehenna;* compare PURGATORY **(3) :** a spiritual state of lasting separation from God or of complete isolation **:** eternal death **b (1) :** a nether domain of the devil and the demons **(2) :** the fallen angels headed by Satan **:** the devil and the demons of hell **:** the powers of evil **c** *Christian Science* **:** ERROR 2b, SIN **2 a :** a place or state of misery, torment, or wickedness ⟨hundreds of gallons of spilled gasoline turn the . . . wreckage into a concentrated ~ of searing flames —H.G. Armstrong⟩ ⟨condemned to go through the ~ of war —F.L. Allen⟩ — used interjectionally to express irritation, irony, incredulity, or surprise ⟨oh ~⟩ ⟨expert, ~! — he's no more an expert than I am⟩; often used as a generalized term of abuse ⟨go to ~⟩ or as a mild oath ⟨to ~ with it⟩ or as an intensive ⟨~ yes⟩; often used with *in* ⟨what in ~ are you doing⟩ or *the* ⟨get the ~ out of here⟩ or *to* ⟨lives way to ~ out in the sticks⟩ ⟨hope to ~ you're right⟩ or *as* ⟨cold as ~⟩ ⟨serious as all ~⟩ ⟨he sure as ~ did it⟩ or in the phrases *hell of a* ⟨in a ~ of a mess⟩ ⟨heard a ~ of a crash⟩ ⟨a good singer and one ~ of an actor⟩ and *hell out of* ⟨scared the ~ out of him⟩ ⟨the big guns smashed ~ out of them⟩ **b :** a place or state of turmoil, disorder, or destruction **:** PANDEMONIUM ⟨all ~ broke loose⟩ **:** HAVOC ⟨raise ~ with the true shape of the facts —John Lardner⟩ ⟨the wind played ~ with the garden⟩ **:** RUIN ⟨said the country was going to ~ in a hack⟩ **c :** a cause of torment, tumult, or havoc; *specif* **:** severe verbal castigation ⟨got ~ from his boss for being late⟩ **d (1) :** unrestrained fun or sportiveness **:** TOMFOOLERY ⟨the children were full of ~ and the house was soon a shambles⟩ **(2) :** the vexations or adventurous satisfaction of an activity — usu. used in the phrase *just for the hell of it* ⟨broke all the windows just for the ~ of it⟩ ⟨hopped a freight just for the ~ of it⟩ **(3) :** the most vexing, pleasing, or notable feature — used with *the* ⟨the ~ of it was that nobody could understand him⟩ ⟨the ~ of the plan is that it works⟩ **3 a** *archaic* **:** a receptacle into which a tailor throws his pieces **b :** HELLBOX **4 :** GAMBLING HOUSE **:** a cheap place of public resort **:** HALL, HOUSE, JOINT ⟨dining . . . in the cheap obscurity of a Soho eating ~ —Aldous Huxley⟩ — **hell and gone :** an extreme or inaccessible distance ⟨no sooner does one build sluice boxes . . . than a freshet occurs and carries them to *hell and gone* —S.E. Morison⟩ — often used for emphasis ⟨he would be the *hell and gone* away from here by now —G.B.Whitlaw⟩ — **hell and high water** *or* **hell or high water :** difficulties of whatever kind or size ⟨will stand by his convictions come *hell or high water*⟩ ⟨led his men through *hell and high water*⟩ — **hell for :** extremely concerned with or insistent on ⟨he was *hell for* efficiency and made life miserable for any man who could not fulfill his duties —H.A.Chippendale⟩ — **hell on :** extremely hard on or destructive to ⟨such a life was *hell on* his digestion and soon brought on an ulcer⟩ — **hell to pay :** the devil to pay ⟨if he's late there'll be *hell to pay*⟩ — **what the hell** — used interjectionally to express carefree indifference or cynical resignation ⟨*what the hell,* I may as well go⟩

²hell \"\ *vi* -ED/-ING/-S **1 :** to behave in a noisy and often dissolute way **:** CAROUSE ⟨Saturday night was their night to ~ a little —H.E.Giles⟩ ⟨come down to the city to ~ around for a weekend —Merle Miller⟩ **2 :** to travel at high speed ⟨a police radio car came ~*ing* down between the elevated pillars, siren blasting —Jack Jones b.1923⟩ ⟨with passengers numbering from two to nine, we ~*ed* all over the countryside —Bill Mauldin⟩

hellabaloo *var of* HULLABALOO

hel·lad·ic \heˈladik\ *adj, usu cap* [L *Helladicus* Greek, fr. Gk *Helladikos,* fr. *Hellad-, Hellas* Greece + *-ikos* -ic] **:** of or relating to the Bronze Age culture of the Greek mainland lasting from about 2500 to 1100 B.C. — compare AEGEAN, GREEK 1

hel·la·do·the·ri·um \ˌhelədōˈthirēəm\ *n, cap* [NL, fr. Gk *Hellad-, Hellas* Greece + NL *-o-* + *-therium*] **:** a genus of extinct Pliocene giraffes of Greece and Asia Minor

hell·and·ite \ˈhelənˌdīt\ *n* -s [G *hellandit,* fr. Amund *Helland* †1918 Norw. geologist + G *-it* -ite] **:** a mineral consisting of a silicate of the cerium metals with aluminum, iron, manganese, and calcium

hell·ben·der \ˈhelˌbendə(r)\ *n* **1 a :** a large voracious aquatic salamander (*Cryptobranchus alleganiensis*) that is common in the streams of the Ohio valley and that attains a length of 18 inches **b :** a related species (*C. bishopi*) of the Ozark region **2** *slang* **:** one that is exceedingly reckless or otherwise extreme

¹hell-bent \ˈ=ˌ=\ *adj* **1 :** stubbornly often recklessly determined **:** dead set ⟨they are *hell-bent* to cut taxes again before election —*New Republic*⟩ ⟨*hell-bent* on having his own way⟩ **2 :** moving at a reckless speed **:** going full tilt ⟨wonder if every next turn won't be good-bye after . . . meeting *hell-bent* trucks —Alfred Powers⟩; *broadly* **:** RECKLESS ⟨*hell-bent* adventure⟩ **3 :** moving willfully or speedily on the way to destruction ⟨a *hell-bent* civilization is about to blow its top —Christopher Morley⟩

²hell-bent \"\ *also* **hell-bent for election** *adv* **:** in a hell-bent manner **:** at full tilt ⟨the 15 . . . mares raced *hell-bent* for the first turn —G.F.T.Ryall⟩

hell-bind \ˈ=ˌ=\ *n* [¹*hell* + *bind* (bine)] **:** DODDER

hell bomb *n, sometimes cap H* **:** HYDROGEN BOMB

hellbox \ˈ=ˌ=\ *n* **:** a receptacle into which a printer throws damaged or discarded type material

hellbroth \ˈ=ˌ=\ *n* **:** a brew for working black magic

hellcat \ˈ=ˌ=\ *n* **1 :** WITCH 1b(2) **2 :** one given to tormenting others; *esp* **:** SHREW

hell–diver \ˈ=,==\ *n* **:** a pied-billed grebe or other rather small grebe

helldog \ˈ=,=\ *n* **:** HELLHOUND

hell driver *n* **:** one that engages in hell driving esp. professionally

hell driving *n* **:** the performance of daredevil stunts with an automobile esp. for the entertainment of spectators

hel·le·bore \ˈheləˌbō(ə)r\ *n* -s [L *helleborus, elleborus,* fr. Gk *helleboros,* perh. fr. *hellos, ellos* fawn + *-boros* (fr. *bibrōskein* to devour); akin to Gk *elaphos* deer — more at ELK, VORACIOUS] **1 a :** a plant of the genus *Helleborus* — see BEAR'S-FOOT 1 **b :** a poisonous herb of the genus *Veratrum* **2 a :** the dried rhizome and root of any medicinal herb of the genus *Helleborus* (as the black hellebores *H. niger* and *H. orientalis* and the green hellebore *H. viridis*) or a powder or extract of this used by the ancient Greeks and Romans in treating mental and other disorders **b :** the dried rhizome and root of a white hellebore (*Veratrum album* or *V. viride*) or a powder or extract of this containing alkaloids (as protoveratrine) used as a cardiac and respiratory depressant and also as an insecticide

hellebore green *n* **:** a moderate olive green that is yellower, lighter, and stronger than forest green (sense 2), cypress, or Lincoln green and greener and stronger than holly green (sense 2)

hellebore red *n* **:** a moderate purplish red that is bluer and darker than average rose, redder and duller than violine pink, and redder and paler than magenta rose

hel·lebo·rine \ˈheləbəˌrīn, heˈlebərən\ *n* -s [NL (in older classifications, a genus of orchids), fr. L, a kind of hellebore, fr. Gk *helleborinē,* fr. *helleboros* + *-inē* (fr. fem. of *-inos* -ine)] **:** any of several orchids: as **a :** a plant of the genus *Cephalanthera* (as *C. rubra*) **b :** a plant of the genus *Epipactis* (as *E. helleborine*) **c :** RATTLESNAKE PLANTAIN

hel·leb·o·rus \heˈlebərəs\ *n, cap* [NL, fr. L, hellebore — more at HELLEBORE] **:** a genus of Eurasian perennial herbs (family Ranunculaceae) having deeply divided leaves and showy flowers with five petaloid sepals

helled *past of* HELL

hel·lene \ˈheˌlēn\ *n* -s [Gk *Hellēn*] **1** *cap* **:** a Greek of the Hellenic period **2** *cap* **:** a Greek of the modern kingdom of Greece **3** *usu cap* **:** a person marked by intellectual or artistic Hellenism

¹hel·len·ic \heˈlenik, -nēk *sometimes* -lēn-\ *adj, usu cap* [Gk *Hellēnikos,* fr. *Hellēn* + *-ikos* -ic] **1 :** GREEK; *specif* **:** of, relating to, or characteristic of Greek history or culture between the first Olympiad in 776 B.C. and the conquests of Alexander ending in 323 B.C. constituting a period of a growing sense of solidarity among the independent city states and of original and influential achievements in politics, art, literature, and philosophy **:** CLASSICAL ⟨the controlled intensity of thought and emotion of the *Hellenic* Athenians was not for the people of Hellenistic times—E.H.Short⟩ **2 :** marked by intellectual or artistic Hellenism ⟨the *Hellenic* temper of modern humanism⟩ — **hel·len·i·cal·ly** \-nək(ə)lē, -nēk-, -lī\ *adv, often cap*

²hellenic \ˈ"\ *n* -s *usu cap* **:** classical Greek; *esp* **:** GREEK 2a

hel·le·nism \ˈheləˌnizəm\ *n* -s *usu cap* [Gk *Hellēnismos* imitation of things Greek, use of pure Greek language, fr. *hellēnizein* to speak Greek, imitate the Greeks, fr. *Hellēn* + *-izein* -ize] **1 :** GRECISM 1 **2 a :** conformity to or imitation of ancient Greek thought, customs, or styles ⟨the *Hellenism* of some Seleucid Jews with their Greek hats and gymnasium exercises⟩ ⟨*Hellenism* in the art of the classical revival of the 18th century⟩ **b :** devotion to Greece or to Greek culture or ideals ⟨an Attic poet noted for his intense *Hellenism*⟩ **3 :** Greek civilization esp. as modified in the Hellenistic period by oriental influences **4 :** a body of humanistic and classical ideals associated with ancient Greece and including reason, the pursuit of knowledge and the arts, moderation, civic responsibility, and bodily development ⟨a revival of *Hellenism* fostered by some British Victorians⟩ — compare HEBRAISM 2 **5 :** the Greeks as a national or cultural group

¹hel·le·nist \-nəst\ *n* -s *usu cap* [Gk *Hellēnistēs,* fr. *hellēnizein*] **1 :** a person living in Hellenistic times not Greek in ancestry but Greek in language, outlook, and way of life; *esp* **:** a hellenized Jew ⟨the *Hellenists* murmured against the Hebrews because their widows were neglected —Acts 6:1 (RSV)⟩ **2 :** a specialist in the language or culture of ancient Greece

²hellenist \ˈ"\ *adj, usu cap* **:** of or relating to Hellenism or Hellenists

hel·le·nis·tic \ˌheləˈnistik, -tēk\ *adj, usu cap* **1 :** of, relating to, or characteristic of the cosmopolitan culture that developed after the conquests of Alexander the Great and passed into Roman culture in about the 2d century A.D., blended Greek and eastern elements (as in art, literature, and philosophy), and used Koine Greek as a common language ⟨the *Hellenistic* belief in the unity of mankind⟩ **2 :** of, relating to, or being the empires of Alexander the Great, the Antigonids, the Seleucids, and the Ptolemies representing an expansion of Greek power and influence eastward as far as India and southward to Egypt during the three centuries between the conquests of Alexander and the eastern conquests of Rome ⟨the *Hellenistic* period⟩ ⟨*Hellenistic* Athens⟩ ⟨the *Hellenistic* monarchies⟩ — compare GREEK 1 **3 :** conforming to or essentially influenced by Hellenistic culture ⟨the Scriptures in Greek for *Hellenistic* Jews⟩ ⟨the conflicting viewpoints of Jewish and *Hellenistic* Christianity⟩ — **hel·le·nis·ti·cal·ly** \-tək(ə)lē, -tēk-, -lī\ *adv, often cap*

hel·le·ni·za·tion \ˌhelənəˈzāshən, -ˌnīˈz-\ *n* -s *often cap* **1 :** the act or process of hellenizing **2 :** the quality or state of being hellenized

hel·le·nize \ˈheləˌnīz\ *vb* -ED/-ING/-S *often cap* [Gk *hellēnizein,* fr. *Hellēn* Greek + *-izein* -ize] *vi* **:** to become Greek or Hellenistic (as in cultural characteristics or language) ~ *vt* **:** to make Greek or Hellenistic in form or culture ⟨~ Roman sculpture⟩ ⟨~ a people⟩; *specif* **:** to alter (a word or phrase) so as to make conform to the distinctive language characteristics of Greek — **hel·le·niz·er** \-zə(r)\ *n* -s *often cap*

helleno- *comb form, usu cap* [Gk *hellēno-,* fr. *Hellēn* Greek] **1 :** the Greeks ⟨*Helleno*centric⟩ ⟨*Helleno*phile⟩ **2 :** Greek and ⟨*Helleno*-Italic⟩

¹hel·ler \ˈhelə(r)\ *n, pl* **hellers** *or* **heller** [G, fr. MHG *hallære, haller, heller,* fr. *Hall,* town in Swabia, Germany where they were first minted + MHG *-ære, -er* -er] **1 :** an old small silver coin first issued in Germany in the 13th century, later debased to billon and finally to copper, and spreading to Austria and Switzerland **2 :** an Austrian unit of value 1893-1925 equal to $\frac{1}{100}$ of the krone; *also* **:** a coin representing this unit last issued in 1916 **3 :** HALER

²hell·er \ˈ"\ *n* -s [¹*hell* + *-er*] *chiefly dial* **:** one that is hard to handle; *esp* **:** a person inclined to make trouble ⟨used to be a ~ — drank a lot and threw his weight around till he got in jail —Warren Leslie⟩

hel·leri \ˈheləˌrī, -ˌrē\ *n* -ES [NL (specific epithet of *Xiphophorus helleri*), after C. *Heller,* 20th cent. tropical fish collector] **1 :** SWORDTAIL **2 :** any of numerous brightly colored topminnows developed in the aquarium by hybridization between two tropical American fishes (*Xiphophorus helleri* and *Platypoecilus maculatus*)

hel·les·pon·tine \ˌheləˈspänt°n, -ānˌtīn\ *adj, usu cap* [*Hellespont,* narrow strait between the Gallipoli peninsula in Europe and Turkey in Asia that connects the Sea of Marmara with the Aegean sea (fr. L *Hellespontus,* fr. Gk *Hellēspontos*) + E *-ine*] **:** of or relating to the Hellespont

¹hellfire \ˈ=ˌ=\ *n* [ME, fr. *hell* + *fire*] **1 :** the fire of hell **:** FIRE AND BRIMSTONE ⟨an old-fashioned Calvinist sermon on ~⟩ **2 :** something that torments like the fire of hell (as burning spite or resentment)

²hellfire \ˈ"\ *adj* **:** FIRE-AND-BRIMSTONE ⟨a ~ preacher⟩ ⟨preached on a ~ topic⟩

hell–fired \ˈ=ˌ=\ *adj* **:** DAMNED — used as an intensive ⟨is so *hell-fired* fussy⟩

hell·flö·te \ˈhelˌflə(r)d·ə, -lǝ̄l\ *n* -s [G, fr. *hell* bright, clear + *flöte* flute] **:** a clear-toned flute organ stop sounding at 8-foot pitch

¹hell–for–leather \ˌ=ˈ=ˌ=\ *adv* **:** in a hell-for-leather manner **:** at full tilt **:** HELL-BENT ⟨galloped *hell-for-leather* down the trail⟩

²hell–for–leather \ˈ"\ *adj* [¹*hell-for-leather*] **:** marked by determined recklessness or great speed or force **:** RIP-ROARING ⟨she swept down the dizzying descent with the verve and *hell-for-leather* dash of a man —*Time*⟩

³hell–for–leather \ˈ"\ *n* **:** wild abandon or frantic haste ⟨became surer of his music . . . learned . . . to take it easy when the crowd did not demand *hell-for-leather* —Harold Sinclair⟩

hell·gram·mite *or* **hell·gra·mite** *or* **hel·gram·mite** \ˈhelgrəˌmīt, *usu* -īd.+V\ *n* -s [origin unknown] **:** a long-lived carnivorous aquatic larva of a large North American insect (*Corydalus cornutus*) or of various related insects that is much used as a fish bait by anglers — called also *dobson, toe-biter*

hellhole \ˈ=ˌ=\ *n* **1 :** the pit of hell **2 :** a place of extreme discomfort or squalor **3 :** a place notorious for its wild or immoral activities

hellhound \ˈ=ˌ=\ *n* [ME *hellehound,* fr. OE *hellehund,* fr. *hell* hell + *hund* dog — more at HELL, HOUND] **1 :** a dog represented in mythology (as of ancient Greece and Scandinavia) as standing guard in the underworld **2 :** a fiendishly evil person

¹hel·li·cat \ˈheləˌkat\ *n* [alter. (perh. influenced by E *hellcat*) of Sc *haloked,* fr. *halok* giddy girl + E *-ed*] *Scot* **:** an irresponsible and wild person

²hellicat \ˈ"\ *adj, Scot* **:** wild and giddy

hel·lier \ˈhelyə(r)\ *n* -s [ME *helyer,* fr. *helen* to hide, conceal, cover + *-yer, -ier* -er — more at HEAL] *dial Eng* **:** a tiler or slater of roofs

helling *pres part of* HELL

hel·lion \ˈhelyən\ *n* -s [prob. alter. (influenced by ¹*hell*) of *hallion*] **:** a disorderly, troublesome, or mischievous person ⟨the young ~s in my neighborhood are only interested in breaking windows and raising a row —*Camera*⟩ ⟨the difficult and usu. thankless work of teaching and mothering swarms of little ~s —J.A.MacEwen⟩

¹hell·ish \ˈhelish, -lēsh\ *adj* [¹*hell* + *-ish*] **:** of, resembling, or befitting hell **:** causing torment **:** DEVILISH ⟨nothing more ~ than warfare within the soul —Frank Yerby⟩ — **hell·ish·ly** \-ləshlē, -li\ *adv* — **hell·ish·ness** \-lishnəs, -lēsh-\ *n* -ES

²hellish \ˈ"\ *adv* **:** in an execrable manner ⟨the child acted ~ all day⟩ — sometimes used as an intensive ⟨a ~ cold day⟩

hellkite \ˈ=ˌ=\ *n* **:** one that shows hellish cruelty

hellmouth \ˈ=ˌ=\ *n, often cap* **:** a property in a medieval mystery or miracle play representing the entrance of hell as the gaping jaws sometimes with moving joints of a monster resembling a whale

¹hel·lo \həˈlō, heˈlō, ˈhe(ˌ)lō, ˈheˈlō; *when a name follows, as in "Hello Bill", often* (ˌ)=ˈ=; *subject to wide intonational variation*\ *interj* [alter. of *hollo*] — used esp. as a familiar greeting or in answering the telephone or to express surprise

²hello \həˈlō, heˈlō, ˈhe(ˌ)lō\ *vi* -ED/-ING/-S **:** to call or say hello

³hello \ˈ"\ *n* -s **:** an expression or gesture of greeting ⟨just dropped in to say ~⟩ ⟨never failed to wave a cheery ~ as he passed⟩

hello girl *n* **:** a female telephone operator

hell on wheels : one noted for hell raising

hell–roaring \ˈ=ˌ==\ *adj* **:** marked by tumultuous violence or carousing

hellroot \ˈ=ˌ=\ *n* **:** SMALL BROOMRAPE

hells *pl of* HELL, *pres 3d sing of* HELL

hell's bells *interj* — used esp. to express impatience or irritation

hell ship *n* **:** a ship characterized by brutal discipline or inhumane living conditions

hell–vine \ˈ=ˌ=\ *n* **:** TRUMPET CREEPER

hell·ward \ˈhelwə(r)d\ *adv* [short for earlier *to hellward,* fr. ME, fr. *to* + *hell* + *-ward*] **:** toward hell

hellweed \ˈ=ˌ=\ *n* **1 :** DODDER **2 :** CORN CROWFOOT **3 :** HEDGE BINDWEED

hell week *n* **:** a period of often rough initiation into a college fraternity

helly *adj, obs* **:** HELLISH

hel·ly's fluid \ˈhelēz-\ *n, usu cap H* [after Konrad *Helly* *b*1875 Swiss pathologist] **:** a fixing fluid consisting of an aqueous solution of mercuric chloride, potassium dichromate, sodium sulfate, and neutral formalin used in microscopy esp. for preservation of the cytoplasm and mitochondria

¹helm \ˈhelm, ˈheu̇m\ *n* -s [ME, fr. OE — more at HELMET] **1 :** HELMET 1; *specif* **:** HEAUME **2** *dial Eng* **a** *or* **helm cloud :** a heavy cloud lying over a mountain top **b** *or* **helm wind :** a gale of wind from the mountains accompanying a helm cloud **3** *dial Brit* **:** a rough shed or shelter for cattle

²helm \ˈ"\ *vt* -ED/-ING/-S [ME *helmen,* fr. OE *helmian,* fr. *helm,* n., helmet] **:** to cover or furnish with a helmet

³helm \ˈ"\ *n* -s [ME *helme,* fr. OE *helma;* akin to OHG *helmo* tiller, MHG *helm, halm, halme* handle, ON *hjalm* rudder, helm, and prob. to OE *sciell* shell — more at SHELL] **1 a :** a lever or wheel controlling the rudder of a ship for steering **:** the tiller or the wheel of a ship; *broadly* **:** the entire apparatus by which a ship is steered **b :** a position of a tiller attached forward of the rudder or a corresponding position of a wheel ⟨gave the command "up ~"⟩ ⟨with ~ hard aport⟩ — compare RIGHT RUDDER, WEATHER HELM **c :** deviation of the position of the helm from the amidships position ⟨15-degree ~⟩ ⟨sometimes no amount of opposite ~ will straighten the boat —C.D.Lane⟩ **2 :** a position of control or of highest executive power (as in an organization) **:** HEAD

⁴helm \ˈ"\ *vt* -ED/-ING/-S **:** to direct with or as if with a helm **:** STEER

hel·met \ˈhelmət, ˈheu̇m-, *usu* -əd.+V\ *n* -s *often attrib* [MF *helmet, heaumet,* dim. of *helme, heaume* helmet, of Gmc origin; akin to OE & OHG *helm* helmet, ON *hjalmr,* Goth *hilms;* akin to OE *helan* to hide, conceal — more at HELL] **1 a :** a covering or enclosing headpiece of ancient or medieval armor — see ARMET, BASINET, MORION, SALLET; ARMOR illustration **b :** a piece of medieval head armor smaller than a heaume and resting on the head **:** CASQUE **c :** a heraldic representation of a helmet depicted above the shield in an achievement and supporting the crest **2 :** any of various protective head coverings usu. made of a hard material (as metal, heavy leather, fiber) to resist impact and supported by bands that prevent direct contact with the head for comfort and ventilation; *specif* **:** one covering the top, back, and sides of the head and often also the neck and having a window for the face and sometimes breathing or radio apparatus (as for a diver) — see CRASH HELMET, WELDER'S HELMET; compare GAS MASK, TOPEE **3 :** a variety of tumbler pigeon having a white ground color and a sharply defined cap and the tail of another color **4 :** something resembling a helmet in form or position: as **a :** a hood-shaped upper sepal or petal of some flowers (as monkshood or snapdragon) **b :** CASQUE 3 **c :** a galea of an insect **5 a :** a close-fitting cap (as of leather or knitted material) covering the top, back, and sides of the head and fastening under the chin — compare BALACLAVA **b :** a woman's small close-fitting brimless hat

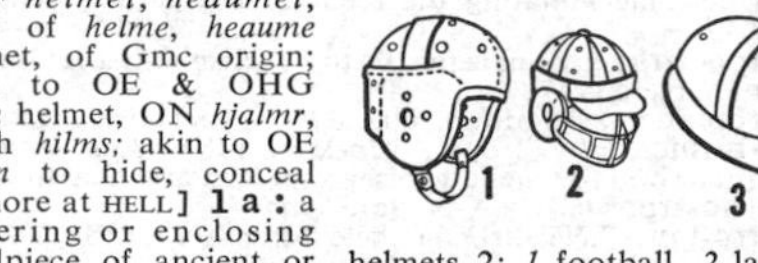

helmets 2: *1* football, *2* lacrosse, *3* polo

helmet bird *n* **1 :** TOURACO **2 :** a Madagascan passerine bird (*Aerocharis prevostii*) having a swollen hooked beak and black-and-chestnut plumage

helmet crab *n* **:** KING CRAB 1

hel·met·ed \-məd·|əd, -mət|\ *adj* **1 :** wearing a helmet **2 :** having a helmet or a helmet-shaped form or structure

helmeted guinea fowl *n* **:** a guinea fowl (*Numida meleagris*) — used esp. of the wild African bird

helmetflower \ˈ=ˌ=ˌ=\ *n* **:** a plant having flowers with helmet-shaped petals or sepals or a flower of such a plant: as **a :** MONKSHOOD **b :** SKULLCAP **c :** a tropical American orchid of the genus *Coryanthes*

helmetlike \ˈ==ˌ=\ *adj* **:** resembling a helmet in shape

helmet liner *n* **:** a stiff fabric or plastic headgear that fits inside a metal helmet and may be worn without the helmet

helmet orchid *n* **1 :** HELMETFLOWER c **2 :** an Australian orchid (*Pterostylis cucullata*) with a galeate lip

helmetpod \ˈ==ˌ=\ *n* **:** TWINLEAF

helmet quail *n* **:** any of several American partridges (as the valley quail and Gambel quail) constituting a genus (*Lophortyx*) distinguished by a forwardly curving crest

helmets *pl of* HELMET

helmet shell *n* **1 :** a gastropod mollusk of the family Cassididae **2 :** the thick-walled shell of the helmet shell often used for cameos

helmet shrike *n* **:** any of various chiefly tropical Old World passerine birds related to and resembling the shrikes but usu. isolated in a separate family (Prionopidae)

helm·holtz coil \ˈhel|mˌhōlts, ˈheu̇|-\ *n, usu cap H* [after Hermann L.F. von *Helmholtz* †1894 Ger. physicist] **:** one of two equal parallel coaxial circular coils in series that are separated from each other by a distance equal to the radius of one coil for producing an approximately uniform magnetic field in the space between the coils

helmholtz double layer *n, usu cap H* [after H.L.F. von *Helmholtz*] **:** ELECTRIC DOUBLE LAYER

helmholtz resonator *n, usu cap H* [after H.L.F. von *Helmholtz*] **:** RESONATOR 1a

helming *pres part of* HELM

hel·minth \ˈhelˌmin(t)th, -mən-\ *n, pl* **helminths** \-n(t)s, -n(t)ths\ [NL *Helminthes*] **:** a parasitic worm (as a roundworm, tapeworm, or leech); *esp* **:** one that parasitizes the intestine of a vertebrate

helminth- *or* **helmintho-** *comb form* [NL, fr. Gk, fr. *helminth-, helmis* intestinal worm, parasitic worm; akin to Gk *eulē* worm, maggot, Toch A *walyi* worms, Gk *eilein* to wind, roll — more at VOLUBLE] **1 :** helminth ⟨*helminth*iasis⟩ ⟨*helmintho*logy⟩ **2 :** shaped like a worm ⟨*helmintho*sporium⟩

hel·min·thes \helˈmin(t)thēz, -nˌthēz\ *n pl, cap* [NL, fr. Gk *helminth-, helmis*] **:** the parasitic worms — used as though a taxon but without taxonomic implications

hel·min·thi·a·sis \ˌhelˌminˈthīəsəs, -ˌmən-\ *n, pl* **helminthia·ses** \-əˌsēz\ [NL, fr. *helminth-* + *-iasis*] **:** infestation with or disease caused by parasitic worms

hel·min·thic \(ˈ)helˈmin(t)thik\ *adj* **:** of or caused by a helminth

hel·min·tho·clad·i·a·ce·ae \helˌmin(t)thōˌkladēˈāsēˌē, -lad-\ *n pl, cap* [NL, fr. *Helminthocladia,* type genus (fr. *helminth-* + Gk *klados* branch + NL *-ia*) + *-aceae* — more at GLADIATOR] **:** a family of red algae (order Nemalionales) having no envelope of vegetative cells formed about the reproductive filaments

hel·min·thoid \helˈminˌthȯid; ˈhelmən-, -ˌmin-\ *adj* [*helminth-* + *-oid*] **:** resembling a helminth **:** WORMLIKE

hel·min·tho·log·i·cal \(ˌ)helˌmin(t)thəˈläjəkəl\ *adj* **:** of or relating to helminthology ⟨~ abstracts⟩

hel·min·thol·o·gist \ˌhelmənˈthäləjəst, -ˌmin-\ *n* -s **:** a specialist in helminthology

hel·min·thol·o·gy \-jē\ *n* -ES [*helminth-* + *-logy*] **:** a branch of zoology that is concerned with helminths; *esp* **:** the study of parasitic worms

hel·min·tho·spo·rin \(ˌ)helˌmin(t)thəˈspōrən\ *n* -s [NL *Helminthosporium* + E *-in*] **:** a dark maroon crystalline phenolic pigment $C_{15}H_{10}O_5$ derived from anthraquinone and formed by the action of certain molds (as *Helminthosporium gramineum*) on sugar

hel·min·tho·spo·ri·um \-rēəm\ *n* [NL, fr. *helminth-* + *-sporium*] **1** *cap* **:** a form genus of saprophytic or parasitic imperfect fungi (family Dematiaceae) having erect conidiophores and elongate, clavate or cylindric, several-septate spores — see BARLEY STRIPE **2** *pl* **helminthospo·ria** \-rēə\ *or* **helminthosporiums :** any fungus of the genus *Helminthosporium* — **hel·min·tho·spo·roid** \(ˌ)=ˌ==ˈspōrȯid\ *adj*

helm·less \ˈhelmləs, ˈheu̇m-\ *adj* **:** lacking a helm

helm port *n* **:** an opening in the counter of a ship for the rudder stock

helm roof *n* [¹*helm*] **:** a 4-faced steeply pitched roof rising to a point from a base of four gables

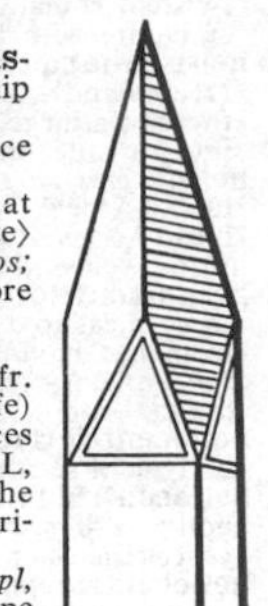
helm roof

helms *pl of* HELM, *pres 3d sing of* HELM

helms·man \ˈhelmzmən, ˈheu̇m-\ *n, pl* **helms·men :** a man at the helm who steers a ship **:** STEERSMAN

helms·man·ship \-ˌship\ *n* **:** the art or practice of steering a ship

¹helo- *comb form* [NL, fr. Gk *helos* — more at HELODES] **:** marsh **:** bog ⟨*helo*bious⟩ ⟨*helo*phyte⟩

²helo- *comb form* [NL, fr. Gk *hēlo-,* fr. *hēlos;* perh. akin to L *vallus* stake, palisade — more at WALL] **:** nail ⟨*Helo*derma⟩ ⟨*Helo*tium⟩

he·lo·bi·ae \heˈlōbēˌē\ *syn of* NAIADALES

he·lo·bi·ous \-bēəs\ *adj* [¹*helo-* + *-bious* (fr. NL *-bius* having a — specified — mode of life) — more at -BIUS] **:** living in marshy places

helo·der·ma \ˌhēlōˈdərmə, ˌhel-\ *n, cap* [NL, fr. ²*helo-* + *-derma*] **:** the type genus of the family Helodermatidae comprising the American gila monsters

he·lo·der·mat·i·dae \ˌ==(ˌ)dərˈmad·əˌdē\ *n pl, cap* [NL, fr. *Helodermat-, Heloderma,* type genus + *-idae*] **:** a small family of lizards having the dorsal scales replaced by rough tuberculated skin and including the American gila monsters and an obscure Bornean lizard

he·lo·des \heˈlō(ˌ)dēz\ *adj* [Gk *helōdēs,* fr. *helos* marsh; akin to Skt *saras* pond] **:** MARSHY

he·lo·dri·lus \ˌhelōˈdrīləs\ *n, cap* [NL, fr. ¹*helo-* + Gk *drilos* worm] **:** a common No. American genus of earthworms (family Lumbricidae) found in rich soil or manure

he·lo·ni·as \həˈlōnēəs\ *n* [NL, irreg. fr. ¹*helo-* + *-ia*] **1** *cap* **:** a genus of bog herbs (family Melanthaceae) of the northeastern U.S. with basal leaves and purple racemose perfect flowers on a tall scape — see SWAMP PINK **2** -ES **:** the dried rhizome and roots of a blazing star (*Chamaelirium luteum*) formerly used as a vermifuge

hel·o·pel·tis \ˌhelōˈpeltəs\ *n* [NL, fr. ¹*helo-* + *-peltis* (fr. Gk *peltē* shield)] **1** *cap* **:** a genus of tropical mirid bugs including several that attack economically important plants **2** -ES **:** any bug of the genus *Helopeltis;* *specif* **:** TEA MOSQUITO

hel·o·phyte \ˈheləˌfīt\ *n* -s [¹*helo-* + *-phyte*] **:** a bog plant; *esp* **:** a perennial marsh plant having its overwintering buds under water — compare HYDROPHYTE

hel·ot \ˈhelət\ *n* -s [L *Helotes,* pl., fr. Gk *Heilōtes*] **1** *usu cap* **:** a member of the lowest social and economic class of ancient Sparta thought to represent the conquered original population and constituting a body of serfs who were attached to the land, could not be sold, could be freed only by the state, were obliged to pay fixed portions of produce to the ruling Spartiates, and were required to serve in the armed forces — compare PERIOECI 2 **2 :** a member of any group of people deprived of rights and privileges and often exploited **:** SERF

he·lo·ti·a·les \həˌlōshēˈā(ˌ)lēz, -ōd·ē-\ *n pl, cap* [NL, fr. *Helotium* + *-ales*] **:** an order of fungi (subclass Euascomycetes) that are characterized by inoperculate asci borne in a disk-shaped to goblet-shaped sessile or stalked apothecium which may be brilliantly colored or dark and dull and that include numerous saprophytes and a few parasites of economically important plants — compare PEZIZALES

hel·ot·ism \ˈheləd·ˌizəm\ *n* -s **1 :** the quality or state of being a helot **:** SERFDOM **2 :** a symbiotic relation of plants or animals in which one functions as the slave of the other (as that between certain species of ants) — compare COMMENSALISM, PARASITISM, SYMBIOSIS

he·lo·ti·um \həˈlōshēəm, -ōd·ē-\ *n, cap* [NL, fr. LGk *hēlōtos* nail-shaped (fr. Gk *hēlos* nail) + NL *-ium*] **:** a genus (the type of the family Helotiaceae) comprising fungi that have inoperculate asci arranged in a hymenial layer in a cup-shaped apothecium with a colored rim of elongate thin-walled hyphae

hel·ot·ry \ˈhelətrē\ *n* -ES **1 :** the helots of a country or of an estate **2 :** the condition of a helot **:** SLAVERY, SERFDOM ⟨permanent white supremacy and permanent black ~ —Basil Davidson⟩

¹help \ˈhelp, ˈheu̇p, *chiefly in southern U S* ˈhep\ *vb* **helped** \-pt\ *or now chiefly dial* **holp** \ˈhō(l)p\ *or* **holped** \-pt\ **helped** *or now chiefly dial* **holp** *or* **hol·pen** \ˈhō(l)pən\ **helping; helps** [ME *helpen,* fr. OE *helpan;* akin to OHG *helfan* to help, ON *hjalpa,* Goth *hilpan,* Lith *šelpti*] *vt* **1 a :** to give assistance or support to **:** AID ⟨agreed to ~ him with his biography —Ruth P. Randall⟩ ⟨from the beginning she had ~*ed* and abetted him —Stuart Cloete⟩ — often used interjectionally ⟨*Help!* I'm drowning⟩ **b :** to assist in attaining ⟨good pitching ~*ed* the team to the American league championship⟩ **2 a :** REMEDY, CURE, RELIEVE ⟨bright curtains ~ a drab room⟩ ⟨aspirin ~*s* a headache⟩ ⟨humor often ~*s* a tense situation⟩ **b** *archaic* **:** to rescue from harm or misfortune **:** SAVE ⟨~ beer that beginneth to sour —Hugh Plat⟩ ⟨~ us from famine —Alfred Tennyson⟩ **c :** to get (oneself) out of a difficulty **:** EXTRICATE ⟨sometimes I fought when I couldn't ~ myself —John Reed⟩ **3 a :** to be of use to **:** BENEFIT ⟨a good speech should either amuse or ~ an audience⟩ ⟨one-way sailing was ~*ed* by monsoons —Anne Dorrance⟩ **b :** to further the advancement of **:** PROMOTE ⟨this dispute certainly did not ~ the negotiations —Theodore Hsi-En Chen⟩ ⟨~*ing* industrial development with two loans —Paul Bareau⟩ **4 a :** to change for the better **:** MEND ⟨people get used to what they can't ~ quicker than they think they're going to —Mary Austin⟩ **b :** to keep oneself from **:** refrain from **:** AVOID ⟨neither of us could ~ laughing —Oscar Wilde⟩ ⟨couldn't ~ seeing it was stuffed with newspaper clippings —James Hilton⟩ **c :** to keep from occurring **:** PREVENT ⟨scolded him for something he couldn't ~⟩ **d :** to be kept from **:** fail in ⟨the campaign against industrial accidents cannot ~ producing results —F.D.Roosevelt⟩ **5 a :** to dispense esp. at a meal **:** SERVE ⟨a loop of gold thread hung down from her sleeve as she ~*ed* the soup —Virginia Woolf⟩ **b :** to serve with food or drink esp. at a meal — often used with *to* ⟨~*ed* his neighbor to the wine⟩ ⟨~*ing* himself . . . to a slice of beef —T.L.Peacock⟩ **6 :** to appropriate for the use of (oneself) ⟨the company had ~*ed* itself to a generous supply of bicycles —P.W.Thompson⟩ **~** *vi* **:** to give aid or support **:** be of use **:** ASSIST ⟨to ~ rather than to blame —A.C.Benson⟩ ⟨every little bit ~*s*⟩ — often used with a following infinitive ⟨this principle may at least ~ to explain —A.O.Wolfers⟩

syn AID, ASSIST: these three verbs are virtually interchangeable in meaning to furnish another person or thing with what is needed to fill an insufficiency or what is needed for the attainment of an end. HELP implies more frequently than the others, however, an advance toward an end ⟨only money could *help* her through the worst of her ordeal —Marcia Davenport⟩ ⟨*help* a team to win a game⟩ ⟨will *help* to combat inflation⟩ ⟨*help* a wounded soldier back to camp⟩ AID often suggests the need of help or relief, often stressing weakness or insufficiency in the one aided and strength in the one aiding ⟨his undergraduate work . . . was *aided* by tuition grants —*Current Biog.*⟩ ⟨a wide variety of literature . . . that will broaden their horizons and *aid* them to sound, democratic decisions —C.M. Wieting⟩ ⟨to *aid* families in distress⟩ ASSIST usu. stresses the secondary role of the one assisting or the subordinate character of the assistance ⟨to *assist* visitors in finding places in hotels and auto courts —*Amer. Guide Series: Nev.*⟩ ⟨the president . . . is *assisted* by an 11-man cabinet —*Americana Annual*⟩ **syn** see in addition IMPROVE

— cannot help but : cannot but **— so help me :** on my word of honor **:** believe it or not ⟨dressed, *so help me,* in pink and purple tights⟩

2help \"\ *n* -s [ME, fr. OE; akin to OHG *helfa, hilfa* help, ON *hjalp* help, OE *helpan* to help] **1 a :** an act or instance of giving aid or support **:** ASSISTANCE ⟨offered his ~ in unloading the baggage⟩ ⟨generous to all who needed ~⟩ ⟨making . . . decisions with the ~ of all significant facts —*College & Univ. Business*⟩ ⟨always tried to be of ~⟩ **b :** the strength or resources employed in giving assistance ⟨the ~ comprised food, clothing, and medicine —J.A.McVann⟩ **2 a :** a useful adjunct **:** source of aid ⟨printed ~*s* to the memory —C.S.Braden⟩ ⟨the singer is a ~ but he is not essential —Deems Taylor⟩ **b :** DEALER HELP **3 :** a possibility of preventing or curing **:** REMEDY ⟨a situation for which there was no ~⟩ **4 a :** one who is in the pay or service of another: (1) **:** ASSISTANT, ALLY ⟨I could get you three or four rupees a month as my ~ —Attia S. Hosain⟩ ⟨now if the ~ of Norfolk and myself . . . will but amount to five-and-twenty thousand —Shak.⟩ (2) *or pl* **help :** a domestic worker or farmhand ⟨I've . . . scrubbed the bathroom floor when the ~ has quit —Ethel Merman⟩ ⟨hired ~ sat at table with the rest of the family —Sherwood Anderson⟩ ⟨the two extra ~*s* we always get in for the birthday —Ngaio Marsh⟩ (3) *pl* **help :** an office or factory worker **:** EMPLOYEE ⟨ran an ad in the ~ wanted column⟩ ⟨one of the ~ in . . . government agencies —*Antioch Rev.*⟩ **b :** the services of a paid worker ⟨they were without ~ again and she had all the work to do —Hamilton Basso⟩ **5 :** HELPING

help·able \-pəbəl\ *adj* **:** capable of being helped

helped *past of* HELP

help·er \-pə(r)\ *n* -s [ME, fr. *helpen* + *-er*] **1 :** one that helps ⟨the most idiomatic class of verbs are the ~*s* —Frederick Bodmer⟩; *specif* **:** an extra locomotive to assist a train (as on a grade) **2 :** HELP 4a; *specif* **:** a relatively unskilled worker who assists another esp. by manual labor ⟨first a ~ and then a journeyman —Walter Bernstein⟩ **3** *usu cap, Islam* **:** a member of the ansar — compare COMPANION 4c

help·ful \-pfəl\ *adj* [ME, fr. *help* + *-ful*] **1 :** of service or assistance **:** USEFUL, SALUTARY ⟨certain ideas are not only agreeable to think about . . . but they are also ~ in life's practical struggles —William James⟩ ⟨to the stomach it is pleasant, wholesome, and ~ —E.J.Banfield⟩ **2 :** CONSTRUCTIVE, ENCOURAGING ⟨a price control picture that is ~ —T.W.Arnold⟩ **— help·ful·ly** \-fəlē, -li\ *adv*

help·ful·ness \-fəlnəs\ *n* -ES **:** the quality or state of being helpful ⟨the . . . ~ of reference books —C.B.Shaw⟩

1helping *n* -s [ME, fr. *helpen* to help + *-ing*] **1** *archaic* **:** an act or instance of giving aid **:** HELP ⟨the law of all true ~ —R.C. Trench⟩ **2 a :** a portion of food **:** SERVING ⟨sent his plate back for a second ~⟩ **b :** something compared to a serving of food **:** PORTION ⟨only bona fide settlers . . . deserved ~*s* from the public domain —Dixon Wecter⟩

2helping *adj* [ME, fr. pres. part. of *helpen*] **1 :** giving aid or support **2 :** AUXILIARY ⟨~ verbs⟩ **— help·ing·ly** *adv*

helping card *n* **:** a queen or jack led in whist in an effort to promote the value of a card in a partner's hand

helping hand *n* **1 :** AID, ASSISTANCE ⟨always ready to lend a *helping hand*⟩ **2 :** a bridge hand containing some strength (as a queen or king) in each of at least three suits but with no biddable suit of its own and with too little strength for a no-trump bid

help·less \-pləs\ *adj* [ME *helpless*, fr. *help* + *-les* -less] **1 :** lacking protection or support **:** DEFENSELESS ⟨as ~ as a flock of shepherdless sheep —W.H.Mallock⟩ **2 :** lacking in effectiveness **:** FUTILE ⟨a ~ medley of indecisions —Hugh Walpole⟩ **3 a :** lacking in strength or vigor **:** incapable of action **:** POWERLESS ⟨fell ill and lay ~ at the mouth of the river —Francis Parkman⟩ ⟨the government . . . drifted ~ in the conflicting currents —Charles & Mary Beard⟩ **b :** lacking power to resist **:** INVOLUNTARY ⟨the tiny spill of pebbles in ~ fall —Richard Llewellyn⟩ **4 :** lacking in comprehension **:** BEWILDERED ⟨blinked at the candle in a ~ way, like a young barn owl —Mary Webb⟩

help·less·ly *adv* **:** in a helpless manner

help·less·ness *n* -ES **:** the quality or state of being helpless

help·mate \-p,māt, *usu* -ād·+V\ *n* [by folk etymology (influence of *mate*) fr. *helpmeet*] **:** one serving as a companion, partner, or assistant; *specif* **:** WIFE ⟨proved a good and faithful ~, assisted me much by attending the shop —Benjamin Franklin⟩

helpmeet \'=,=\ *n* [2*help* + *meet*, adj. (fitting) in *I will make an help meet for him* (Gen 2:18 AV)] **:** HELPMATE ⟨testify that their ~*s* retain that feminine tenderness and loyalty . . . no longer found in my own household —*Atlantic*⟩ ⟨chemistry . . . is the farmer's ~ —*Crops in Peace & War*⟩

help out *vi* **:** to render assistance **:** be of use ⟨won a scholarship which would *help out* —MacKinlay Kantor⟩ **~** *vt* **:** to give aid to ⟨agree to *help him out*⟩

helps *pres 3d sing of* HELP, *pl of* HELP

hel-shoes \'hel,=\ *n pl, usu cap H* [part trans. of ON *helskōr*, fr. *hel* heathen realm of the dead + *skōr* shoes — more at HELL] *Norse mythol* **:** shoes placed on the dead before burial to aid them on the rough road to Hel

hel·sing·fors \'helsiŋ,fȯrz, -sēŋ-, -ō(ə)z\ *adj, usu cap* [fr. *Helsingfors* (Helsinki), Finland] **:** HELSINKI

hel·sin·ki \'hel,siŋkē, -ki, =ˈ==\ *adj, usu cap* [fr. *Helsinki*, Finland] **:** of or from Helsinki, the capital of Finland **:** of the kind or style prevalent in Helsinki

1hel·ter–skel·ter \ˌheltə(r)ˈskeltə(r)\ *adv* [imit.] **1 :** in headlong disorder **:** PELL-MELL ⟨ran *helter-skelter*, getting in each other's way —F.V.W.Mason⟩ **2 :** in random order **:** HAPHAZARDLY ⟨magazines stacked *helter-skelter* on tables —T.H. White b. 1915⟩

2helter–skelter \"\ *n* -s **1 :** a disorderly confusion **:** TURMOIL ⟨the horses set off in a wild *helter-skelter* —J.M.Synge⟩ ⟨*helter-skelter* of conflict, emotion, and group activity —John Gould⟩ **2 :** an external spiral slide around a tower in an amusement park

3helter–skelter \"\ *adj* **1 :** confused and hurried **:** PRECIPITATE ⟨most companies are plagued with *helter-skelter* disorder when that five o'clock whistle blows —*Modern Industry*⟩ **2 a :** HIT-OR-MISS **:** HAPHAZARD ⟨shocked at the *helter-skelter* arrangement of the papers, all mussed and frayed —Jean Stafford⟩ ⟨the *helter-skelter* nondirectional nature of the discussion —John Withall⟩ **b :** FLIGHTY, SCATTERBRAINED ⟨*helter-skelter* attitude of the younger generation —Erle Stanley Gardner⟩

1helve \'helv, 'heuv\ *n* -s [ME, fr. OE *hielfe*; akin to OHG *halb* handle, OE *healf* half — more at HALF] **1 :** a handle of a tool or weapon (as an ax) **:** HAFT **2 :** a lever in a helve hammer that has the hammerhead at its end

2helve \"\ *vt* -ED/-ING/-S [ME *helven*, fr. *helve*, n.] **:** to furnish or fit with a helve

helve hammer *n* **:** a power hammer consisting essentially of a heavy head at one end of a lever lifted by power and dropping by its own weight on work that rests on an anvil — compare STRAP HAMMER, TRIP-HAMMER

hel·vel·la \hel'velə\ *n* [NL, fr. L, a small potherb, fr. *helvus* light-bay-colored + *-ella* (dim. suffix) — more at YELLOW] **1** *cap* **:** a genus (the type of the family Helvellaceae) comprising ascomycetous fungi with the ascocarps stalked, pileate, or saddle-shaped and often thrown into folds **2** -s **:** any fungus of the genus *Helvella* **— hel·vel·lic** \(')=ˈvelik\ *adj*

hel·vel·la·ce·ae \ˌhelvəˈlāsē,ē\ *n pl, cap* [NL, fr. *Helvella*, type genus + *-aceae*] **:** a family of fungi (order Pezizales) that includes various important edible fungi (as the morels) — see HELVELLA **— hel·vel·la·ceous** \ˌ==ˈlāshəs\ *adj*

hel·vel·la·les \-ˈlā(,)lēz\ *n pl, cap* [NL, fr. *Helvella* + *-ales*] *in some classifications* **:** an order of fungi including the Helvellaceae and Geoglossaceae

hel·ve·tia blue \(')helˈvēsh(ē)ə-\ *n, often cap H* [NL *Helvetia* Switzerland] **:** NAPOLEON BLUE

1hel·ve·tian \-shən\ *adj, usu cap* [NL *Helvetia* land of the Helvetii, Switzerland (fr. L *Helvetii*, ancient people of Switzerland + *-ia* -y) + E *-an*] **:** of or relating to the Helvetii or Helvetia **:** SWISS

2helvetian \"\ *n* -s *cap* **:** a native or inhabitant of Switzerland **:** SWISS; *specif* **:** a member of the ancient Helvetii

1hel·vet·ic \(')helˈved·ik\ *adj, usu cap* [L *Helveticus* of the Helvetii, fr. *Helvetii* + *-icus* -ic] **:** HELVETIAN

2helvetic \"\ *n* -s *usu cap* **:** a Swiss Protestant **:** a follower of Zwingli

hel·ve·tii \helˈvēshē,ī\ *n pl, usu cap* [L] **:** an early Celtic people of western Switzerland in the time of Julius Caesar

hel·vid·i·an \(')helˈvidēən\ *adj, usu cap* [*Helvidius* fl A.D.380 Roman heretic + E *-an*] **:** of or relating to the teachings of the Roman layman Helvidius who held that Mary bore children after Jesus

hel·vite \ˈhel,vīt\ *also* **hel·vin** \-,vən\ *or* **hel·vine** \", -,vēn\ *n* -s [*helvite* alter. (influenced by *-ite*) of *helvin*; *helvin, helvine* fr. G *helvin*, fr. L *helvus* light-bay-colored + G *-in* — more at YELLOW] **:** a silicate mineral $(Mn,Fe,Zn)_8Be_6O_{24}S_2$ consisting of sulfide of manganese and beryllium and usu. containing also iron and zinc that is isomorphous with danalite and genthelvite

hel·vo·lic acid \helˈvä|lik-, -vō|\ *n* [ISV *helvol-* (fr. L *helvolus, helveolus* pale yellow, fr. *helvus* light-bay-colored) + *-ic*] **:** FUMIGACIN

helxi·ne \helkˈsīnē, -lˈzī-\ *n, cap* [NL, fr. Gk *helxinē* pellitory, bindweed, fr. *helkein* to drag, pull — more at SULCUS] **:** a genus of plants (family Urticaceae) native to Corsica and Sardinia and cultivated elsewhere as pot plants with small leaves and tiny solitary flowers that form dense mossy mats — see BABY'S TEARS

hel·zel \ˈhelzəl\ *n* -s [Yiddish, dim. of *hals* neck, fr. OHG — more at COLLAR] **:** a skin of the neck of poultry stuffed usu. with fat and flour

1hem \ˈhem\ *pron* [ME, fr. OE *him, heom*, dat. of *hīe* they — more at HE] **1** *dial* **:** THEM **2** *obs* **:** THEMSELVES

2hem \"\ *n* -s [ME *hem, hemm*, fr. OE; akin to ON *hemja* to hem in, restrain, OFris *hemma* to hinder, MHG *hemmen* to hem in, restrain, *hamen* to hem in, restrain, Arm *kamel* to press, squeeze, Russ *kom* lump, ball] **1 a :** a finished edge of a cloth article (as a skirt, sleeve, curtain, napkin, stocking) made by rolling or folding back an edge and stitching it down **b :** an edge usu. folded back and fastened down on articles of sheet metal, plastic, rubber, leather **2 a :** BORDER ⟨bright green ~ of reeds about the ponds —R.M.Lockley⟩ **b :** EDGE ⟨~ of the sea —Shak.⟩ ⟨the polar ~ —Emily Dickinson⟩ **3 :** the raised rim of a volute of an Ionic capital

3hem \"\ *vb* **hemmed; hemmed; hemming; hems** [ME *hemmen*, fr. *hem, hemm*, n.] *vt* **1 a :** to finish with a plain or decorative hem ⟨*hemmed* just above the ankle —*Women's Wear Daily*⟩ **b :** BORDER, EDGE **2 :** to enclose or confine with or as if with a ring around or arc before usu. preventing or hindering access, free activity, growth, or escape — usu. used with *in* ⟨body of water, *hemmed* in on all sides by evergreen forests —*Amer. Guide Series: N. H.*⟩ ⟨the regiment now found itself *hemmed* in by its own mine fields —P.W.Thompson⟩ **~** *vi* **:** to make hems in sewing **syn** see SURROUND

4hem \"\ *vi* **hemmed; hemmed; hemming; hems :** to utter the sound represented by *hem* ⟨*hemmed* ominously as he always did when he was about to relieve his mind —W.A. White⟩ — often used with *haw* ⟨~ and haw and put it off, apparently in the hope that things will pick up —Clifford Aucoin⟩ ⟨*hemmed* and hawed, and then pointed out that the trouble was obviously connected with our consignment —F.W. Crofts⟩

5hem \"; *as an interjection a throat-clearing sound*\ *n* -s [imit.] **:** a vocalized pause in speaking ⟨after clearing the husk in his throat with two or three ~*s* —T.L.Peacock⟩ **:** an instance of uttering this sound ⟨would use a peculiar rap at the door, and give four loud ~*s* —Oliver Goldsmith⟩ — often used interjectionally to call attention, to warn, or to express hesitation or doubt; compare 3HUM

6hem \"\ *archaic and dial var of* HIM

7hem \"\ *dial Eng var of* HAME

8hem \"\ *var of* HEME

hem- *or* **hemo-** *or* **hemi-** *or* **haem-** *or* **haemo-** *comb form* [MF *hemo-*, fr. L *haem-, haemo-*, fr. Gk *haim-, haimo-*, fr. *haima*; perh. akin to ON *seimr* honeycomb, OHG *seim* virgin honey, W *hufen* cream] **:** blood ⟨*hem*arthrosis⟩ ⟨*hem*agglutination⟩ ⟨*hemo*cyte⟩ — the forms *haem-* or *haemo-* are preferred in taxonomic names ⟨*Haem*acanthus⟩ ⟨*Haemo*gregarina⟩

hema- *or* **haema-** *comb form* [NL, fr. Gk *haima* blood] **:** HEM- ⟨*hema*cytometer⟩ ⟨*hema*poiesis⟩ — *haema-* preferred in taxonomic names in biology ⟨*Haema*stoma⟩

hem·a·chate \ˈhemə,kāt\ *n* -s [L *haemachates*, fr. (assumed) Gk *haimachatēs*, fr. Gk *haima* blood + *achatēs* agate — more at AGATE] **:** a light-colored agate like bloodstone with red jasper spots

he·ma·cy·tom·e·ter \ˌhēmə(,)sīˈtämədˑə(r), ,hem-\ *n* [*hema-* + *cyt-* + *-meter*] **:** an instrument for counting blood cells

he·ma·cy·to·zo·on \ˌhē,mə,sīd·əˈzō,än\ *n* [NL, fr. *hema-* + *cyt-* + *-zoon*] **:** HEMOCYTOZOON

he·mad \ˈhē,mad\ *adv* [*hem-* + 2*-ad*] **:** toward the hemal side

he·ma·dynamometer \ˌhēmə, ˌhemə+\ *n* [*hema-* + *dynamometer*] **:** a device for measuring blood pressure

he·ma·fi·brite \ˌhēməˈfī,brīt, ,hem-\ *n* -s [ISV *hema-* + *fibr-* + *-ite*] **:** a mineral $Mn_3(AsO_4)(OH)_3.H_2O$ consisting of basic manganese arsenate

he·mag·glut·i·nate \ˌhēməˈglüd·ə,nāt, ,hem-\ *vt* [*hem-* + *agglutinate*] **:** to cause hemagglutination of

he·mag·glu·ti·na·tion \ˌ=,==ˈnāshən\ *n* [ISV *hem-* + *agglutination*] **:** agglutination of red blood cells

he·mag·glu·ti·nin \ˌ=ˈglüd·ənən\ *or* **he·mo·agglutinin** \ˌhē(,)mō, ˌhe(,)mō+\ *n* [ISV *hem-* + *agglutinin*] **:** an agglutinin that causes hemagglutination

he·mal \ˈhēməl\ *adj* [*hem-* + *-al*] **1 :** of or relating to the blood or blood vessels **2 :** situated on or belonging to the side of the spinal cord where the heart and chief blood vessels are placed **:** VENTRAL — used of vertebrate parts or organs

hemal arch *n* **:** a bony or cartilaginous arch extending ventrally from the spinal column: **a :** the arch formed by a vertebra and an associated pair of ribs **b** (1) **:** an arch on the ventral surface of each caudal vertebra of a lower vertebrate (as a fish or reptile) usu. considered to consist of the extended and ventrally fused parapophyses of the vertebra (2) **:** such an arch together with its dependent hemal spine forming a V-shaped or Y-shaped ventral prolongation of a caudal vertebra — called also *chevron bone*

he·mal·bu·men \ˌhēmalˈbyümən, ,hem-\ *n* [ISV *hem-* + *albumen*] **:** a preparation of blood containing iron albuminate and used in chlorosis and anemia

hemal node *or* **hemal gland** *n* **:** HEMOLYMPH GLAND

he·ma·moe·ba \ˌhēməˈmēbə, ,hem-\ *n* [NL, fr. *hem-* + *amoeba*] **1 :** an organism like an amoeba living in the blood; *esp* **:** MALARIA PARASITE **2 :** LEUKOCYTE

he–man \ˈ=,=\ *n, pl* **he–men :** an obviously strong virile man ⟨the great open spaces, where red-blooded *he-men* still roam —H.L.Mencken⟩ ⟨peppy, poker-playing, sales-hustling *he-men* who are our most characteristic Americans —Sinclair Lewis⟩ ⟨the tough, assured, half-humorous *he-man* who can take his women or leave them alone —Arthur Knight⟩

he·man·gi·ec·ta·sis \hēˌmanjē+\ *n* -ES [NL, fr. *hem-* + *angi-* + *ectasis*] **:** dilatation of blood vessels

he·man·gi·o·endothelioma \hēˌmanjē(,)ō+\ *n* [NL, fr. *hemangio-* (fr. *hemangioma*) + *endothelioma*] **:** an often malignant tumor originating by proliferation of capillary endothelium

he·man·gi·oma \hē,manjēˈōmə\ *n, pl* **hemangiomas** *also* **hemangio·ma·ta** \-məd·ə\ [NL, fr. *hem-* + *angioma*] **:** a usu. benign tumor made up of blood vessels and typically occurring as a purplish or reddish slightly elevated area of skin overlying a network of intercommunicating capillaries — see PORT-WINE STAIN, STRAWBERRY MARK

he·man·gi·o·ma·to·sis \=,==,ōməˈtōsəs\ *n, pl* **hemangioma·to·ses** \-ō,sēz\ [NL, fr. *hemangiomat-*, *hemangioma* + *-osis*] **:** a condition in which hemangiomas are present in several parts of the body

he·man·gi·o·sarcoma \hēˌmanjē(,)ō+\ *n* [NL, fr. *hemangio-* (fr. *hemangioma*) + *sarcoma*] **:** a malignant hemangioma

he·ma·po·di·um \ˌhēməˈpōdēəm, ,hem-\ *or* **he·ma·pod** \ˈhēmə,päd, ˈhem-\ *n, pl* **hemapodia** *also* **hemapodiums** *or* **hemapods** [*hemapodium*, NL, fr. *hema-* + *-podium*; *hemapod* fr. *hema-* + *-pod*; fr. its proximity to the dorsal blood vessel] **:** the dorsal lobe of a parapodium

he·map·o·dous \hēˈmapədəs\ *adj* [*hema-* + *-podous*] **:** of or relating to a hemapodium **:** having hemapodia

he·ma·poi·e·sis \ˌhēmə(,)pȯiˈēsəs, ,hem-\ *n* [NL, fr. *hema-* + *-poiesis*] **:** HEMATOPOIESIS

he·mar·thro·sis \ˌhēmärˈthrōsəs, ,hem-\ *n* [NL, fr. *hem-* + *arthrosis*] **:** hemorrhage into a joint

hemat- *or* **hemato-** *or* **haemat-** *or* **haemato-** *comb form* [L *haemat-*, *haemato-*, fr. Gk *haimat-*, *haimato-*, fr. *haimat-*, *haima* blood — more at HEM-] **:** HEM- ⟨*hemat*oid⟩ ⟨*hemato*crit⟩ — the forms *haemat-* or *haemato-* are preferred in taxonomic names ⟨*Haemato*zoon⟩ ⟨*Haemato*gaster⟩

he·ma·tal \ˈhēməd·əl, ˈhem-\ *adj* [*hemat-* + *-al*] **:** relating to the blood or blood vessels

he·ma·te·in \ˌhēməˈtēən, ,hem-\ *n* -s [ISV *hemat-* + *-ein*] **:** a reddish brown crystalline phenolic quinonoid compound $C_{16}H_{12}O_6$ constituting the essential dye in logwood extracts — see HEMATOXYLIN

he·ma·tem·e·sis \-ˈteməsəs\ *n* -ES [NL, fr. *hemat-* + Gk *emesis* vomiting — more at EMETIC] **:** the vomiting of blood

he·ma·te·met·ic \ˌhēməd·ə̇ˈmed·ik, ˌhem-\ *adj* [fr. NL *hematemesis*, after NL *emesis*: E *emetic*] **:** of or relating to hematemesis

he·ma·therm \ˈhēmə,thərm, ˈhem-\ *n* -s [NL *Hematherma* (pl.), fr. *hema-* + *-therma* (fr. Gk *therma*, neut. pl. of *thermos* warm, hot) — more at WARM] **:** HOMOIOTHERM

he·ma·ther·mal \ˌ==ˈthərməl\ *or* **he·ma·ther·mous** \-məs\ *adj* [*hematherm* + *-al* or *-ous*] **:** HOMOIOTHERMIC

1he·mat·ic \hēˈmad·|ik, -at|, |ēk\ *adj* [Gk *haimatikos*, fr. *haimat-* hemat- + *-ikos* -ic] **1 :** of or relating to blood **2 :** containing blood ⟨a ~ cyst⟩ **3 :** involving or affecting the blood ⟨a ~ crisis⟩ **4 :** having the color of blood **:** SANGUINEOUS

2hematic \"\ *n* -s **:** HEMATINIC

he·ma·tid \ˈhēməd·əd, ˈhem-\ *n* -s [*hemat-* + *-id*] **:** a mature nonnucleated red blood cell

he·ma·ti·dro·sis \ˌhēməd·əˈdrōsəs, ,hem-\ *n* -ES [NL, fr. *hemat-* + *-idrosis*] **:** the excretion through the skin of blood or blood pigments

hem·a·tin \ˈhemədˑən, ˈhēm-\ *n* -s [ISV *hemat-* + *-in*] **1** *or* **hem·a·tine** \-ə,tēn, -ədˑən\ **:** HEMATEIN ⟨~ extract crystals⟩ — used esp. of preparations for use in dyeing; see DYE table I (under *Natural Black 1*) **2 a :** a compound derived from oxidized heme and usu. obtained in aqueous alkaline solutions or as a brownish black or bluish black solid $C_{34}H_{32}N_4O_4FeOH$ by treatment of hemin chloride with alkali; ferriprotoporphyrin hydroxide **b :** any of several similar compounds regarded as formed by the breakdown of hemoglobin esp. in some pathological conditions **c :** any of various similar iron-porphyrin derivatives or closely related pyrrole derivatives — compare HEME 2

1hem·a·tin·ic \ˌheməˈtinik, ˌhēm-\ *n* -s [*hematin* + *-ic*] **:** an agent that tends to stimulate blood-cell formation or to increase the hemoglobin in the blood

2hematinic \"\ *adj* **:** functioning as a hematinic ⟨the ~ value of certain iron salts⟩

hem·a·tin·om·e·ter \ˌhemədˑəˈnäməd·ə(r), ,hēm-\ *n* [ISV *hematin* + *-o-* + *-meter*] **:** HEMOGLOBINOMETER **— hem·a·tin·o·met·ric** \ˌ==dˑənōˈme·trik\ *adj*

hem·a·tite \ˈhemə,tīt, ˈhēm-\ *n* -s [L *haematites*, fr. Gk *haimatitēs* resembling blood, fr. *haimat-*, *haima* blood — more at HEM-] **:** a mineral Fe_2O_3 consisting of ferric oxide and constituting an important iron ore that occurs in splendent metallic-looking rhombohedral crystals, in massive forms, and in red earthy forms (hardness of crystals 5.5–6.5, sp. gr. of crystals about 5.20) — called also *specular iron*; see LIMONITE, RED OCHER

hematite red *n* **:** a dark to dark grayish red

hem·a·tit·ic \ˌ==ˈtid·ik\ *adj* **:** of, containing, relating to, or resembling hematite in substance and color

he·ma·to·bic \ˌ==ˈtōbik\ *or* **he·ma·to·bi·ous** \-bēəs\ *adj* [NL *hematobium* + E *-ic* or *-ous*] **:** living in blood **:** parasitic in blood

he·ma·to·bi·um \ˌhēməˈtōbēəm, ,hem-\ *n, pl* **hemato·bia** \-bēə\ [NL, fr. *hemat-* + *-bium* (fr. Gk *bios* mode of life) — more at QUICK] **:** an organism living in blood

hem·a·to·blast \ˈhemədˑō,blast, ˈhēm-\ *n* [ISV *hemat-* + *-blast*] **1 :** BLOOD PLATELET **2 :** an immature blood cell; *esp* **:** an immature red blood cell **— hem·a·to·blas·tic** \ˌ===ˈblastik\ *adj*

hem·a·to·cele \ˈ===,sēl\ *n* -s [ISV *hemat-* + *-cele*] **:** a blood-filled cavity of the body; *also* **:** the effusion of blood into a body cavity (as the scrotum)

he·ma·to·chrome \ˌkrōm\ *n* [*hemat-* + *-chrome*] **:** an orange or reddish coloring matter found in various algae (as red snow)

hem·a·to·col·pos \ˌhemədˑōˈkäl,päs, ˌhēm-, -lpəs\ *or* **hem·a·to·col·pus** \-lpəs\ *n* -ES [NL, fr. *hemat-* + *-colpos* or *-colpus*] **:** an accumulation of blood within the vagina

he·mat·o·crit \hiˈmad·əkrət, -,krit\ *n* -s [ISV *hemat-* + *-crit* (fr. Gk *kritēs* judge) — more at CRITERION] **1 :** an instrument for determining the relative amounts of plasma and corpuscles in blood usu. by means of centrifugation **2** *or* **hematocrit value :** a percentile ratio of volume of packed red blood cells to volume of whole blood centrifuged by a hematocrit

hem·a·to·cry·al \ˌhemədˑōˈkrīəl, ,hēm-\ *adj* [*hemat-* + *cry-* + *-al*] **:** COLD-BLOODED

hem·a·to·cyte \ˈ===,sīt\ *n* -s [*hemat-* + *-cyte*] **:** HEMOCYTE

he·ma·tog·e·nous \ˌhēməˈtäjənəs, ˌhem-\ *adj* [*hemat-* + *-genous*] **1 :** concerned with the production of blood or of one or more of its constituents ⟨~ functions of the liver⟩ **2 a :** taking place by way of the blood ⟨~ metastasis of a tumor⟩ **b :** spread by way of the blood stream ⟨~ focal infection⟩ ⟨~ tuberculosis⟩

hem·a·to·gone \'hemad·a,gōn, 'hēm-\ *or* **hem·a·to·go·nia** \,==='gōnēa\ *n* -s [NL *hematogonia*, fr. *hemat-* + *-gonia* (fr. Gk *gonē* generation, offspring, seed) — more at GONE (germ cell)] : HEMOCYTOBLAST

he·ma·toid \'hēma,tȯid, 'hem-\ *adj* [Gk *haimatoeidēs*, fr. *haimat-* hemat — + *-eidēs* -oid] : resembling blood

he·ma·toi·din \,=='tȯidan\ *n* -s [ISV *hematoid* + *-in*] : BILIRUBIN

hem·a·to·lite \'hemad·ō,līt, 'hēm-\ *n* -s [ISV *hemat-* + *-lite;* fr. its color; orig. formed as Sw or G *aimatolit*] : a mineral $(Mn,Mg)_4Al(AsO_4)(OH)_8$ consisting of a brownish red aluminum manganese arsenate in rhombohedral crystals (sp.gr. 3.3–3.4)

hem·a·to·log·ic \ˌhemad·ō'läjik, ˌhēm-\ *or* **hem·a·to·log·i·cal** \-jakal\ *adj* : of, relating to, or involving blood

he·ma·tol·o·gist \,hēma'tälajast, ,hem-\ *n* -s : one that specializes in the study of the blood

he·ma·tol·o·gy \-jē\ *n* -ES [*hemat-* + *-logy*] : a branch of biology that deals with the blood and blood-forming organs

he·ma·tol·y·sis \-'tälasas\ *n* [NL, fr. *hemat-* + *-lysis*] : HEMOLYSIS — **hem·a·to·lyt·ic** \ˌhemad·ō'lid·ik, ˌhēm-\ *adj*

he·ma·to·ma \,hēma'tōma, ,hem-\ *n, pl* **hematomas** \-ōmaz\ *also* **hematomata** \-ōmad·a\ [NL, fr. *hemat-* + *-oma*] : a tumor or swelling containing blood

hem·a·tom·e·ter \-'tämad·a(r)\ *n* [ISV *hemat-* + *-meter*] : HEMACYTOMETER

hem·a·to·metra \,hemad·ō'mē·tra, ,hēm-\ *n* -s [NL, fr. *hemat-* + *-metra*] : an accumulation of blood or menstrual fluid in the uterus

hem·a·to·my·e·lia \-d·ō,mī'ēlēa\ *n* -s [NL, fr. *hemat-* + *-myelia*] : a hemorrhage into the spinal cord

hem·a·to·pericardium \ˌhemad·ō, ˌhēm-+\ *n* [NL, fr. *hemat-* + *pericardium*] : HEMOPERICARDIUM

hem·a·to·peritoneum \"+\ *n* [NL, fr. *hemat-* + *peritoneum*] : HEMOPERITONEUM

he·ma·toph·a·gous \ˌhēma'täfagas, ˌhem-\ *adj* [ISV *hemat-* + *-phagous*] : feeding on blood ⟨~ insects⟩ ⟨~ vampire bats⟩

he·ma·toph·a·nite \,=='täfa,nīt\ *n* -s [ISV *hemat-* + *phan-* (prob. fr. Gk *phanos* light, bright) + *-ite;* orig. formed as G *hämatophanit*] : a mineral $Pb_5Fe_4O_{10}(Cl,OH)_2$ consisting of oxychloride lead and iron

hem·a·to·phyte \'hemad·ō,fīt, 'hēm-\ *n* -s [*hemat-* + *-phyte*] : a plant parasite (as a bacterium) of the blood

hem·a·to·plast \-,plast\ *n* -s [*hemat-* + *-plast*] : HEMATOBLAST

hem·a·to·poi·e·sis \,hemad·ō(,)pȯi'ēsas, ,hēm-\ *n* -ES [NL, fr. *hemat-* + *-poiesis*] : formation of blood or of blood cells within the living body

hem·a·to·poi·et·ic system \ˌ===(,)=ˌed·ik-\ *n* [ISV *hemat-* + *-poietic*] : an organic system of the body consisting of the blood and the structures that function in its production

hem·a·to·porphyrin \ˌhemad·ō, ˌhēm-+\ *n* [ISV *hemat-* + *porphyrin*] : any of several isomeric porphyrins $C_{20}H_6N_4$-$(CH_3)_4(CHOHCH_3)_2(CH_2CH_2COOH)_2$ that are hydrated derivatives of protoporphyrins; *esp* : the deep red crystalline pigment obtained by treating hematin or heme with acid

hem·a·to·por·phy·ri·nu·ria \,hemad·ō,pȯrfarā'n(y)ūrēa, ,hēm-\ *n* -s [NL, fr. ISV *hematoporphyrin* + NL *-uria*] : PORPHYRINURIA

hem·a·tor·rha·chis \,hema'tȯrakas, ,hēm-\ *n* -ES [NL, fr. *hemat-* + *-rrhachis*] : hemorrhage into the spinal canal

hem·a·to·salpinx \ˌhemad·ō, ˌhēm-+\ *n* [NL, fr. *hemat-* + *salpinx*] : accumulation of blood in a fallopian tube

hem·a·to·scope \'hemad·ō,skōp, 'hēm-\ *n* [ISV *hemat-* + *-scope*] : an instrument for the spectroscopic examination of blood

hem·a·to·thermal \ˌhemad·ō, ˌhēm-+\ *adj* [*hemat-* + *thermal*] : WARM-BLOODED

he·ma·tox·y·lin \,hēma'täksalan, ,hem-\ *n* -s [ISV *hematoxyl-* (fr. NL *Haematoxylon*, genus of plants, fr. *haemat-* hemat- + *-xylon*) + *-in*] : a colorless to yellowish crystalline phenolic compound $C_{16}H_{14}O_6$ found in logwood and used chiefly as a biological stain because of its ready oxidation to hematein; hydroxy-brazilin

hem·a·to·zoal \ˌhemad·aˌzōal, ˌhēm-\ *adj* : of or relating to hematozoa; *also* : blood-dwelling

hem·a·to·zoan \,==='zōan\ *n* -s [*hematozoon* + *-an*] : HEMATOZOON

hem·a·to·zo·on \-ō,än\ *n, pl* **hemato·zoa** \-ōa\ [NL, fr. *hemat-* + *-zoon*] : a blood-dwelling animal parasite

he·ma·tu·ria \,hēma'tūrēa, -a'tyū-, ,hem-\ *n* -s [NL, fr. *hemat-* + *-uria*] : the presence of blood or blood cells in the urine — compare HEMOGLOBINURIA

he·mau·to·graph \hē'mȯd·a,graf, he'-\ *n* [*hem-* + *auto-* + *-graph*] : a curve that is obtained when a stream of blood from an artery strikes against a piece of moving paper and that is indicative of the variations in blood pressure — **he·mau·to·graph·ic** \ˌ=ˌ=='grafik\ *adj* — **he·mau·tog·ra·phy** \,hēmȯ'tägrafē, ,hem-\ *n* -ES

heme \'hēm\ *also* **hem** \'hem\ *or* **haem** \'hēm, 'hem\ *n* -s [ISV, fr. *hematin*] **1** : a deep red iron-containing pigment $C_{34}H_{32}N_4O_4Fe$ that is obtained from hemoglobin by treatment with acid to remove the globin, that is a ferrous derivative of protoporphyrin, and that readily oxidizes to hematin or hemin — called also *ferroprotoporphyrin, protoheme, reduced hematin* **2** : any of several compounds that are derived from protoporphyrin and iron in either the ferrous or ferric state and that constitute the nonprotein groups of some hemoproteins — compare HEMATIN 2c, HEMIN 2

hem·el·y·tral \he'mela·tral\ *adj* : of or relating to a hemelytron or to hemelytra

hem·el·y·tron \-a-,trän\ *also* **hem·el·y·trum** \-a·tram\ *n, pl* **hemely·tra** \-a·tra\ [NL, fr. *hem-* (fr. *hemi-*) + *elytron* or *elytrum*] **1** : one of the basally thickened anterior wings of various insects (as of Hemiptera) **2** : one of the elytra of a chaetopod worm

hem·en \'heman\ *pron* [ME, alter. of *hem* — more at HEM (them)] *now dial Brit* : THEM — compare ¹HEM

hem·era \'hemara\ *n, pl* **hemerae** \-a(,)rē\ *also* **hemera** [NL, fr. Gk *hēmera* day; akin to Gk *ēmar* day, Arm *aur*] **1** : a stratigraphic zone comprising the time range of a particular fossil species **2** : a period of time during which a race of organisms is at the apex of its evolution

hem·er·a·lope \-ra,lōp\ *n* -s [F *héméralope*, fr. Gk *hēmeralōp-*, *hēmeralōps*] : one affected with hemeralopia

hem·er·a·lo·pia \,==='lōpēa\ *n* -s [NL, fr. Gk *hēmeralōp-*, *hēmeralōps* (fr. *hēmera* day + *alaos* blind + *ōp-*, *ōps* eye) + NL *-ia*] **1** : a defect of vision characterized by reduced visual capacity in bright lights — called also *day blindness* **2** : NYCTALOPIA — **hem·er·a·lopic** \ˌ==='läpik\ *adj*

hem·er·o·baptist \ˌhemarō+\ *n* [ML *Hemerobaptista*, fr. Gk *Hēmerobaptistēs*, fr. *hēmero-* (fr. *hēmera* day) + *baptistēs* baptizer — more at BAPTIST] *usu cap* : one who practices daily or frequent baptism or ceremonial ablution; *specif* : a member of an ancient Jewish sect

¹**hem·er·o·bi·id** \ˌhemarō'bīad\ *adj* [NL *Hemerobiidae*, family of flies, fr. *Hemerobius*, type genus + *-idae*] : of or relating to the genus *Hemerobius* or the family Hemerobiidae

²**hemerobiid** \"\ *n* -s : a hemerobiid fly

hem·er·o·bi·us \,hema'rōbēas\ *n, cap* [NL, fr. Gk *hēmerobios* living for a day, fr. *hēmero-* + *-bios* (fr. *bios* mode of life) — more at QUICK] : a genus (the type of the family Hemerobiidae) of small usu. dark-colored lacewings with wings mottled with smoky brown — compare APHIS LION

hem·er·o·cal·lis \,hemarō'kalas\ *n, cap* [NL, fr. Gk *hēmerokalles*, a kind of lily, fr. *hēmero-* (fr. *hēmera* day) + *-kalles* (fr. *kallos* beauty); fr. the fact that the blossoms close at night — more at CALLI-] : a genus of Eurasian herbs of the family Liliaceae with fibrous fleshy roots, basal linear leaves, and showy flowers in small clusters on naked scapes

he·me·ryth·rin \,hēmā'rithran, ,hem-\ *n* -s [*hem-* + *erythr-* + *-in*] : an iron-containing respiratory pigment in the blood of various invertebrates

¹**hemi-** *in pronunciations below*, ˌ==*=*|heme *or (usu not before vowels)* |hemā *sometimes* |he,mī\ *prefix* [ME, fr. L, fr. Gk *hēmi-* — more at SEMI-] **1** : half of; *esp* : a lateral half of ⟨*hemi*centrum⟩ ⟨*hemi*cerebrum⟩ ⟨*hemi*cardia⟩ **2** : relating to or affecting a half (as a lateral half) of an organ or part or of the whole body ⟨*hemi*plegia⟩ ⟨*hemi*atrophy⟩ **3** *chem* **a** : half in respect to combining ratio ⟨*hemi*basic⟩ **b** : having one half of the molecular weight of a (specified) compound or class of compounds **c** : having one half the number of characteristic groups in a (specified) compound or class of compounds ⟨*hemi*cyanine⟩ **4** *crystallog* : having one half the number of faces ⟨*hemi*hedron⟩

²**hemi-** — see HEM-

-he·mia \'hēmēa, *esp Brit* 'hēmya\ — see -EMIA

hemi·acetal \ˌ== *at* HEMI-+\ *n* [¹*hemi-* + *acetal*] : any of a class of compounds characterized by the grouping >C(OH)-(OR) and usu. formed as intermediate products in the preparation of acetals from aldehydes or ketones ⟨an aldose is a favorable compound for the study of ~s —C.D.Hurd⟩ — see GLYCOSIDE, MONOSACCHARIDE

hemi·anatropous \"+\ *adj* [¹*hemi-* + *anatropous*] : AMPHITROPOUS

hemi·anesthesia \"+\ *n* [NL, fr. ¹*hemi-* + *anesthesia*] : loss of sensation in either lateral half of the body

hemi·a·nop·sia \,==+a'näpsēa\ *also* **hem·i·a·no·pia** \-'nōpēa\ *n* -s [NL, fr. ¹*hemi-* + *an-* ²*a-* + *-opsia* or *-opia*] : blindness in one half of the visual field and affecting one or both eyes

hemi·a·nop·tic \ˌ==='näptik\ *adj* [NL *hemianopsia* + E *optic*] : of or relating to hemianopsia

hemi·ascomycetes \ˌ== *at* HEMI-+\ *n pl, cap* [NL, fr. ¹*hemi-* + *Ascomycetes*] : a subclass of Ascomycetes comprising simple ascomycetous fungi that lack an ascocarp and have asci arising directly from the fertile ascogonium and each containing an indefinite number of spores — see ENDOMYCETALES, TAPHRINALES; compare PROTOASCOMYCETES

hemi·as·co·my·cet·i·dae \"+,a(,)skō,mī,sed·a,dē\ *syn of* HEMIASCOMYCETES

hemi·atrophy \"+\ *n* -ES [NL *hemiatrophia*, fr. ¹*hemi-* + LL *atrophia* atrophy — more at ATROPHY] : atrophy of one half of an organ or part or of the whole body ⟨facial ~⟩ — opposed to *hemihypertrophy*

hemi·auxin \"+\ *n* [¹*hemi* + *auxin*] : an auxin precursor

hemi·azygous vein \"+ . . . -\ *n* [NL *hemiazygos*, fr. ¹*hemi-* + *azygos*] : the left azygous vein passing up on the left side, crossing ventral to the vertebral column, and joining the right azygous vein

hemi·ballism *also* **hemi·ballismus** \"+\ *n, pl* **hemiballisms** *also* **hemiballismuses** [NL *hemiballismus*, fr. ¹*hemi-* + *ballismus*] : violent uncontrollable movements of one lateral half of the body usu. due to hemorrhage in the opposite side of the brain

hemi·ba·sid·i·ae \,==+ba'sidē,ē\ [NL, fr. ¹*hemi-* + *-basidiae* (fr. *basidium*)] *syn of* HEMIBASIDII

hemi·ba·sid·i·a·les \,===,sidē'ā(,)lēz\ [NL, fr. *hemibasidium* + *-ales*] *syn of* USTILAGINALES

hemi·ba·sid·ii \,==='sidē,ī\ *n pl, cap* [NL, fr. ¹*hemi-* + *-basidii* (fr. *basidium*)] *in some classifications* : a subclass of Basidiomycetes comprising fungi with the basidium produced from a resting spore and including the order Ustilaginales or this together with the Uredinales — compare EUBASIDII, HETEROBASIDIOMYCETES

hemi·basidiomycetes \ˌ== *at* HEMI-+\ [NL, fr. *hemi-* + *Basidiomycetes*] *syn of* HEMIBASIDII

hemi·basidium \"+\ *n* [NL, fr. ¹*hemi-* + *basidium*] : the transversely septate promycelium of a smut fungus — compare AUTOBASIDIUM, PROTOBASIDIUM

hemi·benthic *also* **hemi·benthonic** \"+\ *adj* [¹*hemi-* + *benthic* or *benthonic*] : having a planktonic stage or phase ⟨~ animals⟩

hemi·branch \'==+,braŋk\ *n* **1** [NL *Hemibranchii*] : one of the Hemibranchii **2** [¹*hemi-* + *-branch*] : a gill having lamellae or filaments only on one side; *collectively* : the lamellae or filaments on one side of a gill

hemi·branchiate \ˌ== *at* HEMI-+\ *adj* [¹*hemi-* + *branchiate*] **1** : having an incomplete or reduced branchial apparatus **2** : of or relating to the Hemibranchii

hemi·bran·chii \,==+'braŋkē,ī\ *n pl, cap* [NL, fr. ¹*hemi-* + *-branchii* (fr. L *branchia* gill) — more at BRANCHIA] *in some classifications* : a suborder of Thoracostei comprising fishes with an incomplete or reduced branchial apparatus and usu. including the sticklebacks, cornetfishes, bellows fishes, and shrimpfishes

he·mic \'hēmik, 'hem-, -mēk\ *adj* [*hem-* + *-ic*] : of or relating to blood

hemi·car·dia \ˌ== *at* HEMI-+ˌkärdēa\ *n* -s [NL, fr. ¹*hemi-* + Gk *kardia* heart — more at HEART] : a lateral half of a 4= chambered heart

hemi·cellulose \ˌ==+\ *n* [ISV ¹*hemi-* + *cellulose*] : any of various polysaccharides that accompany cellulose and lignin in the skeletal substances of wood and green plants and that resemble cellulose in being insoluble in water and hydrolyzable to simple sugar units by acids but differ from it in being soluble in alkali and presumably of smaller molecular dimensions, in undergoing acid hydrolysis more easily, and in giving rise on hydrolysis not only to glucose but also to uronic acids, xylose, galactose, and other carbohydrates — compare CELLULOSAN, PENTOSAN, POLYURONIDE — **hemi·cellulosic** \"+\ *adj*

hemi·centrum \"+\ *n* [NL, fr. ¹*hemi-* + *centrum*] : a lateral half of the centrum of a vertebra

hemi·ceph·a·lous \"+ˌsefalas\ *or* **hemi·ce·phal·ic** \"+sa'falik\ *adj* [¹*hemi-* + *-cephalous* or *-cephalic*] : having a poorly differentiated but distinct head — used of the larvae of various flies; compare EUCEPHALOUS

hemi·cerebrum \"+\ *n* [NL, fr. ¹*hemi-* + *cerebrum*] : a lateral half of the cerebrum : CEREBRAL HEMISPHERE

hemi·chorda \"+\ [NL, fr. ¹*hemi-* + *chorda* (notochord)] *syn of* HEMICHORDATA

hemi·chordata \"+\ *n pl, cap* [NL, fr. ¹*hemi-* + *chordata*] : a division of Chordata usu. considered both subphylum and class, including the Enteropneusta and Pterobranchia and in some classifications the Phoronidea, and comprising a group of vermiform marine animals that have in the proboscis an outgrowth of the pharyngeal wall which suggests and is probably homologous with the notochord of higher chordates — **hemi·chordate** \"+\ *n or adj*

hemi·cra·nia \ˌ=='krānēa\ *n* -s [LL — more at MIGRAINE] : pain in one side of the head — opposed to *amphicrania*

hemi·cryptophyte \ˌ== *at* HEMI-+\ *n* [ISV ¹*hemi-* + *cryptophyte*] : a perennial plant having its overwintering buds located at the soil surface — **hemi·cryptophytic** \"+\ *adj*

hemi·crystalline \"+\ *adj* [ISV ¹*hemi* + *crystalline*] : partly crystalline : characterized by crystals embedded in an amorphous groundmass

he·mic·tic \hē'miktik\ *adj* [fr. NL *hemixis*, after such pairs as NL *apomixis:* E *apomictic*] : of or relating to hemixis

hemi·cy·cle \ˌ== *at* HEMI- + ,sīkal\ *n* [F *hémicycle*, modif. of L *hemicyclium*, fr. Gk *hēmikyklion*, fr. *hēmi-* ¹hemi- + *kyklos* circle + *-ion* -ium — more at CYCLE] **1** : a half circle : SEMICIRCLE **2** : a curved or approximately semicircular structure or arrangement (as in an arena) : a curving or semicircular form (as of a driveway) ⟨a simple ~ containing the altar —W.K.Sturges⟩ ⟨the ~ of our modern civilization, the horseshoe area where nomadic man first settled down to tend crops —*Nat'l Geographic*⟩

hemi·cyclic \"+\ *adj* [¹*hemi-* + *cyclic*] : having floral leaves partly in whorls and partly in spirals ⟨~ flowers⟩

hemi·dactylous \"+\ *adj* [NL *Hemidactylus* + E *-ous*] : of or relating to the genus *Hemidactylus*

hemi·dactylus \"+\ *n, cap* [NL, fr. ¹*hemi-* + *dactylus*] : a widely distributed genus of geckos having the digits dilated and provided with two rows of lamellae on the underside

hemi·demisemiquaver \"+\ *n* [¹*hemi-* + *demisemiquaver*] : SIXTY-FOURTH NOTE

hemi·dome \'==+,dōm\ *n* [ISV ¹*hemi-* + *dome*] **1** : a pinacoid parallel to the orthoaxis and cutting the vertical axes and clinoaxes in a crystal **2** : a dome that has only two like faces (as an orthodome of a monoclinic crystal)

hemi·dystrophy \ˌ== *at* HEMI- + \ *n* [¹*hemi-* + *dystrophy*] : an unequal development of the two lateral halves of the body

hemi·elytral \"+\ *adj* [NL *hemielytron* + E *-al*] : HEMELYTRAL

hemi·elytron *also* **hemi·elytrum** \"+\ *n* [NL, fr. ¹*hemi-* + *elytron* or *elytrum*] : HEMELYTRON

hemi·ep·es \ˌ==+'e(,)pēz\ *n, pl* **hemiepe** [LL, fr. LGk *hēmiepes*, fr. Gk *hēmi-* ¹hemi- + *-epes* (neut. of *-epēs*, fr. *epos* verse, line, word) — more at VOICE] : a dactylic tripody having a spondaic third foot or lacking the two short syllables of the third foot

hemi·facial \ˌ== *at* HEMI- +\ *adj* [¹*hemi-* + *facial*] : involving or affecting one lateral half of the face ⟨~ spasm⟩

hemi·form \'==+,-\ *n* [¹*hemi-* + *form*] : a rust in which only the urediniial and telial stages are known

he·mig·a·lus \hē'migalas\ *n, cap* [NL, fr. ¹*hemi-* + *-galus* (fr. Gk *galē* weasel) — more at GALEA] : a genus of East Indian civets comprising the banded palm civets (as *H. hardwickii*)

hemi·globin \ˌ== *at* HEMI- +\ *n* [*hem-* + *globin*] : METHEMOGLOBIN

hemi·glyph \'==+,-\ *n* [¹*hemi-* + *glyph*] : the half channel or groove on each edge of a triglyph

hemi·he·dral \ˌ==+ˈhēdral\ *or* **hemi·he·dric** \-rik\ *adj* [¹*hemi-* + *-hedron* + *-al* or *-ic*] **1** *of a crystal* : having half the faces required by complete symmetry — compare HOLOHEDRAL **2** : having the symmetry appropriate to a hemihedral form — **hemi·he·dral·ly** \-ralē\ *adv*

hemi·he·drism \ˌ==+'hē,drizam\ *also* **hemi·he·dry** \-'hēdrē\ *n, pl* **hemihedrisms** *also* **hemihedries** [¹*hemi-* + *-hedron* + *-ism* or *-y*] : the property of crystallizing hemihedrally

hemi·he·dron \-'hēdran\ *n, pl* **hemihedrons** *or* **hemihedra** [NL, fr. ¹*hemi-* + *-hedron*] : a hemihedral form or crystal

hemi·holohedral \ˌ== *at* HEMI- +\ *adj* [¹*hemi-* + *holohedral*] *of a crystal* : having a hemihedral form in which half the octants have the full number of planes ⟨~ tetrahedron ⟨~ sphenoid⟩

hemi·hydrate \"+\ *n* [¹*hemi-* + *hydrate*] : a hydrate containing half a molecule of water to one of the compound forming the hydrate — compare PLASTER OF PARIS — **hemi·hydrated** \"+\ *adj*

hemi·hypertrophy \"+\ *n* [NL *hemihypertrophia*, fr. ¹*hemi-* + *hypertrophia* hypertrophy — more at HYPERTROPHY] : hypertrophy of one half of an organ or part or of the whole body ⟨facial ~⟩ — opposed to *hemiatrophy*

hemi·karyon \"+\ *n* [ISV ¹*hemi-* + *karyon;* orig. formed in G] : a cell nucleus containing the haploid number of chromosomes — opposed to *amphikaryon* — **hemi·kar·y·ot·ic** \"+,karē¦äd·ik\ *adj*

hemi·lateral \"+\ *adj* [ISV ¹*hemi-* + *lateral*] : of or affecting one lateral half of the body

hemi·leia \,==+'līa\ *n, cap* [NL, fr. ¹*hemi-* + *-leia* (fr. Gk *leios* smooth, flat); fr. the shape of the spores — more at LIME] : a genus of rusts (order Uredinales) producing both urediospores and teliospores from a compound spore-bearing stalk

hemi·mel·li·tene \-'mela,tēn\ *n* -s [ISV ¹*hemi-* + *mellite* + *-ene*] : a liquid hydrocarbon $C_6H_3(CH_3)_3$ obtained from coal tar and petroleum; 1,2,3-trimethylbenzene

hemi·mellitic acid \ˌ== *at* HEMI- + . . -\ *n* [ISV ¹*hemi-* + *mellitic*] : a crystalline acid $C_6H_3(COOH)_3$ derived from benzene and having half as many carboxyl groups as mellitic acid; 1,2,3-benzene-tricarboxylic acid

hem·im·er·id \he'mimarad\ *n* -s [NL *Hemimeridae*, family of insects, fr. *Hemimerus*, type genus + *-idae*] : an insect of the genus *Hemimerus*

hem·im·er·oi·dea \he,mima'rȯidēa\ [NL, fr. *Hemimerus* + *-oidea*] *syn of* DIPLOGLOSSATA

hem·im·er·us \he'mimaras\ *n, cap* [NL, fr. ¹*hemi-* + *-merus* (fr. Gk *meros* part) — more at MERIT] : a genus (coextensive with the family Hemimeridae and the order or suborder Diploglossata) comprising small wingless viviparous African insects parasitic on rodents

hemi·metabola \ˌ== *at* HEMI- +\ *n pl, cap* [NL, fr. ¹*hemi-* + *Metabola*] : insects characterized by hemimetabolism

hemi·metabolism *also* **hemi·metabole** *or* **hemi·metaboly** \"+\ *n* [¹*hemi-* + *metabolism* or *metabole* or *metaboly*] : incomplete metamorphosis; *esp* : incomplete metamorphosis in various insects with aquatic larvae in which the young does not resemble the adult

hemi·metabolous *also* **hemi·metabolic** \"+\ *adj* **1** [¹*hemi-* + *metabolous* or *metabolic*] : of or relating to hemimetabolism **2** [NL *Hemimetabola* + E *-ous* or *-ic*] : of or relating to the Hemimetabola

hemi·metamorphic *or* **hemi·metamorphous** \"+\ *adj* [¹*hemi-* + *metamorphic* or *metamorphous*] : of, relating to, or being marked by hemimetamorphosis

hemi·metamorphosis \"+\ *n, pl* **hemimetamorphoses** [NL, fr. ¹*hemi-* + *metamorphosis*] : HEMIMETABOLISM

hemimixis *var of* HEMIXIS

hemi·morph \'==+,mȯrf\ *n* -s [¹*hemi-* + *-morph*] : a hemimorphic form or crystal

hemi·mor·phic \ˌ==+ˈmȯrfik\ *adj* [ISV ¹*hemi-* + *-morphic*] : unsymmetrical in form as regards the two ends of an axis : having a singular and polar axis

hemi·mor·phism \,==+'mȯr,fizam\ *or* **hemi·mor·phy** \'==+,mȯrfē\ *n, pl* **hemimorphisms** *or* **hemimorphies** [ISV ¹*hemi-* + *-morphism* or *-morphy*] : the quality or state of being hemimorphic

hemi·mor·phite \,==+'mȯr,fīt\ *n* -s [ISV *hemimorphic* + *-ite;* orig. formed as G *hemimorphit*] **1** : a mineral $Zn_4Si_2O_7OH.H_2O$ consisting of a basic zinc silicate in usu. white or colorless transparent orthorhombic crystals **2** : SMITHSONITE

hemi·my·aria \"+mī'a(a)rēa\ *n pl, cap* [NL, fr. ¹*hemi-* + *-myaria*] : a suborder of Thaliacea that is coextensive in recent classifications with the family Salpidae

he·min *also* **hae·min** \'hēman\ *n* -s [ISV *hem-* + *-in*] **1 a** *also* **hemin chloride** : a red-brown to blue-black crystalline salt $C_{34}H_{32}N_4O_4FeCl$ derived from oxidized heme but usu. obtained in a characteristic crystalline form from hemoglobin by treatment with hot glacial acetic acid containing sodium chloride; ferriprotoporphyrin chloride — called also *protohemin;* compare BLOOD CRYSTAL, HEMATIN 2a, TEICHMANN'S CRYSTAL **b** : any of a series of salts of which hemin chloride is a member **2** : any of several iron-porphyrin derivatives similar to hemin chloride — compare HEME 2

hem·i·o·la \,hemē'ōla\ *or* **hem·i·o·lia** \-lēa\ *n* -s [LL *hemiolia*, fr. Gk *hēmiolia* ratio of one and a half to one (3:2), fr. *hēmiolia*, fem. of *hēmiolios* in the ratio of one and a half to one (3:2), fr. *hēmi-* ¹hemi- + *-olios* (fr. *holos* whole) — more at SAFE] **1** : the interval of a fifth in medieval music **2** : the rhythmic alteration consisting of three notes in place of two or two notes in place of three

hem·i·ol·ic \ˌ=='älik\ *adj* [L *hemiolius* (fr. Gk *hēmiolios*) + E *-ic*] *in classical prosody* : of, relating to, or characterized by the proportion of three to two; *esp* : characterized by such a proportion between thesis and arsis ⟨a ~ foot⟩

hemi·o·pia \,== *at* HEMI- + 'ōpēa\ *or* **hemi·op·sia** \-'äpsēa\ *n* -s [NL, fr. ¹*hemi-* + *-opia*, *-opsia*] : HEMIANOPSIA — **hemi·op·ic** \ˌ==+ˈäpik, -ˈōp-\ *adj*

hemi·orthotype \ˌ== *at* HEMI- +\ *adj* [*hemi-* + *orth-* + *type*] : MONOCLINIC

hemi·parasite \"+\ *n* [ISV ¹*hemi-* + *parasite*] **1** : a facultative parasite — compare HOLOPARASITE **2** : a parasitic plant that contains some chlorophyll and is therefore capable of photosynthesis (as the mistletoe) — **hemi·parasitic** \"+\ *adj*

hemi·paresis \"+\ *n* [NL, fr. ¹*hemi-* + *paresis*] : muscular weakness or partial paralysis restricted to one side of the body usu. of neural or psychic origin and often transitory — **hemi·paretic** \"+\ *adj*

hemi·penis \"+\ *n* [NL, fr. ¹*hemi-* + *penis*] : one of the paired copulatory organs of lizards and snakes

hemi·plankton \"+\ *n* [NL, fr. ¹*hemi-* + *plankton*] : plankton composed of predominantly plant organisms that at certain seasons come to rest on the bottom — compare HOLOPLANKTON

hemi·ple·gia \,==+'plēj(ē)a\ *n* -s [NL, fr. MGk *hēmiplēgia* paralysis, fr. *hēmi-* ¹hemi- + *-plēgia* -plegia] : paralysis of one lateral half of the body or part of it resulting from injury (as by hemorrhage or disease) to the motor centers of the brain

¹**hemi·ple·gic** \ˌ==+ˈplējik, -jēk\ *adj* [*hemiplegia* + *-ic*] : relating to or marked by hemiplegia

²**hemiplegic** \"\ *n* -s : a hemiplegic individual

hemi·pode \'==+,pōd\ *also* **hemi·pod** \-,päd\ *n* -s [NL *Hemipodius*, genus of birds, fr. Gk *hēmipod-*, *hēmipous* half foot, fr. *hēmi-* ¹hemi- + *pod-*, *pous* foot — more at FOOT] : BUTTON QUAIL

he·mip·pe \hē'mipē\ *n* -s [NL *hemippus* (specific epithet of *Equus hemippus*), fr. ¹*hemi-* + *-ippus* (fr. Gk *hippos* horse) —

more at EQUINE] : a small wild ass (*Equus hemippus*) of Syria and Iraq

hemi·prism \ˈ⸗⸗ at HEMI- + ˌ-\ *n* [ISV ¹*hemi-* + *prism*] **:** a prism consisting of only two parallel faces (as in the triclinic system) **:** a pinacoid cutting two crystallographic axes

he·mip·tera \heˈmiptərə\ *n pl, cap* [NL, fr. ¹*hemi-* + *-ptera*] **1 :** a large order of insects that comprise the true bugs (as the bedbug, squash bug, and chinch bug) and various related insects (as the aphids and mealybugs), that are generally more or less flattened, that have mouthparts adapted to piercing and sucking and usu. two pairs of wings of which the basal part of the anterior pair is thickened and coriaceous and the distal part membranous while the posterior pair is wholly membranous, that undergo an incomplete metamorphosis, and that include many important pests — see HETEROPTERA, HOMOPTERA **2 a** *in some classifications* **:** an order coextensive with Heteroptera **b** *in some esp former classifications* **:** an order including Hemiptera (sense 1) together with Anoplura and Thysanoptera

he·mip·ter·oid \-təˌrȯid\ *adj* [NL *Hemiptera* + E *-oid*] **:** characteristic of or resembling the Hemiptera ⟨~ insect⟩ ⟨~ mouthparts⟩

he·mip·ter·ol·o·gy \⸗ˌ⸗⸗ˈräləjē\ *n* -ES [NL *Hemiptera* + E *-o-* + *-logy*] **:** a branch of entomology that deals with Hemiptera

he·mip·ter·on \-ˈ⸗⸗ˌrän\ *also* **he·mip·ter·an** \-ˌrən\ *n* -S [*hemipteron*, NL, back-formation fr. *Hemiptera*; *hemipteran* fr. NL *Hemiptera* + E *-an*] **:** one of the Hemiptera

he·mip·ter·ous \-ˌrəs\ *adj* [NL *Hemiptera* + E *-ous*] **:** of or relating to the Hemiptera

hemi·pyramid \ˈ⸗⸗ at HEMI- + \ *n* [ISV ¹*hemi-* + *pyramid*] **:** a crystallographic pyramid or inclined prism consisting of only two pairs of parallel faces (as in the monoclinic system)

hemi·quinonoid *or* **hemi·quinoid** \"+\ *adj* [¹*hemi-* + *quinonoid* or *quinoid*] **:** having or relating to a quinonoid arrangement of bonds but only one carbonyl group instead of two

hemi·ramph \ˈ⸗⸗ˌram(p)f\ *n* -S [NL *Hemiramphus*] **:** a halfbeak of the genus *Hemiramphus*

hem·i·ram·phid \ˈ⸗⸗ˈram(p)fəd\ *adj* [NL *Hemiramphidae*, family of halfbeaks, fr. *Hemiramphus*, type genus + *-idae*] **:** HEMIRAMPHINE

hemi·ram·phine \-)ˌfīn, -ˌfən\ *adj* [NL *Hemiramphus* + E *-ine*] **:** of or relating to the genus *Hemiramphus* or the family Hemiramphidae

hemi·ram·phus \ˌ⸗⸗ˈram(p)fəs\ *n, cap* [NL, fr. ¹*hemi-* + *-ramphus* (irreg. fr. Gk *rhamphos* crooked beak, beak)] **:** a widely distributed genus of halfbeaks now usu. made the type of a separate family (Hemirhamphidae) but sometimes esp. formerly included in the family Exocoetidae

hemirhamphus \"\ [NL, fr. ¹*hemi-* + Gk *rhamphos* crooked beak, beak] *syn of* HEMIRAMPHUS

hemi·saprophyte \ˈ⸗⸗ at HEMI- + \ *n* [ISV ¹*hemi-* + *saprophyte*] **:** a partial saprophyte: **a :** an organism usu. a saprophyte but capable of existing as a parasite — compare HOLOSAPROPHYTE **b :** a plant containing a small amount of chlorophyll but obtaining most of its food material from humus — **hemi·saprophytic** \"+\ *adj*

hemi·sect \ˌ⸗⸗+ˈsekt\ *vt* -ED/-ING/-S [¹*hemi-* + *-sect*] **:** to divide along the mesial plane

hemi·section \ˈ⸗⸗ at HEMI- +\ *n* [¹*hemi-* + *section*] **:** a division or dividing along the mesial plane

hemi·sphaeriales \"+\ [NL, fr. ¹*hemi-* + *Sphaeriales*] *syn of* MICROTHYRIALES

hem·i·spher·al \ˌheməˈsfirəl, -fer-\ *adj* **:** HEMISPHERIC

hem·i·sphere \ˈheməˌsfi(ə)r, -iə\ *n* [alter. (influenced by MF *emisphere*) of ME *hemispere, hemisperie*, fr. L *hemisphaerium*, fr. Gk *hēmisphairion*, fr. *hēmi-* ¹hemi- + *sphairion* small sphere (dim. of *sphaira* sphere, ball)] **1 a :** a half of the celestial sphere divided into two halves by the horizon, the celestial equator, or the ecliptic **b** *obs* **:** the sky above the horizon or overhead **c :** a projection on a plane surface of half of the celestial sphere **2 :** REALM, PROVINCE ⟨a ~ of special knowledge⟩ ⟨a ~ of life heretofore unknown to us⟩ ⟨a discovery that was to have important repercussions in the ~*s* of French literary life —*Times Lit. Supp.*⟩ **3 a :** a half of the terrestrial globe esp. as divided by the equator ⟨sailed down over the equator into the southern ~⟩ or into halves one of which contains Europe, Asia, and Africa and the other the Americas ⟨sailed from Europe for the western ~⟩ **b :** a map or projection of one of these halves **c :** the inhabitants of one of these halves of the earth ⟨America's plans did not seem to interest the eastern ~⟩ **4 :** either of two half spheres formed by a plane through a sphere's center **5 :** CEREBRAL HEMISPHERE

hem·i·spher·ec·to·my \ˌ⸗⸗ˌsfiˈrektəmē\ *n* -ES [*hemisphere* + *-ectomy*] **:** surgical removal of a cerebral hemisphere

hem·i·sphered \ˈheməˌsfi(ə)rd\ *adj* **:** having a hemisphere or hemispheric form

hem·i·spher·ic \ˌheməˈsfirik, -fer-, -rēk\ *or* **hem·i·spher·i·cal** \-rəkəl, -rēk-\ *adj* [*hemisphere* + *-ic* or *-ical*] **:** of, relating to, or resembling a hemisphere ⟨a ~ bowl⟩ ⟨~ solidarity⟩ — **hem·i·spher·i·cal·ly** \-rək(ə)lē, -rēk-, -li\ *adv*

hemispherical scale *n* **:** a cosmopolitan soft scale (*Saissetia coffeae*) found in warm countries or as a greenhouse pest

hem·i·sphe·roid \ˌ⸗⸗ˈsfiˌrȯid\ *n* [¹*hemi-* + *spheroid*] **:** one of the halves into which a plane of symmetry cuts a spheroid — **hem·i·sphe·roi·dal** \ˌ⸗⸗ˌsfiˈrȯidᵊl\ *adj*

hem·i·stich \ˈheməˌstik\ *n* [L *hemistichium*, fr. Gk *hēmistichion*, fr. *hēmi-* ¹hemi- + *stichos* line, verse + *-ion* -ium; akin to Gk *steichein* to go — more at STAIR] **:** half a poetic line usu. divided by a caesura (as a metrically independent colon or group of feet of less than regular length)

hem·i·stich·al \ˈ⸗⸗ˈstikəl\ *adj* **:** of, relating to, or written in hemistichs ⟨a ~ division of a verse⟩

hemi·symmetrical \ˈ⸗⸗ at HEMI- +\ *adj* **:** HEMIHEDRAL

hemi·symmetry \"+\ *n* [¹*hemi-* + *symmetry*] **:** the quality or state of being hemisymmetrical

hemi·terpene \"+\ *n* [ISV ¹*hemi-* + *terpene*] **:** a compound C_5H_8 whose formula represents half that of a terpene; *esp* **:** ISOPRENE

hemi·thorax \"+\ *n* [NL, fr. ¹*hemi-* + *thorax*] **:** a lateral half of the thorax

he·mit·ro·pal \heˈmi·trəpəl\ *adj* **:** HEMITROPOUS

¹**hemi·trope** \ˈ⸗⸗ at HEMI- + ˌtrōp\ *adj* [F *hémitrope*, adj. & n., fr. *hémi-* ¹hemi- + *-trope*] **:** half turned round **:** half inverted; *specif* **:** HEMITROPIC

²**hemitrope** \"\ *n* -S [F *hémitrope*] **:** a hemitropic crystal

hemi·trop·ic \ˌ⸗⸗ˈträpik\ *adj, crystallog* **:** having a twinned structure such that one part would be parallel to the other if it were rotated 180 degrees

hemi·tro·pism \ˈ⸗⸗ˌtrōˌpizəm\ *or* **he·mit·ro·py** \hēˈmi·trəpē\ *n, pl* **hemitropisms** *or* **hemitropies** [*hemitropism* fr. ¹*hemitrope* + *-ism*; *hemitropy* fr. F *hémitropie*, fr. *hémi-* ¹hemi- + *tropie* -tropy] **:** the quality or state of being hemitropic

he·mit·ro·pous \ˈ⸗ˈ⸗pəs\ *adj* **1** [¹*hemitrope* + *-ous*] **:** HEMITROPIC **2** [¹*hemi-* + *-tropous*] **:** AMPHITROPOUS

hemi·type \ˈ⸗⸗ at HEMI- + ˌ-\ *n* [¹*hemi-* + *type*] **:** one that is hemitypic

¹**hemi·typic** \ˈ⸗⸗+\ *adj* [¹*hemi-* + *typic*] **:** imperfectly typical

²**hemitypic** \"+\ *n* -S **:** one that is hemitypic

he·mix·is \hēˈmiksəs\ *also* **hemi·mix·is** \ˌ⸗⸗ at HEMI- + ˈmiksəs\ *n* -ES [*hemixis*, NL, contr. of *hemimixis*; *hemimixis*, NL, fr. ¹*hemi-* + *-mixis*] **:** a reorganization process in various ciliated protozoans in which the macronucleus breaks up and a new macronucleus is reconstituted from the fragments without accompanying micronuclear changes — compare ENDOMIXIS

hemi·zo·ic \ˈ⸗⸗+ˈzōik\ *adj* [¹*hemi-* + *-zoic*] **:** having chlorophyll-bearing chromatophores but also ingesting solid food ⟨~ green flagellates⟩ — compare HOLOPHYTIC, HOLOZOIC

hemi·zygote \"+\ *n* [¹*hemi-* + *zygote*] **:** one that is hemizygous

hemi·zygotic \"+\ *adj* **:** HEMIZYGOUS

hemi·zy·gous \ˈ⸗⸗+ˈzīgəs, hēˈmizəgəs\ *adj* [¹*hemi-* + *-zygous*] **:** having or characterized by unpaired genes or a haploid organism or generation ⟨a ~ sex chromosome⟩

hemline \ˈ⸗ˌ⸗\ *n* [²*hem* + *line*] **:** the line formed by the lower edge of a dress, skirt, or coat

hem·lock \ˈhemˌläk\ *n, often attrib* [ME *hemeluc, hemlok, homelok*, fr. OE *hemlic, hymlic*, perh. fr. *hymele* hop plant; akin to MLG *homele* hop plant, ON *humli*; all prob. of Finno-Ugric origin akin to Finn *humala* hop plant & Vogul *qumlix*] **1 a :** any of several poisonous herbs having finely cut leaves and small white flowers; *esp* **:** any of the water hemlocks or the poison hemlock **b :** CONIUM 2 **2** *also* **hemlock fir** *or* **hemlock spruce a :** a tree of the genus *Tsuga* — see CAROLINA HEMLOCK, EASTERN HEMLOCK, MOUNTAIN HEMLOCK, WESTERN HEMLOCK; TREE illustration **b :** the soft coarse light splintery wood of a hemlock tree **3 :** any of several prostrate evergreens of the genus *Taxus*

hemlock chervil *n* **:** a hedge parsley (*Torilis japonica*) that is native to Eurasia but naturalized widely in No. America

hemlock green *n* **:** a dark grayish green that is bluer and deeper than average ivy and bluer and darker than Persian green

hemlock leather *n* **:** leather tanned with hemlock bark or extract

hemlock looper *also* **hemlock spanworm** *n* **:** a greenish looper that is the larva of a rather plain buff or gray geometrid moth (*Lambdina fiscellaria*) of most of No. America, that feeds on hemlock and other conifers and oak, and that is sometimes a serious defoliator

hemlock parsley *n* **:** any of several plants of the genus *Conioselinum* (esp. *C. chinense*) that resemble the poisonous hemlocks but are themselves innocuous

hemlock pitch *n* **:** CANADA PITCH

hemlock sawfly *n* **:** a sawfly (*Neodiprion tsugae*) of western No. America having a larva that is a serious defoliator of western hemlock and occas. other conifers

hemlock storksbill *n* **:** ALFILARIA

hemmed *past of* HEM

hem·mel \ˈheməl\ *n* -S [perh. alter. of ¹*helm* (rough shed)] *dial Brit* **:** a simple shelter usu. in a field for cattle or hay

¹**hem·mer** \ˈhemə(r)\ *n* -S [ME, fr. *hemmen* to hem, border + *-er* — more at ³HEM] **:** one that hems: **a :** a worker who makes hems by hand or machine **b :** a sewing machine attachment for turning under and stitching hems **c :** a tool for turning over the edge of sheet metal

²**hemmer** \"\ *n* -S [⁵*hem* + *-er*] **:** one that hems in speech

hemming *n* -S [fr. gerund of ³*hem*] **:** the act or process of one that hems; *also* **:** HEM

hemo- — see HEM-

hemoagglutinin *var of* HEMAGGLUTININ

he·mo·blast \ˈhēməˌblast, ˈhem-\ *n* [ISV *hem-* + *-blast*] **:** HEMATOBLAST

he·mo·chorial \ˌhēmō, ˌhemō+\ *adj* [*hem-* + *chorial*] *of a placenta* **:** having fetal epithelium bathed in maternal blood ⟨the lower rodents, bats, some insectivores, and most primates including man are ~⟩ — compare ENDOTHELIOCHORIAL, EPITHELIOCHORIAL, SYNDESMOCHORIAL

he·mo·chromatosis \"+\ *n* [NL, fr. *hem-* + *chromatosis*] **:** a disease characterized by widespread deposition of iron-containing pigments (as hemosiderin) in the tissues resulting in bronzing of the skin, associated with cirrhosis of the liver and pancreas and frequently with diabetic symptoms, and occurring usu. in males — called also *bronze diabetes*

he·mo·chrome \ˈhēməˌkrōm, ˈhem-\ *n* -S [ISV *hem-* + *-chrome*] **:** HEMOCHROMOGEN

he·mo·chro·mo·gen \ˌ⸗⸗ˈkrōməˌjen, -jən\ *n* -S [ISV *hemochromo-* (fr. *hemochrome*) + *-gen*] **1 :** a colored compound formed from or related to hemoglobin; *esp* **:** a bright red combination of a nitrogen base (as globin or pyridine) with heme — compare HEMOPROTEIN **2 :** a colored compound of a nitrogenous base with a metal-porphyrin derivative esp. when in the reduced form

he·mo·clas·tic crisis \ˈ⸗⸗ˈklastik-\ *n* [ISV *hem-* + *-clastic* (disintegrating)] **:** an acute transitory alteration of the blood that sometimes accompanies anaphylactic shock and is marked by intense leukopenia with relative lymphocytosis, alteration in blood coagulability, and fall in blood pressure

he·mo·coel *also* **he·mo·coele** \ˈhēməˌsēl, ˈhem-\ *n* -S [*hem-* + *-coele*] **:** a body cavity (as in arthropods) formed by the expansion of parts of the blood-vascular system — **he·mo·coe·lic** \ˈ⸗⸗ˈsēlik\ *adj* — **he·mo·coe·lous** \-ləs\ *adj*

he·mo·coelom \ˌhēmō, ˌhemō+\ *n* [*hem-* + *coelom*] **1 :** the part of the embryonic coelom in which the heart develops **2 :** HEMOCOEL

he·mo·concentration \"+\ *n* [ISV *hem-* + *concentration*] **:** increased concentration of cells and solids in the blood usu. resulting from loss of fluid to the tissues — compare HEMODILUTION

he·mo·co·nia *also* **he·mo·ko·nia** \ˌhēməˈkōnēə, ˌhem-\ *n* -S [NL, fr. *hem-* + Gk *konia* dust — more at INCINERATE] **:** small refractive colorless particles in the blood that are believed to be castoff granules from the cells in the blood or minute globules of fat — called also *blood dust*

he·mo·co·ni·o·sis \ˌ⸗⸗ˌkōnēˈōsəs\ *n, pl* **hemoconio·ses** \-ˈōˌsēz\ [NL, fr. *hemoconia* + *-osis*] **:** a condition in which there is an abnormally high content of hemoconia in the blood

he·mo·culture \ˌhēmō, ˌhemō+\ *n* [ISV *hem-* + *culture*] **:** a culture made from blood to detect the presence of pathogenic microorganisms by providing conditions likely to further their multiplication

he·mo·cu·pre·in \ˌhēmōˈk(y)üprēən, ˌhem-\ *n* -S [ISV *hem-* + *cupr-* + *-ein*] **:** a blue copper-containing protein obtained from red blood cells

he·mo·cy·a·nin \ˌ⸗⸗ˈsīənən\ *n* [ISV *hem-* + *cyan-* + *-in*] **:** a colorless copper-containing respiratory pigment found in solution in the blood plasma of various arthropods and mollusks and converted by oxygen to blue oxyhemocyanin

he·mo·cyte \ˈ⸗⸗ˌsīt\ *n* -S [ISV *hem-* + *-cyte*] **:** a blood cell esp. of an invertebrate animal

he·mo·cy·to·blast \ˌ⸗⸗ˈsīd·əˌblast\ *n* -S [ISV *hemocyto-* (fr. *hemocyte*) + *-blast*] **:** a stem cell for blood-cellular elements; *esp* **:** one considered competent to produce all types of blood cell — **he·mo·cy·to·blas·tic** \ˈ⸗⸗ˌ⸗⸗ˈblastik\ *adj*

he·mo·cy·to·blas·to·sis \ˌhēməˌsīd·əˌblaˈstōsəs, ˌhem-\ *n, pl* **hemocytoblasto·ses** \-ˌōˌsēz\ [NL, fr. ISV *hemocytoblast* + NL *-osis*] **:** lymphocytomatosis of chickens

he·mo·cy·to·gen·e·sis \-d·əˈjenəsəs\ *n* [NL, fr. *hemocyto-* (fr. ISV *hemocyte*) + L *genesis*] **:** the part of hematopoiesis concerned with the formation of blood cells

he·mo·cy·tol·y·sis \ˌ-ˌsīˈtäləsəs\ *n, pl* **hemocytoly·ses** \-əˌsēz\ [NL, fr. *hemocyto-* (fr. ISV *hemocyte*) + NL *-lysis*] **:** a breaking down or dissolution of red blood cells esp. by the action of hypotonic solutions

he·mo·cy·tom·e·ter \-ˈtäməd·ə(r)\ *n* [ISV *hem-* + *cyt-* + *-meter*] **:** HEMACYTOMETER

he·mo·cy·to·zo·on \-ˌsīd·əˈzōˌän\ *n* -S [NL, fr. *hemocyto-* (fr. ISV *hemocyte*) + NL *-zoon*] **:** an animal parasite (as the plasmodium of malaria) living within a blood corpuscle

he·mo·dilution \ˌhēmō, ˌhemō+\ *n* [*hem-* + *dilution*] **:** decreased concentration of cells and solids in the blood usu. resulting from gain of fluid from the tissues (as after hemorrhage) — compare HEMOCONCENTRATION

he·mo·dynamic \"+\ *adj* [ISV *hem-* + *dynamic*] **1 :** of, relating to, or involving hemodynamics **2 :** concerned with or functioning in the mechanics of blood circulation

he·mo·dynamics \"+\ *n pl but sing or pl in constr* [ISV *hem-* + *dynamics*] **1 :** a branch of physiology that deals with circulatory movements and the forces involved in circulation of the blood **2 a :** the forces involved in circulation (as of a particular body part) ⟨renal ~⟩ **b :** hemodynamic effect (as of a drug)

he·mo·endothelial \"+\ *adj* [*hem-* + *endothelial*] *of a placenta* **:** having the fetal villi reduced to bare capillary loops that are bathed in maternal blood ⟨higher rodents are ~⟩

hemoflagellate \"+\ *n* [*hem-* + *flagellate*] **:** a flagellate (as a trypanosome) that is a blood parasite

he·mo·fus·cin \ˌhēmōˈfəsən, ˌhem-\ *n* [ISV *hem-* + *fusc-* (fr. L *fuscus* dark brown) + *-in* — more at DUSK] **:** a yellowish brown pigment found in small amount in some normal tissues and increased amount in certain pathological states (as hemochromatosis)

he·mo·glo·bic \ˈ⸗⸗ˈglōbik\ *adj* [*hemoglobin* + *-ic*] **:** HEMOGLOBINIC

he·mo·glo·bin *also* **hae·mo·glo·bin** \ˈ⸗⸗ˌglōbən, ˌ⸗⸗ˈ⸗⸗\ *n* -S [ISV, short for earlier *hematoglobulin*, fr. *hemato-* (fr. *hematin*) + *globulin*] **1 a :** an iron-containing protein pigment occurring in the red blood cells of vertebrates and functioning primarily in the transport of oxygen from the lungs to the tissues of the body **b :** the dark purplish crystallizable form of this pigment that is found chiefly in the venous blood of vertebrates, that is a conjugated protein composed of heme and globin commonly in a ratio of four molecules of heme to one of globin but that may vary somewhat in different species and in different physiological and pathological states (as in some anemias), that combines loosely and reversibly with oxygen in the lungs or gills to form oxyhemoglobin and with carbon dioxide in the tissues to form carbhemoglobin, that in man is present normally in blood to the extent of 14 to 16 gm. in 100 ml. expressed sometimes on a scale of 0 to 100 with an average normal value (as 15 gm.) taken as 100, and that is determined in blood either colorimetrically or by quantitative estimation of the iron present — symbol *Hb*; called also *ferrohemoglobin, reduced hemoglobin*; compare CARBONYLHEMOGLOBIN, METHEMOGLOBIN **c :** any of numerous chemically similar iron-containing respiratory pigments that occur in cells or usu. free in the plasma of many annelid worms and certain other invertebrates, in some yeasts and other fungi, in the nodules formed on the roots of leguminous plants by nitrogen-fixing bacteria, and elsewhere — compare HEMOPROTEIN **2 :** any of various respiratory pigments consisting of a conjugated protein that has as the nonprotein group either heme or an analogous compound containing a metal — compare MYOGLOBIN — **he·mo·glo·bin·ic** \ˈ⸗⸗ˌglōˈbinik\ *adj* — **he·mo·glo·bi·nous** \ˈ⸗⸗ˈglōbənəs\ *adj*

hemoglobin A *n* **:** the hemoglobin in the red blood cells of normal adult human beings

he·mo·glo·bi·ne·mia \ˌ⸗⸗ˌglōbəˈnēmēə\ *n* -S [NL, fr. ISV *hemoglobin* + NL *-emia*] **1 :** the presence of free hemoglobin in the blood plasma resulting from the solution of hemoglobin out of the red blood cells or from disintegration of the red cells **2 :** AZOTEMIA

he·mo·glo·bi·nom·e·ter \-ˈnäməd·ə(r)\ *n* [ISV *hemoglobin* + *-o-* + *-meter*] **:** an instrument for the colorimetric determination of hemoglobin in blood ⟨visual and photoelectric ~*s*⟩ — **he·mo·glo·bi·nom·e·try** \-mə·trē\ *n* -ES

hemoglobin S *n* **:** the hemoglobin occurring in the red blood cells in sickle-cell anemia and sickle-cell trait and differing from hemoglobin A in its lower solubility and lower isoelectric point

he·mo·glo·bi·nu·ria \-ˈn(y)u̇rēə\ *n* -S [NL, fr. ISV *hemoglobin* + NL *-uria*] **:** the presence of free hemoglobin in the urine — compare HEMATURIA — **he·mo·glo·bi·nu·ric** \ˈ⸗⸗ˌ⸗⸗ˈn(y)u̇rik\ *adj*

he·mo·gram \ˈhēməˌgram, ˈhem-\ *n* [ISV *hem-* + *-gram*] **:** a systematic report of the findings from a blood examination

hemogregarine *var of* HAEMOGREGARINE

he·mo·his·ti·o·blast \ˌhēmōˈhistēōˌblast, ˌhem-\ *n* [ISV *hem-* + *histi-* + *-blast*] **:** a hemocytoblast that is a derivative of the reticuloendothelial system

he·moid \ˈhēˌmȯid\ *adj* [ISV *hem-* + *-oid*] **:** resembling blood **:** HEMATOID

hemokonia *var of* HEMOCONIA

he·mo·lymph \ˈhēmə, ˈheməˌ+ˌ-\ *n* [ISV *hem-* + *lymph*] **:** the circulatory fluid of various invertebrate animals that is functionally comparable to the blood and lymph of vertebrates

he·mo·lymphatic \ˈ⸗⸗+\ *adj* [fr. *hemolymph*, after E *lymph*: *lymphatic*] **:** of, like, or relating to hemolymph or to a hemolymph gland

hemolymph gland *or* **hemolymph node** *n* **:** any of several small chiefly retroperitoneal nodes of tissue resembling lymph nodes but having the lymph spaces replaced in whole or in part by blood sinuses

he·mo·ly·sin \ˌhēməˈlīsᵊn, ˌhem-\ *n* [ISV *hem-* + *lysin*] **:** a substance (as an antibody) that esp. in conjunction with complement causes the dissolution of red blood cells with liberation of the contained hemoglobin

he·mol·y·sis \hēˈmäləsəs\ *n, pl* **hemoly·ses** \-əˌsēz\ [NL, fr. *hem-* + *-lysis*] **:** liberation of hemoglobin from red blood cells; *specif* **:** such a liberation brought about by a specific hemolysin usu. interacting with complement

he·mo·lyt·ic \ˌhēməˈlid·ik, ˌhem-\ *adj* [ISV *hem-* + *-lytic*] **:** of, relating to, involving, or inducing hemolysis ⟨~ antigens⟩

hemolytic anemia *n* **:** anemia characterized by excessive destruction of red blood cells caused by chemical poisoning (as by certain sulfonamide compounds), infections (as malaria or sepsis), cell abnormalities (as sickle-cell anemia), or other agents or factors (as endogenous hemolysins)

hemolytic disease of the newborn : ERYTHROBLASTOSIS FETALIS

hemolytic jaundice *or* **hemolytic icterus** *n* **:** a condition characterized by excessive destruction of red blood cells accompanied by jaundice; *specif* **:** a rare familial anemia characterized by small thick fragile red blood cells which are extremely susceptible to hemolysis, by enlargement of the spleen, and by more or less marked jaundice

he·mo·lyze \ˈhēməˌlīz, ˈhem-\ *vb* -ED/-ING/-S [fr. *hemolysis*, after such pairs as E *analysis: analyze*] *vt* **:** to cause (red blood cells) to dissolve **:** induce hemolysis of **~** *vi* **:** to undergo hemolysis

he·mom·e·ter \hēˈmäməd·ə(r)\ *n* [ISV *hem-* + *-meter*] **:** an instrument for measuring some quality of blood: as **a :** HEMOGLOBINOMETER **b :** HEMADYNAMOMETER **c :** HEMACYTOMETER — **he·mo·met·ric** \ˌhēməˈme·trik, ˌhem-\ *adj* — **he·mom·e·try** \hēˈmämə·trē\ *n* -ES

he·mo·parasite \ˌhēmō, ˌhemō+\ *n* [*hem-* + *parasite*] **:** an animal parasite (as a hemoflagellate or a filarial worm) living in the blood of a vertebrate

he·mop·a·thy \hēˈmäpəthē\ *n* -ES [ISV *hem-* + *-pathy*] **:** a pathological state (as anemia or agranulocytosis) of the blood or blood-forming tissues

he·mo·pericardium \ˌhēmō, ˌhemō+\ *n* [NL, fr. *hem-* + *pericardium*] **:** blood in the pericardial cavity

he·mo·peritoneum \"+\ *n* [NL, fr. *hem-* + *peritoneum*] **:** blood in the peritoneal cavity

he·mo·phage \ˈhēməˌfāj, ˈhem-\ *n* -S [*hem-* + *-phage*] **:** ERYTHROPHAGE

he·mo·pha·gia \ˌ⸗⸗ˈfāj(ē)ə\ *n* -S [NL, fr. *hem-* + *-phagia*] **1 :** an ingestion of blood **2 :** phagocytosis of red blood cells — **he·moph·a·gous** \hēˈmäfəgəs\ *adj*

he·mo·phagocyte \ˌhēmō, ˌhemō+\ *n* [*hem-* + *phagocyte*] **1 :** HEMOPHAGE **2 :** a phagocytic cell of the bloodstream — **he·mo·phagocytic** \"+\ *adj*

¹**he·mo·phile** \ˈhēməˌfīl, ˈhem-\ *adj* [*hem-* + *-phile*] **:** HEMOPHILIC

²**hemophile** \"\ *n* -S [ISV *hem-* + *-phile*] **1 :** HEMOPHILIAC **2 :** a hemophilic organism (as a bacterium)

he·mo·phil·ia \ˌ⸗⸗ˈfilēə\ *n* -S [NL, fr. *hem-* + *-philia*] **:** a tendency to uncontrollable bleeding; *esp* **:** a sex-linked hereditary blood defect of males characterized by delayed clotting of the blood and consequent difficulty in controlling hemorrhage even after minor injuries — compare PSEUDOHEMOPHILIA

¹**he·mo·phil·i·ac** \-lēˌak\ *n* -S [*hemophilia* + *-ac* (fr. Gk *-akos*, adj. suffix)] **:** one affected with hemophilia

²**hemophiliac** \ˈ⸗⸗ˈ⸗⸗ˌ⸗\ *adj* [*hemophilia* + *-ac* (fr. Gk *-akos*, adj. suffix)] **:** HEMOPHILIC

he·mo·phil·ic \-ˈfilik\ *adj* **1** [*hemophilia* + *-ic*] **:** of, like, or affected with hemophilia **2** [*hem-* + *-philic*] **:** tending to thrive in blood ⟨~ bacteria⟩

he·mo·phil·i·oid \-ˈfilēˌȯid\ *also* **he·moph·i·loid** \hēˈmäfəˌlȯid\ *adj* [*hemophili-* or *hemophil-* (fr. *hemophilia*) + *-oid*] **:** resembling hemophilia esp. in exhibiting a tendency to uncontrollable bleeding ⟨a ~ state⟩

he·moph·i·lus \hēˈmäfələs\ *n, cap* [NL, fr. *hem-* + *-philus*] **:** a genus of minute nonmotile gram-negative strictly parasitic hemophilic bacteria (family Parvobacteriaceae) including several important pathogens (as *H. influenzae* associated with human respiratory infections, conjunctivitis, and meningitis, *H. suis* of swine influenza, or *H. ducreyi* of chancroid)

he·mo·poi·e·sis \ˌhēmōˌpȯiˈēsəs, ˌhem-\ *n* -S [NL, fr. *hem-* + *-poiesis*] **:** HEMATOPOIESIS — **he·mo·poi·et·ic** \ˈ⸗⸗ˌpȯiˈed·ik\ *adj*

he·mo·poi·etin \ˌ⸗⸗pȯiˈētᵊn\ *n* -S [ISV *hemopoietic* + *-in*; prob. orig. formed as F *hémopoïétine*] **:** a hypothetical stimulant to blood-cell production possibly equivalent to the antianemic factor or one of its precursors

he·mo·proteidae \ˌhēmō, ˌhemō+\ *syn of* HAEMOPROTEIDAE

he·mo·protein \"+\ *n* [*hem-* + *protein*] **:** a conjugated protein (as hemoglobin, catalase, peroxidase, or cytochrome) whose nonprotein portion is heme or a heme **:** a hemochromogen with a protein combined with heme — compare CHROMOPROTEIN

he·mo·pro·teus \"+\ *syn of* HAEMOPROTEUS

he·mop·toe \hē'mäptəwē\ *n* -s [NL, alter. of *hemoptysis*] **:** hemorrhage from the lungs

he·mop·to·ic \-wik\ *adj* [prob. fr. LL *haemoptoicus* spitting blood, fr. LGk *haimoptoikos*, alter. of Gk *haimoptyikos*, fr. *haimo-* hem- + *-ptyikos* (fr. *ptyein* to spit + *-ikos* -ic) — more at SPEW] **:** of or produced by hemoptysis

he·mop·ty·sis \-təsəs\ *n, pl* **hemopty·ses** \-ə,sēz\ [NL, fr. *hem-* + *-ptysis*] **:** expectoration of blood from some part of the respiratory tract — compare HEMATEMESIS

he·mo·pyrrole \ˌhēmō, ¦hemō+\ *n* [ISV *hem-* + *pyrrole*] **:** a low-melting solid or liquid homologue $C_8H_{13}N$ of pyrrole formed during reduction of hemin or phylloporphyrin with hydriodic acid; 2,3-dimethyl-4-ethyl-pyrrole

¹**hem·or·rhage** \'hem(ə)rij, -rēj\ *n* -s [F & L; F *hémorrhagie*, fr. L *haemorrhagia*, fr. Gk *haimorrhagia*, fr. *haimo-* hem- + *-rrhagia*] **:** a copious discharge of blood from the blood vessels

²**hemorrhage** \"\ *vi* -ED/-ING/-s **:** BLEED

hem·or·rhag·ic \ˌhemə¦rajik\ *adj* [Gk *haimorrhagikos*, fr. *haimorrhagia* hemorrhage + *-ikos* -ic] **:** involving, associated with, or tending to cause hemorrhage ⟨~ retinitis⟩

hemorrhagic diathesis *n* **:** a constitutional tendency to spontaneous often severe bleeding — compare HEMOPHILIA, PURPURA HEMORRHAGICA

hemorrhagic septicemia *n* **:** pasteurellosis of domestic animals usu. due to a bacterium (*Pasteurella multocida*) and typically marked by internal hemorrhages, fever, mucopurulent discharges, and often pneumonia and diarrhea, typical forms being swine plague, shipping fever of cattle and lambs, and fowl cholera

hem·or·rhag·in \ˌ==¦rajən\ *n* -s [ISV *hemorrhage* + *-in*] **:** a toxic substance occurring usu. as a component of various snake venoms and capable of destroying the blood cells and the walls of small blood vessels — compare HEMOLYSIN

hem·or·rhoid \'hem(ə)ˌrȯid\ *n* -s [MF *hemorrhoides*, pl, fr. L *haemorrhoidae*, fr. Gk *haimorrhoides*, fr. *haimorrhoos* flowing with blood, fr. *haimo-* hem- + *-rrhoos* (fr. *rhein* to flow) — more at STREAM] **:** a mass of dilated veins in swollen tissue at the margin of the anus or nearby within the rectum — usu. used in pl.; called also *piles*

¹**hem·or·rhoi·dal** \ˌ==¦rȯidᵊl\ *adj* [F *hémorrhoïdal*, fr. MF, fr. *hemorrhoides* hemorrhoids + *-al*] **1 :** of, relating to, or involving hemorrhoids **2 :** RECTAL

²**hemorrhoidal** \"\ *n* -s **:** a hemorrhoidal part (as an artery or vein)

hemorrhoidal artery *n* **:** one of the arteries supplying the rectal and anal region that consists of a superior which is a continuation of the inferior mesenteric and a middle and inferior which are usu. branches of the hypogastric and pudendal respectively

hemorrhoidal vein *n* **:** any of the veins corresponding to the hemorrhoidal arteries and forming a plexus at the lower rectum and anus

hem·or·rhoid·ec·to·my \ˌhem(ə)ˌrȯi'dektəmē\ *n* -ES [*hemorrhoid* + *-ectomy*] **:** surgical removal of a hemorrhoid

he·mo·salpinx \ˌhēmō, ¦hemō+\ *n* [NL, fr. *hem-* + *salpinx*] **:** HEMATOSALPINX

he·mo·sid·er·in \ˌhēmō'sidərən, ˌhem-\ *n* -s [ISV *hem-* + *sider-* + *-in*] **:** a yellowish brown granular pigment formed by breakdown of hemoglobin, found in phagocytes and in tissues esp. in disturbances of iron metabolism (as in hemochromatosis, hemosiderosis, or some anemias), and composed essentially of colloidal ferric oxide — compare FERRITIN

he·mo·sid·er·o·sis \ˌ==ˌsidə'rōsəs\ *n, pl* **hemosidero·ses** \-ō,sēz\ [NL, fr. ISV *hemosiderin* + NL *-osis*] **:** a pathological condition marked by the deposition of hemosiderin in the tissues as a result of the breakdown of red blood cells — compare HEMOCHROMATOSIS — **he·mo·sid·er·ot·ic** \¦==ˌ==¦räd·ik\ *adj*

he·mo·spo·rid·ia \ˌhēmōspə'ridēə, ˌhem-\ *syn of* HAEMOSPORIDIA

he·mo·sta·sis \ˌhēmə'stāsəs\ *n, pl* **hemosta·ses** \-əˌsēz\ [NL, fr. Gk *haimostasis* styptic, fr. *haimo-* hem- + *-stasis*] **1 :** stoppage or sluggishness of blood flow **2 :** arrest of bleeding (as by a hemostatic agent)

he·mo·stat \'hēməˌstat, 'hem-\ *n* -s **1** [by shortening] **:** HEMOSTATIC **2** [*hem-* + *-stat*] **:** an instrument for compressing a bleeding vessel

¹**he·mo·stat·ic** \¦==¦stad·ik\ *n* -s [LGk *haimostatikos*, n. & adj.] **:** an agent that checks bleeding; *esp* **:** one that shortens the clotting time of blood — compare HEMOSTAT

²**hemostatic** \"\ *adj* [LGk *haimostatikos* good for stopping blood, fr. Gk *haimo-* hem- + *-statikos* -static] **1 :** of or caused by hemostasis **2 :** serving to check bleeding

he·mo·therapy \ˌhēmō, ¦hemō + \ *n* [ISV *hem-* + *therapy*] **:** treatment involving the administration of fresh blood, a blood fraction, or a blood preparation

he·mo·thorax \ˌhēmō, ¦hemō+\ *n* [NL, fr. *hem-* + *thorax*] **:** blood in the pleural cavity

he·mo·toxin \"+\ *n* [ISV *hem-* + *toxin*] **:** HEMOLYSIN

he·mot·ro·phe \hē'mä·trəfē\ *n* -s [*hem-* + *-trophe* (as in *embryotrophe*)] **:** the nutrients supplied to the embryo in placental mammals by the maternal bloodstream after formation of the placenta — compare EMBRYOTROPH, HISTOTROPH

he·mo·zo·on \ˌhēmə'zōˌän, ˌhem-\ *n, pl* **hemo·zoa** \-ōə\ [NL, fr. *hem-* + *-zoon*] **:** HEMATOZOON

hemp \'hemp\ *n* -s *often attrib* [ME *hemp, hempe*, fr. OE

hemp: flowering shoots of *1* staminate plant, of *2*, pistillate plant; *3* staminate flower; *4* pistillate flower; *5* fruit

hænep, henep; akin to MD *hennep* hemp, OHG *hanaf, hanif*, ON *hampr*; prob. all of non-IE origin; akin to the source of Gk *kannabis* hemp & Arm *kanap*] **1 a :** a tall widely cultivated Asiatic herb (*Cannabis sativa*) with tough bast fiber that is used for making cloth, floor covering, and cordage — see BHANG, CANNABIDIOL, CANNABIN, CANNABINOL, CANNABIS, CHARAS, HASHISH; compare GANJA **b :** the fiber of this plant prepared for commercial use **c :** a narcotic drug (as hashish) from hemp **2 :** the useful fiber of any of numerous plants (as jute, abaca, ramie) other than hemp; *also* **:** the plant producing such fiber **3** *archaic* **a :** a gallows rope **b :** HANGING **4 :** a light grayish olive color that is redder and deeper than twine, Quaker gray, or average citron gray

hemp agrimony *n* **:** a coarse European herb (*Eupatorium cannabinum*) with reddish flower heads and sessile leaves

hemp-brake \'=,=\ *n* **:** ⁴BRAKE 1

hemp dogbane *n* **:** INDIAN HEMP 1

hem·pel column \'hempəl-\ *n, usu cap H* [after Walter *Hempel* †1916 Ger. chemist] **:** a vertical column for fractional distillation filled with glass beads and provided with a side tube for exit of the vapors

hemp·en \'hempən\ *adj* [ME, fr. *hemp* + ¹*-en*] **1 :** of, relating to, made of, or like hemp **2** *archaic* **:** of or relating to a hangman's noose or a hanging

hemp family *n* **:** URTICACEAE

hemp nettle *n* **:** a plant of the genus *Galeopsis*; *esp* **:** a coarse bristly Eurasian herb (*G. tetrahit*) having foliage resembling that of the nettle and being common as a weed in the U. S.

hemp palm *n* **:** either of two dwarf fan palms (*Chamaerops humilis* of the Mediterranean region and *Trachycarpus excelsa* of China) the leaves of which yield the fiber African hair

hempseed \'=,=\ *n* [ME, fr. *hemp* + *seed*] **:** the seed of hemp

hempseed oil *n* **:** a light green to brownish yellow drying fatty oil obtained from hempseed and used chiefly in soft soap, paints, and varnishes and in Asia in foods

hemp tree *n* **:** AGNUS CASTUS

hempweed \'=,=\ *n* **1 :** HEMP AGRIMONY **2** *also* **hemp vine :** CLIMBING HEMPWEED

¹**hempy** *or* **hemp·ie** \'hempi\ *n, pl* **hempies** [*hemp* + *-y* or *-ie*] **1** *chiefly Scot* **:** ROGUE, GALLOWS BIRD **2** *chiefly Scot* **:** a lively mischievous young person

²**hempy** *or* **hempie** \"\ *adj, Scot* **:** full of deviltry **:** MISCHIEVOUS

hems *pl of* HEM, *pres 3d sing of* HEM

¹**hemstitch** \'=,=\ *vt* [²*hem* + *stitch*] **:** to embroider (fabric) by drawing out parallel threads and stitching the exposed threads in groups to form various designs

²**hemstitch** \"\ *n* **1** *or* **hemstitching** \'=,==\ **:** decorative needlework similar to drawnwork that is often used on or near stitching lines of hems **2 :** a stitch used in hemstitching

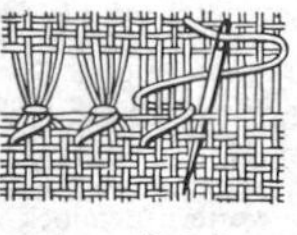

hemstitch 1

hemstitcher \'=,==\ *n* **1 :** a worker who hemstitches by hand or machine **2 :** a sewing-machine attachment for making hemstitching

hen \'hen\ *n* -s *often attrib* [ME, fr. OE *henn*; akin to OHG *henna* hen, OE *hana* rooster — more at CHANT] **1 a :** the female of the domestic fowl; *esp* **:** one that is more than a year old **b :** the female of any of various other birds (as most gallinaceous or domesticated birds) **c :** one who behaves like a hen ⟨there were younger children at home and Minnie was their devoted mother ~ —R.T.Moriarty⟩ **2 a :** the female of various marine animals (as the lobster) and some fishes **b :** HEN FISH **3 :** an esp. older woman who is fussy or officious ⟨grown into a cantankerous old ~⟩ — **a hen on :** a secret plan in preparation **:** something hatching ⟨the higher officials knew there was *a hen on* —Jo Mora⟩

henad \'heˌnad, 'hē,-\ *n* -s [Gk *henad-*, *henas*, fr. *hen*, neut. of *heis* one + *-ad-*, *-as* (fem. suffix denoting connection with); akin to Gk *homos* same — more at SAME, -AD] **:** MONAD 1a

hen and chickens *n, pl* **hens and chickens :** any of several plants having offsets, runners, or proliferous flowers: as **a :** HOUSELEEK **b :** GROUND IVY **c :** an English daisy with proliferous flowers **d :** a plant of the genus *Echeveria*

henbane \'=,=\ *n* [ME, fr. *hen* + *bane*] **1 a :** a poisonous fetid Old World solanaceous herb of the genus *Hyoscyamus* (*H. niger*) having sticky hairy dentate leaves and yellowish brown flowers and yielding hyoscyamine and scopolamine — called also *black henbane* **b :** YELLOW HENBANE **2 :** EGYPTIAN HENBANE

henbill \'=,=\ *n* **1 :** PIED-BILLED GREBE **2 :** AMERICAN COOT

henbit \'=,=\ *n* [*hen* + *bit* (morsel)] **1 :** an annual dead nettle (*Lamium amplexicaule*) with reniform leaves and flowers that are arranged in whorls of 6 to 10 or more and have connivent calyx teeth — called also *bee nettle* **2 :** IVY-LEAVED SPEEDWELL **3 :** BLACK HOREHOUND

hence \'hen(t)s\ *adv* [ME *hennes*, fr. *henne* hence (fr. OE *heonan*) + *-s* (adv. suffix); akin to OS *hinan, hinana* away from here, OHG *hina & hinnan, hinana*, OE *hēr* here — more at HERE] **1 a :** from this place **:** AWAY ⟨how churlishly I bid Lucretia ~ —Shak.⟩ ⟨get thee ~, Satan⟩; *specif* **:** from this world or life ⟨before I go ~ and be no more —Ps 39:13 (AV)⟩ **b** *obs* **:** at an interval in space **:** DISTANT ⟨three quarters of a mile ~ —Shak.⟩ — often used imperatively for *go hence* or *get (you) hence* ⟨hence with your little ones —Shak.⟩ **2 a** *archaic* **:** from now on **:** HENCEFORTH ⟨from ~ I'll love no friend —Shak.⟩ **b :** from this time **:** in the future ⟨a generation ~⟩ **3 :** because of a preceding fact or premise **:** THEREFORE ⟨unorthodox and ~ unpopular doctrines —J.B.Conant⟩ **4 :** from this source or origin ⟨~ the desire to impress public opinion —Hugh Gaitskell⟩ — **from hence** *adv, archaic* **:** HENCE **:** from this place ⟨a fortnight since we set out *from hence* upon a little excursion —Thomas Gray⟩

henceforth \(')=¦=\ *adv* [ME *hennesforth*, fr. *hennes* + *forth*] **:** from this point on — **from henceforth** *adv, archaic* **:** HENCEFORTH ⟨*from henceforth* bear his name whose form thou bearest —Shak.⟩

henceforward *also* **henceforwards** \(')=¦==\ *adv* [ME *hennesforward*, fr. *hennes* + *forward*] **:** HENCEFORTH — **from henceforward** *adv, archaic* **:** HENCEFORTH

henchboy *n* [*hench-* (as in *henchman*) + *boy*] *obs* **:** a boy attendant **:** PAGE

hench·man \'henchmən\ *n, pl* **henchmen** [ME *hengestman, henxtman, henxman* groom, squire, fr. *hengest* stallion, gelding (fr. OE) + *man*; akin to OFris *hanxt, hengst* horse, OHG *hengist* gelding, ON *hestr* stallion, horse, and perh. to W *caseg* mare, Gk *kēkiein* to gush forth, Lith *šokti* to jump, dance; basic meaning: jumping, bubbling] **1 a** *obs* **:** a squire or page to a person of high rank ⟨a little changeling boy to be my ~ —Shak.⟩ **b :** a household servant **:** RETAINER ⟨hear my ~ . . . about to ring the bell for luncheon —William Black⟩ **2 a :** the head gillie of a Scottish chief **b :** a subordinate who is heavily relied upon **:** RIGHT-HAND MAN ⟨the significant look that passes between the suave mastermind and his black-browed ~ —Richard Mallett⟩ **3 a :** a loyal supporter **:** ADHERENT ⟨the *henchmen* of German political and economic reaction —Hillel Silver⟩ **b :** a political follower giving active support; *esp* **:** one whose support is chiefly a matter of personal advantage ⟨a fat, easygoing minor ~ who held a judgeship —Hodding Carter⟩ **c :** an unscrupulous often violent member of a gang **:** HATCHET MAN ⟨a third car full of his armed *henchmen* following behind —F.L.Allen⟩

hen clam *n* [so called fr. the belief that such clams are female only] **1 :** SURF CLAM **2 :** PISMO CLAM

hen curlew *n* **:** a long-billed No. American curlew (*Numenius americanus*) now rare because of excessive hunting

hendeca- *or* **hendec-** *comb form* [Gk *hendeka-, hendek-*, fr. *hendeka*, fr. *hen* (neut. of *heis* one) + *deka* ten — more at HENAD, TEN] **:** eleven ⟨*hendeca*syllable⟩ ⟨*hendec*ane⟩

hen·deca·colic \(¦)hen¦dekə¦kōlik, -¦käl-\ *adj* [*hendeca-* + ²*colon* + *-ic*] *Greek & Latin prosody* **:** made up of eleven cola

hen·de·cane \'hendəˌkān, hen'deˌk-\ *n* -s [*hendeca-* + *-ane*] **:** UNDECANE

hen·deca·se·mic \(¦)hen¦dekə¦sēmik\ *adj* [*hendeca-* + Gk *sēma* sign + E *-ic*] *Greek & Latin prosody* **:** containing or equivalent to eleven short syllables — compare MORA

hen·deca·syllabic \(¦)hen¦dekə+\ *or* **en·deca·syllabic** \(¦)en-\ *adj* [L *hendecasyllabus* + E *-ic*] **1 :** having eleven syllables **2 :** composed of eleven-syllable lines

hen·deca·syllable \hen'dekə+,-, (ˌ)hen,dekə+'-\ *n* [modif. (influenced by *syllable*) of L *hendecasyllabus*, fr. Gk *hendeka* eleven + *syllabē* syllable — more at SYLLABLE] **:** a line of eleven syllables ⟨the ~ is the principal verse in Italian poetry⟩

hen·decyl \(')hen¦desəl, -dēs-\ *n* -s [*hendecane* + *-yl*] **:** UNDECYL

hen·di·a·dys \hen'dīədəs\ *n* -ES [LL *hendiadys, hendiadyoin*, modif. of Gk *hen dia dyoin* one through two] **:** the expression of an idea by two nouns connected by *and* (as *cups and gold*) instead of by a noun and an adjective (as *golden cups*)

hen·don \'hendən\ *adj, usu cap* [fr. *Hendon*, England] **:** of or from the urban district of Hendon, England **:** of the kind or style prevalent in Hendon

hen·eicosane \(')hen+\ *n* -s [ISV *heneicos-* (fr. *hen-* — fr. Gk *hen*, neut. of *heis* one — + *eicosa-*) + *-ane*] **:** a paraffin hydrocarbon $C_{21}H_{44}$; *esp* **:** the white waxy normal heneicosane $CH_3(CH_2)_{19}CH_3$

hen·e·quen *also* **hen·i·quen** \'henəkən, ¦=='ken\ *n* -s [Sp *henequén, heniquén, jeniquén*, prob. fr. Taino] **1 :** a strong yellowish or reddish hard fiber derived from the leaves of a tropical American agave, produced chiefly in Yucatán, and used largely in the production of binder twine — see SISAL **2 :** the agave (*Agave fourcroydes*) that yields henequen

hen feather *n* **:** a feather on the shaft of an arrow set at an angle of 120 degrees from the cock feather

hen-feathered \'=¦==\ *adj* **:** having plumage like that of a hen — used of a male bird that lacks sickle or hackle feathers; distinguished from *cock-feathered*

hen-feathering \'=,=(=)=\ *n* **:** plumage on a cock resembling that of the hen

hen fish *n* **1 :** any of various marine fishes (as the pomfret) **2 :** an adult female fish

hen flea *n* **:** STICKTIGHT FLEA

hen fruit *n, slang* **:** a hen's egg

henge \'henj\ *n* -s [back-formation fr. *Stonehenge*, an assemblage of upright Bronze Age monuments on Salisbury Plain, near Salisbury, England] **:** a circular Bronze Age structure (as of wood) with a surrounding bank and ditch found in England

hen gorse *n, dial Eng* **:** RESTHARROW

heng·yang \'həŋ¦yäŋ, 'heŋ-; 'heŋ¦yaŋ\ *adj, usu cap* [fr. *Hengyang*, China] **:** of or from the city of Hengyang, China **:** of the kind or style prevalent in Hengyang

hen harrier *n* **:** a commonly harrier (*Circus cyaneus*) of which the adult male is largely bluish gray and the female and young male brown above and buff with dark streaks below, the two types differing so much that they are sometimes mistaken for members of different species — compare MARSH HAWK

hen hawk *n* **:** any of several large buteonine hawks that sometimes attack poultry (as the red-tailed hawk and the red-shouldered hawk)

henhearted \'=¦==\ *adj* **:** TIMID, FEARFUL, COWARDLY

hen·ism \'heˌnizəm\ *n* -s [G *henismus*, fr. Gk *hen* (neut. of *heis* one) + G *-ismus* -ism — more at HENAD] **:** SINGULARISM, MONISM 1a

henle's loop *n, usu cap H* **:** LOOP OF HENLE

henle's sheath *n, usu cap H* **:** SHEATH OF HENLE

¹**hen·na** \'henə\ *n* -s [Ar *ḥinnā'* alcanna (*Lawsonia inermis*)] **1 :** an Old World tropical shrub or small tree (*Lawsonia inermis*) with small opposite leaves and axillary panicles of fragrant white flowers used by Buddhists and Muslims in religious ceremonies — called also *Egyptian henna* **2 a :** a reddish brown dye obtained from leaves of the henna plant and used in tinting or dyeing the hair red **b :** a liquid, powder, or paste made by mixing henna with other coloring agents (as metallic lakes, tannin, lampblack) — called also *compound henna* **3 :** a variable color averaging a strong and moderate reddish brown to strong brown

²**henna** \"\ *vt* -ED/-ING/-s **:** to dye with henna

henne·bique \ˌhenə¦bēk, (')en¦b-\ *adj, usu cap* [after François *Hennebique* †1927 Fr. structural engineer] **:** relating to concrete reinforced with steel or iron

hen·nery \'henərē\ *n* -ES [*hen* + *-ery*] **1 :** a poultry farm **2 :** an enclosure or house for poultry

hen·nin \'henən\ *n* -s [MF] **:** a high cone-shaped headdress usu. with a thin veil pendent from the top worn by European women in the 15th century — called also *steeple headdress*

hennin

hen·ny \'henē\ *adj* [*hen* + *-y*] **:** HEN-FEATHERED

heno- *comb form* [Gk, fr. *hen-*, *heis* — more at HENAD] **:** one ⟨*heno*theism⟩

hen·o·the·ism \'henōthēˌizəm, ¦==¦==\ *n* [G *henotheismus*, fr. *heno-* + *-theismus* -theism] **:** the worship of one god without denying the existence of other gods — called also *monolatry*; compare KATHENOTHEISM

hen·o·the·ist \'henōˌthēəst\ *n* [*heno-* + *-theist*] **:** one who practices henotheism — **hen·o·the·is·tic** \¦==ˌthē¦istik\ *adj*

hen party *n* **:** a party for women only

¹**hen·peck** \-k\ *vt* [back-formation fr. *henpecked*] **:** to subject (one's husband) to persistent nagging and attempts to dominate

²**henpeck** \"\ *n* **1 :** a henpecked husband **2 :** an act or instance of henpecking

hen·pecked \'henˌpekt\ *adj* **:** subject to domination or persistent nagging by a wife

hen pepper *n* **:** SHEPHERD'S PURSE

hen pigeon *n* **:** a long-legged erect pigeon with a short tail carried high

hen plant *n* **:** either of two common plantains: **a :** BROAD-LEAVED PLANTAIN 1 **b :** RIBGRASS

¹**hen·ri·cian** \hen'rishən\ *n* -s *usu cap* [in sense 1, fr. ML *Henricianus*, fr. *Henricus* (Henry of Lausanne), 12th cent. Fr. heresiarch + L *-ianus* -ian; in sense 2, fr. NL *Henricianus*, fr. *Henricus* (Henry VIII) †1547 king of England + L *-ianus* -ian] **1 :** a member of a 12th century religious sect in Switzerland and southern France holding that the sacraments are valid only when administered by a priest who lives up to his monastic vows **2 :** an advocate of secular supremacy over the church and of the ecclesiastical reforms instituted during the reign of Henry VIII of England

²**henrician** \(')=¦==\ *adj, usu cap* **1 :** of, relating to, or associated with Henry of Lausanne **2 :** of or relating to Henry VIII of England or the ecclesiastical measures taken during his reign

hen·ri deux faïence \¦äⁿ(ˌ)rē¦də(r)|-, -dē|-, =¦=¦= \ *n, usu cap H&D* [after Henry II (*Henri Deux*) †1559 king of France] **:** SAINT-PORCHAIRE FAÏENCE

hen·ri·et·ta \ˌhenrē'ed·ə\ *or* **henrietta cloth** \¦==¦==-\ *n* -s *usu cap H* [after *Henrietta* Maria †1669 queen consort of Charles I of England] **:** a fine soft twilled fabric for dresses made of wool and sometimes with a silk warp

henroost \'=,=\ *n* **:** a place where fowls roost

hen·ry \'henrē, -ri\ *n, pl* **henrys** *or* **henries** [after Joseph *Henry* †1878 Am. physicist] **1 :** the practical mks unit of inductance equal to the self-inductance of a circuit or the mutual inductance of two circuits in which the variation of one ampere per second results in an induced electromotive force of one volt, the unit being taken as standard in the U. S. **2 :** a unit of inductance that is equal to 1.00049 henries and that was formerly taken as the standard in the U. S. — called also *international henry*

henry's law *n, usu cap H* [after William Henry †1836 Eng. chemist] **:** a fact in physical chemistry: the weight of a gas dissolved by a liquid is proportional to the pressure of the gas

henry system *n, usu cap H* [after Sir Edward *Henry* †1931 Brit. government official] **:** a system of numerical and letter classification of fingerprint patterns that treats the ten fingers as a unit and forms the basis of the majority of identification systems employed in English-speaking countries

hens *pl of* HEN

hens·low's sparrow \'henzˌlōz-\ *n, usu cap H* [after J. S. *Henslow* †1875 Am. botanist] **:** a common No. American sparrow (*Passerherbulus henslowii*) found in old fields

¹**hent** \'hent\ *vt* **hent; hent; henting; hents** [ME *henten*, fr. OE *hentan* — more at HUNT] **1** *dial* **a :** to lay hold on **:** SEIZE, CATCH **b :** to take away **:** carry off **2** *obs* **:** to arrive at **:** REACH ⟨have ~ the gates —Shak.⟩

²**hent** *n* -s [obs. E *hent* art of seizing, fr. ¹*hent*] *obs* **:** conception of an idea or plan **:** INTENT ⟨up, sword, and know thou a more horrid ~ —Shak.⟩

hen·te·ni·an \(')hen·¦tēnēən\ *adj, usu cap* [John Hentenius (Henten) †1566 Fr. theologian who prepared the 1547 edition of the Vulgate + E *-an*] **:** of or relating to the 1547 edition of the Vulgate used for some time as the standard text of the Roman Catholic Church

hen track *or* **hen scratch** *n* **:** an illegible or scarcely legible mark intended as handwriting ⟨covering page after page of ruled yellow foolscap with his inky *hen tracks* —Bruce Bliven b. 1889⟩

hen·tri·a·con·tane \ˌhen·ˌtrīə'kän·ˌtān, -ˌtrēə-\ *n* -s [ISV *hentriacont-* (fr. *hen-* — fr. Gk *hen*, neut. of *heis* one — + *triacont-* — fr. Gk *triakonta* thirty) + *-ane*] **:** a solid paraffin hydrocarbon $C_{31}H_{64}$; *esp* **:** normal hentriacontane $CH_3(CH_2)_{29}CH_3$ found in many natural waxes

henware \'=,=\ *n* **:** BADDERLOCKS

henwife \'=,=\ *n, pl* **henwives :** a woman who raises poultry

he-oak \'=¦=\ *n* **:** BEEFWOOD 1

he·or·to·log·i·cal \(¦)hē¦ȯ(r)d·ᵊl¦äjəkəl\ *adj* **:** of or relating to heortology

he·or·tol·o·gy \ˌhēˌȯ(r)'täləjē\ *n* -ES [Gk *heortē* feast + E *-o-* + *-logy*] **:** a study of religious calendars; *esp* **:** a study of the history and the meaning of the seasons and festivals of the church year

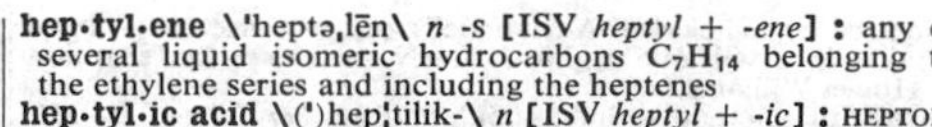

¹hep \ˈhep\ *var of* HIP

²hep \ˈhep, ˈhəp\ *interj* [origin unknown] — used to mark the cadence when troops are marching at attention

³hep \ˈhep\ *or* hip \ˈhip\ *adj* [origin unknown] **1 :** characterized by a keen informed awareness of or interest in what is new or smart **:** extremely alert and knowing ⟨astronautics, to which the small fry have been ~ for quite some time —C.J.Rolo⟩ ⟨you'll go crazy if you start using all that *hip* talk —Stanford Whitmore⟩ **2 :** characterized by a keen interest in and ready responsiveness to jazz ⟨each night after playing with his quintet before ~ audiences he studies classical compositions —Bob Thomas⟩ ⟨listening to recorded jazz with *hip* friends —*Metronome*⟩

HEP *abbr* hydroelectric power

he·par \ˈhē,pär\ *n* -s **1** [NL, fr. LL, liver (organ), fr. Gk *hēpar*] **:** LIVER 6 **2** [LL] **:** LIVER 1

hep·a·rin \ˈhepərən\ *n* -s [ISV *hepar* (organ) + *-in*] **:** a polysaccharide sulfuric acid ester found in liver, lung, and other tissues that prolongs the clotting time of blood by preventing the formation of fibrin and that is used in vascular surgery and in treatment of postoperative thrombosis and embolism

hep·a·rin·iza·tion \,hepərənəˈzāshən, -,nīˈz-\ *n* -s **:** the process of heparinizing

hep·a·rin·ize \ˈhepərə,nīz\ *vt* -ED/-ING/-S [*heparin* + *-ize*] **:** to treat with heparin so as to make the blood nonclotting

hepat- *or* **hepato-** *comb form* [ML, fr. L, fr. Gk *hēpat-, hēpato-*, fr. *hēpat-, hēpar*] **1 :** liver ⟨*hepat*ectomy⟩ ⟨*hepato*logy⟩ **2 :** liver and ⟨*hepato*colic⟩ ⟨*hepato*splenomegaly⟩

hep·a·tec·to·mize \,hepəˈtektə,mīz\ *vt* -ED/-ING/-S **:** to excise the liver of

hep·a·tec·to·my \-,mē\ *n* -ES [*hepat-* + *-ectomy*] **:** excision of the liver or of a part of the liver

¹**he·pat·ic** \həˈpad·ik, -at|, |ēk\ *adj* [L *hepaticus*, fr. Gk *hēpatikos*, fr. *hēpat-, hēpar* liver + *-ikos* -ic; akin to L *jecur* liver, Skt *yakṛt*, Lith *jaknos, jeknos*] **1 a :** of, relating to, or affecting the liver ⟨~ cirrhosis⟩ **b :** resembling the liver in color or form ⟨~ aloes⟩ **2** *archaic* **:** of, relating to, or resembling a liver (sense 6) **3** [NL *Hepaticae*] **:** of or relating to the class Hepaticae

²**hepatic** \ˈ"\ *n* -s [NL *Hepaticae*] **:** a plant of the class Hepaticae **:** LIVERWORT

¹**he·pat·i·ca** \|əkə, |ēkə\ *n* [NL, fr. ML, liverwort, fr. L *hepatica*, fem. of *hepaticus* of the liver; fr. the shape of the lobed leaves] **1 a** *cap* **:** a small genus of perennial herbs (family Ranunculaceae) of the north temperate zone that flower in the early spring and have lobed basal partly evergreen leaves and delicate white, pink, blue, or purplish flowers **b** -s **:** any plant or flower of the genus *Hepatica* **2** -s [ML] **:** a common liverwort (*Marchantia polymorpha*)

²**hepatica** \ˈ"\ *n* -s *usu cap* [NL, fr. L, fem. of *hepaticus*] **:** LINE OF MERCURY

hepatica

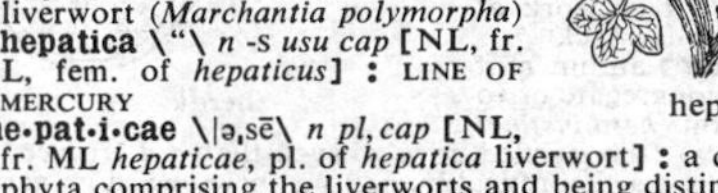

he·pat·i·cae \|ə,sē\ *n pl, cap* [NL, fr. ML *hepaticae*, pl. of *hepatica* liverwort] **:** a class of Bryophyta comprising the liverworts and being distinguished from Musci by the presence of a usu. thalloid gametophyte that is not produced from a protonema, unicellular rhizoids and elaters, and antheridia and archegonia that are borne on the thallus and produce a short-lived and simple sporophyte — compare ANTHOCEROTALES, JUNGERMANNIALES, MARCHANTIALES, SPHAEROCARPALES

hepatic artery *n* **:** the branch of the coeliac artery that supplies the liver with arterial blood

hepatic cell *n* **:** one of the polygonal epithelial cells of the liver that secrete bile

hepatic duct *n* **:** a duct conveying the bile away from the liver and in man and many other vertebrates uniting with the cystic duct to form the common bile duct — see DIGESTION illustration

hepatic line *n, usu cap H* **:** LINE OF MERCURY

he·pat·i·col·o·gist \hə,pad·əˈkäləjəst\ *n* -s **:** a specialist in hepaticology

he·pat·i·col·o·gy \-jē\ *n* -ES [NL *Hepaticae* + E *-o-* + *-logy*] **:** a branch of botany that deals with the Hepaticae

hepatic tanager *n* **:** a common tanager (*Piranga flava hepatica*) of the southwestern U. S. and Mexico

hepatic vein *n* **:** one of the veins that carry the blood received from the hepatic artery and from the portal vein away from the liver and that in man are usu. three in number and open into the inferior vena cava

hep·a·tite \ˈhepə,tīt\ *n* -s [G *hepatit*, fr. *hepat-* (fr. Gk *hēpat-* hepat-) + *-it* -ite; fr. its odor] **:** a barite that becomes fetid when rubbed or heated

hep·a·ti·tis \,hepəˈtīd·əs, -ītəs\ *n* -ES [NL, fr. *hepat-* + *-itis*] **1 :** inflammation of the liver **2 :** a disease or condition characterized by inflammation of the liver: as **a :** INFECTIOUS HEPATITIS **b :** SERUM HEPATITIS

hep·a·ti·za·tion \,hepəd·əˈzāshən, -pə,tīˈz-\ *n* -s [*hepat-* + *-ization*] **:** conversion of tissue (as of the lungs in pneumonia) into a substance resembling liver tissue in which the affected tissue may become solidified

hep·a·tize \ˈhepə,tīz\ *vt* -ED/-ING/-S [*hepat-* + *-ize*] **:** to cause to undergo hepatization ⟨a *hepatized* area of lung tissue⟩

hepato- — see HEPAT-

hep·a·to·cellular \ˌhepəd·ō+\ *adj* [*hepat-* + *cellular*] **:** of or involving hepatic cells ⟨~ jaundice⟩

hep·a·to·cu·pre·in \,hepəd·ōˈk(y)üprēən\ *n* -s [*hepat-* + *cupr-* + *-ein*] **:** a copper-containing protein isolated from ox liver

hep·a·to·fla·vin \-ˈflāvən *also* -lav-\ *n* [*hepat-* + *flavin*] **:** RIBOFLAVIN

hep·a·to·gen·ic \ˌhepəd·ō¦jenik\ *or* **hep·a·tog·e·nous** \ˌhepə¦täjənəs\ *adj* [*hepat-* + *-genic* or *-genous*] **:** produced or originating in the liver

hep·a·to·ma \,hepəˈtōmə\ *n, pl* **hepatomas** \-məz\ *or* **hepatoma·ta** \-məd·ə\ [NL, fr. *hepat-* + *-oma*] **:** a tumor of the liver that is usu. malignant — **hep·a·toma·tous** \¦==¦tämad·əs, -¦tōm-\ *adj*

hep·a·to·me·gal·ic \ˌhepəd·ōmə¦galik\ *adj* **:** of, relating to, or resembling hepatomegaly

hep·a·to·meg·a·ly \,===ˈmegəlē\ *n* -ES [*hepat-* + *-megaly*] **:** enlargement of the liver

hep·a·to·pancreas \ˌhepəd·ō+\ *n* [NL *hepat-* + *pancreas*] **:** a glandular structure (as that of various crustaceans) that combines the digestive function of the vertebrate liver and pancreas — **hep·a·to·pancreatic** \ˈ"+\ *adj*

hep·a·to·portal \ˈ"+\ *adj* [*hepat-* + *portal*] **:** of or relating to the portal circulation of the liver as distinguished from that of the kidneys

hep·a·tos·co·py \,hepəˈtäskəpē\ *n* -ES [Gk *hēpatoskopia* inspection of the liver, fr. *hēpatoskopein* to inspect the liver (fr. *hēpat-* hepat- + *skopein* to inspect, contemplate, view) + *-ia* -y — more at SPY] **:** divination by inspecting the liver of animals

hep·a·to·splenomegaly \ˌhepəd·ō+\ *n* [*hepat-* + *splenomegaly*] **:** coincident enlargement of the liver and spleen

hep·a·to·toxic \ˈ"+\ *adj* [*hepat-* + *toxic*] **:** causing injury to the liver ⟨~ drugs⟩

hepcat \ˈ=,=\ *n* [³*hep* + *cat*] **:** one who is extremely hep ⟨horn-rimmed intellectual ~s with wild black hair —Jack Kerouac⟩; *specif* **:** a player or devotee of hot jazz

hephthalite *usu cap, var of* EPHTHALITE

heph·the·mim·er·al caesura \ˈhefthə¦mimərəl, ¦hepth-\ *n* [LL *hephthemimeris*, fr. Gk *hephthēmimerēs*, adj., containing seven halves, containing three feet and a half (fr. *hepta-* + *hēmi-* hemi- + *meros* part) + E *-al* — more at MERIT] **:** a caesura in classical verse occurring after the seventh half foot

hep·i·al·i·dae \,hēpēˈalə,dē, ,hep-\ *n pl, cap* [NL, fr. *Hepialus*, type genus (irreg. fr. Gk *hēpiolos* moth) + *-idae*] **:** a family of lepidopterous insects comprising the ghost moths and having larvae which burrow in wood or feed on roots

hepped up \ˈhep¦təp\ *adj* **1 :** marked by intense interest or enthusiasm **:** HIPPED — usu. used with *about* ⟨was all *hepped up* about buying some silverware —E.G.Grening⟩ **2 :** marked by lively motion or tempo **:** pepped up **:** JAZZED ⟨*hepped-up* dinner music —*Saturday Rev.*⟩

hep·pen \ˈhepən\ *adj, usu* -ER/-EST [of Scand origin; akin to ON *heppinn* lucky, *happ* good luck — more at HAP (chance)] **1** *dial Brit* **:** NEAT, ATTRACTIVE **2** *dial Brit* **:** DEFT, HANDY

¹**hep·ple·white** \ˈhepəl,(h)wīt\ *adj, usu cap* [after George *Hepplewhite* †1786 Eng. cabinetmaker] **:** of, relating to, or closely imitating a light and elegant style of furniture originating in late 18th century England that is often distinguishable from Sheraton by its greater use of curves (as in the favored shield and heart backs of its chairs), in its preference for concave curves esp. at sideboard corners, in its characteristic detachment of chair backs from the seat rail except for short side posts, and in the sweep of the high arms of its chairs to meet the line of the front legs

²**hepplewhite** \ˈ"\ *n* -s *usu cap* **:** an article of Hepplewhite furniture

hep·ster \ˈhepstə(r)\ *or* **hip·ster** \ˈhip-\ *n* -s [³*hep* or *hip* + *-ster*] **1 :** a devotee of jazz ⟨the orchestra's free style in improvising has impressed at least one longhair as well as the ~s —*Newsweek*⟩ **2** *usu* **hipster :** one who professes hep attitudes or tastes ⟨the ladies and gentlemen of the late watch — the *hipsters* who take the sun as a personal affront —Billy Rose⟩ ⟨the colorful dialogue of the *hipster* —*Saturday Rev.*⟩

Hepplewhite chair

hepta- *or* **hept-** *comb form* [Gk, fr. *hepta* — more at SEVEN] **1 :** seven ⟨*hepta*gon⟩ **2** *chem* **:** containing seven atoms, groups, or equivalents ⟨*hepta*acetate⟩

hep·ta·chlor \ˈheptə,klō(ə)r\ *n* -s [*heptachloro-*, fr. *hepta-* + *chlor-*] **:** a solid insecticide $C_{10}H_5Cl_7$ similar to chlordane

hep·ta·chord \-,kȯrd\ *n* [LL *heptachordus* with seven strings, fr. Gk *heptachordos*, fr. *hepta-* + *-chordos* stringed — more at -CHORD] **1 :** a 7-stringed lyre of ancient Greece **2 :** a diatonic scale of seven notes or tones **3 :** the interval of a seventh

hep·tac·o·sane \hepˈtakə,sān\ *n* -s [ISV *heptacos-* (fr. *hepta-* + *-cos-* — fr. *eicosa-*) + *-ane*] **:** a solid paraffin hydrocarbon $C_{27}H_{56}$; *esp* **:** the normal hydrocarbon $CH_3(CH_2)_{25}CH_3$ occurring in many waxes

hep·tad \ˈhep,tad\ *n* -s [Gk *heptad-, heptas* the number seven, fr. *hepta* seven] **:** a group of seven ⟨a ~ of litanies⟩

hep·ta·dec·ane \,heptəˈde,kān\ *n* -s [ISV *heptadec-* (fr. *hepta-* + *deca-*) + *-ane*] **:** any of several isomeric paraffin hydrocarbons $C_{17}H_{36}$; *esp* **:** the low-melting crystalline normal hydrocarbon $CH_3(CH_2)_{15}CH_3$

hep·ta·dec·a·no·ic acid \ˌheptə¦dekə¦nōik-\ *n* [ISV *heptadecane* + *-oic*] **:** MARGARIC ACID

hep·ta·decyl \,heptəˈdesəl, -dēs-\ *n* [*heptadecane* + *-yl*] **:** any of several univalent radicals $C_{17}H_{35}$ derived from the heptadecanes by removal of one hydrogen atom; *esp* **:** the normal radical $CH_3(CH_2)_{15}CH_2–$

hep·ta·gon \ˈheptə,gän *sometimes* -təgən\ *n* -s [Gk *heptagōnos* heptagonal, fr. *hepta* seven + *-gōnos* (fr. *gōnia* corner, angle) — more at -GON] **:** a plane polygon having seven angles and therefore seven sides

heptagons

hep·tag·o·nal \(ˈ)hep¦tagənᵊl, -taig-\ *adj* **:** having seven angles or sides

hep·ta·hydrate \ˌheptə+\ *n* [*hepta-* + *hydrate*] **:** a compound with seven molecules of water — **hep·ta·hydrated** \ˈ"+\ *adj*

hep·ta·kai·decagon \ˌheptə,kī+\ *n* -s [Gk *heptakaideka* seventeen (fr. *hepta-* + *kai* and + *deka* ten) + E *-gon* — more at TEN] **:** a plane polygon having seventeen angles and therefore seventeen sides

hept·aldehyde \(ˈ)hept+\ *n* [ISV *hepta-* + *aldehyde*] **:** ENANTHALDEHYDE

hep·tam·e·ter \hepˈtaməd·ə(r)\ *n* [*hepta-* + *-meter*] **:** a poetic line of seven feet — **hep·ta·met·ri·cal** \ˌheptə¦metrəkəl\ *adj*

hep·ta·nal \ˈheptə,nal\ *n* -s [*heptane* + *-al*] **:** ENANTHALDEHYDE

hep·tane \ˈhep,tān\ *n* -s [ISV *hepta-* + *-ane*] **:** any of nine isomeric paraffin hydrocarbons C_7H_{16}; *esp* **:** the liquid normal hydrocarbon $CH_3(CH_2)_5CH_3$ occurring in petroleum and as the chief constituent of some pine oils

hep·ta·no·ic acid \ˌheptə¦nōik-\ *n* [*heptane* + *-oic*] **:** ENANTHIC ACID

hep·ta·none \ˈheptə,nōn\ *n* -s [ISV *heptane* + *-one*] **:** a ketone $C_7H_{14}O$ derived from normal heptane

hep·ta·phyllite \ˌheptə+\ *n* [*hepta-* + *phyllite*] **:** any of a group of micas (as muscovite and other light-colored micas) with seven metallic ions per ten oxygen and two hydroxyl ions — compare OCTAPHYLLITE

¹**hep·ta·ploid** \ˈheptə,plȯid\ *adj* [*hepta-* + *-ploid*] **:** having seven times the monoploid number of chromosomes

²**heptaploid** \ˈ"\ *n* -s **:** a heptaploid individual, group, or generation

hep·ta·ploi·dy \ˈ==,plȯidē\ *n* -ES **:** the condition of being heptaploid

hep·tarch \ˈhep,tärk\ *n* -s [*hepta-* + ¹*-arch*] **:** one of the rulers of a heptarchy

hep·tar·chal \(ˈ)hep¦tärkəl\ *or* **hep·tar·chic** \-kik\ *or* **hep·tar·chi·cal** \-kəkəl\ *adj* **:** of, relating to, or constituting a heptarchy

hep·tarchy \ˈhep,tärkē\ *n* -ES [*hepta-* + *-archy*] **1 :** a government by seven persons **2 :** a confederacy of seven Anglo-Saxon kingdoms held to have existed in the 7th and 8th centuries with each kingdom having its own ruler and one of the seven heptarchs sometimes being recognized as overlord

hep·ta·stich \ˈheptə,stik\ *n* -s [*hepta-* + *-stich*] **:** a group, stanza, or poem of seven lines

hep·ta·style \-,stīl\ *also* **hep·ta·sty·lar** \¦==¦stīlə(r)\ *adj* [*hepta-* + *-style, -stylar*] **:** marked by columniation with seven columns across the front — compare DISTYLE

hep·ta·sulfide \ˌheptə+\ *n* [*hepta-* + *sulfide*] **:** a sulfide containing seven atoms of sulfur in the molecule

hep·ta·syllabic \ˌheptə+\ *adj* [*hepta-* + *-syllabic*] **:** consisting of or having seven syllables ⟨a ~ line⟩

hep·ta·syllable \ˈ"+\ *n* [*hepta-* + *syllable*] **:** a poetic line of seven syllables

hept·atomic \ˌhept+\ *adj* [*hepta-* + *atomic*] **1 :** consisting of seven atoms **2 :** having seven replaceable atoms or radicals

hep·ta·tonic \ˌheptə+\ *adj* [*hepta-* + *tonic*] **:** composed of seven musical tones

hep·ta·valent \ˌheptə+\ *adj* [*hepta-* + *valent*] **:** having a valence of seven

hep·tene \ˈhep,tēn\ *n* -s [ISV *hepta-* + *-ene*] **:** any of the three straight-chain heptylenes

hep·ti·tol \ˈheptə,tȯl, -,tōl\ *n* -s [*hepta-* + *-itol*] **:** a heptahydroxy alcohol that is obtained by reducing a heptose or that exists naturally

hep·tode \ˈhep,tōd\ *n* -s [ISV *hepta-* + *-ode*] **:** a vacuum tube with seven electrodes including a cathode, an anode, a control grid, and four additional grids or other electrodes

hep·to·ic acid \(ˈ)hep¦tōik-\ *n* [*heptane* + *-oic*] **:** any of the monocarboxylic acids $C_7H_{13}COOH$ (as enanthic acid) derived from the heptanes

hep·tose \ˈhep,tōs *also* -ōz\ *n* -s [ISV *hepta-* + *-ose*] **:** any of a class of monosaccharides $C_7H_{14}O_7$ containing seven carbon atoms in the molecule and obtainable in various ways from lower sugars

hept·ox·ide \hept+\ *n* [ISV *hepta-* + *oxide*] **:** an oxide containing seven oxygen atoms in the molecule

hep·tran·chi·as \hepˈtraŋkēəs\ *n, cap* [NL, prob. irreg. fr. *hepta-* + *branchiae*] **:** a genus of sharks (family Hexanchidae) having seven pairs of branchial clefts

hep·tu·lose \ˈheptə,lōs, -pchə- *also* -ōz\ *n* -s [*hepta-* + *-ulose*] **:** a ketose $C_7H_{14}O_7$ containing seven carbons in the molecule; *esp* **:** the isomer having the carbonyl group in the beta or 2-position ⟨D-*manno-heptulose* is found in avocados⟩

hep·tyl \ˈheptəl\ *n* -s [ISV *hepta-* + *-yl*] **:** any of several isomeric alkyl radicals C_7H_{15} derived from the heptanes; *esp* **:** the normal radical $CH_3(CH_2)_5CH_2–$

hep·tyl·ene \ˈheptə,lēn\ *n* -s [ISV *heptyl* + *-ene*] **:** any of several liquid isomeric hydrocarbons C_7H_{14} belonging to the ethylene series and including the heptenes

hep·tyl·ic acid \(ˈ)hep¦tilik-\ *n* [ISV *heptyl* + *-ic*] **:** HEPTOIC ACID

hep·tyne *also* **hep·tine** \ˈhep,tīn\ *n* -s [ISV *hepta-* + *-yne* or *-ine*] **:** any of three isomeric straight-chain liquid hydrocarbons C_7H_{12} of the acetylene series

¹**her** [ME *hire*, fr. OE *hiere, hire, hyre*, gen. of *hēo, hīo* she — more at HE] *obs possessive of* ¹SHE

²**her** \R (h)ər, ˈhər, +V ¦hər·; -R (h)ə(r, ¦hə, +V ¦hər· *or* ¦hə *also* ¦hər\ *adj* [ME *hire*, fr. OE *hiere, hire, hyre*, gen. of *hēo, hīo*] **1 a :** of or relating to her or herself as possessor **:** due to her **:** inherent in her **:** associated or connected with her ⟨before she has ~ floor swept —Edna S. V. Millay⟩ ⟨you have not seen Maine until you have seen ~ islands —R.W. Hatch⟩ — compare ¹SHE **b :** of or relating to her or herself as author, doer, giver, or agent **:** effected by her **:** experienced by her as subject **:** that she is capable of ⟨~ paintings⟩ ⟨~ research⟩ ⟨the reason for ~ winning the game⟩ ⟨she did ~ best⟩ **c :** of or relating to her or herself as object of an action **:** experienced by her as object ⟨~ rescuer⟩ ⟨~ exclusion from the club⟩ **d :** that she has to do with or is supposed to possess or to have knowledge or a share of or some interest in ⟨she plays ~ waltzes beautifully⟩ **e :** that is esp. significant for her **:** that brings her good fortune or prominence — used with *day* or sometimes with other words indicating a division of time ⟨it's not only her birthday, it's ~ day⟩ **2** *now dial* **:** -'s — used after a noun or noun phrase designating a female person or something personified as female in place of the possessive ending *'s* ⟨Jane Doe ~ book⟩

³**her** \ˈ"\ *pron, objective case of* SHE [ME *hire*, fr. OE *hiere, hire, hyre*, dat. of *hēo, hīo*] ¹SHE 1, 2, 3: **a** — used as indirect object of a verb ⟨tell ~ the news⟩ **b** — used as object of a preposition ⟨a gift for ~⟩ **c** — used as direct object of a verb ⟨lifted the skiff and slid ~ into the water —Ernest Hemingway⟩ **d** — used in comparisons after *than* and *as* when the first term in the comparison is the direct or indirect object of a verb or the object of a preposition ⟨the dress fits her sister as well as ~⟩ ⟨give me the book rather than ~⟩ ⟨this course of study would be more useful to you than ~⟩ **e** — used in absolute constructions esp. together with a prepositional phrase, adjective, or participle ⟨she was invited to go dancing two or three times a week, and ~ without half as many nice dresses as she really needed⟩ ⟨and ~ being my own child⟩ **f** — used by speakers on all educational levels and by many reputable writers, though disapproved by some grammarians, in the predicate after forms of *be*, in comparisons after *than* and *as* when the first term in the comparison is the subject of a verb, and in other positions where it is itself neither the subject of a verb nor the object of a verb or preposition ⟨it was not ~ one hated but the idea of her —Virginia Woolf⟩ ⟨her sister sings better than ~⟩ ⟨~ and her excuses⟩ **g** — used in substandard speech as the subject of a verb which it does not immediately precede or as part of the compound subject of a verb ⟨~ and John got married⟩ **h** — used with a gerund in combination with other pronouns (as *him*) in the objective case ⟨I can't imagine ~ doing that any more than I can imagine him doing it⟩ **2 :** HERSELF — used reflexively as indirect object of a verb ⟨she bought ~ a hat⟩, object of a preposition ⟨she took her son with ~⟩, or direct object of a verb ⟨she sat ~ down⟩

⁴**her** *like stressed pronunciations at* ²HER\ *n* -s **:** WOMAN, GIRL ⟨four hims and a ~ —Charles Dickens⟩

her *abbr* **1** heraldic; heraldry **2** [L *heres*] heir

hera \ˈherə\ *n, pl* **hera** *or* **heras** *usu cap* **1 :** the peasant segment of the Nyoro people presumed to be cognate with the Bairu **2 :** a member of the Hera people

her·a·bol myrrh *or* **heer·a·bol myrrh** \ˈherə,bōl-\ *n* [origin unknown] **:** the true myrrh of commerce said to be obtained from an East African and Arabian tree (*Commiphora myrrha*)

her·a·cle·an \ˌherə¦klēən\ *or* **her·a·cleian** \-lē(y)ən, -līən\ *adj, usu cap* [*heraclean* fr. L *heracleus* Heraclean (fr. Gk *hērakleios*, fr. *Hēraklēs* Heracles, Hercules, legendary Greek hero) + E *-an*; *heracleian* fr. Gk *hērakleios* + E *-an*] **:** of or relating to the hero Heracles

he·rac·le·on·ite \həˈraklēə,nīt\ *n* -s *usu cap* [*Heracleon*, 2d cent. Gnostic Christian + E *-ite*] **:** a follower of the Gnostic Heracleon of Alexandria

¹**her·a·cle·o·poli·tan** \ˌherə,klēə¦pälətᵊn\ *or* **her·a·cle·op·o·lite** \,==,klē¦äpə,līt\ *adj, usu cap* [*Heracleopolit-, Heracleopolis*, ancient city of Egypt + E *-an* or *-ite*] **:** of or relating to the ancient city of Heracleopolis in northern Egypt — often used of the kings of the IXth and Xth dynasties in Egypt

²**heracleopolitan** \ˈ"\ *n* -s *usu cap* **:** a native or inhabitant of Heracleopolis in northern Egypt

her·a·cle·um \,herəˈklēəm\ *n, cap* [NL, irreg. fr. Gk *hērakleia*, a plant, fr. *Hēraklēs* Hercules] **:** a widely distributed genus of plants (family Umbelliferae) having wing-margined fruit and large umbels of white flowers — see COW PARSNIP

¹**her·a·cli·te·an** \¦herə¦klīd·ēən, -,klī¦tēən\ *also* **her·a·clitic** \-¦klid·ik, -lī|\ *adj, usu cap* [L *heracliteus* Heraclitean (fr. Gk *hērakleiteios*, fr. *Hērakleitos* Heraclitus, 6th-5th cent. B.C. Greek philosopher) + E *-an* or *-ic*] **:** of or relating to the philosopher Heraclitus or his theories

²**heraclitean** \ˈ"\ *also* **heraclitic** \ˈ"\ *n* -s *usu cap* **:** a follower of Heraclitus

her·a·cli·te·an·ism \,==ˈklīd·ēə,nizəm, -,klīˈtē-\ *n* -s *usu cap* **:** a philosophy based on the theory that everything is in flux and nothing remains fixed except the logos which is at once law and a ruling element identified with fire and that the world is made of the four elements fire, water, earth, and air which are continually transmuted into one another in fixed measures

¹**her·ald** \ˈherəld\ *n* -s [ME *heraud, herald*, fr. MF *hiraut, heraut*, fr. an (assumed) Gmc compound (akin to the name *Chariovalda* attested in Tacitus) whose first component is akin to OHG *heri* army, and whose 2d component is akin to OHG *waltan* to have power over, rule — more at HARRY, WIELD] **1 a :** an official at a tournament of arms whose duties consisting orig. of making announcements came to include keeping the scores, interpreting the rules, and marshaling the combatants **b :** an officer whose original duties of a tournament official came to include also the marshaling of other chivalric ceremonials, the making of official announcements, and the carrying of messages to or from rulers or commanders esp. in war with the status of ambassador **c :** such an officer of a monarch or government also having the responsibility for devising, granting, registering, and confirming armorial bearings, this responsibility coming to constitute his chief function as earlier functions became obsolete **:** OFFICER OF ARMS **d :** a member of the second of three grades of officers of arms ranking above a pursuivant and below a king of arms **2 a :** an official crier or messenger having duties similar in one or more respects to those of the herald of medieval and modern Europe ⟨Mercury was the gods' ~⟩ **b :** one (as a soldier) who signals with a trumpet ⟨more chieftains came, with ~s who blew on trumpets that were twelve feet long —Hector Bolitho⟩ **c :** AVANT-COURIER **3 a :** one that precedes or foreshadows **:** HARBINGER, FORERUNNER ⟨flights of ravens . . . are the sure ~s of the approach of the deer —Farley Mowat⟩ ⟨revolutions . . . were the ~s of social changes —R.W.Livingstone⟩ **b** (1) **:** one that conveys news or proclaims **:** ANNOUNCER ⟨hark the ~ angels sing —George Whitefield⟩ ⟨it was the lark, the ~ of the morn —Shak.⟩ (2) **:** one that supports or advocates **:** SPOKESMAN ⟨conspicuous ~ of this enfranchising movement —C.A. Dinsmore⟩ **4 :** a specialist in heraldry **:** HERALDIST **5 :** a European noctuid moth (*Scoliopteryx libatrix*) **6 :** the identifying symbol or monogram of a railroad usu. displayed on its freight cars

²**herald** \ˈ"\ *vt* -ED/-ING/-S **1 :** to give notice of **:** ANNOUNCE, SIGNAL ⟨the publisher ~s a second series —J.N.Hazard⟩ ⟨the approach of a cold air mass . . . is ~ed by a shift of the wind —P.E.James⟩ **2 a :** to bring to public notice **:** PUBLICIZE ⟨one of the most ~ed and most exciting events in the country —T.H.Fielding⟩ **b :** to greet esp. with enthusiasm **:** HAIL ⟨the show was ~ed with a glum essay —E.R.Bentley⟩ ⟨automation has been extravagantly ~ed by some as the threshold to a new Utopia —John Diebold⟩ **3 :** to signal the approach of **:** PRECEDE, FORESHADOW ⟨~ed by a man ringing a bell and

esquired by his clerk —Adrian Bell⟩ ⟨an increase in . . . local quakes in a volcanic region is fairly sure to ~ an eruption —Howel Williams⟩

he·ral·dic \he'raldik, hə'-, -dēk\ *adj* [F *héraldique*, fr. ML *heraldus* (fr. MF *hiraut, heraut*) + F *-ique* -ic] : of or relating to heralds or heraldry ⟨the ~ emblem of the emperor —Ethel Lewis⟩ ⟨the ~ procession moved on in gilded coaches —*Time*⟩ — **he·ral·di·cal·ly** \-dək(ə)lē, -dēk-, -li\ *adv*

her·ald·ist \'herəldəst\ *n* -s : a specialist in heraldry

herald of arms *also* **herald at arms** : ¹HERALD 1

her·ald·ry \'herəldrē, -ri\ *n* -ES [¹*herald* + *-ry*] **1 a** : the art or practice of an officer of arms including the devising, blazoning, and granting of armorial insignia, the investigation of persons' rights to use arms or particular armorial ensigns, the tracing and recording of pedigrees, the settling of questions of precedence, the marshaling of processions, and the supervision of public ceremonies **b** : pomp and elaborate ceremony esp. with display of armorial ensigns : PAGEANTRY ⟨historic ~ of a British coronation⟩ **c** : a branch of knowledge that deals with the history and practice of bearing and displaying armorial ensigns and with the art of describing them : ARMORY **2 a** : armorial ensigns ⟨methods of painting ~ have changed very little —G.W.Eve⟩ **b** : insignia (as military badges or Japanese mons) that resemble or are likened to armorial ensigns ⟨brands are the ~ of the range —J.F. Dobie⟩ **3** *archaic* : the office of an official crier or messenger ⟨I trust my next ~ will be to a more friendly court —E.G. Bulwer-Lytton⟩ **4** *obs* : social rank or precedence ⟨you are more saucy . . . than the commission of your birth and virtue gives you ~ —Shak.⟩ **5** : advance notice or publicity ⟨the play opened with no ~ to speak of⟩

heralds' college *n, cap H&C* : COLLEGE OF ARMS

heralds' office *n, cap H & usu cap O* : COLLEGE OF ARMS

heraldy *n* -ES [ME *heraldie*, fr. *heraud, herald* + *-ie* -y] *obs* : HERALDRY

her·a·path·ite \'herəˌpaˌthīt, -pä,-\ *n* -s [William B. *Herapath* †1868 Eng. chemist + E *-ite*] : a salt of quinine that is obtained by treating the sulfate with iodine in the form of rhomboidal plates capable of polarizing light and that is used as a polarizing agent usu. in the form of small crystals oriented in the same direction in a transparent film

heras *pl of* HERA

he·rat \he'rät\ *or* **he·rati** \-ädē\ *n* -s *usu cap* [fr. *Herat*, Afghanistan, where such rugs are made] **1** : a usu. heavy cotton, silk, or occas. wool Oriental rug of loose texture that is tied with the Ghiordes knot and characterized by a basic pattern of a rosette between two curved leaves that is often much elaborated — compare KHORASSAN **2** : an Ispahan of the 16th and 17th centuries

herb \'(h)ərb, '(h)ōb, '(h)əib\ *n* -s *often attrib* [ME *erbe, herbe*, fr. OF, fr. L *herba*] **1** : a seed-producing annual, biennial, or herbaceous perennial that does not develop persistent woody tissue but dies down at the end of a growing season — compare SHRUB, TREE **2** : a plant or plant part valued for its medicinal, savory, or aromatic qualities ⟨under ~s I have included laurel leaves —J.W.Parry⟩ **3** *archaic* : GRASS, VEGETATION ⟨underfoot the ~ was dry —Alfred Tennyson⟩ **4** : the leafy top of an herbaceous plant considered separately from the root

her·ba·ce·ae \ˌ(h)ər'bāsē,ē\ *n pl, cap* [NL, fr. fem. pl. of L *herbaceus*] *in some esp former classifications* : a phylum comprising all plants that are fundamentally herbaceous and remain so — compare LIGNOSAE

her·ba·ceous \(')(h)ər'bāshəs\ *adj* [L *herbaceus* grassy, fr. *herba* grass, herb + *-aceus* -aceous] **1 a** : of, relating to, or having the characteristics of an herb **b** *of a stem* : having little or no woody tissue and persisting usu. for a single growing season **2** : having the texture, color, or appearance of a leaf ⟨~ sepals⟩ — **her·ba·ceous·ly** *adv* — **her·ba·ceous·ness** *n* -ES

herbaceous border *n* : a permanent flower border consisting primarily of hardy herbaceous perennials but frequently including annuals and biennials

herbaceous grafting *n* : grafting in which both stock and scion are herbaceous (as in grafting a scion of double-flowered gypsophila onto a stock of single-flowered gypsophila)

herbaceous perennial *n* : a plant whose top growth dies down annually but whose crowns, roots, bulbs, or rhizomes survive the winter

herb·age \'(h)ərbij, -)ōb-, -)əib-, -bēj\ *n* -s [ME, fr. MF, fr. *herbe, erbe* + *-age*] **1** : grass and other herbaceous vegetation esp. when used for grazing animals : PASTURE **2** : the succulent parts (as the foliage and young stems) of herbaceous plants **3** : an easement of pasturage on another's ground

her·ba im·pia \ˌ(h)ərbə'impēə\ *n* [L, lit., undutiful or unfilial herb; fr. the fact that small branches shoot out from the top of the main stem and on top of the parent stem] : a cotton rose (*Filago germanica*)

¹**herb·al** \'(h)ərbəl, -)ōb-, -)əib-\ *n* -s [*herb* + *-al* (n. suffix)] **1** : a book in which plants are named, described, and often pictured usu. with special reference to their officinal properties **2** *archaic* : HERBARIUM 1

²**herbal** \"\ *adj* [*herb* + *-al* (adj. suffix)] : of, relating to, or made of herbs

herb·al·ist \-ləst\ *n* -s **1 a** : one that collects, grows, or deals in herbs, esp. medicinal herbs **b** : HERB DOCTOR ⟨described herself as an ~ and dresser of sores —C.J.Brown⟩ **2** *obs* : BOTANIST

herb·al·ize \-ˌlīz\ *vi* -ED/-ING/-S : to collect plants (as medicinal herbs)

her·ba·rism \-bəˌrizəm\ *n* -s [L *herbaria* botany (fr. *herba* grass, herb + *-aria* -ary) + E *-ism*] *archaic* : BOTANY

herbarist *n* -s [L *herbaria* + E *-ist*] *obs* : HERBALIST

her·bar·i·um \ˌ(h)ər'ba(a)rēəm, ˌ(h)ō'-, ˌ(h)əi'-, ˌ(h)ə(r)'-, -ber-,-bär-\ *n, pl* **herbaria** [LL, fr. L *herba* + *-arium* -ary] **1** : a collection of dried plant specimens usu. mounted and systematically arranged for botanical reference **2** : a room, building, or institution housing an herbarium

her·ba·rize \'hərbəˌrīz\ *vi* -ED/-ING/-S [L *herbaria* + E *-ize*] *archaic* : BOTANIZE

¹**her·bar·ti·an** \(')her¦bärd·ēən, ¦hər¦-\ *adj, usu cap* [Johann F. *Herbart* †1841 Ger. philosopher + E *-ian*] : of or relating to the German philosopher Herbart, his doctrines, or esp. the educational system outlined by him and developed by his disciples

²**herbartian** \"\ *n* -s *usu cap* : one who supports or believes in Herbartian doctrines

her·bar·ti·an·ism \ˌ(,)=¦==ˌnizəm\ *n* -s *usu cap* : the doctrines advocated by the German philosopher Herbart and his followers

herb·a·ry \'(h)ərbərē, -)ōb-, -)əib-, -ri\ *n* -ES [*herb* + *-ary*] *archaic* : a garden of herbs or vegetables

herbbane \'=ˌ=\ *n* : BROOMRAPE

herb bar·ba·ra \-'bärb(ə)rə, -'bäb-\ *n, pl* **herbs barbara** *or* **herb barbaras** *usu cap B* [trans. of ML or NL *herba* (*Sanctae*) *Barbarae*, fr. *Barbara* (St. Barbara) 3d cent. Christian martyr] : WINTER CRESS

herb ben·net \-'benət\ *n, pl* **herbs bennet** *or* **herb bennets** [ME *herbe beneit*, fr. MF *herbe beneite, herbe benoite*, fr. ML *herba benedicta*, lit., blessed herb] : a European herb (*Geum urbanum*) with pinnatifid leaves and yellow flowers

herb chris·to·pher \-'kristəfə(r)\ *n, pl* **herbs christopher** *or* **herb christophers** *usu cap C* [trans. of NL or ML *herba* (*Sancti*) *Christophori*, after *Christophorus* (St. Christopher) 3d cent. Christian martyr] **1** : a common European baneberry (*Actaea spicata*) **2** : either of two American baneberries: **a** : WHITE BANEBERRY **b** : RED BANEBERRY **3** : ROYAL FERN **4** : FLEABANE a **5** : MEADOWSWEET 2

herb doctor *n* : one who practices healing by the use of herbs — called also *herbalist*

her·bert river cherry \'hərbərt-\ *n, usu cap H&R* [fr. the *Herbert river*, Australia] : QUEENSLAND CHERRY

herb gerard \-jə'rärd, -'je,rärd\ *n, pl* **herbs gerard** *or* **herb gerards** *usu cap G* [trans. of ML or NL *herba* (*Sancti*) *Gerardi*, after *Gerardus* (St. Gerard) †1120 founder of the Knights of St. John] : GOUTWEED

her·bi·ci·dal \ˌ(h)ərbə¦sīdᵊl\ *adj* **1** : of or relating to an herbicide **2** : having the ability to destroy plants ⟨~ agents⟩

her·bi·cide \'==ˌsīd\ *n* -s [ISV *herbi-* (fr. L, fr. *herba* grass, herb) + *-cide*] : an agent (as a chemical) used to destroy or inhibit plant growth; *specif* : a selective weed killer that is not injurious to crop plants

herbier *comparative of* HERBY

herbiest *superlative of* HERBY

herb·ish \'(h)ərbish\ *adj, now dial* : of, relating to, or resembling herbs

her·biv·o·ra \(ˌ)(h)ər'bivərə\ *n pl* [NL, fr. neut. pl. of *herbivorus*] **1** *cap, in former classifications* : a group of mammals nearly or exactly equivalent to Ungulata and feeding mainly on herbage **2** : herbivorous animals; *esp* : members of the Herbivora

her·bi·vore \'(h)ərbəˌvō(ə)r\ *n* -s [NL *Herbivora*] : a plant-eating animal; *esp* : one of the Herbivora

her·bi·vor·i·ty \ˌ(h)ərbə'vōrəd·ē\ *n* -ES [*herbivorous* + *-ity*] : the quality or state of being herbivorous ⟨the form of the molar teeth . . . is recognizable, but the ~ of the fossil is not thereby determined —Richard Owen⟩

her·biv·o·rous \ˌ(h)ər¦bivərəs, ˌ(h)ər'b-\ *adj* [NL *herbivorus*, fr. L *herbi-* (fr. *herba* grass, herb) + *-vorus* -vorous] **1** : feeding on plants : PHYTOPHAGOUS — used esp. of mammals; compare CARNIVOROUS, OMNIVOROUS **2** : having a stout body-build and a long small intestine : ENDOMORPHIC — opposed to *carnivorous* — **her·biv·o·rous·ly** *adv*

herb·less \'(h)ərbləs\ *adj* : lacking herbs or herbage

herb·let \-lət\ *n* -s *archaic* : a small herb

herblike \'=ˌ=\ *adj* : resembling an herb

herb lily *n* : a plant of the genus *Alstroemeria*

herb mercury *n, pl* **herbs mercury** *or* **herb mercuries** : a Eurafrican annual herb (*Mercurialis annua*) widely naturalized as a weed and having inconspicuous greenish flowers

herb of grace *n, pl* **herbs of grace** [so called fr. the association of *rue* (plant) with *rue* (repentance)] : RUE

herb-of-the-cross \ˌ===¦=\ *n, pl* **herbs-of-the-cross** : EUROPEAN VERVAIN

her·bo·rist \'(h)ərbərəst\ *n* -s [MF *herboriste, herboliste*, irreg. fr. herbe herb (fr. L *herba*) + *-iste* -ist] : HERBALIST

her·bo·ri·za·tion \ˌ==rə'zāshən, -ˌrī'z-\ *n* -s : an excursion for the study or collection of plants

her·bo·rize \'==ˌrīz\ *vi* -ED/-ING/-S [F *herboriser*, fr. *herboriste* + *-iser* -ize] : BOTANIZE

herb·ous \'(h)ərbəs\ *or* **her·bose** \-ˌbōs\ *adj* [L *herbosus*, fr. *herba* grass, herb + *-osus* -ous, -ose] : HERBY

herb par·is \-'parəs\ *n, pl* **herbs paris** *or* **herb parises** *usu cap P* [by folk etymology (influence of *Paris*, France) fr. ML or NL *herba paris*, lit., herb of a couple; fr. the resemblance of its four leaves on a stalk to a true lover's knot] : a European herb (*Paris quadrifolia*) resembling and closely related to the trilliums and commonly reputed to be poisonous

herb patience *n, pl* **herbs patience** : PATIENCE 3

herb rob·ert \-'räbə(r)t\ *n, pl* **herbs robert** *or* **herb roberts** *usu cap R* [trans. of ML *herba Roberti*, prob. *Robertus* (St. Robert) †1067 Fr. ecclesiastic] : a sticky low herb (*Geranium robertianum*) with small reddish purple flowers

herbs *pl of* HERB

herb st. bar·ba·ra \-(ˌ)sānt'bärb(ə)rə, ˌsənt-, -'bäb-\ *n, pl* **herbs st. barbara** *or* **herb st. barbaras**, *usu cap S&B* [trans. of ML or NL *herba* (*Sanctae*) *Barbarae* — more at HERB BARBARA] : WINTER CRESS

herb she·rard \-shə'rärd\ *n, pl* **herbs sherard** *or* **herb sherards** [NL *Sherardia*] : FIELD MADDER

herb so·phia \-sə'fīə, -sō'-, -fēə\ *n, pl* **herbs sophia** *or* **herb sophias** *usu cap S* [prob. fr. NL *sophia* (specific epithet of *Descurainia sophia*), fr. the name *Sophia*] : a hedge mustard (*Descurainia sophia*) with long linear pods

herbst's corpuscle \'herps(ts)-\ *n, usu cap H* : CORPUSCLE OF HERBST

herb tobacco *n* : a mixture of herbs containing coltsfoot (*Tussilago farfara*) and smoked for relieving coughs

herb trinity *n, pl* **herbs trinity** *or* **herb trinities** [trans. of ML or NL *herba trinitatis*] **1** [so called fr. the three-colored flowers] : PANSY **2** [so called fr. the three lobes of the leaf] : HEPATICA 1b

herbwoman \'=ˌ==\ *or* **herbwife** \'=ˌ=\ *n, pl* **herbwomen** *or* **herbwives** : a woman who sells herbs

herby \'(h)ərbē\ *adj* -ER/-EST [*herb* + *-y*] **1** : abounding in herbaceous vegetation **2** : relating to, resembling, or tasting like an herb ⟨a rich ~ flavor⟩

her·cog·a·mous \ˌhər¦kägəməs\ *adj* [Gk *herkos* fence, barrier + E *-gamous*] : incapable of self-fertilization

her·cog·a·my \ˌhər'kägəmē\ *n* -ES [Gk *herkos* + E *-gamy*] : a state in which self-pollination is made impossible by structural obstacles (as in the flowers of orchids)

her·cu·la·ne·an \¦hərkyə¦lānēən\ *adj, usu cap* [*Herculaneum*, ancient city in southwestern Italy + E *-an*] : of or relating to the ancient Roman city of Herculaneum

her·cu·le·an \¦hər¦kyə¦lēən, ¦hər¦kyülēən, ¦hō¦, ¦həi¦, hə(r)-'kyül-ē\ *adj, usu cap* [*Hercules* + E *-an*] **1** : of or relating to Hercules or his feats ⟨*Herculean* labors⟩ **2 a** : of heroic proportions : very large and strong ⟨*Herculean* longshoreman⟩ ⟨the bed was a wide and *Herculean* piece —Ellery Queen⟩ **b** : of extraordinary might or tremendous difficulty : displaying or requiring the strength of a Hercules ⟨*Herculean* exertions⟩ ⟨*Herculean* task⟩ **syn** see HUGE

her·cu·les \'hərkyəˌlēz, 'hōk-, 'həik-\ *n* -ES *usu cap* [after *Hercules*, Greco-Roman mythological hero noted for his great strength and for having accomplished twelve gigantic tasks imposed upon him, fr. L, fr. Gk *Hēraklēs*] : a man of great physical strength ⟨said of him that it was greedy and unfair to be an Adonis and a *Hercules* as well —E.V.Lucas⟩

hercules' allheal \-ˌlē'zōl,hēl\ *n, usu cap H* : a European herb (*Opopanax chironium*) — compare WOUNDWORT

hercules beetle *n, usu cap H* **1** : a very large beetle (*Dynastes hercules*) native to tropical America of which the male being prob. the largest existing insect attains a length of over five inches and bears a long forwardly projecting horn on the thorax and another on the head **2** : RHINOCEROS BEETLE

hercules club *n, usu cap H* : a large Australian whelk (*Pyrazus ebeninus*) with a dark brown nodose shell

hercules'-club \'==ˌ=¦=\ *n, pl* **hercules'-clubs** *usu cap* **1** : any of several prickly shrubs or trees: **a** : an ornamental tree (*Zanthoxylum clava-herculis*) of the southeastern U. S. and the West Indies **b** : either of two shrubs of the Bahamas (*Zanthoxylum coreaceum* or *Caesalpinia bahamensis*) **2** : a gourd (*Lagenaria vulgaris*) with fruit sometimes exceeding five feet in length **3** : a small prickly tree (*Aralia spinosa*) of eastern U. S. — called also *angelica tree, devil's-walking-stick*

hercules stone *n, usu cap H* : LODESTONE

her·cyn·i·an \(¦)hər¦sinēən\ *adj, usu cap* [L *Hercynia* (*silva*) Hercynian forest + E *-an*] **1** : of or relating to an extensive mountain range covered with forests in ancient Germany **2** : of or relating to the folding and mountain building that took place in the eastern hemisphere in late Paleozoic time — see GEOLOGIC TIME table

her·cy·nite \'hərsᵊnˌīt\ *n* -s [G *hercynit*, fr. L *Hercynia* (*silva*), its locality + G *-it* -ite] : a black mineral $FeAl_2O_4$ consisting of an oxide of iron and aluminum and constituting a member of the spinel series

¹**herd** \'hərd, 'hōd, 'həid\ *n* -s [ME *herde, herd*, fr. OE *heord*; akin to OHG *herta* herd, ON *hjǫrth*, Goth *hairda* herd, MW *cordd* troop, Gk *korthys* heap, Skt *śardha* herd, troop] **1 a** : a number of one kind of animal kept together under human care or control: as (1) : a company of one of the larger domestic animals ⟨a ~ of horses⟩ ⟨~s of swine⟩; *esp* : such a company of domestic oxen — often contrasted with *flock* ⟨patriarchs rich in ~s of cattle and flocks of sheep and goats⟩ (2) : a company of one kind of wild or semi-domesticated animals kept or bred for human use ⟨a ~ of ranch mink⟩ ⟨a ~ of laboratory mice⟩ **b** : a congregation of gregarious wild animals: as (1) : a group of one or more kinds of usu. large herbivorous mammals ⟨a ~ of elephants⟩ ⟨~s of antelopes darkening the African veldt⟩ or of marine mammals ⟨the dolphin ~ playing through the swell —Sacheverell Sitwell⟩ ⟨~s of seal coming ashore to bear young⟩ (2) : a school of large fish ⟨grazing on the bottom in ~s like the haddock —Rachel L. Carson⟩ (3) : a flock of large and usu. chiefly terrestrial or aquatic birds ⟨a ~ of swans⟩ ⟨a large ~ of wild turkeys⟩ **2 a** : a group of people usu. having a common bond ⟨entered the troop with the midwinter ~ of tenderfeet —MacKinlay Kantor⟩ **b** : the whole body of mankind : the undistinguished masses : MOB ⟨isolate the individual prophets from the ~ —Norman Cousins⟩; *esp* : society viewed as clinging to a blind conformity of standards and behavior ⟨the ~ of mankind can hardly be said to think; their notions are almost all adoptive —Earl of Chesterfield⟩ ⟨a boarding school where the thirteen-year-old . . . helplessly watches the ~ tearing to shreds the spirit of a nonconformist student —Rose Feld⟩ **3** : a considerable quantity : large number ⟨~s of new cars from America —Christopher Rand⟩

²**herd** \"\ *vi* -ED/-ING/-S [ME *herden*, fr. *herde, herd*, n.] **1 a** : to come together in a herd : feed or run together ⟨animals are in general fond of ~*ing* and grazing in company —Oliver Goldsmith⟩ **b** : to assemble or move in a group ⟨New Yorkers . . . ~*ing* resignedly on subway platforms —Charlotte Devree⟩ ⟨when the bell rang they ~*ed* in together —Oliver La Farge⟩ **2** : to place oneself in a group : ASSOCIATE ⟨it is desirable that young noblemen should ~ —Sir Walter Scott⟩

³**herd** \"\ *n* -s [ME *hierde, hirde, herde*, fr. OE *hyrde, hierde*; akin to OHG *hirti* herdsman, ON *hirthir*, Goth *hairdeis*; derivatives fr. the root of E ¹*herd*] **1 a** : one that herds domestic animals : HERDSMAN — now used chiefly in combination ⟨cow*herd*⟩ ⟨swine*herd*⟩ **b** *dial Brit* : SHEPHERD **2** [⁴*herd*] *West* : a tour of duty as a herdsman ⟨a new ranch hand, on ~ for the first time⟩ ⟨cook had flapjacks ready for the men coming off night ~⟩

⁴**herd** \"\ *vt* -ED/-ING/-S [ME *herden*, fr. *hierde, herde*, n.] **1 a** : to keep (animals) together : LEAD, DRIVE ⟨dogs are often trained to ~ sheep⟩ **b** : to gather, lead, or drive as if in a herd ⟨a nation that ~s fifteen millions of its own citizens into slave labor camps —James Burnham⟩ ⟨seventy-five boys and girls were ~*ed* by six or eight teachers —W.A.White⟩ **2** : to place in a group : ASSOCIATE ⟨~ us with their kindred fools —Jonathan Swift⟩

herdbook \'=ˌ=\ *n* : a book containing the records of one or more herds; *an* official record of the individuals and pedigrees of a recognized breed esp. of cattle or swine

herdboy \'=ˌ=\ *n* **1** : a boy who tends herd or assists a herder **2** : COWBOY 3a

herd·er \-də(r)\ *n* -s [⁴*herd* + *-er*] **1** : HERDSMAN **2** : FLUME RUNNER **3** : a worker who couples and uncouples locomotives in a railroad yard

her·der·ite \'hərdəˌrīt, 'her-\ *n* -s [Baron Siegmund A. W. von *Herder* †1838 Ger. mining official + E *-ite*] : a mineral $CaBe(PO_4)(F,OH)$ consisting of phosphate and fluoride of beryllium and calcium

her·dic \'hərdik\ *n* -s [after Peter *Herdic* †1888 Am. inventor] : a small horse-drawn omnibus of late 19th century America having side seats and an entrance at the back ⟨a ~ load of boys from some dance in town —C.M.Flandrau⟩

herdic

herding *n* -s [fr. gerund of ⁴*herd*] : the act or work of taking care of livestock

herd instinct *n* : an inherent tendency to congregate or to react in unison ⟨*herd instinct* of wild horses⟩ ⟨the startled cows obeyed the *herd instinct* to stampede⟩; *esp* : a theoretical human instinct toward gregariousness and conformity

herds *pl of* HERD, *pres 3d sing of* HERD

herd's-grass *also* **herd grass** \'=ˌ=\ *n, pl* **herd's-grasses** [after John *Herd*, who in 1700 found timothy growing in N. H.] **1** : TIMOTHY **2** [so called fr. its being frequently sown in mixtures with timothy] : REDTOP 1

herds·man \'hərdzmən, 'hōd-, 'həid-\ *n, pl* **herdsmen** [alter. of earlier *herdman*, fr. ME *hirdman, herdman*, fr. OE *hyrdeman*, fr. *hierde, hyrde* herdsman + *man* — more at HERD] : a manager, breeder, or tender of livestock (as cattle or sheep)

herd·wick \'hərˌdwik\ *n* [fr. obs. *herdwick* pasture ground, fr. ME, fr. *hierde, herde* herdsman + *wick*; fr. the breed's having been developed on the herdwicks of the Abbey of Furness in Lancashire, England] **1** *usu cap* : a British breed of very hardy coarse-wooled mountain sheep **2** -s *often cap* : an animal of the Herdwick breed

¹**here** \'hi(ə)r, -iə; "*Come here!*" *is often* kə'mi-\ *adv* [ME, fr. OE *hēr*; akin to OHG *hiar, hier* here, ON & Goth *hēr*, OE *hē* he — more at HE] **1 a** : at this point in space : in this location ⟨turn ~⟩ ⟨if they mean to have a war, let it begin ~ —John Parker⟩ : in this very spot ⟨he is not ~, for he has risen —Mt 28:6 (RSV)⟩ — opposed to *there*; often used interjectionally esp. in answering a roll call or in calling a domestic animal **b** : at this point in time : NOW ⟨~ it's August and summer's nearly over⟩ **2 a** : at this critical point esp. of an argument or development : at this juncture ⟨~ it becomes necessary to bring our concepts together —R.M.Weaver⟩ **b** : in the matter in question : in this case or particular ⟨the essential fact ~ was the division of the Roman empire —Gilbert Highet⟩ **3** : in the present life or state : on earth ⟨happy ~, and more happy hereafter —Francis Bacon⟩ — often used with *below* ⟨implies some endeavor to improve conditions ~ below instead of a single-minded concentration on . . . the next world —Elmer Davis⟩ **4** : to or into this place : HITHER ⟨bring the book ~⟩ **5** — used interjectionally and often reduplicated as an admonitory rebuke ⟨~, that's enough⟩ or soothing encouragement ⟨~ ~, don't cry⟩ — **here goes** — used interjectionally to express resolution or resignation esp. at the beginning of a rash, difficult, or unpleasant undertaking — **neither here nor there** : having no interest or relevance : of no consequence ⟨matters of comfort and convenience that are *neither here nor there* to a real sailing fan⟩

²**here** \"\ *adj* [ME, fr. *here*, adv.] **1** — used for emphasis esp. after a demonstrative pronoun or after a noun modified by a demonstrative adjective ⟨this boy ~ knows what happened⟩ **2** *now substand* — used for emphasis after a demonstrative adjective but before the noun modified ⟨with regard to this ~ robbery —Charles Dickens⟩

³**here** \"\ *n* -s [ME, fr. *here*, adv.] **1** : the present location or juncture : this place ⟨where do we go from ~⟩ ⟨from ~ on the story gets more interesting⟩ — opposed to *there* **2** : immediacy in space abstracted from the other qualities and relations of the immediate experience ⟨a ~ to which we relate all theres —James Ward⟩

⁴**he·re** \'heˌre\ *n* -s [OE *here* army — more at HARRY] : an army in Anglo-Saxon times; *esp* : an army of invaders

hereabouts *or* **hereabout** \¦=ə¦=\ *adv* [ME *her abute*, fr. *her*, *here* here + *abute, about* about] : about or near this place : in this vicinity ⟨the countryside ~⟩ ⟨somewhere ~⟩

¹**hereafter** \(')=¦==\ *adv* [ME *here after*, fr. OE *hēræfter*, fr. *hēr* here + *æfter* after — more at HERE, AFTER] : after this: **a** : after this in order or sequence ⟨here and ~ I am following . . . her own version —S.H.Adams⟩ **b** : after this in time ⟨devise the agencies . . . that will make them impossible ~ —B.N.Cardozo⟩ **c** : in some future time or state ⟨this life is a preparation for life ~ —F.B.Artz⟩ **d** : at the time of taking effect — used with this meaning in a statute and expressly so construed by law in some states of the U. S.

²**hereafter** \=¦==\ *n* -s *sometimes cap* **1** : a time to come : FUTURE **2** : an existence or state beyond this life — often used with *the* ⟨a belief in the ~ is shown in gifts and articles left with the dead in many burials —P.I.Wellman⟩

³**hereafter** \(')=¦==\ *adj, archaic* : FUTURE ⟨that ~ ages may behold what ruin happened in revenge of him —Shak.⟩

here and now *n* : the immediately present space and time : this day and age — used with *the* ⟨although Omar was entirely negative in describing the joys of the hereafter, he was completely positive in enumerating the less doubtful joys of the *here and now* —H. W. Van Loon⟩ ⟨man's obligation is in the *here and now* —W.H.Whyte⟩

here and there *adv* [ME] **1 a** : in one place and another : IRREGULARLY ⟨hills topped *here and there* by white buildings —Fred Zimmer⟩ **b** : from time to time : now and then ⟨only caught a word *here and there*⟩ **2** : hither and thither ⟨roamed *here and there* looking for blueberries⟩

hereat \=ˈ=\ *adv, archaic* [ME *here at*, fr. *here* + *at* (prep.)] : at or because of this

hereaway \¦=ə¦=\ *or* **here·aways** \¦=ə¦wāz\ *adv* [ME *here-away*, fr. *here* + *away*] *now dial* : HEREABOUT

hereby \(')=¦=\ *adv* [ME, fr. *here* + *by* (prep.)] : by this a *obs* : by this place : near here ⟨~ upon the edge of yonder coppice —Shak.⟩ **b** : by this means; *esp* : by means of this act or document ⟨the sum of $800 is ~ authorized to be appropriated for this purpose —*Congressional Record*⟩

heredes *pl of* HERES

he·red·i·ta·ble \hə'redədəbəl, he'-, ¦herə¦did-·\ *adj* [MF, fr. LL *hereditare* to inherit (fr. L. *hered-, heres* heir) + *-abilis* -able — more at HEIR] : HERITABLE

her·e·dit·a·ment \,herə'did·əmənt; hə'redəd-·, he'-\ *n* -s [ML *hereditamentum*, fr. LL *hereditare* + L *-mentum* -ment] *law* : heritable property : lands, tenements, any property corporeal or incorporeal, real, personal, or mixed, that may descend to an heir

he·red·i·tar·i·an \hə,redə'terēən, he,-\ *n* -s [*hereditary* + *-an*] : an advocate of hereditarianism

he·red·i·tar·i·an·ism \-ēə,nizəm\ *n* -s : a doctrine that individual differences may be accounted for primarily on the basis of genetics — compare ENVIRONMENTALISM

he·red·i·tar·i·ly \⸗¦⸗⸗¦terəlē, -li\ *adv* : in an hereditary manner ⟨the members of society who are ~ predisposed toward mental illness —J.F.Cuber & R.A.Harper⟩

he·red·i·tar·i·ness \-rēnəs, -rin-\ *n* -ES : the quality or state of being hereditary

he·red·i·tary \hə'redə,terē, -ri *also* he'-\ *adj* [L *hereditarius*, fr. *hereditas* inheritance + *-arius* -ary — more at HEREDITY] **1 a** : genetically transmitted or capable of being genetically transmitted from parent to offspring ⟨~ factor⟩ ⟨~ disease⟩ — see HEREDITY 2; compare ACQUIRED, CONGENITAL, FAMILIAL **b** : characteristic of or fostered by one's predecessors : ANCESTRAL ⟨~ pride⟩ ⟨~ bravery⟩ ⟨~ feud⟩ **2 a** : descended or capable of descending from an ancestor to an heir at law : received or passing by inheritance or required to pass by inheritance ⟨~ wealth⟩ ⟨~ monarchy⟩ **b** : having title or possession through inheritance ⟨~ sovereign⟩ ⟨~ nobility⟩ **3** : of a kind or status established by tradition ⟨~ enemy⟩ ⟨a ~ reputation for liberality and kindness —Louise P. Kellogg⟩ **4** : of or relating to inheritance or heredity ⟨unless he had the ~ dispositions which he has, he would not behave the way he does —Arthur Pap⟩ ⟨the ~ principle, once a business has been founded, has proved . . . a serviceable method of ensuring fresh supplies of managerial talent —Roy Lewis & Angus Maude⟩ **syn** see INNATE

he·re·di·tas *also* **hae·re·di·tas** \hə'redə,tas\ *n, pl* **hereditates** \⸗,⸗⸗'tād·(,)ēz\ [L] *Roman & civil law* : inheritance or succession : the rights and liabilities to which an heir succeeds : an estate of a deceased person regarded as a juridical person

hereditas ja·cens \-'jā,senz\ *n* [L, lit., lying (inactive) inheritance] *Roman & civil law* : an inheritance not entered upon by the heir : a vacant succession

he·red·i·ty \hə'redəd·ē, -ətē, -i *also* he'-\ *n* -ES [MF *heredité*, fr. L *hereditat-, hereditas*, fr. *hered-, heres* heir + *-itat-, -itas* -ity — more at HEIR] **1 a** : INHERITANCE ⟨their fathers were of yeoman rank, both by ~ and as large freeholders —Charles Partridge⟩ **b** : TRADITION ⟨Bretons are fishermen by ~⟩ **2 a** : the sum of the qualities and potentialities of an individual that are genetically derived from its ancestors : the germinal constitution of an individual **b** : the transmission of qualities from ancestor to descendant (as from parent to child) through a mechanism lying primarily in the chromosomes of the germ cells that in sexually reproducing organisms sorts out in meiosis the genes accumulated in past generations and recombines them during fertilization to produce a new individual conforming to the general pattern of its kind but exhibiting variations dependent both on specific recombination of factors and on interaction between the hereditary potentialities and the environment — compare GALTON'S LAW OF INHERITANCE, LAMARCKISM, MENDEL'S LAW, PANGENESIS, PHENOCOPY, WEISMANNISM

heredo- *comb form* [NL, fr. L *hered-, heres* heir — more at HEIR] : hereditary : hereditarily ⟨*heredo*ataxia⟩ ⟨*heredo*-familial⟩

her·e·ford \'hərfərd, 'hēfəd, 'həifəd *sometimes* 'herəf-\ *n* [fr. county of *Hereford*, England] **1 a** *usu cap* : a breed of hardy red beef cattle with white faces and markings and either horned or polled that originated in Herefordshire, England, but are now extensively raised in the western U.S. and other grazing regions **b** -s *often cap* : an animal of this breed **2a** *usu cap* : an American breed of red and white swine typically having markings similar to those of Hereford cattle **b** -s *often cap* : a hog of this breed

hereford disease *n, cap H* : GRASS TETANY

her·e·ford·shire \'herəfərd,shi(ə)r, -fəd,shiə, -,shə(r), *US* " *or* 'hərf- *or* 'hēf- *or* 'həif-\ *or* **hereford** *adj, usu cap* [fr. *Herefordshire* or county of *Hereford*, Eng.] : of or from the county of Hereford, England : of the kind or style prevalent in Hereford

herefrom \(')⸗¦⸗\ *adv* [¹*here* + *from* (prep.)] *archaic* : from this: **a** : from this place **b** : from this source

he·re·geld \'herə,geld, -,ye-\ *n* -s [OE *heregeld, heregild*, fr. *here* army + *gield, geld, gild* payment, tribute — more at HARRY, GELD] **1** : DANEGELD **2** [ME (Sc dial.) *heregeld, hereyeld, hereȝeld*, prob. fr. OE *heregeld*] *old Scots law* : a due or payment corresponding to the English heriot

herehence *adv* [¹*here* + *hence*] *obs* : from or away from this point or source

herein \(,)⸗¦⸗\ *adv* [ME *herinne, herin*, fr. OE *hērinne*, fr. *hēr* here + *inne* in — more at HERE, IN] : in this: **a** : in this place ⟨~ were many vaulted . . . walks hewn out of the rock —John Ray⟩ ⟨enclosed ~ you will find my check⟩ **b** : in this passage, book, or document ⟨all legislative powers ~ granted —*U.S.Constitution*⟩ **c** : in this fact or particular ⟨~ you war against your reputation —Shak.⟩

hereinabove \⸗¦⸗⸗¦⸗, ¦⸗(,)⸗¦⸗\ *adv* [*herein* + *above*] : above this : at a prior point in this writing or document ⟨payments due said fund, as ~ described —*Nat'l Bituminous Coal Wage Agreement*⟩

hereinafter \¦⸗¦⸗⸗\ *adv* [*herein* + *after*] : after this : in the following part of this writing or document ⟨a behavior to be ~ defined —Edward Sapir⟩ ⟨subject to conditions of this policy as ~ specified⟩

hereinbefore \⸗¦⸗⸗¦⸗, ¦⸗(,)⸗¦⸗\ *adv* [*herein* + *before*] : before this : in the preceding part of this writing or document ⟨oaths ~ directed to be taken by the governor —Martin Wight⟩

hereinbelow \⸗¦⸗⸗¦⸗, ¦⸗(,)⸗¦⸗\ *adv* [*herein* + *below*] : below this : at a subsequent point in this writing or document ⟨which report is ~ set forth in full —*U.S.Code*⟩

he·rem *or* **che·rem** \'kārəm, 'ker-\ *n* -s [Heb *hērem*] : one of three forms of ecclesiastical excommunication pronounced by a rabbi or by the officials of a synagogue or community

he·rend porcelain \'he,rend-\ *n, usu cap H* [fr. *Herend*, town in Hungary where it was made] : Hungarian hard-paste porcelain made since the 18th century and often imitative of other wares

here·ness *n* -ES [*here* + *-ness*] : the state of being here

her·eni·ging *also* **her·ee·ni·ging** \hə'rēnəkiŋ, -əkiŋ\ *n* -s *sometimes cap* [Afrik *hereniging* (formerly spelled *hereeniging*), lit., reunion, reuniting, fr. *herenig* to reunite + *-ing*] : an amalgamation of So. African political parties

hereof \(')⸗¦⸗ *sometimes* -¦äf\ *adv* [ME *herof*, fr. OE *hērof*, fr. *hēr* here + *of* (prep.) — more at HERE, OF] : of this ⟨the twigs ~ are physic —Thomas Fuller⟩; *specif* : of this writing or document ⟨shown in the schedule on the last page ~⟩

hereon \(')⸗¦⸗\ *adv* [ME *heron*, fr. OE *hēron*, fr. *hēr* here + *on* (prep.)] : on this: **a** *archaic* : on this fact or basis ⟨happiness grounded ~ —Nehemiah Grew⟩ **b** : on this writing or document ⟨endorsed ~⟩

hereout \(')⸗¦⸗\ *adv* [ME *herout, herut*, fr. *here* + *out, ut* out (prep.) — more at HERE, OUT] *archaic* : out of this: **a** : out of this place : from here **b** : out of this premise : HENCE

here-right \(')⸗¦⸗\ *adv, dial Eng* : on the spot : right here ⟨let's settle it *here-right* —F.T.Elworthy⟩

he·re·ro \hə're(,)rō, 'herə,rō\ *n, pl* **herero** *or* **hereros** *usu cap* **1 a** : a Bantu people of the central part of South-West Africa — compare DAMARA **b** : a member of the Herero people **2** : the Bantu language of the Herero people

¹**heres** *pl of* HERE

²**he·res** \'hā,rās\ *or* **hae·res** \'hī,-\ *n, pl* **here·des** *or* **haere·des** \⸗'rā,dās\ [L — more at HEIR] *civil law* : the universal successor of a deceased person — called also *heir*

he·re·si·arch \hə'rēzē,ärk, he'-, -rēsē-; 'herəsē,-\ *n* -s [LL *haeresiarcha*, fr. LGk *hairesiarchēs* leader of a sect, leader of a group of heretics, fr. Gk *hairesis* sect & LGk, heresy + Gk *-archēs* -arch — more at HERESY] : an originator or chief advocate of a heresy : leader of a group of heretics ⟨it is not only the lives of saints who leave their mark . . . but the lives of ~s and sinners as well —D.H.Wiest⟩ ⟨became the chief Communist ~ —E.J.Simmons⟩

he·re·si·mach \hə'rēzə,mak, he'-, -rēsə-; 'herəsē,-\ *n* -s [LGk *hairesimachos*, fr. Gk *hairesis* heresy + Gk *-machos* (fr. *machesthai* to fight) — more at HERESY, -MACHY] : an active opponent of heresy and heretics

he·re·si·og·ra·phy \hə,rēzē'ägrəfē, he,-, -rēsē-; ,herəsē-\ *n* -ES [*heresio-* (fr. *heresy*) + *-graphy*] : a treatise on heresy

he·re·si·ol·o·gist \-'äləjəst\ *n* -s : a writer against heresies

he·re·si·ol·o·gy \-jē\ *n* -ES [*heresio-* (fr. *heresy*) + *-logy*] **1** : the study of heresies **2** : a treatise on heresies

he·res ne·ces·sa·ri·us \'hā,rā,snekə'sārēəs\ *n* [LL, lit., heir of necessity] *Roman law* : a slave who is instituted by his master as his heir and who upon his master's death automatically attains his freedom and becomes his heir

her·e·sy \'herəsē, -si\ *n* -ES [ME *eresie, heresie*, fr. OF, fr. LL *haeresis*, fr. LGk *hairesis*, fr. Gk, action of taking, choice, sect, fr. *hairein* to take + *-sis*; perh. akin to Gk *hormē* assault, attack — more at SERUM] **1 a** : adherence to a religious opinion that is contrary to an established dogma of a church : HETERODOXY ⟨was convicted of ~ . . . because of his belief in the preexistence of souls —H.E.Starr⟩ — opposed to *orthodoxy* **b** : a deliberate and obstinate denial of a revealed truth by a baptized member of the Roman Catholic Church — compare INQUISITION 3a **c** : an opinion or doctrine contrary to church dogma ⟨all the great *heresies* . . . in Christianity have been specifically concerned with the relationship of the Son to the Father —Weston La Barre⟩ **2 a** : dissent from a dominant theory or opinion in any field ⟨so much that used to be scientific ~ is now regarded as scientific truth —Elmer Davis⟩ ⟨preaching ~ to the good Jeffersonian progressives of his day —C.B.Forcey⟩ **b** : an opinion or doctrine contrary to the truth or to generally accepted beliefs ⟨our democratic ~ which holds that . . . truth is to be found by majority vote —M.W. Straight⟩ **3** : a group or school of thought centering around a particular heresy ⟨favoring the German school of historians and other *heresies* of similar nature —A.G.Mayous⟩

¹**her·e·tic** \'herə,tik\ *n* -s [ME *eretik, heretik*, fr. MF *eretique, heretique*, adj. & n., fr. LL *haereticus*, fr. LGk *hairetikos*, fr. Gk, able to choose, fr. *hairetos* (verbal of *hairein* to take, *haireisthai* to choose) + *-ikos* -ic] **1 a** : a dissenter from established church dogma : DEVIATIONIST — distinguished from *infidel* **b** : a baptized member of the Roman Catholic Church who deliberately and obstinately disavows a revealed truth **2** : one that dissents from an accepted belief or doctrine of any kind : INNOVATOR, NONCONFORMIST ⟨to delete from history its ~s and its radicals would be to deprive it of that rare quality known as independence of mind —F.C.Neff⟩ ⟨he who resists a mania may be trodden under foot like any other ~ —W.G. Sumner⟩

²**heretic** \", hə'red·|ik, he'-, -ret|, |ēk\ *adj* [ME *eretik, heretik*, fr. MF *eretique, heretique*] : HERETICAL

he·ret·i·cal \hə'red·|əkəl, he'-, -ret|, 'ek-\ *adj* [ML *haereticalis*, fr. LL *haereticus* + L *-alis* -al] **1** : of, relating to, or characterized by religious heresy : HETERODOX ⟨let a church member in good standing dare to utter ~ opinions on theology . . . his scalp is in danger —L.L.Rice⟩ — opposed to *orthodox* **2** : of, relating to, or characterized by departure from accepted beliefs or standards : RADICAL, UNORTHODOX ⟨we must have a spirit of tolerance which allows the expression of all opinions, however ~ they may appear —J.B.Conant⟩ ⟨many critics regard individualism in art as an ~ innovation —John Dewey⟩ — **he·ret·i·cal·ly** \-k(ə)lē, -li\ *adv* — **he·ret·i·cal·ness** \-kəlnəs\ *n* -ES

he·ret·i·cate \-,kāt\ *vt* -ED/-ING/-S [ML *haereticatus*, past part. of *haereticare*, fr. LL *haereticus*] **1** : to pronounce or denounce as heretical **2** : to denounce as a heretic : make a heretic of — **he·ret·i·ca·tion** \⸗,⸗⸗'kāshən\ *n* -s

he·ret·i·ca·tor \⸗'⸗⸗,kād·ə(r)\ *n* -s : one that hereticates

hereto \(,)⸗¦⸗\ *adv* [ME *herto*, fr. *her, here* here + *to* (prep.)] : to this writing or document ⟨the chart ~ attached⟩

¹**here·to·fore** \¦hir|d·ə¦fō(ə)r, |hiə|, |tə-, -fō(ə)r, -ōə, -ó(ə)\ *adv* [ME *heretofore, heretoforn*, fr. *here* + *tofore, toforn* before, fr. OE *tōforan*, fr. *tō* to + *foran* before, fr. *fore* — more at TO, FORE] : before this : up to this time : HITHERTO ⟨I tell you now what we have ~ kept secret from you —A.C. Whitehead⟩

²**heretofore** \"\ *adj* [ME *heretoforn*, fr. *heretoforn*, adv.] *archaic* : PREVIOUS ⟨in his ~ voyages —Nathaniel Hawthorne⟩

he·re·to·ga \,herə'tōgə, '⸗⸗,⸗⸗\ *also* **her·e·togh** \'herə,tōk\ *n* -s [ME & OE; ME *heretogh*, fr. OE *heretoga*; akin to OFris *hertoga* leader of an army, duke, OS *heritogo*, OHG *herizoho, herizogo*, ON *hertogi*; all fr. a prehistoric Gmc compound whose constituents are akin respectively to OE *here* army and to OE *togian* to draw, drag, and that is prob. a trans. of Gk *stratēlatēs* leader of an army — more at HARRY, TOW] : the leader of an army or commander of militia in Anglo-Saxon England

heretrix *var of* HERITRIX

hereunder \(,)⸗¦⸗⸗\ *adv* [ME, fr. *here* + *under* (prep.)] : under this: **a** : under this written statement : subsequently in this writing or document : BELOW ⟨I subjoin ~ a brief description of the seven-year bean —*Farmer's Weekly*⟩ **b** : under this agreement : in accordance with the terms of this document ⟨registration of copyright . . . ~ shall not exempt the copyright proprietor from the deposit of copies —Richard Wincor⟩

hereunto \⸗'⸗(,)⸗, ¦⸗(,)⸗¦⸗\ *adv* [¹*here* + *unto* (prep.)] : to this; *esp* : to this writing or document ⟨we ~ affix our signatures⟩

hereupon \¦⸗⸗¦⸗\ *adv* [ME *herupon*, fr. *her, here* here + *upon* (prep.)] : on this : at or as a sequel to this : immediately after this ⟨the warning whistle sounded and ~ the last passengers scrambled aboard⟩

herewith \(,)⸗¦⸗\ *adv* [ME *herwith*, fr. OE *hērwith*, fr. *hēr* here + *with*] : with this: **a** : with this communication : accompanying this writing or document; *specif* : enclosed in this envelope ⟨you will find my check ~⟩ **b** : with this proof : by this : in this way ⟨~ the principle is established —A. L.Kroeber⟩

he·rez \hə'rez\ *n* -ES *usu cap* [fr. *Herez*, Iran, where such rugs are made] : a usu. large heavy cotton or wool Oriental rug of coarse texture and variable quality made in northwestern Iran and characterized by strong angular design and an ivory background

he·re·zeld \'herə,yeld\ *n* -s [alter. (ȝ being taken as z) of ME (Sc dial.) *heregeld, hereyeld, hereȝeld* — more at HEREGELD] : HEREGELD 2

heried *past of* HERY

heries *pres 3d sing of* HERY

herile *adj* [L *herilis, erilis*, fr. *herus, erus* master + *-ilis* -ile] *obs* : of or relating to a master

he·ring image \'hā|riŋ-, 'he|\ *n, usu cap H* [after Ewald *Hering* †1918 Ger. physiologist and psychologist] : a first positive afterimage in a succession of visual afterimages resulting from a brief light stimulus and appearing in the same hue as the original sensation

her·i·ot \'hereēət\ *n* -s [ME *heriet, heriot*, fr. OE *heregeatwe, heregeatwa*, pl., military equipment, fr. *here* army + *geatwe, geatwa*, pl., equipment — more at HARRY] *Eng law* : a feudal duty or tribute due under English law to a lord upon the death of a tenant and consisting orig. of the horses and arms lent by the lord to his man, later of the best beast or chattel of the tenant, and in modern times (as surviving in copyhold tenures) of such a chattel as the custom of the manor enables the lord to take or of a money payment — distinguished from *relief*; compare HEREGELD 2, THIRDINGS

her·i·ot·able \-ēəd·əbəl\ *adj* : subject to payment of a heriot

heriot service *n* : a heriot reserved as an incident of the tenure of an estate in fee simple granted in free tenure before 1290

her·i·ta·bil·i·ty \,herəd·ə'biləd·ē, -rətə-, -lətē, -i\ *n* -ES : the quality or state of being heritable

¹**her·i·ta·ble** \'herəd·əbəl, -rətə-\ *adj* [ME, fr. MF, fr. *heriter* to inherit + *-able*] **1** : capable of being inherited or of passing by inheritance : INHERITABLE **2** *Scots law* : of or relating to heritage or heritables **3** : HEREDITARY ⟨~ character⟩ ⟨~ office⟩ ⟨a viruslike agent transmitting ~ mammary tumors to young sucklings —*Lancet*⟩

²**heritable** \"\ *n* -s : a piece of heritable property — usu. used in pl.

heritable bond *or* **heritable security** *n, Scots law* : a form of bond or obligation carrying a yearly profit, secured upon land, treated as heritable, and now essentially like the English and American mortgage of real property

her·i·ta·bly \-blē,-bli\ *adv* : by right of inheritance

her·i·tage \'herəd·ij, -ətij *sometimes* -rə,tāj\ *n* -s [ME, fr. MF, fr. *heriter* to inherit (fr. LL *hereditare*, fr. L *hered-, heres* heir) + *-age* — more at HEIR] **1 a** *law* : real and other property that descends to an heir as distinguished from personal property that passes to an executor or administrator : PATRIMONY **b** *Scots law* : immovable property as distinguished from movable or personal property **2 a** : something transmitted by or acquired from a predecessor : INHERITANCE, LEGACY ⟨rich ~ of folklore⟩ ⟨a ~, a shrine, their history in stone —*Britain Today*⟩ ⟨war had left its ~ of poverty —Rose Macaulay⟩ ⟨the corn crop is a ~ from the Indians —*Annual Report of Ill. Power Co.*⟩ **b** : TRADITION ⟨a . . . party whose ~ is vision and boldness —M.W.Straight⟩ ⟨institutions . . . adapted to varying national ~s —S.P.Hayes b.1910⟩ **3** : BIRTHRIGHT ⟨the ~ of natural freedom was long since cast away —V.L.Parrington⟩

her·i·tance \-rəd·ən(t)s, -ətə-\ *n* -s [ME *heritaunce*, fr. MF *heritance*, fr. *heriter* + *-ance*] *archaic* : HERITAGE, INHERITANCE

her·i·tie·ra \,herə'tirə\ *n, cap* [NL, after C.L.L'*Héritier* de Brutelle †1800 Fr. botanist] : a small genus of Australasian trees (family Sterculiaceae) yielding hard heavy durable wood

her·i·tor \'herəd·ə(r), -rətə-\ *n* -s [alter. of ME *heriter*, fr. MF *eretier, heritier*, fr. L *hereditarius*, hereditary — more at HEREDITARY] **1** : INHERITOR **2** *Scots law* : the owner in fee of heritable property or in parochial law of such real property in a parish as is subject to public burdens

her·i·trix *or* **her·e·trix** \'herə·(,)triks\ *n, pl* **heritri·ces** \,herə·'trī(,)sēz\ *or* **heritrix·es** \'herə·,triksəz\ : a female heritor

herl \'hər(·ə)l\ *n* -s [ME *herle* — more at HARL] **1** : a barb of a feather used in dressing an artificial fly **2** : an artificial fly containing a herl

her·ling \'hərlən, 'her-, -liŋ\ *n* -s [origin unknown] *chiefly Scot* : SEA TROUT 1; *esp* : a young sea trout

herm \'hərm\ *n* -s [L *herma, hermes*, fr. Gk *hermēs* statue of Hermes, herm, fr. *Hermēs*, messenger of the gods] : a statue in the form of a square stone pillar surmounted by a bust or head ⟨a ~ of Themistocles which has been identified by its inscription —*New Internat'l Yr. Bk.*⟩; *esp* : a pillar surmounted by a usu. bearded head of Hermes — compare TERM

her·ma \'hərmə\ *n, pl* **her·mae** \-,mē, -,mī\ *or* **her·mai** \-,mī\ [L] : HERM

her·mae·an \¦hər¦mēən\ *adj, often cap* [L *Hermaeus* (fr. Gk *Hermaios*, fr. *Hermēs*) + E *-an*] : of or relating to Hermes or a herm

her·ma·ic \-māik\ *adj, usu cap* [Gk *Hermaikos*, fr. *Hermaios* + *-ikos* -ic] **1** : HERMETIC 1a **2** : HERMAEAN

her·man·dad \,ermən'dä(th)\ *n, pl* **hermanda·des** \-ä(,)thās\ *sometimes cap* [Sp, brotherhood, fr. *hermano* brother (fr. L *germanus*, fr. *germanus*, adj., having the same parents) + *-dad* (fr. L *-tat-, -tas* -ty) — more at GERMAN] : one of several voluntary organizations formed in Spain during the 13th, 14th, and 15th centuries to maintain public order and resist the depredations of the nobles and later to exercise general police functions

her·mann's fluid \'hərmənz-, 'her,mänz-\ *n, usu cap H* [after Friedrich *Hermann* †1920 Ger. anatomist] : a fixing solution of platinic chloride, osmic acid, and acetic acid used in microscopy for cytological preparations

her·maph·ro·dism \hə(r)'mafrə,dizəm, ,hər'-, hə'-, həi'-\ *n* -s [F *hermaphrodisme*, fr. *hermaphrodite* (fr. L *hermaphroditus*) + *-isme* -ism] : HERMAPHRODITISM

¹**her·maph·ro·dite** \-dīt, *usu* -īd·+V\ *n* -s [ME *hermofrodite*, fr. L *hermaphroditus*, fr. Gk *hermaphroditos*, fr. *Hermaphroditos*, mythological son of Hermes and Aphrodite who became joined in body with the nymph Salmacis] **1 a** : an abnormal individual esp. among the higher vertebrates having both male and female reproductive organs — called also *androgyne* **b** : HOMOSEXUAL **2** : a combination of diverse elements; *specif* : HERMAPHRODITE BRIG **3** : an animal or plant that is normally equipped with both male and female reproductive organs : BISEXUAL ⟨the hydra . . . is a true ~ —Alpheus Hyatt⟩

²**hermaphrodite** \"\ *adj* : HERMAPHRODITIC

hermaphrodite brig *n* : a 2-masted vessel square-rigged forward and schooner-rigged aft — called also *brigantine*

hermaphrodite brig

hermaphrodite caliper *n* : a drawing instrument having one caliper and one divider leg

hermaphrodite duct *n* : a duct for the passage of both eggs and sperm in mollusks having an ovotestis

her·maph·ro·dit·ic \(,)⸗¦⸗¦did·|ik, ¦hər,m-, ¦hə,m-, ¦həi,m-, -¦dit|, |ēk\ *also* **her·maph·ro·dit·i·cal** \|əkəl, |ēk-\ *adj* **1** : of, relating to, or characterized by hermaphroditism **2** : MONOCLINOUS — **her·maph·ro·dit·i·cal·ly** \|ək(ə)lē, |ēk-, -li\ *adv*

her·maph·ro·dit·ish \-¦dīd·|ish, -īt|, |ēsh\ *adj* : HERMAPHRODITIC

her·maph·ro·dit·ism \(,)⸗¦⸗⸗,dīd·,izəm, -,dī,tiz-\ *n* -s : the condition of being a hermaphrodite — compare DIOECISM

her·me·neut \'hərmə,n(y)üt\ *n* -s [Gk *hermēneutēs*, fr. *hermēneuein*] : an interpreter esp. in the early church

her·me·neu·tic \¦hərmə¦n(y)üd·ik\ *or* **her·me·neu·ti·cal** \-d·əkəl\ *adj* [*hermeneutic* fr. Gk *hermēneutikos*, fr. (assumed) *hermēneutos* (verbal of *hermēneuein* to interpret, translate, fr. *hermēneus* interpreter, prob. of non-IE origin) + *-ikos* -ic; *hermeneutical* fr. Gk *hermēneutikos* + E *-al*] : of or relating to hermeneutics : INTERPRETATIVE ⟨use of the ~ principle in the sociology of religion⟩ — **her·me·neu·ti·cal·ly** \-d·ək(ə)lē\ *adv*

her·me·neu·tics \,hərmə'n(y)üd·iks\ *n pl but usu sing in constr, also* **her·me·neu·tic** [Gk *hermēneutikē*, fr. fem. of *hermēneutikos*] : the study of the methodological principles of interpretation and explanation; *specif* : the study of the general principles of biblical interpretation ⟨~ became a weapon in ecclesiastical controversies —J.H.Summers⟩

her·mes \'hər(,)mēz\ *n, pl* **her·mae** \-,mē, -,mī\ *or* **her·mai** \-,mī\ *usu cap* [L — more at HERM] : HERM

¹**her·met·ic** \hə(r)'med·|ik, ¦hər'm-, (')hə¦m-, (')həi¦m-, -et|, |ēk\ *or* **her·met·i·cal** \|əkəl, |ēk-\ *adj* [NL *hermeticus*, fr. *Hermet-, Hermes Trismegistus* Thoth, the Egyptian god of wisdom, fabled author of a number of mystical, philosophical, and alchemistic writings, fr. Gk *Hermēt-, Hermēs trismegistos*, lit., thrice-great Hermes (with whom the Greeks identified Thoth) + L *-icus* -ic, -ical] **1** *sometimes cap* **a** : of or relating to the mystical and alchemical writings or teachings of Thoth, the Egyptian god of wisdom ⟨~ sciences⟩ **b** : relating to or characterized by occultism, alchemy, magic, or whatever is obscure and mysterious : RECONDITE ⟨~ poetry⟩ **2** [so called fr. the belief that Hermes Trismegistus invented a magic seal to keep vessels airtight] **a** : impervious to air : AIRTIGHT ⟨~ seal⟩ ⟨~ compass⟩ **b** : impervious to external influence ⟨as ~ as a nunnery —Eugene MacCown⟩ **3** : of or relating to a herm : HERMAEAN

²**hermetic** \"\ *n* -s **1** : ALCHEMIST **2** : an expounder of hermetic teachings

her·met·i·cal·ly \|ək(ə)lē, |ēk-, -li\ *adv* **1 a** : in an airtight manner ⟨~ sealed suit for use in high-altitude flying —H.G. Armstrong⟩ **b** : in a manner that prevents entry or change ⟨doors ~ sealed to less illustrious callers —Marguerite Steen⟩

⟨two gentlemen of decided and ~ opposite views —Philip Hamburger⟩ **2 :** in an obscure or mystical manner ⟨~ painted in the Cubist discipline —Janet Flanner⟩
her·met·i·cism \(ˌ)ˈmed·əˌsizəm, -etə-\ *n* -s *often cap* **:** HERMETISM
hermetic powder *n* **:** SYMPATHETIC POWDER
her·met·ics \(ˌ)ˈmed·|iks, -et|, |ēks\ *n pl but usu sing in constr, usu cap* **:** HERMETISM
her·me·tism \ˈhərməˌtizəm\ *n* -s [*hermetic* + *-ism*] **1** *usu cap* **:** a system of ideas based on hermetic teachings **2 :** adherence to or practice of hermetic doctrine ⟨it is not . . . willful ~ if the message of their art is veiled and indirect —R.J. Goldwater⟩
her·me·tist \-məd·əst\ *n* -s *usu cap* **:** an adherent to hermetic doctrine or practices
her·mi·no·nes \ˌhərməˈnō(ˌ)nēz\ *or* **her·mi·o·nes** \-mēˈō-, -ˌmīˈō-\ *n pl, usu cap* [L] **:** a division of ancient Teutons described by Tacitus as occupying central and eastern Germany and including interior tribes (as the Hermunduri, Heruli, Suevians, Quadi, Lombards, Vandals)
her·mit \ˈhərmət, ˈhəm-, ˈhəim-, *usu* -əd·+V\ *n* -s *often attrib* [ME *ermite, eremite, hermite, heremite*, fr. OF, fr. LL *eremita*, fr. LGk *erēmitēs*, fr. Gk *erēmitēs*, adj., living in the desert, fr. *erēmia* desert (fr. *erēmos* desolate, lonely + *-ia* -y) + *-itēs* -ite — more at RETINA] **1 a :** one that retires from society and lives in solitude **:** ANCHORITE, RECLUSE ⟨seclusive ~*s* whether in mountain shacks or shuttered brownstone houses⟩ ⟨a ~ nation⟩; *specif* **:** a Christian ascetic living alone in an isolated place in order to devote himself to religious exercises ⟨Christian monasticism from the third century ~*s* of the Egyptian deserts⟩ — compare MONK **b :** a member of a monastic order (as the Carthusians) whose members lead a chiefly eremitical life or of the Hermits of St. Augustine **c** *obs* **:** BEADSMAN ⟨for . . . the late dignities heaped up to them we rest your ~*s* —Shak.⟩ **2 a** (1) **:** any of various plainly colored forest-dwelling tropical hummingbirds constituting the genus *Phaethornis* (2) **:** any of several related hummingbirds **b :** HERMIT CRAB **3 :** a spiced molasses cookie often containing chopped raisins and nuts
¹her·mit·age \-əd·ij, -ətij\ *n* -s [ME *ermitage, hermitage*, fr. OF, fr. *ermite, hermite* + *-age*] **1 a :** the habitation of a hermit ⟨some forlorn and naked ~ remote from all the pleasures of the world —Shak.⟩ **b :** a secluded residence or private retreat **:** HIDEAWAY ⟨retirement to some country ~ —John Buchan⟩ **c :** a house of various monastic orders **:** MONASTERY ⟨Carthusian ~⟩ **2 :** the life or condition of a hermit ⟨when public places like theaters and restaurants are an integral part of city life . . . it is sheer ~ to be forced to forgo both —Evelyn Barkins⟩
²her·mi·tage \ˌ(h)ermēˌtäzh\ *n* -s *usu cap* [fr. Tain-l'*Ermitage*, commune in Drôme dept., France] **1 :** a chiefly red Rhone Valley wine made from grapes grown above the commune of Tain-l'Ermitage **2 :** a wine similar to Hermitage made elsewhere
hermit crab *n* [so called fr. its living in the empty shells of gastropods, like a hermit in a cave] **1 :** any of numerous chiefly marine decapod crustaceans of the families Paguridae and Parapaguridae having somewhat elongated bodies and soft and more or less asymmetrical abdomens, occupying the empty shells of gastropods, and seeking larger shells as they increase in size — compare PURSE CRAB **2 :** one that behaves like a hermit crab ⟨creep out of that shell of gentility, you little *hermit crab* —W.J.Locke⟩

hermit crab in shell

hermit crow *n* [so called fr. its nongregarious habits] **:** CHOUGH
her·mit·ess \ˈhərməd·əs\ *or* **her·mi·tress** \-mə·trəs\ *n* -ES **:** a female hermit
her·mit·ic \(ˈ)hərˈmid·ik\ *or* **her·mit·i·cal** \-d·əkəl\ *adj* **:** of, relating to, or suited for a hermit — **her·mit·i·cal·ly** \-d·ək(ə)lē\ *adv*
her·mit·ize \ˈhərməd·ˌīz\ *vi* -ED/-ING/-S [*hermit* + *-ize*] **:** to live a solitary life
hermit of st. au·gus·tine \-əˈgəstən, -ˌȯˈg-, -ˈȯgəˌstēn\ *usu cap H&S&A* [after *St. Augustine* — more at AUGUSTINIAN] **:** a member of an order of friars established in 1256 by Pope Alexander IV
her·mit·ry \ˈhərmətrē\ *n* -ES [*hermit* + *-ry*] **:** the quality or state of being a hermit **:** ISOLATION
hermits *pl of* HERMIT
her·mit·ship \ˈ==ˌship\ *n* [*hermit* + *-ship*] **:** HERMITRY
hermit thrush *n* **:** a thrush (*Hylocichla guttata faxoni*) of eastern No. America that is dull brown above becoming rufous on the tail and spotted on the breast and is noted for its song; *broadly* **:** any of several related thrushes of western No. America
hermit warbler *n* **:** a warbler (*Dendroica occidentalis*) found from the Rocky mountains to the Pacific and having in the adult male a yellow head, black throat, and gray back
her·mo·dac·tyl \ˈhərməˌdaktᵊl, ˌ==ˈ==\ *or* **her·mo·dac·ty·lus** \ˌ==ˈ=təs\ *n, pl* **hermodactyls** \-tᵊlz\ *or* **hermodacty·li** \-təˌlī\ [ML *hermodactylus*, fr. Gk *hermodaktylon*, fr. *hermo-* (fr. *Hermēs*, messenger of the gods) + *-daktylon* (fr. *daktylos* finger)] **1 :** a root formerly used as a cathartic or for the relief of gout that was prob. derived from an Asiatic colchicum (*Colchicum luteum*) but has been often considered to be or confused with the root of the Mediterranean snake's-head iris **2 :** a plant producing hermodactyls; *broadly* **:** any of several colchicums — compare COLCHICINE
her·mo·ge·nian \ˌhərməˈjēnēən, -nyən\ *n, usu cap* [*Hermogenes*, 2d cent. A.D. Greek rhetorician (fr. L, fr. Gk *Hermogenēs*) + E *-ian*] **:** a disciple of Hermogenes in developing Marcion's doctrine of the eternity of matter
her·mo·glyph·ic \ˌhərməˈglifik\ *also* **her·mog·ly·phist** \(ˌ)hərˈmägləfəst, ˈhərməˌglif-, ˌ==ˈ==\ *n* -s [*hermoglyphic* fr. Gk *hermoglyphikos* of statuary, fr. *hermoglypheus* statuary (fr. *hermēs* herm + *-glypheus*, fr. *glyphein* to carve) + *-ikos* -ic; *hermoglyphist* fr. Gk *hermoglyphikos* + E *-ist* — more at HERM, CLEAVE] **:** one that carves statues; *esp* **:** one that engraves inscriptions on herms
her·mo·sa pink \(ˌ)hərˈmōsə-\ *n* [prob. fr. *hermosa* (*rose*) bourbon rose, fr. Sp *hermosa*, fem. of *hermoso* beautiful, fr. L *formosus* — more at FORMOSITY] **:** a moderate to strong pink that is yellower and lighter than nymph pink and bluer and darker than peachblossom (sense 1)
herms *pl of* HERM
¹hern \ˈhərn\ *n* -s [ME *herne, hirne*, fr. OE *hyrne*; akin to OFris *horne* corner, MLG *hörne*, ON *hyrni* corner, OE *horn* horn — more at HORN] *now dial Eng* **:** NOOK, CORNER
²hern \ˈhərn, ˈhər·ən\ *pron* [ME *hiren*, alter. (influenced by the *-n* in *min* mine, *thin* thine) of *hire* — more at HER] *dial* **:** HERS
³hern *also* **herne** \ˈhern, ˈhərn\ *dial Brit var of* HERON
her·nan·dia \(ˌ)hərˈnandēə\ *n, cap* [NL, fr. Francisco *Hernández* †1578 Span. botanist + NL *-ia*] **:** a genus (the type of the family Hernandiaceae of the order Ranales) of tropical trees having light combustible wood, alternate entire leaves, small paniculate flowers, and drupaceous fruits — **her·nan·di·a·ceous** \(ˌ)=ˌ==ˈāshəs\ *adj*
her·ne \ˈhe(ə)rnə\ *adj, usu cap* [fr. *Herne*, Germany] **:** of or from the city of Herne, Germany **:** of the kind or style prevalent in Herne
her·nia \ˈhərnēə, ˈhən-, ˈhəin-, -nyə\ *n, pl* **herni·as** \-nēəz, -nyəz\ *or* **herni·ae** \-nēˌē\ [L — more at YARN] **:** a protrusion esp. of one of the abdominal viscera through connective tissue or through a wall of the cavity in which it is normally enclosed — called also *rupture* — **her·nial** \-nēəl,-nyəl\ *adj*
her·ni·ar·ia \ˌhərnēˈa(a)rēə\ *n, cap* [NL, fr. L *hernia* rupture + NL *-aria* — more at HERNIA] **:** a genus of small Old World herbs (family Caryophyllaceae) with minute green flowers — see RUPTUREWORT
her·ni·ar·in \-rən\ *n* -s [ISV *herniar-* (fr. NL *Herniaria*, genus name of *Herniaria hirsuta*) + *-in*] **:** a crystalline compound $C_{10}H_8O_3$ found esp. in a rupturewort (*Herniaria hirsuta*); the methyl ether of umbelliferone
¹her·ni·ary \ˈ==ˌerē, -ri\ *adj* [*hernia* + *-ary*] **:** of or relating to hernia or its treatment
²herniary \"\ *n* -ES [NL *Herniaria*] **:** a plant of the genus *Herniaria*
her·ni·ate \-ˌāt, *usu* -ˌād·+V\ *vi* -ED/-ING/-S [*hernia* + *-ate*] **:** to protrude through an abnormal body opening **:** RUPTURE
her·ni·a·tion \ˌ==ˈāshən\ *n* -s **1 :** the act or process of herniating **:** formation of a hernia **2 :** HERNIA
hernio- *comb form* [F, fr. L *hernia* — more at YARN] **:** hernia ⟨*hernio*rrhaphy⟩ ⟨*hernio*tomy⟩
her·ni·or·rha·phy \ˌhərnēˈȯrəfē\ *n* -ES [ISV *hernio-* + *-rrhaphy*] **:** an operation for hernia that involves opening the coverings, returning the contents to their normal place, obliterating the hernial sac, and closing the opening with strong sutures
her·ni·ot·o·my \-ˈäd·əmē\ *n* -ES [F *herniotomie*, fr. *hernio-* + *-tomie* -tomy] **:** the operation of cutting through a band of tissue that constricts a strangulated hernia
he·ro \ˈhē(ˌ)rō, ˈhi(-\ *n* -ES [back-formation fr. *heroes*, pl., fr. ME, fr. L, fr. Gk *hērōes*, pl. of *hērōs*; perh. akin to L *servare* to protect — more at CONSERVE] **1 a :** a mythological or legendary figure endowed with great strength, courage, or ability, favored by the gods, and often believed to be of divine or partly divine descent — compare CULTURE HERO, DEMIGOD **b :** a man of courage and nobility famed for his military achievements **:** an illustrious warrior **c :** a man admired for his achievements and noble qualities and considered a model or ideal **d :** the principal male character in a drama, novel, story, or narrative poem **:** PROTAGONIST **e :** the central figure in an event, action, or period **2** *New York* **:** POOR BOY
¹he·ro·di·an \həˈrōdēən, heˈ-\ *n* -s *usu cap* [ME, fr. LL *Herodianus*, fr. *Herodes* (Herod) †4 B.C. king of Judea + L *-ianus* *-ian*] **:** a member of a political party of biblical times consisting of Jews who were apparently partisans of the Herodian house and together with the Pharisees opposed Jesus
²herodian \"\ *adj, usu cap* **:** of or relating esp. to Herod the Great, king of Judea (37–4 B.C.)
he·rod·o·te·an \həˌrädəˈtēən\ *adj, usu cap* [*Herodotus*, 5th cent. B.C. Greek historian (fr. L, fr. Gk *Hērodotos*) + E *-ean*] **:** of, relating to, or suggestive of the historian Herodotus
heroess *n* -ES [*hero* + *-ess*] *obs* **:** HEROINE
¹he·ro·ic \həˈrōik, heˈ-, hē-, -ōek\ *also* **he·ro·i·cal** \-ōəkəl, -ōek-\ *adj* [L *heroicus*, fr. Gk *hērōikos*, fr. *hērōs* hero + *-ikos* -ic, -ical] **1 a :** belonging to or representative or suggestive of the heroes of antiquity ⟨a ~ culture⟩ ⟨~ society⟩ ⟨the ~ age⟩ **b :** treating of or suitable to or used in the treatment of the heroes of antiquity ⟨~ legends⟩ ⟨~ material⟩ **2 a** (1) **:** arising from, exhibiting, or suggestive of boldness, spirit, or daring ⟨a ~ cavalry charge⟩ ⟨a ~ enterprise⟩ (2) **:** such as is likely to be undertaken only to save life ⟨~ surgery⟩ **:** EXTREME, RADICAL ⟨~ treatment⟩ **b :** supremely noble, altruistic, or self-sacrificing ⟨a ~ gesture⟩ ⟨~ deeds⟩ **3 a :** of impressively generous proportion, size, or volume ⟨a ~ voice⟩ ⟨~ contributions to charity⟩ **b :** larger than life but smaller than colossal ⟨a ~ statue⟩ **c :** having a pronounced effect **:** LARGE, POWERFUL — used chiefly of medicaments or dosage ⟨~ doses⟩ ⟨a ~ drug⟩ **4 :** belonging to or inspired by the literary conventions of Restoration England esp. as found in the works of John Dryden ⟨~ drama⟩
²heroic \"\ *n* -s **1 :** HEROIC VERSE, HEROIC POEM **2 heroics** *pl* **:** vainglorious, unnaturally extravagant, or shamelessly flamboyant conduct, behavior, or expression ⟨avoids all ~*s* . . . in its delineation of a man of dignity —*Newsweek*⟩
he·ro·i·cal·ly \-ōək(ə)lē, -ōek-, -li\ *also* **he·ro·ic·ly** \-kl-\ *adv* **:** in a heroic manner ⟨struggling ~⟩ ⟨~ generous⟩
he·ro·i·cal·ness *n* -ES **:** the quality or state of being heroic **:** HEROICNESS
heroic couplet *n* **:** a couplet of rhyming iambic pentameters often forming a distinct rhetorical as well as metrical unit
he·ro·ic·ness *n* -ES **:** the quality or state of being heroic
he·roi·comic *or* **he·roi·comical** \həˌrōə, heˌ-, hēˌ-, -ōe+\ *adj* [F *héroïcomique*, blend of *héroïque* heroic (fr. L *heroicus*) and *comique* comic, comical, fr. L *comicus* — more at HEROIC, COMIC] **:** comic by being ludicrously noble, bold, or elevated
heroic poem *n* **:** an epic or a poem in epic style
heroic poetry *n* **:** epic poetry esp. celebrating the deeds of a hero
heroic stanza *or* **heroic quatrain** *n* **:** a rhymed quatrain in heroic verse with rhyme scheme *abab*
heroic verse *or* **heroic meter** *n* **1 :** dactylic hexameter — usu. used with special reference to epic verse of classical times **2** *or* **heroic line :** the verse form in which the heroic poetry of a particular language is or according to critical opinion should be composed (as the alexandrine in French and the hendecasyllabic line in Italian) **3 :** the iambic pentameter in rising rhythm used in epic and other serious English poetry during the 17th and 18th centuries
her·oin *also* **her·oine** \ˈhe\|rəwən *sometimes* ˈhi\| *or* \|ˌrōin\ *n* -s [fr. *Heroin*, a trademark] **:** a bitter white crystalline narcotic $C_{21}H_{23}NO_5$ made from morphine but more potent than morphine and because of its addictive properties prohibited by law from being manufactured in or imported into the U.S. and many other countries — called also *diacetylmorphine, diamorphine*
her·o·ine \ˈherəwən *sometimes* ˈhir-\ *n* -s [L *heroina, heroine*, fr. Gk *hērōinē*, fem. of *hērōs* hero — more at HERO] **1 a :** a mythological or legendary woman having the qualities of a hero **b :** a woman admired for her achievements and noble qualities and considered a model or ideal **2 a :** the principal female character in a drama, novel, story, or narrative poem **b :** the central female figure in an event, action, or period
her·oin·ism \ˈhe\|rəwəˌnizəm *sometimes* ˈhi\| *or* \|ˌrōiˌni-\ *n* -s [*heroin* + *-ism*] **:** addiction to heroin **:** habitual use of heroin
hero·ism \ˈherəˌwizəm *also* ˈhir- *or* ˈhēr-\ *n* -s [F *héroïsme*, fr. *héros* hero (fr. L *heros*, fr. Gk *hērōs*) + *-isme* -ism — more at HERO] **1 :** heroic conduct ⟨the ~ of a regiment defending a position⟩ **2 :** the qualities (as courage, bravery, self-sacrifice, unselfishness) of a hero **:** heroic characteristics ⟨a nation famous for the ~ of its leaders⟩
hero·ize \ˈhē(ˌ)rōˌīz, ˈhi(-\ *vb* -ED/-ING/-S [*hero* + *-ize*] *vt* **:** to make heroic **:** treat or represent as a hero ⟨politicians *heroizing* themselves to their constituents⟩ ⟨*heroized* their leader⟩ ~ *vi* **:** to play the hero **:** represent oneself as a hero
he·ro·la \həˈrōlə\ *n* -s [origin unknown] **:** a large yellowish tawny African antelope (*Damaliscus hunteri*) with markings on face and tail
her·on \ˈherən\ *n, pl* **herons** *also* **heron** [ME *heiroun, heroun*, fr. MF *hairon, heron*, of Gmc origin; akin to OE *hrāgra* heron, OHG *heigaro, hreigaro*, ON *hegri*; akin to W *cryg* hoarse, Gk *krikē* it creaked, Lith *krykšti* to shriek, OHG *scrīan* to scream, cry — more at SCREAM] **:** any of various wading birds constituting the family Ardeidae that have a long neck and legs, a long tapering bill with a sharp point and sharp cutting edges, large wings and soft plumage, and the inner edge of the claw of the middle toe pectinate, that exhibit in some species dichromatism and develop in many species special plumes in the breeding season, that frequent chiefly the vicinity of water and feed mostly on aquatic animals which they capture by quick thrusts of the sharp bill, that usu. nest in trees often in communities, and that vary much in size among different species but are not as large as some of the cranes — see GREAT BLUE HERON, GREAT WHITE HERON, LITTLE BLUE HERON; compare EGRET

great blue heron

her·on·ry \-rē, -ri\ *n* -ES [*heron* + *-ry*] **:** a place where herons breed; *also* **:** a community of herons
heron's-bill \ˈ==ˌ=\ *also* **heronbill** \ˈ==ˌ=\ *n, pl* **heron's-bills** *also* **heronbills :** ERODIUM 2
her·on·sew \ˈherənˌsō, -sü\ *n* -s [ME *heronsewe*, fr. MF *heroncel, heronceau* young heron, dim. of *hairon, heron*] *dial Brit* **:** HERON
He·roult \(ˈ)āˈrü\ *trademark* — used for an arc furnace that heats both by radiation and by resistance of the bath and is widely used for making electric steel
hero worship *n* **1 :** veneration of heroes; *specif* **:** the recognition and just evaluation of illustrious individuals as the chief promoters of cultural advance **2 :** excessive adulation
hero-worship \ˈ==ˌ=\ *vt* [*hero worship*] **:** to feel, show, or express hero worship for — **hero-worshiper** \ˈ=ˌ=ˌ==\ *n*
her·pan·gi·na \ˌhərˌpanˈjīnə, ˌhərˈpanjənə\ *n* [NL, fr. *herpes* + *angina*] **:** a contagious disease of children characterized by fever, headache, and a vesicular eruption in the throat and caused by a strain of the Coxsackie virus
her·pes \ˈhər(ˌ)pēz\ *n* -ES [L, fr. Gk *herpēs*, fr. *herpein* to creep — more at SERPENT] **:** any of several virus diseases characterized by the formation of blisters on the skin or mucous membranes — see HERPES SIMPLEX, HERPES ZOSTER
herpes sim·plex \ˌ==ˈsimˌpleks\ *n* [NL, lit., simple herpes] **:** either of two virus diseases marked by groups of watery blisters on the skin or mucous membranes that in one case affect esp. the mouth and lips and in the other esp. the genitalia —see COLD SORE
her·pes·tes \ˌhərˈpe(ˌ)stēz\ *n, cap* [NL, fr. Gk *herpēstēs* animal that walks on all four feet, fr. *herpēstēs*, adj., creeping, fr. *herpein* to creep] **:** a genus of Old World carnivorous mammals (family Viverridae) comprising typical mongooses and sometimes placed in a separate family — **her·pes·tine** \-ˌstən, ˈhərpəˌstīn\ *adj or n*
herpes zos·ter \ˌ==ˈzōstər, -ˈzäs-\ *n* [NL, lit., girdle herpes; *zoster* fr. Gk *zōstēr* girdle; akin to Gk *zōnē* girdle, belt — more at ZONE] **:** an acute inflammation of the sensory ganglia of spinal and cranial nerves that tends to occur late in life, during immunological suppression, or following local skin injury, that is caused by reactivation of the virus causing chicken pox, and that is associated with a vesicular eruption and neuralgic pains along the course of those nerves arising in the affected ganglia — called also *shingles*
herpet- *or* **herpeto-** *comb form* [partly fr. Gk *herpeton* animal that goes on all fours, snake, fr. neut. of *herpetos* creeping, fr. *herpein* to creep; partly fr. L *herpet-, herpes* herpes (also, a kind of animal, prob. a snake), fr. Gk *herpēt-, herpēs*; partly fr. Gk *herpetos* creeping — more at SERPENT] **1 :** reptile or reptiles ⟨*herpeto*fauna⟩ ⟨*herpeto*logy⟩ **2 :** herpes ⟨*herpet*iform⟩ **3 :** creeping ⟨*herpeto*monas⟩
her·pet·ic \(ˌ)hərˈped·ik\ *adj* [*herpet-* + *-ic*] **:** of or relating to herpes ⟨~ virus⟩ ⟨~ pain⟩ **:** resembling herpes ⟨~ lesions⟩
her·pet·i·form \-d·əˌfȯrm\ *adj* [ISV *herpet-* + *-iform*] **:** resembling herpes
her·pe·to·fauna \ˌhərpəd·ō+\ *n* [NL, fr. *herpet-* + *fauna*] **:** reptiles or reptile life esp. of a particular region
her·pe·to·log·ic \ˌhərpəd·əˌläjik\ *or* **her·pe·to·log·i·cal** \-jəkəl\ *adj* **:** of or relating to herpetology — **her·pe·to·log·i·cal·ly** \-jək(ə)lē\ *adv*
her·pe·tol·o·gist \ˌhərpəˈtäləjəst\ *n* -s **:** a specialist in herpetology
her·pe·tol·o·gy \-jē\ *n* -ES [*herpet-* + *-logy*] **:** a branch of zoology that treats of reptiles and amphibians
¹her·pe·tom·o·nad \ˌhərpəˈtäməˌnad\ *adj* [NL *Herpetomonad-, Herpetomonas*] **:** of or relating to the genus *Herpetomonas*
²herpetomonad \"\ *n* -s **:** a flagellate of the genus *Herpetomonas*
her·pe·tom·o·nas \-nəs, -ˌnas\ *n* [NL, fr. *herpet-* + *-monas*] **1** *cap* **:** a genus of flagellates of the family Trypanosomatidae that are parasites of the gut of insects **2** -ES **:** any flagellate of the genus *Herpetomonas*; *also* **:** any member of the Trypanosomatidae that appears to have two flagella due to precocious duplication of the locomotor apparatus
her·pob·del·li·da \ˌhərˌpäbˈdeləda\ [NL, fr. *Herpobdella* genus of leeches (fr. Gk *herpein* to creep + NL *-o-* + *-bdella*) + *-ida*] *syn of* PHARYNGOBDELLIDA
her·po·trich·ia \ˌhərpəˈtrikēə\ *n, cap* [NL, fr. Gk *herpein* to creep + NL *-o-* + *-trichia*] **:** a genus of fungi (family Sphaeriaceae) having perithecia on a brown mycelial layer and including a form (*Herpotrichia nigra*) that is a parasite on conifers
herr \(ˌ)he(ə)r\ *n, pl* **her·ren** \ˌherən, (ˌ)he(ə)rn\ [G, lit., lord, master] *usu cap* **:** MISTER — usu. used preceding the name of a German man
her·ren·volk \ˈherənˌfōk, -fōlk\ *n* -s *often cap* [G, fr. *herr* lord, master + *volk* people, nation] **:** a nationalistic group that believes itself to be racially preeminent and hence fitted to rule over inferior groups
her·ring \ˈheriŋ, -rēŋ\ *n, pl* **herring** *or* **herrings** [ME *hering*, fr. OE *hǣring*; akin to OS *hering* herring, MD *harinc, hareng, herinc*, OHG *hārinc, hering*] **1 :** a valuable food fish (*Clupea harengus*) that reaches a length of about one foot, is extraordinarily abundant in the temperate and colder parts of the north Atlantic where it swims in great schools, feeds chiefly on small crustaceans, and approaches the coasts for spawning where it is caught and preserved in the adult state by smoking or salting and in the young state is extensively canned as sardines; *broadly* **:** a fish of the family Clupeidae — often used in combination ⟨California ~⟩; see ALEWIFE, FALL HERRING, GLUT HERRING **2 :** any of various fishes of families other than Clupeidae that resemble the north Atlantic herring — usu. used in combination; see FRESHWATER HERRING, LAKE HERRING, RAINBOW HERRING
¹herringbone \ˈ==ˌ=\ *n, often attrib* [*herring* + *bone*] **1 :** a pattern resembling the lateral skeletal configuration of a herring; *specif* **:** a pattern (as on a fabric) made up of adjacent rows of parallel lines where any two adjacent rows slope slightly in reverse directions **2 a :** a twilled fabric with a herringbone pattern; *also* **:** a suit made of such a fabric **b :** a herringbone arrangement of materials (as of bricks in a wall) **3 :** a method in skiing of ascending a slope by herringboning; *also* **:** a series of herringbone steps made by herringboning

bricks laid in herringbone pattern

²herringbone \"\ *vt* **1 :** to produce a herringbone pattern on **2 :** to arrange in a herringbone pattern ~ *vi* **1 :** to produce herringbone configurations **2 :** to ascend a slope by toeing out with the ski tips and placing the weight on the inner border of the skis
herringbone bond *n* **:** a bond in masonry in which the bricks form a herringbone pattern
herringbone gear *n* **:** a gear with double helical teeth inclined in reverse directions and making a herringbone pattern
herringbone stitch *n* **:** an ornamental catch stitch
herringbone strutting *n* **:** crossed struts between floor joists
her·ring-cale *or* **her·ring-kale** \ˈ==ˌkāl\ *n* -s **:** a common fish (*Olisthops cyanomelas*) that resembles a wrasse and is found in Australian coastal waters
her·ring·er \-ŋə(r)\ *n* -s [*herring* + *-er*] **:** one that fishes for herrings
herring gull *n* **:** a common large gull (*Larus argentatus*) of the northern hemisphere that in the adult state is largely white with blue-gray mantle and dark wing tips and pink feet and in the immature state is mainly dark brown
herring gutted *adj, of a horse* **:** having a form usu. indicative of inferior quality where the abdomen or barrel narrows sharply toward the flanks
herring hog *n* **:** HARBOR PORPOISE
herring king *n* **:** OARFISH
herring oil *n* **:** a pale yellow to dark-colored fatty oil obtained from herring and used in making soap and fat-liquoring leather
herring pond *n* **:** a great body of water (as the Atlantic ocean or English channel) ⟨have been in perils on the great salt *herring pond* —David Humphreys⟩
herrn·hut·er \ˈhernˌhüd·ər, ˌ=ˈ==\ *n* -s *usu cap* [G, fr. *Herrnhut* (lit., Lord's protection), town near Dresden, Germany founded by the Moravians in 1722] **:** MORAVIAN
¹hers \ˈhərz, ˈhəz\ *pron, sing or pl in constr* [ME *hires, hirs*, fr. *hire* her + *-s* -'s — more at HER] **1 :** her one or her ones — used without a following noun as a pronoun equivalent in meaning to the adjective *her* ⟨what a stricken look was ~ —S.T.Coleridge⟩ ⟨the eternal years of God are ~ —W.C.Bryant⟩; often used after *of* to single out one or more members of a class belonging to or connected with a particular female person or animal ⟨a favorite dessert of ~⟩ ⟨some friends of ~⟩ or merely to identify something or someone as belonging to or connected with a particular female person or animal without any implication of membership in a more extensive class ⟨that face of ~ —Shak.⟩ ⟨those charming manners of ~⟩ **2 :** something that belongs to her **:** what belongs to her ⟨all that is his is ~⟩

²**hers** *pl of* HER

³**hers** \"\ *adj, obs* **:** ²HER 1 — used as the first of two possessive adjectives modifying the same noun ⟨~ and mine adultery —Shak.⟩

her·schel effect \'hərshəl-\ *n, usu cap H* [after John F.W. *Herschel* †1871 Eng. astronomer] **:** a partial destruction of the latent image in photography by action of long wave radiation which is either red or infrared

her·schelian \ˌhər'shelēən, -shel-\ *adj, usu cap* [Sir William *Herschel* †1822 Eng. astronomer + E *-ian*] **:** of or relating to the astronomer Herschel

herschelian telescope *n, usu cap H* **:** a reflecting telescope in which the need for a secondary mirror is avoided by tilting the primary mirror slightly and thereby throwing the focused image to the side where it can be observed without obstruction to the incoming light rays — called also *off-axis reflector*

her·schel·ite \'hərshəˌlīt\ *n* -s [Sir John F. W. *Herschel* + E *-ite*] **:** a chabazite that consists of glassy crystals of complex twinned structure

herse *obs var of* HEARSE

her·self \(h)ə(r)'self\ *pron* [ME *hire self*, fr. OE *hiere self, hire self, hyre self*, dat. of *hēo self, hīo self* she herself — more at HE, SELF] **1 :** that identical female one **:** that identical one regarded as feminine (as by personification) — compare ¹SHE 1; used (1) reflexively as object of a preposition or direct or indirect object of a verb ⟨she devotes a lot of time to her children and very little to ~⟩ ⟨she bought ~ some clothes⟩ ⟨she considers ~ lucky⟩ (2) for emphasis in apposition with *she, who, that*, or a noun ⟨she ~ painted the room⟩ ⟨she did it ~⟩ ⟨the housewife ~ bought the groceries⟩ ⟨the housewife bought the groceries ~⟩ ⟨armies threatened Rome ~⟩ ⟨my mother, who was young once ~⟩ (3) for emphasis instead of nonreflexive *her* as object of a preposition or direct or indirect object of a verb ⟨I looked beside me then, and I saw ~ —Padraic Colum⟩ (4) for emphasis instead of *she* or instead of *she herself* as subject of a verb ⟨she told me that neither her husband nor ~ could attend the meeting⟩ or as predicate nominative ⟨it's ~ she's trying to convince⟩ or in comparisons after *than* or *as* ⟨she met another woman as tall as ~⟩ (5) in absolute constructions ⟨~ an orphan, the authoress shows deep understanding of the problems of the orphan girl whose story she tells⟩ **2 :** her normal, healthy, or sane condition ⟨she came to ~⟩ **:** her normal, healthy, or sane self ⟨ill for a week, she is now ~ again⟩ **3** *Scot* **:** MYSELF, YOURSELF, HIMSELF, ITSELF — used esp. in literary representations of the English spoken by Scottish Highlanders; compare ¹SHE 2 **4** *Irish & Scot* **:** a woman of consequence; *esp* **:** the mistress of the house ⟨where's ~⟩ **5 :** YOURSELF ⟨did she hurt ~⟩ — compare HIMSELF 4

hership *n* [ME, fr. *herien* to harry + *-ship* — more at HARRY] **1** *obs* **:** a warlike raid esp. to steal cattle; *also* **:** the distress caused by such a raid **2** *obs* **:** the loot stolen in a hership

hert·ford·shire *Brit* 'hä(t)fədshiə(r, -ˌshə(r), *US* " *or* 'härtfərd,shi(ə)r *or* -ˌshər *or* 'hərt- *or* 'hōt- *or* 'həit-\ *or* **hertford** *adj, usu cap* [fr. *Hertfordshire* or county of *Hertford*, England] **:** of or from the county of Hertford, England **:** of the kind or style prevalent in Hertford

hertfordshire kindness *n, usu cap H* **:** a favor of the same kind in return

hertz \'hərts, 'hōts, 'həits; 'he(ə)rts, 'heəts\ *n, pl* **hertz** *or* **hertzes** [after Heinrich R. *Hertz* †1894 Ger. physicist] **:** a unit of frequency of a periodic process equal to one cycle per second — abbr. *Hz*

hertz·ian \-sēən\ *adj, sometimes cap* [H. R. *Hertz* + E *-ian*] **:** of, relating to, or developed by the physicist Hertz

hertzian telegraphy *n* **:** telegraphy by means of Hertzian waves **:** RADIOTELEGRAPH

hertzian wave *n, usu cap H* **:** an electromagnetic wave produced by the oscillation of electricity in a conductor (as a radio antenna) and of a length ranging from a few millimeters to many kilometers

hertz oscillator *or* **hertzian oscillator** *n* **:** an inductive and capacitive circuit in which electric oscillations resulting in the emission of Hertzian waves are set up by passage of a spark or otherwise

her·va ma·té \ˌervə'mä(ˌ)tā, -mäd·ə\ *n* [Pg *herva mate, erva mate*, lit., maté plant] **:** MATÉ

herx·hei·mer reaction \'herksˌhīmər-\ *n, usu cap H* [after Karl *Herxheimer* †1944 Ger. dermatologist] **:** an increase in the symptoms of syphilis occurring in some persons when treatment with spirochetícidal drugs is instituted

hery *vt* -ED/-ING/-ES [ME *herien*, fr. OE *herian*; akin to OHG *harēn* to call, Goth *hazjan* to praise] *obs* **:** GLORIFY, PRAISE

her·ze·go·vinian \ˌhertsəgō'vēnēən, ˌhər-, -vin-\ *n* -s *cap* [*Herzegovina*, region in the northwestern Balkan peninsula + E *-ian*] **:** a native of Herzegovina

hes *pl of* HE

hesh \'hesh\ *dial var of* HUSH

hesh·van *also* **hes·van** *or* **ches·van** \'keshvən\ *n* -s *usu cap* [Heb *heshwān*, short for *marḥeshwān* Marheshvan] **:** the 2d month of the civil year or the 8th month of the ecclesiastical year in the Jewish calendar — see MONTH table

he·si·od·ic \ˌhēsē¦ädik *sometimes* ˌhesē- *or* ¦hēzē-\ *adj, usu cap* [*Hesiod*, 8th cent. B.C. Greek poet (fr. Gk *Hēsiodos*) + E *-ic*] **:** of or relating to the poet Hesiod or his simple practical maxims or theology

he·si·o·ne \hə'sīə(ˌ)nē\ *n, cap* [NL, after *Hesione*, Trojan princess of Greek mythology saved from a monster by Hercules, fr. L, fr. Gk *Hēsionē*] **:** a genus (the type of the family Hesionidae) of marine free-swimming polychaete worms having long peristomial cirri and two pairs of eyes

hes·i·tan·cy \'hezəd·ənsē, -zətən-, -si *also* -zət³n- *sometimes* -ztən- *or* 'hesə-\ *or* **hes·i·tance** \-n(t)s\ *n, pl* **hesitancies** *or* **hesitances** [LL *haesitantia*, fr. L, action of stammering, fr. *haesitant-, haesitans* + *-ia* -y] **1 :** the quality or state of being hesitant: as **a :** INDECISION ⟨had lost that nervous ~ that had so troubled her —Elizabeth Goudge⟩ **b :** RELUCTANCE ⟨had no ~ in entering the field of composition —Fannie L. G. Cole⟩ **2 :** an act or instance of hesitating **:** HESITATION ⟨her girlish *hesitancies*, her maidenly delays and refusals —S.H. Adams⟩

hes·i·tant \-nt\ *adj* [L *haesitant-, haesitans*, pres. part. of *haesitare*] **:** given to hesitation **:** tending to hold back (as from fear, indecision, or disinclination) ⟨a ~ fighter⟩ ⟨~ policies⟩
syn SEE DISINCLINED

hes·i·tant·ly *adv* **:** in a hesitant manner

hes·i·tate \'hezəˌtāt *sometimes* 'hezˌtāt *or* 'hesəˌtāt, *usu* -ād·+V\ *vb* -ED/-ING/-S [L *haesitatus*, past part of *haesitare* to stick fast, stammer, hesitate, fr. the stem of *haerēre* to stick; akin to Lith *gaišti* to loiter, delay] *vi* **1 a :** to hold back in doubt or indecision **:** avoid facing a decision, encounter, or problem ⟨the government *hesitated* before each policy⟩ **b :** to hold back from or as if from scruple ⟨~ at treason⟩ **2 :** to delay usu. momentarily **:** PAUSE ⟨a glimpse of a deer as it *hesitated* before disappearing into the underbrush⟩ **3 :** STAMMER ~ *vt* **:** to express in a hesitant manner ⟨choose rather to ~ my opinion than to assert it roundly —J.R.Lowell⟩

syn HESITATE, WAVER, VACILLATE, and FALTER agree in meaning to show irresolution or uncertainty. HESITATE implies a pause or other sign of indecision before acting ⟨no properly qualified student should *hesitate* to apply —*Official Register of Harvard Univ.*⟩ ⟨the young second officer *hesitated* to break the established rule of every ship's discipline —Joseph Conrad⟩ ⟨she *hesitated* a minute and then she said, 'Yes.' —Dorothy Baker⟩ WAVER implies hesitation after having seemed to decide and usu. suggests weakness or retreat from a decision ⟨the great man, who never *wavered* in his faith —H.S.Canby⟩ ⟨he was a good student and possessed an un*wavering* will —Nora Waln⟩ ⟨Henry was in the grip of his own master-passion and he did not *waver* —Francis Hackett⟩ VACILLATE implies prolonged hesitation from inability to reach a decision ⟨the . . . government has been *vacillating* in its policies on such emigration —*Collier's Yr. Bk.*⟩ ⟨I have *vacillated* when I should have insisted; temporized when I should have taken definite action —Ngaio Marsh⟩ FALTER suggests a hesitation or wavering evident in some physical sign of nervousness, lack of courage, or outright fear, as an uncertainty or breaking of the voice ⟨kept the bright excited look upon her face without *faltering* —F. Tennyson Jesse⟩ ⟨his steps perceptibly *falter* —*Times Lit. Supp.*⟩ ⟨his eyes did not flinch and his tongue did not *falter* —Joseph Conrad⟩

hes·i·tat·er *also* **hes·i·ta·tor** \-ād·ə(r), -ātə-\ *n* -s **:** one that hesitates

hes·i·tat·ing·ly \'≈≈ˌ≈≈≈, ˌ≈≈'≈≈≈\ *adv* **:** HESITANTLY

hes·i·ta·tion \ˌhezə'tāshən *sometimes* ˌhesə-\ *n* -s [L *haesitation-, haesitatio*, fr. *haesitatus* + *-ion-, -io* -ion] **1 :** the act or action of hesitating (as by holding back, pausing, or faltering) ⟨~ before decisions⟩ ⟨~ in accepting an offer⟩ **2 :** a faltering in speech **:** STAMMERING **3** *also* **hesitation waltz :** a waltz in which the dancers intersperse at pleasure a gliding movement; *also* **:** the gliding movement in such a waltz

hesitation form *n* **:** a sound (as \ə\, \ə̄\, or \ä̃\ usu. prolonged) or word (as er, uh, mmm, what-you-may-call-it, well) involuntarily or deliberately used while a speaker is uncertain about the fitting expression of his thought or the correct name of a person or object

hes·i·ta·tive \'hezəˌtād·|iv, -zətə|, -zəd·ə|, |t|, |ēv *sometimes* 'heztə| *or* 'hesə-\ *adj* **:** showing or characterized by hesitation — **hes·i·ta·tive·ly** \|əvlē, lēv-, -li\ *adv*

hesp \'hesp\ *dial var of* HASP

hes·ped \'heˌsped\ *n, pl* **hes·pe·dim** \he'spädəm, -ˌdēm\ [Heb *hespēdh*] **:** an oration or eulogy at a Jewish memorial service

hes·pe·ria \he'spirēə, -pēr-\ *n, cap* [NL, fr. L, west, fr. Gk, fr. *hesperos* of the evening, western (fr. *hesperos, hespera* evening) + *-ia* -y — more at WEST] **:** a genus of skipper butterflies that is the type of the family Hesperiidae and includes many small butterflies of the northern hemisphere that are mostly tawny with dark and pale markings

¹**hes·pe·ri·an** \(')≈¦≈rēən\ *adj, usu cap* [L *Hesperia* west + E *-an*] **1 :** WESTERN, OCCIDENTAL **2** [NL *Hesperia* + E *-an*] **:** of or relating to the Hesperiidae

²**hesperian** \"\ *n* -s **1** *usu cap* **:** an inhabitant of the West **:** OCCIDENTAL **2 :** a butterfly of the family Hesperiidae

¹**hes·per·id** \'hespərəd\ *or* **hes·pe·ri·id** \(')he¦spirēəd\ *adj* [NL *Hesperiidae*] **:** of or relating to the Hesperiidae

²**hesperid** *or* **hesperiid** *n* -s **:** an insect of the family Hesperiidae **:** a skipper butterfly

hes·per·i·date \hes'perəˌdāt\ *or* **hes·per·id·e·ous** \ˌhespə'ridēəs\ *adj* [NL *hesperidium* + E *-ate* or *-eous*] **:** of, relating to, or being a hesperidium

hes·per·id·e·an *or* **hes·per·id·i·an** \ˌhespə'ridēən\ *adj, usu cap* [*Hesperides* mythological paradisiacal garden growing golden apples (fr. the *Hesperides*, the nymphs that guard it, fr. L, fr. Gk) + E *-an, -ian*] **:** of, relating to, or having the characteristics of the gardens of the Hesperides

hes·per·i·din \he'sperəd³n, -ˌsperə'din\ *n* -s [NL *hesperidium* + E *-in*] **:** a crystalline bioflavonoid glycoside $C_{28}H_{34}O_{15}$ found in most citrus fruits and esp. in orange peel that yields hesperitin, glucose, and rhamnose on hydrolysis — see CITRIN

hes·per·id·i·um \ˌhespə'ridēəm\ *n, pl* **hesperid·ia** \-ēə\ [NL, fr. the *Hesperides* + NL *-ium*; fr. the myth of the golden apples of the Hesperides] **:** a berry (as an orange or lime) having a leathery rind — see FRUIT illustration

hes·per·i·idae \ˌhespə'rīəˌdē\ *n pl, cap* [NL, fr. *Hesperia*, type genus + *-idae*] **:** a large family of skipper butterflies (superfamily Hesperioidea) comprising the typical skippers — see HESPERIA; compare MEGATHYMIDAE

hes·per·i·nos \ˌhespərə'nōs, -nōs\ *n* -ES [LGk, fr. Gk, adj., of the evening, fr. *hesperos, hespera* evening + *-inos* -ine — more at WEST] **:** the office in the Eastern Church corresponding to vespers in the Western Church

hes·pe·ri·oi·dea \(ˌ)heˌspirē'ȯidēə\ *n pl, cap* [NL, fr. *Hesperia* + *-oidea*] **:** a superfamily of Lepidoptera comprising insects often considered butterflies but usu. distinguished from the typical butterflies by the hooked tips of the widely separated antennae, peculiarities of the wing venation, and the erratic and often very swift flight — see HESPERIIDAE, MEGATHYMIDAE, SKIPPER

hes·per·is \'hespərəs\ *n, cap* [NL, fr. L, dame's violet, fr. Gk, fr. fem. of *hesperios* of the evening, fr. *hesperos, hespera* evening] **:** a genus of biennial or perennial Eurasian herbs (family Cruciferae) having large purple or white racemose flowers — see DAME'S VIOLET

hes·per·i·tin *also* **hes·per·e·tin** \he'sperət³n, -ˌsperə'tin\ *n* -s [prob. irreg. fr. *hesperidin*] **:** a crystalline compound $C_{16}H_{14}O_6$ derived from flavanone and obtained by hydrolysis of hesperidin; a monomethyl ether of eriodictyol

hes·per·or·nis \ˌhespə'rȯrnəs\ *n, cap* [NL, fr. Gk *hesperos* western + NL *-ornis*] **:** a genus of swimming birds (order Hesperornithiformes) from the Cretaceous of Kansas that resemble loons in form, that have teeth in each jaw implanted in a long groove, and that in some cases exceed five feet in length

hes·per·or·nith·i·for·mes \ˌhespə(ˌ)rȯrˌnithə'fȯrˌmēz\ *n pl, cap* [NL, fr. *Hesperornith-, Hesperornis* + *-iformes*] **:** an order of extinct aquatic birds (superorder Odontognathae) including the genus *Hesperornis* and related Cretaceous forms

hesselbach's triangle *n, usu cap H* **:** TRIANGLE OF HESSELBACH

¹**hes·sian** \'heshən, *chiefly Brit* 'hesēən\ *adj, usu cap* [*Hesse*, region or state in southwestern Germany + E *-ian*] **:** of or relating to Hesse or the Hessians

²**hessian** \"\ *n* -s **1** *cap* **a :** a native of Hesse, a region or state in southwestern Germany **b :** a German mercenary often a native of Hesse serving in the British forces during the American Revolution **c :** a mercenary soldier **2 a :** HESSIAN BOOT **b :** HESSIAN ANDIRON **3** *chiefly Midland* **a :** SCAMP, RASCAL — used esp. of a child **b :** a troublesome or meddlesome person — used esp. of a woman **4** *also* **hessian cloth :** BURLAP

hessian andiron *n, usu cap H* **:** an andiron with an upright shaped to represent a Hessian soldier

hessian boot *n, usu cap H* **:** a high boot with a top extending to just below the knee and commonly ornamented with a tassel that was introduced into England by the Hessians early in the 19th century

Hessian boot

hessian crucible *n, usu cap H* **:** a cheap brittle fragile but very refractory crucible composed of the finest fireclay and sand and commonly used for a single heating

hessian fly *n, often cap H* [so called fr. the belief it was brought to America by Hessian soldiers] **:** a small two-winged fly (*Mayetiola destructor*) which is destructive to wheat in America and whose larvae live between the base of the lower leaves and the stalk and suck the juices of the plant

hess image \'hes-\ *n, usu cap H* [after Carl von *Hess* †1923 Ger. ophthalmologist] **:** a third positive afterimage in a succession of visual afterimages resulting from a brief light stimulus

hess·ite \'heˌsīt\ *n* -s [G *hessit*, fr. Henry *Hess* †1850 Swiss chemist in Russia + G *-it* -ite] **:** a mineral Ag_2Te consisting of a lead-gray sectile silver telluride often auriferous and usu. massive

hessonite *var of* ESSONITE

hess's law \'hesəz-\ *n, usu cap H* [after Henry *Hess*] **:** a statement in chemistry: the heat change in a chemical reaction is the same regardless of the number of stages in which the reaction is effected

hest \'hest\ *n* -s [ME *hest, heste*, alter. of *hes*, fr. OE *hǣs*; akin to OE *hātan* to command, call, be called — more at HIGHT] *archaic* **:** COMMAND

hes·thog·e·nous \(')hes¦thäjənəs\ *adj* [irreg. fr. Gk *esthēs* clothing + E *-genous*] **:** having a covering of down when hatched **:** DASYPAEDIC

hesvan *usu cap, var of* HESHVAN

hes·y·chasm \'hesəˌkazəm, 'hezə-\ *n* -s *often cap* [fr. *hesychast*, after such pairs as E *enthusiast: enthusiasm*] **:** hesychastic belief or practice

hes·y·chast \-kast\ *n* -s *often cap* [MGk *hēsychastēs*, fr. LGk, quietist, hermit, fr. Gk *hēsychazein* to be still, keep quiet, fr. *hēsychos* quiet; perh. akin to OE *sīd* long — more at SIDE] **:** one of an Eastern Orthodox ascetic sect of mystics originating among the monks of Mount Athos in the 14th century and practicing a quietistic method of contemplation for the purpose of attaining a beatific vision or similar mystical experience

hes·y·chas·tic \ˌ≈≈¦kastik\ *adj* [Gk *hēsychastikos*, fr. (assumed) Gk *hēsychastos* (verbal of *hēsychazein*) + Gk *-ikos* -ic] **1 :** SOOTHING, CALMING — used esp. of a style of ancient Greek music **2** *often cap* [*hesychast* + *-ic*] **:** of or relating to the hesychasts or their solitary meditative mysticism

¹**het** *var of* HETH

²**het** \'het\ *n* -s *usu cap* **:** CHECHEHET

³**het** \'het, *usu* -ed·+V\ *dial var of* ²HEAT

⁴**het** \"\ *chiefly Scot var of* HOT

⁵**het** \"\ *dial past of* HEAT

he·tae·ra \hə'tirə\ *or* **he·tai·ra** \-'tīrə\ *n, pl* **hetae·rae** \-i(ˌ)rē\ *or* **hetaeras** *or* **hetairas** \-ˌrəz\ *or* **hetai·rai** \-īˌrī\ [Gk *hetaira*, lit., companion, fem. of *hetairos* comrade, companion] **1 :** one of a class of highly cultivated courtesans in ancient Greece **2 :** DEMIMONDAINE ⟨the lady in the canary-colored carriage was New York's first fashionable ~ —*Harper's*⟩ ⟨a hair-pulling fight between two drunken *hetaerae* over a free spender —*Amer. Mercury*⟩

he·tae·rism *or* **he·tai·rism** \-ˌrizəm\ *n* -s [Gk *hetairismos*, fr. *hetaira* + *-ismos* -ism] **1 :** a general system of temporary or continued sexual relations outside wedlock **:** CONCUBINAGE **2 :** a state of society conceived as existing in the past and characterized by the holding of women in common

he·tae·ro·lite \hə'tirəˌlīt\ *n* -s [Gk *hetairos* companion + E *-lite*] **:** a mineral $ZnMn_2O_4$ consisting of a zinc-manganese oxide found with chalcophanite

hetchel *var of* HATCHEL

heter- *or* **hetero-** *comb form* [MF or LL; MF, fr. LL, fr. Gk, fr. *heteros*; akin to Gk *heis, hen* one — more at SAME] **1 :** other than usual **:** other **:** different ⟨*hetero*geneous⟩ ⟨*hetero*dox⟩ ⟨*Heter*anthera⟩ — opposed to *hom-, is-, orth-*, **2 :** for, from, or to a different species ⟨*hetero*agglutinin⟩ **3 a :** containing atoms of different kinds ⟨*hetero*cyclic⟩ **b :** isomeric with or closely related to a (specified) compound ⟨*hetero*xanthine⟩

¹**het·er·akid** \ˌhed·ə¦rakəd, -rak-\ *adj* [NL *Heterakidae*] **:** of or relating to the family Heterakidae; *esp* **:** caused by worms of the genus *Heterakis* ⟨~ transmission of blackhead⟩

²**heterakid** \"\ *n* -s **:** a worm of the family Heterakidae

het·er·aki·dae \ˌ≈≈'rakəˌdē\ *n pl, cap* [NL, fr. *Heterakis*, type genus + *-idae*] **:** a somewhat variably limited family comprising nematode worms with three lips, a small buccal capsule, and usu. a posterior esophageal bulb and sometimes being included in the family Ascaridae — see HETERAKIS

het·er·a·kis \ˌ≈≈'rākəs\ *n, cap* [NL, fr. *heter-* + Gk *akis* pointed object — more at ACIDANTHERA] **:** a genus (the type of the family Heterakidae) of nematode worms including the common cecal worm of chickens and turkeys

het·er·an·drous \ˌhed·ə¦randrəs\ *adj* [*heter-* + *-androus*] **:** having stamens of different length or form — **het·er·an·dry** \'≈≈ˌ≈drē\ *n* -ES

het·er·an·gi·um \ˌ≈≈'ranjēəm\ *n, cap* [NL, fr. *heter-* + *-angium*] **:** a genus of Devonian seed ferns having a protostelic stem resembling that of members of the genus *Gleichenia*

het·er·an·the·ra \-'ran(t)thərə\ *n, cap* [NL, fr. *heter-* + *-anthera*] **:** a genus of aquatic or marsh herbs (family Pontederiaceae) having flowers with a salverform perianth, three stamens, and a many-seeded capsule

het·er·atomic \¦hed·ər+\ *or* **het·ero·atomic** \¦hed·ə(ˌ)rō+\ *adj* [*heter-* + *atomic*] **:** made up of atoms of different kinds

het·er·auxesis \¦hed·ər+\ *n* [NL, fr. *heter-* + *auxesis*] **:** allometric growth — compare ALLOMETRY — **het·er·auxetic** \"+\ *adj*

het·er·axial \"+\ *adj* [*heter-* + *axial*] **:** having three unequal axes perpendicular to each other (as in animals having biradial or bilateral symmetry)

heterecious *var of* HETEROECIOUS

het·er·ism \'hed·əˌrizəm\ *n* -s [*heter-* + *-ism*] **:** variability of animals and plants

het·er·i·za·tion \ˌhed·ərə'zāshən, -ˌrī'z-\ *n* -s [*heter-* + *-ization*] **:** a changing from one form into another

het·ero \'hed·ə(ˌ)rō\ *adj* [*heter-*] **:** relating to or being an atom or element other than the predominating or significant one (as carbon) esp. in a ring of a molecule or compound ⟨~ atoms such as nitrogen or oxygen⟩

het·ero·agglutinin \¦hed·ə(ˌ)rō+\ *n* [*heter-* + *agglutinin*] **:** a hemagglutinin found in serum and reacting with red cells of animals of other species than the one producing the serum

het·ero·autotroph \"+\ *n* [*heter-* + *autotroph*] **:** a heteroautotrophic organism

het·ero·autotrophic \"+\ *adj* [*heter-* + *autotrophic*] **:** requiring a simple organic source of carbon but utilizing inorganic nitrogen for metabolism

het·ero·auxin \"+\ *n* [G, fr. *heter-* + *auxin*] **:** INDOLEACETIC ACID

het·ero·ba·sid·i·ae \ˌhed·ərōbə'sidēˌē\ *n pl, cap* [NL, fr. *heter-* + *-basidiae* (fr. *basidium*)] *in some classifications* **:** a subclass of Basidiomycetes comprising fungi with a basidium that is transversely or vertically septate or forked or has four rounded terminal cells from each of which a sterigma and spore arise and including Tremellales and other orders or being restricted to the order Tremellales — compare EUBASIDIAE, TELIOSPOREAE

het·ero·basidiomycetes \¦hed·ər(ˌ)ō+\ *n pl, cap* [NL, fr. *heter-* + *Basidiomycetes*] **:** a subclass of fungi (class Basidiomycetes) including the rusts, smuts, and jelly fungi that has septate or deeply divided basidia and basidiospores which often germinate to form conidia or similar spores — compare HOMOBASIDIOMYCETES — **het·ero·basidiomycetous** \"+\ *adj*

het·ero·ba·sid·io·my·cet·i·dae \¦≈≈(ˌ)≈bəˌsidē(ˌ)ōˌmī'sed·əˌdē\ *n pl, cap* [NL, fr. *heter-* + *Basidiomycetes* + *-idae*] *syn of* HETEROBASIDIOMYCETES

het·ero·basidium \"+\ *n* [NL, fr. *heter-* + *basidium*] **:** a basidium that is septate or with deep divisions (as in the subclass Heterobasidiomycetes)

het·ero·blas·tic \¦hed·ərō¦blastik\ *adj* [*heter-* + *-blastic*] **1 :** having an indirect embryonic development — opposed to *homoblastic*; compare EMBRYOGENY **2 :** arising from different germ layers — used of functionally similar organs of related animals **3 :** having young and adult forms different ⟨~ leaves of flowering plants⟩ — **het·ero·blas·ty** \'≈≈≈ˌblastē\ *n* -ES

het·ero·cap·sa·les \ˌhed·ə(ˌ)rōˌkap'sā(ˌ)lēz\ *n pl, cap* [NL] **:** an order of yellowish to brownish green algae (class Xanthophyceae) that form amorphous or arborescent palmelloid colonies containing an indefinite number of cells which are capable of reverting to a motile state directly or through zoospore formation — compare HETEROCOCCALES, VOLVOCALES

het·ero·carpus \ˌhed·ərō'kärpəs\ *n, cap* [NL, fr. *heter-* + *carpus*] **:** a genus of bioluminescent prawns occurring in the Indian ocean

heterocaryon *var of* HETEROKARYON

heterocaryosis *var of* HETEROKARYOSIS

het·ero·cellular \¦hed·ə(ˌ)rō+\ *adj* [*heter-* + *cellular*] **:** composed of more than one kind of cell

het·er·oc·era \ˌhed·ə'räsərə\ *n pl, cap* [NL, fr. *heter-* + *-cera*] **:** a division of Lepidoptera consisting of the moths — compare RHOPALOCERA — **het·er·oc·er·ous** \¦≈≈¦≈≈rəs\ *adj*

¹**het·ero·cerc** \'hed·ərōˌsərk\ *n* -s [*heter-* + *-cerc* (fr. Gk *kerkos* tail)] **:** a heterocercal fish

²**heterocerc** \"\ *adj* **:** HETEROCERCAL

het·ero·cer·cal \¦≈≈≈¦sərkəl\ *adj* [*heter-* + *-cercal*] **1 :** having the upper lobe larger than the lower with the end of the vertebral column prolonged and somewhat upturned in the upper lobe — used of the tail fin of various fishes (as sharks) **2 :** having or relating to a heterocercal tail fin — **het·ero·cer·cal·i·ty** \¦hed·ə(ˌ)rōˌsər'kaləd·ē\ *n* -ES

het·ero·charge \'hed·ərō+ˌ-\ *n* [*heter-* + *charge*] **:** a charge on an electret that is of sign opposite to that of the electrode orig. in contact with it — compare HOMOCHARGE

het·er·o·che·lous \¦hed·ərō¦kēləs\ *adj* [*heter-* + *chel-* + *-ous*] *of a crustacean* **:** having the chelae unlike in size and form — **het·er·o·che·ly** \'≈≈≈ˌkēlē\ *n* -ES

het·ero·chlamydeous \¦≈≈(ˌ)≈+\ *adj* [ISV *heter-* + *chlamydeous*] **:** having a perianth whose calyx and corolla are differentiated as to color and texture — compare HOMOCHLAMYDEOUS

het·er·o·chlo·ri·da·les \ˌ≈≈(ˌ)≈ˌklōrə'dā(ˌ)lēz\ *n pl, cap* [NL, fr. *Heterochlorid-, Heterochloris*, genus of algae + *-ales*] **:** an order of yellow-green algae including all members of the Xanthophyceae having flagellated vegetative cells

het·ero·chromatic \¦hed·ə(ˌ)rō+\ *adj* [*heter-* + *chromatic*] **1 :** of, relating to, or having different colors; *specif* **:** having a more or less complex pattern of colors — opposed to *homochromatic* **2 :** made up of various wavelengths or frequencies **:** not monochromatic **3** [*heterochromatin* + *-ic*] **:** of or relating to heterochromatin — **het·ero·chromatism** \"+\ *n* -s

het·ero·chromatin \"+\ *n* [G, fr. *hetero-* heter- + *chromatin*] **:** densely staining chromatin appearing as nodules in or along chromosomes — compare EUCHROMATIN

het·ero·chro·ma·ti·za·tion \ˌhed·ə·rō,krōməd·ə'zāshən, -mə-,tī'z-\ *n* -s [*heterochromat-* (fr. *heterochromatin*) + *-ization*] **:** the state of being or becoming heterochromatic **:** the transformation of genetically active euchromatin to inactive heterochromatin — **het·ero·chromatized** \ˌ≡≡ˈ≡mə,tīzd\ *adj*

het·ero·chrome \ˈ≡≡≡,krōm\ *adj* [ISV *heter-* + *-chrome*] **:** HETEROCHROMATIC

het·ero·chro·mia \ˌ≡≡ˈkrōmēə\ *n* -s [NL, fr. *heter-* + *-chromia*] **:** a difference in coloration in two anatomical structures or two parts of the same structure which are normally alike in color ⟨~ of the iris⟩

het·ero·chromomere \ˈhed·ə(ˌ)rō+\ *n* [*heter-* + *chromomere*] **:** a chromomere of the heterochromatic region of a chromosome; *also* **:** a granule of heterochromatin

het·ero·chromosome \"+\ *n* [ISV *heter-* + *chromosome*] **:** a sex chromosome

het·ero·chro·mous \ˌhed·ərəˈkrōməs\ *or* **het·ero·chro·mic** \-mik\ *adj* [*heter-* + *chrom-* + *-ous* or *-ic*] **:** of different colors

het·er·och·ro·nism \ˌhed·əˈräkrə,nizəm\ *also* **het·er·och·ro·ny** \-ˌnē\ *n, pl* **heterochronisms** *also* **heterochronies** [*heterochronism* fr. NL *heterochronus* heterochronous (fr. *heter-* + Gk *-chronos* -chronous) + E *-ism*; *heterochrony* fr. NL *heterochronia*, fr. *heterochronus* + L *-ia* -y] **1 :** deviation from the typical embryological sequence of formation of organs and parts as a factor in evolution — compare FETALIZATION **2 :** irregularity in time relationships; *specif* **:** the existence of differences in chronaxies among functionally related tissue elements — **het·er·och·ro·nis·tic** \ˌ≡≡ˌ≡≡ˈnistik\ *adj* — **het·er·och·ro·nous** \ˌ≡≡ˈräkrənəs\ *adj*

het·er·och·tho·nous \ˌ≡≡ˈräkthənəs\ *adj* [*heter-* + *-chthonous* (as in *autochthonous*)] **1 :** not indigenous **:** FOREIGN, NATURALIZED ⟨a ~ flora⟩ **2 a :** not formed in the place where it now occurs **:** TRANSPORTED ⟨~ rock⟩ **b :** removed from the original deposit (as by erosion) and reembedded (as certain fossils)

¹het·er·o·clite \ˈhed·ərə,klīt\ *n* -s [MF, n. & adj.] **1** *in the grammar of various languages* **:** a word irregular in inflection; *esp* **:** a noun irregular in declension (as Latin *pecus* having case forms of both third and fourth declensions) **2 :** one that deviates from the common rule or from common forms ⟨modern poetry is not a privilege of ~s —Wallace Stevens⟩

²heteroclite \"\ *adj* [MF or LL; MF, fr. LL *heteroclitus* irregularly inflected, fr. Gk *heteroklitos*, fr. *heter-* + (assumed) Gk *klitos* (verbal of Gk *klinein* to lean, incline, inflect) — more at LEAN] **:** deviating from ordinary forms or rules **:** IRREGULAR, ANOMALOUS, ABNORMAL ⟨a confusing, dusty, ~ accretion of objects —Janet Flanner⟩

het·er·o·clit·ic \ˌ≡≡≡ˈklid·ik\ *adj* **:** marked by irregularity of inflection ⟨many nouns . . . are ~ in one or more cases —F.W. Householder⟩

het·ero·coc·ca·les \ˌhed·ə(ˌ)rō,käˈkā(ˌ)lēz\ *n pl, cap* [NL, fr. *Heterococcus*, genus of algae (fr. *heter-* + *-coccus*) + *-ales*] **:** an order of yellow-green algae including all members of the class Xanthophyceae having the immobile vegetative cells surrounded by a cell wall and incapable of returning to the motile state directly

het·ero·coe·la \ˌhed·ərōˈsēlə\ [NL, fr. *heter-* + *-coela*, neut. pl. of *-coelus* -coelous] *syn of* SYCONOSA

het·ero·coe·lan \ˌ≡≡≡ˈ≡lən\ *adj* [NL *Heterocoela* + E *-an*] **:** of or relating to the Syconosa

het·ero·coe·lous \-ləs\ *adj* [*heter-* + *-coelous*] **1 :** of or relating to vertebrae having saddle-shaped articular surfaces ⟨~ birds⟩ **2** [NL *Heterocoela* + E *-ous*] **:** of or relating to the Syconosa

het·er·o·cont \ˈhed·ərō,känt\ *adj* [NL *Heterocontae*] **:** of or relating to the Heterokontae

heterocontae *syn of* HETEROKONTAE

het·ero·co·tyl·ea \ˌhed·ə(ˌ)rōkəˈtilēə, -ˌkädᵊlˈēə\ [NL, fr. *heter-* + *-cotylea* (fr. Gk *kotylē* cup, small vessel) — more at KETTLE] *syn of* MONOGENEA

het·er·o·crine \ˈhed·ərə,krin, -rīn,-rēn; -ˌkrən\ *adj* [*heter-* + *-crine* (as in *endocrine*)] *of a gland* **:** having both an endocrine and an exocrine secretion **:** MIXED

het·ero·cy·cle \-ˌsīkəl\ *n* [*heter-* + *cycle*] **:** a heterocyclic ring system or a heterocyclic compound

¹het·ero·cyclic \ˌ≡≡≡ˈsīklik, -lēk *also* -sik-\ *adj* [ISV *heter-* + *cyclic*] **:** relating to, characterized by, or being a ring composed of atoms of different elements ⟨furan and quinoline are ~⟩ — distinguished from *isocyclic*

²heterocyclic \"\ *n* **:** a heterocyclic compound or a heterocyclic ring system

het·ero·cyst \ˈhed·ərə,sist\ *n* [ISV *heter-* + *cyst*] **:** one of the large transparent thick-walled cells resembling spores occurring at intervals along the filament in certain filamentous blue-green algae

het·ero·dac·tyl \ˈhed·ərōˈdaktᵊl\ *adj* [ISV *heter-* + *-dactyl* (fr. Gk *daktylos* finger, toe)] **:** HETERODACTYLOUS

het·ero·dac·ty·lism \-tə,lizəm\ *n* -s [*heter-* + *-dactylism*] **1 :** unilateral polydactylism **2 :** a greater degree of polydactylism on one side than on the other

het·ero·dac·ty·lous \-tələs\ *adj* [*heter-* + *-dactylous*] **:** having the first and second toes turned backward ⟨trogons are ~⟩

het·er·od·era \ˌhed·əˈrädərə\ *n, cap* [NL, fr. *heter-* + *-dera* (fr. Gk *derē* neck) — more at DER-] **:** a genus (the type of the family Heteroderidae of the superfamily Tylenchoidea) of minute nematode worms many of which attack the roots and underground stems of various cultivated plants (as sugar beets, potatoes, peas) — compare GOLDEN NEMATODE, ROOT-KNOT NEMATODE

het·er·odon \ˈhed·ərə,dän\ *n, cap* [NL, fr. *heter-* + *-odon*] **:** a genus of small stocky colubrid snakes comprising the No. American hognose snakes

¹het·er·odont \-nt\ *adj* [ISV *heter-* + *-odont*] **1 :** having the teeth differentiated into incisors, canines, and molars ⟨~ mammals⟩ ⟨man is ~⟩ — opposed to *homodont* **2 :** having both cardinal and lateral teeth that fit into depressions on the opposite valve — compare HETERODONTA

²heterodont \"\ *n* -s **:** an animal with heterodont dentition

het·er·odon·ta \ˌ≡≡ˈdäntə\ *n pl, cap* [NL fr. *heter-* + *-odonta*] *in some classifications* **:** an order of Lamellibranchia comprising bivalve mollusks with few hinge teeth but usu. with both lateral and cardinal teeth and with unequal adductor muscles

het·er·odon·ti·dae \-tə,dē\ *n pl, cap* [NL, fr. *Heterodontus*, type genus + *-idae*] **:** a family of small sharks (suborder Squaloidea) having a few recent representatives in warm parts of the Pacific and Indian oceans but known since Jurassic times, bearing two dorsal fins each armed with a spine, and having the posterior teeth arranged in a dense pavement adapted for crushing the shells of mollusks — see HETERODONTUS

het·er·odon·tus \-təs\ *n, cap* [NL, fr. *heter-* + *-odontus* (fr. Gk *odont-*, *odōn* tooth) — more at TOOTH] **:** the type genus of Heterodontidae including most recent representatives of the family — see PORT JACKSON SHARK

het·er·o·dox \ˈhed·ərə,däks, ˈhetər-, ˈhe·tr-\ *adj* [LL *heterodoxus*, fr. Gk *heterodoxos*, fr. *hetero-* heter- + *doxa* opinion — more at DOXOLOGY] **1 :** differing from an established religious point of view: **a :** contrary to acknowledged religious opinion or belief **:** differing from a religious standard or official position **:** UNORTHODOX, HERETICAL ⟨~ sermon⟩ **b :** accepting or teaching heretical or unorthodox opinions or doctrines ⟨the ~ opponent of the established religion has often much more real faith than most of its followers —M.R.Cohen⟩ **2 :** lacking the usual content, qualities, or values **:** not following traditional form or procedure **:** UNCONVENTIONAL ⟨some ~ ideas on books —H.J.Laski⟩ ⟨the societies representing the orthodox practice of medicine have generally succeeded in keeping . . . ~ practitioners out —D.D.McKean⟩ — **het·ero·dox·ly** *adv* — **het·ero·dox·ness** *n* -ES

het·er·o·doxy \-sē,-si\ *n* [Gk *heterodoxia*, fr. *heterodoxos* + *-ia* -y] **1 :** the quality or state of being heterodox **:** departure from orthodoxy ⟨the unbridled ~ of the gay nineties —M.L. Bach⟩ **2 :** a heterodox opinion or doctrine ⟨revived the long-decaying . . . ~ and established it as the religion of the Persian state —H.A.R.Gibb⟩

het·er·od·ro·mous \ˌhed·əˈrädrəməs\ *adj* [*heter-* + *-dromous*] **:** having the genetic spiral of the branches reversed in its direction from that of the main stem ⟨~ leaf arrangement⟩ ⟨a ~ tendril⟩ — compare HOMODROMOUS — **het·er·od·ro·my** \ˌ≡≡ˈ≡≡mē\ *n* -ES

¹het·ero·dyne \ˈhed·ərə,dīn, ˈhetər-,ˈhe·tr-\ *adj* [*heter-* + *dyne*] **:** of or relating to the production of an electrical beat between two radio frequencies one of which usu. is that of a received signal-carrying current and the other that of an uninterrupted current introduced into the apparatus — compare SUPERHETERODYNE

²heterodyne \"\ *vt* -ED/-ING/-S **:** to combine (a radio frequency) with a different frequency so that a beat is produced ⟨a low value of signal frequency (generally about 100 kc), which is subsequently multiplied and *heterodyned* to produce the desired carrier frequency —*Radio Corp. of Amer. Rev.*⟩

¹het·er·oe·cious *or* **het·er·e·cious** \ˌhed·əˈrēshəs\ *adj* [*heter-* + *-oecious* or *-ecious* (fr. Gk *oikia* house + E *-ous*) — more at VICINITY] **:** passing through the different stages in its life cycle on alternate and often unrelated hosts ⟨~ rusts⟩ ⟨~ insects⟩ — contrasted with *homoecious;* compare AUTOECIOUS — **het·er·oe·cious·ly** *adv* — **het·er·oe·cious·ness** *n* -ES — **het·er·oe·cism** \ˌ≡≡ˈrē,sizəm\ *n* -s — **het·er·oe·cy** \ˈ≡≡,rēsē\ *n* -ES

²heteroecious *var of* HETEROICOUS

het·er·oe·cis·mal \ˌhed·əˈrē,sizməl; ˈhed·ərēˈs-, -rəˈ-\ *adj* [*heteroecism* (fr. ¹*heteroecious* + *-ism*) + *-al*] **:** HETEROECIOUS

het·ero·erotic \ˈhed·ə(ˌ)rō+\ *adj* [*heter-* + *erotic*] **:** ALLOEROTIC

het·ero·erotism \"+\ *n* [*heter-* + *erotism*] **:** ALLOEROTISM

het·ero·fermentative \ˈhed·ə(ˌ)rō+\ *adj* [*heter-* + *fermentative*] **:** producing a fermentation resulting in a number of end products — used esp. of lactic-acid bacteria that ferment carbohydrates and produce volatile acids and carbon dioxide as well as lactic acid

het·ero·fermenter \"+\ *n* [*heter-* + *fermenter*] **:** a heterofermentative organism

het·ero·fertilization \"+\ *n* [*heter-* + *fertilization*] **:** double fertilization in a seed plant (as maize) that results in phenotypically and probably genotypically different endosperm and embryo ⟨~ is considered to result when the polar nuclei and the egg fuse with male nuclei of differing genetic constitution⟩

het·ero·gamete \"+\ *n* [ISV *heter-* + *gamete*] **:** either of a pair of gametes that differ in form, size, or behavior, that are characteristic of most multicellular animals and many plants, and that occur typically as large nonmotile oogametes and small motile sperms — compare ISOGAMETE

het·ero·gametic \"+\ *adj* [*heter-* + *gametic*] **1 :** exhibiting heterogamety **:** DIGAMETIC **2 :** of or relating to a heterogamete or to heterogamety

het·ero·gam·e·tism \ˌ≡≡(ˌ)≡ˈgamə,tizəm\ *n* -s **:** HETEROGAMETY

het·ero·gam·e·ty \-məd·ē\ *n* -ES [*heter-* + *gamete* + *-y*] **:** the production by one sex of a species of two types of gametes of which one is destined to produce a male and the other a female

het·er·og·a·mous \ˌhed·əˈrägəməs\ *also* **het·ero·gam·ic** \ˈhed·ərōˈgamik\ *adj* [*heter-* + *-gamous* or *-gamic*] **:** exhibiting or characterized by diversity in the reproductive elements or processes: as **a** *of sexual reproduction* **:** characterized by fusion of unlike gametes; *esp* **:** OOGAMOUS 1 — often used of processes in higher organisms in contrast to *anisogamous;* compare ISOGAMOUS **b :** having heterogamous reproduction **c :** exhibiting alternation of generations in which two kinds of sexual generation (as dioecious and parthenogenetic) alternate **d :** bearing flowers of two kinds (as perfect and pistillate) — used esp. of sedges and composites and opposed to *homogamous*

het·er·og·a·my \ˌhed·əˈrägəmē\ *n* -ES [ISV *heter-* + *-gamy*] **1 :** the condition of being heterogamous — opposed to HOMOGAMY **2 :** heterogamous reproduction

het·ero·gangliate \ˈhed·ə(ˌ)rō+\ *adj* [*heter-* + *gangliate*] **:** having the nerve ganglia more or less widely separated and unsymmetrically situated ⟨~ mollusks⟩

het·er·o·gen \ˈhed·ərəjən,-,jen, ˈhe·tr-\ *n* -s [*heter-* + *-gen*] **:** a group of heterozygous hybrid organisms

het·er·o·gene \-,jēn\ *adj* [Gk *heterogenēs*] *archaic* **:** HETEROGENEOUS

het·er·o·ge·neal \ˌ≡(≡)ˈjēnēəl, -nyəl\ *adj* [ML *heterogeneus* + E *-al*] *archaic* **:** HETEROGENEOUS

het·er·o·ge·ne·i·ty \ˌhed·ərəjəˈnēəd·ē, ˌhetər-, ˌhe·tr-, -rōj-, |ətē, -i *sometimes* -nā| *or* ÷ -nī|\ *n* -ES [ML *heterogeneitas*, fr. *heterogeneus* heterogeneous + L *-itas* -ity] **:** the quality or state of being heterogeneous ⟨speaking by radio may vastly increase the number and ~ of your hearers —H.D.Scott⟩ ⟨the cultural ~ of the area —Mary Tew⟩ ⟨order which prevents variation from becoming a disordered ~ —John Dewey⟩

het·er·o·ge·neous \ˌ≡(≡)ˈjēnēəs, -nyəs, *Brit sometimes* -ˈjen-\ *adj* [ML *heterogeneus*, fr. Gk *heterogenēs*, fr. *hetero-* heter- + *-genēs* born — more at -GEN] **1 :** differing in kind ⟨a ~ population —L.W.Doob⟩ ⟨genetically ~⟩ **2 :** consisting of dissimilar ingredients or constituents ⟨~ substances⟩ ⟨a town may be culturally or economically ~ —*Notes & Queries on Anthropology*⟩ **:** having different values, opinions, or backgrounds ⟨the family is ~ enough to make quite a good party in itself —Rose Macaulay⟩ **3 a :** made up of parts or elements that are not unified, compatible, or proportionate ⟨no ~ hotchpotch but a book with an underlying unity —Roger Pippett⟩ **b :** incapable of comparison in respect to magnitude **:** being incommensurable ⟨volume and area are ~ quantities⟩ **4 :** having different genders in the singular and plural number ⟨Latin *locus* "place", which is masculine but has a neuter plural *loca*, is a ~ noun⟩ **5 :** possessed of unlike quality or meanings **:** DISPARATE ⟨not all the artists who painted . . . him from life were competent, and their results are ~ —J.C.Fitzpatrick⟩ **6 :** not uniform in structure or composition ⟨the ~ earth⟩ ⟨a ~ weld⟩ ⟨tumors which have a ~ composition by reason of structure and presence of necrosis —*Yr.Bk. of Endocrinology*⟩ ⟨the beam of x ray is not . . . monochromatic but ~, containing wavelengths over a large range —*Medical Physics*⟩ **7 :** relating to or occurring in or being a system that is not uniform throughout but consists of phases separated by boundaries (as solid-solid phases, solid-liquid phases, or solid-liquid-vapor phases) ⟨~ reaction⟩ — **het·er·o·ge·neous·ly** *adv* — **het·er·o·ge·neous·ness** *n* -ES

heterogeneous ray *n* **:** a vascular ray consisting of both upright and procumbent cells — compare HOMOGENEOUS RAY

het·ero·gen·er·a·tae \ˌhed·ə(ˌ)rō,jenəˈrād·(ˌ)ē, -ˈrād·(ˌ)ē\ *n pl, cap* [NL, fr. *heter-* + L *generatae* (fem. pl. of *generatus*, past part. of *generare* to generate) — more at GENERATE] **:** a class of brown algae including those having two alternating generations unlike in vegetative structure, the larger sporophyte being often macroscopic and the smaller gametophyte usu. microscopic — compare ISOGENERATAE

het·ero·genesis \ˈhed·ərō+\ *n* [NL, fr. *heter-* + L *genesis*] **1 :** ABIOGENESIS **2 :** ALTERNATION OF GENERATIONS: as **a :** alternation of a dioecious and one or more parthenogenetic generations **b :** alternation of a haploid with a diploid generation

het·ero·genetic \ˌ≡≡(ˌ)≡+\ *adj* [*heter-* + *genetic*] **1 :** relating to or characterized by heterogenesis **2 :** HETEROPHILE

heterogenetic association *n* **:** the pairing in synapsis of genomes from diverse ancestors in a polyploid organism

heterogenetic induction *n, bot* **:** the union of two or more stimuli **:** complex stimulation

het·er·o·gen·ic \ˌhed·ərəˈjenik\ *adj* **1** [*heterogeny* + *-ic*] **:** HETEROGENETIC **2** [*heter-* + *gene* + *-ic*] **:** containing more than one allele of a gene — used of a cell or of population

het·er·og·e·nist \ˌhed·əˈräjənəst\ *n* -s [*heterogeny* + *-ist*] **:** ABIOGENIST

het·er·og·e·nous \ˌ≡≡ˈräjənəs\ *adj* **1** [*heter-* + *-genous*] **:** of other origin **:** not originating within the body — opposed to *autogenous* **2** [ML *heterogenus* diverse, fr. Gk *heterogenēs* — more at HETEROGENEOUS] **:** HETEROGENEOUS 2

heterogenous graft *n* **:** HETEROGRAFT

het·er·og·e·ny \-ˈräjənē\ *n* -ES [*heterogenous* + *-y*] **1 :** a heterogeneous collection or group ⟨the descendants of the ~ of Arab tribes that settled in Samaria —A.N.Williams b.1914⟩ **2** [*heter-* + *-geny*] **:** HETEROGENESIS **3 :** the application of different genders to neuter things

¹het·er·og·nath \ˈhed·ərag,nath\ *adj* [NL *Heterognathi*] **:** of or relating to the Heterognathi

²heterognath \"\ *n* -s **:** ²CHARACIN

het·er·og·na·thi \ˌhed·əˈrägnə,thī\ *n pl, cap* [NL, fr. *heter-* + *-gnathi* (pl. of *-gnathus* -gnathous)] *in some classifications* **:** an order of teleost fishes that resemble members of the family Cyprinidae but have an adipose fin and teeth in the jaws and that comprise Characidae and related families now usu. included in a division of the suborder Cyprinoidea — compare OSTARIOPHYSI

het·er·o·gone \ˈhed·ərə,gōn\ *n* -s [back-formation fr. *heterogony*] **:** a heterogonous plant

het·er·o·gon·ic \ˈhed·ərəˈgänik\ *or* **het·er·og·o·nous** \ˈhed·əˈrägənəs\ *adj* [*heterogony* + *-ic* or *-ous*] **1 :** of, relating to, or characterized by heterogony; *esp* **:** ALLOMETRIC **2 :** being that course of development in which a generation of parasites is succeeded by a free-living generation — used of certain nematode worms; distinguished from *homogonic*

het·er·og·o·nism \ˌhed·əˈrägə,nizəm\ *n* -s [*heterogonous* + *-ism*] **:** HETEROGONY

het·er·og·o·nous·ly *adv* **:** in a heterogonous manner

het·er·og·o·ny \-nē\ *n* -ES [ISV *heter-* + *-gony*] **1 :** the state of having two or more kinds of perfect flowers varying in relative length of androecium and gynoecium — opposed to *homogony;* distinguished from *heteromorphism* **2 a :** ALTERNATION OF GENERATIONS; *esp* **:** alternation of a dioecious and hermaphroditic generation **b :** heterogamous reproduction **c :** ALLOMETRY

het·ero·graft \ˈhed·ərō+,-\ *n* [ISV *heter-* + *graft*] **:** a graft of tissue taken from a donor of one species to be grafted into a recipient of another species ⟨the use of ~s has proved impracticable in cosmetic surgery⟩ — compare AUTOGRAFT, HOMOGRAFT

het·ero·graph·ic \ˌhed·ərəˈgrafik\ *adj* **:** of, relating to, or characterized by heterography — opposed to *homographic*

het·er·og·ra·phy \ˌhed·əˈrägrəfē\ *n* -ES [*heter-* + *-graphy*] **1 :** spelling differing from standard current usage **2 :** spelling in which the same letters represent different sounds in different words or syllables (as in current English orthography)

het·er·og·y·nous \ˌhed·əˈräjənəs\ *or* **het·er·og·y·nal** \-nᵊl\ *adj* [*heterogynous* fr. *heter-* + *-gynous; heterogynal* fr. *heterogynous* + *-al*] **:** having females of more than one kind ⟨bees and ants are ~⟩

het·er·oi·cous \-ˈrȯikəs\ *also* **het·er·oe·cious** \-ˈrēshəs\ *adj* [*heter-* + *-oicous*, *-oecious* (fr. Gk *oikos* dwelling + E *-ous*) — more at VICINITY] **:** having archegonia and antheridia either on the same branch or on different branches of the same plant — compare PAROICOUS, POLYOICOUS

het·ero·karyon *also* **het·ero·caryon** \ˈhed·ərō+\ *n* -s [NL, fr. *heter-* + *karyon* or *caryon*] **:** a cell in the mycelium of a fungus that contains two or more genetically unlike nuclei — compare DIKARYON, HOMOKARYON

het·ero·kary·o·sis *or* **het·ero·cary·o·sis** \ˌ≡≡≡,karēˈōsəs\ *n* -ES [NL, fr. *heter-* + *kary-* or *cary-* + *-osis*] **:** the condition of having cells that are heterokaryons

het·ero·kary·ot·ic *or* **het·ero·cary·ot·ic** \ˈhed·ə(ˌ)rōˌkarēˈäd·ik\ *adj* [*heter-* + *kary-* or *cary-* + *-otic*] **:** of, relating to, or consisting of heterokaryons ⟨a ~ division⟩ ⟨~ mycelia⟩

het·ero·kinesis \ˈhed·ə(ˌ)rō+\ *n* [NL, fr. *heter-* + *-kinesis*] **:** qualitative nuclear division — used of the meiotic reduction division in the heterogametic sex — **het·ero·kinetic** \"+\ *adj*

het·ero·kon·tae \ˌhed·ərōˈkän,tē\ *n pl, cap* [NL, fr. *heter-* + *-kontae* (fr. Gk *kontos* punting pole, fr. *kentein* to prick, goad); fr. the unequal length of the flagella — more at CENTER] *in some classifications* **:** a class of algae equivalent to Xanthophyceae that includes all the yellow-green algae having flagella of unequal length — compare ISOKONTAE

het·ero·lecithal \"+\ *adj* [*heter-* + Gk *lekithos* yolk of an egg + E *-al*] **:** having the yolk unequally distributed — opposed to *homolecithal*

het·er·ol·o·cha \ˌhed·əˈräləkə\ *n, cap* [NL, alter. of *Heteralocha*, fr. *heter-* + *-alocha* (fr. Gk *alochos* spouse, bedfellow, concubine)] *in some classifications* **:** a genus coextensive with *Neomorpha*

het·er·o·log·i·cal \ˈhed·ərəˈläjəkəl\ *also* **het·er·o·log·ic** \-jik\ *adj* [*heterology* + *-ical* or *-ic*] **:** of or relating to or characterized by heterology **:** HETEROLOGOUS — **het·er·o·log·i·cal·ly** \-jək(ə)lē\ *adv*

het·er·ol·o·gous \ˌhed·əˈräləgəs\ *adj* [*heter-* + Gk *logos* proportion, word + E *-ous* — more at LEGEND] **1 :** characterized by heterology **:** consisting of different elements or of like elements in different proportions **:** DIFFERENT **2 :** derived from a different species ⟨~ serum⟩ — compare AUTOLOGOUS, HOMOLOGOUS — **het·er·ol·o·gous·ly** *adv*

heterologous graft *n* **:** HETEROGRAFT

heterologous series *n* **:** a series (as ethane, ethyl alcohol, acetaldehyde, acetic acid) of related derivatives not homologous

heterologous stimulus *n* **:** a stimulus capable of affecting any available sensory end organ and thought to be further capable of being interpreted centrally as a stimulus of the kind to which the end organ is adapted to respond ⟨a blow on the eye acts as a *heterologous stimulus* seen as a flash of light⟩ — compare HOMOLOGOUS STIMULUS

het·er·ol·o·gy \ˌ≡≡ˈräləjē\ *n* -ES [ISV *heter-* + *-logy*] **:** the lack of correspondence of apparently similar bodily parts due to differences in fundamental makeup or origin — compare ANALOGY, HOMOLOGY

het·ero·lysin \ˈhed·ərō+\ *n* [ISV *heter-* + *lysin*] **:** a hemolysin from an animal of a different species

het·er·ol·y·sis \ˌhed·əˈräləsəs\ *n* [NL, fr. *heter-* + *-lysis*] **1 :** destruction by an outside agent; *specif* **:** solution (as of a cell) by lysins or enzymes from another source **2 :** decomposition of a compound into two oppositely charged particles or ions (as X:Y→X⁺ + :Y⁻) — compare HOMOLYSIS — **het·er·o·lyt·ic** \ˈhed·ərōˈlid·ik\ *adj*

het·ero·mal·lous \ˈhed·ərōˈmaləs\ *adj* [Gk *heteromallos* woolly, fr. *hetero-* heter- + *mallos* lock of wool] **:** spreading or turning in different directions — used of leaves of various mosses; opposed to *homomallous*

het·er·o·mas·ti·gote \ˌ≡≡≡ˈmastə,gōt\ *or* **het·er·o·mas·ti·gate** \-ˌgāt\ *adj* [*heteromastigote*, alter. of *heteromastigate*, fr. *heter-* + *mastig-* + *-ate*] **:** having two unlike flagella ⟨~ dinoflagellates⟩

het·er·o·me·les \ˌ≡≡≡ˈmē(ˌ)lēz\ *n, cap* [NL, fr. *heter-* + *-meles* (fr. Gk *mēlon* apple)] *in some classifications* **:** a genus of plants including only the toyon — compare PHOTINIA

het·er·om·er·ous \ˌhed·əˈrämərəs\ *adj* [*heter-* + Gk *meros* part + E *-ous* — more at MERIT] **1 :** unrelated in chemical composition — used of homeomorphous substances **2** *of a flower* **:** having one or more whorls the number of whose members differs from that of the remaining whorls — opposed to *isomerous* **3 :** having a thallus with one or more layers of algal cells ⟨~ lichens⟩ — opposed to *homoeomerous*

het·ero·mesotroph \ˈhed·ərō+\ *n* -s [*heter-* + *mesotroph*] **:** a heteromesotrophic organism

het·ero·mesotrophic \"+\ *adj* [*heter-* + *mesotrophic*] **:** requiring a single organic source of nitrogen and carbon for metabolism

het·ero·metabolic \"+\ *or* **het·ero·metabolous** \"+\ *adj* [*heter-* + *metabolic* or *metabolous*] **:** of or relating to or exhibiting heterometabolism

het·ero·metabolism \"+\ *also* **het·ero·metaboly** \"+\ *n* [*heter-* + *metabolism* or *metaboly*] *of insects* **:** development with incomplete or direct metamorphosis in which the young nymph is fundamentally like the adult and no pupal stage precedes maturity — distinguished from *holometabolism;* compare HEMIMETABOLISM

het·ero·metatrophic \"+\ *adj* [*heter-* + *metatrophic*] **:** requiring complex organic sources of carbon and nitrogen for metabolism — compare HOLOZOIC

het·ero·met·ric \ˈhed·ərōˈme·trik\ *adj* [ISV *heter-* + *-metric*] **:** characterized by diversity of meter

het·er·o·mi \ˌhed·əˈrō,mī\ *n pl, cap* [NL, fr. *heter-* + *-omi* (fr. Gk *ōmos* shoulder) — more at HUMERUS] **:** a small order of cellike deep-sea teleost fishes with a spiny dorsal fin

het·er·o·mor·phic \ˈhed·ərōˈmȯrfik\ *or* **het·er·o·mor·phous** \-fəs\ *adj* [ISV *heter-* + *-morphic* or *-morphous*] **1 :** deviating from the usual form or exhibiting diversity of form: as **a :** having different forms at different stages of development ⟨holometabolic insects and certain plants with complex life cycles are ~⟩ **b :** having different forms in different members of a colony ⟨the polyps of many complex compound jellyfishes are highly ~ being chiefly specialized for feeding, defense, motility, or reproduction⟩ **c :** of irregular or unusual structure **:** of variable shape ⟨the leaves of emergent plants are commonly ~⟩ **d :** unlike in form or size — used specif. of synaptic chromosomes ⟨the X and Y chromosomes constitute a ~ pair⟩ ⟨~ bivalents⟩ **2 :** exhibiting or undergoing heteromorphosis

het·er·o·mor·phism \ˌ⸗⸗⸗ˈmȯrˌfizəm\ *n* -s [ISV *heter-* + *-morphism*] **1 :** the quality or state of being heteromorphic **2 :** dissimilarity in crystal form shown by compounds of similar composition — contrasted with *homeomorphism* and *isomorphism* **3 :** HETEROGONY 1 **4 :** POLYMORPHISM

het·er·o·mor·phite \-ˌfīt\ *n* -s [ISV *heter-* + *morph-* + *-ite*] **:** a mineral $Pb_7Sb_8S_{19}$ consisting of a lead antimony sulfide related closely to füllöppite, plagionite, and semseyite

het·er·o·mor·pho·sis \ˌ⸗⸗⸗ˈmȯrfəsəs\ *n* [NL, fr. *heter-* + *-morphosis*] **1 :** the production in an organism of an abnormal or misplaced part esp. in place of one that has been lost (as the regeneration of a tail in place of a head) — compare HOMOMORPHOSIS **2 a :** the production of a malformed or malplaced tissue or organ **b :** the formation of tissue of a different type from that from which it derives

het·er·o·mor·phy \ˈ⸗⸗⸗ˌmȯrfē\ *n* -ES [ISV *heter-* + *-morphy*] **:** HETEROMORPHISM

het·ero·mya \ˌhed·ərōˈmīə\ [NL, fr. *heter-* + *-mya*] *syn of* HETEROMYARIA

het·ero·my·ar·ia \-ōmīˈa(a)rēə\ *n pl, cap* [NL, fr. *heter-* + *-myaria*] *in some classifications* **:** a division of Lamellibranchia comprising bivalve mollusks having two adductor muscles the anterior one of which is very small — compare ISOMYARIA, MONOMYARIA — **het·er·o·my·ar·i·an** \ˌ⸗⸗⸗ˈ⸗rēən\ *adj*

¹het·er·o·my·id \ˌhed·ərōˈmīəd\ *adj* [NL *Heteromyidae*] **:** of or relating to the Heteromyidae

²heteromyid \ˈ"\ *n* -s **:** one of the Heteromyidae

het·er·o·my·i·dae \ˌ⸗⸗⸗ˈmīəˌdē\ *n pl, cap* [NL, fr. *Heteromys*, type genus + *-idae*] **:** a family of New World rodents having fur-lined external cheek pouches, large eyes, well developed ears, elongated hind limbs and tail adapted to leaping and balancing, and the ability to live on dry food and depending on metabolic water to survive under extreme desert conditions — see POCKET MOUSE

het·ero·mys \ˈ⸗⸗⸗ˌmis\ *n, cap* [NL, fr. *heter-* + *-mys*] **:** the type genus of the family Heteromyidae

het·ero·nemertea \ˌhed·ərō+\ *n pl, cap* [NL, fr. *heter-* + *Nemertea*] **:** an order of Nemertea (class Anopla) comprising long slender forms with cerebral organs and often with caudal cirri — **het·ero·nemertean** \ˈ"+\ *adj or n*

het·ero·nemertini \ˈ"+\ [NL, fr. *heter-* + *Nemertini*] *syn of* HETERONEMERTEA

¹het·er·o·ne·re·id \ˌhed·ərōˈnirēəd\ *adj* [NL *heteronereid-, heteronereis*] **:** of, relating to, or having the characters of a heteronereis

²heteronereid \ˈ"\ *n* -s **:** HETERONEREIS

het·ero·nereis \ˌhed·ərō+\ *n* [NL, fr. *heter-* + *Nereis*] **:** a free-swimming dimorphic sexual individual of certain polychaete worms (family Nereidae) characterized by greatly enlarged eyes, enlarged and modified parapodia and other appendages, and more or less complete obliteration of the internal viscera by masses of developing germ cells

het·er·o·neu·ra \ˌ⸗⸗⸗ˈn(y)u̇rə\ *n pl, cap* [NL, fr. *heter-* + *-neura*] *in some classifications* **:** a suborder of Lepidoptera including those forms in which the venation of the fore wings differs from that of the hind wings — compare HOMONEURA

het·er·on·o·mous \ˌhed·əˈränəməs\ *adj* [G *heteronom* (fr. *heter-* + *-onom*, as in *autonom* autonomous, fr. Gk *autonomos*) + E *-ous* — more at AUTONOMOUS] **1 :** subject to or involving different laws of growth ⟨in most segmented animals . . . the segmentation is ~ —Libbie H. Hyman⟩ **2 :** subject to external controls and impositions **:** originating outside the self or one's own will ⟨nor is the Christian view ~, in the sense that the will is enslaved by the dictates of a despot alien to the self's will —W.W.Beach⟩ — **het·er·on·o·mous·ly** *adv*

het·er·on·o·my \ˌ⸗ˈ⸗⸗mē\ *n* -ES [G *heteronomie*, fr. *heter-* + *-onomie* (as in *autonomie* autonomy, fr. Gk *autonomia*) — more at AUTONOMY] **1 :** a subjection to something else: as **a :** a subordination to the law or domination of another (as in political subjection) **b :** the condition of lacking moral freedom or self-determination ⟨in ~ the will . . . is obeying laws not of its own making —D.D.Runes⟩ — opposed to *autonomy* **2 :** the quality or state of being heteronomous

het·ero·nuclear \ˌhed·ərō+\ *adj* [*heter-* + *nuclear*] **1 :** HETEROCYCLIC **2 :** of or relating to different rings in a chemical compound ⟨~ substitution in naphthalene⟩ **3 :** of or relating to a molecule composed of different nuclei ⟨hydrogen chloride HCl and deuterium hydride HD consist of ~ diatomic molecules⟩

het·er·on·y·mous \ˌhed·əˈränəməs\ *adj* [LGk *heterōnymos*, fr. Gk *hetero-* heter- + *onyma*, *onoma* name — more at NAME] **:** having different designations ⟨parent and child are ~ relatives⟩ — opposed to *homonymous* — **het·er·on·y·mous·ly** *adv*

het·ero·ou·sia \ˌhed·ərōˈüzēə, -üsēə, -üzh(ē)ə, -üsh(ē)ə\ *also* **het·er·ou·sia** \ˌhed·əˈrü-\ *n* [LGk, fr. Gk *hetero-*, heter- heter- + *ousia*] **:** difference in essence or substance

¹het·ero·ou·sian *also* **het·er·ou·sian** \-ən\ *adj* [LGk *heteroousios*, *heterousios* (fr. Gk *hetero-*, *heter-* heter- + *ousia*) + E *-an*] **1 :** having different essential qualities **:** being of a different nature **2** *often cap* **:** of or relating to the heteroousians

²heteroousian \ˈ"\ *also* **heterousian** \ˈ"\ *n* -s *often cap* **:** an Arian holding that the Son was of a different substance from the Father — compare HOMOIOUSIAN, HOMOOUSIAN

het·er·o·path·ic \ˌhed·ərōˈpathik\ *adj* [*heter-* + Gk *pathos* experience, suffering, emotion + E *-ic* — more at PATHOS] **1 :** different in operation or effect ⟨~ laws —J.S.Mill⟩ **2 :** identifying self with another

het·er·o·pel·mous \-ˈpelməs\ *adj* [*heter-* + *-pelmous*] **:** having each of the two flexor tendons of the toes bifid with the branches of one going to the first and second toes and those of the other to the third and fourth toes

het·er·o·pet·al·ous \-ˈped·ᵊləs\ *adj* [*heter-* + *-petalous*] **:** having dissimilar petals

het·er·oph·a·gous \ˌhed·əˈräfəgəs\ *adj* [*heter-* + *-phagous*] **1 :** ALTRICIAL **2 :** feeding or living on two or more hosts at different stages of the life history ⟨digenetic trematodes are ~⟩

het·er·o·phe·my \ˈhed·əräˌfēmē\ *n* -ES [*heter-* + Gk *phēmē* voice, speech (fr. *phanai* to say) + E *-y* — more at BAN] **:** unconscious use of words other than those intended

het·er·o·phil antibody \ˈ⸗⸗rəˌfil-\ *n* **:** an antibody characteristic of human blood during an attack of infectious mononucleosis that agglutinates sheep red blood cells

¹het·er·o·phile \ˈ⸗⸗⸗ˌfīl\ *also* **het·er·o·phil** \-ˌfil\ *or* **het·er·o·phil·ic** \ˌ⸗⸗⸗ˈfilik\ *adj* [*heter-* + *-phile* or *-phil* or *-philic*] **:** reacting serologically with an antigen of another species

²heterophile \ˈ"\ *or* **heterophil** \ˈ"\ *n* -s [*heter-* + *-phile* or *-phil*] **:** NEUTROPHIL — used esp. in veterinary medicine

het·er·oph·o·ny \ˌhed·əˈräfənē\ *n* -ES [Gk *heterophōnia* diversity of note, fr. *heter-* + *-phōnia* -phony] **:** a singing or sounding of the same melody by two or more voices or instruments usu. with some modifications (as in rhythm or ornamentation) by one or both of the performers

het·er·o·pho·ria \ˌhed·ərōˈfōrēə\ *n* -s [NL, fr. *heter-* + *-phoria*] **:** latent strabismus in which one eye tends to deviate either medially or laterally — compare EXOPHORIA — **het·ero·phor·ic** \ˌ⸗⸗⸗ˈfȯrik\ *adj*

het·ero·phy·es \-ˈfī(ˌ)ēz\ *n, cap* [NL, fr. LGk *heterophyēs* of different nature, fr. Gk *heter-* + *phyē* growth, nature; akin to Gk *phyein* to bring forth — more at BE] **:** a genus (the type of the family Heterophyidae) of small digenetic trematode worms infesting the small intestine of dogs, cats, and man in Egypt and much of tropical Asia

¹het·er·o·phy·id \ˌ⸗⸗⸗ˈfīəd\ *adj* [NL *Heterophyidae*, family of trematode worms, fr. *Heterophyes*, type genus + *-idae*] **:** of or relating to the genus *Heterophyes* or family Heterophyidae

²heterophyid \ˈ"\ *n* -s **:** a heterophyid worm

het·ero·phylesis \ˌhed·ə(ˌ)rō+\ *n* [NL, fr. *heter-* + *phylesis*] **:** the quality or state of being heterophyletic

het·ero·phyletic \ˈ"+\ *adj* [*heter-* + *phyletic*] **:** of or relating to or possessing two or more lines of descent

het·er·o·phyl·lous \ˌhed·ərōˈfiləs\ *adj* [*heter-* + *-phyllous*] **1 :** having the foliage leaves of more than one form on the same plant or stem ⟨many eucalypts, pondweeds, and crowfoots are ~⟩ — opposed to *isophyllous* **2 :** having two or more forms of foliation of the septal margins ⟨~ ammonites⟩ — **het·er·o·phyl·ly** \ˈ⸗⸗⸗ˌfilē\ *n* -ES

het·er·o·phyte \ˈhed·ərəˌfīt\ *n* -s [*heter-* + *-phyte*] **:** a plant that is dependent for food materials upon other living or dead plant or animal organisms or their products **:** PARASITE, SAPROPHYTE — compare AUTOPHYTE — **het·er·o·phyt·ic** \ˌ⸗⸗⸗ˈfid·ik\ *adj*

het·er·o·pi·idae \ˌhed·ərōˈpīəˌdē\ *n pl, cap* [NL, fr. *Heteropia*, type genus (fr. *heter-* + *-opia*) + *-idae*] **:** a family of sponges (order Heterocoela) with a distinct dermal cortex pierced by inhalant pores and with subdermal triradiate spicules

het·er·o·pla·sia \-ˈplāzh(ē)ə\ *n* -s [NL, fr. *heter-* + *-plasia*] **1 :** a development of a tissue from tissue of a different kind **2 :** a formation of abnormal tissue or of normal tissue in an abnormal locality

het·er·o·plasm \ˈhed·ərōˌplazəm\ *n* [ISV *heter-* + *-plasm*] **:** tissue formed or growing where it does not normally occur

het·er·o·plas·tic \ˌ⸗⸗⸗ˈplastik\ *adj* [ISV *heter-* + *-plastic*] **1 :** of or relating to heteroplasm or heteroplasty or heteroplasia **2 :** HETEROLOGOUS — **het·er·o·plas·ti·cal·ly** \-tək(ə)lē\ *adv*

het·er·o·plas·ty \ˈ⸗⸗⸗ˌplastē\ *n* -ES [ISV *heter-* + *-plasty*] **1 :** HETEROPLASIA **2 :** a grafting of tissue from an individual of one species into an individual of a different species

¹het·er·o·ploid \-ˌplȯid\ *adj* [ISV *heter-* + *-ploid*] **:** having a chromosome number that is greater or smaller usu. by one than the somatic number characteristic of the species but not a simple multiple of the haploid chromosome number — compare POLYPLOID

²heteroploid \ˈ"\ *n* -s **:** a heteroploid individual

het·er·o·ploi·dy \-dē\ *n* -ES **:** the condition of being heteroploid

het·er·o·pod \-ˌpäd\ *n* -s [NL *Heteropoda*] **:** one of the Heteropoda

het·er·op·o·da \ˌhed·əˈräpədə\ *n pl, cap* [NL, fr. *heter-* + *-poda*] **:** a small division of Pectinibranchia (suborder Taenioglossa) formerly ranked as a separate order and comprising pelagic gastropod mollusks that swim at the surface with the ventral side up with a foot or a part of it forming a median fin and that have a transparent body and a transparent shell or none — **het·er·op·o·dous** \ˌ⸗⸗ˈ⸗⸗dəs\ *adj*

het·er·op·o·dal \ˌ⸗ˈ⸗⸗dᵊl\ *adj* [*heter-* + *pod-* + *-al*] **:** of or relating to nerve cells having different kinds of branches

het·ero·polar \ˌhed·ərō+\ *adj* [ISV *heter-* + *polar*] **1 :** of, relating to, or having unlike poles ⟨~ systems⟩ **2 :** POLAR 5b, IONIC — used esp. of chemical bonds or of crystals; distinguished from *homopolar* — **het·ero·polarity** \ˈ"+\ *n*

het·er·o·poly \ˌhed·ərōˈpälē\ *adj* [ISV *heteropoly-*] **:** containing several groups or ions of different acid-forming elements

heteropoly- *comb form* [ISV *heter-* + *poly-*] **:** containing several groups or ions of different acid-forming elements — in names of complex inorganic acids and their salts ⟨*heteropoly*molybdates such as phosphomolybdates⟩; compare ISOPOLY-

heteropoly acid *n* **:** any of a large group of complex oxygen-containing acids derived from two or more different inorganic acids by elimination of water from two or more molecules of the acids; *esp* **:** an acid regarded as formed by combination of several molecules of an acid anhydride (as molybdenum trioxide or tungsten trioxide) with a second acid that furnishes the central atom (as phosphorus or silicon) of the complex — distinguished from *isopoly acid*

het·ero·polymer \ˌhed·ərō+\ *n* [G, fr. *hetero-* heter- + *polymer*] **:** COPOLYMER

het·er·op·tera \ˌhed·əˈräptərə\ *n pl, cap* [NL, fr. *heter-* + *-ptera*] **:** a suborder of Hemiptera or sometimes a separate order comprising the true bugs — compare HOMOPTERA — **het·er·op·ter·ous** \ˌ⸗⸗ˈ⸗⸗rəs\ *adj*

het·ero·pycnosis \ˌhed·ərō+\ *n* [NL, fr. *heter-* + *pycnosis*] **:** a differential degree of condensation that distinguishes various chromosomes (as sex) or parts of chromosomes in a nucleus — **het·ero·pycnotic** \ˈ"+\ *adj*

het·er·o·scope \ˈhed·ərəˌskōp\ *n* [*heter-* + *-scope*] **:** an apparatus for measuring the range of vision in strabismus — **het·er·os·co·py** \ˌhed·əˈräskəpē\ *n* -ES

¹het·ero·sexual \ˌhed·ərō+\ *adj* [ISV *heter-* + *sexual*] **1 :** of or relating to or characterized by heterosexuality ⟨sexual relationships between individuals of opposite sexes are ~ —A.C.Kinsey⟩ — opposed to *homosexual* **2 :** of or relating to different sexes ⟨~ twins⟩ ⟨a ~ flock of chickens —*Anatomical Record*⟩ ⟨the pairing off . . . is seldom ~ —A.J.Liebling⟩

²heterosexual \ˈ"\ *n* -s **:** a heterosexual individual

het·ero·sexuality \ˈ"+\ *n* [ISV *heter-* + *sexuality*] **:** the manifestation of sexual desire toward a member of the opposite sex ⟨the achievement of a healthy ~ —F.E.Williams⟩

het·er·o·side \ˈhed·ərōˌsīd, ˈ⸗⸗(ˌ)⸗ˌsīd\ *n* -s [ISV *heter-* + *-oside*] **:** a glycoside that on hydrolysis yields a noncarbohydrate as well as a glycose — compare HOLOSIDE

het·er·o·si·pho·na·les \ˌhed·ərōˌsīfəˈnā(ˌ)lēz\ *n pl, cap* [NL, fr. *heter-* + *siphon-* + *-ales*] **:** an order of yellow-green algae comprising the siphonaceous members of the class Xanthophyceae and including the single genus *Botrydium*

het·er·o·sis \ˌhed·əˈrōsəs\ *n, pl* **hetero·ses** \-ōˌsēz\ [NL, fr. Gk *heterōsis* alteration, alter. of *heteroiōsis*, fr. *heteroioun* to alter (fr. *heteroios* different in kind, fr. *heteros* other) + *-ōsis* -osis — more at HETER-] **:** a greater vigor or capacity for growth frequently displayed by crossbred animals or plants as compared with those resulting from inbreeding

het·er·o·site \ˈhed·ərəˌsīt\ *n* -s [F *hétérosite*, fr. Gk *heteros* other, different + F *-ite*] **:** a mineral isomorphous with purpurite and consisting of phosphate of iron and manganese

het·er·o·so·ma·ta \ˌhed·ərōˈsōməd·ə\ *n pl, cap* [NL, fr. *heter-* + *-somata*] **:** an order or other group of teleost fishes consisting of the flatfishes — **het·er·o·so·mate** \ˌ⸗⸗⸗ˈsōˌmāt\ *adj* — **het·er·o·so·ma·tous** \-məd·əs\ *adj*

het·er·o·so·ma·ti \ˌ⸗⸗⸗ˈsōməd·ˌī\ *or* **het·er·o·so·mi** \-ˈsōˌmī\ [NL, fr. *heter-* + *-somati* (fr. Gk *somata*) or *-somi* (pl. of *-somus*)] *syn of* HETEROSOMATA

het·er·o·some \ˈhed·ərəˌsōm\ *n* -s [*heter-* + *-some*] **:** HETEROCHROMOSOME

het·er·o·spo·re·ae \ˌhed·ərōˈspōrēˌē\ *n pl, cap* [NL, fr. *heter-* + *-sporeae* (fr. Gk *spora* seed) — more at SPORE] *in some classifications* **:** a primary subdivision of Pteridophyta including the Lycopodiaceae and Equisetaceae and producing two kinds of asexual spores

het·er·o·spo·ri·um \-rēəm\ *n, cap* [NL, fr. *heter-* + *-sporium*] **:** a form genus of imperfect fungi (family Dematiaceae) with echinulate and 2-septate to several-septate brown conidia

het·er·o·spor·ous \ˌ⸗⸗⸗ˈspōrəs, ˌhed·əˈräspərəs\ *also* **het·er·o·spor·ic** \ˌ⸗⸗rōˈspōrik\ *adj* [*heter-* + *-sporous* or *-sporic*] **:** characterized by heterospory **:** reproducing asexually by heterospory ⟨~ plants⟩; *specif* **:** producing microspores and megaspores ⟨some pteridophytes and all spermatophytes are ~⟩

het·er·o·spo·ry \ˈ⸗⸗rōˌspōrē, ˌ⸗⸗ˈräspərē\ *n* -ES [*heter-* + *-spory*] **1 :** the production of asexual spores of more than one kind **2 :** the development of microspores and megaspores in some ferns and fern allies and in all seed plants — opposed to *homospory*

het·ero·static \ˌhed·ərō+\ *adj* [ISV *heter-* + *static*] **:** of or relating to a method of electrostatic measurement in which one potential is measured by means of a different potential — **het·ero·statically** *adv*

het·er·os·tra·ca \ˌhed·əˈrästrəkə\ [NL] *syn of* HETEROSTRACI

¹het·er·os·tra·can \ˌ⸗ˈ⸗⸗kən\ *adj* [NL *Heterostraci* + E *-an*] **:** of or relating to the Heterostraci

²heterostracan \ˈ"\ *n* -s **:** an animal or fossil of the order Heterostraci

het·er·os·tra·ci \ˌ⸗⸗ˈstraˌsī\ *n pl, cap* [NL, fr. *heter-* + Gk *ostrakon* shell, potsherd — more at OSTRACON] **:** a class or other division of ostracoderms with widely separated nares and eyes and with an exoskeleton which may consist of a few large plates or numerous placoid scales

het·er·o·stroph·ic \ˌhed·ərōˈsträfik\ *adj* **1** [Gk *heterostrophos* + E *-ic*] **:** consisting of strophes differing in metrical form **2** [NL *heterostrophus* + E *-ic*] **:** relating to or marked by heterostrophy ⟨a shell with ~ whorls⟩

het·er·os·tro·phous \ˌhed·əˈrästrəfəs\ *adj* [NL *heterostrophus*] **:** HETEROSTROPHIC 1

het·er·os·tro·phy \ˌ⸗⸗ˈ⸗⸗fē\ *n* -ES [ISV *heter-* + *-strophy* (fr. Gk *strophē* turn)] **:** the quality or state of being coiled in a direction opposite to the usual one

het·er·o·styled \ˈhed·ərōˌstīld\ *adj* [*heter-* + *-styled*] **:** having styles of two or more distinct forms or of different lengths ⟨~ buckwheat⟩ — compare HOMOSTYLED

het·er·o·sty·lism \ˌ⸗⸗⸗ˈstīˌlizəm\ *also* **het·er·o·sty·ly** \ˈ⸗⸗⸗ˌstīlē\ *n, pl* **heterostylisms** *also* **heterostylies** [*heterostylism* fr. *heter-* + *style* + *-ism*; *heterostyly* fr. *heter-* + *-styly*] **:** HETEROGONY 1

het·er·o·sty·lous \ˌ⸗⸗⸗ˈstīləs\ *adj* [*heter-* + *-stylous*] **:** HETEROSTYLED

het·ero·suggestion \ˌhed·ə(ˌ)rō+\ *n* [ISV *heter-* + *suggestion*] **:** suggestion used by one person to influence another

het·ero·syllabic \ˈ"+\ *adj* [*heter-* + *syllabic*] **:** belonging to another syllable or to different syllables

het·ero·syllis \ˈ"+\ *n, pl* **heterosylles** [NL, fr. *heter-* + *Syllis*] **:** a modified sexual form of an annelid of the family Syllidae comparable to a heteronereis

het·er·o·tac·tic \ˌhed·ərōˈtaktik\ *also* **het·er·o·tac·tous** \-təs\ *adj* [*heter-* + *-tactic* or *-tactous* (fr. Gk *taktos* ordered, fixed)] **:** characterized by or exhibiting heterotaxis

het·er·o·tax·ic \-ˈtaksik\ *adj* [NL *heterotaxia* + E *-ic*] **:** HETEROTACTIC

het·er·o·tax·is \ˌ⸗⸗⸗ˈtaksəs\ *also* **het·er·o·tax·ia** \-ksēə\ *n, pl* **heterotax·es** \-kˌsēz\ *also* **heterotax·i·as** \-ksēəz\ [NL, fr. *heter-* + *-taxis* or *-taxia*] **:** abnormal arrangement (as of organs or parts of the body or of geological strata)

het·er·o·taxy \ˈ⸗⸗⸗ˌtaksē\ *n* -ES [NL *heterotaxia*] **:** HETEROTAXIS

het·ero·telic \ˌhed·ərō+\ *adj* [*heter-* + *telic*] **:** existing for the sake of something else **:** having an extraneous end or purpose — contrasted with *autotelic*

het·er·o·thal·lic \ˌhed·ərōˈthalik\ *adj* [*heter-* + *thall-* + *-ic*] **1 :** having two or more genetically incompatible but morphologically similar haploid phases which function as separate sexes or strains — used esp. of certain algae and fungi or of the unisexual spores producing these strains — compare HOMOTHALLIC, MINUS, PLUS **2 :** DIOECIOUS — **het·er·o·thal·lism** \ˌ⸗⸗⸗ˈthaˌlizəm\ *n* -s — **het·er·o·thal·ly** \ˈ⸗⸗⸗ˌthalē\ *n* -ES

het·ero·therm \ˈ⸗⸗⸗ˌthərm\ *n* [*heter-* + *-therm*] **:** POIKILOTHERM

het·er·o·ther·mic \ˌhed·ərōˈthərmik\ *also* **het·ero·ther·mal** \-məl\ *or* **het·ero·ther·mous** \-məs\ *adj* [*heter-* + *thermic* or *thermal* or *-thermous*] **:** POIKILOTHERMIC

het·er·ot·ic \ˌhed·əˈräd·ik\ *adj* [fr. NL *heterosis*, after such pairs as NL *narcosis*: E *narcotic*] **:** of, relating to, or exhibiting heterosis ⟨~ tetraploids⟩ ⟨a ~ modification⟩

het·er·o·to·pia \ˌhed·ərōˈtōpēə\ *also* **het·er·ot·o·py** \ˌhed·əˈräd·əpē\ *n, pl* **heterotopias** *also* **heterotopies** [NL *heterotopia*, fr. *heter-* + *-topia* -topy] **:** displacement in or difference of position: as **a :** deviation of an organ from the normal position **b :** an abnormal habitat **c :** the grafting of tissue into an abnormal location (as skin into the anterior chamber of the eye) — **het·er·o·top·ic** \ˌ⸗⸗⸗ˈtäpik\ *adj* — **het·er·ot·o·pous** \ˌ⸗⸗ˈräd·əpəs\ *adj*

het·ero·transplant \ˌhed·ərō+\ *n* [*heter-* + *transplant*] **:** HETEROGRAFT — **het·ero·transplantation** \ˈ"+\ *n*

het·er·o·trich \ˈ⸗⸗rōˌtrik\ *n* -s [NL *Heterotricha*] **:** one of the Heterotricha

het·er·ot·ri·cha \ˌhed·əˈrä·trəkə\ *n pl, cap* [NL, fr. *heter-* + *-tricha*] **:** a suborder of Spirotricha comprising ciliate protozoans that have uniform or reduced ciliation but no cirri and containing free-living organisms (as members of the genus *Stentor*) as well as commensals and parasites of vertebrate intestines — see BALANTIDIUM

het·er·o·tri·cha·les \ˌhed·ərōˌtrəˈkā(ˌ)lēz\ *n pl, cap* [NL, fr. *heter-* + *trich-* + *-ales*] **:** an order of yellow-green algae comprising all those with cells arranged in simple or branching filaments and including the single family Tribonemaceae

het·er·o·trich·i·da \-rōˈtrikədə\ [NL, fr. *heter-* + *trich-* + *-ida*] *syn of* HETEROTRICHA

het·er·o·tri·cho·sis \-rōtrəˈkōsəs\ *n* [NL, fr. *heter-* + *trich-* + *-osis*] **:** a condition of having hair of variegated color

het·er·ot·ri·chous \ˌhed·əˈrä·trəkəs\ *adj* [prob. fr. NL *heterotrichus*] **:** having the thallus differentiated into a prostrate portion and an upright or projecting system ⟨many algae are ~⟩ — **het·er·ot·ri·chy** \ˌ⸗⸗ˈrä·trəkē\ *n* -ES

het·er·ot·ro·pal \ˌ⸗⸗ˈrä·trəpəl\ *adj* [Gk *heterotropos* of different sort, various + E *-al*] **:** AMPHITROPOUS

het·er·o·troph \ˈhed·ərōˌträf\ *also* **het·er·o·trophe** \-ˌtrōf\ *n* -s [*heter-* + *-troph* or *-trophe* (prob. fr. Gk *trophos* one that feeds)] **:** a heterotrophic individual — **het·er·ot·ro·phism** \ˌhed·əˈrä·trəˌfizəm\ *n* — **het·er·ot·ro·phy** \-ˌfē\ *n* -ES

heterotroph hypothesis *n* **:** a hypothesis in biology: the most primitive first life was heterotrophic — compare AUTOTROPH HYPOTHESIS

het·ero·tro·phic \ˌhed·ərōˈträfik, -ˈtrōf-\ *adj* [*heter-* + *-trophic*] **:** obtaining nourishment from outside sources; *specif* **:** requiring complex organic compounds of nitrogen and carbon for metabolic synthesis ⟨most animals and those plants that do not carry on photosynthesis are ~⟩ — opposed to *autotrophic* — **het·ero·tro·phi·cal·ly** \-fək(ə)lē\ *adv*

het·er·o·tro·pia \ˌ⸗⸗⸗ˈtrōpēə\ *n* -s [NL, fr. *heter-* + *-tropia*] **:** STRABISMUS

het·er·ot·ro·pous \ˌhed·əˈrä·trəpəs\ *adj* [Gk *heterotropos* of different sort, various, fr. *hetero-* heter- + *-tropos* -tropous] **:** AMPHITROPOUS

het·ero·typic \ˌhed·ərō+\ *also* **het·ero·typical** \ˈ"+\ *adj* [*heter-* + *typic* or *typical*] **1 :** of or being the reduction division of meiosis as contrasted with typical mitotic division — compare HOMEOTYPIC **2** *usu* **heterotypical :** of or being a genus containing groups of species showing various degrees of relationship **3 :** different in kind, arrangement, or form ⟨a ~ ecological community⟩ ⟨monkeys paralyzed with one poliomyelitis virus . . . show no . . . antibody . . . to a ~ virus —Isabel M. Morgan⟩ — **het·ero·typically** \ˈ"+\ *adv*

heterousia *var of* HETEROOUSIA

het·ero·xanthine \ˌhed·ərō+\ *also* **het·ero·xanthin** \ˈ"+\ *n* [ISV *heter-* + *xanthine* or *xanthin*] **:** a crystalline compound $C_6H_6N_4O_2$ sometimes found in urine; 7-methyl-xanthine

het·er·ox·e·nous \ˌhed·əˈräksənəs\ *adj* [*heter-* + *-xenous*] **:** infesting more than one kind of host; *esp* **:** requiring at least two kinds of host to complete the life cycle — used of various parasites (as the malaria parasites or the liver flukes)

het·er·o·ze·te·sis \ˌhed·ərōzēˈtēsəs\ *n, pl* **heterozete·ses** \-ˌtēˌsēz\ [NL, fr. *heter-* + Gk *zētēsis* search, inquiry (fr. *zētein* to seek, inquire)] **:** IGNORATIO ELENCHI

het·ero·zygosis \ˌhed·ərō+\ *n* [NL, fr. *heter-* + *zygosis*] **1 :** a union of genetically dissimilar gametes to form a heterozygote **2 :** HETEROZYGOSITY

het·ero·zy·gos·i·ty \ˈ"+zīˈgäsəd·ē\ *n* -ES **:** the state of being a heterozygote — compare HOMOZYGOSITY

het·ero·zygote \ˈ"+\ *n* [*heter-* + *zygote*] **:** an animal or plant that contains genes for both members of at least one pair of allelomorphic characters and that segregates according to Mendel's laws and does not breed true to type with respect to the specified character **:** a heterozygous individual — compare HOMOZYGOTE — **het·ero·zygotic** \ˈ"+\ *adj*

het·er·o·zy·gous \ˌhed·ərōˈzīgəs\ *adj* [*heter-* + *-zygous*] **1 :** of, relating to, or derived from a heterozygote **2 :** producing two types of gametes with respect to one or more allelomorphic characters — opposed to *homozygous* — **het·er·o·zy·gous·ly** *adv*

heth *also* **cheth** *or* **hheth** *or* **kheth** *or* **het** \ˈkāt, -āth, -ās, -et, -eth, -es\ *n* -s [Heb *ḥēth*] **1 :** the eighth letter of the Hebrew alphabet — symbol ח; see ALPHABET table **2 :** the letter of the Phoenician alphabet or of various other Semitic alphabets that corresponds to Hebrew heth

het·man \ˈhetmən\ *n* -s [Pol, commander in chief, fr. G *hauptmann* headman] **:** a cossack leader

het·man·ate \-əˌnāt\ *n* -s **:** the administration of a hetman

HETP \ˌāˌchēˌtēˈpē\ *abbr or n* -s hexaethyl tetraphosphate

Het·ra·zan \ˈhe·trəˌzan\ *trademark* — used for diethylcarbamazine citrate

hets *pl of* HET

het up *adj* [*⁵het*] *chiefly dial* **:** being in a state of excitement **:** worked up **:** ANGRY — used esp. to connote indignation or enthusiasm ⟨had been terrible *het up* over chickadees —Esther Forbes⟩

HEU *abbr* hydroelectric unit

heu·chera \'hyükərə\ *n* [NL, after J. H. von *Heucher* †1747 Ger. botanist] **1** *cap* **:** a genus of No. American herbs (family Saxifragaceae) having basal cordate or orbicular leaves and small panicled flowers with petals entire or lacking **2** -s **:** any plant of the genus *Heuchera*

heu gaze *or* **heu gaze** \hyü'gäz\ [origin unknown] — used as a view halloo in hunting otters

heugh *or* **heuch** \'kyük\ *n* -s [ME *hough, hogh, heuch,* fr. OE *hōh*] **1** *chiefly Scot* **a :** a steep crag or cliff **b :** a ravine or glen with overhanging sides **2** *chiefly Scot* **a :** a shaft of a coal mine **b :** an open coal pit

heu·land·ite \'hyülən,dīt\ *n* -s [Henry *Heuland* 19th cent. Eng. mineral collector + E *-ite*] **:** a zeolite $(Na,Ca)_{4-6}Al_6(Al,Si)_4Si_{26}O_{72}.24H_2O$ consisting of a hydrous aluminosilicate of sodium and calcium often occurring as foliated masses with pearly luster on the cleavage surfaces

¹heu·ris·tic \'(h)yü¦ristik, -yü¦-, -tēk\ *adj* [G *heuristisch,* fr. NL *heuristicus,* fr. Gk *heuriskein* to discover; akin to OIr *fūar* I have found] **:** providing aid or direction in the solution of a problem but otherwise unjustified or incapable of justification ⟨~ techniques⟩ ⟨a ~ assumption⟩ ⟨even vague and dubious assertions can render good services to empirical research as a ~ stimulus —Edgar Zilsel⟩; *specif* **:** of or relating to exploratory problem-solving techniques that utilize self-educating techniques (as the evaluation of feedback) to improve performance ⟨a ~ computer program⟩ — **heu·ris·ti·cal·ly** \-tək(ə)lē, -tēk-, -li\ *adv*

²heuristic \"\ *n* -s [G *heuristik,* fr. NL *heuristica,* fr. fem. of *heuristicus*] **1 :** the science or art of heuristic procedure **2 :** heuristic argument

heurt *or* **heurte** *var of* HURT

heus·ler alloy \'hyüslə(r)-\ *n, usu cap H* [after Conrad *Heusler* 19th cent. Ger. mining engineer and chemist] **1 :** a magnetic alloy composed of the nonmagnetic metals copper, manganese, and tin approximately in the proportions Cu_2MnSn **2 :** any similar magnetic alloy (as one in which tin is replaced by aluminum, arsenic, antimony, bismuth, or boron, or copper is replaced by silver)

hev *dial var of* HAVE

he·vea \'hēvēə\ *n* [NL, fr. Sp *jebe* rubber plant, of AmerInd origin] **1** *cap* **:** a small genus of So. American trees (family Euphorbiaceae) which have trifoliolate leaves, small panicled apetalous flowers, and a capsular fruit and many of which yield latex used in rubber manufacture **2** -s **:** any plant of the genus *Hevea*

¹hew \'hyü\ *vb* **hewed; hewed** *or* **hewn; hewing; hews** [ME *hewen,* fr. OE *hēawan;* akin to OHG *houwan* to hew, ON *hǫggva* to hew, L *cudere* to beat, Toch (A) *kot* to split] *vt* **1 :** to cut with hard or rough blows of a heavy cutting instrument (as an ax, broadsword, or large chisel) ⟨the miners who ~ out the coal —G.B.Shaw⟩ **2 :** to fell (as a tree) by blows of an ax **:** cut down **3 :** to shape, form, create, or bring into being with or as if with hard rough blows or efforts ⟨my own grandparents ~*ed* their farms from the wilderness —J.T. Shotwell⟩ ⟨~ out a rock tomb⟩ ~ *vi* **1 :** to make rough heavy cutting blows (as with an ax) **2 :** ADHERE, CONFORM, STICK ⟨each of his ... masterpieces ~*s* to its stanza form with meticulous accuracy —Clement Wood⟩ ⟨if he is elected ... he will ~ to the constitutional law —*N.Y.Times*⟩ ⟨avoiding sentimentality by ~*ing* doggedly to domestic realism —Roger Pippett⟩ — often used in the phrase *hew to the line* ⟨I learned in a hard school and I know the importance of ~*ing* to the line —Archie Binns⟩ **syn** see CUT

²hew \"\ *now chiefly dial var of* HUE

hew·er \'hyüə(r), 'hyü(ə)r, 'hyüa\ *n* -s [ME, fr. *hewen,* v. + *-er*] **:** a person whose work is hewing ⟨these skilled island ~*s* and masons work with primitive axes, chisels and saws —J.P. O'Donnell⟩ ⟨let them be ~*s* of wood and drawers of water unto all the congregation —Josh 9:21 (AV)⟩ ⟨deserve a better future than being mere ~*s* of wood and drawers of water for the highly industrialized countries —Emilio Abello⟩

hew·ett·ite \'hyüə,tīt\ *n* -s [D. Foster *Hewett* †1971 Am. geologist + E *-ite*] **:** a mineral $CaV_6O_{16}.9H_2O$ consisting of a hydrous calcium vanadate occurring in mahogany-red silky aggregates (sp. gr. 2.5)

hew·gag \'hyü,gag\ *n* [origin unknown] **:** a toy pipe of esp. the latter part of the 19th century resembling a kazoo ⟨sound the bull-roarers, and the ~ —W.A.White⟩

hew·let \'hyülət\ *var of* HOWLET

hewn \'hyün\ *adj* [fr. past part. of ¹*hew*] **1 :** felled, cut, or shaped by hewing (as with an ax) **:** roughly squared ⟨a house built of ~ logs⟩ **2** *of stone* **:** roughly dressed (as with a hammer)

¹hex \'heks\ *vb* -ED/-ING/-ES *vi* [PaG *hexe,* fr. G *hexen,* fr. *hexe,* n.] **:** to practice witchcraft ~ *vt* [PaG *verhexe,* fr. *verfor-* + *hexe,* v.] **1 :** to practice witchcraft upon **:** put a hex on ⟨he can ... ~ him, and he knows it —J.H.Allen⟩ **2 :** to affect as if by an evil spell **:** JINX, QUEER ⟨giving in to an unscientific fear of ~*ing* the whole project —Daniel Lang⟩ ⟨~*es* the acoustics —*Springfield (Mass.) Daily News*⟩

²hex \"\ *n* -ES *often attrib* **1 :** SPELL, ENCHANTMENT, JINX ⟨my grandmother used to say some families had a ~ on them —Sherman Kent⟩ ⟨sung to death in a musical ~ rendered by an enemy —*Newsweek*⟩ ⟨we finally had to come to the conclusion that he had put a ~ on the cars —Linda Braidwood⟩ **2** [PaG *hex* & G *hexe,* fr. MHG *hecse, häxe;* akin to OHG *hagzissa, hagazussa* harpy, witch — more at HAG (harpy)] **:** a person who practices witchcraft **:** WITCH ⟨I couldn't talk to you without twenty old ~*es* watching —Sinclair Lewis⟩

³hex \"\ *adj* [short for *hexagonal*] **:** hexagonal in shape ⟨a bolt with a ~ head⟩

hex *abbr* **1** hexachord **2** hexagon; hexagonal

hexa- *or* **hex-** *comb form* [Gk, fr. *hex* six — more at SIX] **1 :** six ⟨*hexa*tomic⟩ **2 :** containing six atoms, groups, or equivalents ⟨*hex*oxide⟩ ⟨*hexa*acetate⟩

hex·a·bi·ose *or* **hex·o·bi·ose** \,heksə'bī,ōs\ *n* [*hexabiose* fr. *hexa-* + *biose; hexobiose,* ISV *hexo-* (fr. *hexa-*) + *biose*] **:** a disaccharide (as maltose) yielding two hexose molecules on hydrolysis

hex·a·bromide \¦heksə+\ *n* [*hexa-* + *bromide*] **:** a bromide containing six atoms of bromine in the molecule

hex·a·canth \'heksə,kan(t)th\ *or* **hex·a·can·thous** \¦==¦kan(t)thəs\ *adj* [NL *hexacanthus,* fr. *hexa-* + *-acanthus* (fr. Gk *akantha* thorn) — more at ACANTH-] *zool* **:** having six hooks; *specif* **:** constituting the onchosphere of a tapeworm

hexachlor- *or* **hexachloro-** *comb form* [*hexa-* + *chlor-*] **:** containing six atoms of chlorine — compare CHLOR-

hexa·chloride \¦heksə+\ *n* [*hexa-* + *chloride*] **:** a chloride containing six atoms of chlorine in the molecule

hex·a·chlo·ro \¦heksə¦klō(,)rō, -lȯ(-\ *adj* [*hexachlor-*] **:** containing six atoms of chlorine

hex·a·chlo·ro·cyclohexane \¦==¦==+\ *n* [*hexachlor-* + *cyclohexane*] **:** a hexachloro derivative of cyclohexane; *esp* **:** BENZENE HEXACHLORIDE

hex·a·chlo·ro·ethane \"+\ *also* **hex·a·chlor·ethane** \¦heksə,klōr, -lȯr-+\ *n* [ISV *hexa-* + *chlor-* + *ethane*] **:** a colorless toxic crystalline compound C_2Cl_6 of camphoraceous odor made usu. by chlorinating tetrachloroethylene and used esp. in smoke bombs and in the control of liver flukes in ruminants

hex·a·chlo·ro·phene \,heksə'klōrə,fēn, -lȯr-\ *n* -s [*hexachlor-* + *-phene* (fr. *-phenol*)] **:** a crystalline phenolic antibacterial agent $CH_2(C_6HCl_3OH)_2$ made by condensing a trichlorophenol with formaldehyde and used esp. in soap

hexa·chloroplatinate \¦heksə+\ *n* [*hexa-* + *chloroplatinate*] **:** CHLOROPLATINATE

hex·a·chord \'heksə,kȯrd, -ō(ə)d\ *n* [*hexa-* + *-chord*] **1 :** a diatonic series of six tones having a semitone between the third and fourth tones that formed the basic unit of analysis from the 11th to the 18th centuries, seven such overlapping series beginning successively on G, C, and F comprising all of the recognized tones — compare GREAT SCALE, SOLMIZATION **2 :** a 6-stringed musical instrument — **hex·a·chord·ic** \¦==¦kȯrdik\ *adj*

hex·a·con·tane \,heksə'kän,tān\ *n* -s [ISV *hexacont-* (fr. Gk *hexēkonta* sixty) + *-ane*] **:** a solid paraffin hydrocarbon $C_{60}H_{122}$; *esp* **:** the normal hydrocarbon $CH_3(CH_2)_{58}CH_3$

hex·a·co·ral·la \,heksəkə'ralə\ *or* **hex·a·co·ral·lia** \-lēə\ [NL, fr. *hexa-* + L *coralla, corallia* (pl. of *corallum, corallium* coral) — more at CORAL] *syn of* ZOANTHARIA

hex·a·co·sane \,heksə'kō,sān\ *n* -s [ISV *hexacos-* (fr. *hexa-* + *-cos-* — fr. *eicosa-*) + *-ane*] **:** a solid paraffin hydrocarbon $C_{26}H_{54}$; *esp* **:** the normal hydrocarbon $CH_3(CH_2)_{24}CH_3$

hex·ac·ti·nal \¦hek(,)sak¦tīnᵊl, (')hek¦saktənᵊl\ *or* **hex·ac·tine** \(')hek¦sak,tīn, -,tən\ *adj* [*hexa-* + *-actinal* or *-actine*] **:** having six rays (~ sponge spicules)

¹hex·ac·ti·nel·lid \¦hek(,)saktə¦neləd\ *adj* [NL *Hexactinellida*] **:** of, relating to, or characteristic of the Hyalospongiae

²hexactinellid \"\ *n* -s **:** one of the Hyalospongiae

hex·ac·ti·nel·li·da \,=(,)=='neləda\ [NL, fr. *Hexactinella,* genus of sponges (fr. *hexa-* + *actin-* + *-ella*) + *-ida*] *syn of* HYALOSPONGIAE

hex·ac·tin·i·an \¦hek(,)sak¦tinēən\ *adj* [*hexa-* + *actin-* + *-an*] **:** having the tentacles or mesenteries in multiples of six

hex·ad \'hek,sad\ *or* **hex·ade** \-,sād\ *n* -s [LL *hexad-, hexas* the number six, fr. Gk, fr. *hex* six + *-ad-, -as* -ad — more at SIX] **:** a group or series of six

hex·a·decane \¦heksə+\ *n* -s [ISV *hexadec-* (fr. *hexa-* + *deca-*) + *-ane*] **:** any of numerous isomeric hydrocarbons $C_{16}H_{34}$; *esp* **:** CETANE

hex·a·dec·a·no·ic acid \¦heksə¦dekə¦nōik-\ *n* [*hexadecane* + *-oic*] **:** PALMITIC ACID

hex·a·dec·a·nol \,=='dekə,nōl, -,nōl\ *n* -s [*hexadecane* + *-ol*] **:** any of several alcohols $C_{16}H_{33}OH$ derived from cetane; *esp* **:** CETYL ALCOHOL

hex·a·dec·ene \-'de,sēn\ *n* -s [ISV *hexadec-* (fr. *hexa-* + *deca-*) + *-ene*] **:** any of several straight-chain isomeric hydrocarbons $C_{16}H_{32}$ of the ethylene series; *esp* **:** CETENE

hexa·decyl \¦heksə+\ *n* [*hexadecane* + *-yl*] **:** an alkyl radical derived from a hexadecane; *esp* **:** CETYL

hex·ad·ic \(')hek¦sadik\ *adj* [*hexad* + *-ic*] **:** of or relating to a hexad

hex·a·di·ene \,heksə'dī,ēn\ *n* -s [ISV *hexa-* + *-diene*] **:** any of six straight-chain isomeric diolefins C_6H_{10}

hex·a·em·er·al \¦heksə¦emərəl\ *or* **hex·a·em·er·ic** \-rik\ *adj* [*hexaemeron* + *-al* or *-ic*] **:** of or relating to the hexaemeron

hex·a·em·er·on \,=='emə,rän\ *or* **hex·a·hem·er·on** \-'he-\ *n* -s [LL *hexaēmeron,* fr. Gk *hexaēmeron,* fr. neut. of *hexaēmeros* of six days, fr. *hexa-* + *hēmera* day — more at HEMERA] **:** the six days of the creation

hexa·ethyl tetraphosphate \¦heksə+ ... -\ *n* [*hexa-* + *ethyl*] **:** an insecticide $(C_2H_5)_6P_4O_{13}$ obtained synthetically usu. as a yellow liquid mixture containing tetraethyl pyrophosphate — called also *HETP*

hexa·fluoride \"+\ *n* [*hexa-* + *fluoride*] **:** a fluoride containing six atoms of fluorine in the molecule

hex·a·foos \'heksə,füs\ *n, pl* **hexafoos** [PaG *hexefuss,* fr. *hex* witch + *fuss* foot (fr. OHG *fuoz*) — more at HEX, FOOT] **:** a three-toed or triangular mark put on some Pennsylvania barns to keep evil spirits from the cattle or for decoration

¹hex·a·gon \'heksə,gän *sometimes* -səgən\ *n* -s [Gk *hexagōnon,* neut. of *hexagōnos* hexagonal, fr. *hexa-* six (fr. *hex*) + *-gōnos* -cornered, -angled (fr. *gōnia* angle, corner) — more at SIX, -GON] **1 :** a plane polygon of six angles and therefore six sides — see AREA table **2 :** a hexagonal object

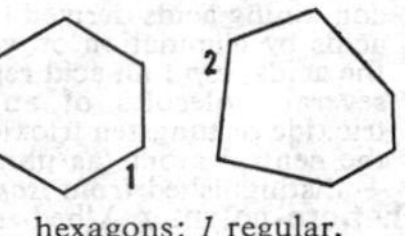

hexagons: *1* regular, *2* irregular

²hexagon \"\ *adj* **:** constituting a hexagon ⟨a ~ tower⟩

hex·ag·o·nal \(')hek¦sagənᵊl, -saig-\ *adj* **1 :** having six angles and six sides **:** six-sided **:** divided into hexagons **2 :** having a hexagon as section or base **3 :** relating or belonging to a hexagonal system — see SCALENOHEDRON illustration — **hex·ag·o·nal·ly** \-ᵊlē, -ᵊli\ *adv*

hexagonal system *n* **:** a crystal system characterized by three equal lateral axes intersecting at angles of 60 degrees and a vertical axis of variable length at right angles (as in the hexagonal prism) — see CRYSTAL SYSTEM illustration

hex·a·gram \'heksə,gram\ *n* [ISV *hexa-* + *-gram*] **:** a figure formed by completing externally an equilateral triangle on each side of a regular hexagon

hexagram

¹hex·a·gram·mid \¦==¦gra,mid\ *adj* [NL *Hexagrammidae*] **:** of or relating to the Hexagrammidae

²hexagrammid \"\ *n* -s **:** a member of the family Hexagrammidae

hex·a·gram·mi·dae \,heksə'gramə,dē\ *n pl, cap* [NL, fr. *Hexagrammos,* type genus + *-idae*] **:** a family of marine carnivorous fishes (order Scleroparei) of the northern Pacific ocean that includes several food fishes — see GREENLING

hex·a·gram·mos \-ə,mäs\ *n, cap* [NL, fr. *hexa-* + *-grammos* (fr. Gk *gramma* line) — more at GRAMMAR] **:** the type genus of the family Hexagrammidae

hex·a·he·dral \¦heksə¦hēdrəl\ *adj* [NL *hexahedron* + E *-al*] **:** having the form of a hexahedron

hexahedral coordination *n* **:** the state or condition of being surrounded by eight atoms whose centers lie at the corners of a hexahedron

hex·a·he·dron \,=='=drən\ *n, pl* **hexahedrons** \-rənz\ *also* **hexahe·dra** \-rə\ [NL, fr. LL, fr. Gk *hexaedron,* fr. neut. of *hexaedros* of six surfaces, fr. *hexa-* + *-edros* (fr. *hedra* base, seat)] **1 :** a polyhedron of six faces **2 :** ¹CUBE 5

hexahemeron *var of* HEXAEMERON

hexahydr- *or* **hexahydro-** *comb form* [ISV *hexa-* + *hydr-*] **:** combined with six atoms of hydrogen — in names of chemical compounds ⟨*hexahydro*benzene⟩

hexa·hydrate \¦heksə+\ *n* [*hexa-* + *hydrate*] **:** a chemical compound with six molecules of water — **hexa·hydrated** \"+\ *adj*

hex·a·hy·dric \¦heksə¦hīdrik\ *adj* [*hexa-* + *-hydric*] **:** HEXAHYDROXY — used esp. of alcohols and phenols

hex·a·hy·drite \,=='hī,drīt\ *n* -s [ISV *hexa-* + *hydr-* + *-ite*] **:** a mineral $MgSO_4.6H_2O$ consisting of a hydrous magnesium sulfate

hexa·hydroxy \¦heksə+\ *adj* [*hexahydroxy-*] **:** containing six hydroxyl groups in the molecule

hexahydroxy- *comb form* [ISV *hexa-* + *hydroxy-*] **:** containing six hydroxyl groups — in names of chemical compounds

hex·a·kis·octahedron \¦heksəkis+\ *n* [NL, fr. Gk *hexakis* six times (fr. *hex* six) + NL *octahedron* — more at SIX] **:** HEXOCTAHEDRON

hex·a·kis·tetrahedron \"+\ *n* [NL, fr. Gk *hexakis* six times + NL *tetrahedron*] **:** HEXTETRAHEDRON

hex·a·mer \'heksəmə(r)\ *n* -s [ISV *hexa-* + *-mer*] **:** a polymer formed from six molecules of a monomer — **hex·a·mer·ic** \¦heksə¦merik\ *adj*

hex·am·er·al \(')hek¦sam(ə)rəl\ *adj* [*hexamerous* + *-al*] **:** HEXAMEROUS

hex·am·er·ous \-rəs\ *adj* [*hexa-* + *-merous*] **1** *bot* **:** consisting of six parts **:** having floral whorls composed of six members **2** *zool* **:** having six parts or parts in multiples of six arranged radially — used esp. of anthozoans in which the tentacles and mesenteries are in multiples of six

hexa·metaphosphate \¦heksə+\ *n* [*hexa-* + *metaphosphate*] **:** a metaphosphate glass; *esp* **:** SODIUM HEXAMETAPHOSPHATE — not used systematically

¹hex·am·e·ter \hek'samədə(r), -mətə-\ *n* [L, fr. Gk *hexametron,* fr. neut. of *hexametros*] **:** a line of six metrical feet or of six dipodies: as **a :** the six-foot dactylic line of Greek and Latin epic poetry in which the first four feet are dactyls or spondees, the fifth a dactyl, and the sixth a spondee (as in Vergil's "Arma virumque cano Trojae qui primus ab oris") **b :** the six-foot dactylic line of English poetry (as in Coleridge's "Strongly it bears us along on swelling and limitless billows")

²hexameter \(')=¦==\ *adj* [L, fr. Gk *hexametros* of six meters, fr. *hexa-* + *-metros* (akin to *metron* measure) — more at MEASURE] **1 :** having six metrical feet — used esp. of dactylic or spondaic verse **2 :** having six dipodies — used esp. of classical iambic, trochaic, or anapestic verse

hex·a·me·tho·ni·um \¦heksəmə'thōnēəm\ *n* -s [NL, fr. *hexa-* + *methonium*] **:** the bivalent substituted ammonium ion $[(CH_3)_3N(CH_2)_6N(CH_3)_3]^{++}$ derived by methylation of hexamethylenediamine; *also* **:** any salt (as the chloride or bromide) containing this ion used as a ganglionic blocking agent in the treatment of hypertension

hexa·methyl \¦heksə+\ *adj* [ISV *hexa-* + *methyl*] **:** containing six methyl groups in the molecule

hexa·methylene \"+\ *n* [ISV *hexa-* + *methylene*] **1 :** CYCLOHEXANE **2 :** the bivalent radical $-CH_2(CH_2)_4CH_2-$ derived from normal hexane by removal of one hydrogen atom from each end carbon atom

hexamethylene·diamine \"+\ *n* [ISV *hexamethylene* + *diamine*] **:** a crystalline base $H_2N(CH_2)_6NH_2$ made by hydrogenation of adiponitrile and used in the manufacture of nylon; 1,6-hexane-diamine

hexa·methylene·tetramine \"+\ *n* [ISV *hexamethylene* + *tetramine*] **:** a crystalline tricyclic weak base $(CH_2)_6N_4$ made by the action of ammonia on formaldehyde and used chiefly as a source of formaldehyde (as in the manufacture of phenolic resins), as a vulcanization accelerator, and in medicine as a urinary antiseptic — called also *hexamine, methenamine*

hex·am·e·trist \hek'samə·trəst\ *n* -s [*hexameter* + *-ist*] **:** one who writes in hexameters

hex·a·mine \'heksə,mēn, hek'samən\ *n* [by contr.] **:** HEXAMETHYLENETETRAMINE

hex·am·i·ta \hek'samədə\ *n, cap* [NL, fr. *hexa-* + *-mita* (fr. Gk *mitos* thread) — more at DIMITY] **:** a genus (the type of the family Hexamitidae) of binucleate zooflagellates having six anterior and two trailing flagella and including free-living forms as well as intestinal parasites of birds (as *H. meleagridis*) and of salmonid fishes (as *H. salmonis*) that are associated with enteritides — compare GIARDIA

hex·am·i·ti·a·sis \hek,samə'tīəsəs\ *n* -ES [NL, fr. *Hexamita* + *-iasis*] **:** infestation with or disease caused by flagellates of the genus *Hexamita*

¹hex·am·i·tid \(')hek¦samədəd\ *adj* [NL *Hexamitidae,* family of zooflagellates, fr. *Hexamita,* type genus + *-idae*] **:** of or relating to the genus *Hexamita* or family Hexamitidae

²hexamitid \"\ *n* -s **:** a member of the genus *Hexamita* or family Hexamitidae

hex·ammine \hek'sa,mēn, -,mən, ,heksə'mēn\ *n* [*hexa-* + *ammine*] **:** an ammine containing six molecules of ammonia

hex·a·nal \'heksə,nal\ *n* -s [*hexane* + *-al*] **:** a volatile liquid aldehyde $CH_3(CH_2)_4CHO$ of irritating odor obtained from several volatile oils (as eucalyptus oil and peppermint oil) — called also *caproaldehyde*

hex·an·chi·dae \hek'saŋkə,dē\ *n pl, cap* [NL, fr. *Hexanchus,* type genus + *-idae*] **:** a family of sharks consisting of many fossil forms and a few living forms that have one dorsal fin and a palatoquadrate which articulates with the postorbital part of the skull

hex·an·chus \hek'saŋkəs\ *n, cap* [NL, fr. *hexa-* + *anchus* (prob. fr. Gk *anchein* to strangle) — more at ANGER] **:** the type genus of the family *Hexanchidae* sometimes considered to include all living members of the family but sometimes restricted to those with six pairs of branchial clefts

hex·ane \'hek,sān\ *n* -s [ISV *hexa-* + *-ane*] **:** any of five isomeric volatile liquid paraffin hydrocarbons C_6H_{14} found in petroleum; *esp* **:** the normal hydrocarbon $CH_3(CH_2)_4CH_3$

hexa·nitrate \¦heksə+\ *n* [*hexa-* + *nitrate*] **:** a compound containing six nitrate groups in the molecule

hexa·ni·tro·diphenylamine \¦heksə¦nī·trō+\ *n* [ISV *hexa-* + *nitro-* + *diphenylamine*] **:** a light-yellow poisonous crystalline compound $[(NO_2)_3C_6H_2]_2NH$ made by nitrating diphenylamine and used as a high explosive — called also *dipicrylamine;* see AURANTIA

hex·a·no·ic acid \¦heksə¦nōik-\ *n* [ISV *hexan-* (fr. *hexane*) + *-oic*] **:** CAPROIC ACID — used in the system of nomenclature adopted by the International Union of Pure and Applied Chemistry

hex·a·no·yl \¦heksə¦nōəl; hek'sanə,wil, -,wēl\ *n* -s [ISV *hexan-* (fr. *hexanoic acid*) + *-oyl*] **:** CAPROYL

hexa·partite \¦heksə+\ *adj* [*hexa-* + *partite*] **:** SEXPARTITE

hexa·petaloid \"+\ *adj* [*hexa-* + *petaloid*] **:** having or being a perianth with six petaloid divisions

hexa·petalous \"+\ *adj* [*hexa-* + *-petalous*] **:** having or being a perianth with six petals

hex·a·pla \'heksəplə\ *n* -s *often cap* [LL, fr. Gk *hexapla,* fr. neut. pl. of *hexaplous, hexaploos* sixfold, fr. *hexa-* + *-plous, -ploos* -fold (as in *diploos* double) — more at DOUBLE] **:** an edition or work in six texts or versions in parallel columns — compare TETRAPLA — **hex·a·plar** \-lə(r)\ *adj, often cap*

hex·a·plar·ic \¦heksə¦plarik\ *also* **hex·a·plar·i·an** \¦==¦pla(a)rēən\ *adj, often cap* **:** of or relating to a hexapla; *esp* **:** of or relating to the edition of the Old Testament compiled by Origen in the 3d century A.D. and consisting of the Hebrew text, a transliteration in Greek, and the Greek versions of Aquila, Symmachus, the Septuagint, and Theodotion

¹hex·a·ploid \'heksə,plȯid\ *adj* [ISV *hexa-* + *-ploid*] **:** sixfold in appearance or arrangement; *specif* **:** having or being six times the monoploid chromosome number ⟨a ~ cell⟩ — compare DIPLOID, HAPLOID, POLYPLOID

²hexaploid \"\ *n* -s **:** a hexaploid individual

hex·a·ploidy \-dē\ *n* -ES **:** the condition of being hexaploid

¹hex·a·pod \'heksə,päd\ *n* -s [Gk *hexapod-, hexapous,* adj., six-footed, fr. *hexa-* + *pod-, pous* foot — more at FOOT] **:** INSECT 1b

²hexapod \"\ *adj* **1 :** six-footed **2 :** of or relating to insects

hex·ap·o·da \hek'sapədə\ *n pl, cap* [NL, fr. *hexa-* + *-poda*] *in some classifications* **:** a class or other division of Arthropoda coextensive with the class Insecta — used esp. when Collembola and Protura are considered with the typical insects

hex·ap·o·dous \-dəs\ *adj* **:** HEXAPOD

hex·ap·o·dy \-dē\ *n* -ES [ISV *hexa-* + *-pody* (as in *dipody*)] **:** a prosodic line or group consisting of six feet

hex·arch \'hek,särk\ *adj* [*hexa-* + *-arch*] *of a root* **:** having six radiating vascular strands ⟨the ~ roots of an onion⟩

¹hex·a·so·mic \¦heksə¦sōmik\ *adj* [*hexa-* + *-somic*] **:** having one chromosome or a few chromosomes hexaploid in otherwise diploid nuclei

²hexasomic \"\ *n* -s **:** a hexasomic individual

hex·as·ter \'hek,sastə(r)\ *n* [NL, fr. *hexa-* + *-aster* (star)] **:** a triaxon sponge spicule usu. with equal rays

hex·as·ter·oph·o·ra \,hek,sastə'räf(ə)rə\ *n pl, cap* [NL, fr. *hexaster* + *-o-* + *-phora*] **:** an order of Hyalospongiae comprising sponges with hexasters but not amphidisks among the spicules

hex·a·stich \'heksə,stik\ *also* **hex·as·ti·chon** \hek'sastə,kän\ *n, pl* **hexastichs** *also* **hex·as·ti·cha** \'=stəkə\ [NL *hexastichon,* fr. ML, prob. fr. Gk *hexastichon,* neut. of *hexastichos* of six rows, of six lines, fr. *hexa-* + *stichos* row, line; akin to Gk *steichein* to go — more at STICH] **:** a group, stanza, or poem of six lines — **hex·a·stich·ic** \¦heksə¦stikik\ *adj*

hex·a·sty·lar \¦heksə¦stīlə(r)\ *adj* **:** HEXASTYLE

¹hex·a·style \'heksə,stīl\ *n* [L *hexastylos,* adj., of six columns] **:** a portico with six columns

²hexastyle \"\ *adj* **:** marked by columniation with six columns across the front — compare DISTYLE

hex·a·sty·los \,heksə'stī,läs\ *n* -ES [NL, fr. L, adj., of six columns, fr. Gk, fr. *hexa-* + *stylos* column, pillar — more at STOIC] **:** a hexastyle building

hexa·syllabic \¦heksə+\ *adj* [Gk *hexasyllabos* (fr. *hexa-* + *syllabē* syllable) + E *-ic* — more at SYLLABLE] **:** comprising six syllables

hexa·syllable \"+\ *n* [*hexa-* + *syllable*] **:** a word of six syllables

hexatetrahedron *var of* HEXTETRAHEDRON

hex·a·teu·chal \¦heksə¦tükəl, -sə¦tyü-\ *adj, usu cap* [*Hexateuch* the first 6 books of the Bible (fr. *hexa-* + *-teuch,* as in *Pentateuch* the first 5 books of the Bible) + E *-al* — more at PENTATEUCHAL] **:** of or relating to the first six books of the Old Testament

hex·atomic \¦heks+\ *adj* [*hexa-* + *atomic*] **1 :** consisting of six atoms **2 :** having six replaceable atoms or radicals

hex·a·tri·a·con·tane \,heksə,trīə'kän,tān\ *n* [ISV *hexatriacont-* (fr. *hexa-* + *triacont-* — fr. Gk *triakonta* thirty) + *-ane*]

: a solid paraffin hydrocarbon $C_{36}H_{74}$; *esp* **:** the normal hydrocarbon $CH_3(CH_2)_{34}CH_3$

hexa·valent \¦heksə+\ *adj* [ISV *hexa-* + *valent*] **:** having a valence of six

hex·ax·on \hek'sak,sän\ *n* [NL, fr. *hexa-* + Gk *axōn* axle, axis — more at AXIS] **:** HEXASTER

hexed *past of* HEX

hex·en·be·sen \'heksən,bāzᵊn\ *n* -s [G, fr. *hexen* (pl. of *hexe* witch) + *besen* broom, fr. OHG *besmo* — more at HEX, BESOM] **:** WITCHES'-BROOM

hex·ene \'hek,sēn\ *n* -s [ISV *hexa-* + *-ene*] **:** any of the three straight-chain hexylenes

hex·er \'heksə(r)\ *n* -s [¹*hex* + *-er*] **:** a person who hexes

hex·e·rei \,heksə'rī\ *n* -s [PaG, fr. G, fr. *hexen* to practice witchcraft + *-erei* -ery (fr. MHG *-erīe*, fr. OF *-erie*) — more at HEX] **:** WITCHCRAFT

hexes *pres 3d sing of* HEX, *pl of* HEX

hex·es·trol *also* **hex·oes·trol** \hek'se,strōl, -rōl\ *n* -s [*hexane* + NL *estrus* or *oestrus* + E *-ol*] **:** a crystalline estrogenic diphenol $[HOC_6H_4CH(C_2H_5)-]_2$ derived from diphenylethane; dihydro-diethylstilbestrol

hex·ine \'hek,sīn\ *archaic var of* HEXYNE

hexing *pres part of* HEX

hex·i·tol \'heksə,tȯl, -,tōl\ *n* -s [*hexose* + *-itol*] **:** any of the hexahydroxy alcohols $HOCH_2(CHOH)_4CH_2OH$ obtainable by reduction of the corresponding hexoses and in some cases (as mannitol and sorbitol) occurring naturally

hex mark *or* **hex sign** *n* **:** a usu. stylized often symbolic design placed on a structure (as a building or an enclosure for animals) for the purpose of warding off evil spirits or simply for its decorative effect — compare HEXAFOOS

hexo·barbital \¦heksō+\ *n* [*hexo-* (fr. *hexa-*) + *barbital*] **:** a crystalline barbiturate $C_{12}H_{16}N_2O_3$ used as a sedative and hypnotic and in the form of its soluble sodium salt as an intravenous anesthetic of short duration

hexo·barbitone \"+\ *n* [*hexo-* (fr. *hexa-*) + *barbitone*] **:** HEXOBARBITAL

hexobiose *var of* HEXABIOSE

hex·octahedral \(¦)heks+\ *adj* [NL *hexoctahedron* + E *-al*] **:** having the shape or symmetry of a hexoctahedron

hex·octahedron \"+\ *n* [NL, fr. *hexa-* + *octahedron*] **:** an isometric crystal having 48 equal triangular faces

hexoctahedron

hex·ode \'hek,sōd\ *n* -s [ISV *hexa-* + *-ode*] **:** a vacuum tube with six electrodes consisting of a cathode, an anode, a control grid, and three additional grids or other electrodes

hex·o·ic acid \(')hek¦sōik-\ *n* [*hexane* + *-oic*] **:** any of the monocarboxylic acids $C_5H_{11}COOH$ (as caproic acid) derived from the hexanes

hexo·kinase \¦heksō+\ *n* [ISV *hexose* + *kinase*] **:** any of several enzymes that occur in living tissues (as muscle, brain, yeast) and are important in carbohydrate metabolism in which they accelerate the phosphorylation of hexoses (as the formation of glucose 6-phosphate from glucose and adenosine triphosphate in the presence of magnesium ions or similar cations)

-hex·ol \'hek,sȯl, -,sōl\ *n suffix* -s [ISV *hexa-* + *-ol*] **:** containing six hydroxyl groups ⟨cyclohexane*-hexol*⟩

hex·one \'hek,sōn\ *n* -s [ISV *hexa-* + *-one*; orig. formed as G *hexon*] **:** METHYL ISOBUTYL KETONE — used esp. of the technical grade

hex·on·ic acid \(')hek¦sänik-\ *n* [ISV *hexa-* + *-onic*] **:** an aldonic acid (as gluconic acid) that contains six carbon atoms in a molecule

hex·os·a·mine \hek¦säsə'mēn\ *n* [ISV *hexose* + *amine*] **:** an amine (as glucosamine) derived from a hexose by replacement of hydroxyl by the amino group

hex·o·san \'heksə,san\ *n* -s [*hexose* + *-an*] **:** any of a class of polysaccharides (as fructosans or glucosans) yielding only hexoses on hydrolysis

hex·ose \'hek,sōs\ *n* -s [ISV *hexa-* + *-ose*] **:** any of a class of monosaccharides $C_6H_{12}O_6$ (as glucose or fructose) containing six carbon atoms in the molecule

hexose phosphate *n* **:** a phosphoric derivative of a hexose (as glucose phosphate) of which two types have been found in living tissues as intermediates of carbohydrate metabolism: **a** *or* **hexose monophosphate :** a mono-phosphoric ester or acylal $C_6H_{11}O_5(OPO_3H_2)$ **b** *or* **hexose diphosphate : a** diphosphoric ester $C_6H_{10}O_4(OPO_3H_2)_2$

hex·oxide \(')heks+\ *n* [*hex-* + *oxide*] **:** an oxide containing six atoms of oxygen in the molecule

hex·partite \(')heks+\ *adj* [*hexa-* + *partite*] *archit* **:** SEXPARTITE

hex·tetrahedral \(¦)heks+\ *adj* [NL *hextetrahedron* + E *-al*] **:** having the shape or symmetry of a hextetrahedron

hex·tetrahedron \"+\ *n* [NL, fr. *hexa-* + *tetrahedron*] **:** a 24-faced crystalline form of the tetrahedral group of the isometric system

hex·u·lose \'heksyə,lōs\ *n* -s [*hexa-* + *-ulose*] **:** a ketose $C_6H_{12}O_6$ (as fructose or sorbose) containing six carbon atoms in the molecule; *esp* **:** the isomer having the carbonyl group in the beta or 2-position; compare GLUCOSE illustration

hex·u·ron·ic acid \¦heksyə¦ränik-\ *n* [*hexa-* + *-uronic*] **1 :** ASCORBIC ACID — now little used **2 :** a uronic acid (as glucuronic acid) derived from a hexose (as glucose)

hex·yl \'heksəl\ *n* -s [ISV *hexa-* + *-yl*] **:** an alkyl radical C_6H_{13} derived from a hexane; *esp* **:** the normal radical $CH_3(CH_2)_4CH_2$—

hex·yl·ene \'heksə,lēn\ *n* -s [ISV *hexyl* + *-ene*] **:** any of several liquid isomeric hydrocarbons C_6H_{12} belonging to the ethylene series and including the hexenes

hex·yl·ic acid \(')hek¦silik-\ *n* [ISV *hexyl* + *-ic*] **:** HEXOIC ACID

hexylresorcinol \¦≈≈¦≈≈,≈\ *n* [*hexyl* + *resorcinol*] **:** a white or yellowish white crystalline phenol $C_6H_{13}C_6H_3(OH)_2$ used in medicine as an antiseptic and internally as an anthelmintic; 1,3-dihydroxy-4-*n*-hexyl-benzene

hex·yne \'hek,sīn\ *n* -s [*hexa-* + *-yne*] **:** any of three isomeric straight-chain hydrocarbons C_6H_{10} of the acetylene series

¹hey \'hā\ *interj* [ME *hei, hey*] — used to call attention or to incite, to express interrogation, surprise, or exultation, or with indefinite meaning in the burden of a song

²hey *var of* HAY

hey cockalorum *n* **:** HIGH COCKALORUM 1

¹hey·day \'hā,dā\ *interj* [fr. earlier *heyda*, alter. of ¹*hey*] *archaic* — used to express frolicsomeness, exultation, or sometimes wonder

²heyday *also* **heydey** \"\ *n* **1** *archaic* **:** high spirits **:** FROLICSOMENESS, WILDNESS, JOY **2 :** a time of highest strength, vigor, or prosperity **:** ACME ⟨in the ~ of his power⟩ ⟨Athens and Venice in their commercial ~ —David Riesman⟩ ⟨during the ~ of the fur trade —Grace L. Nute⟩

¹hey rube *interj* [¹*hey* + *rube*] — used traditionally as a rallying cry among circus or carnival folk in a fight with townspeople

²hey rube *n* **:** a usu. free-for-all fight between circus or carnival folk and townspeople ⟨we found ourselves with an old-fashioned *hey rube* and obliged to move the show on that night —Herbert Gold⟩

hf *abbr* half

HF *abbr* **1** *often not cap* high frequency **2** home fleet **3** home forces

Hf *symbol* hafnium

HFC *abbr* high-frequency current

HFM *abbr* hold for money

hg *abbr* **1** hectogram **2** heliogram

HG *abbr* **1** Her Grace; His Grace **2** High German **3** home guard

Hg *symbol* [NL *hydrargyrum*] mercury

h girder *n, cap H* **:** a girder like an I beam but with wider flanges

hgm *abbr* hectogram

hgt *abbr* height

HH *abbr* **1** Her Highness; His Highness **2** His Holiness

hhd *abbr* hogshead

hheth *var of* HETH

HHG *abbr* household goods

h hinge *n, cap 1st H* **:** a hinge with leaves that when open resemble the letter H

H hinge

h hour *n, usu cap 1st H* [²*h* (abbr. for *hour*)] **:** the hour set for launching a specific tactical operation — compare D DAY, ZERO HOUR

hi \'hī(ē), -ī(i)\ *interj* [ME *hy*] — used to express greeting or to attract attention

HI *abbr* high intensity

hi·a·tal \(')hī¦ād·ᵊl\ *adj* [*hiatus* + *-al*] **1 :** having a rock texture in which the sizes of the individual crystals do not vary in a continuous series but are in two or more series of marked differences **2 :** HIATUS

¹hi·a·tus \hī'ād·əs, -ātəs\ *n* -ES [L, fr. past part. of *hiare* to gape — more at YAWN] **1 a :** a break in or as if in a material object **:** GAP **:** APERTURE ⟨the weedy ~ between the town and the railroad —Willa Cather⟩ ⟨the ~ between the theory and the practice of the party —J.G.Colton⟩ **b :** a gap or passage through an anatomical part or organ; *esp* **:** a gap through which another part or organ passes **2 a :** an interruption or lapse in or as if in time or continuity ⟨the programs that are to fill in during the summer ~ —Saul Carson⟩ ⟨if deposition of sediment should cease everywhere for a time, a natural . . . ~ in the stratigraphic record would result —C.O.Dunbar⟩ ⟨~*es* of thought when certain links in the association of ideas are dropped —Edmund Wilson⟩ **b :** the occurrence of or relationship between two vowel sounds without pause or intervening consonantal sound (as when *beyond* is pronounced without a \y\ sound) **syn** see BREAK

²hiatus \"\ *adj* **1 :** involving a hiatus **2** *of a hernia* **:** having a part that herniates through the esophageal hiatus of the diaphragm

hi·ba arborvitae \'hēbə-\ *n* [Jap *hiba*] **:** a large Japanese evergreen tree (*Thujopsis dolobrata*) that has glossy green leaves with a broad white band on the underside and is used as an ornamental

hi·ba·chi \hē'bächē\ *n* -s [Jap, fr. *hi* fire + *hachi* bowl] **:** a charcoal brazier

hib·ber·tia \hi'bərd·ēə, -rsh(ē)ə\ *n* [NL, fr. George *Hibbert* †1837 Eng. merchant and botanist + NL *-ia*] **1** *cap* **:** a genus of Australasian shrubs (family Dilleniaceae) having showy yellow or white flowers with numerous stamens and five fugacious petals **2** -s **:** any plant of the genus *Hibbertia*

hi·ber·na·cle \'hībə(r),nakəl\ *n* -s [NL *hibernaculum*] **:** HIBERNACULUM 2a ⟨brought forth a frog from his ~ in the leaves —John Burroughs⟩

hi·ber·nac·u·lum \,hībə(r)'nakyələm\ *n, pl* **hibernacu·la** \-lə\ [NL, fr. L, winter residence, fr. *hibernus* of winter, wintry + *-culum* -cle — more at HIBERNATE] **1 :** the winter resting part of a plant (as a bud or underground stem) **2 a :** a shelter that is occupied during the winter by a dormant insect or other animal and that usu. has a characteristic structure for each species — called also *hibernacle* **b :** an encysted bud in a freshwater bryozoan that survives the winter and develops into a colony in the spring **c :** the epiphragm of a snail

hi·ber·nal \(')hī¦bərnᵊl\ *adj* [LL *hibernalis*, fr. L *hibernus* of winter + *-alis* -al] **:** of or relating to winter **:** WINTRY

¹hi·ber·nant \'hībə(r)nənt\ *adj* [L *hibernant-, hibernans*, pres. part. of *hibernare*] **:** HIBERNATING ⟨~ animals⟩

²hibernant \"\ *n* -s **:** an animal that hibernates

hi·ber·nate \'hībə(r),nāt, *usu* -ād·+V\ *vi* -ED/-ING/-S [L *hibernatus*, past part. of *hibernare*, fr. *hibernus* of winter, wintry; akin to L *hiems* winter, Gk *cheimōn*, OSlav *zima*, Skt *himā*] **1 a :** to pass the winter in a torpid or lethargic state; *specif* **:** to pass the winter in a torpid condition in which the body temperature drops to a little above freezing and metabolic activity is reduced nearly to zero — used esp. of various mammals; compare AESTIVATE **b :** to pass the winter in a resting state — used esp. of the spores and winter buds of various plants **2 a :** to pass the winter esp. in a milder climate ⟨six million farmers lived close enough to Florida to ~ there easily —Alva Johnston⟩ **b :** to be or become inactive or dormant ⟨a few mots survive, to ~ in the mind, and come out again on an early summer day —Osbert Sitwell⟩

hibernating gland *n* **:** a tissue found beneath the skin of the back or abdomen of various mammals that consists of brownish fat cells in a network of vascular connective tissue and serves as a storage for food

hi·ber·na·tion \,hībə(r)'nāshən\ *n* -s **1 :** the act of hibernating ⟨a new concept of the relation between food and ~ of the black bear —R.E.Trippensee⟩ **2 :** the state of one that hibernates ⟨came out of his comfortable ~ to make his first political pronouncement since his retirement —*Time*⟩ — opposed to *aestivation*

hi·ber·na·tor \'hībə(r),nād·ə(r), -ātə-\ *n* -s **:** one that hibernates

¹hi·ber·nian \(')hī¦bərnēən, -bən-, -bəin-, -nyən\ *adj, usu cap* [*Hibernia* Ireland (fr. L) + E *-an*] **1 :** of, relating to, or characteristic of Ireland **2 :** of, relating to, or characteristic of the Irish

²hibernian \"\ *n* -s *usu cap* **:** a native or inhabitant of Ireland **:** IRISHMAN

hibernian green *n, often cap H* **:** a dark yellowish green that is yellower and paler than holly green (sense 1), lighter and stronger than deep chrome green, and yellower, lighter, and stronger than average hunter green — called also *paradise green*

hi·ber·nian·ism \hī'bərnēə,nizəm, -bən-, -bəin-, -nyə-\ *n* -s *usu cap* **:** HIBERNICISM

hi·ber·ni·cism \-nə,sizəm\ *n* -s *usu cap* [ML *Hibernicus* Irish (fr. *Hibernia* + L *-icus* -ic) + E *-ism*] **:** something characteristically Irish; *specif* **:** IRISH BULL

hi·ber·ni·cize \-,sīz\ *vt* -ED/-ING/-S *often cap* [ML *Hibernicus* + E *-ize*] **:** to make Irish **:** express in an Irish way

hiberno- *comb form, usu cap* [*Hibernia*] **1 :** Irish and ⟨*Hiberno*-Celtic⟩ **2 :** Ireland ⟨*Hibernology*⟩

hi·bis·cus \hī'biskəs, hə'-\ *n* [NL, fr. L, *hibiscum, hibiscus* marshmallow] **1** *cap* **:** a large widely distributed genus of herbs, shrubs, or small trees (family Malvaceae) with dentate or lobed leaves and large showy flowers — see CHINA ROSE, KENAF, ROSE OF SHARON **2** -ES **:** any plant or flower of the genus *Hibiscus*

hi·bi·to \(h)ē'bē(,)tō\ *n, pl* **hibito** *or* **hibitos** *usu cap* [Sp, of AmerInd origin] **1 a :** an extinct Cholonan people of northwestern Peru **b :** a member of such people **2 :** the language of the Hibito people

hibsch·ite \'hip,shīt\ *n* -s [Joseph E. *Hibsch* *b*1882 Czech mineralogist + E *-ite*] **:** a mineral $Ca_3Al_2(SiO_4)_2(OH)_4$ consisting of a calcium aluminum silicate-hydroxide

hic *often read as* 'hik\ *interj* [imit.] — used to express the sound of a hiccup

hicaco *var of* ICACO

hic·a·tee *or* **hic·o·tee** \'hikə,tē, ,≈≈'≈\ *or* **hic·o·tea** \,hikə'tāə\ *n* -s [Sp *hicotea, jicotea*, prob. fr. Taino *icotea, icota*] **:** a West Indian freshwater tortoise (*Chrysemys palustris*)

hic·can *also* **hi·can** \(')hi¦kan, -kän\ *n* -s [*hickory* + *pecan*] **:** the nut of a tree produced by hybridizing a hickory and a pecan

hic·cius doc·cius \¦hiksh(ē)əs'däksh(ē)əs, ¦hiksēəs'däksēəs\ *n* [perh. modif. of L *hic est doctus* this is the learned man] *archaic* **:** a juggler's formula

¹hic·cup *or* **hic·cough** \'hi¦kəp *sometimes* 'hē| *or* |,kəp *or* |,kȯf *or* |,käf\ *n* -s [*hiccup* of imit. origin; *hiccough* by folk etymology (influence of *cough*) fr. *hiccup*] **1 :** a spasmodic inspiratory movement of the diaphragm involuntarily checked by a sudden closure of the glottis that produces a characteristic sound **2** *or* **hiccups** *pl but sometimes sing in constr* **:** an attack of hiccuping ⟨severe ~*s* is sometimes seen after operation —*Lancet*⟩ ⟨intractable ~ . . . may be successfully treated —*Jour. Amer. Med. Assoc.*⟩

²hiccup *also* **hiccough** \"\ *vb* **hiccuped** *also* **hiccupped** *also* **hiccoughed; hiccuped** *also* **hiccupped** *also* **hiccoughed; hiccuping** *also* **hiccupping** *also* **hiccoughing; hiccups** *also* **hiccoughs** *vi* **1 :** to have or suffer from hiccups **:** make a hiccup **2 :** to make a sound suggestive of hiccups ⟨the locomotive ~*ed* and belched a gobbet of smoke into the air —S.H. Adams⟩ ~ *vt* **:** to speak with or as if with hiccups — usu. used with *out* ⟨was ~*ing* out the lines —W.M.Thackeray⟩

hic·cup–nut \'≈(,)≈,≈\ *n* **1 :** the seed of an ornamental southern African red-flowering shrub (*Combretum bracteosum*) **2 :** the plant that bears hiccup-nuts

hicht \'hi<u>k</u>t\ *Scot var of* HEIGHT

hichu *var of* ICHU

hic ja·cet \(')hik'jāsət, (')hēk'yäkət\ *n* -s [L, here lies] **:** an inscription on a tombstone **:** EPITAPH ⟨among the knightly brasses of the graves, and by the cold *hic jacets* of the dead —Alfred Tennyson⟩

¹hick \'hik\ *n* -s [fr. *Hick*, nickname for *Richard*] **:** an awkward, rude, unsophisticated, or provincial person ⟨their dullest gags, especially written down for the ~*s* —Edmund Wilson⟩ ⟨the immemorial game of luring ~*s*, tired businessmen and holidaymakers into their shows —Sheldon Cheney⟩ **syn** see BOOR

²hick \"\ *adj* **:** of, relating to, or having the characteristics of a hick **:** suggestive of hicks **:** COUNTRY ⟨a ~ town⟩

³hick \"\ *n* -s [imit.] **:** HICCUP 1

⁴hick \"\ *vi* -ED/-ING/-S **:** HICCUP 1

¹hick·ey *also* **hicky** \'hikē, -ki\ *n, pl* **hickeys** *also* **hickies** [origin unknown] **1 a :** a threaded coupling used to attach an electrical fixture to an outlet box **b :** a device for bending pipe and conduit **2 :** a contrivance or device whose name is unknown or forgotten **:** GADGET ⟨that little ~ with the rubber roller on a handle —*Bagpipe*⟩

²hickey \"\ *n* -s [origin unknown] **1 :** PIMPLE **2 :** a defect in a negative or printing plate

hick joint *n* [perh. fr. the name *Hick*] **:** a joint finished flush with the surface of masonry

¹hick·o·ry \'hik(ə)rē, -ri\ *n* -ES [short for *pokahickory*, fr. Virginia *pawcohiccora* food prepared fr. pounded nuts and water] **1 a :** an American tree of the genus *Carya* — see HICKORY NUT; TREE illustration **b :** the valuable hard wood of various hickories **2 :** a switch or cane used typically for punishing a child **3 :** a rapid gait **:** CLIP **4 a :** any of various Australian trees (as the featherwood or various members of the genera *Acacia* and *Eucalyptus*) **b :** the wood of an Australian hickory

²hickory \"\ *adj* **1 :** of, relating to, or made of hickory ⟨a ~ chair⟩ **2 a :** marked by firmness or toughness ⟨the old general, with all his ~ characteristics —Washington Irving⟩ **b :** marked by the absence of religious zeal or devotion **:** religiously indifferent or lukewarm

³hickory \"\ *vt* -ED/-ING/-ES **:** to give a whipping to **:** CANE, SWITCH

hickory acacia *n* **:** an Australian acacia (*Acacia leprosa*) with hard reddish brown wood

hickory bark beetle *also* **hickory bark borer** *n* **:** a small beetle (*Scolytus quadrispinosus*) that burrows beneath the bark of various hickories

hickory borer *n* **:** any of various beetles whose larvae live under the bark or in the wood of hickories

hickory elm *n* **:** ROCK ELM 1

hickoryhead \'≈(≈)≈,≈\ *n* **:** RUDDY DUCK

hickory horned devil *n* **:** a caterpillar that has a greenish body, red head, and four large curved anterior spines and is the larva of the regal moth

hickory midge *n* **:** a gallfly (*Caryomyia caryae*) that forms globular galls on the leaves of various hickories; *broadly* **:** a member of the genus *Caryomyia*

hickory nut *n* **:** the oblong or nearly orbicular nut or fruit of the hickory that is usu. compressed on the sides, sharp-pointed at the apex, and enclosed in a 4-valved husk

hickory oak *n* **:** CANYON LIVE OAK

hickory pine *n* **1 :** BRISTLECONE PINE **2 :** TABLE-MOUNTAIN PINE

hickory poplar *n* **:** TULIP TREE 1

hickory shad *n* [so called fr. the similarity of the stomachs to hickory nuts] **1 :** FALL HERRING **2 :** GIZZARD SHAD

hickory shirt *also* **hickory** *n* **:** a shirt made of a strong twilled cotton fabric with vertical stripes and used esp. for work clothing

hickory shuckworm *n* **:** a small white brown-headed grub that is the larva of an olethreutid moth (*Laspeyresia caryana*) and that feeds in the developing fruits of hickory and pecan

hickory wattle *n* **:** a Queensland acacia (*Acacia aulacocarpa*)

hicks *pl of* HICK, *pres 3d sing of* HICK

hicks·ite \'hik,sīt\ *n* -s *usu cap* [Elias *Hicks* †1830 Am. Quaker minister + E *-ite*] **:** a member of a liberal branch of Quakers who emphasize the Inner Light at the expense of historical Christianity and the Bible

hicks yew *or* **hicks' yew** \'hiks(əz)-\ *n, usu cap H* [fr. *Hicks* nurseries, Westbury, L.I.] **:** a hybrid yew (*Taxus media hicksii*) having a columnar shape and ascending branches

hick·wall \'hi,kwȯl\ *n* [ME *hygh-whele*, prob. of imit. origin] *dial Eng* **:** GREEN WOODPECKER

hicky *var of* HICKEY

hi·co·ria \hi'kōrēə\ [NL, modif. of E *hickory*] *syn of* CARYA

hicotee *or* **hicotea** *var of* HICATEE

hid \'hid\ *adj* [ME, fr. past part. of *hiden* to hide — more at HIDE] **:** HIDDEN ⟨like the ~ scent in an unbudded rose —John Keats⟩

hid·abil·i·ty \,hīdə'biləd·ē\ *n* **1 :** the quality or state of being hidable **2 :** ability to obscure ⟨paints of superior durability, ~, and color-holding qualities —*Amer. Builder*⟩

hid·able \'hīdəbəl\ *adj* **:** capable of being hidden ⟨jewels are such ~ trifles —*English Digest*⟩

hid·age \'hīdij\ *n* -s [ML *hidagium*, fr. *hida* hide (fr. ME *hyde*) + *-agium* -age] *old Eng law* **1 :** a tax or tribute paid to the royal exchequer for every hide of land **2 :** the value or measure assessed as a basis for hidage

hi·dal·go \hi'dal(,)gō, ē'<u>th</u>äl-\ *n* -s *often cap* [Sp, fr. OSp *fijo dalgo*, lit., son of something, son of riches or property] **:** a member of the lower nobility of Spain

hid·at·ed \'hī,dād·əd\ *adj* [NL *hidatus* (past part. of *hidare* to measure in hides, fr. ML *hida* hide) + E *-ed*] **:** measured in hides

hid·a·tion \hī'dāshən\ *n* -s [NL *hidatus* + E *-ion*] **:** a measuring in or assessing by hides

hi·dat·sa \hi'dätsə, -dat-\ *n, pl* **hidatsa** *also* **hidatsas** *usu cap* **1 a :** a Siouan people of the Missouri River valley in No. Dakota related to the Crow — compare GROS VENTRE **b :** a member of such people **2 :** the language of the Hidatsa people

hid·den \'hidᵊn\ *adj* [fr. past part. of ²*hide*] **1 :** being out of sight or off the beaten track **:** CONCEALED ⟨pulling a ~ switch —D.J.Ingle⟩ ⟨a ~ Broadway restaurant —Scott Fitzgerald⟩ **2 :** UNEXPLAINED, UNDISCLOSED, OBSCURE, SECRET ⟨rendering . . . apparent that which is ~ —Matthew Arnold⟩ ⟨rid your mind of any ~ hates or grudges —W.J.Reilly⟩; *specif* **:** not shown in the accounts or not shown on the books under the usual heading ⟨~ assets⟩ **3 :** obscured by something that makes recognition difficult **:** covered up ⟨~ vowel⟩ ⟨clouds race across the ~ moon⟩ ⟨~ transfers of dollars, the largest item being the estimated $125 million spent by U. S. troops in Germany —*Americana Annual*⟩ — **hid·den·ly** *adv* — **hid·den·ness** \-ᵊn(n)əs\ *n* -ES

hidden fifth *n* **:** an unsounded musical interval of a fifth that is implied by the similar up or down motion of two voice parts and that if sounded would produce consecutive fifths

hidden hunger *n* **:** a nutritional deficiency caused by lack of balance in an otherwise full diet ⟨*hidden hunger* is suffered by cats . . . permitted to eat only liver —Doris Bryant⟩

hid·den·ite \'hidᵊn,īt\ *n* -s [William E. *Hidden* †1918 Am. mineralogist + E *-ite*] **:** a transparent yellow to green spodumene valued as a gem — compare KUNZITE

hidden octave *n* **:** an unsounded musical interval of an octave that is implied by the similar up or down motion of two voice parts and that if sounded would produce consecutive octaves

hidden pensioner *n* **:** an employee no longer performing at peak efficiency but retained in service at a wage exceeding his value to the employer

hidden quantity *n, Latin prosody* **:** the quantity of a hidden vowel so situated that its natural quantity is not determinable by scansion (as when it comes before a double consonant or before two or more consecutive consonants other than a mute and a liquid in the same word)

hidden reserve *n* **:** SECRET RESERVE

¹hide \'hīd\ *n* -s [ME *hyde*, fr. OE *hīgid, hīd*; akin to OE *hīwan* members of a household — more at HOME] **:** any of various old English units of land area; *esp* **:** a unit of 120 acres used in the Domesday Book — see CARUCATE, SULUNG

²hide \"\ *vb* **hid** \'hid\ **hidden** \'hidᵊn\ *or* **hid; hiding** \'hīdiŋ\ **hides** \'hīdz\ [ME *hiden*, fr. OE *hȳdan;* akin to MIr *codal* skin, Gk *keuthein* to conceal, Skt *kuhara* cave, OE *hȳd* hide, skin — more at ⁴HIDE] *vt* **1 a :** to deposit in a place of concealment **:** put out of sight **:** SECRETE ⟨~ a key under a doormat⟩ **b :** to conceal for shelter or protection **:** SHIELD ⟨Rock of Ages, cleft for me, let me ~ myself in thee —A.M. Toplady⟩ **2 :** to withhold from someone or from public knowledge **:** keep secret ⟨fled to her room to ~ her grief —Andrew Meredith⟩ ⟨to keep a secret, you must also ~ the fact that you have one to keep —Piero Compton⟩ **3 a :** to screen from view or from detection by the senses **:** cover up ⟨a thick mantle of glacial deposits ~*s* the solid rocks —L.D. Stamp⟩ ⟨the purling water was nearly *hidden* by the birr of wings —Sacheverell Sitwell⟩ ⟨sugar coating ~*s* the taste of pills⟩ **b :** to submerge in something that makes comprehension difficult **:** BURY 3b, OBSCURE ⟨pokes fun at some of his colleagues who ~ their important messages in language only intelligible to other professors —*Word Study*⟩ ⟨facts *hidden* in folklore⟩ ~ *vi* **1 a :** to remain out of sight **:** become concealed ⟨*hid* in the island bushes is a frigate —H.S.Canby⟩ ⟨spongy bogs . . . *hiding* here and there in the woods —John Muir †1914⟩ **b :** to go into or remain in concealment to evade authority or pursuit ⟨fewer places for violators to ~ —*Newsweek*⟩ — often used with *out* or *up* ⟨people who do not wish to have any contact with the military government authorities are . . . *hiding* out on farms —Nora Waln⟩ ⟨went back to the ranch kind of slow to give me time to ~ up —C.T.Jackson⟩ **2 :** to seek protection or evade responsibility **:** take refuge — usu. used with *behind* ⟨~*s* behind dark glasses, hoping to avoid being recognized⟩ ⟨heads of companies who are not . . . gift-minded ~ behind their boards of directors —*Saturday Rev.*⟩ **syn** see CONCEAL — **hide one's face from :** to turn away from **:** IGNORE ⟨I will forsake them and *hide my face from* them, and they will be devoured —Deut 31:17 (RSV)⟩ — **hide one's head 1** *obs* **:** to take shelter or refuge ⟨alack the heavy day when such a sacred king should *hide his head* —Shak.⟩ **2 :** to keep silent for fear of reproach ⟨the pessimists *hid their heads* at the opening of the new century —Oscar Handlin⟩ — **hide one's light under a bushel :** to be excessively modest **:** conceal one's abilities **:** shrink from public notice ⟨a fine poet who *hid her light under a bushel*⟩

³hide \"\ *n* -s **1 :** a hiding place ⟨knew his ~ had to be very good to elude the scrutiny of the local liquor raiders —*Springfield (Mass.) Union*⟩ **2** *Brit* **:** ³BLIND 2 ⟨in shooting at driven lions it is best to wait until they have passed the ~ —James Stevenson-Hamilton⟩

⁴hide \"\ *n* -s *often attrib* [ME *hid, hide*, fr. OE *hȳd;* akin to OHG *hūt* skin, hide, ON *hūth* skin, hide, L *cutis* skin, Gk *kytos* hollow vessel, *skytos* skin, leather, OPruss *keuto* shell, covering, Skt *skunāti* he covers; basic meaning: to cover, conceal] **1 a :** the outer covering of an animal **:** COAT ⟨bald patches of rock like the ~ of a bison when it is shedding —Norman Mailer⟩ **b :** a raw or tanned pelt taken from an adult of one of the larger animals (as a cow) as distinguished from a skin of one of the smaller or younger animals (as a goat or calf) ⟨calfskins . . . produce a softer leather than cattle ~*s* —G.S. Brady⟩ **c :** a piece of dressed pelt used as material for a manufactured article **:** LEATHER ⟨ladies' luggage set, in English ~ —*advt*⟩ **2 a :** the skin of a human being ⟨the had a certain hard brownness of ~ . . . a horny quality in his face and hands —Arthur Morrison⟩ ⟨much of the industrial plant was doubtless built out of the ~*s* of the people —W.O. Douglas⟩ **b :** a covering aspect or front that gives protection against outside pressure ⟨too tough a ~ to have hurt feelings⟩ **c :** LIFE ⟨such strategy often saved the ~ of the Grand Old Party —Dixon Wecter⟩ — **hide or hair** *or* **hide nor hair :** a vestige or trace of a missing person or object ⟨a wife he hadn't seen *hide or hair* of in over 20 years —H.L.Davis⟩ ⟨turned the closet inside out but couldn't find *hide or hair* of the beach umbrella⟩ ⟨no one has seen *hide nor hair* of him since —*Time*⟩

hide 1b: *a b d c* butt; *A B d b, A B c a* bends; *a b f g* shoulder; *E, E,* belly; *D, D,* cheeks; *F* head

⁵hide \"\ *vt* -ED/-ING/-S **:** to give a beating to **:** FLOG ⟨victualed him and clothed him and *hided* him for his own good when he needed it —S.H.Adams⟩

hide and coop *n* [*coop* fr. *coop*, interj. used by players to call out from their hiding places] **:** HIDE-AND-SEEK

¹hide-and-seek \ˌ==ˈ=\ *n* **1** *or* **hide-and-go-seek** \ˌ==(ˌ)=ˈ=\ **:** a children's game in which one player blinds his eyes and after giving the others time to hide goes looking for and tries to catch them — called also *hide-and-coop, hy spy, I spy* **2 :** a procedure resembling the game of hide-and-seek usu. by involving reciprocal deception or evasion ⟨rumrunners playing *hide-and-seek* with government agents —*Amer. Guide Series: Fla.*⟩

²hide-and-seek \"\ *vi* [¹*hide-and-seek*] **:** to play at hide-and-seek ⟨opposing planes *hide-and-seeking* in the darkness —F.V.Drake⟩

¹hideaway \ˈ==ˌ=\ *n* -s [fr. *hide away*, v.] **1 :** a place of retreat or concealment **:** REFUGE ⟨intimate, private ~*s* —P.E. Deutschman⟩ ⟨a ~ . . . used to secrete slaves on the Underground Railway —*Amer. Guide Series: Md.*⟩ **2 :** a small secluded restaurant or place of entertainment ⟨dine-and-dance places, exclusive ~*s* —*Emporia (Kans.) Gazette*⟩

²hideaway \"\ *adj* [fr. *hide away*, v.] **:** CONCEALED, SECLUDED ⟨~ bed⟩ ⟨~ restaurant⟩

hidebound \ˈ=ˌ=\ *adj* [⁴*hide* + *bound*] **1 a :** having a dry skin lacking in pliancy and adhering closely to the underlying flesh and usu. also a rough and lusterless coat esp. as an accompaniment to disease — used of domestic animals **b :** having scleroderma — used of human beings **c :** having the bark so close and constricting that it impedes growth — used of trees **2 a** *obs* **:** sparing in expenditure **:** MISERLY **b :** having an inflexible or ultraconservative character **:** BIGOTED, NARROW ⟨a nature sometimes ~ and selfish and narrow to the last degree —G.G.Coulton⟩ ⟨the most ~ bureaucrat could not have been more obsoletely reactionary, uninventive, and obstructive —G.B.Shaw⟩ ⟨judicial proceedings should not be ~ by arbitrary rules handed down from the past —K. W.Colgrove⟩ — **hide·bound·ness** \ˈhīdˌbau̇ndnəs *also* -ndnəs\ *n* -ES

hideland \ˈ=ˌ=\ *n* [¹*hide* + *land*] **:** ¹HIDE

hide·less \ˈhīdləs\ *adj* [⁴*hide* + *-less*] **:** lacking a hide or skin

hid·eos·i·ty \ˌhidēˈäsəd-ē\ *n* -ES [fr. *hideous*, after such pairs as E *curious : curiosity*] **:** a hideous thing **:** HIDEOUSNESS ⟨the high-water mark of ~ —*Architectural Rev.*⟩ ⟨this vile incrustation of *hideosities* —Dan Wickenden⟩

hid·eous \ˈhidēəs *sometimes* ÷ˈhijəs\ *adj* [alter. (influenced by such words as *courteous*) of ME *hidous*, fr. OF *hisdos, hidous, hideus*, fr. *hisde, hide* terror] **1 a :** offensive to the sight **:** GRUESOME, UGLY ⟨one man still living in ~ squalor among the bones of his fellow travelers —Mabel R. Gillis⟩ ⟨a ~ congeries of fuming kilns —V.S.Pritchett⟩ ⟨writers concerning the warthog generally commence by enlarging upon its ~ appearance —James Stevenson-Hamilton⟩ ⟨a lampshade . . . too ~ for anyone in their senses to buy —W.H.Auden⟩ **b :** offensive to another of the senses **:** FRIGHTFUL, TERRIBLE ⟨the ~ gasping struggle the asthmatic woman was making to get her breath —Leslie Ford⟩ ⟨during the summer this south-ward-facing row of buildings must be ~ with heat —G.R. Stewart⟩ **c :** appallingly large **:** MONSTROUS ⟨the great scar on a mountainside left by the racing snow, and the ~ mass of snow and soil and rock . . . on the valley floor —Russell Henderson⟩ **2 a :** offensive to the mind or to the moral sense **:** HATEFUL, SHOCKING ⟨monstrous and ~ thoughts —J.C.Powys⟩ ⟨a ~ pattern of injustice —Paul Blanshard⟩ **b :** EMBARRASSING, LUDICROUS, DISMAYING ⟨I am in ~ straits about the . . . performance of a play of mine —G.B.Shaw⟩ ⟨a ~ accident attended the serving of the dessert —Jean Stafford⟩ **syn** see UGLY

hid·eous·ly *adv* **:** in a hideous manner ⟨~ snarling white plaster lions —Mollie Panter-Downes⟩

hid·eous·ness *n* -ES **:** the quality or state of being hideous

hideout \ˈ=ˌ=\ *n* -s [fr. *hide out*, v.] **:** a place of refuge, retreat, or concealment ⟨spiriting his lovely client off to a little ~ that he has —Wolcott Gibbs⟩ ⟨had stopped to refuel their car while taking him to their ~ —*Fingerprint Identification*⟩

hideout gun *n* **:** a handgun that can be easily concealed upon the person

hide powder *n* **:** powdered hide usu. specially prepared and standardized for use in the analysis of tannins and tanning materials

hid·er \ˈhīdə(r)\ *n* -s [ME, fr. *hiden* to hide + *-er* — more at HIDE] **:** one that hides

hide rope *n* **1 :** a rope plaited from strips of green hide **2 :** a fiber rope used for tying baled goods (as hides)

hides *pl of* HIDE, *pres 3d sing of* HIDE

hide splitter *n* **:** one that separates the grain layer from the flesh layer of a hide

hide spreader *n* **:** one that spreads raw hides one on top of another to form a pack for curing

hidey-hole *or* **hidy-hole** \ˈhīdēˌhōl\ *n* [alter. of earlier *hiding-hole*] **:** HIDEAWAY 1

¹hiding *n* -s [ME *hidinge*, fr. *hiden* to hide + *-inge* -ing] **1 :** the act or action of hiding; *esp* **:** a withdrawal from one's usual haunts to evade authority or secure privacy ⟨having got into difficulties with the government for his press reports and cartoons, he went into ~ —*Irish Digest*⟩ **2 :** a place or means of concealment ⟨take me to that ~ in the hills —Alfred Tennyson⟩

²hiding *n* -s [fr. gerund of ⁵*hide*] **:** an infliction of physical punishment **:** BEATING ⟨a fighter . . . who had been taking ~*s* in the gymnasium —*Sporting Life*⟩ ⟨the roof of a van really takes a ~ in all weathers —Keith Winser⟩; *esp* **:** WHIPPING ⟨put her over my knee and gave her a ~ —Saul Bellow⟩

hiding power *n* **:** the ability of a paint or painting material to obscure the surface upon which it is applied — distinguished from *coverage*

¹hid·lings \ˈhidlənz, -liŋz\ *or* **hid·lins** \-lənz\ *adv* [ME *hidlinges*, fr. *hid* (past part. of *hiden* to hide) + *-linges* -lings — more at HIDE] *chiefly Scot* **:** in a clandestine manner **:** SECRETLY — usu. used with *in*

²hidlings \"\ *or* **hidlins** \"\ *adj, chiefly Scot* **:** SECRET, CLANDESTINE

hidr- *or* **hidro-** *comb form* [NL, fr. Gk *hidrōs* sweat — more at SWEAT] **:** of or by means of perspiration **:** of the sweat glands ⟨*hidr*adenitis⟩ ⟨*hidro*cystoma⟩

hidrad·e·ni·tis \ˌhiˌdradᵊnˈīd-əs, ˌhī,-\ *n* [NL, fr. *hidr-* + *adenitis*] **:** inflammation of a sweat gland

hi·dro·sis \hiˈdrōsəs, hīˈ-\ *n, pl* **hidro·ses** \-ōˌsēz\ [NL, fr. Gk *hidrōsis*, fr. *hidrōt-*, *hidrōs* sweat + *-sis*] **:** excretion of sweat **:** PERSPIRATION

hi·drot·ic \(ˈ)=ˈdräd·ik\ *adj* [Gk *hidrōtikos*, fr. *hidrōt-*, *hidrōs* sweat + *-ikos* -ic] **:** causing perspiration **:** DIAPHORETIC, SUDORIFIC

¹hie \ˈhī\ *vb* **hied; hied; hying** *or* **hieing** \ˈhīiŋ\ **hies** [ME *hien*, fr. OE *hīgian* to strive, be eager, hasten; akin to OSw *hikka* to pant, Norw, to sob, Russ *sigat'* to jump, Skt *śīghra* quick] *vi* **:** to go quickly **:** HASTEN ⟨thither we advise you to ~ —*New Yorker*⟩ ~ *vt* **:** to cause (oneself) to go quickly ⟨*hied* myself to the post office —H.A.Chippendale⟩

²hie \ˈhē\ *chiefly Scot var of* HIGH

hie·lan *or* **hie·land** \ˈhēlən(d), -nt\ *Scot var of* HIGHLAND

hield *vi* -ED/-ING/-S [ME *helden, heelden, hielden* — more at HEEL] *obs* **:** TILT, LEAN, HEEL ⟨let it be laid in a dish ~*ing* toward the one side —Peter Morwen⟩

hie·le·man *or* **hee·la·man** *or* **hei·la·man** \ˈhēləmən\ *n* -s [native name in Australia] **:** an elongated wooden shield used by Australian aborigines

hielmite *var of* HJELMITE

hi·emal \ˈhīəməl\ *adj* [L *hiemalis*, fr. *hiem-*, *hiems* winter + *-alis* -al — more at HIBERNATE] **:** of or relating to winter **:** WINTRY

hieng \hēˈeŋ\ *n, pl* **hieng** *or* **hiengs** *usu cap* **1 :** a mountain people of Cambodia **2 :** a member of the Hieng people

hie on *vt* **:** to rouse to quick action **:** urge on ⟨*hie on* a hound⟩

hier- *or* **hiero-** *comb form* [LL, fr. Gk, fr. *hieros* powerful, supernatural, holy, sacred — more at IRE] **:** sacred **:** holy ⟨*hier*archy⟩ ⟨*hiero*glyph⟩

hiera *pl of* HIERON

hi·er·a·cite \ˈhīərəˌsīt, hīˈerəˌs-, ˌhīəˈrāˌs-\ *or* **hi·er·a·cian** \ˌhīəˈrāshən\ *n* -s *usu cap* [*Hieracite* fr. LL *Hieracita*, fr. *Hieracas*, 4th cent. A.D. Egyptian ascetic + L *-ita* -ite; *Hieracian* fr. *Hieracas* + E *-ian*] **:** a follower of the ascetic Hieracas

hi·er·a·ci·um \ˌhīəˈrāshēəm\ *n* [NL, fr. Gk *hierakion* hawkweed, fr. *hierak-*, *hierax* hawk, fr. *hienai* to hurry — more at VIA] **1** *cap* **:** a very large and nearly cosmopolitan genus of weedy perennial herbs (family Compositae) having simple often basal leaves and heads of yellow or reddish orange ray flowers — see ORANGE HAWKWEED **2** *pl* **hieracia** *also* **hieraciums :** any plant of the genus *Hieracium*

hi·er·a·co·sphinx \ˌhīəˈrākə+ˌ-\ *n* [Gk *hierako-* (fr. *hierak-*, *hierax* hawk) + E *sphinx*] **:** a hawk-headed sphinx

hi·era pic·ra \ˌhīərəˈpikrə\ *n* [ML, lit., powerful or sacred antidote] **:** a cathartic powder made of aloes and canella bark

hi·er·arch \ˈhīəˌrärk, -ˌräk *also* ˈhīˌr-\ *n* -s [MF or ML; MF *hierarche*, fr. ML *hierarcha*, fr. Gk *hierarchēs*, fr. *hier-* + *-archēs* -arch] **1 :** a religious leader holding high office or vested with controlling authority **:** chief prelate **:** HIGH PRIEST ⟨the important central painting . . . shows the apostolic succession of ~*s* —W.E.Needham⟩ ⟨steps taken by the British East India Company to . . . establish relations with the Tibetan ~*s* —Beatrice D. Miller⟩ **2 :** one having authority or pontifical dignity resembling that of a hierarch ⟨former ministers, generals, blackshirt ~*s* —Janet Flanner⟩ ⟨proceed with the utmost decorum and in what the ~*s* . . . considered the best of Senate tradition —*N.Y. Times Mag.*⟩

hi·er·ar·chal \ˌhīəˈrärkəl, -ˈräk- *also* (ˈ)hīˈr-\ *or* **hi·er·ar·chi·al** \-kēəl\ *adj* **:** HIERARCHICAL — **hi·er·ar·chal·ly** \ˌ==ˈ=kəlē, (ˈ)=ˈ=kəlē, -li\ *or* **hi·er·ar·chi·al·ly** \-kēəlē, -li\ *adv*

hi·er·ar·chi·cal \-kəkəl, -kēk-\ *or* **hi·er·ar·chic** \-kik, -kēk\ *adj* [MF or ML; MF *hierarchique*, fr. ML *hierarchicus*, fr. *hierarchia* + L *-icus* -ic, -ical] **1 :** of, relating to, or controlled by a religious hierarchy ⟨the liturgy of the mass presupposes . . . the ~ order of church and society corresponds to the divine hierarchy —Jacob Taubes⟩ **2 a :** of an authoritarian or aristocratic character **:** STRATIFIED ⟨although the ~ federal arrangement is typical, there are many organizations which are unitary —D.D.McKean⟩ ⟨only a ~ society with a leisure class at the top can produce works of art —*Partisan Rev.*⟩ **b :** having the power to control **:** INFLUENTIAL ⟨a denial . . . due to pressure from a political or ~ source interfering with the due course of judicial proceedings —M.R.Cohen⟩ **3 :** of or relating to a classification of people according to artistic, social, economic, or other criteria ⟨a ~ feeling has grown up in Italy about the standings of the artists —R.M.Coates⟩ ⟨the ~ status of a child in relation to other members of the family —Norman Cameron⟩ ⟨the tailor, department head, and floor supervisor were summoned, appealed to, and appalled in *hierarchic* succession —Marvin Barrett⟩ **4 :** of, relating to, or constituting a related series **:** SEQUENTIAL ⟨the ~ arrangement of cultures constructed by the 19th century anthropologists —Henry Orenstein⟩ — **hi·er·ar·chi·cal·ly** \-k(ə)lē, -kēk-, -li\ *adv*

hi·er·ar·chism \ˈhīəˌrärˌkizəm, -ˌräk- *also* ˈhīˌr- *n* -s **:** the system or authority of a hierarchy

hi·er·ar·chi·za·tion \(ˌ)=(ˌ)=kəˈzāshən, -ˌkīˈz-\ *n* -s **1 :** the act or process of establishing a hierarchy ⟨~ . . . leads to a clear-cut stratification of all members of any organized group —P.A.Sorokin⟩ **2 :** the quality or state of being a hierarchy ⟨the traditional ~ of the three orders of abstraction —F.G. Connolly⟩

hi·er·ar·chize \ˈhīəˌrärˌkīz, -ˌräk- *also* ˈhīˌr-\ *vt* -ED/-ING/-S **:** to arrange hierarchically ⟨*hierarchized* systems of organization —C.H.Page⟩

hi·er·ar·chy \ˈhīəˌrärkē, -ˌräk-, -ki *also* ˈhīˌr-\ *n* -ES [ME *ierarchie*, fr. MF *ierarchie, hierarchie*, fr. ML *hierarchia*, fr. LGk, fr. Gk *hierarchēs* + *-ia* -y] **1 :** a rank or order of holy beings — *see* CELESTIAL HIERARCHY **2 :** a form of government administered by an authoritarian group ⟨the company town implies a ~ despotically, if benevolently, guiding the lives of those beneath —W.H.Whyte⟩ ⟨the ~ relates all units in vertical levels of responsibility —J.E.Pate⟩; *esp* **:** control exercised by a priesthood ⟨unlimited centralization of ecclesiastical ~ —A.C.N.Gallenga⟩ **3 a :** an authoritarian body of religious officials organized by rank and jurisdiction ⟨the priest, with the ~ at his back, was in theory almost everything to his people —G.G.Coulton⟩ ⟨three cardinals and 65 bishops attended the annual meeting of the American ~ —*Official Catholic Yearbook*⟩ ⟨the power . . . of the great Buddhist ~ is nothing less than stupendous —Edith Hamilton⟩ **b :** a controlling group of any kind ⟨when all power is centered in the top ~ of a single party, there is none left over to serve as a check against the ruling class —A.M.Schlesinger b.1917⟩ ⟨officials at the pinnacle of the mobilization ~ —*Wall Street Jour.*⟩ ⟨the publisher who has . . . exceeded his proper function by becoming the head and dictator of the newspaper ~ —Alistair Cooke⟩ ⟨at the bottom of the ~ of managerial personnel are the foremen —Kurt Braun⟩ ⟨rising steadily in the ~ of the local Boy Scouts —Brendan Gill⟩ **4 a :** the classification of a group of people with regard to ability or economic or social standing ⟨the function of true criticism is to establish a definite ~ among the great artists of the past —C.W.Shumaker⟩ ⟨continuous waves of new immigrants, each pushing the preceding waves upward in the ethnic ~ —Richard Hofstadter⟩ ⟨the seating arrangement was an accurate index of the Hollywood ~ —Budd Schulberg⟩ **b :** a group of people so classified ⟨made his way into the ~ of business families in Montreal —Hugh MacLennan⟩ **c :** the status attaching to such a group ⟨the social ~ that may be associated with possessions —Ruth Benedict⟩; *specif* **:** a graded series of social statuses or class levels ⟨upper and lower class ~ in a community⟩ **5 a :** the arrangement of objects, elements, or values in a graduated series ⟨the ~ of occupations is based on the degree of skill and responsibility they entail⟩ ⟨government officials determine the ~ of importance of affairs of state⟩ **b :** a series of objects, elements, or values so arranged ⟨the Supreme Court is the head of a ~ of federal courts —Felix Frankfurter⟩ ⟨in the multicellular organism there is a ~ of levels — cells, tissues, organs —A.B.Novikoff⟩; *specif, logic* **:** a series the members of which are grouped in accordance with a principle (as of importance, perfection or priority) ⟨~ of values⟩ ⟨an ontological ~ in which the objects of knowledge are arranged in an ascending order of reality —George Boas⟩ **c :** the stratification so achieved ⟨a rigid ~ of clubs —R.M.Lovett⟩; *specif* **:** a table of statistical correlations having a constant proportional relationship and graded from high to low

¹hi·er·at·ic \ˌhīəˈrad·ik *also* (ˈ)hīˈr-\ *adj* [L *hieraticus*, fr. Gk *hieratikos*, fr. (assumed) *hieratos* (verbal of *hierasthai* to be a priest, fr. *hieros* powerful, supernatural, holy, sacred) + *-ikos* -ic — more at IRE] **1 :** written in, constituting, or belonging to a cursive form of ancient Egyptian writing simpler and less pictorial than the hieroglyphic ⟨only those who served in the temples knew the secret of the ~ writing —W.M.James⟩ — see DEMOTIC 2 **2** *also* **hi·er·at·i·cal** \-d·əkəl\ **:** of, relating to, or associated with priestly functions **:** SACERDOTAL ⟨the gestures ~ as if from some slow and ancient ritual —Hallam Tennyson⟩ ⟨~ art of the church —Herbert Read⟩ ⟨the powerful ~ sculpture of the Aztecs —B.D. Wolfe⟩ — **hi·er·at·i·cal·ly** \-d·ək(ə)lē\ *adv*

²hieratic \"\ *n* -s **:** a cursive form of ancient Egyptian writing ⟨the oldest dated papyrus . . . is written in ~ —H.B.Van Hoesen & F.K.Walter⟩

hi·er·a·tite \ˈhīərəˌtīt\ *n* -s [It, fr. *Hiera* (Vulcano), one of the Lipari islands, Italy + It *-ite*] **:** a mineral K_2SiF_6 consisting of potassium fluosilicate found as grayish concretions in the fumaroles of Vulcano

-hi·er·ic \ˌhīˈerik, -rēk\ *adj comb form* [Gk *hieron* (*osteon*) sacrum (fr. hieron — neut. of *hieros* powerful, sacred — + *osteon* bone) + E *-ic* — more at IRE] **:** having (such) a sacrum ⟨dolicho*hieric*⟩ ⟨platy*hieric*⟩

hiero- — see HIER-

hi·er·och·loe \ˌhīəˈräklə(ˌ)wē\ *n, cap* [NL, fr. *hier-* + Gk *chloē* young grass] **:** a genus of aromatic perennial grasses native to temperate and cold regions having spikelets with a perfect terminal floret and two staminate florets — see HOLY GRASS

hi·er·oc·ra·cy \-kräsē\ *n* -ES [*hier-* + *-cracy*] **:** government by ecclesiastics **:** HIERARCHY

hi·er·o·crat·ic \ˌhī(ə)rəˈkrad·ik\ *or* **hi·er·o·crat·i·cal** \-d·əkəl\ *adj* [fr. *hierocracy*, after such pairs as E *democracy: democratic, democratical*] **:** of or relating to government by ecclesiastics (as priests or prelates)

hi·er·o·dule \ˈhī(ə)rəˌd(y)ül, hīˈer-\ *n* -s [LL *hierodulus*, fr. Gk *hierodoulos*, fr. *hier-* + *doulos* slave] **:** a slave attached to the service of a temple; *esp* **:** a sacred prostitute in ancient Greece

hi·er·o·du·lic \ˌhī(ə)rəˈd(y)ülik, (ˌ)hīˌer-\ *adj* **:** of or relating to a hierodule

¹hi·er·o·glyph \ˈhī(ə)rəˌglif, -rō-\ *n* -s [F *hiéroglyphe*, fr. MF *hieroglyphe*, back-formation fr. *hieroglyphique*] **1 :** a character used in a system of hieroglyphic writing ⟨Maya ~*s* were sculptured or . . . incised on stone stelae —J.E.S.Thompson⟩ esp. in ancient Egypt ⟨~*s* often occur on monuments written vertically and from left to right —J.E.M.White⟩ — compare IDEOGRAM **2 :** something that resembles a hieroglyph in form or symbolism ⟨the river glistened in a ~ across the country —D.H.Lawrence⟩ ⟨at the corners of her eyes and mouth were written the decipherable ~*s* of disillusion —Helen Howe⟩ ⟨symbolic ~*s* consisting of nothing more than a few brush strokes —*Times Lit. Supp.*⟩

²hieroglyph \"\ *vt* -ED/-ING/-S **:** to express in or inscribe with hieroglyphs ⟨the first ~*ed* sarcophagus we had yet seen —Amelia B. Edwards⟩

¹hi·er·o·glyph·ic \ˌ==(=)=ˈglifik, -fēk\ *or* **hi·er·o·glyph·i·cal** \-fəkəl, -fēk-\ *adj* [*hieroglyphic* fr. MF *hieroglyphique*, fr. LL *hieroglyphicus*, fr. Gk *hieroglyphikos*, fr. *hier-* + *glyphikos* of carving; *hieroglyphical* fr. MF *hieroglyphique* + E *-al* — more at GLYPHIC] **1 a :** written in, constituting, or belonging to that form of ancient Egyptian writing in which the characters are for the most part recognizable pictures of objects — compare DEMOTIC, HIERATIC **b :** written in, constituting, or belonging to any system of writing in which the characters are to a substantial degree recognizable pictures ⟨finest of the three surviving Maya ~ books —J.E.S.Thompson⟩ **2 :** inscribed with hieroglyphic characters ⟨~ obelisk⟩ **3 :** resembling hieroglyphic in form ⟨coleus mosaic — causing . . . ~ markings on leaves —*Experiment Station Record*⟩, symbolism ⟨~ emblem⟩, or illegibility ⟨the most ~ of prescriptions —H.V. Morton⟩ ⟨*hieroglyphical* entries in thick, half-obliterated pencil —Bram Stoker⟩ — **hi·er·o·glyph·i·cal·ly** \-fək(ə)lē, -fēk-, -li\ *adv*

²hieroglyphic \"\ *n* -s **1 :** HIEROGLYPH 1 **2 :** a system of hieroglyphic writing ⟨a German philologist . . . started the decipherment of Hittite ~ —C.J.Rolo⟩; *specif* **:** the picture script of the ancient Egyptian priesthood ⟨the elaborate ~ . . . was too slow and laborious a method of writing for the needs of everyday business —J.H.Breasted⟩ — often used in pl. but sing. or pl. in constr. **3 :** something that resembles a hieroglyphic in form, symbolic content, or difficulty of decipherment ⟨the frightening ~*s* of . . . shorthand —*advt*⟩ ⟨the traditional ~ that was said to identify for tramps the houses where meals were certain —Ben Riker⟩ ⟨the *hieroglyphic*-covered blackboard —Philip Hamburger⟩

hieroglyphics (Egyptian)

³hieroglyphic *vt* [²*hieroglyphic*] *obs* **:** HIEROGLYPH

hieroglyphic hittite *n, usu cap both Hs* **:** a language related to cuneiform Hittite and known from inscriptions in the Hittite hieroglyphic writing — see INDO-EUROPEAN LANGUAGES table

hi·er·o·glyph·ist \ˌ==(=)ˈglifəst, ˈ=(=)=ˌ==; ˌhīəˈräglәf-, hīˈrä-\ *n* -s **:** a writer of hieroglyphics

hi·er·o·gram \'hī(ə)rə,gram\ *n* [*hier-* + *-gram*] **:** a sacred emblem or graphic symbol

hi·er·o·gram·mat \,hī(ə)rə'gramət, -,mat\ *or* **hi·er·o·gram·mate** \-,mət, -,māt\ *n* -s [Gk *hierogrammateus,* fr. *hier-* + *grammateus* scribe, fr. *grammat-, gramma* letter, writing — more at GRAMMAR] **:** a writer of sacred records esp. in hieroglyphics

hi·er·o·gram·mat·ic \,hī(ə)rəgrə'mad·ik\ *or* **hi·er·o·gram·mat·i·cal** \-d·əkəl\ *adj* [*hier-* + Gk *grammat-, gramma* letter, writing + E *-ic, -ical*] **:** of or relating to hierograms

hi·er·o·graph \'hī(ə)rə,graf, -rȧf\ *n* [*hier-* + *-graph*] **:** HIEROGRAM — **hi·er·o·graph·ic** \¦=(=)=¦grafik\ *or* **hi·er·o·graph·i·cal** \-fəkəl\ *adj*

hi·er·og·ra·phy \,hīə'rägrəfē, hī'r-\ *n* -ES [LGk *hierographia,* fr. Gk *hier-* + *-graphia* -graphy] **:** descriptive writing on sacred subjects **:** a treatise on religion

hi·er·ol·a·try \-älə·trē\ *n* -ES [*hier-* + *-latry*] **:** worship of saints or sacred things

hi·er·o·log·ic \¦hī(ə)rə¦läjik\ *or* **hi·er·o·log·i·cal** \-jəkəl\ *adj* **:** of or relating to hierology

hi·er·ol·o·gist \,hīə'räləjəst, hī'r-\ *n* -s **:** one skilled in hierology

hi·er·ol·o·gy \-jē\ *n* -ES [*hier-* + *-logy*] **1 :** a body of knowledge of sacred things **:** the literary or traditional embodiment of the religious beliefs of a people ⟨the ~ of Greece⟩ **2 :** HAGIOLOGY

hi·er·o·mon·ach \,hī(ə)rō'mänək, -ä,nak; ,hīə'rämə,nak\ *n* -s [LGk or MGk *hieromonachos,* fr. Gk *hier-* + *monachos* monk — more at MONK] **:** HIEROMONK

hi·er·o·monk \'hī(ə)rō,məŋk\ *n* [part. trans. of LGk or MGk *hieromonachos*] **:** a monk of the Eastern Church who is also a priest

hi·er·on \'hīə,rän\ *n, pl* **hi·era** \-ərə\ [Gk, fr. neut. of *hieros* holy, sacred — more at IRE] **:** a consecrated place (as a temple) in ancient Greece

hi·er·o·nym·ic \¦hī(ə)rə¦nimik\ *also* **hi·er·o·nym·i·an** \-mēən\ *adj, usu cap* [Eusebius *Hieronymus* (St. Jerome) †420 church father + E *-ic* or *-ian*] **:** of, relating to, or composed by St. Jerome ⟨the *Hieronymic* version of the Bible⟩

hi·er·on·y·mite \,hīə'ränə,mīt, hī'r-\ *also* **hi·er·o·nym·i·an** \,hī(ə)rə'nimēən\ *n* -s *usu cap* [Eusebius *Hieronymus* + E *-ite* or *-ian*] **:** a member of any of various hermit orders named in honor of St. Jerome

hi·er·o·phant \'hī(ə)rə,fant; hī'erə,fant, -,fənt\ *n* -s [LL *hierophanta, hierophantes,* fr. Gk *hierophantēs,* fr. *hier-* + *-phantēs* (fr. *phainein* to reveal, show, make known) — more at FANCY] **1 :** a priest in ancient Greece ⟨a ~ . . . dressed in a fawn skin, with a crown of poplar leaves —L.P.Smith⟩; *specif* **:** the chief priest of the Eleusinian mysteries **2 a :** a spokesman or interpreter ⟨the ~ of Beauty, the dedicated poet of the cult —F.R.Leavis⟩ ⟨the molder and ~ of the national life —Van Wyck Brooks⟩ **b :** a leading advocate ⟨sociologists have long been ~s of methodology —R.K.Merton⟩

hi·er·o·phan·tic \¦hī(ə)rə¦fantik, (¦)hī¦er-\ *adj* [Gk *hierophantikos,* fr. *hierophantēs* + *-ikos* -ic] **:** of, relating to, or resembling a hierophant — **hi·er·o·phan·ti·cal·ly** \-tək(ə)lē\ *adv*

hi·er·o·sol·y·mi·tan \,hī(ə)rō¦sälə¦mītᵊn\ *adj, usu cap* [LL *Hierosolymitanus,* fr. *Hierosolyma* Jerusalem (fr. Gk *Hierosolyma*) + L *-ita* -ite + *-anus* -an] **:** of or relating to the city of Jerusalem

hi·er·ur·gi·cal \¦hīə¦rərjəkəl, (')hī¦r-\ *adj* **:** of or relating to hierurgy

hi·er·ur·gy \'hīə,rərjē, -ī,rər-\ *n* -ES [Gk *hierourgia,* fr. *hierourgos* sacrificing priest (fr. *hier-* + *-ergos,* fr. *ergon* work) + *-ia* -y] **:** an act or rite of worship **:** LITURGY

hies *pl of* HIE, *pres 3d sing of* HIE

hifalutin *var of* HIGHFALUTIN

¹hi-fi \'hī'fī\ *n* -s [*high fidelity*] **1 :** HIGH FIDELITY **2 :** the equipment needed to play high-fidelity recordings ⟨to own *hi-fi* is to join a community of music lovers —Brooks Atkinson⟩ **3 :** the practice of listening to high-fidelity recordings as a pastime ⟨up to the present, *hi-fi* has been largely . . . the hobby of the enthusiastic amateur —Thomas Heinitz⟩

²hi-fi \'=¦=\ *adj* **1 :** of or relating to hi-fi ⟨*hi-fi* fan⟩ ⟨*hi-fi* range⟩ **2 :** characterized by high fidelity ⟨*hi-fi* recording⟩ **3 :** designed to reproduce hi-fi recordings ⟨*hi-fi* phonograph⟩

hi-flash \'hī¦=\ *adj* [*high flash*] **:** having a high flash point — used esp. of solvents ⟨*hi-flash* naphtha⟩

hig·gle \'higəl\ *vi* **higgled; higgled; higgling** \-g(ə)liŋ\ **higgles** [prob. alter. of ¹*haggle*] **:** to bargain for small advantages (as in buying and selling) **:** HAGGLE, CHAFFER ⟨the purchaser *higgling* about the odd cent —Walt Whitman⟩

¹hig·gle·dy-pig·gle·dy *also* **hig·gle·ty-pig·gle·ty** \¦higəld|ē-¦pigəld|ē, -lt| . . . lt|, |ī, . . . |ī\ *adv* [origin unknown] **:** in confusion **:** without order or coherence **:** TOPSY-TURVY ⟨everything was heaped *higgledy-piggledy* on the luggage racks —Leonide Zarine⟩

²higgledy-piggledy *also* **higgléty-piggléty** \"\ *adj* **:** CONFUSED, JUMBLED ⟨a *higgledy-piggledy* patchwork of . . . overlapping powers —F.D.Roosevelt⟩

hig·gler \'hig(ə)lə(r)\ *n* -s **:** an itinerant peddler **:** HAWKER ⟨is as a rule sold to ~s —T.D.Marsh⟩ ⟨belonged to a local ~ . . . a man that used the roads buying poultry for resale —F.M. Ford⟩

¹high \'hī\ *adj* -ER/-EST [ME *hegh, hey, high,* fr. OE *hēah;* akin to OHG *hōh* high, ON *hār,* Goth *hauhs* high, L *cacumen* top, point, OIr *cūar* bent, crooked, Skt *kucati* he contracts, bends, curves; basic meaning: bending] **1 a** (1) **:** having a relatively great upward extension **:** LOFTY ⟨a ~ tree⟩ ⟨a ~ mountain⟩ (2) **:** being at or rising to a considerable elevation above the ground or other base **:** ELEVATED ⟨a ~ leap⟩ ⟨a ~ plateau⟩ (3) **:** of, relating to, or located on highlands or a plateau ⟨*High* Asia⟩ (4) *of a person* **:** TALL (5) **:** having a specified altitude or elevation ⟨a new office building 10 stories ~⟩ — often used in combination ⟨knee-*high*⟩ ⟨sky-*high*⟩ (6) **:** articulated with some part of the tongue close to the palate ⟨\ē\, \i\, \ü\, and \u\ are ~ vowels⟩ (7) **:** pitched above shoulder height ⟨a ~ ball⟩ **b** (1) **:** advanced toward its acme or fullest extent ⟨it was now ~ June —Guy McCrone⟩ **:** advanced toward its most active or culminating period ⟨an Italian vacation during the ~ season —*N.Y. Times*⟩; *specif* **:** constituting the late, fully developed, or most creative stage or period (as of an artistic style or career or historical movement) ⟨*High* Baroque⟩ ⟨*High* Gothic⟩ ⟨the ~ period of William Faulkner's work —M.D.Geismar⟩ ⟨the ~ middle ages⟩ (2) none too early **:** verging on lateness — usu. used in the phrase *high time* ⟨~ time . . . that your mother came home —Isa Glenn⟩ (3) **:** acute in pitch **:** SHARP, SHRILL ⟨a ~ tone⟩ ⟨a ~ alto voice⟩ ⟨she heard the ~ giggles of the . . . young men —Louis Auchincloss⟩ **:** RAISED, LOUD ⟨"halt!" he called in a ~ voice⟩; *also* **:** of or relating to those musical notes or tones in the three-line or thrice-accented octave esp. in singing ⟨she sang a ~ C easily⟩ (4) **:** long past **:** ANCIENT, REMOTE ⟨the use of which goes back . . . to a ~ antiquity —Edward Clodd⟩ (5) **:** being far toward one of the poles with the equator as base — used chiefly in the phrase *high latitude* (6) **:** being near the wind — used of a ship or its head when pointing close to the wind (7) **:** being toward the middle or near the end of a series of compounds ⟨~*er* alcohols containing six or more carbon atoms⟩ (8) **:** having a complex organization **:** greatly differentiated or developed phylogenetically — usu. used in the comparative degree of advanced types of animals and plants ⟨the ~*er* algae⟩ ⟨the ~*er* apes⟩ (9) **:** sexually mature and active ⟨~ males of the species⟩ (10) **:** exhausted of nearly all air or gas ⟨~ vacuum⟩ **c** (1) **:** of relatively great degree, size, or amount ⟨gambling for ~ stakes⟩ ⟨unemployment was ~⟩ ⟨the ~ cost of living⟩ ⟨enjoyed a ~ standard of living⟩ ⟨moved at a ~ speed⟩ ⟨going into the market at the time of ~ business —Samuel Johnson⟩ ⟨an automobile engine having ~ compression⟩ (2) **:** dear in price **:** EXPENSIVE ⟨everything is so ~ nowadays⟩ (3) **:** VIOLENT, STRONG, VEHEMENT ⟨a ~ wind came up⟩ ⟨the ~ passions of this hour⟩ **:** marked by high waves ⟨a ~ sea⟩ (4) **:** containing a relatively great amount ⟨a food ~ in iron⟩ (5) **:** having more value than another card ⟨the queen is ~*er* than the jack⟩ **:** capable of taking a trick ⟨the nine is ~⟩ (6) **:** giving the highest ratio of propeller-shaft to engine-shaft speed and the lowest multiplication of torque ⟨a ~ transmission gear⟩ ⟨in ~ gear⟩ **d** (1) **:** INTENSE, EXTREME ⟨people of ~ anxiety —Vance Packard⟩ ⟨~ disfavor in her face —Edna Ferber⟩ ⟨the boys were in ~ glee —H.A. Chippendale⟩ ⟨the ~ brilliance of this gem⟩ ⟨my . . . uncle's ~ disapproval —Joyce Cary⟩ ⟨the ~ seriousness . . . and the sound scholarship which inform his work —C.I.Glicksberg⟩ ⟨his hopes were ~⟩ (2) **:** RICH, LUXURIOUS ⟨indulged in a brief but reckless period of ~ living —H.M.Skala⟩ (3) **:** marked by a pink or rosy glow or flush **:** FLORID ⟨a large, personable widow, with a . . . ~ complexion —Dorothy Sayers⟩ ⟨a sturdy, handsome, *high*-colored woman —Carl Van Doren⟩; *also* **:** BRIGHT, PRONOUNCED ⟨fall styles in ~ shades —*N. Y. Times*⟩ ⟨~ flesh tints play a major part in the tonal organization of the picture —Bernard Smith⟩ (4) **:** strong-scented **:** slightly tainted ⟨should cook game when it is ~⟩; *also* **:** MALODOROUS, STINKING ⟨dead . . . had been there since yesterday, and they were plenty ~ —Shelby Foote⟩ ⟨found their blankets a little ~ for civilized noses —Jackson Burgess⟩ (5) **:** INTENSIVE ⟨made their localities into symbols of ~ farming —A.W.Smith⟩ ⟨the first systematic efforts at ~ breeding —E.D. Ross⟩ **2 :** elevated or advanced in rank, quality, or character: as **a** (1) **:** of exalted social or political standing **:** ARISTOCRATIC, POWERFUL ⟨~ society consisting of the Spaniards and Creoles of property —C.L.Jones⟩ ⟨mainly concerned with Roman ~ life —William Murray⟩ ⟨a ~ official of the government⟩ (2) **:** of the first or great consequence **:** IMPORTANT, SUPREME ⟨primarily a parliament is a ~ court of justice —A.F.Pollard⟩ ⟨~ preparations were necessary for this journey —Herbert Hoover⟩ **:** GRAVE, SERIOUS ⟨a ~ insult⟩ ⟨aroused ~ displeasure⟩ **:** CRITICAL, CLIMACTIC ⟨at this ~ hour of Australia's history —W.F.Hambly⟩ ⟨the ~ moments were the start in the freshness of morning —John Buchan⟩ ⟨the ~ point of the novel is the escape⟩ ⟨the ~ spot of the Republican doings will come Friday night —*Spokane (Wash.) Spokesman-Rev.*⟩ (3) **:** relating to matters of the first importance **:** conducted on an exalted political or social level ⟨offered a fertile field for ~ intrigue —Carl Bridenbaugh⟩ ⟨born into the world of ~ politics⟩ (4) **:** rating or ranking as best, first, or most eligible ⟨the ~ man among entrants in the tryout⟩ ⟨if a bidder should be the ~ bidder on a facility —*U. S. Code*⟩ **b** (1) **:** morally or spiritually exalted **:** NOBLE, EDIFYING ⟨a man of ~ character⟩ ⟨met his death in the ~ Roman fashion —John Buchan⟩ ⟨writing is a ~ calling —Cyril Connolly⟩ ⟨good intent and ~ purpose are not enough —D.D.Eisenhower⟩ ⟨~ thinking and plain living⟩ (2) **:** intellectually or artistically of the first order **:** EXCELLENT ⟨the ~ tradition of the European fairy story and folk tale —*Brit. Book News*⟩ ⟨a theatrical production of ~ quality⟩ (3) **:** preeminent among or surpassing other civilizations or societies by some criteria ⟨the ~ civilizations of Middle America and the Andean Highlands —Holger Cahill⟩ (4) **:** characterized by sublime, heroic, or stirring events or subject matter **:** intensely moving **:** EXCITING ⟨a tale of ~ adventure⟩ ⟨~ romance and profound sympathy for the proletariat appear side by side in the poetry —*Encyc. Americana*⟩ ⟨the act in which she faces her accusers is ~ drama⟩ ⟨the ~ tragedy ends with both . . . dying but clasping each other's hands —Leslie Rees⟩ (5) **:** depending not so much on situation as on fine characterization and witty dialogue ⟨~ comedy⟩ (6) **:** conforming to some standard of correctness or excellence in speech or grammar ⟨the ~ Arabic of the Koran —J.C.Swaim⟩ (7) **:** not of the ordinary or routine sort **:** EXTRAVAGANT, BOISTEROUS ⟨an hour for ~ . . . nonsense —Elinor Wylie⟩ ⟨held ~ revelry at the castle that night⟩ ⟨along with her went excitement and ~ occasion —Nadine Gordimer⟩ **c :** difficult to comprehend or master **:** RECONDITE, ABSTRUSE ⟨when it comes to philosophy, ~ thought, and the eternal verities —Bergen Evans⟩ **3 a** (1) **:** indicating or reflecting anger **:** WRATHFUL ⟨saw there were going to be ~ words —Dodie Smith⟩ ⟨threatening them in very ~ language —George Willison⟩ (2) **:** ARROGANT, OVERBEARING, IMPERIOUS ⟨carry things with a ~ hand —John Buchan⟩ ⟨you certainly take a very ~ tone —Louis Auchincloss⟩ (3) **:** PRETENTIOUS, AMBITIOUS ⟨a ~ boast, but it is true —W.R.Inge⟩ ⟨makes ~ claims for his invention⟩ **b** (1) **:** ZEALOUS, EAGER, FAVORABLE, KEEN — usu. used with *on* ⟨is unusually ~ on her next venture —Lewis Funke⟩ ⟨has been particularly ~ on him —*Newsweek*⟩ (2) **:** extreme, devoted, or rigid in advocacy or practice esp. in matters of doctrine or ceremony ⟨hated as the leader of ~ toryism —*Brit. Book News*⟩; *specif, usu cap* **:** HIGH CHURCH **c** (1) **:** ELATED, GAY, CHEERFUL ⟨she hadn't the ~ spirits which endear grown-ups to healthy children —Joseph Conrad⟩ ⟨had a ~ old time together⟩ ⟨his heart was ~ as he entered the old homestead⟩ ⟨those were the ~ days —Sinclair Lewis⟩ (2) **:** hysterically or feverishly excited or gay **:** keyed up ⟨so ~ from nervous tension . . . they need half a dozen drinks to sober down —Alfred Bester⟩ ⟨like a ~ patient after shock treatment —Joseph Hitrec⟩ (3) **:** INTOXICATED, DRUNK ⟨getting ~*er* all the time by nipping at . . . martinis —Daniel Curley⟩ ⟨~ as a kite⟩; *also* **:** excited or stupefied by a narcotic substance (as heroin)

syn TALL, LOFTY: HIGH, the most general of these terms, implies marked extension upward, usu. from a base or foundation, or placement at a conspicuous height above the ground or above some lower level taken as the norm ⟨a *high* building⟩ ⟨a *high* cliff⟩ ⟨a *high* cupboard⟩ In extension it is often used to indicate a great degree of what it modifies or to stress a certain moral elevation ⟨a *high* color⟩ ⟨a *high* volume of sound⟩ ⟨a *high* purpose⟩ TALL applies to what rises or grows high by comparison with others of its kind, esp. when it is small in breadth as compared to its height ⟨a *tall* man⟩ ⟨a *tall* flagpole⟩ LOFTY, suggesting a greater, more imposing altitude than HIGH or TALL, has a much wider figurative than literal application carrying the idea of moral grandeur, dignity, or stature or of superciliousness ⟨a *lofty* mountain⟩ ⟨a *lofty* position in the church⟩ ⟨a *lofty* plane of conversation⟩ ⟨a *lofty* attitude toward servants⟩

²high \"\ *adv* -ER/-EST [ME *heghe, heye, highe, high,* fr. OE *hēah, hēage,* fr. *hēah,* adj.] **:** in a high manner: as **a** (1) **:** at or to a great distance or altitude ⟨after a cup of tea we walked a little ~*er* —John Seago⟩ ⟨climbed ~ on the ladder⟩ ⟨the waves dashed ~⟩ — often used in combination ⟨a *high*-climbing vine⟩ (2) **:** far up toward the source ⟨allow passage of . . . vessels as ~ as Albany —Herman Beukema⟩ — usu. used with *up* ⟨lives ~ up the river⟩ **b :** in or to a high position, amount, or degree ⟨prices have gone too ~⟩ ⟨that young man is aiming ~⟩ ⟨how ~ can one rise in this organization⟩ ⟨delay had cost ~ in bitterness —*Time*⟩ — often used in combination ⟨a *high*-ranking official⟩ **c :** RICHLY, LUXURIOUSLY ⟨has gay reunions . . . and lives ~ —J.W.Krutch⟩ — often used in the phrases *high off the hog* or *high on the hog* ⟨the new America is eating too ~ on the hog for its own good —*Newsweek*⟩

³high \"\ *n* -s [ME *hegh, hey, high,* fr. *hegh, hey, high,* adj.] **:** an elevated place or region: as **a :** HILL, KNOLL ⟨flat as a table top, without a single ~ or low —Harold Sinclair⟩ **b :** the upper region **:** the space overhead **:** SKY — usu. used with *on* ⟨each lifted on ~ his knife —A.C.Whitehead⟩ ⟨watched the birds wheeling on ~⟩ **c :** HEAVEN — used with *on* ⟨a judgment from on ~ —C.S.Kilby⟩ **d :** a region of high barometric pressure **:** ANTICYCLONE **2 a :** a high point **:** a top level **:** HEIGHT, ACME ⟨carrying snobbery to new . . . ~s —Leslie Charteris⟩ ⟨a ~ of 38 was due today . . . the weatherman forecast —*Cleveland (Ohio) Plain Dealer*⟩; *specif* **:** the highest price paid for a security during a specified period ⟨the daily ~⟩ **b :** the transmission gear giving the highest ratio of propeller-shaft to engine-shaft speed and the lowest multiplication of torque and consequently the highest speed of travel of an automotive vehicle **c** (1) **:** the highest trump that has been dealt in any game of the all-fours family (2) **:** the highest-ranking combination of upcards in stud poker **3 :** people of a class regarded as socially superior ⟨you find scoundrels among both the ~ and the low⟩ **4 :** HIGH SCHOOL ⟨she learned bookkeeping in ~ —John O'Hara⟩ **5** *slang* **:** the excited or stupefied state produced by a narcotic substance (as heroin)

high altar *n* [ME] **:** the principal altar in a church

high analysis *adj, of a fertilizer* **:** containing more than 20 percent of total plant nutrients

high and dry *adv* **1 :** out of the reach of the current or tide **:** out of water — used of a ship aground above water **2 :** in a helpless or abandoned position **:** without recourse ⟨millions of old people were left *high and dry* —M.A.Abrams⟩ ⟨resting *high and dry* on a bed of concrete —Dana Burnet⟩

high and low *adv* **:** upstairs and downstairs **:** EVERYWHERE ⟨looked for it *high and low*⟩

high-and-mighty \¦=¦==¦==\ *adj* **:** characterized by arrogance **:** IMPERIOUS ⟨rivermen . . . who had been *high-and-mighty* now were sitting on drift logs, literally, wondering what was coming next —Frederick Way⟩

high-angle fire *n* **:** cannon fire delivered at elevations greater than that for the maximum range

high-back \'=¦=\ *adj, of a vowel* **:** high and back

¹highball \'=,=\ *n* [¹*high* + *ball*] **1 a** [so called fr. the fact that in early RR practice a metal ball was raised on a pole as a go-ahead signal to the engineer] **:** a railroad signal for a train to proceed at full speed **b :** a fast train **2 :** a drink of spirituous liquor mixed with water or more often a carbonated beverage (as seltzer or ginger ale) and served in a tall glass usu. with ice ⟨applejack ~⟩ ⟨whiskey ~⟩

²highball \"\ *vi* **:** to go at full or high speed ⟨see how safely they ~ with a full load —*Civil Engineering*⟩ ⟨a ~*ing* express train⟩ ~ *vt* **:** to drive at full or high speed ⟨how we ~*ed* those camions up —Christopher Morley⟩

high·ball·er \'=,=ə(r)\ *n* [¹*highball* (signal) + *-er*] **:** SIGNALMAN

high bar *n* **:** a horizontal bar adjusted above head height and used as a support in some gymnastic exercises

high beam *n* **:** the focus of a vehicle headlight that sends the light forward for maximum long-range illumination of the road ahead and is intended for driving in open country — contrasted with *low beam*

high beams *n pl, New Eng* **:** LOFT

high·be·lia \hī'bēlyə, -lēə\ *n* -s [¹*high* (in contrast to *lo-,* punningly taken as *low*) + *lobelia*] **:** any of various tall-growing American lobelias; *esp* **:** GREAT LOBELIA

high·bind·er \'hī,bīndə(r)\ *n* -s [fr. the *Highbinders,* a gang of vagabonds in New York City *ab*1806] **1 a :** THUG, GANGSTER, RUFFIAN ⟨this gang of ~s were supposed to be enforcing the law —Julien Hyer⟩ **b :** HATCHET MAN; *specif* **:** a member of an organized band of Chinese professional killers operating in the Chinese quarter of an American city **2 :** a person who engages in fraudulent or shady activities **:** CONFIDENCE MAN, SWINDLER ⟨employ the saliva test on horses to guard against ~s injecting stimulants —C.B.Davis⟩ ⟨the ~ boys of the last Florida boom —Robert Moses⟩; *specif* **:** a corrupt or scheming politician ⟨the county payroll has 2,200 experienced vote raisers, many of them ~s of the lowest degree —*Nation*⟩

high·bind·ing \-diŋ\ *n* **:** SKULDUGGERY, FRAUD ⟨the techniques of larceny and ~ —R.H.Rovere⟩ ⟨the aroma of ~ will not down —R.B.McKerrow⟩

high blood pressure *n* **:** HYPERTENSION

high blower *n* **:** a horse that produces blowing esp. during exercise

high-blown \'=¦=\ *adj* **:** inflated esp. with conceit **:** PRETENTIOUS ⟨*high-blown* but slightly mystifying verse —Stuart Keate⟩

high blueberry *n* **:** HIGHBUSH BLUEBERRY

high-boiling \'=¦==\ *adj* **:** boiling at a relatively high temperature

highborn \'=¦=\ *adj* **:** of noble birth

highboy \'=,=\ *n* **:** a high chest of drawers mounted on a base which has legs of considerable length and usu. several drawers esp. in style between 1690 and 1780 — compare BONNET TOP, LOWBOY

highboy

high-braced \'=¦=\ *adj, archery* **:** HIGH-STRUNG

high brass *n* **1 :** brass containing at least 33 percent zinc — compare LOW BRASS **2 :** high-ranking officers or officials ⟨the living honorees weren't always political or military or railroad *high brass* —B.A.Botkin & A.F.Harlow⟩ ⟨doesn't know enlisted men and their opinion of *high brass* —G.W.Johnson⟩

highbred \'=¦=\ *adj* **1 :** marked by high birth or breeding **:** coming from superior stock ⟨the ~ descendant of an ancient baron —Sir Walter Scott⟩ ⟨a ~ dog⟩ **2 :** having the characteristics of or associated with high birth or breeding **:** REFINED ⟨the grand manner and ~ ways of the society he frequented —J.R.Lowell⟩

¹highbrow \'=,=\ *n* [¹*high* + *brow*] **:** a person who possesses or has pretensions to strong intellectual interests or superiority **:** one who regards aloofly or contemptuously manifestations of mass culture **:** EGGHEAD ⟨~s . . . despise soap operas and are repelled by the success stories in popular magazines —W. O.Aydelotte⟩ ⟨~s who believe that . . . art is for art's sake —A.J.Toynbee⟩

²highbrow \"\ *adj* **:** of, relating to, or appropriate to a highbrow **:** having or giving the appearance of strong intellectual interests or superiority ⟨liking jazz or not liking jazz is almost equally ~ today —Roger Angell⟩ ⟨a Chinese scholar can be ineffably ~ —E.R.Hughes⟩ ⟨the magazine . . . will be uncompromisingly ~ —*Time*⟩

high-browed \'=¦=\ *adj* **1 :** having a high brow **2 :** HIGHBROW ⟨the *high-browed* literary critics⟩

high·brow·ism \'hī,braù,izəm\ *n* -s **:** the state of mind associated with a highbrow **:** self-conscious intellectual superiority **:** INTELLECTUALISM

high-brown \'=¦=\ *adj* **:** being a high yellow

highbush \'=¦=\ *adj* **:** forming a notably tall or erect bush ⟨~ willows⟩ **:** borne on a highbush plant ⟨the ~ berries are larger and sweeter⟩

highbush blueberry *n* **1 :** any of several tall-growing blueberries of eastern No. America; *esp* **:** a highly variable moisture-loving shrub (*Vaccinium corymbosum*) that has deciduous ovate to broadly lanceolate leaves, whitish or pinkish flowers, and bluish to blackish edible fruit usu. with a distinct bloom and that is the source of most cultivated blueberries — compare EVERGREEN BLUEBERRY, RABBITEYE **2 :** the fruit of a highbush blueberry

highbush cranberry *n* **:** CRANBERRY BUSH 2

highbush huckleberry *n* **:** BLACK HUCKLEBERRY

high-card pool *n* **:** RED DOG 3

high-central \'=¦=¦==\ *adj, of a vowel* **:** high and central

high chair \'=¦=\ *n* **:** a child's chair with long legs, a feeding tray, and a footrest

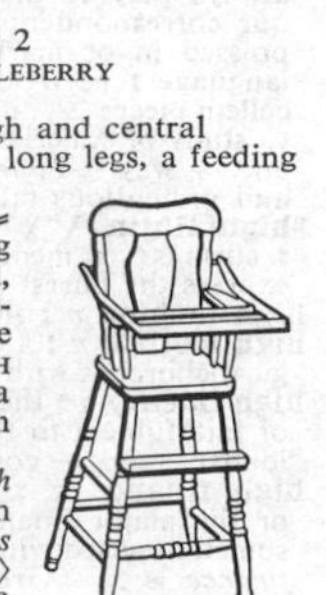

high chair

high church *adj, usu cap H&C* [back-formation fr. *high churchman*] **:** tending toward or stressing sacerdotal, liturgical, ceremonial, traditional, and Catholic elements as appropriate to the life of the Christian church — compare LOW CHURCH

high churchman *n, often cap H&C* **:** a person who adheres to High Church principles

high-class \'=¦=\ *adj* [fr. the phrase *high class*] **:** of a class rated as superior in high degree **:** FIRST-CLASS ⟨modern *high-class* accommodations⟩ ⟨a *high-class* mechanic⟩

high-climber \'=¦==\ *n* **1 :** CLIMBER 1a **2 :** HIGH RIGGER

high cockalorum *n* **1** *Brit* **:** a boys' game of leapfrog — used as a shout during the game **2 :** a person with pretensions to great importance **:** a high-and-mighty person **:** BIG SHOT ⟨placed himself as the *high cockalorum* of the universe —J.F.Stevens⟩

high command *n* **1 :** the supreme headquarters of a military force **2 :** the supreme leadership or decision-making group of any organization ⟨the Republican *high command* attempted to repair this damage —*New Yorker*⟩

high commission *n* **1 :** a group of persons delegated supreme authority and responsibility for the performance of some duty or the execution of some trust ⟨the Allied *High Commission* for Germany⟩ **2 :** the office or jurisdiction of a high commissioner ⟨the Western Pacific *high commission* includes the Gilbert and Ellice Islands Colony —Martin Wight⟩

high commissioner *n* **1 :** a representative of one country stationed in another; *esp* **:** a representative of the government of one British Commonwealth country in the capital of another with representational functions broadly similar to those of an ambassador — compare AGENT-GENERAL **2 a :** the chief officer of a colonial territory or dependency **b :** the chief representative officer in a mandate, protectorate, or trust territory **3 :** the chief officer of an international commission or other agency ⟨the United Nations *high commissioner* for refugees⟩

high council *n* **:** a body of 12 high priests in the Mormon Church presided over by the stake presidency and having executive and judicial authority within the stake — compare APOSTLE

high-count \ˈ=ˌ=\ *adj* **:** having a large number of warp and weft yarns to the square inch ⟨a *high-count* percale sheeting⟩ — compare THREAD COUNT

high court *n* **:** a superior court: as **a :** SUPREME COURT **b :** an Australian court that is the highest and has power of judicial review of legislation

high court of justice *usu cap H&C&J* **:** the system of superior courts having the highest general criminal and civil jurisdiction in England and Wales and including divisions corresponding to the formerly independent courts now constituting it — compare ADMIRALTY 3, CHANCERY 1a, COURT OF COMMON PLEAS 1, COURT OF KING'S BENCH, EXCHEQUER 2, PROBATE COURT

high court of justiciary *usu cap H&C&J* **:** the supreme court having jurisdiction over criminal cases in Scotland ⟨their trial began in the *High Court of Justiciary* in Edinburgh —David Masters⟩ — compare COURT OF SESSION

high cranberry *n* **:** CRANBERRY BUSH 2

high crime *n* **1 :** a crime of an infamous nature contrary to public morality but not technically constituting a felony; *specif* **:** an offense which the U.S. Senate deems to constitute adequate grounds for removal of the president, vice-president, or any civil officer as a person unfit to hold public office and deserving of impeachment **2 :** a crime of a serious or aggravated nature

[1]**high-cut** \ˈ=ˌ=\ *adj* [*high* + *cut*] **1 :** cut high up **2 :** having a high top — used of a boot

[2]**high-cut** \ˈ=ˌ=\ *n* **:** a laced boot reaching well up the calf of the leg

high daddy *n* **:** HIGHBOY

high day *n* [ME] **:** HOLY DAY, FEAST DAY

highday *interj* [by alter.] *obs* **:** HEYDAY

high-dried \ˈ=ˌ=\ *adj* **:** deprived of an unusually high percentage of its moisture by drying or baking

highdried \ˈ=ˌ=\ *n* -S [*high-dried*] **:** RED HERRING

high dutch *n, cap H&D* **1 :** HIGH GERMAN **2 :** the literary Dutch of the Netherlands in contrast to Afrikaans or Low Dutch

high-duty \ˈ=ˌ==\ *adj* [fr. the phrase *high duty*] **1** *of a machine* **:** being capable of doing a large amount of work in a specified time ⟨a *high-duty* drill⟩ **2 :** constituting products subject to a relatively high tax ⟨*high-duty* goods⟩

high enema *n* **:** an enema in which the injected material reaches the colon — compare LOW ENEMA

high·er \ˈhī(ə)r, -īə\ *comparative of* HIGH

higher arithmetic *n* **:** the general theory of numbers

higher bacterium *n* **:** any of numerous bacteria of comparatively complex organization — often contrasted with *eubacterium*

higher certificate *n* **:** HIGHER SCHOOL CERTIFICATE

higher criticism *n* **:** the literary-historical study of the Bible that seeks to determine such factors as authorship, date, place of origin, circumstances of composition, purpose of the author, and the historical credibility of each of the various biblical writings together with the meaning intended by their authors — compare LOWER CRITICISM

higher degree *n* **:** ADVANCED DEGREE

higher education *n* **:** education beyond the secondary level **:** education provided by a college or university

higher functional calculus *n* **:** functional calculus in which quantification is applied not only to individual variables but also to functional and propositional variables — called also *functional calculus of the second order*

higher fungus *n* **:** any of numerous fungi with hyphae well-developed, septate, and usu. at some stage of development interwoven into a compact tissue esp. in the fruiting body (as in Ascomycetes, Basidiomycetes and Fungi Imperfecti) — compare LOWER FUNGUS

higher institution *n* **:** an educational institution of collegiate or more advanced grade

higher law *n* **:** a principle of divine or moral law that is considered to be superior to constitutions and enacted legislation

higher learning *n* **:** education, learning, or scholarship on the collegiate or university level

higher mammal *n* **:** any of the placental or eutherian mammals; *esp* **:** a member of the Educabilia

higher mathematics *n pl but sing in constr* **:** mathematics of more advanced content than ordinary arithmetic and algebra, geometry, trigonometry, and beginning calculus

higher school certificate *n* **:** a certificate awarded on the successful completion of an examination taken by British secondary-school students who are preparing to enter a university

higher thought *n, usu cap H&T* **:** NEW THOUGHT

higher-up \ˌ==ˈ=\ *n* -S [fr. the phrase *higher up*] **:** a superior officer or official **:** a chief leader or agent in an organization ⟨brought to the attention of the *higher-ups* in the . . . State Department —Lindsay Rogers⟩

high·est \ˈhīəst\ *superlative of* HIGH

highest common factor *n* **:** the largest integer or polynomial of highest degree that is an exact divisor of each of two or more integers or polynomials respectively

high explosive *n* **:** a detonating explosive (as trinitrotoluene) used for its shattering effect

[1]**high·fa·lu·tin** \ˌhīfəˈlüt°n\ *also* **high·fa·lu·ting** \", -üd·liŋ, -üt|, |ēŋ\ *or* **hi·fa·lu·tin** *adj* [perh. fr. [1]*high* + alter. of *fluting*, pres. part. of [2]*flute*] **1 :** characterized by or reflecting an attitude of self-importance or superciliousness **:** PRETENTIOUS ⟨~ people like the kind of fine ladies his wife was always playing bridge with —Nathaniel La Mar⟩ ⟨impress our correspondents by ~ letterheads —H.F.Ellis⟩ **2 :** expressed in or marked by the use of high-flown bombastic language **:** POMPOUS ⟨has written perhaps half a dozen excellent pieces . . . and a great deal of ~ bathos —H.L.Mencken⟩ ⟨a study of American adolescence done in a rather high-toned and ~ way —*Time & Tide*⟩ ⟨pretentious idealism or just ~ and pretentious talk —William Chomsky⟩

[2]**highfalutin** \"\ *n* -S **:** high-flown pretentious language **:** BOMBAST ⟨a medium . . . in which dramatic characters can express the purest poetry without ~ —T.S.Eliot⟩

high fashion *n* **:** HIGH STYLE

high festival *n* **:** a church festival observed in the more liturgical churches with full ceremonial

high fidelity *n* **:** the reproduction of sound with a high degree of faithfulness to the original (as by a radio or phonograph loudspeaker) — compare HI-FI

high finance *n* **:** large and complex financial operations or the major financial institutions that engage in them — sometimes used with an implication of unethical practice ⟨*high finance* is . . . Greek to most people —J.R.Aswell & E.J. Michelson⟩

high five *n* **:** [3]CINCH

high flanker *n* **:** a male horse with incompletely descended testes

highflier *or* **highflyer** \ˈ=ˌ=\ *n* **1 :** one that flies high **2** *archaic* **:** one who is uncompromisingly orthodox or extreme in point of doctrine; *esp* **:** one who is extreme in supporting the claims to authority of the Church of England **:** HIGH CHURCHMAN **3 :** FLIER 6 ⟨took a ~ in watermelons that year —F.B.Gipson⟩

high-flown \ˈ=ˌ=\ *adj* **1 :** being high above the ordinary level of thought or sentiment **:** ELEVATED, EXALTED ⟨argue in terms of *high-flown* ideals —Oliver Franks⟩ **2 :** having a turgid or inflated character **:** BOMBASTIC, PRETENTIOUS ⟨*high-flown* talk of preserving the moral tone of the school —Leslie Rees⟩ ⟨the usual inflated rhetoric and *high-flown* vocabulary —James Yaffe⟩

high-flying \ˈ=ˌ==\ *adj* **1 :** rising to a considerable height ⟨displaying *high-flying* hoofs and thrashing tails —Court Paige⟩ **2 a :** inflated or pretentious in style, content, or ambition **:** HIGH-FLOWN ⟨a *high-flying* dissertation on the means to attain a social revolution —Wilfred Fienburgh⟩ ⟨*high-flying* proposals⟩ **b :** having an extremely lofty or metaphysical character **:** being too abstract or remote from human affairs **:** TRANSCENDENTAL ⟨directed against the intuitional, or *high-flying* school —C.N.Feidelson⟩ ⟨mocked the *high-flying* . . . Platonists —P.D.Partner⟩

high forest *n* [trans. of G *hochwald*] **:** a forest from seed — compare COPPICE

high frequency *n* **:** a frequency that is relatively high; *specif* **:** a radio frequency in the middle range of the radio spectrum — see RADIO FREQUENCY table

high-frequency \ˈ=ˌ===\ *adj* [*high frequency*] **1 :** occurring very frequently ⟨drills based on the repetition of *high-frequency* words⟩ **2 :** relating to high frequency: as **a :** involving a radio wave of high frequency — used esp. of sound waves and vibrations **b :** SUPERSONIC 1

high-frequency telephony *n* **:** an art or process of telephonic communication by means of carrier currents over electric conductors (as transmission lines) through the use of transmitting and receiving equipment like those used in radio

high-front \ˈ=ˌ=\ *adj, of a vowel* **:** high and front

high gear *n* **1 :** [3]HIGH 2b **2 :** a state of intense or maximum activity ⟨the political campaign will move into *high gear* —G.C.Wright⟩ ⟨operations went into *high gear* last year —*N.Y. Times*⟩

high german *n, cap H&G* [trans. of G *hochdeutsch*] **1 :** German as natively used in southern and central Germany — see MIDDLE HIGH GERMAN, OLD HIGH GERMAN; compare BENRATH LINE, LOW GERMAN **2 :** [3]GERMAN 2b

high german consonant shift *n, usu cap H&G* **:** CONSONANT SHIFT 2

high grade *n* **:** something that is of superior grade: as **a :** ore of high value or of relatively high value as compared with the average ore in a specific mine **b :** a grade animal that in conformation and economic qualities approximates the breed to which its known purebred ancestors belong

[1]**high-grade** \ˈ=ˌ=\ *adj* [*high grade*] **:** of superior grade or quality ⟨*high-grade* writing⟩ ⟨*high-grade* manganese⟩: as **a :** being securities or other investments involving little or no risk and affording a relatively assured income ⟨*high-grade* bonds⟩ **b :** being near the upper extreme of the range in which it may occur ⟨a *high-grade* moron approaches normality⟩ ⟨a *high-grade* hydrocephalic exhibits maximum deformity⟩ — compare LOW-GRADE

[2]**high-grade** \"\ *vt* [*high grade*] **:** to steal (rich ore) from a mine; *also* **:** to mine only (the rich ore) — **high-grader** \ˈ=ˌ==\ *n* — **high-grading** \ˈ=ˌ==\ *n*

high-ground willow oak *n* **:** TURKEY OAK c

high-grown \ˈ=ˌ=\ *adj* **1 :** grown tall **2 :** covered with tall vegetation ⟨a *high-grown* slope⟩ **3** *of coffee* **:** grown at a high altitude

high-handed \ˈ=ˌ==\ *adj* **:** OVERBEARING, ARBITRARY ⟨*high-handed* behavior⟩ — **high-hand·ed·ly** *adv* — **high-hand·ed·ness** *n* -ES

high hat *n* **1 :** BEAVER 3 **2** *usu* **high-hat** \ˈ=ˌ=\ **:** one who assumes an attitude of superiority **:** SNOB, SWELL ⟨amid the gasps of the *high-hats* he . . . threw in his lot with the British Labor Party —*New Republic*⟩

[1]**high-hat** \ˈ=ˌ=\ *adj* [*high hat*] **:** supercilious or snobbish in attitude or manner **:** ARISTOCRATIC ⟨*high-hat* over the type of job she wants —*Springfield (Mass.) Union*⟩ ⟨cold, impersonal, a trifle *high-hat* —*Nation*⟩

[2]**high-hat** \"\ *vt* [*high hat*] **:** to look down one's nose at **:** treat snobbishly **:** SNUB ⟨*high-hatted* her . . . when they were sober —Edmund Wilson⟩ ⟨the literati tended to *high-hat* the first issues —Jay Franklin⟩

high heal-all *n* **:** WOOD BETONY 2

high-hearted \ˈ=ˌ==\ *adj* [ME *highe herted*] **1 :** full of courage or nobility **:** HIGH-SPIRITED ⟨*high-hearted* language —Archibald MacLeish⟩ **2 :** full of gaiety **:** INSOUCIANT, LIGHTHEARTED ⟨a *high-hearted* junket —*Huntting's Monthly List*⟩ — **high-heart·ed·ly** *adv* — **high-heart·ed·ness** *n* -ES

high-high \ˈ=ˌ=\ *adj, of tide* **:** higher than the normal high

high-hold·er \ˈ=ˌhōldə(r)\ *also* **high-hole** \ˈ=ˌhōl\ *or* **high-hol·er** \ˈ=ˌhōlə(r)\ *n* [by folk etymology fr. ME *hygh-whele*, prob. of imit. origin] *dial* **:** [3]FLICKER

high holiday *or* **high holy day** *n, usu cap both Hs & D* **:** either of the Jewish religious holidays Rosh Hashanah and Yom Kippur observed respectively on the 1st and the 10th of Tishri with particular solemnity

high horse *n* **1 :** an unyielding, pretentious, or arrogant mood **:** a high and mighty air or attitude ⟨when he . . . saw the desperate need for more men, he came down off his *high horse* —J.F.Dobie⟩ ⟨wanted to get on her *high horse* and treat him as if he were nothing —William Heuman⟩ **2 :** a sulky or resentful mood, air, or attitude ⟨on your *high horse* because he didn't praise your mince —Arnold Bennett⟩

high-house \ˈ=ˌ=\ *n* **:** a trap house on the left side of a skeet range that projects the target from a point 10 feet from the ground — called also *hi-trap;* compare LOW-HOUSE

high hurdles *n pl but sing or pl in constr* **:** a track event of 120 yards or 110 meters distance with ten 3 ft. 6 in. hurdles to be surmounted — compare LOW HURDLES

high iron *n* **:** a main-line railroad track

high·ish \ˈhīish\ *adj* **:** rather high ⟨with a ~ collar and a black cord necktie —*New Yorker*⟩

high-jack *var of* HIJACK

high jinks *also* **hi·jinks** *or* **high jinx** \ˈhīˈjiŋ(k)s\ *n pl* **1 :** an old Scottish game of forfeits at drinking **2 :** boisterous or noisy sport **:** HORSEPLAY ⟨the juvenile *high jinks* of a college reunion —John Mason Brown⟩ ⟨the officers and men . . . were indulging in *high jinks* ashore —H.C.Ickes⟩

high jump *n* **:** a jump for height in a track or field contest either from a standing position or from a running start

high jumper *n* **:** an athlete who participates in the high jump

high jumping *n, pl* **high jumpings :** the act or action of performing the high jump

high-key \ˈ=ˌ=\ *adj* **:** having or producing light tones only with little contrast — used of a photographic print or subject or of the lighting of a photographic subject

[1]**high·land** \ˈhīlənd *sometimes* -ˌland *or* -ˌlaa(ə)nd\ *n* [ME, fr. *high* + *land*] **1 :** elevated or mountainous land **2** *usu cap* [[2]*Highland*] **:** WEST HIGHLAND

[2]**highland** \"\ *adj* **1 :** of or relating to a highland **:** inhabiting or growing in a highland **2** *usu cap* [fr. the *Highlands*, northern part of Scotland] **:** of, related to, or typical of the Highlands of Scotland ⟨typically *Highland* . . . a strange mixture of pride and tenderness, of poverty and generosity —Ian Finlay⟩

high·land·er \-də(r)\ *n* -S **1 :** an inhabitant of a highland **2** *usu cap* **:** an inhabitant of the Highlands of Scotland — compare LOWLANDER

highland fling *n, usu cap H* **:** a Scottish folk dance that is performed usu. by three or four persons, with nimble footwork and low kicks

highland pony *n, usu cap H* **:** a comparatively large hardy pony native to the Highlands of Scotland and some adjacent islands

high-lead \ˈ=ˌlēd\ *n* **:** SPAR TREE

high-lead logging *n* **:** HIGH-LINE LOGGING

high-level \ˈ=ˌ==\ *adj* **1 :** carried out or engaged in at a high altitude ⟨were ordered to take to the slit trenches if the *high-level* attack developed —*Coast Artillery Jour.*⟩ **2 a :** of, involving, or engaged in by persons of high position, rank, or achievement ⟨a *high-level* staff to set up and supervise a political and operational training center —S.K.Padover⟩ ⟨time to push the proposal for a *high-level* conference —Drew Middleton⟩ ⟨*high-level* discussions of the control of atomic energy —C.L.Sulzberger⟩ **b :** holding high position or rank ⟨*high-level* government officials will meet . . . to discuss the outlook for aluminum —T.E.Mullaney⟩

[1]**highlight** \ˈ=ˌ=\ *n* [[1]*high* + *light*] **1 a :** the lightest spot or area (as in a painting or engraving) **:** a spot or any of several spots in a modeled drawing or painting that receives the greatest amount of illumination **b :** a bright part of a photographic picture or subject represented by a considerable density in the negative and by nearly clear paper or other support in the print **2 :** an event, detail, topic, or accomplishment of major significance or special interest ⟨one of the ~*s* of the fashionable London season —Emily Hahn⟩ ⟨more analysis will be written . . . later but here are some ~*s* —*Kiplinger Washington Letter*⟩ ⟨these are only ~*s:* he also wrote . . . several volumes of verse, numerous short stories —E.P. Earnest⟩

[2]**highlight** \"\ *vt* **1 :** to illuminate with vivid distinctness **:** throw a strong light upon ⟨designed for general store lighting and to ~ featured merchandise —*Electrical World*⟩ ⟨matches flared, momentarily ~*ing* the faces —*Nat'l Geographic*⟩ **2 :** to paint out the highlight areas of (a halftone negative); *also* **:** to etch away the light dots in the corresponding areas of (a printing plate) — compare DROP OUT **3 a :** to center attention upon **:** cause to loom large in importance or urgency **:** EMPHASIZE, STRESS ⟨these publications . . . ~*ed* the deficiencies of the current freshman program —T.F.Dunn⟩ ⟨~ a major factor in the Hemisphere's aid program —*Atlantic*⟩ **b :** to constitute a highlight or distinctive feature of ⟨the slang that ~*s* his dialogue —Bennett Cerf⟩ ⟨three new talents . . . ~*ed* the year —*Britannica Bk. of the Yr.*⟩

highlight halftone *n* **:** DROPOUT 3

highlighting \ˈ=ˌ==\ *n* **1 :** the act or effect of casting a highlight upon or giving prominence to something ⟨~ is accomplished by the use of high-powered . . . spotlights —H.F.Helvenston⟩ **2 :** additional illumination for enhancing the highlights on a photographic subject

high-line \ˈ=ˌ=\ *adj* **:** being a fisherman or fishing boat with a large or the largest catch ⟨*high-line* vessels sometimes average 400,000 pounds per man —*Commercial Fishing*⟩

highline \ˈ=ˌ=\ *n* **1 :** a high-voltage electric transmission line **2 :** a line or cable strung between ships or from ship to shore (as for the transfer of cargo or crew)

high-line logging *n* **:** logging in which the logs with one end in the air are hauled in by a highline cable

highliner \ˈ=ˌ==\ *n* **:** a high-line fisherman or fishing boat

high-lived \ˈ=ˈlīvd\ *adj, of a horse* **:** HIGH-SPIRITED ⟨a horse of kind disposition but very *high-lived* —J.L.Hervey⟩

high liver *n* **:** one that lives luxuriously

high·lone \ˈhīˌlōn\ *adv* [by alter.] *dial* **:** ALONE ⟨the baby has just learned to stand ~⟩

high lonesome *n, dial* **:** DRUNK, BENDER, SPREE ⟨got on a *high lonesome* and told the barkeeper his business —J.F.Dobie⟩

highlow \ˈ=ˌ=\ *n, dial chiefly Eng* **:** an ankle-high laced boot

high-low \ˈ=ˈ=\ *n* **1 :** a come-on or echo in bridge or whist in which the play of an unnecessarily high card is later confirmed by the play of a lower card of the same suit **2 :** a game of poker in which the highest ranking and lowest ranking hands divide the pot equally

high-low-jack \ˌ=ˌ=ˈ=\ *n* **:** any of several card games derived from all fours (as cinch, pitch, seven-up) in each of which there are special scoring values for winning the highest trump in play, the lowest trump in play, the jack of trumps, and either the ten of trumps or the most points with ace counting 4, king 3, queen 2, and jack 1

high·ly *adv* [ME *heghly, heyly, highly*, fr. OE *hēalīce*, fr. *hēah* high + *-līce* -ly — more at HIGH] **1 :** in or to a high place, level, or rank ⟨only a few ~ placed persons . . . know the entire story —H.L.Stimson⟩ **2 a :** in or to a high degree, amount, or extent **:** EXTREMELY, INTENSELY ⟨a ~ interesting article⟩ ⟨a ~ successful play⟩ ⟨a ~ educated woman⟩ **b :** at a high rate or wage ⟨a ~ paid skilled worker⟩ **3 a :** in a noble or elevated manner **:** SOLEMNLY ⟨let us now and here ~ resolve to . . . march along the path of real progress —F.D. Roosevelt⟩ **b :** with high approval or favor **:** FAVORABLY ⟨does not think ~ of many of his films —*Current Biog.*⟩

highly-strung \ˌ==ˈ=\ *adj* **:** HIGH-STRUNG

high mallow *n* **:** a common biennial hirsute mallow (*Malva sylvestris*) native to Europe and naturalized in the eastern U.S. having an erect stem, long-petioled leaves and rose-purple flowers with darker veins

high mass *n, often cap H&M* [ME] **:** a mass that is sung and not said by a priest with the assistance of a deacon and subdeacon and characteristically with incense, music, and greater ceremonial than in a low mass

high-melting \ˈ=ˌ==\ *adj* **:** melting at a relatively high temperature

high milling *n* **:** a process of making flour from grain by several successive grindings and intermediate sorting

high-minded \ˈ=ˌ==\ *adj* **1** *archaic* **:** PROUD, ARROGANT **2 :** of or marked by or reflecting elevated principles and feelings ⟨a *high-minded* man⟩ ⟨*high-minded* talk⟩ — **high-mind·ed·ly** *adv* — **high-mind·ed·ness** *n* -ES

high-mixed \ˈ=ˌ=\ *adj, of a vowel* **:** high and central

high moor *n* **:** a boggy acid upland area characterized by abundant heaths and sphagnum

high-muck-a-muck \ˈhīˌmək|ēˌmək, |ə|-\ *or* **high-muckety-muck** \|əd·ē|-\ *n* [by folk etymology fr. Chinook Jargon *hiu muckamuck* plenty to eat] **:** a person of high station or importance; *esp* **:** such a person marked by arrogance or conceit

high·ness *n* -ES [ME *heghnes, heynes, highnes*, fr. OE *hēahnes, hēanes*, fr. *hēah* high + *-nes* -ness — more at HIGH] **1 :** the quality or state of being high **:** ELEVATION, LOFTINESS ⟨the ~ of a flooded river⟩ **2 :** a person of honor — used as a title given to kings, princes, or other persons of exalted rank ⟨His Royal *Highness* the Prince of Wales⟩

high noon *n* **1 :** precisely noon **2 :** the most advanced, flourishing, or creative stage or period ⟨the *high noon* of his genius —John Pfeiffer⟩ ⟨the *high noon* of mid-Victorian liberalism —*Times Lit. Supp.*⟩

high-octane \ˈ=ˌ=ˌ=\ *adj* **1 :** having a high octane number (as at least 80) and hence good antiknock properties ⟨*high-octane* aviation gasoline⟩ **2 :** of extreme degree **:** HIGH-POWERED **:** high quality ⟨aquavit, that *high-octane* Swedish liqueur —Bill Hosakawa⟩ ⟨verbs produced by back-formation are usually challenged by *high-octane* purists —H.L. Mencken⟩

high-pass filter *n* **:** an electric-circuit filter that transmits only frequencies above a prescribed frequency limit

high-pitched \ˈ=ˌ=\ *adj* **:** having a high pitch: as **a** (1) **:** being lofty in tone or thought ⟨the magazine was a little *high-pitched* intellectually —R.G.Martin⟩ (2) **:** marked by or exhibiting strong feeling or intense sensibility **:** AGITATED ⟨*high-pitched* denunciations —James Gray⟩ ⟨a *high-pitched* religiosity —Roger Fry⟩ ⟨that restless *high-pitched* life —Gertrude Atherton⟩ **b :** pitched in a high key or register ⟨the composition was too *high-pitched* for the singer⟩ ⟨spoke in a *high-pitched* voice⟩ **c :** inclining steeply ⟨a *high-pitched* roof⟩

high place *n* [ME] **:** a temple or altar used by the ancient Semites and built usu. on a hill or elevation

highpockets \ˈ=ˌ==\ *n pl but sing in constr* **:** a very tall lank man

high polymer *n* **:** a macromolecular substance (as polystyrene or cellulose) consisting of molecules that are large multiples of units of low molecular weight

high port *n* **:** a cross-body position in which a rifle is carried while a soldier is charging or jumping

high-powered *also* **high-power** \ˈ=ˈ=\ *adj* **:** having high power or quality: as **a :** having great drive, energy, or capacity **:** DYNAMIC ⟨import *high-powered* professional talent to help him —T.H.White b. 1915⟩ ⟨many *high-powered* executives . . . work themselves to death —Bruce Bliven b. 1889⟩ **b** *usu* *high-power* using a cartridge with a bullet heavy enough and having a muzzle velocity high enough for hunting deer and larger game ⟨a *high-power* rifle⟩

[1]**high-pressure** \ˈ=ˌ==\ *adj* [fr. the phrase *high pressure*] **1 a :** having, involving, or operating at a high or comparatively high pressure ⟨a *high-pressure* automobile tire⟩ **b :** having a high barometric pressure **2 a :** using or characterized by forceful methods of selling **:** AGGRESSIVE, INSISTENT ⟨a *high-pressure* salesman⟩ ⟨*high-pressure* blurbs about toothpaste —*Amer. Guide Series: N.Y.*⟩ — compare LOW-PRESSURE **b :** imposing or involving severe strain or tension ⟨the . . . stresses of *high-pressure* occupations —*Fortune*⟩ ⟨the *high-pressure* merry-go-round of big business administration —*Current Biog.*⟩

[2]**high-pressure** \"\ *vt* [fr. the phrase *high pressure*] **:** to urge to a course of action with insistent, importunate, or forceful arguments **:** overcome the resistance of by such methods ⟨don't try to *high-pressure* me —Edwin Corle⟩ ⟨beware of salesmen who seek to *high-pressure* you into precipitate purchases —*Assoc. of Better Business Bureaus*⟩ ⟨*high-pressuring* the elected representatives of the people —Karl Schriftgiesser⟩

high-pressure area *n* : ³HIGH 1d
high priest *n* [ME *hege prest*] **1 :** a chief priest; *esp* **:** the head of the Jewish priesthood in ancient times **2 :** a priest of the Melchizedek priesthood in the Mormon Church **3 :** a principal officer of a Masonic chapter **4 :** the head of a movement or chief expounder of a doctrine ⟨the philosophical *high priests* of modern education —M.B.Smith⟩
high priestess *n* **:** a female high priest
high priesthood *n* **:** the priesthood of a high priest; *specif* **:** the Melchizedek priesthood of the Mormon Church
high–priestly \ˈ=ˌ=\ *adj* [*high priest* + *-ly*] **:** of, relating to, or having the characteristics of a high priest
high–proof \ˈ=ˌ=\ *adj* **:** highly rectified **:** very strongly alcoholic ⟨*high-proof* spirits⟩
high relief *n* [trans. of F *haut-relief*] **:** sculptural relief in which half or more than half of the natural circumference of the modeled form projects from the surrounding surface — distinguished from *bas-relief*
high renaissance *n, usu cap H&R* **:** the artistic style of the first half of the 16th century in western Europe esp. as manifested in Rome and Florence and characterized by heroic centralized composition, technical mastery of drawing and conception, and a mature humanistic content
high rigger *n* **1 :** a logger who rigs spar trees — called also *high-climber* **2 :** a worker who erects high ladders for acrobatic performances
highroad \ˈ=ˌ=\ *n* **1** *chiefly Brit* **:** HIGHWAY **2 :** the best approach **:** an easy way ⟨there is no one ~ to literary appreciation —Geoffrey Bullough⟩ ⟨the direct ~ to salvation —*New Republic*⟩
high roller *n* **1 :** one who spends freely in fast or luxurious living ⟨one wealthy cowman . . . who was always a *high roller* in town —Ross Santee⟩ **2 :** one who gambles recklessly or for high stakes ⟨round up some . . . *high rollers* to fade his bets —C.B.Davis⟩
highs *pl of* HIGH
¹**high school** *n* **1 :** a secondary school usu. public-supported and usu. organized on a 3-year or 4-year basis and comprising several divisions (as college preparatory, commercial, vocational, general) **2** *Brit* **:** a college preparatory school **3 :** a school specializing in adult education often professional or technical but sometimes liberal — compare FOLK HIGH SCHOOL
²**high school** *n* [trans. of F *haute école*] **:** a system of advanced exercises in horsemanship
high school·er \ˈ=ˌskülə(r)\ *n* **:** a high school student
high sea *n* **:** the open part of the sea or ocean: as **a :** the sea or ocean lying outside the territorial waters or maritime belts of a country — usu. used in pl. **b :** the part of the sea or ocean within which transactions are subject to court of admiralty jurisdiction — usu. used in pl.
high–sighted *adj, obs* **:** looking upward **:** HAUGHTY
high sign *n* **:** SIGNAL; *esp* **:** a warning or informing signal given stealthily or with gestures — usu. used in the phrase *give the high sign* ⟨gave her the *high sign* when the plainclothes police . . . had gone off to supper —Ida A. R. Wylie⟩
high–sounding \ˈ=ˌ==\ *adj* **:** POMPOUS, IMPOSING ⟨*high-sounding* but barren title —J.L.Motley⟩
high–speed \ˈ=ˌ=\ *adj* **1 :** operated or adapted for operation at high speed **2 :** suitable for or relating to the production of short-exposure photographs of rapidly moving objects or events of short duration (as for analytical measurement or study) ⟨*high-speed* film⟩ ⟨*high-speed* photography⟩
high–speed steel *n* **:** an alloy tool steel which when heat-treated retains much of its hardness and toughness at red heat thus enabling tools made of it to cut at high speeds even though red-hot through friction
high–speed turn *n* **:** TEMPO TURN
high–spirited \ˈ=ˌ===\ *adj* **:** characterized by a bold, energetic, or lofty spirit **:** having ardor or fire **:** not dull or apathetic ⟨a *high-spirited* tomboy of a child —Katharine Scherman⟩ — **high–spirit·ed·ly** *adv* — **high–spirit·ed·ness** *n* -ES
high–step \ˈ=ˌ=\ *vi* [back-formation fr. *high-stepper*] **:** to move with a high step ⟨*high-stepping* across the sand —Nadine Gordimer⟩
high–stepper \ˈ=ˌ==\ *n* **:** one that steps high; *esp* **:** a spirited horse that moves with a high step
high–stepping \ˈ=ˌ==\ *adj* **1 :** moving with a high step ⟨a *high-stepping* horse⟩ **2 :** given to the pursuit of pleasure **:** living fast or wild ⟨a *high-stepping* town with plenty of fun for all —Helene Huff⟩
high–stick·ing \ˈ=ˌstikiŋ\ *n* **:** the act of carrying the blade of the stick at an illegal height in the game of ice hockey
high street *n* [ME *hege strete, heighe strete*, fr. OE *hēahstrǣt*, fr. *hēah* high + *strǣt* street — more at HIGH, STREET] *Brit* **:** a main or principal street
high–strung \ˈ=ˌ=\ *adj* **1 :** being in a state of tense or extreme sensibility **:** highly sensitive or nervous ⟨a *high-strung* person⟩ ⟨dogs . . . are *high-strung* creatures —Joyce Cary⟩ **2** *of an archery bow* **:** having a distance greater than a fistmele between handle and bowstring
high style *n* **:** the newest in fashion or design often with extreme lines and usu. adopted by a limited number of people — called also *high fashion*
¹**hight** \ˈhīt, *Scot* ˈhikt\ *vb past* [ME *highten*, fr. *hehte, heet, highte* (past of *hoten*), fr. OE *heht*, past of *hātan* to command, promise, call, be called; akin to OHG *heizzan* to command, promise, call, ON *heita*, Goth *haitan*, and prob. to L *ciēre* to put in motion, move, Gk *kiein* to go away, travel, *kinein* to set in motion, Skt *cyavate* he moves, goes away; basic meaning: to set in motion] **1** *archaic* **:** CALLED, NAMED ⟨Childe Harold was he ~ —Lord Byron⟩ **2** *chiefly Scot* **:** pledged as security **b :** PROMISED
²**hight** *var of* HEIGHT
high table *n* **:** an elevated table in the dining room of a British college for use by the master and fellows of the college and distinguished guests
hightail \ˈ=ˌ=\ *vi* **:** to move at full speed or rapidly esp. in making a getaway **:** clear out ⟨a young purse snatcher ~*ing* up a steep hill —Elgar Dolson⟩ — often used with *it* ⟨~*ed it* straight through town —Eudora Welty⟩ ⟨where Washington and his troops made their final stand before ~*ing* it across the Hudson —Bernard Kalb⟩ ⟨~*ed* it off with another man —Shelby Foote⟩
high tea *n, Brit* **:** a meal served between five and six o'clock usu. with meat, salad, stewed fruit, cakes or cookies, and with tea
high–temperature \ˈ=ˌ=. . .\ *adj* **:** operating or carried out at high temperatures ⟨*high-temperature* furnaces⟩ ⟨*high-temperature* carbonization of coal⟩
high–temperature cement *n* **:** a cement capable of resisting high temperatures without fusing, softening, or spalling and suitable for the bonding of refractory materials
high–temperature short–time method *n* **:** FLASH PASTEURIZATION
high–tension \ˈ=ˌ==\ *adj* **:** having a high voltage or relating to apparatus to be used at high voltage — used esp. to indicate thousands of volts
high–test \ˈ=ˌ=\ *adj* **:** meeting a high standard; *esp* **:** HIGH-OCTANE — used esp. of gasoline and naphtha
high–test hypochlorite *n* **:** CALCIUM HYPOCHLORITE b
high tide *n* **1 :** the tide when it is high water **2 :** the culminating point **:** CLIMAX ⟨it was, perhaps, *high tide* of the . . . movement, its greatest hour —J.B.Martin⟩
hightoby \ˈ=ˌ==\ *n* [short for earlier *hightobyman*, fr. thieves' argot *hightoby* highway, highway robbery (fr. ¹*high* + *toby*) + *man*] *Brit* **:** HIGHWAYMAN
high–toned \ˈ=ˌ=\ *also* **high–tone** \ˈ=ˌ=\ *adj* **1 a :** having a high moral or intellectual tone or quality **:** DIGNIFIED ⟨Jefferson's *high-toned* . . . and yet devastating reply —C.G. Bowers⟩ ⟨the London *Times* . . . and other *high-toned* publications —H.L.Mencken⟩ **b :** of superior social rank, manners, or breeding **:** ARISTOCRATIC ⟨the *highest-tone* plantation owners in this state —Lillian Hellman⟩ ⟨discreet, decorous, and *high-toned* establishments —Eugene Burr⟩ ⟨has just admitted to its *high-toned* studbook a new breed of dog —*New Yorker*⟩ **2 :** marked by pretensions to superior social status **:** putting on airs **:** PRETENTIOUS, HIGH-FLOWN ⟨*high-toned* insincerity —David Gascoyne⟩
high treason *n* [ME *hye treasoune*] **1 :** treason against the sovereign or the state — the state being in old English law the highest offense against the state — compare PETIT TREASON **2 :** TREASON
highty–tighty \ˌhīd·ē¦tīd·ē\ *adj* [by alter.] **:** HOITY-TOITY ⟨had a *highty-tighty* way that repulsed me —W.A.White⟩
¹**high–up** \ˈ=¦=\ *adj* [²*high* + *up*] **:** of high rank or status ⟨*high-up* officers on both sides —M.A.Hancock⟩
²**high–up** \"\ *n, pl* **high–ups :** a person of high rank or status ⟨the *high-ups* in London and America —Frederick Howard⟩
highveld \ˈ=ˌ=\ *n* [part trans. of Afrik *hoogveld*, fr. *hoog* high + *veld* field, veldt] *southern Africa* **:** plateau land with an elevation of about 4000 feet used esp. for grazing
high–warp \ˈ=ˌ=\ *adj* **:** having the warp threads hung or strung vertically ⟨*high-warp* tapestry⟩
high water *n* **1 a :** water at its utmost flow or greatest elevation; *specif* **:** the water of the sea, a lake, or river at its ordinarily highest level or flow **b :** the time of such elevation **2 :** FRESHET ⟨wanted a new house after a *high water* on the river carried her old one away —Shirley A. Grau⟩
high–water \ˈ=ˌ==\ *adj* [*high water*] **:** unusually short; *esp* **:** having or being trousers that are unfashionably short ⟨an ancient *high-water* suit —Sinclair Lewis⟩ ⟨bought me *high-water* pants —Calder Willingham⟩
high–water line *or* **high–water mark** *n* **1 a :** the line of the shore of the sea or of a lake or river to which the waters usu. reach at high water: (1) **:** the line that marks the limit of the rise of the medium tides of the sea between the spring and neap tides (2) **:** the line that marks the limit of the soil so affected by the water of a lake or river as to have a nature and vegetation distinct from that of the banks **b :** a mark showing the highest level reached by a body of water **2** *usu high-water mark* **:** the highest point **:** ACME ⟨the *high-water mark* of a girl's social career —Hamilton Basso⟩
high–water shrub *n* **:** MARSH ELDER 2
highway \ˈ=ˌ=\ *n* -S *often attrib* [ME *heghewei, highway*, fr. OE *hēiweg, hēahweg*, fr. *hēah* high + *weg* way — more at HIGH, WAY] **1 a :** a road or way on land or water that is open to public use as a matter of right whether or not a thoroughfare **:** a public road or way (as a footpath, road, or waterway) including the right-of-way — compare PRIVATE WAY **b :** such a road or way established and maintained (as by a state) in accordance with law **c :** a main direct road (as between one town or city and another) — sometimes contrasted with *byway* **2 :** a primary or well-known aspect or field ⟨the ~*s* and byways of literature⟩
highway bond *n* **:** a bond issued by a taxing jurisdiction the proceeds of which are for the construction of highways
highway engineer *n* **:** an engineer whose training or occupation is in highway engineering
highway engineering *n* **:** a branch of civil engineering dealing with the planning, location, design, construction, and maintenance of highways and with the regulations and control devices employed in highway traffic operations
high·way·man \ˈ=ˌ=mən *sometimes* (ˈ)=ˌ=\ *n, pl* **highwaymen :** a person who robs on the public road **:** a highway robber
highway post office *n* **:** a bus carrying mail which is sorted in transit
highway robbery *n* **1 :** robbery committed on or near a public highway esp. against travelers **2 :** excessive profit or advantage derived from a business transaction
highwheeler \ˈ=ˌ==\ *n* **:** a steam locomotive with large driving wheels for high-speed passenger-train service
high wine *n* **:** distilled spirits containing a high percentage of alcohol — usu. used in pl.
high wire *n* **:** a tightrope considerably higher above ground than the one ordinarily used
high–wrought \ˈ=ˌ=\ *adj* **1 :** wrought with fine art or skill **:** ELABORATE ⟨the recipient of these *high-wrought* epistles —*Times Lit. Supp.*⟩ **2 :** worked up or agitated to a high degree ⟨a *high-wrought* passion⟩
high yellow *n* **:** a mulatto or colored person of light-yellow color
HIH *abbr* Her Imperial Highness; His Imperial Highness
hi·jack *or* **high–jack** \ˈhī,jak\ *vt* [origin unknown] **1 a** (1) **:** to steal by stopping a vehicle carrying contraband, illicit, or stolen goods ⟨~ a truckload of bootleg whiskey —*Emporia (Kans.) Gazette*⟩ (2) **:** to stop in transit and steal the cargo of ⟨~ a truck near the foot of the mountain⟩ (3) **:** to hold up and rob in the manner of one who hijacks ⟨attempted to ~ us for the jewelry right in daylight —Frank O'Leary⟩ **b :** to steal or rob as if by hijacking ⟨accused of ~*ing* half a million marks' worth of textiles —Joseph Wechsberg⟩ ⟨connives against the republic and has to flee the country in a ~*ed* airplane —Harvey Swados⟩ ⟨reputedly ~*ed* the less intrepid gentry of their ill-got booty and their slaves —*N.Y. Herald Tribune*⟩ **c :** KIDNAP ⟨about sixty thousand Kanakas were enticed or ~*ed* to Australia —Alan Moorehead⟩ **2 a :** to subject to extortion or swindling ⟨has deliberately set out to . . . ~ the American people through uncontrolled profits and inflation —Philip Murray †1952⟩ **b :** COERCE, FORCE ⟨~*ing* buyers into purchasing unwanted accessories —N.K.Teeters & J.O.Reinemann⟩
hi·jack·er *or* **high–jack·er** \-kə(r)\ *n* **:** one that hijacks ⟨repair-bill ~*s* —*Road & Track*⟩ ⟨~*s* stole . . . over $20 million worth of cargo from trucks —*Business Week*⟩
hijinks *var of* HIGH JINKS
hij·ra *or* **hij·rah** \ˈhijrə\ *n* -S [Ar *hijrah*, lit., flight] **:** HEGIRA
¹**hike** \ˈhīk\ *vb* -ED/-ING/-S [perh. akin to ¹*hitch*] *vt* **1 a** *dial chiefly Eng* **:** to raise or toss with the horns **:** GORE **b** *dial Brit* **:** to toss up and down **:** SWING **2 :** to move, pull, or raise often with a jerk or other sudden motion ⟨*hiked* him out —Adrian Bell⟩ ⟨*hiked* himself onto my bed⟩ ⟨*hiking* their dresses above their knees —E.D.Radin⟩ ⟨sections *hiked* into place by cranes —*Newsweek*⟩ **3 :** to increase in amount esp. sharply or suddenly ⟨~ taxes on luxury goods⟩ ⟨~ rents⟩ **4 :** to cause to hike ⟨*hiked* himself off to work⟩ **:** guide or lead on a hike ⟨*hiked* them until their feet hurt⟩ ~ *vi* **1 a :** MARCH, TRAMP, WALK ⟨*hiked* 10 miles that day⟩ ⟨you have to park the car . . . and ~ in —Linda Braidwood⟩; *esp* **:** to go on a long walk or march for pleasure or exercise ⟨loves to ~⟩ ⟨arranged to spend the weekend *hiking*⟩ **b** *dial chiefly Eng* **:** to go away **:** DECAMP — usu. used with *off* or *out* **c :** to journey or travel by any means ⟨~ on skis through snow and dark —Carl Jonas⟩ ⟨borrowed some money and *hiked* over to Paris⟩ **2** *dial Brit* **:** to toss up and down **:** JOLT, JOUNCE, SWAY **3 :** to rise or go up as if by being pulled **:** work upward out of place ⟨no shrinking, no sagging, no *hiking* —*N.Y.Times*⟩ — usu. used with *up* ⟨her skirt and slip had *hiked* up in back —Ralph Chapman⟩
²**hike** \"\ *n* -S **1 :** TRAMP, MARCH; *esp* **:** a long walk undertaken for pleasure or exercise **2 :** a lifting or a moving upward (as of a quantity, amount, degree) **:** INCREASE, RISE ⟨a 10 percent ~ in taxes⟩ ⟨called for a ~ in production⟩ ⟨wage ~*s*⟩
hik·er \-kə(r)\ *n* -S **:** one that hikes; *esp* **:** a person who goes on a hike for pleasure or exercise
hi·ku·li \(h)iˈkülē\ *n* -S [Huichol] **:** PEYOTE
hila *pl of* HILUM
hi·lar \ˈhīlə(r)\ *adj* [NL *hilum* + E *-ar*] **:** of, relating to, or located near a hilum
¹**hi·lar·ia** \həˈla(a)rēə, hīˈ-\ *n* -S *usu cap* [L, fr. neut. pl. of *hilaris*] **:** an imperial Roman festival of the cult of Cybele held on the vernal equinox to celebrate the renewal of life on earth in the spring symbolized by the resurrection of the god Attis
²**hilaria** \"\ *n, cap* [NL, irreg. fr. Auguste de Saint-Hilaire †1853 Fr. botanist + NL *-ia*] **:** a small genus of grasses of the southwestern U. S. and Mexico having a terminal spike with the spikelets in threes — see CURLY MESQUITE
hi·lar·i·ous \həˈlar(a)rēəs, -ler-, -lār- *also* (ˈ)hī¦l-\ *adj* [modif. (influenced by E *-ious*) of L *hilarus, hilaris*, fr. Gk *hilaros* — more at SILLY] **:** marked by hilarity **:** affording or given to hilarity **:** LUDICROUS, MERRY, MIRTHFUL ⟨serious plays . . . alternated with ~ broad comedy —W.P.Eaton⟩ ⟨a joyous, light-hearted, and ~ mode of life —C.A. and Mary Beard⟩
hi·lar·i·ous·ly *adv* **:** in a hilarious manner
hi·lar·i·ous·ness *n* -ES **:** HILARITY
hi·lar·i·ty \həˈlarəd·ē, -ətē, -i *also* hīˈ- *or* -ler-\ *n* -ES [MF *hilarité*, fr. L *hilaritat-, hilaritas*, fr. *hilarus, hilaris* + *-itat-, -itas* -ity] **1 :** temperate gaiety **:** CHEER, CHEERFULNESS ⟨wine gives not light, gay, ideal ~ but tumultuous, noisy, clamorous merriment —Samuel Johnson⟩ **2 :** boisterous merriment **:** intense mirth or laughter ⟨in a continual gale of ~⟩
hil·a·ry·mas \ˈhil(ə)rēməs\ *n* -ES *usu cap* [ME *Hillarimesse*, fr. St. *Hilary* †*ab* A.D. 367 bishop of Poitiers + ME *messe* mass — more at MASS] **:** the feast of St. Hilary on January 13 in the Anglican calendar and January 14 in the Roman Catholic calendar
hil·a·ry term \ˈhilərē-\ *n, usu cap H* [after St. *Hilary*] **1** *chiefly Brit* **a :** the term from January 11 to 31 during which the superior courts of England were formerly open — compare EASTER TERM, MICHAELMAS TERM **b** *also* **hilary sitting :** the sitting of the High Court of Justice of England between January 11 and the Wednesday before Easter **2** *chiefly Brit* **:** the second academic term in a British university beginning in mid January and ending before Easter
hilch \ˈhilch, -lsh\ *vi* -ED/-ING/-ES [prob. alter. of Sc *hilt* to limp, alter. of ²*halt*] *chiefly Scot* **:** to hobble along **:** LIMP
hil·de·brand·ine \ˌhildə¦brandən, -n,dīn\ *also* **hil·de·brand·ian** \-ndēən\ *adj, usu cap* [*Hildebrand* (Pope Gregory VII), Ital. prelate + E *-ine* or *-ian*] **1 :** of or relating to Hildebrand esp. with reference to his drastic reforms of church government and his assertion of papal supremacy over the lower clergy and civil authorities **2 :** adhering to the principles of Hildebrand ⟨the *Hildebrandine* party⟩
¹**hil·ding** \ˈhildiŋ\ *adj* [perh. fr. pres. part. of *hild, hyld*, obs. var. of *hield*] *archaic* **:** lacking moral principles, convictions, or courage **:** BASE
²**hilding** \"\ *n* -S *archaic* **:** a hilding person
hil·gard·ite \ˈhil,gär,dīt, -gər-\ *n* -S [Eugene W. *Hilgard* †1916 Amer. geologist + E *-ite*] **:** a mineral $Ca_8(B_6O_{11})_3Cl_4.4H_2O$ consisting of hydrous chloride and borate of calcium occurring in colorless monoclinic domatic crystals
hili *pl of* HILUS
hi·lif·er·ous \(ˈ)hī¦lif(ə)rəs\ *adj* [ISV *hili-* (fr. NL *hilum*) + *-ferous*] **:** bearing a hilum
hil·i·gay·non *also* **hil·i·gai·non** \ˌhiləˈgīnən\ *n, pl* **hiligaynon** *or* **hiligaynons** *also* **hiligainon** *or* **hiligainons** *usu cap* [native name on Panay] **1 a :** a Bisayan people inhabiting Panay and part of Negros, Philippines **b :** a member of the Hiligaynon people **2 :** an Austronesian language of the Hiligaynon people related to but not mutually intelligible with Cebuan and frequently considered a dialect of Bisayan
¹**hill** \ˈhil\ *n* -S *often attrib* [ME *hill, hul*, fr. OE *hyll*; akin to OE *holm* island, OS *holm* hill, ON *hōlmr* island, L *collis* hill, *culmen* top, *celsus* high, Gk *kolōnos* hill, Lith *kelti* to lift up, and perh. to OE *heall* stone, rock, ON *hallr* stone, Goth *hallus* rock, cliff, and perh. to Skt *kūṭa* hammer, mallet; basic meaning: rising, raising] **1 :** a natural elevation of land of local area and well-defined outline: **a :** a more or less rounded elevation as contrasted with a peaked or precipitous one — compare BUTTE, MESA **b :** a conspicuous elevation in a comparatively flat country ⟨the seven ~*s* on which Rome was built⟩ **c** (1) **:** any of the inferior elevations of a rugged country **:** an elevation higher than a rise and lower than a mountain (2) **hills** *pl* **:** a range or group of hills ⟨visited the Black ~*s* and the Rocky mountains⟩ **d :** hilly country ⟨a ~ district⟩ ⟨~ people⟩ — often used in pl. ⟨lives in the ~*s*⟩ **2 :** a heap or mound of earth or other material reared by human or animal agency ⟨the ~*s* of a prairie dogs' town⟩ **3 :** a group of several seeds or plants planted in one hole ⟨sow five seeds to each ~⟩ ⟨a ~ of beans⟩ **4 :** an incline esp. in a road **:** SLOPE ⟨trucks laboring up the long ~⟩ **5** *dial* **:** dry land surrounded by swamp, marsh, or water **:** solid ground **6 :** an elevation on any surface **:** RIDGE ⟨the ~*s* and hollows of the cobblestone pavement⟩ — **over the hill :** past the peak **:** on the downgrade ⟨I was *over the hill* as far as moneymaking was concerned —W.A.White⟩ — compare *go over the hill* at GO OVER
²**hill** \"\ *vt* -ED/-ING/-S **1 :** to form into a heap ⟨~ up soil around roses⟩ **2 :** to heap or draw earth around or upon ⟨~*ed* the potatoes⟩
³**hill** \"\ *vt* -ED/-ING/-S [ME *hulen, hilen, hillen*, prob. fr. ON *hylja* to hide, cover; akin to OHG *hullen* to cover, Goth *huljan* to cover, OE *helan* to hide, conceal — more at HELL] *dial Eng* **:** to protect by covering **:** HIDE
hill–and–dale \ˌ==ˈ=\ *adj* [fr. the phrase *(over) hill and dale*] *of a phonograph record* **:** having a groove of varying depth
¹**hill·bil·ly** \ˈhil,bilē, -li, ˈ=ˌ==\ *n* -ES [¹*hill* + *Billy*, nickname for *William*] **1 :** a person from a backwoods area (as the mountains of the southern U.S.) — often used disparagingly **2 :** a hillbilly song
²**hillbilly** \"\ *adj* **1 :** of or relating to a hillbilly **:** suggestive of hillbillies **2 :** relating to or characterized by hillbilly music
hillbilly music *n* **1 :** folk songs and folk style of singing and playing of the southern U. S. **2 :** any music deriving from or imitating folk style or the style of the western cowboy esp. as exploited commercially — called also *country music*
hillbird \ˈ=ˌ=\ *n* **1 :** UPLAND PLOVER **2 :** FIELDFARE
hill climb *n* **:** a road race over a hilly course held by an automobile or motorcycle club
hillcrest \ˈ=ˌ=\ *n* **:** the top line of a hill
hillculture \ˈ=ˌ==\ *n* -S [trans. of D *bergcultuur*] **:** agriculture utilizing erosion-preventing crops that are ecologically and economically best suited for sloping or hilly land
hill–drop \ˈ=ˌ=\ *adj* **:** planting a full hill at desired intervals ⟨a *hill-drop* corn planter⟩
hil·le·brand·ite \ˈhilə,bran,dīt, ˌ==ˈ=ˌ=\ *n* -S [William F. *Hillebrand* †1925 Amer. chemist + E *-ite*] **:** a mineral $Ca_2SiO_3(OH)_2$ consisting of a hydrous calcium silicate occurring in white masses
hil·lel·ite \ˈhi,le,līt\ *n* -S *usu cap* [*Hillel* †A.D. 9 Jewish teacher + E *-ite*] **:** an adherent of the liberal and humanitarian principles of interpretation of the Jewish law developed by Rabbi Hillel and opposed by the Shammaites
hill·er \ˈhilə(r)\ *n* -S **:** an attachment to a cultivator or plow for hilling plants
hill fox *n* **:** a fox (*Vulpes himalaicus*) that has fur of a pale fulvous color and is found in the mountains of India
hill grub *n* **:** a larva of the antler moth (*Cerapteryx graminis*) that is often destructive to pasture grasses in England
hill holder *n* **:** a device other than a hand brake that keeps a motor vehicle from backing down an incline when the foot is removed from the brake pedal; *esp* **:** such a device connected to a clutch pedal to keep the brakes applied as long as the clutch pedal is depressed
hill indexing *n, pl* **hill indexings :** indexing by preplanting a potato of each hill
hil·li·ness \ˈhilēnəs, -lin-\ *n* -ES **:** the quality or state of being hilly
hill·man \ˈhilmən\ *also* **hills·man** \-lzm-\ *n, pl* **hillmen** *also* **hillsmen :** a man native to or inhabiting a hilly or mountainous often isolated area and typically differing markedly in outlook, customs, and speech from a man of the plains
hill myna *n* **:** an Asiatic starling (*Gracula religiosa*) that is black with a white spot on the wings and a pair of flat yellow wattles on the head and is often tamed and taught to pronounce words
hi·lo *or* **hil·loa** \həˈlō, ˈhi(,)lō, ˈhiˈlō — *see* HELLO\ *archaic var of* HELLO
hil·lock \ˈhilək\ *n* -S [ME *hilloc*, fr. *hill* + *-oc* -ock] **:** a small hill **:** MOUND — **hill·ocked** \-kt\ *adj* — **hill·ocky** \-kē\ *adj*
hillock tree *n* **:** an Australian shrub (*Melaleuca hypericifolia*) with showy spikes of red flowers
hill of beans : something of negligible importance or value — used chiefly in negative constructions ⟨doesn't amount to a *hill of beans*⟩ ⟨not worth a *hill of beans*⟩
hill partridge *n* **1 :** any of numerous partridges of southern Asia and the East Indies that constitute a genus (*Arborophila*) of the family Phasianidae — called also *tree partridge* **2 :** SPUR FOWL
hill planter *n* **:** a machine that is used for planting seed (as corn) in hills
hill reaction \ˈhil-\ *n, usu cap H* [after Robin *Hill*, Brit. chemist] **:** a photochemical liberation of oxygen from water by cells or cell fragments containing chlorophyll that is equivalent to the photochemical phase of plant photosynthesis
hills *pl of* HILL, *pres 3d sing of* HILL
hillside \ˈ=ˌ=\ *n, often attrib* [ME *hulle syde*, fr. *hulle, hill* hill + *syde, side* side] **:** a part of a hill between the summit and the foot ⟨a green valley whose ~*s* . . . are a mass of yellow buttercups —*Amer. Guide Series: Minn.*⟩ ⟨pell-mell down the ~ streets —Sherwood Anderson⟩
hillside plow *n* **:** SWIVEL PLOW

hillslope \ˈ≈,≈\ *n* **:** HILLSIDE

hills–of–snow \ˌ≈≈ˈ≈\ *n, pl* **hills–of–snow :** a Japanese hydrangea (*Hydrangea arborescens grandiflora*) with large clusters of snow-white sterile flowers

hill star *n* **:** any of several hummingbirds comprising the genus *Oreotrochilus* and inhabiting parts of the Andes

hill station *n* **:** a village or government post (as in India) situated in the hills or low mountain ranges and serving usu. as a health resort in the hot season

hill tit *n* **:** any of numerous small Asiatic singing birds of *Siva, Leiothrix,* and related genera

hilltop \ˈ≈,≈\ *n* **:** the highest part of a hill

hil·lul ha·shem \kəˈlülhəˈshām\ *n* -s [Heb *ḥillūl hashshēm* desecration of the name (of God)] **:** an act in contravention of Jewish religious or ethical principles that is regarded as an offense to God — compare KIDDUSH HASHEM

hillwort \ˈ≈,≈\ *n* **:** WILD THYME

hilly \ˈhilē, -li\ *adj* -ER/-EST [ME, fr. *hill* + *-y*] **1 :** abounding with hills **2 :** inclining like a hill **:** of the character of a hill **:** STEEP

hi·lo grass \ˈhē(ˌ)lō-\ *n* [Hawaiian *hilo*] **:** a sour grass (*Paspalum conjugatum*) that is common in the Hawaiian islands and is often a troublesome weed because of its ability to cover vast areas in a short time

hil·sa \ˈhilsə *also* -l(t)sə\ *n* -s [Hindi *hilsā,* fr. Skt *iliśa, illiśa*] **:** a valuable anadromous herring (*Clupea ilisha*) of India resembling a shad

¹**hilt** \ˈhilt\ *n* -s [ME, fr. OE; akin to OS *helta* oar handle, OHG *helza* hilt, ON *hjalt* hilt, W *cleddyf* sword, OE *healt* lame — more at HALT] **1 :** a handle of a sword or dagger **2 :** the handle of any weapon or of a tool (as a miner's pick) — **to the hilt** *or* **up to the hilt :** to the very limit **:** FULLY, COMPLETELY ⟨mortgaged the farm *up to the hilt*⟩ ⟨proved its importance *to the hilt*⟩

hilt

²**hilt** \"\ *dial past of* HOLD

³**hilt** \"\ *dial var of* HOLD

hi·lum \ˈhīləm\ *n, pl* **hi·la** \-lə\ [NL, fr. L, trifle] **1 a :** a scar on a seed (as a bean) marking the point of attachment of the ovule to the funiculus **b :** the nucleus of a starch grain **c :** a small lateral outgrowth on a basidiospore near the point of its attachment to the sterigma on which it was borne **2 :** a mark or notch in or opening from a bodily part suggesting the hilum of a bean: as **a :** the part of a gland or of certain other organs where the blood vessels, nerves, or ducts leave and enter ⟨the ~ of the kidney⟩ ⟨the ~ of the lung⟩ **b :** a small opening in the statoblast of a sponge

hi·lus \-ləs\ *n, pl* **hi·li** \-ˌlī\ [NL, alter. of *hilum*] **:** HILUM 2a

¹**him** \(h)im, ˈhim, ˌēm\ *pron, objective case of* HE [ME, fr. OE, dat. of *hē* he — more at HE] **1 :** ¹HE 1, 2, 3, 4: **a** — used as indirect object of a verb ⟨friends who have given ~ the most sympathy —W.M.Thackeray⟩ **b** — used as object of a preposition ⟨we may not fight a duel with Death nor engage in controversy with ~ —W.L.Sullivan⟩ **c** — used as direct object of a verb ⟨I know ~⟩ **d** — used in comparisons after *than* and *as* when the first term in the comparison is the direct or indirect object of a verb or the object of a preposition ⟨the jacket fits you as well as ~⟩ ⟨give me the book rather than ~⟩ ⟨this treatment would be more beneficial to you than ~⟩ **e** — used in absolute constructions esp. together with a prepositional phrase, adjective, or participle ⟨I met him down near the river, at the height of the first run of fish, and ~ without his rod —Alasdair Carmichael⟩ ⟨~ being such a fool, the Fool Killer heard about him —Helen Eustis⟩ **f** — used by speakers on all educational levels and by many reputable writers though disapproved by some grammarians in the predicate after forms of *be,* in comparisons after *than* and *as* when the first term in the comparison is the subject of a verb, and in other positions where it is itself neither the subject of a verb nor the object of a verb or preposition ⟨it was ~⟩ ⟨she is as tall as ~⟩ ⟨~ and his promises!⟩ **g** — used in substandard speech and formerly also by reputable writers as the subject of a verb which it does not immediately precede or as part of the compound subject of a verb ⟨damned be ~ that first cries "Hold, enough!" —Shak.⟩ ⟨~ and his wife was real old-timers —Vance Randolph⟩ **h** — used like the adjective *his* with a gerund by speakers and writers on all educational levels though disapproved by some grammarians ⟨what do you think of ~ becoming a doctor⟩ **2 :** HIMSELF — used reflexively as indirect object of a verb ⟨he went to his . . . tailor . . . and got ~ a . . . gray spring suit —W.A.White⟩, object of a preposition ⟨he couldn't decide whether to have the package delivered or take it with ~⟩, or direct object of a verb ⟨a child that . . . finds ~ suddenly in his mother's arms again —Nathaniel Hawthorne⟩

²**him** \ˈhim\ *n* -s **:** MAN, BOY ⟨four ~s and a her —Charles Dickens⟩

HIM *abbr* Her Imperial Majesty; His Imperial Majesty

hi·ma \ˈhēmə\ *also* **hu·ma** \ˈhümə\ *n, pl* **hima** *or* **himas** *also* **huma** *or* **humas** *usu cap* **1 :** a Bantu-speaking pastoral people who constitute the ruling segment of the population of the Uganda kingdoms of Nyankole, Nyoro, and Toro and an inferior class among the Ganda people, are found also in Ruanda and on the western shore of Lake Albert in the Congo, and are supposed to be cognate in origin with the Tusi and perhaps the Galla and Somali **2 :** a member of the Hima people

hima·laya berry \ˌhiməˈlāə-; həˈmäl(ə)yə-, -ˈmäl, ˌlēə-; *sometimes* ˌhiməˈläyə- *or* -ˈlāyə- *or* -ˈlīə-\ *n, usu cap H* [fr. the *Himalayas,* mountain range between Nepal and Tibet] **:** a European blackberry (*Rubus procerus*) introduced and naturalized in the U.S. and having leaves strongly whitened beneath with dense felty tomentum

himalaya honeysuckle *n, usu cap H* **:** a Himalayan shrub honeysuckle (*Leycesteria formosa*) of the family Caprifoliaceae with drooping spikes of purplish flowers

¹**hima·layan** *pronunc at* HIMALAYA BERRY +n\ *adj, usu cap* [*Himalayas* + E *-an*] **1 :** of, relating to, or characteristic of the Himalayas **2 :** extremely large ⟨was responsible for a *Himalayan* blunder⟩

²**himalayan** \"\ *n* **1** *or* **himalayan rabbit** *usu cap H* **a :** a breed of small white domesticated rabbits with black nose, feet, tail, and ear tips **b** -s *often cap H* **:** a rabbit of this breed **2** -s **:** total or partial restriction of pigmentation to the cooler parts of the body (as tail, paws, face, ears) occurring as one of a polygenic series of variants in mammalian coat color dominant to albinism but recessive to chinchilla and the wild type and exhibited in typical form in the Himalayan rabbit and less perfectly in the Siamese cat

himalayan barley *n, usu cap H* **:** an Asiatic barley (*Hordeum vulgare trifurcatum*) having the awns represented by short furcate branches

himalayan black bear *n, usu cap H* **:** BLACK BEAR 2

himalayan cedar *n, usu cap H* **:** DEODAR

himalayan cypress *n, usu cap H* **:** BHUTAN CYPRESS

himalayan fir *n, usu cap H* **:** a very large evergreen tree (*Abies spectabilis*) of the mountains of northern India that is cultivated for its majestic habit and luxuriant foliage

himalayan hare *n, usu cap H* **:** a large long-eared hare (*Lepus oiostolus*) that is usu. silvery brown with the tail white above and is found at high elevations in Tibet

himalayan lilac *n, usu cap H* **:** a shrub (*Syringa emodi*) of the mountains of northern India that has pale-lilac or white flowers

himalayan pine *n, usu cap H* **:** a Himalayan tree (*Pinus excelsa*) with wide-spreading branches and drooping bluish-gray leaves — called also *Asiatic white pine*

himalayan rhubarb *n, usu cap H* **:** an East Indian herb (*Rheum emodi*) that is one of the sources of emodin — called also *Indian rhubarb*

himalayan snow cock *n, usu cap H* **:** a snow cock (*Tetraogallus himalayensis*) having a chestnut pectoral band and a white chest with black bars

himalayan spruce *n, usu cap H* **:** a spruce (*Picea smithiana*) of the Himalayan region that is cultivated for ornament

hima·lo–chinese \ˌhiməˌlō, həˈmä(ˌ)lō(- + \ *adj, usu cap H&C* [*Himalo-,* fr. *Himalayas*] **:** BURMO-CHINESE

hi·man·to·pus \həˈmantəpəs\ *n, cap* [NL, fr. Gk *himantopous,* a kind of water bird, fr. *himant-, himas* thong, strap + *-o-* + *pous* foot] **:** a genus of wading birds comprising the stilts

hi·mat·i·on \həˈmadēˌän, -ēən\ *n* -s [Gk, dim. of *himat-, hima, heimat-, heima* garment, fr. *hennynai* to clothe — more at WEAR] **:** a long loose outer garment of ancient Greece consisting of a rectangular cloth worn by both men and women usu. with one end pulled over the left shoulder from the rear and the remainder going round the back, under the right arm and across the front and draped over the left arm or shoulder — compare CHITON, CHLAMYS, PEPLOS, TRIBON

himation

hi·me·ji \həˈmäjē\ *adj, usu cap* [fr. *Himeji,* Japan] **:** of or from the city of Himeji, Japan **:** of the kind or style prevalent in Himeji

hime·ne *also* **himi·ne** \ˈhēməˌnā, ˈhim-\ *n* -s [Tahitian, Hawaiian, & Marquesan *himene,* fr. E *hymn*] **:** a native song or hymn of French Oceania

himp \ˈhimp\ *vi* -ED/-ING/-S [prob. akin to G dial. *hümpen, himpen* to limp] *dial Eng* **:** LIMP

him·self \(h)imˈ≈, ēmˈ≈\ *pron* [ME, fr. OE *him selfum,* dat., him himself, fr. *him* + *selfum,* dat. of *self* — more at SELF] **1 :** that identical male one **:** that identical one regarded as masculine (as by personification) **:** that identical one whose sex is unknown or immaterial — compare ¹HE; used (1) reflexively as object of a preposition or direct or indirect object of a verb ⟨everyone must look out for ~⟩ ⟨in those days Providence was still busying ~ with everybody's affairs —Arnold Bennett⟩ ⟨he got ~ a new suit⟩; (2) for emphasis in apposition with *he, who, that,* or a noun ⟨he ~ informed me⟩ ⟨he informed me ~⟩ ⟨the composer ~ conducted the symphony⟩ ⟨the composer conducted the symphony ~⟩ ⟨criticizing the king's advisers and the king ~⟩ ⟨the judge, who had once been a lawyer ~⟩; (3) for emphasis instead of nonreflexive *him* as object of a preposition or direct or indirect object of a verb ⟨his income supports his wife and ~⟩; (4) for emphasis instead of *he* or instead of *he himself* as subject of a verb ⟨he was never influenced in art by any fashions save those ~ created —Osbert Sitwell⟩ or as predicate nominative ⟨he has only one loyal disciple and that is ~⟩ or in comparisons after *than* or *as* ⟨he associated mainly with people younger than ~⟩; (5) in absolute constructions ⟨~ simple, fair-minded, unhappy, he comes in contact with the more extravagant varieties of Americans abroad —Carl Van Doren⟩ **2 :** his normal, healthy, or sane condition ⟨he came to ~⟩ **:** his normal, healthy, or sane self ⟨ill for some time, he is now ~ again⟩ **3** *Irish & Scot* **:** a man of consequence; *esp* **:** the master of the house ⟨she has . . . breakfast on the table before ~ is up —Cahir Healy⟩ **4 :** YOURSELF — used in speaking to or as if to a baby ⟨did he hurt ~⟩; used in some English dialects in addressing a boy or a person of higher or lower social status than the speaker; compare ¹HE 4

¹**him·yar·ite** \ˈhimyəˌrīt\ *n* -s *usu cap* [*Himyar,* a legendary ancient king in Yemen + E *-ite*] **1 a :** an Arab people of antiquity dwelling in southern Arabia **b :** a member of such people **2 :** an Arab of a group of related ancient peoples of southern Arabia that included besides the Himyarites proper the Sabaeans and Minaeans, that had a civilization of great antiquity, and that were completely absorbed by northern Arabs by the time of Muhammad

²**himyarite** \"\ *or* **him·yar·it·ic** \ˌ≈≈ˈridik\ *adj, usu cap* **:** of or relating to the ancient Himyarites or their language

himyaritic \"\ *or* **himyarite** \"\ *n* -s *usu cap* **:** the language of the Himyarites occurring in inscriptions ranging from about 700 B.C. to A.D. 550

¹**hin** \ˌ(h)ən, ˌ(h)ēn\ *pron* [ME, fr. OE *hine,* accus. of *hē* he — more at HE] *dial chiefly Eng* **:** HIM

²**hin** \ˈhin, -ē-\ *n* -s [Heb *hīn,* fr. Egypt *hnw*] **:** an ancient Hebrew unit of measure for liquids equal to about a gallon and a half

hi·na·lea \ˌhēnəˈlāə\ *n* -s [Hawaiian] **:** a brilliantly marked convict fish (*Hepatus triostegus*) of the Hawaiian islands that is often used for food

hi·nau \ˈhēˌnaù\ *n* -s [Maori] **:** a New Zealand timber tree (*Elaeocarpus dentatus*) whose bark yields a useful dye

hi·na·ya·na \ˌhēnəˈyänə, -ēnēˈ(y)ä-\ *n* -s *cap* [Skt *hīnayāna,* lit., lesser vehicle, fr. *hīna* left behind, inferior, lesser (fr. *hīyate* he is left) + *yāna* action of going, vehicle, fr. *yāti* he goes; akin to *jahāti* he leaves — more at GO, JANITOR] **:** the smaller more conservative branch of Buddhism dominant in Ceylon, Burma, Thailand, and Cambodia and characterized by adherence to the Pali scriptures and to the nontheistic nonspeculative ideal of self-purification to nirvana through contemplative and moral effort esp. as an arhat — called also *Little Vehicle, Pali Buddhism, Southern Buddhism, Theravada;* compare MAHAYANA

hi·na·ya·nist \-nəst\ *n* -s *usu cap* **:** an adherent of Hinayana — **hi·na·ya·nis·tic** \ˌ≈≈(ˌ)≈ˈnistik\ *adj, usu cap*

¹**hind** \ˈhīnd\ *n, pl* **hinds** *also* **hind** [ME *hinde,* fr. OE *hind;* akin to OHG *hinta* hind, ON *hind,* Gk *kemas* young deer, Skt *śáma* hornless; basic meaning: hornless] **1 :** a female of the red deer — compare HART, STAG **2 :** any of various typically spotted groupers — see RED HIND, ROCK HIND, SPECKLED HIND

²**hind** \"\ *n* -s [ME *hine* servant, farmhand, fr. OE *hīna,* gen. of *hīwan,* pl., members of a household — more at HOME] **1 a :** a farm laborer in northern England and Scotland; *esp* **:** a skilled farm worker who is provided with a cottage on the farm as a home for himself and his family **b :** an English farm manager **:** BAILIFF **2 :** an unsophisticated countryman **:** HICK, RUSTIC

³**hind** \", *before consonants & in "hind end" often* -n\ *adj* [ME *hint,* prob. back-formation fr. OE *hinder,* adv., behind, *hindan,* adv., from behind, behind, & *hindema* last; akin to OHG *hintar,* prep., behind, *hintaro,* adj., rear, *hintana,* adv., from behind, behind, ON *hindri* last, Goth *hindana,* adv., behind, beyond, *hindar,* prep., behind, beyond, and prob. to OE *hē* he — more at HE] **:** of or forming the part that follows or is behind **:** BACK, REAR ⟨the dog's ~ legs⟩ ⟨the handkerchief in his ~ pocket⟩ — compare FORE — **on one's hind legs :** taking an indignant or determinedly independent attitude ⟨got up *on my hind legs* . . . and sounded off —Saul Bellow⟩

⁴**hind** \ˈhīnd\ *n* -s **:** HINDQUARTER ⟨a ~ of beef⟩

hind·ber·ry \ˈhīn(d)- — *see* BERRY\ *n* [fr. (assumed) ME *hindberie,* fr. OE (akin to OHG *hintberi* raspberry), fr. *hind* + *berie* berry — more at BERRY] **:** EUROPEAN RASPBERRY

hindbrain \ˈ≈,≈\ *n* **1 a :** the posterior of the three primary divisions of the vertebrate brain or the parts developed from it including the cerebellum, pons, and medulla oblongata **b :** METENCEPHALON 1 — distinguished from *myelencephalon* **c :** MYELENCEPHALON **2 :** the posterior segment of the brain of an invertebrate (as an insect) **:** TRITOCEREBRUM

hindcast \ˈ≈,≈\ *n* **:** a statistical calculation determining probable past conditions (as of marine wave characteristics at a given place and time)

hind end *see* ³HIND\ *n* **1 :** a part that follows behind **:** REAR ⟨the *hind end* of a train⟩ **2 :** BUTTOCKS, RUMP

¹**hin·der** \ˈhində(r)\ **hindered; hindered; hindering** \-d(ə)riŋ\ **hinders** *vb* [ME *hindren, hinderen,* fr. OE *hindrian;* akin to OHG *hintarōn* to hinder, ON *hindra,* and prob. to OE *hinder* behind — more at HIND] *vt* **1** *obs* **:** to do harm to **:** IMPAIR, DAMAGE ⟨fight against Jerusalem, and to ~ it —Neh 4:3 (AV)⟩ **2 :** to make slow or difficult the course or progress of **:** RETARD, HAMPER ⟨policies that will further or ~ the cause of independence⟩ ⟨was greatly ~*ed* in his efforts by bad weather⟩ **3 :** to keep from occurring, starting, or continuing **:** hold back **:** PREVENT, CHECK — often used with *from* ⟨machines are sometimes ~*ed* by speed from delivering their best performance —Edith Diehl⟩ ⟨could not ~ himself from dwelling upon it —Stephen Crane⟩ **4 :** to interfere with the activity of (a group or molecule of a compound) esp. as a result of space relationships — compare BLOCK 1g, STERIC HINDRANCE ~ *vi* **:** to delay, impede, or prevent action **:** be a hindrance ⟨uncertain whether it would help or ~⟩

syn IMPEDE, OBSTRUCT, BLOCK, BAR, DAM: HINDER indicates a checking or holding back from acting, moving, or starting, often with harmful or annoying delay or interference ⟨shallow water and constantly shifting sandbars at the mouth of the Mississippi impeded navigation and *hindered* the full development of New Orleans as a port —*Amer. Guide Series: La.*⟩ ⟨after the war German physicists maintained that the Nazis *hindered* research on a bomb, permitting only work toward an atomic power plant —*Current Biog.*⟩ IMPEDE suggests checking motion or progress by or as if by clogging or fettering so that forward activity is difficult ⟨he looked at her, startled, and placed his hand on hers, *impeding* the rapidity of her embroidery needle —Rose Macaulay⟩ ⟨action is *impeded* by a multitude of rules and regulations drawn up by the agency itself —E.M.Eriksson⟩ OBSTRUCT indicates hindering free and easy passage by obstacles in the way or by interference ⟨at some point below the Danish camp he *obstructed* the course of the Lea, so that the Danish ships could not be brought downstream —F.M.Stenton⟩ ⟨charged with *obstructing* the military in the execution of duty —Francis Stuart⟩ ⟨the restriction of the power of the House of Lords to *obstruct* legislation —Alfred Plummer⟩ BLOCK indicates complete obstruction to egress, passage, or exit ⟨roads *blocked* by the storm⟩ ⟨the steamer Heilo, which, having run aground, was *blocking* the entrance to Corinto harbor —*Current Biog.*⟩ ⟨a polyglot of diagnostic labels and systems, effectively *blocking* communication and the collection of medical statistics —G.N.Raines⟩ BAR is often a close synonym for BLOCK; it may indicate a purposive blocking or suggest a prohibiting that renders a physical obstacle unnecessary ⟨streetcars that, if not quite medieval, *bar* the road to the hurrying traveler —*N. Y. Times*⟩ ⟨to *bar* further immigration of aliens⟩ DAM may apply to obstructing whatever flows or may be thought of as flowing ⟨*dam* up the waters⟩ ⟨instances in which the bile ducts are blocked so that the bile is *dammed* back —Morris Fishbein⟩ ⟨the nun in her cell lost in contemplation is but inspired by a desire which, *dammed* in its earthly course, rises and rises to unimaginable heights —Francis Stuart⟩

²**hinder** \"\ *n* -s **:** accidental interference esp. by an opponent in some games (as handball and squash) that prevents a fair and unobstructed chance to return a ball

³**hind·er** \ˈhīndə(r), *dial Brit* " *or* ˈhində- *or* ˈhin(t)ə-\ *adj* [ME, prob. fr. OE *hinder,* adv., behind — more at HIND] **1 :** situated behind or at or in the rear **:** BACK, HIND ⟨a long oval forward part and a taillike ~ portion —R.E.Coker⟩ **2** *dial Brit* **:** YONDER

⁴**hind·er** \ˈhīndə(r), *Brit* " *or* ˈhində- *or* ˈhin(t)ə-\ *n* -s *chiefly dial* **:** BUTTOCKS

hindering impediment *n* **:** IMPEDIENT IMPEDIMENT

hin·der·ing·ly *adv* **:** in a hindering manner

hin·der·lands *or* **hin·der·lings** *or* **hin·der·lins** \ˈhindərlənz, ˈhin(t)ə-\ *n pl* [*hinderlands* alter. of *hinderlins, hinderlings; hinderlins, hinderlings* fr. ³*hinder* + *-lings* or *-lins* (alter. of *-lings*)] *Scot* **:** BUTTOCKS

hind·er·most \ˈhīndə(r)ˌmōst, *chiefly Brit* -məst\ *adj* [alter. (influenced by *most*) of ME *hindermest,* fr. ³*hinder* + *-mest* -most] *archaic* **:** HINDMOST

hin·der·some \ˈhində(r)səm\ *adj* [¹*hinder* + *-some*] *now dial* **:** likely to hinder **:** TROUBLESOME

hind–foremost \ˈ≈ˈ≈(ˌ)≈\ *adv* **:** with the hind part before **:** in reverse order

hindgut \ˈ≈,≈\ *n* **1 :** the posterior part of the alimentary canal of a vertebrate embryo **2 :** the portion of the posterior intestine of an invertebrate formed by an infolding of the ectoderm

¹**hin·di** \ˈhin(ˌ)dē\ *n* -s *cap* [Hindi *hindī,* fr. *Hind* India, fr. Per] **1 a :** a literary language of northern India usu. written in the Devanagari alphabet that is the official language of several states in India and is scheduled to become the official language of the republic **b :** a complex of vernacular dialects of northern India for which Hindi is the usual literary language **2 :** a member of a cultural group inhabiting the middle and upper Ganges-Jumna valley, speaking a Hindi dialect, and characterized by dark skin, tall stature, and long head

²**hindi** \"\ *adj, usu cap* **:** of or relating to northern India or its language ⟨*Hindi* troops⟩ ⟨*Hindi* dialects⟩

hind kidney *n* **:** METANEPHROS

hind·ley's screw \ˈhī(n(d)lēz-, ˈhi(\ *n, usu cap H* [after Henry *Hindley,* 18th cent. Eng. clockmaker] **:** an endless screw or worm shaped like an hourglass to fit a part of the circumference of a worm wheel so as to increase the bearing area and thereby diminish the wear — called also *hourglass screw*

hind·most \ˈhīn(d)ˌmōst, *chiefly Brit* -məst\ *adj* [³*hind* + *-most*] **:** farthest in or toward the rear **:** most remote **:** LAST

hindneck \ˈ≈,≈\ *n* **:** NAPE — used chiefly of birds

hindquarter \ˈ≈,≈≈\ *n* **1 :** the back half of a side of beef, veal, mutton, or lamb including a leg and usu. one or more ribs **2 hindquarters** *pl* **:** the hind biped of a quadruped; *broadly* **:** all the structures of a quadruped that lie posterior to the attachment of the hind legs to the trunk including the hind legs, rump, and posterior part of the back

hin·drance *also* **hin·der·ance** \ˈhind(ə)rən(t)s\ *n* -s [ME *hinderaunce,* fr. *hindren, hinderen* to hinder + *-aunce* -ance — more at HINDER] **1 :** the state of being hindered ⟨his rebellion against . . . his tremor of knee and ~ of speech —Glenway Wescott⟩ **2 :** the action of hindering ⟨~ of industry by too easily obtained patents —*Jour. of Patent Office Society*⟩ **3 :** something that hinders **:** BLOCK, DRAWBACK ⟨sunken hulks that are a ~ to navigation⟩

hinds *pl of* HIND

hindsaddle \ˈ≈,≈≈\ *n* **:** a wholesale cut of veal, lamb, or mutton consisting of undivided hindquarters and usu. including one pair of ribs — compare FORESADDLE

hind shank *n* **:** a cut of beef, veal, or mutton from the upper part of a hind leg

¹**hindside** \ˈ≈,≈\ *n* [³*hind* + *side*] *chiefly dial* **:** the back side ⟨she had her dress on ~ to⟩ ⟨put on his clothes ~ before⟩

²**hindside** \"\ *prep, chiefly dial* **:** BEHIND

hindsight \ˈ≈,≈\ *n* **1 :** a rear sight of a firearm **2 :** perception of the nature and demands of an event after it has happened ⟨that ~ is better than foresight is axiomatic⟩

¹**hin·du** *also* **hin·doo** \ˈhin(ˌ)dü\ *n* -s [Per *Hindū,* fr. *Hind* India, fr. OPer *Hindu* — more at INDIA] **1** *usu cap* **:** an adherent of Hinduism **2** *cap* **:** a native or inhabitant of India

²**hindu** *also* **hindoo** \"\ *adj, usu cap* **1 :** of, relating to, or characteristic of the Hindus ⟨a *Hindu* poet⟩ **2 :** of, relating to, or characteristic of Hinduism ⟨*Hindu* gods⟩

hin·du·ism \-ü,izəm\ *n* -s **1** *usu cap* **:** a complex body of social, cultural, and religious beliefs and practices evolved in and largely confined to the Indian subcontinent and marked by a caste system, an outlook tending to view all forms and theories as aspects of one eternal being and truth, a belief in ahimsa, karma, dharma, samsara, and moksha, and the practice of the way of works, the way of knowledge, or the way of devotion as the means of release from the round of rebirths **:** the way of life and form of thought of a Hindu — compare AVATAR, BHAKTI, BRAHMANISM, JNANA-MARGA, KARMA-MARGA **2** *usu cap* **:** a religious philosophy based on Hinduism **3** *cap* **:** the dominant cultic religion of India marked by participation in one of the bhakti sects (as Vaishnavism, Sivaism, Shaktism)

hin·du·ize \-ü,īz\ *vt* -ED/-ING/-S *often cap* **:** to bring into conformity with Hinduism **:** make Hindu (as in customs, outlook, or religion)

hindu numeral *or* **hindu–arabic numeral** *n, usu cap H&A* **:** ARABIC NUMERAL

¹**hin·du·stani** \ˌhindüˈstanē, -dəˈ-, -tän-,-tän-, -ni\ *also* **hin·do·stani** \", -dōˈ-\ *n* -s *cap* [Hindi *Hindūstānī,* fr. Per *Hindūstān* India] **1 :** Hindi, Urdu, and various vernacular dialects of northern India comprising a group of which literary Hindi and Urdu are considered diverse written forms **2 :** the dialect of Delhi and the region to the northeast of Delhi **3 :** a form of speech allied to Urdu but less divergent from Hindi, used in some urban areas and formerly in the British army, and commonly written in the Roman alphabet

²**hindustani** \ˌ≈≈ˈ≈≈\ *also* **hindostani** \ˌ≈≈ˈ≈≈\ *adj, usu cap* **:** of or relating to Hindustan or its people or Hindustani

hind wing *n* **:** a posterior wing of an insect

¹**hine** *obs var of* HIND

²hi·ne \'hē(,)nä\ *n* -s [native name in Burma] : a male Indian elephant without tusks or tushes — compare TUSKER
hi·ney *var of* ²HEINIE
¹hing \'hiŋ\ *dial var of* HANG
²hing \"\ *dial past of* HANG
³hing \"\ *n* -s [Hindi *hīg*, fr. Skt *hiṅgu*] : ASAFETIDA
¹hinge \'hinj\ *n* -s *often attrib* [ME *heng, heeng, hyng;* akin to MD *henge, hengene* hook, handle, MLG *henge* hinge; derivatives fr. the root of E *hang*] **1 a :** a jointed or flexible device on which a door, lid, or other swinging part turns comprising typically a pair of metal leaves joined through the knuckles by a pin — see BUTT HINGE, CLEANING HINGE, H HINGE, HOOK-AND-EYE HINGE, PIANO HINGE **b :** a flexible ligamentous joint (as of a bivalve shell) **c** (1) **:** a paper or muslin joint, stub, or guard in a bound book that strengthens or permits the free flexing of a section, insert leaf, or map (2) **:** ¹JOINT 2d **d :** a small piece of thin gummed paper used in fastening a stamp in an album or on a sheet — called also *mount* **2** *obs* **a :** the earth's axis **b :** a cardinal point of the compass **3 :** something on which a development turns or depends **:** a basic issue or determining factor **:** TURNING POINT **4 :** a strategic point or line in the battle position of an army **5 :** HINGE LINE
²hinge \"\ *vb* -ED/-ING/-S *vt* **1 :** to attach by or furnish with hinges **2 :** to mount (a stamp) with a hinge **:** fasten a hinge to (a stamp) ~ *vi* **:** to be contingent or dependent on a single cardinal point or sole decisive consideration — used with *on* or *upon* ⟨a decision on which success or irrevocable failure *hinged* —Bernard De Voto⟩ **syn** see DEPEND
hingecorner \'=,==\ *n* **:** a hinged corner (as on a box or packing case)
hinged–back tortoise *n* **:** any of various grotesque tropical African tortoises that constitute a genus *Kinixys* of the family Testudinidae and have the posterior part of the carapace hinged
hinged frame *n* **:** a revolver frame hinged forward of the trigger to allow the forward portion of the frame to be rocked forward so as to expose the cylinder for loading and cleaning
hinged·ly \'hinj(ə)dlē\ *adv* **:** by means of hinging ⟨each of said inner panels being ~ connected to an end of one of the inner panels —*Modern Packaging*⟩
hinge fault *n* **:** a fault in the earth's surface in which displacement increases in one direction from a hinge line
hinge joint *n* **:** a joint that permits motion in one plane; *esp* **:** GINGLYMUS
hinge·less \'hinjləs\ *adj* **:** having no hinge
hinge line *also* **hinge** *n* **1 a :** an imaginary line on the earth's surface which can be regarded as a boundary between a stable region and one undergoing upward or downward movement **b :** a line around which one wall of a fault may appear to have rotated with respect to the other wall **2 :** the dorsal edge or border of a bivalve shell on which the hinge is situated
hinge plate *n* **1 :** the part of each valve that supports the hinge teeth in a bivalve mollusk **2 :** the part of a brachiopod that bears the sockets of the dorsal valve
hing·er \'hinjə(r)\ *n* -s **:** one that makes or puts on hinges
hinge tooth *n* **:** a projection of one valve of a bivalve shell that is located near the hinge line and that fits into a corresponding indentation in the other valve
hinging post *n* **:** GATEPOST
hin·gle \'hiŋəl\ *n* -s [ME *hengle;* akin to MD *hengel* fishhook, MLG & MHG, hook, handle; derivatives fr. the root of E *hang*] *dial Eng* **:** the part (as a gate hinge or pot handle) by which something hangs
hink *n* -s [prob. of Scand origin; akin to ON *hinkr* hesitation, fr. *hinka* to limp, fr. MLG *hinken;* akin to OE *hincian* to limp, OHG *hinkan* to limp, ON *skakkr* crooked, askew — more at SHANK] *obs* **:** HESITATION, FALTERING
hin·kum·boo·by \'hiŋkəm,bübē\ *n* [fr. *hinkumbooby* (in the refrain *hinkumbooby round about*), prob. fr. Sc *hinkum* mischievous child + *booby*] *chiefly Scot* **:** a singing game similar to looby-loo
hin·most \'hinməst, -,mōst\ *dial Brit var of* HINDMOST
hin·na \'hinə\ [Sc *hin-* (fr. *hae*) + *na*] *Scot* **:** have not
hin·ner \'hinər\ *Scot var of* ³HINDER
hin·ney *or* **hin·ny** *or* **hin·nie** \'hinī\ *dial Brit var of* HONEY
hin·ni·tes \hi'nīd·(,)ēz\ *n, cap* [NL, fr. L *hinnus* + NL *-ites*] **:** a genus of scallops (family Pectinidae) containing forms that become attached to the substrate with consequent thickening and modification of the shell to resemble that of an oyster and including the rock oyster (*H. giganteus*) of the Pacific coast of No. America
hin·ny \'hinē\ *n* -ES [modif. of L *hinnus*, prob. modif. (influenced by L *hinnire* to neigh, of imit. origin) of Gk *ginnos, innos*, prob. of non-IE origin] **:** a hybrid between a stallion and an ass that differs from the mule in having a more bushy tail, in having a body disproportionately large in comparison with the legs, and in being of a gentler disposition
hi·no·ki \hə'nōkē\ *or* **hinoki cypress** *n* -s [Jap *hinoki*, lit., fire tree] **1 :** SUN TREE **2 :** the wood or fiber of the hinoki
hins *pl of* HIN
hins·dal·ite \'hinz,dā,līt, -,dəl-\ *n* -s [*Hinsdale* county, Colo., its locality + E *-ite*] **:** a mineral $(Pb,Sr)Al_3(PO_4)(SO_4)(OH)_6$ consisting of a basic lead and strontium aluminum sulphate and phosphate occurring in coarse crystals and masses
¹hint \'hint\ *n* -s [prob. alter. of obs. *hent* act of seizing — more at HENT] **1** *archaic* **:** an occasion that can be taken advantage of **:** OPPORTUNITY ⟨look about you ere the ~ be past —Alexander Ross⟩ **2 a :** a suggestion for action given in an indirect or summary manner ⟨a list of helpful ~s for new students⟩ **b :** a statement conveying by implication what it is preferred not to say explicitly ⟨dropping ~s . . . of something mysterious and important about to happen —Sherwood Anderson⟩ ⟨his failure for some years to declare himself definitely in the struggle against the Nazis laid him open to . . . ~s of cowardice —H.J.Muller⟩ **3 :** a usu. slight indication of the approach, existence, or nature of something **:** SIGN, FOREWARNING, CLUE ⟨when the . . . beat of a tom-tom rose without ~ or introduction —William Beebe⟩ ⟨I can give only a ~ of the treasures to be found in the . . . museum —Dana Burnet⟩ **4 :** a very small amount **:** SUGGESTION ⟨friendly and cheerful with just the right ~ of respect —Margaret Kennedy⟩ **:** SUSPICION ⟨carry out this task . . . without ~ of favoritism —Peyton Boswell⟩ **:** DASH ⟨turnip greens seasoned with a ~ of vinegar⟩ ⟨a ~ of nutmeg and a suspicion of orange-flower water —Elinor Wylie⟩ **5** *Scot* **:** MOMENT, INSTANT
²hint \"\ *vb* -ED/-ING/-S *vt* **1 :** to seek to convey by a hint **:** to bring to mind by a slight reference or allusion rather than a full or explicit expression ⟨~ a suspicion⟩ ⟨~*ed* that he would like to be invited⟩ ⟨your father ~*ed* that the school wasn't good enough for you —Mary Austin⟩ **2 :** to indicate or reveal in the manner of a hint ⟨mighty ruins around the city ~ a better past —Curtis Dahl⟩ **:** PRESAGE, FORESHADOW, SUGGEST ⟨a cool, bright day, ~*ing* Indian summer —John Muir⟩ **3 :** to cause to go by hinting **:** send by a hint ⟨~ them along tactfully . . . toward the stuff that counts —Christopher Morley⟩ ~ *vi* **1 :** to make an indirect suggestion, allusion, or reference **:** give a hint ⟨~ broadly for the coveted invitation⟩ ⟨the face of the old retainer ~*ed* of things still untold —T.B.Costain⟩ — usu. used with *at* ⟨finally caught on to what he was ~*ing* at⟩ ⟨little gusts of wind ~*ed* at the storm to follow⟩ **2** *Scot* **:** to go about slyly or furtively esp. in order to further one's own interests **:** slink about or watch quietly **syn** see SUGGEST
³hint \"\ *adj* -ER/-EST [by alter.] *Scot* **:** HIND
⁴hint \"\ *prep, Scot* **:** BEHIND
⁵hint \"\ *n* -s **1** *Scot* **:** BACK, REAR **2** *Scot* **:** a furrow left between two ridges in plowing
⁶hint \"\ *vi* -ED/-ING/-S *Scot* **:** to plow up the furrow that is left to the last between two ridges **:** finish a ridge in plowing
hint·er \'hintə(r)\ *n* -s **:** one that hints
hin·ter·hand \'hintə(r)+,-\ *n* [G, fr. *hinter* rear, last + *hand*] **:** ENDHAND
hin·ter·land \'hintə(r),land, -laa(ə)nd\ *n* [G, fr. *hinter* rear + *land*] **1 a :** a region behind a coast or other usu. specified place ⟨the herdsmen have tended to avoid the immediate ~ of the coast —Walter Fitzgerald⟩; *specif* **:** the territory extending inland from a coastal colony (as along a river system or to the recognized boundary of another territory) over which the colonial power is sometimes held to possess sovereignty **b :** a region that provides supplies for the nation controlling it ⟨the vast ~ Nazi Germany has conquered in eastern and southern Europe —*New Republic*⟩ **c :** a region remote from cities and towns **:** WILDERNESS ⟨when this section, then a rough and rugged ~, was first being settled —*Amer. Guide Series: Minn.*⟩ **d :** a part of a country or region lying beyond any or all of its metropolitan or cultural centers **:** INTERIOR, STICKS ⟨by various profound thinkers in the ~ and by their counterparts in New York —G.J.Nathan⟩ ⟨steer the American out of the capital cities abroad and into the ~s, into the country pubs and . . . village taverns —Horace Sutton⟩ **2 :** the area often including satellites of which a city is the economic or cultural center **:** an urban zone of influence ⟨sometimes the ~s of different seaports overlap —W.G.Moore⟩ **3 :** a little-known sometimes contributory area of knowledge **:** FRONTIER ⟨a ~ of surgery hitherto neglected by the regular practitioner —W.T. Stead⟩ **:** BACKGROUND ⟨taught . . . to read around a subject, to understand its ~ —Hewlett Johnson⟩
hint·ing·ly *adv* **:** in a hinting manner
hin·ton test \'hint°n-, -ntən-\ *n, usu cap H* [after William A. *Hinton* b1883 Am. physician] **:** a blood-serum test for syphilis
hin·tze·ite \'hin(t)sə,īt\ *n* -s [G *hintzeit*, fr. Carl A. F. *Hintze* †1916 Ger. mineralogist + G *-it* -ite] **:** KALIBORITE
hi·o·don \'hīə,dän\ *n, cap* [NL, irreg. fr. *hy-* + *-odon*] **:** a genus (the type of the family Hiodontidae) of No. American freshwater fishes comprising the mooneyes — **hi·o·dont** \-nt\ *adj or n*
h ion *n, cap H* **:** HYDROGEN ION
hiort·dahl·ite \'yō(r)t,dä,līt, -,dəl-\ *n* -s [Norw *hiortdahlit*, fr. T. H. *Hiortdahl* †1925 Norw. chemist + Norw *-it* -ite] **:** a rare mineral $(Ca,Na)_{13}Zr_3Si_9(O,OH,F)_{33}$ consisting essentially of a sodium calcium zirconium silicate containing also fluorine and occurring as pale yellow tabular triclinic crystals
¹hip \'hip\ *also* **hep** \'hep\ *n* -s [ME *hepe, heppe, hipe*, fr. OE *hēope;* akin to OS *hiopo* bramble, OHG *hiafo, hiufa, hiefa* hip, bramble, Norw dial. *hjupa*, Dan *hyben*, and perh. to OPruss *kaāubri* thorn] **:** the ripened false fruit of a rosebush (as the dog rose) that consists of a fleshy receptacle enclosing numerous achenes
²hip \'hip\ *n* -s *often attrib* [ME *hip, hippe, hepe*, fr. OE *hype;* akin to OHG *huf* hip, Goth *hups* hip, L *cubitus, cubitum* elbow, *cubare* to lie down, Gk *kybos* cube, cubical die, vertebra, hollow before the hip (in cattle), OE *hēah* high — more at HIGH] **1 a** (1) **:** the laterally projecting region of each side of the lower or posterior part of the mammalian trunk that is formed by the lateral parts of the pelvis and upper part of the femur together with the fleshy parts covering them **:** HAUNCH (2) **:** HIP JOINT 1 **b :** COXA 2 **2 a :** the external angle formed by the meeting of two sloping sides or skirts of a roof that have their wall plates running in different directions **b** *also* **hip joint :** the junction between an inclined end post and the top chord of a truss **c :** HIP RAFTER — **on the hip** *archaic* **:** at a disadvantage ⟨feeling that she had the culprit *on the hip* —Anthony Trollope⟩
³hip \"\ *vt* **hipped; hipped; hipping; hips 1 :** to strain, injure, or fracture the hip of — usu. used of livestock **2 a :** to throw (an opponent) over one's hip in wrestling **:** throw by a cross-buttock **b :** to bump with one's hip (as in checking a sports opponent) ⟨I took a throw from the outfield, . . . *hipped* him, and he went sprawling to the right of the plate —G.R. Tebbetts⟩ **c :** to support or carry on the hip ⟨he loaded his small revolver and *hipped* it —Christopher Morley⟩ **3 :** to make (as a roof) with a hip
⁴hip \"\ *vb* **hipped; hipped; hipping; hips** [ME *hippen, huppen;* akin to OE *hoppian* to hop — more at HOP] *vi, now dial Brit* **:** to hop esp. on one foot ~ *vt, dial Brit* **:** to pass over **:** MISS, SKIP
⁵hip \"\ *n* -s [by shortening & alter.] *archaic* **:** HYPOCHONDRIA ⟨you have caught the ~ of your hypochondriac wife —Richard Cumberland †1811⟩
⁶hip \"\ *vt* **hipped; hipped; hipping; hips :** to make depressed, worried, or hypochondriac ⟨I rather would hearten than ~ thee —Elizabeth B. Browning⟩
⁷hip \"\ *interj* [origin unknown] — usu. used to begin a cheer ⟨~ ~ hooray⟩
⁸hip *var of* HEP
hip and thigh *adv* **:** OVERWHELMINGLY, UNSPARINGLY ⟨smote him *hip and thigh* with great slaughter —Judg 15:8 (RSV)⟩
hip–and–valley roof *n* **:** a roof so shaped as to have both hips and valleys — compare HIP ROOF
hip bath *n* **:** SITZ BATH
hip·ber·ry \'hip-—*see* BERRY\ *n* **:** ¹HIP
hipbone \'=,=\ *n* [ME *hipboon*, fr. *hip* + *boon* bone — more at BONE] **:** INNOMINATE BONE
hip boot *n* **:** a boot reaching to the hips that is worn esp. by fishermen
hip girdle *n* **:** PELVIC GIRDLE
hip joint *n* **1 :** the articulation between the femur and the innominate bone **2 :** ²HIP 2b
hip knob *n* **:** a finial, ball, or other ornament at the intersection of the hip rafters and the ridge of a roof
hiplength \'=,=\ *adj* **:** extending to or over the hips ⟨a ~ coat⟩
hip·less \'hipləs\ *adj* **:** having or seeming to have no hips
hipline \'=,=\ *n* **:** the line formed by the lower edge of a hiplength garment or by measuring the hip at its fullest part
hip lock *n* **:** a cross-buttock in which a headlock is held throughout the maneuver

hip boot

hipp- *or* **hippo-** *comb form* [L, fr. Gk, fr. *hippos* — more at EQUINE] **:** horse ⟨*hippo*gastronomy⟩ ⟨*hipp*uric acid⟩
hip·pa \'hipə\ [NL, alter. of L *hippus*, a sea fish, fr. Gk *hippos*, lit., horse] *syn of* EMERITA
hip·parch \'hi,pärk\ *n* -s [Gk *hipparchos, hipparchēs*, fr. *hipp-* + *-archos, -archēs* -arch] **:** a commander of cavalry in ancient Greece
hip·par·i·on \hi'pa(a)rē,än, -ēən\ *n* [NL, fr. Gk, pony, dim. of *hippos* horse] **1** *cap* **:** a genus of extinct Miocene and Pliocene three-toed mammals related to but not now considered direct ancestors of the horse **2** -s **:** any animal or fossil of the genus *Hipparion*
hip·pe·as·trum \,hipē'astrəm\ *n* [NL, fr. Gk *hippeus* horseman, (fr. *hippos*) + *astron* star; fr. the equitant leaves and the star-shaped flowers — more at STAR] **1** *cap* **:** a genus of tropical American bulbous plants (family Amaryllidaceae) that are widely cultivated for their showy white to crimson flowers and that are sometimes included in the genus *Amaryllis* **2** -s **:** any amaryllis of the genus *Hippeastrum*
¹hipped \'hipt\ *adj* [²*hip* + *-ed*] **1 :** having hips ⟨a ~ roof⟩ — often used in combination ⟨a broad-*hipped* person⟩ **2 :** HIPSHOT
²hipped \'hipt\ *adj* [⁵*hip* + *-ed*] **1 :** marked by worry, depression, or hypochondria ⟨with his bad habits and his domestic grievances he became completely ~ —H.W.Longfellow⟩ ⟨felt ~ because no one . . . bothered about his claret-colored ribbon —Philip Gibbs⟩ **2 :** absorbed or interested to an extreme or unreasonable degree **:** OBSESSED — usu. used with *on* ⟨married to a girl who is ~ on psychoanalysis —Bennett Cerf⟩
hip·pe·la·tes \,hipə'lād·(,)ēz\ *n, cap* [NL, fr. Gk *hippelatēs* horse driver, fr. *hipp-* + *elatēs* driver (fr. *elaunein* to drive); fr. the large spurs] **:** a genus of small black American eye gnats (family Chloropidae) including some that are held to be vectors of pinkeye and yaws
hip·pen *or* **hip·pin** \'hipən\ *n* -s [²*hip* + *-en* or *-in* (alter. of *-ing*)] *dial* **:** a baby's diaper
hip·pe·ty–hop *or* **hip·pi·ty–hop** \'hipəd·ē'häp\ *or* **hip·pe·ty–hop·pe·ty** *or* **hip·pi·ty–hop·pi·ty** \-äpəd·ē\ *adv (or adj)* [irreg. fr. ⁴*hip* + *hop*] **:** with a hopping rhythm or motion ⟨the rabbit went *hippety-hop* across the lawn⟩ ⟨rising and falling in their saddles, with a *hippity-hop* motion —Laura Krey⟩
hip·peu·tis \hi'pyüd·əs\ *n, cap* [NL, prob. fr. Gk *hippeutēs* horseman, fr. *hippos* horse — more at EQUINE] **:** a genus of freshwater snails (family Planorbidae) that are occas. the intermediate hosts of some medically important flukes
hip·pic \'hipik\ *adj* [Gk *hippikos*, fr. *hippos* horse + *-ikos* -ic] **:** of or relating to horses or horse racing ⟨the chief English ~ events of the season —*Punch*⟩
hip·pid·i·on \hi'pidē,än, -ēən\ *n, cap* [NL, fr. Gk *hippidion*, dim. of *hippos*] **:** a genus of extinct Pleistocene horses of Argentina and Brazil
hip·pid·i·um \-ēəm\ [NL, alter. of *Hippidion*] *syn of* HIPPIDION
hippier *comparative of* HIPPY
hippiest *superlative of* HIPPY
hipping *pres part of* HIP
hip·pio·spongia \,hipē(,)ō+\ *n, cap* [NL, alter. of *Hippospongia*] **:** a genus of sponges (family Spongiidae) containing numerous important commercial sponges
hip·pish \'hipish\ *adj* [⁵*hip* + *-ish*] **:** characterized by or suffering from worry, depression, or hypochondria **:** HIPPED
hip·ple \'hipəl\ *n* -s [ME *heepil, hypil*, dim. of *heep, hepe* heap — more at HEAP] *dial Eng* **:** a small heap; *esp* **:** a small haycock
hip·po \'hi(,)pō\ *n* -s [by shortening] **:** HIPPOPOTAMUS
hippo- — see HIPP-
hip·po·bos·ca \,hipə'bäskə\ *n, cap* [NL, fr. *hipp-* + *-bosca* (fr. Gk *boskein* to feed)] **:** the type genus of the family Hippoboscidae
¹hip·po·bos·cid \;==¦bäs(k)əd\ *adj* [NL *Hippoboscidae*] **:** of or relating to the Hippoboscidae
²hippoboscid \"\ *n* -s **:** a fly of the family Hippoboscidae
hip·po·bos·ci·dae \,==¦bäs(k)ə,dē\ *n pl, cap* [NL, fr. *Hippobosca*, type genus + *-idae*] **:** a family of winged or wingless dipterans that comprise the louse flies, are bloodsucking parasites on birds and mammals, and are larviparous bringing forth single advanced larvae from time to time which almost immediately pupate — compare SHEEP KED
hip·po·camp \'hipə,kamp\ *n* [Gk *hippokampos*] **:** HIPPOCAMPUS 1
hip·po·cam·pal \¦==¦kampəl\ *adj* [NL *hippocampus* + E *-al*] **:** of or relating to the hippocampus
hippocampal convolution *or* **hippocampal gyrus** *n* **:** a convolution of the cerebral cortex that borders the hippocampus and contains elements of both archipallium and neopallium
hippocampal fissure *n* **:** DENTATE FISSURE
hip·po·cam·pine \¦=¦kam,pīn, -pən\ *adj* [NL *Hippocampus* + E *-ine*] **:** of or relating to sea horses
hip·po·cam·pus \,==kampəs\ *n* [NL, fr. Gk *hippokampos* sea horse, legendary sea monster, fr. *hippo-* hipp- + *kampos* sea monster] **1** *pl* **hippocam·pi** \-m,pī\ **:** a legendary creature with the head and forequarters of a horse and the tail of a dolphin or fish **2** *pl* **hippocampi :** a curved elongated ridge extending over the floor of the descending horn of each lateral ventricle of the brain, consisting of gray matter covered on the ventricular surface with white matter, and forming the larger part of the archipallium **3** *cap* **:** a genus of fishes (family Syngnathidae) consisting of the typical sea horses
hip·po·cas·ta·na·ce·ae \,hipə,kastə'nāsē,ē\ *n pl, cap* [NL, fr. *Hippocastanum*, type genus in former classifications (fr. *hipp-* + Gk *kastanon* chestnut) + *-aceae*] **:** a family of trees (order Sapindales) having opposite palmately lobed leaves, showy flowers in large clusters, and nutlike seeds encased in a leathery capsule and including the buckeyes
hip·po·centaur \,hipə+\ *n* [L *hippocentaurus*, fr. Gk *hippokentauros*, fr. *hippo-* hipp- + *kentauros* centaur] **:** CENTAUR
hip·po·cras \'hipə,kras, -krəs\ *n* -ES [ME *ypocras*, after *Hippocras, Hypocras, Ypocras* Hippocrates †ab377 B.C. Greek physician, its legendary inventor; prob. fr. his name's having been falsely analyzed as Gk *hypo* under + *krasis* mixture] **:** an aromatic highly spiced wine of medieval Europe
hip·po·crat·ea \,hipə'krad·ēə\ *n, cap* [NL, after *Hippocrates*] **:** a genus (the type of the family Hippocrateaceae) of tropical trees or twining shrubs having a 3-lobed capsule with winged seeds — see WOOD ALMOND
hip·po·crat·e·a·ce·ae \,==,krad·ē'āsē,ē\ *n pl, cap* [NL, fr. *Hippocratea*, type genus + *-aceae*] **:** a family of tropical shrubs or trees (order Sapindales) having opposite leaves and small 5-parted flowers — **hip·po·crat·e·a·ceous** \¦==,==¦āshəs\ *adj*
hip·po·crat·ic \¦hipə¦krad·ik, -atl, ¦ēk\ *also* **hip·po·crat·i·cal** \|əkəl, |ēk-\ *adj, usu cap* [LL *Hippocraticus*, fr. *Hippocrates* (fr. Gk *Hippokratēs*) + *-icus* -ic, -ical] **:** of or relating to Hippocrates or to the school of medicine that took his name
hippocratic facies *n, usu cap H* **:** the face as it appears near death and in some debilitating conditions marked by sunken eyes and temples, pinched nose, and tense hard skin
hippocratic finger *n, usu cap H* **:** a clubbed finger
hippocratic oath *n, usu cap H* **:** an oath embodying a code of medical ethics that is usu. taken by those about to begin medical practice
hip·poc·ra·tism \hi'päkrə,tizəm\ *n* -s *usu cap* [*Hippocrates* + E *-ism*] **:** the medical doctrine of the Hippocratic school
hip·po·crene \'hipə,krēn, ,=='krēnē\ *n* -s *usu cap* [fr. *Hippocrene*, a fountain in ancient Greece that was fabled to have burst forth when the ground was struck by the hoof of the winged horse Pegasus and that was supposed to be a source of poetic inspiration, fr. L, fr. Gk *Hippokrēnē*, fr. *hippo-* hipp- + *krēnē* fountain] **:** poetic inspiration ⟨we shrink from a cup of the purest *Hippocrene* after the critics' solar microscope —J.R. Lowell⟩ ⟨a loiterer by the waves of *Hippocrene* —O.W.Holmes †1894⟩
hip·po·crep·i·form \¦hipə¦krepə,fȯrm\ *adj* [*hipp-* + Gk *krēpis* boot + E *-form* — more at CREPIDULA] **:** shaped like a horseshoe
¹hip·po·drome \'hipə,drōm\ *n* -s [MF, fr. L *hippodromos*, fr. Gk, fr. *hippo-* hipp- + *dromos* racecourse — more at -DROME] **1 :** an oval stadium for horse and chariot races in ancient Greece **2 a :** an arena for equestrian performances **b** (1) **:** a spectacle presented in a hippodrome (2) **:** an activity suggesting such a spectacle **3 :** a sports contest with a predetermined winner
²hippodrome \"\ *vi* -ED/-ING/-S **1 :** to arrange or fix a sports contest whose winner is predetermined **2 :** to act as if in a hippodrome **:** attract attention by or as if by spectacular performance
hip·po·drom·ic \¦==¦drämik, -rōm-\ *adj* **:** of, relating to, or having the characteristics of a hippodrome
hip·po·glos·sus \,hipə'gläsəs, -lȯs-\ *n, cap* [NL, fr. *hipp-* + *-glossus* (fr. Gk *glōssa* tongue) — more at GLOSS] **:** a genus of flatfishes containing the typical halibuts and sometimes being made to be the type of a separate family but usu. included in the Pleuronectidae
hip·po·griff \'hipə,grif\ *n* -s [F *hippogriffe*, fr. It *ippogrifo*, fr. *ippo-* (fr. L *hippo-* hipp-) + *grifo* griffin, fr. L *gryphus* — more at GRIFFIN] **:** a legendary animal having the foreparts of a winged griffin and the body and hindquarters of a horse
hip·po·griffin \¦hipə+\ *n* [by alter. (influenced by *griffin*)] **:** HIPPOGRIFF
¹hip·poid \'hi,pȯid\ *adj* [NL *Hippoidea*] **:** of or relating to the Hippoidea
²hippoid \"\ *n* -s **:** a mammal of the group Hippoidea
hip·poi·dea \hi'pȯidēə\ *n pl, cap* [NL, fr. *hipp-* + *-oidea*] *in some classifications* **:** a division of perissodactylous mammals comprising the Equidae and extinct related forms
hip·po·lith \'hipə,lith\ *or* **hip·po·lite** \-,līt\ *n* -s [NL *hippolithus*, fr. *hipp-* + *-lithus* -lith, -lite] **:** a concretion from the intestines of the horse
hip·pol·o·gy \hi'päləjē\ *n* -ES [ISV *hipp-* + *-logy*] **:** the study of the horse
hip·pol·y·te \hi'pälə(,)tē\ *n, cap* [NL, after *Hippolyte*, Amazon in Greek mythology, fr. Gk *Hippolytē*] **:** a common and widely distributed genus (the type of the family Hippolytidae) of small prawns having the abdomen sharply bent at the third segment — **hip·pol·y·tid** \-,təd\ *adj or n*
hip·pom·a·nes \hi'pämə,nēz\ *n* -ES [L, fr. Gk, fr. *hippo-* hipp- + *-manes* (fr. *mainesthai* to rage, be furious) — more at MIND] **:** a growth found on the forehead of a newborn foal and held in antiquity to be aphrodisiac
hip·po·mo·bile \¦hipəmō¦bē(ə)l, ,=='mō,b-\ *n* [*hipp-* + *-mobile* (as in *automobile*)] **:** a horse-drawn vehicle
hip·po·mor·pha \,hipə'mȯrfə\ *n pl, cap* [NL, fr. *hipp-* + *-morpha*] **:** a suborder of Perissodactyla comprising horses, asses, zebras, and many extinct related forms
¹hip·po·nac·te·an \¦hipə,nak¦tēən, -¦nakte-\ *adj, usu cap* [L *Hipponacteus* of Hipponax (fr. *Hipponact-, Hipponax*, 6th cent. B.C. Greek poet reputed to have invented the choliamb, fr. Gk *Hippōnakt-, Hippōnax*) + E *-an*] **:** of or relating to Hipponax or to the verse forms ascribed to him; *specif* **:** CHOLIAMBIC
²hipponactean \"\ *n* -s *usu cap* **:** a Hipponactean verse; *specif* **:** a hypercatalectic form of glyconic

hipponactean distich *n, usu cap H* : a distich composed of a catalectic trochaic dimeter and iambic trimeter

hip·po·pathology \ˌhi(ˌ)pō+\ *n* [*hipp-* + *pathology*] : the pathology of the horse

hip·poph·a·ë \hiˈpäfē,ē\ *n, cap* [NL, fr. L *hippophaes*, fr. Gk, spurge] : a genus of thorny deciduous Old World shrubs (family Eleagnaceae) including the sea buckthorn

hip·poph·a·gism \hiˈpäfəˌjizəm\ *n* -s [*hipp-* + *-phagism*] : HIPPOPHAGY

hip·poph·a·gist \-jəst\ *n* -s [*hippophagy* + *-ist*] : one that eats horseflesh — **hip·poph·a·gis·ti·cal** \hiˌpäfəˈjistəkəl\ *adj*

hip·poph·a·gous \(ˈ)hiˈpäfəgəs\ *adj* [*hipp-* + *-phagous*] : eating horseflesh

hip·poph·a·gy \-ˈfəjē\ *n* -ES [*hipp-* + *-phagy*] : the act or practice of eating horseflesh

hip·po·pod \ˈhipəˌpäd\ *n, pl* **hippopods** \-dz\ *or* **hippop·o·des** \hiˈpäpəˌdēz\ [*hipp-* + *-pod*] : a legendary creature having the body of a man and the legs of a horse

hip·po·po·tam·ic \ˌhi(ˌ)pōpəˈtamik, ˌhipəpəˈ-; ˌhipəˈpäd·ə-(ˌ)mik\ *or* **hip·po·po·ta·mi·an** \ˌhi(ˌ)pōpəˈtāmēən, ˌhipəpəˈ-\ *adj* : of, relating to, or resembling the hippopotamus; *specif* : UNWIELDY

hip·po·pot·a·mus \ˌhipəˈpäd·əməs, -ätəm-\ *n* [L, fr. Gk, fr. *hippo-* hipp- + *potamos* river, fr. *petesthai* to fly, dart, rush — more at FEATHER] **1** *pl* **hip·popotamus·es** \-səz\ *or* **hippopota·mi** \-ˌmī, -(ˌ)mē\ : any of various large herbivorous four-toed chiefly aquatic mammals of the order Artiodactyla with an extremely large head and mouth, bare and very thick skin, and short legs; *esp* : a member of the genus *Hippopotamus* (as *H. amphibius*) formerly common in most rivers of Africa that is except for the elephant the bulkiest existing quadruped and has long canine and incisor teeth that yield a good quality of ivory **2** *cap* [NL, fr. L] : a genus (the type of the family Hippopotamidae) of mammals that includes the typical hippopotamuses

hippopotamus

hippos *pl of* HIPPO

hip·po·si·de·ros \ˌhi(ˌ)pōsəˈdirəs, -ˌsīˈd-\ *n, cap* [NL, fr. *hipp-* + Gk *sidēros* iron, object made of iron] : a large genus (the type of the family Hipposideridae) of horseshoe bats comprising some 40 species and ranging from northwest Africa to the Philippines and Australia

hip·po·spongia \ˌhipə+\ [NL, fr. *hipp-* + *Spongia*] *syn of* SPONGIA

hip·po·ti·grine \ˌhipəˈtīgrən, -ˌgrīn\ *adj* [NL *Hippotigris*, subgenus of *Equus* containing the zebras (fr. *hipp-* + Gk *tigris* tiger) + E *-ine* — more at TIGER] : of or relating to the zebra

hip·pot·o·my \hiˈpäd·əmē\ *n* -ES [ISV *hipp-* + *-tomy* (as in *anatomy*)] : the anatomy of the horse

hip·pot·ra·gine \hiˈpä·trəˌjīn, -əˌgīn, -əjən, -əgən\ *adj* [NL *Hippotragus* + E *-ine*] : of or relating to the genus *Hippotragus* or to any of the antelopes belonging to it

hip·pot·ra·gus \-rəgəs\ *n, cap* [NL, fr. *hipp-* + Gk *tragos* he-goat] : a genus of large antelopes with long annulated backwardly curved horns that includes the sable and roan antelopes and the extinct blaubok

hip·pu·rate \hiˈpyu̇ˌrāt, ˈhipyəˌr-\ *n* -s [ISV *hippuric* + *-ate*] : a salt or ester of hippuric acid

hip·pu·ric acid \(ˈ)hiˈpyu̇rik-\ *n* [*hipp-* + *-uric*] : a white crystalline nitrogenous acid $C_6H_5CONHCH_2COOH$ formed in the liver as a detoxication product of benzoic acid and present in the urine of herbivorous animals and in small quantity in human urine — called also *benzoylglycine*

hip·pu·ri·case \hiˈpyu̇rəˌkās, -āz\ *n* -s [ISV *hippuric* + *-ase*] : HISTOZYME

hip·pu·ris \hiˈpyu̇rəs\ *n, cap* [NL, fr. Gk *hippouris* horsetail fr. *hipp-* + *-ouris* (fr. *oura* tail)] : a widely distributed genus of small-flowered aquatic herbs (family Haloragaceae) with single erect stems and verticillate leaves

hip·pu·rite \ˈhipyəˌrīt\ *n* -s [NL *Hippurites*] : a mollusk or fossil of the genus *Hippurites*

hip·pu·ri·tes \ˌhipyəˈrīd·(ˌ)ēz\ *n, cap* [NL, fr. *hipp-* + *ur-* (tail) + *-ites*] : a genus (the type of the family Hippuritidae) of aberrant marine bivalve mollusks that are confined to the Cretaceous and whose lower valve is conical, usu. longitudinally ribbed, and attached by its apex and whose upper valve is depressed conic with a nearly central umbo — **hip·pu·rit·ic** \ˌ==ˈrid·ik\ *adj* — **hip·pu·ri·tid** \-ˈrid·əd\ *adj or n* — **hip·pu·ri·toid** \-ˈrīd-ˌȯid\ *adj*

hip·pus \ˈhipəs\ *n* -ES [NL, fr. Gk *hippos* horse, eye complaint — more at EQUINE] : a spasmodic variation in the size of the pupil of the eye caused by a tremor of the iris

-hippus \ˈ"\ *n comb form* [NL, fr. Gk *hippos*] : horse — in generic names esp. in paleontology ⟨*Eohippus*⟩

hip·py \ˈhipē\ *adj, usu* -ER/-EST : having or resembling large hips ⟨farthingales . . . to make the hips seem *hippier* and the waist tinier —*Britannica Bk. of the Yr.*⟩

hip rafter *n* : the rafter extending from the wall plate to the ridge and forming the angle of a hip roof

hip roll *n* : a tile or strip that covers the angle of a hip roof

hip roof *n* : a roof having sloping ends and sloping sides — compare HIP-AND-VALLEY ROOF

hips *pl of* HIP, *pres 3d sing of* HIP

hip-shot \ˈ=,=\ *adj* **1** : having the hip dislocated **2** : having one hip lower than the other ⟨spun slowly toward the long mirror . . . and posed ∼ like a model —Crary Moore⟩

hipster *var of* HEPSTER

hip tile *n* : a tile for covering the hip of a roof

hip vertical *n* : a vertical member whose upper end is at the hip of a truss

hip roof

hir·able *or* **hire·able** \ˈhīrəbəl\ *adj* : capable of being hired : available for hire

hi·ra·do ware \həˈrä(ˌ)dō-\ *n, usu cap H* [fr. *Hirado*, town and island of Japan where such porcelain is manufactured] : a Hizen porcelain characteristically decorated in underglaze blue with a design showing children playing under a fir tree

hi·ra·ga·na \ˌhirəˈgänə\ *n* -s [Jap, lit., flat kana] : the cursive script that is one of two sets of symbols in which Japanese kana is written — compare KATAKANA

hir·car·rah \hərˈkärə\ *n* -s [Per *harkāra*, fr. *har* every, all (fr. OPer *haruva-*) + *kār* work, deed, fr. MPer, fr. OPer *kar-* to do, make] *India* : COURIER, SPY

hirch *var of* HIRTCH

hir·cine \ˈhərˌsīn, -ˌsᵊn\ *adj* [L *hircinus*, fr. *hircus* he-goat + *-inus* -ine; perh. akin to L *horrēre* to bristle — more at HORROR] : of, relating to, or suggestive of a goat; *esp* : resembling a goat in smell

hir·co·cer·vus \ˌhərkōˈsərvəs\ *n* -ES [LL, fr. L *hircus* he-goat + *cervus* stag; trans. of Gk *tragelaphos*, fr. *tragos* he-goat + *elaphos* stag] : a legendary creature that is half goat and half stag

hir·die–gir·die \ˈhirdiˈgirdi, ˈhərdiˈgər-\ *adv* [alter. of *hiddie-giddie*, fr. ME (Sc) *hiddy-giddy*, prob. redupl. (influenced by *hed*, head) of *giddy*] *dial Brit* : TOPSY-TURVY

hir·dum–dir·dum \ˈhirdəmˈdirdəm, ˈhərdəmˈdər-\ *n* [prob. redupl. (influenced by *heard*) of *dirdum*] *dial Brit* : UPROAR

¹hire \ˈhī(ə)r, ˈhīə\ *n* -s [ME, fr. OE *hȳr*; akin to OFris *hēre* tax, lease, rent, OS *hūra*, *hūria*, MLG & MD *hūre*] **1 a** : payment for the temporary use of something ⟨the heaviest single item of government expenditure is . . . the ∼ of the money we borrowed for the war —G.B.Shaw⟩ **b** : payment for labor or personal services : WAGES ⟨the laborer is worthy of his ∼ —Lk 10: 7 (AV)⟩ **2 a** (1) : the act of hiring ⟨the government office which controlled the ∼ of coolies —Dillon Ripley⟩ (2) : an instance of such act ⟨the monthly base compensation payroll . . . is $70,000 as the result of new ∼s and merit and length-of-service increases —*U.S.Code*⟩ **b** : the state of being hired : EMPLOYMENT ⟨men of every political leaning are in the ∼ of big corporations —Robert Shaplen⟩ **syn** see WAGE — **for hire** *also* **on hire** : available for use or service in return for payment ⟨a coal lighter which plies *for hire* up and down the Meuse —H.J.Laski⟩ ⟨a thrashing machine went *on hire* from farm to farm —Flora Thompson⟩

²hire \ˈ"\ *vb* -ED/-ING/-S [ME *hiren*, fr. OE *hȳrian*; akin to OFris *hēra* to lease, MLG & MD *huren*; denominatives fr. the root of E ¹*hire*] *vt* **1 a** : to engage the personal services of for a fixed sum : employ for wages ⟨many clergy fought in person, and others *hired* substitutes —G.G.Coulton⟩ ⟨the leader . . . ∼s staff people to think up the ideas —W.H.Whyte⟩ — sometimes used with *away* or *on* ⟨can ∼ them away from any company . . . if you offer them a few more dollars —W.J.Reilly⟩ ⟨the crew was fully *hired* on —John Hersey⟩ **b** : to engage the temporary use of for a fixed sum ⟨came down with a hundred people in four private cars and *hired* a whole floor of the . . . hotel —Scott Fitzgerald⟩ ⟨*hired* a car for the afternoon —Elizabeth Bowen⟩ **c** *archaic* : BORROW ⟨she can ∼ the money, and I know she will pay you —A.D.McFaul⟩ **2 a** : to grant the personal services of for a fixed sum — often used with *out* ⟨have been *hiring* themselves out as practical consultants —Vance Packard⟩ ⟨the colonel had *hired* out most of his slaves —Winston Churchill⟩ **b** : to grant the temporary use of for a fixed sum ⟨bored-looking camels which they ∼ to visitors as props for exotic snapshots —Mollie Panter-Downes⟩ — often used with *out* ⟨the town council *hired* out chairs for visitors —B.L.K.Henderson⟩ **3** : to pay for having (something done) ⟨my father . . . had to ∼ all his share of the farm work done —W.A.White⟩ — *vi* : to accept employment ⟨asked me if I would ∼ with him to tend shop and keep books —John Woolman⟩ — **hire one's time** : to pay one's master for the right to use one's time for one's own gain

hired girl *n* : a woman employed as a domestic; *specif* : one living in a farm household who helps around the house and performs light farm chores

hired hand *n* : FARMHAND

hired man *n* : a man employed to do odd jobs about a house, estate, or farm; *esp* : FARMHAND

hire in *vi* : to accept employment and begin to work ⟨most of the guys . . . who've *hired in* over the past fourteen years —Warner Bloomberg⟩

hire·less \ˈhī(ə)rləs, -īəl-\ *adj* : receiving no payment or reward ⟨preaching . . . in most of the great towns as an ∼ volunteer —S.T.Coleridge⟩

hire·ling \-liŋ,-lēŋ\ *n* -s *often attrib* **1** : one who is hired; *esp* : one whose motives and interests in serving another are chiefly gainful ⟨was murdered by ∼s in the service of foreign powers —Stoyan Christowe⟩ **2** : one whose motives are venal or mercenary ⟨baser ∼s who live by lies on good men's lives —Lord Byron⟩ **3** : a horse for hire ⟨went to a neighboring livery stable to look for ∼s —Evelyn Waugh⟩

hire on *vi* : to find or accept employment ⟨doubtful that he could *hire on* as a Hollywood extra —F.B.Gipson⟩

hire out *vi* : to accept employment ⟨young Englishman who *hired out* as a photographer —Marcus Duffield⟩

hire purchase *n* **1** *chiefly Brit* : a contract of hire with an option of purchase in which a person hires goods for a specified period and at a fixed rent with the added condition that if he retains the goods for the full period and pays all the installments of rent as they become due the contract shall determine and the title vest absolutely in him and that if he chooses he may at any time during the term surrender the goods and be quit of any liability for future installments upon the contract — compare CONDITIONAL SALE **2** *chiefly Brit* : the practice of buying by hire purchase

hir·er \ˈhīrə(r)\ *n* -s [ME, fr. *hiren* to hire + *-er*] : one that hires

hiring *n* -s [ME, fr. gerund of *hiren* to hire — more at HIRE] : the contract or relationship between the parties to a transaction in which one hires the services or property of the other

hiring hall *n* : a union-operated employment agency or placement office where registered applicants are referred to jobs (as in the shipping industry) on a rotation basis — compare SHAPE-UP

hir·ling \ˈhərlən, ˈhir-, -liŋ\ *var of* HERLING

hir·mos *or* **heir·mos** \irˈmȯs\ *n, pl* **hir·moi** *or* **heir·moi** \-ˈmē\ [LGk *heirmos*, fr. Gk, series, sequence, connection; akin to Gk *eirein* to fasten together — more at SERIES] : a troparion, hymn, or canticle with a fixed rhythm and melody that is used as a standard rhythmic and melodic pattern for other troparia in the canon of the Eastern Church

hirn \ˈhərn, -i-\ *var of* ¹HERN

hir·ne·o·la \(ˌ)hərˈnēələ\ [NL, dim. of L *hirnea* jug] *syn of* AURICULARIA

hiro·shi·ma \ˌhirəˈshēmə, -rō-; həˈrōshəmə, -ˈrish-,-ˈrōsh-; *Jap approximately* hiˈrōˈshē(ˌ)mä\ *adj, usu cap* [fr. *Hiroshima*, Japan] : of or from the city of Hiroshima, Japan : of the kind or style prevalent in Hiroshima

¹hir·ple \ˈhirpəl\ *vi* -ED/-ING/-S [ME (Sc dial.) *hirplen*] *chiefly Scot* : to walk with a limp : HOBBLE

²hirple \ˈ"\ *n* -s *Scot* : LIMP

hirsch·sprung's disease \ˈhirsh,pru̇ŋz-\ *n, usu cap H* [after Harold *Hirschsprung* †1916 Dan. physician] : congenital megacolon

¹hir·sel *also* **hir·sle** \ˈhirsəl\ *n* -s [ME *hirsill*, fr. ON *hirzla*, *hirthsla* safekeeping, custody, fr. *hirtha* to guard sheep, fr. *hirthir* shepherd — more at HERD] **1** *Scot* : a flock of sheep **2** *Scot* : the land grazed by a flock of sheep ⟨like a poor lamb that has wandered from its own native ∼ —Sir Walter Scott⟩ **3** *Scot* : a large number or quantity : MULTITUDE

²hirsel *also* **hirsle** \ˈ"\ *vt* **hirseled** *or* **hirselled** *also* **hirsled**; **hirseled** *or* **hirselled** *also* **hirsled**; **hirseling** *or* **hirselling** *also* **hirsling**; **hirsels** *also* **hirsles** *Scot* : to arrange in or as if in flocks

³hirsel *also* **hirsle** \ˈ"\ *vb* **hirseled** *or* **hirselled** *also* **hirsled**; **hirseled** *or* **hirselled** *also* **hirsled**; **hirseling** *or* **hirselling** *also* **hirsling**; **hirsels** *also* **hirsles** [origin unknown] *vi* **1** *Scot* : to move along a surface awkwardly : SLITHER **2** *Scot* : to move clumsily or with difficulty : SCRAMBLE **3** *Scot* : to move with a rustling or grating noise ∼ *vt, Scot* : to cause to move awkwardly or with difficulty

hirst \ˈhirst\ *n* -s [ME *hirst*, *hurst* grove, knoll — more at HURST] **1** *Scot* **a** : a barren unproductive plot of ground **b** : a sandbank in a river **2** *Scot* : a great number or quantity **3** *Scot* : the part of the floor of a mill where the millstones turn in their framework

hirst·ie \ˈhirsti\ *adj* [*hirst* + *-ie* (Sc var. of *-y*)] *Scot* : BARE, BARREN

hir·su·tal \(ˈ)hərˈsüd·ᵊl\ *adj* [L *hirsutus* + E *-al*] : of or relating to the hair

hir·sute \ˈhərˌsüt, ˈhi(ə)rˌs-, ˈhə̄ˌs-, ˈhəiˌs-, ˈhiəˌs-, (ˌ)=ˈ=, *usu* -üd.+V\ *adj* [L *hirsutus*; akin to L *hirtus* rough, shaggy, *horrēre* to bristle — more at HORROR] **1 a** : rough with hair or bristles : HAIRY, SHAGGY ⟨the dog's master patted the ∼ fellow —Horace Sutton⟩ **b** *biol* : pubescent with coarse stiff hairs **c** : covered with feathers that resemble hair **2** : of, relating to, or having the characteristics of hair — **hir·sute·ness** *n* -ES

hir·su·tel·la \ˌhər(ˌ)süˈtelə, ˌhir-\ *n, cap* [NL, fr. L *hirsutus* + NL *-ella*] : a genus of basidiomycetous fungi of uncertain taxonomic position that are associated with and believed to be parasitic upon various insects

hir·su·ti·es \(ˌ)hərˈsüshēˌēz, hir-\ *n, pl* **hirsuties** [NL, fr. L *hirsutus*] : HIRSUTISM

hir·sut·ism *pronunc at* HIRSUTE + ˌizəm\ *n* -s [ISV *hirsute* + *-ism*] : excessive growth of hair of normal or abnormal distribution : HYPERTRICHOSIS

hir·su·tu·lous \(ˌ)hərˈsüchələs, ˈhir-\ *adj* [*hirsute* + *-ulous*] : minutely or slightly hirsute

¹hirtch \ˈhirch\ *vi* -ED/-ING/-ES [origin unknown] **1** *Scot* : to shudder with or as if with cold **2** *Scot* : to walk with a jerky hobbling motion

²hirtch \ˈ"\ *n* -ES *Scot* : HITCH

hir·tel·la \(ˌ)hərˈtelə, hir-\ *n, cap* [NL, fr. L *hirtus* + NL *-ella*] : a genus of chiefly tropical American shrubs or small trees (family Rosaceae) having axillary or terminal racemes of small white or purplish flowers with numerous stamens

hir·tel·lous \(ˌ)hərˈteləs, ˈhir-\ *adj* [L *hirtus* + *-ellus* (diminutive suffix)] : finely hirsute ⟨thickened ∼ leaves⟩

hiru·din \ˈhir(y)ədən, həˈrüdᵊn\ *n* -s [fr. *Hirudin*, a trademark] : a preparation of the active principles of the buccal glands of a leech used to retard or prevent the clotting of blood

hir·u·din·ea \ˌhir(y)əˈdinēə\ *n pl, cap* [NL, fr. *Hirudin-*, *Hirudo*] : a class of hermaphroditic aquatic, terrestrial, or parasitic annelid worms distinguished by a coelom nearly obliterated by connective tissue and reduced to a series of vascular sinuses, by modification of the hindmost segments into a sucking disk, and by the absence of parapodia and setae — compare GNATHOBDELLIDA, PHARYNGOBDELLIDA, RHYNCHOBDELLIDA — **hir·u·din·e·an** \ˌ==ˈdinēən\ *adj or n*

hir·u·din·ei \ˌ==ˈdinēˌī\ [NL, fr. *Hirudin-*, *Hirudo*] *syn of* HIRUDINEA

hir·u·di·ni·a·sis \ˌhir(y)ədəˈnīəsəs, həˌrüdᵊnˈī-\ *n, pl* **hirudi·nia·ses** \-ˈīəˌsēz\ [NL, fr. *Hirudin-*, *Hirudo* + *-iasis*] : infestation with leeches

hir·u·din·i·dae \ˌhir(y)əˈdinəˌdē\ *n pl, cap* [NL, fr. *Hirudin-*, *Hirudo*, type genus + *-idae*] : a family of aquatic leeches that have 5-ringed segments, 5 pairs of eyes, and usu. 3-toothed jaws and that include the common medicinal leech

hi·ru·di·nize \həˈrüdᵊnˌīz\ *vt* -ED/-ING/-S : to retard or prevent the coagulation of (blood) by the injection of hirudin

hi·ru·do \həˈrü(ˌ)dō\ *n, cap* [NL, fr. L, leech] : a genus (the type of the family Hirudinidae) of the order Gnathobdellida that includes the common medicinal leech

¹hirun·dine \həˈrəndən, -ˌdīn; ˈhirənˌdīn\ *adj* [L *hirundo* swallow + E *-ine*] : of, relating to, or resembling the swallow

²hirundine \ˈ"\ *n* -s [NL *Hirundinidae*] : ¹SWALLOW 1

hir·un·din·i·dae \ˌhirənˈdinəˌdē\ *n pl, cap* [NL, fr. *Hirundin-*, *Hirundo*, type genus (fr. L, swallow) + *-idae*] : a family of passerine birds consisting of the swallows and martins — **hi·run·di·nous** \həˈrəndənəs\ *adj*

¹his [ME, fr. OE, gen. of *hē* he — more at HE] *obs possessive of* ¹HE

²his \(h)iz, ˈhiz, ēz\ *adj* [ME, fr. OE, gen. of *hē*] **1 a** : of or relating to him or himself as possessor : due to him : inherent in him : associated or connected with him ⟨a wise man who built ∼ house upon the rock —Mt 7: 24 (RSV)⟩ ⟨the western ocean in one of the very worst of ∼ moods —Cicely F. Smith⟩ ⟨did he bump ∼ little head⟩ — compare ¹HE **b** : of or relating to him or himself as author, doer, giver, or agent : effected by him : experienced by him as subject : that he is capable of ⟨reading Shakespeare's histories as well as ∼ comedies and tragedies⟩ ⟨∼ promise⟩ ⟨success attributed to ∼ having been prompt⟩ ⟨he ran ∼ fastest⟩ **c** : of or relating to him or himself as object of an action : experienced by him as object ⟨he awaited ∼ confirmation by the senate⟩ ⟨a secret combination against a person with the object of ∼ hurt or injury —H.E.Scudder⟩ **d** : that he has to do with or is supposed to possess or to have knowledge or a share of or some special interest in ⟨the boy who knows ∼ baseball —David Dempsey⟩ ⟨he enthusiastically supports ∼ local symphony —*Amer. Guide Series: Minn.*⟩ **e** : that is esp. significant for him : that brings him good fortune or prominence — used with *day* or sometimes with other words indicating a division of time ⟨this was ∼ day and the treat was on him —H.A.Chippendale⟩ **2** *obs* : ITS — used as late as the 17th century with no implied personification ⟨if the salt have lost ∼ savor, wherewith shall it be salted? —Mt 5: 13 (AV)⟩ **3** *archaic* : 's — used after a noun or noun phrase in place of the possessive ending *'s* ⟨at the tide of Christ ∼ birth —Thomas Fuller⟩ ⟨in George the First ∼ time —W.M.Thackeray⟩ ⟨Billy Bones, ∼ fancy —R.L.Stevenson⟩

³his \ˈhiz\ *pron, sing or pl in constr* [ME, fr. OE, gen. of *hē*] **1** : his one or his ones — used without a following noun as a pronoun equivalent in meaning to the adjective *his* ⟨if my brother had my shape, and I had ∼ —*Shak.*⟩ ⟨my dog is large and ∼ is small⟩ ⟨your eyes are blue and ∼ are brown⟩; often used after *of* to single out one or more members of a class belonging to or connected with a particular male person or animal ⟨a friend of ∼⟩ ⟨four or five books of ∼⟩ or merely to identify something or someone as belonging to or connected with a particular male person or animal without any implication of membership in a more extensive class ⟨that overbearing manner of ∼⟩ ⟨those big feet of ∼⟩ **2** : something that belongs to him : what belongs to him ⟨all that is ∼ is hers⟩

his *abbr* history

hish \ˈhish\ *dial var of* HISS

his heels *n pl but sing or pl in constr* : a jack that is turned up as the starter in cribbage and that scores two points for the dealer

his·ing·er·ite \ˈhisiŋəˌrīt, ˈhizi-\ *n* -s [G *hisingerit*, fr. Wilhelm *Hisinger* †1852 Swed. geologist + G *-it* -ite] : a mineral perhaps $Fe_2Si_2O_5(OH)_4.2H_2O$ consisting of a black amorphous iron ore that is a hydrous ferric silicate

his·lop·ite \ˈhizləˌpīt, ˈhisl-\ *n* -s [Stephen *Hislop* †1863 Eng. missionary to India and amateur geologist + E *-ite*] : a bright green Indian calcite

hisn *or* **his'n** \ˈhizᵊn\ *pron* [ME *hysene*, alter. (influenced by the *-n* in *min* mine, *thin* thine) of *his*] *dial* : HIS

his·pa \ˈhispə\ *n* [NL, irreg. fr. L *hispidus* rough, hairy, bristly] **1** *cap* : a genus (often the type of the family Hispidae) of spiny Old World beetles with larvae that are leaf miners **2** -s : a beetle of *Hispa* or various closely related genera

his·pan·ic \(ˈ)hiˈspanik, -nēk\ *adj, usu cap* [L *Hispanicus*, fr. *Hispania* Spain, Iberian peninsula + L *-icus* -ic] : relating to or derived from the people, speech, or culture of Spain or of Spain and Portugal; *often* : LATIN-AMERICAN ⟨the folklore of *Hispanic* groups⟩ — **hispanic-american** \ˈ"+\ *adj, usu cap H&A*

his·pan·i·cism \hiˈspanəˌsizəm\ *n* -s *usu cap* : a word, phrase, or mode of expression distinctive of Spanish esp. when it appears in an English context

his·pan·i·cist \-səst\ *n* -s *usu cap* : HISPANIST

his·pan·i·ci·za·tion \(ˌ)=ˌ==səˈzāshən, -ˌsīˈz-\ *n* -s *often cap* : the act or a process of hispanicizing

his·pan·i·cize \=ˈ==ˌsīz\ *vt* -ED/-ING/-S *often cap* : to make Spanish: **a** : to cause to acquire a quality, qualities, traits or outlook distinctive of Spanish culture or Spaniards ⟨to ∼ the conquered Indians⟩ **b** : to modify (language or a particular word or expression) to conform to language characteristics distinctive of Spanish ⟨"beisbol" is *hispanicized* "baseball"⟩ **c** : to bring under the control of Spain or Spaniards ⟨the government was *hispanicized*⟩

his·pa·ni·dad \ēspänēˈthä(th)\ *n* -s *often cap* [Sp, fr. *hispánico* Hispanic (fr. L *Hispanicus*) + *-dad* -ty (fr. L *-tat-*, *-tas*)] : hispanism esp. as adapted to fascist purposes and used for the undermining of U.S. influence in Latin America

his·pan·io·lize \hiˈspanyəˌlīz, ˌhispənˈyō,l-\ *vt* -ED/-ING/-S *often cap* [modif. (influenced by *Hispanic*) of Sp *españolizar*, fr. *español* Spanish (fr. — assumed — VL *Hispaniolus*, fr. L *Hispania* Spain) + *-izar* -ize] : HISPANICIZE

his·pa·nism \ˈhispəˌnizəm\ *n* -s *often cap* [Sp *hispanismo*, fr. *hispano* Spanish, Hispanic (fr. L *Hispanus*) + *-ismo* -ism] **1** : the Spanish and Latin-American movement to reassert the spiritual and cultural unity of Spain and the Latin-American countries and promote the return to classic Spanish culture and Spanish supremacy in Latin America — compare HISPANIDAD **2** : a linguistic feature of Spanish origin or due to Spanish influence

his·pa·nist \-nəst\ *n* -s *usu cap* [Sp *hispanista*, fr. *hispano* + *-ista* -ist] : a scholar specially informed in the Spanish or Portuguese languages or Spanish or Portuguese literature, linguistics, or civilization

his·pa·ni·za·tion \ˌhispənəˈzāshən, -ˌnīˈz-\ *n* -s *often cap* [Sp *hispanización*, fr. *hispanizar* + *-ación* -ation] : HISPANICIZATION

his·pa·nize \ˈhispəˌnīz\ *vt* -ED/-ING/-S *often cap* [Sp *hispanizar*, fr. *hispano* + *-izar* -ize] : HISPANICIZE

his·pano \hiˈspa(ˌ)nō, -ˈpä(-, -pā(-; ˈhispəˌnō\ *n* -s *cap* [short for *Hispano-American*] : a native or resident of the southwestern U.S. descended from Spaniards settled there before annexation

hispano- *comb form, usu cap* [Sp *hispano*, fr. L *Hispanus*] : Spanish and ⟨*Hispano*-German⟩ : Spanish ⟨*hispanophile*⟩

hispano-moresque \=ˈ==, ˈ=(ˌ)=+\ *adj, usu cap H&M* **1** : of, relating to, or produced in the era of Moorish ascendancy in Spain — used chiefly of art or cultural objects (as pottery, textiles) **2** *of a rug* : antique and oriental and found in Spain

his·pan·o·phile \hiˈspanəˌfīl\ *also* **his·pano·phil** \-ˌfil\ *n* -s *often cap* [*Hispano-* + *-phile, -phil*] **:** one partial to Spain or esp. fond of Spanish culture or civilization

[1]**his·per·ic** \(ˈ)hiˈsperik\ *adj, usu cap* [fr. *Hisperica famina,* 6th cent. Latin work written in Ireland in the Hisperic style] **:** belonging to or constituting a style of Latin writing that probably originated in Ireland in the 6th century and that is characterized by extreme obscurity intentionally produced by periphrasis, coinage of new words, and very liberal use of loanwords to express quite ordinary meanings

[2]**hisperic** \"\ *n* -s *cap* **:** Hisperic Latin

his·pid \ˈhispəd\ *adj* [L *hispidus;* prob. akin to L *horrēre* to bristle — more at HORROR] **:** rough or covered with bristles, stiff hairs, or minute spines ⟨a ~ leaf⟩ — **his·pid·i·ty** \hiˈspidəd·ē\ *n* -ES

his·pid·u·lous \(ˈ)hiˈspijələs\ *also* **his·pid·u·late** \-lət, -ˌlāt\ *adj* [*hispid* + *-ulous* or *-ulate* (fr. *-ulous* + *-ate*)] **:** minutely hispid

his·pine \ˈhiˌspīn, -ˌspən\ *adj* [NL *Hispa* + E *-ine*] **:** of or related to the genus *Hispa*

[1]**hiss** \ˈhis\ *vb* -ED/-ING/-ES [ME *hissen,* of imit. origin] *vi* **:** to make a sharp sibilant sound: as **a :** to make the sound by which an animal (as a goose or snake) indicates alarm, fear, or irritation ⟨the kitten ~*ed* at sight of the dog⟩ **b :** to make such a sound as an expression of hatred, passion, or disapproval ⟨the crowd booed and ~*ed*⟩ **c :** to escape or move with a hissing sound ⟨the wind ~*ed* about the caves⟩ — used esp. of substances under pressure ⟨steam ~*ing* from the kettle's spout⟩ ⟨air ~*ed* from the faulty valve⟩ ~ *vt* **1 :** to condemn or express contempt or dislike for by hissing ⟨~*ed* the speaker from the stage⟩ **2 :** to utter with a hissing sound ⟨~ dispraise⟩ ⟨sibilants should be clearly ~*ed*⟩

[2]**hiss** \"\ *n* -ES **1 :** a prolonged sibilant sound like that of the speech sound \s\ or \z\: as **a :** any of various animal sounds usu. indicative of alarm, fear, or irritation ⟨startled by the sharp ~ of a snake⟩ **b :** the sound made by steam or other gas escaping through a narrow opening **c** (1) **:** the friction that characterizes the utterance of a voiceless fricative consonant (2) **:** a voiceless fricative; *specif* **:** \s\ — compare BUZZ **2 :** a hiss used as an expression of dislike, disapprobation, or contempt ⟨~*es* rose from all parts of the audience⟩

[3]**hiss** \"\ *or* **hissing** *adj* **:** being or involving the sibilant \s\ or \z\ ⟨~ sibilants of Georgian speech⟩ — compare HUSH

hiss·able \ˈhisəbəl\ *adj* **1 :** uttered with a hiss **2 :** deserving to be hissed

his·self \(h)i(z)ˈ⸗, ē(z)ˈ⸗\ *also* **his·sel** \-ˈsel\ *pron* [ME *his self,* fr. *his* + *self*] *substand* **:** HIMSELF ⟨when he come to ~ they told him it was a Union hospital —Helen Eustis⟩

hiss·er \ˈhisə(r)\ *n* -s [ME, fr. *hissen* + *-er*] **:** one that hisses

hissing *n* -s [ME, fr. gerund of *hissen* to hiss] **1 :** an act or instance of emitting a hiss **2 :** an occasion of contempt **:** an object of scorn ⟨the priests, because of their breaches of the restrictions . . . made their calling a reproach and a ~ —A.M. Young⟩

hissing adder *or* **hissing snake** *also* **hissing viper** *n* **:** HOGNOSE SNAKE

hiss·ing·ly *adv* **:** in a hissing manner **:** with a sound of hissing

hissy \ˈhisē\ *n* -ES [origin unknown] *Southwest* **:** a fit of temper **:** TANTRUM

[1]**hist** \s *often prolonged and usu with* p *preceding and/or* t *or a glottal stop following; often read as* ˈhist\ *interj* [origin unknown] — used to demand attention or quietly to attract a person's attention

[2]**hist** \ˈhīst\ *dial var of* HOIST

hist- *or* **histo-** *comb form* [F, fr. Gk *histos* mast, beam of a loom, loom, web, fr. *histanai* to cause to stand — more at STAND] **:** tissue ⟨*hist*amine⟩ ⟨*histo*physiology⟩

hist *abbr* **1** histology **2** historian; historic; historical; history

his·ta·mi·nase \hiˈstaməˌnās, ˈhistəm-, -āz\ *n* -s [ISV *histamine* + *-ase*] **:** a flavoprotein enzyme occurring widely in plant and animal tissues (as in the kidney and small intestine) and capable of oxidizing histamine and various diamines (as putrescine) — called also *diamine oxidase*

his·ta·mine \ˈhistəˌmēn, -ˌmən\ *also* **his·ta·min** \-ˌmən\ *n* -s [ISV *hist-* + *amine*] **:** a crystalline base $C_3H_3N_2CH_2CH_2NH_2$ that is found in ergot and other plants and usu. combined in animal tissues, that is formed from histidine by decarboxylation, and that is held to be responsible for the dilation and increased permeability of blood vessels which play a major role in allergic reactions; 4(or 5)-imidazole-ethylamine — see ANTIHISTAMINE, GASTRIN — **his·ta·min·ic** \ˌ⸗⸗ˈminik\ *adj*

histamine flare *n* **:** an allergic tissue reaction to histamine manifested by local flushing of the skin

his·ta·min·er·gic \ˌ⸗⸗məˈnərjik\ *adj* [ISV *histamine* + *-ergy* + *-ic*] **1** *of autonomic nerve fibers* **:** liberating histamine **2** *of autonomic nerve fibers* **:** activated by histamine

his·tamino·lyt·ic \ˌ⸗⸗ˌmēnəˈlid·ik, -ˌmin-; hiˌstamənəˈl-\ *adj* [ISV *histamine* + *-o-* + *-lytic*] **:** breaking down or tending to break down histamine ⟨~ action of blood plasma⟩

histe \ˈhīst\ *dial var of* HOIST

his·ter \ˈhistə(r)\ *also* **hister beetle** *n* -s [NL *Hister,* genus of beetles, fr. L *hister* actor, fr. Etruscan; fr. the fact that these beetles play dead when disturbed] **:** a beetle of the family Histeridae

[1]**his·ter·id** \-tərəd\ *adj* [NL *Histeridae*] **:** of or relating to the Histeridae

[2]**histerid** \"\ *n* -s **:** HISTER

his·ter·i·dae \hiˈsterəˌdē\ *n pl, cap* [NL, fr. *Hister,* type genus + *-idae*] **:** a family of rather sluggish dark-colored and often shining beetles that live chiefly in decaying organic matter and have larvae which prey on other insects and insect larvae

histi- *or* **histio-** *comb form* [Gk *histion* web, cloth, sail, dim. of *histos* mast, beam of a loom, loom, web — more at HIST-] **1 :** sail ⟨*Histio*pterus⟩ **2 :** tissue ⟨*histio*cyte⟩

his·ti·dase \ˈhistəˌdās, -āz\ *n* -s [ISV *histidin* + *-ase*] **:** an enzyme occurring esp. in the liver of vertebrates that is capable of deaminating histidine to form urocanic acid

his·ti·dine \-ˌdēn, -dən\ *also* **his·ti·din** \-dən\ *n* -s [ISV *hist-* + *-idine, -idin;* orig. formed as G *histidin*] **:** a crystalline basic amino acid $C_3H_3N_2CH_2CH(NH_2)COOH$ that is essential in the nutrition of the rat, is synthesized by microorganisms and by plants, and is formed by the decomposition of most proteins (as globin); 4(or 5)-imidazole-alanine

hist·ie \ˈhisti\ *var of* HIRSTIE

his·tio·cyte \ˈhistēəˌsīt\ *n* -s [ISV *histi-* + *-cyte*] **:** a phagocytic tissue cell that may be fixed or freely motile, is derived from the reticuloendothelial system, and resembles the monocyte with which it is sometimes identified — called also *clasmatocyte, macrophage* — **his·tio·cyt·ic** \ˌ⸗⸗⸗ˈsid·ik\ *adj*

his·tio·cy·to·ma \ˌ⸗⸗(ˌ)⸗sīˈtōmə\ *n, pl* **histiocytomas** \-məz\ *also* **histiocyto·ma·ta** \-məd·ə\ [NL, fr. ISV *histiocyte* + NL *-oma*] **:** a tumor consisting predominantly of histiocytes, being usu. nonmalignant, and occurring esp. in young male dogs

his·tio·cy·to·sis \-ˈtōsəs\ *n, pl* **histiocyto·ses** \-ōˌsēz\ [NL, fr. ISV *histiocyte* + NL *-osis*] **:** abnormal multiplication of histiocytes; *broadly* **:** a condition characterized by such multiplication

his·ti·oid \ˈhistēˌȯid\ *adj* [ISV *histi-* + *-oid*] **:** HISTOID

his·ti·ol·o·gy \ˌhistēˈäləjē, -ji\ *n* -ES [by alter.] **:** HISTOLOGY

his·ti·oph·a·gous \ˌ⸗⸗ˈäfəgəs\ *adj* [*histi-* + *-phagous*] **:** feeding on tissues ⟨~ protozoans⟩

his·tio·phor·i·dae \ˌhistēəˈfȯrəˌdē\ [NL, fr. *Histiophorus,* type genus (fr. *histi-* + *-phorus*) + *-idae*] *syn of* ISTIOPHORIDAE

his·ti·op·ter·i·dae \ˌ⸗⸗ˌäpˈterəˌdē\ *n pl, cap* [NL, fr. *Histiopterus,* type genus (fr. *histi-* + *-pterus*) + *-idae*] **:** a family of deep-sea percoid fishes with compressed body, rough scales, and strong fin spines — see BOARFISH

histo- — see HIST-

his·to·blast \ˈhistəˌblast\ *n* [ISV *hist-* + *-blast*] **:** a cell or cell group possessing broad histogenetic capacity: as **a :** HISTIOCYTE **b :** IMAGINAL DISK

his·to·chemical \ˌhi(ˌ)stō+\ *adj* [*hist-* + *chemical*] **:** of, relating to, or by means of histochemistry — **his·to·chemical·ly** \"+\ *adv*

his·to·chemistry \"+\ *n* [ISV *hist-* + *chemistry*] **:** a science that deals with the chemical constitution of living cells and tissues by combining the techniques of biochemistry and histology

his·to·chem·o·graph \ˌhi(ˌ)stōkeməˌgraf, -rȧf\ *n* [*hist-* + *chem-* + *-graph*] **:** a picture or pattern produced on a photographic plate by the chemical action of a histological specimen in contact with the emulsion — **his·to·che·mog·ra·phy** \-ˌkeˈmägrəfē, -ˌkə'-\ *n* -ES

his·to·cyte \ˈhistəˌsīt\ *n* -s [ISV *hist-* + *-cyte*] **1 :** HISTIOCYTE **2 :** a cell (as in various lower invertebrates) with highly developed capacity to form tissues

his·to·gen \-təjən, -ˌjen\ *n* -s [ISV *hist-* + *-gen*] **:** a zone or clearly delimited region of primary tissue in or from which the specific parts of a plant organ are believed to be produced — see DERMATOGEN, PERIBLEM, PLEROME; HISTOGEN THEORY; compare CALYPTROGEN, CORPUS, TUNICA

his·to·genesis \ˌhistə+\ *n* [NL, fr. *hist-* + L *genesis*] **:** the formation and differentiation of tissues ⟨the ~ of floral organs⟩ ⟨~ of a neoplasm⟩

his·to·ge·net·ic \ˌhistəjəˈned·ik\ *adj* [*hist-* + *genetic*] **1 :** of or relating to histogenesis **2 :** of or relating to histogenetics — **his·to·ge·net·i·cal·ly** \-d·ək(ə)lē\ *adv*

his·to·ge·net·ics \-d·iks\ *n pl but sing or pl in constr* **:** a branch of genetics concerned with the genetic significance and basis of somatic variation (as in the production of bud sports and graft hybrids)

his·to·gen·ic \ˌ⸗(ˌ)⸗ˈjenik\ *adj* [ISV *hist-* + *-genic*] **:** producing tissue

histogen theory *n* **:** a theory in botany: a growing point (as of a stem or root) consists of three histogens each of which gives rise to a different tissue — see DERMATOGEN, PERIBLEM, PLEROME

his·tog·e·ny \hiˈstäjənē\ *n* -ES [ISV *hist-* + *-geny*] **:** HISTOGENESIS

his·to·gram \ˈhistəˌgram\ *n* -s [fr. Gk *histos* mast, pole, web + E *-gram*] **:** a representation of a frequency distribution by means of rectangles whose widths represent class intervals and whose areas are proportional to the corresponding frequencies

his·tog·ra·phy \hiˈstägrəfē\ *n* -ES [ISV *hist-* + *-graphy*] **:** description of bodily tissue

his·toid \ˈhiˌstȯid\ *adj* [ISV *hist-* + *-oid*] **1 :** resembling the normal tissues ⟨~ tumors⟩ **2 :** developed from or consisting of but one tissue

his·to·log·i·cal \ˌhistəˈläjəkəl, -jēk-\ *also* **his·to·log·ic** \-jik,-jēk\ *adj* **:** of or relating to histology or to the microscopic structure of the tissues of organisms ⟨~ studies⟩ ⟨the ~ picture in Bright's disease⟩ — **his·to·log·i·cal·ly** \-jək(ə)lē, -jēk-, -li\ *adv*

his·tol·o·gist \hiˈstäləjəst\ *n* -s **:** a specialist in histology

his·tol·o·gy \-jē, -ji\ *n* -ES [F *histologie,* fr. *hist-* + *-logie* -logy] **1 :** a branch of anatomy that deals with the minute structure of animal and vegetable tissues as discernible with the microscope **:** microscopic anatomy — compare CYTOLOGY **2 :** a treatise on histology **3 :** tissue structure or organization (as of an organism) ⟨the ~ of a fetus⟩ ⟨the ~ of the pancreas⟩

his·tol·y·sis \-ləsəs\ *n* [NL, fr. *hist-* + *-lysis*] **1 :** the breakdown of bodily tissues **2 :** the process by which in the pupa of a holometabolous insect many or most of the larval organs dissolve into a creamy material and leave intact only various groups of cells out of which new organs for the imago are formed

his·to·lyt·ic \ˌhistəˈlid·ik\ *adj* [fr. NL *histolysis,* after such pairs as E *analysis : analytic*] **:** of, relating to, or inducing histolysis

his·tol·y·zate \hiˈstäləˌzāt\ *n* -s [irreg. fr. NL *histolysis* + E *-ate*] **:** a product of tissue lysis

his·to·metabasis \ˌhi(ˌ)stō+\ *n* [NL, fr. *hist-* + *metabasis*] **:** fossilization in which the minute details of texture of the organism are retained

his·tom·o·nad \hiˈstäməˌnad\ *n* [NL *Histomonad-, Histomonas*] **:** a protozoan of the genus *Histomonas*

his·tom·o·nal \(ˈ)hiˈstämənᵊl\ *adj* **:** of, relating to, or caused by histomonads ⟨~ diarrhea⟩

his·tom·o·nas \⸗ˈ⸗⸗ˌnəs, -ˌnas\ *n, cap* [NL, fr. *hist-* + *monas*] **:** a genus of zooflagellates (family Mastigamoebidae) that exhibit both amoeboid and flagellate phases, are parasites in the liver and intestinal mucosa of chickens, turkeys, and various other birds and are usu. considered to include a single species (*H. meleagridis*) that is the causative agent of blackhead

his·tomo·ni·a·sis \(ˌ)hiˌstäməˈnīəsəs, ˌhistəmə-\ *n* -ES [NL, fr. *Histomonas* + *-iasis*] **:** infection with or disease caused by protozoans of the genus *Histomonas* **:** BLACKHEAD 3

his·tone \ˈhiˌstōn\ *n* -s [ISV *hist-* + *-one*] **:** any of various simple proteins that are soluble in water but insoluble in dilute ammonia, that yield a high proportion of basic amino acids on hydrolysis but are less strongly basic than protamines, and that are found esp. in some glandular tissues (as thymus) combined with deoxyribonucleic acid

his·to·pathologic *or* **his·to·pathological** \ˌhi(ˌ)stō+\ *adj* **:** of or relating to histopathology ⟨a ~ process⟩ **:** involving the methods of histopathology ⟨a ~ examination⟩ — **his·to·path·o·log·i·cally** \"+\ *adv*

his·to·pathologist \"+\ *n* **:** a pathologist who specializes in the detection of the effects of disease on body tissues; *esp* **:** one who identifies neoplasms by their histological characteristics

his·to·pathology \"+\ *n* [ISV *hist-* + *pathology*] **1 :** a branch of pathology concerned with the tissue changes characteristic of disease **2 :** the tissue changes that affect a part or accompany a disease ⟨~ of the eye⟩ ⟨~ of tuberculosis⟩

his·to·physiology \"+\ *n* [*hist-* + *physiology*] **1 :** a branch of physiology concerned with the function and activities of tissues **2 :** structural and functional tissue organization (as of a body part) ⟨the ~ of the thyroid gland⟩

his·to·plas·ma \ˌhistəˈplazmə\ *n* [NL, fr. *hist-* + *plasma*] **1** *cap* **:** a genus of fungi (family Coccidioidaceae) usu. considered to consist of a single widespread species (*H. capsulatum*) of fungi that cause histoplasmosis, live parasitically as heavily encapsulated yeastlike cells in blood, lymph, or various tissues, and grow saprophytically (as on nutritive media) as a mycelium that produces both conidia and chlamydospores **2** -s **:** any fungus of the genus *Histoplasma*

his·to·plas·min \-mən, ˈ⸗⸗ˌ⸗\ *n* -s [ISV *histoplasm-* (fr. NL *Histoplasma,* genus name of *Histoplasma capsulatum*) + *-in*] **:** a sterile filtrate of a culture of a fungus (*Histoplasma capsulatum*) used in a cutaneous test for histoplasmosis

his·to·plas·mo·sis \-ˌplazˈmōsəs\ *n, pl* **histoplasmo·ses** \-ōˌsēz\ [NL, fr. *Histoplasma* (genus name of *Histoplasma capsulatum*) + *-osis*] **:** a disease that is endemic in the Mississippi and Ohio river valleys of the U.S., is caused by infection with a fungus (*Histoplasma capsulatum*), and is marked by benign involvement of lymph nodes of the trachea and bronchi usu. without symptoms or by severe progressive generalized involvement of the lymph nodes and the reticuloendothelial system with fever, anemia, leukopenia and often with local lesions (as of the skin, mouth, or throat)

his·to·ri·an \hiˈstōrēən, -tȯr- *sometimes* -tär-\ *n* -s [MF *historien,* fr. L *historia* narrative, history + MF *-en* -an — more at HISTORY] **1 :** a writer of history; *esp* **:** one that produces a work of scholarly synthesis as distinguished from a compilation or chronicle ⟨an ~ and not a mere chronicler —*Times Lit. Supp.*⟩ **2 :** CHRONICLER

his·to·ri·at·ed \-rēˌād·əd\ *adj* [ML *historiatus* (past part. of *historiare* to tell a story in pictures, fr. LL, to relate, fr. L *historia* narrative, history) + E *-ed* — more at HISTORY] **:** adorned with figures (as flowers, animals) having significance rather than purely decorative elements (as scrolls, diapers) — used orig. of the elaborately decorated initials of books and manuscripts and now chiefly of a symbolic representational manner of presenting supplementary information on a map or chart

[1]**his·tor·i·cal** \hiˈstȯrəkəl, -tär-, -rēk-\ *or* **his·tor·ic** \-rik, -rēk\ *adj* [*historical* fr. L *historicus* (fr. Gk *historikos* exact, precise, historical, fr. *historia* inquiry, information, narrative, history + *-ikos* -ic) + E *-al; historic* fr. L *historicus* — more at HISTORY] **1** *usu historical* **a :** of, relating to, or having the character of history esp. as distinguished from myth or legend ⟨an ~ event⟩ ⟨the ~ middle ages were quite unlike those of fiction⟩ **b :** based on or dealing with history ⟨~ studies⟩ **:** true to history **:** accurate in respect to history ⟨reproducing the manners of the period with ~ fidelity⟩ **c :** used in the past and reproduced in historical presentations **d :** based on, resulting from, or acknowledged to be true because of past events or experiences ⟨the ~ necessity for space of growing populations⟩ **2** *usu historic* **a :** important, famous, or decisive in history ⟨*historic* battlefields⟩ ⟨*historic* buildings⟩ **b :** having considerable importance, significance, or consequence ⟨an *historic* occasion⟩ **3 a :** SECONDARY 1e **b** *usu historical* **:** DIACHRONIC ⟨~ grammar⟩ ⟨~ linguistics⟩

[2]**historical** \"\ *n* -s **:** a novel, play or motion picture based upon history

historical cost *n* **1 :** a cost computed after production from records made concurrently with various steps of production — contrasted with *predetermined cost* and *standard cost* **2 :** the value at which a capital asset is recorded on the books representing the outlay of money or its equivalent given in exchange at the time of acquisition ⟨depreciation is based on *historical cost* rather than on replacement value⟩ **3 :** the original cost of a property in a public utility

historical criticism *n* **:** criticism in the light of historical evidence — compare HIGHER CRITICISM

historical geology *n* **:** a branch of geology that deals with the chronology of the events in the earth's history

historical infinitive *n* **:** the present infinitive used with a subject nominative as a finite verb in place of a past indicative

his·tor·i·cal·ly \-rək(ə)lē, -rēk-, -li\ *adv* **1 :** in accordance with or in respect to history ⟨an ~ accurate account⟩ **:** as a matter of history ⟨popular leaders have ~ appeared when the needs and tensions were great enough⟩ **2 :** in the course of history **:** in past times or previous dealings ⟨all employees whom an employer has ~ treated together —*U.S.Code*⟩

historical materialism *n* **:** the part of dialectical materialism dealing with the history of society and holding that ideas and institutions develop as the superstructure of a material economic base, that the course of history is dominated by the struggle of competing classes, and that the final dialectical stages comprise the development of capitalism, the dictatorship of the proletariat, and after the withering away of the state the emergence of a classless society

historical method *n* **:** a technique of presenting information (as in teaching or criticism) in which a topic is considered in terms of its earliest phases and followed in an historical course through its subsequent evolution and development

his·tor·i·cal·ness \-kəlnəs\ *n* -ES **:** the quality or state of being historical

historical novel *n* **:** a novel having as its setting a period of history and usu. introducing some historical personages and events

historical perfect *n* **:** the perfect tense when used in Latin to express action completed in an indefinite past

historical present *n* **:** the present tense used in telling of past events

historical school *n* **1 :** a school of economics developed in Germany in the middle of the 19th century that emphasizes institutional factors in society and pursues a systematic investigation of the development of economic institutions — compare CLASSICAL 3b(3) **2 :** a school of legal philosophy that emphasizes the relation of the evolution of law to the historical milieu and minimizes the importance of arbitrary human action and of natural processes to its development **3 :** a school of ethnology that emphasizes empirical study of the historical continuity of a specific culture or culture area as contrasted with comparative study of diverse or related cultures or culture areas

historical sociology *n* **:** a branch of sociology concerned with study of the origins, stages, and laws of social life and social institutions

his·tor·i·cism \hiˈstȯrəˌsizəm, -tär-\ *n* -s **1 a :** a theory that all sociocultural phenomena are historically determined, that all truths are relative, that there are no absolute values, categories, or standards, and that the student of the past must enter into the mind and attitudes of past periods, accept their point of view, and avoid all intrusion of his own standards or preconceptions **b :** the practice of writing or treating history in accordance with such a theory **c :** a theory of history holding that the development of human society is a process governed by inexorable laws of change operating independently of human wills or wishes **2 a :** a strong or exaggerated concern with or respect for the institutions and traditions of the past ⟨stands for ~ and empiricism in the tradition of Burke —*Times Lit. Supp.*⟩ **b :** the use of or undue reliance upon historical forms or styles in art esp. in architectural design

[1]**his·tor·i·cist** \-ˌsəst\ *n* -s [fr. *historicism,* after such pairs as E *baptism : baptist*] **:** an advocate of historicism

[2]**historicist** \"\ *adj* **:** of, relating to, or based on historicism

his·to·ric·i·ty \ˌhistəˈrisəd·ē, -ətē, -i\ *n* -ES [prob. fr. F *historicité,* fr. L *historicus* + F *-ité* -ity] **1 :** the quality or state of being historic esp. as distinct from the mythological or legendary **2 :** a condition of being placed in the stream of historical developments; *also* **:** a result of such placement

his·tor·i·cize \hiˈstȯrəˌsīz, -tär-\ *vb* -ED/-ING/-S *vt* **1 :** to render historic **:** give an appearance of historical verity or significance to ⟨the traditional myth of the god's victory over the dragon . . . is *historicized* as the triumph of Yahweh over the enemies of Israel —Philip Wheelwright⟩ **2 :** to make dependent on historicism esp. as a basis for action or an explanation of occurrences ⟨various disciplines also have been nationalized and over-*historicized* —Christian Gauss⟩ ~ *vi* **:** to use historical material or depend on historicism ⟨the nationalist and *historicizing* spirit of the 19th century —G.M.J. Moser⟩

historico- *comb form* [NL, fr. L *historicus* — more at HISTORICAL] **:** historical **:** historical and ⟨*historico*philosophical⟩ ⟨*historico*social⟩

his·tor·i·co·critical \hiˌstȯrə(ˌ)kō, -tär-, -rē(-+\ *adj* **:** based on or involving the use of techniques of both historian and critic ⟨an ~ examination of religion⟩ — **his·tor·i·co·critical·ly** \"+\ *adv*

his·to·ried \ˈhist(ə)rēd, -rid\ *adj* **:** related in or as history **:** having a history **:** HISTORICAL

his·to·ri·ette \hiˌstōrēˈet, -tȯr-, ⸗ˌ⸗⸗ˈ⸗\ *n* -s [F, fr. L *historia* narrative, history + F *-ette* (dim. suffix) — more at HISTORY] **:** a short history or story

his·to·ri·fy \hiˈstȯrəˌfī, -tär-\ *vt* -ED/-ING/-S [*history* + *-fy*] **:** to record in or as history

historio- *comb form* [MF, fr. LL, fr. Gk, fr. *historia* inquiry, information, narrative, history — more at HISTORY] **:** history ⟨*historio*metric⟩ ⟨*historio*grapher⟩

his·to·ri·og·ra·pher \(ˌ)hiˌstōrēˈägrəfə(r), -tȯr- *sometimes* -tär-\ *n* -s [MF *historiographeur,* fr. LL *historiographus* (fr. Gk *historiographos,* fr. *historio-* + *-graphos* writer, fr. *graphein* to write) + MF *-eur* -or — more at CARVE] **1 :** a writer of history **:** HISTORIAN **2 :** a person appointed to write a history or to record the continuing history of a country, group, or institution **:** an official historian ⟨since 1924 has been ~ of the Protestant Episcopal Diocese of Virginia —*Christian Century*⟩

his·to·ri·og·ra·pher·ship \-ˌship\ *n* **:** the office of historiographer

his·to·ri·o·graph·ic \hiˌstōrēəˈgrafik, -tȯr- *sometimes* -tär-\ *also* **his·to·ri·o·graph·i·cal** \-fəkəl\ *adj* **:** of or relating to historiography — **his·to·ri·o·graph·i·cal·ly** \-fək(ə)lē\ *adv*

his·to·ri·og·ra·phy \(ˌ)hiˌstōrēˈägrəfē, -tȯr- *sometimes* -tär-\ *n* -ES [MF *historiographie,* fr. Gk *historiographia,* fr. *historio-* + *-graphia* -graphy] **1 a :** the writing of history; *esp* **:** the writing of history based on the critical examination of sources, the selection of particulars from the authentic materials, and the synthesis of particulars into a narrative that will stand the test of critical methods **b :** the principles, theory, and history of historical writing ⟨a course in ~⟩ **2 :** the product of historical writing **:** a body of historical literature ⟨no single work in our ~ has moved more Englishmen —*Times Lit. Supp.*⟩ ⟨for most of the 9th century northern ~ shrinks to a few disconnected annals —F.M.Stenton⟩

his·to·ri·ol·o·gy \-ˈäləjē\ *n* -ES [*historio-* + *-logy*] **:** the study or knowledge of history

his·to·rism \ˈhistəˌrizəm\ *n* -s [G *historismus,* fr. *historie* history (fr. L *historia*) + G *-ismus* -ism] **:** HISTORICISM 1

[1]**his·to·ry** \ˈhist(ə)rē, -ri\ *n* -ES [L *historia,* fr. Gk *historia* inquiry, information, narrative, history, fr. *historein* to inquire into, examine, relate (fr. *histor-, histōr* judge) + *-ia* -y; akin to Gk *idein* to see — more at WIT] **1 :** a narrative of events connected with a real or imaginary object, person, or career **:** TALE, STORY; *esp* **:** such a narrative devoted to the exposition of the natural unfolding and interdependence of the events treated ⟨carefully recording the ~ of our vacation for father⟩ ⟨a ~ of passion, greed, and retribution⟩ **2 a :** a systematic written account comprising a chronological record

of events (as affecting a city, state, nation, institution, science, or art) and usu. including a philosophical explanation of the cause and origin of such events — usu. distinguished from *annals* and *chronicle* **b :** a treatise presenting systematically related natural phenomena (as of geography, animals, or plants) ⟨an illustrated ~ of British birds⟩ **c :** an account of a sick person's family and personal background, his past health, and present illness **3 :** a branch of knowledge that records and explains past events as steps in the sequence of human activities **:** the study of the character and significance of events — usu. used with a qualifying adjective ⟨medieval ~⟩ ⟨European ~⟩ **4** [MF *histoire* story, history, picture, fr. L *historia*] **a** (1) *obs* **:** a pictorial representation of an historical subject (2) *or* **history painting :** painting esp. popular in the 17th and 18th centuries in which a complex of figures conveys a story or message usu. based on history or legend **b** (1) *obs* **:** DRAMA 1 (2) **:** a drama based on historical events **5 a :** the events that form the subject matter of a history **:** a series of events clustering about some center of interest (as a nation, a department of culture, a natural epoch or evolution, a living being or a species) upon the character and significance of which these events cast light **b :** the character and significance of such a center of interest — compare LIFE HISTORY **c** *broadly* **:** past events ⟨that's all ~ now⟩; *esp* **:** those events involving or concerned with mankind **d :** previous treatment, handling, or experience (as of a metal) ⟨the results of heat treating will depend in part on the previous ~ of the specimen⟩ ⟨thermal ~ may modify photoelectric reactivity of certain compounds⟩ ⟨there was a ~ of repeated exposure to near-freezing temperature that might explain the mutation⟩

[2]**history** \"\ *vt* -ED/-ING/-ES [ME *historien*, fr. MF *historier*, fr. LL & ML *historiare* — more at HISTORIATED] **1** *obs* **:** NARRATE, RECOUNT **2** *obs* **:** to decorate with an historical record or scenes from history

his·to·ry·less \-lə̇s\ *adj* **:** having no history or no recorded history or no history worthy of record

historymaker \'=(=)=,==\ *n* **:** one that by acts, ideas, or existence modifies the course of history

history of religions : the objective study of the origin and historical development of the religions of mankind — compare COMPARATIVE RELIGION

history painting *n* **1 :** HISTORY 4a(2) **2 :** the practice or techniques of painting histories

his·to·toxic \¦histə+\ *adj* [ISV *hist-* + *toxic*] **1 :** toxic to tissues ⟨~ agents⟩ **2 :** of, relating to, or caused by a histotoxin ⟨the development of a ~ anoxia⟩

his·to·toxin \"+\ *n* [*hist-* + *toxin*] **:** any of various poisonous substances formed in specific body tissues and usu. deleterious to the body in which they are formed

his·to·troph \'histə,träf, -rȯf\ *or* **his·to·trophe** \-rōf\ *n* -s [F *histotrophe*, fr. *hist-* + *-trophe* (fr. Gk *trophos* one that feeds or rears)] **:** all materials supplied for nutrition of the embryo in viviparous animals from sources other than the maternal bloodstream — compare EMBRYOTROPH, HEMOTROPHE

his·to·trop·ic \¦histə¦träpik\ *adj* [*hist-* + *-tropic*] **:** exhibiting or characterized by histotropism ⟨~ parasites⟩

his·tot·ro·pism \hi'stä·trə,pizəm\ *n* [*hist-* + *-tropism*] **:** attraction (as of a parasite) to a particular kind of tissue

his·to·zo·ic \¦histə¦zōik\ *adj* [*hist-* + *-zoic*] **:** living in the tissues of a host ⟨~ parasites⟩

his·to·zyme \'histə,zīm\ *n* [ISV *hist-* + *-zyme*] **:** an enzyme widely distributed in mammalian tissues that is capable of splitting acyl groups from hippuric acid and other acylated amino acids or from peptides — called also *hippuricase*

his·trio \'histrē,ō\ *n* -s [L, alter. of *hister*, fr. Etruscan] **:** ACTOR

his·tri·ob·del·lea \,histrē,äb'delēə\ *n pl, cap* [NL, fr. L *histrio* actor + NL *-bdellea* (fr. Gk *bdella* leech)] **:** a small group of segmented invertebrate animals that are intermediate in some respects between the Aschelminthes and the Annelida and that are all parasitic on marine crustaceans

his·tri·on \'histrē,än\ *n* -s [MF, fr. L *histrion-*, *histrio*] **:** ACTOR

[1]**his·tri·on·ic** \¦histrē¦änik, -nēk\ *also* **his·tri·on·i·cal** \-nə̇kəl, -nēk-\ *adj* [LL *histrionicus*, fr. L *histrion-*, *histrio* + *-icus* -ic] **1 :** of or relating to actors, acting, or the theater ⟨an able actor ever seeking ~ perfection⟩ **2 :** deliberately affected **:** THEATRICAL, STAGED ⟨her heart attacks were as ~ as her sister's fits of temper⟩ — **his·tri·on·i·cal·ly** \-nə̇k(ə)lē, -nēk-, -li\ *adv*

[2]**histrionic** \"\ *n* -s **1 :** ACTOR **2 histrionics** *pl but sometimes sing in constr* **a :** theatrical performances **b :** staged or stagy conduct or exhibition of temperament usu. intended to produce some particular effect or response in others

his·tri·on·i·cus \,histrē'änə̇kəs\ *n, cap* [NL, fr. LL, adj., histrionic; fr. their handsome plumage] **:** a genus of ducks including only the harlequin duck

his·tri·o·nism \'histrēə,nizəm\ *n* -s **:** THEATRICALITY

his·trix \'histriks\ [NL, alter. of *Hystrix*] *syn of* HYSTRIX

[1]**hit** \'hit, *usu* -id·+V\ *vb* **hit; hit; hitting; hits** [ME *hitten*, fr. ON *hitta* to hit upon, meet up with, hit; perh. akin to OE *hentan* to pursue, attack, seize — more at HUNT] *vt* **1 a :** to reach or get at by striking with or as if with a sudden blow ⟨~ a ball⟩ ⟨be ~ by adversity⟩ **b :** to come in quick forceful contact with ⟨the ball ~ the house and bounced off⟩ **2 a :** to cause to come into sudden forceful contact ⟨~ his hand against the wall⟩ ⟨~ the stick against the railing⟩ **b :** to deliver (a blow) usu. in a vigorous or violent manner **:** STRIKE **c :** to strike a blow at or to ⟨~ the table suddenly⟩ ⟨~ the boy in the eye⟩ **3 a :** to affect esp. strongly and to the detriment or distress of ⟨life had never ~ her very hard —Nevil Shute⟩ ⟨drought ~ the range country early that year⟩ **b :** to criticize adversely **:** CENSURE ⟨no prime minister in our history has been ~ so hard by a biographer who knew him —*Times Lit. Supp.*⟩ **4 :** to make a request of or a claim or demand upon (as for a loan or a job) ⟨~ his friend for 10 dollars⟩ — often used with *up* ⟨~ up his father's friends for work⟩ **5 a :** to come upon, find, or discover by or as if by chance or accident ⟨spent years in prospecting without ever *hitting* gold⟩ **b :** to meet with, reach, or experience by or as if by chance or accident ⟨after several weeks of travel, we ~ our first snowstorm⟩ ⟨~ a run of bad luck⟩ **6 :** to reach or attain by or as if by hitting: as **a :** to accord with usu. exactly and purposely ⟨writing that ~*s* the public taste precisely⟩ **b :** to act in precise accord with ⟨~ a musical cue⟩ **c :** to reach as a rate, standard, or level ⟨a car that can ~ 100 mph.⟩ ⟨prices ~ an all-time high⟩ ⟨when you ~ the middle sixties⟩ **d** *of fish* **:** to bite at or on **:** TAKE ⟨in certain times of the season fish will only ~ live bait⟩ **e :** to appear in or on (as for public sale, consumption, use) ⟨sweet corn ~*s* the markets in New England in midsummer⟩ ⟨a magazine that ~*s* the newsstands early in the month⟩ ⟨morning papers often ~ the streets in the late evening⟩ ⟨this recording will ~ the jukeboxes soon⟩ **f** *of an author* **:** to achieve publication in ⟨took him some time to ~ the better magazines⟩ **g :** to be reported in ⟨~ the front pages⟩ **h :** to impinge on or command the attention of ⟨advertising techniques designed to ~ the subconscious mind⟩ **i :** STRESS, EMPHASIZE ⟨always ~ the message-bearing words firmly⟩ ⟨inclined to ~ the wrong syllable⟩ **j :** to arrive at, in, or on usu. for a brief or transitory stay ⟨arranged to ~ town two days before his brother⟩ ⟨when the first forces ~ the beach⟩ ⟨planned on *hitting* all the new night spots⟩ **k** (1) **:** to reach or strike (as a target) for a score in a game or contest ⟨unbelievable ability to ~ the basket⟩ (2) **:** to succeed in making (a scoring play) ⟨~ three goals before their opponents were well warmed up⟩ (3) *slang* **:** to win in a lottery or game of chance or acquire as if by so winning ⟨~ first prize⟩ ⟨an act that didn't ~ the big money until he took it to New York⟩ — often used with *for* and the thing or the amount gained ⟨~ the numbers pool for $2000⟩ ⟨~ the company education fund for a year in technical school⟩ **l** *slang* (1) **:** to go, lie, or drop on or upon usu. suddenly or at once ⟨~ the deck⟩ (2) **:** to get onto and begin to move along or travel on ⟨~ the road⟩ ⟨~ the right path⟩ **7 :** to capture with precision (as a mood, an idea, a personal characteristic in a description or representation) ⟨none of these analyses seems quite to ~ the main characteristic —R.D.Ellmann⟩ **8 :** to set in operation or cause to function by or as if by striking or touching ⟨~ the lights⟩ ⟨*hitting* slow chords on a guitar⟩ ⟨had to ~ the brakes suddenly⟩ **9 :** to indulge in (as liquor) esp. excessively, habitually, or compulsively ⟨had been *hitting* the bottle for days⟩ **10 a :** to deal another card to (a player at blackjack) **b :** to have another card dealt to (a hand in blackjack) **c :** FILL *vt* 7 ~ *vi* **1 :** to strike or strike out at something with or as if with a sudden blow (as of the fist or a missile) ⟨in the third round he began *hitting* wildly⟩ ⟨*hitting* only about once in five shots⟩ **2 a :** to come into forcible contact with something ⟨when he fell, he ~ hard⟩ — often used with *against* ⟨tipped over and ~ against the wall and was damaged⟩ **b :** ATTACK ⟨guessed at where they would ~, and the date of D day —Dan Levin⟩ **c** *of a fish* **:** STRIKE *vi* 15b **d :** to arrive with a disturbing or damaging effect ⟨a heavy storm that ~ just at sundown⟩ ⟨had been still in school when the bad times ~⟩ ⟨the grippe ~ unusually severely that year⟩ **3 a :** to meet or reach something aimed at or desired **:** succeed in attaining or obtaining something often by or as if by chance — often used with *on* or *upon* ⟨~ on a solution⟩ ⟨~ upon a satisfactory explanation⟩ **b :** to draw or be dealt a valuable card in poker ⟨drew to an inside straight and ~⟩ **c :** to hit a blot **4** *of a crop, now dial* **:** to germinate, grow, or yield well **5** *obs* **:** to be in agreement **:** SUIT — used with *with* ⟨the scheme ~ so exactly with my temper —Daniel Defoe⟩ **6 :** to direct one's course **:** direct oneself ⟨~ for the nearest lunchroom⟩ ⟨in spring the peddlers ~ up the coast with packs and carts⟩ **7** *of an internal-combustion engine* **:** to fire the charge in the cylinders **8 a :** to be a winner (as in a lottery) **b :** to make a score (as in a game) **syn** see STRIKE — **hit a blot 1 :** to capture a man exposed on a point in backgammon **2 :** to find a flaw (as in a policy or argument) — **hit for six 1** *Brit* **:** to hit for six runs in cricket **2** *Brit* **:** to hit hard **:** DEFEAT, TROUNCE — **hit it off :** to associate agreeably **:** get along well **:** have a mutually congenial relationship ⟨had *hit it off* from the very start⟩ — **hit it up :** to work, play, or perform with speed, animation, or abandon ⟨the band was already *hitting it up* when we arrived⟩ — **hit one's stride :** to reach one's best speed or performance **:** exhibit maximum competence or capability — **hit the books** *or* **hit one's books :** to study esp. with intensity — **hit the bricks** *slang* **:** to go on strike **:** walk out — **hit the hay** *or* **hit the sack** *slang* **:** to go to bed — **hit the high points** *or* **hit the high spots :** to touch on or at the most important or salient points or places ⟨a lecture that *hit* only *the high points* of the subject⟩ ⟨with only three days in town the best we could do was *hit the high spots*⟩ — **hit the jackpot** *slang* **:** to be or become notably and usu. unexpectedly successful — **hit the nail on the head :** to perform effectively or be effective **:** be exactly right — **hit the roof** *also* **hit the ceiling :** to give vent to a burst of anger or angry protest — **hit the silk** *slang* **:** to parachute from an airplane — **hit the spot :** to give complete or special satisfaction — used esp. of food or drink

[2]**hit** \"\ *n* -s [ME *hete*, fr. *hitten*, v.] **1 a :** a blow striking an object aimed at — contrasted with *miss* ⟨scored a ~ on his first try⟩ ⟨two ~*s* and three misses out of five tries⟩ **b :** an impact of one thing against another **:** COLLISION **2 a :** a stroke of luck **:** a fortunate chance ⟨answered the questions correctly by a series of lucky ~*s*⟩ **b :** a theatrical production, book, or song that is conspicuously successful or popular; *broadly* **:** anything that is exceedingly popular, pleasing, or successful ⟨this new style is a big ~ with the high-school set⟩ **c :** a win in various gambling games ⟨a string of 20 ~*s* on a pinball machine⟩ **3 :** a censorious, sarcastic, or telling remark or statement ⟨took a sharp ~ at grasping politicians⟩ **4 :** a backgammon game won after the opponent has removed some of his men **5** *dial* **:** a bountiful crop — used esp. of fruit **6 :** a stroke in various games by which a ball is hit so as to result in a score, advancement of a runner, or some other advantage; *specif, in baseball* **:** BASE HIT **7** *printing* **:** IMPRESSION 6b ⟨even two ~*s* of white ink didn't quite seem to cover the green cloth —*Book Production*⟩

[3]**hit** \(¦)hit, *usu* -id·+V\ *obs or dial var of* IT

hit-and-miss \¦==¦=\ *adj* **:** sometimes hitting or corresponding in position and sometimes not **:** RANDOM, HIT-OR-MISS

hit-and-run \¦==¦=\ *adj* **1 :** being or relating to a baseball play in which a base runner starts for the next base as the pitcher starts to pitch and the batter attempts to hit the ball **2 a** (1) *of the driver of a vehicle* **:** guilty of leaving the scene of an accident without stopping to render assistance or to comply with legal requirements (2) **:** caused by, resulting from, or involving a hit-and-run driver ⟨increasing numbers of *hit-and-run* deaths⟩ ⟨a *hit-and-run* accident⟩ **b :** involving or intended for quick specific action or results rather than permanent use ⟨small *hit-and-run* units of troops⟩ ⟨*hit-and-run* merchandising⟩

hit-and-runner \"ə(r)\ *n* **:** one that hits and runs away; *esp* **:** a hit-and-run driver

[1]**hitch** \'hich\ *vb* -ED/-ING/-ES [ME *hytchen*] *vt* **1 :** to move with jerks or jerkily ⟨~*ing* his chair closer to the table⟩ **2 a :** to catch or fasten by or as if by a hook or a knot ⟨~*ed* his horse to the top rail of the fence⟩ **b :** to connect (a vehicle or implement) with a source of motive power ⟨~ a rake to a tractor⟩ or to attach (a source of motive power) to a vehicle or instrument ⟨~ the horses to the wagon⟩ **c** *slang* **:** to join in marriage **3 :** to introduce into a literary work esp. irrelevantly or by obvious straining ⟨can't avoid ~*ing* in a word or two about personal responsibility⟩ **4 :** HITCHHIKE ⟨could ~ a ride on their trucks —Dillon Ripley⟩ ~ *vi* **1 :** to move interruptedly or with halts and jerks usu. due to an obstruction or impediment **:** HOBBLE ⟨~*ed* slowly along on his cane⟩ **2 a :** to become entangled or made fast **:** become linked or yoked ⟨presumably these infinitesimal particles ~*ed* together to become matter⟩ **b** *slang* **:** to become joined in marriage — often used with *up* ⟨decided to ~ up⟩ **3 :** HITCHHIKE ⟨could not risk ~*ing* back —James Jones⟩ — **hitch horses** *archaic* **:** to act or be in agreement **:** HARMONIZE — usu. used with *together*

[2]**hitch** \"\ *n* -ES **1 :** a sudden movement or pull **:** JERK, TWITCH ⟨gave his trousers a ~⟩ **2 a :** HOBBLE, LIMP ⟨a ~ in his gait⟩ **b** *dial* **:** CRICK ⟨had a ~ in his back⟩ **3 :** a sudden halt or stop (as from an accident) **:** ENTANGLEMENT, OBSTRUCTION, STOPPAGE, IMPEDIMENT ⟨a ~ in the performance⟩ **4 :** the act or fact of catching hold of or on something (as a hook) **5 :** a connection between a vehicle or implement and a detachable source of motive power (as a tractor or a horse) **6** *slang* **:** a period of military service; *broadly* **:** a sharply delimited period in one's life ⟨served a three-year ~ in prison⟩ ⟨put in a ~ with the diplomatic service after leaving the army⟩ **7 :** a recess cut in rock to support the end of a timber in mining or tunneling operations **8 :** any of various knots used to form a temporary loop or noose in a line or to secure a line temporarily to an object; *sometimes* **:** HALF HITCH **9 :** HITCHHIKE, LIFT 5b ⟨get a ~ into town —Irwin Shaw⟩

[3]**hitch** \"\ *n* -ES [origin unknown] **:** a minnow (*Lavinia exilicauda*) with silvery sides and dark back that occurs in streams about San Francisco and Monterey and reaches a length of 12 inches

hitch and kick *n* **:** a standing high jump in which the jumper springs from, kicks with, and alights on the same foot

hitch·cock chair *also* **hitchcock** \'hich,käk\ *n, usu cap H* [after Lambert H. *Hitchcock* †1852 Am. furniture manufacturer] **:** a turned usu. rush-seated chair with legs often and back always slightly bent with a top rail and back posts above the seat, and with a finish usu. of black paint and stenciled decoration

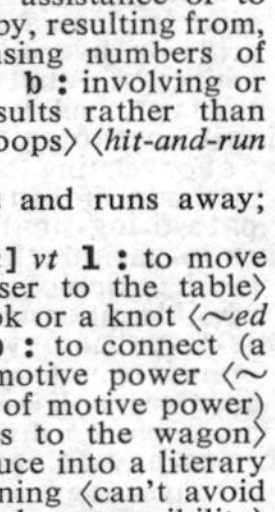

Hitchcock chair

hitch·er \'hichə(r)\ *n* -s **:** one that hitches or catches (as a boat hook)

[1]**hitchhike** \'=,=\ *vb* [[2]*hitch* + *hike*] *vi* **:** to travel by securing free rides from passing vehicles or in transport available by chance ⟨boys *hitchhiking* home from school⟩ ⟨soldiers *hitchhiking* back to their base in a military plane⟩ ~ *vt* **1 :** to proceed or progress on (as a course or way) by hitchhiking ⟨*hitchhiked* his way to the Pacific coast⟩ **2 :** to obtain (a ride) as a hitchhiker ⟨*hitchhiked* a lift on the next plane out⟩

[2]**hitchhike** \"\ *n* **1 :** a trip made by hitchhiking **2** *or* **hitch·hik·er** \"ə(r)\ **:** a brief commercial that follows a radio or television program and usu. advertises a secondary product of the sponsor

hitch·hik·er \"ə(r)\ *n* **:** one that hitchhikes

hitch·i·ly \'hichə̇lē, -li\ *adv* **:** in a hitchy manner **:** JERKILY

hitching *pres part of* HITCH

hitching bar *n* **:** HITCHRACK

hitching post *n* **:** a fixed and often elaborate standard to which a horse or team can be fastened to prevent straying — compare HITCHRACK

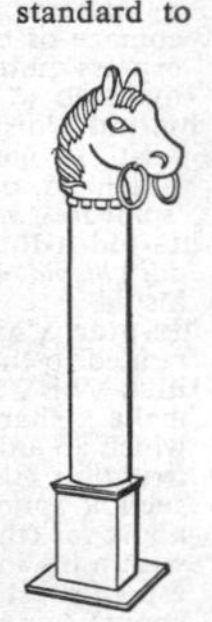

hitching post

hitch·i·ti \'hichəd·ē\ *n, pl* **hitchiti** *or* **hitchitis** *usu cap* **1 a :** a Muskogean people of Georgia, member of the Creek confederacy **b :** a member of such people **2 :** the language of the Hitchiti people

hitch kick *n* **1 :** a running motion executed by a broad jumper while in the air to increase the distance of his jump **2 :** HITCH AND KICK

hitch pin *n* **:** one of a row of slanting metal pins in a piano action to which the strings are attached at the ends opposite the tuning pins

hitchrack \'=,=\ *n* **:** a fixed horizontal rail to which a horse or team can be fastened to prevent straying — compare HITCHING POST

hitch up *vi* **:** to harness a draft animal or team and make it fast (as to a wagon or implement) ⟨we *hitched up* and were on our way before sunrise⟩

hitchy \'hichē, -chi\ *adj* -ER/-EST **:** having impeded movement **:** JERKY

hithe \'hīth, -th\ *n* -s [ME *hythe*, fr. OE *hȳth;* akin to OS *hūth* port] **:** a small port or harbor esp. on a river — now used chiefly in place names

[1]**hith·er** \'hithə(r)\ *adv* [ME *hider*, *hither*, fr. OE *hider;* akin to ON *hethra* here, Goth *hidre* hither, L *citro* hither, *citra* on this side — more at HE] **1 :** to this place ⟨bring ~ your sick and sorrowful⟩ ⟨~ came the children to play⟩ — compare *hence*, *thither* **2** *obs* **:** to this point, source, conclusion, design **:** HERETO

[2]**hither** \"\ *adj* [ME *hider*, *hither*, fr. *hider*, *hither*, adv.] **1 :** being on the side next or toward the person speaking **:** NEARER ⟨on the ~ side of the hill⟩ — compare FARTHER, THITHER **2** *of time* **:** EARLIER

hither and thither *adv* [ME *hider and thider*, fr. OE] **:** to and fro **:** backward and forward **:** in various and usu. random directions ⟨roving *hither and thither*⟩

hither-and-thither \¦===¦==\ *vi* -ED/-ING/-S [*hither and thither*] **:** to move confusedly or at random

hither and yon *also* **hither and yond** *adv* **:** HITHER AND THITHER

hith·er·most \'==,mōst *also chiefly Brit* -,məst\ *adj* [[2]*hither* + *-most*] **:** nearest on this side

[1]**hith·er·to** \'==,tü, ,=='=\ *adv* [ME *hiderto*, fr. *hider* (adv.) + *to* (prep.)] **1 :** up to this time **:** as yet **:** until now ⟨~ unknown resources⟩ **2 :** to this place ⟨the appointed delegates shall come ~⟩

[2]**hitherto** \"\ *adj* **:** existing or done hitherto **:** PREVIOUS, PRIOR ⟨our ~ experience suggests⟩

hith·er·ward \'==,wə(r)d\ *also* **hith·er·wards** \-dz\ *adv* [ME *hiderward*, *hitherwarde*, fr. OE *hiderweard*, fr. *hider* hither + *-weard* -ward] **:** toward this place **:** HITHER

hit·le·ri·an \(')hit¦lirēən\ *adj, usu cap* [Adolf *Hitler* †1945 dictator of Germany + E *-ian*] **:** of, relating to, or suggestive of Adolf Hitler or his regime in Germany ⟨a *Hitlerian* disregard of human rights⟩

hit·ler·ism \'hitlə,rizəm\ *n* -s *usu cap* [A. *Hitler* + E *-ism*] **:** the extreme nationalistic doctrines of the German National Socialist party under the leadership of Adolf Hitler, from about 1930 **:** NAZISM

[1]**hit·ler·ite** \-rīt, *usu* -īd·+V\ *n* -s *usu cap* [A. *Hitler* + E *-ite*] **:** an adherent of Hitlerism

[2]**hitlerite** \"\ *adj, usu cap* **:** HITLERIAN

hit·less \'hitlə̇s\ *adj, of a baseball player or team* **:** making no base hits

hit off *vt* **:** to characterize precisely and usu. satirically ⟨in a brilliant metaphor . . . *hits* himself *off* with terrible accuracy —V.S.Pritchett⟩ ⟨really *hits off* the contours and hierarchies of an English village with an amusing slyness —H.J.Laski⟩; *broadly* **:** IMITATE ⟨*hits off* an old turkey-gobbler to perfection⟩ ~ *vi* **:** to be in harmony or agreement **:** ACCORD ⟨soft shade that will *hit off* with anything⟩ ⟨his late arrival *hit off* perfectly with our plan⟩

hit-off \'=,=\ *n* -s [*hit off*] **:** a clever imitation ⟨did an amusing *hit-off* of his brother⟩

hit or miss *adv* **:** without regard to accuracy or precision **:** at random **:** in a happy-go-lucky fashion

hit-or-miss \¦==¦=\ *adj* [*hit or miss*] **:** unpredictable and uncertain usu. through lack of care, forethought, system, or plan **:** marked by indifferent, ill-considered, or empirical expediency ⟨making all allowances for the *hit-or-miss* element in affirmations of a general kind —*Times Lit. Supp.*⟩; *broadly* **:** having no fixed or predetermined pattern ⟨a *hit-or-miss* carpet⟩ **syn** see RANDOM

hit out *vi* **:** to aim angry often random blows ⟨*hit out* and . . . caught him right between the eyes —H.A.Chippendale⟩ ⟨*hitting out* at injustice and prejudice⟩

hit parade *n* [fr. *Your Hit Parade*, a service mark] **:** a group or listing of transitorily most popular items of a particular kind (as popular songs)

hi-trap \'hī,=\ *n* [alter. of *high* + *trap*] **:** HIGH-HOUSE

hit-run \'=¦=\ *adj* **:** HIT-AND-RUN 2

hits *pres 3d sing of* HIT, *pl of* HIT

hit-skip \'=¦=\ *adj* **:** HIT-AND-RUN 2

hit·ta·ble \'hid·əbəl, -itə-\ *adj* **:** capable of being hit

hit·ter \'hid·ə(r), -itə-\ *n* -s **:** one that hits

hit theory *n* **:** a theory in genetics: the mutafacient action of mutagenically active radiations depends upon the taking up of an effective amount of the radiation by a sensitive region of the cell

hitting *pres part of* HIT

[1]**hit·tite** \'hi,t¦īt, 'hid·,¦, *usu* ¦īd·+V\ *n* -s *usu cap* [Heb *Ḥittī* (fr. Hitt *ḫatti*) + E *-ite*] **1 :** a member of the aboriginal population of the ancient city or country of Khatti in eastern Asia Minor **2 a :** a member of a conquering people in Asia Minor and later in Syria whose origin is not certainly known, whose characteristic features, the sloping forehead and large aquiline nose, as preserved in Hittite and Egyptian reliefs, seem to have been derived from the autochthonous Hittites, and whose empire in the 2d millennium B.C. rivaled the Babylonian and Egyptian **b :** an Indo-European or Indo-Hittite language of this people known from a large body of texts in cuneiform writing largely found at Bogazköy in central Asia Minor — compare HIEROGLYPHIC HITTITE; see INDO-EUROPEAN LANGUAGES table

[2]**hittite** \"\ *adj, usu cap* **:** of or relating to the Hittites or their language

hittite hieroglyph *n, usu cap 1st H* **1 hittite hieroglyphs** *pl* **:** a system of writing known from inscriptions from Asia Minor and esp. northern Syria dating from about 1500 B.C. to about 600 B.C. and composed of pictorial symbols partly ideographic and partly phonetic in which the language Hieroglyphic Hittite was written **2 :** a character in the Hittite hieroglyphs

hittite hieroglyphic *n, usu cap 1st H* **:** HITTITE HIEROGLYPH

hit·tit·ol·o·gy \,hi,tīd·'äləjē, ,hid·,īd·'ä-, ,hi,tī'tä-\ *also* **hit·tol·o·gy** \hi'tä-\ *n* -ES *usu cap* [*Hittito-* or *Hitto-* (fr. [1]*Hittite*) + *-logy*] **:** a branch of knowledge concerned with Hittite philology, archaeology, and history

hit·ty-mis·sy \¦hid·ē¦misē\ *adv* (*or adj*) [irreg. fr. *hit or miss* + *-y*] **:** HIT OR MISS

hit wicket *adj, of a batsman in cricket* **:** having broken the wicket with the bat or some part of the person in making a stroke at a ball — used in the phrase *out, hit wicket;* abbr *hw*

[1]**hive** \'hīv\ *n* -s [ME *hive*, *heve*, fr. OE *hȳf;* akin to ON *hūfr* hull of a ship, L *cupa* tub, cask, Gk *kypellon* cup, *kypros*, a measure for grain, Skt *kūpa* hole, cave, OE *hēah* high — more at HIGH] **1 :** a container for housing honeybees now usu. consisting of a base, a lower rectangular hive body containing removable frames for brood, one or more upper supers that provide room for the storage honey, and a weather-

tight cover — called also *beehive;* compare BEE GUM, SKEP **2 :** the bees of one hive **3 :** something resembling a hive: as **a** *obs* **:** a head covering suggesting a plaited skep **b :** a dwelling place **:** a center of family life ⟨forced out of the family ~ by the excess of hands and the deficiency of land —H.E.Scudder⟩ **c :** a center of activity or a place swarming with busy occupants ⟨the teeming ~ of a great railroad station⟩ ⟨a ~ of political unrest⟩ **d :** a source or point of origin ⟨the ~ from which these barbarians came lay far to the north⟩

²**hive** \"\ *vb* -ED/-ING/-S *vt* **1 a :** to collect into, place in, or cause to enter a hive ⟨*hived* 7 swarms of wild bees⟩ **b :** to shelter in or as if in a hive ⟨these rascals that the city ~*s*⟩ **2 a :** to store up in a hive ⟨a strong colony in a good season may ~ 100 pounds of honey⟩ **b :** to gather and accumulate for future need **:** lay up in store ⟨why did they penuriously ~ and distribute water —Norman Douglas⟩ — sometimes used with *up* or *away* ⟨*hiving* away the extra dollars⟩ ~ *vi* **1 a** *of bees* **:** to enter and take possession of a hive ⟨the swarm *hived* readily⟩ **b :** to reside or gather like bees in close association ⟨the multitudes that ~ in city apartments⟩ **2 :** to secrete oneself or shut oneself up — usu. used with *up* ⟨*hiving* up in an old camp to sit out the storm⟩

³**hive** \"\ *n* -S [back-formation fr. *hives*] **:** an urticarial wheal **:** a lesion of hives

hive bee *n* **:** a domestic honeybee

hive body *n* **:** the brood chamber of a hive

hive·less \'hīvləs\ *adj* **:** having no hive

hive off *vi* **:** to break away from a group like a swarm from a hive of bees ⟨a portion of a nation *hives off* to a new territory and builds a new nationalism of its own —R.M.MacIver⟩

hiv·er \'hīvə(r)\ *n* -S **:** one that hives

hives \'hīvz\ *n pl but sing or pl in constr* [origin unknown] **1 :** URTICARIA **2 :** an eruptive skin disease

hive syrup *n* **:** compound syrup of squill formerly employed as an emetic in croup and as an expectorant

hive tool *n* **:** a blunt metal chisel that has the end opposite the blade bent at right angles to the shaft and is used by beekeepers to separate supers and to scrape away propolis from parts of the hive

hive tool

hive vine *n* **:** PARTRIDGEBERRY

hive·ward \'hīvwə(r)d\ *or* **hive·wards** \-dz\ *adv* **:** toward a hive ⟨bees flying ~ in a straight line⟩

hi·vite \'hī,vīt\ *also* **hiv·vite** \'hi,v-\ *n* -S *usu cap* **:** a member of one of the ancient Canaanite peoples who were conquered by the Israelites

hi·wi hi·wi \,hēwē'hēwē\ *n* [Maori] **:** a small marine spiny-finned food fish (*Chironemus fergussoni*) of New Zealand

hi·ya \'hīyə\ *interj* [alter. of *how are you*] — used as an informal greeting

hi·zen ware \'hē,zen-, ˌ=ˈ=-\ *n, usu cap H* [fr. *Hizen,* old province of Kyushu Island, Japan] **:** pottery and esp. porcelain (as Imari, Hirado, or Nabeshima wares) produced in Hizen

hizz \'hiz\ *obs or dial var of* HISS

hiz·zie \'hizi\ *Scot var of* HUSSY

HJ *abbr* [L *hic jacet*] here lies

hjelm·ite *also* **hielm·ite** \'(h)yel,mīt, hē'el-\ *n* -S [Sw *hjelmit,* fr. P. J. *Hjelm* †1813 Swedish chemist + Sw *-it* -ite] **:** a black mineral that contains yttrium, iron, manganese, uranium, calcium, columbium, tantalum, tin, and tungsten oxide, is often metamict, and has uncertain affinities — compare SAMARSKITE, TAPIOLITE

hjelm·slev·ian \(')(h)yelmz¦levēən, -eüm-,- m(p)¦sl-\ *adj, usu cap* [Louis *Hjelmslev* b1899 Dan. linguist + E *-ian*] **:** belonging to or characteristic of the linguistic methods or terminology of Louis Hjelmslev

HJR *abbr* House joint resolution

HJS *abbr* [L *hic jacet sepultus*] here lies buried

hkf *abbr* handkerchief

hl *abbr* hectoliter

HL *abbr* **1** height-length **2** *often not cap* [L *hoc loco*] in this place; [L *hujus loci*] of this place **3** horizontal line **4** House of Lords

h l hinge *n, cap 1st H&L* **:** H AND L HINGE

hm *abbr* hectometer

HM *abbr* **1** half morocco **2** handmade **3** harbor master **4** harmonic mean **5** headmaster; headmistress **6** heavy mobile **7** Her Majesty; Her Majesty's; His Majesty; His Majesty's **8** *often not cap* [L *hoc mense*] in this month; [L *hujus mensis*] of this month **9** home missions

hmd *abbr* humid

HMD *abbr* hydraulic mean depth

HMG *abbr* **1** heavy machine gun **2** Her Majesty's Government; His Majesty's Government

hmlt *abbr* hamlet

HMP *abbr* **1** handmade paper **2** [L *hoc monumentum posuit*] he erected this monument

HMS *abbr* **1** Her Majesty's Service; His Majesty's Service **2** Her Majesty's Ship; His Majesty's Ship

hnd *abbr* **1** hand **2** hundred

hndbk *abbr* handbook

¹**ho** \'hō\ *interj* [ME] — used typically to express surprise or delight or indignation or derision or to attract attention and esp. postpositively to attract attention to something specified ⟨land ~⟩; often used postpositively as a rallying cry with a specified direction or destination ⟨westward ~⟩

²**ho** \"\ *v imper* [ME, fr. OF *ho* halt, stop] — a call intended to stop a movement or an action; compare WHOA

³**ho** \"\ *vi, dial Eng* **:** ³HONE

⁴**ho** \"\ *n, pl* **ho** *or* **hos** *usu cap* **1 a :** a people of the northeastern part of the Indian subcontinent south of the Ganges plain **b :** a member of such people **2 :** the Munda language of the Ho people

ho *abbr* house

HO *abbr* **1** head office; home office **2** holy day of obligation **3** hostilities only

Ho *symbol* holmium

hoactzin *var of* HOATZIN

¹**hoar** \'hō(ə)r, 'hȯ(ə)r, -ōə, -ȯ(ə)\ *adj* [ME *hor, hoor,* fr. OE *hār;* akin to OHG *hēr* gray, old, ON *hārr* gray, old, Gk *kirrhos* orange yellow, Skt *śiti* white] *archaic* **:** HOARY ⟨whose beard with age is ~ —S.T.Coleridge⟩

²**hoar** \"\ *n* -S [ME *hor, hoor,* fr. *hor, hoor,* adj.] **1** *archaic* **:** HOARINESS **2 a :** a hoary coating ⟨the thick ~ of dust which had accumulated on their shoes —Thomas Hardy⟩ **b :** HOARFROST, RIME

¹**hoard** \'hō(ə)rd, 'hȯ(ə)rd, 'hōəd, 'hȯ(ə)d\ *n* -S [ME *hord,* fr. OE; akin to OHG *hort* treasure, ON *hodd,* Goth *huzd* treasure, Gk *kysthos* vulva, OE *hȳdan* to hide — more at HIDE] **1 :** a collection or accumulation or amassment of something usu. of special value or utility that is put aside for preservation or safekeeping or future use often in a greedy or miserly or otherwise unreasonable manner and that is often kept hidden or as if hidden **:** a supply or stock or fund of something that is stored up and closely and often jealously guarded ⟨a ~ of money⟩ ⟨a ~ of provisions⟩ ⟨a ~ of facts⟩; *often* **:** TREASURE ⟨dug up a ~ of gold and jewels⟩ ⟨a ~ of old coins⟩ **2** *obs* **:** the place where a hoard is kept **:** REPOSITORY; *specif, obs* **:** TREASURY

²**hoard** \"\ *vb* -ED/-ING/-S [ME *horden,* fr. OE *hordian,* fr. *hord,* n.] *vt* **1 :** to collect or accumulate or amass into a hoard **:** lay up a hoard of ⟨~*ing* their money and refusing to make even reasonable expenditures⟩ **2 :** to keep (as a desire) hidden and in reserve and allow to develop or become strengthened ⟨she ~*ed* her intention —Virginia Woolf⟩ ⟨the people outside disperse their affections, you ~ yours, you nurse them into intensity —Joseph Conrad⟩ ~ *vi* **:** to lay up a hoard; *esp* **:** to practice hoarding **syn** see ACCUMULATE

³**hoard** \"\ *n* -S [alter. of earlier *hourd,* prob. fr. F dial., scaffold, scaffolding, fr. OF *hourt* scaffold, scaffolding, platform, of Gmc origin; akin to OHG *hurd* hurdle — more at HURDLE] **:** ²HOARDING 1

hoard·er \-ə(r)\ *n* -S **:** one that hoards

¹**hoard·ing** \'hōrdiŋ, 'hȯr-, -dēŋ\ *n* -S [fr. gerund of ²*hoard*] **1 :** the greedy or miserly accumulation and storing or hiding of money or goods **2 :** something hoarded — usu. used in pl. ⟨the ~*s* of a lifetime⟩

²**hoarding** \"\ *n* -S [³*hoard* + *-ing*] **1 :** a temporary board fence put about a building being erected or repaired **2** *Brit* **:** BILLBOARD

hoard·ing·ly *adv* **:** in a manner marked by hoarding **:** in a greedy or miserly manner

hoarfrost \'=,=\ *n* [ME *horforst,* fr. *hor, hoor* hoar + *forst, frost* frost] **:** FROST 1c(1)

hoar-green \'=¦=\ *adj* **:** grayish white with greenish cast

hoarhead \'=,=\ *n* [ME *horheed,* fr. *hor, hoor* hoar + *heed* head] *archaic* **:** one having a hoary head

hoarhound *var of* HOREHOUND

hoar·i·ly \'hōrəlē, 'hȯr-, -li\ *adv* **:** in a hoary manner

hoar·i·ness \-rēnəs, -rin-\ *n* -ES **:** the quality or state of being hoary

hoarse \'hō(ə)rs, 'hȯ(ə)rs, -ōəs, -ȯ(ə)s\ *adj, usu* -ER/-EST [ME *hors,* alter. (perh. influenced by *harsk* harsh) of earlier *hos,* fr. OE *hās;* akin to OHG *heis* hoarse, ON *hāss,* OE *hāt* hot — more at HOT] **1 :** marked by a relatively low harsh or husky often muffled or laboriously forced quality of sound having little or no resonance **:** not clear or smooth or musical in tone **:** rough-sounding **:** RAUCOUS, GRATING, RASPING, CROAKING ⟨the ~ voice of a person with a cold⟩ ⟨the ~ sound made by a frog⟩ ⟨the ~ cry of a crow⟩ **2 :** having a hoarse voice or cry **:** making hoarse sounds ⟨had caught a cold and was quite ~⟩ ⟨~ from too much talking⟩ ⟨~ with emotion⟩ **syn** see LOUD

hoarse·ly *adv* **:** in a hoarse manner **:** with a hoarse voice or cry or sound or tone

hoars·en \'hōrsᵊn, 'hȯr-, 'hōəs-, 'hȯ(ə)s-\ *vb* **hoarsened; hoarsened; hoarsening** \-s(ᵊ)niŋ\ **hoarsens** *vt* **:** to make hoarse ⟨it agitated their bodies and ~*ed* their voices —Walter O'Meara⟩ ~ *vi* **:** to become hoarse ⟨the deep voice ~*ed* —E.C.Marston⟩

hoarse·ness \-snəs\ *n* -ES [alter. (influenced by *hoarse*) of ME *hosnes,* fr. OE *hāsnys,* fr. *hās* hoarse + *-nys, -nes* -ness] **:** the quality or state of being hoarse

hoarstone \'=,=\ *n* [ME *horeston, harestan,* fr. OE *hār stān,* fr. *hār* hoar + *stān* stone] **1** *Brit* **:** a stone used anciently to mark boundaries **2** *Brit* **:** a stone erected anciently as a memorial (as of an event)

hoary \'hōrē, 'hȯr-, -ri\ *adj, usu* -ER/-EST **1 a :** gray or white; *specif* **:** gray or white with age ⟨nodded his ~ head⟩ **b** (1) **:** having hair that is gray or white with age ⟨a ~ old man⟩ (2) **:** CANESCENT 2 (3) *of a plant* **:** having grayish or whitish leaves **2 a** (1) **:** very old **:** ANCIENT ⟨~ legends⟩; *esp* **:** impressively or venerably old ⟨the ~ walls of the castle⟩ ⟨the ~ figure of the prophet⟩ (2) **:** so old or so familiar as to be without freshness and sparkle ⟨~ jokes⟩ or devoid of interest or ability to stimulate ⟨~ clichés⟩ ⟨~ half-truths⟩ **:** TRITE, STALE, HACKNEYED **b :** far removed in time past **:** REMOTE ⟨~ antiquity⟩

hoary alder *n* **:** SPECKLED ALDER

hoary alyssum *n* **:** a tall leafy perennial European plant (*Berteroa incana*) with gray-green foliage, entire leaves, and pubescent pods that is naturalized in No. America and is sometimes troublesome as a weed

hoary bat *n* **:** a rather large migratory bat (*Lasiurus cinereus*) having yellowish or brown hair tipped with white

hoary cinquefoil **:** SILVERY CINQUEFOIL

hoary cress *or* **hoary peppergrass** *or* **hoary pepperwort** *n* **:** a perennial cruciferous European herb (*Cardaria draba*) with clasping stem leaves, clusters of small white flowers, and reniform or cordate depressed pods that is naturalized widely in America and often becomes a troublesome weed in the western U.S.

hoary-haired \'=¦=¦=\ *adj* **:** having hoary hair

hoary-headed \'=¦=¦=\ *adj* **:** having a hoary head

hoary marmot *n* **:** a large gray marmot (*Marmota pruinosa*) of northwestern No. America — called also *mountain badger*

hoary pea *n* **:** a plant of the genus *Tephrosia; esp* **:** GOAT'S RUE

hoary plantain *n* **1 :** a widely distributed Old World perennial plantain (*Plantago media*) that is naturalized in No. America and has a flat rosette of finely hirsute leaves and a tall scape bearing inconspicuous whitish fragrant flowers **2 :** a No. American annual or biennial plantain (*P. virginica*) with long soft hairs on the leaves

hoary puccoon *n* **:** a No. American perennial herb (*Lithospermum canescens*) with hairy foliage

hoary redpoll *n* **:** HORNEMANN'S REDPOLL

hoary vervain *n* **:** a densely white hairy perennial herb (*Verbena stricta*) of central No. America with showy purplish blue spicate flowers

hoary willow *n* **:** a white-leaved No. American shrub (*Salix candida*)

¹**hoast** \'hōst\ *n* -S [ME *host, hoost,* fr. ON *hōsti;* akin to OE *hwōsta* cough, OHG *huosto* cough, Skt *kāsate* he coughs] *dial Brit* **:** COUGH

²**hoast** \"\ *vb* -ED/-ING/-S [ME *hosten,* fr. ON *hōsta;* akin to ON *hōsti,* n.] *dial Brit* **:** COUGH

hoa·tzin \wä(t)'sēn\ *or* **hoac·tzin** \wäk(t)'s-\ *also* **hoa·cin** \wä's-\ *n, pl* **hoatzins** \-ēnz\ *also* **hoatzi·nes** \-ē(,)nās\ *or* **hoac·tzins** \-ēnz\ *also* **hoactzi·nes** \-ē(,)nās\ [AmerSp, fr. Nahuatl *uatzin* pheasant] **:** a crested bird (*Opisthocomus hoazin*) of tropical So. America constituting the suborder Opisthocomi of the Galliformes that is somewhat smaller than a pheasant and that has olivaceous plumage marked with white above and that has a disagreeable strong musky smell and the young of which have a well-developed claw on the first and second fingers of the wing by means of which they climb about — called also *stinkbird*

¹**hoax** \'hōks\ *vt* -ED/-ING/-ES [prob. by contr. of *hocus*] **:** to trick into believing or accepting or doing something **:** play upon the credulity of so as to bring about belief in or acceptance of what is actually false and often preposterous **:** take in **:** DELUDE, DUPE, MISLEAD, VICTIMIZE ⟨~*ed* them into thinking the diamonds were genuine⟩ ⟨eager to ~ people into swallowing propaganda⟩ ⟨even the experts were ~*ed*⟩ **syn** see DUPE

²**hoax** \"\ *n* -ES **1 :** an act intended to trick or dupe **:** a piece of trickery **:** IMPOSTURE ⟨played a ~ on the miners —*New Republic*⟩ ⟨~*es* have occurred even in the present century —R.W.Murray⟩ **2 :** something accepted or believed in through trickery **:** something established by fraud or fabrication ⟨the book was once thought to be based on actual experience, but it is now recognized as a literary ~⟩ ⟨Piltdown man is one of the biggest ~*es* ever launched on the scientific world⟩

¹**hob** \'häb\ *n* -S [ME *hob, hobbe,* fr. *Hobbe,* nickname of *Robert* or *Robin*] **1** *now dial Eng* **a :** a clownish lout **b :** RUSTIC **2** *now dial Eng* **:** HOBGOBLIN, ELF **3 :** a male ferret — **play hob 1 :** to cause mischief **:** make trouble **:** cause an upset **:** cause confusion or disruption or havoc — usu. used with *with* ⟨would disorganize his life and *play hob* with his standard of living —John Lardner⟩ **2 :** to take liberties **:** make free — usu. used with *with* ⟨a biased book that *plays hob* with historical fact⟩ — **raise hob 1 :** to play hob — usu. used with *with* ⟨the war . . . *raised hob* with international trade —*Harper's*⟩ **2 a :** to show extreme irritation or wrath ⟨his . . . wife was getting on his nerves and he was *raising* unaccountable *hob* —V.P.Hass⟩ — often used with *with* ⟨*raised hob* with him for being late⟩ **b :** to be riotous (as with intoxication or glee) and cause a rumpus ⟨going to go out tonight and *raise hob*⟩

²**hob** \"\ *n* -S [origin unknown] **1 :** a level projection (as of brickwork, stone, or iron) at the back or side of an open fireplace on which something (as a kettle) can be placed to be kept warm **2** *archaic* **a :** a peg or stake used as a target in quoits and similar games **b :** a game in which such a peg or stake is used **3 :** HOBNAIL **4 a** (1) **:** a cutting tool consisting of a fluted steel worm that is used in a milling machine for cutting the teeth of worm wheels or screw chasers or other tool devices or used in a gear hobber for hobbing the teeth of gear wheels (2) **:** MASTER TAP (3) **:** SELLERS HOB (4) **:** an engraved steel block that is casehardened and used to impress an embossing die or a die-casting die — called also *hub* **b :** LEADER 1d

³**hob** \"\ *vt* **hobbed; hobbed; hobbing; hobs 1 :** to furnish with hobnails **2 a :** to cut (as the teeth of worm wheels) with a hob **b :** to impress (as an embossing die) with a hob

¹**hob and nob** \¦häbə(n)¦näb\ *interj* [prob. alter. of earlier *hob or nob,* alter. of *hab or nab* — more at HABNAB] *archaic* — used as an informal toast in convivial drinking

²**hob and nob** \"\ *also* **hob a nob** \"\ *adv (or adj) archaic* **:** in a close and friendly relationship **:** in a warmly companionable relationship

³**hob and nob** \"\ *or* **hob-a-nob** \"\ *archaic var of* ¹HOBNOB

ho·bart \'hō,bärt\ *adj, usu cap* **:** of or from Hobart, the capital of Tasmania **:** of the kind or style prevalent in Hobart

hob·ba·de·hoy *or* **hob·ba·dy·hoy** \¦häbədē¦hȯi\ *also* **hob·ber·de·hoy** \-bə(r)d-\ *archaic var of* HOBBLEDEHOY

hob·ber \'häbə(r)\ *n* -S **1 :** a machine used for hobbing; *also* **:** the operator of such a machine **2 :** a pitched horseshoe or quoit leaning against a stake or peg without ringing it — called also *leaner*

¹**hobbes·ian** \'häbzēən\ *adj, usu cap* [Thomas *Hobbes* †1679 Eng. philosopher + E *-ian*] **:** of or relating to Hobbes or Hobbism

²**hobbesian** \"\ *n* -S *usu cap* **:** HOBBIST

hobbied *past of* HOBBY

hobbies *pres 3d sing of* HOBBY, *pl of* HOBBY

hob·bil \'häbəl\ *n* -S [alter. of obs *hoball,* prob. fr. ¹*hob*] *now dial Eng* **:** a stupid individual **:** DOLT

hob·bism \'hä,bizəm\ *n* -S *usu cap* **:** the philosophical system of Hobbes; *esp* **:** Hobbes' political theory maintaining that man has a natural right to self-preservation and happiness and that the clashing interests and desires of individuals must be controlled by a strong government esp. of a monarchist constitution

¹**hob·bist** \'häbəst\ *n* -S *usu cap* **:** a follower of Hobbes or advocate of Hobbism

²**hobbist** \"\ *adj, usu cap* **:** HOBBESIAN

¹**hob·ble** \'häbəl\ *vb* **hobbled; hobbled; hobbling** \-b(ə)liŋ\ **hobbles** [ME *hoblen;* akin to MD *hobbelen* to turn, roll] *vi* **1 :** to move along unsteadily or with great difficulty or uncertainty **:** advance waveringly or laboriously or painfully **:** limp along **:** move lamely **:** struggle along ⟨the crippled ship managed to ~ into port⟩ ⟨try to ~ along to the end of the school term⟩; *specif* **:** to walk with a halting labored typically up-and-down movement often marked by lurching or wobbling ⟨saw an old man *hobbling* down the street⟩ ⟨*hobbling* along on his crutches⟩ **2** *of an arrow* **:** to wobble in flight ~ *vt* **1 :** to cause to hobble **:** make lame **:** CRIPPLE ⟨was *hobbled* by an ankle injury⟩ **2** [prob. alter. of *hopple*] **a :** to tie or otherwise fasten together the legs of (as a horse) to prevent straying or to keep under control **:** FETTER ⟨*hobbled* the horses before turning them loose⟩ **b :** to interfere with the free movement or advance of **:** HAMPER, OBSTRUCT, IMPEDE ⟨felt himself *hobbled* by his parents' lack of understanding⟩ ⟨*hobbling* factory production by inefficient methods⟩

²**hobble** \"\ *n* -S **1 :** a hobbling movement or hobbling manner of walking ⟨had a bad ~ —Adrian Bell⟩ **2** *archaic* **:** an awkward or perplexing situation **3 a :** something used for tying the legs (as of a horse) esp. to prevent straying **:** FETTER **b :** something that restrains or hampers ⟨censorship and other ~*s* of free expression⟩ **4 :** HOBBLE SKIRT

hobblebush \'=,=\ *n* [²*hobble* + *bush;* fr. the hindrance caused by its drooping branches] **:** a shrub (*Viburnum alnifolium*) of northern No. America that has long straggling branches and opposite double-toothed leaves — called also *American wayfaring tree*

hobbled *adj* [fr. past part. of ¹*hobble*] *West* **:** tied together beneath the belly of a horse — used of stirrups

hob·ble·de·hoy \¦häbəldē¦hȯi\ *n* -S [origin unknown] **:** a usu. awkward callow adolescent male **:** a gawky youth

hobble out *vt* **:** to attach hobbles to (as a horse) and allow to wander about esp. in a pasture ⟨had *hobbled out* some horses not far from his cabin —Ross Santee⟩ ⟨and *hobbled* the animals *out* to graze —Fred Gipson⟩

¹**hob·bler** \-b(ə)lə(r)\ *n* -S [¹*hobble* + *-er*] **:** one that hobbles

²**hob·bler** \'häb(ə)lə(r)\ *n* -S [alter. (perh. influenced by ¹*hobble*) of *hoveler*] **:** an unlicensed boat pilot or a freelance longshoreman in some parts of southern England

hob·ble·shew \'häbəl,shü\ *or* **hob·ble·show** \-,shō\ *var of* HUBBLESHEW

hobble skirt *n* [²*hobble*] **:** a skirt with bottom fullness constricted at the ankles by a band

hob·ble·te·hoy \¦häbəltē¦hȯi\ *or* **hob·by·de·hoy** \-bēdē¦-\ *archaic var of* HOBBLEDEHOY

hob·bling·ly *adv* [*hobbling* (pres. part. of ¹*hobble*) + *-ly*] **:** with a hobbling movement **:** LAMELY

hob·bly \'häb(ə)li\ *adj* [*hobble* + *-y*] *dial Brit* **:** having a rough uneven surface

¹**hob·by** \'häbē, -bi\ *n* -ES [ME *hoby, hobyn,* perh. fr. *Hobbin,* nickname of *Robert* or *Robin*] **1** *or* **hobby horse** *archaic* **:** a small or medium-sized light horse esp. of Irish origin having a gentle ambling pace **2** *archaic* **:** HOBBYHORSE 1,3 **3 a :** HOBBYHORSE 4a **b :** a specialized pursuit (as stamp collecting, painting, woodworking, gardening) that is outside one's regular occupation and that one finds particularly interesting and enjoys doing usu. in a nonprofessional way as a source of leisure-time relaxation; *broadly* **:** any favorite pursuit or interest **4** *archaic* **:** DANDY HORSE

²**hobby** \"\ *vi* -ED/-ING/-ES **:** to follow a hobby **:** have a hobby ⟨*hobbied* in photography for many years⟩

³**hobby** \"\ *n* -ES [ME *hoby,* modif. of MF *hobé,* fr. OF, alter. of *hobel,* perh. fr. *hobeler* to skirmish, prob. fr. MD *hobbelen* to turn, roll — more at HOBBLE] **:** a small falcon (*Falco subbuteo*) widely distributed in the Old World and formerly trained for hawking and flown at small birds (as larks)

hobbyhorse \'==,=\ *n* **1 a :** a figure designed to resemble a horse and made of light material (as wickerwork) that is fastened about the waist of a dancer (as in the morris dance or in Spanish or Javanese dance rituals) who dances about imitating the movements of a high-spirited horse **b :** a dancer wearing this figure and performing a dance associated with it **2** *obs* **:** BUFFOON **3 a :** a child's plaything which consists typically of a stick having an imitation horse's head at one end and sometimes wheels at the other and which the child straddles and pretends to ride — called also *stick horse* **b :** one of the horses on a merry-go-round **c :** ROCKING HORSE **d :** a toy horse suspended by springs from a frame **4 a :** something (as a pet idea or favorite topic or special object of concern) with which one is preoccupied or to which one constantly reverts ⟨this is one of his political ~*s*⟩; *specif* **:** a cranky obsession **b** *archaic* **:** HOBBY 3b **5 :** DANDY HORSE

hobbyhorse 3a

hob·by·ist \'häbēəst, -biə-\ *n* -S [¹*hobby* + *-ist*] **1** *archaic* **:** one that is preoccupied with a pet idea or cranky obsession **2 :** one that has one or more hobbies; *esp* **:** one that is particularly fond of cultivating hobbies

hobby lantern *n* [¹*hob* + *-y*] *dial Eng* **:** WILL-O'-THE-WISP

hob ferret *n* **:** ¹HOB 3

hobgoblin \'=,==\ *n* [¹*hob* + *goblin*] **1 :** a goblin esp. when conceived of as mischievous or impish **2 :** BOGEY 3 ⟨unreason has taken the place of evil as the ~ of a rational society —Albert Hubbell⟩ **:** BUGABOO ⟨a foolish consistency is the ~ of little minds —R.W.Emerson⟩

hobnail \'=,=\ *n, often attrib* [²*hob* + *nail*] **1 :** a short nail with a large head and a sharp point that is used esp. for studding soles of heavy shoes (as work shoes) **2** *archaic* **:** a countrified often loutish individual **:** CLODHOPPER ⟨troops of ~*s* clumping to church —W.M.Thackeray⟩ **3 a :** a pattern consisting of small tufts usu. closely spaced (as on some bedspreads) or of similarly spaced bosses often having the shape of diamonds (as in some vases and other objects made of pressed glass) **b :** one of the tufts or bosses used in such a pattern

hobnailed \'=,näld\ *adj* **1 :** studded with or as if with hobnails ⟨~ boots⟩ **2 a :** marked by the wearing of heavy shoes or boots studded with hobnails ⟨~ laborers⟩ ⟨the ~ entry of investigating officialdom into the classroom —M.H.Bernstein⟩ **b :** countrified or rustic in tone ⟨~ to the feeling⟩

hobnail liver *also* **hobnailed liver** *n* **1 :** the liver as it appears in one form of cirrhosis in which it is shrunken and hard and covered with small projecting nodules **2 :** the cirrhosis associated with hobnail liver **:** LAENNEC'S CIRRHOSIS o \'häb,näb\ vi hobnobbed; hobnobbed; hobnob-hobnobs [alter. of habnab] 1 archaic : to drink sociably onvivially — often used with with 2 a : to associate iliarly : go about in an easy informal companionship num around — often used with with ⟨once hobnobbed with ings and princes⟩ ⟨have hobnobbed ever since they were boys⟩ b : to talk informally and freely to or with someone : speak familiarly — usu. used with with : CHAT ⟨officials have long enjoyed the practice of hobnobbing with newspapermen —Douglass Cater⟩ — hob·nob·ber \-näbə(r)\ n -s

²hobnob \"\ n -s : an informal sociable meeting and chat : GET-TOGETHER ⟨going to have a quiet little ~ with them⟩

¹ho·bo \'hō(,)bō\ n, pl hoboes also hobos [perh. alter. of

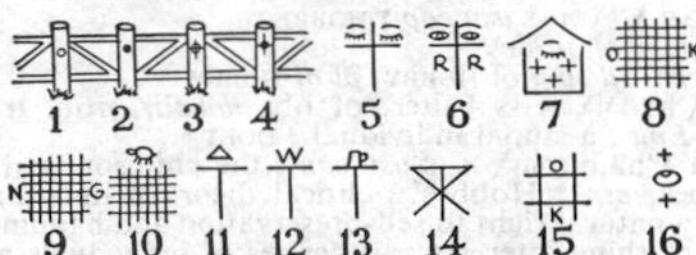

common symbols used by hoboes: *1* good for a handout, *2* cranky woman or bad dog, *3* not generous, *4* stay away, *5* police not hostile, *6* police hostile; *R R* used for railroad police, *7* jail good for a night's lodging, *8* clean jail, *9* jail food no good, *10* unclean jail, *11* jail has rock pile, *12* jail is a workhouse, *13* saloons in town, *14* town is hostile, *15* streets good for begging, *16* plainclothes detectives here

ho, boy, a call used in the northwestern U.S. in the 1880's by railway mail handlers when delivering mail] 1 : a migratory worker 2 a : one that is homeless and usu. penniless and that leads a largely vagrant life often by choice and that occas. works at odd jobs : TRAMP b : ⁷BUM 1a, 1b syn see VAGABOND

²hobo \"\ vi -ED/-ING/-ES : to live or travel in the manner of a hobo ⟨spent two years ~*ing* around the country⟩

ho·bo·he·mia \,hō(,)bō'hēmēə\ n [blend of *hobo* and *bohemia*] 1 : a usu. run-down urban district in which hoboes congregate 2 : a fringe group of society made up of hoboes : the hobo realm — ho·bo·he·mi·an \ˌ=(,)=ˈhēmēən\ adj or n

ho·bo·ism \'hō(,)bō,izəm\ n -s : the condition of being a hobo

¹hob or nob \,häbə(r)'näb\ var of ¹HOB AND NOB

²hob or nob archaic var of ¹HOBNOB

hobs pl of HOB, pres 3d sing of HOB

hob·son–job·son \'häbsən'jäbsən\ n -s usu cap H&J [Anglo-Indian modif. (influenced by the Eng. surnames Hobson and Jobson) of Ar *yā Ḥasan! yā Ḥusayn!* O Hasan! O Husain! (cry repeated at the Muharram festival as an expression of mourning for Hasan and Husain, grandsons of Muhammad, killed in the early struggles between the Sunni and Shiʿa parties)] : assimilation of the sounds of a word or words foreign to a language into the sounds of a word or words coined or already existent in the language (as Spanish *cucaracha* has become English *cockroach* or as English *riding coat* has become French *redingote*) ⟨the law of *Hobson-Jobson* has played a great role in the evolution of surnames —R.F. Barton⟩ — compare FOLK ETYMOLOGY

hob·son's choice \'häbsənz-\ n, usu cap H [after Thomas Hobson †1631 Eng. liveryman; fr. his practice of requiring every customer to take the horse which stood nearest the door] 1 : an apparent freedom to take or reject something offered when in actual fact no such freedom exists : an apparent freedom of choice where there is no real alternative: a : the forced acceptance of something whether one likes it or not (as in a so-called free election where only one candidate is proposed) b (1) : the necessity of accepting something objectionable through the fact that one would otherwise get nothing at all (as an underpaid job rather than no job at all) (2) : the necessity of accepting one of two or more equally objectionable things (as enslavement or annihilation by a conquered people) 2 : something that one must accept through want of any real alternative : the object of a Hobson's choice ⟨military unity . . . is . . . a *Hobson's choice* which all accept —V.D.Hurd⟩

hob tap n [²hob] : MASTER TAP

hob·thrush \'häb,thrəsh\ n [prob. irreg. fr. ¹hob + obs. E *thurse* goblin, fr. ME *thirs* malevolent supernatural being, fr. OE *thyrs* demon; akin to OHG *duris* giant, ON *thurs*] dial Eng : HOBGOBLIN

hoc \'häk\ n -s [F, perh. fr. L, this, neut. of *hic* this] : a card game in which the holder gives certain cards any value

¹hoch \'häk, -ō-\ chiefly Scot var of HOCK

²hoch \'hōk\ interj, often cap [G, lit., high, fr. OHG *hōh* — more at HIGH] — used to express salutation and approval

hoche·laga \,(,)h|äsh(ə)'lagə, |ōsh-, |ȯsh, -lä-\ n, pl hochelaga or hochelagas usu cap 1 : an extinct Iroquoian people located on the site of present Montreal 2 : a member of the Hochelaga people

hoch·moor \'hōk+,-\ adj [G *hoch* high + *moor* fen, swamp, fr. OHG *muor* — more at MOOR] : being or growing on various acid peats or peaty soils ⟨the ~ soils along the Baltic coast⟩

höchst \'hə(r)kst, 'hōk-, 'hek- Ger 'hœkst or -œk-\ adj, often cap [*Höchst*, former city (now part of Frankfurt am Main) in western Germany] : of, relating to, or being an 18th century German clayware including both faience and hard-paste porcelain often modeled after natural objects and usu. enamel-decorated

¹hock \'häk\ n -s [ME *hocke*, fr. OE *hoc*] : any of several mallows of the genera *Althaea* and *Malva* — now used only in holly*hock*

²hock \"\ vb -ED/-ING/-S [ME *hocken* to celebrate Hocktide, fr. *hocke-, hoke-* (in *hockedai, hokeday* Hockday)] vt, archaic : to tease or harass after a manner formerly customary at Hocktide ~ vi : to behave in a brash rambunctious manner suitable to Hocktide

³hock \"\ n -s [prob. alter. of *hook*] chiefly Brit : a strong usu. handled hook used esp. for cargo handling or for hanging meat

⁴hock \"\ n -s [alter. of ME *hoch, hough*, fr. OE *hōh* heel; akin to ON *hāsin* hock, sinew, Skt *kaṅkāla* skeleton] 1 a : the tarsal joint or its region in the hind limb of a digitigrade quadruped (as the horse) that corresponds to the ankle of man but is elevated and bends backward and that is a compound joint containing a number of small bones and having a prominence at the back caused by the calcaneum and corresponding to the heel of man — see COW illustration b : the corresponding joint of a fowl's leg — called also *knee*; see COCK illustration 2 : a small cut of meat from either the front or hind leg just above the foot — used esp. of pork ⟨pork ~s and sauerkraut⟩ 3 chiefly dial : the hip and thigh — often used in pl. ⟨so hipless . . . his pants . . . forever slipping down around his ~*s* —F.B. Gipson⟩

⁵hock \"\ vt -ED/-ING/-S : to disable by cutting the tendons of the hock : HAMSTRING

⁶hock \"\ n -s often cap [modif. of *Hochheimer* fr. *Hochheim*, Germany, its locality] chiefly Brit : RHINE WINE 1

⁷hock \"\ n -s [D *hok* pen (for animals), hovel, prison] 1 a : restraint of goods usu. as a pledge for a loan ⟨put his winter overcoat into ~⟩ ⟨had difficulty getting the technical supplies out of ~ with the customs⟩ b slang : PRISON ⟨will be 10 years before he gets out of ~⟩ 2 [Afrik *hok*, fr. D] *Africa* : a small or temporary building or enclosure ⟨a chicken ~⟩ — in hock : PAWNED ⟨his watch was *in hock*⟩ : in debt ⟨the company was heavily *in hock* to the banks⟩

⁸hock \"\ vt -ED/-ING/-S : to pledge as security for a loan : PAWN

⁹hock \"\ n -s [perh. short for *hockelty*] : the last card in a faro dealing box

hock·day \'häk,dā\ or hoke·day \'hōk-\ n, usu cap [ME *hockedai, hokeday*] 1 : the second Tuesday after Easter celebrated in England before the 18th century with rough sport and humorous play orig. for the collection of funds for community purposes — called also *Hock Tuesday* 2 : the second Monday after Easter — called also *Hock Monday*

hock disease n [⁴hock] : perosis of the young chicken or turkey

hock·el·ty \'häkəltē\ n -ES [origin unknown] : ⁹HOCK

¹hock·er \'häkə(r)\ n -s : one that hocks

²hocker \"\ vi -ED/-ING/-S [modif. of Norw dial. *hokra* to crouch, fr. ON *hūka* to squat] dial Eng : to behave or move in an awkward flustered manner

hock·et or ho·quet \'häkət\ n -s [ME *hocket* obstacle, fr. MF *hoquet*, of imit. origin] 1 : HICCUP 2 *in medieval music* : an interruption of a voice part by interjected rests resulting in a broken musical line; *also* : a composition using such an interruption as a contrapuntal device

¹hock·ey \'häkē, -ki\ n -s often attrib [perh. fr. MF *hoquet* shepherd's crook, dim. of *hoc* hook, of Gmc origin; akin to MD *hoec* corner — more at HOOK] 1 : a game in which two parties of players provided with sticks curved or hooked at the end seek to drive a ball or other small object through opposite goals: as a : FIELD HOCKEY b : ICE HOCKEY 2 : HOCKEY STICK

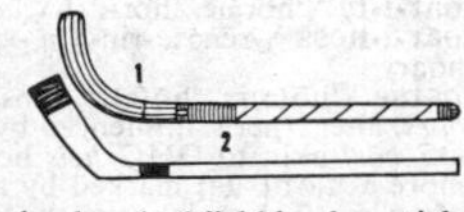

hockey 1: *1* field hockey stick, *2* ice hockey stick

²hockey \"\ n -ES [earlier *hocky*, prob. fr. LG *hokk* pile of sheaves (fr. MLG *hocke*; akin to MD *hocke*, ME *hock* pile, ON *hūka* to squat) + E *-y* — more at HAWKER] 1 chiefly dial : HARVEST HOME 2 chiefly dial : a harvest-home supper

³hock·ey \", 'hōk-,'hīk-\ n -ES [origin unknown] chiefly Midland : EXCREMENT, FECES

⁴hockey \"\ vi -ED/-ING/-S chiefly Midland : DEFECATE

hock·ey·ist \'häkēəst, -ki|\ also hock·ey·ite \|,īt\ n -s : a hockey player

hockey skate n : a tubular skate made with a short curved blade and a shoe giving support and protection to the foot and ankle and worn esp. by ice hockey players

hockey skate

hockey stick n : a curved or angled stick used in playing hockey

hocking pres part of HOCK

hock·ing ale \'häkiŋ-\ n [ME *hokyng*, gerund of *hoken, hocken* to celebrate Hocktide — more at HOCK] archaic : ale for the Hocktide festival

hock leg n [⁴hock] : a cabriole having a broken curve on the inner side of the knee — see LEG illustration

hock monday \'häk-\ n, usu cap H&M [ME *hoc Monday*, fr. *hoc-, hocke-, hoke-* (in *hockedai, hokeday* Hockday) + *Monday*] : HOCKDAY 2

hock money \"+\ n, usu cap H [ME *hockemoney*, fr. *hocke-, hoke-* + *money*] archaic : money collected at Hocktide

hocks pl of HOCK, pres 3d sing of HOCK

hock shop n [⁷hock] : PAWNSHOP

hocktide \'=,=\ n, usu cap [ME *hoketyde*, fr. *hoke-* + *tyde, tide* time, season — more at TIDE] : Hock Monday and Hock Tuesday

hock tuesday n, usu cap H&T [ME *hoke Tuesday*, fr. *hoc-, hocke-, hoke-* (in *hockedai, hakeday* Hockday) + *Tuesday*] : HOCKDAY 1

hocs pl of HOC

¹ho·cus \'hōkəs\ n, pl hocuses or hocusses [short for *hocus-pocus*] 1 obs a : CONJURER, CHEAT, DECEIVER b : CHEATING, TRICKERY, FRAUD 2 : drugged liquor

²hocus \"\ vt hocused or hocussed; hocused or hocussed; hocusing or hocussing; hocuses or hocusses 1 : DECEIVE, CHEAT 2 a : ADULTERATE, DRUG ⟨~*ed* liquor⟩ b : to ply with stupefying drugs

¹ho·cus-po·cus also ho·kus-po·kus \,hōkəs'pōkəs\ n -ES [prob. invented by jugglers in imitation of Latin] 1 a obs : JUGGLER, TRICKSTER b archaic : a juggler's trick or art : SLEIGHT OF HAND 2 : words or a formula used (as by jugglers) in pretended incantations without regard to the usual meaning 3 : nonsense or sham used or intended to cloak deception ⟨the *hocus-pocus* of city politics⟩; *broadly* : something that confuses, misleads, or is difficult to comprehend ⟨the tape recordings, through some electronic *hocus-pocus*, will retain all the visual quality of the original telecast —*Newsweek*⟩

²hocus-pocus \"\ vb hocus-pocussed or hocus-pocused hocus-pocussed or hocus-pocused; hocus-pocussing or hocus-pocusing; hocus-pocusses or hocus-pocuses vi : to play the part of a conjurer; *broadly* : TRICK, CHEAT ~ vt : to play tricks on : TRICK, BEFOOL ⟨got through *hocus-pocussing* the jury —Shelby Foote⟩

¹hod \'häd\ n -s [prob. fr. MD *hodde*; akin to MHG *hotte*, *hotze* cradle, G dial. *hotteln, hotzeln* to shake, Lith *kutėti* to shake up, ME *schuderen* to shudder — more at SHUDDER] 1 : a tray or trough with a pole handle that is borne on the shoulder for carrying mortar, brick, or similar loads 2 : a utensil for holding or carrying coal : COAL SCUTTLE

²hod \"\ vi hodded; hodded; hodding; hods [prob. imit.] Scot : to bob up and down : JOG

³hod \'hōd\ vb [by alter.] Scot : HIDE

⁴hod \'häd, -ō-\ dial Eng var of HOLD

ho·dag \'hō,dag\ n -s [origin unknown] : a mythical animal reported chiefly from Wisconsin and Minnesota, noted for its ugliness, lateral horns, and hooked tail, and reputed to be outstanding in both ferocity and melancholy

hod carrier n : a laborer employed in carrying bricks, mortar, concrete, or plaster to supply bricklayers, stonemasons, cement finishers, or plasterers on the job

hod·den \'häd°n\ n -s [origin unknown] chiefly Scot : coarse cloth of undyed wool

hodden grey n, dial Brit : HODDEN; *esp* : hodden prepared from a mingling of white or light fleeces with a small proportion of natural black wool

hod·dle \'häd°l\ vi -ED/-ING/-S [prob. by alter.] Scot : WADDLE

hoddy-doddy \'hädē'dädē\ n, pl hoddy-doddies [prob. alter. and redupl. of *dodman, hodmadod*] 1 dial Eng a : GARDEN SNAIL b : a snail shell 2 archaic a : a short and stout person b (1) : a henpecked man (2) : CUCKOLD c : FOOL, BLOCKHEAD, SIMPLETON

hod·dy·poll \'==,pōl\ n -s [*hoddy-* (fr. *hoddy-doddy*) + *poll*] 1 : a fumbling inept person 2 obs : CUCKOLD

hod·ful \'häd,fu̇l\ n, pl hodfuls also hodsful : the quantity that may be carried at one time in a hod ⟨a ~ of coal⟩; *broadly* : a considerable quantity : LOTS ⟨had ~*s* of fun⟩

hodge \'häj\ n -s [ME *Hoge*, nickname of *Roger*] : an English rustic or farm laborer

¹hodge·podge \'häj,päj\ n -s [alter. of *hotchpotch*] 1 : a heterogeneous mixture often of incongruous and ill-suited elements : MIXTURE, MEDLEY 2 : HOTCHPOTCH 1

²hodgepodge \"\ vt -ED/-ING/-S : to make into a hodgepodge

hodg·kin's disease \'häjkənz-\ n, usu cap H [after Thomas *Hodgkin* †1866 Eng. physician] : a disease of unknown cause that is characterized by progressive enlargement of lymph glands, spleen, and liver and by progressive anemia and that in some respects suggests an inflammatory or tumorous process

hodg·kin·son·ite \'häjkənsə,nīt\ n -s [H. H. *Hodgkinson* Am. mineralogist + E *-ite*] : a mineral $MnZn_2SiO_5.H_2O$ consisting of a hydrous zinc manganese silicate that occurs in the form of pink to reddish brown crystals

ho·di·er·nal \,hōdē'ərn°l, 'häd-\ adj [obs. E *hodiern* hodiernal (fr. L *hodiernus*, fr. *hodie* today, contr. of *hoc die* this day) + E *-al*] : of this day

hodja var of KHOJA

hod·ma·dod \'hädmə,däd\ n -s [alter. and redupl. of *dodman*] 1 dial Eng a : SNAIL; *esp* : GARDEN SNAIL b : a snail shell 2 dial Eng a : a deformed or clumsy person 3 dial Eng : SCARECROW

hod·man \'hädmən\ n, pl hodmen [¹hod + man] chiefly Brit : HOD CARRIER; *broadly* : one whose duties are mere routine assistance : HACK

ho·do·graph \'hädə,graf, 'hōd-, -ràf\ n [Gk *hodos* path + E *-graph* — more at CEDE] : a path described by the extremity of a vector drawn from a fixed origin and representing the linear velocity of a moving point — ho·do·graph·ic \'==grafik\ adj

ho·do·scope \'==,skōp\ n [Gk *hodos* path + E *-scope*] : an instrument for tracing the paths of cosmic-ray or other ionizing particles by means of ion counters in close array

hods pl of HOD, pres 3d sing of HOD

¹hoe \'hō\ n -s [ME *hogh*, fr. OE *hōh*; prob. akin to OE *hōh* heel — more at ⁴HOCK] obs : PROMONTORY, HILL, CLIFF — used in English place names ⟨on the *Hoe* at Plymouth⟩

²hoe \"\ n -s [ME *howe*, fr. MF *houe*, fr. OF, of Gmc origin; akin to MD *houwe* mattock, OHG *houwa*; derivative fr. the verb represented by OHG *houwan* to hew — more at HEW] 1 a : an agricultural implement that usu. consists of a thin flat blade set transversely on a long handle and is used esp. for cultivating, weeding, or loosening the earth around plants b : an implement that functions like a hoe and is arranged with a wheel and one or two handles for more rapid cultivation c : a one-horse tillage implement for cultivating between rows (as of vines or bushes) ⟨a berry ~⟩ ⟨a grape ~⟩ d : any of various cultivating or weeding implements usu. for use with animal or mechanical draft — see ROTARY HOE, SPRING HOE, SPRING-TRIP HOE, WHEEL CULTIVATOR 2 2 : an implement or tool felt to resemble or serving a purpose like that of a hoe: as a : a rake designed for stirring up a furnace fire b : an instrument for spreading and mixing mortar, concrete, or similar substances c : BACKHOE

hoe 1a

³hoe \"\ vb hoed; hoed; hoeing; hoes [ME *howwen*, fr. *howe*, n.] vi : to use a hoe : work with a hoe ⟨was ~*ing* in the field by the road⟩ ~ vt : to weed, cultivate, or thin (a crop) with a hoe ⟨~ out the strawberries⟩ : remove (weeds) by hoeing ⟨soon have to ~ the weeds from the corn⟩ : dress or cultivate (land) by hoeing ⟨*hoed* 7 acres with a spring hoe⟩

⁴hoe \"\ n -s [E dial. (Shetland) *ho*, of Scand origin; akin to ON *hār* dogfish, shark, tholepin — more at HAYE] chiefly Scot : SPINY DOGFISH

hoecake \'=,=\ n [²hoe + cake; fr. its being baked on the blade of a hoe] 1 chiefly South & Midland : a small cake made of cornmeal, water, and salt usu. cooked before an open fire 2 chiefly South & Midland : a hoecake to which shortening has been added and which is usu. baked on a griddle or in an oven

hoe culture also hoe agriculture or hoe cultivation n : the growing of crops by hand methods including use of a hoe for stirring the soil

hoedown \'=,=\ n -s [³hoe + down] 1 a : a lively old-time dance; *esp* : SQUARE DANCE 1 b : a lively hillbilly tune played usu. to accompany folk or square dancing 2 a : an informal dancing party at which hoedowns are danced b slang : a loud or spectacular affair (as a social or theatrical event)

hoe drill n : a seed drill with hoeing devices for opening furrows

hoeg·bom·ite \'hōgbə,mīt, 'hāg-\ n -s [Sw *högbomit*, fr. Arvid Gustaf *Högbom*, 20th cent. Swed. scientist + Sw *-it* -ite] : a mineral $Mg(Al,Fe,Ti)_4O_7$(?) consisting of an oxide of magnesium, aluminum, iron, and titanium

ho·er \'hōə(r), -ōr\ n -s : one that hoes

hoer·nes·ite \'hərnə,sīt, 'hōr-\ n -s [G *hörnesit*, fr. Moritz *Hoernes* †1868 Austrian paleontologist + G *-it* -ite] : a mineral $Mg_3As_2O_8.8H_2O$ consisting of hydrous magnesium arsenate occurring as crystals resembling gypsum

hoff·man clamp \'häfmən, 'hȯf|\ n, usu cap H [prob. fr. the name *Hoffman*] : a pinchcock for flexible tubing controlled by a screw

hoffmann's anodyne n, usu cap H [after Friedrich *Hoffmann* †1742 Ger. physician] : COMPOUND SPIRIT OF ETHER

hoffmann's drops n pl, usu cap H [after Friedrich *Hoffmann* †1742] : SPIRIT OF ETHER

hof·mann reaction or hofmann rearrangement \'häl|fmən-, 'hȯ|, 'hō|\ n, usu cap H [after August Wilhelm von *Hofmann* †1892 Ger. chemist] : the conversion of an acid amide $RCONH_2$ to an amine RNH_2 with one less carbon atom by treatment with sodium hypobromite

Hoffman clamp

hofmann's violet n, usu cap H : any of several violet dyes that are alkylated fuchsines made by treating rosaniline with an alkyl halide (as ethyl iodide)

hof·meis·ter series \'häl,fmīstə(r), 'hȯ|, 'hō|\ n, usu cap H [after Franz *Hofmeister* †1922 Austro-Ger. physiological chemist] : an arrangement of salts, anions, or cations in descending order of their effect upon a physical phenomenon (as the swelling of gelatin) — called also *lyotropic series*

¹hog \'hȯg, -ä-\ n, pl hogs also hog often attrib [ME *hogge*, fr. OE *hogg*, perh. of Celt origin; akin to W *hwch* hog, Corn *hoch* — more at sow] 1 a : a domestic swine : PIG, SOW, BOAR; *esp* : an adult or a growing animal weighing more than 120 pounds — compare PORK b Brit : ²BARROW c : a wild boar; *broadly* : any of various animals of the family Suidae — usu. used in combination ⟨the wart*hogs* and river ~*s* are tropical relatives of our domestic swine⟩ 2 usu hogg Brit a : a young sheep usu. less than or about a year in age and not yet shorn; *also* : wool from such a sheep b : a young domestic animal (as a bullock) of similar age — often used in combination ⟨several good *hogg* colts⟩ 3 : a person felt to resemble a hog esp. in selfishness, gluttony, or filthiness — often used in combination 4 or hogg slang a Brit : SHILLING b : DIME 5 : a curling stone that fails to pass the hog score 6 : a machine with revolving cutters for reducing bulk material (as waste lumber or animal carcasses) to small bits — called also *hogger* 7 : a frame of timber or a heavy flat rough broom hauled along a ship's bottom under water to clean it 8 : an agitator for mixing and stirring pulp in papermaking 9 slang : a railroad locomotive — on the hog slang : having no funds : BROKE

²hog \"\ vb hogged; hogged; hogging; hogs vt 1 : to cut (a horse's mane) short : ROACH 2 : to clean the bottom of (a ship) with a hog 3 a : to cause to arch like the back of a hog b : to cause (as a ship or timber) to bow up in the middle and sag at the ends usu. as a result of improper loading or supporting 4 a Brit : to winter over (young sheep) b : to utilize (an unharvested crop) by turning in hogs to feed — often used with *down* or *off* ⟨got a drove of gilts to ~ down the corn⟩ ⟨it would be cheaper to ~ off that piece than to harvest it⟩ 5 a : to take, grasp, or retain selfishly or in excess of one's due or need ⟨don't ~ the light, I want to read too⟩ ⟨*hogging* everything in sight⟩ b : to consume voraciously — usu. used with *down* ⟨*hogged* down his dinner and rushed out⟩ ⟨finished the book next day, *hogging* it down in great gulps —Bruce Marshall⟩ 6 : to play (a curling stone) so as not to pass the hog score 7 : to tear up or shred (bulk material) into bits with a hog ~ vi 1 : to become curved upward in the middle like a hog's back — used esp. of a ship or its bottom or keel 2 : to act like a hog esp. in taking more than one's share

ho gage \'(')hō'gāj\ n, usu cap H&O [*half o gage*] : a scale of ⅛ inch to one foot used in model railroading for trains and track layout with a distance between rails of ⅝ inch

ho·gan \'hō,gän, -gàn, -gan\ n -s [Navaho *hogan*, fr. *ho-*, deictic prefix + *-gan* dwelling] : a conical, hexagonal, or octagonal dwelling characteristic of the Navaho Indian made with a door traditionally facing east and constructed of logs and sticks covered with mud, sods, or adobe or sometimes of stones — compare LODGE 8a

hog and hominy n : pork and Indian corn; *broadly* : meager or very plain and simple food

hogan–mogan obs var of HOGEN-MOGEN

ho·garth chair \'hō,gärth, -gàth-\ n, usu cap H [after William *Hogarth* †1764 Eng. painter] : any of certain 18th century English side chairs, usu. with hooped back and cabriole legs

ho·garth·ian \(')hō'gärthēən, -gàth-\ adj, usu cap [William *Hogarth* + E *-ian*] : relating to, characteristic of, or suggesting Hogarth or his work ⟨a thoroughly *Hogarthian* attitude⟩ ⟨*Hogarthian* cartoons of the human scene —*Dial*⟩

hogarth's line n, usu cap H [after William Hogarth, who considered it the essence of beauty] : an S-shaped line used for decorative and compositional purposes esp. in painting and engraving

hogback \'=,=\ n 1 : an arched back suggesting that of a hog ⟨most of the sunfishes have ~*s*⟩ 2 : something felt to resemble the back of a hog in outline or section: as a : a ridge of land formed by the outcropping edges of tilted strata; *broadly* : a ridge with a sharp summit and steeply sloping sides b : a sharp rise in the floor of a coal mine c : HOGFRAME

hog-backed \ˈ=ˌ=\ *or* **hogback** \ˈ=ˌ=\ *adj* **:** having an arched back or prominence ⟨a *hog-backed* island in the channel⟩
hog badger *n* **:** HOG-NOSED BADGER
hog banana *n* **:** a rather large coarse-textured red-skinned banana that is usu. eaten cooked
hog bean *n* **:** HENBANE 1
hogbite \ˈ=ˌ=\ *n* **:** GUM SUCCORY 1
hog brace *n* **:** HOGFRAME
hog brake *n* **:** BRACKEN 1b
hog cane *n* **:** SALT REED GRASS
hog chain *n* **:** a chain or a tie rod used in a ship to prevent hogging
hogchoker \ˈ=ˌ==\ *also* **hogchoke** \ˈ=ˌ=\ *n* **:** a small American sole (esp. *Achirus fasciatus*) of no market value
hog cholera *n* **:** a highly infectious often fatal virus disease of swine characterized by fever, loss of appetite, diarrhea, petechial hemorrhages esp. in the kidneys and lymph glands, and in chronic cases intestinal ulceration often complicated by secondary infection with the necrotic enteritis bacterium
hog clover *n* **:** BUR CLOVER
hog constable *n* **:** HOGREEVE
hog corn *n* **:** poor quality Indian corn
hog-corn ratio *n* **:** CORN-HOG RATIO
hog cranberry *n* **1 :** CROWBERRY 1a **2 :** BEARBERRY 1
hog deer *n* **:** a white-spotted deer (*Axis porcinus* syn. *Hyelaphus porcinus*) of India about two feet high at the withers
hog-dressed \ˈ=ˌ=\ *adj, of a meat animal* **:** bled and eviscerated but having the skin left on the carcass
[1]**hogen-mogen** \ˌhōgənˈmōgən\ *n* -s *usu cap H&M* [prob. alter. of D *hoogmogend* all-powerful] **1** *obs* **:** a person of consequence or one who affects authority **2** *archaic* **:** HOLLANDER; *collectively* **:** the people of Holland — often used disparagingly
[2]**hogen-mogen** \ˈ"\ *adj, usu cap H&M* **1** *obs* **a :** HIGH-AND-MIGHTY **b** *of liquor* **:** STRONG **2** *archaic* **:** DUTCH
hog feeder *n* **:** an operator who feeds bulk material into and supervises a shredding or mincing hog — called also *hogger*
hog fennel *n* **:** a plant of *Oxypolis* or the closely related genus *Lomatium*
hogfish \ˈ=ˌ=\ *n* see PLURAL *note* **1 :** any of various fishes felt to resemble a hog: as **a :** a large West Indian and Florida wrasse (*Lachnolaimus maximus*) often used for food **b :** a pigfish (*Orthopristis chrysopterus*) **c :** LOG PERCH **d :** a large red spiny-headed European marine scorpion fish (*Scorpaena scorfa*) **2** *obs* **a :** PORPOISE **b :** MANATEE
hog flu *n* **:** SWINE INFLUENZA
hogframe \ˈ=ˌ=\ *n* **:** a trussed frame extending fore and aft esp. in American river and lake steamers, being usu. above deck, and reaching to the ends to increase longitudinal strength and stiffness and prevent hogging — called also *hogback, hogging frame*
hog fuel *n* **:** ground up or powdered wood used for fuel
hogg *var of* HOG
hog·gas·ter \ˈhȯgəstə(r), ˈhäg-\ *n* -s [ME *hogaster*, fr. *hogge* hog + L *-aster* (dim. suffix) — more at HOG] **1** *archaic* **:** a boar in its third year **2** *archaic* **:** HOG 2a
hogged \ˈhȯgd, -ä-\ *adj* **1 :** raised in the center or falling away at the ends or sides **:** HOG-BACKED — used esp. of a ship or of a road that is sharply convex in section **2** *of a horse's mane* **:** cut short **:** ROACHED
hoggee *var of* HOGGY
[1]**hog·ger** \ˈhägər, ˈhȯg-\ *n* -s [origin unknown] **1** *chiefly Scot* **:** a stocking made without a foot and worn as a gaiter **2** *chiefly Scot* **:** an old stocking used for keeping money
[2]**hog·ger** \ˈhȯgə(r), ˈhäg-\ *n* -s [partly fr. [1]*hog* + *-er*; partly fr. [2]*hog* + *-er*] **1 a :** a machine tool that takes heavy cuts at high speed **b :** HOG 6 **2 a** *slang* **:** a locomotive engineer — called also *hoghead* **b :** HOG FEEDER
hog·ger·el \ˈhäg(ə)rəl\ *n* -s [ME (Sc dial), dim. of *hogge* hog, sheep — more at HOG] *Brit* **:** a young sheep; *usu* **:** HOG 2a
hog·gery \ˈhȯg(ə)rē, ˈhäg-, -ri\ *n* -ES **1 :** a place where hogs are kept **:** PIGGERY, HOG HOUSE **2 :** hoggish character or manners **:** gross animality **:** GREED
hog·get \ˈhägət\ *n* -s [ME, fr. [1]*hog* + *-et*] *chiefly Brit* **:** HOG 2a
hog·gin *also* **hog·ging** \ˈhȯgən, ˈhäg-, -giŋ\ *n* -s [origin unknown] **:** a material composed of screenings or siftings of gravel or of a mixture of loam, coarse sand, and fine gravel
hogging *pres part of* HOG
hogging frame *or* **hogging girder** *n* **:** HOGFRAME
hogging line *n* **:** a line or chain used to draw a collision mat into position over a damaged area of a ship's hull
hog·gish \ˈhȯgish, ˈhäg-, -gēsh\ *adj* **:** like a hog esp. in gluttony or selfishness — compare PIGGISH, SWINISH — **hog·gish·ly** *adv* — **hog·gish·ness** *n* -ES
hoggs *pl of* HOGG
hog gum *n* **1 a :** a gum resin obtained from a West Indian tree (*Moronobea coccinea*) of the family Guttiferae **b :** a similar product obtained from other trees (as *Rhus metopium*) **c :** TRAGACANTH; *also* **:** a similar gum (as bassora or kutira) **2 :** any of various tropical trees chiefly of the families Anacardiaceae and Guttiferae that produce hog gum or are associated or confused with trees producing hog gum
hog·gy *or* **hog·gee** \ˈhȯgē, ˈhäg-\ *n, pl* **hoggies** *or* **hoggees** [prob. fr. [1]*hog* + *-y* or *-ee* (alter. of *-y*)] **:** a towpath driver for the early 19th century barge transportation system in parts of the eastern U.S.
hog·head \ˈhȯgˌhed, ˈhäg-\ *n, slang* **:** HOGGER 2a
hogherd \ˈ=ˌ=\ *n* [ME] **:** SWINEHERD
hog hook *n* **:** a hook with a transverse handle for handling a hog carcass while scalding it
hog house *n* **:** a building in which hogs are housed **:** PIGPEN, STY; *esp* **:** a building with facilities for housing a number of hogs under one roof
hog in *vi, of a cutting tool* **:** to dig in and take a bigger cut than intended with a possible stalling of the machine or breaking of the tool
hog in armor : one self-conscious or ill at ease in fine clothes
hog-killing \ˈ=ˌ==\ *or* **hog-killing time** *n, dial* **:** a jolly or riotous party
hog latin *n, usu cap L* **:** PIG LATIN
hogleg \ˈ=ˌ=\ *n, chiefly West* **:** a large single-action revolver of the type carried in the West by cowboys and frontiersmen
hoglike \ˈ=ˌ=\ *adj* **:** like or like that of a hog ⟨a heavy ∼ face⟩
hog lily *n* **:** SPATTERDOCK
hog line *n* **:** HOG SCORE
hog·ling \ˈhȯgliŋ, ˈhäg-\ *n* -s [ME, fr. *hog* + *-ling*] **1** *obs* **:** PIGLET **2** *dial Brit* **:** LAMB
hog lot *n* **:** an enclosure usu. with housing in which hogs are reared or fattened for market
hog louse *n* **:** a large sucking louse (*Haematopinus suis*) that is parasitic on the hog and in some areas is associated with the transmission of swine pox
hog·man \ˈ=mən\ *n, pl* **hogmen 1 :** a raiser of or attendant on hogs **:** a hog farmer **:** SWINEHERD **2 :** HOG FEEDER
hog·ma·nay *also* **hag·me·na** \ˌhägməˈnā\ *n* -s *sometimes cap* [origin unknown] **1** *Scot* **:** NEW YEAR'S EVE **2 :** a traditional Scottish celebration at New Year's Eve: **a :** the going about of children from house to house singing and asking for gifts usu. of cakes or nuts **b :** the going about from house to house with the intention of being the first visitor **3 :** a cake, gift, or treat given at New Year's Eve
hog-maned \ˈ=ˌmānd\ *adj* **:** having a short bristly mane **:** ROACHED
hog millet *n* **:** MILLET 1a
hog mol·ly \-ˌmälē\ *n* **1** *or* **hog mullet :** HOG SUCKER **2 :** LOG PERCH
hog money *n* **:** early 17th century copper coins of Bermuda bearing the image of a hog and valued from twopence to a shilling
hog-mouthed fry \ˈ=ˌ=\ *n* **:** a small fish (*Anchoviella choerostomus*) that resembles an anchovy and is common at Bermuda
hognose \ˈ=ˌ=\ *adj* **:** having a rounded cutting edge — used of a cutting or boring tool
hog-nosed badger \ˈ=ˌ=\ *n* **:** a large short-legged Asiatic badger (*Arctonyx collaris*) with white fur tipped with black and white markings on face, neck, tail, and ears — called also *sand badger*
hog-nosed skunk *n* **:** a large stocky white-backed skunk (*Conepatus mesoleucus*) of southwestern No. America with a short white tail and a naked muzzle; *also* **:** any of several closely related So. American skunks — called also *white-backed skunk*
hog-nosed viper *n* **:** any of several small tropical American pit vipers (genus *Bothrops*) related to the fer-de-lance but with short fangs and venom of low toxicity
hognose snake *or* **hog-nosed snake** *n* **:** any of certain moderate-sized stout-bodied No. American snakes that constitute the genus *Heterodon*, are perfectly harmless though often reputed deadly prob. because of the threatening way in which they dilate the neck, flatten the head, and hiss and blow when startled, and are noted for the habit of rolling over on the back and playing dead when their threatening display is ineffective — called also *blowing adder, flatheaded adder, puffing adder, sand viper, spreading adder*
hognut \ˈ=ˌ=\ *n* **1 :** EARTHNUT 1a **2 :** PIGNUT 2 **3 :** JAMAICA COBNUT
ho·go \ˈhō(ˌ)gō\ *n* -s [modif. of F *haut goût* high savor or flavor] *now dial Eng* **:** a notably strong flavor or smell
hog oiler *n* **:** a device that automatically applies oil or insecticide to the skin of a hog that rubs against it
hog out *vt* **1 :** to cut (metal) out of a piece of work at very high speeds and very fast feeds **2 :** to machine (as a part) from a billet of size and shape such that the removal of much metal is necessary in order to achieve the shape desired
hog peanut *n* **:** a plant of the genus *Amphicarpa* that is usu. considered to constitute a single variable species (*A. bracteata*), is widely distributed in eastern and central No. America, and produces abundant subterranean fruits, each containing a single edible seed which resembles a peanut, is much relished by hogs, and was formerly important in Amerindian dietary — called also *wild peanut*
hogpen \ˈ=ˌ=\ *n* **:** PIGPEN 1
hog perch *n* **:** LOG PERCH
hog plum *n* **1 :** a tree of the genus *Spondias; esp* **:** a tropical American tree (*S. mombin*) sometimes cultivated for its edible yellow fruits which resemble plums **2 :** POISON-WOOD 1 **3 :** the Chickasaw plum or other wild plum of the southern U.S. **4 :** FALSE SANDALWOOD 1
hog potato *n* **1 :** a small or inferior potato often boiled for hog feed **2 a :** MAN-OF-THE-EARTH **b :** DEATH CAMAS
hog pox *n* **:** SWINE POX 2
hogreeve \ˈ=ˌ=\ *n* -s **:** a former New England town officer responsible for the impounding of stray hogs
hog ring *n* **1 :** a split metal ring usu. with beveled points that can be pushed through the median cartilage of the nose of a pig and there locked to prevent rooting or to serve as a means of leading the animal **2 :** an upholstery fastener resembling a hog ring — **hog-ringer** \ˈ=ˌ==\ *n*

hog rings 1

hog-round \ˈ=ˌ=\ *adv (or adj)* **:** at a flat rate **:** without grading ⟨sometimes it is wiser to sell *hog-round*⟩ ⟨a common custom on southern cotton markets for buyers to take everything *hog-round* on a middling basis —Clarence Poe⟩
hogs *pl of* HOG, *pres 3d sing of* HOG
hog's-back \ˈ=ˌ=\ *n* **:** HOGBACK
hog's-bean \ˈ=ˌ=\ *n, pl* **hog's-beans 1 :** HENBANE **2 :** SEA STARWORT
hog score *n* **:** a line that is marked across a curling rink 7 yards in front of each tee and that a stone must pass or be removed from the ice — called also *hog line;* see CURLING illustration
hog scraper *n* **:** a circular concave metal disk with a sharp rim suitable for scraping the bristles from a hog carcass and a handle often in the form of a candle holder in the center of its convex surface; *also* **:** a candlestick with a hog-scraper base
hog's fennel *n* **1 :** a European sulphurweed (*Peucedanum officinale* or a closely related species) **2 :** MAYWEED 1
hog's-haw \ˈ=ˌ=\ *n, pl* **hog's-haws :** a hawthorn (*Crataegus brachyacantha*) of the southern U.S.
hogs·head \ˈhȯgzˌhed, ˈhäg-, *sometimes* -zəd *dial* -zət\ *n* [ME *hoggeshed*, fr. *hogges* (gen. of *hogge* hog) + *hed* head — more at HOG, HEAD] **1 :** a large cask or barrel; *esp* **:** one containing from 63 to 140 gallons — abbr. *hhd* **2 :** any of various units of capacity equal to the amount a hogshead will hold: as **a :** a U.S. unit equal to 63 gallons **b :** a British unit equal to 54 imperial gallons or 64.85 U.S. gallons **3 :** something (as an unpleasing person) felt to resemble the head of a hog
hog's head cheese \ˈhȯgzˌhed-, ˈhäl, =ˈ=-\ *n, dial* **:** HEADCHEESE
hog sheer *n* **:** the deck curve of a ship in which the middle portion of the deck is higher than the ends
hog·skin \ˈ=ˌ=\ *n* **1 :** PIGSKIN 1 **2 :** an article (as a saddle or a pair of gloves) made of pigskin
hog's-meat \ˈ=ˌ=\ *n, pl* **hog's-meats 1 :** a small chiefly tropical American herb (*Boerhavia coccinea*) with sticky foliage and reddish flowers **2 :** a tropical American ornamental vine (*Aristolochia grandiflora*) with poisonous roots
hog snake *n* **:** HOGNOSE SNAKE
hog's-potato \ˈ=ˌ=(ˌ)=\ *n, pl* **hog's-potatoes :** HOG POTATO 2
hogs·teer \ˈhȯgzˌti(ə)r, ˈhäg-, -gˌst-\ *n* [alter. of *hoggaster*] **:** a wild boar in his third year
hog sucker *n* **:** a No. American fish (*Hypentelium nigricans*) of the family Catostomidae that is brassy olive marked with brown, is widely distributed in warm clear shallow streams, and in some areas is used as food — called also *hog molly*
hog-tie \ˈ=ˌ=\ *vt* **1 :** to make (a thrown animal) helpless by tying the hind legs together and then to one or both front legs with a short line ⟨*hog-tying* calves for branding⟩ **2 :** to make (as a person) helpless ⟨financial institutions . . . damned for *hog-tying* the region's economy —*Frontier*⟩ ⟨a police force *hog-tied* by graft and corruption⟩ **syn** see HAMPER
hog wallow *n* **1 a :** a depression in land made by the wallowing of swine **b :** a similar depression said to be due to heavy rains **2 :** a land surface characterized by numerous low rounded mounds — usu. used in pl.
hogwash \ˈ=ˌ=\ *n* [ME *hoggyswasch*, fr. *hoggys* (gen. of *hogge* hog) + *wasch* wash — more at HOG, WASH] **1 a :** SWILL 1a, SLOP 4a(1) **b :** poor or flavorless food or drink **2 :** something (as writing or propaganda) that is insipid, worthless, or lacking in real substance ⟨the ∼ of political oratory⟩
hogweed \ˈ=ˌ=\ *n* **:** any of various weeds or coarse plants: as **a :** RAGWEED 2 **b :** KNOTWEED **c :** DOG FENNEL **d :** HORSEWEED **e** *Brit* (1) **:** COW PARSNIP (2) **:** HEDGE PARSLEY
hog-wild \ˈ=ˌ=\ *adj* **:** free from restraint and often disorderly or foolish ⟨*hog-wild* enthusiasm⟩ **:** overenthusiastic and often extravagant or intemperate ⟨legislatures gone *hog-wild* on spending⟩
hog wire *n* **1 :** barbed wire having 4-pointed barbs and weighing about 400 pounds per mile **2 :** heavy woven fencing with the meshes smaller at the bottom and usu. with the bottom-most wire barbed

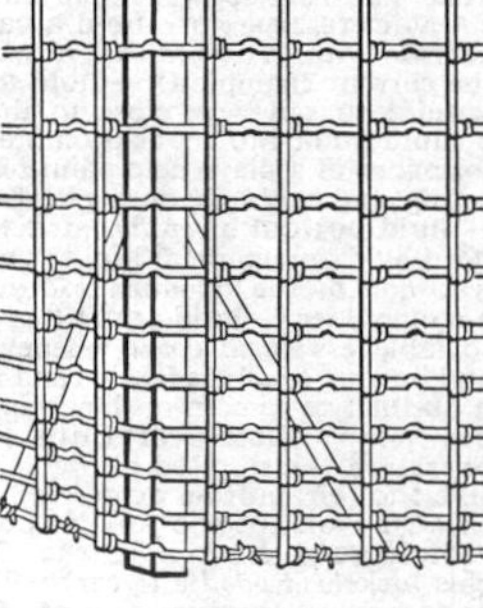

hog wire 2

hogwort \ˈ=ˌ=\ *n* **:** an annual silvery green weed (*Croton capitatus*) of the southeastern U.S. — called also *woolly croton*
hog-wrestle \ˈ=ˌ==\ *n, slang* **:** an informal dance (as a country dance) sometimes marked by coarse vulgar conduct
hoh \ˈhō\ *n, pl* **hoh** *or* **hohs** *usu cap* **1 :** an Indian people of the Olympic Peninsula, Washington, speaking the Quileute language **2 :** a member of the Hoh people
ho·he \ˈhō(ˌ)hā\ *n, pl* **hohe** *or* **hohes** *usu cap* **:** ASSINIBOIN
[1]**ho·hen·stau·fen** \ˈhōən,s(h)taùfən, ˌ=ˈ==\ *adj, usu cap* **:** of or relating to a German princely family of Swabian origin that furnished sovereigns of the Holy Roman Empire from 1138–1254 and of Sicily from 1194–1266
[2]**hohenstaufen** \ˈ"\ *n* -s *usu cap* **:** a member of the Hohenstaufen family; *esp* **:** a Hohenstaufen sovereign
[1]**ho·hen·zol·lern** \ˈhōən,z|älə(r)n, -ōən(t)s|, |ōl-, ˌ=ˈ==\ *adj, usu cap* **:** of or relating to a German princely family founded about the 11th century that furnished kings of Prussia from 1701–1918 and German emperors from 1871–1918
[2]**hohenzollern** \ˈ"\ *n* -s *usu cap* **:** a member of the Hohenzollern family; *esp* **:** a Hohenzollern sovereign
ho·hen·zol·lern·ism \-ə(r)ˌnizəm\ *n* -s *usu cap* **:** Prussianism as developed under and exemplified by the Hohenzollern rulers of Germany
hohl·flö·te \ˈhōlˌflād·ə, -lǣd·ə, *G* -lœtə\ *or* **hohl·flute** \-flüt, *usu* -üd·+V\ *n* -s [*hohlflöte* fr. G, fr. *hohl* hollow (fr. OHG *hol*) + *flöte* flute; *hohlflute* part trans. of G *hohlflöte* — more at HOLE, DOPPELFLÖTE] **:** a pipe-organ flute stop usu. in 8-foot pitch with a dull hollow quality
hoh·mann·ite \ˈhōməˌnīt\ *n* -s *usu cap* [G *hohmannit*, fr. Thomas *Hohmann*, its discoverer + G *-it* -ite] **:** a mineral $Fe_2(SO_4)_2(OH)_2 \cdot 7H_2O$ consisting of a hydrated basic ferric sulfate
ho·ho·kam \ˈhōhōˌkäm, hōˈhōkəm\ *adj, usu cap* [Pima *húhukam* ancient one] **:** of or belonging to a prehistoric desert culture of southwestern U.S. centering in the Gila valley of Arizona and contemporaneous with the Anasazi culture to the north and characterized by irrigated agriculture, large pit houses, good pottery, decorative bone and shell ornaments, and use of cremation
ho-hum \ˈhōˈhəm\ *adj* [imit.] **:** dull and routine **:** UNINTERESTED, UNINTERESTING ⟨held one *ho-hum* job after another⟩ ⟨looked on in *ho-hum* unconcern —*Springfield (Mass.) Union*⟩ — often used interjectionally
hoi *var of* HOY
[1]**hoick** \ˈhȯik\ *vt* -ED/-ING/-S [prob. alter. of [1]*hike*] **1** *chiefly dial* **:** to yank or pull with a jerk ⟨before you could have counted ten, I was ∼*ed* out of my job —Vincent Sheean⟩ **2 :** to cause (an airplane) to climb steeply
[2]**hoick** \ˈ"\ *n* -s **:** a rough or jerky movement in rowing
[3]**hoick** \ˈ"\ *vi* -ED/-ING/-S [imit.] **:** to clear the throat **:** HAWK
hoicks \ˈhȯiks\ *also* **hoick** \-k\ *interj* [origin unknown] — used chiefly to urge on hounds
hoigh *n* -s [prob. alter. of *hoy*] *obs* **:** a state of excitement
hoi pol·loi \ˌhȯipəˈlȯi, *chiefly Brit* hȯiˈpälˌȯi\ *n pl* [Gk *hoi polloi* the many] **1 :** ordinary people **:** the general populace **:** MULTITUDE, MASSES ⟨strain so hard in making their questions comprehensible to *hoi polloi* —S.L.Payne⟩ ⟨burlesque performance . . . for the *hoi polloi* —Henry Miller⟩ **2 :** people of distinction or wealth or elevated social status **:** ELITE
hoise \ˈhȯiz\ *vt* **hoised** \-zd\ *or* **hoist** \-ȯist\ **hoised** *or* **hoist; hoising; hoises** [alter. of earlier *heise*, prob. fr. MD *hischen* or (assumed) MLG *hissen* (whence LG *hissen*), of imit. origin] **1** *dial* **:** to raise upward or into the air by means of a tackle **:** HOIST ⟨∼ the mainsail⟩ **2** *dial* **:** to lift and carry off — **hoist with one's own petard** *or* **hoist by one's own petard :** blown up by one's own bomb; *usu* **:** victimized or hurt by one's own scheme
[1]**hoist** \ˈhȯist, *chiefly dial* ˈhīst\ *vb* -ED/-ING/-S [alter. of *hoise*] *vt* **:** RAISE, LIFT, ELEVATE: as **a :** to raise into position by means of tackle ⟨∼ all sails⟩ ⟨∼*ed* the mate's boat aboard⟩ **b :** to raise (a flag or a hoist of flags) often as a formal indication of possession or sovereignty **c :** to move from one place to another by or as if by lifting ⟨groaned as they ∼*ed* him into the ambulance⟩ ⟨∼*ing* himself out of bed⟩ **d** *slang* **:** to pick up and drink ⟨decided to ∼ a few with the boys⟩ **e :** to cause to be or become higher or greater ⟨the war ∼*ed* prices⟩ **f** *slang* **:** STEAL ∼ *vi* **1 :** to become hoisted **:** RISE ⟨the load ∼*s* well with the new tackle⟩ ⟨let it ∼ right up to the upper block⟩ **2 :** to pull on a rope in hoisting something ⟨∼ until it's near the top⟩ — often used with *away* **syn** see LIFT
[2]**hoist** \ˈ"\ *n* -s **1 :** an act of hoisting **:** LIFT, BOOST ⟨gave him a ∼ over the wall⟩ **2 :** an apparatus (as a mechanical tackle or hydraulic lift) by which things are hoisted: as **a** *chiefly Brit* **:** a freight or other service elevator **b :** CHAIN HOIST **3 a :** the extent to which something can be hoisted or its mass or dimension when hoisted ⟨a sail with a 30-foot ∼⟩ ⟨a ∼ of several tons⟩ **b** (1) **:** the perpendicular edge or height of a flag when viewed flying or as if flying from a staff — compare [2]FLY 6c (2) **:** the part of the field of a flag that adjoins the staff **c :** the height or depth of a square sail except a course **:** the length of a fore-and-aft sail or staysail as measured along the luff **4 a :** a string of flags hoisted or to be hoisted as a signal usu. from one ship to another **b :** a message or information conveyed by such a hoist
hoist·er \-tə(r)\ *n* -s **:** one that hoists; *esp* **:** a mechanical apparatus for hoisting or one who operates it
hoisting pad *n* [*hoisting* fr. gerund of [1]*hoist*] **:** metal fittings on a boat for attaching hoisting equipment
hoisting tower *n* **:** a temporary elevator shaft of scaffolding used to hoist materials on building-construction work
hoist·man \-tmən\ *n, pl* **hoistmen** [[2]*hoist* + *man*] **:** the operator of a hoist **:** ENGINEMAN
hoistway \ˈ=ˌ=\ *n* **:** a passage (as an elevator shaft) through or along which a thing may be hoisted
hoit \ˈhȯit\ *n* -s [E dial. *hoit*, v., to romp, play the fool] *dial Brit* **:** a lazy stupid person
[1]**hoi·ty-toi·ty** \ˌhȯid·ēˈtȯid·ē, ˌhīd·ēˈtīd·ē\ *n* -ES [redupl. of *hoity*, fr. E dial. *hoit*, v.] **1 a** *obs* **:** thoughtless or frivolous or giddy behavior **b :** affectation of superiority **:** patronizing pomposity **2 :** a hoity-toity person
[2]**hoity-toity** \ˈ"\ *adj* **1 :** THOUGHTLESS, FRIVOLOUS, GIDDY, FLIGHTY ⟨very *hoity-toity* of me not to know that royal personage —W.S.Maugham⟩ **2 :** affecting superiority **:** haughty and patronizing **:** POMPOUS ⟨*hoity-toity* airs and graces⟩ ⟨an inflated *hoity-toity* manner⟩
ho-ja \ˈō(ˌ)hä\ *n* -s [Sp, leaf, fr. L *folia*, pl. of *folium* leaf — more at BLADE] *Southwest* **:** a piece of corn husk formerly used for rolling cigarettes
hok \ˈhäk\ *n* -s [Afrik *hak*, fr. D *hok* hutch, hovel, fr. MD *hocke* corn, grain — more at HOCK] *Africa* **:** a small enclosure (as for storage) **:** PEN
ho·kal·tec·an \ˌhōˌkalˈtekən, ˌhōkəl-\ *n, pl* **hokaltecan** *or* **hokaltecans** *usu cap* [by alter.] **:** HOKAN-COAHUILTECAN
ho·kan \ˈhōkən\ *also* **ho·ka** \-kə\ *n, pl* **hokan** *or* **hokans** *also* **hoka** *or* **hokas** *usu cap* [coined 1913 by Roland B. Dixon †1934 and Alfred L. Kroeber †1960 Am. anthropologists] **1 :** a language stock centering in California comprising the Chimarikan, Esselenian, Kulanapan, Quoratean, Shastan, Yuman, and Yanan families **2 :** a language phylum generally considered as comprising the Hokan stock plus Chumashan, Jicaquean, Salinan, Serian, Supanecan, Tequistlatecan, and Washoan
hokan-coahuiltecan \ˌhōkən+\ *n, usu cap H&C* **:** the Hokan language phylum enlarged by the inclusion of Coahuiltecan and sometimes Karankawa and Tonkawan — called also *Hokaltecan*
hokan-siouan \ˈ"+\ *n, usu cap H&S* **:** a language phylum comprising the Hokan, Supanecan, and Coahuiltecan language stocks
[1]**hoke** \ˈhōk\ *n* -s [by shortening] **:** HOKUM
[2]**hoke** \ˈ"\ *vt* -ED/-ING/-S *slang* **:** to give a false quality or value to **:** FAKE — usu. used with *up* ⟨tired of these *hoked-up* excuses⟩
hokeday *usu cap, var of* HOCKDAY
[1]**ho·key** \ˈhōkē\ *interj* [origin unknown] — used as a mild oath
[2]**hok·ey** \ˈ"\ *adj* [irreg. fr. *hokum* + *-y*] *slang* **:** marked by hokum **:** being characterized by or the product of hoking **:** hoked up ⟨a ∼ version of an old favorite⟩
hokey-pokey \ˌhōkēˈpōkē\ *n* -s [prob. alter. of *hocus-pocus*] **1** *slang* **:** HOKUM, BUNKUM, MONKEY BUSINESS **2 :** ice cream packaged in small portions (as between sweet wafers or in a paper cup) and sold by street vendors or peddlers
hokh·mah *or* **hok·mah** *or* **chok·mah** \ˈkōk(ˌ)mä, =ˈ=\ *n* -s *usu cap, often attrib* [Heb *hokhmāh* wisdom] **:** WISDOM 4
hok·ku \ˈhō(ˌ)kü, ˈhä(-\ *n, pl* **hokku** [Jap, fr. *hok* beginning, first + *ku* hemistich] **1 :** a fixed lyric form of Japanese origin having three short unrhymed lines of five, seven, and five syllables and being typically epigrammatic or suggestive — compare HAIKU **2 :** a lyric in hokku form

hok-lo \'hō(,)klō, 'hä(-\ *n, pl* **hok-lo** *or* **hok-los** *usu cap* [Chin (Cant), man from Fukien, fr. *hok* Fukien + *lo* man, person] **:** a member of a people with a distinctive dialect that inhabit sectors of northeastern Kwangtung including Swatow and parts of adjacent southern Fukien including Amoy and that have migrated in large numbers to Formosa and various countries of southeast Asia

ho·kum \'hōkəm\ *n* -s [prob. blend of ¹*hocus-pocus* and *bunkum*] **1 :** a device found to elicit a display of mirth or sentimental emotion from an audience and therefore deliberately used to impel persons to a desired action **2 :** something worthless or untrue **:** BUNKUM

hokus-pokus *var of* HOCUS-POCUS

hol \'häl\ *n* -s [by shortening] *Brit* **:** HOLIDAY

hol- *or* **holo-** *comb form* [ME *holo-*, fr. OF, fr. L *hol-, holo-*, fr. Gk, fr. *holos* — more at SAFE] **1 a :** complete **:** entire **:** total ⟨*holo*graph⟩ ⟨*holo*parasite⟩ **b :** completely **:** totally **:** throughout ⟨*hol*arthritic⟩ ⟨*holo*branchiate⟩ ⟨*holo*axial⟩ ⟨*holo*crystalline⟩ **c :** without division **:** forming one piece ⟨*holo*gnathous⟩ ⟨*hol*orhinal⟩ **2 a :** similar **:** homogeneous ⟨*holo*morph⟩ **b :** similarly **:** homogeneously ⟨*holo*gamous⟩ **3** *usu holo-* **:** containing the highest possible number of hydroxyl groups — in names of inorganic acids ⟨*holo*phosphoric acid $P(OH)_5$ or H_5PO_5⟩ ⟨*holo*quinonoid⟩

hol *abbr* hollow

ho·la \'ō(,)lä\ *interj* [Sp] — used esp. among Latin Americans to attract attention or to shout encouragement or exultation

hol·andric \(')häl, (')hōl+\ *adj* [ISV *hol-* + *andric*] **1 a :** inherited solely in the male line **b :** transmitted by a gene or genes in the nonhomologous portion of the Y chromosome **2 :** having the full number of testes characteristic of a group — compare METANDRIC

hol·an·dry \'hä,landrē, 'hō,-\ *n* -ES **:** the quality or state of being holandric

hol·arctic \(')häl, (')hōl+\ *adj* [*hol-* + *arctic*] **1 :** of or relating to the arctic regions **2** *usu cap* **:** of, relating to, or being the biogeographic realm or region that includes the northern parts of the Old and the New World and comprises the Palaearctic and Nearctic regions or subregions

holard \'hä,lärd, 'hō,-\ *n* -s [*hol-* + Gk *ardein* to water] **:** the entire water content of the soil — compare CHRESARD, ECHARD

hol·as·pid·e·an \,hä,la;spidēən, ;hō,-\ *adj* [*hol-* + *aspid-* + *-ean*] **:** having a single series of large scutes on the posterior side of the tarsus (as in the true larks)

hol·bein stitch \'hō|l,bīn *sometimes* 'hä|\ *n, usu cap H* [after Hans Holbein †1543 Ger. artist; fr. the kind of embroidery seen in his paintings] **:** a running stitch worked twice often in different colors on the same line to make a continuous reversible pattern

Holbein stitch

hol·boell's grebe \'hōl,bůlz-\ *n, usu cap H* [after Carl P. *Holboell* †1856 Dan. civil servant] **:** RED-NECKED GREBE

hol·co·dont \'hälkə,dänt\ *adj* [ISV *holc-* (fr. Gk *holkos* furrow) + *-odont*] **:** having the teeth set in a long continuous groove

hol·co·no·ti \,hälkə'nōd·,ī, -d·(,)ē\ *n pl, cap* [NL, fr. *holco-* (fr. Gk *holkos* furrow) + *-noti* (fr. Gk *nōton* back) — more at NATES] **:** the Embiotocidae regarded as an independent order of fishes

hol·cus \'hälkəs\ *n, cap* [NL, fr. L, wall barley (*Hordeum murinum*), fr. Gk *holkos* wall barley, furrow — more at SULCUS] **:** a genus of Old World grasses widely naturalized in America with velvety pubescence and deciduous spikelets — see VELVET GRASS

¹**hold** \'hōld *dial sometimes* -lt\ *vb* **held** \'held\ *or dial past* **hilt** \'hilt\ **held** *or archaic* **hold·en** \'hōldən\ **holding; holds** \'hōl(d)z\ [ME *holden*, fr. OE *healdan, haldan*; akin to OHG *haltan* to hold, ON *halda*, Goth *haldan* to tend cattle, L *celer* rapid, Gk *kellein* to run a ship to land, Skt *kālayati* he drives, holds, carries] *vt* **1 a :** to retain in one's keeping **:** maintain possession of **:** not give up or relinquish **:** POSSESS, HAVE ⟨*held* property worth millions⟩ ⟨~ several slaves as household servants⟩ ⟨~*s* the title to the property⟩ ⟨~*s* the power to hire or fire at will⟩ **b :** to retain or occupy by force **:** defend and not retreat from ⟨the soldiers *held* the bridge against all attacks⟩ **c :** to keep control of or authority or jurisdiction over ⟨wished to ~ the territory because of the fur trade⟩ **d :** to have power over **:** affect strongly and unremittingly ⟨a pleasurable excitement *held* him —D.G.Gerahty⟩ ⟨invalidism *held* him for eight years —J.C.Archer⟩ **e :** to have possession of the privileges, benefits, or perquisites of ⟨~*s* the eastern seaboard under an authorization granted by the manufacturer of the goods⟩ **f :** to use or keep as a threat or as a means of gaining advantage **2 :** to impose restraint upon or limit in motion or action ⟨the bushing *held* the drive shaft so that it had no play whatsoever⟩: as **a :** to refrain from producing (as speech or noise) ⟨~ your talk, man⟩ **b** (1) **:** to keep back **:** not loose **:** not let go ⟨~ the dogs so the strangers can pass⟩ (2) **:** STAY, ARREST ⟨~ him with a glance⟩ ⟨a strange compunction *held* his hand as he raised it to strike⟩ ⟨tried to ~ him from an action he would always regret⟩ (3) **:** DELAY ⟨*held* the curtain for an hour until the arrival of the royal carriage at the theater⟩ (4) **:** to stop the action of usu. temporarily ⟨time must be allowed . . . for ~*ing* the press while waiting for the sheet to dry —F.W.Hoch⟩ **c** (1) **:** to keep from advancing or succeeding in attack ⟨were able to ~ the enemy⟩ (2) **:** to keep (as an opposing team) from gaining an advantage ⟨the weaker team *held* the stronger during the first half⟩ **d :** to restrict or limit (as in amount of variation, advance, gain, loss) by acting to control or oppose ⟨*held* the sound to one level of loudness⟩ ⟨*held* the army to only a few miles' gain⟩ ⟨*held* the opposing team to only two runs⟩ **e :** to bind legally or morally **:** CONSTRAIN ⟨~ a man to his word⟩ — often used with an adjective complement ⟨~ a man responsible for his actions⟩ ⟨~ the men accountable for all money spent⟩ **f** *Scot* **:** to oppress by affliction **:** keep down **:** hold down **g :** DETAIN ⟨*held* him in conversation for ten minutes before letting him go⟩ **h :** RESTRICT, LIMIT ⟨bouts have been *held* to three 1½-minute rounds —Barrett McGurn⟩ **i :** to tense muscles in order to brace (oneself) ⟨had to ~ himself against the swaying and bumping of the coach⟩ **j :** to keep (a herd of cattle) together in a unit ⟨out ~*ing* the herd while the rest were eating⟩ **3** *obs* **:** to abide by (as a promise) or keep inviolate (as a faith) **4 a :** to have or keep in the grasp ⟨~ a child's hand⟩ ⟨~ a pocketbook tightly⟩ ⟨this volume is a joy to ~ as well as to read —J.M.Chase⟩ **b** (1) **:** to keep as if in a grasp **:** cause to be or remain in a particular situation, position, or relation, within certain limits, or of a particular quality ⟨~ a person in suspense⟩ ⟨~ an emotion under rigid control⟩ ⟨~ a ladder steady⟩ ⟨~ a child in check⟩ ⟨~ himself in readiness⟩ ⟨the stern demands of necessity *held* men in their grip —V.L.Parrington⟩ ⟨the searchlight . . . caught and *held* them in its glare —Nevil Shute⟩ (2) **:** to place and usu. not allow to move ⟨~ a pad of gauze to a wound⟩ ⟨~ your hand against my cheek⟩ **:** FIX ⟨*held* his eyes steadily on the picture⟩ **c** (1) **:** SUPPORT, SUSTAIN ⟨the building was *held* by concrete underpinning⟩ ⟨roof will ~ a deadweight of 94 inches of snow —*Monsanto Mag.*⟩ ⟨~*s* his seventy-two years easily⟩ (2) **:** to keep (as a bank of dirt) from eroding, collapsing, or washing away ⟨pines and other hardy trees were planted to ~ the sand —George Farwell⟩ **d** (1) **:** RETAIN ⟨struggling to ~, or to capture, the allegiance of the British people —F.A.Ogg & Harold Zink⟩ ⟨the parents still ~ the children's affection⟩ ⟨the suit ~*s* its press well⟩ ⟨a plastic that will ~ any shape you press it into⟩ **:** to retain by not vomiting ⟨unable to take a bite of food or ~ it on his stomach when it was forced upon him —F.B.Gipson⟩ **:** retain by not discharging ⟨the metal *held* the electrical charge for a long time⟩ (2) **:** to keep in custody **:** keep as a prisoner ⟨the cops agreed that the death was accidental, and did not ~ him —*Time*⟩ **e** (1) **:** to have in one's keeping **:** STORE ⟨another consideration was the cost of storing type — we certainly could not afford to ~ it forever —B.L.Stratton⟩ **:** keep on file or record ⟨the title is *held* at the registry of deeds⟩ (2) **:** RESERVE ⟨called the hotel and asked them to ~ a room for him⟩ ⟨*held* a few seats in case some visiting celebrities turned up⟩ **f :** BEAR, CARRY, COMPORT ⟨something unbending and strong, peasantlike, in the way he ~*s* himself —Madaleine Chapsal⟩ **g** (1) **:** to maintain in being or action **:** keep up without interruption, diminution, or flagging **:** SUSTAIN, PRESERVE ⟨~ one's course due north⟩ ⟨~ silence⟩ (2) **:** to maintain in a given condition (as of temperature, pressure, or humidity) or stage of processing (3) **:** to maintain a given condition in (4) **:** to maintain the articulation of (a speech sound) or the production of (as a note in music) ⟨the vowel in *feet* is not *held* as long as the vowel in *feed*⟩ **h :** to keep the uninterrupted interest, attention, or devotion of **:** keep from other interests, attractions, or places ⟨the play *held* the audience for over three hours⟩ ⟨a community that . . . ~*s* young people and offers inducements to them to stay and help build a greater hometown —J.C.Penney⟩ ⟨newspaper editing did not ~ him long —A.H.Meneely⟩ ⟨wants to ~ her husband while resisting his domination —H.M.Parshley⟩ **i :** to keep (as a letter or package) from being delivered usu. temporarily ⟨asked the post office to ~ his mail until he returned⟩ **j :** to cover (the ears) so as to prevent hearing ⟨when I spoke she *held* her ears —Eudora Welty⟩ **k :** to constitute or provide adequate satisfaction for ⟨enough food to ~ him for a week⟩ ⟨had had enough of high causes and noble sacrifice to ~ them for a long time —F.L.Allen⟩ **l** (1) **:** not to veer or alter from ⟨the car *held* 70 miles an hour for 20 miles⟩ ⟨prices had *held* the same level for a month⟩ ⟨had trouble ~*ing* his course⟩ (2) **:** to be free of marked bouncing, swerving, or skidding on ⟨a car that ~*s* the road well at any speed⟩ **m :** to make an exhibition of or call persistently to one's consciousness ⟨trying to entertain his audience by ~*ing* his betters to ridicule⟩ **n :** to fix on and not turn away from ⟨for a few minutes the flashlight *held* the canoe, then lost it —Erle Stanley Gardner⟩ **5 a** (1) **:** to receive and retain ⟨the can ~*s* gasoline⟩ **:** have within **:** CONTAIN ⟨the cemetery which *held* the bodies of his family for seven generations back⟩ ⟨the room *held* only Victorian furniture⟩ ⟨the envelope which *held* his ticket —J.P.Marquand⟩ (2) **:** to have or retain within its limits as if in a container ⟨throw into a word every trace of meaning it can ~ —C.S.Kilby⟩ ⟨the cast *held* some noted singers⟩ ⟨could ~ large quantities of verse in his mind without effort⟩ (3) **:** to keep within moderate bounds the characteristic intoxicating effects of (an alcoholic liquor) ⟨drank heavily but *held* it well⟩ **b** (1) **:** to be able or designed to receive and retain or contain ⟨a special container to ~ flammable liquids⟩ ⟨the basket that *held* outgoing mail was empty⟩ (2) **:** ACCOMMODATE ⟨the hotel could ~ over 300 guests⟩ ⟨sleeping platforms ran the length of the side walls in two tiers, ~*ing* eight men —Meridel Le Sueur⟩ **c :** to be marked or characterized by as an essential feature ⟨the volume *held* an historical rather than a literary interest⟩ ⟨its steeply pitched gable roof ~*s* one dormer —*Amer. Guide Series: Md.*⟩ ⟨a scene that *held* many fond memories for him⟩ ⟨the famous hymn of creation . . . ~*s* an awesome vastness of mood —Emma Hawkridge⟩ **d :** to provide or have in reserve as a reward ⟨the story ~*s* a happy ending for everybody⟩ ⟨the tournament ~*s* a nice prize for the winner⟩ ⟨would like to know what the future ~*s*⟩ **6 a :** HARBOR, EXPERIENCE ⟨~ a feeling⟩ ⟨a nation for whom we all ~ a good deal of admiration⟩ ⟨~*s* no sympathy for criminals⟩ **b :** ACCEPT ⟨~ a point of view⟩ **:** BELIEVE ⟨~ a theory⟩ ⟨~ opposing opinions⟩ **:** subscribe to ⟨the aesthetic philosophy we happen to ~ —C.I.Glicksberg⟩ **c** (1) **:** CONSIDER, REGARD, THINK, JUDGE ⟨*held* that the action was dishonest⟩ ⟨*held* calculus to be too difficult for that age group⟩ ⟨*held* by many to be the greatest contemporary tennis player⟩ ⟨the expression of those truths *held* to be self-evident —F.B. Millett⟩ (2) **:** to decide in a judicial ruling ⟨the court *held* that the man was sane⟩ (3) **:** ESTEEM, VALUE ⟨the story is that he *held* it so lightly that he lost the land on one turn of the cards —*Amer. Guide Series: N.C.*⟩ **d :** to have or maintain in judgment or regard ⟨~ someone in contempt⟩ ⟨~ a parent in honor⟩ **7 a :** to engage in with someone else or with others **:** do by concerted action ⟨the student body *held* games in the afternoon⟩ **b :** CONVOKE, CONVENE ⟨the king *held* an assembly of all his courtiers⟩ ⟨the second court session was *held* in the afternoon⟩ **:** arrange for and have in a united action ⟨the company *held* a feast to celebrate victory⟩ **:** schedule and assemble or meet ⟨some classes were *held* in the evening⟩ **8 a :** to be or stand in (as a relative position) ⟨~*s* second place in the city golf tournament⟩ ⟨urban redevelopment continues to ~ an important place in planning programs —*Collier's Yr. Bk.*⟩ **b :** to have earned or been appointed, promoted, or elected to and now occupy (as an office) ⟨~*s* a captaincy in the navy⟩ ⟨~*s* a secretaryship in the club⟩ ⟨*held* the presidency for two terms⟩ **c :** to have earned or been awarded (as an academic degree) ⟨~*s* an M.D. from one of the best medical schools⟩ ⟨~*s* a German Ph.D.⟩ ⟨~*s* a medal of honor⟩ **9** *now dial Brit* **:** BET, WAGER **10 a** *obs* **:** to handle so as to guide or manage (as reins or a gun) **b :** POINT, AIM, DIRECT — used with *on* ⟨*held* a gun on the grocer while an accomplice robbed the till⟩ **11** *obs* **:** to endure or bear up under (as rough handling or invidious comparison) ~ *vi* **1 a :** to maintain position **:** not retreat **:** remain unconquered or unsubdued ⟨the troops *held* in the face of repeated attacks⟩ **b** (1) **:** to continue or remain esp. as is or of the same kind or quality **:** LAST ⟨winter *held* until the middle of March⟩ ⟨his anger *held* for several days⟩ ⟨the output of copper *held* at the level of the year before⟩ ⟨hoping that the good weather would ~⟩ **:** not change or alter ⟨we can go if the present circumstances ~⟩ ⟨our luck *held* and we won⟩ ⟨the habit of a lifetime *held* —John Buchan⟩ — often used with *up* ⟨the good weather *held* up for several days⟩ (2) **:** to endure a test or trial ⟨their courage *held* against all odds⟩ — often used with *up* ⟨if his interest ~*s* up⟩ **2 a :** to maintain a grasp on or a connection with something **:** remain fastened to something (as by a strap) **:** keep hold ⟨the anchor *held* in the rough sea⟩ **:** not slip **:** not lose a grip **:** CLING ⟨felt his rubber soles grip and ~⟩ **b** *of a female mammal* **:** to hold to service **:** CONCEIVE **3 :** to derive right or title (as to the possession of lands or as land to be held) — usu. used with *of* or *from* ⟨*held* of the crown by an outright gift⟩ **4 :** to bear or carry oneself ⟨a man who *held* aloof from strangers⟩ ⟨asked the boy to ~ still⟩ **5 :** to be or remain valid **:** APPLY ⟨the rule ~*s* only in special cases⟩ **:** prove consistent or acceptable to reason or logic ⟨the theory does not ~ under analysis⟩ **6 :** to go ahead **:** continue as one has been going ⟨the travelers *held* on their way⟩ ⟨*held* south for several miles⟩ **:** not veer or fluctuate in progress or forward movement ⟨the plane *held* steadily on its course by automatic control⟩ **7 :** to restrain or withhold oneself **:** cease or forbear an intended or threatened action **:** HALT, STOP, PAUSE ⟨wished that he might ~ a while and stop his incessant chatter⟩ **8 :** to take place ⟨went . . . to the place where the funeral service was ~*ing* —John Bennett⟩ ⟨annual show and sale of highland ponies ~*s* on Monday —*Scotsman*⟩ **9 :** to pause in archery between drawing and loosing an arrow **10 :** to hold copy (as in proofreading) **syn** see CONTAIN, HAVE, KEEP — **hold a brief :** to act as or be a counsel in a legal case ⟨had *held* several important *briefs*⟩ — **hold a brief for :** ADVOCATE, DEFEND — **hold a candle to :** to qualify for comparison with ⟨asserted that no wrestler could *hold a candle to* the current champion⟩ — **hold a close wind** *or* **hold a good wind :** to sail very close to the wind making little leeway — **hold book :** to act as prompter during a rehearsal or a performance of a play ⟨help paint scenery, carry props, do a little acting, and *hold book* during performances —Maurice Zolotow⟩ — **hold bottom** *of an anchor* **:** to hold in holding ground — **hold by :** to remain faithful to **:** hold to or be devoted to ⟨those who *hold by* the humanist tradition⟩ — **hold copy :** to work as a copyholder — **hold court :** to act with marked and courtly sociableness ⟨*held court* whenever he was in public nodding and bowing to all his friends and acquaintances⟩ — **hold down a claim :** to remain on land claimed so as to establish one's ownership — **hold everything :** to stop or cease an action or operation — usu. used as a command or exhortation — **hold fire :** to refrain from expressing oneself or from taking action ⟨*held fire* on specific foreign policy questions —*N.Y.Times*⟩ — **hold good 1 :** to hold true **2 :** to hold up **:** ENDURE, LAST ⟨his luck *held good* all year⟩ — **hold hands :** to go hand in hand esp. as an expression of affection — **hold in demesne** *law* **:** to hold in one's own possession or power — **hold one's breath 1 :** to cease breathing momentarily (as from fear) **2 :** to be in extreme suspense ⟨*held her breath* all during the examination for fear the child would not pass⟩ — **hold one's ground :** to maintain a position ⟨the speaker calmly *held his ground* in the face of angry opposition⟩ — **hold one's horses** *slang* **:** to stop action or talk for a moment **:** wait or be patient for a minute — usu. used as a command or exhortation — **hold one's own :** to maintain one's position **:** prove at least equal to opposition ⟨proved able to *hold their own* under heavy attack⟩ ⟨the lighter boy *held his own* well against the heavier boxer⟩ — **hold one's peace :** to keep silent **:** keep one's thoughts to oneself ⟨felt it would do no good to complain so *held his peace*⟩ — **hold one's tongue :** to keep silent ⟨told the boy sharply to *hold his tongue*⟩ — **hold tack with 1** *of a boat* **:** to keep on the same tacks as and change tacks with (another boat) **2 :** to keep up with (as in activity) — **hold the bag** *also* **hold the sack 1 :** to be or be left empty-handed or with only the most undesirable items of a group of apportioned items **2 :** to bear alone and in full a responsibility that should properly have been shared by others ⟨when the police began to investigate, five of the men left the country leaving the sixth *holding the bag*⟩ — **hold the boards :** to hold the stage — **hold the field 1 :** to maintain a position in a field of play or an arena of contest **2 :** to remain dominantly before the public ⟨a doctrine which *held the field* for quite five hundred years —R.W.Southern⟩ — **hold the fort 1 :** to maintain a firm position usu. against opposition ⟨found himself *holding the fort* against a solid block of opponents of the plan⟩ **2 :** to take care of usual affairs ⟨a skeleton staff was left to *hold the fort* at the office during the Saturday morning —Dorothy Sayers⟩ — **hold the line :** to keep things as they are without undesirable alteration ⟨*holding the line* on the price of electrical appliances despite increased costs⟩ ⟨*hold the line* on present taxes⟩ — **hold the market :** to buy or sell in order to maintain prices as they are — **hold the stage :** to continue to be produced — used of a play — **hold the wind :** to sail close to the wind without making much leeway — **hold to 1 a :** to remain steadfast, attached, or faithful to **:** adhere to ⟨*hold to* an established plan⟩ ⟨*hold to* one's purpose⟩ ⟨*hold to* one's family in all circumstances⟩ **b :** to subscribe to **:** BELIEVE ⟨those who *hold to* the doctrine of spontaneous generation —J.B.Conant⟩ **2 :** to stay close to or on (as a particular course) ⟨the new ships *hold* closely *to* the major trade lanes —R.H.Brown⟩ — **hold to account :** to hold responsible ⟨*hold* all salesmen *to account* for the money spent on company business⟩ — **hold to service** *of a domestic animal* **:** to become pregnant **:** SETTLE — **hold true :** to remain true or valid esp. under changed circumstances ⟨the theory *holds true* in all applications⟩ — **hold up one's head :** to conduct oneself in a normally unashamed manner ⟨if they found out that she had cheated, she would be unable to *hold up her head* again⟩ — **hold water 1 a :** to retain water without leaking **b :** to be whole, consistent, or valid **:** stand up under criticism or analysis ⟨an accusation which would *hold water* in a court of law —Michael Howard⟩ ⟨an explanation that would not *hold water* if the true facts were known⟩ **2 :** to hold oars steady in the water usu. at right angles to the direction of movement to check headway — **hold with :** to agree with (as a principle) or approve of (as a practice) ⟨political methods that few would *hold with*⟩

²**hold** \'hōld, *dial often* -lt\ *n* -s [ME *hold, holde* hold, possession, land that is held, property, fr. OE *heald, hald* protection, keeping, fr. *healdan, haldan* to hold] **1 a :** a place of temporary shelter or refuge; *also* **:** a lair or a lurking place (as of a fish) **b :** STRONGHOLD **2 a :** CONFINEMENT, CUSTODY **b :** a place of confining **:** PRISON **3 a** (1) **:** the act or the manner of holding or grasping (as in the hands or arms) ⟨released his ~ on the man's arm⟩ ⟨has a strong ~ for a small man⟩ **:** GRASP ⟨took a firm ~ on the club⟩ **:** CLASP, GRIP ⟨in his arms his ~ was tight and reassuring⟩ — often used idiomatically without an article as object of *catch, get, have, seize, take* ⟨got ~ of the oar and was pulled out of the water⟩ ⟨seized ~ as the rope brushed his fingers⟩ ⟨held out a hand and waited until the child took ~⟩ ⟨took ~ of the knob and opened the door⟩ ⟨the boy's sneakers suddenly took ~ and stopped him from sliding off the roof⟩ ⟨saw that the climber had ~ of the rope before he began to haul on it⟩ (2) **:** a manner of grasping an opponent in wrestling ⟨knee ~*s* and body presses⟩ **b** (1) **:** a nonphysical bond, grip, or clasp which attaches, restrains, or constrains or by or through which something is affected, controlled, dominated, or possessed — often used with *on, upon,* or *over* ⟨afraid they might lose their ~ on the domestic market —*Sydney (Australia) Bull.*⟩ ⟨yet the ~ of the public school upon the middle-class mind has not weakened —Roy Lewis & Angus Maude⟩ ⟨the father had a strong ~ over his children⟩ and often used idiomatically without an article as object of *catch, get, have, seize, take* ⟨the newspapers got ~ of the story⟩ ⟨after a moment of panic he got ~ of himself⟩ ⟨seized ~ and stepped up production 50 percent⟩ ⟨in the confusion of contradictory ideas we did not know what philosophy he had ~ of⟩ (2) **:** an action, expedient, or device for achieving an end ⟨arguing that in . . . politics no ~*s* are barred —*New Republic*⟩ **c :** conscious grasp **:** full comprehension — used with *on* or *upon* ⟨at the point of sleep one loses his ~ on the real world⟩ ⟨how weak was his ~ upon character —Roger Fry⟩ **4 :** something that may be grasped as a support ⟨climbed up the rock using some ledges and jutting pieces as ~*s*⟩ **5 :** a pause between the completion of the draw and the release of the arrow in archery **6 a :** FERMATA **b :** a rhythmic lengthening of a word or syllable or a symbol used to indicate this **c :** the time between the onset and the release of a vocal articulation **7 :** a sudden motionless posture at the end of a dance or dance phrase **8 a :** an order or indication that something is to be reserved ⟨put a ~ on all the hotel rooms still unoccupied⟩ **b :** an order or indication that some action is to be delayed ⟨announced a ~ on all takeoffs until the weather cleared⟩ **c :** a notation on a depositor's account to indicate that the balance or a portion thereof should not be paid out **d :** a recommendation indicating that a stock has long-term and fundamental values but is not considered a desirable present purchase for near-term appreciation

³**hold** \" \ *n* -s [fr. (assumed) ME *hold*, alter. (prob. influenced by ME ²*hold*) of ME ¹*hole*] **1 a :** the interior of a ship below decks; *esp* **:** the cargo deck of a ship **b :** the interior of a plane; *esp* **:** the cargo compartment of a plane **2 a :** a division of the interior esp. the cargo deck of a ship **b :** a division of the interior of a plane esp. for cargo

⁴**hold** \" \ *n* -s [OE, fr. ON *hölthr* free landowner, man; akin to OE *hæle, hæleth* man, hero, OS *helith* man, hero, ON *halr* man, and perh. to Skt *kalya* healthy — more at CALLI-] **:** an officer of high rank in the Danelaw corresponding to the high reeve of the Anglo-Saxons

hold·able \'hōldəbəl\ *adj* **:** capable of being held **:** of a size or character that makes holding convenient or desirable

holdall \'ₛ,ₛ\ *n* -s [¹*hold* + *all*] **:** a container for miscellaneous articles; *esp* **:** an often cloth traveling case or bag

hold away *vi* **1** *Scot* **:** to remain at a distance **:** hold off **2** *chiefly Scot* **:** to continue on one's way

hold back *vb* [¹*hold* + *back*] *vt* **1 a :** to keep in check **:** RESTRAIN, CURB ⟨had to *hold* the children *back* from running out into the street⟩ **b :** to keep from advancing to the next stage, grade, or level ⟨followed the policy of *holding* any child *back* who could not read adequately⟩ **2 a :** to retain in one's keeping ⟨*held* a large sum *back* to cover costs of handling⟩ **b :** to keep to oneself ⟨who is at liberty to speak and *hold* nothing *back* —F.L.Paxson⟩ **3 :** to shade (a portion of an image in photography) while printing to reduce the density ~ *vi* **:** to keep oneself from doing, feeling, or indulging in something **:** hold aloof ⟨*held back* from making a complete statement about his political position⟩ ⟨were asked to *hold back* on food deliveries during the shortage⟩ ⟨when they asked the child to come in he *held back*⟩ **syn** see KEEP

holdback \'ₛ,ₛ\ *n* [*hold back*] **1 :** a device (as an iron catch on a carriage shaft with a looped strap) to enable a horse to back or hold back a vehicle **2 :** one of several devices for holding something back or open: as **a :** a device (as a specially constructed hinge) for holding a door, shutter, or casement window open **b :** TIEBACK **3 a :** the act of holding something back or of holding back on something (as work or production) ⟨ordered a ~ until negotiations looked more auspicious⟩ **b :** something held back or withheld often temporarily

hold beam *n* **:** a beam placed in the hold of a ship to supply usu. transverse structural strength

hold-clear \'ₛ;ₛ\ *n* -s [fr. the phrase *hold clear*] **:** a device for holding a railroad signal in any position other than its most restrictive

hold down *vb* [¹*hold* + *down*] *vt* **1 a :** to keep in subjection ⟨conquered them but had no success in *holding* them *down*⟩ **b :** RESTRAIN, CURB ⟨noisy despite all efforts to *hold* them *down*⟩ **2 :** to retain continuously and handle competently (as a job) **:** hold and keep ⟨a man who had *held down* some significant political positions⟩ **3 :** to take care of ⟨some friends *held down* his grocery business while he was sick⟩ **~** *vi* **:** to limit oneself ⟨he is not stopping smoking but *holding down* to three cigarettes a day⟩ — **hold down on :** to keep down or low ⟨*held down on* the price he was willing to pay⟩

hold–down \ˈ=ˌ=\ *n* -S [*hold down*] **:** a clamp or other device for holding a part down against another part (as a sheet against the bed of a press or a battery against the bottom of its container)

holden *archaic past part of* HOLD

hol·den·ite \ˈhōldəˌnīt\ *n* -S [Albert F. *Holden* †1913 Am. mining engineer + E *-ite*] **:** a mineral $(Mn,Ca)_4(Zn,Mg,Fe)_2(AsO_4)(OH)_5O_2$ consisting of a basic manganese zinc arsenate with minor calcium, magnesium, and iron and occurring as red orthorhombic crystals at Franklin, New Jersey

¹hold·er \ˈhōldə(r)\ *n* -S [ME, fr. *holden* to hold + *-er*] **1 :** one that holds something: as **a** (1) **:** POSSESSOR, OWNER — often used in combination ⟨slave*holder*⟩ ⟨job*holder*⟩ (2) **:** one who holds any estate in land **:** a person in constructive possession of land having the right of immediate possession thereto which he can exercise without hindrance **:** a tenant in his own right or under another in actual possession of land **b :** a person in possession of and legally entitled to receive payment of a bill, note, or check **:** the payee, endorsee in possession, or the bearer of a bill, note, or check — compare HOLDER IN DUE COURSE **c :** a worker who holds articles during an industrial process **d :** one who has won or been awarded and reaps the benefits of a scholarship or fellowship **e :** one who has won, earned, or been awarded a trophy, title, or degree ⟨the ~ of a tennis championship⟩ ⟨was ~ of several swimming cups⟩ ⟨the ~ of a college degree in animal husbandry⟩ **2 :** a device or contrivance by which or a container in which something is held ⟨umbrella ~⟩ ⟨a flower ~⟩: as **a :** either of two loops attached to reins for holding a pulling horse **b :** a thick protective cloth pad for grasping hot utensils **c :** a narrow tubular device often used by smokers for holding a cigarette or cigar while smoking it **d :** a flat lightproof container in which photographic films or plates may be held for use in a camera **e :** a device that resembles a safety pin and is used in knitting for holding stitches temporarily to keep them from dropping **3 :** something (as a strap or rail) which one may grasp for support or for steadying oneself **4 :** a device by which something (as a door or shutter) is held back or open

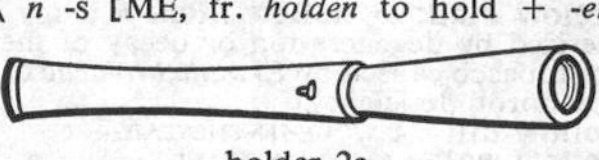
holder 2c

²holder \"\ *n* -S [ME, fr. (assumed) ME *hold* + ME *-er* — more at ³HOLD] **:** a worker in the hold of a ship

holder–forth \ˌ=ˈ=\ *n, pl* **holders–forth :** one that holds forth **:** PREACHER, RANTER

holder in due course : the holder of a negotiable instrument that is complete and regular on its face who takes it in good faith and for value before it is overdue and without notice of its dishonor or of any infirmity in it or of any defect in the title of the person negotiating it

holder–on \ˌ==ˈ=\ *n, pl* **holders–on** *or* **holder–ons 1 :** a worker who bucks rivets **2 :** a pneumatic tool used in place of a dolly to back up rivets while they are being headed

holder process *n* **:** HOLDING METHOD

holder–up \ˌ==ˈ=\ *n, pl* **holders–up** *or* **holder–ups :** one that holds something up; *specif* **:** a man who holds up the setting punch in riveting

holdfast \ˈ=ˌ=\ *n* -S *often attrib* [fr. the phrase *hold fast*] **1 :** something that secures, holds in place, or supports: as **a** (1) **:** a rhizoidal base resembling a sucker but without absorption cells by which the thallus of many algae (as seaweeds) is attached to its support (2) **:** a discoid extremity of a tendril in certain plants (as the Virginia creeper) by which the vines fix themselves to flat surfaces **b :** an organ (as the acetabulum of a trematode or the scolex of a tapeworm) by which a parasitic animal attaches itself to its host **2 :** something to which something else (as a guy line or tackle) may be secured firmly **3 :** an actinomycotic tumor of the jaw — not used technically

hold·fast·ness \ˈhōl(d)ˌfas(t)nəs, -faas-,-fais-,-fȧs-\ *n* -ES **:** the tendency to keep a firm often stubborn hold (as on a position or possession) **:** TENACITY, PERSISTENCE

hold forth *vb* [ME *holden forth*, fr. *holden* to hold + *forth*] *vt* **:** OFFER, EXHIBIT, PROPOUND ⟨*hold forth* the hopes of better times to come⟩ ⟨*hold* it *forth* that one can cure all ailments of the spirit⟩ **~** *vi* **1 :** to speak out in public esp. at length **:** HARANGUE, PREACH — often used disparagingly **2 :** to conduct one's affairs ⟨a group of nuclear physicists now *holding forth* at their annual convention⟩ **3 :** to take place **:** undergo performance ⟨a region in which every variety of winter sports *holds forth*⟩

hold in *vb* [ME *holden in*, fr. *holden* to hold + *in*] *vt* **:** to keep in check **:** RESTRAIN, CURB ⟨the rider had a hard time *holding* his horse *in*⟩ **~** *vi* **:** to restrain oneself **:** keep silent ⟨wanted to speak but thought better of it and *held in*⟩

¹holding *n* -S [ME *holdyng*, gerund of *holden* to hold] **1 :** the act of one that holds or takes hold **:** HOLD, GRIP, CLASP **2 :** something that is held: as **a :** land held esp. by a vassal of a superior **:** TENEMENT ⟨small ~*s* of less than 5 acres — *Americana Annual*⟩ **b :** an actual judgment or ruling of a court upon any issue of law raised in a case **:** the actual final decision of a court on the particular facts of a given case as distinguished from the dictum ⟨difficult to find a recent . . . enactment that equals in impact and scope this judicial ~ — J.P.Roche & M.M.Gordon⟩ **c :** any property that is owned or possessed — usu. used in pl. ⟨record-breaking frozen fish ~*s* totaled 179 million pounds —*Americana Annual*⟩ ⟨the ~*s* of American libraries —*Current Biog.*⟩ **3 :** something that holds **:** a means of holding **:** ATTACHMENT, CONNECTION **4 :** personal contact esp. with the hands or arms that retards or interferes with the movement of an opponent in some sports (as basketball, football, soccer) **5 :** a company or enterprise owned or controlled by a holding company

²holding *adj* [ME *holdyng*, pres. part. of *holden* to hold] **1 :** effecting a delay **:** being a hindrance or interference ⟨a ~ action to prevent the passage of more drastic control legislation —E.P.Hutchinson⟩ **2 :** designed for usu. temporary storage or retention ⟨a ~ refrigerator at a railhead⟩ ⟨a ~ pen for the horses⟩ ⟨shunted the cars onto the ~ track⟩

holding attack *n* **:** a secondary attack designed to hold an enemy in position in a military envelopment

holding company *n* **:** a company that owns part or all of one or more other companies for purposes of control — compare INVESTMENT COMPANY

holding fund *n* **:** a sum of money allotted or set aside for investment usu. for noncommercial purposes (as scholarships or grants-in-aid)

holding ground *n* **:** bottom that an anchor can hold in

holding method *n* **:** a method of pasteurization in which a fluid (as milk or fruit juice) is heated to not less than 143° F for at least 30 minutes

holding–out partner \ˌ=ˈ=-\ *n* **:** NOMINAL PARTNER

holding–up hammer \ˌ=ˈ=-\ *n* **:** a riveter's dolly

hold·man \ˈhōl(d)mən\ *n, pl* **holdmen :** a dock worker who works in a ship's hold in loading or unloading a ship

hold off *vb* [ME *holden of*, fr. *holden* to hold + *of* off] *vt* **1 a :** to keep at a distance ⟨a tendency to *hold* people *off*⟩ **b :** WITHSTAND ⟨*held* all enemy attacks *off*⟩ **2 :** POSTPONE, DELAY ⟨*held off* going to see a doctor⟩ ⟨tries to *hold off* making decisions⟩ **~** *vi* **1 a :** to keep aloof ⟨a tendency to *hold off* from people⟩ **b :** ABSTAIN ⟨*held off* from smoking for a month⟩ **2 :** to hold back **:** HESITATE ⟨*held off* from answering directly⟩

hold–off \ˈ=ˌ=\ *n* -S [*hold off*] **:** the act or period of holding off **:** a delay or period of delay or postponement

hold on *vi* [ME *holden on*, fr. *holden* to hold + *on*] **1 a :** to go on **:** maintain a course **:** CONTINUE ⟨*held on* in their route until they arrived at a river⟩ **b :** to remain unconquered or undefeated ⟨felt they could *hold on* under siege for at least two months⟩ **2 a :** to maintain one's position **:** hold on to something **:** hang on ⟨a ledge where the tree roots could *hold on*⟩ **b :** to delay action (as in making a sale) ⟨wanted to sell but *held on*, hoping for a rise in price⟩ **3 :** to wait a minute **:** STOP, CEASE — used esp. in the imperative ⟨the man became irritated at the speaker and finally cried, "*Hold on!*"⟩ — **hold on to 1 a :** to keep in the grasp esp. with persistence ⟨the child *held on to* the man's hand tightly⟩ ⟨*held on to* what he had with desperation⟩ **b :** to keep control of ⟨*held on to* his temper⟩ ⟨had a hard time *holding on to* himself⟩ **2 a :** not to relinquish **:** not give up or abandon ⟨she *held on to* a quiet plan of her own —Margaret Deland⟩ **b :** to continue to produce (as a sound) or sing (as a note) ⟨*held on to* the final chord for a long time⟩

hold out *vb* [¹*hold* + *out*] *vt* **1 a :** to reach or stretch out ⟨the cook *held* a plate of food *out* to him⟩ ⟨*held* his hand *out* with a smile⟩ **b :** OFFER, PROFFER ⟨a job that seemed to *hold* many more opportunities *out* to him than his old one⟩ ⟨could *hold out* no hope of advancement⟩ **2 :** to make out to be **:** REPRESENT ⟨*held* himself *out* as a trained pharmacist⟩ **3 a** *archaic* **:** to keep up **:** CONTINUE, MAINTAIN **b** *obs* **:** SUSTAIN **c** *archaic* **:** to defend against a foe **4 :** to retain possession of (a card) secretly for the purpose of cheating or deceiving in a game (as poker) **~** *vi* **1 a :** to remain unsubdued by opposing forces **:** not yield or give way **:** LAST, ENDURE ⟨the garrison under siege *held out* for almost a month⟩; *also* **:** to continue to operate **:** not fail ⟨prayed the engine would *hold out* until we got home⟩ **b :** to refuse to come to an agreement or make a settlement until certain terms are met ⟨*held out* for a shorter working day⟩ **2 :** to hang out ⟨a gang of adolescents who *hold out* at the corner drug store⟩ — **hold out on 1 :** to withhold something from ⟨she didn't tell me she was rich; she's been *holding out on* me⟩ **2 :** to withhold a part or the whole of ⟨threatened to *hold out on* his sister's dividends if she didn't pose —*Fortune*⟩

holdout \ˈ=ˌ=\ *n* -S [*hold out*] **1 :** the act or an instance of holding out: as **a :** a holding out by a negotiator to try to force concessions **b :** the act of secreting one or more cards of a pack for private use in a gambling game **2 :** a mechanism designed to assist a holdout in a game of cards **3 :** something held out **4 :** one that holds out (as in negotiations or an anticipated action) ⟨there was one ~ among the negotiators⟩ ⟨expected her to go from the movies to television but she remained a ~⟩

hold over *vb* [¹*hold* + *over*] *vi* **1 :** to continue in occupancy of land or exercise the powers of office beyond the limits of the term set or fixed **2 :** to continue into the succeeding beat or measure — used of a note or tone **3 :** to continue to exist **:** REMAIN, LAST, ENDURE ⟨no rancor *held over* through the years —W.A.White⟩ **~** *vt* **1 a :** to keep for future action **:** POSTPONE ⟨*held* the picnic *over* until better weather came⟩ ⟨*held over* several bills until the next session⟩ **b :** to keep in one's possession or as part of one's knowledge **:** RETAIN **:** not lose ⟨a conviction *held over* from school days —Robertson Davies⟩ **2 a :** to retain in possession or occupancy esp. of a post or office from an earlier term or period **:** keep on ⟨department heads who had been *held over* from the previous administration⟩ **b :** to renew or prolong the engagement of (as a performer or an act) **:** CONTINUE ⟨*held* the acrobats *over* for a second week⟩ ⟨a smash hit *held over* by popular demand⟩ **3 :** to continue (as the production of a note) into the succeeding beat or measure

¹holdover \ˈ=ˌ==\ *n* -S [*hold over*] **1 :** one that holds over or is held over: as **a :** one that remains in office after the departure of his associates **b :** CARRY-OVER 2 **c :** a tree left in cutting as a reserve for a future crop or a tree remaining after fire or wind damage **d :** HANGOVER 2a **e :** an act or a performer whose engagement is immediately continued **f :** a team member remaining on a team from a past season ⟨a backfield consisting of a new man and three ~*s*⟩ **2 :** a cell where one is held for appearance before a court

²holdover \"\ *adj* **1 :** of, belonging to, or being a holdover ⟨a team with four ~ players⟩ ⟨the city has a ~ mayor although almost all other officials are new⟩ **2** *plant pathol* **:** permitting survival of a pathogenic organism under unfavorable conditions ⟨a ~ canker⟩ ⟨a ~ stage⟩

holds *pres 3d sing of* HOLD, *pl of* HOLD

hold together *vt* **1 :** to preserve as a unit **:** keep from separating into component parts ⟨only rubber bands *held* the toy *together*⟩ **:** preserve from disintegrating or falling ⟨only the force of the man's will *held* the company *together* in the last five years⟩ ⟨are of different inspirations but all *held together* by a remarkable unity —*Amer. Guide Series: Conn.*⟩ **2 :** to keep from nervous or mental collapse ⟨the novelist's attempt to *hold* himself *together* —Pat Frank⟩ **~** *vi* **:** to remain loyal to each other **:** preserve a unanimity of feeling or action ⟨we have only to *hold together* to go safely through the dark valley —Sir Winston Churchill⟩

hold up *vb* [ME *holden up*, fr. *holden* to hold + *up*] *vt* **1 a** (1) **:** RAISE, LIFT ⟨*hold* your hand *up* if you wish the chairman to recognize you⟩ ⟨*hold up* the object so it can be seen more clearly⟩ (2) **:** SUPPORT, SUSTAIN ⟨the underpinnings were not adequate to *hold* the house *up*⟩ ⟨the confiscated money *held* the toppling regime *up* for only a short time⟩ **b :** HOLD *vt* 4m **c :** to expose or call to attention as something one subscribes to, advocates, or lives by ⟨*held* a high standard *up* for his colleagues to follow⟩ ⟨*held up* the Old Testament in opposition to 18th century rationalism —William Petersen⟩ **2 a :** to rein in **:** CHECK, HALT ⟨*hold up* a horse⟩ **b :** to prevent (a fox or cub) from leaving a covert thus assuring a find and kill in fox hunting **c :** to stop, delay, or impede the course or advance of ⟨the accident *held* the traffic *up* for an hour⟩ ⟨a storm that *held* deliveries *up* for a day⟩ ⟨felt that she was *holding* her husband *up* in his career⟩ **3 :** to refuse to play (the winning card of a suit led) **4 :** to rob at gun's point ⟨*held* a gas station *up* and got away with several thousand dollars⟩ ⟨plotting to *hold up* a bank⟩ **~** *vi* **1 a** (1) **:** to remain undismayed or unsubdued (as under attack or misfortune) ⟨was determined to *hold up* for her children's sake⟩ ⟨*hold up* under attack⟩ (2) **:** to keep from falling **:** not to collapse, crumble, or fall apart ⟨an industry that *held up* well in the depression⟩ **b :** to prove true, accurate, or valid ⟨much depends on how well the weather forecasts *hold up*⟩ ⟨wondered if the charges would *hold up* in court⟩ **c :** to prove effective **:** PREVAIL ⟨despite attempts to countermand them, the provisions of the old charter *held up*⟩ **2 a :** to keep up **:** not fall behind or lose ground **:** hold out ⟨even the smaller children *held up* pretty well until the last mile⟩ **b :** to retain interest or artistic effectiveness esp. over an extended period of time ⟨a book that *holds up* well⟩ **3 :** to stop an action or postpone an intended action ⟨planned a picnic but the rain forced us to *hold up*⟩ **4 :** to keep from raining **:** remain clear ⟨a beautiful day, if it only *holds up*⟩ — **hold up on 1 :** DELAY, POSTPONE ⟨ran out of money and had to *hold up on* all plans to travel⟩ **2 :** to hold back (sense 2a) ⟨the court *held up on* the money until the estate was totally settled⟩

holdup \ˈ=ˌ=\ *n* -S [*hold up*] **1 :** the act or process of holding something up: as **a :** a robbery at the point of a gun **b :** a delay or a stopping of something ⟨a week's ~ in the completion of the plans⟩; *specif* **:** the delay or keeping back of a liquid during fractional distillation or reflex extraction with solvents or of a gas in fluidization **c :** the saving for later use of a card that could win the current trick in a bridge game **2 :** an instance of extortion **3 :** a place where livestock may be temporarily held on a range

holdup man *n* **:** a criminal who commits a holdup ⟨had mistaken the gendarme for a *holdup man* —H.A.Chippendale⟩

hold yard *n* **:** a yard for holding railroad cars or trains convenient for immediate use

¹hole \ˈhōl\ *n* -S [ME, hole, hollow place, hold (of a ship), fr. OE *hol* hole, hollow place (fr. neut. of *hol*, adj., hollow) & OE *holh* hole, hollow; akin to OHG *hol*, adj., hollow, ON *holr*, adj., hollow, Goth *ushulon* to hollow out, L *caulis* stalk of a plant, Gk *kaulos* stem, and perh. to Skt *kulyā* brook, ditch; basic meaning: hollow] **1 a :** an opening into or through anything **:** APERTURE, PERFORATION ⟨a ~ in a roof⟩ ⟨shot a ~ through a board⟩ ⟨entered the shed through a ~ in the side⟩ ⟨fishing through a ~ in the ice⟩ **b :** a pocket of a pool table ⟨dropped the eight ball in the corner ~⟩ **c :** an opening in a defensive football lineup (as a space between players or created by a player who is out of position or has been blocked) that offers an opportunity for an offensive player to advance the ball **2 a :** a hollow place **:** a cavity in a solid body or area ⟨a ~ in an apple⟩ ⟨a ~ in the hillside⟩: as (1) **:** a hollow in the ground **:** EXCAVATION, PIT, CAVE ⟨the steam shovel had dug a large ~⟩ (2) **:** a hollow in the ground filled with soft material (3) **:** a deep place in a body of water (4) **:** a mine, a well, or other shaft dug or drilled in the earth **b :** an unfilled or blank area (as in a page or column printed or to be printed) ⟨expand your story to fill an 18-line ~⟩ **c :** the hold of a ship **d :** a sense of loss or persistent yearning for something lost — usu. used in the phrase *to make a hole in* ⟨the loss of his daughter made quite a ~ in the man's life⟩ **e** (1) **:** a defect that exists in a crystal (as of a semiconductor) due to an electron having left its normal position in one of the crystal bonds and that is equivalent in many respects to a positively charged particle (2) **:** VACANCY 7 **f :** an air pocket as it affects an aircraft usu. causing it to drop suddenly **3 a :** an underground habitation or lurking place usu. excavated **:** DEN, BURROW ⟨the fox in his ~⟩ ⟨a rabbit ~⟩ **b :** a prison cell esp. for solitary confinement **4 a :** FLAW, FAULT ⟨looking for ~*s* in his character⟩ **b :** a weak spot or inconsistency (as in a line of reasoning) ⟨his stories are full of ~*s* since he does not explain how his characters get from one psychological state to another⟩ ⟨ingenious theory in which . . . there are many ~*s* —V.S.Pritchett⟩ **c :** an oversight or inadequate provision (as in a law, statute, treaty, or agreement) that permits significant evasions ⟨stop up the manifest ~*s* in the neutrality laws —R.M.Lovett⟩ **5 a :** a small cavity or perforation of significance in various games: as (1) **:** a small cavity into which a marble is to be played in any of various marble games (2) **:** a usu. lined cavity 4½ inches in diameter and 4 or more inches deep in a putting green into which the ball is to be played in a game of golf **b** (1) **:** the unit of play from a tee to its corresponding hole in a game of golf (2) **:** the fairway from a tee to its corresponding green on a golf course (3) **:** the score made in playing the ball from the tee into the hole in a game of golf **6 a :** a mean, dingy, or small and disreputable place esp. of lodging or habitation ⟨lived in some ~ or other across the tracks⟩ ⟨the ladies' cabin . . . is a dreadful ~ — Rachel Henning⟩ **b :** a place that one finds objectionable or offensive **7 :** a small bay **:** COVE **8 :** an awkward embarrassing position **:** FIX ⟨the loss of so competent an assistant put him in a ~ for a little while⟩ ⟨the noble heroes that got the rebels out of a ~ at the battle of Long Island —Kenneth Roberts⟩ **:** a losing position ⟨the ball team dropped the next two games which put them in the ~ by five games⟩; *esp* **:** a position of debt or financial loss ⟨in the ~ to the tune of several thousand dollars⟩ ⟨lent him some money to get him temporarily out of a ~⟩ **9** *West* **:** a level grassy mountain valley — usu. used in place names ⟨Jackson *Hole*⟩ **10 :** a side track branching from a main line of a railroad — **in the hole 1 a :** FACEDOWN — used of a hole card in stud poker **b :** having a score below zero **2 a :** next but one to bat in a ball game **b** *of a pitcher* **:** having pitched more balls than strikes to a batter **c** *of a batter* **:** having two strikes against him

²hole \"\ *vb* -ED/-ING/-S [ME *holen*, fr. OE *holian*; akin to OHG *holōn* to hollow out, ON *hola*, Goth *ushulon*; denominative fr. the root of OE *hol* hole] *vt* **1 :** to make a hole in (as by cutting, digging, boring, or shooting at) **:** PERFORATE, PIERCE ⟨*holing* the fence posts to take the crosspieces⟩ ⟨the ship was *holed* along the waterline by enemy fire⟩ **2 a :** to drive (as an animal or ball) into a hole ⟨the dogs *holed* the fox⟩ ⟨*holed* the ball in a single shot⟩ **b :** to place in a hole **3 :** to undercut (the coal) in a bed in coal mining **~** *vi* **1 :** to make a hole in something; *esp* **:** to excavate or undercut in coal mining **2 a :** to go or get into a hole **b** *of a train* **:** to take a side track so that an oncoming train can pass on the main track

hole·able \ˈhōləbəl\ *adj* **:** capable of being holed esp. in one stroke

hole–and–corner \ˌ=ˈ=ˈ==\ *also* **hole–in–corner** \ˈ=ˈ=ˈ==\ *adj* **1 :** hidden from public view esp. for reprehensible reasons **:** CLANDESTINE, UNDERHAND ⟨carrying on a *hole-and-corner* intrigue —*Times Lit. Supp.*⟩ ⟨done behind my back in a *hole-and-corner* fashion —Dorothy Sayers⟩ ⟨following a *hole-in-corner*, semiconspiratorial existence —*N. Y. Times*⟩ **2 :** belonging to the peripheral unimportant activities of life **:** INSIGNIFICANT ⟨marriage degenerated into a *hole-and-corner* existence in which spirit and intellect played no part —Olive Arden⟩ ⟨a *hole-and-corner* life in some obscure community —H.G.Wells⟩

hole board *n* **:** COMBER BOARD

hole card *n* **1 :** a card in stud poker that is properly dealt facedown and that the holder need not expose before the showdown — called also *down card* **2 :** a possession, action, or power that carries often unexpected weight in negotiations or other relationships and that is held in reserve or used to its most strategic advantage

ho·lec·ty·pi·na \hōˌlektəˈpīnə\ *n pl, cap* [NL, fr. *Holectypus*, genus of sea urchins (fr. *hol-* + Gk *ektypos* worked in relief) + *-ina*] **:** a suborder of extinct sea urchins (order Exocycloida) having a central peristome, an excentric periproct, an Aristotle's lantern, and nonpetaloid ambulacra and found in Jurassic, Cretaceous, and Eocene strata

¹ho·lec·ty·poid \hōˈlektəˌpȯid\ *adj* [NL *Holectypoida*] **:** of or relating to the Holectypina

²holectypoid \"\ *n* -S [NL *Holectypoida*] **:** a sea urchin of the suborder Holectypina

ho·lec·ty·poi·da \hōˌlektəˈpȯidə\ [NL, fr. *Holectypus* + *-oida*] *syn of* HOLECTYPINA

hole–high \ˈ=ˈ=\ *adj* **:** stopping or resting on a line that is roughly even with the hole one is playing toward — used of an approach shot in golf

hole in *vi* **:** to take refuge or lodging **:** put up for the night ⟨stopped traveling and *holed in* at a motel⟩

hole in one : ¹ACE 4

hole–in–the–wall \ˈ===ˌ=\ *n, pl* **holes–in–the–wall :** a small and insignificant place esp. difficult to locate ⟨in the jewelry business and ran a *hole-in-the-wall* you could barely squeeze into⟩ ⟨a *hole-in-the-wall* patent-medicine manufacturer⟩

hole·less \ˈhōlləs\ *adj* [*hole* + *-less*] **:** having no hole or aperture

hole out *vt* **1 :** to play (the ball) into the cup in a game of golf **2 :** to complete a hole in golf for ⟨his second putt *holed* him *out* for a six⟩ **~** *vi* **:** to play one's ball into the cup in a game of golf

holeproof \ˈ=ˌ=\ *adj* **1 a :** designed to be proof against holes worn in by ordinary use ⟨~ stockings⟩ **b :** having no flaws or weak points ⟨the evidence against the prisoner was ~⟩ **2 :** designed to prevent evasion or subversion — used of a law, statute, provision, or system ⟨asked them to formulate laws that were ~ and would stop graft and corruption in the city⟩

hol·er \ˈhōlə(r)\ *n* -S [²*hole* + *-er*] **1 :** one that digs or fashions holes **2 :** one that has a specified number of holes — used in combinations ⟨the golf course was only a nine-*holer*⟩ ⟨the outhouse was a two-*holer*⟩

holes *pl of* HOLE, *pres 3d sing of* HOLE

hole saw *n* **:** CROWN SAW

hole through *vi* **:** to connect two underground tunnels by removing the rock that divides them

hole up *vi* **1 :** to take refuge or shelter in a hole or cave or as if in one **:** seek protection ⟨gone upstate to where her people were . . . figured on *holing up* with them for a while until she got over being afraid —R.F.Mirvish⟩ ⟨*holed up* in caves until they were blasted out by tommy gun and dynamite —*Newsweek*⟩ **2 :** to go into hiding ⟨breaks jail and *holes up* in an isolated turkey ranch —*Newsweek*⟩ ⟨badmen who *holed up* in badlands where others dared not venture —*Ford Times*⟩ **~** *vt* **1 a :** to place in or as if in a refuge, a shelter, or a hiding place ⟨during the wartime absence of her husband . . . she was *holed up* with two small sons on a farm —*New Yorker*⟩ **b :** IMPRISON ⟨the gunman *holed* them *up* in the house for two days⟩ **2 :** to hold up or delay esp. for a long time ⟨housing legislation is *holed up* in a Senate committee —*Time*⟩

holey \ˈhōlē, -li\ *adj* [ME *holly*, fr. *hole*, *hol* hole + *-y*] **:** having a hole or being full of holes ⟨wearing a ~ bathing suit —*Time*⟩

holey dollar *n* **:** a Spanish piece of eight or dollar having a round hole in its center, bearing the denomination 5 shillings, and current in Australia 1813–29 — called also *colonial dollar, pierced dollar, ring dollar*

hol·ger niel·sen method \'hōlgə(r)'nēlsən-\ *n, usu cap H&N* [after *Holger Nielsen* †1955 Dan. army officer who originated it] **:** BACK PRESSURE–ARM LIFT METHOD

hol ha·mo·ed *or* **chol ha·mo·ed** \ˌkōlhä'mōəd\ *n pl, sometimes cap* [Heb *ḥol ha-mo'ed*, lit., the secular portion of the festival] **:** the four intermediate semiholidays between the first two and last two full festival days of Passover; *also* **:** the five intermediate days between the first two and last two days of Sukkoth

ho·li \'hōlē\ *n* -s *usu cap* [Hindi *holī*, fr. Skt *holikā*] **:** a Hindu spring festival characterized by boisterous and usu. ribald revelry including esp. the throwing of colored water and powder

ho·lia \'hōlēə\ *n* -s [origin unknown] **:** HUMPBACK SALMON

¹hol·i·day \'hälə,dā, *chiefly Brit* -ˌdi\ *n* -s [ME, fr. OE *hāligdæg*, fr. *hālig* holy + *dæg* day — more at HOLY, DAY] **1 :** HOLY DAY **2 a :** a day on which one is exempt from one's usual labor or vocational activity ⟨had a ~ on the day the boss's daughter was married⟩ **b :** a time of release from work **:** FESTIVITY, CELEBRATION — usu. used in the phrase *to make holiday* ⟨the people who are making ~ flock to the beaches⟩ **c** *chiefly Brit* **:** VACATION ⟨everybody is on ~ in August —Joy Packer⟩ ⟨went on ~ for two weeks⟩ — often used in pl. with *the* ⟨worried about how to keep the child occupied for the ~*s*⟩ **d :** a period of exemption (as from a tax or from fear) ⟨tax ~*s* up to ten years —J.P.McEvoy⟩ ⟨gave myself a ~ from sad forebodings —Mary B. Chesnut⟩ **:** a period of relief ⟨a ~ from periodical literature —Aldous Huxley⟩ **3 a :** a day marked by a general cessation from work as an act of public commemoration of some event and often accompanied by public ceremonies and parades — see LEGAL HOLIDAY, NATIONAL HOLIDAY **b :** a good time **:** a festive occasion ⟨massacring soldiers to make a despot's ~ —H.R.G.Greaves⟩ **4 :** a spot accidentally left uncovered on a coated or painted surface

²holiday \"\ *adj* **:** of, belonging to, or befitting a holiday **:** FESTIVE, CAREFREE ⟨~ reading⟩ ⟨wearing ~ clothes⟩ ⟨a face with a ~ look⟩ ⟨~ atmosphere on the excursion boat⟩

³holiday \"\ *vi* **:** to take or spend a holiday esp. in a journey or at a resort ⟨~*ing* in the country⟩

holiday disease *n* [so called fr. its frequent occurrence after holidays as a result of overexertion] **:** azoturia of horses

hol·i·day·er \'hälə,dāə(r)\ *n* -s [³*holiday* + *-er*] **:** one on a holiday **:** VACATIONER ⟨~*s* who want to lead the fairly simple life for their all too short two-week break —Marvin Schwartz⟩

holiday flag *n* **:** the largest size of the national flag flown (as at U.S. Navy shore installations and Marine Corps posts) on national holidays and special occasions — compare GARRISON FLAG

holidaymaker \'==(,)=,==\ *n* **:** HOLIDAYER ⟨boatloads of ~*s* —*Nat'l Geographic*⟩

hol·i·days \'hälə,dāz\ *adv* **:** on holidays **:** on any holiday

holier *comparative of* HOLY

¹holier-than-thou \'====;=\ *adj* [compar. of ¹*holy*] **:** marked by an objectionable air of usu. pious superiority ⟨preserved always an infuriating *holier-than-thou* attitude toward his erring younger brother⟩ ⟨loudly prayed with a *holier-than-thou* expression on his face —G.W.Benson⟩

²holier-than-thou \'====;=\ *n* -s **:** one that is holier-than-thou ⟨his success in self-reform turned him into a *holier-than-thou* before his less successful friends⟩

holiest *superlative of* HOLY

ho·li·ly \'hōlǝlē\ *adv* [ME, fr. *holy* + *-ly*] **:** in a holy manner **:** PIOUSLY

¹ho·li·ness \'hōlēnǝs, -lin-\ *n* -ES [ME *holynesse*, fr. OE *hālignes*, fr. *hālig* holy + *-nes* -ness — more at HOLY] **1 :** the quality or state of being holy **:** SANCTITY, SAINTLINESS ⟨the ~ of the saints⟩ ⟨the ~ of the consecrated place⟩ — often used as a title for various high religious dignitaries ⟨His *Holiness* Pope Pius XII⟩ ⟨His *Holiness* the Dalai Lama⟩ **2 :** a state of moral and spiritual perfection **:** complete sanctification **:** SINLESSNESS; *specif* **:** a state of sinlessness that according to some small religious groups is bestowed as a blessing on a Christian believer following conversion and is often a prerequisite of salvation

²holiness \"\ *adj, often cap* **:** emphasizing a perfectionist doctrine of holiness as a prerequisite of salvation ⟨the group was Arminian, Pentecostal, and *Holiness*⟩

holiness body *or* **holiness church** *n, often cap H* **:** one of numerous small religious groups in America emphasizing a perfectionist doctrine of holiness

holing *pres part of* HOLE

holis *pl of* HOLI

hol·ish·kes \'hȯlishkǝz\ *n pl* [Yiddish] **:** stuffed cabbage

ho·lism \'hō,lizǝm\ *n* -s [*hol-* + *-ism*] **1 :** the philosophic theory first formulated by Jan C. Smuts that the determining factors in nature are wholes (as organisms) which are irreducible to the sum of their parts and that the evolution of the universe is the record of the activity and making of these wholes **2 :** a theory or doctrine according to which a whole cannot be analyzed without residue into the sum of its parts or reduced to discrete elements — compare GESTALT PSYCHOLOGY, ORGANICISM

ho·list \'hōlǝst\ *n* -s [*hol-* + *-ist*] **:** an advocate of holism or holistic principles ⟨a ~ who denied that the English state, for example, is a logical construction out of individual people, and who asserted that it is an organism which develops, and responds to challenges, according to holistic laws —J.W.N. Watkins⟩

ho·lis·tic \(')hō'listik\ *adj* **1 :** of, relating to, or based on holism **2 a :** in accordance with a theory of holism or conceptions advocated by holism ⟨the ~ strain in his thinking⟩ **b :** emphasizing the organic or functional relation between parts and wholes ⟨a ~ rather than an atomistic approach to the study of culture⟩ — **ho·lis·ti·cal·ly** \-tǝk(ǝ)lē\ *adv*

holk \'hōk\ *var of* ²HOWK

¹holl \'häl\ *adj* [ME, fr. OE *hol* — more at HOLE] *dial Eng* **:** HOLLOW

²holl \"\ *n* -s [ME, fr. OE *hol*, fr. neut. of *hol*, adj., hollow] **:** a hollow place: as **a :** *dial Eng* **:** DITCH **b** *obs* **:** a ship's hold

¹hol·land \'hälǝnd\ *n* -s *often cap* [ME *holand*, fr. *Holand*, county in the Netherlands, fr. MD *Holland*] **1 a :** a linen shirting of former times made in the Netherlands **b :** a cotton or linen fabric in plain weave usu. heavily sized or glazed and used for window shades, bookbinding, clothing **2 :** a smooth glazed or unglazed finish for cotton fabrics to make them opaque or semiopaque **3 :** ²DUTCH 1b

²holland \"\ *adj, usu cap* [fr. *Holland* the Netherlands, kingdom in northwestern Europe] **1 :** NETHERLANDS **2 :** of or belonging to a landholding company organized in Holland about 1791 to sell land in western New York state to settlers ⟨*Holland* purchase⟩

hol·lan·daise \ˌhälǝn'dāz\ *n* -s **:** GOULASH 2a

hollandaise sauce *also* **hollandaise** *n* -s [part trans. of F *sauce hollandaise*, lit., Dutch sauce, fr. *sauce* + *hollandaise*, fem. of *hollandais* Dutch, fr. *Hollande* Holland, country in northwestern Europe] **:** sauce made of butter, yolks of eggs, and lemon juice or vinegar

holland blue *n, often cap H* **:** a dark blue that is redder and duller than Peking blue or Flemish blue and greener and less strong than Japan blue — called also *canton, orion*

hol·land·er \'hälǝndǝ(r)\ *n* -s **1** *cap* **a :** a native or inhabitant of the Netherlands **b :** a Dutch ship **2** *often cap* **:** DUTCH CLINKER **3** *often cap* [so called fr. its invention in the Netherlands] **:** a paper-pulp beater typically consisting of an iron roll set with steel blades and revolving in an oval tub

holland gin *n, usu cap H* **:** HOLLANDS

hol·land·ite \'hälǝn,dīt\ *n* -s [Sir Thomas H. *Holland* †1947 Brit. geologist + E *-ite*] **:** a mineral $MnBaMn_6O_{14}$ consisting of a crystallized manganate of barium and manganese from central India

hol·lands \'hälǝn(d)z\ *n, usu cap* [modif. of D *hollandsch* Dutch, fr. *hollandsch genever* Dutch gin] **:** gin made in the Netherlands

hol·lan·tide \'hälǝn·,tīd\ *n, usu cap* [by shortening & alter.] *dial Eng* **:** ALLHALLOWTIDE

¹hol·ler \'hälǝ(r)\ *vb* **hollered; hollered; hollering** \-l(ǝ)riŋ\ **hollers** [alter. of ²*hollo*] *vi* **1** *chiefly dial, of a bird or animal* **:** to utter its characteristic cry or call ⟨spring frogs were ~*ing* in the marsh last night⟩ **2 a :** to make a loud noise ⟨the children were seeing who could ~ the loudest⟩ **b :** to shout or cry out to attract attention or summon someone ⟨~ for help⟩ or in pain or fear ⟨heard his brothers ~*ing* as they were killed —G.F.Weisel⟩ or in enthusiasm or exuberance ⟨baseball fans ~*ing* for the team⟩ **3 :** GRIPE, COMPLAIN, GRUMBLE ⟨people will always ~ about an increase in taxes⟩ ~ *vt* **1 a :** to express by hollering ⟨~ encouragement⟩ **b :** to call out (a word or phrase) ⟨~ uncle⟩ ⟨~ bloody murder⟩ **2** *chiefly dial* **:** to call or summon by hollering — often used with *out* ⟨wake up first in the morning and ~ out the ranch hands⟩

²holler \"\ *n* -s **1 :** a shout or outcry esp. of joy or exuberance ⟨with a whoop and a ~ the winners left⟩ or to attract attention or summon aid **2 :** GRIPE, COMPLAINT ⟨the new law brought a ~ from the minority⟩ **3 :** an American Negro work song freely improvised usu. in terms of the particular occupation of the moment and often without words ⟨cornfield ~⟩ — compare JUBILEE 8

³holler \"\ *chiefly dial var of* HOLLOW

holler guy *n, slang* **:** a member of a team who unofficially but effectively assumes responsibility for the success of the team during a game by the direction of play or by constant encouraging chatter

hollering *adj* [fr. pres. part. of ¹*holler*] **:** marked by or as if by shouting ⟨~ headlines . . . were always about murder of one sort or another —William Saroyan⟩

hollering distance *n, dial* **:** HAILING DISTANCE

hol·ler·ith machine \'hälǝrǝth-\ *also* **hollerith** *n* -s *usu cap H* [after Herman *Hollerith*, 19th cent. inventor] **:** a machine for tabulating and sorting punched cards and tabulating data from them

hollies *pl of* HOLLY

hol·lin *or* **hol·len** \'hälǝn\ *n* -s [ME *holen, holyn*, fr. OE *holen, holegn* — more at HOLLY] *dial Brit* **:** HOLLY

¹hol·lo \'hä(,)lō, hä'lō, hǝ'lō\ *or* **hol·la** \'hälǝ; hä'lä, hǝ'l-, -'lä\ *or* **hol·loo** \'hä(,)lü, hä'lü, hǝ'lü\ *also* **hol·loa** \'hä(,)lō, hä'lō, hǝ'lō\ *interj* [origin unknown] **1** — used to attract attention **2** — used as a call of encouragement or jubilation

²hollo \"\ *or* **holla** \"\ *or* **holloo** \"\ *also* **holloa** \"\ *vb* -ED/-ING/-ES *vi* **:** to cry hollo **:** call out **:** HOLLER ~ *vt* **1 a :** to call or cry hollo to **:** attract the attention of **b :** to call encouragement to **2 :** to utter loudly **:** HOLLER ⟨that reeling man . . . ~*ing* bawdy inanities —C.C.Morrison⟩

³hollo \"\ *or* **holla** \"\ *or* **holloo** \"\ *also* **holloa** \"\ *n, pl* **hollos** *or* **holloes** *or* **hollas** *or* **holloos** *also* **holloas :** an exclamation or call of hollo ⟨listening to the ~*s* of the fox hunters⟩ **:** HOLLOING, SHOUTING, HOLLER

hol·long \'hä,lȯŋ\ *n* -s [Assamese *holoṅ* large] **:** an East Indian timber tree (*Dipterocarpus pilosus*) having resinous decay-resistant wood

¹hol·low \'hä(,)lō, -lǝ *often* -lǝw+V\ *adj, often* -ER/-EST [ME *holwe, holg, holh*, fr. *holg, holh* hole, den, fr. OE *holh* hole, hollow — more at HOLE] **1 a :** constituting a depression or a low or excavated place ⟨a ~ spot in the road⟩ ⟨the force of the meteor's fall made a ~ place in the open plain⟩ **:** curved or rounded inward **:** CONCAVE ⟨the dish was covered by a ~ piece of metal⟩ **:** SUNKEN ⟨~ temples⟩ **b :** marked by hollows or sunken areas ⟨his face became gaunter and more ~ with each passing year⟩ **c** *of the sea* **:** having deep-troughed waves **d :** having a concave face or surface — used of various tools esp. when designed for curved work ⟨~ adz⟩ ⟨~ auger⟩ ⟨~ punch⟩ **2 a** (1) **:** having an empty space or cavity within **:** not solid ⟨a ~ tree⟩ ⟨~ sphere⟩ (2) *of a two-dimensional figure* **:** being in outline only **:** not filled in **:** consisting partly of unfilled spaces ⟨~ letters⟩ **b :** EMPTY ⟨a ~ walnut⟩ ⟨a ~ feeling in the stomach⟩ **c** (1) **:** devoid of worth, value, significance, or substance ⟨a ~ victory⟩ ⟨a ~ gain⟩ ⟨the whole celebration seems strangely ~ and unreal —W.F.Hambly⟩ ⟨the ~ position taken by the opposition⟩ **:** lacking in qualities that give substance, worth, or moral or intellectual solidity ⟨men of social significance but essentially ~⟩ (2) **:** devoid of any significant ideas, principles, or purposes ⟨we are the ~ men —T.S.Eliot⟩ ⟨a ~ generation of youths⟩ **d :** having hollow spaces in the interior; *esp* **:** having a net area less than 75 percent of the gross area — used of a masonry unit (as a brick or building tile) **3 a :** sounding or reverberating like a sound made in a cave or large empty enclosure **:** muffled and sepulchral **:** breathy and lacking in overtones **:** producing confused echoes ⟨the car in the empty garage started with a ~ roar⟩ ⟨the ~ echo of the monkeys' call —M.P.O'Connor⟩ ⟨the ~ subdued sound of the wind outside —Robert Murphy⟩ **b :** making or being a sound of or as if of beating on a hollow enclosure ⟨the ~ drumming of horses' hooves on the bridge⟩ **4 :** marked by insincerity or lack of good faith ⟨a ~ greeting to an enemy⟩ ⟨a ~ promise⟩ **:** FALSE, DECEITFUL, TREACHEROUS ⟨a ~ heart⟩ ⟨a ~ truce⟩ ⟨talk about war aims sounded ~ to them —F.L. Allen⟩ **5 :** COMPLETE, THOROUGH **syn** see VAIN

²hollow \"\ *vb* -ED/-ING/-S [ME *holwen*, fr. *holwe*, adj.] *vt* **1 a :** to make hollow **:** form an indentation or concavity in — usu. used with *out* ⟨~ out half of a coconut shell⟩ ⟨~*ed* a place out in the cliffside where he could hide⟩ **b :** to make concave or cause to be curved or rounded inward ⟨the can cover must be cut in two, and each half so ~*ed* as to fit around the pipe —Emily Holt⟩ ⟨the short double woolly scarf which you could ~ into a cap —Fred Majdalany⟩ **c** (1) **:** to gouge, dig, or scrape the inside out of — usu. used with *out* ⟨~*ed* out a stump and filled it with concrete⟩ (2) **:** GUT — often used with *out* ⟨dozens of dead cities, their insides ~*ed* out by dynamite and fire —Norman Cousins⟩ **2 :** to form by hollowing something out ⟨rain barrels ~*ed* out from trees —Robert Shaplen⟩ **:** EXCAVATE — usu. used with *out* ⟨engineers ~*ed* out a tunnel through the mountain⟩ ~ *vi* **:** to become hollow ⟨her cheeks ~*ed* suddenly as she sucked in her breath⟩

³hollow \"\ *n* -s [¹*hollow*] **1 :** a low spot surrounded by elevations **:** a depressed or low part of a surface **:** CONCAVITY, CHANNEL, BASIN ⟨driving down through the ~ in the road⟩ ⟨the ~ of the hand⟩; *esp* **:** a small valley **:** RAVINE, NOTCH, DINGLE **2 a :** an unfilled space within anything **:** CAVITY, HOLE ⟨in the ~ of a tree⟩ **b :** an area marked by such a space or cavity ⟨the horse buses rumble by, dropping a note as their hooves strike the ~ of the bridge —*Times Lit. Supp.*⟩ ⟨pounding on the ~ of the wall⟩

⁴hollow \"\ *adv* [¹*hollow*] **:** HOLLOWLY ⟨the attacks on him rang ~ because he had proved his honesty and integrity⟩

holloware \'=(,)=,=\ *n* [by alter.] **:** HOLLOW WARE

hollow back *n* **:** a book back in which the backs of the sections are affixed to the backbone of the cover only at the joints, the separation sometimes being made by a flattened tubular lining of paper or cloth; *also* **:** a book so bound or a style of binding featuring this construction — called also *open back, spring back;* compare TIGHT BACKBONE; see SPINE illustration

hollow cabochon *n* **:** a cabochon with a concave back

hollow charge *n* **:** an explosive which concentrates its force in one direction (as in a projectile designed to blow a hole through armor plate)

hollow-cut \'=(,)=¦=\ *adj* **:** made with a pile cut in graduated lengths for a corded effect — used of normally even-pile fabrics (as velveteen)

hollow-faced bat \'==,=-\ *n* **:** any of various Asiatic or African bats (genus *Nycteris*) with a basin-shaped depression in the front of the skull that is margined by fleshy foliate outgrowths

hollow-ground \¦=(,)=¦=\ *adj* **:** ground so as to have a concave surface behind the cutting edge ⟨a *hollow-ground* razor⟩ ⟨a *hollow-ground* blade of a skate⟩

hollow handle *n* **:** a haft of a piece of silver flatware molded of two hollow halves soldered together and fastened to the shank of the object (as a knife or a serving fork or spoon)

hollow heart *n* **:** an abnormal condition of potato tubers which is usu. the result of rapid and uneven growth and in which the central tissue ruptures and leaves a cavity

hollow horn *n* **:** debility in cattle popularly attributed to the hollowness of their horns

hollow-horned \¦=(,)=¦=\ *adj* **1 :** having permanent horns with a bony core into which the frontal sinuses often extend to form air spaces (as in cattle, sheep, goats, and true antelopes) **2** *of lumber* **:** HONEYCOMBED

hollow-horning \'=(,)=,==\ *n, of lumber* **:** HONEYCOMBING

hol·low leg *n, slang* **:** an unusual capacity for alcoholic drinks

hol·low·ly *adv* **:** in a hollow manner ⟨the sound echoed ~ in the cave⟩

hollow mill *n* **:** a milling cutter with three or more cutting edges enclosing and revolving around the cylindrical workpiece

hol·low·ness *n* -ES [ME *holowenesse*, fr. *holwe, holowe* hollow + *-nesse* -ness] **:** the quality or state of being hollow ⟨testing the wall for ~ by tapping on it lightly⟩ ⟨the ~ and trickery of these appeals —F.D.Roosevelt⟩ ⟨the ~, the sham, the silliness of the empty pageant —Oscar Wilde⟩

hollow newel *n* **:** an opening in the center of a winding staircase in place of a newel-post, the stairs being supported each step by those below, and all held in place by the wall — called also *open newel;* distinguished from *solid newel*

hollow newel stair *n* **:** OPEN-NEWEL STAIR

hollow organ *n* **:** any visceral organ that has the form of a hollow tube or pouch (as the stomach or intestine) or that includes a cavity which subserves a vital function (as the heart or bladder)

hollow square *n* **:** a formation of troops in former military tactics in the shape of a square with the sides each usu. consisting of several ranks of soldiers and the middle holding the officers and the colors

hollow stalk *or* **hollow stem** *n* **:** any plant disease characterized by degeneration or decay of the pith of the stalk (as of tobacco caused by *Erwinia aroideae* or of cauliflower caused by boron deficiency)

hollow tail *n* **:** WOLF-IN-THE-TAIL

hollow wall *n* **:** CAVITY WALL

hollow ware *n* **:** articles (as of pottery, glass, or metal) that have volume and significant depth ⟨cups, bowls, and pots are typical *hollow ware*⟩ — distinguished from *flatware*

holls *pl of* HOLL

hol·lus·chick \'häləs,chik\ *n, pl* **holluschick·ie** \-kē\ [modif. of Russ *kholostyak* bachelor] **:** a young male fur seal

hol·ly \'hälē, -li\ *n* -ES *often attrib* [ME, fr. OE *holegn, holen;* akin to OHG *hulis* holly, ON *hulfr*, MIr *cuilenn*] **1 a :** a tree or shrub of the genus *Ilex* (as English holly or American holly) — see CHINESE HOLLY, INKBERRY 1; compare MATÉ **b :** the foliage or branches of this tree or shrub used for esp. Christmas decoration **2 :** a tree whose leaves resemble those of holly (as *Prunus ilicifolia* and *Photinia arbutifolia* of California, members of the genus *Olearia* of New Zealand, or the holm oak) **3 :** SEA HOLLY

European holly

holly bay *n* **1 :** LOBLOLLY BAY **2 :** EVERGREEN MAGNOLIA

holly family *n* **:** AQUIFOLIACEAE

holly fern *n* **:** any of certain ferns having fronds of a texture and glossy surface suggesting holly: as **a :** an evergreen fern (*Polystichum lonchitis*) of the north temperate zone **b :** a Californian fern (*Polystichum aculeatum*) that is often cultivated for ornament **c :** a tropical Old World fern (*Cyrtomium aculeatum*)

hollygrape \'==,=\ *n* **:** OREGON GRAPE

holly green *n* **1 :** a dark yellowish green that is greener, stronger, and very slightly darker than average palm green, greener, lighter, and stronger than deep chrome green or average hunter green, and greener and deeper than golf green **2 :** a moderate olive green that is yellower and paler than forest green and yellower, lighter, and stronger than cypress or Lincoln green

hol·ly·hock \'hälē,häk, -li,-, -,hȯk\ *n* -s [ME *holihoc*, fr. *holi*, *holy* holy + *hoc* hock (mallow)] **1 :** a tall perennial Chinese herb (*Althaea rosea*) cultivated in gardens as a biennial with large coarse rounded leaves and showy flowers in a large terminal spike **2 :** a deep purplish red that is bluer and deeper than Harvard crimson (sense 2) or American beauty and redder and duller than magenta (sense 2a)

hollyhock delphinium *n* **:** any of various cultivated larkspurs with narrow flower clusters forming spires

hollyhock tree *n* **:** an Australian shrub (*Hibiscus splendens*) with showy rose-colored flowers

holly laurel *n* **:** ISLAY

holly leaf miner *n* **:** a small black fly (*Phytomyza ilicis*) having a yellowish larva that tunnels in the leaves of various hollies

holly–leaved barberry \¦==¦=-\ *or* **hollyleaf barberry** \'==-,=-\ *n* **:** OREGON GRAPE

holly–leaved cherry *or* **hollyleaf cherry** *n* **:** ISLAY

holly oak *n* **:** an oak (as the holm oak) with leaves like holly

holly rose *n* **:** a West Indian shrub (*Turnera ulmifolia*) with showy yellow flowers

¹hol·ly·wood \'hälē,wu̇d, -li,-\ *n, usu cap* [fr. *Hollywood*, district in the city of Los Angeles, California] **1 a :** the American motion-picture industry ⟨a lawyer speaking for *Hollywood* before an investigating committee⟩ **b :** a place constituting a center for a motion-picture industry ⟨there are many *Hollywoods* besides the one in California —*N.Y. Times*⟩ **2 :** something produced by or befitting the American motion-picture industry or its productions ⟨pure *Hollywood* —Will Irwin & T.M.Johnson⟩

²hollywood \"\ *adj, usu cap* **1 :** of or from Hollywood, a district of Los Angeles, Calif. **:** of the kind or style prevalent in Hollywood ⟨a *Hollywood* fashion⟩ **2 :** of, relating to, produced by, or characteristic of the American motion-picture industry esp. as centered in Los Angeles, Calif., and vicinity ⟨a *Hollywood* film technique⟩

hollywood bed *n, usu cap H* **1 :** a bed consisting of a mattress on a box spring supported by 4 or 6 low legs and sometimes having an upholstered headboard separately fastened to a wall **2 :** any bed on a low frame and without a footboard, corner posts, and sometimes a headboard

Hollywood bed

hollywood gin *or* **hollywood** *n, usu cap H* [so called fr. its introduction by the motion-picture colony in Hollywood] **:** a method of scoring in gin rummy whereby each deal is scored as though part of three different games

¹hol·ly·wood·ian \ˌhälē'wu̇dēən, -li'-\ *n* -s *cap* **:** a native or resident of Hollywood, Calif.; *also* **:** a person employed in the Hollywood motion-picture industry

²hollywoodian \¦==¦===\ *adj, cap* **:** of or befitting Hollywood or Hollywoodians

hol·ly·wood·ish \'hälē,wu̇dish\ *adj, usu cap* **:** HOLLYWOODIAN ⟨*Hollywoodish* klieg lights and grinding cameras —*Newsweek*⟩ ⟨a *Hollywoodish* sort of bombast —Moses Smith⟩

hol·ly·wood·ite \'==,wu̇,dīt\ *n* -s *cap* **:** HOLLYWOODIAN

hol·ly·wood·ize \-,dīz\ *vt* -ED/-ING/-S *often cap* **:** to make (as an author or his writings) conform to standards set up by the American motion-picture industry ⟨does not believe that the author can be completely *Hollywoodized* —A.A.VanDuym⟩

hollywood palm *n, usu cap H* **:** a glabrous perennial (*Kalanchoe verticillata*) of southern Africa that is used as an ornamental pot plant and that has long linear leaves mottled with violet brown and terminal clusters of salmon to scarlet flowers

hol·ly·woody \-ūdē\ *adj, usu cap* **:** characterized by the less desirable qualities attributed to motion pictures as produced by Hollywood ⟨the story was called thick and *Hollywoody* —Janet Flanner⟩

¹holm *or* **holme** \'hōm *also* -ōlm\ *n* -s [ME, fr. OE *holm*, fr. ON *holmr* small island; akin to OE *holm* sea, OS *holm* hill, OE *hyll* hill — more at HILL] **1** *Brit* **:** a small island in a river or lake or near the mainland — often used in place names **2** *chiefly Brit* **:** low flat land near a river **:** BOTTOMS

²holm \"\ *n* -s [ME, alter. of *holen* holly, fr. OE — more at HOLLY] **:** HOLM OAK

holm·berry \'=- — *see* BERRY\ *n* [²*holm* + *berry*] **:** the berry of the butcher's-broom

holmes·ian \'hōmzēən *also* -ōlm-\ *adj* [Sherlock *Holmes*, a detective in stories by Sir Arthur Conan Doyle †1930 Brit. writer + E *-ian*] *usu cap* **:** of, belonging to or suggesting the detective Sherlock Holmes

holmes light \'hōmz- *also* -ōlmz-\ *or* **holmes signal** *n, usu cap H* [prob. fr. the name *Holmes*] **:** a signaling device that consists of a case containing impure calcium phosphide and a float and that when thrown into water generates hydrogen phosphides that take fire spontaneously

holm·gang \'hō(l)m,gaŋ\ *n* [ON *hōlmganga*, fr. *hōlmr* small island + *ganga* act of going; akin to OE *gang* act of going — more at GANG] *archaic* : a duel esp. on an island

holm·gren yarn test \'hōm\|grən, -,gren- *also* -ōlm\|\ *also* **holm·gren test** *n, usu cap H* [after Alarik Frithiof *Holmgren* †1897 Swed. physiologist] : a method of testing color vision by the use of colored wool yarns

holmi·um \'hō(l)mēəm\ *n* -s [NL, fr. *Holmia* (latinized form of *Stockholm*, Sweden) + NL *-ium*; fr. the locality near which minerals rich in yttrium are found] : a trivalent metallic element of the rare-earth group that occurs with yttrium (as in gadolinite) and that forms cream-colored or yellow compounds which are among the most highly magnetic known — symbol *Ho;* see ELEMENT table

holm oak *n* [²holm] **1** : an evergreen oak (*Quercus ilex*) of southern Europe with leaves resembling those of holly **2** : the hard wood of the holm oak

holm·quist·ite \'hōm,kwi,stīt *also* -ōlm-\ *n* -s *usu cap* [Sw *hölmquistit*, fr. Per Johan *Hölmquist*, Swed. scientist + Sw *-it* -ite] : a mineral $(Na,K,Ca)Li(Mg, Fe)_3Al_2Si_8O_{22}(OH)_2$ consisting of an alkali and a silicate of iron, magnesium, lithium, and aluminum and related to hornblende

holm tree *n* [ME *holme tre*, fr. ²*holm* + *tree*] : HOLM OAK

holo- — see HOL-

holo·axial \¦hälō, ¦hōlō+\ *adj* [*hol-* + *axial*] *of a crystal system* : having all the axes of symmetry possible

holo·baptist \"+\ *n* [*hol-* + *Baptist*] : IMMERSIONIST

holo·basidium \"+\ [NL, fr. *hol-* + *basidium*] *syn of* AUTOBASIDIUM

holo·benthic \"+\ *adj* [*hol-* + *benthic*] : inhabiting the deep sea during all stages of life

hol·o·blas·tic \¦hälō¦blastik, ¦hōl-\ *adj* [ISV *hol-* + *-blastic*] *of an egg* : undergoing complete cleavage as a result of the absence of an impeding mass of yolk material : having cleavage planes that divide the whole egg into distinct and separate though coherent blastomeres — opposed to *meroblastic* — **hol·o·blas·ti·cal·ly** \-tək(ə)lē\ *adv*

hol·o·branch \'häla,braŋk, 'hōl-\ *n* -s [NL, fr. *hol-* + *-branch*] : a fish gill in which the branchial arch has two rows of lamellae or filaments — compare HEMIBRANCH 2

hol·o·car·pic \¦hälō¦kärpik, ¦hōl-\ *adj* [*hol-* + *-carpic*] **1** : having the whole thallus developed into a fruiting body or sporangium ⟨~ algae⟩ ⟨~ fungi⟩ **2** : lacking rhizoids and haustoria — compare EUCARPIC

hol·o·car·pous \-pəs\ *adj* [*hol-* + *-carpous*] : HOLOCARPIC 1

holo·caust \'hälə\|,kȯst, 'hōl- *also* 'hōl- *or* \|,käst *sometimes* -lē\| *or* -li\| *or* \|,kəst\ *n* -s [ME, fr. OF *holocauste*, fr. LL *holocaustum*, fr. Gk *holokauston*, neut. of *holokaustos* burnt whole, fr. *hol-* + *kaustos* burnt, fr. *kaiein* to burn — more at CAUSTIC] **1** : a burnt sacrifice : a sacrificial offering wholly consumed by fire **2** : a complete or thorough sacrifice or destruction esp. by fire ⟨burned all his books and paper in a giant ~⟩ ⟨thousands of enemy troops consumed in the ~ —Upton Sinclair⟩ ⟨an atomic global ~ —J.B.Conant⟩ — **holo·caus·tic** \¦==-¦kȯstik, -tēk *also* -¦käs-\ *adj*

holo·cellulose \¦hälō, ¦hōlō+\ *n* [ISV *hol-* + *cellulose*; orig. formed in G] : the total polysaccharide fraction of wood or straw and the like that is made up of cellulose and all of the hemicelluloses and that is obtained by removing the extractives and the lignin from the original natural material

hol·o·cene \'hälə,sēn, 'hōl-\ *adj, usu cap* [ISV *hol-* + *-cene*] : RECENT 3

hol·o·cen·trid \,hälō'sen·trəd, ,hōl-\ *n* -s [NL *Holocentridae*] : a fish of the family Holocentridae

hol·o·cen·tri·dae \-rə,dē\ *n pl, cap* [NL, fr. *Holocentrus*, type genus + *-idae*] : a family of tropical marine fishes closely related to and in old classifications included in the Berycidae

hol·o·cen·trus \-rəs\ *n, cap* [NL, fr. *hol-* + *-centrus* (fr. Gk *kentros* sharp point, fr. *kentein* to prick, goad) — more at CENTER] : the type genus of the family Holocentridae containing certain typical squirrelfishes

hol·o·ceph·a·la \,hälō'sefələ, ,hōl-\ [NL, fr. *hol-* + *-cephala*] *syn of* HOLOCEPHALI

¹**hol·o·ceph·a·lan** \¦==¦==lən\ *or* **hol·o·ce·pha·li·an** \¦hälōsə-¦fālēən, ¦hōl-\ *adj* [NL *Holocephali* + E *-an* or *-ian*] : of or relating to the subclass Holocephali

²**holocephalan** \"\ *or* **holocephalian** \"\ *n* -s : a fish of the subclass Holocephali

hol·o·ceph·a·li \¦hälō¦sefə,lī, ¦hōl-\ *n pl, cap* [NL, fr. *hol-* + *-cephali*] : a subclass of Chondrichthyes that is sometimes made a separate class, includes the recent chimaeras and certain chiefly extinct related fishes some of which date from Devonian time, and is distinguished by a cartilaginous skeleton, gill clefts covered by a fold of skin, high compressed head with small narrow mouth and the dentition reduced to broad flat plates, and a body tapering off into a long tail — **hol·o·ceph·a·lous** \¦==¦sefələs\ *adj*

hol·o·cho·a·nite \¦hälō¦kōə,nīt, ¦hōl-\ *n* -s [NL *Holochoanites*, suborder of nautiloids in some classifications, fr. *hol-* + Gk *choanē* funnel (fr. *chein* to pour) + NL *-ites* -ite — more at FOUND] : a fossil nautiloid in which the funnels about the siphuncle extend from one septum to the next — **hol·o·cho·a·nit·ic** \¦==,==¦nid·ik\ *adj*

ho·loch·ro·al \hə'läkrəwəl\ *adj* [*hol-* + Gk *chrōs* skin, color + E *-al* — more at GRIT] : having compound eyes with the visual area covered by a continuous cornea — used esp. of certain trilobites

hol·o·clas·tic \¦hälō¦klastik, ¦hōl-\ *adj* [ISV *hol-* + *-clastic*] : being or belonging to ordinary sedimentary rocks as distinguished from tuffs or pyroclastic rocks

hol·o·coe·not·ic \¦hälōsē¦näd·ik, ¦hōl-\ *adj* [*hol-* + *coen-* + *-otic*] : acting in concert — used of the impact of a complex environment on living organisms

hol·o·crine \'häləkrən, 'hōl-, -ə,krīn\ *adj* [ISV *hol-* + *-crine* (fr. Gk *krinein* to separate, decide) — more at CERTAIN] : producing a secretion consisting of altered secretory cells; *also* : produced by a holocrine gland — compare MEROCRINE

holo·crystalline \¦hälō, ¦hōlō+\ *adj* [ISV *hol-* + *crystalline*] : completely crystalline : made up wholly of crystals or crystalline particles — used of a rock (as granite)

hol·o·dac·tyl·ic \¦hälō(,)dak¦tilik, ¦hōl-\ *adj* [MGk *holodaktylos* (fr. Gk *hol-* + *daktylos* dactyl) + E *-ic*] *of a hexameter* : having all the feet dactyls except the last

hol·o·dis·cus \,hälō'diskəs, ,hōl-\ *n, cap* [NL, fr. *hol-* + *-discus*] : a small genus of shrubs (family Rosaceae) of western No. America that resemble spirea and have flowers in a pendant pyramidal panicle and achenes enclosed in the calyx

holo·enzyme \¦hälō, ¦hōlō+\ *n* [ISV *hol-* + *enzyme*] : a complete active enzyme consisting of an apoenzyme combined with its coenzyme

holo·gamete \"+\ *n* [*hol-* + *gamete*] : a hologamous gamete

ho·log·a·mous \hə'lägəməs\ *adj* [*hol-* + *-gamous*] **1** : having gametes of essentially the same size and structural features as vegetative cells — used of various flagellates, ciliates, diatoms, and desmids **2** : having the entire thallus developing into a gametangium — used of thalloid plants, esp. fungi

ho·log·a·my \-mē\ *n* -ES [*hol-* + *-gamy*] : the condition of being hologamous

hol·o·go·nia \,hälə'gōnēə, ,hōl-\ *n pl, cap* [NL, fr. *hol-* + *-gonia* (fr. Gk *gonos* offspring, procreation, genitals) — more at GON-] *in some classifications* : an order of Nematoda comprising forms in which the germinal area extends the whole length of the gonad — compare TELOGONIA — **hol·o·gon·ic** \¦==-¦gänik\ *adj*

holo·gonidium \¦hälō, ¦hōlō+\ *n* [NL, fr. *hol-* + *gonidium*] : SOREDIUM

¹**hol·o·graph** \'hälə,graf, 'hōl-\ *n* [LL *holographus* written entirely in one's own hand, fr. LGk *holographos*, fr. Gk *hol-* + *-graphos* written, writing (fr. *graphein* to write) — more at CARVE] : a document (as a letter, deed, or will) wholly in the handwriting of the person from whom it proceeds and whose act it purports to be

²**holograph** \"\ *or* **hol·o·graph·ic** \¦==¦grafik\ *or* **hol·o·graph·i·cal** \-fəkəl\ *adj* : being a holograph : written entirely in one's own hand

holographic will *n* : a testamentary instrument that is written entirely by the testator in his own handwriting and signed by him and that even if unattested is usu. recognized as a valid will in most jurisdictions

holo·gynic \¦hälō, ¦hōlō+\ *adj* [ISV *hol-* + *gynic*] : inherited solely in the female line, presumably through transmission as a recessive factor in the nonhomologous portion of the X chromosome — **ho·log·y·ny** \hə'läjənē\ *n* -ES

hol·o·he·dral \¦hälō¦hēdrəl, ¦hōl-\ *adj* [*hol-* + Gk *hedra* seat + E *-al* — more at SIT] *of a crystal* : having all the faces required by complete symmetry — compare HEMIHEDRAL, TETARTOHEDRAL — **hol·o·he·drism** \,==¦hē,drizəm\ *n* -s — **hol·o·he·dry** \-ēdrē\ *n* -ES

hol·o·he·dron \,==¦hēdrən\ *n, pl* **holohedrons** *or* **holohedra** [NL, fr. *hol-* + *-hedron*] : a holohedral crystal form

holo·hemihedral \¦hälō, ¦hōlō+\ *adj* [*hol-* + *hemihedral*] : belonging to, presenting, or being hemihedral crystal forms

holo·hyaline \"+\ *adj* [*hol-* + *hyaline*] *of a rock* : wholly glassy

ho·lo·ku \hō'lōkü\ *n* -s [Hawaiian *holokū*] : a woman's long one-piece gown usu. made with some fitting and a train and worn esp. in Hawaii

holo·mastigote \¦hälō, ¦hōlō+\ *adj* [*hol-* + *mastigote*] : having many flagella scattered evenly over the body

holo·metabola \"+\ *n pl, cap* [NL, fr. *hol-* + *Metabola*] *in some classifications* : a group comprising all insects that have complete metamorphosis

holo·metabolic \"+\ *adj* [*hol-* + *metabolic*] : HOLOMETABOLOUS

holo·metabolism \"+\ *n* [*hol-* + Gk *metabolē* change + E *-ism* — more at METABOLISM] *of an insect* : development with complete metamorphosis — distinguished from *heterometabolism*; compare AMETABOLISM — **holo·metabolous** \"+\ *adj*

holo·metaboly \"+\ *n* [ISV *hol-* + *metaboly*] : HOLOMETABOLISM

hol·o·mic·tic \¦hälō¦miktik, ¦hōl-\ *adj* [*hol-* + *-mictic* (fr. Gk *miktos* mixed; akin to Gk *misgein* to mix) — more at MIX] *of a lake* : undergoing a complete circulation that extends to the deepest parts during overturn

hol·o·mor·pho·sis \,hälō'mȯrfəsəs, ,hōl- *sometimes* -ō,mȯr-'fōsəs\ *n, pl* **holomorpho·ses** \-,sēz\ [NL, fr. *hol-* + *-morphosis*] : the complete regeneration of a lost part

hol·o·my·ar·i·an \¦hälō(,)mī¦a(a)rēən, ¦hōl-\ *also* **hol·o·my·ar·i·al** \-əl\ *adj* [NL *Holomyaria*, division of nematode worms in some classifications (fr. *hol-* + *-myaria*) + E *-an* or *-al*] *of a nematode worm* : having the muscle layer continuous or divided into two longitudinal zones without true muscle cells

holo·nephros \¦hälō, ¦hōlō+\ *n* [NL, fr. *hol-* + *-nephros*] : a hypothetical generalized vertebrate kidney consisting of a single nephric tubule in each trunk segment of either side of the body

holo·parasite \"+\ *n* [ISV *hol-* + *parasite*; orig. formed as G *holoparasit*] : an obligate parasite — compare HEMIPARASITE — **holo·parasitic** \"+\ *adj*

hol·o·pho·tal \¦hälə¦fōd·ᵊl, ¦hōl-\ *adj* [*hol-* + *phot-* + *-al*] : of or relating to a holophote; *esp* : reflecting the whole of the light from a light source in a given direction

hol·o·phote \'==,fōt\ *n* -s [back-formation fr. *holophotal*] : an optical apparatus for collecting and throwing in a desired direction by means of lenses or reflectors a large amount of the light from a source (as a lighthouse lamp)

holo·phrase \'hala,frāz, 'hōl-\ *n* [*hol-* + *phrase*] : a single word expressing a complex of ideas; *also* : HOLOPHRASIS

ho·loph·ra·sis \hə'läfrəsəs\ *n, pl* **holophra·ses** \-,sēz\ [*hol-* + Gk *phrasis* expression, phrase] : the expression of a complex of ideas by a single word; *also* : HOLOPHRASE

hol·o·phrasm \'hälə,frazəm, 'hōl-\ *n* -s [fr. *holophrastic*, after such pairs as E *spasm*: *spastic*] : HOLOPHRASE

hol·o·phras·tic \¦==¦frastik\ *adj* [ISV *hol-* + *-phrastic* (fr. Gk *phrastikos* expressive, fr. *phrazein* to express) — more at PHRASE] : of or relating to holophrasis : equivalent to a whole phrase : expressing a complex of ideas in a single word

hol·o·phyt·ic \¦hälō¦fid·ik, ¦hōl-\ *adj* [*hol-* + *-phytic*] : obtaining food after the manner of a green plant : PHOTOAUTOTROPHIC — opposed to *holozoic*; compare HEMIZOIC

hol·o·plank·ton \,hälō'plaŋktən, ,hōl-\ *n* [ISV *hol-* + *plankton*] : plankton composed of organisms that pass their whole life floating, drifting, or swimming weakly in the water — compare HEMIPLANKTON — **hol·o·plank·ton·ic** \¦==(,)plaŋk¦tänik\ *adj*

hol·o·plast \'hälō,plast, 'hōl-\ *n* -s [*hol-* + *-plast*] : paneling made of plastic-impregnated paper tubes with a variety of surfaces

hol·op·neus·tic \¦häləp¦n(y)üstik, ¦hōl-\ *adj* [ISV *hol-* + *-pneustic* (fr. Gk *pneustikos* of or for breathing, fr. — assumed — Gk *pneustos* — verbal of Gk *pnein* to breathe — + Gk *-ikos* -ic) — more at SNEEZE] : having all the spiracles or tracheal stigmata open — distinguished from *apneustic*; used of various insects

hol·optic \(')häl, (')hōl+\ *adj* [*hol-* + *optic*] *of a two-winged fly* : having the compound eyes contiguous in front — compare DICHOPTIC

¹**hol·op·tych·i·an** \¦häləp¦tikēən, ¦hōl-\ *adj* [NL *Holoptychius* + E *-an* (adj. suffix)] : ¹HOLOPTYCHIID

²**holoptychian** \"\ *n* -s [NL *Holoptychius* + E *-an* (n. suffix)] : ²HOLOPTYCHIID

¹**hol·op·tych·i·id** \-ēəd\ *adj* [NL *Holoptychiidae*] : of or relating to the Holoptychiidae

²**holoptychiid** \"\ *n* -s [NL *Holoptychiidae*] : a fish of the family Holoptychiidae

hol·op·ty·chi·idae \,häləptə'kīə,dē, ,hōl-\ *n pl, cap* [NL, fr. *Holoptychius*, type genus + *-idae*] : a family of Devonian fishes (order Rhipidistia) having unossified vertebrae, teeth of complicated structure, and the body covered with imbricating cycloid enameled scales

hol·op·tych·i·us \,==¦tikēəs\ *n, cap* [NL, fr. *hol-* + *-ptychius* (fr. Gk *ptych-*, *ptyx* fold) — more at PTYCH-] : the type genus of Holoptychiidae

holo·rhinal \¦hälō, ¦hōlō+\ *adj* [*hol-* + *rhinal*] *of a bird* : having the anterior border of the nasal bones not deeply cleft — opposed to *schizorhinal*

holo·saprophyte \"+\ *n* [ISV *hol-* + *saprophyte*; orig. formed in G] : a totally saprophytic organism : an obligate saprophyte — compare HEMISAPROPHYTE

holo·sericeous \"+\ *adj* [*hol-* + *sericeous*] : covered with silky hair : entirely sericeous

hol·o·side \'hälə,sīd, 'hōl-\ *n* -s [ISV *hol-* + *-oside*] : a glycoside that yields only glycoses on hydrolysis — compare HETEROSIDE

holo·siderite \¦hälō, ¦hōlō+\ *n* [ISV *hol-* + *siderite*] : meteoric iron or a meteorite consisting of metallic iron without stony matter

holo·siphonate \"+\ *adj* [*hol-* + *siphonate*] : having a completely tubular siphon — used of the Dibranchia

hol·o·so·ma·ta \,hälō'sōməd·ə, ,hōl-, -'säm-\ *n pl, cap* [NL, fr. *hol-* + Gk *-somata*] *in some classifications* : a division of ascidians comprising compound ascidians with zooids of which the bodies are not divided into regions and sometimes including the simple ascidians — **hol·o·som·a·tous** \¦==-¦sämad·əs, -¦sōm-\ *adj*

hol·o·spondaic \¦hälō, ¦hōlō+\ *adj* [*hol-* + *spondaic*] : made up wholly of spondees

¹**ho·los·te·an** \hə'lästēən\ *or* **ho·los·te·ous** \-ēəs\ *adj* [NL *Holostei* + E *-an* or *-ous*] : of or relating to fishes of the order Holostei

²**holostean** \"\ *n* -s : a fish of the order Holostei

ho·los·tei \-ē,ī\ *n pl, cap* [NL, fr. *hol-* + *-ostei* (fr. Gk *osteon* bone) — more at OSSEOUS] *in many classifications* : an order of ganoid fishes having a well-developed bony skeleton and approaching teleosts in structure now usu. restricted to the gars (family *Lepisosteidae*) and various extinct genera (as *Lepidotes* and *Semionotus*) but sometimes extended to include the bowfin and related fishes or made a superorder including the teleosts — compare CYCLOGANOIDEI, GINGLYMODI

holo·steric \¦hälō, ¦hōlō+\ *adj* [ISV *hol-* + *steric*] : wholly solid — used of a barometer (as the aneroid) constructed without the use of liquids

ho·los·te·um \hə'lästēəm\ *n, cap* [NL, fr. Gk *holosteon*, a plant, fr. *hol-* + *osteon* bone] : a Eurasian genus of plants (family Caryophyllaceae) resembling chickweed and having the flowers in cymes like umbels — see JAGGED CHICKWEED

hol·o·sto·ma·ta \,hälō'stōməd·ə, ,hōl-, -täm-\ *n pl, cap* [NL, fr. *hol-* + *-stomata*] *in many classifications* : a suborder of Digenea coextensive with the family Strigeidae

hol·o·stom·a·tous \¦==¦stäməd·əs, -tōm-\ *adj* [*hol-* + *-stomatous*] : having the margin of the aperture entire and more or less circular ⟨~ gastropod shells⟩

hol·o·stome \'hälə,stōm, 'hōl-\ *adj or n* [NL *Holostomata*] : STRIGEID

ho·los·to·mous \hə'lästəməs\ *adj* [*hol-* + *-stomous*] : HOLOSTOMATOUS

hol·o·sty·lic \¦hälō¦stīlik, ¦hōl-\ *adj* [*hol-* + *-stylic*] : having the jaws connected directly with the cranium ⟨~ chimaeras⟩ — compare AUTOSTYLIC

holo·symmetric \¦hälō, ¦hōlō+\ *or* **holo·symmetrical** \"+\ *adj* [*hol-* + *symmetric, symmetrical*] : HOLOHEDRAL — **holo·symmetry** \"+\ *n*

holo·systematic \"+\ *adj* [*hol-* + *systematic*] : HOLOHEDRAL

holo·systolic \"+\ *adj* [ISV *hol-* + *systolic*] : relating to an entire systole

holo·thecal \"+\ *adj* [*hol-* + *thecal*] : BOOTED 2

holo·thoracic \"\ *adj* [*hol-* + *thorac-* + *-ic*] : having the three parts of the thorax closely united ⟨~ insects⟩ — compare SCHIZOTHORACIC

hol·o·thu·ria \,hälō'thu̇rēə, ,hōl-\ *n, cap* [NL, fr. L, a water polyp, fr. Gk *holothourion*] **1** : a Linnaean genus containing various rather wormlike aquatic animals (as some gephyreans and holothurians) originally thought to be modified mollusks **2** : a large cosmopolitan genus of holothurians that is the type of the family Holothuriidae and is characterized by the presence of scattered more or less papillate pedicels — compare TREPANG

hol·o·thu·ri·ae \-ē,ē\ [NL, fr. *Holothuria*] *syn of* HOLOTHURIOIDEA

¹**hol·o·thu·ri·an** \¦==¦thu̇rēən\ *adj* [NL *Holothuria* + E *-an*] : belonging to the Holothurioidea

²**holothurian** \"\ *n* -s : one of the Holothurioidea : SEA CUCUMBER

hol·o·thu·rid·ea \,hälōthə'ridēə, ,hōl-\ *or* **hol·o·thu·roi·da** \-'rȯidə\ [NL, fr. *Holothuria* + *-idea* or *-oida*] *syn of* HOLOTHURIOIDEA

hol·o·thu·ri·idae \-'rīə,dē\ *n pl, cap* [NL, fr. *Holothuria*, type genus + *-idae*] : a large cosmopolitan family (order Aspidochirota) of holothurians that includes all those of economic importance — see HOLOTHURIA

¹**hol·o·thu·ri·oid** \¦hälō¦thu̇rē,ȯid, ¦hōl-\ *adj* [NL *Holothurioidea*] : ¹HOLOTHURIAN

²**holothurioid** \"\ *n* -s [NL *Holothurioidea*] : ²HOLOTHURIAN

hol·o·thu·ri·oi·dea \,==,==¦ȯidēə\ *n pl, cap* [NL, fr. *Holothuria* + *-oidea*] : a class of echinoderms comprising the sea cucumbers and having a more or less elongate form usu. with well-marked bilateral symmetry and differentiated dorsal and ventral surfaces, a flexible but tough and muscular body with the skeleton reduced to scattered ossicles or spicules, a water-vascular system with radial ambulacral vessels and tube feet for creeping, respiratory trees, Cuvierian organs, and strong branched tentacles about the mouth — compare TREPANG

hol·o·thu·roi·dea \,hälōthə'rȯidēə, ,hōl-\ [NL, irreg. fr. *Holothuria* + *-oidea*] *syn of* HOLOTHURIOIDEA

hol·o·trich \'hälə-,trik, 'hōl-\ *n* -s [NL *Holotricha*] : a protozoan of the order Holotricha

ho·lot·ri·cha \hə'lä·trəkə\ *n pl, cap* [NL, fr. *hol-* + *-tricha*] : a large order of uniformly ciliated euciliate protozoans without adoral zone, usu. with a cytostome, and with holozoic or saprozoic nutrition — **ho·lot·ri·chal** \-kəl\ *or* **ho·lot·ri·chous** \-kəs\ *adj* — **ho·lot·ri·chous·ly** *adv*

hol·o·trich·i·da \,hälō'trikədə, ,hōl-\ [NL, fr. *Holotricha* + *-ida*] *syn of* HOLOTRICHA

holo·type \'hälə,tīp, 'hōl-\ *n* [*hol-* + *type*] **1** : the single specimen designated by an author as the type of a species or lesser taxon at the time of establishing a group — compare LECTOTYPE **2** : the type of a species or lesser taxon designated at a date later than that of establishing a group or by another person than the author of the taxon — compare NEOTYPE — **holo·typ·ic** \¦==¦tipik\ *adj*

hol·o·zo·ic \¦hälō¦zōik, ¦hōl-\ *adj* [*hol-* + *-zoic*] : obtaining food after the manner of most animals by ingesting complex organic matter : HETEROTROPHIC — opposed to *holophytic*; compare HEMIZOIC

holp *now chiefly dial past of* HELP

holped *now chiefly dial past of* HELP

holpen *now chiefly dial past part of* HELP

hols *pl of* HOL

hol·stein–friesian \'hōl,z,tēn, -l,st- *also* -tīn *or NewEng* 'hälə-(,)stēn\ *or* **holstein** *n* [fr. *Holstein*, region of NW Germany, its later locality + *Friesian*] **1** *usu cap H&F* : a breed of large dairy cattle orig. from northern Holland and Friesland that produce large quantities of comparatively low-fat milk and that are usu. black and white in irregular patches **2** -s *often cap H&F* : any animal of the Holstein-Friesian breed

¹**hol·ster** \'hōlztə(r), -l(t)st-\ *n* -s [D; akin to OE *heolstor* darkness, cover, ON *hulstr* case, Goth *hulistr* veil, OE *helan* to conceal — more at HELL] **1** : a usu. leather case for a pistol that is often open at the top to facilitate quick withdrawal, that often conforms to the pistol's shape, and that is usu. carried at the belt or under one arm or often at the front of a saddle **2** **holsters** *pl* : housings or standards for a set of rolls in steel manufacturing

holster 1

²**holster** \"\ *vt* **holstered; holstered; holstering** \-t(ə)riŋ\ **holsters** : to place in a holster

holster stock *n* : a pistol holster that can be attached to the pistol to form a shoulder stock

¹**holt** \'hōlt\ *n* -s [ME, fr. OE; akin to OHG *holz* wood, ON *holt*, L *clades* destruction, Gk *klados* twig — more at GLADIATOR] **1** *now dial* **a** : a small woods : COPSE **b** : a wooded hill or rise **2** : a planted grove of osiers or willows

²**holt** \"\ *n* -s [ME, alter. of ²*hold*] **1** ²HOLD 3 **2** *dial Brit* : a den or lair esp. of a burrowing animal (as an otter)

ho·lus-bo·lus \¦hōləs¦bōləs\ *adv* [prob. redupl. of *bolus*] : all at once : ALTOGETHER ⟨gulped it down, *holus-bolus*⟩ ⟨existing economic system was taken over *holus-bolus* —A.J.Brewer⟩

¹**ho·ly** \'hōlē, -li\ *adj* -ER/-EST [ME *holy*, *hooly*, *haly*, fr. OE *hālig*; akin to OHG *heilag* holy, ON *heilagr*, Goth *hailags*, OE *hāl* whole — more at WHOLE] **1** **a** : set apart and dedicated to the service or worship of God or a god : HALLOWED, SACRED ⟨~ vessels⟩ ⟨the ~ priesthood⟩ **b** : dedicated to or laying claim to being dedicated to a sacred or selfless purpose ⟨gave money to various ~ causes⟩ **2** **a** (1) : perfect in righteousness and divine love : infinitely good : worthy of complete devotion and trust : commanding one's fullest powers of adoration and reverence ⟨the ~ Lord God Almighty⟩ (2) : of or befitting something that is perfect or worthy in this way ⟨a smile of ~ sweetness —George Meredith⟩ **b** : spiritually whole, sound, or perfect : of unimpaired innocence or proved virtue : pure in heart : GODLY, PIOUS — often used in mild oaths ⟨my ~ aunt⟩ **3** **a** : venerated because of association with someone or something holy ⟨~ relics⟩ ⟨the ~ cross⟩ **b** *of a saint or saintly person* : worthy of veneration ⟨~ martyrs⟩ **c** : to be treated with veneration or the utmost respect ⟨to him every action of the campaign was ~⟩ **d** : being awesome, frightening, or beyond belief ⟨the child was a ~ terror⟩ ⟨so frightened he had the ~ horrors⟩ **4** : not capable of being approached with impunity : filled with mysterious, superhuman, and potentially fatal power : dangerously powerful if violated ⟨some words are considered so ~ they must never be spoken aloud —Stuart Chase⟩

²**holy** \"\ *n* -ES [ME *holi*, adj., fr. OE] **1** [trans. of LL *sanctus*] : a holy place : SANCTUARY **2** *obs* : SAINT **3** *cap* : ²GOD 1 ⟨into the presence of the *Holy*⟩

holy ark *n, often cap H&A* : ARK 3

holy basil *n* : a basil (*Ocimum sanctum*) found in the tropics of the Old World that is extensively naturalized in tropical America and that in India is held sacred to Vishnu

holy bread *n* [ME *holy brede*] **1** : bread consecrated in the Eucharist **2** : bread provided for the Communion service **3** : ANTIDORON

holy cats *interj* — used as an exclamation of surprise, amazement, or bewilderment

holy clover *n* : SAINFOIN 1

holy communion *n, usu cap H&C* : COMMUNION 2

holy cow *interj* — used as an exclamation of surprise, amazement, or bewilderment
holy cross day *n, usu cap H&C&D* : HOLY-ROOD DAY 2
holy day *n* [ME *haly day*, fr. OE *hāligdæg* — more at HOLIDAY] **1 :** a day set aside as having special religious significance to be commemorated by religious services, feasting, or fasting; *specif* : HOLY DAY OF OBLIGATION **2** *archaic* : HOLIDAY
holy day of obligation 1 : one of the days on which Roman Catholics are obliged to hear mass and abstain from servile work ⟨Sunday is a common *holy day of obligation*⟩ **2 :** one of the days on which communicants of the Episcopal Church are obliged to take Communion
holy dollar *n* [by alter.] : HOLEY DOLLAR
holy doors *n pl, often cap H&D* : the doors and esp. the central doors in the iconostasis in an Eastern church that separate the bema from the main part of the church — called also *royal doors*
holy family *n, usu cap H&F* : a painting or piece of sculpture in which the infant Jesus and the Virgin are represented attended by sacred personages (as St. Joseph, the infant St. John Baptist, St. Elisabeth, and St. Anne or angels or fathers of the church)
holy father *n, usu cap H&F* : POPE 1a
holy fire *n* [ME *holy fuyre*, trans. of L *sacer ignis*] *archaic* : ERYSIPELAS
holy ghost *n, cap H&G* [ME *holi gost*, fr. OE *hālig gāst*, trans. of LL *spiritus sanctus*, trans. of Gk *pneuma hagion*, trans. of Heb *ruah ha-qodesh* holy spirit] : HOLY SPIRIT
holy ghost flower *also* **holy ghost orchid** *or* **holy ghost** *n, usu cap H&G* [so called fr. the resemblance of part of the flower to a dove, a symbol of the Holy Ghost] : DOVEFLOWER
holy grail *n, usu cap H&G* : ²GRAIL
holy grass *n* [so called fr. the custom in northern Europe of strewing it before church doors on saints' days] : any of several sweet-scented grasses of the genus *Hierochloe; esp* : SWEET GRASS
holy green *n* : TERRE VERTE 2
holy herb *n* [trans. of LGk *hierobotanē*] **1 :** YERBA SANTA **2 :** HOLY BASIL **3 :** VERVAIN 1
holy innocents' day *n, usu cap H&I&D* : the day of December 28 commemorating the children slain by Herod after he had been told by the Magi of the birth of a king of the Jews
holy joe *n, usu cap H&J, slang* : PARSON, CHAPLAIN
holy jumper *n, usu cap H&J* : JUMPER 1a
holy kiss *n* [trans. of LL *osculum sanctum*, trans. of Gk *philēma hagion*] : KISS OF PEACE
holy lamb *n, usu cap H&L* : AGNUS DEI 1
holy mackerel *interj* — used as an exclamation of surprise or amazement
holy moses *interj, usu cap H & M* — used as an exclamation of surprise or amazement
holy mysteries *n pl, usu cap H&M* : the liturgy in the Eastern Church
holy of holies [ME *holi of halowes*, trans. of LL *sanctum sanctorum*, trans. of Gk *to hagion tōn hagiōn*, trans. of Heb *qōdhesh haqqōdhāshīm*] **1 a :** the innermost chamber of a Jewish temple **b :** the bema in an Eastern Orthodox church : SANCTUARY **c :** a very sacred place ⟨father's study was always considered the *holy of holies* by the children⟩ **2 :** something considered as if very sacred ⟨defeated that legislative *holy of holies*, a veterans' pension bill —*Newsweek*⟩
holy oil *n* [ME *holi oylle*] **1 :** CHRISM 1a **2 :** olive oil blessed by a bishop or in an Eastern church by a priest — see OIL OF CATECHUMENS, OIL OF THE SICK **3 :** the oil taken from the lamps at the grave of a saint or in an Eastern church from the lamps at the altar and used for various blessings
holy one *n* **1** *cap H&O* : ²GOD a(1) ⟨the Lord, the *Holy One* of Israel —Isa 10:20 (RSV)⟩ **2** *often cap H&O* : ANGEL ⟨and behold, a watcher, a *holy one*, came down from heaven —Dan 4:13 (RSV)⟩ **3** *cap H&O* : CHRIST 1 ⟨the *Holy One* of God —Mk 1:24 (RSV)⟩
holy order *n, often cap H&O* [ME] **1 :** MAJOR ORDER **2 holy orders** *pl* : ORDINATION **3 :** ORDER 1a(2) — usu. used in pl.
holy people *n, usu cap H&P* : the supernatural beings of the sacred world who in the religion of the Navahos have great power to help or harm humans — contrasted with *Earth People*
holy place *n* **1 :** a place set apart for religious rites; *specif* : the larger chamber of the Jewish tabernacle and temple separated from the holy of holies by a veil **2 :** a place made sacred by association : SHRINE; *specif* : one of various places (as of the birth, death, resurrection, and ascension of Jesus) of religious pilgrimage
holy pole *n* [prob. alter. of *holey pole;* fr. its hollow stems] : ANT TREE
holy roller *n, usu cap H&R* **1 :** one of a minor religious sect in the U. S. and Canada whose meetings are often characterized by frenzied excitement — often taken to be offensive **2 :** one of various religious groups resembling the Holy Rollers — often taken to be offensive
holy-rood day *n, usu cap H&R&D* [ME *holi rode dei*] **1 :** the 3d day of May on which occurs the feast of the Invention of the Cross **2 :** September 14 — called also *Holy Cross Day*
holy sacrament *n, usu cap H&S* [ME] : SACRAMENT 2
holy saturday *n, usu cap H&S* [ME] : the Saturday immediately preceding the festival of Easter : the vigil of Easter
holy scripture *n, usu cap H&S* [ME] : BIBLE 1, 5
holy scriptures *n pl, usu cap H&S* : BIBLE 1, 5
holy smoke *interj* — used to express surprise or amazement ⟨*holy smoke!* You'd think a man 26 years old . . . would have more sense —E.J.Curran⟩
holy spear *n* : ¹LANCE 2c
holy spirit *n, cap H&S* [ME *hooli spirit*, trans. of LL *spiritus sanctus*] : the active presence of God in human life constituting the third person of the Trinity — called also *Holy Ghost*
¹holystone \ˈ==,=\ *n* [¹*holy* + *stone;* prob. fr. the fact that seamen likened it to a prayer book or bible] : a soft sandstone used to scrub a ship's decks
²holystone \"\ *vb* : to scrub with a holystone
holy synod *n* : a governing body in an autocephalous church being composed usu. of several bishops representing the whole episcopate of the particular church under the presidency of the primate
holy table *n, usu cap H&T* : the altar or communion table
holy thistle *n* **1 :** BLESSED THISTLE 1 **2 :** MILK THISTLE 1
holy thursday *n, usu cap H&T* [ME, fr. OE *hālig thunresdæg*] **1** ASCENSION DAY **2 :** MAUNDY THURSDAY
holytide \ˈ==,=\ *n* [ME *halitide*, fr. *hali* holy + *tide*] : a time devoted to religion
holy tree *n* : CHINABERRY 2
holy unction *n, often cap H&U* [ME *hooly unctioun*] : a ceremonial in Eastern Orthodox and various Catholic non-Roman churches of anointing with oil the dead or those in imminent danger of dying
holy war *n* **1 :** a war waged for what is regarded as a holy purpose **2 :** JIHAD
holy water *n* [ME, fr. OE *hāligwæter*, fr. *hālig* holy + *wæter* water] : water blessed by a priest and used as a purifying sacramental in church and home
holy-water sprinkler *n* : MORNING STAR 2
holy week *n, usu cap H&W* : the week before Easter in which the passion of Christ is commemorated among Christians
holy well *n* : a well or spring venerated often from pagan times for reputed healing properties
holy writ *n* [ME, fr. OE *hālige writu* holy writings] **1** *usu cap H&W* : BIBLE 1 **2 :** a writing that is taken to be as sacred as the Bible ⟨the potpourri of special nostrums . . . became a kind of political *holy writ* —N.E.Long⟩
holy year *n, usu cap H&Y* : a jubilee year
hom- *or* **homo-** *comb form* [L, fr. Gk, fr. *homos* — more at SAME] **1 :** one and the same : similar : alike ⟨*homo*geneous⟩ ⟨*hom*onym⟩ — opposed to *heter-* **2 :** homologous with a (specified) organic compound esp. with a formula containing one carbon and two hydrogen atoms CH_2 more than the compound to whose name the prefix is added ⟨*homo*serine $HOCH_2CH_2CH(NH_2)COOH$⟩ **3 :** from the same species : corresponding in type of structure ⟨*homo*graft⟩ ⟨*homo*lysin⟩
ho·ma \ˈhōmə\ *n* -s [Av *haoma* haoma, plant that is the source of haoma and is conceived as the tree of life — more at SOMA] **1 :** HAOMA **2** *or* **hom** \ˈhōm\ [*hom* fr. Per *hōm*, fr. Av *haoma*] : a stylized tree pattern originating in Mesopotamia as a symbol of the tree of life and used esp. in Persian textiles
¹hom·age \ˈ(h)ämij, -mēj\ *n* -s [ME *omage, homage*, fr. OF *omage, hommage*, fr. *om, omme, homme* man, vassal (fr. L *homin-, homo* man) + *-age;* akin to OE *guma* man, OHG *gomo*, ON *gumi*, Goth *guma* man, OPruss *smoy* human being, Toch B *śaumo* human being, L *humus* earth — more at HUMBLE] **1 a :** a feudal solemn public ceremony by which in return for a fief (as a tenancy of land) a man acknowledges himself the man or vassal of a lord and recognizes the rights and duties inherent in this relationship — compare COMMENDATION 4, FEALTY 1, LIEGE **b :** the relationship between a feudal lord and his man **c :** an act done or payment made in meeting the obligations of vassalage **2 :** a body of persons bound under feudal law by homage; *specif* : the body of tenants attending a manorial court or those acting as jury **3 a :** reverential regard : RESPECT, DEFERENCE ⟨the ~ that matter pays to spirit —Clive Bell⟩; *esp* : respect shown by external action : OBEISANCE ⟨then the ~ of . . . peers; and again the air was lively with the trumpets and drums —Hector Bolitho⟩ **b :** flattering attention : TRIBUTE ⟨turned to look at the young woman . . . and permitted himself the ~ of a smile —Guy McCrone⟩ ⟨the present pamphlet is a modest . . . ~ to one of the leading linguists of our times —André Martinet⟩ **syn** see HONOR
²homage \"\ *vt* -ED/-ING/-S [MF *hommager*, fr. *hommage*] : to pay homage to
homage blue *n* : a dark purplish blue that is slightly less strong and very slightly darker than Scotch blue and slightly less strong and very slightly lighter than national flag blue
hom·ag·er \-jə(r)\ *n* -s [ME *omager*, fr. MF *omagier, hommagier*, fr. *omage, hommage* + *-ier* -er] **1 :** one that pays homage **2 :** one who holds land by fief; *specif* : one of the tenants of a manor
homal- *or* **homalo-** *comb form* [NL, fr. Gk, fr. *homalos;* akin to Gk *homos* same — more at SAME] **1 :** flat : even ⟨*homalo*sternal⟩ **2 :** equal ⟨*homalo*graphic⟩
ho·ma·li·um \hōˈmalēəm, -māl-\ *n, cap* [NL, fr. *homal-* + *-ium*] : a large widely distributed genus of tropical trees (family Flacourtiaceae) including several that yield hard heavy durable timber used for construction or cabinetwork — see ARANGA
ho·mal·o·do·the·ri·um \hō,malədōˈthirēəm\ *n, cap* [NL, irreg. fr. *homal-* + Gk *odont-, odōn* tooth + NL *-therium* — more at TOOTH] : a genus of extinct So. American Miocene herbivorous mammals (order Notoungulata) the size of a small ox with the teeth comparatively undifferentiated, the 5-toed feet ending in heavy blunt claws, and the forefeet adapted for digging
homalographic *var of* HOMOLOGRAPHIC
hom·a·lo·no·tus \,häməlōˈnōdəs\ *n, cap* [NL, fr. *homal-* + *-notus*] : a genus of Silurian and Devonian trilobites having long indistinctly 3-lobed bodies
¹hom·a·lop·sid \;häməˈläpsəd\ *adj* [NL *Homalopsidae*] : of or relating to the Homalopsidae
²homalopsid \"\ *n* -s : a snake of the family Homalopsidae
hom·a·lop·si·dae \,==ˈ=sə,dē\ *n pl, cap* [NL, fr. *Homalopsis*, type genus (fr. *homal-* + *-opsis*) + *-idae*] : a family of venomous opisthoglyphous water snakes of southeastern Asia and northern Australia that are often included as a subfamily in the family Colubridae
ho·man's sign \ˈhōmənz-\ *n, usu cap H* [after John *Homans* †1954 Am. surgeon] : pain in the calf of the leg upon dorsiflexion of the foot with the leg extended that is diagnostic of thrombosis in the deep veins of the area
ho·mar·i·dae \hōˈmarə,dē\ *n pl, cap* [NL, fr. *Homarus*, type genus + *-idae*] : a family of decapod crustaceans (tribe Astacura) comprising the large-clawed lobsters
hom·a·rus \ˈhämərəs\ *n, cap* [NL, fr. F *homard* lobster, fr. MF, of Scand origin; akin to ON *humarr* lobster — more at CAMBARUS] : a genus of decapod crustaceans including the common lobsters of Europe and No. America and the little Cape lobster (*H. capensis*) of southern Africa and with the related genus *Nephrops* constituting a family (Homaridae or Nephropidae)
hom·atomic \;hōm, ;häm+\ *adj* [*hom-* + *atomic*] : consisting of like atoms
hom·atropine \(ˈ)hōm, (ˈ)häm+\ *n* [ISV *hom-* + *atropine*] : a poisonous crystalline ester $C_{16}H_{21}NO_3$ of tropine and mandelic acid used (as in the form of its hydrobromide) for dilating the pupil of the eye
hom·axial \(ˈ)hōm, (ˈ)häm+\ *or* **hom·ax·o·ni·al** \;=ˈak;sōnēəl\ *also* **hom·ax·on·ic** \-ˈ;sänik\ *adj* [*hom-* + *axial* or *-axonial, -axonic* (fr. Gk *axon-, axōn* axle, axis + E *-ial* or *-ic*) — more at AXIS] *biol* : having all the axes equal
¹hombre *var of* OMBRE
²hom·bre \ˈämbrē, ˈəm-, -m(,)brā\ *n* -s [Sp, man, fr. L *homin-, homo* — more at HOMAGE] : GUY ⟨that conceited ~ . . . will be riding in here —Zane Grey⟩ ⟨bad ~s held up the stagecoach⟩
hom·burg \ˈhäm,bərg, -bōg,-bəig *also* -bůrg *or* -bůəg\ *n* -s [fr. *Homburg*, town near Wiesbaden, Germany, where such hats were first made] *often cap* : a man's hat of smooth-finished felt with a stiff curled ribbon-bound brim and a high tapered crown creased lengthwise

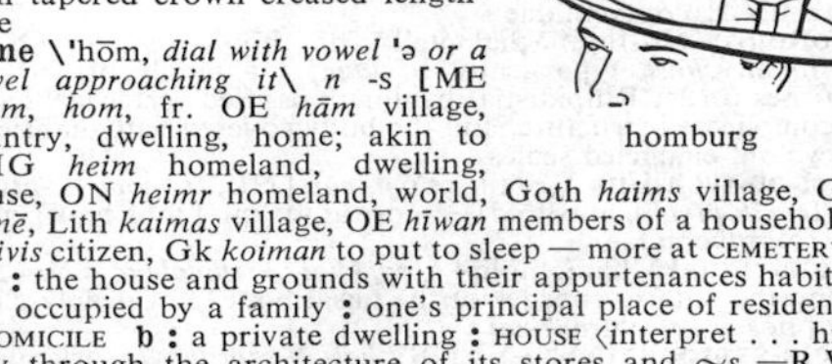
homburg

¹home \ˈhōm, *dial with vowel* ˈə *or a vowel approaching it*\ *n* -s [ME *hoom, hom*, fr. OE *hām* village, country, dwelling, home; akin to OHG *heim* homeland, dwelling, house, ON *heimr* homeland, world, Goth *haims* village, Gk *kōmē*, Lith *kaimas* village, OE *hīwan* members of a household, L *civis* citizen, Gk *koiman* to put to sleep — more at CEMETERY] **1 a :** the house and grounds with their appurtenances habitually occupied by a family : one's principal place of residence : DOMICILE **b :** a private dwelling : HOUSE ⟨interpret . . . history through the architecture of its stores and ~s —R.W. Howard⟩ **c :** the refuge or usual haunt of an animal ⟨the pool at the foot of the rapids is . . . the ~ of big trout —Alexander MacDonald⟩ **2 :** one's abode after death ⟨I'm but a stranger here, heaven is my ~ —T.R.Taylor⟩ **3 a :** the social unit formed by a family living together in one dwelling ⟨a man establishes a ~ and makes use of a specific piece of land —P.E. James⟩ **b :** the family environment to which one is emotionally attached : focus of domestic affections ⟨~ is where the heart is⟩ **4 a :** a familiar or suitable setting : congenial environment ⟨finds no spiritual ~ in the gang —John Brooks⟩ ⟨the theater would have been the proper ~ for his characters and plots —L.O.Coxe⟩ **b :** normal environment : HABITAT ⟨California is the ~ of the redwood⟩ ⟨the ~ of petroleum is in sedimentary rocks —A.M.Bateman⟩ **c :** center of cultivation : FOCAL POINT ⟨concept of a university as the ~ of learning —J.B. Conant⟩ **5 a :** the country or place of origin ⟨Britain is the ~ of railroads —Richard Joseph⟩ ⟨in the ~ of the direct primary —F.L.Paxson⟩; *specif* : MOTHER COUNTRY ⟨people . . . from the old ~s moved into the same pursuits because they had brought across similar skills —Oscar Handlin⟩ **b :** center or base of operations : LOCATION, HEADQUARTERS ⟨the amphitheater . . . will be the ~ of one of two festival companies —E.B.Radcliffe⟩ ⟨the four largest national broadcasting networks . . . have their ~ in the city —*Amer. Guide Series: N. Y.*⟩ ⟨the pilot . . . heads for ~ —*Newsweek*⟩ **6 :** an establishment taking the place of a home — see NURSING HOME, TOURIST HOME; compare FUNERAL HOME **7 a :** the objective toward which a player progresses in certain active sports (as baseball) or toward which he moves his pieces in various board games (as backgammon) **b :** an area in which a player is safe from attack **c :** one's original position in a square-dance set **d** (1) **:** either of two lacrosse positions nearest the opponent's goal (2) **:** a player assigned to either of these positions — compare INSIDE HOME, OUTSIDE HOME — **at home** \ətˈhōm *sometimes chiefly Brit & NewEng* əˈtōm\ **1 a :** in one's own house or home ⟨generally to be found *at home* in the morning⟩ **b :** ready to receive callers ⟨the newly wed couple will be *at home* after June 15⟩ **2 a :** in the country of origin : on the domestic front ⟨totalitarianism is despotic *at home* and expansionist abroad —George Fischer⟩ **b :** in the mother country ⟨people . . . *at home* and throughout the Commonwealth —Wendell Willkie⟩ **3 a :** in a familiar or congenial relationship : relaxed and comfortable : at ease ⟨a pleasant manner that soon made me feel *at home*⟩ ⟨he is . . . *at home* among the diplomatic and fashionable circles —Peggy Durdin⟩ **b :** in harmony with the surroundings : acclimated to the environment ⟨in the universities where basic research is most *at home* —M.H.Trytten⟩ ⟨*at home* in surf, the young abound in rock pools —J.L.B.Smith⟩ **4 :** on familiar ground : COMPETENT, KNOWLEDGEABLE ⟨*at home* in Italian opera —George Jellinek⟩ ⟨the sciences of biology and psychology in which the author is masterfully *at home*⟩
²home \"\ *adv* [ME *hoom, hom, home*, fr. OE *hām*, acc. of *hām*, n.] **1 a :** to or at one's principal place of residence ⟨go ~ on the bus⟩ ⟨stay ~ and practice the piano⟩ **b :** to one's family ⟨writes ~ once a week⟩ **c :** to or at the focus of one's sympathies ⟨has deserted the speculative heights . . . and is back ~ among the sweet and profound bums —Paul Pickrel⟩ **2 :** to or at the country or place of origin ⟨ordering diplomats ~ from various parts of the world⟩ ⟨customs differ from those back ~⟩; *specif* : to the mother country ⟨ordinances passed in the colonies are periodically transmitted ~⟩ **3 a :** to the final or closed position : to the full or ultimate limit ⟨drive a nail ~⟩ ⟨shove ~ a bolt⟩; *specif* : into position for loosing from a bow ⟨draw an arrow ~⟩ **b** (1) **:** to or toward a ship or its interior ⟨haul an anchor ~⟩ (2) **:** from the sea onto the shore ⟨the wind is blowing ~⟩ **c :** to an ultimate objective (as the finish line) in a game or sport : to the end of a course ⟨he had 33 on the outward nine and 35 coming ~ —*N. Y. Times*⟩ **d :** to a successful, rewarding, or winning end ⟨if the long shot comes ~ —Richard Scammon⟩ ⟨when my ship comes ~⟩ **4 a :** to the center of consciousness or sensitivity ⟨insights . . . whose truth strikes ~ to any candid and reflective mind J.H.Randall⟩ ⟨the full significance of this discovery was brought ~ to him —J.B.Conant⟩ **b :** to the point of uncovering underlying facts or truths ⟨questions are asked, parried, pressed ~ —R.W.Speaight⟩
³home \"\ *adj* [¹*home*] **1 :** of, relating to, or adjacent to a home ⟨the recent decline in ~ building⟩ ⟨yearned for some ~ cooking⟩ ⟨tramped with him over his ~ acres —Witmer Stone⟩ **2 a :** of or relating to the country or place of origin : DOMESTIC, NATIVE ⟨~ industry⟩ ⟨~ city⟩ ⟨~ language⟩; *specif* : of or relating to the mother country ⟨gap between the ~ and the Kenya points of view —Lionel Fleming⟩ **b :** of or relating to the vicinity of the home : LOCAL ⟨after finishing a preparatory course in the ~ academy . . . attended Yale College —F.L. Riley⟩ **c :** of or relating to a headquarters or base of operations ⟨~ territory⟩; *esp* : of an athletic team ⟨will close their ~ season today —*N.Y.Times*⟩ **3 a :** reaching the mark physically or emotionally : well-aimed and effective ⟨dispatched the bull with a dexterous ~ thrust⟩ ⟨this was a very ~ question —A.R.Smith⟩ **b :** being in proximity to or constituting the objective in a game or sport ⟨in Saturday's race he was forced . . . wide at the ~ turn —*Sydney (Australia) Bull.*⟩ ⟨the counter is moved around the board and up the path to the ~ space⟩ **4 :** ORIGINAL, NORMAL — used of the position of a machine or its parts ⟨the cylinder travels past the ~ position, and is then pushed back . . . against a catch —John Southward⟩
⁴home \"\ *vb* -ED/-ING/-S [¹*home*] *vi* **1 a :** to go or return home ⟨a plane ~s to its carrier⟩ ⟨when school is out a boy ~s to his dog and his marbles⟩; *specif, of an animal* : to return accurately to its home or natal area from a distance ⟨a pigeon ~s to its loft⟩ ⟨a salmon ~s to the stream in which it was spawned⟩ **b :** to move toward an objective by following a beam or landmark — usu. used with *on* or *in* ⟨picked up a radio beam and *homed* on it toward the fiord —Sloan Wilson⟩ ⟨mariners . . . sought the dark spires of Oakland's redwoods to ~ on —J.W.Noble⟩ ⟨with one engine out of action, the aircraft turned back and *homed* in on the . . . radio beacon —*U.N.Bull.*⟩ **c :** to become guided to a target by an emanation from it — usu. used with *on* or *in* ⟨the new long-range electric torpedo . . . ~s on the noise of the target ship's propellers —*N.Y.Times*⟩ ⟨keep the missile *homing* in on the source of heat —*Newsweek*⟩ **2 :** to have a home or headquarters ⟨several fine publishers have *homed* in that marvelous city —H.G.Merriam⟩ ~ *vt* **1 :** to send to or provide with a home ⟨radar installations . . . *homed* friendly aircraft to land bases —*Crowsnest*⟩ ⟨hidden pools and much wider creeks each of which *homed* its cranes —I.L.Idriess⟩ **2 :** to teach (a pigeon) to return to a loft
home- *or* **homeo-** *or* **homoe-** *or* **homoeo-** *also* **homoi-** *or* **homoio-** *comb form* [L & Gk; L *homoeo-*, fr. Gk *homoi-, homoio-*, fr. *homoios*, fr. *homos* — more at SAME] : like : similar ⟨*homeo*pathy⟩ ⟨*homoeo*graphy⟩ ⟨*homoio*thermic⟩
home-and-home \;==ˈ=\ *adj* : taking place alternately on the home grounds of competing teams or participants engaged in successive contests or contests related by being on the same schedule ⟨*home-and-home* series⟩
home base *n* **1 :** HOME PLATE **2 :** HOME 5b **3 :** HOME 7a
homebody \ˈ=,==\ *n* : one whose life centers around the home and its activities : STAY-AT-HOME ⟨he and his wife are *homebodies:* they love to read and listen to records —*Time*⟩
homeborn \ˈ=;=\ *adj* : home produced : INDIGENOUS ⟨~ hockey players breaking up the Canadian monopoly⟩
¹homebound \ˈ=,=\ *adj* [¹*home* + ⁴*bound*] : confined to the home ⟨~ invalid⟩ ⟨the old segmented family structure of the working father and the ~ mother —Anna & Arnold Silverman⟩
²homebound \ˈ=;=\ *adj* [¹*home* + ¹*bound*] : going homeward ⟨~ traveler⟩ ⟨became eligible for redeployment and were shipped to ~ outfits —W.J.Statoff⟩
homebred \ˈ=;=\ *adj* **1 :** HOMEBORN **2** *archaic* : having little experience outside the home : UNSOPHISTICATED
home brew *n* **1 :** an alcoholic beverage made at home or with homemade equipment usu. by trial-and-error methods **2 :** something formulated at home ⟨puritanism in rural England was never a *home brew;* it was always imported from the town —H.J.Massingham⟩
home car *n* : a freight car on the tracks of the railroad line to which it belongs — contrasted with *foreign car*
homecoming \ˈ=;==\ *n* -s [ME *homcomyng*, fr. *hom* home + *comyng* coming] **1 :** a return to or arrival at one's home ⟨take off for Lisbon on his last ~ —Henry La Cossitt⟩ ⟨dramatic moment of the bride's ~ —Sinclair Lewis⟩ **2 a :** the return of a group of people to a place formerly frequented or regarded as home ⟨a holiday celebrating the ~ of . . . illustrious natives —Thomas Sugrue⟩ **b :** an occasion for or celebration of such a return ⟨traveled halfway across the continent to be present at his college ~⟩
homecraft \ˈ=,=\ *n* : the household arts (as cooking); *esp* : handcrafts (as weaving) that may be practiced at home
home demonstration *n* : a demonstration of a new or useful method of performing a household task; *specif* : a demonstration given to women in rural areas by an agent of a government extension service
home economics *n pl but usu sing in constr* : the theory and practice of homemaking; *specif* : a field of study and research forming part of an academic curriculum of formal subjects and practical skills (as in nutrition, clothing, child care, home furnishing and decoration, household accounts, family and community relationships) necessary for good home management and family life
home economist *n* : a specialist in home economics
home edition *n* : CITY EDITION
home factor *n* : DOMESTIC FACTOR
homefelt \ˈ=,=\ *adj, archaic* : felt in one's own breast : INWARD, PRIVATE
home folks *n pl* : the people of one's home locality; *esp* : the members of one's immediate family
home freezer *n* : FREEZER 1d(2)
home fried potatoes *n pl* : COTTAGE FRIED POTATOES
home front *n* : a sphere of civilian activity directly or indirectly supporting the armed forces of a nation at war by production and supply of war materiel, civilian defense, and the preservation of public order and morale ⟨in somber contrast to the tinsel prosperity of the *home front* —Oscar Handlin⟩
homegrown \ˈ=;=\ *adj* **1 :** grown or produced at home or in the vicinity of the home : NATIVE, LOCAL ⟨~ corn⟩ ⟨~ bacon⟩ ⟨~ wool⟩ ⟨smoked bad ~ cigarettes —Upton Sinclair⟩ ⟨put up with ~ amateur talkers during most of the season —H.W. Wind⟩ **2 :** produced or located in or characteristic of the

home country or place of origin : DOMESTIC, INDIGENOUS ⟨~ politician⟩ ⟨~ literature⟩ ⟨~ industry⟩ ⟨a delightful mixture of ~ raffishness and imported elegance —Peggy Durdin⟩

home guard *n* : a force organized often on a volunteer basis for local defense or home protection esp. when the regular army is in a combat area — compare HOME RESERVE

home guardsman *n, pl* **home guardsmen** : a member of a home guard

home industry *n* : a gainful employment carried on in the home

homekeeping \ˈ⸗,⸗⸗\ *adj* : STAY-AT-HOME

home key *n* : one of the eight keys for the characters *asdf* and *jkl;* on which the fingers normally rest in starting position for touch typing — called also *guide key*

home·land \ˈhōm,land, -aa(ə)nd *also* -,lənd\ *n* **1** : country of origin : native land ⟨represents his ~ in international competition⟩; *specif* : MOTHER COUNTRY ⟨urged to . . . support the ~ — although many of them never had been citizens —Oscar Handlin⟩ **2** : chief place of residence : region in which one's home is located ⟨appetizing dishes from her ~, the Pennsylvania Dutch country —V.O.Williams⟩

home·less \-ləs\ *adj* : having no home or permanent place of residence ⟨the ~, unhappy, uprooted look of a displaced person —John Mason Brown⟩ — **home·less·ly** *adv*

home·less·ness *n* -ES : the quality or state of being homeless

homelife \ˈ⸗,⸗\ *n* : the domestic routine or way of living ⟨television will change the ~ of America —L.A.Appley⟩

homelike \ˈ⸗,⸗\ *adj* : having the qualities associated with family living : simple and wholesome : INVITING ⟨a ~ meal⟩ ⟨the hotel tries to create a ~ atmosphere⟩ — **home·like·ness** *n*

home·li·ness \ˈhōmlēnəs, -lin-\ *n* -ES [ME *hoomlynesse*, fr. *hoomly* homely + *-nesse* -ness] : the quality or state of being homely: **a** : COZINESS, INTIMACY **b** : lack of elegance, beauty, or refinement **c** : SIMPLICITY ⟨voters attracted by his ~ of speech⟩

¹**home·ly** \-lē,-li\ *adj* -ER/-EST [ME *hoomly, homly*, fr. *hoom, hom* home + *-ly* (adj. suffix) — more at HOME] **1** : HOMEY **2 a** : established on a friendly footing : INTIMATE — often used with *with* ⟨asked them to . . . dinner at our house and they came and were ~ with us —*Times Lit. Supp.*⟩ **b** : frequently encountered : COMMONPLACE, FAMILIAR ⟨translates the issue into ~ terms and makes the point beyond all doubt —Robert Bendiner⟩ ⟨an English garden full of the old ~ plants —David Ewen⟩ **3** : of a sympathetic character : KINDLY ⟨nature, the ~ nurse . . . has her own ways of comforting —G.G.Coulton⟩ **4 a** : natural and unaffected : SIMPLE ⟨~ courtesy⟩ ⟨a pastorale written in ~ muted prose about life on a farm —*New Yorker*⟩ **b** : free from ornament or complexity : PLAIN ⟨~ food⟩ ⟨shrines that are simple, quaint, ~ and common —J.C.Powys⟩ ⟨so many bizarre forms of dinosaur that these are almost ~ by comparison —W.E. Swinton⟩ **c** : free from ambiguity : DIRECT ⟨~ vigor of expression⟩ **d** : lacking in elegance or sophistication ⟨a ~ audience drawn from the surrounding farms⟩ **5** : lacking in physical beauty or proportion : plain-featured : UNATTRACTIVE ⟨an awkward, lanky giant whose ~ countenance was surmounted by a shock of rough black hair —Allan Nevins & H.S.Commager⟩ ⟨make possible retirement of at least two or three of the buildings . . . downright ~ to behold —B.F.Wright⟩ **syn** see PLAIN

²**homely** *adv* [ME *hoomly, homly*, fr. *hoom, hom* + *-ly* (adv. suffix)] *obs* : in a homely way : FAMILIARLY, KINDLY : RUDELY

home·lyn \ˈhōmlən, ˈhäm-\ *also* **homelyn ray** *n* -S [origin unknown] : a European ray (*Raja maculata*)

homemade \ˈhō,mād *also* -ōm\m-\ *adj* **1 a** : made or prepared in the home or on the premises ⟨~ bread⟩ ⟨~ skis⟩ **b** : constructed, produced, or acquired by one's own efforts ⟨~ jalopy⟩ ⟨this obviously ~ memoir —*New Yorker*⟩ ⟨a major with . . . a ~ education —Mari Sandoz⟩ **2** : of domestic origin or manufacture : NATIVE ⟨~ Saturday Reviews and Yankee Athenaeums —H.L.Mencken⟩ ⟨~ typewriters⟩

homemaker \ˈ⸗,⸗⸗\ *n* **1** : one that makes a home : one whose occupation is household and family management — usu. used of a wife and mother as distinguished from a paid housekeeper **2** : a welfare worker placed by a social agency to take care of a family during the absence or illness of the mother

homemaking \ˈ⸗,⸗⸗\ *n* : the creation and maintenance of a wholesome family environment — compare HOME ECONOMICS

home mission *n* : a religious mission conducted within the nation or national territories of the sponsoring church or organization — called also *national mission*; compare FOREIGN MISSION

home missionary *n* : a missionary appointed to a home mission

homeo- — see HOME-

ho·meo·blas·tic \ˌhōmēō¦blastik, ¦häm-\ *adj* [ISV *home-* + *-blastic*; orig. formed as G *homöoblastisch*] : having a texture corresponding to the equigranular in igneous rock and grains of approximately equal size — used of metamorphic rock

ho·meo·chromatic \ˌ⸗mē(ˌ)ō+\ *adj* [*home-* + *chromatic*] : of similar color

ho·meo·och·ro·nous \ˌhōmē¦äkrənəs, ¦häm-\ *adj* [*home-* + *-chronous*] : recurring at the same period of life in succeeding generations — used of organs, traits, or other characters; compare HETEROCHRONISM 1

ho·meo·crystalline \ˌhōmē(ˌ)ō, ¦häm-+\ *adj* [ISV *home-* + *crystalline*; orig. formed as G *homöokrystallinisch*] : having the crystals of the constituent minerals equally developed : GRANITIC

home office *n* : principal business location or base of operations : HEADQUARTERS ⟨the branch manager had a telegram from the *home office* informing him of price changes⟩ ⟨the diplomat cables the *home office* for instructions⟩

ho·me·ol·o·gy \ˌhōmēˈäləjē, ˌhäm-\ *n* -ES [*home-* + *-logy*] : SIMILARITY, LIKENESS

ho·meo·morph \ˈ⸗mēə,mȯrf\ *n* -S [ISV *home-* + *-morph*] : an individual bearing a superficial resemblance to another; *specif* : a crystalline substance exhibiting homeomorphism

ho·meo·mor·phic \ˌ⸗⸗⸗¦mȯrfik\ *adj* [*home-* + *-morphic*] **1** : characterized by homeomorphism; *specif* : topologically equivalent — used of geometric figures **2** : HOMOMORPHIC

ho·meo·mor·phism \-,fizəm\ *n* -S [ISV *homeomorphous* + *-ism*] **1** : a near similarity of crystalline forms between unlike chemical compounds — compare HETEROMORPHISM 2 **2** : a function that is a one-to-one mapping between sets such that both the function and its inverse are continuous and that in topology exists for geometric figures which can be transformed one into the other by an elastic deformation

ho·meo·mor·phous \-fəs\ *adj* [Gk *homoiomorphos* of like form, fr. *homoio-* home- + *-morphos* -morphous] **1** : manifesting homeomorphism **2** : HOMOMORPHOUS

ho·meo·mor·phy \ˈ⸗⸗⸗,⸗fē\ *n* -ES [*home-* + *-morphy*] : HOMOMORPHY

ho·meo·path \-,path\ *n* -S [G *homöopath*, fr. *homöo-* home- + *-path*] : a believer in or practitioner of homeopathy

ho·meo·path·ic \ˌ⸗⸗⸗¦pathik\ *adj* [G *homöopathisch*, fr. *homöo-* home- + *-pathisch* -pathic] **1** : of or relating to the belief in or practice of homeopathy ⟨~ remedy⟩ **2** : of a diluted or analogous nature ⟨a ~ abolitionist, intellectually persuaded rather than emotionally —W.A.White⟩ — **ho·meo·path·i·cal·ly** \-thək(ə)lē\ *adv*

homeopathic magic *n* : IMITATIVE MAGIC

ho·me·op·a·thy \ˌhōmēˈäpəthē, ˌhäm-\ *n* -ES [G *homöopathie*, fr. *homöo-* home- + *-pathie* -pathy] : a system of medical practice that treats a disease by the administration of minute doses of a remedy that would in healthy persons produce symptoms of the disease treated — compare ALLOPATHY

ho·meo·pla·sia \ˌ⸗mēō¦plāzh(ē)ə\ *n* -S [NL, fr. *home-* + *-plasia*] : a growth of tissue similar to normal tissue

ho·meo·plas·tic \ˌ⸗⸗⸗¦plastik\ *adj* [*home-* + *-plastic*] : formed by or related to homeoplasia

homeosis *var of* HOMOEOSIS

ho·me·osmotic \ˌhōmē, ¦hämē+\ *adj* [*home-* + *osmotic*] : having a relatively constant bodily osmotic pressure that is maintained independent of the osmotic pressure of the external environment — compare POIKILOSMOTIC

ho·meo·sta·sis \ˌhōmēō'stāsəs, ˌhäm-, -'stasəs; -mē'ästəsəs\ *n* -ES [NL, fr. *home-* + *-stasis*] **1** : a tendency toward maintenance of a relatively stable internal environment in the bodies of higher animals through a series of interacting physiological processes (as the maintenance of a fairly constant degree of body heat in the face of widely varying external temperatures) **2** : a tendency toward maintenance of a relatively stable psychological condition of the individual with respect to contending drives, motivations, and other psychodynamic forces **3** : a tendency toward maintenance of relatively stable social conditions among groups with respect to various factors (as food supply and population among animals) and to competing tendencies and powers within the body politic, to society, or to culture among men

ho·meo·stat·ic \ˌ⸗mēō¦stad·ik\ *adj* [*home-* + *-static*] : related to or characterized by homeostasis

homeotherm, homeothermic, homeothermy *var of* HOMOIOTHERM, HOMOIOTHERMIC, HOMOIOTHERMY

homeotic *var of* HOMOEOTIC

ho·meo·transplant \ˌhōmē(ˌ)ō, ¦häm-+\ *or* **ho·moio·trans·plant** \hȯ¦mȯiō+\ *n* [*home-* + *transplant*] : HOMOGRAFT

¹**ho·meo·type** \ˈhōmēə, ˈhäm+,-\ *n* [*home-* + *type*] : a biological specimen that has been carefully compared with and identified with an original or primary type

²**homeotype** \"\ *adj* : HOMEOTYPIC

ho·meo·typic *also* **ho·meo·typical** \ˌ⸗⸗⸗+\ *adj* [*home-* + *typic, typical*] : being or relating to the second or equational meiotic division — compare HETEROTYPIC, MEIOSIS

homeowner \ˈ⸗,⸗⸗\ *n* : one that owns a home

ho·meo·zo·ic \ˌhōmēō¦zōik, ¦häm-\ *adj* [ISV *home-* + *-zoic*] : of, relating to, or being one or more biogeographic regions throughout which the forms of life are the same or similar

homeplace \ˈ⸗,⸗\ *n* : a family home or its location

home plate *n* : a 5-sided slab of whitened rubber that is 17 inches wide and anchored flush with the ground at the apex of the baseball diamond, that determines the width of the strike zone, and that must be touched by a base runner in order to score a run — called also *home, home base, platter, rubber*; see BASEBALL illustration

home port *n* **1** : the port from which a ship hails or from which it is documented **2 a** : the port from which a man-of-war normally operates **b** : the dockyard in which a ship in the British navy is commissioned and refitted

home position *n* : HOME 7c

¹**ho·mer** \ˈhōmə(r)\ *also* **cho·mer** \ˈkō-\ *n* -S [Heb *ḥōmer*] : an ancient Hebrew unit of capacity for dry or liquid measure equal to about 10½ or in later times 11½ bushels or about 100 gallons

²**hom·er** \ˈhōmə(r)\ *n* -S [¹*home* + *-er*] **1** : HOMING PIGEON **2 a** : HOME RUN **b** *slang* : a sports official who favors the home team

³**homer** \"\ *vi* **homered; homered; homering** \-m(ə)riŋ\ **homers** : to hit a home run

home rails *n pl* : shares of domestic railroads offered on the London Stock Exchange

home range *n* : the area to which an animal confines his activities — compare TERRITORY

home remedy *n* : a simply prepared medication or tonic often of unproven effectiveness administered without prescription or professional supervision — compare FOLK MEDICINE

home reserve *n* : a part of the organized armed forces of a country whose members live at home, carry on their usual vocations, and except for occasional calls for drill or instruction are liable to call only in emergency — called also *militia, national guard, territorial reserve*; compare HOME GUARD

ho·me·ria \hōˈmirēə\ *n, cap* [NL, fr. *Homer*, Greek poet + NL *-ia*] : a genus of southern African herbs (family Iridaceae) that resemble tulips and are sometimes poisonous to cattle — see CAPE TULIP

ho·me·ri·an \hōˈmirēən, -mēr-\ *adj, usu cap* [*Homer* + E *-ian*] : HOMERIC

ho·mer·ic \hōˈmerik, -rēk\ *adj, usu cap* [L *Homericus*, fr. Gk *Homērikos*, fr. *Homēros* Homer, traditional Greek epic poet who prob. lived *ab* the 8th cent. B.C. + Gk *-ikos* -ic] **1** : of or relating to the Greek poet Homer, his age, or his writings ⟨classical *Homeric* conception of death —Alfred Einstein⟩ **2** : of epic proportions : HEROIC, GARGANTUAN ⟨*Homeric* feats of reporting —Stanley Walker⟩ ⟨~ laughter⟩ — **ho·mer·i·cal·ly** \-rək(ə)lē, -rēk-, -li\ *adv, often cap*

ho·mer·i·can \-rəkən\ *adj, usu cap* [L *Homericus* + E *-an*] *archaic* : HOMERIC

homeric simile *n, usu cap H* : EPIC SIMILE

ho·mer·ist \ˈhōmərəst\ *n* -S *usu cap* : a specialist in Homer and his epics

home road *n* : the railroad owning or leasing a car in freight-car interchange

ho·mer·ol·o·gist \ˌhōmə'räləjəst\ *n* -S *usu cap* : a specialist in Homerology

ho·mer·ol·o·gy \-jē\ *n* -ES *usu cap* [*Homer* + *-o-* + *-logy*] : a study of Homer's poems and of his life and times

homeroom \ˈ⸗,⸗\ *n* **1** : a schoolroom where pupils of the same class or grade but often with different academic programs report at the opening of school and meet informally under the guidance of a teacher to conduct class business, plan and organize group activities, and discuss individual and group problems **2** : a group of pupils assigned to the same homeroom

home row *n* : the bank of keys on a typewriter containing the home keys

home rule *n* **1 a** : self-government esp. with regard to local and internal legislation by the inhabitants of a dependent or federated country or territory or colony ⟨split the Liberal party over the issue of *home rule* for Ireland —C.J.Friedrich⟩; *specif, Brit* : dominion status **b** : the political theory or principle of self-government **2 a** : partial municipal autonomy granted to some cities whereby they are authorized to frame their own charters and manage their own affairs within limits set by the state esp. as to taxation, finance, police, and education **b** : limited authority granted by a state to a county esp. with regard to the determination of its organizational structure

home ruler *n* : one that advocates home rule; *specif, often cap H&R* : an advocate or supporter of Irish home-rule policy

home run *n* : a hit in baseball that enables the batter to make a complete circuit of the bases and score a run

homes *pl of* HOME, *pres 3d sing of* HOME

home scrap *n* : steel scrap that is utilized within the plant where it originates

homeseeker \ˈ⸗,⸗⸗\ *n* : one that seeks a home; *esp* : a pioneer in search of land on which to settle ⟨excitement caused by the advent of ~*s* from the eastern states —*Atlantic*⟩

homesick \ˈ⸗,⸗\ *adj* [back-formation fr. *homesickness*] **1** : longing for home and family while absent from them ⟨the boy was ~ his first week at camp⟩ **2** : yearning for a familiar or sympathetic environment ⟨that stretch of blue water was the one thing he was ~ for —Willa Cather⟩ ⟨~ for their comparatively carefree nineteenth-century past —A.J.Toynbee⟩

home·sick·ness *n* -ES [trans. of G *heimweh*] : the quality or state of being homesick : NOSTALGIA

home signal *n* : a railroad signal placed at the beginning of a block to indicate whether or not the block is clear — compare DISTANT SIGNAL

homesite \ˈ⸗,⸗\ *n* **1** : a location suitable for a home ⟨divided the lakefront into ~*s*⟩ **2** : the location of a home ⟨stayed in their bombed-out ~*s* —M.W.Childs⟩

¹**homespun** \ˈ⸗,⸗\ *adj* [¹*home* + *spun*] **1 a** : spun or made at or as if at home ⟨~ cloth⟩ ⟨turn out woven and knitted goods on hand machines that preserve the ~ quality —J.M.Mead⟩ **b** : made of homespun or of a fabric resembling homespun ⟨yeomanry . . . turned out in their working clothes and ~ country garbs —Washington Irving⟩ ⟨other popular cotton suiting choices include . . . ~ types that have weave interest —*Women's Wear Daily*⟩ **2 a** : of or relating to the common people : PLEBEIAN, UNSOPHISTICATED ⟨~ tastes⟩ ⟨~ virtues⟩ ⟨both still assume the air of ~ country boys —T.H.White b.1915⟩ : FOLKSY ⟨oozed with idiosyncrasy, naïveté and ~ humor —E.S.Turner⟩ ⟨prose which varies from the movingly lyrical to the designedly ~ —Clifton Fadiman⟩ **b** : of unaffected simplicity : UNPRETENTIOUS ⟨dresses up his thoughts in very plain ~ garments —William Clark⟩ ⟨~, kindly, shrewd men whose strength resided in their neighborliness —Norman Cousins⟩ **c** : plain and direct : PRACTICAL, STRAIGHTFORWARD ⟨will make a good ~ wife —Thomas Hardy⟩ ⟨managed the affairs of local government with the same ~ skill that went to their farming —V.L.Parrington⟩ ⟨circumstances which brought forth . . . a ~ nationalism —A.G.Mazour⟩

²**homespun** \"\ *n* -S **1 a** : a loosely woven usu. woolen or linen fabric handloomed in the home from uneven hand-spun yarns **b** : a machine-made tweedy material of a plain weave and spongy texture usu. made from irregular woolen, cotton, rayon, or linen yarns and used for outer garments and upholstery **2** : a character or utterance possessing the rustic simplicity of homespun ⟨instead of the silken splendor of the upper middle classes he gives us the ~ of the poor —Grace Frank⟩

¹**home·stead** \ˈhōmz,ted, -m,st- *also* -,təd *or* -,stəd\ *n* [¹*home* + *stead*] **1 a** : the home and land of a family; *esp* : ancestral home ⟨coming into possession . . . of the old Abbot ~ "Three Beeches" —Witmer Stone⟩ **b** : a private residence : HOUSE ⟨a seventeenth-century farm ~ with thatched roof —A.N. Whitehead⟩ **c** : the living quarters on a ranch in Australasia ⟨a good station to manage because the ~ is near the middle —Nevil Shute⟩ **2 a** : a tract of land usu. consisting of 160 acres acquired from U.S. public lands by filing a record and living on and cultivating the tract ⟨these fences marked the boundaries of the small ~*s* which had recently been claimed —Agnes M. Cleaveland⟩ **b** : the land and buildings on such a tract occupied as a home for the owner and his family and more or less legally protected in some jurisdictions from the claims of creditors against both the owner and his surviving spouse and minor children — see HOMESTEAD LAW

²**homestead** \"\ *vt* : to acquire or occupy as a homestead under a homestead law ⟨lacked the experience needed to ~ virgin territory —R.A.Billington⟩ ~ *vi* : to acquire or settle on land under a homestead law ⟨the original settler in the area . . . has lived there since he ~*ed* back in 1902 —Byron Fish⟩

home·stead·er \-də(r)\ *n* -S **1** : one who seeks or establishes a homestead under a homestead law ⟨announced that the lands ceded by the Cherokee tribes . . . would be thrown open to ~*s* —*Amer. Mercury*⟩ **2** : the possessor of a homestead

homestead law *n* **1** : a law conferring special privileges or exemptions upon owners of homesteads; *esp* : a law exempting a homestead from attachment or sale under execution for general debts **2** : any of several legislative acts authorizing the sale of public lands to settlers

homestead lease *or* **homestead selection** *n, Austral* : a leasehold tenure; *esp* : one created by the Crown Land Acts of 1884 and subsequent legislation

home·ster \ˈhōmztə(r), -mst-\ *n* -S [¹*home* + *-ster*] *Brit* **1** : a member of the home team in an athletic contest **2** : HOMEBODY

homestretch \ˈ⸗¦⸗\ *n* **1** : the part of a racecourse between the last curve and the winning post — compare BACKSTRETCH **2** : the final stage (as of a project) ⟨reached the ~ on his thesis with two weeks to spare⟩

home study *n* : a course of instruction administered by mail and carried on in the student's home — compare CORRESPONDENCE SCHOOL

home table *n* : the side of the inner table in backgammon into which a player moves his stones before bearing off

hometown \ˈ⸗¦⸗\ *n, often attrib* : the city or town of one's birth or principal residence ⟨returned to his ~ to stay⟩

home truth *n* **1** : an unpleasant fact that jars the sensibilities ⟨*home truths* demand utterance but not in a scolding voice or a tone edged with arrogance —H.M.Wriston⟩ **2** : a statement of undisputed fact

home visitor *n* : a caseworker who helps children to adjust to school and community life through individual guidance based on information gathered by visits with parents, teachers, and schoolmates

¹**home·ward** \ˈhōmwə(r)d\ *or* **home·wards** \-dz\ *adv* [ME *homward, homwards*, fr. OE *hāmweard*, fr. *hām* home + *-weard* -ward — more at HOME] : in the direction of one's house or place of origin : toward home ⟨battling my way ~ one dark night against the wind and rain —L.P.Smith⟩

²**homeward** *adj* : being or going in the direction of home ⟨a few belated ~ figures were hurrying along —Michael Foster⟩

home·ward·ly *adv* : HOMEWARD

homework \ˈ⸗,⸗\ *n* **1** : work done at home; *specif* : remunerative employment carried on in the home usu. on a piecework basis ⟨the wife and mother . . . tries to eke out the scanty income by ~ —Mabel Elliott & Francis Merrill⟩ **2 a** : an assignment given to a student to be completed outside of the classroom ⟨hurried to finish his ~ so he could play ball⟩ **b** : preparatory reading or research (as for a discussion) ⟨put in . . . two days on ~ prior to each meeting —Dwight Macdonald⟩

homeworker \ˈ⸗¦⸗⸗\ *n* : one that carries on remunerative employment in the home ⟨concealed the existence of ~*s* who were not paid proper overtime wages —*Progressive Labor World*⟩

hom·ey *also* **homy** \ˈhōmē, -mi\ *adj* -ER/-EST [¹*home* + *-y*] **1** : having an air of comfortable intimacy or domesticity : COZY, FAMILIAR ⟨took a chair by the fire and looked round the ~ room with a sigh of relief —*Strand Mag.*⟩ ⟨just the right size teapot . . . in the regular old brownware, very ~ —*New Yorker*⟩ **2 a** : having an air of simple informality or hospitality usu. associated with home : FRIENDLY, UNPRETENTIOUS ⟨lends a ~ touch —*Vanity Fair*⟩ ⟨private power companies traveling under the ~ alias of "local interests" —Leland Olds⟩ **b** : of a family nature : INTIMATE ⟨like the candidate to answer a few ~ questions designed to elicit the lowdown on his wife and relatives —Claud Cockburn⟩ **c** : FOLKSY ⟨written in the excruciatingly ~ prose that is so often confused with the American vulgate —W.H.Whyte⟩ — **hom·ey·ness** *or* **hom·i·ness** \-mēnəs, -min-\ *n* -ES

homi·ci·dal \ˌhämə¦sīdᵊl *also* ˈhōm-\ *adj* : of, relating to, or having a tendency toward homicide : MURDEROUS — **homi·ci·dal·ly** \-dᵊlē, -dᵊli\ *adv*

homi·cide \ˈhämə,sīd *also* hōm-\ *n* -S [in sense 1, fr. ME, fr. MF, fr. L *homicida*, fr. *homi-* (fr. *homo* human being, man) + *-cida* -cide (killer); in sense 2, fr. ME, fr. MF, fr. L *homicidium*, fr. *homi-* + *-cidium* -cide (killing) — more at HOMAGE] **1** : a person who kills another person : MANSLAYER ⟨the ~ must observe a rigorous taboo —J.G.Frazer⟩ **2 a** : a killing of one human being by another ⟨tabloid headlines about the latest ~⟩; *specif* : a killing of a human being through human agency ⟨charged with drunken driving and vehicle ~⟩ **b** : a squad of detectives that specializes in solving murders ⟨the boys in ~ will get all the details —Thurston Scott⟩

homi·cid·i·ous \ˌ⸗⸗¦sidēəs\ *adj* [L *homicidium* + E *-ous*] *archaic* : HOMICIDAL

homi·culture \ˈhämə, ˈhōmə + ,-\ *n* [L *homi-* (fr. *homo* man) + E *culture*] : scientific physical improvement of mankind

hom·i·lete \ˈhämə,lēt\ *n* -S [Gk *homilētēs* disciple, scholar, fr. *homilein*] : HOMILIST

hom·i·let·ic \ˌ⸗⸗¦led·ik\ *adj* [LL *homileticus*, fr. Gk *homilētikos* affable, social, fr. *homilētos* (verbal of *homilein* to consort with, talk with, address, make a speech) + *-ikos* -ic — more at HOMILY] **1** : of the nature of a homily : resembling a sermon **2** : of or relating to homiletics : HORTATORY

hom·i·let·i·cal \-d·əkəl\ *adj* [in sense 1, fr. Gk *homilētikos* + E *-al*; in sense 2 fr. LL *homileticus* + E *-al*] **1** *obs* : of or relating to friendly companionship : SOCIAL **2** : HOMILETIC — **hom·i·let·i·cal·ly** \-k(ə)lē\ *adv*

hom·i·let·ics \ˌ⸗⸗'led·iks\ *n pl but sing in constr* [Gk *homilētikē* art of conversation, fr. fem. of *homilētikos*] **1** : the art of preaching ⟨have on occasion made ~ a substitute for statecraft —J.M.Blum⟩ **2** : a branch of theology that deals with homilies or sermons ⟨a lecturer in ~⟩

ho·mil·i·ary \hä'milē,erē\ *n* -ES [ML *homiliarium*, fr. LL *homilia* homily + L *-arium* -ary] : a book of homilies

hom·i·list \ˈhäməlәst\ *n* -S [*homily* + *-ist*] : one who prepares or delivers a homily

hom·i·lite \-,līt\ *n* -S [G or Sw *homilit*, fr. Gk *homilein* + G or Sw *-it* -ite] : a mineral $(Ca,Fe)_3Al_5B_2Si_2O_{16}$ consisting of a black or blackish brown iron calcium borosilicate

hom·i·lize \-,līz\ *vi* -ED/-ING/-S [*homily* + *-ize*] : to deliver a homily : PREACH

hom·i·ly \ˈhäməlē, -li\ *n* -ES [alter. (influenced by LL *homilia*) of ME *omelie*, fr. MF, fr. LL *homilia*, fr. LGk, fr. Gk, conversation, discourse, fr. *homilein* to consort with, talk with, address, make a speech, fr. *homilos* crowd, assembly) + *-ia* — more at MILITATE] **1** : a discourse on a religious theme esp. delivered to a congregation during a church service

⟨ideas derived from *homilies* and the common teaching of the church —W.P.Ker⟩ **2 :** a lecture or discussion on a moral theme : ADMONITION ⟨the criminal of old was given copious drafts of exhortation and ~ administered . . . by reformers —B.N.Cardozo⟩

homin- *or* **homini-** *comb form* [L *homin-, homo* — more at HOMAGE] : man : human ⟨*hominine*⟩ ⟨*hominiform*⟩ ⟨*hominisection*⟩

hom·i·nal \ˈhämənᵊl\ *adj* [*homin-* + *-al*] : of, relating to, or constituted by man as a species : HUMAN ⟨the vegetable, animal, and ~ kingdoms⟩

hominess *var of* HOMEYNESS

¹homing *n* -s [fr. gerund of ⁴*home*] **1 a :** an accurate return of an animal to a known place (as a home range) **b :** a tendency to return to a known place as a facet of animal behavior ⟨~ is a well-known characteristic of salmon⟩ ⟨~ is an acquired skill operating through topographical memory —*Biol. Abstracts*⟩ **2 :** navigation toward an objective by maintaining a constant bearing on a radio beam or other point of reference ⟨for ~ a loop antenna located perpendicular to the center line of the aircraft is used —*Aircraft Navigation Manual*⟩

²homing *adj* [fr. pres. part. of ⁴*home*] **1 :** home-returning; *specif* : habitually returning to a known place ⟨shad are ~ fish⟩ **2 :** guiding or being guided to an objective ⟨~ beacon⟩ ⟨an acoustic ~ torpedo which, attracted by the submarine's noise, would follow it down and detonate on contact —R.S.Benson⟩

homing pigeon *n* : a racing pigeon sometimes used for carrying messages and trained to return to its loft from distances up to 500 miles or more by being released at gradually increased distances from home — compare CARRIER PIGEON

¹hom·i·nid *also* **hom·o·nid** \ˈhämənəd, -ˌnid\ *or* **ho·min·i·an** \hōˈminēən\ *n* -s [*hominid* fr. NL *Hominidae; homonid* alter. of *hominid; hominian* fr. NL *Homin-, Homo* + E *-ian*] : one of the Hominidae : a manlike creature : MAN ⟨fossil ~s . . . are already quite uniformly assignable to our present genus *Homo* —W.M.Krogman⟩

²hominid \"\ *also* **hominian** \"\ *adj* : of, relating to, or characterizing the Hominidae ⟨regarding man as emerging from a welter of genetically related ~ types —Weston LaBarre⟩

ho·min·i·dae \hōˈminəˌdē\ *n pl, cap* [NL, fr. *Homin-, Homo*, type genus + *-idae*] : a family of mammals (order Primates) to which man and his ancestors belong : a family of animals consisting of mankind — see HOMO, MAN 1b(2), PITHECANTHROPUS

hom·i·nine \ˈhäməˌnīn, -mən\ *adj* [*homin-* + *-ine*] : HUMAN

hom·i·nism \-ˌnizəm\ *n* -s [*homin-* + *-ism*] : pragmatic humanism that regards man as only a highly differentiated animal

hom·i·niv·o·rous \ˌ≈≈ˈniv(ə)rəs\ *adj* [*homin-* + *-vorous*] : man-eating

¹hom·i·noid \ˈhäməˌnȯid\ *adj* [NL *Hominoidea*] **1 :** of, relating to, or characterizing the Hominoidea **2 :** resembling the Hominidae : MANLIKE

²hominoid \"\ *n* -s : one of the Hominoidea : an animal resembling man

hom·i·noi·dea \ˌ≈≈ˈnȯidēə\ *n pl, cap* [NL, fr. *Homin-, Homo* + *-oidea*] **1** *in some classifications* : a major division of Primates segregating *Homo* and related fossil forms from the great apes **2 :** a superfamily of Anthropoidea comprising the great apes and the recent and fossil hominids as distinguished from the lower Old World monkeys — compare CERCOPITHECIDAE

hom·i·ny \ˈhämənē, -ni\ *n* -ES [prob. fr. a word of Algonquian origin whose 1st constituent is unknown and whose 2d constituent is akin to Natick *-minne* small fruit, grain (used in all names given to prepared corn)] : kernels of hulled corn (as white flint corn) with the germ removed and either whole or ground — see HOMINY GRITS; compare ¹GRIT 2a

hominy grits *n pl but sing or pl in constr* : hominy in uniform granular particles

hom·ish \ˈhōmish\ *adj* [¹*home* + *-ish*] : HOMEY — **hom·ish·ness** *n* -ES

hommock *var of* HUMMOCK

¹ho·mo \ˈhō(ˌ)mō\ *n, cap* [NL, fr. L, man, human being — more at HOMAGE] : the genus of man : a genus of mammals consisting of mankind that is the type and sole surviving member of the family Hominidae and is usu. held to include a single recent species (*H. sapiens*) comprising all surviving and various extinct men — see MAN 1b(2)

²homo \"\ *n* -s [by shortening] *slang* : HOMOSEXUAL

homo- *in pronunciations below*, ˈ≈ = ˌhō(ˌ)mō *or* ˌhä(ˌ)mō *or* -ˌmə\ — see HOM-

homo alieni juris \ˈhō(ˌ)mō+\ *n* [L] : a man under the control of another — opposed to *homo sui juris*

homo·basidiomycetes *pronunc at* HOMO- +\ *n pl, cap* [NL, fr. *hom-* + *Basidiomycetes*] : a subclass of Basidiomycetes comprising fungi with nonseptate and nondivided basidia and basidiospores that usu. germinate directly to form a mycelium and including the gill fungi, pore fungi, coral fungi, and bird's-nest fungi and the puffballs and stinkhorns — compare HETEROBASIDIOMYCETES

homo·ba·sid·io·my·cet·i·dae \ˌ≈(ˌ)≈bəˌsidē(ˌ)ōˌmīˈsed·əˌdē\ *syn of* HOMOBASIDIOMYCETES

homo·basidium \"+\ *n* [NL, fr. *hom-* + *basidium*] : AUTOBASIDIUM

homo·blas·tic \ˌ≈≈ˈblastik\ *adj* [*hom-* + *-blastic*] : having a direct embryonic development : arising from cells of the same kind; *specif* : having the embryo similar in appearance to the adult plant and developing directly from the fertilized seed — **homo·blas·ty** \ˈ≈≈ˌtē\ *n* -ES

homocaryon *var of* HOMOKARYON

¹homo·centric *also* **homo·central** *pronunc at* HOMO- +\ *adj* [NL *homocentricus*, fr. Gk *homokentros* concentric (fr. *homo-* hom- + *-kentros*, fr. *kentron* center) + L *-icus* -ic — more at CENTER] : having the same center ⟨~ spheres⟩; *specif* : diverging from or converging toward a common center — used of light rays forming a pencil

²homocentric \"\ *adj* [L *homo* man, human being + E *-centric* — more at HOMAGE] : centered on man ⟨the universe is not ~ —Junjiro Takakusu⟩ — **homo·centrically** \"+\ *adv*

homo·cercal *pronunc at* HOMO- +\ *adj* [*hom-* + *-cercal*] **1 :** having the upper and lower lobes approximately symmetrical and the vertebral column ending at or near the middle of the base — used of the tail fin of various fishes (as most teleosts) **2 :** having or relating to a homocercal tail fin — compare ISOCERCAL

homo·charge \"+ˌ-\ *n* [*hom-* + *charge*] : a charge on an electret that is of the same sign as that of the electrode orig. in contact with it — compare HETEROCHARGE

homo·chlamydeous \"+\ *adj* [*hom-* + *chlamydeous*] : having a perianth whose inner and outer series are similar or not differentiated into calyx and corolla ⟨the lily has a typical ~ perianth⟩ — compare ACHLAMYDEAE

homo·chromatic \"+\ *adj* [*hom-* + *chromatic*] **1 :** of or relating to one color **2** *of an afterimage* : having approximately the same hues as an original image — opposed to *heterochromatic*

homo·chromosome \"+\ *n* [*hom-* + *chromosome*] : AUTOSOME

ho·moch·ro·nous \(ˈ)hōˈmäkrənəs, (ˈ)häˈ-\ *adj* [*hom-* + *-chronous*] : HOMEOCHRONOUS

homo·clime *pronunc at* HOMO- + ˌ-\ *n* [*hom-* + *clime*] : a climatically similar environment; *specif* : a region climatically similar to another specified region ⟨New World ~s of certain parts of Australia⟩

homo·cli·nal \ˌ≈≈ˈklīnᵊl\ *adj* : of or relating to a homocline

homo·cline \ˈ≈≈ˌklīn\ *n* -s [*hom-* + *-cline*] : a layer of stratified rock (as one limb of an anticline or syncline) in which the strata dip consistently in one general direction though the angle of dip may vary greatly from place to place — compare MONOCLINE

homo·coe·la \ˌ≈≈ˈsēlə\ [NL, fr. *hom-* + *-coela* (fr. neut. pl. of *-coelus* -coelous)] *syn of* ASCONOSA

homo·cyclic \ˌ≈≈+\ *adj* [*hom-* + *cyclic*] : ISOCYCLIC

homo·cysteine \"+\ *n* [*hom-* + *cysteine*] : a crystalline amino acid $HSCH_2CH_2CH(NH_2)COOH$ held to be formed by demethylation of methionine in the animal organism; α-amino-γ-mercapto-butyric acid

homo·cystine \"+\ *n* [*hom-* + *cystine*] : a crystalline amino acid $[-SCH_2CH_2CH(NH_2)COOH]_2$ formed by oxidation of homocysteine

homo·dermic \"+\ *adj* [*hom-* + *dermic*] *biol* : originating from the same germ layer — **homo·der·my** \ˈ≈≈ˌdərmē\ *n* -ES

homo·dont \ˈ≈≈ˌdänt\ *adj* [ISV *hom-* + *-odont*] : having all the teeth similar in form ⟨the porpoise is a ~ animal⟩ — opposed to *heterodont*

ho·mod·ro·mal \hōˈmädrəməl, häˈ-\ *adj* [NL *homodromus* + E *-al*] : HOMODROMOUS

ho·mod·ro·mous \-məs\ *or* **homo·drome** \ˈhōməˌdrōm, ˈhäm-\ *adj* [NL *homodromus*, fr. *hom-* + *-dromus* -dromous] : having the genetic spiral following the same direction in both stem and branches — compare HETERODROMOUS

ho·mod·ro·my \hōˈmädrəmē, häˈ-\ *n* -ES [ISV *homodromous* + *-y*] : the quality or state of being homodromous

homo·dynamic *pronunc at* HOMO- +\ *adj* [*hom-* + *dynamic*] : producing a continuous succession of generations until interrupted by adverse circumstances (as cold or lack of food) — used of an insect

homo·dyne \ˈ≈≈ˌdīn\ *adj* [*hom-* + *dyne*] : of or relating to the process of detecting a radio wave by the aid of a locally generated current or wave of exactly the same frequency as that of the incoming wave ⟨~ reception⟩ — see ZERO BEAT

homoe- *or* **homoeo-** — see HOME-

ho·moe·an \(ˈ)hōˌmēən, (ˈ)häˌ-, ˈ≈ˌmē-\ *or* **ho·moi·an** \(ˈ)≈ˌmȯi(y)ən\ *n* -s *often cap* [*Homoean* fr. NL *Homoeus* (fr. Gk *homoios* like) + E *-an; Homoian* fr. Gk *homoios* + E *-an* — more at HOME-] : a member of an Arian party holding to the doctrine that the Son is like the Father though not in essence — compare ANOMOEAN, APOLLINARIAN, HOMOIOUSIAN

ho·moe·cious \(ˈ)hōˈmēshəs, (ˈ)häˈ-\ *adj* [*hom-* + Gk *oikia* house + E *-ous* — more at VICINITY] : having the same host during the entire life cycle — used esp. of a beetle parasitic in the nest of an ant — contrasted with *heteroecious*; compare AUTOECIOUS

ho·moe·om·er·al \ˌhōmēˈämərəl, ˌhäm-\ *adj* [Gk *homoiomerēs* consisting of equal parts (fr. *homoio-* home- + *-merēs*, fr. *meros* part) + E *-al* — more at MERIT] *prosody* : having like or corresponding parts

ho·moeo·me·ria \ˌhōˌmēəməˈrīə, ˌhä,-, ˌ≈ˌmē(ˌ)ōm-, -ˈmirēə\ *n, pl* **homoeomeri·ae** \-rīˌē, -rēˌē\ [L] : HOMOEOMERY — **ho·moeo·me·ri·an** \-rīən,-rēən\ *n* -s — **ho·moeo·me·ri·an·ism** \-əˌnizəm\ *n* -s

ho·moeo·mer·ic \ˌ≈ˌ≈ˈmerik, ˌ≈≈≈ˈ-, -mir-\ *or* **ho·moeo·mer·i·cal** \-rəkəl\ *adj* [*homoeomery* + *-ic, -ical*] **1 :** of or relating to homoeomery **2 :** consisting of homogeneous parts or particles **3** *usu* **homoeomeric** [Gk *homoiomerēs* + E *-ic*] : HOMOEOMERAL

¹homoe·om·er·ous \ˌhōmēˈämərəs, ˌhäm-\ *adj* [Gk *homoiomerēs* + E *-ous*] **1 :** having the algal cells scattered throughout the thallus ⟨~ lichens⟩ — opposed to *heteromerous* **2** [*homoeomery* + *-ous*] : HOMOEOMERIC 1, 2 **3 :** HOMOEOMERAL

²homoeomerous \"\ *adj* [*home-* + Gk *mēros* thigh + E *-ous*] : having the sciatic artery developed as the main artery of the thigh — used of a bird

ho·moe·om·ery \ˌ≈ˈ≈≈rē\ *n* -ES [L *homoeomeria*, fr. Gk *homoiomereia*, fr. *homoiomerēs* + *-eia* -y] **1 :** one of an infinite number of homogeneous ultimate particles of matter constituting through their combination and separation everything in the world **2 :** an Anaxagorean theory postulating homoeomeries

ho·moe·o·sis *or* **ho·me·o·sis** \ˌhōmēˈōsəs, ˌhäm-\ *n* -ES [NL, fr. Gk *homoiōsis* assimilation, resemblance, fr. *homoioun* to make like, become like (fr. *homoios* like) + *-sis* — more at HOME-] *biol* : an assumption by one part or structure in a series of a form characteristic of another member of the series ⟨with a wing of the fore-wing type in place of one of the normal hind wings, it provides an extreme instance of ~ —G.E.Hyde⟩ — compare HETEROMORPHOSIS

ho·moeo·te·leu·tic \ˌhōmēətəˈlüd·ik, ˌhä,-; ˌhōmē(ˌ)ōtə-, ˌhäm- *also* -təlˈyü-\ *adj* [Gk *homoioteleutos* having the same ending (fr. *homoio-* home- + *-teleutos*, fr. *teleutē* end) + E *-ic* — more at TELEUT-] **1 :** having the same or similar endings ⟨~ words⟩ **2** [*homoeoteleuton* + *-ic*] : due to homoeoteleuton ⟨~ error⟩

ho·moeo·te·leu·ton \ˌ≈≈təˈlüˌtän *also* -təlˈyü-\ *n* -s [LL, fr. Gk *homoioteleuton*, fr. neut. of *homoioteleutos*] : an occurrence in writing of the same or similar endings near together (as in neighboring clauses or lines) whether happening by chance or done for rhythmical effect ⟨~ is a frequent cause of omissions in copying⟩

homoe·ot·ic *also* **home·ot·ic** \ˌhōmēˈäd·ik, ˌhäm-\ *adj* [fr. NL *homoeosis, homeosis*, after such pairs as NL *hypnosis: E hypnotic*] : of or relating to homoeosis

ho·moe·ot·o·py \ˌ≈≈ˈäd·əpē\ *n* -ES [*home-* + *-topy*] : HOMOEOTELEUTON

homo·erotic \ˌhō(ˌ)mō, ˌhä(ˌ)mō+\ *adj* [*hom-* + *erotic*] **1 :** involving or characterized by homoeroticism ⟨the ~ level of development⟩ **2 :** HOMOSEXUAL

homo·eroticism *also* **homo·erotism** \"+\ *n* [*hom-* + *eroticism* or *erotism*] **1 :** the tendency to obtain libidinal gratification from a member of one's own sex **2 :** HOMOSEXUALITY

homo fa·ber \ˌhō(ˌ)mōˈfäbə(r), -ˌbe(ə)r; -ˈfābə-\ *n* [NL, lit., skillful man] **1 :** man the maker or creator **2** *in Bergsonism* : man as engaged in transforming both himself morally and material things — contrasted with *homo sapiens*

homo·fermentative \ˌhō(ˌ)mō, ˌhä(-+\ *adj* [*hom-* + *fermentative*] : producing a fermentation resulting wholly or principally in a single end product — used esp. of economically important lactic-acid bacteria that ferment carbohydrates to lactic acid

homo·fermenter \"+\ *n* [*hom-* + *fermenter*] : a homofermentative organism

homo·gametic *pronunc at* HOMO- +\ *adj* [*hom-* + *gametic*] : forming one kind of germ cell; *esp* : having an X chromosome in all gametes — compare DIGAMETIC, HETEROGAMETIC

ho·mog·a·mous \hōˈmägəməs, häˈ-\ *or* **homo·gam·ic** *pronunc at* HOMO- + ˈgamik\ *adj* [*hom-* + *-gamous, -gamic*] : characterized by or relating to homogamy

ho·mog·a·my \hōˈmägəmē, häˈ-\ *n* -ES [G *homogamie*, fr. *homo-* hom- + *-gamie* -gamy] **1 a :** a state of having flowers alike throughout (as in the heads of chicory and related plants or the spikes of many sedges) — opposed to *heterogamy* **b :** the maturing of the stamens and pistils at the same period — used of a perfect or monoclinous flower **2 a :** reproduction within an isolated group perpetuating qualities by which it is differentiated from the larger group of which it is a part — compare APOGAMY **b :** the mating of like with like whether selection is determined by physical or cultural similarities or both

homo·gangliate *pronunc at* HOMO- +\ *adj* [*hom-* + *gangliate*] : having symmetrically arranged nervous ganglia ⟨~ annelid worms⟩ ⟨~ arthropods⟩

ho·mo·gen \ˈ≈≈jən, -ˌjen\ *n* -s [*hom-* + *-gen*] *biol* **1 :** a group having a common origin **2 :** one of two or more homogenous organs or parts

ho·mog·e·nate \hōˈmäjəˌnāt, həˈ-, -nət\ *n* -s [*homogenize* + *-ate*] : a substance that has been homogenized; *esp* : biological tissue that has been finely divided (as by a grinder) and thoroughly mixed ⟨liver ~⟩ — compare MACERATE

homo·ge·neal \ˌhōməˈjēnyəl, -nēəl *sometimes* ˌhäm-\ *adj* [ML *homogeneus* + E *-al*] : HOMOGENEOUS

homo·ge·ne·ity \ˌhōməjəˈnēəd·ē, -mōj-, -ətē, -i *sometimes* ˌhäm- *or* -nāə- *or* -niə-\ *n* -ES [ML *homogeneitas*, fr. *homogeneus* + *-itas* -ity] : the quality or state of being homogeneous

ho·mo·ge·neous \ˌ≈≈ˈjēnēəs, -nyəs, *Brit sometimes* -ˈjen-\ *adj* [ML *homogeneus, homogenus*, fr. Gk *homogenēs*, fr. *homo-* hom- + *-genēs* (fr. *genos* kind, race) — more at SAME, KIN] **1 a :** of a similar kind or nature : COMPARABLE, EQUIVALENT ⟨the three schools . . . are relatively ~ —B.F.Wright⟩ **b :** having no discordant elements : CONSISTENT, COMPATIBLE ⟨everything about her was ~: her looks, her possessions, the way in which she dressed —Osbert Sitwell⟩ ⟨country people . . . whose manners and morals were ~ with those of the country itself —Van Wyck Brooks⟩ **2 a :** of uniform structure or composition throughout ⟨~ granite⟩ ⟨~ sand deposits . . . laid down under steady conditions of wind —R.A.Bagnold⟩; *specif* : relating to, occurring in, or being a system that contains no internal physical boundaries ⟨~ system⟩ ⟨~ catalysis⟩ **b :** of a single type : showing no variation ⟨bituminous coal is often treated as a ~ product —G.G.Somers⟩ ⟨customary to speak of the Asian mind as though it were ~ —Iqbal Singh⟩; *specif* : MONOCHROMATIC **2 c :** consisting of uniform elements (as of people or groups with similar background) ⟨~ nation⟩ ⟨~ community⟩ ⟨the sound of a full consort of viols is rich and ~ —Robert Donington⟩ **3 :** of the same mathematical degree or dimensions in every term in the symbols considered ⟨a ~ equation⟩ **4 :** HOMOGENOUS 1 — **ho·mo·ge·neous·ly** *adv* — **ho·mo·ge·neous·ness** *n* -ES

homogeneous equilibrium *n* : equilibrium in a homogeneous system

homogeneous ray *n* : a vascular ray consisting of only upright or only procumbent cells — compare HETEROGENEOUS RAY

homogeneous reaction *n* : reaction in a homogeneous system

homogeneous reactor *n* : a nuclear reactor in which the fuel is distributed (as by being dissolved in a liquid) uniformly or approximately uniformly throughout the moderator material

homogeneous roof *n* : a roof (as a concrete dome) forming a solid shell of one material

homo·genesis *pronunc at* HOMO- +\ *n* [NL, fr. *hom-* + *genesis*] : production of offspring that resemble the parents — compare HETEROGENESIS 2

homo·genetic *or* **homo·genetical** \"+\ *adj* [*hom-* + *genetic, genetical*] : HOMOGENOUS

homo·gen·ic \"+\ *adj* [*hom-* + *genic*] **1 :** HOMOGENOUS **2 :** having only one allele of a gene or genes — used of a gamete or of a population

ho·mog·e·ni·za·tion \hōˌmäjənəˈzāshən, hə,-, hä,-, -ˌnīˈz-\ *n* -s **1 :** the quality or state of being homogenized **2 :** the act or process of homogenizing

ho·mog·e·nize \≈ˈ≈≈ˌnīz\ *vb* -ED/-ING/-S [*homogenous* + *-ize*] *vt* **1 a :** to blend (diverse elements) into a smooth mixture ⟨after these two main ingredients . . . have been thoroughly *homogenized* —D.A.Dearle⟩ **b :** to blend as if by homogenizing : make homogeneous ⟨trying to legislate decency or ~ social relations by law —Malcolm Moos⟩ **c :** to anneal (an alloy) for a long time at a high temperature to make more nearly uniform in chemical composition throughout **2 a :** to reduce to particles of uniform size evenly distributed ⟨~ peanut butter⟩ ⟨a large fragment of cocoon . . . was cut into small pieces and *homogenized* into tiny fragments in water —*Science*⟩; *specif* : to grind (tobacco leaves) into a pulp and compress into a sheet for use as binder **b :** to reduce the particles of (a liquid) to uniform size and distribute them evenly ⟨~ paint⟩ — compare EMULSIFY **c :** to break up the fat globules and other solids of (milk or cream) by means of a homogenizer ~ *vi* : to attain a uniform state or consistency through reduction or blending ⟨heat causes the product to ~⟩

homogenized *adj* **1 :** reduced to small evenly distributed particles ⟨~ baby food⟩ ⟨~ cosmetics⟩ **2 :** of unvarying uniformity : HOMOGENEOUS ⟨Americans are anything but a standard ~ article —David Davidson⟩

ho·mog·e·niz·er \-zə(r)\ *n* -s : one that homogenizes; *esp* : a machine that forces a substance through fine openings against a hard surface for the purpose of blending or emulsification — compare COLLOID MILL, EMULSIFIER

ho·mog·e·nous \-ˌnəs\ *adj* [ML *homogenus* of the same kind — more at HOMOGENEOUS] **1 :** of, relating to, or exhibiting homogeny **2 :** HOMOPLASTIC 2 **3 :** HOMOGENEOUS

homo·gen·tis·ic acid *pronunc at* HOMO- +ˌjenˈtizik-\ *n* [*homogentisic* ISV *hom-* + *gentisic* (in *gentisic acid*)] : a crystalline acid $C_6H_3(OH)_2CH_2COOH$ formed as an intermediate in the metabolism of phenylalanine and tyrosine and found esp. in the urine in cases of alkaptonuria

ho·mog·e·ny \hōˈmäjənē, həˈ-, häˈ-\ *n* -ES [Gk *homogeneia*, fr. *homogenēs* of the same kind + *-ia* -y — more at HOMOGENEOUS] : correspondence between parts or organs due to descent from the same ancestral type : HOMOLOGY — opposed to *homoplasy*

homo·gone *pronunc at* HOMO- +ˌgōn\ *adj* [*hom-* + *-gone*] : HOMOGONOUS

homo·gon·ic \ˌ≈≈ˈgänik, -ˈgōn-\ *adj* [*hom-* + *-gonic* (fr. *-gone* + *-ic*)] : being that course of development in which one generation of parasites immediately succeeds another — used of various nematode worms; distinguished from *heterogonic*

ho·mog·o·nous \hōˈmägənəs, həˈ-, häˈ-\ *adj* : of or relating to homogony — **ho·mog·o·nous·ly** *adv*

ho·mog·o·ny \-nē\ *n* -ES [*hom-* + *-gony*] : a condition of having only one kind of flowers with the androecium and gynoecium of uniform relative length — opposed to *heterogony*

homo·graft *pronunc at* HOMO- +ˌ-\ *n* [*hom-* + *graft*] : a graft of tissue taken from a donor of the same species as the recipient — compare HETEROGRAFT

homo·graph \ˈhäməˌgraf, ˈhōm-, -raa(ə)f,-raif,-rȧf\ *n* [*hom-* + *-graph*] : one of two or more words spelled alike but differing in derivation or meaning or pronunciation (as *fair*, market and *fair*, beautiful; *lead*, to conduct and *lead*, metal) — called also *homonym*

homo·graph·ic \ˌ≈≈ˈgrafik\ *adj* [*hom-* + *-graphic*] **1 :** of, relating to, or consisting of a homograph **2 :** employing a single and separate character to represent each sound : PHONETIC — opposed to *heterographic*

ho·mog·ra·phy \häˈmägrəfē, hōˈ-,-fi\ *n* -ES [*hom-* + *-graphy*] : homographic spelling

homo·he·dral *pronunc at* HOMO- +ˈhēdrəl *sometimes chiefly Brit* ˈhed-\ *adj* [*hom-* + *-hedral*] : having equal or corresponding faces; *also* : HOLOHEDRAL

homoi- *or* **homoio-** — see HOME-

homoian *often cap, var of* HOMOEAN

ho·moio·genetic \hōˌmȯiō+\ *adj* [*home-* + *genetic*] : having the ability to induce the formation of a similar part when grafted into an undetermined field ⟨the ~ inducing of a new neural tube by a neural tube graft⟩ — used of a determined part of an embryo

ho·moio·me·ria \hōˌmȯi(y)əməˈrīə, ˌhōmēōm-, ˌhämēōm-, -ˈmirēə\ *n, pl* **homoiomeri·ae** \-rīˌē, -rēˌē\ [Gk *homoiomereia* — more at HOMOEOMERY] : HOMOEOMERY — **ho·moio·me·ri·an** \-rīən,-rēən\ *n* -s — **ho·moio·me·ri·an·ism** \-əˌnizəm\ *n* -s

ho·moi·osmotic \(ˌ)hōˌmȯi, (ˌ)häˌ- +\ *adj* [*home-* + *osmotic*] : having a bodily osmotic regulating mechanism and having body fluids that differ in osmotic pressure from the surrounding medium or from sea water ⟨~ animals include all the land and freshwater vertebrates⟩ — compare POIKILOSMOTIC

ho·moio·te·leu·ton \hōˌmȯi(y)ətəˈlüˌtän *also* -təlˈyü-\ *n* -s [Gk — more at HOMOEOTELEUTON] : HOMOEOTELEUTON

ho·moio·therm \hōˈmȯi(y)əˌthərm\ *or* **homeo·therm** \ˈhōmēə,-, ˈhäm-\ *n* -s [*home-* + *-therm*] : a homoiothermic organism

ho·moio·ther·mic \hōˌmȯi(y)əˈthərmik\ *or* **homeo·ther·mic** \ˌhōmēō-, ˌhäm-\ *also* **ho·moio·ther·mal** \hōˌmȯi(y)əˈthərməl\ *adj* [*home-* + *-thermic, thermal*] : having a relatively uniform body temperature maintained nearly independent of the environmental temperature : WARM-BLOODED

ho·moio·ther·my \hōˈmȯi(y)əˌthərmē\ *or* **homeo·ther·my** \ˈhōmēə,-, ˈhäm-\ *also* **ho·moio·ther·mism** \hōˌmȯi(y)əˈthərˌmizəm\ *n, pl* **homoiothermies** *or* **homeothermies** *also* **homoiothermisms** [*home-* + *-thermy* or *-thermism* (fr. *therm-* + *-ism*)] : the state of being homoiothermic : warm-blooded condition or state

homoiotransplant *var of* HOMEOTRANSPLANT

ho·moi·ou·sia \ˌhōˌmȯiˈüzēə, -ˈüsēə, -ˈüzh(ē)ə, -ˈüsh(ē)ə\ *n* -s [NL, fr. LGk *homoiousios* + L *-ia* -y] : similarity but not identity in essence or substance : essential likeness

¹ho·moi·ou·sian \-ən\ *n* -s *often cap* [LGk *homoiousios* of like substance (fr. Gk *homoi-* home- + *-ousios*, fr. *ousia* substance, being) + E *-an* (n. suffix)] : one that accepts the homoiousian doctrine

²homoiousian \"\ *adj* [LGk *homoiousios* + E *-an* (adj. suffix)] **1 a :** holding to the doctrine that the Son is essentially like the Father but not of the same substance **b :** of or relating to the doctrine of homoiousia — distinguished from *homoousian*; compare HETEROOUSIAN **2 :** of or relating to the homoiousians **3 :** of or relating to homoiousia

ho·moi·ou·sian·ism \-əˌnizəm\ *n* -s : the doctrines and beliefs of the homoiousians

ho·moi·ou·sious \-ˌsəs\ *adj* [LGk *homoiousios*] : HOMOIOUSIAN

homo·karyon *also* **homo·caryon** *pronunc at* HOMO- +\ *n* -s [NL, fr. *hom-* + *karyon*] : a cell in the mycelium of a fungus that contains two or more genetically identical nuclei — compare DIKARYON, HETEROKARYON

homo·kary·osis or **homo·cary·osis** \ˌ≈≈ˌkarēˈōsə̇s\ *n* -ES [NL, fr. *homokaryon, homocaryon* + *-osis*] : the condition of having homokaryons

homo·kary·ot·ic or **homo·cary·ot·ic** \ˌ≈≈ˌ≈≈¦äd·ik\ *adj* [irreg. fr. NL *homokaryon, homocaryon* + E *-ic*] **1** : of, relating to, or being part of a homokaryon ⟨~ nuclei⟩ **2** : involving or consisting of homokaryons : exhibiting homokaryosis ⟨a ~ mycelium⟩ ⟨~ development⟩

homo·lateral *pronunc at* HOMO- + \ *adj* [ISV *hom-* + *lateral*] : IPSILATERAL

homo·lecithal \"+ \ *adj* [*hom-* + *lecithal*] : having the yolk small in amount and nearly uniformly distributed — used of an egg; opposed to *heterolecithal;* compare ALECITHAL

ho·mo le·ga·lis \ˌhō(ˌ)mōlə̇ˈgalə̇s, -gäl-,-gāl-\ *n* [ML] : one whose status as a citizen or member of a community is recognized in law : a legal person

ho·mol·o·gate \hōˈmäləˌgāt\ *vb* -ED/-ING/-S [ML *homologatus,* past part. of *homologare,* fr. Gk *homologein* to agree, fr. *homologos* agreeing — more at HOMOLOGOUS] *vt* **1** : to agree with : SANCTION ⟨~ the act of an ally⟩ **2** : APPROVE, ALLOW, CONFIRM ⟨a party to an adverse judgment ~*s* it by failure to appeal⟩ **3** *Scots law* : to cause (a document or transaction that is defective or informal) to be validated : RATIFY **4** : to confirm officially (some aspect of the performance of an airplane, as speed, altitude, duration) ~ *vi* : to be or act in accord : AGREE, CONCUR — **ho·mol·o·ga·tion** \≈ˌ≈≈ˈgāshən\ *n* -S

homo·log·i·cal *pronunc at* HOMO- + ¦läjə̇kəl\ *also* **homo·log·ic** \-jik\ *adj* [*homology* + *-ical, -ic*] : relating to or characterized by homology : HOMOLOGOUS — **homo·log·i·cal·ly** \-jə̇k(ə)lē\ *adv*

ho·mol·o·gize \hōˈmäləˌjīz, hə'-\ *vb* -ED/-ING/-S [*homologous* + *-ize*] *vi* : to be homologous : CORRESPOND ⟨a man's arm ~*s* with a dog's foreleg⟩ ~ *vt* **1** : to make homologous ⟨~ one set of rules with another⟩ **2** : to demonstrate the homology of (as parts)

ho·mol·o·giz·er \-zə(r)\ *n* -S : one that homologizes

homolo·gou·me·na \ˌhäməlōˈgümənə, hōˌmäl-\ *also* **homolo·gu·me·na** \-ˈg(y)ü-\ *n pl* [LGk *homologoumena,* fr. Gk, neut. pl. of *homologoumenos,* pres. passive part. of *homologein* to agree, fr. *homologos*] : books of the New Testament acknowledged as authoritative and canonical from the earliest time — compare ANTILEGOMENA

ho·mol·o·gous \hōˈmäləgəs, hə'-\ *adj* [Gk *homologos* agreeing, fr. *hom-* hom- + *-logos* (fr. *legein* to speak) — more at LEGEND] **1** : of, relating to, or characterized by homology: as **a** : having the same relative position, proportion, value, or structure : CORRESPONDING ⟨~ constituents in logically equivalent . . . sentences —Arthur Pap⟩ **b** (1) : corresponding in structure or origin — compare ANALOGOUS 2a (2) : of like genic constitution — used of allelic chromosomes **c** : belonging to or consisting of a chemical series whose members exhibit homology **d** : showing geometrical homology **2** : derived from or developed in response to organisms of the same species ⟨a ~ tissue graft⟩ ⟨bacteria suspended in a ~ serum⟩ — compare AUTOLOGOUS, HETEROLOGOUS — **ho·mol·o·gous·ly** *adv*

homologous graft *n* : HOMOGRAFT

homologous serum hepatitis or **homologous serum jaundice** *n* : SERUM HEPATITIS

homologous stimulus *n* : an agent (as light or sound) that is the normal stimulus of a sense organ and is able to produce its specialized stimulation only when acting on the organ adapted to receive it — compare HETEROLOGOUS STIMULUS

homologous theory *n* : a theory in botany: the sporophyte and gametophyte in plants are essentially alike, the sporophyte having developed by direct modification of the gametophyte — compare ANTITHETIC THEORY

homologous twin *n* : IDENTICAL TWIN

homolo·graph·ic \¦häməlō¦grafik, hōˌmäl-\ *or* **hom·a·lo·graph·ic** \¦häməl-\ *adj* [modif. of F *homalographique,* fr. *homalo-* homal- + *-graphique* -graphic] : preserving the mutual relations of parts esp. as to size and form

homolographic projection *n* : an equal-area map projection — compare MOLLWEIDE PROJECTION

homo·logue *or* **homo·log** \ˈhōməˌlȯg, ˈhäm- *also* -läg\ *n* -S [fr. *homologous,* after such pairs as E *analogous: analogue*] **1** : one that exhibits homology ⟨interlingual ~⟩ ⟨~*s* of the ethylene series⟩ ⟨corresponding sides of similar polygons are ~*s* of each other⟩ ⟨pectoral fin, wing, and arm are ~*s*⟩ **2** : a homologous chromosome or pair of chromosomes

ho·mol·o·gy \hōˈmäləjē, hə'-, -ji\ *n* -ES [Gk *homologia* agreement, fr. *homologos* agreeing + *-ia* -y — more at HOMOLOGOUS] **1** : a similarity often attributable to common origin : AFFINITY ⟨the anthropologist is in the curious position of dealing with . . . striking *homologies* not necessarily due to historical contact —Edward Sapir⟩ **2 a** : likeness short of identity in structure or function between parts of different organisms due to evolutionary differentiation from the same or a corresponding part of a remote ancestor ⟨the structural relation between the wing of a bird and the pectoral fin of a fish is a familiar example of ~⟩ — distinguished from *analogy* **b** : correspondence in structure between different parts of the same individual **3 a** : the relation existing between chemical compounds in a series whose successive members have in composition a regular difference esp. of one carbon and two hydrogen atoms CH_2 (as in the series of alcohols beginning with methyl alcohol CH_3OH, ethyl alcohol C_2H_5OH, propyl alcohol C_3H_7OH) **b** : the relation existing among elements in the same group of the periodic table (as the elements of the halogen group) **4** : a one-to-one correspondence of two coplanar geometrical figures whereby the junction lines of correspondent points are copunctal in the center of homology and the junction points of correspondent lines are collinear on the axis of homology

ho·mol·o·sine projection \hōˈmäləˌsīn-\ *n* [*homolographic* +

homolosine projection

sine] : an equal-area interrupted map projection that combines the sinusoidal projection for latitudes up to 40° with the homolographic for areas poleward of these latitudes

ho·mol·y·sis \hōˈmäləsə̇s\ *n* [NL, fr. *hom-* + *-lysis*] : the decomposition of a chemical compound into two neutral atoms or radicals (as X:Y → X· + Y·) — compare HETEROLYSIS — **homo·lyt·ic** \ˌhōmə¦lid·ik, ˌhäm-\ *adj*

homo·mal·lous *pronunc at* HOMO- + ¦maləs\ *adj* [*hom-* + *-mallous* (as in *heteromallous*)] : uniformly curving to one side — used of the leaves of mosses; opposed to *heteromallous*

ho·mo men·su·ra \ˌhō(ˌ)mōˌmenˈsürə\ *n* [L, lit., man the measure] : a doctrine first propounded by Protagoras holding that man is the measure of all things, that everything is relative to human apprehension and evaluation, and that there is no objective truth

homo·metrical *pronunc at* HOMO- + \ *adj* [*hom-* + *metrical*] : having the same meter — **homo·metrically** \"+ \ *adv*

homo·mor·phic \ˌ≈≈+¦mȯrfik\ *adj* [*hom-* + *-morphic*] **1** : of, relating to, or characterized by homomorphism or homomorphy **2** : alike in form or size — used specif. of synaptic chromosomes; compare HETEROMORPHIC 1d

homo·mor·phism \ˌ≈≈¦fizəm\ *n* -S [ISV *hom-* + *-morphism*] : likeness in form: as **a** : HOMOMORPHY **b** : the state of having perfect flowers of only one type — distinguished from *heterogony* — **homo·mor·phous** \ˌ≈≈¦≈fəs\ *adj*

homo·mor·pho·sis \ˌ≈≈ˈmȯrfəsə̇s *sometimes* -ˌmȯrˈfōsə̇s\ *n* [NL, fr. *hom-* + *-morphosis*] : regeneration by an organism of a part similar to one that has been lost — compare HETEROMORPHOSIS

homo·mor·phy \ˈ≈≈ˌfē\ *n* -ES [ISV *hom-* + *-morphy*] : similarity of form (as in external characters) with different fundamental structure : superficial resemblance between organisms of different groups due to convergence — opposed to *homophyly,* compare HOMOLOGY 2a

homo·neu·ra \ˌ≈≈ˈn(y)ürə\ *n pl, cap* [NL, fr. *hom-* + *-neura*] : a suborder of primitive Lepidoptera including those forms in which the venation is alike in the two pairs of wings — compare HETERONEURA

homonid *var of* HOMINID

ho·mon·o·mous \(ˈ)hōˈmänəməs, (ˈ)hä¦-\ *adj* [Gk *homonomos* under the same laws, fr. *homo-* hom- + *-nomos* (fr. *nomos* usage, custom, law) — more at NIMBLE] : similar in function and structure and developed to a like degree — used of metameric parts and animals ⟨a few insects have nearly ~ legs and wings⟩ — **ho·mon·o·mous·ly** *adv*

homo·nuclear *pronunc at* HOMO- + \ *adj* [*hom-* + *nuclear*] **1** : of or relating to the same ring in a chemical compound ⟨~ substitution in naphthalene⟩ **2** : of or relating to a molecule composed of like nuclei (as hydrogen H_2 or nitrogen N_2)

homo·nym \ˈhäməˌnim, ˈhōm-\ *n* -S [L *homonymum* the same word used to denote different things, fr. Gk *homōnymon,* fr. neut. of *homōnymos* having the same name] **1 a** : HOMOPHONE **b** : HOMOGRAPH **c** : one of two or more words spelled and pronounced alike but different in meaning (as *pool* of water and *pool* the game) **2** : NAMESAKE **3** : a taxonomic designation rejected because the identical term has been used to designate another group of the same rank — compare SYNONYM

homo·nym·ic \ˌ≈≈¦nimik\ *adj* : of, relating to, or being homonyms — **homo·nym·i·ty** \ˌ≈≈≈ˈnimәd·ē\ *n* -ES

ho·mon·y·mous \hōˈmänəməs, hä'-\ *adj* [L *homonymus,* fr. Gk *homōnymos* having the same name, fr. *homo-* hom- + *-ōnymos* (fr. *onyma, onoma* name) — more at NAME] **1 a** : having two or more different significations : AMBIGUOUS — used chiefly of words **b** : having the same designation ⟨the state and its capital are ~⟩ — opposed to *heteronymous* **c** : HOMONYMIC **2 a** : standing in the same relation; *specif* : relating to or being a convergence of the eyes such that the object is beyond the fixation point resulting in double vision with the right-eye image to the right of the left-eye image ⟨~ diplopia⟩ **b** : UNILATERAL ⟨~ hemianopia⟩ — **ho·mon·y·mous·ly** *adv*

ho·mon·y·my \-mē\ *n* -ES [LL *homonymia* identity of name, fr. Gk *homōnymia,* fr. *homōnymos* + *-ia* -y] : the quality or state of being homonymous

homo·osis \ˌhōmōˈōsə̇s, ˌhäm-\ *n* -ES [NL, fr. *hom-* + *-osis*] : development in one part of an organism of a structure normally produced in another part

homo·ou·sia \ˌ≈≈¦üzēə, -üsēə, -üzh(ē)ə, -üsh(ē)ə\ *n* -S [NL, fr. LGk *homoousios* + L *-ia* -y] : identity in essence or substance

¹homo·ou·sian \-ən\ *n* -S *often cap* [modif. (influenced by LGk *homoousios*) of LL *homousianus,* adj. & n., fr. LGk *homoousios* of the same substance (fr. Gk *homo-* hom- + *ousios,* fr. *ousia* substance) + L *-anus* -an] : one that accepts the homoousian doctrine of the Nicene Creed

²homoousian \"\ *adj* **1 a** : holding to the doctrine of the Nicene Creed that the Son of God is of the same essence or substance with the Father **b** : of or relating to the doctrine of homoousia — distinguished from *homoiousian;* compare HETEROOUSIAN **2** : of or relating to the homoousians **3** : of or relating to homoousia

homo·ou·sian·ism \-əˌnizəm\ *n* -S : the doctrines and beliefs of the homoousians

homo·ou·si·on \-üz(h)ēˌän, -üs(h)-\ *n* -S *often cap* [Gk, acc. masc. sing. of *homoousios*] : a theological doctrine holding that Christ is of one substance with God ⟨the very existence of Christianity . . . was at stake over the *Homoousion* —C.H. Turner⟩

homo·pet·al·ous \ˌ≈≈¦pedᵊləs\ *adj* [ISV *hom-* + *-petalous*] : having petals alike

homo·phone \ˈhäməˌfōn, ˈhōm-\ *n* [ISV *hom-* + *-phone*] **1** : one of two or more words pronounced alike but different in meaning or derivation or spelling (as *all* and *awl; to, too,* and *two; rite, write, right,* and *wright*) — called also *homonym* **2** : a character or group of characters pronounced the same as another character or group ⟨η, ι, υ, ει, and οι are ~*s* in modern Greek, all being pronounced \ē\⟩

homo·phon·ic \ˌ≈≈¦fänik\ *adj* [Gk *homophōnos* + E *-ic*] **1** : sounding alike or being of the same musical pitch : UNISONOUS **2** : relating to homophony : MONOPHONIC — compare POLYPHONIC **3** : having all musical parts moving in the same rhythm — **homo·phon·i·cal·ly** \-nə̇k(ə)lē\ *adv*

ho·moph·o·nous \hōˈmäfənəs, hä'-, hə'-\ *adj* [Gk *homophōnos,* fr. *homo-* hom- + *-phōnos* (fr. *phōnē* sound, voice) — more at BAN] **1** : HOMOPHONIC 1 **2** *also* **homo·phone** \ˈhäməˌfōn, ˈhōm-\ : being a homophone

ho·moph·o·ny \hōˈmäfənē, hä'-, hə'-\ *n* -ES [Gk *homophōnia,* fr. *homophōnos* + *-ia* -y] **1** : sameness of sound : the quality or state of being homophonous **2 a** : UNISON **b** : MONODY 4a — compare POLYPHONY **c** : composition in which the voice or instrumental parts move in one rhythm in chordal style

homo·phyletic *pronunc at* HOMO- + \ *adj* [ISV *hom-* + *phyletic;* orig. formed as G *homophyl*] : relating to homophyly : belonging to the same race

ho·moph·y·ly \hōˈmäfəlē\ *n* -ES [ISV *hom-* + *phyl-* + *-y;* orig. formed as G *homophylie*] : resemblance due to common ancestry — opposed to *homomorphy*

homo·pla·sia \≈≈ *at* HOMO- + ˈplāzh(ē)ə\ *or* **homo·pla·sis** \-ˈplāsə̇s\ *n, pl* **homopla·sias** \-āzh(ē)əz\ *or* **homopla·ses** \-āˌsēz\ [NL, fr. *hom-* + *-plasia, -plasis*] : HOMOPLASY

homo·plas·tic \ˌ≈≈¦plastik\ *adj* [ISV *hom-* + *-plastic*] **1** : of or relating to homoplasy ⟨~ organ⟩ **2** : of, relating to, or derived from another individual of the same species ⟨~ graft⟩ — **homo·plas·ti·cal·ly** \-tə̇k(ə)lē\ *adv*

homo·plasy \ˈ≈≈ˌplāsē, -lasē; hōˈmäpləsē, hä'-\ *n* -ES [*hom-* + *-plasy*] : correspondence between parts or organs acquired as the result of parallel evolution or convergence — opposed to *homogeny*

homo·ploid \ˈ≈≈ˌplȯid\ *adj* [*hom-* + *-ploid*] : exhibiting similar degrees of ploidy

homo·polar \ˌ≈≈+ \ *adj* [ISV *hom-* + *polar*] **1** : having the poles of the primary axis alike **2** : alike in both senses (as AB and BA) with respect to physical or other property — used of a direction in crystals; compare CENTER OF SYMMETRY 2 **3 a** : relating to, characterized by, or being a union of atoms of like state as regards polarity : NONPOLAR, NONIONIC — distinguished from *heteropolar;* compare IONIC, POLAR **b** : UNIPOLAR ⟨~ dynamo⟩ — **homo·polarity** \"+ \ *n*

homopolar generator *n* : a generator producing direct current without reversals of potential or resort to commutation

homopolar machine *n* : ACYCLIC MACHINE

homo·polymer *pronunc at* HOMO- + \ *n* [*homogeneous* + *polymer*] : a polymer (as polyethylene, polyvinyl acetate) containing only units of one single monomer

homo·polymerization \"+ \ *n* : the process of homopolymerizing

homo·polymerize \"+ \ *vi* -ED/-ING/-S [*homopolymer* + *-ize*] : to form a homopolymer

ho·mop·tera \hōˈmäptərə\ *n pl, cap* [NL, fr. *hom-* + *-ptera*] : a large and important suborder of Hemiptera (sometimes considered a separate order) comprising the cicadas, lantern flies, leafhoppers, spittle insects, treehoppers, aphids, psyllas, whiteflies, and scales all of which have a small prothorax and sucking mouthparts consisting of a jointed beak and undergo an incomplete metamorphosis — compare HETEROPTERA — **ho·mop·ter·an** \-rən\ *adj* — **ho·mop·ter·ous** \-rəs\ *adj*

ho·mop·ter·ist \-rə̇st\ *n* -S [NL *Homoptera* + *-ist*] : a specialist on or student of the Homoptera

ho·mop·ter·on \-ˌrän\ *n* -S [NL, back-formation fr. *Homoptera*] : one of the Homoptera

ho·mor·elaps \hōˈmȯrəˌlaps\ [NL, prob. irreg. fr. *hom-* + *Elaps*] *syn of* ELAPS

hom·organic \ˌhōm, ˌhäm+\ *adj* [*hom-* + *organic*] : sharing one or more of the articulating vocal organs : articulated with the same basic closure or constriction but differentiated by one or more modifications ⟨\p\, \b\, and \m\ are ~, contact of the two lips being common to all three⟩

homos *pl of* HOMO

ho·mo sapi·ens \ˌhō(ˌ)mōˈsapēˌenz, -sāp- *also* -ēˌenz *or* -ēˌen(t)s\ *n* [NL, a biological species, fr. *Homo* + *sapiens* (specific epithet), fr. L, wise — more at SAPIENT] **1** *usu cap H* : MANKIND 1 **2** *pl* **homo sapiens** : sentient, conscious, thinking man — contrasted with *homo faber*

homo·sce·das·tic *pronunc at* HOMO- + s(k)ə̇¦dastik\ *adj* [*hom-* + LGk *skedastikos* able to scatter, fr. Gk *skedastos* capable of being scattered (fr. *skedannynai* to scatter) + *-ikos* -ic — more at SHATTER] : having equal standard deviations ⟨~ statistical distributions⟩ — **homo·sce·das·tic·i·ty** \ˌ≈(ˌ)≈-ˌs(k)ēˌdaˈstisəd·ē\ *n* -ES

¹ho·mo·sexual \ˌhōmə, -mō + \ *adj* [*hom-* + *sexual*] **1** : of, relating to, or being of the same sex ⟨~ twins⟩ **2 a** : of, relating to, or exhibiting homosexuality ⟨~ tendency⟩ ⟨~ act⟩ — opposed to *heterosexual* **b** : involving, characterized by, or based on homosexuality ⟨a child's ~ phase⟩

²homosexual \"\ *n* -S : one who is inclined toward or practices homosexuality

ho·mo·sexualist \ˌ≈≈+ \ *n* : HOMOSEXUAL

ho·mo·sexuality \"+ \ *n* **1** : atypical sexuality characterized by manifestation of sexual desire toward a member of one's own sex **2** : erotic activity with a member of one's own sex — compare LESBIANISM **3 a** : a stage in normal psychosexual development occurring during prepuberty in the male and during early adolescence in the female during which libidinal gratification is sought with members of one's own sex **b** : the extent to which one's libido is fixated at a homoerotic level

ho·mo sig·no·rum \ˌhō(ˌ)mōsigˈnōrəm\ *n* [NL, lit., man of signs] : a conventionalized figure often found in old almanacs showing a man surrounded by signs of the zodiac from which lines point to the parts of the body thought to be subject to their influence

ho·mo·spor·ous *pronunc at* HOMO- + ¦spōrəs; (ˈ)hō¦mäspərəs, (ˈ)hä¦-\ *adj* [*hom-* + *-sporous*] : characterized by homospory — compare PROTHALLIUM

homo·spory \ˈ≈≈ˌspōrē, ≈ˈ≈ˌsparē\ *n* -ES [*hom-* + *-spory*] : the production by various plants (as the club mosses and horsetails) of asexual spores of only one kind — opposed to *heterospory*

ho·mos·te·us \hōˈmästēəs, hä'-\ *n, cap* [NL, fr. *hom-* + *-osteus*] : a genus of very large flattened Devonian fishes (subclass Arthrodira) having slender toothless jaws

homo·styled *pronunc at* HOMO- + ˌstīld\ *also* **homo·sty·lic** \ˌ≈≈¦stīlik\ *or* **homo·sty·lous** \-ləs\ *adj* [*homostyled* fr. *hom-* + *styled; homostylic* fr. *hom-* + *style* + *-ic; homostylous* fr. *hom-* + *-stylous*] : having styles all of one length — compare HETEROSTYLED

homo·sty·ly \ˈ≈≈ˌstīlē\ *n* -ES [ISV *hom-* + *-styly;* orig. formed as G *homostylie*] : HOMOGONY

ho·mo sui juris \ˌhō(ˌ)mō+\ *n* [L] : a man under his own control — opposed to *homo alieni juris*

homo·tac·tic *pronunc at* HOMO- + ¦taktik\ *adj* [*hom-* + *-tactic*] : HOMOTAXIAL

homo·tax·e·ous \-¦taksēəs\ *adj* [NL *homotaxis* + E *-eous*] : HOMOTAXIAL

homo·tax·ia \ˌ≈≈ˈtaksēə\ *n* -S [NL, fr. *hom-* + *-taxia*] : HOMOTAXIS

homo·tax·i·al \ˌ≈≈¦taksēəl\ *adj* [NL *homotaxis* + E *-al*] : of or relating to homotaxis — **homo·tax·i·al·ly** \-əlē\ *adv*

homo·tax·is \ˌ≈≈¦taksə̇s\ *n* [NL, fr. *hom-* + *-taxis*] : similarity in arrangement; *esp* : similarity in fossil content and in order of arrangement of stratified deposits that are not necessarily contemporaneous

homo·taxy \ˌ≈≈ˌtaksē\ *n* -ES [NL *homotaxia*] : HOMOTAXIS

homo·thal·lic *pronunc at* HOMO- + ¦thalik\ *adj* [*hom-* + *thall-* + *-ic*] **1** : having only one haploid phase producing genetically compatible gametes — used esp. of algae and fungi or of the spores producing such a phase; compare HETEROTHALLIC **2** : MONOECIOUS

homo·thal·lism \ˌ≈≈ˈthaˌlizəm\ *n* -S : the quality or state of being homothallic

ho·mo·therm \ˈ≈≈ˌthərm\ *n* -S [*hom-* + *-therm*] : HOMOIOTHERM

homo·ther·mous \ˌ≈≈¦thərməs\ *also* **homo·ther·mal** \-məl\ *or* **homo·ther·mic** \-mik\ *adj* [*hom-* + *-thermous, thermal, thermic*] : HOMOIOTHERMIC

homo·thet·ic \ˌ≈≈¦thed·ik\ *adj* [ISV *hom-* + Gk *thetikos* fit for placing; orig. formed as F *homothétique* — more at THETIC] : similar and similarly oriented — used of geometric figures

homo·top·ic \-¦täpik\ *adj* [*hom-* + Gk *topos* place + E *-ic*] **1** : relating to the same or corresponding places or parts ⟨~ tumors⟩ **2** : HOMEOMORPHIC — **ho·mot·o·py** \hōˈmäd·əpē\ *n* -ES

homo·transplant *pronunc at* HOMO- + \ *n* [*hom-* + *transplant*] : HOMOGRAFT — **homo·transplantation** \"+ \ *n*

ho·mot·ro·pous \hōˈmäˌtrəpəs\ *or* **ho·mot·ro·pal** \-pəl\ *adj* [F *homotrope* (fr. *homo-* hom- + *-trope*) + E *-ous* or *-al*] : having the radicle directed toward the hilum ⟨~ seeds⟩

homo·typ·al *pronunc at* HOMO- + ¦tīpəl\ *adj* : of or relating to a homotype

homo·type \ˈ≈≈+ \ *n* [*hom-* + *type*] **1** : a part or organ of the same fundamental structure as another : HOMOLOGUE ⟨the right arm is the ~ of the right leg⟩ ⟨one arm is the ~ of the other⟩ **2** : HOMEOTYPE

homo·typ·ic \ˌ≈≈¦tipik\ *or* **homo·typ·i·cal** \-pə̇kəl\ *adj* **1** : of or relating to a homotype **2** : being the equational division of meiosis — **homo·typ·i·cal·ly** \-pə̇k(ə)lē\ *adv*

homo·typy \ˈ≈≈ˌtīpē\ *n* -ES [ISV *hom-* + *-typy*] : the relation existing between homotypes : SERIAL HOMOLOGY

homo·zygosis \ˌ≈≈+ \ *n* [NL, fr. *hom-* + *zygosis*] **1** : the union of gametes identical for one or more pairs of genes : the act or process of becoming a homozygote **2** : HOMOZYGOSITY

homo·zygosity \"+ \ *n* -ES : the quality or state of being a homozygote — compare HETEROZYGOSITY

homo·zygote \"+ \ *n* [ISV *hom-* + *zygote*] : an animal or plant containing either but not both members of at least one pair of allelomorphic characters : an individual that breeds true to type and is termed pure with respect to a specified character — compare HETEROZYGOTE, MENDEL'S LAWS — **homo·zygotic** \"+ \ *adj*

homo·zy·gous \"+¦zīgəs\ *adj* **1** : possessing genes for only one member of at least one pair of allelomorphic characters **2** : producing only one type of gamete with respect to a specified character — opposed to *heterozygous* — **homo·zy·gous·ly** *adv*

hom·rai \ˈhōmˌrī, ˈhäm-\ *or* **homu·rai** \-məˌrī\ *n* -S [Nepali *hōgrāyo*] : a large hornbill (*Buceros bicornis*) of India and southeastern Asia

homs \ˈhōmz, -m(p)s\ *adj, usu cap* [fr. *Homs,* Syria] : of or from the city of Homs, Syria : of the kind or style prevalent in Homs

homuncio *n* -ES [L, dim. of *homin-, homo* man — more at HOMAGE] *obs* : HOMUNCULUS

ho·mun·cu·lar \(ˈ)hōˌməŋkyələ(r)\ *adj* [*homunculus* + *-ar*] : resembling or characteristic of a homunculus

ho·mun·cu·lus \≈ˈ≈≈ləs\ *n, pl* **homuncu·li** \-ˌlī\ [L, dim. of *homin-, homo* man] : a little man : DWARF : MANIKIN; *specif* : a manikin that is artificially produced in a cucurbit by an alchemist

homy *var of* HOMEY

hon \ˈhən\ *n* -S [short for *honey*] : SWEETHEART, DEAR ⟨you're a great old girl, ~ —Sinclair Lewis⟩

hon *abbr* honor; honorable; honorary; honored

ho·nan \ˈhōˈnan\ *n* -S [fr. *Honan,* province in China where it was originally made] : a lustrous lightweight silk material resembling pongee now widely imitated in other fibers

honble *abbr* honorable

hon·da \ˈhändə\ *also* **hon·do** \-n(ˌ)dō\ *n* -S [Sp *honda* sling, fr. L *funda,* perh. fr. Gk *sphendonē*] : a metal, knotted, or spliced eye at one end of a lariat through which the other end is passed to form a running noose or lasso

hon·do \ˈhän(ˌ)dō\ *n* -S [Sp, bottom, fr. L *fundus* — more at BOTTOM] : a broad low-lying arroyo in the southwestern U.S.

¹hon·du·ran \(ˈ)hän¦d(y)ürən, -ür-\ *adj, usu cap* [*Honduras* + E *-an* (adj. suffix)] : of, relating to, or characteristic of Honduras

²honduran \"\ *n* -S *cap* [*Honduras* + E *-an* (n. suffix)] : a native or inhabitant of Honduras

¹hon·du·ra·ne·an *also* **hon·du·ra·ni·an** \¦händ(y)ə¦rānēən\

adj, usu cap [irreg. fr. *Honduras* + E *-ean, -ian,* vars. of *-an* (adj. suffix)] : HONDURAN

²**honduranean** *or* **honduranian** \"\ *n* -s *usu cap* [irreg. fr. *Honduras* + E *-ean, -ian,* vars. of *-an* (n. suffix)] : HONDURAN

hon·du·ras \(')hän¦d(y)ůrəs, -)ůr-\ *adj, usu cap* [fr. *Honduras,* republic in Central Amer.; British *Honduras,* crown colony in Central Amer.] : of or from Honduras : of the kind or style prevalent in Honduras : HONDURAN

honduras bark *n, usu cap H* [fr. Rep. of *Honduras,* its locality] : CASCARA AMARGA

honduras cedar *n, usu cap H* : SPANISH CEDAR

honduras mahogany *n, usu cap H* **1** : an important Central American timber tree (*Swietenia macrophylla*) closely related to true mahogany **2** : MAHOGANY 1a(2)

honduras rosewood *n, usu cap H* : a valuable dark streaked wood from one or more Central American trees of the genus *Dalbergia* (as *D. stevensonii* and *D. cubilquitzensis*)

¹**hone** \'hōn\ *n* -s [ME, fr. OE *hān* stone; akin to ON *hein* whetstone, L *cos,* Gk *kōnos* cone, Skt *sisāti* he sharpens, *sana* whetstone] **1 a** : a fine-grit stone used for sharpening a cutting implement (as a razor) — compare OILSTONE, WHETSTONE **b** : an artificial stone covered with an abrading substance and used for sharpening **2** : a tool for enlarging holes to precise tolerances and controlling finishes esp. of internal cylindrical surfaces by means of a mechanically rotated and expanded abrasive **3** : a drag for dressing and smoothing a road surface (as gravel)

²**hone** \"\ *vt* -ED/-ING/-S **1** : to sharpen with or as if with a hone : WHET ⟨learned to ~ and strop his razor correctly —G.S.Perry⟩ ⟨*honed* his antlers sharp as knives —D.C.Peattie⟩ ⟨the Yankee character was *honed* sharp right here —Bernard DeVoto⟩ **2** : to enlarge or smooth with a hone ⟨cylinder bodies are bored and then *honed* to a mirror finish —*Mechanical Engineering*⟩ ⟨the walls of the vestibule are lined with *honed* pink stone from Mankato —*Amer. Guide Series: Minn.*⟩

³**hone** \"\ *vi* -ED/-ING/-S [MF *hoigner* to murmur, grumble, perh. alter. (influenced by *groigner* to grumble, fr. L *grunnire* to grunt) of *honir, honnir* to dishonor, of Gmc origin; akin to OE *hīenan, hȳnan* to abase, OHG *hōnen* to revile, Goth *haunjan* to abase; causative-denominative fr. a Gmc adjective represented by OE *hēan* lowly, abject, Goth *hauns* humble; akin to OHG *hōna* scorn, ON *hāth* act of jeering, Gk *kauros* bad, Latvian *kauns* disgrace — more at GRUNT] **1** *now dial* : to grumble and moan **2** *now dial* : LONG, YEARN — usu. used with *for* or *after* ⟨'tis vain, 'tis vain, my dear young man, to ~ for Barbara Allen —*Barbara Allen*⟩

hon·er \-nə(r)\ *n* -s [²*hone* + *-er*] : one that hones

¹**hon·est** \'änəst\ *adj, sometimes* -ER/-EST [ME *honest, honeste,* fr. OF *honeste,* fr. L *honestus* honorable, decent, handsome, fr. *honos, honor* esteem, honor] **1 a** : free from fraud or deception : LEGITIMATE, TRUTHFUL ⟨make an ~ dollar⟩ ⟨an atmosphere still magically colored by gentility, culture and ~ wealth —Winston Brebner⟩ ⟨the first need is for ~ and candid presentation of the facts —Dean Acheson⟩ **b** : of unquestioned authenticity : GENUINE, REAL ⟨making ~ stops at stop signs —*Christian Science Monitor*⟩ ⟨when it's not making ~ rain . . . it's misting from the marshes or fogging from the sea —T.H.Fielding⟩ — often used intensively in hyphened combination with *to* and an object ⟨the first *honest*-to-God American beauty I had seen in four months —Tom O'Reilly⟩ ⟨a real *honest*-to-goodness Cape Cod lobster stew —M.F.Leonard⟩ **c** (1) : free of ostentation or pretense : HUMBLE ⟨younger sons . . . were often apprenticed to some ~ trade —Wallace Clare⟩ (2) : free of ornament or disguise : PLAIN ⟨a cafeteria which . . . serves really good ~ food —C.M.Smith⟩ **2 a** *obs* : of good repute : ESTIMABLE **b** : virtuous in the eyes of society : REPUTABLE ⟨the fortune . . . made the woman ~, as her second protector immediately married her —G.L.Phillips⟩ **c** *chiefly Brit* : GOOD, WORTHY ⟨an ~ fellow, who did his best to please⟩ ⟨I keep six ~ serving-men —Rudyard Kipling⟩ **3 a** : of a creditable nature : PRAISEWORTHY ⟨workers who would not take the trouble to turn out an ~ job —Roy Lewis & Angus Maude⟩ **b** *obs* : of good reputation : RESPECTABLE ⟨now let's go to an ~ alehouse and sing Old Rose —Izaak Walton⟩ **4 a** : characterized by integrity : adhering to principle : UPRIGHT ⟨~ merchants⟩ ⟨no ~ prostitute would have had the face to ask the prices they asked —Robert Graves⟩ **b** : frank and straightforward : SINCERE ⟨early in life I had to choose between ~ arrogance and hypocritical humility —F.L.Wright⟩ ⟨an ~ appeal to the people was the last thing desired by the Federalists —V.L.Parrington⟩ **c** : direct and uncomplicated : INNOCENT, SIMPLE ⟨the ~ sleep of any tired child —Alice Marriott⟩ ⟨the ~ average playgoer simply wants to be told what play is best worth going to—for him —C.E.Montague⟩ **syn** see UPRIGHT

²**honest** \"\ *vt* -ED/-ING/-S *obs* : to make honest or honorable : JUSTIFY

³**honest** \"\ *adv* : HONESTLY ⟨I have ever found thee ~ true —Shak.⟩ ⟨~ I won't tell⟩ — often used intensively in hyphened combination with *to* and an object ⟨knowing I was *honest*-to-goodness off and away —Helen Eustis⟩

honest injun *adv, usu cap I* : on my word of honor : HONESTLY

hon·est·ly *adv* [ME, fr. ¹*honest* + *-ly*] : in an honest manner : with honesty

hon·est·ness *n* -ES [ME *honestnes,* fr. ¹ *honest* + *-nes* -ness] : the quality or state of being honest

hone·stone \'=,=\ *n* : a stone suitable for making hones for sharpening; *also* : a hone made from such a stone

hon·es·ty \'änəstē, -ti\ *n* -ES [ME *honeste* estimable character, honor, fr. OF *honesté,* fr. L *honestat-, honestas,* fr. *honestus* honorable] **1** *obs* : estimable character; *esp* : CHASTITY ⟨the honor of a maid is her name; and no legacy is so rich as ~ —Shak.⟩ **2 a** : fairness and straightforwardness of conduct : INTEGRITY ⟨was not greatly pleased with Lincoln, though admitting his ~ and fair capability —W.C.Ford⟩ **b** : adherence to the facts : freedom from subterfuge or duplicity : TRUTHFULNESS, SINCERITY ⟨~ is the best policy⟩ ⟨the field worker depends on the ~ of the people for correct replies —J.M.Mogey⟩ ⟨a film of rare ~ and heart —Arthur Knight⟩ ⟨peaceable life in all godliness and ~ —1 Tim 2:2 (AV)⟩ **3** [so called fr. the semitransparent pods] : a European plant of the genus *Lunaria* (esp. *L. annua*) — called also *satinpod*

honesty clause *n* : FULL REPORTING CLAUSE

hone·wort \'hōn,-\ *n* [*hone-* (of unknown origin) + *wort*] : any of several plants of the family Umbelliferae: as **a** : STONE PARSLEY **b** : a perennial herb (*Cryptotaenia canadensis*) with thin three-foliolate leaves and small white flowers — called also *wild chervil*

¹**hon·ey** \'hənē, -ni\ *n, pl* **hon·eys** *or* **hon·ies** \-nēz,-niz\ [ME *hony,* fr. OE *hunig;* akin to OHG *honag* honey, ON *hunang,* L *canicae* bran, Gk *knēkos* tawny, and perh. to Skt *kāñcana* gold] **1 a** : a sweet viscid material that is elaborated out of the nectar of flowers in the honey sac of various kinds of bees and stored in the nest for use during the winter as food for the larvae or esp. in the case of the honeybee for the colony and that has a flavor and color depending largely on the plants from which the nectar is gathered with that of clover being esp. esteemed by man for whom as for certain wild animals honey constitutes a favorite article of food — compare HONEYCOMB, INVERT SUGAR **b** : a sweet fluid resembling honey that is collected or elaborated by various other insects — compare HONEY ANT, HONEYDEW **2 a** : SWEETHEART, DEAR — often used as a term of endearment **b** : something superlative in appearance, excellence, complexity, or degree ⟨a ~ of a full-length coat . . . in white American broadtail —Lois Long⟩ ⟨incidental romance and a ~ of an Indian battle at the end —Muriel Burns⟩ ⟨it must have been a ~ with the complicated distilling columns, the automatic controls, the valves and pressure tanks —Joseph Starobin⟩ ⟨if there is a postwar depression . . . it will be a ~ —George Soule⟩ **3** : the quality or state of being sweet : SWEETNESS : something that is sweet ⟨coaxed him with ~ in her voice⟩ ⟨seduced by the ~ of admiration⟩ **4** *pharmacy* : any of various preparations consisting of simple mixtures of medicaments with honey ⟨borax ~⟩ **5** : a sweet syrupy liquid (as maple syrup) with a flavor resembling honey — see APPLE HONEY **6** *or* **honey yellow** : a dark grayish yellow that is redder, stronger, and slightly lighter than California green, redder, stronger, and slightly lighter than olivesheen, and very slightly redder than yellowstone — called also *middle stone* **7** : HONEY LOCUST

²**honey** \"\ *vb* **hon·eyed** *also* **hon·ied** \-nēd,-nid\ **honeyed** *also* **honied; honeying; honeys** *also* **honies** [ME *honien,* fr. *hony,* n.] *vt* **1** : to sweeten with or as if with honey **2 a** : to call one "honey" as a term of endearment ⟨their husbands were ~*ing* . . . them all the time —Thomas Hart⟩ **b** : to speak ingratiatingly to : FLATTER ⟨the station master . . . ~*ed* him up the steps of the last coach —Thomas Wood †1950⟩ ~ *vi* **1** : to use blandishments or cajolery — often used with *up* ⟨by ~*ing* up to his landlady got his socks darned and his buttons sewn on⟩ **2** : to be flattering or obsequious : FAWN ⟨rough to common men but ~*ing* at the whisper of a lord —Alfred Tennyson⟩

³**honey** \"\ *adj* **hon·i·er** \-nēə(r), -niə-\ **hon·i·est** \-nēəst, -niə-\ *adj* [ME *hony,* fr. *hony,* n.] **1** : of or relating to honey or its production ⟨~ cake⟩ **2 a** : resembling honey (as in color or sweetness) ⟨among the walking shoes is one of ~ or black alligator —*New Yorker*⟩ ⟨the ~ peace in old poems —Robinson Jeffers⟩ **b** *archaic* : DEAR ⟨my good sweet ~ lord —Shak.⟩

honey agaric *n* : HONEY MUSHROOM

honey ant *n* : any of various ants some of whose workers serve as receptacles for the storage of honey which they are able to regurgitate from their greatly distended abdomens when it is needed to feed other members of the colony

honey badger *n* : RATEL

honey bag *n* : HONEY SAC

honeyballs \'=,=,=\ *n pl* : BUTTONBUSH

honey balm *n* : a sweet-scented mint (*Melittis melissophyllum*) of central and southern Europe

honey bear *n* **1** : KINKAJOU **2** : SLOTH BEAR

honeybee \'=,=,=\ *n* : any of certain social honey-producing

honeybees: *1* queen, *2* drone, *3* worker

bees of *Apis* and related genera; *esp* : a native European bee (*Apis mellifera*) that is kept for its honey and wax in most parts of the world, has developed into several races differing in size, color, disposition, and productivity, and has escaped to the wild wherever suitable conditions prevail — compare BLACK BEE, CARNIOLAN BEE, DRONE, HONEYCOMB, ITALIAN BEE, QUEEN BEE, WORKER

honey beige *n* : DORADO 2

honey bell *n* : an African shrub (*Mahernia verticillata*) of the family Sterculiaceae having sweet honey-yellow flowers and used as an ornamental

hon·ey·ber·ry \'=,=- — *see* BERRY\ *n* **1** : the fruit of either of two trees having sweetish berries: as **a** : an Old World hackberry (*Celtis australis*) **b** : GENIP 2 **2** : a tree that bears honeyberries

honeybird *also* **honeybine** \'=,=,=\ *n* : WOODBINE 1

honey bird *n* **1** : HONEY GUIDE **2** : HONEY EATER

honeyblob \'=,=,=\ *n, Brit* : GOOSEBERRY

honey-blonde \'=¦=¦=\ *adj* : HONEY 2a

honeybloom \'=,=,=\ *n* : SPREADING DOGBANE

honey bread *n* : CAROB 1

honeybunch *or* **honeybun** \'=,=,=\ *n* : HONEY 2a

honey buzzard *n* : a European hawk (*Pernis apivorus*) related to the kites and feeding on insects and small reptiles and often tearing up nests of wasps and bumblebees to eat their larvae — called also *honey kite*

honey clover *n* **1** : WHITE SWEET CLOVER **2** : KURA CLOVER

¹**honeycomb** \'=,=,=\ *n, often attrib* [ME *honycomb,* fr. OE *hunigcamb,* fr. *hunig* honey + *camb* comb — more at ¹HONEY, COMB] **1 a** : a mass of hexagonal prismatic wax cells varying in size according to their use built by honeybees in their nest or hive to contain their brood and stores of honey — compare BEESWAX **b** : a mass of cells containing honey used as an article of food ⟨pats of butter stamped with a swan, and slabs of ~ —Mary Webb⟩ **2** : a flaw in metal due to imperfect casting, corrosion, or the abrasive action of gunpowder ⟨a scratch or spot of ~ in the grooves renders the rifle completely useless for match-shooting —W.W.Greener⟩ **3 a** : something that resembles a honeycomb in structure or appearance ⟨a ~ of pigeonholes stuffed with old letters —Berton Roueché⟩ ⟨a ~ of dark, roofed-in arcades —Mollie Panter-Downes⟩ ⟨is experimenting with metal ~ made of stainless steel —Reid Hale⟩ ⟨a red ~ of fire burning far into a great pine root —Eve Langley⟩; *specif* : a building facade having a multicellular pattern of repeated units **b** (1) : a weave with a small allover pattern of raised squares, oblongs, or diamonds with indented centers formed by long floats (2) : a reversible fabric of this weave made usu. of cotton or wool and used for clothing or towels — called also *waffle cloth* **c** *or* **honeycomb stomach** : RETICULUM 1 **d** : HONEYCOMB SPONGE

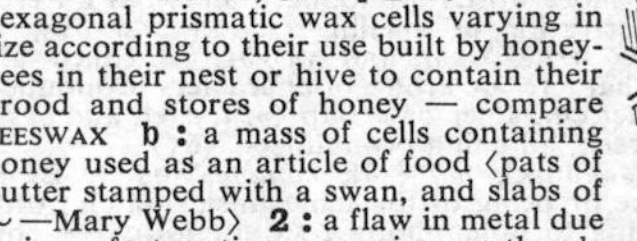

honeycomb 1a

²**honeycomb** \"\ *vt* **1 a** : to cause to be full of cavities like a honeycomb : make into a tissue of holes separated by thin walls or partitions : PIT ⟨both substances eat and ~ the pipe —Emily Holt⟩ ⟨the tunnels of the subways ~ rocks and rivers and skyscrapers —*Amer. Guide Series: N. Y. City*⟩ ⟨the limestone country hereabouts is ~*ed* with caves and grottoes —Tom Marvel⟩ **b** : to make into a checkered pattern : FRET ⟨the 650,000-odd peasant settlements which ~ the countryside —Daniel & Alice Thorner⟩ ⟨blouses are ruched and ~*ed* in alternating panels⟩ **2 a** : to penetrate into every part of : FILL, INFILTRATE ⟨a book that has been ~*ed* with classical allusions⟩ ⟨the . . . government is ~*ed* with spies —T.H.White b.1915⟩ **b** : SUBVERT, WEAKEN ⟨the gigantic edifice of prices was ~*ed* with speculative credit —F.L.Allen⟩ ~ *vi* : to become pitted, checked, or cellular in structure or appearance ⟨acids cause boiler metal to ~⟩ ⟨the cliff opened . . . before the girl, ~*ing* into archways and steep flights of stairs —Kay Boyle⟩

honeycomb coral *n* : a fossil coral of *Favosites* or a related genus

honeycombing *n* : internal cracking or checking in lumber due to imperfect seasoning and often not visible on the surface — called also *hollow-horning*

honeycomb ringworm *n* : FAVUS

honeycomb sponge *n* : a fine soft-fibered commercial sponge (*Hippospongia equina elastica*) of a massive form occurring in the Mediterranean and Red seas

honeycomb stitch *n* : any of various decorative stitches used in smocking, lacemaking, or knitting to form a honeycomb pattern

honeycomb tripe *n* : TRIPE 1a(2)

honeycreeper \'=,=,=\ *n* : any of numerous small bright-colored oscine birds constituting the family Coerebidae found in tropical and subtropical America — see BANANA QUIT; compare CREEPER 4, HONEY EATER

honeycup \'=,=,=\ *n* : SENSITIVE PEA

hon·ey·dew \'hənē,d(y)ü, -ni,-\ *n* **1** : a saccharine deposit found on the leaves of many plants that is secreted usu. by aphids or scales but sometimes by a fungus esp. of the genus *Claviceps* **2** : something as sweet as honeydew or as honey ⟨on ~ hath fed, and drunk the milk of paradise —S.T.Coleridge⟩ ⟨a gentle ~ of a southern girl —Raymond Walters b.1912⟩ **3** : tobacco moistened with molasses **4** : a moderate orange that is redder and paler than Persian orange, redder and paler than ocher brown, and redder, stronger, and slightly darker than average apricot **5** : HONEYDEW MELON

hon·ey·dewed \-üd\ *adj* : covered with honeydew ⟨~ foliage⟩

honeydew melon *n* : a smooth-skinned white, greenish white, or pale yellow muskmelon derived from the winter melon and having greenish very sweet flesh

honeydrop \'=,=,=\ *n* : a drop of honey or something like a drop of honey in sweetness

honey eater *n* : any of several oscine birds that constitute the family Meliphagidae, are found mostly in the south Pacific, and have a long protrusible tongue adapted for extracting nectar and small insects from flowers — called also *honeysucker;* see BELLBIRD, FLYING COACHMAN, FRIARBIRD, STITCHBIRD, WATTLEBIRD; compare HONEYCREEPER

hon·eyed *also* **hon·ied** \-nēd,-nid\ *adj* [ME *honied,* fr. past part. of *honien* to honey] : sweetened with or as if with honey ⟨stilling the ~ air —Walter de la Mare⟩ ⟨many a wily rogue beguiles with ~ tongue —Peggy Bennett⟩ — **hon·eyed·ly** *adv* — **hon·eyed·ness** *n* -ES

honey extractor *n* : EXTRACTOR 1c

honeyflow \'=,=,=\ *n* : a supply or period of availability of floral nectar suitable for bees to convert into honey ⟨some swarming was evident . . . due to the heavy ~ —*Canadian Bee Jour.*⟩ ⟨the ~ . . . began during the latter part of June —*Western Canada Beekeeper*⟩

honeyflower \'=,=,=\ *n* : any of several flowers yielding nectar copiously: as **a** : a plant of the genus *Melianthus* **b** : either of two Australian shrubs (*Protea mellifera* or the related *Lambertia formosa*) **c** : BEE ORCHIS **d** : a sweet sultan (*Centaurea moschata*)

honeyflower family *n* : MELIANTHACEAE

hon·ey·fug·gle \'hənē,fəgəl\ *also* **hon·ey·fo·gle** \-fōg-\ *or* **hon·ey·fu·gle** \-f(y)üg-\ *vb* -ED/-ING/-S [perh. fr. ¹*honey* + E dial. *fugel* to cheat, trick] *vt* **1** *chiefly dial* **a** : DECEIVE, CHEAT, COZEN **b** : to obtain by cheating or deception : FINAGLE **2** **2** *chiefly dial* : FLATTER, CAJOLE, BLANDISH ~ *vi, chiefly dial* : to ingratiate or seek to ingratiate oneself so as to cheat or deceive

honey gland *n* : NECTARY

honey gold *n* : a moderate yellow that is redder and deeper than colonial yellow or mustard yellow and greener and stronger than brass

honey grass *n* **1** : MOLASSES GRASS **2** : MELIC GRASS

honey guide *n* **1** : any of several small plainly colored nonpasserine birds of the family Indicatoridae esp. of the genera *Indicator* and *Prodotiscus* that inhabit Africa, the Himalayas, and the East Indies and include some that lead men or lower animals to the nests of bees — compare BARBET **2** : a spot or stripe of a different color from the rest of the corolla that is found on the petals of many flowers and is assumed to act as a guide to insects in their quest of nectar

honeying *pres part of* HONEY

honey kite *n* : HONEY BUZZARD

hon·ey·less \'hənēləs\ *adj* : lacking honey

honey locust *n* **1 a** (1) : a tall usu. spiny No. American tree (*Gleditsia triacanthos*) that has bipinnate leaves, small greenish flowers in drooping racemes followed by long twisted pods containing seeds resembling beans and separated by a sweet edible pulp, and very hard durable reddish or reddish brown wood (2) : LOCUST 3a(2) (3) : CLAMMY LOCUST **b** : the wood of a honey locust **2 a** : MESQUITE 1a; *esp* : any of various large arborescent tropical American mesquites with strong heavy wood **b** : the wood of such a tropical American mesquite

honey mesquite *n* : MESQUITE 1a

¹**hon·ey·moon** \'hənē,mün, -ni,-\ *n, often attrib* [¹*honey* + *moon* (month); fr. the idea that the first month of marriage is the sweetest] **1 a** : a trip or vacation taken by a newly married couple ⟨has planned ~*s* for more than 60,000 newlyweds —Walter Winchell⟩ ⟨a popular ~ resort⟩ ⟨obviously a ~ couple⟩ **b** : a period usu. of exceptional compatibility immediately following marriage ⟨made their ~ last a lifetime⟩ **2** : a period of unusual harmony following the establishment of a new relationship ⟨today . . . congress thwarts the president, after a brief ~ in each administration —Irving Brant⟩ ⟨the ~ period of war alliance —Merle Fainsod⟩

²**honeymoon** \"\ *vi* -ED/-ING/-S : to spend a honeymoon ⟨had a fashionable wedding and ~*ed* in Bermuda⟩ — **hon·ey·moon·er** \-ünə(r)\ *n* -s

honeymoon bridge *n* : any of several forms of auction or contract bridge for two players

honeymouthed *also* **honeylipped** \'=¦=¦=\ *adj* : sweet or cajoling in speech ⟨cajoled him with ~ flattery until his suspicion was quieted —John Bennett⟩

honey mushroom *or* **honey fungus** *n* : an edible agaric (*Armillaria mellea*) commonly associated with the roots of trees : SHOESTRING FUNGUS — called also *honey agaric*

honeymyrtle \'=,=,==\ *n* : an Australian tree of the genus *Melaleuca*

honey of rose *pharmacy* : a mixture of fluid extract of rose and purified honey

honey palm *n* : COQUITO PALM

honey plant *n* : any of numerous flowering plants that furnish nectar suitable for the making of honey by insects; *specif* : a plant of the genus *Hoya*

honeypod \'=,=,=\ *n* **1** : MESQUITE 1a **2** : a pod of a mesquite

honey possum *or* **honey mouse** *n* : a small chestnut-brown long-muzzled phalanger (*Tarsipes spencerae*) of southwestern Australia that feeds upon nectar and small insects

honeypot \'=,=,=\ *n* [ME *hony pot,* fr. *hony* honey + *pot*] **1** : a receptacle for honey: **a** : one of the isolated waxen vessels constructed by some wild bees **b** : a glass or crockery container for table use ⟨early blown ~*s* or jam pots have high lids, deep rims, and solid finials —C.W.Drepperd⟩ **2** **honeypots** *pl* : a game in which a child (called the *honeypot*) with his hands clasped under his hams is swung backward and forward by his arms until his grip relaxes in order to find his weight which is reckoned at a pound for each swing **3** : a flower head of a southern African shrub (*Protea cynaroides*) which when open is shaped like a pot and consists of an involucre of showy bracts surrounding a head of small flowers **4 a** : HONEY ANT **b** : a replete of a honey ant

honeypot ant *n* : HONEY ANT

honeys *pl of* HONEY, *pres 3d sing of* HONEY

honey sac *or* **honey stomach** *n* : a distention of the esophagus of a bee in which the honey is elaborated : CROP 2c

honeyscented gum \'=,=,=-\ *n* : YELLOW BOX

honey shucks *n pl but usu sing in constr, also* **honey shuck** : HONEY LOCUST

honey-stalks \'=,=,=\ *n pl* : HONEYSUCKLE CLOVER

honeysuck \'=,=,=\ *n* [ME *honysouke,* fr. OE *hunisūce,* fr. *huni-, hunig* honey + *-sūce* (fr. *sūcan* to suck) — more at ¹HONEY, SUCK] *now dial* : HONEYSUCKLE

honeysucker \'=,=,=\ *n* : HONEY EATER

honeysuckle \'=,=,=\ *n* -s [ME *honysoukel,* alter. of *honysouke*] **1** *obs* : clover or its flowers **2 a** : a plant of the genus *Lonicera* — see WOODBINE 1 **b** : a shrub or tree of the genus *Banksia* (esp. *B. integrifolia*) — see AUSTRALIAN HONEYSUCKLE **3** : any of several other plants with tubular flowers abounding in honey: as **a** : BUSH HONEYSUCKLE **b** : COLUMBINE **c** : HONEYFLOWER **d** : PINXTER FLOWER **e** : SWAMP AZALEA **4** : REWAREWA

honeysuckle apple *n* : SWAMP APPLE

honeysuckle clover *n, chiefly dial* : a clover (as red clover or white Dutch clover) that is rich in nectar

honeysuckled \'=,=,=\ *adj* : covered with honeysuckle

honeysuckle family *n* : CAPRIFOLIACEAE

honeysuckle ornament *n* : ANTHEMION

honey-sweet \'=¦=¦=\ *adj* [ME *hony sweete,* fr. OE *hunigswēte,* fr. *hunig* honey + *swēte* sweet] : sweet with or as if with honey ⟨*honey-sweet* blossoms⟩ ⟨*honey-sweet* voice⟩

honeysweet \'=,=,=\ *n* [*honey-sweet*] : a white woolly perennial herb (*Tidestromia oblongifolia*) of the desert region of the U.S. forming broad flat mats and having stems and involucral bracts that often turn reddish with age and honey-scented yellow flowers

honey-tongued \'=¦=¦=\ *adj* : SMOOTH-TONGUED

honey tree *n* **1** : a forest tree that harbors wild bees and honey **2** : JAPANESE RAISIN TREE

honey tube *n* : either of a pair of small cornicles borne on the dorsal part of one of the abdominal segments of many aphids and formerly believed to secrete honeydew

honey vine *n* : SAND VINE

honeywood \'=,=,=\ *n* : a Tasmanian shrub (*Bedfordia salicina*) of the family Compositae having white foliage and heads of yellow flowers

honeywort \'=,=,=\ *n* **1** : a European plant of the genus *Cerinthe* (esp. *C. retorta*) often cultivated for its flowers which yield much honey **2** : a sweet-scented crosswort (*Galium cruciatum*)

honey yellow *n* : HONEY 6

hong \'häŋ, 'hȯŋ\ *n* -s [Chin (Cant) *hōng* row, mercantile

firm, guild] : a commercial establishment or house of foreign trade in China ⟨clippers . . . known equally in Canton ~s and European countinghouses —*Nat'l Geographic*⟩
hong kong \'häŋ,käŋ, 'hȯŋ,kȯŋ, (')=¦=\ *adj, usu cap H&K* [fr. *Hong Kong*, British crown colony in southeastern China] : of or from the British crown colony of Hong Kong : of the kind or style prevalent in Hong Kong
¹honied *var of* HONEYED
²honied *past of* HONEY
honier *comparative of* HONEY
honies *pl of* HONEY, *pres 3d sing of* HONEY
honiest *superlative of* HONEY
honing *pres part of* HONE
hon·i·ton \'hänət°n, 'hən-\ *or* **honiton lace** *n, usu cap H* [fr. *Honiton*, municipal borough in Devonshire, England] : any of various laces made orig. at Honiton, England; *esp* : a bobbin lace with designs of foliage, figures, or flowers, joined by brides or appliquéd to machine-made net
¹honk \'häŋk, -ȯ- *sometimes* -ə-\ *n* -s [imit.] **1** : the cry of a goose **2** : a sound resembling the cry of a goose
²honk \"\ *vb* -ED/-ING/-s *vi* **1** : to utter the characteristic cry of a goose ⟨northbound geese ~ overhead —Corey Ford⟩ **2** : to make a noise resembling the cry of a goose ⟨seals ~*ing* and splashing in a tank⟩ ⟨a fogbound ship ~*s* mournfully⟩ ~ *vt* : to cause (as a horn) to make a honk ⟨pulled up in front of the house and ~*ed* his horn⟩ ⟨finished her tears and ~*ed* her nose into the . . . handkerchief —Peggy Bennett⟩
honk·er \-kə(r)\ *n* -s : one that honks; *specif* : CANADA GOOSE
honky-tonk \'häŋkē,täŋk, 'hȯŋkē,tȯŋk, 'hoŋkē,toŋk, -ki-, ,=='=\ *n* -s *often attrib* [origin unknown] : a cheap nightclub or dance hall : DIVE 2 ⟨a row of brothels, gin mills and *honky=tonks* —Robert O'Brien⟩ ⟨a real *honky-tonk* joint, with hillbilly music and pinball machines going full blast —A.L.Davis⟩
hon·ni·a·sont \'hänēə,sänt\ *n, pl* **honniasont** *or* **honniasonts** *usu cap* **1** : an Iroquoian people of the valley of the upper Ohio river and its tributaries **2** : a member of the Honniasont people
hono·lu·lan \,hän°l'ülən, -nə'lü- *also* ,hōn-\ *n* -s *cap* [*Honolulu*, Hawaii + E *-an*] : a native or inhabitant of Honolulu
hono·lu·lu \¦=='=(,)lü *sometimes* -,lə\ *adj, usu cap* [fr. *Honolulu*, Hawaii] : of or from Honolulu, the capital of Hawaii : of the kind or style prevalent in Honolulu
¹hon·or \'änə(r)\ *n* -s *see -or in Explan Notes, often attrib* [ME *onour, honour, honor* fr. OF *onur, honur, honeur, honor*, fr. L *honor-, honos* or *honor*] **1 a** : good name or public esteem : REPUTATION, GLORY ⟨a national administration of such integrity . . . that its ~ at home will ensure respect abroad —D.D.Eisenhower⟩ ⟨a prophet is not without ~ except in his own country —Mt 13:57 (RSV)⟩ **b** : outward respect or admiration : RECOGNITION, DEFERENCE ⟨a dinner in ~ of the football coach⟩ ⟨treat the clergy with ~⟩ **2** : a special prerogative : PRIVILEGE ⟨I have the ~ to inform you⟩ ⟨the second artist . . . to be accorded the ~ of designing the annual Christmas seal —*Phoenix Flame*⟩ **3** : a person of superior standing or importance — now used esp. as a title for and in a mode of address to certain holders of high office (as judges and mayors of cities) ⟨if Your *Honor* please⟩ ⟨His *Honor* presided⟩ **4 a** : one that is of intrinsic value : ASSET ⟨he is an ~ to his profession⟩ **b** *obs* : one that decorates : ORNAMENT ⟨the woods, in scarlet ~*s* bright —William Cowper⟩ **5** : an evidence or symbol of distinction : mark of respect or admiration: as **a** : an exalted title or rank ⟨elected United States Senator in 1794 and governor of Maryland . . . he declined both ~*s* — *Amer. Guide Series: Md.*⟩ **b** (1) : BADGE, DECORATION ⟨among his ~*s* is the Order of the Golden Fleece⟩ (2) a ceremonial rite or observance ⟨the general was buried with full military ~*s*⟩ (3) **honors** *pl* : drum ruffles and trumpet flourishes and the national anthem or other music played during a ceremony when troops are presented **c** *archaic* : a gesture of deference : BOW ⟨they . . . made their ~*s* very prettily as they passed by us —Samuel Richardson⟩ **d honors** *pl* : social courtesies or civilities esp. as when rendered by a host ⟨the president did the ~*s* and the new club member acknowledged each introduction with a gracious nod⟩ ⟨handed him the carving knife, and asked him to do the ~*s* of the table⟩ **e** (1) : an academic grade, distinction, or award conferred on a superior student by a school or college ⟨received her B.A. with first class ~*s* from the University of London —B.F.Wright⟩ ⟨gained a first with ~*s* in mathematics —Lois I. Woodville⟩ (2) *or* **honors** *pl but sing in constr* : a course of study either supplementing or replacing a regular course, open to students of superior ability, and usu. culminating in an examination or thesis to determine eligibility for a degree with special distinction ⟨~ study gives to seniors . . . an opportunity to do independent study and research in their major field —*Bull. of Bates College*⟩ ⟨British universities offer two types of courses in the faculties of arts and science: an ~*s* course . . . and an ordinary, pass, or general course —I.L.Kandel⟩ **f** : an accolade for supremacy in a contest or field of competition ⟨the debating team won regional ~*s*⟩ ⟨airlines vie for commercial ~*s*⟩ **g** : an achievement award earned by a camp fire girl ⟨Camp Fire's method of giving individual recognition is the ~ bead —*Camp Fire Girl*⟩ **6** : CHASTITY, PURITY, VIRGINITY — used of a woman ⟨fought fiercely for her ~ and her life —Barton Black⟩ **7 a** : a holding of a large amount of land including numerous manors **b** : the seignorial franchise or jurisdiction annexed to such a holding **8 a** : adherence to high standards of justice and responsibility : ethical conduct : INTEGRITY ⟨code of ~⟩ ⟨an acute sense of ~ in private and business matters —Edith Wharton⟩ — compare BUSHIDO, NOBLESSE OBLIGE **b** : one's word given as a guarantee of performance **9 a** (1) *or* **honor-card** : an ace, king, queen, jack, or ten (2) : the ace, king, queen, jack, or ten of the trump suit in bridge or any ace when the contract is no-trump considered from the standpoint of its scoring value (3) : the ace, king, queen, or jack of the trump suit in whist (4) : the scoring value of honors held in bridge or whist — usu. used in pl. (5) **honors** *pl* : HONOR SCORE **b** : the privilege of playing first; *specif* : the privilege of driving a golf ball first from the tee that is granted the winner of the previous hole or the last unhalved hole **c** : one of 28 special-value tiles in the game of Mah-Jongg
syn HONOR, HOMAGE, REVERENCE, DEFERENCE, and OBEISANCE agree in signifying respect or esteem shown to another or claimed by him as a right. HONOR can apply to the recognition of one's title to great respect or to the expression of that respect ⟨to hold a statesman in high *honor*⟩ ⟨some member of the family there to see you get your *honor* —Agnes S. Turnbull⟩ ⟨to accept the *honor* the university proffered him⟩ HOMAGE adds the idea of accompanying praise or tribute esp. from one owing allegiance ⟨the ostentatious *homage* paid by state officials to bishops —*Times Lit. Supp.*⟩ ⟨brought up in the veneration of a man so truly worthy of *homage* —Matthew Arnold⟩ ⟨the *homage* which man owes his Creator —M.W.Baldwin⟩ REVERENCE implies profound respect usu. colored by love, devotion, or awe ⟨a *reverence* for all things sacred⟩ ⟨they rather produce in man thoughtfulness, *reverence*, a sense, confused yet precious, of the boundless importance of the unseen world —Charles Kingsley⟩ ⟨a *reverence* for government —Sherwood Anderson⟩ DEFERENCE implies a yielding or submitting to another's judgment or preference out of respect or reverence ⟨the attitude of *deference* which Elizabethan children were taught to cultivate toward their fathers —G.E.Dawson⟩ ⟨the magistrate and the clergyman . . . were conceded a *deference* which superior education, and not superior birth, compelled —H.E.Scudder⟩ OBEISANCE implies a show of honor or reverence by or as if by bowing or kneeling, often applying to a self-humbling gesture in confession of defeat or subjection ⟨the court is also showing great *obeisance* to the wishes of the executive and administrative branches —*New Republic*⟩ ⟨continually making humble *obeisance* to supercilious superiors —A.E.Wier⟩ ⟨unfortunate growing things . . . found that they were clipped, mowed, segregated, pruned, espaliered and generally bullied into *obeisance* —T.H.Robsjohn-Gibbings⟩
syn see in addition FAME
²honor \"\ *vt* **honored**; **honored**; **honoring** \-n(ə)riŋ\ **honors** *see -or in Explan Notes* [ME *onouren, honouren*, fr. OF *onurer, honurer, honeurer*, fr. L *honorare*, fr. *honor-, honos* or *honor*] **1 a** : to show high regard or appreciation for : pay tribute to : EXALT, PRAISE ⟨~ your father and your mother —Exod 20:12 (RSV)⟩ ⟨he has been ~*ed* at half a dozen public luncheons and banquets —J.A.Morris b. 1904⟩ **b** : to confer a distinction upon ⟨the only Englishman in all history that the world ~*s* with the surname of Great —Kemp Malone⟩ ⟨in addition to his French decorations, he was ~*ed* by the governments of Great Britain, Italy, Belgium, Serbia, and Venezuela —J.J.Senturia⟩ **2** : to be a credit to : ADORN ⟨the quality of his statesmanship would ~ any country⟩ **3 a** : to treat with consideration : RECOGNIZE, RESPECT ⟨federal bill . . . to ~ state commitments of addicts —D.W.Maurer & V.H. Vogel⟩ ⟨truck drivers were ~*ing* the picket line —*Springfield (Mass.) Union*⟩ **b** : to live up to or fulfill : carry out ⟨~ a treaty⟩ ⟨~ a contract⟩; *specif* : to accept and comply with the terms of ⟨~ a check⟩ ⟨~ a requisition . . . for the surrender of a violator —P.G.Auchampaugh⟩ **4** : to salute with a bow usu. at the beginning or at the end of a square dance ⟨~ your partner⟩
¹hon·or·able \'änər(ə)bəl, -nrəb-\ *adj, see -or in Explan Notes* [ME *honourable, honorable*, fr. MF, fr. L *honorabilis*, fr. *honorare* + *-abilis* -able] **1 a** *obs* : up to a standard of respectability (as in quality, size, amount) : DECENT, CONSIDERABLE ⟨when he plays at tables, chides the dice in ~ terms —Shak.⟩ **b** : deserving of honor : ADMIRABLE, DIGNIFIED ⟨judges are ~ for their high calling⟩ ⟨marriage is an ~ estate —*Bk. of Com. Prayer*⟩ **2** : conferring honor ⟨won an ~ mention for verse⟩ **3 a** : of great renown : ILLUSTRIOUS ⟨comes of a family ~ for centuries⟩ **b** *usu cap* (1) : belonging to a family or having a rank entitled to honor — used as a courtesy title for the younger children of earls and for all children of viscounts and barons and for maids of honor and also given to the wife of any man having a courtesy title; abbr. *Hon.*; compare MOST HONORABLE, RIGHT HONORABLE (2) : being of high eminence or dignity — used in the U.S. as a title or in a mode of reference for members of congress and of state legislatures, cabinet officers and their assistants, commissioners of bureaus, heads of state departments, judges, mayors of cities, and various other high government officials; abbr. *Hon.* **4 a** : doing credit to the possessor ⟨~ wounds⟩ **b** : consistent with an untarnished reputation ⟨~ dismissal⟩ ⟨~ peace terms⟩ **5** : characterized by integrity : ETHICAL, UPRIGHT ⟨Brutus is an ~ man —Shak.⟩ ⟨~ in all his dealings⟩ ⟨assured her that his intentions were ~⟩ **syn** see UPRIGHT
²honorable \"\ *n* -s *see -or in Explan Notes* [ME *honourable, honorable*, fr. *honourable, honorable*, adj.] **1 a** : any of various members of British noble families ⟨a host of little cousins, lords and ~*s* for playmates —*Time*⟩ **b** : any of various high British governmental officials to whom the title of Honorable is officially applied **2** : a person of rank or distinction ⟨the guest list was studded with judges, congressmen, and other ~*s*⟩
honorable discharge *n* : a formal release given a member of the armed forces at the conclusion (as by expiration of his enlistment) of a period of honest and faithful service
hon·or·able·ness \-ləs\ *also* **hon·or·abil·i·ty** \,än(ə)rə'biləd·ē\ *n* -ES : the quality or state of being honorable
honorable ordinary *n, heraldry* : an ordinary as distinguished from a subordinary
hon·or·ably \'änər(ə)blē, -nrəb-, -li\ *adv* [ME *honourably, honorably*, fr. *honourable, honorable*, adj. + *-y*] : in an honorable manner : with honor ⟨dealt ~ with his opponent⟩ ⟨was ~ discharged from the marine corps⟩
hon·or·and \¦änə¦rand, -raa(ə)nd\ *n* -s [fr. L *honorandus*, gerundive of *honorare* to honor — more at HONOR] : one that is awarded an honor (as an honorary degree)
hon·or·ar·i·ly \¦änə¦rerəlē, -li\ *adv* : in an honorary manner
hon·o·rar·i·um \,änə'rerēəm, -'ra(a)r-, -'rār-\ *n, pl* **honorar·ia** \-ēə\ *also* **honorariums** [L, fr. neut. of *honorarius* honorary] : an honorary payment or reward usu. given as compensation for services on which custom or propriety forbids any fixed business price to be set or for which no payment can be enforced at law ⟨supplementing his income by *honoraria* from speaking engagements⟩ ⟨the medal carries an ~ of $500⟩
¹hon·or·ary \'änə,rerē, -eri\ *adj* [L *honorarius*, fr. *honor* honor + *-arius* -ary — more at HONOR] **1 a** : having or conferring distinction ⟨~ scholar⟩ ⟨~ bridesmaid⟩ ⟨~ engineering society⟩ **b** : COMMEMORATIVE ⟨~ plaque⟩ ⟨wrote an ~ ode for the centennial⟩ **2 a** : conferred in recognition of achievement or service without the usual prerequisites, duties, or obligations : TITULAR ⟨does not really tell us what it is like to hold an ~, though honorable, position in a domain where once his word was law —Richard Griffith⟩ ⟨two hard-earned degrees . . . and several ~ ones —A.W.Griswold⟩ **b** : UNPAID, UNREMUNERATIVE, VOLUNTARY ⟨~ secretary⟩ ⟨in the Australian theater play-writing remains very largely an ~ task and consequently a luxury —Leslie Rees⟩ **3** : dependent on honor for fulfillment : MORAL — used esp. of an obligation
²honorary \"\ *n* -ES [L *honorarium*] **1** *archaic* : HONORARIUM **2** [by shortening] : an honorary society ⟨elected to . . . the senior men's ~ —Neil Stueck⟩ **3** [*honorary* (degree)] : an honorary degree or its recipient
honorary canon *n* : a cleric appointed to assist occas. in the services of a cathedral but not residentiary and not entitled to stipend or vote in the chapter — compare MAJOR CANON
honorary trust *n* : a transfer of property for a designated noncharitable purpose that empowers the transferee to apply the property to the designated purpose or else to surrender it to the one making the transfer or to his estate and that is not enforceable as a trust because it does not benefit a specific ascertainable existing person
honor attendant *n* **1** : BRIDESMAID **2** : MAID OF HONOR 2
honor camp *n* : a work camp of trusted prisoners conducted under an honor system
honor-card \'==,=\ *n* : HONOR 9a(1)
honor court *n, Eng feudal law* : a court held for an honor as a whole
honored *adj* **1** : held in honor : RESPECTED **2** : accorded recognition
hon·or·ee \¦änə¦rē\ *n* -s : one that receives an honor
hon·or·er \'änərə(r)\ *n* -s [ME *honurer*, fr. *onouren, honouren, honuren* to honor + *-er* — more at HONOR] : one that honors
honor guard *n* : GUARD OF HONOR
hon·o·ri·al \(')ä¦nōrēəl\ *adj* [¹*honor* + *-ial*] : of or relating to a seignorial holding under English feudal law
¹hon·or·if·ic \¦änə¦rifik, -fēk\ *also* **hon·or·if·i·cal** \-fəkəl, -fēk-\ *adj* [*honorific* fr. L *honorificus*, fr. *honorare* to honor; *honorifical* fr. L *honorificus* + E *-al*] **1** : conferring or conveying honor ⟨~ social status commonly attaches to membership in a recognized profession —D.D.McKean⟩ ⟨a largely honorary but distinctly ~ post —*Time*⟩ ⟨the elaborate set of ~ words used to people of rank —Margaret Mead⟩ **2** : belonging to or constituting a class of grammatical forms used in speaking to or about a social superior — **hon·or·if·i·cal·ly** \-fək(ə)lē, -fēk-, -li\ *adv*
²honorific \"\ *n* -s **1** : an honorific term of address esp. when used by an Oriental to convey verbal respect ⟨a leader in the movement to abolish caste distinctions — he has officially repudiated the hereditary . . . ~ of "Pandit" before his name —Robert Trumbull⟩ **2** : an honorific word or form
honoring *pres part of* HONOR
ho·no·ris cau·sa \(h)ä,nōr'əskau̇sə, (h)ə,n-, (h)ō,n-, (h)ō,n-, -nȯr-, -kau̇(,)sä, -kau̇(,)zä *sometimes* -kȯzə\ *adv (or adj)* [L] : as a token of respect or honor; *esp* : in recognition of distinctions or accomplishments not achieved in course ⟨degrees conferred *honoris causa*⟩ ⟨the degree of doctor of laws *honoris causa*⟩
hon·or·less \'änə(r)ləs\ *adj, see -or in Explan Notes* : lacking honor
honor point *n* **1** : a point in an escutcheon of arms approximately midway between the middle chief point and the fess point — see POINT illustration **2 honor points** *pl* : HONOR SCORE 1
honor price *n* : a price paid by an offender or his kinsmen to the injured person or his kinsmen under ancient Irish law — compare CRO, ERIC, GALANAS
honor roll *n* : a roster of names of persons deserving honor: as **a** : a list of pupils achieving academic distinction **b** : a public memorial listing the names of local citizens who have served in the armed forces
honors *pl of* HONOR, *pres 3d sing of* HONOR
honor score *n* **1** : a score that does not count toward game in contract bridge — called also *honor points, honors* **2** : a space provided on a contract bridge score sheet for recording extra tricks, penalties, and bonuses
honor society *n* : a society for the recognition of scholarly achievement esp. at the undergraduate level in colleges and universities
honors of war : courtesies granted a vanquished enemy (as the privilege of marching out from a camp or town armed and with colors flying)
honor system *n* : a system granting freedom from customary surveillance (as to students or prisoners) with the understanding that those who are so freed will be bound by their honor to observe regulations ⟨prison farms operated under the *honor system*⟩; *specif* : a system of conducting examinations without faculty supervision
honor trick \'==,=\ *n* : a high card or combination of high cards having a specified trick-winning expectancy and used as a basis for evaluating the strength of a contract bridge hand — called also *quick trick*
hon·our \'änə(r)\ *chiefly Brit var of* HONOR
hon·tish \'häntish\ *adj* [origin unknown] *dial Eng* : HAUGHTY
hony *abbr* honorary
honyak *or* **honyock** *usu cap, var of* HUNYAK
¹hoo *obs var of* HO
²hoo *dial var of* WHO
³hoo \'hü\ *interj* [origin unknown] — used chiefly to express an emotional reaction (as of surprise or triumph) or as a call
⁴hoo \(')hü\ *chiefly Scot var of* HOW
⁵hoo \"\ *var of* ⁴HOW
¹hooch \'hük\ *interj, chiefly Scot* [origin unknown] — used to express emotion (as excitement, elation)
²hooch \'hüch\ *n* -ES [short for *hoochinoo*] *slang* : alcoholic liquor esp. when inferior, obtained illicitly, or made surreptitiously
hoochie-coochie *or* **hoochy-koochy** *var of* HOOTCHY=KOOTCHY
hoo·chi·noo \'hüchə,nü, ,=='=\ *n* -s [fr. the *Hoochinoo* Indians, a Tlingit people of Alaska that made such liquor, fr. Tlingit *Hutsnuwu*, lit., grizzly bear fort] : a distilled liquor made by Alaska Indians
¹hood \'hu̇d\ *n* -s [ME *hood, hod*, fr. OE *hōd*; akin to OFris *hōd* head covering, *hōde* guard, protection, OHG *huot* head covering, helmet, *huota* guard, protection, ON *höttr* head covering, and perh. to L *cassis* helmet, MIr *cais* love; basic meaning: protecting, covering] **1 a** (1) : a covering usu. of cloth or leather for the head and neck and sometimes the shoulders that is attached to a garment or worn separately and is made with a loose or close-fitting opening for the face — see COWL 1, FRENCH HOOD (2) : a flexible covering of mail worn by an armored man usu. under a helmet or dependent from a steel cap esp. to protect the neck (3) : the head covering of an ecclesiastical garment; *esp* : a monk's cowl (4) : a protective covering for the head and face that often extends below the shoulders, is made of various resistant materials, and is used by persons exposed to special hazards (as heat, fumes, radiation) **b** : a covering for a hawk's head and eyes **c** : a covering for a horse's head; *also* : BLINDER **2** : something felt to resemble a hood: as **a** (1) : an ornamental fold at the back of an ecclesiastical vestment (2) : an ornamental scarf that is worn over an academic gown so as to swathe the neck and hang loose or form a closed pouch in back and that indicates by its color the wearer's college and often his degree or field of specialization — see ACADEMIC COSTUME **b** : a color marking or crest on the head of an animal or an expansion of the head that occupies the position of or suggests a hood ⟨a cobra spreading his ~⟩ — compare HOODED **c** (1) : a cap of foam on water (2) : the upper fine-textured part of a batholith **d** (1) : a hood=shaped upper petal of some flowers (as of monkshood) — called also *helmet* (2) : a thickened structure that replaces the awn in barleys **e** : an unblocked usu. cone-shaped hat body of felt, straw, or other material **3** : a covering that protects or obscures like a hood: as **a** *chiefly Brit* (1) : a covering of earth and hay or straw over a heap of produce (2) : a thatch or shelter of straw over a beehive (3) : CAPSHEAF 1 **b** : a cap over the top of a chimney; *esp* : a metal cap designed to secure constant draft by turning with the wind **c** (1) : a top cover for the body of a vehicle (as a carriage or perambulator) that is usu. flexible and designed to be folded back when desired (2) *Brit* : the top of an automobile; *esp* : a fabric top for a convertible **d** (1) : a projecting cover above a hearth forming the upper part of a fireplace and confining and directing smoke to its flue (2) : an enclosure or cover (as a canopy or booth) for exhausting by means of a draft disagreeable or noxious fumes, sprays, smoke, or dusts ⟨installed a ~ over the kitchen range⟩ (3) : the part of a furnace cupola shell above the charging hole (4) : BONNET 2e(4) **e** : a covering or porch for a companion hatch or other opening on a boat **f** : a projecting canopy on a building (as over a door or window) **g** : the endmost plank of a strake or plate of a shell strake, reaching the stem or stern of a wooden ship or both stem and stern **h** (1) : a protective cowl or cover for mechanical devices or parts of them (2) : the removable metal covering over the engine of an automobile — called also *bonnet* **i** : a covering over the front of a stirrup **j** : a covering that protects and supports the connections of a suspended electric lighting unit **k** (1) : an arched or rounded top on furniture (2) : the case enclosing the dial and works of some tall clocks **l** : a metal band that holds the reel of a fishing rod in position on the reel seat **m** : a protective cover (as of metal, paper, or plastic) fitted over the lip or top of a container and used esp. to maintain sterile or sanitary conditions of the unopened package **4** : HOODED SEAL

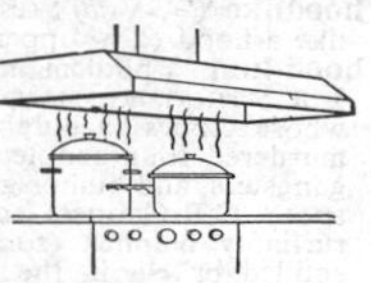

hood 3(d)2

²hood \"\ *vt* -ED/-ING/-s [ME *hooden, hoden*, fr. *hood, hod*, n.] **1** : to cover or furnish with a hood ⟨one must ~ the young hawk early in his training⟩ **2** : to cover over or obscure (as for protection or concealment) : HIDE ⟨~*ing* the flashlight with his hand⟩; *esp* : to partially close (the eyes or eyelids) ⟨~*ed* her eyes against the sun⟩
³hood \'hu̇d, -ü-\ *n* -s [short for *hoodlum*] *slang* : HOODLUM: as **a** : a gangster or racketeer **b** : a gunman or strong-arm man
-hood \,hu̇d, *after voiceless consonants sometimes* ,u̇d *as in* 'prē,stu̇d *one pronunciation of "priesthood"*\ *n suffix* -s [ME *-hod, -hode*, fr. OE *-hād*; akin to OFris&OS *-hēd*, suffix denoting state or condition, OHG *-heit*; all fr. a prehistoric Gmc word represented by OE *hād* person, rank, state, condition, OHG *heit* person, rank, state, condition, ON *heithr* honor, Goth *haidus* manner, way; akin to OE *hādor* bright, clear, OHG *heitar*, ON *heithr*, and prob. to L *caesius* bluish gray, *caelum* sky, heaven, Skt *citra* variegated, bright, *ketu* brightness, light; basic meaning: bright] **1** : state : condition : quality : character ⟨boy*hood*⟩ ⟨girl*hood*⟩ ⟨hardi*hood*⟩ ⟨unlikeli*hood*⟩ **2** : an instance of a specified state, condition, quality, or character ⟨false*hood*⟩ **3** : individuals sharing a specified state, condition, quality, or character ⟨brother*hood*⟩
hoodcap \'=,=\ *n* : HOODED SEAL
hood clock *also* **hooded clock** *n* : a wall or mantel clock having the movement enclosed in a case and the weights and pendulum if weight-driven exposed to view
hooded *adj* [ME *hoded, hooded*, fr. *hod, hood* + *-ed*] **1 a** : covered or furnished with a hood or something resembling a hood **b** : having the awn replaced by a trifurcate hood — used of some cereal grasses **2 a** : shaped like a hood **b** : rolled in expanded conical form with a reflexed tip : CUCULLATE — used of plant organs ⟨arums with ~ spathes⟩ **3 a** : having the head conspicuously different in color from the rest of the body — used chiefly of birds **b** : having a crest on the head that suggests a hood ⟨~ seals⟩ **c** *of a cobra* : having the skin at each side of the neck capable of expansion by movements of the ribs — **hood·ed·ness** *n* -ES
hooded crow *n* **1** : a European crow (*Corvus cornix*) that is black with gray back and underparts and is closely related to the carrion crow **2** *India* : HOUSE CROW
hooded gull *n* **1** : BLACK-HEADED GULL; *esp* : a common European gull (*Larus ridibundus*)

hooded ladies' tresses *n pl but sing or pl in constr* **:** a native orchid (*Spiranthes romanzoffiana*) that is widely distributed in northern No. America and occurs occas. in Ireland and eastern Asia and that has spikes of small creamy or straw-colored almond-scented flowers with sepals and petals partly fused into an upward arching hood
hooded merganser *or* **hooded sheldrake** *n* **:** a small No. American merganser (*Lophodytes cucullatus*) having a high vertical nearly circular crest on the head of the adult male
hooded milfoil *n* **:** PURPLE BLADDERWORT
hooded oriole *n* **:** an oriole (*Icterus cucullatus*) of the southwestern U.S. and Mexico that occurs in several races and is distinguished by the yellow head and black throat of the male
hooded pitcher plant *n* **:** a yellow-flowered pitcher plant (*Sarracenia minor*) of the southeastern U.S. having variegated trumpet-shaped leaves with green and purple veins and white or yellowish blotches and with the orifice closely covered by an arched hood
hooded rat *n* **:** a strain of the black rat developed in captivity and characterized by a white body and black head
hooded seal *n* **:** a large seal (*Cystophora cristata*) of the north Atlantic distinguished by a large inflatable sac upon the fore-part of the head of the male
hooded snake *n* **:** COBRA
hooded tern *n* **:** LITTLE TERN
hooded top *n* **:** BONNET TOP
hooded violet *n* **:** a usu. purple-flowered tufted violet (*Viola cucullata*) of No. America having the young leaves rolled in and the lateral petals bearded
hooded warbler *n* **:** an American warbler (*Wilsonia citrina*) having in the male the forehead, ear coverts, and lower parts gamboge yellow and the rest of the head, neck, and chest black
hood·ie *also* **hoody** \'hu̇di, 'hēdi, 'hēdi\ *n, pl* **hoodies** [¹*hood* + *-ie, -y*] **1 a** *or* **hoodie crow :** HOODED CROW 1 **b :** CARRION CROW **2** *dial Brit* **:** a hooded gull (*Larus ridibundus*)
hooding *pres part of* HOOD
hooding end *or* **hood end** *n* **:** the end of a hood of a ship that enters the rabbet in the stempost or sternpost
hood·less \'hu̇dləs\ *adj* **:** lacking a hood ⟨an African ~ cobra⟩
hoodlike \'=,=\ *adj* **:** resembling a hood ⟨a ~ crest⟩ **:** enclosing like a hood ⟨a ~ upper petal⟩
hood·lum \'hüdləm *also* 'hu̇d-\ *n* -s [origin unknown] **1 a :** THUG, RUFFIAN, MOBSTER; *esp* **:** a small-time criminal whose crimes include acts of violence ⟨a gang of ~s had murdered four people —J.A.Michener⟩ ⟨a ~ . . . works for gangsters, and bumps guys off after they have been put on the spot —C.R.Cooper⟩ **b :** one who behaves in an uncouth or ruffianly manner ⟨some of the tenderest scenes . . . were spoiled by ~s in the gallery —*Amer. Guide Series: Wash.*⟩ **c :** a young ruffian or street loafer **:** a rowdy or misbehaved child or adolescent ⟨that kid was a real ~, . . . shot craps and everything —*Lamp*⟩ **2** *West* **a** *or* **hoodlum wagon :** a wagon used at roundup to carry bedding and miscellaneous supplies **b :** the driver of a hoodlum, usu. serving also as cook's helper
hood·lum·ish \-mish\ *adj* **:** like or typical of a hoodlum ⟨~ louts⟩ ⟨~ behavior⟩
hood·lum·ism \-lə,mizəm\ *n* -s **:** conduct typical of a hoodlum **:** rough rowdy behavior **:** delinquency or criminality marked esp. by gross disregard for the rights of others
hood·man-blind \,hu̇dmən'=\ *n, archaic* **:** BLINDMAN'S BUFF
hoodmold \'=,=\ *also* **hood molding** *n* **:** a molding that projects over the head of an arch and forms the outermost member of the archivolt **:** DRIPSTONE

hoodmold

¹**hoo·doo** \'hü(,)dü\ *n* -s [of African origin; akin to Hausa *hu³du³ba¹* to arouse resentment against someone] **1 :** VOODOO **2 a :** something that brings or is associated with the occurrence of bad luck **:** JINX, JONAH — compare MASCOT **b :** bad luck **3 a :** a natural column or pinnacle of rock common in parts of western No. America that results from weathering or erosion and occurs in varied and often fantastic forms **b :** EARTH PILLAR
²**hoodoo** \"\ *adj* **1 :** of, relating to, or being a hoodoo ⟨~ priests⟩ ⟨a ~ fetish⟩ **2 a :** persistently unlucky as if under a spell ⟨a ~ ship⟩ **:** JINXED **b :** bringing or associated with bad luck ⟨when that ~ planet crops up in a horoscope⟩
³**hoodoo** \"\ *vt* -ED/-ING/-S **:** to cast a spell on **:** bring to misfortune by occult means; *broadly* **:** be a source of misfortune to
hoo·doo·ism \-,izəm\ *n* -s **:** VOODOOISM
hoods *pl of* HOOD, *pres 3d sing of* HOOD
-hoods *pl of* -HOOD
hoodsheaf \'=,=\ *n* [¹*hood* + *sheaf*] **:** CAPSHEAF 1
¹**hood·wink** \'hu̇,dwiŋk\ *vt* [¹*hood* + *wink*] **1** *archaic* **:** to blind by covering the eyes **:** BLINDFOLD **2** *obs* **:** to hide out of sight or mind **3 :** to deceive by false appearance **:** impose upon ⟨such an easy person to ~⟩ ⟨packages designed to ~ buyers⟩ **syn** see DUPE
²**hoodwink** \"\ *n* **1 :** the act of hoodwinking **2 :** a device for concealing or dissembling (as a mask or blindfold) **:** BLIND
hood·wink·er \-kə(r)\ *n* **:** one that hoodwinks
hoodwise \'=,=\ *adv* [¹*hood* + *-wise*] **:** in the manner of or so as to serve the purpose of a hood ⟨held a newspaper ~ over her hat⟩
hoodwort \'=,=\ *n* **:** MAD-DOG SKULLCAP
hoo·ey \'hüē, -üi\ *n* -s [origin unknown] **:** something false or unacceptable **:** HOKUM, NONSENSE — often used interjectionally
¹**hoof** \'hu̇f, 'hüf\ *n, pl* **hooves** \|vz\ *or* **hoofs** \|fs\ [ME, fr. OE *hōf;* akin to OFris & OS *hōf* hoof, OHG *huof*, ON *hōfr* hoof, Skt *śapha* hoof, claw, Av *safa-* horse's hoof] **1 a :** a curved covering of horn that protects the front of or more or less extensively encloses the ends of the digits of an ungulate mammal and that corresponds to a nail or claw — see COW illustration **b :** a hoofed foot esp. of a horse or other equine — compare CLOVEN FOOT **c :** FOOT; *esp* **:** a large, heavy, or ill-managed human foot ⟨heard those *hooves* on the stair⟩ **2** *now chiefly dial* **:** a hoofed animal; *usu* **:** a hoofed domestic mammal ⟨hadn't a ~ fit to dress⟩ **3 :** one of the smaller and more angulate plates (as a marginal plate) of the shell of the hawksbill turtle; *also* **:** the tortoise shell composing these plates — used chiefly commercially — **on the hoof 1** *of meat animals* **:** LIVING, LIVEWEIGHT ⟨10 cents a pound *on the hoof*⟩ ⟨*on the hoof* meat is supplied —*Nat'l Geographic*⟩ **2** *of persons* **:** in ordinary condition **:** without an opportunity for any special show ⟨meeting people *on the hoof* across a sales counter⟩ ⟨executives expert at judging men *on the hoof*⟩
²**hoof** \"\ *vb* -ED/-ING/-S *vt* **1 :** WALK ⟨~*ed* a mile to school each day⟩ ⟨~*ing* it to town⟩ **2 :** KICK, TRAMPLE ⟨buffalo ~*ed* up the dust⟩ ⟨colts ~*ing* the sod⟩ **3 :** to put out by or as if by kicking **:** throw out **:** EJECT, BOOT ⟨uncle got me ~*ed* out of that —F.M.Ford⟩ ~ *vi* **:** to move on the feet (as in walking, tramping, or dancing); *esp* **:** to execute noisy rhythmic footwork (as in tap-dancing)
hoof-and-mouth disease *n* **:** FOOT-AND-MOUTH DISEASE
hoofbeat \'=,=\ *n* **:** the sound of a hoof striking the ground or other hard surface ⟨~s fading in the distance⟩
hoofbound \'=,=\ *adj* **:** having a dry and contracted hoof that occasions pain and lameness
hoofed \,hu̇ft, -üft\ *adj* **1 :** having hoofs **:** UNGULATE — often used in combination ⟨cloven-*hoofed*⟩ **2** *of a shoe* **:** having a broad rounded front
hoofed locust *n* [so called fr. the fact that sheep closely crop the vegetation when they graze] **:** SHEEP — usu. used disparagingly by cattlemen
hoof·er \'hu̇fə(r), -üf-\ *n* -s **1 :** one that travels on foot **2** *slang* **:** DANCER; *esp* **:** a professional dancer (as in vaudeville or a chorus)
hoof foot *n* **:** a furniture foot in the form of a usu. cloven hoof
hoof·i·ness \-fēnəs, -fin-\ *n* -ES **:** the quality or state of being hoofed
hoof·less \-fləs\ *adj* **:** lacking hooves
hoof·let \-lət\ *n* -s [¹*hoof* + *-let*] **:** a small hoof; *esp* **:** FALSE HOOF

hoof foot

hooflike \'=,=\ *adj* **:** resembling a hoof; *esp* **:** having the horny texture of a hoof ⟨~ calluses⟩

hoof-pick \'=,=\ *n* **:** a hooked implement used to remove foreign objects from a hoof
hoofprint \'=,=\ *n* **:** an impression or hollow made by a hoof
hoofrot \'=,=\ *n* **:** FOOT ROT 2
hoog·aars \'hō,gärs\ *n, pl* **hoogaars** \", -rz\ [D, fr. *hoog* high + *aars* buttocks] **:** a Dutch sloop
hoo-ha \'hü,hä\ *n* -s [origin unknown] **:** HULLABALOO
¹**hook** \'hu̇k\ *n* -s [ME *hok, hook*, fr. OE *hōc;* akin to OFris *hōk* corner, MD *hoec* fishhook, corner, OE *haca* bolt, OHG *hāko* hook, Icel *haki* hook, ON *haka* chin, MIr *ailcheng* rake, stand for weapons, Lith *kengė* hook, latch] **1 a** (1) **:** an implement for cutting grass or grain **:** SICKLE, SCYTHE (2) **:** an implement for cutting or lopping **:** BILLHOOK **b :** a hand fork with the tines turned nearly at right angles to the handle ⟨a potato ~⟩ ⟨manure ~*s*⟩ **c :** a curved metal prong attached to a leather wristband for tearing the husks from an ear of corn **2 a :** a piece of metal or other hard or tough material formed or bent into a curve or at an angle for catching, holding, sustaining, or pulling something ⟨a ~ for fastening a gate⟩ ⟨a ~ for filing papers⟩ **b :** any of various hooked objects: as (1) **:** BREASTHOOK (2) **:** an artificial replacement for the hand made in the form of a hook (3) **:** an instrument used in surgery to take hold of tissue ⟨crypt ~⟩ ⟨chordotomy ~⟩ (4) **:** the part of a hook and eye that is bent over to form a finger that fits into the eye (5) **:** a long pole with a hooked end by which one in the wings can reach out and pull a performer off the stage — often used in the phrase *get the hook* (6) **:** FIRE HOOK **3 a :** FISHHOOK; *broadly* **:** any angling device or lure capable of taking but one fish at a time **b :** something designed to attract and ensnare **4 :** a part of a hinge that is fixed to a post and on which the part that is fixed to a door or gate hangs and turns **5 :** something felt to resemble a hook: as **a :** a sharp bend or curve (as in a stream) or a spit or narrow cape of sand or gravel turned landward at the outer end ⟨wave action may build spits into ~*s*⟩ **b** (1) **:** an angular or recurved mark (as a written character or an element in one) (2) **:** EAR ⟨the ~ of lower-case g or q⟩ (3) **:** ⁵FLAG 3a (4) **:** PARENTHESIS 3a — used in printing; usu. in pl. **c** (1) **:** a recurved part or appendage of a plant or animal ⟨burrs clinging by their ~*s*⟩ (2) *or* **hook bone :** the projecting angle of the hipbone of cattle — usu. used in pl. ⟨a good covering of flesh over the ~*s*⟩ **d :** the angle between the face of a tooth and a line to the center of a circular saw or to a line perpendicular to the back of a band saw **e :** ANCHOR **f hooks** *pl, slang* **:** FINGERS ⟨just let me get my ~*s* on him⟩ **g :** a lever by which a device (as a fire-alarm box) is actuated **h :** a mobile wrecking crane; *broadly* **:** a wreck train or car mounting a crane **6 a :** an act or instance of hooking ⟨the cow gave a sudden ~ and ripped his sleeve⟩ **b :** a flight of a ball (as in golf, cricket, bowling, baseball) that deviates from a straight course in a direction opposite to the dominant hand of the player projecting it; *also* **:** a ball following such a course — compare SLICE, SPIN **c :** a short blow delivered with a circular motion by a boxer while the elbow remains bent and rigid **7 :** CROOK 2b — **by hook or by crook** *also* **by hook or crook :** by any means **:** fairly or unfairly ⟨determined to win *by hook or by crook*⟩ — **drop off the hooks** *or* **slip off the hooks** *Brit* **:** DIE — **off the hook** *adv (or adj)* **:** out of a difficulty or trouble ⟨counted on his friends to get him *off the hook*⟩ — **off the hooks** *obs* **:** disordered in mind or body **:** UNHINGED, DERANGED — **on one's own hook :** on one's own account or responsibility **:** without authorization or assistance **:** by oneself **:** INDEPENDENTLY

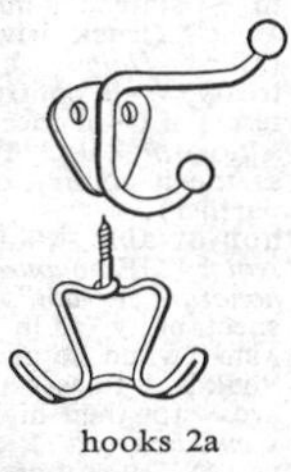
hooks 2a

²**hook** \"\ *vb* -ED/-ING/-S [ME *hoken*, fr. *hok, hook*, n.] *vt* **1 :** to give the form of a hook to **:** CROOK ⟨~*ed* an arm about the stanchion⟩ **2 a :** to make fast with or as if with a hook or hooks ⟨~ a dress⟩ **b :** to seize, capture, or hold with a hook ⟨~*ed* a large trout⟩ **c :** to secure or catch as if with a hook ⟨~*ed* herself a husband⟩: as (1) *slang* **:** to reduce to a complete loss of self-control **:** make wholly dependent — usu. used in passive ⟨~*ed* by the morphine habit⟩ (2) *slang* **:** to entrap into improper, undesirable, or foolish activity ⟨when the sucker listens he's half ~*ed*⟩ (3) **:** to hold (a dancing partner) by interlocking feet or elbows; *also* **:** to interlock (feet or elbows) in dancing **3 a :** to seize and draw with or as if with a hook ⟨~*ed* the logs out of the channel⟩ **b :** to take by stealth **:** STEAL, PILFER ⟨~*ing* apples from the tree⟩ **4 :** to strike or pierce with the points of the horns **:** GORE **5 a :** to make (as a rug) by drawing loops of thread, yarn, or cloth through a coarse fabric with a hook **b :** to so draw (as yarn) in forming a pattern ⟨~*ed* heavy woolen rags into an ombré pattern⟩ **6 a :** to strike (a boxing opponent) with a hook **b :** to strike or throw (as a golf ball or bowling ball) so that a hook results — compare FADE, SLICE **c :** to hit (a bowled cricket ball) to leg with a stroke in which the bat swings upward and in a leg direction **d** (1) **:** to intercept (the ball) in rugby and propel backward with the heel of the boot from the front line of the scrum (2) **:** to gain possession of (the ball) in soccer by reaching out, intercepting, and drawing with the foot ~ *vi* **1 :** to bend sharply so as to form a hook **:** CURVE ⟨the beak ~*s* strongly downward⟩ **2** *slang* **:** to make off **:** LEAVE, DEPART ⟨~*ed* for home⟩ — usu. used with formulary *it* ⟨~ it, the cops are coming⟩ **3 :** to secure or fasten by or as if by a hook ⟨a dress that ~*s* in back⟩ **4 a :** to make an attack with the horns ⟨the bull ~*ed* at his handler⟩ **b :** to deliver a hook in boxing ⟨~*ing* expertly but without much power⟩ **5 a** *of a ball* **:** to travel in or be a hook ⟨the ball ~*ed* badly but bounced onto the fairway⟩ **b** *of a player* **:** to hook a ball ⟨~*ed* into the rough⟩ **c :** to score or attempt to score in basketball with a hook shot
hookah *also* **hooka** \'hu̇kə, 'hükə\ *n* -s [Ar *huqqah* round box, casket, bottle of a water pipe] **:** a pipe for smoking that has a long flexible tube whereby the smoke is cooled by passing through water — compare NARGILEH
hook-and-butt joint *n* **:** a scarf joint formed to resist tension
hook and eye *n* **:** a two-part fastening device (as on a garment or a door) consisting of a wire hook that catches over a bar or into a loop of wire — see FASTENER illustration
hook-and-eye \,=='=\ *adj* [*hook and eye*] **:** having religious scruples against the wearing of buttons ⟨a *hook-and-eye* sect⟩
hook-and-eye hinge *n* **:** a hinge intended for use on a gate and consisting of an L-shaped hook secured to one member (as the gatepost) and fitted into an eye-shaped loop or screw hook secured to the other member (as the gate)

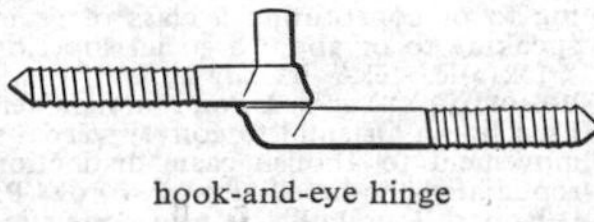
hook-and-eye hinge

hook and ladder *n* **1** *or* **hook-and-ladder truck :** LADDER TRUCK **2** *or* **hook-and-ladder company :** LADDER COMPANY
hook-and-liner \,=='==\ *n* **:** a boat (as a tuna clipper) for fishing with hook and line
hook·a·roon \,hu̇kə'rün\ *n* -s [¹*hook* + *-aroon* (as in *pickaroon*)] **:** ²PICKAROON
hook-bill \'=,=\ *n* **:** a parrot or a closely related bird (as a cockatoo or parrakeet) esp. when domesticated
hook-billed \'=,bild\ *adj* **:** having a strongly curved bill or jaws ⟨a *hook-billed* salmon⟩
hook bolt *n* **:** a bolt hooked at one end and threaded at the other to receive a nut

hook bolts

hook bones *n* **:** HOOK 5c(2)
hook check *n* **:** a technique of gaining possession of an ice-hockey puck or diverting it to a teammate by hooking it away from the opponent with one's stick
hook climber *n* **:** a plant (as a climbing rose) that climbs by hooks or prickles

hooked \'hu̇kt\ *adj* **1 :** having the form of a hook ⟨the ~ bill of a bird of prey⟩ **2 :** provided with a hook or hooks ⟨a fireman's ~ ax⟩ **3 :** made by hooking ⟨a ~ design⟩ ⟨~ carpets⟩ **4** *slang* **:** addicted to narcotics **:** having reached a state of physical dependence on narcotics —
hooked·ness \'hu̇k(t)nəs, -kədn-\ *n* -ES
hooked rug *n* **:** a rug formed by hooking into a strong coarse fabric back loops (as of yarn or strips of cloth) to form a surface pile
¹**hookem-snivey** \,hu̇kəm'snivi\ *n* -s [fr. earlier *hook and snivey*, prob. fr. *hook* (to steal)] *dial chiefly Eng* **:** TRICKERY, DECEIT
²**hookem-snivey** *adj, dial chiefly Eng* **:** DECEITFUL, TRICKY
¹**hook·er** \'hu̇kə(r)\ *n* -s [²*hook* + *-er*] **1 a :** one that hooks esp. habitually ⟨that cow is a bad ~⟩ **b** *slang* **:** THIEF, PICKPOCKET **c** [fr. the fact that they fasten their clothes with hooks rather than buttons] *usu cap* **:** one of the Amish Mennonites **d :** a worker that uses a hook or hooking device to fasten, move, handle, or form articles with which he works: as (1) **:** a logger that fastens logs to hooks, cables, or tongs by which they may be skidded or loaded (2) **:** a steelworker that guides billets in a rolling mill (3) **:** a sponge fisher that detaches sponges with a sponge hook (4) **:** a maker of hooked rugs (5) **:** an operator of a machine for folding and measuring cloth **e :** a player in the front row of a rugby scrum who hooks the ball **2** *slang* **:** DRINK; *esp* **:** a copious drink of liquor ⟨a ~ of hard cider⟩ **3** [prob. fr. ²*hook* (to entrap) + *-er*] *slang* **:** PROSTITUTE
²**hooker** \"\ *n* -s [D *hoeker*, fr. earlier *hoeckboot*, fr. MD *hoecboot* fishing boat, fr. *hoec* fishhook + *boot* boat — more at HOOK] **1 :** a Dutch boat with two masts **2 :** a fishing boat with one mast used on the coasts of England and Ireland **3 :** an old, outmoded, or clumsy boat
hooker cell \"-\ *n, usu cap H* [after Albert H. Hooker †1936 Am. electrochemist] **:** a cell that has graphite anodes and wire-screen cathodes covered with asbestos diaphragms and that is used for making sodium hydroxide and chlorine by electrolysis of sodium chloride
hoo·ke·ri·a·les \(,)hu̇r,kirē'ā(,)lēz\ *n pl, cap* [NL, fr. *Hookeria*, genus of mosses (fr. Sir William J. Hooker †1865 Eng. botanist + NL *-ia*) + *-ales*] **:** an order of usu. pleurocarpous mosses with branched prostrate gametophores, asymmetrical leaves often with two midribs, and capsules with a double peristome
hooker-out \,=='=\ *n, pl* **hookers-out** [*hook out*, v. + *-er*] **1 :** a tonger in a wireworks **2 :** STICKMAN 1c(1)
hooker's green *n, usu cap H* [after William Hooker †1832 Eng. botanical painter] **1 :** a green pigment consisting of a mixture of Prussian blue and gamboge **2 :** a moderate to strong green that is yellower and less strong than spearmint
hooker's orchid *n, usu cap H* [after Sir William J. Hooker †1865 Eng. botanist] **:** a long-spurred orchid (*Habenaria hookeri*) having basal leaves and petals connivent under the upper sepal
hooke's law \'hu̇ks-\ *n, usu cap H* [after Robert Hooke †1703 Eng. scientist] **:** a statement of elasticity: the stress within an elastic solid up to the elastic limit is proportional to the strain responsible for it
hookey *var of* HOOKY
hook gage *n* **:** an instrument for measuring the rise or drop in elevation of a liquid (as water in a reservoir) from a previously recorded level by means of a pointed hook that is directly connected to a fixed part containing a scale (as a vernier) and is submerged and moved gradually until its point just pierces the surface of the liquid from beneath when the measurement is taken
hook-headed spike \'=,==-\ *n* **:** a spike with extended head to hook over the base of a railroad rail and secure it to a tie
hookier *comparative of* HOOKY
hookiest *superlative of* HOOKY
hooking *pres part of* HOOK
hooking iron *n* **:** a hand tool with a pointed metal blade for removing caulking from seams (as of a boat)
hook·ish \'hu̇kish\ *adj* **:** somewhat hooked ⟨a prominent ~ nose⟩
hook ladder *n* **:** POMPIER LADDER
hook·less \-kləs\ *adj* **:** having no hooks
hook·let \-klət\ *n* -s [¹*hook* + *-let*] **:** a small hook ⟨a circle of ~*s* on the tapeworm scolex⟩ — see ECHINOCOCCUS illustration
hooklike \'=,=\ *adj* **:** resembling a hook esp. in recurved form or in ability to grasp and hold ⟨~ thorns⟩
hook·man \'hu̇kmən, -,man\ *n, pl* **hookmen :** a worker that uses a gaff or a cant hook (as in handling logs or fish)
hook money *n* **:** Persian larin money
hooknose \'=,=\ *n* **:** an aquiline nose
hook order *n* **:** a pattern of social organization within a herd of cattle that is characterized by the right of any member to hook one of lower status without fear of retaliation and its submission to hooking by one of higher rank — compare PECK ORDER
hook pass *n* **:** a basketball pass executed in a manner similar to that of a hook shot
hook rope *n* **:** a rope with a hook on the end used esp. on shipboard for clearing and handling lines
hook rug *n* **:** HOOKED RUG
hooks *pl of* HOOK, *pres 3d sing of* HOOK
hook screw *n* **:** SCREW HOOK
hookshop \'=,=\ *n* [²*hook* (to entrap) + *shop*] *slang* **:** BROTHEL 2
hook shot *n* **:** a clear or bank shot in basketball in which a player shoots sideways for the basket by bringing the ball up over his head in an arc with the far hand and releasing it in a usu. flat trajectory
hook slide *n* **:** a foot-first slide to a base in a baseball game in which the runner with both legs extended throws his body to either side to avoid the baseman and hooks the base with the inside foot
hook squid *n* **:** any of certain squids (*Enoploteuthis* and related genera) in which the acetabula of the sessile arms are modified into a formidable armament of hooks
hook strip *n* **:** a horizontal strip or band of wood supporting a series of hooks (as for hanging hats and coats)
hookswinging \'=,==\ *n* **:** a voluntary ritual torture in which the individual is suspended by hooks inserted into the muscles of the back
hook tender *n* **:** a working foreman in charge of a crew yarding logs
hooktip \'=,=\ *or* **hook-tip moth** *n* **:** a moth of the family Drepanidae
hook·um \'hu̇kəm\ *n* -s [Hindi *hukm*, fr. Ar, decision, judgment] *India* **:** COMMAND, ORDER; *esp* **:** an official paper giving instructions
hook·um·pake \'hu̇kəm,pāk\ *n* -s [imit.] *Midland* **:** WOODCOCK 1a(2)
hookum-snivey *var of* HOOKEM-SNIVEY
hook up *vi* **:** to attach a horse or other source of draft to a vehicle ⟨*hooked up* and drove to the meadow⟩ ~ *vt* **1 :** to attach (as a team) to a vehicle **2 :** to install in or connect into a suitable environment to function as part of a system ⟨*hooked* the big parlor heater *up* each fall⟩ ⟨*hook* the gas *up*⟩ ⟨finished *hooking up* the new bathroom⟩ **3** *dial* **:** MARRY ⟨arranged to have the parson *hook* them *up*⟩
hookup \'=,=\ *n* -s [*hook up*] **1 :** a group or number of items cooperating or acting together: as **a :** an assemblage (as of apparatus or circuits) used for a specific purpose (as radio transmission or reception); *also* **:** the general scheme or plan of such an assemblage **b :** a sequence or arrangement of communicating and usu. interacting parts (as the steering gear or brake mechanism of an automobile) ⟨the stoker ~ on the furnace⟩ **2 :** the establishment of a hookup **:** a linking of two or more items into an interacting whole: as **a :** an assembling of parts into a functional whole ⟨finished the ~ of the new pump⟩ **b :** a midair recoupling of a parasite fighter airplane to the belly of the bomber from which it was previously launched **3 :** the end of a line transposed to the line above and preceded by a left-hand bracket ⟨~*s* are sometimes necessary in narrow-measure setting⟩ **4 :** a state of cooperation or alliance between diverse and often supposedly mutually antagonistic elements ⟨explaining the ~ between politics and crime⟩ ⟨a ~ designed to protect the sovereignty of small nations⟩

ho·oku·pu \ˌhōə'kü(ˌ)pü\ *n* -s [Hawaiian *ho'okupu*] **:** a Hawaiian ceremonial presentation of gifts formerly offered as tribute to a chief
hookweed \'≈,≈\ *n* **:** SELF-HEAL
hookworm \'≈,≈\ *n* **1 :** any of numerous parasitic nematode worms (family Ancylostomatidae) having strong buccal hooks or plates for attaching to the host's intestinal lining and including serious bloodsucking pests of man, many domestic and wild mammals, and a few birds — see ANCYLOSTOMA **2 :** *or* **hookworm disease :** disease caused by hookworms **:** ANCYLOSTOMIASIS
hook·wormy \"ē\ *adj* **:** infested by hookworms
hook wrench *or* **hook spanner** *n* **:** a wrench having a hook at the end (as for turning a bolt head or nut)
¹hooky \'hùkē, -ki\ *adj* -ER/-EST [¹*hook* + -*y*] **1 :** full of or covered with hooks **2 :** resembling or having the form of a hook
²hooky \"\ *or* **hook·ey** \"\ *n, pl* **hookies** *or* **hookeys** [prob. fr. ²*hook* (to make off) + -*y*] **:** TRUANT — used chiefly in the phrase *play hooky*
hool \'hœl, -üe-\ *Scot var of* HULL
ho·olau·lea \ˌhōˌōˌlaù'lāə\ *n* -s [Hawaiian *ho'olaule'a*, fr. *ho'o* to make + *lau* much + *le'a* gaiety] **:** a Hawaiian celebration or festival
hoo·let \'hülət\ *chiefly Scot var of* HOWLET
hoo·ley \'hülē\ *n* -s [origin unknown] **:** an Irish party usu. with music
hoo·ley-ann \ˌhülē'an\ *also* **hoo·li·an** \", (')hül'yan\ *n* -s [origin unknown] *West* **:** a throw with a lariat in which the loop is well spread and settles from above on its objective
hoo·li·gan \'hüləgən, -lēg-\ *n* -s *often attrib* [perh. after an Irishman named *Hooligan fl* 1898 in Southwark, London, England] **1 :** HOODLUM 1 **2 :** a person that as a representative of some special interest (as a political or racial philosophy) attempts to override the legal and human rights of other people **3 :** a gambling game played with 10 dice in which a player attempts to throw a selected number 26 or more times in 13 throws
hoo·li·gan·ism \-gəˌnizəm\ *n* -s **:** lawless disorderly conduct typical of hooligans; *often* **:** VANDALISM
hoo·li·han \'hüləˌhan\ *vt* **hoolihanned; hoolihanned; hoolihanning; hoolihans** [prob. fr. the name *Hoolihan*] *West* **:** to bring down (a steer) in bulldogging by leaping well forward on the horns rather than by twisting
hoo·lock \'hüˌläk, -ˌlək\ *n* -s [native name in Assam (state in northeastern India) or Burma] **:** a small gibbon (*Hylobates hoolock*) of Assam and upper Burma; *broadly* **:** a gibbon of the genus *Hylobates*
¹hoo·ly \'hœli\ *adv* [ME *holy*, of Scand origin; akin to ON *hōfliga* fairly, with moderation, fr. *hōfligr* moderate, fr. *hōf* moderation, proportion + -*ligr* -ly; akin to ON *hefja* to lift — more at HEAVE] *chiefly Scot* **:** in a slow, careful, or gentle manner
²hooly \"\ *adj* [ME (Sc dial.) *huly*, of Scand origin; akin to ON *hōfligr* moderate] *chiefly Scot* **:** SLOW, CAREFUL
ho·oma·li·ma·li \ˌhōˌōmälē'mälē\ *n* -s [Hawaiian *ho'omalimali*] *Hawaii* **:** something designed primarily to attract favorable attention **:** SOFT SOAP
hoon \'hün, -ù-\ *n* -s [Hindi *hūn, hun*] *India* **:** PAGODA 2
hoondee *or* **hoondi** *var of* HUNDI
¹hoop \'hüp, -ü-\ *n* -s *often attrib* [ME *hop, hoop*, fr. OE *hōp*; akin to OFris *hōp* ring, band, MD *hoep* ring, band, hoop, Lith *kabė* hook, and perh. to OIr *camm* crooked — more at CHANGE] **1 a :** a strip of wood or metal bent in a circular form and united at the ends that is used esp. for holding together the staves of containers (as casks, tubs, barrels) — see BARREL illustration **b :** such a hoop or a substitute used as a plaything — compare HULA HOOP **2 :** something felt to resemble a hoop **:** a circular figure or object esp. when serving or viewed as a retaining band **:** RING, CIRCLET: as **a :** FINGER RING **b :** either or both members of an embroidery hoop **c :** one of the cylindrical forgings that are concentric with the tube and that are shrunk in rows upon the tube, jacket, or inner layer in the construction of a built-up gun **d :** CHEESE HOOP **e :** a large circle of light material usu. supporting a sheet of paper through which performers leap in various spectacular shows (as in a circus) **f :** a piece of cane looped at one end for handing messages to the crew of a moving railroad train **g :** the rim of a basketball basket; *broadly* **:** the entire basket **3 :** a circle or series of graduated circles of whalebone, metal, or other flexible material inserted into a petticoat or joined by tapes and used to expand a woman's skirt ⟨wore ~*s* under ruffled white mull⟩ **4 a** *dial Eng* **:** an old unit of capacity (as for grain) varying from ¼ peck to 4 pecks **b** *obs* **:** the quantity of drink contained between adjacent hoops of a hooped quart pot **5 hoops** *pl* **:** light strip steel folded up like a skein of wool into lengths of 14 feet **6 :** a croquet wicket **7 :** a shoulder yoke used for carrying loads

hoop 3

²hoop \"\ *vb* -ED/-ING/-S [ME *hoopen*, fr. *hop, hoop*, n.] *vt* **1 a :** to bind, enclose, or fasten (as a barrel) with hoops **b :** CLASP, ENCLOSE, SURROUND **2 a :** to place on or in a hoop ⟨~*ing* her embroidery⟩ ⟨~ curds in the making of cheese⟩ **b :** to score at basketball ⟨~*ed* 5 points to win the game⟩ **3 :** to give the form of a hoop or partial hoop to ⟨a measuring worm ~*ing* his back⟩ ⟨~*ed* the backs of the chairs in a graceful arch⟩ ~ *vi* **1 :** to assume the form of a hoop or partial hoop ⟨the cat's back ~*ed* under his hand⟩ **2 :** to keep a hula hoop revolving about the body
³hoop \'hüp, -ù-\ *archaic var of* WHOOP
⁴hoop *n* -s [MF *huppe*, fr. L *upupa*, of imit. origin like Gk *epop-, epops* hoopoe, G dial *huppupp*] *obs* **:** HOOPOE
hoop ash *n* **1 :** BLACK ASH 1 **2 :** HACKBERRY
hoop back \'≈,≈\ *n* **:** a back (as of a Windsor chair) formed by a bent piece of wood fitted with vertical spindles
hoop dance *n* **:** a male exhibition dance with hoops performed among Indian peoples and imitators from New Mexico to the Great Lakes
hoop driver *n* **:** a tool for setting and tightening hoops (as on a barrel)
hooped *adj* **1 :** made with or shaped like a hoop ⟨a ~ chair back⟩; *esp* **:** having a full rounded contour ⟨a horse with well-*hooped* ribs⟩ **2 :** having, wearing, or enclosed by a hoop ⟨a ~ skirt⟩ ⟨graceful ~ dancers⟩ ⟨~ curds ripening into cheese⟩
hooped·ness \-p(t)nəs, -pədn-\ *n* -ES **:** the quality or state of being hooped

hoop back

hoopee *var of* WHOOPEE
¹hoop·er \'hüpə(r), 'hùp-\ *n* -s **:** one that hoops: as **a :** a man or machine that makes or applies hoops (as to barrels or tubs) **b :** a worker that stretches skins (as sealskins) over a hoop-shaped frame for curing or processing **c :** HOOPSTER
²hooper *or* **hooper swan** *var of* WHOOPER SWAN
hoop·erat·ing *or* **hooper rating** \ˌhüpə'rād·iŋ, ˌhüp-, -ät|, |ēŋ\ *n* -s *usu cap H* [after Claude E. *Hooper* †1954 Am. statistician] **:** a percentage indication of the number of radios or television sets tuned to a particular program at a particular time ⟨rain on a Sunday raises *Hooperatings* —Saul Carson⟩ ⟨the most glamorous, high *Hooperating* show on the air —Frederic Wakeman⟩
hoop fastener *n* **:** a special nail for securing the hoops of a barrel
hoo·pid salmon \'hüpəd-, 'hùp-\ *also* **hoopid** *n* -s [origin unknown] **:** SILVER SALMON
hoop·ing \'hüpiŋ, 'hùp-\ *n* -s [¹*hoop* + -*ing*] **1 :** stock for making hoops **2 :** HOOPS; *esp* **:** a set of hoops used together ⟨the ~ on this barrel is too slack⟩
hoop iron *n* **:** iron in thin strips used for or suitable for use as barrel hoops ⟨arrowheads of sharpened *hoop iron*⟩
hoop·la *also* **houp-la** \'hüˌplä, 'hù-, -lä\ *n* -s [F *houp-là*, interj.] **1 a :** excited commotion ⟨the ~ occasioned . . . by the report —C.J.Rolo⟩; *often* **:** gay or rowdy excitement ⟨holiday ~ and parties⟩ **b :** gaudy, artificial, or pretentious show **:** TO-DO ⟨opportunities for plenty of romantic ~ in a costume drama —John McCarten⟩ ⟨launched the new promotion in a blaze of ~⟩ **c :** something (as utterances) designed to bewilder or confuse ⟨official ~ about the back of organized crime being broken —Joseph LeBaron⟩ **:** BUNKUM, BALLYHOO **2** [influenced in meaning by ¹*hoop*] **:** a game in which novelty items are won by tossing rings over them
hoople \'hüpəl, 'hùp-\ *n* -s [D *hoepel*, dim. of *hoep* hoop, fr. MD — more at HOOP] *dial* **:** HOOP; *esp* **:** a child's hoop for play
hoop·less \-pləs\ *adj* **:** lacking a hoop ⟨an old ~ barrel⟩
hooplike \'≈,≈\ *adj* **:** like a hoop **:** ARCHED, ROUNDED
hoop·man \'hüpmən, 'hùp-\ *n, pl* **hoopmen :** a basketball player
hoop net *n* **:** an elongated cylindrical net supported by one or more hoops and fitted with one or more valves resembling funnels through which fishes may enter but not escape that is used esp. in rivers or other waters where fishes tend to move along regular paths
hoo·poe *also* **hoo·poo** \'hü(ˌ)pü, -pō\ *n* -s [imit. alter. of ⁴*hoop*] **:** any of certain Old World nonpasserine birds (family Upupidae) having a slender decurved bill; *esp* **:** a widely distributed bird (*Upupa epops*) of Europe, Asia, and northern Africa that is of the size of a large thrush with a handsome erectile semicircular crest and cinnamon-colored and black plumage and feeds on insects and other small invertebrates found about decaying organic matter — see WOOD HOOPOE
hoop-petticoat daffodil *also* **hoop-petticoat narcissus** *n* **:** a small early-flowering narcissus (*Narcissus bulbocodium*) that has yellow conical to bell-shaped flowers borne singly, is native from southern France to Morocco, and is widely grown as a rock-garden plant
hoop pine *n* **:** an araucaria (*Araucaria cunninghamii*) of Australia and New Guinea that yields a valuable light soft even-textured wood
hoop pole *n* **:** a straight slender length of green sapling wood usu. of hickory or white oak that was formerly used as stock for barrel hoops
hoop ring *n* **:** a finger ring in the form of a plain or ornamented band or with low-mounted stones along the band
hoops *pl of* HOOP, *pres 3d sing of* HOOP
hoopskirt \'≈,≈\ *n* **1 :** an underskirt stiffened with or as if with hoops **2 :** a full outer skirt expanded by petticoats or hoops
hoop snake *n* **1** *chiefly South and Midland* **:** a fabled snake of extremely venomous character that rolls itself up with its tail in its mouth to proceed at great speed in the manner of a hoop and destroys both animal and plant life with a sting in the end of its tail **2 :** either of two harmless brightly colored burrowing colubrid snakes chiefly of the southeastern U.S.: **a :** a large snake (*Farancia abacura*) that is blue black above and largely red below and has a sharp nonvenomous spine at the end of its tail — called also *horn snake* **b :** RAINBOW SNAKE
hoop·ster \'hüpstə(r), 'hùp-\ *n* -s [¹*hoop* + -*ster*] **1 :** a basketball player **2 :** one that keeps a hula hoop revolving
hoopstick \'≈,≈\ *n* **1 a :** HOOP POLE **b :** a light framing member for a carriage or wagon hood **2 :** a stick for rolling a child's play hoop
hoop withe *or* **hoop withy** *n* **1 :** a tropical Old World shrub (*Colubrina asiatica*) the fruits of which are used as fish poison in the Philippines **2 :** a tropical American shrub of a genus (*Trichostigma*) of the family Phytolaccaceae (esp. *T. octandrum*)
hoopwood \'≈,≈\ *n* **1 :** BLACK ASH 1 **2 :** a winterberry (*Ilex laevigata*)
hoorah *or* **hooray** *var of* HURRAH
hoorah's nest *or* **hooraw's nest** *var of* HURRAH'S NEST
hoo·roosh \hə'rüsh\ *n* -ES [imit.] **:** a wild, hurried, or excited state or situation **:** CONFUSION ⟨such a ~ as we had getting to the docks⟩
¹hoose \'hüs\ *chiefly Scot var of* HOUSE
²hoose *also* **hooze** \'hüz\ *n* -s [prob. akin to E *wheeze*] **1** *dial Eng* **:** a dry cough **:** WHEEZING, WHEEZE **2 :** verminous bronchitis of cattle, sheep, and goats caused by larval strongylid roundworms irritating the bronchial tubes and producing a dry hacking cough — called also *husk*
³hoose *or* **hooze** \"\ *vi* -ED/-ING/-S *dial Eng* **:** WHEEZE
hoose·gow *also* **hoos·gow** \'hüsˌgaù\ *n* -s [Sp *juzgado* panel of judges, tribunal, courtroom, fr. past part. of *juzgar* to judge, fr. L *judicare* — more at JUDGE] *slang* **:** JAIL, LOCKUP, GUARDHOUSE, PRISON
¹hoosh \'hüsh\ *interj* [origin unknown] — used esp. in driving away animals
²hoosh \"\ *vt* -ED/-ING/-ES [perh. alter. of *hoise*] *chiefly Irish* **:** BOOST, LIFT
³hoosh \"\ *n* -ES *chiefly Irish* **:** HOIST, BOOST
⁴hoosh \"\ *n* -ES [origin unknown] **:** a thick soup
¹hoo·sier \'hüzhə(r)\ *n* -s [perh. alter. of E dial. *hoozer* anything large of its kind] **1 :** an awkward, unhandy, or unskilled person; *esp* **:** an ignorant rustic **2** *usu cap* **:** INDIANAN — used as a nickname
²hoosier \"\ *adj, usu cap* **:** of or relating to Indiana or its people ⟨the *Hoosier* state⟩
³hoosier \"\ *vi* -ED/-ING/-S *slang* **:** to loaf on or botch a job
hoo·sier·ism \-zhəˌrizəm\ *n* -s *usu cap* **:** a turn of speech typical of or peculiar to natives of a geographic area centered on Indiana
¹hoot \'hüt, *usu* -üd·+V\ *vb* -ED/-ING/-S [ME *houten, hoten*, of imit. origin] *vi* **1 :** to utter a loud shout; *usu* **:** to cry out or shout in contempt ⟨matrons and girls shall ~ at thee no more —John Dryden⟩ **2 a :** to make the natural throat noise of an owl **b :** to make a sound resembling the hoot of an owl — used esp. of other birds or mammals **3 :** to make a loud clamorous mechanical sound — used esp. of a siren and similar devices ⟨foghorns ~*ing* in the gloom⟩ ~ *vt* **1 a :** to assail with contemptuous cries or other expressions of disapproval or contempt ⟨men of goodwill ~*ed* by rowdies⟩ **b :** to check, interrupt, or drive out by hooting ⟨~*ed* down the speaker⟩ ⟨~*ing* unpopular actors off the stage⟩ **2 :** to express in or by hoots ⟨~*ed* his disapproval⟩
²hoot \"\ *n* -s **1 :** a loud inarticulate shout or noise; *esp* **:** a derisive cry ⟨gave a ~ of contempt⟩ **2 a :** the cry of an owl **b :** a sound (as of a motor horn) suggesting this cry **3 :** a very small amount **:** BIT, TRIFLE, WHIT — used chiefly in negative constructions and esp. with the indefinite article ⟨don't care a ~ what you decide⟩ ⟨she didn't really give two ~*s* about me —Eric Soames⟩
³hoot \"\ *or* **hoots** \-ts\ *interj* [origin unknown] *chiefly Scot* — used to express impatience, mild dissatisfaction, or objection and often in combination ⟨~ awa⟩ ⟨~ mon⟩
⁴hoot \"\ *n* -s [Maori *utu* price, requital] *slang Austral* **:** MONEY
hoo·ta·ma·gan·zy \ˌhüd·əməˌganzē\ *n* -ES [by alter.] **:** HOODED MERGANSER
hootch *var of* ²HOOCH
hootchy-kootchy *or* **hootchie-kootchie** \ˌhüchē'küchē, |hüchi|küchi\ *also* **hootchy-kootch** \-|küch\ *or* **hoochie-coochie** *or* **hoochy-koochy** *n, pl* **hootchy-kootchies** *also* **hootchy-kootches** *or* **hoochie-coochies** *or* **hoochy-koochies** [perh. alter. of *hula-hula*] **:** COOCH
hoo·te·nan·ny *or* **hoot·nan·ny** *also* **hoo·ta·nan·ny** \'hütᵊnˌanē, 'hütˌna-, ≈(ə)'≈≈\ *n* -ES [origin unknown] **1 a** *chiefly dial* **:** THING, GADGET; *usu* **:** a device or piece of mechanical equipment — used esp. when the standard name is unknown ⟨the ~ that goes on top of the carburetor⟩ **b** *usu hootnanny* **:** a device for holding a crosscut saw in position while sawing a log from the under side **2** *usu hootenanny* **:** a gathering at which folksingers entertain often with the audience joining in
hoot·er \'hüd·ə(r), -ütə-\ *n* -s **1 :** one that hoots: as **a** *chiefly Brit* **:** a whistle, siren, or other device (as on an automobile or in a factory) for producing a loud hooting noise **b :** a bird (as an owl or blue grouse) that has a hooting call **2 :** ²HOOT 3
hoot·ing·ly *adv* **:** in the manner of a hoot ⟨sounded ~ in the empty hall⟩ **:** to the point of hooting ⟨~ astonished⟩
hoot owl *n* **:** OWL; *esp* **:** any of various owls (as the tawny owl of Europe or the barred owl of America) having a loud hooting call
hooved \'hüvd, -ü-\ *adj* **:** having or characterized by hooves ⟨the ~ mammals⟩ **:** HOOFED — often used in combination ⟨strong-*hooved*⟩
hoo·ver apron \'hüvə(r)-\ *n* [after Herbert *Hoover* †1964 31st president of the U.S.; fr. its popularity among home gardeners when Hoover was food administrator in World War I] **:** a woman's coverall in the form of a dress that closes by a tie at the waist and has an overlapping reversible front
hoo·ver·crat \'hüvə(r)ˌkrat\ *n* -s *usu cap* [Herbert *Hoover* + E *democrat*] **:** a Democrat of the southern U.S. voting for or supporting Herbert Hoover in the presidential election of 1928 — **hoo·ver·crat·ic** \|≈≈'krad·ik\ *adj, usu cap*
hoo·ver·ism \'hüvəˌrizəm\ *n* -s *often cap* [Herbert *Hoover* + E -*ism*] **:** a system or views formulated by or attributed to Herbert Hoover
hoo·ver·ize \-ˌrīz\ *vb* -ED/-ING/-s *often cap* [Herbert *Hoover* + E -*ize*; fr. his policy as U.S. food administrator 1917–19] *vi* **:** to economize esp. in the use of food ~ *vt* **:** to be saving of or sparing in the use of (food)
hoo·ver·ville \-və(r)ˌvil\ *n, usu cap* [Herbert *Hoover* + E -*ville* (final constituent in many names of towns); fr. the prevalence of such housing during his presidency] **:** a collection of ramshackle dwellings erected upon a dump or urban wasteland and occupied by dispossessed, unemployed, or migratory persons
hooves *pl of* HOOF
¹hop \'häp\ *vb* **hopped; hopped; hopping; hops** [ME *hoppen*, fr. OE *hoppian*; akin to MHG *hupfen, hüpfen, hopfen* to hop, ON *hoppa* to hop, OE *hype* hip — more at HIP] *vi* **1 a :** to move by a quick springy leap or in a series of leaps **:** JUMP ⟨chalked out a hopscotch game and began to ~ around its squares —Dorothy C. Fisher⟩ ⟨~ on a fast-moving train⟩; *esp* **:** to move by leaping with all feet off the ground ⟨a . . . bird came *hopping* around —Francis Birtles⟩ **b :** to jump on one foot or move about in such manner ⟨requiring the applicant to ~ on the toes of each foot —H.G.Armstrong⟩ **c :** BOUNCE, REBOUND ⟨the ball *hopped* around the playing field⟩ **2 a :** to emerge with a quick elastic movement suggestive of a leap ⟨*hopped* out of bed bright and early⟩ ⟨*hopped* out of the car and opened the door for the lady⟩ **b :** to move or go quickly **:** make a quick trip **:** RUN ⟨do you want to ~ down to the store —Oakley Hall⟩ ⟨*hopped* down to the city for the day⟩; *specif* **:** to make a flight usu. of short duration ⟨Western Airlines . . . ~*s* all over the West —Gladwin Hill⟩ ⟨~*s* to Miami for Christmas —Phil Gustafson⟩ **c** *slang chiefly Brit* **:** to go away **:** SCRAM ⟨state your business and get *hopping* —Ruth Park⟩ — usu. used with *it* ⟨no, thanks . . . got to ~ it —Richard Llewellyn⟩ **3 :** to set about doing something — usu. used in the phrase *hop to it* ⟨lots of work to be done . . . you'd better ~ to it —Gordon Webber⟩ **4 :** to make a verbal attack **:** give a tongue-lashing ⟨expect them to make . . . mistakes and don't ~ all over them when they do —W.J.Reilly⟩ ~ *vt* **1 a :** to jump over ⟨the men *hopped* the rails and were in the boats —H.A.Chippendale⟩ **b :** to give a hopping motion to ⟨*hopped* the ball up and down⟩ **c :** to get upon by or as if by hopping **:** climb aboard ⟨~ a freight⟩ ⟨*hopped* a street car —John Dos Passos⟩ **d :** HITCHHIKE ⟨~ a ride⟩ **2 a :** to transport in an airplane from one point to another ⟨the heaviest machinery can be *hopped* over the Andes —*Skyways*⟩ ⟨save . . . travel time by *hopping* them for short distances —*Time*⟩ **b :** to cross by airplane ⟨fears about air armadas *hopping* the Atlantic —S.L.A.Marshall⟩ **3** *slang* **:** to attack physically or verbally **:** JUMP ⟨~ an enemy aircraft⟩ **4 :** to wait on **:** give service to **:** TEND, SERVE ⟨you're here to ~ bells —Calder Willingham⟩ ⟨young girls and boys in uniform *hopping* cars —Horace McCoy⟩ ⟨did you think I was going to . . . ~ bar for the rest of my life —Maritta Wolff⟩
²hop \"\ *n* -s **1 a :** an instance of hopping **:** a short brisk leap esp. on one leg **b** (1) **:** BOUNCE, REBOUND ⟨the shortstop took it on the first ~⟩ ⟨one mortar shell hit a tree, took a freak ~ —Mack Morriss⟩ (2) **:** a slight, sudden elevation taken by a fast pitched ball in its course of flight **2 :** DANCE, BALL ⟨formal and informal ~*s* —*Career for Tomorrow*⟩ ⟨going to the junior *hop*⟩; *also* **:** a party with dancing **3 a :** a flight in an airplane usu. of short duration ⟨made his dramatic ~ to Paris last week —*New Republic*⟩ **b :** a usu. short or quick trip or excursion ⟨supplement their rations with ~*s* across the border —Richard Joseph⟩ ⟨weekend ~*s* to Paris —Sinclair Lewis⟩ ⟨required long ~*s* on bad trains —Virginia D. Dawson and Betty D. Wilson⟩ **c :** a ride given by a passing vehicle ⟨~*s* most of the way, and a little walking —J.A. Michener⟩ — **on the hop** *adv (or adj), Brit* **:** in the act **:** with the goods **:** by surprise or unawares — usu. used in the phrase *catch on the hop* ⟨would never catch him *on the hop* —*Sydney (Australia) Bull.*⟩ ⟨that flood of customers caught them *on the hop* —Fred Majdalany⟩
³hop \"\ *n* -s *often attrib* [ME *hoppe*, fr. MD; akin to OS *feldhoppo* hop, OHG *hopfo* hop, Norw *hupp* tassel, OE *scēaf* sheaf — more at SHEAF] **1 a :** a twining Eurasian vine (*Humulus lupulus*) with 3-lobed or 5-lobed leaves and small greenish dioecious flowers that is widely cultivated in America, occurs often as an escape, and is sometimes confused with a native hop plant (*H. Americanus*) **b hops** *pl* **:** the ripened and dried pistillate cones of hop used chiefly to impart a bitter flavor to malt liquors and also in medicine as a tonic **2** *slang* **:** a narcotic drug; *esp* **:** OPIUM
⁴hop \"\ *vb* **hopped; hopped; hopping; hops** *vt* **1 :** to impregnate with hops **2 a** (1) **:** to drug or stimulate with drugs **:** DOPE ⟨I'm not drunk . . . I'm *hopped* to the eyes —Ernest Hemingway⟩ — usu. used with *up* ⟨maybe he was *hopped* up on dope of some sort —Shirley A. Grau⟩ (2) **:** to administer a stimulant to (a race horse) **b :** to stimulate or excite by any means **:** ROUSE — used with *up* ⟨used those alumni banquets to ~ everybody up —Millard Lampell⟩ ⟨*hopped* up by the music —Morley Callaghan⟩ **c :** to increase the power of (an engine) or the power of the engine of (a vehicle) beyond an original rating — used with *up* ⟨~ up the motor⟩ ~ *vi* **:** to gather or grow hops
ho·pak \'hōˌpak\ *n* -s [Ukrainian — more at GOPAK] **:** GOPAK
hop aphid *n* **:** a widely distributed aphid (*Phorodon humuli*) that feeds on the growing shoots of hops and other cultivated plants — called also *hop fly, hop louse*
hop back *n* **:** a brewing vat into which the wort is run after boiling in the copper and which has a perforated false bottom for straining off the hops — called also *hop jack*
hopbine *or* **hopbind** \'≈,≈\ *n* **:** BINE a
hopbush \'≈,≈\ *n* **:** a shrub or tree of the genus *Dodonaea* — see AKEAKE 1
Hop·cal·ite \'häpkəˌlīt\ *trademark* — used for a granular mixture of specially prepared manganese dioxide with other oxides used as a catalyst esp. for removing carbon monoxide from air by oxidation or for detecting carbon monoxide in gas analysis
hop clover *n* **1 :** any of several plants of the genus *Trifolium* with heads of yellow flowers resembling hop **2 :** BLACK MEDIC
¹hope \'hōp\ *vb* -ED/-ING/-S [ME *hopen*, fr. OE *hopian*; akin to OFris *hopia* to hope, MLG & MD *hopen*, MHG *hoffen* to hope, and perh. to OE *hoppian* to hop — more at HOP] *vi* **1 :** to cherish a desire with expectation ⟨~*s* for great things from his son⟩ **2** *archaic* **:** to place confidence or trust — usu. used with *in* ⟨I ~ in thy word —Ps 119:81 (RSV)⟩ ~ *vt* **1 a :** to desire with expectation or with belief in the possibility of obtaining **:** cherish hope of ⟨what I have been longing for, though I never *hoped* it —Rachel Henning⟩ **b :** DESIRE, TRUST ⟨~ and expect to be back in my laboratory —E.J.Simmons⟩ ⟨~ he'll let us in⟩ **2** *Midland* **:** WISH ⟨all *hoped* him well —H.E.Giles⟩ **syn** see EXPECT — **hope against hope :** to hope without any basis for expecting fulfillment
²hope \"\ *n* -s [ME, fr. OE *hopa*; akin to OFris, MLG, & MD *hope*, MHG *hoffe*; derivatives fr. the root of E ¹*hope*] **1** *archaic* **:** TRUST, RELIANCE ⟨all my ~ is in the Lord⟩ **2 a :** desire accompanied with expectation of obtaining what is desired or belief that it is obtainable ⟨wished but not with ~ —John Milton⟩ ⟨all ~ is dead⟩ ⟨are in ~*s* of an early recovery⟩ **b :** one on whom hopes are centered ⟨the team's only ~ for victory⟩ **c :** a source of hopeful expectation **:** PROMISE ⟨viewed America as the land of ~⟩ **d :** something that is hoped for **:** an object of hope ⟨the arrival of reinforcements was their last forlorn ~⟩ ⟨a healthy family is the ~ . . . of every homemaker —Mary S. Switzer⟩
³hope \"\ *n* -s [ME, fr. OE *hop*, akin to OE *hype* hip — more at HIP] **1** *now chiefly dial* **:** a piece of arable land surrounded by waste; *esp* **:** one surrounded by swamp or marsh **2** *dial chiefly Brit* **:** a broad upland valley sometimes rounded and often with a stream running through it **3** *now dial* **:** a small bay or inlet

ho·pea \'hōpēə\ *n, cap* [NL, after John *Hope* †1786 Sc. physician and botanist] **:** a genus of tropical trees (family Dipterocarpaceae) with simple leaves, usu. fragrant flowers with one-sided spikes or racemes, and often hard heavy wood — compare MERAWAN

hope chest *n* **1 :** a young woman's accumulation of clothes and domestic furnishings (as silver, linen) kept in or as if in a chest in anticipation of her marriage — compare BOTTOM DRAWER **2 :** a box for use as a hope chest

¹hope·ful \'hōpfəl\ *adj* [²*hope* + *-ful*] **1 :** full of hope or agreeable expectation **:** inclined to hope **:** happily expectant **2 :** having qualities which inspire hope **:** giving promise of good or of success ⟨a ~ prospect⟩ — **hope·ful·ly** \-fəlē, -li\ *adv* — **hope·ful·ness** *n* -ES

²hopeful \"\ *n* -S **:** a person who aspires hopefully or expectantly to become or achieve something ⟨before the convention . . . meets the various presidential ~*s* have set up headquarters —D.D.McKean⟩ ⟨not all who want to write can go to universities . . . a large army of ~*s* is scattered all over the land —Edward Uhlan⟩

hope·ite \'hō,pīt\ *n* -S [Thomas C. *Hope* †1844 Scot. chemist + E *-ite*] **:** a mineral $Zn_3(PO_4)_2.4H_2O$ consisting of a hydrous phosphate of zinc (sp. gr. 2.76–2.85)

hope·less \'hōpləs\ *adj* **1 a** (1) **:** devoid of hope **:** having no expectation of good **:** DESPAIRING ⟨girls feel ~ if they haven't a marriage at least in sight —Sidonie M. Gruenberg⟩ ⟨three lonely and ~ old women —Upton Sinclair⟩ ⟨was never ~ of anybody —Margaret Deland⟩ (2) **:** reflecting or indicating lack of hope ⟨gazed with lusterless, ~ eyes —Jack London⟩ **b :** not susceptible of remedy or cure **:** INCURABLE ⟨should be aware of his responsibility if he declares a . . . patient ~ —*Jour. Amer. Med. Assoc.*⟩ **c :** being beyond redemption **:** offering no prospect of change or improvement ⟨the dream of every magazine writer who is not a ~ hack —Raymond Chandler⟩ ⟨as an actor he is really ~⟩ ⟨a ~ extrovert, giving herself completely and trustingly to everyone —*Holiday*⟩ ⟨a ~ Anglophile —Richard Joseph⟩ **2 a :** giving no ground for hope **:** promising nothing desirable **:** DESPERATE ⟨the situation looked ~ indeed —C.B.Nordhoff & J.N.Hall⟩ **b :** incapable of solution, management, or accomplishment **:** IMPOSSIBLE, INSOLUBLE ⟨a ~ task⟩ ⟨had a ~ jumble of papers on my hands —*Phoenix Flame*⟩ ⟨the defective . . . whose redemption is ~ —B.N.Cardozo⟩ ⟨worked at depths that seemed ~ fifty years ago —Waldemar Kaempffert⟩ ⟨in ~ conflict with religion —R.W.Murray⟩ ⟨lucidity ~ to find amid all the cluttering detail of advanced works —*Geog. Journal*⟩ **syn** see DESPONDENT

hope·less·ly *adv* **:** in a hopeless manner

hope·less·ness *n* -ES **:** the quality or state of being hopeless

hop·er \'hōpə(r)\ *n* -S [ME, fr. *hopen* to hope + *-er*] **:** one that hopes

hopes *pres 3d sing of* HOPE, *pl of* HOPE

hope·well \'hōp,wel\ *or* **hope·well·ian** \(')hōp¦welēən\ *adj, usu cap* [after Cloud *Hopewell*, 19th cent. Am. farmer on whose Ohio farm type stations were found] **:** of or belonging to the most advanced of the mound-building cultures of No. America centered in the Ohio and Illinois river valleys and characterized by large complex earthworks and burial mounds, artistic excellence in artifacts, and frequent cremation of the dead

hop flea beetle *n* **:** a small flea beetle (*Psylliodes punctulata*) sometimes injurious to hops

hop flour *or* **hop meal** *n* **:** LUPULIN

hop fly *n* **:** HOP APHID

hophead \'=,=\ *n* [³*hop* + *head*] *slang* **:** a drug addict

hop hornbeam *n* **:** a tree of the genus *Ostrya; esp* **:** an American tree (*O. virginiana*) with fruiting clusters resembling hops

ho·pi \'hō(,)pē, -,pi\ *n, pl* **hopi** *also* **hopis** *usu cap* [Hopi *Hópi*, lit., good, peaceful] **1 a :** a Shoshonean people of Pueblo Indians in northeastern Arizona **b :** a member of such people **2 :** the language of the Hopi people **3 :** FRENCH BEIGE

hoping *pres part of* HOPE

hop·ing·ly *adv* **:** in a hopeful manner ⟨regarded me ~⟩

hopi way *n, usu cap H&W* **:** the ethical and behavioral code of the Hopi people depicted dramatically in the annual ceremonial cycle and including rules for each of the roles which a person of either sex and at the various age levels is expected to assume throughout life

hop jack *n* **:** HOP BACK

hop kiln *n* **:** a kiln for drying hops

¹hop·kins·ian \hŭp'kinzēən\ *n* -S *usu cap* [Samuel *Hopkins* †1803 Am. clergyman + *-ian*] **:** a follower of the clergyman Samuel Hopkins who taught a rigorous form of Calvinistic theology

²hopkinsian \(')=¦==\ *adj, usu cap* **:** of or relating to Hopkinsians or to Hopkinsianism

hop·kins·ian·ism \='==ə,nizəm\ *n* -S *usu cap* **:** the theology taught by Samuel Hopkins holding that one must submit unconditionally to the will of God and be willing to be damned if the glory of God requires it

hop·lite \'hä,plīt\ *n* -S [Gk *hoplitēs*, fr. *hoplon* tool, weapon, piece of armor (fr. *hepein* to care for, prepare) + *-itēs* -ite — more at SEPULCHER] **:** a heavily armed infantry soldier of ancient Greece equipped with helmet, cuirass, greaves, shield, spear, and sword

hoplo- *comb form* [NL, fr. Gk *hopl-*, *hoplo-* tool, weapon, piece of armor, fr. *hoplon*] **:** heavily armed **:** having powerful offensive members — used chiefly in zoological taxa ⟨*Hoplonemertea*⟩

hop·lo·car·i·da \,häplō'karədə\ *n pl, cap* [NL, fr. *hoplo-* + *-carida* (fr. Gk *karid-*, *karis* shrimp, prawn)] **:** a division of Malacostraca coextensive with an order Stomatopoda of tropical marine burrowing crustaceans comprising the mantis shrimps and having a reduced capelike carapace, a large powerful abdomen, five pairs of anteriorly directly thoracic maxillipeds of which the second pair form greatly enlarged raptorial arms, and enlarged swimming appendages on the abdomen with large branching gills on the exopodites

hop·lo·ceph·a·lus \-'sefələs\ *n, cap* [NL, fr. *hoplo-* + *-cephalus*] **:** a genus of moderately venomous Australian elapid snakes

hop·lo·nemertea \¦häplō+\ *n pl, cap* [NL, fr. *hoplo-* + *Nemertea*] **:** an order of Nemertea (class Enopla) comprising variable forms with the proboscis armed with stylets and with an intestinal cecum — **hop·lo·nemertean** \"+\ *adj*

hop·lo·nemertini \"+\ [NL, fr. *hoplo-* + *Nemertini*] *syn of* HOPLONEMERTEA

hop·lo·pho·ne·us \,häplə'fōnēəs\ *n, cap* [NL, fr. *hoplo-* + Gk *phonios* murderous] **:** a genus of primitive sabertooths from the Oligocene and Miocene of western No. America having the large heads and canines of later forms but small brains and a grasping forefoot

hop louse *n* **:** HOP APHID

hop marjoram *n* **:** CRETAN DITTANY

hop medic *n* **:** BLACK MEDIC

hop merchant *n* **:** a comma butterfly (*Polygonia comma*)

hop mildew *n* **1 :** either of two parasitic fungi attacking the hop: **a :** a powdery mildew (*Sphaerotheca humuli*) **b :** a downy mildew (*Peronoplasmopara humuli*) **2 :** disease of hops caused by a hop mildew

hop oil *also* **hops oil** *n* **:** a brownish yellow aromatic essential oil obtained from hops and used chiefly in flavoring cereal beverages

hop–o'–my–thumb \¦häpəmə'thəm, -,mī-\ *n, pl* **hop–o'–my–thumbs :** a very diminutive person **:** DWARF, PYGMY

¹hopped *past of* HOP

²hopped *adj* **:** impregnated with hops

hopped–up \'=¦=\ *adj* [fr. past part. of *hop up*, v.] **1 a :** being under the stimulating or stupefying influence of a narcotic drug **:** DOPED ⟨when . . . not *hopped-up*, she had a certain pride in her bearing —Polly Adler⟩ **b** (1) **:** full of enthusiasm **:** ENTHUSIASTIC, EXUBERANT, AROUSED, ROUSED, EXCITED ⟨all *hopped-up* over the visit —Danton Walker⟩ ⟨squeaking past an obstinate, *hopped-up* . . . team —*Official Basketball Guide*⟩ (2) **:** dressed up **:** EMBELLISHED ⟨this *hopped-up* image of plantation life —Manny Farber⟩ **2 :** having its engine power increased beyond the original rating ⟨a *hopped-up* hot rod —*Science Newsletter*⟩

¹hop·per \'häpə(r)\ *n* -S [ME, fr. *hoppen* to hop + *-er* — more at HOP] **1 :** one that hops: as **a :** a leaping insect (as a leafhopper, grasshopper, or froghopper); *specif* **:** an immature hopping form usu. of an insect that is winged as an adult (as the larva of a cheese fly or a young grasshopper or locust) **b** (1) **:** a person who makes flights or trips of usu. short duration ⟨the first island-*hopper* in the Caribbean —*Newsweek*⟩ (2) **:** one who flits about from one place of a specified kind to another of the same kind — usu. used in combination ⟨a table-*hopper*⟩ ⟨a bar*hopper*⟩ **c :** a batted ball which rebounds from the ground **2 a :** a chute, box, or receptacle usu. funnel-shaped with an opening at the lower part for delivering material (as grain, fuel, or coal) **b :** something like or likened to a hopper in form or function as: (1) **:** any of the compartments of a hopper frame or the hopper frame itself (2) **:** a feeder for animals; *esp* **:** one from which food flows automatically from an enclosed reservoir to the compartment from which it is eaten **c :** a box usu. on the desk of the clerk or other official of a legislative body into which a proposed bill is dropped **d :** the process of realization or preparation — used in the phrase *in the hopper* ⟨your show is in the ~ and you might just as well . . . not worry —E.J.Kahn⟩ ⟨a plan for exempting . . . small businesses from wage controls is in the ~ —*Washington Report*⟩ **3 a :** a ship used esp. to convey mud, gravel, or sand dredged from harbors out to sea and constructed with a full midship section from which the cargo is discharged through the bottom **b :** HOPPER CAR **c** (1) **:** a tank holding water or other liquid and having a device for releasing its contents through a pipe at the bottom (2) **:** a toilet bowl

²hopper \"\ *n* -S [³*hop* + *-er*] **1 :** a hop picker **2 :** a brewery worker who pours dried hops into casks **3 :** an inverted pyramid or cone through which malt passes to the grinding mill in the brewing process

hopper boy *n* **:** a revolving rake used in flour milling to spread and stir freshly ground flour for cooling before it is bolted

hopperburn \'==,=\ *n* **:** a browning and shriveling of potato foliage associated with the feeding of the potato leafhopper — compare TIPBURN

hopper car *n* **:** a freight car with a floor sloping to one or more hinged doors or hoppers for discharging bulk contents (as coal, ore, sand) by gravity and with a permanent roof and roof hatches when used for carrying bulk commodities (as cement) which must be kept dry

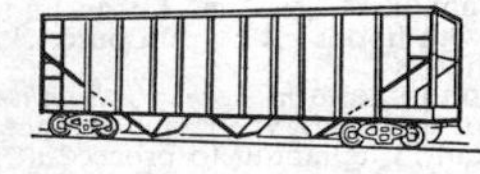
hopper car

hopper closet *n* **:** a toilet with a hopper

hopper crystal *n* **:** a funnel-shaped crystal

hop·per·doz·er \'häpə(r),dōzə(r)\ *n* [¹*hopper* + *-dozer* (as in *bulldozer*)] **:** a device for catching and destroying insects (as grasshoppers) that is drawn on runners across a field and has a shield against which insects jump and fall into a pan containing kerosene or oil

hopper frame *n* **:** a window frame that has superimposed fanlights opening inward and is used esp. in hospitals — called also *hospital light*

hoppergrass \'==,=\ *n* [by alter.] *dial* **:** GRASSHOPPER

hop·per·man \'==mən\ *n, pl* **hoppermen 1 :** a member of the crew of a hopper barge **2 :** a worker who adjusts and attends hoppers

hop·pet \'häpət\ *n* -S [obs. E *hopper* basket, seed-basket (fr. ME, fr. *hoppen* to hop + *-er*) + *-et* — more at HOP] *dial Eng* **:** BASKET, BUCKET

¹hop·ping \'häpiŋ, -pēŋ\ *pres part of* HOP

²hopping \"\ *adj* **1 :** journeying or flitting about from one place of a specified kind to another place of the same kind — usu. used in combination ⟨thus began a frenetic show-*hopping* existence —*N.Y.Times*⟩ **2 :** moving about busily **:** working hard **:** intensely active **:** BUSY ⟨intrigue and foul play keep the captain ~ —Andrea Parke⟩ ⟨the drivers were kept ~ to cover . . . 66 square miles —*Crowsnest*⟩ **3 :** extremely angry **:** FURIOUS

³hopping \"\ *adv* **:** EXTREMELY, VIOLENTLY — used in the phrase *hopping mad* ⟨apt to get ~ mad and bring suit —Margaret Nicholson⟩ ⟨~ mad when we discovered that barbed wire —W.A.White⟩

hopping dick *n, usu cap D* **:** a Jamaican thrush (*Turdus aurantius*) resembling a blackbird (*Turdus merula*)

hop·ping·ly *adv* **:** in a hopping manner ⟨flown ~ away —Israel Zangwill⟩

hoppin john \'häpən-\ *also* **hopping john** *n, usu cap J* **:** a stew of cowpeas, rice, and bacon or salt pork esp. popular in the southern states and traditionally served on New Year's Day

¹hop·ple \'häpəl\ *vt* **hoppled; hoppled; hoppling** \-p(ə)liŋ\ **hopples** [prob. fr. ¹*hop* + *-le*] **:** to fetter the feet of (as a horse or cow) **:** HOBBLE

²hopple \"\ *n* -S **:** a fetter used for grazing horses or cattle or a leg harness usu. of leather to control the gait of trotting or pacing horses — used chiefly in pl.

¹hop·py \'häpē, -pi\ *adj* -ER/-EST [³*hop* + *-y*] **1 :** abounding in hops **2 :** having the bitter taste of hops — used esp. of ale or beer

²hoppy \"\ *n* -ES *slang* **:** a drug addict

³hoppy \"\ *adj* -ER/-EST [²*hop* + *-y*] **:** characterized by a hopping step or movement ⟨a restless, ~ Frenchman —Ludwig Bemelmans⟩ ⟨a lively little blue crane with a ~ leg —I.L. Idriess⟩

hops *pres 3d sing of* HOP, *pl of* HOP

hopsack \'=,=\ *n* [ME *hopsak* sack for hops, fr. *hoppe* hop + *sak* sack] **:** HOPSACKING 2

hopsacking \'=,==\ *n* [³*hop* + *sacking*] **1 :** material of hemp and jute used esp. as bagging by hop growers **2 :** a rough-surfaced clothing fabric loosely woven of various fibers in an open basket weave

hopsage \'=,=\ *n* [³*hop* + *sage*] **:** any of certain low shrubs of alkaline regions of western No. America that constitute the genus *Grayia* of the family Chenopodiaceae and are locally important native browse plants; *esp* **:** an erect much-branched shrub (*G. spinosa*) having the flowers in dense terminal spikes, the fruiting bracts broadly rounded and often tinged with red, and forming a cluster resembling the strobilus of a hopvine

¹hopscotch \'=,=\ *n* [¹*hop* + *scotch* (line)] **:** a child's game of many variations in which a player tosses a small flat stone or similar object consecutively into the lined and numbered areas of a figure outlined upon the ground, hops on one foot through the figure and back to the area in which the stone lies, picks up the stone, and hops on out trying to avoid errors (as stepping on a line or losing balance)

²hopscotch \"\ *vi* **:** to move with or as if with the hopping step used in the game of hopscotch ⟨children ~ between the tables —Willie S. Ethridge⟩

9 10 8 7 5 6 4 3 2 1

one form of hopscotch figure

hops oil *var of* HOP OIL

hop, step, and jump *n* **:** a field event in which the participants cover as much ground as possible by a hop, stride, and jump in succession usu. after a running start

hop·toad \'häp,tōd\ *also* **hop·py·toad** \-pē,-\ *n, chiefly dial* **:** TOAD

hop tree *n* [³*hop*] **:** a small American tree (*Ptelea trifoliata*) having 2-seeded samaras as fruits

hop trefoil *n* **:** HOP CLOVER

hopvine \'=,=\ *n* **1 :** the twining stem of the hop **:** HOPBINE **2 :** a hop plant

hopyard \'=,=\ *n* **:** a hop field

hoquet *var of* HOCKET

hor *abbr* **1** horizon; horizontal **2** horological; horology

¹ho·ra *also* **ho·rah** *or* **hor·ra** \'hōrə, 'hȯrə\ *n* -S [NHeb & Romanian; NHeb *hōrāh*, fr. Romanian *horă*, fr. Turk *hora*] **1 :** a folk dance of Romania and Israel in which dancers form a circle, lock arms, and dance to the left or right with grapevine steps and hops **2 :** music to which the hora is danced

²hora \"\ *n* -S [native name in Ceylon] **:** a tree (*Dipterocarpus zeylanicus*) of Ceylon with reddish brown strong heavy wood

ho·ra·ry \'hōrərē\ *adj* [ML *horarius*, fr. L *hora* hour + *-arius* -ary — more at HOUR] *archaic* **:** of or relating to an hour **:** noting the hours

ho·ra·tian \hə'rāshən, hō'-,hȯ'- *also* -shēən\ *adj, usu cap* [L *Horatianus*, fr. *Horatius* Horace (Quintus Horatius Flaccus) †8 B.C. Latin poet + L *-anus* -an] **:** of or relating to the poet Horace or resembling his poetic style (as in finish of form and aptness of diction)

ho·ra·tio al·ger \hə¦rā(,)shō¦alj'ə(r), -āshē,ō-\ *adj, usu cap H&A* [after *Horatio Alger* †1899 Am. clergyman and author of juvenile fiction] **:** of, relating to, or resembling the works of Horatio Alger in which success is achieved through self-reliance and hard work ⟨their own *Horatio Alger* myth of honest poor boy rises to riches —James Jones⟩

horde \'hō(ə)rd, 'hȯ(ə)rd, -ōəd, -ȯ(ə)d\ *n* -S [MF, G & Pol; MF & G *horde*, fr. Pol *horda*, of Mongolic origin; akin to Mongolian *ordu*, *orda* court, camp, horde, Kalmuck *orda*] **1 a** (1) **:** a clan or tribal group of Tatar or other Mongolian nomadic tent dwellers claiming exclusive hunting or grazing rights over a defined area (2) **:** a people or tribe of nomadic life **b :** a usu. small and typically nomadic social group composed of allied or related family groups occupying a common territory; *esp* **:** such a group among the Australian aborigines **c :** a hypothetical primordial social unit comprised of a number of families ⟨the primitive ~ posited by evolutionists⟩ **2 :** an unorganized or loosely organized mass of individuals **:** a vast number **:** CROWD, SWARM, AGGLOMERATION ⟨circling ~*s* of mixed insects —B.J.Haimes⟩ ⟨unpolluted . . . by their brief contact with the touristic ~ —Arnold Bennett⟩ ⟨~*s* of Irish . . . came to the American shore —*Amer. Guide Series: N.Y.*⟩ ⟨most companies today take ~*s* of pictures —W.B.Eidson⟩ **syn** see CROWD

hor·de·in \'hȯ(r)dēən\ *n* -S [F *hordéine*, fr. L *hordeum* barley + F *-ine*] **:** a prolamin found in the seeds of barley

hor·de·nine \-də,nēn, -,nən\ *n* -S [ISV *horden-* (fr. L *hordeum*) + *-ine*; orig. formed in F] **:** a crystalline alkaloid $HOC_6H_4CH_2CH_2N(CH_3)_2$ found in germinating barley and in mescal

hor·de·o·lum \hȯ(r)'dēələm\ *n, pl* **hordeo·la** \-lə\ [NL, alter. of LL *hordeolus*, dim. of L *hordeum* barley] **:** ⁴STY

hor·de·um \'hȯ(r)dēəm\ *n* [NL, fr. L, barley; akin to OHG *gersta* barley, Gk *kri*, Alb *drith*, and prob. to L *horrēre* to bristle — more at HORROR] **1** *cap* **:** a widely distributed genus of grasses having the flowers in dense spikes often with long-awned glumes and the one-flowered spikelets in clusters of two or three at each joint of the rachis — see BARLEY **2** -S **:** any grass of the genus *Hordeum*

hore·hound *or* **hoar·hound** \'hō(ə)r,haůnd, 'hȯ(ə)r-, 'hōə,h-, 'hȯ(ə),h-\ *n* [by folk etymology fr. ME *horhoune*, fr. OE *hārhūne*, fr. *hār* hoary + *hūne* horehound — more at HOAR] **1 a :** a European aromatic mint (*Marrubium vulgare*) that is naturalized in the U.S., has pubescent leaves and small axillary flowers, has a very bitter taste, and is used as a tonic and anthelmintic — called also *white horehound* **b :** an extract or confection made from this plant and used as a remedy for coughs and colds **2 :** any of several labiates resembling horehound in appearance — used with an attributive or qualifying adjective ⟨black ~⟩ ⟨water ~⟩

horehound bug *n* **:** a widespread orange and black Australian bug (*Agonoscelis rutila*) destructive to the foliage of horehound and other crop plants

ho·rite \'hōr,īt\ *n* -S *usu cap* **1 :** a cave-dwelling people of the biblical period prior to the time of Abraham that inhabited the Dead sea region of the eastern Mediterranean **2 :** a member of the Horite people

¹ho·ri·zon \hə'rīz°n\ *n* -S [alter. (influenced by LL *horizon*) of ME *orisonte*, *orizon*, fr. LL *horizont-*, *horizon*, fr. Gk *horizont-*, *horizōn*, fr. pres. part. of *horizein* to separate, part, bound, define, fr. *horos* boundary, limit + *-izein* -ize; akin to L *urvus* circumference of a city, Oscan *uruvú* boundary] **1 a :** a circle that bounds the part of the earth's surface visible from a given point **:** an apparent junction of earth and sky **b** (1) **:** a great circle 90 degrees from the zenith and constituting the equator of the horizon system of coordinates (2) **:** the circle in which a plane perpendicular to the direction of gravity intersects the celestial sphere (3) **:** the plane tangent to the earth's surface at the observer's position (4) **:** a level mirror (as the surface of mercury in a shallow vessel or a plane reflector adjusted to the true level artificially) used esp. in observing altitudes — called also *artificial horizon*, *false horizon* **c** *or* **horizon line :** an imaginary line in a picture on which is projected the point of sight or station point of the spectator and which in a landscape replaces the natural horizon — compare PERSPECTIVE **d** (1) **:** the fullest range or widest limit of perception, interest, appreciation, knowledge, or experience ⟨the ~ of the human intellect has widened wonderfully during the past hundred years —C.W.Eliot⟩ ⟨your ~ contracts, your mind's eye is focused upon a small circle of . . . details —Jan Struther⟩ (2) **:** the range or limit of hope or expectation or a visible and seemingly attainable end or object lying within or upon it **:** GOAL, PROSPECT ⟨youth . . . demands of life some hope and ~ —John Buchan⟩ ⟨China with its ~*s* of industrialization and trade —M.W.Straight⟩ **2 a :** the geological deposit of a particular time, usu. identified by distinctive fossils **:** a stratigraphic level or position in the geologic column **:** a natural soil layer; *also* **:** ZONE **b :** any of the reasonably distinct layers of soil or its underlying material seen in a vertical section or profile of land and gradually developed as a result of natural soil-forming processes (as the incorporation of organic matter with disintegrated rock material) — see A-HORIZON, B-HORIZON, C-HORIZON, D-HORIZON **c** (1) **:** a cultural area or level of development indicated by widely separated groups of artifacts showing cultural similarities (as in specific styles or objects) (2) **:** a period of time indicated by a particular level of development in an excavated site **3 :** HORIZON BLUE 2 **syn** see RANGE

²horizon \"\ *vt* -ED/-ING/-S **:** to limit by a horizon

ho·ri·zon·al \-z(°)nəl\ *adj* **:** of or relating to a horizon **:** having a horizon ⟨the functional significance of a ~ diffusion —*Amer. Antiquity*⟩ ⟨never has the opportunity for the individual career been so exalted . . . so ~ —S.N.Behrman⟩

horizon blue *n* **1 :** a variable color averaging a light greenish blue to blue **2** *also* **horizon :** a greenish white

horizon clubber *n* [*Horizon Club* + *-er*] **:** a member of Horizon Club, the senior program of the Camp Fire Girls for girls in the ninth grade through high school or about 15 through 18

horizon coordinate *n* **:** any member of a system of celestial coordinates based on the horizon of the observer with azimuth being the primary coordinate and altitude the secondary coordinate

ho·ri·zon·less \-z°nləs\ *adj* **:** devoid of a horizon **:** HOPELESS ⟨it was a ~ grind —Philip Hamburger⟩

horizon system of coordinates : a system of celestial coordinates based on the observer's horizon with its coordinates being altitude and azimuth

¹hor·i·zon·tal \¦hȯrə¦zänt°l, ¦här-\ *adj* [LL *horizont-*, *horizon* + E *-al*] **1 a :** of, relating to, or situated near the horizon **b :** parallel to the horizon **:** being on a level **:** FLAT ⟨a ~ line⟩ ⟨a ~ surface⟩ **c :** measured or contained in a plane of the horizon ⟨~ distance⟩ **d :** placed or operating chiefly along a plane parallel to the horizon — used esp. of machines and mechanical devices ⟨a ~ escapement⟩ **e** *bot* **:** situated in a plane at a right angle to the plane of the primary axis ⟨~ branches⟩ **f** *of a stamp* **:** having a rectangular shape with the longer sides forming the top and bottom **2 a :** applied equally or uniformly to all individuals in a group **:** OVERALL, GENERAL ⟨~ rate increases⟩ ⟨demands for ~ slashing of local government costs —O.K.Armstrong⟩ ⟨the increased ~ spread of buying power —Bud Wilson⟩ **b :** relating to, uniting, or consisting of individuals of similar type or on the same level: as (1) **:** consisting of two or more economic units on the same level of production or distribution ⟨his gigantic ~ and vertical combination of business ventures is efficiently run —Claire Sterling⟩ ⟨a ~ merger⟩ (2) **:** of, relating to, or comprising persons of similar status ⟨a union made up of meat cutters or railroad engineers . . . would be considered ~ —J.F.Cuber⟩ ⟨it must be . . . ~, in the sense of uniting students of similar ages —*General Education in a Free Society*⟩ ⟨~ strata . . . based upon the social values that are attached to occupation, education, place of residence in the community, and associations —August Hollingshead⟩ (3) **:** relating to the motion of a succession of musical notes or tones forming a melodic line or part — **hor·i·zon·tal·ly** \-ᵊlē, -ᵊli\ *adv*

²horizontal \"\ *n* -s **:** something that is horizontal; *esp* **:** a horizontal line ⟨the mood of quiet is emphasized by the ~*s* of the lake —S.M.Green⟩

horizontal bar *n* **1 :** a bar fixed in horizontal position for gymnastic exercise **2 :** an event in gymnastic competition

horizontal engine *n* **:** an engine with horizontal line of stroke

horizontal fault *n* **:** a fault in the earth's crust with no vertical displacement

horizontal intensity *n* **:** the horizontal component of the intensity of the earth's magnetic field

hor·i·zon·tal·i·ty \ˌhȯrəˌzän·ˈtaləd·ē, ˌhär-\ *n* -ES **:** the quality or state of being horizontal ⟨his houses have a pronounced ~ —J.M.Richards⟩

hor·i·zon·tal·ize \ˌhȯrəˈzäntᵊlˌīz, ˌhär-\ *vt* -ED/-ING/-S **:** to arrange horizontally ⟨information with which to scale and ~ the model —*U.S. Army Tech. Manual*⟩

horizontal kiln *n* **:** a kiln that has its axis in a horizontal as opposed to a vertical position with the materials being processed moved through by the slight slope and rotation of the kiln itself or carried through on conveyors

horizontal ladder *n* **:** a ladder of wood or metal held in a horizontal position usu. by upright supports and used in a gymnasium or on a playground for suspension exercises esp. for the development of arm and shoulder-girdle strength

horizontal ladder

horizontal parallax *n* **:** the maximum geocentric parallax observed when the celestial body is at the horizon

horizontal pendulum *n* **:** a pendulum that oscillates in a horizontal plane (as a compass needle on its pivot)

horizontal section *n* **:** a section representing an object as cut horizontally through its center

horizontal structure *n* **:** POLYPHONY 1 — compare VERTICAL STRUCTURE

horizontal training *n* **:** the operation of training fruit trees or grapevines so that the branches will spread out laterally in a horizontal direction — compare ESPALIER

hor·key \ˈhȯrkē\ *var of* ²HOCKEY

horizontal training of a tree

horloge *var of* HOROLOGE

hor·me \ˈhȯr(ˌ)mē\ *n* -s [G, fr. Gk *hormē* impulse, attack, assault — more at SERUM] **:** vital energy as an urge to purposive activity

hor·mic \-ˌmik\ *adj* **:** of or relating to horme; *specif* **:** purposively directed toward a goal ⟨~ activities of the organism⟩

hormic psychology *n* **:** psychology concerned with the purposive factor or force in behavior

hor·mi·go \(h)ȯ(r)ˈmē(ˌ)gō\ *n* -s [AmerSp, fr. Sp *hormiga* ant, fr. L *formica* — more at PISMIRE] **1 :** ANT TREE **2 :** QUIRA

hor·mism \ˈhȯ(r)ˌmizəm\ *n* -s [*horme* + *-ism*] **:** HORMIC PSYCHOLOGY

hor·mo·den·dron \ˌhȯ(r)məˈdendrən\ *syn of* HORMODENDRUM

hor·mo·den·drum \-rəm\ *n, cap* [NL, fr. Gk *hormos* chain, necklace (fr. *eirein* to fasten) + *dendron* tree — more at SERIES, DENDR-] **:** a form genus of imperfect fungi (family Dematiaceae) having dull brownish to black spores produced in chains resembling trees

hor·mo·gon \ˈhȯ(r)məˌgän\ *or* **hor·mo·gone** \-ˌgōn\ *n* -s [NL *hormogonium*] **:** HORMOGONIUM

hor·mo·go·na·les \ˌhȯ(r)mägōˈnā(ˌ)lēz\ *n pl, cap* [NL, fr. *hormogonium* + *-ales*] **:** an order of filamentous blue-green algae having the capacity to form hormogonia

hor·mo·go·ni·um \ˌhȯ(r)məˈgōnēəm\ *n, pl* **hormogo·nia** \-ēə\ [NL, fr. Gk *hormos* + *gonium*] **:** a portion of a filament between two heterocysts in many blue-green algae that becomes detached as a reproductive body — **hor·mog·o·nous** \(ˈ)hȯ(r)ˈmägənəs\ *adj*

hor·mo·nal \(ˈ)hȯ(r)ˈmōnᵊl\ *adj* [ISV *hormone* + *-al*] **:** of, relating to, or effected by hormones — **hor·mo·nal·ly** \-ᵊlē\ *adv*

hor·mone \ˈhȯrˌmōn, ˈhȯ(ə)ˌ-\ *n* -s [Gk *hormōn*, pres. part. of *horman* to stir up, set in motion, fr. *hormē* impulse, attack, assault — more at SERUM] **1 :** a specific organic product of living cells that, transported by body fluids or sap, produces a specific effect on the activity of cells remote from its point of origin **:** internal secretion **:** AUTACOID; *esp* **:** such a product exerting a stimulatory or excitatory effect on a cellular activity — compare AUXIN, CHALONE, PLANT HORMONE **2 :** a synthetic substance that resembles a naturally occurring hormone in producing a specific biological effect — compare GROWTH REGULATOR

hormonelike \ˈ=,=,=\ *adj* **:** resembling a hormone esp. in physiological action

hor·mon·ic \(ˈ)hȯ(r)ˈmänik, -mōn-\ *adj* **:** HORMONAL

hor·mon·iza·tion \ˌhȯ(r)ˌmōnəˈzāshən\ *n* -s **:** the process of hormonizing

hor·mon·ize \ˈhȯ(r)ˌmōˌnīz\ *vt* -ED/-ING/-S [*hormone* + *-ize*] **:** to treat with a hormone; *specif* **:** to castrate chemically — compare CAPONETTE

hor·mo·noid \ˈhȯ(r)məˌnȯid, -ˌmōn-\ *adj* **:** resembling that of a hormone

hor·mo·spore \ˈhȯrməˌspō(ə)r\ *n* [NL *hormogonium* + E *spore*] **:** a terminally borne hormogonium in some blue-green algae with cells modified in shape and having exceptionally thick walls

¹horn \ˈhȯ(ə)rn, ˈhȯ(ə)n\ *n* -s [ME, fr. OE; akin to OHG & ON *horn*, Goth *haurn*, L *cornu* horn, *cerebrum* brain, Gk *keras* horn, Skt *śṛṅga*] **1 a** (1) **:** one of the paired bony processes that arise from the upper part of the head of many ungulate mammals, that function chiefly as weapons, and that in cattle and related forms are usu. present in both sexes and are unbranched and permanent with a bony core anchored to the skull and a sheath of horn and in deer are solid deciduous bony outgrowths usu. branching and usu. present only in the male — see ANTLER; COW illustration (2) **:** a horned animal (3) **:** a part like an animal's horn attributed to a divine or supernatural being and esp. to the devil **b :** a natural projection or excrescence from an animal that resembles or suggests a horn: as (1) **:** a projection (as the casque of a hornbill) from the beak of a bird (2) **:** a tuft of feathers on the head of a bird (as a horned owl) (3) **:** a projection from the head or thorax of an insect or from the head of a reptile or fish (4) **:** a sharp spine in front of the fins of a fish (as a horned pout) (5) **:** one of the tentacles of a snail **c** (1) **:** the tough fibrous material derived from epithelial tissue and consisting chiefly of keratin with which the horns of cattle and related animals are covered (2) **:** any similar substance (as that which forms the hoof crust of horses, sheep, cattle) (3) **:** a manufactured product (as a plastic resembling horn) (4) **:** a bow tip made of horn into which the bowstring nock is cut (5) **:** HORN SPOON 2 **d :** the hollow horn of an animal used as a drinking cup ⟨handed him a ~ filled with red Chilean wine —*Time*⟩ or for holding other liquid or substance (as ink or powder); *also* **:** DRINK ⟨did sometimes take a ~ when he thought it would do him good —*Atlantic*⟩ **e :** CORNUCOPIA **2 :** something resembling or suggestive of a horn: as **a :** one of the curved ends of a crescent; *esp* **:** a cusp of the moon when crescent-shaped **b** (1) **:** a body of land or water shaped like a horn (2) **:** a sharp peak in a rugged mountain region **c** (1) **:** a horn-shaped part of a device or mechanism (as a blacksmith's anvil or a horning press); *specif* **:** a part of a shoemaking machine over which a shoe is placed when being tacked, nailed, pegged, and in some instances sewed (2) **:** one of the outer ends of a ship's crosstrees; *also* **:** one of the points of the jaws of a gaff or boom (3) **:** a high pommel of a saddle; *also* **:** either of the projections on a lady's saddle for supporting the leg — see STOCK SADDLE illustration (4) **:** a short lever attached to a control surface of an airplane by means of which it is operated (5) *or* **horn antenna :** a radio antenna in which a metallic envelope that is usu. a rectangular cross-section wave guide flares out to project a signal into space (6) **:** a tube of varying sectional area used in some types of loudspeaker **d :** an erect penis — usu. considered vulgar **e :** CORNU **3 a :** a musical wind instrument formed from the horn of an animal (as an ox or ram); *specif* **:** SHOFAR **b** (1) **:** a brass wind instrument employing the lips as the vibrating medium (as the trumpet, saxhorn, tuba) or a plastic, wood, or metal imitation used as a children's toy (2) **:** FRENCH HORN (3) **:** a wind instrument (as the saxophone, clarinet, trombone) used in a jazz band **c** (1) **:** a usu. electrically operated device (as on an automobile or a diesel locomotive or in a factory) that makes a noise like that of a horn and is used for sounding a warning signal (2) **:** AIR HORN **4 a :** a means of defense **:** source of strength **:** POWER, GLORY, PRIDE ⟨The Lord is . . . the ~ of my salvation —Ps 18:2 (RSV)⟩ ⟨the election of a prominent layman . . . will help to elevate the ~ of the church —A.W.Long⟩ **b** [so called fr. the old custom of cutting the spurs from cockerels when they were castrated and implanting them in the comb, where they would grow into hornlike members that made it easy to pick out the capons, capons being frequent symbols of cuckoldry] **:** an imaginary horn supposedly growing upon the head of a cuckold and regarded as an emblem of his state — usu. used in pl. **c :** one of the equally disadvantageous alternatives presented by a dilemma ⟨to get off the ~*s* of this dilemma will not be easy —*Atlantic*⟩

²horn \"\ *adj* [ME, fr. *horn*, n.] **:** of or resembling horn or a horn; *esp* **:** composed or made of horn or a similar substance (as a plastic) ⟨~ spectacles⟩

³horn \"\ *vb* -ED/-ING/-S [¹*horn*] *vt* **1 :** CUCKOLD **2 a :** to butt or gore with the horns **b :** to drive with the horns — used with *out* or *off* ⟨the young bull who had come to ~ the old one out of the herd —*Omnibook*⟩ **3 a** (1) **:** to wedge or fasten (as a boom or spar of a ship) as if between horns ⟨~ the boom in a crotch⟩ (2) **:** to install (the frame of a ship) square to the keel after allowing for the keel's declivity **b :** to press or hammer (a piece of metal) on the horn of an anvil **4** *dial Eng* **:** to proclaim or spread the news of ~ *vi*, *dial Eng* **:** to talk in a gossipy manner

horn alligator *n* **:** leather from an alligator's back

horn angle *n* **:** a figure formed by two plane curves tangent to each other on the same side of their mutual tangent line

hornbeam \ˈ=,=\ *n* [¹*horn* + *beam*; fr. its hard, smooth, close-grained wood — more at BEAM] **1 :** a tree of the genus *Carpinus*: as **a :** an Old World tree (*C. betulus*) with smooth gray bark, hardy white wood, and leaves resembling those of the beech **b :** a similar tree (*C. caroliniana*) of America **2 :** HOP HORNBEAM **3 :** PLANER TREE

hornbill \ˈ=,=\ *n* **:** any of various large bulky omnivorous chiefly arboreal birds of Africa, southern Asia, and the East Indies constituting the suborder Bucerotes and having plumage that is predominantly black and white and an enormous bill that is usu. surmounted by a horny casque

horn·blende \ˈhȯrnˌblend, ˈhȯ(ə)n-\ *n* -s [G, fr. *horn* horn (fr. OHG) + *blende* blende — more at HORN, BLENDE] **1 :** a mineral approximately $Ca_2Na(Mg,Fe)_4(Al,Fe,Ti)_3Si_6O_{22}(O,OH)_2$ consisting of the common black, dark green, or brown variety of aluminous amphibole, containing considerable iron, and occurring as distinct crystals and in columnar, fibrous, and granular form **2 :** AMPHIBOLE

horn·blen·dic \(ˈ)hȯ(r)nˈblendik\ *adj* **:** containing hornblende in quantity **:** resembling or related to hornblende

horn·blend·ite \ˈ=ˌblenˌdīt\ *n* -s [*hornblende* + *-ite*] **:** a granular igneous rock composed almost entirely of hornblende

horn·blend·iza·tion \ˌhȯ(r)nˌblendəˈzāshən\ *n* -s **:** the transformation of a rock into hornblende by replacement processes

horn block *n* **:** PEDESTAL 3a

hornbook \ˈ=,=\ *n* **1 :** a child's primer formerly in use consisting typically of a sheet of parchment or later of paper mounted on a thin wooden board and protected by a sheet of transparent horn and having on it the alphabet and other rudiments such as the digits and often the Lord's Prayer — compare BATTLEDORE 3 **2 :** a rudimentary treatise ⟨~*s* of political theory —V.O.Key⟩

horn cell *n* **:** a nerve cell lying in one of the gray columns of the spinal cord

horn chestnut *n* **:** WATER CHESTNUT

horn·church \ˈhȯrnˌchərch\ *adj, usu cap* [fr. *Hornchurch*, urban district, England] **:** of or from the urban district of Hornchurch, England **:** of the kind or style prevalent in Hornchurch

horn–core \ˈ=,=\ *n* **:** the bony inner shaft of a typical horn (as that of a cow)

horn dance *n* **:** a dance of Abbots Bromley, Staffordshire, England, with characters and patterns similar to those of the morris and distinguished by men carrying antlers

horned \ˈhȯ(ə)rnd, ˈhȯ(ə)nd *sometimes when not in combination* -nəd\ *adj* [ME, fr. OE *horn* + *-ed*] **1 :** having horns ⟨a mythical ~ beast, the unicorn⟩ — often used in combination ⟨long-*horned*⟩ **2 :** having a process or appendage resembling a horn **3 :** having a part shaped like a horn ⟨the ~ moon —S.T.Coleridge⟩

horned adder *n* **:** HORNED VIPER

horned bladderwort *n* **:** a No. American bog or aquatic herb (*Stomoisia cornuta*) with stems and minute linear leaves underground and solitary or few yellow showy irregular flowers on a slender naked scape

horned cattle *n* **:** cattle with horns; *specif* **:** bovine animals (as cows, bulls, steers)

horned crab *n* **:** a decorator crab (*Stenocionops furcata*)

horned dace *n* **:** a common No. American cyprinid fish (*Semotilus atromaculatus*)

horned frog *n* **1 :** any of various So. American frogs constituting a genus (*Ceratophrys*) of the family Leptodactylidae and usu. having triangular processes on the eyelids **2 :** HORNED TOAD

horned grebe *n* **:** a grebe (*Podiceps auritis*) that is widely distributed in northern parts of the northern hemisphere, is chiefly dark above and silky white below, and is distinguished when in breeding plumage by a glossy black head banded on either side with gold which encloses the eye and terminates in a brief ear tuft

horned hazel *n* **:** BEAKED HAZEL

horned hog *n* **:** BABIRUSA

horned hummer *n* **:** SUN GEM

horned iguana *n* **:** a Haitian iguana (*Metopoceras cornutus*) having three hornlike scales on the head

horned lark *n* **:** a small lark (*Eremophila alpestris*) and its subspecies widely distributed in the northern hemisphere

horned lizard *n* **:** HORNED TOAD

horned milfoil *n* **:** PURPLE BLADDERWORT

horned·ness \ˈhȯrnədnės, -n(d)nės, ˈhȯ(ə)n-\ *n* -ES **:** the quality or state of being horned

horned owl *n* **:** any of various owls (as the American great horned owl) having conspicuous tufts of feathers on the head

horned pheasant *n* **:** CRIMSON TRAGOPAN

horned pondweed *n* **:** a submerged aquatic weed (*Zannichellia palustris*)

horned poppy *n* **:** a yellow-flowered Eurasian herb (*Glaucium flavum*) adventive in the U. S.

horned pout *n* **:** BULLHEAD 1b; *esp* **:** a common bullhead (*Ameiurus nebulosus*) of the eastern U. S. which has been introduced into streams of the Pacific coast — called also *Sacramento cat*

horned puffin *n* **:** a puffin of the north Pacific having a small fleshy appendage resembling a horn on the eyelid

horned rattlesnake *n* **:** SIDEWINDER

horned ray *n* [so called fr. its cephalic fins or processes] **:** a ray of the family Mobulidae **:** DEVILFISH, MANTA

horned rush *n* **:** any of various sedges of the genus *Rhynchospora*; *esp* **:** a tall sedge (*R. corniculata*) of the eastern U. S. with a long-beaked achene

horned screamer *n* **:** a screamer (*Anhima cornuta*) of northern So. America with a long slender yellowish white process resembling a horn on the forehead — compare CRESTED SCREAMER

horned shark *n* **:** a small California shark (*Heterodontus francisci*) related to the bullhead of Australia

horned snake *n* **1 :** HORNED VIPER **2 :** HOOP SNAKE

horned toad *n* **:** any of various small harmless insectivorous lizards constituting the genus *Phrynosoma* (family Iguanidae) of the dry sandy plains of the western U. S. and Mexico and having several hornlike spines on the head and a broad flat body covered with spiny scales

horned violet *n* [so called fr. the elongated spur of the corolla] **:** TUFTED PANSY

horned viper *n* **:** a common desert-dwelling viper (*Aspis cornutus*) of Egypt and Asia Minor distinguished by a horny scale resembling a spike above each eye — compare ASP

horned wavey *n* **:** ROSS'S GOOSE

hor·ne·mann's redpoll \ˈhȯ(r)nəˌmänz-\ *n, usu cap H* [after Friedrich K. *Hornemann* †1801 Ger. explorer] **:** a redpoll (*Carduelis hornemanni*) of Europe with a small and pale breast and rump

hor·ne·oph·y·ton \ˌhȯ(r)nēˈäfəˌtän\ *n, cap* [NL, fr. *horneo-* (fr. E *horn*) + *phyton*] **:** a genus of Devonian fossil plants (family Rhyniaceae) similar to those of the genus *Rhynia* but smaller and lacking vascular tissue in the rhizome and considered to be one of the earliest forms of vascular land plants

horn·er \ˈhȯrnər\ *n* -s [ME, fr. ¹*horn* + *-er*] **1 :** one who works or deals in horn **2 :** one who blows a horn **3** *obs* **:** one who cuckolds another man **4** *slang* **:** one who inhales heroin

hor·ne·ro \(h)ȯ(r)ˈne(ˌ)rō\ *n* -s [AmerSp, fr. Sp, baker, fr. *horno* oven (fr. L *furnus*) + *-ero* -er; fr. the fact that its nest resembles an oven — more at FURNACE] **:** BAKER BIRD

hor·ner's method \ˈhȯrnərz-\ *n, usu cap H* [after William G. *Horner* †1837 Eng. mathematician] **:** a numerical method of successive approximations used for computing to any number of decimal places an approximate value of any real root of an algebraic equation with real coefficients

horner's syndrome *n, usu cap H* [after Johann F. *Horner* †1886 Swiss ophthalmologist] **:** a syndrome marked by sinking in of the eyeball, contraction of the pupil, drooping of the upper eyelid, and vasodilation and anhidrosis of the face, and caused by injury to the cervical sympathetic innervation

hor·net \ˈhȯrnət, ˈhȯ(ə)n-, *usu* -əd·+V\ *n* -s [ME *hernet*, *harnette*, fr. OE *hyrnet*; akin to OS *hornut* hornet, OHG *hurnuz*, *hornaz*, MD *horsel*, L *crabro* hornet, Lith *širšė* wasp, and prob. to OE *horn* — more at HORN] **:** any of the larger social wasps of the family Vespidae that are vigorous strong-flying insects with powerful stings, usu. construct nests of macerated wood pulp resembling paper, and feed on both animal and vegetable matter — see GIANT HORNET, WHITE-FACED HORNET; compare YELLOW JACKET

white-faced hornet

hornet's nest *n* **:** a troublesome situation **:** angry reaction ⟨must have known that his frank comments . . . would stir up a *hornet's nest* —*U. S. Investor*⟩

horn·fels \ˈhȯrnˌfelz\ *n, pl* **hornfels** [G, fr. *horn* horn (fr. OHG) + *fels* cliff, rock, fr. OHG *felis*, *felisa* — more at HORN, FELL] **:** a fine-grained silicate rock produced by contact metamorphism

hornfish \ˈ=,=\ *n* **:** a fish of the family Triacanthidae

horn fly *n* **:** a small black European blood-sucking two-winged fly (*Haematobia irritans*) introduced into No. America and other cattle-raising areas that clusters about the horns of cattle or hovers about their backs and causes great irritation by its bites

horn gap *n* **:** an arc gap formed by two horn-shaped electrodes that diverge so that the arc extinguishes itself

hornier *comparative of* HORNY

horniest *superlative of* HORNY

horn·i·fy \ˈhȯ(r)nəˌfī\ *vt* -ED/-ING/-ES [¹*horn* + *-ify*] **:** to make hard like horn; *specif* **:** to make keratotic ⟨*hornified* skin⟩

horn·i·ly \ˈhȯ(r)nəlē\ *adv* **:** in a horny manner

horn in *vi* **:** to participate without invitation or often consent **:** butt in **:** INTRUDE ⟨*horned in* with advice⟩ ⟨*horn in* on a deal⟩

¹horning *pres part of* HORN

²horn·ing \ˈhȯrniŋ\ *n* -s *chiefly North* **:** SHIVAREE

horning press *or* **horn press** *n* **:** a punch press with a horn by means of which the seams on hollow tinware are closed

horn·ist \ˈhȯrnəst\ *n* -s **:** a performer on a French horn

hor·ni·to \(h)ȯ(r)ˈnēd·(ˌ)ō\ *n* -s [Sp, dim. of *horno* oven — more at HORNERO] **:** a low oven-shaped mound in volcanic regions that emits smoke and vapors

horn knot *n* **:** SPIKE KNOT

horn·less \ˈ=ləs\ *adj* **:** having no horn

horn·less·ness *n* -ES **:** the condition of being hornless

horn lightning arrester *n* **:** a lightning arrester in which the spark gap is formed by two wires that diverge like a pair of horns — see LIGHTNING ARRESTER illustration

hornlike \ˈ=,=\ *adj* **1 :** having the form of a horn esp. in being elongated, pointed, and protruding ⟨a ~ process⟩ **2 :** resembling horn **:** CORNEOUS, HORNY, KERATINOUS

horn mercury *n* [so called fr. its horny appearance when fused] **:** CALOMEL

horn of plenty : CORNUCOPIA

horn owl *n* **:** HORNED OWL

hornpie \ˈ=,=\ *n* [¹*horn* + *pie*; fr. the tufted feathers on its head] *dial Eng* **:** LAPWING

hornpipe \ˈ=,=\ *n* [ME fr. *horn* + *pipe*] **1 a :** a single reed wind instrument popular in England and thought to be of Celtic origin consisting of a wooden or bone pipe with holes at intervals along its length and with the bell and mouthpiece usu. made of horn — compare PIBGORN, STOCKHORN **b :** a lively country dance tune in 3/2, 3/4, or 4/4 time orig. played on this instrument **2 :** a lively folk dance of the British Isles usu. performed by a single person and orig. accompanied by hornpipe playing **3 :** a tune in the rhythm of a hornpipe

horn poppy *n* **:** HORNED POPPY

hornpout \ˈ=,=\ *n* **:** HORNED POUT

horn quicksilver *n* [so called fr. its horny appearance when fused] **:** native calomel

horn–rimmed \ˈ=ˈ=\ *adj* **:** having rims of horn

horn–rims \ˈ=,=\ *n pl* **:** spectacles with horn rims ⟨a stocky girl with *horn-rims* —William DuBois⟩

horns *pl of* HORN, *pres 3d sing of* HORN

horn shark *n* **:** HORNED SHARK

horn shell *n* **:** a snail of the genus *Cerithidea*

horn silver *n* [trans. of Sw *hornsilver*] **:** CERARGYRITE

horn snake *n* **:** HOOP SNAKE

horn socket *n* **:** a fishing tool consisting of a cone which seizes broken rods or tools in bored wells

horn spoon *n* **1 :** a spoon made of horn — used chiefly interjectionally in the phrase *by the great horn spoon* ⟨cookies, by the great *horn spoon* —Hamlin Garland⟩ **2** *also* **horn :** a small receptacle like a trough made from a section of cow horn and used for careful washing tests in gold mining

hornstone \ˈ=,=\ *n* [trans. of G *hornstein*] **:** a mineral consisting of a variety of quartz much like flint but more brittle

horn·swog·gle *also* **horn·swag·gle** \ˈhȯ(r)nˌswägəl\ *vt* -ED/-ING/-S [origin unknown] **:** BAMBOOZLE, HOAX ⟨continued to ~ the trading public right and left —F.L.Allen⟩

horn·swog·gled *also* **horn·swag·gled** \-ld\ *adj* **:** DAMNED 2a ⟨I'll be ~ if they didn't owe him $400 then —*N.Y. Sun*⟩

horntail \ˈ=,=\ *n* **:** any of various insects constituting a family (Siricidae) of Hymenoptera related to the typical sawflies but having larvae that burrow in woody plants and on the females a stout hornlike ovipositor for depositing the egg within the plant

horn timber *n* **:** a timber extending aft from the sternpost to the transom of a ship and forming the central support of the stern

hornweed \ˈ=,=\ *n* **:** HORNWORT

hornworm \ˈ=,=\ *n* **:** a larva of various hawkmoths (as a tobacco worm) having a hornlike tail process

hornwort \ˈ=,=\ *n* **1 :** a plant of the genus *Ceratophyllum* **2 :** a plant of the order Anthocerotales

horn wrack *n* **:** a bryozoan of the genus *Flustra*

horny \ˈhȯrnē, ˈhȯ(ə)nē, -ni\ *adj* -ER/-EST [ME, fr. ¹*horn* + *-y*] **1 a :** of or made of horn or of a hornlike substance ⟨after the ~ material has been cut away —Morris Fishbein⟩ **b :** HARD, CALLOUS ⟨his feet were ~ and scarred —W.S.Maugham⟩ — often used in combination ⟨*horny*-handed⟩ **c :** compact and homogeneous with a dull luster like that of flint or of an animal's horn — used of the texture of a mineral **2 :** having horns or hornlike projections **3** [¹*horn* (erect penis) + -*y*] **:** easily excited sexually — usu. considered vulgar

horny coral *n* **:** GORGONIAN

hornyhead chub *also* **hornyhead** \'ˌˌ,ˌ\ *n* **:** a common chub (*Nocomis biguttatus*) of the larger streams from Pennsylvania to Wyoming and south to Alabama distinguished by the males having the head covered with conical hornlike processes during the breeding season

horny laminae *n pl* **:** laminae on the inside of the wall of an animal's hoof

horny sponge *n* **:** a sponge lacking spicules but having a spongin skeleton that is more or less horny

ho·ro·ka·ka \ˌhȯrəˈkäkə\ *n* -s [Maori] **:** a prostrate woody Australasian herb (*Mesembryanthemum australe*)

hor·o·loge \'hȯrəˌlōj, 'här-, -läj\ *or* **hor·loge** \'hȯrˌl-\ *n* -s [ME *orloge, oriloge, horologe*, fr. MF, fr. L *horologium*, fr. Gk *hōrologion*, fr. *hōro-* (fr. *hōra* period of time, time of day) + -*logion* (fr. *legein* to gather, speak, tell) — more at HOUR, LEGEND] **:** a timekeeping device; *esp* **:** an early or primitive one (as a sundial or an early clock using a foliot)

ho·rol·o·ger \həˈräləjə(r)\ *n* -s [*horology* + -*er*] **:** HOROLOGIST

hor·o·log·ic \ˌhȯrəˈläjik, ˌhär-, -jēk\ *also* **hor·o·log·i·cal** \-jəkəl, -jēk-\ *adj* [ML *horologicus*, fr. MGk *hōrologikos*, fr. Gk *hōrologion* + -*ikos* -ic, -ical] **:** of or relating to a horologe or horology — **hor·o·log·i·cal·ly** \-jək(ə)lē, -jēk-, -li\ *adv*

ho·ro·lo·gion \ˌȯrəˈlōˌyōn\ *n* [MGk *hōrologion*, fr. Gk, timepiece] **:** a liturgical book in the Eastern Church containing the daily offices corresponding to the Western breviary

ho·rol·o·gist \həˈräləjəst\ *n* -s **:** a person skilled in the practice or theory of horology **:** a maker of clocks or watches

hor·o·lo·gium \ˌhȯrəˈlōj(ē)əm\ *n*, *pl* **horolo·gia** \-ə\ [L] **1 :** TIMEPIECE **2** [ML, fr. MGk *hōrologion*] **:** HOROLOGION

¹**ho·rol·o·gy** \həˈräləjē\ *n* -ES [ME *horologie*, fr. L *horologium*] **:** TIMEPIECE

²**horology** \"\ *n* -ES [Gk *hōro-* + E -*logy*] **1 :** the science of measuring time **2 :** the principles and art of constructing instruments for indicating time

ho·rom·e·try \həˈrämə·trē\ *n* -ES [Gk *hōro-* + E -*metry*] **:** HOROLOGY 1

ho·ro·pi·to \ˌhȯrəˈpēd·(ˌ)ō\ *n* -s [Maori] **:** NEW ZEALAND PEPPER TREE

ho·rop·ter \həˈräptə(r), 'hȯˌr-\ *n* -s [F *horoptère*, fr. Gk *horos* boundary + *optēr* one that looks; akin to Gk *opsesthai* to be going to see — more at HORIZON, OPTIC] **:** the locus of points in external space whose images are formed on corresponding places of the two retinas and which are therefore seen single — **hor·op·ter·ic** \ˌhȯˌräpˈterik\ *adj*

¹**hor·o·scope** \'hȯrəˌskōp, 'här-\ *n* [MF, fr. L *horoscopus*, fr. Gk *hōroskopos*, fr. *hōro-* + *skopos* observer; akin to Gk *skopein* to view, watch — more at SPY] **:** a diagram representing the twelve mundane houses and showing the relative positions of planets and signs of the zodiac at a particular time used by astrologers to foretell the events of a person's life or to answer horary questions ⟨cast a ~ in order to determine the exact day and hour at which a vessel should weigh anchor — G.L. Kittredge⟩; *specif* **:** NATIVITY

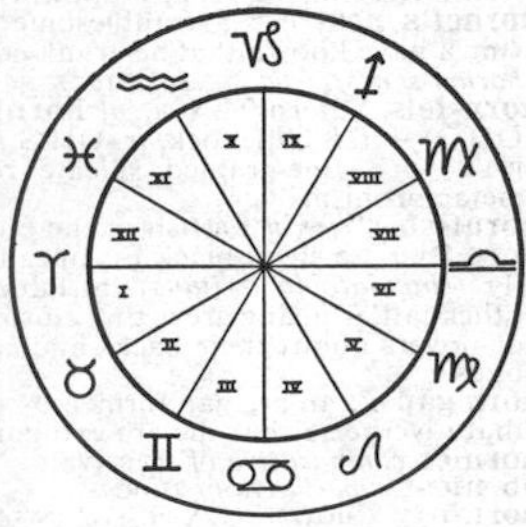

horoscope

²**horoscope** \"\ *vb* -ED/-ING/-S *vi* **:** to make horoscopes ~ *vt* **:** to cast the horoscope of — **hor·o·scop·er** \-pə(r)\ *n* -s

hor·o·scop·ic \ˌˌˈskäpik, -kōp-, -pēk\ *adj* [L *horoscopicus*, fr. Gk *hōroskopikos*, fr. *hōroskopos* + -*ikos* -ic] **:** of or relating to a horoscope

hor·o·tel·ic \ˌhȯrəˈtelik\ *adj* **:** of or relating to horotely

hor·o·tely \'ˌˌ,lē\ *n* -ES [Gk *horos* boundary, limit + *telos* end, consummation, degree of completion, state of maturity + E -*y* — more at HORIZON, WHEEL] **:** biological evolution at rates within the range or rate distribution usual for a given group of plants or animals — compare BRADYTELY, TACHYTELY

horra *var of* HORA

hor·ren·dous \hȯˈrendəs, hä'-, hə'-\ *adj* [L *horrendus*, fr. gerundive of *horrēre* to bristle, tremble — more at HORROR] **:** being such as to inspire horror **:** DREADFUL, FEARFUL, FRIGHTFUL, HORRIBLE ⟨began slapping some ~ taxes on these huge estates —A.C.Spectorsky⟩ ⟨a . . . ~ blending of Hollywood and history —Charles Lee⟩ — **hor·ren·dous·ly** *adv*

hor·rent \'hȯrənt, 'här-\ *adj* [L *horrent-, horrens*, pres. part. of *horrēre*] *archaic* **:** standing up like bristles **:** covered with bristling points **:** BRISTLED, BRISTLING ⟨~ with figures in strong relief —Thomas De Quincey⟩

hor·ri·bi·le dic·tu \hȯˌribəˌlēˈdik(ˌ)tü, hä,-, hə,-\ [L] **:** horrible to say ⟨there is, *horribile dictu*, no mention of the fact that he was president of Harvard —*Times Lit. Supp.*⟩

¹**hor·ri·ble** \'hȯrəbəl, 'här-\ *adj* [ME *orrible, horrible*, fr. MF, fr. L *horribilis*, fr. *horrēre* to bristle, tremble, shudder + -*ibilis* -ible — more at HORROR] **1 :** marked by or conducive to horror **:** likely to arouse fear, dread, or abhorrence ⟨coconuts in the ~ likeness of a head shrunken by headhunters —Sinclair Lewis⟩ ⟨her hearers derived a ~ enjoyment from . . . her wrath —Charles Dickens⟩ **2 :** extremely unpleasant or disagreeable **:** conducive to feelings of acute dislike, disgust, or repulsion ⟨of all horrors in this blessed town, snow is the most ~ —W.M.Thackeray⟩ ⟨the weather is always ~ when I travel —Aldous Huxley⟩ **syn** see FEARFUL

²**horrible** \"\ *adv* [ME *orrible, horrible*, fr. *orrible, horrible*, adj.] **:** to an extreme degree **:** HORRIBLY, EXCEEDINGLY ⟨she was ~ mad⟩

³**horrible** \"\ *n* -s [¹*horrible*] **:** a horrible person or thing; *specif* **:** a person fantastically garbed (as for a masquerade or holiday parade) — usu. used in pl. ⟨the ~*s*, grotesquely costumed children, will parade along a few . . . streets —*Time*⟩ — see ANTIQUES AND HORRIBLES

hor·ri·ble·ness *n* -ES [ME *orriblenesse, horriblenesse*, fr. *orrible, horrible* + -*nesse* -ness] **:** the quality or state of being horrible

hor·ri·bly \-blē, -bli\ *adv* **:** in a horrible manner

hor·rid \'hȯrəd, 'här-\ *adj, sometimes* -ER/-EST [L *horridus*, fr. *horrēre*] **1** *archaic* **:** ROUGH, RUGGED, BRISTLING **2 a :** being such as to inspire horror **:** DREADFUL, HIDEOUS, SHOCKING ⟨performed a ~ . . . rite of that strange magic —Emma Hawkridge⟩ **b :** inspiring disgust or repulsion **:** very offensive **:** NASTY ⟨gave her a loud . . . smack on the back, with ~ familiarity — Liam O'Flaherty⟩ ⟨he's a ~ person⟩ — **hor·rid·ly** *adv* — **hor·rid·ness** *n* -ES

hor·rif·ic \hȯˈrifik, hä'-, hə'-\ *adj* [MF *horrifique*, fr. L *horrificus*, fr. *horrēre* to bristle, tremble, shudder + -*ificus* -ific — more at HORROR] **:** dreadful to behold or contemplate **:** inspiring horror or fear **:** HORRIFYING, HORRIBLE ⟨this ~ picture of conditions in the mining industry —*Brit. Book News*⟩ ⟨~ black headlines in our daily papers —Charles Jackson⟩ **syn** see FEARFUL

hor·rif·i·cal·ly \-fək(ə)lē\ *adv* **:** in a horrific manner

hor·ri·fi·ca·tion \ˌhȯrəfəˈkāshən, ˌhär-\ *n* -s [L *horrificare* to horrify + E -*tion* — more at HORRIFY] **1 :** the act of horrifying or condition of being horrified **2 :** something that horrifies ⟨his two overcoats making him look like a mountain of ~ — Arthur Miller⟩

hor·ri·fied \'ˌˌ,fīd\ *adj* **:** filled with or marked or attended by a sensation, appearance, or attitude of horror **:** expressing or reflecting horror ⟨we were ~, frightened, and angry at the same time —W.A.White⟩ ⟨strained his eyeballs in a ~ stare at vacancy —G.D.Brown⟩ ⟨grip the reader with a . . . ~ fascination —Norman Birkett⟩ — **hor·ri·fied·ly** \-ī(ə)dlē, -li\ *adv*

hor·ri·fy \'hȯrəˌfī, 'här-\ *vt* -ED/-ING/-ES [L *horrificare*, fr. *horrificus* horrific — more at HORRIFIC] **:** to cause to feel horror **:** strike with horror ⟨smoking right through soup, fish, meat, salad, and dessert in a way to ~ the epicure —Frances Perkins⟩ ⟨may ~ some employers who are still living in the nineteenth century —Roy Lewis & Angus Maude⟩ **syn** see DISMAY

hor·ri·fy·ing·ly *adv* **:** in a horrifying manner **:** so as to horrify

hor·rip·i·late \hȯˈripəˌlāt\ *vt* -ED/-ING/-S [back-formation fr. *horripilation*] **:** to produce horripilation in (as by sudden fear) ⟨a strange, wild, *horripilating* tale —R.C.Lewis⟩

hor·rip·i·la·tion \(ˌ)ˌˌˌˈlāshən\ *n* -s [LL *horripilation-, horripilatio*, fr. L *horripilatus* (past part. of *horripilare* to bristle, be shaggy, fr. *horrēre* + *pilus* hair) + -*ion-*, -*io* -ion — more at PILE] **:** a bristling of the hair of the head or body (as from disease, terror, or chilliness) **:** GOOSEFLESH

¹**hor·ror** \'hȯrə(r), 'här-\ *n* -s [ME *orrour, horrour*, fr. MF *orror, horror, horreur*, fr. L *horror* action of trembling or shuddering, terror, horror, fr. *horrēre* to bristle, tremble, shudder + -*or*; akin to OE *gorst* gorse, Gk *chēr* hedgehog, *chersos* dry land, mainland, OIr *garb* rough, Skt *harṣate* he becomes stiff, resists, shudders; basic meaning: stiffening] **1 a :** a painful emotion of intense fear, dread, or dismay **:** CONSTERNATION ⟨I saw astonishment giving place to ~ on the faces of the people about me —H.G.Wells⟩ ⟨only to find to my ~ that the dealer knew its value as well as I —H.J.Laski⟩ **b :** intense aversion or repugnance ⟨shrank from the task with all the ~ of a well-bred English gentleman —Virginia Woolf⟩ ⟨the Spanish ~ of any taint of Moorish blood —A.H.Quinn⟩ **2 a :** the quality of inspiring horror **:** repulsive, horrible, or dismal quality or character ⟨statements emphasizing the ~ of this disclosure —Elmer Davis⟩ ⟨sat in silence . . . contemplating the ~ of their lives —Liam O'Flaherty⟩ **b :** something (as an experience, event, or object) that inspires horror **:** something that is horrible ⟨for him the reef was not a beautiful thing but a ~ —Alan Moorehead⟩ ⟨I know that this Nazi ~ has to be destroyed —Upton Sinclair⟩ ⟨made speeches, and hired lawyers, but was unable to avert the ~ —Alva Johnston⟩ **c horrors** *pl* (1) **:** a state of extreme nervous depression or apprehension **:** BLUES, NERVES ⟨smells and . . . sounds which could give one the ~*s* —Marcia Davenport⟩ ⟨his nervous breakdowns, the attacks of the ~*s* he is known to have suffered from —V.S.Pritchett⟩ ⟨one of their best batsmen was in the ~*s* —Ray Robinson⟩ (2) **:** DELIRIUM TREMENS ⟨came home roaring drunk and that night had the ~*s*⟩ **syn** see FEAR

²**horror** \"\ *adj* **:** specializing in or marked by themes or incidents of extreme violence, cruelty, or weird or macabre quality **:** calculated to inspire feelings of dread or horror **:** BLOODCURDLING ⟨some ~ stories from the Old Testament — J.C.Swaim⟩ ⟨an Elizabethan ~ play —Geoffrey Grigson⟩ ⟨has the strange fascination of a ~ novel —Alfred Frankfurter⟩ ⟨~ comics⟩

horror–struck \'ˌˌ,ˌ\ *adj* **:** struck with horror ⟨stood *horror-struck* as they watched . . . their own city destroyed —*Nashville Tennessean*⟩

horror va·cui \ˌˌˌˈvakyəˌwī\ *n* [NL, horror of a vacuum] **:** horror of empty spaces; *esp* **:** an aversion to empty spaces in artistic designs ⟨the Germans share this *horror vacui*, but there is always a marked spatial curiosity in their ornament — Nikolaus Pevsner⟩

hor·ry \'häri\ *adj* [ME *hory*, fr. OE *horig*, fr. *horh* filth, phlegm; akin to OFris *hore* mud, filth, OS *horu, horo* dirt, filth, OHG *horo* dirt, filth, ON *horr* nasal mucus — more at CORYZA] *now dial Eng* **:** disgustingly dirty **:** FOUL

¹**hors con·cours** \ˌȯr,kōⁿˈkü(ə)r\ *adv* [F, outside of competition] **:** in the manner of one that does not compete ⟨finished too late to enter competition . . . and was shown *hors concours* —R.F.Hawkins⟩

²**hors concours** \"\ *adj* [F, outside of competition] **1 :** excluded from competition ⟨artists . . . who had already received a medal . . . were *hors concours* —John Rewald⟩ **2 :** being without equal or rival **:** SUPREME ⟨these practitioners of the art . . . salute her as *hors concours* —J.M.Murry⟩

hors de com·bat \ˌȯrdəˌkōⁿˈbä\ *adv* (*or adj*) [F] **:** out of the combat **:** in a disabled condition ⟨the master of that art is able . . . to put an untrained antagonist completely *hors de combat* —Lafcadio Hearn⟩ ⟨with the president *hors de combat* and . . . on the verge of complete retirement —R.H.Rovere⟩

hors d'oeuvre \ȯrˈdərv, ȯ(ə)ˈdərv; ȯ(ə)ˈdēv; *sometimes* ȯrˈdev\ *n*, *pl* **hors d'oeuvres** *also* **hors d'oeuvre** \-v(z)\ [F *hors d'œuvre* something nonessential, side dish, hors d'oeuvre, fr. the phrase *hors d'œuvre*, nonessential, lit., outside of work] **:** any of various savory foods (as olives, anchovies, or spiced crab apples) usu. served as appetizers at the beginning of a meal — usu. used in pl.; compare CANAPE 1

¹**horse** *R* 'hȯ(ə)rs, -*R* 'hȯ(ə)s, *dial R* 'hōs *or* 'hä(r)s –*R* 'häs\

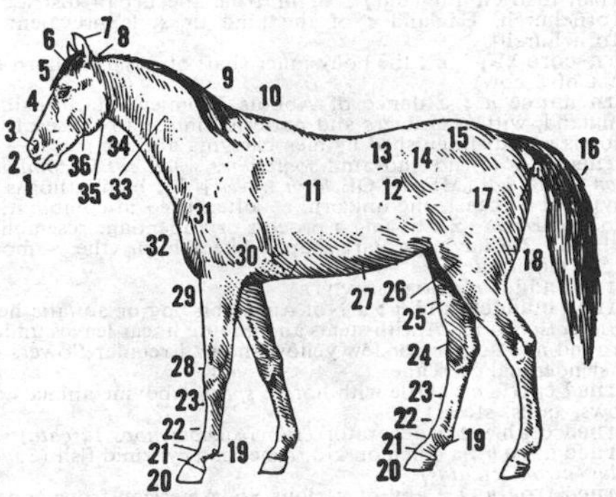

parts of the horse: *1* mouth, *2* nose, *3* nostril, *4* face, *5* forehead, *6* forelock, *7* ear, *8* poll, *9* mane, *10* withers, *11* ribs, *12* flank, *13* loin, *14* haunch, *15* croup, *16* tail, *17* thigh, *18* buttock, *19, 19* fetlocks, *20, 20* hooves, *21, 21* coronets, *22, 22* pasterns, *23, 23* cannons, *24* hock, *25* gaskin, *26* stifle, *27* belly, *28* knee, *29* forearm, *30* elbow, *31* shoulder, *32* breast, *33* neck, *34* throatlatch, *35* lower jaw, *36* cheek

n, *pl* **horses** *also* **horse** [ME *hors*, fr. OE; akin to OFris *hors, hars* horse, OS *hros, hers*, OHG *hros*, ON *hross*, and perh. to ON *hrata* to stagger, fall — more at CARDINAL] **1 a** (1) **:** a large solid-hoofed herbivorous mammal (*Equus caballus*) domesticated by man since a prehistoric period and used as a beast of burden, a draft animal, or for riding, and distinguished from the other existing members of the genus *Equus* and family Equidae by the long hair of the mane and tail, the usual presence of a callosity on the inside of the hind leg below the hock, and other less constant characters (as the larger size, larger hooves, more arched neck, small head, short ears) (2) **:** a horse over 14.2 hands tall — compare COLT, PONY (3) **:** RACEHORSE ⟨play the ~*s*⟩ **b** (1) **:** the male of the horse **:** STALLION; *sometimes* **:** a gelding as distinguished from an entire male (2) **:** a stallion four years old or older — used in the terminology of the U.S. Trotting Association **c** (1) **:** any of various extinct animals closely related to the horse (2) **:** any member of the family Equidae **2 :** any of several devices: as **a :** a hook-shaped tool used in making embossed or hammered work **b** (1) **:** FOOTROPE (2) **:** a breastband or similar protection for a sailor in an exposed position (3) **:** TRAVELER 3b (4) **:** JACKSTAY 1 **c :** a frame usu. with legs used for supporting something (as planks, a staging, clothing) **:** TRESTLE; *specif* **:** a sloping frame used in printing for holding paper about to be printed **d :** a notched board to support the steps of a staircase **e** (1) **:** SIDE HORSE (2) **:** LONG HORSE **3** *horse pl* **:** HORSEMEN ⟨the whole party of 1500 ~ —H.A.Shield⟩; *esp* **:** CAVALRY ⟨a regiment of ~⟩ **4 a :** a mass of the same geological character as the wall rock occurring within a vein; *esp* **:** a body of useless rock within an ore deposit **b :** a mass of rock enclosed between two branches of a fault or vein **5 a :** HORSEPOWER **b** *slang* **:** HEROIN ⟨went back on the ~ —*Police Dragnet*⟩ — **from the horse's mouth :** from the original source **:** from an unimpeachable source ⟨information he had just obtained . . . *from the horse's mouth* —*Newsweek*⟩

²**horse** \"\ *vb* -ED/-ING/-S [ME *horsen*, fr. *hors*, n.] *vt* **1 a :** to provide with a horse; *specif* **:** to provide horses for (a vehicle) **b :** to place on a horse **2 a :** to lift, pull, or push roughly or by main force ⟨*horsing* him around in the snow —Theodore Morrison⟩ ⟨sweating gunners *horsed* their pieces into action — Bruce Catton⟩ **b :** to hang (leather) on a horse to drain — often used with *up* **3 :** to subject to horseplay **:** play a joke on **:** KID ⟨if there was nothing else to do, you could ~ the . . . newspaper vendor —Wallace Stegner⟩ ~ *vi* **1** *of a mare* **:** to be in heat **:** be willing to take a stallion **2 :** to engage in horseplay **:** PLAY, FOOL — usu. used with *around* ⟨I ~ around quite a lot, just to keep from getting bored —J.D.Salinger⟩ ⟨I never ~ around much with the women —Norman Mailer⟩ **3 :** to read a proof by comparing it directly with copy

³**horse** \"\ *adj* [¹*horse*] **1 a :** of or relating to a horse **b :** hauled or powered by a horse ⟨a ~ barge⟩ **2 :** large or coarse of its kind ⟨~ corn⟩ **3 :** mounted on horseback ⟨~ dragoons⟩; *also* **:** used by or designed for mounted troops ⟨~ barracks⟩

horse aloes *n* **:** CABALLINE ALOES

horse–and–buggy \ˌˌˌˈˌˌ\ *adj* **1 :** of or relating to the era before the advent of the automobile and other socially revolutionizing major inventions ⟨devotes a lovingly lavish amount of space to *horse-and-buggy* days —A.W.Derleth⟩ ⟨having been born in the *horse-and-buggy* era —J.N.Hall⟩ **2 :** clinging to outworn attitudes or ideas **:** hopelessly outmoded **:** OLD-FASHIONED ⟨*horse-and-buggy* thinking⟩ ⟨the *horse-and-buggy* naval strategists of yesterday —F.H.Gervasi⟩

horse ant *n* **:** a large red mound-building ant (*Formica rufa*) of Europe and No. America

horse apples *n pl, chiefly dial* **:** dried horse droppings

¹**horseback** \'ˌˌ,ˌ\ *n* [ME *horsback*, fr. *hors* horse + *back*] **1 :** the back of a horse **2 a :** a natural ridge of sand, gravel, or rock **:** HOGBACK **b :** a mound, ridge, bank, or parting of barren rock in a coal seam

²**horseback** \"\ *adv* **:** on horseback

horse·back·er \"ə(r)\ *n* **:** a person on horseback

horse balm *n* **1 :** an erect smooth perennial strong-scented herb (*Collinsonia canadensis*) of eastern No. America with serrate pointed leaves and a loose panicle of yellowish flowers — called also *horseweed* **2 :** a plant of the genus *Monarda*

horsebane \'ˌ,ˌ\ *n* **:** a European water dropwort (*Oenanthe phellandrium*)

horsebean \'ˌ,ˌ\ *n* **1 :** BROAD BEAN 1 **2 :** a West Indian bean of the genus *Canavalia* **3 :** JERUSALEM THORN 2

horse block *n* **:** a block or platform for use in mounting or dismounting from a horse or entering or leaving a vehicle

horse boat *n* **:** a boat for conveying horses and cattle

horse bot *also* **horse bee** *n* **:** HORSE BOTFLY; *specif* **:** the larval stage of a horse botfly

horse botfly *n* **:** any of several botflies chiefly attacking horses; *esp* **:** a cosmopolitan cloudy-winged form (*Gasterophilus intestinalis*) that glues its eggs to the hairs esp. of the forelegs whence they are taken into the mouth where they hatch into young bots and pass into the stomach and become attached to the lining

horse box *n* **:** a railroad car or trailer for transporting horses (as racers)

horseboy \'ˌ,ˌ\ *n, Brit* **:** HOSTLER

horse brass *n* **:** a brass ornament fastened to a martingale

horsebreaker \'ˌˌ,ˌˌ\ *n* **:** one who breaks or trains horses

horse brier *n* **:** GREENBRIER

horsebrush \'ˌ,ˌ\ *n* **:** any of several plants of the genus *Tetradymia* (family Compositae) that occur on rangelands in the western U.S. and are a major cause of bighead of American sheep

horsebush \'ˌ,ˌ\ *n, in the Bahama islands* **:** any of several plants: as **a :** a West Indian tree (*Peltophorum adnatum*) of the family Leguminosae with densely brown-tomentose foliage and racemose yellow flowers **b :** an annual weedy herb (*Heliotropium parviflorum*) with spicate white flowers **c :** a West Indian sticky shrub (*Gundlachia corymbosa*) of the family Compositae with alternate leaves and many small white flowers in corymbose heads

horse cane *n* **:** GREAT RAGWEED

horsecar \'ˌ,ˌ\ *n* **1 :** a railroad car or streetcar drawn by horses **2 :** a car fitted for transporting horses

horse cassia *n* **1 :** an East Indian cassia (*Cassia marginata*) with long pods containing a black cathartic pulp used as a horse medicine **2 :** CANAFISTULA 2

horse cavalry *n* **:** cavalry mounted on horses as distinct from mechanized cavalry

horse chestnut *n* [so called fr. the use of its nut to treat respiratory ailments in horses] **1 a :** a large Asian tree of the genus *Aesculus* (*A. hippocastanum*) that was introduced into Europe in the 16th century and is widely cultivated as an ornamental and shade tree and naturalized as an escape in much of the temperate zone and that has a rough bark, coarse branches, opposite palmately compound leaves, and predominantly white flowers in showy terminal clusters which are followed by large glossy brown seeds enclosed in a coarsely prickly bur; *broadly* **:** any of several trees of the genus *Aesculus* —see BUCKEYE, TREE illustration **b :** the seed of a horse chestnut **2 :** a dark grayish brown that is deeper and very slightly redder than average chocolate brown and deeper and very slightly yellower than African brown

horse–chestnut family *n* **:** HIPPOCASTANACEAE

horsecloth \'ˌ,ˌ\ *n* **:** a cloth for a covering or trapping of a horse

horse conch *n* **:** a massive conch (*Fasciolaria gigantea*) of the warm western Atlantic, the animal being bright red and enclosed in a yellowish spired shell as much as two feet in length

horse coper *n, Brit* **:** a horse dealer; *esp* **:** a dishonest one ⟨a timber buyer was thought to hold the same kind of reputation as a *horse coper* —F.D.Smith & Barbara Wilcox⟩

horse·cors·er *or* **horse·cours·er** \'ˌ,kȯrsər, -,kȯr-\ *n* [¹*horse* + obs. *corser, courser* horsedealer, fr. *corse* (to barter) or *course* (var. of *corse*) + -*er*] *archaic* **:** a dealer in horses; *esp* **:** a tricky dealer

horse crab *n* **1 :** KING CRAB **2 :** either of two very large crabs (*Telmessus cheiragonus* and *Erimacrus isenbeckii*) widely distributed in waters of moderate depths along the coasts of the northern Pacific ocean

horse crevalle *n* **:** BLUE RUNNER

horsed *past of* HORSE

horse daisy *n* **1 :** DAISY 1b **2 :** MAYWEED 1

horse dance *n* **1 :** a dance of No. American Indians imitating the rearing of a horse **2 :** a dance executed on either a hobbyhorse or a live horse

horse devil *n* **:** a wild indigo (*Baptisia lanceolata*) of the southern U.S. that when dried and withered is rolled about by the wind sometimes frightening horses

horse doctor *n* **1 :** one who doctors horses **:** VETERINARIAN **2 :** an inadequately trained or incompetent doctor

horse elder *n* **:** ELECAMPANE

horse–eye \'ˌ,ˌ\ *or* **horse–eye bean** *n* **1 :** a seed of the cowhage (*Mucuna pruriens*); *also* **:** the plant itself **2 :** OXEYE BEAN **3 :** a seed of the hyacinth bean

horse–eye jack *also* **horse–eyed jack** \'ˌ,ˌ-\ *n* **:** any of several carangid food fishes: as **a :** a blue and silver carangid fish (*Caranx latus*) of the tropical western Atlantic **b :** BIGEYED SCAD

horseface \'ˌ,ˌ\ *n* **:** a long homely face

horse family *n* **:** EQUIDAE

horsefeathers \'ˌ,ˌ\ *n pl, slang* **:** NONSENSE, BALDERDASH — often used interjectionally

horse fiddle *n, chiefly dial* **:** a noisemaking device based on the principle of a rosined bow drawn across a string

horsefish \'ˌ,ˌ\ *n, pl* **horsefish** *or* **horsefishes 1 a :** MOONFISH a **b :** SAUGER **c :** a sea horse (genus *Hippocampus*) **d :** a dusky rough-skinned southern African scorpaenid fish (*Congiopodus torvus*) **2 :** KING CRAB 1

horseflesh \'ˌ,ˌ\ *n* **1 :** the flesh of a horse esp. when slaughtered for food **2 :** horses considered esp. with reference to riding, driving, or racing **3 :** any of several hard often reddish West Indian timbers: as **a :** SABICU **b :** the wood of a bully tree (*Manilkara bidentata*) **c :** the wood of black mangrove

horseflesh mahogany *n* **1 :** any of several hard mottled tropical American woods that somewhat resemble mahogany

2 : a tree (as *Peltophorum adnatum* or *Hieronyma caribaea*) that yields horseflesh mahogany
horseflesh ore *n* [so called fr. its reddish color when newly fractured] *dial Eng* **:** BORNITE
horsefly \ˈ=,=\ *n* **1 :** any of numerous rather large stocky swift-flying two-winged flies constituting the family Tabanidae having in the female a piercing proboscis with which they suck the blood of animals (as horses and cattle) inflicting painful bites — compare CHRYSOPS, GREENHEAD **2 :** any of several other flies annoying to horses (as the horse tick *Hippobosca equina*)
horsefly weed *n* [so called fr. its supposed ability to drive away horseflies] **:** INDIGO BROOM
horse gentian *n* **:** a plant of the genus *Triosteum; esp* **:** FEVERROOT
horse gowan *n* **1 :** DAISY 1b **2 :** CHAMOMILE **3 :** DANDELION **4 :** any of several plants of the genera *Crepis* and *Hypochaeris*
horse gram *or* **horse grain** *n* **:** a twining herb (*Dolichos biflorus*) of the tropics of the Old World that is cultivated in India for fodder with the seeds being used as food
horsehair \ˈ=,=\ *n, often attrib* [ME *hors her,* fr. *hors* horse + *her* hair — more at HAIR] **1 a :** a hair of a horse esp. from the mane or tail **b :** a quantity of such hairs **2 :** HAIRCLOTH
horsehair blight *n* **:** a disease of tea and other tropical plants caused by a fungus (*Marasmius equicrinis*) the mycelium of which hangs in black festoons from the branches
horsehair lichen *n* **:** any of several lichens esp. of the genus *Alectoria* with a thallus consisting of filaments resembling hair — called also *horsetail lichen*
horsehair snake *or* **horsehair worm** *n* **:** a free-living adult gordioid worm
horsehead \ˈ=,=\ *n* **:** MOONFISH a
horse·heal *or* **horse·heel** \ˈ=,hē(ə)l\ *n* [by folk etymology fr. ME *horselne, horshelne, horshelyn,* fr. OE *horselene, horshelene,* fr. *hors* horse + *elene, eolone* elecampane, fr. ML *elena* (*campana*) — more at HORSE, ELECAMPANE] **:** ELECAMPANE
horsehide \ˈ=,=\ *n* **1 :** the hide of a horse or colt or leather made from either — compare CORDOVAN **2 :** BASEBALL 2
horse hoe *n* **:** a horse-drawn surface cultivator
horsehoof \ˈ=,=\ *n, pl* **horsehoofs** [ME *horshoof,* fr. *hors* horse + *hoof*] **:** COLTSFOOT
horsehoof clam *n* **:** a large tropical clam (*Hippopus hippopus*) related to and much resembling the giant clam (*Tridacna derasi*) — called also *horseshoe clam*
horsekeeper \ˈ=,==\ *n* [ME *horskepare,* fr. *hors* horse + *kepare, keper* keeper] **:** one who has charge of horses **:** GROOM
horse knacker *n* **:** KNACKER
horse knob *or* **horse knop** *n* **:** KNAPWEED
horse latitudes *n pl* **:** either of two belts or regions in the neighborhood of 30° N. and 30° S. latitude characterized by high pressure, calms, and light baffling winds; *esp* **:** that part of the northern belt which is over the Atlantic ocean
horselaugh \ˈ=,=\ *n* **:** a loud boisterous laugh **:** GUFFAW
horseleech \ˈ=,=\ *n* [ME *horsleche,* fr. *hors* horse + *leche* leech — more at LEECH] **:** a common European leech (*Haemopis gulo*) that feeds chiefly on worms; *also* **:** any of several related No. American leeches
horse·less carriage \ˈ=ləs-\ *n* **:** AUTOMOBILE — used esp. of early models
horselike \ˈ=,=\ *adj* **:** resembling a horse
horse louse *n* **1 :** a sucking louse (*Haematopinus asini*) found on horses and other equines **2 :** any of several biting lice infesting horses
horse mackerel *n* **1 :** any of several large scombroid fishes: as **a :** BLUEFIN TUNA **b :** CHILE BONITO **2 :** any of various large fishes of the family Carangidae; *esp* **:** a large Atlantic food fish (*Trachurus trachurus*)
horse·man \ˈ=mən\ *n, pl* **horsemen** [ME *horsman,* fr. *hors* horse + *man*] **1 a :** a rider on horseback **b :** one skilled in managing horses **2 :** a breeder or raiser of horses
horse·man·ship \-,ship\ *n* **:** the art of riding horseback **:** equestrian skill **:** MANEGE
horsemeat \ˈ=,=\ *n* **:** the flesh of the horse esp. for use as food ⟨a ~ butcher⟩ ⟨~ is important in the diet of mink⟩
horsemint \ˈ=,=\ *n* [ME *horsminte* fr. *hors* + *minte* mint] **:** any of various coarse mints: as **a :** WATER MINT **b :** a plant of the genus *Monarda; esp* **:** a tall erect perennial herb (*M. punctata*) with petioled lanceolate leaves somewhat hairy beneath and heads of purple-spotted creamy flowers subtended by purplish or whitish bracts
horse-mule \ˈ=,=\ *n* **:** a male mule
horse mushroom *n* **:** a rather coarse edible mushroom (*Agaricus arvensis*) with a hollow stem, pale gills, and a broad white cap — compare MEADOW MUSHROOM
horse mussel *n* **:** a large coarse marine mussel (*Modiolus modiolus*) found on the shores of northern Europe and America; *also* **:** any similar closely related species
horse nettle *n* **:** a coarse prickly weed (*Solanum carolinense*) common in eastern and southern U.S., having white or pale= purple flowers and bright-yellow fruit resembling berries — called also *ball nettle, bull nettle*
horse opera *n* **:** a motion picture or radio or television play having its scene laid in the western U.S. and usu. having cowboys as its principal characters
horse parlor *n* **:** a place where betting on horses is carried on
horse piece *n* **:** one of the large pieces into which blubber is cut before mincing
horse pistol *n* **:** a large pistol formerly carried by horsemen
¹horseplay \ˈ=,=\ *n* [¹*horse* + *play*] **:** rough or boisterous play
²horseplay \ˈ"\ *vi* **:** to engage in horseplay ⟨~*ed* around with the boys —Betty Smith⟩
horseplayer \ˈ=,==\ *n* [¹*horse* + *player*] **:** one who habitually bets on horse races
horseplaying \ˈ=,==\ *n* [¹*horse* + *playing*] **:** betting on horse races
horse plum *n* **1 :** AMERICAN PLUM **2 :** CANADA PLUM
horsepond \ˈ=,=\ *n* **:** a pond for watering horses
horse post *n* **1 :** a hitching post **2 a :** a mail carrier who makes his deliveries on horseback **b :** a mail service performed by such carriers
horsepower \ˈ=ˌ=\ *n* **1 a :** the power that a horse exerts in pulling **b :** a machine worked by a horse **2 :** a standard unit of power equal in the U.S. to 746 watts and nearly equivalent to the English gravitational unit of the same name that equals 550 foot-pounds of work per second — compare BRAKE HORSEPOWER, INDICATED HORSEPOWER
horsepower-hour \ˈ=ˌ=ˈ=\ *n* **:** the work performed or energy consumed by working at the rate of one horsepower for one hour, being equal to 1,980,000 foot-pounds
horsepox \ˈ=,=\ *n* **:** a virus disease of horses related to cowpox and marked by a vesiculopustular eruption of the skin esp. on the pasterns and sometimes by a vesiculopapular inflammation of the buccal mucosa — called also *equine variola*
horse purslane *n* **:** a coarse tropical American fleshy weed (*Trianthema portulacastrum*) of the family Aizoaceae
horse racer *n* **1 :** one who keeps horses for racing **2 :** JOCKEY **3 :** a devotee of horse racing
horse racing *n* **:** the racing of horses as a sport
horseradish \ˈ=,==\ *n* **1 a :** a tall coarse white-flowered herb (*Armoracia lapathifolia*) native to Europe and widely cultivated **b :** the pungent root of horseradish **c :** KERGUELEN CABBAGE **2 :** a condiment made of the grated root of the horseradish plant often moistened with vinegar or a similar substance
horseradish tree *n* **1 :** an East Indian tree (*Moringa oleifera*) that has a horseradish-flavored root and is cultivated throughout the tropics for its elongated capsular fruit which when young is pickled or cooked as a vegetable and for its seeds which yield ben oil **2 :** any Australian tree of the genus *Codonocarpus* (family Phytolaccaceae) having pungent leaves suggesting the flavor of horseradish or mustard
horse rake *n* **:** a horse-drawn rake
horse room *n* **:** a bookmaker's establishment which provides information on horse races and opportunity to bet on them
horses *pl of* HORSE, *pres 3d sing of* HORSE
horse savin *n* **:** COMMON JUNIPER
horse sense *n* **:** plain shrewd unsophisticated common sense ⟨juries seldom accept purely scientific evidence if it seems in conflict with everyday *horse sense* —E.M.Lustgarten⟩ **syn** see SENSE

horseshit \ˈ=,=\ *n* **1 :** horse droppings — usu. considered vulgar **2 :** BUNK, NONSENSE — usu. considered vulgar
¹horseshoe \ˈ=,=\ *n* [ME *hors sho,* fr. *hors* + *sho* shoe] **1 :** a shoe for horses usu. consisting of a narrow plate of iron conformed to the rim of a horse's hoof **2 :** something (as a valley or other physical feature) shaped like a horseshoe ⟨the town . . . stood in the mouth of a ~ —John Buchan⟩ ⟨the vast ~ of hills surrounding the central plains —D.G.E.Hall⟩ **3 horseshoes** *pl* **:** a game like quoits played with horseshoes or with horseshoe-shaped pieces of metal which are thrown from one peg in the ground toward another 40 feet away with the object of ringing or coming close to the peg

underside of typical horseshoes: *1* plain shoe, *2* shoe with toe and heel calks

²horseshoe \ˈ"\ *vt* **1 :** to furnish with horseshoes **:** put shoes on (a horse) **2 :** to put in the shape of a horseshoe; *specif* **:** to make (an architectural arch) like a horseshoe
³horseshoe \ˈ"\ *adj* **1 :** shaped like a horseshoe ⟨a ~ curve⟩ ⟨the ~ bend of a river⟩ **2** *of an arch* **:** having an intrados that widens above the springing before narrowing to a rounded or pointed crown — see ARCH illustration
horseshoe bat *n* **:** any of several bats of the Old World (families Rhinolophidae and Hipposideridae) having a more or less horseshoe-shaped leaf on the nose
horseshoe clam *n* **:** HORSEHOOF CLAM
horseshoe crab *n* **:** KING CRAB
horseshoe kidney *n* **:** congenital partial fusion of the kidneys resulting in a horseshoe shape
horseshoe nail *n* **:** a thin pointed nail with heavy flaring head that is used to fix a horseshoe to the hoof
horseshoe plate *n* **:** a plate around a ship's rudder stock that is shaped like a horseshoe and designed to prevent water from entering the rudder trunk
horseshoer \ˈ=,==\ *n* **:** one who makes horseshoes or shoes horses; *specif* **:** BLACKSMITH 1b
horseshoe snake *n* **:** a harmless colubrid snake (*Zamenis hippocrepis*) of Spain and Africa
horseshoe vetch *n* **:** a European herb (*Hippocrepis comosa*) of the family Leguminosae with yellow umbellate flowers succeeded by flattened pods that separate into horseshoe-shaped joints
horseshoe violet *n* **:** BIRD'S-FOOT VIOLET
horse show *n* **:** a competitive exhibition of horses and vehicles esp. as an annual fashionable event
horsesickness \ˈ=,==\ *n* **:** AFRICAN HORSE SICKNESS
horse's neck *n* **:** a tall drink consisting of ginger ale or ginger ale and a liquor served iced in a large tumbler with a spiral of lemon peel hanging over the rim
horse sorrel *n* **1 :** a European water dock (*Rumex hydrolapathum*) **2 :** SHEEP SORREL 1
horse sponge *n* **:** a sponge of the genus *Hippiospongia*
horse stinger *n, dial Eng* **:** DRAGONFLY
horse sugar *n* **:** SWEETLEAF
horse syphilis *n* **:** DOURINE
horsetail \ˈ=,=\ *n* [ME *horse tayle* fr. *horse, hors* + *tayle, tail*] **1 :** the tail of a horse **2 :** a plant of the genus *Equisetum*
horsetail agaric *or* **horsetail fungus** *n* **:** SHAGGYMANE
horsetail corn *n* **:** INDIAN CORN
horsetail family *n* **:** EQUISETACEAE
horsetail lichen *n* **:** HORSEHAIR LICHEN
horsetaillike \ˈ=,=,=\ *adj* **:** resembling a plant of the genus *Equisetum*
horsetail milkweed *n* **:** WHORLED MILKWEED
horsetail tree *n* **:** a tree of the genus *Casuarina; esp* **:** a tree (*C. equisetifolia*) planted in the southern and southwestern U.S. that is used for windbreaks and planting on sand dunes and as an ornamental
horse thistle *n* [ME *hors thistel,* fr. *hors* + *thistel* thistle] **:** PRICKLY LETTUCE
horse thyme *n, dial Eng* **:** WILD BASIL
horse tick *n* **1 :** a louse fly attacking horses — compare HIPPOBOSCIDAE **2 :** any tick attacking horses
horse trade *n* **1 :** a swap of horses usu. accompanied by bargaining and compromise **2 :** negotiation accompanied by shrewd bargaining and usu. by reciprocal concessions **:** practical compromise ⟨a political *horse trade*⟩ ⟨his *horse trades* with foreign governments have been masterpieces of commercial diplomacy —J.D.Ratcliff⟩
horse-trade \ˈ=,=\ *vi* [back-formation fr. *horse trading* & *horse trader*] **:** to engage in a horse trade
horse trader *n* **:** one who engages in horse trading
horse trading *n* **:** the act or practice or an instance of making a horse trade ⟨the . . . foreign ministers had finally gotten down to *horse trading* —*Newsweek*⟩ ⟨lively *horse trading* in . . . smoke-filled back rooms —*N.Y. Herald Tribune*⟩
horse·tree \ˈ=(,)trē, -,tri\ *n, dial Eng* **:** WHIFFLETREE
horse violet *n* **:** BIRD'S-FOOT VIOLET
horseweed \ˈ=,=\ *n* **1 :** a common No. American weed (*Erigeron canadensis*) with linear leaves and small discoid heads of yellowish flowers **2 :** HORSE BALM **3 :** GREAT RAGWEED **4 :** WILD LETTUCE 1b(3)
¹horsewhip \ˈ=,=\ *n* [¹*horse* + *whip*] **:** a whip for horses
²horsewhip \ˈ"\ *vt* **:** to flog with a horsewhip
horsewoman \ˈ=,==\ *n, pl* **horsewomen 1 :** a woman horseback rider **2 :** a woman skilled in riding horseback or in caring for or managing horses
horsewood \ˈ=,=\ *n* **:** SEA GRAPE 1b
horse wrangler *n* **:** a ranch hand who takes care of the saddle horses
hors·ey *also* **horsy** *pronunc at* ¹HORSE + ē *or* i\ *adj* **horsier; horsiest 1 :** relating to, resembling, or suggestive of a horse ⟨bounced the boy on his knee in a ~ manner —Wright Morris⟩ ⟨not ~ or masculine, but a woman of whom one could be proud —Kathleen Freeman⟩ **2 :** addicted to or having to do with horses or horse racing or characteristic of the manners, dress, or tastes of horsemen ⟨the ~ set⟩ ⟨a ~, flashy, tweedy sort of man —Lewis Mumford⟩
hors·ford·ite \ˈhȯ(r)sfə(r),dīt\ *n* -s [Eben N. *Horsford* †1893 Am. chemist + E *-ite*] **:** a mineral Cu_5Sb consisting of a massive silver-white copper antimony alloy (sp. gr. 8.8)
hors·i·ly *pronunc at* ¹HORSE + əlē *or* əli\ *adv* **:** in a horsey manner
hors·i·ness \-sēnəs, -sin-\ *n* -ES **:** the quality or state of being horsey
horsing *adj* [fr. pres. part. of ²*horse*] *of a mare* **:** being in heat
horst \ˈhȯ(ə)rst\ *n* -s [G, thicket, eyrie, horst, fr. OHG *hurst* thicket — more at HURST] **:** a tract or block of the earth's crust separated by faults from adjacent tracts or blocks that have been relatively depressed — compare GRABEN
hort *abbr* horticultural; horticulture
hor·ta·tion \hȯ(r)ˈtāshən\ *n* -s [L *hortation-, hortatio,* fr. *hortatus* (past part. of *hortari* to urge, exhort) + *-ion-, -io* -ion — more at YEARN] **:** EXHORTATION
hor·ta·tive \ˈhȯ(r)d·əd·iv\ *adj* [LL *hortativus,* fr. L *hortatus* + *-ivus* -ive] **:** giving exhortation **:** ADVISORY, EXHORTATIVE — **hor·ta·tive·ly** \-d·əvlē\ *adv*
hor·ta·to·ri·ly \ˌ=ˌ=ˈtȯrəlē\ *adv* **:** in a hortatory manner
hor·ta·to·ry \-)d·ə,tōrē\ *adj* [LL *hortatorius,* fr. L *hortatus* + *-orius* -ory] **:** giving or characterized by exhortation **:** EXHORTATORY, HORTATIVE
hor·tense blue \ˈhȯr,ten(t)s-, =ˈ=-\ *n, often cap H* [prob. fr. the name *Hortense*] **:** PRUSSIAN BLUE 2
hortense violet *n, often cap H* [prob. fr. the name *Hortense*] **:** a moderate purple that is bluer and duller than heliotrope (sense 4a), bluer, lighter, and stronger than average amethyst, and bluer, stronger, and slightly lighter than manganese violet
hor·ti·cul·tur·al \ˌhȯ(r)d·əˈkəlch(ə)rəl, -)tə|-\ *adj* **1 :** relating to horticulture **2 :** produced under cultivation (as by breeding) — compare BOTANICAL — **hor·ti·cul·tur·al·ly** \-rəlē, -li\ *adv*
horticultural bean *n* **:** a shell bean characterized by pods splashed with carmine or red and white and by white or buff= colored seeds marked with red
horticultural variety *n* **:** a variety of plant that has originated under cultivation as distinct from a botanical variety
hor·ti·cul·ture \ˈhȯ(r)d·ə,kəlchə(r), -)tə,- *also* ,==ˈ==\ *n* [L

hortus garden + E *-i-* + *culture* — more at YARD] **:** the cultivation of an orchard, garden, or nursery on a small or large scale **:** the science and art of growing fruits, vegetables, flowers, or ornamental plants — compare FLORICULTURE, OLERICULTURE, POMOLOGY
hor·ti·cul·tur·ist \ˌ==ˈkəlch(ə)rəst\ *n* **:** a specialist in horticulture
hor·ton·o·lite \hȯ(r)ˈtänᵊl,īt, ˈhȯ(r)tᵊn-\ *n* -s [Silas R. *Horton,* 19th cent. Am. mineralogist + E *-o-* + *-lite*] **:** a mineral $(Fe,Mg,Mn)_2SiO_4$ of the olivine series consisting of a dark silicate of iron, magnesium, and manganese
hor·to·ri·um \hȯ(r)ˈtōrēəm, -tȯr-\ *n, pl* **hortoriums** \-ēəmz\ *or* **horto·ria** \-ēə\ [NL, fr. L *hortus* + *-orium* -ory] **:** an institution or museum for the collection, preservation, and study of horticultural specimens
hor·tu·lan \ˈhȯ(r)chələn\ *adj* [L *hortulanus,* fr. *hortulus* small garden (dim. of *hortus* garden) + *-anus* -an] **:** of or relating to a garden
hortulan plum *n* [NL *hortulana* (specific epithet of *Prunus hortulana*), fr. L, fem. of *hortulanus*] **:** a wild-goose plum (*Prunus hortulana*)
hor·tus sic·cus \ˌhȯ(r)d·ə(s)ˈsikəs\ *n* [NL, lit., dry garden] **:** a collection of dried botanical specimens **:** HERBARIUM
hos *pl of* HO
ho·sack·ia \hōˈsakēə, -ˈza-\ *n, cap* [NL, fr. David *Hosack* †1835 Am. botanist + NL *-ia*] **:** a large genus of mostly western No. American herbs (family Leguminosae) having pinnate leaves, yellow or red flowers, and linear flat pods
¹ho·san·na \hōˈzanə *sometimes* -zä- *or* -zȧ-\ *n* -s [ME *osanna,* fr. LL, fr. Gk *hōsanna,* fr. Heb *hōshīʽāh nnā* save now, we pray] **:** an expression of enthusiastic praise **:** ACCLAMATION ⟨the law was passed with a considerable fanfare of editorial ~*s* —Herbert Asbury⟩ ⟨men with loud ~*s* will confess her greatness —John Milton⟩ — used interjectionally as a cry of acclamation and adoration ⟨*hosanna!* Blessed be he who comes in the name of the Lord —Mk 11: 9 (RSV)⟩
²hosanna \"\ *vt* -ED/-ING/-S **:** to acclaim with or as if with shouts of "hosanna" **:** APPLAUD ⟨the act of him who has been ~*ed* as if he were a savior —Henry Angus⟩
¹hose \ˈhōz\ *n, pl* **hose** *or* **hoses** [ME, fr. OE *hosa* stocking, husk; akin to OS, OHG, & ON *hosa* leg covering, Gk *kystis* bladder, OE *hȳd* hide — more at HIDE] **1** *pl* **hose a** (1) **:** a cloth leg covering that reaches down to the ankle and sometimes covers the foot ⟨footless athletic ~ worn over socks are part of a baseball uniform⟩ (2) **:** STOCKING, SOCK ⟨a pair of ~⟩ — usu. used in pl. **b** (1) **:** a close-fitting garment similar to tights that covers the body from the waist to and sometimes including the feet and is usu. attached to a doublet by points ⟨eight times thrust through the doublet, four through the ~ —Shak.⟩ (2) **:** short breeches often reaching to the knee — see TRUNK HOSE **2** *now dial Brit* **:** a sheath enclosing an inflorescence (as a spathe or the ensheathing leaves about the developing spike of a cereal grass) **3** *pl sometimes* **hoses a :** a flexible tube (as of rubber, plastic, or fabric) for conveying fluids (as air, steam, powdered coal, or water from a faucet or hydrant) **b :** such a tube with nozzle and attachments **c :** the tubing as material **4 :** HOSEL

hose 3a

²hose \"\ *vt* -ED/-ING/-S [ME *hosen,* fr. *hose,* n.] **1** *archaic* **:** to provide with hose for the legs **2 a :** to spray or water with a hose ⟨~ the garden⟩ **b :** to wash or drench with water from a hose — usu. used with *down* ⟨the bridge . . . had been *hosed* down by the fire department —*N.Y.Times*⟩
hose·bird \ˈhōz,bərd\ *n* [prob. alter. of *whore's brood*] *dial Eng* **:** RASCAL, RAPSCALLION
hose bridge *or* **hose jumper** *n* **:** a contrivance that permits traffic to pass over or under lines of fire hose
hose cart *or* **hose wagon** *also* **hose truck** *or* **hose carriage** *n* **:** a wheeled vehicle for carrying fire hose
hose clip *n* **:** a device for clamping or supporting a hose
hose cock *or* **hose bib** *n* **1 :** SILL COCK **2 :** PINCHCOCK
hose company *n* **:** a company of men who bring and manage hose in fire fighting
hose-in-hose \ˌ==ˈ=\ *n* **:** a double flower in which one corolla appears to be within another (as in various daturas and primulas)
ho·sel \ˈhōzəl\ *n* -s [¹*hose* + *-el*] **:** a socket in the head of a golf club into which the shaft is inserted — see GOLF illustration
hose·less \ˈhōzləs\ *adj* **:** having no hose to wear
hose·man \-mən, -,man\ *n, pl* **hosemen :** one who uses, tends, or repairs hose; *esp* **:** a fireman who belongs to a hose company
hos·en \ˈhōzᵊn\ *now dial pl of* HOSE
hose net *n, chiefly Scot* **:** a fishnet shaped like a stocking
hosepipe \ˈ=,=\ *n* **:** HOSE 3
ho·sha·na *or* **ho·sha·nah** \hōˈshä(,)nä, -,nə\ *n, pl* **hoshanoth** *or* **hosha·not** \-,nōt(h), -ōs\ [Heb *hōshīʽāh nnā,* lit., save now, we pray] **1 :** a cry of entreaty in the liturgical litany chanted in the synagogue on Sukkoth esp. during the processional circuits around the altar on Hoshana Rabbah **2 :** the prayer chanted on Hoshana Rabbah
hoshana rab·bah *or* **hoshanah rab·bah** *or* **hoshana rab·ba** \-ˈrä(,)bä, -,bə\ *n, usu cap H&R* [Aram *hōshaʽnā rabbā*] **:** the 7th day of the Festival of Sukkoth observed on the 21st day of Tishri with special prayers and ceremonies in the synagogue by Orthodox and Conservative Jews
ho·sier \ˈhōzhə(r)\ *n* -s [ME *hosyere,* fr. *hose* + *-yere* -ier] **:** one who deals in hosiery
ho·siery \ˈhōzh(ə)rē, -ri, ÷ -z(ə)-\ *n* -ES *often attrib* [*hosier* + *-y*] **1 :** HOSE 1a **2** *chiefly Brit* **:** KNITWEAR
hos·pice \ˈhäspəs\ *n* -s [F, fr. L *hospitium* hospitality, lodging, inn, fr. *hospit-, hospes* host, stranger, guest — more at HOST] **1 :** an establishment providing rest or entertainment for travelers; *esp* **:** one kept by a religious order **2 :** a lodging for students, young workers, or the underprivileged often maintained by a religious order — compare HOSTEL
hos·pi·ta·ble \hä'spid·əbəl, ˈhä,spi|, |tə-, *also* ˈhäspə| *sometimes* hȯ's- *or* ˈhȯ(,)s- *or* hə'spi|\ *adj* [NL *hospitabilis,* fr. L *hospitare* to be a guest, lodge + *-abilis* -able] **1 a :** marked by or given to generous and cordial reception and entertainment of guests or strangers ⟨they are ~ . . . : give a guest everything, and leave him free to do as he likes —Bram Stoker⟩ ⟨this ~, talkative man who was everywhere bustling about, trying to be of service —O.E.Rölvaag⟩ **b :** promising or suggesting generous and cordial welcome and entertainment ⟨wrote off immediately on his return to his inn the most ~ of invitations —W.M.Thackeray⟩ ⟨small incommunicable mysteries . . . chambered in their inner hearts and guarded by their ~ faces —A.T.Quiller-Couch⟩ **c :** offering a pleasant or sustaining environment **:** not hostile ⟨hard sandstone ridges carry a soil sufficiently ~ for forest growth —*Amer. Guide Series: N.J.*⟩ ⟨the British Isles enjoy a ~ climate, but the British gardener does not have life too easy —Emily Hahn⟩ **2 :** marked by ready or willing receptivity (as of new ideas) **:** favorably disposed esp. to the new or strange ⟨keep the mind open and ~ to new evidence on any side of the question —W.J.Reilly⟩ ⟨freedom to inquire and teach . . . provides a climate more ~ to fresh vision —Sidney Hook⟩ **syn** see SOCIAL
hos·pi·ta·ble·ness *n* -ES *archaic* **:** the quality or state of being hospitable
hos·pi·ta·bly \-blē, -bli\ *adv* **:** in a hospitable manner
¹hos·pi·tal \ˈhäˌspid·ᵊl, |tᵊl *also* |ˌspə| *sometimes* ˈhȯ|\ *n* -s *often attrib* [ME, fr. OF, fr. LL *hospitale,* fr. L, bedroom, fr. neut. of *hospitalis* of a guest, hospitable, fr. *hospit-, hospes* host, stranger, guest + *-alis* -al — more at HOST] **1** *archaic* **:** HOSPICE 1 ⟨an adjacent ~ founded by the princess . . . for the reception of pilgrims —Horace Walpole⟩ **2 :** a charitable institution for the needy, aged, infirm, or young; *specif* **:** one for the education of the young ⟨received his formal education at Christ's *Hospital* in London⟩ **3 a :** an institution or place where sick or injured persons are given medical or surgical care — usu. used in British English without an article when the object of a preposition ⟨so badly wounded that he died in ~ —*Manchester Guardian Weekly*⟩ ⟨diagnosed frostbitten toes and removed him immediately to ~ —Alexander Tewnion⟩; compare CLINIC, SANATORIUM **b :** a place for the care and treatment of sick or injured animals **4 :** a

workshop for the repair of any of various small objects ⟨a doll ~⟩ ⟨a fountain-pen ~⟩

²hospital *adj* [L *hospitalis*] *obs* : HOSPITABLE

hospital apprentice *n* : an enlisted man in the U. S. Navy training to be a hospitalman

hospital bed *n* : a bed with a frame in three sections equipped with mechanical spring parts that permit raising the head end, foot end, or middle as required

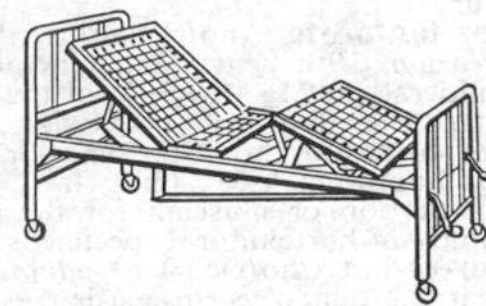
hospital bed

hospital corpsman *n* : a petty officer of the U. S. Navy performing general medical duties, giving first aid, and serving as a technician and assistant to the medical officer

hos·pi·tal·er *or* **hos·pi·tal·ler** *pronunc at* HOSPITAL + ə(r), ˌ=ˈ===\ *n* -s [ME *hospitalier, hospiteler,* fr. MF *hospitalier,* fr. ML *hospitalarius,* fr. LL *hospitale* hospice + L *-arius* -ary — more at HOSPITAL] **1** *usu cap* : a member of a religious military order established in Jerusalem in the 12th century and revived as an honorary society in 1879 by Leo XIII — called also *Knight of Malta, Knight of Rhodes, Knight of St. John of Jerusalem* **2** : a member of any of numerous religious orders chiefly concerned with the care of the sick or needy **3** : a chaplain of a London hospital

hospital fever *n* : typhus fever or fever associated with hospital gangrene prevalent in hospitals before the development of modern sanitation

hospital gangrene *n* : gangrene prevalent in crowded hospitals before the development of modern sanitation

hos·pi·tal·ism \-ˌlizəm\ *n* -s **1 a** : the factors and influences (as of system or custom) that adversely affect the health of hospitalized persons **b** : the effect of such factors on mental or physical health **2** : the physical and mental effects on infants and children resulting from their living in foundling homes

hos·pi·tal·i·ty \ˌhäspəˈtaləd·ē, -ətē, -i *sometimes* ˌhȯs-\ *n* -ES [ME *hospitalite,* fr. MF *hospitalité,* fr L *hospitalitat-, hospitalitas,* fr. *hospitalis* of a guest, hospitable + *-itat-, -itas* -ity — more at HOSPITAL] **1 a** : the cordial and generous reception and entertainment of guests or strangers socially or commercially ⟨built a house, and later a tavern . . . whose ~ was known to thousands —*Amer. Guide Series: Vt.*⟩ ⟨the meaning of country ~ . . . extends far beyond threshold and board —Louise D. Rich⟩ **b** : an instance of hospitality — usu. used in pl. ⟨convivial and domestic *hospitalities* —R.W. Emerson⟩ **2** : ready receptivity esp. to new ideas and interests ⟨hope to give ~ on my walls to new and promising American talent —Bennett Cerf⟩ ⟨the great tradition in poetry has always offered ~ to ideas —J.L.Lowes⟩

hos·pi·tal·iza·tion \ˌ=(ˌ)===ˈzāshən, -ˌīˈz-\ *n* -s **1** : the act or process of being hospitalized ⟨pain persisted constantly through a two-day period, finally necessitating ~ —*Jour. Amer. Med. Assoc.*⟩ **2** : the period of stay in a hospital ⟨drug treatment shortened the length of ~ —*Today's Health*⟩ ⟨entitled to ~ for two weeks —*Newsweek*⟩

hospitalization insurance *n* : insurance that provides benefits to cover or partly cover hospital expenses — see HOSPITAL SERVICE CONTRACT

hos·pi·tal·ize \ˈ=(ˌ)==ˌīz\ *vt* -ED/-ING/-S : to place in a hospital as a patient — compare INSTITUTIONALIZE ⟨the child was *hospitalized* at once for diagnosis and treatment —*Jour. Amer. Med. Assoc.*⟩

hospital light *n* : HOPPER FRAME

hos·pi·tal·man \ˈ=(ˌ)== mən\ *n, pl* **hospitalmen** : an enlisted man in the U. S. Navy performing general medical duties

hospital service contract *n* : hospitalization insurance that provides for payment of actual hospital charges within specified limits as contrasted with cash benefits

hospital ship *n* : a ship equipped as a hospital; *esp* : one constructed or assigned specif. to assist the wounded, sick, and shipwrecked in time of war in accordance with international law

hospital train *n* : a railway train equipped for the transport of sick and wounded military personnel

hos·pi·tious \(ˈ)häˈspishəs\ *adj* [L *hospitium* hospitality, lodging, inn + E *-ous* — more at HOSPICE] *archaic* : HOSPITABLE

hos·pi·ti·um \häˈspishēəm, -id·ē-\ *n, pl* **hospi·tia** \-ēə\ [L] **1** : HOSPICE 1 **2** *chiefly Brit* : HOSTEL 2a (1)

hos·po·dar \ˈhäspəˌdär\ *n* -s [Romanian, fr. Ukrainian, fr. *hospod'* lord, master; akin to OSlav *gospodĭ, gospodinŭ* lord, master — more at GOSPODIN] : a governor of Moldavia and Walachia under Turkish rule

¹host \ˈhōst\ *n* -s [ME *ost, oost, host, hoost,* fr. OF *ost, host,* fr. LL *hostis,* fr. L, stranger, enemy — more at GUEST] **1 a** : a large number of men gathered for war : ARMY ⟨the destruction of Pharaoh's ~ in that sea —W.L.Sperry⟩ ⟨walls that must be directly stormed by the ~*s* of courage —A.E.Stevenson b.1900⟩ **2 a** : ANGELS ⟨a multitude of the heavenly ~ praising God —Lk 2:13 (RSV)⟩ **b** : the sun, moon, and stars ⟨all the ~ of heaven —Deut 4:19 (RSV)⟩ **3** : a very large number : a great quantity : MULTITUDE, MYRIAD ⟨a whole ~ of children began to push at the door —Ernest Beaglehole⟩ ⟨hotel with its long lobbies filled with . . . ~*s* of rocking chairs —Marjory S. Douglas⟩ ⟨writing a ~ of accumulated book reviews —H.J.Laski⟩ ⟨a whole ~ of national monuments, military parks, memorials, and cemeteries —C.L.Wirth⟩

²host \"\ *vi* -ED/-ING/-S : to gather in a host : assemble usu. for a hostile purpose

³host \"\ *n* -s [ME *oste, hoste* host, guest, fr. OF, fr. L *hospit-, hospes* host, stranger, guest, fr. *hostis* stranger, enemy] **1 a** : INNKEEPER **b** : one who receives or entertains guests or strangers socially or commercially ⟨ourself will mingle with society and play the humble ~ —Shak.⟩ **2 a** : a living animal or plant affording subsistence or lodgment to a parasite — see ALTERNATE HOST, DEFINITIVE HOST, INTERMEDIATE HOST **b** : the larger, stronger, or dominant one of a commensal or symbiotic pair **c** (1) : an individual into which a tissue or part is transplanted from another (2) : an individual in whom an abnormal growth (as a cancer) is proliferating **3** : a mineral or rock that is older than other minerals or rocks introduced into it or formed within or adjacent to it

⁴host \"\ *vb* -ED/-ING/-S [ME *osten, hosten,* fr *oste, hoste,* n.] *vi, obs* : LODGE ⟨go bear it to the Centaur, where we ~, and stay there —Shak.⟩ ~ *vt* **1** : to receive or entertain socially : serve as host to ⟨will ~ the cadets during their visit —*Springfield (Mass.) Daily News*⟩ **2 a** : to receive or entertain guests at : serve as host at ⟨the garden party he had ~*ed* last spring —*Saturday Rev.*⟩ ⟨~*ed* the shower, at which 70 relatives were present to meet the bride —*Sacramento (Calif.) Bee*⟩ **b** : EMCEE ⟨successfully ~*ed* a series of television programs⟩

⁵host \"\ *n* -s [ME *oste, hoste,* fr. MF *osté, hosté,* back-formation fr. *ostez, hostez,* pl. of *ostel, hostel* — more at HOSTEL] *obs* : LODGING — used in the phrase *at host* ⟨lay at ~ . . . in the Centaur —Shak.⟩

⁶host \"\ *n* -s *usu cap* [ME *oste, hoste,* fr. MF *oiste, hoiste,* fr. LL & L; LL *hostia* Eucharist, fr. L, sacrifice] **1** : the eucharistic wafer or bread before or after consecration **2** *obs* : SACRIFICE

hos·ta \ˈhōstə, ˈhäs-\ *n* [NL, after Nicolaus T. *Host* †1834 Austrian botanist] **1** *cap* : a genus of Asiatic perennial herbs (family Liliaceae) that have ribbed basal leaves often blotched or bordered with white and scapes of white, blue, or lilac flowers and that are widely cultivated as ornamentals **2** -s : any plant of the genus *Hosta*

hos·tage \ˈhästij, -tēj *sometimes* ˈhȯs-\ *n* -s [ME *ostage, hostage,* fr. OF, fr. *oste, hoste* host, guest + *-age* — more at HOST] **1 a** *obs* : the state of a person given or kept as a pledge pending the fulfillment of an agreement, demand, or treaty ⟨if he stand in ~ for his safety —Shak.⟩ **b** : a person in such a state ⟨two boys . . . had been held as ~*s* for seven years —*N.Y. Times*⟩ **c** : a pledge, security, or guarantee usu. of good faith or intentions ⟨you know now your ~*s*: your uncle's word and my firm faith —Shak.⟩ **2** *archaic* : HOSTEL, INN **syn** see PLEDGE

hos·tage·ship \-ˌship\ *n* -s : the quality or state of a hostage

host·al \ˈhōstᵊl\ *adj* [³*host* + *-al*] : relating to hosts ⟨a parasite with wide ~ range⟩

¹hos·tel \ˈhästᵊl\ *n* -s [ME *ostel, hostel,* fr. OF, fr. LL *hospitale* hospice — more at HOSPITAL] **1** : a public house for entertaining or lodging travelers : INN ⟨folks used to ride up the bumpy road . . . to dine at the little ~ —Hodding Carter⟩ **2 a** *chiefly Brit* : housing maintained by a public or private organization or institution: (1) : DORMITORY 2 (2) : a rest home or rehabilitation center for the chronically ill, the aged, or the physically handicapped (3) : living quarters for newly arrived immigrants **b** : one of a system of supervised inexpensive lodgings or shelters for use by youth esp. on hiking or bicycling trips — called also *youth hostel* **3** *obs* : TOWN HOUSE

²hos·tel \"*, dial* -səl\ *vi* -ED/-ING/-S [ME *hostelen,* fr. *hostel,* n.] **1** *dial Eng* : LODGE **2** : to travel usu. by foot or by bicycle staying at hostels overnight ⟨hundreds of outdoor-minded vacationers will ~ alone or in independent groups of two or three this summer —Phil Spelman⟩

hos·tel·er \-stələ(r), *in sense 1* " *or* -slə-\ *n* -s [ME *osteler, hosteler,* fr. OF *ostelier, hostelier,* fr. *ostel, hostel* + *-ier*] **1** : one that lodges or entertains guests or strangers: **a** : the officer in charge of guests in a religious house **b** *archaic* : INNKEEPER **2 a** : one residing in a hostel **b** : one that goes hosteling

hos·tel·ry \ˈhästᵊlrē *sometimes* ˈhäsəl-\ *n* -ES [ME *ostelrie, hostelrie,* fr. MF *ostelerie, hostelerie,* fr. *ostel, hostel* + *-erie* -ery] : a place where food and lodging are available to the traveler : INN, HOTEL ⟨a large wooden-porched building with mansard roof is a typical ~ of the Civil War period —*Amer. Guide Series: Vt.*⟩

¹host·ess \ˈhōstəs\ *n* -ES [ME *ostesse, hostesse,* fr. OF, fr. *oste, hoste* host, guest + *-esse* -ess — more at HOST] **1** : a female innkeeper ⟨had a good understanding with the brother of mine ~ —Washington Irving⟩ **2** : a woman who receives and entertains guests socially ⟨successful party giving amounts to little more than the friendly enthusiasm of the host and ~ —Emily Post⟩ **3** : one whose job is to serve patrons: as **a** : a woman in charge of a public dining room who seats diners and ensures pleasant and efficient service **b** : a woman who directs social activities at a hotel or resort **c** (1) : a woman employed by a railroad or bus line to give personal service to passengers (2) : AIR HOSTESS **d** : a woman who acts as social partner in a dance hall or nightclub

²hostess \"\ *vb* -ED/-ING/-ES *vi* : to act as hostess ⟨had to arrange for the afternoon she was ~*ing* —W.L.George⟩ ~ *vt* : to serve as hostess at ⟨enjoyed ~*ing* the party⟩

hostess cart *n* : DINNER WAGON, TEA CART

hostess gown *n* : a dressy negligee or housecoat worn esp. for informal entertainment at home

hostess house *n* : an establishment at military installations for the lodging and entertainment of visitors

host·ess-ship \ˈhōstə(sh)ˌship, -təsˌsh-\ *n* : the position or role of hostess

¹hos·tile \ˈhäˌstᵊl *also* ˌstīl *or* ˌ(ˌ)stil *sometimes* ˈhȯ\ *adj* [MF or L; MF, fr. L *hostilis,* fr. *hostis* stranger, enemy + *-ilis* -ile — more at GUEST] **1 a** : of or relating to an enemy ⟨a ~ army⟩ ⟨~ territory⟩ ⟨turned the guns toward a ~ position⟩ **b** : marked by malevolence and a desire to injure ⟨might commit some ~ act, attempt to strike me or choke me —Jack London⟩ **c** : marked by antagonism or unfriendliness ⟨the instinct of Americans has always been ~ to the alignment of classes in political parties —H.S.Commager⟩ **d** : marked by resistance esp. to new ideas : unfavorable esp. to the new or strange ⟨are ~ to the idea of literature for the sake of enjoyment —M.R.Cohen⟩ **e** : offering an unpleasant or forbidding environment : not hospitable ⟨searching the ~ glaring desert for gold —*Amer. Guide Series: Ariz.*⟩ ⟨maps of the area indicated the ~ character of the land —C.L. Walker⟩ **2 a** : of or relating to an opposing party in a legal controversy ⟨~ claim⟩ **b** : adverse to the interests of an owner or possessor of property ⟨~ use⟩ ⟨~ title⟩ **c** *of a witness* : subject to cross-examination because of evident hostility shown during direct examination

²hostile \"\ *n* -s : one that is hostile; *esp* : an American Indian unfriendly to whites ⟨ought to have guessed the ~*s* would try to come in here —Alan LeMay⟩

hostile embargo *n* : a government's embargo on the movement of enemy ships — compare CIVIL EMBARGO

hostile fire *n* : a fire that is not confined in a receptacle specif. made to contain fire — used in fire-insurance contracts; compare FRIENDLY FIRE

hos·tile·ly \-tᵊl(l)ē, -tīl|, -til(l)|, |i\ *adv* : in a hostile manner

hos·tile·ness \-ᵊlnəs, -īln-, -iln-\ *n* -ES : the quality or state of being hostile

hostile possession *n* : ADVERSE POSSESSION

hos·til·i·ty \häˈstiləd·ē, -ətē, -i *sometimes* hȯˈ-\ *n* -ES [MF or LL; MF *hostilité,* fr. LL *hostilitat-, hostilitas,* fr. L *hostilis* + *-itat-, -itas* -ity] **1 a** : a hostile or antagonistic state ⟨the civilized south and the barbarous north stood in perpetual ~ —Kemp Malone⟩ **b** (1) : hostile action ⟨the Spanish expedition encountered ~ . . . and was forced to flee —R.W.Murray⟩ (2) **hostilities** *pl* : overt acts of warfare : WAR ⟨the outbreak of *hostilities*⟩ **2** : antagonism, opposition, or resistance in thought or principle : ANIMOSITY ⟨there was tension, there was ~ and envy in the air —Theodor Reik⟩ ⟨~ to annexation has different grounds in different places —B.K.Sandwell⟩ **syn** see ENMITY

hos·ti·mel·la \ˌhästəˈmelə\ *n, cap* [NL, fr. *Hostim,* Czechoslovakia, its locality + NL *-ella*] : a form genus of fossil plants based on naked sporangia that are now commonly believed to be the fruiting structures of plants of the genus *Asteroxylon*

host·ing \ˈhōstiŋ\ *n* -s [ME, fr. ¹*host* + *-ing*] **1 a** : the mustering of armed men **b** : a hostile incursion or encounter ⟨strange to us it seemed . . . that angel should with angel war, and in fierce ~ meet —John Milton⟩ **2** : GATHERING ⟨the good people who come out about this time of night to hold their ~ on the hills —O.S.J.Gogarty⟩

hos·tler \(ˈ)(h)äslə(r) *sometimes* ˈhəs-\ *n* -s [ME *osteler, hosteler, hostler* innkeeper, hostler — more at HOSTELER] **1 a** *also* **os·tler** \ˈäs-\ : one who takes care of horses at an inn or stable : GROOM **b** : one who is in charge of the horses or mules used in an industry : STABLEMAN **2 a** : one who takes charge of a railroad locomotive after a run : one who moves and services locomotives in enginehouse or roundhouse territory **b** : one employed in the storage garage of a transportation company to assist with the moving about and servicing of trucks or buses **c** : a worker who cleans, oils, or otherwise services machines (as cranes, dinkeys, boilers) that are in almost constant use

hostler's control *n* : a simplified throttle provided to move the unit of a diesel locomotive not equipped with a regular engineer's control

host·less \ˈhōstləs\ *adj* [³*host* + *-less*] : having no host

hos·tling \ˈ(h)äsliŋ *sometimes* ˈhəs-\ *n* -s [perh. alter. of *hosteling,* gerund of ²*hostel*] : the act or process of handling a locomotive between runs that includes taking it to the enginehouse and delivering it to the road crew

host·ly \ˈhōstlē\ *adj* [³*host* + *-ly*] : of or appropriate to a host ⟨still so young-looking that people did not instinctively lay upon him ~ duties —John Updike⟩

hos·try \ˈhästrē\ *n* -ES [ME *ostrie, hostrie,* fr. MF *osterie, hosterie,* fr. *oste, hoste* host, guest + *-erie* -ery — more at HOST] *archaic* : HOSTELRY

hosts *pl of* HOST, *pres 3d sing of* HOST

¹hot \ˈhät, *usu* -äd·+V\ *adj* **hotter**; **hottest** [ME *hoot, hot,* fr. OE *hāt;* akin to OFris & OS *hēt* hot, OHG *heiz,* ON *heitr* hot, Goth *heito* fever, Lith *kaĩsti* to get hot] **1** : having heat in a degree exceeding normal body heat : having a relatively high temperature : giving or capable of giving a sensation of heat : capable of burning, searing, or scalding ⟨~ stove⟩ ⟨~ forehead⟩ **2 a** : ARDENT, FIERY ⟨~ blood of youth⟩ ⟨~ tempers⟩ : VEHEMENT ⟨~ words were exchanged⟩ **b** : VIOLENT, RAGING ⟨~ battle⟩ **c** : URGENT, FEVERISH ⟨messengers sent in ~ haste⟩ **d** (1) *of an animal* : being in heat (2) : LUSTFUL, LECHEROUS **e** : ZEALOUS, EAGER ⟨~ for reform⟩ ⟨~ patriot⟩ ⟨~ baseball fan⟩ ⟨~ fisherman⟩ **f** (1) *of jazz* : ecstatic and emotionally exciting and usu. marked by complex rhythms and free contrapuntal improvisations on the melody — often contrasted with *sweet* (2) *of a jazz performer* : stimulated and inspired to complete rhythmic and melodic freedom **3 a** : having the sensation of an uncomfortable degree of body heat : too warm for comfort ⟨~ and tired⟩ ⟨I'm too ~ in this sweater⟩ **b** : causing discomfort or distress through excessive warmth or humidity ⟨~ climate⟩ ⟨this room is ~ and stuffy⟩ ⟨~ sunshine⟩ **c** (1) : naturally or constitutionally possessing heat — used in medieval physiology, natural philosophy, and astrology to name one of the qualities of the four elements (2) *of a sign of the zodiac* : having a hot complexion **4 a** : having or retaining the heat of cooking ⟨this pudding is best when served ~⟩ ⟨will you have ~ or iced coffee⟩ **b** : not yet grown cool or stale : newly made or received : FRESH ⟨news ~ from the press⟩ ⟨following a ~ scent⟩; *also* : close to something pursued or sought ⟨~ on the trail of the murderer⟩ ⟨guess again, you're getting *hotter*⟩ **c** : suggestive of heat ⟨~ smell of burning rubber⟩ ⟨~ sound of buzzing flies⟩ or of burning or glowing objects ⟨I like ~ colors . . . hot orange and red and shocking pink —Mitzi Gaynor⟩ **d** (1) *of type* : made by the casting of hot metal into a mold (2) : using type so made ⟨~ composition⟩ — compare COLD **e** : uncomfortable to an intolerable or dangerous degree : UNSAFE ⟨the police were making the town too ~ for him⟩ **5** : PUNGENT, PEPPERY, BITING ⟨~ sauce⟩ ⟨~ pickles⟩ **6** : showing energy or activity in an unusual degree: as **a** : of intense and immediate interest ⟨~ news story⟩ ⟨~ scandal⟩ **b** : unusually lucky or successful ⟨~ streak at poker⟩ or favorable ⟨the dice are ~ for me tonight⟩ **c** : temporarily capable of unusual performance (as in a sport) ⟨any one of half a dozen golfers might get ~ and win this tournament⟩ ⟨~ favorite in the race⟩ **d** *of merchandise or securities* : readily salable : enjoying current popularity ⟨~ items in women's wear⟩ **e** (1) : very good — used as a generalized term of approval ⟨a real ~ lawyer⟩ ⟨he's ~ in math⟩ (2) *slang* : ABSURD, UNBELIEVABLE ⟨wants to fight the champion? that's a ~ one⟩ **7** : having or charged with high energy: as **a** : electrically charged; *esp* : charged with high voltage **b** *of a cartridge* : having a powder load which gives a high muzzle velocity and corresponding high chamber pressure and flat trajectory — used esp. of hand-loaded ammunition **c** : RADIOACTIVE ⟨~ material⟩; *also* : dealing with radioactive material ⟨~ laboratory⟩ **d** *of an airplane* : FAST; *esp* : characterized by a high landing speed **8 a** : stolen or otherwise illegally obtained ⟨~ jewels⟩ ⟨~ bonds⟩; *also* : CONTRABAND **b** : wanted by the police : fugitive from justice **c** *of a commodity* : prohibited by law or agreement from being shipped or handled ⟨~ oil⟩

²hot \"\ *adv* [ME *hoote, hote,* fr. OE *hāte,* fr. *hāt,* adj.] : HOTLY ⟨the sun shines ~ —Shak.⟩ ⟨*hot*-glowing coals⟩ ⟨took a club and gave it to him ~ and heavy⟩

³hot \"\ *n* -s [ME *hoot, hot,* fr. *hoot, hot,* adj.] **1** *dial* : HEAT **2** : HOT DOG

⁴hot \"\ *vb* **hotted; hotted; hotting; hots** [¹*hot*] *vi, chiefly Brit* : to become warm or heated — usu. used with *up* ⟨fresh air ~*s* up quickly⟩ ⟨the argument had *hotted* up considerably⟩ ~ *vt, chiefly Brit* : WARM, HEAT; *specif* : to warm over (food) — usu. used with *up* ⟨there's some stew and dumplings left I can ~ up in a minute —Victoria Lincoln⟩

⁵hot \"\ *n* -s [ME *hott,* fr. OF *hotte, hote,* of Gmc origin; akin to G dial. *hutte, hotte* basket, pannier, MHG *hotte, hotze* cradle — more at HOD] **1** *now dial Eng* : a basket for carrying earth or manure **2** *dial Brit* : a little heap or pile (as of manure) **3** *obs* : a padded sheath for the spur of a gamecock

hot air *n* : empty talk : unsubstantiated and often boastful statements ⟨used to talk a lot of *hot air* about medicine —A.J. Cronin⟩ ⟨threats both ways are just *hot air,* big talk and face saving —*Kiplinger Washington Letter*⟩

hot-air engine *n* : an engine using heated air as the working substance

hot-air furnace *n* : a heating unit enclosed in a casing from which warm air is circulated through the building in ducts by gravity convection or by fans

hotbed \ˈ=ˌ=\ *n* **1** : a bed of soil enclosed in a low glass frame heated by fermenting manure or by other means and used for forcing or for raising early seedlings — compare COLD FRAME **2** : a place or environment which favors rapid growth or development ⟨~ of crime⟩ **3** : a frame or area in a rolling mill on which hot bars or rails are laid to cool

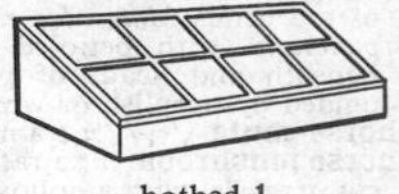
hotbed 1

hot-blast stove *n* : an apparatus used to preheat the blast for an iron blast furnace and consisting of firebrick passages which alternately receive heat from burning gas and then give up this heat to the incoming blast

hotblood \ˈ=ˌ=\ *n* : one that is hotblooded: as **a** : one having strong passions or a quick temper **b** : THOROUGHBRED 1b

hot-blooded \ˈ=ˈ==\ *adj* **1** : having hot blood : EXCITABLE, HIGH-SPIRITED, ARDENT, PASSIONATE **2 a** *of a horse* : having Arab or Thoroughbred ancestors **b** *of a horse and other livestock* : of pure or superior breeding — **hot-blood·ed·ness** *n* -ES

hotbox \ˈ=ˌ=\ *n* **1** : a journal bearing (as of a railroad car) overheated by friction **2** : SWEATBOX 2

hot-brain \ˈ=ˌ=\ *n, archaic* : HOTHEAD

hot-brained \ˈ=ˈ=\ *adj, archaic* : HOTHEADED

hot bread *n* : bread, rolls, biscuits, or muffins served still hot from baking — usu. used in pl.

hot-bulb \ˈ=ˌ=\ *adj* : having an ignition system in which the charge is ignited by spraying it into a separate chamber kept above the ignition temperature of the charge by the heat of compression — used of a semidiesel engine

hot buttered rum *n* : a hot drink consisting of rum and water spiced and sweetened and served with a lump of butter floating on the surface

hot cake *n* : GRIDDLE CAKE

hot cap *n* : a paper or plastic cap set over growing plants in early spring for protection from frost

hot-cathode \ˈ=ˌ==\ *adj* : operated by thermionic emission from a heated cathode ⟨*hot-cathode* tube⟩

hotch \ˈhäch\ *vb* -ED/-ING/-ES [prob. fr. MF *hocher* to shake, fr. OF *hochier,* of Gmc origin; akin to MHG *hotteln, hotzeln* to shake — more at HOD] *vi* **1** *dial Brit* : to shake, jog, and wiggle : FIDGET **2** *dial Brit* : to change position or shift weight to make room : HITCH ~ *vt, chiefly Scot* : to cause to shake or shift

hot·cha \ˈhä(ˌ)chä, -ˌchə\ *n* -s [prob. irreg. fr. ¹*hot*] *slang* : hot jazz ⟨band began to play the blatant ~ —John Fante⟩

hot chisel *n* : a chisel used in cutting hot metal

hotch·pot \ˈhächˌpät\ *n* [ME *hochepot,* fr. MF, fr. OF, fr. *hochier* to shake + *pot* — more at HOTCH, POTAGE] **1** : HOTCHPOTCH 1 **2** : HODGEPODGE 1 **3** [AF *hochepot,* fr. OF, hotchpotch] : a throwing into a common lot of property for equality of division which requires that advancements to a child be made up to the estate by contribution or by an accounting : COLLATION 5

hotch·potch \-ˌpäch\ *n* -ES [alter. of *hotchpot*] **1 a** : a thick soup of barley, peas, and other vegetables, and often also meat **b** : a stew of meat and vegetables **2** *chiefly Brit* : HODGEPODGE 1 **3** : HOTCHPOT 3

hot cockles *n pl but sing in constr* : a game in which one player covers his eyes and tries to guess who strikes him

hot corner *n* : the fielding position of the third baseman in baseball

hot cross bun *n* : a raisin bun marked with a cross made of sugar frosting traditionally served on Good Friday

hot deck *n* : a pile of logs from which logs are hauled to the mill as soon as they are cut and yarded — compare COLD DECK

hot dish *n* : CASSEROLE 3 ⟨had a *hot dish* and salad for lunch⟩

¹hot dog *n* [prob. so called fr. the fancied resemblance of a frankfurter to a dachshund] : a cooked frankfurter usu. served in a long split roll and garnished with mustard, onion, or other savory substance

²hot dog *interj* — used to express approval or gratification

hot-draw \ˈ=ˌ=\ *vt* : to draw (as metal or nylon) while hot or with application of heat

¹ho·tel \(ˈ)hōˈtel\ *n* -s [F *hôtel,* fr. OF *ostel, hostel* — more at

HOSTEL] **1** *archaic* **:** a city mansion of a person of rank or wealth **2 a :** a house licensed to provide lodging and usu. meals, entertainment, and various personal services for the public **:** INN **b :** a building of many rooms chiefly for overnight accommodation of transients and several floors served by elevators, usu. with a large open street-level lobby containing easy chairs, with a variety of compartments for eating, drinking, dancing, exhibitions, and group meetings (as of salesmen or convention attendants), with shops having both inside and street-side entrances and offering for sale items (as clothes, gifts, candy, theater tickets, travel tickets) of particular interest to a traveler, or providing personal services (as hairdressing, shoe shining), and with telephone booths, writing tables, and washrooms freely available

²hotel \"\ *vt* **hotelled; hotelled; hotelling; hotels :** to lodge at a hotel

³hotel \"\ *usu cap* — a communications code word for the letter *h*

hotel car *n* **:** a railroad car with facilities for preparing and serving food and for sleeping

hô·tel de ville \(,)(h)ō,teldə'vēl\ *n, pl* **hôtels de ville** \-l(z)d-\ [F] **:** a town hall in France and other European countries

ho·tel dieu \l'dyə(r), -yō\ *n, pl* **hotels dieu** \-l(z)'d-\ *cap D* [F *hôtel-Dieu*, fr. OF *ostel Dieu*, fr. *ostel, hostel* hostel, hospice + *Dieu* God, fr. L *deus* — more at HOSTEL, DEITY] **:** a medieval hospital

ho·tel·dom \hō'teldəm\ *n* -s **:** hotels and hotel workers ⟨you can't talk connectedly to anybody except . . to a minor part of ~ and of officialdom —Laura Z. Hobson⟩

ho·tel·ier \hō·'telyə(r); ,ōt³l'yā, ,ōt-\ *n* -s [F *hôtelier*, fr. OF *ostelier, hostelier* — more at HOSTELER] **:** HOTELKEEPER

hotelkeeper \(')ˌˌˌ\ *n* **:** a proprietor or manager of a hotel

ho·tel·less \hō'teləs\ *adj* **:** lacking a hotel ⟨some parts of the country are nearly ~⟩

hotel lock *n* **:** a knob lock that can be operated by a master key

ho·tel·man \(')ˌˌmən, -,man\ *n, pl* **hotelmen :** HOTELKEEPER

hotel rack *n* **:** the unsplit rib section of a foresaddle of lamb

hot flash *or* **hot flush** *n* **:** a sudden usu. brief sensation of heat and reddening of the skin accompanying sudden dilation of skin capillaries usu. associated with endocrine imbalance esp. that accompanying menopause

¹hotfoot \'hät,fu̇t, *usu* -u̇d.+V\ *adv* [ME *hot fot*] **:** in haste **:** without delay **:** HASTILY ⟨sent ambassadors ~ to the Turk —Francis Hackett⟩ ⟨drove his vessel ~ for the Boston pier —Mary H. Vorse⟩

²hotfoot \"\ *vi* **:** to go hotfoot **:** HASTEN, HURRY — usu. used with *it* ⟨~*ing* it north . . . with a Texas posse on its heels —W.F.Harris⟩ ~ *vt* **:** to give (someone) a hotfoot **:** GOAD

³hotfoot \"\ *n, pl* **hotfoots** [¹*hot* + *foot*] **1 :** a practical joke in which a match is surreptitiously inserted in the side of a victim's shoe and lighted **2 a :** a stinging rebuke **:** INSULT, TAUNT ⟨administers one intellectual ~ after another to the Philistine public —Edgar Johnson⟩ **b :** GOAD, SPUR ⟨has given tradition-bound Baltimore a ~ —*Newsweek*⟩

hot-galvanize \'ˌˌˌ\ *vt* **:** to galvanize by dipping in molten zinc

hot-gospeler \'ˌˌˌˌ\ *n* **:** an evangelical preacher **:** REVIVALIST

hothead \'ˌˌ\ *n* **:** a hotheaded person

hotheaded \'ˌˌˌ\ *adj* **1 :** having a hot head (as from drinking) **2 :** FIERY, HASTY, IMPETUOUS — **hot·head·ed·ly** *adv* — **hot·head·ed·ness** *n* -ES

hothearted \'ˌˌˌ\ *adj* **:** HOTHEADED

¹hothouse \'ˌˌ\ *n* [¹*hot* + *house*] **1** *obs* **:** TURKISH BATH **2** *obs* **:** BROTHEL **3 :** a room or building kept heated for drying something (as green pottery) **4 :** a greenhouse maintained at a high temperature for the culture of tender or tropical plants and other plants (as cucumbers and tomatoes) requiring such a temperature **5 :** SWEAT HOUSE 1 **6 :** HOTBED 2 ⟨the prose is a ~ of clichés —*New Yorker*⟩ ⟨the great city is . . . a ~ of decadence and of every perversion —François Bondy⟩

²hothouse \"\ *adj* **1 :** grown in a hothouse **:** artificially cultivated ⟨~ grapes⟩ **2 :** having the qualities of a plant raised in a hothouse **:** lacking normal resistance to cold or adversity **:** SOFT, DELICATE, DECADENT ⟨~ voluptuousness⟩ ⟨her father . . . was a brittle, ~ sort of creature —Frederick Prokosch⟩

hothouse lamb *n* **:** the meat of a lamb born out of the normal lambing season and usu. marketed during the period from January to March

ho·tis test \'hōd-əs-\ *n, usu cap H* [after R. P. *Hotis* †1935 Amer. agricultural marketing specialist] **:** a test for the presence of the common streptococcus of bovine mastitis in milk made by incubating a sample of milk with the aniline dye bromcresol purple, the appearance of yellow patches or coloration being indicative of the presence of the organism

hot lead *n* **:** fired bullets **:** GUNFIRE ⟨settled arguments with *hot lead*⟩

hot logging *n* **:** logging in which the logs are taken from stump directly to stream landing or mill — compare COLD DECK

hot·ly *adv* **:** in a hot or fiery manner **:** ARDENTLY, EAGERLY, PUNGENTLY, VIOLENTLY, HASTILY, LUSTFULLY

hotmelt \'ˌˌ\ *n* **:** a fast-drying nonvolatile adhesive made of synthetic resins and plasticizers and applied hot in the molten state

hot money *n* **:** money of foreign ownership deposited or invested to avoid depreciation and constituting a threat to national currency and credit by being liable to sudden withdrawal — called also *funk money*

hot·ness *n* -ES **1 :** the quality or state of being hot **:** the sensation of heat **2 :** TEMPERATURE ⟨a thermometer measures the ~ of an object⟩

hot·not \'hät,nät\ *n* -s *usu cap* [Afrik] *Africa* **:** HOTTENTOT

hot oven *n* **:** a baking oven heated to a temperature between 400° and 450° F

hot pack *n* **:** absorbent material (as a blanket or squares of gauze) wrung out in hot water, wrapped around the body or a portion of the body, and covered with dry material to hold in the moist heat ⟨*hot pack* for an infected arm⟩

hot-pack method *n* **:** a method of canning in which food is partly cooked in an open kettle before being put in containers and then sterilized as in the cold-pack method

hot pants *n pl* **:** EAGERNESS, IMPETUOSITY; *esp* **:** impatient sexual desire ⟨still got *hot pants* for her, if you want to call that love —Mary McCarthy⟩

hot papa *n, slang* **:** HOT SUITMAN

hot pepper *n* **1 :** any of various capsicum fruits (as cayenne) that contain significant amounts of capsaicin, are characterized by marked pungency, usu. have rather thin walls, and vary in form from spherical to greatly elongated — compare SWEET PEPPER **2 :** a plant (as a bird pepper or cone pepper) that bears hot peppers

hot plate *n* **1 :** a heated iron plate (as on a cooking range) for cooking or for keeping food warm **2 :** a simple portable gas or electric heater for heating liquids or laboratory materials or for cooking in limited spaces **3 :** a food plate with a hot-water jacket for keeping food warm (as for infants or invalids)

hot plates: electric, *A;* gas, *B*

hot pond *n* **:** a log pond kept open by means of hot water and steam

hot pot *n* **:** a stew of meat and vegetables

hot potato *n* **:** a question or issue that involves unpleasant or dangerous consequences for anyone dealing with it ⟨bingo parties and church raffles have . . . developed into such a *hot potato* that everyone concerned now is seeking some easy solution —*N.Y. Times*⟩

¹hot-press \'ˌˌ\ *n* **1 :** a calendering machine in which paper or cloth is glossed by being pressed between glazed boards and hot metal plates **2 :** a hydraulic oil press in which the contents are kept hot by steam radiators

²hot-press \'ˌˌ\ *vt* **1 :** to gloss (paper or cloth) or to express (oil) by combined heat and pressure **2 :** to press (wood or metal) while hot

hot press *n, Brit* **:** a small heated room for drying laundry

hot-presser \'ˌˌˌ\ *n* **:** one that operates a hot-press

hot pursuit *n* **:** fresh pursuit esp. across state or territorial lines

hot-quench \'ˌˌ\ *vt* **:** to quench (a metal) in a hot bath (as of molten salt, lead, or oil)

hot rock *n* **:** a highly skilled or daredevil airplane pilot

hot rod *n* **:** an automobile rebuilt or modified for high speed and fast acceleration

hot rod·der \-ˌräd·ə(r)\ *n* **1 :** a hot-rod driver, builder, or enthusiast **2 :** one who drives a car in a showy or reckless manner

hot roll *n, West* **:** BEDROLL

hot-roll \'ˌˌ\ *vt* **:** to roll (metal) while hot or with the application of heat — compare COLD-ROLL

hots *pl of* HOT, *pres 3d sing of* HOT

hot saw *n* **:** a power saw for cutting hot metal — distinguished from *cold saw*

hot seat *n* **1** *slang* **:** ELECTRIC CHAIR **2 :** a position of uneasiness or embarrassment or anxiety **:** a position involving oppressive responsibility ⟨on the *hot seat*, directing a half-million dollar gamble —Mark Stroock & Percy Knauth⟩ ⟨kept Iran on a political *hot seat* —*Armed Forces Talk*⟩ **3** *slang* **:** an ejection seat in an airplane

hot-short \'ˌˌ\ *adj, of metal* **:** short or brittle when heated beyond a red heat — compare COLD-SHORT, RED-SHORT — **hot-short·ness** *n*

hot shot *n* **:** shot heated to redness in order to set fire to buildings or ships

¹hotshot \'ˌˌ\ *n* [¹*hot* + *shot*] **1 a :** a fast freight usu. hauling merchandise or perishables in scheduled service **b :** a very fast airplane or vehicle **2** *slang* **:** a skillful, showy, and aggressive person; *esp* **:** one holding a position of importance by exercise of skill, showiness, and aggression **3 a :** a skilled workman **b :** a skilled performer in a sport (as golf, basketball, baseball) that involves shooting or aiming **4 :** one trained to fight forest fires in remote areas

²hotshot \"\ *adj* **1** *slang* **:** highly skilled, fast-working, or showy; *also* **:** important or successful by exercise of skill, adroitness, or showiness ⟨a ~ surgeon with more business than he can handle⟩ **2** *of a freight carrier* **:** NONSTOP, THROUGH, FAST ⟨a ~ freight train⟩

hot slaw *n* **:** coleslaw prepared with a cooked dressing

hot spot *n* **1 :** a place that is hotter than the surrounding surface: as **a :** a spot in the intake manifold of an internal-combustion engine which is heated by the exhaust gases to aid in the vaporization of the fuel **b :** an overheated spot in the combustion chamber tending to cause preignition **c :** a place in the shell of a furnace hotter than the rest **d :** an uncooled portion of a combustion chamber against which a charge is sprayed for ignition in a semidiesel engine **2 :** a region of high forest-fire frequency **3 a :** an area in a plastered wall containing alkaline salts that cause paper and paints to discolor **b :** an area on a negative or print representing excessive illumination of a part of the subject **c :** an area of excessive illumination (as on a subject or on the easel of an enlarger) in a pictorial reproduction **4 :** a center of night life **:** NIGHTCLUB

hot-spot \'ˌˌ\ *vt* [*hot spot*] **:** to check a forest fire at hot spots

hot spring *n* **:** THERMAL SPRING; *esp* **:** a spring with water above 98° F

hotspur \'ˌˌ\ *n* [ME *hatspore*, fr. *hat, hoot, hot* hot + *spore* spur — more at HOT, SPUR] **:** a rash hotheaded impetuous man

hot stove league *n* **:** sports followers (as of baseball) gathering for off-season discussion ⟨first place a baseball fan might look for some good, between-seasons, *hot stove league* reading —J.K.Hutchens⟩

hot stuff *n, slang* **:** something or someone unusually good or extraordinary or formidable ⟨in surf casting . . . the man who can average one hundred yards is *hot stuff* —*Fisherman's Encyc.*⟩

hot stuff man *n* **:** a bakery worker who removes baked goods from pans

hot suit·man \-'süitmən\ *n, pl* **hot suitmen :** a man esp. equipped to rescue the crew of a burning airplane

hot-swage \'ˌˌ\ *vt* **:** to swage (metal) while hot

hot·sy-tot·sy \'hätsē'tätsē\ *adj* [coined *ab*1926 by Billie De Beck †1942 Am. cartoonist] *slang* **:** comfortably stable or secure **:** PERFECT, OK ⟨had a quarrel, but everything is *hotsy-totsy* now⟩

hott \'hät\ *var of* ⁵HOT

hotted *past of* HOT

hot-tempered \'ˌˌˌ\ *adj* **:** having a quick or violent temper

hot·ten \'hät³n\ *vb* -ED/-ING/-S [¹*hot* + -*en*] *vt, dial* **:** HEAT ⟨~ up the soup, ma⟩ ~ *vi, dial* **:** to grow hot **:** become angry or lively ⟨warmed and then ~*ed* to his subject —Adria Langley⟩

hot·ten·tot \'hät³n,tät, *usu* -äd-+V\ *n* -s [Afrik *Hottentot, Hotnot*] **1** *usu cap* **a :** a people of southern Africa apparently akin to both the Bushmen and the Bantus and having moderately negroid features, typically very long heads, and prominent buttocks — see GRIQUA, NAMA **b :** a member of such people **2** *usu cap* **:** the Khoisan language of the Hottentot people **3 :** a common So. African marine sparid food fish (*Pachymetopon blochii*)

hottentot apron *n, usu cap H* **:** an excessive development of the labia minora occurring in Hottentot women

hottentot bread *or* **hottentot's bread** *n, usu cap H* **1 :** ELEPHANT'S-FOOT 1 **2 :** the thick edible rootstock of elephant's-foot

hottentot bustle *n, usu cap H* **:** STEATOPYGIA

hottentot fig *or* **hottentot's fig** *n, usu cap H* **:** a low-growing woody southern African perennial (*Carpobrotus edulis*) of the family Aizoaceae that has angular stems, opposite succulent leaves united at the base, and large yellow or purplish rose flowers, that is cultivated as a ground cover, and that sometimes occurs as an escape in the southwestern U.S.

¹hotter *comparative of* HOT

²hot·ter \'hätə(r)\ *vi* -ED/-ING/-S [perh. fr. Flem *hotteren* to shake; akin to MHG *hotteln, hotzeln* to shake — more at HOD] **1** *dial Brit* **a :** to shake esp. with rage or laughter **b :** to move shakily **:** JOLT **c :** to crowd together in confusion **2** *dial Brit* **a :** RUMBLE ⟨~*ing* thunder⟩ **b :** to talk incoherently **:** MUTTER, MUMBLE, STAMMER

³hotter \"\ *n* -s **1** *dial Brit* **:** the act or motion of hottering **2** *dial Brit* **:** a swarm or heap of things

hottest *superlative of* HOT

hotting *pres part of* HOT

hot·tish \'häd·ish\ *adj* **:** somewhat hot

hot·to·nia \hä'tōnēə\ *n, cap* [NL, fr. Peter *Hotton* †1709 Dutch botanist + NL -*ia*] **:** a genus of aquatic herbs (family Primulaceae) with submerged crowded leaves and small white or purplish racemose flowers — see FEATHERFOIL

hot top *n* **:** a feedhead for an ingot mold

hot-trod \'ˌˌ\ *n* **1** *Scot* **:** the pursuit with hounds and horn in old border forays **2** *Scot* **:** the signal for such pursuit

hot up *vi* **1 :** to grow hot, lively, or exciting ⟨the gossip began to *hot up* —*Life*⟩ **2 :** to speed up ⟨the air raids began to *hot up* about the beginning of February —George Orwell⟩ ~ *vt* **1 :** AROUSE, ANNOY ⟨getting him all *hotted up* —Lord Beaverbrook⟩ **2 :** to make livelier or speedier ⟨a protest against . . . the genteel *hotting up* of Shakespearean productions robbed of all poetry —Stephen Spender⟩

hot-walker \'ˌˌˌ\ *n* **:** one employed to cool out horses ⟨got odd jobs as a *hot-walker* and exercise boy —*Time*⟩

hot wall *n* **:** a wall provided with heating flues for hastening the growth or ripening of fruit

hot war *n* **:** an armed conflict **:** a shooting war — compare COLD WAR

hot water *n* **:** a dangerous or distressing predicament **:** TROUBLE, DIFFICULTY ⟨primitive people take exception to a camera . . . so that indiscriminate snapshooting has landed more than one explorer in *hot water* —W.W.Howells⟩

hot-water bag *or* **hot-water bottle** *n* **1 :** a stoppered rubber bag or earthenware bottle filled with hot water to provide warmth **2** *Brit* **:** HEATING PAD ⟨electric *hot-water bottles*⟩

hot-water heating *n* **:** central heating by means of hot water circulated through pipes or radiators

hot-water treatment *n* **:** a treatment of plants or plant parts for the eradication of parasites (as loose smut of wheat) involving immersion in water at a temperature above the thermal death point of the parasite but below that of the host

hot-water bag

hot wave *n* **:** a period of relatively high temperatures; *specif* **:** one caused by the southerly winds in front of an advancing cyclone or by the accumulating heat in a stagnant anticyclone — called also *heat wave*

hot well *n* **1 :** HOT SPRING **2 :** a reservoir in a condensing steam-engine or turbine installation for receiving the warm condensed steam drawn from the condenser

hot-wire \'ˌˌ\ *adj* **:** operated by the thermal expansion of a wire through which an electric current is passed or by the convective cooling (as by air) of a wire heated by passage through it of an electric current, the expansion or contraction of the wire usu. deflecting a pointer ⟨*hot-wire* ammeter⟩ ⟨*hot-wire* anemometer⟩

hot-work \'ˌˌ\ *vt* **:** to roll, forge, press, or shape (metal) while hot

hou·ba·ra \hü'bärə\ *n* -s [Ar *hubārā* bustard] **:** a bustard (*Chlamydotis undulata* syn. *Houbara undulata*) of northern Africa or its eastern form (*C. u. macqueenii*) found in Persia, India, and sometimes in England — called also *ruffed bustard*

houdah *var of* HOWDAH

hou·dan \'hü,dan, ü'dä⁽ⁿ⁾\ *n* -s *usu cap* [F, fr. *Houdan*, village in northern France where it was developed] **:** a domestic fowl of a French breed of medium size with a V-shaped leaf comb, mottled black-and-white or pure-white plumage and crest, and five toes

hou·die \'hau̇dī\ *var of* HOWDIE

hou·dry process \'hüdrē-\ *n, usu cap H* [after Eugene *Houdry* *b*1892 Am. engineer] **:** a cracking process for making high-octane gasoline by passing oil vapors through a fixed bed of an aluminum silicate catalyst in the form of pellets

houf \'hau̇f\ *var of* HOWF

¹hough \'häk, 'hōk\ *n* -s [ME *hoch, hough* — more at HOCK] *chiefly Scot* **:** ⁴HOCK

²hough \"\ *vt* -ED/-ING/-S [ME *houghen*, fr. *hough*, n.] *now chiefly Scot* **:** HAMSTRING ⟨thou shalt ~ their horses, and burn their chariots —Josh 11:6 (AV)⟩

hough·er \'häkə(r)\ *n* -s **:** one that hamstrings cattle; *specif* **:** one of a band of lawbreakers in Ireland that hamstrung cattle

hough·ma·gan·dy \,hōkmə'gandī\ *n* -ES [perh. irreg. fr. ¹*hough* + *canty*] *Scot* **:** FORNICATION

hou·here \'hō'herə\ *n* -s [Maori] **1** *NewZeal* **:** RIBBONWOOD 1 **2** *NewZeal* **:** RIBBON TREE

hounce \'hau̇ns\ *n* -s [origin unknown] *dial Eng* **:** an ornament on the collar of a cart horse

¹hound \'hau̇nd\ *n* -s [ME, fr. OE *hund*; akin to OHG *hunt* dog, ON *hundr*, Goth *hunds*, L *canis*, Gk *kyōn*, Skt *śvā*] **1 a :** DOG **b :** a dog of any of various breeds used in the chase that have typically large drooping ears and a deep voice and follow their prey by scent **c** *Brit* **:** FOXHOUND **2 :** a mean or despicable person ⟨that low-down, sneaking ~⟩ **3 a :** DOGFISH 1 **b** *Newfoundland* **:** OLD-SQUAW **4 :** one of the chasers in the game hare and hounds **5 :** one closely attached to a habit or pursuit **:** ADDICT ⟨autograph ~⟩ ⟨an expert lens ~ —H.H.Miller⟩ — often used in combinations ⟨booze*hound*⟩ ⟨chow*hound*⟩

²hound \"\ *vt* -ED/-ING/-S [ME (Sc dial.) *hounden*, fr. *hound*, n.] **1 a :** to hunt, chase, or track with hounds or as if with hounds **b :** to pursue unrelentingly ⟨was ~*ed* by his creditors⟩ **:** heckle or harass unceasingly ⟨~*ed* from office by the press⟩ **2 :** to set on the chase **:** incite to pursuit ⟨~ a dog at a hare⟩ — often used with *on* ⟨~ on pursuers⟩ **syn** see BAIT

³hound \"\ *n* -s [ME *hune, hownde*, of Scand origin; akin to ON *hūnn* cube, knob at the top of a masthead, young of an animal, bear cub — more at CAVE] **1 hounds** *pl* **:** the framing at the masthead of a ship for supporting the heel of the topmast and the upper parts of the lower rigging **2 :** a sidebar connecting the tongue of a wagon with the forecarriage or the reach with the hind carriage in order to give additional rigidity to those parts

hound band *n* **:** an iron band at the mast hounds of a ship for attaching the shrouds

hound color *n* **:** a color pattern typical of hound breeds and consisting of black and tan distributed in clearly defined patches on a white ground

hound dog *n, chiefly South* **:** HOUND

hound·er \'hau̇ndə(r)\ *n* -s **:** one that hounds

houndfish \'ˌˌ\ *n* [ME, fr. *hound* + *fish*] **1 :** DOGFISH 1 **2 :** NEEDLEFISH

hound·ing \'hau̇ndiŋ\ *n* -s [³*hound* + -*ing*] **:** the portion of a mast between the hounds and deck or of a bowsprit between the cap and gammon iron

hound·ish \'hau̇ndish\ *adj* **:** of, relating to, or having the characteristics of a hound ⟨a mongrel with a vaguely ~ look⟩

houndman \'hau̇n(d)mən\ *n, pl* **houndmen :** a keeper of hounds

hound-marked \'ˌˌ\ *adj* **:** marked with hound color

hound music *n* **:** the baying of hounds on a scent

houndsbane \'hau̇n(d)zˌˌ\ *n* -s **:** HOREHOUND

houndsberry *n* [ME *houndesberye*, fr. *hound* + *berye* berry — more at BERRY] **1** *obs* **:** BLACK BRYONY **2** *obs* **:** BLACK NIGHTSHADE

houndsfoot \'ˌˌ\ *n* -s [¹*hound* + *foot*; intended as trans. of G *hundsfott* or D *hondsvot*, lit., dog's vulva] *archaic* **:** a worthless rascal

houndshark \'ˌˌ\ *n* **:** DOGFISH 1

hound's-tongue \'ˌˌ\ *n, pl* **hound's-tongues** [ME *houndestunge*, fr. OE, fr. *hund* dog + *tunge* tongue — more at HOUND, TONGUE] **1 :** any of various coarse plants of the genus *Cynoglossum* (esp. *C. officinale*) having tongue-shaped leaves and reddish flowers succeeded by nutlets covered with barbed prickles **2 :** YELLOW CLINTONIA

houndstooth check *or* **hound's-tooth check** \'ˌˌ-\ *n* **:** a small broken-check pattern; *also* **:** a fabric woven in this pattern

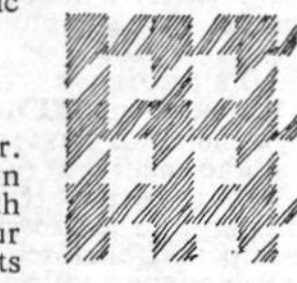

houndstooth check

houndy \'hau̇ndē\ *adj* **:** HOUNDISH

houpe *var of* ⁴HOOP

houp-la *var of* HOOPLA

houppe·lande \'hü,pländ, ˌˌ\ *n* -s [F, fr. OF *hoppelande*] **:** a loose belted overgown of the 14th and 15th centuries usu. with long wide sleeves, dagged edges, a fur lining, and full-length skirt often with slits in it

hour \'au̇(ə)r, 'au̇ə, *esp in the South* 'au̇wə(r\ *n* -s [ME *our, hour*, fr. OF *ore, ure, hore, hure, heure*, fr. LL & L; LL *hora* canonical hour, fr. L, season of the year, time of day, part of the day, hour, fr. Gk *hōra* — more at YEAR] **1 hours** *pl* **a :** the times of the day ecclesiastically set for prayer (as matins and vespers) — see CANONICAL HOUR **b :** the prayers appointed for such times ⟨book of ~*s*⟩ **2 a** *obs* **:** the 12th part of the time between sunrise and sunset or between sunset and sunrise and hence of varying duration **b :** the 24th part of a mean solar day **:** 60 minutes of mean solar time **3 a :** the time of day expressed in hours and minutes as indicated by a timepiece ⟨the ~ is half past ten⟩ ⟨what are you doing here at this ~⟩; *specif* **:** the number of full hours elapsed since noon or midnight ⟨the clock has just struck the ~⟩ **b :** the time reckoned from midnight to midnight — used chiefly in the armed services ⟨dinner would come about 1700 ~*s* —*Infantry Jour.*⟩ ⟨a conference at 0900 ~*s*⟩ **4 a :** a fixed, stated, or customary time or period of time ⟨~*s* of business⟩ ⟨during his leisure ~*s*⟩ ⟨cocktail ~⟩ **b :** a particular time ⟨help in his ~ of need⟩ ⟨hottest ~*s* of the day⟩ **c hours** *pl* **:** time of going to bed ⟨late ~*s* ruined his health⟩ ⟨keep early ~*s* out here in the country⟩ **5 :** one twelfth of a natural day or of a natural night as determined by sunrise and sunset and assigned in astrology to the special influence of a planet — called also *inequal hour, planetary hour* **6 a :** 60 minutes of sidereal time **b :** an angular unit of right ascension equal to 15 degrees measured along the equinoctial **7 :** a unit of measure of work equal to the normal amount done in an hour (as a token of presswork) **8 :** a measure of distance estimated by the time normally taken to cover it ⟨the city was two ~*s* away⟩ **9 a :** a class session or period ⟨~ tests, lasting fifty minutes each, are given several times during the semester⟩ **b :** CREDIT HOUR, SEMESTER HOUR ⟨three-*hour* course⟩ — **after hours** *adv* **1 a :** after the close of the regular working day ⟨worked on his invention at home *after hours*⟩ **b :** after classroom hours **2 :** after the legal closing time set for a public place (as a saloon) — **on the hour** *adv* **:** at exactly the full hour ⟨from 8 a.m. to 10 p.m. trains leave every hour *on the hour*⟩

hour·age \'au̇(ə)rij\ *n* -s **:** aggregate working or traveling time in hours
hour angle *n* **:** the angle between the celestial meridian of an observer and the hour circle of a celestial object measured westward from the meridian — compare MERIDIAN ANGLE
hour circle *n* **1 :** a circle of the celestial sphere passing through the two poles **2 :** the circle upon an equatorial telescope mounted perpendicular to the polar axis and graduated in hours and subdivisions of hours of right ascension **3 :** a small metal circle attached to the pole of an artificial globe and divided into 24 parts to mark differences of time at different places
¹hourglass \'ˌ=,=\ *n* [*hour* + *glass*] **1 :** an instrument for measuring time consisting of a glass vessel having two symmetrical compartments from the uppermost of which a quantity of sand, water, or mercury occupies an hour in running through a small aperture into the lower one and an hour returning when the instrument is turned upside down **2 :** the space of time measured by an hourglass

hourglass

²hourglass \"\ *adj* **:** shaped like an hourglass ⟨~ waistline⟩ ⟨~ contraction of the stomach⟩ ⟨~ tumor⟩
hourglass screw *or* **hourglass worm** *n* **:** HINDLEY'S SCREW
hourglass spider *n* **:** a black widow or a closely related spider
hourglass stomach *n* **:** a stomach divided into two communicating cavities by a circular constriction usu. caused by the scar tissue around an ulcer
hour hand *n* **:** the index showing the hour on a timepiece
hou·ri *or* **hu·ri** \'hu̇rē, 'hürē, 'hau̇rē, –i\ *n* -s [F *houri*, fr. Per *hūrī*, fr. Ar *ḥūrīyah*, sing. of *ḥūr* (in *ḥūr al-'ayn* fair black-eyed women)] **1 :** one of the dark-eyed virgins of perfect beauty that in Muslim belief live with the blessed in paradise **2 :** a voluptuously beautiful young woman
hour·less \'=ləs\ *adj* **:** being outside of time **:** TIMELESS
hour line *n* **:** a dial line for indicating the hour
hour–long \'=¦=\ *adj* **:** lasting for an hour ⟨*hour-long* radio program⟩
¹hour·ly *pronunc at* HOUR + lē *or* li\ *adv* [ME, fr. *hour* + *-ly* (adv. suffix)] **1 :** at or during every hour **:** FREQUENTLY **:** CONTINUALLY ⟨strife, which ~ was renewed —John Dryden⟩
²hourly \"\ *adj* [*hour* + *-ly* (adj. suffix)] **1** *obs* **:** happening within an hour **:** BRIEF, RECENT **2 :** happening or done every hour **:** occurring hour by hour **:** renewed hour by hour **:** FREQUENT, CONTINUAL ⟨~ train service⟩ ⟨in ~ expectation of the rain's stopping⟩ **3 :** using an hour as the unit for determining an amount (as for reckoning wages) ⟨engaged and paid on an ~ basis⟩
hourly–rated \¦=¦=\ *adj* **:** receiving a fixed wage of a certain amount per hour — contrasted with *salaried*
hours *pl of* HOUR
hour wheel *n* **:** the wheel in a timepiece that carries the hour hand
hou·sa·ton·ic \ˌhüsə'tänik, -üzə-\ *n* -s *usu cap* [fr. the *Housatonic* river, Mass. & Conn.] **:** STOCKBRIDGE
¹house \'hau̇s; *sing. possessive* -au̇səz, -au̇zəz\ *n, pl* **hous·es** \-au̇zəz *chiefly substand* -au̇səz\ *often attrib* [ME *hous*, fr. OE *hūs*; akin to OHG & ON *hūs* house, Goth gud*hūs* temple, and prob. to OE *hȳd* hide — more at HIDE] **1 a :** a structure intended or used for human habitation **:** a building that serves as one's residence or domicile esp. as contrasted with a place of business **:** a building containing living quarters for one or a few families — sometimes used at law of a room or other part of such a building; see BUNGALOW, COTTAGE, MANSION; APARTMENT BUILDING, BOARDINGHOUSE, DWELLING HOUSE, LODGING HOUSE, ROOMING HOUSE, TENEMENT HOUSE; compare APARTMENT, HOME, HOMESTEAD, HOTEL, INN, TENEMENT **b :** regular existence in or as if in a house ⟨left home to set up ~ in another town⟩ ⟨children imitating their elders by playing ~⟩ **c :** a place of habitation, rest, or abode ⟨~ of death⟩ ⟨fleshly ~ of the soul⟩ **d** *dial Eng* **:** the chief living room (as the kitchen) of a farmhouse or cottage **2 a :** something (as a shell, nest, den) that serves an animal for shelter or habitation ⟨muskrat ~⟩ **b :** a building in which something is kept or stored ⟨carriage ~⟩ ⟨reptile ~⟩ ⟨a ~ for hens⟩ **3 a :** MUNDANE HOUSE **b :** a zodiacal sign regarded as the seat of a planet's greatest influence — called also *mansion, planetary house* **c** *obs* **:** a square on a chessboard **d :** the circular area 12 feet in diameter surrounding the tee within which a curling stone must rest in order to count **4 a** *archaic* **:** those who dwell in the same house **:** HOUSEHOLD ⟨himself believed and his whole ~ —Jn 4:53 (AV)⟩ **b :** a family of ancestors, descendants, and kindred **:** a race of persons from the same stock; *esp* **:** a noble family ⟨the great ~*s* of England⟩ **5 a :** the residence of a religious community **b :** the members of a religious community **6 a :** a college in a university **b :** a hall or dormitory in a college or school ⟨~ dinner⟩; *also* **:** the students in a hall or dormitory ⟨~ team⟩ **7 a :** one of the estates of a kingdom or other government assembled in parliament or legislature **:** a body of men united in a legislative capacity ⟨the *House* of Lords⟩ *also* **:** a quorum of such a body — see HOUSE OF ASSEMBLY, HOUSE OF COMMONS, HOUSE OF DELEGATES, HOUSE OF REPRESENTATIVES **b :** the building or the chamber in which such a body holds its sessions **8 :** a body of men forming a deliberative or consultative assembly esp. of an ecclesiastical or a collegiate character ⟨~ of bishops⟩ ⟨~ of convocation⟩ **9 a :** a business organization **:** FIRM, PARTNERSHIP ⟨banking ~⟩ ⟨~ of tea importers⟩ ⟨printing ~⟩ ⟨publishing ~⟩ **b** (1) **:** the operators of a gambling game **:** the management of a gambling establishment ⟨a percentage of each pot goes to the ~⟩ (2) **:** a gambling establishment **:** CASINO **10 a :** HOTEL, RESTAURANT, BARROOM ⟨have a drink on the ~⟩ **b :** BROTHEL **11 a :** a building for dramatic or musical performances **:** THEATER **b :** an audience esp. in a theater ⟨playing to small ~*s*⟩ ⟨a good ~ at the opening⟩ ⟨I'll concentrate on acting, because I don't have to count the ~ —*Newsweek*⟩ **12 :** a structure rising above the deck of a tanker or cargo ship that encloses living quarters or the bridge **13** *archaic Brit* **:** WORKHOUSE — used with *the* **14 :** a clump of trees or shrubs growing on a slight elevation in a Florida prairie **15** *Brit* **:** any of several lotto or keno games
²house \'hau̇z, *chiefly substand* -au̇s\ *vb* -ED/-ING/-S [ME *housen*, fr. OE *hūsian*, fr. *hūs* house] *vt* **1 a :** to provide with a permanent dwelling place or living quarters ⟨trying to feed and ~ his family⟩ **b :** to lodge or shelter temporarily ⟨guests were *housed* in a separate cottage⟩ **:** find shelter for **c :** to confine within a house ⟨*housed* with a bad cold⟩ — often used with *up* ⟨*housed* up all day in these four walls⟩ **d :** to store in a house ⟨~ garden tools in a shed⟩ **2 a :** to encase, enclose, or shelter as if by putting in a house ⟨so timorous a soul *housed* in so impressive a body —A.W.Long⟩ **b :** to stow or secure in a safe place ⟨~ the upper spars of a ship⟩ ⟨~ a yacht for the winter⟩ **c :** to cover (a deck) with a roof **3 :** to serve as shelter for **:** CONTAIN ⟨those caves may ~ snakes⟩ ⟨library ~*s* thousands of volumes⟩ ⟨former stately homes now ~ professional and business offices⟩ **4 :** to provide (as a play or opera) with a theater **5 :** to fit (as machinery or gears) with shrouds or protective walls or housings **6 a :** to cut a housing in (as a timber) **b :** to insert into or put together by means of a housing ~ *vi* **1 :** to take shelter **:** find refuge **:** LODGE, DWELL, HARBOR ⟨graze where you will, you shall not ~ with me —Shak.⟩ — used often with *up* ⟨~ up in a cave for the winter⟩ **2** *of a planet* **:** to have position in a mundane house or a mansion
³house \'hau̇s, -au̇z\ *n, pl* **hous·es** \-au̇zəz,-au̇səz\ [ME *houce, house*, fr. MF *houce, housse*, of Gmc origin; akin to MHG *hulst, hulft* covering, OE *heolstor* darkness, cover — more at HOLSTER] **:** ²HOUSING
⁴house \'hau̇z, -au̇s\ *vt* -ED/-ING/-S **:** to cover with or as if with a housing **:** CAPARISON ⟨a gaily *housed* horse⟩
house agent *n, chiefly Brit* **:** a real-estate broker or agent
house amish *n, usu cap A* **:** Amish Mennonites who have no churches, who purposely avoid owning church property, and who worship in the various homes of members on a rotating basis
house ant *n* **:** any of various ants common in human dwellings — compare PHARAOH ANT
house arrest *n* **:** confinement often under guard to one's house or quarters or a hospital instead of in a jail or prison
house bill *n* **:** a bill originating in the U.S. House of Representatives
house board *n* **:** a display board on the front of a theater
¹houseboat \'=,=\ *n* [¹*house* + *boat*] **1 :** a barge fitted up with cabins and designed for use as a dwelling or for leisurely cruising in quiet waters **2 :** a yacht having sleeping accommodations for several people

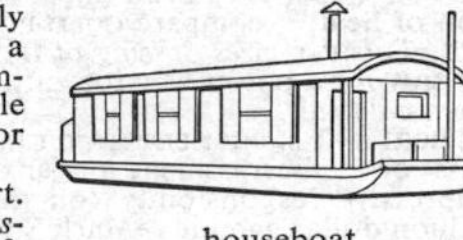
houseboat

²houseboat \"\ *vi* **:** to live or cruise in a houseboat
housebote \'=,=\ *n* -s [part. trans. of (assumed) ME *housbote* (whence ML *husbota* & AF *ousbote*), fr. ME *hous* house + *bote* repair, deliverance — more at BOOT] **:** wood allowed to a tenant for repairing a house — compare ESTOVERS
housebound \'=,=\ *adj* **:** confined to the house ⟨bad weather kept us ~ for days⟩ ⟨~ with a severe cold⟩
houseboy \'=,=\ *n* **:** HOUSEMAN 1
¹house·break \'hau̇s,brāk\ *vi* [back-formation fr. *housebreaker* & *housebreaking*] **:** to commit housebreaking
²housebreak \"\ *vt* [back-formation fr. *housebroken*] **1 :** to train (an animal or a baby) to live in a domestic environment with respect to sanitary habits **2 a :** to teach acceptable social manners to **:** accustom to indoor living **:** make tractable or polite **b :** to break the spirit of **:** TAME, SUBDUE
house·break·er \-kə(r)\ *n* [ME *housbreker*, fr. *hous* house + *breker* breaker] **1 :** one that commits housebreaking **2** *chiefly Brit* **:** one that pulls down old buildings **:** WRECKER
housebreaking \'=,==\ *n* [¹*house* + *breaking*] **1 :** an act of breaking open and entering with a felonious purpose the dwelling house of another by day or night — compare BURGLARY **2 :** an act of pulling down old buildings
housebroken \'=,==\ *or* **housebroke** \'=,=\ *adj* **:** trained to live in a house **:** adjusted to indoor conditions ⟨~ dog⟩ ⟨~ plant⟩
housebuilder \'=,==\ *n* **:** one whose business is to build houses
house–building rat \'=,==-\ *n* **:** a large Australian rat (*Leporillus conditor*) that builds a large nest of sticks
houseburn \'=,=\ *n* **:** an injury to tobacco leaves in the curing barn resulting from fungus activity caused by excess moisture — compare POLE ROT
house car *n* **1 :** an enclosed freight car (as a boxcar, refrigerator car, stockcar) **2 :** a railroad car for handling goods to be loaded or unloaded at a freight house
housecarl \'=,=\ *also* **hus·carl** \'hüs,-\ *n* [OE *hūscarl*, fr. ON *hūskarl*, fr. *hūs* house + *karl* carl — more at HOUSE, CARL] **:** a member of the small standing army or bodyguard of a Danish or early English king or noble
house cat *n* **:** CAT 1a
house centipede *n* **:** a widespread long-legged centipede (*Scutigera coleoptrata*) common in damp sheltered places (as the cellars of buildings) and believed to be valuable as a destroyer of flies, roaches, and other noxious insects
house·clean \'hau̇,sklēn\ *vb* [back-formation fr. *housecleaning*] *vi* **1 :** to remove dirt and accumulated rubbish from a house, room, or building **:** clean a house and its furniture **2 :** to get rid of unwanted or useless or obnoxious items or people **:** clean house ~ *vt* **1 :** to set (a house or room) in order by thorough cleaning of surfaces and furnishings **2 :** to improve or reform (as an administrative department) by ridding of undesirable people or inefficient practices
housecleaner \'=,==\ *n* [*house* + *cleaner*] **:** one that housecleans
housecleaning \'=,==\ *n* [*house* + *cleaning*] **1 :** the removal of dirt and rubbish from a house esp. after long accumulation ⟨spring ~⟩ **2 :** the act of improving or reforming by removal of undesirable, inefficient, or corrupt elements ⟨a thorough ~ which will sweep away the cobwebs of learning and clear our attics of academic lumber —Marjorie Nicolson⟩ ⟨urged that a thorough ~ was needed to rid the business of sharp practices —*Advertising Age*⟩
housecoat \'=,=\ *n* **:** an informal garment for wear around the house: as **a :** a woman's one-piece usu. long-skirted garment that has a front closing and is similar in cut to a dressing gown or negligee ⟨wearing . . . an emerald-green taffeta ~ —Edmund Wilson⟩ **b :** a man's lounging coat or jacket usu. of fine material (as silk or velvet) — compare SMOKING JACKET
housecraft \'hau̇s,kraft\ *n, Brit* **:** HOUSEHOLD ART
house cricket *n* **:** any of various crickets living in or about dwellings; *esp* **:** a widely distributed American cricket (*Acheta domesticus*)
house crow *n* **:** a common crow (*Corvus splendens*) of India familiar as a scavenger and resembling the hooded crow of Europe
housed *past of* HOUSE
house detective *or* **house dick** *n* **:** one who is employed by a department store, hotel, or place of entertainment to prevent disorderly or improper conduct of patrons
housedoor \'=,=\ *n* **:** the front or main door of a house
house drain *n* **:** the horizontal drain in a basement that receives the waste discharge from stacks and extends a few feet outside the foundation — called also *building drain, collection line*
house dramatist *n* **:** a writer of plays for a particular theater
housedress \'=,=\ *n* **:** a dress with simple lines suitable for work about the house and made usu. of a washable printed fabric
house dust *n* **:** an airborne respiratory allergen of uncertain origin found about houses and held to be the chief cause of nonseasonal hay fever
house·fast \'hüs,fast\ *adj, chiefly Scot* **:** HOUSEBOUND
housefather \'=,==\ *n* **:** the father or male head of any collection of persons living together as a family; *specif* **:** a man in charge of a dormitory, hall, or hostel for young people or children
house finch *n* **:** a small redheaded finch (*Carpodacus mexicanus*) closely related to the purple finch and represented by several races in the western U.S. and Mexico including the common familiar house finch (*C. m. frontalis*) that often nests about houses and is a good singer
house flag *n* **1 :** a flag with an emblem denoting a commercial house or line to which a merchant ship belongs **2 :** the personal flag of a yacht owner
housefly \'=,=\ *n* **1 :** a two-winged fly (*Musca domestica*) with mouthparts adapted for lapping or sipping that is found in all habitable parts of the world, being often a most abundant and familiar insect about human habitations during the warm part of the year and acting as a mechanical agent in transmitting diseases (as typhoid fever) by alighting on infected substances and then on food **2 :** any of various flies of similar appearance or habitat (as the lesser housefly or the stable fly)
housefront \'=,=\ *n* **:** the facade of a house
house·ful \'hau̇,sfu̇l\ *n* -s **:** as much or as many as a house will accommodate ⟨~ of guests⟩
house fungus *n* **:** any of several saprophytic fungi (as *Coniophora cerebella* and *Merulius lacrymans*) developing upon and rotting wood exposed to moisture in houses
housefurnishings \'=,===\ *n pl* **:** furnishings for a house; *esp* **:** small articles of household equipment (as kitchen utensils)
house girl *n* **:** HOUSEMAID
house god *n* **:** HOUSEHOLD GOD
houseguest \'=,=\ *n* **:** a guest staying overnight or longer
househeating \'=,==\ *n* **1 :** HOUSEWARMING **2 :** central heating of a dwelling
¹house·hold \'hau̇,sōld, -au̇s,hō-\ *n* [ME *houshold*, fr. *hous* house + *hold*] **1** *obs* **a :** the maintaining of a house **:** HOUSEKEEPING **b :** household goods and chattels **2 :** those who dwell under the same roof and compose a family **:** a domestic establishment; *specif* **:** a social unit comprised of those living together in the same dwelling place **3 households** *pl* **:** ALL-PURPOSE FLOUR
²household \"\ *adj* [ME *houshold*, fr. *houshold*, n.] **1 :** of or relating to a household **:** DOMESTIC ⟨~ tasks⟩ **2 :** FAMILIAR **:** COMMON ⟨~ remedy⟩ ⟨~ legend⟩
household ammonia *n* **:** dilute ammonia water for household use often containing small amounts of detergents
household art *n* **:** one of the arts or techniques (as cooking, sewing, baby care) concerned with the maintenance and care of a household — usu. used in pl.
household economics *n pl but usu sing in constr* **:** HOME ECONOMICS
house·hold·er \-də(r)\ *n* [ME *housholder*, fr. *hous* + *holder*] **1 :** the master or head of a family **:** one who occupies a house or separate tenement with his family or alone **2 :** FREEHOLDER
house·hold·er·ship \-(r),ship\ *n* **:** the position or status of a householder
household franchise *n* **:** the right of voting in parliamentary and other elections in Great Britain restricted before 1918 to householders
household god *n* **1 household gods** *pl* **:** LARES AND PENATES **2 :** a deeply respected or revered person, thing, idea, or custom ⟨the Victorian *household gods* Respectability, Prudery and Humbug squat smugly on their pedestals —*N.Y.Herald Tribune*⟩
house·hold·ing \-diŋ\ *n* [ME *housholding*, fr. *hous* + *holding*, gerund of *holden* to hold — more at HOLD] **:** the management or occupation of a house or tenement
house·hold·ry \-drē\ *n* -ES **:** HOUSEHOLDING, DOMESTIC ECONOMY, HOUSEKEEPING
household stuff *n, archaic* **:** housefurnishings and furniture
household troops *n pl* **:** troops appointed to attend and guard a sovereign or his residence
household word *n* **:** a common word or phrase **:** BYWORD ⟨*penicillin* has become a new *household word* —W.E.Swinton⟩
house·keep \'hau̇,skēp\ *vi* [back-formation fr. *housekeeping* & *housekeeper*] **:** to keep house **:** act as housekeeper; *esp* **:** to prepare meals regularly for oneself and family ⟨a large cafeteria for those who do not wish to ~ —Diana Rice⟩
house·keep·er \-pə(r)\ *n* [ME *howskepare*, fr. *hows, hous* house + *kepare, keper* keeper — more at KEEPER] **1** *archaic* **:** HOUSEHOLDER **2** *obs* **:** one who exercises hospitality **3 a :** a woman who is employed on a permanent basis to do the work in a private home either supervised by or taking the place of a housewife ⟨she came as a general domestic but we gave her the status of ~ —Margo Fischer⟩ **b :** a woman who is employed in a hotel or an institution to supervise the cleaning personnel **4 :** one in charge of a house **:** CARETAKER, JANITOR
housekeeping \'=,==\ *n* [*house* + *keeping*] **1** *archaic* **:** the state of occupying a dwelling house as a householder **2 :** the care or management of domestic concerns **:** the management of a house and home affairs **3 :** the physical care and control of industrial or state property to ensure maintenance, proper and full utilization, and disposition
¹housel *n* -s [ME, fr. OE *hūsel* sacrifice, Eucharist; akin to Goth *hunsl* sacrifice, and prob. to Av *spənta-* holy, Lith *šventas*] *archaic* **:** the Eucharist or the act of administering or receiving it
²housel *vt* -ED/-ING/-S [ME *houselen*, fr. OE *hūslian*, fr. *hūsel*, n.] *archaic* **:** to administer the Eucharist to
houseleek \'=,=\ *n* [ME *howsleke*, fr. *hows, hous* house + *leke, lek* leek — more at HOUSE, LEEK] **:** a plant of the genus *Sempervivum*: as **a :** a common European succulent (*S. tectorum*) found on old walls and roofs and having pink flowers and leaves clustered in a basal rosette which produces numerous offsets **b :** a plant (*S. soboliferum*) having the offsets produced high among the leaves of the rosette
house·less \'hau̇slǝs\ *adj* [ME *housles*, fr. *hous* + *-les* -less] **1 :** destitute of the shelter of a house **:** SHELTERLESS, HOMELESS ⟨~ wanderer⟩ **2 :** destitute of houses ⟨~ desert⟩ — **house·less·ness** *n* -ES
house·let *n* -s \-lǝt\ **:** a very small house
houselights \'=,=\ *n pl* **:** the lights that illuminate the spaces in a theater occupied by an audience before and after performance on the stage ⟨the ~ went down and the footlights came up —W.L.White⟩ ⟨the ~ darkened and the curtain rose —Thyra S. Winslow⟩
houseline \'=,=\ *n* [so called fr. the use of small tarred lines to wrap around large ropes] **:** a light rope made of three strands left-laid and used for seizing
house machine *n* **:** a mechanical device for laying and forming rope
house magazine *n* **:** HOUSE ORGAN
house·maid \'hau̇s,mād\ *n* **:** a female servant employed to do housework
house·maid·ing \-diŋ\ *n* -s **:** the work of a housemaid
housemaid's knee *n* [so called fr. its frequent occurrence among servant girls who work a great deal on their knees] **:** a swelling over the knee due to an enlargement of the bursa in the front of the patella
house·man \'hau̇smǝn\ *n, pl* **housemen 1 :** one hired to perform general work or the heavy duties about a house, hotel, or similar establishment — called also *houseboy* **2 :** an attendant in a gambling house who sells and cashes in chips, collects house fees from players, explains rules, or plays games for the house **3 a :** HOUSE DETECTIVE **b :** BOUNCER 3 **4** *chiefly Brit* **:** ⁴INTERN 1b
house martin *n* **:** ²MARTIN 1
housemaster \'=,==\ *n* **:** a master in charge of a house in a boys' boarding school
housemastership \'=,==,=\ *n* **:** the position of a housemaster
housemate \'=,=\ *n* **:** one that lives in the same house with another
housemistress \'=,==\ *n* **1 :** a mistress of a house **2 :** a woman in charge of a house in a girls' boarding school
house mite *n* **:** CLOVER MITE
house money *n* **:** money used or set aside for household expenses
house mosquito *n* **:** any of various mosquitoes frequenting houses; *esp* **:** a widespread mosquito (*Culex pipiens*) of Europe and No. America
house moss *n, dial* **:** rolls of soft dust that commonly collect on floors and under furniture
housemother \'=,==\ *n* **:** a mother of a family **:** a woman living at the head of a household or small community; *specif* **:** a woman acting as hostess, chaperon, and often as housekeeper in a dormitory, hall, or hostel where young people or children reside
house mouse *n* **:** a mouse that frequents houses; *esp* **:** a common nearly cosmopolitan usu. gray mouse (*Mus musculus*) that lives and breeds about buildings and is important as a consumer of human food, as a vector of diseases, and as an experimental animal
hous·en \'hau̇z³n\ *dial pl of* HOUSE
house of assembly : a legislative body or the lower house of a legislature (as in the American colonies and various British colonies, protectorates, and countries of the Commonwealth)
house of assignation : a house maintained and used for illicit sexual intercourse **:** BROTHEL
house of cards : CARDHOUSE
house of commons : the lower house of a legislative body in some countries (as Great Britain, Canada)
house of correction : an institution where persons are confined who have committed a minor offense and are considered capable of reformation — compare REFORMATORY
house of delegates : the lower house of the legislature of some states (as Virginia, Maryland)
house of detention 1 : a place where prisoners and occasionally witnesses are detained pending a criminal trial **2 :** DETENTION HOME
house officer *n, Brit* **:** ⁴INTERN 1b
house of god *cap G* [trans. of LL *domus Dei*] **:** TEMPLE, CHURCH — called also *house of prayer, house of worship*
house of ill fame *or* **house of ill repute :** BROTHEL
house of issue : an investment bank that originates new security offerings for public distribution or joins with other houses in purchase groups that underwrite such offerings
house of life : HOUSE OF THE ASCENDANT
house of mercy 1 : a charitable institution for lodging, relieving, or reclaiming those in distress or disgrace **2 :** HOSPITAL
house of office [ME *hous of offyce*] *obs* **:** a building or room (as a kitchen or pantry) used for domestic purposes; *esp* **:** PRIVY
house of refuge : a charitable institution for giving shelter and protection to the homeless or destitute
house of representatives : the lower house of the legislature of many countries and states

house of the ascendant [ME *hous of the ascendent*] **:** the first mundane house
house of worship *or* **house of prayer :** HOUSE OF GOD
house organ *n* **1 :** a publication typically in magazine format issued periodically by a business concern to further its interest among employees and sales personnel or among agents and customers **2 :** a publication put out by or for a professional group with relevant matter of special interest
house painter \ˈ=,==\ *n* **:** one whose business or occupation is painting houses
houseparent \ˈ=,==\ *n* **:** one of a married couple in charge of a dormitory, hall, or hostel where children or young people reside **:** HOUSEFATHER, HOUSEMOTHER
house party *n* **:** a gathering and entertainment lasting over one or more nights of a party of guests usu. in a house in the country; *also* **:** the guests in a house
housephone \ˈ=,=\ *n* **:** a telephone that is connected to the switchboard of a building (as a hotel or apartment house) but not directly to the exchange
house physician *n* **:** a physician who is employed by and lives in a hospital — compare ⁴INTERN 1b, RESIDENT
house place *n, dial* **:** ¹HOUSE 1d
houseplant \ˈ=,=\ *n* **:** a plant grown or kept indoors
housepride \ˈ=,=\ *n* **:** pride in one's house or housekeeping
house–proud \ˈ=,=\ *adj* **:** proud of one's house or housekeeping
hous·er \ˈhaùzə(r)\ *n* -s [²*house* + *-er*] **1 :** one that promotes or administers housing projects **2 :** HOUSEBOAT
house–raising \ˈ=,==\ *n* **:** the joint erection of a house or its framework by a gathering of neighbors
house rat *n* **:** any of several rats (as the black rat) common about dwellings
houseroom \ˈ=,=\ *n* **:** space for accommodation in a house **:** LODGING ⟨getting food, raiment, and ~ for three people ashore —Joseph Conrad⟩
house rule *n* **:** a rule applying to a game only among a certain group or in a certain place (as a gambling house)
houses *pl of* HOUSE, *pres 3d sing of* HOUSE
house seat *n* **:** a seat (as in a theater) reserved by the management for special guests
house sewer *n* **:** a prolongation of a house drain extending from a few feet outside a foundation to a connection with a public sewer in the street or alley — called also *building sewer*
house shrew *n* **:** a common European shrew (*Crocidura russula*) sometimes found in barns and other outbuildings
house slipper *n* **:** a slipper for indoor wear — compare BEDROOM SLIPPER
housesmith \ˈ=,=\ *n* **:** an ironworker who assists in erecting a steel skeleton or other steelwork used in buildings
house snake *n* **1 :** MILK SNAKE **2 :** any of several harmless African colubrid snakes (genus *Boaedon*) that live chiefly on mice and rats
house sparrow *n* **:** a sparrow (*Passer domesticus*) native to most of Europe and parts of Asia that has been intentionally introduced into America, Australia, New Zealand, and elsewhere to destroy insects and caterpillars although it feeds largely upon grain seeds — called also *English sparrow*
house spider *n* **:** any of various spiders (as members of the genus *Tegenaria*) that habitually live in buildings
house staff *n* **:** the resident physicians and surgeons in a hospital
house steward *n* **:** one employed to manage the domestic affairs of a large household or a club
house surgeon *n* **:** a surgeon fully qualified in his specialty and resident in a hospital
house–to–house \ˌ==ˈ=\ *adj* **:** made or applying successively to all the residences in an area ⟨a *house-to-house* canvass for signatures⟩
housetop \ˈ=,=\ *n* **:** the roof of a house; *esp* **:** the level surface of a flat roof — **from the housetops** *adv* **:** for all to hear **:** PUBLICLY, OPENLY ⟨shouted *from the housetops* that our defenses were fully adequate —F.D.Roosevelt⟩
house track *n* **:** a railroad track alongside or inside a freight house for loading and unloading cars **:** STATION TRACK
house trailer *n* **:** a trailer that can be used as living quarters
house–train \ˈ=,=\ *vt, chiefly Brit* **:** ²HOUSEBREAK
house trap *n* **:** a trap in the house drain for preventing the entrance of gases from a sewer
house·ward \ˈhaùswə(r)d\ *adv* **:** toward the house **:** HOMEWARD

house trailer

housewares \ˈ=,=\ *n pl* **:** HOUSEFURNISHINGS
housewarming \ˈ=,==\ *n* **:** a party to celebrate the taking possession of a house or premises
¹**house·wife** \ˈhaù,swīf *or esp in sense 2* ˈhəzəf *or* ˈhəsəf\ *n, pl* **house·wives** \-īvz,-əfs\ [ME *houswif,* fr. *hous* house + *wif* woman, wife — more at HOUSE, WIFE] **1 :** a married woman in charge of a household; *specif* **:** a married woman who occupies herself with the domestic affairs of her household and who engages in no employment for pay or profit **2 :** a pocket-size container (as a bag or roll of cloth) for carrying small articles (as thread, needles, scissors) — called also *hussy*
²**housewife** \ˈhaù,swīf\ *vb* -ED/-ING/-S *vt, archaic* **:** to manage with skill and economy **:** HUSBAND ~ *vi, archaic* **:** ECONOMIZE
house·wife·li·ness \-īflēnəs -lin-\ *n* -ES **:** the quality or state of being housewifely
house·wife·ly \-īflē, -li\ *adj* **:** relating, belonging, or appropriate to a housewife ⟨~ virtues⟩ ⟨~ indignation over high prices⟩ **:** DOMESTIC, THRIFTY
house·wife·ry \ˈhaù,swīf(ə)rē, -ri, *chiefly Brit* -swəf-\ *n* -ES [ME *houswiferie,* fr. *houswif* + *-erie* -ery] **:** the business of a housewife **:** HOUSEKEEPING
house·wif·ish \-,swīfish\ *adj* **:** belonging or appropriate to a housewife **:** DOMESTIC, PETTY
housework \ˈ=,=\ *n* **:** the work of housekeeping (as kitchen work, sweeping, scrubbing)
houseworker \ˈ=,==\ *n* **:** one that does general housework for wages **:** HOUSEMAID
housewrecker \ˈ=,==\ *n* **:** WRECKER 1b
house wren *n* **:** a common wren (*Troglodytes aedon*) that nests about houses and walls throughout the U.S. and migrates south in winter
housewright \ˈ=,=\ *n* **:** a builder of wooden houses **:** a house carpenter
housey–housey *or* **housie–housie** \ˌhaùsiˈhaùsi\ *n* -s [¹*house* + *-ie* or *-ey* (var. of *-ie*)] *Brit* **:** HOUSE 15
¹**hous·ing** \ˈhaùziŋ, -zēŋ\ *n* -s [ME; partly fr. *hous,* n., house + *-ing;* partly fr. gerund of *housen* to house — more at HOUSE] **1 :** SHELTER, LODGING **2 a :** the act of putting under shelter **b :** the act of living in a house **3 :** dwellings provided for numbers of people or for a community ⟨~ for the aged⟩ **4 a :** something that covers or protects (as of boards over a ship's deck) **b :** a case or enclosure esp. for a machine or part, an instrument, a lamp ⟨the differential ~ on an automobile⟩ **c :** a tube or cylindrical sleeve or casing (as an enclosed bearing) in which a shaft revolves **5 :** a portion of a mast that is beneath the deck or of a bowsprit that is inboard **6 a :** the space taken out of a structural member (as a timber) to admit the insertion of part of another — compare MORTISE **b :** a hollowed space (as a niche) for holding a piece of sculpture **7** [perh. fr. D *huizing* (fr. *huis* house + *-ing*) or LG *hüsing,* fr. *hus* house + *-ing*)] **:** HOUSELINE
²**housing** \ˈ"\ *n* -s [ME, fr. *house* housing + *-ing* — more at HOUSE] **1 :** an ornamental cover for a horse's saddle **2 housings** *pl* **:** TRAPPINGS, ORNAMENTATION
housing development *n* **:** a group of individual dwellings or of apartment houses commonly of similar design and built and leased under one management — compare COLONY 4c
housing estate *n, Brit* **:** HOUSING DEVELOPMENT
housing project *n* **:** a publicly supported and administered housing development planned usu. for low-income families
hous·ton \ˈ(h)yüstən\ *adj, usu cap* [fr. *Houston,* Tex.] **:** of or from the city of Houston, Texas ⟨a *Houston* shopping center⟩ **:** of the kind or style prevalent in Houston
hous·to·nia \(h)yüˈstōnēə, hüˈ-,hauˈ-\ *n* [NL, fr. William *Houston* †1733 Scot. botanist + NL *-ia*] **1** *cap* **:** a genus of No. American herbs (family Rubiaceae) with entire leaves and small blue, lilac, or white tubular lobed flowers — see BLUET **2** -s **:** any plant of the genus *Houstonia*
hous·to·ni·an \(h)yüˈstōnēən\ *n* -s *cap* [*Houston,* Tex. + E *-ian*] **:** a native or resident of Houston, Texas
hous·ton's fold *or* **houston's valve** \ˈ(h)yülstənz-, ˈhül, ˈhaù|\ *n, usu cap H* [after John *Houston* †1845 Irish surgeon] **:** any of the valvular folds in the lining of the rectum
hout·ing \ˈhaùdiŋ\ *n* -s [D, fr. MD *houtic,* perh. fr. *hout* wood; akin to OHG *holz* wood — more at HOLT] **:** an anadromous fish (*Coregonus oxyrhynchus*) of the North sea that ascends rivers and estuaries of northwestern Europe to spawn
hou·tou \ˈhü(,)tü\ *n* -s [modif. of Arawak *hotoli,* of imit. origin] **:** a So. American motmot (*Momotus momota*)
hou·va·ri \ˌ(h)üvəˈrē\ *n* -s [AmerSp *huvari, hurivari*] **:** a severe thunderstorm with strong land breezes in the West Indies
ho·va \ˈhōvə, ˈhüv-\ *n, pl* **hova** *or* **hovas** *usu cap* **1 a :** the dominant native people of central Madagascar **b :** a member of such people — compare MALAGASY **2 :** the language of the Hova people
¹**hove** *past of* HEAVE
²**hove** *vb* -ED/-ING/-S [fr. *hove,* past of *heave*] *vi, archaic* **:** RISE, HEAVE ~ *vt, archaic* **:** to lift or swell up **:** RAISE
³**hove** \ˈhōv\ *dial Eng var of* HALF
⁴**hove** *vi* -ED/-ING/-S [ME *hoven*] *obs* **:** HOVER 1, 4
hoved *dial past of* HEAVE
¹**hov·el** \ˈhəvəl *sometimes* ˈhäv-\ *n* -s [ME] **1** *chiefly dial* **:** an open shed or canopy for sheltering livestock or protecting produce **2 a :** TABERNACLE **b :** a niche like those that replace pinnacles on some Gothic churches and shelter statues **3 a :** a shed or open-roofed shelter for human beings **b :** a poor cottage **:** a small mean house **:** HUT **4 :** a large conical or conoidal brick structure within which a firing kiln is built
²**hovel** \ˈ"\ *vt* **hoveled** *or* **hovelled; hoveled** *or* **hovelled; hoveling** *or* **hovelling** \-v(ə)liŋ\ **hovels 1 :** to put in a hovel **:** provide with a roof ⟨~ thee with swine, and rogues forlorn —Shak.⟩ **2 :** to shape (as a chimney) like a hovel or hut
³**hov·el** \ˈhävəl *also* ˈhəv-\ *vb* **hoveled** *or* **hovelled; hoveled** *or* **hovelled; hoveling** *or* **hovelling; hovels** [back-formation fr. *hoveler*] *vt, Brit* **:** to aid (a ship) by pilotage, unloading, or landing passengers ~ *vi, Brit* **:** to aid ships in the capacity of a hoveler
hov·el·er *or* **hov·el·ler** \-v(ə)lə(r\ *also* **huf·fler** \ˈhəflə(r\ *n* -s [origin unknown] **1 :** a usu. unlicensed coast boatman who does odd jobs in assisting ships or goes out to wrecks to land passengers or secure salvage **2 :** a boat that is used by a hoveler
¹**ho·ven** \ˈhōvən\ *archaic & dial past part of* HEAVE
²**hoven** \ˈ"\ *adj* [fr. archaic past part. of *heave*] **:** afflicted with bloat
³**hoven** \ˈ"\ *n* -s **:** BLOAT 2
ho·ve·nia \hōˈvēnēə\ *n, cap* [NL, fr. David ten *Hove* †1787 Dutch senator + connective *-n-* + NL *-ia*] **:** a genus of Asiatic trees or shrubs (family Rhamnaceae) having alternate serrate leaves, small greenish flowers, and indehiscent fruit
¹**hov·er** \ˈhəvə(r) *also* ˈhäv-\ *vb* **hovered; hovered; hovering** \-v(ə)riŋ\ **hovers** [ME *hoveren,* freq. of *hoven* to hover] *vi* **1 a :** to hang fluttering in the air or on the wing ⟨the hawk ~*ed* searching the ground below⟩ **:** remain floating or suspended about or over a place or object ⟨clouds of smoke ~*ed* over the building⟩ **b** *of an airplane* **:** to maintain altitude without forward motion **2 a :** to hang about **:** move to and fro near a place threateningly, watchfully, uncertainly, irresolutely ⟨doormen annoy me . . . ~*ing* anxiously over people —Evelyn Barkins⟩ ⟨the shark was still ~*ing* about —Francis Birtles⟩ ⟨the thermometer ~*ed* around 90⟩ ⟨the boat ~*ed* outside the three-mile limit⟩ **b :** to be in a state of uncertainty, irresolution, or suspense ⟨when he was hesitating or ~*ing* over a word —David Abercrombie⟩ ⟨~*ing* uncomfortably behind a cigar —Tennessee Williams⟩ ⟨the country ~*ed* on the brink of famine⟩ **3 :** to crouch in hiding **:** COWER ⟨as if a gash had been torn in the web of restraint behind which she forced him to ~ —Marcia Davenport⟩ ⟨the bathtub fell . . . and crushed the woman ~*ing* in the cellar —*Springfield (Mass.) Union*⟩ **4** *dial Brit* **:** WAIT, LINGER ~ *vt* **1** *obs* **:** to flutter (the wings) so as to remain suspended in air **2 :** to brood over ⟨a hen ~*s* her chicks⟩
²**hover** \ˈ"\ *n* -s **1 :** the act or state of hovering ⟨the sweep and ~ of the pale birds —Mary H. Vorse⟩ ⟨the smoke from the croft house rises, a ~ of peat-scented blue —Naomi Mitchison⟩ **2 :** a group of trout **3 a** *dial* **:** a shelter (as an overhanging bank or hedge) for an animal or fish **b :** a floating island of vegetation **4 :** a canopy or other device for holding the heat of a brooder near the floor or ground so that it is available to young birds or animals cared for in the brooder
hov·er·er \-vərə(r)\ *n* -s **:** one that hovers
hover fly *n* **:** a syrphus fly or other fly that hovers in air
hover hawk *n* **:** a kestrel (*Falco tinnunculus*)
hovering *adj* **:** SUSPENDED, UNCERTAIN, WAVERING, POISED — **hov·er·ing·ly** *adv*
hovering accent *or* **hovering stress** *n* **:** distribution of energy, pitch, or duration in two adjacent syllables in some utterance of verse when a heavy syllable occurs next to a syllable bearing the metrical ictus so that for perception the stress seems to be divided or diffused nearly equally over both (as *cornfield* in the line "that o'er'/the green'/cornfield/did pass'")
hovering act *n* [fr. gerund of ¹*hover*] **:** an act prohibiting or regulating the roving or hovering of domestic or foreign ships within certain limits; *esp* **:** an act providing for the boarding of foreign ships and inspection of cargo manifests outside the three-mile limit (as within four leagues of the coast) in order to enforce revenue or security laws esp. for protection of the commerce of a coastal nation
hoverplane \ˈ=,=\ *n, Brit* **:** HELICOPTER
hove to *adv (or adj)* [fr. past part. of *heave to*] **:** in a stationary position with head to wind **:** at a standstill ⟨ore freighters *hove to* in the fog —Richard Bissell⟩ ⟨lying *hove to* on the fishing bank⟩
Ho·vis \ˈhōvəs\ *trademark* — used for a wheat flour or bread made from it that includes wheat germ made inactive by heating
¹**how** \(ˈ)haù\ *adv* [ME *hou, how,* adv & conj., fr. OE *hū;* akin to OFris *hū, hō* how, OS *hū, hwō,* OHG *hwuo* how, OE *hwā* who — more at WHO] **1 a :** in what manner or way ⟨~ explain behavior so contrary to the principles of good authorship —G.M.Fess⟩ ⟨the continuing problems of . . . ~ to say what we mean —Stuart Chase⟩ ⟨learn ~ to enter a room properly⟩ ⟨tell him ~ to do it⟩ — often used as an intensive ⟨~ they laughed⟩ **b :** by what means or process ⟨at his wit's end regarding ~ to support himself —C.S.Forester⟩ ⟨question of ~ to increase the benefits under the . . . Retirement System —W.J.Kennedy⟩ **c** *obs* **:** SOMEHOW, ANYHOW ⟨by ransom or ~ else —John Milton⟩ **2 a :** to what extent, degree, number, or amount ⟨~ little we know of human motives⟩ ⟨~ far can he be trusted⟩ **b :** by what measure or quantity ⟨concerned with ~ much to eat⟩ ⟨decided ~ deep to cut⟩ ⟨~ hard do you plan to make it⟩ **3 a :** in what state, condition, or plight ⟨~ are things at home⟩ ⟨~ are you⟩ ⟨~ are you off for money⟩ **b :** at what price ⟨~ is the market today⟩ **4 a :** for what reason or excuse ⟨in the face of his own knowledge, ~ can he make such a statement —Weston LaBarre⟩ **:** for what possible or plausible reason ⟨~ could he have said that⟩ — often used with *ever* ⟨~ can I ever leave you⟩ **b :** from what cause **:** WHY ⟨~ did you come to sell your house⟩ **5 a :** *archaic* **:** by what name or designation ⟨~ art thou called —Shak.⟩ **b :** with what meaning **:** to what effect ⟨~ are we to interpret such behavior⟩ **6 a :** what in that case **:** what then ⟨~ if, when I am laid into the tomb, I awake before the time —Shak.⟩ ⟨~ if I had denounced you when you forced your way in there —Max Peacock⟩ **b :** WHAT — used to introduce or imply a question ⟨~ about the other one, do you want it too⟩ ⟨~ say you, maiden, will you wed —W.S.Gilbert⟩ or in requests to repeat what has not been understood ⟨~ is that again⟩ **c** *dial* **:** what did you say **7** — used to express surprise or admiration ⟨~ co you like that⟩ — **and how** — used as an intensive ⟨prices are going up, *and how*⟩ — **how about :** what do you say to or think of ⟨*how about* a game of tennis⟩ **:** would you like to have ⟨*how about* some more pie⟩ or give ⟨*how about* a couple of dollars until payday⟩ or agree to ⟨well, *how about* it, are you coming⟩ — **how come :** how does it happen that **:** WHY ⟨*how come* you're here so early⟩ — **how do you do :** HELLO — used to express a polite greeting or formal salutation face-to-face — **how so :** how is that so **:** what do you mean **:** WHY ⟨it won't work? *how so*⟩
²**how** \ˈ"\ *conj* [ME *hou, how*] **1 a** (1) **:** the way or manner in which ⟨it was odd ~ writers never seemed to have anything to do except write —Martha Gellhorn⟩; *also* **:** the state or condition in which (2) **:** to what degree or extent ⟨knows ~ small the town is⟩ (3) **:** of the way or manner in which ⟨be careful ~ you talk⟩ **b :** THAT ⟨told them ~ he had a situation —Charles Dickens⟩ **2 :** in whatever way or manner **:** AS ⟨a reader can shift his attention ~ he likes —William Empson⟩
³**how** \ˈhaù\ *n* -s [¹*how*] **1 :** the manner or method in which something is done or comes about ⟨most of the film is devoted to the grim ~*s* and not the difficult whys of battle —John McCarten⟩ **2 :** a question concerning manner or method ⟨the eternal whys and ~*s* of small children —Jeanne Massey⟩
⁴**how** \ˈhü\ *n* -s [ME *houwe, how,* fr. OE *hūfe* — more at CYPHELLA] **1** *Scot* **:** COIF, HOOD; *esp* **:** NIGHTCAP **2** *Scot* **:** an infant's caul
⁵**how** \ˈhaù\ *n* -s [ME, fr. ON *haugr* hill; akin to OHG *houg* hill, ON *hār* high — more at HIGH] *now dial Eng* **:** a low hill **:** MOUND, HILLOCK — used chiefly in place names
⁶**how** \ˈ"\ *interj* [ME] **1** *now chiefly dial* — used to attract attention or express greeting ⟨~ now, my masters!⟩ or to urge on (as a sheep dog) ⟨~ sheep!⟩ **2** *chiefly Scot* — used to express pain or grief
⁷**how** \ˈhaù\ *var of* HOWE
⁸**how** \ˈhaù\ *interj* [of Siouan origin; akin to Dakota *háo,* Omaha *hau*] — used as a greeting esp. in imitation of American Indian speech
⁹**how** \ˈ"\ *usu cap* — a communications code word for the letter *h*
how *abbr* howitzer
how·ard·ite \ˈhaùə(r),dīt\ *n* -s [Luke *Howard* †1864 Eng. meteorologist + E *-ite*] **:** a stony meteorite composed essentially of anorthite, olivine, and bronzite
¹**how·be·it** \(ˈ)haùˈbēət\ *adv* [ME *how be it*] **:** be it as it may **:** NEVERTHELESS ⟨~, the whole problem . . . cannot be solved —G.A.Llano⟩
²**howbeit** \ˈ"\ *conj* **:** ALTHOUGH ⟨are highly ingenious . . . and pleasantly diverting, ~ in certain passages of somewhat low-brow content —Ben Crisler⟩
¹**howd** \ˈhaùd\ *vi* -ED/-ING/-S [origin unknown] *chiefly Scot* **:** to move from side to side or up and down
²**howd** \ˈ"\ *n* -s **:** a lurching rocking movement
how·dah *or* **hou·dah** \ˈhaùdə\ *n* -s [Hindi *hauda,* fr. Ar *haudaj*] **:** a seat or covered pavilion on the back of an elephant or camel
how·der \ˈhaùdər\ *vt* -ED/-ING/-S [freq. of *howd*] *chiefly Scot* **:** to heap or crowd together **:** HUDDLE
how·die *or* **how·dy** \ˈhaùdi\ *n, pl* **howdies** [origin unknown] *chiefly Scot* **:** MIDWIFE
how do \(ˈ)haùdˈdü\ *interj* [short for *how do you do*] *dial* — used to express greeting

howdah

how–do–you–do *also* **how–d'ye–do** *or* **how–de–do** \ˌhaùdəyəˈdü, -dəyēˈdü, ˌhaùdēˈdü, -aùdiˈdü, (ˈ)haùdˈdü\ *n* [fr. the phrase *how do you do?* or *how d'ye do?*] **:** an embarrassing situation **:** a troublesome fix ⟨this is a pretty *how-do-you-do*⟩
¹**how·dy** \ˈhaùdē, -di\ *interj* [alter. of *how do*] — used to express greeting
²**howdy** \ˈ"\ *vb* -ED/-ING/-ES *vt, dial* **:** to say the words *how do you do* to ~ *vi, dial* **:** to exchange greetings
¹**howe** \ˈhaù\ *n* -s [ME (northern dial.) *how,* alter. of *holl* — more at HOLL] **1** *chiefly Scot* **:** HOLLOW, DEPRESSION; *esp* **:** VALLEY **2** *Scot* **:** the middle part of a night or of winter
²**howe** \ˈ"\ *adj* [ME (northern dial.) *how,* alter. of *holl* — more at HOLL] *Scot* **:** HOLLOW, DEEP
³**howe** \ˈ"\ *adv, Scot* **:** in a hollow voice ⟨it spak right ~, my name is Death —Robert Burns⟩
⁴**howe** \ˈhō, ˈhaù\ *dial Eng var of* HOE
how·ea \ˈhaùēə\ *n, cap* [NL, fr. Lord *Howe* island, in the southwestern Pacific] **:** a genus of feather palms having papery spathes and flowers each with 30 to 40 stamens and sunken in pits on the spadix that are succeeded by fruits resembling pecans
ho·wei·tat \(ˌ)hōˌwāˈtat\ *n, pl* **howeitat** *or* **howeitats** *usu cap* **1 :** a Bedouin people of northern Arabia **2 :** a member of the Howeitat people
¹**how·el** \ˈhaù(ə)l\ *n* -s [prob. fr. LG *höwel* plane, fr. MLG *hövel;* akin to OHG *hubil* hill, OE *hȳf* beehive — more at HIVE] **1 :** a cooper's plane having a convex sole for smoothing the insides of casks and for chamfering, crozing, and chiming **2 :** a rounded cut above and below the croze in a barrel stave
²**howel** \ˈ"\ *vt* **howeled** *or* **howelled; howeled** *or* **howelled; howeling** *or* **howelling; howels :** to smooth with a howel
how·ell \ˈhaù(ə)l\ *n* -s *usu cap* [after E. C. *Howell* †1907 Am. journalist and whist expert] **1 :** HOWELL SYSTEM **2 a :** a duplicate game conducted by the Howell system **b :** a game of duplicate bridge in which match-point scoring is used
howell–jol·ly body \-zhōˈlē, -ˈjälē-\ *n, usu cap H&J* [after William H. *Howell* †1945 Am. physiologist and Justin M. J. *Jolly* †1953 Fr. physician] **:** one of the basophilic granules that are probably nuclear fragments, that sometimes occur in red blood cells, and that indicate by their appearance in circulating blood that red cells are leaving the marrow while incompletely mature (as in certain anemias)
howell settlement *n, usu cap H* [after E. C. *Howell*] **:** a method of scoring in the game of hearts whereby after the play of each deal each player puts into a pot for every heart he has taken as many chips as there are other players in the game and withdraws from the pot the number of chips representing the difference between 13 and the number of hearts he has taken
howell system *or* **howell movement** *n, usu cap H* [after E. C. *Howell*] **:** a method of conducting a game of duplicate bridge or whist so that each pair plays one set of boards against each other pair — compare MITCHELL MOVEMENT
howe truss \ˈhaù-\ *n, usu cap H* [after William *Howe* †1852 Am. inventor] **:** a truss having vertical and diagonal members between the upper and lower horizontal members

Howe truss

how·ev·er \haù-ˈ(w)evə(r)\ *conj* [ME, fr. *how* + *ever*] **1a :** in whatever manner or way ⟨can go ~ he likes⟩ **b :** no matter to what degree or extent ⟨~ much he gives her, she wants more⟩ **2** *archaic* **:** ALTHOUGH ⟨*howe'er* thou art a fiend, a woman's shape doth shield thee —Shak.⟩
²**however** *adv* **1a :** to whatever degree or extent ⟨has done this for ~ many thousands of years —Emma Hawkridge⟩ ⟨every device, ~ paltry, was resorted to —W.H. Prescott⟩ **b :** in whatever manner or way ⟨shall serve you, sir, truly, ~ else —Shak.⟩ **2 :** in spite of that **:** on the other hand **:** BUT ⟨it still seems possible, ~, that conditions will improve⟩ ⟨I would like to go; ~, I think I'd better not⟩ **3** *archaic* **:** at all events **:** at least **:** in any case **4 :** how in the world ⟨~ did you manage it⟩
¹**howf** *or* **howff** \ˈhaùf\ *n* -s [D *hof* enclosure, burial ground, garden, resort; akin to OE *hof* enclosure, court, dwelling, temple, OHG, court, garden, landed property, ON, enclosure, roofed temple, OE *hȳf* beehive — more at HIVE] **1** *chiefly Scot* **:** a dwelling place **2** *chiefly Scot* **:** an accustomed haunt or resort; *specif* **:** a favorite tavern
²**howf** *or* **howff** \ˈ"\ *vi* -ED/-ING/-S **1** *Scot* **a :** to take up one's abode **:** LODGE **b :** to make frequent visits **2** *Scot* **:** to take shelter
how·go·zit curve \haùˈgōzət-\ *n* [alter. of the phrase *how goes it?*] **:** a running graph of the progress of an airplane flight involving the distance covered, fuel consumed, and time elapsed and enabling the pilot to determine the equitime point
how·ish \ˈhaùish\ *adj* [short for *I don't know howish,* fr. the phrase *I don't know how* + *-ish*] *archaic* **:** feeling vaguely ill
how·it·zer \ˈhaùətsə(r)\ *n* -s [D *houwitser,* fr. G *haubitze,* fr.

MHG *haufnitz* ballista, fr. Czech *houfnice*] **:** a cannon shorter than a gun of the same caliber employed to fire projectiles at medium muzzle velocities at relatively high angles of elevation at a target (as enemy artillery behind a ridge) which cannot be reached by flat-trajectory weapons

[1]**howk** \'hōk\ *dial Brit var of* HAWK

[2]**howk** \"\ *vb* -ED/-ING/-S [ME *holken;* akin to MLG *holken* to hollow out; derivatives fr. the root of OE *hol* hollow — more at HOLE] *vt, dial Brit* **:** to hollow out **:** EXCAVATE, DIG — often used with a preposition ⟨lobsters had got at it . . . and ~*ed* pieces out of it —E.F.Benson⟩ ~ *vi, dial Brit* **:** DIG ⟨the dog was ~*ing* in the yard⟩

howk·it \'hau̇kət\ *adj* [fr. Sc past part. of [2]*howk*] *Scot* **:** dug up **:** hollowed out

[1]**howl** \'hau̇l, *esp before pause or consonant* -au̇əl\ *vb* -ED/-ING/-S [ME *houlen;* akin to MD *hūlen* to howl, MHG *hiulen, hiuweln* to howl, OHG *hūwila* owl, Gk *kōkyein* to shriek, wail, lament, Skt *kauti* he cries out] *vi* **1 :** to utter or emit a loud sustained doleful sound or outcry characteristic of dogs and wolves ⟨wolves ~*ing* in the arctic night⟩ ⟨the only sound is a melancholy wind ~*ing* —John Buchan⟩ **2 :** to cry out or exclaim with lack of restraint and prolonged loudness through strong impulse, feeling, or emotion ⟨the scalded men ~*ing* in agony⟩ ⟨the hungry mob ~*ed* about the Senate house, threatening fire and massacre —J.A.Froude⟩ ⟨proctors ~*ing* at the blunder⟩ **3 :** to go on a spree or rampage ⟨this is my night to ~⟩ ~ *vt* **1 :** to utter or announce noisily with unrestrained demonstrative outcry ⟨newsboys ~*ing* the news⟩ **2 :** to affect, effect, or drive by adverse outcry — used esp. with *down* ⟨supporters of the Administration . . . ready to ~ down any suggestion of criticism —*Wall Street Jour.*⟩ **syn** see ROAR

[2]**howl** \"\ *n* -S **1 :** a loud protracted mournful rising and falling cry characteristic of a dog or a wolf **2 a :** a prolonged cry of distress **:** WAIL **b :** a yell or outcry of disappointment, rage, or protest **3 :** PROTEST, COMPLAINT ⟨raise a ~ over high taxes⟩ ⟨set up a ~ that he was being cheated⟩ **4 :** something that provokes laughter ⟨his act was a ~⟩ **5 :** a noise produced in an electronic amplifier usu. by undesired regeneration of alternating currents of audio frequency **:** OSCILLATION — called also *squeal*

howl·er \'hau̇lə(r)\ *n* -S **1 :** one that howls; *specif* **:** a professional wailer for the dead **2 :** HOWLER MONKEY **3 :** a glaringly stupid and ridiculous blunder esp. in the use of words ⟨his autobiography is spotted with ~*s* such as his description of the winter of 1938–39 as one of "peaceful preparation for war" —Geoffrey Parsons †1956⟩ **4 :** an electric buzzer **syn** see ERROR

howler monkey *or* **howling monkey** *n* **:** any of various So. and Central American monkeys having a long prehensile tail and a peculiar enlargement of the hyoid and laryngeal apparatus enabling them to make remarkable howling noises and constituting the genus *Alouatta*

howl·et \'hau̇lət, *dial Brit* 'hül-\ *n* -S [ME *howlat, howlott,* prob. fr. *oule, owle, howle* owl + *-at, -ott* (vars. of *-et*) — more at OWL] **1** *now dial* **:** OWL, OWLET **2** *dial Brit* **:** a noisy dirty person

howling *adj* **1 :** producing, filled with, or marked by howling ⟨~ storm⟩ **2 :** WILD, SAVAGE, DESOLATE ⟨~ wilderness⟩ **3 :** very great **:** EXTREME, PRONOUNCED ⟨~ success⟩ — **howl·ing·ly** *adv*

how·lite \'hau̇,līt\ *n* -S [Henry *How* †1879 Canadian mineralogist + E *-lite*] **:** a mineral $Ca_2SiB_5O_9(OH)_5$ consisting of a white nodular or earthy calcium borosilicate

howm \'hau̇m\ *chiefly Scot var of* [1]HOLM

how·rah \'hau̇rə\ *adj, usu cap* [fr. *Howrah,* India] **:** of or from the city of Howrah, India **:** of the kind or style prevalent in Howrah

hows *pl of* HOW

how's about [by alter.] *substand* **:** how about

how·ship's lacuna \'hau̇,ships-\ *n, usu cap H* [after John *Howship* †1841 Eng. anatomist] **:** a groove or cavity containing osteoclasts in bone that is undergoing absorption

how·so \'hau̇(,)sō\ *adv* [ME, fr. *how* + *so*] *archaic* **:** HOWEVER

how·so·ev·er \¦hau̇sə¦wevə(r), -(,)sō¦ev-\ *adv* [ME, fr. *how* + *so* + *ever*] **1 :** in what manner soever **:** to whatever degree or extent ⟨I am glad he's come, ~ he comes —Shak.⟩ **2** *archaic* **:** HOWEVER

how·som·ev·er \¦hau̇sə¦mevə(r)\ *adv* [alter. of *howsoever*] *chiefly dial* **:** HOWSOEVER, NEVERTHELESS, HOWEVER

how–to \'=¦tü\ *adj* [fr. *how to* in phrases like *how to make a birdhouse*] **:** giving practical instruction and advice (as on a craft, trade, hobby) ⟨publishing paperbound books, mostly of a *how-to* nature —*Publishers' Weekly*⟩ ⟨the magazine has a regular *how-to* section⟩

hox \'häks\ *vt* -ED/-ING/-ES [ME *hoxen,* fr. *hox* hock sinew, fr. OE *hōhsinu,* fr. *hōh* heel + *sinu, seonu* sinew — more at HOCK, SINEW] **1 :** HAMSTRING **2 :** to pester by following **:** HARASS, ANNOY

[1]**hoy** *or* **hoi** \'hȯi\ *interj* [ME] — used in greeting or in calling attention or in driving animals or to express surprise or alarm

[2]**hoy** \"\ *n* -S **:** HAIL, SHOUT, CALL ⟨better give that boat a ~⟩

[3]**hoy** \"\ *n* -S [ME *hoy, hoye,* fr. MD *hoei*] **1 :** a small usu. sloop-rigged coasting ship formerly used in conveying passengers and goods from place to place or as a tender to larger ships in port **2 :** a heavy barge used for weighty or bulky cargo

[1]**hoya** \'hȯi(y)ə\ *n* [NL, after Thomas *Hoy* †1821 Eng. gardener] **1** *cap* **:** a large genus of climbing Australasian shrubs (family Asclepiadaceae) having fleshy leaves and nectariferous flowers with a rotate corolla and a star-shaped crown — see WAX PLANT, HONEY PLANT **2** -S **:** any plant of the genus *Hoya*

[2]**hoya** \"\ *n* -S [AmerSp, fr. Sp, large hole, pit, ditch, valley, fr. L *fovea* small pit] **:** a valley or basin high in rugged mountains (as the Andes)

[1]**hoy·den** \'hȯidᵊn\ *n* -S [perh. fr. obs. D *heiden* country lout, fr. MD *heidijn, heiden* heathen, one that lives on a heath; akin to OE *hǣthen* heathen — more at HEATHEN] **1** *obs* **:** a rude clownish youth **2 :** a girl or woman of loud, boisterous, or carefree behavior **:** TOMBOY ⟨dancing in public with a troop of country ~*s* —Thomas Hardy⟩

[2]**hoyden** \"\ *vi* -ED/-ING/-S **:** to act like a hoyden

[3]**hoyden** \"\ *adj, of a girl* **:** RUDE, ILL-BRED, ROISTERING

hoy·den·ish \-ᵊnish\ *adj* **:** LIVELY, TOMBOYISH, UNLADYLIKE ⟨horsey, ~, six feet tall and far from shrinking —Sara H. Hay⟩

hoy·den·ism \-ᵊn,izəm\ *n* -S **:** unladylike or tomboyish behavior

[1]**hoyle** \'hȯil, *esp before pause or consonant* -ȯiəl\ *n* -S [origin unknown] **:** a natural object (as a molehill) used as an archery mark at short range

[2]**hoyle** \"\ *n* -S *often cap* [after Edmond *Hoyle* †1769 Eng. writer on games] **:** an encyclopedia of card games and usu. other indoor games; *esp* **:** a book of rules accepted as standard or authoritative

hoyle shooting *n* [[1]*hoyle*] **:** an archery pastime like roving except that the marks are always at short range

hoy·man \'hȯimən\ *n, pl* **hoymen :** one who owns or navigates a hoy

HP *abbr* **1** half pay **2** handmade paper **3** high-pass **4** high power **5** high pressure **6** high priest **7** hire purchase **8** horizontal parallax **9** *often not cap* horsepower **10** house physician **11** House of Parliament

HPH *abbr, often not cap* horsepower-hour

h–pile \'=,=\ *n, cap H* **:** a steel pile having an H-shaped cross section

HPO *abbr* highway post office

h pole *n, cap H* **:** a telegraph pole built up of two parallel poles braced together

hps *abbr* harpsichord

HQ *abbr* **1** headquarters **2** *often not cap* [L *hoc quaere*] look for this; see this

hr *abbr* hour

HR *abbr* **1** high resistance **2** high run **3** home rule **4** home run **5** House of Representatives

hrd *abbr* hard

hr factor \(')ā'chär-\ *n, usu cap H* **:** an agglutinogen present in Rh-negative blood and apparently reciprocally related to the Rh factor

HRH *abbr* Her Royal Highness; His Royal Highness

HRIP *abbr* [L *hic requiescit in pace*] here rests in peace

hrt *abbr* heart

hrtwd *abbr* heartwood

HS *abbr* **1** hemstitched **2** [L *hic sepultus; hic situs*] here is buried **3** high school **4** high speed **5** *often not cap* [L *hoc sensu*] in this sense **6** honorary secretary **7** house surgeon

h's *or* **hs** *pl of* H

h–scope \'=,=\ *n, usu cap H* **:** a radarscope on which signals appear as two dots joined by a line whose slope indicates the angle of elevation — compare B-SCOPE

hse *abbr* house

HSE *abbr* [L *hic sepultus est; hic situs est*] here is buried

h section *n, cap H* **:** a rolled structural metal section with an H-shaped cross section and wide flanges

hsg *abbr* housing

HSH *abbr* Her Serene Highness; His Serene Highness

h–shaped \'=,=\ *adj, cap H* **:** having the shape of a capital H

hsia \'shē'ä\ *n, usu cap H* [Chin (Pek) *hsia*[4]] **1 :** the first dynasty of China said to have been founded by the legendary emperor Yu **2** -S **:** the people of the Hsia dynasty

hsi–fan \'shē'fän\ *n, pl* **hsi–fan** *usu cap H&F* [Chin (Pek) *hsi*[1] *fan*[1] fr. *hsi*[1] west, western + *fan*[1] foreign, barbarous] **:** any of several east Tibetan peoples on the western border of China

hsin \'shin\ *n* -S [Chin (Pek) *hsin*[4]] *Confucianism* **:** the cardinal virtue faithfulness or veracity

hsiung–nu \shē'u̇ŋ'nü\ *n, pl* **hsiung–nu** *usu cap H&N* [Chin (Pek) *hsiung*[1] *nu*[2], fr. *hsiung*[1] cruel, fierce + *nu*[2] slave, servant] **:** an ancient horse-using people related to or identical with the Huns, including the Jung and Ti peoples of Chinese history, and recorded in Chinese annals as being a powerful nation and in the 3d century B.C. occupying all the country between the Caspian sea and the Great Wall and dominating much of Mongolia

HSM *abbr* Her Serene Majesty; His Serene Majesty

h–stretcher \'=,==\ *n, cap H* **:** a common leg brace for furniture consisting of two stretchers from front to back joined by a central crossbar

H-stretcher

ht *abbr* **1** heat **2** height

HT *abbr* **1** half time **2** herd test **3** high-tension **4** high tide **5** *often not cap* [L *hoc tempore*] at this time **6** *often not cap* [L *hoc titulo*] under this title

HTA *abbr* heavier than air

htg *abbr* heating

HTH *abbr* high-test hypochlorite

hu \'hü\ *n, pl* **hu** *or* **hus** *usu cap* [Chin (Pek) *hu*[2], lit., dewlap of an ox] **:** an ancient Tatar people of northwest China related to the Hsiung-Nu

hua \'hyüə\ *n, cap* [NL] **:** a genus of freshwater snails of eastern Asia (family Thiaridae) including important intermediate hosts of the Chinese liver fluke and the human lung fluke

huabi *usu cap, var of* HUAVE

hua·ca \'wäkə\ *or* **gua·ca** \'gw-\ *n* -S [Sp *guaca, huaca,* fr. Quechua *wáka*] **:** an ancient Peruvian sacred object: **a :** GOD, SPIRIT **b :** any object (as a mountain, animal, shrine, or artifact) inhabited by a god or spirit **:** FETISH — compare MANITOU, NAGUAL, ZEMI **c :** a pre-Columbian ruin (as a tomb or burial mound)

hua·co \-(,)kō\ *n* -S [Sp *guaco, huaco,* fr. Quechua *wáko, wáku,* fr. *wáka*] **:** a pre-Columbian relic of Peru (as an object discovered in a tomb)

hua·ji·llo \wä'hē(,)(y)ō\ *also* **hua·ji·lla** \-ē(y)ə\ *n* -S [MexSp *guajillo, huajillo, guajilla, huajilla,* dim. of *guaje* gourd, fr. Nahuatl *huaxin*] **:** either of two honey plants from Texas and adjacent Mexico: **a :** a spiny shrub (*Pithecolobium brevifolium*) **b :** a sweet-scented shrub (*Acacia berlandieri*)

hualapai *or* **hualpai** *usu cap, var of* WALAPAI

hualpi *usu cap, var of* WALPI

hua·mu·chil \wä'mü,chēl\ *or* **gua·mu·chil** \gw-\ *also* **cua·mu·chil** \kw-\ *n* -S [MexSp *guamúchil, huamúchil, cuamúchil* — more at CAMACHILE] **:** CAMACHILE

huanaco *var of* GUANACO

huan·ca·pam·pa \,wäŋkə'pämpə\ *n, pl* **huancapampa** *or* **huancapampas** *usu cap* [Sp, fr. *Huancapampa* (now *Huancabamba*), region of Peru] **:** CHINCHAISUYU

hua·nu·co coca \'wänə,kō-\ *n, usu cap H* [AmerSp (Peru) *huánuco,* prob. fr. *Huánuco,* town and department in Peru] **:** COCA 2a

hua·pan·go \wä'päŋ(,)gō\ *n* -S [MexSp, a festival celebrated in the state of Veracruz, dance typical of this festival, huapango, fr. *Huapango,* town in Veracruz, Mexico] **:** a fast and complicated Mexican couple dance that is usu. performed on a wooden platform to accentuate the rhythmic beating of heels and toes

hua·ra·che \wə'rächē\ *also* **gua·ra·che** \"\ *or* **hua·ra·cho** \-(,)chō\ *n* -S [MexSp *guarache, huarache*] **:** a low-heeled sandal; *esp* **:** a sling-backed sandal having an upper made of interwoven leather thongs

huarache

hua·ri \'wä(,)rē\ *n, pl* **huari** *or* **huaris** *usu cap* [Pg, of AmerInd origin] **1 a :** an Indian people of western Mato Grosso, Brazil **b :** a member of such people **2 :** the language of the Huari people

hua·ri·zo \wä'rē(,)zō, -ē(,)sō\ *n* -S [AmerSp] **:** the offspring of a male llama and a female alpaca

huar·pe \'wär(,)pā\ *n, pl* **huarpe** *or* **huarpes** *usu cap* [Sp, of AmerInd origin] **1 a :** a group of Indian peoples of western Argentina including the Allentiac of the San Juan province **b :** a member of such peoples **2 :** a language family consisting of the languages spoken by the Huarpe peoples — **huar·pe·an** \-pēən\ *adj or n, usu cap*

huasima *var of* GUACIMO

huas·tec *or* **huax·tec** \'wä,stek\ *also* **huas·teca** \wä'stākə, -tekə\ *or* **huas·te·co** \-(,)kō\ *n, pl* **huastec** *or* **huastecs** *or* **huaxtec** *or* **huaxtecs** *usu cap* [Sp *guasteco, guaxteco, huasteco, huaxteco,* of AmerInd origin] **1 a :** an Indian people of the states of San Luis Potosí, Veracruz, and Tamaulipas, Mexico **b :** a member of such people **2 :** the Mayan language of the Huastec people — **huas·tecan** \(')wä¦stäkən, -tek-\ *adj, usu cap*

hua·ve \'wävē\ *or* **hua·bi** \", -äbē\ *n, pl* **huave** *or* **huaves** *or* **huabi** *or* **huabis** *usu cap* [Sp, of AmerInd origin] **1 a :** an Indian people of the region between the lagoons and the Gulf of Tehuantepec, Oaxaca, Mexico **b :** a member of such people **2 :** the language of the Huave people that is without proven affinities — **hua·ve·an** \-vēən\ *adj, usu cap*

huayule *var of* GUAYULE

[1]**hub** \'həb\ *n* -S [prob. alter. of [2]*hob*] **1 a :** the usu. cylindrical central part of a wheel **:** NAVE — compare AXLE BOX **b :** the central part of a propeller or motor-driven fan to which the blades are attached ⟨raising the propeller ~ above water so that we could get the prop off —K.M.Dodson⟩ **2 a :** a chief center of activity **:** FOCAL POINT ⟨heart, ~, and pivot of this new Virginia Metropolis is the Pentagon —A.W.Atwood⟩ ⟨Indianapolis . . . became the ~ of a rail center with lines running in all directions —R.H.Brown⟩ ⟨this fact must serve as the ~ of the analysis —*Political Science Quarterly*⟩ ⟨the ~ of every hemoglobin molecule is one atom of iron —D.C. Peattie⟩ ⟨Boston Statehouse is the ~ of the solar system —O.W.Holmes †1894⟩; *specif* **:** a center of circulation in architectural planning ⟨the dwelling has a novel ~ floor plan, permitting easy access between rooms —*N.Y. Herald Tribune*⟩ **b :** a durable marker placed at an important point of a survey for use (as in triangulation) **3 a :** a steel punch from which a working die for a coin or medal is made and which in modern processes bears the design as cut by a reducing machine copying the engraver's model **b :** [2]HOB 4a(4) **c :** MASTER TAP **d** (1) **:** a boss that resembles the hub of a wheel (2) **:** BARREL 3d **e :** a piece in a lock that is turned by the knob spindle passing through it and that moves the bolt **4 :** a ridge on the backbone of a book (as a leather-bound book) formed by a sewing cord or a strip of cardboard **:** [1]BAND 5b(1) **5 :** a connection or point of confluence: as **a** (1) **:** a short coupling used to join pipes in plumbing (2) *also* **hubb :** BELL 5i **b :** a hole on the panelboard of a piece of electrical equipment into which a wire is plugged **:** electrical contact **c :** the enlarged base by which a hollow needle (as for a hypodermic) may be attached to a syringe or other device **syn** see CENTER

[2]**hub** \"\ *vt* **hubbed; hubbed; hubbing; hubs :** [3]HOB 2b

[3]**hub** \"\ *adj, usu cap* [fr. *the Hub,* nickname for Boston, Mass.] *chiefly NewEng* **:** of or relating to the city of Boston, Mass. ⟨*Hub* officials⟩

hu·ba·bo \(h)ü'bä(,)bō\ *n, pl* **hubabo** *or* **hubabos** *usu cap* [Sp, of AmerInd origin] **1 :** an Indian people of the northern part of the Dominican Republic **2 :** a member of the Hubabo people

hu·bam clover \'hyü,bam-\ *also* **hubam** *n* -S *often cap H* [Harold DeMott *Hughes* *b*1882 Am. agronomist, its discoverer + *Alabama,* state in the U.S., source of the seed for the experimental plot in which it was discovered] **:** an annual variety (*Melilotus alba annua*) of sweet clover

hub–and–spigot joint \,=='==-\ *n* **:** BELL-AND-SPIGOT JOINT

hubba–hubba \¦həbə¦həbə\ *interj* [origin unknown] — used to express approval, excitement, or enthusiasm

hub·bard squash \'həbə(r)d-\ *also* **hubbard** *n* -S *usu cap H* [prob. fr. the name *Hubbard*] **:** any of various winter squashes having the fruit generally ovoid and pointed at the end away from the stem, the skin smooth to strongly warted, and ranging in color from dark green to orange

hub·bell·ite \'həbə,līt\ *n* -S [fr. *Hubbellite,* a trademark] **:** an oxychloride cement that contains finely powdered copper, is fungicidal and germicidal, possesses high tensile strength and adhesive properties, and is resistant to abrasion

hub·ber \'həbə(r)\ *n* -S [[1]*hub* + *-er*] **:** one that sinks hobs into steel for die stamping

hub·bite \'hə,bīt\ *n* -S *usu cap* [the *Hub,* nickname for Boston + E *-ite*] **:** BOSTONIAN

hub·ble \'həbəl\ *n* -S [prob. short for *hubbleshew*] *dial Brit* **:** HUBBUB, UPROAR

hubble–bubble \¦həbəl¦bəbəl\ *n* -S [redupl. of *bubble*] **1 :** WATER PIPE 2; *esp* **:** a rudimentary water pipe sometimes consisting merely of a bowl mounted on a coconut in which there is a hole that serves as a mouthpiece — compare HOOKAH, NARGILEH **2 :** a burble of sound or flurry of activity **:** COMMOTION ⟨for hours a merry but rather tedious *hubble-bubble,* suggesting liquor, was heard ascending from the cabin skylight —R.A.W.Hughes⟩ ⟨the *hubble-bubble* of spring-cleaning —*Manchester Guardian Weekly*⟩

hub·ble·shew *or* **hub·ble·show** \'həbəl,shō, -shü\ *n* -S [perh. fr. obs. Flem *hobbel-sjobbel, hobbel-sobbel* in an uproar, confusedly] *chiefly Scot* **:** UPROAR, TUMULT, COMMOTION

hub·bly \'həb(ə)lē\ *adj* [alter. of *hobbly*] **:** having an uneven surface **:** ROUGH ⟨a ~ road⟩ ⟨a ~ sea⟩

hub·bub \'hə,bəb\ *n* -S [prob. of Celt origin; akin to ScGael *ub ub, ubub,* an interj. of contempt] **1 :** a noisy confusion of sound **:** DIN, UPROAR ⟨a ~ of cocks crowing and children shouting —Alan Moorehead⟩ ⟨~ of an orchestra tuning up⟩ **2 :** a state of tumultuous confusion or excitement **:** TURMOIL ⟨swarmed onto the field in a wild ~ after winning the game⟩ ⟨the animated excitement and ~ that gives the . . . institution its friendly vitality —Aline B. Saarinen⟩ ⟨it behoves culture to . . . save the individual in the midst of this industrial ~ —J.C. Powys⟩ **3 :** an Indian game resembling dice played with bones and a tray — used by New England settlers **syn** see DIN

hub·bu·boo *or* **hub·ba·boo** \¦həbə¦bü\ *n* -S [prob. of Celt origin like *hubbub*] **:** HUBBUB 1, 2

hub·by \'həbē, -bi\ *n* -ES [by alter.] **:** HUSBAND — not often in formal use

hubcap \'=,=\ *n* **:** a removable metal cap screwed or clamped over the end of an axle; *esp* **:** such a cap used on the wheel of a motor vehicle

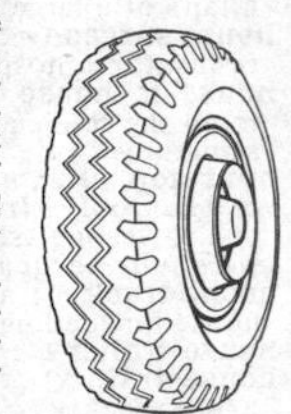
hubcap on an automobile wheel

hu·bris \'h(y)übrə̇s\ *also* **hy·bris** \'hīb-\ *n* -ES [Gk *hybris* — more at OUT] **:** overweening pride or self-confidence **:** ARROGANCE ⟨the very best critics of the past have made so many blunders . . . that our own critics today should be careful to avoid ~ —*Times Lit. Supp.*⟩ — contrasted with *sophrosyne*

hu·bris·tic \hyü'bristik\ *adj* [Gk *hybristikos,* fr. *hybristēs* violent, wanton, insolent man (fr. *hybris*) + *-ikos* -ic] **:** INSOLENT, VAIN, ARROGANT — **hu·bris·ti·cal·ly** \-tə̇k(ə)lē\ *adv*

hubs *pl of* HUB, *pres 3d sing of* HUB

hu·chen \'hükən, -k̲-\ *also* **huch** \-k,-k̲\ *n* -S [G] **:** a large elongate predacious game fish (*Hucho hucho*) of the Danube that resembles the Atlantic salmon but may attain a weight of 130 pounds

huch·nom \'hüchnəm\ *n, pl* **huchnom** *or* **huchnoms** *usu cap* [Yuki] **1 a :** an Indian people of the Eel river valley in northwestern California **b :** a member of such people **2 :** the Yuki dialect of the Huchnom people

hu·cho \'h(y)ü(,)kō\ *n* [NL, fr. G *huchen, huch*] **1** *cap* **:** a European genus of large riverine fishes (family Salmonidae) that are closely related to the salmons and trouts of the genus *Salmo* from which they are distinguished esp. by the absence of teeth along the median line of the hyoid bone **2** -S **:** any fish of the genus *Hucho; esp* **:** HUCHEN

[1]**huck** \'hək\ *vi* -ED/-ING/-S [ME *hukken,* prob. back-formation fr. *hukster, hokster* huckster — more at HUCKSTER] *now dial Eng* **:** HIGGLE, BARGAIN

[2]**huck** \"\ *n* -S [ME *hokebone* — more at HUCKLE] *chiefly dial* **:** HIP, HAUNCH

[3]**huck** \"\ *n* -S [by shortening] **:** HUCKABACK

[4]**huck** \"\ *n* -S [by alter.] *dial* **:** HUSK

huck·a·back \'həkə,bak, -,bək\ *n* -S [origin unknown] **1 :** a textured weave in which yarns are floated on a plain ground to form small allover patterns **2 :** an absorbent durable cotton, linen, or cotton and linen fabric with a huckaback weave used chiefly for towels

huck·le \'həkəl\ *n* -S [akin to ME *hokebone* hip, haunch, and perh. to ON *hūka* to squat — more at HAWKER] **:** HIP, HAUNCH

huckleback \'==,=\ *n* **:** HUMPBACK

[1]**huck·le·ber·ry** \'həkəl- — *see* BERRY\ *n* [perh. alter. of *hurtleberry*] **1 a :** an edible dark-blue to black berry with 10 hard bony nutlets that is typically smaller and more acid than a blueberry **b :** any of several No. American shrubs of the genus *Gaylussacia* (esp. *G. baccata*) whose fruit is a huckleberry — see BOX HUCKLEBERRY **2 :** BLUEBERRY 1: as **a :** a dark-fruited as distinguished from a blue-fruited blueberry **b :** WHORTLEBERRY 1 **c :** a stiff evergreen shrub (*Vaccinium ovatum*) with edible garnet to black berries and glossy foliage much used as greenery in floral arrangements and decorations

[2]**huckleberry** \"\ *vi* **:** to pick or look for huckleberries ⟨go ~*ing*⟩

huckleberry family *n* **:** ERICACEAE

huckleberry oak *n* **:** a low, spreading, often prostrate shrub (*Quercus vaccinifolia*) of southwestern U.S. with slender branches and green leaves that resemble those of the huckleberry

hucklebone \'==,=\ *n* **1 :** HIPBONE, HOOK 5c(2) **2 :** TALUS **3** *archaic* **:** KNUCKLEBONE 2

[1]**huck·ster** \'həkstə(r)\ *n* -S [ME *hukster, hokster,* fr. MD *hokester, hoekster,* fr. *hoeken,* *hoeken* to peddle, bear on the back, squat + *-ster* — more at HAWKER] **1 :** one that sells goods along the street or from door to door **:** HAWKER, PEDDLER **2 a** *archaic* **:** one that buys to resell at a profit **:** MIDDLEMAN **b :** one that acts primarily from mercenary motives **3 a :** one that produces advertising material for commercial clients **:** ADMAN ⟨home is not the plastic chromium dream . . . the ~*s* promised to them —R.W.Kenny⟩; *specif* **:** one that prepares or delivers commercials for radio or television ⟨~*s* speak only to sponsors; and sponsors don't speak at all, they read sales charts —Walter Goodman⟩ ⟨a syrupy-voiced ~ proclaiming the virtues of Dinkelspiel's Deodorant —Bennett Cerf⟩ **b :** one that employs persuasive showmanship to make a sale or attain an objective ⟨the most adroit ~ of $1000 trinkets in our time —Maurice Zolotow⟩ ⟨minds taught to respond without reflection to the slogans of our political ~*s* —*New Republic*⟩

[2]**huckster** \"\ *vb* **huckstered; huckstered; huckstering** \-t(ə)riŋ\ **hucksters** *vi* **:** HAGGLE ⟨~ over prices on the

black market⟩ ~ *vt* **1 :** to deal in or bargain over **:** retail for profit ⟨~ fresh eggs⟩ ⟨~ real estate⟩ ⟨~ his services⟩ **2 :** to promote by showmanship ⟨a store where cheap stuff is ballyhooed and ~*ed* into seeming richness —C.W.Dreppard⟩

huck·ster·er \-t(ə)rə(r)\ *n* -s *archaic* **:** HUCKSTER

huckstering *n* -s [fr. gerund of ²*huckster*] **:** the activities or occupation of a huckster

huck·ster·ism \-tə,rizəm\ *n* -s **:** persuasive showmanship in advertising or selling **:** COMMERCIALISM 2 ⟨sponsoring the Metropolitan Opera broadcasts . . . without the faintest trace of bad taste or ~ —Howard Taubman⟩ ⟨the unashamed ~ practiced by our present government —R.L.Riggs⟩

hud \'həd\ *n* -s [ME *hudde*] *dial Eng* **:** a husk or hull esp. of a berry

hud·ders·field \'hədə(r)z,fēld\ *adj, usu cap* [fr. *Huddersfield*, England] **:** of or from the county borough of Huddersfield, England **:** of the kind or style prevalent in Huddersfield

¹**hud·dle** \'həd³l\ *vb* **huddled; huddled; huddling** \-d(³)liŋ\ **huddles** [prob. fr. or akin to ME *hoderen* to huddle together, wrap up; prob. akin to ME *hiden* to hide — more at HIDE] *vt* **1** *Brit* **:** to throw together or complete carelessly or hurriedly ⟨things happened as in a badly directed moving picture, all *huddled*, all hurried —Donn Byrne⟩ — often followed by a directional adverb ⟨the solemnities had to be *huddled* through at express speed —*Manchester Examiner*⟩ ⟨weakness . . . to ~ up his stories rather than to wind them off to an orderly conclusion —George Saintsbury⟩ **2 :** to conceal from view **:** cover up ⟨political deaths are *huddled* and secret —*Time & Tide*⟩ **3 a :** to mass together **:** CROWD ⟨give me your tired, your poor, your *huddled* masses yearning to breathe free —Emma Lazarus⟩ ⟨ours is a nation in which military and civilian targets are *huddled* together —D. H. McLachlan⟩ ⟨all over the country people are *huddled* round their radios —F.L.Allen⟩ **b :** to draw (oneself) together **:** CROUCH ⟨the men *huddled* themselves low against the wind —A.J.Cronin⟩ ⟨she was *huddled* in his cot, trying to keep warm —Gertrude Atherton⟩ **4** *dial chiefly Eng* **:** HUG, EMBRACE **5 a** *archaic* **:** to herd into or out of a place in a disorderly mass ⟨we were *huddled* out like a flock of sheep, by a file of soldiers —Frederick Marryat⟩ **b :** to pull on unceremoniously or wrap oneself closely in (clothes) ⟨she *huddled* her purple woolen coat round her —Rumer Godden⟩ — often used with *on* ⟨I *huddled* on my clothes —A.T.Quiller-Couch⟩ ~ *vi* **1 a :** to gather in a group **:** press close together **:** ASSEMBLE, BUNCH ⟨passengers . . . ~ like sheep at entrance gates —Bennett Cerf⟩ ⟨an opera chorus ~*s* round a few haughty soloists —G.B. Shaw⟩ ⟨little printers' cafés . . . ~ near the thundering presses —Francis Aldor⟩ **b :** to curl up **:** CROUCH ⟨*huddled* in the lee of a rock, trying to get a little protection from the wind —H.D. Quillin⟩ ⟨a long gray cat *huddled* watchfully in the window —Katherine A. Porter⟩ — often used with *up* ⟨*huddled* up, closed his eyes, and went quite . . . peacefully to sleep —James Hilton⟩ **c :** to dress oneself hurriedly or wrap something around oneself ⟨hip-length coat, with a big collar to ~ —Lois Long⟩ **2** *obs* **:** to act in a precipitate manner ⟨fools ~ on, and always are in haste —Nicholas Rowe⟩ **3 a :** to hold a consultation **:** CONFER ⟨worried financiers *huddled* to discuss the possible effects of the blow on California's economy —*Newsweek*⟩; *specif* **:** to gather behind the scrimmage line in a football game in order to receive the play (as from the quarterback) for the next down **b :** to pause for thought in a bridge game

²**huddle** \"\ *n* -s **1 a :** a close-packed group **:** JUMBLE, BUNCH ⟨~*s* of cows and sheep⟩ ⟨the ugly ~ of weather-beaten shacks and wharves where the fishermen kept their tackle —L.C. Douglas⟩ ⟨~ of meaningless words —Edith Sitwell⟩ ⟨the four harpooners, the cooper, and myself were sitting in a ~ in the steerage —H.A.Chippendale⟩ **b :** a shapeless mass **:** LUMP ⟨a ~ of black against the starlight —Marjory S. Douglas⟩ **2 :** CONFUSION, DISARRAY, MUDDLE ⟨equally free from the dullness of slow or the hurry and ~ of quick time —Earl of Chesterfield⟩ **3 a :** MEETING, DISCUSSION, CONFERENCE ⟨spent some eight hours in a ~ with a dozen laymen and priests —M.E.Bennett⟩ ⟨secret ~*s* were held by five leading Republicans —*Newsweek*⟩ ⟨a ~ of social scientists put the finishing touches on a massive study of American life —F.L.Allen⟩ — often used in the phrase *go into a huddle* ⟨at the end of the bout the judges go into a ~ to determine the winner⟩ ⟨she went into a series of ~*s* with cheese experts —Harry Thompson⟩ ⟨go into a ~ with yourself about it —Mary D. Gillies⟩ **b :** a strategy conference of football players behind the line of scrimmage **c :** a long pause for thought by a bridge player before he bids or plays ⟨went into a ~ before making his first discard —Oswald Jacoby⟩

hud·dler \'həd(³)lə(r)\ *n* -s **:** one that huddles

huddling *adj* **:** in a huddle or hurry **:** JUMBLED, RUSHING ⟨horsemen charged the ~ crowd⟩ ⟨the ~ and tumultuous brook —Sir Walter Scott⟩ — **hud·dling·ly** *adv*

hud·dup \(,)hə'dəp, -dap; hə'rəp, hə'rəp\ *v imper* [perh. alter. of *get up*] — used as a command to horses or oxen to go ahead or go faster

¹**hu·di·bras·tic** \¦hyüdə¦brastik\ *adj, usu cap* [*Hudibras*, mock-heroic satirical poem in octosyllabic couplets by Samuel Butler †1680 Eng. poet + E *-tic* (as in *fantastic*)] **1 :** written in humorous octosyllabic couplets **2 :** smartly and sportively burlesque **:** MOCK-HEROIC — **hu·di·bras·ti·cal·ly** \-tək(ə)lē\ *adv, usu cap*

²**hudibrastic** \"\ *n* -s **:** an octosyllabic couplet used in humorous verse

hud·son bay pine \'hədsən,bā-\ *n, usu cap H&B* [fr. *Hudson bay* or *Hudson's bay*, inland sea in northern Canada] **:** JACK PINE 1

hudson bay sable *n, usu cap H&B* **:** AMERICAN SABLE

hud·so·nia \,həd'sōnēə\ *n* [NL, fr. William *Hudson* †1793 Eng. botanist + NL *-ia*] **1** *cap* **:** a genus of low heathlike No. American herbs (family Cistaceae) with hoary or villous foliage and usu. bright yellow flowers **2 :** any plant of the genus *Hudsonia*

hud·so·ni·an \,həd¦sōnēən\ *adj, usu cap* [*Hudson* (*bay*) + E *-ian*] **1 :** of or relating to Hudson bay **2 :** of, relating to, or being a subdivision of the biogeographic Boreal zone extending across No. America from Labrador to Alaska, being bounded to the south and in certain high mountain regions by the isotherm indicating a mean temperature of 57.2° Fahrenheit during the 6 hottest weeks of the year, and marking the northern extent of the coniferous forest belt

hudsonian chickadee *n, usu cap H* **:** CHICKADEE

hudsonian curlew *n, usu cap H* **:** the No. American variety (*Numenius phaeopus hudsonicus*) of the whimbrel

hudsonian godwit *n, usu cap H* **:** an American godwit (*Limosa haemastica*) with a long slightly upturned bill and underparts that are finely black barred during the spring

hudson's bay blanket *n, usu cap H&B* **:** a heavy woolen blanket with one or more broad stripes usu. black on a red ground or varicolored on a white ground at each end to indicate its weight

¹**hue** \'hyü\ *n* -s [ME *hewe* appearance, shape, kind, color, fr. OE *hīw*, *hēow*; akin to ON *hȳ* fine hair, down, Goth *hiwi* form, appearance, OE *hār* hoary — more at HOAR] **1 :** SHAPE, COMPLEXION, ASPECT ⟨a ghost town in modern ~ —*Springfield (Mass.) Union*⟩ ⟨songs . . . of a sad and somber ~ —William Black⟩ ⟨political parties of every ~ —Louis Wasserman⟩ **2 a :** COLOR 1; *esp* **:** gradation of color ⟨the work of an inspired painter can reveal to us the ~*s* and shades of twilight —Colin Clark⟩ **b :** the attribute of colors that permits them to be classed as red, yellow, green, blue, or an intermediate between any contiguous pair of these — used in psychology; see COLOR 1b **c :** hue in the Munsell color system — used in psychophysics; see the Color Charts explanation at COLOR **syn** see COLOR

²**hue** \"\ *vb* -ED/-ING/-S [ME *hewen* to form, fashion, color, fr. OE *hīwian*, fr. *hīw*, n.] *vt* **:** TINGE ⟨*hued* their sight with rainbow beauty —Peggy Bennett⟩ ~ *vi* **:** to take on color **:** become colored ⟨in highlights it *hued* to dull silver gray —William Beebe⟩

³**hue** \"\ *vb* -ED/-ING/-S [ME *huwen*, fr. OF *huer* to shout, hoot, fr. *hu*, interj. used esp. to apprise of danger] *vi, now dial* **:** to make outcry **:** SHOUT ~ *vt, obs* **:** to shout at **:** drive with shouts

⁴**hue** \"\ *n* -s [ME *hew*, *hu*, fr. OF *hue*, outcry, noise, fr *huer*] **:** SHOUT, OUTCRY

hue and cry *n* [⁴*hue*] **1 a :** a loud outcry used in the pursuit of felons and joined and taken up by all who heard it in the pursuit **b :** the pursuit of a felon or a written proclamation for the capture of a felon or the finding of stolen goods **2 :** a clamor of pursuit or protest ⟨had visions of sheriffs . . . posses and *hue and cry* —Esther Forbes⟩ ⟨conservative politicians joined in the *hue and cry* against the school —Hunter Mead⟩ **3 :** HUBBUB ⟨the unloading . . . was being conducted with a *hue and cry*, with raucous bangs and crashes —Jean Stafford⟩

hueb·ner·ite \'hēbnə,rīt, 'hyüb-\ *n* -s [G *hübnerit*, fr. Adolf *Hübner*, 19th cent. Ger. foundry superintendent + G *-it* -ite] **:** a mineral $MnWO_4$ consisting of manganese tungstate, having a brownish red to nearly black color, occurring in columnar or foliated masses, and being isomorphous with wolframite

hue circle *or* **hue circuit** *also* **hue cycle** *n* **:** COLOR CIRCLE

hued \¦hyüd\ *adj* [ME *hewed* formed, fashioned, colored, fr. OE *gehīwod*, *hīwod*, past part. of *gehīwian*, *hīwian* to hue — more at HUE] **:** COLORED — usu. used in combination ⟨green-*hued*⟩ ⟨rich, many-*hued* prose —Ray Corsini⟩

hue·ful \'hyüfəl\ *adj* **:** having hue and saturation **:** CHROMATIC

hue·huetl \(')wā¦(h)wāt³l\ *n* -s [MexSp, fr. Nahuatl] **:** an ancient vertically cylindrical Mexican Indian drum usu. hollowed from a tree trunk and fitted with a skin head

hue·less \'hyüləs\ *adj* [ME *heweles* shapeless, colorless, fr. OE *hīwlēas*, fr. *hīw* appearance, shape, kind, color + *-lēas* -less — more at HUE] **1 :** COLORLESS **2 :** having no hue **:** GRAY — **hue·less·ness** *n* -ES

huemul *var of* GUEMAL

huer·ta \'wer(,)tä\ *n* -s [Sp, large vegetable garden or orchard, fr. *huerto* small vegetable garden or orchard, fr. L *hortus* garden — more at YARD] **:** a piece of highly cultivated land (as for an orchard) in Spain

¹**huff** \'həf\ *vb* -ED/-ING/-S [imit.] *vi* **1 a :** to emit puffs (as of air or steam) **:** BLOW, PANT ⟨he ~*ed* and he puffed and he blew the house down —*Three Little Pigs*⟩ ⟨another tug ~*s* quietly somewhere down below —W.V.Anderson⟩ **b :** to progress with puffing ⟨the first cyclists ~*ed* into sight —*Time*⟩ **2 a :** to speak in a threatening and bombastic manner **:** make empty threats **:** BLUSTER, RANT ⟨faced with new wage demands, management ~*s* about spiraling costs and the dangers of inflation⟩ ⟨children will soon discover that this is only ~*ing* and puffing on your part —H.R.Litchfield & L.H.Dembo⟩ **b** (1) **:** to react indignantly **:** speak resentfully **:** SNAP, STORM ⟨the father ~*s* and puffs and says, "Do you think I'm made of money" —Peter DeVries⟩ (2) **:** to behave indignantly **:** FLOUNCE ⟨resigned in pique and ~*ed* off to London —Janet Flanner⟩ **3** *archaic* **:** to become angry **:** take offense ⟨the woman has ~*ed* and won't trust me —Frederick Marryat⟩ **4** *now dial* **:** to expand in size **:** ENLARGE ⟨the bread ~*s*⟩ **5 :** to remove an opponent's checker from the board for failure to make a possible jump ~ *vt* **1 a :** to blow into **:** INFLATE, PUFF ⟨it ~*s* air steadily . . . through its hollow shaft —*Newsweek*⟩ ⟨their buying ~*ed* low-priced motor shares —*Time*⟩ **b :** to accomplish with puffing ⟨~*ed* himself up and stumped out of the room —Jackson Burgess⟩ **2** *archaic* **:** to treat with contempt **:** BULLY ⟨quarreling with his bread and butter and ~*ing* the waiter —Washington Irving⟩ **3 :** to make angry or petulant **:** PROVOKE, ANNOY ⟨this astounding rigidity of custom ~*ed* the king —Francis Hackett⟩ **4 :** to remove (an opponent's checker) from the board for failure to make a possible jump

²**huff** \"\ *n* -s **1 :** ²PUFF 1a ⟨at the moment of firing he might actually turn his face away from his sights to avoid the ~ from the pan —Odell & Willard Shepard⟩ **2 :** a fit of anger or pique ⟨in an . . . unprecedented display of parliamentary ~, refused to join the traditional procession —Mollie Panter-Downes⟩ — usu. used in the phrase *in a huff* ⟨the dissenting experts will secede in a ~ —Ernst Pulgram⟩ ⟨if you encounter a person who's in a ~ about something, you'd better wait until he cools off —W.J.Reilly⟩ **3** *obs* **a :** an attitude or display of arrogance ⟨quell . . . the ~ of the proud —Randle Cotgrave⟩ **b :** an arrogant or conceited person ⟨this young ~ commanded a sergeant to pay him respect —William Darrell⟩ **4** *dial Eng* **:** light leavened pastry **b :** HUFF CAP 1 **5 :** an act of huffing in checkers **syn** see OFFENSE

³**huff** \"\ *adj, dial* **:** HUFFED, OFFENDED

¹**huffcap** \'ˌ=ˌ=\ *n* -s [¹*huff* + *cap*] **1** *obs* **:** strong ale **2** *obs* **:** SWAGGERER, BULLY

²**huffcap** \"\ *adj* **1** *obs* **:** INTOXICATING **2** *archaic* **:** SWAGGERING ⟨a ~ hero . . . mouthed and strutted out his hour on the stage —A.C.Swinburne⟩

huff·i·ly \'həfəlē, -li\ *adv* **:** in a huffy manner

huff·i·ness \-fēnəs, -fin-\ *n* -ES **:** the quality or state of being huffy

huff·ing·ly *adv, archaic* **:** in an arrogant or sulky manner

huff·ish \'həfish\ *adj* **:** ARROGANT, SULKY **syn** see IRRITABLE

¹**huf·fle** \'həfəl\ *vi* -ED/-ING/-S [¹*huff* + *-le*] *now dial Eng* **:** to blow in gusts ⟨the winds do ~ queerer tonight than ever afore —Thomas Hardy⟩

²**huffle** \"\ *n* -s **:** GUST ⟨five haggard pines . . . knuckle together against the ~*s* of wind —Leah B. Drake⟩

huffler *var of* HOVELER

huff-snuff *n* -s [¹*huff* + *snuff*] *obs* **:** SWASHBUCKLER

huffy \'həfē, -fi\ *adj* -ER/-EST [²*huff* + *-y*] **1 :** HAUGHTY, ARROGANT ⟨relapsed into . . . ~ complacency —*Harper's*⟩ **2 a :** roused to indignation **:** IRRITATED, SULKY ⟨stayed ~ a good while —Mark Twain⟩ — usu. used with *get* ⟨now don't get ~ if I offer a frank criticism⟩ **b :** easily offended **:** TOUCHY ⟨not ~ and crabbed like yourself —Augusta Gregory⟩ **syn** see IRRITABLE

¹**hug** \'həg\ *vb* **hugged; hugged; hugging; hugs** [perh. of Scand origin; akin to ON *hugga* to comfort, soothe; akin to OE *hycgan* to think, consider, understand, OHG *huggen* to think, ON *huga* & *hyggja*, Goth *hugjan*, and perh. to Gk *kyknos* swan — more at CYGNET] *vt* **1 a :** to press tightly **:** CLUTCH ⟨the grip of her knees *hugging* Saidi's hot, rippling withers —L.C.Douglas⟩; *specif* **:** to clasp within the arms ⟨hurries down the gangplank to ~ his waiting wife⟩ ⟨she sat up in bed and *hugged* her knees —Louis Auchincloss⟩ **b :** to squeeze between the forelegs ⟨discounting the chances of being . . . *hugged* to death in the claws of a 9-foot anteater —George Weller⟩ **2 a** *archaic* **:** to show fondness for ⟨*hugged* the authors as his bosom friends —John Arbuthnot⟩; *specif* **:** to curry favor with ⟨refused to fight, on the ground that his opponent had been guilty of *hugging* attorneys —T.B.Macaulay⟩ **b :** CONGRATULATE, FELICITATE ⟨*hugged* ourselves that we hadn't had to be told —A.N.Whitehead⟩ **c :** to cling to or hold fast **:** CHERISH, KEEP ⟨~ our half belief in ghosts —W.W. Howells⟩ ⟨*hugged* his miseries like a sulky child —John Buchan⟩ ⟨an effort to ~ all credit to himself —Jonathan Daniels⟩ **3 :** to stay close or adhere to ⟨the road ~*s* the river⟩ ⟨this blast . . . helps the normal airflow ~ the contour of the flap —Richard Witkin⟩ ⟨collars either ~ the neck or stand away —*Women's Wear Daily*⟩ ⟨berries ~ the stem⟩ ⟨skaters ~ the bonfire⟩ ⟨a sailboat ~*s* the wind⟩ ⟨the faint aroma . . . *hugged* them like smog —Sally Benson⟩ **4** *dial Eng* **:** to carry with difficulty **:** LUG ~ *vi* **1 :** to press together **:** CROWD ⟨in groups that *hugged* together —Francis Hackett⟩ **2 a :** to embrace or adhere closely ⟨they *hugged* and kissed⟩ ⟨the revolving part is *hugging* closely against one side —Terrell Croft⟩ **b :** to crush a victim by squeezing with the forelegs ⟨'tis a bear's talent not to kick but ~ —Alexander Pope⟩ — **hug one's chains :** to be glad of servitude

²**hug** \"\ *n* -s **1 :** an affectionate embrace ⟨gave him a motherly ~⟩ **2 :** a crushing or restraining grasp ⟨bitter ~ of mortality —Walt Whitman⟩

¹**huge** \'hyüj *also* 'yüj\ *adj* -ER/-EST [ME *huge*, *hoge*, modif. of OF *ahuge*, *ahoge*] **:** very large or extensive: as **a :** of great size or area **:** GIGANTIC, VAST ⟨the two ships settled . . . to the bottom, each with a ~ hole in her hull —T.E.Cooney⟩ ⟨~ organizations like the American Express Company —Richard Joseph⟩ ⟨a ~ country estate⟩ ⟨~ number of stories —G.B. Saul⟩ **b :** of sizable scale or degree **:** ENORMOUS ⟨the days of the NRA when there was ~ government spending —T.W. Arnold⟩ ⟨~ popular demand for higher education —V.S. Pritchett⟩ ⟨glowered . . . from under his heavy brows with a ~ disgust —G.D.Brown⟩ ⟨turns . . . a dismal failure into a ~ success —Jeanne Massey⟩ **c :** of limitless scope or character **:** UNBOUNDED ⟨his ~ personal talent —Virgil Thomson⟩ ⟨go through rubbish heaps and find rings and scissors and broken noses buried in the ~ past —Virginia Woolf⟩ ⟨~ sense of destiny —Henry Wallace⟩

syn VAST, IMMENSE, ENORMOUS, ELEPHANTINE, MAMMOTH, GIANT, GIGANTIC, GIGANTEAN, COLOSSAL, GARGANTUAN, HERCULEAN, CYCLOPEAN, TITANIC, BROBDINGNAGIAN: HUGE is a rather general term indicating extreme largeness, usu. in size, bulk, or capacity ⟨an enormous volume of heavy, inky vapor, coiling and pouring upward in a *huge* and ebony cumulus cloud —H.G.Wells⟩ ⟨the Texan question and Mexican War made *huge* annexations of Southwestern territory certain —Allan Nevins & H.S.Commager⟩ VAST denotes extreme largeness or broadness, esp. of extent or range ⟨the Great Valley of California, a *vast* elliptical bowl averaging 50 miles in width and more than 400 miles long —*Amer. Guide Series: Calif.*⟩ ⟨consider the *vast* varieties of religions ancient and modern —M.R.Cohen⟩ IMMENSE suggests size far in excess of ordinary measurements or accustomed concepts ⟨an *immense* quill, plucked from a distended albatross' wing —Herman Melville⟩ ⟨found the balloon at an *immense* height indeed, and the earth's convexity had now become strikingly manifest —E.A. Poe⟩ ⟨the *immense* waste of war —D.W.Brogan⟩ ENORMOUS also indicates a size or degree exceeding accustomed bounds or norms ⟨heavy wagons, *enormous* loads, scarcely any less than three tons —*Amer. Guide Series: Calif.*⟩ ⟨the princes of the Renascence lavished upon private luxury and display *enormous* amounts of money —Lewis Mumford⟩ ELEPHANTINE suggests the cumbersome or ponderous largeness of the elephant ⟨similar *elephantine* bones were being displayed . . . as relics of the "giants" mentioned in the Bible —R.W.Murray⟩ ⟨*elephantine* grain elevators —*Amer. Guide Series: N.Y.*⟩ MAMMOTH is similar to ELEPHANTINE ⟨her parties were . . . *mammoth* — she rarely invited fewer than 100 people —*Time*⟩ ⟨a *mammoth* cyclotron —G.F.Whicher⟩ GIANT indicates unusual size or scope ⟨loaded with a typical unit of *giant* industrial equipment, the new car weighs more than a million pounds —*Pa. Railroad Annual Report*⟩ ⟨his *giant* intellect⟩ GIGANTIC and the less common GIGANTEAN are close synonyms of GIANT, perhaps more likely to be used in metaphorical extensions ⟨*gigantic* jewels that a hundred Negroes could not carry —G.K.Chesterton⟩ ⟨a justice of the Supreme Court . . . however *gigantic* his learning and his juridic rectitude —H.L.Mencken⟩ COLOSSAL may suggest vast proportion ⟨three sets of *colossal* figures of men and animals . . . the largest man is 167 feet long —*Amer. Guide Series: Calif.*⟩ ⟨the sun blazed down . . . the heat was *colossal* —C.S.Forester⟩ GARGANTUAN suggests the hugeness of Rabelais's Gargantua and is often used in reference to appetites and similar physical matters ⟨*gargantuan* breakfasts . . . pigs' knuckles and sauerkraut, liver and bacon, ham and eggs, beef stew —Edna Ferber⟩ HERCULEAN suggests the superhuman power of the Greek hero Hercules or the superhuman difficulties of his famous labors ⟨a *Herculean* task confronted them. Some 1700 miles of track had to be laid through a wilderness —Allan Nevins and H.S.Commager⟩ CYCLOPEAN suggests the superhuman size and strength of the Cyclops of Greek mythology ⟨*cyclopean* masonry, consisting of very large blocks of stone —*Scientific American*⟩ TITANIC suggests colossal size and, often, primitive earth-shaking strength ⟨*titanic* water fronds speedily choked both those rivers —H.G. Wells⟩ ⟨it was his *titanic* energy that broke the fetters of medievalism —M.R.Cohen⟩ BROBDINGNAGIAN suggests the hugeness of the inhabitants of Brobdingnag in *Gulliver's Travels* ⟨a brand-new *Brobdingnagian* hotel —Benjamin D'Israeli⟩

²**huge** \"\ *adv* [ME, fr. *huge*, *hoge*, adj.] **:** HUGELY ⟨the sky was swelling ~ with the last dusk —John Dos Passos⟩

huge·ly *adv* [ME, fr. *huge*, *hoge* + *-ly*] **:** in a huge manner **:** EXTREMELY, IMMENSELY ⟨a ~ interesting account —Bernard De Voto⟩ ⟨~ successful work —Roger Shattuck⟩ ⟨children enjoyed themselves ~ in games —Rex Ingamells⟩

huge·ness *n* -ES [ME *hugenes*, fr. *huge*, *hoge* huge + *-nes* -ness] **:** the quality or state of being huge **:** IMMENSITY

huge·ous \-jəs\ *adj* [¹*huge* + *-ous*] **:** HUGE — **huge·ous·ly** *adv*

huger *comparative of* HUGE

hugest *superlative of* HUGE

hug·ga·ble \'həgəbəl\ *adj* **:** of a kind that invites hugging **:** CUDDLESOME ⟨a ~ teddy bear⟩

hugged *past of* HUG

hug·ger \'həgə(r)\ *n* -s **:** one that hugs

¹**hug·ger-mug·ger** \'həgə(r),məgə(r), ¦=ˌ=¦=ˌ=\ *n* [origin unknown] **1 :** the act or practice of concealment **:** SECRECY ⟨had always had the impression that sex was sin . . . here it was treated without any *hugger-mugger* or snickering —A.W.Long⟩ **2 :** a disorderly jumble **:** CONFUSION, MUMBO JUMBO ⟨engage in the *hugger-mugger* of international politics and moneymaking —H.R.Isaacs⟩ ⟨apart from the effect of all this unwholesome *hugger-mugger* on their minds, there was the greater tragedy that they were being shortchanged educationally —Victor Boesen⟩

²**hugger-mugger** \"\ *adv* **:** in secrecy or confusion

³**hugger-mugger** \"\ *adj* **1 :** of a clandestine nature **:** SECRET ⟨an eventual *hugger-mugger* hanging —P.H.Newby⟩ **2 :** of a confused or disorderly nature **:** JUMBLED ⟨readers will be puzzled by what at first appears a completely *hugger-mugger* haphazard arrangement — Ralph Abercrombie⟩

⁴**hugger-mugger** \"\ *vb* **hugger-muggered; hugger-muggered; hugger-muggering** \-g(ə)riŋ\ **hugger-muggers** *vt* **:** to keep secret **:** hush up ~ *vi* **1 :** to act or confer stealthily **2 :** to muddle around

hugger-muggery \-g(ə)rē, -ri\ *n* -ES **:** HUGGER-MUGGER 1

hugging *adj* **:** tending to hug **:** CLINGING — **hug·ging·ly** *adv*

hug·gle \'həgəl, 'hùg-\ *vt* **huggled; huggled; huggling** \-g(ə)liŋ\ **huggles** [freq. of ¹*hug*] *dial Eng* **:** HUG, CUDDLE

hug-me-tight \'=ˌ=ˌ=\ *n* -s **1 :** a woman's short close-fitting bed jacket or undergarment usu. knitted of wool and sleeveless **2 :** a woman's short wraparound jacket

hug-me-tight 1

hu·go·esque \¦(h)yü(,)gō¦esk\ *adj, usu cap* [Victor *Hugo* †1885 Fr. writer + E *-esque*] **:** of, relating to, or characteristic of Victor Hugo or his works

hu·go·nis \(h)yü'gōnəs\ *n* -ES [NL (specif. epithet of *Rosa hugonis*), after Father *Hugo* — more at FATHER HUGO'S ROSE] **:** FATHER HUGO'S ROSE

hugo rose *n, usu cap H* [after Father *Hugo*] **:** FATHER HUGO'S ROSE

hugs *pres 3d sing of* HUG, *pl of* HUG

hu·gue·not \'hyügə,nät *sometimes* -nòt, + V *usu* -äd· *or* -òd·; *sometimes* -nō\ *n, pl* **huguenots** \-äts, -òts, -ō(z)\ *usu cap* [MF, fr. (Geneva dial.) *huguenot* Genevan partisan of an alliance with Fribourg and Bern as a means of preventing annexation by Savoy, alter. (after Besançon *Hugues* †1532 leader of the movement in Geneva to prevent annexation by Savoy) of *eidgnot*, fr. G (Swiss dial.) *eidgnoss* confederate, fr. MHG *eitgenōz*, fr. *eit* oath (fr. OHG *eid*) + *genōz* comrade, fr. OHG *ginōz*; akin to OHG *niozzan* to use, enjoy — more at OATH, NEAT] **:** a French Protestant in the 16th and 17th centuries **:** a member of the Reformed or Calvinistic communion — **hu·gue·not·ic** \¦==¦näd·ik, -nòt, ¦t¦, ¦ēk\ *adj, usu cap* — **hu·gue·not·ism** \'==,näd·,izəm, -,nòt, ¦,tiz-, -,nō,tiz-\ *n* -s *usu cap* **:** the doctrines and practices of the French Huguenots

huh *typically a snort or a strong h-sound followed by an m-sound or by the vowel* 'ə *usu nasalized, the last part varying in intonation; often read as* 'hə\ *interj* [imit. of a grunt] — used typically to express surprise, disbelief, or disgust or to request repetition or confirmation of something just said

hüh·ner·ko·bel·ite \'h(y)ünə(r)¦kōbə,līt\ *n* -s [*Hühnerkobel*, region in Bavaria, Germany, its locality + E *-ite*] **:** a mineral $(Na,Ca)(Fe,Mn)_2(PO_4)_2$ consisting of phosphate of sodium, calcium, iron, and manganese and being isomorphous with varulite

huh·ner test \'h(y)ünə(r)-\ *n, usu cap H* [after Max *Huhner* †1947 Am. surgeon] **:** a test used in sterility studies that involves postcoital examination of aspirated vaginal and intracervical fluid to determine the presence or survival of spermatozoa in these areas

hu·hu \'hü(,)hü\ *n* -s [Maori] **:** a large creamy white roundheaded grub that is the larva of a yellowish brown New Zealand beetle (*Prionoplus reticularis*), bores in dead trees and timber, and was formerly much used as food by the Maori

hui \'hü(,)ē\ *n* -s [Hawaiian] **1** *Hawaii* **a :** PARTNERSHIP, SYNDICATE ⟨efforts by mainland capital to gain control of

Hawaiian Airlines are believed to have been thwarted by a local ~ that has secretly bought close to 70,000 shares —*Honolulu Advertiser*⟩ **b :** CLUB, ASSOCIATION ⟨the ~ is an organization of civic-minded . . . women who cooperate in furthering the interests of the Y.W.C.A. —*Honolulu Star-Bull.*⟩ **2** [Hawaiian & Maori] **:** community gathering **:** ASSEMBLY ⟨when the ~ broke up at 4 p.m. the issue was still in doubt —*New Zealand Jour. of Agric.*⟩

hu·ia \ˈhüyə\ *also* **huia bird** *n* -s [Maori *huia*] **:** a bird (*Neomorpha acutirostris* or *Heteralocha acutirostris*) related to the starlings, confined to a small region in the mountains of New Zealand, and having black white-tipped tail feathers prized by Maori chiefs and worn as insignia of rank

hui·chol \wēˈchōl\ *n, pl* **huichol** \″\ *or* **huicho·les** \-ōlēz, -ō(ˌ)lās\ *usu cap* [Sp, of AmerInd origin] **1 a :** a Nahuatlan people of the mountains between Zacatecas and Nayarit, Mexico **b :** a member of such people **2 :** the language of the Huichol people

huid \ˈhœd, -üe-\ *Scot var of* HOOD

huil \ˈhœl, -üe-\ *Scot var of* HULL

hui·lie \ˈhœli\ *var of* HOOLY

hui·pil \wēˈpēl\ *n, pl* **huipils** \-lz\ *or* **huipi·les** \-(ˌ)lās\ [MexSp, fr. Nahuatl *huipilli*] **:** a straight slipover one-piece garment that is made by folding a rectangle of material end to end, sewing up the straight sides but leaving openings near the folded top for the arms, and cutting a slit or a square in the center of the fold to furnish an opening for the head, is often decorated with embroidery, and is worn as a blouse or dress by women chiefly in Mexico and Central America

hui·pi·lla \wēˈpē(y)ə\ *n* -s [MexSp] **:** PINGUIN

hui·sa·che \wēˈsächē\ *n* -s [MexSp, fr. Nahuatl *huixachi*, fr. *huitztli* thorn + *izachi* abundant] **:** a thorny shrub or small tree (*Acacia farnesiana*) found abundantly in the southern U.S. and throughout tropical regions and having fragrant yellow flowers used in making perfumery — called also CASSIE

huis·co·yol \ˌwēskəˈyōl\ *n* -s [MexSp, fr. Nahuatl *huitzcoyolli*, fr. *huitztli* thorn + *coyolli, coyulli*, a nut-bearing palm] **:** a shrubby Central American palm (*Bactris subglobosa*) that forms impenetrable thickets

huis·quil \ˈwēˌskēl\ *or* **guis·quil** \ˈgw-\ *n* -s [AmerSp *huisquil, güisquil*] **:** CHAYOTE

hui·tain \wēˈtān, *F* wʸētaⁿ\ *n, pl* **huitains** \-ānz, -aⁿ(z)\ [MF, fr. *huit* eight (fr. L *octo*) + *-ain*, fr. L *-anus* -an — more at EIGHT] **1 :** OCTASTICH **2 :** OCTAVE 2b

hukama *pl of* HAKIM

huke \ˈhyük\ *n* -s [ME *huyke, huke*, fr. MD *huik*] **1 :** a medieval hooded cloak worn orig. by women but later by both sexes **2 :** a late medieval close-fitting gown for either sex

hu·ki·lau \ˌhükēˈlau̇\ *n* -s [Hawaiian, fr. *huki* pull + *lau* net] *Hawaii* **:** a seine-fishing party often involving large numbers of people and much revelry

¹hu·la \ˈhülə\ *also* **hula-hula** \ˈ==ˈ==\ *n* -s [Hawaiian] **1 :** a sinuous mimetic Polynesian dance of conventional form and topical adaptation performed by men and women singly or together and usu. accompanied by chants and rhythmic drumming ⟨the ~ was in essence a magical ritual designed to bring rain and cause fertility —E.S.C.Handy⟩ ⟨a lovely brown maiden performed a ~ in the aisle of the cabin to entertain the passengers —Horace Sutton⟩ **2 :** the music to which a hula is performed ⟨snatches of ~*s* being sung —Armine von Tempski⟩

²hula \″\ *vi* -ED/-ING/-S **:** to dance a hula

³hula \″\ *n, pl* **hula** *or* **hulas** *usu cap* **1 a :** a people of the Territory of Papua **b :** a member of such people **2 :** the Austronesian language of the Hula people

Hula–Hoop *trademark* — used for a hoop made usu. of plastic or rubber for twirling about the body by movements like those of the hula

hula–hoop \ˈ==ˌ=\ *vi* [*Hula-Hoop*] **:** to twirl a Hula-Hoop hoop about one's body

hula skirt *n* **:** a grass skirt worn by a hula dancer or an imitation of such a skirt ⟨a young girl, wearing a *hula skirt* of cellophane, came to the car and took their order —Speed Lamkin⟩

hula skirt

hulch *adj* [origin unknown] *obs* **:** HUMPED ⟨a man with a ~ back —Charles Cotton⟩

hule *var of* ULE

hul gul *var of* HULL-GULL

¹hulk \ˈhəlk\ *n* -s [ME *hulke*, fr. OE *hulc*, fr. ML *holcas, hulca*, fr. Gk *holkas* barge, trading vessel, fr. *helkein* to pull, drag, tow — more at SULCUS] **1 :** SHIP; *specif* **:** a heavy ship of clumsy build ⟨the colossal ~ was the Great Eastern, the forerunner of today's ocean liners —James Dugan⟩ **2 :** one that is bulky or unwieldy ⟨faced by a ~ of a man, well over six feet tall and professionally broad-shouldered —William Phillips b. 1878⟩ ⟨towering ~*s* of two vast apartment houses —Lewis Mumford⟩ ⟨the black ~*s* of the mountains across the bay —H.T.DeSa⟩ **3** *obs* **:** HULL ⟨her ~ painted over with sparkling vermilion —James Hayward⟩ **4 a :** the body of an old wrecked or dismantled ship unfit for sea service ⟨for a clubhouse the boys used an abandoned ~ they found on the waterfront⟩ **b :** an abandoned wreck or shell ⟨the ~*s* of British tanks rusting in the fields —J.A.Phillips⟩ ⟨once-glittering halls were left empty ~*s* —*Foreign Affairs*⟩ ⟨the moribund ~ of the Spanish Empire —J.H.Plumb⟩ **c :** a ship used as a prison ⟨a celebrated lock picker . . . serving time in a prison ~ —Rufus Jarman⟩ — usu. used in pl. ⟨every prisoner sent to the ~*s* —Kenneth Roberts⟩

²hulk \″\ *vb* -ED/-ING/-S *vi* **1** *dial Eng* **:** to move lazily or ponderously ⟨~*s* up from his chair by the hearth —Emmett Gowen⟩ **2 :** to appear impressively large or massive **:** BULK, LOOM ⟨the smoking port and Vesuvius ~*ing* beyond —William Sansom⟩ ⟨a horned owl coasted into a perch on a dead tree stub, and it ~*ed* there against the sky —Hugh Fosburgh⟩ ~ *vt* **:** to condemn to or lodge in a hulk

³hulk \″\ *vt* -ED/-ING/-S [alter. of *holk* to hollow out — more at HOWK] *dial* **:** DISEMBOWEL

hulking *adj* [¹*hulk* + *-ing*] **:** of great size or powerful build **:** HUSKY, MASSIVE ⟨a big ~ figure of a man with thick shoulders and no neck worth mentioning —Claudia Cassidy⟩ ⟨three ~ battleships —Norris Houghton⟩

hulky \ˈhəlkē, -ki\ *adj* -ER/-EST [¹*hulk* + *-y*] **:** HULKING

¹hull \ˈhəl\ *n* -s [ME *hul, hull, hole*, fr. OE *hulu*; akin to OHG *helawa* oat chaff, *hala* hull, OE *helan* to conceal — more at HELL] **1 a :** the outer covering of a fruit or seed (as the husk of a grain or nut or the pod of the pea) **b :** the persistent calyx or involucre that subtends some fruits (as the strawberry) **2** *dial Eng* **:** HUT, HOVEL, SHED **3 a** (1) **:** the frame or body of a ship exclusive of masts, yards, sails, and rigging — see SHIP illustration (2) *obs* **:** HULK 4a **b** (1) **:** the portion of a flying boat which furnishes buoyancy when in contact with the water and to which the main supporting surfaces and other parts are attached (2) **:** the main structure of a rigid airship consisting of a covered elongated framework which encloses the gasbags and supports the cars and equipment **c :** the armored body of a vehicle ⟨casting . . . huge steel tank ~*s* in a single piece —G.H.Johnston⟩ ⟨the ~ of an armored car is . . . of lighter-weight plate —*Principles of Automotive Vehicles*⟩ **4 :** COVERING, CASING: as **a :** the shell of a crustacean ⟨shrimp ~*s* and heads are used as fertilizer⟩ **b :** a film of water encasing a soil particle **c** (1) **:** an empty ammunition shell case ⟨hot, spent cartridge ~*s* would be showering all over —Thomas Anderson⟩ (2) **:** CARTRIDGE ⟨won the national crown for the second time with a variety of . . . .22 ~*s* —Charles Askins b.1907⟩

²hull \″\ *vb* -ED/-ING/-S [ME *holen, hullen*, fr. *hole, hul, hull*, n.] *vt* **1 a :** to remove the husks or shells of **:** SHUCK ⟨~ peas⟩ ⟨~ pecans⟩ ⟨~ oysters⟩ **b :** to remove the outer skin of **:** DECORTICATE ⟨~ kernels of corn⟩ ⟨~ coffee beans⟩ ⟨~ barley⟩ **c :** to remove the calyx of ⟨~ strawberries⟩ **2 :** to pierce or strike the hull of (as a ship) ~ *vi* **1 :** to float or drift with sails furled **:** lie ahull **2** *archaic* **:** IDLE ⟨I am to ~ here a little longer —Shak.⟩

³hull \″\ *adj, usu cap* [fr. *Hull*, England] **:** of or from the county borough of Hull, or Kingston upon Hull, England **:** of the kind or style prevalent in Hull

¹hul·la·ba·loo *also* **hul·la·bal·loo** \ˈhələbəˌlü, ˌ===ˈ= *sometimes* -lēb- *or* -lib-\ *or* **hel·la·bal·loo** \ˈhel-, ˌhel-\ *n* -s [perh. irreg. fr. *hallo* + Sc *baloo*, interj. used to hush children] **1 :** a babel of noise and confusion **:** HUBBUB ⟨didn't whisper because there was such a ~ down in the cut that nobody could hear him anyhow —J.B.Benefield⟩ **2 :** an excited clamor or controversy **:** UPROAR ⟨this attempt was accompanied by a big propaganda ~ —*Cavalry Jour.*⟩ ⟨a terrific ~ at the Met this season over the merits of these rival supersopranos —Winthrop Sargeant⟩ **syn** see DIN

²hullabaloo \″\ *vb* -ED/-ING/-S *vi* **:** to make a hullabaloo ~ *vt* **:** BALLYHOO 2

hull down *adv (or adj)* **1** *of a ship* **a :** at such a distance that only the superstructure is visible ⟨had cleared with a leading wind . . . and was *hull down* long before dark —Raymond McFarland⟩ **b :** with main deck awash ⟨one ship . . . after another went *hull down* into the sucking tide —D.C.Peattie⟩ **2** *of a tank or other armored vehicle* **:** in a place of concealment but in position to observe the enemy and deliver fire ⟨were standing *hull down* behind a hillock and on each of their turrets was a figure staring forward through field glasses —Peter Rainier⟩

hulled barley *n* **:** barley in which the husks adhere to the kernel — called also *Scotch barley*

hulled corn *n* **:** whole grain corn from which the hulls have been removed by soaking or boiling in lye water — see HOMINY

hull·er \ˈhələ(r)\ *n* -s **:** one that hulls: as **a :** a machine that removes the hulls from grain, nuts, or castor beans **b :** a machine that threshes clover and separates the seeds from the hulls **c :** a small hand tool for removing hulls from strawberries

huller c

hul·let \ˈhələt, ˈhu̇l-\ *var of* HOWLET

hull-gull *or* **hul gul** \ˈhəlˌgəl\ *n* [origin unknown] **:** a children's game in which one player guesses how many beans or other small objects are in another's handful and gives up or receives beans according as his guess is high, low, or exact

hull insurance *n* **:** insurance protecting the owners against loss caused by damage or destruction of waterborne craft or aircraft

hul·lion \ˈhəlyən\ *var of* HALLION

hull–less *or* **hul·less** \ˈhəlləs\ *adj* **1 :** having no hull **2 a** *of barley* **:** having the kernels free within the husk **b** *of popcorn* **:** having short thick ears and pointed kernels with a white tender seed coat

hul·lo \(ˌ)həˈlō, ˈhə(ˌ)lō, ˈhəˈlō\ *chiefly Brit var of* HELLO

hullock *n* -s [origin unknown] *obs* **:** a small piece of sail kept standing to hold a ship's head to the wind in a storm

hul·loo \(ˌ)həˈlü, ˈhə(ˌ)lü, ˈhəˈlü\ *var of* HALLO

hu·lock \ˈhü-\ *also* **hulock gibbon** *or* **hulock monkey** *n* -s [*hulock* fr. native name in Assam or Burma] **:** HOOLOCK

hul·site \ˈhəl(t)ˌsīt\ *n* -s [Alfred *Hulse* Brooks †1924 Am. scientist + E *-ite*] **:** a mineral $(Fe,Ca,Mg)_4(Fe,Sn)_2B_2O_{10}$(?) consisting of a hydrous iron calcium magnesium tin borate

hul·ver \ˈhəlvə(r)\ *n* -s [ME *hulver, holver*, fr. ON *hulfr* — more at HOLLY] *dial Eng* **:** HOLLY

¹hum \ˈhəm\ *vb* **hummed; hummed; humming; hums** [ME *hummen*; akin to MHG *hummen* to hum, D *hommelen* to hum, *hommel* bumblebee, OHG *humbal*] *vi* **1 a :** to utter a sound like or suggestive of that of the speech sound \m\ prolonged **:** continue voicing a nasal on one pitch or on varying pitches ⟨~ in time to the music⟩; *esp* **:** to utter such a sound to express dissent, approval, surprise, or embarrassment ⟨*hummed* and hawed and finally blurted out his views⟩ **b :** to make the natural noise of an insect (as a bumblebee) in motion ⟨a bee *hummed* by —Zane Grey⟩ ⟨mosquitoes *humming* —R.A.W. Hughes⟩ **c :** to make a low prolonged sound like that of an insect **:** DRONE, BUZZ ⟨the top ~*s*⟩ ⟨the snoring of his grandfather *hummed* like the coming of wasps —Elizabeth Enright⟩ ⟨a kettle was *humming* on a small gas stove —Ellen Glasgow⟩ ⟨electric power lines ~ —*Lamp*⟩ **d :** to give forth a low murmuring indistinct sound from the blending of many voices ⟨the sound of children's voices with which the house was always *humming* —J.M.Brinnin⟩ **e :** to produce a continuous blend of nonvocal sounds ⟨all night the printing plants *hummed* —Bill Davidson⟩ ⟨shrapnel and bullets *hummed* through the brush —Dave Richardson⟩ ⟨once, this place had *hummed* with noise: the ring of hammer upon anvil, the rasping of the saws that hewed the oak logs —Elizabeth Goudge⟩ **f :** to have an internal humming ⟨my head ~*s*⟩ **2 :** to be very active as if noisily ⟨steel and other industries are *humming* along at much higher rates of operation —R.M.Blough⟩ ⟨the business started to ~ —Isabelle M. Hoover⟩ ⟨to make the free world ~ with full productive activity —Max Ascoli⟩ ~ *vt* **1 :** to sing with the lips closed and without articulation ⟨~ a tune⟩ **2 :** to affect by humming ⟨*hummed* me to sleep⟩ ⟨~ herself to rest⟩ **:** express by humming ⟨*hummed* his displeasure⟩

²hum \″\ *n* -s [ME, fr. *hummen*, v.] **:** the act of humming or the sound made by humming ⟨a ~ of approbation⟩: as **a :** a low monotonous noise (as of bees in flight or a whirling wheel) **:** DRONE, BUZZ **b :** the confused noise (as of a crowd or machinery) heard at a distance ⟨the ~ of industry⟩ ⟨the high-pitched ~ of swift power belts —*Amer. Guide Series: Ark.*⟩ **c :** the humming of a melody; *also* **:** MELODY **d :** an undesired audio signal in the output of a piece of electronic equipment usu. of low frequency resulting from direct pickup of a power signal or the residual power signal in a power supply

³hum \″; *interjectionally often a prolonged* m *sometimes preceded by* h\ *n* -s [imit.] **:** an inarticulate nasal sound or murmur (as from embarrassment or hesitation) ⟨after some evasive ~*s* he gave his answer⟩ — often used interjectionally to express hesitation or doubt, dissent, deliberation, or embarrassment; compare ⁴HEM

⁴hum \ˈhəm\ *n* -s [short for ¹*humbug*] **:** HUMBUG

⁵hum \″\ *vt* **hummed; hummed; humming; hums** [short for ²*humbug*] **:** HUMBUG

⁶hum \ˈhüm\ *n* -s [Serbo-Croatian, hill] **:** an isolated residual hill or mass of limestone (as in a region of karst topography)

hum *abbr* **1** [NL *humaniora*] the humanities **2** humor; humorous

hu·ma \ˈhümə\ *usu cap, var of* HIMA

¹hu·man \ˈhyümən *also* ˈyü-\ *adj, sometimes* -ER/-EST [ME *humayne, humain*, fr. MF *humain*, fr. L *humanus*, fr. *hum-* (akin to L *homo* man, human being) + *-anus* -an — more at HOMAGE] **1 a :** of or relating to man **:** characteristic of man ⟨~ voices⟩ ⟨vulnerability of the ~ body⟩ **b :** primarily or usu. harbored by, affecting, or attacking man ⟨~ appendicitis⟩ ⟨the common ~ flea⟩ **2 a :** being a man **:** consisting of men ⟨contrived for the destruction of the ~ species —Tobias Smollett⟩ ⟨the ~ race⟩ ⟨some special quality in the ~ beings who have made this particular transition —A.J.Toynbee⟩ **b :** of or relating to the social life or collective relations of mankind ⟨~ progress⟩ ⟨~ history and evolution⟩ ⟨in the course of ~ events —*U.S. Declaration of Independence*⟩ **3 :** characteristic of or relating to man in his essential nature: as **a :** of, relating to, or resembling man or his attributes in distinction from the lower animals ⟨to be ~ is to understand, to evaluate, to choose, to accept responsibility —Lewis Mumford⟩ ⟨the gregarious impulses of ~ beings —J.B.Conant⟩ **b :** of or relating to man as distinguished from the superhuman, from the divine, or from nature **:** belonging to finite intelligence and powers ⟨to err is ~; to forgive, divine —Alexander Pope⟩ ⟨there are no absolutes and man must content himself with being ~ —H.E.Clurman⟩ **c :** susceptible to, representative of, or exemplifying the range of feelings, strengths, or weaknesses of which man is capable ⟨a very ~ world, filled with joy and sorrow, innocence and evil⟩ ⟨for all his stiff outward bearing, he is very ~⟩ ⟨the story of the ascent is a great ~ document⟩ ⟨far too ~ a creature to care much for art —Max Beerbohm⟩ **d :** having to do with, portraying, or arising from the small or large joys, sorrows, passions, struggles, or other interest-provoking experiences or situations of individual persons ⟨~ comedy⟩ ⟨full of the milk of ~ kindness —Shak.⟩ ⟨those *human*-interest yarns —Erle Stanley Gardner⟩ ⟨no business like book retailing for ~ interest —Allan McMahan⟩ ⟨a careful history of the ~ side of the whole case —M.R.Cohen⟩ ⟨nearly all these books contain the same ~ stories about the Queen —*N.Y. Times Book Rev.*⟩ **4 :** symbolized in a representation of the zodiac or in a configuration of the stars by a man (as Aquarius), woman (as Virgo), or child (as Gemini) **5 :** HUMANE ⟨balance her sharp tongue and uncertain moods against her warmly ~ disposition —Havelock Ellis⟩ **6 :** having some of the characteristics of a living person **:** like a human ⟨the nearest of blood to me a d the ~*est* was not a person nor a villager —H.D.Thoreau⟩ ⟨the woods began to open up, and the country looked more ~ —Willa Cather⟩ ⟨the statue is more ~ than the beings at his feet —Clifton Fadiman⟩ ⟨the humbler aspects of our cities are more ~ than the skyscrapers —Walter Pach⟩ **7 :** consisting of members of the family Hominidae **:** HOMINID ⟨the several fossil ~ genera⟩ **8 :** unpredictably fallible or erratic **:** not behaving by known law **:** ENIGMATIC ⟨must always consider the ~ element⟩ ⟨Americans like other human beings are bewilderingly ~ —Max Lerner⟩ ⟨such an inconsistency is very ~ —P.E.More⟩

²human \″\ *n* -s **:** a human being ⟨sprung of ~*s* that inhabit earth —George Chapman⟩ ⟨incomprehensible to us ~*s* —William James⟩ ⟨no ~ since Adam —G.W.Cable⟩ ⟨the least developed of all ancestral ~*s* —A.L.Kroeber⟩ ⟨what has been found true about rats may be applied to ~*s* —E.E.Slosson⟩ ⟨like most of us lazy and indecisive ~*s* —T.H.Fielding⟩ ⟨as completely scientific and objective an approach as a ~ is capable of —R.A.Hall b. 1911⟩ ⟨two thousand million ~*s* —G.H.T.Kimble⟩

human botfly *n* **:** a large fly (*Dermatobia hominis*) of the family Cuterebridae that has brown wings and bluish body, is widely distributed in tropical America, and undergoes its larval development subcutaneously in man and other mammals

hu·mane \(ˈ)hyüˈmān *also* (ˈ)yü-\ *adj, sometimes* -ER/-EST [ME *humayne, humain* — more at HUMAN] **1** *obs* **:** HUMAN **2 :** marked by compassion, sympathy, or consideration for other human beings or animals ⟨a ~ warden⟩ ⟨~ treatment of laboratory animals⟩ ⟨a ~ attitude⟩ **3 :** of, relating to, or characterized by broad humanistic culture **:** HUMANISTIC ⟨~ studies⟩ ⟨painting was the first ~ art to develop here —Virgil Thomson⟩

human ecology *n* **:** a branch of sociology that studies the relationship between a human community and its environment; *specif* **:** the study of the spatial and temporal interrelationships between men and their economic, social, and political organization

hu·mane·ly *adv* **:** in a humane manner

hu·mane·ness \-ānnəs\ *n* -ES **:** the quality or state of being humane

human engineering *n* **1 :** management of human beings and affairs esp. in industry with a view to securing satisfactory adjustment esp. in terms of maximum work efficiency and job satisfaction **2 :** ERGONOMICS

human equation *n* **:** the factor of human strength or weakness that needs to be considered in predicting the outcome of any social, political, economic, or mechanical process operated by human agency

humaner *comparative of* HUMAN *or of* HUMANE

humane society *n, often cap H&S* **1** *chiefly Brit* **:** a lifesaving society **2 :** a society concerned with the promotion of humane conduct or ideals or having charitable or philanthropic ends ⟨the *Humane Society* is a child-caring agency —A.E.Fink⟩; *specif* **:** a society for the prevention of cruelty to animals

humanest *superlative of* HUMAN *or of* HUMANE

human geography *n* **:** ANTHROPOGEOGRAPHY

hu·man·ics \hyüˈmaniks *also* yü-\ *n pl but sing in constr* **:** a subject that treats of human nature or human affairs

hu·man·i·o·ra \(ˌ)(h)yüˌmanēˈōrə\ *n pl* [NL *humaniora* (*studia*), lit., more humane studies] **:** humanistic studies **:** HUMANITIES ⟨on the borderland between science and the ~ —*Chronica Botanica*⟩

hu·man·ism \ˈ(h)yüməˌnizəm\ *n* -s [¹*human* + *-ism*; in some senses prob. fr. F *humanisme* or G *humanismus*] **1 a :** devotion to the humanities **:** literary culture **b** *often cap* **:** the learning or cultural impulse that is characterized by a revival of classical letters, an individualistic and critical spirit, and a shift of emphasis from religious to secular concerns and that flowered during the Renaissance **2 :** devotion to human welfare **:** interest in or concern for man **:** HUMANITY, HUMANITARIANISM ⟨born in a city tenement, he early acquired the kind of ~ that is humanitarian —Donald Davidson⟩ ⟨wrote that medicine was a social science and urged doctors to participate in the battles of ~ —B.J.Stern⟩ **3 :** a doctrine, set of attitudes, or way of life centered upon human interests or values: as **a :** a philosophy that rejects supernaturalism, regards man as a natural object, and asserts the essential dignity and worth of man and his capacity to achieve self-realization through the use of reason and scientific method — called also *naturalistic humanism, scientific humanism*; compare INSTRUMENTALISM, PRAGMATISM **b** *often cap* **:** a religion subscribing to these beliefs **:** RELIGIOUS HUMANISM **c :** a philosophy advocating the self-fulfillment of man within the framework of Christian principles — called also *Christian humanism*; see INTEGRAL HUMANISM **4 :** NEW HUMANISM

¹hu·man·ist \-nəst\ *n* -s [prob. fr. MF *humaniste*, fr. L *humanus* + MF *-iste* -ist] **1 a :** a person who pursues the study of the humanities ⟨accused by ~*s* of having an exclusive interest in social sciences —*Publ's Mod. Lang. Assoc. of Amer.*⟩ ⟨called for a greater understanding betweed scientists and ~*s* —*Science*⟩ **b :** an adherent or practitioner of Renaissance humanism; *specif* **:** a Renaissance scholar devoting himself to the study of classical letters **2 :** a person who is devoted to human welfare **:** one who is marked by a strong interest in or concern for man **:** HUMANITARIAN ⟨a ~, a lover of all sorts of people —*Yale Rev.*⟩ ⟨a ~, who felt deeply about inequality . . . wherever he saw it —Max Lerner⟩ **3 a** *often cap* **:** a person who subscribes to the doctrines of scientific humanism; *specif* **:** a member of a religious society or cult subscribing to such doctrines **b :** a person who subscribes to a form of philosophical humanism **c :** NEW HUMANIST

²humanist \″\ *or* **hu·man·is·tic** \ˌ==ˈnistik, -tēk\ *adj* **1 a :** of or relating to Renaissance humanism or humanists ⟨the *humanistic* revival of learning⟩ **b :** of, relating to, or concerned with the humanities **:** CULTURAL ⟨the fact that *humanistic* subjects . . . have a part in the development of the students —*Science*⟩ ⟨Greek . . . the most exacting *humanist* study —Robert Birley⟩ **2 :** of or relating to philosophical or religious humanism in any of its forms ⟨what we need is a *humanistic* religion . . . man-centered and comfortable —R.C. Hartnett⟩ ⟨supernaturalist and *humanist* strategies of motivation —K.D.Burke⟩ ⟨the *humanist* belief in continuous emergent evolution —Wendell Thomas⟩ **3 :** marked by or expressive of devotion to human welfare or strong interest in or concern for man **:** HUMANITARIAN ⟨the liberal approach has been a *humanist* approach —M.W.Straight⟩ ⟨incorporate the socialist idealism of Russia with the *humanist* individualism of America —Cyril Connolly⟩ ⟨respect and *humanistic* regard for all other members of our species —Weston La Barre⟩

hu·man·is·ti·cal·ly \ˌ==ˈnistək(ə)lē, -tēk-, -li\ *adv* **:** in a humanistic manner

¹hu·man·i·tar·i·an \(ˌ)hyüˌmanəˈterēən, (ˌ)yü-, -taar-, -tār-\ *n* -s [*humanity* + *-arian*] **:** a person who is actively concerned in promoting human welfare and esp. social reform **:** PHILANTHROPIST

²humanitarian \(ˌ)=ˌ==ˈ===\ *adj* **:** of, relating to, or characteristic of humanitarians or humanitarianism **:** zealously concerned for or active in the promotion of human welfare and esp. of social reform **:** PHILANTHROPIC, HUMANE ⟨to use the A-bomb was wrong on ~ grounds —E.M.Zacharias⟩ ⟨a refreshing example of . . . ~ zeal —Benjamin Farrington⟩ ⟨a hard, stern race . . . little responsive to ~ appeal —V.L. Parrington⟩

hu·man·i·tar·i·an·ism \-ēəˌnizəm\ *n* -s **:** concern for human welfare esp. as expressed through philanthropic activities and interest in social reforms **:** the practice or display of humanitarian principles ⟨extended their ~ to include the Indian tribes —H.M.Hyman⟩

hu·man·i·ty \hyüˈmanəd·ē, -ətē, -i *also* yü-\ *n* -ES [ME *humanite*, fr. MF *humanité*, fr. L *humanitat-, humanitas*, fr. *humanus* human, humane + *-itat-, -itas* -ity — more at HUMAN] **1 :** the quality or state of being humane **:** kind or generous behavior or disposition **:** COMPASSION, BENEVOLENCE ⟨which she had intended to do with beautiful mercy, a lovely ~ —Elizabeth Taylor⟩ ⟨bespeaking ~ for the enemy in the midst of a bloody struggle —C.G.Bowers⟩ **2 a :** the totality of attributes which distinguish man from other beings **:** the condition of being human : essential human quality or character ⟨very ape-looking, but with many marks of an incipient ~ —J.S.Weiner⟩ ⟨man's ~ consists of his . . . labor power —Hannah Arendt⟩ ⟨seem coldly to deny him a common ~ —Philip Woodruff⟩ ⟨committed to a belief in the ~ of all men and women —Brendan Sexton⟩ **b humanities** *pl* (1) : human attributes or qualities ⟨his work has the ripeness of the 18th century, and its rough *humanities* —Pamela H. Johnson⟩ (2) : things pleasing to human tastes or sensibilities ⟨it has *humanities*: many mirrors, for example, which augment the numbers of the guests —Philip Wylie⟩ **3** [ML *humanitas*, fr. L] **a** *archaic* : the study of classical language and literature **b** *in Scottish universities* : Latin language and literature **c humanities** *pl* : the branches of learning regarded as having primarily a cultural character and usu. including languages, literature, history, mathematics, and philosophy **4 a** : the totality of human beings : the human race : MANKIND ⟨a fierce compassion for the woes of ~ —Maurice Bowra⟩ **b** : PEOPLE, MEN ⟨the packed mass of ~ below would swing . . . with the movement of the ship —C.S.Forester⟩

hu·man·ization \ˌhyümənəˈzāshən, -ˌnīˈz- *also* ˌyü-\ *n* -s : the act or process of humanizing : the fact or condition of being humanized ⟨an increasing ~ of the industrial process —E.M.Erikson⟩ ⟨the changes in the carved figures well illustrate the growing ~ of the divine and the saintly —G.C. Sellery⟩

hu·man·ize \ˈ=ˌnīz\ *vb* -ED/-ING/-S [F *humaniser*, fr. MF, fr. L *humanus* + MF *-iser* -ize] *vt* **1 a** : to give a human character or aspect to : treat or regard as human : represent in human form ⟨there is no worship here, . . . but nevertheless they ~ the crocodiles —W.W.Howells⟩ **b** : to adapt or make congenial to human nature, sensibilities, or use : make more sympathetic or responsive to human needs or desires ⟨dedicated himself . . . to the *humanizing* of business and finance —George Wolf⟩ **2** : to make humane : make gentle : SOFTEN, REFINE, CIVILIZE ⟨nations have feebly tried to ~ and regulate war —Vera M. Dean⟩ ⟨New England was appointed to guide the nation, to . . . ~ it —Van Wyck Brooks⟩ ~ *vi* **1** : to become humane **2** : to have or spread a civilizing influence ⟨it is the function of women to ~ —M.F.A.Montagu⟩

humankind \ˈ==ˌ=\ *n sing but sing or pl in constr* : the human race : MANKIND

humanlike \ˈ==ˌ=\ *adj* : like or resembling humans : like or resembling that of humans ⟨salmon . . . live a ~ existence —June Collins⟩ ⟨very ~ gods inhabit a . . . delightful heaven —Edith Hamilton⟩

hu·man·ly *adv* **1 a** : from the viewpoint of man : as concerns the human aspect ⟨lesser known but more ~ and historically interesting phase of his character —*Publ's Mod. Lang. Assoc. of Amer.*⟩ ⟨dramatic action that is at once ingenious, ~ illuminating, and true —Leslie Rees⟩ ⟨operate a successful organization both economically and ~ —*Current Biog.*⟩ **b** : within the range of human capacity ⟨policy that will insure, so far as it is ~ possible to do so, high employment —A.E.Stevenson b.1900⟩ **2** : in a human manner : after the manner of man ⟨what . . . children need most sorely is to be made ~ articulate —George Sampson⟩ ⟨men want more than merely to live . . . they want to live ~ —Ludwig Von Mises⟩

human nature *n* [ME *nature humayne*, fr. MF *nature humaine*] : the nature of man: **a** : the complex of behavioral patterns, attitudes, and ideas which man has acquired socially — called also *cultural nature* ⟨socially conditioned *human nature* . . . the qualities of the personality that make it like other personalities within the same society —A.L.Kroeber⟩ **b** : the complex of fundamental dispositions and traits of man sometimes considered innate ⟨belief that "you can't change *human nature*" —A.Van Duym⟩

hu·man·ness \-mən(n)əs\ *n* -ES : the quality or state of being human ⟨we miss the humanity, or ~, that would inspire us to love or to hate his people —*New Yorker*⟩ ⟨the public image of you lacks warmth, and depth, and ~ —Stewart Alsop⟩

¹hu·man·oid \-məˌnȯid\ *adj* [¹*human* + *-oid*] : having human characters esp. as opposed to anthropoid

²humanoid \"\ *n* -s : a humanoid being ⟨the ~s and the anthropoids part company between a million and two million years ago —J.A.Thomson⟩

human relations *n pl but usu sing in constr* **1** : the social relations between human beings esp. when being investigated **2** : a study of the human problems arising from organizational and interpersonal relations in industry esp. with reference to the employer-employee relationship and the interaction between personal traits, group membership, and productive efficiency **3** : a course, study, or program designed to develop better interpersonal and intergroup adjustments

humans *pl of* HUMAN

hu·mate \ˈhyüˌmāt\ *n* -s [*humic* + *-ate*] : a salt or ester of a humic acid

humbird \ˈ=ˌ=\ *n* : HUMMINGBIRD

¹hum·ble \ˈhəmbəl *also* ˈəm-\ *adj* -ER/-EST [ME *umble, humble*, fr. OF, fr. L *humilis* low, slight, humble, fr. *humus* earth, ground + *-ilis* -ile; akin to Gk *chthōn* earth, *chamai* on the ground, Skt *kṣam* earth, ground] **1 a** : having a low opinion of one's own importance or merits : modest or meek in spirit, manner, or appearance : not proud or haughty ⟨essentially ~ . . . and self-effacing, he achieved the highest formal honors and distinctions —B.K.Malinowski⟩ ⟨to them even the president was ~ —Sinclair Lewis⟩ ⟨a spot where a man feels his own insignificance and may well learn to be ~ —Samuel Butler †1902⟩ **b** : reflecting, expressing, or offered in a humble spirit ⟨my *humblest* apologies for the long wait —T.B. Costain⟩ ⟨beg to submit my ~ notion —Vicki Baum⟩ ⟨hear my ~ cry —Fanny J. Crosby⟩ ⟨loathed his cringing look and ~ smile⟩ **2 a** : ranking low in the social or political scale ⟨a man of ~ origin⟩ ⟨all civil servants, no matter how ~, should be disenfranchised —J.H.Plumb⟩ ⟨a ~ fisherman⟩ **b** : ranking low in some hierarchy or scale : INSIGNIFICANT ⟨in the study of the life of animals, however ~, we are studying . . . our own complex human life —W.E.Swinton⟩ ⟨the ~ weeds of the field⟩ ⟨the giant stellar family of which our sun is a ~ member —George Gamow⟩ **c** : of inferior value or worth : not costly or luxurious : MEAN, BASE, UNPRETENTIOUS ⟨chief clerks have mahogany desks; to the others is relegated the *humbler* walnut —H.J.Laski⟩ ⟨artisans . . . who work by hand with gold, silver, and the *humbler* metals —*New Yorker*⟩ ⟨the ~ fare of any Mexican peon —Green Peyton⟩ : of modest dimensions or proportions ⟨freighters using the same slips as the ~ powerboats of small fishermen —*Amer. Guide Series: Mass.*⟩ ⟨equally ~ were the beginnings of . . . the important State Department of Agriculture —*Amer. Guide Series: N.Y.*⟩

syn MEEK, MODEST, LOWLY: HUMBLE suggests absence of vanity and pride, feeling of weakness or lack of worth, self-depreciation, or an abject attitude and demeanor ⟨love hath made her *humble*, and her race doth she forget, and her noble and mighty heart —William Morris⟩ ⟨she prays there as the light goes out, prays with an *humble* heart, and walks home shrinking and silent —W.M.Thackeray⟩ ⟨the cook drew himself up in a smugly *humble* fashion, a deprecating smirk on his face —Jack London⟩ MEEK may suggest patient, subdued, retiring mildness and gentleness, sometimes even a spiritless, cowed submissiveness ⟨the most modest, silent, sheep-faced and *meek* of little men —W.M.Thackeray⟩ ⟨her father, of course, was the lion of the party, but seeing that we were all *meek* and quite willing to be eaten, he roared to us rather than at us —Samuel Butler †1902⟩ MODEST may contrast with *brash* or *self-assertive*; without any implication of abjectness or submissiveness, it may imply unobtrusive lack of boastfulness or conceited or jealous demand for recognition ⟨a simple, *modest*, retiring man —F.D.Roosevelt⟩ ⟨the anthropologist is entirely proper and *modest* in refusing as an anthropologist to make judgments on other cultural beliefs with respect to their epistemological truth —Weston La Barre⟩ LOWLY, close to *humble*, may stress complete lack of worldly pretentiousness ⟨a monk of Lindisfarne, so simple and *lowly* in temper that he traveled on foot —J.R.Green⟩ ⟨you hold aloof from me because you are rich and lofty — and I poor and *lowly* —W.S. Gilbert⟩

²humble \"\ *vt* **humbled; humbled; humbling** \-b(ə)liŋ\ **humbles** [ME *humblen*, fr. *humble*, adj.] **1** : to make humble in spirit or manner : bring down the pride or arrogance of ⟨having *humbled* your heart . . . you may find him —Francis Yeats-Brown⟩ ⟨*humbled* himself before the rich and great⟩ **2** : to destroy the power, independence, or prestige of : defeat decisively : DEGRADE, ABASE ⟨the great marshal *humbled* his enemies in a swift, brilliantly conducted campaign⟩ ⟨it was now the turn of the Church to be *humbled*⟩

humble-bee \ˈhəmbəlˌbē\ *n* [ME *humbylbee*, fr. *humbyll-* (akin to MD *hommel* bumblebee) + bee — more at HUM, BEE] : BUMBLEBEE

hum·ble·ness *n* -ES [ME *humblenesse*, fr. *humble* + *-nesse* -ness] : the quality or state of being humble : HUMILITY

humble pie *n* [*humbles*] **1 a** : a meat pie formerly made of the inferior parts of a deer and served to the huntsman and other servants **b** : a meat pie made of the humbles of a hog **2** [influenced in meaning by ¹*humble*] : submission, apology, or retraction esp. made under pressure or in humiliating circumstances : HUMILIATION ⟨would it mean such a deal of *humble pie*? —Margery Sharp⟩ — often used in the phrase *eat humble pie* ⟨forced to eat *humble pie* —H.W.Van Loon⟩ ⟨before I'd go and eat *humble pie* to the sergeant . . . he might break my neck —Henry Lapham⟩

humble plant *n* : SENSITIVE PLANT 1

humbler *comparative of* HUMBLE

hum·bles \ˈhəmbəlz\ *n pl* [by folk etymology fr. *umbles*] : the heart, liver, kidneys, and other small pieces of a deer or of a hog — compare HUMBLE PIE 1

humblest *superlative of* HUMBLE

humbling *adj* : tending to humble : causing humbleness ⟨a ~ sense of our power —A.E.Stevenson b.1900⟩ — **hum·bling·ly** *adv*

hum·bly \ˈhəmblē, -li *also* ˈəm-\ *adv* [ME *umbly, humbly, humblely*, fr. *umble, humble* + *-ly*] : in a humble manner: as **a** : with humility : with a humble aspect or bearing ⟨must say ~ to the haughty dealers —Pearl Buck⟩ **b** : in a humble position or condition ⟨strategically, though ~ placed, he holds the job of official translator —Ralph de Toledano⟩

hum·boldt·ine \ˈhəmˌbōlˌtēn, -ltᵊn\ *n* -s [F *humboldtine*, fr. Baron Alexander von *Humboldt* †1859 Ger. naturalist and traveler + F *-ine*] : a mineral $FeC_2O_4.2H_2O$ consisting of ferrous oxalate

hum·boldt·ite \-ˌlˌtīt\ *n* -s [in sense 1, fr. Alex. von *Humboldt* + E *-ite*; in sense 2, fr. G *humboldtit*, modif. of F *humboldtine*] **1** : DATOLITE **2** : HUMBOLDTINE

hum·boldt's lily \ˈhəmˌbōlts-\ *n, usu cap H* [after Alex. von *Humboldt*] : a Californian bulbous herb (*Lilium humboldtii*) with showy orange-red purple-spotted flowers

¹hum·bug \ˈhəmˌbəg\ *n* -s [origin unknown] **1 a** : something designed to deceive and mislead : QUACKERY, HOAX, FRAUD, IMPOSTURE ⟨contrived so many delicious ~s to foist on the gullible public —R.L.Taylor⟩ **b** : a person who usu. willfully deceives or misleads others as to his true condition, qualities, or attitudes : one who passes himself off as something that he is not : SHAM, HYPOCRITE, IMPOSTOR ⟨denounced as ~s the playwrights who magnify the difficulties of their craft —*Times Lit. Supp.*⟩ ⟨he's no doctor; he's a ~⟩ **c** : an attitude or spirit of pretense and deception or self-deception ⟨in all his ~, in all his malice and hollowness —Mary Lindsay⟩ **d** : something empty of sense or meaning : DRIVEL, NONSENSE ⟨a frightful lot of ~ talked about glasses —L.B.Somerville-Large⟩ ⟨academic ~⟩ **2** *Brit* : a peppermint candy **syn** see IMPOSTURE

²humbug \"\ *vt* : impose on : DECEIVE, CAJOLE, HOAX ⟨*humbugged* me into buying his worthless stock⟩ ⟨*humbugged* by their doctors, pillaged by their tradesmen —G.B.Shaw⟩ ~ *vi* : to play the part of a humbug

hum·bug·gery \-ˌbəg(ə)rē, -ri\ *n* -ES : HUMBUG

hum·ding·er \ˌhəmˈdiŋə(r)\ *n* -s [prob. alter. of ¹*hummer*] : something extraordinary or of striking excellence ⟨a ~ in the . . . tradition of fantastic humor —Sarah C. Gross⟩ ⟨a sandstorm roared in, a real ~ —Shine Philips⟩

¹hum·drum \ˈhəmˌdrəm\ *adj* [irreg. redupl. of ¹*hum*] : having a routine or commonplace character : lacking interest, excitement, or sparkle : MONOTONOUS, WORKADAY, PROSAIC ⟨makes rather ~ use of a good idea —Eric Keown⟩ ⟨the more ~ aspects of military life, like drill, neatness, and organization —Blair Clark⟩ ⟨the ~ problem of making ends meet —*Amer. Guide Series: Mass.*⟩

²humdrum \"\ *n* : the quality or state of being humdrum ⟨the ordinary, average day, with its good human ~ —C.E.Montague⟩ ⟨give him that very experience of the ~ of clerical life —Compton Mackenzie⟩

hum·dud·geon \ˌhəmˈdəjən\ *or* **hum·dur·geon** \-dərjən\ *n* -s [prob. fr. ⁴*hum* + *dudgeon*] **1** *Scot* : a loud complaint or noise ⟨the auld carline went . . . on top of her head, making such a *humdudgeon* —Hugh McCrae⟩ **2** *Scot* : an imaginary illness or pain

¹hum·ean *or* **hum·ian** \ˈhyümēən\ *adj, usu cap* [David *Hume* †1776 Scot. philosopher + E *-an* or *-ian*] : of, like, or relating to the philosophical system or methods of the philosopher Hume esp. his philosophical skepticism

²humean *or* **humian** \"\ *n* -s *usu cap* : a follower of the philosophy of Hume

hu·mect \hyüˈmekt\ *vb* -ED/-ING/-S [L *humectare, umectare*, fr. *humectus, umectus* moist, fr. *humēre, umēre* to be moist — more at HUMOR] *archaic* : MOISTEN

¹hu·mec·tant \-ktənt\ *adj* [L *humectant-, humectans, umectant-, umectans*, pres. part. of *humectare, umectare*] : MOISTENING ⟨~ properties⟩

²humectant \"\ *n* -s : a substance that promotes retention of moisture (as glycerol, various glycols, sorbitol)

hu·mec·tate \-kˌtāt\ *vb* -ED/-ING/-S [L *humectatus, umectatus*, past part. of *humectare, umectare*] *archaic* : MOISTEN

hu·mec·ta·tion \ˌhyüˌmekˈtāshən\ *n* -s [LL *humectation-, humectatio, umectation-, umectatio*, fr. L *humectatus, umectatus* + *-ion-, -io* -ion] **1** *archaic* : the action or process of moistening **2** *archaic* : the quality or state of being moist

¹hu·mer·al \ˈhyümərəl\ *adj* [prob. fr. F *huméral*, fr. MF *humeral*, fr. NL *humerus* + MF *-al*] **1** : of, relating to, or situated in the region of the humerus : BRACHIAL **2** [LL *humeralis, umeralis*, fr. L *humerus, umerus* + *-alis* -al] : of or belonging to the shoulder ⟨the ~ horny plates or any of several scales on the plastron of turtles⟩ **3** : of, relating to, or being any of several body parts that are analogous in structure, function, or location to the humerus or shoulder ⟨the ~ anterior basal angle of an insect's wing⟩ ⟨the ~ anterior corner of the thorax of a two-winged fly⟩

²humeral \"\ *n* -s **1** : a large bone that forms part of the shoulder girdle of certain fishes not homologous with the humerus **2** : a humeral part (as a scale or plate)

humeral veil *n* [trans. of ML *velum humerale*] : an oblong veil or scarf of the same material as the vestments that is worn around the shoulders at high mass by a subdeacon when he holds the paten between the offertory and pater noster and by a priest when he carries the monstrance in a procession or raises it to give the benediction

humero- *comb form* [ISV, fr. NL *humerus*] : humeral and ⟨*humero*dorsal⟩

hu·mer·us \ˈhyümərəs\ *n, pl* **humeri** \-əˌrī\ [NL, fr. L *humerus, umerus* upper arm, shoulder; akin to ON *āss* mountain ridge, Goth *ams* shoulder, Gk *ōmos*, Toch A *es*, Skt *aṃsa*] **1** : the long bone of the upper arm or forelimb : the longest bone of the upper extremity articulating above by a rounded head with the glenoid fossa, having below a broad articular surface divided by a ridge into a medial pulley-shaped portion and a lateral rounded eminence that articulate with the ulna and radius respectively, and providing various processes and modified surfaces for the attachment of muscles **2** : the shoulder region of an insect; *also* : any of various structures located in this region (as the coxa of a foreleg or the lateral angle of the prothorax)

hu·met \hyüˈmet\ *n* -s [origin unknown] : a heraldic bar or a fess couped at its ends

hu·met·ty \hyüˈmed·ē\ *also* **hu·met·tée** \", ˌhyüməˈtā\ *adj* [*humet* + *-y* or *-ée* (fr. MF *-é*, past part. ending of some verbs) — more at -EE] *heraldry* : couped at the extremities

hum·hum \ˈhəmˌhəm\ *n* -s [Ar *hammām* bath; fr. its use as toweling] : a coarse cotton cloth formerly imported from India

humian *usu cap, var of* HUMEAN

hu·mic \ˈhyümik\ *adj* [prob. fr. F *humique*, fr. NL *humus* + F *-ique* -ic] : relating to or composed at least in part of organic matter : relating to or derived from humus

humic acid *n* : any of various organic acids that are insoluble in alcohol and organic solvents and are obtained from humus

hu·mid \ˈhyüməd *also* ˈyü-\ *adj* [F or L; MF *humide*, fr. L *humidus, umidus*, fr. *humēre, umēre* to be moist or damp — more at HUMOR] : containing or characterized by perceptible moisture : DAMP, MOIST, VAPOROUS ⟨~ air⟩ ⟨a hot ~ climate⟩ **syn** see WET

hu·mid·i·fi·ca·tion \(h)yüˌmidəfəˈkāshən\ *n* -s [fr. *humidify*, after such pairs as E *identify: identification*] : the process of making humid

hu·mid·i·fi·er \=ˈ==ˌfī(ə)r, -īə\ *n* -s **1** : a device for supplying or maintaining humidity **2** : a textile or tobacco worker who tends a humidifying system to keep the moisture content of rooms at the desired level

hu·mid·i·fy \-ˌfī\ *vt* -ED/-ING/-ES [prob. fr. F *humidifier*, fr. *humide* humid + *-ifier* -ify] : to make humid (as the atmosphere) : MOISTEN

hu·mid·i·stat \-dəˌstat\ *n* -s [*humidity* + *-stat*] : an instrument for regulating or maintaining the degree of humidity — called also *hygrostat*

hu·mid·i·ty \hyüˈmidəd·ē, -ətē, -i *also* yü-\ *n* -ES [ME *humidite*, fr. MF *humidité*, fr. LL *humiditas, umiditas*, fr. L *humidus, umidus* moist, damp + *-itat-, -itas* -ity — more at HUMID] : a moderate degree of wetness (as of a solid surface or the air) perceptible to the eye or to touch : MOISTURE, DAMPNESS — see ABSOLUTE HUMIDITY, RELATIVE HUMIDITY

hu·mid·ly *adv* : in a humid manner : WETLY ⟨eyes . . . beaming ~ through their dark lashes —*Dublin Bk. of Irish Verse*⟩

hu·mi·dor \ˈhyüməˌdȯ(ə)r, -ȯ(ə) *also* ˈyü-\ *n* -s [*humid* + *-or*] : a case or enclosure (as for storing cigars) in which the air is kept properly humidified : *also* : a contrivance (as a tube containing moistened sponges) placed in a case to keep the air moist

hu·mi·fi·ca·tion \ˌhyüməfəˈkāshən\ *n* -s [NL *humus* + E *-i-* + *-fication*] : the process of the formation of humus

hu·mi·fied \ˈhyüməˌfīd\ *adj* [NL *humus* + E *-ified* (fr. *-ify* + *-ed*)] : converted into humus ⟨~ organic matter⟩

hu·mi·fuse \-ˌfyüs\ *adj* [ISV *humi-* (fr. L *humus* earth, ground) + L *fusus*, past part. of *fundere* to pour — more at FOUND] : spread over the surface of the ground : PROCUMBENT ⟨~ plant stems⟩

hu·mil·i·ate \hyüˈmilēˌāt, *also* yü-, *usu* -ād·+V\ *vt* -ED/-ING/-S [LL *humiliatus*, past part. of *humiliare*, fr. L *humilis* low, humble — more at HUMBLE] : to reduce to a lower position in one's own eyes or the eyes of others : injure the self-respect of : HUMBLE, MORTIFY ⟨insulted and *humiliated* his darling niece —Hilaire Belloc⟩

humiliating *adj* : lowering one's position or dignity : HUMBLING, MORTIFYING ⟨a ~ peace⟩ — **hu·mil·i·at·ing·ly** *adv*

hu·mil·i·a·tion \(ˌ)=ˌ=lēˈāshən\ *n* -s [ME *humiliacioun*, fr. MF *humiliation*, fr. LL *humiliation-, humiliatio*, fr. *humiliatus* + L *-ion-, -io* -ion] **1 a** : the act of humiliating ⟨His incarnation was the ~ of His godhead —R.J.Wilberforce⟩ **b** : the state of being humiliated ⟨what submission, what cringing and fawning, what servility, what abject ~ —Charles Dickens⟩ **2** : an instance of humiliation ⟨watched China undergo one ~ after another —E.P.Snow⟩

hu·mil·i·a·tive \=ˈ=lēˌād·iv, -lēəd-\ *adj* : tending to humiliate : causing humiliation

hu·mil·i·ty \hyüˈmiləd·ē, -ətē, -i *also* yü-\ *n* -ES [ME *humilite*, fr. MF *humilité*, fr. L *humilitat-, humilitas*, fr. *humilis* low, humble + *-itat-, -itas* -ity — more at HUMBLE] **1** : the quality or state of being humble in spirit : freedom from pride or arrogance ⟨we all need . . . ~ in the face of what we do not understand —Nicola Chiaromonte⟩ **2** *New Eng* : any of several snipes

hu·min \ˈhyümən\ *n* -s [G, fr. NL *humus* + G *-in*] : any of various dark-colored insoluble usu. amorphous substances formed in many reactions: as **a** : a substance obtained from humus (as the residue from treatment with cold alkali) **b** : a pigment formed in the acid hydrolysis of protein containing tryptophan — compare MELANOIDIN

hu·mir·ia \hyüˈmirēə\ *n, cap* [NL, modif. of Pg *umiri* umiri — more at UMIRI] : a genus (the type of the family Humiriaceae) of So. American balsam-yielding trees with small cymose flowers

hu·mir·i·a·ce·ae \=ˌ==ˈāsēˌē\ *n pl, cap* [NL, fr. *Humiria*, type genus + *-aceae*] : a family of tropical American and African trees or shrubs (order Geraniales) by some treated as a subfamily of the Linaceae but having bilocular anthers and numerous stamens — **hu·mir·i·a·ceous** \(ˌ)=ˌ==ˈāshəs\ *adj*

hum·ism \ˈhyüˌmizəm\ *n* -s *usu cap* [David *Hume* + E *-ism* — more at HUMEAN] : the philosophical system or methods of Hume; *esp* : philosophical skepticism according to which it is impossible to demonstrate any necessary connection between occurrences

hu·mit \ˈhyüməṭ\ *n* -s [short for *humiture*] : the unit used in expressing humiture ⟨a humiture of 68 ~s⟩

hum·ite \ˈhyüˌmīt\ *n* -s [Sir Abraham *Hume* †1838 Eng. mineral collector + E *-ite*] : a white, yellow, brown, or red mineral $Mg_7Si_3O_{12}(F,OH)_2$ consisting of a basic magnesium silicate containing fluorine that is brittle and of vitreous to resinous luster, that is found in the masses ejected from Vesuvius and elsewhere, and is related to chondrodite, norbergite, and olivine (hardness 6–6.5; sp. gr. 3.1–3.2)

humite group *n* : a group of isomorphous minerals consisting of olivine, chondrodite, humite, and clinohumite and closely resembling one another in chemical composition, physical properties, and crystallization

hu·mi·ture \ˈhyüməˌchü(ə)r\ *n* -s [blend of *humidity* and *temperature*] : a combined measurement of temperature and humidity computed in integers by adding the temperature in degrees Fahrenheit to the relative humidity and dividing by two and choosing the next integer if a fraction of ½ is left over (when the temperature is 75° F and the relative humidity is 60 percent the ~ is 68)

hum·lie \ˈhəmli\ *n* -s [*hummel* + *-ie*] *Scot* : a polled domestic bovine : DODDIE

hum·ma·ble \ˈhəməbəl\ *adj* : capable of or lending itself to being hummed ⟨a ~ melody, a catchy tune —John Mason Brown⟩

hummed *past of* HUM

¹hum·mel *also* **hum·ble** \ˈhəməl\ *adj* [ME *hommyll*; akin to LG *hummel* polled animal] **1** *Scot* : AWNLESS — used of grain **2** *Scot* : HORNLESS — used of cattle or stags

²hummel *also* **humble** \"\ *vt* **hummeled** *or* **hummelled** *also* **humbled; hummeled** *or* **hummelled** *also* **humbled; hummeling** *or* **hummelling** *also* **humbling** \-m(ə)liŋ\ **hummels** *also* **humbles** *chiefly Scot* : to separate (barley or oats) from the awns and tips of hull

³hummel \"\ *n* -s **1** *chiefly Scot* : HUMLIE **2** *chiefly Scot* : a hornless stag

hum·mel·er *or* **hum·mel·ler** \-m(ə)lə(r)\ *n* -s : one that hummels

¹hum·mer \ˈhəmə(r)\ *n* -s [¹*hum* + *-er* (n. suffix)] **1** : one that hums; *specif* : HUMMINGBIRD **2** : HUMDINGER ⟨the early pace was certainly a ~ —G.F.T.Ryall⟩ — **on the hummer** **1** *dial* : not in working order **2** *dial* : not well : under the weather

²hum·mer \ˈhəmə(r), ˈhům-\ *vb* [freq. of ¹*hum*] *dial Brit* : MURMUR, MUMBLE

humming *adj* [ME, fr. pres. part. of *hummen* to hum — more at HUM] **1** : DRONING, BUZZING ⟨the ~ sound of telephone wires⟩ **2** : extremely busy : BOOMING, BRISK ⟨the tobacco warehouses . . . are ~ centers of activity —*Amer. Guide Series: N.C.*⟩ — **hum·ming·ly** *adv*

hummingbird \ˈ=ˌ=ˌ=\ *n* : any of numerous nonpasserine birds constituting a family (Trochilidae) that is noted for the small size of most species and the brilliant iridescent plumage of the males which in some forms have remarkable crests, neck tufts, or elongated tail feathers, and being anatomically related to the swifts and like them having narrow wings with long primaries but a slender bill and a very extensile tongue

hummingbird moth *n* : HAWKMOTH

hummingbird sage *n* : CRIMSON SAGE

hummingbird's trumpet *n* : CALIFORNIA FUCHSIA

¹hum·mock \ˈhəmək\ *or* **hom·mock** \ˈhäm-\ *n* -s [alter. of ³*hammock*] **1** : a rounded or conical knoll or hillock : a slight rise of ground above a level surface **2** : a ridge or pile of ice (as in an ice field or floe) **3** : HAMMOCK 2

[2]**hummock** \"\ *vb* -ED/-ING/-S : to form into hummocks esp. on an ice field

hum·mocky \-kē,-ki\ *adj* : abounding in hummocks : resembling a hummock : UNEVEN ⟨a ~ road⟩ ⟨~ fields⟩ ⟨stopped by ~ ice —T.H.Manning⟩

hum·mum \'hə(,)məm\ *also* **hum·mums** \-)məmz\ *n, pl* **hummums** *usu cap* [fr. the *Hummums*, a 17th cent. bathhouse in Covent Garden, London, England, fr. Turk *hamam*, fr. Ar *hammām* bath] : TURKISH BATH

hum note *n* : the humming tone given by the whole mass of a vibrating bell sounding an octave below its fundamental note — called also *hum tone*

[1]**hu·mor** \'(h)yümə(r)\ *n* -S *see -or in Explan Notes* [ME *humour*, fr. MF *humeur*, fr. ML & L; ML *humor* humor of the body, fr. L *humor, umor* moisture, fluid; akin to MD *wac* damp, wet, ON *vökr* damp, L *humēre, umēre* to be moist or damp, *uvidus* damp, moist, Gk *hygros* wet, Skt *ukṣati* he sprinkles, he moistens] **1 a** (1) : a normal functioning fluid or semifluid of the body (as the blood, lymph, or bile) esp. of vertebrates (2) : a secretion that is itself an excitant of activity (as certain hormones) — see NEUROHUMOR **b** (1) *in medieval physiology* : a fluid or juice of an animal or plant; *specif* : one of the four fluids entering into the constitution of the body and determining by their relative proportions a person's health and temperament — see BLACK BILE, BLOOD, PHLEGM, YELLOW BILE (2) : constitutional or habitual disposition, character, or bent : TEMPERAMENT ⟨are you an agreeable person? Have you a pleasant ~? —Alfred Buchanan⟩ ⟨every word they spoke . . . attested to their mutual love, the combining of their ~*s* —Djuna Barnes⟩ ⟨the women were horrified or admiring, as their ~ moved them —Edith Wharton⟩ (3) : temporary state of mind : TEMPER, MOOD ⟨not in a ~ to hear you further —Thomas Hardy⟩ ⟨in excellent ~⟩ ⟨after the execution . . . the ~ of the court involuntarily changed —Francis Hackett⟩ (4) : a sudden, unpredictable, or unreasoning inclination : CAPRICE, WHIM, FANCY ⟨a very frolicsome and tricky creature . . . full of wild fantastic ~*s* —W.H.Hudson †1922⟩ ⟨conceived the ~ of impeaching casual passersby . . . and wreaking vengeance on them —Charles Dickens⟩ ⟨victims of nature's cataclysmic ~*s*, dust storms and drought —Julian Dana⟩ (5) **humors** *pl* : actions revealing the oddities or quirks of human temperament : whimsical or fantastic actions : VAGARIES ⟨the ~*s* and small details of ordinary life —John Erskine †1951⟩ **c** *obs* : MOISTURE, VAPOR ⟨the ~*s* of the dank morning —Shak.⟩ **2 a** : that quality in a happening, an action, a situation, or an expression of ideas which appeals to a sense of the ludicrous or absurdly incongruous : comic or amusing quality ⟨the ~ of his plight⟩ ⟨the delightful ~ of a book⟩ **b** : the mental faculty of discovering, expressing, or appreciating ludicrous or absurdly incongruous elements in ideas, situations, happenings, or acts : droll imagination or its expressions ⟨the man is completely without ~⟩ — compare WIT **c** : the act of or effort at being humorous : something (as an action, saying, or writing) that is or is designed to be humorous ⟨his heavy ~ fell completely flat⟩ ⟨never read any ~ above the so-called comics —Ellie Tucker⟩ ⟨a ~ magazine⟩ **syn** see MOOD, WIT — **out of humor** *adv* : in a bad humor : out of sorts

[2]**humor** \"\ *vt* **humored**; **humored**; **humoring** \-m(ə)riŋ\ **humors** *see -or in Explan Notes* **1** : to comply with the humor of : soothe or content by indulgence or compliance : INDULGE ⟨one must discover and ~ his weaknesses —H.M. Parshley⟩ **2** : to comply with the nature of : adjust matters to the peculiarities or exigencies of : adapt oneself to ⟨yielding to, and ~*ing* the motion of the limbs and twigs —William Bartram⟩ **syn** see INDULGE

hu·mor·al \-mərəl\ *adj* [MF, fr. ML *humoralis*, fr. *humor* + L *-alis* -al — more at HUMOR] : of, relating to, proceeding from, or involving a bodily humor — now often used of endocrine factors as opposed to neural or somatic ⟨~ control of sugar metabolism⟩

hu·mored \¦(h)yümə(r)d\ *adj* : having a specified humor — now used only in combination ⟨a good-*humored* child⟩ ⟨a bad-*humored* man⟩ — **hu·mored·ly** *adv*

hu·mor·esque \¦(h)yümə¦resk\ *n* -S [G *humoreske*, fr. *humor* (fr. E) + *-eske* -esque] : a musical composition typically whimsical or fanciful in character : CAPRICCIO

hu·mor·ist \'(h)yümərəst\ *n* -S [MF *humoriste*, fr. *humeur* humor + *-iste* -ist] **1** *archaic* : a person subject to humors or whims : one who has some peculiarity or eccentricity of character which he indulges in odd or whimsical ways **2** : a person given to the display or enjoyment of humor: as **a** : a person with a strong sense of humor : a facetious person : JOKER, WAG ⟨two local ~*s* go in . . . to make a goat of the doctor —*Sydney (Australia) Bull.*⟩ **b** : a writer specializing in or noted for the quality of his humor ⟨a great and powerful ~⟩

hu·mor·is·tic \¦==¦ristik\ *adj* : HUMOROUS ⟨that book was to be ~ and undoubtedly . . . would have amused many people —Felix Reichmann⟩

hu·mor·less \'(h)yümə(r)ləs\ *adj* **1** : lacking in humor ⟨heavy, ~, slow-moving, methodical —T.H.Fielding⟩ **2** : offered, said, or done in dead seriousness : reflecting the lack of a sense of humor ⟨~ memorizing of 500 dates . . . for a three-hour third-degree oral examination —L. Ruth Middlebrook⟩ ⟨this ~ proposal aroused covert snickers⟩ — **hu·mor·less·ly** *adv* — **hu·mor·less·ness** *n* -ES

hu·mor·ous \'(h)yüm(ə)rəs\ *adj* [MF *humereux*, fr. *humeur* + *-eux* -ous] **1** *archaic* : subject to or governed by humor or caprice : CAPRICIOUS, WHIMSICAL **2** *obs* : MOIST, HUMID, WATERY **3 a** : full of or characterized by humor : FUNNY, JOCULAR ⟨a ~ poem⟩ ⟨earned part of his way through college by selling ~ drawings —*Current Biog.*⟩ ⟨stories in a ~ vein⟩ **b** : possessing, indicating, or expressive of a sense of humor : given to the display or appreciative of humor ⟨short, rotund, with . . . ~ brown eyes —R.M.Lovett⟩ ⟨a very kindly and rather ~ man —O.W.Holmes †1935⟩ ⟨vented a low ~ laugh —Thomas Hardy⟩ ⟨studied his own life . . . with a shrewd and ~ eye —Harrison Smith⟩ **syn** see WITTY

hu·mor·ous·ly *adv* : in a humorous manner

hu·mor·ous·ness *n* -ES : the quality or state of being humorous

hu·mor·some \-mə(r)səm\ *adj* : full of humors : WHIMSICAL

humour *Brit var of* HUMOR

hu·mous \'(h)yüməs\ *adj* [NL *humus* + E *-ous*] : of or relating to humus : containing a relatively large amount of humus ⟨~ soils⟩

[1]**hump** \'həmp\ *n* -S [akin to Fris *hompe* lump, chunk, D *homp* lump, chunk, MLG *hump* bump, ON *aptrhuppr* flank of an animal, Norw dial. *hupp, hump* flank of an animal, L *incumbere* to lie down, Gk *kymbē* drinking cup, bowl, boat, Skt *kumbha* pot, OE *hype* hip — more at HIP] **1** : a rounded protuberance: as **a** : the protuberance formed by a crooked back in human beings **b** : a fleshy protuberance on the back of an animal (as a camel, bison, or whale) **2** *Brit* : a fit of depression or sulking ⟨enough to give anyone the ~ to see him now —Samuel Butler †1902⟩ **3 a** (1) : MOUND, HUMMOCK (2) : a conspicuous bulge or protruding section of coastline ⟨the ~ of Brazil⟩ (3) : a mountain range or mountain that has to be crossed — used chiefly in aeronautics ⟨over the ~ from Chile to Buenos Aires⟩ ⟨the Himalayan ~⟩ **b** : an elevation in a railroad switch yard up one side of which the cars are pushed by an engine and down the other side of which they are switched by gravity to their proper tracks **4 a** : a difficult, trying, or critical phase (as of an undertaking) — often used in the phrase *over the hump* ⟨in the production of machine tools the Soviet Union is over the ~ —P.E.Mosely⟩ **b** : strenuous exertion or effort : GO, HUSTLE — often used in the phrases *on the hump* ⟨my duties keep me pretty much on the ~ —*New Yorker*⟩ and *get a hump on* ⟨nowadays even ministers of the gospel know how to get a ~ on —J.W.Krutch⟩

[2]**hump** \"\ *vb* -ED/-ING/-S *vt* **1** : to exert (oneself) ⟨last year he had to ~ himself and make over a million —*Fortune*⟩ **2** : to make humpbacked : HUNCH ⟨stood ~*ed* with pain —F.B. Gipson⟩ **3** *chiefly Brit* : to put or carry on the back or shoulder ⟨we ~*ed* our barracks bags, piled in the wet trucks —H.D. Skidmore⟩ ⟨rose at six in the morning to ~ coal . . . to the neighbors' homes —*Books of the Month*⟩; *also* : to carry in any way ⟨helped . . . ~ in the crates of beer —Audrey Barker⟩ **4** : to sort (freight cars) in a classification yard and assemble in trains by means of a hump **5** : to copulate with — usu. considered vulgar ~ *vi* **1 a** : to exert oneself : HUSTLE, HURRY ⟨will have to ~ to get through . . . tomorrow —Richard Bissell⟩ ⟨keeps me ~*ing* even with three assistants —C.E. Lovejoy⟩ ⟨~ along and do your chores —Howard Troyer⟩ **b** : to move swiftly or at top speed : RACE ⟨it's moving southeast and ~*ing* toward the north —*Springfield (Mass.) Daily News*⟩ ⟨really ~*ing* along ahead of that tail wind —Norman Carlisle⟩ **2** : to rise in a hump : form a hump ⟨the . . . highway ~*s* and dips in a manner which discourages fast driving —*Amer. Guide Series: Conn.*⟩ ⟨~*s* up to 11,600 feet —A.H. Brown⟩

humpback \'=,=\ *n* **1** : a crooked back : a humped back : KYPHOSIS **2** : a humpbacked person : HUNCHBACK **3 a** *also* **humpback whale** : a whalebone whale of the genus *Megaptera* related to the rorquals but having very long flippers, being black above and white below, attaining large size, but yielding inferior whalebone and oil **b** (1) : HUMPBACK SALMON (2) : the black sea bass (*Centropristes striatus*)

humpbacked \'=¦=\ *adj* : having a humped back

humpbacked whitefish *n* : an Alaskan whitefish (*Coregonus nelsoni*)

humpback grunt *n* : YELLOW GRUNT

humpback salmon *also* **humpbacked salmon** *n* : a small salmon (*Oncorhynchus gorbuscha*) which ascends Pacific coast rivers of Asia and of America from California to Alaska

humpback sucker *n* : a large sucker (*Xyrauchen texanus*) of the Colorado basin reputed to attain a weight of 7 pounds

humped \'həm(p)t\ *adj* : having a hump : HUMPBACKED

humped cattle *n* : domestic cattle developed from an Indian species (*Bos indicus*) and characterized by a hump of fat and muscle above the shoulders : Brahman cattle : domestic zebus

[1]**humph** *typically a snort or a strong h-sound followed by a contemptuously intoned m-sound or vowel 'ə the 'ə usu nasalized; often read as* 'həm(p)f\ *n* -S [imit. of a grunt] : a sound expressive of doubt or contempt ⟨voiced many a skeptical ~ —*Time*⟩ — often used as an interjection

[2]**humph** \'həm(p)f\ *vb* -ED/-ING/-S *vi* : to utter a humph ⟨~*ed* and shagged upstairs —Feike Feikema⟩ ~ *vt* : to utter in a tone suggestive of a humph ⟨might as well give one to the Queen of England, ~*ed* a correspondent —Horace Sutton⟩

humping track *n* : a yard track for sorting freight cars by humping

hump·less \'həmpləs\ *adj* : having no hump

hump rider *n* : a yardman who rides and brakes cars in hump yards not equipped with car retarders

humps *pl of* HUMP, *pres 3d sing of* HUMP

hump-shouldered \'=¦==\ *adj* : having a humped shoulder ⟨their life preservers making them appear *hump-shouldered* —H.D.Skidmore⟩

hump sore *n* : infestation of the skin of Indian cattle by a filarial worm (*Stephanofilaria assamensis*); *also* : the hide-damaging lesions it causes esp. about the hump and neck

hump speed *n* : the speed of a seaplane during takeoff at which the water resistance reaches a maximum

hump·ty \'həm(p)ti\ *n* -ES [perh. after *Humpty*-Dumpty] *Brit* : a low soft cushioned seat ⟨the dean, curled on a ~, was frankly listening —Dorothy Sayers⟩

hump·ty–dump·ty \¦həm(p)tē¦dəm(p)tē, -ti . . . ti\ *n* -ES *often cap H&D* [after *Humpty-Dumpty*, egg-shaped nursery-rhyme character who fell from a wall and broke into bits] : something that once damaged can never be repaired or made operative again ⟨the exchange crisis . . . that brought the *Humpty-Dumpty* of currency stabilization tumbling —*Atlantic*⟩ ⟨people fled into their suddenly *Humpty-Dumpty* world —Robert O'Brien⟩

[1]**humpy** \'həmpē, -pi\ *adj* -ER/-EST [[1]*hump* + *-y*] : full of humps or bunches : covered with protuberances : HUMPED

[2]**hum·py** \"\ *n* -ES [native name in Australia] *Austral* : a small, primitive, or ramshackle dwelling : SHANTY, SHACK, HUT

hump yard *n* : a railroad switch yard having a hump

hums *pres 3d sing of* HUM, *pl of* HUM

humstrum \'=,=\ *n* -S [[1]*hum* + *strum*] **1** : a crude fiddle; *broadly* : any out-of-tune musical instrument **2** : HURDY-GURDY

hum tone *n* : HUM NOTE

hu·mu·hu·mu·nu·ku·nu·ku·a·pu·aa \,hüməˈhüməˌnükə ˈnükəˌäpəˈwäˌä\ *n* -S [Hawaiian] : a small Hawaiian triggerfish

hu·mu·lene \'hyümyə,lēn\ *n* -S [ISV *humul-* (fr. NL *Humulus*) + *-ene*] : a liquid sesquiterpene $C_{15}H_{24}$ in hop oil and clove oil — called also *alpha-caryophyllene*

hu·mu·lone \-,lōn\ *or* **hu·mu·lon** \-,län\ *n* -S [ISV *humul-* (fr. NL *Humulus*) + *-one*] : a bitter crystalline antibiotic $C_{21}H_{30}O_5$ obtained from lupulin

hu·mu·lus \-ləs\ *n, cap* [NL, fr. ML, hop (plant), prob. of Gmc origin; akin to OE *hymele* hop, MLG *homele*, ON *humli*] : a genus of herbaceous vines (family Urticaceae) with palmate leaves and pistillate flowers in clusters resembling catkins or cones — see [3]HOP

hu·mus \'(h)yüməs\ *n* -ES [NL, fr. L, earth, ground — more at HUMBLE] : a brown or black complex and varying material formed by the partial decomposition of vegetable or animal matter : the organic portion of soil

[1]**hun** \'hən\ *n* -S [LL *Hunni*, pl.] **1** *cap* : a member of a nomadic Mongolian people who were driven westward from Mongolia about A.D. 200 and obtaining control of a large portion of central and eastern Europe under Attila about the middle of the 5th century forced even Rome to pay tribute until their power was terminated by their defeat at Châlons in 451 and the death of Attila in 453 — compare EPHTHALITE **2 a** *often cap* : a person who is wantonly destructive : VANDAL **b** *usu cap* : GERMAN; *esp* : a German soldier in World War I or World War II ⟨the recoiling Hitlerites and *Huns* are redoubling their ruthless cruelties —*Britannica Bk. of the Yr.*⟩ — usu. used disparagingly

[2]**hun** \"\ *n* -S [by shortening] *usu cap* : HUNGARIAN PARTRIDGE

hun *abbr* hundred

[1]**hu·na·nese** \¦hünə¦nēz, -ēs\ *adj, usu cap* [*Hunan*, province in China + E *-ese*] : of or relating to the province of Hunan

[2]**hunanese** \"\ *n, pl* **hunanese** *cap* : a native or inhabitant of Hunan

[1]**hunch** \'hənch\ *vb* -ED/-ING/-ES [origin unknown] *vi* **1** : to push, thrust, or move oneself forward ⟨~*ed* along for a short spell of safe steps —T.B.Costain⟩ ⟨heavy shoulders . . . ~*ed* through the open door —S.H.Adams⟩ **2 a** : to assume a bent or crooked posture esp. in sitting : bend one's body into an arch or hump ⟨a technical sergeant ~*es* in a tiny cubicle —*Fortune*⟩ ⟨gripped the wheel, ~*ing* over it —Gregor Felsen⟩ ⟨folded his hands on the table and ~*ed* forward —Hugh MacLennan⟩ **b** : to draw or compress oneself into a ball : curl up ⟨~*ed* up on the rug —Margery Allingham⟩ ⟨~ beneath the covers, in my curled red ball of darkness —Randall Jarrell⟩ **c** : HUDDLE, SQUAT ⟨we ~*ed* close to the damp earth —H.D.Skidmore⟩ ⟨the home ~*es* on a one-acre point of land —*Springfield (Mass.) Union*⟩ ⟨the mountains ~*ed* around the valley —Helen Rich⟩ **d** : to rise so as to form a hump or arch : REAR ⟨the sea ~*ed* up and hurled itself on the . . . land —H.E.Rieseberg⟩ ⟨his shoulder ~*ed* convulsively —Bernard DeVoto⟩ **3** : FUDGE 2a ~ *vt* **1** : PUSH, JOSTLE, SHOVE ⟨I would ~ my chair . . . closer to my dear and only cronies —Mary Nash⟩ ⟨tugboats . . . ~*ed* their ocean-going charges to the quayside —Newman Bumstead⟩ **2** : to thrust or bend so as to form a hump or arch : CROOK, ARCH ⟨the crow ~*ed* its shoulders, like an old woman seeking comfort in her moldy coat —Edita Morris⟩ ⟨kept his . . . body ~*ed* slightly forward —Tennessee Williams⟩ ⟨if you ~ yourself up . . . it is probably due to self-consciousness or fatigue —*Farmer's Weekly (So. Africa)*⟩ : HUDDLE ⟨~*ed* ourselves into a little group in the corner⟩

[2]**hunch** \"\ *n* -ES **1** : the act or an instance of hunching : PUSH ⟨give him a good ~ with your foot —Abraham Tucker⟩ **2** [prob. back-formation fr. *hunchbacked*] **a** : a rounded protuberance : HUMP ⟨his back carried a huge ~ —William Scoresby †1857⟩ **b** : a thick piece : LUMP ⟨barter it for a ~ of cake —Flora Thompson⟩ **3** : a strong intuitive feeling ⟨expressed her ~ that the photograph had slid off the desk —*Saturday Rev.*⟩; *esp* : a strong intuitive feeling as to how something (as a course of action) will turn out ⟨on a ~, resolved to establish a rail and shipping terminus here —*Amer. Guide Series: Texas*⟩

hunchback \'=,=\ *n* [back-formation fr. *hunchbacked*] **1** : a back with a hunch or hump : KYPHOSIS **2** : a hunchbacked person

hunchbacked \'=¦=\ *adj* [perh. fr. [1]*hunch* + *-backed* (fr. [1]*back* + *-ed*)] : HUMPBACKED

hund \'hən(d), -ü-,-ü-\ *dial var of* HOUND

hund *abbr* hundred

hun·der \'hən(d)ə(r)\ *or* **hun·dert** \-(d)ə(r)t\ *dial var of* HUNDRED

hun·di *also* **hoon·dee** *or* **hoon·di** \'hündē\ *n* -S [Hindi *hundī*] : a negotiable instrument, bill of exchange, or promissory note of India used esp. in the internal finance of trade

[1]**hun·dred** \'həndrəd, ÷ -ndə(r)d, *rapid* -nə(r)d, *dial or substand* -nə(r)t\ *n, pl* **hundreds** *or* **hundred** [ME, fr. OE; akin to OFris *hundred, hunderd* hundred, OS *hunderod*, ON *hundrath*; all fr. a prehistoric WGmc-NGmc compound whose constituents are akin respectively to OE *hund* hundred and Goth *garathjan* to count; akin to OHG *hunt* hundred, OS & Goth *hund*, L *centum*, Gk *hekaton*, Skt *śatam*; all fr. a prehistoric word derived fr. the root of E *ten* — more at TEN, REASON] **1** : 10 tens : twice 50 : five twenties : five score : the square of ten — see NUMBER table **2 a** : 100 units or objects ⟨a total of a ~⟩ **b** : a group or set of 100 ⟨arranged by ~*s*⟩ **3 a** : the numerable quantity symbolized by the arabic numerals 100 **b** : the letter C **4** : the number occupying the position three to the left of the decimal point in the Arabic notation (as 9 in the number 2968) — usu. used in pl. **5 a** : any of various British units of quantity for commercial items (as for 120 boards, 120 nails, or 140 pecks or 35 bushels of lime) **b** : HUNDREDWEIGHT **6 a** : a hundred-pound note **b** : a hundred-dollar bill **7 a** : a division of a county orig. English but later established also in certain British possessions and formerly having its own local court **b** : the body of landholders and residents of a hundred **8** : **hundreds** *pl* — used in combination to designate a specified century ⟨the early fifteen-*hundreds*⟩ — **by the hundred** *or* **by the hundreds** : in great numbers ⟨examples can be found *by the hundreds* —H.S. Morrison⟩

[2]**hundred** \"\ *adj* [ME, fr. OE, fr. *hundred*, n.] : being 100 in number ⟨a ~ years⟩ — usu. preceded by *a, an*, or a numeral (as *one, four*)

[1]**hun·dred·fold** \¦=¦fōld\ *adv* [ME, fr. [2]*hundred* + *-fold*] : by 100 times ⟨increased a ~⟩ ⟨increased one ~⟩ — usu. preceded by *a, an*, or a numeral (as *one, four*)

[2]**hundredfold** \"\ *adj* [ME, fr. [2]*hundred* + *-fold*] : being 100 times as large, as great, or as many as some understood size, degree, or amount : very great — usu. preceded by *a, an*, or a numeral (as *one, four*)

hundred–legs \'==,=\ *n pl but sing or pl in constr* : CENTIPEDE

[1]**hundred–percent** \¦===¦=\ *adj* **1** : PERFECT, UNALLOYED, GENUINE **2** : THOROUGHGOING, UNQUESTIONABLE ⟨the resources of the *hundred-percent* American —*The Bookman*⟩

[2]**hundred–percent** \"\ *adv* : without qualification or reservation : ENTIRELY, COMPLETELY ⟨a *hundred-percent* pure wool⟩

hundred–percent·er \"ə(r)\ *n* -S [*hundred-percent (American)* + *-er*] : a thoroughgoing, unqualified, and often blatant nationalist; *esp* : a self-proclaimed opponent of foreign alliances, influences, and interests ⟨the vociferous nationalism of the *hundred-percenters* . . . is always most eloquent when it is about to be most rowdy —Walter Lippmann⟩ ⟨could never be a *hundred-percenter* as long as he did not possess an American birth certificate —*Amer. Mercury*⟩

hundred–percent·ism \-,izəm\ *n* -S : the beliefs and practices of a hundred-percenter ⟨laws . . . passed under the stress of antialien phobia and *hundred-percentism* —*Christian Century*⟩

[1]**hun·dredth** \'həndrə|dth, 'hən(d)ə(r)|, |tth\ *adj* [ME *hundreth*, fr. *hundred* + *-th*] **1** : being number 100 in a countable series ⟨the ~ day⟩ — see NUMBER table **2** : being one of a hundred equal parts into which anything is divisible ⟨a ~ share of the money⟩

[2]**hundredth** \"\ *n, pl* **hundredths** \-dths, -t(th)s\ **1** : number 100 in a countable series **2** : the quotient of a unit divided by 100 : one of 100 equal parts of anything

hundredweight \'==,=\ *n, pl* **hundredweight** *or* **hundredweights** : any of various units of weight ranging from 100 to about 120 pounds: as **a** : a unit equal to 100 pounds — called also *short hundredweight* **b** *Brit* : a unit equal to 112 pounds — called also *long hundredweight*; see MEASURE table **c** : METRIC HUNDREDWEIGHT

hung *past of* HANG

[1]**hun·gar·i·an** \,həŋ'ga(a)rēən, -ger-,-gar-\ *n* -S *cap* [*Hungary*, country in central Europe + E *-an*] **1 a** : a native or inhabitant of Hungary : MAGYAR **b** : one that is of Hungarian descent **2** : the language of the Magyars : MAGYAR 2

[2]**hungarian** \¦=¦===\ *adj, usu cap* **1** : of, relating to, or characteristic of Hungary **2** : of, relating to, or characteristic of the people of Hungary

hungarian balsam *n, usu cap H* : a resin from the Swiss mountain pine

hungarian blue *n, often cap H* : AZURITE BLUE

hungarian brome *or* **hungarian forage grass** *n, usu cap H* : AWNLESS BROMEGRASS

hungarian goulash *n, usu cap H* : GOULASH

hungarian grass *or* **hungarian millet** *n, usu cap H* : FOXTAIL MILLET

hungarian green *n, often cap H* : MALACHITE GREEN 3

hungarian gypsy scale *n, usu cap H* : a musical scale having a whole step between steps 1 and 2, half steps between 2 and 3, 4 and 5, 5 and 6, 7 and 8, and augmented seconds between 3 and 4, and 6 and 7 — compare HARMONIC MINOR SCALE

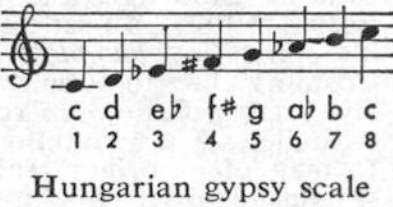

Hungarian gypsy scale

hungarian lilac *n, usu cap H* : a central European shrub (*Syringa josikaea*) having lilac-violet flowers in upright clusters and with the lobes of the corolla nearly upright

hungarian paprika *also* **hungarian pepper** *n, usu cap H* **1** : a paprika produced in Hungary from peppers of slight pungency and distinctive flavor; *esp* : one produced from the fleshy fruit freed from seeds and stalk — see KING'S PAPRIKA **2** : a plant producing peppers suitable for making Hungarian paprika

hungarian partridge *n, usu cap H* : a common European partridge (*Perdix perdix*)

hungarian vetch *or* **hungarian clover** *n, usu cap H* : a European vetch (*Vicia cannonica*) introduced into the Pacific Northwest as a hay, forage, and silage crop esp. on heavy clay soils and having stems and leaves with hair which give the plants a gray color

hun·ga·ry \'həŋgərē, -ri\ *adj, usu cap* [fr. *Hungary*, country in central Europe] : of or from Hungary : of the kind or style prevalent in Hungary : HUNGARIAN

hungary blue *n, often cap H* : COBALT BLUE 2

[1]**hun·ger** \'həŋgə(r)\ *n* -S [ME, fr. OE *hungor*; akin to OHG *hungar* hunger, ON *hungr*, Goth *hūhrus* hunger, Gk *kenkei* he is hungry, Skt *kāṅksati* he desires, Lith *kanka* pain; basic meaning: burning, hurting] **1 a** : a craving, desire, or urgent need for food **b** : an uneasy sensation occasioned normally by the lack of food and resulting directly from stimulation of the sensory nerves of the stomach by the contraction and churning movement of the empty stomach **c** : a weakened disordered condition brought about by prolonged lack of food ⟨die of ~⟩ **2** : FAMINE ⟨the great ~*s* and . . . pestilences of the past —*Times Lit. Supp.*⟩ **3** : a strong desire or craving ⟨a ~ for knowledge⟩ ⟨land ~⟩ **4** : a craving for or deterioration from lack of a specified substance ⟨potash ~⟩ — used esp. of plants

[2]**hunger** \"\ *vb* **hungered**; **hungered**; **hungering** \-g(ə)riŋ\ **hungers** [ME *hungrin, hungeren*, fr. OE *hyngran*; akin to OHG *hungaren* to hunger, ON *hungra*, Goth *huggrjan* to hunger, OE *hungor*, n., hunger] *vi* **1** : to feel or be oppressed by hunger ⟨the poor ~, yet are not fed⟩ **2** : to have an eager desire : LONG ⟨the world today ~*s* for ideals⟩ ~ *vt* : to make hungry : force by hunger ⟨the besiegers ~*ed* the garrison into surrender⟩ **syn** see LONG

hunger flower *n* : a whitlow grass (*Draba incana*) growing in dry soil

hunger grass *n* : SLENDER FOXTAIL

hungering *adj* : having the sensation of hunger ⟨a ~ man⟩ — **hun·ger·ing·ly** *adv*

hun·ger·ly \'həŋgə(r)lē\ *adj, archaic* : having a hungry look

hunger strike *n* **:** the action of one esp. a prisoner who refuses to eat anything or enough to sustain life so as to obtain compliance with his demands

hunger-strike \ˈ==,=\ *vi* [hunger strike] **:** to engage in a hunger strike

hungerweed \ˈ==,=\ *n* **1 :** CORN CROWFOOT **2 :** SLENDER FOXTAIL

hung over *adj* [fr. *hangover*, n., after *hung*, past part. of *hang*, v.] **:** suffering from a hangover ⟨the next morning after the party everybody was *hung over*⟩

hun·gri·ly \ˈhəŋgrəlē, -li\ *adv* [ME, fr. *hungry* + *-ly*] **:** in a hungry manner **:** with avidity **:** LONGINGLY, EAGERLY ⟨looking ~ to the day of cheaper power —Gordon Dean⟩ ⟨I read ~ —Jan Valtin⟩

hun·gri·ness \-grēnəs, -grin-\ *n* -ES **:** the quality or state of being hungry

hun·gry \ˈhəŋgrē, -gri, *chiefly in substand speech* -ŋr-, *dial* ˈhȯŋ-\ *adj* -ER/-EST [ME, fr. OE *hungrig*, fr. *hungor* hunger + *-ig* -y — more at HUNGER] **1 a :** feeling hunger **:** feeling distress from lack of food **:** having a keen appetite ⟨the ~ children trooped into the house⟩ **b :** marked by famine or lack of food ⟨gloom reigned in the ~ countryside⟩ ⟨the ~ days of the great famine⟩ ⟨listen, Captain, this town is ~ —John Hersey⟩ **c :** reflecting or indicating hunger or keen appetite ⟨stand at the row of pastries with a ~ look⟩ **2 :** having, reflecting, or characterized by an ardent desire or craving **:** longing eagerly **:** AVID ⟨~ for affection⟩ ⟨with a kind of ~ fervor —Robertson Davies⟩ ⟨~ for jobs and patronage —H.F.Wilkins⟩ — often used in combination ⟨a land-*hungry* people⟩ ⟨the fuel-*hungry* East⟩ ⟨a trade-*hungry* nation⟩ **3 :** not rich or fertile **:** POOR, BARREN ⟨a ~ soil⟩ ⟨~ ore⟩

hungry rice *n* **:** FUNDI

hungryroot \ˈ==,=\ *n* **:** the root of the spikenard (sense 2a)

hung up \ˌhəŋˈəp\ *adj* [fr. past part. of *hang up*] **:** DELAYED, DETAINED ⟨was *hung up* at the office and missed his train⟩

hunia \ˈhünēə\ *n* -S [prob. native name in India] **:** a tall long-legged sheep used in southern Asia as a fighting and pack animal

[1]hunk \ˈhəŋk\ *n* -S [Flem *hunke*; perh. akin to D *homp* lump, chunk — more at HUMP] **:** a large lump or piece ⟨a ~ of bread⟩ ⟨~*s* of iron⟩

[2]hunk \"\ *also* **hunky** \ˈhəŋkē, -ki\ *adj* [fr. obs. E dial. (New York) *hunk* goal, home (in games), fr. D *honk*, fr. MD *honc* corner, hiding place; akin to WFris *honck*, *honcke* house, hiding place] **1** *slang* **:** ALL RIGHT **:** HUNKY-DORY, OK **2** *slang* **:** EVEN — usu. used with *get* ⟨getting ~ on him —J.B.Benefield⟩ ⟨we'll get ~ with him good —S.F.Eckfeld⟩ ⟨"I'll get ~," I whispered —Harold Robbins⟩

[1]hun·ker \ˈhəŋkə(r)\ *vi* **hunkered; hunkered; hunkering** \-k(ə)riŋ\ **hunkers** [perh. of Scand origin; akin to ON *hokra* to crouch, creep, *hūka* to squat — more at HAWKER] **:** CROUCH, SQUAT — usu. used with *down* ⟨~*ed* down around the deerskin which they were scraping —Kenneth Roberts⟩ ⟨~*ed* down on his heels —Luke Short⟩

[2]hunker \"\ *n* -S [origin unknown] **1** *usu cap* **:** a member of the conservative section of the Democratic party in New York, 1845–1848 **2 :** a conservative in any respect **:** a person opposed to change or innovation ⟨to this day there are ~*s* . . . who object to it —H.L.Mencken⟩

hun·kers \-kə(r)z\ *n pl* [[1]*hunker* + *-s*] **:** HAUNCHES ⟨perched there on his ~ —Gerard Perry⟩

hunks \ˈhəŋks\ *n pl but sing or pl in constr* [origin unknown] **:** a surly ill-natured person **:** a covetous sordid man **:** MISER ⟨some old ~ of a sea captain —Herman Melville⟩ ⟨all the prudence and selfishness of an old ~ —Thomas Gray⟩

hun·ky *also* **hun·kie** \ˈhəŋkē, -ki\ *n, pl* **hunkies** *often cap* [prob. shortening & alter. of *Hungarian* + *-y*, *-ie*] **:** a person of central or east European birth or descent; *esp* **:** an industrial worker of such birth or descent — usu. used disparagingly

hunky-dory \ˌhəŋkēˈdōrē, -kəˈd-, -ki...ri, -dȯr-\ *adj* [*hunky* (var. of [2]*hunk*) + *-dory* (origin unknown)] **:** quite satisfactory **:** FINE ⟨everything was *hunky-dory*⟩

hun·nic \ˈhənik, -nēk\ *adj, usu cap* [ML *Hunnicus*, fr. LL *Hunni* Huns + L *-icus* -ic] **:** HUNNISH

hun·nish \-nish, -nēsh\ *adj, usu cap* [*Hun* + *-ish*] **:** of, like, or relating to the Huns **:** BARBAROUS — **hun·nish·ness** *n* -ES *usu cap*

huns *pl of* HUN

[1]hunt \ˈhənt\ *vb* -ED/-ING/-S [ME *hunten*, fr. OE *huntian*; akin to OE *hentan* to attack, seize, OHG *herihunda* battle spoils, ON *henda* to grasp, OSw *hinna* to attain, reach, Goth *frahinthan* to take captive] *vt* **1 a :** to follow or search for (game or prey) for the purpose and with the means of capturing or killing **:** pursue (game or prey) for food or in sport ⟨~ buffalo⟩ ⟨wolves ~ large prey only in packs⟩; *esp* **:** to pursue with weapons and often with trained animals **b :** to use or manage in the search for game ⟨~*s* a pack of dogs⟩ **2 a :** to pursue, follow, or track (a person) esp. with the object of capture — often used with *down* ⟨surviving patriots . . . were ~*ed* down in legal manner and put to death —J.A.Froude⟩ **b :** to try to find, locate, or obtain esp. by sustained or careful search or effort ⟨missing persons are ~*ed* by the police⟩ ⟨he's ~*ing* a job⟩ **c :** to find, uncover, or obtain after diligent search — used with *up*, *out*, or *down* ⟨~*ing* out recondite meanings in poems —Howard M. Jones⟩ ⟨~*ed* up a lot of valuable new evidence⟩ **3 :** to drive or chase esp. by hounding, harrying, or persecuting ⟨members of the colonial council . . . were ~*ed* from their homes —J.T.Adams⟩ **4 :** to traverse or go over in quest of game or quarry ⟨~*s* the swamp for moths —J.D. Hart⟩ ~ *vi* **1 :** to take part in a hunt **:** pursue game **2 :** to attempt to find, uncover, or obtain something esp. by diligent search — used with *for* or *after* ⟨~ for a lost wallet⟩ ⟨~*ing* for a street address⟩ ⟨ideas would not come to me if I went out to ~ for them —Ellen Glasgow⟩ **3 :** to oscillate alternately to each side of a neutral point or to run alternately faster and slower instead of steadily because of insufficient stability controls — used esp. of a device or machine ⟨sudden changes of load frequently cause the governor to ~, i.e., to open too wide, then close too far, and so on —S.H.Mortensen & Sterling Beckwith⟩ ⟨~*ing*, in electrical engineering, is a periodic increase or decrease in the speed of synchronous machinery operating in parallel, such as generators or motors —F.D.Jones⟩ ⟨a magnetic compass . . . must be damped to prevent lengthy oscillation or ~*ing* —Benjamin Dutton⟩ **4** *of a bell* **:** to shift continuously up or down in the order of striking in change ringing **syn** see SEEK

[2]hunt \"\ *n* -S [ME *hunte*, fr. *hunten*, v.] **1 :** the act, practice, or an instance of hunting **:** CHASE ⟨the ~ is up; the morn is bright and gray —Shak.⟩ **2 :** an association of huntsmen **:** a number of persons with horses and dogs engaged in hunting or riding to hounds ⟨a gate was being held open . . . and the ~ was streaming through —Adrian Bell⟩ **3 :** an instance of hunting (as in a mechanical device) **4 :** a regular course followed by each bell up or down the striking order in change ringing

hunt·able \ˈhəntəbəl\ *adj* **:** capable of being hunted

hunt and peck *n* **:** a mode of typing in which one looks at the keyboard and uses random fingering ⟨types fast and accurately, by *hunt and peck* —Brendan Gill⟩ — compare TOUCH SYSTEM

huntaway \ˈ==,=\ *adj* [fr. *hunt away*, v.] *NewZeal, of a dog* **:** trained to follow after and drive on a flock of sheep

hunted *adj* **1 :** being the object of a search, pursuit, or persecution ⟨a ~ man⟩ ⟨a ~ minority⟩ **2 :** reflecting or expressing the terror or fears of one who is hunted ⟨the prisoner's face lost its ~, hopeless look —Julian Dana⟩ ⟨a glitter of apprehension in her ~ eyes —Edith Wharton⟩ — **hunt·ed·ly** *adv*

hunt·er \ˈhəntə(r)\ *n* -S [ME, fr. *hunten* + *-er*] **1 a :** a person who hunts game **:** HUNTSMAN **b :** a dog used or trained for hunting **c :** a horse used or adapted for use in hunting; *esp* **:** one exhibiting endurance, speed, and ability to carry weight and trained for facility in cross-country work and jumping **2 :** a person who hunts or searches diligently or systematically for something ⟨~*s* with camera —S.H.Holbrook⟩ ⟨~*s* after the philosopher's stone —M.R.Cohen⟩ — often used in combination ⟨sensation-*hunters*⟩ **3 a :** a large Jamaican cuckoo (*Hyetornis pluvialis*) **b :** HUNTING SPIDER **4 :** a pocket watch having a hunting case **5 :** HUNTER GREEN

hunter green *or* **hunter's green** *n* **:** a variable color averaging a dark yellowish green that is yellower and duller than holly green (sense 1), greener and stronger than deep chrome green, and greener and duller than golf green — called also *elephant green*

hunter-killer \ˌ==ˈ==\ *adj* **:** of or relating to a coordinated air-sea operation against enemy submarines ⟨a *hunter-killer* group⟩

hun·ter's canal \ˈhəntə(r)z-\ *n, usu cap H* [after John *Hunter* †1793 Scot. surgeon] **:** an aponeurotic canal in the middle third of the thigh through which the femoral artery passes

hunter's moon *n* **:** the full moon after the harvest moon

hunter's pink *n* **:** any of several vivid or strong reds used for hunting jackets

hunth *abbr* hundred thousand

[1]hunting *n* -S [ME, fr. OE *huntung*, fr. *huntian* to hunt + *-ung* -ing] **1 :** the act, practice, or an instance of chasing, taking, or killing wild and esp. game animals **:** CHASE **2 :** the act, practice, or an instance of trying to find or obtain esp. by diligent search or effort ⟨the bibliographical ~ that lies behind any research work —H.N.Southern⟩ ⟨have had little time for book-*hunting* —H.J.Laski⟩

[2]hunting *adj* [fr. pres. part. of [2]*hunt*] **1 :** given to or interested in hunting ⟨a ~ man⟩; *also* **:** PREDACIOUS ⟨a ~ wasp⟩ **2 :** of, relating to, or used or adapted for use in hunting ⟨a ~ saddle⟩

hunting boot *n* **:** a heavy strong boot often extending to the knee and commonly laced from the instep to the top

hunting box *n, chiefly Brit* **:** a hunting lodge

hunting case *n* **:** a watchcase with a hinged cover to protect the crystal from accidents (as on the hunting field)

hunting cat *or* **hunting leopard** *n* **:** CHEETAH

hunting crow *n* **:** any of several tropical Asiatic long-tailed crested birds (genus *Kitta*) that resemble jays and have predominantly pale green, red, or sometimes yellow plumage and red bill and feet

hunting dog *n* **1 :** a dog used in hunting game **2 a :** AFRICAN HUNTING DOG **b :** DHOLE

hun·ting·don elm \ˈhəntiŋdən-\ *n, usu cap H* **:** an erect vigorous hybrid ornamental tree (*Ulmus hollandica vegetata*) with usu. forked stems and pubescent branches

hun·ting·don·shire \-ˌshi(ə)r, -iə, -ˌshə(r)\ *or* **hun·ting·don** *adj, usu cap* [fr. *Huntingdonshire* or *Huntingdon* county, England] **:** of or from the county of Huntingdon, England **:** of the kind or style prevalent in Huntingdon

huntingdon willow *n, usu cap H* **:** WHITE WILLOW 1

hunting ground *n* **:** a place or area used for hunting; *specif* **:** a region in which game is hunted ⟨the planting of waterfowl food in the public *hunting grounds* —J.B.Robson⟩ ⟨the *hunting ground* of a peaceful tribe⟩ — compare HAPPY HUNTING GROUND

hunting horn *n* **:** a signal horn used in the chase; *specif* **:** a long conical tube coiled in a large circle and having a large flaring end and a trumpet mouthpiece — compare FRENCH HORN

hunting knife *n* **:** a large stout knife used to skin and cut up game and sometimes to dispatch game

hunting knife

hunting seat *n, chiefly Brit* **:** a hunting lodge of some pretensions

hunting shirt *n* **:** a shirt worn for hunting; *esp* **:** a long jacket resembling a shirt and usu. of fringed deerskin worn by frontiersmen

hunting shirt

hunting spider *n* **:** any of several spiders that hunt their prey instead of catching it in a web **:** WOLF SPIDER

hun·ting·ton's chorea \ˈhəntiŋtənz-\ *n, usu cap H* [after George *Huntington* †1916 Am. neurologist] **:** hereditary chorea developing in adult life and ending in dementia

hunting tooth *n* **:** a tooth in the larger of two geared wheels which makes its number of teeth prime to the number in the smaller wheel with the object of equalizing wear

hunting watch *n* **:** HUNTER 4

hunt·ress \ˈhən-trəs\ *n* -ES [ME *hunteresse*, fr. *hunter* + *-esse* -ess] **:** a female hunter; *specif* **:** one who follows the chase

hunts *pres 3d sing of* HUNT, *pl of* HUNT

hunts·man \ˈhən(t)smən\ *n, pl* **huntsmen 1 :** HUNTER 1a **2 :** a person who manages a hunt and looks after the hounds esp. in fox hunting

huntsman's-cup \ˈ==ˌ=\ *n, pl* **huntsman's-cups :** PITCHER PLANT a

huntsman's-horn \ˈ==ˌ=\ *n, pl* **huntsman's-horns :** a pitcher plant (*Sarracenia flava*) of the southern U.S.

hunt's-up \ˈhən(t)ˌsəp\ *n, pl* **hunt's-ups 1 :** a tune played on a hunting horn to call out the hunters; *also* **:** a rousing song or tune **2 :** a pipers' tune used by Christmas waits

hunt table *n* **:** a low table usu. semicircular in shape

hunt the slipper : a circle game in which players attempt to pass a slipper from one to another without being discovered by the player who is it

hun·yak \ˈhənˌyak, ˈhün-,ˈhün-, -yak\ *or* **hun·yock** \-yäk\ *also* **hon·yak** \ˈhän-\ *or* **hon·yock** \-yäk\ *n* -S *usu cap* [by alter (influence of *Polack*)] **:** HUNKY —usu. used disparagingly

hu·on pine \ˈhyüən-\ *n, usu cap H* [fr. *Huon* river, Tasmania] **:** a large Tasmanian timber tree (*Dacrydium franklinii*) with light yellow aromatic wavy-grained wood used for carving and shipbuilding

[1]hup \ˈhəp\ *interj* [origin unknown] **1** — used to urge on a horse **2** — used as a command (1) to a horse to turn to the right or (2) to a dog to down

[2]hup \"\ *vb* **hupped; hupped; hupping; hups** *vt, chiefly dial* **:** to turn (a horse) to the right ~ *vi, of a dog* **:** DOWN ⟨promptly *hupped* . . . at a handler's command —*Amer. Field*⟩

hu·pa \ˈhüpə\ *n, pl* **hupa** *or* **hupas** *usu cap* **1 a :** an Athapaskan people of the Trinity river valley, California **b :** a member of such people **2 :** a language of the Hupa and Chilula peoples

hup·pah *or* **chup·pah** \ˈkúpə, -(ˌ)pä, kuˈpä\ *n, pl* **hup·poth** *or* **hup·pot** \ˈkuˌpōt(h), -ōs, ˌ=ˈ=\ *also* **huppahs** [Heb *huppāh* cover, canopy] **:** a canopy under which bride and groom stand during a Jewish wedding ceremony

hu·ra \ˈhyürə\ *n, cap* [NL, prob. modif. of Carib *urari* sandbox tree] **:** a genus of tropical American trees (family Euphorbiaceae) having milky juice, monoecious flowers, and capsular fruit

hur·cheon \ˈhərchən\ *n* -S [ME *hirchoun*, *hurcheoun* — more at URCHIN] **1** *chiefly Scot* **:** HEDGEHOG **2** *chiefly Scot* **:** URCHIN

hurcn *abbr* hurricane

hurd·en \ˈhərdən\ *var of* HARDEN

hur·dies \ˈhərdiz\ *n pl* [origin unknown] *dial Brit* **:** BUTTOCKS, RUMP

[1]hur·dle \ˈhərdᵊl, ˈhəd-, ˈhəid-\ *n* -S [ME *hirdel*, *hurdel*, fr. OE *hyrdel*; akin to OHG *hurd* hurdle, ON *hurth* door, Goth *haurds* door, L *cratis* wickerwork, hurdle, Gk *kartalos* basket, Skt *kṛnatti* he spins, *cṛtati* he ties, and perh. to L *crassus* thick; basic meaning: to twist] **1 a :** a portable panel of wattled twigs, osiers, or withes and stakes, or sometimes of iron or rails, used for fencing in land or livestock, reinforcing a wall or breastwork, or spanning a bog or ditch **b :** a frame or sled formerly used in England for dragging traitors to a place of execution **c :** an artificial barrier over which men or horses leap in a race **2 :** something that acts as a barrier **:** OBSTACLE ⟨once you have passed the final ~ — an interview with a selection board —E.O.Hauser⟩ ⟨one of the worst ~*s* a staff man faces is the vale of distrust that exists between echelons of command —W.H.Whyte⟩ ⟨a session of the foreign ministers . . . removed the final ~*s* in the way of a peace conference —A.H.Vandenberg †1951⟩ **3 a hurdles** *pl* **:** HURDLE RACE **b :** a jump made after the last approach step and carrying a diver to the end of the board in a running dive

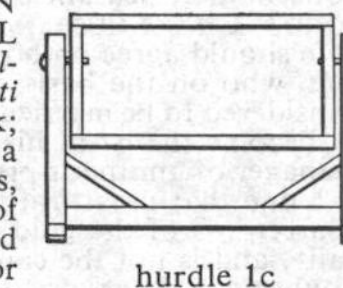

hurdle 1c

[2]hurdle \"\ *vb* **hurdled; hurdled; hurdling** \-d(ᵊ)liŋ\ **hurdles** *vt* **1 :** to fence in or reinforce with hurdles **2 :** to leap over (an obstacle) while running **3 :** to get across or past **:** OVERCOME, SURMOUNT ⟨only the boldest pioneers would ~ a pathless wilderness —R.A.Billington⟩ ⟨student performers . . . had to ~ a series of competitive auditions —*Collier's*⟩ ⟨engineers . . . wrestle with the multitude of problems to be *hurdled* in the construction of thruway spurs —*N.Y.Times*⟩ ~ *vi* **:** to leap over an obstacle while running; *specif* **:** to run a hurdle race

hurdle gate *n* **:** the crosspiece of a track hurdle that swings up to form a high hurdle or down to form a low hurdle

hur·dler \-d(ᵊ)lə(r)\ *n* -S [[1]*hurdle* + *-er*] **1 :** one that makes hurdles ⟨authoritative minds in postwar Britain are recognizing the value of the . . . thatcher, ~, and kindred craftsmen in the total national economy —Mary E. Jones⟩ **2 :** one that runs in hurdle races ⟨the ~ is actually a sprinter until he reaches the first hurdle —W.H.O'Connor⟩

hurdle race *n* **1 :** a track event in which artificial barriers must be leaped — called also *hurdles*; compare HIGH HURDLES, LOW HURDLES **2 :** a horse race over a flat course equipped with movable hurdles — compare STEEPLECHASE

hurdle racer *n* **:** a horse trained for hurdle racing

hurdlework \ˈ==,=\ *n* **:** work made of hurdles **:** WICKERWORK

hurds \ˈhərdz\ *n pl* [ME *herdes*, *hurdes* (pl.), fr. OE *heordan* (pl.); akin to OE *-heord* hair of a woman's head, ON *haddr* hair of a woman's head, Gk *keskeon* tow, Russ *kosa* braid] **:** the coarse parts of flax or hemp that adhere to the fiber after it is separated — called also *hards*

hurdy-gurdist \ˌhərdēˈgərdəst\ *or* **hurdy-gurdy·ist** \ˌ==-ˈ=dēəst\ *n* -S **:** a hurdy-gurdy player

hur·dy-gur·dy \ˌhərdēˈgərdē, ˈhədēˈgədē, ˈhəidēˈgəidē, -di...di\ *n* -ES [prob. imit.] **1 :** a stringed musical instrument resembling a lute in which the sound is produced by the friction of a rosined wheel turned by a crank against the strings and the pitches are varied by a set of mechanical keys **2 a :** BARREL ORGAN 1 **b :** STREET PIANO **3 :** a crank or windlass used to haul in heavy trawls or lines in deep-sea fishing

hurdy-gurdy 1

hure \ˈhyü(ə)r\ *n* -S [ME, fr. OF, cap, head of a wild animal] **1 :** a close-fitting cap **2** [F, fr. OF] **:** the head of a boar, wolf, or bear

hu·reau·lite \ˈhyü(ˌ)rōˌlīt, hyəˈr-\ *n* -S [F, fr. *Hureaux*, north of Limoges, France + F *-lite*] **:** a mineral $H_2Mn_5(PO_4)_4.4H_2O$ consisting of a hydrous manganese phosphate having a yellowish, orange-red, rose, or grayish color, and occurring in prismatic monoclinic crystals or massive

hur·gi·la \(ˌ)hərˈgēlə\ *n* -S [Hindi *hargilā*, *hargīlā*, lit., bone swallower, fr. *har*, *hār* bone + *gīlā* swallower, fr. Skt *gilati*, *girati* he swallows — more at VORACIOUS] **:** ADJUTANT BIRD

huri *var of* HOURI

hur·kle \ˈhərkəl\ *vi* -ED/-ING/-S [ME *hurkelen*, *hurklen*; akin to D *hurken* to squat, MLG *hurken*, MHG *hūren*] *now dial Brit* **:** to draw up the limbs and crouch or squat

[1]hurl \ˈhərl *esp before pause or consonant* ˈhər·əl; ˈhōl, ˈhəil\ *vb* -ED/-ING/-S [ME *hurlen*, prob. of imit. origin] *vi* **1 a :** to move rapidly or violently **:** RUSH, HURTLE ⟨sent the car ~*ing* over the roads —Sherwood Anderson⟩ ⟨a myriad senseless atoms . . . go ~*ing* forever through the infinite inane —P.E.More⟩ **b :** WHIRL ⟨now I've plenty money I'll make the tavern ~, a bottle of good brandy and on each arm a girl —Carl Sandburg⟩ **2** *chiefly Scot* **:** to wheel or drive in a vehicle esp. with a heavy or clumsy movement ⟨now and then we'll ~ in a coach —Robert Tannahill⟩ **3 a :** to play the game of hurling **b** *baseball* **:** PITCH ~ *vt* **1 a :** to impel with great vigor **:** DRIVE, THRUST ⟨could ~ his great strength into the ax head —Irving Bacheller⟩ ⟨~*ing* its mighty breakers upon the rocky ramparts —*Amer. Guide Series: Mich.*⟩ ⟨the forces that were to be ~*ed* against the Turks —N.T.Gilroy⟩ **b :** to impel (oneself) violently or impetuously ⟨he ~*ed* himself around the corner against the squall . . . with almost drunken violence —Liam O'Flaherty⟩ ⟨the characteristic wholeheartedness with which he continued to ~ himself at life —John Mason Brown⟩ **2 :** to throw down or out with violence ⟨~ the tyrant from his throne⟩ **3 a :** to throw or cast forcefully **:** FLING ⟨for forty-five minutes a battleship and lesser ships ~*ed* salvo after salvo at the field —H.L.Merillat⟩ ⟨a jet of gas . . . ~*s* strings of drill pipe and massive tools upwards —*Irish Digest*⟩ ⟨literally ~*ing* the ring I had given her in my face —Rex Ingamells⟩ **b** *obs* **:** to throw in wrestling **c** *baseball* **:** PITCH ⟨both ~*ed* scoreless ball for five innings —*Los Angeles* (*Calif.*) *Examiner*⟩ **4 :** to send or utter with vehemence ⟨~*ed* crisp piercing shrieks at the train —William Beebe⟩ ⟨publishers . . . took a delight in ~*ing* back at the tyro any copy he was venturesome enough to offer —A.W.Long⟩ ⟨he suddenly began to ~ reproaches down on her where she sat a little below him —Josephine Pinckney⟩ **5** *chiefly Scot* **:** to wheel or drive (a vehicle) **:** TRUNDLE **syn** see THROW

[2]hurl \"\ *n* -S [ME *hurl*, *hurle* swirl of water, strife, fr. *hurlen*, v.] **1 a :** a forceful throw or thrust; *specif* **:** a rushing swirl of water ⟨the halt and ~ of an angry, crashing, tempestuous seaway —C.C.Shaw⟩ **b** *Scot* **:** a downward rush (as of stones on a hill) **2 :** the stick used in the Irish game of hurling

[3]hurl \ˈhərl\ *dial Brit var of* WHIRL

hurl·bar·row \ˈhərlˌbärə\ *n* [[1]*hurl* + *barrow*] *chiefly Scot* **:** WHEELBARROW

hurlbat \ˈ=,=\ *n* [ME *hurlebat*, fr. *hurlen* to hurl + *bat*] **1** *obs* **:** either of two ancient Roman weapons: **a :** [3]CESTUS **b :** a short javelin having a thong by which it could be recovered after it was hurled **2 a :** a bat used in a game of hurling and popular in Tudor England **b :** [2]HURL 2

hurlement *n* -S [[1]*hurl* + *-ment*] *obs* **:** TUMULT, CONFUSION

hurl·er \ˈhərlər; ˈhələ(r, ˈhəil-\ *n* -S **:** one that hurls: as **a :** one that takes part in a game of hurling **b :** a baseball pitcher

hurl·ey *also* **hurly** \-lē\ *n, pl* **hurleys** *also* **hurlies** [[1]*hurl* + *-y*] **1 :** HURLING **2 :** the stick or the ball used in the game of hurling

hur·ley-house \ˈhərliˌhüs\ *n* [*hurley-* (prob. fr. [2]*hurl* + *-y*) + *house*] *Scot* **:** a large dilapidated house

hurling *n* -S [fr. gerund of [1]*hurl*] **1 :** an early form of football popular esp. in Cornwall in which each side tries to throw or carry the ball to its own goal or to get it beyond the parish boundary **2 :** an Irish game resembling field hockey in which teams of 15 players use a broad-bladed stick to catch, balance and run with, or hurl a 9″ to 10″ ball in an effort to score by hurling the ball over or under a crossbar between goalposts

hur·ly \ˈhərlē\ *n* -ES [prob. short for [1]*hurly-burly*] **:** CONFUSION, UPROAR, TUMULT

[1]hurly-burly \ˌhərlēˈbərlē, ˈhəlēˈbəlē, ˈhəilēˈbəilē, -liˈ...li\ *n* -ES [prob. alter. & redupl. of *hurling* (gerund of [1]*hurl*)] **1 :** CONFUSION, TURMOIL, TUMULT, UPROAR ⟨through all the *hurly-burly* of the days immediately preceding election —A.D.H. Smith⟩ ⟨men and women relaxing after a hard day in the *hurly-burly* of the garment district —Al Hine⟩ ⟨delighted in the *hurly-burly* of her uninhibited conversation —Ellery Sedgwick⟩ **2 :** an act or instance of tumult **:** MELEE ⟨in the *hurly-burly* the poet is seized by the enemy —Donald Davidson⟩

[2]hurly-burly \"\ *adj* **:** TUMULTUOUS, CONFUSED ⟨outrageous clothes and *hurly-burly* antics —G.E.Fox⟩

[3]hurly-burly *adv, obs* **:** in a hurly-burly manner

hu·ro \ˈhyü(ˌ)rō\ *n, cap* [NL *Huron-*, *Huro*, fr. Lake *Huron*, lake partly in Michigan and partly in Ontario, Canada] *in some classifications* **:** a genus of sunfishes containing solely the largemouth black bass which is now usu. included in *Micropterus*

[1]hu·ron \ˈhyürən, -yür-, -ˌrän\ *n, pl* **huron** *or* **hurons** *usu cap* [F, lit., boor, fr. MF, fr. *hure* disheveled head of hair, head of a wild animal] **1 a :** an Iroquoian people orig. of the St. Lawrence valley and Ontario and later of the midwestern U.S. **b :** a member of such people **2 :** the language of the Huron people

[2]huron \"\ *n* -S [NL *Huron-*, *Huro*] **:** LARGEMOUTH BLACK BASS

[3]hu·ron \üˈrōn, -rȯn\ *n* -S [AmerSp *hurón*, fr. Sp, ferret, fr. ML *furon-*, *furo*, fr. LL, cat, thief, fr. L *fur* thief — more at FURTIVE] **:** a grison (*Grison vittatus*) or related animal of So. America

hu·ro·ni·an \hyüˈrōnēən\ *adj, usu cap* [Lake *Huron* (north of which the system was first differentiated)] **:** of or relating to a division of the Proterozoic — see GEOLOGIC TIME table

hur·ple *var of* HIRPLE

[1]hur·rah \həˈrō, (ˈ)hüˈr-, hüˈr-, -rä, -rȧ\ *or* **hoo·ray** *also* **hur·ray** \-rā\ *interj* [perh. fr. G *hurra*, prob. fr. MHG *hurrā*, fr.

hurre (imper. of *hurren* to move quickly, of imit. origin) + *ā*, interj.] — used to express joy, approbation, or encouragement

²**hurrah** \"\ *or* **hoorah** \"\ *also* **hooray** \-rā\ *n* -s **1 a :** a display of excitement or acclamation : FANFARE ⟨many institutions were just being founded with the ~ of circuses coming to town —Ernestine Evans⟩ ⟨the everyday business of war as opposed to its ~ and heroism —*New Republic*⟩ **b :** ENTHUSIASM ⟨whose tireless ~ occasionally lifts the . . . book into some sort of magic while he is on the stage —Kappo Phelan⟩ **2 a :** FUSS, CONTROVERSY ⟨raised a big ~ over her reckless extravagance⟩ **b :** RAILLERY ⟨the crew rode them hard, but it was the sort of good-humored ~ that made a kid feel he was one of the bunch —F.B.Gipson⟩ **3 :** SPREE

³**hurrah** \"\ *also* **hoorah** \"\ *or* **hooray** \"\ *vb* -ED/-ING/-S *vi* **1 :** to shout hurrah : CHEER **2 :** to behave in a lively or boisterous way : ROMP **3 :** TEASE ~ *vt* **:** HARASS, SCOLD

hurrah bush *n* **:** FETTERBUSH 1

hurrah's nest \-rōz-,-räz-,-rāz-\ *also* **hoorah's nest** \"\ *or* **hoo·raw's nest** \"\ *n* **:** an untidy heap : MESS ⟨in spite of all efforts, the lockers generally become a *hurrah's nest* . . . a place for everything and nothing in its place —S.S.Rabl⟩; *specif* **:** a tangle of debris blocking a trail or stream

hurr-bur \ˈhər,bər\ *n* -s [prob. redupl. of ¹*burr*] **:** BURDOCK

hur·ri \ˈhu̇rē\ *also* **har·ri** \ˈhärē\ *n, pl* **hurri** *or* **hurris** *usu cap* [Akkadian *hurri*] **:** HURRIAN

hur·ria \ˈhərēə\ *n pl, cap* [NL] **:** a small genus of East Asian broad-snouted water snakes (family Homalopsidae)

hur·ri·an \ˈhu̇rēən\ *n* -s *usu cap* **1 a :** an ancient non-Semitic people prominent in northern Mesopotamia, Syria, and eastern Asia Minor about 1500 B.C. and regarded by some scholars as identical with the Horites **b :** a member of such people **2 :** the language of the Hurrian people

hur·ri·cane \ˈhər·ə,kān, ˈhə·r\, \ē,k-, \i,k- *also* \ēkən *or* \əkən *or* \ikən\ *n* -s *often attrib* [Sp *huracán*, fr. Taino *hurakán*, fr. *hura* wind, to blow away] **1 a :** a tropical cyclone with winds of 73 miles per hour or greater but rarely exceeding 150 miles per hour, usu. accompanied by rain, thunder, and lightning, and esp. prevalent from August to October in the tropical No. Atlantic and tropical Western Pacific but occas. moving into temperate latitudes — see BEAUFORT SCALE table; compare TYPHOON **b :** something resembling a hurricane esp. in violence : STORM ⟨the noise rose to a ~ —Dorothy C. Fisher⟩ ⟨a rushing ~ of blows struck him as he stood up —Donn Byrne⟩ ⟨the damage done by emotional ~*s* is not confined to the object of wrath —J.A.O'Brien⟩ **2** *dial* **:** an area where trees have been blown down by a hurricane or tornado ⟨there was a place about eight miles east of Bloomington which was known for many years as the ~ —J.A.Woodburn⟩ **syn** see WIND

hurricane bird *n* **:** FRIGATE BIRD

hurricane deck *or* **hurricane roof** *n* **:** AWNING DECK, PROMENADE DECK

hurricane globe *or* **hurricane glass** *also* **hurricane shade** *n* **:** a glass chimney placed over a candle to keep it from being blown out by the wind — see HURRICANE LAMP

hurricane lamp *n* **1** *or* **hurricane lantern :** an oil lantern having a glass chimney with a perforated metal lid that permits the egress of air but protects the flame from high winds and used usu. on shipboard and to mark outdoor construction projects — called also *tornado lantern* **2 :** a candlestick equipped with a hurricane globe **3 :** an electric lamp equipped with a hurricane globe instead of a shade

hurricane lamp 2

hurricane–proof \ˈ==(,)=;=\ *adj* **:** able to withstand a hurricane

hurricano *n* -ES [modif. of Sp *huracán* hurricane] *obs* **1 :** WATERSPOUT **2 :** HURRICANE

hurried *adj* [fr. past part. of ¹*hurry*] **1 a :** characterized by speed : FAST ⟨~ rush of a locomotive⟩ **b :** characterized by commotion : TUMULTUOUS ⟨~ life of a city⟩ **2 a :** done or working under pressure ⟨gave ~ last-minute instructions to the crew⟩ ⟨a shorter version for the ~ reader⟩ **b :** done with excessive haste : HASTY ⟨the ~ funeral was a shocking indignity —A.M.Young⟩; *specif* **:** executed so hastily as to be perfunctory ⟨it is a short book, but never sparse or ~ —D.C.DeJong⟩ — **hur·ried·ness** *n* -ES

hur·ried·ly \ˈhər·ədlē, ˈhə·r|, |ēd-, -li\ *adv* **:** in a hurried manner : QUICKLY, HASTILY

hur·ri·er \|ēə(r)\ *n* -s **:** one that hurries or causes to hurry

hur·ri·some \ˈhərisəm\ *adj* (*or adv*) [¹*hurry* + *-some*] *dial Eng* **:** HASTY, RUSHED

hur·rite \ˈhu̇,rīt\ *n* -s *usu cap* [*Hurri* + *-ite*] **:** HURRIAN

hur·rock \ˈhərək\ *n* [perh. of Scand origin; akin to ON *hörgr* pile of stones, shrine; akin to OE *hearg* shrine, OHG *harug* sacred grove, shrine, and perh. to OE *heard* hard — more at HARD] *dial Eng* **:** a heap of stones or rubbish

¹**hur·ry** \ˈhər·|ē, ˈhə·r|, |i\ *vb* -ED/-ING/-ES [perh. fr. ME *horyen*; prob. of imit. origin like MHG *hurren* to move quickly] *vt* **1 a :** to carry or cause to go fast : SPEED ⟨an ambulance *hurried* him to the hospital⟩ ⟨the quest to discover whither modern science is ~*ing* us —Howard M. Jones⟩ ⟨fishing for either species don't ~ your lure —L.S.Marceau⟩ **b** *archaic* **:** to impel to rash or precipitate action ⟨that hard-to-be-governed passion of youth *hurried* me frequently into intrigues with low women —Benjamin Franklin⟩ **2** *dial Eng* **:** to cause distress to : HARASS ⟨I've been very much *hurried* this morning; for I've just learned of the death of my old friend —A.B.Evans⟩ **3 a :** to impel to greater speed : QUICKEN, PROD ⟨heard the train coming and *hurried* his pace⟩ ⟨used his spurs to ~ the horse⟩ ⟨hates to be *hurried* at mealtime⟩ **b :** to speed up the progress or completion of : EXPEDITE ⟨~ dinner by doing the meat in the pressure cooker⟩ ⟨electronic machines ~ the sorting of data⟩ ⟨cultural exchange can ~ the development of world understanding⟩; *specif* **:** to perform with undue haste ⟨some of the most perfect passages are *hurried* over as if they were a mistake on the composer's part —Warwick Braithwaite⟩ ~ *vi* **:** to move or act with haste : go fast : RUSH ⟨we'll have to ~ if we want to see the curtain go up⟩ ⟨sheep . . . stared at her through the ~*ing* snowflakes —Ellen Glasgow⟩ — often used with an adverb to lend emphasis or indicate direction ⟨~ up or you'll miss the train⟩ ⟨small launches ~*ing* back and forth —Tom Marvel⟩ ⟨a stiff northwest wind was blowing and patches of clouds *hurried* by —H.H.Arnold & I.C.Eaker⟩ ⟨the nation *hurried* forward along the path of . . . consolidation —V.L.Parrington⟩ **syn** see SPEED

²**hurry** \"\ *n* -ES **1 a :** DISTURBANCE, TUMULT, COMMOTION ⟨the incessant ~ and trivial activity of daily life . . . seem to prevent, or at least discourage, quiet and intense thinking —C.W.Eliot⟩; **b** *dial Brit* **:** DISPUTE, RUCTION **2 a** *obs* **:** disturbance of mind : mental turmoil ⟨there is nothing like hurrying the body, to divert the ~ of the mind —Francis Fuller⟩ **b** *now dial* **:** a minor illness **3 :** a recurrent agitation of sound ⟨the ~ of water or languor of sand —Michael Sayers⟩ **4 a :** excessive haste : PRECIPITANCE ⟨the blind ~ of the universe —Bertrand Russell⟩ **b :** a state of eagerness or urgency : RUSH ⟨it was going to be a wonderful party and she was in a ~ to get there⟩ ⟨they were all good reporters; but they were all in too big a ~, for fear somebody else would beat them to it —Elmer Davis⟩ **5 :** a tremolo in the strings or a roll on the drum accompanying an exciting situation in dramatic music **syn** see HASTE — **in a hurry** *adv* **:** in a short time or at a fast rate : HURRIEDLY, SPEEDILY ⟨they are not translations to be read *in a hurry*; they do not yield their charm easily —T.S. Eliot⟩ ⟨the new grammar can be taught *in a hurry* by a nonlinguist —MacCurdy Burnet⟩

¹**hurry-burry** \ˌhəri̇ˈbəri\ *n* -ES [redupl. (influenced by *hurly-burly*) of ²*hurry*] *Scot* **:** HURLY-BURLY

²**hurry-burry** \"\ *adv, Scot* **:** in a hurly-burly manner

hurry call *n* **:** an emergency summons

hurry-durry *adj* [redupl. of ²*hurry*] *obs, of weather* **:** windy and rainy

hurrying *adj* [fr. pres. part. of ¹*hurry*] **:** swiftly moving : HASTENING — **hur·ry·ing·ly** *adv*

¹**hurry-scurry** *or* **hurry-skurry** \ˌhər·ē¦skər·ē, ¦hə·r| . . . ə·r|ē, |i| . . . |i\ *adv* (*or adj*) [redupl. (prob. influenced by ¹*helter-skelter*) of ²*hurry*] **:** in or with disorderly haste : HELTER-SKELTER

²**hurry-scurry** *or* **hurry-skurry** \"\ *n* -ES **:** a confused rush : TURMOIL

hurry-up \ˈ==;=\ *adj* [fr. *hurry up*, v.] **1 a :** of an emergency nature : RUSH ⟨*hurry-up* call⟩ ⟨*hurry-up* job⟩ **b :** equipped to respond to an emergency ⟨*hurry-up* wagon⟩ **2 :** speeded up : completed in a hurry : HASTY ⟨*hurry-up* breakfast⟩ ⟨*hurry-up* briefing⟩

hur·sin·ghar \ˌhərsinˈgär\ *n* -s [Hindi *harsiṅgār, hārsiṅgār, hārsiṅghār*] **:** an East Indian tree (*Nyctanthes arbortristis*) of the family Oleaceae with flowers that yield a dye used as a substitute for saffron

hurst *also* **hyrst** \ˈhərst\ *n* -s [ME *hurst*, fr. OE *hyrst*; akin to OS & OHG *hurst* thicket, OIr *crann* tree, and perh. to Gk *prinos* holm oak] **1 a :** a grove or wooded knoll — often used in combination in place names ⟨Elm*hurst*⟩ **b** *heraldry* **:** a clump of trees **2 :** a bank or piece of rising ground; *esp* **:** a sandbank in a river

¹**hurt** \ˈhər|t, ˈhə|, ˈhəi|, *usu* |d+V\ *vb* **hurt** *or dial* **hurted**; **hurt** *or dial* **hurted**; **hurting**; **hurts** [ME *hurten, hirten* to cause or allow to strike, injure, prob. fr. OF *hurter* to collide with, prob. of Gmc origin; akin to ON *hrūtr* ram (male sheep); akin to ON *hjörtr* hart — more at HART] *vt* **1 a :** to afflict with bodily pain : INJURE, WOUND ⟨the hot sand ~*s* my feet⟩ ⟨was badly ~ in the wreck⟩ ⟨got ~ in a bombing raid⟩ **b :** to do physical or material harm to : DAMAGE, IMPAIR ⟨the submarine is ~ by heavy depth charges⟩ ⟨the walkout is not ~*ing* service as much as the strikers hoped⟩ **c :** to do substantial or fundamental harm to : WEAKEN ⟨the story is ~ but not ruined by too many long descriptive passages⟩ **2 a :** to cause pain or anguish to : DISTRESS, OFFEND ⟨disillusions of the mind ~ less than disillusions of the heart —W.L.Sullivan⟩ ⟨was ~ by their lack of confidence in him⟩ ⟨it ~*s* me to think of all that land wasted —Ellen Glasgow⟩ **b :** to be detrimental to : CHECK, HAMPER ⟨the charges of graft will ~ his chances in the fall election⟩ ⟨a good wife can't help a husband as much as a bad wife can ~ one —W.H.Whyte⟩ ~ *vi* **1 a :** to feel pain or frustration : ACHE, SUFFER ⟨her hand . . . ~ from lugging the suitcase —John Dos Passos⟩ ⟨knocked a young heifer in the head because he . . . figured she had ~ long enough —Caroline Miller⟩ ⟨atomic-energy programs are ~*ing* from lack of enough scientific help —*Newsweek*⟩ **b** *chiefly Midland* **:** to be in need : WANT **2 :** to cause damage or distress : do harm ⟨hit the aggressor . . . where it will ~ most —D.H.McLachlan⟩ ⟨essential needs abroad must be met even if it ~*s* at home —J.S.Carson⟩ ⟨the rain may hold off but it won't ~ to take your umbrella⟩ **syn** see INJURE

²**hurt** \"\ *n* -s [ME *hurte, hurt, hirt*, prob. fr. OF *hurte* shock of a collision, stroke, blow, fr. *hurter* to collide with] **1 :** a wounding blow or stroke : cause of injury or damage ⟨the superiority . . . of the United States was a ~ to British prestige —Bernard Brodie⟩ ⟨this tower of granite, weathering the ~*s* of so many ages —R.W.Emerson⟩ **2 a :** a bodily injury or wound ⟨rattleweed, made into a tincture, is better than arnica for ~*s* of every sort —Emily Holt⟩ **b :** mental distress or anguish : RESENTMENT, SUFFERING ⟨are apt to be exasperated, and say things in immediate ~ which a little later they realize they do not wholly mean —A.E.Sutherland⟩ ⟨her sympathy eased his ~⟩ **3 :** WRONG, HARM, DISADVANTAGE, DETRIMENT ⟨his soul-stuff, by working on which a sorcerer may do the man himself grievous ~ —J.G.Frazer⟩ ⟨subordinating cosmic to moral considerations, to the ~ of both —M.R.Cohen⟩ **syn** see INJURY

³**hurt** \"\ *adj* [ME, fr. past part. of *hurten*, v.] **1 :** injured in body or spirit : WOUNDED, RESENTFUL ⟨ambulances . . . quickly dispose of ~ men and women —J.C.Powys⟩ ⟨an air of ~ innocence⟩ ⟨hoped to avoid ~ feelings over rejection of the plan⟩ **2 :** physically impaired : DAMAGED ⟨~ book sale⟩ ⟨restore ~ land with woods, game cover, and water —Russell Lord⟩

⁴**hurt** *also* **heurt** *or* **heurte** \ˈhərt\ *n* -s [MF *heurte*, prob. fr. *heurter* to collide with, knock, fr. OF *hurter* to collide with; perh. fr. the idea that it represents the mark of a blow] *heraldry* **:** a roundel azure

hurt·able \ˈhərd·əbəl\ *adj* **:** capable of being hurt

¹**hur·ter** \ˈhərd·ər\ *n* -s [ME *hurtur, hurtour* metal reinforcement for the shoulder of an axle, fr. AF *hurteuer*, fr. OF *hurter* to collide with] *archaic* **:** BUFFER, REINFORCEMENT; *esp* **:** a bumper that stops the wheels of a gun carriage as the piece is run into battery

²**hurt·er** \"\ *n* -s [¹*hurt* + *-er*] *archaic* **:** one that injures

hurt·ful \ˈhərtfəl, ˈhət-, ˈhəit-\ *adj* **:** causing injury or suffering : DAMAGING, PAINFUL ⟨regarded as ~ to the profession —H.A. Wagner⟩ ⟨~ to low-income classes —*Dun's Rev.*⟩ ⟨the crippled child hobbling to catch up was a ~ sight⟩ — **hurt·ful·ly** \-fəlē, -li\ *adv* — **hurt·ful·ness** *n* -ES

¹**hurt·ing** \ˈhərd·iŋ\ *n* -s [ME *hurtinge, hirtinge* injury, hurt, gerund of *hurten, hirten* to cause or allow to strike, injure] *chiefly dial* **:** PAIN, DISTRESS

²**hurting** *adj* [fr. pres. part. of ¹*hurt*] **:** PAINFUL, DISTRESSING ⟨his breath came in ~ gasps⟩

¹**hur·tle** \ˈhər|d·ᵊl, ˈhə|, ˈhəi|, |tᵊl\ *vb* **hurtled**; **hurtled**; **hurtling** \|d·ᵊliŋ, |t(ᵊ)liŋ\ **hurtles** [ME *hurtlen* to collide, cause or allow to strike, freq. of *hurten* to cause or allow to strike] *vi* **1** *archaic* **:** to meet violently : hit with impact : COLLIDE ⟨together *hurtled* both their steeds —Edward Fairfax⟩ **2 :** to progress with the sound or suddenness of violent motion : CLATTER, CRASH ⟨boulders *hurtled* down the cliffs⟩ ⟨the morning gun . . . sent its echoes *hurtling* through the coco palms —G.P.Insh⟩ ⟨stubbed his foot against the doorjamb and *hurtled* into the hall —Liam O'Flaherty⟩ **3 :** to move rapidly : dash headlong : RUSH, SHOOT ⟨you can ~ along at supersonic speeds —Irwin Edman⟩ ⟨somehow he had *hurtled* past the propellers' blades —*Time*⟩ ⟨the country was *hurtling* toward disaster —Sidney Warren⟩ ~ *vt* **1 :** to propel violently : CATAPULT, FLING ⟨the subway ~*s* hordes of workers daily into lower Manhattan⟩ ⟨Indians ~ flaming arrows over the stockade wall⟩ ⟨when he ~*s* himself into a dance —John Mason Brown⟩ **2** *dial Eng* **:** CROUCH

²**hurtle** \"\ *n* -s **:** an act of hurtling : THROW, COLLISION

hur·tle·ber·ry \ˈhərd·ᵊl- — *see* BERRY\ *n* [ME *hurtilberye*, fr. *hurtil-* (irreg. fr. OE *horte* whortleberry) + *berye* berry] **1** *archaic* **:** BLUEBERRY 1; *esp* **:** WHORTLEBERRY 1 **2** *archaic* **:** HUCKLEBERRY 1

hurt·less \ˈhərtləs\ *adj* [ME *hurtles*, fr. *hurte, hurt, hirt* wounding blow + *-les* -less] **1 :** free from harm : UNHURT **2 :** incapable of inflicting injury : HARMLESS — **hurt·less·ly** *adv* — **hurt·less·ness** *n* -ES

hurtling *adj* [fr. pres. part. of ¹*hurtle*] **:** characterized by rushing violence : SPEEDING, TUMULTUOUS — **hurt·ling·ly** *adv*

hurts *pres 3d sing of* HURT, *pl of* HURT

hus *pl of* HU

¹**hus·band** \ˈhəzbənd\ *n* -s [ME *housbonde, husbonde* husbandman, married man, master of a house, fr. OE *hūsbonda* master of a house, fr. ON *hūsbōndi*, fr. *hūs* house + *bōndi* householder, peasant owning his own land — more at HOUSE, BOND] **1** *obs* **:** HUSBANDMAN 1 **2 a :** a married man ⟨~ and wife should agree on how to budget the family income⟩ **b :** a man who on the basis of his tribal or societal institutions is considered to be married ⟨under the levirate a man was obliged to become the ~ of his brother's widow⟩ **3 a** *archaic* **:** the manager of another's property : STEWARD **b :** SHIP'S HUSBAND **4 :** one that uses thriftily or saves for future use : HOARDER ⟨barren ~*s* of the gold —S.V.Benét⟩ ⟨speaks his whole mind gaily, and is not the cautious ~ of a part —W.B.Yeats⟩

²**husband** \"\ *vt* -ED/-ING/-S [ME *husbonden*, fr. *housbonde, husbonde*, n.] **1** *archaic* **:** to plow and grow crops on (land) : CULTIVATE **2 a :** to take care of : utilize to advantage : MANAGE ⟨the ancient Nile is controlled at its source . . . and its waters are to be ~*ed* for the benefit of the farmers —Elizabeth II⟩; *specif* **:** to equip, supply, and maintain (a ship) **b :** to use sparingly or hold back for future use : CONSERVE, SAVE ⟨one's strength or resources⟩ ⟨~ their air strength . . . for the best nights, rather than risk losses from the weather —A.A.Michie⟩ ⟨toys . . . ~*ed* for the benefit of baby —Robert Grant †1940⟩ **3** *archaic* **:** to marry or find a husband for

hus·band·age \-dij\ *n* -s **:** a commission paid to a ship's husband by the owners for managing its affairs

hus·band·er \-də(r)\ *n* -s **:** one that husbands

hus·band·land \ˈhəzbən(d)lənd\ *n* [ME *husbondeland*, fr. *housbonde, husbonde* + *land*] **1 a :** the holding of a manorial tenant **b :** a quantity of arable land equal to two bovates : VIRGATE **2 :** the land occupied and tilled by the tenants of a manor as distinguished from the demesne lands

hus·band·less \ˈhəzbən(d)ləs\ *adj* **:** having no husband

hus·band·like \-(d),līk\ *adj* **:** HUSBANDLY 1b

¹**husbandly** *adv* [ME, fr. ¹*husband* + *-ly* (adv. suffix)] *obs* **:** in a thrifty manner : ECONOMICALLY

²**hus·band·ly** \ˈhəzbən(d)lē, -li\ *adj* [¹*husband* + *-ly* (adj. suffix)] **1 a** *obs* **:** of or relating to a farmer or farming **b :** consistent with good farm management practice **2 :** of, relating to, or befitting a husband : MARITAL **3** *obs* **:** THRIFTY, FRUGAL

hus·band·man \ˈhəzbən(d)mən\ *n, pl* **husbandmen** [ME *housbondeman*, fr. *housbonde* + *man*] **1 :** one that plows and cultivates land : FARMER ⟨where the menace of erosion has become most manifest . . . both landlords and tenants have become *husbandmen* under grave handicaps —Russell Lord⟩ ⟨the parable of the *husbandmen* in St. Mark's Gospel —Leonardo Olschki⟩ **2** *Brit* **:** a rural laborer : FARMHAND **3 :** a specialist in a branch of farm husbandry ⟨dairy ~⟩ ⟨poultry ~⟩

hus·band·ry \ˈhəzbəndrē, -ri\ *n* -ES [ME *housbondrie*, fr. *housbonde* + *-rie* -ry] **1** *obs* **:** the care of a household : domestic management ⟨I commit into your hands the ~ and manage of my house until my lord's return —Shak.⟩ **2 a :** the judicious use of resources : CONSERVATION, THRIFT ⟨this careful ~ of his remaining powers —W.V.T.Clark⟩ ⟨borrowing dulls the edge of ~ —Shak.⟩ **b :** the control or use of resources : MANAGEMENT ⟨problems of soil conservation and ~ of water resources —*Brit. Book News*⟩ **3 :** the cultivation or production of plants and animals : AGRICULTURE, FARMING ⟨some dealt in corn, others in sheep and wool, others in a mixed ~ —G.M. Trevelyan⟩ ⟨commercial farming has not displaced subsistence ~ —J.M.Mogey⟩ **4** *obs* **:** the tenantry or husbandland of a manor **5 :** the scientific control and management of a specified branch of farming ⟨more limited experimental work is also being carried out in . . . animal ~ —C.J.Bishop⟩

hus·band·ry·man \ˈ===mən\ *n, pl* **husbandrymen :** HUSBANDMAN 3

huscarl *var of* HOUSECARL

¹**hush** \ˈhəsh, *when imperative* " *or* sh *often prolonged*\ *vb* -ED/-ING/-ES [back-formation fr. ²*husht*, taken as a past participle] *vt* **1 :** to repress the agitation or clamor of : LULL, SILENCE, CALM, QUIET ⟨sleep . . . ~*ed* by solemn-sounding waterfalls —John Muir †1914⟩ ⟨his movement ~*ed* the courtroom —B.A.Williams⟩ **2 :** to gloss over or put at rest : MOLLIFY, QUELL ⟨their protests are mild and . . . can be easily ~*ed* —Paul Blanshard⟩ ⟨brings her flowers to ~ his conscience⟩ ⟨his wife . . . serves him quickly and silently, ~*ing* signs of disorder in the children —H.A.Overstreet⟩ — often used with *up* ⟨this contradiction is ~*ed* up —L.A.Fiedler⟩ **3 :** to keep from public knowledge : treat confidentially : SUPPRESS ⟨police attempt to ~ the crime —*Books of the Month*⟩ — usu. used with *up* ⟨the story of her disgrace was ~*ed* up —Edith Sitwell⟩ ⟨trying to ~ it up, but it was plain suicide —Vicki Baum⟩ ~ *vi* **:** to become quiet : grow still ⟨the crowd ~*ed*, and she sang —Franc Shor⟩ — used in the imperative to enjoin silence or urge moderation of sound ⟨~, baby, go to sleep⟩ ⟨~, boys, the party's getting noisy⟩

²**hush** \ˈhəsh\ *adj* **1 :** devoid of sound : SILENT, STILL ⟨everything was . . . ~ as midnight about the house —Laurence Sterne⟩ **2 :** designed to prevent the dissemination of certain information ⟨~ money⟩ ⟨a ~ policy concerning any faults . . . in the American economy —Jerome Frank⟩ **3** *or* **hushing** [fr. the use of a prolonged \sh\ sound in hushing (enjoining silence)] **:** being the sibilants \sh\ and \zh\ — compare HISS

³**hush** \"\ *n* -ES **1 a :** silence or freedom from agitation : STILLNESS, CALM ⟨sickroom ~⟩ ⟨cathedral ~ of the deep woods⟩ ⟨a ~ and a solemnity about the proceedings —Hugh Walpole⟩ **b :** a suspension of noise or activity : CESSATION, LULL ⟨after a time there came a profound ~ and out of the stillness a woman's voice rose —Lyle Saxon⟩ **2 :** restriction of information : SECRECY ⟨prompted the policy of ~ in regard to the presence of the disease on their properties —*Australasian*⟩

⁴**hush** \ˈhu̇sh, ˈhəsh\ *vb* -ED/-ING/-ES [imit.] *vi, dial Brit* **:** to gush forth in a rapid stream : RUSH ~ *vt, dial Eng* **:** to expose (ore) by washing a hillside with water under pressure : FLUSH — **hush·ing** \-shən, -shiŋ\ *n* -s

⁵**hush** \"\ *n* -ES *dial Brit* **:** a rushing sound as of wind or water; *specif* **:** a swell of the sea

hush·a·by *or* **hush-a-bye** \ˈhəshə,bī\ *v imper* [¹*hush* + connective *-a-* + ²*bye*] **:** be still and go to sleep — used to soothe a child to sleep

hushed \ˈhəsht\ *adj* [fr. past part. of ¹*hush*] **1 a :** free of noise or agitation : CALM, STILL ⟨~ silence of the reading room⟩ **b :** marked by suspension of noise or activity : reduced to silence ⟨~ attention of the spectators —L.P.Stryker⟩ ⟨an atmosphere of ~ suspense⟩ **2 :** marked by secrecy or caution : CONFIDENTIAL, DISCREET ⟨~ meeting of political strategists⟩ ⟨counseled his clients in ~ tones⟩ — **hushed·ly** \-shədlē, -shtlē, -li\ *adv*

hush·ful \ˈhəshfəl\ *adj* [³*hush* + *-ful*] **:** full of silence : QUIET — **hush·ful·ly** \-fəlē\ *adv*

¹**hush-hush** \ˈ=;=\ *vt* [fr. *hush! hush!*, repeated imperative use of ¹*hush*] **1 :** to enjoin to silence ⟨was *hush-hushed* by army censors when he started to report soldier opinion on the issue⟩ **2 :** HUSH *vt* 3

²**hush-hush** \"\ *adj* **:** marked by secrecy or concealment : kept from public knowledge : SECRET, CONFIDENTIAL ⟨a specific cure for one of the *hush-hush* diseases, gonorrhea —*Science News Letter*⟩ ⟨decreed an end to the . . . *hush-hush* atmosphere that has shielded major presidential policies —Ray Tucker⟩; *specif* **:** subject to official censorship ⟨military intelligence, cryptography, secret chemical corps projects and other *hush-hush* assignments —Sidney Shalett⟩ ⟨of all air corps planes, this is the most *hush-hush* —D.C.Cooke⟩

³**hush-hush** \"\ *n* **:** a policy or atmosphere of concealment : SECRECY, SUPPRESSION ⟨the *hush-hush* surrounding new car design⟩ ⟨after decades of *hush-hush*, the problem of mental illness is now being openly discussed⟩; *specif* **:** CENSORSHIP ⟨wartime *hush-hush* concerning plane losses⟩

hush puppy *n* [¹*hush* + *puppy*; fr. its occasional use as food for dogs] *chiefly South* **:** a cornmeal bread shaped into small cakes and fried in deep fat — usu. used in pl.; compare CORN DODGER

¹**husht** \ˈhəsht\ *interj* [ME *huissht*] *archaic* — used to enjoin silence

²**husht** \"\ *adj* [ME *hussht*, fr. *huissht*, interj.] *archaic* **:** HUSHED

hush tube *n* **:** a tube for conducting the inflow beneath the surface of the water in a flush tank to reduce noise

husi *var of* JUSI

¹**husk** \ˈhəsk\ *n* -s [ME *husk, huske*, prob. modif. of MD *huuskijn, huusken* small house, small cover, fr. *huus* house, cover + *-kijn, -ken* -kin; akin to OE *hūs* house — more at HOUSE] **1 a :** the outer covering of a kernel or seed esp. when dry and membranous : the chaff of grain : HULL, POD; *specif* **:** CAROB 1b ⟨with the ~*s* that the swine did eat —Lk 15:16 (AV)⟩ **b :** one of the leaves enveloping an ear of corn : BRACT ⟨corn roasted in the ~*s*⟩ **2 a :** something that resembles a husk : an outer layer or empty framework : SHELL ⟨much of the remote past is conserved in the ~ of convention —Norman Lewis⟩ ⟨the wind . . . blew through that eerie ~ of a room —Edita Morris⟩ **b** *slang* **:** GUY, FELLOW ⟨you're some ~ —Sinclair Lewis⟩ **c :** a classic drop ornament made of whorls of conventionalized foliage usu. in diminishing series and used esp. in an 18th century style of furniture introduced by Robert Adam **3 a :** the outer skin or shell of an animal ⟨the sea floor is littered with the discarded ~*s* of small crustaceans⟩ **b :** a supporting framework: as (1) **:** the decorative covering around the holder that supports the socket and bulb of an electric lamp (2) **:** a frame supporting the arbor of a large circular saw

husk 2c

²**husk** \"\ *vt* -ED/-ING/-S **:** to remove the outer skin or covering of : PEEL, STRIP ⟨~ rice⟩ ⟨~ corn⟩ ⟨~ a coconut⟩ ⟨would ~ it of its religious and political bias —S.E.Hyman⟩

³**husk** \"\ *n* -s [prob. fr. obs. *husk*, v., to have a dry cough, of imit. origin] **1 :** HOOSE ⟨an outbreak of ~ was observed in a flock of 200 sheep —*Veterinary Bull.*⟩ **2 :** HUSKINESS

⁴**husk** \"\ *vb* -ED/-ING/-S *vi* **:** to become husky ⟨tried to keep

his voice from ~*ing* with emotion⟩ **~** *vt* **:** to utter in a husky voice ⟨the sultry singer in the cabaret ~*s* out the latest ballad⟩

1hus·ka·naw \ˈhəskə,nȯ\ *or* **hus·ka·naw·ing** \-ōiŋ\ *n* -s [of Algonquian origin; akin to Natick *wuskenoo* he is young] **:** an initiation rite for youths at puberty practiced by various Indians of Virginia and including fasting and the use of narcotics

2huskanaw \"\ *vt* -ED/-ING/-S **:** to subject to a huskanaw

husk corn *n* **:** POD CORN

husked *adj* [ˈ*husk* + -*ed*] **1 :** covered with a husk **2** [fr. past part. of *2husk*] **:** stripped or deprived of the husk

husk·ened \ˈhəskənd\ *adj* [prob. irreg. fr. *2husky* + -*en* + -*ed*] **:** HUSKY

husk·er \ˈhəskə(r)\ *n* -s **:** one that husks: as **a :** a participant in a cornhusking **b :** HUSKING GLOVE **c :** HUSKER-SHREDDER

husker-shredder \ˈ==ˌ==\ *n* **:** a power machine that husks corn ears and cuts up the husks and stalks for fodder

husk·i·ly \ˈhəskəlē, -li\ *adv* **:** in a husky manner

husk·i·ness \-kēnəs, -kin-\ *n* -ES **:** the quality or state of being husky

husking *n* -s [fr. gerund of *2husk*] **1 :** an act or process of peeling or stripping off an outer layer ⟨the ~ of coffee beans⟩ ⟨corn ready for ~⟩ **2** *also* **husking bee :** a neighborly gathering of farm families to husk corn ⟨~*s*, berry-pickings and winter sleigh rides —Van Wyck Brooks⟩

husking glove *n* **:** a glove with metal plates and hooks on the palm and palm side of the fingers that is used in husking corn

husking peg *or* **husking pin** *n* **:** a peg of wood or metal strapped or tied to the hand as an aid in husking corn

husk-tomato *n* **:** GROUND-CHERRY

1husky \ˈhəskē, -ki\ *adj* -ER/-EST [*1husk* + -*y*] **1 :** containing or full of husks ⟨the kernels are plump and not very ~ —*Farmers Weekly (So. Africa)*⟩ **2 :** of the nature of a husk **:** MEMBRANOUS, RATTLING, EMPTY ⟨the nut is contained in a ~ shell —S.J.Watson⟩ ⟨his footfalls were ~ in cinders —Richard Llewellyn⟩ ⟨repeated that ~ phrase so often —Willa Cather⟩

2hus·ky \"\ *adj* -ER/-EST [prob. fr. *3husk* + -*y*] **:** dry or roughened as with emotion **:** HOARSE ⟨the voices of the chief women mourners had become worn and ~ —J.A.Lomax⟩ ⟨~ voices bawled at the yokes of steers —Carl Sandburg⟩ ⟨makes all the instruments sound powerful but ~ —Virgil Thomson⟩

3hus·ky \"\ *adj* -ER/-EST [prob. fr. *1husk* + -*y*; prob. fr. the toughness and harsh texture of a corn husk] **1 :** big and muscular **:** BURLY, ROBUST ⟨a crew of ~ lumberjacks⟩ **2 a :** of sizable proportions or vigorous potential **:** LARGE, POWERFUL ⟨a ~ $19 million in the like period last year —Mitchell Gordon⟩ ⟨a big, ~, honestly built . . . power cruiser —*Yankee*⟩ ⟨there still was a ~ United Nations army left in Korea —A.J. Liebling⟩ **b :** having or producing strength **:** STURDY ⟨a ~ beef stew⟩

4husky \"\ *n* -ES **:** one that is husky or powerful ⟨foremen looked over the *huskies* crowded in these rooms to pick their crews —*Amer. Guide Series: Minn.*⟩ ⟨these four breeds of engines are *huskies* —R.M.Neal⟩

5husky \"\ *n* -ES *sometimes cap* [prob. by shortening & alter. fr. *Eskimo*] **1** *dial* **:** an Eskimo of Labrador and northeastern Canada or his language ⟨a huge whale . . . which the old-time *huskies* had killed with harpoons and lances —D.B.Putnam⟩ — sometimes taken to be offensive **2 a :** a heavy-coated working dog (as an Eskimo dog or malamute) of the New World arctic region used esp. as a sled dog **b :** SIBERIAN HUSKY

hu·so \ˈhyü(,)sō, -)zō\ *n* -s [ML, fr. OHG *hūso*; akin to Norw dial. *huse* fish skull, ON *hauss* skull, OE *hȳd* hide, skin; prob. fr. the armored head — more at HIDE] **1 :** BELUGA 1 **2 :** HUCHEN

huss \ˈhəs\ *n* -ES [alter. of ME *husk, huske*] *dial* **:** DOGFISH

hus·sar \(,)həˈz‖är, ‖ȧ(r *sometimes* -ˈs‖\ *n* -s [Hung *huszár* hussar, (obs.) highway robber, fr. Serb *husar, gusar* pirate, fr. ML *cursarius* — more at CORSAIR] **1 a** *often cap* **:** a horseman of the Hungarian light cavalry organized in the 15th century **b :** a member of the light cavalry of various European armies usu. distinguished by a brilliant much-decorated uniform often featuring the dolman and the busby **c :** a member of certain now mechanized European cavalry units **2 :** any of several brilliantly colored snappers (family Lutjanidae) — see YELLOW-BANDED HUSSAR

hussar monkey *n* **:** PATAS

hus·ser·li·an \(ˈ)hu̇ˈsərlēən, -ser-\ *adj, usu cap* [Edmund *Husserl* †1938 Ger. philosopher + E -*ian*] **:** of or relating to the German philosopher Husserl or his theories ⟨*Husserlian* phenomenology⟩

1huss·ite \ˈhə,sīt, ˈhu̇,-\ *n* -s *usu cap* [NL *hussita*, fr. John *Huss* †1415 Bohemian religious reformer + L -*ita* -ite] **:** a member of the Bohemian religious and nationalist movement originating with John Huss, marked by advocacy of the Wycliffite doctrines of clerical purity and poverty and the supremacy of the Bible and by insistence upon communion in both bread and wine for the laity, and split after the death of Huss into the Calixtin and Taborite parties — compare LOLLARD 2

2hussite \"\ *adj, usu cap* **:** of, relating to, or characteristic of John Huss or the Hussites

huss·it·ism \-ˌīd,izəm\ *also* **huss·ism** \-,sizəm\ *n* -s *usu cap* [*hussitism* fr. *1hussite* + -*ism*; *hussism* fr. John *Huss* + E -*ism*] **:** the beliefs and practices of the Hussites

hus·sy *also* **hus·sey** \ˈhəzē, ˈhəs‖, ‖i\ *or* **huz·zy** \ˈhəz‖\ *n* -ES [alter. of *housewife*] **1** *obs* **:** the female head of a house **:** HOUSEWIFE **2 :** a lewd or brazen woman **:** JADE **3 :** a saucy or mischievous girl **:** MINX **4** *dial* **:** HOUSEWIFE 2

hus·ting \ˈhəstiŋ, -tēŋ\ *n* -s [ME, fr. OE *hūsting*, fr. ON *hūsthing*, fr. *hūs* house + *thing* assembly — more at HOUSE, THING] **1 :** a deliberative assembly or council in early medieval England; *esp* **:** one called by a king or other leader **2 a** *or* **hustings** *pl but sing in constr* **:** a court held in London before the lord mayor, recorder, and sheriffs or aldermen **b hustings** *pl but sing in constr or* **hustings court :** a local court in some cities in Virginia **3** *or* **hustings** *pl but sing in constr* **:** the upper end or dais of the guildhall where the London husting sits **4 a** *or* **hustings** *pl but sing in constr* **:** a raised platform from which candidates for the British Parliament were formerly nominated and from which they addressed their constituency **b :** the proceedings at a parliamentary election **5 hustings** *pl but sing or pl in constr* **a :** an election platform **:** STUMP ⟨the charge . . . is expected to resound from political ~*s* throughout the land —*Foreign Policy Bull.*⟩ **b :** an act or process of electioneering ⟨an election which has generated far more excitement than the usual off-year ~*s* —*Saturday Rev.*⟩ ⟨the rough give-and-take of the ~*s* —*Yale Rev.*⟩

1hus·tle \ˈhəsəl\ *vb* **hustled; hustled; hustling** \-s(ə)liŋ\ **hustles** [D *husselen, hutselen* to shake, toss, fr. MD *hutselen*, freq. of *hutsen* to shake; akin to G dial. *hotteln, hotzeln* to shake — more at HOD] *vt* **1 :** to shake or jar together in confusion **:** JOSTLE ⟨~ pennies in a hat⟩ **2 a :** to crowd or push roughly **:** SHOVE ⟨in the cell into which we were *hustled* were forty or fifty Negroes —R.M.Lovett⟩; *specif* **:** to jostle with intent to rob ⟨they ~ old gentlemen; the old gentleman glances down, his watch is gone —E.M.Forster⟩ **b :** to convey forcibly or hurriedly ⟨grabbed him by the arm and *hustled* him out the door —John Dos Passos⟩ ⟨~ freight aboard the scow —N.C.McDonald⟩ ⟨allow himself to be *hustled* across the frontier —F.A.Ogg & Harold Zink⟩ **c :** to urge forward precipitately ⟨~ the tourist from one museum to the next⟩ ⟨~ your horse and don't say die —W.S.Gilbert⟩ ⟨trying to ~ history along —N.E.Nelson⟩ **3 a :** to obtain by energetic activity **:** GATHER, EARN ⟨*hustled* new customers —*Time*⟩ ⟨*hustled* himself a job as a section hand —Pearl Puckett⟩ **b :** to exert pressure on **:** sell or promote business with **:** WORK ⟨a waiter has to learn . . . that he must not ~ the customers —Robert Sylvester⟩ ⟨they ~ them for drinks —A.J.Liebling⟩ ⟨played it safe by *hustling* both sides of the street —Nelson Algren⟩ **c :** to deprive of one's possessions by force or fraud **:** ROB, CHEAT ⟨made the rounds of lovers' lanes . . . *hustling* the occupants of parked cars —C.L.Lamson⟩ ⟨~*s* schoolboys out of their lunch money with phony dice —Nelson Algren⟩; *specif* **:** to lure into a gambling game **~** *vi* **1 :** PUSH, SHOVE, PRESS ⟨curious throngs ~ to the scene of the crime⟩ ⟨someone *hustled* against him in the crowd⟩ **2 :** to move or act with vigorous speed **:** bestir oneself energetically **:** HURRY ⟨urged her to ~ across the street before the light changed⟩ ⟨ten miles of track a day were laid by *hustling* crews —R.A. Billington⟩ **3 a :** to make strenuous efforts to secure money or business ⟨our quartet was out *hustling* . . . and we knew we stood good to take in a lot of change before the night was over —Louis Armstrong⟩ ⟨diesel boats ~ at the docks —H.G. Nickels⟩ **b :** to solicit for prostitution ⟨there are fewer girls working in houses than there are *hustling* on the streets —Polly Adler⟩ **4 :** to obtain money by fraud or deception **:** SWINDLE; *specif* **:** to lure a victim into a crooked gambling game

2hustle \"\ *n* -s **1 :** an act of jostling or shoving **2 a :** energetic activity ⟨increase of leisure, diminution of ~, are the ends to be sought —Bertrand Russell⟩ ⟨the ~ and bustle in construction of motels —A.L.Himbert⟩ **b :** a hurried motion **:** MOVE ⟨get a ~ on to stockpile these essential materials —*Congressional Record*⟩ **3** *slang* **a :** an income-producing activity **:** JOB **b (1) :** an act or instance of fraud **:** SWINDLE, RACKET **(2) :** HUSTLER

hustle-bustle \ˈ==ˈ==\ *n* **:** energetic confusion

hustle-cap \ˈ==,=\ *n* [*1hustle* + *cap*] **:** a game of pitch and toss in which coins are shaken in a cap

hus·tle·ment \ˈhəsəlmənt\ *n* -s [ME *ostelement, hustilment* article of furniture, fr. MF *ostillement, oustillement*, fr. OF *ustillement*, fr. *ustil* article of furniture, tool, utensil, prob. fr. (assumed) VL *usitilia* (pl.) utensils, alter. of L *utensilia* — more at UTENSIL] *now dial* **:** household goods **:** FURNITURE, KNICKKNACKS — often used in pl.

hus·tler \ˈhəs(ə)lə(r)\ *n* -s **1 a :** a pickpocket's accomplice **b :** one who obtains money by fraudulent means **:** petty racketeer; *specif* **:** a professional gambler **c :** PROSTITUTE **2 :** an active, enterprising, sometimes unscrupulous individual **:** GO-GETTER, LIVE WIRE **3 a :** VENDOR **b :** one that delivers or transports **c :** a pottery worker who carries greenware to the kiln shed or other place of processing **4** *New Zeal* **:** a tillage implement with tines used to stir the soil

hustling *adj* [fr. pres. part. of *1hustle*] **1 :** characterized by hustling activity **:** ENERGETIC **2 :** soliciting or productive of illicit gain; *specif* **:** WHORING

1hut \ˈhət, *usu* -əd.+V\ *n* -s [MF *hutte* temporary dwelling of simple construction, of Gmc origin; akin to OHG *hutta* temporary dwelling of simple construction; akin to OE *hȳd* hide, skin — more at HIDE] **1 a :** a temporary structure used as living quarters for troops esp. in a theater of operations **b :** a rudimentary structure erected by the army for a special purpose (as a field aid station) **c :** a room or building used as a recreation center for troops in World War I **2 a :** an often small and temporary dwelling of simple construction **:** COTTAGE, SHACK ⟨sod ~⟩ ⟨the simplest of the primitive dwellings of the colonists were conical ~*s* of branches, rushes, and turf —Fiske Kimball⟩ **b** *Austral* **:** a house for shearers or other laborers on a ranch **c :** a simple shelter from the elements ⟨bathing ~⟩ ⟨round a winding road you come to a small ~ and a turnstile —Fred Streeter⟩ ⟨small wooden ~*s* inside which fishermen . . . can sit in comparative comfort with a portable stove while waiting for a nibble from far below the frozen surface —James Montagnes⟩; *specif* **:** overnight cabin ⟨hostel ~*s*⟩ ⟨mountain ~*s*⟩

2hut \"\ *vb* **hutted; hutted; hutting; huts** *vt* **:** to provide with usu. temporary living quarters **:** HOUSE, BILLET ⟨were no sooner *hutted* than we were on the march —S.W.Mitchell⟩ **~** *vi* **:** to become housed or quartered **:** LODGE ⟨his troops *hutted* among the heights —Washington Irving⟩

1hutch \ˈhəch\ *n* -ES [ME *hucche, huche*, fr. OF *huche*] **1 a :** a chest or compartment for storage **:** BIN, LOCKER **b :** a low cupboard with doors usu. surmounted by two open shelves **2 a :** a pen or coop for an animal **:** CAGE ⟨provided a ~ for them in the garden —T.E.Donne⟩ **b :** a cageful of animals ⟨kept . . . a ~ or two of hare —Joyce Warren⟩ **3 :** a cramped or flimsy shelter for a man **:** SHACK, SHANTY **4 a :** a car on low wheels in which coal is drawn and hoisted out of a mine pit **b (1) :** the bottom compartment of an ore-dressing jig **(2) :** the mineral product that collects there

hutch 1b

2hutch \"\ *vt* -ED/-ING/-ES **1** *archaic* **:** to put away or store in a hutch **:** HOARD **2 :** to wash (ore) in a box or jig

3hutch *adj* [perh. alter. of *hulch*] *obs* **:** HUMPED

hutch burn *n* **:** an inflammation of the skin of rabbits esp. on the hind feet and adjacent parts associated with unclean urine-soiled cages

hutch·e·so·ni·an \ˌhəchəˈsōnēən\ *adj, usu cap* [Francis *Hutcheson* †1746 Scot. philosopher + E -*ian*] **:** of or relating to the theories of the Scottish philosopher Francis Hutcheson

hutch·et \ˈhəchət\ *n* -s [MF *huchet*, fr. *hucher* to cry out, fr. OF *huchier*, prob. of imit. origin] **:** a hunter's horn **:** BUGLE 2

hutch·in·so·ni·an teeth *or* **hutchinsonian incisors** \ˌhəchənˈsōnēən-\ *n pl, often cap H* [*hutchinsonian* fr. Sir Jonathan *Hutchinson* + E -*ian*] **:** HUTCHINSON'S TEETH

hutch·in·son·ite \ˈhəchənsə,nīt\ *n* -s [Arthur *Hutchinson* †1937 Eng. mineralogist + E -*ite*] **:** a mineral $(Pb,Tl)_2(Cu,Ag)As_5S_{10}$ consisting of sulfide of lead, copper, and arsenic, with thallium and silver replacing variable amounts of lead and copper, and occurring in small red orthorhombic crystals

hutch·in·son's teeth \ˈhəchənsənz-\ *also* **hutchinson teeth** *n pl but sing or pl in constr, usu cap H* [after Sir Jonathan *Hutchinson* †1913 Eng. surgeon] **:** peg-shaped teeth having a crescentic notch in the cutting edge and occurring esp. in children with congenital syphilis

hutchinson's triad *n, usu cap H* **:** a triad of symptoms comprising Hutchinson's teeth, interstitial keratitis, and deafness and occurring in children with congenital syphilis

hutch·ins's goose \ˈhəchənz(əz)-\ *n, usu cap H* [after Thomas *Hutchins* †1790 Eng. attaché of the Hudson's Bay Company] **:** a variety (*Branta canadensis hutchinsii*) of the Canada goose closely resembling but smaller than the typical form, breeding in arctic America and migrating south through the U.S., but being rare east of the Mississippi

hutch table *n* **:** a combination table and chest whose top can be tilted back to convert the unit into a chair or settee

hut circle *n* **:** a ring of stones or earth marking the site of a prehistoric dwelling

hu·tia *also* **ju·tia** \(h)üˈtēə\ *n* -s [Sp *hutia* & AmerSp *jutia*, fr. Taino *hutia*] **:** any of several large edible hystricomorph rodents that constitute two West Indian genera (*Capromys* and *Geocapromys*) and a related So. American genus (*Procapromys*), are closely related to the coypus, and are now extinct over much of their range

hutkeeper \ˈ=,==\ *n, Austral* **:** the man in charge of a hut on a ranch

hut·man \ˈhətmən\ *n, pl* **hutmen :** a member of the staff of an overnight hut for hikers

hutmaster \ˈ=,==\ *n* **:** the manager of an overnight hut for hikers

hut·ment \ˈhətmənt\ *n* -s [*2hut* + -*ment*] **1 a :** a collection of huts **:** ENCAMPMENT **b :** the act or process of housing people in huts **2 :** HUT; *specif* **:** a prefabricated portable army housing unit usu. made of plywood and accommodating 16 to 20 men

huts *pl of* HUT, *pres 3d sing of* HUT

hutted *adj* [fr. past part. of *2hut*] **:** consisting of or supplied with huts ⟨single-story ~ wards —*Lancet*⟩ ⟨a ~ camp⟩

hut·te·ri·an brethren \,həˈtirēən-, hü‖, hu̇‖\ *n, cap H&B* [*hutterian* fr. Jakob *Hutter* (or *Huter*) †1536 Moravian Anabaptist + E -*ian*] **:** a Mennonite sect of northwestern U.S. and Canada living in communities and holding property in common

hut·ter·ite *also* **hu·ter·ite** \ˈhəd·ə,rīt, ˈhü‖, ˈhu̇‖\ *n* -s *usu cap* **:** a member of the Hutterian Brethren

hutting *pres part of* HUT

1hut·to·ni·an \,həˈtōnēən\ *adj, usu cap* [James *Hutton* †1797 Scot. geologist + E -*ian*] **:** of or relating to the views of the Scottish geologist James Hutton

2huttonian \"\ *n* -s *usu cap* **:** an adherent of Huttonian theories (as uniformitarianism) of geology — **hut·to·ni·an·ism** \-ēə,nizəm\ *n* -s *usu cap*

hut·ton·ite \ˈhət°n,īt\ *n* -s [Colin O. *Hutton* †1971 Am. geologist born in New Zealand + E -*ite*] **:** a mineral $ThSiO_4$ consisting of monoclinic silicate of thorium dimorphous with thorite

hut·ton's vireo \ˈhət°nz-\ *n, usu cap H* [prob. fr. the name *Hutton*] **:** a vireo (*Vireo huttoni*) of western No. America having a dull olive back and dingy white underparts

hut·ton·weed \-°n,wēd\ *n* [prob. fr. the name *Hutton*] **:** WILD TEASEL

hu·tu \ˈhü(,)tü\ *n, pl* **hutu** *or* **hutus** *usu cap* **:** RUNDI

hu·tukh·tu *or* **hu·tuk·tu** \hüˈtu̇k(,)tü\ *n* -s *often cap* [Mongolian *khutuktu* eminent, fr. *khutuk* eminence] **:** a Lamaist dignitary believed to be an incarnation of Buddha; *specif* **:** the spiritual ruler of Mongolia

hut urn *n* **:** a prehistoric cinerary urn shaped like a round hut with a conical roof and found esp. in southern Italy

hu·tzul *also* **hu·zul** \hüt'sül\ *n, pl* **hutzul** *or* **hutzuls** *usu cap* **1 :** a mountain people of the high Carpathians in Slovakia, Ruthenia, and Poland speaking a Ruthenian dialect **2 :** a member of the Hutzul people

hux·le·ian *also* **hux·ley·an** \ˈhəkslēən, ,=ˈ==\ *adj, usu cap* [Thomas H. *Huxley* †1895 Eng. biologist *or* Aldous L. *Huxley* *b*1894 Eng. novelist and critic + E -*an*] **:** of or relating to the English biologist Thomas H. Huxley or his novelist grandson Aldous Huxley

huy·ge·ni·an eyepiece \(ˈ)hīˈgēnēən-, (ˈ)hȯi-\ *also* **huy·gens eyepiece** \ˈhīgənz-, ˈhȯi-\ *or* **huy·ghe·ni·an eyepiece** *n, usu cap H* [*huyghenian* irreg. fr. Christian *Huygens* (or *Huyghens*) †1695 Du. physicist + E -*ian*] **:** a compound eyepiece used esp. with achromatic objectives that consists of two plano-convex lenses separated by a diaphragm with the convex sides facing the objective

huy·gens' principle *also* **huy·ghens' principle** \ˈ=,gənz(əz)-\ *n, usu cap H* **:** a principle in physics: every point of an advancing wave front is a new center of disturbance from which emanate independent wavelets whose envelope constitutes a new wave front at each successive stage of the process

huz \(ˌ)(h)əz, (ˌ)(h)üz\ *pron* [by alter.] *dial Brit* **:** US

huzz \ˈhəz\ *vi* -ED/-ING/-ES [imit.] **:** BUZZ

1huz·zah *or* **huz·za** \(,)həˈzä, -zȧ\ *n* -s [origin unknown] **:** a cheer or shout of applause **:** HURRAH — often used interjectionally to express joy or approbation

2huzzah *or* **huzza** \"\ *vb* -ED/-ING/-S *vi* **:** to shout huzzah **:** HURRAH **~** *vt* **:** APPLAUD, CHEER

huzzy *var of* HUSSY

HV *abbr* **1** high velocity **2** high voltage

hvy *abbr* heavy

HW *abbr* **1** high water **2** highway **3** hit wicket **4** hot water

hwan \ˈ(h)wän\ *n, pl* **hwan** [Korean] **:** a former monetary unit of So. Korea established in 1953 and replaced in 1962 by the won

HWL *abbr* high-water line

HWM *abbr* high-water mark

hwy *abbr* highway

hy- *or* **hyo-** *comb form* [NL, fr. Gk *hyo-* upsilon (Υ, υ), fr. *y, hy* upsilon] **1 :** connecting with the hyoid arch ⟨*hyo*glossus⟩ **2 :** hyoid and ⟨*hyo*thyroid⟩

hy *abbr* **1** heavy **2** henry

hy·a·cinth \ˈhīə,sin(t)th, -,sən-\ *n, pl* **hyacinths** \-n(t)s, -n(t)ths\ [L *hyacinthus*, a precious stone, a flowering plant, fr. Gk *hyakinthos*] **1 a :** a precious stone of the ancients sometimes held to be the sapphire **b (1) :** a transparent red or brownish zircon sometimes used as a gem **(2) :** a red or brownish essonite used as a gem **2 a :** a plant of the ancients held to be the Turk's-cap lily, iris, larkspur, or gladiolus **b (1) :** a plant of the genus *Hyacinthus*; *esp* **:** the common garden hyacinth (*H. orientalis*) widely grown for the beauty and fragrance of its flowers — see ROMAN HYACINTH **(2) :** any of several other plants of the family Liliaceae — usu. used with preceding qualifier; see SUMMER HYACINTH, WATER HYACINTH **3 :** a light violet to moderate purple **4 :** PURPLE GALLINULE

hyacinth 2b(1)

hyacinth bacteriosis *n* **:** a destructive bacterial disease of the hyacinth caused by a bacterium (*Xanthomonas hyacinthi*) that attacks both dry bulbs and growing plants

hyacinth bean *n* **:** a large twining vine (*Dolichos lablab*) that is native to the Old World tropics, has dark purple racemes of pealike flowers, and is widely grown as an ornamental, less often as a source of fodder, and sometimes for its edible pods and seeds

hyacinth blue *n* **:** a deep purplish blue that is slightly bluer than mazarine blue, redder and paler than average sapphire (sense 2a), and redder, lighter, and stronger than cyanine blue (sense 1b)

hy·a·cin·thi·an \,hīəˈsin(t)thēən\ *adj* **:** HYACINTHINE

hy·a·cin·thine \,hīəˈsin(t)thən, -n,thīn\ *adj* [L *hyacinthinus*, fr. Gk *hyakinthinos*, fr. *hyakinthos* hyacinth + -*inos* -ine] **1 :** having any one of the four colors hyacinth, hyacinth blue, hyacinth violet, or hyacinth red **2 a :** of, relating to, or resembling the hyacinth ⟨his ~ locks descend in wavy curls —Alexander Pope⟩ **b :** adorned or decorated with hyacinths ⟨with ~ chaplet crowned —Francis Fawkes⟩

hyacinth red *n* **:** a grayish reddish orange that is slightly lighter than Etruscan red and yellower and darker than Persian melon

hyacinth squill *n* **:** an ornamental bulbous Mediterranean plant (*Scilla hyacinthoides*) with lilac-purple flowers

hy·a·cin·thus \,hīəˈsin(t)thəs\ *n, cap* [NL, fr. L, a flowering plant] **:** a genus of Old World bulbous and scapose herbs (family Liliaceae) having flowers in terminal mostly compact racemes and a bell-shaped corolla with a prominent tube and short limb — see HYACINTH

hyacinth violet *n* **:** a deep purple that is bluer and slightly darker than petunia violet, redder than pontiff, bluer, lighter, and stronger than imperial purple (sense 2), and bluer and paler than dahlia purple (sense 2)

1hy·ae·na \hīˈēnə\ *var of* HYENA

2hyaena \"\ *n, cap* [NL, fr. L, hyena — more at HYENA] **:** the type genus of the family Hyaenidae

hy·ae·nan·che \,hīəˈnaŋkē\ *n, cap* [NL, fr. L *hyaena* hyena + NL -*anche* (fr. Gk *anchein* to strangle); fr. the use of the fruit in poisoning hyenas — more at HYENA, ANGER] **:** a genus of trees (family Euphorbiaceae) of southern Africa with coriaceous whorled leaves, cymose staminate flowers, and solitary pistillate flowers

hy·ae·narc·tos \-ˈnärk,täs\ *n, cap* [NL, fr. L *hyaena* hyena + Gk *arktos* bear — more at ARCTIC] **:** a genus of large Old World Pliocene and Pleistocene bears

hy·ae·nid \hīˈēnəd, -ˈen-\ *n* -s [NL *Hyaenidae*] **:** one of the Hyaenidae

hy·aeni·dae \hīˈēnə,dē, -ˈen-\ *n pl, cap* [NL, fr. *Hyaena*, type genus + -*idae*] **:** a family of carnivorous mammals comprising the hyenas and usu. the aardwolf

hy·aeno·don \hīˈēnə,dän, -ˈen-\ *n* [NL *Hyaenodont-, Hyaenodon*, fr. *Hyaena* + -*odont-*, -*odon* -odon] **1** *cap* **:** the type genus of Hyaenodontidae comprising extinct carnivorous mammals from Eocene, Oligocene, and possibly Miocene deposits of Eurasia, Africa, and No. America **2** -s **:** a mammal of the genus *Hyaenodon*

1hy·aeno·dont \-ˌänt\ *adj* [NL *Hyaenodontidae*] **:** of or relating to the Hyaenodontidae

2hyaenodont \"\ *n* -s [NL *Hyaenodontidae*] **:** an animal of the family Hyaenodontidae

hy·aeno·don·ti·dae \,hī,ēnəˈdäntə,dē, -,en-\ *n pl, cap* [NL, fr. *Hyaenodont-, Hyaenodon*, type genus + -*idae*] **:** a family of typically rather slender long-skulled, more or less digitigrade clawed extinct carnivores of the suborder Creodonta varying from a few inches in length to the size of some of the recent large cats (as the leopard)

hy·aeno·don·toid \(,)=ˈ==ˈdän,tȯid\ *adj* [NL *Hyaenodontidae* + E -*oid*] **:** of, relating to, or resembling the Hyaenodontidae

hyal- *or* **hyalo-** *comb form* [LL, glass, fr. Gk, fr. *hyalos* transparent stone, glass] **1** : glass : glassy ⟨*hyal*escent⟩ ⟨*hyalo*crystalline⟩ **2** : transparent or translucent substance ⟨*hyalo*gen⟩

hy·a·les·cence \ˌhīə'lesᵊn(t)s\ *n* -s [*hyal-* + *-escence*] : the quality or state of being hyalescent

hy·a·les·cent \ˌ==ˈlesᵊnt\ *adj* [*hyal-* + *-escent*] : becoming or appearing hyaline

¹hy·a·line \ˈhīələn, -əˌlīn\ *adj* [LL *hyalinus*, fr. Gk *hyalinos*, fr. *hyalos* transparent stone, glass + *-inos* -ine] **1** : of, resembling, or consisting of glass ⟨a glimpse of bay below, a rock-set ~ circlet —Sybille Bedford⟩ **2 a** *biol* : transparent or nearly so ⟨a ~ membrane⟩ **b** *mineralogy* (1) : GLASSY (2) : lacking crystallinity : AMORPHOUS

²hy·a·line \"\, *in sense 2* -əˌlēn *or* -ələn\ *n* -s **1** : something transparent (as the smooth sea or the clear atmosphere) ⟨the morning is as clear as diamond or as ~ —Sacheverell Sitwell⟩ **2** *or* **hy·a·lin** \-ələn\ [prob. ISV *hyal-* + *-ine* or *-in*] **a** : a nitrogenous substance closely related to chitin that forms the main constituent of the walls of hydatid cysts and yields a sugar on decomposition **b** : any of several similar translucent substances collecting around cells, capable of being stained by eosin, and yielding a carbohydrate as a cleavage product

hyaline cartilage *n* [¹*hyaline*] : translucent bluish white cartilage that has the cartilage cells embedded in an apparently homogeneous matrix, is the commonest type of cartilage present in joints and in respiratory passages, and forms most of the fetal skeleton

hyaline cast *n* [¹*hyaline*] : a renal cast characterized by homogeneity of structure

hyaline degeneration *n* [¹*hyaline*] : tissue degeneration chiefly of connective tissues in which structural elements of affected cells are replaced by homogeneous translucent material that stains intensely with acid dyes

hy·a·lin·iza·tion \ˌhīələnəˈzāshən\ *n* -s : the process of becoming hyalinized or the state of being hyaline

hy·a·lin·ize \ˈhīələˌnīz\ *vi* -ED/-ING/-S [¹*hyaline* + *-ize*] : to become hyaline; *esp* : to undergo hyaline degeneration

hy·al·i·no·crystalline \ˌhīˌal(ˌ)nō+\ *adj* [ISV ¹*hyaline* + *-o-* + *crystalline*; orig. formed as G *hyalinokristallin*] *of rock* : having a texture partly glassy and partly crystalline

hy·a·li·no·sis \ˌhīələˈnōsəs\ *n, pl* **hyalino·ses** \-ōˌsēz\ [NL, fr. LL *hyalinus* hyaline + NL *-osis*] **1** : HYALINE DEGENERATION **2** : a condition characterized by hyaline degeneration

hy·a·lite \ˈhīəˌlīt\ *n* -s [G *hyalit*, fr. Gk *hyalos* transparent stone, glass + G *-it* -ite] : a colorless opal that is sometimes clear as glass and sometimes translucent or whitish and that occurs as globules or crusts lining cavities or cracks in rocks

hy·a·lithe \ˈhīəˌlith, -ˌlīth\ *n* -s [prob. modif. (influenced by E *-lith*) of F *hyalite* hyalithe, hyalite, fr. G *hyalit* hyalite] : an opaque glass that resembles porcelain and is sometimes used as a gemstone

hyalo- — see HYAL-

hy·a·lo·basalt \ˌhīə(ˌ)lō+\ *n* [ISV *hyal-* + *basalt*; orig. formed in G] : BASALT GLASS

hy·a·lo·crystalline \"+\ *adj* [*hyal-* + *crystalline*] : HYALINOCRYSTALLINE

hy·al·o·gen \hīˈaləjən, -ˌjen\ *n* -s [ISV *hyal-* + *-gen*; prob. orig. formed in G] : any of several insoluble substances related to mucoids that are found in many animal structures (as hydatid cysts or sponges) and that yield hyalines on hydrolysis

hy·a·loid \ˈhīəˌlȯid\ *adj* [Gk *hyaloeidēs*, fr. *hyalos* glass + *-eidēs* -oid] *anat* : GLASSY, TRANSPARENT

hyaloid membrane *n* : a very delicate membrane enclosing the vitreous humor of the eye

hy·al·o·mere \hīˈaləˌmi(ə)r\ *n* -s [*hyal-* + *-mere*] : the pale nonrefractile portion of a blood platelet — compare CHROMOMERE

hy·a·lom·ma \ˌhīəˈlämə\ *n, cap* [NL, fr. *hyal-* + *-omma*] : an Old World genus of ticks that attack wild and domestic mammals and sometimes man, produce severe lesions by their bites, and often serve as vectors of viral and protozoal diseases

hy·a·lo·mucoid \ˌhīə(ˌ)lō+\ *n* [*hyal-* + *mucoid*] : a mucoprotein in the vitreous humor

hy·a·lo·ne·ma \ˌhīəlōˈnēmə\ *n, cap* [NL, fr. *hyal-* + *-nema*] : a genus of hyalosponges having a long stem composed of very long slender transparent siliceous fibers twisted together like the strands of a cord

hy·al·o·phane \hīˈaləˌfān\ *n* -s [G *hyalophan*, fr. *hyal-* + *-phan* -phane] : a mineral $BaAl_2Si_2O_8$ consisting of a monoclinic feldspar isomorphous with and resembling adularia

hy·a·lo·pi·lit·ic \ˌhīə(ˌ)lōˌpīˈlid·ik\ *adj* [ISV *hyalopilit-* (fr. G *hyalopilitisch* hyalopilitic, fr. *hyal-* + Gk *pilos* felt + G *-it* -ite + *-isch* -ish, fr. OHG *-isc*) + *-ic* — more at PILE (hair)] : composed of or characterized by innumerable slender microlites embedded in glass ⟨~ structure is frequently found in basic lavas⟩

hy·alo·plasm \hīˈaləˌplazəm, ˈhīəlō,-\ *n* -s [prob. fr. G *hyaloplasma*, fr. *hyal-* + *-plasma* -plasm] : the clear apparently homogeneous ground substance of cytoplasm that is essentially the continuous phase of a multiple-phase colloidal system

hy·a·lo·plas·ma \ˌhīəlōˈplazmə\ *n* [prob. fr. G] : HYALOPLASM

hy·a·lo·sid·er·ite \ˌhīəlōˈsidəˌrīt\ *n* [G *hyalosiderit*, fr. *hyal-* + Gk *sidēros* iron + G *-it* -ite] : an olivine containing much iron

hy·alo·sponge \hīˈalōˌspənj, ˈhīəl-\ *n* [NL *Hyalospongiae*] : one of the Hyalospongiae

hy·a·lo·spon·gea \ˌhīəlōˈspənjēə, -pän-\ [NL, fr. *hyal-* + *-spongea* (irreg. fr. L *spongia* sponge) — more at SPONGE] *syn of* HYALOSPONGIAE

hy·a·lo·spon·gia \"\ [NL, fr. *hyal-* + *-spongia*] *syn of* HYALOSPONGIAE

hy·a·lo·spon·gi·ae \-ēˌē\ *n pl, cap* [NL, fr. *hyal-* + *-spongiae*] : a class of Porifera comprising sponges with 6-rayed siliceous spicules, no surface epithelium, and the choanocytes restricted to finger-shaped chambers — see GLASS SPONGE

hy·a·lo·te·kite \ˌhīəlōˈtēˌkīt\ *n* -s [Sw *hyalotekit*, fr. *hyal-* + Gk *tēkein* to melt + Sw *-it* -ite; fr. the fact that it fuses to a clear glass — more at THAW] : a mineral approximately $(Pb,Ca,Ba)_4BSi_6O_{17}(OH,F)$ consisting of a borosilicate and fluoride of lead, barium, and calcium found in crystalline masses

hy·al·uro·nate \ˌhīəˈlu̇rəˌnāt\ *n* -s [ISV *hyaluronic* + *-ate*] : a salt or ester of hyaluronic acid

hy·al·uron·ic acid \ˌhīəlu̇ˈränik-\ *n* [*hyaluronic* ISV *hyal-* + *-uronic*] : a viscous mucopolysaccharide acid that occurs chiefly in connective tissues or their derivatives — compare MUCOITINSULFURIC ACID

hy·al·uron·i·dase \ˌ===ˈränəˌdās, -āz\ *n* -s [ISV *hyaluronid-* (fr. *hyaluronic acid*) + *-ase*] : an enzyme that splits hyaluronic acid and thus lowers the viscosity of the acid and facilitates the spreading of fluids through tissues either advantageously (as in the absorption of drugs) or disadvantageously (as in the dissemination of infection), that occurs in many normal tissues, in malignant growths, in invasive bacteria, and in certain venoms but is usu. prepared from mammalian testes, and that is used esp. to aid in the dispersion of fluids (as local anesthetics) injected subcutaneously for therapeutic purposes — called also *spreading factor*

hyb *abbr* hybrid

hy·blae·an \(ˈ)hīˈblēən\ *adj, usu cap* [L *hyblae*us of Hybla (fr. Gk *hyblaios*, fr. *Hybla*, ancient town in Sicily famous for the excellence of its honey) + E *-an*] : MELLIFLUOUS, HONEYED ⟨golden and *Hyblaean* eloquence —A.C.Swinburne⟩

¹hyb·o·dont \ˈhībəˌdänt\ *adj* [NL *Hybodont-*, *Hybodus*] : of or relating to the genus *Hybodus* or family Hybodontidae

²hybodont \"\ *n* -s [NL *Hybodont-*, *Hybodus*] : a hybodont shark

hyb·o·dus \-ədəs\ *n, cap* [NL *Hybodont-*, *Hybodus*, fr. Gk *hybos* hump + NL *-odont*, *-odus*] : a large genus (the type of the family Hybodontidae) of extinct sharks existing from the Trias to the Lower Cretaceous that are usu. included among the Squaloidea but are sometimes placed with related extinct forms in a separate suborder of the order Pleurotremata

hy·bo·sis \hīˈbōsəs, hə'-\ *n, pl* **hybo·ses** \-ōˌsēz\ *also* **hybosises** [NL, fr. Gk *hybos* hump + NL *-osis*] : a virus disease of cotton in which the leaves are reduced and distorted

¹hy·brid \ˈhībrəd, *substand* -ˌbred\ *n* -s [L *hybrida* animal whose parents belong to different varieties or to different species, person whose parents belong to different ethnic groups, prob. of non-IE origin; akin to the source of L *imbr-*, *imber* offspring of a tame sheep and a wild sheep] **1** : an offspring of two animals or plants of different races, breeds, varieties, species, or genera; *specif* : an individual produced by union of gametes from parents of different genotype — compare CROSSBREED, MENDEL'S LAW, MULE **2** : a person or group produced by the blending of two diverse cultures or traditions ⟨the cultural ~ occupies a marginal position between two cultures⟩ ⟨every civilized group . . . has been a ~ —H.J.Muller⟩ **3 a** : one that is heterogeneous in origin or composition : COMPOSITE ⟨most of the tools are original designs or ~s evolved from established forms —Victor Boesen⟩ ⟨the vice-president is a ~ in the government, being both an executive and legislative officer —Arthur Krock⟩ **b** : LOANBLEND

²hybrid \"\ *adj* **1 a** : marked by heterogeneity in origin, composition, or appearance : COMPOSITE ⟨difficulties with normal English are . . . its ~ vocabulary and the irregularities of English spelling —G.A.Miller⟩ **b** : being a linguistic hybrid ⟨a ~ term⟩ **2** : of, relating to, or resulting from the union of gametes from parents of different genotype ⟨the high percentage of intermarriage, however, has made the population . . racially ~ —*Current Biog.*⟩ **3** : having characteristics resulting from the blending of two diverse cultures or traditions ⟨a remarkable ~ culture in which Norse and Irish elements are inextricably combined —F.M.Stenton⟩

hy·bri·da \ˈhībrədə\ *n, pl* **hybri·dae** \-rəˌdē\ [NL, fr. L] : an interspecific hybrid

hybrid clover *n* : ALSIKE CLOVER

hybrid coil *n* : a transformer having three windings two of which are in series to facilitate maintenance of voltage balance to ground

hybrid corn *n* **1** : a corn resulting from crossbreeding; *specif* : the grain of Indian corn developed by hybridizing two or more inbred strains **2** : the plant that is grown from the grain of hybrid corn and that conforms to a standard of desirable characteristics including increased size, yield, or disease resistance but whose own grain produces an inferior progeny

hy·brid·ism \ˈhībrəˌdizəm\ *n* -s [ISV *hybrid* + *-ism*] **1** : HYBRIDITY **2** : the fusion of diverse cultures or traditions ⟨the ~ of Puerto Rico combines both No. American and Spanish culture⟩

hy·brid·ist \-dəst\ *n* -s [*hybrid* + *-ist*] : HYBRIDIZER

hy·brid·i·ty \hīˈbridəd·ē, -ətē, -i\ *n* -ES [ISV *hybrid* + *-ity*] : the quality or state of being hybrid

hy·brid·iz·able \ˈhībrəˌdīzəbəl, ˌ==ˈ==\ *adj* **1** : capable of producing a hybrid by crossing with another species or form **2** : reproducible by hybridization

hy·brid·iza·tion \ˌhībrədəˈzāshən, -ˌdīˈz-\ *n* -s : the act or process of hybridizing or the state of being hybridized

hy·brid·ize \ˈhībrəˌdīz\ *vb* -ED/-ING/-S [*hybrid* + *-ize*] *vt* : to cause to produce hybrids : CROSS, INTERBREED ⟨laid out ranches . . . where they could fatten and ~ their stock —R.A.Billington⟩ ~ *vi* : to produce hybrids ⟨the possibility . . . that Homo sapiens and Neanderthal were *hybridizing* in northwest India or central Asia prior to the third interglacial —J.E.Weckler⟩

hy·brid·iz·er \-zə(r)\ *n* -s : one that hybridizes ⟨is a noted botanist and ~ of native iris —*Wild Flower*⟩

hy·brid·ous \ˈhībrədəs\ *adj* : HYBRID

hybrid perpetual *or* **hybrid perpetual rose** *n* : any of certain cultivated bush roses derived chiefly from the bourbon and characterized by vigorous hardy growth, a tendency to recurrent blooming, and good-sized often fragrant flowers borne singly or in groups of two to five — see HYBRID TEA

hybrid polyantha *n* : FLORIBUNDA

hybrid rock *n* : a rock formed by the mixing of two magmas or by the assimilation of the intruded by the intruding rock

hybrids *pl of* HYBRID

hybrid swarm *n* : a variable local population at the junction of the range of two interfertile species or subspecies resulting from extensive interbreeding and hybridization

hybrid tea *or* **hybrid tea rose** *n* : any of numerous cultivated bush roses derived chiefly from crosses of tea roses and hybrid perpetuals and characterized by intermediate hardiness and vigor, strongly recurrent bloom, and long pointed buds followed by large usu. scentless flowers borne singly or in groups of two to five

hybrid vigor *n* : unusual vigor associated with hybridity : HETEROSIS

hybris *var of* HUBRIS

hyd *abbr* **1** hydraulic; hydraulics **2** hydrographic; hydrography **3** hydrostatic; hydrostatics

hy·dan·to·ic acid \ˌhīˌdanˈtōik-\ *n* [*hydantoic* ISV *hydrogen* + *allantoic*] : a white crystalline acid $NH_2CONHCH_2COOH$ obtained esp. by boiling hydantoin with alkalies

hy·dan·to·in \hīˈdantəwən\ *n* -s [ISV *hydrogen* + *allantoin*; prob. orig. formed in G] **1** : a crystalline weakly acidic compound $C_3H_4N_2O_2$ that is a di-oxo derivative of imidazole with a sweetish taste, that is found in beet juice and made synthetically (as by the action of hydriodic acid on allantoin), and that is used in organic synthesis **2** : a derivative of the hydantoin compound (as diphenylhydantoin)

hy·dan·to·in·ate \-əˌnāt\ *n* -s [*hydantoin* + *-ate*] : a salt of hydantoin or one of its derivatives

hydat- *or* **hydato-** *comb form* [prob. fr. NL, fr. Gk, fr. *hydat-*, *hydōr* — more at WATER] : water ⟨*Hydat*ina⟩ ⟨*hydato*genesis⟩

hy·da·thode \ˈhīdəˌthōd\ *n* -s [ISV *hydat-* + *-hode* (fr. Gk *hodos* way, road); prob. orig. formed in G — more at CEDE] : an epidermal structure in higher plants functioning in the exudation of water; *specif* : an opening in the epidermis resembling a stoma below which is a chamber usu. filled or bordered by thin-walled loosely arranged cells — called also *water pore*, *water stoma*; see GUTTATION, WATER GLAND

hy·da·tid \ˈhīdəd·əd, -īdətəd\ *n* [prob. fr. (assumed) NL *hydatid-*, *hydatis*, fr. Gk, watery vesicle, fr. *hydat-*, *hydōr* water] **1** *also* **hydatid cyst** : a larval tapeworm typically comprising a fluid-filled sac from the inner walls of which develop daughter cysts and scolices but occas. forming an uncircumscribed proliferating spongy mass that actively invades and metastasizes in the host's tissues — see ECHINOCOCCUS; compare COENURUS, CYSTICERCOID, CYSTICERCUS **2 a** : an abnormal cyst or cystic structure; *esp* : HYDATIDIFORM MOLE **b** : HYDATID DISEASE

hydatid disease *n* : a form of echinococcosis caused by the development of hydatids of a tapeworm (*Echinococcus granulosus*) in the tissues esp. of the liver or lungs of man and certain animals

hy·da·tid·i·form \ˌhīdəˈtidəˌfȯrm\ *also* **hy·dat·i·form** \(ˈ)hīˈdad·əˌfȯrm\ *adj* [*hydatidiform* prob. alter. (influenced by *hydatid*) of *hydatiform*; *hydatiform* ISV *hydat-* (fr. *hydatid*) + *-iform*; prob. orig. formed as F *hydatiforme*] : resembling a hydatid : CYSTIC

hydatidiform mole *n* : a mass in the uterus consisting of enlarged edematous degenerated placental villi growing in clusters resembling grapes and usu. associated with death of the fetus

hy·da·tid·o·cele \ˌhīdəˈtidəˌsēl\ *n* -s [NL, prob. fr. (assumed) NL *hydatid-*, *hydatis* + NL *-o-* + *-cele*] : a tumorous condition of the scrotum caused by local infestation with echinococcus larvae

hydatid of mor·ga·gni \-mȯ(r)ˈgänyē\ *usu cap M* [after Giovanni B. *Morgagni* †1771 Ital. physician] **1** : a small stalked or pedunculated body found between the testicle and the head of the epididymis in the male or attached to the fimbriae of the fallopian tube or the broad ligament in the female and considered to be a remnant of the duct of the pronephros or of the upper end of the müllerian duct **2** : a small unstalked or sessile body found in the same situation in the male only and considered to be a remnant of the müllerian duct

hy·da·tid·o·sis \ˌhīdəˌtiˈdōsəs\ *n, pl* **hydatid·oses** \-ōˌsēz\ [NL, prob. fr. (assumed) NL *hydatid-*, *hydatis* + NL *-osis*] : ECHINOCOCCOSIS; *specif* : HYDATID DISEASE

hy·dat·i·na \hīˈdatᵊnə\ *n, cap* [NL, fr. *hydat-* + *-ina*] : a genus of stout-bodied naked rotifers (order Monogononta)

hy·da·to·genesis \ˌhīdə(ˌ)tō +\ *n* [*hydat-* + *genesis*] **1** : the crystallization of minerals in certain rocks by the water present in a magma; *esp* : the process of depositing minerals in veins from aqueous solutions **2** : the crystallization of salt or gypsum from normal aqueous solutions

hy·da·to·genetic \"+\ *adj* [fr. *hydatogenesis*, after E *genesis*: *genetic*] : HYDATOGENIC

hy·da·to·gen·ic \ˌhīdətōˈjenik\ *or* **hy·da·tog·e·nous** \ˌhīdəˈtäjənəs\ *adj* [G *hydatogen* hydatogenic (fr. *hydat-* + *-gen* -genic, -genous, fr. Gk *-genēs* born) + E *-ic* or *-ous* — more at -GEN] **1** : crystallized from or deposited by aqueous solutions **2** : of or relating to hydatogenesis

hy·da·to·mor·phic \ˌhīdətōˈmȯrfik\ *adj* [G *hydatomorph*ose crystallization from aqueous solutions (fr. *hydat-* + *-morphose* -morphosis) + E *-ic*] : of, relating to, or produced by crystallization from aqueous solutions — **hy·da·to·mor·phism** \ˌ===ˈmȯrˌfizəm\ *n* -s

hy·da·to·pneumatolytic \ˌhīdə(ˌ)tō +\ *or* **hy·da·to·pneumatic** \"+\ *adj* [*hydatopneumatolytic* fr. *hydat-* + *pneumatolytic*; *hydatopneumatic* fr. *hydat-* + *pneumatic*] *of ore deposits* : formed by the joint agency of water and vapor

hy·der·a·bad \ˈhīd(ə)rəˌbad, -ˌbäd, ˌ=(=)=ˈ=\ *adj, usu cap* **1** [fr. *Hyderabad*, city in south central India] : of or from the city of Hyderabad, India : of the kind or style prevalent in Hyderabad **2** [fr. *Hyderabad*, city in southwest Pakistan] : of or from the city of Hyderabad, Pakistan : of the kind or style prevalent in Hyderabad

hyd·na·ce·ae \hidˈnāsēˌē\ *n pl, cap* [NL, fr. *Hydnum*, type genus + *-aceae*] : a family of fungi (order Agaricales) that are distinguished by a hymenium spread out over teeth, spines, or warty emergences or a fleshy, woody, or leathery fruiting body and that include several which cause rot in timbers and a few which are edible

hyd·no·car·pic acid \ˌhidnəˈkärpik-\ *n* [*hydnocarpic*, ISV *hydnocarp-* (fr. NL *Hydnocarpus*) + *-ic*] : a low-melting unsaturated acid $C_5H_7(CH_2)_{10}COOH$ occurring as the glyceride in chaulmoogra oil and hydnocarpus oil; 11-(2-cyclopenten-1-yl)-undecanoic acid

hyd·no·car·pus \ˌ==ˈkärpəs\ *n* [NL, fr. *hydno-* (fr. Gk *hydnon* truffle) + *-carpus*] **1** *cap* : a genus of Indo-Malayan trees (family Flacourtiaceae) with alternate leaves, small dioecious racemose flowers, and capsular fruits — compare CHAULMOOGRA **2** -ES : any tree of the genus *Hydnocarpus*

hydnocarpus oil \ˌ==ˈ==-\ *n* : a fatty oil obtained from seeds of trees of the genus *Hydnocarpus* (esp. *H. wightiana*) — compare CHAULMOOGRA OIL

hyd·noid \ˈhidˌnȯid\ *adj* [NL *Hydnum* + E *-oid*] : of, relating to, or characteristic of the genus *Hydnum*

hyd·no·ra \hidˈnōrə, ˈhidnərə\ *n, cap* [NL, irreg. fr. Gk *hydnon* truffle] : a genus (the type of the family Hydnoraceae) of African root parasites having soft spines on the inner surface of the perianth lobes resembling those of the hymenium of a fungus of the genus *Hydnum*

hyd·no·ra·ce·ae \ˌhidnəˈrāsēˌē\ *n pl, cap* [NL, fr. *Hydnora*, type genus + *-aceae*] : a family of African and Argentinian highly modified flowering plants (order Aristolochiales) that are parasitic on the roots of other plants and consist of a branched subterranean system of leafless rhizoid shoots from which large succulent solitary flowers are sent up to the surface of the ground — compare RAFFLESIACEAE — **hyd·no·ra·ceous** \ˌ==ˈrāshəs\ *adj*

hyd·num \ˈhidnəm\ *n, cap* [NL, fr. Gk *hydnon* truffle] : the type genus of the family Hydnaceae

hydr- *or* **hydro-** *comb form* [alter. (influenced by L *hydr-*, *hydro-*) of ME *ydr-*, *ydro-*, fr. OF *ydr-* & MF *ydro-*, fr. L *hydr-*, *hydro-*, fr. Gk, fr. *hydōr* — more at WATER] **1 a** : water ⟨*hydro*gel⟩ ⟨*hydro*electricity⟩ **b** : hydraulic ⟨*hydro*press⟩ **2** : water-loving organism — chiefly in generic names ⟨*Hydr*acarina⟩ ⟨*Hydro*dictyon⟩ **3 a** : hydrogen : containing hydrogen ⟨*hydr*iodic acid⟩ ⟨*hydro*borate⟩ **b** *now usu* **hydro-** : combined with hydrogen — esp. in names of organic compounds ⟨*hydro*quinidine⟩ **c** : combined with water by hydration ⟨*hydr*acrylic acid⟩ or by hydrolysis ⟨*hydro*cellulose⟩ **4** : characterized by an accumulation of fluid in a (specified) bodily part ⟨*hydro*nephrosis⟩ **5 a** : combined with water — in names of minerals ⟨*hydro*hetaerolite⟩ **b** : characterized by addition of water or its constituents — in names of varieties of minerals ⟨*hydro*mica⟩ **6** [NL, fr. *Hydra* (genus of polyps)] : hydroid ⟨*hydro*medusa⟩ ⟨*hydr*orhiza⟩

hy·dra \ˈhīdrə\ *n* [alter. (influenced by L *Hydra*) of earlier *idre* complicated evil thing, fr. ME *Ydre*, *Ydra* Hydra (mythical many-headed serpent slain by Hercules that grew two heads in place of each one that was cut off unless the wound was cauterized), fr. MF & L; MF *Ydre* Hydra, fr. L *Hydra*, fr. Gk; akin to Gk *hydros* water snake — more at OTTER] **1** -s : a many-sided problem or obstacle that presents new difficulties each time one aspect of it is solved or overcome **2** [NL, fr. L *Hydra* (mythical serpent)] **a** -s : any of a number of small freshwater hydrozoan polyps constituting *Hydra* and related genera, usu. living attached to sticks, leaves, or other submerged objects, and consisting of a simple tube with a mouth at one extremity surrounded by a circle of tentacles with which to capture food, the young developing either from eggs or as buds that become detached from the side of the parent after differentiating **b** *cap* : a common genus of hydras

hy·dra·car·i·an \ˌhīdrəˈka(a)rēən\ *n* -s [ISV *hydracar-* (fr. NL *Hydracarina*) + *-ian*] : one of the Hydrachnellae

hy·dra·ca·ri·na \ˌhīˌdrakəˈrīnə, -ˈrēnə\ [NL, fr. *hydr-* + *Acarina*] *syn of* HYDRACHNELLAE

hy·drac·a·rine \(ˈ)hīˈdrakəˌrīn, -ˌrēn, -ˌrən\ *adj* [NL *Hydracarina*] : of or relating to the Hydrachnellae

hy·drach·nel·lae \ˌhīˌdrakˈneˌlē\ *n pl, cap* [NL, fr. *Hydrachna* + *-ellae* (pl. of *-ella*)] : a superfamily or higher group of Acarina comprising freshwater and marine mites that are usu. rather large and often bright red, that have two pairs of eyes, tarsi usu. with two claws and without an empodium, and chelicerae with a sickle-shaped movable digit, and that with few exceptions breathe by means of a well-developed tracheal system — see HALACARIDAE, HYDRACHNIDAE

hy·drach·nid \hīˈdraknəd\ *n* -s [NL *Hydrachnidae*] : one of the Hydrachnidae : WATER MITE

hy·drach·ni·dae \-nəˌdē\ *n pl, cap* [NL, fr. *Hydrachna*, type genus (fr. *hydr-* + Gk *achna*, *achnē* foam, chaff) + *-idae* — more at EAR] *in some classifications* : a large family of water mites (group Hydrachnellae) that includes all the common free-living mites of fresh water and a few parasites of the gills of mollusks and that is now usu. broken up into numerous separate families

hy·drach·noi·dea \ˌhīˌdrakˈnȯidēə\ [NL, fr. *Hydrachna* + *-oidea*] *syn of* HYDRACHNELLAE

hy·dra·coral \ˈhīdrə+\ *n* [perh. irreg. fr. NL *Hydrocorallinae*] : HYDROCORAL

hy·drac·ry·late \hīˈdrakrəˌlāt, ˌhīdrəˈkriˌl-\ *n* -s [ISV *hydracrylic* + *-ate*] : a salt or ester of hydracrylic acid

hy·dracryl·ic acid \ˌhīdrəˈkrilik-\ *n* [*hydracrylic* ISV *hydr-* + *acrylic*] : a syrupy acid $HOCH_2CH_2COOH$ that is isomeric with lactic acid and decomposes easily on heating into acrylic acid

hy·drac·ry·lo·ni·trile \ˌhīˌdrakrə(ˌ)lōˈnīˌtrəl, -ˌtrēl, -ˌtrīl\ *n* [*hydr-* + *acrylonitrile*] : ETHYLENE CYANOHYDRIN

hy·drac·tin·ia \ˌhīˌdrakˈtinēə\ *n, cap* [NL, fr. *hydr-* + *Actinia*] : a genus of marine hydroids that have separate and distinctive polyps for nutritive, reproductive, and defensive functions borne on a dense encrusting coenosarc and that are commonly associated with shells containing hermit crabs — **hy·drac·tin·i·an** \ˌ==ˈtinēən\ *adj or n*

hydraemia *var of* HYDREMIA

hy·dra·gogue *also* **hydragog** \ˈhīdrəˌgäg\ *n* -s [obs. *hydragogue*, adj., causing a watery discharge from the bowels, fr. LL *hydragogus*, fr. Gk *hydragōgos*, fr. *hydr-* + *agōgos* leading, drawing forth — more at -AGOGUE] : a cathartic that causes copious watery discharges from the bowels

hydra–headed \ˌ==ˈ==\ *adj* [*Hydra*, mythical many-headed serpent + *headed* — more at HYDRA] : having many centers or branches ⟨a *hydra-headed* organization⟩ ⟨passive but *hydra-headed* resistance —Edward Crankshaw⟩

hy·dral·a·zine \hīˈdraləˌzēn, -ˌzən\ *n* -s [prob. fr. *hydr-* + *phthalazine*] : a crystalline base $C_8H_5N_2NHNH_2$ used in the treatment of hypertension; 1-hydrazino-phthalazine

Hydra–Matic \ˌhīdrəˈmad·ik\ *trademark* — used for an automobile transmission having a fluid coupling and automatic gear-shifting controls

hy·dram·ni·os \hīˈdramnēˌäs\ *also* **hy·dram·ni·on** \-ˌän\ *n*

[NL, fr. *hydr-* + *amnios* or *amnion*] **:** excessive accumulation of the amniotic fluid
hy·dran·gea \hī'drānjə *sometimes* -ran- *or* -raan-, *chiefly in substand speech* ˌhīdə'r-\ *n* [NL, fr. *hydr-* + *-angea* (fr. Gk *angeion* vessel); prob. fr. the shape of the seed capsule — more at ANGI-] **1** *cap* **:** a large genus of widely distributed shrubs and one woody vine (family Saxifragaceae) with opposite leaves and corymbose clusters of usu. showy flowers — compare HYDRANGEACEAE **2** -s **:** a plant of the genus *Hydrangea* having ample white or tinted flower clusters in which all or most of the flowers are sterile: as **a :** a shrub (*H. macrophylla*) commonly grown in greenhouses **b :** a hardy fall-blooming shrub (*H. paniculata* or its variety *H. paniculata grandiflora*) **3 :** the dried rhizome and roots of the wild hydrangea (*Hydrangea arborescens*) formerly used in pharmacy as a diuretic
hydrangea blue *n* **:** a pale purplish blue that is deeper and slightly redder than starlight blue and bluer and deeper than haze blue, moonstone blue, or Ontario violet
hy·dran·ge·a·ce·ae \(ˌ)hīˌdrānjē'āsēˌē, -ran-,-raan-\ *n pl, cap* [NL, fr. *Hydrangea*, type genus + *-aceae*] *in some classifications* **:** a family of shrubs and trees (order Rosales) that are now usu. included in Saxifragaceae
hydrangea family *n* **:** SAXIFRAGACEAE
hydrangea pink *n* **:** a moderate pink that is yellower and less strong than arbutus pink, yellower and paler than blossom pink, and paler than chalk pink — called also *aurore*
hydrangea red *n* **:** a grayish red that is bluer and duller than Pompeian red or bois de rose, yellower and less strong than blush rose, and yellower and duller than appleblossom
hy·drant \'hīdrənt\ *n* -s [*hydr-* + *-ant* (n. suffix)] **1 :** a discharge pipe with a valve and spout at which water may be drawn from the mains of waterworks — called also *fireplug* **2 :** FAUCET
hy·dranth \'hīˌdran(t)th\ *n* -s [ISV *hydr-* + *-anth* (fr. Gk *anthos* flower) — more at ANTHOLOGY] **:** one of the nutritive zooids of a hydroid colony, each having a mouth, digestive cavity, and tentacles
hy·drarch \'hīˌdrärk\ *adj* [*hydr-* + *-arch* (adj. comb. form)] **:** originating in water — used of an ecological succession; compare HYDROSERE, MESARCH, XERARCH

hydrant

hy·drar·gil·lite \hī'drärjəˌlīt\ *n* [*hydr-* + *argillite*] **1 :** WAVELLITE **2 :** GIBBSITE
hy·drar·gyr·ia \ˌhī(ˌ)drär'jirēə\ *also* **hy·drar·gy·ri·a·sis** \hīˌdrärjə'rīəsəs\ *n, pl* **hydrargyrias** *also* **hydrargyriases** [NL, fr. *hydrargyrum* + *-ia* or *-iasis*] **:** MERCURIALISM
hy·drar·gy·rism \hī'drärjəˌrizəm\ *n* -s [ISV *hydrargyr-* (fr. NL *hydrargyrum*) + *-ism*] **:** MERCURIALISM
hy·drar·gy·rum \-ˌrəm\ *n* -s [NL, alter. of L *hydrargyrus*, fr. Gk *hydrargyros*, fr. *hydr-* + *argyros* silver — more at ARGENT] **:** MERCURY — symbol *Hg*
hy·drar·thro·sis \ˌhī(ˌ)drär'thrōsəs\ *n, pl* **hydrarthro·ses** \-ōˌsēz\ [NL, fr. *hydr-* + *arthr-* + *-osis*] **:** a watery effusion into a joint cavity
hydras *pl of* HYDRA
hy·drase \'hīˌdrās, -āz\ *n* -s [*hydr-* + *-ase*] **:** an enzyme that promotes addition of water to its substrate or removal of water therefrom
hy·dras·tine \hī'draˌstēn, -ˌstən\ *also* **hy·dras·tin** \-ˌstən\ *n* -s [ISV *hydrast-* (fr. NL *Hydrastis*) + *-ine* or *-in*] **:** a bitter crystalline alkaloid $C_{21}H_{21}NO_6$ derived from isoquinoline that is an active constituent of hydrastis and berberis preparations and is the parent compound of narcotine
hy·dras·ti·nine \hī'drastəˌnēn, -ˌnən\ *n* -s [ISV *hydrastine* + *-ine*; prob. orig. formed as G *hydrastinin*] **:** a crystalline base $C_{11}H_{13}NO_3$ formed by the oxidation of hydrastine and useful in controlling uterine hemorrhage; 5-(methylamino-ethyl)-piperonal
hy·dras·tis \hī'drastəs\ *n* [NL, prob. irreg. fr. *hydr-*] **1** *cap* **:** a genus of herbs (family Ranunculaceae) having palmately lobed leaves and small greenish apetalous flowers — see GOLDENSEAL **2** -ES **:** the dried rhizome and roots of the goldenseal (*Hydrastis canadensis*) formerly used in pharmacy as a bitter tonic
¹hy·drate \'hīˌdrāt, -drət, *usu* -d.+V\ *n* -s [ISV *hydr-* + *-ate* (n. suffix)] **:** a product of hydration: as **a :** a compound or complex ion formed by the union of water with some other substance and represented as actually containing water **:** a solvate containing molecules of water — compare WATER OF CRYSTALLIZATION, WATER OF HYDRATION ⟨Glauber's salt is a ~⟩ ⟨the aluminum ion forms a ~ $[Al(H_2O)_6]^{+++}$⟩ **b :** a compound containing hydroxyl ⟨camphene ~ $C_{10}H_{17}OH$⟩ **:** HYDROXIDE ⟨calcium ~⟩ — used chiefly commercially
²hy·drate \-ˌdrāt\ *vb* -ED/-ING/-S [ISV *hydr-* + *-ate* (v. suffix)] *vt* **1 :** to cause to take up or combine with water or with hydrogen and hydroxyl in the proportion in which they form water (as by chemical reaction or by adsorption) **:** subject to hydration — compare AQUATE **2 :** to maintain or restore the normal proportion of fluid in the body of esp. by oral or intravenous administration **3 :** to subject (paper pulp) to prolonged beating esp. in making glassine and greaseproof papers in order to increase moisture resistance ~ *vi* **:** to take up or combine with water or with hydrogen and hydroxyl **:** undergo hydration
hydrated *adj* [fr. past part. of ²*hydrate*] **1 :** containing combined water (as in a hydrate) **:** HYDROUS **2** *of paper pulp* **:** subjected to prolonged beating to make moisture-resistant paper
hydrated alumina *n* **:** ALUMINUM HYDROXIDE
hydrated lime *n* **:** a dry white powder consisting essentially of calcium hydroxide obtained by treating lime with water — called also *slaked lime*
hy·dra·tion \hī'drāshən\ *n* -s [²*hydrate* + *-ion*] **1 :** the act or process of combining with water: as **a :** the introduction of additional fluid into the body ⟨~ sometimes helps to reduce the concentration of toxic substances in the tissues⟩ **b :** a chemical reaction in which water takes part with the formation of only one product ⟨~ of ethylene to ethyl alcohol⟩; *esp* **:** a reaction in which water takes part in the form of intact molecules ⟨~ of sodium sulfate to the decahydrate⟩ — compare HYDROLYSIS, SOLVATION **c :** the addition of water to a calcium aluminate powder to produce cement **2 :** the quality or state of being hydrated: as **a :** the condition of having adequate fluid in the body tissues **b :** a physical change in paper fibers due to adsorption and imbibition of water caused by prolonged beating
hy·dra·tor \'hīˌdrād·ə(r)\ *n* -s [²*hydrate* + *-or*] **:** one that hydrates
hy·dra·trop·ic acid \ˌhīdrə¦träpik-\ *n* [*hydratropic* ISV *hydr-* + *atropic* being an alpha-phenyl-acrylic acid $CH_2{:}C(C_6H_5)COOH$ obtainable by the decomposition of atropine (ISV *atrop-* — fr. *atropine* — + *-ic*)] **:** a colorless liquid acid $C_6H_5CH(CH_3)COOH$ obtained by reduction of alpha-phenyl-acrylic acid; α-phenyl-propionic acid
hydra–tuba \'≈≈'≈\ *n* [*hydra* (polyp) + *tuba* (horn); fr. the similarity in shape to a trumpet] **:** SCYPHISTOMA
hy·drau·cone \'hīdrōˌkōn\ *n* [*hydraulic* + *cone*] **:** a draft tube symmetrical with the axis of a water turbine and enlarging in diameter at the lower end where the water impinges upon a horizontal slab as it enters the tailrace
hydrauli *pl of* HYDRAULUS
¹hy·drau·lic \hī'drȯlik, -lēk *also* -räl-\ *n* -s [L *hydraulicus*, adj.] **:** a hydraulic machine or device ⟨brakes are four-wheel ~s —*Motor Life*⟩; *specif* **:** HYDRAULIC ORGAN
²hy·drau·lic \(')≈¦≈≈\ *adj* [L *hydraulicus* being a hydraulic organ, fr. Gk *hydraulikos*, fr. *hydraulis* hydraulic organ (fr. *hydr-* + *-aulis*, fr. *aulos* reed instrument like an oboe) + *-ikos* -ic — more at ALVEOLUS] **1 :** operated, moved, or effected by means of water **2 a :** of or relating to hydraulics ⟨~ engineer⟩ **b :** of or relating to water or other liquid in motion ⟨~ erosion . . . of shore reef fronts —*Scientific Monthly*⟩ **3 :** operated by the resistance offered or the pressure transmitted when a quantity of water, oil, or other liquid is forced through a comparatively small orifice or through a tube — used of a mechanism ⟨~ buffer⟩ ⟨~ turbine⟩ ⟨~ equipment⟩ ⟨~ system⟩; *also* **:** relating to a device operated in this way ⟨~ pressure⟩ ⟨~ action⟩ **4 :** hardening or setting under water ⟨~ mortar⟩ ⟨~ bond⟩ — **hy·drau·li·cal·ly** \-lək(ə)lē, -lēk-, -li\ *adv*
³hydraulic \≈'≈≈\ *vt* **hydraulicked; hydraulicked; hydraulicking; hydraulics :** to subject to the action of a powerful stream or jet of water or excavate in this manner **:** SLUICE
hydraulic brake *n* **:** a brake (as for a motor vehicle) in which

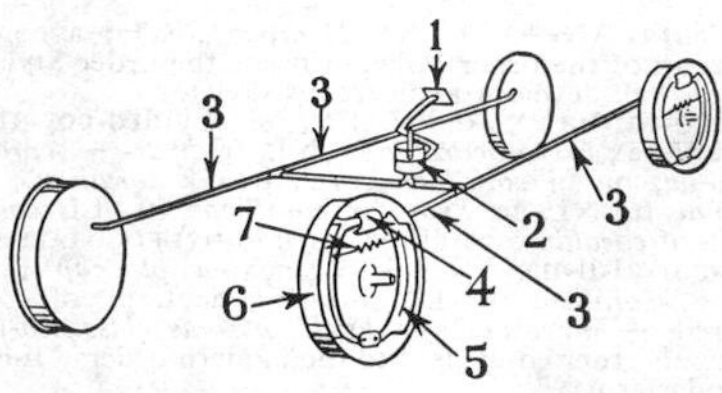

four-wheeled hydraulic brake system: *1* pedal; *2* master cylinder containing piston; *3, 3, 3, 3,* lines to each wheel; *4* wheel cylinder containing opposed pistons; *5* shoe; *6* drum; *7* return spring

the braking force is applied through a mechanism operated like a small hydraulic press
hydraulic cement *n* **:** a cement that is capable of hardening under water — see PORTLAND CEMENT, POZZOLANA
hydraulic classification *n* **:** the sorting of small particles (as of ground ore) by allowing them to settle against rising currents of fresh water of different velocities
hydraulic coupling *n* **:** FLUID COUPLING
hydraulic dredge *n* **:** a floating dredge using a centrifugal pump to draw mud or saturated sand (as from a river channel) and discharge it elsewhere
hydraulic elevator *n* **:** an elevator operated by the weight or pressure of water — see HYDRAULIC PLUNGER ELEVATOR, HYDRAULIC ROPE-GEARED ELEVATOR
hydraulic engineering *n* **:** a branch of civil engineering that deals with the use and control of flowing water (as for power or in placer mining)
hydraulic–fill dam *n* **:** a dam constructed by washing earthy materials into place
hydraulic fluid *n* **:** a fluid usu. of low viscosity (as oil or glycerol but seldom water) used in a hydraulically operated mechanism ⟨*hydraulic fluid* in a brake cylinder⟩
hydraulic gradient *or* **hydraulic grade line** *n* **:** a line joining the points of highest elevation of water in a series of vertical open pipes rising from a pipeline in which water flows under pressure
hy·drau·lic·i·ty \ˌhī(ˌ)drȯ'lisəd·ē\ *n* -ES [ISV ²*hydraulic* + *-ity*] **:** the capacity which hydraulic cements or their ingredients have for hardening under water
hydraulic jack *n* **:** a jack designed on the principle of the hydraulic press
hydraulic jump *n* **:** a sudden usu. turbulent rise of water flowing rapidly in an open channel where it encounters an obstruction or change in the channel slope
hy·drau·lick·er \hī'drȯlikə(r)\ *n* -s [¹*hydraulic* + *-er*] **:** one that operates a hydraulic mechanism; *specif* **:** a worker who shapes hats in a hydraulic press
hydraulic lift *n* **:** HYDRAULIC ELEVATOR; *esp* **:** one used for lifting motor vehicles (as for servicing in a garage)
hydraulic lime *n* **:** a hydraulic cementitious product made by burning hydraulic limestone
hydraulic limestone *n* **:** a limestone containing silica and alumina and yielding a lime that will harden under water
hydraulic mean depth *n* **:** HYDRAULIC RADIUS
hydraulic mining *n* **:** mining by the action of powerful jets of water — compare PLACER MINING
hydraulic oil *n* **:** an oil used as a hydraulic fluid
hy·drau·li·con \hī'drȯləˌkän\ *n* -s [Gk *hydraulikon organon*] **:** HYDRAULUS
hydraulic organ *n* [trans. of Gk *hydraulikon organon*, fr. *hydraulikon* (neut. of *hydraulikos* being a hydraulic organ) + *organon* organ — more at HYDRAULIC] **:** HYDRAULUS
hydraulic packing *n* **:** packing made of a material that is highly resistant to the action of water esp. under high pressure
hydraulic plunger elevator *n* **:** a hydraulic elevator having a steel-tube plunger several feet longer than the travel of the car encased in a cylinder sunk into the ground and actuated by water pressure assisted by a counterweight and controlled by valves operated from the car, the water being forced out as the car descends
hydraulic press *n* **:** a machine in which great force with slow motion is communicated to a large plunger by means of liquid forced into the cylinder in which it moves by a piston pump of small diameter to which the power is applied — called also *Bramah press, hydrostatic press*
hydraulic radius *n* **:** the ratio of the cross-sectional area of a channel or pipe in which a fluid is flowing to the wetted perimeter of the conduit
hydraulic ram *n* **1 :** a pump that forces running water to a higher level by utilizing the kinetic energy of flow, only a small portion of the water being so lifted by the velocity head of a much larger portion when the latter is suddenly checked by the closing of a valve **2 :** the larger output piston of a hydraulic press or similar machine
hydraulic rope–geared elevator \-'≈,≈-\ *n* **:** a hydraulic elevator in which one end of a system of ropes and sheaves is attached to the elevator car and the other end to a piston operating in a cylinder
hy·drau·lics \hī'drȯliks, -lēks *also* -räl-\ *n pl but usu sing in constr* **:** a branch of science that deals with practical applications (as the transmission of energy or the effects of flow) of water or other liquid in motion

hydraulic ram: *1* original flow, *2* output pipe, *3* air chamber, *4* check valve

hydraulic sprayer *n* **:** a machine for the large-scale application of insecticides or fungicides to crops in the form of a spray — compare MIST BLOWER
hy·drau·lus \hī'drȯləs\ *n, pl* **hydrauli** *or* **hydrauluses** [L, fr. Gk *hydraulos* hydraulic organ, fr. *hydr-* + *aulos* reed instrument like an oboe — more at ALVEOLUS] **:** an ancient Roman pipe organ using water under pressure as a means of compressing the air
hydraz- *or* **hydrazo-** *comb form* [ISV, fr. *hydrazine*] **1 :** related to hydrazine ⟨*hydrazide*⟩ **2** *usu hydrazo-* **:** containing the bivalent radical –NHNH– derived from hydrazine by removal of one hydrogen atom from each nitrogen atom — esp. in names of compounds in which the radical is united to two hydrocarbon radicals ⟨*hydrazo*toluene⟩
hy·dra·zide \'hīdrəˌzīd, -zəd\ *n* -s [ISV *hydraz-* + *-ide*] **:** any of a class of chemical compounds $RCONHNH_2$ resulting from the replacement by an acid radical of hydrogen in hydrazine or in one of its derivatives ⟨acetic ~⟩ — compare PHENYLHYDRAZIDE
hy·draz·i·dine \hī'drazəˌdēn, -dən\ *n* -s [ISV *hydrazine* + *-idin*] **:** an organic base of the general formula $RC(=NH)NHNH_2$ or $RC(=NNH_2)NH_2$ formed by the action of hydrazine on an imido ester — compare AMIDINE
hy·dra·zine \'hīdrəˌzēn, -zən\ *n* -s [ISV *hydr-* + *az-* + *-ine*; orig. formed as G *hydrazin*] **:** a colorless fuming corrosive strongly reducing liquid compound NH_2NH_2 that is a weaker base than ammonia, that is usu. made by dehydration of hydrazine hydrate, and that is used chiefly as a component of fuels for rocket and jet engines and in making salts (as the sulfates) and organic derivatives; *also* **:** an organic base (as phenylhydrazine) derived from this compound
hydrazine hydrate *n* **:** a colorless liquid base $N_2H_4.H_2O$ made usu. by reaction of sodium hypochlorite and ammonia or urea and used for the same purposes as hydrazine
hy·dra·zin·i·um \ˌhīdrə'zinēəm\ *n* -s [ISV *hydrazine* + *-ium*] **:** either of two cations derived from hydrazine; *esp* **:** the univalent cation $NH_2NH_3^+$ ⟨~ chloride NH_2NH_3Cl or hydrazine hydrochloride $NH_2NH_2.HCl$⟩
hydrazino- *comb form* [ISV, fr. *hydrazine*] **:** containing the univalent radical NH_2NH– derived from hydrazine by removal of one hydrogen atom ⟨1-*hydrazino*phthalazine⟩
hy·dra·zo·ate \ˌhīdrə'zōˌāt\ *n* -s [*hydrazoic* + *-ate*] **:** a salt of hydrazoic acid **:** AZIDE
hy·draz·o·benzene \hī¦drazō, ¦hīdrəzō+\ *n* [ISV *hydraz-* + *benzene*] **:** a crystalline compound $C_6H_5NHNHC_6H_5$ obtained by alkaline reduction of nitrobenzene or azobenzene and capable of being converted into aniline by reduction, into azobenzene by oxidation, and into benzidine by rearrangement in the presence of hydrochloric acid
hy·dra·zo·ic acid \¦hīdrə¦zōik-\ *n* [*hydrazoic* fr. *hydr-* + *az-* + *-ic*] **:** a colorless volatile poisonous explosive liquid HN_3 that when pure has an unbearable odor, is made usu. by reaction of nitrous oxide with fused sodium amide or of hydrazine hydrate with ethyl nitrite in alkaline alcoholic solution, and yields explosive salts of heavy metals (as lead azide) — called also *azoimide*
hy·dra·zone \'hīdrəˌzōn\ *n* -s [ISV *hydraz-* + *ketone*; orig. formed as G *hydrazon*] **:** any of a class of compounds containing the grouping >C=NNHR formed by the action of hydrazine or a substituted hydrazine (as phenylhydrazine) on a compound containing the carbonyl group (as an aldehyde or ketone) ⟨acetone ~ $(CH_3)_2C{:}NNH_2$⟩ — see OSAZONE; compare AZINE 2
hy·dra·zo·ni·um \ˌhīdrə'zōnēəm\ *n* -s [ISV *hydraz-* + *-onium*] **:** HYDRAZINIUM
hy·dre·mia *also* **hy·drae·mia** \hī'drēmēə\ *n* -s [NL, fr. *hydr-* + *-emia*] **:** an abnormally watery state of the blood — **hy·dre·mic** *also* **hy·drae·mic** \(')hī¦drēmik\ *adj*
hy·dren·ceph·a·lus \ˌhī(ˌ)dren'sefələs\ *also* **hy·dren·ceph·a·ly** \-lē\ *n* -ES [*hydrencephalus* fr. NL, fr. *hydr-* + *-encephalus*; *hydrencephaly* ISV *hydr-* + *-encephaly*] **:** HYDROCEPHALUS
hy·dria \'hīdrēə\ *n, pl* **hydri·ae** \-ēˌē\ [L, fr. Gk, fr. *hydōr* water — more at WATER] **:** an ancient Greek or Roman water jar characterized by horizontal side handles and a vertical back handle and in the earlier form an angular and abrupt shoulder — compare KALPIS
¹hy·dric \'hīdrik\ *adj* [ISV *hydr-* + *-ic*] **:** relating to or containing hydrogen

hydriae

²hydric \"\ *adj* [*hydr-* + *-ic*] **:** characterized by, relating to, or requiring an abundance of moisture ⟨a ~ habitat⟩ ⟨~ plants⟩ — compare MESIC, XERIC — **hy·dri·cal·ly** \-rək(ə)lē\ *adv*
-hy·dric \¦hīdrik, -rēk\ *adj suffix* [ISV *hydr-* + *-ic*] **1** *archaic* **:** containing acid hydrogen ⟨*dihydric*⟩ **2 :** containing hydroxyl — esp. in terms relating to classes of alcohols and phenols ⟨hexa*hydric* alcohols⟩
hy·drich·thys \hī'drikthəs\ *n, cap* [NL, fr. *hydr-* + *-ichthys*] **:** a genus of colonial hydrozoans parasitic on the skin and tissues of fish
hy·dri·dae \'hīdrəˌdē\ [NL, fr. *hydr-* + *-idae*] *syn of* HYDROPHIDAE
hy·dride \'hīˌdrīd, -drəd\ *n* -s [ISV *hydr-* + *-ide*] **1** *archaic* **:** HYDROXIDE **2 :** a binary compound of hydrogen usu. with a more electropositive element or radical
hy·dri·do·borate \¦hīdrədō+\ *n* [short for *tetrahydridoborate*] **:** BOROHYDRIDE
hy·dri·form \'hīdrəˌfȯrm\ *adj* [prob. fr. (assumed) NL *hydriformis*, fr. NL *Hydra* + *-iformis* -iform] **:** resembling a polyp of the genus *Hydra*
-hy·drin \'hīdrən\ *n comb form* -s [ISV *hydr-* + *-in*] **:** chemical compound containing halogen or cyanogen in place of alcoholic hydroxyl esp. of only part of the hydroxyl ⟨iodo*hydrin*⟩
hy·drin·dene \hī'drinˌdēn\ *n* [ISV *hydr-* + *indene*] **:** INDAN
hy·dri·od·ic acid \¦hīdrē¦ädik-\ *n* [*hydriodic* ISV *hydr-* + *iodic*] **:** a strong liquid acid HI that resembles hydrochloric acid chemically but in addition is a strong reducing agent and that is formed by solution of hydrogen iodide in water
hy·dri·o·dide \hī'drīəˌdīd, -dəd\ *n* [ISV *hydriodic* + *-ide*] **:** a compound of hydriodic acid ⟨pyridine ~⟩ — distinguished from *iodide*; compare HYDROCHLORIDE
hy·dri·on \'hīdrēˌän\ *n* [*hydr-* + *ion*] **:** HYDROGEN ION
hy·dri·o·taph·ia \ˌhīdrēō'tafēə\ *n* -s [NL, fr. *hydrio-* (fr. Gk *hydria* water jar, cinerary urn) + *-taphia* (fr. Gk *taphē* burial); akin to Gk *thaptein* to bury — more at HYDRIA, EPITAPH] **:** URN BURIAL
hydri·ote \'hidrēˌōt, 'hīd-\ *n, usu cap* [*Hydra*, Greek island in the Aegean sea + E *-i-* + *-ote*] **:** a native or inhabitant of the Greek island of Hydra
¹hy·dro \'hī(ˌ)drō\ *n* -s **1** [short for ²*hydropathic*] *Brit* **a :** a hotel that caters to people taking a water cure **b :** an establishment that furnishes water cures **:** SPA **2** [short for *hydroelectric*] **a** *chiefly Canada* **:** hydroelectric power **b :** a hydroelectric power plant
²hydro \"\ *adj* [by shortening] **:** HYDROELECTRIC ⟨~ power⟩
³hydro \"\ *adj* [*hydr-*] **:** HYDROGEN **:** combined with hydrogen ⟨~ derivatives⟩
hydro- *in pronunciations below* ¦≈≈=¦hī(ˌ)drō *or* -ˌdrə\ — see HYDR-
hy·droa \hī'drōə\ *n* -s [F, prob. modif. (influenced by F *hydr-*, fr. L) of Gk *hidrōa* (pl.) prickly heat, fr. *hidrōs* sweat — more at SWEAT] **:** an itching usu. vesicular eruption of the skin; *esp* **:** one induced by exposure to light
hy·dro·ab·i·et·yl alcohol \ˌ≈≈ *at* HYDRO- + ə'bīəlˌtēl- *or* 'abēə|\ *n* [*hydroabietyl* fr. *hydr-* + *abiet-* (fr. *abietic acid*) + *-yl*] **:** a soft viscous resinous substance obtained by hydrogenation of the methyl ester of rosin and used esp. as a plasticizer
hy·dro–airplane \¦hī(ˌ)drō+\ *n* **:** SEAPLANE
hy·dro·alcoholic \"+\ *adj* [*hydr-* + *alcohol* + *-ic*] **:** of or relating to water and alcohol ⟨~ solutions⟩
hy·dro·aromatic \"+\ *adj* [ISV *hydr-* + *aromatic*] **:** derived from the aromatic compounds by adding hydrogen to the ring **:** ALICYCLIC ⟨cyclohexane is a ~ compound formed by hydrogenating benzene⟩
hy·dro·atmospheric \"+\ *adj* [*hydr-* + *atmosphere* + *-ic*] **:** of or relating to both water and air
hy·dro·basaluminite \"+\ *n* [*hydr-* + *basaluminite*] **:** a mineral $Al_4(SO_4)(OH)_{10}.36H_2O$ consisting of hydrous sulfate and hydroxide of aluminum
hy·dro·bat·i·dae \ˌ≈≈+'bad·əˌdē\ *n pl, cap* [NL, fr. *Hydrobates*, type genus (fr. *hydr-* + *-bates*) + *-idae*] **:** a family of birds consisting of the storm petrels
hy·dro·benzoin \¦≈≈ *at* HYDRO- +\ *n* [ISV *hydr-* + *benzoin*; orig. formed in G] **:** a crystalline compound $(C_6H_5CHOH)_2$ formed by action of sodium amalgam on benzaldehyde and yielding benzoin on oxidation
hy·dro·biological \"+\ *adj* [*hydrobiology* + *-ical*] **:** of or relating to hydrobiology
hy·dro·biology \"+\ *n* [ISV *hydr-* + *biology*; prob. orig. formed as G *hydrobiologie*] **:** the biology of bodies or units of water; *esp* **:** LIMNOLOGY
hy·dro·bomb \'≈≈+ˌ-\ *n* [*hydr-* + *bomb*] **:** an aerial torpedo propelled by a rocket engine after entering the water
hy·dro·boracite \¦≈≈+'-\ *n* [obs. G *hydroboracit* (now *hydroborazit*), fr. G *hydr-* + ML *borac-*, *borax* borax + G *-it* -ite] **:** a mineral $CaMgB_6O_{11}.6H_2O$ consisting of a white hydrous calcium magnesium borate and occurring in fibrous and foliated masses
hy·dro·borate \"+'-\ *n* [short for *tetrahydroborate*] **:** BOROHYDRIDE
hy·dro·bromic acid \¦≈≈ *at* HYDRO- + . . . -\ *n* [*hydrobromic* ISV *hydr-* + *bromic*] **:** a strong liquid acid HBr that is formed by solution of hydrogen bromide in water, that resembles hydrochloric acid chemically but in addition is a weak reducing agent, and that is used chiefly in making bromides and as a catalyst
hy·dro·bromide \¦≈≈+'-\ *n* [ISV *hydrobromic* + *-ide*] **:** a compound of hydrobromic acid — distinguished from *bromide* ⟨pyridine ~ $C_5H_5N.HBr$⟩; compare HYDROCHLORIDE

hy·dro·cal·u·mite \"+ˈkalyə,mīt\ *n* [*hydr-* + *c-* (fr. *calcium*) + *alum-* (fr. *aluminum*) + *-ite*] **:** a colorless to light green mineral $Ca_2Al(OH)_7.3H_2O$ consisting of hydrous hydroxide of calcium and aluminum

hy·dro·car·bon \ˈ⸗⸗ *at* HYDRO- +\ *n* [*hydr-* + *carbon*] **:** any of a large class of organic compounds containing only carbon and hydrogen, comprising paraffins, olefins, members of the acetylene series, alicyclic hydrocarbons (as cyclic terpenes and steroid hydrocarbons), and aromatic hydrocarbons (as benzene, naphthalene, biphenyl), and occurring in many cases in petroleum, natural gas, coal, and bitumens — **hy·dro·car·bo·na·ceous** \"+\ *adj*

hy·dro·car·bon·ate \"+\ *n* [ISV *hydr-* + *carbonate*] **:** BICARBONATE

hydrocarbon cement *n* **:** a cement containing bitumen

hy·dro·car·bon·ic \"+\ *or* **hy·dro·car·bon·ous** \"+\ *adj* **:** of, relating to, or of the nature of a hydrocarbon

hydrocarbon oil *n* **:** any of various oily liquids consisting chiefly or wholly of mixtures of hydrocarbons (as petroleum or many of its products) — compare MINERAL OIL

hy·dro·car·y·a·ce·ae \,⸗⸗+,karēˈāsē,ē\ *n pl, cap* [NL, fr. *hydr-* + *cary-* + *-aceae*] *in some classifications* **:** a family coextensive with the Trapaceae — **hy·dro·car·y·a·ceous** \ˈ⸗⸗,⸗⸗ˈāshəs\ *adj*

hy·dro·cau·line \ˈ⸗⸗ *at* HYDRO- +ˈkȯ,līn, -,lən\ *adj* [*hydrocaulus* + *-ine*] **:** resembling a hydrocaulus

hy·dro·cau·lus \,⸗⸗+ˈkȯləs\ *n, pl* **hydrocau·li** \-ȯ,lī\ [NL, fr. *hydr-* + Gk *kaulos* stem — more at HOLE] **:** the simple or branched stem of a hydroid

hy·dro·cele \ˈ⸗⸗+,sēl\ *n* -s [L, fr. Gk *hydrokēlē*, fr. *hydr-* + *kēlē* tumor — more at -CELE] **:** an accumulation of serous fluid in a sacculated cavity esp. the scrotum

hy·dro·cellulose \ˈ⸗⸗ *at* HYDRO- +\ *n* [ISV *hydr-* + *cellulose*; prob. orig. formed in F] **:** a substance obtained as a gelatinous mass or a fine powder by the partial hydrolysis of cellulose usu. by means of acids

¹hy·dro·ce·phal·ic \ˈ⸗⸗+sə̇ˈfalik\ *adj* [*hydrocephalus* + *-ic*] **:** relating to, characterized by, or exhibiting hydrocephalus

²hydrocephalic \"\ *n* -s **:** one that is afflicted with hydrocephalus

hy·dro·ceph·a·loid \"+ˈsefə,lȯid\ *adj* [*hydrocephalus* + *-oid*] **:** resembling hydrocephalus

hy·dro·ceph·a·lous \-,ləs\ *adj* [*hydrocephalus* + *-ous*] **:** having hydrocephalus

hy·dro·ceph·a·lus \,⸗⸗+ˈsefələs\ *also* **hy·dro·ceph·a·ly** \-lē\ *n* -ES [*hydrocephalus* fr. LL, hydrocephalus, hydrocephalous, fr. Gk *hydrokephalos* characterized by hydrocephalus, fr. *hydr-* + *-kephalos* -cephalous; *hydrocephaly* prob. fr. F *hydrocéphalie*, fr. *hydrocéphale* hydrocephalus (fr. LL *hydrocephalus*) + *-ie* -y] **1 :** an abnormal increase in the amount of cerebrospinal fluid within the cranial cavity, with expansion of the cerebral ventricles, enlargement of the skull esp. the forehead, and atrophy of the brain **2 :** a condition resulting from or an individual affected with such an increase in the cerebrospinal fluid

hy·dro·ce·ram·ic \ˈ⸗⸗+sə̇ˈramik\ *adj* [prob. fr. F *hydrocéramique*, fr. *hydrocérame* pottery vessel employed for cooling liquid by evaporation of what exudes (fr. *hydr-* + Gk *keramos* pottery, jar) + *-ique* -ic] **:** made of clay that remains porous after firing — used of pottery vessels employed for cooling liquid by evaporation of what exudes; compare GOGLET

hy·dro·ce·rus·site \,⸗⸗+sə̇ˈrə,sīt\ *n* [Sw *hydrocerussit*, fr. *hydr-* + *cerussit* cerussite, fr. G *zerussit*] **:** a mineral $Pb_3(OH)_2(CO_3)_2$ consisting of a basic lead carbonate that crystallizes in thin colorless hexagonal plates

hy·dro·char·i·da·ce·ae \,⸗⸗+,karəˈdāsē,ē\ [NL, irreg fr. *Hydrocharis* + *-aceae*] *syn of* HYDROCHARITACEAE

hy·dro·char·i·da·ceous \ˈ⸗⸗,⸗⸗ˈdāshəs\ *adj* [NL *Hydrocharidaceae* + E *-ous*] **:** HYDROCHARITACEOUS

hy·droch·a·ris \hīˈdräkərə̇s\ *n, cap* [NL, fr. *hydr-* + Gk *charit-, charis* grace, beauty; akin to Gk *chairein* to rejoice — more at YEARN] **:** a small genus (the type of the family Hydrocharitaceae) of Old World aquatic herbs with petioled floating leaves — see FROGBIT

hy·dro·char·i·ta·ce·ae \,⸗⸗ *at* HYDRO- +,karəˈtāsē,ē\ *n pl, cap* [NL, fr. *Hydrocharit-, Hydrocharis*, type genus + *-aceae*] **:** a family of very simple widely distributed nearly stemless aquatic herbs (order Naiadales) with a 6-parted perianth and somewhat fleshy fruit — see ELODEA, VALLISNERIACEAE — **hy·dro·char·i·ta·ceous** \ˈ⸗⸗,⸗⸗ˈtāshəs\ *adj*

hydrochinone *or* **hydrochinon** *var of* HYDROQUINONE

hy·dro·chlo·ric acid \ˈ⸗⸗ *at* HYDRO- + . . . -\ *n* [*hydrochloric* ISV *hydr-* + *chloric*] **:** a strong corrosive irritating liquid acid HCl that is formed by solution of hydrogen chloride in water and is normally present in dilute form in gastric juice, that is usu. made by the action of sulfuric acid on salt, and that is widely used in industry (as for pickling metals) and in the laboratory — called also *muriatic acid*

hy·dro·chlo·ride \,⸗⸗+ˈ-\ *n* [ISV *hydrochloric* + *-ide*] **:** a compound of hydrochloric acid — used esp. with the names of organic bases for convenience in naming salts; distinguished from *chloride* ⟨pyridine ~, $C_5H_5N.HCl$ is the same as pyridinium chloride, C_5H_6NCl⟩

hy·dro·chlo·ri·nate \ˈ⸗⸗ *at* HYDRO- +\ *vt* [*hydr-* + *chlorinate*] **:** to treat or combine with hydrochloric acid or hydrogen chloride ⟨~ rubber⟩ — **hy·dro·chlo·ri·na·tion** \"+\ *n*

hy·dro·choe·rus \,⸗⸗+ˈkirəs, -ˈkēr-\ *n, cap* [NL, fr. *hydr-* + *-choerus*] **:** a genus consisting of the capybara

hy·dro·cho·le·re·sis \ˈ⸗⸗ *at* HYDRO- +\ *n* [NL, fr. *hydr-* + *choleresis*] **:** increased production of watery liver bile without necessarily increased secretion of bile solids — compare CHOLERESIS

¹hy·dro·cho·le·ret·ic \"+\ *adj* [fr. *hydrocholeresis*, after such pairs as E *diuresis*: *diuretic*] **:** of, relating to, or characterized by hydrocholeresis

²hydrocholeretic \"\ *n* **:** an agent that produces hydrocholeresis

hy·dro·chore \ˈ⸗⸗+,kō(ə)r\ *n* -s [*hydr-* + *-chore*] **:** a plant that depends primarily on water for the distribution of its seeds or spores — compare ANEMOCHORE

hy·dro·cho·ry \-ōrē\ *n* -ES [*hydrochore* + *-y*] **:** dissemination of seeds or plants by water

hy·dro·cin·cho·nine \ˈ⸗⸗ *at* HYDRO- +\ *n* [ISV *hydr-* + *cinchonine*] **:** CINCHOTINE

hy·dro·cin·na·mal·de·hyde \,⸗⸗+,sinəˈmaldə,hīd\ *n* [*hydrocinnamic* + *aldehyde*] **:** an oily liquid compound $C_6H_5CH_2CH_2CHO$ that has a floral odor, occurs in species of cinnamon, and is used in perfumes

hy·dro·cin·nam·ic acid \ˈ⸗⸗ *at* HYDRO- + . . . -\ *n* [*hydrocinnamic* ISV *hydr-* + *cinnamic*] **:** a white crystalline acid $C_6H_5CH_2CH_2COOH$ obtained from cinnamic acid by hydrogenation; β-phenyl-propionic acid

hy·dro·cla·di·um \,⸗⸗+ˈklādēəm\ *n, pl* **hydrocla·dia** \-ēə\ [NL, fr. *hydr-* + Gk *kladion* twig, dim. of *klados* branch — more at GLADIATOR] **:** one of the small branchlets bearing the hydrothecae in a colony of plumularian hydroids

hy·dro·clas·tic \ˈ⸗⸗ *at* HYDRO- +ˈklastik\ *adj* [*hydr-* + *-clastic*] **:** clastic through the agency of water — used of fragmental rocks deposited by the agency of water; compare PYROCLASTIC

hy·dro·cleis \ˈ⸗⸗+,klīs *or* -,klās\ *n, cap* [NL, fr. *hydr-* + Gk *kleis* key — more at CLOSE] **:** a small genus of Brazilian aquatic herbs (family Butomaceae) with broad leaves and solitary showy yellow flowers — see WATER POPPY

hy·dro·cleys \"\ *syn of* HYDROCLEIS

hy·dro·climate \ˈ⸗⸗ *at* HYDRO- +\ *n* [*hydr-* + *climate*] **:** the varied physical factors (as temperature, pH, density, turbidity) and often associated chemical factors (as concentration of certain ions) that characterize a particular aquatic habitat

hy·dro·codimer \"+\ *n* [*hydr-* + *codimer*] **:** hydrogenated codimer containing octanes

hy·dro·coele *or* **hy·dro·coel** \ˈ⸗⸗+,sēl\ *n* -s [*hydr-* + *-coele*] **:** the water-vascular system of an echinoderm or the pouch or cavity in the embryo from which it develops

hy·dro·colloid \ˈ⸗⸗ *at* HYDRO- +\ *n* [*hydr-* + *colloid*] **:** any of several substances that yield gels with water (as alginic acid salts, agar, carrageenin, and related polysaccharide gums) and that are used esp. as protective colloids and as impression materials in dentistry — **hy·dro·colloidal** \"+\ *adj*

hy·dro·col process \ˈhīdrə,kȯl-\ *n, usu cap H* [prob irreg. fr. *hydr-* (hydrogen)] **:** a modified Fischer-Tropsch process for producing chiefly high-octane gasoline from natural gas

hy·dro·cooler \ˈ⸗⸗ *at* HYDRO- + ,-\ *n* **:** an apparatus used in hydrocooling

hy·dro·cooling \"+,-\ *n* **:** the process of removing heat from freshly harvested fruits and vegetables by bathing them in ice water

hy·dro·coral \ˈ⸗⸗+\ *n* [NL *Hydrocorallia*] **:** a compound hydrozoan of the order Milleporina or the order Stylasterina having a well-developed calcareous skeleton

hy·dro·co·ral·lia \,⸗⸗+kəˈralēə\ *or* **hy·dro·cor·al·li·nae** \-,kȯrəˈlī,nē\ [*Hydrocorallia* fr. NL, fr. *hydr-* + *-corallia* (fr. L *corallia*, pl. of *corallium* coral, fr. Gk *korallion*); *Hydrocorallinae* fr. NL, fr. *hydr-* + *-corallinae* (fr. LL *corallinae*, fem. pl. of *corallinus* coral red)] *syn of* HYDROCORALLINA

hy·dro·cor·al·li·na \,⸗⸗+,kȯrəˈlīnə\ *n pl, cap* [NL, fr. *hydr-* + *-corallina* (fr. LL *corallina*, neut. pl. of *corallinus* coral red) — more at CORALLINE] *in some classifications* **:** a hydrozoan order equivalent to the modern orders Millepora and Stylasterina

¹hy·dro·cor·al·line \ˈ⸗⸗ *at* HYDRO- ˈkȯrə,līn, -,lən\ *adj* [NL *Hydrocorallina*] **:** of or relating to the Hydrocorallina

²hydrocoralline \"\ *n* -s [NL *Hydrocorallina*] **:** a hydrozoan of the order Hydrocorallina **:** MILLEPORE, STYLASTER

hy·dro·cortisone \"+\ *n* [*hydr-* + *cortisone*] **:** a crystalline hormone $C_{21}H_{30}O_5$ occurring in the adrenal cortex and also prepared synthetically that is a dihydro derivative of cortisone and is used similarly; 17-hydroxycorticosterone — called also *cortisol*

hy·dro·cotarnine \"+\ *n* [ISV *hydr-* + *cotarnine*; prob. orig. formed as G *hydrokotarnin*] **:** a crystalline alkaloid $C_{12}H_{15}NO_3$ obtained from opium and also formed by the reduction of cotarnine

hy·dro·cot·y·le \,⸗⸗+ˈkäd·ᵊlē\ *n, cap* [NL, fr. *hydr-* + Gk *kotylē* cup; prob. fr. the watery habitat and the cuplike shape of the leaves — more at KETTLE] **:** a genus of low creeping widely distributed herbs (family Umbelliferae) with crenate peltate leaves and umbellate flowers — see MARSH PENNYWORT

hy·dro·cracking \ˈ⸗⸗+,-\ *n* **:** the cracking of hydrocarbons in the presence of hydrogen

hy·droc·te·na \hīˈdräktənə\ *n, cap* [NL, fr. *hydr-* + *-ctena* (fr. Gk *kten-, kteis* comb) — more at PECTINATE] **:** a genus of trachyline medusae resembling ctenophores

hy·dro·cyanic acid \ˈ⸗⸗ *at* HYDRO- + . . . -\ *n* [*hydrocyanic* ISV *hydr-* + *cyanic*] **:** a very weak poisonous liquid acid HCN or HNC that is formed by solution of hydrogen cyanide in water, is readily made by the action of an acid on a cyanide, and is used chiefly in fumigating against insects, rats, and mice and in organic synthesis — called also *prussic acid*

hy·dro·cyanide \,⸗⸗+ˈ-\ *n* [ISV *hydrocyanic* + *-ide*] **:** a compound of hydrocyanic acid — distinguished from *cyanide*; compare HYDROCHLORIDE

hy·dro·cycle \ˈ⸗⸗+,-\ *n* [*hydr-* + *cycle*] **:** a cycle for riding on water

hy·dro·cyclist \"+,-\ *n* [*hydrocycle* + *-ist*] **:** one that rides a hydrocycle

hy·droc·y·on \hīˈdräsē,än\ *n, cap* [NL, fr. *hydr-* + Gk *kyōn* dog — more at HOUND] **:** a genus of large African carnivorous freshwater fishes of the family Characidae — compare TIGER FISH

hy·dro·dam·a·lis \,⸗⸗ *at* HYDRO- + ˈdamələ̇s\ *n, cap* [NL, fr. *hydr-* + Gk *damalis* heifer; akin to Gk *damalēs* young bull — more at DAMA] **:** a genus of aquatic mammals that includes only the Steller's sea cow and is now usu. placed in the family Dugongidae but was formerly made type of a separate family

hy·dro·dic·ty·on \-ˈdiktē,än\ *n, cap* [NL, fr. *hydr-* + Gk *diktyon* net, fr. *dikein* to throw — more at DISH] **:** a genus (the type of the family Hydrodictyaceae) of unicellular freshwater green algae of the order Chlorococcales that associate in colonies of cylindrical multinucleate cells joined by their ends into pentagonal meshes which are linked in a continuous elongate saccular network often reaching a length of 20 centimeters

hy·dro·dynamic \ˈ⸗⸗ *at* HYDRO- +\ *also* **hy·dro·dynamical** \"+\ *adj* [*hydrodynamic* fr. NL *hydrodynamicus*, fr. *hydr-* + *dynamicus* of or relating to power, fr. Gk *dynamikos* powerful; *hydrodynamical* fr. NL *hydrodynamicus* + E *-al* — more at DYNAMIC] **:** of or relating to hydrodynamics — **hy·dro·dy·namically** \"+\ *adv*

hy·dro·dy·nam·ics \,⸗⸗+dīˈnamiks\ *n pl but usu sing in constr* [NL *hydrodynamica*, fr. neut. pl. of *hydrodynamicus* hydrodynamic] **:** a branch of hydromechanics that deals with the motion of fluids and the forces acting on solid bodies immersed in fluids and in motion relative to them — compare HYDROSTATICS

hy·dro·electric \ˈ⸗⸗ *at* HYDRO-+\ *adj* [ISV *hydr-* + *electric*] **:** of, relating to, or employed in the production of electricity by waterpower

hy·dro·electricity \"+\ *n* [*hydr-* + *electricity*] **:** electricity produced by water power

hy·dro·ex·tract \,⸗⸗+ikˈstrakt, -ek-\ *vt* [back-formation fr. *hydroextractor*] **:** to treat with a hydroextractor — **hy·dro·ex·trac·tion** \-akshən\ *n*

hy·dro·extractor \ˈ⸗⸗ *at* HYDRO-+\ *n* [*hydr-* + *extractor*] **:** a usu. centrifugal machine for extracting water (as from yarn or cloth)

hy·dro·ferrocyanic acid \"+ . . . -\ *n* [*hydroferrocyanic* ISV *hydr-* + *ferrocyanic* (as in *ferrocyanic acid*)] **:** FERROCYANIC ACID

hy·dro·fin·ing \ˈ⸗⸗+,fīniŋ\ *n* [*hydr-* + *-fining* (fr. *refining*)] **:** a process for improving the quality of gasoline and other petroleum products by treating with hydrogen in the presence of a catalyst at a temperature below that at which decomposition takes place — compare HYDROFORMING

hy·dro·flap \ˈ⸗⸗+,-\ *n* [*hydr-* + *flap*] **:** an adjustable planing surface on a fuselage or seaplane hull used to provide a pitching moment to counteract the tendency of an aircraft to dive on its first contact with the water

hy·dro·fluoric acid \ˈ⸗⸗ *at* HYDRO- + . . .-\ *n* [*hydrofluoric* ISV *hydr-* + *fluoric*; prob. orig. formed as F *hydrofluorique*] **:** a weak poisonous liquid acid HF that is formed by solution of hydrogen fluoride in water, that resembles hydrochloric acid chemically but attacks silica and silicates (as glass or porcelain) forming gaseous silicon tetrafluoride and must therefore be handled and stored in equipment of steel, lead, rubber, wax, or other nonsilicate materials, and that is used chiefly in making other fluorine compounds, in polishing and etching glass, and in pickling metals

hy·dro·flu·or·ide \,⸗ˈ-\ *n* [ISV *hydrofluoric* + *-ide*] **:** a compound of hydrofluoric acid — distinguished from *fluoride*; compare HYDROCHLORIDE

hy·dro·fluosilicic acid \ˈ⸗⸗ *at* HYDRO-+ . . .-\ *n* [*hydrofluosilicic* ISV *hydr-* + *fluosilicic*] **:** FLUOSILICIC ACID

hy·dro·foil \ˈ⸗⸗+,-\ *n* [*hydr-* + *foil*] **1 :** a flat or curved plane surface designed to obtain reaction upon its surfaces from the water through which it moves ⟨ships of all sizes may be effectively stabilized against rolling . . . by the use of controlled ~s —F.D.Braddon⟩ — compare AIRFOIL, HYDROPLANE **2 :** an underwater plate or fin attached by struts to a seaplane (where it is retractable) or to a speedboat for lifting the hull clear of the water as speed is increased

hy·dro·form·ate \,⸗⸗+ˈfȯr,māt\ *n* [*hydroforming* + *-ate*] **:** a product obtained by hydroforming

hy·dro·form·er \ˈ⸗⸗+,fȯrmər\ *n* [*hydroforming* + *-er*] **:** the unit in a petroleum refinery in which hydroforming is carried out

hy·dro·form·ing \-miŋ\ *n* -s [*hydr-* + *-forming* (fr. *reforming*)] **:** a process for producing high-octane gasoline or aromatic hydrocarbons (as toluene, xylenes) by dehydrogenation and aromatization of petroleum naphthas usu. containing a high ratio of naphthenes in a stream of added hydrogen and in the presence of a catalyst at elevated temperature

hy·dro·for·myl·a·tion \,⸗⸗+,fȯ(r)məˈlāshən\ *n* -s [*hydr-* + *formyl* + *-ation*] **:** the addition of a hydrogen atom and a formyl group to the molecule of a compound containing a double bond by reaction with hydrogen and carbon monoxide, the chief product being one or more aldehydes — compare OXO PROCESS

hy·dro·fuge \ˈ⸗⸗+,fyüj\ *adj* [ISV *hydr-* + *-fuge*; prob. orig. formed in F] **:** shedding water — used of the pubescent coating of many aquatic insects

hy·dro·garnet \ˈ⸗⸗ *at* HYDRO- +\ *n* [*hydr-* + *garnet*] **:** one of a group of minerals of the general formula $A''_3B'''_2(SiO_4)_{3-x}(OH)_{4x}$ that are isomorphous with various garnets — compare HIBSCHITE

hy·dro·gel \ˈ⸗⸗+,jel\ *n* [*hydr-* + *-gel* (fr. *gelatin*)] *chem* **:** a gel in which the liquid is water

hy·dro·gen \ˈhīdrəjən, -rēj-\ *n* -s [F *hydrogène*, fr. *hydr-* (water) + *-gène* -gen; fr. the fact that water is generated by its combustion] **:** a nonmetallic univalent element that is the simplest and lightest of the elements, that is normally a colorless odorless highly flammable diatomic gas, that occurs in the free state only sparsely on the earth and in its atmosphere though abundantly in the sun, many stars, and nebulae, and in combination as a constituent of innumerable compounds from many of which it can be readily prepared (as from water by electrolysis, from natural gas or other hydrocarbons by reaction with steam or by pyrolysis, from acids by reaction with active metals), and that is used chiefly in synthesis (as of ammonia and methanol), in reducing or hydrogenating a variety of compounds (as in hardening oils to fats), as a mixture with oxygen or as atomic hydrogen in producing very high temperatures (as in welding), as liquid hydrogen for rocket fuel and in producing very low temperatures, and in filling balloons — symbol *H*; see DEUTERIUM, ELEMENT table, ORTHO-HYDROGEN, PARA-HYDROGEN, SYNTHESIS GAS, TRITIUM

hydrogen arsenide *n* **:** ARSINE

hy·dro·gen·ase \-jə,nās, hīˈdräjə,-\ *n* -s [ISV *hydrogen* + *-ase*] *biochem* **:** an enzyme that promotes the formation and utilization of gaseous hydrogen and occurs esp. in bacteria

hy·dro·gen·ate \-āt, *usu* -ād·+V\ *vt* -ED/-ING/-s [*hydrogen* + *-ate*] **1 :** to combine with hydrogen ⟨~ a vegetable oil to a fat⟩ **2 :** to treat with or expose to hydrogen ⟨~ rosin⟩ — compare HARDEN *vt* 1a — **hy·dro·gen·a·tor** \-ād·ə(r)\ *n* -s

hy·dro·gen·a·tion \,hīdrəjəˈnāshən, hī,dräjəˈ-\ *n* -s [ISV *hydrogen* + *-ation*] **:** the process of hydrogenating: as **a :** the addition of hydrogen to the molecule of an unsaturated organic compound usu. in the presence of a catalyst (as nickel) and often at elevated temperature and pressure ⟨~ of benzene to cyclohexane⟩ **b :** a decomposition (as of hydrocarbons) at high temperature and pressure with addition of hydrogen to the molecules formed **:** HYDROGENOLYSIS ⟨~ of coal to gasoline and oils⟩ — called also *destructive hydrogenation*

hydrogen bomb \ˈ⸗⸗⸗-\ *n* **:** a bomb whose violent explosive power is due to the sudden release of atomic energy resulting from the union of light nuclei (as of hydrogen atoms) at very high temperature and pressure to form helium nuclei — called also *fusion bomb*

hydrogen bond *n* **:** a linkage through hydrogen of two electronegative atoms esp. fluorine, oxygen, or nitrogen with one side of the linkage usu. being a conventional covalent bond (as the –O–H bond in water H–O–H or alcohol R–O–H) and the other side being primarily electrostatic in character ⟨the stable hydrogen fluoride ion HF_2^- or $[F^-H^+F^-]^-$ is held together by a *hydrogen bond*⟩ — see ASSOCIATION 7

hydrogen bromide *n* **:** a colorless irritating gas HBr that fumes in moist air and yields hydrobromic acid when dissolved in water and that is formed as a by-product in the bromination of organic compounds but is usu. made by the direct union of hydrogen and bromine vapor or by the reaction of bromine, red phosphorus, and water

hydrogen chloride *n* **:** a colorless pungent nonflammable poisonous gas HCl that fumes strongly in moist air and yields hydrochloric acid when dissolved in water and that is obtained primarily as a by-product of the chlorination of organic compounds or by burning hydrogen in chlorine

hydrogen cyanide *n* **:** a very poisonous mobile volatile liquid or gas HCN or HNC that has an odor of bitter almonds, that occurs in many plants usu. combined as glycosides (as amygdalin) and also in coke-oven gas, that can be synthesized from ammonia and carbon monoxide or from ammonia, oxygen or air, and natural gas, and that yields hydrocyanic acid when dissolved in water

hydrogen dioxide *n* **:** HYDROGEN PEROXIDE

hydrogen electrode *n* **:** an electrode composed typically of platinum black on platinum over which a stream of hydrogen is bubbled and that under specified conditions serves as the standard electrode with an assigned potential of zero to which all other electrode potentials are referred for purposes of comparison

hydrogen fluoride *n* **:** a colorless mobile fuming corrosive poisonous liquid or gas HF or (HF)*n* that yields hydrofluoric acid when dissolved in water, is made usu. by the action of sulfuric acid on fluorite, and is used chiefly in the manufacture of fluorine and fluorides and as a catalyst esp. in the alkylation of branched-chain paraffins with olefins to produce superior motor fuels — called also *anhydrous hydrofluoric acid*

¹hy·dro·gen·ic \ˈ⸗⸗ *at* HYDRO- +ˈjenik\ *adj* [*hydr-* + *-genic*] **1 :** formed by the agency of water ⟨dinosaur footprints in ~ rock⟩ **2 :** developed under the dominant influence of water (as in a cold humid region) ⟨~ soil⟩

²hydrogenic \"\ *adj* [ISV *hydrogen* + *-ic*] **:** resembling hydrogen in nuclear composition

hy·dro·gen·ide \ˈhīdrəjə,nīd, hīˈdräjə,-\ *n* -s [*hydrogen* + *-ide*] **:** HYDRIDE

hydrogen iodide *n* **:** a heavy colorless gas HI that fumes in moist air and yields hydriodic acid when dissolved in water and that is usu. made by the direct catalytic union of hydrogen and iodine vapor or by the reaction of iodine, red phosphorus, and water

hydrogen ion *n* **1 :** the cation H^+ of acids consisting of a hydrogen atom whose electron has been transferred to the anion of the acid and existing in aqueous solution as a hydronium ion **:** PROTON **2 :** HYDRONIUM

hydrogen–ion concentration *n* **:** the concentration of hydrogen ions in a solution expressed usu. in moles per liter or in pH units and used as a measure of the acidity of the solution ⟨indicator dyes for narrow ranges of *hydrogen-ion concentration*⟩

hy·dro·ge·ni·um \,hīdrəˈjenēəm\ *n* -s [NL, fr. E *hydrogen* + NL *-ium*] **:** HYDROGEN

hy·dro·gen·ize \ˈhīˈdräjə,nīz, ˈhīdrəjə,-\ *vt* -ED/-ING/-s **:** HYDROGENATE

hy·dro·gen·ol·y·sis \,hīdrəjəˈnäləsə̇s\ *n* [*hydrogen* + *-o-* + *-lysis*] **:** a chemical reaction analogous to hydrolysis in which hydrogen plays a role similar to that of water **:** destructive hydrogenation ⟨~ of hydrazine to ammonia⟩

hy·dro·gen·om·o·nas \,hīdrəjəˈnäməˌnas\ *n, cap* [NL, fr. ISV *hydrogen* + NL *-o-* + *-monas*] **:** a genus of short rod-shaped soil bacteria (family Methanomonadaceae) that are facultative autotrophs capable of oxidizing hydrogen to form water and using carbon dioxide as a source of carbon for growth

hy·drog·e·nous \(ˈ)hīˈdräjənəs\ *adj* **:** of, relating to, or containing hydrogen

hydrogen oxide *n* **:** WATER

hydrogen peroxide *n* **:** a colorless syrupy explosive corrosive compound H_2O_2 that has a bitter metallic taste and causes blisters on the skin, that is prepared in aqueous solutions in various ways (as by the electrolysis of sulfuric acid and hydrolysis of the persulfuric acid formed, by the action of acid on barium peroxide, or by the autoxidation of anthraquinone derivatives) and can be concentrated usu. by distillation, and that is used chiefly in dilute form as a bleach and antiseptic and in more concentrated forms as an oxidizing agent and propellant (as for rockets)

hydrogen selenide *n* **:** a colorless flammable poisonous gas H_2Se that has a disagreeable odor, resembles hydrogen sulfide, and is usu. formed by the action of acids on selenides

hydrogen sulfide *n* **:** a colorless flammable very poisonous gas H_2S that has a disagreeable odor suggestive of rotten eggs and is slightly soluble in water to give a weakly acidic solution, that is formed by putrefaction esp. of animal matter, that is found also in many mineral waters, in most volcanic gases, and in most natural gas and petroleum deposits and is formed in many industrial processes (as coking of coal) usu. as an objectionable impurity, that is recovered as a by-product from many of these sources or is prepared by the action of an acid on a metallic sulfide or by synthesis from hydrogen and sulfur vapor, and that is used chiefly in making elemental sulfur, sulfuric acid, and other sulfur compounds and in analysis as a precipitant for metallic ions

hy·dro·geology \ˈ≈≈ *at* HYDRO- +\ *n* [F *hydrogéologie,* fr. *hydr-* + *géologie* geology] **1 :** a branch of geology concerned with the occurrence and utilization of surface and ground water and with the functions of water in modifying the earth esp. by erosion and deposition **2 :** the phenomena with which hydrogeology deals

hy·dro·glider \ˈ≈≈+ˌ-\ *n* **:** a glider equipped with floats

hy·drog·no·sy \hīˈdrägnəsē\ *n* -ES [ISV *hydr-* + *-gnosy*] **:** the history and description of the waters of the earth

hy·dro·graph \ˈ≈≈ *at* HYDRO- +ˌgraf\ *n* [*hydr-* + *-graph*] **1 :** a mechanism for recording on a chart the changing level of water (as in a well, reservoir, stream) **2 :** a chart produced by this mechanism

hy·drog·ra·pher \hīˈdrägrəfə(r)\ *n* -S [*hydrography* + *-er*] **:** a specialist in hydrography

hy·dro·graph·ic \ˈ≈≈ *at* HYDRO- +ˈgrafik\ *also* **hy·dro·graph·i·cal** \-fəkəl\ *adj* [*hydrographic* fr. F *hydrographique,* fr. MF, fr. *hydr-* + *-graphique* -graphic (fr. LL *-graphicus*); *hydrographical* fr. MF *hydrographique* + E *-al*] **:** of or relating to hydrography — **hy·dro·graph·i·cal·ly** \-fək(ə)lē\ *adv*

hydrographic basin *n* **:** the drainage area of a stream

hydrographic surveying *n* **:** surveying of coastlines, bays, harbors, and of the ocean bed

hy·drog·ra·phy \hīˈdrägrəfē\ *n* -ES [MF *hydrographie,* fr. *hydr-* + *-graphie* -graphy (fr. L *-graphia*)] **1 :** the description and study of seas, lakes, rivers, and other waters: as **a :** the measurement of flow and investigation of the behavior of streams esp. with reference to the control or utilization of their waters **b :** the measurement of tides and currents esp. as an aid in navigation **c :** the surveying, sounding, and charting of bodies of water **2 :** bodies of water or a representation of them on a map

hy·dro·grossularite \ˈ≈≈ *at* HYDRO- +\ *n* [*hydr-* + *grossularite*] **:** a mineral $Ca_3Al_2(SiO_4)_{3-x}(OH)_{4x}$, consisting of silicate of calcium and aluminum in which silicon is partly replaced by hydrogen with *x* near ½ **:** one of the hydrogarnets intermediate between grossularite (x=0) and hibschite (x=1)

hy·dro·halide \"+\ *n* [*hydr-* + *halide*] **:** a compound (as a hydrochloride) with one of the halogen acids **:** a hydrogen halide

hy·dro·halite \"+\ *n* [G *hydrohalit,* fr. *hydr-* + *halit* halite, fr. NL *halites*] **:** a mineral $NaCl.2H_2O$ consisting of a hydrated chloride of sodium formed only from salty water below the freezing temperature of pure water

hy·dro·hetaerolite \"+\ *n* [*hydr-* + *hetaerolite*] **:** a mineral of uncertain composition approximately $Zn_2Mn_4O_8.H_2O$ consisting of a hydrous oxide of zinc and manganese

hy·dro–hotel \ˈhī(ˌ)drō+\ *n* [ˈ*hydro* + *hotel*] *Brit* **:** HYDRO 1a

¹**hy·droid** \ˈhīˌdrȯid\ *also* **hy·droidean** \(ˈ)hīˈdrȯidēən\ *adj* [*hydroid* fr. NL *Hydroida; hydroidean* fr. NL *Hydroidea* + E *-an* (adj. suffix)] **:** of or relating to the Hydroida or Hydrozoa **:** resembling a polyp of the genus *Hydra*

²**hydroid** \"\ *also* **hydroidean** \"\ *n* -S [*hydroid* fr. NL *Hydroida; hydroidean* fr. NL *Hydroidea* + E *-an* (n. suffix)] **1 :** one of the Hydroida **:** HYDROZOAN **2 :** the polyp form of a hydrozoan as distinguished from the medusa form — see HYDROMEDUSA

¹**hy·droi·da** \hīˈdrȯidə\ *n pl, cap* [NL, fr. *Hydra,* included genus + *-oida*] **:** an order of Hydrozoa comprising forms alternating a well-developed asexual polyp generation with a generation of free medusae or of abortive medusoid reproductive structures on the polyps — *see* LEPTOMEDUSAE

²**hydroida** \"\ [NL, fr. *Hydra,* included genus + *-oida*] *syn of* HYDROZOA

hydroid coral *n* **:** HYDROCORAL

hy·droi·dea \hīˈdrȯidēə\ [NL, fr. *Hydra* + *-oidea*] *syn of* HYDROIDA

hy·droi·des \hīˈdrȯi(ˌ)dēz\ *n, cap* [NL, prob. fr. *Hydra* (genus of polyps) + *-oides* (fr. L *-oides* -oid)] **:** a genus of tube-dwelling marine polychaete worms frequently present in the fouling of ship bottoms

hydroid polyp *n* **:** HYDROPOLYP

hy·dro·kinetic \"+\ *adj* [*hydr-* + *kinetic*] **:** of or relating to the motions of fluids or the forces which produce or affect such motions — opposed to *hydrostatic*

hy·dro·kinetics \"+\ *n pl but usu sing in constr* [*hydr-* + *kinetics*] **:** a branch of kinetics that deals with liquids — compare HYDRAULICS

hy·drol \ˈhīˌdrȯl, -rōl\ *n* -S [*hydr-* + *-ol*] **1 a :** the simple water molecule H_2O **b :** a polymer $(H_2O)_n$ of this molecule **2 :** a secondary alcohol (as benzhydrol) esp. of the aromatic series **3** [prob. irreg. fr. *hydr-*] *also* **hydrol syrup :** a light brown syrupy mother liquor from the manufacture of dextrose used in the fermentation industries

hy·dro·lase \ˈhīdrəˌlās\ *n* -S [ISV *hydrol* (fr. E) + *-ase*] **:** a hydrolytic enzyme (as an esterase)

hy·drol·a·try \hīˈdrälə·trē\ *n* -ES [*hydr-* + *-latry*] **:** the worship of water

hy·dro·lea \hīˈdrōlēə\ *n, cap* [NL, fr. *hydr-* + L *olea* olive; fr. the watery habitat and the resemblance of the leaves to those of the olive — more at OLEA] **:** a genus of blue-flowered perennial herbs (family Hydrophyllaceae) of warm regions having entire leaves and flowers with two distinct styles and bilocular ovaries and capsules

hy·dro·lith \ˈ≈≈ *at* HYDRO- +ˌlith\ *n* -S [ISV *hydr-* + *-lith;* prob. orig. formed as F *hydrolithe*] **:** CALCIUM HYDRIDE

hy·dro·log·ic \ˌhīdrəˈläjik\ *or* **hy·dro·log·i·cal** \-jəkəl\ *adj* [*hydrologic* ISV *hydrology* + *-ic; hydrological* fr. NL *hydrologia* hydrology + E *-ical*] **:** of or relating to hydrology — **hy·dro·log·i·cal·ly** \-jək(ə)lē\ *adv*

hydrologic cycle *n* **:** a complex sequence of conditions through which water naturally passes from water vapor in the atmosphere through precipitation upon land or water surfaces and ultimately back into the atmosphere as a result of evaporation and transpiration

hy·drol·o·gist \hīˈdräləjəst\ *n* -S [*hydrology* + *-ist*] **:** a specialist in hydrology

hy·drol·o·gy \-jē\ *n* -ES [NL *hydrologia,* fr. L *hydr-* + *-logia* -logy] **1 :** a science dealing with the properties, distribution, and circulation of water; *specif* **:** the study of water on the surface of the land, in the soil and underlying rocks, and in the atmosphere, particularly with respect to evaporation and precipitation **2 :** the physical factors studied by hydrologists (as precipitation, stream flow, snow melt, groundwater storage, and evaporation) ⟨the ~ of Mexico⟩

hy·dro·lube \ˈ≈≈ *at* HYDRO- +ˌ-\ *n* [*hydr-* + *lube*] **:** any of various nonflammable hydraulic fluids having a water-glycol base

hy·dro·lymph \"+ˌ-\ *n* [*hydr-* + *lymph*] **:** a watery circulatory fluid that substitutes for blood or hemolymph in some of the lower invertebrates (as jellyfishes)

hy·drol·y·sate \hīˈdräləˌsāt\ *also* **hy·drol·y·zate** \-ˌzāt\ *n* -S [*hydrolysis* or *hydrolyze* + *-ate*] **:** a product of hydrolysis

hy·drol·y·sis \hīˈdräləsəs\ *n* [ISV *hydr-* + *-lysis*] **:** a chemical reaction of water in which a bond in the reactant other than water is split and hydrogen and hydroxyl are added with the formation usu. of two or more new compounds, some types of hydration however often being included ⟨~ of a salt to an acid and a base⟩ ⟨~ of an ester to an acid and an alcohol⟩ — compare SAPONIFICATION, SOLVOLYSIS

hy·dro·lyte \ˈ≈≈ *at* HYDRO- +ˌlīt\ *n* -S [*hydr-* + *-lyte*] **:** a substance subjected to hydrolysis

hy·dro·lyt·ic \ˌ≈≈+ˈlid·ik\ *adj* [ISV *hydr-* + *-lytic*] **:** of, relating to, or causing hydrolysis

hy·dro·lyz·able \ˈhīdrəˌlīzəbəl\ *adj* [ISV *hydrolyze* + *-able*] **:** capable of hydrolyzing or of being hydrolyzed ⟨compounds containing ~ groups⟩

hy·dro·lyze *also* **hy·dro·lyse** \ˈhīdrəˌlīz\ *vb* -ED/-ING/-S [ISV, fr. *hydrolysis,* after such pairs as E *analysis: analyze*] *vt* **:** to subject to hydrolysis ~ *vi* **:** to undergo hydrolysis

hy·dro·lyz·er \-zə(r)\ *n* -S **:** a piece of equipment in which hydrolysis is carried out ⟨starch ~s⟩

hy·dro·magnesite \ˈ≈≈ *at* HYDRO- +\ *n* [G *hydromagnesit,* fr. *hydr-* + *magnesit* magnesite, fr. F *magnésite*] **:** a mineral $Mg_4(OH)_2(CO_3)_3.3H_2O$ consisting of a basic magnesium carbonate occurring in the form of small white crystals or chalky crusts

hy·dro·man·cer \ˈhīdrəˌman(t)sə(r)\ *n* -S [alter. (influenced by *hydromancy*) of ME *idromauncer,* fr. *ydromancye* hydromancy + *-er*] **:** one that engages in hydromancy

hy·dro·man·cy \-sē, -si\ *n* -ES [alter. (influenced by L *hydromantia*) of ME *ydromancye,* fr. MF *ydromancie,* fr. L *hydromantia,* fr. (assumed) Gk *hydromanteia,* fr. Gk *hydr-* + *manteia* divination — more at -MANCY] **:** divination by water or other liquid (as by visions seen therein or the ebb and flow of tides)

hy·dro·mechanics \ˈ≈≈ *at* HYDRO- +\ *n pl but usu sing in constr* [ISV *hydr-* + *mechanics*] **:** a branch of mechanics that deals with the equilibrium and motion of fluids and of solid bodies immersed in them

hy·dro·medusa \"+\ *n, pl* **hydromedusae** [NL, fr. *hydr-* + *medusa*] **:** a medusa that is produced as a bud from a hydroid (as of the orders Anthomedusae and Leptomedusae) and that constitutes the sexual generation of this hydroid and produces new asexual polyps from eggs and sperm

hy·dro·medusae \"+\ *n pl, cap* [NL, fr. *hydr-* + *medusae* (pl. of *medusa*)] **:** a formerly recognized subclass of Hydrozoa nearly coextensive with Hydrozoa as now restricted

¹**hy·dro·medusan** \"+\ *or* **hy·dro·medusoid** \"+\ *adj* [NL *hydromedusa* or *Hydromedusae* + E *-an* (adj. suffix) or *-oid*] **:** of or relating to a hydromedusa or the Hydromedusae

²**hydromedusan** \"\ *n* -S [NL *Hydromedusae* + E *-an* (n. suffix)] **:** one of the Hydromedusae

³**hydromedusan** \"\ *n* -S [NL *hydromedusa* + E *-an* (n. suffix)] **:** HYDROMEDUSA

hy·dro·mel \ˈhīdrəˌmel\ *n* -S [alter. (influenced by LL *hydromel*) of ME *ydromel,* fr. MF & LL; MF *ydromel,* fr. LL *hydromel,* fr. L *hydromeli,* fr. Gk, fr. *hydr-* + *meli* honey — more at MELLIFLUOUS] **1 :** a liquor consisting of honey diluted in water which upon fermentation becomes mead **2** *pharmacy* **:** a laxative containing honey and water

hy·dro·meningitis \ˈ≈≈ *at* HYDRO- +\ *n* [NL, fr. *hydr-* + *meningitis*] **:** meningitis with serous effusion

hy·dro·metallurgical \"+\ *adj* [*hydrometallurgy* + *-ical*] **:** of or relating to hydrometallurgy — **hy·dro·metallurgically** \"+\ *adv*

hy·dro·metallurgy \"+\ *n* [ISV *hydr-* + *metallurgy*] **:** treatment of ores by wet processes (as leaching and accompanying operations)

hy·dro·metamorphism \"+\ *n* [*hydr-* + *metamorphism*] **:** the alteration of rock by the addition, subtraction, or exchange of material brought or carried in solution by water and without the influence of high temperature or pressure — compare DYNAMOMETAMORPHISM

hy·dro·meteor \"+\ *n* [ISV *hydr-* + *meteor*] **:** a product of the condensation of atmospheric water vapor (as fog, rain, hail)

hy·dro·meteorological \"+\ *adj* [*hydrometeorology* + *-ical*] **:** of or relating to hydrometeorology

hy·dro·meteorology \"+\ *n* [*hydr-* + *meteorology*] **:** a branch of meteorology having to do with water in the atmosphere esp. as precipitation

hy·drom·e·ter \hīˈdräməd·ə(r)\ *n* [*hydr-* + *-meter*] **:** an instrument for measuring the specific gravity of a liquid commonly consisting of a thin glass or metal tube graduated to indicate either specific gravities or percentages of solution constituents and weighted so that it floats upright — compare ALCOHOLOMETER, NICHOLSON'S HYDROMETER

hy·dro·me·tra \ˈ≈≈ *at* HYDRO- +ˈmē·trə\ *n* -S [NL, fr. *hydr-* + *-metra*] **:** an accumulation of watery fluid in the uterus

hy·dro·met·ric \ˌhīdrəˈme·trik\ *or* **hy·dro·met·ri·cal** \-rəkəl\ *adj* [*hydrometric* ISV *hydrometr-* (fr. NL *hydrometria* hydrometry) + *-ic; hydrometrical* fr. NL *Hydrometria* + E *-ical*] **:** of or relating to hydrometry

hy·drom·e·trid \hīˈdräməˌtrəd\ *adj* [NL *Hydrometridae*] **:** of or relating to the Hydrometridae

hy·dro·met·ri·dae \ˌ≈≈ *at* HYDRO- +ˈme·trəˌdē\ *n pl, cap* [NL, fr. *Hydrometra,* type genus (fr. *hydr-* + *-metra,* fr. Gk *metrein* to measure, traverse, fr. *metron* measure) + *-idae* — more at MEASURE] **:** a family of small slender long-legged semiaquatic bugs closely related to the water striders

hy·drom·e·try \hīˈdrämə·trē\ *n* -ES [NL *hydrometria,* fr. *hydr-* + *-metria* -metry] **:** the measurement of specific gravity esp. of a liquid

hy·dro·mica \ˈ≈≈ *at* HYDRO- +\ *n* [*hydr-* + *mica*] **:** any of several varieties of muscovite that are less elastic and more unctuous than mica and have a pearly luster and some of which contain more water and less potash than ordinary muscovite — **hy·dro·micaceous** \"+\ *adj*

hy·dro·morphic \ˌ≈≈+ˈmȯrfik\ *adj* [*hydr-* + *-morphic*] **:** of or relating to an intrazonal soil (as the waterlogged soil of a bog area) characterized by an excess of moisture — compare CALOMORPHIC, HALOMORPHIC

hy·dro·mys \ˈ≈≈+ˌmis\ *n, cap* [NL, fr. *hydr-* + *-mys*] **:** a genus of myomorph rodents comprising the Australian beaver rats

hy·dro·negative \ˈ≈≈ *at* HYDRO- +\ *adj* [*hydr-* + *negative*] **:** characterized by negative hydrotaxis or hydrotropism

hy·dro·ne·phro·sis \ˌ≈≈+nəˈfrōsəs\ *n* [NL, fr. *hydr-* + *nephrosis*] **:** cystic distension of the kidney caused by the accumulation of urine in the kidney pelvis as a result of obstruction to outflow and accompanied by atrophy of the kidney structure and cyst formation

hy·dro·ne·phrot·ic \ˌ≈≈≈ˈfräd·ik\ *adj* [fr. NL *hydronephrosis,* after such pairs as NL *hypnosis:* E *hypnotic*] **:** affected with hydronephrosis

hy·dro·nitrogen \ˈ≈≈ *at* HYDRO- +\ *n* [*hydr-* + *nitrogen*] **:** a compound of hydrogen and nitrogen (as ammonia, hydrazine, hydrazoic acid)

hy·dro·ni·um \hīˈdrōnēəm\ *n* -S [ISV *hydr-* + *-onium*] **:** a hydrated hydrogen ion; *esp* **:** OXONIUM — used chiefly in inorganic chemistry ⟨~ perchlorate $[H_3O]^+[ClO_4]^-$⟩; called also *hydrogen ion*

hy·dron·y·my \hīˈdränəmē\ *n* -ES [ISV *hydr-* + *-onymy*] **:** names of bodies of water

¹**hy·dro·path·ic** \ˌhīdrəˈpathik, -thēk\ *adj* [ISV *hydropathy* + *-ic*] **:** of or relating to hydropathy or to an establishment where it is obtainable ⟨advocating and using a ~ system for the cure of fevers —*Amer. Guide Series: Vt.*⟩ — **hy·dro·path·i·cal·ly** \-thək(ə)lē, -thēk-, -li\ *adv*

²**hydropathic** \"\ *n* -S *Brit* **:** a water-cure resort or establishment

hy·drop·a·thy \hīˈdräpəthē, -thi\ *n* -ES [ISV *hydr-* + *-pathy;* prob. orig. formed as G *hydropathie*] **:** a method of treating disease by copious and frequent use of water both externally and internally — compare HYDROTHERAPY

hy·dro·pericardium \ˈ≈≈ *at* HYDRO- +\ *n* [NL, fr. *hydr-* + *pericardium*] **:** an excess of watery fluid in the pericardial cavity

hy·dro·period \"+\ *n* **:** the period during which a soil area is waterlogged ⟨upland swamps with a 5-month ~⟩

hy·dro·peritoneum \"+\ *n* [NL, fr. *hydr-* + *peritoneum*] **:** ASCITES

hy·dro·peroxide \"+\ *n* [ISV *hydr-* + *peroxide*] **:** a compound of an element or radical with the univalent group —OOH ⟨sodium ~ NaOOH⟩

hy·dro·phane \ˈ≈≈+ˌfān\ *n* -S [*hydr-* + *-phane*] **:** a semitranslucent variety of opal that becomes translucent or transparent on immersion in water

hy·droph·a·nous \hīˈdräfənəs\ *adj* [*hydrophane* + *-ous*] **:** made transparent by immersion in water

hy·droph·i·dae \hīˈdräfəˌdē\ *n pl, cap* [NL, fr. *Hydrophis,* type genus + *-idae*] **:** a family of aquatic snakes that comprises the sea snakes and was formerly considered to constitute a subfamily of the family Colubridae

hy·dro·phi·idae \ˌhīdrəˈfīəˌdē\ [NL, fr. *Hydrophis* + *-idae*] *syn of* HYDROPHIDAE

hy·dro·phil \ˈhīdrəˌfil\ *n* -S [obs. *hydrophil,* adj., hydrophytic, fr. NL *hydrophilus* water-loving] **:** HYDROPHYTE

hy·dro·phil·ic \ˌ≈≈ˈfilik\ *also* **hy·dro·phile** \ˈ≈≈ˌfīl\ *adj* [*hydrophilic* fr. NL *hydrophilus* water-loving + E *-ic; hydrophile* fr. NL *hydrophilus*] **:** of, relating to, or having a strong affinity for water ⟨~ colloids swell in water and are relatively stable⟩ **:** readily wet by water ⟨cotton is a ~ fiber⟩ — opposed to *hydrophobic;* compare HYGROSCOPIC, LIPOPHILIC, LYOPHILIC, ORGANOPHILIC

hydrophilic ointment *n, pharmacy* **:** an ointment base easily removable with water

hy·droph·i·lid \hīˈdräfələd\ *adj* [NL *Hydrophilidae*] **:** of or relating to the Hydrophilidae

hy·dro·phil·i·dae \ˌhīdrəˈfiləˌdē\ *n pl, cap* [NL fr. *Hydrophilus,* type genus (fr. *hydr-* + *-philus*) + *-idae*] **:** a large family of diving beetles that are mostly of scavenging or predaceous habits and of elliptical form and black color and that live chiefly in quiet pools and carry with them a film of air for respiration

hy·droph·i·lism \hīˈdräfəˌlizəm\ *n* -S [*hydrophilous* + *-ism*] **:** HYDROPHILY

hy·droph·i·lite \hīˈdräfəˌlīt\ *n* -S [G *hydrophilit,* fr. *hydr-* + Gk *philos* loving + G *-it* -ite; fr. the fact that it is very hygroscopic] **:** a mineral $CaCl_2$ of very rare occurrence consisting of native calcium chloride

hy·droph·i·lous \hīˈdräfələs\ *adj* [NL *hydrophilus* water-loving, fr. *hydr-* + *-philus* -philous, fr. Gk *philos* loving — more at -PHILOUS] **1 :** pollinated by the agency of water **2 :** HYDROPHYTIC

hy·droph·i·ly \-lē\ *n* -ES [*hydrophilous* + *-y*] **:** the quality or state of being hydrophilous

hy·dro·phis \ˈhīdrəfəs\ *n, cap* [NL, fr. *hydr-* + *-ophis*] **:** the type genus of the family Hydrophidae comprising sea snakes of the western and southern Pacific ocean

hy·dro·phobe \ˈhīdrəˌfōb\ *n* -S [LL *hydrophobus* one that has hydrophobia, fr. *hydrophobus,* adj., having hydrophobia, fr. Gk *hydrophobos,* fr. *hydr-* + *-phobos* -phobous] **:** one that is averse to or sheds water

hy·dro·pho·bia \ˌ≈≈ˈfōbēə\ *n* [LL, fr. Gk, fr. *hydr-* + *-phobia*] **1 :** a morbid dread of water **2 :** RABIES

hydrophobia skunk *also* **hydrophobia cat** *n, Southwest* **:** LITTLE SPOTTED SKUNK

hy·dro·pho·bic \ˌ≈≈ˈfōbik *also* -ˈfäb-\ *adj* [LL *hydrophobicus* characterized by hydrophobia, fr. Gk *hydrophobikos,* fr. *hydrophobia* + *-ikos* -ic] **1 :** of, relating to, or suffering from hydrophobia **2 :** resistant to or avoiding wetting ⟨most insects have ~ cuticle⟩ **3** *also* **hydrophobe** [*hydrophobe* fr. LL *hydrophobus* having hydrophobia, fr. Gk *hydrophobos*] **a :** of, relating to, or having a lack of affinity for water ⟨~ colloids are relatively unstable⟩ **b :** not readily wet by water ⟨nylon is a ~ fiber⟩ — opposed to *hydrophilic;* compare LIPOPHILIC, LYOPHOBIC — **hy·dro·pho·bic·i·ty** \ˌhīdrəfōˈbisəd·ē\ *n* -ES

hydrophobous *adj* [LL *hydrophobus* having hydrophobia] *obs* **:** HYDROPHOBIC

hy·dro·phone \ˈ≈≈ *at* HYDRO- + ˌfōn\ *n* [*hydr-* + *-phone*] **:** an electroacoustic transducer for listening to sound transmitted through water ⟨detection of submarines by ~⟩ ⟨underwater seismic surveying by ~⟩

hy·dro·phore \"+ˌfō(ə)r\ *n* -S [*hydr-* + *-phore*] **:** an instrument for obtaining specimens of water (as in a river, lake, or ocean) from any desired depth

hy·dro·pho·ria \ˌ≈≈+ˈfōrēə, -ˈfȯr-\ *n* -S [Gk, fr. *hydr-* + *-phoria* act of carrying — more at -PHORIA] **:** an act of carrying water; *specif* **:** a scene on a Greek water jar showing women carrying water from a fountain

hy·dro·phyl·la·ce·ae \ˌ≈≈+fəˈlāsēˌē\ *n pl, cap* [NL, fr. *Hydrophyllum,* type genus + *-aceae*] **:** a family of chiefly No. American herbs or undershrubs (order Polemoniales) having a cymose often helicoid inflorescence and usu. numerous ovules in each cell of a capsular fruit — see HYDROPHYLLUM, PHACELIA — **hy·dro·phyl·la·ceous** \ˌ≈≈≈ˈlāshəs\ *adj*

hy·dro·phyl·li·um \ˌ≈≈+ˈfilēəm\ *n, pl* **hydrophyl·lia** \-ēə\ [NL, fr. *hydr-* + *-phyllium* (fr. Gk *phyllion* small leaf, dim. of *phyllon* leaf) — more at BLOW (to blossom)] **:** one of the leaflike organs regarded as greatly modified zooids that cover other zooids of many siphonophores

hy·dro·phyl·lum \ˌ≈≈+ˈfiləm\ *n, cap* [NL, fr. *hydr-* + *-phyllum*] **:** a genus of No. American herbs (family Hydrophyllaceae) having lobed or pinnate deeply and sharply toothed leaves and bell-shaped cymose flowers

hy·dro·phyte \ˈ≈≈+ˌfīt\ *n* -S [ISV *hydr-* + *-phyte*] **:** a plant growing in water: **a :** a vascular plant growing wholly or partly in water; *esp* **:** a perennial aquatic plant having its overwintering buds under water — compare HELOPHYTE **b :** a plant requiring an abundance of water for growth and growing in water or in soil too waterlogged for most other plants to survive — compare MESOPHYTE, XEROPHYTE — **hy·dro·phyt·ic** \ˌ≈≈ˈfid·ik\ *adj*

hy·droph·y·ton \hīˈdräfəˌtän\ *n, pl* **hydrophy·ta** \-fəd·ə\ [NL, fr. *hydr-* + Gk *phyton* plant — more at PHYT-] **:** a common support connecting the zooids of a hydroid colony usu. including a hydrorhiza and a hydrocaulus — **hy·droph·y·tous** \-fəd·əs\ *adj*

hy·drop·ic \hīˈdräpik\ *also* **hy·drop·i·cal** \-pəkəl\ *adj* [*hydropic* alter. (influenced by L *hydropicus*) of ME *ydropike, idropik,* fr. MF *ydropique,* fr. L *hydropicus,* fr Gk *hydrōpikos,* fr. *hydrōp-, hydrōps* hydrops + *-ikos* -ic; *hydropical* fr. L *hydropicus* + E *-al*] **1 :** of, relating to, or exhibiting hydrops; *esp* **:** EDEMATOUS **2 :** characterized by swelling and imbibition of fluid — used of a type of cellular degeneration — **hy·drop·i·cal·ly** \-pək(ə)lē\ *adv*

¹**hy·dro·plane** \ˈ≈≈ *at* HYDRO- +ˌ-\ *n* [*hydr-* + *plane*] **1 :** a hydrofoil or any surface (as of an airplane pontoon) having a similar shape and tendency **2 a :** a speedboat equipped with hydrofoils or having a stepped bottom that provides more than one lifting surface so that the hull is raised wholly or partially out of the water as the boat attains forward speed **b :** DIVING PLANE **3 :** SEAPLANE — not used technically

²**hydroplane** \"\ *vi* **1 :** to skim over the water with the hull either clear of the surface or barely immersed **2 :** to drive or ride in a hydroplane

hy·dro·planula \ˌ≈≈+\ *n* [NL, fr. *hydr-* + *planula*] **:** a larval stage of a coelenterate intermediate between the planula and actinula stages

hy·dro·pneumatic \"+\ *adj* [ISV *hydr-* + *pneumatic*] **:** of, relating to, or operating by means of both water and air or other gas ⟨a ~ elevator⟩

hy·dro·pneumothorax \"+\ *n* [NL, fr. *hydr-* + *pneumothorax*] **:** the presence of gas and serous fluid in the pleural cavity

hy·dro·polyp \"+\ *n* [ISV *hydr-* + *polyp*] **1 :** a polyp of a hydrozoan **2 :** HYDRULA 2

hy·dro·pon·ic \ˌhīdrəˈpänik\ *adj* [fr. *hydroponics,* after such pairs as E *geoponics: geoponic*] **:** of or relating to hydroponics — **hy·dro·pon·i·cal·ly** \-nək(ə)lē\ *adv*

hy·dro·pon·i·cist \ˌ≈≈ˈpänəsəst\ *n* -S **:** a specialist in hydroponics

hy·dro·pon·ics \ˌ≈≈ˈpäniks\ *n pl but usu sing in constr* [*hydr-* + *-ponics* (as in *geoponics*)] **:** the growing of plants in nutrient solutions with or without sand, gravel, or other inert medium to provide mechanical support

hy·dro·positive \ˈ≈≈ *at* HYDRO- +\ *adj* [*hydr-* + *positive*] *biol* **:** characterized by positive hydrotaxis or hydrotropism

hy·drop·o·tes \hīˈdräpəˌtēz\ *n, cap* [NL, fr. Gk *hydropotēs* water drinker, fr. *hydr-* + *potēs* drinker; akin to Gk *pinein* to drink — more at POTABLE] **:** a genus of deer consisting of a small Chinese species (*H. inermis*) having no antlers

hydropower \ˈ≈≈+\ *n* [²*hydro* + *power*] **:** hydroelectric power

hy·dro·press \ˈ≈≈ *at* HYDRO- + ˌ-\ *n* **:** HYDRAULIC PRESS

hy·drops \ˈhīˌdräps\ *also* **hy·drop·sy** \-sē, -si\ *n* -ES [*hydrops* fr. L, fr. Gk *hydrōps; hydropsy* alter. (influenced by L *hydropisis*) of earlier *idropesie,* fr. ME *ydropesie,* fr. OF *idropisie,* fr. L *hydropisis,* modif. of Gk *hydrōps* — more at DROPSY] **1 :** EDEMA **2 :** distention of a hollow organ with fluid ⟨~ of the gall bladder⟩ **3** *or* **hydrops fetalis :** congenital erythroblastosis

hy·dro·quinine \ˈ≈≈ *at* HYDRO- +\ *n* [ISV *hydr-* + *quinine*] **:** a bitter crystalline antipyretic alkaloid $C_{20}H_{26}N_2O_2$ found with quinine in cinchona bark and usu. present in commercial quinine; dihydro-quinine

hy·dro·quinone \"+\ *also* **hy·dro·chinone** \"+\ *or* **hy·dro·chi·non** \ˌ≈≈+ˈkiˌnän\ *n* [ISV *hydr-* + *quinone;* orig. formed as G *hydrochinon*] **:** a white crystalline strongly reducing phenol $C_6H_4(OH)_2$ occurring naturally in the form of the glucoside arbutin, made usu. by reduction of quinone, and used chiefly as a photographic developer, as an antioxidant esp. for fats and oils, and as a stabilizer and inhibitor (as in the polymerization of vinyl compounds); *para*-dihydroxy-benzene — see QUINHYDRONE

hy·dro·rhi·za \ˌ≈≈+ˈrīzə\ *n, pl* **hydrorhi·zae** \-ī(ˌ)zē\ [NL, fr. *hydr-* + *-rhiza*] **:** a rootstock or decumbent stem by which a hydroid is attached to other objects — **hy·dro·rhi·zal** \¦==¦rīzəl\ *adj*

hy·dror·rhea \,==+'rēə\ *n* -s [NL, fr. *hydr-* + *-rrhea*] **:** a profuse watery discharge (as from the nose)

hy·dro·rubber \¦== *at* HYDRO- +\ *n* [*hydr-* + *rubber*] *chem* **:** a substance $(C_5H_{10})_x$ obtained as an elastic or tough inelastic mass by catalytic hydrogenation of rubber

hydros *pl of* HYDRO

hy·dro·salpinx \"+\ *n* [NL, fr. *hydr-* + *salpinx*] **:** abnormal distension of one or both fallopian tubes with fluid usu. due to inflammation

hy·dro·scope \'==+,skōp\ *n* [ISV *hydr-* + *-scope;* prob. orig. formed as It *idroscopio*] **:** a device for enabling a person to see an object at a considerable distance below the surface of water by means of a series of mirrors enclosed in a steel tube — compare WATER GLASS — **hy·dro·scop·ic** \¦==¦skäpik\ *also* **hy·dro·scop·i·cal** \-pəkəl\ *adj*

hy·dro·separator \¦== *at* HYDRO- +\ *n* [*hydr-* + *separator*] **:** a settling tank (as for an industrial process) in which solids in suspension are separated from the suspending liquid

hy·dro·sere \'==+,-\ *n* **:** an ecological sere originating in an aquatic habitat

hy·dro·silicate \¦== *at* HYDRO- +\ *n* [ISV *hydr-* + *silicate*] **:** a hydrous silicate

hy·dro·ski \'==+,-\ *n* **:** a sometimes retractable hydrofoil attached below the fuselage of a seaplane to accelerate take-offs and simplify landings

hy·dro·sol \"+,sōl, -,säl\ *n* [*hydr-* + *-sol* (fr. *solution*)] *chem* **:** a sol in which the liquid is water

hy·dro·some \"+,sōm\ *also* **hy·dro·so·ma** \,==+'sōmə\ *n* -s [NL *hydrosoma,* fr. *hydr-* + *-soma*] **:** the entire colony of a compound hydrozoan **:** HYDROID

hy·dro·sphere \'==+,-\ *n* [ISV *hydr-* + *sphere*] **1 :** the aqueous vapor of the entire atmosphere **2 :** the aqueous envelope of the earth including oceans, lakes, streams, and underground waters and the aqueous vapor in the atmosphere

hy·dro·spire \"+,-\ *n* [*hydr-* + *spire* (coil)] **:** a flattened calcareous pouch or tube on either side of the middle line of the inner surface of the ambulacra of a blastoid, located within the cavity of the calyx, opening on the exterior by a small aperture, and presumed to form part of the respiratory system — **hy·dro·spi·ric** \¦==¦spīrik\ *adj*

hy·dro·stat·ic \¦==+¦stad·|ik, -at|, |ēk-\ *also* **hy·dro·stat·i·cal** \-|əkəl, |ēk-\ *adj* [*hydrostatic* prob. fr. NL *hydrostaticus,* fr. *hydr-* + *staticus* static; *hydrostatical* prob. fr. NL *hydrostaticus* + E *-al* — more at STATIC] **:** of or relating to liquids at rest or to the pressures they exert or transmit — opposed to *hydrokinetic* — **hy·dro·stat·i·cal·ly** \|ək(ə)lē, |ēk-, -li\ *adv*

hydrostatic arch *n* **:** an arch designed to bear at each point a pressure proportional to the depth below a datum line

hydrostatic balance *n* **:** a balance for weighing a substance in water to ascertain its specific gravity

hydrostatic bed *n* **:** WATER BED

hydrostatic head *n* **:** a measure of pressure at a given point in a liquid in terms of the vertical height of a column of the liquid which would produce the same pressure

hydrostatic press *n* **:** HYDRAULIC PRESS

hydrostatic pressure *n* **:** pressure exerted by or existing within a liquid at rest with respect to adjacent bodies

hy·dro·stat·ics \¦== *at* HYDRO- + 'stad·iks\ *n pl but usu sing in constr* [prob. fr. NL *hydrostatica,* fr. neut. pl. of *hydrostaticus* hydrostatic] **:** a branch of physics that deals with the characteristics of liquids at rest and esp. with the pressure in a liquid or exerted by a liquid on an immersed body — compare HYDRODYNAMICS

hy·dro·stome \'==+,stōm\ *n* -s [*hydr-* + *-stome*] **:** the mouth of a hydroid

hy·dro·sulfide \¦== *at* HYDRO- +\ *n* [ISV *hydr-* + *sulfide*] **:** a compound derived from hydrogen sulfide by the replacement of half its hydrogen by an element or radical ⟨potassium ~ KSH⟩ — compare MERCAPTAN

hy·dro·sul·fite \,==+'səl,fīt\ *n* [ISV *hydrosulfurous* + *-ite*] **:** a salt of hydrosulfurous acid; *esp* **:** SODIUM HYDROSULFITE — not used scientifically; called also *dithionite, hyposulfite*

hy·dro·sulfureted \¦== *at* HYDRO- +\ *or* **hy·dro·sulfuretted** \"+\ *adj* [*hydr-* + *sulfureted, sulfuretted,* past part. of *sulfuret*] **:** combined or impregnated with hydrogen sulfide

hy·dro·sulfuric acid \" + . . . -\ *n* [*hydrosulfuric* ISV *hydr-* + *sulfuric*] **:** HYDROGEN SULFIDE

hy·dro·sulfurous acid \" + . . . -\ *n* [*hydrosulfurous* ISV *hydr-* + *sulfurous*] **:** an unstable acid $H_2S_2O_4$ known only in aqueous solution formed by reducing sulfurous acid or in the form of salts — not used scientifically; called also *dithionous acid, hyposulfurous acid*

hy·dro·tac·tic \¦==+¦taktik\ *adj* [fr. NL *hydrotaxis,* after such pairs as NL *chemotaxis*: E *chemotactic*] **:** of or relating to hydrotaxis

hy·dro·tal·cite \,==+'tal,sīt\ *n* -s [G *hydrotalkit,* fr. *hydr-* + *talk* talc (prob. fr. MF *talc*) + G *-it* -ite] **:** a pearly-white mineral $Mg_6Al_2(OH)_{16}(CO_3).4H_2O$ consisting of hydrous aluminum and magnesium hydroxide and carbonate

hy·dro·taxis \¦== *at* HYDRO- +\ *n* [NL, fr. *hydr-* + *-taxis*] **:** a taxis in which moisture is the directive factor

hy·dro·the·ca \,==+'thēkə\ *n* [NL, fr. *hydr-* + L *theca* sheath, case — more at TICK] **:** a cup-shaped extension of the perisarc in hydroids of the group Leptomedusae that surrounds and protects the hydranths when they are contracted — **hy·dro·the·cal** \¦==¦thēkəl\ *adj*

hy·dro·therapeutic \¦== *at* HYDRO- +\ *or* **hy·dro·thera·peutical** \"+\ *adj* [*hydr-* + *therapeutic, therapeutical*] **:** of, relating to, or involving the methods of hydrotherapy

hy·dro·therapeutics \"+\ *n pl but usu sing in constr* [*hydr-* + *therapeutics*] **:** HYDROTHERAPY

hy·dro·therapist \"+\ *n* [*hydrotherapy* + *-ist*] **:** a specialist in hydrotherapy

hy·dro·therapy \"+\ *n* [ISV *hydr-* + *therapy*] **:** the treatment of disease or disability by the external application of water ⟨~ by cold compresses to reduce fever⟩ ⟨~ of crippled limbs in a whirlpool bath⟩

hy·dro·thermal \"+\ *adj* [ISV *hydr-* + *thermal;* orig. formed in G] **:** of or relating to hot water — used esp. of the formation or metamorphism of minerals by the action of hot solutions rising up through the earth's crust from a cooling magma

hy·dro·tho·rax \,==+'thōr,aks, -'thȯ,ra-\ *n* [NL, fr. *hydr-* + L *thorax*] **:** an excess of serous fluid in the pleural cavity; *esp* **:** an effusion resulting from a failing circulation (as in heart disease or from lung infection)

hy·dro·trop·ic \¦==+¦träpik\ *adj* [ISV *hydr-* + *-tropic*] **1 :** exhibiting or characterized by hydrotropism **2** *chem* **:** relating to or causing hydrotropy ⟨~ solvents⟩ — **hy·dro·trop·i·cal·ly** \-pək(ə)lē\ *adv*

hy·drot·ro·pism \hī'drä·trə,pizəm\ *n* [ISV *hydr-* + *-tropism*] **:** a tropism (as in many plant roots) in which water or water vapor constitutes the orienting factor

hy·drot·ro·py \-rəpē\ *n* -ES [ISV *hydr-* + *-tropy*] *chem* **:** solubilization of a sparingly soluble substance in water brought about by an added agent

hy·dro·tungstite \¦== *at* HYDRO- +\ *n* [*hydr-* + *tungstite*] **:** a mineral $H_2WO_4.H_2O$ consisting of hydrous tungstic acid

hy·dro·turbine \,==+'-\ *n* **:** a hydraulic turbine

hy·dro·type \'==+,tīp\ *n* [ISV *hydr-* + *type*] **:** a positive printing process in photography that uses a gelatin-coated plate containing dichromate on which appears after the plate has been exposed to light under a positive and then soaked in a dye solution a positive image of dye that is transferred to a sheet of paper coated with soft gelatin

hy·dro·ureter \¦== *at* HYDRO-+\ *n* [NL, fr. *hydr-* + *ureter*] **:** abnormal distension of the ureter with urine

hy·drous \'hīdrəs\ *adj* [*hydr-* + *-ous*] **:** containing water **:** WATERY; *specif* **:** HYDRATED

hydrous wool fat *n* **:** LANOLIN a

hy·dro·vane \'== *at* HYDRO-+,vān\ *n* [*hydr-* + *vane*] **1 :** HYDROFOIL **2 :** DIVING PLANE

hy·drox·am·ic acid \,hī,dräk¦samik-\ *n* [*hydroxamic* ISV *hydroxy-* + *am-* (fr. *amide*) + *-ic*] **:** any of a class of weak acids (as RCONHOH) that are acylated derivatives of hydroxylamine

hy·drox·ide \hī'dräk,sīd\ *n* [ISV *hydr-* + *oxide*] **1 :** the univalent anion OH^- consisting of one atom of hydrogen and one of oxygen **2 a :** an ionic compound of hydroxide with an element or group **b :** any of various hydrated oxides (as aluminum hydroxide) regarded as containing hydroxide

hydroxide ion *or* **hydroxyl ion** *n* **:** HYDROXIDE[1]

hydroximino- *comb form* [*hydroxy-* + *imin-*] **:** isonitroso-

hydroxo- *comb form* [*hydroxyl* + *-o-*] **:** containing hydroxyl as a coordinated group ⟨potassium *hydroxo*stannate $K_2Sn(OH)_6$⟩ ⟨*hydroxo*cobalamin⟩ — compare HYDROXY-

hy·drox·o·ni·um \,hī,dräk'sōnēəm\ *n* -s [*hydroxy-* + *-onium*] **:** HYDRONIUM

hy·droxy \(')hī¦dräksē\ *adj* [*hydroxy-*] **:** relating to or containing hydroxyl ⟨~ molecule⟩ — compare -HYDRIC 2, HYDROXY-

hydroxy- *or* **hydrox-** *comb form* [ISV, fr. *hydroxyl,* fr. E] **:** hydroxyl **:** containing hydroxyl esp. in place of hydrogen — in names of chemical compounds or radicals ⟨*hydroxy*alkyl⟩ ⟨*hydrox*amic acid⟩ — compare HYDROXO-

hy·droxy·acetic acid \(¦)hī¦dräksē+ . . . -\ *n* **:** GLYCOLIC ACID

hydroxy acid *n* **:** an acid (as lactic acid, tartaric acid, salicylic acid) having one or more hydroxyl groups in the molecule in addition to that present in the acid group itself

hydroxy amine *n* **:** AMINO ALCOHOL

hydroxyamino- *or* **hydroxamino-** *comb form* [*hydroxy-* + *amin-*] **:** containing the univalent radical –NHOH of hydroxylamine

hy·droxy·benzoic acid \(¦)hī¦dräksē+ . . .-\ *n* [*hydroxybenzoic* ISV *hydroxy-* + *benzoic*] **:** any of three crystalline monohydroxy derivatives HOC_6H_4COOH of benzoic acid: as **a :** the colorless para-substituted acid used in making several of its esters that are effective preservatives — called also *para-hydroxybenzoic acid, p-hydroxybenzoic acid* **b :** SALICYLIC ACID

hy·droxy·butyrate \"+\ *n* **:** a salt or ester of hydroxybutyric acid

hy·droxy·butyric acid \"+ . . .-\ *n* **:** a hydroxy derivative $C_3H_6(OH)COOH$ of butyric acid; *esp* **:** the beta derivative $CH_3CHOHCH_2COOH$ found in the blood and urine esp. in conditions of impaired metabolism — see KETONE BODY

hy·droxy·citronellal \"+\ *n* **:** a liquid hydroxy aldehyde $(CH_3)_2C(OH)(CH_2)_3CH(CH_3)CH_2CHO$ obtained by hydration of citronellal and used in perfumery to impart an odor of lily of the valley

hy·droxy·corticosterone \"+\ *n* **:** a hydroxy derivative of corticosterone; *esp* **:** HYDROCORTISONE

hy·droxy·de·oxy·corticosterone \'hī,dräksē¦dē,äksē +\ *or* **hy·droxy·des·oxy·corticosterone** \-'de,zäksē, -'de,sä-+\ *n* [*hydroxy-* + *deoxy-* or *desoxy-* + *corticosterone*] **:** a crystalline steroid hormone $C_{21}H_{30}O_4$ occurring in the adrenal cortex

hy·droxy·ethyl \(¦)hī¦dräksē+\ *n* **:** a hydroxy derivative of ethyl; *esp* **:** the beta or 2-derivative $HOCH_2CH_2-$

hy·droxy·eth·yl·a·tion \(,)hī,dräksē,ethə'lāshən\ *n* -s [*hydroxyethyl* + *-ation*] **:** the introduction of a hydroxyethyl group into a compound usu. by reaction with ethylene oxide

hydroxy ketone *n* **:** a hydroxy derivative of a ketone

hy·droxy·yl \hī'dräksəl\ *n* -s [*hydr-* + *ox-* + *-yl*] **1 :** the chemical group or ion OH that consists of one atom of hydrogen and one of oxygen, is neutral or positively charged, and is characteristic esp. of oxygen acids, alcohols, glycols, phenols, and hemiacetals **2 :** HYDROXIDE 1

hy·drox·yl·amine \hī¦dräksələ¦mēn; ,hī,dräk'silə,mēn, -,mən\ *n* [ISV *hydroxyl* (fr. E) + *amine*] **:** a colorless low-melting crystalline unstable compound NH_2OH that is a weaker base than ammonia and forms stable crystalline salts with acids, that is made by reaction of its salts with alkali, and that is used chiefly as a reducing agent and as an intermediate — see OXIME

hy·drox·yl·ammonium \(¦)hī¦dräksəl+\ *n* [ISV *hydroxyl* (fr. E) + *ammonium*] **:** the univalent cation $HONH_3^+$ derived from hydroxylamine and present in its salts which are obtainable by hydrolysis of a primary nitroparaffin (as nitromethane) with water and a strong acid ⟨~ chloride $HONH_3Cl$ or hydroxylamine hydrochloride $NH_2OH.HCl$⟩

hy·drox·yl·apatite \"+\ *or* **hy·droxy·apatite** \(¦)hī¦dräksē+\ *n* [*hydroxylapatite* fr. G *hydroxylapatit,* fr. *hydroxyl* (fr. E) + *apatit* apatite; *hydroxyapatite* fr. *hydroxy-* + *apatite*] **:** apatite containing hydroxyl: as **a :** apatite in which hydroxyl predominates over fluorine, chlorine, and carbonate **b :** calcium phosphate hydroxide $Ca_5(OH)(PO_4)_3$ — see CALCIUM PHOSPHATE 1b(2)

hy·drox·yl·ate \hī'dräksə,lāt\ *vt* -ED/-ING/-S [*hydroxyl* + *-ate*] **:** to introduce hydroxyl into (a compound or radical) usu. by replacement of hydrogen — **hy·drox·yl·ation** \hī,dräksə'lāshən\ *n* -s

hydroxyl-herderite \==¦==,=\ *n* [*hydroxyl* + *herderite*] **:** a mineral $CaBe(PO_4)(OH)$ consisting of phosphate and hydroxide of calcium and beryllium and being isomorphous with herderite

hy·drox·yl·ic \,hī,dräk¦silik\ *adj* [ISV *hydroxyl* (fr. E) + *-ic*] **:** of or relating to hydroxyl

hy·droxy·methyl \(¦)hī¦dräksē+\ *n* **:** the univalent radical $HOCH_2-$ derived from methanol by removal of one hydrogen atom attached to carbon — called also *methylol*

hy·droxy·meth·yl·ation \(,)hī,dräksē,methə'lāshən\ *n* -s [*hydroxymethyl* + *-ation*] **:** the introduction of a hydroxymethyl group into a compound

hy·droxy·naphthoic acid \(¦)hī¦dräksē+ . . .-\ *n* **:** any of several crystalline acids $C_{10}H_6(OH)COOH$ derived from the naphthols: as **a :** a yellow acid derived from beta-naphthol and used as an intermediate for azo dyes and pigments — called also *beta-hydroxynaphthoic acid, 3-hydroxy-2-naphthoic acid;* see DYE table I (under *Developer 8*), NAPHTHOL AS **b :** a white to reddish acid derived from alpha-naphthol and used as an analytical reagent — called also *1-hydroxy-2-naphthoic acid*

hy·droxy·proline \"+\ *n* **:** a crystalline amino acid HOC_4H_7NCOOH obtained in the levorotatory L-form esp. by hydrolysis of gelatin or collagen — called also *4-hydroxyproline*

hy·droxy·quinoline \"+\ *n* **:** any of seven hydroxy derivatives of quinoline; *esp* **:** OXINE

hy·droxy·tryptamine \"+\ *n* -s [ISV *hydroxy-* + *tryptamine*] **:** SEROTONIN

hy·drox·y·zine \hī'dräksə,zēn\ *n* -s [*hydroxy-* + *piperazine*] **:** a tranquilizer and antihistamine $C_{21}H_{27}ClN_2O_2$ that is an ether alcohol derived from piperazine

hy·dro·zinc·ite \,hīdrō'ziŋ,kīt\ *n* [G *hydrozinkit,* fr. *hydr-* + *zink* zinc + *-it* -ite] **:** a mineral $Zn_5(OH)_6(CO_3)_2$ consisting of a basic zinc carbonate occurring as white, grayish, or yellowish masses or crusts (sp. gr. 3.58–3.8)

hy·dro·zoa \,hīdrə'zōə\ *n pl, cap* [NL, fr. *hydr-* (hydroid) + *-zoa*] **:** a class of coelenterates that includes various simple and compound polyps and jellyfishes having no stomodaeum or gastric tentacles and differing widely in appearance, structure, and habits, some being attached polyps which have no free-swimming stage, others being always free-swimming and the majority having an alternation of a free-swimming sexual generation with an attached asexual generation — see HYDROIDA, MILLEPORINA, SIPHONOPHORA, STYLASTERINA, TRACHYLINA

[1]**hydrozoan** \¦==¦zōən\ *or* **hydrozoal** \-ōəl\ *adj* [NL *Hydrozoa* + E *-an* (adj. suffix) *or -al* (adj. suffix)] **:** of or relating to the Hydrozoa

[2]**hydrozoan** \"\ *n* -s [NL *Hydrozoa* + E *-an* (n. suffix)] **:** one of the Hydrozoa

hy·dro·zo·on \,==¦zō,än\ *n, pl* **hydro·zoa** \-ōə\ *or* **hydrozoons** [NL, fr. *hydr-* + *-zoon*] **:** HYDROZOAN

hy·dru·la \'hīdrələ\ *n* -s [NL, dim. of *hydra* (hydrozoan polyp)] **1 :** a hypothetical primitive polyp of simple type **2 :** a developmental phase of many coelenterates (as hydroids) in which they have the form of a simple polyp

hy·dru·ra·ce·ae \,hī,drü'rāsē,ē\ *n pl, cap* [NL, fr. *Hydrurus,* type genus + *-aceae*] **:** a family of algae (order Chrysocapsales) that includes the genus *Hydrurus* and related forms when these are considered to be algae rather than protozoans

hy·drur·ga \hī'drürgə\ *n, cap* [NL, irreg. fr. *hydr-*] **:** a genus of mammals (family Phocidae) comprising the leopard seal

hy·dru·rus \hī'drürəs\ *n, cap* [NL, fr. *hydr-* + *-urus*] **:** a genus of colonial plantlike flagellates (order Chrysomonadina) occurring as sticky foul-smelling branched feathery greenish brown tufts in cold flowing water — see HYDRURACEAE

hydt *abbr* hydrant

hy·e·na *also* **hy·ae·na** \hī'ēnə\ *n* -s [L *hyaena,* fr. Gk *hyaina,* fr. *hys* hog — more at sow] **1 :** any of several large strong nocturnal carnivorous Old World mammals constituting the family Hyaenidae, having a long thick neck, large head, powerful jaws, rough coat, and four-toed feet with nonretractile claws, and feeding largely on carrion — compare CAVE HYENA **2** *Austral* **:** TASMANIAN WOLF

striped hyena

hyena dog *n* **:** AFRICAN HUNTING DOG

hy·e·nia \hī'ēnēə\ *n, cap* [NL, fr. *Hyen,* locality near Nord Fjord, western Norway, near which the fossils on which the genus is based were discovered + NL *-ia*] **:** a genus of small Devonian fossil plants (order Hyeniales) having horizontal rhizomes bearing aerial shoots with small bifurcated leaves in whorls and pendulous terminal sporangia

hy·e·ni·a·les \(,)hī,ēnē'ā(,)lēz\ *n pl, cap* [NL, fr. *Hyenia* + *-ales*] **:** an order of Devonian sphenopsid plants known only in the fossil state — see CALAMOPHYTON, HYENIA

hy·enic *or* **hy·aenic** \(')hī¦ēnik, -¦en-\ *adj* [*hyena, hyaena* + *-ic*] **:** of, relating to, or like a hyena

hy·e·ni·form \(')hī¦ēnə,fȯrm\ *adj* [*hyena* + *-iform*] **:** HYENOID

hy·e·noid \hī'ē,nȯid\ *adj* [*hyena* + *-oid*] **:** resembling a hyena

hyenoid dog *n* **:** any of several No. American Miocene and Pliocene carnivorous mammals constituting *Borophagus* and related genera of the family Canidae and being intermediate in character between the true dogs and the hyenas

hyet- *or* **hyeto-** *comb form* [Gk, fr. *hyetos;* akin to Gk *hyei* it is raining — more at SUCK] **:** rain ⟨*hyet*al⟩ ⟨*hyeto*meter⟩ ⟨*hyeto*graphy⟩

hy·e·tal \'hīəd·ᵊl\ *adj* **:** of or relating to rain, rainfall, or rainy regions

hy·et·o·graph \hī'ed·ə,graf, -rȧf\ *n* [ISV *hyet-* + *-graph*] **1 :** a chart showing average annual rainfall **2 :** HYETOMETROGRAPH

hy·et·o·graph·ic \(,)hī¦ed·ə¦grafik\ *also* **hy·et·o·graph·i·cal** \-fəkəl\ *adj* [*hyetography* + *-ic, -ical*] **:** of or relating to hyetography — **hy·et·o·graph·i·cal·ly** \-fək(ə)lē\ *adv*

hy·e·tog·ra·phy \,hīə'tägrəfē\ *n* -ES [ISV *hyet-* + *-graphy*] **:** scientific description of the geographical distribution of rain

hy·et·o·log·i·cal \(,)hī¦ed·ᵊl¦äjəkəl\ *adj* [*hyet-* + *-logy* + *-ical*] **:** of or relating to hyetology

hy·e·tol·o·gy \,hīə'täləjē\ *n* -ES [*hyet-* + *-logy*] **:** a branch of meteorology that deals with precipitation (as of rain and snow)

hy·e·tom·e·ter \-ämədə(r)\ *n* [*hyet-* + *-meter*] **:** RAIN GAGE

hy·e·to·met·ro·graph \,hīətō'me·trə,graf, -rȧf\ *n* [*hyet-* + *metr-* (measure) + *-graph*] **:** a self-registering rain gage

hyg *abbr* hygiene

hy·ge·ian \(')hī¦jēən\ *adj* [*Hygeia,* ancient Greek goddess of health (fr. L *Hygea,* fr. Gk *Hygieia,* fr. *hygieia* health, fr. *hygiēs* sound, healthy) + E *-an*] **1** *usu cap* **:** of or relating to Hygeia, the ancient Greek goddess of health **2 :** of or relating to health or to medical practice

hy·ge·ist \'hījēəst\ *n* -s [Gk *hygeia* health (alter. of *hygieia*) + E *-ist*] **:** HYGIENIST

hy·giene \'hī,jēn *sometimes* =¦=\ *n* -s [F *hygiène* & NL *hygiena, hygieina,* fr. Gk *hygieinē,* fem. of *hygieinos* healthful, relating to health, fr. *hygiēs* sound, healthy, fr. a prehistoric compound whose first and second constituents respectively are akin to OIr *so-* good, well, OSlav *sŭdravŭ* healthy, Av *hu-* good, well, Skt *su* and to Lith *gyvas* living — more at QUICK] **1 :** the science which deals with the establishment and maintenance of health in the individual and the group ⟨took a course in municipal ~⟩ **2 :** conditions or practices conducive to health ⟨infant mortality was very high because of bad ~ and the lack of nourishing foods —P.E.James⟩

hy·gien·ic \,hījē'enik, (')hī¦jen-, -nēk *also* (')hī¦jēn-\ *also* **hy·gien·i·cal** \-nəkəl, -nēk-\ *adj* [prob. fr. F *hygiénique,* fr. *hygiène* hygiene + *-ique* -ic, -ical] **:** of, relating to, or conducive to health or hygiene **syn** see HEALTHFUL

hy·gien·i·cal·ly \-nək(ə)lē, -nēk-, -li\ *adv* **:** in a hygienic manner

hy·gien·ics \,hījē'eniks, hī'jen- -nēks *also* hī'jēn-\ *n pl but sing in constr* **:** HYGIENE 1

hy·gien·ist \(')hī¦jēnəst, (')hī¦jen-, *also* ¦hījē¦en- *or* 'hījən-\ *n* -s [ISV *hygiene* + *-ist*] **:** a specialist in hygiene; *esp* **:** one skilled in a specified branch of hygiene ⟨dental ~⟩ ⟨mental ~⟩

hygr- *also* **hygro-** *comb form* [Gk, fr. *hygros* moist, wet — more at HUMOR] **1 :** humidity **:** moisture **:** moist ⟨*hygr*ic⟩ ⟨*hygro*stat⟩ ⟨*hygro*phobia⟩ ⟨*hygro*phyte⟩ **2 :** moisture and **:** of or relating to moisture and ⟨*hygro*thermal⟩

hy·gric \'hīgrik\ *adj* [ISV *hygr-* + *-ic*] **:** of, relating to, or containing moisture

hy·grine \'hī,grēn, -grən\ *n* -s [ISV *hygr-* + *-ine;* orig. formed as G *hygrin*] **:** a colorless liquid ketonic alkaloid $C_8H_{15}NO$ derived from pyrrolidine and obtained from coca leaves

hy·gro·deik \'hīgrə,dīk\ *n* -s [*hygr-* + *-deik* (fr. Gk *deiknynai* to show) — more at DICTION] **:** a hygrometer having wet-bulb and dry-bulb thermometers and an adjustable index for determining relative humidity

hy·gro·expansivity \¦hī(,)grō+\ *n* **:** expansivity due to moisture or humidity

hy·gro·graph \'hīgrə,graf, -rȧf\ *n* [ISV *hygr-* + *-graph*] **:** an instrument for recording automatically variations in the humidity of the atmosphere

hy·grol·o·gy \hī'gräləjē\ *n* -ES [ISV *hygr-* + *-logy*] **:** a branch of physics that deals with the phenomena of humidity

hy·gro·ma \hī'grōmə\ *n, pl* **hygromas** \-məz\ *or* **hygro·ma·ta** \-məd·ə\ [NL, fr. *hygr-* + *-oma*] **1 :** a cystic tumor of lymphatic origin **2 :** a cyst esp. of the knee of cattle caused by injury or infection

hy·grom·e·ter \hī'grämədə(r)\ *n* [prob. fr. F *hygromètre,* fr. *hygr-* + *-mètre* -meter] **:** any of several instruments for measuring the humidity of the atmosphere — see DEW-POINT HYGROMETER, HAIR HYGROMETER, PSYCHROMETER

hy·gro·met·ric \¦hīgrə¦me·trik\ *also* **hy·gro·met·ri·cal** \-rəkəl\ *adj* [prob. fr. F *hygrométrique,* fr. *hygrométrie* hygrometry + *-ique* -ic, -ical] **1 :** of or relating to hygrometry or to humidity **2 :** HYGROSCOPIC — **hy·gro·met·ri·cal·ly** \-rək(ə)lē\ *adv*

hygrometric water *n* **:** water in a mineral that can be released by raising its temperature to 110° C

hy·grom·e·try \hī'grämə·trē\ *n* -ES [F *hygrométrie,* fr. *hygr-* + *-métrie* -metry] **:** a science that deals with the measurement of humidity esp. of the atmosphere

hy·groph·i·la \hī'gräfələ\ *n* [NL, fr. *hygr-* + *-phila*] **1** *cap* **:** a genus of aquatic herbaceous or woody plants (family Acanthaceae) having leaves resembling those of the willow **2** -s **:** any plant of the genus *Hygrophila*

hy·gro·phile \'hīgrə,fīl\ *or* **hy·gro·phil·ic** \¦==¦filik\ *adj* [*hygrophile* fr. F, fr. *hygr-* + *-phile; hygrophilic* prob. fr. F *hygrophile* + E *-ic*] **:** HYGROPHILOUS

hy·groph·i·lous \(')hī¦gräfələs\ *adj* [prob. fr. F *hygrophile* + E *-ous*] **:** living or growing in moist places

hy·gro·phyte \'hīgrə,fīt\ *n* -s [ISV *hygr-* + *-phyte*] **1 :** a plant living under conditions of plentiful moisture **2 :** HYDROPHYTE — **hy·gro·phyt·ic** \¦==¦fid·ik\ *adj*

hy·gro·scope \'hīgrə,skōp\ *n* [*hygr-* + *-scope*] **:** an instrument that shows changes in humidity (as of the atmosphere) — compare HYGROMETER

hy·gro·scop·ic \¦==¦skäpik\ *adj* [*hygroscope* + *-ic*] **1 a :** readily taking up and retaining moisture ⟨glycerol is ~⟩ ⟨~ soils⟩ ⟨common salt is slightly ~⟩ — compare DELIQUESCENT, HYDROPHILIC **b :** taken up and retained under certain conditions of humidity and temperature — used of moisture ⟨~ water is not removed from clay by drying at 110° C⟩ **2 a** *bot* **:** sensitive to moisture ⟨~ tissues⟩ ⟨~ organs⟩ **b :** induced by moisture ⟨turgor movements are ~⟩ — **hy·gro·scop·i·cal·ly**

\-pək(ə)lē\ *adv* — **hy·gro·sco·pic·i·ty** \ˌhīgrəˌskō'pisəd·ē\ *n* -ES

hygroscopic cell *n* **:** BULLIFORM CELL

hygroscopic coefficient *n* **:** the percentage of water that is absorbed and held in equilibrium by a soil in a saturated atmosphere

hygroscopic moisture *or* **hygroscopic water** *n* **:** moisture held firmly as a film on soil particles and not responding to capillary action

hy·gro·stat \'hīgrəˌstat\ *n* -s [*hygr-* + *-stat*] **:** HUMIDISTAT

hy·gro·thermal \ˌhīgrə+\ *adj* [*hygr-* + *thermal*] **:** of or relating to a combination of moisture and heat

hy·gro·ther·mo·graph \ˌhīgrə'thərməˌgraf\ *n* [*hygr-* + *therm-* + *-graph*] **:** an instrument that records both humidity and temperature on the same chart

hying *pres part of* HIE

hyk·sos \'hikˌsōs, -sīs, -sōs, -ˌsəs\ *adj, usu cap* [Gk *Hyksōs*, dynasty ruling Egypt, fr. Egypt *ḥq'š'sw* ruler of the countries of the nomads] **:** of or relating to a Semite dynasty ruling Egypt from about 1650 to 1580 B.C. and known as the Shepherd kings

hyl- *or* **hylo-** *comb form* [Gk, wood, matter, fr. *hylē* wood, forest, material, matter] **1 :** matter **:** material ⟨*hylo*morphism⟩ ⟨*hylo*morphous⟩ **2 :** wood ⟨*hylo*phagous⟩ **:** forest ⟨*Hylocichla*⟩

hy·la \'hīlə\ *n* [NL, fr. Gk *hylē* wood, forest] **1** *cap* **:** a large genus (the type of the family Hylidae) of arciferous amphibians comprising the typical toads that have swollen terminal phalanges resembling claws and forming adhesive pads adapted to an arboreal habitat **2** -s **:** any amphibian of the genus *Hyla; broadly* **:** TREE TOAD

hy·lam \(')hī¦läm\ *n, pl* **hylam** *or* **hylams** *usu cap* **1 a :** a people of southeastern China derived from intermarriage between the Chinese and the Li tribesmen of the island of Hainan **b :** a member of such people **2 :** the language of the Hylam people

hy·le \'hī(ˌ)lē\ *n* -s [LL, matter, fr. Gk *hylē* wood, matter; perh. akin to OE *syll* sill — more at SILL] *philos* **:** whatever receives form or determination from outside itself **:** MATTER; *esp* **:** CHAOS 2

hy·le·an \(')hī¦lēən\ *adj* [prob. fr. G *Hyläa*, region of tropical rain forest in the basin of the Amazon river in So. America (fr. Gk *Hylaia*, forested region on what is now the Dnieper river in the Ukraine, fr. *hylaia*, fem. of *hylaios* of the forest, wild, fr. *hylē* wood, forest) + E *-an*] **:** covered with forest **:** WOODED

hy·leg \'hīˌleg\ *n* -s [modif. of Per *hailāj* material body] **:** the astrological position of the planets at the time of birth

hy·le·gi·a·cal \ˌhīlə¦jīəkəl\ *adj* [irreg. fr. *hyleg*] **:** of or relating to a hyleg

hy·le·mya \ˌhīlə'mīə\ *n, cap* [NL, fr. Gk *hylē* wood, forest + *mya, myia* fly — more at MIDGE] **:** a genus of two-winged flies (family Anthomyiidae) including numerous species having larvae that are maggots (as the onion maggot) boring in economically important plants

hy·lic \'hīlik\ *adj* [LL *hylicus*, fr. Gk *hylikos*, fr. *hylē* wood, matter + *-ikos* -ic] **1 :** of or relating to matter **:** MATERIAL, CORPOREAL ⟨~ wants⟩ **2 :** of or relating to the lowest of the three Gnostic divisions of mankind — compare ²PSYCHIC 3, ²PNEUMATIC 1

hy·lid \'hīləd\ *n* -s [NL *Hylidae*] **:** a tree toad of the family Hylidae

hy·li·dae \'hīləˌdē\ *n pl, cap* [NL, fr. *Hyla*, type genus + *-idae*] **:** a large family of predominantly arboreal rather slender-bodied frogs with elongated hind limbs, rounded adhesive disks on the digits, and the thumbs not enlarged in the male — see TREE TOAD

hy·lob·a·tes \hī'läbəˌtēz\ *n, cap* [NL, fr. *hyl-* + *-bates*] **:** a genus of primates comprising the typical gibbons that with the siamang and extinct related forms make up a subfamily of Pongidae or in some classifications a separate family

hy·lo·cereus \ˌhīlō+\ *n, cap* [NL, fr. *hyl-* + *Cereus*] **:** a genus of climbing sometimes epiphytic tropical American cacti with angular stems and mostly white very showy fragrant flowers — see NIGHT-BLOOMING CEREUS

hy·lo·cich·la \ˌhīlō'sikla\ *n, cap* [NL, fr. *hyl-* + Gk *kichlē* thrush; akin to Gk *chelidōn* swallow — more at CELANDINE] **:** a genus of thrushes containing the wood thrush, hermit thrush, veery, and other American species

hy·lo·co·mi·um \-'kōmēəm\ *n, cap* [NL, fr. *hyl-* + Gk *komē* hair + NL *-ium*] **:** a small genus of mostly feathery mosses of the family Hypnaceae

hy·lo·des \hī'lō(ˌ)dēz\ [NL, fr. *Hyla* + *-odes*] *syn of* ELEUTHERODACTYLUS

hy·loid \'hīˌlȯid\ *adj* [NL *Hyla* + E *-oid*] **:** resembling or belonging to the family Hylidae

hy·lo·mor·phic *also* **hy·le·mor·phic** \ˌhīlə¦mȯrfik\ *adj* [*hylomorphism, hylemorphism* + *-ic*] **:** of, relating to, or based on hylomorphism

hy·lo·mor·phism *also* **hy·le·mor·phism** \ˌ⁼⁼'mȯ(r)ˌfizəm\ *n* -s [*hylomorphism* fr. *hyl-* + *morph-* + *-ism; hylemorphism* alter. (influenced by Gk *hylē* matter) of *hylomorphism*] *Aristotelianism* **:** a doctrine that corporeal beings consist of a combination of Aristotelian forms and primordial matter

hy·lo·mor·phous \¦⁼⁼mȯrfəs\ *adj* [*hyl-* + *-morphous*] **:** having a material form

hy·lo·mys \'hīləˌmis\ [NL, fr. *hyl-* + *-mys*] *syn of* ECHINOSOREX

hy·loph·a·gous \(')hī¦läfəgəs\ *adj* [*hyl-* + *-phagous*] *zool* **:** eating wood ⟨~ insects⟩

hy·lo·theism \¦hīlō+\ *n* [*hyl-* + *theism*] **:** a doctrine equating God with matter — compare MATERIALISM

hy·lo·the·ist \"+\ *n* [*hyl-* + *-theist*] **:** an advocate of hylotheism — **hy·lo·the·istic** \"+\ *adj*

hy·lot·o·mous \(')hī¦lädəməs\ *adj* [Gk *hylotomos*, fr. *hyl-* + *tomos* cutting, sharp, fr. *temnein* to cut — more at TOME] *zool* **:** cutting wood ⟨~ insects⟩

hy·lo·zo·ic \¦hīlə¦zōik\ *adj* [*hyl-* + *zo-* + *-ic*] **:** of or relating to hylozoism

hy·lo·zo·ism \ˌ⁼⁼'zōˌizəm\ *n* [*hyl-* + *zo-* + *-ism*] **:** a doctrine that all matter is animated — used esp. of the theories of early Greek philosophers

hy·lo·zo·ist \ˌhīlə'zōəst\ *n* -s [*hyl-* + *zo-* + *-ist*] **:** an advocate of hylozoism

hy·lo·zo·is·tic \¦hīləzō¦istik\ *adj* [*hyl-* + *zo-* + *-istic*] **:** of, relating to, or having the characteristics of hylozoism or the hylozoists

¹hy·men \'hīmən\ *n* -s [L, fr. Gk *hymēn* wedding song, fr. *Hymēn* Hymen, god of marriage (lit., a wedding cry); perh. akin to Gk *hymnos* hymn, song of praise] **1** *archaic* **:** MARRIAGE **2** *archaic* **:** a wedding song

²hymen \"\ *n* -s [LL, fr. Gk *hymēn* membrane, caul; prob. akin to Skt *syūman* band, thong, L *suere* to sew — more at SEW] **:** a fold of mucous membrane partly closing the orifice of the vagina — called also *maidenhead*

hymen- *or* **hymeno-** *comb form* [NL, fr. Gk, fr. *hymen-*, *hymēn* membrane, caul] **:** hymen **:** membrane ⟨*hymeno*tomy⟩ ⟨*Hymeno*ptera⟩

hy·me·naea \ˌhēmə'nēə\ *n, cap* [NL, prob. fr. L *hymenaeus* wedding song, marriage] **:** a genus of tropical American timber trees (family Leguminosae) having large white or purplish flowers in panicles and pinnate leaves consisting of a single pair of large thick glossy leaflets — see COURBARIL

hy·me·na·ic meter \¦⁼⁼¦nāik-\ *n* [LL *hymenaicum metrum*] **:** a dactylic dimeter — symbol -⏑⏑|-⏑⏑

hy·men·al \'hīmənᵊl\ *adj* [²*hymen* + *-al*] **:** of, relating to, or affecting the hymen

¹hy·me·ne·al \¦hīmə¦nēəl\ *adj* [L *hymenaeus* marriage, wedding song (fr. Gk *hymenaios*, fr. *Hymen-, Hymēn* Hymen) + E *-al*] **:** of or relating to marriage **:** NUPTIAL — **hy·me·ne·al·ly** \-ēəlē, -li\ *adv*

²hymeneal \"\ *n* -s **1 hymeneals** *pl, archaic* **:** NUPTIALS **2** *archaic* **:** a wedding hymn

hymenean *n* -s [L *hymenaeus* wedding, wedding song + E *-an*] *obs* **:** ¹HYMEN

hy·me·ni·al \(')hī¦mēnēəl\ *adj* [NL *hymenium* + E *-al*] **:** of or relating to the hymenium

hymenial layer *n* **:** HYMENIUM

hy·me·nif·er·ous \ˌhīmə¦nif(ə)rəs\ *adj* [NL *hymenium* + E *-ferous*] **:** having a hymenium

hy·me·ni·um \hī'mēnēəm\ *n, pl* **hyme·nia** \-nēə\ *or* **hymeniums** [NL, fr. *hymen-* + *-ium*] **:** a spore-bearing layer in fungi or their fruiting bodies (as apothecia or the sporophores of agarics) consisting of a group of asci or basidia often interspersed with paraphyses, setae, and other sterile structures

hy·me·no·cal·lis \ˌhīmənō'kaləs\ *n, cap* [NL, fr. *hymen-* + *-callis* (fr. Gk *kallos* beauty); fr. the delicate texture of the perianth — more at CALLI-] **:** a genus of tropical and subtropical American bulbous plants (family Amaryllidaceae) with linear basal leaves and umbels of usu. white or pink but sometimes yellow tubular flowers — compare PERUVIAN DAFFODIL

hy·me·no·chae·te \-'kēd·(ˌ)ē\ *n, cap* [NL fr. *hymen-* + Gk *chaitē* long flowing hair — more at CHAETA] **:** a genus of fungi (family Thelephoraceae) having a corky or leathery sporophore and a hymenium which appears downy because of the many simple cystidia projecting from it — see BROWN ROOT DISEASE

hy·me·no·gas·tra·ce·ae \-(ˌ)nōˌga'strāsēˌē\ *n pl, cap* [NL, fr. *Hymenogastr-*, *Hymenogaster*, type genus (fr. *hymen-* + *-gaster*) + *-aceae*] **:** a family of basidiomycetous fungi of the order Hymenogastrales forming subterranean irregularly globose sporophores — see FALSE TRUFFLE, RHIZOPOGON

hy·me·no·gas·tra·les \-ā(ˌ)lēz\ *n pl, cap* [NL, fr. *Hymenogastr-*, *Hymenogaster*, genus of fungi + *-ales*] **:** an order of gasteromycetous fungi (subclass Homobasidiomycetes) having a distinct basidiocarp with a usu. fleshy or waxy gleba which remains closed at least until after the basidia have discharged the basidiospores

hy·men·oid \'hīməˌnȯid\ *adj* [Gk *hymenoeidēs*, fr. *hymeno-* hymen- + *-eidēs* -oid] **:** MEMBRANOUS

hy·me·no·lep·i·did \¦hīmənō¦lepəˌdid\ *adj* [NL *Hymenolepididae*, family of tapeworms, fr. *Hymenolepid-*, *Hymenolepis*, type genus + *-idae*] **:** of or relating to the genus *Hymenolepis* or family Hymenolepididae

hy·me·nol·e·pis \ˌ⁼⁼'näləpəs\ *n, cap* [NL, fr. *hymen-* + *-lepis*] **:** a genus of small taenioid tapeworms (type of the family Hymenolepididae) including numerous comparatively innocuous parasites (as the dwarf tapeworm of man) of birds and mammals that usu. require insect intermediate hosts but may be able in some cases (as the dwarf tapeworm) to complete the life cycle in a single host by means of a hexacanth which hatches in the intestine, invades a villus, and there develops into a cysticercoid which ultimately escapes and develops into an adult tapeworm in the lumen of the intestine

hy·me·no·lichenes \¦hīmənō+\ *n pl, cap* [NL, fr. *hymen-* + *Lichenes*] **:** a subgroup of Lichenes comprising lichens in which the fungal component is a hymenomycete and being coextensive with the group Basidiolichenes

hy·me·no·my·cete \-ˌmīˌsēt, -ˌmī¦sēt\ *n* -s [NL *Hymenomycetes*] **1 :** a fungus of the order Agaricales **2 :** a fungus having a fruiting body with a definite hymenium

hy·me·no·my·ce·tes \-ˌmīˌsēd·(ˌ)ēz\ *n pl, cap* [NL, fr. *hymen-* + *-mycetes*] *in some classifications* **:** a subclass of Basidiomycetes coextensive with the order Agaricales

hy·me·no·my·ce·tous \-sēd·əs\ *adj* [*hymen-* + *-mycetous*] **:** of, relating to, or being a hymenomycete **:** having a hymenium

hy·meno·phore \hī'menəˌfō(ə)r, 'hīmənō,-\ *also* **hy·me·noph·o·rum** \ˌhīmə'näfərəm\ *n, pl* **hymenophores** \-ˌfō(ə)rz\ *also* **hymenopho·ra** \-äf(ə)rə\ [NL *hymenophorum*, fr. *hymeno-* (irreg. fr. *hymenium*) + *-phorum*] **1 :** the hymenium-bearing portion of the sporophore in fungi **2 :** SPOROPHORE

hy·me·no·phyl·la·ce·ae \ˌhīmə(ˌ)nōfə'lāsēˌē\ *n pl, cap* [NL, fr. *Hymenophyllum*, type genus + *-aceae*] **:** a family of ferns having delicate fronds with sessile sporangia on a receptacle resembling a bristle and surrounded by a cup-shaped, tubular, or 2-valved involucre — **hy·me·no·phyl·la·ceous** \¦⁼⁼(ˌ)⁼⁼¦lāshəs\ *adj*

hy·me·no·phyl·li·tes \ˌ⁼⁼(ˌ)⁼fə'līd·(ˌ)ēz\ *n pl, cap* [NL, fr. *Hymenophyllum*, genus of ferns + *-ites* -ite] **:** a genus of fossil ferns of the Carboniferous and perhaps of more recent age bearing a superficial resemblance to the existing genus *Hymenophyllum*

hy·me·no·phyl·lum \ˌ⁼⁼⁼'filəm\ *n, cap* [NL, fr. *hymen-* + *-phyllum*] **:** a genus (the type of the family Hymenophyllaceae) of tropical hygrophytic and usu. epiphytic ferns distinguished from *Trichomanes* by having the valves of the involucre bearing the sporangia separate

hy·me·nop·ter \¦hīmə¦näptə(r)\ *n* -s [NL *Hymenoptera*] **:** HYMENOPTERON

hy·me·nop·tera \-'näptərə\ *n pl, cap* [NL, fr. Gk, neut. pl. of *hymenopteros* membrane-winged, fr. *hymeno-* (fr. *hymen-*, *hymēn* membrane, caul) + *-pteros* -pterous — more at HYMEN] **:** an extensive order of highly specialized insects that include the bees, wasps, ants, ichneumons, sawflies, gall wasps, and related forms, that often associate in large colonies with complex social organization, that have usu. four membranous wings typically with a thickened dark spot near the anterior edge of the forewings, the abdomen generally borne on a slender pedicel, and in the female complex ovipositors at the posterior end of the body which may be modified into sawing, boring, or piercing organs or in one group converted into a sting, and that undergo complete metamorphosis, the larva being usu. a footless grub — **hy·me·nop·ter·ous** \¦⁼⁼¦⁼t(ə)rəs\ *adj*

hy·me·nop·ter·ist \ˌ⁼⁼'⁼tərəst\ *n* -s *or* **hy·me·nop·ter·ol·o·gist** \ˌ⁼⁼ˌ⁼⁼'räləjəst\ *n* -s **:** a specialist in the Hymenoptera

hy·me·nop·ter·ol·o·gy \ˌ⁼⁼ˌ⁼⁼'räləjē\ *n* -ES [ISV *hymenoptero-* (fr. NL *Hymenoptera*) + *-logy*; prob. orig. formed as F *hyménoptérologie*] **:** a branch of entomology concerned with Hymenoptera

hy·me·nop·ter·on \ˌ⁼⁼'⁼təˌrän, -ˌrən\ *also* **hy·me·nop·ter·an** \-tərən\ *n, pl* **hymenop·tera** \-tərə\ [*hymenopteron* fr. NL *Hymenopteron*, sing. of *Hymenoptera*; *hymenopteran* fr. NL *Hymenoptera* + E *-an*] **:** one of the Hymenoptera

hy·men·ot·o·my \ˌhīmə'näd·əmē\ *n* -ES [ISV *hymen-* + *-tomy*; prob. orig. formed as F *hyménotomie*] **:** surgical incision of the hymen

hymens *pl of* HYMEN

hy·met·ti·an \(')hī¦med·ēən\ *also* **hy·met·tic** \-d·ik\ *adj, usu cap* [L *Hymettius* (fr. *Hymettus*, mountain near Athens, Greece fr. Gk *Hymēttos*) + E *-an* or *-ic*] **:** of or relating to Mount Hymettus ⟨*Hymettian* marble⟩ ⟨*Hymettian* honey⟩

¹hymn \'him\ *n* -s *often attrib* [ME *ymne, hympne*, partly fr. OE *ymen, hymen*, fr. L *hymnus* and partly fr. MF *himpne*, fr. ML *hympnus*, fr. L *hymnus* and partly fr. OF *ymne*, fr. ML *ymnus*, fr. L *hymnus*; L *hymnus* fr. Gk *hymnos* song of praise] **1 a :** a song of praise to God ⟨grows into the chorus . . . with its triumphal ~: Lift up your heads, O ye gates —J.P.Larsen⟩ **b :** a metrical composition adapted for singing in a religious service ⟨collection of ~s, carols, anthems, gospel songs —*Saturday Rev.*⟩ **2 :** a song of praise or joy ⟨in jolly ~s they praise the god of wine —John Dryden⟩ **3 :** something resembling a hymn esp. in expressing praise **:** PAEAN ⟨this prose ~ of contentment in simple and external things —Douglas Bush⟩ ⟨the plot of this ~ to American domesticity —Jack Weeks⟩ ⟨painted a ~ to the wonder of light —Lewis Mumford⟩

²hymn \"\ *vb* **hymned; hymned; hymning** \'himiŋ *sometimes* -mniŋ\ **hymns** *vt* **:** to sing the praises of **:** EXTOL ⟨still ~s his love of the earth and proclaims his faith in the race that inhabits it —B.R.Redman⟩; *specif* **:** to worship in song ~ *vi* **:** SING ⟨the lark ~s on high⟩; *specif* **:** to sing a hymn ⟨the choir ~s softly in the chancel⟩

¹hym·nal \'himnəl\ *n* -s [ME *hymnale*, fr. ML *hymnale, hymnare*, fr. L *hymnus* hymn + *-ale* (neut. of *-alis* -al) or *-are* (neut. of *-aris* -ar)] **:** a collection of church hymns **:** HYMNBOOK

²hymnal \"\ *adj* [L *hymnus* hymn + E *-al*] **:** of or relating to a hymn ⟨a ~ rite⟩

hym·na·ry \'himnərē\ *also* **hym·nar·i·um** \him'na(a)rēəm\ *n, pl* **hymnaries** \-nərēz\ *also* **hymnar·ia** \-na(a)rēə\ [ML *hymnarium*, fr. L *hymnus* hymn + *-arium* -ary] **:** ¹HYMNAL

hymn board *also* **hymn tablet** *n* **:** a usu. wooden tablet that holds removable numerals and is hung on a wall or pillar of a church to inform the congregation of the numbers of the hymns and responsive readings for a service of worship

hymn board

hymnbook \'⁼ˌ⁼\ *n* **:** ¹HYMNAL

hymner \'himə(r), -mnə-\ *n* -s **:** one that sings hymns

hym·nic \'himnik\ *adj* **:** of, relating to, or having the characteristics of a hymn ⟨~ praise⟩ ⟨~ prose⟩

hym·nist \-nəst\ *n* -s **:** a writer of hymns

hymn·less \'himləs\ *adj* **:** lacking a hymn

hymnlike \'⁼ˌ⁼\ *adj* **:** resembling or suggesting a hymn

hym·no·dist \'himnədəst\ *n* -s [LL *hymnodia* hymnody + E *-ist*] **:** HYMNIST

hym·no·dy \-dē\ *n* -ES [LL *hymnodia*, fr. Gk *hymnōidia*, fr. *hymnōidein* to sing a hymn or song of praise (fr. *hymnos* hymn, song of praise + *aeidein* to sing) + *-ia* -y — more at ODE] **1 :** the singing of hymns **2 :** the writing of hymns ⟨a pioneer in Byzantine ~, whose compositions were to come into extensive use —K.S.Latourette⟩ **3 a :** a study of hymns and their composition ⟨an authority on ~⟩ **b :** a body of hymns of a specified kind or period ⟨~ of the early church⟩

hym·nog·ra·pher \him'nägrəfə(r)\ *n* -s [Gk *hymnographos* (fr. *hymnos* hymn + *-graphos* -graph) + E *-er*] **1 :** a writer on hymnography **2 :** HYMNIST

hym·nog·ra·phy \-fē\ *n* -ES [*hymnographer* + *-y*] **1 :** an exposition and bibliography of hymns **2 :** HYMNODY

hym·no·log·ic \¦himnə¦läjik\ *or* **hym·no·log·i·cal** \-jəkəl\ *adj* **:** of or relating to hymnology — **hym·no·log·i·cal·ly** \-jək(ə)lē\ *adv*

hym·nol·o·gist \him'näləjəst\ *n* -s **:** HYMNIST

hym·nol·o·gy \-jē\ *n* -ES [Gk *hymnologia* singing of hymns, fr. *hymnos* song of praise, hymn + *-logia* -logy] **:** HYMNODY

hymns *pl of* HYMN, *pres 3d sing of* HYMN

hyne \'hīn\ *adv* [ME, prob. alter. of ME (northern dial.) *hethen*, fr. ON *hethan* hence; akin to OE *heonan* hence — more at HENCE] *now dial Eng* **:** HENCE

hy·no·bi·idae \ˌhīnō'bīəˌdē\ *n pl, cap* [NL, fr. *Hynobius*, type genus (fr. *hyno-* — perh. fr. Gk *hynis* plowshare — + NL *-bius*) + *-idae*] **:** a small family of primitive Asiatic salamanders (suborder Cryptobranchoidea) sometimes included in the Ambystomidae from which they can be distinguished by more adult skull characters, smaller size, and short saccular egg pouches

¹hyo- — see HY-

²hyo- *comb form* [L&Gk; L, fr. Gk, fr. *hys* swine — more at SOW (swine)] **:** derived from or related to swine ⟨*hyo*deoxycholic⟩

hyo·branchial \¦hīō+\ *adj* [*hy-* + *branchial*] **:** of, relating to, or joining the hyoid and branchial arches

hyo·bran·chi·um \ˌhīō'braŋkēəm\ *n, pl* **hyobran·chia** \-ēə\ [NL, fr. *hy-* + *-branchium* (fr. Gk *branchion* gill) — more at BRANCHIA] **:** a typically somewhat Y-shaped bone that serves to support the tongue and tongue muscles in a snake and is considered to result from fusion of the hyoid and remnants of the branchial arches

hyo·deoxycholic acid *or* **hyo·desoxycholic acid** \¦hī-(ˌ)ō+ . . . -\ *n* [ISV ²*hyo-* + *deoxy-* or *desoxy-* + *cholic*] **:** a crystalline bile acid $C_{22}H_{37}(OH)_2COOH$ found in the bile of the pig and wild boar; 3,6-dihydroxy-cholanic acid

hy·o·don [NL, fr. *hy-* + *-odon*] *syn of* HIODON

hyo·epiglottic *also* **hyo·epiglottidean** \¦hī(ˌ)ō+\ *adj* [*hy-* + *epiglottic* or *epiglottidean*] **:** connecting the hyoid bone and epiglottis

hyo·glossal \¦hīō+\ *adj* [*hy-* + *glossal*] **1 :** of or relating to the tongue and hyoid arch **2** [NL *hyoglossus* + E *-al*] **:** of or relating to the hyoglossus

hyo·glos·sus \ˌ⁼⁼'gläsəs, -lȯs-\ *n, pl* **hyoglos·si** \-ˌsī\ [NL, fr. *hy-* + *-glossus* (fr. Gk *glōssa* tongue) — more at GLOSS] **:** a flat muscle on each side of the tongue connecting it with the body and greater cornu of the hyoid

hy·oid \'hīˌȯid\ *also* **hy·oi·dal** \(')hī¦ȯidᵊl\ *or* **hy·oi·de·an** \-dēən\ *adj* [*hyoid* fr. NL *hyoides* hyoid bone; *hyoidal* fr. *hyoid* + *-al; hyoidean* fr. NL *hyoides* + E *-an*] **1 :** of, relating to, or being the hyoid bone **2 :** of, relating to, or being the second postoral visceral arch from which the hyoid bone of the higher vertebrates is in part formed

hyoid bone *also* **hyoid** *n* -s [NL *hyoides*, fr. Gk *hyoeidēs*, adj., shaped like the letter upsilon (Υ, υ), being the hyoid bone, fr. *hyo-* (fr. *y, hy* upsilon) + *-eidēs* -oid] **:** a bone or complex of bones situated at the base of the tongue and developed from the second and third visceral arches, supporting the tongue and its muscles, and being in man a U-shaped structure placed horizontally with the convexity forward, two large cornua directed backward, and two lesser cornua directed upward and backward

hy·ol·i·thes \hī'äləˌthēz\ *n, cap* [NL, prob. fr. *hy-* + *-lithes* (fr. Gk *lithos* stone)] **:** a genus of Paleozoic swimming pteropod mollusks esp. common in the Cambrian — **hy·ol·i·thid** \-ˌthəd\ *adj or n*

hyo·mandibula \¦hī(ˌ)ō+\ *n* -s [NL, fr. *hy-* + LL *mandibula*] **1 :** the hyomandibular arch **2 :** a bone or cartilage derived from the hyomandibular arch

¹hyo·mandibular \"+\ *adj* [*hy-* + *mandibular*] **:** of or derived from the hyoid arch and mandible; *specif* **:** being or relating to the dorsal segment of the hyoid arch

²hyomandibular \"\ *n* -s **:** a bone or cartilage derived from the dorsal hyoid arch, being part of the articulating mechanism of the lower jaw in fishes, and forming the columella or stapes of the ear of higher vertebrates

hyo·mental \¦hīō+\ *adj* [*hy-* + *mental* (of the chin)] **:** of or relating to the hyoid bone and chin

hyo·plastron \"+\ *n, pl* **hyoplastra** [*hy-* + *plastron*] **:** the second lateral bony plate in the plastron of most turtles — called also *hyosternum*

hyo·scapular \"+\ *adj* [*hy-* + *scapular*] **:** of or relating to the hyoid bone and scapula

hy·o·scine \'hīəˌsēn, -ˌsən\ *n* -s [ISV *hyosc-* (fr. NL *Hyoscyamus*, genus that produces it) + *-ine*; orig. formed as G *hyoscin*] **:** SCOPOLAMINE; *esp* **:** the levorotatory form of scopolamine

hy·o·scy·a·mine \ˌhīə'sīəˌmēn, -mən\ *n* -s [G *hyoscyamin*, fr. NL *Hyoscyamus* (genus that produces it) + G *-in* -ine] **:** a poisonous crystalline alkaloid $C_{17}H_{23}NO_3$ known in three optically isomeric forms **:** the ester of tropine and tropic acid; *esp* **:** the levorotatory form of this alkaloid that readily yields the racemic form atropine (as by treatment with alkali), that occurs in henbane, belladonna, and various other plants of the family Solanaceae (as species of *Datura*), and that is more active than atropine in most pharmacological effects and is used similarly (as in sedation and in relieving spasms)

hy·o·scy·a·mus \-məs\ *n* [NL, fr. L, henbane, fr. Gk *hyoskyamos*, lit., swine's bean, fr. *hyos* (gen. of *hys* swine) + *kyamos* bean — more at SOW (swine)] **1** *cap* **:** a genus of poisonous Eurasian herbs (family Solanaceae) having simple leaves, somewhat irregular flowers, and circumscissile capsular fruit — see HENBANE **2** -ES **:** the dried leaves of the henbane containing the alkaloids hyoscyamine and scopolamine and used as an antispasmodic and sedative

hyo·sternal \¦hīō+\ *adj* [*hy-* + *sternal*] **1 :** of or relating to the hyoid bone and sternum **2** [NL *hyosternum* + E *-al*] **:** of or relating to the hyosternum

hyo·sternum \"+\ *n, pl* **hyosterna** [NL, fr. *hy-* + *sternum*] **:** HYOPLASTRON

hyo·strongylus \"+\ *n, cap* [NL, fr. ²*hyo-* + *Strongylus* (genus of parasitic nematode worms)] **:** a genus of nematode worms (family Trichostrongylidae) including the common small red stomach worm (*H. rubidus*) of swine

hy·o·sty·lic \¦hīō¦stīlik\ *adj* [*hy-* + *-stylic*] **:** having the jaws connected with the cranium by the hyomandibular ⟨a large majority of fishes are ~⟩ — **hyo·sty·ly** \'⁼⁼ˌ⁼lē\ *n* -ES

hy·o·there \'hīōˌthi(ə)r\ *n* -s [NL *Hyotherium*] **:** a member of the genus *Hyotherium*

hy·o·the·ri·um \ˌhīō'thirēəm\ *n, cap* [NL, fr. ²*hyo-* + *-therium*] **:** a genus of swine of the Miocene and lower Pliocene on the direct ancestral line of the modern wild boar and domestic swine

hyo·thyreoid \¦hīō+\ *adj* [*hy-* + *thyreoid*] **:** THYROHYOID

hyo·thyroid \"+\ *adj* [*hy-* + *thyroid*] **:** THYROHYOID

hyp *n* -s [by shortening] *obs* **:** HYPOCHONDRIA

hyp- — see HYPO-

hyp *abbr* hypothesis; hypothetical

hyp·abyssal \¦hip+\ *adj* [ISV *hypo-* + *abyssal*; orig. formed as G *hypabyssisch*] **:** of or relating to a fine-grained igneous rock intermediate in texture between the plutonites and extrusive rocks and usu. formed at a moderate distance below the surface

hyp·acu·sic \¦hipə¦kyüsik, -kü-\ *or* **hyp·acou·sic** \-kü-\ *adj* [NL *hypacusia, hypacousia* defective hearing (fr. *hypo-* + *-acusia, -acousia*) + E *-ic*] **:** slightly deaf — used esp. of partial deafness associated with lessened irritability of the auditory nerve

hy·pae·thral \hī'pēthrəl, hə'-\ *adj* [L *hypaethrus* in the open air, uncovered (fr. Gk *hypaithros*, fr. *hypo-* + *-aithros* — fr. *aithēr* ether, heaven, air) + E *-al* — more at ETHER] **1** *of an ancient temple* **:** having a roofless central space — opposed to *cleithral* **2 :** open to the sky **3 :** OUTDOOR

hyp·algesia \¦hip, ¦hīp+\ *also* **hyp·al·gia** \hi'palj(ē)ə, hī'-\ *n* [NL, fr. *hypo-* + *algesia* or *-algia*] **:** diminished sensitivity to pain

hyp·al·lac·tic \¦hipə¦laktik, ¦hīp-\ *adj* [Gk *hypallaktikos*, fr. (assumed) Gk *hypallaktos* (verbal of Gk *hypallassein* to interchange, exchange) + Gk *-icos* -ic] **:** of, relating to, or of the nature of hypallage

hy·pal·la·ge \hi'palə(,)jē, hī'-\ *n* -s [LL, fr. Gk *hypallagē*, lit., interchange, fr. *hypallassein* to interchange, fr. *hypo-* + *allassein* to change (fr. *allos* other) — more at ELSE] **:** interchange in syntactic relationship between two terms (as in "you are lost to joy" for "joy is lost to you")

hy·pan·dri·um \hi'pandrēəm, hī'-\ *n, pl* **hypan·dria** \-ēə\ [NL, fr. *hypo-* + *andr-* + *-ium*] **:** a plate or modified area underlying the genitalia of a male insect; *esp* **:** the fused coxites of the ninth abdominal segment when these form a ventral covering plate for the genitalia

hy·pan·thi·al \(')hi¦pan(t)thēəl, (')hī¦-\ *adj* **:** of, relating to, or of the nature of a hypanthium

hy·pan·thi·um \≈'≈thēəm\ *n, pl* **hypan·thia** \-ēə\ [NL, fr. *hypo-* + *anth-* + *-ium*] **:** an enlargement of the usu. cup-shaped receptacle bearing on its rim the stamens, petals, and sepals of a flower and often enlarging and surrounding the fruits (as in the rose hip) — called also *calyx tube*

hy·pan·trum \hi'pan·trəm, hī'-\ *n, pl* **hypan·tra** \-rə\ [NL, fr. *hypo-* + LL *antrum* cavity in the body — more at ANTRUM] **:** a notch on the neural arch at the anterior ends of the vertebrae of various reptiles that articulates with the hyposphene — compare ZYGANTRUM

hy·pa·pan·te \,ēpə,pan'dē\ *n* -s *cap* [LL or LGk; LL *hypapante*, fr. LGk *hypapantē*, lit., meeting, fr. Gk *hypapantan* to meet, fr. *hypo-* + *apantan* to meet — more at APANTESIS] **:** a feast celebrated by the Eastern Orthodox Church on February 2 commemorating primarily the presentation of Jesus and his meeting Simeon and Anna in the temple and secondarily the purification of the Virgin Mary — compare CANDLEMAS

hyp·apophysis \¦hip, ¦hīp+\ *n, pl* **hypapophyses** [NL, fr. *hypo-* + *apophysis*] **:** a ventral process or element of a vertebra: as **a :** a hemal spine **b :** HYPOCENTRUM

hy·par·chic \(')hi¦pärkik, (')hī¦-\ *adj* [*hypo-* + *-archic* (as in *autarchic*)] **:** affected by adjacent genes — used of genes in mosaic tissues that do not manifest their effect if epistatic genes are present in adjacent tissues; compare AUTARCHIC

hyp·arterial \¦hip, ¦hīp+\ *adj* [*hypo-* + *arterial*] **:** situated below an artery — used of branches of the bronchi given off below the pulmonary artery; compare EPARTERIAL

hy·pas·pist \hi'paspəst\ *n* -s [Gk *hypaspistēs*, fr. *hypaspizein* to serve as shield bearer, fr. *hypo-* + *aspis* shield + *-izein* -ize — more at ASPID-] **:** SHIELD BEARER; *esp* **:** a Macedonian shield bearer

hyp·automorphic \¦hip, ¦hīp+\ *adj* [*hypo-* + *automorphic*] **1 :** HYPIDIOMORPHIC **2 :** SUBHEDRAL

hyp·axial \(')hip, (')hīp+\ *also* **hyp·axonic** \(¦)hip, (¦)hīp+\ *adj* [*hypaxial* fr. *hypo-* + *axial*; *hypaxonic* fr. *hypo-* + Gk *axon-, axōn* axle, axis + E *-ic* — more at AXIS] **:** beneath the axis of the vertebral column

hype \'hīp\ *n* -s [short for *hypodermic*] **1** *slang* **:** HYPODERMIC **2** *slang* **:** a narcotics addict

hy·per \'hīpə(r)\ *vi* -ED/-ING/-S [origin unknown] *chiefly NewEng* **:** BUSTLE, HURRY ⟨must ~ about —J.R.Lowell⟩

hyper- *prefix* [alter. (influenced by L *hyper-*) of ME *iper-*, fr. LL *hyper-*, fr. L, fr. Gk, fr. *hyper* — more at OVER] **1 :** over **:** above **:** beyond **:** SUPER- ⟨*hyper*barbarous⟩ ⟨*hyper*emphasis⟩ **2 :** overmuch **:** excessively **:** EXTRA- ⟨*hyper*critical⟩ ⟨*hyper*sensitive⟩ **3 a :** excessive in extent or quality ⟨*hyper*esthesia⟩ ⟨*hyper*emesis⟩ **b :** located above ⟨*hyper*apophysis⟩ **4** *in ancient Greek music* **a :** being the upper octave in a disdiapason ⟨*hyper*lydian⟩ **b** *of an interval* **:** measured upward ⟨*hyper*diapason⟩

hy·pera \'hīpərə\ *n, cap* [NL, fr. Gk *hypera* upper rope, brace (of a ship), fr. *hyper* above, over] **:** a large genus of small often mottled or hairy weevils whose legless larvae feed destructively on numerous crop plants (as legumes) and have ventral ridges that function as legs — compare ALFALFA WEEVIL, CLOVER LEAF WEEVIL

hy·per·acid \¦hīpə(r)+\ *adj* [*hyper-* + *acid*] **:** excessively acid **:** containing more than the normal amount of acid ⟨a ~ secretion⟩ — **hy·per·acidity** \"+\ *n* -ES

hy·per·active \"+\ *adj* [*hyper-* + *active*] **:** excessively or pathologically active

hy·per·adre·no·cor·ti·cism \,≈≈ə,drēnō'kȯ(r)d·ə,sizəm, -,drēn-\ *n* -S [*hyper-* + *adrenocortical* + *-ism*] **1 :** the presence of excess adrenocortical products in the body **2 :** the syndrome resulting from hyperadrenocorticism that is often a complication of medication with adrenal hormones, fractions, or stimulants

hyperaemia *var of* HYPEREMIA

hyperaesthesia *var of* HYPERESTHESIA

hy·per·algesia \¦hīpə(r)+\ *n* [NL, fr. *hyper-* + *algesia*] **:** increased sensitivity to pain or enhanced intensity of pain sensation — **hy·per·algesic** \"+\ *adj*

hy·per·apophysis \"+\ *n, pl* **hyperapophyses** [NL, fr. *hyper-* + *apophysis*] **:** a process on the dorsal side of a vertebra that projects laterally and backward

hy·per·azotemia \"+\ *n* [NL, fr. *hyper-* + *azotemia*] **:** the presence of abnormal amounts of nitrogenous substances in the blood

hy·per·bar·ic \¦hīpə(r)¦barik\ *adj* [*hyper-* + Gk *baros* weight + E *-ic* — more at GRIEVE] **:** having a specific gravity greater than that of cerebrospinal fluid — used of solutions for spinal anesthesia; opposed to *hypobaric*

hy·per·ba·ton \hī'pərbə,tän\ *n, pl* **hyperbatons** \-nz\ *or* **hyperba·ta** \-bəd·ə\ [L, fr. Gk, fr. neut. of *hyperbatos* transposed, inverted, fr. *hyperbainein* to step over, scale, fr. *hyper-* + *bainein* to step, walk — more at COME] **:** a transposition or inversion of idiomatic word order (as "echoed the hills" for "the hills echoed")

hy·per·bilirubinemia \¦hīpə(r)+\ *n* [NL, fr. *hyper-* + *bilirubinemia*] **:** BILIRUBINEMIA

hy·per·bo·la \hī'pərbələ, -pəb-,-pəib-\ *n, pl* **hyperbolas** \-ləz\ *or* **hyperbo·lae** \-,lē, -,lī\ [NL, fr. Gk *hyperbolē* hyperbola, excess] **:** a plane curve generated by a point so moving that its distance from a fixed point divided by its distance from a fixed line is a positive constant greater than 1 **:** a curve formed by a section of a right circular cone when the cutting plane makes a greater angle with the base than the cone's side makes

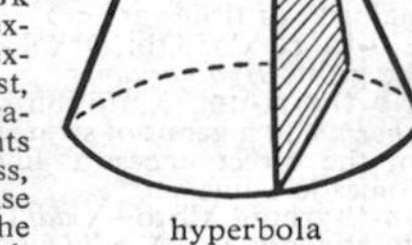

hyperbola

hy·per·bo·le \-(,)lē\ *n* -s [L, fr. Gk *hyperbolē* hyperbole, excess, extravagance, fr. *hyperballein* to exceed, fr. *hyper-* + *ballein* to cast, throw — more at DEVIL] **:** extravagant exaggeration that represents something as much greater or less, better or worse, or more intense than it really is or that depicts the impossible as actual (as "mile-high ice-cream cones") — opposed to *litotes*

¹hy·per·bol·ic \¦hīpə(r)¦bälik, -lēk\ *also* **hy·per·bol·i·cal** \-lәkəl, -lēk-\ *adj* [*hyperbolic* fr. LL *hyperbolicus*, fr. Gk *hyperbolikos* excessive, fr. *hyperbolē* hyperbole, excess + *-ikos* -ic; *hyperbolical*, alter. (influenced by L *hyper-*) of ME *iperbolicalle*, fr. LL *hyperbolicus* + ME *-alle, -al* -al] **:** of, characterized by, or given to hyperbole ⟨a ~ style⟩ — **hy·per·bol·i·cal·ly** \-lәk(ə)lē, -lēk-, -li\ *adv*

²hyperbolic \"\ *also* **hyperbolical** \"\ *adj* [*hyperbolic* fr. NL *hyperbola* + E *-ic*; *hyperbolical* fr. Gk *hyperbolē* hyperbola, excess + E *-ical*] **:** of, relating to, or analogous to a hyperbola

hyperbolic cosecant *n* **:** the hyperbolic function that is analogous to the cosecant and defined by the equation $\operatorname{csch} x = \frac{1}{\sinh x}$ — abbr. *csch*

hyperbolic cosine *n* **:** the hyperbolic function that is analogous to the cosine and defined by the equation $\cosh x = \frac{e^x + e^{-x}}{2}$ — abbr. *cosh*

hyperbolic cotangent *n* **:** the hyperbolic function that is analogous to the cotangent and defined by the equation $\coth x = \frac{\cosh x}{\sinh x}$ — abbr. *coth*

hyperbolic function *n* **:** any of a set of six functions analogous to the trigonometric functions but related to the hyperbola in a way similar to that in which trigonometric functions are related to a circle

hyperbolic geometry *n* **:** geometry that adopts all of Euclid's axioms except the parallel axiom, this being replaced by the axiom that through any point in a plane there pass more lines than one that do not intersect a given line in the plane

hyperbolic navigation *n* **:** a system of radio navigation (as loran) in which the time difference between receipt of signals from two stations of known position determines a line of position in the form of a hyperbola

hyperbolic paraboloid *n* **:** a saddle-shaped quadric surface whose sections by planes parallel to one coordinate plane are hyperbolas while those sections by planes parallel to the other two are parabolas if proper orientation of the coordinate axes is assumed

hyperbolic secant *n* **:** the hyperbolic function that is analogous to the secant and defined by the equation $\operatorname{sech} x = \frac{1}{\cosh x}$ — abbr. *sech*

hyperbolic sine *n* **:** the hyperbolic function that is analogous to the sine and defined by the equation $\sinh x = \frac{e^x - e^{-x}}{2}$ — abbr. *sinh*

hyperbolic tangent *n* **:** the hyperbolic function that is analogous to the tangent and defined by the equation $\tanh x = \frac{\sinh x}{\cosh x}$ — abbr. *tanh*

hy·per·bo·lism \hī'pərbə,lizəm, -pəb-,-pəib-\ *n* -s [*hyperbole* + *-ism*] **:** HYPERBOLE

hy·per·bo·list \-ləst\ *n* -s **:** a user of hyperbole ⟨humorists and ~s —John Hersey⟩

hy·per·bo·lize \-,līz\ *vb* -ED/-ING/-S *vi* **:** to indulge in hyperbole ~ *vt* **:** to exaggerate to a hyperbolic degree ⟨~ the esthetic modes of the moment —*Times Lit. Supp.*⟩ ⟨portions of this account have been *hyperbolized* —John Mendelsohn⟩

hy·per·bo·loid \-,lȯid\ *n* -s [NL *hyperbola* + E *-oid*] **:** a quadric surface whose sections by planes parallel to one coordinate plane are ellipses while those sections by planes parallel to the other two are hyperbolas if proper orientation of the coordinate axes is assumed — **hy·per·bo·loi·dal** \≈¦≈≈¦lȯid°l\ *adj*

hyperboloid of revolution : the surface generated by a hyperbola rotating about one of its axes

¹hy·per·bo·re·al \¦hīpə(r)¦bōrēəl, -bȯr-\ *adj* [L *Hyperborei* + E *-al*] *archaic* **:** HYPERBOREAN

¹hy·per·bo·re·an \-ēən, -,bə¦rē-\ *adj* [L *Hyperborei*, ancient legendary people living in the far north (fr. Gk *Hyperboreoi*, *Hyperboreioi*, fr. *hyper-* + *boreioi*, masc. pl. of *boreios* northern, of the north wind, fr. *Boreas* north, northwind) + E *-an* — more at BOREAS] **1 :** of, relating to, or inhabiting an extreme northern region **:** FRIGID, FROZEN ⟨drags us out of our ~ gloom into the South —John Davenport⟩ **2 :** of or relating to any of the arctic peoples of Asia or No. America

²hyperborean \"\ *n* -s *often cap* **1 :** a member of an arctic people (as the Chukchi and Koryak of northeastern Asia and the Eskimo of No. America) **2 :** one who lives in a cool northern climate ⟨we are *Hyperboreans* — we know well enough how far off we live —W.A.Kaufmann⟩

hy·per·brachycephal \¦hīpə(r)+\ *n* [*hyper-* + *brachycephal*] **:** a hyperbrachycephalic person

hy·per·brachycephalic \"+\ *adj* [*hyper-* + *brachycephalic*] **:** having a very round or broad head with a cephalic index of over 85

hy·per·brachycephaly \"+\ *n* **:** the quality or state of being hyperbrachycephalic

hy·per·brachycranial *or* **hy·per·brachycranic** \"+\ *adj* [*hyper-* + *brachycranial* or *brachycranic*] **:** having a very round or broad skull with a cranial index of 85 to 90

hy·per·brachycrany \"+\ *n* [ISV *hyper-* + *brachycrany*] **:** the quality or state of being hyperbrachycranial

hy·per·brachyskelic \"+\ *adj* [*hyper-* + *brachyskelic*] **:** having the length of the legs less than three-fourths that of the trunk with a skelic index below 75

hy·per·cal·ce·mia *also* **hy·per·cal·cae·mia** \,hīpə(r),kal'sēmēə\ *n* [NL, fr. *hyper-* + *calcemia, calcaemia* calcium in the blood (fr. *calc-* + *-emia, -aemia*)] **:** an excess of calcium in the blood — **hy·per·cal·ce·mic** \¦≈≈¦≈¦sēmik\ *adj*

hy·per·cap·nia \,hīpə(r)'kapnēə\ *n* [NL, fr. *hyper-* + *-capnia*] **:** the presence of excessive amounts of carbon dioxide in the blood — **hy·per·cap·nic** \¦≈≈¦≈nik\ *adj*

hy·per·catalectic \¦≈≈+\ *adj* [LL *hypercatalecticus*, fr. *hypercatalectus* (fr. Gk *hyperkatalēktos*, fr. *hyper-* + *katalēktos* catalectic) + *-icus* -ic — more at CATALECTIC] **:** of, relating to, or exhibiting hypercatalexis

hy·per·catalexis \"+\ *n* [NL, fr. *hyper-* + *catalexis*] **:** occurrence of an additional syllable at the end of a line of verse after the line is metrically complete; *esp* **:** occurrence of a syllable after the last complete dipody in verse measured by dipodies

hy·per·cathexis \"+\ *n* [NL, fr. *hyper-* + *cathexis*] **:** excessive concentration of desire upon a particular object

hy·per·ce·men·to·sis \,hīpə(r),sē,men·'tōsəs\ *n, pl* **hyper·cemento·ses** \-ō,sēz\ [NL, fr. *hyper-* + *cementum* + *-osis*] **:** excessive formation of cementum at the root of a tooth

hy·per·chamaerrhine \¦hīpə(r)+\ *adj* [ISV *hyper-* + *chamaerrhine*; orig. formed as G *hyperchamärrhin*] **:** having a very short broad nose with a nasal index of 58 or above

hy·per·chamaerrhiny \"+\ *n* [ISV *hyper-* + *chamaerrhiny*] **:** the quality or state of being hyperchamaerrhine

hy·per·chlor·hy·dria \¦≈≈,klōr'hīdrēə\ *n* -s [NL, fr. *hyper-* + *-chlorhydria* hydrochloric acid in the gastric juice (fr. *chlor-* + *hydr-* + *-ia*)] **:** the presence of a greater than typical proportion of hydrochloric acid in gastric juice that occurs in many normal individuals but is esp. characteristic of various pathologic states (as ulceration) — compare ACHLORHYDRIA, HYPOCHLORHYDRIA

hy·per·cholesteremia *or* **hy·per·cholesterolemia** \¦≈≈+\ *n* [NL, fr. *hyper-* + *cholesteremia* or *cholesterolemia* (fr. E *cholesterin* + NL *-emia*)] **:** the presence of excess cholesterol in the blood — **hy·per·cho·les·ter·e·mic** \¦≈≈kə,lestə¦rēmik\ *or* **hy·per·cho·les·ter·ol·e·mic** \-tə(,)rōl¦ēmik, -(,)rōl-\ *adj*

hy·per·chro·ma·tism \,≈≈'krōmə,tizəm\ *n* -s [*hyper-* + *chromatin* + *-ism*] **:** the development of excess chromatin or of excessive nuclear staining esp. as a part of a pathologic process

hy·per·chromatosis \¦hīpə(r)+\ *n* [NL, fr. *hyper-* + *chromatosis*] **1 :** HYPERCHROMIA 2 **2 :** HYPERCHROMATISM

hy·per·chro·mia \,≈≈'krōmēə\ *n* -s [NL, fr. *hyper-* + *-chromia*] **1 :** excessive pigmentation (as of the skin) **2 :** a state of the red blood cells marked by increase in the hemoglobin content — **hy·per·chro·mic** \¦≈≈¦mik\ *adj*

hyperchromic anemia *n* **:** any of various anemias (as pernicious anemia) that are characterized by abnormally high color index, increase of hemoglobin in individual red blood cells, and marked reduction in the number of red blood cells and alteration and irregularity in their form and that are associated with deficiency or unavailability of an antianemic factor — compare HYPOCHROMIC ANEMIA

hy·per·conjugation \¦≈≈+\ *n* [*hyper-* + *conjugation*] **:** resonance in an organic chemical structure that involves as part of the resonance hybrid the separation of a proton from a methyl or other alkyl group situated next to an electron-deficient unit (as a double bond or carbonium ion), the electrons released by the proton tending to move toward the electron-deficient function with resultant stabilization of the entire structure (as in a trisubstituted propylene $H{-}CH_2CR{=}CR_2 \longleftrightarrow H^+ CH_2{=}CR{-}CR_2^-$) — called also *no-bond resonance*

hy·per·conscious \"+\ *adj* [*hyper-* + *conscious*] **:** excessively aware **:** acutely conscious ⟨~ of strain or falsity —Elizabeth Bowen⟩ ⟨a politically ~ country —J.E.Burchard⟩

¹hy·per·coracoid \"+\ *n* [*hyper-* + *coracoid*] **:** a hypercoracoid bone

²hypercoracoid \"\ *adj* **:** of, relating to, or being the upper of two bones at the base of the pectoral fin of teleost fishes sometimes regarded as homologous with the scapula of the higher vertebrates

hy·per·correct \"+\ *adj* [*hyper-* + *correct*] **1 :** excessively proper **:** FINICKY ⟨fastidious and ~ to the point of prissiness⟩ **2 :** of, characterized by, or constituting hypercorrection

hy·per·correction \"+\ *n* **:** an alteration of a speech habit on the basis of a false analogy (as when *between you and I* is used by one who is substituting *it is I* for *it is me* or when \'fiŋə(r)\ is used for *finger* by one who is attempting to rid himself of pronunciations like \'siŋgə(r)\ for *singer*)

hy·per·critic \"+\ *n* [*hyper-* + Gk *kritikē* criticism — more at CRITIC] **1** *obs* **:** HYPERCRITICISM **2** [NL *hypercriticus*, n. or adj., fr. *hyper-* + L *criticus*, n. or adj., critic — more at CRITIC] **:** a carping or unduly censorious critic

hy·per·critical \"+\ *also* **hy·per·critic** \"+\ *adj* [*hypercritical* fr. NL *hypercriticus* + E *-al*; *hypercritic* fr. NL *hypercriticus*] **:** meticulously or excessively critical esp. of small and trivial matters **:** overnice in judgment **:** CAPTIOUS, FAULTFINDING ⟨only the critical or ~ grammarian . . . discovers anything wrong in it —Otto Jespersen⟩ ⟨constant ~ belittling of the efforts of others —Harold Rosen & H.E.Kiene⟩ **syn** see CRITICAL

hy·per·critically \"+\ *adv* **:** in a hypercritical manner **:** CAPTIOUSLY, CARPINGLY

hy·per·criticism \"+\ *n* [*hyper-* + *criticism*] **:** captious or carping criticism

hy·per·criticize \"+\ *vt* **:** to criticize excessively ~ *vi* **:** to be hypercritical

hy·per·cry·algesia \,hīpə(r),krī+\ *n* -s [NL, fr. *hyper-* + *cry-* + *algesia*] **:** excessive pain due to cold

hy·per·di·a·lect·ism \,hīpə(r)'dīə,lek,tizəm\ *n* -s [*hyper-* + *dialect* + *-ism*] **:** an attempted dialectical form or pronunciation that overreaches dialectical authenticity — compare HYPERURBANISM

hy·per·dimensional \¦≈≈+\ *adj* [*hyper-* + *dimensional*] **:** of or relating to space of more than three dimensions — **hy·per·dimensionality** \"+\ *n* -ES

hy·per·dolichocephal \"+\ *n* [*hyper-* + *dolichocephal*] **:** a hyperdolichocephalic person

hy·per·dolichocephalic \"+\ *adj* [*hyper-* + *dolichocephalic*] **:** having a very long narrow head with a cephalic index of less than 70

hy·per·dolichocephaly \"+\ *n* **:** the quality or state of being hyperdolichocephalic

hy·per·dolichocranial \"+\ *adj* [ISV *hyper-* + *dolichocranial*] **:** having a very long narrow skull with a cranial index of 65 to 70

hy·per·dolichocrany \"+\ *n* [ISV *hyper-* + *dolichocrany*] **:** the quality or state of being hyperdolichocranial

hy·per·dulia \"+\ *n* [ML, fr. L *hyper-* + ML *dulia*] *Roman Catholicism* **:** veneration of the Virgin Mary as the holiest of creatures — compare LATRIA

hypered *past of* HYPER

hy·per·emesis \¦hīpə(r)+\ *n* [NL, fr. *hyper-* + Gk *emesis* vomiting — more at EMESIS] **:** excessive vomiting

hyperemesis grav·i·dar·um \-,gravə'da(a)rəm\ *n* [NL, lit., excessive vomiting in pregnant women] **:** excessive vomiting during pregnancy

hy·per·e·mia *or* **hy·per·ae·mia** \,hīpə'rēmēə\ *n* -s [NL, fr. *hyper-* + *-emia, -aemia*] **:** excess of blood in a body part (as from active dilation of blood vessels or from obstruction of blood flow) — **hy·per·e·mic** \¦≈≈¦rēmik\ *adj*

hy·per·endemic \¦hīpə(r)+\ *adj* [*hyper-* + *endemic*] **1 :** exhibiting a high and continued incidence — used chiefly of human diseases ⟨~ malaria⟩ **2 :** marked by hyperendemic disease — used of geographic areas ⟨a ~ focus of plague⟩ — **hy·per·endemicity** \"+\ *n* -ES

hy·per·er·gic \¦hīpə¦rərjik\ *adj* **:** having a degree of sensitivity toward an allergen greater than that typical of age group and community — compare NORMERGIC

hy·per·er·gy \'≈≈,≈jē\ *n* [ISV *hyper-* + *allergy*; prob. orig. formed as G *hyperergie*] **:** the quality or state of being hyperergic

hy·per·essence \¦hīpə(r)+\ *n* [*hyper-* + *essence*] **:** a concentrated essence (as of flowers)

hy·per·es·the·sia *or* **hyperaesthesia** \,hīpərəs'thēzhə\ *n* [NL, fr. *hyper-* + *-esthesia, -aesthesia* (as in *anesthesia, anaesthesia*)] **1 :** excessive or pathological sensitivity of the skin or of a particular sense **2 :** heightened perceptiveness of or response to the environment

hy·per·esthetic \¦≈≈+\ *adj* **:** of, relating to, or affected with hyperesthesia

hy·per·es·trin·ism \,hīpə'(r)estrə,nizəm\ *n* -s [*hyper-* + *estrin* + *-ism*] **:** a condition marked by the presence of excess estrins in the body and often accompanied by functional uterine bleeding — compare HYPERESTROGENISM

hy·per·es·tro·gen·ism \-trəjə,nizəm\ *n* -s [*hyper-* + *estrogen* + *-ism*] **:** a condition marked by the presence of excess estrogens in the body

hy·per·euryene \¦hīpə(r)+\ *adj* [*hyper-* + *euryene*] **:** having a very high wide forehead with an upper facial index of less than 45

hy·per·euryeny \"+\ *n* **:** the quality or state of being hypereuryene

hy·per·euryprosopic \"+\ *adj* [G *hypereuryprosop* hypereuryprosopic (fr. *hyper-* + *euryprosop* euryprosopic) + E *-ic*] **:** having a very short broad face with a facial index below 80

hy·per·euryprosopy \"+\ *n* [ISV *hyper-* + *euryprosopy*; prob. orig. formed as G *hypereuryprosopie*] **:** the quality or state of being hypereuryprosopic

hy·per·eutectic \"+\ *adj* [*hyper-* + *eutectic*] **:** containing the minor component in an amount in excess of that contained in the eutectic mixture

hy·per·eutectoid \"+\ *adj* [*hyper-* + *eutectoid*] **1 :** containing the minor component in an amount in excess of that contained in the eutectoid **2** *of steel* **:** containing more than 0.80 percent carbon

hy·per·fo·cal distance \¦hīpə(r)¦fōkəl-\ *n* [ISV *hyper-* + *focal*] **:** the nearest distance upon which a photographic lens may be focused to produce satisfactory definition at infinity

hy·per·form \'hīpə(r)+,-\ *n* [*hyper-* + *form*] **:** a speech form resulting from hypercorrection

hy·per·ga·mous \(')hī¦pərgəməs\ *adj* **:** of, relating to, or constituting hypergamy

hy·per·ga·my \≈'≈≈mē\ *n* -ES [*hyper-* + *-gamy*] **:** marriage into an equal or higher caste or social group — used of Hindu laws forbidding women to marry men of inferior caste

hy·per·geometric *also* **hy·per·geometrical** \¦hīpə(r)+\ *adj* [*hyper-* + *geometric* or *geometrical*] **:** involving, related to, or analogous to operations or series that transcend ordinary geometrical operations or series

hy·per·glob·u·lin·emia \,≈≈,gläbyələ'nēmēə\ *n* -s [NL, fr. *hyper-* + ISV *globulin* + NL *-emia*] **:** the presence of excess globulins in the blood

hy·per·glu·ce·mia \¦hīpə(r),glü'sēmēə\ *n* -s [NL, fr. *hyper-* + *gluc-* + *-emia*] **:** HYPERGLYCEMIA

hy·per·glycemia \¦≈≈+\ *n* [NL, fr. *hyper-* + *glycemia*] **:** excess of sugar in the blood — compare HYPERINSULINISM — **hy·per·glycemic** \"+\ *adj*

hyperglycemic-glycogenolytic factor *n* **:** GLUCAGON

hy·per·gol \'hīpə(r),gȯl, -gōl\ *n* -s [G, fr. *hyp-* (fr. *hyper-*) + *erg-* + *-ol* (fr. L *oleum* oil) — more at OIL] **:** a hypergolic fluid propellant

hy·per·golic \¦≈≈¦gȯlik, -gäl-,-gōl-\ *adj* [*hypergol* + *-ic*] **:** self-igniting upon contact of components without a spark or other external aid — used esp. of a fluid rocket propellant

hy·per·hep·a·rin·emia \ˌ==ˌhepərəˈnēmēə\ *n* -s [NL, fr. *hyper-* + ISV *heparin* + NL *-emia*] **:** the presence of excess heparin in the blood (as from ionizing radiation) usu. resulting in hemorrhage — **hy·per·hep·a·rin·emic** \ˌ==ˌ===ˌ=mik\ *adj*

hy·per·hidrosis \ˈ==+\ *also* **hy·per·idro·sis** \+ə̇ˈdrōsə̇s, -ˌīˈd-\ *n* [NL, fr. *hyper-* + *hidrosis* or *-idrosis*] **:** generalized or localized excessive sweating — opposed to *hypohidrosis*

hy·per·i·ca·ce·ae \hīˌperəˈkāsēˌē\ *n pl, cap* [NL, fr. *Hypericum*, type genus + *-aceae*] *in some classifications* **:** a family of dicotyledonous plants of warm and temperate regions that are distinguished by opposite resinous-dotted leaves, regular flowers with numerous fascicled stamens, and a 3- to 5= loculed ovary and that are often included among the Guttiferae

hy·per·i·ca·les \-ā(ˌ)lēz\ [NL, fr. *Hypericum* + *-ales*] *syn of* PARIETALES

hy·per·i·cin \hīˈperəsə̇n\ *n* -s [ISV *hyperic-* (fr. NL *Hypericum*, genus that produces it) + *-in*] **:** a violet crystalline pigment $C_{30}H_{16}O_8$ from St.-John's-wort that has a red fluorescence and causes hypericism

hy·per·i·cism \-ˌsizəm\ *n* -s [NL *Hypericum*, genus that causes it + E *-ism*] **:** a severe dermatitis of domestic herbivorous animals due to photosensitivity resulting from eating St.-John's-wort — compare FAGOPYRISM

hy·per·i·cum \-rəkəm\ *n, cap* [NL, fr. L *hypericum, hypericon* a plant, St.-John's-wort, fr. Gk *hyperikon, hypereikos*, a plant, St.-John's-wort, prob. fr. *hypo-* + *ereikē* heath, heather — more at BRIER] **:** a large and widely distributed genus of herbs or shrubs (family Guttiferae) that are characterized chiefly by their pentamerous and often showy yellow flowers

hy·per·immune \ˈhīpə(r)+\ *adj* [*hyper-* + *immune*] **:** exhibiting an unusual degree of immunization ⟨~ swine⟩: **a** *of a serum* **:** containing exceptional quantities of antibody **b** *of an antibody* **:** having the characteristics of a blocking antibody

hy·per·immunization \"+\ *n* **:** the process of hyperimmunizing an individual; *also* **:** the resulting state

hy·per·immunize \"+\ *vt* [*hyper-* + *immunize*] **:** to induce a high level of immunity or of circulating antibodies in (as by a long course of injections of antigen, repeated increasing doses of antigen, or the use of adjuvants with the antigen)

hy·per·in \ˈhīpərə̇n\ *n* -s [*hyper-* (fr. NL *Hypericum*, genus that produces it) + *-in*] **:** a glycoside $C_{21}H_{20}O_{12}$ found in various plants (as St.-John's-wort and apples); quercetin 3= galactoside

hy·per·infection \ˈhīpə(r)+\ *n* [*hyper-* + *infection*] **:** repeated reinfection with larvae produced by parasitic worms already in the body due to the ability of various parasites to complete the life cycle within a single host — compare AUTOINFECTION

hypering *pres part of* HYPER

hy·per·in·su·lin·ism \ˌ==ˈ=(=)=ˌizəm\ *n* -s [ISV *hyper-* + *insulin* + *-ism*] **:** the presence of excess insulin in the body resulting in hypoglycemia and often accompanied by weakness, susceptibility to fatigue, tremor, sweating, and other evidences of debility

hy·per·irritability \ˈhīpə(r)+\ *n* [*hyper-* + *irritability*] **:** excessive irritability **:** abnormally great or uninhibited response to stimuli

hy·per·irritable \"+\ *adj* [*hyper-* + *irritable*] **:** marked by hyperirritability

hy·per·keratinization \"+\ *n* [*hyper-* + *keratinization*] **:** HYPERKERATOSIS

hy·per·keratosis \"+\ *n, pl* **hyperkeratoses** [NL, fr. *hyper-* + *keratosis*] **1 :** hypertrophy of the corneous layer of the skin **2 a :** any of various conditions marked by hyperkeratosis **b :** a disease of cattle marked by thickening and wrinkling of the hide and formation of papillary outgrowths on the buccal mucous membranes, often accompanied by watery discharge from eyes and nose, diarrhea, loss of condition, and abortion of pregnant animals, and now believed to result from ingestion of the chlorinated naphthalene of various lubricating oils — called also *X-disease, XX-disease*

hy·per·keratotic \"+\ *adj* [*hyper-* + *keratotic*] **:** of, relating to, or marked by hyperkeratosis

hy·per·kinesis *also* **hy·per·kinesia** \"+\ *n, pl* **hyperkineses** *also* **hyperkinesias** [NL, fr. *hyper-* + *-kinesia* or *-kinesis*] **:** abnormally increased and usu. purposeless and uncontrollable muscular movement; *also* **:** a condition esp. of childhood characterized by this

hy·per·kinetic \"+\ *adj* [*hyper-* + *kinetic*] **:** of, relating to, or marked by hyperkinesia

hy·per·leptene \"+\ *adj* [*hyper-* + *leptene*] **:** having a very high narrow forehead with an upper facial index of 60 or over

hy·per·lepteny \"+\ *n* [*hyper-* + *lepteny*] **:** the quality or state of being hyperleptene

hy·per·leptoprosopic \"+\ *adj* [G *hyperleptoprosop* hyperleptoprosopic (fr. *hyper-* + *leptoprosop*) + E *-ic*] **:** having a very long narrow face with a facial index of 93 and over on the living and of 95 and over on the skull

hy·per·leptoprosopy \"+\ *n* [ISV *hyper-* + *leptoprosopy*; orig. formed as G *hyperleptoprosopie*] **:** the quality or state of being hyperleptoprosopic

hy·per·leptorrhine \ˈhīpə(r)+\ *adj* [*hyper-* + *leptorrhine*] **:** having a very long narrow nose with a nasal index of 40 to 55

hy·per·leptorrhiny \"+\ *n* [*hyper-* + *leptorrhiny*] **:** the quality or state of being hyperleptorrhine

hy·per·leptosome \"+\ *adj* [*hyper-* + *leptosome*] **:** very tall and slender

hy·per·lipemia \"+\ *n* [NL, fr. *hyper-* + *lipemia*] **:** the presence of excess fat or lipids in the blood — **hy·per·lipemic** \"+\ *adj*

hy·per·makroskelic \"+\ *adj* [*hyper-* + *makroskelic*] **:** having extremely long legs in proportion to the trunk with a skelic index of 100 or over

hy·per·mas·tig·i·da \ˌhīpə(r)ˌmaˈstijədə\ [NL, fr. *hyper-* + *mastig-* + *-ida*] *syn of* HYPERMASTIGINA

hy·per·mas·tig·i·na \-jənə\ *n pl, cap* [NL, fr. *hyper-* + *mastig-* + *-ina*] **:** an order (subclass Zoomastigina) of complex cellulose-producing flagellates that have numerous flagella and are symbiotic in the intestine of termites and other wood= consuming insects

¹hy·per·mastigote \ˈhīpə(r)+\ *adj* [*hyper-* + *mastigote*] **:** of or relating to the Hypermastigina

²hypermastigote \"\ *n* -s **:** a flagellate of the order Hypermastigina

hy·per·mature \"+\ *adj* [*hyper-* + *mature*] **:** having passed the stage of full development or differentiation ⟨a ~ cataract⟩

hy·per·metabolism \"+\ *n* [*hyper-* + *metabolism*] **:** metabolism at an increased or excessive rate

hy·per·metamorphic \"+\ *adj* [*hyper-* + *metamorphic*] **:** exhibiting or involving hypermetamorphosis

hy·per·metamorphosis \"+\ *n* [NL, fr. *hyper-* + *metamorphosis*] **:** a method of development in an insect (as the blister beetle) in which the larva passes through numerous instars each markedly diverse from the rest in structure

hy·per·me·ter \hīˈpərmədˑər\ *n* [LL *hypermeter, hypermetrus* hypercatalectic, fr. Gk *hypermetros* beyond measure, beyond the meter, fr. *hyper-* + *-metros* (akin to *metron* measure, meter) — more at MEASURE] **1 :** a hypercatalectic verse **2 :** a period comprising more than two or three cola — called also *hypermetron*

hy·per·metric *or* **hy·per·metrical** \ˈhīpə(r)+\ *adj* [Gk *hypermetros* beyond measure, beyond the meter + E *-ic* or *-ical*] **:** exceeding the normal measure; *specif* **:** having a redundant syllable ⟨a poem with numerous ~ lines⟩

hy·per·me·tron \hīˈpərməˌträn\ *n* -s [NL, fr. Gk, neut. of *hypermetros* beyond the meter, beyond measure] **:** HYPERMETER 2

hy·per·met·rope \ˌhīpə(r)ˈmeˌtrōp\ *n* -s [ISV *hypermetr-* (fr. Gk *hypermetros*) + *-ope*] **:** HYPEROPE

hy·per·me·tro·pia \-ˌmə̇ˈtrōpēə\ *n* -s [NL, fr. Gk *hypermetros* + NL *-opia*] **:** HYPEROPIA — **hy·per·me·tropic** \ˈ==mə̇-ˈträpik, -rōp-\ *adj* — **hy·per·me·tropi·cal** \-pə̇kəl\ *adj* — **hy·per·met·ro·py** \ˌ==ˈme·trəpē\ *n* -ES

hy·per·me·try \hīˈpərmə·trē\ *n* -ES [*hyper-* + *-metry*] **:** the addition of one or more syllables beyond the required measure at the end of a line or other metrical unit

hy·perm·ne·sia \ˌhī(ˌ)pərmˈnēzh(ē)ə\ *n* -s [NL, fr. *hyper-* + *-mnesia*] **:** abnormally vivid or complete memory or the reawakening of impressions long seemingly forgotten (as at a moment of extreme danger) — **hy·perm·ne·sic** \-ēzik,-ēsik\ *adj*

hy·per·morph \ˈhīpərˌmȯrf\ *n* -s [*hyper-* + *-morph*] **1 :** a long-limbed and long-headed person **:** ECTOMORPH — opposed to *hypomorph* **2 :** a mutant gene having a similar but greater effect than the corresponding wild-type gene — compare HYPOMORPH — **hy·per·mor·phic** \ˈ==ˈmȯrfik\ *adj* — **hy·per·mor·phism** \-ˌfizəm\ *n* -s

hy·per·mor·pho·sis \ˌ==ˈmȯrfəsə̇s *sometimes* -ˌmȯrˈfōsə̇s\ *n* [NL, fr. *hyper-* + *-morphosis*] **:** excessive growth of some member of a body

hy·per·motility \ˈhīpə(r)+\ *n* [ISV *hyper-* + *motility*] **:** abnormal or excessive movement; *specif* **:** excessive motility of all or part of the gastrointestinal tract — compare HYPOMOTILITY

hy·per·myotonia \"+\ *n* [NL, fr. *hyper-* + *myotonia*] **:** muscular hypertonicity

hy·per·ne·phro·ma \ˌ==nəˈfrōmə, -neˈ-\ *n, pl* **hypernephromas** \-ōməz\ *or* **hypernephroma·ta** \-mədˑə\ [NL, fr. Gk *hyper-* + *nephr-* + *-oma*] **:** a tumor of the kidney resembling the adrenal cortex in its histological structure

hy·per·nic \ˈ==ˈnik\ *n* -s [*hyper-* + *Nicaragua*, country of Central America] **1 :** any of several tropical American dyewoods (as various brazilwoods or logwood) **2 :** a dye or an extract used in dyeing that is obtained from a hypernic

hy·pero·ar·tia \ˌhīpərōˈärsh(ē)ə, -ärd·ēə\ *n pl, cap* [NL, fr. Gk *hyperōia* palate (fr. fem. of *hyperōios* upper, fr. *hyper* over, above) + NL *-artia* (fr. Gk *artios* complete, perfect); akin to Gk *arti* just, exactly, *arariskein* to fit — more at OVER, ARM] **:** an order of cyclostomi consisting of the lampreys as distinguished from the hagfishes — compare HYPEROTRETA

¹hy·pero·ar·tian \ˈ==ˈärsh(ē)ən, -ärd·ēən\ *adj* [NL *Hyperoartia* + E *-an*] **:** of or relating to the Hyperoartia

²hyperoartian \"\ *n* -s **:** one of the Hyperoartia

hy·pero·ar·tii \ˌ==ˈärshēˌī, -ärd·ēˌī\ [NL, fr. Gk *hyperōia* palate + NL *-artii* (fr. Gk *artios* complete, perfect)] *syn of* HYPEROARTIA

hy·per·on \ˈhīpəˌrän\ *n* -s [prob. fr. *hyper-* + *-on*] **:** an elementary particle that obeys Fermi-Dirac statistics but differs from nucleons in one or more intrinsic quantum properties

hy·per·on·to·morph \ˈhīpəˈräntəˌmȯrf\ *n* -s [*hyper-* + *ont-* + *-morph*] **:** an ectomorphic body type or individual — opposed to *meso-ontomorph*

hy·pero·odon \ˌhīpəˈrōəˌdän\ *n, cap* [NL, fr. Gk *hyperōios* upper + NL *-odon*] **:** a genus of beaked whales distinguished esp. by prominent crests on the maxillary bones

hy·per·ope \ˈhīpəˌrōp\ *n* -s [*hyper-* + *-ope*] **:** one affected with hyperopia

hy·per·opia \ˌ==ˈrōpēə\ *n* -s [NL, fr. *hyper-* + *-opia*] **:** a condition in which visual images come to a focus behind the retina of the eye because of defects in the refractive media of the eye or because of abnormal shortness of the eyeball — called also *farsightedness* — **hy·per·opic** \ˈ==ˈräpik, -rāp-\ *adj*

hy·per·orthognathous \ˈhīpə(r)+\ *adj* [*hyper-* + *orthognathous*] **:** having a very flat facial profile with a facial angle of 93 degrees or above

hy·per·os·mia \ˌhīpəˈräzmēə\ *n* -s [NL, fr. *hyper-* + *-osmia* (as in *anosmia*)] **:** extreme acuteness of the sense of smell — **hy·per·os·mic** \ˈ==ˈ=mik\ *adj*

hy·per·os·to·sis \ˌhīpəˌräˈstōsə̇s\ *n, pl* **hyperosto·ses** \-ōˌsēz\ [NL, fr. *hyper-* + *-ostosis*] **1 :** excessive formation of bone tissue esp. in the skull **2 a :** the condition resulting from hyperostosis **b :** one of the bony outgrowths produced by hyperostosis

hy·per·os·tot·ic \ˈ==ˈstäd·ik\ *adj* [fr. NL *hyperostosis*, after such pairs as NL *exostosis*: E *exostotic*] **:** of, relating to, or affected with hyperostosis

hy·per·o·tre·ta \ˌhīpərōˈtrēd·ə\ *n pl, cap* [NL, fr. Gk *hyperōia* palate (fr. fem. of *hyperōios* upper) + NL *-treta* (fr. Gk *trētos* perforated, fr. *tetrainein* to perforate, pierce) — more at THROW] **:** an order of Cyclostomi including the hagfishes as distinguished from the lampreys — compare HYPEROARTIA

¹hy·per·o·tre·tan \ˈ===ˈtrētᵊn\ *or* **hy·per·o·tre·tous** \-ēd·əs\ *adj* [NL *Hyperotreta* + E *-an* or *-ous*] **:** of or relating to the Hyperotreta

²hyperotretan \"\ *n* -s **:** one of the Hyperotreta

hy·per·o·tre·ti \ˌ===ˈtrēdˌī\ [NL, fr. Gk *hyperōia* palate + NL *-treti* (fr. Gk *trētos* perforated)] *syn of* HYPEROTRETA

hy·per·oxide \ˈhīpə(r)+\ *n* [ISV *hyper-* + *oxide*] **:** a compound containing a relatively large proportion of oxygen; *esp* **:** SUPEROXIDE

hy·per·panchromatic \"+\ *adj* [*hyper-* + *panchromatic*] **:** sensitive to blue and green and highly sensitive to red — used of a photographic film or plate

hy·per·parasite \"+\ *n* [*hyper-* + *parasite*] **:** a parasite that is parasitic upon another parasite **:** a secondary parasite — used esp. of fungi and of hymenopterous insects that attack the primary parasites of other insects — **hy·per·parasitic** \"+\ *adj*

hy·per·parasitism \"+\ *n* [*hyper-* + *parasitism*] **1 :** the quality or state of being hyperparasitic **2 :** parasitism involving excessive numbers of parasites

hy·per·parasitize \"+\ *vt* **:** to live on or in as a hyperparasite

hy·per·par·a·thy·roid·ism \ˌ==ˈ=+ˌizəm\ *n* [ISV *hyper-* + *parathyroid* + *-ism*] **:** the presence of excess parathyroid hormone in the body resulting in disturbance of calcium metabolism with increase in serum calcium and decrease in inorganic phosphorus, loss of calcium from bone, and renal damage with frequent kidney-stone formation

hy·per·path·ia \-ˈpathēə\ *n* -s [NL, fr. *hyper-* + *-pathia*] **1 :** disagreeable or painful sensation in response to a normally innocuous stimulus (as touch) **2 :** a condition in which the sensations of hyperpathia occur — **hy·per·path·ic** \ˈ==ˈpathik\ *adj*

hy·per·peristalsis \ˈ==+\ *n* [NL, fr. *hyper-* + *peristalsis*] **:** excessive or excessively vigorous peristalsis — compare HYPERMOTILITY

hy·per·pha·gia \ˌ==ˈfāj(ē)ə\ *n* -s [NL, fr. *hyper-* + *-phagia*] **:** abnormally increased desire for food frequently resulting from injury to the hypothalamus — compare POLYPHAGIA

hy·per·pha·lan·gism \-fəˈlanˌjizəm, -fāˈ-\ *n* -s [ISV *hyper-* + *phalang-* (fr. NL *phalang-, phalanx*) + *-ism*] **:** the presence of supernumerary phalanges in fingers or toes

hy·per·pharyngeal \ˈ==+\ *adj* [*hyper-* + *pharyngeal*] **:** EPIPHARYNGEAL 2

hy·per·physical \"+\ *adj* [*hyper-* + *physical*] **1 :** being beyond or more than the physical **2 :** independent of the physical or not being within its confines — **hy·per·physically** \"+\ *adv*

hy·per·pi·e·sia \ˌ==pīˈēzh(ē)ə\ *also* **hy·per·pi·e·sis** \-ˌpīˈēsə̇s, -ˈpīəsə̇s\ *n, pl* **hyperpiesias** *also* **hyperpieses** [*hyperpiesia*, NL, fr. *hyper-* + *-piesia* (fr. Gk *piesis* pressure — fr. *piezein* to press — + NL *-ia*); *hyperpiesis*, NL, fr. *hyper-* + Gk *piesis*] **:** HYPERTENSION; *esp* **:** ESSENTIAL HYPERTENSION

¹hy·per·pi·et·ic \ˈ==ˈpīˈed·ik\ *adj* [fr. NL *hyperpiesia*, after such pairs as NL *anesthesia*: E *anesthetic*] **:** marked by hyperpiesia

²hyperpietic \"\ *n* -s **:** a person having hyperpiesia

hy·per·pi·tu·i·ta·rism \ˌ==pəˈtüətəˌrizəm, -pəˈtyü-\ *n* -s [ISV *hyper-* + *pituitar-* (fr. *pituitary*) + *-ism*] **1 :** excessive activity of the pituitary gland esp. in the production of growth= regulating hormones — compare HYPOPITUITARISM **2 :** a growth abnormality dependent on hyperpituitarism (as acromegaly and various gigantisms)

hy·per·pituitary \ˈ==+\ *adj* [*hyper-* + *pituitary*] **:** marked by hyperpituitarism ⟨giant ferns, banana leaves, creepers, and ~ trees —Michael Rosene⟩

hy·per·plane \ˈ==+\ *n* [*hyper-* + *plane*] **:** a figure in hyperspace corresponding to a plane in ordinary space

hy·per·pla·sia \ˌ==ˈplāzh(ē)ə\ *n* -s [NL, fr. *hyper-* + *-plasia*] **:** an abnormal or unusual increase in the elements composing a part (as of the cells of a tissue) — compare HYPERTROPHY, HYPOPLASIA — **hy·per·plas·tic** \ˈ==ˈplastik\ *adj*

hy·per·platycnemic \ˈ==+\ *adj* [*hyper-* + *platycnemic*] *of a shinbone* **:** much flattened laterally with a platycnemic index of less than 55

hy·per·platymeric \"+\ *adj* [*hyper-* + *platymeric*] *of a thighbone* **:** much flattened laterally with a platymeric index of less than 75

¹hy·per·ploid \ˈhīpə(r)ˌplȯid\ *adj* [ISV *hyper-* + *-ploid*] **:** having or being a chromosome number slightly greater than an exact multiple of the monoploid number

²hyperploid \"\ *n* -s **:** a hyperploid organism

hy·per·ploidy \-dē\ *n* -ES [ISV *hyperploid* + *-y*] **:** the quality or state of being hyperploid

hy·per·pnea *also* **hy·per·pnoea** \ˌhīpərˈnēə, -ˌpərpˈnēə\ *n* -s [NL, fr. *hyper-* + *-pnea* or *-pnoea*] **:** abnormally rapid or deep breathing **:** HYPERVENTILATION — compare DYSPNEA, EUPNEA — **hy·per·pne·ic** \ˈ=(ˌ)=ˈnēik\ *adj*

hy·per·predator \ˈhīpə(r)+\ *n* [*hyper-* + *predator*] **:** a predator that preys chiefly on another predatory animal

hy·per·prognathous \"+\ *adj* [*hyper-* + *prognathous*] **:** having exceedingly prominent jaws with a facial profile angle below 70 degrees

hy·per·pro·sex·ia \ˌ==prəˈseksēə\ *n* -s [NL, fr. *hyper-* + Gk *prosexis* attention (fr. *prosechein* to pay attention to, fr. *pros* toward + *echein* to hold) + NL *-ia* — more at PROS-, SCHEME] **:** excessive fixity of attention on a stimulus object

hy·per·pro·throm·bin·emia *or* **hy·per·pro·throm·bin·ae·mia** \-prōˌthrämbə̇ˈnēmēə\ *n* -s [NL, fr. *hyper-* + ISV *prothrombin* + NL *-emia* or *-aemia*] **:** excess of prothrombin in the blood

hy·per·pyretic \ˈ==+\ *adj* [ISV *hyper-* + *pyretic*] **:** of, relating to, or affected with hyperpyrexia

hy·per·pyrexia \"+\ *n* [NL, fr. *hyper-* + *pyrexia*] **:** exceptionally high fever either in comparison to the fever usu. accompanying a particular disease or absolutely (as in heat stroke)

hy·per·re·flex·ia \ˌhīpə(r)rə̇ˈfleksēə\ *n* -s [NL, fr. *hyper-* + E *reflex* + NL *-ia*] **:** overactivity of physiological reflexes

hy·per·resonance \ˈhīpə(r)+\ *n* [*hyper-* + *resonance*] **:** an exaggerated chest resonance heard in various abnormal pulmonary conditions — **hy·per·resonant** \"+\ *adj*

hypers *pres 3d sing of* HYPER

hy·per·secretion \"+\ *n* [ISV *hyper-* + *secretion*] **:** excessive production of a bodily secretion — **hy·per·secretory** \"+\ *adj*

hy·per·sensibility \"+\ *n* [ISV *hyper-* + *sensibility*] **:** HYPERESTHESIA

hy·per·sensitive \"+\ *adj* [*hyper-* + *sensitive*] **1 :** excessively sensitive ⟨extracultivated, ~, delicate manhood —*Saturday Rev.*⟩ **2 a :** abnormally susceptible to an antigen, drug, or other agent — compare ALLERGY 2, ANAPHYLAXIS **b :** reacting violently to attack by a parasite so that sudden death of invaded tissues provides a barrier against further invasion **3 :** of or relating to a photographic emulsion whose speed and sensitivity are increased before the image-forming exposure (as by treatment with ammonia or by exposure to heat or light) — **hy·per·sensitiveness** \"+\ *n* — **hy·per·sensitivity** \"+\ *n*

hy·per·sensitization \"+\ *n* **:** an act or process of hypersensitizing

hy·per·sensitize \"+\ *vt* [*hypersensitive* + *-ize*] **:** to make hypersensitive

hy·per·solid \"+\ *n* [*hyper-* + *solid*] **:** a figure (as a hypersphere) in hyperspace that corresponds to a solid in ordinary three-dimensional space

hy·per·som·nia \ˌhīpə(r)ˈsämnēə\ *n* -s [NL, fr. *hyper-* + *-somnia* (as in L *insomnia*)] **1 :** sleep of excessive depth or duration **2 :** the condition of sleeping for excessive periods at intervals with intervening periods of normal duration of sleeping and waking — compare NARCOLEPSY, SOMNOLENCE

hy·per·sonic \ˈ==+\ *adj* [ISV *hyper-* + *sonic*] **1 :** of, relating to, or being speed five times or more that of sound in air — compare SONIC **2 :** moving, capable of moving, or utilizing air currents that move at hypersonic speed ⟨~ wind tunnel⟩

hy·per·sorp·tion \ˈ==ˈsȯrpshən\ *n* [*hyper-* + *adsorption*] **:** the selective adsorption of various hydrocarbons from gaseous mixtures on activated carbon (as propane from natural gas or ethylene from gases produced in the refining of petroleum)

hy·per·space \ˈ==+\ *n* [ISV *hyper-* + *space*] **1 :** space of more than three dimensions **2 :** space other than ordinary euclidean space

hy·per·spatial \ˈ==+\ *adj* [*hyper-* + *spatial*] **:** of or relating to hyperspace

hy·per·sphere \ˈ==+ˌ-\ *n* [*hyper-* + *sphere*] **:** a sphere that is the analogue in hyperspace of the sphere in ordinary space

hy·per·splenic \ˈ==+\ *adj* **:** marked by hypersplenism

hy·per·splenism \ˌ==ˈspléˌnizəm, -leˌn-\ *n* -s [ISV *hyper-* + *splen-* + *-ism*] **:** a condition marked by excessive destruction of one or more kinds of blood cells in the spleen

hy·per·stereoscopic \ˈ==+\ *adj* [*hyper-* + *stereoscopic*] **:** having an enhanced three-dimensional appearance due to an abnormally large separation between the binocular points of view (as with some prism binoculars or in stereoscopic photographs) — **hy·per·stereoscopy** \"+\ *n*

hy·per·sthene \ˈhīpə(r)ˌsthēn\ *n* -s [F *hypersthène*, fr. *hyper-* + Gk *sthenos* strength — more at ASTHEN-] **:** a mineral $(Mg,Fe)SiO_3$ consisting of an orthorhombic grayish or greenish black or dark brown pyroxene that is a silicate of magnesium and iron isomorphous with enstatite and often has a bronze luster on the cleavage surface — **hy·per·sthenic** \ˈ==ˈsthenik, -thēn-\ *adj*

hy·per·sthe·nite \ˌ==ˈsthēˌnīt\ *n* -s [G *hypersthenit*, fr. *hypersthen* hypersthene (fr. F *hypersthène*) + *-it* -ite] **1 :** a rock composed of hypersthene and labradorite **2 :** pyroxenite composed essentially of hypersthene

hy·per·sthen·iza·tion \-ˌsthenə̇ˈzāshən, -ˌnīˈz-\ *n* -s **:** development of hypersthene by metamorphic processes

hy·per·strophic \ˈ==ˈsträfik *also* -rōf-\ *adj* [*hyper-* + Gk *strophos* twisted band, cord + E *-ic* — more at STROPHE] **:** characterized by a coiling of the shell to the left combined with an asymmetric arrangement of the organs like that of an individual of the same or related species with a shell coiled to the right

hy·per·surface \"+\ *n* [*hyper-* + *surface*] **:** a surface that is the analogue in hyperspace of a surface in three-dimensional space

hy·per·susceptibility \"+\ *n* [*hyper-* + *susceptibility*] **:** the quality or state of being hypersensitive

hy·per·susceptible \"+\ *adj* [*hyper-* + *susceptible*] **:** HYPERSENSITIVE

hy·per·tel·ic \ˈhīpə(r)ˈtelik\ *adj* **:** of, relating to, or exhibiting hypertely

hy·per·tely \hīˈpərd·ᵊlē; ˈhīpərˌtelē, ˌ==ˈ==\ *n* -ES [ISV *hyper-* + *tel-* (end) + *-y*] **:** an extreme degree of imitative coloration or ornamentation not explainable on the ground of utility

hy·per·tense \ˈhīpə(r)+\ *adj* [*hyper-* + *tense*] **:** excessively tense ⟨a furiously ambitious young ~ instructor —Christopher Morley⟩

hy·per·ten·sin \ˌ==ˈten(t)sə̇n\ *n* -s [ISV *hypertension* + *-in*] **:** any of several vasoconstrictor pressor polypeptides formed by partial hydrolysis of hypertensinogen — called also *angiotonin*

hy·per·ten·sin·ase \-sə̇ˌnās, -āz\ *n* -s [ISV *hypertensin* + *-ase*] **:** an enzyme found esp. in the kidney and intestine that inactivates hypertensin

hy·per·ten·sin·o·gen \-ˌtenˈsinəjən, -ˌjen\ *n* -s [ISV *hypertensino-* (fr. *hypertensin*) + *-gen*] **:** a globulin of blood plasma and serum that is produced by the liver and when acted on by renin forms hypertensin

hy·per·tension \ˈ==+\ *n* [ISV *hyper-* + *tension*] **1 :** abnormally high arterial blood pressure: **a :** such blood pressure occurring without apparent or determinable prior organic changes in the tissues possibly because of hereditary tendency, emotional tensions, faulty nutrition, or hormonal influence **b :** such blood pressure with demonstrable organic changes (as in nephritis, diabetes, and hyperthyroidism) **2 :** a systemic condition resulting from hypertension that is either symptomless or is accompanied by nervousness, dizziness, or headache ⟨a morass of ~ and domestic misery —C.J.Rolo⟩

¹hy·per·ten·sive \-ˈten(t)siv, -sēv *also* -səv\ *adj* [ISV *hypertension* + *-ive*] **:** marked by a rise in blood pressure **:** suffering or caused by hypertension

²hypertensive \"\ *n* -s **:** an individual affected with hypertension

Hy·per·therm \ˈ==ˌthərm\ *trademark* — used for an apparatus using hot humid air to produce artificial fever for remedial purposes

hy·per·ther·mia \,ˌ=ˈthərmēə\ *n* -s [NL, fr. *hyper-* + *therm-* + *-ia*] : hyperpyrexia esp. when induced artificially for therapeutic purposes — **hy·per·ther·mic** \ˌ==ˈthərmik\ *adj*

hy·per·thyroid \ˌ==+\ *adj* [ISV *hyper-* + *thyroid*] : of, relating to, or having hyperthyroidism

hy·per·thyroidism \"+\ *n* [ISV *hyper-* + *thyroid* + *-ism*] **1** : excessive functional activity of the thyroid gland **2** : the abnormal condition resulting from hyperthyroidism marked by increased metabolic rate, enlargement of the thyroid gland, rapid heart rate, high blood pressure, and various secondary symptoms — see EXOPHTHALMIC GOITER, GOITER

hy·per·thy·ro·sis \,==,thīˈrōsəs\ *also* **hy·per·thy·re·o·sis** \-,thīrēˈōsəs\ *n, pl* **hyperthyro·ses** *also* **hyperthyreo·ses** \-ō,sēz\ [NL, fr. *hyper-* + *thyr-* or *thyreo-* + *-osis*] : HYPERTHYROIDISM

hy·per·to·nia \,==ˈtōnēə\ *or* **hy·per·tony** \ˈ==,tōnē, hīˈpərtᵊnē\ *n, pl* **hypertonias** *or* **hypertonies** [NL *hypertonia*, fr. *hyper-* + *-tonia* -tony] : HYPERTONICITY

hy·per·tonic \ˌhīpə(r)+\ *adj* [ISV *hyper-* + *tonic*] **1** *of living tissue* : having excessive tone **2** *of a fluid* : having a higher osmotic pressure than a fluid under comparison or used as a standard — compare ISOTONIC

hy·per·tonicity \"+\ *n* : the quality or state of being hypertonic

hy·per·tonus \"+\ *n* [NL, fr. *hyper-* + *tonus*] : HYPERTONICITY

hy·per·trichosis \"+\ *n, pl* **hypertrichoses** [NL, fr. *hyper-* + Gk *trichōsis* growth of hair (fr. *trich-* + *-ōsis* -osis)] : excessive growth of hair

hy·per·trophic \hīpərˈtrō(,)fik; ˌhīpərˈträfik, -rōf-\ *or* **hy·per·tro·phous** \(ˈ)hīˈpərtrəfəs\ *adj* [*hyper-* + *-trophic* or *-trophous*] : of or relating to hypertrophy : affected with or tending to hypertrophy

hypertrophic arthritis *n* : DEGENERATIVE ARTHRITIS

hy·per·tro·phied \(ˈ)hīˈpərtrəfēd\ *adj* : marked by hypertrophy : excessively or abnormally developed : OVERGROWN ⟨~ tonsils⟩ ⟨a ~ carnival —Janet Flanner⟩ ⟨~ capitalists —G.B.Shaw⟩

¹hy·per·tro·phy \=ˈ==fē\ *n* [prob. fr. NL *hypertrophia*, fr. *hyper-* + *-trophia* -trophy] **1** : overgrowth or excessive development of an organ or part (as that resulting from unusually steady or severe use or in compensation for an organic deficiency); *specif* : increase in bulk without increase in the number of constituent elements that is produced by thickening of the muscle fibers ⟨cardiac ~⟩ — compare HYPERPLASIA, HYPOTROPHY **2** : exaggerated growth in size or complexity : excessive enlargement ⟨economic concentration increasing at a parallel rate with business ~ —Paul Johnson⟩ ⟨a certain ~ in the contrapuntal writing making for very complicated listening —K.H.Wörner⟩

²hypertrophy \"\ *vb* -ED/-ING/-ES *vt* : to affect with hypertrophy ~ *vi* : to increase or grow in size beyond the normal ⟨a healthy kidney *hypertrophies* when the other fails⟩ ⟨orthodoxies ~ as inspiration declines⟩

hy·per·urbanism \ˌhīpər+\ *n* -s [*hyper-* + *urban* + *-ism*] : a form, pronunciation, or usage that overreaches correctness in an effort to avoid provincial speech

hy·per·uricemia \ˌhīpə(r)+\ *n* -s [NL, fr *hyper-* + *uric-* + *-emia*] : excess uric acid in the blood (as in gout)

hy·per·ventilation \"+\ *n* [ISV *hyper-* + *ventilation*] : excessive ventilation; *specif* : excessive rate and depth of respiration leading to abnormal loss of carbon dioxide from the blood

hy·per·vi·ta·min·osis \,==,vīd·əməˈnōsəs\ *n, pl* **hypervitamino·ses** \-ō,sēz\ [NL, fr *hyper-* + ISV *vitamin* + NL *-osis*] : an abnormal state resulting from excessive intake of one or more vitamins esp. over a long period of time

hy·per·vol·emia \,hīpə(r)välˈlēmēə\ *n* -s [NL, fr. *hyper-* + *vol-* (fr. E *volume*) + *-emia*] : an excessive volume of blood in the body

hyp·es·the·sia \,hipəsˈthēzh(ē)ə, ,hīp-, -,pes-\ *n* [NL, fr. *hypo-* + *-esthesia* (as in *anesthesia*)] : impaired or lessened tactile sensibility

hy·pha \ˈhīfə\ *n, pl* **hy·phae** \-ī(,)ē\ [NL, fr. Gk *hyphē* web; akin to Gk *hyphos* web — more at WEAVE] **1** : one of the individual threads that make up the mycelium of a fungus, increase by apical growth, and are coenocytic in the Phycomycetes but transversely septate in the Ascomycetes and Basidiomycetes **2** : a simple or branched filamentous outgrowth from the cortex or other inner tissues of various large seaweeds esp. of the order Fucales

hy·phae·ne \hīˈfēnē\ *n, cap* [NL, fr. Gk *hyphainein* to weave — more at WEAVE] : a genus of tropical African fan palms having branching trunks, dioecious flowers, and one-seeded fruits with thick rinds — see DOOM PALM

hy·phaer·e·sis \hīˈferəsəs, *esp Brit* -ˈfi(ə)r-\ *n, pl* **hyphaereses** \-ə,sēz\ [Gk *hyphairesis*, fr. *hyphairein* to take from under, subtract, fr. *hypo-* + *hairein* to take — more at HERESY] : the omission of a sound, letter, or syllable from the body of a word — compare SYNCOPE 2a

hy·phal \ˈhīfəl\ *adj* [NL *hypha* + E ¹*-al*] : of, relating to, or constituting a hypha

hyphal body *n* : an irregularly shaped often thickened fragment formed (as in members of the genus *Entomophthora*) by segmentation of a hypha and sometimes multiplying by fission or budding

hy·phan·tria \hīˈfan·trēə\ *n, cap* [NL, fr. Gk, female weaver, fem. of *hyphantēs* weaver, fr. *hyphainein* to weave] : a genus of arctiid moths including some No. American species having hairy social larvae that are serious pests of trees — see FALL WEBWORM

¹hy·phen \ˈhīfən\ *n* -s [LL & Gk; LL, a diacritical mark (-) used to indicate that two words are to be read as a compound, fr. Gk, fr. *hyph' hen* under one, fr. *hypo* under + *hen* (neut. of *heis* one) — more at UP, SAME] **1** : the punctuation mark - used to divide or to compound words or word elements: **a** : a mark used for division esp. at the end of a line terminating with a syllable of a word that is completed in the next line, between letters or syllables repeated to give the effect of stuttering, sobbing, or halting expression (as in *s-s-sorry*), or between the letters of a word spelled out letter by letter (as in *p-r-o-b-a-t-i-o-n-a-r-y*) **b** : a mark used for compounding esp. in a compound containing a prepositional phrase (as in *mother-in-law*), in a compound adjective (as in *first-rate*), in a compound whose first element is *self* (as in *self-pity*), in a compound whose second element is capitalized (as in *pro-British*), in a compound containing reduplication (as in *bang-bang*), in a spelled-out compound numeral (as in *twenty-five*), in a compound whose meaning differs from that of an otherwise identical word (as in *re-formation*), in a compound containing a vowel otherwise confusingly doubled (as in *co-opt*), or in a compound containing the same letter three successive times (as in *bell-less*) **2** : something resembling a hyphen ⟨the lady whose odd smile is the merest ~ —Karl Shapiro⟩

²hyphen \"\ *vt* **hyphened**; **hyphened**; **hyphening** \-f(ə)niŋ\ **hyphens** : to connect (as two words or the parts of a word) with a hyphen : mark with a hyphen

¹hy·phen·ate \ˈhīfə,nāt, *usu* -ād·+V\ *vt* -ED/-ING/-S [¹*hyphen* + *-ate*] : HYPHEN — **hy·phen·ation** \,hīfəˈnāshən\ *n* -s

²hy·phen·ate \-,nə̇t, ,nāt, *usu* |d·+V\ *n* -s [back-formation fr. *hyphenated* (adj.)] : a hyphenated person; *specif* : a resident or citizen of the U.S. whose recent foreign national origin divides or is believed to divide his patriotic loyalties ⟨the effect of war hysteria upon a household of so-called ~s —*N.Y. Times*⟩ ⟨denounced ~s and called for national preparedness —*Current History*⟩

hyphenated *adj* [fr. past part. of ¹*hyphenate*; fr. the use of hyphenated words (as German-American, Irish-American) to designate foreign-born citizens of the U.S.] : of, relating to, or constituting a person or unit of mixed or diverse composition or origin ⟨~ Canadians —*N.Y. Herald*⟩ ⟨~ activity as both commercial florists and horticultural journalists —Richard Thruelsen⟩

hy·phen·ic \(ˈ)hīˈfenik\ *adj* : of or relating to hyphens

hy·phen·ism \ˈhīfə,nizəm\ *n* -s [¹*hyphen* + *-ism*; fr. the use of hyphenated words (as German-American, Irish-American) to designate foreign-born citizens of the U.S.] : the quality or state of being a hyphenate : the conduct that marks or is ascribed to hyphenates ⟨~ in the United States is almost extinct —E.A.Mowrer⟩

hy·phen·iza·tion \,hīfənə̇ˈzāshən, -,nīˈz-\ *n* -s : the joining of syllables or words with hyphens

hy·phen·ize \ˈhīfə,nīz\ *vt* -ED/-ING/-S : HYPHEN

hy·phes·so·bry·con \hī,fesəˈbrī,kän\ *n, cap* [NL, fr. *hyphesso-* (fr. Gk *hyphēssōn* of lesser stature, fr. *hypo-* + *hēssōn* inferior, less) + *Brycon*, genus of fishes (fr. Gk *brykein* to eat greedily, bite, devour)] : a genus of small brilliantly colored So. American characin fishes including several that are often kept in the tropical aquarium

hypho- *comb form* [NL, fr. Gk *hyphē*, *hyphos* web — more at WEAVE] : web : tissue ⟨*hypho*drome⟩

hy·pho·chyt·ri·a·les \,hīfō,ki·trēˈā(,)lēz\ *n pl, cap* [NL, fr. *Hyphochytrium* genus of fungi (fr. *hypho-* + Gk *chytrion* small pot, cup, dim. of *chytris* small pot, dim. of *chytra* earthen pot) + *-ales* — more at CHYTRA] : a small order of lower fungi (subclass Oomycetes) that in general resemble members of the order Chytridiales but have anteriorly uniflagellate zoospores

hy·pho·mi·cro·bi·a·les \-ā(,)lēz\ *n pl, cap* [NL, fr. *Hyphomicrobium* + *-ales*] : a small order of solitary or colonial chiefly free-living and aquatic sometimes stalked bacteria that reproduce by budding or by budding and longitudinal fission

hy·pho·mi·cro·bi·a·ce·ae \ˌhī(,)fō(,)mī,krōbēˈāsē,ē\ *n pl, cap* [NL, fr. *Hyphomicrobium*, type genus (fr. *hypho-* + *microbium*) + *-aceae*] : a small family of heterotrophic soil or water bacteria (order Hyphomicrobiales) that often have the individual cells linked by fine filaments

hy·pho·my·ce·ta·les \,hī(,)fō,mīsəˈtā(,)lēz\ [NL, fr. *hypho-* + *mycet-* + *-ales*] *syn of* MONILIALES

hy·pho·my·cete \,hīfōˈmī,sēt, ˌ==,=ˈ=\ *n* -s [NL *Hyphomycetes*] : a fungus of the subclass Hyphomycetes

hy·pho·my·ce·tes \,hīfō,mīˈsēd·ēz\ *n pl, cap* [NL, fr. *hypho-* + *-mycetes*] *in some classifications* : a subclass of fungi coextensive with the order Moniliales or including both the Moniliales and the Mycelia Sterilia — **hy·pho·my·ce·tic** \ˌ==,=ˈsēd·ik\ *adj* — **hy·pho·my·ce·tous** \-d·əs\ *adj*

hy·pho·my·co·sis \,hīfō,mīˈkōsəs\ *n* [NL, fr. *Hyphomycetes* + *-osis*] **1** : infection with a hyphomycete **2** : BURSATI 1

hy·pho·po·di·ate \ˌhīfōˈpōdēət, -ē,āt\ *adj* [NL *hyphopodium* + E *-ate*] : having a hyphopodium

hy·pho·po·di·um \,==ˈpōdēəm\ *n, pl* **hyphopo·dia** \-ēə\ [NL, fr. *hypho-* + *-podium*] : a short 1-celled or 2-celled often lobed outgrowth from the mycelium of various ectoparasitic fungi that serves to attach the fungus to the host (as in the sooty molds)

hy·pid·i·o·mor·phic \hīˌpidēōˈmȯrfik\ *adj* [ISV *hypo-* + *idiomorphic*] : partly idiomorphic — used of a rock only some of whose constituents have a distinct crystalline form — **hy·pid·i·o·mor·phi·cal·ly** \-fə̇k(ə)lē\ *adv*

hypn- *or* **hypno-** *comb form* [F *hypn-*, fr. LL, fr. Gk, fr. *hypnos* — more at SOMNOLENT] **1** : sleep ⟨*hypn*agogic⟩ **2** : hypnotism ⟨*hypno*genesis⟩

hyp·na·ce·ae \hipˈnāsē,ē\ *n pl, cap* [NL, fr. *Hypnum*, type genus + *-aceae*] : a family of mosses (order Hypnobryales) that usu. grow in dense mats and have asymmetrical capsules — see HYPNUM — **hyp·na·ceous** \(ˈ)hipˈnāshəs\ *adj*

hyp·na·gog·ic *or* **hyp·no·gog·ic** \ˌhipnəˈgäjik\ *adj* [*hypnagogic* fr. F *hypnagogique*, fr. *hypn-* + *-agogique* (fr. Gk *-agōgikos* as in *paidagōgikos* pedagogic); *hypnogogic*, alter. of *hypnagogic*] : of, relating to, or associated with the drowsiness preceding sleep ⟨~ hallucinations⟩ — opposed to *hypnopompic*

hyp·nea \ˈhipnēə\ *n, cap* [NL, fr. *Hypnum*, genus of mosses] : a genus (the type of the family Hypneaceae) comprising red algae of the order Gigartinales that have a thallus of terete fleshy branches with the tips curving inward like tendrils and that include one (*H. musciformis*) which is occas. used as a source of agar

hyp·no·analysis \ˌhipnō+\ *n* [NL, fr. *hypnosis* + psycho*analysis*] : psychoanalytic psychotherapy that uses hypnosis to facilitate transference by helping to dissolve resistance, assimilate interpretation, and recover repressed memories — compare HYPNOTHERAPY

hyp·no·bryales \"+\ *n pl, cap* [NL, fr. *hypno-* (fr. *Hypnum*, genus of mosses) + *Bryales*] : an order of Musci comprising mosses with a pleurocarpous sporophyte and a capsule usu. inclined at the end of a long seta and with an entire endostome

hyp·no·cyst \ˈhipnə,sist\ *n* [*hypn-* + *-cyst*] **1** : HYPNOSPORE **2** : an encysted form by which various protozoans resist adverse conditions (as cold or drought)

hyp·no·gen·e·sis \,hipnōˈjenəsə̇s\ *n* [NL, fr. *hypn-* + L *genesis*] : the production of a hypnotic state

hyp·no·ge·net·ic \ˌhipnōjəˈned·ik\ *adj* [*hypn-* + *-genetic*] **1** : inducing a hypnotic state **2** : inducing sleep — **hyp·no·ge·net·i·cal·ly** \-d·ə̇k(ə)lē\ *adv*

hyp·nog·e·nous \(ˈ)hipˈnäjənəs\ *adj* [*hypn-* + *-genous*] : HYPNOGENETIC

¹hyp·noid \ˈhip,nȯid\ *adj* [NL *Hypnum* + E *-oid*] : of, relating to, or resembling mosses of the genus *Hypnum* or related forms

²hypnoid \"\ *or* **hyp·noi·dal** \(ˈ)hipˈnȯidᵊl\ *adj* [*hypnoid* fr. NL *hypnosis* + E *-oid*; *hypnoidal* fr. *hypnoid* + *-al*] : of, relating to, or resembling sleep or hypnosis

hyp·nol·o·gy \hipˈnäləjē\ *n* -ES [*hypn-* + *-logy*] : the scientific study of sleep and hypnotic phenomena

hyp·none \ˈhip,nōn\ *n* -s [ISV *hypn-* + *-one*; orig. formed in F] : ACETOPHENONE

hyp·no·pho·bia \,hipnəˈfōbēə\ *or* **hyp·no·pho·by** \ˈ==,=bē\ *n, pl* **hypnophobias** *or* **hypnophobies** [NL *hypnophobia*, fr. *hypn-* + *phobia*] : morbid fear of sleep — **hy·pno·pho·bic** \ˌ==ˈfōbik *also* -ˈfäb-\ *adj*

hyp·no·pom·pic \ˌhipnəˈpämpik\ *adj* [*hypn-* + *pomp-* (fr. Gk *pompē* act of sending, escort, procession) + *-ic* — more at POMP] : dispelling sleep : of, relating to, or associated with the semiconsciousness preceding waking ⟨~ dreams⟩ — opposed to *hypnagogic*

hyp·no·sis \hipˈnōsəs\ *n, pl* **hypno·ses** \-ō,sēz\ [NL, fr. *hypn-* + *-osis*] **1** : a state that resembles normal sleep but differs in being induced by the suggestions and operations of the hypnotizer with whom the hypnotized subject remains in rapport and responsive to his suggestions which may include anesthesia, blindness, hallucinations, and paralysis while suggestions of curative value may also be accepted — compare POSTHYPNOTIC **2** : any of various conditions that resemble sleep — compare CATAPLEXY **3** : HYPNOTISM 1

hyp·no·sperm \ˈhipnə+,-\ *n* [*hypn-* + *sperm*] : HYPNOSPORE

hyp·no·sporangium \ˌhipnō+\ *n* [NL, blend of E *hypnospore* and NL *sporangium*] : a sporangium containing hypnospores

hyp·no·spore \ˈhipnə+,-\ *n* [*hypn-* + *spore*] : a very thick-walled asexual resting spore (as of various green algae) — **hyp·no·spo·ric** \ˌ==ˈspȯrik, -pōr-\ *adj*

hyp·no·therapeutic \ˌhipnō+\ *adj* [fr. *hypnotherapy*, after E *therapy: therapeutic*] : of, relating to, or promoting hypnotherapy

hyp·no·therapy \"+\ *n* [*hypn-* + *therapy*] **1** : the treatment of disease by hypnotism **2** : psychotherapy that facilitates suggestion, reeducation, or analysis by means of hypnosis — compare HYPNOANALYSIS

¹hyp·not·ic \(ˈ)hipˈnäd·|ik, -ät|, |ēk\ *adj* [F or LL; F *hypnotique*, fr. MF, fr. LL *hypnoticus*, fr. Gk *hypnōtikos* inclined to sleep, putting to sleep, soporific, fr. (assumed) Gk *hypnōtos* (verbal of Gk *hypnoun* to put to sleep, sleep, fr. *hypnos* sleep) + Gk *-ikos* -ic — more at SOMNOLENT] **1** : tending to produce sleep : SOPORIFIC **2** [short for *neurohypnotic*] : of or relating to hypnosis or hypnotism : being under, susceptible to, or tending to induce hypnosis ⟨his noble brow and ~ stare —Julian Maclaren-Ross⟩ ⟨the mother's ~ will —Leslie Rees⟩ ⟨~ suspension of all his faculties —Mary Austin⟩

²hypnotic \"\ *n* -s **1** : a drug or other agent that produces or tends to produce sleep : SOPORIFIC **2** : one that is or is capable of being hypnotized

hyp·not·i·cal·ly \|ə̇k(ə)lē, |ēk-, -li\ *adv* : in a hypnotic manner ⟨~ interesting from beginning to end —*Harper's*⟩ : by means of hypnotism ⟨a fictitious meal ~ suggested —P.S.deQ.Cabot⟩

hyp·no·tism \ˈhipnə,tizəm\ *n* -s [short for *neurohypnotism*] **1** : the study of or the act or practice of inducing hypnosis — compare MESMERISM **2** : HYPNOSIS 1

hyp·no·tist \ˈhipnətə̇st, -əd·ə̇st\ *n* -s : one that practices hypnotism

hyp·no·tiz·abil·i·ty \,hipnə,tīzəˈbilə̇d·ē\ *n* : susceptibility to hypnotism

hyp·no·tiz·able \ˈhipnə,tīzəbəl, ˌ==ˈ===\ *adj* : that can be hypnotized

hyp·no·tize *or* **hyp·no·tise** \ˈhipnə,tīz\ *vb* -ED/-ING/-s [*hypnotism* + *-ize* or *-ise*] *vt* **1** : to induce hypnosis in **2** : to deaden (judgment or resistance) by or as if by hypnotic suggestion ⟨gave a passion to his oratory which *hypnotized* criticism —J.H.Plumb⟩ ~ *vi* : to practice hypnosis : use hypnotic art or suggestion

hyp·no·toxin \ˌhipnə+\ *n* [ISV *hypn-* + *toxin*] : a hypothetical hormonal product of brain tissue that is held to induce sleep

hyp·num \ˈhipnəm\ *n* [NL, fr. LGk *hypnon*, a lichen] **1** *cap* : the type genus of the family Hypnaceae comprising mosses with the leaves arranged in three rows — see PLUME MOSS **2** -s : any moss of the genus *Hypnum*

¹hy·po \ˈhī(,)pō\ *n* -s [by shortening] : HYPOCHONDRIA ⟨nor is his spirit drooping with the ~s —*Amer. Mercury*⟩

²hypo \"\ *n* -s [short for *hyposulfite*] : sodium thiosulfate used as a fixing agent in photography

³hypo \"\ *n* -s [short for *hypodermic*] **1** : HYPODERMIC SYRINGE **2** : HYPODERMIC INJECTION **3** : STIMULUS ⟨a sure ~ for car sales —*Hartford (Conn.) Times*⟩

⁴hypo \"\ *vt* -ED/-ING/-s **1** : to administer a hypodermic injection to ⟨purged the calf with laxative, ~*ed* it with penicillin —*Time*⟩ **2** : to stimulate as if with a hypodermic injection : EXCITE, ACCELERATE ⟨tried to ~ her interest —*Saturday Rev.*⟩ ⟨giant giveaways to ~ their sales figures —Bennett Cerf⟩ ⟨prefer their parties ~*ed* occasionally with a new face or figure —Maureen Daly⟩

hypo- *in pronunciations below* ˌ== ˌhī(,)pō *or* -,pə\ *or* **hyp-** *prefix* [alter. (influenced by LL *hypo-*, *hyp-*) of ME *ypo-*, fr. OF, fr. LL *hypo-*, *hyp-*, fr. Gk, fr. *hypo* — more at UP] **1** : under : beneath : down ⟨*hypo*blast⟩ ⟨*hypo*dermic⟩ **2** : less than normal or normally ⟨*hypo*calcemia⟩ ⟨*hypo*chromia⟩ ⟨*hypo*chlorhydric⟩ ⟨*hypo*sensitive⟩ **3** : in a lower state of oxidation : in a low usu. the lowest position in a series of compounds ⟨*hypo*vanadous⟩ ⟨*hyp*oxanthine⟩ **4 a** *in ancient Greek music* (1) : being the lower octave in a disdiapason ⟨*hypo*lydian⟩ (2) *of an interval* : measured downward ⟨*hypo*diapason⟩ **b** *in medieval music* : being in a plagal mode ⟨*hypo*dorian⟩

hy·po·adre·nia \,== *at* HYPO- + əˈdrēnēə\ *also* **hy·po·adre·nal·ism** \-nə,lizəm\ *n* -s [*hypoadrenia* fr. NL, fr. *hypo-* + *adren-* + *-ia*; *hypoadrenalism* fr. *hypo-* + *adrenal* + *-ism*] : decreased activity of the adrenal glands; *specif* : adrenocortical insufficiency

hy·po·aeolian mode \ˌ==+. . .-\ *n* [LL *hypoaeolius* hypoaeolian (fr. — assumed — Gk *hypoaiolios*, fr. Gk *hypo-* + *aiolios* Aeolian, fr. *Aiolis* Aeolis, ancient country in Asia Minor) + E *-an*] : a plagal ecclesiastical mode consisting of a tetrachord and an upper conjunct pentachord represented on the white keys of the piano by an ascending diatonic scale from E to E — see MODE illustration

hy·po·aesthesia \"+\ *chiefly Brit var of* HYPESTHESIA

hy·po·al·bu·min·emia \,==+(,)al,byüməˈnēmēə\ *n* -s [NL, fr. *hypo-* + *albumin-* + *-emia*] : hypoproteinemia marked by reduction in serum albumins

hy·po·allergenic \ˌ==+\ *adj* [*hypo-* + *allergenic*] : having a relatively low capacity to induce hypersensitivity

hypo-alum toning process *n* [²*hypo* + *alum*] : a method of altering a developed silver photographic image to a sepia color by means of a warm solution containing essentially hypo and alum

hy·po·bar·ic \ˌ==+ˈbarik\ *adj* [*hypo-* + Gk *baros* weight + E *-ic* — more at GRIEVE] : having a specific gravity less than that of cerebrospinal fluid — used of solutions for spinal anesthesia; opposed to *hyperbaric*

hy·po·basal \"+\ *adj* [ISV *hypo-* + *basal*] *bot* : situated posterior to the basal wall ⟨the ~ lower segment of a developing embryo⟩ — compare EPIBASAL

hy·po·basidium \"+\ *n* [NL, fr. *hypo-* + *basidium*] : a special cell constituting the base of the basidium in various fungi of the orders Auriculariales and Tremellales in which haploid nuclei fuse and from which the epibasidium arises

hy·po·batholithic \"+\ *adj* [*hypo-* + *batholithic*] : of, relating to, or constituting ore deposits that occur in deeply eroded batholiths

hy·po·benthos \"+\ *n* [NL, fr. *hypo-* + *benthos*] : the fauna of the deep sea

hy·po·blast \ˈ==+,blast\ *n* [*hypo-* + *-blast*] : the endoderm of an embryo

hy·po·blas·tic \ˌ==ˈblastik\ *adj* : of, relating to, or derived from hypoblast : ENDODERMAL

¹hy·po·branchial \ˌ==+\ *adj* [*hypo-* + *branchial*] **1** : situated below the gills : of or relating to the ventral wall of the pharynx; *specif* : of or relating to the endostyle **2** : of, relating to, or being the segment of a branchial arch between the basibranchial and the ceratobranchial

²hypobranchial \"\ *n* -s : a hypobranchial bone or cartilage

hy·po·bro·mite \,==+ˈbrō,mīt\ *n* -s [ISV *hypobrom-* (fr. *hypobromous acid*) + *-ite*] : a salt or ester of hypobromous acid

hy·po·bro·mous acid \ˌ==ˈbrōməs. . .-\ *n* [ISV *hypo-* + *bromine* + *-ous*] : an unstable acid HBrO that resembles hypochlorous acid and is obtained in solution by reaction of bromine water with silver nitrate or in the form of unstable salts by reaction of bromine with alkaline solutions

hy·po·bu·lia \,==+ˈbyülēə\ *n* -s [NL, fr. *hypo-* + *-bulia*] : lowered ability to make decisions or to act — **hy·po·bu·lic** \ˌ==ˈlik\ *adj*

hy·po·cal·ce·mia *also* **hy·po·cal·cae·mia** \,==+,kalˈsēmēə\ *n* -s [NL, fr. *hypo-* + *calcemia*, *calcaemia* calcium in the blood (fr. *calc-* + *-emia*, *-aemia*)] : a deficiency of calcium in the blood — **hy·po·cal·ce·mic** *also* **hy·po·cal·cae·mic** \ˌ==ˌ=ˈmik\ *adj*

hy·po·cap·nia \,==+ˈkapnēə\ *n* -s [NL, fr. *hypo-* + *-capnia*] : deficiency of carbon dioxide in the blood

hy·po·carp \ˈ==+,kärp\ *or* **hy·po·car·pi·um** \,==+ˈkärpēəm\ *n, pl* **hypocarps** \-ps\ *or* **hypocar·pia** \-ēə\ [NL *hypocarpium*, fr. *hypo-* + *-carpium* -carp] : an enlarged sometimes edible peduncle beneath some fruits (as the cashew apple)

hy·po·caust \ˈ==+,kȯst\ *n* -s [L *hypocaustum*, *hypocauston*, fr. Gk *hypokauston*, fr. neut. of *hypokaustos* heated by a hypocaust, fr. (assumed) Gk *hypokaustos*, verbal of Gk *hypokaiein* to light (a fire) under, fr. *hypo-* + *kaiein* to burn — more at CAUSTIC] : a central heating system of an ancient Roman dwelling, public bath, or other building consisting of an underground furnace or fire chamber and a series of tile flues for distribution of the heat

hy·po·cellular \ˌ== *at* HYPO-+\ *adj* [*hypo-* + *cellular*] : containing less than the normal number of cells ⟨~ bone marrow in chronic lead poisoning⟩

hy·po·center \"+\ *n* [*hypo-* + *center*] : the point on the earth's surface directly below the center of a nuclear bomb explosion

hy·po·centrum \"+\ *n, pl* **hypocentra** [NL, fr. *hypo-* + *centrum*] : a ventral part of the body of a vertebra that is usu. wedge-shaped or horseshoe-shaped, consists of the fused lower arcualia of the anterior of the two arches from which each vertebra is formed, and is characteristic of some fishes, stegocephalians, and primitive reptiles — called also *intercentrum*

hy·po·ceph·a·lus \,==+ˈsefələs\ *n, pl* **hypocepha·li** \-fə,lī\ [NL, fr. *hypo-* + *-cephalus* (fr. Gk *kephalē* head) — more at CEPHALIC] : a circular sheet of papyrus containing extracts from the 162d chapter of the Book of the Dead stiffened with plastered linen and placed as an amulet under the head of an ancient Egyptian mummy in the coffin

hy·po·chae·ris \"+ˈkirəs\ *n, cap* [NL, alter. of L *hypochoeris*, a plant, fr. Gk *hypochoiris* succory plant, fr. *hypo-* + *-choiris* (fr. *choiros* young pig, pig) — more at CHAEROPUS] : a large widely distributed genus of milky-juiced herbs (family Compositae) that have basal leaves and scapose yellow flower heads and include some (as the cat's-ear) that are cosmopolitan weeds of open lands

hy·po·chil \ˈ==+,kil\ *or* **hy·po·chil·i·um** \,==+ˈkilēəm\ *n* -s [NL *hypochilium*, fr. *hypo-* + Gk *cheilos* lip + NL *-ium* — more at GILL] : the lower part of the labellum in orchids

hy·po·chil·o·morph \¦⸗⸗+¦kīlə,mȯrf\ *adj* [NL *Hypochilomorphae*] **:** of or relating to the Hypochilomorphae

hy·po·chil·o·mor·phae \,⸗⸗,⸗⸗'mȯr(,)fē\ *n pl, cap* [NL, fr. *hypo-* + *chil-* + *-morphae*] **:** a suborder of Araneida comprising arachnomorph spiders with two pairs of book lungs

hy·po·chloremia \¦⸗⸗ *at* HYPO- +\ *n* [NL, fr. *hypo-* + *chloremia*] **:** abnormal decrease of chlorides in the blood — **hy·po·chlor·e·mic** \"+,klōr¦ēmik\ *adj*

hy·po·chlor·hy·dria \,⸗⸗+,klōr'hīdrēə\ *n* -s [NL, fr. *hypo-* + *chlorhydria* hydrochloric acid in the gastric juice (fr. *chlor-* + *hydr-* + *-ia*)] **:** deficiency of hydrochloric acid in the gastric juice — compare HYPERCHLORHYDRIA — **hy·po·chlor·hy·dric** \¦⸗⸗,⸗¦⸗drik\ *adj*

hy·po·chlorite \¦⸗⸗ *at* HYPO- +\ *n* [ISV *hypochlor-* (fr. *hypochlorous acid*) + *-ite*] **:** a salt or ester of hypochlorous acid: as **a :** SODIUM HYPOCHLORITE **b :** CALCIUM HYPOCHLORITE

hy·po·chlorous acid \¦⸗⸗+...-\ *n* [ISV *hypo-* + *chlorous;* orig. formed as F *hypochloreux*] **:** an unstable strongly oxidizing but weak acid HClO that is obtained in solution along with hydrochloric acid by reaction of chlorine with water or in the form of salts by reaction of chlorine with alkaline solutions and that is used chiefly in the form of salts as an oxidizing agent, bleaching agent, disinfectant, and chlorinating agent

hy·poch·na·ce·ae \,hī(,)päk'nāsē,ē\ [NL, fr. *Hypochnus* + *-aceae*] *syn of* THELEPHORACEAE

hy·poch·nus \hī'päknəs\ [NL, fr. *hypo-* + Gk *chnoos, chnous* dust, fine down; akin to Gk *chnauein* to gnaw, nibble, OE *gnagan* to gnaw — more at GNAW] *syn of* TOMENTELLA

hy·po·choeris \,⸗⸗ *at* HYPO- +'kirəs\ [NL, fr. L, a plant — more at HYPOCHAERIS] *syn of* HYPOCHAERIS

hy·po·chon·der *or* **hy·po·chon·dre** \"+'kändə(r)\ *n* -s [LL *hypochondria*, pl., abdomen] *archaic* **:** HYPOCHONDRIUM

hy·po·chon·dria \,hīpə'kändrēə, -pō'- *sometimes* ,hip-\ *n* -s [NL, fr. LL, pl., abdomen, belly (formerly supposed to be the seat of hypochondria), fr. Gk, fr. *hypochondria*, neut. pl. of *hypochondrios* under the cartilage of the breastbone, fr. *hypo-* + *-chondrios* (fr. *chondros* cartilage, cartilage of the breastbone, granule, grain) — more at GRIND] **:** extreme depression of mind or spirits often centered on imaginary physical ailments ⟨her ~, her insecurity, her staunch integrity, and loneliness —Bosley Crowther⟩ ⟨the present philosophical and political ~ about moral skepticism —Charles Frankel⟩; *specif* **:** HYPOCHONDRIASIS

¹hy·po·chon·dri·ac \¦⸗⸗¦⸗drē,ak\ *adj* [F *hypochondriaque*, adj. & n., fr. MF, fr. Gk *hypochondriakos*, adj., of the abdomen, fr. *hypochondrion*, sing., *hypochondria*, pl., abdomen + *-akos* (adj. suffix)] **1** *also* **hy·po·chon·dri·al** \-ēəl\ **a :** situated below the costal cartilages **b :** of, relating to, or being the two regions of the abdomen lying on either side of the epigastric region and above the lumbar regions — see ABDOMINAL REGION illustration **2** *or* **hy·po·chon·dri·a·cal** \,hīpə¦kən-'drīəkəl, -pō|, |,kän- *sometimes* ¦hip-\ **:** affected, characterized, or produced by hypochondria

²hypochondriac \"\ *n* -s [F *hypochondriaque*] **:** one affected by hypochondria or hypochondriasis ⟨a ~ . . . lives in a world of sick imagination —J.W.Krutch⟩ ⟨some miserable ~ whose interests are bounded by his own ailments —Bertrand Russell⟩

hy·po·chon·dri·a·sis \,hīpəkən'drīəsəs\ *n, pl* **hypochondria·ses** \-ī ə,sēz\ [NL, fr. *hypochondria* + *-iasis*] **:** hypochondria of pathological proportions **:** morbid concern about one's health esp. when accompanied by delusions of physical disease

hy·po·chon·dri·ast \,hīpə'kändrē,ast\ *n* -s [NL *hypochondria* + E *-ast* (as in *enthusiast*)] **:** HYPOCHONDRIAC

hy·po·chon·dri·um \-ēəm\ *n, pl* **hypochon·dria** \-ēə\ [NL, fr. Gk *hypochondrion* abdomen, belly, fr. neut. sing. of *hypochondrios*] **:** either hypochondriac region of the body

hy·po·chordal \¦⸗⸗ *at* HYPO- +\ *adj* [*hypo-* + *chordal*] **:** ventral to the spinal cord

hy·po·chro·mia \,⸗⸗+'krōmēə\ *n* [NL, fr. *hypo-* + *-chromia*] **1 :** deficiency of color or pigmentation **2 :** deficiency of hemoglobin in the red blood cells (as in nutritional anemia)

hy·po·chro·mic \¦⸗⸗¦⸗mik\ *adj* [NL *hypochromia* + E *-ic*] **:** exhibiting hypochromia

hypochromic anemia *n* **:** any of various anemias that are characterized by abnormally low blood color index, deficiency of hemoglobin, and usu. microcytic red blood cells and are associated with lack of available iron, whether by reason of excessive loss (as in hemorrhage), inadequate intake, or faulty assimilation — compare HYPERCHROMIC ANEMIA

hy·po·clei·di·an \¦⸗⸗+¦klīdēən\ *adj* [NL *hypocleidium* + E *-an*] **:** of or relating to a hypocleidium

hy·po·clei·di·um \,⸗⸗'⸗⸗əm\ *n, pl* **hypoclei·dia** \-ēə\ [NL, fr. *hypo-* + Gk *kleidion* small key, dim. of *kleid-, kleis* key, hook, clavicle — more at CLEID-] **:** a median process on the wishbone of many birds often connected with the sternum by a ligament or ossified with it

hy·po·condylar \¦⸗⸗ *at* HYPO- +\ *adj* [*hypo-* + *condylar*] **:** located under or below a condyle

hy·po·cone \'⸗⸗+,-\ *n* [*hypo-* + *cone*] **:** the principal rear inner cusp of a mammalian upper molar

hy·po·con·id \,⸗⸗+'kānəd\ *n* -s [*hypo-* + ²*con-* + *-id*] **:** the principal rear outer cusp of a mammalian lower molar

¹hy·po·coracoid \¦⸗⸗ *at* HYPO- +\ *n* [*hypo-* + *coracoid*] **:** a hypocoracoid bone

²hypocoracoid \"\ *adj* **:** of, relating to, or being the lower of two bones at the base of the pectoral fin attached behind the clavicle and sometimes regarded as homologous with the coracoid of the higher vertebrates

hypoco·rism \hī'päkə,rizəm, hə'-; ,hīpə'kōr,izəm, ,hip-\ *n* -s [LL *hypocorisma* diminutive (n.), fr. Gk *hypokorisma* endearing name, fr. *hypokorizesthai* to call by endearing names, fr. *hypo-* + *korizesthai* to caress (fr. *koros* boy, *korē* girl) — more at CRESCENT] **1 :** a pet name or term of endearment **2 :** the formation or use of pet names ⟨~ is the frequent practice of fond parents⟩ **3 :** BABY TALK 1b ⟨~ is hardly in keeping with human dignity —A.W.Read⟩

¹hypo·co·ris·tic \,hīpəkə¦ristik, ¦hip-; hī¦päk-, hi¦-\ *adj* [Gk *hypokoristikos* diminutive, fr. (assumed) Gk *hypokoristos* (verbal of Gk *hypokorizesthai*) + Gk *-ikos* -ic] **1 :** of, relating to, or used as a pet name or form of baby talk **2 :** forming a hypocoristic word — used of a suffix, abbreviation, or other modification

²hypocoristic \"\ *n* **:** a hypocoristic term

hy·po·cot·yl \'⸗⸗ *at* HYPO- +,käd·ᵊl, ,⸗⸗'⸗⸗\ *n* -s [ISV *hypo-* + *-cotyl*] **:** the part of the axis of a plant embryo or seedling below the cotyledon — compare EPICOTYL, RADICLE

hypocotyl arch *n* **:** the part of the stem that is normally below the cotyledons but in various seedlings (as of the bean) grows at a differential rate and curves so as to be the first structure to appear above the ground

hy·po·cotyledonary \"+\ *adj* [*hypocotyledonary*, ISV *hypo-* + *cotyledonary*] **:** located below the cotyledons

hy·po·cre·a·ce·ae \,⸗⸗+krē'āsē,ē\ *n pl, cap* [NL, fr. *Hypocrea*, type genus (fr. *hypo-* + Gk *kreas* flesh) + *-aceae* — more at RAW] **:** a family of fungi that have brightly colored fleshy or membranous ascocarps, include parasites of economic plants, and are usu. included in Hypocreales but sometimes placed in Sphaeriales and then held to include the Nectriaceae

hy·po·cre·a·les \-'ā(,)lēz\ *n pl, cap* [NL, fr. *Hypocrea*, genus of fungi + *-ales*] **:** an order of fungi (subclass Euascomycetes) closely related to and probably derived from the Sphaeriales — see HYPOCREACEAE

hyp·o·crise *or* **hyp·o·crize** \'hipə,krīz\ *vi* -ED/-ING/-S [F *hypocriser*, fr. MF, fr. OF *ypocrisie* hypocrisy] **:** to act hypocritically

hy·poc·ri·sy \hə'päkrəsē, -si *sometimes* hī'-\ *n* -ES [ME *ipocrisie*, fr. OF *ypocrisie*, fr. LL *hypocrisis*, fr. Gk *hypokrisis* act of playing a part on the stage, hypocrisy, outward show, fr. *hypokrinesthai* to answer, play a part on the stage, act, pretend, fr. *hypo-* + *krinesthai* to dispute, *krinein* to decide, judge — more at CERTAIN] **1 :** the act or practice of pretending to be what one is not or to have principles or beliefs that one does not have ⟨the passing stranger who took such a vitriolic joy in exposing their pretensions and their ~ —Van Wyck Brooks⟩; *esp* **:** the false assumption of an appearance of virtue or religion ⟨may admit that our conventional morality often serves as a cover for ~ and selfishness —Lucius Garvin⟩ **2 :** an act or instance of hypocrisy ⟨the little *hypocrisies* which are so frequently the rule rather than the exception in human contacts —Erle Stanley Gardner⟩

hy·poc·ri·tal \hə'päkrəd·ᵊl, ¦hipə¦krid·ᵊl\ *adj* **:** HYPOCRITICAL

¹hyp·o·crite \'hipə,krit, *usu* -id·+V\ *n* -s [ME *ipocrite*, fr. OF *ypocrite*, fr. LL *hypocrita*, fr. Gk *hypokritēs* actor on the stage, pretender, hypocrite, fr. *hypokrinesthai*] **:** one who pretends to be what he is not or to have principles or beliefs that he does not have; *esp* **:** one who falsely assumes an appearance of virtue or religion ⟨I dare swear he is no ~, but prays from his heart —Shak.⟩

²hypocrite \"\ *adj* [ME *ypocrite*, fr. *ypocrite, ipocrite*, n.] **:** HYPOCRITICAL ⟨our ~ century —Wyndham Lewis⟩

hypocrite plant *n* **:** MEXICAN FIRE PLANT 1

hyp·o·crit·i·cal \¦hipə¦krid·|əkəl, -it|, |ēk-\ *or* **hyp·o·crit·ic** \|ik, |ēk\ *adj* [¹*hypocrite* + *-ical* or *-ic*] **:** of or relating to a hypocrite or hypocrisy **:** DISSEMBLING, FALSE, SPECIOUS ⟨a ~ gesture of modesty and virtue —Robert Graves⟩ — **hyp·o·crit·i·cal·ly** \|ək(ə)lē, |ēk-, -li\ *adv*

hy·po·crystalline \¦⸗⸗ *at* HYPO- +\ *adj* [ISV *hypo-* + *crystalline*] **:** HEMICRYSTALLINE

hy·po·cu·pre·mia *or* **hy·po·cu·prae·mia** \,⸗⸗+,k(y)ü'prēmēə\ *also* **hy·po·cu·pro·sis** \-rōsəs\ *n, pl* **hypocupremias** *or* **hypocupraemias** *also* **hypocuproses** [NL, fr. *hypo-* + *cupr-* + *-emia* or *-aemia* or *-osis*] **1 :** a deficiency in blood copper esp. of a domestic animal **2 :** a diseased condition resulting from a blood-copper deficiency — **hy·po·cu·pre·mic** \¦⸗⸗,⸗¦prēmik\ *adj*

hy·po·cycloid \¦⸗⸗ *at* HYPO- +\ *n* [*hypo-* + *cycloid*] **:** a curve traced by a point on the circumference of a circle rolling internally on another circle — compare EPICYCLOID

hypocycloid *H* traced by point *P* on circle *R* rolling within fixed circle *F*

hy·po·derm \'⸗⸗+,dərm\ *n* [NL *hypoderma* (tissue)] **1 a :** HYPODERMIS 2b **b :** HYPOBLAST **2 :** HYPODERMIS 1

¹hy·po·der·ma \,⸗⸗+'dərmə, -'dəmə, -'dəimə\ *n* [NL, fr. *hypo-* + Gk *derma* skin, fr. *derein* to skin — more at TEAR] **1** *cap* **:** a cosmopolitan genus (the type of the family Hypodermatidae) of two-winged flies that have larvae parasitic in the tissues of vertebrates **2 -s :** an insect or maggot of the genus *Hypoderma*

²hypoderma \"\ *n* [NL, fr. *hypo-* + Gk *derma* skin] **1 :** HYPODERMIS 2b **2 :** HYPODERMIS 1

hy·po·der·mal \¦⸗⸗¦⸗məl\ *adj* [NL *hypoderma* + E *-al*] **:** of or relating to a hypodermis ⟨~ tissues⟩ **:** lying beneath an outer skin or epidermis ⟨~ glands⟩

hy·po·dermatic \¦⸗⸗(,)dər¦mad·ik\ *adj* [*hypo-* + *dermatic* dermal (fr. Gk *dermatikos*, fr. *dermat-* + *-ikos* -ic)] **:** HYPODERMIC — **hy·po·der·mat·i·cal·ly** \-d·ək(ə)lē\ *adv*

¹hy·po·der·mic \,hīpə¦dərmik, -¦dəm-, -¦dəim-, -mēk\ *adj* [ISV *hypo-* + *dermic*] **1 :** of or relating to the parts beneath the skin **2 a :** adapted for use in injecting medication or drugs beneath the skin **b :** administered by injection beneath the skin **3 :** resembling a hypodermic injection in effect **:** ROUSING, STIMULATING ⟨one of the most ~ personalities he had ever known —Robert Rice⟩

²hypodermic \"\ *n* -s **1 :** HYPODERMIC INJECTION **2 :** HYPODERMIC SYRINGE

hy·po·der·mi·cal·ly \-mək(ə)lē, -mēk-, -li\ *adv* **:** in a hypodermic location or manner; *specif* **:** by means of a hypodermic

hypodermic injection *n* **:** an injection made into the subcutaneous tissues

hypodermic medication *n* **:** application of medicaments by injection under the skin

hypodermic needle *n* **1 :** NEEDLE 1c(2) **2 :** a hypodermic syringe complete with needle

hypodermic syringe *n* **:** a small syringe used with a hollow needle for injection of material into or beneath the skin

hypodermic syringe

hypodermic tablet *n* **:** a water-soluble tablet that contains a specified amount of medication and is intended for hypodermic administration

hy·po·der·mis \,⸗⸗'⸗məs\ *n* [NL, fr. *hypo-* + *-dermis*] **1 :** the tissue immediately beneath the epidermis of a plant esp. when lignified, suberized, or otherwise modified to serve as a supporting and protecting layer **2 a :** HYPOBLAST **b :** the cellular layer that underlies and secretes the chitinous cuticle of arthropods and some other invertebrates

hy·po·der·moc·ly·sis \,⸗⸗(,)dər'mäkləsəs\ *n, pl* **hypoder·mocly·ses** \-lə,sēz\ [NL, fr. *hypo-* + *derm-* + *clysis*] **:** subcutaneous injection of fluids (as saline or glucose solution)

hy·po·der·mo·sis \-'mōsəs\ *n* -ES [NL, fr. *hypo-* + *derm-* + *-osis*] **:** infestation with warbles

hy·po·der·mous \¦⸗⸗¦dərməs\ *adj* [NL *hypodermis* + E *-ous*] **:** HYPODERMAL

hy·po·dochmius \¦⸗⸗ *at* HYPO- +\ *n* [NL, fr. *hypo-* + L *dochmius*] **:** a metrical line of three trochees the last of which lacks a final unstressed syllable

hy·po·dorian mode \¦⸗⸗+...-\ *n* [LL *hypodorius* hypodorian (fr. Gk *hypodōrios*, fr. *hypo-* + *Dōrios* Dorian) + E *-an; hypodorian mode*, trans. of Gk *hypodōria harmonia* — more at DORIAN] **1 :** a Greek mode consisting of two disjunct tetrachords represented on the white keys of the piano by a descending diatonic scale from A to A — see GREEK MODE illustration **2 :** a plagal ecclesiastical mode consisting of a tetrachord and an upper conjunct pentachord represented on the white keys of the piano by an ascending diatonic scale from A to A — see MODE illustration

hy·po·dy·namia \,⸗⸗+,dī'namēə, -,dä'-, -nām-\ *n* -s [NL, fr. *hypo-* + *-dynamia*] **:** decrease in strength or power

hy·po·dynamic \¦⸗⸗ *at* HYPO- +\ *adj* [*hypo-* + *dynamic*] **:** marked by or exhibiting hypodynamia

hypoed *past of* HYPO

hy·po·er·gic \¦⸗⸗+¦ərjik\ *adj* **:** having a degree of sensitivity toward an allergen less than that typical of age group and community — compare NORMERGIC

hy·po·ergy \'⸗⸗,ərjē\ *n* -ES [ISV *hypo-* + *allergy*] **:** the quality or state of being hypoergic

hy·po·eutectic \¦⸗⸗+\ *adj* [*hypo-* + *eutectic*] **:** containing the minor component in an amount less than in the eutectic mixture

hy·po·eutectoid \"+\ *adj* [*hypo-* + *eutectoid*] **1 :** containing the minor component in an amount less than that contained in the eutectoid **2** *of steel* **:** containing less than 0.80 percent carbon

hy·po·fer·re·mia *also* **hy·po·fer·rae·mia** \,⸗⸗+,fe'rēmēə\ *n* -s [NL, fr *hypo-* + L *ferrum* iron + NL *-emia* or *-aemia* — more at FARRIER] **1 :** deficiency in blood iron esp of a domestic animal **2 :** a diseased condition resulting from a blood iron deficiency

hy·po·function \¦⸗⸗ *at* HYPO-+\ *n* [*hypo-* + *function*] **:** decreased or insufficient function esp. of an endocrine gland

hypogaeum *var of* HYPOGEUM

hy·pog·a·my \hī'pägəmē, hə'-\ *n* -ES [*hypo-* + *-gamy*] **:** marriage into a lower caste, class, or social group

hy·po·gas·tric \¦⸗⸗ *at* HYPO- + ¦gastrik\ *adj* [F *hypogastrique*, fr. MF, fr. *hypogastre* hypogastrium (fr. Gk *hypogastrion*) + *-ique* -ic] **:** of or relating to the lower median region of the abdomen — see ABDOMINAL REGION illustration

hypogastric artery *n* **:** ILIAC ARTERY 3

hypogastric plexus *n* **:** the sympathetic nerve plexus that supplies the pelvic viscera, lies in front of the promontory of the sacrum, and extends down into two lateral portions

hypogastric vein *n* **:** a vein that accompanies the hypogastric artery, drains the pelvis and the gluteal and perineal regions, and unites with the external iliac vein to form the common iliac vein

hy·po·gas·tri·um \,⸗⸗+'gastrēəm\ *n, pl* **hypogas·tria** \-ēə\ [NL, fr. Gk *hypogastrion*, fr. *hypo-* + *gastr-* + *-ion* -ium] **:** the hypogastric region

hy·po·ge·al \¦⸗⸗+¦jēəl\ *or* **hy·po·ge·ous** \-əs\ *also* **hy·po·ge·an** *or* **hy·po·gae·an** \-ən\ *or* **hy·po·ge·ic** \-ēik\ *adj* [LL *hypogeus* subterranean (fr. Gk *hypogeios, hypogaios*) + E *-al* or *-ous* or *-an* or *-ic*] **1 a** *of a plant or plant part* **:** growing below the surface of the ground; *esp, of a cotyledon* **:** remaining below the ground while the epicotyl elongates **b** *of plant germination* **:** producing hypogeal cotyledons **2 :** living below the surface of the ground — used esp. of an insect; distinguished from *aerial* and *epigeal* **3** *geol* **:** occurring below the surface or within the interior of the earth ⟨~ forces⟩ — **hy·po·ge·al·ly** \-əlē\ *adv*

hy·po·gee \'⸗⸗+jē\ *n* -s [F or L; F *hypogée*, fr. MF, fr. L *hypogeum*] **:** HYPOGEUM

hyp·o·gene \"+,jēn\ *adj* [*hypo-* + *-gene* (as in *epigene*)] **1 :** formed, crystallized, or lying at depths below the earth's surface **:** PLUTONIC — used of various rocks; opposed to *epigene* **2 :** formed by generally ascending solutions — used of ore deposits; opposed to *supergene*

hy·po·gen·e·sis \¦⸗⸗ *at* HYPO-+¦jenəsəs\ *n* [NL, fr. *hypo-* + L *genesis*] **1 :** direct development without alternation of generations **2 :** underdevelopment esp. of an organ or function

hy·po·ge·net·ic \"+jə¦ned·ik\ *adj* **:** of, relating to, or exhibiting hypogenesis

hy·po·gen·ic \"+¦jenik\ *adj* [*hypogene* + *-ic*] **:** of, relating to, or constituting hypogene activity or crystallization ⟨a district under the influence of ~ activities reaches a condition of seismic strain —*Encyclopedia Britannica*⟩

hy·po·gen·i·tal·ism \,⸗⸗+'jenəd·ᵊl,izəm\ *n* -s [ISV *hypo-* + *genital* + *-ism*] **:** subnormal development of genital organs **:** genital infantilism

hy·pog·e·nous \(')hī¦päjənəs, hə'p-\ *adj* [ISV *hypo-* + *-genous*] **1 :** growing on the lower side (as of a leaf) — used esp. of a fungus **2 :** HYPOGENIC

hy·po·ge·um *or* **hy·po·gae·um** \,⸗⸗ *at* HYPO- + 'jēəm\ *n, pl* **hypo·gea** *or* **hypo·gaea** \-ēə\ [L, fr. Gk *hypogeion, hypogaion*, fr. neut. of *hypogeios, hypogaios* subterranean, fr. *hypo-* + *gē, gaia* earth, ground] **1 a :** the subterranean part of an ancient building **:** CELLAR **b :** the underground service galleries of an ancient amphitheater **2 :** an ancient underground burial chamber or series of such rooms **:** CATACOMB

hy·po·glos·sal \¦⸗⸗+¦gläsəl, -lȯs-\ *adj* [NL *hypoglossus* + E *-al*] **:** of, relating to, or constituting the hypoglossal nerve ⟨~ fissure⟩

hypoglossal nerve *also* **hypoglossal** *n* -s **:** either of the 12th and final pair of cranial nerves being a motor nerve arising usu. from three roots in the medulla oblongata and supplying muscles of the tongue and hyoid apparatus in higher vertebrates but being absent in lower forms

hy·po·glos·sus \,⸗⸗'⸗səs\ *n, pl* **hypoglos·si** \-ä,sī, -ȯ,sī\ [NL, fr. *hypo-* + *-glossus* (fr. Gk *glōssa* tongue)] — more at GLOSS] **:** HYPOGLOSSAL NERVE

hy·po·glot·tis \,⸗⸗+'gläd·əs\ *n* [Gk *hypoglōttis*, fr. *hypo-* + *glōtta, glōssa* tongue] **1 :** the underpart of the tongue **2 :** a sclerite adjoining the labium of various beetles

hy·po·glu·ce·mia *also* **hy·po·glu·cae·mia** \,⸗⸗+,glü'sēmēə\ *n* -s [NL, fr. *hypo-* + *gluc-* + *-emia* or *-aemia*] **:** HYPOGLYCEMIA

hy·po·glycemia \¦⸗⸗+\ *n* [NL, fr. *hypo-* + *glycemia*] **:** abnormal decrease of sugar in the blood — see HYPERINSULINISM — **hy·po·glycemic** \"+\ *adj*

hy·pog·na·thous \(')hī¦pägnəthəs\ *adj* [*hypo-* + *-gnathous*] **1 :** having the lower jaw longer than the upper **2 :** having the mouthparts ventrally directed — used esp. of certain insects with biting mouthparts directed downward and often somewhat backward; compare PROGNATHOUS

hy·po·gonadal \¦⸗⸗ *at* HYPO-+\ *adj* **1 :** suffering from or marked by hypogonadism **2 :** marked by or exhibiting deficient development of secondary sexual characteristics

hy·po·gonad·ism \,⸗⸗+'gō,na,dizəm *or* 'gä,n-\ *n* -s [ISV *hypo-* + *gonad* + *-ism*] **1 :** functional incompetence of the gonads esp. in the male with subnormal or impaired production of both hormonal and reproductive elements **2 :** an abnormal state involving gonadal incompetence **:** EUNUCHOIDISM

hy·pog·y·nous \(')hī¦päjənəs\ *adj* [*hypo-* + *-gynous*] **1 :** inserted upon the receptacle or axis below the gynoecium and free from it — used of sepals, petals, and stamens; compare EPIGYNOUS **2** *of a flower* **:** having sepals, petals, or stamens inserted as hypogynous parts — **hy·pog·y·ny** \⸗'⸗⸗nē\ *n* -ES

hy·po·hal·ite \,⸗⸗ *at* HYPO- + 'ha,līt\ *n* [*hypohalous* acid + *-ite*] **:** a salt or ester of a hypohalous acid

hy·po·hal·ous acid \¦⸗⸗¦haləs-\ *n* [*hypo-* + *hal-* + *-ous*] **:** an acid HXO derived from the halogens and including hypochlorous acid, hypobromous acid, and hypoiodous acid

hy·po·hidrosis \¦⸗⸗+\ *n* [NL, fr. *hypo-* + *hidrosis*] **:** abnormally diminished sweating — opposed to *hyperhidrosis*

hy·po·hip·pine \,⸗⸗+'hi,pīn, -,pən\ *n* -s [NL *Hypohippus* + E *-ine* (fr. *-ine*, adj. suffix)] **:** an animal or fossil of the genus *Hypohippus*

hy·po·hip·pus \-,pəs\ *n, cap* [NL, fr. *hypo-* + *-hippus*] **:** a genus of extinct long-necked long-bodied short-limbed horses showing adaptations for life in forests and known from remains found in the Miocene of America and the Pliocene of China

hy·po·hy·al \¦⸗⸗+¦hīəl\ *adj* [*hypo-* + *hyoid* + *-al*] **:** of, relating to, or constituting one or two small elements of each side of the hyoid arch of most fishes between the ceratohyal and the median basihyal

hy·po·hyaline \"+\ *adj* [*hypo-* + *hyaline*] **:** partly glassy — used of rocks

hy·poid \'hī,pȯid\ *adj* [short for *hyperboloid*] **:** utilizing, used for, or relating to hypoid gears ⟨~ rear axle⟩ ⟨~ grease⟩

hypoid gear *also* **hypoid** *n* -s **:** one of a pair of bevel gears that are used esp. in automotive transmissions, are designed so that the axis of the pinion does not intersect the axis of the gear, and have the teeth on the pinion cut spirally and the teeth on the gear cut nonradially

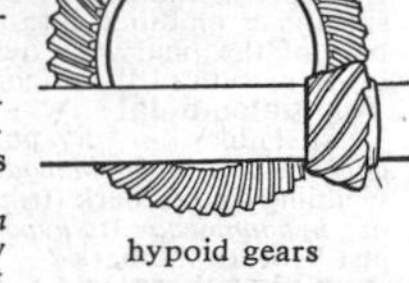

hypoid gears

hypoing *pres part of* HYPO

hy·po·io·dite \,⸗⸗ *at* HYPO- + 'īə,dīt\ *n* -s [ISV *hypo-* + *iod-* + *-ite*] **:** a salt or ester of hypoiodous acid

hy·po·iodous acid \¦⸗⸗+...-\ *n* [ISV *hypo-* + *iodous*] **:** a very unstable very weak acid HIO that resembles hypochlorous acid and is obtained in solution by treating mercury oxide (sense b) with iodine in water or in the form of unstable salts in solution by reaction of iodine with alkali

hy·po·ionian mode \"+...-\ *n* [*hypo-* + L *ionius* Ionian + E *-an* — more at IONIAN] **:** a plagal ecclesiastical mode consisting of a tetrachord and an upper conjunct pentachord represented on the white keys of the piano by an ascending diatonic scale from G to G — see MODE illustration

hy·po·ischium \"+\ *n* [NL, fr. *hypo-* + *ischium*] **:** a small median bony rod passing backward from the ischial symphysis and supporting the ventral wall of the cloaca in most lizards

hy·po·ka·le·mia \,⸗⸗+,kā'lēmēə\ *n* -s [NL, fr. *hypo-* + *kalium* + *-emia*] **:** a deficiency of potassium in the blood —**hy·po·ka·le·mic** \¦⸗⸗,⸗¦⸗mik\ *adj*

hy·po·limnetic \¦⸗⸗ *at* HYPO- +\ *or* **hy·po·lim·ni·al** \"+¦limnēəl\ *adj* [NL *hypolimnion* + E *-etic* or *-ial*] **:** of or relating to a hypolimnion

hy·po·lim·ni·on \,⸗⸗+'limnē,än, -ēən\ *n, pl* **hypolim·nia** \-ēə\ [NL, fr. *hypo-* + Gk *limnion* small lake, dim. of *limnē* lake, sea] **:** the part of a lake below the thermocline made up of water that is stagnant and of essentially uniform temperature except during the period of overturn — compare EPILIMNION

hy·po·lithic \¦⸗⸗+\ *adj* [*hypo-* + Gk *lithos* stone + E *-ic*] *of plants* **:** growing beneath rocks

hy·po·locrian mode \"+...-\ *n* [*hypo-* + *locrian*] **:** a plagal ecclesiastical mode consisting of a tetrachord and an upper conjunct pentachord represented on the white keys of the piano by an ascending diatonic scale from F to F but rarely used because its tetrachord and pentachord comprise respectively the forbidden augmented fourth and diminished fifth — see MODE illustration

hy·po·lydian mode \"+...-\ *n* [LL *hypolydius* hypolydian (fr. Gk *hypolydios*, fr. *hypo-* + *lydios* Lydian) + E *-an; hypolydian mode*, trans. of Gk *hypolydios tonos*] **1 :** a Greek mode consisting of two disjunct tetrachords represented on the white keys of the piano by a descending diatonic scale from F to F — see GREEK MODE illustration **2** : a plagal ecclesiastical mode consisting of a tetrachord and an upper conjunct pentachord represented on the white keys of the piano by an ascending diatonic scale from C to C — see MODE illustration

hy·po·mag·ne·se·mia \ˌ==+ˌmagnə'sēmēə\ *n* -s [NL, fr. *hypo-* + *magnesium* + *-emia*] : deficiency of magnesium in the blood constituting a prime factor in grass tetany or milk fever in cattle — **hy·po·mag·ne·se·mic** \ˌ==ˌ==¦sēmik\ *adj*

hy·po·ma·nia \ˌ==+'mānēə\ *n* [NL, fr. *hypo-* + LL *mania*] : a mild mania esp. when part of a manic-depressive cycle — **hy·po·man·ic** \¦==¦manik\ *adj*

hy·po·menorrhea \¦== *at* HYPO- +\ *n* [NL, fr. *hypo-* + *menorrhea*] : decreased menstrual flow

hy·po·metabolism \"+\ *n* [*hypo-* + *metabolism*] : a state (as in myxedema or hypothyroidism) marked by an abnormally low metabolic rate

hy·po·mixolydian mode \"+...-\ *n* [*hypo-* + *mixolydian* (*mode*)] : a plagal ecclesiastical mode consisting of a tetrachord and an upper conjunct pentachord represented on the white keys of the piano by an ascending diatonic scale from D to D — see MODE illustration

hy·po·moch·li·on \ˌ==+'mäklēˌän\ *n* -s [L, fr. Gk, fr. *hypo-* + *mochlion* small lever, dim. of *mochlos* lever; akin to Gk *mogos* exertion, labor — more at MOGI-] *archaic* : FULCRUM

hy·po·morph \'==+ˌmȯrf\ *n* -s [*hypo-* + *-morph*] **1** : a short-limbed and round-headed person : ENDOMORPH — opposed to *hypermorph* **2** : a mutant gene having a similar but weaker effect than the corresponding wild-type gene — compare HYPERMORPH — **hy·po·mor·phic** \¦==¦mȯrfik\ *adj*

hy·po·mor·pho·sis \ˌ==+'mȯ(r)fəsə̇s *sometimes* +ˌmȯ(r)'fōs-\ *n* [NL, fr. *hypo-* + *-morphosis*] **1** : DEDIFFERENTIATION 1 **2** : inhibition of differentiation (as in an embryo)

hy·po·motility \¦== *at* HYPO- +\ *n* [ISV *hypo-* + *motility*] : abnormal deficiency of movement; *specif* : decreased motility of the stomach or intestine — compare HYPERMOTILITY

hy·po·nas·tic \"+¦nastik\ *adj* [ISV *hyponasty* + *-ic*] : of, relating to, or caused by hyponasty — **hy·po·nas·ti·cal·ly** \-tə̇k(ə)lē\ *adv*

hy·po·nas·ty \'==ˌnastē\ *n* -ES [ISV *hypo-* + *-nasty*; orig. formed as G *hyponastie*] : a nastic movement in which a plant part is bent inward and upward

hy·po·na·tre·mia \ˌ==+nə'trēmēə\ *n* -s [NL, fr. *hypo-* + *natrium* + *-emia*] : deficiency of sodium in the blood

hy·po·nitrite \¦== *at* HYPO- +\ *n* [ISV *hyponitr-* (fr. *hyponitrous acid*) + *-ite*] : a salt or ester of hyponitrous acid

hy·po·nitrous acid \" + . . . -\ *n* [*hypo-* + *nitrous* (*acid*)] : an explosive crystalline weak acid $H_2N_2O_2$ or HON=NOH obtained usu. in the form of its salts by oxidation of hydroxylamine or by reduction of nitrites

hy·po·nome \'==+ˌnōm\ *n* -s [Gk *hyponomē* underground passage, *hyponomos* underground passage, water pipe, conduit, fr. *hyponemesthai* to undermine, fr. *hypo-* + *nemesthai* to inhabit, spread over, be situated upon, middle of *nemein* to distribute, pasture — more at NIMBLE] : the swimming funnel of a cephalopod — **hy·po·nom·ic** \¦==¦nämik\ *adj*

hy·po·nutrition \¦==+\ *n* [*hypo-* + *nutrition*] : UNDERNUTRITION

hy·po·nych·i·al \¦==+¦nikēəl\ *adj* [NL *hyponychium* + E *-al*] **1** : of or relating to the hyponychium **2** : located under a nail

hy·po·nych·i·um \ˌ==='==əm\ *n* -s [NL, fr. *hypo-* + *-onychium*] **1** : the thickened layer of epidermis beneath the free end of a nail **2** : MATRIX 1c

hy·po·nym \'==+ˌnim\ *n* -s [*hypo-* + *-onym*] : NOMEN NUDUM; *specif* : a generic name not based on a recognizable species — **hy·po·nym·ic** \¦==¦nimik\ *adj* — **hy·pon·y·mous** \(ˈ)hī¦pänəməs, hə'p-\ *adj*

hy·po–on·to·morph \¦==+'äntəˌmȯrf\ *n* -s [*hypo-* + *ont-* + *-morph*] : an endomorphic individual

hy·po·ovar·i·an·ism \ˌ==+ˌō'va(a)rēəˌnizəm\ *n* -s [*hypo-* + *ovarian* + *-ism*] : a condition marked by a deficiency of ovarian function : female hypogonadism — compare INFANTILISM

hy·po·parathyroid \¦== *at* HYPO- +\ *adj* [prob. back-formation from *hypoparathyroidism*] : of or affected by hypoparathyroidism

hy·po·par·a·thy·roid·ism \ˌ==+ˌparə'thīˌrȯiˌdizəm\ *n* -s [ISV *hypo-* + *parathyroid* + *-ism*] : deficiency of parathyroid hormone in the body; *also* : the resultant abnormal state marked by low serum calcium and a tendency to chronic tetany

hy·po·par·ia \ˌ==+'pa(a)rēə\ *n pl, cap* [NL, fr. *hypo-* + *-paria* (fr. Gk *pareia* cheek)] : an order of trilobites with marginal facial suture and small pygidium known from the Lower Ordivician through the Cambrian — **hy·po·par·i·an** \¦==¦==ən\ *adj or n*

hy·po·pha·lan·gism \ˌ==+fə'lanˌjizəm\ *n* -s [*hypo-* + *phalange* + *-ism*] : a condition in which the number of phalanges of fingers or toes is less than normal

hy·poph·a·mine \hī'päfəˌmēn, -ˌmə̇n\ *n* [NL *hypophysis* + E *amine*] : either of two hormones obtained from the posterior lobe of the pituitary gland: **a** : OXYTOCIN **b** : VASOPRESSIN

¹hy·po·pharyngeal \¦== *at* HYPO- +\ *adj* [*hypo-* + *pharyngeal*] **1** : located below or in the lower part of the pharynx **2** [fr. NL *hypopharynx*, after NL *pharynx*: E *pharyngeal*] : of or relating to the hypopharynx **3** : of or relating to a bone behind the last functional gill arch in teleost fishes that represents the ceratobranchial of the fifth branchial arch

²hypopharyngeal \"\ *n* : a hypopharyngeal element esp. of bone

hy·po·pharynx \"+\ *n* [NL, fr. *hypo-* + *pharynx*] **1** : an appendage or thickened fold on the floor of the mouth of many insects that resembles a tongue, is very conspicuous in Orthoptera, and is believed to be sensory in function although sometimes modified into a piercing organ **2** : the laryngeal part of the pharynx extending from the hyoid bone to the lower margin of the cricoid cartilage

hy·po·phloe·o·dal \"+ˌflēədᵊl\ *or* **hy·po·phloe·od·ic** \"+flē¦ädik\ *or* **hy·po·phloe·ous** \"+¦flēəs\ *adj* [*hypophloeodal*, *hypophloeodic* fr. *hypo-* + Gk *phloiōdēs* resembling rind or bark (fr. *phloios* bark + *-ōdēs* -ode) + E *-al* or *-ic*; *hypophloeous* fr. *hypo-* + Gk *phloios* + E *-ous*] : living just beneath the bark ⟨~ lichens⟩

hy·po·phosphate \"+\ *n* [ISV *hypophosph-* (fr. *hypophosphoric acid*) + *-ate*] : a salt or ester of hypophosphoric acid

hy·po·phos·pha·te·mia \ˌ==+ˌfäsfə'tēmēə\ *n* -s [NL, fr. *hypo-* + ISV *phosphate* + NL *-emia*] : deficiency of phosphates in the blood that is due to inadequate intake, excessive excretion, or defective absorption and that results in bone defects and other disturbances

hy·po·phosphite \¦==+\ *n* [*hypophosphorous* (acid) + *-ite*] : a salt of hypophosphorous acid

hy·po·phosphoric acid \" + . . . -\ *n* [ISV *hypo-* + *phosphoric*] : an unstable tetrabasic acid $H_4P_2O_6$ usu. obtained in the form of its salts (as by oxidation of red phosphorus in alkaline solution)

hy·po·phosphorous acid \" + . . . -\ *n* [F *hypophosphoreux*, fr. *hypo-* + *phosphoreux* phosphorous] : a low-melting deliquescent crystalline strong monobasic acid H_3PO_2 usu. obtained by acidifying one of its salts and used as a reducing agent

hy·po·phre·nia \ˌ==+'frēnēə\ *or* **hy·po·phre·no·sis** \"+frə'nōsə̇s\ *n, pl* **hypophrenias** \-əz\ *or* **hypophreno·ses** \-ōˌsēz\ [NL, fr. *hypo-* + *-phrenia* or *-phrenosis* (fr. Gk *phren-*, *phrēn* mind, heart + NL *-osis*)] : MENTAL DEFICIENCY — **hy·po·phren·ic** \¦==¦frenik *also* -rēn-\ *adj*

hy·po·phrygian mode \¦==+ . . . -\ *n* [*hypophrygian* (fr. LL *hypophrygius* hypophrygian — fr. Gk *hypophrygios*, fr. *hypo-* + *phrygios* Phrygian, fr. *Phrygia*, ancient country in west central Asia Minor — + E *-an*) + *mode*; trans. of Gk *hypophrygia harmonia*] **1** : a Greek mode consisting of two disjunct tetrachords represented on the white keys of the piano by a descending diatonic scale from G to G — see GREEK MODE illustration **2** : a plagal ecclesiastical mode consisting of a tetrachord and an upper conjunct pentachord represented on the white keys of the piano by an ascending diatonic scale from B to B — see MODE illustration

hy·poph·y·ge \hī'päfə(ˌ)jē, hə'-\ *n* -s [NL, fr. Gk *hypophygē* refuge, recess, fr. *hypo-* + *phygē* flight, fr. *pheugein* to flee — more at FUGITIVE] : a hollow curvature esp. under a Doric capital in some Greek buildings — compare APOPHYGE

hy·po·phyl·lous \¦== *at* HYPO- +¦filəs\ *adj* [*hypo-* + *-phyllous*] : located on the under side of a leaf — compare EPIGENOUS

hy·po·phy·se·al *also* **hy·po·phy·si·al** \(ˌ)hī¦päfə¦sēəl, ¦hīpə-, -¦zē-, ¦hīpə¦fiz-\ *adj* [*hypophyseal*, alter. of *hypophysial*; *hypophysial* fr. NL *hypophysis* + E *-al*] : of or relating to the hypophysis

hy·poph·y·sec·to·mize \(ˌ)hīˌpäfə'sektəˌmīz\ *vt* -ED/-ING/-S : to remove the pituitary gland from

hy·poph·y·sec·to·my \-təmē\ *n* -ES [ISV *hypophys-* (fr. NL *hypophysis*) + *-ectomy*] : surgical removal of the pituitary gland

hy·poph·y·sis \hī'päfəsə̇s\ *n, pl* **hypophyses** \-əˌsēz\ [NL, outgrowth, pituitary body (esp. in *hypophysis cerebri*, lit., outgrowth of the brain), fr. Gk, outgrowth, attachment underneath, process of a bone, fr. *hypophyein* to grow up below, fr. *hypo-* + *phyein* to grow, produce, bring forth — more at BE] **1** *also* **hypophysis ce·re·bri** \-sə'rēˌbrī, -'serə,-\ : PITUITARY GLAND **2 a** : a cell or cells in a seed plant resulting from the transverse division of the next adjoining suspensor cell and giving rise to the tip of the root **b** : APOPHYSIS 2

hypopi *pl of* HYPOPUS

hy·po·pi·al \(ˈ)hī¦pōpēəl, hə'p-\ *adj* [NL *hypopus* + E *-ial*] : of, relating to, or consisting of a hypopus

hy·po·pi·tu·i·ta·rism \ˌ== *at* HYPO- + pə'tüətəˌrizəm, -pə'tyü-\ *n* -s [ISV *hypo-* + *pituitar-* (fr. *pituitary*) + *-ism*] : deficient activity of the pituitary gland esp. in the production of growth-regulating hormones or of those fractions (as the gonadotropic or thyrotrophic hormones) that regulate the secretory activity of other endocrine organs — compare HYPERPITUITARISM

hy·po·pituitary \¦==+\ *adj* [*hypo-* + *pituitary*] : of or relating to pituitary deficiency

hy·pop·i·tys \hī'päpəd·əs, hə'-\ *n, cap* [NL, fr. *hypo-* + Gk *pitys* pine — more at PINE (tree)] *in some classifications* : a genus of plants comprising the pinesaps and including leafless saprophytic herbs with erect stems and racemose flowers that are commonly placed in the genus *Monotropa*

hy·po·plankton \¦== *at* HYPO- +\ *n* [*hypo-* + *plankton*] : the plankton inhabiting the greatest depths esp. immediately over the bottom but sometimes throughout the whole abyssal zone — **hy·po·planktonic** \"+\ *adj*

hy·po·pla·sia \ˌ==+'plāzh(ē)ə\ *n* -s [NL, fr. *hypo-* + *-plasia*] : a condition of arrested development in which an organ or part remains below the normal size or in an immature state — compare HYPERPLASIA

hy·po·plas·tic \¦==¦plastik\ *adj* [*hypo-* + *plastic*] : of, relating to, or marked by hypoplasia

hypoplastic anemia *n* : APLASTIC ANEMIA

hy·po·plastral \¦==+\ *adj* : of or relating to the hypoplastron

hy·po·plastron \"+\ *n* [*hypo-* + *plastron*] : either of the third lateral pair of bony plates in the plastron of most turtles

hy·po·ploid \'==+ˌplȯid\ *adj* [*hypo-* + *-ploid*] : having a chromosome number a little smaller than an exact multiple of the monoploid number

hy·po·pneus·tic \¦==+¦n(y)üstik, ¦hīˌpäp¦-\ *adj* [*hypo-* + *-pneustic*] : having some of the respiratory spiracles lacking or nonfunctional — used chiefly of larval insects

hy·po·po·tas·se·mia \ˌ==+pəˌta'sēmēə\ *n* -s [NL, fr. *hypo-* + *potassium* + *-emia*] : HYPOKALEMIA — **hy·po·po·tas·se·mic** \ˌ===ˌ=¦sēmik\ *adj*

hy·po·pro·sex·ia \ˌ==+prə'seksēə\ *n* -s [NL, fr. *hypo-* + Gk *prosexis* attention (fr. *prosechein* to pay attention to, fr. *pros* toward + *echein* to hold) + NL *-ia*] *psychol* : defective fixity of attention on a stimulus object

hy·po·pro·tein·emia \"+ˌprōˌtē'nēmēə, ˌprōd·ēə'n-\ *n* -s [NL, fr. *hypo-* + ISV *protein* + NL *-emia*] : abnormal decrease of protein in the blood — **hy·po·pro·tein·e·mic** \¦==ˌ===¦nēmik\ *adj*

hy·po·pro·throm·bin·e·mia \ˌ==+(ˌ)prōˌthrämbə'nēmēə\ *n* -s [NL, fr. *hypo-* + ISV *prothrombin* + NL *-emia*] : deficiency of prothrombin in the blood usu. due to vitamin K deficiency or liver disease (esp. obstructive jaundice) and resulting in delayed clotting of blood or spontaneous bleeding (as from the nose or into the skin) — **hy·po·pro·throm·bin·e·mic** \¦==(ˌ)=¦==¦nēmik\ *adj*

hy·pop·ter·on \hī'päptəˌrän, hə'-\ *n, pl* **hypop·tera** \-ərə\ [NL, fr. *hypo-* + Gk *pteron* feather, wing — more at FEATHER] : the tuft of feathers of a bird's wing covering the axillars

hy·pop·ti·lum \hī'päptələm, hə'-\ *n, pl* **hypopti·la** \-lə\ [NL, fr. *hypo-* + Gk *ptilon* wing, feather, down; akin to Gk *petesthai* to fly — more at FEATHER] : AFTERSHAFT

hy·po·pus \'hīpəpəs\ *n, pl* **hy·po·pi** \-ˌpī\ [NL, fr. Gk *hypopous* furnished with feet, fr. *hypo-* + *pous* foot — more at FOOT] : a nonfeeding migratory larva of some mites that attaches itself to and is passively distributed by an animal

hy·po·pyg·i·al \¦== *at* HYPO- + ¦pijēəl\ *adj* [NL *hypopygium* + E *-al*] : of or relating to a hypopygium

hy·po·pyg·i·um \ˌ==+'pijēəm\ *also* **hy·po·py·gid·i·um** \"+pə'jidēəm\ *n, pl* **hypopyg·ia** *also* **hypopygid·ia** \-ēə\ [NL, fr. *hypo-* + *-pygium* (fr. *pyg-* + *-ium*) or *-pygidium* (fr. Gk *pygidion* small rump) — more at PYGIDIUM] : a modified 9th abdominal segment of many insects with which the copulatory apparatus is associated; *esp* : such a modified segment together with the copulatory apparatus of a dipterous insect

hy·po·py·on \hī'pōpēˌän, hə'-\ *n* -s [NL, fr. Gk, ulcer, fr. *hypopyon*, neut. of *hypopyos* suppurative, fr. *hypo-* + *pyon* pus — more at FOUL] : an accumulation of white blood cells in the anterior chamber of the eye

hy·por·che·ma \ˌhīpə(r)'kēmə\ *or* **hyp·or·cheme** \'hīpə(r)ˌkēm\ *n, pl* **hyporchema·ta** \-məd·ə\ *or* **hyporchemes** [Gk *hyporchēma*, fr. *hyporcheisthai* to dance to music, fr. *hypo-* + *orcheisthai* to dance — more at ORCHESTRA] : an ancient Greek choral song and dance usu. in honor of Apollo or Dionysus — **hy·por·che·mat·ic** \¦==kē¦mad·ik\ *adj*

hy·po·rhined \¦== *at* HYPO- +ˌrīnd\ *adj* [*hypo-* + *rhin-* + *-ed*] : having small nostrils

hy·po·ri·bo·fla·vin·o·sis \ˌ==+ˌrībəˌflāvə'nōsə̇s *also* -rib- *or* -lav-\ *n, pl* **hyporiboflavino·ses** \-ōˌsēz\ [NL, fr. *hypo-* + ISV *riboflavin* + NL *-osis*] : ARIBOFLAVINOSIS

hy·por·rhyth·mic \¦==+¦rith̲mik *sometimes* -ithm-\ *adj* [Gk *hyporrhythmos* hyporrhythmic (fr. *hypo-* + *rhythmos* measure, rhythm) + E *-ic* — more at RHYTHM] *in Greek and Latin prosody* : deficient as to rhythm — used of a hexameter in which the end of a word coincides with the end of each foot and which accordingly has no true caesura

hypos *pl of* HYPO, *pres 3d sing of* HYPO

hy·po·scleral \"+\ *adj* [*hypo-* + *scleral*] : located beneath the sclera of the eye

hy·po·scope \'==+ˌskōp\ *n* [*hypo-* + *-scope*] : a military periscope designed for use as a hand instrument or for attachment to a rifle

hy·po·secretion \¦== *at* HYPO- +\ *n* [*hypo-* + *secretion*] : production of a body secretion at an abnormally slow rate or in abnormally small quantities

hy·po·sensitive \"+\ *adj* [*hypo-* + *sensitive*] : exhibiting or marked by deficient response to stimulation — **hy·po·sensitivity** \"+\ *n*

hy·po·sensitization \"+\ *n* [*hypo-* + *sensitization*] : the state or process of being hyposensitized

hy·po·sensitize \"+\ *vt* [*hypo-* + *sensitize*] : to reduce the sensitivity of (an individual) esp. to an allergen : DESENSITIZE

hy·po·spa·dia \ˌ==+'spādēə\ *or* **hy·po·spa·dy** \'==ˌspādē\ *n, pl* **hypospadias** *or* **hypospadies** [NL *hypospadia*, fr. Gk *hypospadias* man with hypospadias] : HYPOSPADIAS

hy·po·spa·di·ac \¦==¦spādēˌak\ *adj* [Gk *hypospadias* man with hypospadias + E *-ac* (as in *elegiac*)] : of or affected with hypospadias

hy·po·spa·di·as \ˌ=='spādēəs\ *n* -ES [NL, fr. Gk, man with hypospadias, fr. *hypo-* + *-spadias* (prob. fr. *spadōn* eunuch, fr. *span* to tear, pluck off, pull, draw) — more at SPAN] : an abnormality of the penis in which the urethra opens on the under surface

hy·po·sphene \'==+ˌsfēn\ *n* [*hypo-* + Gk *sphēn* wedge] : a median wedge-shaped posterior process on the neural arch of the vertebrae of certain extinct reptiles — compare HYPANTRUM

hypospray \'=(ˌ)=ˌ=\ *n* [³*hypo* + *spray*] : a device with a spring and plunger for administering a medicated solution by forcing it in extremely fine jets through the unbroken skin

hy·po·stase \'== *at* HYPO-+ˌstās\ *n* -s [NL *hypostasis*] : a disk of lignified tissue formed at the base of the ovule in certain orders of plants

hy·pos·ta·sis \hī'pästəsə̇s\ *n, pl* **hyposta·ses** \-əˌsēz\ [LL, substance, sediment, fr. Gk, support, sediment, foundation, substance, fr. *hyphistasthai* to support, stand under, fr. *hypo-* + *histasthai* to stand, middle of *histanai* to cause to stand — more at STAND] **1 a** : something that settles at the bottom of a fluid : SEDIMENT, DEPOSIT **b** : the settling of blood in the dependent parts of an organ or body **2 a** *in the original Nicene use* : the essence or substance of the triune Godhead — called also *ousia* **b** *in later use* (1) one of the persons of the Godhead or Trinity (2) : the individual as subject or substance **c** : the whole personality of Christ as distinguished from his human and divine natures **3** *obs* : basis of support : FOUNDATION **4** *philos* **a** *Plotinism* : any of the three aspects or essential principles constituting the Godhead: (1) : the transcendent one (2) : NOUS, SPIRIT (3) : LOGOS, WORLD SOUL **b** *Thomism* : the substance or rational nature of an individual or person; *also* : PERSON, INDIVIDUAL **c** : substance as an ontological entity or category : a self-subsistent reality or mode of being **d** : a hypothetical or conceptual entity : a reified abstraction : HYPOSTATIZATION ⟨as far as the Buddhist ~ of the law is concerned, we should search in vain for a Christian equivalent —Joachim Wach⟩ ⟨for legal purposes a right is only the ~ of a prophecy —Alfred Lief⟩ **5** [NL, fr. LL] : failure of a gene to produce its usual effect when coupled with another gene that is epistatic toward it **6** [NL, fr. LL] : HYPOSTASE **7 a** : the mention of a word, grammatical form, or word group (as *in*, *un-*, *in the dark*) as a linguistic element **b** : a linguistic element so referred to — called also *citation form, quotation noun*

hy·pos·ta·size \hī'pästəˌsīz\ *vt* -ED/-ING/-S [LL *hypostasis* + E *-ize*] : HYPOSTATIZE

hy·po·stat·ic \¦== *at* HYPO-+¦stad·ik\ *adj* [Gk *hypostatikos*, fr. *hypostatos* substantially existing (verbal of *hyphistasthai* to support, stand under) + *-ikos* -ic] **1** *or* **hy·po·stat·i·cal** \-d·ə̇kəl\ : of or relating to substance : ELEMENTAL **2** *or* **hypostatical** [F *hypostatique*, fr. MF, fr. ML *hypostaticus*, fr. Gk *hypostatikos*] : of or relating to theological hypostasis **3** [fr. NL *hypostasis*, after NL *-stasis*: E *-static*] **a** *of a gene* : exhibiting hypostasis in the presence of a corresponding epistatic gene **b** *of a hereditary character* : suppressed by epistasis : appearing recessive to another character due to mediation by a hypostatic gene **4** [fr. LL *hypostasis*, after such pairs as E *emphasis*: *emphatic*] : depending on or due to hypostasis ⟨~ congestion⟩ ⟨~ pneumonia⟩ — **hy·po·stat·i·cal·ly** \-d·ə̇k(ə)lē\ *adv*

hypostatic union *n* [part trans. of F *union hypostatique*, fr. MF] : union in one hypostasis; *esp* : the union of the divine and human natures of Christ in one hypostasis

hy·pos·ta·ti·za·tion \hīˌpästəd·ə̇'zāshən\ *n* -s **1** : an act or instance of hypostatizing : REIFICATION ⟨realism is built on the fallacy of ~, the supposition that an abstract term must somehow have a denotation —T.T.Lafferty⟩ **2** : something that is hypostatized

hy·pos·ta·tize *or* **hy·pos·ta·tise** \hī'pästəˌtīz\ *vt* -ED/-ING/-S [Gk *hypostatos* substantially existing + E *-ize* or *-ise*] : to make into or regard as a hypostasis: **a** : to transform (a conceptual entity) into or construe as a self-subsistent substance ⟨we are told that the conception of God, or the Sacred, or the Mana, or the Totem, is nothing but *hypostatized* society itself —P.A.Sorokin⟩ **b** : to assume as concrete : REIFY ⟨our ingrained habit of *hypostatizing* impressions, of seeing things and not sense-data —Susanne K. Langer⟩

hy·po·sthenia \¦== *at* HYPO-+\ *n* [NL, fr. *hypo-* + Gk *sthenos* strength + NL *-ia* — more at STHENIC] : lack of strength : bodily weakness — **hy·po·sthenic** \"+\ *adj*

hy·pos·the·nu·ria \hīˌpästhə'n(y)u̇rēə\ *n* -s [NL, fr. *hypo-* + Gk *sthenos* strength + NL *-uria*] : the secretion of urine of low specific gravity due to inability of the kidney to concentrate the urine normally — **hy·pos·the·nu·ric** \=¦==¦n(y)u̇rik\ *adj*

hy·pos·to·ma \hī'pästəmə, hə'-\ *n, pl* **hypostomas** \-məz\ *or* **hy·po·sto·ma·ta** \ˌ== *at* HYPO-+'stōməd·ə\ [NL, fr. *hypo-* + *-stoma*] : HYPOSTOME

hy·po·sto·ma·ta \¦== *at* HYPO-+'stōməd·ə\ [NL, fr. *hypo-* + *-stomata*] *syn of* HYPOSTOMIDES

hy·po·sto·mat·ic \¦==+ˌstō¦mad·ik\ *adj* [*hypo-* + *stomatic*] *of a leaf* : having stomata only on the underside

hy·po·stom·a·tous \"+¦stäməd·əs, -tōm-\ *adj* [*hypo-* + *-stomatous*] **1** *of a fish* : having the mouth on the lower side **2** : HYPOSTOMATIC

¹hy·po·stome \'==+ˌstōm\ *n* -s [ISV *hypo-* + *-stome*] : any of several structures associated with the mouth: as **a** : the labrum of a trilobite or crustacean **b** : the manubrium of a hydrozoan **c** : an organ like a rod that arises at the base of the beak in various mites and in ticks

²hypostome \"\ *n* -s [NL *Hypostoma*, genus of fishes, fr. *hypo-* + *-stoma*] : a fish of the order Hypostomides

hy·po·stom·i·des \ˌ==+'stäməˌdēz\ *n pl, cap* [NL, fr. *Hypostoma*, genus of fishes] : an order or suborder of teleost fishes coextensive with the family Pegasidae

hy·pos·to·mous \(ˈ)hī¦pästəməs, hə'p-\ *adj* [*hypo-* + *-stomous*] : HYPOSTOMATOUS

hy·po·stroma \¦== *at* HYPO- +\ *n* [NL, fr. *hypo-* + *stroma*] : a compact mass of hyphae below the true stroma and beneath the host epidermis of a fungus — **hy·po·stromal** \"+\ *adj*

¹hy·po·style \'==+ˌstīl\ *adj* [Gk *hypostylos* resting upon pillars, fr. *hypo-* + *stylos* pillar] : having the roof resting upon rows of columns : constructed by means of columns ⟨~ halls of antiquity⟩

²hypostyle \"\ *n* [¹*hypostyle*] : a hypostyle hall

³hypostyle \"\ *n* [*hypo-* + *style* (cusp)] : a small cusp between the hypocone and metacone of a molar tooth

hy·po·stypsis \¦== *at* HYPO-+\ *n* [NL, fr. *hypo-* + *stypsis*] : mild or moderate astringency

hy·po·styptic \"+\ *adj* [*hypo-* + *styptic*] : mildly or moderately styptic

hy·po·sulfite \"+\ *n* [*hyposulf-* (fr. *hyposulfurous acid*) + *-ite*] **1** : ²HYPO **2** : HYDROSULFITE

hy·po·sulfurous acid \"+ . . . -\ *n* [ISV *hypo-* + *sulfurous* (*acid*)] **1** *archaic* : THIOSULFURIC ACID **2** : HYDROSULFUROUS ACID

hy·po·syllogistic \"+\ *adj* [*hypo-* + *syllogistic*] : having syllogistic value or purpose without the form

hy·po·synergia \"+\ *n* [NL, fr. *hypo-* + *synergia*] : imperfect coordination

hy·po·tac·tic \"+¦taktik\ *adj* [Gk *hypotaktikos*, fr. (assumed) Gk *hypotaktos* (verbal of Gk *hypotassein* to arrange under) + Gk *-ikos* -ic] : of, relating to, or exhibiting hypotaxis

hy·po·tarsus \"+\ *n* [NL, fr. *hypo-* + *tarsus*] : CALCANEUM 2

hy·po·tax·is \ˌ==+'taksə̇s\ *n* [NL, fr. Gk, subjection, submission, fr. *hypotassein* to arrange under, subject, put after, fr. *hypo-* + *tassein* to arrange — more at TACTICS] : syntactic subordination (as by a conjunction) — opposed to *parataxis*

hy·po·tension \¦== *at* HYPO-+\ *n* [ISV *hypo-* + *tension*] **1** : abnormally low arterial blood pressure; *also*: the state of one with such blood pressure **2** : abnormally low pressure of the intraocular fluid

¹hy·po·tensive \"+\ *adj* [ISV *hypotension* + *-ive*] **1** : characterized by or due to hypotension **2** : causing low blood pressure or a lowering of blood pressure ⟨~ drugs⟩

²hypotensive \"\ *n* -s : a person with hypotension

hy·pot·e·nuse \hī'pätᵊnˌ(y)üs *also* -üz\ *also* **hy·poth·e·nuse** \-äthəˌn(y)-\ *n* -s [L *hypotenusa*, fr. Gk *hypoteinousa*, fr. fem. of *hypoteinōn*, pres. part. of *hypoteinein* to subtend, fr. *hypo-* + *teinein* to stretch] : the side of a right-angled triangle that is opposite the right angle; *also* : the length of a hypotenuse

hy·po·thalamic \¦== *at* HYPO-+\ *adj* [*hypo-* + *thalamic*] **1** : located below the thalamus **2** [NL *hypothalamus* + E *-ic*] : of, relating to, or involving the hypothalamus

hypothalamico- *or* **hypothalamo-** *comb form* [*hypothalamico-* fr. *hypothalamic* + *-o-*; *hypothalamo-* fr. NL *hypothalamus*] : hypothalamic and ⟨*hypothalamico*hypophyseal⟩ ⟨*hypothalamo*cortical⟩

hy·po·thalamus \ˌ÷÷+\ *n* [NL, fr. *hypo-* + *thalamus*] **:** a basal part of the diencephalon that lies beneath the thalamus on each side, forms the floor of the third ventricle, and is usu. considered to include vital autonomic regulatory centers and sometimes the posterior pituitary lobe

hy·po·thallus \"+\ *n* [NL, fr. *hypo-* + *thallus*] **1 :** a marginal outgrowth of hyphae from the thallus in crustose lichens **2 :** a residue like a film that remains after the formation of sporangia in the slime molds of the class Myxomycetes

hy·poth·ec \hə̇ˈpäthik, hīˈ-\ *n* -s [F&LL; F *hypothèque*, fr. MF, fr. LL *hypotheca*, fr. Gk *hypothēkē* deposit, pledge, mortgage, fr. *hypotithenai* to deposit as a pledge, put under, propose — more at HYPOTHESIS] **1** *Roman & civil law* **:** an obligation, right, or security given by contract or by operation of law to a creditor over property of the debtor without transfer of possession or title to the creditor — compare PIGNUS, PLEDGE **2** *Scot* **:** AFFAIR, CONCERN

hy·po·theca \ˌ÷÷ *at* HYPO- +\ *n* [NL, fr. *hypo-* + *-theca*] **:** the inner or bottom half or valve of the diatom frustule — compare EPITHECA — **hy·po·thecal** \"+\ *adj*

hy·poth·e·cary \hə̇ˈpäthəˌkerē, hīˈ-\ *adj* [LL *hypothecarius*, fr. *hypotheca* hypothec + L *-arius* -ary] **:** of, relating to, or created or secured by a hypothec ⟨~ right⟩

¹hy·poth·e·cate \hə̇ˈpäthəˌkāt, hīˈ-, *usu* -ād·+V\ *vt* -ED/-ING/-S [ML *hypothecatus*, past part. of *hypothecare* to pledge, fr. LL *hypotheca* pledge, hypothec] **:** to subject to a hypothec **:** to pledge without delivery of title or possession; *specif* **:** to pledge (a ship) by a bottomry bond

²hy·poth·e·cate \hīˈ-\ *vb* -ED/-ING/-S [Gk *hypothēkē* suggestion, counsel, pledge, mortgage + E *-ate*] **:** HYPOTHESIZE

hy·poth·e·ca·tion \hə̇ˌpäthəˈkāshən, (ˌ)hīˌ-\ *n* -s [ML *hypothecation-, hypothecatio*, fr. *hypothecatus* (past part.) + L *-ion-, -io* -ion] **1** *Roman, civil, & maritime law* **:** the act or contract by which property (as real property) is hypothecated **2** *Roman, civil, & maritime law* **:** the right or power of a creditor or claimant over property owned by his debtor or another who has pledged it for the debt to cause the property to be sold to satisfy his claim if payment is defaulted

hypothecation certificate *n* **:** a certificate attached to a bill of exchange empowering the holder to dispose of merchandise if payment or acceptance is refused — called also *letter of hypothecation*

hy·poth·e·ca·tor \-ˈ÷÷ˌkād·ə(r)\ *n* [¹*hypothecate* + *-or*] **:** one that hypothecates

hy·poth·e·ca·tory \-ˈ÷÷ˌkəˌtōrē\ *adj* [¹*hypothecate* + *-ory*] **:** HYPOTHECARY

hy·po·thecium \ˌ÷÷ *at* HYPO- +\ *n* [NL, fr. *hypo-* + *thecium*] **:** a layer of dense hyphal tissue just below the hymenium of lichens and fungi — compare EPITHECIUM

¹hy·po·the·nar \hīˈpäthəˌnär, |ˌnər, ¦hīpə¦thē|\ *n* [NL, fr. Gk, hypothenar of the hand, fr. *hypo-* + *thenar*] **:** the hypothenar eminence

²hypothenar \(ˈ)÷¦÷÷÷\ *also* **hy·po·the·nal** \-thənᵊl, -thēn-\ *adj* **:** of, relating to, or constituting the prominent part of the palm of the hand above the base of the little finger or a corresponding part in the forefoot of an animal

hypothenuse *var of* HYPOTENUSE

hy·po·the·ria \ˌ÷÷ *at* HYPO- + ˈthirēə\ *n pl, cap* [NL, fr. *hypo-* + *-theria*] **:** a hypothetical order including the as yet undiscovered ancestors of the mammals

hy·po·thermal \ˌ÷÷+\ *adj* [*hypo-* + *thermal*] **:** of or relating to a hydrothermal metalliferous ore vein deposited at high temperature — compare EPITHERMAL, MESOTHERMAL

hy·po·ther·mia \ˌ÷÷+ˈthərmēə\ *n* -s [NL, fr. *hypo-* + *-thermia*] **:** subnormal temperature of the body often induced artificially to facilitate cardiac surgery — compare REFRIGERATION

hy·poth·e·sis \hīˈpäthəsə̇s\ *n, pl* **hypothe·ses** \-əˌsēz\ [L, fr. Gk, fr. *hypotithenai* to suppose, propose, put under, fr. *hypo-* + *tithenai* to place, put — more at DO] **1 :** a proposition tentatively assumed in order to draw out its logical or empirical consequences and so test its accord with facts that are known or may be determined ⟨it appears, then, to be a condition of the most genuinely scientific ~ that it be . . . of such a nature as to be either proved or disproved by comparison with observed facts —J.S.Mill⟩ ⟨most of the great unifying conceptions of modern science are working *hypotheses* —Bernard Bosanquet⟩ **2 a :** an assumption or concession made for the sake of argument **b :** an interpretation of a practical situation or condition taken as the ground for action **3 :** the antecedent clause in a conditional statement **4 :** a hypothetical relation **:** the conditioning of one thing by another

hy·poth·e·size \-əˌsīz\ *vb* -ED/-ING/-S *vi* **:** to make a hypothesis ~ *vt* **:** to adopt as a hypothesis **:** ASSUME ⟨we can ~ any value as truth . . . but there are varying probabilities for each hypothesis we make —Lester Guest⟩

¹hy·po·thet·i·cal \ˌhīpə¦thed·ə̇kəl, -etl, |ēk-\ *also* **hy·po·thet·ic** \|ik, |ēk\ *adj* [*hypothetical* fr. LL *hypotheticus* (fr. Gk *hypothetikos*) + E *-al*; *hypothetic* fr. F *hypothétique*, fr. LL *hypotheticus*] **1 :** involving logical hypothesis **:** ASSUMED, CONDITIONAL — distinguished from *categorical* **2 :** of or depending on supposition **:** CONJECTURAL — contrasted with *actual* — **hy·po·thet·i·cal·ly** \|ək(ə)lē, |ēk-, -li\ *adv*

²hypothetical \"\ *n* -s **:** a hypothetical statement or proposition **:** IMPLICATION 2b

hypothetical imperative *n* [trans. of G *hypothetischer imperativ*] **:** an imperative of conduct that springs from expediency or practical necessity rather than from moral law — contrasted with *categorical imperative*

hypothetical question *n* **:** a question based on hypothetical facts concerning which a witness in court is asked for an opinion

hypothetical syllogism *n* [trans. of LL *hypotheticus syllogismus*] **1 :** a syllogism consisting wholly of hypothetical propositions — called also *pure hypothetical syllogism* **2 :** a syllogism consisting partly of hypothetical propositions — called also *mixed hypothetical syllogism*; compare MODUS PONENS, MODUS TOLLENS

hy·po·thet·i·co-deductive \|ə̇kō-\ *adj* [*hypothetic* + *-o-*] **:** of or relating to scientific method in which hypotheses suggested by the facts of observation are proposed and consequences deduced from them so as to test the hypotheses and evaluate the consequences **:** AXIOMATIC

hypothetico-disjunctive *adj* **:** of, relating to, or constituting a logical proposition that combines hypothesis and disjunction

hy·po·thyroid \ˌ÷÷ *at* HYPO- +\ *adj* [*hypo-* + *thyroid*] **:** of, relating to, or affected by hypothyroidism

hy·po·thyroidism \"+\ *n* -s [ISV *hypo-* + *thyroid* + *-ism*] **:** deficient activity of the thyroid gland; *also* **:** a resultant abnormal state marked by lowered metabolic rate and general loss of vigor — compare CRETINISM, MYXEDEMA

hy·po·to·nia \ˌ÷÷+ˈtōnēə\ *or* **hy·pot·o·ny** \hīˈpätᵊnē, hə̇ˈ-\ *n, pl* **hypotonias** *or* **hypotonies** [NL *hypotonia*, fr. *hypo-* + *-tonia*] **:** HYPOTONICITY

hy·po·tonic \ˌ÷÷ *at* HYPO- +\ *adj* [ISV *hypo-* + *tonic*] **1** *of living tissue* **:** having less than the normal tone **2** *of a fluid* **:** having a lower osmotic pressure than a fluid under comparison or used as a standard — compare ISOTONIC

hy·po·tonicity \"+\ *n* **:** the quality or state of being hypotonic

hy·po·tonus \"+\ *n* -ES [NL, fr. *hypo-* + *tonus*] **:** HYPOTONICITY

hy·po·tra·che·li·um \ˌ÷÷+trəˈkēlēəm\ *n* [L, fr. Gk *hypotrachēlion*, fr. *hypo-* + *trachēlos* neck] **:** GORGERIN

hy·po·trem·a·ta \"+ˈtremədə, -rēm-\ *n pl, cap* [NL, fr. *hypo-* + *-tremata*] **:** an order of Chondrichthyes comprising the rays — compare PLEUROTREMATA

hy·po·trich \ˈ÷÷+ˌtrik\ *n* -s [NL *Hypotricha*] **:** one of the Hypotricha

hy·pot·ri·cha \hīˈpä·trəkə\ *n pl, cap* [NL, fr. *hypo-* + *-tricha*] **:** a suborder of Spirotricha comprising ciliates that have cilia only on the ventral surface and usu. fused to cirri and that often have tactile bristles on the dorsum — compare EUPLOTES, OXYTRICHA, STYLONYCHIA — **hy·pot·ri·chous** \(ˈ)÷¦÷÷kəs\ *adj*

hy·po·trich·ia \ˌ÷÷ *at* HYPO- + ˈtrikēə\ *n* -s [NL, fr. *hypo-* + *-trichia*] **:** HYPOTRICHOSIS

hy·po·trich·i·da \-kədə\ [NL, fr. *hypo-* + *trich-* + *-ida*] *syn of* HYPOTRICHA

hy·po·tri·cho·sis \ˌ÷÷+trəˈkōsə̇s\ *n* [NL, fr. *hypo-* + Gk *trichōsis* growth of hair (fr. *trich-* + *-ōsis* -osis)] **:** congenital deficiency of hair — **hy·po·tri·chot·ic** \ˌ÷÷÷¦käd·ik\ *adj*

hy·po·trochanteric \ˌ÷÷ *at* HYPO- +\ *adj* [*hypo-* + *trochanteric*] **:** situated beneath a trochanter

hy·po·trochoid \"+\ *n* [*hypo-* + *trochoid*] **:** a plane curve traced by a point on the radius or extended radius but not on the circumference of a circle rolling on the inside of a fixed circle — compare EPITROCHOID — **hy·po·trochoidal** \"+\ *adj*

hy·pot·ro·phy \hīˈpä·trəfē, həˈ-\ *n* [ISV *hypo-* + *-trophy*] **1 :** subnormal growth — compare HYPERTROPHY **2 :** greater growth of the lower than of the upper side of horizontal or ascending branches or roots — opposed to *epitrophy*

hy·po·tympanic \ˌ÷÷ *at* HYPO- +\ *adj* [in sense 1, fr. *hypo-* + *tympanic*; in sense 2, fr. NL *hypotympanum* + E *-ic*] **1 :** located below the tympanum **2 :** of or relating to the hypotympanum

hy·po·tympanum \"+\ *n* [NL, fr. *hypo-* + *tympanum*] **:** the lower part of the middle ear — compare EPITYMPANUM

hy·po·type \ˈ÷÷+ˌ-\ *n* [*hypo-* + *type*] **:** a specimen of a species not of the original type series but known by published description, figure, or listing

hy·po·typic \ˌ÷÷+\ *or* **hy·po·typical** \"+\ *adj* [in sense 1, fr. *hypo-* + *typic* or *typical*; in sense 2, fr. *hypotype* + *-ic* or *-ical*] **1 :** imperfectly typical **2 :** of or relating to a hypotype

hy·po·ty·po·sis \ˌ÷÷+ˌtīˈpōsə̇s\ *n, pl* **hypotypo·ses** \-ōˌsēz\ [Gk *hypotypōsis*, fr. *hypotypoun* to sketch, outline, fr. *hypo-* + *typoun* to stamp, form (fr. *typos* impression, cast)] **:** vivid picturesque description

hy·po·valve \ˈ÷÷+ˌ-\ *n* [*hypo-* + *valve*] **1 :** one half of the shell of a dinoflagellate **2 :** the hypotheca of a diatom

hy·po·vanadate \ˌ÷÷+\ *n* [ISV *hypo-* + *vanadate*] **:** a salt (as potassium hypovanadate $K_2V_4O_9$) containing tetravalent vanadium in the anion — called also *vanadite*

hy·po·vi·ta·min·osis \ˌ÷÷+ˌvīd·əmə̇ˈnōsə̇s\ *n* -ES [NL, fr. *hypo-* + ISV *vitamin* + NL *-osis*] **:** AVITAMINOSIS

hy·po·vi·ta·min·ot·ic \ˌ÷÷¦÷÷÷¦näd·ik\ *adj* **:** AVITAMINOTIC

hy·po·vo·le·mia \ˌ÷÷+väˈlēmēə\ *n* -s [NL, fr. *hypo-* + *vol-* (fr. E *volume*) + *-emia*] **:** decrease in the volume of the circulating blood — **hy·po·vo·le·mic** \ˌ÷÷¦÷¦lēmik\ *adj*

hy·po·xanthine \ˌ÷÷+\ *n* [ISV *hypo-* + *xanthine*] **:** a purine base $C_5H_4N_4O$ found in plant and animal tissues, formed by hydrolysis of adenine and inosinic acid, and yielding xanthine on oxidation; 6-hydroxy-purine

hy·pox·e·mia \ˌhīˌpäkˈsēmēə\ *n* -s [NL, fr. *hypo-* + ¹*ox-* + *-emia*] **:** deficient oxygenation of the blood

hy·pox·ia \hīˈpäksēə\ *n* -s [NL, fr. *hypo-* + ¹*ox-* + *-ia*] **:** a deficiency of oxygen reaching the tissues of the body whether due to environmental deficiency or impaired respiratory and circulatory organs — **hy·pox·ic** \(ˈ)÷¦sik\ *adj*

hy·pox·is \hīˈpäksə̇s, hə̇ˈ-\ *n, cap* [NL, irreg. fr. *hypo-* + Gk *oxys* sharp — more at OXY-] **:** a genus of small scapose herbs (family Amaryllidaceae) having numerous hairy linear leaves from a corm or short rootstock and umbellate yellow flowers with 6-parted perianth — see STAR GRASS 1

hy·pox·y·lon \hīˈpäksəˌlän\ *n, cap* [NL, fr. *hypo-* + *-xylon*] **:** a genus of fungi (family Xylariaceae) having effuse to hemispherical stromata and including a species (*H. pruinatum*) that causes a canker of poplars — compare XYLARIA

hy·po·zeug·ma \ˌ÷÷ *at* HYPO- + ˈzügmə\ *n* [LL, fr. *hypo-* + L *zeugma*] **:** the joining of several subjects with a single verb

hy·po·zeux·is \"+ˈzüksə̇s\ *n* -ES [LL, fr. LGk, fr. Gk *hypozeugnynai* to subjugate, yoke under, fr. *hypo-* + *zeugnynai* to yoke — more at YOKE] **:** the use in a parallel construction of successive clauses each complete with subject and verb

hy·po·zoic \ˌ÷÷+ˈzōik\ *adj* [ISV *hypo-* + *-zoic*] **:** lying under the fossiliferous systems

hypped \ˈhipt\ *archaic var of* HIPPED

hyp·pish \ˈhipish\ *adj* [*hyp* + *-ish*] **:** affected with hypochondria **:** BLUE, DEPRESSED, MELANCHOLIC

hyps *pl of* HYP

hyps- *or* **hypsi-** *or* **hypso-** *comb form* [in sense 1, fr. Gk, fr. *hypsos*, in sense 2, fr. Gk, fr. *hypsi*; Gk *hypsos* & Gk *hypsi* akin to Gk *hypo* under — more at UP] **1 :** height ⟨*hypso*graphy⟩ **2 :** on high **:** aloft ⟨*hypsi*cephalic⟩ ⟨*hypso*dont⟩

hyp·si·brachycephalic \¦hipsə̇, -sē+\ *adj* [*hyps-* + *brachycephalic*] **:** having a high broad head

hyp·si·brachycephalism \"+\ *n* [*hyps-* + *brachycephalism*] **:** the quality or state of being hypsibrachycephalic

hyp·si·brachycephaly \"+\ *n* [*hypsibrachycephalic* + *-y*] **:** HYPSIBRACHYCEPHALISM

hyp·si·ceph·al \ˌhipsəˈsefəl\ *n* -s [ISV *hyps-* + *-cephal* (as in *dolichocephal*)] **:** a person having a high forehead

hyp·si·ce·phal·ic \ˌhipsə̇sə̇¦falik\ *also* **hyp·si·ceph·a·lous** \¦hipsə¦sefələs\ *adj* [*hyps-* + *-cephalic* or *-cephalous*] **:** having a high forehead with a length-height index of 62.6 or higher — compare HYPSICRANIC

hyp·si·conch \ˈhipsəˌkäŋk, -änch\ *adj* [*hyps-* + *-conch* (fr. L *concha* conch, shell) — more at CONCH] *anthropol* **:** having high orbits with an orbital index of 89 or over — **hyp·si·con·chy** \-äŋkē, -änchē\ *n* -ES

hyp·si·cra·ni·al \¦hipsə¦krānēəl\ *or* **hyp·si·cra·nic** \-nik\ *adj* [G *hypsikran* hypsicranial (fr. *hyps-* + Gk *kranion* cranium) + E *-ial* or *-ic* — more at CRANIUM] **:** having a high skull with a length-height index of 75 or over — **hyp·si·cra·ny** \ˈ÷÷ˌkrānē\ *n* -ES

hyp·si·dolichocephalic \¦hipsə̇, -sē+\ *adj* [*hyps-* + *dolichocephalic*] **:** having a head that is high and narrow or high and long or high, long, and narrow

hyp·si·dolichocephalism \"+\ *n* [*hyps-* + *dolichocephalism*] **:** the quality or state of being hypsidolichocephalic

hyp·si·dolichocephaly \"+\ *n* [*hyps-* + *dolichocephaly*] **:** HYPSIDOLICHOCEPHALISM

hyp·si·dont \ˈhipsəˌdänt\ *adj* [*hyps-* + *-dont* (fr. *-odont*)] **:** HYPSODONT

hyp·sil·i·form \(ˈ)hip¦siləˌfȯrm\ *adj* [*hypsil-* (fr. MGk *hy psilon* upsilon) + *-iform*] **:** HYPSILOID

hyp·si·loid \ˈhipsəˌlȯid\ *adj* [MGk *hypsiloeidēs*, fr. *hy psilon* upsilon, lit., simple y + *-oeidēs* -oid] *anat* **:** resembling a Greek capital letter upsilon in form

hyp·si·loph·o·don \ˌhipsəˈläfəˌdän\ *n, cap* [NL, fr. Gk *hypsilophos* high-crested (fr. *hyps-* + *lophos* crest) + NL *-odon*] **:** a genus (the type of the family Hypsilophodontidae) of small primitive ornithopod dinosaurs of the Wealden of the Isle of Wight

hyp·si·loph·o·dont \ˌ÷÷¦÷÷ˌdänt\ *adj* [NL *Hypsilophodontidae*, family of dinosaurs, fr. *Hypsilophodont-, Hypsilophodon*, type genus + *-idae*] **:** of or relating to the genus *Hypsilophodon* or family Hypsilophodontidae

hyp·si·prym·no·don \ˌhipsəˈprimnəˌdän\ *n, cap* [NL, fr. *hyps-* + Gk *prymnos* endmost, hindmost + NL *-odon*] **:** a genus of marsupial mammals comprising the musk kangaroos

hyp·sis·tar·i·an \¦hipsə¦sta(a)rēən\ *n* -s *usu cap* [LGk *Hypsistarioi*, pl., fr. *hypsistarioi*, pl. of *hypsistarios* worshiping the highest (fr. Gk *hypsistos* highest, fr. *hypsi* on high) + E *-an*] **:** a member of a sect of the 4th to the 9th century in Asia Minor combining heathen, Jewish, and Christian tenets

hyp·si·stenocephalic \¦hipsə̇, -sē+\ *adj* [*hyps-* + *stenocephalic*] **:** having an extremely high narrow head

hyp·si·sten·o·ceph·a·lism \ˌ÷÷+ˌstenəˈsefəˌlizəm\ *n* [*hypsistenocephalic* + *-ism*] **:** the quality or state of being hypsistenocephalic

hyp·si·stenocephaly \¦÷÷+\ *n* [*hyps-* + *stenocephaly*] **:** HYPSISTENOCEPHALISM

hypso- — see HYPS-

hyp·so·chrome \ˈhipsəˌkrōm\ *n* [ISV *hyps-* + *-chrome*] **:** an atom or group that when introduced into a compound causes a visible lightening of color (as from green toward yellow) — contrasted with *bathochrome* — **hyp·so·chro·mic** \ˌ÷÷ˈkrōmik\ *adj*

hyp·so·dont \ˈhipsəˌdänt\ *adj* [*hyps-* + *-odont*] **1** *of teeth* **:** having high or deep crowns and short roots (as the molar teeth of a horse) — compare BRACHYDONT **2 :** having hypsodont teeth

hyp·so·dont·ism \-nˌtizəm\ *n* -s [*hypsodont* + *-ism*] **:** the quality or state of being hypsodont

hyp·so·donty \-ntē\ *n* -ES [*hypsodont* + *-y*] **:** HYPSODONTISM

hyp·sog·ra·phy \hipˈsägrəfē\ *n* -ES [ISV *hyps-* + *-graphy*] **1 :** a branch of geography that deals with the measurement and mapping of the varying elevations of the earth's surface with reference to sea level **2 :** topographic relief or the devices (as color shadings) by which it is indicated on maps

hyp·so·isotherm \¦hip(ˌ)sō+\ *n* [*hyps-* + *isotherm*; trans. of G *höhenisotherme*] **:** an isotherm that is drawn on a vertical section of the atmosphere and sometimes also of the ground to show the distribution of temperature in the vertical

hyp·som·e·ter \hipˈsäməd·ə(r)\ *n* [ISV *hyps-* + *-meter*] **1 :** an apparatus for estimating elevations in mountainous regions from the boiling points of liquids **2 :** any of various instruments used to determine the height of trees by triangulation

hyp·so·met·ric \¦hipsə¦me·trik\ *or* **hyp·so·met·ri·cal** \-rə̇kəl\ *adj* **:** of or relating to hypsometry

hyp·som·e·try \hipˈsämə·trē\ *n* -ES [Gk *hypsos* height + E *-metry*] **:** the science of measuring heights (as with reference to sea level)

hyp·so·phyll \ˈhipsəˌfil\ *n* -s [NL *hypsophyllum* trans. of G *hochblatt*, lit., high leaf), fr. *hyps-* + *-phyllum* -phyll] **:** a floral leaf beneath the sporophylls **:** BRACT, SCALE LEAF — **hyp·so·phyl·lar** \¦÷÷¦filə(r)\ *or* **hyp·so·phyl·lary** \-lərē\ *or* **hyp·so·phyl·lous** \-ləs\ *adj*

¹hy·pu·ral \(ˈ)hī¦pyu̇rəl\ *adj* [*hypo-* + *ur-* (tail) + *-al*] **:** of, relating to, or constituting the bony structure chiefly formed of the expanded and more or less fused hemal spines of the last few vertebrae that supports the caudal fin rays in most teleost fishes

²hypural \"\ *n* -s **:** a hypural bone

hy·ra·ce·um \hīˈrāsēəm\ *n* -s [NL, fr. *hyrac-, hyrax* + *-eum* (as in *castoreum*)] **:** a southern African product somewhat like castoreum said to be excreted by the hyrax and formerly much used as a folk remedy and as a fixative for perfumes

hy·rach·y·us \hīˈrakēəs\ *n, cap* [NL, fr. *Hyrac-, Hyrax*, genus of ungulates + *-hyus* (fr. Gk *hy-, hys* hog, swine) — more at SOW (female hog)] **:** a genus (the type of the family Hyrachyidae) of primitive perissodactyl ungulates related to the rhinoceroses and common in the No. American Eocene

¹hy·rac·id \(ˈ)hī¦rasə̇d\ *adj* [NL *Hyracidae*] **:** of or relating to the Procaviidae

²hyracid \"\ *n* -s **:** a member of the family Procaviidae **:** CONEY

hy·rac·i·dae \hīˈrasəˌdē\ [NL, fr. *Hyrac-, Hyrax* + *-idae*] *syn of* PROCAVIIDAE

hy·rac·i·form \(ˈ)÷¦÷÷ˌfȯrm\ *adj* [NL *hyrac-, hyrax* + E *-iform*] **:** resembling a hyrax

hy·ra·ci·na \ˌhīrəˈsīnə\ [NL, fr. *Hyrac-, Hyrax* + *-ina*] *syn of* HYRACOIDEA

hy·rac·o·don \hīˈrakəˌdän\ *n, cap* [NL, fr. *Hyrac-, Hyrax* + *-odon*] **:** a genus (the type of the family Hyracodontidae) of Eocene and Oligocene perissodactyls related to the rhinoceroses but hornless and of light agile build with all feet three-toed

¹hy·rac·o·dont \(ˈ)÷¦÷÷ˌdänt\ *adj* [NL *Hyracodont-, Hyracodon*] **:** of or relating to the genus *Hyracodon* or family Hyracodontidae

²hyracodont \"\ *n* -s **:** a mammal of the genus *Hyracodon* or family Hyracodontidae

hy·ra·coid \ˈhīrəˌkȯid\ *n* -s [NL *Hyracoidea*] **:** one of the Hyracoidea

hy·ra·coi·dea \ˌ÷÷ˈkȯidēə\ *n pl, cap* [NL, fr. *Hyrac-, Hyrax* + *-oidea*] **:** an order of Old World ungulate mammals that is now restricted to Africa and southwestern Asia and that comprises various extinct animals and the surviving hyraxes which find their nearest living relatives in the elephants and sirenians but in many respects resemble rabbits

hy·ra·co·there \ˈhīrə̇kōˌthir\ *n* -s [NL *Hyracotherium*] **:** an animal or fossil of the genus *Hyracotherium*

hy·ra·co·the·ri·um \ˌ÷÷÷ˈthirēəm\ *n, cap* [NL *Hyrac-, Hyrax* + *-o-* + *-therium*] **:** a genus of lower Eocene perissodactylous mammals about the size of a fox having four-toed forelimbs and three-toed hind limbs and regarded as among the earliest ancestors of the modern horse — see EQUIDAE illustration

¹hy·rax \ˈhīˌraks\ [NL, fr. Gk, mouse, shrewmouse; akin to L *susurrus* hum, murmur — more at SWARM] *syn of* PROCAVIA

²hyrax \"\ *n, pl* **hyraxes** \-ksə̇z\ *also* **hyra·ces** \-īrəˌsēz\ [NL, fr. ¹*Hyrax*] **:** any of certain small mammals that constitute the order Hyracoidea and are characterized by thickset body with short legs and ears and rudimentary tail, feet with soft pads and broad nails, and teeth of which the molars resemble those of the rhinoceros and the incisors those of rodents — called also *coney*

³hyrax \"\ *n* -ES [origin unknown] **:** a microscopic mounting medium of high refractive index that consists of a naphthalene derivative dissolved in benzene or xylol, is used esp. for mounting semiopaque structures (as diatom frustules), and tends to darken but not crystallize with age

hyr·ca·ni·an \¦hər¦kānēən\ *also* **hyr·can** \ˈhərkən\ *adj, usu cap* [*hyrcanian* fr. L *Hyrcanius* Hyrcanian (fr. *Hyrcania*, ancient country or province of Asia) + E *-an*; *hyrcan* fr. L *Hyrcanus* Hyrcanian, fr. Gk *Hyrkanos*, n., Hyrcanian, inhabitant of Hyrcania] **:** of or relating to the ancient land of Hyrcania southeast of the Caspian sea

hyrst *var of* HURST

hy·son \ˈhīsᵊn\ *n* -s [Chin (Peking) *hsi¹ ch'un¹*, lit., flourishing spring] **:** a Chinese green tea made from thinly rolled and twisted leaves

hyson skin *n* **:** the light and inferior leaves separated from hyson by a winnowing machine

hy spy \ˈhī-\ *n* [prob. fr. *hi, spy!* (call used by the hiders in the game as a signal to the searchers to start looking for them), fr. *hi* + *spy*, n.] **:** HIDE-AND-SEEK

hys·sop \ˈhisəp\ *n* -s [ME *ysop*, partly fr. OE *ysope* and partly fr. OF *ysope*; OE & OF, fr. L *hyssopum, hyssopum, hyssopus*, fr. Gk *hyssōpon, hyssōpos*, of Sem origin; akin to Heb *ēzōbh* hyssop, Assyr-Bab *zūpu*, Syriac *zōfā*] **1 a :** a plant used in bunches for purificatory sprinkling rites by the ancient Hebrews **b :** a European mint (*Hyssopus officinalis*) that has highly aromatic and pungent leaves and is often cultivated in gardens as a remedy for bruises **2 a** [prob. fr. ML *hyssopus* (also, the plant), fr. L] **:** ASPERGILLUM **b :** the holy water sprinkled in the asperges

hyssop loosestrife *n* **:** GRASS POLY

hyssop oil *n* **:** an essential oil obtained from hyssop and used chiefly in liqueurs

hyssop skullcap *n* **:** a perennial herb (*Scutellaria integrifolia*) of the eastern U.S. with showy blue flowers

hys·so·pus \ˈhisəpəs, həˈsōp-\ *n, cap* [NL, fr. L, hyssop] **:** a Eurasian genus of perennial herbs or subshrubs (family Labiatae) having floral whorls in bracted spikes — see HYSSOP 1

hyssop violet *n* **:** a grayish purple that is redder and stronger than telegraph blue, bluer and deeper than mauve gray, and bluer, lighter, and stronger than average rose mauve

hys·taz·a·rin \hə̇ˈstazərə̇n\ *n* -s [ISV *hyst-* (fr. Gk *hysteros* latter, later) + *alizarin*; orig. formed in G] **:** a yellow crystalline compound $C_{14}H_6O_2(OH)_2$ produced along with its isomer alizarin by condensation of phthalic anhydride and pyrocatechol; 2,3-dihydroxy-anthraquinone

hyster- *or* **hystero-** *comb form* [F or L; F *hystér-*, fr. MF, fr. L *hyster-*, fr. Gk, fr. *hystera* womb] **1 :** womb ⟨*hyster*ectomy⟩ ⟨*hystero*myoma⟩ **2** [NL, fr. *hysteria*] **a :** hysteria ⟨*hystero*genic⟩ **b :** hysteria and ⟨*hystero*neurasthenia⟩

hys·ter·ec·to·mize \ˌhistəˈrektəˌmīz\ *vt* -ED/-ING/-S **:** to remove the uterus of by surgery

hys·ter·ec·to·my \-ˌmē\ *n* -ES [ISV *hyster-* + *-ectomy*] **:** surgical removal of the uterus

hys·ter·e·sis \ˌhistəˈrēsə̇s\ *n, pl* **hystere·ses** \-ēˌsēz\ [NL, fr. Gk *hysterēsis* shortcoming, deficiency, need, fr. *hysterein* to come late, be behind (fr. *hysteros* later) + *-sis* — more at OUT] **1 a :** the lagging of a physical effect on a body behind its cause (as behind changed forces and conditions) ⟨there is a good deal of ~, that is, a time lag between the cooling and the setting to be expected of the jelly —J.W.McBain⟩ ⟨all manometers must be tested for ~ as well as for sensitivity and natural frequency —H.D.Green⟩ **b :** a lagging of elongation behind tensile stress and of contraction behind release from stress in an elastic solid due to internal friction **c :** a lagging of magnetization and hence of magnetic induction behind magnetic intensity and of demagnetization behind reduction of intensity in a ferromagnetic substance (as iron) **d :** a lagging of electric polarization behind electric intensity and of depolarization behind reduction of intensity in a dielectric **2 a :** the influence of the previous history or treatment of a body on its subsequent response to a given force or changed condition ⟨the influence of the previous treatment of a gel upon its behavior is known as ~ —B.S.Meyer & D.B.Anderson⟩ ⟨a study has been made of the phenomenon of rennet ~, in which the time of coagulation of heated milk is progressively greater with increase in the time interval between heating and addition of rennet —J.S.Fruton⟩ **b :** the changed response of a body that results from this influence ⟨the permeability depends on the past history (magnetically speaking) of the iron, a phenomenon known as ~ —F.W.Sears⟩ **3 :** HYSTERESIS LOSS

hysteresis coefficient *n* **:** the constant in a formula for hysteresis loss that is characteristic of the substance under test

hysteresis loop *n* **:** a cycle of alternating changes involving elastic, magnetic, or dielectric hysteresis; *also* **:** the loop-shaped graph representing such a cycle

hysteresis loss *n* **:** loss of energy in the form of heat due to hysteresis (as in an alternating-current core)

hysteresis motor *n* **:** a synchronous motor that utilizes the hysteresis effect in a solid rotor of permanent-magnet material to achieve synchronism and that is used esp. in sound recording and reproducing machines

hys·ter·et·ic \\¦histə¦red·|ik, -et|, |ēk\\ *adj* [fr. NL *hysteresis,* after such pairs as NL *exegesis:* E *exegetic*] **:** of, relating to, or marked by hysteresis — **hys·ter·et·i·cal·ly** \\|ək(ə)lē, |ēk-, -li\\ *adv*

hys·te·ria \\hə'sterēə, -tir-\\ *n* -s [NL, fr. E *hyster*ic + NL *-ia*] **1 a :** a psychoneurosis that is marked by emotional excitability involving disturbances of the psychic, sensory, vasomotor, and visceral functions **b :** a similar disease of domesticated animals; *specif* **:** CANINE HYSTERIA **2 :** conduct or an outbreak of conduct exhibiting unmanageable fear or emotional excess in individuals or groups ⟨could not fail to destroy his system, never very strong and pitched to ~ from the first —H.M. Ledig-Rowohlt⟩ ⟨weeping generously . . . and wildly giggling, in a ~ which she could not control —Arnold Bennett⟩ ⟨swept up into the systematized ~ of the war —Scott Fitzgerald⟩ ⟨the ghost dance was the religious expression of a social ~ —W.W. Howells⟩ **syn** see MANIA

hys·te·ri·a·ce·ae \\hə,stirē'āsē,ē\\ *n pl, cap* [NL, fr. *Hysterium,* type genus (fr. Gk *hystera* womb + NL *-ium*) + *-aceae*] **:** a family of ascomycetous fungi (order Hysteriales) that is often considered to be derived from the family Sphaeriaceae from which it is distinguished chiefly by the form and method of opening of the ascomata of its members

hys·te·ri·a·gen·ic \\hə¦sterēə¦jenik, -tir-\\ *adj* [NL *hysteria* + E *-genic*] **:** HYSTEROGENIC

hys·te·ri·a·les \\hə,stirē'ā(,)lēz\\ *n pl, cap* [NL, fr. *Hysterium,* genus of fungi + *-ales*] **:** an order of fungi of the subclass Euascomycetes that is characterized by elongated ascomata opening by a longitudinal slit and includes various fungi which cause leaf cast of conifers — see HYSTERIACEAE

1hys·ter·ic \\hə'sterik, (')hi¦s-, -rēk\\ *adj* [L *hystericus* of the womb] **:** HYSTERICAL ⟨raved and ran hither and thither in ~ insanity —W.M.Thackeray⟩

2hysteric \\"\\ *n* -s **1 :** one subject to or suffering from hysteria **2 :** an overemotional or unstable person ⟨Bohemia, which has always been (along with better things) the refuge of fakers, self-deceivers, and ~*s* —C.J.Rolo⟩ ⟨a charlatan, a lucky ~, and a lying demagogue —John Gunther⟩

hys·ter·i·cal \\hə'sterəkəl, (')hi¦s-, -rēk-\\ *adj* [L *hyster*icus hysterical (fr. Gk *hysterikos,* fr. *hystera* womb + *-ikos* -ic) + E *-al;* fr. its being orig. applied to women thought to be suffering from disturbances of the womb] **1 :** of, relating to, or marked by hysteria ⟨during ~ conditions various functions of the human body are disordered —Morris Fishbein⟩ — compare PSYCHOGENIC **2 :** exhibiting unrestrained emotionalism ⟨had absorbed all the serenity of America, and left none for his restless, rickety, ~ countrymen —R.W.Emerson⟩ — **hys·ter·i·cal·ly** \\-rək(ə)lē, -rēk-, -li\\ *adv*

hys·ter·icky \\-rəkē\\ *adj* **:** HYSTERICAL ⟨up I went with all the courage I could muster, but a sort of ~ feeling —W.G. Hammond⟩

hys·ter·ics \\hə'steriks, -rēks\\ *n pl but usu sing in constr, also* **hys·ter·ic** \\-k\\ **:** a fit of uncontrollable laughter or crying **:** HYSTERIA ⟨she'll go all to pieces and start bawling and having ~ —Erle Stanley Gardner⟩

1hys·ter·i·form \\hə'sterə,fȯrm\\ *adj* [ISV *hyster-* + *-iform*] **:** resembling hysteria

2hysteriform \\"\\ *adj* [NL *Hysterium,* genus of fungi + E *-form*] **:** HYSTERIOID

hys·te·ri·oid \\hə'stirē,ȯid\\ *adj* [NL *Hysterium,* genus of fungi + E *-oid* — more at HYSTERIACEAE] **:** BOAT-SHAPED ⟨the ~ apothecia of fungi of the order Hysteriales⟩

hystero- — see HYSTER-

hys·tero·crystalline \\¦histə(,)rō+\\ *n* -s [ISV *hystero-* (fr. Gk *hysteros* latter, later) + *crystalline;* orig. formed as G *hysterokrystallin*] **:** a secondary crystallization in igneous rock

hys·tero-epilepsy \\"+\\ *n* [ISV *hyster-* + *epilepsy*] **:** a hysteria characterized by motor convulsions resembling those of epilepsy — **hys·tero-epileptic** \\"+\\ *adj*

hys·ter·o·gen·ic \\¦histərō¦jenik\\ *adj* [*hyster-* + *-genic*] **:** inducing hysteria

hys·ter·o·gram \\'histərō,gram\\ *n* [*hyster-* + *-gram*] **:** a roentgenogram made by hysterography

hys·ter·o·graph \\-raf,-råf\\ *n* [*hyster-* + *-graph*] **:** HYSTEROGRAM — **hys·ter·o·graph·ic** \\¦==¦grafik\\ *adj*

hys·ter·og·ra·phy \\,histə'rägrəfē\\ *n* -ES [*hyster-* + *-graphy*] **:** examination of the uterus by roentgenography after the injection of an opaque medium

hys·ter·oid \\'histə,rȯid\\ *also* **hys·ter·oi·dal** \\¦==¦rȯidᵊl\\ *adj* [*hysteroid,* ISV *hyster-* + *-oid; hysteroidal* fr. *hysteroid* + *-al*] **:** resembling hysteria

hys·ter·ol·o·gy \\,histə'räləjē\\ *n* -ES [LL *hysterologia,* fr. LGk, fr. Gk *hysteros* latter, later + *-logia* -logy] *archaic* **:** HYSTERON PROTERON

hys·ter·o·mor·phous \\¦histərō¦mȯrfəs\\ *adj* [Gk *hysteros* later, latter + E *-morphous*] **:** of, relating to, or constituting mineral deposits formed on the earth's surface by mechanical or chemical concentration

hys·ter·on pro·ter·on \\'histə,rän'prōd·ə,rän\\ *n* [LL, fr. Gk, lit., later earlier, the latter earlier] **1 :** a figure of speech consisting of reversal of a natural or rational order (as in "then came the thunder and the lightning") **2 :** a logical fallacy consisting in assuming as a premise something that follows from what is to be proved

hys·tero-oophorectomy \\¦histə(,)rō+\\ *n* [*hyster-* + *oophor-* + *-ectomy*] **:** surgical removal of the uterus and ovaries

hys·ter·o·pexy \\'histərō,peksē\\ *n* -ES [ISV *hyster-* + *-pexy*] **:** surgical fixation of a displaced uterus

hys·ter·o·phyte \\'histərō,fīt\\ *n* -S [NL *hysterophytum,* fr. *hyster-* + *-phytum* -phyte] **:** HETEROPHYTE

hys·ter·or·rha·phy \\,histə'rärəfē\\ *n* -ES [ISV *hyster-* + *-rrhaphy*] **1 :** a suturing of an incised or ruptured uterus **2 :** HYSTEROPEXY

hys·ter·or·rhex·is \\,histərō'reksəs\\ *n, pl* **hysterorrhex·es** \\-k,sēz\\ [NL, fr. *hyster-* + *-rrhexis*] **:** rupture of the uterus

hys·ter·o·sal·pin·gog·raphy \\,histərō,sal,piŋ'gägrəfē\\ *n* -ES [ISV *hyster-* + *salping-* + *-graphy*] **:** examination of the uterus and fallopian tubes by roentgenography after injection of an opaque medium

hys·tero-salpingo-oophorectomy \\¦histə(,)rō+\\ *n* [*hyster-* + *salping-* + *oophorectomy*] **:** surgical removal of uterus, oviducts, and ovaries

hys·ter·o·scope \\'histərō,skōp\\ *n* [ISV *hyster-* + *-scope*] **:** an instrument used in inspection of the uterus — **hys·ter·o·scop·ic** \\¦===¦skäpik\\ *adj* — **hys·ter·os·co·py** \\,histə'räskəpē\\ *n* -ES

hys·ter·o·sto·mat·o·my \\,histərō,stō'mad·əmē\\ *n* -ES [F *hystérostomatomie,* fr. *hystér-* hyster- + *stoma-* + *-tomie* -tomy] **:** surgical incision of the uterine cervix

hys·ter·o·tely \\'histərō,telē\\ *n* -ES [Gk *hysteros* latter, later + *telos* end, completion, maturity + E *-y* — more at WHEEL] **:** relatively retarded differentiation of a structure or organ so that it shows a form usu. associated with a stage of development earlier than that shown by the individual plant or animal as a whole — compare PROTHETELY

hys·ter·o·the·ci·um \\,histərō'thēs(h)ēəm\\ *n* [NL, fr. *hyster-* + *-thecium*] **:** a narrow elongated ascocarp opening at maturity by a narrow lengthwise slit

hys·ter·ot·o·my \\,histə'räd·əmē\\ *n* -ES [NL *hysterotomia,* fr. *hyster-* + *-tomia* -tomy] **:** surgical incision of the uterus **:** CESAREAN, HYSTEROSTOMATOMY

hys·tric·i·dae \\hə'strisə,dē\\ *n pl, cap* [NL, fr. *Hystric-, Hystrix,* type genus + *-idae*] **:** a family of Old World hystricomorph rodents comprising the terrestrial porcupines that was formerly extended to include the New World arboreal porcupines — compare ERETHIZONTIDAE

1hys·tri·coid \\'histrə,kȯid\\ *adj* [NL *Hystricoidea*] **:** of or relating to the Hystricoidea

2hystricoid \\"\\ *n* -s **:** a rodent of the superfamily Hystricoidea

hys·tri·coi·dea \\,=='kȯidēə\\ *n pl, cap* [NL, fr. *Hystric-, Hystrix* + *-oidea*] **1** *in some classifications* **:** a major division of hystricomorph rodents equivalent to the Hystricidae **2** *in some classifications* **:** HYSTRICOMORPHA

1hys·tri·co·morph \\'histrəkō,mȯrf\\ *adj* [NL *Hystricomorpha*] **:** of or relating to the Hystricomorpha

2hystricomorph \\"\\ *n* -s **:** a rodent of the suborder Hystricomorpha

hys·tri·co·mor·pha \\,==='mȯrfə\\ *n pl, cap* [NL, fr. *Hystric-, Hystrix* + *-morpha*] **:** a suborder of Rodentia comprising forms distinguished by a zygomatic arch in which the jugal bone forms the center block and including porcupines, guinea pigs, chinchillas, and many others — **hys·tri·co·mor·phic** \\¦===¦mȯrfik\\ *or* **hys·tri·co·mor·phous** \\-fəs\\ *adj*

1hys·trix \\'histriks\\ *n, cap* [NL, fr. L, porcupine, fr. Gk] **:** a genus of terrestrial porcupines that is the type of the family Hystricidae

2hystrix \\"\\ *n, cap* [NL] **:** a genus of perennial grasses (family Gramineae) of No. America, Asia, and New Zealand having loosely flowered spikes with spikelets becoming widely divergent — see BOTTLE BRUSH GRASS

hyte \\'həit\\ *adj* [origin unknown] *Scot* **:** stark raving mad

hy·ther·graph \\'hīthə(r),graf, -råf\\ *also* **hy·ther·o·graph** \\-ərō,-\\ *n* [*hyther-* or *hythero-* (fr. Gk *hydōr* water + *thermē* heat) + *-graph*] **:** a climograph that records temperature and rainfall

Hz *abbr* hertz

hzy *abbr* hazy

¹i \ˈī\ *n, pl* **i's** *or* **is** \ˈīz\ *often cap, often attrib* **1 a :** the ninth letter of the English alphabet **b :** an instance of this letter printed, written, or otherwise represented **c :** a speech counterpart of orthographic *i* (as long *i* in *side*, short *i* in *sit*, or *i* in French *élite*) **2 :** ONE — see NUMBER table **3 :** a printer's type, a stamp, or some other instrument for reproducing the letter *i* **4 :** someone or something arbitrarily or conveniently designated *i* esp. as the ninth in order or class **5 :** something having the shape of the capital letter I **6 :** a unit vector parallel to the x-axis **7** [abbr. for *incomplete*] **a :** a grade assigned by a teacher or examiner rating a student's work as incomplete **b :** one graded or rated with an I

²i \(ˈ)ī, ə, *often* ä *or* a *when unemphatic esp in contracted forms as "I'm" & "I'll"*\ *pron, cap* [ME *ich, i*, fr. OE *ic*; akin to OHG *ih*, ON *ek*, Goth *ik*, L *ego*, Gk *egō, egōn*, Skt *aham*] **1 :** the one who is speaking or writing ⟨*I* shall not want —Ps 23:1 (AV)⟩ — used as a nominative pronoun of the first person singular by one speaking or writing to refer to himself as the doer of an action ⟨*I* will not hurt you⟩ ⟨whither thou goest, *I* will go —Ruth 1:16 (AV)⟩ or the subject of a predicated condition ⟨*I* don't feel very well today⟩ or sometimes in the predicate after forms of *be* ⟨it will not be *I* —D.D.Eisenhower⟩ ⟨it is *I* —Mk 6:50 (AV)⟩ or in comparisons after *than* or *as* when the first term in the comparison is the subject of a verb ⟨you can do it just as well as *I*⟩ ⟨he writes much better than *I*⟩ ⟨thou art stronger than *I* —Jer 20:7 (AV)⟩ or in some absolute or elliptical constructions esp. when not used with a prepositional phrase or an adjective or a participle ⟨who, *I*? You're foolish to say that anyone would do it⟩ or after *but* in a compound subject ⟨no one but *I* could have known —H. G.Wells⟩ — see ME, MINE, MY; compare WE **2 a** *now chiefly substand* **:** ME — used in a compound object ⟨belongs to my mother and *I*⟩ ⟨between you and *I*⟩ ⟨he saw my brother and *I*⟩ **b** *now dial Eng* **:** ME — used emphatically as object of a verb ⟨give poor *I* another chance⟩ or preposition ⟨give the ball to *I*⟩ ⟨my father hath no child but *I* —Shak.⟩ **3 :** the one who acts as authorized spokesman of a social or military system (as an army) ⟨*I* order you to report for duty⟩

³i \ˈī\ *n, pl* **i's** *or* **is** *cap* **1 :** someone possessing and aware of possessing a distinct and personal individuality **:** SELF, EGO ⟨there is but one *I* —Mary B. Eddy⟩ ⟨society has been atomized down to its elemental particles each of which is an *I* —W.P. Webb⟩; *also* **:** the quality or state of possessing such individuality ⟨the crowd is like a community in that it can be any size, the difference being that the We precedes the *I* —Howard Griffin⟩ **2 :** an excessively egotistic person **:** one that uses the first person pronoun excessively ⟨just a big *I*⟩ **3 :** a dichotomous part of one's self ⟨the other *I*⟩

⁴i *or* **i'** \ˌi\ *now chiefly dial var of* IN

⁵i *obs var of* AYE

⁶i *abbr, often cap* **1** [L *id*] that **2** [L *imperator; imperatrix*] emperor; empress **3** imperial **4** incendiary **5** incomplete **6** independent **7** indicated; indicative **8** industrial **9** infantry **10** infield **11** inhibitory **12** initial **13** inner **14** inside **15** inspector **16** instantaneous **17** institute; institution **18** instrumental **19** intelligence **20** interceptor **21** interest **22** international **23** interstate **24** intransitive **25** Iraqi **26** iron **27** island; isle **28** Israeli

⁷i *symbol, cap* **1** iodine **2** candlepower **3** electric current **4** moment of inertia **5** imaginary unit

¹i- *comb form* [*inactive*] **:** inactive (sense c) ⟨*i*-inositol⟩ — usu. joined to second element with a hyphen

²i- *comb form* [by shortening] **:** IS- 2b ⟨*i*-butyl⟩ — usu. joined to second element with a hyphen

-i- [ME, fr. OF, fr. L, thematic vowel of most nouns and adjectives in combination] — used as a connective vowel to join two elements of usu. Latin origin, being either identical with ⟨aur*i*form⟩ or representative of ⟨Herb*i*vora⟩ an original Latin stem vowel or simply inserted ⟨cant*i*lever⟩; compare -O-

¹-ia \ēə, yə, iə\ *n suffix* [NL, fr. L & Gk, suffix forming feminine abstract nouns] **1** -S **:** pathological condition ⟨pneumon*ia*⟩ ⟨hyster*ia*⟩ ⟨diphther*ia*⟩ **2 :** genus of plants or animals ⟨Wistar*ia*⟩ ⟨Osm*ia*⟩

²-ia \"\ *n pl suffix* [NL, fr. L (neut. pl. of *-ius*, adj. ending) & Gk, neut. pl. of *-ios*, adj. ending] **1 :** taxonomic division (as class, order) of plants or animals ⟨Cryptogam*ia*⟩ ⟨Mammal*ia*⟩ **2 :** things belonging to or derived from or relating to (something specified) ⟨Maryland*ia*⟩ ⟨tabloid*ia*⟩

³-ia *pl of* -IUM

IA *abbr* **1** incorporated accountant **2** infected area **3** *often not cap* [L *inter alia*] among other things **4** international angstrom

IAA *abbr* indoleacetic acid

IAC *abbr* **1** industry advisory committee **2** interview-after-combat

-ial \ēəl, yəl, iəl, əl\ *adj suffix* [ME, fr. MF *-iel, -ial*, fr. L *-ialis*, fr. *-i-* + *-alis* -al] **:** ¹-AL ⟨manor*ial*⟩

iamb \ˈī‚am, -‚a(ə)m *also* -mb\ *n, pl* **iambs** \-mz\ [L *iambus*, fr. Gk *iambos*] **1 :** a metrical foot of two syllables unstressed and stressed respectively (as in *above, invent*, and Tennyson's 4-foot line "he watches from his mountain walls") or short and long respectively (as in classical prosody) **:** a disyllabic rising cadence — symbol ◡ –; compare TROCHEE **2 :** verses written in iambs

iam·bel·e·gus \ˌī‚amˈbeləgəs\ *n* -ES [LL, fr. Gk *iambelegos*, fr. *iambos* + *elegos* song of mourning or lamentation, prob. of non-IE origin] **:** a verse used in classical prosody consisting of an iambic dimeter and half an elegiac pentameter

¹iam·bic \īˈambik, -bēk\ *n* -S [L *iambicus*, adj.] **1 :** IAMB **2 :** a piece of usu. satiric verse written in iambs (as that developed by the Ionian Greeks in the period succeeding the epic) **:** a lampoon written in iambs

²iambic \(ˈ)═¦═\ *adj* [L *iambicus*, fr. Gk *iambikos*, fr. *iambos* + *-ikos* -ic] **:** relating to or consisting of iambs or iambics ⟨~ verse⟩ — **iam·bi·cal·ly** \-bək(ə)lē, -bēk-, -li\ *adv*

iam·bist \īˈambəst, ˈ═‚═-\ *n* -S [Gk *iambistēs*, fr. *iambizein* to write iambs, fr. *iambos* + *-izein* -ize] **:** one who writes iambic verse

iam·bog·ra·pher \ˌī‚amˈbägrəfə(r)\ *n* -S [MGk *iambographos* writer of iambs (fr. Gk *iambos* + *-graphos*, fr. *graphein* to write) + E *-er* — more at CARVE] **:** IAMBIST; *esp* **:** one given to or noted for writing iambic lampoons

iam·bus \īˈambəs\ *n, pl* **iambus·es** \-bəsəz\ *also* **iam·bi** \-‚bī\ [L, fr. Gk *iambos*] **:** IAMB

-ian \ēən, yən, iən, ən\ — see -AN

-iana — see -ANA

I and E *abbr* information and education

I and P *abbr* indexed and paged

I and R *abbr* **1** initiative and referendum **2** intelligence and reconnaissance

I and S *abbr* **1** inspection and security **2** inspection and survey

¹ian·thi·na \ēˈan(t)thənə, īˈ-\ [NL, by alter.] *syn of* JANTHINA

²ianthina \"\ *n* -S **:** JANTHINA 2

ian·thine \ēˈan(t)thən, (ˈ)ī¦a-\ *adj* [L *ianthinus* — more at JANTHINA] **:** having a violet color

ian·thi·ni·dae \ˌī‚anˈthinə‚dē\ [NL, fr. *Ianthina*, type genus + *-idae*] *syn of* JANTHINIDAE

ian·thi·nite \ēˈan(t)thə‚nīt, īˈ-\ *n* -S [G *ianthinit*, fr. L *ianthinus* + G *-it* -ite] **:** a mineral $2UO_2.7H_2O$ consisting of a hydrous uranium dioxide and occurring as violet orthorhombic crystals

¹iao \(ˈ)ē¦au̇\ *n* -S [Samoan] **:** WATTLEBIRD 1a

²iao \"\ *n* -S [native name in Hawaii] **:** a small silversides often used as bait in fishing

¹ia·pyg·ian \ˌīəˈpij(ē)ən\ *n* -S *usu cap* [*Iapygia*, ancient region in southeastern Italy (fr. L, fr. Gk) + E *-an*] **1 :** a member of one of several peoples anciently inhabiting the peninsula of Apulia in southeastern Italy **2 :** the language of the Iapygians

²iapygian \ˈ═¦═(═)═\ *adj, usu cap* **:** of or relating to the Iapygians

ia·pyg·i·dae \ˌīəˈpijə‚dē\ [NL, fr. *Iapyg-, Iapyx*, type genus (alter. of *Japyg-, Japyx*) + *-idae*] *syn of* JAPYGIDAE

iarovize *var of* JAROVIZE

IAS *abbr* indicated airspeed

-ias *pl of* -IA

ia·si \ˈyäsh(ē)\ *or* **ias·sy** \ˈyäsē\ *adj, usu cap* [fr. *Iași* (*Jassy*), Romania] **:** of or from the city of Iasi, Romania **:** of the kind or style prevalent in Iasi

-i·a·sis \ˈīəsəs\ *n suffix, pl* **-i·a·ses** \-‚sēz\ [NL, fr. L, fr. Gk, suffix of action, fr. verbs in *-ian, -iazein* (fr. nouns in *-ia* -y) + *-sis*] **:** morbid state or condition **:** disease having characteristics of (something specified) ⟨elephant*iasis*⟩ ⟨satyr*iasis*⟩ **:** disease produced by (something specified) ⟨ancylostom*iasis*⟩ ⟨habronem*iasis*⟩

ias·us \ˈēasəs, īˈ-\ [NL, fr. *Iasus, Iassus*, ancient city of Asia Minor] *syn of* JASUS

iat·mul \ˈyät‚mül\ *n, pl* **iatmul** *or* **iatmuls** *usu cap* **1 :** a Papuan people of the Sepik district, Territory of New Guinea **2 :** a member of the Iatmul people

iat·ric \(ˈ)ī¦a·trik, -rēk\ *also* **iat·ri·cal** \-rəkəl, -rēk-\ *adj* [Gk *iatrikos*, fr. *iatros* healer, physician (fr. *iasthai* to heal) + *-ikos* -ic, -ical; perh. akin to L *ira* anger — more at IRE] **1 :** of or relating to a physician or medical treatment **:** MEDICAL ⟨outstanding ~ ability⟩ **2 :** MEDICINAL, HEALING, CURATIVE ⟨an extract with a remarkable ~ quality⟩

-i·at·ric \ē¦a·trik, -rēk\ *also* **-i·at·ri·cal** \-rəkəl, -rēk-\ *adj comb form* [*-iatric* fr. NL *-iatria* -iatry + E *-ic*; *-iatrical* fr. *-iatric* + *-al*] **:** of or relating to medical treatment **:** of or relating to healing ⟨hydr*iatric*⟩ ⟨psych*iatric*⟩

-i·at·rics \-ks\ *n pl comb form usu sing in constr* [*-iatric* + *-s*] **:** medical treatment **:** healing ⟨gyn*iatrics*⟩ ⟨ped*iatrics*⟩

-iatrist \ˈīə·trəst, ē¦a·trəst\ *n comb form* [*-iatry* + *-ist*] **:** physician **:** healer ⟨psych*iatrist*⟩ ⟨pod*iatrist*⟩

iatro- *comb form* [NL, fr. Gk, fr. *iatros* physician] **1 :** physician **:** medicine **:** healing ⟨*iatro*logy⟩ ⟨*iatro*genic⟩ **2 :** physician and ⟨*iatro*chemist⟩ **:** medicine or healing and ⟨*iatro*physics⟩ ⟨*iatro*-astrological⟩

iat·ro·chemical \ī¦a·trō, ē¦·+\ *adj* [*iatro-* + *chemical*] **:** of or relating to iatrochemistry **:** ¹CHEMICAL 1b

iat·ro·chemist \"+\ *n* [*iatro-* + *chemist*] **:** one believing in or practicing iatrochemistry

iat·ro·chemistry \"+\ *n* [*iatro-* + *chemistry*] **:** chemistry combined with medicine — used of the chemistry of the period about 1525–1660 dominated by the teachings of Paracelsus; compare IATROPHYSICS

iat·ro·gen·ic \ī¦a·trō¦jenik, ē¦-\ *adj* [*iatro-* + *-genic*] **:** induced by a physician — used chiefly of ailments induced in a patient by autosuggestion based on a physician's words or actions during examination — **iat·ro·ge·nic·i·ty** \═‚══jəˈnisəd·ē\ *n* -ES

iat·ro·mathematics \ī¦a·trō, ē¦-+\ *n pl but usu sing in constr* [NL *iatromathematica*, fr. *iatro-* + L *mathematica* mathematics, astrology; after Gk *iatromathēmatikos* one that practices medicine in conjunction with astrology — more at MATHEMATICS] **:** IATROPHYSICS

iat·ro·physicist \"+\ *n, archaic* **:** one who specializes in iatrophysics

iat·ro·physics \"+\ *n pl but usu sing in constr* [ISV *iatro-* + *physics*] **:** physics combined with medicine — used of a school of medicine of the 17th century that explained disease and the activities of the body in terms of physics rather than of chemistry; compare IATROCHEMISTRY

-i·atry \ˈīə·trē, ē¦a·t-, -ri\ *n comb form* -ES [F *-iatrie*, fr. NL *-iatria*, fr. Gk *iatreia* art or action of healing, fr. *iatros* physician + *-eia* -y — more at IATRIC] **:** medical treatment **:** healing ⟨pod*iatry*⟩ ⟨gyn*iatry*⟩ ⟨psych*iatry*⟩

IAZ *abbr* inner artillery zone

ib *abbr* [L *ibidem*] in the same place

IB *abbr* **1** in bond **2** inbound **3** incendiary bomb **4** intelligence branch **5** invoice book

iba \ˈēbə\ *n* -S [Tag] **:** a medium-sized Philippine tree (*Cicca acida*) sometimes cultivated for its edible roundish greenish white fruit

IBA *abbr* indolebutyric acid

ibad \ˈē‚bäd\ *n, pl* **ibad** *or* **ibads** *usu cap* **1 :** an Arab people in Hira between the Euphrates and the Arabian desert **2 :** a member of the Ibad people

iba·dan \ēˈbädᵊn, -bad-\ *adj, usu cap* [fr. *Ibadan*, Nigeria] **:** of or from the city of Ibadan, Nigeria **:** of the kind or style prevalent in Ibadan

iba·dhi \əˈbädē\ *n, pl* **ibadhi** *or* **ibadhis** *usu cap* [after ʿAbdallah ibn-*Ibāḍ*] **:** IBADITE

¹iba·dite *also* **aba·dite** \əˈbä‚dīt\ *n* -S *usu cap* [ʿAbdallah ibn-*Ibāḍ* (*Abāḍ*), 7th cent. Arab religious leader + E *-ite*] **:** a member of an austere Muslim sect found chiefly in the northern part of Africa

²ibadite \"\ *n* -S *usu cap* [*Ibad* + *-ite*] **:** IBAD

iba·loi \¦ēbə¦lȯi\ *n, pl* **ibaloi** *or* **ibalois** *usu cap* **:** NABALOI

iban \(ˈ)ē¦bän\ *n, pl* **iban** *or* **ibans** *usu cap* **1 a :** a Dayak people of Sarawak, Borneo — called also *Sea Dayak* **b :** a member of such people **2 :** the Austronesian language of the Iban people

iba·nag \ˌēbəˈnäg\ *n, pl* **ibanag** *or* **ibanags** *usu cap* **1 a :** a people of northern Luzon inhabiting chiefly the Cagayan valley **b :** a member of such people **2 :** the Austronesian language of the Ibanag people

i bar *n, cap I* **:** a rolled iron or steel bar of I section used in construction work

i beam *n, cap I* **:** a rolled iron or steel beam or a cast steel beam of I section; *also* **:** a built-up beam of I section used esp. in structural ironwork (as in steel-framed buildings) — called also *I girder*

¹ibe·ri·an \īˈbirēən\ *n* -S *cap* [*Iberia*, ancient region of the Caucasus approximately equivalent to modern Georgia (fr. L *Iberia, Hiberia*, fr. Gk *Ibēria*) + E *-an*] **:** a member of one or more peoples anciently inhabiting the Caucasus in Asia between the Black and Caspian seas in the approximate region of the Soviet republic of Georgia and prob. being the ancestors of the Kartvelians

²iberian \(ˈ)═¦═══\ *adj, usu cap* **:** of, relating to, or characteristic of Asiatic Iberia, its inhabitants, or their language **:** GEORGIAN

³iberian \═ˈ═══\ *n* -S *cap* [*Iberia*, peninsula in southwestern Europe that contains Spain and Portugal (fr. L *Iberia, Hiberia*, fr. Gk *Ibēria*) + E *-an*] **1 a :** a member of one or more Caucasoid peoples anciently inhabiting the peninsula comprising Spain and Portugal and the Basque region about the Pyrenees, prob. being related in origin to the Mauretanians and other peoples of the northern part of Africa and early known to the Greeks and later conquered by the Romans, being short and dark and dolichocephalic, and being prob. the builders of the neolithic stone structures (as cairns, dolmens) found esp. in Spain and in the northern part of Africa and in France and Great Britain **b :** a native or inhabitant of Spain or Portugal or the Basque region about the Pyrenees **2 :** one or more of the languages natively spoken by the ancient Iberians

⁴iberian \(ˈ)═¦═══\ *adj, usu cap* **:** of, relating to, or characteristic of the Iberian peninsula, its inhabitants, or their language ⟨tragedy and death are indeed recurrent themes in *Iberian* art —George Woodcock⟩

iberian tortoise *or* **iberian turtle** *n, usu cap I* **:** a common tortoise (*Clemmys leprosa* syn. *Testudo ibera*) of southwestern Europe and northern Africa

ibe·ric \(ˈ)ī¦birik, -ber-\ *adj, usu cap* [L *Ibericus, Hibericus*, fr. *Iberia, Hiberia* Iberia + *-icus* -ic] **:** IBERIAN

ibe·ris \īˈbirəs\ *n, cap* [NL, fr. L, peppergrass, fr. Gk *ibēris*, perh. fr. *Ibēria* (in Europe)] **:** a genus of Old World mostly glabrous plants (family Cruciferae) having entire or pinnatifid sometimes fleshy leaves and flowers with two long and two short petals succeeded by a broad ovate pod, the herbaceous members being often cultivated for their flat-topped clusters of white or purplish flowers — see CANDYTUFT

ibe·rite \ˈībə‚rīt, īˈbi‚r-\ *n* -S [Sw or G *iberit*, fr. *Iberia* (in Europe), its locality + Sw or G *-it* -ite] **:** an alteration product of cordierite

ibero- *comb form, usu cap* [L *Iberus, Hiberus*] **:** Iberian **:** Iberian and ⟨*Ibero*-American⟩

ibero-romance \ī¦birō+\ *n, cap I&R* [*Ibero-* + *Romance*] **1 :** the Romance language of the Iberian peninsula prior to the emergence of Spanish, Portuguese, and Catalan as national languages **2 :** a language group of the Romance division consisting of Spanish, Portuguese, and Catalan

ibex \ˈī‚beks\ *n* [L] **1** *pl* **ibex** *or* **ibex·es a :** one of several wild goats living chiefly in high mountain areas (as the Alps) of the Old World and having large recurved horns transversely ridged in front **b :** a wild goat (*Capra aegagrus*) now found in Asia Minor and supposed to be the progenitor of the domestic goat **c** (1) **:** MOUNTAIN GOAT (2) **:** MOUNTAIN SHEEP **2** *cap* [NL, fr. L] *in some classifications* **:** a genus that comprises the ibex and that is often considered a subgenus of *Capra*

IBI *abbr* invoice book, inwards

ibi·bio \ˌibəˈbē(‚)ō\ *n, pl* **ibibio** *or* **ibibios** *usu cap* **1 a :** a people of southeastern Nigeria **b :** a member of such people **2 :** the language of the Ibibio people, belonging to the Central branch of the Niger-Congo language family

ibid \ˈibəd\ *abbr* [L *ibidem*] in the same place

ibi·dem \ˈibə‚dem, -‚dəm; əˈbīdəm, əˈbēd-, -‚dem\ *adv* [L] **:** in the same place — usu. abbreviated and used (as in a footnote) to avoid repetition of source data (as author, title) in a reference immediately preceding; abbr. *ibid., ib.*

ibid·i·dae \īˈbidə‚dē\ [NL, fr. *Ibid-, Ibis*, genus of birds (fr. L *ibid-, ibis*) + *-idae*] *syn of* THRESKIORNITHIDAE

ibid·i·um \īˈbidēəm\ [NL, fr. L *ibid-, ibis* ibis + NL *-ium*; fr. the shape of the anthers] *syn of* SPIRANTHES

-ibility — see -ABILITY

ibis \ˈībəs *sometimes* ˈēb-\ *n, pl* **ibis** *or* **ibis·es** [L *ibid-, ibis*, fr. Gk *ibis*, fr. Egypt *hby*] **:** any of several wading birds related to the herons and constituting the family Threskiornithidae that inhabit warm regions in both hemispheres and feed on aquatic and amphibious animals and are distinguished by a long slender downwardly curved bill resembling a curlew's bill

ibisbill \ˈ══‚═\ *n* **:** a bluish gray bird (*Ibidorhyncha struthersii*) of central Asia having a long downcurved red bill and resembling a lapwing

-ible — see -ABLE

IBM *abbr or n* -S **:** an intercontinental ballistic missile

ibo \ˈē(‚)bō\ *or* **ig·bo** \ˈig‚bō\ *n, pl* **ibo** *or* **ibos** *or* **igbo** *or* **igbos** *usu cap* **1 a :** a Negro people of the country about the lower Niger **b :** a member of such people **2 :** a Kwa language of the Igbo people used as a language of trade and education in a large area of southern Nigeria

IBO *abbr* invoice book, outwards

ibo·ga·ine \əˈbōgə‚ēn\ *n* -S [ISV *iboga* (fr. NL, specific epithet of *Tabernanthe iboga*, fr. a native name in central Africa) + *-ine*] **:** a crystalline alkaloid hallucinogen $C_{20}H_{26}N_2O$ obtained from the roots, bark, and leaves of an apocynaceous plant (*Tabernanthe iboga*) of equatorial Africa

ibo·li·um privet \īˈbōlēəm-\ *or* **ibo·ta privet** \īˈbōd·ə-\ *n* [*ibolium*, NL (specific epithet of *Ligustrum ibolium*), irreg. fr. Jap *ibota* wax tree + L *oleum* oil — more at OIL] **:** a privet (*Ligustrum ibolium*) produced by hybridizing two privets (*L. obtusifolium* and *L. ovalifolium*) that has pubescent branches and midribs of the under surfaces of the leaves and a glabrous calyx

ib·sen·i·an \(ˈ)ib¦sēnēən, (ˈ)ip¦-, -sen-\ *adj, usu cap* [Henrik *Ibsen* †1906 Norw. poet and dramatist + E *-ian*] **:** of, relating to, or having the characteristics of the playwright Ibsen or his plays

ib·sen·ism \ˈibsə‚nizəm, ˈips-\ *n* -S *usu cap* [Henrik *Ibsen* + E *-ism*] **1 :** dramatic invention or construction characteristic of Ibsen whose plays attack conventional hypocrisies **2 :** adherence to or championship of Ibsen's plays and ideas

¹ib·sen·ite \-‚nīt\ *n* -S *usu cap* [Henrik *Ibsen* + E *-ite*] **1 :** an admirer or devotee of Ibsen **2 :** a dramatist who imitates Ibsen's manner or technique

²ibsenite \"\ *adj, usu cap* **:** IBSENIAN

¹-ic \ˌik, ˌēk; ˌik *in a few words that have a heavy stress on a syllable preceding the penult, as "politic"*\ *adj suffix* [ME *-ik, -ic*, fr. OF & L; OF *-ique*, fr. L *-icus* — more at -Y] **1 :** having the character or form of **:** being ⟨panoram*ic*⟩ ⟨rhomb*ic*⟩ ⟨Samoyed*ic*⟩ **:** consisting of ⟨run*ic*⟩ **2 a :** of or relating to ⟨alderman*ic*⟩ ⟨datur*ic*⟩ ⟨Koran*ic*⟩ **b :** related to, derived from, or containing ⟨alcohol*ic*⟩ — esp. in names of acids and related compounds ⟨bor*ic*⟩ ⟨cinnam*ic*⟩ ⟨ole*ic*⟩ **3 :** in the manner of **:** like that of **:** characteristic of ⟨Byron*ic*⟩ ⟨quixot*ic*⟩ ⟨Puritan*ic*⟩ **4 :** associated or dealing with ⟨Ved*ic*⟩ **:** utilizing ⟨electron*ic*⟩ ⟨atom*ic*⟩ **5 :** characterized by **:** exhibiting ⟨nostalg*ic*⟩ **:** affected with ⟨allerg*ic*⟩ ⟨parapleg*ic*⟩ **6 :** caused by ⟨amoeb*ic*⟩ **7 :** tending to produce ⟨analges*ic*⟩ **8 :** having the highest valence of a (specified) element or a valence relatively higher than in compounds or ions named with an adjective ending in *-ous* ⟨ferr*ic* iron⟩ ⟨sulfur*ic* acid⟩ — compare ¹-ATE 2

²-ic \"\ *n suffix* -S [ME *-ik, -ic*, fr. OF & L; OF *-ique*, fr. L *-icus*, fr. *-icus* (adj. suffix)] **:** one having the character or nature of **:** one belonging to or associated with **:** one exhibiting or affected by ⟨glycon*ic*⟩ **:** one that produces ⟨ecbol*ic*⟩

IC *abbr* **1** immediate constituent **2** *often not cap* in charge **3** index correction **4** information center **5** information circular **6** inspected and condemned **7** interior communications **8** internal combustion **9** internal connection

ica \ˈēkə\ *n, pl* **ica** *or* **icas** *usu cap* [Sp, of AmerInd origin] **1 a :** a Chibchan people of northern Colombia **b :** a member of such people **2 :** the language of the Ica people

icac·i·na·ce·ae \ˌi‚kasəˈnāsē‚ē\ *n pl, cap* [NL, fr. *Icacina*, type genus (fr. ISV *icaco* + NL *-ina*) + *-aceae*] **:** a family of tropical chiefly woody plants of the order Sapindales with alternate leaves, panicled flowers, and drupaceous fruit — **icac·i·na·ceous** \═¦═══¦nāshəs\ *adj*

icaco \ēˈkä‚kō, iˈkā-\ *or* **icaco plum** *also* **hi·caco** \(h)i-\ *n* -S [Sp *icaco, hicaco*, fr. Arawak] **:** COCO PLUM

-i·cal \ə̇kəl, ēk-\ *adj suffix* [ME, fr. LL *-icalis* (as in *clericalis* clerical, *grammaticalis* grammatical, *radicalis* radical) — more at CLERICAL, GRAMMATICAL, RADICAL] **:** -IC ⟨cosm*ical*⟩ ⟨fantast*ical*⟩ — sometimes differing from *-ic* in that adjectives formed with *-ical* have a wider or more transferred semantic range than corresponding adjectives in *-ic* ⟨economic*al*: econom*ic*⟩ ⟨prophet*ical*: prophet*ic*⟩

¹icar·i·an \ī¦ka(a)rēən, (ˈ)i¦k-\ *adj, usu cap* [L *icarius* of Icarus (fr. Gk *ikarios*, fr. *Ikaros* Icarus, Greek mythological character who flew so high on man-made wings that the sun melted them and sent him to destruction) + E *-an*] **:** of, relating to, or characteristic of Icarus: **a :** soaring too high for safety ⟨*Icarian* flight⟩ **b :** inadequate for or incapable of bringing about an ambitious project ⟨*Icarian* methods⟩

²icarian \"\ *adj, usu cap* [F *icarien*, fr. *Icarie*, communistic utopia in *Voyage en Icarie* (1842), novel by Étienne Cabet †1857 Fr. political radical (fr. *Icarie* Icaria, island in the Aegean sea) + F *-en* -an] **:** of, relating to, or constituting a communistic settlement established in the U.S. during the latter half of the 19th century by a group of French immigrants ⟨the last *Icarian* utopia . . . fizzled out in 1895 —*Time*⟩

³icarian \"\ *n* -S *usu cap* [F *icarien*, fr. *icarien*, adj.] **:** a member of an Icarian community

ICAS *abbr* intermittent commercial and amateur service

ICBM *abbr or n* -S **:** an intercontinental ballistic missile ⟨the ~ era —Clay Blair⟩

¹ice \ˈīs\ *n* -S *often attrib* [ME *is*, fr. OE *īs*; akin to OFris, OS, & OHG *īs* ice, ON *īss*, Av *isu-* icy, *aēxa-* cold, and perh. to Russ *ineĭ* frost, Lith *ynis*] **1 a :** water reduced to the solid state by cooling and when pure constituting a nearly colorless brittle substance that in freezing expands about one eleventh in volume, that has a specific gravity of 0.9166 as compared with 1.0 for water at 4°C, that under normal atmospheric pressure is formed at and has a melting point of 0°C or 32°F, that occurs in the common form as hexagonal crystals, and that in large masses is classed as a rock — compare BLUE ICE, FROST, SNOW; HEAT OF FUSION **b :** the layer of frozen water covering a surface (as of a road, rink, or body of water) ⟨broke through the ~⟩ **:** the surface of a sheet of ice ⟨slipped on the ~⟩ ⟨skated down the ~⟩ ⟨an ~ carnival⟩ **2 :** the quality or state of being emotionally cold (as from formality, reserve, embarrassment, or hostility) ⟨perceptibly chilled by the ~ in his voice⟩ ⟨thawed a little of the ~ that held his lady's heart —Robert Murphy⟩ — compare BREAK THE ICE **3 :** a substance resembling ice in appearance or solid form ⟨these hydrogen ~s might well be retained in meteoritic particles —P.M.Millman⟩; *specif* **:** ICING **4 a :** a sweet frozen food containing a fruit juice or other flavoring and usu. served as a dessert or refreshment; *specif* **:** one containing no milk or cream (as a fruit ice or water ice) **b** *Brit* **:** a serving of ice cream; *specif* **:** ICE-CREAM CONE **5** *slang* **:** DIAMONDS ⟨fenced the ~ for the gang⟩; *broadly* **:** JEWELRY

6 *slang* **:** protection money paid by an operator of illicit business ⟨a $20,000,000-a-year bookmaking syndicate that paid out $1,000,000 in ~ to the police —*N.Y. Times*⟩ **7 :** allowance made in directing a curling stone for its deviation from a straight course ⟨make the shot . . . by using the ~ and weight suggested by his skip —Ken Watson⟩ — **on ice** *adv* **1 a :** with every likelihood of being won ⟨with their lead they had the game *on ice*⟩ **b :** with every likelihood of being fulfilled — used of a contract in a card game **2 :** in reserve ⟨put the project *on ice* until funds were sent⟩ ⟨kept the invention *on ice* for 10 years⟩ **3** *slang* **:** in safekeeping ⟨put you *on ice* quietly till they've had time to settle up their affairs —Dorothy Sayers⟩; *specif* **:** in jail or prison ⟨*on ice* pending his appearance in court —*Front Page Detective*⟩ — **on thin ice :** in a situation involving great risk ⟨in opposing mob passions he was *on thin ice*⟩

²**ice** \"\ *vb* -ED/-ING/-s [ME *isen*, fr. *is*, n.] *vt* **1 a :** to coat with or convert into ice ⟨sleet *iced* the turnpike⟩ ⟨weather that *iced* his breath⟩ **b :** to chill esp. by surface contact with ice ⟨~ the champagne before serving⟩ ⟨an *iced* melon⟩ ⟨a frown that *iced* his enthusiasm⟩ **c :** to load or supply with ice ⟨a portable cooler *iced* with cubes from the refrigerator⟩ ⟨stations for *icing* refrigerator cars containing perishables⟩ **2 :** to cover with or as if with icing ⟨~ a cake⟩ ⟨houses *iced* over with multicolored stuccoes —Norman Lewis⟩ **3 :** to put in a secure place or state or in reserve **:** put on ice ⟨sank a free throw . . . to ~ the victory —*Spokane Spokesman-Rev.*⟩ ⟨has frozen all major route applications . . would probably ~ a merger too —*Time*⟩ ~ *vi* **1 :** to become ice cold **:** FREEZE ⟨the two bottles were *icing* in a bucket —Lionel Trilling⟩ **2 a :** to become covered with ice ⟨at the first sign of snow or *icing*, equipment is deployed along the turnpike —*Roads & Streets*⟩ — often used with *up* ⟨the airplane propeller and wings may ~ up⟩ **b :** to have ice form inside — usu. used with *up* ⟨the airplane carburetor *iced* up⟩

-ice \əs\ *n suffix* -s [ME *-ice, -ise*, fr. OF, fr. L *-itius* (masc.), *-itia* (fem.), *-itium* (neut.), suffixes forming adjectives and nouns; akin to Gk *-sios*, Skt *-tya*] **:** act ⟨serv*ice*⟩ **:** quality ⟨just*ice*⟩ **:** condition ⟨coward*ice*⟩

ice age *n* **1 :** a time of widespread glaciation **2** *usu cap I&A* **:** the Pleistocene glacial epoch

ice anchor *n* **:** a small anchor usu. having one fluke and used for mooring a boat to ice

ice apron *n* **:** a wedge-shaped structure for protecting a bridge pier from floating ice

ice ax *n* **:** a mountain-climbing tool that has a pick and adze at one end of a shaft and a spike or a ferrule at the other end and that is used esp. for cutting steps, belaying, and glissading

ice bag *n* **:** a waterproof bag designed to hold cracked ice and used for local application of cold to the body — see ICE CAP, ICE COLLAR

ice bag

ice banner *n* **:** SNOW BANNER

ice barrier *n* **:** the outer margin of the antarctic ice sheet

ice bear *n* **:** POLAR BEAR

ice belt *n* **:** ICE FOOT 1

ice·berg \ˈīs,bərg, -bōg,-bəig\ *n* [prob. part trans. of Dan or Norw *isberg*, fr. *is* ice + *berg* mountain, fr. ON, rock — more at BARROW] **1 a** *archaic* **:** GLACIER **b :** a large mass of land ice broken from a glacier at the edge of a body of water that when afloat has only a small part above the surface and that in the ocean floats with subsurface currents often to great distances — called also *berg;* compare GROWLER, ICE ISLAND **2 :** an emotionally cold person **3 :** something of which only a fraction is observed or explicit ⟨the seven-eighths of the ~ of personality that is submerged and never seen —W.E.Allen⟩

iceberg lettuce *also* **iceberg** *n* **:** any of various crisp freely blanching head lettuces

ice bird *n* **1 :** any of several sea birds that frequent ice floes: as **a :** DOVEKIE 2 **b :** PRION **2 :** an Indian goatsucker (*Caprimulgus asiaticus*)

iceblink \ˈ=,=\ *n* **1 :** a yellowish or whitish glare in the sky over an ice field (as in polar regions) — called also *ice sky;* compare SNOWBLINK, WATER SKY **2 :** a cliff of ice on a coast (as of Greenland)

ice bloom *n* **:** a brownish purple color imparted to ice in some regions by the growth of desmids of the genus *Ancylonema*

ice-blue \ˈ=ˈ=\ *adj* **:** very pale greenish blue like the color seen in a cake of clear ice

iceboat \ˈ=,=\ *n* **1 :** a vehicle similar to a boat that has runners, is propelled on ice by sails or sometimes a propeller or jet propulsion, and is used chiefly for sport; *esp* **:** one having a center timber or long slender hull rigged fore-and-aft with a mainsail and sometimes also a jib and resting on a pivoted steering runner at the stern or bow and two other runners outrigged at each end of a running plank **2 :** ICEBREAKER

iceboat 1

iceboating \ˈ=,==\ *n* **:** the sport of sailing in iceboats

ice·bone \ˈīs,=\ *n* [prob. trans. of D *ijsbeen* (fr. MD *isebeen*, *ijsbeen*) or LG *isbeen*, fr. MLG *isbēn;* both prob. by folk etymology fr. L *ischium* + MD *been* bone or MLG *bēn* — more at ISCHIUM] **:** AITCHBONE

icebound \ˈ=ˈ=\ *adj* **1 :** surrounded with ice so as to be incapable of advancing ⟨an ~ ship⟩ **2 :** surrounded or obstructed with ice so as to hinder access **:** iced in ⟨an ~ coast⟩ **3 :** constricted by inhibitions or taboos ⟨sweet young things whose ~ virtue excited them to . . . sighing and languishing whenever a man was about —Max Peacock⟩

icebox \ˈ=,=\ *n* **:** an insulated cabinet or box having a compartment for ice and used for refrigeration (as of food); *broadly* **:** REFRIGERATOR ⟨an electric ~⟩

icebreaker \ˈ=,==\ *n* **1 :** an ice apron or other structure that protects a bridge pier from floating ice **2 :** a ship designed or equipped (as with a reinforced bow) to make and maintain a channel through the ice **3 :** the right whale of the arctic **4 :** something that breaks the ice on a project or social occasion ⟨pictures of girls . . . intended as an ~ between us and the French officers —Nathaniel Benchley⟩; *specif* **:** MIXER 1c

ice candle *n, dial* **:** ICICLE

ice cap *n* **1 :** an ice bag shaped to be fitted to the head **2 a :** cover of perennial ice and snow (as in the polar regions or on a mountain peak above the snow line); *specif* **:** a glacier forming on an extensive area of relatively level land (as a plateau, or a large part of a continent) and flowing outward from its center ⟨the endless polar *ice cap* was running between eight and eighty feet thick —W.R.Anderson⟩

ice car *n* **:** a railway car that is specially insulated for transporting ice

ice cave *n* **1 :** a cave so protected from the summer heat that ice remains in it throughout all or most of the year **2 :** a cave or tunnel in ice; *esp* **:** one formed in a glacier by meltwater streams

ice cellar *n* **:** an underground room where foods and drinks are kept cool by ice

ice chest *n* **:** ICEBOX

ice chisel *n* **:** a long-handled chisel for cutting holes in ice (as for fishing) or splitting blocks of ice

ice-cold \ˈ=ˈ=\ *adj* **:** extremely cold or impassive ⟨plunged into the *ice-cold* water⟩ ⟨planning all his battles . . . with an *ice-cold* brain —Brian Horrocks⟩

ice collar *n* **:** an ice bag shaped to fit around the neck

ice color *n* [so called fr. its being treated with a diazo solution in the presence of ice] **:** AZOIC DYE

icecraft \ˈ=,=\ *n* **:** skill in traveling on an ice surface or through waters containing floating ice

ice cream \(ˈ)=ˈ=, ˈ=,=\ *n* **1 :** a frozen food containing cream or butter fat, flavoring, sweetening, and usu. eggs; *specif* **:** such a food made smooth by stirring during freezing — distinguished from *mousse* and *parfait* **2 :** a serving of ice cream

ice-cream *adj* [*ice cream*] **:** of a color similar to that of vanilla ice cream — usu. used of clothing ⟨a gentleman in a blue serge coat and *ice-cream* pants —Conrad Richter⟩

ice-cream cone *n* **:** a crisp conical wafer usu. about five inches long holding ice cream

ice-cream cone

ice-cream fork *n* **:** a fork of medium size that has a bowl-shaped or blade-shaped end terminating usu. in three short tines and is used for eating ice cream or sherbets

ice-cream freezer *n* **:** a hand or power operated machine for freezing and stirring ice cream; *specif* **:** a can rotated by a crank within a tub of ice and salt so that the ice-cream mixture in it is stirred by a dasher

ice-cream soda *n* **:** a sweet food drink of soda water, flavored syrup, and ice cream

ice crusher *n* **:** a device for crushing ice; *specif* **:** a kitchen grinder having a hopper, a crank, blades, and a cup and used for crushing ice cubes

ice crystal *n* **:** ICE NEEDLE

ice cube *n* **:** a small block of artificial ice formed in a mold or cut from a larger block and commonly used for icing drinks

iced *adj* **:** containing cracked ice or ice cubes ⟨~ coffee⟩

ice firn *n* **:** a mixture of ice and firn

ice dike *n* **:** a formation of secondary ice in a glacier along a crevice

iced-tea spoon *n* **:** a teaspoon with a very long handle

ice duck *n* **:** any of various ducks found in icy seas; *esp* **:** OLD-SQUAW 1

icefall \ˈ=,=\ *n* **1 :** a frozen waterfall or similar mass of ice **2 :** a falling of ice (as from an iceberg or glacier) **3 :** the mass of jumbled and usu. jagged blocks of ice into which a glacier may break when it moves down a steep declivity

ice feathers *n pl* **:** ¹RIME 2

ice field *n* **1 :** an extensive sheet of sea ice larger than an ice floe **2 :** a large body of glacial ice **:** ICE CAP

icefish \ˈ=,=\ *n* **:** any of several small, shining, more or less translucent fishes: as **a :** a fish of the family Salangidae **b :** CAPELIN **c :** a common No. American smelt (*Osmerus mordax*)

ice fishing *n* **:** fishing through a hole in the ice

ice floe *n* **:** a flat free mass of floating sea ice of usu. visible extent larger than a pan and smaller than an ice field; *broadly* **:** a large floating fragment of sheet ice

ice flower *n* **:** FROST FLOWER 2

ice fog *n* **:** a fog composed of ice particles

ice foot *n* **1 :** a wall or belt of ice frozen to the shore in arctic regions having a base at or below the low-water mark and formed as a result of the rise and fall of the tides, freezing spray, or stranded ice **2 :** the ice at the front of a glacier

ice fork *n* **:** a fork or serrated chisel for splitting or chopping up ice

ice fox *n* **:** ARCTIC FOX

ice-free \ˈ=ˈ=\ *adj* **:** free from ice; *esp* **:** not frozen over in winter ⟨an *ice-free* port⟩

ice front *n* **:** the lower or outer margin of a glacier

ice gland *n* **:** a roughly cylindrical and more or less vertical column of ice in névé

ice green *n* **:** a variable color averaging a very light bluish green that is lighter, stronger, and slightly bluer than spray

ice gull *n* **:** any of several northern gulls; *esp* **:** IVORY GULL

ice hockey *n* **:** a goal game played on an ice rink by two teams of six players on skates whose object is to direct a puck into the opponents' goal with a hockey stick

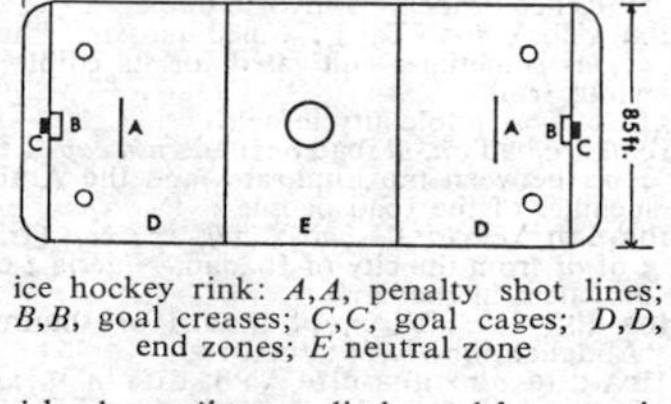

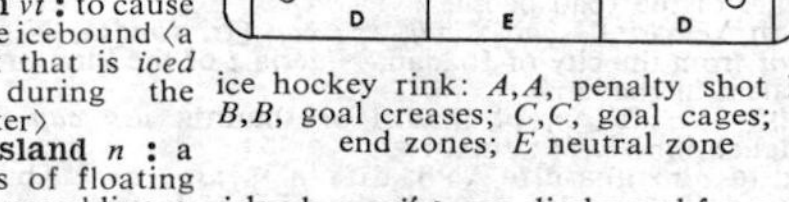

ice hockey rink: *A,A*, penalty shot lines; *B,B*, goal creases; *C,C*, goal cages; *D,D*, end zones; *E* neutral zone

icehouse \ˈ=,=\ *n* **:** a building for storing ice

ice in *vt* **:** to cause to be icebound ⟨a port that is *iced in* during the winter⟩

ice island *n* **:** a mass of floating ice resembling an island; *specif* **:** one discharged from arctic shelf ice that may extend several hundred square miles in area and several hundred feet in depth and floats with a subsurface current around the north pole — compare BARRIER BERG

ice-laid \ˈ=ˈ=\ *adj* **:** deposited by ice ⟨an *ice-laid* boulder till⟩

ice lance *n* **:** an ice tester used by the Eskimo for determining the thickness and therefore the safety of ice

ice·land \ˈīslənd, -,sland, -laa(ə)nd\ *adj, usu cap* [fr. *Iceland*, island between the No. Atlantic and the Arctic oceans, fr. ME *Island*, fr. ON *Īsland*, fr. *īss* ice + *land* — more at ICE, LAND] **:** of or from Iceland **:** of the kind or style prevalent in Iceland **:** ICELANDIC

iceland dog *or* **iceland cur** *n, usu cap I* **:** a breed of small shaggy-haired dogs supposed to have originated in Iceland and kept in England as pets during the 16th and 17th centuries

ice·land·er \ˈī,slandə(r), -slən-, -,slaan-\ *n* -s *cap* [Dan *Islænder*, fr. *Island* Iceland + *-er*] **:** a native or inhabitant of Iceland

iceland gull *n, usu cap I* **:** a large white-winged gull (*Larus leucopterus*) that is similar to but smaller than the glaucous gull and that breeds in the arctic regions and migrates south to northern France and the northern U.S.

¹**ice·lan·dic** \(ˈ)ī¦slandik, -laan-\ *adj, usu cap* [*Iceland* + E *-ic*] **1 a :** of, relating to, or characteristic of Iceland **b :** of, relating to, or characteristic of the Icelanders **2 :** of, relating to, or characteristic of the Icelandic language

²**icelandic** \"\ *n* -s *cap* **:** a Scandinavian language of the Icelandic people — compare OLD ICELANDIC, OLD NORSE; see INDO-EUROPEAN LANGUAGES table

iceland moss *also* **iceland lichen** *n, usu cap I* **:** a lichen (*Cetraria islandica*) with branched flattened partly erect thallus that grows in mountainous and arctic regions and is used (as in Scandinavia) as a medicine or as food for humans and livestock and as a source of glycerol

iceland pony *n, usu cap I* **:** a short stocky hardy usu. chestnut-colored pony developed in Iceland by interbreeding ponies of European origin

iceland poppy *n, usu cap I* **1 :** either of two nearly stemless perennial poppies that tend to grow in a firm close turf: **a :** a subarctic poppy (*Papaver nudicaule*) of both hemispheres that is hairy and somewhat glaucous with pinnately lobed or cleft petioled leaves and fragrant typically yellow and white flowers borne on slender wiry scapes **b :** a similar Old World alpine poppy (*Papaver alpinum*) with white and yellow or often pink or orange flowers and glabrous foliage **2 :** any of various cultivated poppies that are prob. derived from one or the other of the wild Iceland poppies, are commonly grown as biennials or short-lived perennials, and have small or medium-sized single or double flowers chiefly of pastel color — compare SHIRLEY POPPY

iceland sea grass *n, usu cap I* **1 :** a sea lettuce (*Ulva latissima*) **2 :** any of various green algae of the genus *Enteromorpha*

iceland spar *also* **iceland crystal** *n, usu cap I* **:** a transparent calcite the best of which is obtained in Iceland, which easily cleaves into rhombohedrons, and which is used for polariscope prisms because of its strong double refraction

ice·less \ˈīsləs\ *adj* **:** having or using no ice

icelike \ˈ=,=\ *adj* **:** resembling ice

ice line *n* **:** the graph on a phase diagram of the state of equilibrium between ice and water

ice machine *n* **:** a machine for making ice artificially

ice·man \ˈī,sman, -maa(ə)n *also* -,smən\ *n, pl* **icemen 1 :** a man who is skilled in traveling upon ice (as among glaciers) **2 :** one who retails or delivers ice **:** an ice dealer **3 :** one who prepares and cares for an ice rink

ice·man·ship \ˈīsmən,ship\ *n* **:** ICECRAFT

ice milk *n* **:** a frozen food that is soft in texture and is made of skim milk **:** frozen custard

ice needle *n* **:** one of a number of slender ice particles that float in the air in clear cold weather — called also *ice crystal*

ice·ni \ˈīˈsē,nī\ *n pl, usu cap* [L] **:** an ancient British people that under its queen Boadicea revolted against the Romans in A.D. 61 — **ice·ni·an** \(ˈ)ī¦sēnēən\ *or* **icenic** \-nik, (ˈ)ī¦sen-\ *adj, usu cap*

ice pack *n* **1 :** an expanse of pack ice **2 :** crushed ice placed in a suitable container (as an ice bag) or folded in a towel and applied to the body

ice paper *n* **:** a paper coated with an adhesive containing a salt that crystallizes when the coating dries and gives a frosted appearance

ice partridge *n* **:** IVORY GULL

ice petrel *n* **:** an antarctic shearwater (*Adamastor cinereus*)

ice pick *n* **:** a hand tool with a needlelike spike for chipping ice

ice pick

ice pillar *n* **:** a pedestal of glacial ice covered with a stone or debris that has given protection from solar heat and caused the ice to melt less rapidly than that around it

ice pilot *or* **ice master** *n* **:** a pilot trained in navigating amid ice

ice pink *n* **:** a European alpine dwarf herb (*Dianthus glacialis*) with bright red flowers

¹**ice plant** *n* **:** an Old World annual herb (*Mesembryanthemum crystallinum*) that is widely naturalized in warm regions and that has fleshy foliage covered with glistening papillate dots or vesicles; *broadly* **:** FIG MARIGOLD

²**ice plant** *n* **:** a plant where artificial ice is manufactured

ice plow *n* **:** a grooving device resembling a plow that is used in cutting ice (as on a river or pond) into cakes

ice point *n* **:** the temperature at which ice is in equilibrium with air-saturated water at standard atmospheric pressure and which is commonly used as a fixed point in calibrating thermometers and is represented by 0° C or 32° F

icequake \ˈ=,=\ *n* **:** the concussion attending the breaking up of masses of ice

ic·er \ˈīsə(r)\ *n* -s **:** one that ices: as **a :** a worker who covers food (as fresh produce or cases of milk) with ice before shipment **b :** a worker who mixes icing or ices baked goods

ice raft *n* **:** ICE FLOE

ice-raft \ˈ=,=\ *vt* [*ice raft*] **:** to transport on or in an iceberg or other floating ice ⟨a granitic boulder . . . might have reached its present location by *ice-rafting* —*Jour. of Geol.*⟩ ⟨*ice-rafted* sediment⟩

ice river *or* **ice stream** *n* **:** a valley glacier

iceroot \ˈ=,=\ *n* **:** GOLDENSEAL 1

ices *pl of* ICE, *pres 3d sing of* ICE

-ices *pl of* -ICE

ice shed *n* **:** a glacial divide from which ice moves in opposite directions

ice sheet *n* **:** a glacial ice cover **:** ICE CAP ⟨the *ice sheets* on some Greenland promontories⟩; *esp* **:** one (as a continental glacier) spreading outward over a large land area and concealing all or most surface features ⟨the great *ice sheets* covering much of Europe during the ice age⟩

ice shelf *n* **:** SHELF ICE

ice·shock·le \ˈī,shäkəl\ *dial Brit var of* ICICLE

ice show *n* **:** an ice-skating entertainment consisting of various exhibitions (as solo figure skating, group spectacles) often with musical accompaniment

ice skate *n* **1 :** a metal runner or blade attached by a frame to the sole of a shoe for skating on ice **2 a :** SKATE 1a(1) **b :** DOUBLE-RUNNER 2

ice-skate \ˈ=,=\ *vi* **:** to glide on ice skates — **ice skater** *n*

ice sky *n* **:** ICEBLINK

ice storm *n* **:** a storm in which falling rain freezes as soon as it touches any object

ice structure *n* **:** an imperfection consisting usu. of a group of cracks about an included foreign body in a diamond or other gem

ice table *n* **:** GLACIER TABLE

ice tea *n* **:** iced tea

ice tint *n* **:** a very pale green that is yellower and paler than tourmaline, emerald tint, or microcline green

ice tongs *n pl* **1 :** tongs having usu. two handles and hooked points for lifting large blocks of ice **2 :** small tongs often with claw-shaped ends for handling ice in an ice tub

ice tongs 1

ice tub *n* **:** a container (as of silver or glass) shaped like a tub or bowl to hold ice ready for use

ice water *n* **:** chilled or iced water esp. for drinking

ice well *n* **:** a cold storage pit containing a solid cake of ice built up during freezing weather

ice whale *n* **:** the right whale of the arctic

ice yacht *n* **:** ICEBOAT

icg *abbr* icing

¹**ich** \(ˌ)ich, ˌ(ə)ch\ *pron* [ME — more at I] *archaic & dial Brit* **:** I

²**ich** *also* **ick** \ˈik\ *n* -s [by shortening & modif. fr. NL *ichthyophthirius* or *ichthyophthiriasis*] **:** a severe dermatitis of freshwater fish that results from invasion of the skin by a ciliated protozoan (*Ichthyophthirius multifiliis*) and is esp. destructive in the aquarium and hatchery — called also *ichthyophthiriasis, ichthyophthirius*

ich *abbr* ichthyology

ich·a·bod \ˈikə,bäd\ *interj, usu cap* [Heb *ī-khābhōdh* inglorious] — used to express regret for departed glory ⟨a refreshingly cheerful note in the thundering chorus whose burden is "*Ichabod*" —G.W.Johnson⟩

ich-laut \ˈik,laůt\ *n* -s *sometimes cap I* [G, fr. *ich* I + *laut* sound] **:** the voiceless palatal fricative sound represented by the *ch* of German *ich* that is phonemically often allophonic with the ach-laut

ichn- *or* **ichno-** *comb form* [Gk, fr. *ichnos*] **:** footprint **:** track ⟨*ichno*logy⟩

ich·neu·mia \ik'n(y)ümēə\ *n, cap* [NL, fr. L *ichneumon* + NL *-ia*] **:** a genus of African carnivorous mammals (family Viverridae) containing the white-tailed mongooses

ich·neu·mon \-mən\ *n* -s [L, fr. Gk *ichneumōn*, mongoose, small wasp, lit., tracker, fr. *ichneuein* to track, fr. *ichnos* track, footstep; the mongoose so called fr. the ancient belief that it hunted out the eggs of the crocodile; the wasp so called fr. its hunting of spiders] **1 :** MONGOOSE; *esp* **:** the No. African mongoose (*Herpestes ichneumon*) that was highly regarded in ancient times for being supposed to devour crocodiles' eggs **2 :** ICHNEUMON FLY

ich·neu·mo·nes \-mə,nēz\ *n pl, cap* [NL, fr. L, pl. of *ichneumon*] **:** ICHNEUMONOIDEA

ichneumon fly *n* **:** any of a large superfamily (Ichneumonoidea) of hymenopterous insects that have many-jointed antennae, fore wings with a usu. triangular stigma, petiolate abdomen, and in the female a commonly long sheathed ovipositor for use on other insect larvae (as caterpillars) which the larval ichneumon fly burrows in and feeds on and ultimately kills thereby constituting an important natural check on many destructive insects

¹**ich·neu·mo·nid** \(ˈ)=¦=mənəd\ *adj* [NL *Ichneumonidae*] **:** of or relating to the Ichneumonidae

²**ichneumonid** \"\ *n* -s **:** an insect of the family Ichneumonidae

ich·neu·mon·i·dae \,==ˈmänə,dē\ *n pl, cap* [NL, fr. *Ichneumon*, type genus (fr. L) + *-idae*] **:** a family including the typical ichneumon flies that have no costal cell and two recurrent veins in the fore wing

ich·neu·mo·noi·dea \(,)=,=məˈnȯidēə\ *n pl, cap* [NL, fr. *Ichneumon*, genus of ichneumon flies + *-oidea*] **:** a superfamily of Hymenoptera consisting of the ichneumon flies

ich·nite \ˈik,nīt\ *n* -s [*ichn-* + *-ite*] **:** a fossil footprint

ich·no·graph·ic \¦iknə¦grafik\ *or* **ich·no·graph·i·cal** \-fəkəl\ *adj* **:** of or having the form of an ichnography

ich·nog·ra·phy \ikˈnägrəfē\ *n* -ES [L *ichnographia*, fr. Gk, fr. *ichno-* ichn- + *-graphia* -graphy] **:** a horizontal section (as of a building) showing true dimensions according to a geometric scale **:** GROUND PLAN, MAP

ich·no·lite \ˈiknə,līt\ *n* -s [*ichn-* + *-lite*] **:** a fossil footprint

ich·nol·o·gy \ikˈnäləjē\ *n* -ES [*ichn-* + *-logy*] **:** the study of fossil footprints

icho \ˈē(,)chō\ *n* -s [Jap *ichō*] **:** GINKGO

ichor \ˈī,kȯ(ə)r, -ō(ə), -,kə(r)\ *n* -s [LL & Gk; LL, sanies, fr. Gk *ichōr* fluid in the veins of the gods, sanies, prob. of non-IE origin] **1** *Greek mythol* **:** an ethereal fluid taking the place

of blood in the veins of the gods **2 :** a thin watery or blood-tinged discharge (as from an ulcer) — compare SANIES **3 :** a concentrated magma rich in mineralizers
ichor·ous \ˈīkərəs\ *adj* **:** of, resembling, or characterized by ichor **:** THIN, WATERY, SEROUS, SANIOUS
ichs *pl of* ICH
ich·tham·mol \ikˈthaˌmōl, ˈikthə-, -mōl\ *n* -S [ISV *ichthyo*-sulfonate + *ammonium* + *-ol*] **:** a brownish black viscous liquid prepared from a distillate of bituminous schists by sulfonation followed by neutralization with ammonia and used as an antiseptic and emollient
ich·thus \ˈikthəs\ *also* **ich·thys** \-thəs\ *n* -ES [Gk *ichthys* fish; akin to Arm *jukn* fish, Lith *žuvis*, OPruss *suckis*] **:** a representation of a fish used in ancient times as a pagan fertility talisman or amulet or as a Christian symbol for the Greek word *ichthys* interpreted as an acrostic in which the Greek letters are the initials of the words *Iēsous Christos theou hyios sōtēr* meaning Jesus Christ Son of God Savior
ichthy- *or* **ichthyo-** *comb form* [L, fr. Gk, fr. *ichthys*] **:** fish ⟨*ichthyic*⟩ ⟨*ichthyology*⟩
ich·thy·ic \ˈikthē(ˌ)ik, (ˈ)ikˈthīik\ *adj* [*ichthy-* + *-ic*] **:** of or relating to fishes or having the form of a fish
ich·thy·ism \ˈikthēˌizəm\ *or* **ich·thy·is·mus** \ˌ≈≈ˈizməs\ *n, pl* **ichthyisms** *or* **ichthyismuses** [NL *ichthyismus*, fr. *ichthy-* + *-ismus* -ism] **:** poisoning from fish — compare ICHTHYOSARCOTOXISM
ich·thy·ob·del·la \ˌ≈≈ˌäbˈdelə\ *n, cap* [NL, fr. *ichthy-* + *-bdella*] **:** a genus (the type of the family Ichthyobdellidae) of elongated freshwater and marine leeches (order Rhynchobdellida) parasitic on fishes and other vertebrates
¹ich·thy·ob·del·lid \¦≈≈¦≈ˈdeləd\ *adj* [NL *Ichthyobdellidae* family of leeches, fr. *Ichthyobdella*, type genus + *-idae*] **:** of or relating to the genus *Ichthyobdella* or family Ichthyobdellidae
²ichthyobdellid \"\ *n* -S **:** a leech of the genus *Ichthyobdella* or family Ichthyobdellidae
ich·thyo·ceph·a·li \ˌikthēōˈsefəˌlī\ [NL, fr. *ichthy-* + *-cephali*] *syn of* SYNBRANCHOIDEA
ich·thy·o·col *or* **ich·thy·o·coll** \ˈikthēəˌkäl\ *or* **ich·thy·o·col·la** \ˌ≈≈≈ˈkälə\ *n* -S [L *ichthyocolla*, fr. Gk *ichthyokolla*, fr. *ichthy-* + *kolla* glue — more at PROTOCOL] **:** ISINGLASS 1
ich·thy·o·dea \ˌ≈≈ˈōdēə\ *n pl, cap* [NL, fr. *ichthy-* + *-odea*] *in some former classifications* **:** a suborder of Amphibia comprising forms having the gills or gill clefts usu. persistent (as the siren, the congo snake, and members of the genera *Proteus* and *Necturus*) — compare MUTABILIA — **ich·thy·o·di·an** \¦≈≈¦ōdēən\ *adj*
ich·thy·o·dont \ˈikthēəˌdänt\ *n* -S [*ichthy-* + *-odont*] **:** a fossil fish tooth
ich·thyo·dor·u·lite \ˌ≈≈ōˈdȯr(y)əˌlīt\ *also* **ich·thyo·dor·y·lite** \-rə-,-\ *n* -S [*ichthy-* + *dory-* or *doru-* (alter. of *dory-*) + *-lite*] **:** a fossil fin spine, dermal spine, or tubercle of a fish or ichthyoid vertebrate
ich·thyo·fauna \¦≈≈≈+\ *also* **ich·thy·fauna** \ˈikthē+\ *n* [NL, fr. *ichthy-* + *fauna*] **:** the fish life of a region
¹ich·thy·oid \ˈikthēˌȯid\ *adj* [Gk *ichthyoeidēs*, fr. *ichthy-* + *-oeidēs* -oid] **:** resembling a fish — **ich·thy·oi·dal** \¦≈≈ˈȯidᵊl\ *adj*
²ichthyoid \"\ *n* -S **:** an animal that resembles a fish; *specif* **:** one of the Ichthyopsida
ichthyoid blood cell *n* **:** MEGALOBLAST
Ich·thy·ol \ˈikthēˌōl, -ˌȯl\ *trademark* — used for ichthammol
ich·thy·o·lite \ˈikthēəˌlīt\ *n* -S [F *ichtyolithe*, fr. *ichty-* ichthy- + *-lithe* -lite] **:** a fossil fish or fragment of a fish — **ich·thy·o·lit·ic** \¦≈≈¦litik\ *adj*
ich·thy·o·log·i·cal \¦≈≈¦läjəkəl\ *adj* **1 :** of or relating to ichthyology **2 :** PISCINE — **ich·thy·o·log·i·cal·ly** \-jək(ə)lē\ *adv*
ich·thy·ol·o·gist \ˌ≈≈ˈäləjəst\ *n* -S **:** a specialist in ichthyology
ich·thy·ol·o·gy \-jē\ *n* -ES [*ichthy-* + *-logy*] **1 :** a branch of zoology that deals with fishes **2 :** a treatise on fishes
ich·thyo·mor·pha \ˌikthēəˈmȯrfə\ [NL, fr. *ichthy-* + *-morpha*] *syn of* CAUDATA
ich·thyo·mor·phic \¦≈≈≈¦fik\ *also* **ich·thyo·mor·phous** \-fəs\ *adj* [*ichthy-* + *-morphic*, *-morphous*] **:** having the shape or some other feature of a fish ⟨~ idols⟩
ich·thy·oph·a·gi \ˌikthēˈäfəˌjī\ *n pl* [L, pl., fr. Gk *ichthyophagoi*, pl. of *ichthyophagos* fish-eating, fr. *ichthyophagein* to eat fish, fr. *ichthy-* + *phagein* to eat — more at BAKSHEESH] **:** a people (as in ancient times on the African coast of the Red sea) living largely on sea food **:** fish eaters
ich·thy·oph·a·gist \-jəst\ *n* -S **:** one that eats or subsists on fish
ich·thy·oph·a·gous \¦≈≈¦≈≈gəs\ *adj* [Gk *ichthyophagos*] **:** eating or subsisting on fish **:** PISCIVOROUS
ich·thy·oph·thi·ri·a·sis \ˌikthēˌäfthəˈrīəsəs\ *n* [NL, fr. *Ichthyophthirius* + *-iasis*] **:** ICH
ich·thy·oph·thir·i·us \ˌikthēˌäfˈthirēəs\ *n* [NL, fr. *ichthy-* + *-phthirius* (fr. *Phthirius*)] **1** *cap* **:** a genus of oval holotrichous ciliates comprising a single species (*I. multifiliis*) that are parasitic in the skin of various freshwater fishes where they encyst and multiply causing a severe and sometimes fatal inflammation **2** -ES **:** ICH
ich·thy·op·sid \¦≈≈¦äpsəd\ *adj* [NL *Ichthyopsida*] **:** of or relating to the Ichthyopsida
²ichthyopsid \"\ *n* -S **:** a vertebrate of the group Ichthyopsida
ich·thy·op·si·da \ˌ≈≈ˈäpsədə\ *n pl, cap* [NL, fr. *ichthy-* + Gk *opsis* appearance + NL *-ida* — more at OPTIC] *in some esp former classifications* **:** a group of vertebrates comprising the agnathous vertebrates, fishes, and amphibians — compare MAMMALIA, SAUROPSIDA — **ich·thy·op·si·dan** \¦≈≈¦sədən, -dᵊn\ *adj or n*
¹ich·thy·op·te·ryg·ia \ˌ≈≈ˌätəˈrijēə\ *n pl, cap* [NL, fr. *ichthy-* + Gk *pterygia*, pl. of *pterygion* fin] *in some classifications* **:** a subclass of fossil aquatic reptiles occurring from the late Carboniferous through the Jurassic and including the small freshwater Mesosauria and the extremely ichthyoid Ichthyosauria
²ichthyopterygia \"\ [NL, fr. *ichthy-* + Gk *pterygia*] *syn of* ICHTHYOSAURIA
ich·thy·op·te·ryg·i·um \-jēəm\ *n, pl* **ichthyopteryg·ia** \-jēə\ [NL, fr. *ichthy-* + Gk *pterygion* small wing, fin, dim. of *pteryg-*, *pteryx* wing — more at PTERYG-] **:** the vertebrate limb when having the form of a fin whether as a definitive organ or in the course of individual or evolutionary development; *esp* **:** any of the paired fins that are the typical limbs of fishes — compare CHIROPTERYGIUM
ich·thy·or·nis \ˌ≈≈ˈȯrnəs\ *n, cap* [NL, fr. *ichthy-* + *-ornis*] **:** the type genus of Ichthyornithidae comprising extinct birds of the Upper Cretaceous that have biconcave vertebrae, articulated quadrate bones, sharp conical teeth set in sockets, well-developed wings, and a keeled sternum and that are similar in size and probably in habits to a tern
ich·thy·or·ni·thes \ˌ≈≈ˈȯrnəˌthēz, -ˌȯrˈnī(ˌ)thēz\ *n pl, cap* [NL, fr. pl. of *Ichthyornis*] *in some classifications* **:** a superorder of extinct birds coextensive with the order Ichthyornithiformes
ich·thy·or·nith·i·dae \-ˌȯrˈnithəˌdē\ *n pl, cap* [NL, fr. *Ichthyornith-*, *Ichthyornis*, type genus + *-idae*] **:** a family of extinct birds (order Ichthyornithiformes) from the Upper Cretaceous of No. America that comprises the genus *Ichthyornis* and in some classifications *Apatornis* and possibly one other genus
ich·thy·or·nithi·for·mes \-ˌȯrnəthəˈfȯrˌmēz, -ˌȯrˌnith-\ *n pl, cap* [NL, fr. *Ichthyornith-*, *Ichthyornis* + *-iformes*] **:** an order of extinct toothed birds (superorder Odontognathae) coextensive with the family Ichthyornithidae in its broadest scope
ich·thyo·sar·co·tox·ism \ˌikthēōˌsärkəˈtäkˌsizəm\ *n* -S [*ichthy-* + *sarc-* + *tox-* + *-ism*] **:** poisoning from eating the flesh of poisonous fishes — compare ICHTHYISM
ich·thyo·saur \ˈ≈≈≈ˌsȯ(ə)r\ *n* -S [NL *Ichthyosaurus*] **:** a reptile of the order Ichthyosauria
ich·thy·o·sau·ria \ˌ≈≈≈ˈsȯrēə\ *n pl, cap* [NL, fr. *ichthy-* + *-sauria*] **:** an order of Mesozoic marine reptiles most abundant in the Lias having an ichthyoid body, elongated snout, short neck, dorsal and caudal fins, limbs modified into paddles by the flattening of the bones, multiplication of the phalanges and addition of from one to four digits, eyes very large and protected by a ring of bony sclerotic plates, and numerous conical teeth set in grooves and adapted for catching fish — **ich·thyo·sau·ri·an** \¦≈≈≈¦≈rēən\ *adj or n* — **ich·thyo·sau·roid** \-ˌrȯid\ *adj*
¹ich·thyo·sau·rid \¦≈≈≈¦≈rəd\ *adj* [NL *Ichthyosauridae*] **:** of or relating to the Ichthyosauridae
²ichthyosaurid \"\ *n* -S **:** a reptile of the family Ichthyosauridae
ich·thyo·sau·ri·dae \ˌ≈≈≈ˈ≈rəˌdē\ *n pl, cap* [NL, fr. *Ichthyosaurus*, type genus + *-idae*] **:** a family of ichthyosaurs widely distributed in Jurassic and Cretaceous rocks of both hemispheres — see ICHTHYOSAURUS
ich·thyo·sau·rus \-rəs\ *n* [NL, fr. *ichthy-* + *-saurus*] **1** *cap* **:** the type genus of Ichthyosauridae comprising highly variable Jurassic ichthyosaurs and orig. including most of the later ichthyosaurs most of which are now placed in other genera **2** -ES **:** any reptile of the genus *Ichthyosaurus*
ich·thy·o·si·form \¦≈≈ˈōsəˌfȯrm\ *adj* [NL *ichthyosis* + E *-iform*] **:** resembling ichthyosis or that of ichthyosis
ich·thy·o·sis \ˌ≈≈ˈōsəs\ *n, pl* **ichthyo·ses** \-ōˌsēz\ [NL, fr. *ichthy-* — *-osis*] **:** a congenital disease usu. of hereditary origin characterized by skin that is rough, thick, and scaly and resembles that of a fish — called also *fishskin disease*
ich·thy·ot·ic \¦≈≈¦äd·ik\ *adj* **:** of or relating to ichthyosis
ich·thy·ot·o·mi \ˌ≈≈ˈäd·əˌmī\ *n pl, cap* [NL, fr. *ichthy-* + *-tomi* (fr. Gk *temnein* to cut) — more at TOME] **:** a subclass or order of Chondrichthyes comprising chiefly Carboniferous and early Permian sharks having a slender and elongated body with diphycercal tail and archipterygial fins — compare PLEURACANTHUS — **ich·thy·ot·o·mous** \¦≈≈¦äd·əməs\ *adj*
ich·thyo·tox·ism \ˌ≈≈ōˈtäkˌsizəm\ *n* -S [*ichthy-* + *tox-* + *-ism*] **:** ICHTHYISM
ichthys *var of* ICHTHUS
-ich·thys \ˈikthəs\ *n comb form* [NL, fr. Gk *ichthys* — more at ICHTHUS] **:** fish — in generic names chiefly in ichthyology ⟨*Dinichthys*⟩ ⟨*Nemichthys*⟩
ichu \ˈē(ˌ)chü\ *or* **ichu grass** *or* **hi·chu** \ˈ(h)ē-\ *n* -S [Quechua *ichu*] **:** a valuable grass (*Stipa ichu*) of the upper Andes that is used as forage and for thatching
-i·cian \ˈishən\ *n suffix* -S [ME *-icien*, *-ician*, fr. OF *-icien*, fr. L *-ica* (as in *rhetorica* rhetoric) + OF *-ien* -ian — more at RHETORIC] **:** a specialist or practitioner in a (specified) field ⟨*beautician*⟩ ⟨*technician*⟩
ici·ca \əˈsēkə\ *n* -S [Pg, fr. Tupi] **1 :** a tropical American timber tree of the genus *Protium* **2 :** any of several Brazilian gum-producing trees; *esp* **:** BALATA
ici·cle \ˈīˌsikəl, -ˌsək-, -ˌsēk-\ *n* -S [ME *isikel*, fr. *is* ice + *ikel* icicle, fr. OE *gicel*; akin to OHG *ihilla* icicle, ON *jökull* icicle, glacier, *jaki* piece of ice, MIr *aig* ice, W *iâ*] **1 :** a pendent usu. conical mass of ice formed by the freezing of dripping water **2 :** an emotionally unresponsive person **3 :** a long hanging Christmas tree ornament (as a thin strip of lead foil) **4 :** a metal projection forming on the upper inside of a pipe joint during welding
icier *comparative of* ICY
iciest *superlative of* ICY
ic·i·ly \ˈīsəlē, -li\ *adv* **:** in an icy manner ⟨an ~ unenthusiastic audience of . . . bankers —Mollie Panter-Downes⟩
ic·i·ness \ˈīsēnəs, -sin-\ *n* -ES **:** the quality or state of being icy ⟨her voice carried . . . a quality of ~ —Louis Bromfield⟩
¹ic·ing \ˈīsiŋ, -sēŋ\ *n* -S [fr. gerund of ²*ice*] **:** a sweet coating for baked goods usu. made from sugar and butter combined with water, milk, or egg white, flavored, often colored, and often cooked — called also *frosting*
²icing *n* -S [fr. the phrase *icing the puck*] **:** the act or an instance of an ice-hockey player's shooting the puck from within his own defensive zone through the neutral zone and beyond the opponents' goal line
icing station *n* **:** railway facilities for icing refrigerator cars
icing sugar *n, chiefly Brit* **:** CONFECTIONERS' SUGAR
ick *var of* ICH
ick·er \ˈikər\ *n* -S [fr. (assumed) ME (Sc dial.), fr. OE *eher*, var. of *ēar* — more at EAR] *Scot* **:** a head of grain
ick·i·ness \ˈikēnəs\ *n* -ES **:** the quality or state of being icky
ick·le \ˈikəl\ *n* -S [ME *ikel* — more at ICICLE] *dial Eng* **:** ICICLE
icky \ˈikē\ *adj* -ER/-EST [perh. baby-talk alter. of *sticky*] **1 :** STICKY ⟨cooing baby talk at him in an ~ way —Kathleen O'Malley⟩ — often used as a generalized expression of disapproval **2 :** lacking sophistication **:** not hep ⟨music you want to dance to — not wild and not ~ —Ralph Flanagan⟩
icon \ˈīˌkän *sometimes* -ˌkən\ *n* -S [L, fr. Gk *eikōn*, fr. *eikenai* to resemble; perh. akin to Lith *paveikslas* example, *įvykti* to occur, come about] **1 :** a usu. pictorial representation **:** IMAGE **2** [LGk *eikōn*, fr. Gk] **a** *also* **ikon** *or* **ei·kon** \"\ **:** a sacred image venerated in churches and homes of Eastern Christianity depicting Christ, the Virgin Mary, a saint, or some other religious subject in the conventional manner of Byzantine art and typically painted on a small wooden panel often with a repoussé metal cover but also enameled on metal or made of mosaic **b :** an object of uncritical devotion **:** IDOL; *esp* **:** a traditional belief or ideal ⟨the ridiculous drudgery of the Ph.D. and the devotion of university administration to the ~ of that degree —*Times Lit. Supp.*⟩ **3** *in philosophy of language and semiotic* **:** a sign (as a straight line on a map) that signifies by virtue of sharing a property with what it represents (as a straight road) — contrasted with *index* and *symbol* ⟨a photograph, a star chart, a model, a chemical diagram are ~*s*, while the word 'photograph', the names of the stars and of chemical elements are symbols —C.W.Morris⟩
icon- *or* **icono-** *also* **eikon-** *or* **eikono-** *or* **ikon-** *or* **ikono-** *comb form* [Gk *eikon-*, *eikono-*, fr. *eikon-*, *eikōn*] **:** image ⟨*iconism*⟩ ⟨*iconomania*⟩ ⟨*iconometry*⟩
icon *abbr* iconography
¹ico·ni·an \(ˈ)īˈkōnēən\ *adj, usu cap* [*Iconium* (now Konya, Turkey), ancient city of Asia Minor (fr. L) + E *-an*] **:** of or relating to Iconium
²iconian \"\ *n* -S *cap* **:** a native or inhabitant of Iconium
icon·ic \(ˈ)īˈkänik\ *adj* [L *iconicus*, fr. Gk *eikonikos*, fr. *eikon-*, *eikōn* image + *-ikos* -ic — more at ICON] **1 :** of, relating to, or having the character of an icon ⟨~ veneration⟩ ⟨~ theories⟩ ⟨~ signs or conventional signs⟩ **2 :** resembling an icon — **icon·i·cal·ly** \-nək(ə)lē\ *adv* — **ico·nic·i·ty** \ˌīkəˈnisəd·ē\ *n* -ES
icon·o·clasm \īˈkänəˌklazəm\ *n* -S [fr. *iconoclast*, after such pairs as E *baptist*: *baptism*] **:** the doctrine, practice, or attitude of an iconoclast **:** image breaking
icon·o·clast \-ˌklast, -aa(ə)st,-aist\ *n* -S [ML *iconoclastes*, fr. MGk *eikonoklastēs*, lit., image destroyer, fr. Gk *eikono-* icon- + MGk *-klastēs* -clast] **1 a :** one who destroys religious images or opposes their veneration **b** *usu cap* **:** one of a religious party in the Eastern Empire in the 8th and 9th centuries that opposed the use of icons **2 :** one who attacks established beliefs, ideals, customs, or institutions ⟨the blundering cruelty of the tough-minded ~ —Lucius Garvin⟩
icon·o·clas·tic \(ˌ)ī¦≈≈¦klastik, -laas-,-lais-, -tēk\ *adj* **1 :** of or relating to iconoclasm or iconoclasts ⟨~ outbursts associated with the Reformation⟩ ⟨the Byzantine ~ controversy⟩ **2 :** being or befitting an iconoclast **:** marked by or having the character of iconoclasm ⟨an ~ critic of the monarchy⟩ ⟨an ~ article opposing the prevailing educational philosophy⟩ **3 :** tending to produce iconoclasm or overthrow what is established ⟨the ~ influence of modern science⟩ — **icon·o·clas·ti·cal·ly** \-tək(ə)lē, -tēk-, -li\ *adv*
icon·o·dule \īˈkänəˌd(y)ül\ *n* -S [*icon-* + Gk *doulos* slave] **:** one who venerates icons and defends their devotional use
icon·o·du·list \≈ˈ≈≈ˌd(y)üləst, (ˌ)≈¦≈≈ˈ≈≈\ *n* -S [*iconoduly* + *-ist*] **:** ICONODULE
icon·o·du·ly \≈ˈ≈≈ˌlē\ *n* -ES [*icon-* + ML *dulia* veneration — more at DULIA] **:** the veneration of images
ico·nog·ra·pher \ˌīkəˈnägrəfə(r)\ *n* -S [*iconography* + *-er*] **:** a maker or designer of figures or drawings esp. of a conventional or mechanical type
icon·o·graph·ic \(ˌ)ī¦känə¦grafik\ *or* **icon·o·graph·i·cal** \-fəkəl\ *adj* **1 :** of or relating to iconography ⟨experimenting in ~ forms⟩ ⟨~ studies⟩ ⟨analyze . . . his use of *iconographical* types, for the art of the Middle Ages and the Renaissance is rich in symbolism —K.M.Setton⟩ **2 :** representing something by pictures or diagrams ⟨cartographic and ~ items illustrative of colonial history⟩ — **icon·o·graph·i·cal·ly** \-fək(ə)lē\ *adv*
ico·nog·ra·phy \ˌīkəˈnägrəfē\ *n* -ES [Gk *eikonographia* sketch, description, fr. *eikonographein* to describe (fr. *eikon-* icon- + *graphein* to draw, write) + *-ia* -y — more at CARVE] **1 a :** illustration of a subject by pictures or other visual representations ⟨figures . . . to be placed alongside the work of such masters of crustacean ~ —*Nature*⟩ **b :** pictures and other visual representations illustrating or relating to a subject ⟨a discovery adding another portrait to the ~ of Columbus⟩; *specif* **:** art representing religious or legendary subjects by conventional images and symbols ⟨sculptures . . . of the highest importance for the history of both Indian art and Buddhist ~ —V.A.Smith⟩ **c** (1) **:** the imagery selected to convey the meaning of a work of art or the identity of its figures and setting and comprising figures or objects or features often fixed (as in medieval religious art) by convention **:** a set of symbolic forms ⟨the guitar, the wine glass, the playing cards together form an ~ suggestive of pleasant, carefree moments —Aline B. Saarinen⟩ (2) **:** the set of conventions or principles governing such imagery ⟨the types of the Muses in art . . . must wait until the Roman period before their ~ and their roles are definitively codified —J.J.Seznec⟩ **2 :** ICONOLOGY **3 :** a book, list, or other record featuring or dealing with iconography
ico·nol·a·ter \-ˈnäləd·ə(r)\ *n* -S [*icon-* + *-later*] **:** a worshiper of images or icons
ico·nol·a·try \-lə·trē\ *n* -ES [Gk *eikono-* icon- + *-latry*] **:** IMAGE WORSHIP
icono·log·i·cal \(ˌ)ī¦känᵊl¦äjəkəl, ¦īkən-\ *adj* **:** of, relating to, or constituting iconology ⟨~ elaboration of abstract painting⟩
ico·nol·o·gist \ˌīkəˈnäləjəst\ *n* -S **:** a specialist in iconology
ico·nol·o·gy \-jē\ *n* -ES [F *iconologie*, fr. *icono-* icon- + *-logie* -logy] **:** the description, history, or analysis of symbolic art (as in the medieval church) or of artistic symbolism **:** the study of icons or iconography
icono·mat·ic *or* **ikono·mat·ic** \(ˌ)ī¦känə¦mad·ik, ¦īkən-\ *adj* [*icon-* + *onomat-*, *onoma* name + E *-ic* — more at NAME] **:** of or relating to a form of writing believed to be intermediate between picture writing and phonetic writing in which pictures or signs stand not for objects themselves but for their names considered as phonetic elements only — **icono·mat·i·cal·ly** \-d·ək(ə)lē\ *adv*
icono·mat·i·cism \(ˌ)ī¦känəˈmadəˌsizəm, ¦īkən-\ *n* -S **:** iconomatic writing
icon·o·ma·tog·ra·phy *also* **ikon·o·ma·tog·ra·phy** \(ˌ)ī¦känəməˈtägrəfē\ *n* -ES [*iconomatic*, *ikonomatic* + *-o-* + *-graphy*] **:** iconomatic writing
ico·nom·e·ter \ˌīkəˈnäməd·ə(r)\ *n* [ISV *icon-* + *-meter*] **1 :** an instrument for determining the distance of an object of known size or the size of an object at known distance by measuring the image of it produced by a lens of known focal length **2 a :** an instrument that determines the proper objective to be used in taking a picture of given size from a given standpoint and that consists of a diopter and an open rectangular frame sliding on a graduated rod **b :** a direct viewfinder having a metal frame
icono·met·ric \(ˌ)ī¦känə¦me·trik, ¦īkən-\ *adj* **:** of, relating to, or ascertained by iconometry
ico·nom·e·try \ˌīkəˈnäməˌtrē\ *n* -ES [ISV *icon-* + *-metry*] **:** the art of estimating the distance or size of an object by the use of an iconometer
icon·o·scope \īˈkänəˌskōp\ *n* [fr. *Iconoscope*, a trademark] **:** a camera tube containing an electron gun and a photoemissive mosaic screen each cell of which produces a charge proportional to the varying light intensity of the optical image focused on the screen by the camera lenses, these charges being transformed as the beam of electrons from the gun scans the screen into voltages that are subsequently amplified and transmitted as television picture signals — called also *ike*
ico·nos·ta·sis \ˌīkəˈnästəsəs\ *also* **ico·no·stas** \ēˈkōnəˈstäs\ *n, pl* **ico·nostases** \ˌīkəˈnästəˌsēz, ēˌkōnə¦stäsəz\ [*iconostasis* modif. of MGk *eikonostasi*, *eikonostasion*, fr. LGk *eikonostasion* shrine, fr. *eikono-* icon- + *-stasion* (fr. Gk *histanai* to stand); *iconostas* fr. Russ *ikonostas*, fr. MGk *eikonostasi*, *eikonostasion* — more at STAND] **:** a screen or partition with doors and tiers of icons that separates the bema from the nave in Eastern churches
icons *pl of* ICON
icosa- *also* **icosi-** *or* **icos-** *comb form* [Gk *eikosa-*, *eikosi-*, *eikos-*, fr. *eikosi* — more at VICENARY] **:** twenty ⟨*icosahedron*⟩
icosa·he·dral \(ˌ)ī¦kōsə¦hēdrəl, -kās- *sometimes chiefly Brit* -hed-\ *adj* **:** of or having the form of an icosahedron
icosa·he·dron \-drən *sometimes* -ˌdrän\ *n* -S [Gk *eikosaedron*, fr. *eikosa-* icosa- + *-edron* -hedron] **1 :** a polyhedron having 20 faces **2 :** an imaginary polyhedron in the Laban system of dance notation representing the 20 principal movement directions of a dancer in its center

regular icosahedron

icosa·se·mic \-¦sēmik\ *adj* [*icosa-* + *-semic*] *in ancient prosody* **:** having or equal to 20 morae
icosa·sphere \≈ˈ≈≈+,-\ *n* [*icosa-* + *sphere*] **:** a spherical tank for volatile liquids built of twenty steel plates corresponding to the faces of a regular icosahedron
icosi·tetrahedron \ī¦kōsə, -kāsə +\ *n* [*icosi-* + *tetrahedron*] **:** an isometric crystal form with 24 faces; *specif* **:** TRAPEZOHEDRON
icos·te·idae \ˌīˌkäˈstēəˌdē\ *n pl, cap* [NL, fr. *Icosteus*, type genus + *-idae*] **:** a family of deepwater fishes (order Malacichthyes) comprising the ragfishes and having a soft skeleton and skin loose and naked or with small prickles or scales
icos·te·us \īˈkästēəs\ *n, cap* [NL, fr. Gk *eikein* to yield, give way + NL *-osteus* — more at WEAK] **:** the type genus of the family Icosteidae comprising various typical ragfishes of the Pacific ocean
ico·type \ˈīkəˌtīp\ *n* [Gk *eikōs* like (part. of *eikenai* to resemble) + E *type* — more at ICON] **:** a typical specimen of a species accurately identified but not serving as the basis for a published description
-ics \(ˌ)iks, ˌēks\ *n pl suffix but sing or pl in constr* [*-ic* (as in arithmetic) + *-s*; after Gk pl. nouns ending in *-ika*, as *mathēmatika* mathematics] **1** *usu sing in constr* **:** study **:** knowledge **:** skill **:** practice ⟨*optics*⟩ ⟨*linguistics*⟩ ⟨*pediatrics*⟩ ⟨*homiletics*⟩ **2** *usu sing in constr* **:** systematic formulation **:** treatise ⟨*economics*⟩ ⟨*politics*⟩ **3** *usu pl in constr* **:** characteristic actions or activities ⟨*heroics*⟩ ⟨*hysterics*⟩ ⟨*gymnastics*⟩ **4** *usu pl in constr* **:** characteristic qualities, operations, or phenomena ⟨*acoustics*⟩ ⟨*mechanics*⟩ ⟨*phonetics*⟩
ICSH *abbr* interstitial-cell-stimulating hormone
ic·tal \ˈiktᵊl\ *adj, med* **:** of, relating to, or caused by ictus
ic·ta·lu·rus \ˌiktəˈlürəs, -təlˈyü-\ *n, cap* [NL, irreg. fr. *ichthy-* + Gk *ailouros* cat] **:** a genus of large catfishes (family Ameiuridae) of the fresh waters of No. America
icter- *or* **ictero-** [MF or L *icter-*, fr. Gk *ikter-*, fr. *ikteros*] *comb form* **1 :** jaundice ⟨*icterogen*⟩ ⟨*icterohemorrhagic*⟩ ⟨*icteroid*⟩ **2 :** jaundice and ⟨*icteroanemia*⟩
ic·ter·ic \(ˈ)ikˈterik\ *adj* [MF or L; MF *icterique*, fr. L *ictericus*, fr. Gk *ikterikos*, fr. *ikteros* jaundice + *-ikos* -ic; akin to Gk *iktinos* kite, *iktis* yellow-breasted marten] **:** of, relating to, or affected with jaundice
icteric index *var of* ICTERUS INDEX
ic·ter·i·dae \ikˈterəˌdē\ *n pl, cap* [NL, fr. *Icterus*, type genus + *-idae*] **:** a large family of American oscine birds comprising the orioles, the American blackbirds, the bobolinks, and the meadowlarks and having nine primaries, a sharp conical bill, and no rictal bristles
ic·ter·ine \ˈiktəˌrīn, -ˌrən\ *adj* [NL *Icterus* + E *-ine*] **:** resembling or relating to the family Icteridae
icterine warbler *n* **:** a small greenish warbler (*Hippolais icterina*) common in central Europe
ic·ter·i·tious \¦iktə¦rishəs\ *or* **ic·ter·i·tous** \(ˈ)≈¦terəd·əs\ *adj* [*icterus* + *-itious* or *-itous*] **:** of a jaundiced color **:** YELLOW
ic·tero·anemia \¦iktə(ˌ)rō+\ *n* [NL, fr. *icter-* + *anemia*] **:** a disease characterized by jaundice, anemia, and marked destruction of red blood cells and seen esp. in swine
ic·ter·o·gen·ic \¦iktərō¦jenik, (ˌ)ik¦terə¦j-\ *also* **ic·ter·og·e·nous** \ˌiktəˈräjənəs\ *adj* [*icter-* + *-genic*, *-genous*] **:** causing or tending to cause jaundice
ic·tero·hematuria \¦iktə(ˌ)rō+\ *n* -S [NL, fr. *icter-* + *hematuria*] **:** an infectious disease of sheep that is marked by jaundice and caused by a parasitic protozoan (*Babesia ovis*) which destroys red blood cells — compare TEXAS FEVER

ic·ter·oid \'iktə,rȯid\ *adj* [ISV *icter-* + *-oid*] **:** resembling jaundice **:** of a yellow tint like that produced by jaundice

ic·ter·us \'iktərəs\ *n* [NL, fr. Gk *ikteros* jaundice, a yellow bird] **1** -ES **:** JAUNDICE **2** *cap* **:** the type genus of the family Icteridae comprising the American orioles

icterus gravis \-'gravəs, -räv-,-rāv-\ *n* [NL, lit., severe jaundice] **1 :** a condition marked by severe jaundice; *specif* **:** ERYTHROBLASTOSIS **2** *or* **icterus ne·o·na·to·rum** \-,nēənə'tōrəm\ **:** a common fatal disease of newborn mules related to erythroblastosis fetalis in the human and due to sensitization of the horse dam to blood elements derived from the ass sire

icterus index *or* **icteric index** *n* **:** a figure representing the amount of bilirubin in the blood as determined by comparing the color of a sample of test serum with a set of color standards ⟨an *icterus index* of 15 or above indicates active jaundice⟩

ic·tic \'iktik\ *adj* **:** of or relating to an ictus

ic·tid·o·saur \ik'tidə,sȯ(ə)r\ *n* -S [NL *Ictidosauria*] **:** a reptile of the Ictidosauria

ic·tido·sau·ria \(,)ik,tidə'sȯrēə, ,iktədō's-\ *n pl, cap* [NL, fr. Gk *iktid-, iktis* yellow-breasted marten + NL *-o-* + *-sauria*] **:** an order of Reptilia comprising a number of imperfectly known Upper Triassic forms intermediate in character between the therapsids and the most primitive true mammals — compare MICROCONODON

ic·ti·o·bus \ik'tīəbəs\ *n, cap* [NL, irreg. fr. Gk *ichthy-* + Gk *bous* ox, cow (also, a kind of fish) — more at COW] **:** a common genus of buffalo fishes

ic·to·gen·ic \¦iktə¦jenik\ *adj* [*ictus* + *-o-* + *-genic*] *med* **:** giving rise to ictus

ic·to·nyx \'iktə,niks\ *n, cap* [NL, fr. Gk *iktis* yellow-breasted marten + NL *-onyx*] **:** a genus of African mustelid mammals comprising the zorils

ic·tus \'iktəs\ *n* -ES [L, fr. *ictus*, past part. of *icere* to strike; akin to Gk *aichmē* lance, *iktea* wounded, Lith *iešmas* spit, OPruss *aysmis* and perh. to ON *eigin* newly-sprouted seed, MLG *īne* awn] **1 a** (1) **:** recurring stress or beat in a rhythmic usu. metrical series of sounds **:** metrical accent (2) **:** the place of the stress or beat in a metrical foot — compare ARSIS, THESIS **b :** ACCENT 6b **2 a :** a beat or pulsation esp. of the heart **b :** a sudden attack or seizure esp. of apoplexy **:** STROKE

ICW *abbr* interrupted continuous waves

icy \'īsē, -si\ *adj* **icier; iciest;** [¹*ice* + *-y*] **1 a :** covered with, abounding in, or consisting of ice ⟨skidded on the ~ street⟩ ⟨exploring the ~ polar wastes⟩ ⟨the ~ cliffs at the glacier's edge⟩ **b :** intensely cold ⟨~ weather⟩ ⟨an ~ room⟩ **2 :** characterized by coldness (as of manner, influence) **:** CHILLING, FRIGID, COLD ⟨got an ~ stare from the stranger⟩ **3 :** sure to be fulfilled — used of a contract in a card game

¹**id** \'id\ *n* -S [G, short for *idioplasma* idioplasm — more at IDIOPLASM] **:** a hypothetical structural unit of living matter resulting from the successive aggregation of biophores and determinants

²**id** \"\ *n* -S [NL, fr. L, it; trans. of G *es*] **:** the primitive undifferentiated part of the psychic apparatus that reacts blindly on a pleasure-pain level, is the seat of psychic energy, and is the ultimate source of higher psychic components (as ego and superego)

³**id** \"\ *n* -S *often attrib* [¹*-id*] **:** a skin rash that is secondary to a primary infection elsewhere and is considered to be an allergic reaction of the skin to the circulating antigen ⟨a syphilitic ~⟩

¹**-id** \əd, (,)id\ *n suffix* -S [in sense 1, fr. L *-ides*, masc. patronymic suffix, fr. Gk *-idēs*; in sense 2, fr. It *-ide*, fr. L *-id-, -is*, fem. patronymic suffix, fr. Gk; in sense 3, fr. F *-ide*, fr. L *-id-, -is*, fem. patronymic suffix] **1 a :** one belonging to a (specified) natural group or line of descent ⟨Melanes*id*⟩ ⟨Australo*id*⟩ **b :** one belonging to a (specified) dynastic line ⟨Fatim*id*⟩ **2 a :** meteor associated with or radiating from a (specified) constellation or comet ⟨Perse*id*⟩ **b :** variable star of a (specified) source or type ⟨Cephe*id*⟩ **3** *also* **-ide** \,īd, ,əd, (,)id\ **:** skin rash caused by (something specified) ⟨bacter*id*⟩ ⟨syphil*id*⟩

²**-id** \"\ *adj suffix* **:** of, relating to, or characteristic of a (specified) natural group or line of descent ⟨pre-Mongolo*id* artifacts⟩

³**-id** \"\ — see -IDE

⁴**-id** \"\ *n suffix* -S [prob. fr. L *-id-, -is*, formative element of some nouns, fr. Gk] **1 :** structural element of a lower molar or premolar ⟨protocon*id*⟩ **2 :** structure, body, or particle of a (specified) kind ⟨chromat*id*⟩

id *abbr* **1** [L *idem*] the same **2** island

ID *abbr* **1** identification **2** inside diameter; internal diameter **3** inside dimensions **4** intelligence department **5** intradermal

-i·da \ədə\ *n pl suffix* [NL (neut. pl. in form), fr. L- *ides*, patronymic suffix] **:** animals that are or have the form of — in names of higher taxa (as orders and classes) ⟨Scorpion*ida*⟩ ⟨Acar*ida*⟩ ⟨Bero*ida*⟩ — **-i·dan** \ədən, əd°n\ *n or adj suffix*

-i·dae \ə,dē\ *n pl suffix* [NL, fr. L (pl. of *-ides*, masc. patronymic suffix), fr. Gk *-idai*, pl. of *-idēs*, masc. patronymic suffix] **:** members of the family of — in patronymic group names ⟨Alcmaeon*idae*⟩ ⟨Homer*idae*⟩ ⟨Seleuc*idae*⟩; in names of families of animals substituted for the last syllable of the genitive case of the name of the type genus ⟨Aphid*idae* from *Aphis*⟩ ⟨Equ*idae* from *Equus*⟩

¹**idae·an** *or* **ide·an** \(')ī¦dēən\ *adj, usu cap* [L *idaeus* Idaean (fr. Gk *idaios*, fr. *Idē* Mt. Ida in Crete) + E *-an*] **1 :** of, relating to, or dwelling on Mt. Ida in Crete **2 :** of, relating to, or characteristic of the ancient Greek goddess Rhea with whom Mt. Ida was associated

²**idaean** \"\ *adj, usu cap* [L *idaeus* Idaean (fr. Gk *idaios*, fr. *Idē* Mt. Ida in Asia Minor) + E *-an*] **1 :** of, relating to, or dwelling on Mt. Ida in Asia Minor **2 :** of, relating to, or characteristic of the ancient Greek goddess Cybele with whom Mt. Ida was associated

idae·in *also* **ide·in** \ī'dēən\ *n* -S [ISV *idae-, ide-* (fr. NL *vitis-idaea* — specific epithet of the mountain cranberry *Vaccinium vitis-idaea minus* —, fr. L *vitis* vine + *idaea*, fem. of *idaeus*) + *-in*] **:** an anthocyanin pigment obtained in the form of the greenish brown crystalline chloride $C_{21}H_{21}ClO_{11}$ from the skin of red apples and from cranberries and similar fruit; a galactoside of cyanidin

¹**ida·ho** \'īdə,hō\ *adj, usu cap* [*Idaho*, state in the northwestern U.S., prob. of AmerInd origin] **:** of or from the state of Idaho **:** of the kind or style prevalent in Idaho **:** IDAHOAN

²**idaho** \"\ *n, pl* **idahoes** *also* **idahos** *usu cap* **:** an elongated potato rich in starch and suitable for baking that is grown esp. in Idaho

¹**ida·ho·an** \,īdə¦hōən\ *adj, usu cap* [*Idaho* + E *-an*] **:** of, relating to, or characteristic of Idaho or Idahoans

²**idahoan** \"\ *n* -S *cap* **:** a native or resident of Idaho

idaho fescue *n, usu cap I* **:** a tall meadow grass (*Festuca idahoensis*) of central and western No. America with smooth filiform leaves, an open inflorescence, and awns about half as long as the lemmas

idaho white pine *n, usu cap I* **1 :** WESTERN WHITE PINE 1 **2 :** the wood of western white pine

ida·lian \(')ī¦dālēən, -lyən\ *adj, usu cap* [*Idalium*, ancient town in Cyprus + E *-an*] **:** of or relating to the ancient town Idalium that was a center of the worship of Aphrodite

idant \'īd°nt, 'ī¦, ¦,dant\ *n* -S [ISV ¹*id* + *-ant*; orig. formed in G] **:** a hypothetical structural unit arising from an aggregation of ids and forming a basic element of the germ plasm in the Weismannian theory of heredity

id·dings·ite \'idiŋ,zīt\ *n* -S [Joseph P. *Iddings* †1920 Am. geologist + E *-ite*] **:** a mineral consisting of a silicate of calcium, magnesium, and iron of doubtful composition and forming pseudomorphs after olivine

¹**ide** \'īd\ *n* -S [back-formation fr. *ides*] **:** one of the ides

²**ide** \"\ *n* -S [Sw *id* — more at IDE] **:** a European freshwater cyprinid food fish (*Idus idus*) — see ORFE

¹**-ide** \,īd, ,əd, (,)id\ *also* **-id** \əd, (,)id\ *n suffix* -S [G & F; G *-id*, fr. F *-ide* (as in *oxide*) — more at OXIDE] **1 :** binary chemical compound or compound regarded as binary — added to contracted name of the nonmetallic or more electronegative element ⟨iron ox*ide*⟩ ⟨hydrogen sulf*ide*⟩ or radical ⟨am*ide*⟩ ⟨ethox*ide*⟩ **2 a :** chemical compound derived from or related to another (usu. specified) compound ⟨anhydr*ide*⟩ ⟨glycol*ide*⟩ ⟨phthal*ide*⟩ **b :** acetal derivative of a sugar — in names of glycosides replacing final *-e* of the name of the sugar ⟨arabinos*ide*⟩ ⟨cerebros*ide*⟩ — compare -OSIDE **3 :** one of a class of organic esp. naturally occurring compounds ⟨phosphat*ide*⟩ ⟨pept*ide*⟩ ⟨sacchar*ide*⟩ **4 :** chemical element of a series of metallic elements of increasing atomic numbers ⟨actin*ide*⟩ ⟨lanthan*ide*⟩

²**-ide** — see -ID

idea \(')ī¦dēə, (')ī¦diə; *chiefly in southern US* 'ī,dē(ə) *or* 'ī,di(ə); *dial or archaic* (')ī¦dē; *in NewEng extremely frequent with intrusive* r —(')ī¦dēər *or* (')ī¦di(ə)r\ *n* -S [L, fr. Gk, fr. *idein* to see — more at WIT] **1 a :** a presentation of sense, concept, or representation: as (1) *Platonism* **:** an archetype or subsistent form **:** a transcendent universal (2) *Aristotelianism* **:** the form-giving cause **:** FORM (3) *Lockeanism* **:** an immediate object or a compound of immediate objects of sensation or reflection — see COMPLEX IDEA, SIMPLE IDEA (4) *Berkeleianism* **:** an impression of sense or imagination; *esp* **:** PERCEPT (5) *Humism* **:** a representation or construct of memory and association as distinguished from direct impression of sense (6) *Kantianism* **:** a transcendent but nonempirical concept of reason **:** NOUMENON (7) *Hegelianism* **:** the highest category **:** the complete and final product of reason; *also* **:** its realization or embodiment — compare ABSOLUTE **b :** an object of a concept **2 a :** a conception or standard of any perfection **:** IDEAL **b :** a preliminary plan **:** CONCEPTION, DESIGN; *usu* **:** a plan or purpose of action **:** PROJECT ⟨his ~ of going in for law⟩ ⟨a new ~ for decorating the house⟩ **3** *archaic* **:** a visible representation of a conception (as an abstract perfection) or of a design **:** a replica of a pattern or archetype **:** a realized ideal **4 a** *obs* **:** an image or picture recalled by memory **b :** an indefinite or fanciful conception or notion **:** a figment of the imagination **:** FANCY, SUPPOSITION, OPINION ⟨that is a mere ~ of yours⟩ ⟨a head full of absurd ~*s*⟩ ⟨I've an ~ we'll win⟩ **5 :** an object of the mind existing in apprehension, conception, or thought **:** NOTION, THOUGHT, IMPRESSION ⟨a clear ~ of his responsibility⟩ **6 :** a product of reflection or mental concentration **:** a formulated thought or opinion ⟨~*s* on a subject⟩ ⟨clearly defined ~*s*⟩ **7 :** whatever is known, believed, or supposed regarding any object ⟨the child's ~ of air⟩ **8 :** the central or key meaning or the chief end of a particular action or situation ⟨get the ~⟩ — see BIG IDEA **9 :** a musical figure or theme **10** *Christian Science* **:** an image in Mind

syn IDEA, CONCEPT, CONCEPTION, THOUGHT, NOTION, IMPRESSION: IDEA may apply to an image or formulation of something seen or known, of something imagined and visualized, of something vaguely assumed, guessed at, or sensed ⟨practically every American boy who is not tied to his mother's apron strings is going to encounter other boys whose *ideas* of fighting are very different from his own —Margaret Mead⟩ ⟨success with the steamboat inspired Colonel John Stevens to work on the *idea* of a steam railroad —*Amer. Guide Series: N.J.*⟩ ⟨an earlier paper has reviewed the development during the Middle Ages of the *idea* that the Kingdom of France had natural frontiers which it was her right, even her duty, to attain —N.J. G.Pounds⟩ CONCEPT may indicate a fairly definite mental formulation determined by consideration of instances, although the word readily admits of suggesting foundations differing with individuals ⟨thus the popular *concept* of what news was came more and more to be formed upon what news was printed —F.L.Mott⟩ ⟨if his *concept* of the national security he has sworn to defend impels him to dispatch troops into foreign regions and in situations that may involve the United States in war, the sole responsibility is his —Arthur Krock⟩ ⟨the emerging of a fresh *concept* of architecture needed to produce new forms and revitalize tradition —*Amer. Guide Series: Mich.*⟩ CONCEPTION, often interchangeable with CONCEPT, may stress the idea of the mental action of imagining and formulating rather than the notion of its result ⟨the *conception*, building, and profitable sale of the New York, Chicago & St. Louis Railway, commonly known as the Nickel Plate, was in great measure due to him —K.F.Geiser⟩ ⟨the Malays have a whole system of tabooed and substituted words, based as usual on the *conception* of all Nature as animate and sensitive —J.G. Frazer⟩ THOUGHT is a general term but is likely to imply the result of ratiocination, of thinking, reasoning, or meditating, rather than fancying or imagining ⟨the next 10 years Abbot devoted to the final elaboration of his *thought* in abstruse technical form in *The Syllogistic Philosophy* —F.A.Christie⟩ ⟨Adams' first *thought* was that Palmerston wished a quarrel; his second, that it might be connected with a desire for mediation —W.C.Ford⟩ ⟨there are insights which are spoiled by *thought* —Lewis Leary b.1906⟩ NOTION may suggest a vague half-formed idea not resolved by much thought and analysis ⟨the *notion* that primitive languages lack the power of abstraction —A.A.Hill⟩ ⟨the *notion* that history shows a continual progress and especially a progress in the liberation of the individual is amply refuted by many examples —M.R.Cohen⟩ ⟨the British have some queer and quaint *notions* about Americans — some almost as peculiar as our preconceived ideas about them —Richard Joseph⟩ IMPRESSION applies to a first notion frankly lacking in analysis, consideration, and thought ⟨when he steps out on the street his first *impression* is of broad radiating avenues —*Amer. Guide Series: Minn.*⟩ ⟨the additional real difficulty of eliminating all possibility of adding subjective *impressions* to objective findings —W.C.Allee⟩

-id·ea \'idēə\ *n pl suffix* [NL (neut. pl. in form), fr. Gk *-ideus*, n. suffix with quasi-patronymic value] **:** animals that are or have the form of — in names of higher taxa ⟨Car*idea*⟩ ⟨Phoron*idea*⟩

ideaed *also* **idea'd** *pronunc at* IDEA + d\ *adj* **:** having a specified kind of idea or a specified number of ideas ⟨a one-*ideaed* man⟩ ⟨eager bright-*ideaed* students⟩ **:** characterized by ideas ⟨alert ~ men are priceless treasures⟩

idea·is·tic \(,)ī¦dēə¦istik, ¦īdē¦i-\ *adj* **:** relating to, concerned with, or based on ideas esp. as abstract or symbolic matters of mind

¹**ide·al** \(')ī¦dē(ə)l, -diəl\ *adj* [F or LL; F *idéal*, fr. LL *idealis*, fr. L *idea* + *-alis* -al] **1 a :** existing as a mere mental image **:** existing in fancy or imagination only **:** IMAGINARY, HYPOTHETICAL ⟨confusing ~ and concrete things⟩; *broadly* **:** lacking practicality **:** VISIONARY ⟨a purely ~ concept of society⟩ **b :** relating to or constituting mental images, ideas, or conceptions **:** IDEATIONAL, CONCEPTUAL ⟨life and death appeared to me ~ bounds —Mary W. Shelley⟩ **c :** embodying or symbolizing an idea **2 :** of or relating to an ideal or to perfection of kind **:** existing as a perfect exemplar **:** embodying or symbolizing an ideal ⟨~ beauty⟩ ⟨an ~ moral character⟩ **3 :** existing as a patterning or archetypal idea; *usu* **:** of or relating to Platonic ideas **4 :** of or relating to philosophical idealism

²**ideal** \"\ *n* -S [F or G; F *idéal*, fr. G *ideal*, fr. *ideal-* (as in *idealform* ideal form), fr. LL *idealis*, adj.] **1 a :** a conception of something in its highest perfection ⟨a perfect circle is an ~ impossible to construct⟩ **b :** a standard of perfection, beauty, or excellence believed to be capable of realization or attainment ⟨the ~*s* of our civilization⟩ **2 :** one regarded as exemplifying an ideal and often taken as a model for imitation ⟨considered the older man his ~⟩ **3 :** an ultimate object or aim of endeavor **:** GOAL ⟨their ~ was a quiet unhurried life⟩ **4 :** a subset of a ring that contains as an element the sum or difference of any two elements and the product of any element with an element of the ring ⟨the integers ending in 0 are an ~ in the ring of all integers⟩ **syn** see MODEL

ideal engine *n* **:** a heat engine operating on a reversible cycle (as a Carnot cycle)

idea·less *pronunc at* IDEA + ləs\ *adj* **:** lacking an idea or ideas

ideal gas *n* **:** a gas in which there is no attraction between the molecules; *usu* **:** a gas conforming exactly to the ideal-gas law

ideal–gas law *n* **:** GAS LAW c

ide·al·ism \(')ī¦dē(ə),lizəm, -diə,l- *sometimes* 'ī,dēə,- *or* 'ī,diə-\ *n* -S [prob. fr. G or F; G *idealismus*, fr. F *idéalisme*, fr. *idéal* + *-isme* -ism] **1 :** a theory that affirms that mind or the spiritual and ideal is of central importance in reality: as **a :** a theory that regards reality as essentially spiritual or the embodiment of mind or reason esp. by asserting either that the ideal element in reality is dominant (as in Platonism) or that the intrinsic nature and essence of reality is consciousness or reason (as in Hegelianism) — called also *metaphysical idealism* **b :** a theory that identifies reality with perceptibility or denies the possibility of knowing anything except psychical reality and proceeds from the affirmation that the mental life alone is knowable to a dogmatic dualism (as in Cartesianism and Lockeanism) which in metaphysics results in realism, to a subjective idealism in metaphysics (as in Berkeleianism), or to solipsism or skepticism (as in Humism) — called also *epistemological idealism*; see ABSOLUTE IDEALISM, MONISTIC IDEALISM, OBJECTIVE IDEALISM, PERSONAL IDEALISM, PLURALISTIC IDEALISM, SUBJECTIVE IDEALISM, TRANSCENDENTAL IDEALISM **2 a :** the practice of forming ideals or living under their influence **:** tendency to idealize **b :** something that is idealized **:** an ideal representation or experience **3 :** literary or artistic theory or practice that values ideal or subjective types or aspects of beauty more than formal or sensible qualities or that affirms the preeminent value of imagination as compared with faithful copying of nature — opposed to *realism*

¹**ide·al·ist** \-ləst\ *n* -S [¹*ideal* + *-ist*] **1 a :** an adherent of a philosophical theory of idealism **b :** an artist or author who advocates or practices idealism in art or writing **2 :** one whose conduct is influenced or guided by ideals; *usu* **:** one that places ideals before practical considerations **:** VISIONARY, DREAMER

²**idealist** \"\ *adj* **:** IDEALISTIC

ide·al·is·tic \(,)ī¦dē(ə)¦listik, (,)ī¦diə¦l-, -tēk *sometimes* 'ī,dēə¦l- *or* 'ī,diə¦l-\ *adj* **1 :** of, relating to, or advocated by idealists or idealism ⟨~ theories⟩ **2 :** exhibiting, practicing, or characterized by idealism ⟨an ~ man⟩ ⟨an ~ view of life⟩ — **ide·al·is·ti·cal·ly** \-tək(ə)lē, -tēk-, -li\ *adv*

ide·al·i·ty \,īdē'alədē, -di'a-, -ətē, -i\ *n* -ES [¹*ideal* + *-ity*] **1 a :** the quality or state of being ideal **b :** existence only in idea **2 :** something imaginary or idealized **:** an unreal or unrealistic thing or concept **3 :** the poetic or creative faculty — used orig. in phrenology

ide·al·iza·tion \(,)ī,dē(ə)lə'zāshən, -diəl-, -,lī'z- *sometimes* ,ī,dēə,)l- *or* ,ī,diə(,)l-\ *n* -S **1 a :** an act or the process of idealizing **b :** a product of idealizing **2 :** the employment of idealistic methods

ide·al·ize \(')ī¦dē(ə),līz, -diə,l- *sometimes* 'ī,dēə,l- *or* 'ī,diə,l-\ *vb* -ED/-ING/-S *see -ize in Explan Notes* [prob. fr. G *idealisieren*, fr. *ideal* + *-isieren* -ize] *vt* **1 :** to make ideal **:** give an ideal form or value to **:** attribute ideal characteristics and excellences to ⟨tended to ~ her friends⟩ **2 :** to treat (an artistic subject) idealistically ~ *vi* **1 :** to form ideals **2 :** to work idealistically — **ide·al·iz·er** \-zə(r)\ *n* -S

ideal·less *pronunc at* IDEAL + ləs\ *adj* **:** lacking ideals **:** basing conduct and judgments on the everyday realities of life; *broadly* **:** MATERIALISTIC

ide·al·ly *pronunc at* IDEAL + (l)ē *or* (l)i\ *adv* **1 :** in idea or imagination **:** by means of ideas **:** MENTALLY **2 :** in relation to or in the manner of an exemplar, archetype, or pattern **3 a :** conformably to or in respect to an ideal **:** PERFECTLY **b :** for best results or greatest enjoyment, efficiency, or value ⟨~ each meal should be planned in relation both to activity and to other meals of the day⟩ **c :** in accordance with an ideal or typical standard **:** CLASSICALLY

ide·al·ness *n* -ES **:** the quality or state of being ideal ⟨~ of his prose⟩ ⟨the ~ of such aspirations⟩

idealogue *var of* IDEOLOGUE

idealogy *var of* IDEOLOGY

ideal point *n* **:** a point at infinity that in projective geometry is the assumed intersection of any two parallel lines

ideal realism *n* **:** any of various philosophical theories combining idealistic and realistic elements; *specif* **:** a theory combining idealistic epistemology with realistic metaphysics — called also *real idealism*

ideals *pl of* IDEAL

ideal solution *n* **:** a solution in which the interaction between molecules of the components does not differ from the interactions between the molecules of each component; *usu* **:** a solution that conforms exactly to Raoult's law — compare ACTIVITY 6b, ACTIVITY COEFFICIENT, FUGACITY 2b

ideal truth *n* **:** NORMATIVE TRUTH

ideal type *n* **:** an abstraction of features from empirical reality and their embodiment into a unified conceptual scheme of hypothetical validity ⟨sees the *ideal type* of monogamy in Christian marriage —Rodney Needham⟩ ⟨analysis of social situations by the use of *ideal types*⟩

ideal utilitarianism *n* **:** UTILITARIANISM 1b

idea man *n* **:** a person with an unusual capacity for visualizing and formulating new techniques, approaches, products

ideamonger *pronunc at* IDEA + ,-\ *n* **:** one that deals in ideas **:** IDEA MAN

i·de·an *usu cap, var of* IDAEAN

idea·pho·ria \(,)ī,dēə'fōrēə, ,ī,deə-\ *n* -S [NL, fr. L *idea* + NL *-phoria*] **:** capacity for creative thought or imagination

ideas *pl of* IDEA

ideas of reference : a delusion that accompanies certain abnormal mental states in which remarks overheard and people seen seem to be concerned with and usu. inimical to oneself

¹**ide·ate** \'īdē,āt, ī'd-\ *vb* -ED/-ING/-S [*idea* + *-ate*] *vt* **:** to form in idea **:** CONCEIVE, PRECONCEIVE, PREFIGURE; *usu* **:** to have ideas, thoughts, or impressions of **:** remember, imagine, or think of when not in the actual presence of ~ *vi* **1 :** to form an idea **2 :** to invent by working through ideas

²**ide·ate** \'īdē,āt, ī'dēət\ *n* -S [NL *ideatum*] **:** IDEATUM

ide·a·tion \,īdē'āshən\ *n* -S **:** the capacity of the mind to form or entertain ideas; *broadly* **:** the process of entertaining and relating ideas

ide·a·tion·al \¦==¦āshən°l, -āshnəl\ *adj* **:** of, relating to, or produced by ideation; *broadly* **:** consisting of or referring to ideas or thoughts of objects not immediately present to the senses — compare IDEALISTIC, PERCEPTUAL — **ide·a·tion·al·ly** \-n°l¦ē, -nəl¦ē, ¦i\ *adv*

ide·a·tive \ī'dēəd.iv, 'īdē,ād-\ *adj* [¹*ideate* + *-ive*] **:** IDEATIONAL

ide·atum \,īdē'ādəm\ *n, pl* **ide·ata** \-d·ə\ [NL, fr. L *idea* + *-atum*, neut. of *-atus* -ate — more at IDEA] *philos* **:** the actual existence supposed to correspond with an idea

idée fixe \(,)ē,dā'fēks\ *n, pl* **idées fixes** \-ks(əz)\ [F] **:** FIXED IDEA

idée–force \-'fō(ə)rs\ *n, pl* **idées–forces** \-rs(əz)\ [F, fr. *idée* idea + *force*] **:** an idea considered as a real factor in the behavior of an individual or social group and thus in the course of events

idein *var of* IDAEIN

ide·ist \(')ī¦dēəst, 'ī,dēə-\ *n* -S [*idea* + *-ist*] **:** an adherent of an idealistic philosophy; *specif* **:** an advocate of epistemological idealism

idem *with reference to a person* 'ī,dem *or* 'ē,dem, *with reference to a thing* 'ī,dem *or* 'i,dem, *the masculine Latin form having a long* i *& the neuter form a short* i\ *pron* [L, same — more at IDENTITY] **:** something previously mentioned **:** SAME — used chiefly in bibliographies to avoid repetition of author's name and title when a reference to an item immediately follows another to the same item ⟨~ page 30⟩; abbr. *id.*

idem so·nans \¦ī,dem'sō,nanz, ¦i,dem'sō,nän(t)s\ [L] **:** having the same sound — used of a rule in law that the occurrence in a document of a spelling of a material word that is wrong but has the sound of the word intended (as *Lawrance* for *Lawrence* or *Kean* for *Keen*) does not vitiate the instrument

-i·dene \ə,dēn\ *n suffix* -S [ISV ¹*-ide* + *-ene*] **:** radical having two valence bonds at the point of attachment ⟨ethyl*idene* $CH_3CH<$⟩ ⟨eth*idene*⟩ — compare -YLIDENE

¹**ident** \ī'dent\ *n* -S [by shortening] **:** IDENTIFICATION

²**ident** \"\ *vb* -ED/-ING/-S [by shortening] **:** IDENTIFY

iden·ta·code \ī'dentə,kōd, ə'd-\ *n* [*identification* + connective *-a-* + *code*] **:** a means of identification of a pedigreed animal consisting of a tattoo mark that is recorded on both pedigree and certificate of ownership

iden·tic \(')ī¦dentik, ə'd-\ *adj* [prob. fr. ML *identicus*] **:** IDENTICAL ⟨recognition of ~ themes in the apparently incongruous —R.P.Blackmur⟩: as **a :** constituting an action or expression in which two or more governments follow precisely the same course or employ an identical form — compare JOINT 2a(3) **b :** constituting an action or expression in which a government follows precisely the same course or employs identical forms with reference to two or more other governments **syn** see SAME

iden·ti·cal \-təkəl, -tēk-\ *adj* [prob. fr. ML *identicus* (fr. LL *identitas* identity + L *-icus* -ic) + E *-al*] **1 :** expressing or effecting identity — used chiefly of propositions in logic and of equations and operations in mathematics **2 :** being the same **:** having complete identity ⟨the ~ place where we stopped before⟩ — often used with *same* or *very* for emphasis ⟨the same ~ menu⟩ ⟨the very ~ house⟩ **3 a :** showing exact likeness **:** characterized by such entire agreement in qualities and attributes that identity may be assumed — often used with *with* and sometimes with *to* ⟨a replica that is ~ with the original⟩ **b :** very similar **:** having such close resemblance and such minor difference as to be essentially the same **:** appearing or seeming exactly alike ⟨saw the ~ dress on sale for three dollars⟩ ⟨the two plants were ~⟩ — often used with *with* or *to* ⟨his examination paper was ~ to his brother's⟩ ⟨political issues are seldom ~ with religious⟩ **4 :** having the same cause or origin ⟨~ infections⟩ **syn** see LIKE, SAME

identical equation *n* **:** an equation that is satisfied for all values of the literal symbols

iden·ti·cal·i·ty \(ˌ)īˌdentə'kaləd·ē, əˌden-, -lətē, -i\ *n* -ES **:** IDENTICALNESS

iden·ti·cal·ly \-'dentək(ə)lē, -tēk-, -li\ *adv* **:** in an identical manner **:** with complete identity ⟨shoes ~ alike⟩; *specif* **:** for all values of the mathematical symbols involved

iden·ti·cal·ness \-kəlnəs\ *n* -ES **:** the quality or state of being identical

identical points *n pl* **:** points on the retinas of the two eyes that occupy corresponding positions in respect to the retinal centers

identical proposition *n* **:** a proposition in logic whose subject and predicate are identical in meaning and whose affirmation is therefore superfluous ⟨"nothing inconceivable can be conceived" is an *identical proposition*⟩

identical rhyme *n* **:** RIME RICHE

identical twin *n* **:** either member of a pair of twins produced from a single zygote

iden·ti·fi·a·bil·i·ty \(ˌ)īˌdentəˌfīə'biləd·ē, əˌd-, -lətē, -i\ *n* **:** the quality or state of being identifiable

iden·ti·fi·a·ble \⸗'⸗⸗ˌ⸗əbəl, (ˌ)⸗ˌ⸗⸗'⸗əbəl\ *adj* **:** subject to identification **:** capable of being identified — **iden·ti·fi·a·bly** \-blē,-bli\ *adv*

iden·ti·fi·ca·tion \(ˌ)⸗ˌ⸗⸗fə'kāshən\ *n* -S *often attrib* [prob. fr. F, fr. *identité* identity + *-fication* — more at IDENTITY] **1 a :** an act or the action of identifying or the state of being identified **b :** a means of identifying **:** evidence of identity ⟨experienced travelers always carry some ~⟩ ⟨a driver's license is sufficient ~⟩ **2 a :** a mental mechanism wherein the individual gains gratification, emotional support, or relief from anxiety by attributing to himself consciously or unconsciously the characteristics of another person or group **b :** orientation of the self in regard to something (as a familial or ethnic group, class, nation, ideology) with a resulting feeling of close emotional association ⟨the immigrant's ~ with his new country⟩ **3 :** CONDENSATION 5

identification bracelet *n* **:** a bracelet with a narrow plaque for the owner's name

identification tag *n* **:** either of two metal tags worn suspended around the neck by a member of the armed forces and stamped with his name, serial number, and other information

identification bracelet

iden·ti·fi·ca·to·ry \ī'dentəfəkəˌtōrē, ə'd-, ˌīˌden·'tif-, *chiefly Brit* ⸗¦dentifi¦kāt(ə)ri *or* -ā·tri\ *adj* [*identification* + *-ory*] **:** concerned with or serving for identification ⟨~ thinking⟩ ⟨~ traits⟩

iden·ti·fi·er \ī'dentəˌfī(ə)r, ə'd-, -fīə\ *n* -S **:** one that identifies

iden·ti·fy \-fī\ *vb* -ED/-ING/-ES [prob. fr. F *identifier*, fr. *identité* identity + *-fier* -fy — more at IDENTITY] *vt* **1 a :** to cause to be or become identical **:** regard as identical ⟨*identified* their own interests with those of the rulers⟩ **b :** to link in an inseparable fashion **:** make correlative with something ⟨may not rationally ~ itself with any one church⟩ **c :** to conceive as united in spirit, principle, outlook, or interest ⟨*identified* himself with the middle classes⟩; *broadly* **:** to associate or join (as oneself) with some interest (as a business or political party) **2 a :** to establish the identity of ⟨soon *identified* the child⟩ **:** show or prove the sameness of (as with something known, stated, or possessed) ⟨tried to ~ the stolen property as his own⟩ ⟨could not immediately ~ the quotation⟩ **b :** to determine the taxonomic position of (a biological specimen) ⟨*identified* it as a member of the genus *Salix* but could not determine the species⟩ **~** *vi* **:** to be or become the same **:** associate in such a way as to have unity (as of interests, purpose, effect) ⟨our tastes do not always ~⟩ ⟨people long in association tend to ~ with one another⟩ **:** practice identification ⟨to ~ is to share the interests and acts of another person until identification results —C.R.Adams⟩

identifying pronoun *n* **:** a pronoun referring to something as identical with what has been mentioned ⟨*same* is an *identifying pronoun*⟩

iden·tism \-n·ˌtizəm\ *n* -S [*identity* + *-ism*] **:** IDENTITY PHILOSOPHY

iden·ti·ty \ī'den(t)əd·ē, ə'den-, -ətē, -i\ *n* -ES [MF *identité*, fr. LL *identitat-*, *identitas*, irreg. fr. L *idem* same (fr. *is* he) + *-itat-*, *-itas* -ity — more at ITERATE] **1 a :** sameness of essential or generic character in different examples or instances **:** the limit approached by increasing similarity ⟨the ~ of the red in the rug with the red of a brick⟩ **b :** sameness in all that constitutes the objective reality of a thing **:** SELFSAMENESS, ONENESS **:** sameness of that which is distinguishable only in some accidental fashion (as being designated by different names, or the object of different perceptions, or different in time and place) ⟨the ~ of Scott with the author of Waverley⟩ ⟨the sense of ~ arising in shared experience⟩ **c :** an instance of such sameness **2 :** unity and persistence of personality **:** unity or individual comprehensiveness of a life or character ⟨lost consciousness of his own ~⟩ **3 :** the condition of being the same with something described, claimed, or asserted or of possessing a character claimed ⟨establish the ~ of stolen goods⟩ **4** *archaic* **:** individual or real existence **5** *Schellingian philos* **:** reality at its deepest level at which subject and object are one **6 a :** IDENTICAL PROPOSITION **b :** IDENTICAL EQUATION **7** *Austral* **:** CHARACTER 8a **8** *or* **identity element :** an operator that leaves unchanged an element on which it operates ⟨since if zero is added to any integer, the sum is the same integer, zero is an additive ~⟩

identity card *n* **:** a usu. official card bearing identifying data about the individual to whom it pertains

identity philosophy *n* **:** a monistic philosophical theory (as the philosophy of Schelling) that rejects any ultimate bifurcation into spirit and nature or subject and object and finds fundamental unity in the Absolute

identity principle *n* **:** LAW OF IDENTITY

ideo- *comb form* [F *idéo-*, fr. Gk *idea* — more at IDEA] **:** idea ⟨*ideo*crat⟩ ⟨*ideo*genetic⟩ ⟨*ideo*logy⟩

ide·oc·ra·cy \ˌīdē'äkrəsē, ˌid-\ *n* -ES [*ideo-* + *-cracy*] **:** government or social management based on abstract ideas

ideo·ge·net·ic \¦īdē(ˌ)ōjə¦ned·ik, ¦id-\ *adj* [*ideo-* + *-genetic*] **:** originating ideas

ideo·gram \'īdēəˌgram, 'id-, -raa(ə)m *sometimes* ī'dēə- *or* ī'diə-\ *n* [*ideo-* + *-gram*] **1 a :** a picture, a conventionalized picture, or a symbol that symbolizes a thing or an idea but not a particular word or phrase for it **b :** a picture, a conventionalized picture, or a symbol that symbolizes a thing or an idea but not a particular word or phrase for it and that if pictorial symbolizes not the object pictured but some thing or idea that the object pictured is supposed to suggest or emblematize — distinguished from *pictogram* **2 :** a symbol or group of symbols that as used in the writing of a particular language represents usu. a particular morpheme, word, or phrase but without providing separate phonetic representation of the individual phonemes or syllables composing the morpheme, word, or phrase **:** LOGOGRAM a; *specif* **:** a symbol or group of symbols used for convenience in writing an alphabetic language and directly representing a word or phrase or in some instances an idea expressible by any of two or more different words or phrases (as in English *3* read as *three*, + read as *plus*, & read as *and*, $ read as *dollar* or *dollars*, *1960* read as *one thousand nine hundred and sixty* or *nineteen hundred and sixty* or *nineteen sixty*) **3 :** a composite character in Chinese writing made by combining two or more other characters for words of related meaning

ideo·gram·ic *or* **ideo·gram·mic** \¦⸗⸗⸗¦gramik, ⸗¦⸗⸗-\ *adj* **:** of, relating to, or characterized by the use of ideograms

ideo·gram·mat·ic \-ˌgrə'mad·|ik, -at|, |ēk\ *adj* [*ideogram* + *-atic* (as in *epigrammatic*)] **1 :** being an ideogram **2 :** IDEOGRAMIC

ideo·graph \'⸗⸗⸗ˌgraf, ⸗'⸗⸗-, -raa(ə)f,-raif,-råf\ *n* [*ideo-* + *-graph*] **:** IDEOGRAM

ideo·graph·ic \¦⸗⸗⸗¦grafik, ⸗¦⸗⸗-, -fēk\ *adj* [*ideo-* + *-graphic*] **1 :** consisting of or characterized by the use of ideograms ⟨an ~ script⟩ ⟨the ~ stage in the development of writing⟩ **2 :** being an ideogram ⟨an ~ sign⟩ **3 :** of or relating to an ideogram ⟨these characters had sometimes an ~, and sometimes a phonetic value —David Diringer⟩ — **ideo·graph·i·cal·ly** \-fək(ə)lē, -fēk-, -li\ *adv*

ide·og·ra·phy \ˌīdē'ägrəfē, id-, -fi\ *n* -ES [*ideo-* + *-graphy*] **1 :** the use of ideograms **2 :** the representation of ideas by graphic symbols

ideo·log·i·cal \¦īdēə¦läjəkəl, ¦id, -jēk- *sometimes* ¦ēd-\ *or* **ideo·log·ic** \-jik,-jēk\ *also* **idea·log·i·cal** \-dēə¦l-\ *adj* **1 :** of, relating to, or based on ideology ⟨~ conflict⟩ **2 :** relating to or concerned with ideas ⟨an ~ application of a theory⟩ **3 :** symbolically suggestive of an idea or mood ⟨~ drama⟩ — **ideo·log·i·cal·ly** \-jək(ə)lē, -jēk-, -li\ *adv*

ide·ol·o·gist \ˌīdē'äləjəst, ˌid- *sometimes* ˌēd-\ *n* -S [F *idéologiste*, fr. *idéologie* + *-iste* -ist] **1 a :** a specialist in the science of ideas **:** a student of the origin and nature of ideas **b :** an advocate or adherent of a particular system or doctrine of ideology **2 :** IDEOLOGUE 1

ide·ol·o·gize \-ˌjīz\ *vt* -ED/-ING/-S [*ideology* + *-ize*] **1 :** to interpret or formulate ideologically ⟨the dogged tendency of our time to ~ all things into grayness —Lionel Trilling⟩ **2 :** to cause (as an individual or a social institution) to accept or conform to a particular ideology ⟨planners who attempt to alter and ~ the fundamental character of our culture⟩

ideo·logue *also* **idea·logue** \'īdēəˌlȯg, 'id-, ī'dē- *also* -läg\ *n* -S [F *idéologue*, back-formation fr. *idéologie*] **1 :** THEORIST, DREAMER, VISIONARY **2 :** IDEOLOGIST 1b

ide·ol·o·gy \ˌīdē'äləjē, ˌid-, -ji *sometimes* ˌēd-\ *also* **ide·al·o·gy** \", -ē'al-\ *n* -ES [F *idéologie*, fr. *idéo-* ideo- + *-logie* -logy] **1 a :** a branch of knowledge concerned with the origin and nature of ideas **b :** a theory in philosophy advocated by Destutt de Tracy (1754–1836): ideas originate from sensation **2 :** visionary speculation **:** idle theorizing; *often* **:** an impractical theory or system of theories **3 a :** a systematic scheme or coordinated body of ideas or concepts esp. about human life or culture **b :** a manner or the content of thinking characteristic of an individual, group, or culture ⟨bourgeois ~⟩ ⟨medical, legal, and other professional *ideologies*⟩ ⟨kept his ~ inviolate⟩ **c** (1) **:** the integrated assertions, theories, and aims that constitute a sociopolitical program ⟨a national ~ that was not static but altered with altering circumstances⟩ (2) **:** an extremist sociopolitical program or philosophy constructed wholly or in part on factitious or hypothetical ideational bases

ideo·motor \¦īdēə, ¦id- +-\ *adj* [ISV *ideo-* + *motor*] **1** *of movement or action* **:** resulting from the impingement of ideas on the system **:** not reflex **2 :** of, relating to, or concerned with ideomotor activity ⟨~ theory⟩ ⟨~ suggestions⟩

ideo·pho·bia \ˌ⸗⸗⸗'fōbēə\ *n* [NL, fr. *ideo-* + *-phobia*] **:** fear or distrust of ideas or of reason

ideo·plas·tic \¦⸗⸗ō¦plastik\ *adj* [ISV *ideo-* + *-plastic;* orig. formed as F *idéoplastique*] **1 :** modified by mental activity ⟨~ factors in digestion⟩ **2** *of an art form* **:** rendered symbolic or conventional through the mental remodeling of natural subjects — **ideo·plas·tic·i·ty** \-ˌpla¦stisəd·ē\ *n*

ideo·type \'⸗⸗⸗+ˌ-\ *n* [*ideo-* + *type*] **:** a specimen collected from other than the type locality but identified as belonging to a particular taxon by the author of that taxon

ides \'īdz\ *n pl but sing or pl in constr* [MF, fr. L *idus*, prob. of non-IE origin] **:** the 15th day of March, May, July, or October or the 13th day of any other month in the ancient Roman calendar; *broadly* **:** this day and the seven days preceding it counting backward toward the nones — compare CALENDS

-ides *pl of* -IDE

ide·sia \ī'dēzh(ē)ə\ *n* [NL, fr. Evert I. *Ides*, 17th cent. German-born Dutch statesman and traveler in the service of Russia + NL *-ia*] **1** *cap* **:** a monotypic genus (family Flacourtiaceae) comprising a single Asiatic tree (*I. polycarpa*) that has a broad spreading head, large alternate long-petioled cordate leaves, and large terminal panicles of apetalous flowers followed by fleshy orange red berries and that is widely grown as an ornamental where the climate is relatively mild **2** -S **:** any plant of the genus *Idesia*

id·gah \'id(ˌ)gä\ *n* -S [Per *'īdgāh*, fr. *'īd* feast (fr. Ar) + Per *-gāh* place, fr. MPer *gās*, fr. OPer *gāthu-;* akin to Av *gātav-* place, Skt *gātu* going, way, course] **:** a place set apart for public prayers on the two chief Muslim feasts

-idia *pl of* -IDIUM

idi·acan·thus \ˌidēə'kan(t)thəs\ *n*, *cap* [NL, fr. Gk *idios* + NL *-acanthus*] **:** a genus (the type of the family Idiacanthidae) of black deep-sea stomiatoid fishes that include a number of typical dragonfish

id·i·asm \'idēˌazəm\ *n* -S [Gk *idiasmos* peculiarity, fr. *idiazein* to be peculiar, fr. *idios* one's own, private, peculiar — more at IDIOT] **:** an individual mannerism (as in literary style)

id·ic \'idik\ *adj* [[1]*id* + *-ic*] **:** relating to or consisting of ids ⟨~ constituents of germ plasm⟩

idig·bo \ə'digˌbō, 'ēdigˌbō\ *n* -S [native name in Africa] **1 :** an African tree (*Terminalia worensis*) valued for its light yellow wood **2 :** the wood of the idigbo

-i·din \ədən, əd°n\ *or* **-i·dine** \əˌdēn, ədən, əd°n\ *n suffix* -S [ISV [1]*-ide* + *-in, -ine*] **:** chemical compound related in origin or structure to another compound: as **a** *usu -idin* **:** aglycon of a glycoside ⟨pelargon*idin* from pelargonin⟩ **b** *usu -idine* **:** completely hydrogenated form of a cyclic base ⟨pyrrol*idine* from pyrrole⟩ ⟨thiazol*idine* from thiazole⟩ **c** *usu -idine* **:** base obtained otherwise than by hydrogenation ⟨tolu*idine* or tol*idine* from toluene⟩ ⟨guan*idine* from guanine⟩

idio- *comb form* [Gk, fr. *idios* — more at IDIOT] **1 :** one's own **:** personal **:** separate **:** distinct ⟨*idio*type⟩ ⟨*idio*syncrasy⟩ **2 :** self-produced **:** arising within ⟨*idio*lysin⟩ ⟨*idio*reflex⟩ ⟨*idio*pathic⟩ ⟨*idio*ventricular rhythm⟩

id·io·adaptation \¦idē(ˌ)ō\ *n* [*idio-* + *adaptation*] **:** evolutionary modification involving progressive specialization that results in more perfect adaptation of an organism to a particular environment with corresponding loss of adaptability to new or changing environment

id·io·an·drospo·rous \¦idē(ˌ)ō¦andrə¦spōrəs, -¦an¦dräspər-\ *adj* [*idio-* + *androspore* + *-ous*] *of an alga* **:** bearing androspores and oogonia on separate filaments — compare GYNANDROSPOROUS

id·io·biology \¦idē(ˌ)ō+\ *n* [ISV *idio-* + *biology;* orig. formed as G *idiobiologie*] **:** a branch of biology concerned with the study of organisms as individuals

id·io·blap·sis \ˌidēō'blapsəs\ *n* -ES [NL, fr. *idio-* + Gk *blapsis* damage, fr. *blaptein* to damage] **:** a hypothetical familial allergy presumably manifested in alteration of pulse rate following the ingestion of an allergenic food

id·io·blap·tic \¦⸗⸗⸗¦⸗tik\ *adj* [*idio-* + Gk *blaptikos* hurtful, fr. *blaptein* + *-ikos* -ic] **:** of or relating to idioblapsis

id·io·blast \'idēəˌblast\ *n* [ISV *idio-* + *-blast;* orig. formed in G] **1 a :** an isolated plant cell (as a sclereid) that differs markedly in form, contents, or wall structure from neighboring cells **b :** a hypothetical structural unit of a living cell — compare BIOPHORE **2 :** a crystal in a metamorphic rock that is bounded by its own faces, looks like a phenocryst, but is of later growth — **id·io·blas·tic** \¦idēə¦blastik\ *adj*

id·io·chromatic \¦idē(ˌ)ō+\ *adj* [ISV *idio-* + *chromatic*] **:** colored inherently and characteristically **:** having a distinctive and constant coloration ⟨copper sulfate is an ~ substance⟩ — used esp. of minerals; compare ALLOCHROMATIC 1

id·io·chromatin \"+\ *n* [ISV *idio-* + *chromatin*] **:** the part of the chromatin of a cell that is thought to transmit genes and function in reproduction — compare TROPHOCHROMATIN

id·io·chromosome \"+\ *n* [ISV *idio-* + *chromosome*] **:** SEX CHROMOSOME

id·i·oc·ra·sy \ˌidē'äkrəsē\ *n* -ES [LGk *idiokrasia*, prob. MS var. of Gk *idiosynkrasia* idiosyncrasy — more at IDIOSYNCRASY] **:** peculiarity of constitution **:** IDIOSYNCRASY

id·i·o·crat·ic \¦idēə¦krad·ik\ *or* **id·i·o·crat·i·cal** \d·əkəl *also* |ək\ *adj* [fr. *idiocrasy*, after such pairs as E *apostasy: apostatic, apostatical*] **:** IDIOSYNCRATIC — **id·i·o·crat·i·cal·ly** \-d·ək(ə)lē\ *adv*

id·i·o·cy \'idēəsē, -si\ *n* -ES [fr. *idiot*, after such pairs as E *accurate: accuracy*] **1 :** extreme mental deficiency commonly due to incomplete or abnormal development of the brain and usu. congenital or due to arrest of development following disease or injury in early childhood **2 a :** something notably stupid or foolish ⟨the usual bureaucratic *idiocies* —W.M. Hitzig⟩ **b :** something so light, frothy, and trivial that it is usu. considered silly ⟨amused by his amiable *idiocies*⟩

id·io·cy·cloph·a·nous \¦idē(ˌ)ō¦sī¦kläfənəs\ *adj* [ISV *idio-* + *cycl-* + *phan-* (fr. Gk *phainein* to show) + *-ous* — more at FANCY] **:** IDIOPHANOUS

id·io·genesis \¦idēə+\ *n* [NL, fr. *idio-* + *genesis*] **:** spontaneous origin (as of disease)

id·io·genetic \"+\ *adj* [*idio-* + *-genetic*] **:** originating spontaneously ⟨an apparently ~ disorder⟩

id·io·glos·sia \ˌidēə'gläsēə, -lȯs-\ *n* -S [NL, fr. *idio-* + *-glossia*] **:** a condition in which the affected person pronounces his words so badly as to seem to speak a language of his own

id·io·gram \'idēəˌgram\ *n* [ISV *idio-* + *-gram*] **:** a diagrammatic representation of a chromosome complement or karyotype

id·io·graph \-ˌgraf, -råf\ *n* [LGk *idiographon* autograph, fr. neut. of Gk *idiographos* specially written, in the author's handwriting, fr. *idio-* + *-graphos* (fr. *graphein* to write) — more at CARVE] **:** a mark or signature peculiar to an individual

id·io·graph·ic \¦⸗⸗⸗¦grafik\ *adj* [ISV *idio-* + *-graphic;* orig. formed as G *idiographisch*] **:** relating to, involving, or dealing with the concrete, individual, or unique ⟨considering history an ~ discipline⟩ — contrasted with *nomothetic*

id·io·kinetic \¦idē(ˌ)ō+\ *adj* [*idio-* + *kinetic*] *of movement* **:** induced by activity of the pyramidal tracts of the brain

id·io·lalia \ˌidēō'lālēə, -lal-\ *n* -S [NL, fr. *idio-* + *-lalia*] **:** IDIOGLOSSIA

id·i·o·lect \'idēəˌlekt\ *n* -S [*idio-* + *-lect* (as in *dialect*)] **:** the language or speech pattern of one individual at a particular period of his life

id·i·om \'idēəm\ *n* -S [MF & LL; MF *idiome*, fr. LL *idioma*, fr. Gk *idiōma* peculiarity, peculiarity of style, idiom, fr. *idiousthai* to appropriate, fr. *idios* one's own, private, peculiar — more at IDIOT] **1 a :** the language proper or peculiar to a people or to a district, community, or class **:** TONGUE, DIALECT **b :** the syntactical, grammatical, or structural form peculiar to a language **:** the genius, habit, or cast of a language **2 :** an expression established in the usage of a language that is peculiar to itself either in grammatical construction (as *no, it wasn't me*) or in having a meaning that cannot be derived as a whole from the conjoined meanings of its elements (as *Monday week* for "the Monday a week after next Monday"; *many a* for "many taken distributively"; *had better* for "might better"; *how are you?* for "what is the state of your health or feelings?") **3 :** a style or form of artistic expression (as in painting, writing, composing) that is characteristic esp. of an individual, a period or movement, or a medium or instrument ⟨an interesting orchestral ~⟩ ⟨surrealist ~⟩ ⟨imagination has its specific hereditary ~*s* —George Santayana⟩ **syn** see LANGUAGE

id·i·om·at·ic \¦idēə¦mad·|ik, -at|, |ēk\ *also* **id·i·om·at·i·cal** \|əkəl, |ēk-\ *adj* [LGk *idiōmatikos* peculiar, characteristic, fr. Gk *idiōmat-*, *idiōma* + *-ikos* -ic, -ical] **1 :** of, relating to, or conforming to idiom ⟨~ fluency in speech and writing⟩ ⟨a highly ~ concerto⟩ ⟨~ English⟩ **2 :** peculiar to a particular group or individual **:** INDIVIDUAL ⟨one person acting in his ~ purposeful fashion to evoke a response from another —John Dewey⟩ ⟨grows to value the physical sex life per se rather than as a symbol of ~ relationships —F.S.Chapin⟩ ⟨how vigorous and ~ was the native life —John Buchan⟩ — **id·i·o·mat·i·cal·ly** \|ək(ə)lē, |ēk-, -li\ *adv* — **id·i·o·mat·ic·ness** \|iknəs, |ēk-\ *n* -ES

id·i·om·e·ter \ˌidē'äməd·ə(r)\ *n* [*idio-* + *-meter*] **:** an instrument for ascertaining the personal equation of an astronomical observer

idiom neutral *n*, *usu cap I&N* **:** an artificial language partially derived from Volapük and having a vocabulary consistently selected on the basis of the maximum internationality of the roots

id·i·om·og·ra·phy \ˌidēə'mägrəfē\ *n* -ES [F *idiomographie*, fr. *idiome* idiom + *-o-* + *-graphie* -graphy — more at IDIOM] **:** the description of idiom

id·i·om·ol·o·gy \-'mäləjē\ *n* -ES [*idiom* + *-o-* + *-logy*] **:** the study of idiom

id·io·morph \'idēəˌmȯrf\ *n* -S [*idio-* + *-morph*] **:** a pattern of repeated letters in cryptography ⟨the ~ PXLXAP fits the probable word STATES⟩ — compare ISOMORPH C

id·io·mor·phic \¦⸗⸗⸗¦mȯrfik\ *adj* [Gk *idiomorphos* + E *-ic*] **1 :** having the proper form or shape **:** AUTOMORPHIC — used of minerals the growth of whose crystals in a rock has not been interfered with; contrasted with *allotriomorphic* **2 :** of, relating to, or being an idiomorph — **id·io·mor·phi·cal·ly** \-fək(ə)lē\ *adv*

id·io·mor·phism \ˌ⸗⸗⸗'⸗ˌfizəm\ *n* -S [*idiomorphic* + *-ism*] **:** the condition of being idiomorphic (sense 1)

id·io·mor·phous \¦⸗⸗⸗¦⸗fəs\ *adj* [Gk *idiomorphos* having a form of its own, fr. *idio-* + *-morphos* -morphous] **:** IDIOMORPHIC 1

id·io·muscular \¦idē(ˌ)ō+\ *adj* [ISV *idio-* + *muscular*] **:** relating to muscular tissue exclusively; *esp* **:** originating in muscle ⟨~ contraction⟩

-idion — see -IDIUM

id·i·o·path·ic \¦idēə¦pathik\ *adj* **1 :** peculiar to the individual **:** INNATE ⟨~ sensitivity⟩ **2 :** arising spontaneously or from an obscure or unknown cause **:** PRIMARY ⟨~ epilepsy⟩ — **id·i·o·path·i·cal·ly** \-thək(ə)lē\ *adv*

id·i·op·a·thy \ˌidē'äpəthē\ *n* -ES [Gk *idiopatheia*, fr. *idio-* + *-patheia* -pathy] **:** an idiopathic anomaly or disease

id·i·oph·a·nous \¦idē¦äfənəs\ *adj* [*idio-* + *phan-* (fr. Gk *phainein* to show) + *-ous* — more at FANCY] *of a crystal* **:** exhibiting interference figures without the aid of a polariscope

id·io·phone \'idēəˌfōn\ *n* [G *idiophon*, fr. *idio-* + *-phon* -phone] **:** a musical instrument (as a bell, gong, rattle) the source of whose sound is the vibration of its elastic constituent material unmodified by any special tension (as in a drum) — **id·io·phon·ic** \¦⸗⸗⸗¦fänik\ *adj*

id·io·plasm \'idēəˌplazəm\ *n* [ISV *idio-* + *-plasm;* orig. formed as G *idioplasma*] **:** the part of protoplasm held to function specif. in transmission of hereditary properties and commonly equated with chromatin — opposed to *trophoplasm* — **id·io·plas·mat·ic** \¦⸗⸗⸗¦plaz¦mad·ik\ *or* **id·io·plas·mic** \-zmik\ *adj*

id·io·retinal \¦idē(ˌ)ō+\ *adj* [*idio-* + *retinal*] **:** peculiar to the retina; *specif* **:** originating subjectively in the retina ⟨~ light⟩

id·i·or·rhythmic \¦idēə+\ *adj* [LGk *idiorrhythmos* (fr. Gk *idio-* + *rhythmos* measured motion, measure, proportion) + E *-ic* — more at RHYTHM] *Eastern Church* **:** SELF-REGULATING — used of (1) monks that live separately, hold property, work individually in supporting themselves, and though members of a monastery supervised by an elected council are not under direct daily supervision or (2) of monasteries so organized

id·i·or·rhyth·mism \ˌ⸗⸗⸗'rit͟hˌmizəm\ *n* -S **:** a system of monastic self-regulation in the Eastern Church — compare IDIORRHYTHMIC

id·i·o·se·pi·idae \ˌidē(ˌ)ōsə'pīəˌdē\ *n pl*, *cap* [NL, fr. *Idiosepion* or *Idiosepius*, type genus (fr. *idio-* + Gk *sēpion* cuttlefish bone) + *-idae* — more at SEPIA] **:** a family of squids that includes a single tiny squid (*Idiosepius pygmaeus* or *Idiosepion pygmaeum*) of the Indian ocean which lacks an internal shell and is considerably less than an inch in length

id·io·some \'idēəˌsōm\ *n* -S [*idio-* + *-some*] **:** any of several specialized cellular organelles: as **a :** IDIOBLAST 1b **b :** ACROSOME **c :** an area of modified cytoplasm surrounding a centrosome **d :** SEX CHROMOSOME

id·i·o·syn·cra·sy *also* **id·i·o·syn·cra·cy** \ˌidēə'siŋkrəsē, -dēō'-, -sink-, -rəsi\ *n* [Gk *idiosynkrasia*, fr. *idio-* + *-synkrasia* (fr. *synkrasis* action of commingling or blending — fr. *synkerannynai* to commingle, blend, fr. *syn-* + *kerannynai* to mingle, mix — + *-ia* -y) — more at CRATER] **1 :** characteristic peculiarity of habit or structure **2 a :** a peculiarity of physical or mental constitution or temperament **:** a characteristic distinguishing an individual; *broadly* **:** ECCENTRICITY **b :** individual hypersensitiveness (as to a drug or food) ⟨anemia accompanying the use of a sulfa drug is usually considered to be due to ~⟩

¹id·i·o·syn·crat·ic \¦idēə¦sin¦krad·|ik, -dē(,)ō¦s-, -siŋ¦-, -at|, |ēk\ *adj* [fr. *idiosyncrasy*, after such pairs as E *apostasy: apostatic*] **1 a :** peculiar to the individual ⟨an ~ gesture⟩ **b :** of, relating to, or resulting from idiosyncrasy ⟨~ response to a drug⟩ ⟨~ disease⟩ **2 :** marked by idiosyncrasy : ECCENTRIC ⟨is so ~ in his literary judgments that it is impossible to think of him as a sound critic —*Saturday Rev.*⟩ — **id·i·o·syn·crat·i·cal·ly** \|ək(ə)lē, |ēk-, -li\ *adv*

²idiosyncratic \"\ *n* -s : one that is idiosyncratic

¹id·i·ot \'idēə|t, *chiefly dial* 'ijə| *or* 'ējə|; *usu* |d·+V\ *n* -s [ME, fr. MF *idiote*, fr. L *idiota*, fr. Gk *idiōtēs* person in a private station, person without professional knowledge, ignorant person, common man, fr. *idios* one's own, private, peculiar; akin to L *sed, se* without, *sui* of oneself — more at SUICIDE] **1** *obs* : an ignorant or unschooled person : a simple unlearned person : CLOWN 1 **2 :** a person afflicted with idiocy; *specif* : a feebleminded person that has a mental age not exceeding three years and accordingly requires complete custodial care **3 a :** a silly simple person : SIMPLETON, BLOCKHEAD ⟨he means well but he is such an ~⟩ **b :** a person who fails to exhibit normal or usual sense, discrimination, or judgment esp. at a particular time or in respect to a particular subject ⟨I don't know why I was such an ~⟩ ⟨a perfect ~ about budgeting⟩ **c :** a professional fool : JESTER **4** [Gk *idiōtēs*] *obs* : a person in private station or one not schooled in a trade or profession : LAYMAN **syn** see FOOL

²idiot \"\ *adj* [ME, fr. *idiot* (n.)] **1 :** IDIOTIC **2 :** fit for, typical of, or suitable to idiots : being such as an idiot might be expected to have, engage in, display ⟨~ terror⟩ ⟨those ~ hats⟩ ⟨such ~ war⟩

idiot board *n* : a device (as a projection of a script) used to prompt a television speaker and placed out of camera range

id·i·ot·cy \'idēətsē, -si\ *n* -ES ['*idiot* + *-cy*] **1 :** IDIOCY 1 **2 :** something worthy of an idiot : utter folly

id·i·ot·ic \¦idē¦äd·|ik, -ät|, |ēk\ *adj* [LL *idioticus* unskilled, rude, simple, fr. Gk *idiōtikos* private, unprofessional, ordinary, fr. *idiōtēs* + *-ikos* -ic] **1 :** relating to or like an idiot **2 :** characterized by idiocy : FOOLISH, SENSELESS

id·i·ot·i·cal \|əkəl, |ēk-\ *adj* [LL *idioticus* + E *-al*] **1** *obs* : lacking education : IGNORANT, UNSCHOOLED **2 :** IDIOTIC 2

id·i·ot·i·cal·ly \|ək(ə)lē, |ēk-, -li\ *adv* **1 :** like an idiot : in an idiot or idiotic way ⟨behaved ~⟩ **2 :** ABSURDLY, RIDICULOUSLY ⟨~ cheap⟩

id·i·ot·i·cal·ness \-kəlnəs\ *n* -ES : extreme stupidity or foolishness

id·i·ot·ism \'idēəd·,izəm, -ēə,ti-\ *n* -s [in sense 1, fr. MF *idiotisme*, fr. L *idiotismus* common or vulgar manner of speaking, fr. Gk *idiōtismos* way of a common man, manner of speech of a common man, fr. *idiōtēs* common man + *-ismos* -ism; in sense 2, fr. ¹*idiot* + *-ism* — more at IDIOT] **1 a** *obs* : IDIOM 1 **b :** IDIOM 2 **2** *archaic* : IDIOCY

id·i·ot·ize \-əd·,īz, -ə,tīz\ *vt* -ED/-ING/-S ['*idiot* + *-ize*] : to make a fool of : cause to become or behave like an idiot

id·i·ot·ry \-ətrē, -ri\ *n* -ES ['*idiot* + *-ry*] *chiefly Scots law* : IDIOCY

idiot savant *pronunc at* IDIOT + *pronunc at* SAVANT, *or* ē,dyōsə'väⁿ\ *n, pl* **idiots savants** \-n(t)s, -äⁿ(z)\ [F, lit., skilled idiot] : a person that is in general mentally defective but that displays unusual aptitude or brilliance in some special field

idiot's delight *n* : any of various solitaire card games

idiot sheet *also* **idiot card** *n* : a large card bearing usu. hand-lettered words or phrases for prompting a speaker or actor during a telecast — compare IDIOT BOARD

id·i·o·zome \'idēə,zōm\ *n* -s [ISV *idio-* + Gk *zōma* girdle — more at ZONE] : ACROSOME

id·i·tol \'idə,tōl, -tȯl\ *n* -s [ISV *idose* + *-itol*] : a sweet crystalline hexahydroxy alcohol $C_6H_{14}O_6C_6H_8(OH)_6$ obtained by a reduction of idose or sorbose

-id·i·um \'idēəm\ *also* **-id·i·on** \-ē,än, -ēən\ *n suffix, pl* **-idi·ums** \-ēəmz\ *or* **-id·ia** \-ēə\ *also* **idions** [NL, fr. Gk *-idion*, dim. suffix] : small one : lesser one ⟨anther*idium*⟩ ⟨chrom*idium*⟩

¹idle \'īdᵊl\ *adj* **idler** \-d(ᵊ)lə(r)\ **idlest** \-d(ᵊ)ləst\ [ME *idel* (also, empty, void), fr. OE *īdel*; akin to OFris *īdel* empty, worthless, vain, OS *īdal*, OHG *ītal*] **1 a :** lacking worth or basis : leading to nothing : GROUNDLESS, USELESS ⟨~ theorizing⟩ ⟨an ~ rumor⟩ ⟨it would be ~ to argue further⟩ **b :** having no particular reason for existing or occurring : light, casual, and superficial ⟨~ chatter⟩ ⟨took an ~ glance about⟩ ⟨asked out of ~ curiosity⟩ **2 a :** not occupied or employed: as (1) *of a person* : having no employment or business : UNEMPLOYED ⟨closed factories and ~ workmen⟩ (2) *of a period of time* : marked by want of activity esp. of a useful or constructive nature : WASTED ⟨passed his ~ days in sloth⟩ ⟨that ~ hour just before dusk⟩ (3) *of a thing* : not turned to normal or appropriate use ⟨~ tenements⟩ : not called into active service ⟨~ capital⟩ **b** (1) : given to rest or ease : seeking to avoid labor or employment : TRIFLING, LAZY, SLOTHFUL ⟨a careless ~ worker⟩ ⟨~ boys playing in the streets⟩ (2) : having no regular occupation or evident lawful means of support ⟨answer to the charge of being an ~ person⟩ (3) : IDLING ⟨an engine running at fast ~ speed⟩ **3** *now dial Eng* **a :** LIGHTHEADED, FOOLISH **b :** MISCHIEVOUS **syn** see INACTIVE, VAIN

²idle \"\ *vb* **idled; idled; idling** \-d(ᵊ)liŋ\ **idles** *vi* **1 :** to lose or spend time in idleness ⟨*idling* in the garden⟩; *esp* : to move idly ⟨*idled* along the stream bank⟩ **2 :** to run disconnected or unloaded so that power is not used for external or useful work — used esp. of a motor, engine, pulley wheel ~ *vt* **1 :** to spend (as time) in idleness — often used with *away* ⟨*idling* away a pleasant summer day⟩ **2 :** to make or leave idle ⟨cutbacks in orders that *idled* thousands of workers⟩ ⟨the common cold ~*s* more people than any other disease⟩ **3 :** to cause to idle ⟨~ a motor⟩

³idle \"\ *n* -s [²*idle*] : an act or instance or the state of idling ⟨an engine running at ~⟩

idleby *n* -s [¹*idle* + *-by* (as in the name *Crosby*)] *obs* : IDLER

idleheaded \¦=¦==\ *adj* **1 :** FOOLISH, STUPID, SILLY **2** *obs* : out of one's head : DELIRIOUS, CRAZY

idle·hood \'īdᵊl,hu̇d\ *n, archaic* : IDLENESS

idle·man \-,mən\ *n, pl* **idlemen** *archaic* : a man of substance who does not need to work for a living

idle·ness *n* -ES [ME *idelnesse* (also, vanity) fr. OE *īdelnes*, fr. *īdel* + *-nes* -ness] : the quality or state of being idle (as through lack of worth, occupation, employment, industry) ⟨the ~ of our search⟩ ⟨increasing ~ in the auto industry⟩ ⟨a person of unbelievable ~⟩; *also* : an instance of such idleness ⟨our yesterday's ~ forgotten⟩

idler \'īd(ᵊ)lə(r)\ *n* -s **1 :** one that idles or is unoccupied : one that spends his time in inaction : a lazy person **2 a :** IDLER GEAR **b :** IDLER PULLEY **c :** IDLER WHEEL **3 :** a member of a ship's crew that has constant day duties and keeps no night watch **4 :** an empty railroad car placed between two cars that support a load; *also* : an empty flatcar placed at either end of a loaded flatcar to take the overhang but not the weight of a projecting load **5 :** a member of a fish-dressing gang who washes gutted fish or a wharf laborer who carries fish and supplies to the cleaners and removes scrap

idler gear *n* **1 :** a gear placed between a driving and a driven gear to transfer motion without change of direction or gear ratio **2 :** a gear for support or guidance instead of power transmission

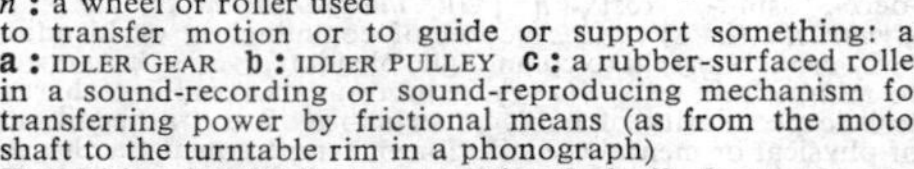
idler gear

idler pulley *n* : a guide or tightening pulley for a belt or chain (as in a conveyor system)

idler wheel *also* **idle wheel** *n* : a wheel or roller used to transfer motion or to guide or support something: as **a :** IDLER GEAR **b :** IDLER PULLEY **c :** a rubber-surfaced roller in a sound-recording or sound-reproducing mechanism for transferring power by frictional means (as from the motor shaft to the turntable rim in a phonograph)

idleset \'==,=\ *n* ['*idle* + *set* (setting)] *chiefly Scot* : IDLENESS

idlesse \'īdləs, īd'les\ *n* -s ['*idle* + ME *-esse* (as in *richesse* wealth) — more at RICHES] : IDLENESS

idling *n* -s : the act of one that idles

idly \'īd(ᵊ)lē, -li\ *adv* [ME *idilly*, fr. OE *īdellīce*, fr. *īdel* idle + *-līce* -ly — more at IDLE] : in an idle manner: as **a :** INEFFECTUALLY, VAINLY **b :** LAZILY, INDOLENTLY; *broadly* : without especial interest or effort : CASUALLY **c** *obs* : FOOLISHLY, INCOHERENTLY

ido \'ē(,)dō\ *n* -s *cap* [Esperanto, offspring, fr. Gk *-idēs*, patronymic suffix] : an international artificial language produced by modification of Esperanto

ido·crase \'īdō,krās, 'id-, -āz\ *n* -s [F, fr. Gk *eidos* form, shape + *krasis* mixture, fr. *kerannynai* to mix — more at IDYLL, CRATER] : a mineral $Ca_{10}(Mg,Fe)_2Al_4Si_9O_{34}(OH)_4$ that is a complex silicate of calcium, magnesium, iron, and aluminum — called also *vesuvianite*

idol \'īdᵊl\ *n* -s *often attrib* [ME *idel, idol*, fr. OF *idele, idle, idole*, fr. LL *idolum*, fr. Gk *eidōlon* phantom, image, image of a god; akin to Gk *eidos* shape, form — more at WISE] **1 a :** an image of a divinity : a representation or symbol of a deity or any other being or thing made or used as an object of worship; *broadly* : a false god : a heathen deity **b :** an image (as of a saint) used in Christian worship **2 a** *obs* : an appearance, aspect, or likeness of something **b** *obs* : EFFIGY, STATUE **c** *obs* : PRETENDER, IMPOSTOR **3 :** a form or appearance visible but without substance : an incorporeal image or phantom ⟨sense perception is explained, after the manner of Democritus, by ~*s* or images or thin filmlike forms, which emanate from the objects around us —Frank Thilly⟩ **4 :** something or someone on which the affections are strongly and often excessively set : an object of passionate devotion : a person or thing greatly loved or adored **5 :** a false notion or conception : FALLACY, IDOLUM 2

idol·a·ter \ī'dälad·ə(r), -ətə- *sometimes* ə'dä-\ *n* -s [alter. (influenced by MF *idolatre*) of ME *idolatrer, idolatrour*, fr. MF *idolatre* (fr. LL *idololatres*, fr. Gk *eidōlolatrēs*, fr. *eidōlon* idol + *-latrēs* -later) + ME *-er* or *-our* -or — more at IDOL] **1 :** a worshiper of idols : one that pays divine honors to an image, statue, or natural object as a representation of deity **2 :** a person that devotes intense or excessive and often blind affection, adoration, or admiration to an object not normally or usu. a subject of worship ⟨no undiscriminating ~ of Great Britain —B.J.Hendrick⟩

idol·a·tress \-lə·trəs\ *n* -ES : a female idolater

idol·a·tric \(')ī¦dälə·(,)trik, ¦īdə¦la·tr-\ *also* **ido·lat·ri·cal** \¦īdə¦la·trəkəl\ *adj* [ML *idolatricus*, fr. *idolatria* idolatry + L *-icus* -ic, -ical] : IDOLATROUS

idol·a·trize \ī'dälə,trīz *sometimes* ə'd-\ *vb* -ED/-ING/-S [*idolatry* + *-ize*] *vi* : to worship idols : pay idolatrous worship ~ *vt* : to make an idol of : IDOLIZE — **idol·a·triz·er** \-zə(r)\ *n* -s

idol·a·trous \(')ī¦dälə·trəs *sometimes* ə'd-\ *adj* **1 :** of or relating to idolatry: as **a :** being or resembling idolatry ⟨~ veneration for antiquity⟩ **b :** given to or practicing idolatry ⟨an ~ worshiper⟩ — **idol·a·trous·ly** *adv* — **idol·a·trous·ness** *n* -ES

idol·a·try \-=ˈ=lə·trē, -ri\ *n* -ES [ME *idolatrie*, fr. OF, fr. ML *idolatria*, alter. of LL *idololatria*, fr. Gk *eidōlolatreia*, fr. *eidōlon* + *latreia* -latry] **1 a :** the worship of a physical object as a god; *esp* : such worship of a made image **b :** the giving of absolute religious devotion and ultimate trust to something that is not God **2 :** immoderate attachment or devotion to or veneration for something : respect or love that approaches that due a divine power **3** *obs* : an object of idolatry

idol·ism \'īdᵊl,izəm\ *n* -s **1 a :** the worship of idols **b :** IDOLIZATION **2 :** IDOLUM 2

idol·ist \-,əst\ *n* -s *archaic* : IDOLATER 1

idol·i·za·tion \,īdᵊlə'zāshən, -ᵊlī'z-\ *n* -s : the act of idolizing or state of being idolized ⟨the ~ to which they were subjected⟩

idol·ize \'īdᵊl,īz\ *vb* -ED/-ING/-S *see -ize in Explan Notes vt* : to make an idol of : worship idolatrously; *broadly* : to love to excess : reverence to adoration ⟨~ gold⟩ ⟨boys at just the right age for *idolizing* military or sports heroes⟩ ~ *vi* : to practice idolatry — **idol·iz·er** \-zə(r)\ *n* -s

idolo- *also* **eidolo-** *comb form* [LL & Gk; LL *idolo-*, fr. Gk *eidōlo-*, fr. *eidōlon* — more at idol] : idol : image ⟨*idolo*cracy⟩ ⟨*idolo*mania⟩ ⟨*idolo*clastic⟩

idololatry *n* -ES [LL *idololatria* — more at IDOLATRY] *obs* : IDOLATRY

idol shepherd *n* : a counterfeit or worthless shepherd ⟨woe to the *idol shepherd* that leaveth the flock —Zech 11:17 (AV)⟩ — compare SHEPHERD 2

idols of the cave [trans. of NL *idola specus*] : idola due to individual peculiarities or prejudices — compare IDOLUM 2

idols of the forum *or* **idols of the market** [trans. of NL *idola fori*] : idola due to human factors (as language) — compare IDOLUM 2

idols of the theater [trans. of NL *idola theatri*] : idola due to traditional doctrines and methods — compare IDOLUM 2

idols of the tribe [trans. of NL *idola tribus*] : idola due to human nature itself or to the tribe or race of man (as anthropomorphic projections) — compare IDOLUM 2

ido·lum \ī'dōləm\ *n, pl* **ido·la** \-lə\ [in sense 1, fr. L & Gk; L, phantom, image, fr. Gk *eidōlon* phantom, image, idol; in sense 2, NL, fr. LL, idol, fr. Gk *eidōlon* — more at IDOL] **1 :** EIDOLON **2 :** a form of false thinking : FALLACY, IDOL 5; *specif* : one of the four varieties of fallacy distinguished by Francis Bacon in his *Novum Organum* (1620) — compare IDOLS OF THE CAVE, IDOLS OF THE FORUM, IDOLS OF THE THEATER, IDOLS OF THE TRIBE

ido·ne·i·ty \,īdə'nēəd·ē\ *n* -ES [ML *idoneitas*, fr. L *idoneus* + *-itas* -ity] *archaic* : the quality or state of being idoneous : SUITABILITY, FITNESS

ido·ne·ous \(')ī¦dōnēəs\ *adj* [L *idoneus*] *archaic* : FIT, APPROPRIATE, SUITABLE, PROPER

idos *pl of* IDO

idose \'ī,dōs, 'i,d- *also* -ōz\ *n* -s [ISV *id-* (fr. ISV *idonic* — *acid* — $C_6H_{12}O_7$, fr. L *idem* same + ISV *gulonic*) + *-ose* — more at IDENTITY] : a sugar $C_6H_{12}O_6$ epimeric with gulose and obtainable along with gulose by synthesis from xylose

ido·tea \ī'dōd·ēə\ [NL, irreg. fr. Gk *Eidothea*, a sea goddess] *syn of* IDOTHEA

idothea \ī'dōthēə, -däth-\ *n, cap* [NL, alter. of *Idotea*] : a large and widely distributed genus (the type of the family Idotheidae) of small marine cursorial isopods

i doubt it \=ˈ==\ *n, cap first I* : a card game in which each player tries to be first to empty his hand by laying down a number of cards and calling them the rank it is his turn to play (as two, ten, ace), discarding them if no one says "I doubt it" or if his claim is proved correct, but having to take up all discards on the table if it is shown that he included cards not called for

IDR *abbr* infantry drill regulations

id·ri·a·lite \'idrēə,līt\ *n* -s [F *idrialite*, fr. *Idria* (Idrija), Yugoslavia + F *-lite*] : a mineral prob. $C_{43}H_{32}O$ occurring as a crystalline hydrocarbon and melting at 205° C

-i·dro·sis \ə'drōsəs\ *n comb form, pl* **-idro·ses** \-ō,sēz\ [NL, fr. Gk *-idrōsis*, fr. *hidrōsis* act of sweating, fr. *hidroun* to sweat (fr. *hidrōs* sweat) + *-sis* — more at SWEAT] : a specified form of sweating ⟨chrom*idrosis*⟩ ⟨brom*idrosis*⟩ ⟨hyper*idrosis*⟩

ids *pl of* ID

-ids *pl of* -ID

¹id·u·mae·an *or* **id·u·me·an** \¦idyə¦mēən, ¦ijə¦-, ¦idə¦-\ *n* -s *usu cap* [*Idumaea* or *Idumea*, ancient region south of the Dead sea in Palestine (fr. L *Idumaea*, fr. Gk *Idoumaia*) + E *-an*] : EDOMITE

²idumaean \"\ *adj, usu cap* : of or relating to the Edomites : EDOMITIC

idun·it \(')ī¦dənət\ *n* -s [alter. of *I done it*] : an autobiographical or confessional account usu. of a sensational character

idyll *or* **idyl** \'īdᵊl, *chiefly Brit* 'id-\ *n* -s [L *idyllion, idyllium*, fr. Gk *eidyllion*, dim. of *eidos* shape, form, literary form; akin to Gk *idein* to see — more at WIT] **1 a :** a short descriptive poem usu. dealing with pastoral or rural life : ECLOGUE **b :** a simple descriptive work either in poetry or prose that deals with rustic life or pastoral scenes or suggests a mood of peace and contentment **c :** a narrative poem (as Tennyson's *Idylls of the King*) treating more or less fully an epic, romantic, or tragic theme **2 a :** a lighthearted carefree episode or one of such pastoral charm and simplicity as to be a fit subject for a poetic idyll **b :** a romantic or amorous interlude **3 :** a pastoral or romantic musical composition

idyl·lic \(')ī¦dilik, -lēk *sometimes* ə'd-\ *adj* **1 :** of, relating to, or being an idyll **2 :** pleasing or picturesque in its natural simplicity ⟨romantic memories of a lost cause threw an ~ haze over earlier times —V.L.Parrington⟩ — **idyl·li·cal·ly** \-lək(ə)lē, -lēk-, -li\ *adv*

idyll·ist \'īdᵊləst, *chiefly Brit* 'id-\ *n* -s : a composer of idylls : an idyllic writer

idyl·li·um \ī'dilēəm, ə'd-\ *also* **idyl·li·on** \-ē,än, -ēən\ *n, pl* **idyl·lia** \-ēə\ [L — more at IDYLL] *archaic* : IDYLL

ie \'ē(,)ā\ *or* **ieie** \'ē(,)ā'ē(,)ā\ *n* -s [Hawaiian] **1 :** a Pacific Islands screw pine (*Freycinetia arborea*) having prop roots which yield a fiber **2 :** a mat or basket made of the fiber of the ie

-ie *also* **-y** *or* **-ey** \ē, i\ *n suffix, pl* **-ies** *or* **-eys** [ME (Sc) *-ie*] **1 a :** little one : dear little one ⟨bird*ie*⟩ ⟨boot*ie*⟩ ⟨Jean*ie*⟩ **b —** in names of articles of feminine apparel ⟨night*ie*⟩ ⟨pant*ie*⟩ **2 :** one belonging to : one having to do with ⟨book*ie*⟩ ⟨deck*ie*⟩ ⟨hack*ie*⟩ ⟨town*ie*⟩ **3 :** one of (such) a kind or quality ⟨bigg*ie*⟩ ⟨cut*ie*⟩ ⟨smart*ie*⟩ ⟨tough*ie*⟩ ⟨dark*ey*⟩

ie \th̲ad·'iz, -a'tiz; (')ī¦ē\ *abbr* [L *id est*] that is

IE *abbr or n* -s : industrial engineer

IE *abbr* **1** Indo-European **2** initial equipment **3** inside edge

¹-ier — see ²-ER

²-ier *comparative of* -Y

³-ier \'i(ə)r, ¦iə\ *n suffix* -s [MF — more at -EER] : person belonging to, connected with, or engaged in ⟨cash*ier*⟩ ⟨gondol*ier*⟩

ier·oe \,ēə'rōi\ *n* -s [ScGael *iarogh*] *Scot* : a great-grandchild

-ies *pl of* -Y

-iest *superlative of* -Y

¹if \(,)if, ,əf, f, *chiefly dial* (¦)ef\ *conj* [ME *yif, if*, fr. OE *gif*; akin to OFris *jef, ef* if, OS *ef* if, whether, OHG *ibu*, *oba* if, whether, Goth *ibai* whether, and perh. to L *is* he, that — more at ITERATE] **1 a :** in the event that : in case ⟨~ the train is on time, we'll meet him⟩ ⟨the news ~ false will prove distressing⟩ **b :** allowing, conceding, or granting that ⟨~ he actually did commit the crime⟩ **c :** SUPPOSING ⟨~ the money were right here on the table, you couldn't count it⟩ **d :** so long as : on condition that ⟨~ any part of the plan succeeds, you will get the credit⟩ ⟨~ you can keep your head when all about are losing theirs —Rudyard Kipling⟩ **2 :** WHETHER ⟨not knowing ~ the candidate had the necessary qualifications⟩ ⟨asked ~ the mail had come⟩ ⟨doubts ~ two and two make four —Matthew Prior⟩ **3 —** used to introduce an exclamation expressing a wish ⟨~ it would only rain⟩ **4 :** even though : although perhaps ⟨an interesting ~ untenable argument⟩ ⟨~ we are broke, still we got our money's worth⟩ — **if anything** *adv* : on the contrary even : perhaps even : possibly even ⟨despite reports, conditions had *if anything* worsened⟩ ⟨*if anything* you ought to apologize⟩

²if \'if\ *n* -s **1 :** CONDITION ⟨an argument with too many ~*s* in it⟩ : STIPULATION ⟨a contract weakened by ~*s*⟩ **2 :** SUPPOSITION ⟨a theory full of ~*s*⟩

IF *abbr* **1** in full **2** *often not cap* intermediate frequency **3** *often not cap* [L *ipse fecit*] he did it himself

ifa·fa lily \ə'fäfə-\ *n, usu cap I* [*ifafa* fr. native name in southern Africa] : a bulbous scapose southern African herb (*Cyrtanthus mackenii*) of the family Amaryllidaceae used as an ornamental and having linear leaves and drooping waxy whitish or yellowish flowers in a terminal umbel

if-bet \'=,=\ *n* : a bet placed with a bookmaker whereby a bettor has money on a horse in a subsequent race provided his horse in an earlier race wins

if-clause \'=,=\ *n* : a conditional clause — compare THEN-CLAUSE

ife \'ēfə\ *n* -s [Pg, fr. native name in Angola] : a tropical African bowstring hemp (*Sansevieria cylindrica*) the cylindrical leaves of which yield a strong cordage fiber

-if·er·ous \¦if(ə)rəs\ *adj comb form* [ME, fr. L *-ifer* (fr. *-i-* + *-fer*) & MF *-ifere* (fr. L *-ifer*) + ME *-ous* — more at -FER] : -FEROUS

IFF *abbr or n* -s [abbr. of *identification, friend or foe*] : the electronic equipment or the system used to identify approaching craft as friendly or hostile ⟨was identified by his *IFF*⟩

if·fen \'ifən\ *conj* [by alter.] *dial* : IF

if·fy \'ifē, -fi\ *adj, sometimes* -ER/-EST [¹*if* + *-y*] : abounding in contingencies or unknown qualities or conditions : UNCERTAIN ⟨an ~ question⟩ ⟨some very ~ political steps —*New Republic*⟩

ifil *var of* IPIL

if money \'=,==\ *n, pl* **if moneys** *or* **if monies** : money from earnings on one race automatically applied to a subsequent race when an if-bet is placed

-i·form \ə,fȯrm, -ō(ə)m\ *adj comb form* [MF & L; MF *-iforme*, fr. L *-iformis*, fr. *-i-* + *-formis* -form] : -FORM

i formation *n, cap I* : an offensive football formation in which the quarterback, fullback, and one or both halfbacks line up behind the center and perpendicular to the line

-i·for·mes \ə'fȯr,mēz, -ō(ə),-\ *n pl comb form* [NL, fr. L, masc. & fem. pl. of *-iformis* -iform] : ones having (such a) form — in taxonomic names of animals ⟨Anser*iformes*⟩

IFR *abbr* instrument flight rules

ifrit \'i,frēt, ə'f-\ *n* -s [Ar *'ifrīt* — more at AFREET] : AFREET

ifs *pl of* IF

if–then \'=¦=\ *adj* : CONDITIONAL, HYPOTHETICAL ⟨an *if-then* proposition⟩

ifu·gao \,ēfü'gaủ\ *n, pl* **ifugao** *or* **ifugaos** *usu cap* [Sp, fr. a native name in the Philippines] **1 a :** a people inhabiting northern Luzon, Philippines **b :** a member of such people **2 :** the Austronesian language of the Ifugao people

-i·fy \ə,fī\ *vb suffix* -ED/-ING/-ES [ME *-ifien*, fr. OF *-ifier*, fr. L *-ificare*, fr. *-i-* + *-ficare* -fy] : -FY

IG *abbr* **1** inspector general **2** intendant-general

iga·la \ē'gälə\ *also* **iga·ra** \-ärə\ *n, pl* **igala** *or* **igalas** *also* **igara** *or* **igaras** *usu cap* **1 :** a Yoruba-speaking people on the Niger at its confluence with the Benue in Nigeria **2 :** a member of the Igala people

ig·bira *or* **ig·ba·ra** \'igbərə\ *n, pl* **igbira** *or* **igbiras** *or* **igbara** *or* **igbaras** *usu cap* **1 :** a Negro people of the Benue river region **2 :** a member of the Igbira people

igbo *usu cap, var of* IBO

ig·dyr \ig'di(ə)r\ *n, pl* **igdyr** *or* **igdyrs** *usu cap* **1 :** a nomadic Turkoman people in Turkmenistan, Soviet Union, by the Caspian sea **2 :** a member of the Igdyr people

-ig·er·ous \¦ij(ə)rəs\ *adj comb form* [L *-iger* (fr. *-i-* + *-ger* -gerous) + E *-ous*] : -GEROUS

igi·gi \ē'jējē\ *n pl* [Assyr-Bab, fr. Sumerian] : a group of heavenly spirits under the god Anu in Babylonian religion

i girder *n, cap I* : I BEAM

ig·loo *also* **ig·lu** \'i(,)glü\ *n* -s [Eskimo *iglu, igdlu* house] **1 a :** an Eskimo house usu. made of sod, wood, or stone when permanent or of snow blocks in the shape of a dome when built for temporary purposes **b :** a building shaped like a dome: as (1) : a magazine for storing munitions (2) : a hut for housing poultry **2 :** a cavity in the snow shaped like a dome and made by a seal over its breathing hole in the ice

igloo 1a

ign *abbr* **1** ignition **2** [L *ignotus*] unknown

ignaro *n* -s *often cap* [after *Ignaro*, character in *The Faerie Queene* by Edmund Spenser †1599 Eng. poet] *obs* : IGNORAMUS

ig·na·tia \ig'nāsh(ē)ə\ *n* -s [NL, fr. *ignatii* (specific epithet of *Strychnos ignatii*), after Saint *Ignatius*, 1st–2d cent. Christian prelate, bishop of Antioch] : the dried ripe seeds of the St.-Ignatius's-bean used like nux vomica

¹ig·na·tian \(')ig¦nāsh(ē)ən\ *adj, usu cap* [St. *Ignatius* of Loyola (Íñigo de Oñez y Loyola) †1556 Span. soldier & ecclesiastic + E *-an*] **a :** of or relating to St. Ignatius of Loyola **b :** of or relating to the Society of Jesus founded by St. Ignatius of Loyola **2** [St. *Ignatius*, bishop of Antioch + E *-an*] : of, relating to, or characteristic of St. Ignatius, bishop of Antioch

²ignatian \"\ *n* -s *usu cap* **1 :** a follower of St. Ignatius, bishop of Antioch **2 :** a follower of St. Ignatius of Loyola

ig·na·tius bean \ig'nāsh(ē)əs-\ *n, usu cap I* : SAINT-IGNATIUS'S-BEAN

ig·ne·ous \'ignēəs\ *adj* [L *igneus*, fr. *ignis* fire; akin to Skt *agni* fire, Lith *ugnis*, OSlav *ognĭ*] **1 :** of, relating to, resembling, or suggestive of fire : containing fire : FIERY ⟨an ~ desert atmosphere⟩ **2 :** relating to, resulting from, or suggestive of the intrusion or extrusion of magma or the activity of volcanoes

igneous fusion *n* **:** fusion by heat alone unassisted by solution in the water of crystallization

igneous rock *n* **:** rock formed by solidification of a molten magma — compare PLUTONIC ROCK, VOLCANIC ROCK

ig·ne·ri \ig'nerē\ *or* **ine·ri** \ə'-\ *n, pl* **igneri** *or* **igneris** *or* **ineri** *or* **ineris** *usu cap* [F, fr. Carib] **1 a :** an aboriginal Arawakan people of the Lesser Antilles **b :** a member of such people **2 :** the language of the Igneri people

ig·nes·cent \(')ig'nes°nt\ *adj* [L *ignescent-, ignescens,* pres. part. of *ignescere* to catch fire, fr. *ignis* fire] **1 :** capable of emitting sparks ⟨~ stone⟩ **2 :** INFLAMMATORY, VOLATILE ⟨an ~ personality⟩

igni- *comb form* [L, fr. *ignis* — more at IGNEOUS] **:** fire **:** burning ⟨*igni*ferous⟩ ⟨*igni*puncture⟩

ig·nis fat·u·us \ˌignəs'fachəwəs\ *n, pl* **ig·nes fat·u·i** \-ˌnēz-'fachəˌwī\ [ML, lit., foolish fire] **1 :** a light that sometimes appears in the night usu. over marshy ground and that is often attributable to the combustion of marsh gas — called also *jack-o'-lantern, will-o'-the wisp* **2 :** a deceptive or false goal **:** a misleading ideal ⟨the *ignis fatuus* of a world without wars⟩

ig·nit·abil·i·ty *also* **ig·nit·ibil·i·ty** \(ˌ)igˌnīd·ə'bilәd·ē\ *n* -ES **:** the quality or state of being ignitable ⟨the ~ of coal⟩

ig·nit·able *also* **ig·nit·ible** \(')ig'nīd·əbəl\ *adj* **:** capable of being ignited

[1]**ignite** *adj* [L *ignitus*] *obs* **:** intensely hot **:** FIERY, ARDENT

[2]**ig·nite** \ig'nīt, *usu* -īd·+V\ *vb* -ED/-ING/-S [L *ignitus,* past part. of *ignire* to ignite, fr. *ignis* fire] *vt* **1 :** to subject to fire or intense heat; *specif* **:** to render luminous by heat **2 a :** to set aflame ⟨~ paper⟩; *also* **:** KINDLE ⟨~ a fire⟩ **b :** to cause (a fuel mixture) to burn ⟨a rocket . . . ~*ed* by remote control —Milton Bracker⟩ **3 :** to heat up **:** EXCITE, INFLAME ⟨oppression that *ignited* the hatred of the people⟩ ~ *vi* **1 :** to catch fire **:** begin to burn ⟨slowly the fire *ignited*⟩ **2 :** to begin to glow **:** become luminescent

ig·nit·er *or* **ig·ni·tor** \-īd·ə(r)\ *n* -S **:** one that ignites: as **a :** a charge usu. of black gunpowder used to facilitate the ignition of a propelling charge and sometimes of a bursting charge **b :** a device for igniting fuel mixture (as in an internal-combustion engine, a jet engine, or a rocket engine) **c :** a separately energized electrode used for restriking the arc in an ignitron

ig·ni·tion \ig'nishən\ *n* -S **1 :** the act or action of igniting: as **a** (1) **:** subjection to the action of fire or intense heat **:** setting fire **:** KINDLING (2) **:** an analytical procedure of heating an inorganic substance with free access to air — compare INCINERATION **b :** the setting fire to a single point of the charge in the explosion of a charge of powder for ballistic purposes **2 :** the process or means of igniting a fuel mixture (as in an internal-combustion engine, a rocket engine, or an oil-burning furnace)

ignition charge *n* **:** a small charge usu. of black powder used to facilitate the ignition of the main charge

ignition temperature *or* **ignition point** *n* **:** the lowest temperature at which a combustible substance when heated (as in a bath of molten metal) takes fire in air and continues to burn — called also *autogenous ignition temperature;* compare FIRE POINT

ignition tube *n* **:** a heavy-walled test tube of hard glass for examining the behavior of heated samples

ig·ni·tron \ig'nīˌträn\ *n* -S [*igni-* + *-tron*] **:** a mercury-containing half-wave-rectifier tube in which the arc is restruck at the beginning of each cycle by a special electrode separately energized by an auxiliary circuit

ig·no·bil·i·ty \ˌignō'biləd·ē\ *n* [L *ignobilitas,* fr. *ignobilis* + *-itas* -ity] **:** the quality or state of being ignoble

ig·no·ble \(')ig'nōbəl\ *adj* [L *ignobilis,* fr. *i-* (fr. *in-* [1]in-) + *gnobilis, nobilis* noble — more at NOBLE] **1 :** of low birth or common origin **:** PLEBEIAN ⟨an ~ mob⟩ **2 :** displaying, motivated by, or characterized by baseness or meanness **:** DESPICABLE ⟨~ laws⟩ ⟨~ purposes⟩

ignoble hawk *n* **:** a short-winged hawk that rakes for its prey **:** ACCIPITER — used chiefly in the technical language of falconry

ig·no·ble·ness *n* **:** IGNOBILITY

ig·no·bly \-blē,-bli\ *adv* **:** in an ignoble manner

ig·no·min·i·ous \ˌignə'minēəs\ *adj* [MF or L; MF *ignominieux,* fr. L *ignominiosus,* fr. *ignominia* + *-osus* -ous] **1 :** marked by, full of, or characterized by disgrace or shame **:** DISHONORABLE ⟨an ~ fate⟩ ⟨an ~ peace treaty⟩ **2 :** deserving of shame or infamy **:** DESPICABLE ⟨~ language⟩ **3 :** HUMILIATING, DEGRADING ⟨~ labor⟩

ig·no·min·i·ous·ly *adv* **:** in an ignominious manner

ig·no·min·i·ous·ness *n* -ES **:** the quality or state of being ignominious

ig·no·my \'ignəˌminē, -mini *also* -ˌmən- *or* əg'nämən-\ *n* -ES [MF or L; MF *ignominie,* fr. L *ignominia,* fr. *ig-* (as in *ignorare* to be ignorant of, ignore) + *nomin-, nomen* name + *-ia* -y — more at IGNORE, NAME] **1 :** deep personal disgrace ⟨the ~ of prison⟩ **2 :** disgraceful or dishonorable conduct, quality, or action ⟨~ of abandoning his comrades⟩ **syn** see DISHONOR

ig·no·my \'ignəmē\ *n* -ES [modif. of MF *ignominie* or L *ignominia*] *archaic* **:** IGNOMINY

ig·nor·able \(')ig'nōrəbəl, -nȯr-\ *adj* **:** capable of being ignored

ig·no·ra·mus \ˌignə'rāməs *sometimes* -ram-\ *n* -ES [NL, fr. L, we do not know, 1st pl. pres. indic. of *ignorare* to be ignorant of — more at IGNORE] **1 :** an endorsement formerly written on a bill of indictment by a grand jury when it considered the evidence insufficient to warrant the finding of a true bill; *also* **:** a bill returned with such an endorsement **2** [after *Ignoramus,* an ignorant lawyer in *Ignoramus* (1615), play by George Ruggle †1622, Eng. playwright] **:** an utterly ignorant person **:** DUNCE

ignoramus waltz *n* **:** an easy two-step waltz

ig·no·rance \'ignərən(t)s\ *n* -S [ME *ignoraunce,* fr. OF *ignorance,* fr. L *ignorantia,* fr. *ignorant-, ignorans* + *-ia* -y] **:** the quality or state of being ignorant ⟨~ of facts⟩

ig·no·rant \-nt\ *adj* [ME *ignoraunt,* fr. MF *ignorant,* fr. L *ignorant-, ignorans,* pres. part. of *ignorare* to be ignorant of, ignore — more at IGNORE] **1 a :** destitute of knowledge **:** UNINSTRUCTED, UNLEARNED ⟨an ~ society⟩ **b :** resulting from or exhibiting lack of perception, knowledge, or intelligence ⟨~ errors⟩ ⟨~ public spokesmen⟩ **2 a :** UNAWARE, UNINFORMED ⟨frauds palmed off on an ~ public⟩ — often used with *of* or *in* ⟨~ of the true significance of the news⟩ **b :** INNOCENT, GUILELESS ⟨~ hope⟩ **3 a :** UNCIVILIZED, BACKWARD, UNENLIGHTENED ⟨~ absolutism⟩ **b :** PRIMITIVE, CRUDE ⟨~ devices⟩ **syn** ILLITERATE, UNLETTERED, UNEDUCATED, UNTAUGHT, UNTUTORED, UNLEARNED, NESCIENT: IGNORANT indicates a lack of knowledge, either in general or of a particular point ⟨a population of uncivilized peasants, *ignorant,* illiterate, superstitious, cruel, and land hungry —G.B.Shaw⟩ ⟨the disputants on both sides were *ignorant* of the matter they were disputing about —Havelock Ellis⟩ ILLITERATE is now most commonly used in reference to inability to read and write or to gross unfamiliarity with the written language and the world of learning ⟨*illiterate* in the sense that they could not read or write, or . . . functionally *illiterate* in the sense that they were unable to understand what they read —I.L.Kandel⟩ ⟨as near *illiterate* as one can be who can read and write, her grammar and spelling being equally uncertain —H.S.Canby⟩ UNLETTERED stresses the fact of unfamiliarity with reading and writing or with written learning, often without any implication of condemnation ⟨even written in English, a paper like this would answer every purpose; for the *unlettered* natives, standing in great awe of the document, would not dare to molest us —Herman Melville⟩ ⟨*unlettered* provincials who knew their nets, or trades, or farms, but could hardly be expected to follow the Emperor's physician in his theories of Greek science —J.R. Perkins⟩ UNEDUCATED and UNTAUGHT simply indicate lack of formal schooling; the latter is sometimes used to describe natural spontaneity ⟨*untaught* graces⟩ UNTUTORED is sometimes used to refer to the unschooled condition of primitives ⟨the poor Indian, whose *untutored* mind —Alexander Pope⟩ ⟨taught so many flat lies that their false knowledge is more dangerous than the *untutored* natural wit of savages —G.B. Shaw⟩ UNLEARNED may suggest lack of much learning or ignorance of advanced subjects ⟨such generosity becomes, in effect, a cruel sentimentality, when it crowds the profession with thousands of unwanted persons, most of them relatively unskilled and *unlearned* —Robert Evett⟩ NESCIENT may apply to a deep, determined, or invincible ignorance of what is outside one's immediate ken ⟨most men are not intended to be any wiser than their cocks and bulls — duly scientific of their yard and pasture, peacefully *nescient* of all beyond —John Ruskin⟩

ig·no·ran·tism \-nt·ˌizəm, -n·ˌti-\ *n* -S [F *ignorantisme,* fr. *ignorant* + *-isme* -ism] **:** OBSCURANTISM ⟨fascism . . . founding its educational policy on basic ~ —D.F.Fleming⟩

ig·no·rant·ly *adv* [ME *ignorauntly,* fr. *ignoraunt* + *-ly*] **:** in an ignorant manner

ig·no·rant·ness *n* -ES **:** the quality or state of being ignorant

ig·no·ra·tio elen·chi \ˌignə'räd·ē,ōə'leŋˌkē\ *n* [L, lit., ignorance of proof; trans. of Gk *elenchou agnoia*] **:** a fallacy in logic of supposing that the point at issue is proved or disproved by an argument which proves or disproves something not at issue; *also* **:** an argument based on such a fallacy

ig·no·ra·tion \ˌignə'rāshən\ *n* -S [L *ignoration-, ignoratio,* fr. *ignoratus* (past part. of *ignorare*) + *-ion-, -io* -ion] **1 :** complete or utter ignorance ⟨the ~ of the true relation of each organism to its environment —A.N.Whitehead⟩ **2** [*ignore* + *-ation*] **:** an act or action of ignoring ⟨changed from complete ~ of my presence to an almost pathetic agreement with every word I said —H.J.Laski⟩

ig·nore \ig'nō(ə)r, -'nȯ(ə)r, -ōə, -ō(ə)\ *vt* -ED/-ING/-S [F *ignorer,* fr. L *ignorare,* fr. *ignarus* ignorant, unknown, fr. *i-* (fr. *in-* [1]in-) + *gnarus* knowing, known; akin to L *gnoscere, noscere* to know — more at KNOW] **1** *archaic* **:** to be ignorant of **2 :** to refuse to take notice of ⟨~ a friendly gesture⟩ **:** shut the eyes to ⟨~ public abuses⟩ **:** disregard willfully ⟨~ evidence⟩ **3 :** to reject or throw out (a bill of indictment) as false or ungrounded — compare IGNORAMUS 1 **syn** see NEGLECT

ig·nor·er \ig'nōrə(r)\, -nȯr-\ *n* -S **:** one that ignores

ignote *adj* [L *ignotus,* fr. *i-* (fr. *in-* [1]in-) + *gnotus, notus* known, past part. of *gnoscere, noscere* to know] *obs* **:** UNKNOWN

ig·o·rot \ˌēgə'rōt, ˈ≐≐ˌ≐\ *n, pl* **igorot** *or* **igorots** *usu cap* **1 a :** any of several related peoples inhabiting the mountains of northwestern Luzon, Philippines: (1) **:** a people inhabiting the Mountain Province south of Kalinga (2) **:** KANKANAI (3) **:** NABALOI (4) **:** BONTOK **b :** a member of any of these peoples **2 :** any of the Austronesian languages of the Igorot peoples

IGS *abbr* imperial general staff

igua·na \ə'gwänə, ē'-\ *n* [Sp, fr. Arawak *iwana*] **1 a** *also* **gua·na** \'gwänə\ -S **:** any of a number of large herbivorous chiefly tropical American lizards (family Iguanidae) being typically dark-colored with a serrated dorsal crest and a gular pouch, attaining a length of several feet, and serving as an important article of human food in their native habitat **b** *cap* [NL, fr. Sp] **:** the type genus of Iguanidae **2** *also* **gua·na** \'gwänə\ *or* **gua·no** \-ä(ˌ)nō\ -S **:** any of various large lizards: as **a :** LACE LIZARD **b :** TUATARA

[1]**igua·nid** \ə'gwänəd, ē'-\ *adj* [NL *Iguanidae*] **:** of or relating to the Iguanidae

[2]**iguanid** \"\ *n* -S **:** a lizard of the family Iguanidae

Igua·ni·dae \-nəˌdē\ *n pl, cap* [NL, fr. *Iguana,* type genus + *-idae*] **:** a large family of chiefly New World lizards including the iguanas and many of the small inoffensive lizards (as the pine lizard and horned toads) of the U.S. and being distinguished from the related Agamidae by possession of pleurodont dentition

igua·no·don \-ˌdän\ *n, cap* [NL, fr. Sp *iguana* + NL *-odon*] **:** a genus of large herbivorous ornithischian dinosaurs (type of a family Iguanodontidae) from the early Cretaceous of Belgium and England having the head compressed, the jaws probably provided with a horny covering in front like that of a turtle but with numerous spatulate serrated teeth farther back, and the forelimbs comparatively small and provided with large three-toed hind limbs used chiefly in walking and a large heavy tail which doubtless assisted in standing upright — **igua·no·dont** \-nt\ *adj or n*

igua·no·don·toi·dea \≐ˌ≐≐ˌdän'tȯidēə\ *or* **igua·no·don·tia** \≐ˌ≐≐'dänch(ē)ə\ [NL, fr. *Iguanodont-, Iguanodon* + *-oidea* or *-ia*] *syn of* ORNITHOPODA

[1]**igua·noid** \ə'gwäˌnȯid, ē'-\ *adj* [*iguana* + *-oid*] **:** of or relating to an iguana or the iguanas

[2]**iguanoid** \"\ *n* -S **1 :** a lizard like an iguana **2 :** a lizard of the family Iguanidae

igua·pe \ē'gwä(ˌ)pā\ *n* -S [fr. *Iguape,* fishing port and river in Brazil] **:** CANDLENUT 1

IGY *abbr* international geophysical year

IH *abbr, often not cap* inside height

i-head \'≐ˌ≐\ *adj, cap I* **:** having valves in the cylinder head ⟨an *I-head* gasoline engine⟩

[1]**ihi** \'ē(ˌ)hē\ *n* -S [Maori *hihi*] **:** STITCHBIRD

[2]**ihi** \"\ *n* -S [Maori *ihe*] **:** either of two important New Zealand food fishes (order Synentognathi): **a :** a halfbeak (*Hemiramphus intermedius*) **b :** a skipper (*Scombresox forsteri*)

ih·lat \ē'lät\ *n, pl* **ihlat** *or* **ihlats** *usu cap* **1 :** an orig. nomadic Sunnite people of Persia **2 :** a member of the Ihlat people

ih·le·ite \'ēləˌīt, -lē-,\ *n* -S [G *ihleit,* fr. M. *Ihle,* 19th cent. Bohemian superintendent of mines + G *-it* -ite] **:** COPIAPITE

IHP *abbr, often not cap* indicated horsepower

ih·ram \ē'räm\ *n* -S [Ar *iḥrām*] **1 :** a state of consecration assumed by Muslims on pilgrimage to Mecca **2 :** the ceremonially plain clothing worn by Muslims on pilgrimage

IHS *or* **IHC** *or* **JHS** *or* **YHS** *symbol* [LL IHS, IHC, fr. Gk IHC, IHΣ (the capitalized forms of the Greek letters iota, eta, and sigma), short for *Iēsous* Jesus] — used as a Christian symbol and monogram for *Jesus*

IHVH *var of* YHWH

II *abbr* **1** indorsement irregular **2** inventory and inspection

i iron *n, cap 1st I* **:** I BAR

ii·wi \ē'ēwē\ *n* -S [Hawaiian *'i'iwi*] **:** an Hawaiian honeycreeper (*Vestiaria coccinea*) with chiefly bright vermilion plumage formerly used in making feather cloaks

ijo \'ē(ˌ)jō\ *also* **ijaw** \-jȯ\ *n, pl* **ijo** *or* **ijos** *also* **ijaw** *or* **ijaws** *usu cap* **1 a :** a Negro people of the Niger delta **b :** a member of such people **2 :** the language of the Ijo people **3 :** a branch of the Niger-Congo language family containing only the Ijo language

ijo·lite \'ē(y)əˌlīt, 'iyə,-\ *n* -S [Swed *Ijo,* river and village in Finland + E *-lite*] **:** a granular igneous rock consisting chiefly of nephelite and augite typically with calcite, apatite, and titanite accessories

ik·a·ry \'ikərē\ *n* -ES [Russ *ikra*] *archaic* **:** CAVIAR

ikat \'ēˌkät\ *n* -S [Malay, tying-up, fastening, binding (as yarns prior to dyeing)] **1 :** a technique of fabric decoration common in Malaya, Indonesia, and Latin America in which warp and sometimes also weft yarns are tied-and-dyed before weaving **2 :** a fabric of tied-and-dyed design **:** CHINÉ

ike \'īk\ *n* -S [by alter. and shortening] **:** ICONOSCOPE

ikh·wan \ik'wän\ *n pl, usu cap* [Ar *ikhwān,* lit. brethren] **:** Muslim brethren united by the ties of common membership in the Wahhabi sect of central Arabia

ikmo *var of* ITMO

ikon *var of* ICON

ikon- *or* **ikono-** — see ICON-

il *abbr* illustrated; illustration; illustrator

IL *abbr* **1** including loading **2** inside left **3** *often not cap* inside length **4** interline

il- — see IN-

-il \əl, °l, (ˌ)il\ *also* **-ile** \", ˌēl, ˌīl\ *n suffix* -S [G *-il* & F *-ile,* prob. fr. F *-ile* & L *-ilis* -ile, adj. suffix] **:** substance related to (something specified) ⟨benz*il*⟩

i·la \'ēlə\ *n, pl* **ila** *or* **ilas** *usu cap* **1 a :** a Bantu-speaking people of northern Rhodesia **b :** a member of such people **2 :** a Bantu language of the Ila people

ila·ma \ə'lämə\ *n* -S [MexSp, fr. Nahuatl *ilamatzapotl,* fr. *ilamatl* old woman + *tzapotl* sapodilla; fr. the fancied resemblance of the fruit to an old woman's head] **1 :** a tropical American tree (*Annona diversifolia*) grown in the southern U.S. that has a whitish fruit with pinkish tinge **2 :** the fruit of the ilama

ilang-ilang *or* **ylang-ylang** \ˌēˌläŋ'ēˌläŋ\ *n* -S [Tag] **1 :** a tree (*Canangium odoratum*) of the Malay archipelago, the Philippines, and adjacent areas that has very fragrant greenish yellow flowers **2 :** a perfume distilled from the flowers of the ilang-ilang tree

ilang-ilang oil *n* **:** a yellowish essential oil that has a fine floral odor, is obtained chiefly in the Philippines and on Réunion Island from the flowers of the ilang-ilang tree, and is used in perfumes, cosmetics, and soaps — compare CANANGA OIL

ila·va \ə'lävə\ *or* **ila·van** \-vən\ *n* -S *usu cap* [Tamil & Malayalam *īravan*] **1 :** a large caste of cultivators in southern India **2 :** a member of the Ilava caste

ile- *also* **ileo-** *comb form* [NL *ileum*] **1 :** ileum ⟨*ileo*stomy⟩ **2 :** ileal and ⟨*ileo*cecal⟩

[1]**-ile** \əl, °l, ˌīl, (ˌ)il\ *adj suffix* [ME, fr. MF, fr. L *-ilis*] **:** of, relating to, suited for, or capable of ⟨contract*ile*⟩ ⟨expans*ile*⟩

[2]**-ile** \"\ *n suffix* -S [prob. fr. *-ile* (as in *quartile,* n. — quartile aspect — and *sextile,* n.)] **:** segment of a (specified) size in a frequency distribution ⟨cent*ile*⟩ ⟨dec*ile*⟩

[3]**-ile** — see -IL

il·e·al \'ilēəl\ *also* **il·e·ac** \-ēˌak\ *adj* [*ile-* + *-al* or *-ac*] **:** of, relating to, or involving the ileum

il·e·i·tis \ˌilē'īd·əs\ *n, pl* **il·e·it·i·des** \-'id·əˌdēz\ [NL, fr. *ile-* + *-itis*] **:** inflammation of the ileum — see REGIONAL ILEITIS

il·eo·cecal \ˌilē(ˌ)ō+\ *adj* [*ile-* + *cecal*] **:** of, related to, or involving both ileum and cecum ⟨the ~ region⟩

ileocecal valve *n* **:** the valve formed by two folds of mucous membrane at the opening of the ileum into the large intestine

il·eo·colic artery \"+. . .-\ *n* [*ile-* + *colic*] **:** a branch of the superior mesenteric supplying the terminal part of the ileum and the beginning of the colon

ileocolic valve *n* **1 :** ILEOCECAL VALVE **2 :** a circular valvular ridge between small intestine and colon in animals (as amphibians) that lack a cecum

ileon *n* -S [ME, modif. of L *ile, ilium, ileum* groin] *obs* **:** ILEUM

il·e·os·to·my \ˌilē'ästəmē\ *n* -ES [ISV *ile-* + *-stomy*] **1 :** an operation to create an artificial anus by making an opening from the ileum through the abdominal wall **2 :** the orifice made by ileostomy

ileostomy bag *n* **:** a container designed to receive feces discharged through an ileostomy

iles·ite \'īlˌzīt\ *n* -S [M.W.*Iles* †1890 Am. mineralogist + E *-ite*] **:** a mineral $(Mn,Zn,Fe)SO_4.4H_2O$ consisting of a green hydrous manganese zinc iron sulfate

il·e·um \'ilēəm\ *n, pl* **il·ea** \-ēə\ [NL, fr. L *ile, ilium, ileum* groin, viscera; prob. akin to Gk *ilia* female genitals, *ilion* female pubes, and perh. to Pol *jelito* intestine, sausage, Russ *liton'ya* third stomach of ruminants] **:** the last division of the small intestine constituting the part between the jejunum and large intestine, in man forming the last three fifths of the part of the small intestine beyond the end of the duodenum, and being smaller and thinner-walled than the jejunum with fewer circular folds but more numerous Peyer's patches

il·e·us \'ilēəs\ *n* -ES [L, fr. Gk *eileos, ileos,* from *eilein, illein* to roll] **:** obstruction of the bowel; *specif* **:** a condition that is commonly marked by painful distended abdomen, vomiting of dark or fecal matter, toxemia, and dehydration and that results when the intestinal contents back up because peristalsis fails although the lumen is not occluded — called also *paralytic ileus*

ilex \'īˌleks\ *n* [ME, fr. L, prob. of non-IE origin like Gk (Macedonian dial.) *ilax* holm oak] **1** -ES **:** HOLM OAK **2** [NL, fr. L] **a** *cap* **:** a large genus of widely distributed trees and shrubs (family Aquifoliaceae) having small flowers and berries — see HOLLY **b** -ES **:** any plant of this genus

il·ford \'ilfə(r)d\ *adj, usu cap* [fr. *Ilford,* England] **:** of or from the municipal borough of Ilford, England **:** of the kind or style prevalent in Ilford

ilia *pl of* ILIUM

il·i·ac \'ilēˌak\ *adj* [NL *ilium* + E *-ac* (fr. L *-acus,* adj. suffix, fr. Gk *-akos*)] **1** *archaic* **:** ILEAL **2 :** of or relating to the ilium **:** located in the region of the ilium ⟨~ bone⟩ ⟨~ graft⟩ — see ABDOMINAL REGION illustration

iliac artery *n* **1 :** either of the large arteries supplying blood to the lower trunk and hind limbs and arising by bifurcation of the aorta which in man occurs at the level of the fourth lumbar vertebra to form one vessel for each side of the body — called also *common iliac artery* **2 :** the outer branch of either iliac artery that passes beneath Poupart's ligament to become the femoral artery — called also *external iliac artery* **3 :** the inner branch of either common iliac artery that soon breaks into several branches and supplies blood chiefly to the pelvic and gluteal areas — called also *hypogastric artery, internal iliac artery*

iliac crest *n* **:** the thick curved upper border of the ilium

iliac fascia *n* **:** an aponeurotic layer lining the back part of the abdominal cavity and covering the psoas and iliacus muscles

iliac fossa *n* **:** the inner concavity of the ilium

iliac index *n* **:** the anthropometric ratio of the distance between the iliac spines and that between the topmost margin of the crest of the ilium and the lowest margin of the acetabulum multiplied by 100

il·i·a·cus \ə'līəkəs\ *n, pl* **ilia·ci** \-īəˌsī\ [NL, fr. *ilium*] **:** a muscle that flexes the thigh or bends the pelvis and lumbar region forward, has its origin from the iliac fossa, iliac crest, the base of the sacrum, and adjoining parts, and is inserted into the outer side of the tendon of the psoas major, the capsule of the hip joint, and the lesser trochanter of the femur

iliac vein *n* **:** any of three veins on each side of the body corresponding to and accompanying the iliac arteries

il·i·ad \'ilēəd *also* -ēˌad\ *n* -S *often cap* [fr. the *Iliad,* ancient Greek epic poem dealing with the siege of Troy and attributed to Homer, fr. L *Iliad-, Ilias,* fr. Gk *Iliad-, Ilias,* lit., of Ilium, fr. *Ilion* Troy] **1 :** a long narrative; *esp* **:** an epic in the Homeric tradition ⟨the farmer has inspired no ringing saga or ~ —*Scribner's*⟩ **2 a :** a series of martial exploits regarded as suitable for epic commemoration ⟨who leaving his glad school days . . . joined England's bitter *Iliad* —Margaret Wilson⟩ **b :** a series of miseries or disasters ⟨opens another *Iliad* of woes to Europe —Edmund Burke⟩

il·i·ad·ic \ˌilē'adik\ *adj* **1** *usu cap* **:** of or relating to the *Iliad* of Homer **2** *often cap* **:** of, relating to, or being an iliad ⟨*iliadic* adventures during wartime⟩

il·i·a·hi \ˌēlē'āhē\ *n* -S [Hawaiian] **:** an Hawaiian sandalwood tree (*Santalum freycinetianum*) yielding an aromatic wood

il·i·al \'ilēəl\ *adj* [NL *ilium* + E *-al*] **:** ILIAC

[1]**il·i·an** \'ilēən\ *adj, usu cap* [*Ilium* (Troy), ancient city in northwestern Asia Minor + E *-an*] **:** of or relating to ancient Troy

[2]**ilian** \"\ *n* -S *cap* **:** an inhabitant of ancient Troy

ili·au \ˌēlē'aů\ *n* -S [Hawaiian, lit., hideebound] **:** a destructive disease of young sugarcane endemic in Hawaii caused by a fungus (*Gnomonia iliau*) and characterized by binding of the leaf bases tightly about the stem

il·i·ca·ce·ae \ˌilə'kāsēˌē\ [NL, fr. *Ilic-, Ilex,* type genus + *-aceae*] *syn of* AQUIFOLIACEAE

ili·ma \ē'lēmə\ *n* -S [Hawaiian *'ilima*] **:** a small shrub of the genus *Sida* (esp. *S. fallax*) commonly bearing tiny yellow or orange flowers that are often used in Hawaiian leis

ilio- *comb form* [NL *ilium*] **:** iliac and ⟨*ilio*costal⟩ ⟨*ilio*pelvic⟩

il·i·o·cos·ta·lis \ˌilēō,kä'stāləs, -tal-, -täl-\ *n* -ES [NL, fr. *ilio-* + LL *costalis* rib, fr. L *costa* rib + *-alis* (fr. *-alis* -al, adj. suffix)] **:** the lateral division of the sacrospinalis muscle that helps to keep the trunk erect and consists of a part from the ilium to the lower ribs which draws the trunk to the same side or depresses the ribs, a part from the lower to the upper ribs which draws the trunk to the same side and approximates the ribs, and a part from the ribs to the cervical transverse processes which draws the neck to the same side and elevates the ribs — called also respectively *iliocostalis lumborum, iliocostalis dorsi, iliocostalis cervicis*

il·io·femoral ligament \ˌilē(ˌ)ō+. . .-\ *n* [ISV *ilio-* + *femoral*] **:** a ligament that extends from the anterior inferior spine of the ilium to the intertrochanteric line of the femur and divides below into two branches

il·io·hypogastric nerve \"+. . .-\ *n* [ISV *ilio-* + *hypogastric*] **:** a branch of the first lumbar nerve distributed to the iliohypogastric regions

ilioinguinal nerve \"+. . .-\ *n* [*ilio-* + *inguinal*] **:** a branch of the first lumbar nerve distributed to the ilioinguinal regions

il·io·lumbar artery \"+...-\ *n* [*ilio-* + *lumbar*] **:** a branch of the posterior trunk of the iliac artery (sense 3)

iliolumbar ligament *n* **:** a ligament connecting the transverse process of the last lumbar vertebra with the iliac crest

il·io·pectineal eminence \"+...-\ *n* [*ilio-* + *pectineal*] **:** an eminence indicating the junction of the ilium and the pubis

iliopectineal line *n* **:** a line or ridge on the inner surface of the innominate bone marking the border between the true and false pelvis

il·io·psoas \¦ilēō'sōəs, -ē'äpsəwəs\ *n* [NL, fr. *ilio-* + *psoas*] **:** a muscle consisting of the iliacus and psoas major muscles

il·io·pso·at·ic \¦ilē(,)ōsō¦ad·ik, -ē¦äpsə¦wa-\ *adj* **:** of or relating to the iliopsoas

il·io·tibial band \¦ilē(,)ō+...-\ *n* [*ilio-* + *tibial*] **:** a downward continuation of the fascia lata that resembles a tendon and is inserted into the lateral tuberosity of the tibia

il·i·um \'ilēəm\ *n, pl* **il·ia** \-ēə\ [NL, fr. L *ilium, ileum, ile* groin, viscera — more at ILEUM] **1 :** the dorsal and upper one of the three bones composing either lateral half of the pelvis being in man broad and expanded above and narrower below where it joins with the ischium and pubis to form part of the acetabulum **2** *archaic* **:** ILEUM

¹ilk \'ilk, 'iu̇k\ *pron* [ME *ilk, ilke,* fr. OE *ilca* same, fr. a prehistoric compound whose constituents are akin respectively to Goth *is* he and OE *gelīc* like — more at ITERATE, LIKE] *now chiefly Scot* **:** SAME — used with preceding *that* esp. in the names of landed families ⟨Grant of that ~ means Grant of Grant⟩

²ilk \"\ *n* -S **:** FAMILY, SORT, KIND — often used disparagingly ⟨determinists, materialists, agnostics, behaviorists and their ~ —John Dewey⟩ **syn** see TYPE

³ilk \"\ *adj* [ME, adj. & pron., fr. OE *ylc, ǣlc* — more at EACH] *chiefly Scot* **:** EACH, EVERY

⁴ilk \"\ *pron* [ME] *chiefly Scot* **:** EACH

il·ka \'ilkə\ *adj* [ME *ilka, ilkan,* fr. *ilk* each + *a, an* (indef. art.)] *chiefly Scot* **:** EACH, EVERY ⟨and ~ bird sang o' its luve —Robert Burns⟩

ilka day *n, Scot* **:** WEEKDAY

¹ill \'il\ *adj* **worse** \'wərs, -ōs, -əis\ *also sometimes and in sense 2c often* **ill·er** \'ilə(r)\ *or substand* **wors·er** \'wərsə(r), -ōs-,-əis-\ **worst** \'wərst, -ōst, -əist\ *also sometimes and in sense 2c often* **ill·est** \'iləst\ [ME *ill, ille,* fr. ON *illr*] **1 a** *now chiefly Scot* **:** immoral or vicious or corrupt or otherwise morally reprehensible **b :** resulting from or accompanied by or evidencing an evil, malicious, or malevolent intention ⟨~ deeds that wrecked their lives⟩ **c :** that imputes evil to or implies evil in something referred to **:** that ascribes evil to or assumes evil in something referred to ⟨an ~ opinion of everything they did⟩ ⟨attaching an ~ significance to what was said⟩ ⟨in ~ repute⟩ **2 a :** that causes or is accompanied by pain or discomfort or inconvenience or that is otherwise disagreeable ⟨died an ~ death⟩ ⟨the ~ smells of a fish market⟩ ⟨had an ~ taste⟩ **b :** that causes or tends to result in harm **:** HURTFUL, INJURIOUS, PERNICIOUS ⟨its ~ effects were felt for many generations —Gilbert Highet⟩ ⟨a decision that can have only ~ results⟩ ⟨did them an ~ service⟩ **c** (1) **:** affected with some ailment **:** INDISPOSED **:** not being in good health **:** AILING, UNWELL, SICK ⟨is ~ with a fever⟩ ⟨incurably ~ with cancer —*Time*⟩ **:** UNSOUND, FAILING ⟨suffers from chronically ~ health⟩ **:** UPSET, DISORDERED ⟨emotionally ~⟩ ⟨mentally ~⟩ (2) **:** affected by nausea often to the point of vomiting **:** NAUSEATED, SICK ⟨thought she would be ~ after the ride on the roller coaster⟩ **3 a :** that is not suited to circumstances or that is not to one's advantage **:** UNPROPITIOUS, UNTOWARD, UNLUCKY ⟨its leaders were choosing an ~ moment for a revolution —J.A.Froude⟩ **:** not promising well **:** INAUSPICIOUS ⟨an ~ omen⟩ **:** marked by unfavorable events **:** contrary to one's hopes and expectations ⟨had a discouraging run of ~ luck⟩ **b :** that involves difficulties with regard to the accomplishment of an objective **:** HARD, TROUBLESOME ⟨beauty is intangible, vague, ~ to be defined —M.F.Tupper⟩ **:** so difficult as to make effort useless **:** POINTLESS ⟨it is ~ prophesying; but one has hope of a regeneration of our literature—*Yale Rev.*⟩ **4 a :** that is not up to an accepted standard of worth or ability **:** notably imperfect or unsatisfactory **:** quite faulty **:** INFERIOR, DEFECTIVE ⟨a period of ~ management⟩ ⟨an ~ specimen of humanity⟩ **b :** that is not up to an accepted standard of propriety **:** UNPOLISHED, CRUDE, BOORISH ⟨~ manners⟩ ⟨~ behavior⟩ **c** *archaic* **:** notably unskillful or inexpert or inefficient **:** MALADROIT ⟨I am ~ at describing female apparel —Charles Lamb⟩ **5 a :** UNFRIENDLY, HOSTILE ⟨~ feeling that culminated in bloody feuds⟩ **b :** HARSH, CRUEL ⟨~ treatment of minorities⟩ **c** *now chiefly dial* (1) *of an animal* **:** dangerously fierce **:** FEROCIOUS, SAVAGE (2) *of a person* **:** cantankerous and irritable **:** CROSS, SURLY, GRUMPY **syn** see BAD

²ill \"\ *adv* **worse** \"\ **worst** \"\ [ME *ille,* fr. ON *illa,* fr. *illr,* adj.] **1 a :** with displeasure or offense ⟨the remark was ~ received⟩ **b :** in an unfriendly or harsh or malevolent manner ⟨were ~ treated during their stay⟩ **c :** in such a way as to reflect unfavorable estimation of something referred to or to cast aspersion or blame on something referred to ⟨spoke very ~ of them⟩ ⟨however ~ he might think of that general —John Buchan⟩ **2 :** in a reprehensible manner ⟨an *ill-spent* youth⟩ **3** *now dial Eng* **:** to a grave extent **:** SERIOUSLY ⟨was ~ hurt⟩ **4 a :** not to any real extent **:** not really **:** HARDLY, SCARCELY **:** by the narrowest margin or none at all ⟨can ~ afford further expense⟩ ⟨they were soon ~ content —A.M. Young⟩ **b :** only with great trouble or difficulty ⟨except in matters of doctrine Pilgrim and Puritan consorted ~ together —V.L.Parrington⟩ **5 a :** UNADVANTAGEOUSLY, UNPROPITIOUSLY, UNLUCKILY ⟨warned them that it would go ~ with them if they insisted⟩ ⟨the whole affair turned out ~⟩ **b :** in a faulty or inefficient or otherwise defective manner **:** IMPERFECTLY, INEFFECTIVELY ⟨the economic irresponsibility of prison life left me ~ equipped to live up to my good intentions —Frank O'Leary⟩ ⟨has been bad propaganda, ~ calculated to achieve its objects —G.E.G.Catlin⟩ — often used in combination ⟨*ill-smelling*⟩ esp. with adjectives in *-ed* ⟨*ill-prepared*⟩

³ill \"\ *n* -S [ME, fr. *ill, ille* (adj.)] **1 a** (1) **:** the reverse of good **:** EVIL ⟨not knowing whether the outcome would be for good or for ~⟩ ⟨if ~ should befall her —E.T.Thurston⟩ (2) *archaic* **:** the reverse of virtue **:** WICKEDNESS **b** *archaic* **:** the reverse of a good act **:** a wicked deed **2 a** *archaic* **:** CALAMITY, DISASTER **b :** MISFORTUNE, DISTRESS ⟨a morbid fear of some future ~⟩ **c** (1) **:** AILMENT, SICKNESS ⟨measles and other ~*s* of childhood⟩ (2) **:** something that bothers or disturbs or afflicts ⟨once again society is asking the papers to remedy a social ~ by suppressing the facts —Herbert Brucker⟩ **:** DIFFICULTY, TROUBLE, DISORDER ⟨political and economic ~*s*⟩ **3 :** something (as an opinion, a remark) that reflects unfavorable estimation or casts aspersion or blame ⟨spoke no ~ of them⟩ **syn** see EVIL

ill *abbr* **1** illuminated; illumination **2** illustrated; illustration; illustrator **3** [L *illustrissimus*] most illustrious

-il·la \'ilə\ *n suffix, pl* **-illae** *or* **-illas** [NL, alter. of L *-ella*] **:** -ELLA ⟨*Spongilla*⟩

illaborate *adj* [L *illaboratus,* fr. *in-* ¹in- + *laboratus,* past part. of *laborare* to labor — more at LABOR] *obs* **:** carelessly done **:** ROUGH

ill-advised \¦=¦==\ *adj* **:** not well counseled **:** IMPRUDENT, RASH: **a :** acting without wise and sufficient counsel or deliberation ⟨would be *ill-advised* to accept the offer⟩ **b :** following upon or resulting from or showing a lack of wise and sufficient counsel or deliberation ⟨*ill-advised* efforts⟩ ⟨tactics that were *ill-advised*⟩ ⟨*ill-advised* laws⟩ — **ill-advisedly** \¦=¦===\ *adv*

il·lae·nus \ə'lēnəs\ *n, cap* [NL, fr. Gk *illaenein* to squint] **:** a genus of Ordovician and Silurian trilobites

ill-affected \¦=¦==\ *adj* **1** *archaic* **:** not well disposed **:** alienated in disposition **2** *obs* **:** not healthy **:** AILING, DISEASED

il·la·nun \ēl'yü(,)nün\ *n, pl* **illanun** *or* **illanuns** *usu cap* [Maranao *Ilanun,* fr. *i-* from + *lanaw* lake + *-n* suffix denoting a people or language] **1 :** the Maranao people of northern Borneo and of the southwest coastal area of the island of Mindanao in the Philippines **2 :** a member of the Illanun people

¹il·lapse \ə'laps\ *n* -S [L *illapsus* infusion, influx, fr. *illapsus,* past part. of *illabi* to fall into, flow into, fr. *in-* ²in- + *labi* to fall, slide — more at SLEEP] **:** INFLUX, ACCESSION ⟨the ~ of the Spirit at Pentecost —B.J.Kidd⟩

²illapse \"\ *vi* -ED/-ING/-S [L *illapsus,* past part.] *archaic* **:** FLOW, GLIDE, SLIP

il·laq·ue·ate \ə'lakwē,āt\ *vt* -ED/-ING/-S [L *illaqueatus,* past part. of *illaqueare* to trick, enmesh, ensnare, fr. *in-* ²in- + *laqueare* to ensnare, fr. *laqueus* noose, snare — more at DELIGHT] *archaic* **:** SNARE

ill at ease *adj* **:** not feeling easy **:** UNCOMFORTABLE, ANXIOUS ⟨back of all our lives is the somber setting of a world *ill at ease* and beset by perils —Agnes Repplier⟩ ⟨and wandered around rather *ill at ease* among swirls and eddies of people I didn't know —Scott Fitzgerald⟩

il·la·tion \ə'lāshən\ *n* -S [LL *illation-, illatio,* fr. L, action of bringing in, fr. *illatus* (suppletive past part. of *inferre* to bring in, infer, fr. *in-* ²in- + *latus,* suppletive past part. of *ferre* to carry) + *-ion-, -io* -ion — more at TOLERATE, BEAR] **1 :** the action of inferring **:** INFERENCE **2 :** something inferred

¹il·la·tive \'iləd·iv, ə'lād·iv\ *n* -S [LL *illativum* conclusion, fr. neut. of *illativus*] **1 a :** a word (as *therefore*) or phrase (as *as a consequence*) expressing the formation of or introducing an inference **b :** ILLATION 2 **2** [L *illatus* + E *-ive*] **a :** a grammatical case used in some languages (as Hungarian) that expresses a relationship of motion into or direction toward **b :** a word having the inflection of this case

²illative \"\ *adj* [LL *illativus,* fr. L *illatus* + *-ivus* -ive] **1 a :** expressing the formation of or introducing an inference ⟨an ~ conjunction⟩ **b :** having the nature of, dependent on the use of, or arrived at by inference ⟨an ~ conclusion⟩ ⟨~ reasoning⟩ ⟨the ~ relation between what is asserted in two or more propositions —M.R.Cohen⟩ **c :** of or relating to inference **:** marked by the use of or by ability in drawing an inference ⟨the ~ faculty of the human mind⟩ **2** [L *illatus* + E *-ive*] **:** of, relating to, or having the nature of an illative ⟨an ~ case ending⟩ — **il·la·tive·ly** \-d·əvlē\ *adv*

il·laudable \(')i(l), ə+\ *adj* [L *illaudabilis,* fr. *in-* ¹in- + *laudabilis* laudable — more at LAUDABLE] **:** deserving no praise or commendation ⟨an ~ way of acting⟩ — **il·laudably** \"+\ *adv*

il·la·war·ra ash \¦ilə¦wärə-\ *n, usu cap I* [fr. *Illawarra* district, New South Wales, Australia] **:** an Australian timber tree (*Elaeocarpus cyaneus*) with racemose flowers and blue globular fruit

illawarra mountain pine *n, usu cap I* **:** an Australian cypress pine (*Callitris cupressiformis*)

ill-being \¦=¦==\ *n* **:** the condition of being unprosperous or otherwise below a desirable standard of living — opposed to *well-being*

ill blood *n* **:** BAD BLOOD

ill-boding \¦=¦==\ *adj* **:** boding evil **:** INAUSPICIOUS

ill-bred \¦=¦=\ *adj* **1 :** showing (as by rudeness, boorishness) the results of poor upbringing **:** lacking good manners **:** IMPOLITE, UNCIVIL, RUDE, LOUTISH ⟨*ill-bred* remarks⟩ ⟨*ill-bred* behavior⟩ **2 :** inferior (as in physical characteristics) by reason of being the offspring of mismatched parents ⟨an *ill-bred* animal⟩

ill-come \'il(,)kəm\ *adj* **:** UNWELCOME ⟨wondered what this *ill-come* visitor might be seeking —Rafael Sabatini⟩

ill-conditioned \¦=¦==\ *adj* **:** having a bad temper or mean disposition **:** SURLY, IRRITABLE ⟨three hours after shaving he developed a dark smear about the lips which made him look . . . treacherous and *ill-conditioned* —John Wain⟩ ⟨some *ill-conditioned,* growling fellow —Charles Dickens⟩

ill-contrived \¦=¦=\ *adj, chiefly Scot* **:** ILL-CONDITIONED

ill convenience *n, archaic* **:** INCONVENIENCE

ill convenient *adj, archaic* **:** INCONVENIENT

ill-deed·ie \'=¦dēdi\ *adj* [ME *ille-dedy,* fr. *ille ded* ill deed + *-y*] *Scot* **:** given to evil deeds or to making trouble

ill-disposed \¦=¦=\ *adj* **:** not well disposed **:** UNSYMPATHETIC **:** alienated in disposition

ill-doer \¦=¦==\ *n* **:** one that does evil

ill-doing \¦=¦==\ *n* **:** the action of perpetrating evil **:** the action of doing or furthering wrong

ill ease *n* **:** UNEASINESS

il·lec·e·bra·ce·ae \ə,lesə'brāsē,ē\ [NL, fr. *Illecebrum,* type genus (fr. L *illecebra* attraction, fr. *illicere* to entice, fr. *in-* ²in- + *-licere,* fr. *lacere* to entice) + *-aceae* — more at DELIGHT] *syn of* CORRIGIOLACEAE

il·legal \(')i(l), ə+\ *adj* [F or ML; F *illégal,* fr. ML *illegalis,* fr. L *in-* ¹in- + *legalis* legal — more at LEGAL] **:** contrary to or violating a law or rule or regulation or something else (as an established custom) having the force of law **:** UNLAWFUL, ILLICIT ⟨the ~ use of taxpayers' money⟩ ⟨~ trade restrictions⟩ ⟨an ~ trial⟩ ⟨an ~ pitching technique in baseball⟩ ⟨an ~ chess move⟩ — compare NONLEGAL — **il·legally** \"+\ *adv*

illegal abortion *n* **:** abortion artificially induced for reasons other than medical

il·legality \¦i(l)+\ *n* [F or ML; F *illégalité,* fr. ML *illegalitat-, illegalitas,* fr. *illegalis* + L *-itat-, -itas* -ity] **1 :** the quality or state of being illegal ⟨the ~ of the contract was evident⟩ **2 :** an illegal action or procedure ⟨the right to resist ~⟩

il·legalization \(¦)i(l), ə+\ *n* **:** the action of illegalizing ⟨~ of gambling, drinking, and prostitution did not destroy the demand —H.D.Lasswell⟩

il·legalize \(')i(l), ə+\ *vt, see -ize in Explan Notes* **:** to make or declare illegal ⟨~*s* excessive or discriminatory initiation fees —*Newsweek*⟩

il·legibility \(¦)i(l), ə+\ *n* **:** the quality or state of being illegible

il·legible \(')i(l), ə+\ *adj* [¹in- + *legible*] **1 :** incapable of being read or deciphered **:** not legible ⟨injured his right hand in football, making his handwriting almost ~ —E.S.Bates⟩ ⟨no way of knowing by his ~ face whether he told the truth or not —Jean Stafford⟩ **2 :** not readable because of language or content ⟨a mediaeval jargon that is now but little less ~ than Coptic —J.B.Cabell⟩ — **il·legibly** \"+\ *adv*

il·legitimacy \¦i(l)+\ *n* **1 :** the quality or state of being illegitimate **2 :** BASTARDY 2

¹il·legitimate \"+\ *adj* [¹in- + *legitimate*] **1 a :** not recognized by law as lawful offspring **:** BASTARD; *usu* **:** born of parents not married to each other **b :** conceived in fornication or adultery **2 :** not rightly deduced or inferred **:** ILLOGICAL ⟨an ~ inference⟩ ⟨an ~ supposition⟩ **3 :** departing in some way from the regular or expected **:** IRREGULAR, ERRATIC ⟨~ unions between broken chromosomes —*Encyc. Britannica*⟩ ⟨~ pollination⟩ **4 a :** contrary to or violating a law or regulation **:** ILLEGAL **:** not sanctioned by law **:** UNWARRANTED ⟨an ~ seizure of power⟩ ⟨an ~ government⟩ **b :** not authorized by good usage **:** not widely accepted **:** not reputable ⟨an ~ phrase⟩ **c** *of a taxon* **:** published either validly or invalidly but not according with the rules of the relevant international code — **il·legitimately** \"+\ *adv*

²il·legitimate \"+\ *vt* **:** to make or declare or prove to be illegitimate **:** BASTARDIZE ⟨testimony that would certainly ~ her older son⟩

³illegitimate *like* ¹ILLEGITIMATE\ *n* -S **:** a person that is in some way illegitimate or that is regarded as illegitimate; *esp* **:** BASTARD

il·legitimation \¦i(l)+\ *n* **1 :** the action of illegitimating **2** *obs* **:** the state of being illegitimate **:** ILLEGITIMACY

il·legitimatize \"+\ *vt* **:** ILLEGITIMATE

il·le·ism \'ilē,izəm\ *n* -S [L *ille* he, that one, that + E *-ism* — more at LARIAT] **:** excessive use of the pronoun *he* esp. in reference to oneself

il·le·ist \-,əst\ *n* -S [L *ille* + E *-ist*] **:** one who makes excessive use of the pronoun *he* esp. in reference to himself

iller *comparative of* ILL

illest *superlative of* ILL

ill fame *n* [ME] **:** bad repute; *esp* **:** reputation for immorality or vice ⟨a house of *ill fame*⟩ — **ill-famed** \¦=¦=\ *adj*

illfare \¦=,=\ *n* **:** the condition of faring badly or of not being well off ⟨no regard for the ~ of the workers —W.J.H.Sprott⟩ — opposed to *welfare*

ill-fared \¦=¦=\ *adj* **:** that has fared badly **:** UNSUCCESSFUL, INAUSPICIOUS ⟨it is surely going too far to assume that the *ill-fared* arrangement was wholeheartedly supported —G.A. Craig⟩

ill-faring \¦=¦==\ *adj* **:** faring badly

ill-fated \¦=¦==\ *adj* **1 :** having or destined to an evil fate **:** UNFORTUNATE, HAPLESS ⟨an *ill-fated* army⟩ ⟨an *ill-fated* ship⟩ ⟨started out on the *ill-fated* expedition⟩ **2 :** that causes or marks the beginning of misfortune or bad luck ⟨an *ill-fated* suggestion⟩ ⟨met them in an *ill-fated* hour⟩ **syn** see UNLUCKY

ill-favored \¦=¦==\ *adj* **1 :** unattractive or disagreeable in physical appearance **:** unpleasant to look at ⟨an *ill-favored* old man⟩ ⟨her *ill-favored* features⟩; *esp* **:** having an unattractive or ugly face **2 :** that gives offense or arouses resentment **:** OBJECTIONABLE ⟨an *ill-favored* word that no one likes⟩ ⟨*ill-favored* behavior⟩ **syn** see UGLY

ill-given \¦=¦==\ *adj, chiefly Scot* **:** ILL-DISPOSED

ill-gotten \¦=¦==\ *also* **ill-got** \¦=¦=\ *adj* **:** obtained dishonestly or otherwise unlawfully or unjustly ⟨*ill-gotten* wealth⟩ ⟨*ill-gotten* gains⟩

illguide \¦=¦=\ *vt, Scot* **:** to treat or handle badly **:** MISMANAGE

ill humor *n* **:** a disagreeable mood marked by surliness and irritability **:** CROSSNESS ⟨was in an *ill humor* and sulked⟩ — **ill-humored** \¦=¦==\ *adj* — **ill-hu·mored·ly** \¦=¦===\ *adv*

¹il·liberal \(')i(l), ə+\ *adj* [MF or L; MF, fr. L *illiberalis* unworthy of a freeman, ignoble, stingy, fr. *in-* ¹in- + *liberalis* worthy of a freeman, noble, generous — more at LIBERAL] **:** not liberal: as **a** *archaic* (1) **:** lacking a liberal education **:** UNSCHOOLED (2) **:** lacking culture and refinement **:** marked by rude manners or behavior **:** COARSE, VULGAR **b :** requiring or emphasizing physical dexterity rather than intellectual ability **:** not belonging to or having the qualities of the liberal arts ⟨trades and other ~ occupations⟩ ⟨an ~ education⟩ **c** *archaic* **:** not generous **:** STINGY **d** (1) **:** not broad-minded **:** having a constricted narrow viewpoint or outlook so as often to be small-minded or pettily prejudiced or bigoted **:** INTOLERANT ⟨the ~ or fanatically intolerant spirit which war psychology always engenders —M.R.Cohen⟩ ⟨~ thinking⟩ (2) **:** opposed to liberalism ⟨~ tendencies⟩ — **il·liberally** \"+\ *adv*

²illiberal \"+\ *n* **:** one that is illiberal; *esp* **:** one that is opposed to liberalism

il·liberalism \"+\ *n* **:** opposition to liberalism

il·liberality \(¦)i(l), ə+\ *n* [MF or L; MF *illiberalité,* fr. L *illiberalitat-, illiberalitas* conduct unworthy of a freeman, ignobility, stinginess, fr. *illiberalis* + *-itat-, -itas* -ity] **:** the quality or state of being illiberal

il·liberalize \(')i(l), ə+\ *vt* **:** to make illiberal

il·licit \(')i(l), ə+\ *adj* [L *illicitus,* fr. *in-* ¹in- + *licitus* lawful — more at LICIT] **:** not permitted **:** not allowed **:** UNLAWFUL ⟨~ trade⟩ — **il·lic·it·ly** \"+\ *adv*

illicit process *n* **:** a fallacy of distribution in which a term is distributed in a conclusion that has not been distributed in the premises

il·lici·um \ə'lis(h)ēəm, -likē-\ *n* [NL, fr. L, allurement] **1** *cap* **:** a small genus of evergreen trees (family Magnoliaceae) with aromatic persistent leaves and nodding yellow or purplish flowers — see CHINESE ANISE, STAR ANISE **2** *pl* **il·licia** \-ēə\ *or* **illiciums :** the first spine of the dorsal fin of a pediculate fish migrated to the upper lip and transformed into a complex tentacle that serves as a lure to attract other fish within range of the capacious jaws

illighten *vt* [by alter. (influence of ²*in-*)] *obs* **:** ENLIGHTEN

il·limitability \(¦)i(l), ə+\ *n* **:** the quality or state of being illimitable

¹il·limitable \(')i(l), ə+\ *adj* [¹*in-* + *limitable*] **:** incapable of being limited or bounded **:** MEASURELESS ⟨the ~ reaches of space and time⟩ — **il·limitableness** \"+\ *n* — **il·limitably** \"+\ *adv*

²illimitable \"\ *n* -S **:** something illimitable ⟨the ~*s* that are the past and the future⟩

illimitate *adj* [LL *illimitatus,* fr. L *in-* ¹in- + *limitatus,* past part. of *limitare* to limit — more at LIMIT] *obs* **:** UNLIMITED

il·limitation \(¦)i(l), ə+\ *n* [¹*in-* + *limitation*] **:** the quality or state of being unlimited **:** freedom from limitation

il·limited \(')i(l), ə+\ *adj* [¹*in-* + *limited*] *archaic* **:** free from limitation or restraint **:** UNBOUNDED ⟨in a fullhearted evensong of joy ~ —Thomas Hardy⟩ — **il·limitedly** \"+\ *adv, archaic* — **il·limitedness** \"+\ *n, archaic*

il·lin·i·um \ə'linēəm\ *n* -S [NL, fr. *Illinois* + NL *-ium*] **:** chemical element 61 — a name now superseded by *promethium*

il·li·noi·an \¦ilə¦nȯi(y)ən\ *adj, usu cap* [*Illinois* (state) + E *-an*] **:** belonging to the third glacial stage during the glacial epoch in No. America

¹il·li·nois \¦ilə¦nȯi *sometimes* ¦el- *or esp in southern Illinois & in the southern US* -ȯiz\ *n, pl* **illinois** \-ȯi(z)\ *usu cap* [F, of Algonquian origin; akin to Miami *alänia* man, Shawnee *hilenawe*] **1 a :** a confederacy of Indian peoples of Illinois and Iowa and Wisconsin **b :** a member of such peoples **2 :** an Algonquian language of the Illinois and Miami peoples

²illinois \"\ *adj, usu cap* [*Illinois,* state in the north central U.S., fr. ¹*illinois*] **:** of or from the state of Illinois **:** of the kind or style prevalent in Illinois **:** ILLINOISAN

¹il·li·nois·an \¦==¦nȯi(y)ən, -ȯizⁿn\ *also* **il·li·nois·ian** \-ȯizhən, -zēən\ *or* **il·li·noi·an** \-ȯi(y)ən\ *adj, usu cap* [*Illinois* + E *-an, -ian*] **1 :** of, relating to, or characteristic of the state of Illinois **2 :** of, relating to, or characteristic of the people of Illinois

²illinoisan \"\ *also* **illinoisian** \"\ *or* **illinoian** \"\ *n* -S *cap* **:** a native or resident of Illinois

illinois gooseberry *n, usu cap I* **:** MISSOURI GOOSEBERRY

illinois nut *n, usu cap I* **:** PECAN

¹il·li·pe \'ilə(,)pē\ [NL, fr. Malayalam *ilippa* — more at ILLUPI] *syn of* MADHUCA

²illipe *or* **illipi** *var of* ILLUPI

illipe butter *n* **:** any of various vegetable fats: as **a :** MOWRAH BUTTER **b** *or* **illipe tallow :** BORNEO TALLOW — used esp. in the chocolate industry

il·liquid \(')i(l), ə+\ *adj* [¹*in-* + *liquid*] **1 :** not being cash or readily convertible into cash ⟨~ holdings⟩ **2 :** deficient in liquid assets ⟨an ~ bank⟩ — **il·liquidity** \¦i(l)+\ *n*

il·lite \'i,līt\ *n* -S [*Illinois* (state) + E *-ite*] **1 :** a group of minerals found in clays and having essentially the crystal structure of muscovite **2 :** one of the minerals of the illite group; *esp* **:** the mineral having the composition of muscovite or of a hydrated muscovite but giving a line-poor X-ray powder pattern — **il·lit·ic** \(')i¦lid·ik, -līd-\ *adj*

il·literacy \(')i(l), ə+\ *n* **1 :** the quality or state of being illiterate; *esp* **:** inability to read or write **2 :** a mistake or crudity (as in reading, writing, or speaking) made by or typical of one who is illiterate

¹il·literate \"+\ *adj* [L *illiteratus,* fr. *in-* ¹in- + *litteratus* lettered, learned — more at LITERATE] **1 :** having little or no education **:** UNLETTERED, IGNORANT; *esp* **:** unable to read or write ⟨a largely ~ population⟩ **2 a :** showing or marked by a lack of familiarity with language and literature **:** deficient in literary background **:** UNCULTURED ⟨an ~ speaker⟩ ⟨an ~ magazine⟩ ⟨an ~ style of writing⟩ **b :** violating generally accepted usage patterns of speaking or writing in such a way as to indicate ignorance or lack of culture ⟨~ words and phrases⟩ ⟨~ pronunciations⟩ **3 :** showing or marked by a lack of acquaintance with the fundamentals or background of a particular field of knowledge ⟨musically ~⟩ ⟨politically ~⟩ **syn** see IGNORANT

²illiterate \"+\ *n* **:** an illiterate person; *esp* **:** a person unable to read or write

il·literately \"+\ *adv* **:** in an illiterate manner

il·literateness \"+\ *n* -ES **:** ILLITERACY

ill-judged \¦=¦=\ *adj* **:** UNWISE, INJUDICIOUS ⟨ponderous and *ill-judged* irony —E.M.Forster⟩

ill-judging \¦=¦==\ *adj* **1** *archaic* **:** judging faultily or uncritically **2** *archaic* **:** judging hostilely or malevolently

ill-kempt \¦=¦kem(p)t\ *adj* [²*ill* + *-kempt* (as in *unkempt*)] **:** UNKEMPT ⟨untidy and *ill-kempt,* he looked perfectly at home —W.S.Maugham⟩

ill-looked \¦=¦lu̇kt\ *adj, archaic* **:** not pleasant in appearance

ill-looking \¦=¦==\ *adj* **:** not pleasant in appearance

ill-mannered \¦=¦==\ *adj* **:** marked by bad manners **:** UNCIVIL ⟨an *ill-mannered* guest⟩ **syn** see RUDE

illmo *abbr* [It *illustrissimo*] most illustrious

ill-natured \¦=¦==\ *adj* **1 :** having or showing a malevolent or spiteful disposition ⟨*ill-natured* people say . . . that his hair . . . is a wig —W.M.Thackeray⟩ **2 :** having or showing a bad temper or peevish disposition **:** CROSS, SURLY ⟨is pretty *ill-natured* until he's had his coffee⟩ — **ill-natured·ly** \"lē, -li\ *adv*

ill·ness \'ilnəs\ *n* -ES **1** *obs* **a** : WICKEDNESS, DEPRAVITY **b** : DISAGREEABLENESS, UNPLEASANTNESS **2** : an unhealthy condition of the body or mind : MALADY ⟨a severe ~⟩
il·local \(')i(l), ə+\ *adj* [LL *illocalis*, fr. L *in-* ¹in- + LL *localis* local — more at LOCAL] : not confined to a particular place ⟨the spirit that God is ~⟩ — **il·locality** \¦i(l)+\ *n*
ill off *adv* (*or adj*) : BADLY OFF ⟨were not so *ill off* by the modest standards of that day —G.M.Trevelyan⟩
il·logic \(')i(l), ə+\ *n* [¹*in-* + *logic*] : the quality or state of being illogical : lack of logic ⟨an argument that was full of ~⟩
il·logical \"+\ *adj* [¹*in-* + *logical*] **1** : not observing the principles of logic : reasoning unsoundly through ignorance or negligence of logic ⟨the speaker seemed most ~ as he developed his argument⟩ **2** : contrary to or devoid of logic ⟨this policy was extremely ~ —Aidan Mulloy⟩ ⟨~ resentment against a group of his friends —W. F. de Morgan⟩ — **il·logically** \"+\ *adv* — **il·logicalness** \"+\ *n*
il·logicality \(')i(l), ə+\ *n* **1** : ILLOGIC ⟨the scientist rebels against the ~ of such reasoning —J.M.Grant⟩ **2** : an instance of illogic : a piece of illogic ⟨the book is full of *illogicalities*⟩
ill–omened \'=¦==\ *adj* : having or marked by bad omens : INAUSPICIOUS, UNLUCKY ⟨it was to be an *ill-omened* day for them⟩
il·loricate *or* **il·loricated** \(')i(l), ə+\ *adj* [¹*in-* + *loricate*, *loricated*] : having no lorica ⟨~ rotifers⟩
ills *pl of* ILL
ill–seen \'=¦=\ *adj, archaic* : not well regarded or thought of
ill–set \'=¦=\ *adj* **1** : not well set : poorly set or placed **2** *chiefly Scot* : SPITEFUL
ill–sorted \'=¦==\ *adj* **1** : not well matched : badly suited ⟨an *ill-sorted* couple⟩ **2** *Scot* : DISPLEASED
ill–starred \'=¦=\ *adj* : ILL-FATED ⟨an *ill-starred* romance⟩ ⟨the holiday was *ill-starred* from the outset —Bennett Cerf⟩ **syn** see UNLUCKY
ill–tempered \'=¦==\ *adj* : having a bad temper : SURLY, IRRITABLE ⟨*ill-tempered* and tyrannical to his sister —Catherine M. Brown⟩ — **ill–temperedly** *adv* — **ill–temperedness** *n* -ES
illth \'ilth *also* -ltth\ *n* -S [¹*ill* + *-th* (as in *wealth*)] **1** : the condition of being economically unprosperous or miserable ⟨the glaring disparity between the state's natural wealth and its human ~ —*Christian Century*⟩ **2** : something that produces or is symptomatic of illth ⟨much of the goods on our shelves is wealth rather than ~ —*Nation*⟩
ill–treat \'=¦=\ *vt* : to treat cruelly or improperly : MALTREAT ⟨they do not *ill-treat* the butlers —C.G.Harper⟩ — **ill–treatment** \'=¦==\ *n*
il·lu·ci·date \ə'lüsə,dāt *also* əl'yü-\ *vt* -ED/-ING/-S [²*in-* + L *lucidus* clear + E *-ate* — more at LUCID] *archaic* : ELUCIDATE
il·lude \ə'lüd *also* əl'yüd\ *vt* -ED/-ING/-S [ME *illuden*, fr. MF or ML; MF *illuder*, fr. ML *illudere*, fr. L, to mock or jeer at — more at ILLUSION] **1 a** : DELUDE, DECEIVE ⟨in order to ~ him regarding the paternity of the child —R.F.Hawkins⟩ **b** : to subject to an illusion ⟨at the cinema I am . . . completely *illuded* —J.E.Agate⟩ **2** [L *illudere*] *obs* : MOCK, DERIDE **3** *archaic* : to escape from : ELUDE ⟨glad to ~ the burdens of the day —George Crabbe †1832⟩
il·luk \'ilək, -,lük\ *or* **illuk grass** *n* -S [prob. native name in Malaya] : COGON
il·lume \ə'lüm *also* əl'yüm\ *vt* -ED/-ING/-S [short for *illumine*] **1** *archaic* **a** : to make bright with or as if with light : light up ⟨the beams yet filter through, *illuming* the wide spaces beneath —W.H.Hudson †1922⟩ **b** : ENLIGHTEN ⟨calculated . . . to ~ the minds of all classes of mankind —George Borrow⟩ **2** *obs* : IGNITE, KINDLE
il·lu·mi·na·bil·i·ty \=,===ˈbiləd·ē, -ətē, -i\ *n* : the capability of being illuminated
il·lu·mi·na·ble \-mənəbəl\ *adj* [LL *illuminabilis*, fr. L *illuminare* to illuminate + *-abilis* -able — more at ILLUMINATE] : capable of being illuminated
il·lu·mi·na·graph·ic \=¦===¦grafik\ *adj* [*illumination* + *-graphic*] *of a camera* : designed for photographing the image formed by a convex mirror for recording the sources and intensities of light affecting a specific area
il·lu·mi·nance \='==nən(t)s\ *n* -S [*illuminate* + *-ance*] : ILLUMINATION 2
¹il·lu·mi·nant \-nənt\ *n* -S [L *illuminant-*, *illuminans*, pres. part. of *illuminare*] : something that illuminates; *esp* : something (as gas, petroleum, an electric lamp) that gives physical light
²illuminant \"\ *adj* [L *illuminant-*, *illuminans*] : that illuminates : ILLUMINATING, ENLIGHTENING
¹il·lu·mi·nate \-nət, *usu* -nəd·+V\ *adj* [ME, fr. L *illuminatus*, past part.] **1** *archaic* : made bright with light ⟨leaves ~ with autumnal hues —H.W.Longfellow⟩ **2** *archaic* : being or claiming to be intellectually or culturally or spiritually enlightened to a superior extent
²il·lu·mi·nate \ə'lümə,nāt *also* əl'yü-; *usu* -ād·+V\ *vt* [L *illuminatus*, past part. of *illuminare*, fr. *in-* ²in + *luminare* to light up, fr. L *lumin-*, *lumen* light — more at LUMINARY] **1 a** (1) : to give physical light to : supply with light : light up ⟨*illuminated* a picture that hung on the wall —G.B.Shaw⟩ : make bright with light : bathe in light ⟨destroyers ~ the little boats with their searchlights —H.W.Baldwin⟩ (2) : to light up artificially with usu. brilliant lights or decorative lighting effects ⟨the city was *illuminated* in celebration of the victory⟩ ⟨the fountains are beautifully *illuminated* at night⟩ (3) : to make luminous or shining ⟨the beautiful smile that slowly ~*s* her face —Vernon Jarratt⟩ **b** : to give spiritual or intellectual light to : enlighten spiritually or intellectually ⟨bought a couple of books for the train to Edinburgh, but I can't say I was greatly *illuminated* —H.J.Laski⟩ **c** *archaic* : to set alight : KINDLE ⟨the butler . . . *illuminated* the antique Gothic chandelier —W.M.Thackeray⟩ **2** : to make clear : clear up : remove obscurity from : ELUCIDATE ⟨worked out and *illuminated* broad principles of constitutional interpretation —W.P.M.Kennedy⟩ ⟨historical insight clarifies and *illuminates* the critical activity of a period —C.I.Glicksberg⟩ **3** : to make illustrious or glorious ⟨brilliant achievements that ~ that era⟩ : make resplendent ⟨splendid tapestries and paintings *illuminated* the walls⟩ **4** : to decorate (as a letter or part of a page) with gold or silver or brilliant colors or with often elaborate designs or miniature pictures ⟨beautiful *illuminated* manuscripts of the middle ages⟩
³il·lu·mi·nate \-,nət, *usu* -nəd·+V\ *n* -S [NL *illuminati*, pl.] *archaic* : a person possessing or claiming to possess unusual enlightenment
il·lu·mi·na·ti \=,=='näd·(,)ē, -'nä, ¦(,)t¦, ¦i *also* -'nā,tī\ *n pl* [It & NL; It, fr. NL, fr. L, masc. pl. of *illuminatus*, past part. of *illuminare*] **1** *usu cap* **a** : ALUMBRADOS **b** : members of an 18th century German secret society professing deistic and republican principles **2** : persons who are or who claim to be unusually enlightened ⟨make the enjoyment of poetry primarily an affair of the ~ —J.L.Lowes⟩
illuminating *adj* : that illuminates; *esp* : highly informative ⟨an ~ lecture⟩ ⟨an ~ remark⟩ ⟨an ~ illustration⟩ — **il·lu·mi·nat·ing·ly** *adv*
illuminating engineer *n* : an engineer specializing in illuminating engineering
illuminating engineering *n* : a branch of engineering that deals with planning the lighting systems of new buildings and outdoor areas (as streets, parking lots) and the study and correction of old lighting installations
illuminating gas *n* : a gas (as coal gas or carbureted water gas) used for lighting
illuminating projectile *n* : a projectile that bursts by the action of a time fuze so as to eject a pyrotechnic element that is usu. held suspended by a parachute after ejection and that lights up terrain — compare STAR SHELL
il·lu·mi·na·tion \ə,lümə'nāshən *also* əl,yü-\ *n* -S [ME *illuminacioun*, fr. MF & LL; MF *illumination*, fr. LL *illumination-*, *illuminatio*, fr. L *illuminatus* (past part. of *illuminare* to illuminate) + *-ion-*, *-io* -ion — more at ILLUMINATE] **1** : the action of illuminating or condition of being illuminated: as **a** : spiritual or cultural or intellectual enlightenment ⟨claimed she had received divine ~⟩ ⟨found great ~ in the lecture⟩ **b** (1) : a giving of physical light or the state of being lighted up ⟨the brilliant ~ of the room⟩ (2) : decorative lighting or lighting effects ⟨~ of the city in celebration of the victory⟩ **c** : decoration (as of an initial letter, a text) by the art of illuminating ⟨was much interested in the ~ of manuscripts⟩ **2** : the luminous flux per unit area on an intercepting surface at any given point — called also *illuminance* **3** : one of the decorative features used in the art of illuminating or in decorative lighting ⟨marveled at the intricate designs and other ~*s* of the manuscript⟩ ⟨the city was resplendent in its many ~*s*⟩
il·lu·mi·na·tism \=¦==,nə,tizəm\ *n* -S [NL *illuminati* + E *-ism*] : ILLUMINISM
il·lu·mi·na·tist \=¦==¦näd·əst, -¦nä¦, ¦tə- *also* -¦nā¦: ='==,nətə-\ *n* -S [NL *illuminati* + E *-ist*] : ILLUMINIST
il·lu·mi·na·tive \='==,nād·¦iv, -,nə¦, ¦t¦, ¦ēv *also* ¦əv\ *adj* : of, relating to, or producing illumination ⟨had arrived at what is called the ~ stage of mysticism⟩ : ILLUMINATING ⟨had an ~ talk with the scientist⟩
il·lu·mi·na·to \=,=='näd·(,)ō, -'nä¦, ¦(,)tō\ *sing of* ILLUMINATI
il·lu·mi·na·tor \='==,nād·ə(r), -ātə- *also* =,=='nā,tō(ə)r *or* -ō(ə)\ *n* -S [LL, fr. L *illuminatus* (past part. of *illuminare* to illuminate) + *-or*] : one that illuminates: as **a** : one that enlightens intellectually or culturally or spiritually **b** : a device that gives physical light or that is used to direct light to a specific area or that is used to concentrate or reflect light **c** : one that practices the art of illuminating esp. manuscripts
il·lu·mine \='=mən\ *vt* -ED/-ING/-S [ME *illuminen*, fr. MF or L; MF *illuminer*, fr. L *illuminare* — more at ILLUMINATE] : ILLUMINATE
il·lu·min·er \-mənə(r)\ *n* -S [alter. of ME *illuminour*, fr. *illuminen* + *-our* -or] : ILLUMINATOR
il·lu·mi·nism \-mə,nizəm\ *n* -S [NL *illuminati* + E *-ism*] **1** : belief in or claim to a personal intellectual or cultural or spiritual superiority not accessible to mankind in general **2** *usu cap* : beliefs or claims viewed as forming the doctrine or principles of the Illuminati
il·lu·mi·nist \-,nəst\ *n* -S *often attrib* [NL *illuminati* + E *-ist*] **1** : one that professes illuminism **2** *usu cap* : one of the Illuminati
il·lu·mi·nom·e·ter \=,=='nämәd·ə(r)\ *n* [*illumination* + *-o-* + *-meter*] : a photometer for measuring illumination usu. by the brightness of an illuminated surface
il·lu·pi \'ilə,pī, -(,)pē\ *also* **il·li·pe** \-(,)pē\ *or* **il·li·pi** *or* **il·lu·pie** \-,pī, -(,)pē\ *n* -S [Tamil *iluppai* & Malayalam *ilippa*] : an important East Indian tree (*Madhuca malabrorum*) whose leaves and juice and bark are used medicinally and whose nuts yield oil and whose very sweet flowers are eaten dried or cooked with other foods — compare MAHUA
illus *abbr* illustrated; illustration; illustrator
ill–usage \'='==\ *n* : harsh, unkind, or abusive treatment : MALTREATMENT ⟨my wits sharpened by hunger and *ill-usage* —W.J.Locke⟩
ill–use \'=¦=\ *vt* : MALTREAT, ABUSE ⟨those who he thought had stolen his ideas or otherwise *ill-used* him —*William & Mary Quarterly*⟩
il·lu·sion \ə'lüzhən *also* əl'yü-\ *n* -S [ME *illusioun*, fr. MF *illusion*, fr. LL *illusion-*, *illusio*, fr. L, action of mocking, jeering, fr. *illusus* (past part. of *illudere* to mock or jeer at, fr. *in-* ²in- + *ludere* to play, mock, jeer) + *-ion-*, *-io* -ion — more at LUDICROUS] **1 a** *obs* : the action of deceiving or attempting to deceive **b** (1) : the state or fact of being intellectually deceived or deluded or misled by others or by oneself either intentionally or unintentionally in such a way as to have false impressions or ideas marked by the attribution of more to something or less to something than is actually the case : MISAPPREHENSION, MISCONCEPTION, DELUSION, FANCY ⟨the happy ~*s* of youth⟩ (2) : an instance of such deception or delusion ⟨a dreamy life that was filled with one ~ after another⟩ **2 a** (1) : a misleading image presented to the vision : false show; *specif* : APPARITION ⟨these were all an ~ and a phantasma, a thing that appeared, but did not really exist —F.W.Robertson⟩ (2) : something that deceives or deludes or misleads intellectually in such a way as to produce false impressions or ideas that exaggerate or minimize reality or that attribute existence to what does not exist or nonexistence to what does exist ⟨most modern great men are mere ~*s* sprung out of a national hunger for greatness —Sherwood Anderson⟩ **b** (1) : perception of something objectively existing in such a way as to cause or permit misinterpretation of its actual nature either because of the ambiguous qualities of the thing perceived or because of the personal characteristics of the one perceiving or because of both factors ⟨heat rays shimmering on the road produced the ~ of pools of water⟩ ⟨the horizontal lines cause an optical ~, making the object appear in a different position from what it really is in —Richard Jefferies⟩ (2) : HALLUCINATION 1a (3) : a pattern capable of reversible perspective **3** : a fine plain transparent bobbinet or tulle usu. of silk and used for veils, trimmings, dresses

optical illusions: figure *A*: *a* is actually equal to *b*; figure *B*: either side *a* or side *b* may appear nearer the observer; figure *C*: *o* may be regarded as either the near or the far corner of the block

il·lu·sion·al \-zhən³l, -zhnəl\ *adj* : ILLUSIONARY
il·lu·sion·ary \-zhə,nerē, -ri\ *adj* : of, relating to, marked by, or producing illusion ⟨~ stage effects⟩
il·lu·sioned \-zhənd\ *adj* : having illusions ⟨~ lovers⟩
il·lu·sion·ism \-zhə,nizəm\ *n* -S **1** : a theory or doctrine affirming that the phenomenal world is wholly or nearly wholly illusory **2** : the use of or propensity for the use of often extreme illusionary effects esp. in art and decoration (as in the use of a technique in painting whereby an object represented appears nearer an observer than the surface on which it is painted)
il·lu·sion·ist \-,nəst\ *n* -S *often attrib* **1** : an adherent of the theory or doctrine of illusionism **2** : one that produces illusionary effects: as **a** : a painter or sculptor or architect whose work is marked by illusionism **b** : a ventriloquist or sleight-of-hand performer or magician
il·lu·sion·is·tic \=¦=zhə¦nistik\ *adj* : of, relating to, or marked by illusionism ⟨~ devices have been abundant in sculpture —P.A.Sorokin⟩
il·lu·sion·less \='=zhənləs\ *adj* : free from illusion ⟨the cold neon light of a modern novelist's ~ imagination —*N.Y. Herald Tribune Bk. Rev.*⟩
il·lu·sive \='=s¦iv, ¦ēv *also* -z¦ *or* ¦əv\ *adj* [*illusion* + *-ive*] : ILLUSORY — **il·lu·sive·ly** \¦əvlē, ¦ēv-, -li\ *adv* — **il·lu·sive·ness** \¦ivnəs, ¦ēv- *also* ¦əv-\ *n* -ES
il·lu·so·ri·ly \ə'lüs(ə)rəlē, -üz(-, -li *also* əl'yü-\ *adv* : in an illusory manner
il·lu·so·ri·ness \-rēnəs, -rin-\ *n* -ES : the quality or state of being illusory
il·lu·so·ry \-rē, -ri\ *adj* [LL *illusorius* mocking, deceptive, fr. L *illusus* (past part. of *illudere* to mock or jeer at) + *-orius* -ory — more at ILLUSION] : of, relating to, or marked by illusion : based on or producing illusion : DECEPTIVE, UNREAL ⟨a tense period of ~ peace⟩ ⟨filled with ~ hopes⟩ **syn** see APPARENT
illusory appointment *n* : an appointment of a nominal or disproportionately small share of property to one of a class (as to one among several brothers) regarded as void in courts of equity because fraudulently defeating the intent of the original donor (as a deceased father) of the power of appointment
il·lus·trat·able \'ilə,strād·əbəl, -ātəb- *also* ə'lə,s-\ *adj* : capable of being illustrated
¹il·lus·trate \'ilə,strāt, ə'lə,s-; *usu* -ād·+V\ *vb* -ED/-ING/-S [L *illustratus*, past part. of *illustrare*, fr. *in-* ²in + *lustrare* to purify, make bright, fr. *lustrum* — more at LUSTRUM] *vt* **1** *obs* **a** : to enlighten intellectually or culturally or spiritually **b** : to give physical light to : light up **2 a** *archaic* : to make illustrious : confer honor or distinction on **b** *obs* (1) : to make luminous or bright (2) : ADORN **3 a** : to make clear : remove obscurity from : make intelligible : CLARIFY, ELUCIDATE ⟨*illustrated* the new theory by careful references to what was already known⟩ **b** (1) : to make clear by giving examples or instances ⟨used many examples to ~ his lecture on what had been accomplished⟩ (2) : to make clear by reason of being an example or instance : serve as an example or instance of ⟨a national hero who embodies and ~*s* the nation's passionate love of freedom⟩ **c** (1) : to make clear or more helpful or attractive by furnishing or combining with apt visual features (as photographs, charts, slides) or other sensory aids (as recordings of music, speech) ⟨the author has *illustrated* the book with some excellent pictures⟩ ⟨*illustrated* the lecture on the history of art with a couple of short films and some color slides⟩ ⟨discussed some aspects of jazz and *illustrated* the talk with tape recordings⟩ (2) : to make clear or more helpful or attractive by reason of being an apt visual feature or other sensory aid ⟨a wealth of photographs ~ the book⟩ **d** : to provide with visual features (as photographs) or other sensory aids (as recordings) ⟨the book is very well *illustrated*⟩ ⟨a beautifully *illustrated* magazine⟩ **4** : to show to advantage : set in a clear light : clearly exhibit : DEMONSTRATE ⟨the gaiety we too often associate with levity of character is, as the French ~ it, a necessity of mental health —W.C.Brownell⟩ ⟨honoring and *illustrating* the supreme worth of freedom —Agnes Repplier⟩ ⟨a situation that ~*s* the need for tolerance⟩ ~ *vi* : to make something clear by furnishing an example or instance ⟨the speaker hesitated and then said he would endeavor to ~⟩
²illustrate *adj* [L *illustratus*] **1** *obs* : RESPLENDENT **2** *obs* : ILLUSTRIOUS
illustrated *n* -S *chiefly Brit* : a newspaper or magazine or other periodical marked by the inclusion of much pictorial material
il·lus·tra·tion \,ilə'strāshən *sometimes* ə,lə's-\ *n* -S [ME *illustracione*, fr. MF *illustration*, fr. L *illustration-*, *illustratio*, fr. *illustratus* + *-ion-*, *-io* -ion] **1 a** : the action of illustrating or condition of being illustrated **b** *obs* (1) : intellectual or cultural or spiritual enlightenment (2) : physical illumination **c** *archaic* : the action of making or condition of being made illustrious or honored or distinguished ⟨admirably translated by himself in ~ of Shelley —T.L.Peacock⟩ **2** : something that serves to illustrate: as **a** : an example or instance that helps make something clear ⟨gave an ~ of what he meant⟩ **b** : a picture or drawing or diagram or some other sensory aid that helps make something (as a book, a lecture) clear or more helpful or attractive **syn** see INSTANCE
il·lus·tra·tion·al \¦=='strāshən³l, -shnəl *sometimes* ə¦lə¦s-\ *adj* : of, relating to, or having the character of illustration : serving to illustrate : ILLUSTRATIVE ⟨~ technique⟩ ⟨a purely ~ drawing⟩
il·lus·tra·tive \ə'ləstrəd·¦iv, ¦t¦ *sometimes* ə'lə,strā¦ *or* 'ilə,strā¦ *or* ¦ēv *or* ¦əv\ *adj* : that illustrates : serving to illustrate ⟨plenty of ~ material is to be found in the book⟩ ⟨an ~ anecdote⟩ ⟨a remark that was ~ of his attitude toward life⟩ — **il·lus·tra·tive·ly** \¦əvlē, ¦ēv-, -li\ *adv*
il·lus·tra·tor \'ilə,strād·ə(r), -ātə- *also* ə'lə,s-\ *n* -S [LL, fr. *illustratus* (past part. of *illustrare* to illustrate) + *-or* — more at ILLUSTRATE] : one that illustrates; *specif* : an artist that makes illustrations (as for books, magazines, advertising copy)
il·lus·tra·to·ry \ə'ləstrə,tōrē, -tór-, -ri\ *n* -ES : ILLUSTRATIVE
il·lus·tri·ous \ə'ləstrēəs\ *adj* [L *illustris* (prob. back-formation fr. *illustrare* to illustrate) + E *-ous* — more at ILLUSTRATE] **1** : notably or brilliantly outstanding because of dignity (as of birth, rank, position) or because of achievements or actions or because of qualities possessed : very distinguished : greatly respected : EMINENT, FAMOUS ⟨a man who comes of an ~ family⟩ ⟨the ~ heroes of antiquity⟩ ⟨~ accomplishments⟩ **2** *archaic* **a** : shining brightly with light **b** : clearly evident — **il·lus·tri·ous·ly** *adv* — **il·lus·tri·ous·ness** *n* -ES
il·lu·vial \(')i¦lüvēəl, -vyəl *also* (')il¦yü-\ *adj* [²*in-* + *-luvial* (as in *alluvial*)] : of, relating to, or marked by illuviation or illuviated materials or areas ⟨~ soil⟩
il·lu·vi·ate \i'lüvē,āt *also* il'yü-\ *vi* -ED/-ING/-S [²*in-* + *-luviate* (as in *alluviate*)] : to undergo illuviation
il·lu·vi·a·tion \(,)=,=='āshən\ *n* -S [²*in-* + *-luviation* (as in *alluviation*)] : accumulation of dissolved or suspended soil materials in one area or horizon as a result of eluviation from another
il·lu·vi·um \='=vēəm\ *n, pl* **illuviums** \-ēəmz\ *or* **illu·via** \-ēə\ [NL, fr. ²*in-* + *-luvium* (as in *alluvium*)] : material leached from one soil horizon and deposited in another — compare ALLUVIUM, COLLUVIUM
ill will *n* [ME, part trans. of ON *illvili*, fr. *illr* ill + *vili* will — more at ILL] : unfriendly feeling : ANIMOSITY, HOSTILITY ⟨a growing *ill will* between the two countries⟩ ⟨bore them no *ill will*⟩ **syn** see MALICE
ill–willer \'=¦==\ *n, archaic* : one that has an unfriendly disposition toward something specified ⟨an *ill-willer* to the human race —Thomas Hood †1845⟩
ill–will·ie \'=¦wili\ *adj* [ME (Sc dial.), fr. *ill will* + *-ie*] *chiefly Scot* : having an unfriendly disposition
ill–wish \'=¦=\ *vt* **1** *dial Eng* : to wish evil or ill to **2** *dial Brit* : to put an evil spell on : BEWITCH, HEX
il·ly \'il(l)ē, -)i\ *adv* [¹*ill* + *-ly*] : BADLY, ILL ⟨never were two beings more ~ assorted —Washington Irving⟩ ⟨his ~ concealed pride —Della Lutes⟩
¹il·lyr·i·an \ə'lirēən\ *adj, usu cap* [*Illyria*, ancient country on the eastern shore of the Adriatic sea (fr. L, fr. Gk) + E *-an*] **1 a** : of, relating to, or characteristic of ancient Illyria **b** : of, relating to, or characteristic of the Illyrians **2** : of, relating to, or characteristic of the Illyrian languages
²illyrian \"\ *n* -S *cap* **1** : a native or inhabitant of ancient Illyria **2 a** : the Indo-European languages of the Illyrians poorly attested and hence not certainly classified — see INDO-EUROPEAN LANGUAGES table **b** *obs* : SERBO-CROATIAN
il·lyr·ic \-rik\ *adj, usu cap* [L *illyricus*, fr. Gk *illyrikos*, fr. *Illyria* + Gk *-ikos* -ic] : ILLYRIAN
il·men·ite \'ilmə,nīt\ *n* -S [G *ilmenit*, fr. *Ilmen* range, Ural Mts., U.S.S.R. + G *-it* -ite] : a usu. massive iron-black mineral $FeTiO_3$ of submetallic luster that is an important ore of titanium and is a compound of iron and titanium and oxygen and may sometimes occur in rhombohedral crystals with very close crystal-structural relations to hematite
il·meno·rutile \¦ilmə(,)nō+\ *n* [G *ilmenorutil*, fr. *Ilmen* range + G *-o-* + *rutil* rutile] : black rutile containing niobium
ilmo *abbr* [It *illustrissimo*] most illustrious
ILO *abbr. often not cap* in lieu of
ilo·ca·no *or* **ilo·ka·no** \,ēlō'kä(,)nō\ *n, pl* **ilocano** *or* **ilocanos** *or* **ilokano** *or* **ilokanos** *usu cap* [Sp *ilocano*, fr. *iloko* (native name in the Philippines) + Sp *-ano* -an] **1 a** : a major people inhabiting northern Luzon in the Philippines **b** : a member of such people **2** : the Austronesian language of the Ilocano people
ilo·ilo \¦ēlō¦ē(,)lō\ *adj, usu cap* [fr. *Iloilo*, Philippines] : of or from the city of Iloilo in the Philippines : of the kind or style prevalent in Iloilo
ilo·ko \ē'lō(,)kō\ *n, pl* **iloko** *or* **ilokos** *usu cap* [native name in the Philippines] : ILOCANO
i lon·ga \'ī'lòŋgə\ *n* [L, long i] : a taller variety of the letter *i* used occas. in writing Latin in classical times to indicate the sound \ē\ as contrasted with \i\
ilon·got \(,)ē,lòŋ'gōt\ *n, pl* **ilongot** *or* **ilongots** *usu cap* [native name in the Philippines] **1 a** : a people inhabiting northern Luzon in the Philippines **b** : a member of such people **2** : the Austronesian language of the Ilongot people
ilot \'īlət\ *var of* ISLOT
il più forte \ēl'pyü+\ *adj* (*or adv*) [It] : very loud : as loud as possible — used as a direction in music
il più piano \"+\ *adj* (*or adv*) [It] : very soft : as soft as possible — used as a direction in music
ILS *abbr* instrument landing system
il·se·mann·ite \'il(t)səmə,nīt, 'ilzə-\ *n* -S [G *ilsemannit*, fr. J. C. *Ilsemann* †1822 Ger. mining commissioner + G *-it* -ite] : a mineral $Mo_3O_8.nH_2O$(?) consisting of black, blue-black, or blue earthy massive hydrous oxide or perhaps sulfate of molybdenum
il·va·ite \'ilvə,īt\ *n* -S [G *ilvait*, fr. *Ilva* (Elba), Ital. island in the Mediterranean + G *-it* -ite] : a silicate $CaFe_3Si_2O_8(OH)$ of iron and calcium and sometimes manganese related to epidote and occurring in black prismatic crystals and columnar masses (hardness 5.5–6, sp. gr. 4.0)
il·y·san·thes \,ilə'san(t)(,)thēz\ *n, cap* [NL, fr. Gk *ilys* mud + NL *-anthes*] : a genus of low herbs (family Scrophulariaceae) with opposite leaves and small solitary usu. purplish flowers — see FALSE HEDGE HYSSOP

il·y·si·idae \ˌiləˈsīəˌdē\ [NL, fr. *Ilysia*, genus of burrowing snakes (fr. Gk *ilys* mud + NL *-ia*) + *-idae*; akin to OSlav *ilŭ* mud] + *-idae*] *syn of* ANILIIDAE

im- — see IN

im *abbr* immature

IM *abbr* **1** imperial measure **2** inner marker **3** intramuscular

¹im·age \ˈimij, -mēj\ *n* -s [ME, fr. OF, short for *imagene*, fr. L *imagin-, imago*; akin to L *imitari* to imitate] **1 :** a reproduction of a person or thing: as **a :** STATUE **b** (1) **:** DEVICE, EMBLEM (2) **:** a figure used as a talisman or amulet esp. in conjurations (as by sorcerers in casting spells) **c** (1) **:** PICTURE, PORTRAIT (2) **:** a sculptured or fabricated object of symbolic value **:** IDOL; *specif* **:** a holy picture (as an ikon) **2 :** a thing actually or seemingly reproducing another: as **a** (1) **:** the optical counterpart of an object produced by a lens, mirror, or other optical system and being the geometric figure made up of the foci corresponding to the points of the object — see REAL IMAGE, VIRTUAL IMAGE (2) **:** an analogous phenomenon in some field other than optics ⟨an acoustic ~⟩ ⟨an electric ~⟩ **b :** any likeness of an object produced on a photographic material **3 :** exact likeness **:** SEMBLANCE **4 a :** a tangible or visible representation **:** INCARNATION ⟨a civil servant who is the ~ of conscientiousness⟩ **b** *archaic* **:** an illusory appearance **:** APPARITION **5 a** (1) **:** a mental picture **:** IMPRESSION ⟨a soldier haunted by ~s of battle⟩ ⟨~s, as contrasted with sensations, are the responses during a narrative —Bertrand Russell⟩ (2) **:** a mental conception held in common by members of a group and being symbolic of a basic attitude and orientation toward something (as a person, class, racial type, political philosophy, or nationality) ⟨the Frenchman's ~ of America⟩ **b :** the memory of a perception in psychology that is modified by subsequent experience and that contains both intellectual and emotional elements elicited by intrapsychic and extrapsychic stimuli; *also* **:** the representation of a stimulus object on a receptor mechanism **c :** IDEA, CONCEPT ⟨conflicting ~s of good and evil⟩ **6 :** a markedly vivid, effective, or graphic representation or description ⟨the set for the play being the ~ of a New England village⟩ **7 a :** something concrete or abstract introduced (as in a poem or speech) to represent something else which it strikingly resembles or suggests (as the use of *sleep* for *death*) — compare EMBLEM, SYMBOL **b :** a figure of speech (as a metaphor or simile) **:** TROPE **8 :** a person who is strikingly like another person in appearance, manner, or thought ⟨a son who is the ~ of his father⟩

²image \"\, *chiefly in pres part* -məj\ *vt* -ED/-ING/-S **1 :** to describe or portray in language esp. in an effective or vivid manner **2 :** to call up a mental picture of **:** IMAGINE ⟨we no longer ~ the native landscape in the terms beloved of Rossetti and Tennyson —Vincent Buckley⟩ **3 a :** REFLECT, MIRROR ⟨a face *imaged* in a mirror⟩ **b :** to make appear (as in desired form) **:** PROJECT ⟨film *imaged* on a screen⟩ **4 a :** to create a representation of **:** DEPICT, PORTRAY ⟨a national hero *imaged* in bronze on a village green⟩ **b** (1) **:** to create or produce a suggestion of **:** ADUMBRATE ⟨a symphony *imaging* the beauty of nature⟩ (2) **:** to represent symbolically **:** stand as a symbol of ⟨acres of headstones *imaging* the losses of war⟩

image dissector *n* **:** a camera tube resembling the iconoscope and having the electronic image focused electromagnetically through an aperture and voltages that are subsequently amplified and transmitted as television-picture signals being produced by electron multiplication

im·age·less \-ləs\ *adj* **:** characterized by absence of mental images ⟨an ~ thought⟩

image orthicon *n* **:** a camera tube that is similar to the iconoscope or the orthicon and uses secondary emission and electron multiplication to produce the voltages that are subsequently amplified and transmitted as television-picture signals

im·ag·er \ˈimijə(r), -mēj-\ *n* -s **:** one that images **:** a vivid describer or portrayer

im·ag·ery \-j(ə)rē, -ri\ *n* -ES [ME *imagerie*, fr. MF, fr. *image* + *-erie* -ery] **1 :** the product of image makers (as a statue, emblem, or idol) **:** IMAGES; *also* **:** the art of making images **2** *obs* **:** IMAGE WORSHIP **3 :** ornate or heightened description or figures of speech; *specif* **:** the often peculiarly individual concrete or figurative diction used by a writer in those portions of his texts where he wishes to produce a particular effect (as a special emotional appeal or a train of intellectual associations) ⟨Shakespeare's ~⟩ **4 :** mental images; *esp* **:** the products of imagination ⟨psychotic ~⟩

images *pl of* IMAGE, *pres 3d sing of* IMAGE

image slicer *n* **:** an attachment for a stellar spectrograph comprised of a system of very small mirrors that direct strips of light from various portions of the star-image disk so that they pass through the narrow slit of the spectrograph thereby increasing the intensity of the star's spectrum several times

image space *n* **:** a space in connection with an optical system each of whose points is an image of a corresponding point in the object space

image tube *n* **:** CAMERA TUBE

image worship *n* **:** the worship of images as the special residence of a divine spirit or supernatural power **:** IDOLATRY

imag·in·able \əˈmaj(ə)nəbəl\ *adj* [ME, fr. LL *imaginabilis*, fr. L *imaginari* to imagine + *-abilis* -able — more at IMAGINE] **:** capable of being imagined **:** CONCEIVABLE ⟨the biggest lies ~⟩ ⟨any ~ situation⟩ — **imag·in·able·ness** \-nəs\ *n* -ES — **imag·in·ably** \-blē, -bli\ *adv*

imagi·nal \əˈmajənᵊl\, *in sense 4* -māgən- *or* -mägən- *or* -māgən- *or* -majən- *or* -majən-\ *adj* [*imagine* + *-al*] **1 :** of or relating to imagination ⟨~ objects⟩ **2** [LL *imaginalis*, fr. L *imagin-, imago* image + *-alis* -al — more at IMAGE] **:** of or relating to an image ⟨the idea of weeping can be translated into its ~ equivalent, as rain —K.D.Burke⟩ **3** [NL *imagin-, imago* + E *-al*] **:** relating to mental images **4** [NL *imagin-, imago* + E *-al*] **:** of or relating to the insect imago

imaginal disk *also* **imaginal bud** *n* **:** one of the clusters of undifferentiated cells in the larvae and pupae of some insects from which the wings, legs, and other organs of the adult are formed

imaginal type *n* **:** a tendency of an individual to have images arising predominantly from one or another sense (as from vision, hearing, or taste)

imaginant *n* -s [L *imaginant-, imaginans*, pres. part. of *imaginari* to imagine — more at IMAGINE] *obs* **:** IMAGINER

imag·i·nar·i·ly \əˌmajəˈnerəlē, -li, ˌiˌ==ˈ===\ *adv* **:** in an imaginary manner

imag·i·nar·i·ness \əˈ==ˌnerēnəs, -rin-\ *n* -ES **:** the quality or state of being imaginary

¹imag·i·nary \əˈmajəˌnerē, -ri\ *adj* [ME, fr. L *imaginarius*, fr. *imaginari* to imagine + *-arius* -ary] **1 a :** having no real existence **:** existing only in imagination or fancy **:** UNREAL, FANCIED, FICTITIOUS, HYPOTHETICAL ⟨to guard the cattle against their real and their ~ foes, the wolves and the witches —J.G. Frazer⟩ **b :** formed, characterized, or ascribed outside the evidence of reality **:** shaped, endowed, or attributed imaginatively or arbitrarily ⟨the statue of John Harvard . . . is an ~ likeness; no portrait of Harvard is known to exist —*Amer. Guide Series: Mass.*⟩ **2** *obs* **:** of the nature of or suggesting an image **3** *obs* **:** IMAGINATIVE **4 :** containing or related to the imaginary unit

syn FANCIFUL, VISIONARY, FANTASTIC, CHIMERICAL, QUIXOTIC: IMAGINARY stresses lack of reality; it indicates an existence, formation, or ascription by imagination, not fact ⟨those nervous persons who may be terrified by *imaginary* dangers are often courageous in the face of real danger —Havelock Ellis⟩ In relation to things, FANCIFUL indicates formation or conditioning by free, unrestrained fancy or imagination; in relation to people, it indicates a tendency to give free rein to the imagination ⟨*fanciful* tale of his own exploits tells how he was carried, wounded, down the mountainside in a big buckskin bag tied to the back of a wrinkled squaw —*Amer. Guide Series: Calif.*⟩ ⟨one may perhaps without being too *fanciful* see in his art something of the magic of the Celt —Irving Babbitt⟩ VISIONARY applies to a person given to seeing visions or to the ideas and notions from visions rather than real facts and hence impractical, wild, and impossible of fulfillment or fruition ⟨planning, as his *visionary* father might have done, to go to Brazil to pick up a fortune —Carl Van Doren⟩ ⟨unless, therefore, our philosophic vision receives technical development . . . it may rightly be condemned as unsubstantial and *visionary* —M.R.Cohen⟩ FANTASTIC and its variant FANTASTICAL heighten the notion of extravagant fancy far transcending the usual, ordinary, or real ⟨one of those eoan errors to which we are subject before the clear commonplace of daylight orders and moderates our tenebrous and *fantastical* imaginations —Rose Macaulay⟩ ⟨a *fantastic* world inhabited by monsters of iron and steel —Louis Bromfield⟩ ⟨two heroes may mangle each other in every impossible and *fantastic* way, beyond the bounds of the faintest shadow of verisimilitude —H.O.Taylor⟩ CHIMERICAL suggests the wild, utterly unreal, and extravagantly imaginary characteristics of creations of classical mythology ⟨the defeat was more complete, more humiliating . . . the hopes of revival more *chimerical* —*Times Lit. Supp.*⟩ ⟨as *chimerical* as a specter —Bernard Smith⟩ QUIXOTIC describes completely unrealistic and impractical devotion to romantic or chivalric ideals ⟨was *quixotic*, and would not permit a secret service and spies —G.K.Chesterton⟩ ⟨among the last *quixotic* acts of his life was an attempt to set up a Greek academy for aspiring authors —Alfred Kreymborg⟩ ⟨be so *quixotic* as to stand upon principles at the risk of losing the business —R.M.Cunningham⟩

²imaginary \"\ *n* -ES **1** *obs* **:** a figment of imagination **2 :** a complex number (as $2+3i$) whose imaginary part is not zero

imaginary number *n* **:** IMAGINARY 2

imaginary part *n* **:** the part of a complex number (as "3i" in $2+3i$) that has the imaginary unit as a factor

imaginary unit *n* **:** the positive square root of minus 1 **:** $+\sqrt{-1}$ — symbol *i*

imag·i·na·tion \əˌmajəˈnāshən\ *n* -s [ME *imaginacioun*, fr. MF *imagination*, fr. L *imagination-, imaginatio*, fr. *imaginatus* (past part. of *imaginari* to imagine) + *-ion-, -io* -ion — more at IMAGINE] **1 :** an act or process of forming a conscious idea or mental image of something never before wholly perceived in reality by the imaginer (as through a synthesis of remembered elements of previous sensory experiences or ideas as modified by unconscious mechanisms of defense); *also* **:** the ability or gift of forming such conscious ideas or mental images esp. for the purposes of artistic or intellectual creation ⟨our simple apprehension of corporeal objects, if present, is sense; if absent, is ~ —Joseph Glanvill⟩ **2 a :** creative ability **:** GENIUS ⟨the great ~s of literature⟩ **b :** ability to confront and deal with a problem **:** RESOURCEFULNESS ⟨the attempt shows suggestions of the ~ that the situation demands⟩ **3** *obs* **:** a plotting or scheming esp. of evil **:** PLOT ⟨all their vengeance and all their ~s against me —Lam 3:60 (AV)⟩ **4 a :** a mental image, conception, or notion formed by the action of imagination **b :** a creation of the mind; *esp* **:** an idealized or poetic creation ⟨the gory ~s of folk poetry⟩ **c :** fanciful or empty assumption ⟨idle ~s⟩ **5 :** popular or traditional belief **:** usual or accepted conception ⟨the Magna Charta . . . has operated in the meaning given it in ~ rather than by its literal contents —John Dewey⟩

syn FANCY, FANTASY, PHANTASY: IMAGINATION, freer of derogatory connotations than the other terms, is the most comprehensive, applying to the power of creating, in the mind or in an outward form as in a literary work, images of things once known but absent, of things never seen or never seen in their entirety, of things actually nonexistent, of things created new from diverse old elements, or of things perfected or idealized; it may carry the implication of mere tricky concoction, as of things unreal or odd, but is more frequently nearer the other extreme in suggesting the genuine artist's gift of perceiving more deeply or essentially and creating the interestingly and the significantly new and vital ⟨all youth lives much in reverie; thereby the stronger minds anticipate and rehearse themselves for life in a thousand *imaginations* —H.G.Wells⟩ ⟨*imagination* being little else than another name for illusion —Samuel Butler⟩ ⟨the *imagination* is able to manipulate nature as by creating three legs and five arms but it is not able to create a totally new nature —Wallace Stevens⟩ ⟨the production of vivid images, usually visual images . . . is the commonest and the least interesting thing which is referred to by *imagination* —I.A.Richards⟩ ⟨a product of fancy rather than imagination — if one accepts fancy as decorative and *imagination* as creative —Pamela L. Travers⟩ ⟨*imagination*, in his opinion, gets at relationships that are true at the deepest level of experience —F.A.Pottle⟩ ⟨*imagination* is something akin to what it was in Wordsworth, a means of deepest insight and sympathy —Roy Pascal⟩ ⟨it is only through *imagination* that men become aware of what the world might be —Bertrand Russell⟩ FANCY now usu. suggests the power to conceive and give expression to images of things removed from reality, usu. of things purely, sometimes frivolously though often delightfully, imaginary, often contrasting with IMAGINATION in suggesting a more superficial often factitious power of inventing the novel or unreal by recombining existing elements as opposed to the imagination's gift of grasping a deeper, more organic reality ⟨like all weak men of a vivid *fancy*, he was constantly framing dramas of which he was the towering lord —G.D.Brown⟩ ⟨the associative faculty performs, to a varying extent in individual cases, constantly shifting arrangements and rearrangements of the data of observation, thought, feeling . . . which Coleridge distinguishes from imagination by the word *fancy* —George Whalley⟩ ⟨in a creative artist the imagination functions . . . in three ways. It is partly mere *fancy*, which moves happily into make-believe —K.P.Kempton⟩ FANTASY or PHANTASY suggests the power of unrestrained, often extravagant or delusive, fancy, stressing the unreal more than *fancy*; PHANTASY is used more frequently than FANTASY in the technical sense of image-making power in general ⟨hard to say where the actuality ends and the *fantasy* begins in these sketches of life —B.C.L.Keelan⟩ ⟨fairy stories and *fantasy* are phenomenally popular —Lavinia R. Davis⟩ ⟨an appealing *fantasy*, though its appeal does not lie in what is fantastic about it. It lies in what is realistic and homely —*Time*⟩ ⟨a *fantasy* . . . may be distinguished from the representation of something that actually exists, but it is not opposed to "reality" and not an "escape" from reality. Thus, the idea of a rational society, or the image of a good house to be built, or the story of something that never happened, is a fantasy —Lionel Trilling⟩ ⟨this mechanical man or robot idea has been decidedly overdone in the writings of *fantasy* —C.C. Furnas⟩ ⟨a mixture . . . of comic *phantasy*, improbable adventure and rainbow colors —G.E.Fox⟩ ⟨a novelist is a person who has a highly developed gift of *phantasy* —Bernard De Voto⟩ ⟨its invention is based on the extinction of a wish *phantasy* belonging to the period of puberty —D.F.Tait⟩

imag·i·na·tion·al \-shənᵊl, -shnəl\ *adj* **:** of, relating to, involving, caused by, or suggestive of the imagination

imag·i·na·tive \əˈmaj(ə)nəd·iv, -jəˌnā|, |t|, |ēv *also* |əv\ *adj* [ME, fr. MF *imaginatif*, fr. *imagination* + *-if* -ive] **1 :** of or relating to the imagination: as **a :** created, inspired, guided, or drawn from the imagination and not from known facts or sources ⟨an ~ biography⟩ **b :** tending to provoke, excite, or enliven the imagination ⟨a few ~ comments⟩ **c** (1) **:** able to handle new or difficult problems **:** RESOURCEFUL ⟨a young and ~ general⟩ (2) **:** imbued with or showing an ability to draw conclusions, suggest hypotheses, make comparisons, or create systems ⟨an ~ interpretation of a poem⟩ ⟨an ~ critic⟩ ⟨~ research⟩ (3) **:** full of freshness, originality, or vividness ⟨~ patterns⟩ **d :** devoid of truth **:** FALSE ⟨the report of his death was wholly ~⟩ **2 :** of or relating to images; *esp* **:** showing a distinctive or fine command of artistic images ⟨~ diction⟩

imag·i·na·tive·ly \|əvlē, -li\ *adv* **:** in an imaginative manner ⟨a play produced ~⟩ ⟨an ~ planned garden⟩

imag·i·na·tive·ness \|ivnəs, |ēv- *also* |əv-\ *n* -ES **:** the quality or state of being imaginative

imag·i·na·tor \əˈmajəˌnād·ə(r)\ *n* -s [L *imaginatus* (past part. of *imaginari*) + E *-or*] **:** one that imagines; *esp* **:** a person who creates (as an artistic or intellectual work)

imag·ine \əˈmajən *sometimes* -maaj-; *when "I" precedes or when imperative & sentence-initial often* ˈm-\ *vb* **imagined; imagined; imagining** \-j(ə)niŋ\ **imagines** [ME *imaginen*, fr. MF *imaginer*, fr. L *imaginari*, fr. *imagin-, imago* image — more at IMAGE] *vt* **1 :** to form an idea of **:** create a mental image of ⟨~ accidents at every turn⟩ **2 :** to create by or as if by the imagination **:** FABRICATE ⟨*imagining* stories to fool the public⟩ **3 :** THINK, SUPPOSE, GUESS ⟨I ~ it will rain⟩ ~ *vi* **1** *obs* **:** PONDER, MEDITATE **2 :** to use the imagination; *specif* **:** to form images or conceptions **3 :** SUPPOSE, THINK

syn see THINK

imag·in·er \-j(ə)nə(r)\ *n* -s [ME, fr. *imaginen* + *-er*] **:** one that imagines

imaging *pres part of* IMAGE

im·ag·ism \ˈimiˌjizəm, -mēˌ-, -məˌ-\ *n* -s **:** a movement in poetry (as in America and England before World War I) advocating concrete language and figures of speech, modern subject matter, freedom in the use of meter, and avoidance of romantic or mystic themes — compare SYMBOLISM

¹im·ag·ist \-jəst\ *n* -s [*¹image* + *-ist*] **:** one that follows the precepts of imagism

²im·ag·ist \"\ *or* **im·ag·is·tic** \ˌ==ˈjistik, -tēk\ *adj* **:** of or relating to imagism — **im·ag·is·ti·cal·ly** \-tək(ə)lē, -tēk-, -li\ *adv*

ima·go \əˈmā(ˌ)gō, -mä(-, -mȧ(-\ *n, pl* **imagoes** *or* **imag·i·nes** \-māgəˌnēz; -mägəˌnēz, -mȧg-, -ˌnās; -majəˌnēz, -maj-\ [NL, fr. L, image — more at IMAGE] **1 :** an insect in its final adult sexually mature usu. winged state — compare LARVA, NYMPH, PUPA **2 :** a conception of the parent that is retained in the unconscious, elaborated by infantile phantasies, and bound with the affect pertaining to the infantile period; *also* **:** an idealized mental image of any person including the self

imam \əˈmäm, (ˈ)ē¦-, -mam\ *n* -s [Ar *imām*] **1 :** the prayer leader of a mosque **2 :** the caliph who is the spiritual and secular head of Islam **3 :** one of the twelve divinely inspired leaders of the Shi'a appointed to guide men; *also* **:** one of their earthly representatives descended from Muhammad and appointed head of the Muslim community **4 :** one of the founders of the four orthodox schools of Muslim jurisprudence; *also* **:** any authoritative Muslim scholar who founds a school of interpretation or is followed as an authority in theology and law **5 :** any of various sovereign princes that claim descent from Muhammad and that exercise spiritual and temporal leadership over a Muslim region

imam·ate \-ˌāt\ *n* -s *often cap* **1 :** the office of an imam **2 :** the region or country ruled over by an imam ⟨the ~ of Yemen⟩

imami \-ē\ *n* -s [Ar *imāmī*, fr. *imām*] *usu cap* **:** TWELVER

iman·to·phyl·lum \(ˌ)iˌmantəˈfiləm\ [NL, irreg. fr. Gk *himanto-* (fr. *himant-, himas* thong) + NL *-phyllum*] *syn of* CLIVIA

ima·ret \əˈmärət\ *n* -s [Turk, fr. Ar *'imārah* building] **:** an inn or hospice in Turkey

ima·ri ware \əˈmärē-\ *n, usu cap I* [fr. *Imari*, Japan, where it is made] **:** a Hizen porcelain characteristically decorated in red, green, and blue with a design of bamboo and cherry blossoms or hedges of brushwood growing out of stylized rocks

im·balance \(ˈ)im+\ *n* [*¹in-* + *balance*] **:** absence of balance: as **a** (1) **:** loss of parallel relation between the optical axes of the eyes caused by faulty action of the extrinsic muscles and often resulting in diplopia (2) **:** absence of biological equilibrium (as in a gland) **b :** lack of balance between segments of a nation's economy (as between debit and credit in international payments or between costs and prices) **c :** a disproportion between the number of males and females in a population

imbarn *vt* -ED/-ING/-S [*²in-* + *barn* (n.)] *obs* **:** to gather into or store in a barn **:** GARNER

im·base \əm+\ *var of* EMBASE

im·bat \(ˈ)imˈbät\ *n* -s [Turk] **:** a cooling etesian wind in the Levant (as in Cyprus)

im·ba·uba \ˌimbəˈübə\ *also* **im·ba·ubao** \-ü,baů\ *n* -s [Pg *ambaúba, imbaúba, umbaúba*, fr. Tupi *ambauba, umbauba*] **:** TRUMPETWOOD

im·be \(ˈ)imˈbā\ *n* -s [Pg *imbé*, fr. Tupi] **1 :** a cordage fiber derived from the stems of an epiphytic Brazilian plant (*Philodendron imbe*) **2 :** the plant that yields imbe fiber

¹im·be·cile \ˈimbəsəl *also* -(ˌ)sil *or* -ˌsīl, *chiefly Brit* -ˌsēl\ *adj* [MF *imbecille*, fr. L *imbecillus* weak, weak-minded, fr. *in-* ¹in- + *-becillus* (perh. fr. *bacillus, bacillum* small staff) — more at BACILLUS] **1** *archaic* **:** WEAK, FEEBLE **2** [F *imbécile*, fr. L *imbecillus*] **a :** of, relating to, or befitting an imbecile **b :** markedly inane, idiotic, foolish, or stupid — used as a generalized term of contempt

²imbecile \"\ *n* -s [F *imbécile*, fr. *imbécile*, adj] **1 :** one marked by mental deficiency: as **a :** one who has a less-than-normal average intelligence and intellectual capacity that is usu. above that of an idiot but below that of a moron **b :** a feebleminded person who has a mental age of approximately three to seven years and who requires special care and supervision in the performance of routine daily tasks of self-care (as feeding and clothing himself) **2 :** FOOL, IDIOT — used as a generalized term of contempt **syn** see FOOL

im·be·cile·ly \-əl(l)ē, -il(l)ē, -īl|, |i\ *adv* **:** in an imbecile manner

im·be·cil·ic \ˌimbəˈsilik, -ilēk\ *adj* **:** characteristic or suggestive of an imbecile ⟨an ~ grin⟩ ⟨~ conclusions⟩

im·be·cil·i·ty \ˌimbəˈsiləd·ē, -lətē, -i\ *n* -ES [MF *imbecillité*, fr. L *imbecillitat-, imbecillitas* weakness, weak-mindedness, fr. *imbecillus* + *-itat-, -itas* -ity] **1 a :** the quality or state of being weak **b :** INCAPACITY, INABILITY ⟨~ of judgment⟩ **2** [F *imbécillité*, fr. L *imbecillitat-, imbecillitas*] **:** the quality or state of being mentally weak — compare MENTAL DEFICIENCY **3 a :** complete nonsense **:** utter foolishness ⟨the ~ of trying to live without food⟩; *also* **:** FUTILITY **b :** something that is foolish or absurd

imbed *var of* EMBED

imbellious *also* **imbellic** *adj* [L *imbellis* (fr. *in-* ¹in- + *-bellis*, fr. *bellum* war) + E *-ous* or *-ic* — more at BELLICOSE] *obs* **:** not warlike

im·bibe \əmˈbīb\ *vb* -ED/-ING/-S [in sense 1, fr. ME *enbiben*, fr. MF *embiber*, fr. L *imbibere* to drink in, conceive, fr. *in-* ²in- + *bibere* to drink; in other senses, fr. L *imbibere* — more at POTABLE] *vt* **1** *archaic* **:** to cause to absorb liquid **:** SOAK **2 a :** to receive into the mind and retain **:** ASSIMILATE ⟨~ moral principles⟩ **b :** to assimilate (as gas, light, or heat) or take into solution **3 a :** to consume by drinking ⟨~s vast quantities of strong coffee⟩ **b :** to drink in **:** ABSORB ⟨plants can ~ as much nourishment through their leaves as via their roots —F.J.Taylor⟩ ⟨a sponge *imbibing* moisture⟩ ~ *vi* **1 :** DRINK 2 **2 a :** to take in or up liquid **b :** to absorb or assimilate moisture, gas, light, or heat

im·bib·er \-bə(r)\ *n* -s **:** one that imbibes

im·bi·bi·tion \ˌimbəˈbishən, -m,bīˈbi-\ *n* -s [in sense 1, fr. ME *imbybycyon*, fr. MF *imbibition*, fr. L *imbibitus* (past part. of *imbibere*) + MF *-ion*; in other senses, fr. L *imbibitus* + E *-ion*] **1** *obs* **a :** saturation with or solution in liquid **b :** mixture of solid and liquid by such imbibition **2 :** the act or action of imbibing: as **a :** the taking up and sorption of fluid by a colloidal system resulting in swelling and offering a possible explanation of certain biological phenomena (as the retention of water by desert plants) — compare OSMOSIS 1, SYNERESIS 2 **b :** IMBIBITION PROCESS

im·bi·bi·tion·al \ˌ==ˌ=ˈbishənᵊl, -shnəl\ *adj* **:** of, relating to, or characterized by imbibition

imbibition process *n* **:** a process by which a photographic print is produced by absorption of a water-soluble dye by a relief image or a differentially absorbing image in gelatin or a similar medium or in which a previously formed dye image is transferred by absorption from one to another layer

im·bi·rus·sú \ˌimbərəˈsü, -rüˈsü\ *n* -s [Pg *embiruçú, embirussú*, fr. Tupi *embirussú, imbirussú*, fr. *embira, imbira* embira + *-ussú* big] **:** a timber tree of So. and Central America that is an undetermined species of the genus *Bombax* and that bears pods yielding a brownish fiber similar to kapok

imbitter *var of* EMBITTER

imbosom *var of* EMBOSOM

imbound *var of* EMBOUND

imbrace *obs var of* EMBRACE

imbreviate *vt* -ED/-ING/-S [ML *imbreviatus*, past part. of *imbreviare*, fr. L *in-* ²in- + ML *brevis, breve* brief — more at BRIEF (n.)] *obs* **:** to write or enter in the form of a brief **:** ENROLL, REGISTER

im·brex \ˈimˌbreks, -ˌbriks\ *n, pl* **imbri·ces** \-brəˌsēz, -əˌkās\ [L] **1 :** a curved roof tile used esp. by the ancient Romans **:** PANTILE **2** [NL, fr. L] **:** one of the scales or subdivisions of imbricated ornament

¹im·bri·cate \ˈimbrəkə|t, -rēk-, -rəˌkā|\ *usu* |d·+V\ *adj* [LL *imbricatus*, past part. of *imbricare* to cover with imbrices, fr. L *imbric-, imbrex* (fr. *imbr-, imber* rain) + *-atus* -ate; akin to

Gk *ombros* rain, Skt *abhra* cloud, Arm *amb*, and perh. to L *nebula* mist, vapor, cloud — more at NEBULA] **1 :** lying lapped over each other in regular order in the manner of tiles or shingles on a roof — used esp. of bud scales, involucral bracts, fish scales **2 :** overlapping at the margins — used esp. of leaves in the bud — **im·bri·cate·ly** *adv*

²im·bri·cate \-rə,kāt, *usu* -ād.+V\ *vb* -ED/-ING/-S [LL *imbricatus*, past part.] *vt* **:** to cause (as tiles or layers of tissue in closing a wound) to overlap ~ *vi* **:** OVERLAP

imbricated snout beetle *n* **:** a small light-colored weevil (*Epicaerus imbricatus*) destructive to many vegetables and fruits

imbricated texture *n* **:** a texture in certain minerals (as tridymite) resembling overlapping plates

im·bri·ca·tion \,imbrə'kāshən\ *n* -S **1 :** an overlapping esp. of tiles or shingles or of successive layers of tissue in the closure of a wound **2 :** a decoration or pattern showing imbrication

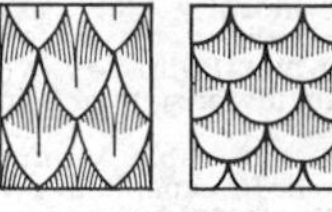
imbrication 1

im·bro·glio \əm'brōl(,)yō, -rōl-\ *or* **em·bro·glio** \", em-\ *n* -S [It *imbroglio*, fr. *imbrogliare* to entangle, confuse, embroil, fr. OIt, fr. MF *embrouiller* — more at EMBROIL] **1 :** a confused mass **:** CONGLOMERATION ⟨an ~ of papers and books⟩ **2 a :** an intricate or complicated situation (as in a drama or novel) **b :** an acutely painful or embarrassing misunderstanding ⟨an ~ between foreign ministers⟩ **c :** a violently confused or bitterly complicated altercation **:** EMBROILMENT ⟨an ~ over misuses of public funds⟩ **3 :** a musical passage designed to effect confusion by sharply contrasting the rhythm and meter (as between the voice parts in an opera)

im·brue \əm'brü\ *or* **em·brue** \", em-\ *vt* -ED/-ING/-S [ME *enbrewen*, *embrowen*, prob. fr. MF *abrevrer*, *abreuver*, *embevrer* to soak, drench, fr. (assumed) VL *abbiberare*, fr. L *ad-* + (assumed) VL *biberare* to give to drink, fr. L *bibere* to drink — more at POTABLE] **:** DRENCH ⟨a nation *imbrued* with the blood of executed men⟩

imbrued *adj* **:** stained with blood

im·brute \əm+\ *also* **em·brute** \əm, em+\ *vb* -ED/-ING/-S [²*in-* or ¹*en-* + *brute* (n.)] *vi* **:** to sink to the level of a brute **:** become bestial ~ *vt* **:** to degrade to the level of a brute **:** BRUTALIZE

im·bue \əm'byü\ *also* **em·bue** \", em-\ *vt* -ED/-ING/-S [L *imbuere* to dye, wet, moisten, prob. fr. *in-* ²in- + *-buere* (of unknown origin)] **1 :** to tinge or dye deeply ⟨a landscape deeply *imbued* with shadow⟩ **2 :** to cause to become penetrated **:** IMPREGNATE, PERMEATE ⟨a statesman *imbued* with a deep sense of national pride⟩ **syn** see INFUSE

im·bu·ia *or* **em·bu·ia** *also* **im·bu·ya** \əm'bü(y)ə\ *n* -S [Pg] **1 :** any of several Brazilian timber trees of the genera *Nectandra* and *Phoebe* (family Lauraceae) **2 :** the light to dark brown lustrous durable often strikingly figured wood of the imbuias that is readily polished and much used for fine cabinetwork — called also *Brazilian walnut*

im·er·i·na \,imə'rēnə\ *n, pl* **imerina** *or* **imerinas** *usu cap* **:** HOVA

im·er·i·nite \,imə'rē,nīt\ *n* -S [F *imerinite*, fr. *Imerina*, province of Madagascar, its locality + F *-ite*] **:** a monoclinic amphibole $Na_2(Mg,Fe)_6Si_8O_{22}(O,OH)_2$ that is related to richterite and occurs in colorless to blue acicular crystals **:** a basic silicate of sodium, iron, and magnesium

im·er·i·tian \,imə'rishən\ *also* **im·er·e·tian** \-rēsh-\ *n* -S *cap* [*Imeritia* or *Imeretia*, district of Georgian S.S.R. in the southern Caucasus + E *-an*] **1 :** a Georgian-speaking people of Imeritia **2 :** a member of the Imeritian people

im·hoff tank \'im,hōf-, -hōf-\ *n, usu cap I* [after Karl *Imhoff* *b*1876 Ger. engineer] **:** a tank for sewage clarification consisting of an upper or sedimentation chamber with sloping floor leading to slots through which the solids settle to the lower sludge-digestion chamber

imid- *or* **imido-** *comb form* [ISV, fr. *imide*] **1** *now usu* **imido- :** containing the bivalent group =NH characteristic of imides united to or in one or two radicals of acid character ⟨*imido*carbonic acid $HN{=}C(OH)_2$⟩ ⟨*imido*disulfuric acid $HN(SO_2OH)_2$⟩ ⟨*imidate*⟩ — distinguished from *imin-* **2 :** IMIN- — now less used than formerly

imidaz- *or* **imidazo-** *comb form* [ISV, fr. *imidazole*] **:** imidazole ⟨7-*imidazo* [4.5-*d*] pyrimidine⟩

im·id·azole \,imə'da,zōl, -,da'z-\ *n* [ISV *imid-* + *azole*] **1 :** a white crystalline heterocyclic base $C_3H_4N_2$ made by the action of ammonia and formaldehyde on glyoxal and isomeric with pyrazole; 1,3-diazole — called also *glyoxaline*; compare STRUCTURAL FORMULA **2 :** any of a large class of derivatives of imidazole including histidine and histamine

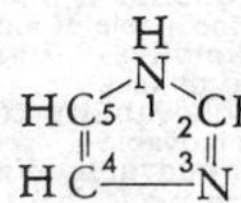
imidazole 1

im·id·az·o·line \,imə'dazə,lēn\ *n* -S [*imidazole* + *-ine*] **:** any of three dihydro derivatives $C_3H_6N_2$ of imidazole; *also* **:** a derivative of these — called also *glyoxalidine*

im·id·az·o·lyl \-zə,lil\ *n* -S [ISV *imidazole* + *-yl*] **:** any of four univalent radicals $C_3H_3N_2$ derived from imidazole by removal of one hydrogen atom

im·ide \'i,mīd, -,məd\ *n* -S [ISV, alter. of *amide*] **1 :** any of a class of compounds derived from ammonia by replacement of two hydrogen atoms by a metal ⟨calcium ~ CaNH⟩ ⟨lithium ~ Li_2NH⟩ — called also *metallic imide* **2 :** any of a class of compounds derived from ammonia by replacement of two hydrogen atoms by one bivalent acid radical or by two univalent acid radicals; *esp* **:** a cyclic compound (as phthalimide, saccharin) containing a bivalent acyl radical — called also *acid imide*; compare AMIDE — **imid·ic** \(')i¦midik\ *adj*

imidic acid *n* [ISV *imide* + *-ic*] **:** any of various acids characterized by the presence of the imido group; *esp* **:** one of a class of organic acids containing a carboxyl group in which the carbonyl oxygen atom is replaced by an imido group and having the general formula RC(=NH)OH but known only in the form of derivatives (as esters or acid chlorides)

im·i·do \'imə,dō\ *adj* [*imid-*] **1 :** relating to or containing the group =NH or a substituted group =NR united to one or two radicals of acid character — distinguished from *imino* **2 :** IMINO

imido ester *n* **:** an ester of an imidic acid

imid·o·gen \ə'midəjən, -,jen\ *n* -S [F *imidogène*, fr. *imid-* + *-gène* -gen] **:** a bivalent radical =NH derived from ammonia esp. as detected in the free state — compare IMIDO, IMINO

imin- *or* **imino-** *comb form* [ISV, fr. *imine*] **:** containing the bivalent group =NH characteristic of imines united to or in a nonacid bivalent radical ⟨*imino*porphyrins⟩ — distinguished from *imid-*

im·in·az·ole \,imə'na,zōl, -,na'z-\ *n* [*imin-* + *azole*] IMIDAZOLE

im·ine \'i,mēn, -,mən\ *n* -S [ISV, alter. of *amine*] **:** any of a class of compounds (as ethylenimine) derived from ammonia by replacement of two hydrogen atoms by a bivalent hydrocarbon radical or other nonacid organic radical — distinguished from *amine*

im·i·no \'imə,nō\ *adj* [*imin-*] **:** relating to or containing the group =NH or a substituted group =NR united to a radical other than an acid radical — distinguished from *imido*

imino ether *n* **:** IMIDO ESTER

imit *abbr* imitation; imitative

im·i·ta·bil·i·ty \,imədə'bilədē, -mətə-, -lətē, -i\ *n* **1 :** the quality or state of being imitable **2 :** the power of exhibiting Platonic imitation

im·i·ta·ble \-əbəl\ *adj* [MF, fr. L *imitabilis*, fr. *imitari* + *-abilis* -able] **1 :** capable of being imitated or copied ⟨the music is curiously devoid of those analyzable — and ~ — features —Winthrop Sargeant⟩ **2 :** worthy of imitation — **im·i·ta·ble·ness** *n* -ES

im·i·tan·cy \'imədənsē, -mətə-, -si\ *n* -ES [*imitate* + *-ancy*] **:** tendency to imitation **:** IMITATIVENESS

im·i·tant \-nt\ *n* -S [L *imitant-*, *imitans*, pres. part. of *imitari*] **:** something that imitates **:** a counterfeit or substitute article or product

im·i·tate \'imə,tāt, *usu* -ād.+V\ *vt* -ED/-ING/-S [L *imitatus*, past part. of *imitari* — more at IMAGE] **1 :** to follow as a pattern, model, or example **:** copy or strive to copy (as in acts, manners, conduct) **:** assume the form or likeness of ⟨drama that ~s life⟩ **2 :** to produce a likeness of (as in form, character, color, qualities, conduct, manners) **:** REPRODUCE, COPY **3 :** to be or appear like **:** resemble in external appearance ⟨paper finished to ~ leather⟩ **4 a :** MIMIC, MOCK ⟨~ another's intonations⟩ ⟨*imitating* his father's halting walk⟩ **b :** to exhibit or assume mimicry of **:** MIMIC 4 ⟨chameleons *imitating* their background⟩ ⟨the viceroy butterfly is said to ~ the monarch⟩ **5** *dial Eng* **:** ATTEMPT, ENDEAVOR — usu. followed by an infinitive ⟨that colt will ~ to throw you, give him a chance⟩ **syn** see COPY

im·i·tat·ee \,imə,tād·¦ē, -ā¦tē\ *n* -S [*imitate* + *-ee*] **:** one that is imitated

im·i·ta·tion \,imə'tāshən, *attrib* ¦==¦==\ *n* -S *often attrib* [L *imitation-*, *imitatio*, fr. *imitatus* + *-ion-*, *-io* -ion] **1 :** an act or instance of imitating **:** an assumption of or mimicking of the form of something that serves or is regarded as a model ⟨~ is the sincerest form of flattery⟩ ⟨the ~ of leaves by certain butterflies is unbelievably perfect⟩ ⟨a style developed in ~ of classic models⟩ **2 :** something that is made or produced as a copy **:** an artificial likeness **:** COUNTERFEIT ⟨risible ~s of his schoolfellows⟩ ⟨a convincing ~ of colonial architecture⟩ **3 a :** a literary work or composition designed to reproduce the style or manner of another author **b :** a free translation or an adaptation or parody esp. when involving transformation of cultural, social, or temporal situation **4 :** the repetition in a voice part of the melodic theme, phrase, or motive previously found in another part **5 a** *in Platonism* **:** the process through which a sensible object is informed by or participates in a subsistent idea or transcendent archetype — compare PARTICIPATION **b** *in Aristotelianism* (1) **:** the artistic simulation of anything as it is actually (2) **:** its representation as it is ideally or as it ought to be **6 a :** the execution of an act supposedly as a direct response to the perception of another person performing the act **b :** the assumption of the modes of behavior observed in other individuals

im·i·ta·tion·al \,imə¦tāshən³l, -shnəl\ *adj* **:** relating to, marked by, or employed in imitation ⟨~ propensities⟩

imitation art paper *n* **:** a paper that is heavily filled with clay and given a high finish on the calenders

imitation brick *n* **:** brick made of material other than clay or shale but having the same appearance

imitation leather *n* **:** a material (as a coated fabric, rubber or plastic composition, or paper) made and finished to resemble genuine leather

im·i·ta·tive \'imə,tād|iv, -məd·əl, |t|, |ēv *also* |əv\ *adj* [LL *imitativus*, fr. L *imitatus* + *-ivus* -ive] **1 a :** marked by imitation **:** exhibiting some of the qualities of or formed after a model, pattern, or original ⟨acting is an ~ art⟩ **b :** ONOMATOPOEIC ⟨~ words intended to reproduce or represent a natural sound⟩ **c :** exhibiting mimicry **2 :** inclined to imitate **:** given to imitation ⟨man is an ~ being⟩ **3 :** imitating something superior **:** COUNTERFEIT — **im·i·ta·tive·ly** \|əvlē, |li\ *adv* — **im·i·ta·tive·ness** \|ivnəs, |ēv- *also* |əv-\ *n* -ES

imitative magic *n* **:** magic based on the assumption that a desired result (as rain, the death of an enemy) can be brought about or assured by mimicking it — called also *homeopathic magic*; compare SYMPATHETIC MAGIC

im·i·ta·tor \'imə,tād·ə(r), -ātə-\ *n* -S [L, fr. *imitatus* (past part. of *imitari* to imitate) + *-or* — more at IMAGE] **:** one that imitates **:** one that gives or produces imitations

im·i·ta·tress \,imə¦tā·trəs\ *also* **im·i·ta·trix** \-riks\ *n, pl* **imitatress·es** \-rəsəz\ *also* **imitatri·ces** \,==¦tā·trə,sēz, -,tə'trī(,)sēz\ *or* **imitatrix·es** \,==¦tā·triksəz\ **:** a female imitator

im·mac·u·la·cy \ə'makyələsē, -si\ *n* -ES **:** the quality or state of being immaculate

im·mac·u·late \-lət, *usu* -ləd·+V\ *adj* [ME *immaculat*, fr. L *immaculatus*, fr. *in-* ¹in- + *maculatus*, past part. of *maculare* to spot, stain — more at MACULATE] **1 :** having no stain or blemish **:** SPOTLESS, UNDEFILED, PURE ⟨an ~ heart⟩ **2 :** containing no flaw, fault, or error ⟨an ~ book⟩ **3 a :** lacking any spot, soil, or smirch **:** spotlessly clean ⟨his linen was ~⟩ **b** *biol* **:** having no colored spots or marks — **im·mac·u·late·ly** *adv* — **im·mac·u·late·ness** *n* -ES

immaculate conception *n* [trans. of ML *immaculata conceptio*] **1** *usu cap I & C* **:** a conception in which the offspring is immediately and constantly preserved free from original sin by divine grace — used of the conception of the Virgin Mary in the womb of Saint Anne and made an article of faith of the Roman Catholic Church by Pius IX; distinguished from *virgin birth* **2 :** conception not preceded by sexual intercourse; *broadly* **:** production of something without evident source or origin ⟨the naturalist must insist that reason is not of *immaculate conception* —H.J.Muller⟩

im·malleable \(')i(m), ə+\ *adj* [¹*in-* + *malleable*] **:** lacking malleability **:** UNYIELDING, RIGID

im·manacle \ə+\ *vt* [²*in-* + *manacle* (n.)] *archaic* **:** MANACLE, FETTER

im·mane \(')i¦mān, ə'm-\ *adj* [L *immanis*, fr. *in-* ¹in- + *manis*, *manus* good — more at MATURE] **1** *archaic* **:** vast in size or extent **:** HUGE **2** *archaic* **:** extremely cruel **:** INHUMAN

im·ma·nence \'imənən(t)s\ *n* -S **1 :** the state or quality of being indwelling or inward or of not going beyond a particular domain **:** INHERENCE: as **a :** the condition of being in the mind or experientially given **b** *in Kantianism* **:** the condition of being within the limits of possible experience — contrasted with *transcendence* **2 :** the indwelling presence of God in the world

im·ma·nen·cy \-nənsē, -si\ *n* -ES **1 :** IMMANENCE **2 :** the doctrine of immanence; *esp* **:** the principle that God is immanent in the world — distinguished from *transcendence*

im·ma·nent \-nənt\ *adj* [LL *immanent-*, *immanens*, pres. part. of *immanēre* to remain in place, inhabit, fr. *in-* ²in- + L *manēre* to remain — more at MANSION] **1 a :** remaining or operating within the subject considered **:** INDWELLING, INHERENT, INTRINSIC ⟨considering both ~ and external factors in social evolution⟩ ⟨in many cults . . . objects of cult are the temporary abodes of spirits; when the spirits are ~ the objects receive ceremonial treatment —*Notes & Queries on Anthropology*⟩ **b** *of a mental event* **:** confined to consciousness or to the mind **:** SUBJECTIVE ⟨a cognition is an ~ act of mind —William Hamilton †1856⟩ — contrasted with *transcendent* **2 :** being or characterizing the relation of the world to mind according to various philosophies — **im·ma·nent·ly** *adv*

im·ma·nen·tal \,imə¦nent³l\ *adj* **:** relating to the doctrine of immanence **:** affirming and emphasizing the indwelling presence of God in the world ⟨an ~ religion⟩

immanent cause *n, Spinozism* **:** a cause originating and evolving within an entity ⟨God is the *immanent cause* of all things rather than the transient cause —*transl*⟩ — contrasted with *transient cause*

im·ma·nent·ism \'imənənt·,izəm, -nən·,ti-\ *n* -S **1 :** an epistemological theory according to which the relation of the world to the mind of an individual is one of immanence **2 :** any of several theories according to which the relation of God, mind, or spirit to the world including individuals is one of immanence ⟨the high ~ or near pantheism of Emerson and of the whole transcendentalist school owed not a little to oriental thought —C.S.Braden⟩

im·ma·nent·ist \-nəntəst, -,nen-\ *n* -S **:** an advocate of immanentism

im·ma·nen·tis·tic \¦imənən·¦tistik\ *or* **im·ma·nent·ist** \'imənəntəst, -,nen-\ *adj* **:** relating to or characteristic of immanentism

im·ma·nent·iza·tion \,imənəntə'zāshən, -,nentə'z-, -,nənt-,ī'z-\ *n* -S **:** the process of rendering immanent

im·manifest \(')i(m), ə+\ *adj* [¹*in-* + *manifest*] **:** not manifest

im·manity *n* -ES [L *immanitas*, fr. *immanis* immane + *-itas* -ity — more at IMMANE] *obs* **:** MONSTROSITY

im·mantle \ə+\ *vt* [²*in-* + *mantle* (n.)] **:** to cover or encircle with or as if with a mantle

im·marble *var of* EMMARBLE

im·mar·ces·ci·ble *or* **im·mar·ces·si·ble** \¦i(m)mär¦sesəbəl\ *adj* [LL *immarcescibilis*, fr. L *in-* ¹in- + LL *marcescibilis* withering, fr. L *marcescere* to wither, fade away + *-ibilis* -ible — more at MARCESCENT] **:** IMPERISHABLE, INDESTRUCTIBLE — **im·mar·ces·ci·bly** *or* **im·mar·ces·si·bly** \-blē\ *adv*

im·marginate \(')i(m), ə+\ *adj* [¹*in-* + *marginate*] **:** lacking a definite margin

immask *vt* [²*in-* + *mask* (n.)] *obs* **:** to cover with or as if with a mask **:** DISGUISE

im·material \¦i(m)+\ *adj* [ME *immateriel*, fr. MF, fr. LL *immaterialis*, fr. L *in-* ¹in- + LL *materialis* material — more at MATERIAL] **1 :** not consisting of matter **:** INCORPOREAL, SPIRITUAL, DISEMBODIED ⟨in making mind purely ~ . . . the body ceases to be living —John Dewey⟩ ⟨ghosts and other ~ entities⟩ **2** *obs* **:** having little body or substance **:** FLIMSY **3 a :** of no substantial consequence **:** UNIMPORTANT ⟨wholly ~ whether he stays or not⟩ ⟨the exact form of government appears ~ —Aidan Mulloy⟩ **b :** not material or essential to a legal matter or case — **im·materially** \"+\ *adv* — **im·materialness** \"+\ *n*

im·materialism \"+\ *n* **1 :** immaterial state or being **2 :** a philosophical theory that views external bodies as being of the essence of mind; *specif* **:** BERKELEIANISM

im·materialist \"+\ *n* **:** an advocate of philosophical immaterialism

im·materiality \"+\ *n* **:** the quality or state of being immaterial; *also* **:** something immaterial

im·materialize \"+\ *vt* **:** to render immaterial or incorporeal

im·ma·te·ri·als \-lz\ *n pl* **:** immaterial or incorporeal things

im·matriculate \,i+\ *vt* [ML *immatriculatus*, past part. of *immatriculare* to join, fr. L *in-* ²in- + ML *matricula* — more at MATRICULATE] *archaic* **:** MATRICULATE, ENROLL

im·matriculation \,i+\ *n* [prob. fr. G *immatrikulation*, fr. ML *immatriculatus* + G *-ion*] **:** an act, state, or process of being enrolled (as in an official register) ⟨lands on which a native title can be shown are put through a process of ~; a tax is then levied —F.M.Keesing⟩

¹im·mature \¦i(m)+\ *adj* [L *immaturus*, fr. *in-* ¹in- + *maturus* mature — more at MATURE] **1** *archaic* **:** PREMATURE, UNTIMELY **2 a :** lacking complete growth, differentiation, or development ⟨poor thin ~ soils⟩ ⟨~ animals⟩ **:** UNRIPE ⟨~ fruit⟩ **b** (1) **:** having capacities or potentialities for attaining but not yet having attained a definitive form or state ⟨~ talents⟩ ⟨a vigorous but ~ school of art⟩ **:** CRUDE, UNFINISHED (2) *of a topographic feature* **:** predictably due to undergo further changes **:** not having attained maturity — used esp. of valleys and drainages while most of the area is well above base-level **c :** exhibiting less than a normal or expected degree of maturity ⟨emotionally ~ adults⟩ ⟨the alcoholic is an ~, maladjusted individual —W.L.Wilkins⟩ — **im·maturely** \"+\ *adv* — **im·matureness** \"+\ *n*

²im·mature \"+\ *n* -S **:** an immature individual; *esp* **:** a young bird that has molted the juvenal plumage but has not yet acquired complete adult plumage

im·matured \"+\ *adj* [¹*in-* + *matured*, past part. of *mature*] **:** IMMATURE

im·maturity \"+\ *n* [L *immaturitas*, fr. *immaturus* + *-itas* -ity] **1 :** the state or quality of being immature ⟨emotional and cultural ~⟩ ⟨the ~ of such coarse mineral soils⟩ **2 :** something that is immature ⟨childish *immaturities*⟩ ⟨always within his *immaturities* is the saving grace of his willingness . . . to accept responsibility —*Times Lit. Supp.*⟩

im·measurability \(¦)i(m)+\ *n* **:** the quality or state of being immeasurable

im·measurable \(')i(m)+\ *adj* [ME *ynmesurable*, fr. *yn-* ¹in- + *mesurable* measurable — more at MEASURABLE] **:** incapable of being measured **:** IMMENSURABLE; *broadly* **:** indefinitely extensive **:** ILLIMITABLE — **im·measurableness** \"+\ *n* — **im·measurably** \"+\ *adv*

im·measured \"+\ *adj* [¹*in-* + *measured*] **:** IMMEASURABLE, VAST

im·mechanical \¦i(m)+\ *adj* [¹*in-* + *mechanical*] *archaic* **:** not mechanical **:** UNTECHNICAL

im·me·di·a·cy \ə'mēdēəsē, -si, *chiefly Brit* -mējə- *or* -mēdyə-\ *n* **1 :** the quality or state of being immediate; *usu* **:** freedom from or absence of an intervening medium **:** direct presence **:** DIRECTNESS, CONTIGUITY ⟨the ~ of personal experience —*London Calling*⟩ ⟨television has on occasion furnished a startling ~ . . . to news reports —F.L.Mott⟩ — opposed to *mediacy* **2 :** something that is immediate ⟨the ~ of our need⟩ — usu. used in pl. ⟨the *immediacies* of life⟩ **3 :** the state or relation under feudal law of being immediate lord or vassal **4 a :** the direct content of consciousness or consciousness itself as distinguished from what consciousness represents or mediates a knowledge of **b :** direct awareness or presentations of sense as contrasted with what is added by memory and association or thought **c :** the quality of something that is self-evident or intuited as contrasted with something that is arrived at by thought or reason

im·me·di·ate \ə'mēdēət, *usu* |d·+V; *chiefly Brit* -mējət *or* -mēdyət\ *adj* [LL *immediatus*, fr. L *in-* ¹in- + *mediatus* mediate — more at MEDIATE] **1 a :** acting or being without the intervention of another object, cause, or agency **:** DIRECT, PROXIMATE ⟨the ~ cause of death⟩ **b :** of or relating to psychic immediacy **:** being or occurring without reference to other states or factors **:** INTUITIVE ⟨~ knowledge⟩ **2** *of relations between persons* **a :** having no individual intervening **:** being next in line or relation **:** not secondary or remote ⟨the ~ parties to the quarrel⟩ ⟨only the ~ family was present⟩ ⟨you are most ~ to our throne —Shak.⟩ **b :** standing in or being the relation of vassal and lord when the one holds directly of the other **3 a :** occurring, acting, or accomplished without loss of time **:** made or done at once **:** INSTANT ⟨an ~ need for help⟩ ⟨~ expenses⟩ ⟨agreed to an ~ marriage⟩ **b** *of time* **:** near to or related to the present ⟨sometime in the ~ past⟩ ⟨the ~ future is uncertain⟩ **4 :** characterized by contiguity **:** existing without intervening space or substance ⟨bring the chemicals into ~ contact very cautiously⟩; *broadly* **:** being near at hand **:** not far apart or distant ⟨hid the money in the ~ neighborhood⟩

immediate annuity *n* **:** an annuity which is purchased with a single premium and on which the initial payment is made to the annuitant within the first year

immediate constituent *n* **:** any of the two or three meaningful parts directly forming a larger expression

immediate inference *n* **1 :** an inference drawn from a single premise **2 :** the operation of drawing an inference from a single premise

¹im·me·di·ate·ly *pronunc at* IMMEDIATE +lē *or* li; *or* ÷-mēdət-\ *adv* [ME *immediatly*, fr. LL *immediatus* + ME *-ly*] **1 :** without intermediary **:** in direct connection or relation **:** CLOSELY ⟨~ contiguous⟩ ⟨~ away from the shore⟩ **2 :** without interval of time **:** without delay **:** STRAIGHTWAY ⟨~ after the meeting⟩ ⟨come home ~⟩

²immediately \"\ *conj* **:** as soon as ⟨~ his intentions are understood, he may leave⟩

im·me·di·ate·ness *pronunc at* IMMEDIATE +nəs\ *n* -ES **:** the quality or state of being immediate **:** IMMEDIACY ⟨the ~ of their relationship⟩

im·me·di·a·tism \-ə,tizəm\ *n* -S **1 :** IMMEDIATENESS **2 :** a policy or practice of gaining a desired end by immediate action; *specif* **:** a policy advocating the immediate abolition of slavery **3 :** an epistemological theory that views the object of perception as directly knowable

im·me·di·a·tist \-əd·əst, -ətə-\ *n* -S **:** one that advocates or believes in immediatism

im·medicable \(')i(m)+\ *adj* [L *immedicabilis*, fr. *in-* ¹in- + *medicabilis* medicable — more at MEDICABLE] **:** being such as cannot be healed or remedied **:** INCURABLE ⟨this ~ evil⟩ — **im·medicably** \"+\ *adv*

im·mel·mann \'iməlmən, -l,män\ *vi* -ED/-ING/-S *often cap* [*Immelmann* (*turn*)] **:** to execute an Immelmann turn

immelmann turn *also* **immelmann** *n, usu cap I* [after Max *Immelmann* †1916 Ger. aviator] **:** a maneuver in which an airplane is first made to complete half of a loop and is then rolled half of a complete turn — called also *reverse turn*

im·melodious \¦i(m)+\ *adj* [¹*in-* + *melodious*] **:** not melodious

im·memorable \(')i(m)+\ *adj* [L *immemorabilis*, fr. *in-* ¹in- + *memorabilis* memorable — more at MEMORABLE] **1 :** not memorable **2 :** IMMEMORIAL — **im·memorably** \"+\ *adv*

im·memorial \¦i(m)+\ *adj* [prob. fr. F *immémorial*, fr. MF *immemorial*, fr. *in-* ¹in- + *memorial* — more at MEMORIAL] **:** extending beyond the reach of memory, record, or tradition **:** indefinitely ancient ⟨existing from time ~⟩ ⟨a chapel of ~ age —Andrew Lang⟩ ⟨~ elms —Alfred Tennyson⟩ — **im·memorially** \"\ *adv*

¹im·mense \ə'men(t)s\ *adj, sometimes* -ER/-EST [MF, fr. L *immensus* immeasurable, boundlesss, vast, fr. *in-* ¹in- + *mensus*, past part. of *metiri* to measure — more at MEASURE] **1** : marked by greatness in size, amount, number, degree, force, significance; *often* : transcending usual procedures of measuring and estimating ⟨the Los Angeles Aqueduct . . . like an ~ snake along the base of the mountains —*Amer. Guide Series: Calif.*⟩ ⟨thousands of lakes and ponds afford congenial haunts for ~ numbers of water birds —*Amer. Guide Series: Minn.*⟩ ⟨the ~ relief of the armistice —Mary Austin⟩ **2** : supremely good : EXCELLENT, FINE ⟨the reading has been ~ . . . started on the *Odyssey* and read six books with uncritical joy —H.J.Laski⟩ **syn** see HUGE

²immense \"\ *n* -s : immense space, extent, or number : IMMENSITY ⟨the dark ~ of air —Alfred Tennyson⟩

im·mense·ly *adv* : to an immense degree : VERY, EXCEEDINGLY

im·mense·ness *n* -ES : the quality or state of being immense : IMMENSITY

im·men·si·ty \-n(t)səd·ē, -ətē, -i\ *n* -ES [ME *immensitee*, fr. MF or L; MF *immensité*, fr. L *immensitat-, immensitas*, fr. *immensus* + *-itat-, -itas* -ity] **1 a** : immeasurable or boundless size, quantity, or degree : vastness in extent or bulk : unlimited extension ⟨the starry ~ of the heavens⟩ **b** : greatness of scope ⟨the ~ of this concept⟩ ⟨undertook a task of grave ~⟩ **2** : something that is immense : vast or infinite being, existence, or space ⟨the gigantic temples of Egypt, those massive *immensities* of granite —Edith Hamilton⟩ ⟨the mountain reared its white ~ before us⟩

im·mensurability \(ˌ)i(m)+\ *n* [ML *immensurabilitas*, fr. LL *immensurabilis* + L *-itas* -ity] : the quality or state of being immensurable

im·mensurable \(ˈ)i(m)+\ *adj* [LL *immensurabilis*, fr. L *in-* ¹in- + LL *mensurabilis* measurable — more at MEASURABLE] : not capable of being measured; *esp* : vastly large — **im·mensurableness** \"+\ *n* -ES

im·mensurate \(ˈ)i(m)ˈmen(t)s(ə)rət, -mench(ə)-\ *adj* [LL *immensuratus*, fr. L *in-* ¹in- + LL *mensuratus*, past part. of *mensurare* to measure — more at MENSURABLE] : UNMEASURED, UNLIMITED

im·merd \iˈmərd\ *vt* -ED/-ING/-S [²*in-* + L *merda* dung; akin to Gk *smordoun* to copulate, OSlav *smrŭděti* to stink, and prob. to L *mordēre* to bite — more at SMART] *archaic* : to cover with ordure

im·merge \(ˈ)i(m)ˈmərj\ *vb* [L *immergere* — more at IMMERSE] *vt, archaic* : to plunge (something) into, under, or within a fluid or other medium : IMMERSE ~ *vi* **1 a** *obs* : to plunge into a fluid **b** : to plunge into or immerse oneself in something ⟨no need to ~ further into this topic⟩ **2** *obs, of a celestial body* : to disappear by passing behind some obscuring agent (as a horizon or another celestial body)

im·mer·gence \-jən(t)s\ *n* : act of immerging

immerit *n* [¹*in-* + *merit*] *obs* : lack of worth : DEMERIT

immerited *adj* [¹*in-* + *merited*] *obs* : UNDESERVED

im·mer·sal \əˈmərsəl, -məs-,-məis-\ *n* -s [*immerse* + *-al*] : the state of being immersed ⟨his complete ~ in affairs of state⟩

im·merse \əˈmərs, -məs, -məis\ *vb* -ED/-ING/-S [L *immersus*, past part. of *immergere*, fr. *in-* ²in- + *mergere* to dip, merge — more at MERGE] *vt* **1 a** (1) : to plunge or dip into a liquid ⟨~ the cut beans in boiling water to blanch⟩ ⟨test the temperature before *immersing* yourself in the pool⟩ (2) : to baptize by immersion **b** : to enclose in something : EMBED, INCLUDE, SINK, BURY ⟨fossils *immersed* in sandstone⟩ ⟨the lower half of the cuttings should be *immersed* in moist sand⟩ **2** : to engross the attention of : engage deeply : ABSORB ⟨~s himself completely in his work⟩ ⟨has been *immersed* almost all his life in the business of the law —M.R.Cohen⟩ ~ *vi* : to become absorbed : PLUNGE, SINK **syn** see DIP

immersed *adj* : submerged in or as if in a fluid: as **a** : completely engrossed **b** (1) *of a bodily structure* : completely embedded in or sunk below the surface of another part or organ (2) *of the capsule of a moss* : covered by the perichaetium **c** *of a plant* : growing wholly under water

immersed wedge *n* : the wedge-shaped portion of a ship that becomes immersed when the ship rolls

im·mers·ible \-səbəl\ *adj* : capable of being immersed

im·mer·sion \-mər|zhən, -məl, -məi|, |sh-\ *n* -s [LL *immersion-, immersio*, fr. L *immersus* + *-ion-, -io* -ion] : an act of immersing or a state of being immersed: as **a** (1) : a sinking or plunging usu. into or within a fluid : DIPPING ⟨the sense of chill that follows ~ of the hand in a volatile liquid⟩ (2) : submersion in water for the purpose of Christian baptism : baptism by complete submersion of the person in water — compare AFFUSION, ASPERSION **b** : disappearance of a celestial body either by passing behind another (as in the occultation of a star by the moon) or by passing into its shadow (as in the eclipse of a satellite) — compare EMERSION **c** : SIMPLE IMMERSION

im·mer·sion·al \-zhənᵊl, -zhnəl, -sh-\ *adj* : of, relating to, or occurring through immersion ⟨~ baptism⟩

immersion cup *n* : a cup used for examining a gem immersed in a liquid of high refractive index

immersion foot *n* : a painful condition of the feet marked by inflammation and stabbing pain and followed by discoloration, swelling, ulcers, and numbness due to prolonged exposure to moist cold usu. without actual freezing — compare TRENCH FOOT

immersion heater *n* : a usu. electric unit for heating a liquid by immersion

immersion heater

im·mer·sion·ism \-zhəˌnizəm, -sh-\ *n* -s : a doctrine that immersion is essential to Christian baptism : the practice of baptism by immersion

im·mer·sion·ist \-nəst\ *n* -s : one that advocates or practices immersionism

immersion lens *or* **immersion objective** *n* : an objective of short focal distance designed to work with a drop of liquid (as oil or water) between front lens and cover glass

immersion liquid *n* : a liquid of known refractive index used by gemmologists to reduce refraction of light at the surfaces of a gem and facilitate examination of the interior

immesh *var of* ENMESH

im·methodical *also* **im·methodic** \ˌi(m)+\ *adj* [¹*in-* + *methodical, methodic*] : lacking method or order : not methodical ⟨a careless ~ program⟩ — **im·methodically** \"+\ *adv*

im·metrical \(ˈ)i(m)+\ *adj* [¹*in-* + *metrical*] : lacking meter : UNMETRICAL ⟨a harsh ~ line of verse⟩ — **im·metrically** \"+\ *adv*

im·meu·bles \ēmœbl(ᵊ), -b(lə)\ *n pl* [F, pl. of *immeuble* piece of fixed property, fr. MF, fr. *immeuble* immovable (in *biens immeubles* immovable property), fr. OF *immobile*, fr. L *immobilis* — more at IMMOBILE] : a class of property under French law that consists essentially of immovables — compare MEUBLES

im·mie \ˈimē\ *n* -s [*imm-* (fr. *imitation agate*) + *-ie*] : MARBLE 2a; *esp* : a glass marble streaked with colors

¹im·mi·grant \ˈiməgrənt, -mēg- *sometimes* -ˌgrant *or* -ˌgraa(ə)nt\ *n* -s [L *immigrant-, immigrans*, pres. part. of *immigrare*] : one that immigrates: **a** : a person that comes to a country for the purpose of permanent residence — compare EMIGRANT **b** : a plant or animal that appears and becomes established in an area in which it was previously unknown

²immigrant \"\ *adj* : of, relating to, or composed of immigrants ⟨an ~ fauna⟩ ⟨department concerned with ~ affairs⟩ : IMMIGRATING ⟨~ birds⟩

im·mi·grate \ˈiməˌgrāt\ *vb* [L *immigratus*, past part. of *immigrare* to remove, go in, fr. *in-* ²in- + *migrare* to migrate — more at MIGRATE] *vi* : to come to dwell or settle : to enter and usu. become established ⟨white blood cells ~ to the site of the injury⟩; *esp* : to come into a country of which one is not a native for the purpose of permanent residence ~ *vt* : to bring in or send as immigrants

im·mi·gra·tion \ˌiməˈgrāshən\ *n* -s *often attrib* **1** : an act or instance of immigrating; *specif* : a going into a country for the purpose of permanent residence **2** : a party of immigrants; *broadly* : the number of immigrants arriving during a given period

im·mi·gra·tion·al \ˌiməˈgrāshənᵊl, -shnəl\ *adj* : relating to or concerned with immigration

immigration pressure *n* : the effect on the makeup of a natural population of recurrent immigrations of individuals capable of interbreeding with the original stock

im·mi·gra·to·ry \ˈiməgrəˌtōrē, -mēg-, -ȯr-, -ri\ *adj* : of, relating to, or constituting immigration ⟨~ movements of populations⟩

immind *vt* [²*in-* + *mind* (n.)] *obs* : REMIND

im·mi·nence \ˈimənən(t)s\ *n* -s [L *imminentia*, fr. *imminent-, imminens* + *-ia* -y] **1** *also* **im·mi·nen·cy** \-nənsē, -si\ -ES : the quality or state of being imminent **2** : something that is imminent; *usu* : impending evil or danger

im·mi·nent \-nənt\ *adj* [L *imminent-, imminens*, pres. part. of *imminēre* to project, threaten, fr. *in-* ²in- + *-minēre* (akin to L *mont-, mons* mountain) — more at MOUNT] **1** : ready to take place : near at hand : IMPENDING ⟨our ~ departure⟩; *usu* : hanging threateningly over one's head : menacingly near ⟨in ~ jeopardy⟩ ⟨this ~ danger⟩ **2** : IMMANENT — **im·mi·nent·ly** *adv* — **im·mi·nent·ness** *n* -ES

im·min·gle \i+\ *vb* [²*in-* + *mingle*] : BLEND, INTERMINGLE

im·mi·nu·tion \ˌiməˈn(y)üshən\ *n* -s [L *imminution-, imminutio*, fr. *imminutus* (past part. of *imminuere* to lessen, fr. *in-* ²in- + *minuere* to lessen) + *-ion-, -io* -ion — more at MINOR] *archaic* : DIMINUTION

im·miscibility \(ˌ)i(m)+\ *n* : inability to mix or become homogeneous

im·miscible \(ˈ)i(m)+\ *adj* [¹*in-* + *miscible*] : incapable of mixing or being mixed : unable to blend or attain homogeneity ⟨makes separate polyphonic lines more ~ by writing them sometimes in different keys —Joseph Kerman⟩ — used esp. of liquids ⟨~ solvents⟩; compare INCOMPATIBLE — **im·miscibly** \"+\ *adv*

im·mis·er·i·za·tion \iˌmizərəˈzāshən, -ˌrīˈz-\ *n* -s [²*in-* + *miserable* + *-ization*; intended as trans. of G *verelendung*] : act of making or state of becoming miserable; *esp* : IMPOVERISHMENT ⟨the ~ of the proletariat⟩

im·mis·sion \(ˈ)iˈmishən\ *n* [L *immission-, immissio*, fr. *immissus* past part. of *immittere* to send in (fr. *in-* ²in- + *mittere* to send) + *-ion-, -io* -ion — more at SMITE] **1 a** *archaic* : an act of sending or letting in : INJECTION, ADMISSION, INTRODUCTION **b** *obs* : something introduced **2** : COMMIXTURE 2

im·mit \iˈmit\ *vt* **immitted; immitted; immitting; immits** [L *immittere*] *archaic* : to send or let in : INJECT, ADMIT, INTRODUCE

im·mitigable \(ˈ)i(m)+\ *adj* [LL *immitigabilis*, fr. L *in-* ¹in- + *mitigare* to mitigate + *-abilis* -able — more at MITIGATE] : not capable of being mitigated, softened, lessened, or appeased ⟨such ~ evil⟩ — **im·mitigableness** \"+\ *n* -ES — **im·mitigably** \"+\ *adv*

im·mix \iˈmiks\ *vt* [back-formation fr. *immixed* mixed in, fr. ME *immixte*, fr. L *immixtus*, past part. of *immiscēre* to mix in, fr. *in-* ²in- + *miscēre* to mix — more at MIX] : to mix intimately : mix in or up : COMMINGLE

im·mix·able \(ˈ)i(m)ˈmiksəbəl\ *adj* [¹*in-* + *mixable*] : IMMISCIBLE

im·mixture \i+\ *n* [L *immixtus* + E *-ure*] : the act of immixing : the quality or state of being immixed : an intimate mixture

im·mobile \(ˈ)i(m), ə+\ *adj* [ME *in-mobill*, fr. L *immobilis*, fr. *in-* ¹in- + *mobilis* movable — more at MOBILE] : incapable of being moved : IMMOVABLE, FIXED, STABLE; *broadly* : UNMOVING, MOTIONLESS

im·mo·bi·lism \əˈmōbəˌlizəm\ *n* -s [F *immobilisme*, fr. *immobile* (fr. L *immobilis*) + *-isme* -ism] : a governmental policy characterized by compromise and moderation often to the point of ignoring basic issues and stagnation of progressive trends

im·mo·bi·list \-ləst\ *n* -s : one who advocates immobilism

im·mobility \ˌi(m)+\ *n* [MF *immobilité*, fr. LL *immobilitat-, immobilitas*, fr. L *immobilis* + *-itat-, -itas* -ity] : the quality or state of being immobile : FIXEDNESS; *broadly* : MOTIONLESSNESS

im·mobilization \(ˌ)i(m), ə+\ *n* [F *immobilisation*, fr. *immobiliser* + *-ation*] : the act of immobilizing or state of being immobilized: as **a** (1) : quiet rest in bed for a prolonged period used in the treatment of disease (as tuberculosis) (2) : fixation (as by a plaster cast) of a body part usu. to promote healing in normal structural relation **b** : loss of evolutionary plasticity due to existence in a relatively constant environment resulting in elimination of mutations and variability

im·mobilize \(ˈ)i(m), ə+\ *vt, see -ize in Explan Notes* [F *immobiliser*, fr. *immobile* + *-iser* -ize] : to make immobile : fix in place or position : render incapable of movement: as **a** : to interfere with or prevent freedom of movement or effective use of (as military forces or equipment) ⟨our planes were *immobilized* by bad weather⟩ ⟨the enemy was *immobilized* by lack of transport⟩ **b** : to fix (as a body part) so as to reduce or eliminate motion usu. by means of a cast or splint, by strapping, or by strict bed rest ⟨*immobilizing* a fractured bone by a cast and continuous traction⟩ ⟨~ an injury⟩ ⟨the patient was *immobilized* for three months⟩ **c** (1) : to withhold (specie) from circulation to serve as security for other money (2) : to convert (circulating capital) into fixed capital

im·mo·bi·liz·er \"ə(r)\ *n* : one that immobilizes

im·moderacy \(ˈ)i(m), ə+\ *n* -ES : IMMODERATENESS

im·moderate \"+\ *adj* [ME *immoderat*, fr. L *immoderatus*, fr. *in-* ¹in- + *moderatus*, past part. of *moderare* to moderate — more at MODERATE] **1** : lacking in moderation : exceeding just, usual, or suitable bounds : EXTRAVAGANT, UNREASONABLE ⟨~ demands⟩ ⟨an ~ speed⟩ ⟨~ appetites⟩ ⟨an ~ theorist⟩ **2** *obs* **a** : characterized by excess : INTEMPERATE **b** : having no limits : BOUNDLESS **syn** see EXCESSIVE

im·moderately \"+\ *adv* [ME, fr. *immoderat* + *-ly*] : without moderation : to an immoderate degree

im·moderateness \"+\ *n* : the quality or state of being immoderate

im·moderation \(ˌ)i(m), ə+\ *n* [MF *immoderacion*, fr. L *immoderation-, immoderatio*, fr. *in-* ¹in- + *moderation-, moderatio* moderation — more at MODERATION] : lack of moderation

im·modest \(ˈ)i(m), ə\ *adj* [L *immodestus*, fr. *in-* ¹in- + *modestus* modest — more at MODEST] : lacking or deficient in modesty: as **a** : failing in the reserve or restraint that decorum or custom requires ⟨brash ~ boasting⟩ ⟨the ~ claims of the billboards⟩ **b** : deficient in sexual modesty : not conforming to the sexual mores of a particular time or place : BRAZEN, INDECENT ⟨a thoroughly ~ costume⟩ ⟨~ conduct⟩ — **im·modestly** \"\ *adv*

im·modesty \"+\ *n* [L *immodestia*, fr. *immodestus* + *-ia* -y] **1** : lack of modesty, delicacy, or decent reserve : FORWARDNESS, BOLDNESS **2** : lack of decency : IMPROPRIETY, UNCHASTITY

im·modulated \"+\ *adj* [¹*in-* + *modulated*] : lacking modulation

im·mo·late \ˈiməˌlāt, *usu* -ād·+V\ *vt* -ED/-ING/-S [L *immolatus*, past part. of *immolare*, fr. *in-* ²in- + *mola* spelt grits; fr. the ancient custom of sprinkling victims with sacrificial salted meal; akin to *molere* to grind — more at MILL] **1** : to offer in sacrifice (as to a deity); *esp* : to kill as a sacrificial victim **2** : to sacrifice or abnegate (as oneself) usu. in the interests of some cause or objective ⟨the end to which she has *immolated* all her affections —T.L.Peacock⟩ ⟨*immolating* himself for his family's sake⟩ **3** : KILL, DESTROY ⟨the millions *immolated* in war⟩ ⟨a party of [African] hunting dogs would assuredly chase and ~ any single domestic canine —James Stevenson-Hamilton⟩

im·mo·la·tion \ˌiməˈlāshən\ *n* -s [L *immolation-, immolatio*, fr. *immolatus* + *-ion-, -io* -ion] **1** : the act of immolating or state of being immolated **2** : something that is immolated

im·mo·la·tor \ˈiməˌlād·ə(r), -ātə-\ *n* -s [L, fr. *immolatus* + *-or*] : one that immolates

im·mo·ment \i+\ *or* **im·momentous** \ˌi(m)+\ *adj* [¹*in-* + *moment* (n.) *or momentous*] : TRIFLING, UNIMPORTANT

im·moral \(ˈ)i(m), ə+\ *adj* [¹*in-* + *moral*] : not moral : inconsistent with purity or good morals : contrary to conscience or moral law : WICKED, LICENTIOUS ⟨an ~ man⟩ ⟨such ~ acts⟩; *broadly* : opposed to, critical of, or in conflict with generally or traditionally held moral principles ⟨refusal to acknowledge the boundaries set by convention is the source of frequent denunciations of art as ~ —John Dewey⟩ — compare UNMORAL

im·moralism \"+\ *n* [G *immoralismus*, fr. *immoral* (fr. F or E) + *-ismus* -ism] : an ethical viewpoint (as that of Nietzsche) that would institute a new scale of values in opposition to the traditional

im·moralist \"+\ *n* **1** : an advocate or practicer of immorality **2** : an advocate of immoralism

im·morality \ˌi(m)+\ *n* [¹*in-* + *morality*] **1** : the quality or state of being immoral : VICE, WICKEDNESS; *esp* : UNCHASTITY **2** : an immoral act or practice

im·moralize \(ˈ)i(m), ə+\ *vt* : to make immoral : DEMORALIZE

im·morally \"+\ *adv* : in an immoral manner : with immorality

im·mor·ta·bil·i·ty \(ˌ)iˌm,mȯ(r)d·əˈbiləd·ē, əˌm-\ *n* : the quality or state of being capable of attaining or fit for immortality

im·mor·ta·ble \(ˈ)i(m)ˈmȯ(r)d·əbəl, əˈm-\ *adj* [*immortal* + *-able*] : capable of attaining immortality

¹im·mortal \(ˈ)i(m), ə+\ *adj* [ME, fr. L *immortalis*, fr. *in-* ¹in- + *mortalis* mortal — more at MORTAL] **1** : not mortal : exempt from liability to die ⟨the ~ gods⟩ **2** : connected with or relating to immortality ⟨I have ~ longings in me —Shak.⟩ **3** : destined to persist through the ages : exempt from oblivion : IMPERISHABLE, ABIDING ⟨those ~ words⟩ ⟨his fame ~⟩

²immortal \"\ *n* **1 a** : an immortal being : one exempt from death **b immortals** *pl, often cap* : the gods of the Greek and Roman pantheon **2 a immortals** *pl, often cap* : a body of troops immortal in some way: as (1) : the royal bodyguard of ancient Persia whose number was always kept full (2) : troops famous for gallant behavior in war (3) : troops that never see war **b** : a person (as an author) whose fame is lasting **c** *usu cap* : any of the 40 members of the Académie française **3 a** *in Confucianism* : an ideal human being of antiquity **b** *in Taoism* : one that has reached a divine state that is the highest to which man can attain **c** : a Chinese saint **4** *also* **immortal hand** : a stud-poker hand that is sure to win

im·mortalism \"+\ *n* : a doctrine of or belief in the soul's immortality

im·mortalist \"+\ *n* : one that affirms a belief in immortalism

im·mor·tal·i·ty \ˌi(m),mȯ(r)ˈtaləd·ē, -lətē, -i *sometimes* ə,mȯ(r)- *or* ˌimə(r)-\ *n* [ME *immortalite*, fr. MF *immortalité*, fr. L *immortalitat-, immortalitas*, fr. *immortalis* + *-itat-, -itas* -ity] : the quality or state of being immortal: as **a** : exemption from death or annihilation : unending existence : everlasting life ⟨the ~ of the soul⟩ ⟨human ~⟩ **b** : exemption from oblivion : lasting fame ⟨the ~ of these stirring words⟩ ⟨his deeds have earned him ~ in the hearts of men⟩

im·mor·tal·iz·able \i(m)ˈmȯ(r)d·ᵊlˌīzəbəl, əˈm-, -)tᵊl-, (ˌ)=-, ˌ=ˈ===\ *adj* : capable of being immortalized

im·mor·tal·iza·tion \=ˌ===əˈzāshən, -ˌīˈz-\ *n* -s [F *immortalisation*, fr. *immortaliser* to immortalize + *-ation*] : the act or process of making immortal; *also* : the state of being made immortal

im·mor·tal·ize \=ˈ===ˌīz\ *vt* -ED/-ING/-S *see -ize in Explan Notes* [MF *immortaliser*, fr. *immortal* (fr. L *immortalis*) + *-iser* -ize — more at IMMORTAL] : to make immortal: **a** : to cause to live or exist forever : endow with everlasting life **b** : to exempt from oblivion : perpetuate in fame

im·mor·tal·iz·er \"ə(r)\ *n* -s : one that immortalizes something; *esp* : a writer who preserves in his work something of the present for posterity

im·mortally \(ˈ)i(m), ə+\ *adv* **1** : ETERNALLY, EVERLASTINGLY, FOREVER, PERPETUALLY **2** : to a superhuman or excessive degree : INFINITELY

im·mor·telle \ˌi,mȯ(r)ˈtel, ə,=ˈ=\ *n* -s [F, fr. fem. of *immortel* immortal, fr. L *immortalis* — more at IMMORTAL] **1** : EVERLASTING 3 **2** *or* **immortelle tree** : any of various coral trees; *esp* : a large red-flowered tree (*Erythrina micropteryx*) widely used in tropical America as an ornamental and as a shade tree in cacao plantations

im·mortification \(ˌ)i(m)+\ *n* [F, fr. MF, fr. ML *immortificatus* disciplined, fr. L *in-* ²in- + LL *mortificatus*, past part. of *mortificare* to mortify — more at MORTIFY] *archaic* : a lack of discipline (as of bodily appetites and desires)

im·motile \(ˈ)i(m), ə+\ *adj* [¹*in-* + *motile*] : lacking motility : incapable of movement — **im·motility** \ˌi(m)\ *n*

im·motive \(ˈ)i(m)+\ *adj* [¹*in-* + *motive*] : UNMOVING, IMMOVABLE

im·movability \(ˌ)i(m), ə+\ *n* : the quality or state of being immovable

¹im·movable *also* **im·moveable** \(ˈ)i(m), ə+\ *adj* [ME *immovable*, fr. ¹*in-* + *movable*] **1** : incapable of being moved : firmly fixed : FAST ⟨the ~ hills⟩; *broadly* : not moving or not intended to be moved : STATIONARY **2 a** : STEADFAST, UNALTERABLE, UNYIELDING ⟨an ~ purpose⟩ **b** : not capable of being moved in feeling or sympathies : UNIMPRESSIBLE, IMPASSIVE ⟨a stern ~ man⟩ **3** : not liable to be removed : permanent in place or tenure : FIXED ⟨an ~ estate⟩ — **im·movableness** \"+\ *n*

²immovable *also* **immoveable** \"\ *n* **1** : one that cannot be moved **2 immovables** *pl, Roman & civil law* **a** : lands, houses thereon, and all things adhering or belonging there by nature (as trees, minerals) or by act of man (as planted crops, fertilizer) — compare ACCESSION 2c **b** : all personal property permanently attached to immovable property that cannot be removed without injury to the latter — see FIXTURE 2c **c** : all personal property placed on immovable property by the owner for its service, improvement, or exploitation **d** : an interest or estate in immovable property **3** *Scots law* : heritable property as opposed to movable property

immovable feast *n* : an ecclesiastical feast that always occurs on the same day of the year

immovable fixture *n* : FIXTURE 2c(1)

im·movably \(ˈ)i(m), ə+\ *adv* [ME, fr. *immovable* + *-ly*] : so as to be incapable of movement or of being moved ⟨hills brooding ~ over the town⟩

im·mund \əˈmənd\ *adj* [L *immundus*, fr. *in-* ¹in- + *mundus* clean — more at MOTHER (dregs)] : UNCLEAN, FILTHY — **im·mun·di·ty** \-dəd·ē\ *n* -ES

¹im·mune \əˈmyün\ *adj* [L *immunis* exempt from public service, exempt, fr. *in-* ¹in- + *-munis* (fr. *munia* services, obligations) — more at MEAN (common)] **1 a** : FREE, EXEMPT ⟨~ from further taxation⟩ ⟨a book is a tool . . . and should be as ~, almost, from decoration as a crowbar or a cartridge —Holbrook Jackson⟩ **b** : PROTECTED, GUARDED — usu. used with *from* or *against* ⟨~ from political pressures by reason of his office⟩ ⟨a full life is ~ against boredom⟩ **2** [F *immun*, fr. L *immunis*] : not susceptible or responsive — usu. used with *to* ⟨~ to all pleas⟩ ⟨the Soviet Union has not been ~ to the pressures of coexistence —L.S.Feuer⟩ ⟨a streptococcus ~ to antibiotics⟩; *esp* : having a high degree of natural or acquired resistance to a disease ⟨~ to diphtheria⟩ **3 a** : having or producing antibodies to a corresponding antigen or hapten ⟨an ~ serum⟩ **b** : produced in response to the presence of a corresponding antigen ⟨~ agglutinins⟩ **4** *of cotton yarn* : treated so as to repel the usual dyes for cotton

²immune \"\ *n* -s : an immune individual

immune body *n* : ANTIBODY

im·muned \-nd\ *adj* [¹*immune* + *-ed*] : IMMUNIZED — used chiefly of domestic animals

immune globulin *or* **immune serum globulin** *n* : globulin from the blood of a person or animal immune to a particular disease

immune serum *n* : ANTISERUM

im·mun·ist \əˈmyünəst, ˈimyən-\ *n* -s [F *immuniste*, fr. *immun* + *-iste* -ist] : one that enjoys an immunity (as from service or payment of some due)

im·mu·ni·ty \əˈmyünəd·ē, -ətē, -i\ *n* -ES [L *immunitas*, fr. *immunis* + *-itas* -ity] **1 a** : freedom or exemption from a charge, duty, obligation, office, tax, imposition, penalty, or service esp. as granted by law to a person or class of persons **b** : a freedom granted to a special category of persons from the normal burdens and duties arising out of a legal relationship with other persons ⟨legislative ~⟩ ⟨judicial ~⟩ **2** *obs* **:** unrestrained license or an instance of it **3 a :** lack of susceptibility (as to a natural hazard) ⟨this alloy has complete ~ to rust⟩ ⟨no one has assured ~ from error⟩ **b :** freedom from or security against something noxious or injurious ⟨the long ~ of America from outside threats or dangers —D.W. Brogan⟩ **4** [F *immunité*, fr. *immun* + *-ité* -ity] **:** a condition of being able or the capacity to resist a particular disease esp. through preventing development of a pathogenic microorganism or by counteracting the effects of its products — see ACTIVE IMMUNITY, ACQUIRED IMMUNITY, NATURAL IMMUNITY, PASSIVE IMMUNITY

im·mu·ni·za·tion \ˌimyə|nə'zāshən, |ˌnī'z- *also* ə̇ˌmyü|\ *n* -s **:** the creation of immunity usu. against a particular disease ⟨~ against smallpox⟩; *esp* **:** treatment of an organism for the purpose of making it immune to subsequent attack by a particular pathogen

im·mu·nize \'imyəˌnīz\ *vt* -ED/-ING/-S *see -ize in Explan Notes* [G *immunisieren*, fr. *immun* immune (fr. F) + *-isieren* -ize — more at IMMUNE] **:** to make immune ⟨the best known examples . . . are in semiarid regions, a circumstance that has *immunized* the scarps from attack by vigorous consequent rivers —C.A.Cotton⟩; *esp* **:** to cause to produce antibodies against an antigen or hapten

immuno- *comb form* [ISV, fr. *immune*] **1 :** physiological immunity ⟨*immuno*logy⟩ **2 :** immunologic ⟨*immuno*chemistry⟩ **:** immunologically ⟨*immuno*compatible⟩ **:** immunology and ⟨*immuno*genetics⟩

im·mu·no·biologic *also* **immunobiological** \¦imyə(ˌ)nō, ə̇¦myü(ˌ)nō+\ *adj* [*immuno-* + *biologic, biological*] **:** of or relating to the physiological reactions characteristic of the immune state ⟨~ anomalies in leprosy —*Biol. Abstracts*⟩ — **im·mu·no·biology** \"+\ *n*

im·mu·no·chemical \"+\ *adj* [*immuno-* + *chemical*] **:** of or relating to immunochemistry — **im·mu·no·chemically** \"+\ *adv*

im·mu·no·chemist \"+\ *n* [*immuno-* + *chemist*] **:** a specialist in immunochemistry

im·mu·no·chemistry \"+\ *n* [ISV *immuno-* + *chemistry*] **:** a branch of chemistry that deals with substances (as antibodies, antigens, or haptens) and reactions as concerned in the phenomena of immunity-antibody production

im·mu·no·gen \ə̇'myünəjə̇n, -ˌjen\ *n* -s [fr. *Immunogen*, a trademark] **:** an antigen that produces an immune response (as antibody production)

im·mu·no·genesis \¦imyə(ˌ)nō, ə̇¦myü(ˌ)nō+\ *n* [NL, fr. *immuno-* + *genesis*] **:** immunity production

im·mu·no·genetic *also* **immunogenetical** \"+\ *adj* [*immuno-* + *genetic, genetical*] **:** of or relating to immunogenetics

im·mu·no·genetics \"+\ *n pl but sing or pl in constr* [*immuno-* + *genetics*] **:** a branch of immunology concerned with the interrelations of heredity, disease, and the immune system esp. with regard to the way in which the genetic information required to produce the great diversity of antibodies required by the immune system is stored in the genome, transmitted from one generation to the next, and expressed in the organism

im·mu·no·gen·ic \"+¦jenik\ *adj* [*immuno-* + *-genic*] **:** relating to or producing an immune response — compare ANTIGENIC — **im·mu·no·gen·i·cal·ly** \-nə̇k(ə)lē\ *adv* — **im·mu·no·ge·nic·i·ty** \-jə̇'nisəd·ē\ *n* -ES

im·mu·no·log·ic \"+¦läjik\ *also* **im·mu·no·log·i·cal** \-jə̇kəl\ *adj* **:** of or relating to immunology — **im·mu·no·log·i·cal·ly** \-jə̇k(ə)lē\ *adv*

im·mu·nol·o·gist \ˌimyə'näləjə̇st\ *n* -s **:** a specialist in immunology

im·mu·nol·o·gy \-jē\ *n* -ES [ISV *immuno-* + *-logy*] **1 :** a science that deals with the phenomena and causes of immunity **2 :** a treatise on immunology

im·mu·no·therapy \¦imyə(ˌ)nō, ə̇¦myü(ˌ)nō+\ *n* [ISV *immuno-* + *therapy*] **:** treatment of or prophylaxis against disease that is based on the production of antibodies and induction of immunity and that chiefly employs antigens or antigenic preparations (as antisera, toxoids, vaccines)

im·mu·no·transfusion \"+\ *n* [ISV *immuno-* + *transfusion*] **:** transfusion of blood from a donor in whom there has been stimulated the production of antibodies for an infectious agent affecting the recipient

im·mu·ra·tion \ˌimyə'rāshən\ *n* -s **:** act of immuring or state of being immured

im·mure \ə̇'myu̇(ə)r, -u̇ə\ *vt* -ED/-ING/-S [ML *immurare*, fr. L *in-* [2]in- + *murus* wall — more at MURAL] **1** *obs* **:** to enclose or fortify with a wall **2 a :** to enclose within or as if within walls ⟨*immured* in an isolated outpost⟩ ⟨scientists who ~ themselves in special research⟩ **b :** to shut up **:** IMPRISON, INCARCERATE ⟨a fairy princess *immured* in a tower⟩ **3 :** to build into a wall ⟨an ancient altar half-*immured*⟩; *esp* **:** to punish by entombing within a wall or between walls ⟨a nun who broke her vow might be *immured*⟩ ⟨*immuring* these heretics⟩

im·mure·ment \-u̇(ə)rmənt, -u̇əm-\ *n* -s **:** the quality or state of being immured ⟨the ~ within colleges of the artist, the poet in residence —Marcus Cunliffe⟩

im·musical \(')i(m), ə+\ *adj* [[1]*in-* + *musical*] **:** INHARMONIOUS, UNMUSICAL, DISCORDANT — **im·musically** \"+\ *adv*

im·mutability \(¦)i(m), ə+\ *n* [L *immutabilitas*, fr. *immutabilis* immutable + *-itas* -ity] **:** the quality or state of being immutable

im·mutable \(')i(m), ə+\ *adj* [ME, fr. L *immutabilis*, fr. *in-* [1]in + *mutabilis* mutable — more at MUTABLE] **:** not capable or susceptible of change **:** INVARIABLE, UNALTERABLE ⟨~ laws⟩ — **im·mutableness** \"+\ *n* — **im·mutably** \"+\ *adv*

immutation *n* [L *immutation-*, *immutatio*, fr. *immutatus* (past part. of *immutare* to change, alter, fr. *in-* [2]in- + *mutare* to change) + *-ion-*, *-io* -ion — more at MUTABLE] *obs* **:** CHANGE, ALTERATION, MUTATION

immy *abbr* immediately

imo·chagh *also* **imo·shagh** \¦ēmō¦shäg\ *n* -s *usu cap* **:** a member of the southern branch of the Tuareg people

imo·hagh \¦ēmō¦häg\ *n* -s *usu cap* **:** a member of the northern branch of the Tuareg people

imo·ni·um \(')i¦mōnēəm, (')ī¦m-\ *n* -s [*im*ine + ammo*nium*] **:** ammonium in which a bivalent radical is a substituent

imou pine \'ēˌmü-\ *n* [prob. native name in New Zealand] *NewZeal* **:** RIMU

[1]imp \'imp\ *n* -s [ME *impe*, fr. OE *impa*, fr. *impian* — more at [2]IMP] **1 a** *obs* **:** SHOOT, BUD, SLIP; *also* **:** GRAFT **b** *archaic* **:** OFFSPRING, PROGENY, CHILD, SCION **2 a** *archaic* **:** an evil or malicious child **b :** a small demon, devil, or wicked spirit ⟨~*s* released from a sorcerer's bottle —William Peden⟩ **c :** a mischievous child **:** URCHIN ⟨as disagreeable a young ~ as you'd ask to see —G.B.Shaw⟩

[2]imp \"\ *vt* -ED/-ING/-S [ME *impen*, fr. OE *impian*; akin to OHG *impfōn* to graft; both fr. a prehistoric OHG-OE word derived fr. (assumed) VL *imputare* (whence OF *enter* to graft), fr. L *in-* [2]in- + *putare* to cut, prune — more at PAVE] **1** *archaic* **:** to graft into or on **:** IMPLANT **2 a :** to graft or repair (a wing, tail, or feather) with a feather to improve a falcon's flying capacity **b** *archaic* **:** to fasten wings on or to **:** equip with wings **c** *archaic* **:** to eke out **:** REPAIR, INCREASE, EQUIP

imp *abbr* **1** imperative **2** [L *imperator; imperatrix*] emperor; empress **3** imperfect **4** imperial **5** implement **6** import; imported; importer **7** important **8** impression **9** imprimatur **10** [L *imprimis*] in the first place **11** imprint **12** improved; improvement

[1]im·pact \(ˌ)im¦pakt\ *vb* -ED/-ING/-S [L *impactus*, past part. of *impingere* to strike or push at or against — more at IMPINGE] *vt* **1 a :** to fix firmly by or as if by packing or wedging ⟨a substance ~*ed* in the upper intestine⟩ ⟨the mule lay . . . ~*ed* in the loam —Ben Johnson⟩ **b :** to press together or mix into a clotted, wedged, or tightly bound mass ⟨goblets of clay and drops of sweat ~*ed* into a hot mulch —*Time*⟩ ⟨puns that can ~ the scabrous with the sublime in a word —Eleanor Clark⟩ **c :** to press down and wedge or force in or under ⟨the golden nuggets of wisdom being ~*ed* in tons of verbosity —Dwight Macdonald⟩ **d :** to fill up **:** CROWD, CONGEST ⟨~*s* the area with military and defense workers and their families —Tait Trussell⟩ **2 a :** to have an impact upon **:** make contact with **:** impinge upon ⟨the images ~*ing* the human retina —T.H. Benton †1975⟩ **b :** to drive or transmit with a forceful impact ⟨the critic who . . . is supposed to ~ his messianic visions of jazz perfection to musicians struggling at his feet —*Saturday Rev.*⟩ ~ *vi* **:** to have an impact ⟨the world did not ~ upon me until I got to the post office —Christopher Morley⟩ **:** impinge or make contact esp. forcefully ⟨image the ~*ing* ball splashing into the loose mass of surface balls —R.A.Bagnold⟩ ⟨how will total war ~ on such a poet —*Times Lit. Supp.*⟩

[2]im·pact \'imˌpakt\ *n* -s **1 a :** the act of impinging or striking (as of one body against another or of a stream squarely against a fixed or moving surface) **b :** a forceful contact, collision, or onset **:** the degree or concentration of force in a collision **:** the impetus communicated in or as if in a collision ⟨felt the terrific ~ of the blow⟩ ⟨air rendered incandescent by the vehemence of the ~*s* of the electrons against its molecules —K.K.Darrow⟩ **2 :** the force of impression of one thing on another: **a :** the notable ability to arouse and hold attention and interest **:** the power of impressing ⟨a way of securing a maximum of dramatic ~ on the reader —W.M.Frohock⟩ **b :** a concentrated force producing change **:** an esp. forceful effect checking or forcing change **:** an impelling or compelling effect ⟨the ~ of modern science and technology upon society as a whole —Harrison Brown⟩ ⟨the ~ of terror⟩ ⟨the environmental ~ of industrial pollution⟩ ⟨loses the ~ of the basic story in a maze of philosophies —Whitney Betts⟩; *also* **:** the degree of such force ⟨American youth in the early 1930s felt spiritually paralyzed by the ~ of confusing events —J.W. Chase⟩

syn BRUNT, COLLISION, CLASH, SHOCK, BUMP, JOLT, JAR, IMPINGEMENT, PERCUSSION, CONCUSSION: IMPACT now commonly suggests the driving impetus or momentum in or as if in a collision or the dynamic force in impressing or compelling change ⟨the aunt's home shook at the *impact* and the windows were smashed —Norman Cousins⟩ ⟨the *impact* of world war on the lives of countless millions —R.H.Jackson⟩ BRUNT now indicates the major part of the force of an onset, collision, jar, stress, or strain ⟨a number of the leaders had . . . fled from the persecution, leaving the little people to bear its *brunt* —Maurice Samuel⟩ ⟨the national financial panic was felt throughout the state, but it was Duluth that bore the *brunt* of the disaster . . . it was rendered almost totally bankrupt —*Amer. Guide Series: Minn.*⟩ COLLISION implies a forceful running together of more or less complex things through accident and with resulting harm, or a sharp opposition or conflict ⟨the *collision* between two ships in a fog⟩ ⟨the buyers and sellers of capital could do almost as they pleased with it, no matter how much damage a *collision* between them might bring about —F.L.Allen⟩ CLASH suggests a noisy, metallic striking together, a sharp skirmish or brawl, or a sharp direct variance, opposition, or contrast ⟨roll of cannon and *clash* of arms —Alfred Tennyson⟩ ⟨fishermen from the Michigan mainland . . . violently opposed further settlement by the Mormons. *Clashes* occurred at several places —*Amer. Guide Series: Mich.*⟩ ⟨a *clash* or conflict between his demands and the strict limitations upon the supply⟩ SHOCK may refer to a very forcible onslaught or violent collision literally or figuratively ⟨the *shock* of the cavalry charge⟩ ⟨the discoveries of physical science came as a *shock* to the general mind of Europe —Laurence Binyon⟩ ⟨the *shock* of physical dislocation effected a very considerable modification of old attitudes —John Dewey⟩ BUMP indicates a sudden thudding blow, esp. one checking forward progress with some force ⟨a *bump* on the head⟩ ⟨the springs were broken by the bad *bump* during the detour⟩ JOLT refers to an abrupt violent blow or movement tending to shake, agitate, or unsettle, or, figuratively, to a shock or major surprise ⟨newly picked fruit being bruised by the *jolts* of shipment⟩ ⟨we have no offensive naval policy . . . I fear there will be some horrible *jolts* in the future —F.D. Roosevelt⟩ JAR usu. refers to some wrenching dislodgment or break in continuity ⟨the bottles were cracked by the *jars* they underwent in shipment⟩; it may refer to an agitation or shaking up ⟨the fall gave him a *jar*⟩ IMPINGEMENT now is less likely to indicate violent collision than lighter overlaying or more subtle infringement or penetration ⟨each little *impingement* of sound struck on her consciousness —Adria Langley⟩ PERCUSSION, more common in technical than in general language, may suggest a sharp, purposive tapping or knocking ⟨musical instruments that sound by *percussion*, as the drum⟩ CONCUSSION, which may mean a blow or collision, is now more likely to suggest the shattering effects, including noise, of a collision or explosion, or the stunning, weakening effect of a heavy blow ⟨from the shelter survivors heard the *concussions* of the bombing raid⟩ ⟨suffered a *concussion* in the collision⟩

impact bomb *n* **:** a bomb that detonates on striking an object

impacted *adj* **1 :** driven together (as the broken ends of a fractured bone) **2 a :** wedged into a passage (as a fetus in the birth canal, a calculus in a duct, a foreign body in the larynx) **b** *of a tooth* **:** wedged between the jawbone and another tooth ⟨~ and unerupted normal teeth are excised —K.H. Thoma⟩

impacted crop *n* **:** CROP-BOUND

impact extrusion *n* **:** a process in which metal is forced by a quick blow to flow around a punch; *also* **:** the product so formed

im·pact·ful \'=ˌ=fəl, ='=-\ *adj* **:** having a forceful impact **:** producing a marked impression ⟨some of the most ~ heroines of current films —Martha Wolfenstein & Nathan Leites⟩

im·pac·tion \im'pakshən\ *n* -s [LL *impaction-*, *impactio*, fr. L *impactus* + *-ion-*, *-io* -ion] **:** the act of becoming or the state of being impacted; *specif* **:** lodgment or an instance of lodgment of something (as a tooth or feces or calculi) in a body passage or cavity ⟨fecal ~⟩ ⟨~ of the rumen⟩

im·pact·ite \'imˌpakˌtīt\ *n* -s [[2]*impact* + *-ite*] **:** a glassy object produced by fusion of rock or meteoritic fragments by the heat developed from the impact of a meteorite on the earth's surface

im·pac·tive \(')im¦paktiv\ *adj* **1 :** having an impact or marked effect ⟨the ~ wonder that is in natural things —R.L.Cook⟩ ⟨the ~ scrutiny of strange faces —Scott Fitzgerald⟩ **2 :** resulting from impact ⟨~ shocks —G.L.Riddell⟩

im·pac·tor *or* **im·pact·er** \-tə(r)\ *n* -s **:** a machine (as a steam hammer or a pile driver) or part that operates by striking blows

impact parameter *n* **:** the perpendicular distance from the center of the force field to the initial path of the particle deflected by the field in nuclear scattering

impact pressure *n* **:** DYNAMIC PRESSURE

impact strength *n* **:** the resistance of a material (as metal or ceramic ware) to fracture by a blow, expressed in terms of the amount of energy absorbed before fracture

impact test *n* **:** a test for determining the impact strength of a material ⟨the *impact test* of the pottery was made with a dropping metal ball⟩

impact tube *n* **:** a Pitot tube having its orifice headed directly into an oncoming stream of fluid

impact wrench *n* **:** an electrically or pneumatically operated wrench that gives a rapid succession of sudden torques

impaint *vt* [[2]*in-* + *paint* (n.)] *obs* **:** PAINT, DEPICT

[1]im·pair \im'pa(a)|(ə)r, -pe|, |ə\ *vb* -ED/-ING/-S [ME *empeiren*, *empairen*, *impairen*, fr. MF *empeirer*, *emperer*, *empirer*, fr. OF *empeirier*, *empirier*, fr. (assumed) VL *impejorare*, fr. L *in-* [2]in- + LL *pejorare* to make worse — more at PEJORATIVE] *vt* **:** to make worse **:** diminish in quantity, value, excellence, or strength **:** do harm to **:** DAMAGE, LESSEN ⟨the output of produce was ~*ed* by the cold weather⟩ ⟨~ their health by wild living⟩ ⟨had to teach so many pupils it ~*ed* his own musical career⟩ ⟨his pleasure was ~*ed* by worry about money⟩ ~ *vi*, *obs* **:** DETERIORATE **syn** see INJURE

[2]impair \"\ *n* -s *archaic* **:** IMPAIRMENT, INJURY

[3]im·pair \'imˌpa(a)|(ə)r, -pə|, |ə\ *n* -s [F, fr. *impair* odd, fr. L *impar* — more at IMPAR] **:** the odd numbers in roulette when a bet is made on them ⟨made a large bet on ~⟩

im·pair·able \im'pa(a)rəbəl, -per-\ *adj* **:** capable of being impaired

impaired life *or* **impaired risk** *n* **:** a person whose physical condition according to insurance ratings is below that required for life insurance at standard rates

im·pair·er \-rə(r)\ *n* -s **:** one that impairs ⟨lack of confidence is often an ~ of efficiency⟩

im·pair·ment \-a(a)|(ə)rmənt, -e|, |əm-\ *n* -s [ME *empeirment*, fr. MF *empeirement*, fr. OF, fr. *empeirier*, to impair + *-ment* — more at IMPAIR] **:** the act of impairing or the state of being impaired **:** INJURY ⟨physical and mental diseases and ~*s* of man —*Current Biog.*⟩ **:** DETERIORATION ⟨any ~ . . . of his bodily vigor through sickness or age —J.G.Frazer⟩ **:** LESSENING ⟨an ~ of the pain⟩

im·pala *also* **im·pal·la** \im'palə, -pälə\ *n*, *pl* **impalas** *or* **impala** *also* **impallas** *or* **impalla** [Zulu] **:** a large African antelope (*Aepyceros melampus*) of a brownish bay color, white below, with a black crescentic stripe on the haunch, the male being distinguished by slender annulated lyrate horns

impala lily *n* **:** a succulent-stemmed shrub (*Adenium multiflorum*) of the family Apocynaceae of southern Africa with showy pink and white flowers borne after the leaves fall

im·palatable \(')im+\ *adj* [[1]*in-* + *palatable*] **:** UNPALATABLE

im·pale \ə̇m'pāl, *esp before pause or consonant* -āəl\ *also* **em·pale** \ə̇mˌem-\ *vt* [MF & ML; MF *empaler*, fr. ML *impalare*, fr. L *in-* [2]in- + *palus* stake, pole — more at POLE] **1** *archaic* **a :** to enclose with poles, stakes, or a palisade **b :** to hem in **:** ENCLOSE, SURROUND, CONFINE, ENCIRCLE **2 a :** to pierce or pierce through with a pole or with something pointed; *esp* **:** to torture or kill by fixing on a sharp stake **b :** to fix in a position by piercing or piercing through with something pointed or to cause to be so fixed ⟨the head . . . *impaled* upon the bowsprit of his sloop —Nike Anderson⟩ ⟨having some man rush at you so that he *impaled* his chest upon the ice pick —Erle Stanley Gardner⟩ ⟨a butterfly *impaled* by a pin —Louis Bromfield⟩ **c :** to fix in a position as if by piercing or piercing through in such a manner **:** fix in a position of defeat or helplessness or one from which there is no escape or retreat ⟨*impaled* itself on a dilemma —S.W.Chapman⟩ ⟨a question on which . . . he had always been insecurely *impaled* —Marcia Davenport⟩ ⟨*impaled* his victim neatly with his logic —V.L.Parrington⟩ **d :** to deflate by telling logic or biting wit **3 :** to join or conjoin in heraldry by impalement

im·pale·ment \-mənt\ *n* -s [MF *empalement*, fr. *empaler* + *-ment*] **1 :** the act of impaling or the state of being impaled: as **a** (1) *archaic* **:** ENCLOSING, ENCIRCLING, CONFINING (2) **:** the union of two or more coats of arms side by side on a heraldic shield divided palewise **b :** a piercing or piercing through with a pale, spike, or other pointed thing (as for fixing in a position or by an accidental fall) **c** (1) **:** a placing or a being placed in an inescapable and awkward position (as of defeat or helplessness) (2) **:** a deflating or a being deflated by telling logic or biting wit **2 :** an enclosing fence or palisade

im·palpability \(¦)im+\ *n* **:** the quality or state of being impalpable

[1]im·palpable \(')im+\ *adj* [[1]*in-* + *palpable*] **1 a :** incapable of being felt by the touch ⟨an ~ pulse⟩ **:** not palpable **:** INTANGIBLE ⟨as ~ as a dream —Nathaniel Hawthorne⟩ ⟨the ~ aura of power that emanated from him —Osbert Sitwell⟩ **b :** extremely fine so that no grains or grit can be felt ⟨an ~ cloud⟩ ⟨an ~ powder⟩ ⟨the ~ mud —*Encyc. Britannica*⟩ **2 :** not readily apprehended by the mind ⟨an ~ beauty of style⟩ — **im·palpably** \"+\ *adv*

[2]impalpable \"\ *n* -s **:** something impalpable ⟨an intellectual, dealing eternally in ~*s*⟩

im·panate \im'panə̇t, 'impəˌnāt\ *or* **im·pa·nat·ed** \'impəˌnād·ə̇d\ *adj* [*impanate* fr. ML *impanatus*, fr. L *in-* [2]in- + L *panis* bread + *-atus* -ate; *impanated* fr. ML *impanatus* + E *-ed* — more at FOOD] **:** embodied in bread in impanation

im·pa·na·tion \ˌimpə'nāshən\ *n* -s [ML *impanation-*, *impanatio*, fr. *impanatus* impanate + L *-ion-*, *-io* -ion] **1 :** the inclusion of the body of Christ in the eucharistic bread in a hypostatic union without change in either substance — compare INVINATION **2 :** the Christian theological doctrine affirming the real presence of Christ in the Eucharist by impanation and invination — compare CONSUBSTANTIATION, TRANSUBSTANTIATION

im·pa·na·tor \'impəˌnād·ə(r)\ *n* -s [ML, fr. *impanatus* + L *-or*] **:** one holding the doctrine of impanation

im·panel \ə̇m+\ *also* **em·panel** \ə̇m, em+\ *vt* [[2]*in-* or [1]*en-* + *panel* (n.)] **:** to enter in or on a panel **:** enroll (as a list of jurors) in a court of justice

im·papy·rat·ed \ˌimpə'pīˌrād·ə̇d, im'papəˌr-\ *adj* [[2]*in-* + *papyrus* + *-ate* + *-ed*] **:** recorded on or as if on papyrus

im·par \'imˌpär\ *adj* [NL, fr. L, unequal, uneven, fr. *in-* [1]in- + *par* equal — more at PAIR] *anat* **:** UNPAIRED, AZYGOUS

im·paradise \ə̇m+\ *or* **em·paradise** \ə̇mˌem+\ *vt* [[2]*in-* or [1]*en-* + *paradise* (n.)] **1 a :** to put in paradise ⟨an *imparadised* saint⟩ **b :** to make supremely happy **:** transport with delight or joy ⟨*imparadised* in her lover's arms⟩ **2 :** to convert into a paradise

imparalleled *adj* [[1]*in-* + *paralled*] *obs* **:** UNPARALLELED

im·paripinnate \(¦)im+\ *adj* [NL *imparipinnatus*, fr. L *impar* + NL *-i-* + *pinnatus* pinnate — more at PINNATE] **:** ODD-PINNATE

im·parisyllabic \(¦)im+\ *adj* [L *impar* + E *-i-* + *-syllabic*] **:** not having the same number of syllables in all declensional cases ⟨the Latin words *lapis, lapidis* and *mens, mentis* are ~⟩

im·parity \(')im+\ *n* [LL *imparitas*, fr. L *impar* + *-itas* -ity] **:** difference esp. of degree, rank, excellence, number **:** INEQUALITY, DISPARITY

impark *vt* [ME *imparken*, fr. AF *emparker*, fr. OF *en-* [1]en- + *park, parc* — more at PARK] **1** *obs* **a :** to enclose or confine in a park **b :** ENCLOSE **2** *obs* **:** to enclose (as woods) for a park

im·parl \ə̇m'pärl\ *or* **em·parl** \ə̇mˌem-\ *vi* -ED/-ING/-S [ME *enparlen*, fr. MF *emparler*, fr. *en-* [1]en- + *parler* to speak — more at PARLEY] **:** to have an imparlance **:** confer esp. regarding settlement of a dispute

im·par·lance \-lən(t)s\ *n* [AF *emparlance*, fr. MF *emparler* + *-ance*] **1** *obs* **:** mutual discourse **:** CONFERENCE, DISCUSSION **2 a :** time formerly given to a party before pleading in a lawsuit for making an amicable settlement **b :** the delay or continuance of a suit **c :** a petition or leave for such a delay

im·part \ə̇m'pär|t, -på|, *usu* |d·+V\ *vb* [MF&L; MF *impartir*, fr. L *impartire*, *impertire*, fr. *in-* [2]in- + *partire* to divide, part — more at PART] *vt* **1 :** to give or grant (what one has or of what one has) or give rise to (in another) by contact, association, or influence ⟨~*ed* his fortune to the needy⟩ ⟨his manner of speaking ~*ed* authority to a mediocre plan⟩ ⟨the chief hope of ~*ing* a new direction and purpose to the lives of prisoners —*Times Lit. Supp.*⟩ **:** COMMUNICATE, TRANSMIT ⟨his very position ~*ed* a political significance to whatever he did⟩ ⟨their elegance was ~*ed* to the passengers . . . who were forced to sit ramrod straight —*Fortnight*⟩ ⟨a sudden motion ~*ed* to the air —*Encyc. Americana*⟩ ⟨the musician ~*ed* a lyric quality to the piece⟩ ⟨~ knowledge to students⟩ **2 :** to communicate the knowledge of **:** DISCLOSE ⟨told to ~ what he knew to the police⟩; *esp* **:** to give utterance to **:** reveal in writing or speaking ⟨~*ed* her plans to him in their talk⟩ ⟨~*ed* the events in a letter⟩ ~ *vi* **:** GIVE, BESTOW ⟨the aspect of receiving, and the aspect of ~*ing* —S.W.Rowland & Brian Magee⟩

im·par·ta·tion \ˌimˌpär'tāshən, -på't-\ *n* -s **:** the act of imparting or the state of being imparted

im·partial \(')im, əm+\ *adj* [[1]*in-* + *partial*] **:** not partial; *esp* **:** not favoring one more than another **:** treating all alike **:** UNBIASED, EQUITABLE ⟨in any criminal trial . . . the jury may be ~ but it is never neutral —M.C.Bernays⟩ ⟨law shall be uniform and ~ —B.N.Cardozo⟩ **syn** see FAIR

impartial chairman *n* **:** an arbitrator, referee, or umpire jointly employed by union and management to interpret or to resolve differences arising out of the terms of a labor agreement

im·partiality \(¦)im, əm+\ *n* **:** the quality or state of being impartial **:** freedom from bias or favoritism **:** DISINTERESTEDNESS, FAIRNESS ⟨the ~ of the scientific spirit —John Dewey⟩ ⟨with wonderful ~, the play admits shenanigans and sentiment —*Time*⟩

im·partially \(')im, əm+\ *adv* **:** in an impartial manner **:** without bias or special favor ⟨smiled at them both ~ —T.B. Costain⟩

im·par·tial·ness *n* -ES **:** the quality or state of being impartial

im·partibility \(¦)im+\ *n* **:** the quality or state of being impartible

im·partible \(')im+\ *adj* [LL *impartibilis*, fr. L *in-* [1]in- + *partibilis* partible — more at PARTIBLE] **:** not partible **:** not subject to partition ⟨decided that the office should be held jointly by his two sisters, an absurd decision which ignored the historic principle that great offices of state are ~ —G.H. White⟩ ⟨an ~ inheritance⟩ — **im·partibly** \"+\ *adv*

im·participable \ˌim+\ *adj* [¹*in-* + *participable*] **:** not participable **:** incapable of being shared ⟨an ~ office⟩

im·par·tite \(ˈ)imˈpärˌtīt\ *adj* [LL *impartitus*, fr. L *in-* ¹in- + *partitus*, past part. of *partire* to divide — more at PART] **:** UNDIVIDED

im·part·ment \imˈpärtmənt\ *n* -s **:** the act of imparting or something that is imparted **:** COMMUNICATION, TRANSMISSION

im·passability \(ˌ)im+\ *n* **:** the quality or state of being impassable ⟨stopped by the complete ~ of the road⟩

im·passable \(ˈ)im+\ *adj* [¹*in-* + *passable*] **:** incapable of being passed: as **a :** incapable of being traveled, traveled through, or crossed ⟨an ~ road⟩ ⟨an ~ jungle⟩ ⟨an ~ river⟩ **b :** incapable of being put into circulation ⟨counterfeit bills so crude they were ~⟩ **c :** INSURMOUNTABLE ⟨an ~ obstacle to discussion⟩ — **im·passableness** \"+\ *n* — **im·passably** \"+\ *adv*

im·passe \ˈimˌpas, -paa(ə)s, -pais, -päs *also* imˈp- *or* ˈamˌp- *or* amˈp-\ *n* -s [F, fr. *in-* ¹in- + *-passe* (fr. *passer* to pass — more at PASS)] **1 :** an impassable road or way **:** BLIND ALLEY, CUL-DE-SAC **2 a :** a predicament affording no obvious escape ⟨placed himself in an impossible ~ by at one and the same time attacking the heads of the party and recognizing its supreme authority —*Times Lit. Supp.*⟩ **b :** DEADLOCK ⟨negotiations between the two parties had reached an ~ since neither side would compromise in any way⟩

im·passibility \(ˌ)im, əm+\ *n* -ES [ME *impassibilite*, fr. MF or LL; MF *impassibilité*, fr. LL *impassibilitat-, impassibilitas*, fr. *impassibilis* + *-itat-, -itas* -ity] **:** the quality or state of being impassible ⟨the ~ or aloofness she showed sometimes toward me —Mary McCarthy⟩

im·passible \əm, (ˈ)im+\ *adj* [ME, fr. MF or LL; MF, fr. LL *impassibilis*, fr. L *in-* ¹in- + *passibilis* passible — more at PASSIBLE] **1 a :** incapable of suffering or of experiencing pain ⟨the Godhead is ~, for where there is perfection and unity, there can be no suffering —Aldous Huxley⟩ **b :** incapable of being harmed **:** inaccessible to injury ⟨as ~ as a ghost —Walker Percy⟩ **2 :** incapable of feeling **:** IMPASSIVE, UNFEELING, COLD ⟨the murderer stood ~ gazing down at his victim⟩ — **im·pas·si·bly** \-əblē, -li\ *adv*

im·pas·sion \əmˈpashən, -paash-,-paish-\ *vt* **impassioned; impassioned; impassioning** \-sh(ə)niŋ\ **impassions** [prob. fr. It *impassionare*, fr. *in-* ²in- (fr. L) + *passione* passion, fr. LL *passion-, passio* — more at PASSION] **:** to move or affect strongly **:** arouse the feelings or passions of ⟨dampens the ardor of the most ~*ed* newcomer —*Amer. Guide Series: Tenn.*⟩ ⟨the ideal of an elected emperor that ~*ed* the revolutionaries —Norbert Mühlen⟩ **:** fill with passion or mark by evidence of strong feeling ⟨public speaking is more ~*ed* than private speaking —A.T. Weaver⟩

¹im·pas·sion·ate \-sh(ə)nət, *usu* -əd.+V\ *adj* [It *impassionato*, past part. of *impassionare*] **:** IMPASSIONED — **im·pas·sion·ate·ly** *adv*

²im·pas·sion·ate \-shəˌnāt, *usu* -ād.+V\ *vt*, *archaic* **:** IMPASSION

³im·passionate \(ˈ)im+\ *adj* [¹*in-* + *passionate*] *archaic* **:** without passion or feeling **:** DISPASSIONATE

im·pas·sioned \əmˈpashənd, -paash-,-paish-\ *adj* **:** actuated or characterized by or filled with passion or zeal **:** showing great warmth of feeling **:** ARDENT ⟨an ~ oration⟩ ⟨the expression of ~ love of ideal beauty —Richard Garnett †1906⟩ **syn** PASSIONATE, ARDENT, FERVENT, FERVID, PERFERVID: IMPASSIONED indicates intense, strong, and fiery feeling demanding expression ⟨much would I have given to have understood some of his *impassioned* bursts; when he tossed his arms overhead, stamped, scowled, and glared, till he looked like the very Angel of Vengeance —Herman Melville⟩ ⟨as his *impassioned* language did its work the multitude rose into fury —J.A.Froude⟩ PASSIONATE applies to vehemence or violence of emotion sometimes extinguishing rationality ⟨he heard for the first time mamma's *passionate* appeal to him never to let Judy forget mamma —Rudyard Kipling⟩ ⟨may profess Socialism or Communism in *passionate* harangues from one end of the country to the other, and even suffer martyrdom for it —G.B. Shaw⟩ ⟨it had not been condemned in the court of human reason, but lynched outside of it by the *passionate* and uncompromisingly ruthless war spirit, common to Communists and Fascists —M.R.Cohen⟩ ARDENT is almost always complimentary and may apply to the fiery or warm expression of lasting intense zeal and militancy ⟨an *ardent* Jeffersonian, vigorously partisan in the pulpit —H.E.Starr⟩ ⟨a man of violent temper, strong prejudices and an *ardent* Tory had left Virginia because of the unpopularity he had stirred up there against himself —*Amer. Guide Series: Md.*⟩ FERVENT may connote a depth and intensity of glowing feeling, often sustained and steady ⟨a strong and popular preacher, *fervent*, sometimes fiery, inclined to speak everywhere as though addressing a congregation —J.A.Faulkner⟩ ⟨a *fervent* loyalty such as soldiers feel for a general who leads them in some cause dear to all —Rebecca West⟩ FERVID may apply to a warmly or even feverishly expressed emotion, often spontaneous and always intense ⟨because his *fervid* manner of lovemaking offended her English phlegm —Arnold Bennett⟩ ⟨the most *fervid* and momentous oratory of Revolutionary days —*Amer. Guide Series: Mass.*⟩ PERFERVID may suggest extreme emotional excitement, sometimes overwrought or factitious ⟨in his *perfervid* flag-waving moments —S.H.Adams⟩

im·pas·sioned·ly \-n(ə)dlē, -li\ *adj* **:** in an impassioned manner

im·pas·sioned·ness \-n(d)nəs\ *n* -ES **:** the quality or state of being impassioned ⟨the ~ of his plea for mercy⟩

im·passive \əm, (ˈ)im+\ *adj* [¹*in-* + *passive*] **1 :** devoid of passion, feeling, or receptivity to impression: **a** *archaic* **:** unsusceptible to pain, suffering, injury, or harm **:** INVULNERABLE **b :** unsusceptible to physical feeling **:** INSENSIBLE, INANIMATE ⟨a dial cut in ~ stone —Virginia Woolf⟩ **c :** unsusceptible to or destitute of emotion **:** UNIMPRESSIONABLE ⟨the violet pallor of death . . . enveloped her in an ~ remoteness —Ellen Glasgow⟩ ⟨a large dull ~ man⟩ **2 :** giving no sign of feeling or emotion **:** EXPRESSIONLESS ⟨beneath a reserved and ~ surface, a highly nervous and sensitive person —Havelock Ellis⟩ ⟨a cold ~ stare —Charles Dickens⟩ **3 :** not moving in any way **:** MOTIONLESS ⟨we can load up a piece of amber . . . with the greatest possible excess of negative charge, and still it remains absolutely ~ in the presence of a magnet —K.K.Darrow⟩ **syn** STOIC, APATHETIC, PHLEGMATIC, STOLID: IMPASSIVE applies to one who shows no passion, emotion, sensation, or noticeable interest in situations in which such a reaction might be expected ⟨the veil of *impassive* reserve with which I concealed the whole of my intimate personal life —Havelock Ellis⟩ ⟨I watched the man's face while Nelson was relating the story, but he remained *impassive*, showing neither interest in nor concern for our plight —C.B.Nordhoff & J.N.Hall⟩ STOIC may suggest an indifference to pain or pleasure, perhaps through a conscious schooling of oneself in fortitude ⟨it sums up not only the cataclysm of a world, but also the *stoic* and indomitable temper that endures it —J.L.Lowes⟩ ⟨a *stoic* atmosphere of fortitude in adversity —Orville Prescott⟩ APATHETIC may describe a puzzling, remiss, or blameworthy indifference or a preoccupation with something else that precludes normal interest and reactions ⟨enforcement of the liquor laws was lax, and sentiment was *apathetic* to the evils of excessive drinking —C.A.Dinsmore⟩ ⟨the row of stolid, dull, vacant plowboys, ungainly in build, uncomely in face, lifeless, *apathetic* —Samuel Butler †1902⟩ PHLEGMATIC describes a temperament or disposition not given to ready emotional reaction or similar response ⟨the religious mysticism that lurked in the heart of primitive Puritanism found no response in his *phlegmatic* soul —V.L.Parrington⟩ STOLID implies an accustomed heavy or cloddish obtuse imperceptive and incurious lack of interest, emotion, or other response ⟨an agricultural parish, peopled by *stolid* Saxon rustics, in whom the temperature of religious zeal was little, if at all, above absolute zero —Aldous Huxley⟩ ⟨watched for an expression of hatred, or pity, or horror, on the faces of the multitude. No emotion whatsoever was displayed —nothing but *stolid* indifference —V.G.Heiser⟩

im·passively \"+\ *adv* **:** in an impassive manner ⟨submitted ~ to arrest —*Time*⟩

im·passiveness \"+\ *n* **:** IMPASSIVITY

im·passivity \ˌim+\ *n* **:** the quality or state of being impassive **:** a lack or absence of feeling or expression ⟨behind her ~ lay passionate growing anxiety —Marcia Davenport⟩ ⟨his majestic ~ contrasting with the overt astonishment with which a row of savagely ugly attendant chiefs grinned —G.B.Shaw⟩

im·paste \imˈpāst\ *vt* [It *impastare*, fr. *in-* ²in- (fr. L) + *pasta* dough, paste, fr. LL — more at PASTE] **1 :** to make into a paste **2 :** to decorate by impasto

im·pas·to \imˈpa(ˌ)stō, -pä-,-paa-,-pà-\ *n* -s *often attrib* [It, fr. *impastare*] **:** the thick application of a pigment to a canvas or panel in painting ⟨~ tempera —Ralph Mayer⟩ ⟨~ effects —*Yankee*⟩; *also* **:** the body of pigment so applied ⟨paint laid on in so thick an ~ that it appears almost in bas-relief —R.M. Coates⟩

im·pa·ter·nate \ˌimpəˈtərnət\ *adj* [¹*in-* + *paternal* + *-ate*] **:** fatherless as a result of parthenogenetic development

im·patience \(ˈ)im, əm+\ *n* [ME *impacience*, fr. OF & L; OF *impacience, impatience*, fr. L *impatientia*, fr. *impatient-, impatiens* + *-ia* -y] **:** the quality or state of being impatient: as **a :** restlessness or chafing of spirit (as under irritation, delay, or opposition) ⟨~ of restraint⟩ **b :** manifest disapproval or intolerance ⟨~ of delay or incompetence⟩ **:** manifest unwillingness to be tolerant ⟨~ with red tape and outworn procedure —R.M.Dawson⟩ **c :** restless or eager desire or longing ⟨~ to get his mark completed on time⟩

im·patiency \"+\ *n* [L *impatientia*] *archaic* **:** IMPATIENCE

im·pa·tiens \əmˈpāshənz, -shēˌenz, -shən(t)s\ *n* [NL, fr. L, adj., impatient; fr. the fact that the ripe pods burst open and scatter their seeds when slight pressure is applied] **1** *cap* **:** a large genus of widely distributed annual plants (family Balsaminaceae) with watery juice, irregular spurred or saccate flowers, and dehiscent capsules — see BALSAM 4, JEWELWEED **2** *or* **impatience**, *pl* **impatiens** *or* **impatiences :** any plant of the genus *Impatiens*

¹im·patient \(ˈ)im, əm+\ *adj* [ME *impacient*, fr. MF *impacient, impatient*, fr. L *impatient-, impatiens*, fr. *in-* ¹in- + *patient-, patiens* patient — more at PATIENT] **1 a :** not patient **:** restless or short of temper esp. under irritation, delay, opposition **:** FRETFUL ⟨an ~ mood⟩ ⟨an ~ disposition⟩ ⟨the temper of the youth of his country is violent, ~, and revolutionary —Louis Fischer⟩ **b :** not bearing with composure **:** INTOLERANT ⟨~ of poverty or delay⟩ ⟨~ of this prolonged parting from their pets —F.D.Smith & Barbara Wilcox⟩ ⟨~ of preaching without practice —A.J.Russell⟩ **:** showing quickly an unwillingness to be unconcerned or tolerant (as with something one dislikes or disapproves of) ⟨~ with anything like dishonesty —W.L.Frierson⟩ **2 :** prompted by or giving evidence of impatience ⟨an ~ speech⟩ ⟨~ restlessness⟩ ⟨an ~ honesty —S.H.Adams⟩ **3 a :** restlessly or eagerly desirous **:** ANXIOUS ⟨~ to see his sweetheart⟩ ⟨quite ~ for the concert evening —Jane Austen⟩ ⟨~ to know what did occur —E.K. Brown⟩ ⟨~ for home —E.A.Weeks⟩ **b :** marked by intolerance of delay ⟨an ~ wait⟩ ⟨~ hours⟩ **4** *obs* **:** UNENDURABLE — **im·patiently** \"+\ *adv* — **im·patientness** \"+\ *n*

²impatient \"\ *n* **:** one that is impatient

impatronize *vt* [MF *impatroniser*, fr. *in-* ²in- + *patron* patron, master + *-iser* -ize — more at PATRON] *obs* **:** to give or take possession of

im·pavid \(ˈ)im+\ *adj* [L *impavidus*, fr. *in-* ¹in- + *pavidus* fearful — more at PAVID] *archaic* **:** FEARLESS — **im·pavidly** \"+\ *adv*

im·pawn \im+\ *vt* [²*in-* + *pawn* (n.)] *archaic* **:** to put in pawn

im·pay·able \aⁿpāyābl(ᵊ), -b(lə)\ *adj* [F, fr. MF, incapable of being paid, fr. *in-* ¹in- + *payable* — more at PAYABLE] **:** PRICELESS, INVALUABLE

¹im·peach \əmˈpēch\ *vt* -ED/-ING/-ES [ME *empechen*, fr. MF *empecher*, fr. OF *empeechier*, fr. LL *impedicare* to entangle, fetter, fr. L *in-* ²in- + *pedica* fetter, fr. *ped-, pes* foot — more at FOOT] **1** *obs* **:** HINDER, PREVENT, IMPEDE **2 a :** to bring an accusation (as of wrongdoing or impropriety) against **:** charge with a crime or misdemeanor; *specif* **:** to charge (a public official) before a competent tribunal with misbehavior in office **:** arraign or cite for official misconduct ⟨~ the president⟩ ⟨~ a circuit-court judge⟩ **b :** to inform against or give incriminating evidence against **:** accuse or aid in accusing **:** peach on **c :** to challenge, impugn, or charge as having some fault esp. as biased, venal, not credible, or invalid ⟨the testimony of the 1850 federal census . . . ~*es* the accuracy of his memory —Dixon Wecter⟩ ⟨in a state of mind to ~ the justice of the republic —Charles Dickens⟩ ⟨~ the testimony of a witness⟩ **3 :** to convict of impropriety, misdemeanor, misconduct in office, or bias, venality, or invalidity; *also* **:** to cause (an official) to be removed from office because of such a conviction **syn** see ACCUSE

²impeach *n*, *obs* **:** IMPEACHMENT

im·peach·able \-chəbəl\ *adj* **1 :** capable of being impeached **:** chargeable with misconduct, inadequacy, or other fault which might lead to being impeached **2 :** capable of being used as the charge in an impeachment ⟨an ~ offense⟩

im·peach·ment \-chmənt\ *n* -s [ME *empechement*, fr. MF, fr. *empecher* + *-ment*] **:** the act or result of impeaching: as **a** *obs* **:** HINDRANCE, OBSTRUCTION, IMPEDIMENT **b** *obs* **:** INJURY, HARM, DAMAGE **c :** a calling into question or discrediting (as the purity of one's motives or one's honesty) ⟨the ~ of his character⟩ ⟨the ~ of the witness's testimony⟩ **d :** a calling to account for some high crime or offense before a competent tribunal **:** ARRAIGNMENT; *esp* **:** the arraignment (as of a public official) for misconduct while in office **e** (1) **:** conviction of bias, venality, invalidity, or other fault (2) **:** conviction of misconduct and usu. removal from office — **without impeachment of waste** *of a tenant* **:** exempt from suit for waste committed — used in a real estate lease

im·pearl \əm+\ *or* **em·pearl** \əm,em+\ *vt* [prob. fr. MF *emperler*, fr. *en-* ¹en- + *perle* pearl — more at PEARL] **:** to form into pearls or into the likeness of pearls; *also* **:** to form of or adorn with or as if with pearls

im·pec·ca·bil·i·ty \(ˌ)imˌpekəˈbiləd·ē, əm-, -lət, -i\ *n* **:** the quality or state of being impeccable ⟨have never pretended to ~ —George Meredith⟩

im·pec·ca·ble \(ˈ)imˈpekəbəl, əmˈp-\ *adj* [L *impeccabilis*, fr. *in-* ¹in- + *peccare* to sin + *-abilis* -able — more at PECCANT] **1 :** not capable of sinning or liable to sin **:** exempt from the possibility of wrongdoing ⟨no soul is absolutely ~ —F.W. Robertson⟩ **2 :** free from fault or blame **:** FLAWLESS, IRREPROACHABLE ⟨women of ~ character and honorable life —Herbert Mitgang⟩ ⟨this masterly record . . . written with ~ discretion and understanding —John Hayward b.1905⟩ ⟨an ~ figure in trim dinner jacket and starched shirt —Truman Capote⟩ — **im·pec·ca·ble·ness** \-bəlnəs\ *n* -ES — **im·pec·ca·bly** \-blē, bli\ *adv*

im·pec·can·cy \-kənsē, -si\ *n* [LL *impeccantia*, fr. L *in-* ¹in- + LL *peccantia* sinfulness — more at PECCANCY] **:** the quality or state of being impeccant **:** SINLESSNESS

im·pec·cant \-nt\ *adj* [¹*in-* + *peccant*] **:** free from error or fault **:** SINLESS

im·pectinate \(ˈ)im+\ *adj* [¹*in-* + *pectinate*] **:** not pectinate

im·pecuniary \ˌim+\ *adj* [¹*in-* + *pecuniary*] *archaic* **:** IMPECUNIOUS

im·pe·cu·nios·i·ty \ˌimpəˌkyünēˈäsəd·ē, -pē,-, -nˈyä-, -sətē, -i\ *n* -ES **:** IMPECUNIOUSNESS

im·pe·cu·nious \ˌimpəˈkyünyəs, -pēˈ-, -nēəs\ *adj* [¹*in-* + obs. E *pecunious* rich, fr. ME *pecunyous*, fr. L *pecuniosus*, fr. *pecunia* money + *-osus* -ose — more at FEE] **:** having very little or no money usu. habitually **:** INDIGENT, PENNILESS ⟨this eager ~ young man who has fared so richly in his poverty —Edith Wharton⟩ **syn** see POOR

im·pe·cu·nious·ly *adv* **:** in an impecunious manner ⟨an ~ situated family⟩ ⟨plodding his way ~ through life⟩

im·pe·cu·nious·ness *n* -ES **:** the quality or state of being impecunious **:** INDIGENCE, POVERTY

im·pe·cu·ni·ty \ˌimpəˈkyünəd·ē, -pēˈ-, -nətē, -i\ *n* -ES [*impecunious* + *-ty*] **:** IMPECUNIOUSNESS

imped *past of* IMP

im·ped·ance \əmˈpēdᵊn(t)s\ *n* -s [*impede* + *-ance*] **1 a :** the apparent opposition in an electrical circuit to the flow of an alternating current that is analogous to the actual electrical resistance to a direct current and that is the ratio of effective electromotive force to the effective current **b :** the resistance to passage of a substance (as water or water vapor) through a film **2 :** the ratio of the pressure to the volume displacement at a given surface in a sound-transmitting medium

impedance bond *n* **:** an iron-core coil of low resistance and relatively high reactance used on electrified railroads to provide a continuous path around insulated joints for the return propulsion current and to confine the alternating-current signaling energy to its own track circuit

impedance bridge *n* **:** BRIDGE

im·pede \əmˈpēd\ *vt* -ED/-ING/-S [L *impedire*, fr. *in-* ²in- + *-pedire* (fr. *ped-, pes* foot) — more at FOOT] **:** to interfere with or get in the way of the progress of ⟨storms *impeded* the vessels —*Amer. Guide Series: N.C.*⟩ ⟨are further *impeded* in our work by financial stringency —C.A.Robinson⟩ **:** hold up **:** BLOCK ⟨the departure was *impeded* by heavy rain⟩ ⟨his progress was *impeded* by sickness and poverty⟩ **:** detract from ⟨no heavy weight of fable *impedes* the reader's enjoyment —Elizabeth Janeway⟩ **syn** see HINDER

im·pe·di·ent impediment \əmˈpēdēənt-\ *n* [*impedient* fr. L *impedient-*, impediens, pres. part. of *impedire*] **:** a bar to marriage that is an obstacle to the marriage if known but that does not make the marriage void after it has been solemnized — called also *hindering impediment*

im·ped·i·ment \əmˈpedəmənt\ *n* -s [L *impedimentum*, fr. *impedire* + *-mentum* -ment] **1 a :** the act or state of being impeded **:** OBSTRUCTION ⟨trying to determine where the ~*s* of growth lay in the life cycle⟩ **b :** something that impedes **:** HINDRANCE, BLOCK ⟨some ~ lay between him and advancement⟩ ⟨the destruction of all ~*s* to love —C.D.Lewis⟩ ⟨strove to get ahead despite all ~*s* in his path⟩; *esp* **:** an organic obstruction to speech ⟨some small ~ slowed his conversation⟩ **2 impediments** *pl*, *archaic* **:** IMPEDIMENTA **3 a :** a bar to the formation of a contract arising out of the lack of capacity of one of the parties (as from minority or want of sufficient mental capacity) **b :** a bar or hindrance (as lack of sufficient age, lack of genuine consent) to a lawful marriage sometimes resulting in complete nullity of marriage without any decree or declaration or in the marriage being voidable by the injured party — see ABSOLUTE IMPEDIMENT, DIRIMENT IMPEDIMENT, IMPEDIENT IMPEDIMENT, PROHIBITIVE IMPEDIMENT, RELATIVE IMPEDIMENT **syn** see OBSTACLE

im·ped·i·men·ta \əmˌpedəˈmentə, ˌim-\ *n pl* [L, pl. of *impedimentum* impediment] **:** things that impede or hinder progress or movement; *esp* **:** baggage, equipment, or supplies ⟨the photographer left all his ~ in the hall⟩ ⟨the supply trains dropped the ~ at convenient stopping places on the army's route⟩ ⟨clubs, bag, cart, umbrella, spiked shoes and all the other ~ of the golfer⟩

im·ped·i·men·tal \(ˌ)imˌpedəˈmentᵊl, əmˌ-\ *adj*, *archaic* **:** being an impediment **:** HINDERING, OBSTRUCTIVE

im·ped·i·tive \(ˈ)imˈpedəd·iv, əmˈp-\ *adj* [F *impéditif*, fr. MF *impeditif*, fr. L *impeditus* (past part. of *impedire* to impede) + MF *-if* -ive — more at IMPEDE] **:** tending to impede **:** hindering or causing a hindrance **:** OBSTRUCTIVE

im·pe·dor \əmˈpēdə(r)\ *n* -s [*impede* + *-or*] **:** an electric-circuit element that introduces impedance

im·pel \əmˈpel\ *vt* **impelled; impelled; impelling; impels** [L *impellere*, fr. *in-* ²in- + *pellere* to drive — more at FELT] **1 a :** to urge or drive by force or constraint ⟨*impelled* out of England . . . by religious dissension —Evelyn Wrench⟩ **:** exert strong moral pressure on or affect with marked moral compulsion in a particular direction ⟨*impelled* to resist oppressive laws⟩ ⟨felt *impelled* to tolerate what he intensely disliked⟩ ⟨continued to write, *impelled* by profit instead of vision and recollection —*Saturday Rev.*⟩ **b :** to create or generate by force or constraint ⟨land hunger *impelled* the deceit, trickery, bribery which whites practiced upon the red man —H.M. Hyman⟩ ⟨his symphonies and symphonic poems are *impelled* by picturesque Celtic folklore —Norman Demuth⟩ **2 :** to impart motion to **:** give a physical impulse to **:** PROPEL ⟨*impelling* a wheelbarrow along the street —Nathaniel Hawthorne⟩ **syn** see MOVE

¹im·pel·lent \(ˈ)imˈpelənt, əmˈp-\ *adj* [L *impellent-, impellens*, pres. part. of *impellere*] **:** IMPELLING

²impellent \"\ *n* -s **:** something that impels

im·pel·ler *also* **im·pel·lor** \əmˈpelə(r)\ *n* -s **1 :** one that impels **2 :** ROTOR 1a, 1b; *also* **:** a blade of a rotor — see JET ENGINE illustration

impelling *adj* **:** markedly effective **:** FORCEFUL ⟨an ~ personality⟩ ⟨an ~ skill as a teller of tales⟩ — **im·pel·ling·ly** *adv*

im·pend \əmˈpend\ *vi* -ED/-ING/-S [L *impendēre*, fr. *in-* ²in- + *pendēre* to hang — more at PENDANT] **1** *archaic* **:** to hang suspended (as over one's head) ⟨a profuse crop of hair ~*ing* over the top of his face —Thomas Hardy⟩ **:** jut out and seem to hang suspended ⟨the crags . . . now begin to ~ terribly over your way —Thomas Gray⟩ **2 a :** to threaten from near at hand or as in the immediate future **:** MENACE ⟨trouble ~*ed* over the entire enterprise⟩ **b :** to be imminent **:** give promise of occurring in the immediate future ⟨went indoors because rain ~*ed*⟩ **:** be about to occur ⟨the most critical contests ~ —Cabell Phillips⟩

impendence *or* **impendency** *n*, *pl* **impendences** *or* **impendencies** *obs* **:** the quality or state of being impending

im·pend·ent \-dənt\ *adj* [L *impendent-, impendens*, pres. part. of *impendēre*] **:** IMPENDING

impending *adj* **:** that is about to occur **:** IMMINENT ⟨an ~ crisis⟩ ⟨an ~ storm⟩ ⟨~ danger⟩

im·penetrability \(ˌ)im, əm+\ *n* **1 :** the quality or state of being impenetrable **2 :** the property of matter from which two portions of matter cannot occupy the same space at the same time

im·penetrable \(ˈ)im, əm+\ *adj* [ME *impenetrabel*, fr. MF *impenetrable*, fr. L *impenetrabilis*, fr. *in-* ¹in- + *penetrabilis* penetrable — more at PENETRABLE] **1 a :** incapable of being penetrated or pierced **:** not admitting the passage of other bodies **:** not to be entered **:** IMPERVIOUS ⟨an ~ shield⟩ ⟨an ~ forest⟩ ⟨an ~ barrier⟩ **b :** inaccessible to knowledge, reason, sympathy **:** not to be moved by logic or other method of persuasion **:** UNIMPRESSIBLE ⟨an ~ heart⟩ ⟨an ~ stupidity⟩ **c :** incapable of being dealt with in a way that brings a usu. warm, cordial, or unguarded response ⟨an ~ reserve⟩ ⟨an ~ gloom⟩ **2 :** incapable of being comprehended **:** INSCRUTABLE, UNFATHOMABLE ⟨an ~ mystery⟩ ⟨a child speaking in an ~ language of its own⟩ **3 :** having the property of impenetrability ⟨~ matter⟩ — **im·penetrableness** \"+\ *n* — **im·penetrably** \"+\ *adv*

im·penetrate \əm+\ *vt* [²*in-* + *penetrate*] **:** to penetrate thoroughly ⟨power to isolate and ~ Poland and the Balkan States —John Gunther⟩ **syn** see PERMEATE

im·penetration \(ˌ)im, əm+\ *n* **:** the act of impenetrating or the state of being impenetrated

im·penitence *also* **im·penitency** \(ˈ)im, əm+\ *n* [LL *impaenitentia*, fr. *impaenitent-, impaenitens* + L *-ia* -y] **:** the quality or state of being impenitent **:** failure or refusal to repent

¹im·penitent \"+\ *adj* [LL *impaenitent-, impaenitens*, fr. L *in-* ¹in- + *paenitent-, paenitens* penitent — more at PENITENT] **:** not penitent **:** not repenting of sin **:** not contrite — **im·penitently** \"+\ *adv* — **im·penitentness** \"+\ *n* -ES

²impenitent \"\ *n* **:** one that is impenitent

imper *abbr* imperative

im·pe·ra·ta \ˌimpəˈräd·ə\ *n*, *cap* [NL, after Ferrante *Imperato* †1625 It. apothecary] **:** a genus of tropical grasses having slender erect culms and a narrow panicle with spikelets surrounded by long silky hairs — see COGON

im·per·ate \ˈimpəˌrāt\ *vt* -ED/-ING/-S [L *imperatus*, past part. of *imperare* to command — more at EMPEROR] **:** COMMAND, GOVERN — **im·per·a·tion** \ˌimpəˈrāshən\ *n* -s

²imperate *adj* [L *imperatus*] *obs*, *of an act* **:** COMMANDED — contrasted with *elicit*

im·per·a·ti·val \(ˌ)imˌperəˈtīvəl, əm-\ *adj* **:** of or relating to the grammatical imperative **:** expressing an imperative meaning **:** having an imperative function — **im·per·a·ti·val·ly** \-vəlē\ *adv*

¹im·per·a·tive \əmˈperəd·|iv, -rət|\ *adj* [LL *imperativus*, fr. L *imperatus* (past part. of *imperare* to command) + *-ivus* -ive — more at EMPEROR] **1 a :** of, relating to, or being the grammatical mood that expresses the will to influence the behavior of another (as in a command, entreaty, or exhortation) — compare INDICATIVE **b :** expressive of or being a command, entreaty, or exhortation ⟨an ~ rule of conduct⟩ ⟨an ~ tone of voice⟩ **:** commanding often imperiously ⟨an ~ manner⟩ ⟨~ persons rush about giving orders⟩ ⟨"you must let me speak," said the woman, in an ~ voice —A. Conan Doyle⟩ **c :** restraining, controlling, and directing ⟨the democratic instinct is in France too ~ —W.C.Brownell⟩ **2 :** not to be avoided or evaded : URGENT, OBLIGATORY, BINDING, COMPULSORY ⟨an ~ duty⟩ ⟨an ~ engagement⟩ **syn** see MASTERFUL, PRESSING

²imperative \"\ *n* -s **1 :** the imperative mood or a verb form or verbal phrase expressing it ⟨an ~ of the verb⟩ **2 :** COMMAND, ORDER ⟨a sheep dog emits ~s to his flock hardly distinguishable from those that the shepherd employs toward him —Bertrand Russell⟩; *also* : RULE, GUIDE ⟨lived by certain simple ~s⟩ **3 a :** an obligatory act or duty ⟨the social ~s of our time —M.J.Rosenberg⟩ ⟨it is an ~ that we try again before giving up⟩ **b :** an imperative judgment, proposition, or statement — see CATEGORICAL IMPERATIVE, HYPOTHETICAL IMPERATIVE **c :** NECESSITY, NEED ⟨the terrible ~ of reaching the springs —D.L.Morgan⟩ ⟨the sheer ~ of survival —*New Republic*⟩ **d :** an unavoidable fact compelling or insistently calling for action ⟨the ~s of physical battle —*N.Y. Herald Tribune Bk. Rev.*⟩ ⟨economic ~s⟩ **e :** a quality or aspect that gives authority or obligatoriness or that demands action ⟨the ~ of law is not simply the ~ of grammatical form —Glenn Negley⟩ ⟨by the conscious direction of the people quite apart from the ~ of events —T.K.Finletter⟩

im·per·a·tive·ly \|əvlē, -li\ *adv* **:** in an imperative manner

im·per·a·tive·ness \|ivnəs\ *n* -ES **:** the quality or state of being imperative

im·pe·ra·tor \ˌimpəˈrädˌər, ˌ==ˈräˌtȯ(ə)r\ *n* -s [L — more at EMPEROR] **:** supreme leader esp. of the ancient Romans : COMMANDER, EMPEROR — **im·per·a·to·ri·al** \(ˌ)imˌperəˈtōrēəl\ *adj*

imperatorious *adj* [L *imperatorius*, fr. *imperator* + *-orius* -ory] *obs* : IMPERATORIAL

im·per·a·tor·ship \ˌimpəˈräd·ər,ship\ *n* **:** the position of imperator

im·perceivable \ˌim+\ *adj* [¹*in-* + *perceivable*] *archaic* : IMPERCEPTIBLE

im·perceptibility \ˌim+\ *n* **:** the quality or state of being imperceptible

¹im·perceptible \ˌim+\ *adj* [MF, fr. ML *imperceptibilis*, fr. L *in-* ¹in- + LL *perceptibilis* perceptible — more at PERCEPTIBLE] **:** not perceptible: **a :** not capable of being perceived by a sense or of affecting a sense ⟨color is ~ to the touch⟩ ⟨made an almost ~ gesture of assent⟩ **b :** not capable of being perceived or discriminated mentally ⟨the difference between the two propositions was ~ to him⟩ **c :** extremely slight, gradual, or subtle ⟨saw him grow up by ~ gradations⟩ — **im·perceptibleness** \"+\ *n* -ES — **im·perceptibly** \"+\ *adv*

²imperceptible \"\ *n* -s **:** something that is imperceptible

im·perception \ˌim+\ *n* [¹*in-* + *perception*] **:** a lack of perception

im·perceptive \"+\ *adj* [¹*in-* + *perceptive*] **:** not perceptive : UNPERCEIVING : lacking perception ⟨~ persons have been intolerably bored by masterpieces —*N.Y.Herald Tribune*⟩ ⟨stupid and ~ of even the grossest differences between foods⟩ — **im·perceptiveness** \"+\ *n* — **im·perceptivity** \"+\ *n*

im·percipience \ˌim+\ *n* **:** the quality or state of being unperceptive : lack of perception

im·percipient \"+\ *adj* [¹*in-* + *percipient*] : UNPERCEPTIVE ⟨agitated by the strangely ~ criticisms of his work —Hesketh Pearson⟩

im·per·ence \ˈimpərən(t)s\ *n* -s [by alter.] *substand Brit* : IMPUDENCE

imperf *abbr* **1** imperfect **2** imperforate

¹im·perfect \(ˈ)im, əm+\ *adj* [alter. (influenced by L *imperfectus*) of ME *imperfit*, *imparfit*, fr. MF *imparfait*, fr. L *imperfectus*, fr. *in-* ¹in- + *perfectus* perfect — more at PERFECT] **1 a :** falling short of perfection : not perfect (as in form, development, or function) : not complete in parts or attributes : not satisfying the standard or ideal : DEFECTIVE, INADEQUATE, INCOMPLETE ⟨had only an ~ understanding of his task⟩ ⟨in the ~ light of the moon —Anthony Trollope⟩ ⟨what an ~ husband he had always been —H.G.Wells⟩ ⟨~ mortals⟩ ⟨drainage of the region is ~ —*Jour. of Geol.*⟩ **b :** DICLINOUS **2 :** of, relating to, or being a verb tense used to designate a continuing state or an incomplete action esp. in the past **3 a** *in medieval church music* (1) **:** twofold rather than threefold in time value — used of notation; compare PERFECT (2) **:** having a duple rather than triple rhythm — used of a rhythmic mode **b :** DIMINISHED 2 **4 :** not enforceable at law : lacking some essential element required by law : depending for fulfillment upon moral rather than legal duty ⟨an ~ obligation⟩ : enforceable only under certain conditions : DEFEASIBLE ⟨an ~ mortgage⟩ ⟨an ~ grant avoidable by the government⟩ — **im·perfectly** \"+\ *adv* — **im·perfectness** \"+\ *n* -ES

²imperfect *vt, obs* **:** to make imperfect

³im·perfect \(ˈ)im, əm+\ *n* **:** an imperfect tense; *also* **:** the verb form expressing it

imperfect cadence *n* **1 :** an authentic or plagal cadence in which the third or the fifth of the final chord appears in the soprano part or in which one or both of the cadential chords are inverted — compare PERFECT CADENCE; see CADENCE illustration **2 :** HALF CADENCE

imperfect competition *n* **:** competition among sellers of inhomogeneous products in which the sellers are sufficiently few in number so that each exerts an influence upon the market : limited competition

imperfect diphthong *n* : PARTIAL DIPHTHONG

im·perfected \(ˌ)im, əm+\ *adj* [¹*in-* + *perfected*] **:** not perfected : IMPERFECT — **im·perfectedly** \"+\ *adv*

imperfect flower *n* **:** a diclinous flower

imperfect fungus *n* **:** a fungus of which only the conidial stage is known : one of the Fungi Imperfecti

im·perfectibility \(ˌ)im, əm+\ *n* [¹*in-* + *perfectibility*] **:** the quality or state of being imperfectible

im·perfectible \(ˌ)im, əm+\ *adj* [¹*in-* + *perfectible*] **:** incapable of being made perfect

im·perfection \ˌim+\ *n* [ME *imperfeccioun*, fr. MF or LL; MF *imperfection* fr. LL *imperfection-*, *imperfectio*, fr. L *imperfectus* + *-ion-*, *-io* -ion — more at IMPERFECT] **1 a :** the quality or state of being imperfect : lack of perfection : INCOMPLETENESS ⟨dissatisfied with the ~ of man⟩ ⟨saw the ~ of the dress⟩ **b :** the quality or aspect in which something is incomplete : DEFICIENCY, FAULT, BLEMISH ⟨tried to cover up the ~s in the cloth⟩ **2** *in medieval church music* **a :** duple time **b :** the occasional division of a triple measure into two equal parts **3 a :** a sheet that is rejected because of faulty printing; *also* **:** a replacement for such a sheet **b :** a printed or folded book section or a complete gathered or sewed but unbound book that has been rejected for any reason **4 :** a piece of type cast to fill a deficiency in a type font

¹im·perfective \(ˌ)im, əm+\ *adj* [¹*in-* + *perfective*] *of a verb form or aspect* **:** expressing action as incomplete or without reference to completion : expressing action as continuing : expressing action as reiterated : DURATIVE — opposed to *perfective* — **im·perfectivity** \"+\ *n*

²imperfective \"\ *n* **:** the imperfective aspect or form of a verb

imperfect number *n* **:** a number (as 15) that is not equal to the sum of its divisors — compare PERFECT NUMBER; see ABUNDANT NUMBER, DEFICIENT NUMBER

imperfect stage *n* **:** any of various conidial or asexual stages in the life history of a fungus

imperfect usufruct *n* **:** the right of usufruct allowed in a thing consumed in the using — called also *quasi usufruct*

im·perforata \(ˌ)im, əm+\ *n pl, cap* [NL, fr. ¹*in-* + *Perforata*] *in some classifications* **:** a division of the Foraminifera having imperforate shells

¹im·perforate \(ˈ)im, əm+\ *adj* [¹*in-* + *perforate*] **1 :** not perforated : having no opening or aperture; *specif* **:** lacking the normal opening ⟨an ~ anus⟩ **2** *of a stamp or a sheet of stamps* **:** lacking perforations or rouletting **3 :** having the umbilicus obliterated by the later whorls — used of various spiral shells

²imperforate \"\ *n* -s **:** an imperforate stamp

im·perforated \(ˈ)im, əm+\ *adj* [¹*in-* + *perforated*] : IMPERFORATE

im·perforation \(ˌ)im, əm+\ *n* [F, fr. *in-* ¹in- + *perforation* — more at PERFORATION] **:** the quality or state of being without perforation

¹im·pe·ri·al \(ˈ)imˈpirēəl, əmˈp-, -pēr-\ *adj* [ME *emperial*, *imperial*, fr. MF, fr. LL *imperialis*, fr. L *imperium* command, supreme authority, empire + *-alis* -al — more at EMPIRE] **1 a :** of or relating to an empire or an emperor esp. of a particular or implicit empire ⟨the national poet of the empire, in whom ~ patriotism found its highest expression —James Bryce⟩ ⟨~ Caesar⟩ ⟨his view was ~ rather than provincial —Carl Bridenbaugh⟩ **b :** of, relating to, or befitting supreme authority or one that exercises it : of the rank of or suitable to an emperor or supreme ruler : ROYAL, SOVEREIGN **c :** of or relating to a state as governing or being supreme over colonies, dependencies, or many subdivisions; *specif, usu cap* **:** of or relating to Britain as such a state ⟨make an essential contribution . . . to New Zealand and *Imperial* history —*Notes & Queries*⟩ ⟨British *Imperial* communications —*Brit. Book News*⟩ **d :** HAUGHTY, REGAL, COMMANDING, IMPERIOUS ⟨stood there, tall, broad, ~ —Donn Byrne⟩ ⟨the rigid, ~ hyacinth —Rebecca West⟩ ⟨humoring us with her fatigued ~ smiles —Arnold Bennett⟩ **2 a :** of superior or unusual size or excellence ⟨a rich man living on an ~ diet⟩ ⟨grow from the little old town of the nineties to the ~ city that stands there now —W.A.White⟩ ⟨a homicidal mania on an ~ scale —Ellery Sedgwick⟩ **b :** of fancy quality — used as a designation for various commercial products **c :** SELF-AGGRANDIZING, GRANDIOSE ⟨thoughts that were partly dreams . . . ~, childish dreams —Audrey L. Barker⟩ **3** *of a measure or weight* **:** being the British legal standard : belonging to the official British series of weights and measures ⟨the ~ gallon⟩ — **im·pe·ri·al·ly** \-ēəlē, -li\ *adv* — **im·pe·ri·al·ness** \-ēəlnəs\ *n* -ES

²imperial \"\ *n* -s **1 :** a medieval silk and gold fabric of oriental origin **2** *usu cap* [Russ, prob. fr. Pol *imperjal*, a kind of coin, fr. ML *imperialis*, a medieval coin, fr. LL *imperialis*, adj., imperial] **:** an adherent of the Holy Roman emperor or a soldier of his troops : IMPERIALIST **3 :** a person of imperial rank : EMPEROR, EMPRESS **4 :** a size of paper usu. 23 x 31, 22½ x 29, or 22 x 30 inches **5 :** a game similar to piquet but having a trump; *also* **:** any of several scoring combinations in the game **6 a :** a luggage case for the top of a coach **b :** the top, roof, or second-story compartment of a coach or carriage, esp. a diligence **7 :** a gold coin of imperial Russia worth 10 rubles when first issued in 1745 and 15 rubles from 1897–1917 **8** [F *impériale*, fr. fem. of *impérial* imperial, fr. LL *imperialis*; fr. the beard worn as a young man by Napoleon III †1873 emperor of France] **:** a pointed beard growing below the lower lip **9 :** something of unusual size or excellence **10 :** a dark reddish purple that is lighter and stronger than average plum (sense 6a), bluer and stronger than violet carmine or average grape wine, and bluer and deeper than royal purple (sense 1) — called also *Cotinga purple*

imperial 8

imperial blue *n* **:** a deep blue that is greener and deeper than Yale blue, greener, lighter, and stronger than royal (sense 8b), and greener and stronger than Napoleon blue

imperial bushel *n* : BUSHEL 1b

imperial city *n* **1 :** a city (as Rome) that is the seat of empire **2 :** a city that is an immediate vassal of the emperor of the Holy Roman Empire

imperial crown *n, often cap I, sometimes cap C* **1 :** a crown emblematic of independent sovereignty: as **a :** the crown in the royal regalia of England that is used for the crowning in the coronation ceremony, that consists of a circlet of gold heightened with four crosses formée alternately with four fleurs-de-lis and has two arches rising from the crosses and surmounted by a mound and a cross formée, and that is ornamented with precious stones — called also *St. Edward's crown* **b :** the crown of an emperor or of an empire **2 :** a conventionalized representation of an imperial crown; *esp* **:** a figure of a crown in the style of the imperial crown of England often used as an emblem of the sovereignty of the British monarch or as a heraldic bearing **3 :** IMPERIAL STATE CROWN

imperial crown of state *often cap I&C&S* : IMPERIAL STATE CROWN

imperial dome *or* **imperial roof** *n* **:** a pointed dome or roof the vertical section of which is an ogee

imperial eagle *n* **:** an eagle (*Aquila heliaca*) of southern Europe and Asia the adult of which is dark brown with white shoulder patches — called also *king eagle*

imperial gallon *n* : GALLON 1b

imperial green *n* **1 :** PARIS GREEN 2b **2 :** EMERALD GREEN

im·pe·ri·al·ism \əmˈpirēəˌlizəm, -pēr-\ *n* -s **1 a :** the power or the government of an emperor : imperial authority : an imperial system ⟨the ~ of Caesar⟩ ⟨educational ~ —*Current Biog.*⟩ **b :** an imperial quality ⟨with dramatic ~ and disarming gentility . . . the epitome of mysterious womanhood —Louise Mace⟩ **2 a :** the policy, practice, or advocacy of seeking or the acquiescing in the extension of the control or empire of a nation by the acquirement of new territory or dependencies esp. when lying outside the nation's natural boundaries, by the extension of its rule over other races of mankind (as where commerce demands the protection of the flag), or by the closer union of more or less independent parts (as for war, copyright, or internal commerce) **b :** any extension of power or authority or an advocacy of such extension ⟨union ~ —S.H.Slichter⟩ ⟨cultural ~⟩

¹im·pe·ri·al·ist \-ləst\ *n* -s [¹*imperial* + *-ist*] **1 :** one that adheres to an emperor or to his party; *esp* **:** one loyal to the Holy Roman Empire **2 :** one who favors or practices imperialism

²imperialist \"\ *or* **im·pe·ri·al·is·tic** \(ˌ)imˌ===ˈlistik, əm-, -tēk\ *adj* **:** of, relating to, practicing, or favoring imperialism ⟨the great faiths . . . are *imperialistic*, going out to bring into the fold others than those people among whom they grew up —W.W.Howells⟩ ⟨an ~ war⟩ ⟨*imperialistic* in seeking to convert almost the whole of political science to his own interests —David Easton⟩ ⟨autocratic control and *imperialistic* expansion —Sigmund Neumann⟩ ⟨*imperialistic* policies of aggression along the weaker races —Lewis Mumford⟩ — **im·pe·ri·al·is·ti·cal·ly** \-tək(ə)lē, -tēk-, -li\ *adv*

im·pe·ri·al·iza·tion \=,===ləˈzāshən, -ˌlīˈz-\ *n* -s **:** the act of imperializing or the state of being imperialized

im·pe·ri·al·ize \=ˈ===ə,līz\ *vt* -ED/-ING/-S **:** to make imperial : invest with an imperial quality or character : bring to the form of an empire

imperial jade *n, usu cap I* : ³JADE 1a

imperially crowned *adj, of a heraldic bearing* **:** crowned with an imperial crown

imperial mammoth *also* **imperial elephant** *n* **:** the largest known mammoth (*Archidiskidon imperator*) of the American Pleistocene reaching a height of 14 feet

imperial moth *n* **:** a large American saturniid moth (*Eacles imperialis*) marked with yellow, lilac, or purplish brown whose rough hairy larva feeds esp. on maple, sumach, and pine trees

imperial pigeon *n* **:** any of various very large Asiatic and Australasian pigeons that constitute a distinct subfamily of Columbidae — compare NUTMEG PIGEON

imperial preference *n* **:** the preferential lowering of tariff rates accorded in the British Commonwealth to its members

imperial purple *n* **1 :** a grayish violet **2** *of textiles* **:** a deep purple that is redder and duller than hyacinth violet or petunia violet and redder and less strong than dahlia purple (sense 2)

imperial red *also* **imperial scarlet** *n* **:** vermilion or a color resembling it

imperials *pl of* IMPERIAL

imperial state crown *n, usu cap I&S&C* **:** an English royal crown worn on various state occasions that is more richly jeweled than the imperial crown but lighter in weight and usu. remade for successive sovereigns — called also *state crown*

imperial stone *n* **:** a light olive brown that is deeper than drab or sponge and deeper and slightly redder than average mustard tan

imperial tea *n* **:** a high-grade Chinese green tea made usu. from older leaves

imperial woodpecker *n* **:** a woodpecker (*Campephilus imperialis*) of northern Mexico that has black plumage with white markings on the wings and neck, a red crest in the male, and a white bill and that is the largest woodpecker known, the male being about two feet in length

imperial yellow *n* : YELLOW OCHER

im·peril \əm+\ *vt* **imperiled** *or* **imperilled; imperiled** *or* **imperilled; imperiling** *or* **imperilling; imperils** [²*in-* + *peril* (n.)] **:** to bring into peril : expose to danger of imminent harm or loss : endanger or threaten danger to ⟨a jungle of aggressive power politics which ~*s* . . . the healing of the wounds of war —Mark Starr⟩ ⟨people whose investments were ~*ed* —G.W.Johnson⟩ ⟨stray mines . . . began to turn up off the Pacific coast, ~*ing* commercial shipping —Alan Hynd⟩ **syn** see VENTURE

im·per·il·ment \-mənt\ *n* -s **:** the act of imperiling or the state of being imperiled ⟨cut down on the convoy escort to the ~ of shipping everywhere⟩

im·pe·ri·ous \(ˈ)imˈpirēəs, əmˈp-, -pēr-\ *adj* [L *imperiosus*, fr. *imperium* command, supreme authority, empire + *-osus* -ous — more at EMPIRE] **1 a** *obs* : IMPERIAL 1 a, 1b **b :** COMMANDING, DOMINANT, LORDLY ⟨sweeps through her social duties with ~ kindness —Margaret Landon⟩ **c** *obs* : MAJESTIC, STATELY **2 :** ARROGANT, OVERBEARING, DOMINEERING **3 :** IMPERATIVE, URGENT, COMPELLING ⟨at the mercy of the most ~ of instincts, of passions, and of intoxications —Arthur Symons⟩ ⟨so ~ became the commercial demand —Lewis Mumford⟩ **syn** see MASTERFUL

im·pe·ri·ous·ly *adv* **:** in an imperious manner ⟨drew him ~ apart from the others —George Meredith⟩ ⟨clung to authority as ~ as a king who refuses to abdicate —Ellen Glasgow⟩

im·pe·ri·ous·ness *n* -ES **:** the quality or state of being imperious

im·perishability \(ˌ)im, əm+\ *n* **:** the quality or state of being imperishable

¹im·perishable \(ˈ)im, əm+\ *adj* [¹*in-* + *perishable*] **:** not perishable : not subject to decay : enduring permanently : INDESTRUCTIBLE ⟨an ~ monument⟩ ⟨~ fame⟩ ⟨peace is not ~ —M.W.Straight⟩ ⟨an ~ memory⟩ — **im·perishableness** \"+\ *n* — **im·perishably** \"+\ *adv*

²imperishable \"\ *n* **:** something imperishable ⟨a classic to take its place among the ~*s*⟩

im·pe·ri·um \əmˈpirēəm, -per-, -pēr-\ *n* -s [L, command, supreme authority, empire — more at EMPIRE] **1 a** (1) **:** supreme power or absolute dominion esp. over a large area ⟨surrender the showy shadow of ~ to secure the solid substance of colonial loyalty and cooperation —Oliver Benson⟩ (2) **:** regulatory powers or control ⟨had relinquished all ~ . . . over the land in question —*U. S. Code*⟩ ⟨existing governments had exhausted their ~ —Walter Lippmann⟩ **b :** an area over which such power or dominion is exercised : TERRITORY, EMPIRE ⟨the portentous ~ of the cartels —R.M.MacIver⟩ **2 a :** the right to command : the right of jurisdiction which includes the right to employ the force of the state to enforce the laws : executive power : SOVEREIGNTY **b** *Roman law* **:** the power to hear and determine cases and to give judgments — compare DOMINIUM, JURISDICTION

imperium in im·pe·rio \-ˌinəmˈpirēˌō, -per-, -pēr-\ *n* [NL] **:** a government, power, or sovereignty within a government, power, or sovereignty

im·permanence *or* **im·permanency** \(ˈ)im+\ *n* [¹*in-* + *permanence*, *permanency*] **:** the quality or state of being impermanent ⟨the ~ . . . of all the dear world of beauty —C.E.Montague⟩ ⟨the sense of the ~ of things, the transitoriness of life —Laurence Binyon⟩ ⟨the foolishness of love and the *impermanency* of all human relationships —Lafcadio Hearn⟩

im·permanent \"+\ *adj* [¹*in-* + *permanent*] **:** not permanent : not lasting : TRANSIENT ⟨politics is an ~ factor of life —James Thurber⟩ : UNSTABLE ⟨broken homes, ~ family life —Bingham Dai⟩ : soon destroyed ⟨~ log and palm cottages raised on stilts above the bayous —*Amer. Guide Series: La.*⟩ — **im·permanently** \"+\ *adv*

im·permeability \(ˌ)im, əm+\ *n* **:** the quality or state of being impermeable

im·per·me·a·bi·li·za·tion \(ˌ)imˌpərmēəˌbiləˈzāshən, -ˌbələˈz-, -bəˌlīˈz-\ *n* -s [F *imperméabilisation*, fr. *imperméabiliser* + *-ation*] **:** the act of impermeabilizing something

im·per·me·a·bi·lize \=ˈ===bəˌlīz\ *vt* -ED/-ING/-S [F *imperméabiliser*, fr. LL *impermeabilis* + F *-iser* -ize] **:** to make impermeable esp. to liquids

im·permeable \(ˈ)im, əm+\ *adj* [LL *impermeabilis*, fr. L *in-* ¹in- + LL *permeabilis* permeable — more at PERMEABLE] **:** not permeable : not permitting passage (as of a fluid) through its substance : IMPASSABLE, IMPERVIOUS ⟨an ~ stone⟩ ⟨a coat ~ to rain⟩ ⟨an ~ layer of scum⟩ — **im·permeableness** \"+\ *n* — **im·permeably** \"+\ *adv*

im·permissibility \ˌim+\ *n* **:** the quality or state of being impermissible

im·permissible \"+\ *adj* [¹*in-* + *permissible*] **:** not permissible ⟨his secret and legally ~ objective —B.N.Meltzer⟩ ⟨has taken ~ liberties —J.D.Clarkson⟩ — **im·permissibly** \"+\ *adv*

impers *abbr* impersonal

im·personable \(ˈ)im, əm+\ *adj* [¹*in-* + *personable*] **:** not personable : UNATTRACTIVE

¹im·personal \"+\ *adj* [LL *impersonalis*, fr. L *in-* ¹in- + LL *personalis* personal — more at PERSONAL] **1 a** (1) *of a verb* **:** not predicated of a personal or determinate subject : denoting the action of an unspecified agent and hence used with no expressed subject (as *methinks*) or with a merely formal subject (as *is raining* in *it is raining*) (2) **:** consisting of either an indefinite pronoun and an impersonal verb (as *it is raining* or French *on dit*) or the expletive *there* and such a verb (as *there is* in *there is fog ahead*) **b** *of a pronoun* : INDEFINITE **c** *of a proposition* **:** having an indeterminate subject **2 a** (1) **:** having no personal reference or connection : not referring or belonging to any particular person ⟨when I say that a belief is ~ I mean that those desires which enter into its causation are universal human desires, and not such as are peculiar to the person in question —Bertrand Russell⟩ ⟨the brightly ~ sunshine —K.M.Dodson⟩ ⟨an ~ coat of arms⟩ (2) **:** not engaging the human personality or person ⟨the machine as compared with the hand tool is an ~ agency —John Dewey⟩ **b :** not representing or existing as a person : not having personality ⟨nature becomes an ~ slave —W.H.Auden⟩ **c :** not primarily affecting or involving the emotions of the person who has it ⟨an ~ interest in law⟩ ⟨the ~ attitude of a doctor⟩ — **im·personally** \"+\ *adv*

²impersonal \"\ *n* **:** something impersonal; *specif* **:** an impersonal verb

im·personalism \(ˈ)im, əm+\ *n* **1 :** IMPERSONALITY ⟨the ~ of research in the sciences⟩ ⟨the trend toward ~ in office relations⟩ **2 :** the policy of being impersonal in relations with other persons or of maintaining impersonal relations among a group

im·personality \(ˌ)im, əm+\ *n* [¹*impersonal* + *-ity*] **1 :** the lack or absence of a personal or human character ⟨the ~ of natural law⟩ **2 :** the quality or state of not involving personal feelings or the emotions or of being unemotional and disinterested ⟨marveled at the ~ of the thinking of so passionate a man⟩ ⟨the emotional detachment and ~ required of a good playwright —Leslie Rees⟩ ⟨so much ~, so much coldness and emphasis on technique —Manny Farber⟩ **3 a :** the quality or state of not involving, not being activated by, or not tracing to a personal agent ⟨the ~ of the popular ballad⟩ ⟨the ~ of the machine⟩ **b :** a quality or state marked by an absence or suppression of human expression or a minimizing of the significance of personality ⟨the ~ of society⟩ ⟨the ~ of the world money market⟩ **c :** the quality of not bearing on only a single or a particular person ⟨the ~, the universality of his remarks⟩ **4 :** something impersonal ⟨forced to deal with *impersonalities* such as the state or the law⟩

im·personalization \(ˌ)im, əm+\ *n* **:** the act of impersonalizing or the state of being impersonalized ⟨the growing ~ of higher civilizations —A.L.Kroeber⟩

im·personalize \(ˈ)im, əm+\ *vt* [¹*impersonal* + *-ize*] **:** to make impersonal ⟨one cannot ~ entirely a cosmic human drama like that war —W.A.White⟩

¹im·per·son·ate \əmˈpərsᵊnˌāt, -pə̄s-, -pəis-, *usu* -ād·+V\ *vt* [²*in-* + *person* + *-ate* (v. suffix)] **1 a** *obs* **:** to give or ascribe the qualities of a person to : PERSONIFY **b** *archaic* : TYPIFY, EXEMPLIFY **2 :** to assume the character of : pretend to be in actuality or personality, appearance, or behavior : PERSONATE ⟨caught trying to ~ an officer⟩ ⟨do not have the correct intonation for the character they are trying to ~ —Samuel Selden⟩ ⟨the dancers *impersonated* animals⟩ **3 a :** to give personal expression to ⟨an actor who could ~ any emotion⟩

b : to give expression to the person of ⟨music to ~ the hero of the opera⟩

²im·per·son·ate \-sᵊnət, *usu* -əd·+V\ *adj* [²*in-* + *person* + *-ate* (adj. suffix)] **:** invested with personality ⟨in the dictator all the forces of evil found an ~ expression⟩

im·per·son·a·tion \əm,ˌ==ˈāshən, ˌim-\ *n* **:** the act of impersonating or the state of being impersonated ⟨arrested for his ~ of an army major⟩ ⟨a man noted for his ~ of women⟩ ⟨the musical ~ of the hero himself —Eric Blom⟩

im·per·son·a·tor \=ˈ==ˌād·ə(r), -ātə-\ *n* **:** one that impersonates; *esp* **:** an entertainer who impersonates an individual, a type of person, an animal, or an inanimate object

im·personification \ˌim+\ *n* [²*in-* + *personification*] **:** EMBODIMENT

im·personify \"+\ *vt* [²*in-* + *personify*] *archaic* **:** to give a personal form or expression to **:** PERSONIFY

im·pertinence *also* **impertinency** \im+, əm+, *or in senses* 1a & 2a ˈim+¦-\ *n* [*impertinence* fr. F, fr. ML *impertinentia*, fr. LL *impertinent-, impertinens* + L *-ia* -y; *impertinency* fr. F *impertinence* + E *-y*] **1 :** the quality or state of being impertinent: as **a :** lack of relevance or appropriateness **:** IRRELEVANCE, UNFITNESS **b :** lack of due respect for others in conduct **:** INCIVILITY, INSOLENCE ⟨the ~, the brashness had gone forever —Katharine F. Gerould⟩ **2 :** something impertinent or an instance of impertinence: **a :** an irrelevant thing or matter ⟨at the climax of high tragedy all scenic adjuncts become an ~ —W.B.Adams⟩ **b :** an impertinent or uncivil act or person ⟨irritated by the man's social faults and ~*s*⟩ ⟨unwilling to scold the young ~ that was his son⟩

¹im·pertinent \(ˈ)im, əm+\ *adj* [ME, fr. MF, fr. LL *impertinent-, impertinens*, fr. L *in-* ¹in- + *pertinent-, pertinens*, pres. part. of *pertinēre* to reach out, extend, pertain — more at PERTAIN] **1 a :** not pertinent **:** not significantly belonging or related to the matter in hand **:** IRRELEVANT, INAPPLICABLE ⟨should rigidly exclude courses of study ~ to their central purposes —H.W.Sams⟩ **b** *obs* **:** not suitable or congruous **:** INAPPROPRIATE **c** *archaic* **:** FRIVOLOUS, FOOLISH **2 :** not restrained within the due or proper bounds esp. of propriety or good breeding in words or actions **:** guilty of or prone to rudeness or incivility ⟨a child taught not to make ~ remarks to his elders⟩ ⟨approach complete strangers, ask them a battery of ~ questions —S.L.Payne⟩

syn IMPERTINENT, OFFICIOUS, MEDDLESOME, INTRUSIVE, OBTRUSIVE: IMPERTINENT implies a concerning of oneself offensively with what is another's business ⟨all that had occurred to make my former interference in his affairs absurd and *impertinent* —Jane Austen⟩ ⟨we were secure from all *impertinent* interference in our concerns —Herman Melville⟩ ⟨something so extremely *impertinent* in entering upon a man's premises, and using them without paying —William Cowper⟩ OFFICIOUS implies an offering of unwelcome or offensive services, attentions, or assistance ⟨cannot walk home from office, but some *officious* friend offers his unwelcome courtesies to accompany me —Charles Lamb⟩ ⟨had no desire to call in a detective for fear the man might become an *officious* nuisance⟩ MEDDLESOME stresses an annoying and usu. prying interference in others' business ⟨turns with scorn upon the Abolitionists and their *meddlesome* interference with the beneficent ways of Providence —V.L.Parrington⟩ ⟨a vain, *meddlesome* vagabond, and must needs pry into a secret which certainly did not concern him —Charles Kingsley⟩ INTRUSIVE applies to one who has or something that reveals a disposition to be unduly curious about another's business ⟨made an inconspicuous fourth in their small world, always at hand yet never *intrusive* —B.A.Williams⟩ ⟨to protect oneself by silence from well-meaning but *intrusive* friends⟩ OBTRUSIVE is like INTRUSIVE but usu. stresses more objectionable actions than a disposition, suggesting an undue, improper, or offensive conspicuousness of interference ⟨she knelt and watched, quietly, without expressing any *obtrusive* concern for his safety —Floyd Dell⟩ ⟨the *obtrusive* attentions of sycophants and henchmen⟩

²impertinent \"\ *n* **:** an impertinent person **:** one that is presumptuous, meddlesome, or insolent

im·per·ti·nent·ly *adv* [ME, fr. *impertinent* + *-ly*] **:** in an impertinent manner ⟨prying ~ into my affairs⟩

im·per·ti·nent·ness *n* -ES **:** IMPERTINENCE

im·per·turb·abil·i·ty \ˌimpər,tərbəˈbiləd·ē\ *n* **:** the quality or state of being imperturbable ⟨no excitement or depression ever disturbed his extraordinary ~⟩

im·per·turb·able \-ˈtərbəbəl\ *adj* [ME, fr. LL *imperturbabilis*, fr. L *in-* ¹in- + *perturbare* to perturb + *-abilis* -able — more at PERTURB] **:** marked by extreme calm, impassivity, assurance, and steadiness **:** unlikely to be disconcerted, agitated, or alarmed ⟨hitherto ~, he now showed signs of alarm⟩ ⟨an ~ self-possession —Albert Dasnoy⟩ **syn** see COOL

im·per·turb·able·ness *n* -ES **:** IMPERTURBABILITY ⟨a certain calm indifference, a certain ~ —J.C.Powys⟩

im·per·turb·ably \-blē\ *adv* **:** in an imperturbable manner ⟨stalked ~ about the streets . . . or stood impassively in doorways —Green Peyton⟩

im·perturbation \(ˌ)im+\ *n* [LL *imperturbation-, imperturbatio*, fr. L *in-* ¹in- + *perturbation-, perturbatio* perturbation — more at PERTURBATION] **:** freedom from agitation **:** CALMNESS, QUIETUDE

im·perturbed \ˌim+\ *adj* [¹*in-* + *perturbed*] **:** not perturbed **:** CALM

im·per·vi·a·ble \(ˈ)im¦pərvēəbəl\ *adj* [alter. (influenced by *impermeable*) of *impervious*] **:** IMPERVIOUS, IMPERMEABLE

im·pervious \(ˈ)im+\ *adj* [L *impervius*, fr. *in-* ¹in- + *pervius* pervious — more at PERVIOUS] **1 a :** not allowing entrance or passage through **:** IMPENETRABLE ⟨waterproofed so that the coat was ~ to rain⟩ ⟨a steel ~ to bullets⟩ **b :** not capable of being damaged or harmed ⟨a carpet material ~ to most rough treatment⟩ **2 :** not capable of being affected or disturbed ⟨a man ~ to criticism⟩ ⟨looked at her, ~ to her tears —Jean Stafford⟩ **:** not open ⟨~ to arguments or facts⟩ — **im·perviously** \"+\ *adv* — **im·perviousness** \"+\ *n*

im·pest \əmˈpest\ *archaic var of* EMPEST

impester *vt* [MF *empestrer* — more at PESTER] *obs* **:** ENTANGLE, EMBARRASS

im·pe·tig·i·nized \ˌimpə¦tijə,nīzd\ *adj* [L *impetigin-, impetigo* + E *-ize* + *-ed*] **:** secondarily covered with crusts — used of skin diseases or lesions ⟨~ dermatitis⟩

im·pe·tig·i·nous \-ˌnəs\ *adj* [LL *impetiginosus*, fr. L *impetigin-, impetigo* + *-osus* -ous] **:** of, relating to, or like impetigo — **im·pe·tig·i·nous·ly** *adv*

im·pe·ti·go \ˌimpəˈtē(ˌ)gō, -tī(-\ *n* -S [L, fr. *impetere* to attack — more at IMPETUS] **:** an acute contagious skin disease characterized by the formation of vesicles, pustules, and yellowish crusts and caused by staphylococci or streptococci transmitted by contact between persons or between healthy and infected skin

im·pe·trate \ˈimpə,trāt\ *vt* -ED/-ING/-S [L *impetratus*, past part. of *impetrare*, fr. *in-* ²in- + *-petrare* (fr. *patrare* to accomplish) — more at PERPETRATE] **1 :** to obtain by request or entreaty **:** PROCURE **2 :** to ask for **:** ENTREAT

im·pe·tra·tion \ˌimpəˈtrāshən\ *n* -S [L *impetration-, impetratio*, fr. *impetratus* + *-ion-, -io* -ion] **1 :** the act of impetrating **:** petition or a procuring by petition **2** *Old Eng law* **:** the act of obtaining from Rome by solicitation a benefice which belonged to the disposal of the king or other lay patron of the realm

im·pe·tra·tive \ˈimpə,trād·iv\ *adj* [LL *impetrativus*, fr. L *impetratus* + *-ivus* -ive] **:** of, relating to, or being impetration **:** consisting of, getting, or tending to get by entreaty

im·pe·tra·to·ry \ˈimpə·trə,tōrē\ *adj* [L *impetratus* + E *-ory*] *archaic* **:** IMPETRATIVE

im·pet·u·os·i·ty \(ˌ)im,pechəˈwäsəd·ē, əm-, -sətē, -i\ *n* -ES [MF *impetuosité*, fr. OF, fr. LL *impetuosus* + OF *-ité* -ity] **1 :** the quality or state of being impetuous ⟨the ~ of his proposal —Louis Auchincloss⟩ **2 :** an impetuous action or impulse ⟨a man driven by impetuosities and whims⟩

im·pet·u·o·so \(ˌ)im,pechəˈwō(ˌ)sō, -)zō\ *adj (or adv)* [It, fr. LL *impetuosus*] **:** IMPETUOUS — used as a direction in music

im·pet·u·ous \(ˈ)imˈpechəwəs, əmˈp-\ *adj* [ME, fr. MF *impetueux*, fr. LL *impetuosus*, fr. L *impetus* + *-osus* -ous] **1 :** marked by force and violence of movement or action **:** FURIOUS ⟨an ~ wind⟩ ⟨with ~ speed⟩ ⟨match his more ~ neighbors working furiously at their hobbies —G.B.Shaw⟩ **2 :** impulsively vehement in feeling ⟨of a very warm and ~ nature, responded to their affection with quite a tropical ardor —W.M.Thackeray⟩ **:** hastily or rashly energetic or passionate ⟨~ in his habits . . . lost his temper and punched another officer in the nose —J.G.Cozzens⟩ ⟨restless, energetic, ~, temperamental, and at times a little irascible —A.W.Long⟩ **syn** see PRECIPITATE

im·pet·u·ous·ly *adv* **:** in an impetuous manner ⟨a stream rushing ~ over rocks⟩

im·pet·u·ous·ness *n* -ES [ME *impetuousnes*, fr. *impetuous* + *-nes* -ness] **:** the quality or state of being impetuous

im·pe·tus \ˈimpəd·əs, -pətəs\ *n* -ES [L, attack, assault, impetus, fr. *impetere* to attack, fr. *in-* ²in- + *petere* to go to or toward, rush at, attack, seek — more at FEATHER] **1 a** (1) **:** a driving or impelling force ⟨trying to discover the ~ behind all this activity⟩ **:** IMPULSE ⟨an intermittent force, each ~ being of only the shortest duration⟩ (2) **:** INCENTIVE, STIMULUS ⟨felt no ~ to do well in school⟩ **b :** stimulation or encouragement resulting in increased activity ⟨gave a good deal of ~ to the musical activity of the city⟩ **2 :** the property possessed by a moving body in virtue of its mass and its motion — used of bodies moving suddenly or violently to indicate the origin and intensity of the motion rather than the quantity or effectiveness

im·pey·an pheasant \ˈimpēən-\ *n* [Sir Elijah *Impey* †1809 Eng. jurist, and Lady *Impey* †1818 his wife, who introduced the bird into England + E *-an*] **:** a monal (*Lophophorus impejanus*) ranging from Afghanistan to Assam

impf *abbr* imperfect

im·phee \ˈim(p)fē\ *n* -S [Zulu *imfe*] **:** any of several African sorghums

im·pi \ˈimpē\ *n* -S [Zulu] **:** a body of Kaffir warriors or other southern African native armed men

im·picture \əm+\ *vt* [²*in-* + *picture* (n.)] *archaic* **:** to represent as if in a picture **:** PORTRAY

im·piety \(ˈ)im, əm+\ *n* [MF *impieté*, fr. L *impietat-, impietas*, fr. *impius* impious + *-tat-, -tas* -ty — more at IMPIOUS] **1 a :** the quality or state of being impious **:** lack of piety **:** IRREVERENCE, UNGODLINESS ⟨~, in denying the gods recognized by the state —J.S.Mill⟩ **b :** UNDUTIFULNESS ⟨guilty of filial ~ in showing no respect for his father's advice⟩ **2 :** an impious act ⟨his sins turned into his *impieties* —William Empson⟩

im·pig·no·rate \əmˈpignə,rāt\ *vt* [LL or ML *impignoratus*, *impigneratus*, past part. of *impignorare, impignerare*, fr. L *in-* ²in- + *pignorare, pignerare* to pledge — more at PIGNORATE] **:** PLEDGE, PAWN, MORTGAGE — **im·pig·no·ra·tion** \=,==ˈrāshən\ *n*

imp·ing \ˈimpiŋ\ *n* -S [ME, fr. gerund of *impen* to graft — more at IMP] **:** the process in falconry of mending a broken pinion by inserting one end of a specially prepared needle into the stub of the feather and the other into the shaft of the original feather or a replacement feather

im·pinge \əmˈpinj\ *vb* -ED/-ING/-S [L *impingere* to strike or push at or against, fr. *in-* ²in- + *-pingere* (fr. *pangere* to fasten, drive in) — more at PACT] *vi* **1 :** to strike or dash esp. with a sharp collision **:** come into sharp contact — usu. used with *on, upon,* or *against* ⟨when an elastic ball ~*s* on another —K.K.Darrow⟩ ⟨I heard the rain ~ upon the earth —James Joyce⟩ ⟨the creak of oarlocks *impinged* on his ear⟩ ⟨something ~*s* violently on your senses —Peggy Durdin⟩ ⟨a strong light *impinging* on the eyes and causing a sudden pain⟩ **2 :** to come into a relationship as if impinging **:** make an impression **:** touch closely or bear directly — usu. used with *on* or *upon* ⟨waiting for the germ of a new idea to ~ upon my mind —Phyllis Bentley⟩ ⟨the objects that *impinged* upon his imagination with the greatest impact —*Times Lit. Supp.*⟩ ⟨in that line of reasoning we ~ upon an abstruse metaphysical problem⟩ ⟨political forces that ~ on everyone's daily life⟩ **3 :** ENCROACH, INFRINGE — usu. used with *on* ⟨*impinging* on other people's rights⟩ ⟨not that I want to ~ on any man's recreation —Ezra Pound⟩ ~ *vt* **:** to cause (as a gas or a flame) to strike ⟨*impinging* live steam on the printed surface —*Chem. & Engineering News*⟩

im·pinge·ment \-mənt\ *n* -S **:** the act of impinging or the state of being impinged upon: as **a :** a sharp collision **:** a striking or dashing against **b :** INFLUENCE, EFFECT, ENCROACHMENT, INFRINGEMENT ⟨the ~ of American power upon Asiatic life without adequate comprehension of the vast complexities of Asiatic politics —Reinhold Niebuhr⟩ ⟨the ~ of Russia's security aims upon interests of Britain or the U. S. —Allan Taylor⟩ **syn** see IMPACT

impingement black *n* **:** CHANNEL BLACK

im·pin·gent \-jənt\ *adj* [L *impingent-, impingens*, pres. part. of *impingere*] **:** IMPINGING ⟨ecological factors ~ upon the production and use of foods —Theodore Stern⟩

im·ping·er \-jə(r)\ *n* -S **:** an instrument for collecting samples of dust or other suspended particles esp. in air by impinging a stream of the suspension on a surface or in a liquid (as water)

impinguate *vt* -ED/-ING/-S [LL *impinguatus*, past part. of *impinguare*, fr. L *in-* ²in- + *pinguis* fat — more at PINGUID] *obs* **:** FATTEN

im·pi·ous \ˈimpēəs, (ˈ)im¦pīəs\ *adj* [L *impius*, fr. *in-* ¹in- + *pius* pious — more at PIOUS] **:** not pious **:** IRREVERENT: **a :** lacking reverence for God, a deity, or for what is sacred **:** PROFANE, IRRELIGIOUS ⟨an ~ life⟩ **b :** lacking in proper respect (as for parents or for something usu. held in general respect) ⟨an ~ son⟩ ⟨an ~ flouting of experience —Donagh MacDonagh⟩ ⟨any alteration in the ceremonies that surrounded Thanksgiving would have been considered ~ and heartbreaking by my mother —John Cheever⟩

syn PROFANE, BLASPHEMOUS, SACRILEGIOUS: IMPIOUS usu. implies extreme disrespect for a divinity or his attributes and manifestations ⟨the *impious* challenge of power divine —William Cowper⟩ ⟨who is there more *impious* than a backsliding priest? —John Steinbeck⟩ PROFANE in this sense may suggest not only the disrespect involved in IMPIOUS but also desecration, intentional or not, of something to be held inviolate ⟨hitherto no liberal statesman has been so audacious as to "imagine the king's death" and lay *profane* hands on the divine right of nations to seek their own advantage at the cost of the rest by such means as the rule of reason shall decide to be permissible —Thorstein Veblen⟩ ⟨I collected bones from charnel houses; and disturbed, with *profane* fingers, the tremendous secrets of the human frame —Mary W. Shelley⟩ BLASPHEMOUS may apply to strong and intentional impiety or profanation fervently expressed or performed or to the harboring and abetting of ideas calculated to lower the awesome dignity of a deity ⟨*blasphemous* conversation⟩ ⟨it is *blasphemous* because it attributes to God purposes which we would not respect even in an earthly parent —J.A.Pike⟩ SACRILEGIOUS commonly may describe any flagrant depredation, disrespect, or contempt ⟨*sacrilegious* in his scandalous burlesques of the gods⟩ All of these words lend themselves to broad and inexact uses.

im·pi·ous·ly *adv* **:** in an impious manner

im·pi·ous·ness *n* **:** IMPIETY

imp·ish \ˈimpish, -pēsh\ *adj* **:** of, relating to, or befitting an imp; *esp* **:** MISCHIEVOUS ⟨the spectacle is weird and grotesque, and suggests something ~ and uncanny —John Burroughs⟩ ⟨took ~ delight in pestering his parents⟩ ⟨the child's ~ face⟩ — **imp·ish·ly** *adv* — **imp·ish·ness** *n* -ES

im·pit·e·ous \(ˈ)im¦pid·ēəs\ *adj* [¹*in-* + *piteous*] **:** PITILESS, CRUEL

impl *abbr* **1** imperial **2** implement

im·placa·bil·i·ty \(ˌ)im,plakəˈbiləd·ē, əm-, -lətē, -i *also* -plāk-\ *n* [LL *implacabilitas*, fr. L *implacabilis* + *-itas* -ity] **:** the quality or state of being implacable ⟨the ~ of his resentments —Jane Austen⟩ ⟨the ~ of a Greek tragedy —Arthur Schlesinger b. 1917⟩

im·placa·ble \(ˈ)im¦plakəbəl, əmˈp- *also* -plāk-\ *adj* [MF or L; MF, fr. L *implacabilis*, fr. *in-* ¹in- + *placabilis* placable — more at PLACABLE] **1 a :** not placable **:** not capable of being appeased or pacified **:** INEXORABLE ⟨an ~ enemy⟩ ⟨an ~ resentment⟩ ⟨single-minded and ~, even unmerciful, in his servitude to the law —M.S.Mayer⟩ **b :** incapable of being significantly changed or modified **:** following a due unalterable course ⟨the ~ lives of plants —Clifford Gessler⟩ ⟨the ~ logic of his career⟩ ⟨the measured, arranged, ~ movement of the universe —A.J.Cronin⟩ **2 :** incapable of being relieved or mitigated ⟨an ~ disease⟩ ⟨the horns of an ~ dilemma —J.C. Powys⟩ ⟨his ~ interest in love —William McFee⟩ ⟨watched that ~ blaze of space as far as the mountainous horizon —D.C.Peattie⟩ — **im·placa·ble·ness** \-bəlnəs\ *n* — **im·placa·bly** \-blē,-bli\ *adv*

im·place·ment \əmˈplāsmənt\ *n* [modif. (influenced by ²*in-*) of F *emplacement* — more at EMPLACEMENT] **:** EMPLACEMENT

im·placentalia \(ˌ)im+\ *n pl, cap* [NL, fr. ¹*in-* + *Placentalia*] *in former classifications* **:** the monotremes and marsupials regarded as a systematic unit characterized by the absence or rudimentary development of a placenta

¹im·plant \əm+\ *also* **em·plant** \əm,em+\ *vt* [²*in-* or ¹*en-* + *plant*] **1 a :** to fix or set securely or deeply ⟨a ruby ~*ed* in a gold ring⟩ **b :** to set or fix as permanent in the consciousness, the psyche, or habit patterns **:** INSTILL, INCULCATE ⟨~ good habits in children⟩ ⟨~ in a person the idea that the end of the world is near⟩ ⟨such a taste . . . simply cannot be ~*ed* —H.L.Mencken⟩ **2** *archaic* **:** PLANT **3 a :** to insert in a living site for growth, formation of an organic union, or absorption **b :** to insert an implant in ⟨100 patients have been ~*ed* with nylon ribbons without complications —U.K.Henschke⟩

syn IMPLANT, INCULCATE, INSTILL can mean, in common, to introduce into the mind. IMPLANT implies teaching and stresses a fixing firmly in the mind of what is taught or advocated ⟨the duty of Congress to see that educational institutions *implant* only sound ideas in the minds of students —Elmer Davis⟩ ⟨the teacher, the parent, or the friend can often do much to *implant* this conviction —C.W.Eliot⟩ ⟨in me especially, she *implanted* a respect for pioneering tradition —Rex Ingamells⟩ ⟨sea voyagers . . . may remain to *implant* their knowledge and practices in the new territory —C.D. Forde⟩ INCULCATE lays stress on repeated persistent efforts to impress on or fix in the mind ⟨it is no part of the duty of a university to *inculcate* any particular philosophy of life —Walter Moberly⟩ ⟨a means of *inculcating* in the conscripts intense patriotism and religious devotion to the state —Chitoshi Yanaga⟩ ⟨the seriousness *inculcated* in men by two cataclysmic world wars —S.P.Lamprecht⟩ INSTILL implies a gradual usu. gentle method of imparting knowledge usu. over a long period of time ⟨the principles which had been *instilled* in her soul from the time she began to speak —Ruth Park⟩ ⟨schools must plan to *instill* not only knowledge, but more of permanent refined interests; not only scholarship, but more of character and social purpose —A.C.Ellis⟩ ⟨a profound sense of public duty will be *instilled* into boys and girls of the governing class as soon as they are able to understand such an idea —Bertrand Russell⟩

²im·plant \ˈim+,-\ *n* **:** something implanted esp. in tissue (as a graft, a small container of radioactive material for treatment of cancer, or a pellet containing hormones to be gradually absorbed)

im·plan·ta·tion \ˌim,planˈtāshən, -laan-,-lān-\ *n* **1 :** the act or process of implanting or the state of being implanted: as **a :** the placement of the root of a tooth in an artificially prepared socket in the jawbone **b** *in placental mammals* **:** the process of attachment of the embryo to the maternal uterine wall **c :** experimental addition of tissue or other material to an intact embryo **d :** medical treatment by the insertion of an implant **2 :** the spontaneous passage of cells esp. of tumors to a new site with subsequent growth — compare METASTASIS

im·plastic \(ˈ)im+\ *adj* [¹*in-* + *plastic*] **:** not plastic **:** not readily molded **:** STIFF — **im·plasticity** \ˌim+\ *n*

im·plausibility \(ˌ)im, əm+\ *n* **1 :** the quality or state of being implausible ⟨put on his guard by the ~ of the man's explanation⟩ **2 :** something implausible

im·plausible \(ˈ)im, əm+\ *adj* [¹*in-* + *plausible*] **:** not plausible **:** having a quality that provokes disbelief ⟨experienced a number of ~ adventures⟩ ⟨gave the teacher an ~ explanation of his absence from school⟩ — **im·plausibleness** \"+\ *n* — **im·plausibly** \"+\ *adv*

im·pleach \əm+\ *vt* [²*in-* + *pleach*] **:** PLEACH, INTERWEAVE

im·plead \əmˈplēd\ *vb* [ME *empleden, impleden*, fr. MF *empleider, emplaider*, fr. OF *empleidier, emplaidier*, fr. *en-* ¹en- + *pleidier, plaidier* to plead — more at PLEAD] *vt* **1 a :** to institute and prosecute a suit against in a court **:** sue or prosecute at law ⟨the government, as a general rule, claims an exemption from being sued in its own courts . . . will not permit itself to be ~*ed* therein —H.M.Hart⟩ **b** *archaic* **:** ACCUSE, IMPEACH **2** *archaic* **:** PLEAD **3 :** to include or incorporate as part of or party to a legal suit or action ⟨modern procedure permits a defendant to ~ . . . a third person —Herbert Peterfreund⟩ ⟨the bond . . . was ~*ed* as a part of the motion for judgment —*Southeastern Reporter*⟩ ~ *vi, archaic* **:** PLEAD

im·plead·able \-dəbəl\ *adj, archaic* **:** capable of being sued or prosecuted at law

im·plead·er \-də(r)\ *n* **1 :** one that impleads **2 :** INTERPLEADER

im·pledge \əm+\ *vt* [²*in-* + *pledge* (n.)] *archaic* **:** PLEDGE

¹im·ple·ment \ˈimpləmənt\ *n* -S [ME, fr. LL *implementum* action of filling up, fr. L *implēre* to fill up, finish (fr. *in-* ²in- + *plēre* to fill) + *-mentum* -ment — more at FULL] **1 a :** an article (as of apparel or furniture) serving to equip ⟨the ~*s* of religious worship⟩ **b :** a tool or utensil forming part of equipment for work ⟨a farm ~⟩ ⟨an ~ of war⟩ ⟨the ~*s* of his trade⟩ ⟨useful ~*s* such as axes, chisels, gouges, arrowheads, pestles and mortars, and ornamented pipes —*Amer. Guide Series: R.I.*⟩ ⟨the need for an ~ to help roll the heavy logs —*McGill News*⟩ **c :** one that serves as an instrument or tool ⟨judges striving to be efficient ~*s* of justice⟩ ⟨the most stringent ~ that could be employed . . . would be withdrawal of safe conduct for Swedish ships plying the Atlantic —*Newsweek*⟩ **2** *Scots law* **:** FULFILLMENT, PERFORMANCE

syn IMPLEMENT, TOOL, INSTRUMENT, APPLIANCE, UTENSIL apply in common to any device usu. relatively simple for performing a mechanical or manual operation. IMPLEMENT applies to anything, usu. a contrivance, necessary to effect an end or perform a task ⟨spades and other gardener's *implements*⟩ ⟨swords, guns, and *implements* of war⟩ ⟨propaganda as an *implement* of cold war⟩ ⟨the quill pen was an early *implement* of communication⟩ TOOL suggests an implement adapted to facilitate a given work, esp. the work of a craftsman or artisan ⟨carpenter's *tools*⟩ ⟨a pipe wrench and other plumber's *tools*⟩ ⟨a new research *tool*, in the form of a bibliography of all the literature on the arctic put out in the last 75 years —*Science*⟩ ⟨reference *tools* like the dictionary and the encyclopedia —*English Language Arts*⟩ ⟨the breeder uses three basic *tools* to bring about the genetic improvement of animals . . . selection, inbreeding, and crossing —*Science in Farming*⟩ INSTRUMENT suggests delicate construction or precision work as in dentistry, surgery, or surveying and may extend beyond mechanical or manual operation as in instruments for recording temperatures or rates of speed or musical instruments or in any more or less precise device for achieving any end ⟨the laboratory *instruments* necessary to careful scientific research⟩ ⟨an oscilloscope and other radio-testing *instruments*⟩ ⟨language is the essential *instrument* for the acquirement and communication of ideas —L.J.Shehan⟩ ⟨in a day when novels were considered *instruments* of Satan —*Amer. Guide Series: N.Y.*⟩ APPLIANCE is used usu. for a device which effects work but which is moved by some power other than or in addition to guidance or control by hand ⟨washing machines, vacuum cleaners, and other household *appliances*⟩ ⟨*appliance* means current-consuming equipment, fixed or portable; for example, heating, cooking, and small motor-operated equipment —*Nat'l Electric Safety Code*⟩ ⟨the clutch cleats for the sheet lines, reefing gears, and many other *appliances* used with the enormous sails —E.J.Schoettle⟩ UTENSIL suggests something useful in accomplishing work, esp. domestic work or work similar to it, and usu. manageable by hand ⟨pipe, pipe cleaners, and other smoking *utensils*⟩ ⟨a rolling pin, a fork, a frying pan and an oven are the *utensils* with which she makes her pie —Gilbert Ryle⟩ ⟨kitchen *utensils*⟩ ⟨fingers were the only eating *utensils* —H.A.Chippendale⟩

²im·ple·ment \-ˌment, -mənt — *see* ²-MENT\ *vt* -ED/-ING/-S **1 a :** to carry out **:** ACCOMPLISH, FULFILL ⟨wondering how he might best ~ his purpose⟩ ⟨continued to clamor for action to ~ the promise —*N.Y.Times*⟩ ⟨a committee to ~ the plans so well formulated⟩; *esp* **:** to give practical effect to and ensure of actual fulfillment by concrete measures ⟨failure to carry out and ~ the will of the majority —Clement Attlee⟩ ⟨an agency created to ~ the recommendation of the committee) ⟨programs to ~ our foreign policy⟩ **b :** to provide instruments or means of practical expression for ⟨survey the problem as a whole and ~ the joint interest in an expanding economy —George Soule⟩ **2 :** SUPPLEMENT **syn** see ENFORCE

im·ple·men·tal \¦==¦ment³l\ *adj* **:** of, relating to, or being an implement or relating to or providing implementation

im·ple·men·ta·ry \-ntərē, -n·trē, -ri\ *adj* **:** providing implementation ⟨~ legislation⟩

im·ple·men·ta·tion \¸==,mən·'tāshən, -(,)men-\ *n* -s **:** the act of implementing or the state of being implemented

im·ple·ment·er *or* **im·ple·men·tor** \'==,mentə(r)\ *n* -s **:** one that implements

im·ple·men·tif·er·ous \¦==(,)=·¦tif(ə)rəs\ *adj* **:** bearing or containing implements ⟨~ strata at an archaeological site⟩

im·ple·tion \əm'plēshən\ *n* -s [LL *impletion-, impletio,* fr. L *impletus* (past part. of *implēre* to fill up) + *-ion-, -io* -ion — more at IMPLEMENT] *archaic* **:** the act of filling or the state of being full

im·pliable \(,)im¦plīəbəl, əm'p-\ *adj* [¹*in-* + *pliable*] **:** not pliable **:** INFLEXIBLE

im·pli·cant \'impləkənt, -lēk-\ *n* -s [L *implicant-, implicans,* pres. part. of *implicare*] **:** something that implies (as a proposition)

¹**im·pli·cate** \-kə̇t, -,kāt, *usu* ¦d·+V\ *adj* [L *implicatus*] **1** *obs* **:** INTERTWINED, ENTANGLED, INVOLVED **2 :** IMPLIED, IMPLICIT ⟨content to let this accusation remain ~ in her questions —Osbert Sitwell⟩

²**im·pli·cate** \-,kāt, *usu* -ād·+V\ *vt* [L *implicatus,* past part. of *implicare* to infold, involve, implicate, engage — more at EMPLOY] **1** *archaic* **:** to fold or twist together **:** INTERWEAVE, ENTWINE ⟨the meeting boughs and *implicated* leaves —P.B. Shelley⟩ **2 :** to involve as a consequence, corollary, or natural inference **:** IMPLY **3 a :** to bring into intimate or incriminating connection **:** involve deeply or unfavorably ⟨evidence *implicating* many high officials in the conspiracy⟩ ⟨an innocent person *implicated* by circumstances in a crime⟩ ⟨all men, even the most virtuous and wise, are *implicated* in historic evil —Reinhold Niebuhr⟩ **b :** to involve in the nature or operation of something **:** connect intimately **:** require or entail as a natural or necessary cause, concomitant, or consequence ⟨local diseases often ~ a general derangement of the system⟩ ⟨each element in life forms part of a cultural mesh: one part *implicates* . . . the other —Lewis Mumford⟩ **syn** see INCLUDE

³**im·pli·cate** *same as adj*\ *n* -s [¹*implicate*] **:** something (as a proposition) implied or involved ⟨made ethics independent of theology and theology a series of ~*s* from the moral life —E.E. Aubrey⟩

im·pli·ca·tion \¸==¦kāshən\ *n* -s [ME *implicacioun,* fr. L *implication-, implicatio,* fr. *implicatus,* + *-ion-, -io* -ion] **1 :** the act of implicating or the state of being implicated: **a** *archaic* **:** a twisting together **:** ENTWINEMENT, INTERWEAVING **b :** close connection, relationship, or involvement (as from long association, logical inevitability, intimate accompaniment) ⟨in the arts, in literature, and in science . . . all these activities were freeing themselves from their religious ~*s* —Stringfellow Barr⟩ ⟨looked upon railroad operation purely in its engineering ~*s* —O.S.Nock⟩; *esp* **:** an incriminating involvement ⟨suspected of ~ in a number of robberies⟩ **2 a :** the act of implying or the state of being implied ⟨no concept that by ~ views a functional bureaucracy as the ruling class can be tolerated —K.A.Wittfogel⟩ ⟨speak of their own language with at least an ~ of disparagement —George Sampson⟩ ⟨whether in words or by ~ —O.W.Holmes †1935⟩ **b :** one of several formal logical relationships or a statement containing propositions in such a relationship: (1) **:** a logical relationship of the form symbolically rendered "if *p* then *q*" in which *p* and *q* are propositions and in which *p* is false or *q* is true or both; *also* **:** a statement in this form — called also *material implication* (2) **:** a logical relationship of the form symbolically rendered "if *p* then strictly *q*" in which *q* is deducible from *p; also* **:** a statement in this form — called also *logical implication, strict implication* **c :** the symbol used to indicate one of these two formal relationships and rendered "if . . . then" or the logical operation implicit in one of them **3 :** something implied ⟨two propositions with a clear ~⟩ **:** INFERENCE ⟨was aware of the ~ to be found in his remarks⟩ **:** SUGGESTION, CONNOTATION ⟨tea is very important in British life, and a spectacular rise in its price does have political ~*s* —Michael Davie⟩ ⟨a book is a bulwark against the ~ of lack of culture —Allan McMahan⟩

im·pli·ca·tion·al \¦==¦kāshən³l, -shnəl\ *adj* **:** IMPLICATIVE — **im·pli·ca·tion·al·ly** \-³l|ē, -əl|, |i\ *adv*

im·plica·tive \'impl·ə,kād·iv, im'plikəd·-\ *adj* **:** of, relating to, or being implication or an implication **:** involving implication ⟨an ~ statement⟩ ⟨an ~ function⟩; *also* **:** tending to implicate — **im·plica·tive·ly** \-d·əvlē\ *adv* — **im·plica·tive·ness** \-d·ivnə̇s\ *n* -ES

im·plica·to·ry \'impləkə,tōrē, im'plik-, *chiefly Brit* ¦implə¦kātəri *or* -ā·tri\ *adj* **:** IMPLICATIVE

im·plic·it \(')im¦plisə̇t, əm'p-, *usu* -ə̇d·+V\ *adj* [L *implicitus,* past part. of *implicare* to infold, involve, implicate, engage — more at EMPLOY] **1** *obs* **:** tangled or twisted together **:** INTERWOVEN **2 a** (1) **:** tacitly involved in something else **:** capable of being understood from something else though unexpressed **:** capable of being inferred **:** IMPLIED — compare EXPLICIT ⟨draws no social conclusions of his own, but they are ~ —Robert Lasch⟩ ⟨the artistic standards of our time are . . . ~ rather than codified —Michael Kitson⟩ (2) **:** involved in the nature or essence of something though not revealed, expressed, or developed **:** POTENTIAL ⟨the oak is ~ in the acorn⟩ ⟨a sculptor may see different figures ~ in a block of stone —John Dewey⟩ ⟨the drama ~ in an idea becomes explicit when it is shown as a point of view which a person holds and upon which he acts —F.J.Hoffman⟩ **b** (1) **:** not appearing overtly **:** confined in the organism ⟨~ behavior⟩ ⟨~ speech⟩ (2) *of a culture* **:** capable of being derived only as an implication from behavior **:** not apparent or overt to the people it characterizes **:** tacit and underlying **3 a :** lacking doubt or reserve **:** UNQUESTIONING, WHOLEHEARTED ⟨~ obedience⟩ ⟨an ~ trust⟩ **b** *obs* **:** UNQUALIFIED, ABSOLUTE ⟨~ ignorance —Francis Bacon⟩ **4** *archaic* **:** marked by an implicit faith, credulity, or obedience — **im·plic·it·ly** *adv* — **im·plic·it·ness** *n* -ES

implicit definition *n* **:** CONTEXTUAL DEFINITION

implicit function *n* **:** a mathematical function defined by means of a relation that is not solved for the function in terms of the independent variable or variables — opposed to *explicit function*

im·plic·i·ty \əm'plisəd·ē\ *n* -ES [prob. fr. F *implicité,* fr. *implicite* implicit (fr. L *implicitus*) + *-té* -ty] **:** the quality or state of being implicit ⟨the strangeness of a man's life and the ~ with which he accepts it —Albert Camus⟩

implied *past of* IMPLY

implied authority *or* **implied agency** *n* **:** authority that is not proved expressly but by inferences and reasonable deductions and that arises out of the language and course of conduct of the principal toward his agent and the agency

implied contract *n* **1 :** a contract inferred to have been entered into by the parties to it from their conduct or from a special relationship existing between them **2 :** QUASI CONTRACT

im·plied·ly \əm'plī(ə)dlē\ *adv* [ME, fr. *implied* (past part. of *implien* to imply) + *-ly* — more at IMPLY] **:** by implication ⟨uncataloged situations will arise and, not being specifically prohibited, will be taken as ~ permitted —W.E.Jackson b. 1919⟩

implied malice *n* **:** malice proved indirectly from all the attendant circumstances when it is impossible to prove the actual state of mind as evincing it — called also *constructive malice;* distinguished from *malice in fact*

implied power *n* **:** a power that is reasonably necessary and appropriate to carry out the purposes of a power expressly granted — usu. used in pl.

implied trust *n* **1 :** a trust created by operation of law for reasons based on considerations of morality, justice, conscience, and fair dealing, or to prevent unjust enrichment **2 :** a trust found by judicial construction to have been intended by the settlor notwithstanding the intent was not clearly manifested in express terms

implied warranty *n* **:** a warranty raised in the operation of law though not expressly made and arising out of a particular transaction for reasons of public policy (as, that a ship chartered is seaworthy, that food sold to people is fit for human consumption, that goods sold are merchantable)

im·plode \əm'plōd\ *vi* -ED/-ING/-S [²*in-* + *-plode* (as in *explode*)] **:** to burst inward ⟨when a vacuum tube breaks it ~*s*⟩

im·plo·ra·tion \,implə'rāshən -lō'r-, -lȯ'r-\ *n* -s [MF or L; MF, fr. L *imploration-, imploratio,* fr. *imploratus* (past part. of *implorare* to implore) + *-ion-, -io* -ion] **:** earnest supplication **:** IMPLORING

im·plore \əm'plō(ə)r, -ȯ(ə)r, -ōə, -ȯ(ə)\ *vb* -ED/-ING/-S [MF or L; MF *implorer,* fr. L *implorare,* fr. *in-* ²*in-* + *plorare* to cry out, wail, lament, prob. of imit. origin] *vt* **1 :** to call upon in supplication **:** urgently petition **:** BESEECH ⟨*implored* his Maker for help out of his trouble⟩ ⟨but don't, I ~ you, let the metropolis monopolize your attention or your time —Richard Joseph⟩ **2 :** to call for or pray for earnestly or in supplication ⟨~ someone else's help in a crisis⟩ ⟨~ another chance to prove his innocence⟩ ⟨asked in a voice that *implored* a favorable answer —Aldous Huxley⟩ ~ *vi* **:** ENTREAT, PRAY ⟨wished he would stop begging and *imploring*⟩ **syn** see BEG

im·plor·ing·ly *adv* **:** in the manner of one that implores **:** BESEECHINGLY

im·plor·ing·ness *n* -ES **:** the quality or state of one that implores

im·plo·sion \əm'plōzhən\ *n* -s [²*in-* + *-plosion* (as in *explosion*)] **1 :** the action of imploding — contrasted with *explosion* **2 a :** APPLOSION **b :** the inrush of air in forming a suction stop

¹**im·plo·sive** \-ōs|iv, |ēv *also* -ōz| *or* |əv\ *adj* [²*in-* + *-plosive* (as in *explosive*)] **:** of, relating to, or being an implosion **:** formed or uttered with implosion — **im·plo·sive·ly** \|əvlē, -li\ *adv*

²**implosive** \"\ *n* -s **:** an implosive consonant **:** SUCTION STOP

im·ploy \əm'plȯi\ *archaic var of* EMPLOY

im·plume \əm+\ *or* **em·plume** \əm,em+\ *vt* [²*in-* or ¹*en-* + *plume* (n.)] **:** to furnish with or as if with plumes

im·plumed \(')im, əm+\ *adj* [¹*in-* + *plumed*] *archaic* **:** having no feathers

implunge *vb* [²*in-* + *plunge*] *obs* **:** PLUNGE

im·plu·vi·um \(')im¦plüvēəm, əm'p-\ *n, pl* **implu·via** \-ēə\ [L, fr. *in-* ²in- + *-pluvium* (fr. *pluere* to rain) — more at FLOW] **:** a cistern or tank in the atrium or peristyle of a house of ancient Rome to receive the water falling through the compluvium

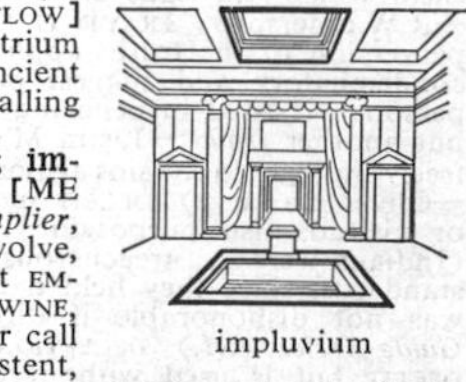
impluvium

im·ply \əm'plī\ *vt* **implied; implied; implying; implies** [ME *emplien, implien,* fr. MF *emplier,* fr. L *implicare* to infold, involve, implicate, engage — more at EMPLOY] **1** *obs* **:** ENFOLD, ENTWINE, ENWRAP **2 a :** to indicate or call for recognition of as existent, present, or related not by express statement but by logical inference or association or necessary consequence ⟨enrollment in the college *implies* willingness on the part of the student to comply with the requirements and regulations of the college —*Bull. of Mt. Saint Mary's College*⟩ ⟨the philosophy of nature which is *implied* in Chinese art —Lawrence Binyon⟩ ⟨democracy *implies* a number of freedoms⟩ ⟨emergency and crisis ~ conflict —H.S.Langfeld⟩ **b :** to involve as a necessary concomitant (as by general or logical implication, by signification, or by very nature or essence) ⟨two propositions may ~ a third⟩ ⟨war *implies* fighting⟩ ⟨an acorn *implies* an oak⟩ **3 :** to convey or communicate not by direct forthright statement but by allusion or reference likely to lead to natural inference **:** suggest or hint at ⟨the girl's evasive answer and burning brow seemed to ~ that her suitor had changed his mind —Edith Wharton⟩ ⟨made me sick to hear him ~ that somebody would make a report against him —Joseph Conrad⟩ ⟨the tone of the book was *implied* by shrewd advertisements —J.D.Hart⟩ **syn** see INCLUDE, SUGGEST

im·pocket \əm+\ *vt* [²*in-* + *pocket* (n.)] *archaic* **:** to keep or put in a pocket

im·po·fo \əm'pō(,)fō\ *n* -s [Zulu *im-pofu*] **:** ELAND

impolder *var of* EMPOLDER

im·policy \əm+\ *n* [¹*in-* + *policy*] **:** the quality or state of being impolitic **:** unsuitableness to the end in view **:** INEXPEDIENCY; *also* **:** an impolitic act

impolished *adj* [¹*in-* + *polished*] *obs* **:** not polished

im·polite \¦im+\ *adj* [L *impolitus* unpolished, unrefined, fr. *in-* ¹in- + *politus* polished, refined — more at POLITE] **:** not polite: **a** *obs* **:** lacking culture, cultivation, polish **b :** lacking in politeness, in etiquette, or in consideration of others **syn** see RUDE

im·po·lite·ly *adv* **:** in an impolite manner **:** RUDELY ⟨~ turning his back on her⟩

im·po·lite·ness *n* **:** the quality or state of being impolite **:** RUDENESS; *also* **:** an impolite act or remark

im·politic \(')im, əm+\ *also* **im·political** \¦im+\ *adj* [¹*in-* + *politic, political*] **:** not politic **:** contrary to or lacking in policy **:** UNWISE, INEXPEDIENT ⟨unjust and ~ discriminations between racial and other classes of citizens —E.P.Hutchinson⟩ ⟨would be manifestly ~ to start a brawl —Max Peacock⟩ — **im·politically** \¦im+\ *adv* — **im·politicalness** \"+\ *n* -ES — **im·politicly** \(')im, əm+\ *adv* — **im·politicness** \"+\ *n* -ES

im·pon·der·a·bil·ia \(,)im,pändərə'bilēə, əm-, -lyə\ *n pl* [NL, fr. neut. pl. of ML *imponderabilis*] **:** IMPONDERABLES ⟨it ignores these ~ without which life is no life, history no history, and people no people —*Amer. Quarterly*⟩

im·ponderability \(¦)im, əm+\ *n* **:** the quality or state of being imponderable

¹**im·ponderable** \(')im, əm+\ *adj* [ML *imponderabilis,* fr. L *in-* ¹in- + LL *ponderabilis* ponderable — more at PONDERABLE] **:** not ponderable **:** incapable of being weighed, measured, or evaluated with exactness ⟨supposed that there was an ~ electrical fluid which pervaded all space —S.F.Mason⟩ ⟨such ~ human factors as one's aesthetic sensitivity —Hunter Mead⟩ — **im·ponderableness** \"+\ *n* -ES — **im·ponderably** \"+\ *adv*

²**imponderable** \"\ *n* **:** an imponderable thing, element, or agency ⟨spiritual ~*s*⟩ ⟨that huge ~ which enters the courtroom: public opinion —Catherine Bowen⟩ ⟨the overriding importance of ~*s* in determining human conduct —John Russell b. 1872⟩

im·ponderous \(')im, əm+\ *adj* [¹*in-* + *ponderous*] **:** having no weight or insignificant weight **:** very light

impone *vt* -ED/-ING/-S [L *imponere* to put upon, impose, fr. *in-* ²in- + *ponere* to put, place — more at POSITION] *obs* **:** STAKE, WAGER

im·po·nent \əm'pōnənt, 'im,p-\ *n* -s [L *imponent-, imponens,* pres. part. of *imponere*] **:** one that imposes

imporous *adj* [¹*in-* + *porous*] *obs* **:** not porous

¹**im·port** \(')im¦pō(ə)r|t, əm'p-, -ȯ(ə)r|, -ōə|, -ȯ(ə)|, *usu* |d·+V\ *vb* -ED/-ING/-S [ME *importen,* fr. L *importare* to bring or carry into, introduce, cause, fr. *in-* ²*in-* + *portare* to carry — more at PORT] *vt* **1 a :** to bear or convey as purport, meaning, information, or portent **:** MEAN, SIGNIFY ⟨his words ~*ed* that some change in plans had to be made⟩ ⟨the verse then would ~ that the riders have let their freedom . . . get out of hand —Warren Carrier⟩ **b** *archaic* **:** EXPRESS, STATE **c :** to involve as a consequence or inevitable concomitant **:** IMPLY ⟨honor ~*s* justice⟩ **2 :** to bring from a foreign or external source **:** introduce from without ⟨food ~*ed* into the city from surrounding farms⟩ ⟨another murder case . . . distinguished by the local animosities sought to be ~*ed* into the trial —H.W. H.Knott⟩ ⟨~*ed* some college boys for the dance⟩; *esp* **:** to bring (as wares or merchandise) into a place or country from another country ⟨a business that ~*ed* toys from Japan⟩ ⟨~*ed* wheat during the grain shortage⟩ ⟨Icelanders . . . ~*ed* the literature of the Continent, translating it into their own tongue —Charlton Laird⟩ ⟨Canada also ~*s* a great many leading scientists —*Report: (Canadian) Royal Commission on Nat'l Development*⟩ — opposed to *export* **3** [MF *importer,* fr. OIt *importare,* fr. L] *archaic* **:** to be of importance or consequence to **:** have to do with **:** have a bearing on **:** CONCERN ~ *vi* [MF *importer*] **:** to be of moment or consequence **:** MATTER ⟨it ~*s* little that we are early or late⟩ **syn** see MEAN

²**im·port** \'im,p-\ *n* -s **1 :** something contained as signification or intention **:** PURPORT, MEANING ⟨trying vainly to fathom the ~ of the speaker's words⟩ ⟨a gesture whose ~ he knew immediately⟩ **2 :** WEIGHT, CONSEQUENCE, SIGNIFICANCE ⟨less concerned about the literary value of his books than about their social ~⟩ ⟨a man of great ~⟩ **3 :** something (as an article of merchandise) brought in from an outside source (as a foreign country) ⟨the car was a British ~ —Frances G. Patton⟩ ⟨chief ~*s* were machinery and vehicles, raw wool and cotton —*Americana Annual*⟩ **4 :** IMPORTATION ⟨a proclamation allowing the ~ of an additional 51 million pounds of peanuts —*Time*⟩ **syn** see IMPORTANCE

¹**importable** *adj* [ME, fr. MF, fr. LL *importabilis,* fr. L *in-* ¹in- + *portare* to carry, bear + *-abilis* -able — more at PORT] *obs* **:** UNENDURABLE, INTOLERABLE

²**im·port·able** \(')im¦pōr|d·əbəl, əm'p-, -pȯ(r)|, -pōə|, |tə-\ *adj* [¹*import* + *-able*] **:** capable of being imported ⟨an ~ article of merchandise⟩

im·por·tance \əm'pȯr|t³n(t)s, -ȯ(ə)|, *chiefly in NewEng & the South* |d·ən- *or* |tən-\ *n* -s [MF, fr. OIt *importanza,* fr. *importante*] **1 a :** the quality or state of being important **:** WEIGHT, SIGNIFICANCE ⟨an event of ~ in the history of the country⟩ ⟨a natural resource of great ~ to industry⟩ **b :** an important aspect or bearing ⟨this feat has several ~*s* —*Time*⟩ **2** *obs* **:** IMPORT, MEANING, SIGNIFICATION **3** *obs* **:** IMPORTUNITY, SOLICITATION **4** *obs* **:** a matter of importance

syn CONSEQUENCE, SIGNIFICANCE, IMPORT, MOMENT, WEIGHT: IMPORTANCE, the most general of these nouns, signifies a quality or state that is of value or influence, often with the implication that this is in someone's opinion ⟨issues which, whilst not the major significance, have some *importance* —*Current History*⟩ ⟨the *importance* of taking a wide, strategic view has prevailed —A.P.Ryan⟩ ⟨her sense of *importance* will help her —H.M.Parshley⟩ ⟨a position of some *importance* in industry⟩ ⟨clusters of huge inverted pleats that add *importance* to the skirt —Lois Long⟩ When used interchangeably with IMPORTANCE, CONSEQUENCE often applies to social rank, public position, or reputation but more generally implies an importance by reason of effects, results, or interrelationships ⟨a man of some *consequence*⟩ ⟨a subscription library in every town of *consequence* in the country —*Amer. Guide Series: Pa.*⟩ ⟨the newspapers have been demanding these things for years, and nothing of any real and lasting *consequence* ever seems to happen —Herman Kogan⟩ SIGNIFICANCE can be used interchangeably with IMPORTANCE or CONSEQUENCE, although in meaning basically *that which is signified* (*to anyone*) it usu. stresses strongly the mere fact of having value or worth and sometimes the relativity of that value or worth ⟨a person of some *significance*⟩ ⟨here, in 1864, occurred a battle of some strategic *significance* —*Amer. Guide Series: Ark.*⟩ ⟨a temper tantrum once in a while should be overlooked for it has little *significance* —H.R.Litchfield & L.H.Dembo⟩ ⟨such trivia take on *significance* only if the reader is able to catch the subtle hints of impending disaster —Leland Miles⟩ ⟨a generation of boys and girls who understand the social *significance* of the family —*Current Biog.*⟩ IMPORT usu. stresses, even more than SIGNIFICANCE, the relativity of the value or worth, bringing out the idea of a significance bearing upon or in relation to person or thing specified or strongly implied ⟨the Contemporary Theater, concentrating on plays of sociological *import* —*Amer. Guide Series: Mich.*⟩ ⟨when we allow our mind to dwell upon such considerations as these, the entire *import* of the illustration changes —John Dewey⟩ ⟨the differences between one variety of man and another, points of negligible *import* in medicine —A.L.Kroeber⟩ ⟨other measures of international *import* upon which he voted —*Current Biog.*⟩ MOMENT, very like SIGNIFICANCE or IMPORT though less frequent in oral communication, usu. suggests worthiness of consideration, often stressing the conspicuousness or self-evidence of the significance or worthiness ⟨some excerpts describe matters of greater *moment* than do others —*Times Lit. Supp.*⟩ ⟨the questions before the Department of State were many and of grave *moment* —W.C.Ford⟩ ⟨the material inequalities of our worldly life will be found to be of no *moment* in the hereafter —P.G.Waris⟩ WEIGHT tends to stress largeness of possible consequence or import as of something that must be taken into account or whose presence does or may seriously alter an outcome ⟨men who take the lead, and whose opinions and wishes have great *weight* with the others —J.G.Frazer⟩ ⟨the author's expertness in the field lends *weight* to his conclusions —H.M.Hyman⟩ ⟨a gap between their appreciation of a man's value at any moment and his real *weight* —Hilaire Belloc⟩ ⟨diplomatic questions remained, but they had no such *weight* as those of the wartime —W.C.Ford⟩

im·por·tan·cy \-nsē, -nsi\ *n* -ES *archaic* **:** IMPORTANCE

im·por·tant \-nt\ *adj* [MF, fr. OIt *importante* (verbal of *importare* to be important), fr. L *important-, importans,* pres. part. of *importare* to bring or carry in, convey, cause — more at IMPORT] **1 a :** marked by or possessing weight or consequence **:** valuable in content or relationship **:** SIGNIFICANT ⟨an ~ day in one's life⟩ ⟨an ~ consideration⟩ ⟨a country producing petroleum in ~ quantities⟩ **b :** significant or large in amount or size ⟨spent ~ money on a small gem for his wife⟩ ⟨an ~ part of the architect's time was devoted to department-store design —*Current Biog.*⟩ **2 a :** giving evidence of or seeming to relate to something of consequence ⟨holding the attorney's letter in his hand, and with so solemn and ~ an air that his wife . . . thought the worst was about to befall —W.M.Thackeray⟩ ⟨took long ~ strides in the direction of the courthouse⟩ **b :** giving evidence of a feeling of personal importance **:** marked by self-complacency, ostentation, or pompousness ⟨an ~ manner⟩ **3** *obs* **:** IMPORTUNATE, URGENT — **im·por·tant·ly** *adv* — **im·por·tant·ness** *n* -ES

im·por·ta·tion \,im,pōr'tāshən, -pȯ(r)'-, -pōə'- *also* -,pə(r)'-\ *n* -s [¹*import* + *-ation*] **1 :** the act or practice of bringing in (as merchandise) from an outside or foreign source ⟨the ~ of goods from Holland⟩ ⟨the ~ of foreign labor⟩ **2 :** IMPORT 3 ⟨the car was an ~ from Italy⟩

import credit *n* **:** a credit which is opened by an importer with a bank in his own country and upon which the exporter he deals with may draw bills of exchange — compare EXPORT CREDIT

imported *past of* IMPORT

imported cabbageworm *n* **:** the larva of the common white cabbage butterfly that is a serious pest of cabbage and related plants

imported currantworm *n* **:** a larval sawfly (*Nematus ribesii*) that is native to Europe but now widespread in No. America and that is very destructive to the foliage of currants, gooseberries, and related plants

im·por·tee \¦im,pōr¦tē, -,pər-\ *n* -s [¹*import* + *-ee*] **:** one that has been imported ⟨~*s* brought in to harvest the cherry crop⟩

im·port·er *pronunc at* ¹IMPORT + ə(r)\ *n* **:** one that imports; *esp* **:** one whose business is the importation and sale of goods from a foreign country

importing *pres part of* IMPORT

imports *pres 3d sing of* IMPORT, *pl of* IMPORT

im·por·tu·na·cy \əm'pȯrchənəsē; ¦impər'tün-, -r'tyün-\ *n* -ES **:** IMPORTUNATENESS

im·por·tu·nate \əm'pȯrchənə̇t; ¦impər¦tünə̇t, -r¦tyü-\ *adj* [prob. fr. ¹*importune* + *-ate*] **1 :** BURDENSOME, TROUBLESOME **2 :** troublesomely urgent **:** unreasonably solicitous **:** overly persistent in request or demand ⟨an ~ petitioner⟩ ⟨an ~ curiosity⟩ ⟨~ requests for assistance⟩ **syn** see PRESSING

im·por·tu·nate·ly *adv* **:** in an importunate manner

im·por·tu·nate·ness *n* -ES **:** the quality or state of being importunate

¹**im·por·tune** \¦impər¦tün, -,pȯr-, -r¦tyün; əm'pȯrchən, -(,)chün\ *adj* [ME, fr. MF & L; MF *importun,* fr. L *importunus* unfit, troublesome, rude, fr. *in-* ¹in- + *-portunus* (as in *opportunus* fit, convenient) — more at OPPORTUNE] **:** IMPORTUNATE — **im·por·tune·ly** *adv*

²**importune** \"\ *vb* -ED/-ING/-S [MF or ML; MF *importuner,* fr. ML *importunare,* fr. L *importunus*] *vt* **1 a :** to press or urge with frequent or unreasonable requests or troublesome persistence ⟨were being *importuned* to try their luck with the play —Claudia Cassidy⟩ ⟨*importuned* many businessmen to come to Washington —John McDonald⟩ **b** *archaic* **:** to request or beg for urgently **2 a :** ANNOY, WORRY, TROUBLE **b :** to make immoral or lewd advances toward ⟨arrested for

importuning a male person in the park⟩ ~ *vi* **1** : to beg, urge, or solicit persistently or troublesomely **2** : to make immoral or lewd advances toward another ⟨fined for *importuning* in a public convenience —T.A.Cullen⟩ **syn** see BEG

im·por·tun·er \-nər\ *n* -s : one that importunes

im·por·tu·ni·ty \ˌimpərˈtünəd·ē, -ˌpȯr-, -rˈtyü-\ *n* -ES [ME *importunite*, fr. MF *importunité*, fr. L *importunitat-, importunitas*, fr. *importunus* + *-itat-, -itas* -ity] : the quality or state of being importunate : pressing or pertinacious solicitation : troublesome pertinacity

im·pose \əmˈpōz\ *vb* -ED/-ING/-S [MF *imposer*, modif. (influenced by *poser* to put, place) of L *imponere* to put upon, impose, deceive, cheat, fr. *in-* ²in- + *ponere* to put, place — more at POSE, POSITION] *vt* **1** *obs* : CHARGE, IMPUTE **2** : to give or bestow (as a name or title) authoritatively or officially **3 a** *obs* : to cause to be burdened : SUBJECT — used with *to* **b** (1) : to make, frame, or apply (as a charge, tax, obligation, rule, penalty) as compulsory, obligatory, or enforcible ⟨~ a duty on a city official⟩ ⟨the obligations *imposed* by international law —*Encyc. Americana*⟩ : LEVY ⟨~ a tax on all unmarried men⟩ : INFLICT ⟨~ punishment upon a traitor⟩ ⟨flying ~s a heavy nervous strain on the individual —H.G. Armstrong⟩ : force one to submit to or come into accord with — usu. used with *on* or *upon* ⟨moved the newspapers to ~ a uniformity upon the written language —Oscar Handlin⟩ ⟨~ their dictates on the smaller nations —Vera M. Dean⟩ ⟨~ restraints upon the children⟩ (2) : to establish forcibly ⟨he *imposed* himself as leader⟩ ⟨~ law and order on a primitive people⟩ ⟨*imposed* a uniform organization over the whole of Lowland Britain —L.D.Stamp⟩ (3) : to make to prevail as a basic pattern, order, or quality ⟨neoclassic styles were *imposed* on the landscape —*Amer. Guide Series: Ariz.*⟩ **c** *archaic* : to lay (as a charge) upon a person **d** : to bring into being : CREATE, GENERATE ⟨the dangers and irritations *imposed* by many railroad grade crossings —*Amer. Guide Series: Minn.*⟩ **4 a** *obs* : to lay (the hands) on in an ecclesiastical rite (as blessing or confirmation) **b** *archaic* : SET, PLACE, PUT, DEPOSIT **c** (1) : to arrange (type or plated pages) on an imposing stone preparatory to locking up in a chase; *sometimes* : to arrange and lock up (pages) (2) : to arrange (the component parts of a nonletterpress printing surface) in a similar manner **5 a** : to force into the company or upon the attention of another ⟨~ oneself upon others⟩ **b** : to inflict by deception or fraud : pass off ⟨~ fake documents upon a gullible public⟩ ⟨so long as imaginary events are not *imposed* upon the reader as historical evidence —J.L. Clifford⟩ ~ *vi* : to take usu. unwarranted advantage of something ⟨I was not formally invited to my friend's party and I would not wish to ~ by going uninvited⟩ **syn** see DICTATE — **impose on** *or* **impose upon 1 a** : to force oneself esp. obnoxiously on (others) **b** *obs* : to encroach or infringe on : INFRINGE **2** : to take unwarranted advantage of : exploit a personal relationship with ⟨got a reputation for *imposing on* friends for their time and money⟩ : ABUSE ⟨did not wish to *impose upon* what privileges he had⟩ **3** : to practice deception on : DECEIVE, DEFRAUD, CHEAT ⟨an attempt to *impose on* the good-natured tolerance of the public —Roger Fry⟩ ⟨succeed in deceiving, and *imposing upon*, others —George Meredith⟩

imposed load *n* : the part of the total load sustained by a structure or member thereof that is applied to it after erection — compare DEAD LOAD

im·pos·er \-zə(r)\ *n* : one that imposes; *esp* : STONEMAN 1

imposing *adj* **1** *archaic* : insistent and exacting **2** *archaic* : DECEPTIVE, TREACHEROUS **3** : impressive because of size, scope, bearing, dignity, or grandeur : COMMANDING ⟨an ~ building⟩ ⟨an ~ appearance⟩ **syn** see GRAND

im·pos·ing·ly *adv* : in an imposing manner; *esp* : IMPRESSIVELY

im·pos·ing·ness *n* -ES : the quality or state of being imposing

imposing stone *or* **imposing table** *or* **imposing surface** *n* : a slab of stone or metal on which matter to be printed is imposed

im·po·si·tion \ˌimpəˈzishən\ *n* [ME *imposicioun*, fr. MF & LL; MF *imposition*, fr. LL *imposition-, impositio*, fr. L *impositus* (past part. of *imponere*) + *-ion-, -io* -ion] **1** : the act of imposing: as **a** : the laying on of the hands as a religious ceremony (as in ordination or confirmation) **b** : a putting, placing, or laying on ⟨the ~ of color on the clear wood⟩ ⟨the ~ of a second layer on the first⟩ **c** : an applying by compelling means ⟨the ~ of rigid censorship⟩ ⟨the ~ of a foreign form on a domestic product⟩ **d** : a levying or assessment (as of a tax or a fine) ⟨the ~ of extra charges for extra services⟩ ⟨the ~ of a high tariff⟩ **e** : the arranging on an imposing stone of matter to be printed **2** : something imposed: as **a** : LEVY, TAX ⟨an ~ of 5000 francs on a coat⟩ **b** *obs* : COMMAND, CHARGE **c** : an excessive, unwarranted, or uncalled-for requirement or burden ⟨severe ~s on her children —John Dollard⟩ **d** : an exercise imposed as punishment on a student (as at an English public school) **3** : the act of imposing upon another or the condition of being imposed upon : DECEPTION ⟨know that their tricks are ~s —W.D.Howells⟩ **4** : the order of arrangement of imposed pages or other matter ⟨the standard ~s are simple multiples of 16 pages —*Plan for a Good Book*⟩

im·pos·i·tor \əmˈpäzəd·ə(r), -z(ə)tə(r)\ *n* -s [*impose* + *-itor* (as in *compositor*)] : STONEMAN 1

im·possibilism \(ˈ)im, əm+\ *n* [L *impossibilis* + E *-ism*] **1** : a political purpose or plan felt to be impossible of achievement **2** : the advocacy of an impossible purpose or plan

¹**im·possibilist** \"+\ *n* [L *impossibilis* + E *-ist*] : an advocate of impossibilism

²**impossibilist** \"\ *adj* : of or relating to impossibilism

im·possibility \(ˌ)im, əm+\ *n* [ME *impossibilite*, fr. MF & LL; MF *impossibilité*, fr. LL *impossibilitat-, impossibilitas*, fr. L *impossibilis* + *-itat-, -itas* -ity] **1** : the quality or state of being impossible: as **a** : IMPRACTICABILITY ⟨never deterred by the seeming ~ of any task⟩ **b** : incapability of being dealt with by reasonable or acceptable means ⟨his cool cheek, his frightful temper, his sheer ~ —James Cameron⟩ ⟨the ~ of the political setup for an honest man⟩ **2** *obs* : INABILITY **3** : something impossible of attainment ⟨a child who always goes after *impossibilities*⟩

¹**im·possible** \(ˈ)im, əm+\ *adj* [ME, fr. MF & L; MF, fr. L *impossibilis*, fr. *in-* ¹in- + *possibilis* possible — more at POSSIBLE] **1 a** : incapable of being or of occurring : not within the realm of the possible : contrary to the nature of reality ⟨an ~ motion⟩ ⟨an ~ creature⟩ **b** (1) : felt to be incapable of being done, attained, or fulfilled : felt to be utterly impracticable ⟨a land ~ of conquest⟩ (2) : extremely and almost insuperably difficult under the circumstances : having little likelihood of accomplishment or completion ⟨spent his time indefatigably doing ~ tasks for the committee⟩ **c** *of a statement* : SELF-CONTRADICTORY **2 a** : out of the question : UNACCEPTABLE ⟨~ coloring in a picture⟩ ⟨an ~ political candidate⟩ : extremely undesirable ⟨relieving ~ and unfair economic conditions —F.D.Roosevelt⟩ ⟨his claret was ~ —Elinor Wylie⟩ : marked by very undesirable qualities ⟨his wife is simply ~ . . . uses perfumery, and has an awful voice —Margaret Deland⟩ **b** : difficult or extremely awkward to deal with or so markedly odd as to be unpleasant or objectionable ⟨a positive genius for collecting ~ people —Ngaio Marsh⟩ ⟨an almost ~ man to have for an enemy —Bruce Catton⟩ — **im·possibleness** \"+\ *n*

²**impossible** \"\ *n* [ME, fr. *impossible*, adj.] : something impossible : IMPOSSIBILITY

im·possibly \"+\ *adv* **1** : in an impossible manner or to an impossible degree ⟨an ~ idealistic young man⟩ **2** : to a degree that causes hardship or prevents a remedy ⟨food and clothing are ~ expensive⟩ ⟨~ far away from all sources of supply —June Platt⟩

¹**im·post** \ˈim,pōst\ *n* [MF, fr. ML *impositum*, fr. neut. of L *impositus*, past part. of *imponere* to put upon, impose — more at IMPOSE] **1** : something imposed or levied : TAX, TRIBUTE, DUTY **2** : the weight carried by a horse in a handicap race

²**impost** \"\ *vt* : to classify (imports) in order to fix import duties

³**impost** \"\ *n* [F *imposte*, fr. MF, fr. OIt *imposta*, fr. fem. of *imposto* (past part. of *imporre* to put upon, impose), fr. L *impositus*] : a block, capital, or molding (as of a pillar, pier, or wall) from which an arch springs — see ARCH illustration

imposterous *adj, obs* : IMPOSTROUS

im·pos·tor *or* **im·pos·ter** \əmˈpästə(r)\ *n* -s [MF & LL; MF *imposteur*, fr. LL *impostor*, fr. L *impostus, impositus* (past part. of *imponere* to put upon, impose, deceive, cheat) + *-or* — more at IMPOSE] : one that practices imposture : one that assumes an identity, character, or title not his own for the purpose of deception : PRETENDER, FRAUD, HUMBUG

im·pos·trous \(ˈ)imˈpästrəs, əmˈp-\ *adj* : of, relating to, or being an imposture : DECEITFUL, FRAUDULENT

impostumate *or* **imposthumate** *vb* -ED/-ING/-S [¹*impostume, imposthume* + *-ate*] *vt, obs* : to affect with an impostume : to cause to have an impostume ~ *vi, obs* : to form an impostume

¹**im·pos·tume** \əmˈpäs(ˌ)chüm, -s(ˌ)t(y)üm, -stəm\ *or* **im·pos·thume** \", -s(ˌ)thüm, -sthəm\ *n* -s [ME *emposteme, empostyme, imposteme*, fr. MF *apostume, empostume*, fr. L *apostema* — more at APOSTEME] **1** *archaic* : ABSCESS, CYST **2** *archaic* : an instance or source of moral corruption

²**impostume** *vb* [ME *empostemen*, fr. *emposteme*, n.] *obs* : IMPOSTUMATE

¹**im·pos·ture** \əmˈpäschə(r)\ *n* [LL *impostura*, fr. L *impostus, impositus* (past part. of *imponere* to put upon, impose, deceive, cheat) + *-ura* -ure — more at IMPOSE] **1** : the act or practice of imposing on or deceiving someone by means of an assumed character or name : the act or conduct of an impostor ⟨careful not to detect cases of malingering . . . and thus placed a premium on ~ —G.E.Fussell⟩ **2** : an instance of imposture ⟨admitted under oath that the whole defense of insanity was an ~ and a sham —B.N.Cardozo⟩

syn CHEAT, FRAUD, DECEIT, DECEPTION, COUNTERFEIT, SHAM, FAKE, HUMBUG, SIMULACRUM: IMPOSTURE applies to any situation in which a spurious object or action is passed off as genuine and bona fide ⟨its values . . . are an *imposture*: pretending to honor and distinction it accepts all that is vulgar and base —Edmund Wilson⟩ CHEAT applies to any abuse of credence and faith by misleading or trickery and also to delusion induced by the victim's credulousness ⟨though the counts allowed the *cheat* for fact . . . and let the tale o' the feigned birth pass for true —Robert Browning⟩ ⟨the *cheat* which still leads us to work and live for appearances —R.W.Emerson⟩ FRAUD is likely to indicate a calculated perversion of the truth; applied to a person it may be less condemnatory and suggest pretence and hypocrisy ⟨many persons persisted in believing that his supposed suicide was but another *fraud* —Justin M'Carthy⟩ ⟨the pious *fraud* who freely indulges in the sins against which he eloquently preaches —Oliver LaFarge⟩ DECEIT indicates anything that deceives or misleads, usu. purposefully, and is strongly condemnatory ⟨Indians were . . . treacherous according to the white man's standards, since they held that the basest trickery or *deceit* was not dishonorable if directed against a foe —*Amer. Guide Series: R.I.*⟩ DECEPTION is often interchangeable with DECEIT but is used without condemnation in reference to sleights and feints and to innocent or natural characteristics likely to mislead ⟨practice gross *deception* on the public with all the earnestness of a moral "crusade" —K.S.Davis⟩ ⟨a fast backfield trained in *deception*⟩ COUNTERFEIT refers to a close imitation or copy of a thing, usu. one made or circulated for dishonest gain ⟨this bill's a *counterfeit*⟩; in reference to persons or ideas or qualities it suggests spurious although close imitation without culpable intent to deceive ⟨not really a married woman and a housemistress but only a kind of *counterfeit* —Arnold Bennett⟩ SHAM is severe in censuring what fraudulently imitates or purports to be a genuine reality ⟨perhaps her devotion to Marcellus was a *sham* and her real intention was that Agrippa should be goaded into putting him out of the way —Robert Graves⟩ ⟨if people would only build on facts, not on *shams* —Ellen Glasgow⟩ FAKE refers to something factitious or assumed with plausible closeness to the original, genuine, or true; it may or may not condemn, depending on culpable intent to deceive ⟨Gaston B. Means's volume, *The Strange Death of President Harding*, . . . bears every imprint of being a thoroughgoing *fake* —S.H.Adams⟩ ⟨he pretends everything is what it is not, he is a *fake* —Katherine A. Porter⟩ HUMBUG indicates elaborate pretense, esp. so flagrant that it approaches transparency ⟨you're a *humbug*, sir . . . I will speak plainer, if you wish it. An imposter, sir —Charles Dickens⟩ ⟨these liars warn't no kings nor dukes, at all, but just low-down *humbugs* and frauds —Mark Twain⟩ SIMULACRUM indicates an image or imitation but usu. lacks the suggestion that it is made to defraud; it may indicate an image utterly wanting in essential substance or reality ⟨nothing but a coat and a wig and a mask smiling below it — nothing but a great *simulacrum* —W.M.Thackeray⟩ ⟨something whose essence was not there at all, a stiff lifeless *simulacrum* —J.C. Powys⟩

²**imposture** *vi, obs* : to practice imposture ~ *vt* **1** *obs* : to show to be an imposture **2** *obs* : DECEIVE

im·pos·tur·ing \-chəriŋ\ *n* : IMPOSTURE 2 ⟨think . . . these concealments and ~s can be exaggerated —John Cheever⟩

im·pos·tur·ous \(ˈ)imˈpäschərəs, əmˈp-\ *adj* : IMPOSTROUS

im·potable \(ˈ)im+\ *adj* [LL *impotabilis*, fr. L *in-* ¹in- + LL *potabilis* potable — more at POTABLE] : not suited for drinking : UNDRINKABLE

im·po·tence \ˈimpə̇d·ən(t)s, ǀtən- *also* ǀtᵊn- *sometimes except in sense b* (ˈ)imˈpō| *or* əmˈpō|\ *also* **im·po·ten·cy** \-nsē,-nsi\ *n, pl* **impotences** *also* **impotencies** [ME *impotence, impotencie*, fr. MF & ML; MF *impotence*, fr. ML *impotentia*, fr. L, lack of self-control, fr. *impotent-, impotens* + *-ia* -y] **1** : the quality or state of being impotent: as **a** : lack of strength : WEAKNESS, FEEBLENESS ⟨the very ~ of the government, the impossibility of doing anything —Upton Sinclair⟩ : HELPLESSNESS ⟨reduce them to intellectual ~ —H.J.Laski⟩ ⟨a small force . . . reduced to ~ a fortress that had been expected to withstand attack for at least 2 weeks —*Military Rev.*⟩ **b** (1) : a physical or psychological abnormal state usu. of a male characterized by inability to copulate — compare STERILITY (2) : STERILITY — not used technically **2** [L *impotentia*] *obs* : lack of self-restraint or self-control

¹**im·po·tent** \-nt\ *adj* [ME, fr. MF & L; MF, fr. L *impotent-, impotens*, fr. *in-* ¹in- + *potent-, potens* potent — more at POTENT] **1 a** : not potent : lacking in power, strength, or vigor : deficient in capacity : WEAK, POWERLESS ⟨he liked to be bad and see them all ~ to correct him —Stuart Cloete⟩ ⟨its ~ ruling classes —Edward Shils⟩ ⟨a relatively ~ preparation of penicillin⟩ ⟨a lame and ~, and a trite, conclusion —Howard M. Jones⟩ **b** : unable to copulate : wanting in procreative power; *broadly* : STERILE — usu. used of males **2** [L *impotent-, impotens*] *obs* : incapable of self-restraint : UNGOVERNABLE, VIOLENT **syn** see STERILE

²**impotent** \"\ *n* : one that is impotent

im·po·tent·ly *adv* : in an impotent manner : FEEBLY, WEAKLY, HELPLESSLY

im·po·tent·ness *n* : IMPOTENCE

¹**im·pound** \əmˈpau̇nd\ *vt* -ED/-ING/-S [²*in-* + *pound* (enclosure)] **1 a** : to shut up in or as if in a pound : CONFINE, ENCLOSE ⟨to catch and ~ stray dogs⟩ ⟨explosive release of the breath which had been ~*ed* in the mouth cavity —A.L. Kroeber⟩ **b** : to seize and hold in the custody of the law ⟨~ stray cattle⟩ ⟨~ the files of a court⟩ ⟨all slave ships that put into Bahama ports were ~*ed* and their cargoes freed —Marjory S. Douglas⟩ **c** : to take possession of : APPROPRIATE **2** : to collect (water) for irrigation, hydroelectric use, flood control, or similar purpose : confine and store (water) in an impound

²**im·pound** \ˈim,p-\ *n* : a reservoir for impounding

im·pound·able \(ˈ)imˈpau̇ndəbəl, əmˈp-\ *adj* : capable of or liable to impoundment

im·pound·ment \əmˈpau̇n(d)mənt\ *also* **im·pound·age** \-ndij\ *n* -s **1** : the act of impounding or the state of being impounded **2** : a body of water formed by impounding (as by a dam); *also* : the quantity of water in such a body

im·pov·er·ish \əmˈpäv(ə)rish, -rēsh, *esp in pres part* -rəsh\ *vt* -ED/-ING/-ES [ME *enpoverisen*, fr. MF *empovriss-*, stem of *empovrir*, fr. *en-* ¹en- + *povre* poor — more at POOR] **1** : to make poor : reduce to poverty or indigence ⟨a family ~*ed* by misfortune and sickness⟩ ⟨a foolish effort to ~ life by robbing men of sustaining vision —M.R.Cohen⟩ ⟨the provinces were ~*ed* of their scientific talent —S.F.Mason⟩ **2** : to exhaust the strength, richness, or fertility of : make sterile ⟨worked the land year after year until it was ~*ed*⟩ **syn** see DEPLETE

impoverished *adj, of a fauna or flora* : represented by few species or individuals : SCANTY

im·pov·er·ish·ment \-mənt\ *n* -s [AF *empoverissement*, fr. MF *empovriss-* + *-ment*] : the act of impoverishing or the state of being impoverished ⟨soil ~⟩ ⟨spiritual ~⟩

impower *obs var of* EMPOWER

impr *abbr* improved; improvement

im·practicability \(ˌ)im, əm+\ *n* **1** : the quality or state of being impracticable **2** : something impracticable

im·practicable \(ˈ)im, əm+\ *adj* [¹*in-* + *practicable*] **1 a** : not practicable : incapable of being performed or accomplished by the means employed or at command : INFEASIBLE ⟨economically ~ to maintain an air force which will provide absolute security —*Nat'l Aviation Policy*⟩ ⟨regretted that his appointment as chaplain . . . was at present ~ —Rose Macaulay⟩ **b** : incapable of being passed, scaled, or conveniently negotiated ⟨an ~ road⟩ ⟨an ~ cliff⟩ **2** *archaic* : UNMANAGEABLE, INTRACTABLE **3** : IMPRACTICAL, UNWISE, IMPRUDENT ⟨the tear is apt to go clear across the sail, making it ~ for you to continue —H.A.Calahan⟩ : lacking common sense in practical matters ⟨given him up for many years as ~ and hopeless —George Meredith⟩ — **im·practicableness** \"+\ *n* — **im·practicably** \"+\ *adv*

im·practical \(ˈ)im, əm+\ *adj* [¹*in-* + *practical*] : not practical: as **a** (1) : not wise to put into or keep in practice or effect : not pleasing to common sense or prudence ⟨slavery, we have been taught, was economically ~ —Carol L. Thompson⟩ (2) : IDEALISTIC ⟨an ~ pipe dream —James Laughlin⟩ : THEORETICAL ⟨an anchorite living austerely and owning little, but rich in ~ and priceless honor —W.L.Sullivan⟩ **b** : incapable of dealing sensibly or prudently with practical esp. economic matters ⟨a totally ~ man who would have starved but for his wife's common sense⟩ **c** : IMPRACTICABLE : incapable of being put into use or effect or of being accomplished or done successfully or without extreme trouble, hardship, or expense ⟨all of the aircraft-engine mufflers . . . have been found ~ —H.G.Armstrong⟩ ⟨feels that any . . . plan might prove so expensive — and so ~ — that he does not intend to try a new one —*Time*⟩ ⟨a totally ~ scheme for making a quick million⟩ ⟨led him to write music that is vocally ~ —A.T.Davison⟩ — **im·practicality** \(ˌ)im, əm+\ *n* — **im·practicalness** \(ˈ)im, əm+\ *n*

im·pre·cate \ˈimprə̇ˌkāt, -rē,-, *usu* -ād.+V\ *vb* -ED/-ING/-S [L *imprecatus*, past part. of *imprecari*, fr. *in-* ²in- + *precari* to ask, entreat, pray — more at PRAY] *vt* **1 a** *archaic* : to call down by prayer : INVOKE **b** : to invoke evil upon : CURSE ⟨*imprecated* the weather when the ink froze in his fountain pen —Stanley Snaith⟩ **2** *archaic* : to beg or pray for ~ *vi* **1** *obs* : to invoke evil **2** : to utter imprecations : CURSE

im·pre·cat·ing·ly \ˈ===ˌ===, ˌ==ˈ===\ *adv* : in the manner of one cursing : with curses

im·pre·ca·tion \ˌ==ˈkāshən\ *n* -s [L *imprecation-, imprecatio*, fr. *imprecatus* + *-ion-, -io* -ion] **1** : the act of imprecating esp. by invoking evil : CURSING **2 a** : PLEA, SUPPLICATION ⟨the ~s to the Lord for forgiveness —W.A.White⟩ **b** : CURSE, MALEDICTION ⟨uttered ~s under his breath⟩

im·preca·to·ry \ˈimprəkəˌtōrē, ˈimprēk-, əmˈprek-, -tȯr-, -ri, *chiefly Brit* ˌimpriˈkātəri *or* -ā·tri\ *adj* : of, relating to, or being imprecation : invoking evil : CURSING

im·precise \ˌim+\ *adj* [¹*in-* + *precise*] : not precise: as **a** : not exact ⟨~ astronomical observation⟩ **b** : vague or indefinite in nature, form, or outline ⟨~ dawn changes to photographic clearness —Han Suyin⟩ ⟨made him a rather ~ officer⟩ — **im·precisely** \"+\ *adv* — **im·preciseness** \"+\ *n*

im·precision \ˌim+\ *n* [¹*in-* + *precision*] : the quality or state of being imprecise : lack of precision ⟨it is the indefiniteness, the ~ of the process that is baffling —Herbert Read⟩ ⟨an ~ of language⟩ : INACCURACY ⟨trying to mark as accurately as possible with tools calibrated with great ~⟩

im·predicable \(ˈ)im, əm+\ *adj* [¹*in-* + *predicable*] : not predicable

im·preg \ˈim,preg\ *n* -s [*impregnated (wood)*] : wood impregnated with a resin so that face checking is reduced and compressional strength and hardness, electrical resistance, and resistance to moisture, acid, and decay are increased

im·pregn \imˈprēn\ *vt* -ED/-ING/-S [LL *impraegnare* — more at IMPREGNATE] *archaic* : IMPREGNATE

im·preg·na·bil·i·ty \(ˌ)im,pregnəˈbilәd·ē, əm-, -lətē, -i\ *n* -ES : the quality or state of being impregnable

¹**im·preg·na·ble** \(ˈ)imˈpregnəbəl, əmˈp-\ *adj* [alter. (influenced by *impregnate*) of earlier *impreignable*, alter. (influenced by such words as *reign, deign*, with silent *g*) of earlier *imprenable*, fr. ME, fr. MF, fr. *in-* ¹in- + *prenable* capable of being captured, fr. *pren-* (stem of *prendre* to take, capture, fr. L *prehendere* to grasp, seize) + *-able* — more at GET] **1** : incapable of being taken by assault : able to resist attack : UNCONQUERABLE, UNASSAILABLE ⟨an ~ fortress⟩ ⟨~ virtue⟩; *also* : incapable of being broken into or escaped from ⟨an ~ cell⟩ **2** : being beyond criticism or question : not subject to higher authority ⟨an ~ social position⟩ ⟨of ~ financial standing⟩ ⟨an ~ reputation for honesty⟩ — **im·pregnableness** \"+\ *n* -ES — **im·pregnably** \"+\ *adv*

²**im·preg·na·ble** \əmˈpregnəbəl\ *adj* [²*impregnate* + *-able*] : capable of being impregnated (as an egg)

¹**im·preg·nant** \əmˈpregnənt\ *adj* [LL *impraegnant-, impraegnans*, pres. part. of *impraegnare*] **1** *obs* : IMPREGNATED, SATURATED, PERMEATED, IMBUED **2** *archaic* : IMPREGNATING

²**impregnant** \"\ *n* -s : an agent (as an oil, plastic, insecticide, resin) used to penetrate another substance (as cloth, paper, plaster, concrete, pulp, wood)

¹**im·preg·nate** \əmˈpregnə̇t, *usu* -nə̇d.+V\ *adj* [LL *impraegnatus*, past part.] : IMPREGNATED

²**im·preg·nate** \əmˈpreg,nāt, ˈim,p-, *usu* -ād.+V\ *vt* -ED/-ING/-S [LL *impraegnatus*, past part. of *impraegnare*, fr. L *in-* ²in- + *praegnas* pregnant — more at PREGNANT] **1 a** (1) : to make pregnant : cause to conceive : get with child or young (2) : to introduce sperm cells into : INSEMINATE **b** : to infuse an active principle into : make fruitful or fertile : FERTILIZE, IMBUE **2 a** : to cause to be filled, imbued, mixed, furnished, or saturated (as with particles of another substance) ⟨~ wood with creosote⟩ ⟨gauze *impregnated* with medicament⟩ ⟨a cake strongly *impregnated* with brandy⟩ ⟨the chamber . . . *impregnated* with the odor of furniture paste —Arnold Bennett⟩ **b** (1) : to mix with : INTERPENETRATE ⟨quicksilver ore ~s sandstone in California —A.M.Bateman⟩ (2) : to have a marked permeating or coloring effect upon ⟨a very notable poem *impregnated* with the pessimism of a time —R.M.Lovett⟩ ⟨criticism . . . richly *impregnated* with history —C.W.Shumaker⟩ **c** : to force by impregnation ⟨plastics *impregnated* into cloth —Jack DeMent⟩ **3** : to influence markedly : INDOCTRINATE ⟨*impregnated* with socialistic ideas⟩ **syn** see PERMEATE

im·preg·na·tion \ˌim,pregˈnāshən\ *n* -s [F or L; F *imprégnation*, fr. MF *impregnation*, fr. ML *impraegnation-, impraegnatio*, fr. LL *impraegnatus* + L *-ion-, -io* -ion] **1** : the act of impregnating or the state of being impregnated: as **a** : a causing to conceive : FECUNDATION, FERTILIZATION **b** : INFUSION, SATURATION **c** : INDOCTRINATION **2** : something with which something else is impregnated: **a** : a mineral concentration consisting of small scattered grains in a rock matrix **b** : IMPREGNANT

im·preg·na·tor \əmˈpreg,nād·ə(r), ˈim,p-, -ātə-\ *n* -s [ML *impraegnator*, fr. LL *impraegnatus* + L *-or*] : one that impregnates: as **a** : an operator of a machine that impregnates (as a fabric with a chemical compound) **b** : an instrument used for artificial insemination

impresa *n* -s [It, undertaking, chivalric deed, heraldic device, motto, fr. fem. of *impreso*, past part. of *imprendere* to undertake, fr. (assumed) VL *imprehendere* — more at EMPRISE] **1** *obs* : DEVICE, EMBLEM **2** *obs* **a** : a sentence usu. accompanying an impresa **b** : MOTTO, PROVERB, MAXIM

im·pre·sar·i·al \ˌimprəˈsärēəl, -sa(a)r-, -sar-, -sår-\ *adj* : of or belonging to an impresario

im·pre·sar·io \ˌ==ˈ=rē,ō\ *n* -s *see sense 1* [It, manager, impresario, fr. *impresa* + *-ario* -ary (fr. L *-arius*)] **1** *pl also* **im·pre·sa·ri** \-ˌrē\ : the projector, manager, or conductor of an opera or concert company **2 :** one who puts on or sponsors an entertainment (as a concert, television show, art exhibition, or sports contest) **3 :** MANAGER, PRODUCER, DIRECTOR ⟨a former beerhall ~ —Upton Sinclair⟩ ⟨an egregious ~ of letters, who kept a squad of writers churning out copy marketed under his signature —C.J.Rolo⟩ ⟨the ~ of the best intelligent conversation to be heard in his time —*Times Lit. Supp.*⟩

im·prescribable \¦im+\ *adj* [[1]*in-* + *prescribe* + *-able*] **:** IMPRESCRIPTIBLE

im·prescriptibility \¦im+\ *n* **:** the quality or state of being imprescriptible

im·prescriptible \¦im+\ *adj* [MF, fr. *in-* [1]*in-* + *prescriptible* — more at PRESCRIPTIBLE] **:** not subject to prescription **:** INALIENABLE ⟨the ~ rights of man⟩; *also* **:** ABSOLUTE — **im·prescriptibly** \"+\ *adv*

imprese *n* -s [MF, fr. OIt *impresa* — more at IMPRESA] *obs* **:** IMPRESA

[1]**im·press** \əm'pres\ *vb* [ME *impressen,* fr. L *impressus,* past part. of *imprimere,* fr. *in-* [2]*in-* + *-primere* (fr. *premere* to press) — more at PRESS] *vt* **1 a :** to apply with pressure so as to press or imprint ⟨~ a signet ring on wax⟩ ⟨the finger-print file . . . in which all 10 fingers are ~*ed* on the card —*FBI Bull.*⟩ **b :** to produce (as a mark or image) by pressure ⟨a perfect spiral ~*ed* on such a cylinder —S.F. Mason⟩ **:** IMPRINT ⟨~ one's name on a metal strip by machine⟩ ⟨~ an odd design on the wood⟩ **c :** to press, stamp, or print in or upon ⟨~*ed* the wax with his seal⟩ **:** mark by or as if by pressure ⟨~ his children with the right attitudes⟩ **2 a :** to produce or imprint an esp. vivid impression of (as on the mind or memory) ⟨~ an idea on the mind⟩ ⟨the general custom for boys to be whipped on certain days to ~ things on their memories —T.B.Costain⟩ ⟨beliefs which have been ~*ed* upon us in our childhood —Frank Thilby⟩ **:** cause to have a strong effect (as of compulsion) ⟨~*ing* his will upon others by sheer force of character —V.L.Parrington⟩ **b :** to produce an impression on **:** affect esp. forcibly or deeply ⟨~ a friend with the sincerity of one's intentions⟩ ⟨~ one favorably⟩ **:** arouse strong feeling (as concern, admiration, dislike) in ⟨the altered manner of his son ~*ed* him strangely —George Meredith⟩ ⟨the bigness of it awed them, the resources ~*ed* them —Joseph Baily⟩ **c :** to mark with an imposed quality or characteristic ⟨~ the poem with the cynicism of his outlook⟩ **3 a** *obs* **:** PRINT ⟨~ the Bible⟩ **b :** to print (a stamp) directly on (a postcard, envelope) ⟨~*ed* with a 2 cent stamp⟩ **4 a :** EXERT ⟨~ a force upon a sail⟩ **b :** to transfer or transmit (as a movement) by communication ⟨~ a motion upon a ball⟩ **c :** to apply (an electromotive force or voltage) to a circuit from an outside source (as a generator) **~** *vi* **:** to produce an impression **:** arouse the strong interest or admiration of another ⟨did not wish to make friends at parties but only to ~ with his sense of personal destiny⟩ ⟨a small child acting up before company in an effort to ~⟩ **syn** see AFFECT

[2]**im·press** \'im,p- *sometimes* əm'p-\ *n* **1 :** the act of impressing or stamping ⟨sealing by the old-time process of ~ —L.F.Middlebrook⟩ **2 a :** a mark made by pressure that produces indentation or embossment **:** IMPRINT ⟨noting the ~ of wheels in lava —Richard Llewellyn⟩ ⟨a matrix in fairly durable metal to receive the ~ of the punch —G.C.Sellery⟩ **b :** an image or figure of something formed by or as if by pressure; *esp* **:** SEAL ⟨the most beautiful seal cuttings are shown on the ~*es* of the old Salem documents —L.F.Middlebrook⟩ **c :** a product of pressure or influence **3 :** a characteristic mark of distinction **:** STAMP ⟨the picture bore the ~ of the artist⟩ **:** distinctive quality ⟨his soft mind had . . . taken an ~ from the society which surrounded him —T.B.Macaulay⟩ ⟨the ~ of a fresh and vital intelligence is stamped unmistakably upon all that is best in his work —Lytton Strachey⟩ **4** *archaic* **:** IMPRESA **5 :** IMPRESSION ⟨his work has made a decided ~ upon our time —W.R.Benét⟩ **:** EFFECT ⟨words are but symbols and, like all symbols, have a varying ~ —Philip Wittenberg⟩ ⟨made his strongest ~ upon the country by his . . . two speeches —G.H.Haynes⟩ ⟨left an enduring ~ on my life, although our relations were always impersonal —A.J. Liebling⟩

[3]**im·press** \əm'p-\ *vt* [[2]*in-* + *press* (take by force)] **1 :** to levy or take by force for public service; *esp* **:** to take or force by impressment (as into naval service) ⟨in searching for British sailors upon our ships, she ~*ed* our own —Owen Wister⟩ **2 a :** to enlist or procure the services or aid of by forcible argument or persuasion ⟨all able-bodied survivors were ~*ed* for the task of finding and caring for the injured —*Amer. Guide Series: Texas*⟩ **b :** to force or forcibly persuade ⟨~*ed* him into a white coat for the Christmas festivities —Nancy Hale⟩

[4]**im·press** \'im,p-, əm'p-\ *n* **:** IMPRESSMENT

[5]**impress** *n* [alter. of [2]*imprest*] *obs* **:** pay in advance

[6]**im·press** \əm'pres\ *vt* [alter. of [1]*imprest*] *archaic* **:** to make an advance payment of (money)

[7]**im·press** \'im,p-, əm'p-\ *n* [alter. of *imprese*] **:** EMBLEM, DEVICE ⟨their shields broken, their ~*es* defaced —Edmund Burke⟩

im·press·able \əm'presəbəl\ *adj* **:** capable of being impressed

im·pressed \əm'prest\ *adj* [ME, fr. past part. of *impressen*] **1 :** deeply or markedly affected by impression **2 a :** lying below the general surface as if stamped into it ⟨~ dots⟩ **b :** having markings lying below the surface ⟨an ~ skin⟩ — **im·pressed·ly** \-sədlē,-stlē, -li\ *adv*

impressed species *n* **:** SENSIBLE SPECIES

impressed stamp *n* **:** a stamp (as for postage or revenue) printed directly on a cover, document, or other paper bearing it — compare EMBOSSED STAMP

impressed watermark *n* **:** an imitation watermark made by pressing rubber letters or a design on the paper web before drying

im·press·ibil·i·ty \(,)im,presə'bilədē, əm-, -lətē, -i\ *n* -ES **:** the quality or state of being impressible

im·press·ible \əm'presəbəl\ *adj* [[1]*impress* + *-ible*] **:** capable of being impressed **:** SUSCEPTIBLE, SENSITIVE — **im·press·ible·ness** \-bəlnəs\ *n* -ES — **im·press·i·bly** \-blē, -bli\ *adv*

im·pres·sion \əm'preshən\ *n* -s [ME *impressioun,* fr. MF *impression,* fr. L *impression-, impressio,* fr. *impressus* (past part of *imprimere* to impress) + *-ion-, -io* -ion — more at IMPRESS] **1 :** the act or process of impressing: as **a** (1) **:** an affecting by stamping, bearing upon, pressing, pressing into, or otherwise exerting a physical force that marks, grooves, embosses, or prints in some way ⟨the worker held the metal firm during the ~ by the die⟩ ⟨a firm ~ of the seal on the wax⟩ (2) *archaic* **:** the printing process **b :** a communicating or giving of a mold, style, trait, or character by an external force or influence ⟨a parent concerned with the ~ of good traits on the mind and personality of his children⟩ **2 :** the effect or product of an impression: as **a** (1) **:** an indentation, stamp, embossment, form, or figure resulting from physical contact usu. with pressure ⟨the strokes became wedge-shaped ~*s* which gave cuneiform its name —Peter Lawrence⟩ ⟨a banking system whose principal features would be a circulation of notes bearing a common ~ —*Encyc. Americana*⟩ ⟨a well-printed book has a sharp, clean ~ —Joseph Blumenthal⟩ (2) *obs* **:** a telling mark or trace (3) **:** a negative imprint in plastic material of the surfaces of the teeth and adjacent portions of the jaw from which a positive likeness may be produced in dentistry (4) **:** METER IMPRESSION **b :** an esp. marked influence or effect on feeling, sense, or mind ⟨the bad dream made a terrible ~ on the child⟩ ⟨the ~ of the ocean was vivid in his mind⟩ ⟨made a favorable ~ on the audience⟩ ⟨the more emotion the reading arouses, the deeper the ~ on the learner —W.F.Mackey⟩ ⟨square chimneys thrusting upward add to the ~ of weight —*Amer. Guide Series: Ark.*⟩ **c** (1) **:** a characteristic trait or feature resulting from influence ⟨the ~ produced by an environment on a person's habits⟩ (2) **:** an effect of alteration or improvement ⟨the fur traders . . . made little permanent ~ on the wilderness —R.A.Billington⟩ ⟨a candle or lamp struggled feebly from a window but made no ~ on the darkness —S.H.Holbrook⟩ **d :** a telling image impressed on the senses or the mind ⟨looking over the steep hills, the first ~ is of an immense void like the sea —Richard Jefferies⟩ ⟨drank in all the new ~*s* eagerly —Havelock Ellis⟩ **3 :** a piece of wax, metal, or other substance on which a seal has been impressed **4** *archaic* **a :** CHARGE, ATTACK **b :** strong effect **:** IMPACT, SHOCK **5** *obs* **:** an atmospheric condition or phenomenon **6 a :** the amount of pressure with which an inked printing surface deposits its ink on the paper in the printing process ⟨each form should be made ready with as light an ~ as practicable —John Southward⟩ **b :** one instance of the meeting of a printing surface and the material being printed ⟨plates badly worn after a million ~*s*⟩; *also* **:** a single print or copy so made **c :** all the copies of a book or other publication printed in one continuous operation from a single makeready ⟨first published in 1939 and now available in a third ~ —*Times Lit. Supp.*⟩ — called also *printing;* compare EDITION **7 :** a usu. indistinct or imprecise notion, remembrance, belief, or opinion ⟨an ~ of familiarity with a face⟩ ⟨the mistaken ~ that they were out of enemy territory⟩ ⟨cold, and mysterious, and ghostly — that is my first and lasting ~ of Mycenae —Mary Chubb⟩ **8 a :** the first coat of color in painting **b :** a coat of paint for ornament or preservation **9 :** an imitation or representation of salient features in an artistic or theatrical medium (as a ballet, painting, or theatrical monologue) ⟨the novel was an ~ of the battle from the point of view of the common soldier⟩; *esp* **:** an imitation in caricature of a noted personality as a form of theatrical entertainment ⟨the comedian gave several ~*s* of famous movie and television stars⟩ **syn** see IDEA

im·pres·sion·abil·i·ty \əmpresh(ə)nə'bilədē, -lətē, -i\ *n* **:** the quality or state of being impressionable **:** susceptibility to impressions ⟨that flabby ~ which is dignified under the name of creative temperament —John O'Hara⟩

im·pres·sion·able \əm'presh(ə)nəbəl\ *adj* [F *impressionnable,* fr. *impression* + *-able*] **:** capable of being easily impressed: **a :** easily influenced or affected ⟨the ~ years of a child's life⟩ ⟨an ~ heart⟩ **b :** capable of being molded or printed on ⟨an ~ plastic material⟩ ⟨paper that was very ~⟩ — **im·pres·sion·able·ness** \-bəlnəs\ *n* -ES — **im·pres·sion·a·bly** \-blē,-bli\ *adv*

im·pres·sion·al \-shənᵊl,-shnəl\ *adj* **:** of, relating to, or being impressions — **im·pres·sion·al·ly** \-ᵊlē,-əlē\ *adv*

im·pres·sion·ary \-shə,nerē\ *adj* **:** IMPRESSIONISTIC

impression cylinder *n* **:** the cylinder of a rotary printing press that carries the paper and impresses it by counterrotation against the inked printing surface on the plate cylinder; *also* **:** the cylinder of a cylinder press

im·pres·sion·ism \əm'preshə,nizəm\ *n* -s [F *impressionnisme,* fr. *impression* + *-isme* -ism] **1 a** *often cap* **:** a theory or practice in painting esp. among French painters of about 1870 of depicting the natural appearances of objects by means of dabs or strokes of primary unmixed colors in order to simulate actual reflected light, the subject matter being generally outdoor scenes painted directly — often contrasted with *expressionism;* compare LUMINISM, NEO-IMPRESSIONISM, PLEIN AIR, POSTIMPRESSIONISM **b :** a rough modeling or texturing of a surface in sculpture to produce a shimmering or scintillating effect **2 a :** the depiction of scene, emotion, or character (as in literature) by the use of detail that is sometimes brief and essential but often of great intricacy and elaborateness and that is intended to achieve a vividness, colorfulness, or effectiveness more by evoking subjective and sensory impressions (as of mood and atmosphere) than by re-creating or representing an objective reality **b :** a style of musical composition designed to create vague impressions and moods through rich and varied harmonies and timbres — often contrasted with *expressionism* **c :** the creation of the impression of a scene or its mood or atmosphere in a drama by the use of undramatic dialogue or nonobjective or symbolic scenery **d :** the creating of a general impression in a movie by the use of a series of shots that have no immediate logical or narrative connection **3 a** (1) **:** a practice in esp. literary criticism of presenting and elaborating one's subjective reactions to a work of art (2) **:** a critical theory that advocates or defends such a practice as the only valid one in criticism **b :** a vague and subjective response (as to a work of art) ⟨her attack is almost always human, rather critical, highly personal, degenerating occasionally into vague ~ —Mark Schorer⟩

im·pres·sion·ist \-sh(ə)nəst\ *n* -s [F *impressionniste,* fr. *impression* + *-iste* -ist] **:** an adherent or follower of impressionism; *specif, usu cap* **:** a member of a group of artists in France who exhibited together between 1874 and 1886 and many of whom practiced impressionism in their painting

im·pres·sion·is·tic \(¦)im¦preshə¦nistik, əm-, -tēk\ *or* **im·pres·sion·ist** \əm'presh(ə)nəst\ *adj* **:** of, belonging to, or being impressionism; *specif, usu cap* **:** of or belonging to the French Impressionists — **im·pres·sion·is·ti·cal·ly** \(¦)im¦preshə¦nistək(ə)lē, əm-, -tēk-, -li\ *adv*

impressions *pl of* IMPRESSION

im·pres·sive \əm'presiv, 'im,p-, -sēv *also* -səv\ *adj* [[1]*impress* + *-ive*] **1** *obs* **:** IMPRESSIBLE **2 :** making or tending to make a marked impression (as because of size, eminence, dignity of bearing, or achievement) **:** having the power to impress **:** notably exciting attention or feeling or arousing awe or admiration ⟨the Grand Canyon of the Colorado, one of the world's most ~ natural wonders —*Amer. Guide Series: Ariz.*⟩ ⟨an ~ speech⟩ ⟨an ~ list of titles to a man's name⟩ ⟨a very ~ play⟩ ⟨the country is ~ for the immensity of the barren reaches and the vast horizons —*Amer. Guide Series: Oregon*⟩ **syn** see MOVING

im·pres·sive·ly \-svlē, -li\ *adv* **:** in an impressive manner ⟨a garrulous young man with ~ complete information on all strata of shipboard life —T.O.Heggen⟩

im·pres·sive·ness \-sivnəs, -sēv- *also* -səv-\ *n* -ES **:** the quality or state of being impressive ⟨the man's ~ was due to his enormous size and thunderous voice⟩

im·press·ment \əm'presmənt\ *n* -s [[3]*impress* + *-ment*] **:** the act of seizing for public use or of impressing into public service ⟨the ~ of sailors⟩ ⟨opposed such measures as the conscription of state officials and ~ of private property —Hallie Farmer⟩

im·pres·sure \-eshə(r)\ *n* [[1]*impress* + *-ure*] **1** *archaic* **:** the act of pressing or impressing **2** *archaic* **a :** an impressed mark **b :** a mental or sensory impression

[1]**im·prest** \əm'prest\ *vt* -ED/-ING/-S [prob. fr. It *imprestare,* fr. *in-* [2]*in-* (fr. L) + *prestare* to lend, fr. L *praestare* to stand before, go surety for, furnish, present — more at PREST] **1** *archaic* **:** to make an advance or loan of (money) **2** *obs* **a :** to make an advance of money to **b :** to draw (as money) by way of advance

[2]**im·prest** \'im,p-\ *n* -s **:** a loan or advance of money: **a :** pay advanced to a soldier or sailor **b :** money advanced from government funds to enable a person to discharge his duties

[3]**imprest** \"\ *adj* **:** advanced or lent esp. as an imprest

[4]**imprest** *n* -s [prob. alter. (influenced by [2]*imprest*) of [4]*impress*] *obs* **:** IMPRESSMENT

[5]**imprest** *vt* -ED/-ING/-S [prob. alter. (influenced by [1]*imprest*) of [3]*impress*] *obs* **:** to impress into army or naval service

imprest accountant *n, Eng law* **:** a person to whom an advance of public money is legally made

imprest fund *n* **:** a sum kept on hand, periodically replenished, and used for small expenditures

im·pri·ma·tur \,imprə'mäd·ə(r), ¦tə- *also* -mā¦\ *n* -s [NL, let it be printed, 3d sing. pres. subj. passive of *imprimere* to print, fr. L, to impress — more at IMPRESS] **1 a :** a license to print or publish (as a book or paper) **b :** approval of that which is published under the circumstances that censorship of the press exists **c :** IMPRINT b(1) **2 a :** SANCTION, APPROVAL ⟨gives its ~ to the shameless attack —Eugene Lyons⟩ **b :** a sign or mark of approval ⟨puts the ~ of approval on the morals and decency of wholesale, universal betting —T.E. Dewey⟩

im·pri·ma·tu·ra \(,)im,primə'türə\ *or* **im·prim·a·ture** \im'primə,chü(ə)r\ *n* -s [modif. of It *imprimitura,* fr. *imprimito* (past part. of *imprimere* to impress, print, stamp, mark, fr. L, to impress) + *-ura* -ure — more at IMPRESS] **:** a thin preliminary glaze applied to the ground in painting

imprime *vt* [prob. fr. [2]*in-* + *prime* (first)] *obs* **:** to separate (as a deer) from the herd

imprimery *n* -ES [F *imprimerie,* fr. MF, fr. *imprimer* to print (fr. NL *imprimare*) + *-erie* -ery — more at IMPRIMATUR] *obs* **:** a printing office

im·pri·mis \im'prīməs, -rēm-\ *adv* [ME *inprimis,* fr. L *in primis* among the first (things)] **:** in the first place — used to introduce a list of items or considerations

[1]**im·print** \əm'print\ *vt* [ME *emprenten, imprenten,* fr. MF *empreinter,* fr. OF, fr. *empreinte* imprint (n.)] **1 a :** to mark by pressure (as a figure on an object or as the object itself with the figure) **:** IMPRESS ⟨a machine to ~ code numbers on metal merchandise⟩ **b** *archaic* **:** PRINT **c :** to add an imprint to ⟨~*ed* statement enclosures⟩ ⟨~ a missing letter⟩ **2 :** to fix indelibly or permanently (as on the memory) ⟨~*ing* her features, her look, her smile, her voice, upon his memory —Edith Sitwell⟩ **3 :** to stamp the characteristics of ⟨~*ing* his own personality on his productions —E.Bentley⟩ **4 :** to establish a response in by imprinting ⟨ducklings of five species were ~*ed* on human beings as their parent-companions at hatching —Margaret M. Nice⟩

[2]**im·print** \'im,p-\ *n* [modif. (influenced by [2]*in-*) of MF *empreinte,* fr. OF, fr. fem. of *empreint,* past part. of *empreindre* to imprint, impress, fr. L *imprimere* to impress, imprint — more at IMPRESS] **:** something imprinted or printed: as **a :** a mark (as a figure or symbol) made by pressure ⟨the footstep left its ~ in the mud⟩ ⟨bore the ~ of a circle and dot in the center —Zane Grey⟩ ⟨an ~ of the town seal on each bond —*Springfield (Mass.) Union*⟩ **b** (1) **:** a publisher's name often with address and date of publication usu. placed in a book at the foot of a title page (2) **:** a printer's name or identifying device usu. placed in a book on the copyright page (3) **:** a dealer's or retailer's name and address printed on matter (as a blotter, catalog, or promotional piece) put out by a wholesaler or supplier (4) **:** a correction (as of a letter that shows imperfectly in a run of printed sheets) struck in by running the printed sheets through the press a second time (5) **:** the name of the manufacturer of a stamp printed in the margin of a sheet or of a single stamp **c :** an indelible distinguishing effect or influence ⟨the teacher left her ~ on several generations of students⟩ ⟨the raw western settlements . . . so strongly marked by the ~ of the industrial process —Sinclair Lewis⟩ ⟨their walk bears a sort of regional ~ —Malcolm Cowley⟩

imprinted stamp *n* **:** a postage or revenue stamp printed directly on the piece of paper on which it is to be used as distinguished from an adhesive stamp

imprinting *n* **:** a rapid learning process that takes place early in the life of a social animal (as a greylag goose) and establishes a behavior pattern involving recognition of and attraction to identifiable attributes of its own kind or of a substitute

im·pris·on \əm'prizᵊn\ *vt* **imprisoned; imprisoned; imprisoning** \-z(ᵊ)niŋ\ **imprisons** [ME *enprisonen, imprisonen,* fr. OF *emprisoner,* fr. *en-* [1]*en-* + *prison* — more at PRISON] **1 :** to put in prison **:** confine in a jail **2 :** to limit, restrain, or confine as if by imprisoning ⟨have ~*ed* its turbulent water between granite walls —Arnold Bennett⟩ ⟨~*s* him with her possessiveness —*Newsweek*⟩ ⟨deftly and with one arm only, he ~*ed* her —Susan Ertz⟩ ⟨~*ed* little sausages in pastry and baked them —Robertson Davies⟩

im·pris·on·able \-z(ᵊ)nəbəl\ *adj* **1 :** capable of being imprisoned **2 :** legally entailing imprisonment as a penalty ⟨an ~ offense⟩

im·pris·on·ment \-zᵊnmənt\ *n* -s [ME *enprisonement, inprisonment,* fr. MF *emprisonnement,* fr. OF, fr. *emprisoner* + *-ment*] **1 :** the act of imprisoning or the state of being imprisoned **:** CONFINEMENT, RESTRAINT **2 :** constraint of a person either by force or by such other coercion as restrains him within limits against his will

im·probability \(¦)im, əm+\ *n* **1 :** the quality or state of being improbable ⟨questioned the ~ of a nuclear accident⟩ **2 :** something improbable

im·probable \(')im,əm+\ *adj* [MF or L; MF, fr. L *improbabilis,* fr. *in-* [1]*in-* + *probabilis* probable — more at PROBABLE] **:** not probable **:** unlikely to be true or to occur **:** not easily believable ⟨an ~ story⟩ ⟨an ~ event⟩ ⟨characters unreal, dialogue artificial, plots highly ~ —C.J.Rolo⟩ — **im·probably** \"+\ *adv*

im·pro·ba·tion \,imprō'bāshən\ *n* [MF, fr. L *improbation-, improbatio* disapprobation, fr. *improbatus* (past part. of *improbare* to disapprove, fr. *in-* [1]*in-* + *probare* to examine, approve, prove) + *-ion-, -io* -ion — more at PROVE] **1** *archaic* **:** DISAPPROVAL **2** [L *improbation-, improbatio*] *Scots law* **:** an act by which falsehood and forgery are proved **:** an action brought for the purpose of having some instrument declared false or forged

im·probative *also* **im·probatory** \əm+\ *adj* **:** of or belonging to improbation

im·probity \(')im,əm+\ *n* [MF or L; MF *improbité,* fr. L *improbitat-, improbitas,* fr. *improbus* bad, dishonest (fr. *in-* [1]*in-* + *probus* good, honest) + *-itat-, -itas* -ity — more at PROVE] **:** lack of probity **:** lack of integrity or rectitude **:** DISHONESTY

im·proficiency \¦im+\ *n* [[1]*in-* + *proficiency*] *archaic* **:** lack of proficiency

im·profitable \(')im,əm+\ *adj* [ME, fr. MF, fr. *in-* [1]*in-* + *profitable* — more at PROFITABLE] **:** UNPROFITABLE

im·progressive \¦im+\ *adj* [[1]*in-* + *progressive*] *archaic* **:** UNPROGRESSIVE — **im·progressively** \"+\ *adv, archaic* — **im·progressiveness** \"+\ *n, archaic*

[1]**im·promp·tu** \əm'präm(p)(,)t(y)ü, -(,)chü\ *adv* [F, fr. L *in promptu* in readiness, at hand] **:** without previous study, preparation, or consideration **:** on the spur of the moment **:** EXTEMPORANEOUSLY ⟨being able to speak ~ and at length on any given subject —Bryan MacMahon⟩ ⟨any cry of contrition that ever came ~ from a human being —C.E.Montague⟩

[2]**impromptu** \"\ *n* -s [F, fr. *impromptu,* adv.] **1 :** something made or done impromptu **:** an extemporaneous composition, address, or remark ⟨the witty ~ must not smack of the midnight oil —Cecil Lavery⟩ **2 a :** a piece of music composed or played impromptu **b :** a musical composition suggesting improvisation

[3]**impromptu** \"\ *adj* [F, fr. *impromptu,* adv.] **1 :** made, done, or formed on or as if on the spur of the moment **:** IMPROVISED, MAKESHIFT ⟨postponements or changes of plan were always ~ —Marcia Davenport⟩ ⟨delegates . . . formed for an ~ parade through the aisle —C.E.Egan⟩ ⟨an ~ bench was made of a long board placed on two chairs and covered with quilts —B.A.Botkin⟩ **2 :** composed or uttered without previous study, preparation, or consideration **:** EXTEMPORANEOUS, UNREHEARSED ⟨an ~ addition to his prepared text —Foster Hailey⟩ ⟨a short ~ speech⟩

[4]**impromptu** \"\ *vb* -ED/-ING/-S [[1]*impromptu*] **:** EXTEMPORIZE, IMPROVISE

im·proper \(')im,əm+\ *adj* [MF *impropre,* fr. L *improprius,* fr. *in-* [2]*in-* + *proprius* own, proper — more at PROPER] **:** not proper: as **a :** not accordant with fact, truth, or right procedure **:** INCORRECT, INACCURATE ⟨arrived at an ~ conclusion from the premises⟩ ⟨charges of bribery, falsification of records, acceptance of ~ fees —*Current Biog.*⟩ **b :** not regularly or normally formed or not properly so called ⟨~ fractions⟩ **c :** not suited to the circumstances, design, or end ⟨an ~ medicine⟩ **d :** not in accord with propriety, modesty, good taste, or good manners **:** INDECOROUS ⟨must not ~ to intrude a dog into the houses of the people they were calling on —Joseph Conrad⟩ ⟨highly ~ to dress ship at any time with college banners —C.D. Lane⟩ **:** INDECENT ⟨guilty of using ~ language⟩ ⟨wearing a scandalously ~ dress⟩ — **im·properly** \"+\ *adv* — **im·properness** \"+\ *n*

improper diphthong *n* **1 :** a vowel digraph **2 :** PARTIAL DIPHTHONG **3 :** an alpha, eta, or omega with an iota subscript

improper fraction *n* **:** a fraction in which the numerator is greater than or equal to the denominator or is of higher or equal degree

improper integral *n* **:** a definite integral whose region of integration includes a point at which the integrand is undefined or tends to infinity or whose region of integration does not have all limits finite

improportion *n, obs* **:** DISPROPORTION — **improportionate** *adj, obs*

improportionable *adj* [[1]*in-* + *proportionable*] *obs* **:** DISPROPORTIONATE

[1]**im·pro·pri·ate** \əm'prōprē,āt\ *vt* -ED/-ING/-S [ML or NL *impropriatus,* past part. of *impropriare,* fr. L *in-* [2]*in-* + *propriare* to appropriate — more at APPROPRIATE] **1** *obs* **:** APPROPRIATE **2 a :** to take over (a benefice or ecclesiastical property) and make one's own ⟨the town which had *impropriated*

the revenues of the church —T.D.Atkinson⟩ **b :** to transfer (monastic property) to lay control or ownership — distinguished from *appropriate*

²im·pro·pri·ate \-ət\ *adj* [NL or ML *impropriatus*] **:** IMPROPRIATED **:** lay as distinguished from clerical

im·pro·pri·a·tion \(,)im,prōprē'āshən, əm-\ *n* -s **1 :** the act of impropriating or state of being impropriate **2 :** something impropriated **:** APPROPRIATION

im·pro·pri·a·tor \əm'prōprē,ād·ə(r)\ *n* -s **:** one to or by whom something is impropriated

im·propriety \¦im+\ *n* [F or LL; F *impropriété*, fr. LL *improprietat-, improprietas*, fr. L *improprius* improper + *-tat-, -tas* -ty — more at IMPROPER] **1 :** the quality or state of being improper ⟨shocked by the ~ of the young man's action⟩ ⟨guilty of ~ of speech and indecency of dress⟩ ⟨saw no ~ in giving preferment to personal friends and relatives —W.E. Stevens⟩ **2 :** something improper **:** an unsuitable or improper act or remark ⟨puns and jokes and pungent *improprieties* —*Times Lit. Supp.*⟩; *specif* **:** an unacceptable use of a word or of language

im·prosperous \(')im,əm+\ *adj* [¹*in-* + *prosperous*] *archaic* **:** not prosperous **:** POOR, UNSUCCESSFUL

im·prov·abil·i·ty \(,)im,prüvə'biləd·ē, əm-, -lətē, -i\ *n* **:** the quality or state of being improvable **:** capability of improving or of being improved

im·prov·able \əm'prüvəbəl\ *adj* [²*improve* + *-able*] **1** *archaic* **:** capable of being profited from or turned to good account **2 :** capable of improving or of being improved **:** susceptible of improvement — **im·prov·able·ness** \-bəlnəs\ *n* — **im·prov·a·bly** \-blē,-bli\ *adv*

¹im·prove \əm'prüv\ *vt* [ME *improven*, fr. MF *improver*, fr. L *improbare* to disapprove, blame, reject — more at IMPROBATION] **1 a** *obs* **:** to show to be wrong **:** CONFUTE **b** *Scots law* **:** to prove false or forged **:** DISPROVE, INVALIDATE **2** *obs* **:** REPROVE, CENSURE

²improve \"\ *vb* [alter. (influenced by *approve*) of earlier *emprou, emprow*, fr. AF *emprouer* to invest profitably, to cultivate profitably, fr. OF *en-* ¹en- + *prou* profit — more at PROW] *vt* **1 a :** to make greater in amount or degree **:** INCREASE, AUGMENT, ENLARGE, INTENSIFY ⟨*improved* the chance that the committee could reach agreement⟩ **b** *obs* **:** to raise the price of **c** *obs* **:** to make (an evil) worse **2 a :** to enhance in value or quality **:** make more profitable, excellent, or desirable ⟨~ the appearance of a display⟩ ⟨~ one's health by exercise⟩ ⟨exhibited an *improved* optical viewfinder —*Americana Annual*⟩ **b** *archaic* **:** to speak on in order to make more generally profitable or turn to better spiritual account **c :** to increase the value of (land or property) by bringing under cultivation, reclaiming for agriculture or stock raising, erecting buildings or other structures, laying out streets, or installing utilities (as sewers) ⟨*improved* farmland⟩ **d** *Scots law* **:** to grant (a lease) for a long term to encourage a tenant in good husbandry **e :** to grade and drain (a road) and apply surfacing material (as gravel, crushed rock, or oil) other than pavement **3** *archaic* **a :** to avail oneself of **:** EMPLOY, USE **b :** OCCUPY **4 a :** to turn to profit or to good account **:** employ to good purpose **:** use to advantage ⟨~ an opportunity to make friends⟩ ⟨~ one's time by studying⟩ **b** *archaic* **:** to cause (money or capital) to yield a profit by investment **5 a :** to turn or convert by improving ⟨~ a nag into a racehorse⟩ **b :** to spend, remove, or dissipate by improvements ⟨a tribe *improved* out of existence⟩ ~ *vi* **1 a :** INCREASE, AUGMENT ⟨the price of cotton is *improving*⟩ ⟨the demand for more commodities *improved*⟩ **b :** to rise in value **:** enhance in price ⟨stocks are *improving*⟩ **2 :** to advance or make progress in what is desirable **:** grow better ⟨the invalid's health *improved* daily⟩

syn IMPROVE, BETTER, AMELIORATE, and HELP mean to correct, make more acceptable, or bring nearer to a higher standard of goodness in part or in some degree. IMPROVE and BETTER are general and interchangeable and are often used of things that are orig. bad or unacceptable ⟨famed for his quick wit and his ability to *improve* a script during a performance —G.S. Perry⟩ ⟨increase his powers of field observation and notation while he *improves* his knowledge of the area —J.F.Hart & Eugene Mather⟩ ⟨*bettering* the general conditions of tenant farmers —*Current Biog.*⟩ ⟨has invariably *bettered* the tunes and often transformed a doggerel text into excellent poetry —*Amer. Guide Series: Tenn.*⟩ AMELIORATE is applied chiefly to things that are unacceptable, esp. conditions difficult to endure or causing suffering, and implies partial relief or alterations that make the conditions more tolerable ⟨*ameliorate* the lot of thousands of victimized human beings —Arnold Bennett⟩ ⟨abolish feudalism or *ameliorate* its vices —W.O. Douglas⟩ ⟨his care in *ameliorating* personality conflicts —Harold Koontz & Cyril O'Donnell⟩ HELP implies a bettering that still leaves room for improvement ⟨*help* farmers meet the fertilizer shortage⟩ ⟨exercises to *help* overcome a speech defect⟩

— **improve on** *or* **improve upon :** to improve or make useful additions or amendments to ⟨an inventor who *improved on* the carburetor system of the automobile⟩ ⟨remembered all the backwoods stories his customers told him — and doubtlessly *improved on* them a little —G.S.Perry⟩

improved cylinder *n* **:** a gun barrel with a choke

improved wood *n* **:** wood that has been strengthened by the filling in or closing of the voids in the cellular structure and by compression under heat

im·prove·ment \-vmənt\ *n* -s [alter. of ME *emprowment* profitable investment, profitable cultivation of land, fr. AF *emprouement*, fr. *emprouer* + OF *-ment*] **1 :** the act or process of improving: as **a :** profitable employment or use ⟨the ~ of one's time in reading⟩ **b :** BETTERMENT ⟨went to college not for a degree but for professional ~⟩ **:** AMELIORATION ⟨the ~ of the patient's state of health⟩ **c :** the enhancement or augmentation of value or quality **:** an increasing of profitableness, excellence, or desirability ⟨an ~ of farm stock⟩ ⟨an ~ of the property by building several outbuildings and a new barn⟩ ⟨an ~ in living standards⟩ **2 a :** the state of being improved; *esp* **:** enhanced value or excellence ⟨saw a great ~ in the man's health and frame of mind⟩ ⟨pleased by the ~ of the transportation system⟩ **b :** an instance of such improvement **:** something that improves in this way: as (1) **:** a permanent addition to or betterment of real property that enhances its capital value and that involves the expenditure of labor or money and is designed to make the property more useful or valuable as distinguished from ordinary repairs — see BENEFICIAL IMPROVEMENT, NECESSARY IMPROVEMENT, VOLUNTARY IMPROVEMENT (2) **:** an alteration or addition to an existing subject of invention or discovery that does not destroy its identity or essential character but accomplishes greater efficiency or economy **:** a modification improving and making more valuable an existing discovery or invention

improvement factor *n* **:** an annual increase in compensation that enables workers to share in the benefits from increased productivity — usu. used in labor negotiations

improvements and betterments insurance *n* **:** insurance for the benefit of a tenant covering improvements made by the tenant to property which he occupies under lease

im·prov·er \əm'prüvə(r)\ *n* **:** one that improves: as **a** *chiefly Brit* (1) **:** an employee who accepts instruction or the opportunity to work in place of wages (2) **:** a worker who has completed an apprenticeship but is not yet qualified as a full-fledged member of a trade or occupation **b :** a device for giving shape to a dress; *esp* **:** BUSTLE **c :** an agent added to improve a substance ⟨potassium bromate is used as a flour ~⟩

im·providence \(')im,əm+\ *n* [MF or LL; MF, fr. LL *improvidentia*, fr. *improvident-, improvidens* + L *-ia* -y] **:** the quality or state of being improvident ⟨unemployment compensation and pensions against ~ in old age —C.O.Gregory⟩

im·provident \(')im,əm+\ *adj* [LL *improvident-, improvidens*, fr. L *in-* ¹in- + *provident-, providens* provident — more at PROVIDENT] **:** not provident **:** lacking foresight or forethought **:** not foreseeing or providing for the future **:** NEGLIGENT, THRIFTLESS ⟨~ throughout his brilliant career . . . in later years became penniless —*Amer. Guide Series: Md.*⟩ ⟨I'm ~; I live in the moment when I'm happy —Edith Wharton⟩ — **im·providently** \"+\ *adv*

im·providentially \(')im,əm+\ *adv* **:** IMPROVIDENTLY

improving *adj* [fr. pres. part. of ²*improve*] **:** morally or intellectually uplifting or designed to be so often to the detriment of any intrinsic excellence ⟨urged his children to read only ~ literature⟩ — **im·prov·ing·ly** *adv*

im·provi·sate \əm'prävə,zāt *sometimes* 'imprəvə̇,z- *or* əm'prävə,sāt\ *vb* -ED/-ING/-S [back-formation fr. *improvisation*] **:** IMPROVISE

im·provi·sa·tion \(,)im,prävə'zāshən, əm- *also* ,imprəvə̇'z- *sometimes* (,)=,prävə'sā- *or* ,imprə,vī'zā- *or* (,)=,prōvə'zā- *or* -ōvə'sā-\ *n* -s [F, fr. *improviser* + *-ation*] **1 :** the act of improvising or the quality or state of being improvised: as **a** (1) **:** extemporaneous composition (as of music or poetry) (2) **:** the extemporaneousness of such composition **b** (1) **:** a course pursued in accordance with no previously devised plan, policy, or consideration ⟨his conduct at the time was merely an ~⟩ ⟨the policy of a democracy thus becomes an eternal ~ —H.L.Mencken⟩ ⟨the flight into the East was not an ~, a sudden, last-minute, desperate measure —A.R. Williams⟩ (2) **:** the extemporaneous quality of such a course ⟨the ~ of the country's relation with foreign powers⟩ **2 :** something improvised or designed to seem improvised **:** IMPROMPTU — **im·provi·sa·tion·al** \-āshən°l,-āshnəl\ *adj*

im·provi·sa·tor *pronunc at* IMPROVISATE + ə(r)\ *n* -s [F or It; F *improvisateur*, fr. It *improvvisatore*, fr. *improvvisato* (past part. of *improvvisare*) + *-ore* -or] **:** IMPROVISER, IMPROVISATORE ⟨he has been a great ~, and that his improvisation is not without merit is proved by his spectacular career —O.D. Tolischus⟩

im·prov·i·sa·to·re \əm,prävəzə'tōrē\ *n, pl* **improvisato·ri** \"\ *or* **improvisatores** \-ēz\ [It *improvvisatore*] **:** IMPROVISER; *esp* **:** one who composes and recites verse extempore

im·prov·i·sa·to·ri·al \əm¦prävəzə¦tōrēəl\ *adj* **:** of or relating to improvisation — **im·prov·i·sa·to·ri·al·ly** \-ēəlē\ *adv*

im·provi·sa·to·ry \əm'prävəzə,tōrē, ,imprə,vīz-, *chiefly Brit* ,imprə,vīzātəri *or* -ā·tri\ *adj* **:** IMPROVISATORIAL

im·prov·i·sa·tri·ce \əm,prävəzə'trēchē\ *n, pl* **improvisatri·ci** \"\ *or* **improvisatrices** \-chēz\ [It *improvvisatrice*, fr. *improvvisatore*] **:** a female improvisatore

im·pro·vise \'imprə,vīz *also* ,=='=\ *vb* -ED/-ING/-S [F *improviser*, fr. It *improvvisare*, fr. *improvviso* unprovided, sudden, extempore, fr. L *improvisus* unforeseen, unexpected, fr. *in-* ¹in- + *provisus* foreseen — more at PROVISO] *vt* **1 :** to compose, recite, or sing esp. in verse or to play on an instrument or act extemporaneously ⟨his cast, who ~ dialogue, gags, and situations as they go along —*Current Biog.*⟩ **2 a :** to bring about, arrange, or make on the spur of the moment or without preparation ⟨the cook . . . hastily *improvised* a supper —Willa Cather⟩ ⟨housed in *improvised* temporary quarters —*Report: (Canadian) Royal Commission on Nat'l Development*⟩ ⟨had to ~ policy always —James Cameron⟩ **b :** to construct or fabricate out of what is conveniently at hand ⟨an *improvised* laboratory —*Current Biog.*⟩ ⟨fish . . . with *improvised* hooks and lines —*Amer. Guide Series: N.Y. City*⟩ ~ *vi* **:** to improvise something esp. in verse or music **:** EXTEMPORIZE

im·pro·vis·er *or* **im·pro·vi·sor** \-zə(r)\ *n* -s **:** one that improvises

¹im·provision \¦im+\ *n* [¹*in-* + *provision*] **:** lack of forethought **:** IMPROVIDENCE

²im·pro·vi·sion \,imprə'vizhən\ *n* [*improvise* + *-ion*] **:** IMPROVISATION

im·pro·vi·so \,imprə'vē(,)zō\ *adv (or adj)* [It *improvviso* — more at IMPROVISE] **:** EXTEMPORE

im·prudence \(')im, əm+\ *n* [MF or L; MF, fr. L *imprudentia*, fr. *imprudent-, imprudens* + *-ia* -y] **1 :** the quality or state of being imprudent **:** lack of caution, circumspection, or due regard to consequences **2 :** an imprudent act

im·prudency \"+\ *n* -ES [L *imprudentia*] *archaic* **:** IMPRUDENCE

im·prudent \(')im, əm+\ *adj* [ME, fr. L *imprudent-, imprudens*, fr. *in-* ¹in- + *prudent-, prudens* prudent — more at PRUDENT] **:** not prudent **:** lacking discretion **:** INJUDICIOUS ⟨very ~ in her parent to encourage her . . . in such idolatry and silly romantic ideas —W.M.Thackeray⟩ ⟨the deep ulcer on my leg . . . renders it ~ to take passage at this time —C.B. Nordhoff & J.N.Hall⟩ ⟨would be ~ for a noneconomist to talk about the details of economic policy —A.M.Schlesinger b.1917⟩ — **im·prudently** \"+\ *adv* — **im·prudentness** \"+\ *n* -ES

imps *pl of* IMP, *pres 3d sing of* IMP

imp·son·ite \'im(p)sə,nīt\ *n* -s [*Impson* valley, Oklahoma + E *-ite*] **:** a mineral consisting of an asphalt much like albertite but almost insoluble in turpentine

impt *abbr* important

imptr *abbr* importer

im·puberty \(')im, əm+\ *n* [ML *impubertas*, fr. L *in-* ¹in- + *pubertas* puberty — more at PUBERTY] **:** the quality or state of not having reached puberty

im·pubic \"+\ *adj* [L *impubes* (fr. *in-* ¹in- + *pubes* adult) + E *-ic* — more at PUBES] **:** not arrived at puberty **:** IMMATURE ⟨toiled in the fields with her ~ children —Thomas Beer⟩

im·pu·dence \'impyəd·ən(t)s *also* -d°n-\ *also* **im·pu·den·cy** \-nsē,-si\ *n, pl* **impudences** *also* **impudencies** [*impudence* fr. ME, fr. L *impudentia*, fr. *impudent-, impudens* impudent + *-ia* -y; *impudency* fr. L *impudentia*] **1 :** the quality or state of being impudent: as **a** *obs* **:** SHAMELESSNESS, INDECENCY **b :** an attitude marked by disrespect or insolence **:** cocky self-assurance **c** *archaic* **:** cool self-possession or self-reliance **2 :** an impudent remark or act ⟨the mother would not endure her son's ~s⟩

im·pu·dent \-nt\ *adj* [ME, fr. L *impudent-, impudens*, fr. *in-* ¹in- + *pudent-, pudens*, pres. part of *pudēre* to feel shame — more at PUDIC] **1** *obs* **:** lacking modesty **2 :** marked by contemptuous or cocky boldness or disregard of others ⟨an arrogant and ~ boy given to insulting strangers⟩ **:** INSOLENT ⟨stood there . . . in an ~ swaggering posture —Helen T. Lowe⟩ **:** FORWARD, DISRESPECTFUL ⟨entertainingly ~ stories —Gerald Bullett⟩ **:** bold and brazen ⟨one of the most ~ miscarriages of justice⟩ **syn** see SHAMELESS

im·pu·dent·ly *adv* **:** in an impudent manner

im·pu·dent·ness *n* -ES **:** IMPUDENCE

im·pu·dic·i·ty \,impyə'disəd·ē, -yü'-\ *n* [MF *impudicité*, fr. L *impudicus* immodest, shameless (fr. *in-* ¹in- + *pudicus* bashful, modest, chaste) + MF *-ité* -ity — more at PUDIC] **:** IMMODESTY, SHAMELESSNESS

im·pugn \əm'pyün\ *vt* -ED/-ING/-S [ME *impugnen, impungnen*, fr. MF *impugner*, fr. L *impugnare*, fr. *in-* ²in- + *pugnare* to fight — more at PUGNACIOUS] **1** *obs* **a :** to assail physically **:** FIGHT **b :** OPPOSE, RESIST **2 :** to assail by words or arguments **:** call into question **:** make insinuations against **:** GAINSAY ⟨~ one's honesty⟩ ⟨~ one's claim to property⟩ ⟨frequent recourse to sword or pistol, whenever honor was ~*ed* —*Amer. Guide Series: La.*⟩ **syn** see DENY

im·pugn·able \-nəbəl\ *adj* **:** capable of being impugned **:** subject to question

im·pugna·tion *n* -s [ME *impugnacioun, impungnacioun*, fr. MF or L; MF *impugnation*, fr. L *impugnation-, impugnatio*, fr. *impugnatus* (past part. of *impugnare* to impugn) + *-ion-, -io* -ion] **1** \,im,pəg'nāshən\ *obs* **:** ATTACK, OPPOSITION **2** \,im,pyü'n-\ *archaic* **:** IMPUGNMENT

im·pugn·ment \əm'pyünmənt\ *n* -s **:** the act of bringing into question or gainsaying or the state of being brought into question or gainsaid

im·puissance \(')im, əm+\ *n* [MF, fr. *in-* ¹in- + *puissance* — more at PUISSANCE] **:** POWERLESSNESS, WEAKNESS

im·puissant \"+\ *adj* [F, fr. MF, fr. *in-* ¹in- + *puissant* — more at PUISSANT] **:** POWERLESS, FEEBLE

¹im·pulse \'im,pəls *also* -lts\ *n* [L *impulsus*, fr. *impulsus*, past part. of *impellere* to impel — more at IMPEL] **1 a :** the act of driving onward with sudden force **:** IMPULSION, THRUST, DRIVE, PUSH **b :** the effect of an impelling force **:** motion produced by a sudden or momentary force **:** IMPETUS ⟨the ~ of the pumping by the heart is carried down so that a finger applied to the artery anywhere near the surface permits a counting of the pulse rate —Morris Fishbein⟩ **c :** a wave of excitation transmitted through certain tissues and esp. nerve fibers and muscles that results in physiological activity or inhibition **d :** an electrical or mechanical action or force usu. of brief duration ⟨the ~s received by the radio set are . . . unimaginably small —A.C.Morrison⟩; *specif* **:** such an action or force actuating an operation (as in a computer) ⟨can be started either by hand or by an air ~ —*Swiss Industry & Trade*⟩ **2 a :** a force so communicated as to produce motion suddenly or immediately ⟨an ~ of the wind⟩: (1) **:** the motive force given by the escape wheel in the driving train of a timepiece to the pendulum or balance (2) **:** the muscular effort initiating a rhythmic dance movement (3) **:** a short directed motion ⟨written with one ~ of the pen —J.R.Gregg⟩ **b :** INCENTIVE ⟨under the ~ of transportation profits —*Amer. Guide Series: Mich.*⟩ **c :** an inspiration or motivation esp. giving a usu. new form or tendency ⟨those who give the religious life a new ~ need disciples to organize the impulse before it runs to seed —Hallam Tennyson⟩ ⟨his more successful stories derive from the same kind of ~ as his poetry —F.R.Leavis⟩ ⟨he received from America fresh artistic ~s —Anatole Chujoy⟩ **3 a :** a sudden spontaneous inclination or an incitement of the mind or spirit arising either directly from feeling or from some outer influence and prompting some usu. unpremeditated action ⟨constitutionally inclined to resist ~ and to take long views —George Santayana⟩ ⟨some uncontrollable ~ . . . may have driven the defendant to the commission of the murderous act —B.N.Cardozo⟩ ⟨act on ~⟩; *also* **:** the force actuated by such a motive or propensity ⟨a man who is driven chiefly by ~⟩ ⟨~s of greed —Bertrand Russell⟩ **b :** a propensity or natural tendency usu. other than rational ⟨a man of good ~s⟩ ⟨the sexual ~⟩ ⟨the fundamental ~ of self-expression —Havelock Ellis⟩ ⟨the systematizing ~, the restless passion for order of the Greeks —John Buchan⟩ ⟨never approaches a new task save with the ~ to postpone it —H.A.Overstreet⟩ **4 a :** the product of the average value of a force and the time during which it acts being a quantity equal to the change in momentum produced by the force if the body acted on is free **b :** PULSE 4a

syn SEE MOTIVE

²im·pulse \", əm'p-\ *vt* [L *impulsus*, past part.] **1 :** to give an impulse to **2 :** to initiate an impulse in (a counter of a computer)

impulse buying *n* **:** the buying of merchandise on impulse rather than from premeditation

impulse charge *n* **:** an explosive used to provide an initial impetus (as to a torpedo)

impulse excitation *n* **:** a method of producing damped alternating current in which the duration of the impressed voltage is short compared with the duration of the current produced — compare QUENCHED GAP

impulse face *n* **:** the lifting plane of one of the club teeth of the escape wheel in a lever-escapement watch or the surface of the pallet stone which is engaged thereby

impulse goods *n* **:** merchandise (as inexpensive or luxury items) likely to be bought on impulse or without significant forethought as opposed to staple or essential goods

impulse movement *n* **:** a clock movement (as of a turret clock) in which the hands are driven by means of energy received by its pendulum in the form of electromagnetic impulses

impulse pallet *n* **:** a pallet stone in a roller of a chronometer balance that receives the driving impulse of the teeth of the escape wheel

impulse pin *n* **:** ROLLER JEWEL

impulse turbine *n* **:** a turbine in which the rotor is driven by fluid jets impinging directly against the blades — compare REACTION TURBINE

im·pul·sion \əm'pəlshən\ *n* -s [ME, fr. MF or L; MF, fr. L *impulsion-, impulsio*, fr. *impulsus* (past part. of *impellere* to impel) + *-ion-, -io* -ion — more at IMPEL] **1 a :** the act of impelling or the state of being impelled **:** the sudden or momentary action of a body in motion impinging on another body **b :** the impelling force or impulse **c :** an onward tendency derived from an impulsion **:** IMPETUS; *specif* **:** a marked or vigorous forward drive of a horse in a gait **2 a :** an influence acting usu. unexpectedly or temporarily on the mind or will and urging to action; *also* **:** an action provoked by such an influence **b :** drive to motor activity or creative effort **c :** IMPULSE 2c **3 :** COMPULSION 2

im·pul·sive \(')im¦pəls¦iv, əm'p-, |ēv *also* -l(t)s| *or* |əv-\ *adj* [prob. fr. MF *impulsif*, fr. *impulsion* + *-if* -ive] **1 :** having the power of or actually driving or impelling ⟨an ~ force⟩ ⟨an ~ influence⟩ **2 a :** actuated by or esp. prone to act on impulse ⟨a houseful of ~ children⟩ ⟨the ~ buying of luxury items⟩ ⟨~, capricious and touchy —D.C.Buchanan⟩ ⟨men's thoughtless or ~ acts —M.R.Cohen⟩ **b :** COMPULSIVE 3 **3 :** acting momentarily ⟨a motor giving the mechanism ~ thrusts⟩ **syn** see SPONTANEOUS

im·pul·sive·ly \|əvlē, -li\ *adv* **:** in an impulsive manner ⟨so happy she flung her arms ~ around his neck and kissed him⟩

im·pul·sive·ness \|ivnə̇s, |ēv- *also* |əv-\ *n* -ES **:** the quality or state of being impulsive ⟨the ~ with which he took up attractive theories —H.E.Scudder⟩

im·pul·siv·i·ty \,im,pəl'sivəd·ē, -vətē, -i *also* -lt's-\ *n* -ES **:** IMPULSIVENESS

impulsor *n* -s [L, fr. *impulsus* (past part.) + *-or*] *obs* **:** one that impels

im·punctate \(')im, əm+\ *adj* [¹*in-* + *punctate*] **:** lacking pores ⟨an ~ brachiopod shell⟩ or impressed punctate markings ⟨a beetle with elytra ~⟩

impunely *adv* [obs. E *impune* unpunished (fr. L *impunis*) + *-ly*] *obs* **:** with impunity

im·pu·ni·bly \(')im¦pyünəblē, əm'p-\ *adv* [L *impunis* + E *-ible* + *-ly*] *archaic* **:** with impunity

im·pu·ni·ty \əm'pyünəd·ē, -nətē, -i\ *n* -ES [MF or L; MF *impunité*, fr. L *impunitat-, impunitas*, fr. *impunis* unpunished (back-formation fr. *impune*, adv., without punishment, fr. *in-* ¹in- + *-pune*, irreg. fr. *poena* punishment, pain) + *-itat-, -itas* -ity — more at PAIN] **:** exemption or freedom from punishment, harm, or loss ⟨trespassing with ~⟩ ⟨many individuals can with apparent ~ remain essentially infants forever, intellectually —Weston La Barre⟩

¹im·pure \(')im, əm+\ *adj* [F & L; F, fr. L *impurus*, fr. *in-* ¹in- + *purus* pure — more at PURE] **1 :** not pure: as **a :** UNCHASTE, LEWD, OBSCENE ⟨~ language⟩ ⟨given to ~ ideas⟩ **b :** containing something unclean **:** DIRTY, FOUL, FILTHY, UNWHOLESOME ⟨~ water⟩ ⟨~ air⟩ **c :** unclean for ceremonial or religious purposes or not purified or hallowed by rites **:** DEFILED, UNHOLY, UNHALLOWED **d :** not accurate **:** not idiomatic ⟨~ Latin⟩ **:** marked by an intermixture of foreign elements ⟨an ~ dialect⟩ or by substandard, incongruous, or objectionable locutions ⟨an ~ style⟩ **e :** mixed or impregnated with an extraneous esp. inferior substance **:** ADULTERATED, UNRECTIFIED ⟨an ~ chemical⟩ ⟨~ food⟩ ⟨an ~ diamond⟩ **f** *of art or decoration* **:** MIXED, BASTARD ⟨an ~ style of ornamentation⟩ **g :** designed to serve a purpose chiefly other than artistic — used of art or an art form (as a poem or painting) ⟨there is ~ poetry, social and political poetry —Jacob Isaacs⟩ **2 :** HETEROZYGOUS — **im·purely** \"+\ *adv* — **im·pureness** \"+\ *n*

²impure *vt, obs* **:** to make impure

im·pu·ri·fy \əm'pyúrə,fī\ *vt* [¹*impure* + *-ify*] **:** to make impure **:** ADULTERATE ⟨a source that is being continually *impurified* by alien additions —Walter de la Mare⟩

im·puritan \(')im, əm+\ *n* [¹*in-* + *puritan*] **:** one who is not a puritan or who is opposed to puritanism

im·purity \(')im, əm+\ *n* [ME *impurite*, fr. L *impuritas*, fr. *impurus* + *-itas* -ity] **1 :** the quality or state of being impure **2 :** something impure (as foul matter or obscene language) or something that makes impure (as a foreign ingredient)

impurple *obs var of* EMPURPLE

imput *var of* INPUT

im·put·abil·i·ty \(,)im,pyüd·ə'biləd·ē, əm-, -ütə'-, -lətē, -i\ *n* **:** the quality or state of being imputable

im·put·able \əm'pyüd·əbəl, -ütə-\ *adj* [F or ML; F, fr. MF, fr. ML *imputabilis*, fr. L *imputare* to impute + *-abilis* -able — more at IMPUTE] **1 :** capable of being imputed **:** ASCRIBABLE, ATTRIBUTABLE, REFERABLE ⟨insofar as he was only acting as an agent the oversight was not ~ to him⟩ ⟨an occasional blurring of outline . . . is ~ to the music rather than the words —*Times Lit. Supp.*⟩ **2** *archaic* **:** capable of being accused or blamed **:** CULPABLE — **im·put·able·ness** \-bəlnəs\ *n* -ES — **im·put·a·bly** \-blē,-bli\ *adv*

im·pu·ta·tion \,impyə'tāshən\ *n* -s [MF or LL; MF, fr. LL *imputation-, imputatio*, fr. L *imputatus* (past part. of *imputare* to impute) + *-ion-, -io* -ion] **1 :** the act of imputing: as **a :** ATTRIBUTION, ASCRIPTION ⟨the ~ of emotions, attitudes, and purposes as an explanation of overt behavior —Ernest Nagel⟩ **b :** ACCUSATION ⟨if . . . told that we are wrong we resent the ~ —J.H.Robinson †1936⟩ **:** INSINUATION ⟨resented the

~ that he had any direct responsibility for what she wrote —Millicent Bell⟩ **c :** the theological attribution of sin or righteousness to one on account of another's sin or righteousness **2 :** something imputed **3 :** the determining of the significance usu. to final profit of an element or factor or of each element or factor in a total industrial or merchandising process

im·pu·ta·tion·al \ˌimpyəˈtāshənᵊl, -shnəl\ *adj* **:** of or relating to imputation

im·pu·ta·tive \əmˈpyüd·əd·ˌiv, -ütət\ *adj* [LL *imputativus*, fr. L *imputatus* + *-ivus* -ive] **:** transferred by imputation ⟨the ~ sin of Adam⟩ — **im·pu·ta·tive·ly** \ˌlivlē, -li\ *adv* — **im·pu·ta·tive·ness** \ˌivnəs\ *n* -ES

im·pute \əmˈpyüt, *usu* -üd.+V\ *vt* -ED/-ING/-S [ME *inputen*, fr. L *imputare*, fr. *in-* ²in- + *putare* to consider, think — more at PAVE] **1 a :** to attribute accusingly **:** lay the responsibility or blame for sometimes falsely or unjustly ⟨accused him of her own fault, in *imputing* to him the wreck of her project —George Meredith⟩ **b :** to credit or ascribe to a person or a cause ⟨*imputing* to me better qualities than I possess⟩ ⟨our vices as well as our virtues have been *imputed* to bodily derangement —B.N.Cardozo⟩ ⟨*imputing* his visit to a wish of hearing that she was better —Jane Austen⟩ often falsely, accusingly, or unjustly ⟨soon began to believe in the opulence *imputed* to me —L.P.Smith⟩ ⟨*imputing* to him a guilt of which he was innocent —Edith Sitwell⟩ ⟨how dare you . . . ~ such monstrous intentions to me —G.B.Shaw⟩ **c :** to make a legal imposition of (as a charge against someone) **d :** to credit by transferal (a virtue or the benefit of a good work) to the account of someone other than the initiating agent **2** *obs* **:** RECKON, CONSIDER, REGARD **3 :** IMPART, GIVE ⟨with his hand he ~s life to clay —Samuel Alexander⟩ **4** *obs* **:** to charge someone with a wrongdoing or crime **syn** see ASCRIBE

imputed *adj* **:** being the value in terms of money or hypothetical income receivable from something one has or owns that would yield real income if one wished (as a house one owns and uses but might rent) ⟨~ rent⟩ ⟨~ income⟩

im·put·ed·ly *adv* **:** by imputation

imputed value *n* **:** the value of a thing determined from its utility rather than by adding the cost of its constituent elements

im·putrescibility \ˌim+\ *n* **:** the quality or state of being imputrescible

im·putrescible \ˌim+\ *adj* [LL *imputrescibilis*, fr. L *in-* ¹in- + LL *putrescibilis* putrescible — more at PUTRESCIBLE] **:** not subject to putrescence **:** not capable of putrefaction

impv *abbr* imperative

impx *abbr* [L *imperatrix*] empress

¹in \(ˈ)in, ən; *usu* ᵊn *after* t, d, s, *or* z *as in "split in two", often* ᵊm *after* p *or* b *as in "up in front", often* ᵊŋ *after* k *or* g *as in "sick in bed", often* n *before* ə *as in "he's in a hurry"*\ *prep* [ME, fr. OE; akin to OHG *in*, prep., in, ON *ī*, Goth *in*, L *in*, Gk *en*, OPruss *en*, Russ *v, vo, vn-*] **1 a** (1) — used as a function word to indicate location or position in space or in some materially bounded object ⟨put the key ~ the lock⟩ ⟨travel ~ Italy⟩ ⟨play ~ the street⟩ ⟨wounded ~ the leg⟩ ⟨read ~ bed⟩ ⟨look up a quotation ~ a book⟩ (2) *chiefly Brit* **:** ON ⟨squatting down ~ his heels —R.M.Daw⟩ ⟨tramcars which run ~ tracks—*Manual of Firemanship (Gt. Brit.)*⟩ ⟨best dwelling house ~ the island —Padraic Fallon⟩ (3) **:** INTO ⟨broke ~ pieces⟩ ⟨called ~ council on many occasions —*U.S.Investor*⟩ ⟨threw it ~ the fire⟩ ⟨wouldn't let her ~ the house —*Springfield (Mass.) Daily News*⟩ **b** (1) — used as a function word to indicate position or location in something immaterial or intangible ⟨saw him ~ my dreams⟩ ⟨the position of the artist ~ society⟩ or the fact of belonging to a group or association ⟨you're ~ the army now⟩ ⟨are you ~ the orchestra⟩ (2) — used as a function word to indicate activity, occupation, or purpose ⟨advanced ~ hot pursuit⟩ ⟨~ search of lost treasure⟩ ⟨~ honor of this event⟩ ⟨what is all this ~ aid of . . . —*Sydney (Australia) Bull.*⟩ (3) — used as a function word to indicate a position or relationship of authority or responsibility ⟨~ charge of the company's affairs⟩ ⟨~ command of the garrison⟩ (4) **:** in the course of ⟨~ cooling this material hardens⟩ ⟨drowned ~ crossing the river⟩ (5) — used as a function word to indicate close connection by way of implication or active participation ⟨~ the plot⟩ ⟨~ an amateur play⟩ (6) — used as a function word to indicate engagement in a business identified with a particular commodity ⟨he's ~ oil, he's ~ rice —Ethel Merman⟩ ⟨her mother's family were . . . ~ butter —Mary Manning⟩ ⟨was ~ buttons but had started to expand into novelties —Mary Barrett⟩ **c** (1) — used as a function word to indicate a material, mental, or moral situation or condition ⟨a house ~ ruins⟩ ⟨a boy ~ love⟩ ⟨he's ~ luck⟩ ⟨~ great pain⟩ ⟨up to his waist ~ water⟩ or an environing condition ⟨the city lay ~ darkness⟩ ⟨basking ~ sunshine⟩ (2) — used as a function word to indicate something that envelops or covers ⟨a book bound ~ buckram⟩ ⟨covered ~ mud —Nevil Shute⟩ ⟨covered ~ . . . cotton plaid —*Spiegel's Catalog*⟩ (3) — used as a function word to indicate a cultivated or natural plant cover ⟨valley bottom is ~ grass —P.E. James⟩ ⟨75 percent of all the cropped land is ~ cereals —Samuel Van Valkenburg & Ellsworth Huntington⟩ ⟨most of the surface is ~ woods or brush —L.E.Klimm⟩ (4) — used as a function word to indicate something that is being worn ⟨a tall man ~ a bowler hat —Christopher Isherwood⟩ ⟨racing the horse ~ blinders⟩; often used to indicate a salient characteristic of what is being worn ⟨a lady ~ black⟩ **d** — used as a function word with an accompanying concrete word to indicate a physiological condition or process (as pregnancy or the condition of producing or yielding) ⟨~ lamb⟩ ⟨a cow ~ milk⟩ **e** (1) — used as a function word with an accompanying concrete word to indicate affluence or easy financial circumstances ⟨the Madrileño ~ the money loves to make a splash —E.D.Hauser⟩ ⟨I am generally ~ cash —Lord Byron⟩ (2) — used as a function word to indicate possession or display of some trait or attribute ⟨a gentleman ~ a gray goatee —Al Hine⟩ ⟨the sheep are ~ wool⟩ ⟨the corn's ~ silk and tassel —G.S.Perry⟩ ⟨~ figure slim —W.H.Hudson †1922⟩ **f :** under the influence of (an alcoholic drink) ⟨when ~ liquor, he would scutter up a tree like a squirrel —S.H.Adams⟩ ⟨~ drink⟩ ⟨~ one's cups⟩ **2 a** (1) **:** within the limits of a space of time expressed or implied ⟨early ~ April⟩ ⟨come ~ time⟩ ⟨~ the days of my childhood⟩ ⟨~ a few minutes he was there⟩ (2) **:** during the course of **:** DURING ⟨~ his long journeys throughout the country —Darcy Ribeiro⟩ ⟨~ all that time I never saw him⟩ (3) **:** during the space of **:** at any time during **:** FOR ⟨the coldest day ~ twenty years⟩ ⟨have not seen him ~ months⟩ **b :** AT ⟨united ~ this time of peril⟩ ⟨vested in the governor acting ~ his discretion —*Achievement in the Gold Coast*⟩ **c** — used as a function word to indicate a proportion or rate ⟨the mix was one ~ twenty —F.W.Crofts⟩ **3 a** (1) — used as a function word to indicate means or instrumentality ⟨scribbled and scratched over . . . ~ pencil or nail —William Faulkner⟩ ⟨caught his coat ~ the gate latch —L.Y.Erskine⟩ ⟨treated ~ moist heat —F.D.Smith & Barbara Wilcox⟩ (2) **:** by virtue of **:** on account of **:** for the reason that ⟨it is also complex, ~ being an integral part of a rich and many-sided mind —E.R.Bentley⟩ ⟨resemble the . . . Uplands ~ the fact that generally they provide an environment unfriendly to human occupancy —Samuel Van Valkenburg & Ellsworth Huntington⟩ — often used in the phrase *in that* ⟨a fallacious argument ~ that it is based on false premises⟩ (3) — used as a function word to indicate material or constituents ⟨a memorial ~ Vermont granite —Bernard De Voto⟩ ⟨tell the court . . . ~ what her cargo consisted —F.W.Crofts⟩ ⟨an artist ~ oils⟩ (4) — used as a function word to indicate degree, extent, or measure ⟨flock to his exhibitions ~ thousands —Herbert Read⟩ ⟨~ the main, we are in agreement⟩ ⟨not discouraged ~ the least⟩ (5) — used as a function word to indicate a class of objects ⟨something ~ a vacuum cleaner —John Steinbeck⟩ ⟨the latest thing ~ cars⟩ **b** — used as a function word to indicate manner, form, or arrangement ⟨buying a pig ~ installments —Dodie Smith⟩ ⟨told ~ confidence⟩ ⟨written ~ French⟩ ⟨carry all your funds ~ traveler's checks —Richard Joseph⟩ **c :** with reference to **:** as concerns ⟨wonder if actors of other countries are as happy ~ their audiences as we are —Phyllis Robbins⟩ ⟨care must be exercised ~ the amount of tannic acid used —C.M.Whittaker & C.C. Wilcock⟩ ⟨~ fall color they have few peers —Laurence Lowry⟩ ⟨Greek ~ language, culture, and religion —Franc Shor⟩ ⟨six feet ~ height⟩ ⟨a library rich ~ manuscripts⟩ ⟨~ the matter of your account⟩ **4 a** — used as a function word to indicate consideration of a thing strictly limited to its own essence, nature, or merits, apart from its relations to others ⟨~ itself, the matter has no importance⟩ ⟨nothing is beautiful ~ itself⟩; compare THING-IN-ITSELF **b** — used as a function word to indicate the specific object, sphere, or aspect to which a qualification is restricted ⟨~ him you have a fine leader⟩ ⟨much remains to be done ~ this field⟩ ⟨a very worthy gentleman, ~ truth⟩ ⟨that we expect ~ persons of your station —W.S. Gilbert⟩ ⟨my trust is ~ the Lord⟩ ⟨believe ~ his good faith⟩ ⟨rich ~ hope —Shak.⟩ **c** (1) **:** WITHIN — used of an inherent quality, attribute, or significance ⟨has no pity ~ him⟩ ⟨there is nothing ~ that story⟩ (2) **:** within the capacity or powers of ⟨if I . . . had anything like that ~ me, it would have made itself felt before now —Hamilton Basso⟩ **d :** in spiritual union with ⟨love one's brothers ~ Christ⟩ **e :** within the grant of **:** in the power or control of ⟨the scholarship is ~ the trustees of the fund⟩ **5 :** in the key of ⟨~ F⟩ — **not in it** *slang* **:** not in the same class **:** hopelessly outclassed ⟨simply is *not in it* as far as skill and brains are concerned⟩

²in \ˈin\ *adv* [ME, fr. OE *in, inn*; akin to OHG *in*, adv., in, ON & Goth *inn*, OE *in*, prep.] **1 a** (1) **:** to or toward the inside esp. of a house or other building **:** into a certain space **:** INSIDE ⟨the door is locked, I can't get ~⟩ ⟨opened the window and climbed ~⟩ ⟨broke ~ and made the arrest⟩ (2) **:** in a particular direction **:** to or toward some destination ⟨drove 20 miles ~ and walked the rest of the way⟩ ⟨flew ~ on the first plane⟩ ⟨it was shank's mare from there ~ —Shelby Foote⟩ (3) **:** into a position of proximity **:** so as to be near some point **:** NEAR ⟨trackless trolleys able to swing ~ to the curb —*Springfield (Mass.) Union*⟩ ⟨the enemy closed ~⟩ **:** at close quarters ⟨advised the infielders to play ~⟩ (4) **:** so as to envelop gradually with something intangible or nebulous ⟨darkness closed ~⟩ ⟨the fog moved ~⟩ **b :** into the midst or into the surface of something so as to form a part ⟨put ~ some sugar⟩ ⟨mix ~ the flour⟩ ⟨paint ~ another figure⟩ — often used in combination ⟨built-*in* stabilizers⟩ **c** (1) **:** to its place ⟨fit a piece ~⟩ (2) **:** so as to conform, agree, or submit **:** into line ⟨fell ~ with our plans⟩ ⟨will he fit ~⟩ **d** (1) **:** to or into a particular place ⟨get your orders ~ early⟩ ⟨called us ~ for a conference⟩ (2) **:** to one's house ⟨had some friends ~ for dinner⟩ ⟨had a girl ~ to serve⟩ **2 a** (1) **:** within a particular place; *esp* **:** within the customary place of residence, practice, or business ⟨is your mother ~⟩ ⟨the doctor will be ~ at 2⟩ (2) **:** in a place that is the goal of a journey or course **:** at one's destination or terminus ⟨the whole whaling fleet was ~ —H.A.Chippendale⟩ ⟨wild riders of the High Plains, ~ from the ranches —*Amer. Guide Series: Texas*⟩ ⟨is the train ~⟩ ⟨two runs ~ last inning⟩ (3) **:** in place or position ⟨is the key ~⟩ ⟨had to climb a ladder because the stairs were not yet ~ —*Current Biog.*⟩ ⟨the footings are already ~ —*Building Estimating & Contracting*⟩ **b** (1) **:** on the interior or inner side **:** WITHIN ⟨shut a person ~⟩ (2) **:** so as to confine or surround ⟨snowed ~⟩ ⟨fence cattle ~⟩ (3) **:** in jail or prison ⟨what offense is he ~ for⟩ (4) *of a ship's sails* **:** in a furled or stowed condition **c** (1) **:** in the position of a participant, accomplice, insider, or observer — usu. used with *on* ⟨it's exciting to be ~ on that —May Sarton⟩ ⟨was ~ on the scheme —E.S.Morgan⟩ ⟨let some members of the diplomatic corps ~ on the government's intention —Sydney Gruson⟩ ⟨bankers who are ~ on current . . . thinking —*Wall Street Jour.*⟩ ⟨time his visit so that he might sit ~ on the Civil War —*Theatre Arts*⟩ (2) **:** in or into participation in a pot by betting as required by the rules ⟨come ~ for three chips⟩ ⟨count me ~⟩ ⟨stay ~ the pot⟩ **d** (1) **:** in office or power ⟨the Tories were ~ again —John Strachey⟩; *also* **:** in the position of having won an election ⟨~ by a landslide⟩ (2) **:** with legal privilege or title **:** in possession — used of a holding, possession, or seisin ⟨~ by descent⟩ (3) **:** in someone's good graces **:** on good terms — usu. used with *with* ⟨~ with the courthouse gang —D.D.McKean⟩ ⟨~ strong with the white folks —Ralph Ellison⟩ (4) **:** in a specified relation as regards favor, esteem, or terms of association ⟨~ bad with the boss⟩ (5) **:** in a position of assured or definitive success ⟨by the end of the performance I was ~ —Emmett Kelly⟩ ⟨why, you're ~, fellow —*Amateur Athlete*⟩; *also* **:** in vogue or style ⟨jewelry is ~ this year —G.A.Wagner⟩ **e** (1) *chiefly Brit* **:** in or into a burning or lighted condition ⟨blow ~ a fire⟩ ⟨the streetlights . . . were ~ —E.M.Lustgarten⟩ (2) **:** in season ⟨strawberries are ~⟩ **:** in cultivation ⟨had some two hundred acres ~ —Eve Langley⟩ **:** in condition to be harvested **:** in mature condition ⟨when cotton is ~ their devotion to the crop alters them completely —*Amer. Guide Series: Ark.*⟩ (3) **:** at bat (as in cricket) ⟨the last man ~⟩ (4) *of an oil well* **:** in or into production ⟨the well has come ~⟩ (5) **:** in effect ⟨rationing by points is over and rationing by the purse is ~ —*Economist*⟩ **f** (1) **:** in one's possession or control **:** at one's disposal **:** at hand ⟨the evidence is not all ~ —W.C.Allee⟩ ⟨the answers aren't ~ —Roscoe Drummond⟩ (2) **:** in a completed or terminated state ⟨when our own crops were ~ —A.W.Barkley⟩ ⟨after harvests are ~⟩ (3) **:** in evidence **:** on hand ⟨October was ~, mild and languorous —Maurice Hewlett⟩ (4) **:** in a specified service or employment ⟨had ~ enough time as mate —H.A.Chippendale⟩ ⟨put ~ a lot of time on that job⟩ **3 :** to the end **:** INDEFINITELY — used as an intensive with *on* ⟨every feeding time from there on ~ —Land Kaderli⟩ — **in for :** certain to experience something, pleasant or unpleasant ⟨*in for* a whale of one hour's entertainment —Goodman Ace⟩ ⟨*in for* a storm⟩ — **in for it 1 :** committed to a course **2 :** certain to suffer punishment or other unpleasant experience ⟨sees us as ineluctably *in for it* —J.W.Krutch⟩ ⟨will be *in for it* if he doesn't get home on time⟩

³in \"\ *vt* **inned; inned; inning; ins** [ME *innen*, fr. OE *innian* to include, go in, fr. *in, inn*, adv.] *now dial chiefly Eng* **:** ENCLOSE, RECLAIM; *also* **:** HARVEST

⁴in \"\ *adj* [²in] **1 a :** that is located inside or within ⟨the ~ part⟩ **b :** that is in position, connection, operation, or power ⟨the ~ party⟩ **c :** having its inning ⟨the ~ team⟩ **2 :** that is directed inward **:** proceeding or bound toward the interior or inner side **:** INCOMING ⟨the ~ train⟩

⁵in \"\ *n* -S [²in] **1 :** one who is in office or power or on the inside ⟨wanted to be an ~ —W.A.White⟩ — usu. used in pl. ⟨a matter of ~s versus outs —L.K.Caldwell⟩ **2 :** INFLUENCE, PULL ⟨enjoyed some sort of ~ with the commandant —Henriette Roosenburg⟩ ⟨must have an ~ someplace —W.R. Burnett⟩ **3 :** a ball hit in bounds in tennis or squash

¹in- *or* **il-** *or* **im-** *or* **ir-** *prefix* [ME, fr. MF, OF, & L; ME *in-* fr. OF, fr. L; ME *il-* fr. MF, fr. L, fr. *in-*; ME *im-* fr. OF, fr. L, fr. *in-*; ME *ir-* fr. OF, fr. L, fr. *in-*; akin to OE *un-* — more at UN-] **:** not **:** NON-, UN- — usu. *il-* before *l* ⟨*il*logical⟩ and *im-* before *b, m,* or *p* ⟨*im*balance⟩ ⟨*im*moral⟩ ⟨*im*provident⟩ and *ir-* before *r* ⟨*ir*reducible⟩ and *in-* before other sounds ⟨*in*active⟩ ⟨*in*apt⟩ ⟨*in*conclusive⟩

²in- *or* **il-** *or* **im-** *or* **ir-** *prefix* [ME, fr. OF, MF, & L; ME *in-* fr. OF *in-, en-*, fr. L *in-*, fr. *in* in, into; ME *il-* fr. MF, fr. L, fr. *in*; ME *im-* fr. MF *im-, em-*, fr. L *im-*, fr. *in*; ME *ir-* fr. L, fr. *in* — more at ¹IN] **1 :** in **:** within **:** inward **:** into **:** toward **:** on ⟨*im*plode⟩ ⟨*ir*radicate⟩ **2 :** ¹EN- ⟨*il*lucidate⟩ ⟨*im*barn⟩ ⟨*im*marble⟩ ⟨*im*panel⟩ ⟨*im*peril⟩ ⟨*in*spirit⟩ — in both senses usu. *il-* before *l*, *im-* before *b, m,* or *p*, *ir-* before *r*, and *in-* before other sounds

³in- *or* **ino-** *comb form* [NL *in-*, fr. Gk, tendon, fr. *in-, is*; prob. akin to L *viēre* to plait — more at WITHY] **:** fiber **:** fibrous tissue ⟨*in*itis⟩ ⟨*in*ogen⟩

-in \ən, ᵊn, ˌin\ *n suffix* -S [F *-ine*, fr. L *-ina* (with long *ī*), fem. of *-inus* (with long *ī*) of or belonging to — more at -INE] **1 a :** neutral chemical compound or compound not distinctly basic or acidic ⟨picrotox*in*⟩ ⟨hematoporphyr*in*⟩ — esp. in names of glycerides ⟨acet*in*⟩ ⟨stear*in*⟩, glycosides ⟨amygdal*in*⟩ ⟨quercitr*in*⟩, proteins ⟨gelat*in*⟩ ⟨insul*in*⟩, and 6-membered heterocyclic compounds ⟨diox*in*⟩; usu. distinguished from *-ine* **b :** enzyme ⟨emuls*in*⟩ ⟨myros*in*⟩ — compare -ASE **c :** antibiotic ⟨penicill*in*⟩ ⟨streptomyc*in*⟩ **2 :** ²-INE 2a, 2b — not used systematically **3 :** pharmaceutical product ⟨niac*in*⟩ ⟨aspir*in*⟩

in *abbr* **1** inch **2** inlet

In *symbol* indium

INA *abbr* international normal atmosphere

¹-i·na \ˈīnə, ˈēnə\ *n suffix, pl* **-ina** [NL, fr. L, fem. sing. and neut. pl. of *-inus* (with long *ī*) ¹-ine] **:** one or ones related to, resembling, or characterized by — in taxonomic names in biology ⟨Acar*ina*⟩ ⟨Clathr*ina*⟩ ⟨Fistul*ina*⟩

²-i·na \ˈēnə *sometimes* ˈīnə\ *also* **-ine** \ˌēn *sometimes* ˌīn\ *n suffix* -S [prob. fr. It *-ina* (dim. suffix), fr. L *-ina* (with long *ī*), fem. of *-inus* (with long *ī*) ¹-ine] **1 :** musical instrument ⟨concert*ina*⟩ ⟨seraph*ine*⟩ **2 :** musical device ⟨aeol*ine*⟩

in·ability \ˌin+\ *n* [ME *inabilite*, fr. MF *inhabilité*, fr. *in-* ¹in- + *habilité* ability — more at ABILITY] **:** the quality or state of being unable **:** lack of ability **:** lack of sufficient power, strength, resources, or capacity ⟨plead an ~ in mathematics —John Dollard⟩

in ab·sen·tia \ˌinabˈsench(ē)ə, ˌinəb-, -sentēə\ *adv* [L] **:** in absence (as of the accused person or of a person receiving a degree) ⟨awarded a degree *in absentia*⟩ ⟨condemned *in absentia*⟩

in·absorbability \ˌin+\ *n* **:** the quality or state of being inabsorbable

in·absorbable \"+\ *adj* [¹in- + *absorbable*] **:** not capable of being absorbed

in ab·strac·to \ˌinəbzˈtrak(ˌ)tō, -bˈst-\ *adv* [L, in the abstract] **:** in or from an abstract point of view **:** in the abstract ⟨the question could not be settled *in abstracto* —Yuen-li Liang⟩ ⟨discovering the problem purely theoretically, *in abstracto* —*Mathematical Biophysics*⟩

in·acceptable \ˌin+\ *adj* [¹in- + *acceptable*] **:** not acceptable

in·accessibility \ˌin+\ *n* [prob. fr. MF *inaccessibilité*, fr. *inaccessible* + *-ité* -ity] **:** the quality or state of being inaccessible

in·accessible \ˌin+\ *adj* [MF or LL; MF, fr. LL *inaccessibilis*, fr. L *in-* ¹in- + LL *accessibilis* accessible — more at ACCESSIBLE] **1 :** not accessible: as **a :** not capable of being reached, entered, or approached ⟨~ except by heavy two-wheeled carts —C.L.Jones⟩ **b :** not capable of being obtained ⟨a rare work, today almost ~⟩ **c :** not easy to form friendly or close relations with **:** not susceptible to advances or influence **:** UNAPPROACHABLE ⟨peculiarly ~ to such questioning —Christine Weston⟩ ⟨a cold ~ figure⟩ **d :** difficult or impossible to comprehend or enter into **:** ABSTRUSE, ESOTERIC ⟨poetry . . . ~ to contemporary criticism —Frederick Morgan⟩ ⟨the novel . . . seems to me among the most ~ —C.J.Rolo⟩ **2 :** reflecting or evidencing inaccessibility ⟨a look which was austere, ~ —Ellen Glasgow⟩ ⟨an air of ~ respectability —John Buchan⟩ — **inaccessibleness** \"+\ *n* — **in·accessibly** \"+\ *adv*

in·accuracy \(ˈ)in, ən+\ *n* [¹in- + *accuracy*] **1 :** the condition of being inaccurate ⟨avoiding muddle and ~ —W.H. Dowdeswell⟩ **2 :** an instance of being inaccurate **:** MISTAKE, ERROR ⟨when all his *inaccuracies* . . . have been acknowledged —D.C.Peattie & Eleanor R. Dobson⟩

in·accurate \(ˈ)in, ən+\ *adj* [¹in- + *accurate*] **:** not accurate: as **a :** containing a mistake or error **:** INCORRECT, ERRONEOUS ⟨an ~ account⟩ **b :** not functioning with accuracy or precision **:** FAULTY, DEFECTIVE ⟨the limbs are useless and sense organs are ~ —Abram Kardiner⟩ ⟨this thermometer is ~⟩ — **in·accurately** \"+\ *adv* — **in·accurateness** \"+\ *n*

in·action \(ˈ)in, ən+\ *n* [¹in- + *action*] **:** lack of action or activity **:** abstention from labor **:** IDLENESS, LETHARGY ⟨impatience with hypocrisy and ~ —Lillian Smith⟩

in·activate \(ˈ)in, ən+\ *vt* [*inactive* + *-ate*] **:** to make inactive: as **a** (1) **:** to destroy certain biological activities of ⟨~ the complement of normal serum by heat⟩ — compare REACTIVATE (2) **:** to cause (as an infective agent) to lose disease-producing capacity ⟨~ bacteria⟩ **b :** to remove (a unit) from the active list of a military service without disbanding — **in·activation** \(ˌ)in, ən+\ *n*

in·active \(ˈ)in, ən+\ *adj* [¹in- + *active*] **:** not active: as **a** (1) **:** marked by deliberate or enforced absence of activity or effort **:** SEDENTARY ⟨forced by illness to lead an ~ life⟩ (2) **:** not given to action or effort **:** not diligent, energetic, or industrious **:** INDOLENT, SLUGGISH ⟨dreamy and ~ by nature⟩ ⟨a very ~ police chief⟩ ⟨the rentier class, an ~ class in the economy —L.R.Klein⟩ **b** (1) **:** being unused or out of use **:** lying idle **:** not functioning ⟨an ~ mine⟩ ⟨an ~ machine⟩ (2) **:** relating to or consisting of officers and enlisted personnel of the armed forces who are not performing or available for military duties ⟨~ list⟩ ⟨~ reserve⟩ ⟨~ status⟩ (3) **:** being a commodity for which there is relatively little demand or in which relatively little trading occurs ⟨active, ~ and obsolete sterling patterns —*Christian Science Monitor*⟩ ⟨~ stocks⟩ (4) *of a disease* **:** not progressing or fulminating **:** QUIESCENT **c** (1) **:** chemically inert **:** UNREACTIVE ⟨~ charcoal⟩ (2) **:** not exhibiting any action on polarized light **:** optically neutral — used of stereoisomeric forms of various substances ⟨~ fructose⟩ ⟨~ camphor⟩; compare MES- 4b, RACEMIC

syn IDLE, INERT, PASSIVE, SUPINE: INACTIVE applies to anyone or anything not in action or not usu. in action (as in operation or use) or at work ⟨*inactive* machines⟩ ⟨an *inactive* child⟩ ⟨an *inactive* charge account⟩ IDLE applies chiefly to persons without occupation at the moment but usu. without occupation as a general or habitual thing, or to their powers, organs, or implements ⟨give work to an *idle* laborer⟩ ⟨an *idle* lathe⟩ ⟨an *idle* mind⟩ ⟨an *idle* pen⟩ INERT implies lack of power in a thing to set it in motion or by itself to produce a given effect, or suggests in a person a general indisposition to activity ⟨aimless accumulation of precise knowledge, *inert* and unutilized —A.N. Whitehead⟩ ⟨this amorphous spreading of responsibility will result in a sort of *inert*, ponderous bureaucracy —Stanley Walker⟩ ⟨would lie for hours on a chaise longue, so *inert* that the folds of chiffon which dripped from her body to the floor hung as steady as if they were stone —Rebecca West⟩ ⟨the greatest menace to freedom is an *inert* people —L.D.Brandeis⟩ PASSIVE implies immobility or a lack of positive reaction when acted upon by an external force or agent, often implying a submissiveness consisting of failure to be provoked to resistance or of a planned avoidance of any action that will give aid to the dominating force or agent ⟨some of those hours were spent in intensive cerebration, some in *passive* listening to lectures —H.M.Wriston⟩ ⟨*passive* obedience to authority⟩ ⟨*passive* resistance to oppression⟩ SUPINE implies abject inertia or passivity, often from indolence ⟨he is *supine*; he accepts his mother's truculence on his behalf with an indolence of temper which distinguishes him in this, as in all matters —Edward Hyams⟩ ⟨political and religious dissension . . . had split a weary and *supine* people into a dozen factions —P.J. Searles⟩

in·actively \"+\ *adv* **:** in an inactive manner

inactiveness \"+\ *n* **:** the quality or state of being inactive

in·activity \ˌin+\ *n* **:** the quality or state of being inactive **:** IDLENESS, SLUGGISHNESS

in·adaptability \ˌin+\ *n* **:** the quality or state of being inadaptable

in·adaptable \ˌin+\ *adj* [¹in- + *adaptable*] **:** incapable of adaptation **:** belonging to a fixed type

in·adaptive \ˌin+\ *adj* [¹in- + *adaptive*] **:** not adaptive

in·adequacy \(ˈ)in, ən+\ *n* [fr. *inadequate*, after *adequate: adequacy*] **:** the quality or state of being inadequate **:** INSUFFICIENCY ⟨~ of unemployment benefits —*Collier's Yr. Bk.*⟩

in·adequate \(ˈ)in, ən+\ *adj* [¹in- + *adequate*] **:** not adequate **:** INSUFFICIENT, DEFICIENT ⟨~ equipment⟩ ⟨~ leadership⟩ *specif* **:** lacking the capacity for psychological maturity ⟨the ~ individual⟩ **:** unable to make adequate social adjustment ⟨an offender coming from an ~ family⟩ ⟨~ parents⟩ — **in·adequately** \"+\ *adv* — **in·adequateness** \"+\ *n* -ES

in·admissibility *also* **in·admissability** \ˌin+\ *n* **:** the quality or state of being inadmissible

in·admissible *also* **in·admissable** \ˌin+\ *adj* [¹in- + *admissible*] **:** not proper to be allowed or received **:** not admissible ⟨~ behavior⟩ — **in·admissibly** \"+\ *adv*

in-a-door bed \ˈ==ˌ=ˌ=-\ *also* **in-a-door** *n* [fr. *In-a-Dor-Bed*, a trademark] **:** MURPHY BED

¹in·adu·nate \ˌinəˈd(y)ünət, (ˈ)iˈnajən-\ *adj* [¹in- + L *adunatus*, past part. of *adunare* to unite, fr. *ad-* + *unus* one — more at ONE] **:** not united; *specif* **:** having the arms completely free from the calyx — used of a crinoid

²inadunate \"\ *n* -S **:** an inadunate crinoid

in·ad·ver·tence \ˌinədˈvərtᵊn(t)s, ˌiˌnad-, -vōt-, -vəit-\ *n* [ML *inadvertentia*, fr. L *in-* ¹in- + *advertent-, advertens* (pres. part. of *advertere* to advert) + *-ia* -y — more at ADVERT] **1 :** the fact or action of being inadvertent; lack of care or attentiveness **:** INATTENTION ⟨mistakes proceed from ~⟩ **2 :** an effect of inattention **:** a result of carelessness **:** an oversight, mistake,

or fault from negligence ⟨annoying misprints and ~s —Tor Ulving⟩
in·ad·ver·ten·cy \-tᵊnsē, -si\ *n* [ML *inadvertentia*] : INADVERTENCE ⟨wars sometimes start through . . . sheer ~ —*Reporter*⟩
in·ad·ver·tent \¦=(,)=¦=ᵊnt\ *adj* [back-formation fr. *inadvertence, inadvertency*] **1** : not turning the mind to a matter : HEEDLESS, NEGLIGENT, INATTENTIVE ⟨an ~ remark⟩ **2** : UNINTENTIONAL ⟨~ violations of trade laws —*Current Biog.*⟩ — **in·ad·ver·tent·ly** *adv*
in·advisability \¦in+\ *n* : the quality or state of being inadvisable
in·advisable \¦in+\ *adj* [¹*in-* + *advisable*] : not advisable : INEXPEDIENT
-i·nae \ˈī(,)nē\ *n pl suffix* [NL, fr. L, fem. pl. of *-inus* -ine] : members of the subfamily of — in recent classifications substituted for the last syllable of the genitive case of the name of the type genus in all names of zoological subfamilies ⟨Fel*inae*⟩ ⟨Melipon*inae*⟩
in·aesthetic \¦in+\ *adj* [¹*in-* + *aesthetic*] **1** : violating aesthetic canons or requirements : deficient in tastefulness or beauty : offensive from lack of beauty ⟨peered through those ~ spectacles —Maurice Cranston⟩ **2** : lacking aesthetic sensibility ⟨~ and quite unintellectual —A.L.Rowse⟩
in·agglutinability \¦in+\ *n* : the quality or state of being inagglutinable
in·agglutinable \"+\ *adj* [¹*in-* + *agglutinable*] : not subject to agglutination : not agglutinable
in·a·ja \,inəˈzhä\ *n* -s [Pg *inajá*, fr. Tupi] : a tall pinnate-leaved Brazilian palm (*Maximiliana regia*) with immense prickle-tipped spathes used for baskets, tubs, and other containers
in·alienability \(¦)in, ən+\ *n* : the quality or state of being inalienable
in·alienable \(ˈ)in, ən+\ *adj* [prob. fr. F *inaliénable*, fr. *in-* ¹in- + *aliénable* alienable — more at ALIENABLE] : incapable of being alienated, surrendered, or transferred ⟨~ human rights⟩ — compare INDEFEASIBLE — **in·alienableness** \"+\ *n* -ES — **in·alienably** \"+\ *adv*
in all *adv* : all told : ALTOGETHER ⟨some 70 ships *in all*⟩ ⟨*in all* we drove more than 40,000 miles⟩
in alt *adv (or adj)* : in the octave beginning with the second G above middle C ⟨ranging up to E *in alt*⟩ — see PITCH illustration
in·alterability \(¦)in, ən+\ *n* : the quality or state of being inalterable
in·alterable \(ˈ)in, ən+\ *adj* [¹*in-* + *alterable*, fr. F *altérable*, fr. *altérer* to alter + *-able* -able] : not alterable : UNALTERABLE — **in·alterably** \"+\ *adv*
in altissimo *adv (or adj)* [It, lit., in the highest] : in the octave beginning with the third G above middle C — see PITCH illustration
in·amissible \¦in+\ *adj* [F or LL; F, fr. LL *inamissibilis*, fr. L *in-* ¹in- + LL *amissibilis* amissible — more at AMISSIBLE] : incapable of being lost
in·am·o·ra·ta \(,)i,naməˈräd·ə, ə,n-\ *n* -s [It *innamorata*, fr. fem. of *innamorato*, past part. of *innamorare* to inspire with love, fr. *in-* ²in- + *amore* love, fr. L *amor* — more at AMOROUS] : a woman with whom one is in love or has intimate relations; *specif* : MISTRESS
in·am·o·ra·to \-ˈäd·(,)ō\ *n* -s [It *innamorato*, fr. past part. of *innamorare*] : a male lover
in-and-in \¦=¦=¦=\ *adv (or adj)* : in repeated generations of the same or closely related stock ⟨families . . . of one blood through mating or marrying *in-and-in* —F.H.Giddings⟩ ⟨this freak of color in range-bred horses is the result of *in-and-in* breeding —Andy Adams⟩
¹**in and out** *adv* **1** : alternately in and out ⟨he's been *in and out* all day⟩ **2** : to the last detail : EXHAUSTIVELY, THOROUGHLY ⟨understands his business *in and out*⟩ ⟨knew each other *in and out* —Virginia Woolf⟩
²**in and out** *n* : an obstacle found in fox hunting and steeplechasing consisting of two fences in close proximity but impossible to clear in the same jump
in-and-out \¦=¦=¦=\ *adj* [¹*in and out*] : now good and now bad in performance ⟨an *in-and-out* showing —*Williams Alumni Rev.*⟩
in-and-out bolt *n* : a bolt running through from outside to inside of a ship's framing
in-and-out bond *n* : a masonry bond formed by headers and stretchers alternating vertically esp. at a corner
in-and-out plating *or* **in-and-out system** *n* : a system of construction for steel ships in which each alternate strake of plating laps over the edge of each adjoining strake
¹**inane** \(ˈ)i¦nān, əˈnān\ *adj, sometimes* -ER/-EST [L *inanis*] **1** : EMPTY, INSUBSTANTIAL ⟨azure of *inanest* space —Walter de la Mare⟩ **2** : lacking significance, meaning or profundity : SHALLOW, VACANT, FATUOUS, SILLY ⟨made some ~ remark about the weather —Joseph Conrad⟩; *also* : reflecting or indicating such condition ⟨an ~ face⟩ **syn** see INSIPID
²**inane** \"\ *n* -s : something that is empty : the emptiness of space ⟨a voyage into the limitless ~ —V.G.Childe⟩
inane·ly *adv* : in an inane manner
inan·ga \ˈē,näŋgä\ *n, pl* **inangas** *or* **inanga** [Maori] : any of several freshwater fishes (family Galaxiidae) of New Zealand and Tasmania
¹**in·animate** \(ˈ)in, ən+\ *adj* [LL *inanimatus*, fr. L *in-* ¹in- + *animatus*, past part. of *animare* to quicken, enliven, endow with breath or soul — more at ANIMATE] **1 a** : not animate : not endowed with life or spirit ⟨the inorganic world is ~⟩ : not endowed with consciousness or animal life ⟨trees are ~⟩ **b** : deprived of consciousness or of life ⟨an ~ body⟩ **c** *of a grammatical gender* : referring typically to dead things or things considered as dead — opposed to *animate* **2** : not animated or lively : DULL, SPIRITLESS ⟨her ~ movement when on the stage —W.B.Yeats⟩ — **in·animately** \"+\ *adv* — **in·animateness** \"+\ *n*
²**inanimate** *vt* [LL *inanimatus*, past part. of *inanimare*, fr. L *in-* ²in- + *animare*] *obs* : ANIMATE
in·a·ni·tion \,inəˈnishən\ *n* -s [ME *in-anisioun*, fr. ML *inanition-, inanitio*, fr. *inanitus* (past part. of *inanire* to make empty, fr. *inanis* empty, inane) + L *-ion-, -io* -ion] : the condition or result of being empty: **a** : the exhausted condition which results from a complete lack of food and water : MARASMUS **b** : absence or loss of social, moral, or intellectual vitality or vigor : LETHARGY ⟨an old society protects itself from ~ by expanding —Lovell Thompson⟩
inan·i·ty \əˈnanəd·ē, -ətē, -i\ *n* -ES [F or L; F *inanité*, fr. L *inanitat-, inanitas*, fr. *inanis* inane + *-itat-, -itas* -ity] **1** : the quality or state of being inane: as **a** : the condition of lacking all substance or content : EMPTINESS, HOLLOWNESS ⟨the present situation in the North is political ~ —J.V.Kelleher⟩ **b** : vapid, pointless, or fatuous character : lack of profundity : meaningless quality : SHALLOWNESS ⟨the ~ and dullness of most conversations —Hunter Mead⟩ ⟨a master who has suffered . . . from the ~ of his interpreters —A.E.Wier⟩ **2** : something that is foolish, trivial, or pointless ⟨fulsome *inanities* —Walker Evans⟩ ⟨the statement was a downright ~⟩
in an·tis \əˈnantə̇s\ *adv* [L, in antae] : between two antas ⟨a Greek Doric entrance *in antis* —Nikolaus Pevsner⟩
in·apparent \¦in+\ *adj* [¹*in-* + *apparent*] : not apparent; *specif* : not apparent clinically — used of subclinical infections
in·appeasable \¦in+\ *adj* [¹*in-* + *appeasable*] : UNAPPEASABLE
in·appetence \(ˈ)in, ən+\ *n* [¹*in-* + *appetence*] : lack of appetite ⟨complained of ~ and slight nausea —*Jour. Amer. Med. Assoc.*⟩ — **in·appetent** \"+\ *adj*
in·applicability \(¦)in, ən+\ *n* : the condition of being inapplicable
in·applicable \"+\ *adj* [¹*in-* + *applicable*] : not applicable : incapable of being applied : not adapted : not suitable — **in·applicableness** \"+\ *n* -ES — **in·applicably** \"+\ *adv*
in·apposite \(ˈ)in, ən+\ *adj* [¹*in-* + *apposite*] : not apposite : not pertinent ⟨so ~, so incongruous as to sound extremely bizarre —*Times Lit. Supp.*⟩ — **in·appositely** \"+\ *adv* — **in·appositeness** \"+\ *n*
in·appreciable \¦in+\ *adj* [prob. fr. F *inappréciable*, fr. MF *inappreciable*, fr. *in-* ¹in- + *appreciable* — more at APPRECIABLE] **1** *archaic* : INVALUABLE **2** : not appreciable : too small to be perceived ⟨became ~ at 615° C. —E.B.Shaud⟩ — **in·appreciably** \"+\ *adv*
in·appreciation \¦in+\ *n* [¹*in-* + *appreciation*] : lack of appreciation ⟨~ of his most vital criticism —F.R.Leavis⟩
in·appreciative \¦in+\ *adj* [¹*in-* + *appreciative*] : not appreciative — **in·appreciatively** \"+\ *adv* — **in·appreciativeness** \"+\ *n* -ES
in·approachable \¦in+\ *adj* [¹*in-* + *approachable*] : not approachable : INACCESSIBLE
in·appropriate \¦in+\ *adj* [¹*in-* + *appropriate*] : not appropriate : UNBECOMING, UNSUITABLE ⟨noise seems ~ in a place of sadness —Franz Boas⟩ — **in·appropriately** \"+\ *adv* — **in·appropriateness** \"+\ *n*
in·apt \(ˈ)in, ən+\ *adj* [¹*in-* + *apt*] : not apt: **a** : not suitable or appropriate ⟨a very ~ analogy⟩ **b** : not qualified or skilled : INEPT, INADEQUATE ⟨unstable, queer, ~ individuals —*Psychological Abstracts*⟩ — **in·apt·ly** *adv* — **in·apt·ness** *n* -ES
in·aptitude \(ˈ)in, ən+\ *n* [¹*in-* + *aptitude*] : lack of aptitude
¹**in·arch** \ən+\ *vt* [²*in* + *arch*] : to form an approach graft of or with ⟨successfully ~*ed* water sprouts to bridge rabbit damage on the apple trees⟩
²**in·arch** \ˈin+,-\ *n* -ES : APPROACH GRAFT; *also* : the plant resulting from a successful approach graft
in·arguable \(ˈ)in, ən+\ *adj* [¹*in-* + *arguable*] : not arguable — **in·arguably** \"+\ *adv*
in·articulata \¦in+\ *n pl, cap* [NL, fr. neut. pl. of *inarticulatus*] : a class of Brachiopoda comprising forms with unhinged usu. chitinophosphatic valves without teeth or sockets and including the orders Atremata and Neotremata
in·articulate \¦in+\ *adj* [LL *inarticulatus*, fr. L *in-* ¹in- + *articulatus*, past part. of *articulare* to utter distinctly — more at ARTICULATE] **1 a** *of a sound* : uttered or formed without the definite articulations which produce intelligible speech ⟨gave a little ~ grunt —Edith Wharton⟩ : indistinctly articulated or pronounced ⟨speech so ~ it resembled a growl⟩ **b** (1) : incapable of speech esp. under stress of emotion : MUTE ⟨almost ~ with excitement —Kenneth Roberts⟩ ⟨almost pathologically shy, he at times became totally ~ —C.B. Forcey⟩ (2) : intense or compelling to the point of preventing speech : not accompanied or attended by speech : incapable of being expressed by speech ⟨dazed with ~ pain —Edith Wharton⟩ ⟨~ misery⟩ (3) : not voiced or expressed : UNSPOKEN ⟨~ judicial notions of rightfulness or wrongfulness of motive —C.O.Gregory⟩ ⟨their ~ major premises —*Times Lit. Supp.*⟩ ⟨expressed the ~ feelings of many scientists —Harrison Brown⟩ **c** (1) : unable to speak coherently, forcefully, or purposefully ⟨remained stupidly ~, saying something noncommittal —Victoria Sackville-West⟩ ⟨~ as most of their class, they could do no more than utter bald phrases —Ruth Park⟩ (2) : having an incoherent or disjointed character ⟨the stumbling, almost ~, speech of the boy —G.W.Russell⟩ **d** : incapable of giving clear and effective expression to one's feelings, ideas, or aspirations in any way ⟨the vast majority of the natives are politically ~ —A.F.Macdonald⟩ **2** [NL *inarticulatus*, fr. ¹*in-* + *articulatus* jointed — more at ARTICULATA] **a** : not jointed : having no distinct body segments ⟨an ~ worm⟩ **b** : lacking a hinge — used esp. of certain brachiopod shells **c** [NL *Inarticulata*] : of, resembling, or relating to the Inarticulata **syn** see DUMB
in·articulately \"+\ *adv* : in an inarticulate manner
in·articulateness \"+\ *n* -ES : the quality or state of being inarticulate
in ar·tic·u·lo mor·tis \,in,närˈtikyə,lōˈmȯrd·ə̇s\ *adv (or adj)* [L] : at the point of death ⟨the king appeared to be *in articulo mortis* —M.A.S.Hume⟩
in·artificial \(¦)in, ən+\ *adj* [L *inartificialis*, fr. *in-* ¹in- + *artificialis* artificial — more at ARTIFICIAL] **1** *archaic* : not characterized by art or skill : CLUMSY, INARTISTIC **2** : not characterized by affectation : ARTLESS, UNAFFECTED, PLAIN — **in·artificially** \"+\ *adv*
in·artistic \¦in+\ *adj* [¹*in-* + *artistic*] : not artistic : not conforming to the principles of art : lacking in taste or appreciation for art — **in·artistically** \"+\ *adv*
-inas *pl of* -INA
in·as·much as \¦inəz¦məchəz\ *conj* [ME *in as muche as*] **1** : in the degree that : insofar as ⟨everything else that is desired is desired *inasmuch as* it leads to pleasure —*Times Lit. Supp.*⟩ **2** : in view of the fact that : for the reason that : SINCE, BECAUSE ⟨should not be used for the relief of pain *inasmuch as* its analgesic value is slight —D.W.Maurer & V.H. Vogel⟩
in·attention \¦in+\ *n* [¹*in-* + *attention*] : failure to pay attention : DISREGARD
in·attentive \¦in+\ *adj* [¹*in-* + *attentive*] : not attentive : HEEDLESS, NEGLIGENT ⟨an ~ student⟩ — **in·attentively** \"+\ *adv* — **in·attentiveness** \"+\ *n*
in·audibility \(¦)in, ən+\ *n* : the quality or state of being inaudible
in·audible \(ˈ)in, ən+\ *adj* [LL *inaudibilis*, fr. L *in-* ¹in- + LL *audibilis* audible — more at AUDIBLE] : not audible : incapable of being heard ⟨his voice was hushed, almost ~ —E. K.Gann⟩ — **in·audibleness** \"+\ *n* -ES — **in·audibly** \"+\ *adv*
¹**in·au·gu·ral** \əˈnȯgyərəl, ÷ -g(ə)rəl\ *adj* [L *inaugurare* + E *-al*] **1** : relating to or performed or pronounced at a formal induction or investiture ⟨new recruits . . . are given an ~ address by their chief superintendent —*Times Lit. Supp.*⟩ ⟨the president's ~ address⟩ : held in connection with such an investiture ⟨an ~ ball⟩ — opposed to *exaugural* **2** : marking the commencement : being the first in a projected series ⟨an ~ meeting of a new historical society⟩ ⟨the ~ performance of a dramatic group⟩ ⟨the ~ run of the new luxury train —*Americas*⟩ ⟨the new association's ~ venture —W.F.Brown b. 1903⟩
²**inaugural** \"\ *n* -s **1** : an inaugural address **2** : the process or ceremony of inaugurating or of being inaugurated ⟨the president's ~ was held inside due to inclement weather⟩ ⟨will continue in that capacity until after the ~ —*N.Y. Times*⟩
in·au·gu·rate \əˈnȯgyə,rāt, ÷ -gə,r-, *usu* -ād·+V\ *vt* [L *inauguratus*, past part. of *inaugurare* to practice augury, to inaugurate, fr. *in-* ²in- + *augurare* to prophesy, augur; fr. the ceremonies connected with the telling of auguries — more at AUGUR] **1** : to introduce or induct into an office with suitable ceremonies or solemnities : invest with power or authority in a formal manner : INSTALL ⟨~ a president⟩ **2** : to begin, introduce, or mark a start or opening of: **a** : to dedicate, consecrate, or observe the opening or beginning of formally, auspiciously, and publicly ⟨a temple *inaugurated* by the emperor⟩ ⟨national assemblies and military expeditions were *inaugurated* by public prayers —G.L.Dickinson⟩ **b** : to start, commence, or institute sometimes publicly, ceremoniously, or formally with the prospect of continuing as a public service or beneficial agency or force ⟨passenger and freight service on the river was *inaugurated* in 1832 —*Amer. Guide Series: Maine*⟩ ⟨various conservation projects in the state have been *inaugurated* —*Amer. Guide Series: Del.*⟩ ⟨compulsory school attendance was not *inaugurated* . . . until 1919 —*Amer. Guide Series: Fla.*⟩ ⟨*inaugurated* the study of Greek —H.O. Taylor⟩ **c** : to begin or bring about the beginning of ⟨turning from the hero to the common man, we *inaugurated* the era of realism —J.W.Krutch⟩ ⟨until the Civil War *inaugurated* a new chapter in Kansas-Missouri relations —W.H.Stephenson⟩ **syn** see BEGIN
in·au·gu·ra·tion \ə,=¦=ˈrāshən\ *n* -s [L *inauguration-, inauguratio*, fr. *inauguratus* + *-ion-, -io* -ion] : the act or an instance of inaugurating: as **a** : investiture by appropriate ceremonies ⟨knighted by the king of Scotland on his ~ —L. G.Pine⟩ **b** : formal initiation, opening, or introduction ⟨~ of a new museum⟩ ⟨~ of a conference on educational problems⟩ **c** : beginning of the operation, use, or practice of something : START, INSTITUTION ⟨~ of a giant calculating machine . . . was announced —*Current Biog.*⟩ ⟨decided to postpone the ~ of fluoridation —J.M.Burns⟩ ⟨~ of scientific systems of tillage —Samuel Van Valkenburg & Ellsworth Huntington⟩
inauguration day *n, usu cap I & D* : a day set for the inauguration of the president of the U. S. now the January 20 but before 1934 the March 4 following the presidential election
in·au·gu·ra·tor \ə=ˈ=,rād·ə(r), -ātə-\ *n* -s : a person who inaugurates
in·auspicious \¦in+\ *adj* [¹*in-* + *auspicious*] : not auspicious : ILL-OMENED, UNLUCKY, UNPROPITIOUS ⟨you come at a singularly ~ moment —Rafael Sabatini⟩ **syn** see OMINOUS
in·auspiciously \¦in+\ *adv* : in an inauspicious manner
in·authentic \¦in+\ *adj* [¹*in-* + *authentic*] : not authentic — **in·authenticity** \(¦)in, ən+\ *n*
in·balance \(ˈ)in+\ *n* [¹*in-* + *balance*] : IMBALANCE ⟨physiological ~ in hyperthyroidism⟩
inbd *abbr* inboard
in·bearing \ˈ=,==\ *adj* [²*in* + *bearing*] *chiefly Scot* : OFFICIOUS
¹**in between** *adv* [²*in* + *between* (adv.)] : BETWEEN ⟨*in between* are the groves of banana trees —Henry Swanzy⟩
²**in between** *prep* [²*in* + *between* (prep.)] : BETWEEN ⟨came *in between* us⟩ ⟨*in between* the houses⟩
¹**in-between** \¦=¦=¦=\ *n* -s [¹*in between*] : INTERMEDIATE, INTERMEDIARY ⟨no *in-betweens*, no compromises —Richard Watts⟩ ⟨for the novice, the expert, or the *in-between* —Johannes Mattern⟩
²**in-between** \"\ *adj* [¹*in between*] : INTERMEDIATE ⟨his *in-between* stand on civil rights —*Newsweek*⟩ ⟨planning to carry *in-between* styles into spring —*N.Y. Times*⟩ ⟨this *in-between* status of the gibbon —Weston La Barre⟩
inblowing \ˈ=¦==\ *adj* [⁴*in* + *blowing* (after *blow in*, v.)] : blowing inward or centripetally ⟨~ winds⟩
¹**inboard** \ˈ=¦=\ *adv* [¹*in* + *board*] **1** : inside the line of a ship's bulwarks or hull : toward the center line of a ship — contrasted with *outboard* **2** : from without inward : toward the inside ⟨pull the throttle ~ —Clay Blair⟩ **3** : in a position closer or closest to the longitudinal axis of an aircraft ⟨flaps located ~ on a wing⟩
²**inboard** \"\ *adj* : located, moving, or being inboard ⟨~ engine⟩ ⟨~ section of a wing⟩
inbond \ˈ=¦=\ *adj* [⁴*in* + *bond* (connection)] : laid across a wall : having bricks or stones laid as headers — opposed to *outbond*
inborn \ˈ=¦=\ *adj* [²*in* + *born*] **1** : born in or with one : implanted by nature : NATURAL ⟨man's ~ desire to fly —H.G. Armstrong⟩ ⟨the ~ conservatism of man⟩ **2** : INHERITED, HEREDITARY ⟨the tendency toward schizophrenia was ~ —*N.Y. Times*⟩ **syn** see INNATE
inbound \ˈ=¦=\ *adj* [²*in* + *bound*] **1** : inward bound ⟨an ~ ship⟩ ⟨~ baggage⟩ — contrasted with *outbound* **2** : relating to inward or inbound traffic ⟨~ station⟩
inbounds line \ˈ=,=\ *n* [fr. the phrase *in bounds*] : either of the broken lines running at right angles to the yard lines and dividing the field of play of a football field into three equal parts — see FOOTBALL illustration
inbreak \ˈ=,=\ *n* [⁴*in* + *break* (after *break in*, v.)] : a breaking in : INROAD, INVASION, INCURSION
inbreathe \ˈ=¦=\ *vt* [²*in* + *breathe*] : to breathe (something) in : INHALE
¹**inbred** \ˈ=¦=\ *adj* [²*in* + *bred*] **1** : bred within ⟨~ worth⟩ ⟨there was in him an ~ goodness —J.A.Froude⟩ **2** : subjected to or produced by inbreeding **syn** see INNATE
²**inbred** \ˈ=,=\ *n* -s : an individual resulting from the mating of closely related parents : a product of inbreeding
in·breed \ˈ=¦=\ *vb* [²*in* + *breed*] *vt* **1** *archaic* : PRODUCE, GENERATE ⟨~ and cherish in a great people the seeds of virtue —John Milton⟩ **2** : to subject to inbreeding — compare CROSSBREED, OUTBREED ~ *vi, of closely related individuals* : to breed together
inbreeding \ˈ=,==\ *n* [fr. gerund of *inbreed*] **1** : the interbreeding of closely related individuals occurring naturally (as in a closed population), as a result of social or religious custom (as in some royal families), or as a deliberately chosen system of breeding (as of cattle or poultry) and serving esp. to preserve and fix desirable characters of and to eliminate unfavorable characters from a suitably selected stock but tending to effect an unwanted decline (as in size, vigor, or fertility) through the fixation of undesirable and often recessive characters when the initial stock is in any way defective — distinguished from *outbreeding;* compare LINEBREEDING **2 a** : confinement to a narrow range of intellectual and cultural resources issuing chiefly from a limited field of specialization ⟨the ~ of ideas —Joseph Pelej⟩ ⟨the ~ of continental philosophy —Max Rieser⟩ ⟨must avoid nationalist ~ —Mark Starr⟩ **b** : employment in an institution or locality of an excessive number of people who received their training there ⟨academic ~ is marked —Dallas Finn⟩
inbring \ˈ=¦=\ *vt* [ME *inbringen*, fr. OE *inbringan* (prob. trans. of L *inferre* to bring in), fr. *in, inn* in (adv.) + *bringan* to bring — more at INFER, BRING] : to bring in; *esp* : to bring into court or to confiscate by legal process in Scots law
inbuilt \ˈ=¦=\ *adj* [²*in* + *built*] : BUILT-IN ⟨the machine has no ~ knowledge of prime numbers —D.R.Hartree⟩
¹**in·bye** *also* **in·by** \ˈin¦bī\ *adv* [²*in* + *bye* (var. of *by*), *by*, adv.] *chiefly Scot* : in an inward direction : INSIDE, WITHIN; *specif* : toward the workings of a mine
²**inbye** *also* **inby** \"\ *adj, chiefly Scot* : situated close by esp. near to the house ⟨the ~ land⟩
³**inbye** *also* **inby** \"\ *n, pl* **inbyes** *Scot* : land situated close by ⟨80 acres of ~⟩
inc *abbr* **1** [L *incisus*] engraved **2** inclosure **3** included; including; inclusive **4** income; incoming **5** incorporated; incorporation **6** increase **7** incumbent
¹**In·ca** \ˈiŋkə\ *n, pl* **incas** *also* **inca** *usu cap* [Sp, fr. Quechua *inka* king, prince, male of royal blood] **1 a** : a ruler of the Incaic Empire prior to the Spanish conquest **b** : a member of this empire's royal house; *broadly* : a person of high rank or exalted position under this empire **2 a** : a small Quechuan people of the valley of Cuzco in Peru that established hegemony over surrounding peoples to form the Incaic Empire from about 1100 until the Spanish conquest in 1531–35 **b** : any of the constituent Quechuan peoples of the Incaic Empire **3** : a member of an Inca people
²**inca** \"\ *adj, usu cap* : INCAIC
In·ca·bloc \-,bläk\ *trademark* — used for a shock-resistant balance jewel mounting and balance staff design in watches
inca bone *n, usu cap I* : the interparietal when developed as a separate bone in the skull (as frequently found in Peruvian mummies)
inca dove *n, usu cap I* : a small dove (*Scardafella inca*) found from Arizona to Central America
in·ca·ic \(ˈ)in¦kāik, (ˈ)iŋ¦-\ *adj, usu cap* [Sp *incaico*, fr. *inca* + *-ico* -ic (fr. L *-icus*)] : of or relating to the Incas or their empire
in·calculability \(¦)in, ən+\ *n* : the quality or state of being incalculable ⟨her alleged ~ turns out to be unscrupulousness which defies all morals —J.C.Blankenagel⟩
in·calculable \(ˈ)in, ən+\ *adj* [¹*in-* + *calculable*] : not capable of being calculated : UNPREDICTABLE ⟨the influence of environment on character is ~ and far-reaching —S.P.B.Mais⟩: as **a** : being beyond calculation : very great ⟨during the last few thousands of years, ~ quantities of hortatory literature have been produced —Aldous Huxley⟩ **b** : not foreseeable or foreseen ⟨justified in the most ~ way —Havelock Ellis⟩ : UNCERTAIN ⟨an ~ temper⟩ — **in·calculableness** \"+\ *n* -ES — **in·calculably** \"+\ *adv*
in·ca·les·cence \,inkəˈlesᵊn(t)s, ,iŋk-\ *n* -s [L *incalescere* + E *-ence*] : incalescent state : a growing warm or ardent
in·ca·les·cent \¦==¦lesᵊnt\ *adj* [L *incalescent-, incalescens*, pres. part. of *incalescere* to become warm, fr. *in-* ²in- + *calescere* to become warm, incho. of *calēre* to be warm — more at LEE] : growing warm : increasing in ardor
in-calf \¦=¦=\ *adj* [¹*in* + *calf*] *of a cow, chiefly Brit* : PREGNANT
in·caliculate \¦in+\ *adj* [¹*in-* + *caliculate*] : having no calyculus ⟨~ corals⟩
inca magic flower *n, usu cap I* : CANTUTA
incamp *obs var of* ENCAMP
¹**in·can** \ˈiŋkən\ *adj, usu cap* [¹*Inca* + *-an*] : INCAIC
²**incan** \"\ *n* -s *usu cap* **1** : an inhabitant or subject of the Incaic Empire **2** : QUECHUA 3a
in·can·desce \,inkənˈdes, -,kan-, -,kaan-\ *vb* -ED/-ING/-S [L *incandescere*] *vi* : to be or become incandescent ~ *vt* : to cause to become incandescent
in·can·des·cence \,=(,)=ˈdesᵊn(t)s\ *n* -s [prob. fr. F, fr. *incandescent*] : the quality or state of being incandescent ⟨a single white flame, an ~ of the passion of avarice —Van Wyck Brooks⟩; *usu* : the glowing of a body due to its high temperature : emission by a hot body of radiation that renders it visible
in·can·des·cent \¦=(,)=¦desᵊnt\ *adj* [prob. fr. F, fr. L *incandescent-, incandescens*, pres. part of *incandescere* to become white, to become hot, fr. *in-* ²in- + *candescere* to become white, to become hot, incho. of *candēre* to shine, be white — more at CANDID] **1 a** : white, glowing, or luminous with intense heat ⟨~ carbon⟩ **b** : strikingly bright, radiant, or clear ⟨all those flowers — the lilies, the roses, and clumps of white flowers

and bushes of burning green —Virginia Woolf⟩ **c :** BRILLIANT, LAMBENT, LUCID ⟨set thoughts aglowing in ~ language — Antonio Iglesias⟩ ⟨~ wit⟩ ⟨one of his ~ masterpieces, the Symphony No. 99 —B.H.Haggin⟩ **d :** GLOWING, HOT, ARDENT ⟨a . . . youth ~ with martial ardor —*Times Lit. Supp.*⟩ **2 :** of, relating to, or being light produced by incandescence **:** producing light by incandescence ⟨the most common artificial light source is the ~ bulb —*This Is Glass*⟩ — compare INCANDESCENT LAMP, MANTLE 7a **syn** see BRIGHT

incandescent lamp *also* **incandescent** *n* -s **:** an electric lamp consisting essentially of a glass or quartz bulb evacuated or filled with an inert gas in which a filament commonly of tungsten gives off light when it is heated to incandescence by an electric current

incandescent light *n* **:** light from a source of incandescence

in·can·des·cent·ly *adv* **:** in an incandescent manner **:** with incandescence

incandescent mantle *n* **:** MANTLE 7a

in·ca·ne·stra·to \\,ēŋ,känə'sträd·(,)ō\\ *n* -s [It *incanestrato, incannestrato,* fr. past part. of *incanestrare, incannestrare* to put into a basket, fr. *in-* (fr. L *in-* ²in-) + *canestro, cannestro* basket, fr. L *canistrum;* fr. its being poured into baskets and sold in this form — more at CANISTER] **:** a sharp white Sicilian cheese that is made of cow's milk often together with goat's milk, seasoned with salt and various spices, and used chiefly grated as a seasoning or garnish

3 2 4 1

incandescent lamp: *1* base, *2* lead-in wire, *3* filament, *4* bulb

in·ca·nous \\ən'kānəs\\ *adj* [L *incanus,* back-formation fr. *incanescere* to become white, fr. *in-* ²in- + *canescere* to become white, incho. of *canēre* to be gray, white — more at CANESCENT] **:** hoary with white pubescence

in·cant \\ən'kant, -aa(ə)nt\\ *vt* [L *incantare*] **1 :** ENCHANT, CHARM **2 :** to utter by way of incantation ⟨~*ing* garbled ritual to cast a spell⟩

in·can·ta·tion \\,in,kan·'tāshən, -kaan-\\ *n* -s [ME *incantacioun,* fr. MF *incantation,* fr. LL *incantation-, incantatio,* fr. L *incantatus* (past part. of *incantare* to enchant) + *-ion-, -io* -ion — more at ENCHANT] **1 a :** a use of spells or verbal charms spoken or sung as a part of a ritual of magic **b :** a ceremonial chanting or reciting of incantations (as for curing disease) **c :** a use of words to obscure rather than illuminate **:** OBFUSCATION ⟨their habit of hypnotizing and magnetizing a subject by the ~*s* of repetitive argument —V.S.Pritchett⟩ **2 a :** a formula of words chanted or recited in a magic ritual for their special virtues or particular effects **b :** words used in the manner of a formula without conscious concern as to their aptness or relevance to a particular situation ⟨the ~*s* of the propagandists⟩ **c :** an expression (as of music or poetry) designed to move rather than amuse or convince ⟨uses repetition as it is used in spell and litany, as an ~ to heighten emotion, and perhaps to bypass reason —*Times Lit. Supp.*⟩ **3 :** MAGIC, SORCERY, ENCHANTMENT — **in·can·ta·tion·al** \\;=;=;'tāshən°l, -shnəl\\ *adj*

in·can·ta·to·ry \\ən'kantə,tōrē\\ *adj* [L *incantatus* + E *-ory*] **:** constituting, employing, dealing with, or suitable for use in incantation ⟨mystic words with ~ power⟩ ⟨an ~ vocal style⟩

in·capability \\(')in, ən+\\ *n* **:** the quality or state of being incapable

¹**in·capable** \\(')in, ən+\\ *adj* [MF, fr. *in-* ¹in- + *capable* — more at CAPABLE] **1 :** lacking capacity, ability, or qualification for the purpose or end in view: as **a** *obs* **:** not able (as because of smallness) to take in, contain, hold, or keep **b** *obs* **:** not able to receive or endure **:** INTOLERANT **c** *archaic* **:** not being in a state to receive so as to be affected or moved or so as to be sensible **:** not receptive **:** not susceptible **d :** not in a state or of a kind to admit **:** not able to admit **:** INSUSCEPTIBLE — now used only with *of* **e :** not able or fit for the doing or performance **:** INCOMPETENT ⟨an ~ helper⟩ ⟨~ of understanding the matter⟩ ⟨~ of doing the work⟩ **2 a :** lacking legal qualification or power esp. because of some fundamental legal disqualification **b :** lacking the personal ability, power, or understanding required in some legal matter; *esp* **:** suffering from such a degree of mental or physical weakness as to require supervision of one's affairs by a court (as through a conservator) — compare INCOMPETENT, INSANE **c :** legally incompetent from any cause — not used technically — **in·capableness** \\"+\\ *n* -ES

²**incapable** \\"\\ *n* -s **:** one that is incapable or inefficient; *esp* **:** a person (as an imbecile or a simpleton) that is so by reason of defective mentality

in·capably \\"+\\ *adv* **:** in an incapable manner **:** without competence or capability; *esp* **:** to a degree that renders incapable ⟨~ drunk⟩

in·capacious \\;in+\\ *adj* [LL *incapac-, incapax* (fr. L *in-* ¹in- + *capac-, capax* capacious) + E *-ious* — more at CAPACIOUS] **1** *obs* **:** having little or insufficient size or capacity **:** CRAMPED, NARROW, STRAIT **2** *archaic* **:** mentally weak **:** lacking perception, insight, or understanding

in·ca·pac·i·tate \\,inkə'pasə,tāt, -paas-, *usu* -ād·+V\\ *vt* [*incapacity* + *-ate*] **1 :** to deprive of capacity or natural power **:** render incapable or unfit **:** DISABLE, DISQUALIFY ⟨age *incapacitated* him for war⟩ **2 :** to deprive of legal requisites or qualification **:** make legally incapable or ineligible ⟨in some states the appointment of a guardian ~*s* the ward from carrying on his business or from marriage⟩

in·ca·pac·i·ta·tion \\;=;=;=;'tāshən\\ *n* **:** the act of incapacitating or state of being incapacitated **:** INCAPACITY

in·capacity \\;in+\\ *n* [F *incapacité,* fr. MF, fr. *in-* ¹in- + *capacité* capacity — more at CAPACITY] **:** the quality or state of being incapable **:** INABILITY, INCAPABILITY; *esp* **:** lack of physical or intellectual power or of natural or legal qualification

in ca·pi·te \\(')in'käpə,tā\\ *adj* [L, in chief] *of a feudal tenant* **:** holding immediately of one's lord; *esp* **:** holding directly of the crown

¹**incapsulate** *var of* ENCAPSULATE

²**in·cap·su·late** \\ən'kapsələt, -,lāt\\ *adj* [²*in-* + *capsule* + *-ate* (adj. suffix)] **:** ENCAPSULATED

¹**in·car·cer·ate** \\ən'kärs(ə)rət, -kȧs-, *usu* -əd·+V\\ *adj* [L *incarceratus*] **:** IMPRISONED

²**in·car·cer·ate** \\-sə,rāt, *usu* -ād·+V\\ *vt* -ED/-ING/-S [L *incarceratus,* past part. of *incarcerare,* fr. *in-* ²in- + *carcer* prison] **1 :** to put in prison **:** IMPRISON **2 :** to shut up or away **:** CONFINE, ENCLOSE ⟨*incarcerated* in his own sensibility —J.P. Bishop⟩

incarcerated *adj, of a hernia* **:** IMPRISONED, CONFINED; *esp* **:** constricted but not strangulated

in·car·cer·a·tion \\(,)in,=='rāshən, ən-\\ *n* -s [LL *incarceration-, incarceratio,* fr. L *incarceratus* + *-ion-, -io* -ion] **1 :** a confining or state of being confined **:** IMPRISONMENT **2 :** abnormal retention or confinement of a body part; *specif* **:** a constriction of the neck of a hernial sac so that the hernial contents become irreducible

in·car·cer·a·tor \\='==,rād·ə(r), -ātə-\\ *n* -s **:** one that incarcerates

in·car·di·nate \\ən'kärd°n,āt\\ *vt* -ED/-ING/-S [LL *incardinatus,* past part. of *incardinare* to ordain as chief priest, fr. L *in-* ²in- + LL *cardinalis,* adj., principal — more at CARDINAL] **1 :** to adopt canonically or to receive formally (a cleric from another diocese) **2 :** to elevate to the cardinalate

in·car·di·na·tion \\(,)in,=d°n'āshən, ən,-\\ *n* -s [LL *incardination-, incardinatio* appointment of a priest, fr. *incardinatus* + L *-ion-, -io* -ion] **:** the act of incardinating a cleric within the enrolled clergy of a diocese

in·car·mined \\ən'kärmənd, -kȧm-, -,mīnd *also* -,mēnd\\ *adj* [²*in-* + *carmine* + *-ed*] **:** RED, REDDENED

in·carn \\ən'kärn\\ *vb* -ED/-ING/-S [ME *incarnen,* fr. MF *incarner,* fr. LL *incarnare* to make flesh, make fleshy, incarnate — more at INCARNATE] *vt, archaic* **:** to cause to heal **:** cover with flesh **~** *vi, archaic* **:** to cause healing **:** become healed **:** heal over

¹**in·car·na·dine** \\ən'kärnə,dīn, -,dən, -,dēn\\ *adj* [MF *incarnadin,* fr. OIt *incarnadino, incarnatino,* fr. *incarnato* flesh-colored (fr. LL *incarnatus,* past part.) + *-ino* -ine (fr. L *inus*)] **1 :** of the color flesh or flesh pink **2 :** of a red hue

²**incarnadine** *also* **en·car·na·dine** \\ən'-,en'-\\ *vt* -ED/-ING/-S **:** to make incarnadine **:** REDDEN; *esp* **:** to dye flesh-colored, pink, red, or crimson

³**incarnadine** \\"\\ *n* -s **:** an incarnadine color

¹**in·car·nate** \\(')in¦kärnə|t, ən'k-, -kȧn-, -,nā|, *usu* |d·+V\\ *adj* [ME *incarnat,* fr. LL *incarnatus,* past part. of *incarnare*] **1 a :** invested with flesh or bodily nature and form, esp. with human nature and form ⟨a monarch . . . regarded as a god ~ —D.L.Oliver⟩ ⟨an ~ spirit⟩ **b :** that is the very type or essence of ⟨purity ~⟩ ⟨that remote valley was peace ~⟩ ⟨confusion ~⟩; *broadly* **:** UTTER, UNSPEAKABLE ⟨a fiend ~⟩ **c :** made manifest or comprehensible **:** EMBODIED ⟨in the . . . United Nations there is now ~ the hope of people everywhere that this world may become one in spirit as it is in fact —H.L.Stimson⟩ **2 :** INCARNADINE — used chiefly of floral colors ⟨~ clover⟩

²**in·car·nate** \\ən'kär,nāt, 'in,k-, -kȧ,n-, *usu* -ād·+V\\ *vb* -ED/-ING/-S [LL *incarnatus,* past part. of *incarnare* to make flesh, make fleshy, incarnate, fr. L *in-* ²in- + *carn-, caro* flesh — more at CARNAL] *vt* **1 :** to make incarnate: as **a :** to give bodily form and substance to ⟨*incarnating* the devil as a serpent⟩ ⟨most peoples have some tradition of spiritual powers that ~ themselves as man⟩ **b :** to give a concrete or actual form to **:** embody in reality or in a more definite ideal form **:** ACTUALIZE ⟨~ a political theory in institutions⟩ ⟨*incarnating* ideals by helping others⟩ **c :** to constitute an embodiment or type of ⟨an international organization that ~*s* all our hopes for lasting peace⟩ ⟨in this man the spirit of the times is *incarnated*⟩ **2** *obs* **:** INCARN **~** *vi, obs* **:** INCARN

in·car·na·tion \\,in,kär'nāshən, -kȧ'n-\\ *n* -s [ME *incarnacioun,* fr. OF *incarnation,* fr. LL *incarnation-, incarnatio,* fr. *incarnatus* + L *-ion-, -io* -ion] **1 :** a clothing or state of being clothed with flesh **:** a taking on of or being manifested in a fleshly body **2 :** an incarnated being or idea: as **a** (1) **:** the embodiment of a deity or spirit in some form of earthly existence (as a person, an animal, or a plant) (2) *usu cap* **:** the union of divinity with humanity in Jesus Christ **b :** a concrete or actual form incorporating or exemplifying a principle, ideal, or other quality or concept **:** EMBODIMENT ⟨this busy grimy port, the very ~ of commerce and industry⟩; *esp* **:** a person showing a trait or typical character to a marked degree ⟨the very ~ of deceit⟩ **3** *archaic* **:** a rosy or red color **:** FLESH 6, CARNATION **4** *archaic* **:** a process or product of healing **5 :** a period of incarnation **:** time passed in a particular bodily form or state ⟨each ~ leading to a higher⟩ ⟨the old building had passed through several ~*s* as church, workshop, stable, and finally tearoom⟩

in·car·na·tion·al \\;=;=;'nāshən°l, -shnəl\\ *adj* **:** of, relating to, or emphasizing incarnation or a doctrine of incarnation ⟨an ~ religion⟩

in·car·na·tion·ist \\;=;=;'nāsh(ə)nəst\\ *n* -s **:** one that believes in the union of divinity with humanity in the person of Jesus Christ

in·car·vil·lea \\,in,kär'vilēə\\ *n* [NL, after Pierre d'*Incarville* †1757 Fr. Jesuit missionary] **1** *cap* **:** a genus of Asiatic herbs (family Bignoniaceae) with racemose trumpet-shaped flowers **2** -s **:** any plant of the genus *Incarvillea*

incas *pl of* INCA

incase *var of* ENCASE

incast \\'=,=\\ *n* [⁴*in* + *cast* (after *cast in,* v.)] *dial Eng* **:** something added for good measure

incautelous *adj* [¹*in-* + *cautelous*] *obs* **:** INCAUTIOUS

in·caution \\(')in, ən-\\ *n* [¹*in-* + *caution*] **:** lack of caution **:** CARELESSNESS, HEEDLESSNESS

in·cautious \\"+\\ *adj* [¹*in-* + *cautious*] **:** lacking in caution **:** INJUDICIOUS, HEEDLESS, CARELESS, RASH ⟨an ~ step⟩ ⟨~ talk⟩ ⟨an ~ reader⟩ — **in·cautiously** \\"+\\ *adv* — **in·cautiousness** \\"+\\ *n*

in·ca·va·tion \\,inkə'vāshən\\ *n* -s [L *incavatus* (past part. of *incavare* to hollow out, fr. *in-* ²in- + *cavare* to hollow out, fr. *cavus* hollow) + *-ion-, -io* -ion — more at CAVE] **:** a hollow thing or place

incave *obs var of* ENCAVE

in·ca·vo \\ēŋ'kä(,)vō, ən'kā(-\\ *n* -s [It, lit., cavity, hollow, fr. *incavare* to make hollow, fr. L] **:** the part of an intaglio that is incised

ince *abbr* insurance

in·celebrity \\;in+\\ *n* [¹*in-* + *celebrity*] **:** lack of celebrity

in·cend \\ən'send\\ *vt* -ED/-ING/-S [L *incendere* to kindle, set on fire — more at INCENSE] *archaic* **:** INFLAME, EXCITE

in·cen·di·a·rism \\ən'sendēə,rizəm\\ *n* -s **1 :** a deliberate and unjustifiable setting of fire to property — compare ARSON, PYROMANIA **2 :** incendiary behavior ⟨party ~⟩

in·cen·di·a·rist \\-,rəst\\ *n* -s **:** INCENDIARY 1

¹**in·cen·di·ary** \\-dē,erē, -ri\\ *n* -ES [L *incendiarius,* adj. & n., fr. *incendium* conflagration (fr. *incendere* to kindle, set afire) + *-arius* -ary — more at INCENSE] **1 a :** a person who deliberately sets fire to a building or other property **b :** an incendiary agent (as a bomb) **2 :** a person who excites or inflames factions and promotes quarrels or sedition **:** AGITATOR, EXCITER **3** *obs* **:** an exciting or causative factor esp. of something bad or unpleasant

²**incendiary** \\"\\ *adj* [L *incendiarius*] **1 :** of, relating to, or involving a deliberate burning of property ⟨~ fires⟩ ⟨an ~ crime⟩ **2 a :** tending to excite or inflame factions, sedition, or quarrels **:** INFLAMMATORY, SEDITIOUS ⟨an ~ speech⟩ ⟨~ literature⟩ **b :** sexually stimulating ⟨an ~ blonde⟩ **3 a :** igniting combustible materials spontaneously ⟨an ~ agent⟩ **b :** relating to, being, or involving the use of an explosive missile containing chemicals that ignite on bursting ⟨~ grenade⟩ ⟨~ warfare⟩ — see INCENDIARY BOMB

incendiary bomb *n* **:** a bomb that contains an incendiary agent (as jellied gasoline) and is designed to kindle fires at its objective — called also *fire bomb*

in·cen·di·um \\ən'sendēəm\\ *n, pl* **incen·dia** \\-ēə\\ [ML, fr. L, conflagration] *Roman law & Roman Dutch law* **:** a crime corresponding to but of wider scope than arson in the English common law

in·cen·sa·tion \\,in,sen'sāshən, ,in(t)sən'-\\ *n* -s [LL *incensatus* (past part. of *incensare*) + E *-ion*] **:** the action of censing

¹**in·cense** \\'in,sen(t)s *sometimes* -,sən-\\ *n* -s [ME *encens, incense,* fr. OF *encens,* fr. LL *incensum* incense, fr. L, neut. of *incensus,* past part. of *incendere* to kindle, set on fire, irritate, fr. *in-* ²in- + *-cendere* to burn (akin to L *candēre* to shine, be glowing hot, be white) — more at CANDID] **1 :** material (as gums or woods) used to produce a fragrant odor when burned **2 :** the perfume or the smoke exhaled from spices and gums when burned in celebrating religious rites or as an offering to a deity; *broadly* **:** a pleasing scent or fragrance **3 :** pleasing attention **:** HOMAGE, FLATTERY **syn** see FRAGRANCE

²**in·cense** \\" *sometimes* ən'sen-\\ *vb* -ED/-ING/-S [ME *encensen, incensen,* fr. MF *encenser,* fr. LL *incensare,* fr. *incensum*] *vt* **1 a :** to apply or offer incense to **:** burn incense before **b :** to burn or offer as an incense offering **2 a :** to perfume with or as if with incense **:** SCENT **b** *archaic* **:** FLATTER **~** *vi* **:** to burn or offer incense

³**in·cense** \\(')in¦sen(t)s, ən's-\\ *vt* -ED/-ING/-S [ME *encensen,* fr. MF *incenser,* fr. L *incensus,* past part. of *incendere* to kindle, set on fire, irritate — more at ¹INCENSE] **1** *obs* **a :** to set fire to **:** KINDLE **b :** to consume with fire **:** BURN **2 a** *archaic* **:** to excite (a passion or an emotion) into activity **:** cause to become aroused **b** *obs* **:** to inflame (a person) with a passion or emotion **c :** to cause to be extremely angry **:** arouse the wrath or indignation of ⟨such careless waste *incensed* her⟩ **3** *obs* **:** to urge to some course or action

⁴**incense** *var of* INSENSE

incense burner *n* **:** one that burns incense; *specif* **:** a vessel (as a stationary vase) for holding burning incense — compare CENSER

incense cedar *n* **:** any of various trees of the genus *Libocedrus; esp* **:** a tall tree (*L. decurrens*) of the No. American Pacific coast with a light soft straight-grained wood that is highly resistant to moisture, foliage suggesting that of a cypress, and cinnamon red bark — called also *pencil cedar, red cedar, white cedar*

incensed *adj* [fr. past part. of ³*incense*] **1 :** ANGERED, ENRAGED, INDIGNANT **2** *of a heraldic figure* **:** represented as enraged usu. by means of fire issuing from mouth and eyes

incense juniper *n* **:** a European juniper (*Juniperus thurifera*) with paired awl-shaped leaves whitened on the upper surface and fragrant wood that is sometimes burned as incense

in·cense·less \\'=(,)=ləs\\ *adj* **:** employing no incense ⟨~ churches⟩

in·cense·ment \\ən'sen(t)smənt\\ *n* -s **:** the state of being incensed **:** intense anger or indignation

incense shrub *n* **:** INDIAN CURRANT 2

incense tree *n* **:** any of various chiefly tropical trees (as members of the genera *Commiphora, Boswellia,* and *Protium*) that produce fragrant gums or resins

incense wood *n* **:** the fragrant wood of either of two tropical American trees (*Protium heptaphyllum* and *P. guianense*)

in·cen·so·ry \\'in,sen(t)s(ə)rē, ən's-; 'insən,sōrē\\ *n* -ES [ML *incensorium,* fr. neut. of LL *incensorius* having burning power, fr. L *incensus* (past part. of *incendere* to kindle) + *-orius* -ory — more at INCENSE] **:** CENSER, THURIBLE

incenter \\'=,==\\ *n* [⁴*in* + *center*] **:** the center of a circle inscribed in a triangle or of a sphere inscribed in a tetrahedron

¹**in·cen·tive** \\ən'sentiv, -tēv *also* -t-əv\\ *n* -s [ME, fr. LL *incentivum,* fr. neut. of L *incentivus*] **:** something that incites or has a tendency to incite to determination or action **:** something (as fear or hope of reward) that constitutes a motive or spur **:** INDUCEMENT ⟨money is still a major ~ in most occupations⟩ ⟨his father's promise of a bicycle was a real ~ to harder study⟩ **syn** see MOTIVE

²**in·cen·tive** \\(')in¦s-, ən's-\\ *adj* [LL *incentivus,* fr. L, setting the tune, fr. *incentus* (past part. of *incinere* to set the tune, fr. *in-* ²in- + *-cinere,* fr. *canere* to sing) + *-ivus* -ive — more at CHANT] **1 a :** serving to encourage, rouse, or move to action **:** STIMULATIVE **:** motivative in a particular direction or course ⟨increasing needs are often ~ to invention⟩ ⟨this charming book is ~ to further study⟩ **b** (1) **:** designed to enhance or improve production esp. in industry ⟨~ pay⟩ ⟨disadvantages of an ~ system⟩ (2) **:** concerned with, based on, or employing incentive measures or techniques in business or industry ⟨~ management⟩ ⟨long-term ~ experience⟩ ⟨~ studies⟩ **2** *obs* **:** serving to set on fire **:** KINDLING — **in·cen·tive·ly** \\-təvlē, -li\\ *adv*

incentive wage *n* **:** a wage based on the number of units produced by a factory pieceworker — compare BONUS SYSTEM

¹**in·cept** \\ən'sept\\ *vb* -ED/-ING/-S [L *inceptus,* past part. of *incipere* — more at INCEPTION] *vt* **1** *archaic* **:** BEGIN, COMMENCE, UNDERTAKE **2** [influenced in meaning by L *capere* to take] **:** to take in: as **a :** INGEST ⟨phagocytes ~*ing* foreign particles⟩ **b :** to receive as a member **~** *vi* **:** to obtain an advanced degree and therewith the right to teach or practice a learned profession — now used only at Cambridge University

²**in·cept** \\'in,sept\\ *n* -s **:** ANLAGE

in·cep·tion \\ən'sepshən\\ *n* -s [L *inception-, inceptio,* fr. *inceptus* (past part. of *incipere* to begin, fr. *in-* ²in- + *-cipere,* fr. *capere* to take) + *-ion-, -io* -ion — more at HEAVE] **1 :** an act, process, or instance of beginning (as of an institution, organization, or concept) **:** COMMENCEMENT, INITIATION **2 :** an act of incepting: as **a :** a public lecture in which the candidate for a master's degree in a medieval university demonstrated his learning and competence to teach **b :** INGESTION **syn** see ORIGIN

¹**in·cep·tive** \\-tiv\\ *n* -s [LL *inceptivus,* adj.] **:** INCHOATIVE

²**in·cep·tive** \\(')in¦s-, ən's-\\ *adj* [LL *inceptivus,* fr. L *inceptus* (past part. of *incipere* to begin) + *-ivus* -ive — more at INCEPTION] **1 a :** BEGINNING **b :** relating to a beginning **2 :** INCHOATIVE 2 — **in·cep·tive·ly** \\-tə̇vlē\\ *adv*

in·cep·tor \\ən'septə(r), 'in,s-\\ *n* -s [ME, fr. L, beginner, fr. *inceptus* + *-or*] **1** *Brit* **:** one that incepts at a university **2 :** one that begins or introduces

in·cer·tae se·dis \\in¦ker,tī'sādəs, in,sərd·ē'sēdəs\\ *adv* [L, of uncertain place] **:** in an uncertain position **:** without assurance of relationship — used of taxa ⟨the Acanthocephala have often been placed *incertae sedis* among the Nemathelminthes⟩

incertain *adj* [MF, fr. *in-* ¹in- + *certain*] *obs* **:** UNCERTAIN — **incertainly** *adv, obs* — **incertainty** *n, obs*

in·certitude \\(')in, ən+\\ *n* [MF, fr. LL *incertitudo,* fr. L *in-* ¹in- + LL *certitudo* certitude — more at CERTITUDE] **:** UNCERTAINTY: **a :** absence of assurance or confidence **:** DOUBT, INDECISION **b :** uncertain or insecure condition

in·ces·san·cy \\ən'ses°nsē, -nsi\\ *n* -ES **:** the quality or state of being incessant

in·ces·sant \\(')in¦ses°nt, ən's-\\ *adj* [ME *incessaunt,* fr. LL *incessant-, incessans,* fr. L *in-* ¹in- + *cessant-, cessans,* pres. part. of *cessare* to delay — more at CEASE] **1 :** continuing or following without interruption **:** UNCEASING ⟨~ rains⟩ ⟨this ~ chatter⟩ **2** *obs* **:** EVERLASTING **syn** see CONTINUAL

in·ces·sant·ly *adv* [ME *incessauntly,* fr. *incessaunt* + *-ly*] **1 :** in an unceasing manner or course **:** without intermission or relief **:** CONTINUALLY ⟨the question ran ~ through his mind —Arnold Bennett⟩ ⟨poor and uncomfortable persons toiling ~ to create riches —G.B.Shaw⟩ **2** *archaic* **:** at once **:** IMMEDIATELY

in·ces·sant·ness *n* -ES **:** the quality or state of being incessant

in·ces·sion \\ən'seshən\\ *n* [LL *incession-, incessio* pace, gait, fr. L *incessus* (past part. of *incedere* to go along, move forward, fr. *in-* ²in- + *cedere* to go, proceed) + *-ion-, -io* -ion — more at CEDE] *archaic* **:** movement onward or forward

in·cest \\'in,sest\\ *n* -s [ME, fr. L *incestus* unchastity, incest (fr. *incestus* impure, unchaste, fr. *in-* ¹in- + *-cestus,* fr. *castus* pure, chaste) & *incestum,* fr. neut. of *incestus* — more at CASTE] **1 :** sexual intercourse or interbreeding between closely related individuals esp. when they are related or regarded as related (as by reason of affinity or membership in a tribal kinship, group, or clan) within degrees wherein marriage is prohibited by law or custom — compare ENDOGAMY, EXOGAMY, INBREEDING **2 :** the statutory crime of cohabitation, marriage, or sexual intercourse without marriage of parties related to each other within the degrees of consanguinity or often of affinity within which marriage is prohibited by law

in·ces·tu·ous \\(')in¦ses(h)chəwəs, ən's-, -)chəs\\ *adj* [LL *incestuosus,* fr. L *incestus* incest + *-osus* -ous] **1 a :** constituting or involving incest ⟨an ~ relation⟩ ⟨~ unions⟩ **b :** of, relating to, or guilty of incest ⟨these ~ beasts⟩ **c :** begotten by incest ⟨~ offspring⟩ **2 :** INGROWN, DERIVATIVE, IMITATIVE — **in·ces·tu·ous·ly** *adv* — **in·ces·tu·ous·ness** *n* -ES

¹**inch** \\'inch\\ *n* -ES *often attrib* [ME *inch, inche,* fr. OE *ince, ynce,* fr. L *uncia* twelfth part, ounce, inch — more at OUNCE] **1 :** a unit of length equal to 1/36 yard or formerly to the length of 3 grains of barley placed end to end ⟨a 6-*inch* rule⟩ ⟨a width of six ~*es*⟩— see MEASURE table **2 :** a small amount, distance, or degree (as of time or space) **:** a narrow margin or little bit ⟨escaped death by an ~⟩ ⟨couldn't see an ~ before them in the storm⟩ **3 inches** *pl* **:** STATURE, HEIGHT ⟨wore raised heels to make the most of his ~*es*⟩ ⟨a man of his ~*es* would be noticeable in any crowd⟩ **4 a :** a fall (as of rain or snow) sufficient to cover a surface or to fill a gage to the depth of one inch ⟨two ~*es* of rain⟩ **b :** a degree of atmospheric or other pressure sufficient to balance the weight of a column of mercury or other specified liquid one inch high in a barometer or manometer ⟨an atmospheric pressure of 30 ~*es*⟩ **c :** WATER-INCH **d** *chiefly Midland* **:** one twelfth of the light period of a day ⟨worked a full 12 ~*es* getting in the hay⟩ **e :** COLUMN INCH — **by inches** *also* **inch by inch** *adv* **:** very gradually or slowly — **by inch of candle :** by auction in which bidding is open only while a small piece of candle burns — **every inch** *adv* **:** to the utmost degree **:** ENTIRELY ⟨looks *every inch* a winner⟩ — **within an inch of :** almost to the point of **:** nearly to **:** very near ⟨broke down when we were *within an inch of* our destination⟩ ⟨came *within an inch of* death⟩

²**inch** \\"\\ *vb* -ED/-ING/-ES *vi* **:** to advance or retire by small degrees ⟨~*ed* back from the lip of the crevasse⟩; *broadly* **:** to move slowly or in little increments ⟨~*ing* along the slippery ridge⟩ ⟨Canada and the U.S. are ~*ing* back to the unity of action achieved 10 years ago —M.W.Straight⟩ ⟨prices are ~*ing* down⟩ **~** *vt* **1 :** to cause to advance or retire by small degrees ⟨~*ed* himself nearer⟩; *broadly* **:** to cause to move slowly or in little increments ⟨~*ing* their feet slowly over the ice⟩ ⟨~*ing* not only the U.S. but the United Nations forward into a war that did not have to be fought —H.L.Ickes⟩ **2** *obs* **:** to give sparingly **:** deal out in small amounts

³**inch** \\"\\ *n* -ES [ME *inch, ynche,* fr. ScGael *innis;* akin to OIr *inis* island, W *ynys,* Bret *enez*] **1** *now dial* **:** ISLAND — often used in the names of small islands off the coast of Scotland ⟨*Inchcolm*⟩ ⟨*Inchkeith*⟩ **2** *now dial* **:** low grassy ground by a river

inch *abbr* inchoative

inchant *obs var of* ENCHANT

incharitable *adj* [ME, fr. ¹*in-* + *charitable*] *obs* **:** UNCHARITABLE

incharity *n* [¹*in-* + *charity*] *obs* **:** lack of charity

inchase *archaic var of* ENCHASE

inched \ˈincht\ *adj* [¹*inch* + *-ed*] **:** having or measuring a specified number of inches ⟨a 4-*inched* hook⟩

inch·er \ˈinchə(r)\ *n* -s [¹*inch* + *-er*] **:** something having a dimension of a specified number of inches; *specif* **:** a gun having a bore of a specified number of inches — usu. used in combination with a numeral ⟨heard the 14-*inchers* firing on the coast⟩

in chief *adj* **1 :** heading a staff **:** LEADING — often used in combination ⟨editor-*in-chief*⟩ **2 :** PRIMARY, BASIC, INITIAL ⟨evidence *in chief*⟩ ⟨a fabric dutiable on its *in chief* value of wool⟩

inch·ling \ˈinchliŋ\ *n* -s [¹*inch* + *-ling*] **:** a small being of a kind likely to grow larger ⟨drew in a netful of ~*s*⟩

inch·ma·ree clause \ˈinchmə,rē-\ *n, usu cap I* [after *Inchmaree*, Brit. steamer; fr. its formulation as a result of the sinking of the Inchmaree in Liverpool harbor March, 1884] **:** a clause in a marine insurance policy on the hull of a ship that assuming the owners and managers of the ship have exercised due diligence makes the underwriter liable for loss or damage to hull or machinery arising from the negligence of the master, charterers, mariners, engineers or pilots from explosions, bursting of boilers, breakage of shafts, or any latent defect in hull and machinery, from contact with aircraft or land conveyances, or from any accident at docking facilities (as when loading or unloading or entering a dry dock)

inch·meal \ˈ≈ˌmē(ə)l\ *adv* [¹*inch* + *-meal* (as in *piecemeal*)] **:** little by little **:** GRADUALLY — often used with *by*

¹**in·cho·ate** \(ˈ)inˈkōət, ənˈkō-, ˈinkə,wāt\ *adj* [L *inchoatus*, *incohatus*, past part. of *inchoare*, *incohare* to begin (lit., to hitch up), fr. *in-* ²in- + *cohum* strap fastening a plow beam to the yoke; perh. akin to Bret *morgo* hame, W *mynci* hame, OE *haga* hedge — more at HEDGE] **:** being recently begun or undertaken **:** INCIPIENT **:** being partly but not fully in existence or operation **:** INCOMPLETE: as **a :** imperfectly formed or formulated **:** DISORDERED, INCOHERENT, UNORGANIZED ⟨the general plan is ~ and incoherent, and the particular treatments disconnected —Hilary Corke⟩ ⟨the solar system . . . far out from the hub of this great wheel of stars and ~ dust and gas —L.C. Eiseley⟩ ⟨vague consumer longings and ~ needs —J.S.Gambs⟩ **b** *of a legal right or instrument or interest* **:** not yet perfected **:** not yet made certain or specific **:** not yet vested **:** INCIPIENT, EXPECTANT, POTENTIAL, CONTINGENT, IMPERFECTED ⟨an ~ right of dower⟩ ⟨an ~ equity⟩ ⟨an instrument that the law requires to be recorded is an ~ instrument until it is recorded —Besse May Miller⟩ — **in·cho·ate·ly** *adv* — **in·cho·ate·ness** *n* -ES

²**in·cho·ate** \ˈinkə,wāt, ənˈkō,āt\ *vb* -ED/-ING/-S [L *inchoatus*, *incohatus*, past part. of *inchoare*, *incohare*] *vt, archaic* **:** to cause to begin ~ *vi, archaic* **:** to make a beginning **:** START

in·cho·a·tion \,inkəˈwāshən\ *n* -s [LL *inchoation-*, *inchoatio*, *incohation-*, *incohatio*, fr. L *inchoatus*, *incohatus* + *-ion-*, *-io* -ion] **:** an act of beginning **:** COMMENCEMENT, INCEPTION

¹**in·cho·a·tive** \(ˈ)inˈkōəd·iv, ənˈk-\ *n* -s [LL *inchoativum*, *incohativum*, fr. neut. of *inchoativus*, *incohativus*] **:** an inchoative verb

²**inchoative** \"\ *adj* [LL *inchoativus*, *incohativus*, fr. L *inchoatus*, *incohatus* + *-ivus* -ive] **1 :** INITIAL, FORMATIVE ⟨~ stages⟩ **2 :** denoting the beginning of an action, state, or occurrence — used of certain verbs (as *begin*, *set out*, *get*, *awake*) or of certain verb forms (as *tremesco* "I begin to tremble" and some other Latin verbs in *-sco*) — **in·cho·a·tive·ly** \-d·əvlē\ *adv*

in·chon \(ˈ)inˈchän\ *adj, usu cap* [fr. *Inchon*, Korea] **:** of or from the city of Inchon, Korea **:** of the kind or style prevalent in Inchon

inch-ounce *n* **1 :** a unit of work equal to the work done in raising one ounce against the force of gravity through a distance of one inch **2 :** a unit of moment equal to the moment of a force of one ounce acting at a distance of one inch from a center of moments

inch plant *n* **:** a wandering Jew (*Tradescantia fluminensis*) that is often grown as a house plant

inch-pound \ˈ≈ˈ≈\ *n* **:** one twelfth of a foot-pound

inch-ton \ˈ≈ˈ≈\ *n* **:** a unit of energy or work that is equal to the work done in raising one ton against the force of gravity the height of one inch

¹**inchworm** \ˈ≈ˌ≈\ *n* [¹*inch* + *worm*] **:** LOOPER 1

²**inchworm** \"\ *vb* **:** CRAWL

in·cide \ənˈsīd\ *vb* -ED/-ING/-S [L *incidere* — more at INCISE] *vi* **1** *archaic* **:** CUT, INCISE **2** *obs* **:** to cause loosening or resolution ~ *vt* **1** *archaic* **:** to cut into (as a lesion or tissue) **2** *archaic* **:** to cause loosening or resolution of (as phlegm)

in·ci·dence \ˈin(t)sədən(t)s *also* -dᵊn- *or* -,den-\ *n* -s [ME, fr. MF, fr. LL *incidentia*, fr. L *incident-*, *incidens* + *-ia* -y] **1** *now chiefly dial* **:** INCIDENT **2 a :** an act or the fact or manner of falling upon or affecting **:** OCCURRENCE ⟨diseases of domestic ~ —*Science*⟩ ⟨control of both the ~ of expense and the meeting of expense must lie primarily in the hands of management⟩ **b :** rate, range, or amount of occurrence or influence ⟨a rising ~ of poverty⟩; *sometimes* **:** the rate of occurrence of new cases of a particular disease in a population being studied — compare PREVALENCE **3 :** the falling of a tax upon a person who is unable to shift it onto someone else and who therefore bears the money burden of the tax ⟨the ultimate ~ of most corporation taxes is on the consumer⟩ — compare DIRECT TAX **4 a :** the arrival of something (as a projectile or a ray of light) at a surface **b :** ANGLE OF INCIDENCE 2

incidence wire *n* **:** STAGGER WIRE

incidency *obs var of* INCIDENCE

¹**in·ci·dent** \-nt\ *n* -s [ME, fr. MF, fr. ML *incident-*, *incidens*, fr. L, pres. part. of *incidere* to fall into, fall on, meet up with, occur, happen, fr. *in-* ²in- + *-cidere* (fr. *cadere* to fall) — more at CHANCE] **1 a :** an occurrence of an action or situation felt as a separate unit of experience **:** an occurrence or sometimes a situation or thing taking place as part of a larger continuum but unimportant or nonessential **:** HAPPENING ⟨conflict is an inevitable ~ in any active system of cooperation —Lewis Mumford⟩ **b :** an accompanying minor occurrence or condition **:** CONCOMITANT ⟨Madison's view . . . that taxation is a necessary ~ anyway to the exercise of any power —C.P.Curtis⟩ **c :** an occurrence noticeably varying a set or accustomed course or routine **:** an uncommon happening ⟨to remain at variance with his wife seemed to him a considerable ~ —Joseph Conrad⟩ **d :** an occurrence calling forth a sequel **:** a motivating event or situation **:** FACTOR ⟨the ~ of that conflict was slavery, but it was not its true cause —*Congressional Record*⟩ **e :** a happening or related group of happenings subordinate to a main narrative plot ⟨the melodrama and the romance . . . must be made up of swift successions of startling ~ —E.G.Sutcliffe⟩ **f :** a frequent, accustomed, or routine occurrence unworthy of note or comment ⟨a quite ordinary ~ of daily life —Arnold Bennett⟩ **2 a :** a contretemps, fracas, disturbance, or other action likely to lead to grave consequences esp. in matters diplomatic ⟨repeated minor ~*s* led finally to the danger of open combat at the boundary —*Amer. Guide Series: Maine*⟩ **b :** a military situation marked by fighting without formally declared war ⟨the Korea ~⟩ **c** *chiefly Brit* **:** a bomb explosion or other sudden violent disturbance ⟨air-raid wardens checking on ~*s*⟩ **3 a :** something dependent upon, appertaining or subordinate to, or accompanying something else of greater or principal importance ⟨an alimony agreement may be an ~ of a divorce proceeding⟩ **b :** something arising or resulting from something else of greater or principal importance ⟨a power to employ a broker may be an ~ of an express power to sell real estate⟩ **syn** see OCCURRENCE

²**incident** \"\ *adj* [ME, fr. L *incident-*, *incidens*, pres. part.] **1 a :** occurring or likely to occur esp. as a minor consequence or accompaniment ⟨confusion ~ to a quick change⟩ **:** associated or naturally related or attaching ⟨the privileges ~ to increased rank⟩ **b** *obs* **:** PERTINENT, APPOSITE, LIABLE, SUBJECT **2** *archaic* **:** occurring accidentally and without essential relationship **:** INCIDENTAL **3** *law* **:** dependent on or appertaining to another thing **:** directly and immediately relating to or involved in something else though not an essential part of it **4 a :** falling or striking on something — used esp. of light rays on a plane **b :** acting from without **:** EXTERNAL ⟨attacks by ~ forces⟩ **syn** see LIABLE

¹**in·ci·den·tal** \ˌ≈≈ˈdentᵊl\ *adj* [¹*incident* + *-al*; prob. influenced in meaning by ML *incidenter* incidentally, adv., fr. L *incident-*, *incidens*] **1 :** subordinate, nonessential, or attendant in position or significance: as **a :** occurring merely by chance or without intention or calculation **:** occurring as a minor concomitant ⟨allowing a few dollars extra for ~ expenses⟩ ⟨the ~ gain which such a policy may win —J.A.Hobson⟩ ⟨man may be an ~ host of the sheep liver fluke⟩ **b :** being likely to ensue as a chance or minor consequence — usu. used with *to* ⟨labor problems ~ to rapidly expanding factories —*Amer. Guide Series: Mass.*⟩ **c :** lacking effect, force, or consequence **:** not receiving much consideration or calculation ⟨a cool, purely ~, and passive contempt —Herman Melville⟩ **d :** presented purposefully but as though without consideration or intention; *often* **:** DIGRESSIVE ⟨an ~ allusion, purposely thrown out, to the day of the week—Charles Dickens⟩ **2 :** met or encountered casually or by accident **:** CHANCE ⟨~ traveling companions⟩ ⟨an ~ shipboard acquaintance⟩ **syn** see ACCIDENTAL

²**incidental** \"\ *n* -s **1 :** something that is incidental **:** a subordinate or incidental item ⟨no such ~ as personal sensibilities can be allowed to interfere with the overall plan of the survey⟩ **2 incidentals** *pl* **:** minor items (as of expense) that are not particularized ⟨a bill for tuition and ~*s*⟩

in·ci·den·tal·ist \ˌ≈≈ˈdentᵊləst\ *n* -s **:** one that is more concerned with the minutiae of incident than with broad overall views or concepts

in·ci·den·tal·ly \ˌ≈≈ˈdentlē, -tᵊlē, -li\ *adv* **1 :** by chance **:** as a matter of minor import **:** CASUALLY ⟨in this discussion grave questions were ~ brought up⟩ **2 :** by way of interjection or digression **:** in passing **:** PARENTHETICALLY ⟨touching ~ on the waterpower values⟩ ⟨another leading industry, ~, has quadrupled its business in five years⟩

incidental music *n* **:** descriptive music played or to be played during the action of a play to heighten a situation or project a mood (as of a battle, a storm, a death scene) or to relate directly to stage action (as a song or a dance); *broadly* **:** any music related to a play (as an overture or entr'acte) — compare BACKGROUND MUSIC

in·ci·den·tal·ness \ˌ≈≈ˈdentᵊlnəs\ *n* -ES **:** the quality or state of being incidental **:** CONCOMITANCE

in·ci·dent·less \ˈin(t)sədəntləs, -dᵊn-, -,den-\ *adj* **:** free from incident **:** UNEVENTFUL

in·ci·dent·ly \ˈin(t)sədəntlē, -dᵊn-, -li, ˌ≈≈ˈdent- — *in sense 2 always the last*\ *adv* **1 :** so as to be incident **2 :** INCIDENTALLY

inciding *pres part of* INCIDE

in·ci·en·so \,in(t)sēˈen(t)(,)sō\ *n* -s [AmerSp, fr. Sp, incense, fr. L *incensum* — more at INCENSE] **:** a shrubby encelia (*Encelia farinosa*) of rocky desert uplands of the southwestern U. S. and adjacent Mexico that has grayish green to almost white tomentose foliage and showy cymes of yellow flowers and that produces a resin that has been used as incense, in folk medicine, and in varnish

in·cin·er·ate \ənˈsinə,rāt, *usu* -ād·+V\ *vb* -ED/-ING/-S [ML *incineratus*, past part. of *incinerare*, fr. L *in-* ²in- + *ciner-*, *cinis* ashes; akin to Gk *konis*, *konia* ashes, dust; basic meaning: to rub, scratch, tickle] *vt* **:** to cause to burn to ashes **:** consume by or as if by fire ⟨*incinerating* the trash⟩ ~ *vi* **:** to be or become completely burned ⟨paper and dry leaves ~ easily⟩

in·cin·er·a·tion \(,)in,sinəˈrāshən, ən,-\ *n* -s [ML *incineration-*, *incineratio*, fr. L *incineratus* (past part. of *incinerare* to incinerate) + *-ion-*, *-io* -ion] **:** the act of incinerating or the state of being incinerated **:** CREMATION; *esp* **:** an analytical procedure of heating an organic substance with free access to air until only its ash remains — compare IGNITION

in·cin·er·a·tor \ə≈ˈ≈,rād·ə(r), -ātə-\ *n* -s **:** one that incinerates; *esp* **:** a furnace or a container for incinerating waste materials

incinerators

¹**in·cip·i·a·tive** \ənˈsipē,ād·iv, -ēəd·-\ *adj* [*incipient* + *-ative*] *of a verb form or aspect* **:** expressing action about to begin or just beginning — compare HABITUATIVE

²**incipiative** \"\ *n* -s **:** an incipiative form of a verb

in·cip·i·en·cy \ənˈsipēənsē, -si\ *also* **in·cip·i·ence** \-ēən(t)s\ *n, pl* **incipiencies** *also* **incipiences :** the state or fact of being incipient **:** BEGINNING, COMMENCEMENT

in·cip·i·ent \(ˈ)inˈsipēənt, ənˈs-\ *adj* [L *incipient-*, *incipiens*, pres. part. of *incipere* to begin, fr. *in-* ²in- + *-cipere* (fr. *capere* to take) — more at HEAVE] **:** beginning to be or become apparent **:** COMMENCING, INITIAL ⟨the ~ stage of a fever⟩ ⟨~ light of day⟩ ⟨~ civil disorders⟩ — **in·cip·i·ent·ly** *adv*

incipient species *n* **:** a natural population that is more or less interfertile with another related population but is inhibited from interbreeding in nature by some specific barrier — compare ECOSPECIES

incipient wilting *n* **:** partial and temporary loss of turgor in a plant that occurs in the presence of adequate soil moisture and is associated with excessive water loss through transpiration

in·ci·pit \ˈin(t)səpət, ˈiŋkə-, *esp in senses b & c* ˈinchə-\ *n* -s [L, it begins, 3d pers. sing. pres. indic. of *incipere*] **:** BEGINNING: as **a :** the introductory words or part of a medieval manuscript or early printed book ⟨reproducing two ~*s* with superb miniatures —Raphael Levy⟩ — compare EXPLICIT **b :** the opening words of the text in a Gregorian chant or psalm tone sung usu. by the cantor **c :** the word given at the beginning of the tenor in a cantus-firmus motet that serves as a reference to the tenor's origin in the liturgy

in·circumscription \ˌin+\ *n* [LL *incircumscription-*, *incircumscriptio*, fr. *incircumscriptus* not circumscribed (fr. L *in-* ¹in- + *circumscriptus*, past part. of *circumscribere* to circumscribe) + L *-ion-*, *-io* -ion — more at CIRCUMSCRIBE] *archaic* **:** the quality or state of being free from bounds or limits

incircumspect *adj* [LL *incircumspectus*, fr. L *in-* ¹in- + *circumspectus*, past part. of *circumspicere* to look around, be cautious — more at CIRCUMSPECT] *obs* **:** IMPRUDENT, INDISCREET — **incircumspection** *n, obs* — **incircumspectly** *adv, obs*

incis *abbr* [L *incisus*] engraved

in·ci·sal \(ˈ)inˈsīzəl\ *adj* [L *incisus* + E *-al*] **:** CUTTING ⟨the ~ edge of a tooth⟩

in·cise \(ˈ)inˈsīz, -īs\ *vb* -ED/-ING/-S [MF or L; MF *inciser*, fr. L *incisus*, past part. of *incidere*, fr. *in-* ²in- + *-cidere* (fr. *caedere* to cut) — more at CONCISE] *vi*, *obs* **:** to make an incision ~ *vt* **1 :** to cut into **:** make an incision in ⟨*incised* the swollen tissue⟩ **2 a :** to carve figures, letters, or devices into **:** ENGRAVE ⟨~ a tablet with an inscription⟩ **b :** to produce (as letters, figures, or devices) by carving into a surface ⟨~ an inscription on a monument⟩ **3 a :** to produce (a narrow steep-walled valley) by downward erosion ⟨caused the streams to ~ their valleys —C.O.Dunbar⟩ **b :** to lower (itself) by eroding a deeper channel ⟨the streams then *incised* themselves to the new baselevel —C.O.Dunbar⟩ **c :** to intersect as a deep narrow cut ⟨more than twenty different submarine canyon systems ~ the continental border —J.C.Crowell⟩

incised *adj* **1 a :** CUT-IN, CARVED, ENGRAVED ⟨~ ornamentation⟩; *esp* **:** decorated with incised figures ⟨~ pottery⟩ **b** *of a cut or wound* **:** made with or as if with a sharp knife or scalpel **:** clean and well defined **2 :** having a margin that is deeply and sharply and more or less irregularly notched ⟨an ~ leaf⟩

incised meander *n* **:** the curve of a winding river with steep slopes on both sides rising to a former floodplain and usu. interpreted as due to rejuvenation of a meandering stream but prob. also formed by a combination of vertical and lateral erosion in a single cycle of valley development — compare ENTRENCHED MEANDER

in·ci·si·form \inˈsīzə,fȯrm, -īsə-\ *adj* [*incisor* + *-iform*] **:** having the form of or resembling a typical incisor tooth **:** shaped for cutting

in·ci·sion \ənˈsizhən\ *n* -s [ME *inscicioun*, fr. MF & L; MF *incision*, fr. L *incision-*, *incisio*, fr. *incisus* + *-ion-*, *-io* -ion] **1 a :** a separation of parts made or such as might be made by a cutting or pointed instrument (as a notch in the margin of a leaf or of an insect's wing) **b :** CLEFT, CUT, GASH; *specif* **:** an incised wound made by a surgeon into the tissues or an organ (as in reaching a site of injury or establishing drainage) ⟨an abdominal ~⟩ **2 :** an act or action of incising (as into a substance) ⟨a Pliocene uplift which caused valley ~ —A.M. Bateman⟩ ⟨the surgeon's skillful ~ of the tissues⟩ **3 :** the quality or state of being incisive (as in comprehension or action) **:** ACUTENESS, PENETRATION

in·ci·sive \(ˈ)inˈsīs|iv, ənˈsī-, |ēv *also* |əv *sometimes* -īz|\ *adj* [ML *incisivus*, fr. L *incisus* + *-ivus* -ive] **1 :** having a cutting edge or piercing point **:** facilitating cutting or piercing ⟨as sharp and ~ as the stroke of a fang —T.B.Costain⟩ **2 :** marked by sharpness and penetration esp. in keen clear unmistakable resolution of matter at issue or in pointed decisive effectiveness of presentation ⟨the clear, ~ genius which could state in a flash the exact point at issue —A.N.Whitehead⟩ ⟨the . . . ~ irony . . . serves to put the literary crackpots in their proper place —S.C.Chew⟩ **3 :** of, relating to, or situated near the incisors

syn CLEAR-CUT, CRISP, TRENCHANT, CUTTING, BITING: INCISIVE indicates a keen penetration and sharp presentation that is effective or decisive ⟨Bismarck's will had not that *incisive*, rapier quality, that quality of highly tempered steel — flexible, unbreakable, of mortal effect, decisive, a sword — which had Richelieu's —Hilaire Belloc⟩ CLEAR-CUT indicates either unmistakably clear and lucid outlining, analysis, or presentation, or finite certainty defying disbelief or question ⟨this *clear-cut* and consistent political creed is set forth throughout with the lucidity and brevity that makes a first-class popular orator —*Times Lit. Supp.*⟩ ⟨the current decision . . . was neither *clear-cut* nor definite . . . it appeared to be an attempted compromise —*N.Y. Times*⟩ CRISP in this series has a variety of suggestions: keenness, freshness, clarity, animation, terseness, vigor, sureness, effectiveness ⟨a languorous work . . . with occasional interludes of *crisp* brilliance —Anthony West⟩ ⟨*crisp* epigrams —George Santayana⟩ TRENCHANT suggests sharp penetrating acuteness often in criticism or detraction and may suggest sarcastic asperity ⟨a *trenchant* critic of the rising capitalism, delighting in exposing the fallacies of the new economics and in pricking the bladders of political reputations —V.L.Parrington⟩ CUTTING and BITING apply to sharp sarcasm, ridicule, or detraction; the former may suggest a tendency to wound by penetrating acuteness, the latter a mordant, implacable harshness ⟨the *cutting* sarcasm . . . the cruel epigrams and occasional harsh witticisms —Jack London⟩ ⟨domineering and censorious of any that stood in his way, with a *biting* wit, although he mellowed somewhat as he grew older —T.D.Bacon⟩

incisive bone *n* **:** PREMAXILLA

incisive foramen *n* **:** a pit or in some animals two pits just behind the incisor teeth transmitting the nasopalatine nerves and the greater palatine artery

incisive fossa *n* **:** a depression on the front of the maxillary bone above the incisor teeth

in·ci·sive·ly \|əvlē, -li\ *adv* **:** in an incisive manner: as **a :** CUTTINGLY ⟨outspokenly and ~ critical —W.A.Taylor⟩ **b :** with exactitude and precision ⟨high-court judges of long experience cannot ~ say how many laws are still in force —Mark Priestley⟩ ⟨enabled him to prove ~ that the concept of a Jewish race was erroneous —W.D.Wallis⟩

in·ci·sive·ness \|ivnəs, |ēv- *also* |əv-\ *n* -ES **:** the quality or state of being incisive; *esp* **:** concise precision of utterance or action

in·ci·sor \ənˈsīzə(r), ˈin,s- *sometimes* -īsə-\ *n* -s *often attrib* [NL, fr. LL, one that cuts, fr. L *incisus* + *-or*] **:** a tooth adapted for cutting; *esp* **:** one of the cutting teeth in mammals arising from the premaxillary bone of the upper jaw in front of the canines when canines are present or one of the corresponding teeth of the lower jaw — see DENTITION illustration

in·ci·su·ra \,in,sīˈzhürə, ,in(t)səˈzh-\ *or* **in·ci·sure** \ənˈsīzhə(r)\ *n, pl* **incisu·rae** \-ü,rē\ *or* **incisures** [L *incisura*, fr. *incisus* + *-ura* -ure] **:** a notch, cleft, or fissure esp. of a body part or organ — **in·ci·sural** \ˌin,sīˈzhürəl, ˌin(t)səˈzh-; (ˈ)inˈsīzhərəl\ *adj*

¹**in·cit·ant** \ənˈsītᵊnt\ *adj* [L *incitant-*, *incitans*, pres. part. of *incitare* to incite] **:** INCITING, CAUSATIVE, STIMULATING ⟨~ of infection⟩ ⟨an ~ factor⟩

²**incitant** \"\ *n* -s **:** an inciting agent; *esp* **:** a factor (as an infective agent) that is the essential causative agent of a particular disease ⟨where the fungal ~ is present mildew is likely to damage foliage in cold wet weather⟩

in·ci·ta·tion \,in,sīˈtāshən, ,in(t)səˈ-\ *n* -s [MF, fr. L *incitation-*, *incitatio*, fr. *incitatus* (past part. of *incitare* to incite) + *-ion-*, *-io* -ion] **1 :** an act of inciting **:** STIMULATION **2 :** something that incites to action **:** INCITEMENT, INCENTIVE ⟨provocative statements that were an open ~ to violence⟩

in·cite \ənˈsīt, *usu* -īd·+V\ *vt* -ED/-ING/-S [MF *inciter*, fr. L *incitare*, fr. *in-* ²in- + *citare* to put in movement, summon — more at CITE] **1 :** to move to a course of action **:** stir up **:** spur on **:** urge on ⟨*inciting* the people to rebel⟩ ⟨*incited* to further effects by his mother's enthusiasm⟩ **2 :** to bring into being **:** induce to exist or occur ⟨such behavior is likely to ~ retaliation⟩ ⟨organisms that readily *incited* antibody formation⟩

syn INSTIGATE, FOMENT, ABET: INCITE may indicate both an initiating, a calling into being or action, and also a degree of prompting, furthering, encouraging, or nurturing of activity ⟨his projects for *inciting* war between the two countries⟩ ⟨posters scattered by the thousands throughout the eastern states and Europe to *incite* immigration —*Amer. Guide Series: Minn.*⟩ ⟨their tutors had *incited* them to dig deeply in the older sources of learning⟩ ⟨did I see a young lady in want of a partner, gallantry would *incite* me to offer myself as her devoted knight —T.L.Peacock⟩ INSTIGATE implies initiating or encouraging others to initiate actions or feelings, often questionable actions initiated with dubious intention ⟨pogroms *instigated* or connived at by the government as a safety valve for popular discontent —W.R.Inge⟩ ⟨a comparative study, *instigated* by the director of the investigation, which classifies a series of nonliterate cultures⟩ FOMENT indicates persistent inciting, esp. of something thought of as seething or boiling ⟨radicals *fomenting* a rebellion⟩ ⟨race theories are indeed not only a modern invention to explain such group conflicts, but also a means for *fomenting* them —M.R.Cohen⟩ ABET is likely to indicate seconding, encouraging, or aiding some action already begun, esp. a questionable activity ⟨aiding and *abetting* a friend in obtaining money under false pretenses⟩ ⟨the general, *abetted* by the excited aide-de-camp, made a fatal error⟩ ⟨the will to achieve perfection, though not so rare as it sounds, is all too rarely *abetted* by leisure —Harry Levin⟩

in·cite·ment \-ītmənt\ *n* -s **1 :** the act of inciting or the state of being incited ⟨through emotional ~ of each other . . . they discover paths they need to know —Kathleen Sproul⟩ **2 :** something that incites **:** INCENTIVE ⟨an ~ to further progress⟩

in·cit·er \-īd·ə(r), -ītə-\ *n* -s **:** one that incites

in·cit·ing·ly *adv* **:** so as to incite **:** in an inciting manner

in·ci·tive \(ˈ)inˈsīd·iv, ənˈs-\ *adj* **:** tending to incite **:** expressive of incitement

in·ci·to·ry \-d·ərē\ *adj* **:** serving to excite **:** STIMULATORY

incity \(ˈ)≈ˈ≈≈, ˈ≈,≈≈\ *adj* [fr. the phrase *in city*] **:** lying wholly within or serving the area within a city ⟨~ and suburban bus lines⟩ ⟨the ~ edition of the paper⟩

in·civic \(ˈ)≈+\ *adj* [¹*in-* + *civic*] **:** lacking civic responsibility

in·civil \"+\ *adj* [MF, fr. LL *incivilis*, fr. L *in-* ¹in- + *civilis* civil — more at CIVIL] **:** RUDE, BARBAROUS

in·civility \ˌin+\ *n* [MF *incivilité*, fr. LL *incivilitat-*, *incivilitas*, fr. *incivilis* + L *-itat-*, *-itas* -ity] **1** *obs* **:** INCIVILIZATION **2 :** the quality or state of being uncivil **:** ill-bred behavior **:** DISCOURTESY, RUDENESS ⟨it is gross ~ to refuse to answer when spoken to⟩ ⟨never before met with such ~⟩ **3 :** a rude or ill-bred act ⟨tired of his constant *incivilities*⟩

in·civilization \(ˌ)in+\ *n* [¹*in-* + *civilization*] **:** the state of being uncivilized

in·civism \(ˈ)in+\ *n* [F *incivisme*, fr. *in-* ¹in- + *civisme* civism — more at CIVISM] **:** lack of civic-mindedness or of patriotism

incl *abbr* **1** inclosure **2** included; including; inclusive

incld *abbr* included

inclasp *var of* ENCLASP

incle *var of* INKLE

in-clearing \ˈ≈,≈≈\ *n* [⁴*in*] *Brit* **:** the checks received for payment by a bank during the process of clearing

in·clem·en·cy \(ˈ)in, ən+\ *n* [L *inclementia*, fr. *inclement-*, *inclemens* + *-ia* -y] **:** the quality or state of being inclement: as **a :** severity of weather **:** STORMINESS ⟨the ~ of the exposed slope⟩ **b :** harshness or cruelty of action or disposition ⟨an honest man but with great ~ of spirit⟩

in·clem·ent \(ˈ)in¦klemənt, ən'k- *sometimes* 'inkləmənt\ *adj* [L *inclement-, inclemens*, fr. *in-* ¹in- + *clement-, clemens* clement — more at CLEMENT] **:** lacking clemency: as **a** *of the elements or weather* **:** physically severe **:** HARSH, ROUGH, STORMY ⟨~ weather⟩; *also* **:** marked by such weather ⟨an ~ day⟩ **b :** severe in temper or action **:** UNMERCIFUL, RIGOROUS ⟨the harsh sentence of an ~ judge⟩ — **in·clem·ent·ly** *adv* — **in·clem·ent·ness** *n* -ES

in·clin·able \ən'klīnəbəl\ *adj* [ME, fr. MF *enclinable, inclinable*, fr. *encliner, incliner* to incline + *-able* — more at INCLINE] **1 a :** having an inclination toward something **:** DISPOSED ⟨had formerly been very ~ to dissipation⟩ **b :** disposed to favor or think well of **:** FAVORABLE ⟨~ to our pleas⟩ **2 :** having a tendency **:** tending to or toward ⟨somewhat ~ to corpulence⟩ ⟨a heavy soil but ~ to bake and dry out⟩ **3 :** capable of being inclined ⟨an ~ punch press⟩

in·cli·na·tion \ˌinklə'nāshən, ˌiŋk-\ *n* -S [ME *inclinacioun*, fr. MF *inclination*, fr. L *inclination-, inclinatio*, fr. *inclinatus* (past part. of *inclinare*) + *-ion-, -io* -ion] **1 :** an act or the action of bending or inclining: as **a :** a bending forward of the head or body (as in respect, greeting, or acknowledgment) **:** BOW, NOD ⟨acknowledged his greeting with a slight ~⟩ **b :** a tilting of something **2 a** *obs* **:** natural disposition **:** NATURE, CHARACTER **b** *obs* **:** a turning of the mind in a particular direction **:** ATTENTION **c :** a particular disposition of mind or character **:** PROPENSITY, BENT ⟨a man of fixed ~*s*⟩; *usu* **:** favorable disposition esp. toward a particular thing, activity, or end **:** LIKING, DESIRE ⟨a strong ~ toward study⟩ ⟨an ~ to make the best of things⟩ **3 a :** direction or trend out of the true vertical or horizontal ⟨the ~ of a column⟩ ⟨the roadbed had considerable ~⟩ **b :** amount of deviation from the vertical or horizontal **:** degree or rate of slope or slant **:** GRADE ⟨an ~ of 20 degrees⟩ **c :** an inclined surface **:** SLOPE, INCLINE ⟨worked their way down the steep ~⟩ **d** (1) **:** the angle determined by two lines or planes ⟨the ~ of two rays of light⟩ (2) *in plane analytic geometry* **:** the angle made by a line with the x-axis measured counterclockwise from the positive direction of that axis **4 a :** a tendency to a particular aspect, state, character, or action ⟨men judge by the complexion of the sky the state and ~ of the day —Shak.⟩ ⟨some ~ to snow⟩ ⟨the clutch had an ~ to slip⟩ **b :** something to which one is inclined **:** an object of habit or favor **:** LIKING **5 :** DIP 3b **6 :** ENCLISIS — **in·cli·na·tion·al** \¦≈≈¦nāshənᵊl, -shnəl\ *adj*

inclination of an orbit : the angle between the plane of the orbit and the plane of the ecliptic

in·cli·na·tor \'≈≈ˌnād·ə(r)\ *n* -S [*inclination* + *-or*] **:** a stand with rockers for inclining a carboy to the required angle for pouring

in·cli·na·to·ry \ən'klīnəˌtōrē\ *adj* [L *inclinatus* + E *-ory*] **:** tending to incline or capable of inclining ⟨the ~ power of a dowsing rod⟩

¹**in·cline** \ən'klīn\ *vb* -ED/-ING/-S [ME *inclinen, enclinen*, fr. MF *encliner, incliner*, fr. L *inclinare*, fr. *in-* ²in- + *clinare* to bend — more at LEAN] *vi* **1 :** to bend the head or body forward **:** BOW ⟨*inclining* toward the speaker to hear more clearly⟩ **2 :** to lean, tend, or become drawn esp. toward an opinion or course of conduct **:** favor an opinion, a course of conduct, or a person ⟨~ as we grow older more and more to traditional ways⟩ ⟨his heart *inclined* to the child⟩ **3 :** to deviate from a line, direction, or course **:** LEAN ⟨converging lines ~ toward each other⟩; *specif* **:** to deviate from the vertical or horizontal ⟨the shaft ~*s* almost 30 degrees⟩ ⟨snow-laden birches *inclining* over the road⟩ **4** *of a military formation* **:** to march or move obliquely to the front so as to gain ground on the flank as well as forward ~ *vt* **1 :** to cause to stoop or bow **:** BEND ⟨*inclining* her head in greeting⟩ **2 :** to orient in the direction of **:** impart a trend toward, liking for, or interest in **:** influence in favor of something (as a course, interest, view) ⟨increasing knowledge ~*s* one to further study⟩ ⟨tried to ~ him to help⟩ **3 :** to cause to deviate physically esp. from the horizontal or vertical **:** arrange in a slanting position **:** give a bend, slope, or slant to ⟨rays of light are *inclined* in passing through a medium of high refractive index⟩ ⟨*inclining* the rake against the fence⟩ **4 :** to heel (a ship) experimentally to determine stability or center of gravity — **incline one's ear :** to listen with favor **:** hear and approve

²**in·cline** \'inˌklīn, ən'k-\ *n* -S **:** an ascending or descending inclined plane **:** GRADE, GRADIENT, SLOPE: as **a :** an inclined mine shaft or inclined portion of an otherwise vertical shaft — compare ADIT **b** (1) **:** a railway track and supporting structure on a grade extending from an adjustable apron or bridge at a transfer slip (2) **:** a railway built on a slope on which cars are raised and lowered by means of a mechanically operated cable

in·clined \ən'klīnd *or esp in sense 2* 'in,k-\ *adj* [ME *enclined, inclined*, fr. past part. of *enclinen, inclinen*] **1 :** having inclination, disposition, or tendency **:** well disposed **2 a :** having a leaning or slope usu. from the vertical or horizontal ⟨an ~ roadway⟩ ⟨an ~ stem⟩ **b :** making an angle with a line or plane

inclined plane *n* **1 :** a plane surface that makes an oblique angle with the plane of the horizon **:** a sloping plane **2 :** an inclined track on which trains or boats are raised or lowered from one level to another

incline man *n* **:** DILLYMAN

in·clin·er \ən'klīnə(r), 'in,k-\ *n* -S **:** one that inclines

¹**inclining** *n* -S [ME *enclining, inclining*, fr. gerund of *enclinen, inclinen*] **1 :** INCLINATION, DISPOSITION **2** *archaic* **:** those who incline toward (as a person or a cause) **:** PARTY, FOLLOWING

²**in·clin·ing** \ən'klīniŋ, 'in,k-, -nēŋ\ *adj* [fr. pres. part. of ¹*incline*] **:** LEANING, BENT: as **a** *of a plant part* **:** bent out of a perpendicular position ⟨an ~ stem⟩ **b :** ENCLITIC 1

in·cli·nom·e·ter \ˌinklə'nämәd·ə(r), -ˌklī'n-\ *n* [²*incline* + *-o-* + *-meter*] **1 :** an apparatus for determining the direction of the earth's magnetic field with reference to the plane of the horizon — see DIP CIRCLE, EARTH INDUCTOR **2 :** a machinist's clinometer **3 a :** an instrument for indicating the inclination to the horizontal of an esp. longitudinal axis of a ship or an airplane; *broadly* **:** any of various instruments for indicating inclination (as of the base of an oil well) **b :** an instrument giving the attitude of an airplane with reference to true gravity — called also *absolute inclinometer*

in·clip \ən+\ *vt* [²*in* + *clip*] *archaic* **:** CLASP, ENCLOSE

incln *abbr* inclusion

incloister *obs var of* ENCLOISTER

inclose *var of* ENCLOSE

in·clud·able *or* **in·clud·ible** \ən'-klüdəbəl\ *adj* **:** capable of being included **:** proper or suitable for inclusion

in·clude \ən'klüd\ *vt* -ED/-ING/-S [ME *includen, encluden*, fr. L *includere*, fr. *in-* ²in- + *-cludere* (fr. *claudere* to close) — more at CLOSE] **1 :** to shut up **:** CONFINE, ENCLOSE, BOUND ⟨the nutshell ~*s* the kernel⟩ ⟨that divine spark *included* in every human being⟩ **2 a :** to place, list, or rate as a part or component of a whole or of a larger group, class, or aggregate ⟨*included* a sum for tips in his estimate of expenses⟩ **b :** to take in, enfold, or comprise as a discrete or subordinate part or item of a larger aggregate, group, or principle ⟨in search of a formula which should cover everything . . . even if it *included* more than I wished —T.S.Eliot⟩ **3** *obs* **:** to bring to an end **:** TERMINATE

syn SUBSUME, EMBRACE, COMPREHEND, IMPLY, INVOLVE, IMPLICATE: INCLUDE and SUBSUME agree in indicating the enclosure or containment by a larger class or whole of a smaller class or specific item or part. INCLUDE, the more common term, may call more attention to the single item or smaller class by stressing the fact of its existence or the fact of its not having been overlooked ⟨it would not be argued today that the power to regulate does not *include* the power to prohibit —O.W. Holmes †1935⟩ ⟨numerous pretty things, or things supposed to be pretty . . . *including* such absurdities as paper knives with fretwork handles —Herbert Spencer⟩ SUBSUME, orig. a technical term in logic and still an erudite term, may call more attention to the larger class or more comprehensive principle, may stress the fact of its existence ⟨free verse . . . is a larger rhythmic movement which *subsumes* other rhythms —J.L. Lowes⟩ ⟨I suggest that in every beautiful building its uses, its representative elements, are indeed *subsumed* into the form —Samuel Alexander⟩ EMBRACE may sometimes suggest marked effort at enclosing; it may be used with that which is vast or is quite varied n designation or classification ⟨Virginia . . . *embraced* in its possessions the present states of West Virginia, Kentucky, Ohio, Illinois, Indiana, Michigan, and Wisconsin —C.G.Bowers⟩ ⟨freedom of speech . . . *embraces* all discussion which enriches human life and helps it to be more wisely led —Zechariah Chafee⟩ COMPREHEND may suggest a noteworthy range or scope in which something is enclosed or held ⟨to find universal law, to *comprehend* all experience in a closed system —W.R.Inge⟩ ⟨to *comprehend* in a single view polities of the most varied and discrepant character —G.L. Dickinson⟩ IMPLY, INVOLVE, and IMPLICATE indicate somewhat similar relationships. IMPLY suggests drawing attention by inference to a certain existence or relationship, not by direct statement ⟨ordinarily imitation is enough to *imply* that the matter imitated is important at least to the sale of the goods —O.W.Holmes †1935⟩ It is applicable to what is logically inferential but not absolutely certain ⟨it would be argued that culture *implies* a certain freedom from parochialism —Bertrand Russell⟩ INVOLVE, on the other hand, may apply to more certain relationship and connection since it may postulate a necessary effect or consequence ⟨in every genuine metaphysical debate some practical issue, however conjectural or remote, is *involved* —William James⟩ ⟨faith *involves* an act of the will —W.R.Inge⟩ IMPLICATE postulates through one actuality or existence the fact of another but fails to suggest an effect or consequence ⟨purpose *implicates* in the most organic way an individual self —John Dewey⟩ ⟨colors are sumptuous and rich just because a total organic resonance is deeply *implicated* in them —John Dewey⟩ ⟨a catalyzing agent has been compared to a parson, who marries others without participating in the event himself. He is *implicated*, but not *involved* —L.K.Anspacher⟩

in·clud·ed \ən'klüdəd, 'in,k-\ *adj* **:** ENCLOSED, CONFINED, EMBRACED ⟨an ~ angle⟩: as **a :** not projecting beyond the mouth of the corolla — used of a stamen and pistil; opposed to *exserted* **b** *of a lower jaw* **:** overlapped by the upper jaw — **in·clud·ed·ness** *n* -ES

included phloem *n* **:** phloem tissue lying within the secondary xylem (as in the wood of some dicotyledons)

included sapwood *n* **:** masses or streaks of tissue in heartwood that have the appearance and characteristics of sapwood

in·clud·er \ən'klüdə(r)\ *n* -S **:** one that includes

in·clud·ing \ən'klüdiŋ, 'in,k-, -dēŋ\ *adj* **:** serving to enclose or cover ⟨an ~ membrane⟩

in·cluse \'in,klüs, ən'k-, -üz\ *n* -S [ME, fr. L *inclusus*, fr. past part. of *includere* to enclose, include — more at INCLUDE] **:** a recluse who is voluntarily immured (as in a cave, hut, or isolated cell)

in·clu·sion \ən'klüzhən\ *n* -S [L *inclusion-, inclusio*, fr. *inclusus* + *-ion-, -io* -ion] **1 :** the act of including or the state of being included ⟨the ~ of domestic . . . reforms in the social program of the government —H.C.Atyeo⟩ **2 :** something that is included: as **a :** a gaseous, liquid, or solid and usu. minute foreign body enclosed in the mass of a mineral **b :** a passive product of cell activity (as a starch grain) visible within the protoplasm **c :** solid and usu. minute foreign particles (as of slag) enclosed in a solid metal **3 :** a relation between two classes that obtains when all members of the first are also members of the second — contrasted with *membership*

inclusion body *n* **:** a rounded or oval intracellular body that consists of elementary bodies in a matrix, is characteristic of certain virus diseases, and is believed to represent a stage in the multiplication of the virus

inclusion disease *n* **:** a virus disease of infants marked by the presence of inclusion bodies in the nucleus and cytoplasm of cells in the organs most affected (as lungs, liver, brain)

in·clu·sive \ən'klüs|iv, 'in,k-, |ēv *also* -üz| *or* |əv\ *adj* [ML *inclusivus*, fr. L *inclusus* + *-ivus* -ive] **1 :** ENCLOSING, ENCOMPASSING ⟨~ walls⟩: as **a :** broad in orientation or scope ⟨the concept of history adopted . . . is modern and ~ —C.V.Woodward⟩ ⟨dance is not as ~ an art as literature —George Balanchine⟩ **b :** covering or intended to cover all items, costs, or services ⟨an ~ fee⟩ **c** *of a Protestant Christian church* **:** extending fellowship to Protestant Christians without regard to rigidly sectarian barriers **d** *in grammar* **:** referring to the speaker and another or some others including the hearer **2 :** comprehending the stated limits or extremes ⟨from Monday to Friday ~⟩ — opposed to *exclusive* — **in·clu·sive·ly** \|əvlē, -li\ *adv* — **in·clu·sive·ness** \|ivnəs, |ēv- *also* |əv-\ *n* -ES

inclusive of *prep* **:** containing as an integral part ⟨the whole cost *inclusive of* materials⟩

in·coagulable \¦in+\ *adj* [¹*in-* + *coagulable*] **:** incapable of coagulating

in·coercible \"+\ *adj* [¹*in-* + *coercible*] **1 :** incapable of being controlled, checked, or confined ⟨the ~ power of the ballot⟩ **2 a :** not reducible to a liquid by pressure — compare PERMANENT GAS **b** *archaic* **:** incapable of being confined in or excluded from vessels — used of a so-called imponderable fluid (as heat, light, electricity)

in·cog \'in,käg, ən'k-\ *adv or adj or n* [by shortening] **:** INCOGNITO

in·cog·i·ta·bil·i·ty \(¦)in,kăjəd·ə¦biləd·ē, ən,≈≈≈'≈≈≈\ *n* **:** the quality or state of being incogitable

in·cogitable \(ˈ)in, ən+\ *adj* [L *incogitabilis* unthinking, unthinkable, fr. *in-* ¹in- + *cogitabilis* cogitable — more at COGITABLE] **:** impossible to accept or believe **:** UNTHINKABLE, INCONCEIVABLE

incogitancy *n* -ES [L *incogitantia*, fr. *incogitant-, incogitans* + *-ia* -y] *obs* **:** lack of thought or of the power of thinking **:** THOUGHTLESSNESS

in·cog·i·tant \(ˈ)in¦kăjəd·ənt, ən'k-\ *adj* [L *incogitant-, incogitans*, fr. *in-* ¹in- + *cogitant-, cogitans*, pres. part. of *cogitare* to cogitate — more at COGITATE] **1 :** failing in due consideration of proper or relevant factors **:** inattentive and heedless **:** THOUGHTLESS, INCONSIDERATE **2 :** INCOGITATIVE

in·cogitative \(ˈ)in, ən+\ *adj* [¹*in-* + *cogitative*] **:** lacking the ability to think

¹**in·cog·ni·ta** \÷ˌin,käg'nēd·ə, ÷-ētə *also* ən'kägnəd·ə *or* -nətə\ *adv (or adj)* [It, fem. of *incognito*] **:** INCOGNITO — used only of a woman

²**incognita** \"\ *n* -S [It, fr. *incognita*, adj.] **:** a woman in disguise; *esp* **:** one concealing her real quality or state under some unobtrusive appearance

¹**in·cog·ni·to** \÷ˌin,käg'nēd·(ˌ)ō, ÷-ē(ˌ)tō *also* ən'kägnə,tō\ *adv (or adj)* [It, fr. L *incognitus* unknown, fr. *in-* ¹in- + *cognitus*, past part. of *cognoscere* to know — more at COGNITION] **1 :** with one's identity concealed or assumed to be concealed; *esp* **:** in a capacity other than one's official capacity or under a name or title not calling for special recognition — used esp. of a personage of note ⟨the baron turned out to be a king ~⟩ **2 :** without recognition **:** UNKNOWN, UNIDENTIFIED ⟨the Neanderthal skull from Gibraltar, which had lain ~ since its discovery —Jacquetta and Christopher Hawkes⟩

²**incognito** \"\ *n* -S [It, fr. *incognito*, adj.] **1 :** one who is appearing or living incognito **2 :** the state or disguise of an incognito or incognita **3 :** the character assumed by an incognito or incognita

in·cognizable \(¦)in, ən+\ *adj* [¹*in-* + *cognizable*] **:** incapable of being recognized, known, or distinguished

in·cognizance \(ˈ)in, ən+\ *n* **:** lack of awareness, recognition, or knowledge

in·cognizant \"+\ *adj* [¹*in-* + *cognizant*] **:** lacking awareness or consciousness — used with *of* ⟨not ~ of the impression he was creating⟩

in·cog·nos·ci·bil·i·ty \ˌin,käg,näsə'biləd·ē\ *n* -ES **:** the quality or state of being incognoscible

in·cognoscible \(¦)in, ən+\ *adj* [LL *incognoscibilis*, fr. L *in-* ¹in- + LL *cognoscibilis* cognoscible — more at COGNOSCIBLE] **:** INCOGNIZABLE

in·coherence *or* **in·coherency** \¦in+\ *n* [¹*in-* + *coherence, coherency*] **1 :** the quality or state of being incoherent: as **a :** lack of cohesion or adherence **b :** lack of continuity or relevance **:** INCONGRUITY, INCONSISTENCY **2 :** something that is incoherent ⟨tearful *incoherencies*⟩

in·coherent \¦in+\ *adj* [¹*in-* + *coherent*] **:** lacking coherence: as **a :** lacking physical coherence or adhesiveness **:** consisting of discrete elements **:** LOOSE ⟨a dangerous slope covered with ~ shale⟩ **b :** lacking orderly continuity or relevance **:** INCONGRUOUS, INCONSISTENT ⟨a turgid ~ presentation⟩ **c :** lacking clarity or intelligibility usu. by reason of some emotional stress ⟨a voice ~ with rage⟩ ⟨a man ~ from sorrow⟩ **d :** lacking normal coordination **:** clumsy and fumbling ⟨a halting ~ gait⟩ **e :** occurring in mixed series or differing from normal patterns of language — used in cryptology of a key or an alphabet — **in·coherently** \"+\ *adv* — **in·coherentness** \"+\ *n* -ES

in·cohering \"+\ *adj* [¹*in-* + *cohering*, pres. part. of *cohere*] **:** lacking physical coherence

in·cohesion \¦in+\ *n* [¹*in-* + *cohesion*] **:** INCOHERENCE; *esp* **:** lack of orderly effective interaction between human groups ⟨difficulties resulting from the ~ of the desert nomads⟩

in·cohesive \¦in+\ *adj* [¹*in-* + *cohesive*] **1 :** INCOHERENT **:** lacking integration **2 :** tending to disrupt ⟨certain ~ social forces⟩

in·coincidence \¦in+\ *n* [¹*in-* + *coincidence*] **:** failure to conform or agree

in·coincident \"+\ *adj* [¹*in-* + *coincident*] **:** not coinciding

in·combustible \¦in+\ *adj or n* [ME, prob. fr. MF, fr. *in-* ¹in- + *combustible* — more at COMBUSTIBLE] **:** NONCOMBUSTIBLE — not used technically

¹**in·come** \'in,kəm, *chiefly attrib also* 'in,k- *sometimes* 'iŋ,k-\ *n* -S *often attrib* [ME, entry, arrival, fr. *in* + *come*, *cume* action of coming (after *comen in* to come in) — more at DOWNCOME, COME] **1** *archaic* **:** an act or an instance of coming in **:** ENTRANCE, ADVENT, INFLUX **2** *dial Brit* **a :** a place of entry **b :** INCOMER **3 :** something that comes in as an increment or addition usu. by chance **4 a :** a gain or recurrent benefit that is usu. measured in money and for a given period of time, derives from capital, labor, or a combination of both, includes gains from transactions in capital assets, but excludes unrealized advances in value **:** commercial revenue or receipts of any kind except receipts or returns of capital — see EARNED INCOME, GROSS INCOME, NET INCOME, UNEARNED INCOME; compare PROFIT, WAGE **b :** the value of goods and services received by an individual in a given period of time — compare WEALTH

²**income** \"\ *n* -S [⁴*in* + *come* (as in *oncome*)] *dial Brit* **:** TUMOR, ABSCESS

income account *n* **1 :** an account in which items of income or revenue are recorded **2** *or* **income statement :** a financial statement of a business showing the details of revenues, costs, expenses, losses, and profits for a given period grouped under appropriate headings — called also *profit and loss statement*

income basis *n* **:** a basis of reckoning income (as from investments, profits) according to the percentage that the interest or revenue bears to the actual cost with no allowance being made for the fact that payment at maturity is to be at par ⟨a bond yielding 3-percent interest on its par value and bought at 60 is on an *income basis* of 5 percent⟩

income bond *n* **:** a bond that is entitled to receive interest only if earned and declared by the board of directors in accordance with its indenture provisions

in·come·less \-ləs\ *adj* **:** having no income

incomer \'in,kəmə(r)\ *n* **:** one that comes in: as **a** *dia chiefly Brit* **:** one that comes from another place **:** IMMIGRANT, STRANGER; *esp* **:** a new tenant **b :** a game bird or a trapshooting target that comes toward the shooter

income splitting *n* **:** an assigning of income for purposes of taxation in equal shares to two or more persons (as husband and wife) irrespective of which one actually received the income

income tax *n* **1 :** a tax on the net income of an individual or business concern (as a corporation) **2 a :** a tax on gross income often levied as a payroll tax by a city **b :** a tax on gross operating revenue (as of a public utility)

¹**in·com·ing** \'in,kəmiŋ, -mēŋ\ *n* [ME, fr. *in-* + *coming* (after *comen in* to come in)] **1 :** the act of coming in **:** ARRIVAL ⟨all these ~*s* and outgoings disturbed our daily routine⟩ **2 :** money or other gains received **:** REVENUE, INCOME — usu. used in pl.

²**incoming** \"\ *adj* [²*in* + *coming* (after *come in*, v.)] **:** coming in: as **a :** taking or coming to occupy a place, position, or status formerly held by another ⟨his ~ tenant⟩ ⟨see what the ~ Congress will do⟩ **b :** arriving at a usual, proper, or normal destination ⟨~ waves⟩ **:** ACCRUING ⟨~ orders⟩ **c :** STARTING, BEGINNING, ENTERING ⟨high hopes for the ~ year⟩ ⟨all ~ freshmen⟩

in·commensurability \¦in+\ *n* [prob. fr. MF *incommensurableté*, fr. ML *incommensurabilitat-, incommensurabilitas*, fr. LL *incommensurabilis* + L *-itat-, -itas* -ity] **:** the quality or state of being incommensurable ⟨a genuine ~ between the individual and the universal —M.R.Cohen⟩

¹**in·commensurable** \¦in+\ *adj* [prob. fr. MF, fr. LL *incommensurabilis*, fr. L *in-* ¹in- + LL *commensurabilis* commensurable — more at COMMENSURABLE] **:** not commensurable **:** having no common measure ⟨quantities are ~ when no third quantity can be found that is an aliquot part of each⟩; *broadly* **:** lacking a common basis of comparison in respect to a quality (as value, size, excellence) normally subject to comparison — **in·com·men·su·ra·bly** \-əblē, -li\ *adv*

²**incommensurable** \"\ *n* -S **:** something that is incommensurable; *esp* **:** any of two or more quantities having no common measure

in·commensurate \¦in+\ *adj* [¹*in-* + *commensurate*] **:** not commensurate: as **a :** INCOMMENSURABLE **b :** INADEQUATE ⟨means ~ to our wants⟩ ⟨~ attention⟩

in com·mer·cio \ˌinkə'mərshē,ō\ *adj* [L, lit., inside of commerce] *Roman & civil law* **:** subject to private ownership — opposed to *extra commercium*

in·com·mis·ci·ble \ˌinkə¦misəbəl\ *adj* [LL *incommiscibilis*, fr. L *in-* ¹in- + LL *commiscibilis* able to be mixed together, fr. L *commiscere* to mix together + *-ibilis* -ible — more at COMMIX] **:** IMMISCIBLE

incommodate *vt* -ED/-ING/-S [L *incommodatus*, past part. of *incommodare*] *obs* **:** INCOMMODE

in·commodation \(¦)in, ən+\ *n* **:** DISCOMFORT, INCONVENIENCE, ANNOYANCE

¹**in·com·mode** \ˌinkə¦mōd\ *vt* -ED/-ING/-S [MF *incommoder*, fr. L *incommodare*, fr. *incommodus* inconvenient, disagreeable, fr. *in-* ¹in- + *commodus* convenient — more at COMMODE] **1 a :** to give inconvenience or distress to **:** put out **:** DISCOMMODE ⟨such delays often *incommoded* passengers⟩ **b :** DISTURB, MOLEST ⟨should any player of the fielding side ~ the striker by any noise or motion —*Laws of Cricket*⟩ **2** *archaic* **:** IMPEDE, HANDICAP, OBSTRUCT

²**incommode** *adj* [F, fr. L *incommodus*] *obs* **:** INCONVENIENT

in·commodious \¦in+\ *adj* [¹*in-* + *commodious*] **:** tending to inconvenience: as **a** *archaic* **:** UNPLEASANT, DISAGREEABLE **b** *archaic* **:** UNCOMFORTABLE, HAMPERING **c** *obs* **:** HARMFUL, DAMAGING **d** *obs* **:** UNSUITABLE, IMPROPER **e :** offering inadequate accommodation **:** unpleasantly small and cramped ⟨an ~ little hall bedroom⟩ — **in·com·mo·di·ous·ly** *adv* — **in·com·mo·di·ous·ness** *n* -ES

in·commodity \¦in+\ *n* [ME *incommoditee*, fr. MF *incommodité*, fr. L *incommoditat-, incommoditas*, fr. *incommodus* + *-itat-, -itas* -ity] **1** *obs* **:** the quality or state of being incommodious **2 :** something that causes inconvenience, annoyance, or discomfort — usu. used in pl. ⟨an inconvenient, ill-balanced house . . . its unsuitability as a public building is intensified by such *incommodities* —Claud Phillimore⟩

in·communicability \"+\ *n* **:** the quality or state of being incommunicable

in·communicable \"+\ *adj* [MF or LL; MF, fr. LL *incommunicabilis*, fr. L *in-* ¹in- + LL *communicabilis* communicable — more at COMMUNICABLE] **1 :** incapable of being communicated: as **a :** not subject to sharing or division ⟨the ~ authority of the crown⟩ **b :** impossible to recount or utter **:** INEFFABLE ⟨an ~ vision⟩ ⟨into the unspeakable and ~ prison of this earth —Thomas Wolfe⟩ **2 :** unwilling or unable to communicate **:** TACITURN, RESERVED, WITHDRAWN ⟨a troubled man, ~ and abstracted⟩ **3 :** lacking means of communication ⟨his nature is ~ — he resembles neither dog nor man —Pamela L. Travers⟩ — **in·com·mu·ni·ca·ble·ness** \-nəs\ *n* -ES — **in·communicably** \"+\ *adv*

in·com·mu·ni·ca·do *also* **in·co·mu·ni·ca·do** \ˌinkə,myünə'kä(,)dō, -kā(-\ *adv (or adj)* [Sp *incomunicado*, fr. past part. of *incomunicar* to deprive of communication, fr. *in-* ¹in- (fr. L) + *comunicar* to communicate, fr. L *communicare* to share, impart, partake — more at COMMUNICATE] **:** without means of communication ⟨it had sometimes brought good luck for people to be politically ~ —A.N.Whitehead⟩; *esp* **:** in solitary confinement ⟨held ~ for 10 days⟩

in·communicated *or* **in·communicating** \¦in+\ *adj* [¹*in-* + *communicated* or *communicating*] *archaic* **:** lacking communication

in·communicative \"+\ *adj* [¹*in-* + *communicative*] **:** UNCOMMUNICATIVE 2

in·com·mut·abil·i·ty \¦inkə,myüd·ə'biləd·ē\ *n* -ES [LL *incommutabilitas*, fr. L *incommutabilis* + *-itas* -ity] **:** the quality or state of being incommutable

in·commutable \¦in+\ *adj* [ME, fr. L *incommutabilis*, fr. *in-* ¹in- + *commutabilis* commutable — more at COMMUTABLE] **:** not commutable: **a :** not subject or liable to alteration **:** UNCHANGEABLE **b :** not able to substitute one for another **:** UNEXCHANGEABLE ⟨these ~ skills⟩ **:** not interchangeable ⟨when two sounds are ~ their phonetic difference prevents their being classed under one phoneme —C.E.Bazell⟩ — **in·com·mut·a·bly** \-blē,-bli\ *adv*

in·compact \(¦)in, ən+\ *adj* [¹*in-* + *compact*] **:** loosely ordered or organized **:** lacking coherence or firm integration

in·comparability \(¦)in, ən+\ *n* **:** the quality or state of being incomparable

in·comparable \(¦)in, ən+\ *adj* [ME, fr. MF, fr. L *incomparabilis*, fr. *in-* ¹in- + *comparabilis* comparable — more at COMPARABLE] **1 :** of such quality as to be beyond comparison **:** having no equal **:** eminent beyond comparison **:** MATCHLESS, PEERLESS, TRANSCENDENT ⟨this ~ scholar⟩ ⟨a heavenly, an ~ week of rest and pleasure⟩ **2 :** not suitable for comparison **:** lacking such common bases or points of reference as make comparison useful, informative, or valid — usu. used with *with* or *to* ⟨this report is ~ with the earlier reports because of the use of different breakdowns of data⟩

in·com·pa·ra·ble·ness *n* -ES **:** INCOMPARABILITY

in·comparably \(¦)in, ən+\ *adv* [ME, fr. *incomparable* + *-ly*] **:** to an incomparable degree **:** beyond comparison **:** EXCEPTIONALLY

incompass *obs var of* ENCOMPASS

in·compassionate \¦in+\ *adj* [¹*in-* + *compassionate*] **:** lacking compassion — **in·compassionately** \"+\ *adv*

in·compatibility \¦in+\ *n* [F *incompatibilité*, fr. MF, fr. *incompatible*] **1 :** the quality or state of being incompatible **:** inability to function or exist in the presence of something else: as **a :** inability to exist in peaceful harmony; *esp* **:** lack of adjustment in marriage **b :** a relation between dignities or public offices such that proper and faithful performance of the duties and exercise of the powers of one is inconsistent with such performance and exercise in another on the part of the same individual **c** (1) **:** lack of interfertility between two plants following pollination (as from characteristics of the pollen) (2) **:** inability of stock and scion to unite successfully in a graft **d :** the exclusion in igneous rock crystallization under conditions of equilibrium of one member of a pair of minerals by the presence of the other member **2 incompatibilities** *pl* **:** mutually antagonistic things or qualities **:** INCOMPATIBLES ⟨the inherent *incompatibilities* of dog and cat⟩

¹**in·compatible** \"+\ *adj* [MF & ML; MF, fr. ML *incompatibilis*, fr. L *in-* ¹in- + ML *compatibilis* compatible — more at COMPATIBLE] **1 :** incapable of being held by one person at one time — used of offices, dignities, or benefices that would make mutually conflicting demands on a holder **2 a :** incapable of appearing or of being thought together or of entering into the same system, theory, or practice ⟨~ ideas⟩ **:** incapable of harmonious combination **:** INCONGRUOUS ⟨~ colors⟩ **:** incapable of harmonious association or of acting in accord **:** DISAGREEING ⟨~ persons⟩ **b** (1) *of drugs or medicaments* **:** unsuitable for use together because of chemical interaction or antagonistic physiological effects — compare SYNERGISTIC (2) *of blood or serum* **:** unsuitable for use in a particular transfusion because of the presence of agglutinins against the recipient's red blood cells **c** *in logic* (1) *of two propositions* **:** not both true — compare STROKE 14 (2) *of terms* **:** not consistently predicable of the same subject — compare ALTERNATIVE DENIAL **d** *of mathematical equations* **:** incapable of being satisfied by the same set of values for the unknowns **e :** incapable of blending into a stable homogeneous mixture — used esp. of solids or solutions ⟨ester gum is ~ with cellulose acetate when formulated into a lacquer —*Glossary of Industrial Coating Terms*⟩ — compare IMMISCIBLE **3** *obs* **:** INTOLERANT — **in·com·pat·i·ble·ness** \-nəs\ *n* -ES — **in·compatibly** \¦in+\ *adv*

²**incompatible** *n* -S **:** one that is incompatible — usu. used in pl.

in·compensated \(')in+\ *adj* [¹*in-* + past part. of *compensate*] **:** lacking compensation; *esp* **:** lacking physiological compensation

in·compensation \(¦)in, ən+\ *n* [¹*in-* + *compensation*] **:** lack of physiological compensation ⟨cardiac ~⟩ — **in·compensatory** \¦in+\ *adj*

in·competence \(')in, ən+\ *n* [F *incompétence*, fr. MF, fr. *in-* ¹in- + *compétence* — more at COMPETENCE] **:** the state or fact of being incompetent: as **a :** lack of physical, intellectual, or moral ability **:** INSUFFICIENCY, INADEQUACY ⟨his ~ was absolute⟩ **b :** lack of legal qualification or fitness ⟨the ~ of an intoxicated man to drive an automobile⟩ **c :** the inability of an organ to perform its function adequately ⟨aortic ~ may lead to enlargement of the heart⟩

in·competency \"+\ *n* [MF *incompétence* + E *-y*] **1 a :** the quality of being incompetent ⟨the ~ typical of idiots⟩ **b incompetencies** *pl* **:** incompetent acts or behavior ⟨the *incompetencies* of such immature executives⟩ **2 :** INCOMPETENCE **3 :** the absence of jurisdiction of a court or judge to determine a civil law case

¹**in·competent** \"+\ *adj* [MF, *incompétent*, fr. *in-* ¹in- + *compétent* — more at COMPETENT] **1 a :** lacking the qualities (as maturity, capacity, initiative, intelligence) necessary to effective independent action **b** (1) **:** lacking specific qualifications to perform a legal function or duty or exercise a legal right — often used without implication of any kind with respect to personal fitness; distinguished from *incapable* ⟨a wife is usually considered ~ to testify against her husband in a criminal case⟩ (2) **:** not acceptable in court because obtained from a legally incompetent source ⟨~ testimony⟩ ⟨~ evidence⟩ **:** INADMISSIBLE **c :** exhibiting or characterized by organic incompetence ⟨an ~ mitral valve⟩ **d :** inadequate to or unsuitable for a particular purpose expressed or implied ⟨certain genotypes are phenotypically ~⟩ ⟨an ~ system of government⟩ ⟨pipes ~ to carry a full head of steam⟩ **2 :** being or forming strata and rock structures that have not the rigidity or strength to transmit particular stresses but that crush or flow under them — **in·competently** \"+\ *adv*

²**incompetent** \"\ *n* -S **:** one that is incompetent: as **a :** a person incapable of managing his affairs because of mental deficiency or immaturity ⟨children and idiots are ~*s* in the eyes of the law⟩ **b :** one incapable of doing properly what is required (as in a particular position) ⟨~*s* in public office⟩

incompetible *adj* [¹*in-* + *competible*] *obs* **:** UNSUITABLE

in·com·plet·abil·i·ty \¦inkəm,plēd·ə'biləd·ē\ *n* -ES **:** the quality or state of being incompletable

in·com·plet·able \¦inkəm¦plēd·əbəl\ *adj* [¹*in-* + *completable* capable of being completed, fr. *complete* + *-able*] **:** impossible to finish or bring to completion — **in·com·plet·able·ness** *n* -ES

in·complete \¦in+\ *adj* [ME *incompleet*, fr. LL *incompletus*, fr. *in-* ¹in- + L *completus* complete — more at COMPLETE] **:** lacking a part or parts or not having all parts arranged in final or functional order **:** UNFINISHED, IMPERFECTED: as **a** *of a flower* **:** lacking one or more sets of floral organs — compare COMPLETE, DICLINOUS **b :** SYNCATEGOREMATIC **c** *of a fertilizer* **:** containing two but not all three of the fertilizing agents nitrogen, phosphorus, and potassium **d** *of a football pass* **:** not legally caught

incomplete antibody *n* **:** BLOCKING ANTIBODY

in·completed \¦in+\ *adj* [¹*in-* + *completed*] **:** INCOMPLETE

in·com·plete·ly *adv* **:** in an incomplete manner or to an incomplete degree **:** not wholly, perfectly, or fully ⟨~ grown crops⟩ ⟨words ~ understood⟩

in·com·plete·ness *n* **:** the quality or state of being incomplete

incomplete pupa *n* **:** PUPA LIBERA

incomplete symbol *n* **:** a sign, word, or expression (as the quotation sign or the word *or*) that systematically contributes to the meaning of expressions in which it occurs but has no independent or separable meaning

in·completion \¦in+\ *n* [¹*in-* + *completion*] **1 :** lack of completion **2 :** an incomplete pass in football

in·complex \(¦)in, ən+\ *adj* [ML *incomplexus*, fr. L *in-* ¹in- + *complexus*, past part. of *complecti* to entwine around, embrace — more at COMPLEX] **:** lacking complexity **:** SIMPLE

incompliable *adj* [¹*in-* + *compliable*] *obs* **:** UNCOMPLIANT

in·compliance *or* **in·compliancy** \¦in+\ *n* [¹*in-* + *compliance, compliancy*] **:** the quality or state of being incompliant **:** OBSTINACY

in·compliant \"+\ *adj* [¹*in-* + *compliant*] **1 :** lacking compliance **:** not cooperative and yielding **2** *of a material thing* **:** lacking pliability **:** STIFF, RESISTANT — **in·compliantly** \"+\ *adv*

in·complicate \(')in, ən+\ *adj* [¹*in-* + *complicate*] **:** SIMPLE, UNCOMPLICATED

incomplying *adj* [¹*in-* + pres. part. of *comply*] *obs* **:** free from compliance or yielding

incomposed *adj* [¹*in-* + *composed*] **1** *obs* **:** lacking calmness and composure **:** DISTURBED, DISORDERED **2** *obs* **:** not made up of diverse elements **:** SIMPLE

in·composite \(¦)in, ən+\ *adj* [L *incompositus*, fr. *in-* ¹in- + *compositus*, past part. of *componere* to put together — more at COMPOSE] **1 :** lacking separable or distinguishable parts **2** *of a number* **:** PRIME

in·compossibility \¦in+\ *n* **:** the quality or state of being incompossible

in·compossible \¦in+\ *adj* [ML *incompossibilis*, fr. L *in-* ¹in- + ML *compossibilis* compossible — more at COMPOSSIBLE] **:** not mutually possible **:** INCONSISTENT, INCOMPATIBLE

in·comprehending \(¦)in, ən+\ *adj* [¹*in-* + *comprehending*] **:** lacking comprehension or lacking in comprehension — **in·comprehendingly** \"+\ *adv*

in·comprehensibility \(¦)in, ən+\ *n* **:** the quality or state of being incomprehensible

¹**in·comprehensible** \(¦)in, ən+\ *adj* [ME, fr. L *incomprehensibilis*, fr. *in-* ¹in- + *comprehensibilis* comprehensible — more at COMPREHENSIBLE] **1** *archaic* **:** having or subject to no limits **:** ILLIMITABLE ⟨an infinite and ~ substance —Richard Hooker⟩ **2 a :** impossible to comprehend **:** lying above or beyond the reach of the human mind ⟨the ~ mysteries of creation⟩ **b :** being beyond the powers of comprehension of a particular mind **:** UNINTELLIGIBLE ⟨an ~ subject to him⟩ **c :** being beyond ordinary comprehension **:** UNFATHOMABLE ⟨~ moods⟩ ⟨a whimsical ~ person⟩ **3** *obs* **:** impossible to catch or hold — **in·com·pre·hen·si·ble·ness** \-nəs\ *n* -ES — **in·comprehensibly** \¦in+\ *adv*

²**incomprehensible** \"\ *n* -S **:** something incomprehensible

in·comprehension \(¦)in, ən+\ *n* [¹*in-* + *comprehension*] **:** lack of comprehension or understanding ⟨their ~ of violence, their terror of social upheaval —A.M.Schlesinger b.1917⟩

in·comprehensive \"+\ *adj* [¹*in-* + *comprehensive*] **1 :** lacking comprehensiveness; *esp* **:** deficient in mental grasp **2** *obs* **:** INCOMPREHENSIBLE — **in·comprehensively** \"+\ *adv*

in·compressibility \¦in+\ *n* **:** the quality or state of being incompressible

in·compressible \"+\ *adj* [¹*in-* + *compressible*] **:** incapable of being compressed; *broadly* **:** resisting compression — **in·com·press·ible·ness** \-nəs\ *n* -ES — **in·com·press·ibly** \-əblē, -li\ *adv*

incompt *adj* [L *incomptus*, fr. *in-* ¹in- + *comptus*, past part. of *comere* to adorn — more at COMPT] *obs* **:** UNKEMPT, UNPOLISHED

in·computable \¦in+\ *adj* [¹*in-* + *computable*] **:** greater than can be computed or enumerated **:** very great — **in·com·put·ably** \-əblē, -li\ *adv*

incommunicado *var of* INCOMMUNICADO

in·concealable \¦in+\ *adj* [¹*in-* + *concealable*] **:** impossible to hide

in·conceivability \¦in+\ *n* **1 :** the quality or state of being inconceivable **2 :** something inconceivable

in·conceivable \¦in+\ *adj* [¹*in-* + *conceivable*] **1 :** falling outside the limit of what can be comprehended, accepted as true or real, or tolerated: as **a :** impossible to comprehend in the absence of actual experience or knowledge **:** UNIMAGINABLE ⟨color is ~ to those born blind⟩ **b :** impossible to entertain in the mind **:** UNTHINKABLE ⟨it is ~ that a thing can both be and not be⟩ **c :** impossible to accept as an article of faith **:** INCREDIBLE, UNBELIEVABLE ⟨it is ~ that God should wantonly inflict suffering⟩ **2 :** hard to believe or believe in ⟨it is ~ that such losses should continue⟩ ⟨~ losses of revenue⟩ — **in·conceivableness** \"+\ *n* — **in·conceivably** \"+\ *adv*

inconciliable *adj* [¹*in-* + *conciliable*] *obs* **:** IRRECONCILABLE

in·concinnity \¦in+\ *n* [L *inconcinnitas*, fr. *in-* ¹in- + *concinnitas* concinnity — more at CONCINNITY] **:** lack of suitability or congruity **:** awkward or unsuitable form or character

in·concinnous \"+\ *adj* [L *inconcinnus*, fr. *in-* ¹in- + *concinnus* concinnous — more at CONCINNITY] *archaic* **:** marked by inconcinnity

inconcludent *adj* [¹*in-* + *concludent*] *obs* **:** INCONCLUSIVE

in·con·clu·si·ble \¦inkən¦klüzəbəl\ *adj* [¹*in-* + obs. *conclusible*, fr. L *conclusus* (past part. of *concludere* to conclude) + E *-ible* — more at CONCLUDE] **:** impossible to bring to an end ⟨an ~ argument⟩

in·conclusive \¦in+\ *adj* [¹*in-* + *conclusive*] **:** leading to no conclusion or to no definite result, decision, or end ⟨such ~ arguments⟩ ⟨a long and ~ war⟩ — **in·conclusively** \"+\ *adv* — **in·conclusiveness** \"+\ *n*

inconcoct *or* **inconcocted** *adj* [*inconcoct* fr. ¹*in-* + obs. *concoct* digested, matured, fr. L *concoctus*, past part. of *concoquere* to boil together; *inconcocted* fr. ¹*in-* + *concocted*, past part. of *concoct* — more at CONCOCT] *obs* **:** not matured **:** UNDIGESTED — **inconcoction** *n*, *obs*

in·concrete \(¦)in, ən+\ *adj* [LL *inconcretus*, fr. L *in-* ¹in- + *concretus*, past part. of *concrescere* to grow together — more at CONCRETE] **:** vague and diffuse **:** ABSTRACT

in·condensable \¦in+\ *adj* [¹*in-* + *condensable*] **:** incapable of being condensed

in·con·dite \ən'kändət, -,dīt\ *adj* [L *inconditus*, fr. *in-* ¹in- + *conditus*, past part. of *condere* to put together, fr. *com-* + *-dere* to put — more at DO] **1 :** badly organized or put together **:** lacking finish or polished form — used chiefly of an utterance ⟨valuable factual information obscured by turgid ~ prose⟩ **2 :** lacking in manners **:** CRUDE, UNPOLISHED

in·conducive \¦in+\ *adj* [¹*in-* + *conducive*] **:** not conducive **:** having no tendency toward

In·co·nel \'iŋkə,nel\ *trademark* — used for an alloy of approximately 80 percent nickel, 14 percent chromium, and 6 percent iron

in·conformable \¦in+\ *adj* [¹*in-* + *conformable*] **:** failing or unwilling to conform ⟨the rebels were ~ to all compromise⟩ ⟨conduct wholly ~ to our principles⟩ — **in·conformably** \"+\ *adv*

in·conformity \"+\ *n* [¹*in-* + *conformity*] **:** lack of conformity **:** NONCONFORMITY

in·confused \¦in+\ *adj* [¹*in-* + *confused*] **:** free from confusion **:** having the elements distinct **:** CLEAR-CUT — **in·confusedly** \"+\ *adv*

in·congenerous \"+\ *adj* [¹*in-* + *congenerous*] *archaic* **:** not belonging to the same group or kind

in·congruence \(¦)in, ən+\ *n* [LL *incongruentia*, fr. L *incongruent-*, *incongruens* + *-ia* -y] **:** INCONGRUITY

in·congruent \"+\ *adj* [L *incongruent-*, *incongruens*, fr. *in-* ¹in- + *congruent-*, *congruens*, pres. part. of *congruere* to come together, coincide, agree — more at CONGRUOUS] **1 :** lacking congruity **:** INCONGRUOUS, UNSUITABLE **2 :** not corresponding in shape and curvature — used of opposed articular surfaces in joints **3 :** relating to the melting point of a molecular compound at which it decomposes into a new solid phase and a liquid of different composition — compare CONGRUENT 3

in·congruently \"+\ *adv* **:** in an incongruent manner

in·congruity \¦in+\ *n* [MF or LL; MF *incongruité*, fr. LL *incongruitat-*, *incongruitas*, fr. *incongruus* + L *-itat-*, *-itas* -ity] **1 :** the quality or state of being incongruous **:** lack of congruity **:** INCONSISTENCY, INHARMONY, DISAGREEMENT **2 :** something that is incongruous **:** a thing that lacks harmonious or rational relation to its environment ⟨Victorian *incongruities* in a typically mid-20th-century setting⟩

in·congruous \(')in, ən+\ *adj* [LL *incongruus*, fr. L *in-* ¹in- + *congruus* congruous — more at CONGRUOUS] **:** lacking congruity: as **a :** characterized by lack of harmony, consistency, or compatibility with one another ⟨~ colors⟩ ⟨~ desires⟩ **b :** characterized by disagreement or lack of conformity with something ⟨conduct ~ with avowed principles⟩ **c :** characterized by inconsistency or inharmony of its own parts or qualities ⟨an ~ story⟩ **d :** characterized by lack of propriety or suitableness ⟨~ manners⟩ — **in·congruously** \"+\ *adv* — **in·congruousness** \"+\ *n*

in·conjunct \(¦)in, ən+\ *adj* [LL *inconjunctus* unconnected, fr. L *in-* ¹in- + *conjunctus*, past part. of *conjungere* to join together — more at CONJOIN] *archaic*, *of celestial bodies or zodiacal signs* **:** lacking conjunction

in·connected \¦in+\ *adj* [¹*in-* + *connected*] **:** DISCONNECTED ⟨halting ~ ideas⟩

in·connection \"+\ *n* [¹*in-* + *connection*] *archaic* **:** DISCONNECTION

in·con·nu \¦inkə¦n(y)ü, ¦iŋk-; ¦aⁿkȯ¦nü\ *n* -S [F, fr. *in-* ¹in- + *connu*, past part. of *connaître* to know, fr. L *cognoscere* — more at COGNITION] **1 :** an unknown person **:** STRANGER **2 :** a large oily soft-fleshed food fish (*Stenodus mackenzii*) related to the whitefish and found in Alaska, northwestern Canada, and adjoining Siberian waters

in·conquerable \(')in, ən+\ *adj* [¹*in-* + *conquerable*] **:** UNCONQUERABLE

in·conscience \(')in, ən+\ *n* **:** the quality or state of being inconscient

in·conscient \"+\ *adj* [prob. fr. F, fr. *in-* ¹in- + *conscient*, fr. L *conscient-*, *consciens*, pres. part. of *conscire* to know, be conscious — more at CONSCIENCE] **1 a :** lacking consciousness **:** MINDLESS ⟨inanimate ~ things —Percy Winner⟩ **b :** lacking full awareness **:** ABSTRACTED ⟨he had passed, ~, full gaze the wide-banded irises —Ezra Pound⟩ **2 :** not involving or based on the action of consciousness ⟨holding creation to be the outcome of ~ natural laws⟩ — **in·consciently** \"+\ *adv*

in·con·scio·na·ble \(')in¦känch(ə)nəbəl, ən'k-\ *adj* [¹*in-* + *conscionable*] **:** UNCONSCIONABLE

in·conscious \(')in+\ *adj* [LL *inconscius*, fr. L *in-* ¹in- + *conscius* conscious — more at CONSCIOUS] **:** UNCONSCIOUS

in·consecutive \¦in+\ *adj* [¹*in-* + *consecutive*] **:** lacking in sequence and order ⟨formless ~ essays he produced by grouping . . . a miscellany of scattered reflections —*New Yorker*⟩ **:** not arranged in order of occurrence ⟨the entries in the Chronicle are ~ and some of them must have been written appreciably later than the events which they relate —F.M.Stenton⟩ — **in·consecutively** \"+\ *adv* — **in·con·sec·u·tive·ness** \-ivnəs\ *n*

in·consequence \(')in, ən+\ *n* [L *inconsequentia*, fr. *in-* ¹in- + *consequentia* consequence — more at CONSEQUENCE] **1 :** the quality or state of being inconsequent: as **a :** lack of just or logical inference or argument **:** ILLOGICALITY **b :** lack of sequence **:** INCONSECUTIVENESS, IRRELEVANCE **2 :** character or mood marked by inconsequence ⟨Sterne propagates his ~, while his suavity and ease of style die with him —J.L.Lowes⟩ ⟨the ~*s* of the Boston mind —Henry Adams⟩

in·consequent \"+\ *adj* [LL *inconsequent-*, *inconsequens*, fr. L *in-* ¹in- + *consequent-*, *consequens* consequent — more at CONSEQUENT] **1 a :** lacking logical order or ordered sequence of thought or reasoning ⟨it is unfortunate that such a significant book should be so slipshod and ~ —*Saturday Rev.*⟩ **:** ILLOGICAL, INCONSISTENT ⟨a premise based on ~ reasoning⟩ **b :** following no natural sequence **:** INCONSECUTIVE ⟨the string of ~ statements to which she had treated them —Ngaio Marsh⟩ **2 :** marked or characterized by a lack of logic or relevancy ⟨these ~ fellows who would lower taxes but increase public expenditure⟩ **3 :** of no consequence **:** lacking worth, significance, or importance ⟨the gay, debauched, quite ~ lad was managed like a puppet —Hilaire Belloc⟩ ⟨futile ~ dreams⟩ — **in·consequently** \"+\ *adv*

in·con·se·quen·tia \,in,kän(t)sə'kwench(ē)ə\ *n pl* [LL, neut. pl. of *inconsequens*] **:** matters of no grave moment or significance **:** TRIVIA ⟨the ~ of daily life⟩

in·consequential \(¦)in, ən+\ *adj* **1 :** not regularly following from the premises; *broadly* **:** IRRELEVANT **2 :** INCONSEQUENT 3 — **in·consequentiality** \"+\ *n* — **in·consequentially** \"+\ *adv*

in·considerable \¦in+\ *adj* [MF, fr. *in-* ¹in- + *considerable*, fr. ML *considerabilis* — more at CONSIDERABLE] **1** *obs* **:** too great to be considered or reckoned **2 a :** unworthy of consideration **:** TRIVIAL ⟨their duties were ~⟩ ⟨earned and spent a not ~ amount of money⟩ ⟨exercised no ~ influence⟩ **b :** SMALL, PETTY ⟨passed his life in an ~ village⟩ ⟨~ size⟩ **3** *obs* **:** INCONSIDERATE, CARELESS — **in·con·sid·er·a·ble·ness** \-nəs\ *n* -ES — **in·considerably** \¦in+\ *adv*

in·con·sid·er·a·cy \,inkən'sid(ə)rəsē\ *n* -ES [fr. *inconsiderate*, after such pairs as E *accurate: accuracy*] *archaic* **:** INCONSIDERATENESS

¹**in·considerate** \¦in+\ *adj* [L *inconsideratus*, fr. *in-* ¹in- + *consideratus*, past part. of *considerare* to consider — more at CONSIDER] **1 :** not adequately considered **:** ILL-ADVISED, RASH, PRECIPITATE ⟨hasty and ~ conclusions⟩ **2 a :** acting or tending to act without due or reasonable deliberation **:** HEEDLESS, THOUGHTLESS, CARELESS ⟨some ~ person repeats like a parrot that if you gave everybody the same amount of money —G.B.Shaw⟩ ⟨that ~, wandering, featherheaded race —L.P.Smith⟩ ⟨exploring the carving with ~ fingers⟩ **b :** failing in regard for the rights or feelings of others **:** indifferent to propriety or courtesy ⟨a gross ~ man⟩ ⟨shockingly ~ behavior⟩ **3** *obs* **:** not held in consideration or esteem — **in·considerately** \"+\ *adv* — **in·con·sid·er·ate·ness** *n* -ES

²**in·considerate** \"\ *n* -S **:** an inconsiderate person

in·consideration \¦in+\ *n* [LL *inconsideration-*, *inconsideratio*, fr. L *inconsideratus* + *-ion-*, *-io* -ion] **:** the quality or state of being inconsiderate **:** INCONSIDERATENESS

in·considered \¦in+\ *adj* [¹*in-* + *considered*] **:** INCONSIDERATE 1

in·consistency *also* **in·consistence** \¦in+\ *n* [¹*in-* + *consistency, consistence*] **1 :** the quality or state of being inconsistent; as **a :** lack of agreement, consonance, harmony, or compatibility **b :** lack of stability, uniformity, or steadiness **2 a :** something that is inconsistent **b :** an instance of inconsistent character or condition

in·consistent \¦in+\ *adj* [¹*in-* + *consistent*] **1 :** lacking consistency **:** INCOMPATIBLE, INCONGRUOUS, INHARMONIOUS: as **a** *of propositions, ideas, beliefs* **:** so related that both or all cannot be true or containing parts so related ⟨~ statements⟩ **b :** so related to something premised or understood that it cannot be true if what is thus assumed is true ⟨an ~ conclusion⟩ **2** *of a person* **a :** incoherent or illogical in thought or actions **:** believing incompatibles or acting in incongruous ways **b :** logically inconsequent **:** lacking in continuity of belief or purpose; *broadly* **:** INCONSTANT, CHANGEABLE, FICKLE **3** *of aesthetic relations* **:** not handled or developed so as to form a harmonious whole **:** INCONSONANT ⟨~ composition⟩ **4 :** INCONGRUOUS, INCOMPATIBLE, IRRECONCILABLE — used of immaterial qualities ⟨wisdom is not ~ with mirth⟩ **5 :** INCOMPATIBLE 2d — **in·consistently** \"+\ *adv* — **in·con·sist·ent·ness** *n* -ES

in·consolable \¦in+\ *adj* [L *inconsolabilis*, fr. *in-* ¹in- + *consolabilis* able to be comforted, fr. *consolari* to console + *-abilis* -able — more at CONSOLE] **:** incapable of being consoled **:** grieved beyond comfort **:** utterly disconsolate — **in·con·sol·able·ness** \-nəs\ *n* -ES — **in·con·sol·ably** \-əblē, -li\ *adv*

in·consonance \(')in+\ *n* **:** lack of consonance or harmony of sound, action, or thought **:** DISAGREEMENT

in·consonant \"+\ *adj* [¹*in-* + *consonant*] **:** not consonant or agreeing **:** INCONSISTENT, DISCORDANT

in·conspicuous \¦in+\ *adj* [L *inconspicuus*, fr. *in-* ¹in- + *conspicuus* conspicuous — more at CONSPICUOUS] **1** *obs* **:** INVISIBLE **2** *obs* **:** not obvious to the mental eye **:** INDISCERNIBLE, IMPERCEPTIBLE **3 :** not readily noticeable **:** hardly discernible **:** not prominent or striking — **in·conspicuously** \"+\ *adv* — **in·conspicuousness** \"+\ *n*

inconstance *n* [ME *inconstaunce*, fr. MF *inconstance*, fr. L *inconstantia*] *obs* **:** INCONSTANCY

in·constancy \(')in+\ *n* [L *inconstantia*, fr. *inconstant-*, *inconstans* + *-ia* -y] **1 :** the quality or state of being inconstant **:** lack of constancy: as **a :** CHANGEABLENESS, FICKLENESS **b :** lack of uniformity **:** VARIABILITY **c** *obs* **:** INCONSISTENCY **2 :** an instance of changeableness or of variability

¹in·con·stant \"+\ *adj* [ME, fr. MF, fr. L *inconstant-, inconstans,* fr. *in-* ¹in- + *constant-, constans* constant — more at CONSTANT] **1 :** marked by lack of constancy **:** likely to change frequently often without apparent or cogent reason **:** given to change of character, inclination, purpose, or location ⟨unjust I may have been . . . but never ~ —Jane Austen⟩ **2** *obs* **:** INCONSISTENT

syn FICKLE, CAPRICIOUS, MERCURIAL, UNSTABLE: INCONSTANT suggests a tendency to frequent change, often without good reason ⟨for people seldom knew what they would be, young men especially, they are so amazingly changeable and *inconstant* —Jane Austen⟩; it is often used in reference to persons incapable of steadfastness in love or in reference to changeable climatic and meteorological developments ⟨supposing now . . . this lover of yours was not the sort of man we all take him to be, and that he was to turn out false, or *inconstant* —Anthony Trollope⟩ ⟨places where the soil was fertile but the rainfall uncertain and the rivers shallow and *inconstant* —A.M. Schlesinger b.1888⟩ FICKLE intensifies notions of pointless, even perverse, changeability and incapacity for steadfastness ⟨she is *fickle!* How she turns from one face to another face — and smiles into them all —Edna S. V. Millay⟩ ⟨but bitter experience soon taught him that lordly patrons are *fickle* and their favor not to be relied on —Aldous Huxley⟩ ⟨the next morning was gay with *fickle* sun-showers; it was a harlequin day, a strayed reveler from April —Elinor Wylie⟩ CAPRICIOUS is less derogatory than FICKLE but suggests motivation by caprice, whim, or fancy making for unexpected change ⟨he seemed heartless and *capricious*, as ready to drop you as he had been to take you up —George du Maurier⟩ ⟨the more *capricious* incidence of sexual passion —Lewis Mumford⟩ ⟨the *capricious* severity of a mere despot —J.R.Green⟩ ⟨a *capricious* and malevolent race of savages —Bernard De Voto⟩ MERCURIAL in this sense is likely to suggest changeability in mood, esp. rapid rise from discouragement to mirth or elation, or to suggest a versatility of gifts ⟨Allnutt's *mercurial* spirits could hardly help rising under the influence of Rose's persistent optimism —C.S. Forester⟩ ⟨*mercurial*, euphoric, he could blaze into hectic social events and become a rather too brash and boyish "life and soul of the party" —*Times Lit. Supp.*⟩ UNSTABLE, a less colorful word, indicates an incapacity to remain stable or steady, with many changes and fluctuations ⟨of some meddling, bold fanatic, mind *unstable*, weird, erratic —Sophia A. Jamieson⟩ ⟨the occupation [of mining] in general is an *unstable* one —Lewis Mumford⟩ ⟨the blots of shade and flakes of light upon the countenances of the group changed shape and position endlessly. All was *unstable*, quivering as leaves, evanescent as lightning —Thomas Hardy⟩

²inconstant \"\ *n* **:** one that is inconstant

in·con·stant·ly *adv* **:** in an inconstant manner **:** without constancy

in·con·stant·ness *n* -ES **:** the quality or state of being inconstant

in·consumable \¦in+\ *adj* [¹*in-* + *consumable*] **1 :** not capable of being consumed or destroyed (as by fire) **2 :** satisfying human wants without being directly consumed in so doing ⟨machinery is commonly thought of as ~⟩ — **in·con·sum·ably** \-blē,-bli\ *adv*

inconsumptible *adj* [¹*in-* + *consumptible* capable of being consumed, fr. L *consumptus* (past part. of *consumere* to consume) + E *-ible* — more at CONSUME] *obs* **:** INCONSUMABLE

in-contact \(ˈ)=ˈ=,=\ *n* [fr. the phrase *in contact*] **:** an individual that has lived in close association with another and has thereby been exposed to infection with a disease with which that other is affected

in·con·tam·i·na·ble \¦inkən¦tam(ə)nəbəl\ *adj* [LL *incontaminabilis,* fr. L *in-* ¹in- + LL *contaminabilis* capable of contamination, fr. L *contaminare* to contaminate + *-abilis* -able — more at CONTAMINATE] **:** impossible to contaminate

in·con·tam·i·nate \-mənət\ *adj* [L *incontaminatus,* fr. *in-* ¹in- + *contaminatus,* past part. of *contaminare* to contaminate] **:** free from contamination **:** PURE, UNDEFILED

in·con·test·abil·i·ty \,inkən,testəˈbiləd·ē\ *n* -ES **:** the quality or state of being incontestable

in·con·test·able *or* **in·con·test·ible** \¦inkən¦testəbəl\ *adj* [*incontestable* fr. F, fr. *in-* ¹in- + *contestable* capable of being contested, fr. *contester* to contest + *-able; incontestible,* alter. of *incontestable* — more at CONTEST] **1 :** not subject to being disputed, called in question, or controverted ⟨~ evidence⟩ **:** offering no grounds for doubt **:** INDUBITABLE, UNDOUBTED ⟨an ~ genius⟩ **2 :** being such that payment of claims cannot be disputed by a life insurance company for any cause except nonpayment of premiums or other reason specifically stated in the contract when the contract has been in force for a stipulated period (as one or two years) and when an insurable interest existed at its inception — **in·con·test·able·ness** *n* -ES

incontestable clause *n* **:** a clause in a life insurance policy providing the conditions under which the policy is incontestable

in·con·test·a·bly \-blē,-bli\ *adv* **:** in an incontestable manner or to an incontestable degree or level **:** CERTAINLY, INDUBITABLY

incontested *adj* [¹*in-* + past part. of *contest*] *obs* **:** UNDISPUTED

in·continence \(ˈ)in, ən+\ *n* [ME, fr. MF or L; MF, fr. L *incontinentia,* fr. *incontinent-, incontinens* + *-ia* -y] **1 :** lack of restraint **:** inability or disinclination to resist desire or impulse; *esp* **:** SALACIOUSNESS, DISSOLUTENESS ⟨fell into a life of sexual and alcoholic ~⟩ **2 :** inability to retain a bodily discharge (as urine) voluntarily

in·continency \"+\ *n* [ME, fr. L *incontinentia*] **1 :** INCONTINENCE **2 :** an act of incontinence; *esp* **:** illicit sexual intercourse — usu. used in pl. ⟨the record of his manifold *incontinencies*⟩

in·continent \"+\ *adj* [ME, fr. MF or L; MF, fr. L *incontinent-, incontinens,* fr. *in-* ¹in- + *continent-, continens* continent — more at CONTINENT] **1 :** marked by incontinence **:** lacking control **:** UNRESTRAINED ⟨the thunderous drumming ~ downpour —Gertrude Diamant⟩; *esp* **:** sexually dissolute ⟨the ~ man's evil appetite —J.E.Hankins⟩ **2 :** unable to retain a bodily discharge (as urine) voluntarily

¹in·continently \"+\ *also* **incontinent** *adv* [*incontinently* fr. MF *incontinent* + E *-ly; incontinent* fr. ME, fr. MF, fr. LL *in continenti*] **1 :** at once **:** without delay **:** IMMEDIATELY ⟨~ turned and fled⟩ **2 :** with unceremonious haste **:** PELL-MELL ⟨fled ~ until I reached a herd's cottage —John Buchan⟩

²incontinently \"\ *adv* [*incontinent* (adj.) + *-ly*] **:** in an incontinent or unrestrained manner: as **a :** LEWDLY, LOOSELY **b :** without due or reasonable consideration ⟨making the speech he had ~ promised⟩

in·continuous \¦in+\ *adj* [¹*in-* + *continuous*] **:** not continuous

in·controllable \"+\ *adj* [¹*in-* + *controllable*] **:** UNCONTROLLABLE

in·controllably \"+\ *adv* **:** UNCONTROLLABLY

in·controvertible \(¦)in, ən+\ *adj* [¹*in-* + *controvertible*] **:** not open to question **:** INDISPUTABLE, CERTAIN ⟨~ evidence⟩ ⟨it seemed ~ that he had deceived his friend⟩ — **in·contro·vertibly** \"+\ *adv*

in con·tu·ma·ci·am \¦in,käntəˈmākē,äm\ *adv* [L, lit., in contumacy] **:** in contempt of or in disobedience to an order or summons of a court — used chiefly in ecclesiastical law of one who has refused to submit to or appear in a court and who is thereupon convicted or condemned in his absence

¹in·convenience \¦in+\ *n* [ME, fr. LL *inconvenientia,* fr. L *inconvenient-, inconveniens* + *-ia* -y] **1 :** the quality or state of being inconvenient: as **a** *obs* **:** INCONGRUITY, UNSUITABLENESS, IMPROPRIETY **b** *obs* **:** HARM, MISCHIEF, MISFORTUNE, TROUBLE; *also* **:** an injury esp. when general or public as distinguished from an injury to one or a few **c :** the quality or state of being unsuited or unadapted to personal needs or comfort **:** DISADVANTAGE, DISCOMFORT ⟨the ~ of his quarters⟩ **2 :** something that is inconvenient **:** something that gives trouble, embarrassment, or uneasiness **:** something that disturbs or impedes **:** DISADVANTAGE, HANDICAP ⟨loss of this extra income was a serious ~⟩ ⟨found the daily trip an ~⟩

²inconvenience \"\ *vt* **:** to subject to inconvenience **:** INCOMMODE

in·conveniency \¦in+\ *n* [LL *inconvenientia*] **:** INCONVENIENCE

¹in·convenient \"+\ *adj* [ME, fr. MF, fr. L *inconvenient-, inconveniens,* fr. *in-* ¹in + *convenient-, conveniens,* convenient — more at CONVENIENT] **1** *obs* **a :** not agreeing **:** INCONGRUOUS, IRRATIONAL **b :** not suitable **:** UNFIT **c :** morally unbecoming **:** IMPROPER **2 :** not convenient **:** giving trouble, uneasiness, or annoyance **:** DISADVANTAGEOUS, INOPPORTUNE ⟨an ~ house⟩ ⟨a most ~ arrangement⟩ — **in·conveniently** \"+\ *adv* — **in·con·ve·nient·ness** *n* -ES

²inconvenient *n* -S [ME, fr. *inconvenient,* adj.] *obs* **:** something inconvenient: as **a :** INCONGRUITY, INCONSISTENCY, ABSURDITY **b :** an unbecoming or improper act **c :** INCONVENIENCE

in·conversable \¦in+\ *adj* [¹*in-* + *conversable*] **:** UNCOMMUNICATIVE, RESERVED

in·conversant \(¦)in, ən+\ *adj* [¹*in-* + *conversant*] **:** lacking experience in or familiarity with

in·convertibility \¦in+\ *n* **:** the quality or state of being inconvertible — used chiefly of foreign exchange

in·convertible \"+\ *adj* [prob. fr. LL *inconvertibilis,* fr. L *in-* ¹in- + *convertibilis* changeable — more at CONVERTIBLE] **:** not capable of being changed into or exchanged for something else ⟨the alchemists were unwilling to accept the ~ nature of elemental metals⟩: **a** *of paper money* **:** not exchangeable on demand for specie **b** *of a currency* **:** not exchangeable for a foreign currency — **in·con·vert·ibly** \-əblē, -li\ *adv*

in·convincible \¦in+\ *adj* [prob. fr. LL *inconvincibilis,* fr. L *in-* ¹in- + *convincibilis* able to be convinced, fr. L *convincere* to convince + *-ibilis* -ible — more at CONVINCE] **:** incapable of being convinced

incony *adj* [origin unknown] *obs* **:** PRETTY

in·cooperative \¦in+\ *adj* [¹*in-* + *cooperative*] **:** lacking in cooperation or in ability or will to cooperate ⟨the patient's family was wholly ~⟩ **:** UNCOOPERATIVE

in·coordinate *also* **in·coordinated** \"+\ *adj* [¹*in-* + *coordinate, coordinated*] **:** lacking coordination **:** not coordinate

in·coordination \¦in+\ *n* [ISV ¹*in-* + *coordination*] **:** lack of coordination; *esp* **:** lack of coordination of muscular movements resulting from loss of voluntary control and usu. associated with disease — compare ATAXIA

in·coronate *also* **in·coronated** \ən+\ *adj* [*incoronate* fr. ML *incoronatus,* past part. of *incoronare* to crown, fr. L *in-* ²in- + *coronare* to crown; *incoronated* fr. ²*in-* + *coronated* — more at CROWN] **:** CROWNED, CORONATED

in·coronation \"+\ *n* [ML *incoronation-, incoronatio,* fr. *incoronatus* + L *-ion-, -io* -ion] **:** CORONATION

in·corporable \ənˈkō(r)p(ə)rəbəl\ *adj* [L *incorporare* + E *-able*] **:** capable of being incorporated

in·corporal \(ˈ)in, ən+\ *adj* [L *incorporalis,* fr. *in-* ¹in- + *corporalis* corporal — more at CORPORAL] **:** INCORPOREAL

¹in·cor·po·rate \ənˈkō(r)pə,rāt, *usu* -ād·+V\ *vb* -ED/-ING/-S [ME *incorporaten,* fr. LL *incorporatus,* past part. of *incorporare,* fr. L *in-* ²in- + *corpor-, corpus* body — more at MIDRIFF] *vt* **1 a :** to unite with or introduce into something already existent usu. so as to form an indistinguishable whole that cannot be restored to the previously separate elements without damage ⟨the complex processes by which food is *incorporated* with living tissues⟩ ⟨the committee recommended that we ~ several new rules into the bylaws⟩ **b :** to admit to membership in a corporation; *esp* **:** to admit (a person) to the rank, status, and privileges of an advanced degree at a British university on the basis of possession of a like degree earned at another institution **2 a :** to combine (ingredients) into one consistent whole **:** unite intimately (as into a new substance or presentation) ⟨*incorporated* his ideas in a monograph on classical philology⟩ **:** blend, combine, or mingle thoroughly to form a homogeneous product ⟨mechanically *incorporating* the materials into a smooth uniform paste⟩ **b :** to bring together in an association; *specif* **:** to form into a corporation recognized by law as an entity and having particular functions, rights, duties, and liabilities **3 :** to give material form to **:** EMBODY **~** *vi* **1 :** to become unified with something into a composite whole ⟨these ideas gradually *incorporated* with existing religious beliefs to form a new philosophy⟩ **2 a** *archaic* **:** to mingle together so as to form a new whole **b :** to form or become a corporation ⟨they will ~ as soon as they have a little more capital⟩

²in·cor·po·rate \ənˈkōrp(ə)rət, -ō(ə)p-, *usu* -əd·+V\ *adj* [ME *incorporat,* fr. LL *incorporatus,* past part.] **1 :** made one body or united in one body **:** intimately united or blended **:** EMBODIED ⟨the doctrines ~ in scriptural writings⟩ **2 a :** formed into a corporation **:** INCORPORATED ⟨an ~ municipality⟩ **b** *obs, of people* **:** associated as members of a corporation

³in·cor·po·rate \(ˈ)in¦kōrp(ə)rət, ən'k-\ *adj* [LL *incorporatus,* fr. L *in-* ¹in- + *corporatus,* past part. of *corporare* to make into a body — more at CORPORATE] *archaic* **:** INCORPOREAL, SPIRITUAL

incorporated *adj* **:** united in one body **:** formed into a corporation **:** made a legal entity

in·cor·po·rat·ed·ness *n* -ES **:** the quality or state of being incorporated **:** INCORPORATION

incorporated territory *n* **:** a portion of the domain of the U.S. that does not constitute and is not a part of any state but that is considered a part of the U.S. proper and is entitled to all the benefits of the Constitution that are not specifically reserved to the states ⟨Arizona, Oklahoma, and New Mexico were all *incorporated territories* before attaining statehood⟩

incorporating *adj* **1 :** serving to incorporate **:** uniting in one body **2** *of language or grammar* **:** POLYSYNTHETIC

incorporating union *n* **:** a union of two or more states into one political whole ⟨the association of the several sovereign states of Germany into the German Empire can be considered an *incorporating union*⟩

in·cor·po·ra·tion \(,)in,kō(r)pəˈrāshən, ən-\ *n* [ME *incorporacioun, incorperacioun,* fr. LL *incorporation-, incorporatio,* fr. *incorporatus* (past part. of *incorporare* to incorporate) + L *-ion-, -io* -ion — more at INCORPORATE] **1 :** an act of incorporating or the state of being incorporated: as **a :** a union of something with an existing whole into a new intimate and usu. permanent new whole ⟨~ of plasticizer with a resin⟩ ⟨~ of the conquered territory into the empire⟩ **b :** a union of diverse things into a whole **:** intimate mingling **:** COMBINATION, SYNTHESIS ⟨the ~ of these rough notes into a coherent report⟩ **c :** a creation of a corporation or esp. of a legal corporate entity **d :** INCARNATION, EMBODIMENT **2 a** *obs* **:** a charter of incorporation **b :** an incorporated association or entity **:** CORPORATION **3 :** the process of word and sentence formation characteristic of incorporating languages

incorporation by reference : a doctrine in law: the terms of a contemporaneous or earlier writing, instrument, or document capable of being identified can be made an actual part of another writing, instrument, or document by referring to, identifying, and adopting the former as part of the latter

in·cor·po·ra·tive \ənˈkō(r)pə,rād·|iv, -p(ə)rə|, |t|, |ēv *also* |əv\ *adj* **:** incorporating or tending to incorporate: as **a** *of language* **:** AGGLUTINATIVE, POLYSYNTHETIC **b** *of a state* **:** growing by taking over and incorporating adjacent territories ⟨the Russian Empire was a typical ~ state⟩

in·cor·po·ra·tor \-pə,rād·ə(r), -ātə-\ *n* **:** one that incorporates: as **a :** any of the persons who join as original members in incorporating a company **:** a member at any time of a corporation aggregate **:** a corporator in a corporation having no capital stock **:** a promoter of a corporation named as an original member **b :** a member of one British university who is incorporated in another

in·cor·po·ra·tor·ship \-,ship\ *n* -S **:** membership in a corporation

¹in·corporeal \¦in+,=¦===\ *adj* [L *incorporeus* (fr. *in-* ¹in- + *corporeus* of the body) + E *-al* — more at CORPOREAL] **1 :** not corporeal **:** having no material body or form **:** not consisting of matter **:** IMMATERIAL **2 :** of, relating to, or characteristic of beings who lack material substance ⟨~ speed⟩ ⟨that ~ music⟩ **3 :** of, relating to, or constituting a right that has no physical existence but that issues out of corporate property which has a physical existence and that concerns or is annexed to or exercisable in relation to such property (as stocks, bonds, mineral rights, patents) **:** existing only in contemplation of law ⟨an ~ hereditament⟩ — **in·corporeality** \¦in+\ *n* — **in·corporeally** \"+,=¦===\ *adv*

²incorporeal \"\ *n* **:** something that is incorporeal **:** an immaterial or spiritual being

incorporeal chattel *n* **:** CHOSE IN ACTION

in·cor·po·re·i·ty \,in,kō(r)pəˈrēəd·ē\ *n* [*incorporeal* + *-ity*] **:** the quality or state of being incorporeal **:** IMMATERIALITY; *also* **:** an incorporeal attribute or entity

incorporeous *adj* [L *incorporeus*] *obs* **:** INCORPOREAL 1

in·corpsed \ənˈkō(ə)rpst\ *adj* [²*in-* + *corpse* + *-¹ed*] **:** made one with **:** incorporated into

in·correct \¦in+\ *adj* [ME, fr. MF or L; MF, fr. L *incorrectus,* fr. *in-* ¹in- + *correctus,* past part. of *corrigere* to correct — more at CORRECT] **1** *obs* **:** not corrected or chastened ⟨it shows a will most ~ to heaven —Shak.⟩ **2 :** failing to agree with a copy or model or with established rules **:** INACCURATE, FAULTY ⟨a careless ~ transcription⟩ ⟨an ~ edition⟩ **3 a :** failing to agree with the requirements of duty, morality, or propriety **:** UNBECOMING, IMPROPER ⟨~ behavior⟩ ⟨this neglect was most ~⟩ **b :** not acceptable to the best taste ⟨gray flannels are ~ for tennis⟩ **4 :** failing to coincide with the truth **:** INACCURATE, IMPRECISE ⟨your answers are all ~⟩ **5** *of a word or expression* **:** formed or used in violation of grammatical principles

in·correctly \"+\ *adv* **:** in an incorrect manner

in·correctness \"+\ *n* **:** the quality or state of being incorrect

in·correspondence *or* **in·correspondency** \(¦)in+\ *n* [¹*in-* + *correspondence, correspondency*] **:** lack of correspondence or harmony

in·corrigibility \(¦)in, ən+\ *n* **:** the quality or state of being incorrigible

¹in·corrigible \"+\ *adj* [ME, fr. LL *incorrigibilis,* fr. L *in-* ¹in- + *corrigere* to correct + *-ibilis* -ible — more at CORRECT] **:** incapable of being corrected or amended: as **a** (1) **:** bad beyond the possibility of correction or rehabilitation **:** utterly bad or depraved ⟨an ~ criminal⟩ ⟨such ~ conduct⟩ (2) **:** *of a child* **:** persistently bad **:** DELINQUENT ⟨a training school for ~ boys⟩ **b** *archaic* **:** INCURABLE, IRREMEDIABLE **c :** requiring no improvement or alteration **:** being perfect as formed or formulated ⟨his judgment is not infallible or ~ —T.D.Weldon⟩ ⟨~ truth⟩ **d :** UNMANAGEABLE, UNRULY ⟨~ hair⟩ **e** (1) **:** unwilling to change or to give something up ⟨an ~ traveler⟩ ⟨an ~ amateur mechanic⟩ (2) **:** not readily altered **:** STRONG, INTENSE ⟨felt an ~ optimism⟩ ⟨irritating ~ self-assurance⟩

²incorrigible \"\ *n* -S **:** something incorrigible; *esp* **:** an incorrigible person

in·cor·ri·gi·ble·ness \-nəs\ *n* -ES **:** the quality or state of being incorrigible

in·corrigibly \(ˈ)in, ən+\ *adv* **:** in an incorrigible manner

in·corrodable *also* **in·corrodible** \¦in+\ *adj* [*incorrodable* alter. of *incorrodible; incorrodible* fr. ¹*in-* + *corrodible*] **:** impervious to corrosion

in·corrupt *also* **in·corrupted** \"+\ *adj* [*incorrupt* fr. ME, fr. L *incorruptus,* fr. *in-* ¹in- + *corruptus* past part. of *corrumpere* to corrupt; *incorrupted* fr. ¹*in-* + past part. of *corrupt* — more at CORRUPT] **:** free from corruption: as **a** *obs* **:** not affected with decay **:** not putrefied or rotten **:** SOUND **b :** INCORRUPTIBLE **c :** not defiled or depraved **:** PURE, SOUND, UNTAINTED, UPRIGHT, HONEST **d :** free from error ⟨an ~ edition prepared from the original text⟩ — **in·corruptly** \"+\ *adv* — **in·corruptness** \"+\ *n*

in·corruptibility \¦in+\ *n* [ME *incorrumptibiletee,* fr. LL *incorruptibilitas,* fr. *incorruptibilis* incorruptible + L *-itas* -ity] **:** the quality or state of being incorruptible

¹in·corruptible \"+\ *adj* [ME, fr. MF or LL; MF, fr. LL *incorruptibilis,* fr. L *in-* ¹in- + LL *corruptibilis* corruptible — more at CORRUPTIBLE] **:** incapable of corruption: as **a :** not subject to decay or dissolution ⟨gold is ~ by most chemical agents⟩ **b :** incapable of being bribed or morally corrupted **:** inflexibly just and upright

²incorruptible \"\ *n* -S **:** something that is not subject to corruption; *esp* **:** something of spiritual nature

in·cor·rupt·ible·ness \-nəs\ *n* **:** INCORRUPTIBILITY

in·cor·rupt·ibly \-əblē, -li\ *adv* **:** in an incorruptible manner

in·corruption \¦in+\ *n* [ME *incorruption-, incorruptio,* fr. L *in-* ¹in- + *corruption-, corruptio* corruption — more at CORRUPTION] **1** *archaic* **:** the quality or state of being free from physical decay **2 :** freedom from corrupt practices **:** UPRIGHTNESS, HONESTY

incounter *obs var of* ENCOUNTER

incourage *obs var of* ENCOURAGE

incr *abbr* increase; increased; increasing

¹incrassate *vb* -ED/-ING/-S [LL *incrassatus,* past part. of *incrassare,* fr. L *in-* ²in- + *crassare* to thicken, fr. *crassus* thick — more at HURDLE] *obs* **:** THICKEN, INSPISSATE — **incrassation** *n* -S

²in·cras·sate \ənˈkra,sāt\ *also* **in·cras·sat·ed** \-ād·əd\ *adj* [LL *incrassatus*] **1 :** THICKENED **2** *of a plant or animal structure* **:** SWOLLEN, INFLATED ⟨an ~ cell wall⟩

in·creas·able \(ˈ)in¦krēsəbəl, ən'k-\ *adj* **:** capable of being increased ⟨his income was no way ~⟩

¹in·crease \(ˈ)in¦krēs, ən'k-\ *vb* -ED/-ING/-S [ME *encresen, incresen,* fr. MF *encreiss-,* stem of *encreistre, encroistre,* fr. L *increscere,* fr. *in-* ²in- + *crescere* to grow — more at CRESCENT] *vi* **1 :** to become greater in some respect (as in size, quantity, number, degree, value, intensity, power, authority, reputation, wealth) **:** GROW, ADVANCE, WAX — opposed to *decrease* ⟨his wealth *increased* over the years⟩ ⟨*increasing* in knowledge through study⟩ **2 :** to multiply by the production of young **:** be prolific ⟨the herd ~*s* yearly⟩ **3** *of a Latin noun or adjective* **:** to have a syllable more in the genitive than in the nominative (as in *rex, regis*) **~** *vt* **1 :** to make greater in some respect (as in bulk, quantity, extent, value, or amount) **:** add to **:** ENHANCE ⟨~ his possessions⟩ **2** *archaic* **:** to cause to be richer, more prosperous, or more powerful **:** ENRICH, PROMOTE **3 :** to add (a stitch) to knitting by knitting twice in the same stitch (as in the front and the back of the stitch)

syn ENLARGE, AUGMENT, MULTIPLY: INCREASE intransitively may carry the idea of progressive growth in numbers, size, amount, quantity or intensity ⟨our population is *increasing*⟩ ⟨prices *increased* on all necessities —*Collier's Yr. Bk.*⟩ ⟨the rice yield to the acre *increased* with improved methods —*Amer. Guide Series: Texas*⟩; transitively this notion is not so prominent ⟨the trustees *increased* salaries⟩ ENLARGE suggests expansion or extension of any sort ⟨to *enlarge* a building⟩ ⟨*enlarging* the farm⟩ ⟨*enlarging* the personnel of the department⟩ ⟨the abundant opportunities which the aesthetic realm provides to *enlarge* our experience —Hunter Mead⟩ ⟨early New England life when strong men enjoyed religion and *enlarged* their minds by profound metaphysical discussion —C.A.Dinsmore⟩ AUGMENT intransitively may suggest further growth, development, or increase of something already grown or developed ⟨the literature of cryptography, both in the form of secret government manuals and openly published books, had *augmented* enormously since 1880 —Fletcher Pratt⟩; transitively it may suggest addition to sufficiency or ampleness ⟨the city police, *augmented* by special deputies, were also called out —*Amer. Guide Series: Tenn.*⟩ ⟨by their weight, which was *augmented* by laying a number of old rails on the top, these slabs have the effect of preventing any tendency for the clay to work up —O.S.Nock⟩ MULTIPLY intransitively may suggest increase by natural generation ⟨in those days the Anglo-American stock, a very fine one, *multiplied* like rabbits —W.R. Inge⟩ ⟨mosquitoes *multiply* rapidly⟩; in all uses it is likely to indicate increasing manifold ⟨skins which would *multiply* Mr. Astor's wealth —Meridel Le Sueur⟩ ⟨those ships had *multiplied* until their very numbers were menacing —Kenneth Roberts⟩

²in·crease \ˈin,krēs *also* ən'k-\ *n* -S [ME *encres, incres,* fr. *encresen, incresen,* v.] **1 :** act of increasing: as **a :** addition or enlargement in size, extent, quantity, number, intensity, value, substance **:** AUGMENTATION, GROWTH, MULTIPLICATION ⟨an ~ of knowledge⟩ **b** *obs* **:** production of young **:** PROPAGATION **c** *obs* (1) **:** growth in wealth, dignity, or influence **:** ADVANCEMENT (2) **:** the rising of flood or tidal waters **2 :** something that results from or is produced by increasing **:** an addition or increment **:** something that is added to the original stock by augmentation or growth (as progeny, issue, offspring, produce, profit, interest)

increased *adj* **:** subjected to augmentation **:** made or become greater ⟨~ time for study⟩ ⟨the ~ wealth of the nation⟩ — **in·creased·ly** \(ˈ)in¦krēsədlē, ən'k-, -stl-, -li\ *adv*

increaseful *adj, obs* **:** full of increase **:** PRODUCTIVE

in·crease·ment \(ˈ)in¦krēsmənt, ən'k-\ *n* -S [ME *encresement,* fr. *encresen* to increase + *-ment*] *archaic* **:** INCREASE

in·creas·er \-sə(r)\ *n* -s **:** one that increases: as **a :** an agent that causes something to increase ⟨these ~*s* of public turmoil⟩ **b** *archaic* **:** one that promotes or furthers something (as a cause, a group) **c :** a plant or animal that tends to multiply freely ⟨several of the new glads proved to be excellent ~*s*⟩ **d :** a coupling for joining a pipe to another of larger diameter

increaser d: *1* smaller pipe, *2* increaser, *3* larger pipe

increasing *adj* **:** becoming progressively greater ⟨to an ~ degree⟩ ⟨settlers came in in ~ numbers⟩

increasing function *n* **:** a mathematical function whose value algebraically increases as the independent variable algebraically increases over a given range

in·creas·ing·ly *adv* **:** to an increasing degree **:** more and more ⟨became ~ apparent⟩ ⟨~ of the opinion —W.H.Camp⟩

in·cre·ate \ˈinkrēˌāt, ənˈkrēət\ *adj* [ME *increat*, fr. LL *increatus*, fr. L *in-* ¹in- + *creatus*, past part. of *creare* to create — more at CRESCENT] **:** UNCREATED, SELF-EXISTENT — **in·cre·ate·ly** *adv*

in·creative \(ˈ)in, ən+\ *adj* [¹*in-* + *creative*] **:** incapable of creating

in·credibility \(ˈ)in, ən+\ *n* **1 :** the quality or state of being incredible ⟨the sheer ~ of this situation⟩ **2 :** something that is incredible ⟨all these tales and *incredibilities*⟩

in·credible \(ˈ)in, ən+\ *adj* [ME, fr. L *incredibilis*, fr. *in-* ¹in- + *credibilis* credible — more at CREDIBLE] **1 a :** surpassing belief **:** too extraordinary and improbable to admit of belief ⟨an ~ cost⟩ **b :** hard to believe real or true **:** UNLIKELY, IMPROBABLE ⟨the children's appetite was ~⟩ **2** *obs* **:** INCREDULOUS, UNBELIEVING — **in·credibleness** \"+\ *n* — **in·credibly** \"+\ *adv*

in·creditable \"+\ *adj* [¹*in-* + *creditable*] *archaic* **:** not creditable

in·credulity \ˌin+\ *n* [ME *incredulite*, fr. L *incredulitas*, fr. *incredulus* + *-itas* -ity] **:** the quality or state of being incredulous **:** a withholding or refusal of belief **:** DISBELIEF

in·credulous \(ˈ)in, ən+\ *adj* [L *incredulus*, fr. *in-* ¹in- + *credulus* credulous — more at CREDULOUS] **1 :** indisposed to admit or accept what is related as true ⟨~ of such statements⟩ **2 :** caused by disbelief or incredulity ⟨an ~ stare⟩ **3** *obs* **:** not to be believed **:** INCREDIBLE — **in·credulously** \"+\ *adv* — **in·credulousness** \"+\ *n*

in·creep \ˈ≈,≈\ *vi* [ME *increpen*, fr. ²*in* + *crepen* to creep — more at CREEP] **:** to enter bit by bit or by slow degrees **:** creep in ⟨the ~*ing* frost⟩

in·cremation \ˌin+≈ˈ≈≈\ *n* [²*in* + *cremation*] **:** CREMATION

in·cre·ment \ˈiŋkrəmənt, ˈink-\ *n* -s [ME, fr. L *incrementum*, fr. *increscere* to increase + *-mentum* -ment — more at INCREASE] **1 :** an increasing or growth in bulk, quantity, number, or value **:** ENLARGEMENT, INCREASE **2 a :** something that is gained or added **:** an added quantity or character **b :** one of a series of regular consecutive additions of like or proportional size or value — compare UNEARNED INCREMENT **c :** one of a series of minute additions **:** a slight or imperceptible augmentation **3 :** increase in volume or value of a forest or its products during a given period **4 a :** a positive or negative change in the value of one or more of a set of variables **b :** an amount of powder packed in a bag that may be added to or removed from the propelling charge of semifixed or separate loading ammunition to permit fire at varying ranges and with varying angles of impact

in·cre·men·tal \ˌ≈≈ˈmentᵊl\ *adj* **:** of, relating to, constituting, or resulting from increments, increase, or growth

incremental repetition *n* **:** repetition in each stanza after the first of part of the preceding stanza — used esp. of popular ballads

increment borer *n* **:** ACCRETION BORER

in·cre·pa·tion \ˌinkrəˈpāshən\ *n* -s [MF or LL; MF, fr. LL *increpation-*, *increpatio*, fr. L *increpatus* (past part. of *increpare* to make a noise, upbraid, fr. *in-* ²in- + *crepare* to crack, creak, break) + *-ion-*, *-io* -ion — more at RAVEN] *archaic* **:** CHIDING, REBUKE, REPROOF

¹**in·crescent** \(ˈ)in, ən+\ *n* [L *increscent-*, *increscens*, pres. part.] **:** an increscent representation of the moon

²**increscent** \"+\ *adj* [L *increscent-*, *increscens*, pres. part. of *increscere* to increase — more at INCREASE] **1 :** becoming greater by gradual augmentation **:** INCREASING **2** *of the moon* **:** WAXING; *specif* **:** having the horns pointing to the dexter side

increscent

in·cre·tion \(ˈ)inˌkrēshən, ən-\ *n* -s [ISV ²*in-* + *secretion*] **1 :** internal secretion **:** secretion into the blood or tissues rather than into a cavity or outlet of the body **2 :** a product of internal secretion **:** AUTACOID, HORMONE — **in·cre·tion·ary** \-shəˌnerē\ *adj*

in·cre·to·ry \(ˈ)inˈkrēdərē, ənˈk-\ *adj* [²*in-* + *secretory*] **:** ENDOCRINE ⟨~ organs⟩

in·crim·i·nate \ənˈkriməˌnāt, *usu* -ād·+V\ *vt* [LL *incriminatus*, past part. of *incriminare*, fr. L *in-* ²in- + *crimin-*, *crimen* crime — more at CRIME] **1 a :** to charge with a crime or fault ⟨he *incriminated* the other boys to the teacher⟩ **b :** to furnish evidence or proof of circumstances tending to show the guilt of ⟨the testimony certainly ~*s* the brother⟩ ⟨those feathers under the cage are enough to ~ the cat⟩ **c :** to involve (as oneself) in a criminal prosecution or the risk of one ⟨unwilling to testify for fear of *incriminating* himself⟩ **2 :** to charge with involvement in or establish as sharing responsibility for some undesirable effect or result ⟨eye gnats have been *incriminated* in some outbreaks of pinkeye⟩ ⟨poor lighting is often *incriminated* in eyestrain⟩ **syn** see ACCUSE

in·crim·i·na·tion \(ˌ)inˌkriməˈnāshən, ənˌk-\ *n* [LL *incrimination-*, *incriminatio*, fr. *incriminatus* + L *-ion-*, *-io* -ion] **:** the act of incriminating or the state of being incriminated

in·crim·i·na·tor \≈ˈ≈≈ˌnād·ə(r), -ātə-\ *n* **:** one that incriminates

in·crim·i·na·to·ry \-ˌnəˌtōrē, -tȯrē, -ri\ *adj* **:** tending to incriminate

incroach *obs var of* ENCROACH

¹**incross** \ˈ≈,≈\ *n* [⁴*in* + *cross* (n.)] **1 :** an individual produced by crossing inbred lines of the same breed or strain — compare INCROSSBRED **2 :** an instance or act of crossing inbred lines of the same breed or strain

²**incross** \ˈ≈,≈\ *vt* [²*in* + *cross* (v.)] **:** to interbreed (inbred lines of a breed or strain)

incrossbred \ˈ≈ˈ≈,≈\ *n* [⁴*in* + *crossbred*] **:** an individual produced by crossing inbred lines of separate breeds or strains — compare INCROSS

incrossbreed \ˌ≈ˈ≈,≈, ˈ≈ˈ≈,≈\ *vt* [²*in* + *crossbreed*] **:** to cause (inbred lines of different breeds or strains) to interbreed

in·crotchet \ən+\ *vt* [²*in-* + *crotchet* (n.)] *archaic* **:** to enclose in brackets

in·croy·a·ble \aⁿkrwäyäbl(ᵊ), -b(lə)\ *n* -s [F, fr. *incroyable*, adj., incredible, fr. MF, fr. *in-* ¹in- + *croyable* credible, fr. *croire* to believe (fr. L *credere*) + *-able*; fr. their extravagant dress and speech — more at CREED] **:** a French dandy of the late 18th century **:** DANDY, FOP

incruent *also* **incruental** *or* **incruentous** [*incruent*, *incruentous* fr. L *incruentus*, fr. *in-* ¹in- + *cruentus* bloody; *incruental* fr. L *incruentus* + E *-al*] *adj*, *obs* **:** UNBLOODY

incrust *var of* ENCRUST

incrustant *var of* ENCRUSTANT

¹**in·crus·tate** \ənˈkrəˌstāt, ˈinˌk \ *vt* -ED/-ING/-S [L *incrustatus*, past part. of *incrustare* — more at ENCRUST] **:** ENCRUST

²**in·crus·tate** \ənˈk-\ *adj* [L *incrustatus*] **1 :** formed into or like a crust **2 :** having a crust

in·crus·ta·tion \ˌinˌkrəsˈtāshən\ *or* **en·crus·ta·tion** \ˌen,-\ *n* [L *incrustation-*, *incrustatio*, fr. *incrustatus* + *-ion-*, *-io* -ion] **1 :** the act of encrusting or state of being encrusted **:** formation of a crust **2 a :** a crust or hard coating of something upon or within a body **b :** a growth or accumulation (as of habits, opinions, customs) resembling an encrusting layer **3 :** a covering or inlaying (as of marble or mosaic) attached to masonry by cramp irons or cement **4 :** something applied as an overlay or inlay ⟨~ of diamonds⟩

in·cu·bate \ˈiŋkyəˌbāt, ˈink-, *usu* -ād·+V\ *vb* -ED/-ING/-S [L *incubatus*, past part. of *incubare* to lie upon, hatch, fr. *in-* ²in- + *cubare* to lie down, lie upon — more at HIP] *vt* **1 :** to sit upon (eggs) so as to hatch by the warmth of the body in the manner of most birds **:** BROOD **2 :** to maintain (as eggs, embryos of animals, or bacteria) under prescribed and usu. controlled conditions (as of temperature and moisture) favorable for hatching or development esp. in an incubator **3 :** to maintain (a chemically active system) under controlled conditions for the development of a reaction **4 :** to cause to develop **:** give form and substance to ⟨*incubated* the new idea for a while before giving it to his supervisor⟩ ~ *vi* **1 :** to sit on eggs **:** BROOD **2 :** to undergo incubation ⟨the cultures must ~ for five more days⟩ **3 :** to acquire form and substance **:** DEVELOP ⟨the plan *incubated* slowly on his nightly walks from work⟩

in·cu·ba·tion \ˌ≈≈ˈbāshən\ *n* -s [L *incubation-*, *incubatio*, fr. *incubatus* + *-ion-*, *-io* -ion] **1 :** the act or process of incubating (as eggs, bacteria, or milk) ⟨during the ~ of the culture⟩ **2 :** the act or an instance of brooding over something in order to give it form and substance ⟨definitely named the four stages of creative thought as preparation, ~, illumination, and verification —R.S.Woodworth⟩ **3 :** the period between the infection of a plant or animal by a pathogen and the manifestation of the disease it causes **4 :** a rite among the ancient Greeks and Romans of sleeping on a skin or on the ground in order to enter into communion with the chthonic gods through dreams

in·cu·ba·tion·al \ˌ≈≈ˈbāshənᵊl, -shnəl\ *adj* **:** of or relating to incubation

incubation period *n* **:** the period of brooding or incubating required to bring an egg to hatching; *broadly* **:** the length of incubating required to attain a desired or expected result ⟨many children's diseases have an *incubation period* of less than one week⟩

INCUBATION PERIODS

BIRD	DAYS	BIRD	DAYS
canary	14	ostrich	42
common fowl	21	peafowl	28
duck	28	pheasant	21–24
goose	28–32	pigeon	17–18
guinea fowl	26–28	swan	42
muscovy duck	35–37	turkey	28

in·cu·ba·tist \ˈ≈≈ˌbātəst\ *n* -s *Brit* **:** a poultry hatcheryman

in·cu·ba·tive \-ād·iv\ *adj* **:** of or relating to incubation ⟨~ technique⟩ **:** characteristic of or marked by incubation ⟨~ period⟩

in·cu·ba·tor \-ād·ə(r), -ātə-\ *n* -s **:** one that incubates: as **a :** an apparatus by which eggs are hatched artificially consisting essentially of an insulated cabinet containing the eggs in trays or drawers, a source of artificial heat and of moisture, and controls to maintain a desired level of heat and moisture **b :** an apparatus for the maintenance of controlled conditions of heat and usu. moisture (as for the cultivation of microorganisms) **c :** an apparatus for housing premature or sick babies in an environment of controlled humidity, oxygen supply, and temperature

incubator bird *n* **:** MEGAPODE

in·cu·ba·to·ri·um \ˌ≈≈bəˈtōrēəm, (ˌ)inˌkyübəˈt-\ *n*, *pl* **incubato·ria** \-rēə\ *also* **incubatoriums** [NL, fr. L *incubatus* (past part. of *incubare* to lie upon, hatch) + *-orium* -ory — more at INCUBATE] **1 :** the ventral brooding pouch of a monotreme **2 :** MARSUPIUM 1a(1)

in·cu·ba·to·ry \ˈiŋkyəbəˌtōrē, ˈink-, ˈ≈≈ˌbād·ərē, ənˈkyübə,-tȯrē\ *adj* **:** relating to or serving for incubation

in·cu·bous \ˈiŋkyəbəs, ˈink-\ *adj* [L *incubare* to lie upon + E *-ous* — more at INCUBATE] **1** *of leaves* **:** being so arranged that the anterior margin of each overlaps the posterior margin of the next younger **2 :** having incubous leaves ⟨~ liverworts⟩ — compare SUCCUBOUS

in·cu·bus \-bəs\ *n*, *pl* **incu·bi** \-ˌbī\ *also* **incubuses** [ME, fr. LL, fr. L *incubare* to lie upon, hatch] **1 :** an evil spirit believed to lie upon persons in their sleep and esp. to have sexual intercourse with women by night — compare SUCCUBUS **2 :** NIGHTMARE 2 **3 :** a person or thing that oppresses or burdens like a nightmare ⟨the security council — free for once from the ~ of the veto — was able to act swiftly and decisively —C.P.Romulo⟩

incud- *or* **incudo-** *comb form* [NL *incud-*, *incus*] **:** incus **:** incus and ⟨*incudectomy*⟩ ⟨*incudomalleal*⟩

in·cu·date \ˈiŋkyəˌdāt, |n|, (ˈ)≈ˈkyüdət\ *also* **in·cu·dal** \-dᵊl\ *adj* [*incud-* + *-ate* or *-al*] **1 :** of or relating to the incus **2 :** having an incus

incudes *pl of* INCUS

in cuerpo *adv (or adj)* [modif. of Sp *en cuerpo*, lit., in body] **1** *obs* **a :** in clothing that exposes the shape of the body **b :** in dishabille **2** *obs* **:** without clothing **:** in a naked or uncovered state

in·cul·cate \ənˈkəlˌkāt, ˈin(ˌ)kə-, *usu* -ād·+V\ *vt* -ED/-ING/-S [L *inculcatus*, past part. of *inculcare*, lit., to tread on, fr. *in-* ²in- + *-culcare* (fr. *calcare* to tread on, trample, fr. *calc-*, *calx* heel) — more at CALK] **1 :** to teach and impress by frequent repetitions or admonitions **:** urge on or fix in the mind ⟨they *inculcated* these principles at every opportunity⟩ ⟨the current emotional religious revivals *inculcated* an enthusiasm for its strong feelings and vivid scenes —J.D.Hart⟩ — often used with *in* or *into*, sometimes with *upon* ⟨social pressures ~ behavior patterns in the young⟩ ⟨the techniques of plumbing were gradually *inculcated* upon his mind⟩ **2 :** to cause (as a person) to become impressed or instilled with something ⟨teachers who fail to ~ students with love of knowledge⟩ ⟨*inculcated* with every virtue⟩ — **in·cul·ca·tive** \ˈin(ˌ)kəlˌkād·iv, ənˈkə-\ *adj* — **in·cul·ca·to·ry** \ənˈkəlkəˌtōrē, ¦in(ˌ)kəl¦kād·ərē\ *adj* **syn** see IMPLANT

in·cul·ca·tion \ˌin(ˌ)kəlˈkāshən\ *n* -s [LL *inculcation-*, *inculcatio*, fr. L *inculcatus* + *-ion-*, *-io* -ion] **:** an act of inculcating **:** teaching and impressing by frequent repetitions or admonitions

in·cul·ca·tor \ənˈkəlˌkād·ə(r), ˈin(ˌ)kə-, -ātə-\ *n* -s [LL, fr. L *inculcatus* + *-or*] **:** one that inculcates

in·culpability \(ˈ)in, ən+\ *n* **:** the quality or state of being free from blame **:** INNOCENCE

in·culpable \(ˈ)in, ən+\ *adj* [LL *inculpabilis*, fr. L *in-* ¹in- + *culpabilis* culpable — more at CULPABLE] **:** free from guilt **:** BLAMELESS, INNOCENT — **in·culpably** \"+\ *adv*

in·cul·pate \ənˈkəlˌpāt, ˈin(ˌ)kə-, *usu* -ād·+V\ *vt* -ED/-ING/-S [LL *inculpatus*, fr. L *in-* ²in- + *culpatus*, past part. of *culpare* to blame — more at CULPABLE] **:** to impute guilt to **:** involve or implicate in a charge of misconduct **:** BLAME, INCRIMINATE ⟨his whole behavior tended to ~ him⟩ ⟨*inculpating* his brother to escape punishment himself⟩ — **in·cul·pa·tion** \ˌin-(ˌ)kəlˈpāshən\ *n* -s — **in·cul·pa·tive** \ˈin(ˌ)kəlˌpād·iv; (ˈ)in¦kəlpəd-, ənˈk-\ *adj* — **in·cul·pa·to·ry** \ənˈkəlpəˌtōrē, *chiefly Brit* ¦in(ˌ)kəl¦pātəri, -ā·tri\ *adj*

in·cult \(ˈ)inˈkəlt, ənˈk-\ *adj* [L *incultus*, fr. *in-* ¹in- + *cultus*, past part. of *colere* to cultivate — more at WHEEL] **1** *archaic* **:** lacking the order that depends on tillage and cultivation **2 :** lacking finish or polish **:** CRUDE, DISORDERED — used esp. of literary style or its products or producers **3 :** lacking ease or smoothness of manner **:** UNCULTURED, RUDE, COARSE ⟨had not been an ~ sort of man . . . he was quiet and sensitive —F.M. Ford⟩

in·cul·ti·vate \(ˈ)in¦kəltəˌvāt\ *also* **in·cul·ti·vat·ed** \-ād·əd\ *adj* [*incultivate*, fr. ¹*in-* + ML *cultivatus*, past part. of *cultivare* to cultivate; *incultivated*, fr. ¹*in-* + *cultivated* — more at CULTIVATE] *archaic* **:** UNCULTIVATED

in·culture \(ˈ)in+\ *n* [¹*in-* + *culture*] *archaic* **:** lack of culture

in·cum·bence \ənˈkəmbən(t)s\ *archaic var of* INCUMBENCY

in·cum·ben·cy \-bənsē, -si\ *n* -ES **1 :** the quality or state of being incumbent: as **a** *archaic* **:** a condition of bearing upon or overshadowing **b** *archaic* **:** the quality of being morally incumbent or incumbent as a correlate of something else **c :** the state of occupying a particular position (as a benefice or office) ⟨the mere ~ of the Labour party in the seats of authority —Edward Shils⟩ **2 :** something that is incumbent: as **a** *archaic* **:** a burdening or oppressive weight **b :** a duty, obligation, or responsibility incumbent usu. as a correlate of some position or relationship held ⟨felt it an ~ as his older brother to rebuke him⟩ ⟨these varied *incumbencies* of the father of a family⟩ **3 :** the sphere of action or period of office of an incumbent ⟨during an ~ of over 30 years⟩ ⟨six years of senatorial ~ —S.H.Adams⟩

¹**in·cum·bent** \-bənt\ *n* -s [ME, fr. L *incumbent-*, *incumbens*, pres. part. of *incumbere* to lie down on, give attention to, fr. *in-* ²in- + *-cumbere* to lie down (akin to L *cubare* to lie down) — more at HIP] **1 a :** the holder of an ecclesiastical benefice ⟨an archdiocese of which he was the first ~ —R.P.Casey⟩ **b :** the holder of an office esp. a public or academic office ⟨the holdover Republican ~*s*⟩ ⟨the last ~ of the professorship⟩ **2 :** one that occupies **:** OCCUPANT ⟨the previous ~*s* insisted that the house was haunted⟩ ⟨the modified bloomer . . . [makes] the lower part stay put, no matter how the ~ sprawls —Lois Long⟩

²**incumbent** \"\ *adj* [L *incumbent-*, *incumbens*] **1 a :** lying or resting on something else esp. so as to exert a downward pressure **:** bearing down **b :** lying upon or apposed to — used either of cotyledons folded so that the hypocotyl is applied to the back of one of them or of an anther lying against the side of a filament but attached at only one point; compare ACCUMBENT 2 **c** *of a geologic stratum* **:** SUPERIMPOSED, OVERLYING **d** *of a bird's hind toe* **:** so placed that its whole length rests on the ground when the bird is standing — opposed to *insistent* **2** *obs* **:** busily engaged **:** ASSIDUOUS **3 :** falling or imposed as a duty, responsibility, or obligation — usu. used with *on* or *upon* ⟨~ on us to help⟩ ⟨demands ~ upon his position⟩ **4 :** having the status of an incumbent ⟨his duties while ~ of the secretaryship⟩; *esp* **:** occupying a specified office or position at a time expressed or implied ⟨defeated the ~ governor by a large plurality⟩ **5 a** *archaic* **:** bending over **:** OVERHANGING **b** *obs* **:** IMPENDING, THREATENING **c :** bent over so as to rest on or touch an underlying surface ⟨~ hairs on the body of an insect⟩

in·cum·bent·ly *adv* **:** in the manner of a duty, responsibility, or obligation

in·cum·ber \ənˈkəmbə(r)\ *var of* ENCUMBER

in·cu·na·ble \ənˈkyünəbəl\ *n* -s [F, fr. NL *incunabulum*] **:** INCUNABULUM

in·cu·nab·u·lar \ˌinkyə¦nabyələ(r)\ *adj* **:** relating to or typical of incunabula ⟨an ~ form of musical expression⟩

in·cu·nab·u·list \ˌ≈≈ˈ≈≈ləst\ *n* -s **:** one that makes a special study of incunabula

in·cu·nab·u·lum \-ləm\ *n*, *pl* **incunabu·la** \-lə\ [in sense 1, L *incunabula* swaddling clothes, cradle, origin, birthplace, fr. *in-* ¹in- + *cunae* cradle + *-bulum* (n. suffix); in other senses, fr. NL, back-formation fr. L *incunabula* — more at CEMETERY] **1** *incunabula*, *pl* **:** earliest stages **:** BEGINNINGS, INFANCY ⟨the resulting symposium . . . outgrew its *incunabula* —*Times Lit. Supp.*⟩ **2 a :** a book printed before 1501 — called also *cradle book*, *fifteener* **b :** a work of art or of human industry of an early epoch **c :** a record, example, or memento of the early period of an art or human activity ⟨old record catalogs . . . any of the *incunabula* of . . . jazz —Ralph de Toledano⟩ **3 :** the cocoon of an insect

in·cur *R* ənˈkər, + *vowel* -kər-; *-R* -kə̄, + *suffixal vowel* -kər- *also* -kə̄r, + *vowel in a following word* -kər- *or* -kə̄ *also* -kə̄r\ *vb* **incurred**; **incurred**; **incurring**; **incurs** [L *incurrere*, lit., to run into, fr. *in-* ²in- + *currere* to run — more at CURRENT] *vt* **1 :** to meet or fall in with (as an inconvenience) **:** become liable or subject to **:** bring down upon oneself ⟨*incurred* large debts to educate his children⟩ ⟨fully deserving the penalty he *incurred*⟩ **2** *obs* **:** to render liable or subject to **:** BRING, ENTAIL ~ *vi* **1 :** to fall as a part or lot, within a scope, or during or at a time **2** *archaic* **:** to occur as a result **:** become involved **:** ACCRUE

in·curability \(ˈ)in, ən+\ *n* **:** the quality or state of being incurable **:** INCURABLENESS

¹**in·curable** \(ˈ)in, ən+\ *adj* [ME, fr. MF or LL; MF, fr. LL *incurabilis*, fr. L *in-* ¹in- + *curabilis* curable — more at CURABLE] **1 :** impossible to cure ⟨an ~ disease⟩ **2 :** admitting of no remedy or correction ⟨~ optimism⟩ **:** being a thing specified beyond any possibility of alteration or control ⟨these ~ busybodies⟩

²**incurable** \"\ *n* -s **:** a person diseased beyond cure

in·cur·able·ness *n* -ES **:** the quality or state of being incurable

in·cur·ably \-blē, -bli\ *adv* **:** in an incurable manner **:** to an incurable degree ⟨an ~ social nature⟩

in·curiosity \(ˈ)in, ən+\ *n* [prob. fr. F *incuriosité*, fr. LL *incuriositat-*, *incuriositas*, fr. L *incuriosus* + *-itat-*, *-itas* -ity] **:** the quality or state of being incurious **:** INCURIOUSNESS

in·curious \(ˈ)in, ən+\ *adj* [L *incuriosus*, fr. *in-* ¹in- + *curiosus* curious — more at CURIOUS] **1 :** not curious or inquisitive **:** having no care or interest **:** INATTENTIVE, CARELESS ⟨a dull ~ gaze⟩ **2 a** *archaic* **:** done without care or nicety **:** HOMELY, COARSE **b** *obs* **:** not particular, fastidious, or critical **3** *archaic* **:** devoid of interest **:** dull and unappealing **:** not remarkable or attractive of attention **syn** see INDIFFERENT

in·curiously \"+\ *adv* **:** in an incurious manner **:** without curiosity or interest

in·cu·ri·ous·ness *n* **:** the quality or state of being incurious **:** lack of curiosity or interest

in·cur·ment \ənˈkərmənt, -kə̄m-\ *n* -s **:** the act of incurring or state of being incurred ⟨prevented the ~ of further debts⟩ ⟨~ of guilt⟩

in·cur·ra·ble \-ˈkər·əbəl *also* -ˈkə̄rə-\ *adj* **:** capable of being incurred

in·cur·rence \-ˈkər·ən(t)s *also* -ˈkə̄rə-\ *n* -s **:** the act or process of incurring ⟨~ of new responsibilities⟩

in·cur·rent \-nt\ *adj* [L *incurrent-*, *incurrens*, pres. part. of *incurrere* to run into, incur — more at INCUR] **:** running in: as **a :** occurring within a given time **b :** giving passage to a current that flows inward ⟨the ~ siphon of a bivalve mollusk⟩ ⟨an ~ pore on a sponge⟩ — see CLAM illustration

in·cur·sion \ənˈkər|zhən, -kə̄|, -kəi|, *chiefly Brit* |shən\ *n* -s [ME, invasion, fr. MF or L; MF, fr. L *incursion-*, *incursio*, fr. *incursus* (past part. of *incurrere* to run into, attack, incur) + *-ion-*, *-io* -ion — more at INCUR] **1 :** an entering into a territory with hostile intention **:** a sudden invasion **:** a predatory or harassing inroad **:** RAID ⟨partners in the Suez ~ —*Newsweek*⟩ **2 a :** a running, bringing, or entering in or into ⟨~ of water through a weakened seam⟩ ⟨his only ~ into the arts⟩ ⟨the inevitable ~ of new techniques⟩ **b :** such action involving vigorous, forceful, or determined effort ⟨the barrier should have been sufficient to protect the adjoining owner against the ~*s*, not of all pigs, but of pigs of average vigor and obstinacy —B.N.Cardozo⟩ ⟨a very sudden ~ of "ah" into London speech between 1780 and 1790 —C.H.Grandgent⟩

in·cur·sion·ary \-zhəˌnerē, -sh-, -ri\ *adj* **:** entering by or engaging in incursion **:** INVADING ⟨~ clays⟩ ⟨traces of this ~ nomad people⟩

in·cur·sion·ist \-zh(ə)nəst, -sh-\ *n* -s **:** a maker of an incursion **:** INVADER

in·cur·sive \(ˈ)in¦kərsiv, ənˈk-\ *adj* [L *incursus* + E *-ive*] **:** making incursions **:** INVASIVE, AGGRESSIVE

¹**in·cur·var·i·id** \¦inˌkər¦va(a)rēəd\ *adj* [NL *Incurvariidae*] **:** of or relating to the family Incurvariidae

²**incurvariid** \"\ *n* -s **:** a moth of the family Incurvariidae

in·cur·va·ri·idae \ˌinˌkərvəˈrīəˌdē\ *n pl*, *cap* [NL, fr. *Incurvaria*, type genus (fr. L *incurvus* curved in — fr. *in-* ²in- + *curvus* curved — + NL *-aria*) + *-idae*] **:** a small family of minute inconspicuous moths usu. having larvae that are initially leaf miners and later casebearers

¹**in·cur·vate** \ˈin(ˌ)kərˌvāt, ənˈk-\ *vb* -ED/-ING/-S [L *incurvatus*, past part. of *incurvare*, fr. *in-* ²in- + *curvare* to curve (fr. *curvus* curved) — more at CROWN] *vt* **:** to turn from a straight line or course **:** BEND, CROOK **:** cause to curve inward — used chiefly as past participle ⟨the gracefully *incurvated* column⟩ ~ *vi*, *obs* **:** to curve inward **:** BOW

²**in·cur·vate** \ˈin(ˌ)kərˌvāt, (ˈ)in¦kərvət\ *adj* [L *incurvatus*] **:** having an inward curvature **:** INCURVED

in·curvation \¦in+\ *n* [L *incurvation-*, *incurvatio*, fr. *incurvatus* + *-ion-*, *-io* -ion] **1 :** the act, fact, or process of incurving or state of being incurved **:** CURVATURE, INCURVATURE **2** *obs* **:** GENUFLECTION, BOW

in·curvature \(ˈ)in+\ *n* [L *incurvatus* + E *-ure*] **:** the act, fact, or process of curving inward or state of being curved inward

¹**in·curve** \(ˈ)in+\ *vb* [L *incurvare*] *vt* **:** to bend so as to curve

: CURVE, CROOK; *esp* : to bend so that the resulting curve projects inward ~ *vi* : to bend or curve inward ⟨the corners ~ gracefully⟩

²**incurve** \"\ *n* [⁴*in* + *curve*] **1** : a curving in ⟨clasped the jewel with a graceful ~ of the hands⟩ **2** : something that curves in ⟨the ~ at the head of the bay⟩; *esp* : DROP 2a(3)

in·cus \'iŋkəs, -,küs\ *n, pl* **in·cu·des** \iŋ'k(y)ü(,)dēz, 'iŋkyə,dēz\ [NL, fr. L, anvil, fr. *incudere* to incuse, stamp, strike] **1 a** : the middle of a chain of three small bones in the ear of mammals — called also *anvil;* see EAR illustration **b** : the median Y-shaped structure in the mastax of a rotifer upon which the mallei work **2** : an anvil-shaped top of a thundercloud

¹**in·cuse** \(')in¦kyüz, -üs\ *adj* [L *incusus,* past part. of *incudere* to incuse, stamp, fr. *in-* ²in- + *cudere* to beat, stamp — more at HEW] : formed by stamping or punching in — used chiefly of old coins or features of their design

²**incuse** \"\ *n* -s : an incuse space, design, or lettering on a coin

³**in·cuse** \-üz\ *vt* -ED/-ING/-S [L *incusus*] : to punch or stamp in (as lettering or a design on a coin) : impress by striking

in·cuse·ly *adv* : in the form of an incuse or an incuse square

incuse square *n* : a sunken square on various ancient Greek coins with or without a raised design inside it

in cus·to·dia le·gis \,in,kü'stōdēə'lāgəs\ *adv* [L] : in the custody of the law

¹**ind-** *or* **indo-** *comb form, usu cap* [Gk, India, of or connected with India, fr. *indos* of or connected with India, fr. *Indos* India (subcontinent in southern Asia), Indus (river in the northwestern part of the Indian subcontinent) — more at INDIA] **1** : India or the East Indies ⟨*Indo*phile⟩ : of or connected with India or the East Indies ⟨*ind*aconitine⟩ ⟨*Indo*-Briton⟩ ⟨*Indo*-African⟩ **2** : of or connected with the Indus river ⟨*Indo*-Gangetic⟩ **3** : Indo-European ⟨*Indo*-Hittite⟩

²**ind-** *or* **indi-** *or* **indo-** *comb form* [ISV, fr. L *indicum* — more at INDIGO] **1** : indigo ⟨*ind*ole⟩ ⟨*indi*rubin⟩ ⟨*indo*phenin⟩ **2** : resembling indigo (as in color) ⟨*ind*amine⟩ ⟨*indo*phenol⟩

ind *abbr* **1** independence; independent **2** index; indexed **3** indicated; indicative; indicator **4** indigo **5** indirect **6** induction **7** industrial; industry

in·da·ba \in'däbə\ *n* -s [Zulu *in-daba* matter, affair] **1** *southern Africa* : a conference esp. among representatives of native tribes : PARLEY, TALK **2** *Brit* : a gathering for camping or conference

in·da·con·i·tine \,ində'känə,tēn, -,tən\ *n* [¹*ind-* + *aconitine*] : a crystalline alkaloid $C_{34}H_{47}NO_{10}$ found in an herb (*Aconitum chasmanthum*) native to India

in·da·gate \'ində,gāt\ *vt* -ED/-ING/-S [L *indagatus,* past part. of *indagare,* fr. *indagin-, indago* examination, investigation, act of enclosing or surrounding, fr. OL *indu* in, within + L *agere* to drive — more at INDIGENOUS, AGENT] *archaic* : to search into : INVESTIGATE — **in·da·ga·tion** \,==ˈgāshən\ *n* -s *archaic* — **in·da·ga·tor** \'==,gād·ə(r)\ *n* -s *archaic*

In·da·lone \'ində,lōn\ *trademark* — used for butopyronoxyl

in dam *adv (or adj), of a domestic animal* : in the fetal state ⟨pigs sold *in dam*⟩

in·da·mine \'ində,mēn, -,mən\ *n* [ISV ²*ind-* + *amine;* orig. formed as G *indamin*] : any of a class of organic bases that are amino-phenyl derivatives of quinone diimine, that in the form of salts are unstable blue and green dyes, and that are used chiefly as intermediates for azine dyes (as safranines); *esp* : the simplest base $NH_2C_6H_4N{=}C_6H_4{=}NH$ that is the parent compound of the class

in·dan \'in,dan\ *also* **in·dane** \-,dān\ *n* -s [ISV *ind*ene + *-an* or *-ane*] : an oily cyclic hydrocarbon C_9H_{10} obtained by reducing indene — called also *hydrindene*

indanger *obs var of* ENDANGER

in·dan·throne \in'dan,thrōn\ *n* -s [obs. E *indanthrene* indanthrone (ISV ²*ind-* + *-anthrene;* prob. orig. formed as G *indanthren*) + E *-one*] : a blue anthraquinone-azine dye that is the parent compound of several halogenated dyes — see DYE table I (under *Vat Blue 4*)

in·dart \ən+\ *vt* [²*in* + *dart,* v.] *archaic* : to cause (as a dart) to be hurled or thrust into something

in·da·zole \'ində,zōl\ *n* [ISV *indole* + *azole;* orig. formed as G *indazol*] **1** : a feebly basic crystalline bicyclic compound $C_7H_6N_2$ made by pyrolysis of *ortho*-hydrazino-cinnamic acid; benzo-pyrazole **2** : a derivative of indazole

indear *obs var of* ENDEAR

in·de·bi·ta·tus assumpsit \ən,debə'tād·əs-\ *n* [NL, lit., being indebted he undertook] : COMMON ASSUMPSIT

inde blue \'ind-\ *n* [ME *inde,* n., indigo blue, fr. OF *inde,* adj., indigo-blue, fr. L *indicum,* n., indigo — more at INDIGO] : INDIGO 3

in·debt \ən'det\ *vt* -ED/-ING/-S [back-formation fr. *indebted*] *archaic* : to place (as oneself) under an obligation (as of returning something borrowed)

in·debt·ed \ən'ded·əd, -etəd\ *adj* [alter. (influenced by ²*in-* and *debt*) of ME *endetted,* modif. (influenced by ME *-ed,* adj. suffix forming past participles) of OF *endeté,* past part. of *endeter* to involve in debt, fr. *en-* ¹en- + *dette, dete* debt — more at DEBT] **1** : being under the obligation of paying or repaying money : owing money : held to payment or repayment ⟨was heavily ~ to the bank for loans extended to him —A.C.Cole⟩ **2** : owing gratitude (as for a favor received or kind act done) or recognition (as of a useful service) to another ⟨felt deeply ~ to her for having given him a home⟩

in·debt·ed·ness *n* -ES **1 a** : the condition of being indebted ⟨should provide for the refinancing of mortgage and other ~ —F.D.Roosevelt⟩ ⟨the ~ was canceled —P.N.Garber⟩ **b** : the extent to which one is indebted ⟨admitted his deep ~ to the accomplishments of those who preceded him⟩ **2** : something (as a sum of money) that is owed ⟨Hawthorne's literary *~es* are . . . chiefly to English writers —*Publ's Mod. Lang. Assoc. of Amer.*⟩ **syn** see DEBT

in·debt·ment \-'detmənt\ *n* -s *archaic* : INDEBTEDNESS

indecence *n* -s [prob. fr. F *indécence,* fr. L *indecentia*] *obs* : INDECENCY

in·de·cen·cy \ən'dēsᵊnsē, (')in-, -nsi\ *n* [L *indecentia,* fr. *indecent-, indecens* indecent + *-ia* -y] **1** : the quality or state of being indecent **2** : something (as a word or an action or a manner of behavior) that is indecent : an offense against decency ⟨innocent and shameless like a child's *indecencies* —W.A.White⟩

in·de·cent \-ᵊnt\ *adj, sometimes* -ER/-EST [MF or L; MF *indécent,* fr. L *indecent-, indecens,* fr. *in-* ¹in- + *decent-, decens* decent] **1** : not decent: as **a** : altogether unbecoming : contrary to what the nature of things or what circumstances would dictate as right or expected or appropriate : hardly suitable : UNSEEMLY ⟨hurried away with ~ haste⟩ **b** : not conforming to generally accepted standards of morality : tending toward or being in fact something generally viewed as morally indelicate or improper or offensive : being or tending to be obscene ⟨an ~ gesture⟩ ⟨~ language⟩ ⟨an ~ costume⟩ **2** *archaic* : unpleasant to look at : UNSIGHTLY, UNCOMELY — **in·de·cent·ly** *adv*

indecent assault *n* : an immoral act or series of acts exclusive of rape or an attempt to commit rape committed by a male against the person of a female without her consent

indecent exposure *n* : intentional exposure of part of one's body (as the genitals) in a place where such exposure is likely to be an offense against the generally accepted standards of decency in a community

in·de·cid·ua \,ində'sijəwə\ *n pl, cap* [NL, fr. ¹*in-* + L *decidua,* neut. pl. of *deciduus* deciduous] : NONDECIDUATA

in·de·cid·u·ate \,==¦==wət\ *adj* [NL *indeciduatus,* fr. ¹*in-* + *deciduatus* deciduate] *of a placenta* : having the maternal and fetal elements associated but not fused so that no maternal tissue is carried off in the placenta at parturition

in·de·cid·u·ous \-wəs\ *adj* [¹*in-* + *deciduous*] : not deciduous ⟨~ leaves⟩ : EVERGREEN ⟨~ trees⟩

in·de·ci·pher·able \,ində¦sif(ə)rəbəl, -dē¦-\ *adj* [¹*in-* + *decipherable*] : that cannot be deciphered ⟨an ~ inscription⟩ ⟨making people whose inner life has seemed to us ~ emerge as human and understandable —C.J.Rolo⟩ — **indecipherableness** *n* -ES — **in·de·ci·pher·ably** \-blē, -li\ *adv*

in·de·ci·sion \,ində¦sizhən, -dē¦-\ *n* [F *indécision,* fr. *indécis* irresolute, undecided (fr. MF *indecis* not yet settled, fr. LL *indecisus,* fr. L *in-* ¹in- + *decisus,* past part. of *decidere* to decide, settle) + *-ion*] : a wavering between two or more possible courses of action : VACILLATION, IRRESOLUTION : inability or failure to arrive at a decision ⟨in a constant state of ~⟩ ⟨halted before the door in ~ —James Joyce⟩

in·decisive \¦in+\ *adj* : not decisive: as **a** : not being of such a sort as would definitely settle something or make something final : INCONCLUSIVE ⟨a drawn-out ~ war⟩ **b** : marked by or prone to indecision : WAVERING, VACILLATING, IRRESOLUTE : unable or failing to arrive at a decision ⟨an ~ state of mind⟩ ⟨a timid ~ sort of individual⟩ **c** : not clearly marked out : not definite : INDISTINCT, UNFIXED, VAGUE ⟨~ boundaries between right and wrong⟩ ⟨an outline that was blurred and ~⟩ — **in·de·ci·sive·ly** *adv* — **in·de·ci·sive·ness** *n*

¹**in·de·clin·able** \¦ində¦klīnəbəl, -dē¦-\ *adj* [MF, fr. LL *indeclinabilis,* fr. L *in-* ¹in- + LL *declinabilis* capable of being inflected, fr. L *declinare* to inflect grammatically + *-abilis* -able — more at DECLINE] : having no grammatical inflections : used without case endings ⟨some Latin nouns are ~⟩

²**indeclinable** \"\ *n* -s : an indeclinable word

in·de·com·po·ni·ble \¦in,dēkəm¦pōnəbəl\ *adj* [¹*in-* + *decompon-* (fr. L *de* from, down, away + *componere* to compose, put together) + *-ible* — more at DE-, COMPOUND] *archaic* : INDECOMPOSABLE

in·de·com·pos·able \-¦pōzəbəl\ *adj* [¹*in-* + *decomposable*] : not capable of being broken up into component parts ⟨a substance that resists analysis and is apparently ~⟩

in·de·co·rous \ən'dekərəs, (')in¦d- *also* -krəs ¦ində¦kōr-, -dē¦-, -kòr-\ *adj* [L *indecorus,* fr. *in-* ¹in- + *decorus* decorous] : not decorous : not proper : conflicting with accepted standards of propriety or good taste or good breeding ⟨an ~ remark⟩ ⟨~ behavior⟩ — **in·dec·or·ous·ly** *adv* — **in·dec·or·ous·ness** *n*

in·de·co·rum \¦ində¦kōrəm, -dē¦k-, -kòr-\ *n* [L, neut. of *indecorus* indecorous] **1** : something (as an action) that is indecorous : an offense against decorum ⟨an ~ for which she refused to forgive him⟩ **2** : the quality or state of being indecorous : lack of decorum : IMPROPRIETY ⟨the general ~ of their lives —Lionel Trilling⟩

in·deed \ən'dēd\ *adv* [ME *in dede,* fr. ¹*in* + *dede* deed] **1 a** : in very fact : without any question : in truth : TRULY, CERTAINLY, ASSUREDLY, POSITIVELY ⟨was ~ glad to see her⟩ — used as an intensive often postpositively ⟨was glad ~⟩ ⟨was a king ~⟩ ⟨found themselves in real trouble ~⟩ and sometimes to reiterate a remark of another speaker ⟨you may well ask who knows how it will end; who knows, ~⟩; often used as an interjection to express irony or disbelief or surprise **b** : by all means : by any means — used to emphasize a reply or remark made in answer to an actual or implied question ⟨yes ~ I intend to go⟩ ⟨no ~ they aren't away⟩ **c** : REALLY, HONESTLY — used interrogatively to indicate that one seeks confirmation from a speaker that a statement just made by the speaker is really true ⟨~? You would like to go home?⟩ **2** : in reality : so far as the truth of the matter is concerned : in actual fact — used to indicate or emphasize that something stated or about to be stated is true and is at the same time opposed to something stated or about to be stated or implied that it is either untrue or merely external or apparent ⟨what seems to be cause for grief is ~ a reason for joy⟩ ⟨they were ~ heroes, though the world failed to recognize them as such⟩ **3** : all things considered : as a matter of fact : so far as that goes — used to confirm or amplify something stated ⟨he likes to have things his own way; ~, he can be quite a tyrant⟩ ⟨she is quite stupid, ~ a simpleton⟩ **4** : ADMITTEDLY, UNDENIABLY ⟨the problems involved are ~ serious ones, but I am convinced they can be solved⟩

in·deedy \-'dēdē, -di\ *adv* [by alter.] : INDEED 1b — not in formal use

indef *abbr* indefinite

in·de·fat·i·ga·bil·i·ty \¦ində,fad·ig(ə)bil·əd·ē, -dē,-, -at¦, ¦ēg-, -ətē, -i\ *n* : the quality or state of being indefatigable

in·de·fat·i·ga·ble \¦==¦==gəbəl\ *adj* [MF, fr. L *indefatigabilis,* fr. *in-* ¹in- + *defatigare* to fatigue, tire (fr. *de* from, down, away + *fatigare* to tire) + *-abilis* -able — more at FATIGUE] : incapable of being fatigued : that continues or proceeds unremittingly and without becoming wearied : UNTIRING, UNWEARYING ⟨an ~ worker⟩ ⟨has ~ patience⟩ — **in·de·fat·i·ga·ble·ness** *n* -ES — **in·de·fat·i·ga·bly** \-blē, -li\ *adv*

in·de·fea·si·bil·i·ty \¦ində,fēzə¦bil·əd·ē, -dē,f-, -ətē, -i\ *n* -ES : the quality or state of being indefeasible

in·de·fea·si·ble \¦==¦fēzəbəl\ *adj* [¹*in-* + *defeasible*] : not defeasible : not capable of or not liable to being annulled or voided or undone : that cannot be forfeited ⟨an ~ right to freedom⟩ ⟨an ~ claim to the title⟩ — compare INALIENABLE — **in·de·fea·si·bly** \-blē, -li\ *adv*

in·de·fec·ti·bil·i·ty \¦ində,fektə¦bil·əd·ē, -(,)dē,-, -ətē, -i\ *n* : the quality or state of being indefectible

in·de·fec·ti·ble \¦==¦fektəbəl\ *adj* [¹*in-* + *defectible*] **1** : not subject to failure or decay : LASTING : that will not and cannot collapse or be done away with ⟨an ~ friendship⟩ ⟨maintained that the church is ~⟩ **2** : free from and incapable of defects or error : having no shortcomings : free of faults : FLAWLESS ⟨possessed what appeared to be a sort of ~ wisdom⟩ ⟨a spokesman who could hardly be considered ~⟩ — **in·de·fec·ti·bly** \-blē, -li\ *adv*

in·defective \¦in+\ *adj* [¹*in-* + *defective*] **1** *archaic* : free from defects : FAULTLESS, FLAWLESS **2** *archaic* : INDEFECTIBLE 1 — **in·de·fec·tive·ly** *adv, archaic*

in·de·fen·si·bil·i·ty \¦ində,fen(t)sə¦bil·əd·ē, -(,)dē,-, -ətē, -i\ *n* : the quality or state of being indefensible

in·de·fen·si·ble \¦==¦fen(t)səbəl\ *adj* [¹*in-* + *defensible*] : not defensible: **a** (1) : incapable of being maintained as right or valid : UNTENABLE ⟨an ~ viewpoint⟩ ⟨an ~ argument⟩ (2) : incapable of being justified or excused : UNJUSTIFIABLE, INEXCUSABLE ⟨~ error⟩ ⟨~ behavior⟩ ⟨an ~ waste of public funds⟩ **b** : incapable of being secured or protected against physical force or attack ⟨a totally ~ city⟩ — **in·de·fen·si·bly** \-blē, -li\ *adv*

indeficiency *n* [*indeficient* + *-cy*] *obs* : the quality or state of being unceasing or unfailing

indeficient *adj* [MF, fr. LL *indeficient-, indeficiens,* fr. L *in-* ¹in- + *deficient-, deficiens,* pres. part. of *deficere* to be lacking — more at DEFICIENT] *obs* : UNCEASING, UNFAILING

in·definability \¦in+\ *n* : the quality or state of being indefinable

¹**in·definable** \¦in+\ *adj* [¹*in-* + *definable*] : not definable: **a** : incapable of being precisely or readily described : not easily put into words ⟨an ~ feeling of terror⟩ **b** : incapable of being precisely or readily given a logical analysis ⟨an abstract concept that seems ~⟩ **c** : incapable of being precisely or readily given a semantic analysis ⟨prepositions often have a relationship to words with which they are used that is purely functional and ~⟩ **d** (1) : not clearly recognizable or ascertainable : UNCERTAIN ⟨a bent, dignified peasant of ~ age —Marcia Davenport⟩ (2) : lacking a clear outline or definitely set limits : not precisely or readily located or fixed or marked off : INDETERMINATE, VAGUE ⟨an area with ~ boundaries⟩ ⟨the lights of the December evening bathing his face with little splashes that left his eyes and mouth almost ~ —E.L.Wallant⟩ — **in·de·fin·able·ness** *n* -ES — **in·definably** \"+\ *adv*

²**indefinable** \"\ *n* -s : something (as a word or concept) that is indefinable

¹**in·definite** \(')in+, ən, (')in+\ *adj* [L *indefinitus,* fr. *in-* ¹in- + *definitus,* past part. of *definire* to limit, determine — more at DEFINITE] : not definite: as **a** (1) *of a grammatical modifier or a pronoun* : typically designating an unidentified or not immediately identifiable person or thing ⟨*some* in "some books" is an ~ modifier⟩ ⟨*anyone* is an ~ pronoun⟩ ⟨the ~ articles *a* and *an*⟩ (2) *of an adjective form or set of adjective forms* : STRONG 16b (3) *of a verb form or set of verb forms in French* : typically denoting completed occurrence of an action — usu. used in the phrase *past indefinite* ⟨*j'ai dit* "I said" contains a past ~ verb⟩ (4) *of a verb form or set of verb forms in English* : denoting an action as neither completed nor continuing ⟨*saw* in "I saw the show" is the past ~ of *see*⟩ — compare PERFECT 5, PROGRESSIVE 7 **b** : being of a nature that is not or cannot be clearly determined : not precise : VAGUE, OBSCURE, UNCERTAIN, AMBIGUOUS ⟨what he really meant to say remains ~⟩ **c** (1) : having no exact limits : indeterminate in extent or amount : not clearly fixed ⟨sentenced to an ~ prison term⟩ ⟨an area with ~ boundaries⟩ ⟨an ~ number of people⟩ (2) : not narrowly confined or restricted ⟨~ extent⟩ : continuing with no immediate end being fixed : UNLIMITED ⟨planned to spend an ~ period in Europe⟩ **d** *of floral organs* (1) : numerous and not easy to determine by reason of being neither constant in number nor in multiples of the petal number (2) : RACEMOSE — **in·def·i·nite·ly** *adv* — **in·def·i·nite·ness** *n*

²**indefinite** \"\ *n* : something that is indefinite; *esp* : a word that is grammatically indefinite ⟨*a, some,* and other *~s*⟩

indefinite failure of issue : a failure of issue which determines an estate and for which no time or period is fixed in the devise — called also *general failure of issue*

indefinite integral *n, of a function of a variable* : a function whose derivative is a given function

indefinite proposition *n* : a statement in logic whose subject is a common term with nothing to indicate distribution or nondistribution (as "the Chinese eat rice")

indefinite sentence *n* : INDETERMINATE SENTENCE

indefinite term *n* : an unlimited negative term in logic

in·definitive \¦in+\ *adj* [¹*in-* + *definitive*] : not definitive : not clearly fixed : INDETERMINATE — **in·de·fin·i·tive·ly** *adv* — **in·de·fin·i·tive·ness** *n*

in·de·fin·i·tude \,ində'finə,tüd, -dē'-, -ə,tyüd\ *n* -s [fr. *indefinite,* prob. after E *infinite: infinitude*] : INDEFINITENESS

in·de·flec·ti·ble \¦ində¦flektəbəl\ *adj* [¹*in-* + *deflect* + *-ible*] : that cannot be deflected ⟨~ courage⟩ — **in·de·flec·ti·bly** \-blē\ *adv*

in·dehiscence \¦in+\ *n* [fr. *indehiscent,* after E *dehiscent: dehiscence*] : the quality or state of being indehiscent

in·dehiscent \"+\ *adj* [¹*in-* + *dehiscent*] : not dehiscent : remaining closed at maturity ⟨~ fruits⟩ — see FRUIT illustration

in·deliberate \¦in+\ *adj* [¹*in-* + *deliberate*] : not deliberate : marked by lack of forethought or intention ⟨an ~ remark⟩ — **in·de·lib·er·ate·ly** *adv* — **in·de·lib·er·ate·ness** *n* — **in·deliberation** \"+\ *n*

in·del·i·bil·i·ty \(,)in,delə'bilədē, -ətē, -i\ *n* -ES : the quality or state of being indelible

in·del·i·ble \ən'deləbəl, (')in¦d-, (')in¦deləbəl\ *adj* [ML *indelibilis,* alter. (influenced by L *-ibilis* -ible) of L *indelebilis,* fr. *in-* ¹in- + *delebilis* delible] **1** : that cannot be removed, washed away, or erased ⟨an ~ stain⟩ ⟨an ~ mark⟩ : that cannot be effaced or obliterated : PERMANENT, LASTING ⟨made an ~ impression on his mind⟩ **2** : that makes marks that cannot easily be removed (as by erasing) ⟨an ~ pencil⟩; *specif* : not attacked by strong acids or alkalies and so not easily removed by washing ⟨india ink is ~⟩ ⟨bought some ~ ink⟩ — **in·del·i·bly** \-blē, -li\ *adv*

in·delicacy \ən, (')in+\ *n* [¹*in-* + *delicacy*] **1** : the quality or state of being indelicate ⟨~ of speech⟩ ⟨~ of behavior⟩ **2** : something (as a coarse expression) that is indelicate ⟨a rollicking tale full of *indelicacies*⟩

in·delicate \"+\ *adj* [¹*in-* + *delicate*] : not delicate: **a** (1) : lacking in or offending against propriety : IMPROPER, RUDE, UNREFINED ⟨~ behavior⟩ (2) : verging on the indecent : COARSE, GROSS ⟨an ~ anecdote⟩ **b** : marked by or showing a lack of feeling for the sensibilities of others : TACTLESS ⟨an ~ allusion to her family's poverty⟩ — **in·del·i·cate·ly** *adv* — **in·del·i·cate·ness** *n*

in·dem·ni·fi·ca·tion \ən,demnəfə'kāshən\ *n* -s [fr. *indemnify,* after such pairs as E *amplify: amplification*] **1 a** : the action of indemnifying ⟨~ of the countries that had suffered the worst damage⟩ **b** : the condition of being indemnified ⟨did not lose hope of ~⟩ **2** : INDEMNITY 2b ⟨paid an enormous ~⟩

in·dem·ni·fi·ca·tor \=¦===,kād·ə(r)\ *n* -s [fr. *indemnification,* after such pairs as E *creation: creator*] : INDEMNIFIER

in·dem·nif·i·ca·to·ry \ən,dem¦nifəkə,tōrē\ *adj* [fr. *indemnification,* after such pairs as E *explanation: explanatory*] : of, relating to, or designed for indemnification ⟨~ court action⟩

in·dem·ni·fi·er \ən'demnə,fī(ə)r\ *n* -s : one that indemnifies or that is under obligation to indemnify

in·dem·ni·fy \-,fī\ *vt* -ED/-ING/-ES [L *indemnis* unharmed + E *-fy*] **1 a** : to secure or protect against hurt or loss or damage : give indemnity to ⟨a plan for *~ing* workers against time lost through illness⟩ **b** : to exempt from incurred penalties or liabilities ⟨was made a partner and *indemnified* against his previously overdrawn accounts⟩ **2** : to make compensation to for incurred hurt or loss or damage ⟨*indemnified* the town for the buildings that had been bombed⟩ **syn** see PAY

in·dem·ni·tee \=¦=nə¦tē\ *n* -s [*indemnity* + *-ee* (person furnished with a specified thing)] : one that is indemnified or that is entitled to be indemnified

in·dem·ni·tor \=ˈ=nəd·ə(r), -ətə(r)\ *n* -s [*indemnity* + *-or*] : INDEMNIFIER

in·dem·ni·ty \ən'demnəd·ē, -ətē, -i\ *n* -ES [ME *indempnyte,* fr. MF *indemnité,* fr. L *indemnitat-, indemnitas,* fr. *indemnis* unharmed (fr. *in-* ¹in- + *damnum* damage, harm) + *-tat-, -tas* -ty — more at DAMN] **1 a** : security or protection against hurt or loss or damage ⟨a plan that offered ~ against further financial loss⟩ **b** : exemption from incurred penalties or liabilities ⟨received ~ for his overdrawn accounts⟩ **2 a** : INDEMNIFICATION 1 **b** : something (as a sum of money paid in compensation) that indemnifies ⟨had to pay a large ~⟩

in·dem·ni·za·tion \=,=nə'zāshən\ *n* -s [F *indemnisation,* fr. *indemniser* to indemnify (fr. MF, fr. *indemne* unharmed — fr. L *indemnis* — + *-iser* -ize) + *-ation*] : INDEMNIFICATION

in·demonstrability \¦in+\ *n* : the quality or state of being indemonstrable

in·demonstrable \¦in+\ *adj* [¹*in-* + *demonstrable*] : incapable of being demonstrated : not subject to proof ⟨a theory that seems valid but is ~⟩ — **in·demonstrably** \"+\ *adv*

indemy *abbr* indemnity

in·dene \'in,dēn\ *n* -s [ISV *indole* + *-ene;* prob. orig. formed as G *inden*] : a liquid readily polymerizable hydrocarbon C_9H_8 obtained from coal tar by distillation or from petroleum by cracking and used chiefly in making resins — compare COUMARONE-INDENE RESIN

indenize *vt* [alter. (influenced by ²*in-*) of *endenize*] *obs* : ENDENIZEN

¹**in·dent** \ən'dent\ *vb* -ED/-ING/-S [ME *indenten, endenten,* fr. MF *endenter,* fr. OF, fr. *en-* ¹en- + *dent* tooth, fr. L *dent-, dens* — more at TOOTH] *vt* **1 a** : to cut or otherwise divide (a sheet of parchment or paper carrying two or more copies esp. of a deed or contract) so that sections having one or more edges with angular projections or a scalloped or curved outline are produced, each section being later fitted if necessary to the section having an exactly tallying edge as proof that the sections are parts of an original authentic document ⟨an *~ed* deed⟩ **b** : to draw up (as a deed or contract) in two or more exactly corresponding copies ⟨*~ing* the agreement⟩ **2 a** (1) : to cut into or notch the edge of in such a way as to produce a scalloped outline or one with angular projections ⟨an *~ed* stick⟩ (2) : to cut into (as a board) for the purpose of mortising or dovetailing **b** : to penetrate the edge of in such a way as to produce an outline marked by one or more recesses ⟨the coastline is *~ed* by the sea into a succession of small bays —Han Suyin⟩ **3 a** *obs* : to come to a formal or express agreement about **b** : INDENTURE ⟨*~ed* servants⟩ **4** : to set (as a line of a paragraph) in from a left-hand margin or sometimes from a right-hand margin ⟨*~ing* the first word of a paragraph⟩ ⟨*~ed* the column of figures one inch from the right-hand margin⟩ **5** : to join together (as two boards) by or as if by mortises or dovetails **6** *chiefly Brit* : to order by an indent ⟨*~ed* guns and ammunition⟩ ⟨*~ing* books⟩ ~ *vi* **1** *obs* : to make a formal or express agreement ⟨thus would I have ecclesiastical and civil historians ~ about the bounds and limits of their subjects —Thomas Fuller⟩ **2** *obs* : to wind in and out : ZIGZAG **3** : to form an indentation ⟨the long line of coast with its series of *~ing* bays —*Amer. Guide Series: N.J.*⟩ **4** *chiefly Brit* : to make out an indent for something ⟨*~ing* for books⟩ — **indent on** *or* **indent upon 1** *chiefly Brit* : to make an official requisition on ⟨*indented on* the governor for food⟩ **2** *chiefly Brit* : to draw on ⟨*indenting on* reserves to cover the deficit in the budget⟩

²**in·dent** \ən'dent, 'in,dent\ *n* -s **1 a** : INDENTURE 1 **b** : a certificate of indebtedness (as of interest on the public debt) issued by the federal or a state government in the late 18th or early 19th century **2** *chiefly Brit* **a** : an official requisition (as for supplies) **b** : a purchase order for goods esp. when sent from a foreign country **3** : INDENTION

³**indent** \"\ *vb* -ED/-ING/-S [ME *endenten,* fr. ¹*en-* + *denten* to dent — more at DENT] *vt* **1** : to force inward (as by striking or

pressing) so as to form a depression (as a dent or hollow) ⟨~*ing* a pattern in a metal surface⟩ **2 :** to form a depression (as a dent or hollow) in the surface of by or as if by striking or pressing ⟨~*ing* the pillow with his head⟩ : make an indentation in ⟨wore tight-fitting pince-nez which ~*ed* the sides of his nose in two red grooves —O.S.J.Gogarty⟩ **~** *vi* : DENT ⟨this asphalt ~*s* easily⟩

⁴indent \"\ *n* -s : INDENTATION ⟨the damp grass was everywhere marked with the ~*s* of his sharp hooves —Llewelyn Powys⟩

in·den·ta·tion \,in,den'tāshən\ *n* -s [¹*indent* + *-ation*] **1 a :** an angular cut (as a notch) or something resembling such a cut in an edge ⟨~*s* along the edge of a leaf⟩ **b :** a usu. deep recess (as in a coastline) ⟨many bays pockmark the coast with ~*s*⟩ **2 :** the action of indenting or condition of being indented **3** [³*indent* + *-ation*] **:** a usu. small surface depression (as a dent or hollow) made by or as if by striking or pressing ⟨noticed that the metal was covered with ~*s*⟩ **4 :** INDENTION 2

in·dent·ed·ly \ən'dentədlē\ *adv* [*indented* (past part. of ³*indent*) + *-ly*] **:** by indentation : in intaglio ⟨a design made ~ in the surface of the stone⟩

in·dent·er *or* **in·den·tor** \-'dentə(r)\ *n* -s [partly fr. ¹*indent* + *-er* or *-or*, partly fr. ³*indent* + *-er* or *-or*] **:** one that indents: **a** *usu* **indentor :** one that orders by an indent (sense 2) **b :** an object (as of diamond, carbide, hard steel) having a pointed or rounded tip that is forcibly pressed against the surface of a metal so as to test for hardness and resistance to indentation

in·den·tion \-'denchən\ *n* -s [¹*indent* + *-ion*] **1** *archaic* **:** INDENTATION 1 **2 a :** the action of indenting (as a line of a paragraph) or condition of being indented **b :** the blank space produced by indenting

¹in·den·ture \ən'denchə(r)\ *n* -s [ME *endenture, indenture,* fr. MF *endenture,* fr. OF, fr. *endenter* to indent (a document) + *-ure* — more at ¹INDENT] **1 a** (1) **:** a document (as a deed or contract) or a section of a document that is indented (sense 1a) (2) **:** a document (as a deed or contract) or a copy of a document that is not indented (sense 1a) but that is usu. formal and under seal and executed in two or more copies (3) **:** a contract binding one person to work for another for a given period of time (as an apprentice for a master craftsman or a new immigrant for an established colonist) — usu. used in pl. **b :** a document (as an inventory, voucher) that is not indented (sense 1a) and that may or may not be executed in two or more copies and that is formal or official and authenticated and prepared for purposes of control **2** *obs* **:** a zigzag course (as of one running) **3 :** INDENTATION 1 **4** [³*indent* + *-ure*] **:** INDENTATION 3

²indenture \"\ *vt* -ED/-ING/-S **1 :** to bind (as an apprentice) by indentures **2** *archaic* **:** to make an indentation (sense 3) in

indentured labor *n* [*indentured* fr. past part. of ²*indenture*] **:** CONTRACT LABOR 2

in·den·ture·ship \-ˌship\ *n* [¹*indenture* + *-ship*] **:** the condition of being indentured ⟨completed the three years of his ~⟩

in·dependable \ˌin+\ *adj* [¹*in-* + *dependable*] **:** UNDEPENDABLE

in·de·pen·dence \ˌində'pendən(t)s, -dē'-\ *n* [fr. *independent,* after such pairs as E *competent: competence*] **1 :** the quality or state of being independent : FREEDOM, LIBERTY ⟨their declaration of ~⟩ ⟨national ~⟩ ⟨political ~⟩ ⟨intellectual ~⟩ ⟨~ from the mother country⟩ ⟨enjoyed ~ of outside control⟩ **2** *archaic* **:** COMPETENCE 2 ⟨had a considerable ~, besides two good livings —Jane Austen⟩ **3 :** a grayish to dark purplish blue that is redder and stronger than flag blue

independence day *n, usu cap I&D* **:** a day set aside for public celebration of an anniversary connected with the beginnings of national independence; *specif* **:** July 4 observed as a legal holiday in the U.S. commemorating the adoption of the Declaration of Independence in 1776

in·de·pen·den·cy \-dənsē, -si\ *n* [*independent* + *-cy*] **1 :** INDEPENDENCE 1 **2** *usu cap* **a :** a religious movement originated in England by Robert Browne (1550?–?1633) who taught that a church consists of a body of believers bound by a covenant to God and each other and that it is independent of any higher ecclesiastical authority **b :** CONGREGATIONALISM 2 **3** *archaic* **:** COMPETENCE 2 **4 :** an independent political state (as a country, a nation)

¹in·de·pen·dent \ˌ==ˈ=dənt\ *adj* [¹*in-* + *dependent*] **1 :** not dependent: as **a** (1) **:** not subject to control by others : not subordinate : SELF-GOVERNING, AUTONOMOUS, FREE ⟨an ~ nation⟩ ⟨was ~ of outside control⟩ (2) **:** not affiliated with or integrated into a larger controlling unit (as a business unit) ⟨an ~ retail store⟩ (3) **:** originating from outside a given unit (as a business unit) ⟨the corporation hired ~ auditors to check its books⟩ or made by individuals from outside a given unit ⟨an ~ audit⟩ **b** (1) **:** not requiring or relying on something else (as for existence, operation, efficiency) : not contingent : not conditioned ⟨an ~ conclusion⟩ ⟨~ action⟩ ⟨two effects that are quite ~ of each other⟩ (2) **:** being or acting free of the influence of something else ⟨an ~ witness⟩ ⟨conducting an ~ investigation⟩ (3) **:** not looking to others for one's opinions or for the guidance of one's conduct : not biased by others : acting or thinking freely or disposed to act or think freely ⟨an ~ mind⟩ ⟨leading an ~ life⟩ ⟨an ~ journal of opinion⟩ (4) **:** not bound by or committed definitively to a political party : exercising a totally free political choice ⟨an ~ voter⟩ **c** (1) **:** not requiring or relying on others (as for support, supplies, a livelihood) ⟨was altogether ~ of the praise or condemnation of others⟩ ⟨an ~ source of revenue⟩ ⟨the job made him ~ of his parents⟩ (2) **:** not needing to work for a living : having a competence ⟨spent most of his time traveling idly about, having been ~ for years⟩ (3) **:** that is enough to free from the necessity of working for a living : making up a competence ⟨a gentleman of ~ means⟩ **d** (1) **:** refusing to look to others for help : disliking or refusing to accept assistance or to be under obligation to others ⟨too ~ to accept charity⟩ (2) **:** showing a desire for or love of freedom and absence of constraint : marked by impatience with or annoyance at restriction ⟨a bold and ~ manner of acting⟩ ⟨had an ~ air about her⟩ **2** *usu cap* **:** of, relating to, or holding the doctrines of the Independents ⟨an *Independent* church⟩ **3 a :** MAIN 6 ⟨an ~ clause⟩ **b :** ISOLATIVE — used of sound change **c :** that is neither derivable from nor incompatible with another statement ⟨an ~ proposition in logic⟩ **syn** see FREE

²independent \"\ *n* **1** *usu cap* **:** an adherent of Independency **2 :** one that is independent ⟨free-lance artists and other ~*s*⟩ ⟨large corporations and the smaller ~*s*⟩; *esp* **:** one that is not bound by or definitively committed to a political party ⟨one third of the voters classify themselves as ~*s* —E.S.Griffith⟩

independent audit *n* **:** an audit made by usu. professional auditors who are wholly independent of the company where the audit is being made — contrasted with *internal audit*

independent baptist *n, usu cap I&B* **:** a member of a pacifist Baptist sect organized in 1927

independent chuck *n* **:** a chuck for holding work by means of four jaws that may be moved separately

independent component *n* **:** a component in a physical-chemical system that may be varied without fixing the condition of the system

independent contractor *n* **:** one that contracts to do work or perform a service for another and that retains total and free control over the means or methods used in doing the work or performing the service

in·de·pen·dent·ly *adv* **:** in an independent manner : without dependence on another : FREELY ⟨living ~⟩ ⟨thinking and acting ~⟩

independently of *prep* **:** without regard to : apart from : aside from : irrespective of ⟨*independently of* what you may think, I have my own convictions⟩ ⟨it aims rather at persuading the people, *independently of* what the state may or may not want —M.R.Masani⟩

independent chuck

independent of *prep* **:** independently of ⟨*independent of* how others felt, they were sure they were right⟩ ⟨obligation . . . to obey a law, *independent of* those resources which the law provides for its own enforcement —R.P.Ward⟩

independent variable *n* **:** a mathematical variable not dependent on other variables

independing *adj* [¹*in-* + *depending* (pres. part. of *depend*)] *obs* **:** INDEPENDENT

in·deprivable \ˌin+\ *adj* [¹*in-* + *deprivable*] *archaic* **:** INALIENABLE

in·der·bo·rite \ˌindər'bō,rīt, -bȯ,-\ *n* -s [Russ *inderborit,* fr. Lake *Inder,* Kazakhstan, U.S.S.R., its locality + Russ *bor-* + *-it* -ite] **:** a mineral $CaMgB_6O_{11}.11H_2O$ consisting of a hydrous borate of calcium and magnesium

in·der·ite \'ində,rīt\ *n* -s [Russ *inderit,* fr. Lake *Inder,* Kazakhstan, U.S.S.R., its locality + Russ *-it* -ite] **:** a mineral $Mg_2B_6O_{11}.15H_2O$ consisting of a hydrous borate of magnesium

in·describability \ˌin+\ *n* **1 :** the quality or state of being indescribable **2 :** something indescribable

¹in·describable \"+\ *adj* [¹*in-* + *describable*] **:** that cannot be described: **a :** that cannot be described with precision : too vague or indefinite or intangible or complex to be described ⟨a strange ~ feeling —J.C.Powys⟩ **b :** that is beyond description : that surpasses description : too extreme or too much beyond experience to be adequately described ⟨filled with ~ joy⟩ ⟨scenes of ~ horror⟩ — **in·de·scrib·able·ness** *n* -ES — **in·describably** \"+\ *adv*

²indescribable \"\ *n* -s **1 :** something indescribable ⟨a box full of curious trinkets and other ~*s*⟩ **2 indescribables** *pl, archaic slang* **:** TROUSERS

indesert *n* [¹*in-* + ³*desert*] *obs* **:** the quality or state of being undeserving : lack of merit

¹in·designate \ən, (ˈ)in+\ *adj* [¹*in-* + L *designatus,* past part. of *designare* to point out, designate] **:** not quantified ⟨an ~ proposition in logic⟩

²indesignate \"\ *n* -s **:** an indesignate term or proposition in logic

indesinent *adj* [LL *indesinent-, indesinens,* fr. L *in-* ¹in- + *desinent-, desinens,* pres. part. of *desinere* to leave off, cease — more at DESINENT] *obs* **:** UNCEASING

in·destructibility \ˌin+\ *n* **:** the quality or state of being indestructible ⟨the ~ of matter⟩

in·de·struc·ti·ble \ˌində'strəktəbəl, -dē'-\ *adj* [prob. fr. LL *indestructibilis,* fr. L *in-* ¹in- + *destructus* (past part. of *destruere* to tear down, destroy) + *-ibilis* -ible — more at DESTROY] **:** not destructible : incapable of being destroyed ⟨any belief more ~ than the belief in the ultimate triumph of justice —Robert Lynd⟩ — **in·de·struc·ti·ble·ness** *n* -ES — **in·de·struc·ti·bly** \-blē, -li\ *adv*

in·detectable \ˌin+\ *adj* [¹*in-* + *detectable*] **:** not detectable

in·determinable \ˌin+\ *adj* [¹*in-* + *determinable*] **:** not determinable: **a** *obs* **:** not subject to limitation **b :** incapable of being definitely decided or settled ⟨would have raised a host of delicate and ~ questions —Leslie Stephen⟩ **c :** incapable of being definitely fixed ⟨handed out free shoes and clothes to ~ thousands —Dwight Macdonald⟩ or ascertained ⟨a questionable and ~ relationship —Jacob Viner⟩ — **in·de·ter·min·able·ness** *n* — **in·determinably** \"+\ *adv*

in·determinacy \ˌin+\ *n* [*indeterminate* + *-cy*] **:** INDETERMINATION

indeterminacy principle *n* **:** UNCERTAINTY PRINCIPLE

in·determinate \ˌin+\ *adj* [ME *indeterminat,* fr. LL *indeterminatus,* fr. L *in-* ¹in- + *determinatus,* past part. of *determinare* to limit, determine — more at DETERMINE] **:** not determinate : not definitely determined : not clearly established : not fixed : not settled : INDEFINITE, UNCERTAIN, VAGUE, INDISTINCT: as **a** (1) **:** not precisely fixed in extent or size or number or nature ⟨a material used in an ~ number of varieties⟩ ⟨a huge container of ~ volume⟩ ⟨an insect of ~ sex⟩ (2) **:** lacking precision of meaning : semantically vague or unfixed ⟨an ~ and obscure phrase⟩ **b :** not fixed beforehand : not known in advance ⟨their future remains ~⟩ ⟨when the rebellion will occur is ~⟩ **c :** not leading to a definite end or result ⟨an ~ debate⟩ : remaining doubtful and unclear ⟨an ~ point of law⟩ **d** (1) **:** not limited as to the number of possible solutions ⟨an ~ problem in mathematics⟩ (2) *of a number* **:** not limited to one fixed value or to a series of fixed values — opposed to *determinate* **e :** not predetermined by some external force : not constrained : acting freely : SPONTANEOUS ⟨maintaining that moral choice is ~⟩ **f** (1) **:** having a capacity for indefinite elongation : not exhibiting determinate growth ⟨~ plants⟩ ⟨an ~ stem⟩; *esp* **:** RACEMOSE ⟨an ~ inflorescence⟩ (2) **:** having no critical photoperiod **g :** phonetically neutral ⟨an ~ vowel⟩ — **in·de·ter·mi·nate·ly** *adv* — **in·de·ter·mi·nate·ness** *n*

indeterminate cleavage *n* **:** cleavage in which all the early cleavage cells possess the potencies of the entire zygote — compare DETERMINATE CLEAVAGE

indeterminate equation *n* **:** an equation in which the unknown quantities admit of an infinite number of values or sets of values

indeterminate form *n* **:** any of the seven undefined expressions

$$\tfrac{0}{0},\ \tfrac{\infty}{\infty},\ 0\cdot\infty,\ \infty-\infty,\ 0^0,\ \infty^0, \text{ and } 1^\infty$$

that a mathematical function may assume by formal substitution

indeterminate growth *n* **:** growth in which a plant axis is not limited by development of a terminal flower bud or other reproductive structure and so continues to elongate indefinitely (as in racemose inflorescence) — compare DETERMINATE GROWTH

indeterminate sentence *n* **:** a punitive sentence that fixes the term or amount of punishment only within certain limits and leaves the exact term or amount of punishment to be determined by administrative authorities

in·determination \ˌin+\ *n* [*indeterminate* + *-ion*] **:** the quality or state of being indeterminate

in·determined \ˌin+\ *adj* [¹*in-* + *determined* (past part. of *determine*)] *archaic* **:** INDETERMINATE

in·determinism \ˌin+\ *n* [¹*in-* + *determinism*] **1 :** a theory that the will is free and that deliberate choice and the action following such choice are not completely or not at all determined by or predictable from antecedent causes — compare DETERMINISM **2 :** the quality or state of being indeterminate; *esp* **:** UNPREDICTABILITY

in·determinist \"+\ *n* [fr. *indeterminism,* after such pairs as E *determinism: determinist*] **:** one that holds the theory of indeterminism

in·deterministic \"+\ *adj* **:** of or relating to indeterminism ⟨a mere ~ account of the moral life —Alexander Darroch⟩

in·devotion \ˌin+\ *n* [¹*in-* + *devotion*] *archaic* **:** lack of devotion

in·devout \ˌin+\ *adj* [ME *indevout* (trans. of LL *indevotus*), fr. ¹*in-* + *devout*] **:** not devout — **in·de·vout·ly** *adv*

¹in·dex \'in,deks\ *n, pl* **indexes** \-ksəz\ *or* **in·di·ces** \-ˌdə,sēz\ *see sense 8* [L *indic-, index,* fr. *indicare* to point out, indicate — more at INDICATE] **1 :** INDEX FINGER 1, FOREFINGER **2 :** ALIDADE c **3 a :** a usu. alphabetical list that includes all or nearly all items (as topics, names of people and places) considered of special pertinence and fully or partially covered or merely mentioned in a printed or written work (as a book, catalog, or dissertation), that gives with each item the place (as by page number) where it may be found in the work, and that is usu. put at or near the end of the work **b** (1) **:** CARD INDEX (2) **:** STEP INDEX (3) **:** TAB INDEX (4) **:** THUMB INDEX **c :** a computer-processed usu. alphabetical list esp. of bibliographical information; *esp* **:** a bibliographical analysis of groups of publications that is usu. published periodically ⟨*Index* Medicus⟩ **4 :** something that serves as a pointer or indicator: as **a :** a pointer (as of metal, plastic, wood) that moves along a graduated scale (as of a weighing machine) or that remains fixed while the scale moves past its tip **b :** one of the hands on a timepiece **c :** the gnomon of a sundial **5** *obs* **:** DIRECT 1 **6 a :** something (as a manner of speaking or acting, a distinctive physical feature) in another person or thing that leads an observer to surmise a particular fact or draw a particular conclusion : SIGN, TOKEN, INDICATION ⟨her fatuous laugh is an ~ of her pygmy intelligence⟩ ⟨the fertility of the land is an ~ of the country's wealth⟩ **b :** a sign whose specific character is causally dependent on the object to which it refers but independent of an interpretant ⟨a bullet hole in a fence is an ~ that a shot has been fired⟩ — contrasted with *icon* and *symbol* **7 a :** a list of restricted or prohibited or otherwise proscribed material ⟨an ~ of forbidden books⟩ **b** *usu cap* **:** INDEX LIBRORUM PROHIBITORUM **8** *pl usu* **indices :** a number or symbol or expression written to the left or right of and above or below or otherwise associated with another number or symbol or expression to indicate use or position in an arrangement or expansion or to indicate a mathematical operation to be performed ⟨the *indices* 2 and 3 used to locate the element a_{23} in the second row and third column of a determinant⟩ ⟨3 is the ~ in the expression $\sqrt[3]{5}$ to specify a cube root of 5⟩ **9** *or* **index mark :** a character ☞ used to direct particular attention (as to a note or paragraph) and as the seventh in series of the reference marks — called also *fist, hand* **10 a :** a ratio or other number derived from a series of observations and used as an indicator or measure (as of a condition, property, or phenomenon) ⟨a discrepancy ~ based on the differences between the students' predicted and attained honor-point ratios —*Educational & Psychological Measurement*⟩ ⟨the ~ of variation . . . is obtained by considering the positive differences between every pair of incomes in the group and averaging these differences —*Economica*⟩ ⟨an ~ is a measurable aspect of society which indicates the extent to which certain more complex aspects are present —Mabel Elliott & Francis Merrill⟩; *specif* **:** INDEX NUMBER ⟨the ~ of industrial production increased from 113.2 in December 1950 to 122.0 by November 1951 (1946 = 100) —*Americana Annual*⟩ — see CONSUMER PRICE INDEX, DOW-JONES INDEX; INDEX OF REFRACTION **b :** the ratio of one dimension of a thing (as an anatomical structure) to another dimension — see CEPHALIC INDEX **11 :** a miniature indication of denomination and value often printed on the corners of playing cards to make it unnecessary to view the full face of each card

index 11

²index \"\ *vb* -ED/-ING/-ES *vt* **1 a :** to provide (as a book) with an index ⟨the book will be ~*ed* in its next edition so as to make it more useful⟩ **b :** to list (as the contents of a book) in an index ⟨all persons and places mentioned are carefully ~*ed*⟩ **2 a :** to serve as an index of ⟨wrinkles ~ advancing age⟩ **b :** to point to : INDICATE ⟨a compass needle that ~*es* true north⟩ **3 :** to move (a machine or a piece of work held in a machine tool) so that a specific operation (as the cutting of gear teeth) will be repeated at definite intervals of space **4 :** to determine the fertility or yielding ability or disease resistance or some other character of (a plant or seed) by planting and testing a sample in advance of release for general use — used esp. of potatoes ⟨~*ing* potato eyes⟩ ⟨~*ing* a potato of each hill⟩ **~** *vi* **:** to index something

index bar *n* **:** the movable arm of a sextant

index center *n* **:** one of a pair of machine-tool centers or jaws provided with means of rotating a piece of work by predetermined equal amounts (as in cutting gear teeth)

index crank *n* **:** the crank of an index head whose turning a specified amount transmits through gearing a definite angular movement to the index-head spindle

in·dex·er \-sə(r)\ *n* -s **1 :** one that makes an index or works at indexing **2 a :** one who operates a machine for cutting index indentations into pages (as of reference books) **b :** one who prepares material (as reference books) for a machine that cuts index indentations or who prepares material for the insertion of index tabs

index ex·pur·ga·to·ri·us \-ikˌspərgə'tōrēəs, -ek-, -ȯr-\ *n, pl* **indices expurgato·rii** \-rē,ī, -rē,ē\ [NL, expurgatory index] **1** *sometimes cap I&E* **:** a list of proscribed material (as books) **2** *usu cap I&E* **:** a list of books once separately published and now included in the Index Librorum Prohibitorum that gives titles of works forbidden by church authority to Roman Catholics pending revision or deletion of some sections

index finger *n* **1 :** the digit next to the thumb : FOREFINGER **2 :** INDEX 9

index forest *n* **:** a forest that in density, volume, and increment reaches the highest average in a given locality

index fossil *n* **:** a fossil that is usu. of narrow time range and wide spatial distribution and that is used in the identification of related geologic formations (as in locating new petroleum reserves)

index finger 1

index glass *n* **:** the mirror on the index bar of a sextant or similar instrument

index hand *n* **:** a pointer or hand for indicating something (as a reading on a dial) : INDICATOR

index head *or* **indexing head** *n* **:** a headstock attachable to the table of a milling machine, planer, or shaper on which work may be mounted by a chuck or centers for indexing

in·dex·i·cal \ən'deksəkəl, (ˈ)in'd-,\ *adj* [¹*index* + *-ical*] **:** of, relating to, or resembling an index ⟨an ~ errors⟩ ⟨~ lists⟩

in·dex·i·cal·ly \-sək(ə)lē\ *adv* [¹*index* + *-ical* + *-ly*] **:** by way of an index : in the manner of an index ⟨what is ~ referred to —C.W.Morris⟩

in·dex·less \'in,deksləs\ *adj* **:** having no index ⟨an ~ book⟩

index li·bro·rum pro·hib·i·to·rum \-lī'brōrəmprō,hibə'tōrəm, -ȯr-\ *n, pl* **indices librorum prohibitorum** [NL, index of prohibited books] **1** *sometimes cap I&L&P* **:** a list of proscribed books **2** *usu cap I&L&P* **:** a list of books condemned in whole or in part as dangerous to faith or morals by church authority and forbidden to Roman Catholics — compare INDEX EXPURGATORIUS

index liquid *n* **:** a liquid of known refractive index used (as in crystallography) in the determination of the refractive index of powdered substances with a microscope

index map *n* **:** a map that shows (as by enclosing a small area in a rectangle on a large map) the location of one or more small areas in relation to a larger area and that typically points up special features in the small areas about which information is desired

index mark *n* **:** INDEX 9

index number *n* **:** a number used to indicate change in magnitude (as of cost, price, or volume of production) as compared with the magnitude at some specified time usu. taken as 100 ⟨if the cost of an item in 1930 was one and one half as much as its cost in 1913, its *index number,* relative to 1913, was 150⟩ ⟨relative *index numbers* representing changes in price level of the particular type of asset being considered would be used for the purpose of converting fixed assets to current dollar values —*Accountants Digest*⟩ — used esp. in statistics

index of refraction : the ratio of the velocity of light or other radiation in the first of two media to its velocity in the second as it passes from one into the other, the first medium being usu. taken to be a vacuum — called also *refractive index*

index percent *n* **:** the increase in value of a tree or of a forest due to the combined volume, quality, and price increments and expressed as an annual percent of its present value

index plane *also* **index horizon** *n* **:** a surface (as the top of a sedimentary bed) used in working out geological structure

index plate *n* **:** a graduated circular plate or one with circular rows of holes differently spaced that is used in machines (as for graduating circles or cutting gear teeth)

index re·rum \-'rērəm\ *n, pl* **indices rerum** [NL, index of things] **:** an index of topics covered (as in a book)

index species *n* **:** a plant or animal species so highly adapted to a particular kind of environment that its presence is sufficient indication that a habitat under investigation belongs to the kind to which the species is adapted

index table *n* **:** a horizontal index head

in·dexterity \ˌin+\ *n* [¹*in-* + *dexterity*] **:** lack of dexterity

index ver·bo·rum \-(ˌ)vər'bōrəm, -bȯr-\ *n, pl* **indices verborum** [NL, index of words] **:** an index of words or terms (as those discussed in a book)

indi- — see IND-

¹in·dia \'indēə *chiefly Brit* -dyə\ *adj, usu cap* [fr. *India,* republic and subcontinent (including the Republic of India and Pakistan) in southern Asia, fr. L *India,* subcontinent in southern Asia, fr. Gk, fr. *Indos* India (subcontinent in southern Asia), Indus (river in the northwestern part of the Indian subcontinent), fr. OPer *Hindu* India; akin to Skt *sindhu* river, Indus, region of the Indus] **1 :** of or from the subcontinent of India : of the kind or style prevalent in the subcontinent of India : INDIAN **2 :** of or from the Republic of India : of the kind or style prevalent in the Republic of India

2india \"\ *usu cap* — a communications code word for the letter *i*

india buff *n, often cap I* : a light yellowish brown that is redder, lighter, and stronger than khaki, yellower than walnut brown, and yellower and paler than cinnamon

india drugget *n, usu cap I* : DRUGGET 3

india gum *usu cap I, var of* INDIAN GUM

india ink *n, often cap 1st I* [so called fr. a belief that it was made in India] **1** : a black pigment (as specially prepared lampblack mixed with a glutinous binder and sometimes perfume) in the form of sticks or cakes and used in drawing and lettering **2** : a fluid ink consisting usu. of a fine suspension of india-ink pigment in a liquid medium (as water containing a gum) — called also *China ink, Chinese ink*

india malacca *n, usu cap I* : any of several rattan palms of the genus *Calamus* used for making walking sticks

in·dia·man \-mən\ *n, pl* **indiamen** *usu cap* : a merchant ship formerly used in trade with India; *esp* : a large sailing ship used in this trade

1in·di·an \'indēən *chiefly Brit* -dyən, *in sense 2 chiefly dial* 'injən *or sometimes* 'in(,)din\ *n* -s *cap* [prob. fr. (assumed) ML *Indianus*, fr. ML *indianus*, adj.] **1 a** : a native or inhabitant of the subcontinent of India or of the East Indies — compare PAKISTANI **b** : one of the native languages of the subcontinent of India or of the East Indies **2 a** [so called fr. the belief on the part of Columbus that the lands discovered by him in 1492 and later were part of Asia] : AMERICAN INDIAN **b** : one of the native languages of American Indians

2indian \"\ *adj, usu cap* [prob. fr. ML *indianus*, fr. L *India*, subcontinent in southern Asia + *-anus* -an (adj. suffix)] **1 a** (1) : of, relating to, or characteristic of the subcontinent of India or the East Indies (2) : of, relating to, or characteristic of one of the peoples of the subcontinent of India or the East Indies **b** : of, relating to, or characteristic of one of the native languages of the subcontinent of India or the East Indies **c** (1) : ORIENTAL 4 (2) : of, relating to, or constituting the subregion of the biogeographical Oriental region that includes Ceylon and the subcontinent of India north to the Himalayas and west to the Persian gulf or sometimes these areas excepting Ceylon and the adjacent part of the subcontinent of India **2 a** [after 1*indian* 2a] : of, relating to, or characteristic of the American Indians **b** : of, relating to, or characteristic of one of the native languages of American Indians **3** : of, relating to, or characteristic of the West Indies

1in·di·ana \¦indē¦anə\ *adj, usu cap* [fr. *Indiana*, state in the north central U. S., fr. NL *indiana*, fem. of *indianus*, adj., Indian (sense 2a), fr. ML, Indian (sense 1a)] : of or from the state of Indiana ⟨*Indiana* writers⟩ : of the kind or style prevalent in Indiana : INDIANAN

2indiana \"\ *n, often cap* [fr. *Indiana*, state in the north central U. S.] : a vivid purplish red that is redder, lighter, and stronger than rubellite and bluer and deeper than malmaison rose

indiana ballot *n, usu cap I* [so called fr. its adoption by Indiana in 1889] : an Australian ballot upon which the names of candidates are placed in separate columns according to their party affiliations with the party name and sometimes emblem at the top of each column — called also *party-column ballot;* compare MASSACHUSETTS BALLOT, OFFICE-BLOCK BALLOT

indian agent *n, usu cap I* : an official representative of the U. S. federal government to American Indian tribes esp. on reservations

in·di·an·a·ite \,indē'anə,īt\ *n* -s [*Indiana*, state in the north central U. S., its locality + E *-ite*] : a variety of halloysite

indiana limestone *n, usu cap I* [so called fr. its quarrying site in southern Indiana] : a usu. gray or buff oolitic Mississippian limestone of the lower Carboniferous that is uniform and easily worked and widely used for building

indian almond *n, usu cap I* [2*indian* 1] : MALABAR ALMOND

1in·di·an·an \¦indē¦anən\ *or* **in·di·an·i·an** \-¦anēən, -nyən\ *adj, usu cap* [*Indiana* + E *-an, -ian* (adj. suffix)] **1** : of, relating to, or characteristic of the state of Indiana **2** : of, relating to, or characteristic of the people of Indiana

2indianan \"\ *or* **indianian** \"\ *n* -s *cap* [*Indiana* + E *-an, -ian* (n. suffix)] : a native or resident of Indiana

indian antelope *n, usu cap I* [2*indian* 1] : BLACK BUCK 1

in·di·an·ap·o·lis \¦indēə¦nap(ə)ləs *sometimes* -di¦-\ *adj, usu cap* : of or from Indianapolis, the capital of Indiana ⟨an *Indianapolis* lawyer⟩ : of the kind or style prevalent in Indianapolis

in·di·an·a·pol·i·tan \,indē,anə'pälət°n\ *n* -s *cap* [fr. *Indianapolis*, after such pairs as E *metropolis: metropolitan*] : a native or resident of Indianapolis, Indiana

indian apple *n, usu cap I* [2*indian* 2] : MAYAPPLE

indian arrow *n, usu cap I* [2*indian* 2] : 2WAHOO a

indian arrowroot *n, usu cap I* [2*indian* 1] **1 a** : a tropical American arrowroot (*Maranta arundinacea*) **b** : starch from this arrowroot — called also *West Indian arrowroot* **2** [2*indian* 1] **a** : a stemless perennial herb (*Tacca leontopetaloides*) widely cultivated in the tropics for its starchy tuberous rootstock **b** : starch from this plant — called also *East Indian arrowroot*

indian arrowwood *n, usu cap I* [2*indian* 2] **1** : FLOWERING DOGWOOD **2** : 2WAHOO a

indian azalea *n, usu cap I* [2*indian* 1] **1 a** : a somewhat bristly evergreen Japanese azalea (*Rhododendron indicum*) with paired or solitary bright red or rosy red flowers containing 5 stamens **b** : a hairy or bristly evergreen Chinese azalea (*Rhododendron simsii*) with large clustered rosy red to dark red flowers containing 10 stamens **2** : any of numerous usu. tender cultivated azaleas that have single or double flowers in many colors and color combinations and that have been developed by selection from and hybridization of the Chinese Indian azalea and other evergreen azaleas

indian balm *n, usu cap I* [2*indian* 2] : PURPLE TRILLIUM

indian barberry *n, usu cap I* [2*indian* 1] : any of several deciduous barberries of southern Asia including some (as *Berberis aristata*) that are occas. cultivated — see DYER'S BARBERRY

indian bark *n, usu cap I* [2*indian* 2] : EVERGREEN MAGNOLIA

indian bean *n, usu cap I* **1 a** : a No. American catalpa (*Catalpa bignonioides*) with flat pods resembling beans **b** : a pod of this catalpa **2** : the fruit of the groundnut **3** : HYACINTH BEAN

indian beech *n, usu cap I* : an Asiatic tree (*Pongamia glabra*) of the family Leguminosae that has glossy pinnate leaves and racemose creamy-white scented flowers and that is used as a shade tree and as the source of an oil used for illumination

indian beet *n, usu cap I* [2*indian* 2] : WILD LUPINE

indian berry *n, usu cap I* [2*indian* 1] : COCCULUS INDICUS

indian birch *n, usu cap I* : a Himalayan tree (*Betula utilis*) with bark resembling that of the common paper birch

indian bison *n, usu cap I* [2*indian* 1] : GAUR

indian bitters *n, usu cap I* : an American magnolia (*Magnolia fraseri*) having a bitter bark formerly used as a tonic

indian blanket *n, usu cap I* **1** : a blanket made by American Indians or made in imitation of Indian designs — compare NAVAHO BLANKET **2** : an annual herb (*Gaillardia pulchella*) of the central U. S. that has showy yellow flower heads marked with scarlet or purple in the center

indian block *n, usu cap I* : a close-quarter block used in lacrosse in which the stick is directed across the opponent's stick

indian blue *n, usu cap I* [2*indian* 1] : INDIGO 3

indian blue pine *n, usu cap I* [2*indian* 1] : BHOTAN PINE

indian boys and girls *n pl, usu cap I* [2*indian* 2] : DUTCHMAN'S-BREECHES

indian bread *n, usu cap I* [2*indian* 2] **1** : CORN BREAD **2** : TUCKAHOE 2

indian breadroot *n, usu cap I* [2*indian* 2] : BREADROOT 1

indian bridle *n, usu cap I* [2*indian* 2] : a rope bridle in which the cord passes from the animal's mouth through a loop about its throat

indian brown *n, usu cap I* [prob. fr. 2*indian* 1] : OLD ENGLISH BROWN

indian buffalo *n, usu cap I* : an upland buffalo of eastern Asia kept for draft and milk production esp. in areas where the true water buffalo does not thrive

indian bullfrog *n, usu cap I* : a large loud-voiced frog (*Rana tigrina*) of India and Malaysia

indian butter *n, usu cap I* : butter derived from the Himalayan butter tree — called also *phulwa butter*

indian cane *n, usu cap I* [2*indian* 1] **1** : INDIAN SHOT **2** : the stem of the turmeric **3** : BAMBOO

indian cedar *n, usu cap I* [2*indian* 1] **1** : DEODAR **2** [2*indian* 2] : HOP HORNBEAM **3** [2*indian* 2] : SPANISH CEDAR **4** : TOON

indian cherry *n, usu cap I* [2*indian* 2] **1** : YELLOW BUCKTHORN **2** : JUNEBERRY

indian chickweed *n, usu cap I* [2*indian* 2] : CARPETWEED

indian chief *n, usu cap I* [2*indian* 2] : SHOOTING STAR 2

indian cigar tree *n, usu cap I* [2*indian* 2] : INDIAN BEAN 1

indian civet *n, usu cap I* [2*indian* 1] : ZIBET

indian clover *n, usu cap I* [2*indian* 2] : a plant of the genus *Trifolium* (esp. *T. dichotomum*)

indian club *n, usu cap I* [2*indian* 1] : a fairly heavy club (as of wood or metal) shaped like a large bottle or tenpin and swung about usu. with one in each hand to strengthen the muscles of the arms

Indian club

indian cobra *n, usu cap I* : a very venomous cobra (*Naja naja*) that is found esp. about settled areas and dwellings in southern and eastern Asia and eastward to the Philippines, that is yellowish to dark brown usu. with spectacle-shaped black and white markings on the expansible hood, and that sometimes reaches a length of 6 feet — called also *spectacled cobra*

indian cockle *n, usu cap I* [2*indian* 1] : COCCULUS INDICUS

indian cork tree *n, usu cap I* : an East Indian timber tree (*Millingtonia hortensis*) of the family Bignoniaceae that yields an inferior cork and is used for decoration

indian corn *n, usu cap I* [2*indian* 2] **1** : a tall cereal grass (*Zea mays*) bearing kernels on typically large ears and long cultivated in America **2 a** : the ripened ears of Indian corn **b** : the kernels of Indian corn widely used as food for human beings and livestock

indian couch grass *n, usu cap I* [2*indian* 1] : BERMUDA GRASS

indian creeper *n, usu cap I* [2*indian* 2] : TRUMPET CREEPER

indian cucumber *or* **indian cucumber root** *n, usu cap I* : a small American herb (*Medeola virginiana*) of the lily family with a white succulent rootstock and with leaves in two whorls of which the upper whorl subtends an umbel of small greenish yellow flowers

indian cup *n, usu cap I* [2*indian* 2] **1** : a plant of the genus *Sarracenia; esp* : PITCHER PLANT a **2** : CUP PLANT

indian currant *n, usu cap I* **1 a** : a No. American shrub (*Symphoricarpos orbiculatus*) **b** : the red fruit of this shrub resembling a berry **2** : a shrub (*Ribes glutinosum*) of the Pacific coast of No. America with showy racemose red flowers and black fragrant fruit

indian devil *n, usu cap I* [2*indian* 2] : WOLVERINE 1a

indian doctor *n, usu cap I* [2*indian* 2] **1** : MEDICINE MAN **2** : a white man professing himself a medical practitioner and resorting chiefly to the use of medicinal herbs

indian dye *n, usu cap I* [2*indian* 2] : GOLDENSEAL

indian ebony *n, usu cap I* [2*indian* 1] : a tree of the genus *Diospyros; esp* : a green ebony (*Diospyros melanoxylon*)

indian elephant *n* [2*indian* 1] *usu cap I* : ASIATIC ELEPHANT

indian elm *n, usu cap I* [2*indian* 2] : SLIPPERY ELM 1

indian fiber *n, usu cap I* [2*indian* 2] : PIASSAVA 1

indian fig *n, usu cap I* [2*indian* 1] **1** : BANYAN **2** [2*indian* 2] **a** : any of several plants of the genus *Opuntia*: as (1) : a tropical American prickly pear (*Opuntia ficus-indica*) (2) : an eastern No. American prickly pear (*Opuntia compressa*) **b** : the edible acid fruit of one of these plants

1indian file *n, usu cap I* [2*indian* 2; fr. the Indian practice of going through woods in single file] : SINGLE FILE ⟨along this road the inhabitants slowly moved in *Indian file* —*Newsweek*⟩

2indian file *adv, usu cap I* : in single file ⟨where two people have to walk *Indian file* —Elizabeth Montizambert⟩

indian fire *n, usu cap I* [2*indian* 1] : BENGAL LIGHT 1

indianfish \'==,=\ *n* [2*indian* 2] **1** : an angelfish (*Pomacanthus paru*) of the western Atlantic from Florida to Brazil **2** : WARMOUTH

indian fog *n, usu cap I* [2*indian* 2] : DWARF HOUSELEEK

indian frankincense *n, usu cap I* [2*indian* 1] : FRANKINCENSE 1

indian game *n, usu cap I&G* [2*indian* 1; fr. its having been produced by crossing English game fowl with Indian and Sumatran game fowl] : CORNISH 2

indian gift *n, usu cap I* : something given by an Indian giver

indian giver *n, usu cap I* [2*indian* 2] : one who gives something to another and then takes it back or expects an equivalent in return

indian giving *n, usu cap I* : the type of giving typical of an Indian giver

indian gooseberry *n, usu cap I* [2*indian* 1] : EMBLIC

indian grass *n, usu cap I* [2*indian* 2] : WOOD GRASS 1

indian gravelroot *n, usu cap I* [2*indian* 2] : JOE-PYE WEED

indian gum *also* **india gum** *n, usu cap I* [2*indian* 1 or *india* + *gum*] **1** : GHATTI GUM **2** : STERCULIA GUM; *esp* : the common karaya gum of India

indian harvest *n, usu cap I* [2*indian* 2] *obs* : a harvest of Indian corn

indian hawthorn *n, usu cap I* [2*indian* 1] : an ornamental evergreen shrub (*Raphiolepis indica*) with sharp-serrate leaves and racemes of pink-tinged white flowers

indian hemp *n, usu cap I* [2*indian* 2] **1 a** : a No. American dogbane (*Apocynum cannabinum*) that yields a tough fiber formerly used in cordage; *broadly* : DOGBANE 1 — compare RHEUMATISM WEED **2** [2*indian* 1] : HEMP 1 **3** [2*indian* 1] : an Indian mallow (*Abutilon theophrasti*) **4** [2*indian* 1] : SUNN **5** : SWAMP MILKWEED

indian–hemp resin *n, usu cap I* [*indian hemp* (sense 2) + *resin*] : CHARAS

indian hen *n, usu cap I* [2*indian* 2] **1** : AMERICAN BITTERN **2** : PILEATED WOODPECKER

indian hippo *n, usu cap I* [2*indian* 2 + *hippo* (perh. alter. of 1*hypo*)] **1** : INDIAN PHYSIC 1 **2** : the rhizome and roots of Indian hippo used as a mild emetic

indianian *usu cap, var of* INDIANAN

indian ink *n, usu cap I* [2*indian* 1; fr. a belief that it was made in India] *Brit* : INDIA INK

indian ipecac *n, usu cap I* [2*indian* 1] **1 a** : an Asiatic vine (*Tylophora asthmatica*) resembling milkweed **b** : the root of this vine **2** [2*indian* 2] : INDIAN PHYSIC **3** [2*indian* 2] : IPECAC 1

in·di·an·ism \'indēə,nizəm, -dyə,n-\ *n* -s *usu cap* **1** : the qualities or culture distinctive of or felt to be distinctive of Indians, esp. of American Indians **2 a** : action or policy directed toward furthering the interests and culture of Indians, esp. of American Indians **b** : specialized interest in or emulation or glorification of the arts and crafts and other achievements of Indians, esp. of American Indians **3** : a word or phrase distinctive or felt to be distinctive of the speech of Indians, esp. of American Indians

in·di·an·ist \-nəst\ *n* -s *usu cap* : a specialist in or advocate of Indianism

in·di·an·iza·tion \,indēənə'zāshən\ *n* -s *usu cap* : the act or process of indianizing or the state of being indianized

in·di·an·ize \'indēə,nīz\ *vt* -ED/-ING/-s *see -ize in Explan Notes, often cap* [2*indian* 1&2 + *-ize*] **1** : to make Indian (as in manner of behavior or in culture or appearance) : cause to have Indian characteristics : adapt to Indian conditions or practices ⟨contact with Indians gradually *indianized* some of the settlers⟩ **2** : to cause (as the staff of a government agency) to be made up largely or wholly of Indians

indian jacana *n, usu cap I* [2*indian* 1] : PHEASANT-TAILED JACANA

indian jalap *n, usu cap I* [2*indian* 1] : TURPETH 1

indian jujube *n, usu cap I* [2*indian* 1] **1** : a shrub or small tree (*Ziziphus mauritiana*) of southeastern Asia cultivated in the southeastern U.S. **2** : the globose dark red fruit of the Indian jujube

indian kale *n, usu cap I* [2*indian* 2] : any of several large-leaved arums (family Araceae) with edible farinaceous rootstocks: as **a** : TARO **b** : YAUTIA

indian laburnum *n, usu cap I* [2*indian* 1] : DRUMSTICK TREE

indian lacquer *n, usu cap I* : a natural black varnish obtained in Ceylon and the subcontinent of India as an exudation from the marking nut or a related tree (*Holigarna longifolia*)

indian ladder *n, usu cap I* [2*indian* 2] : a ladder made of or as if of a small tree so trimmed that several inches of each branch are left as a support for the foot

indian lake *n, usu cap I* [prob. fr. 2*indian* 1] **1** : a red lake prepared from lac dye and formerly used by painters **2** *often cap I* : a dark to deep purplish red that is bluer and slightly lighter than magenta (sense 2c)

indian lamb *n, usu cap I* [2*indian* 1] : the pelt of the young of an Indian sheep of Persian type usu. white with a looser curl to the hair than Persian lamb and usu. dyed gray before use

indian laurel *also* **indian laurelwood** *n, usu cap I* **1** : an Asiatic tree (*Persea indica*) that produces canary wood **2** : any of various trees of the genus *Terminalia* (esp. *T. alata* and *T. tomentosa*)

indian lettuce *n, usu cap I* [2*indian* 2] **1** : ROUND-LEAVED WINTERGREEN **2** : AMERICAN COLUMBO **3** : a succulent herb (*Montia perfoliata*) of the Pacific coast of No. America; *broadly* : a plant of the genus *Montia* (as blinks)

indian licorice *n, usu cap I* : an East Indian twining herb (*Abrus precatorius*) with pinnate leaves and axillary clusters of small purple flowers and a root that is used as a substitute for licorice — see JEQUIRITY

indian lilac *n, usu cap I* [2*indian* 1] **1** : CHINABERRY 2 **2** : CRAPE MYRTLE

indian lotus *n, usu cap I* : an aquatic plant (*Nelumbo nucifera*) native to eastern Asia and widely cultivated for its foliage and large pink flowers — compare LOTUS 3

indian madder *n, usu cap I* **1** : an East Indian plant (*Rubia cordifolia*) used for dyeing in the Orient — called also *munjeet* **2** : CHAY

indian mahogany *n, usu cap I* [2*indian* 1] **1** : TOON **2 a** : ROHUN **b** : the wood of rohun

indian maize *n, usu cap I* [2*indian* 2] : INDIAN CORN

indian mallow *n, usu cap I* [2*indian* 1] **1** : any of several abutilons; *esp* : a tall annual herb (*Abutilon theophrasti*) that has velvety cordate leaves and yellow flowers, yields a long strong fiber for which it is sometimes cultivated, and is native to India but widely naturalized as an escape in warm and temperate regions — called also *velvetleaf* **2** [2*indian* 2] : a tropical American weed (*Sida spinosa*) with pale yellow or orange flowers that has been introduced into the U.S. and is found esp. in the southern U.S.

indian maple *n, usu cap I* : a Himalayan maple (*Acer caesium*) with large palmate leaves

indian meal *n, usu cap I* [2*indian* 2] : CORNMEAL

indian meal moth *n, usu cap I* [*indian meal* + *moth*] : a small variably marked pyralid moth (*Plodia interpunctella*) having an equally variably colored larva that feeds on cereal products and other dried foods and by its extensive webbing destroys more than it consumes

indian melon *n, usu cap I* [2*indian* 2] : BARREL CACTUS

indian millet *n, usu cap I* [2*indian* 1] **1** : DURRA **2** : PEARL MILLET 1 **3** [2*indian* 2] : SILKGRASS 2

indian moccasin *n, usu cap I* [2*indian* 2] : STEMLESS LADY'S-SLIPPER

indian mound *n, usu cap I* [2*indian* 2] : one of the mounds of the Mound Builders

indian mulberry *n, usu cap I* **1** : an East Indian shrub or small tree (*Morinda citrifolia*) with axillary heads of flowers and pulpy fruit **2 a** : WHITE MULBERRY **b** : a related mulberry (*Morus indica*)

indian mustard *n, usu cap I* : an Asiatic mustard (*Brassica juncea*) that has pods growing at an angle with their stems and that is used as a potherb and is widely naturalized as a weed — called also *leaf mustard*

indian nut *n, usu cap I* [2*indian* 1] **1** : BETEL NUT **2** [2*indian* 2] : PINE NUT 2

indian oak *n, usu cap I* [2*indian* 1] **1** : TEAK **2** : any of several oaks (esp. *Quercus dilatata*) of India

indian ocher *n, usu cap I* [2*indian* 1] : INDIAN RED 1a

indian orange *n, often cap I* [prob. fr. 2*indian* 1] : a vivid reddish orange that is paler than international orange and redder and darker than golden poppy or chrome orange

indian ox *n, usu cap I* [2*indian* 1] : ZEBU

indian paint *n, usu cap I* [2*indian* 2] **1** : BLOODROOT 1 **2** : STRAWBERRY BLITE **3** : HOARY PUCCOON

indian paintbrush *n, usu cap I* [2*indian* 2] **1** : any of various American plants of the genus *Castilleja; esp* : a widely distributed annual or biennial (*C. coccinea*) of the eastern U.S. that usu. has bright scarlet floral bracts — called also *painted cup* **2** : ORANGE HAWKWEED

indian paint fungus *n, usu cap I* [2*indian* 2] : a tooth fungus (*Echinodontium tinctorum*) that causes heartrot in fir or spruce or western hemlock

indian pangolin *n, usu cap I* [2*indian* 1] : a scaly anteater (*Manis crassicaudata* syn. *Phatages crassicaudata*) with heavily scaled tail and feet and small ears

indian pea *n, usu cap I* [2*indian* 1] **1** : PIGEON PEA **2** : GRASS PEA

indian peacock *or* **indian peafowl** *n, usu cap I* [2*indian* 1] : the common domesticated peafowl (*Pavo cristatus*) which is native to India and Siam and in which the wings of the male are largely barred in black and buff — compare JAPANNED PEACOCK

indian pear *n, usu cap I* [2*indian* 2] : JUNEBERRY

indian physic *n, usu cap I* **1** : either of two American herbs (*Gillenia trifoliata* and *G. stipulata*) with emetic roots **2** : INDIAN BITTERS **3** : INDIAN HEMP 1

indian pine *n, usu cap I* [2*indian* 2] : LOBLOLLY PINE 1

indian pink *n* [2*indian* 1] **1** *usu cap I* **a** : CHINA PINK **b** *or* **indian pinkroot** [2*indian* 2] : PINKROOT a **c** [2*indian* 2] *West Indies* : CYPRESS VINE **d** [2*indian* 2] : GAYWINGS **e** [2*indian* 2] : INDIAN PAINTBRUSH 1 **f** [2*indian* 2] : any of several wild pinks of the genera *Silene* and *Lychnis* **g** [2*indian* 2] : CARDINAL FLOWER **2** *often cap I* : a light reddish brown that is redder, lighter, and stronger than copper tan or monkey skin and redder and duller than peach tan

indian pipe *n, usu cap I* [2*indian* 2; perh. fr. the use of its pithy stems by American Indians for the stems of tobacco pipes] : a leafless saprophytic herb (*Monotropa uniflora*) native to Asia and the U.S. that is waxy white and turns black in drying and has a solitary nodding flower that becomes erect in fruit; *broadly* : SWEET PINESAP

indian–pipe family *n, usu cap I* : PYROLACEAE

indian pitcher *n, usu cap I* [2*indian* 2] : PITCHER PLANT a

indian plantain *n, usu cap I* : any of various plants of the genus *Cacalia* that have leaves resembling those of plantains

indian plum *n, usu cap I* [2*indian* 1] **1 a** : any of several tropical trees of the genus *Flacourtia* (esp. *F. indica*) — compare GOVERNOR'S PLUM **b** : the edible rather acid plum-shaped fruit of one of these trees **2** [2*indian* 2] : OSOBERRY

indian plume *n, usu cap I* [2*indian* 2] : BUTTERFLY WEED 1

indian–plum family *n, usu cap I* : FLACOURTIACEAE

indian poke *n, usu cap I* : AMERICAN HELLEBORE 1

indian pony *n, usu cap I* **1** : an unimproved typically small hardy vigorous not esp. graceful horse of western No. America descended from stock introduced by Spaniards and redomesticated by Indians that is valuable as a utility range horse and for crossbreeding — compare MUSTANG, QUARTER HORSE **2** : 1PINTO

indian posy *n, usu cap I* **1** : any of several American everlastings (as *Anaphalis margaritacea* and *Gnaphalium obtusifolium*) **2** : BUTTERFLY WEED 1

indian potato *n, usu cap I* : any of several American plants with edible tuberous roots: as **a** : GROUNDNUT 2a **b** : GIANT SUNFLOWER **c** : BREADROOT 1 **d** : a yamp (*Carum gairdneri*)

indian puccoon *n, usu cap I* [2*indian* 2] : HOARY PUCCOON

indian pudding *n, usu cap I* [2*indian* 2] : a pudding usu. made of cornmeal, milk, sugar, butter, molasses, and spices and baked and served as a dessert

indian purple *n, often cap I* [prob. fr. 2*indian* 1] : a dark purplish red that is paler and slightly redder than pansy purple, redder and paler than raisin, bluer and paler than Bokhara, and redder and less strong than Schoenfeld's purple

indian python *n, usu cap I* : a very large python (*Python molurus*) of southeastern Asia that is mottled with dark blotches on an olive to pinkish tan ground

indian red *n* [2*indian* 1] **1** *usu cap I* **a** : a yellowish red ferruginous earth containing hematite and used as a pigment — called also *Persian red* **b** : any of various light red to purplish brown iron oxide pigments made by calcining iron salts (as copperas) **2** *often cap I* **a** : a strong reddish brown that is redder and slightly darker than Venetian red — called also *Japanese red, Prussian red* **b** : a moderate reddish

brown — called also *Chinese red, Majolica earth, Persian earth, Persian red, scarlet ocher, Spanish brown*
indian redroot *n, usu cap I* [²*indian* 2] : REDROOT
indian redwood *n, usu cap I* [²*indian* 1] **1** : INDIAN MAHOGANY 2 **2** : SAPPANWOOD
indian reed *n, usu cap I* [²*indian* 1] **1** : INDIAN SHOT **2** [²*indian* 2] : a tall American grass (*Cinna arundinacea*) resembling reed **3** [²*indian* 2] : WOOD GRASS 1
indian rhubarb *n, usu cap I* [²*indian* 1] **1** : HIMALAYAN RHUBARB **2** [²*indian* 2] : a stout herb (*Peltiphyllum peltatum*) of the family Saxifragaceae of the Pacific coast of No. America with leaves that have edible petioles
indian rice *n, usu cap I* [²*indian* 2] : WILD RICE 1a
indian ricegrass *n, usu cap I* [²*indian* 2] : SILK GRASS 2
indian robin *n, usu cap I* : any of various songbirds of India resembling or related to the English robin
indian root *n, usu cap I* [²*indian* 2] **1** : INDIAN PHYSIC **2** : SPIKENARD 2a
indian rosewood *n, usu cap I* [²*indian* 1] **1** : BLACKWOOD b **2** : SISSOO
indian runner *n, usu cap I&R* [²*indian* 1; fr. a belief that it originated in India] : a breed of small upright domestic ducks noted for their egg production and known in fawn and white or pure white or penciled varieties
indians *pl of* INDIAN
indian saffron *n, usu cap I* [²*indian* 1] **1** : SAFFLOWER 1 **2** : ZEDOARY
indian sage *n, usu cap I* [²*indian* 2] : BONESET 1
indian sago palm *n, usu cap I* [²*indian* 1] : JAGGERY PALM
indian salad *n, usu cap I* : a waterleaf (*Hydrophyllum virginianum*) of the eastern U.S. with divided leaves and cymose bell-shaped flowers that are white or violet
indian sandalwood *n, usu cap I* [²*indian* 1] : SANDALWOOD 1a
indian sanicle *n, usu cap I* [²*indian* 2] : WHITE SNAKEROOT
indian sarsaparilla *n, usu cap I* **1** : an East Indian shrub (*Hemidesmus indicus*) of the family Asclepiadaceae **2** : the root of Indian sarsaparilla used as a substitute for sarsaparilla
indian's-dream \'═══'═\ *n, pl* **indian's-dreams** *usu cap I* [*indian's* (gen. of ¹*indian* 2)] **1** : CLIFF BRAKE **2** : OREGON CLIFF BRAKE
indian senna *n, usu cap I* [²*indian* 1] : TINNEVELLY SENNA
indian shamrock *n, usu cap I* [²*indian* 2] : PURPLE TRILLIUM
indian shoe *n, usu cap I* [²*indian* 2] **1** : STEMLESS LADY'S-SLIPPER **2** : YELLOW LADY'S-SLIPPER
indian shot *n, usu cap I* [²*indian* 1] : a plant of the genus *Canna* (esp. *C. indica*) that has hard black seeds about the size of buckshot
indian sign *n, usu cap I* [prob. fr. ²*indian* 2] **1** : a magic spell for immobilizing or making powerless an opponent or rival ⟨have put the *Indian sign* on that team and beaten them nearly every game⟩ or for subjecting another to one's full control or slightest whims or desires ⟨she's put the *Indian sign* on every bachelor in town⟩ — usu. used with *the* **2** : HEX, JINX ⟨thought the cow had got the *Indian sign* when it wouldn't give any more milk⟩
indian slipper *n, usu cap I* [²*indian* 2] : STEMLESS LADY'S-SLIPPER
indian soap *or* **indian soap-plant** *n, usu cap I* [²*indian* 2] : SOAPBERRY TREE 1
indian squill *n, usu cap I* [²*indian* 1] : squill from an herb of the genus *Urginea* (esp. *Urginea indica*) that is the official source of the drug in Great Britain
indian strawberry *n, usu cap I* [prob. fr. ²*indian* 1] **1** : a low East Indian herb (*Duchesnea indica*) naturalized in eastern No. America and resembling the true strawberry but having yellow flowers and tasteless involucrate fruit **2** [prob. fr. ²*indian* 2] : STRAWBERRY BLITE
indian summer *n, usu cap I* [²*indian* 2] **1** : a period of warm or mild weather late in autumn or in early winter usu. characterized by a clear or cloudless sky and by a hazy or smoky appearance of the atmosphere esp. near the horizon **2** : a period of tranquillity or happiness or prosperity or other generally favorable conditions occurring for the first time or more usu. anew toward the latter part or end of something ⟨if the nineteen-twenties constituted a sort of *Indian summer* of the old order —F.L.Allen⟩ ⟨life in the *Indian summer* of Czarist Russia —John Davenport⟩ ⟨an *Indian summer* of wartime literature —*Blackwood's*⟩ ⟨the *Indian summer* of her widowhood —Dixon Wecter⟩
indian tan *n, often cap I* [²*indian* 2] : AZTEC 3
indian tapir *n, usu cap I* : a tapir (*Tapirus indicus*) that is blackish with a broad white area on the body and that is found in Sumatra and the Malay peninsula
indian tea *n, usu cap I* [²*indian* 2] **1** : a yaupon (*Ilex vomitoria*) **2** : NEW JERSEY TEA **3** : LABRADOR TEA a
indian teakettle *n, usu cap I* [²*indian* 2] : PITCHER PLANT
indian thistle *n, usu cap I* [²*indian* 2] : WILD TEASEL
indian tobacco *n, usu cap I* [²*indian* 2] **1** : an American wild lobelia (*Lobelia inflata*) with small blue flowers and inflated capsules formerly used as an antispasmodic **2** [prob. fr. ²*indian* 1] : HEMP **3** : a wild tobacco (*Nicotiana rustica*) **4** : a plant of the genus *Antennaria*; *esp* : a common cat's-foot (*A. plantaginifolia*) of eastern No. America
indian turmeric *n, usu cap I* [²*indian* 2] : GOLDENSEAL
indian turnip *n, usu cap I* [²*indian* 2] **1 a** : JACK-IN-THE-PULPIT 1 **b** : the acrid root of the jack-in-the-pulpit **2** : BREADROOT
indian warrior *n, usu cap I* [²*indian* 2; fr. its brilliant red crest] : a lousewort (esp. *Pedicularis densiflora* and *P. bracteosa*) of the western U.S.
indian wayfaring tree *n, usu cap I* : a Himalayan shrub (*Viburnum cotinifolium*) with roundish leaves and showy flowers
indian wheat *n, usu cap I* [²*indian* 2] **1** : INDIAN CORN **2** [prob. fr. ²*indian* 1] : TARTARIAN BUCKWHEAT **3** : any of several plants of the genus *Plantago* (esp. *P. fastigiata*)
indian whort *n, usu cap I* [²*indian* 2] : BEARBERRY 1
indian wick·a·pe \-'wikəpē\ *n, usu cap I* [²*indian* 2] : LEATHERWOOD
indian wickup *or* **indian wicopy** *n, usu cap I* [²*indian* 2] : FIREWEED b
indian wild dog *n, usu cap I* [²*indian* 1] : DHOLE
indian wolf *n, usu cap I* : a light-colored wolf (*Canis pallipes*) that is widely distributed in desert and upland areas from the northern part of the subcontinent of India westward to northern Arabia and Iran and that is often considered to constitute an Asiatic race of the common wolf of Europe
indian-wrestle \'═══'═\ *vb, usu cap I* [back-formation fr. *indian wrestling*] : to engage in Indian wrestling
indian wrestling *n, usu cap I* [²*indian* 2] **1** : wrestling in which two wrestlers lie side by side on their backs in reversed position locking their near arms and raising and locking the corresponding legs and attempt to force each other's leg down and turn the other wrestler on his face **2 a** : wrestling in which two wrestlers stand face to face gripping usu. their right hands and setting the outsides of the corresponding feet tightly against each other and attempt to force each other off balance **b** : wrestling in which two wrestlers sit face to face gripping usu. their right hands, setting corresponding elbows firmly on a surface (as the top of a table), and holding the length of the arm from the elbow to the hand tightly against each other and attempt to force each other's arm down
indian yellow *n* [²*indian* 1] **1** *usu cap I* : a yellow coloring matter: as **a** : a pigment made from the evaporated urine of cows fed on mango leaves — called also *piuri* **b** : COBALT YELLOW 1 **c** : a brilliant yellow pigment made from Naphthol Yellow S and used in coatings for paper and in distemper colors **2** *often cap I* : a moderate to strong orange yellow that is slightly lighter than Dutch orange — called also *purree, snowshoe*
india oilstone *n, usu cap I* **1** : a manufactured abrasive material **2** : a grinding wheel or whetstone or similar tool made of India oilstone
india paper *n, usu cap I* [so called fr. a belief that it originally came fr. India] **1** *also* **india proof paper** : a smooth thin delicate but not glossy paper esp. suitable for taking full-bodied impressions (as proofs of engravings, woodcuts) **2** : a smooth thin tough opaque printing paper — called also *Bible paper*
india print *n, usu cap I* : a plain lightweight cotton cloth that usu. has hand-blocked Indian designs in rich colors on a natural ground and is used esp. for bedspreads, drapes, or skirts
india red *n, often cap I* : a deep reddish brown — called also *Arabian red, red robin*
india rubber *n, often cap I* **1** : RUBBER 2a **2 a** : RUBBER 3a **b** : RUBBER 1b(3)
india-rubber tree *or* **india-rubber plant** *also* **india-rubber fig** *n, often cap I* : a rubber plant (*Ficus elastica*)
india-rubber vine *n, often cap I* : a woody vine (*Cryptostegia grandiflora*) sometimes cultivated as a source of rubber
india tan *n, often cap I* : RUSSIAN CALF
india tint *n, usu cap I* : a light shade of buff often used in coated paper and ordinary book paper
india wheat *n, usu cap I* : TARTARIAN BUCKWHEAT
¹**In·dic** \'indik\ *adj, usu cap* [L *indicus*, fr. Gk *indikos*, fr. *Indos* India (subcontinent in southern Asia), Indus (river in the northwestern part of the Indian subcontinent) + *-ikos* -ic — more at INDIA] **1** : of or relating to the subcontinent of India : INDIAN **2** : of, relating to, or constituting Indic
²**indic** \"\ *n, cap* : a branch of the Indo-European language family containing Sanskrit, Pali, the Prakrits, and related modern languages of India, Pakistan, and Ceylon (as Hindi, Urdu, Sinhalese) — see INDO-EUROPEAN LANGUAGES table
³**indic** \"\ *adj* [*ind*ium + *-ic*] : of or relating to indium
indic *abbr* indicated; indicative; indicator
in·di·can \'ində,kan\ *n* -S [L *indicum* indigo + E *-an*] **1** : a colorless crystalline glucoside $C_{14}H_{17}NO_6$ occurring esp. in indigo plants and in woad and yielding indoxyl and glucose on hydrolysis — see INDIGO 1a **2** : the sulfuric acid ester $C_8H_6NOSO_3H$ of indoxyl or the crystalline potassium salt of this ester occurring in urine and other animal fluids as a derivative of the indole formed in the alimentary canal and yielding indigo on oxidation
in·di·cant \-dəkənt\ *n* -S [obs. *indicant*, adj., serving to indicate, fr. L *indicant-, indicans*, pres. part. of *indicare* to indicate] : something that serves to indicate ⟨a paragraph printed with a directional arrow before it as an ~⟩
in·di·cat·able \'ində,kād·əbəl, -dē,-, -ātə-, ,══'═══\ *adj* : capable of being indicated
in·di·cate \'ində,kāt, -dē,-, *usu* -ād.+V\ *vt* -ED/-ING/-S [L *indicatus*, past part. of *indicare*, fr. *in-* ²in- + *dicare* to proclaim, dedicate — more at DICTION] : to point out or point to or toward with more or less exactness : show or make known with a fair degree of certainty: as **a** (1) : to show the probable presence or existence or nature or course of : give fair evidence of : be a fairly certain sign or symptom of : reveal in a fairly clear way ⟨their laughter *indicated* their happiness⟩ ⟨his reply *indicated* total disagreement⟩ ⟨*indicated* his impatience by shrugging⟩ ⟨an anecdote that ~s the kind of people they were⟩ ⟨a fever that ~s severe illness⟩ (2) : to demonstrate or suggest the probable necessity or advisability of ⟨conflicting findings ~ further neurological research —*Collier's Yr. Bk.*⟩ ⟨increased luggage space is *indicated* for the family car —R.F.Loewy⟩ ⟨radical surgery is *indicated* in advanced cancer⟩ (3) : to show the general outlines of in advance : sketch beforehand : PRESAGE ⟨his enthusiasm ~s a bright future for him⟩ **b** : to act as a more or less exact index of : show or suggest the probable extent or degree of ⟨their records must ~ ability to do successful academic work —*Bull. of Bates Coll.*⟩ ⟨their popularity is *indicated* by the warm welcome they receive everywhere⟩ **c** : to state or express in a brief or cursory way : state or express without going into great detail : SUGGEST, INTIMATE, HINT ⟨the commission also *indicated* it might take action —*Wall Street Jour.*⟩ ⟨*indicated* a willingness to negotiate —*World*⟩ ⟨the general outlines of it can be *indicated* —R.L.Duffus⟩ **d** : to show the general position or direction of ⟨a map ~s where the ship was sunk⟩ : direct attention to with more or less preciseness (as by pointing with the finger or making a gesture) ⟨*indicated* the tray of sandwiches —Kay Boyle⟩ : point at ⟨the hands of the clock *indicated* noon⟩
syn INDICATE, BETOKEN, ATTEST, BESPEAK, ARGUE, PROVE can mean, in common, to give evidence of, or serve as a ground for, a valid or reasonable inference or an action validated by the inference. INDICATE signifies to serve as a sign or symptom pointing to (the inference or action), stressing only a general, usu. unspecified, connection between subject and object ⟨to assume that Ginger's invitation *indicated* something serious —Clarissa F. Cushman⟩ ⟨the results thus obtained are believed to be the first to *indicate* a possible magnetic effect directly attributable to a solar eclipse —H.D. Harradon⟩ ⟨the results of the physical examination *indicated* some sort of antibiotic medication⟩ BETOKEN stresses the idea of visible or otherwise perceivable evidence or portent ⟨the air with which she looked at the heathmen *betokened* a certain unconcern at their presence —Thomas Hardy⟩ ⟨towering business buildings, great warehouses, and numerous factories *betoken* its importance —*Amer. Guide Series: N.C.*⟩ ATTEST usu. implies the more or less indisputable nature of the evidence ⟨Washington's strong, natural love of children, nowhere *attested* better than in his expense accounts —J.C. Fitzpatrick⟩ ⟨the skill with which they executed these tasks *attested* to their considerable executive talents —R.A.Billington⟩ ⟨the fighting had been hard and continuous, that was *attested* by all the senses —Ambrose Bierce⟩ BESPEAK is interchangeable with *indicate* though it stresses possibly a little more the role of the subject as evidence or token ⟨a freshness and an originality that *bespeak* the intellectual vigor and intuition that he possessed —D.G.Mandelbaum⟩ ⟨a glint of pride in her eyes that *bespoke* her new dignity —Mary Lasswell⟩ ARGUE usu. stresses a reasonable or logical connection between subject and object ⟨his evasion, of course, was the height of insolence, but it *argued* unlimited resource and nerve —Rudyard Kipling⟩ ⟨a becoming deference *argues* deficiency in self-respect —A.N.Whitehead⟩ ⟨what a mistake to say that complexity *argues* culture —Norman Douglas⟩ PROVE is to demonstrate or make manifest the truth of (a conclusion), suggesting the inferential validity of the relationship between subject and object ⟨to become a writer was, however, in Thoreau's mind; his verses *prove* it, his journal proves it —H.S.Canby⟩ ⟨to them, faith is a belief in something which cannot be *proven* and understood rationally —Erich Fromm⟩ ⟨many studies have *proved* that the failure of an employee is seldom due to his lack of ability —W.J.Reilly⟩
indicated airspeed *n* : the airspeed of an airplane as indicated on an airspeed indicator : the airspeed in an atmosphere of standard sea-level density that would give rise to a dynamic pressure equal to that encountered
indicated altitude *n* : the height above sea level as read on an altimeter
indicated horsepower *n* : the power developed in the cylinders of an engine as calculated from the average pressure of the working fluid, the piston area, the stroke, and the number of working strokes per minute
in·di·ca·tion \,ində'kāshən, -dē'-\ *n* -S [MF, fr. ML *indication-, indicatio* action of pointing out, fr. L, valuation, price, fr. *indicatus* (past part. of *indicare* to indicate) + *-ion-, -io* -ion] **1** : the action of indicating **2 a** : something (as a signal, sign, suggestion) that serves to indicate ⟨refusal to accept the gift was an ~ of her displeasure⟩ ⟨gave no ~ that he heard me⟩ ⟨an ~ of what they could expect⟩; *specif* : a symptom or particular circumstance that indicates the advisability or necessity of (as a specific medical treatment or procedure) ⟨postpartum hemorrhage is the chief ~ for the use of ergot preparations and derivatives —C.H.Thienes⟩ **b** : something that is indicated as advisable or necessary ⟨in case of collapse the immediate ~ is artificial respiration —*Jour. Amer. Med. Assoc.*⟩ **3** : the degree indicated in a specific instance or at a specific time on a graduated physical instrument (as a thermometer) : READING **4** : suggestion (as by the use of conventionalized techniques or symbols) of architectural features (as in a drawing) rather than detailed representation of such features ⟨cross-hatching is used as an ~ of brick⟩
¹**in·dic·a·tive** \ən'dikəd·iv, -kətiv\ *adj* [MF *indicatif*, fr. LL *indicativus*, fr. L *indicatus* (past part. of *indicare* to indicate) + *-ivus* -ive] **1** : of, relating to, or constituting a verb form or set of verb forms that represents an attitude toward or concern with a denoted act or state as an objective fact : of, relating to, or constituting a verb form or set of verb forms used invariably in simple declarative sentences and in questions that can be answered by simple declarative sentences and often also in a great variety of other situations ⟨the ~ mood⟩ ⟨*is writing* in "is he writing now" is an ~ verb form⟩ — compare IMPERATIVE, SUBJUNCTIVE **2** : that indicates : that points out more or less exactly : that reveals fairly clearly or suggests or intimates ⟨the situation was ~ of the fear, bordering on panic, which had seized the people —F.D.Roosevelt⟩ — **in·dic·a·tive·ly** *adv*
²**indicative** *n* -S **1** : the indicative mood of a language ⟨*writes* is in the ~⟩ **2** : a form in the indicative mood ⟨*writes* is an ~⟩
in·di·ca·tor \'ində,kād·ə(r), -dē,k-, -ātə-\ *n* [NL, fr. L *indicatus* (past part. of *indicare* to indicate) + *-or*] **1** -S : one that indicates: as **a** : an index hand (as on a dial) : POINTER **b** (1) : a pressure gauge (2) : an instrument for automatically making a diagram that indicates the pressure in and volume of the working fluid of an engine throughout the cycle so that the horsepower and other characteristics may be deduced **c** : a speed counter for an engine **d** : a registering dial (as on a dial telegraph) **e** : ANNUNCIATOR 2a **2** -S **a** : a substance (as a dye) used to show visually usu. by its capacity for color change the condition of a solution with respect to the presence of free acid or alkali or some other substance (as in detecting the end point of a titration) ⟨litmus and phenolphthalein are acid-base ~s⟩ ⟨oxidation-reduction ~s⟩ **b** : TRACER ⟨radioactive ~s⟩ **3 a** *cap* [NL, fr. LL] : the type genus of the family Indicatoridae — see HONEY GUIDE **b** -S : any bird of the genus *Indicator* : HONEY GUIDE **4** -S [so called fr. a belief that its occurrence indicates that there is ginseng nearby] : VIRGINIA GRAPE FERN **5** -S : an organism or a kind of organism (as a species) or an ecological community that is so strictly associated with particular environmental conditions that its presence is indicative of the existence of these conditions in a particular environment **6** -S : a narrow pyritiferous seam the intersections of which with auriferous quartz veins are usu. accompanied by an ore shoot in the vein **7** -S : a deciphering instruction accompanying a message: as **a** : a code or cipher designation of the key **b** : INTERRUPTER b
indicator card *or* **indicator diagram** *n* : the diagram made by an indicator (sense 1b(2))
in·di·ca·tor·i·dae \,indəkə'tōrə,dē\ *n pl, cap* [NL, fr. *Indicator*, type genus + *-idae*] : a family of birds (order Piciformes) that comprises the honey guides and is sometimes considered a subfamily of Capitonidae
indicator telegraph *n* : NEEDLE TELEGRAPH
in·di·ca·to·ry \ən'dikə,tōrē, *chiefly Brit* ¦indi¦kātəri *or* -ā·tri\ *adj* [LL *indicatorius*, fr. L *indicatus* (past part. of *indicare*) + *-orius* -ory] : INDICATIVE 2
in·dica·trix \,ində'kā·triks, ən'dikə·(,)t-\ *n* -ES [NL, fem. of LL *indicator* — more at -TRIX] : an ellipsoid whose axes are proportional to the principal refractive indices of a crystal and from which various optical properties of the crystal may be deduced
in·di·ca·vit \,ində'kāvət\ *n* -S [L, he has indicated, 3d pers. sing. perf. indic. act. of *indicare* to indicate — more at INDICATE] : a writ of prohibition from a common-law court commanding the removal to that court of a case pending in an ecclesiastical court and prohibiting the ecclesiastical court from exercising any further jurisdiction
indices *pl of* INDEX
in·di·cia \ən'dish(ē)ə\ *n, pl* **indicia** *or* **indicias** [L, pl. of *indicium* sign, mark, fr. *indicare* to point out, indicate] **1 a** : a distinctive mark that indicates or that is felt to indicate the nature or quality or existence or reality of something : INDICATION, SIGN, TOKEN, CRITERION ⟨he had in fact all the ~ of divinity —Wallace Stevens⟩ ⟨many ~ of truth —J.E.Davies⟩ ⟨the real ~ of civilization —H.J.Laski⟩ ⟨press opinion and other ~ of public sentiment —H.H.Sprout⟩ **b** : a significant or apparently significant fact or piece of evidence connected with or deduced from a set of circumstances and giving rise to conjectures having some probability of accord with the truth ⟨studied her belongings carefully but could discover no ~ as to what had become of her⟩ **2 a** (1) : a postal marking (as on bulk mail or business reply envelopes) often imprinted on mail or on labels to be affixed to mail and used in place of postage stamps to indicate prepayment of postage (as by use of a postage meter or by receipt of a special permit) (2) : a postal marking or verbal statement often imprinted on mail or on labels to be affixed to mail and used to indicate the class or type of a piece of mail or to give directives (as with regard to the proper place for an address) or some other information (as that a piece of mail may be opened for inspection by a postmaster) **b** : an identifying marking or verbal statement used to single out one thing from another ⟨each object had a tag carrying its ~⟩ or to serve as directional guides ⟨each card in the file has ~ that show the location of each book on the shelf⟩
in·di·cial \(')in¦dishəl, ən'd-\ *adj* [*indicia* + *-al*] **1** : of, relating to, or having the nature of an indication : INDICATIVE ⟨a remark ~ of their pride⟩ **2** [L *indic-, index* index finger, index + E *-ial*] **a** : of, relating to, or having the nature of an index ⟨an ~ glossary⟩ **b** : of or relating to the index finger — **in·di·cial·ly** \-shəlē\ *adv*
in·dic·i·ble \-isəbəl\ *adj* [MF, fr. LL *indicibilis*, fr. L *in-* ¹in- + *dicere* to say + *-ibilis* -ible — more at DICTION] : UNSPEAKABLE, INEXPRESSIBLE
in·di·ci·um \ən'dishēəm\ *n, pl* **indicia** *or* **indiciums** [L, sign, mark] : INDICIA 1
indico *obs var of* INDIGO
in·di·co·lite \ən'dikə,līt\ *n* -S [F, fr. *indico-* (fr. L *indicum* indigo) + *-lite* — more at INDIGO] : an indigo-blue variety of tourmaline
¹**in·dict** \ən'dīt, *usu* -īd.+V\ *vt* -ED/-ING/-S [alter. (influenced by ML *indictare* to indict, fr. AF *enditer*) of earlier *indite, endite*, fr. ME *inditen, enditen*, fr. AF *enditer*, fr. OF, to write down, compose — more at INDITE] **1** : to charge with some wrong or fault or inadequacy usu. formally and after carefully weighing the matter and as if summoning for trial : bring a charge against : formally accuse; *esp* : to attack by accusation and condemn ⟨I ~ those citizens whose easy consciences condone such wrongdoings —F.D.Roosevelt⟩ **2** : to charge with a crime by the finding or presentment of a jury (as a grand jury) in due form of law ⟨was ~*ed* for murder⟩ ⟨were ~*ed* with conspiracy to defraud⟩ **syn** see ACCUSE
²**indict** *vt* -ED/-ING/-S [MF *indicter*, fr. *indict* decreed, fr. L *indictus*, past part. of *indicere*, fr. *in-* ²in- + *dicere* to say — more at DICTION] *obs* : PROCLAIM, DECREE
in·dict·able \-əbəl\ *adj* [¹*indict* + *-able*] **1** : subject to being indicted : liable to indictment ⟨~ as he might be for bad taste —Oscar Cargill⟩ **2** : that makes one liable to indictment ⟨an ~ offense⟩ — **in·dict·ably** \-blē,-bli\ *adv*
in·dict·ee \(,)in,dīd·'ē, ən-, ═'═(,)═\ *n* -S [alter. (influenced by ¹*indict*) of *enditee*, fr. *endite* (earlier form of ¹*indict*) + *-ee*] : one that is indicted
in·dic·tion \ən'dikshən\ *n* -S [ME *indiccioun*, fr. LL *indiction-, indictio*, fr. L, proclamation, fr. *indictus* (past part. of *indicere* to proclaim) + *-ion-, -io* -ion] **1 a** : a 15-year cycle used as a chronological unit in several ancient and medieval systems — see ROMAN INDICTION **b** (1) : the edict of a Roman emperor establishing the valuation for assessing a property tax at the beginning of each 15-year cycle (2) : the tax or subsidy levied by this edict **2** [L *indiction-, indictio*] *archaic* : PROCLAMATION — **in·dic·tion·al** \-shənᵊl, -shnəl\ *adj*
in·dict·ment \ən'dītmənt\ *n* -S [alter. (influenced by ML *indictare* to indict, fr. AF *enditer*) of earlier *indytement, enditement*, fr. ME *enditement*, fr. AF *enditement*, fr. *enditer* to indict + OF *-ment* — more at INDICT] **1 a** : the action of indicting; *specif* : the legal process by which a bill of indictment is preferred to and presented by a jury (as a grand jury) **b** : the state of being indicted **2** : a formal written statement framed by the prosecuting authority of a state and found by a jury (as a grand jury) charging a person with an offense — compare BILL OF INDICTMENT **3** *Scots law* : a process of bringing a person to trial for a crime at the instance of the lord advocate
in·dict·or *or* **in·dict·er** \ən'dīd·ə(r), -ītə-\ *n* -S [*indictor* alter. (influenced by ML *indictare* to indict) of earlier *endightour*, fr. ME *enditour*, fr. AF, fr. *enditer* to indict + OF *-our* -or; *indicter* alter. (influenced by ML *indictare* to indict) of earlier *inditer*, fr. ME *inditer*, *enditer*, alter. (influenced by ME *-er*) of *enditour*] : one that indicts

in·die \ˈindē\ *n* -s [by shortening & alter. fr. *independent*] *slang* **:** something (as a motion-picture company, a radio or television station) that is independent

¹in·dienne \ˌandēˈen\ *n* -s [F, fr. fem. of *indien* Indian, fr. ML *indianus* — more at INDIAN] **:** a light cotton fabric with designs painted or printed in imitation of designs used orig. in subcontinental India

²indienne \"\ *adj, often cap* [F, fem. of *indien* Indian] **:** seasoned (as with curry) in East Indian style ⟨rice ~⟩

in·dif·er·ous \(ˈ)inˈdif(ə)rəs\ *adj* [*indium* + *-ferous*] **:** containing indium

in·dif·fer·ence \ənˈdifərn(t)s, -f(ə)rən-, *-R sometimes* -fən-\ *n* [MF, fr. L *indifferentia* lack of difference, fr. *indifferent-, indifferens* indifferent + *-ia* -y] **1 a :** the quality or state of being indifferent ⟨an age of ~ to religion⟩ **b :** a manifestation or instance of this quality ⟨was much distressed by his ~ toward her⟩ **2 a** *archaic* **:** lack of difference or distinction between two or more things ⟨journeys discover to us the ~ of places —R.W.Emerson⟩ **b :** absence of compulsion to or toward one thing or another ⟨maintaining the freedom of the will and its ~⟩

indifference curve *n* **:** a curve used in economics to indicate all possible comparative quantities of goods or services equally demanded by or of equal use to a consumer

in·dif·fer·en·cy \-nsē\ *n* [L *indifferentia*] *archaic* **:** INDIFFERENCE

¹in·dif·fer·ent \(ˈ)inˈdifərnt, ənˈd-, -f(ə)rənt, *-R sometimes* -fənt\ *adj* [ME, fr. MF or L; MF, fr. L *indifferent-, indifferens* neither good nor bad, unconcerned, fr. *in-* ¹in- + *different-, differens*, pres. part. of *differre* to carry apart, be different — more at DIFFERENT] **1 :** marked by impartiality **:** UNBIASED, UNPREJUDICED ⟨an ~ judge in a trial⟩ ⟨the jurors remained ~⟩ ⟨a remarkably ~ critic⟩ **2 a** (1) **:** that is looked upon as not mattering one way or another **:** that is regarded as being of no significant importance or value **:** that is viewed with neutrality ⟨what others think is altogether ~ to him⟩ (2) **:** that actually does not matter one way or the other **:** that actually lacks significant importance or value **:** that is of little consequence **:** that is unimportant or immaterial ⟨whether you choose to do it or not is a matter that is quite ~⟩ **b :** that has nothing that calls for sanction or condemnation in either observance or neglect **:** that may be done or not done or observed or not observed with no importance or value one way or the other ⟨ceremonies that are considered essential in some religious sects and ~ in others⟩ ⟨revived an ~ custom⟩ **3 a** (1) **:** marked by no special liking for or dislike of something ⟨she always seemed ~ to the arrival of visitors⟩ (2) **:** marked by no special preference for one thing over another **:** not inclined to one thing more than another ⟨was ~ to their acceptance or rejection of her invitation⟩ ⟨were ~ about which book you would decide to give them⟩ **b :** marked by a total or nearly total lack of interest in or concern about something **:** dully unconcerned or unfeeling **:** UNMOVED, LISTLESS, APATHETIC ⟨was ~ to suffering and poverty⟩ ⟨remained ~ to her pleas⟩ ⟨seemed unaffected and quite ~ in the presence of beauty⟩ **4 :** neither excessive nor defective (as in size, extent, intensity) **:** MODERATE, AVERAGE ⟨had a couple of hills of ~ height to climb⟩ ⟨the wind was blowing with a negligible ~ strength⟩ ⟨inherited an ~ fortune⟩ **5 a** (1) **:** neither good nor bad **:** deserving neither praise nor censure **:** PASSABLE, MEDIOCRE, UNIMPRESSIVE ⟨does ~ work at the office⟩ ⟨turned in an ~ performance of the role⟩ (2) **:** that has a morally neutral nature **:** that is neither right nor wrong ⟨many human acts are viewed as ~⟩ **b :** not very good **:** rather bad **:** fairly poor **:** INFERIOR ⟨with an ~ voice like hers she shouldn't even attempt singing⟩ ⟨has ~ qualifications for the job⟩ **6** *now chiefly dial* **:** marked by poor general health **:** SICKLY **7 :** characterized by lack of active quality **:** NEUTRAL ⟨an ~ chemical⟩ ⟨the ~ part of a magnet⟩ **8 a :** UNDIFFERENTIATED ⟨~ tissues of the human body⟩ **b :** capable of development in more than one direction ⟨~ blastema cells⟩; *esp* **:** not yet embryologically determined

syn UNCONCERNED, INCURIOUS, ALOOF, DETACHED, UNINTERESTED, DISINTERESTED: INDIFFERENT, often interchangeable with others of this group, may imply uninterested neutrality of attitude or marked lack of feeling, inclination, preference, or prejudice ⟨a soldier rigidly bound by his oath to the state and *indifferent* to the political ends to which his services might be put —Gordon Harrison⟩ ⟨nature had no sympathy with our hopes and fears, and was completely *indifferent* to our fate —L.P.Smith⟩ ⟨to be *indifferent* to any circumstances — to be quite thoughtless as to drafts and chills, careless of heat —Richard Jefferies⟩ UNCONCERNED suggests personal lack of interest, feeling, or being moved or worried or otherwise affected, perhaps arising from insensitiveness, selfishness, or stoicism ⟨how could one, knowing the warmth and beauty of living bodies, of all the glory and tenderness the world might show, go plodding *unconcerned* through life; go plodding unconcerned yoked to a life and a companionship unvarying, savorless, and without hope of gusto —James Boyd⟩ INCURIOUS may suggest lack of normal curiosity or of intellectual capacity for interest ⟨indifferent to technique, abnormally *incurious*, in fact, of all the means of the literary art —Van Wyck Brooks⟩ ⟨the faintly pained, heavy, *incurious* unamazement of cattle —R.P.Warren⟩ ALOOF applies to a show of indifference arising from great temperamental reserve, a cold, forbidding character, or a sense of superiority or disdain ⟨with a glassily *aloof* expression as though afraid he might be subjected to some unwelcome, impertinent advance by strangers —Claud Cockburn⟩ ⟨always quite *aloof* from the ordinary social life of the town —Arnold Bennett⟩ DETACHED may indicate a calm objective lack of feeling coming from absence of prejudice or selfishness ⟨Iceland, which cool island remained a little *detached* about the war —Rose Macaulay⟩ ⟨looking at him with a peculiarly *detached* and interested air —Sherwood Anderson⟩ ⟨from the cool and *detached* point of view she had attained, life appeared to her to be essentially comic —Ellen Glasgow⟩ UNINTERESTED simply indicates the fact of lack of interest ⟨*uninterested* in the election⟩ DISINTERESTED is often used with this general meaning despite efforts to restrict its application to objectivity, freedom from personal interests, especially financial, and impartiality ⟨teaching the letters of the alphabet to her wiggling and supremely *disinterested* little daughter —C.L.Sulzberger⟩ ⟨the *disinterested* advice of a parting friend, who can possibly have no personal motive to bias his counsels —J.C.Fitzpatrick⟩

²indifferent \"\ *n* -s **1 a :** one that is indifferent (as in religion or politics) **b :** a morally indifferent act **2 :** a plant or a kind of plant (as a species) that has relatively unspecialized requirements and may occur more or less by chance in a variety of habitats or ecological communities — compare INDICATOR 5

³indifferent \"\ *adv, archaic* **:** INDIFFERENTLY

in·dif·fer·ent·ism \-nt-ˌizəm, -n-ˌti-\ *n* -s [F *indifférentisme*, fr. *indifférent* that is looked upon as not mattering one way or another (fr. MF *indifferent*) + *-isme* -ism] **1 a :** INDIFFERENCE; *esp* **:** a consciously nurtured spirit or attitude or philosophy of indifference (as toward religion) **b :** the principle or conviction that differences in religious beliefs are essentially unimportant **:** ADIAPHORISM; *specif* **:** the principle or conviction that one religion is as good as another **2 :** IDENTITY PHILOSOPHY

in·dif·fer·ent·ist \-ntəst\ *n* -s [F *indifférentiste*, fr. *indifférent* + *-iste* -ist] **:** one that is marked by or adheres to indifferentism

in·dif·fer·ent·ly *adv* **:** in an indifferent manner

in·di·gen \ˈindəjən, -ˌjen\ *also* **in·di·gene** \-ˌjēn\ *n* -s [L *indigena*] **1** *usu* **indigene :** NATIVE 8a **2 :** a biological species that is known from both wild and cultivated forms — compare CULTIGEN

in·di·gence \ˈindəjən(t)s, -dēj-\ *n* -s [ME, fr. MF, fr. L *indigentia*, fr. *indigent-, indigens* + *-ia* -y] **1** *archaic* **:** DEFICIENCY **2 :** poverty that is severe or total **:** NEEDINESS

in·di·gen·cy \-jənsē, -si\ *n* -ES [L *indigentia*] **:** INDIGENCE

in·dig·e·nist \ənˈdijənəst\ *n* -s [Sp *indigenista*, fr. *indigena* native (fr. L *indigena*) + *-ista* -ist (fr. L)] **:** an advocate of Indianism esp. in Latin America

in·dig·e·ni·za·tion \ə‚ˌ=nəˈzāshən, -ˌnīˈz-\ *n* -s **:** the action or process of indigenizing

in·dig·e·nize \=ˈ==ˌnīz\ *vt* -ED/-ING/-S [*indigenous* + *-ize*] **1 :** to cause to have indigenous characteristics **:** adapt to indigenous conditions or practices ⟨an excellent way of *indigenizing* what would otherwise remain a foreign system —F.M.Keesing⟩ **2 :** to cause to be made up chiefly of an indigenous personnel ⟨*indigenizing* the teaching staff of a school⟩

in·dig·e·nous \ənˈdijənəs\ *adj* [LL *indigenus*, fr. L *indigena*, n., native, fr. OL *indu, endo* in, within (akin to Gk *endina* entrails, Hitt *anda* within, into) + L *-gena* (akin to L *gignere* to beget); OL *indu, endo* and its cognates all fr. a prehistoric IE or Indo-Hittite compound whose first constituent is represented by L *in* and whose second constituent is akin to L *de* from, down, away — more at IN, DE-, KIN] **:** NATIVE: **a** (1) **:** not introduced directly or indirectly according to historical record or scientific analysis into a particular land or region or environment from the outside ⟨Indians were the ~ inhabitants of America⟩ ⟨species of plants that are ~ to that country⟩ (2) **:** originating or developing or produced naturally in a particular land or region or environment ⟨an interesting example of ~ architecture⟩ ⟨a people with a rich ~ culture⟩ (3) **:** of, relating to, or designed for natives ⟨the establishment of ~ schools⟩ **b :** INBORN, INNATE, INHERENT ⟨a type of behavior that is ~ to human beings⟩ **syn** see NATIVE

in·dig·e·nous·ly *adv* **:** in an indigenous manner

¹in·di·gent \ˈindəjənt, -dēj-\ *adj* [ME, fr. MF, fr. L *indigent-, indigens*, pres. part. of *indigēre* to need, lack, fr. OL *indu, endo* in + *egēre* to need, be needy, lack; akin to OHG *ekrōdi* thin, weak, ON *ekla* scarcity] **1 :** being in a condition of indigence **:** being poor usu. without being destitute **:** IMPOVERISHED, NEEDY ⟨helping the ~ by means of medical insurance⟩ **2 a** *archaic* **:** DEFICIENT **b** *archaic* **:** totally lacking in something specified ⟨tangible parts ~ of moisture —Francis Bacon⟩ **c** *obs* **:** being in need of something specified ⟨naturally ~ of protection —Richard Steele⟩ **syn** see POOR

²indigent \"\ *n* -s **:** one that is indigent

in·di·gest \ˌindəˈjest, -ˌdī-, ənˈdī‚j-\ *adj* [ME, immature, fr. L *indigestus* confused, not arranged, fr. *in-* ¹in- + *digestus*, past part. of *digerere* to digest] **1** *archaic* **:** not carefully thought out or arranged **2** *archaic* **:** FORMLESS

in·digested \ˌin+(ˌ)=ˈ==\ *adj* [¹*in-* + *digested*, past part. of *digest*] **1** *archaic* **a :** not carefully thought out or arranged **b :** FORMLESS **2** *archaic* **:** not having undergone digestion

in·digestibility \ˌin+\ *n* **:** the quality of being indigestible

¹in·digestible \"+\ *adj* [LL *indigestibilis*, fr. L *in-* ¹in- + LL *digestibilis* digestible] **:** that cannot be digested or that is not easily digested: **a :** not capable of being assimilated as food or not easily or comfortably assimilated as food ⟨green bananas are ~⟩ **b** (1) **:** not capable of being assimilated by the mind or not easily or comfortably assimilated by the mind **:** incomprehensible or nearly incomprehensible ⟨an ~ mass of facts⟩ (2) **:** that is repugnant to the mind or sensibilities **:** intellectually or aesthetically unendurable or nearly unendurable ⟨a book full of ~ pedantry⟩ ⟨clashing colors that make the painting quite ~⟩ — **in·di·gest·ibly** \-blē, -bli\ *adv*

²indigestible \"\ *n* -s **:** something indigestible

in·di·ges·tion \ˌindəˈjes(h)chən, -ˌdī-\ *n* [ME *indygestyon*, fr. MF *indigestion*, fr. LL *indigestion-, indigestio*, fr. L *in-* ¹in- + *digestion-, digestio* digestion — more at DIGESTION] **1 :** inability to digest something or difficulty in digesting something: **a :** inability to assimilate or difficulty in assimilating food **:** incomplete or imperfect assimilation of food **:** DYSPEPSIA ⟨troubled with chronic ~⟩ **b :** inability to assimilate or difficulty in assimilating something other than food **:** incomplete or imperfect assimilation of something other than food ⟨the uniform impression created everywhere . . . was staleness on the part of the teachers, ~ on the part of the students —Benjamin Fine⟩ **2 :** a case or attack of indigestion ⟨spoke of various ~s she had suffered —Booth Tarkington⟩ ⟨a comment that I would get an ~ from so much mental nourishment —Rafael Sabatini⟩

in·digestive \ˌin+\ *adj* [¹*in-* + *digestive*] **:** DYSPEPTIC ⟨an ~ single woman —Charles Dickens⟩

indigitate *vb* -ED/-ING/-S [ML *indigitatus*, past part. of *indigitare* (influenced in meaning by L *digitus* finger), fr. L *indigitare*, *indigetare* to invoke (a deity), fr. *indiget-, indiges* native deity, fr. OL *indu, endo* in, within + *-iget-, -iges* (perh. fr. L *agere* to drive, lead, act) — more at INDIGENOUS, AGENT, TOE] *obs* **:** INDICATE

in·dign \(ˈ)inˈdīn, ənˈd-\ *adj* [ME *indigne*, fr. MF, fr. L *indignus*] **1** *archaic* **:** UNWORTHY, UNDESERVING **2** *obs* **a :** UNBECOMING, DISGRACEFUL **b :** not merited **:** UNDESERVED

in·dig·nance \ənˈdignən(t)s\ *n* -s *archaic* [fr. *indignant*, after such pairs as E *abundant: abundance*] **:** INDIGNATION

in·dig·nan·cy \-gnənsē, -si\ *n* -ES [*indignant* + *-cy*] *archaic* **:** INDIGNATION

in·dig·nant \ənˈdignənt\ *adj* [L *indignant-, indignans*, pres. part. of *indignari* to be indignant, be offended, fr. *indignus* unworthy, fr. *in-* ¹in- + *dignus* worthy — more at DECENT] **1 :** filled with or marked by indignation ⟨grew suddenly quite ~ about the matter —James Hilton⟩ ⟨~ at the injustice —W. M.Thackeray⟩ ⟨were ~ over their mistreatment⟩ ⟨felt quite ~ with them⟩ **2 :** arising from or prompted by or indicative of indignation ⟨wrote an ~ letter⟩ ⟨looked at her with an ~ frown⟩ **syn** see ANGRY

in·dig·nant·ly *adv* **:** with indignation **:** in a manner indicative of indignation ⟨~ denied the accusation⟩

in·dig·na·tion \ˌin(ˌ)digˈnāshən, -ˌdēg-\ *n* -s [ME *indignacioun*, fr. MF & L; MF *indignation*, fr. L *indignation-, indignatio*, fr. *indignatus* (past part. of *indignari* to be indignant) + *-ion-, -io* -ion] **:** typically intense deep-felt resentment or anger aroused by annoyance at or displeasure with or scorn over something that actually is or is felt to be unjust or unworthy or mean ⟨aroused public ~⟩ ⟨~ at the injustice⟩ ⟨~ over the wrong they had suffered⟩ ⟨could feel only ~ with his children⟩ ⟨~ against the ill-treatment of human beings —Leslie Rees⟩ **syn** see ANGER

indignation meeting *n* **:** a meeting held for the purpose of expressing and discussing grievances ⟨the new law was objectionable to nearly everyone and there were numerous *indignation meetings*⟩

indignify *vt* [¹*in-* + *dignify*] *obs* **:** DISHONOR

indignities to the person : misconduct (as habitual incivility or ridicule or neglect) by a spouse constituting grounds for divorce in some states that makes the life of an offended spouse intolerable and burdensome, subverts the family relationship, and evidences the settled hatred of the offending spouse

in·dig·ni·ty \ənˈdignəd·ē, -ətē, -i\ *n* [L *indignitat-, indignitas*, fr. *indignus* unworthy + *-itat-, -itas* -ity] **1** *obs* **:** lack or loss of dignity or honor **2 a :** something that offends against one's personal dignity or self-respect **:** something humiliating or injurious to one's self-esteem **:** INSULT, OUTRAGE ⟨forced to suffer one ~ after another⟩ **b :** treatment that offends against or is humiliating or injurious to one's personal dignity or self-respect ⟨treated them with ~⟩ **3** *obs* **:** INDIGNATION **syn** see AFFRONT

in·di·go \ˈindəˌgō, -dē-\ *n, pl* **indigos** *or* **indigoes** [It *indaco* & It dial. (northern) *indigo, endego*, fr. L *indicum*, fr. Gk *indikon*, fr. neut. of *indikos* Indic — more at INDIC] **1 a :** a blue vat dye that was obtained orig. from plants (as indigo plants or woad) by hydrolysis of the indican present and oxidation by air of the resulting indoxyl and that unless specially purified contained other substances (as indirubin) besides the principal coloring matter — called also *natural indigo* **b** *or* **indigo blue :** the principal coloring matter $C_{16}H_{10}N_2O_2$ of natural indigo that is synthesized as a blue crystalline powder with a coppery luster usu. by oxidation of synthetic indoxyl with air in the presence of alkali and that is used chiefly as a vat dye for cotton and wool — called also *indigotin, synthetic indigo;* see DYE table I (under *Vat Blue 1*); compare INDIGO WHITE, STRUCTURAL FORMULA **c :** any of several blue vat dyes derived from or closely related to indigo **2 a :** INDIGO PLANT **b :** any of various plants resembling the indigo plant **3** *or* **indigo blue :** a variable color averaging a dark grayish blue that is redder and deeper than night blue — called also *inde blue, Indian blue*

indigo 1b

²indigo \"\ *or* **indigo-blue** \ˈ==(ˌ)=ˈ=\ *adj* **:** being of the color indigo

indigo bird *n* **:** INDIGO BUNTING

indigo blue B *or* **indigo blue R** *n, usu cap I & B* **:** a vat dye — see DYE table I (under *Vat Blue 35*)

indigo broom *n* **:** a wild indigo (*Baptisia tinctoria*) having bright yellow flowers and trifoliolate leaves with cuneate leaflets

indigo brown *n* **:** a brown substance found in crude natural indigo

indigo bunting *n* **:** a common small finch (*Passerina cyanea*) of the eastern U. S. marked by indigo-blue coloration in the male

indigobush \ˈ==ˌ(ˌ)=ˌ=\ *n* **1 :** FALSE INDIGO 1 **2 :** SMOKE TREE 2 **3 :** MOCK LOCUST

indigo carmine *n* **1 :** a soluble blue dye that is the sodium salt of indigodisulfonic acid and is used chiefly as a biological stain and food color but is no longer used to any extent as a textile dye — called also *Indigotine IA* **2 :** a strong greenish blue that is bluer and duller than grotto, greener and duller than cobalt blue, and greener and darker than average cerulean blue (sense 1a) — called also *chemic blue, duck blue*

indigo copper *n* **:** COVELLITE

in·di·go·disulfonic acid \ˈ==(ˌ)=+ . . . -\ *n* [*indigodisulfonic* ISV *indigo* + *disulfonic*] **:** a water-soluble disulfonic acid $C_{16}H_8N_2O_2(SO_3H)_2$ obtained by treating indigo with concentrated sulfuric acid — called also *indigo extract, 5,5'-indigotindisulfonic acid*

indigo extract *n* **1 :** INDIGODISULFONIC ACID **2 :** INDIGO CARMINE

in·di·gof·era \ˌindəˈgäf(ə)rə\ *n, cap* [NL, fr. ISV *indigo* + NL *-fera* (fr. L, fem. of *-fer*, adj. comb. form) — more at -FER] **:** a genus of tropical herbs and shrubs (family Leguminosae) having odd-pinnate leaves and flowers with keel petals laterally spurred — see INDIGO PLANT

in·di·gof·er·ous \ˌ==ˈgäf(ə)rəs\ *adj* [¹*indigo* + *-ferous*] **:** yielding indigo

in·di·goid \ˈ==ˌgȯid\ *adj* [ISV ¹*indigo* + *-oid*] **:** related to or resembling indigo esp. in chemical structure and dyeing properties ⟨the ~ character of a blue pigment⟩

indigoid dye *or* **indigoid vat dye** *also* **indigoid** *n* -s **:** any of a class of vat dyes characterized by the same chromophore as indigo (sense 1b) — compare THIOINDIGOID DYE

in·dig·o·lite \ənˈdigəˌlīt\ *n* -s [by alter. (influenced by ¹*indigo*)] **:** INDICOLITE

indigo plant *n* **1 :** a plant that yields indigo: as **a :** any of several plants of the genus *Indigofera* (as *I. tinctoria* of Africa and India, *I. anil* of So. America, *I. auriculata* of Arabia and Egypt) **b :** an East Indian woody vine (*Marsdenia tinctoria*) that yields rank indigo **c :** an Asiatic herb (*Polygonum tinctorium*) **2 a :** an Australian plant (as the Darling pea) of the genus *Swainsona* **b :** BOX BRIER

indigos *pl of* INDIGO

indigo snake *n* **:** a large blue-black colubrid snake (*Drymarchon corais couperi*) of the southern U. S. sometimes reaching a length of almost eight feet — called also *gopher snake*

in·di·go·sol \ˈ==ˌ=ˌsäl\ *n* -s [fr. *Indigosol*, a trademark] **:** any of various solubilized vat dyes (as that derived from indigo white)

indigo thorn *n* **:** SMOKE TREE 2

in·di·got·ic \ˌindəˈgäd·ik\ *adj* [ISV ¹*indigo* + connective *-t-* + *-ic*] **:** of, relating to, or being of the color of indigo

in·di·go·tin \ənˈdigətən, -gəd·ən, -gətᵊn, ˌindəˈgōtᵊn\ *n* -s [ISV ¹*indigo* + connective *-t-* + *-in*] **1 :** INDIGO 1b **2** *or* **indigotine IA** \"+ˌīˈā\ *usu cap* **:** INDIGO CARMINE — see DYE table I (under *Acid Blue 74*)

indigotindisulfonic acid \"+ . . . -\ *n* [*indigotindisulfonic* fr. *indigotin* + *disulfonic*] **:** INDIGODISULFONIC ACID

indigo weed *n* **:** INDIGO BROOM

indigo white *n, sometimes cap I & W* **:** a pale yellow crystalline compound $C_{16}H_{12}N_2O_2$ obtained by reduction of indigo and easily changed back to it by oxidation — called also *leucoindigo;* see DYE table I (under *Vat Blue 1*)

indiligent *adj* [L *indiligent-, indiligens*, fr. *in-* ¹in- + *diligent-, diligens*, pres. part. of *diligere* to esteem highly, love — more at DILIGENT] **1** *obs* **:** INATTENTIVE, HEEDLESS **2** *obs* **:** LAZY, IDLE

in·direct \ˌin+\ *adj* [ME, fr. ML *indirectus*, fr. L *in-* ¹in- + *directus* direct] **:** not direct: as **a** (1) **:** deviating from a direct line or course **:** not proceeding straight from one point to another **:** proceeding obliquely or circuitously **:** ROUNDABOUT ⟨following an ~ route across the continent⟩ (2) **:** not going straight to the point **:** not proceeding to an intended end by the most direct course or method ⟨making ~ but perfectly legitimate inquiries into his prospects —Mary Austin⟩ **b :** not straightforward and open **:** tending to mislead **:** DECEITFUL, DISHONEST ⟨seemed to me to be an untrustworthy ~ individual⟩ **c :** not directly aimed at or achieved ⟨doubtless they had some not clearly recognized ~ purpose in mind⟩ **:** not resulting directly from an action or cause ⟨there will be many ~ consequences of their stupidity⟩ **d** (1) **:** stating what a real or supposed original speaker said without directly quoting the actual words and marked by changes that conform the statement grammatically to the words of the one making the statement ⟨the words *he could come* in the sentence "he said that he could come" are an ~ quotation⟩ ⟨~ discourse⟩ ⟨an example of an ~ question is *how she was* in the statement "he asked her how she was"⟩ (2) *of the object of a verb* **:** being the secondary goal of an action ⟨*borrower* in "I gave the borrower the book" is an ~ object⟩ (3) *of a passive verb or verb form* (a) **:** having a subject that becomes an indirect object when the verb is made active (as *he* in the statement "he was given a book by them" becomes *him* in "they gave him a book") ⟨*was given* in "he was given a book" is an ~ passive⟩ (b) **:** constituting a passive verb phrase made up of a verb and prepositional adverb of such a kind that when the verb phrase is made active the prepositional adverb is necessarily retained as a preposition having an object that is the word that had been used as subject of the passive verb phrase ⟨the passive verb phrase *was shot at* in the statement "the fugitive was shot at by the police" is an ~ passive that is made active in the statement "the police shot at the fugitive"⟩ **e :** HETEROXENOUS — **in·directly** \"+\ *adv* — **in·directness** \"+\ *n*

indirect contempt *n* **:** CONSTRUCTIVE CONTEMPT

indirect cost *also* **indirect charge** *n* **:** a cost that is not identifiable with a specific product, function, or activity — contrasted with *direct cost*

indirect development *n* **:** biologic development accompanied by a metamorphosis

indirect evidence *n* **:** evidence that establishes immediately collateral facts from which the main fact may be inferred **:** CIRCUMSTANTIAL EVIDENCE

indirect exchange *n* **1 :** exchange (as of checks, drafts) between three or more places **2 :** exchange in which rates give the value of the unit of home currency in terms of foreign currencies — compare FIXED EXCHANGE

indirect fire *n* **:** gunfire by indirect aiming at a target not visible from the gun

indirect initiative *n* **:** the legislative initiative where a proposed measure is considered by the legislature and goes to the people by referendum if the legislature rejects it — distinguished from *direct initiative*

in·di·rec·tion \ˌindəˈrekshən *also* -ˌdī-\ *n* [*indirect* + *-ion*] **1 a :** lack of straightforwardness and openness **:** DECEITFULNESS, DISHONESTY ⟨unable to tolerate their double-dealing and ~⟩ **b :** something (as an act, a statement) marked by lack of straightforwardness or by deceitfulness ⟨hated diplomatic ~s —*Rev. of Reviews*⟩ **2 a** (1) **:** indirect action or movement or procedure **:** a roundabout course or means or method ⟨free from moralizing even by ~ —Lavinia R. Davis⟩ ⟨usurp the executive power by ~ —R.W.Ginnane⟩ (2) **:** an action or procedure or method marked by suggestion and free of direct obvious expression ⟨creative experiments in ~ —Louis Untermeyer⟩ **b :** lack of clear-cut action or movement toward a definite objective **:** lack of direction **:** aimless wandering about ⟨a foreign way of writing ruined by its ~⟩ ⟨a bizarre and pathetic ~ —St. Clair McKelway⟩ ⟨a querulous old woman who seemed to be always in a dither of ~⟩ **c :** something (as an act, a statement, a method) marked by indirection ⟨a suave and elegant little comedy of ~s —*Time*⟩

indirect labor *n* **1 :** labor (as clerks, repair men, maintenance men) applied indirectly to a product in the manufacturing process so that the cost is not computable in, identifiable with, or chargeable directly to the specific product — compare DIRECT LABOR **2 :** the wages paid to workers who are classed as indirect labor

indirect laying *n* **:** the laying of an artillery piece with the line of sighting indirectly upon a target not visible from the gun

indirect lighting *n* **:** lighting in which the source of light is concealed and the light emitted is diffusely reflected (as by the ceiling or a wall panel)

indirect material *n* **:** material (as tools, cleaning supplies, lubricating oil) used in manufacturing processes which does not become an integral part of the product and the cost of which is not identifiable with or directly chargeable to it — compare DIRECT MATERIAL

indirect method of difference : a method of scientific induction devised by J. S. Mill according to which if two or more instances in which a phenomenon occurs have only a single circumstance in common and two or more instances in which it does not occur have nothing in common except the absence of the circumstance, the circumstance in which the two sets of instances differ is the effect, cause, or necessary part of the cause of the phenomenon

indirect process *n* **:** a process involving production of pig iron from which metal is then made — compare DIRECT PROCESS

indirect reduction *n* **1 :** the process of reducing a syllogistic argument to the first figure by taking the contradictory of the conclusion as a premise and getting the contradictory of one premise as the new conclusion — contrasted with *direct reduction* **2** *also* **indirect proof :** a reductio ad absurdum

indirect rein *n* **:** the use of a rein that can be pressed against a horse's neck on the side opposite the direction in which it is required to move — compare DIRECT REIN

indirect selling *n* **:** a selling through middlemen

indirect syllogism *n* **:** a syllogism that results from another by indirect reduction

indirect tax *n* **:** a tax exacted indirectly from a person other than the one on whom the ultimate burden of the tax is expected to fall ⟨excise and customs duties are generally included under *indirect taxes*⟩

indirect vision *n* **:** vision resulting from rays of light falling upon peripheral parts of the retina

in·di·ru·bin \ˌində'rübən\ *n* -s [2*ind-* + *rub-* (fr. L *ruber* red) + *-in* — more at RED] **:** a dark red crystalline compound $C_{16}H_{10}N_2O_2$ isomeric with indigo (sense 1b) found in natural indigo but usu. made by reaction of indoxyl with isatin

in·dis·cern·ibil·i·ty \ˌində̇ˌs|ərnə'biləd·ē, |ən-, |əin-, -lətē, -i *also* -ˌz|\ *n* -ES **:** the quality or state of being indiscernible

1**in·discernible** \ˌin+\ *adj* [1*in-* + *discernible*] **:** incapable of being discerned: **a :** not visible or perceptible ⟨his features were ~ —G.B.Shaw⟩ **b :** incapable of being recognized as distinct ⟨thought that good was ~ from evil⟩ — **in·discern·ible·ness** \"+\ *n* — **in·discernibly** \"+\ *adv*

2**indiscernible** \"\ *n* -s **:** something indiscernible; *specif* **:** something that cannot be recognized as distinct

in·discerpible \ˌin+\ *adj* [1*in-* + *discerpible*] *archaic* **:** INDISCERPTIBLE

in·dis·cerp·ti·bil·i·ty \ˌində̇ˌsərptə'biləd·ē, -də̇ˌzər-\ *n* -ES **:** the quality or state of being indiscerptible

in·discerptible \ˌin+\ *adj* [1*in-* + *discerptible*] **:** not discerptible **:** not subject to being separated into parts ⟨simple and ~ entities —James Ward⟩

in·disciplinable \(ˌ)in, ən+\ *adj* [1*in-* + *disciplinable*] **:** not subject to or capable of being disciplined ⟨full of ~ energy⟩

in·discipline \(ˈ)in, ən+\ *n* [1*in* + *discipline*] **:** lack of discipline ⟨coping with ~ and laxity —Cecil Sprigge⟩

in·disciplined \"+\ *adj* [1*in-* + *disciplined* (past part. of *discipline*)] **:** UNDISCIPLINED ⟨~ imagination —Joseph Conrad⟩

in·discoverable \ˌin+\ *adj* [1*in-* + *discoverable*] **:** UNDISCOVERABLE

in·discreet \"+\ *adj* [ME *indiscrete*, fr. MF & LL; MF *indiscret*, fr. LL *indiscretus*, fr. L, indistinguishable, not separated, fr. *in-* 1in- + *discretus*, past part. of *discernere* to separate, distinguish between — more at DISCERN] **1 :** not discreet: as **a :** IMPRUDENT, INJUDICIOUS, UNTACTFUL, INCONSIDERATE ⟨an ~ question⟩ ⟨~ behavior⟩ **b :** not carefully restrained **:** UNWARY, INCAUTIOUS ⟨an ~ display of interest⟩ **2** *Scot* **:** UNCIVIL, IMPOLITE — **in·discreetly** \"+\ *adv* — **in·discreetness** \"+\ *n*

in·discrete \"+\ *adj* [L *indiscretus*] **:** not discrete **:** not separated into distinct parts ⟨an ~ mass of material⟩

in·dis·cre·tion \ˌində̇'skreshən *sometimes* ÷ -rēsh-\ *n* [ME *indiscrecioun*, fr. MF *indiscretion*, fr. LL *indiscretion-*, *indiscretio*, fr. *indiscretus* indiscreet + L *-ion-*, *-io* -ion] **1 :** lack of discretion: as **a :** IMPRUDENCE, INJUDICIOUSNESS, UNTACTFULNESS, INCONSIDERATENESS ⟨warned him against ~ in his conversation⟩ **b :** lack of careful restraint **:** UNWARINESS, INCAUTION ⟨spoke calmly to her and without ~⟩ **2 :** something (as an act, procedure, remark) marked by lack of discretion ⟨had destroyed his political career by an ~ —Gamaliel Bradford⟩; *specif* **:** an act at variance with the accepted morality of a society ⟨careful not to mention the ~*s* of her earlier life⟩ **3** *Scot* **:** INCIVILITY, IMPOLITENESS

in·discriminate \ˌin+\ *adj* [1*in-* + *discriminate*] **1 a** (1) **:** not marked by discrimination **:** not marked by careful distinction **:** not evidencing discernment ⟨~ reading habits⟩ ⟨~ viewing of television programs⟩ ⟨launched ~ destruction⟩ (2) **:** HAPHAZARD, RANDOM, HIT-AND-MISS, SWEEPING ⟨~ application of a law⟩ ⟨~ censure⟩ (3) **:** UNRESTRAINED, PROMISCUOUS ⟨~ sexual intercourse⟩ **b** (1) **:** not separated into distinct parts **:** JUMBLED, CONFUSED ⟨the babble of the crowd was an ~ mixture of several languages⟩ (2) **:** MOTLEY, HETEROGENEOUS ⟨a book filled with an ~ assortment of pictures⟩ **2 :** not exercising discrimination or discernment **:** not making careful distinctions **:** not carefully choosing **:** UNDISCRIMINATING ⟨a hospitable but not ~ host —Sarah G. Bowerman⟩ — **in·discriminately** \"+\ *adv* — **in·discriminateness** \"+\ *n*

in·discriminating \"+\ *adj* [1*in-* + *discriminating*] **:** UNDISCRIMINATING — **in·discriminatingly** \"+\ *adv*

in·discrimination \ˌin+\ *n* [1*in-* + *discrimination*] **1 :** an act or instance of not discriminating or discerning ⟨greater ~*s* than were possibly his —Marguerite Young⟩ **2 :** the quality of not discriminating or the condition of not being discriminated **:** lack of discrimination ⟨show habitual ~ in the choice of their friends⟩ ⟨the various parts of the book are marked by ~⟩

in·discriminative \ˌin+\ *adj* [1*in-* + *discriminative*] **:** UNDISCRIMINATING — **in·discriminatively** \"+\ *adv*

in·discriminatory \"+\ *adj* [1*in-* + *discriminatory*] **:** not discriminatory

in·discussible \"+\ *adj* [1*in-* + *discussible*] **:** not capable of being discussed ⟨the problem has now become ~⟩

in·dis·pens·abil·i·ty \ˌində̇ˌspen(t)sə'biləd·ē, -lətē, -i\ *n* **:** the quality or state of being indispensable

1**in·dis·pens·able** \ˌin+\ *also* **in·dis·pens·ible** \"\ *adj* [1*in-* + *dispensable*] **1 :** that cannot be set aside or neglected or disregarded ⟨his ~ duty to help them⟩ ⟨an ~ obligation⟩ **2 :** that cannot be dispensed with **:** that is absolutely necessary or requisite or essential **:** that cannot be done without ⟨their assistance was ~⟩ ⟨an ~ book in this field⟩ ⟨was an ~ worker⟩ ⟨freedom to read is one of the ~ conditions of a democratic society —W.S.Dix⟩ **syn** see NEEDFUL

2**indispensable** \"\ *n* -s **1 :** something indispensable ⟨needed clothing and food and other ~*s*⟩ **2 indispensables** *pl*, *archaic* **:** TROUSERS

in·dispensableness \ˌin+\ *n* **:** INDISPENSABILITY

in·dis·pens·ably \ˌində̇'spen(t)səblē, -li\ *adv* **:** without the possibility of being dispensed with **:** to an absolutely necessary extent ⟨help that is ~ required⟩

in·dis·pose \ˌində̇'spōz\ *vt* [prob. back-formation fr. *indisposed*] **1 a :** to put out of the proper condition for something **:** make unfit ⟨not to get one's sleep . . . ~*s* one more or less for the day —Edward FitzGerald⟩ **b :** to cause to be disinclined **:** make averse ⟨felt the science of mathematics to ~ the mind to religious belief —J.H.Newman⟩ **2** *archaic* **:** to cause to be in poor physical health **3** *archaic* **:** to cause to be hostile **:** make unfriendly

in·dis·posed \-zd\ *adj* [ME, not prepared for, unfitted, malevolently inclined, fr. 1*in-* + *disposed*] **1 :** being usu. temporarily in poor physical health; *esp* **:** somewhat unwell usu. temporarily ⟨refused to see him because, she said, she felt ~⟩ **2 :** not being in the proper disposition for something **:** AVERSE ⟨you know how ~ tenant farmers are to doing their share of work —Ellen Glasgow⟩ **3** *archaic* **:** having an unsympathetic or unfriendly or hostile attitude toward something **syn** see DISINCLINED

in·dis·posed·ness \ˌində̇'spōzə̇dnə̇s, -z(d)n-\ *n* -ES **:** INDISPOSITION

in·disposition \(ˌ)in, ən+\ *n* [ME *indisposicioun* unfitness, prob. fr. *indisposed* unfitted, after ME *disposed: disposicioun* disposition] **:** the condition of being indisposed: **a** (1) **:** DISINCLINATION ⟨a certain ~ to face reality⟩ (2) *archaic* **:** lack of sympathy **:** UNFRIENDLINESS, HOSTILITY **b :** a usu. temporary condition of poor health; *esp* **:** a usu. temporary condition of being somewhat unwell ⟨has fully recovered from her recent ~⟩

in·disputability \(ˌ)in, ən+\ *n* **:** the quality or state of being indisputable

in·disputable \(ˌ)in, ən+\ *adj* [LL *indisputabilis*, fr. L *in-* 1in- + *disputabilis* disputable] **1 :** that cannot be disputed or called into question **:** that is beyond argument **:** UNQUESTIONABLE, INCONTESTABLE, UNDENIABLE, INDUBITABLE ⟨gave ~ proof that he had been there⟩ ⟨these are facts that are clearly ~⟩ **2 :** truly existing **:** existing beyond the possibility of doubt or denial **:** REAL, ACTUAL ⟨the first ~ author I ever met —W.T.Scott⟩ ⟨secured against aggression by ~ law —Sir Winston Churchill⟩ — **in·disputableness** \"+\ *n* — **in·disputably** \"+\ *adv*

in·disputed \ˌin+\ *adj* [1*in-* + *disputed*, past part. of *dispute*] *archaic* **:** UNDISPUTED

in·dissociable \"+\ *adj* [1*in-* + *dissociable*] **:** that cannot be dissociated ⟨a problem that parallels the other one and is ~ from it⟩ — **in·dis·so·cia·bly** \-blē,-bli\ *adv*

in·dissolubility \(ˌ)in, ən+\ *n* **:** the quality or state of being indissoluble ⟨maintaining the ~ of marriage⟩

in·dissoluble \"+\ *adj* [1*in-* + *dissoluble*] **:** not dissoluble: as **a :** incapable of being annulled or undone or broken **:** perpetually binding or obligatory **:** perpetually lasting **:** PERMANENT ⟨an ~ contract⟩ ⟨bound by ~ vows⟩ **b** (1) **:** incapable of being dissolved into separate elements or particles **:** incapable of being decomposed or disintegrated ⟨a hard ~ mass of material⟩ (2) **:** incapable of being dissolved in a liquid **:** INSOLUBLE ⟨a substance that is ~ in water⟩ (3) *archaic* **:** incapable of being melted or liquefied **:** INFUSIBLE — **in·dis·sol·u·ble·ness** \-nə̇s\ *n* -ES — **in·dis·sol·u·bly** \-blē,-bli\ *adv*

in·dissolvable \ˌin+\ *adj* [1*in-* + *dissolvable*] *archaic* **:** INDISSOLUBLE

in·distinct \"+\ *adj* [L *indistinctus*, fr. *in-* 1in- + *distinctus* distinct] **1 :** not distinct: as **a :** not sharply outlined or separable **:** BLURRED, CONFUSED ⟨buildings that were ~ in the fog⟩ **b :** FAINT, DIM ⟨far away he saw the ~ light of a lantern⟩ **c :** not clearly perceived **:** not clearly recognizable or understandable **:** UNCERTAIN ⟨a peculiar ~ thumping sound⟩ ⟨could hear the ~ murmur of the crowd outside her window⟩ **2** *archaic* **:** UNDISCRIMINATING — **in·distinctly** \"+\ *adv* — **in·distinctness** \"+\ *n*

in·distinction \ˌin+\ *n* [1*in-* + *distinction*] **1** *archaic* **:** failure to make distinctions **2 :** absence of identifying or individualizing qualities **:** INDISTINGUISHABLENESS ⟨the leaves' shadows had a curious grayness and ~ —P.D.Boles⟩

in·distinctive \"+\ *adj* [1*in-* + *distinctive*] **1 :** UNDISCRIMINATING **2 :** marked by a lack of individualizing qualities ⟨an ~ group of weather-beaten shacks —Fred Beck⟩ — **in·distinctively** \"+\ *adv* — **in·distinctiveness** \"+\ *n*

in·distinguishability \ˌin+\ *n* **:** the quality or state of being indistinguishable

in·distinguishable \"+\ *adj* [1*in-* + *distinguishable*] **:** not distinguishable: as **a :** lacking clearly distinguishable parts or a clearly distinguishable outline **:** indeterminate in shape or structure ⟨an ~ mass of material⟩ ⟨~ forms seen in the mist⟩ **b :** not capable of being clearly perceived **:** not clearly recognizable or understandable **:** not discernible ⟨the two specimens are actually different from each other, but the differences are almost ~⟩ **c** (1) **:** not capable of being discriminated **:** lacking identifying or individualizing qualities ⟨a colorless person quite ~ from the colorless mass of humanity⟩ (2) **:** not capable of being analyzed into clearly separate and distinct parts ⟨an ~ blend of happiness and sorrow⟩ — **in·distinguishableness** \"+\ *n* — **in·distinguishably** \"+\ *adv*

in·distinguished \"+\ *adj* [1*in-* + *distinguished*] **:** UNDISTINGUISHED

in·distributable \"+\ *adj* [1*in-* + *distributable*] **:** not capable of being distributed

in·disturbance \"+\ *n* [1*in-* + *disturbance*] *archaic* **:** freedom from disturbance **:** TRANQUILLITY

1**in·dite** \ən'dīt, *usu* -īd·+V\ *vb* -ED/-ING/-S [ME *enditen*, fr. OF *enditer* to write down, compose, tell, make known, fr. (assumed) VL *indictare* to make known, proclaim, fr. L *indictus*, past part. of *indicere* to proclaim, fr. *in-* 2in- + *dicere* to say — more at DICTION] *vt* **1 a :** to make up or compose (as a poem or story) ⟨~ four lines of verse⟩ ⟨~ an epistle⟩ **b :** to give literary or formal expression to **c :** to put down in writing ⟨~ a message to a friend⟩ **2** *obs* **:** to dictate or prescribe esp. the exact verbal form for (something to be repeated or copied) **3** *obs* **:** INVITE ~ *vi* **:** COMPOSE, WRITE — **in·dit·er** \-īd·ə(r), -ītə-\ *n* -S

2**indite** \"\ *archaic var of* 1INDICT

in·dite·ment \-mənt\ *n* -s **:** the act of inditing or the process of being indited **:** COMPOSITION

in·di·um \'indēəm\ *n* -s [NL, fr. ISV 2*ind-* + NL *-ium;* fr. the two indigo-blue lines in its spectrum] **:** a soft malleable easily fusible silvery white metallic element that is resistant to tarnishing and resembles aluminum and gallium in being chiefly trivalent, that occurs in very small quantities in sphalerite and other ores, and that is used chiefly as a plating for lead-coated silver bearings for airplanes — symbol *In;* see ELEMENT table

in·divertible \ˌin+\ *adj* [1*in-* + *divert* + *-ible*] **:** not to be diverted or turned aside — **in·di·vert·ibly** \-blē,-bli\ *adv*

individable *adj* [1*in-* + *dividable*] *obs* **:** INDIVISIBLE

individua *pl of* INDIVIDUUM

1**in·di·vid·u·al** \ˌində'vij(ə)wəl, -jəl\ *adj* [ME *indyvyduall*, fr. ML *individualis* indivisible, individual, fr. L *individuus* indivisible (fr. *in-* 1in- + *dividuus* divided, divisible, fr. *dividere* to divide) + *-alis* -al — more at DIVIDE] **1** *obs* **a :** not divisible **:** of one essence or nature **b :** not to be parted **:** INSEPARABLE **2 a :** of, belonging to, arising from, or possessed or used by an individual ⟨~ traits⟩ ⟨~ possessions⟩ ⟨the secular, modern . . . belief in ~ human rights —A.J.Toynbee⟩ ⟨~ self-reliance⟩ ⟨no private adventures, no purely ~ experiences —J.W.Krutch⟩ **b :** being an individual **:** marked by a distinctness and a complexity within a unity that characterizes organized things, concepts, organic beings, and persons **c :** intended for one person ⟨served the pudding in ~ portions⟩ **:** designed to accommodate enough for one person ⟨a small ~ baking dish⟩ **:** applying to one person ⟨an ~ policy in life insurance⟩ **3 :** existing as a separate and distinct entity **:** SINGLE, SINGULAR, PARTICULAR ⟨dolls, with movable legs and arms, glass eyes, and ~ teeth —Green Peyton⟩ ⟨a bookseller . . . handling ~ copies of net books —James Britton⟩ ⟨consists of 96 island units (comprising some 2,141 ~ islands and coral atolls) —*Americana Annual*⟩ **4** *archaic* **:** SELFSAME, IDENTICAL **5 a :** having marked individuality **:** being peculiar, striking, or uncommon enough in character to be easily identified or distinguished ⟨an ~ style of writing⟩ ⟨the odor from the dump was so putrid in so ~ a way that it was quite impossible to describe —Jean Stafford⟩ **b :** serving to distinguish or identify **c :** DISTINCTIVE, PECULIAR ⟨a threshold of susceptibility which is ~ to each system —G.W.Gray b. 1886⟩ **syn** see CHARACTERISTIC, SPECIAL

2**individual** \"\ *n* -s **1 :** a single or particular being or thing or group of beings or things: as **a :** a particular being or thing as distinguished from a class, species, or collection ⟨the primary subject matter of literature is precisely all that science leaves out: the ~, the particular, the concrete —H.J.Muller⟩ (1) **:** a single human being as contrasted with a social group or institution ⟨the rights of the ~⟩ ⟨countries in distress, like ~*s* in ill health, are inclined to be quarrelsome —Samuel Van Valkenburg & Ellsworth Huntington⟩ (2) **:** a single organism as distinguished from a group **b :** a particular person ⟨a rather odd ~⟩ ⟨attempting to capture rather than kill their enemies, in order that the supply of ~*s* for human sacrifice might be augmented —R.W.Murray⟩ **c :** the product of a single fertilization — called also *genetic individual* **d :** all the vegetative progeny of an organism exhibiting alternation of generations — called also *genetic individual;* compare CLONE **e :** a single chemical substance — compare MIXTURE 2a **2 :** an indivisible entity or a totality which cannot be separated into parts without altering the character or significance of these parts **3** *archaic* **:** SELF, PERSONALITY **4** *logic* **a :** something that cannot have instances **:** PARTICULAR **b :** something referred to by a proper name; *specif* **:** something referred to by a name or variable of the lowest logical type in a formalized language or calculus **5 :** a tournament in contract bridge in which each player changes partners after each round so that one person rather than a pair or team may be determined as winner

individual bond *n* **:** a fidelity bond specifying a single person as principal — compare BLANKET BOND

in·di·vid·u·al·ism \ˌində'vij(ə)wəˌlizəm, -jəˌl-\ *n* -s [F *individualisme*, fr. ML *individualis* individual + F *-isme* -ism] **1 a** (1) **:** the ethical doctrine or principle that the interests of the individual himself are or ought to be paramount in determination of conduct **:** ethical egoism; *also* **:** conduct guided by the principle (2) **:** the conception that all values, rights, and duties originate in individuals and that the community or social whole has no value or ethical significance not derived from its constituent individuals **b** (1) **:** the doctrine which holds that the chief end of society is the promotion of individual welfare and the chief end of moral law is the development of individual character; *also* **:** conduct or practice guided by such a doctrine (2) **:** a theory or policy having primary regard for individual rights and esp. maintaining the political and economic independence of the individual or maintaining the independence of individual initiative, action, and interests (as in industrial organization or in government); *also* **:** conduct or practice guided by such a theory or policy — compare COLLECTIVISM, PATERNALISM, SOCIALISM **c :** any vigorous and independent striving toward an individual goal or any markedly independent assertion of individual opinions esp. without regard for others or in defiance of an institution or larger authority **2 a :** INDIVIDUALITY ⟨the ~ of the backwoodsman —Theodore Roosevelt⟩ **b :** an individual peculiarity **:** IDIOSYNCRASY **3 :** the philosophical doctrine that reality is constituted of individual entities (as the monads of Leibniz) **4 :** an association of two nutritionally interdependent organisms which produces a distinct individual unlike either of the components in form and conditions of life (as in lichens)

in·di·vid·u·al·ist \-ˌlə̇st\ *n* -s [F *individualiste*, fr. ML *individualis* + F *-iste* -ist] **1 :** one that pursues a markedly independent course in thought or action **:** one that speaks or acts with marked individuality ⟨he is apt to be an ~ who has never mastered the important arts of political cooperation and teamwork —R.E.Fitch⟩ ⟨an ~, independent to excess, in conflict with . . . society —H.S.Canby⟩ ⟨a race of ~*s* acknowledging no authority save that of their flintlocks —Deneys Reitz⟩ **2 :** one that advocates or practices individualism ⟨the ~ . . . was soon transformed into a collectivist —Alexander Brady⟩

in·di·vid·u·al·is·tic \ˌ==ˌ=(=)=ˈlistik, -tēk\ *or* **individualist** *adj* **:** of, belonging to, or being individualism or an individualist: as **a :** favoring or allowing individualism ⟨the ~ polity of churches congregationally organized enables any single company of Christians to call and to ordain their own minister —W.L.Sperry⟩ **b :** consisting of individualism ⟨Spinoza's ethics is ~ in the sense that its fundamental motive is the desire for individual perfection or happiness —Frank Thilly⟩ ⟨~ theory . . . that the state, being a necessary evil, should be strictly limited to the preservation of order and the protection of the rights of the individual —W.S.Sayre⟩ **c :** arising from individualism in theory or practice ⟨transferring the democratic tradition from ~ to collectivist economic foundations — Paul Woodring⟩ **d :** characterized by marked individuality ⟨erratic and strongly ~ personalities —*Book-of-the-Month Club News*⟩ ⟨peculiarly ~ interior paintings —*Time*⟩ — **in·di·vid·u·al·is·ti·cal·ly** \ˌ==ˌ=(=)=ˈlistə̇k(ə)lē, -tēk-, -li\ *adv*

in·di·vid·u·al·i·ty \ˌ==ˌvijə'waləd·ē, -lətē, -i\ *n* -ES **1 a :** the total character peculiar to and distinguishing an individual from others **:** the complex of characteristics serving to individualize or set off a person or a thing from others **:** distinctive character ⟨believed that one was born with a particular biochemical ~ just as one was born with a certain physical and psychological personality —*Lancet*⟩ ⟨only slowly does the child become aware of his ~⟩; *esp* **:** a markedly individual or distinctive quality ⟨though he had no great . . . originality, there was a delicate ~ in his gracious and homely pictures —Havelock Ellis⟩ **b :** an individual or individualizing quality ⟨managed to give the borrowed product a distinctive national ~ —A.L.Kroeber⟩ ⟨white wines, which have considerable ~ —*N.Y. Times*⟩ ⟨they were strikingly alike in gifts and tastes, but each had marked ~ of character —H.E.Starr⟩ ⟨the ~ or, better, the personality of each instrument of the orchestra —Nicolas Nabokov⟩ **c :** PERSONALITY ⟨quietened her by sheer force of ~ —Arnold Bennett⟩ ⟨not only is the author unknown, but in the pure ballad there is no trace of his ~ —*Encyc. Americana*⟩ **2** *archaic* **:** INDIVISIBILITY, INSEPARABILITY **3 a :** an individual characteristic ⟨the effort . . . of getting the *individualities* of a fresh group of people into one's head, is becoming every year harder for me —A.C.Benson⟩ **b :** an individual thing; *esp* **:** an individual person **4 :** the quality or state of existing as an individual or of constituting an individual **:** separate or distinct existence ⟨the great artist can transcend his own ~ —Harold Nicolson⟩ **5 :** the tendency to pursue one's course with marked independence or self-reliance **:** INDIVIDUALISM ⟨distinguished by a strong streak of ~ and independence, the counterpart probably of the same pioneer spirit which originally marked the commerce and industry of the New World —W.T. & Barbara Fitts⟩ **syn** see DISPOSITION

in·di·vid·u·al·iza·tion \-ˌvij(ə)wələ̇'zāshən, -jəl-, -ˌlī'z-\ *n* -s **1 :** the act of individualizing or the state of being individualized **2 :** a program of correctional or penal treatment for a delinquent or adult offender which is coordinated with expert information regarding his personal history and rehabilitative needs

in·di·vid·u·al·ize \-'vij(ə)wəˌlīz, -jəˌl-\ *vt* -ED/-ING/-S [1*individual* + *-ize*] **1 a :** to make individual in character **:** invest with individuality ⟨the trace of huskiness in her voice . . . proved to be an asset, helping to ~ her screen personality —*Current Biog.*⟩ ⟨the city is further *individualized* by the many university buildings —*Amer. Guide Series: Mich.*⟩ ⟨the population . . . inevitably becomes depersonalized on the one hand, *individualized* on the other —A.L.Kroeber⟩ **b :** to treat or notice individually **:** PARTICULARIZE, SPECIFY **c :** DISTINGUISH ⟨the sounds were *individualized* by sharpness of tone, incisiveness of utterance —William Beebe⟩ **2 :** to put into the hands or management of an individual ⟨more and more of our savings are institutionalized rather than *individualized* —R.R.Nathan⟩ **3 :** to adjust or adapt (as a treatment or justice) to the needs or the special circumstances of an individual — **in·di·vid·u·al·iz·er** \-īzə(r)\ *n* -s

individual key *n* **:** CHANGE KEY

individual liberty *n* **:** the liberty of those persons who are free from external restraint in the exercise of those rights which are considered to be outside the province of a government to control — compare CIVIL LIBERTY, POLITICAL LIBERTY

in·di·vid·u·al·ly \-'vijəlē, -j(ə)wəlē, -li\ *adv* **:** in an individual manner; as **a** *obs* **:** INDIVISIBLY, INSEPARABLY **b** *obs* **:** in respect to individual identity **c :** one by one, SINGLY, SEPARATELY ⟨the students went in ~ to consult about their programs⟩ ⟨~ constructed houses⟩ **d :** with markedly individual qualities or characteristics ⟨each of the artists paints ~⟩ **e :** as an individual **:** PERSONALLY ⟨whatever action the state takes will affect me ~⟩

individual medley *n* **:** a swimming race in which each competitor swims one third of the total course with the backstroke, one third with the breaststroke, and one third freestyle

individual psychology *n* [trans. of G *individualpsychologie*] **:** a modification of psychoanalysis developed by the Austrian psychologist Alfred Adler emphasizing feelings of inferiority and a will to power as the primary motivating forces in human behavior

individual variable *n, logic* **:** a variable which may be replaced by a name or a description of an individual

[1]**in·di·vid·u·ate** \ˌində'vij(ə)wə̇\|t, -jəˌwā\|, *usu* \|d·+V\ *adj* [ML *individuatus*, past part. of *individuare* to individuate] **1 :** UNDIVIDED, INSEPARABLE **2** *obs* **:** INDIVIDUALIZED

[2]**in·di·vid·u·ate** \-jəˌwāt, *usu* -ād·+V\ *vt* -ED/-ING/-S [ML *individuatus*, past part. of *individuare*, fr. L *individuus* indivisible — more at INDIVIDUAL] **1 :** to give individuality to **:** distinguish from others of the same species ⟨the characters that . . . ~ him from all other writers —George Saintsbury⟩ **2 :** to form into a distinct entity **:** give individual form to ⟨symbolism of language which ~*s* a man's private memories —D.G.Mitchell⟩

in·di·vid·u·a·tion \-ˌvijə'wāshən\ *n* -S [ML *individuation-*, *individuatio*, fr. *individuatus* (past part. of *individuare*) + L *-ion-*, *-io* -ion] **:** the act or process of individuating or the state of being individuated: as **a** (1) **:** the development of the individual from the universal or the determination of the individual in the general ⟨in scholastic philosophy the principle of ~ was variously held to be matter, form, and particularity of the subject in time and space⟩ (2) **:** the process by which individuals in society become differentiated from one another, come to occupy different statuses and roles, and tend to lose group or class identity (3) **:** regional differentiation along a primary embryonic axis **:** field formation — contrasted with *evocation;* compare INDUCTOR **b :** existence as a person or individual **:** INDIVIDUALITY

individuity *n* -ES [LL *individuitat-*, *individuitas*, fr. L *individuus* indivisible + *-itat-*, *-itas* -ity] **1** *obs* **:** INDIVISIBILITY **2** [ML *individuitat-*, *individuitas*, fr. LL, indivisibility] *obs* **:** INDIVIDUALITY

in·di·vid·u·um \ˌində'vijəwəm\ *n, pl* **individ·ua** \-wə\ *or* **individuums** [LL, fr. L, indivisible entity, atom, fr. neut. of *individuus* indivisible] **1 :** an individual instance or an individual being as distinguished from a group of similar instances or beings **2** [L] **:** an indivisible entity; *specif* **:** ATOM 1a

in·divisibility \¦in+\ *n* **:** the quality or state of being indivisible

[1]**in·divisible** \"+\ *adj* [ME *indyvysible*, fr. LL *indivisibilis*, fr. L *in-* [1]in- + LL *divisibilis* divisible] **:** not divisible **:** not separable into parts ⟨the ~ responsibility of school and college in matters of general education —A.W.Griswold⟩ ⟨one nation, ~ —Francis Bellamy⟩ ⟨reality is one and ~ —C.D.Lewis⟩ — **in·divisibleness** \"+\ *n* — **in·di·vis·i·bly** \-blē,-bli\ *adv*

[2]**indivisible** \¦in+\ *n* -S **:** something indivisible; *specif* **:** a mathematical quantity that is assumed to admit of no further division

in·division \"+\ *n* [ML *indivision-*, *indivisio*, fr. L *in-* [1]in- + *division-*, *divisio-* division] **:** the state of being undivided **:** ONENESS

indm *abbr* indemnity

in·do \'in(ˌ)dō\ *n* -S *usu cap* [D, short for *Indo-Europeaan*, fr. *ind-* [1]ind- + *Europeaan* European, fr. L *europaeus* European (adj.) + D *-aan* -an (n. suffix) — more at EUROPEAN] **:** a native or inhabitant of Indonesia who has a Western education and is of mixed European usu. Dutch and Indonesian descent

indo- — see IND-

in·do-african \¦in(ˌ)dō+\ *adj, usu cap I&A* **:** of, relating to, or constituting a terrestrial biogeographic realm that includes intertropical Asia and intertropical Africa

[1]**indo-aryan** \"+\ *adj, usu cap I&A* **1 :** of, relating to, or characteristic of Indo-Aryans **2 :** of, relating to, or characteristic of one of the Aryan languages of India

[2]**indo-aryan** \"\ *n, cap I&A* **1 :** a member of one of the peoples of India of Aryan speech and physique characterized by tall stature, dolichocephaly, fair complexion with dark hair and eyes, plentiful beard, and narrow and prominent nose — compare INDIAN 1a **2 :** one of the early Indo-European invaders of Persia, Afghanistan, and India **3 :** the Indo-European languages of India and Pakistan as a group

in·do-briton \¦in(ˌ)dō+\ *n, cap I&B* **:** a person born in India of mixed Indian and British descent

indo-burmese \"+\ *adj, usu cap I&B* **:** BURMO-CHINESE

[1]**in·do-chinese** \"+\ *adj, usu cap I&C* [*Indochina*, region in southeastern Asia + E *-ese*] **1 a :** of, relating to, or characteristic of Indochina — usu. used of the countries Cambodia, Laos, and Vietnam comprised in the former French Indochina but sometimes of the region comprising all the countries of southeastern Asia: Burma, Malaya, Thailand, Cambodia, Laos, and Vietnam **b :** of, relating to, or characteristic of the Indo-Chinese esp. of Cambodia, Laos, and Vietnam **2** [[1]*ind-* + *chinese*] **:** of, relating to, characteristic of, or constituting the Tibeto-Burman, Thai, Chinese, and various neighboring languages **3** [[1]*ind-* + *chinese*] **:** BURMO-CHINESE

[2]**indo-chinese** \"\ *n, cap I&C* **1 :** a native or inhabitant of Indochina — usu. used of the people of the countries Cambodia, Laos, and Vietnam comprised in the former French Indochina but sometimes of the peoples of southeastern Asia including also those of Burma, Malaya, and Thailand **2 :** an assumed family of languages comprehending Tibeto-Burman, Thai, Chinese, and various neighboring groups

indocibility *n* **:** the quality or state of being indocible

indocible *adj* [LL *indocibilis*, fr. L *in-* [1]in- + LL *docibilis* docible] **:** UNTEACHABLE

in·docile \(')in, ən+\ *adj* [MF, fr. L *indocilis*, fr. *in-* [1]in- + *docilis* docile] **:** unwilling or indisposed to be taught, trained, or disciplined **:** not easily instructed or controlled **:** UNRULY ⟨a large, ~, irresponsible, domineering man —G.P.Elliott⟩

in·docility \¦in+\ *n* [*indocile* + *-ity*] **:** the quality or state of being indocile **:** UNTEACHABLENESS, INTRACTABLENESS

in·doc·tri·nate \ə̇n'däktrə̇ˌnāt, *usu* -ād·+V\ *vt* -ED/-ING/-S [prob. fr. *indoctrine* + *-ate*, v. suffix] **1 a :** to give instructions esp. in fundamentals or rudiments **:** TEACH ⟨the function of *indoctrinating* youth was given to and accepted by . . . the family and the priesthood —L.O.Garber & W.B.Castetter⟩ ⟨the recruits were *indoctrinated* for a month and then sent to specialist schools⟩ **b :** to imbue or make markedly familiar (as with a skill) ⟨*indoctrinated* themselves with the teamwork of attack —Ira Wolfert⟩ **2 :** to cause to be impressed and usu. ultimately imbued (as with a usu. partisan or sectarian opinion, point of view, or principle) ⟨had to be *indoctrinated* with the will to win —J.P.Baxter b.1893⟩ ⟨*indoctrinating* young people with alien ideologies⟩ **:** cause to be drilled or otherwise trained (as in a sectarian doctrine) and usu. persuaded ⟨~ the immigrants in a new way of life⟩ — **in·doc·tri·na·tor** \-ād·ə(r), -ātə-\ *n* -S

in·doc·tri·na·tion \(ˌ)inˌdäktrə̇'nāshən, ənˌd-\ *n* -S [*indoctrinate* + *-ion*] **1 :** the act or process of indoctrinating or the state of being indoctrinated ⟨the proper and adequate ~ of a newly received prisoner is one of the most important points of the rehabilitation program —W.H.Maglin⟩ ⟨evidence of attempts at subversive ~ or disloyal teaching —B.F.Wright⟩ ⟨~ can be smuggled in . . . in the name of democratic education —F.C.Neft⟩ **2 :** something with or in which one is indoctrinated ⟨freedom of minds, the maxims of logic and experimental proof, of intellectual honesty, of tolerance and persuasion . . . constitute a body of ~ to which no objection can consistently be raised —R.B.Perry⟩ — **in·doc·tri·na·tion·al** \(¦)=¦==¦nāshənᵊl, -shnəl\ *adj*

indoctrine *vt* -ED/-ING/-S [alter. (influenced by E [2]*in-*) of ME *endoctrinen*, fr. MF *endoctriner*, fr. OF, fr. *en-* [1]en- + *doctrine* (n.)] *archaic* **:** INDOCTRINATE

in·doc·tri·ni·za·tion \ə̇nˌdäktrənə̇'zāshən, -ˌnī'z-\ *n* -S **:** INDOCTRINATION

in·doc·tri·nize \ə̇n'däktrə̇ˌnīz\ *vt* -ED/-ING/-S [*indoctrinate* + *-ize*] **:** INDOCTRINATE

[1]**in·do-dravidian** \¦in(ˌ)dō+\ *adj, usu cap I&D* **:** of, relating to, or characteristic of Indo-Dravidians

[2]**indo-dravidian** \"\ *n, cap I&D* **:** a member of a composite people resulting from intermixture between the native Dravidians of India and the Aryan invaders but having some elements of the Munda-speaking racial group

[1]**indo-european** \¦in(ˌ)dō+\ *adj, usu cap I&E* [Gk *ind-*, *indo-* India, of or connected with India + E *european* — more at IND-] **:** of, relating to, characteristic of, or constituting the Indo-European languages

[2]**indo-european** \"\ *n, cap I&E* **1 a :** the Indo-European languages **b :** the unrecorded prehistoric language from which the Indo-European languages are descended **2 a :** a speaker of Indo-European (sense 1b) **b :** a member of a people whose original tongue is one of the Indo-European languages **3 :** one who is a native or inhabitant of a country of southeastern Asia and esp. Indochina and who is of European or part-European origin or descent **:** EURASIAN

indo-euro·pe·an·ist \¦=(ˌ)=ˌ=='==əst\ *n* -S *cap I&E* **:** a specialist in Indo-European linguistics

indo-european languages *n pl, usu cap I&E* **:** a family of languages comprising those spoken in most of Europe and in the parts of the world colonized by Europeans since 1500 and also in Persia, the subcontinent of India, and some other parts of Asia

INDO-EUROPEAN LANGUAGES

BRANCH	GROUP	LANGUAGES AND MAJOR DIALECTS[1]			PROVENIENCE
		ANCIENT	MEDIEVAL	MODERN	
GERMANIC	East		*Gothic*		eastern Europe
	North		*Old Norse*	Icelandic Faeroese Norwegian Swedish Danish	Iceland Faeroe islands Norway Sweden Denmark
	West		*Old High German* *Middle High German*	German	Germany, Switzerland, Austria
				Yiddish	Germany, eastern Europe
			Old Saxon *Middle Low German*		Northern Germany
			Middle Dutch	Dutch Afrikaans	Netherlands So. Africa
			Middle Flemish *Old Frisian*	Flemish Frisian	Belgium Netherlands, Germany
			Old English *Middle English*	English	England
CELTIC	Continental	*Gaulish*			Gaul
	Brythonic		*Old Welsh* *Middle Welsh*	Welsh	Wales
			Old Cornish *Middle Breton*	*Cornish* Breton	Cornwall Brittany
	Goidelic		*Old Irish* *Middle Irish*	Irish Gaelic	Ireland
				Scottish Gaelic *Manx*	Scotland Isle of Man
ITALIC	Osco-Umbrian	*Oscan* *Umbrian* *Sabellian*			ancient Italy
	Latinian or Romance[2]	*Venetic* *Lanuvian* *Faliscan* *Praenestine* Latin			ancient Italy
				Portuguese Spanish Judeo-Spanish	Portugal Spain Mediterranean lands
			Old Provençal *Old French* *Middle French*	Catalan Provençal French	Spain (Catalonia) southern France France, Belgium, Switzerland
				Haitian Creole Italian Rhaeto-Romanic Sardinian *Dalmatian* Romanian	Haiti Italy, Switzerland Switzerland, Italy Sardinia Adriatic coast Romania, Balkans
Poorly preserved and of uncertain affinities within Indo-European, "Thraco-Phrygian", "Illyrian", etc.		*Ligurian* *Messapian* *Illyrian* *Thracian* *Phrygian*			ancient Italy ancient Italy Balkans Balkans Asia Minor
Albanian				Albanian	Albania, southern Italy
Greek		Greek ("Ancient Greek")	Greek ("Byzantine Greek", "Middle Greek")	Greek ("Modern Greek", "New Greek")	Greece, the eastern Mediterranean
Baltic			*Old Prussian*	Lithuanian Latvian	East Prussia Lithuania Latvia
SLAVIC	South		Old Church Slavonic	Slovene Serbo-Croatian (Serbian, Croatian) Macedonian Bulgarian	Yugoslavia Yugoslavia Macedonia Bulgaria
	West		*Old Czech*	Czech Slovak Polish Kashubian Wendish *Polabian*	Czechoslovakia Czechoslovakia Poland Poland Germany Germany
	East		*Old Russian*	Russian Ukrainian Belorussian	Russia Ukraine White Russia
Armenian			Armenian ("Old Armenian")	Armenian ("Modern Armenian")	Asia Minor, Caucasus
IRANIAN	West	*Old Persian*			ancient Persia
			Pahlavi Persian ("Classical Persian")	Persian ("Modern Persian")	Persia (Iran)
				Kurdish Baluchi Tajiki	Persia, Iraq, Turkey West Pakistan central Asia
	East	Avestan			ancient Persia
			Sogdian *Khotanese*		central Asia central Asia
				Pashto	Afghanistan, West Pakistan
				Ossetic	Caucasus
INDIC	Dard			Shina Khowar Kafiri Kashmiri	upper Indus valley Kashmir
	Sanskritic	Sanskrit Pali *Prakrits*	*Prakrits*		India
				Lahnda Sindhi Panjabi Rajasthani Gujarati Marathi Konkani Oriya Bengali Assamese Bihari Hindi Urdu Nepali Sinhalese Romany	western Punjab Sind Panjab Rajasthan Gujarat western India western India Orissa Bengal Assam Bihar northern India Pakistan, India Nepal Ceylon uncertain
Tocharian			*Tocharian A* *Tocharian B*		central Asia
The following is sometimes considered as another branch of Indo-European, and sometimes as coordinate with Indo-European, the two together constituting Indo-Hittite					
Anatolian		*Hittite* *Luwian* *Palaic* *Hieroglyphic Hittite* *Lydian* *Lycian*			ancient Asia Minor

[1]Italics denote dead languages. Listing of a language only in the ancient or medieval column but in roman type indicates that it survives only in some special use, as in literary composition or liturgy

[2]Romance is normally applied only to medieval and modern languages; Latinian is normally applied only to ancient languages

in·do·gae·an *or* **in·do·ge·an** \ˌindōˈjēən\ *adj, usu cap* [NL *Indogaea*, Oriental biogeographic realm or region (fr. ¹*ind-* + *-gaea*) + E *-an*] : ORIENTAL

indo–gangetic \ˌin(ˌ)dō+\ *adj, usu cap I&G* : of or relating to the area drained by the Indus and Ganges rivers esp. the lowland plain south of the Himalayas

in·dogen·ide \ˈindəjəˌnīd; ənˈdäjəˌn-, -ˌnəd\ *n* -s [ISV *indogen* bivalent nitrogen-containing radical C_8H_5NO (ISV ²*ind-* + *-gen*) + *-ide*] : a compound that is an alkylidene substitution product of indoxyl formed by reaction of indoxyl with an aldehyde or ketone

¹**in·do–germanic** \ˌin(ˌ)dō+\ *adj, usu cap I&G* [trans. of G *indogermanisch*] : INDO-EUROPEAN

²**indo–germanic** \"\ *n, cap I&G* : INDO-EUROPEAN 1

in·do–hittite \ˌin(ˌ)dō+\ *n, cap I&H, often attrib* [¹*ind-* + *hittite*] **1** : a language family comprehending Indo-European and Anatolian — see INDO-EUROPEAN LANGUAGES table **2 a** : a hypothetical parent language of Indo-European and Anatolian

¹**indo–iranian** \"+\ *adj, usu cap both Is* : of, relating to, characteristic of, or constituting a subfamily of the Indo-European languages that consists of the Indic and the Iranian branches

²**indo–iranian** \"\ *n, cap both Is* **1 a** : the Indo-Iranian languages **b** : the unrecorded prehistoric language from which the Indo-Iranian languages are descended **2 a** : a speaker of Indo-Iranian (sense 1b) **b** : a member of a people whose original tongue is one of the Indo-Iranian languages

indol- *or* **indolo-** *comb form* [ISV, fr. *indole*] **1** : indole ⟨*in-doloid*⟩ **2** : containing an indole ring fused on one side to one side of another ring ⟨*indolo*quinoline⟩

in·dole \ˈinˌdōl\ *n* -s [ISV ²*ind-* + *-ole*; orig. formed as G *indol*] **1** : a crystalline compound C_8H_7N that is found esp. in jasmine oil, civet, and coal tar and along with skatole in the intestines and feces as a decomposition product of proteins containing tryptophan, that may be formed by reductive distillation of indigo with zinc, and that in spite of its unpleasant odor when concentrated is used as a trace component of floral perfumes (as jasmine, gardenia, or lilac) — compare STRUCTURAL FORMULA **2** : a derivative of indole

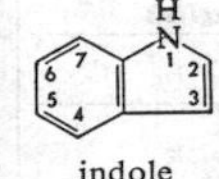

indole

indoleacetic acid \ˌ=ˌ==ˈ==-\ *n* [*indoleacetic* fr. *indole* + *acetic*] : a crystalline plant hormone $(C_8H_6N)CH_2COOH$ present in urine, made synthetically, and used to promote growth and rooting of plants — called also *beta-indolylacetic acid, 3-indoleacetic acid, heteroauxin*; see AUXIN

indolebutyric acid \ˌ=ˌ==ˈ==-\ *n* [*indolebutyric* fr. *indole* + *butyric*] : a crystalline acid $(C_8H_6N)CH_2CH_2CH_2COOH$ similar to indoleacetic acid in its effects on plants

in·do·lence \ˈindələn(t)s\ *n* -s [F, fr. L *indolentia* freedom from pain, fr. *in-* ¹in- + *dolentia* pain, fr. *dolent-, dolens* (pres. part. of *dolēre* to feel pain, grieve) + *-ia* -y — more at CONDOLE] **1** *or* **indolency** -ES *obs* **a** : insensibility or indifference to pain **b** : freedom from pain or a tranquillity of mind marked by neither pain nor pleasure : apathetic ease **2** *med* **a** : a condition of causing little or no pain ⟨deceptive ~ of the tumor⟩ **b** : a condition of growing or progressing slowly **c** : slowness in healing **3** : laziness or inactivity arising from a love of ease or aversion to work : indisposition to labor : SLOTH ⟨the hot moist air of the tropics spreads a feeling of lethargy and ~ over everything that moves —G.H.Reed b.1887⟩ ⟨~, tardiness or even downright opposition to improvements —*Farmer's Weekly (So. Africa)*⟩ ⟨literary ~, mere unwillingness to take the necessary pains —Brand Blanshard⟩

¹**in·do·lent** \-nt\ *adj* [LL *indolent-, indolens* insensitive to pain, fr. L *in-* ¹in- + *dolent-, dolens* (pres. part. of *dolēre*)] **1** *med* **a** : causing little or no pain ⟨an ~ tumor⟩ **b** (1) : growing or progressing slowly ⟨leprosy is an ~ infectious disease⟩ (2) : slow to heal ⟨an ~ ulcer⟩ **2 a** : constantly indulging in ease : chronically averse to labor and exertion ⟨a goad for an ~ writer —Van Wyck Brooks⟩ ⟨old and fat and ~ —A.E.Stevenson †1965⟩ **b** : conducing to or encouraging laziness or avoidance of exertion ⟨the ~ heat of the afternoon⟩ **c** : giving evidence of or exhibiting indolence ⟨an ~ sigh —Willard Robertson⟩ ⟨an ~ amiability⟩ **syn** see LAZY

²**indolent** \"\ *n* -s : one that is indolent ⟨thousands of scoundrelly ~s lived there despising any honest toil —P.I.Wellman⟩

in·do·lent·ly *adv* : in an indolent manner

in·do·line \ˈindəˌlēn, -lən\ *n* -s [ISV *indol-* + *-ine*; prob. orig. formed as G *indolin*] : a liquid base C_8H_9N that is a stronger base than indole and is obtained from indole by reduction; 2,3-dihydro-indole

in·do·log·i·cal \ˌindəˈläjəkəl\ *adj, often cap* : of or relating to Indology

in·dol·o·gist \ənˈdäləjəst\ *n* -s *often cap* : a specialist in Indology

in·dol·o·gy \-jē\ *n* -ES *usu cap* [¹*ind-* + *-logy*] : the study of India and its people (as through its languages, literature, history, philosophy, customs, antiquities)

in·do·lyl \ˈindəˌlil, -lēl\ *n* -s [ISV *indol-* + *-yl*] : the univalent radical C_8H_6N derived from indole by removal of one hydrogen atom

indolylacetic acid \ˌ=ˌ==ˈ==-\ *n* [*indolylacetic* fr. *indolyl* + *acetic*] : INDOLEACETIC ACID

in·do–malay \ˌin(ˌ)dō+\ *adj, usu cap I&M* : INDO-MALAYAN 1

¹**indo–malayan** \"+\ *adj, usu cap I&M* **1** : of or relating to the insular and mainland areas of southeastern Asia **2** : of or relating to the Malayan biogeographic subdivision : MALAYAN

²**indo–malayan** \"\ *n, cap I&M* : a member of one of the major ethnic groups that embrace the inhabitants of mainland and insular southeastern Asia including the island chains from Indonesia through the Ryukyus

in·dom·i·ta·bil·i·ty \(ˌ)inˌdämədəˈbilədē, ən-, -mətə-, -lətē, -i\ *n* -ES : the quality or state of being indomitable

in·dom·i·ta·ble \ənˈdämədəbəl, -mətə-\ *adj* [LL *indomitabilis*, fr. L *in-* ¹in- + *domitare* to tame + *-abilis* -able — more at DAUNT] : incapable of being subdued : INTRACTABLE ⟨~ courage⟩ ⟨an ~ will⟩ — **in·dom·i·ta·ble·ness** \-nəs\ *n* -ES — **in·dom·i·ta·bly** \-blē,-bli\ *adv*

in·do·ne·sia \ˌindəˈnēzhə *also* -ēsh| *or* -ēzē|\ *adj, usu cap* [fr. *Indonesia*, country (also called the Republic of Indonesia) and archipelago (also called the Malay Archipelago or Malaysia) off the southeast coast of Asia] : of or from Indonesia : of the kind or style prevalent in Indonesia : INDONESIAN

¹**in·do·ne·sian** \|ən\ *n* -s *cap* [*Indonesia* + E *-an* (n. suffix)] **1** : MALAYSIAN 1 **2** : PROTO-MALAY **3 a** : a native or inhabitant of the Republic of Indonesia **b** : the language based on Malay that is the national language of the Republic of Indonesia

²**indonesian** \"\ *adj, usu cap* [*Indonesia* + E *-an* (adj. suffix)] **1** : of or relating to the Republic of Indonesia, the Malay archipelago, or Indonesians **2** : of, relating to, or constituting the subfamily of Austronesian languages spoken chiefly in the Malay peninsula and archipelago

in·door \ˈin,=, ənˈ=\ *adj* [alter. (influenced by E ¹*in*) of obs. E *within-door*, adj., fr. the phrase *within door* in a building] : of or relating to the interior of a building ⟨an ~ scene⟩ ⟨an ~ swimming pool⟩: as **a** : of or relating to something done inside a building ⟨an ~ sport⟩ **b** : designed for use indoors ⟨an ~ dress⟩ **c** : living inside an institution ⟨~ paupers⟩ : given within an institution ⟨~ relief⟩ **d** : inclined to stay indoors ⟨Americans have become an ~ people —J.M.Fitch⟩

indoor baseball *n* : softball played indoors

in·doors \(ˈ)inˈ=, ənˈ=\ *adv* [alter. (influenced by E ¹*in*) of *withindoors*] **1** : in a building ⟨worked ~ all afternoon⟩ ⟨stayed ~ during the storm⟩ **2** : into a building ⟨went ~ as soon as it began to rain⟩

in·do–pacific \ˌin(ˌ)dō+\ *adj, usu cap I&P* : of or relating to the Indo-Malayan areas of the Pacific ocean ⟨an *Indo-Pacific* fish⟩ ⟨*Indo-Pacific* coral reefs⟩

in·do·phe·nin \ˌindəˈfēnən, ənˈdäfənən\ *n* [ISV ²*ind-* + *phene* + *-in*; fr. a belief that it was a derivative of benzene; orig. formed in G] : a blue crystalline compound $C_{24}H_{14}N_2O_2S_2$ formed by reaction of thiophene with isatin and sulfuric acid and used as a color test for the presence of thiophene in technical benzene

in·do·phenol \ˌindō+\ *n* [ISV ²*ind-* + *phenol*; prob. orig. formed in G] : any of a class of blue or green dyes derived from quinone imines and used chiefly as intermediates for sulfur dyes and as dyes formed in color photography; *esp* : the simplest phenol $HOC_6H_4N{=}C_6H_4{=}O$

in·do·planorbis \ˌin(ˌ)dō+\ *n, cap* [NL, fr. ¹*ind-* + *Planorbis*] : an Asiatic genus of freshwater snails (family Planorbidae) of veterinary importance as an intermediate host of the bovine blood fluke and other trematode worms

in·dore \(ˈ)inˈdō(ə)r, ənˈd-\ *adj, usu cap* [fr. *Indore*, city in central India] : of or from the city of Indore, India : of the kind or style prevalent in Indore

in·do red MV-6632 \ˈin(ˌ)dō-\ *n, usu cap I&R* [perh. fr. ²*ind-*] : an organic pigment — see DYE table I (under *Pigment Red 87*)

indorse *var of* ENDORSE

indos *pl of* INDO

indow *obs var of* ENDOW

in·dox·yl \ənˈdäksəl, ˈinˌd-\ *n* -s [ISV ²*ind-* + hyd*roxyl*; prob. orig. formed in G] : a yellow crystalline phenolic compound $(C_8H_6N)OH$ that has a strong fecal odor, that occurs combined in plants and animals but is usu. made from phenylglycine by heating with sodamide, and that on oxidation yields indigo; 3-hydroxy-indole — see INDICAN

in·draft \ˈin,=\ *n* [⁴*in* + *draft*] **1** *obs* : an opening into land from the sea : INLET **2 a** : a drawing or pulling in : an inward attraction **b** : an inward flow or current (as of air or water)

in·drape \ənˈ=\ *vt* [²*in-* + *drape*] *archaic* : to make into cloth : WEAVE

¹**indrawing** \ˈ=ˌ==\ *n* [ME *indrawinge*, fr. *in* + *drawinge*, gerund of *drawen* to draw (after ME *drawen in*, v., to draw in)] : the act of drawing in or inward

²**indrawing** \"\ *adj* [²*in* + *drawing*, pres. part. of *draw* (after *draw in*, v.)] : drawing in or inward

indrawn \ˈ=ˌ=\ *adj* [²*in* + *drawn*, past part. of *draw* (after *draw in*, v.)] **1** : drawn in ⟨an ~ breath⟩ **2** : tending to reserve, taciturnity, or egocentricity ⟨an aloof, aristocratic, ~ man —W.S.White⟩ ⟨seen as selfish, ~ —*Times Lit. Supp.*⟩

indre *abbr* indenture

indrench *vt* [²*in-* + *drench*] *obs* : DRENCH, DROWN

in·dri \ˈindrē\ *n* [F, fr. Malagasy *indry* look!; prob. fr. an erroneous belief by the French naturalist Pierre Sonnerat (†1814), who observed the animal in its native habitat about 1780, that the natives were uttering its name when in fact they were only calling attention to its presence] **1** *cap* : a genus of lemurs that is the type of the family Indridae **2** : the largest of the lemurs of Madagascar (*Indri brevicaudatus*) about two feet long with a rudimentary tail and brightly marked in black and white

¹**in·drid** \-drəd\ *adj* [NL *Indridae*] : of or relating to the indris

²**indrid** \"\ *n* -s [NL *Indridae*] : INDRI

in·dri·dae \-drəˌdē\ *n pl, cap* [NL, fr. *Indri*, type genus + *-idae*] : a family of lemurs comprising the indri, avahi, sifaka, and various related extinct forms

¹**in·dris** \ˈindrəs\ *syn of* INDRI

²**indris** \"\ *n* -ES : INDRI 2

indsl *abbr* industrial

in·dubious \(ˈ)in, ən+\ *adj* [perh. fr. L *indubius*, fr. *in-* ¹in- + *dubius* dubious] *archaic* : INDUBITABLE, CERTAIN

in·du·bi·ta·bil·i·ty \(ˌ)inˌd(y)übədəˈbilədē, ən-, -bətə-, -lətē, -i\ *n* -ES : the quality or state of being unquestionable : CERTAINTY ⟨the English empiricists tended to lean on the ~ of the facts given —S.C.Pepper⟩

¹**in·du·bi·ta·ble** \ˌ=ˈ=ˌ==bəl\ *adj* [F or L; F, fr. L *indubitabilis*, fr. *in-* ¹in- + *dubitabilis* dubitable] : not dubitable : not open to question or doubt : too evident to be doubted : UNQUESTIONABLE ⟨there is a core of ~ knowledge in education, but most of the teacher's task consists in imparting methods for understanding what is still unknown —Zechariah Chafee⟩ — **in·du·bi·ta·ble·ness** *n* -ES

²**indubitable** \"\ *n* -s : something that is indubitable

in·du·bi·ta·bly \-blē,-bli\ *adv* : without any doubt : UNQUESTIONABLY ⟨it is ~ true that the civilization of the West . . . has been evolving for centuries —G.C.Sellery⟩

in·duce \ənˈd(y)üs\ *vt* -ED/-ING/-S [ME *enducen, inducen*, fr. L *inducere*, fr. *in-* ²in- + *ducere* to lead — more at TOW] **1 a** : to move and lead (as by persuasion or influence) ⟨powers of persuasion that would have *induced* the atheist to religion⟩ : prevail upon : INFLUENCE, PERSUADE ⟨was unable to ~ his customers to try the product⟩ ⟨condition which had *induced* many persons to emigrate from the old country —John Dewey⟩ **b** : to inspire, call forth, or bring about by influence or stimulation ⟨the gift had been solicited or *induced* by the plaintiff —R.N.Wilkin⟩ ⟨the menace of *induced* immigration —H.M.Diamond⟩ **2** *archaic* **a** : to bring in (as a practice, condition, custom) : INTRODUCE **b** : ADDUCE **3 a** : to bring on or bring about : EFFECT, CAUSE ⟨anesthesia *induced* by drugs⟩ ⟨prices that will cover the costs and ~ the production —*Defense Against Recession*⟩ ⟨an antivitamin . . . was shown to ~ gross malformation in the young —*Americana Annual*⟩ ⟨believed the Christianity . . . *induced* kindliness in men —H.J.Laski⟩: as (1) *embryol* : to cause the formation of ⟨the optic cup *induces* lens in the adjacent ectoderm⟩ (2) : to produce (as an electric current, an electric charge, or magnetic polarity) by induction (3) *psychol* : to arouse by indirect stimulation ⟨~ a contrast color⟩ **b** : AROUSE ⟨music *induces* in us concepts that are vague —H.A.Overstreet⟩ ⟨*induced* a nostalgia for New England in persons who never saw the place —Mark Van Doren⟩ **4** : to conclude or infer from particulars or by induction — contrasted with *deduce* **5** *obs* : to draw on : OVERSPREAD

syn PERSUADE, PREVAIL: INDUCE may indicate overcoming indifference, hesitation, or opposition, usu. by offering for consideration persuasive advantages or gains that bring about a desired decision ⟨well-meaning but misguided professors and teachers felt they were fulfilling their vocations by *inducing* brilliant boys and girls to flee the drudgery of the country and enter the elite professions —*Irish Digest*⟩ ⟨Burt, aided by his father and friends, *induced* Congress to aid his state in building such a canal —C.W.Mitman⟩ PERSUADE may suggest a winning over by an appeal, entreaty, or expostulation addressed as much to feelings as to reason ⟨*persuade* management to recognize collective bargaining —*Current Biog.*⟩ ⟨deputed by the firm of lawyers to *persuade* her to resume her married life —Anthony Powell⟩ PREVAIL may be used in situations in which strong opposition or reluctance is overcome by sustained argument and entreaty ⟨a group of citizens of all parties had *prevailed* on him to enter the race —*Current Biog.*⟩ ⟨I will go now and try to *prevail* on my mother to let me stay with you —G.B.Shaw⟩ ⟨*prevailed* upon the men in the sloop to sail up the river again, to rescue any survivors —Marjory S. Douglas⟩

induced development *n* [*induced* fr. past part. of *induce*] : EPIGENESIS 1

induced draft *n* : a draft produced by a suction steam jet or fan on the stack side of a furnace

induced drag *n* : the portion of the wing drag induced by or resulting from the generation of the lift

induced investment *n* : investment in inventories and equipment which is derived from and varies with changes in final output — distinguished from *autonomous investment*

induced radioactivity *n* : ARTIFICIAL RADIOACTIVITY

induced reaction *n* : a chemical reaction that proceeds more rapidly than it ordinarily would because of the influence of a second and faster reaction in the same system

in·duce·ment \-mənt\ *n* -s **1 a** : the act or process of inducing ⟨put into effect a system of ~ to encourage workers to turn out more work⟩ **b** : a quality or state which induces (as to action) or lures or entices ⟨the ~ of philosophy was that it freed one from a sense of enslavement to circumstance⟩ **2 a** : something that induces : a motive or consideration that leads one to action ⟨reward is an ~ to effort⟩ ⟨offer larger ~s to students to do good work⟩ **b** *in Roman, Scots, and civil law* : the consideration, reason, or motive for entering into a contract or the benefit or advantage furnished in a contractual bargain **3 a** *obs* : INTRODUCTION, PREFACE **b** : matter presented by way of introduction or background to explain the principal allegations of a legal cause, plea, or defense — distinguished from *surplusage* **4** : COLLOQUIUM 2 **syn** see MOTIVE

in·duc·er \-sə(r)\ *n* -s : one that induces; *specif* : the part of a centrifugal blower or compressor that feeds air into the axial region of the impeller

in·du·ci·ae \ənˈd(y)üshēˌē\ *n pl* [L *induciae, indutiae* truce, pause] **1** : a delay allowed for the performance of a legal obligation: as **a** *in Roman, civil, English, or Scots law* (1) *or* **induciae le·ga·les** \-ləˈgā(ˌ)lēz\ : time granted to a party to appear in answer to a summons or citation (2) : time granted for the preparation of a case for trial **b** *in old maritime law* : a period of 20 days after the safe arrival of a vessel under bottomry allowed for the sale of the cargo and the payment of the creditor's claim **2** *in international law* : a truce or cessation of hostilities : ARMISTICE

in·duc·ible \ənˈd(y)üsəbəl\ *adj* : capable of being induced

inducing *pres part of* INDUCE

in·du·cive \-siv\ *adj, archaic* : tending to induce

in·duct \ənˈdəkt\ *vt* -ED/-ING/-S [ME *inducten*, fr. ML *inductus*, past part. of *inducere*, fr. L, to lead in, introduce, induce — more at INDUCE] **1 a** : to put in formal possession of a benefice or living ⟨has taken orders and been ~*ed* to a small country living —Nathaniel Hawthorne⟩ **b** : to put in office with appropriate ceremonies : INSTALL ⟨was ~*ed* as president of the college⟩ **c** : to admit as a member ⟨~ three men into a scholastic society⟩ **d** : to introduce or initiate esp. into something secret or demanding special knowledge ⟨~*ing* neophytes into the mysteries of a cult⟩ ⟨~ a youngster into the use of his language —Stuart Chase⟩ **e** (1) : to enroll for training or service under a selective-service act (2) : to bring into federal service as part of the National Guard of the U.S. **2** : LEAD, CONDUCT ⟨swung the leaves of the door at just the right angle that ~*ed* you to the café —Mary Austin⟩

in·duc·tance \-ən(t)s\ *n* -s [*induction* + *-ance*] **1** : a property of an electric circuit by which an electromotive force is induced in it by a variation of current either (1) in the circuit itself or (2) in a neighboring circuit, which is expressed in henrys and is dependent upon the size, shape, and relative positions of the circuits and upon the proximity of magnetic materials, and which in electrical theory plays a role analogous to that of inertia in mechanics — called also respectively (1) *self-inductance* and (2) *mutual inductance* **2** : a circuit or a device possessing inductance

inductance coil *n* : REACTOR 3

in·duct·ee \ˌ(ˌ)inˌdəkˈtē, ənˌ-, ˌ=ˈ=ˌ=\ *n* -s : a person brought up for induction esp. into one of the armed forces or one who is to be or has been so inducted

in·ductile \(ˈ)in, ən+\ *adj* [¹*in-* + *ductile*] : not ductile : INFLEXIBLE, UNYIELDING

in·duc·tion \ənˈdəkshən\ *n* -s [ME *inducciouп*, fr. AF or ML; AF *induccion*, fr. ML *induction-, inductio*, fr. *inductus* (past part. of *inducere* to induct) + L *-ion-, -io* -ion] **1** : the act or process of inducting, the state of being inducted, or an instance or product of induction: as **a** (1) : a formal or symbolic and ceremonial bringing into or introducing to actual possession (as of an office) ⟨my ~ into the presidency —F.D.Roosevelt⟩ (2) *Eng. eccl. law* : the ceremony of giving the actual possession of an ecclesiastical living or its temporalities to a clergyman already presented and instituted **b** : an initial experience : an exposure that introduces one to something previously mysterious or unknown : INITIATION ⟨six weeks of hard physical effort was his ~ into the arts of war⟩ ⟨this grade of exercise supplies easy ~ to the technique for learners —J.M. Mitchell⟩ **c** : an official usu. formal and ceremonial admittance (as to membership in a club) ⟨awaiting his acceptance by and ~ into the secret order⟩ **d** : the formality by which a civilian is inducted into military service under the provisions of a draft law **2** [ME *inducciouп*, fr. MF or ML; MF *induction* reasoning from a part to a whole, fr. L *induction-, inductio* (trans. of Gk *epagōgē*), fr. *inductus* (past part. of *inducere* to lead in, introduce, induce) + *-ion-, -io* -ion] **a** : an instance of reasoning from a part to a whole, from particulars to generals, or from the individual to the universal : a conclusion arrived at by reasoning from a part to a whole, from particulars to generals, or from the individual to the universal : INFERENCE 2 **b** (1) : reasoning from a part to a whole, from particulars to generals, or from the individual to the universal — compare BACONIAN INDUCTION, ENUMERATIVE INDUCTION, EPAGOGE (2) : a process of mathematical demonstration in which the general validity of a law is inferred from its observed validity in particular cases by proving that if the law holds in a certain case it must hold in the next and therefore in succeeding cases **3** [L *induction-, inductio* action of introducing, fr. *inductus* (past part. of *inducere* to lead in, introduce, induce) + *-ion-, -io* -ion] **a** : a preface, prologue, or introductory scene esp. of an early English play **b** *obs* : something that leads into something else **c** *obs* : an initial step or action **4** [L *induction-, inductio* action of introducing] : the act or process of introducing, the state of being introduced, or an instance or product of introducing: as **a** : the act of bringing forward or adducing (as facts or particulars) **b** : the act of causing, initiating, or bringing on or about esp. at an early time or to a preliminary degree ⟨~ of labor⟩; *specif* : the establishment of an initial state of anesthesia often with an agent other than that used subsequently to maintain the anesthetic state **c** : the production of an electric charge, magnetism, or electromotive force in an object (as an electric conductor, a magnetizable body, an electric circuit) by the proximity without contact of a similarly energized body or by the variation of a magnetic flux — see ELECTROMAGNETIC INDUCTION, ELECTROSTATIC INDUCTION, MAGNETIC INDUCTION, MUTUAL INDUCTION, SELF-INDUCTION **d** : arousal by indirect stimulation (as contrast colors from parts of the retina adjacent to a directly stimulated area) **e** : the inspiration of the fuel-air charge from the carburetor into the combustion chamber of an internal-combustion engine **f** : the sum of the processes by which the fate of embryonic cells is determined and morphogenetic differentiation brought about

induction accelerator *n* : BETATRON

induction coil *n* : an apparatus for obtaining intermittent high voltage often used to produce spark discharges and consisting of a primary coil through which the direct current flows, a mechanical or electrical interrupter, and a secondary coil of a larger number of turns in which the high voltage is induced

induction compass *n* : a compass the indications of which depend on the current generated in a coil revolving in the earth's magnetic field

induction furnace *n* : an electric furnace heated by a current which is caused to flow through the charge by electromagnetic induction — compare ARC FURNACE

induction–harden \ˌ=ˈ=ˌ=ˈ=\ *vt* : to harden (a ferrous alloy) by heating above the transformation temperature by means of electromagnetic induction and then cooling as rapidly as necessary

induction heating *n* : a process of heating by means of an electric current that is caused to flow through the material to be heated or through its container (as a crucible) by electromagnetic induction — compare DIELECTRIC HEATING

induction machine *n* **1** : an electric machine operating by electrostatic induction **2** : an alternating-current machine (as an induction motor or induction generator) in which primary and secondary windings rotate with respect to each other and in which energy is transferred from one circuit to the other circuit by electromagnetic induction

induction motor *n* : any of several alternating-current motors in which the torque is produced by the reaction between a varying or rotating magnetic field that is generated in stationary field magnets and the current that is induced in the coils or circuits of the rotor

induction period *n* **1** : the time that elapses between the immersion of an exposed photographic emulsion in a developer and the appearance of the photographed image **2** : a period at the beginning of some chemical reactions during which little or no action takes place (as in the oxidation of fats by air because of the presence of antioxidants)

inductions *pl of* INDUCTION

in·duc·tive \(ˈ)inˈdəktiv, ənˈd-, -tēv *also* -təv\ *adj* [in sense 1, fr. ML *inductivus*, fr. L *inductus* (past part. of *inducere* to induce) + *-ivus* -ive; in other senses, fr. *induction*, after such pairs as E *deduction: deductive* — more at INDUCE] **1** : leading on : drawing on : INDUCING, TEMPTING ⟨~ to the sin of Eve —John Milton⟩ **2** : of or relating to logical induction ⟨the ~ method⟩ ⟨~ reasoning⟩ : employing the methods of induction ⟨~ science⟩ **3 a** : of, relating to, or produced or operated by electrical induction **b** : of, relating to, or having inductance esp. mutual inductance **4** : INTRODUCTORY, PREFATORY **5** : involving the action of an inductor ⟨~ effect of chordamesoderm⟩ **:** tending to produce induction ⟨~ reactions in the embryo⟩ — **in·duc·tive·ly** \-təvlē, -li\ *adv* — **in·duc·tive·ness** \-tivnəs, -tēv- *also* -təv-\ *n* -ES

inductive coupler *n* **:** a mutual inductor used in radio apparatus to provide coupling between two circuits

inductive coupling *n* **:** electrical coupling in which the influence is that of mutual induction usu. between two coils close together or wound on a common core

inductive inference *n* **:** INDUCTION 2b(1)

inductive logic *n* **:** a branch of logic that deals with induction; *esp* **:** the logic or theory of the methods and reasonings of empirical science

inductive reactance *n* **:** the part of the reactance of an alternating-current circuit that is due to inductance

in·duc·tiv·ism \ən'dəktə,vizəm\ *n* -S **:** a policy or the practice of using an inductive method or of stressing induction in one's methods

in·duc·tiv·ist \-,vəst\ *n* -S **:** one that is characterized by or advocates inductivism

in·duc·tom·e·ter \,in,dək'tämәd·ə(r)\ *n* [*induction* + *-o-* + *-meter*] **:** a variocoupler calibrated in units of inductance

in·duc·tor \ən'dəktə(r)\ *n* -S [partly fr. *induct* + *-or;* partly prob. fr. *induction,* after such pairs as E *conduction: conductor*] **1 :** one that inducts; *esp* **:** a person who inducts another into an office or benefice **2 a :** an inductance coil or reactor **b :** a mass of iron used in certain magnetic train-control devices **3 :** a substance that increases the rate of a chemical reaction and that is used up during the reaction — distinguished from *catalyst* **4 :** a substance capable under certain circumstances of inducing a specific type of development in embryonic or other undifferentiated tissue ⟨chordamesoderm acts on embryonic ectoderm as an ~ of neural tissue⟩ — compare COMPETENCE 5

inductor compass *n* **:** INDUCTION COMPASS

inductor generator *n* **:** a generator that induces voltage in a fixed armature by rotation of a rotor magnetized by current through a fixed field coil

in·duc·to·ri·um \,in,dək'tōrēəm\ *n* -S [NL, fr. *induct-* (fr. ISV *induction*) + *-orium*] **:** a battery-operated apparatus containing induction coils used for producing a continuous pulsing electric current or a single pulse of current (as for physiological or pharmacological experiments)

in·duc·to·ther·my \ən'dəktə,thərmē\ *n* -ES [blend of *Inductotherm* (a trademark) and E *-thermy*] **:** fever therapy by means of an electromagnetic induction field with the body or a part of it acting as a resistance

inducts *pres 3d sing of* INDUCT

indue *var of* ENDUE

in·dulge \ən'dəlj\ *vb* -ED/-ING/-S [L *indulgēre* to grant as a favor, be courteous, be kind, fr. *in-* ²in- + *-dulgēre* (prob. akin to OE *tulge* firmly, well, OS *tulgo* very, Goth *tulgus* firm, steadfast, Gk *dolichos* long, Skt *dirgha*); basic meaning: long, enduring] *vt* **1** *archaic* **:** to grant as a favor **:** BESTOW in concession or in compliance with a wish or request — usu. used in the passive ⟨a privilege seldom *indulged* to ordinary men⟩ **2 a :** to give free rein to ⟨*indulging* idle conjectures as to what might be the news —Rafael Sabatini⟩ ⟨likes to ~ a taste for the difficult —*Current Biog.*⟩ ⟨an excellent place to ~ a normal curiosity about clocks and watches —Ellwood Kirby⟩; take unrestrained pleasure in **:** yield to **:** GRATIFY ⟨~ a taste for exotic dishes⟩ **b :** to allow (oneself) unrestrained pleasure (as in the gratification of a normally restrained habit or desire) or unrestrained freedom (as in the expression of a normally restrained feeling) ⟨*indulged* himself in the delights of leisure⟩ ⟨~ oneself in eating and drinking⟩ ⟨*indulging* herself in histrionics⟩ **3 a :** to yield to the desire of or be forbearing in respect to out of favor or kindness under circumstances where one would not usually yield **:** gratify by unusual compliance **:** allow to proceed or act free from the restraints one would ordinarily impose **:** HUMOR ⟨~ a convalescing child in whatever he wishes to eat⟩ ⟨*indulged* her husband until he would not lift a finger around the house⟩ **:** favor in a way that pampers or treats with undue liberality ⟨a time when schoolboys were less *indulged* with pocket money than they seem to be nowadays —Archibald Marshall⟩ **b :** to grant an indulgence to or on ~ *vi* **:** to indulge in something ⟨offered him a drink but he protested that he did not ~⟩ — **indulge in 1 :** to gratify one's taste or desire for ⟨prone to *indulge in* too many evenings of pleasure⟩ ⟨*indulging in* candy and ice cream⟩ ⟨*indulging in* the bad habit of swearing⟩ **2 :** to give free rein to ⟨*indulge in* heated argument and violent language⟩ **3 :** to engage in ⟨all birds *indulge in* some seasonal movement —W.H.Dowdeswell⟩ ⟨*indulging in* the curious hobby of raising tropical fish —*Times Lit. Supp.*⟩ **:** UNDERTAKE ⟨those who *indulge in* high-altitude flights and suffer from a mild degree of oxygen want —H.G.Armstrong⟩

syn INDULGE, PAMPER, HUMOR, SPOIL, BABY, and MOLLYCODDLE can mean, in common, to treat a person or his desires or feelings with unusual or special usu. undue favor or attention. INDULGE with a personal object implies extreme compliance and often weakness in gratifying another's wishes or desires which have little claim to fulfillment ⟨I wanted to *indulge* him in all his particular food fancies and very soon the air in the apartment became almost visible with the reek of garlic sausage, smoked kippers and cheeses of strong character —Virginia D. Dawson & Betty D. Wilson⟩ ⟨grandmamma is always wanting to see them, for she humors and *indulges* them to such a degree, and gives them so much trash and sweet things, that they are sure to come back sick —Jane Austen⟩ PAMPER implies inordinate gratification of an appetite or taste esp. for luxuries or for what is softening in its physical or moral effects ⟨he preserved without an effort the supremacy of character and mind over the flesh he neither starved nor *pampered* —G.L.Dickinson⟩ ⟨no country can afford to *pamper* snobbery —G.B.Shaw⟩ ⟨*pamper* a child with rich foods and constant solicitude⟩ HUMOR implies an unusual attention to or a voluntary yielding to what are regarded as another's whims or caprices, often suggesting a purposeful sometimes patronizing accommodation to another's moods ⟨*humoring* a pet fawn which had a predilection for soap and cigarette butts —Ray Corsini⟩ ⟨the tone of your voice, when you speak, is too gentle, as if you were *humoring* the vagaries of a blind man's mind —Ben Hecht⟩ ⟨*humor* a customer for the sake of making a sale⟩ SPOIL implies a foolish or excessive indulging or pampering and throws stress upon its injurious effects upon the character or disposition ⟨the new queen played with and *spoiled* the little stepdaughter —Edith Sitwell⟩ ⟨he had been a noisy boastful youth and had been *spoiled* by his father —Sherwood Anderson⟩ BABY implies excessive attentions, as to one unable to care for himself and needing the assistance of a mother or nurse; when applied to one presumably capable, it carries the idea of treating with excessive usu. foolish care or carefulness ⟨if he thinks I'm going to spend my days catering to his whims, *babying* him and watching over him like a child, he's mistaken —Helen S. Rush & Mary Sherkanowski⟩ ⟨your old records will last longer with this new device to *baby* them —*Coronet*⟩ MOLLYCODDLE is the strongest of this group in implying inordinate attention and suggesting a ridiculously undue care for another's health or physical comfort or for the relieving of the strain or hardship he presumably, usu. fictitiously, suffers or may suffer ⟨a mother who *mollycoddles* her children by constantly dosing them, keeping them in when it's at all cold or damp and away from other children for fear of germs⟩ ⟨protests against the policy of *mollycoddling* prisoners —J.F.Steiner & R.M.Brown⟩

indulged *past of* INDULGE

¹**in·dul·gence** \-jən(t)s\ *also* **in·dul·gen·cy** \-nsē,-nsi\ *n, pl* **indulgences** *also* **indulgencies** [*indulgence* in sense 1 fr. ME, fr. MF, fr. ML *indulgentia,* fr. L, quality or state of being indulgent, kindness, complaisance, fr. *indulgent-, indulgens* indulgent + *-ia* -y; *indulgence* in sense 2a fr. ME, fr. L *indulgentia; indulgence* in other senses fr. L *indulgentia; indulgency* in sense 1 fr. ML *indulgentia; indulgency* in other senses fr. L *indulgentia*] **1 :** remission of the temporal punishment including canonical penances and esp. purgatorial atonement that according to Roman Catholicism is due by divine justice for sins whose eternal punishment has been remitted and whose guilt has been pardoned by the reception of the sacrament of penance **2 :** the act of indulging or the state of being indulgent: as **a :** a special often excessive leniency (as toward a sick child) **:** HUMORING ⟨had learned to treat his moody child with ~⟩ **:** any treatment marked by forbearance ⟨a crotchety old man who expected more ~ than he deserved⟩ **b :** FONDNESS, LIKING ⟨his ~ for the government of England —H.J. Laski⟩ **c :** benign tolerance ⟨mocking elegance that has little respect but much ~ for the foibles of man —Claudia Cassidy⟩ **3 a :** an indulgent act **:** a favor granted or an instance of forbearance ⟨sorry she allowed the children all the ~*s* she had in the past⟩ **b** (1) *sometimes cap* **:** a grant or offer of certain religious liberties as special favors made by Charles II and James II to Protestant dissenters and Roman Catholics (2) **:** the permission given during the same reigns to Scotch Presbyterian ministers to hold services **c :** an extension of time for payment or performance granted as a favor — compare MORATORIUM **4 :** the act of indulging in something or the thing indulged in ⟨a commendable degree of ~ in outdoor sports⟩ ⟨excessive ~ in daydreaming⟩ ⟨acquired that habit of romantic reading which was to be a lifetime ~ —H.S.Canby⟩ ⟨his trips abroad were almost the only ~*s* he had ever allowed himself⟩ ⟨had to be content with the weekly ~ of an ice-cream soda⟩ **:** gratification of a kind usu. forbidden or frowned on or to a degree usu. considered excessive; *esp* **:** SELF-GRATIFICATION, SELF-INDULGENCE

²**indulgence** \"\ *vt* -ED/-ING/-S *Roman Catholicism* **:** to attach an indulgence to (as an act or an object's use) ⟨*indulgenced* prayers⟩

in·dul·gent \-nt\ *adj* [L *indulgent-, indulgens,* pres. part. of *indulgēre* to indulge] **:** indulging, prone to indulge, or characterized by indulgence ⟨a smile of ~ pity such as one might grant to a mistaken child —Jane Addams⟩ **:** benignly tolerant **:** FORBEARING **:** markedly permissive ⟨indictments and civil pleadings are viewed with ~ eyes —B.N.Cardozo⟩ ⟨more appreciative of his success, more ~ of his shortcomings —Nathaniel Hawthorne⟩ **syn** see FORBEARING

in·dul·gent·ly *adv* **:** in an indulgent manner ⟨very often the young girl who goes wrong is dishonored, whereas the misconduct of the wife is viewed ~ —H.M.Parshley⟩

in·dulg·er \-jə(r)\ *n* -S **:** one that indulges

indulges *pres 3d sing of* INDULGE

indulging *pres part of* INDULGE

in·du·line \'ind(y)ə,lēn, -,lən\ *n* -S *usu cap* [ISV *ind-* + *-ule* + *-ine*] **:** any of a class of blue or violet dyes related to the safranines: as **a :** a reddish to greenish blue dye derived from phenosafranine and made by heating amino-azobenzene and aniline in the presence of hydrochloric acid — called also *Induline Spirit Soluble;* see DYE table I (under *Solvent Blue 7*) **b :** a water-soluble acid dye made by sulfonating the free base obtained by treating Induline Spirit Soluble with alkali — see DYE table I (under *Acid Blue 20*)

in·dult \'in,dəlt, ən'd-\ *n* -S [ME (Sc), fr. ML *indultum,* fr. LL, grant, privilege, fr. L, neut. of *indultus,* past part. of *indulgēre* to grant as a favor — more at INDULGE] **:** a special privilege granted by ecclesiastical authority for a definite or indefinite period of time; *specif,* **indults** *pl* **:** general faculties granted in the Roman Catholic Church by the pope to bishops and others to act in cases not otherwise permitted

in·dul·to \ən'dül(,)tō\ *n* -S [Sp, license, exemption, fr. ML *indultum* indult] *archaic* **:** INDULT

in·du·ment \'ind(y)əmənt\ *n* -S [L *indumentum* garment, fr. *induere* to put on, don (fr. *ind-* — fr. OL *indu, endo* in — + *-uere* — as in *exuere* to take off) + *-mentum* -ment — more at INDIGENOUS, EXUVIAE] **1** *archaic* **:** CLOTHING, GARMENT, INVESTITURE **2** [NL *indumentum,* fr. L] **:** INDUMENTUM

in·du·men·tum \,==ˈmentəm\ *n, pl* **indumen·ta** \-tə\ *or* **indumentums** [NL, fr. L] **1 :** the entire feathery covering of a bird **2 :** a dense woolly pubescence (as on a leaf or an insect)

in·du·na \ən'dünə\ *n* -S [Zulu *in-duna* government officer] **:** a headman or councilor of an African people esp. the Zulus

in·duplicate \ən +\ *adj* [prob. fr. (assumed) NL *induplicatus,* fr. L *in-* ²in- + *duplicatus* bent, doubled up, doubled, past part. of *duplicare* to double — more at DUPLICATE] **1 :** having the edges bent abruptly toward the axis — used of the parts of the calyx or corolla in a bud **2 :** having the edges rolled inward and then arranged about the axis without overlapping — used of leaves in a bud

indurance *obs var of* ENDURANCE

¹**in·du·rate** \'ind(y)ərət, ən'd(y)ůr-\ *adj* [ME *indurat,* fr. L *induratus,* past part. of *indurare*] **:** physically or morally hardened ⟨this man whom enemies describe as cold-blooded and ~ to public opinion —M.L.Bach⟩

²**in·du·rate** \'ind(y)ə,rāt, *usu* -ād·+V\ *vb* -ED/-ING/-S [L *induratus,* past part. of *indurare,* fr. *in-* ²in- + *durare* to harden, fr. *durus* hard — more at DURE] *vt* **1 :** to make unfeeling, stubborn, or obdurate ⟨the instability of many religionists . . . ~*s* secular men in their impiety —Isaac Taylor⟩ **2 :** to make hardy **:** INURE ⟨had been *indurated* to want, exposure and toil —A.W.Tourgee⟩ **3 :** to make hard: as **a :** to make into a compact hard rock mass by the action of heat, pressure, or cementation ⟨conglomerates are the *indurated* equivalents of gravel —F.J.Pettijohn⟩ **b :** to increase the fibrous elements of **:** make sclerosed ⟨*indurated* tissue⟩ **4 :** to establish firmly **:** make deep-rooted **:** CONFIRM ⟨the *indurated* goat habit . . . every family keeps a goat —Ellery Sedgwick⟩ ~ *vi* **1 :** to grow hard **:** HARDEN **2 :** to become established or deep rooted

in·du·ra·tion \,ind(y)ə'rāshən\ *n* -S [ME *induracion,* fr. MF or LL; MF *induration,* fr. LL *induration-, induratio,* fr. L *induratus* + *-ion-, -io* -ion] **1 :** the act or process of growing hard or the state of having grown hard: as **a :** hardness or inflexibility of character, manner, or feeling **:** OBSTINACY, OBDURATENESS, CALLOUSNESS **b :** the act of becoming inured (as to drudgery) ⟨~ to hackwork —*Saturday Rev.*⟩ **c :** the process by which a rock or rock material is indurated **d :** an increase in the fibrous elements in tissue commonly associated with inflammation and marked by loss of elasticity and pliability **:** SCLEROSIS **2 :** a hardened mass or formation

in·du·ra·tive \'ind(y)ə,rād·iv, ən'd(y)ůrəd·-\ *adj* **:** of, relating to, or producing induration

in·du·rite \'ind(y)ə,rīt\ *n* -S [²*indurate* + *-ite*] **:** a smokeless powder made by treating guncotton with nitrobenzene

indus *abbr* industrial; industry

in·du·sial \ən'd(y)üzēəl, -zh(ē)əl\ *adj* [*indusium* + *-al*] **:** of, relating to, or being an indusium

in·du·si·um \-z(h)ēəm\ *n, pl* **indu·sia** \-zēə, -zh(ē)ə\ [NL, fr. L, woman's undergarment, tunic, perh. fr. *induere* to put on — more at INDUMENT] **1 a :** an outgrowth of the leaf which covers or invests the sori in many ferns **b :** a cuplike fringe of collecting hairs surrounding the stigma in the Goodeniaceae **c :** the annulus in some fungi esp. when skirtlike (as in members of the genus *Dictyophora*) **2 :** a membrane serving as a covering; *esp* **:** AMNION

¹**in·dus·tri·al** \ən'dəstrēəl\ *adj* [partly fr. MF, produced by systematic labor, fr. *industrie* employment involving skill (fr. L *industria* diligence) + *-al;* partly fr. F *industriel* of or belonging to industry (esp. manufacturing), fr. *industrie* industry (fr. L *industria* diligence) + *-el* -al, fr. L *-alis* — more at INDUSTRY] **1 :** of or belonging to industry: as **a :** being in or part of industry ⟨~ work⟩ ⟨an ~ employment⟩ **b :** being or constituting an industry ⟨an ~ enterprise⟩ **c :** characterized by highly developed industries or being chiefly dependent economically upon industry ⟨an ~ nation⟩ **d :** engaged in industry or in industries esp. at manual labor ⟨the ~ classes⟩ **e :** derived from human industry rather than from natural advantages only or from profit only ⟨~ wealth⟩ ⟨an ~ crop⟩ **f :** belonging to or aiding those engaged in industry ⟨~ wages⟩ ⟨~ safety⟩ ⟨~ training⟩ **g :** produced by an organized industry ⟨~ products⟩ **h :** used or designed or developed for use in industry ⟨~ fabrics⟩ ⟨an ~ diamond⟩ ⟨wrapping, building, and other ~ papers⟩ **2 :** belonging to industrial life or accident and health insurance

²**industrial** \"\ *n* -S **1 a :** one that is employed in a manufacturing industry **b :** a company engaged in industrial production or service **2 industrials** *pl* **:** stocks or bonds of industrial companies **3 :** something industrial (as an industrial diamond) as opposed to something else that is of the same class of things but used or designed for use for a nonindustrial purpose

industrial accession *n, Roman, civil, & Scots law* **:** accession brought about by human industry as opposed to some natural process

industrial accident *n* **:** an accident occurring during the course of employment

industrial accident and health insurance *n* **:** accident and health insurance usu. written in small amounts and subject to frequent premium payments and covering persons exposed to the hazard of occupational injury

industrial alcohol *n* **:** alcohol for industrial use; *usu* **:** ethyl alcohol either mixed only with water or denatured — see DENATURED ALCOHOL

industrial art *n* **:** a subject taught in elementary and secondary schools that aims at developing a manual skill, a familiarity with tools and machines, or an acquaintance with industrial processes and design

industrial bank *n* **:** a financial institution deriving funds from the sale of investment certificates and from deposits made by individual savers and investing such funds in personal loans often secured by a comaker note or chattel mortgage

industrial carrier *n* **:** a means of transportation owned, controlled, or operated by one or more industries as a private, exclusive, or common carrier

industrial center *n* **:** a Salvationist institution that provides work (as the salvaging of waste materials) and an opportunity for rehabilitation for homeless or handicapped men

industrial chemistry *n* **:** chemistry in its industrial applications esp. to processes in manufacturing and the arts and to commercial production of chemicals

industrial democracy *n* **:** the determination of a company's policies affecting the welfare of its workers by joint action of management and worker representatives

industrial design *n* **:** design concerned with the appearance of three-dimensional machine-made products; *also* **:** the study of the principles of such design

industrial designer *n* **:** one that works at industrial design

industrial disease *n* **:** OCCUPATIONAL DISEASE

industrial engineer *n* **:** a specialist in industrial engineering

industrial engineering *n* **:** the application of engineering principles and training and the techniques of scientific management to the maintenance of a high level of productivity at optimum cost in industrial enterprises (as by analytical study, improvement, and installation of methods and systems, operating procedures, quantity and quality measurements and controls, safety measures, and personnel administration)

industrial geography *n* **:** a branch of geography that deals with the location of industries, the geographic factors that influence their location and development, the raw materials used in them, and the distribution of their finished products

industrial hygiene *n* **:** a science devoted to the protection and improvement of the health and well-being of workers in their vocational environment

industrial insurance *n* **1 a :** INDUSTRIAL LIFE INSURANCE **b :** INDUSTRIAL ACCIDENT AND HEALTH INSURANCE **2 :** WORKMEN'S COMPENSATION INSURANCE

in·dus·tri·al·ism \-ēə,lizəm\ *n* -S [F *industrialisme,* fr. *industrial-* (fr. *industriel* industrial) + *-isme* -ism — more at INDUSTRIAL] **:** social organization in which industries and esp. large-scale industries are dominant — compare CAPITALISM, COMMERCIALISM, MILITARISM

¹**in·dus·tri·al·ist** \-,ləst\ *n* -S [F *industrialiste* advocate of industrialism, fr. *industrial-* (fr. *industriel*) + *-iste* -ist] **:** one owning or engaged in the management of an esp. large-scale industry; *esp* **:** MANUFACTURER

²**industrialist** \"\ *adj* [F *industrialiste,* fr. *industrialiste,* n.] **:** of, relating to, or characterized by industrialism

in·dus·tri·al·iza·tion \=,===lə'zāshən, -,lī'z-\ *n* -S **:** the act or process of industrializing or the state of being industrialized

in·dus·tri·al·ize \='===,līz\ *vb* -ED/-ING/-S — *see -ize in Explan Notes* [F *industrialiser,* fr. *industrial-* (fr. *industriel*) + *-iser* -ize] *vt* **:** to make industrial **:** convert to industrialism ~ *vi* **:** to become industrial **:** become converted to industrialism ⟨country has been steadily *industrializing* —Eric Goldman⟩

industrial life insurance *n* **:** life insurance which is written upon individual lives in small amounts and for which the premiums are collected weekly or monthly by agents

in·dus·tri·al·ly \-ēəlē, -li\ *adv* **:** in or by means of industry

in·dus·tri·al·ness \-ēəlnəs\ *n* -ES **:** the quality or state of being industrial

industrial park *n* **:** an area that is at a distance from the center of a city and that is designed (as by homogeneous architecture) esp. for a community of industries and businesses

industrial property *n* **:** intangible property rights (as ownership of a trademark or patent) connected with agriculture, commerce, and industry

industrial psychology *n* **:** the application of the findings and methods of experimental, clinical, and social psychology to industrial problems (as personnel selection and training) — compare PSYCHOTECHNOLOGY

industrial railroad *n* **:** a short railroad feeder owned or controlled and operated by an industrial concern — called also *tap line*

industrial relations *n pl* **:** the dealings or relationships of a usu. large business or industrial enterprise with its own workers, with labor in general, with governmental agencies, or with the public or the relationships between industries or large businesses

industrial revolution *n* [prob. trans. of F *révolution industrielle*] **1 :** an economic revolution (as in England beginning in 1760) characterized by a marked acceleration in the output of industrial goods correlative with the introduction of power-driven machinery into industry and consequent decline of handwork and domestic production **2 :** a marked general alteration in industrial or production methods in the direction of machine production and away from manual labor or personal control

industrial school *n* **:** a school specializing in the teaching of the industrial arts; *specif* **:** a public institution of this kind for juvenile delinquents

industrial sociology *n* **:** sociological analysis directed at institutions and social relationships within and largely controlled or affected by industry

industrial store *n* **:** COMPANY STORE

industrial union *n* **:** a labor union that admits to membership workmen in an industry irrespective of their occupation or craft — called also *vertical union*

in·dus·tri·ous \ən'dəstrēəs\ *adj* [MF *industrieux,* fr. L *industriosus* diligent, fr. *industria* diligence + *-osus* -ose] **1** *obs* **:** SKILLFUL, CLEVER, INGENIOUS **2 :** perseveringly active **:** ZEALOUS ⟨~ in seeking out and questioning new arrivals —Gilbert Armitage⟩ **3 :** characterized by industry: as **a :** marked by steady dependable energetic work **:** not lazy **:** DILIGENT ⟨an ~ worker⟩ ⟨an ~ group of campaigners⟩ **b :** constantly, regularly, or habitually occupied **:** BUSY ⟨an ~ housewife whose tasks seemed never-ending⟩ **c :** conducive to purposeful work or enterprise ⟨an ~ home environment⟩ **4** *obs* **:** characterized by design or purpose **:** INTENTIONAL **syn** see BUSY

in·dus·tri·ous·ly *adv* **:** in an industrious manner

in·dus·tri·ous·ness *n* -ES **:** the quality or state of being industrious ⟨a prosperity credited largely to the ~ of the people⟩

in·dus·try \'in(,)dəstrē, -ri *sometimes* ən'd-\ *n* -ES [ME *industrie,* fr. MF, skill, employment involving skill, fr. L *industria* diligence, fr. *industrius* diligent, fr. OL *indostruus,* fr. *indu, endo* in, within + *-struus* (akin to L *struere* to arrange, build) — more at INDIGENOUS, STRUCTURE] **1** *obs* **a :** SKILL, CLEVERNESS **b :** a use or application of skill or cleverness **2 a :** diligence in an employment or pursuit **:** steady attention to business ⟨all his long years of service gone . . . all his ~ and diligence thrown away —James Joyce⟩ ⟨sewing with no great amount of ~ on pieces of white material —Lillian Hellman⟩ **b :** habitual or constant work or effort ⟨a man of fine mental powers . . . unceasing ~, and simple charm —C.B.Fisher⟩ ⟨he had immense ~ but he didn't know how to think —Archibald Marshall⟩ **3 a :** systematic labor esp. for the creation of value ⟨had left the country . . . to live by his own ~ in England —Charles Dickens⟩ **b :** a department or branch of a craft, art, business, or manufacture **:** a division of productive or profit-making labor; *esp* **:** one that employs a large personnel and capital esp. in manufacturing ⟨put his money into an ~ that sold its goods on an international scale⟩ ⟨all the large *industries* in the city⟩ **c :** a group of productive or profit-making enterprises or organizations that have a similar technological structure of production and that produce or supply technically substitutable goods, services, or sources of income ⟨the automobile ~⟩ ⟨the air transport ~⟩ ⟨the poultry ~⟩ ⟨the smuggling of gold, liquor, and other contraband has become a secondary ~ —James Reach⟩ ⟨the tourist ~⟩ **d :** manufacturing activity as a whole ⟨conditions that were auspicious for the nation's ~⟩ ⟨an energetic promoter of New England ~ —*Current Biog.*⟩ **4 a :** a well-developed technique of a people esp. as evidenced in archaeological discoveries **b :** an assemblage of prehistoric implements giving clear evidence that they were used by one group of men

in·dwell \(ˈ)in, ən+\ *vb* [ME *indwellen* to inhabit, fr. ²*in* + *dwellen* to dwell] *vi* **:** to exist as an inner activating spirit, force, or principle ⟨a creative power ~*ing* in the world —Lawrence Binyon⟩ ⟨a divinity ~*ing* in nature —V.L. Parrington⟩ **~** *vt* **:** to exist within or inhabit as an activating spirit, force, or principle ⟨a life of God ~*s* the universe —J.H.Randall⟩ ⟨endowed with or *indwelt* by some supernatural power —E.A.Nida⟩

in·dwell·er \"ə(r)\ *n* [ME, fr. *indwellen* + *-er*] **1 a :** INHABITANT **b :** SOJOURNER **2 :** an inner spirit, force, or principle

indwelling *adj* **1 :** existing or residing as an inner activating spirit, force, or principle ⟨an ~ divinity —B.B.Cohen⟩ ⟨an ~ goodness⟩ **2 :** left for a period of time within an organ or passage to maintain drainage, prevent obstruction, or provide a route for administration of food or drugs — used of a catheter or similar tube

in·dyl \ˈindᵊl, -,dil\ *n* -s [by shortening] **:** INDOLYL

¹-ine \,īn, ,ən, (,)in, ,ēn\ *adj suffix* [ME *-ine, -in*, fr. MF *-in* & L *-inus* (with long *i*), *-inus* (with short *i*); MF *-in* partly fr. L *-inus* (with long *i*) of or belonging to; MF *-in* partly fr. L *-inus* (with short *i*) made of, of or belonging to, fr. Gk *-inos* — more at -EN] **1 :** of, belonging to, or relating to ⟨estuar*ine*⟩ **2 :** made of **:** like ⟨opal*ine*⟩

²-ine \,ēn, ,ən\ *n suffix* -s [ME *-ine, -in*, fr. MF & L; MF *-ine*, fr. L *-ina* (with long *i*), fem. of *-inus* (with long *i*) of or belonging to] **1 :** ¹-ITE 4 ⟨hatchett*ine*⟩ **2 :** chemical substance: as **a :** chemical element — in names of the halogens ⟨astat*ine*⟩ ⟨chlor*ine*⟩ **b** (1) **:** basic carbon compound — in names of alkaloids ⟨quin*ine*⟩ or other organic nitrogenous bases ⟨anil*ine*⟩ ⟨guanid*ine*⟩ including six-membered ring compounds ⟨pyrid*ine*⟩ and intermediate hydrogenated forms of cyclic compounds ⟨pyrrol*ine*⟩ ⟨thiazol*ine*⟩ — usu. distinguished from *-in* (2) **:** carbon compound containing a basic group — in names of amino acids ⟨glyc*ine*⟩ ⟨cyst*ine*⟩ **c :** mixture of chemical compounds — esp. in commercial names (as of mixtures of hydrocarbons) ⟨gasol*ine*⟩ ⟨keros*ine*⟩ **d :** -YNE **e :** hydride ⟨ars*ine*⟩ **3 :** -IN 1a — not used systematically **4 :** commercial product or material ⟨glass*ine*⟩

³-ine — see ²-INA

⁴-ine \ˈēn\ *n suffix* -s [ME *-ina, -ine, -in* (in feminine given names), fr. OE *-ina* (in feminine given names), fr. L *-ina* (with long *i*, in feminine names such as *Agrippina*), fr. fem. of *-inus* (with long *i*) of or belonging to] **:** female person ⟨chor*ine*⟩ ⟨dud*ine*⟩

-in·e·ae \ˈinē,ē\ *n pl suffix* [NL, fr. L, fem. pl. of *-ineus* (as in *gramineus* gramineous)] **:** plants including those of (such) a genus ⟨Abiet*ineae*⟩ **:** plants characterized by (such) a feature ⟨Dinocaps*ineae*⟩ — in names of botanical suborders

in·earth \ən+\ *vt* [²*in-* + *earth* (n.)] *archaic* **:** BURY, INTER

¹in·ebri·ant \əˈnēbrēənt\ *n* -s [L *inebriant-, inebrians*, pres. part. of *inebriare* to make drunk] **:** INTOXICANT

²inebriant \"\ *adj* [L *inebriant-, inebrians*, pres. part. of *inebriare*] **:** INTOXICATING

¹in·ebri·ate \-brē,āt, *usu* -ād.+V\ *vt* -ED/-ING/-S [L *inebriatus*, past part. of *inebriare*, fr. *in-* ²in- + *ebriare* to intoxicate, fr. *ebrius* drunk — more at SOBER] **1 :** to make drunk **:** INTOXICATE **2 :** to disorder the senses of **:** exhilarate as if by liquor **:** deprive of sense and judgment ⟨*inebriated* by his own verbosity —N.A.Jones⟩

²in·ebri·ate \-brēət, -ē,āt, *usu* \d.+V\ *adj* [L *inebriatus*] **1 :** INTOXICATED, DRUNK **2 :** addicted to drinking to excess

³inebriate \"\ *n* -s **:** one who is drunk or intoxicated; *esp* **:** an habitual drunkard ⟨an asylum for ~*s*⟩

inebriated *adj* **:** exhilarated or confused by or as if by alcohol **:** TIPSY, INTOXICATED ⟨drinking steadily . . . getting neither more nor less ~ —Herman Melville⟩ ⟨~ with the exuberance of his own verbosity —Benjamin Disraeli⟩ **syn** see DRUNK

in·ebri·a·tion \ə,nēbrēˈāshən\ *n* -s [LL *inebriation-, inebriatio*, fr. *inebriatus* + *-ion-, -io* -ion] **1 :** the action of inebriating or the condition of being inebriated **2 :** habitual intoxication **:** DRUNKENNESS

in·ebri·ety \,inəˈbrīəd·ē, -ītē, \i\ *n* [prob. blend of *inebriation* and *ebriety*] **:** INEBRIATION, INTOXICATION ⟨the only opportunities for ~ were the visits to town —P.A. Rollins⟩ **:** DRUNKENNESS ⟨public facilities for dealing with ~ —Robert Straus & R.G.McCarthy⟩

in·ebri·ous \əˈnēbrēəs\ *adj* [perh. blend of *inebriation* and obs. E *ebrious* addicted to drink, drunk, fr. L *ebrius* drunk] **1** *obs* **:** INEBRIATING **2 :** INEBRIATED, INTOXICATED **3 :** addicted to drink

ined *abbr* [L *ineditus*] unpublished

in·edible \(ˈ)in, ən+\ *adj* [¹*in-* + *edible*] **:** not edible **:** not fit for food

in·ed·i·ta \(ˈ)iˈnedəd·ə, -ətə\ *n pl* [NL, fr. L, neut. pl. of *ineditus* not made known, fr. *in-* ¹in- + *editus*, past part. of *edere* to proclaim, publish — more at EDITION] **:** unpublished literary material

in·edited \(ˈ)in, ən+\ *adj* [NL *ineditus* + E *-ed*] **:** UNPUBLISHED ⟨~ document⟩ ⟨~ letters⟩

in·educabilia \(ˌ)in, ən+\ *n pl, cap* [NL, fr. ¹*in-* + *Educabilia*] *in former classifications* **:** a superorder of placental mammals including the bats, rodents, edentates, and insectivores in which the brain is less developed than in the Educabilia

in·educability \"+\ *n* **:** the quality or state of being ineducable

in·educable \(ˈ)in, ən+\ *adj* [¹*in-* + *educable*] **:** incapable of being educated; *esp* **:** mentally retarded or psychologically disturbed so as to be unable to benefit from education provided for the normal majority

in·education \(ˌ)in, ən+\ *n* [¹*in-* + *education*] **:** lack of education

in·ef·fa·bil·i·ty \(,)i,nefəˈbiləd·ē, ə,n-, -lətē, -i\ *n* -ES **:** the quality or state of being ineffable

¹in·effable \(ˈ)in, ən+\ *adj* [ME, fr. MF, fr. L *ineffabilis*, fr. *in-* ¹in- + *effabilis* effable — more at EFFABLE] **1 :** incapable of being expressed in words **:** UNUTTERABLE, INDESCRIBABLE ⟨~ joy⟩ ⟨~ torture⟩ **:** UNSPEAKABLE ⟨~ disgust⟩ ⟨~ bungler⟩ **2 :** not to be uttered **:** TABOO ⟨the ~ name of Jehovah⟩ — **in·ef·fa·ble·ness** \-nəs\ *n* -ES — **in·ef·fa·bly** \-blē,-bli\ *adv*

²ineffable \"\ *n* -s **:** something that is ineffable

in·ef·face·abil·i·ty \,inə,fāsəˈbiləd·ē\ *n* -ES **:** the quality or state of being ineffaceable **:** INDELIBILITY

in·effaceable \ˌin+\ *adj* [prob. fr. F *ineffaçable*, fr. MF, fr. *in-* ¹in- + *effaçable* effaceable (fr. *effacer* to efface + *-able*) — more at EFFACE] **:** not effaceable **:** INDELIBLE, INERADICABLE — **in·ef·face·ably** \-blē,-bli\ *adv*

¹in·effective \ˌin+\ *adj* [¹*in-* + *effective*] **1 :** not producing or incapable of producing an intended effect ⟨~ remedy⟩ **2 :** not capable of performing the required work or duties **:** INCAPABLE ⟨~ figurehead⟩ ⟨~ troops⟩ **3 :** lacking in aesthetic merit ⟨~ design⟩ — **in·effectively** \"+\ *adv* — **in·effectiveness** \"+\ *n*

²ineffective \"\ *n* **:** an ineffective person or thing **:** one unfit for service (as in an army)

¹in·effectual \ˌin+\ *adj* [ME, fr. ¹*in-* + *effectual*] **:** not effectual **:** not producing the proper or usual effect **:** INEFFECTIVE, FUTILE, UNAVAILING ⟨~ attempt⟩ ⟨~ expedient⟩ ⟨~ protests⟩ — **in·effectually** \"+\ *adv* — **in·effectualness** \"+\ *n*

²ineffectual \"\ *n* -s **:** INEFFECTIVE ⟨a program of training for the ~*s* —Eugene Davidoff⟩

in·effectuality \ˌin+\ *n* **:** the quality or state of being ineffectual

in·efficacious \(ˌ)in, ən+\ *adj* [¹*in-* + *efficacious*] **:** not efficacious **:** lacking the power to produce a desired effect **:** INADEQUATE — **in·efficaciously** \"+\ *adv* — **in·efficaciousness** \"+\ *n*

in·efficacity \"+\ *n* [¹*in-* + *efficacity*] **:** INEFFICACY

in·efficacy \(ˈ)in, ən+\ *n* [LL *inefficacia*, fr. L *inefficac-, inefficax* inefficacious (fr. *in-* ¹in- + *efficac-, efficax* efficacious) + *-ia* -y — more at EFFICACIOUS] **:** lack of power to produce a desired or the proper effect **:** INEFFECTUALNESS ⟨~ of laws in preventing crime⟩

in·efficiency \ˌin+\ *n* [¹*in-* + *efficiency*] **:** the quality, state, or fact of being inefficient **:** lack of power or energy sufficient for a desired effect **:** INCAPACITY ⟨the ugliness and ~ of legal prose —Malcolm Muggeridge⟩ ⟨operations . . . common to all printing processes have hidden in them great *inefficiencies* and enormous waste —P.R.Russell⟩

¹in·efficient \"+\ *adj* [¹*in-* + *efficient*] **:** not efficient: **a :** not producing the effect intended or desired **:** INEFFICACIOUS, INSUFFICIENT ⟨~ measures⟩ **b :** wasteful of time or energy in performing work ⟨statistics show that retailing . . . is ~ —*Wall Street Jour.*⟩ **c :** incapable of or indisposed to the effective performance of duties ⟨~ workman⟩ — **in·efficiently** \"+\ *adv*

²inefficient \"\ *n* -s **:** an inefficient person

in·egalitarian \ˌin+\ *adj* [¹*in-* + *egalitarian*] **:** marked by disparity in economic and social standing ⟨assumed that society would be aristocratic and ~ . . . that there would be a sufficiently large class of persons with independent incomes —Christopher Hollis⟩

in·elaborate \ˌin+\ *adj* [¹*in-* + *elaborate*] **:** not elaborate **:** SIMPLE

in·elastic \"+\ *adj* [¹*in-* + *elastic*] **1 :** not elastic **:** slow to react or respond to changing conditions ⟨~ price structure⟩ ⟨~ demand for a commodity⟩ **2 :** INFLEXIBLE, RIGID, UNYIELDING — **in·elasticity** \"+\ *n*

inelastic collision *n, physics* **:** a collision in which part of the kinetic energy of the colliding particles changes into another kind of energy (as radiation)

inelastic scattering *n, physics* **:** scattering of material particles due to collisions in which the total kinetic energy of the colliding particles increases or decreases

in·elegance \(ˈ)in, ən+\ *n* **:** the quality or state of being inelegant **:** lack of elegance **:** lack of refinement, beauty, or polish (as in language, manners)

in·elegancy \"+\ *n* **1** *archaic* **:** INELEGANCE **2 :** something that is inelegant ⟨*inelegancies* of prose style⟩

in·elegant \"+\ *adj* [MF *inelegant*, fr. L *inelegant-, inelegans*, fr. *in-* ¹in- + *elegant-, elegans* elegant — more at ELEGANT] **:** not elegant **:** deficient in beauty, polish, refinement, grace, or ornament **:** lacking in something that correct taste requires — **in·elegantly** \"+\ *adv*

in·eligibility \(ˌ)in, ən+\ *n* **:** the condition or fact of being ineligible

¹in·eligible \(ˈ)in, ən+\ *adj* [F *inéligible*, fr. *in-* ¹in- + *éligible* — more at ELIGIBLE] **1 :** not eligible **:** not qualified to be chosen for an office **:** not worthy to be chosen or preferred ⟨~ for marriage⟩ ⟨~ for the football team⟩ **2 :** not expedient or desirable ⟨shawls will be brought by injudicious mothers at precisely the most ~ moments —W.L.Alden⟩

²ineligible \"\ *n* **:** one that is ineligible

ineligible paper *n* **:** notes and bills that do not meet the requirements for discount or rediscount by the Federal Reserve banks

in·eliminable \ˌin+\ *adj* [¹*in-* + *eliminable*] **:** incapable of being eliminated or excluded

in·eloquent \(ˈ)in, ən+\ *adj* [¹*in-* + *eloquent*] **:** not eloquent **:** lacking in eloquence — **in·eloquently** \"+\ *adv*

in·eluc·ta·bil·i·ty \,inə,ləktəˈbiləd·ē\ *n* -ES **:** the quality or state of being ineluctable ⟨~ of fate⟩

in·eluc·ta·ble \ˌinəˈləktəbəl\ *adj* [L *ineluctabilis*, fr. *in-* ¹in- + *eluctari* to struggle out + *-abilis* -able — more at ELUCTATION] **:** not to be avoided, changed, or resisted **:** INESCAPABLE, INEVITABLE ⟨~ facts of human existence⟩ ⟨~ conclusions of logical deduction⟩ — **in·eluc·ta·bly** \-blē,-bli\ *adv*

in·elud·ible \ˌinəˈlüdəbəl\ *adj* [¹*in-* + *elude* + *-ible*] **:** INESCAPABLE — **in·elud·ibly** \-blē,-bli\ *adv*

in·enar·ra·ble \ˌinēˈnarəbəl\ *adj* [ME, fr. MF *inenarrable*, fr. L *inenarrabilis*, fr. *in-* ¹in- + *enarrabilis* capable of being explained, fr. *enarrare* to explain in detail + *-abilis* -able — more at ENARRATION] **:** incapable of being narrated **:** INDESCRIBABLE, INEFFABLE ⟨~ mystery of artistic creation —N.E.Nelson⟩

in·ept \(ˈ)iˈnept, əˈn-\ *adj* [F *inepte*, fr. L *ineptus*, fr. *in-* ¹in- + *aptus* apt — more at APT] **1** *archaic* **:** not apt or fit — often used with *to* or *for* **2 :** not apt for the occasion **:** likely to fail in its purpose **:** out of place **:** INAPPROPRIATE ⟨an ~ and highly artificial comparison —Donald Wayne⟩ ⟨the square is one of those anomalous, shabby-ornate, ~, and pitifully pretentious places —Thomas Wolfe⟩ **3 :** lacking sense or reason **:** FOOLISH, PREPOSTEROUS ⟨it is ~, absurd, downright silly, to argue that in a world torn by . . . convulsions . . . literature can hide away in a hothouse —J.T.Farrell⟩ **4 a :** lacking in skill or aptitude for a particular role or task ⟨an ~ farmer . . . too easily distracted by contemplation —H.V.Gregory⟩ ⟨often a little ~, clumsy about the practical things of life —Rumer Godden⟩ **b :** generally incompetent **:** INADEQUATE, BUNGLING ⟨they found many English officers blundering . . . the brave but ~ Braddock would have done well to take . . . Washington's advice —Allan Nevins & H.S.Commager⟩ **5** *Scots law* **:** NULL, VOID **syn** see AWKWARD

in·ep·ti·tude \əˈneptə,tüd, -ptə-,tyüd\ *n* -s [L *ineptitudo*, fr. *ineptus* inept + *-i-* + *-tudo* -tude] **1 :** UNFITNESS, UNSUITABLENESS ⟨~ of a comparison⟩ ⟨~ that ought to have kept him out of business —Van Wyck Brooks⟩ **2 :** a foolish action or utterance **:** ABSURDITY

in·ept·ly \-ptlē, -li\ *adv* **:** in an inept manner

in·ept·ness \-p(t)nəs\ *n* -ES **:** the quality or state of being inept

in·equable \(ˈ)in, ən+\ *adj* [L *inaequabilis*, fr. *in-* ¹in- + *aequabilis* equable — more at EQUABLE] **:** not evenly distributed **:** not uniform **:** UNFAIR

in·equal \"+\ *adj* [ME, fr. L *inaequalis*, fr. *in-* ¹in- + *aequalis* equal, fr. *aequus* even, equal] **1** *archaic* **:** UNEQUAL **2 :** uneven in quality ⟨library of several ~ books —Holbrook Jackson⟩

inequal hour *n* [ME] **:** HOUR 5

in·equalitarian \ˌin+\ *adj* [fr. *inequality* + *-arian* (as in *equalitarian*)] **:** INEGALITARIAN ⟨privileged and leisured class, the product of a thoroughly ~ order of society —Walter Moberly⟩

in·equality \"+\ *n* [MF *inequalité*, fr. L *inaequalitat-, inaequalitas*, fr. *inaequalis* + *-itat-, -itas* -ity] **1 :** the quality of being unequal or uneven **:** lack of equality: as **a :** UNEVENNESS ⟨hampered by the ~ of the ground⟩ **b :** social disparity ⟨combination of democracy with ~ —H.S.Commager⟩ **c :** disparity of distribution ⟨~ of income⟩ or opportunity ⟨educational ~⟩ **d :** VARIABLENESS, CHANGEABLENESS ⟨~ of temperament⟩ ⟨~ of the climate⟩ **2 :** an instance of being unequal (as in position, proportion, evenness, regularity) ⟨*inequalities* of a surface⟩ **3 :** an irregularity or a deviation in the motion of a planet or satellite; *also* **:** the amount of such deviation **4 :** a statement of inequality between two quantities usu. with a sign of inequality (as $<$ or $>$ or $\neq$ signifying respectively *is less than, is greater than, is not equal to*) between them ($2<3$, $4>1$, and $a \neq b$ are *inequalities*) **5 :** difference in height of successive high or low tides due chiefly to the moon's declination — called also *diurnal inequality*

in·equigranular \(ˌ)in, ən+\ *adj* [¹*in-* + *equigranular*] **:** having or characterized by crystals of different sizes ⟨a rock of ~ texture⟩

in·equilateral \"+\ *adj* [¹*in-* + *equilateral*] **1 :** having the two ends unequal ⟨~ bivalve mollusk⟩ **2 :** having the convolutions of the shell wound obliquely around an axis

in·equitable \(ˈ)in, ən+\ *adj* [¹*in-* + *equitable*] **:** not equitable **:** not just **:** contrary to principles of equity **:** UNFAIR ⟨~ taxation⟩ ⟨~ division of an estate among the heirs⟩ — **in·equitableness** \"+\ *n* — **in·equitably** \"+\ *adv*

in·equity \"+\ *n* [¹*in-* + *equity*] **1 :** lack of equity **:** INJUSTICE, UNFAIRNESS **2 :** an instance of injustice or unfairness ⟨adequate authority to correct maladjustments and *inequities* in wage rates —H.S.Truman⟩

in·equivalve \"+\ *also* **in·equi·valved** \-lvd\ *adj* [¹*in-* + *equi-* + *valve* or *valved* (fr. *valve* + *-ed*)] *of a bivalve mollusk or its shell* **:** having the valves unequal in size and form

in·eradicable \ˌin+\ *adj* [¹*in-* + *eradicate* + *-able*] **:** incapable of being eradicated ⟨~ superstitions⟩ — **in·eradicableness** \"+\ *n* -ES — **in·eradicably** \"+\ *adv*

in·erasable \"+\ *adj* [¹*in-* + *erase* + *-able*] **:** incapable of being erased — **in·eras·able·ness** \-nəs\ *n* -ES — **in·eras·ably** \-blē,-bli\ *adv*

in·er·get·ic \ˌin(,)ərˈjed·ik\ *also* **in·er·get·i·cal** \-d·əkəl\ *adj* [¹*in-* + *energetic*] *archaic* **:** lacking energy

ineri *usu cap, var of* IGNERI

in·er·mia \əˈnərmēə\ [NL, fr. L, neut. pl. of *inermis* unarmed, defenseless, fr. *in-* ¹in- + *-ermis* (fr. *arma* arms) — more at ARM] *syn of* SIPUNCULOIDEA

in·er·mi·cap·si·fer \ə,nərməˈkapsəfər\ *n, cap* [NL, fr. L *inermis* + *capsi-* (fr. L *capsa* chest, case) + *-fer* — more at CASE] **:** a genus of tapeworms (family Anoplocephalidae) parasitic in African and Central American rodents and occas. in man

in·errability \(ˌ)in, ən+\ *n* **:** INFALLIBILITY

in·errable \(ˈ)in, ən+\ *adj* [L *inerrabilis*, fr. *in-* ¹in- + *errabilis* errable, fr. *errare* to err + *-abilis* -able — more at ERR] **:** incapable of erring **:** UNERRING **syn** see INFALLIBLE

in·errancy \"+\ *n* **:** exemption from error **:** INFALLIBILITY ⟨doctrine of the ~ of scripture writings —*Interpreter's Bible*⟩

in·errant \"+\ *adj* [L *inerrant-, inerrans* inerrant, fr. *in-* ¹in- + *errant-, errans*, pres. part. of *errare* to err — more at ERR] **1** *obs* **:** INERRATIC **2 :** free from error or mistake **:** UNERRING **syn** see INFALLIBLE

in·errantly \"+\ *adv* **:** INFALLIBLY, UNERRINGLY

in·erratic \ˌin+\ *adj* [¹*in-* + *erratic*] **:** not erratic or wandering **:** following a set course **:** FIXED ⟨~ star⟩

inerring *adj* [¹*in-* + *erring*] *obs* **:** UNERRING

¹in·ert \(ˈ)iˈnərt, əˈn-, -nə̄l, -nəi|, *usu* \d.+V\ *adj* [L *inert-, iners* unskilled, idle, motionless, fr. *in-* ¹in- + *art-, ars* skill, art — more at ARM] **1 :** not having the power to move itself ⟨the Newtonian world which was composed of units, or atoms, that were material, ~, and all alike —S.F.Mason⟩ ⟨~ ammunition⟩ **2 :** not having or manifesting active properties **:** not affecting other substances when in contact with them **:** chemically unreactive **:** powerless for an expected or desired biological effect ⟨~ drug⟩ **:** NEUTRAL **3 :** very slow to move or act **:** LIFELESS, SLUGGISH, INDOLENT ⟨~ bureaucrats⟩ ⟨~ contemplation of television programs⟩ ⟨politically ~ citizenry⟩ **4** *of a paint pigment* **:** possessing little or no hiding power when ground in oil **syn** see INACTIVE

²inert \"\ *n* -s **:** an inert person, constituent, or material: as **a :** a noncombustible gas (as nitrogen or carbon dioxide) present in a gaseous fuel **b :** EXTENDER 1a (1)

in·ert·ance \ˈtᵊn(t)s\ *n* -s **:** ACOUSTIC INERTANCE

inert gas *n* **1 :** a gas (as nitrogen or carbon dioxide) that is normally chemically inactive esp. in not burning or supporting combustion **2 a :** one of the group of gases comprising helium, neon, argon, krypton, xenon, and sometimes radon **b :** a member of the helium group — called also *noble gas, rare gas*

in·er·tia \əˈnərshə, -nəsh-,-nəish- *also* -shēə\ *n, pl* **iner·tias** \-əz\ *also* **iner·ti·ae** \-shē,ē\ [NL, fr. L, lack of skill, idleness, laziness, fr. *inert-, iners* + *-ia* -y] **1 a :** a property of matter by which it remains at rest or in uniform motion in the same straight line unless acted upon by some external force, any change in the motion being measured by the acceleration of the center of mass ⟨~ carried the train past the station⟩ **b :** an analogous property of other physical quantities (as electricity) ⟨electromagnetic ~⟩ **2 :** indisposition to motion, exertion, or action **:** INERTNESS ⟨the Soviets had to overcome the deep-rooted conservatism and ~ of the peasants —A.R. Williams⟩ **:** resistance to change ⟨social ~, the tendency of animals to continue repeating the same action in the same place —W.C.Allee⟩ **3 :** lack of activity **:** SLUGGISHNESS — used esp. of the uterus in labor when its contractions are weak or irregular **4 :** the period of exposure before there is a detectable effect upon a photographic emulsion

in·er·tial \-sh(ē)əl\ *adj* [NL *inertia* + E *-al*] **:** of, relating to, or of the nature of inertia ⟨~ resistance to change of direction⟩

inertial force *n* **:** a force opposite in direction to an accelerating force acting on a body and equal to the product of the accelerating force and the mass of the body

inertial guidance *or* **inertial navigation** *n* **:** guidance (as of a missile or aircraft) by means of self-contained automatically controlling devices that respond to inertial forces

inertial mass *n* **:** mass as determined by impact experiments in accordance with the law that the masses of bodies are inversely proportional to the velocities which a given force will impart to them in a given time

inertial system *n* **:** a frame of reference with respect to which Newton's laws of motion are valid

inertia starter *n* **:** an internal-combustion engine starter that utilizes the energy of a spinning flywheel set in motion by means of a hand crank or electric motor

in·er·tion \-shən\ *n* -s [¹*inert* + *-ion* (as in *exertion*)] *archaic* **:** INERTNESS, QUIETUDE

in·ert·ly *adv* **:** in an inert manner **:** PASSIVELY, LIFELESSLY

in·ert·ness *n* -ES **:** the quality or state of being inert **:** lack of activity **:** PASSIVITY ⟨chemical ~ makes glass a good food container⟩

in·erudite \(ˈ)in, ən+\ *adj* [L *ineruditus*, fr. *in-* ¹in- + *eruditus* learned, skilled, experienced — more at ERUDITE] **:** not erudite **:** IGNORANT

-ines *pl of* -INE

in·escapable \ˌin+\ *adj* [¹*in-* + *escape* + *-able*] **:** incapable of being avoided, ignored, or denied ⟨the ~ mark of his genius —F.R.Leavis⟩ **:** UNAVOIDABLE **:** necessarily present or to be reckoned with **:** following of strict logical necessity or moral compulsion **:** INEVITABLE ⟨~ that a man must owe economic obligations to his wife and to his children —Weston La Barre⟩ ⟨continuity in design appears to be ~ —J.E.Gloag⟩ — **in·es·cap·able·ness** \-nəs\ *n* -ES — **in·es·cap·ably** \-blē,-bli\ *adv*

in·esculent \(ˈ)in, ən+\ *adj* [¹*in-* + *esculent*] **:** not esculent **:** INEDIBLE

in·escutcheon *also* **in·escucheon** \ˌin+\ *n* [⁴*in* + *escutcheon, escucheon*] **:** a small escutcheon borne within a shield

inescutcheon

ines·ite \ˈīnə,sīt, ˈin-, -,zīt\ *n* -s [G *inesit*, fr. Gk *ines* (pl. of *is* sinew, tendon) + G *-it* -ite — more at WITHY] **:** a mineral $Ca_2Mn_7Si_{10}O_{28}(OH)_2.5H_2O$ consisting of a pale red hydrous manganese calcium silicate, in small prismatic crystals or massive (hardness 6, sp. gr. 3.03)

in es·se \ˈəˈnesē\ *adv (or adj)* [ML] **:** in actual existence — contrasted with *in posse*

¹in·essential \ˌin+\ *adj* [¹*in-* + *essential*] **1 :** having no essence or being **2 :** not essential **:** UNESSENTIAL, NONESSENTIAL

²inessential \"\ *n* **:** something that is not essential **:** UNESSENTIAL

in·essentiality \ˌin+\ *n* **:** the quality or state of being inessential

¹in·es·sive \əˈnesiv\ *adj* [L *inesse* to be in (fr. *in-* ²in- + *esse* to be) + E *-ive* — more at IS] *of a grammatical case* **:** denoting position or location within

²inessive \"\ *n* **:** the inessive case of a substantive

in·es·ti·ma·bil·i·ty \(,)i,nestəməˈbiləd·ē, ə,n-\ *n* -ES **:** INESTIMABLENESS

in·estimable \(ˈ)in, ən+\ *adj* [ME, fr. MF, fr. L *inaestimabilis*, fr. *in-* ¹in- + *aestimabilis* estimable — more at ESTIMABLE] **1 :** incapable of being estimated or computed ⟨~ errors⟩ **2 :** too valuable or excellent to be measured or appreciated **:** above all price ⟨has performed an ~ service for his country⟩ — **in·estimable·ness** \"+\ *n* — **in·es·ti·ma·bly** \-blē,-bli\ *adv*

in·euphonious \ˌin+\ *adj* [¹*in-* + *euphonious*] **:** not euphonious **:** harsh in sound

in·evaporable \"+\ *adj* [¹*in-* + *evaporable*] **:** incapable of being reduced in volume by evaporation

in·eva·si·ble \ˌinəˈvāzəbəl, -āsə-\ *adj* [¹*in-* + L *evasus* (past part. of *evadere* to evade) + E *-ible* — more at EVADE] **:** INEVITABLE

in·evidence \(ˈ)in, ən+\ *n* **1** *obs* **:** lack of evidence or manifestation **2 :** the state or fact of being inevident

in·evident \"+\ *adj* [LL *inevident-, inevidens*, fr. L *in-* ¹in-

+ *evident-, evidens* evident — more at EVIDENT] : not evident : not clear or obvious

in·ev·i·ta·bil·i·ty \(,)i,nevəd·ə'bilәd·ē, ə,n-, -v(ə)tə'-, -lәtē, -i\ *n* -ES : the quality or state of being inevitable ⟨habits . . . seem to have all of the ~ that belongs to the movement of the fixed stars —John Dewey⟩ ⟨less inclined to accept the ~ of servitude —Ray Lewis & Angus Maude⟩

¹in·ev·i·ta·ble \ə'nevəd·əbəl, -v(ə)təb-\ *adj* [ME, fr. L *inevitabilis*, fr. *in-* ¹in- + *evitabilis* evitable — more at EVITABLE] **1** : incapable of being avoided or evaded ⟨~ result⟩ ⟨~ day of reckoning⟩ : being or seeming to be in the natural order of things or foreordained ⟨~ phrase⟩ ⟨landscape, as an ~ expression of the Romantic spirit —F.J.Mather⟩ ⟨once we admit . . . that war is natural and ~ —Vera M. Dean⟩ **2** : certain to occur or to confront one ⟨allowing for the ~ delays of such a journey⟩ ⟨the ~ gas stations at every crossroad⟩ ⟨over the pine mantel . . . were the ~ antlers —Gertrude Atherton⟩ — **in·ev·i·ta·ble·ness** \-nəs\ *n* -ES — **in·ev·i·ta·bly** \-blē, -bli\ *adv*

²inevitable \"\ *n* -S : something that is inevitable ⟨should the symptoms of aging be studied as the natural ~*s* of a cyclic process —Louis Berman⟩

inevitable accident *n, law* : an accident that could not have been foreseen or prevented by the due care and diligence of any human being involved in it : an accident caused by forces beyond the power of any human being involved to foresee or overcome by the exercise of ordinary prudence — compare ACT OF GOD

in·exact \¦in+\ *adj* [F, fr. *in-* ¹in- + *exact* — more at EXACT] **1** : not exact : not precisely correct or true : INACCURATE ⟨~ translation⟩ **2** : not rigorous and careful ⟨~ reasoner⟩ — **in·exactly** \"+\ *adv* — **in·exactness** \"+\ *n*

in·exactitude \"+\ *n* [F, fr. *in-* ¹in- + *exactitude* — more at EXACTITUDE] **1** : lack of exactitude or precision : the quality of being inexact or inaccurate **2** : an instance of inexactness

in ex·cel·sis \,inək'selsəs, ,i(,)nek-, -ks'kel-,-ks'chel-,-k'shel-\ *adv* [L] : in the highest degree : SUPERLATIVELY ⟨he had *in excelsis* what some people term . . . the legal mind —*Blackwood's*⟩

in·excitability \¦in+\ *n* : calmness of temper

in·excitable \"+\ *adj* [¹*in-* + *excitable*] **1** : not readily excited or aroused **2** *of a nerve* : not subject to excitation : not responsive to stimulation

in·excusability \"+\ *n* -ES **1** : the quality of being inexcusable **2** : something that is inexcusable

in·excusable \"+\ *adj* [L *inexcusabilis*, fr. *in-* ¹in- + *excusabilis* excusable — more at EXCUSABLE] : not excusable : being without excuse or justification ⟨~ carelessness⟩ — **in·excusableness** \"+\ *n* — **in·excusably** \"+\ *adv*

in·executable \(¦)in, ən+\ *adj* [¹*in-* + *executable*] : impossible of execution or performance : IMPRACTICABLE

in·execution \"+\ *n* [prob. fr. F *inexécution*, fr. MF *inexecution*, fr. *in-* ¹in- + *execution* — more at EXECUTION] : failure to carry out (as an order) or enforce (as a law) : NONPERFORMANCE

in·exertion \¦in+\ *n* [¹*in-* + *exertion*] : lack of exertion or effort : INDOLENCE, LAZINESS

in·exhausted \"+\ *adj* [¹*in-* + *exhausted*] *archaic* : that is not exhausted

in·exhaustibility \"+\ *n* : the quality or state of being inexhaustible : UNFAILINGNESS

in·exhaustible \"+\ *adj* [¹*in-* + *exhaust* + *-ible*] : not exhaustible: as **a** : incapable of being used up : UNFAILING ⟨~ supplies of coal⟩ ⟨an ~ spring⟩ **b** : incapable of being wearied or worn out ⟨~ fertility of invention⟩ ⟨~ patience⟩ — **in·ex·haust·ible·ness** \-nəs\ *n* -ES — **in·ex·haust·ibly** \-blē, -bli\ *adv*

in·exhaustive \¦in+\ *adj* [¹*in-* + *exhaustive*] **1** *archaic* : INEXHAUSTIBLE **2** : not exhaustive — **in·exhaustively** \"+\ *adv*

in·exhaustless \"+\ *adj* [¹*in-* + *exhaustless*] *archaic* : EXHAUSTLESS

in·exigible \(')in, ən+\ *adj* [¹*in-* + *exigible*] : not exigible

in·exist \¦in+\ *vi* [²*in-* + *exist*] *archaic* : to exist in something else : INHERE

¹in·existence \"+\ *n* [¹*in-* + *existence*] : NONEXISTENCE

²inexistence \"\ *n* [²*in-* + *existence*] *archaic* : INHERENCE

¹in·existent \¦in+\ *adj* [LL *inexistent-, inexistens*, fr. L *in-* ²in- + *exsistent-, existent-, exsistens, existens*, pres. part. of *exsistere, existere* to exist — more at EXIST] *archaic* : INHERENT

²inexistent \"\ *adj* [LL *inexistent-, inexistens*, fr. L *in-* ¹in- + *existent-, exsistent-, existens, exsistens*] : not having being : NONEXISTENT

in·ex·o·ra·bil·i·ty \(,)i,neks(ə)rə'bilәd·ē, ə,n-, -lәtē, -i *also* -negz(- *sometimes* ,inig,zōr- *or* ,i(,)neg,zōr- *or* ¦zōr-\ *n* -ES [L *inexorabilitas*, fr. *inexorabilis* + *-itas* -ity] : the quality of being inexorable ⟨moral world of humans does not behave with the same rigor and ~ as the physical world —Weston La Barre⟩

in·ex·o·ra·ble \(')i¦neks(ə)rəbəl, ə'n- *also* -negz(- *sometimes* ¦inig¦zōr- *or* ¦i(,)neg¦zōr- *or* -¦zōr-\ *adj* [L *inexorabilis*, fr. *in-* ¹in- + *exorabilis* exorable, fr. *exorare* to prevail upon, persuade (fr. *ex-* ¹ex- + *orare* to speak, plead, pray) + *-abilis* -able — more at ORATION] : not to be persuaded or moved by entreaty or prayer : UNYIELDING, INFLEXIBLE, RELENTLESS ⟨~ doom⟩ ⟨~ logic⟩ ⟨~ necessity⟩ ⟨~ opponent⟩ — **in·ex·o·ra·ble·ness** \-nəs\ *n* -ES — **in·ex·o·ra·bly** \-blē, -bli\ *adv*

in·expansible \¦in+\ *adj* [¹*in-* + *expansible*] : not expansible

in·expectancy \"+\ *n* [¹*in-* + *expectancy*] : lack of expectancy ⟨it isn't surfeit alone but ~ which makes entertainment so feeble —J.M.Barzun⟩

in·expectant \"+\ *adj* [¹*in-* + *expectant*] : lacking expectation ⟨small ~ audience⟩

in·expediency *or* **in·expedience** \"+\ *n* [¹*in-* + *expediency, expedience*] : the quality or fact of being inexpedient

in·expedient \"+\ *adj* [¹*in-* + *expedient*] **1** : not expedient : not likely to achieve a purpose or bring success : INADVISABLE, UNPROFITABLE ⟨to rely on a deterrent that will bring the maximum of suffering to all mankind is immoral as well as ~ —Denis Healey⟩ **2** : INCONVENIENT ⟨it was occasionally ~ to carry about measuring chains —Rudyard Kipling⟩ — **in·expediently** \"+\ *adv*

in·expensive \"+\ *adj* [¹*in-* + *expensive*] : not expensive : reasonable in price : CHEAP — **in·expensively** \"+\ *adv* — **in·expensiveness** \"+\ *n*

in·experience \"+\ *n* [MF, fr. LL *inexperientia*, fr. L *in-* ¹in- + *experientia* experience — more at EXPERIENCE] : lack of practical experience : lack of knowledge of the ways of the world or of a particular kind of work or activity

in·experienced \"+\ *adj* : lacking practical experience : UNTRAINED, UNTRIED, GREEN

¹in·expert \(¦)in, ən+\ *adj* [ME *inexperte*, fr. MF *inexpert*, fr. L *inexpertus*, fr. *in-* ¹in- + *expertus*, past part. of *experiri* to try — more at EXPERIENCE] **1** : INEXPERIENCED **2** : not expert : not skilled or dexterous — **in·expertly** \"+\ *adv* — **in·expertness** \"+\ *n*

²in·expert \ən+\ *n* : an inexpert person : NOVICE

in·expiable \(')in, ən+\ *adj* [L *inexpiabilis*, fr. *in-* ¹in- + *expiare* to expiate + *-abilis* -able — more at EXPIATE] **1** : not capable of being expiated or atoned for : UNFORGIVABLE ⟨~ offense⟩ **2** *obs* : IMPLACABLE, UNAPPEASABLE — **in·ex·pi·a·ble·ness** \-nəs\ *n* -ES — **in·ex·pi·a·bly** \-blē,-bli\ *adv*

in·expiate \"+\ *adj* [LL *inexpiatus*, fr. L *in-* ¹in- + *expiatus*, past part. of *expiare*] **1** : not expiated **2** *obs* : not appeased

in·explainable \¦in+\ *adj* [¹*in-* + *explainable*] : INEXPLICABLE

in·explicability \(¦)in, ən+\ *n* -ES : the quality of being inexplicable

in·explicable \"+\ *adj* [MF, fr. L *inexplicabilis*, fr. *in-* ¹in- + *explicabilis* explicable — more at EXPLICABLE] **1** *obs* : incapable of being unfolded or unraveled : INEXTRICABLE **2** : not explicable : incapable of being explained, interpreted, or accounted for ⟨~ action⟩ ⟨~ mystery⟩ — **in·ex·plica·ble·ness** \-nəs\ *n* -ES — **in·ex·plica·bly** \-blē,-bli\ *adv*

in·explicit \¦in+ (,)=¦==\ *adj* [¹*in-* + *explicit*] : not explicit — **in·ex·plic·it·ly** *adv* — **in·ex·plic·it·ness** *n*

in·explosive \¦in+\ *adj* [¹*in-* + *explosive*] : not liable to explode

in·exportable \(¦)in, ən+\ *adj* [¹*in-* + *exportable*] : not capable of being exported : not suitable for export

in·expressibility \¦in+\ *n* -ES : the quality of being inexpressible

in·expressible \"+\ *adj* [¹*in-* + *expressible*] : not capable of being expressed : INDESCRIBABLE, INEFFABLE ⟨~ delight⟩ : UNUTTERABLE, UNSPEAKABLE ⟨~ villainy⟩ — **in·ex·press·ible·ness** \-nəs\ *n* -ES — **in·ex·press·ibly** \-blē,-bli\ *adv*

in·ex·press·ibles \,==¦==bəlz\ *n pl, archaic* : TROUSERS

in·expressive \¦in+\ *adj* [¹*in-* + *expressive*] **1** *obs* : INEXPRESSIBLE **2** : lacking expression : not expressive : DULL, WOODEN ⟨~ face⟩ **3** : lacking meaning ⟨~ music⟩ ⟨~ gestures⟩ — **in·expressively** \"+\ *adv* — **in·expressiveness** \"+\ *n*

in·ex·pugna·bil·i·ty \,inik,spyünə'bilәd·ē, ,i(,)nek-,-,spəgnə-\ *n* -ES : IMPREGNABILITY

in·expugnable \¦in+\ *adj* [MF, fr. L *inexpugnabilis*, fr. *in-* ¹in- + *expugnabilis* expugnable — more at EXPUGNABLE] **1** : incapable of being taken by assault or subdued by force : IMPREGNABLE ⟨his position though strong was not ~ —G.B. Sansom⟩ **2** : incapable of being overthrown or driven out ⟨most common and ~ error of criticism —Meyer Schapiro⟩ : STABLE, FIXED ⟨~ hatred⟩ — **in·ex·pugna·ble·ness** \-nəs\ *n* -ES — **in·ex·pugna·bly** \-blē,-bli\ *adv*

in·ex·pung·ibil·i·ty \¦=(,)=,==¦bilәd·ē\ *n* -ES : the quality or state of being inexpungible : INERADICABLENESS, INDELIBILITY ⟨~ of popular myths⟩

in·ex·pung·ible *also* **in·ex·punge·able** \¦inik¦spənjəbəl, ¦i(,)nek-\ *adj* [¹*in-* + *expunge* + *-ible, -able*] : incapable of being obliterated or got rid of ⟨~ scent of a bottle of perfume he had . . . broken —Louis Auchincloss⟩

in·extended \¦in+\ *adj* [¹*in-* + *extended*] : lacking extension : not occupying space

in·extensibility \"+\ *n* [¹*in-* + *extensibility*] : incapability of being drawn out or stretched ⟨~ of a rope⟩

in·extensible \"+\ *adj* [¹*in-* + *extensible*] : not extensible : incapable of being stretched

in·extensile \"+\ *adj* [¹*in-* + *extensile*] : not extensible

in·extension \"+\ *n* [¹*in-* + *extension*] : lack of extension

in·extensional \"+\ *adj* : marked by or relating to absence of stretching out

inextensional deformation *n* : a bending of a surface that preserves unchanged the length of each line element and the measure of curvature at every point

in·extensive \¦in+\ *adj* [¹*in-* + *extensive*] : not extensive

in ex·ten·so \,inik'sten(t)(,)sō, ,i(,)nek-\ *adv* [L] : at length rather than in summary ⟨the details of all the observations will be reported *in extenso* elsewhere —*Science*⟩

in·exterminable \¦in+\ *adj* [LL *inexterminabilis*, fr. L *in-* ¹in- + LL *exterminabilis* capable of being exterminated, exterminable, fr. L *exterminare* to exterminate + *-abilis* -able — more at EXTERMINATE] **1** *obs* : INTERMINABLE **2** : incapable of extermination

in·extinct \"+(,)=¦=\ *adj* [L *inexstinctus, inextinctus*, fr. *in-* ¹in- + *exstinctus, extinctus*, past part. of *exstinguere, extinguere* to extinguish — more at EXTINGUISH] : UNEXTINGUISHED

in·extinguishable \¦in+\ *adj* [¹*in-* + *extinguishable*] : not extinguishable ⟨~ flame⟩ : UNQUENCHABLE, IRREPRESSIBLE ⟨~ hope⟩ ⟨~ laughter⟩ — **in·extinguishably** \"+\ *adv*

in·ex·tir·pa·ble \(¦)i¦nekstərpəbəl, ə'n-; ¦i(,)nek¦s-\ *adj* [F or L; F, fr. L *inexstirpabilis, inextirpabilis*, fr. *in-* ¹in- + *exstirpare, extirpare* to extirpate + *-abilis* -able — more at EXTIRPATE] : not capable of being extirpated : INERADICABLE — **in·ex·tir·pa·ble·ness** \-nəs\ *n* -ES

in ex·tre·mis \,inik'strāməs, ,i(,)nek-, -rēm-\ *adv* [L] : in extreme circumstances : in desperate case; *esp* : at the point of death

in·extricability \(¦)in, ən+\ *n* -ES : the quality or state of being inextricable ⟨~ of form and content —Peter Viereck⟩

in·extricable \"+\ *adj* [MF or L; MF, fr. L *inextricabilis*, fr. *in-* ¹in- + *extricabilis* extricable — more at EXTRICABLE] **1** : not permitting extrication : forming a maze or tangle from which it is impossible to get free **2 a** : incapable of being disentangled or untied ⟨~ knot⟩ ⟨~ unity⟩ **b** : UNSOLVABLE ⟨~ confusion⟩ **3** : INTRICATE, INVOLVED : highly elaborated ⟨~ design⟩ — **in·ex·trica·ble·ness** \-nəs\ *n* -ES — **in·ex·trica·bly** \-blē,-bli\ *adv*

inf *abbr* **1** infantry **2** inferior **3** infield; infielder **4** infinitive **5** infinity **6** infirmary **7** information **8** infra **9** infused; infusion

inface \'=,=\ *n* [⁴*in* + *face*] : the steeper of the two slopes of a cuesta

in fa·cie cu·ri·ae \-'fāshē,ē'kyürē,ē\ *adv* [ML] : before or in the presence of the court

infall \'=,=\ *n* [⁴*in* + *fall*] **1** : INCURSION ⟨~ of pirates⟩ **2** : INLET, CONFLUENCE, JUNCTION **3** : a falling into or on ⟨~ of meteorites⟩ ⟨~ of a cavern roof⟩

in·fallibilism \(')in+\ *n* **1** : support of or adherence to the dogma of papal infallibility **2** : a belief that scientific laws are not subject to change — opposed to *fallibilism*

in·fallibilist \"+\ *n* **1** : one who believes in infallibility; *esp* : a supporter of the dogma of papal infallibility **2** : one who believes that scientific laws are not subject to change

in·fallibility \(¦)in+\ *n* [ML *infallibilitas*, fr. *infallibilis* infallible + L *-itas* -ity] : the quality or state of being infallible

in·fallible \(')in, ən+\ *adj* [ML *infallibilis*, fr. L *in-* ¹in- + LL *fallibilis* fallible — more at FALLIBLE] **1** : not fallible : incapable of error : UNERRING ⟨~ marksman⟩ ⟨~ ear for pitch in music⟩ ⟨~ memory⟩ **2** : not liable to mislead, deceive, or disappoint : SURE, CERTAIN, INDUBITABLE ⟨~ remedy⟩ ⟨his accent is an almost ~ index of his family background and education —Richard Joseph⟩ ⟨~ scheme for making money⟩ **3** : incapable of error in defining doctrines touching faith or morals

syn INERRABLE, INERRANT, UNERRING: INFALLIBLE describes that which is exempt from possibility of error or mistake or that which has been errorless ⟨no mathematician is *infallible*; he may make mistakes —A.S.Eddington⟩ ⟨believed in an *infallible* Bible —W.W.Sweet⟩ INERRABLE and INERRANT are erudite synonyms for INFALLIBLE sometimes used in its stead to escape connotations arising from the discussion of papal infallibility; the latter may imply that whatever is described has not so far erred ⟨the Church was ubiquitous, omniscient, theoretically *inerrant* and omnicompetent —G.G.Coulton⟩ ⟨at the moment we lack, in all English-speaking countries, the *inerrant* literary sense which gave us the Prayer Book Collects, often quite as beautiful in translation as in the original Latin —W.L.Sperry⟩ UNERRING may imply freedom from error coupled with sureness, reliability, and exactness ⟨an *unerring* marksman⟩ ⟨a man's language is an *unerring* index of his nature —Laurence Binyon⟩ ⟨the *unerring* scent of the hounds in pursuit —George Meredith⟩

in·fal·li·ble·ness *n* : INFALLIBILITY

in·fallibly \"+\ *adj* : without fail : SURELY, CERTAINLY ⟨must make the proper use of his opportunities or he will ~ perish —A.C.McGiffert⟩

in·fam·a·tory \ən'famə,tōrē, -tȯr-\ *adj* [ML *infamatorius*, fr. L *infamatus* (past part. of *infamare*) + *-orius* -ory] *archaic* : DEFAMATORY

in·fame \ən'fām\ *vt* -ED/-ING/-S [ME *enfamen*, fr. MF *enfamer, infamer*, fr. L *infamare*, fr. *infamis*] *archaic* : DEFAME

in·fa·mize \'infə,mīz\ *vt* -ED/-ING/-S [*infamous* + *-ize*] *archaic* : to make infamous : DEFAME

in·fa·mous \'infəməs\ *adj* [ME *infamis, infamous*, fr. L *infamis*, fr. *in-* ¹in- + *-famis* (fr. *fama* fame) — more at FAME] **1** : having a reputation of the worst kind : notorious as being of vicious, contemptible, or criminal character : DETESTABLE, ABHORRENT ⟨one of the most ~ spies and bullies of all time —*Time*⟩ ⟨~ outlaw⟩ ⟨~ traitor⟩ ⟨~ dog has got every vice except hypocrisy —W.M.Thackeray⟩ **2** : causing or bringing infamy : deserving hatred or detestation ⟨~ conduct⟩ ⟨~ vices⟩ ⟨~ treatment of prisoners⟩ ⟨men to whom totalitarianism is ~ —Jerome Frank⟩ ⟨most ~ of quack nostrums —*Time*⟩ **3** : having a bad name as being associated with something disgraceful or detestable ⟨the street outside Newgate had not obtained one ~ notoriety that has since attached to it —Charles Dickens⟩ **4** : convicted of an offense judged infamous ⟨~ person⟩ **syn** see VICIOUS

infamous crime *n* : a crime judged infamous because it constitutes treason or a felony, because it involves moral turpitude of a nature that creates a strong presumption that the one guilty is unworthy of belief in a court of law, or because it subjects the one guilty to infamy ⟨no person shall be held to answer for a capital or otherwise *infamous crime*, unless on a presentment or indictment of a grand jury, except in cases arising in the land or naval forces, or in the militia, when in actual service in time of war or public danger —*U.S.Constitution*⟩

infamous crime against nature : SODOMY

in·fa·mous·ly *adv* : in an infamous manner : in a manner deserving infamy ⟨how ~ he treats his wife —George Meredith⟩ : ATROCIOUSLY ⟨just as the work was nearly completed, being ~ done, it fell down again —L.H.Chambers⟩

in·fa·my \'infəmē, -mi\ *n* -ES [ME *infamye*, fr. MF *infamie*, fr. L *infamia*, fr. *infamis* + *-ia* -y] **1 a** : a lasting, widespread, and deep-rooted evil reputation brought about by something criminal, shocking, or brutal : the highest degree of dishonor ⟨a series of treacherous murders added to his ~⟩ **b** : an indication of such notoriety : strong condemnatory utterance **2 a** : an extreme and publicly known criminal, shocking, or brutal act ⟨an ~ greater than any mutiny⟩ **b** : the state or condition of being rightly and widely known for such an act ⟨his name will live in ~ for this night's work⟩ **3** : the public disgrace or loss of character and honor or loss of civil or political rights incurred by a person convicted of an infamous crime **syn** see DISHONOR

in·fan·cy \'infənsē, -si\ *n* -ES [ME, fr. L *infantia*, fr. *infant-, infans* infant + *-ia* -y] **1** : the state or period of being an infant : the first part of life : early childhood — called also *babyhood* **2** : the beginning or early period of existence ⟨mechanical engineering was then in its ~ —O.S.Nock⟩ ⟨~ of a city⟩ **3** : the legal status of an infant or one under age or under the age of twenty-one years : NONAGE, MINORITY **4** : the initial or very early stage (as of a river) in a cycle of erosion

infang *n* -S [by shortening] *obs* : INFANGTHIEF

in·fang·thief \'infəŋ,thēf\ *n* [ME *infangenthef, infangthef*, fr. OE *infangenethēof, infangenthēof*, fr. *in, inn* in + *fangen* (past part. of *fōn* to seize, capture) + *thēof* thief — more at IN, PACT, THIEF] : a medieval franchise of exercising jurisdiction over a thief caught within the limits to which the franchise was attached : the right of the lord of a manor to judge a thief taken within the seigniory of such lord — distinguished from *outfangthief*

in·fans \'in,fanz\ *n, pl* **infan·tes** \ən'fan·,tēz\ [L] *civil law* : a child under seven years of age : a child not having the ability to speak

¹in·fant \'infənt\ *n* -S [ME *enfaunt, infaunt*, fr. MF *enfant*, fr. L *infant-, infans*, fr. *infant-, infans*, adj., incapable of speech, young, fr. *in-* ¹in- + *fant-, fans*, pres. part. of *fari* to speak — more at BAN] **1 a** : a child in the first year of life : BABY **b** : a child several years of age **2 a** : a person who is not of full age : MINOR **b** *common law* : a person under the age of 21 — see AGE 3 **3** *Brit* : a pupil in an infant school

²infant \"\ *adj* **1** : of, relating to, exemplifying, or being in infancy or young childhood ⟨~ king⟩ ⟨~ martyr⟩ **2** : being in an early stage of development : not matured or fully developed ⟨~ fruit⟩ ⟨~ navy⟩; *esp* : needing protection and care ⟨~ animals⟩ ⟨our ~ steel industry⟩

¹in·fan·ta \ən'fantə\ *n* -S [Sp & Pg, fem. of *infante*] **1** : a daughter of the king and queen of Spain or Portugal **2** : the wife of an infante

²infanta \"\ *adj, of a fashion in dress* : derived from Velasquez's portraits of 17th century Spanish princesses and usu. having wide skirts with side extensions

in·fan·te \ən'fan·,tā\ *n* -S [Sp & Pg, lit., infant, fr. L *infant-, infans*] : a son of the king and queen of Spain or Portugal who is not the eldest — compare PRINCIPE

in·fant·hood \'infənt,hu̇d\ *n* : INFANCY

in·fan·ti·ci·dal \ən¦fantə¦sīdᵊl\ *adj* : relating to the killing of infants

¹in·fanticide \ən'fantə,sīd\ *n* -S [LL *infanticidium*, fr. L *infant-, infans* infant + *-i-* + *-cidium* -cide (killing) — more at INFANT] **1** : a killing of a newly or recently born child **2** : a practice of killing infants — compare ABORTION 1, FETICIDE

²infanticide \"\ *n* -S [LL *infanticida*, fr. L *infant-, infans* + *-i-* + *-cida* -cide (killer)] : one that kills an infant

in·fan·tile \'infən,tīl *also* -n·təl *sometimes* -n,tēl *or* -n(,)til\ *adj* [prob. fr. F, fr. L *infantilis*, fr. *infant-, infans* infant + *-ilis* -ile] **1** : of or relating to infants or infancy ⟨~ disease⟩ ⟨~ state⟩ **2** : suitable to an infant : characteristic of an infant : very immature : CHILDISH ⟨~ level of entertainment⟩ ⟨~ tantrum⟩ **3** : affected with infantilism **4** *of topography* : being in a very early stage of development presumably following an uplift or equivalent change with respect to base level ⟨~ stream⟩ ⟨~ mountain range⟩

infantile myxedema *n* : CRETINISM

infantile paralysis *n* : POLIOMYELITIS

infantile sexuality *n* : needs and strivings in early childhood for libidinal gratification : pregenital eroticism

in·fan·ti·lism \'infən·tə,lizəm *sometimes* ən'fantᵊl,i-\ *n* -S [ISV *infantile* + *-ism*] **1** : a condition of being abnormally childlike : a retention of childish physical, mental, or emotional qualities in adult life; *esp* : failure to attain sexual maturity **2** : an act or expression characteristic of lack of maturity : PUERILITY ⟨~*s* of thought⟩ ⟨the ~ of selfishness —Agnes E. Meyer⟩

in·fan·ti·lis·tic \¦infəntə¦listik\ *adj* : abnormally immature : showing infantile behavior

in·fan·til·i·ty \,infən'tiləd·ē\ *n* -ES [ML *infantilitas*, fr. L *infantilis* infantile + *-itas* -ity] : the quality or state of being infantile : CHILDISHNESS

in·fan·tine \'infən,tīn, -tēn\ *adj* [F *infantin*, fr. MF, alter. (influenced by L *infant-, infans* infant) of *enfantin*, fr. OF, fr. *enfant* infant + *-in* -ine — more at INFANT] : INFANTILE ⟨~ wailing⟩ : CHILDISH

infant mortality *n* : the rate of deaths occurring in the first year of life

in·fan·try \'infəntrē, -ri\ *n* -ES [MF & OIt; MF *infanterie*, fr. OIt *infanteria*, fr. *infante* infant, boy, footman, foot soldier (fr. L *infant-, infans* infant) + *-eria* -ry — more at INFANT] **1 a** : soldiers trained, armed, and equipped to fight on foot **b** : a branch of an army composed of such soldiers **c** : an infantry regiment ⟨the 8th *Infantry*⟩ **d** : MOONLIGHT BLUE **2** [influenced in meaning by ¹*infant*] : a body of children

in·fan·try·man \-mən\ *n, pl* **infantrymen** : an infantry soldier : FOOT SOLDIER

infant's breath \'==¦=\ *n* **1** : WILD MADDER 2a **2** : MONEYWORT

infant school *n, Brit* : PRESCHOOL, KINDERGARTEN

in·farct \'in,färkt, ən'f-\ *n* -S [L *infarctus*, past part. of *infarcire, infercire* to stuff, stuff full, fr. *in-* ²in- + *farcire* to stuff, fill — more at FARCE] : an area of coagulation necrosis in a tissue (as of the heart) resulting from obstruction of the local circulation by a thrombus or embolus

in·farct·ed \ən'färktəd\ *adj* : affected with infarction ⟨~ kidney⟩

in·farc·tion \-kshən\ *n* -S : the producing of an infarct

in·fare \'in,fa(ə)r, -fe(ə)r\ *n* [ME *infer, infair* entrance, infare, fr. OE *infær* entrance, fr. *in, inn* in + *fær* way, journey, fr. *faran* to go, travel — more at IN, FARE] *chiefly dial* : a feast and reception for a newly married couple usu. at the home of the groom's family a day or two after the wedding

infatigable *adj* [L *infatigabilis*, fr. *in-* ¹in- + *fatigare* to fatigue + *-abilis* -able] *obs* : INDEFATIGABLE

¹in·fat·u·ate \ən'fachəwət\ *adj* [ME, fr. L *infatuatus*, past part.] : marked by infatuation : INFATUATED ⟨knowing the inwardness of that grand, ~ gabble —R.P.Warren⟩

²in·fat·u·ate \-chə,wāt, *usu* -ād·+V\ *vt* -ED/-ING/-S [L *infatuatus*, past part. of *infatuare*, fr. *in-* ²in- + *fatuus* foolish, fatuous — more at FATUOUS] **1** *obs* : to turn (as counsel) into foolishness or show to be foolish : FRUSTRATE **2** : to make foolish : affect with folly : weaken the intellectual powers of or deprive of sound judgment ⟨the toys that ~ men —R.W. Emerson⟩ **3** : to inspire with a foolish and extravagant love or desire ⟨you have *infatuated* this boy to such an extent that he would agree with you in anything —W.J.Locke⟩

³in·fat·u·ate \-,wət\ *n* -S [¹*infatuate*] : an infatuated person

in·fat·u·at·ed \ən'fachə,wād·əd\ *adj* : possessed with or marked by a strong attachment or foolish or unreasoning love or desire ⟨a man absolutely ~ and delivered over to certain

destruction —F.R.Leavis⟩ ⟨how ~ she was with her lover, and how regardless of what anyone could say to her on the subject —Anthony Trollope⟩
in·fat·u·at·ed·ly *adv* : in an infatuated manner
in·fat·u·a·tion \ən,fachəˈwāshən\ *n* -s [LL *infatuation-, infatuatio,* fr. L *infatuatus* + *-ion-, -io* -ion] **1** : the act of infatuating or state of being infatuated : strong and unreasoning attachment esp. to something unworthy of attachment ⟨an ~ with the rare that is the mark of a limited understanding —D.C.Peattie⟩ ⟨a sentimentalizing and transitory ~ for India —Paul Potts⟩ ⟨American ~ with big cars and big engines —Eugene Jaderquist⟩ ⟨the victim of a ridiculous ~ —John Morrison⟩ ⟨if they would turn aside from their cinquecento ~ —Norman Douglas⟩ **2** : something that infatuates : the object of an unreasoning or foolish attachment ⟨the heady ~ of speed —Ray Hare⟩
in·fat·u·a·tor \-ˌ-ˌ-ˌwād·ə(r)\ *n* -s : one that infatuates
in·faust \ənˈfau̇st, -ˈfȯst\ *adj* [F or L; F *infauste,* fr. L *infaustus,* fr. *in-* ¹in- + *faustus* lucky; akin to L *favēre* to be favorable — more at FAVOR] : not favorable : UNLUCKY, UNPROPITIOUS
in·feasibility \(ˌ)in+\ *n* : IMPRACTICABILITY
in·feasible \(ˈ)in+\ *adj* [¹*in-* + *feasible*] : not feasible : IMPRACTICABLE — **in·fea·si·ble·ness** *n*
¹**infect** *adj* [ME, fr. MF or L; MF, fr. L *infectus,* past part. of *inficere*] *archaic* : INFECTED
²**in·fect** \ənˈfekt\ *vb* -ED/-ING/-S [ME *infecten,* fr. L *infectus,* past part. of *inficere* to stain, dye, taint, infect, fr. *in-* ²in- + *-ficere* (fr. *facere* to do, make) — more at DO] *vt* **1** : to taint with decaying matter : contaminate with a disease-producing substance, germs, or bacteria ⟨~ a lancet⟩ **2 a** : to communicate a pathogen or a disease to (an individual or organ) ⟨clouds of mosquitoes ~*ed* the unprotected troops with malaria parasites⟩ **b** *of a pathogenic organism* : to invade (an individual or organ) usu. by penetration — often used only of the actual penetration of the pathogen as distinguished from its subsequent growth in the host ⟨the polio virus probably usually ~*s* man through the nasal mucous membrane⟩; compare INFECTION 2 **3** : to communicate or affect as if by some subtle contact: as **a** : to taint by communication of something noxious or pernicious ⟨he is deeply upset and manages to ~ her with a sense of guilt —*London Calling*⟩ ⟨intellectuals . . . become agents of discontent who ~ rich and poor, high and low —Irving Howe⟩ **b** : to work upon or seize upon so as to induce sympathy, belief, or support ⟨~*ed* everyone with his zeal for nature —Van Wyck Brooks⟩ ⟨an exuberance that tends to ~ the whole enterprise —E.J.Kahn⟩ **4** *obs* : DYE, STAIN **5** : INFEST ⟨fish ~*ed* with parasites⟩ ⟨condemned liver ~*ed* with flukes⟩ **6** : to subject (a whole cargo of an owner) to forfeiture because a part is contraband **7** : to induce a change in quality in (the sound of a neighboring syllable) ~ *vi* : to become infected ⟨didn't pay any attention to it because I never ~ —Ernest Hemingway⟩
¹**in·fect·ant** \ənˈfektənt\ *adj* [²*infect* + *-ant*] : producing infection : INFECTING ⟨~ power⟩
²**infectant** *n* -s : an agent of infection (as a bacterium or virus)
infected *adj* **1** : having undergone infection ⟨~ wound⟩ **2** : CONTAMINATED ⟨obliged to go into ~ rooms—Jane Austen⟩ — **in·fect·ed·ness** *n* -ES
in·fect·ibil·i·ty \ən,fektəˈbiləd·ē\ *n* -ES : susceptibility to infection
in·fect·ible \ənˈfektəbəl\ *adj* [*infect* + *-ible*] : capable of being infected
in·fec·tion \ənˈfekshən\ *n* -s [ME *infeccioun,* fr. MF & LL; MF *infection,* fr. LL *infection-, infectio,* fr. L *infectus* + *-ion-, -io* -ion] **1** : the act or result of affecting or infecting injuriously: **a** : contamination or pollution of matter (as air or water) **b** : corruption of character, morals, faith, loyalty ⟨focal point of moral and political ~⟩ **2** : an act or process of infecting ⟨syphilis ~ is chiefly venereal⟩; *also* : the establishment of a pathogen in its host after invasion **3** : the state produced by the establishment of an infective agent in or on a suitable host ⟨hampered by an ~ in his foot⟩ : a contagious or infectious disease ⟨among the more serious ~*s* of childhood are scarlet fever and meningitis⟩ **4** : an infective agent (as a fungus, bacterium, or virus) : material contaminated with an infective agent and capable of causing disease **5** : the communication of emotions or qualities through example or contact ⟨from such people . . . goes forth the ~ of goodwill —W.F.Hambly⟩ ⟨always open to the ~ of the holiday mood —Mary Austin⟩ **6** : the subjecting of an entire cargo to forfeiture because of the contraband nature of part of it **7** : the influence on a speech sound of a vowel sound next following or preceding **8** : the acquisition of inductive power by embryonic cells through diffusion from adjacent organizer
infection–exhaustion psychosis *n* : any one of a group of mental disorders characterized esp. by delirium and mental confusion and occurring in connection with infections, fevers, and exhausted states
infection hypha *or* **infection thread** *n* : the hypha of a parasitic fungus that penetrates the host and establishes an infection
infection period *also* **infection stage** *n* : the period from the first evident manifestation of an infectious disease to the final host reaction — used chiefly in plant pathology
in·fec·tious \ənˈfekshəs\ *adj* [*infection* + *-ous*] **1 a** : capable of causing infection : INFECTIVE ⟨a carrier remains ~ without himself showing signs of disease⟩ ⟨viruses and other ~ agents⟩ **b** : communicable by infection ⟨an ~ disease⟩ — compare CONTAGIOUS **2** : CORRUPTING, CONTAMINATING, VITIATING, DEMORALIZING ⟨fear is exceedingly ~ : children catch it from their elders —Bertrand Russell⟩ ⟨they say cowardice is ~ —R.L.Stevenson⟩ **3** : capable of being easily diffused or spread : readily communicated : CATCHING, SYMPATHETIC ⟨his own delight in his great theme is ~ —Ernest Newman⟩ ⟨~ excitement⟩ **4** *obs* : INFECTED **5** *of contraband goods* : having the effect of subjecting the entire cargo to forfeiture — **in·fec·tious·ly** *adv* — **in·fec·tious·ness** *n* -ES
infectious abortion *n* : CONTAGIOUS ABORTION
infectious anemia *n* : a serious often fatal virus disease of horses and mules marked by intermittent fever, depression, weakness, jaundice, and mucosal hemorrhages and frequently by anemia — called also *swamp fever*
infectious bronchitis *n* **1** : a virus disease of chickens marked by inflammation of the bronchial tubes and abundant secretion of mucus interfering with respiration and causing gasping and choking that is often fatal in young birds and in adults seriously interferes with egg production — compare INFECTIOUS LARYNGOTRACHEITIS **2** : any of various infective diseases of the bronchial tubes (as in horses or cows)
infectious bulbar paralysis *n* : PSEUDORABIES
infectious chlorosis *n* : a general chlorosis or a variegation due to a virus that can be transmitted from chlorotic to normal green plants by budding, grafting, or insect vectors
infectious disease *n* : a disease caused by the entrance into and growth and multiplication in the body of bacteria, protozoans, fungi, or analogous organisms (as filterable viruses) — compare CONTAGIOUS DISEASE
infectious ectromelia *n* : MOUSEPOX
infectious enterohepatitis *n* : BLACKHEAD 3
infectious equine encephalomyelitis *n* : ENCEPHALOMYELITIS
infectious hepatitis *n* **1** : an acute usu. benign hepatitis caused by a single-stranded RNA virus that does not persist in the blood serum and is transmitted esp. in food and water contaminated with infected fecal matter — called also *catarrhal jaundice*; compare SERUM HEPATITIS **2** : WEIL'S DISEASE
infectious jaundice *n* **1** : INFECTIOUS HEPATITIS **2** : WEIL'S DISEASE
infectious laryngotracheitis *n* : a severe highly contagious and often fatal virus disease of chickens affecting chiefly adult birds and taking the form of an inflammation of the trachea and larynx often marked by local necrosis and hemorrhage and by the formation of purulent or cheesy exudate interfering with breathing — compare INFECTIOUS BRONCHITIS, NEWCASTLE DISEASE
infectious mastitis *n* : BOVINE MASTITIS
infectious mononucleosis *n* : an acute infectious disease of unknown cause characterized by fever, malaise and prostration, swelling of lymph glands, and lymphocytosis and seen chiefly in children and young adults — called also *glandular fever, lymphadenosis*
infectious necrotic hepatitis *n* : BLACK DISEASE
infectious sinusitis *n* : a virus disease of turkeys marked by inflammation of the lining of the infraorbital sinuses resulting in great distention of the sinuses and by exudate that interferes with vision and indirectly with nutrition
infectious vaginitis *n* : EPIVAGINITIS
in·fec·tive \ənˈfektiv\ *adj* [ME, fr. ML *infectivus,* fr. L *infectus* (past part. of *inficere* to stain, dye, taint, infect) + *-ivus* -ive — more at INFECT] **1** : producing infection : able to produce infection : INFECTING **2** : affecting others : INFECTIOUS — **in·fec·tive·ness** *n* -ES
in·fec·tiv·i·ty \,in,fekˈtivəd·ē\ *n* -ES : the quality of being infective : the ability to produce infection; *specif* : a tendency to spread rapidly from host to host — distinguished from *virulence*
in·fec·tor \ənˈfektə(r)\ *n* -s : one that infects
infects *pres 3d sing of* INFECT
in·fec·tum \ənˈfektəm\ *n* -s [NL, fr. L, neut. of *infectus* undone, unfinished, fr. *in-* ¹in- + *-fectus* (fr. *factus,* past part. of *facere* to do, make) — more at DO] : an aspectual category of tenses in Latin which includes all that indicate that action or state is in progress in contrast with those tenses which indicate that action or state is completed — compare PERFECTUM
infectuous *adj* [ME, fr. L *infectus* + ME *-ous*] *obs* : INFECTIOUS
in·fecund \(ˈ)in+\ *adj* [ME *infecounde,* fr. L *infecundus,* fr. *in-* ¹in- + *fecundus* fruitful — more at FEMININE] : not fecund
in·fecundity \ˌin+\ *n* [L *infecunditas,* fr. *infecundus* + *-itas* -ity] : lack of fecundity
infeeble *obs var of* ENFEEBLE
¹**infeed** \ˈ-ˌ-\ *n* [⁴*in* + *feed* (n.)] **1 a** : a feed for infeeding a tool or wheel **b** : a mechanism for feeding material into a machine ⟨back goes into the ~ of washing machine —*Manila Times*⟩ **2** : the process of infeeding
²**infeed** \"\ *vt* [²*in* + *feed* (v.)] : to feed (a tool or wheel) into work (as on a lathe) in a direction normal to that of the axis about which the work revolves
in·feft \inˈfeft\ *vt* **infeft** *also* **infefted**; **infeft** *also* **infefted**; **infefting**; **infefts** [ME (Sc dial.) *infeften,* alter. of *enfeffen* to enfeoff — more at ENFEOFF] *Scots law* : to invest with or give symbolical possession of inheritable property — **infeftment** *n* -s
in·felicific \(ˌ)in+\ *adj* [¹*in-* + *felicific*] : not productive of happiness : productive of unhappiness
in·felicitous \ˌin+\ *adj* [¹*in-* + *felicitous*] : not felicitous: **a** : UNFORTUNATE ⟨~ remark⟩ **b** : not appropriate in application : AWKWARD ⟨~ phrase⟩ **c** : DEFECTIVE, IMPERFECT ⟨~ typesetting due to illegible copy⟩ — **in·fe·lic·i·tous·ly** *adv* — **in·fe·lic·i·tous·ness** *n*
in·felicity \ˌin+\ *n* [ME *infelicite,* fr. L *infelicitas,* fr. *infelic-, infelix* unfortunate, unhappy (fr. *in-* ¹in- + *felic-, felix* fruitful, happy) + *-itas* -ity — more at FEMININE] **1** : the quality or state of being infelicitous: **a** : UNHAPPINESS, WRETCHEDNESS, MISFORTUNE ⟨confusion and ~ of her emotions —Elinor Wylie⟩ **b** : lack of suitableness or appropriateness **2** : something (as an act or word) that is infelicitous ⟨examined for *infelicities* before printing —E.P.Cheyney⟩
infelt \ˈ-ˌ-\ *adj* [²*in* + *felt*] *archaic* : felt inwardly : HEARTFELT
in·feminine \(ˈ)in+\ *adj* [¹*in-* + *feminine*] : UNFEMININE
infeodation *var of* INFEUDATION
infeoff *obs var of* ENFEOFF
in·fer \R ənˈfər, + *vowel* -fər·; -R -fə̄, + *suffixal vowel* -fər· *also* -fər, + *vowel in a following word* -fər· *or* -fə̄ *also* -fər\ *vb* **inferred**; **inferred**; **inferring**; **infers** [MF or L; MF *inferer,* fr. L *inferre* to carry or bring into, attack, enter, introduce, cause, deduce, fr. *in* ²in- + *ferre* to carry, bring — more at BEAR] *vt* **1** *obs* **a** : to bring about : PROCURE **b** : to bring upon one : INFLICT **c** : CONFER **2** : to derive by reasoning or implication : conclude from facts or premises ⟨we see smoke and ~ fire —L.A.White⟩ : accept or derive as a consequence, conclusion, or probability ⟨task of physical science is to ~ knowledge of external objects from a set of signals passing along our nerves —A.S.Eddington⟩ ⟨the child ~*s* the existence of an environment which is not part of itself —James Jeans⟩ — compare IMPLY **3** : GUESS, SURMISE ⟨given some utterance, a person may ~ from it all sorts of things which neither the utterance nor the utterer implied —I.A. Richards⟩ ⟨as may be *inferred* from the picture, travel through this type of forest was comparatively easy —C.B.Hitchcock⟩ **4 a** : to lead to as a conclusion or consequence : involve as a normal outcome of thought ⟨democracy ~*s* such loving comradeship —Walt Whitman⟩ **b** : to point out : INDICATE ⟨this doth ~ the zeal I had to see him —Shak.⟩ — compare IMPLY **5** : to give reason to draw an inference concerning : HINT ⟨did not take part in the debate except to ask a question *inferring* that the constitution must be changed —*Manchester Guardian Weekly*⟩ ⟨complain of the American accent, *inferring* that American culture is unworthy of notice —W.C.Greet⟩ **6** *obs* : to bring in : INTRODUCE ~ *vi* : to draw inferences ⟨men have been thinking for ages . . . have observed, *inferred,* and reasoned in all sorts of ways and to all kinds of results—John Dewey⟩
syn DEDUCE, CONCLUDE, JUDGE, GATHER: INFER indicates arriving at an opinion or coming to accept a probability on the basis of available evidence, which may be slight ⟨the population of Gloucester may readily be *inferred* from the number of houses which King found in the returns of hearth money —T.B.Macaulay⟩ ⟨your letter has just arrived and allows me to *infer* that you are as well as ever —O.W. Holmes †1935⟩ ⟨most of the material in this book was spoken before it was printed, as may perhaps be *inferred* from the style —Elmer Davis⟩ DEDUCE adds to INFER implications of ordered logical thought processes used in the study of logic to draw a specific inference from a general principle, in popular use to infer a truth from analysis of evidence ⟨for the apprehension of new elements requires a sensitive perception and familiarity with new details and cannot be *deduced* from established principles —M.R.Cohen⟩ ⟨a register at the head of the stairs on a wooden shelf. The last entry was in pencil, three weeks previous as to date, and had been written by someone with a very unsteady hand. I *deduced* from this that the management was not overparticular —Raymond Chandler⟩ CONCLUDE may indicate attaining to a fact, truth, or belief after ordered consideration following through with necessary consequences of evidence weighed or facts observed ⟨do not *conclude* that all state activities will be state monopolies —G.B.Shaw⟩ ⟨*concluded* that all of the senses were of equal value in obtaining knowledge of the world, and that with one sense alone "the understanding has as many faculties as with the five joined together" —S.F. Mason⟩ JUDGE stresses careful, critical examination of evidence in attempting to arrive at a wise or fit conclusion ⟨there is a unifying as well as a discriminating phase of judgment — technically known as synthesis in distinction from analysis. This unifying phase, even more than the analytic, is a function of the creative response of the individual who *judges* —John Dewey⟩ ⟨the lawfulness or unlawfulness of taking part in deeds of violence must be *judged* on the merits of each particular case —W.R.Inge⟩ GATHER implies conclusion by reflection but not pondering on impressions formed from cumulative evidence ⟨piecing together classical tradition and references in Egyptian and Hebrew records, we *gather* that for some three centuries onwards from 1600 B.C. Phoenicia was a dependency of the Pharaohs —Edward Clodd⟩ ⟨that I myself believe there may be more than one kind of good poetry might, I think, have been *gathered* from that paragraph of mine which Professor Grierson then quotes —F.R.Leavis⟩
in·fer·able *also* **in·fer·ible** *or* **in·fer·ri·ble** \-ˈfərəbəl *also* ˈinf(ə)rə- *or* ənˈfərə-\ *adj* : capable of being inferred ⟨portion most used by travelers . . . for reasons ~ from the map —R.H.Brown⟩ — **in·fer·ably** \-blē\ *adv*
in·fer·ence \ˈinf(ə)rən(t)s *also* -fərn-\ *n* -s [ML *inferentia,* fr. L *inferent-, inferens* (pres. part. of *inferre*) + *-ia* -y] **1** : the act or process of inferring : the act of passing from one or more propositions, statements, or judgments considered as true to another the truth of which is believed to follow from that of the former ⟨this reasoning . . . is . . . stronger than some modern ~*s* of science —Henry Adams⟩ ⟨~*s* are made, but implications are discovered⟩ — see IMMEDIATE INFERENCE, MEDIATE INFERENCE; compare DEDUCTION 1, INDUCTION 2b, TRANSFORMATION RULE **2** : something that is inferred : DEDUCTION 2; *esp* : a proposition or conclusion arrived at by inferring ⟨the following ~*s* may be fairly drawn from these facts⟩ **3** : the premises and conclusion that represent a process of inferring or that form the determinants of a belief ⟨the conviction that action should be based not on shadowy ~ . . . but on solid fact —C.W.Eliot⟩
in·fer·en·tial \ˌinfəˈrenchəl\ *adj* [ML *inferentia* + E *-al*] **1** : relating to, involving, or resembling inference ⟨~ judgment⟩ ⟨~ procedure⟩ **2** : deduced or deducible by inference ⟨~ evidence of his departure⟩
in·fer·en·tial·ly \-chəlē, -li\ *adv* : by way of inference : through inference ⟨answers to these questions are only ~ contained in this latest biography —Bosley Crowther⟩
¹**in·fe·ri·or** \ənˈfirēə(r), -ˈfēr-, (ˈ)inˈf-\ *adj* [ME, fr. L, comp. of *inferus* low, situated beneath — more at UNDER] **1** : situated lower down or nearer what is regarded as the bottom or base : LOWER, NETHER ⟨~ latitudes⟩ ⟨~ rock strata⟩ **2 a** : of lower degree or rank ⟨was a member of an ~ caste⟩ ⟨a major is ~ to a colonel⟩ **b** : of low degree or rank ⟨~ classes of society⟩ **3 a** : of less importance, value, or merit : of poorer quality ⟨the child . . . considers himself ~ to the adult figures —G.S.Blum⟩ ⟨declined to an ~ position among the world powers⟩ ⟨~ chess move⟩ ⟨easily beat his ~ opponent⟩ **b** *of a railroad train* : required to yield right of way in the absence of specific orders **c** : of poor quality : MEDIOCRE : SECOND-RATE ⟨furniture of ~ workmanship⟩ ⟨~ pupil⟩ ⟨~ violinist⟩ **4 a** *of a part of the upright body* : situated below another and esp. another similar part — compare SUPERIOR 6a ⟨~ vena cava⟩ ⟨~ meatus of the nose⟩ ⟨~ rectus muscle of the eye⟩ **b** *of a part of the quadrupedal body* (1) : situated in a more posterior position (2) : situated more ventrad than another and esp. another similar part : VENTRAL **5** *of a part of a plant* **a** : situated below another organ: (1) *of a calyx* : free from the ovary (2) *of an ovary* : adnate to the calyx or other floral envelope **b** : ABAXIAL **c** : situated low on the stipe **6** : SUBSCRIPT ⟨~ letter⟩ ⟨~ number⟩ — used usu. postpositionally ⟨for "H_2O" read "H, 2 ~, O"⟩; contrasted with *superior*
²**inferior** \"\ *n* -s **1** : a person or thing inferior to another (as in worth, status, or importance) ⟨disdainful of his social ~*s*⟩ **2** : a subscript character (as in printing)
inferior alveolar artery *n* : a branch of the internal maxillary artery that is distributed to the mucous membrane of the mouth and through the mandibular canal to the teeth of the lower jaw
inferior alveolar canal *n* : MANDIBULAR CANAL
inferior alveolar nerve *n* : a branch of the mandibular division of the fifth cranial nerve that passes into the mandibular canal to the teeth of the lower jaw
inferior alveolar vein *n* : the vein accompanying the inferior alveolar artery
inferior colliculus *n* : either member of the posterior and lower pair of quadrigeminate bodies together constituting one of the lower coordinating centers for hearing
inferior conjunction *n* : a conjunction in which a lesser or secondary celestial body passes nearer the observer than the primary body around which it revolves ⟨*inferior conjunction* of Venus to the sun⟩ — see CONFIGURATION illustration
inferior court *n* : a court having limited and specified rather than general jurisdiction — compare SUPERIOR COURT
inferior good *n* : a commodity the consumption of which decreases as its price declines or as the income of consumers rises because of the increased income available to buy preferred though more expensive commodities
in·fe·ri·or·i·ty \(ˌ)in,firēˈȯrəd·ē, -fēr-, -ˈär-, -ətē, -i\ *n* -ES [MF or ML; MF *inferiorité,* fr. ML *inferioritat-, inferioritas,* fr. L *inferior* + *-itat-, -itas* -ity — more at INFERIOR] **1** : the state of being inferior : a lower state or condition ⟨making you feel her superiority, your ~; how poor she was; how rich you were —Virginia Woolf⟩ **2** : sense of being inferior ⟨adolescence's indecisive shames and *inferiorities* —Ruth Park⟩
inferiority complex *n* [prob. trans. of G *minderwertigkeitskomplex*] : an acute sense of personal inferiority resulting either in timidity or through overcompensation in exaggerated aggressiveness; *broadly* : sense of being inferior or at a disadvantage : lack of assurance
inferior laryngeal *n* : a branch of the vagus nerve that supplies most of the muscles of the larynx
in·fe·ri·or·ly *adv* **1** : in an inferior manner or to an inferior degree **2** : in a lower position
inferior maxillary nerve *n* : MANDIBULAR NERVE
inferior oblique *n* : OBLIQUE 2b(2)
inferior olive *n* : a large gray nucleus that forms a lateral eminence on the medulla oblongata and has connections with the thalamus, cerebellum, and spinal cord
inferior planet *n* : a planet whose orbit lies within that of the earth
inferior tide *n* : the tide corresponding to the moon's transit of the lower meridian
inferior valve *n* : the valve by which certain bivalve mollusks become attached to an object or surface
¹**in·fer·nal** \ənˈfərnᵊl, -ˈfə̄n-, -ˈfəin-\ *adj* [ME, fr. OF, fr. LL *infernalis,* fr. *infernus* hell (fr. L *infernus* lower, lying beneath, of the lower regions) + L *-alis* -al; akin to L *inferus* low, situated beneath — more at UNDER] **1** : relating or belonging to a nether world of the dead and of earth deities : CHTHONIC — compare HADES **2 a** : relating to or inhabiting hell ⟨~ fires⟩ ⟨~ spirit⟩ **b** : resembling or suitable to hell or the character of its inhabitants : HELLISH, DIABOLICAL, FIENDISH ⟨~ scheme⟩ ⟨~ wickedness⟩ **3** : DAMNABLE, DAMNED ⟨~ nuisance⟩ ⟨~ gadget⟩ ⟨~ racket⟩ — **in·fer·nal·ly** \-ᵊlē, -ᵊli\ *adv*
²**infernal** \"\ *n* -s **1** *archaic* : an infernal person or thing — usu. used in pl. **2 infernals** *pl, obs* : the infernal regions : HELL
infernal blue *n* : SCOTCH BLUE
infernal machine *n* : a machine or apparatus designed to explode and destroy life or property : a concealed or disguised bomb
in·fer·no \ənˈfər(,)nō, -ˈfə̄(,)-, -ˈfəi(,)-\ *n* -s [It, hell (esp. as the title of one of the books of the *Divina Commedia,* long allegorical & philosophical poem by Dante Alighieri †1321 Ital. poet), fr. LL *infernus* — more at INFERNAL] **1** : a place or a state of torment and suffering ⟨the ~ of the passions —Edmund Wilson⟩ ⟨~ of war⟩ ⟨~ of seething misery and poverty —G.B.Shaw⟩ **2** : a place that resembles or suggests hell in being dark, noisy, chaotic, lawless ⟨the factory seemed an ~ of dirt and noise⟩ ⟨plunge into the ~ of the engine room —Joseph Whitehill⟩ **3** : intense heat ⟨roaring ~ of the blast furnace⟩ : CONFLAGRATION ⟨girders melted in the ~⟩
infero- *comb form* [L *inferus* low, situated beneath — more at UNDER] **1** : on the underside ⟨*infero*branchiate⟩ **2** : below and ⟨*infero*lateral⟩
in·fe·ro·branchiate \ˌinfə(,)rō+\ *adj* [*infero-* + *branchiate*] : having the gills on the sides under the mantle margin ⟨~ mollusk⟩
inferred *past of* INFER
in·fer·rer \ənˈfərə(r) *also* -ˈfə̄rə(r\ *n* -s : one that infers
inferrible *var of* INFERABLE
inferring *pres part of* INFER
infers *pres 3d sing of* INFER
in·fertile \(ˈ)in, ən+\ *adj* [MF, fr. LL *infertilis,* fr. L *in-* ¹in- + *fertilis* fertile — more at FERTILE] : not fertile or productive : BARREN ⟨~ egg⟩ ⟨~ soil⟩ **syn** see STERILE
in·fertility \ˌin+\ *n* [F *infertilité,* fr. LL *infertilitat-, infertilitas,* fr. *infertilis* infertile + *-itat-, -itas* -ity] : the quality or state of being infertile : BARRENNESS, STERILITY
in·fest \ənˈfest\ *vt* -ED/-ING/-S [MF *infester,* fr. L *infestare,* fr. *infestus* hostile — more at DARE] **1** *archaic* : to attack or harass persistently : WORRY, ANNOY **2 a** : to visit persistently or in large numbers : OVERRUN, HAUNT ⟨street ~*ed* with children⟩ ⟨lawn ~*ed* with weeds⟩ ⟨~*ed* with ghosts and poltergeists⟩ **b** : to live in or on as a parasite — used esp. of metazoan parasites of animals ⟨the flea that ~*s* cats⟩ ⟨horses ~*ed* with worms⟩
in·fes·tant \-tənt\ *n* -s : one that infests: as **a** : a visible parasite **b** : any of the smaller organisms (as clothes moth,

flour beetle, vinegar eel) that attack fabrics or processed foods or liquids

in·fes·ta·tion \ˌin(ˌ)feˈstāshən\ *n* -s [MF, fr. LL *infestation-, infestatio*, fr. *infestatus* (past part. of *infestare* to infest) + *-ion-, -io* -ion] **1 :** the act of infesting ⟨protecting grain against ~⟩ **:** PLAGUE, ANNOYANCE **2 :** something that infests **:** SWARM ⟨~ of grasshoppers⟩ **3 :** the state of being infested esp. with metazoan parasites in or on an animal or plant body

¹infester *vt* [²in- + *fester* (v.)] *obs* **:** to cause to fester

²in·fest·er \ənˈfestə(r)\ *n* -s [*infest* + *-er*] **:** one that infests

in·fes·tious \ənˈfes(h)chəs\ *adj* [*infest* + *-ious* (as in *infectious*)] **:** INFESTING ⟨to certain ~ bipeds any graft is legitimate —H.L.Ickes⟩

¹in·fes·tive \ənˈfestiv\ *adj* [*infest* + *-ive*] **:** likely to infest **:** TROUBLESOME ⟨~ weeds⟩

²in·festive \(ˈ)in+\ *adj* [¹in- + L *festivus* festive — more at FESTIVE] **:** not festive **:** MIRTHLESS

in·festivity \ˌin+\ *n* [¹in- + *festivity*] **:** lack of festivity **:** MIRTHLESSNESS, DULLNESS

in·fest·ment \ənˈfestmənt\ *n* -s *archaic* **:** INFESTATION

infestuous *adj* [*infest* + *-uous* (as in *infectuous*)] *obs* **:** MISCHIEVOUS, HARMFUL

in·feu·da·tion *also* **in·feo·da·tion** \ˌinfyüˈdāshən\ *n* -s [ME *infeodacioun*, fr. ML *infeudation-, infeudatio, infeodation-, infeodatio*, fr. *infeudatus, infeodatus* (past part. of *infeudare, infeodare* to enfeoff, fr. *in-* ²in- + *feudum, feodum* feoff) + L *-ion-, -io* -ion — more at FEUD] **1 :** ENFEOFFMENT **2 :** a granting of tithes to laymen

in·fib·u·late \ənˈfibyəˌlāt\ *vt* -ED/-ING/-S [L *infibulatus*, past part. of *infibulare* to infibulate, practice infibulation upon, fr. *in-* ²in- + *fibulare* to pin, buckle together, fr. *fibula* — more at FIBULA] **:** to fasten with or as if with a buckle or clasp

in·fib·u·la·tion \(ˌ)inˌfibyəˈlāshən\ *n* -s [L *infibulatus* + E *-ion*] **:** an act or practice of fastening by ring, clasp, or stitches the labia majora in girls and the prepuce in boys in order to prevent sexual intercourse

in·fi·cete \ˈinfəˌsēt\ *adj* [L *inficetus, infacetus*, fr. *in-* ¹in- + *facetus* courteous, elegant, witty, facetious] **:** not witty **:** HEAVY-FOOTED

¹in·fi·del \ˈinfədᵊl, -əˌdel\ *n* -s [MF *infidele*, adj. & n., fr. LL *infidelis*, fr. L, untrustworthy, unfaithful, fr. *in-* ¹in- + *fidelis* faithful — more at FEAL] **1 :** one that is not a Christian or opposes Christianity **2 a :** an unbeliever in respect to a particular religion **b :** one that acknowledges no religious belief — distinguished from *heretic* **3 :** one that does not believe (as in something specified or understood) **:** SKEPTIC, DISBELIEVER

²infidel \"\ *adj* [MF *infidele*] **1 a :** not holding the faith of a given religion; *esp* **:** non-Christian ⟨the ~ nations⟩ ⟨an ~ Saracen⟩ **b :** opposing or traitorous to Christianity ⟨~ writers⟩ ⟨an ~ sect⟩ **2 :** relating to or characteristic of unbelief or unbelievers ⟨~ tract⟩

in·fi·del·ic \ˌinfəˈdelik\ *or* **in·fi·del·i·cal** \-ləkəl\ *adj* **:** INFIDEL 2

in·fi·del·i·ty \ˌinfəˈdelədē, -ətē, -i *sometimes* -ˌfīˈ-\ *n* [MF *infidelité*, fr. LL & L; LL *infidelitat-, infidelitas* disbelief in Christianity, heathenism, fr. L, unfaithfulness, fr. *infidelis* + *-itat-, -itas* -ity] **1 :** lack of faith or belief in a religion **:** state or character of being infidel **2** *archaic* **:** SKEPTICISM, INCREDULITY **3 a :** breach of trust **:** unfaithfulness to a charge or a moral obligation **:** DISLOYALTY, PERFIDY **b :** marital unfaithfulness or an instance of it ⟨made no secret of his many *infidelities*⟩ **4 :** failure to reproduce (as a text or a model) exactly; *also* **:** an instance of such failure ⟨numerous *infidelities* in the translation⟩ ⟨~ in size also made printing from . . . plastic plates a hazard —*Graphic Arts Rev.*⟩

infield \ˈ=ˌ=\ *n* [⁴in + *field*] **1 a :** a field near a farmhouse **b :** land regularly manured and used year after year for the same crop (as hay or fruit) **2 a** (1) **:** the area of a cricket field relatively near the wickets (2) **:** a fieldsman stationed there — contrasted with *outfield* **b** (1) **:** the area of a baseball or softball field enclosed by the three bases and home plate **:** DIAMOND (2) **:** the defensive positions comprising first base, second base, shortstop, and third base ⟨a strong ~⟩ — contrasted with *outfield* **3 :** the area enclosed by a racetrack or running track

in·field·er \-də(r)\ *n* **1 :** a fielder stationed in the infield in cricket **2 :** a baseball player who covers a position in the infield

infield fly *n* **:** a fair fly ball other than a line drive or an attempted bunt that can be handled by an infielder and that is declared an automatic out if it occurs at a time when there are less than two outs and when runners are occupying first and second or first, second, and third bases

in·fields·man \-l(d)zmən\ *n* **:** INFIELDER 1

in fi·eri \(ˈ)inˈfēərē\ *adj* [ML] **1 :** being in process of accomplishment **:** PENDING **2 :** beginning to have existence **:** not yet completely formed

infighter \ˈ=ˌ==\ *n* [⁴in + *fighter*] **:** one that practices or is skilled at infighting ⟨able political ~⟩

infighting \ˈ=ˌ==\ *n* -s [⁴in + *fighting*] **1 a :** fighting or boxing at close range ⟨his bowie . . . was the unexcelled weapon for ~—*Amer. Guide Series: Ark.*⟩ **b :** fighting (as between rivals) that is not openly acknowledged or conducted **2 :** fighting without rules **:** rough-and-tumble fighting

infill \ˈ=ˌ=\ *vt* [²in- + *fill*] **:** to fill in ⟨fractures . . . broadened by ice growth within them . . . and then ~ed from above as the ice melted —*Jour. of Geol.*⟩

infilling \ˈ=ˌ==\ *n* **:** material used (as in building) to fill in space between structural members ⟨steel skeleton with an ~ of brickwork⟩

infilter \=ˈ==\ *vi* [²in + *filter*] **:** to filter or sift in

¹in·fil·trate \ənˈfilˌtrāt, ˈin(ˌ)fil- *also* -ˌfəl-, *usu* -ād.+V\ *vb* [²in- + *filtrate*] *vt* **1 :** to cause something (as a liquid) to enter by penetrating the interstices of ⟨~ tissue with a local anesthetic⟩ **2 :** to pass into or through (a substance) by filtering or permeating **3 :** to advance (troops) by sending single men or small groups through gaps or weak points in the enemy line **4 :** to enter or become established in (as an organization) gradually or unobtrusively and in large numbers ⟨parties which labor leaders accused of being . . . *infiltrated* by extreme nationalists —Clifton Daniel⟩ ~ *vi* **1 :** to enter, permeate, or pass through a substance by filtering ⟨many Hebrew idioms have *infiltrated*, in translated forms, into various Jewish dialects —William Chomsky⟩ **2** *of troops* **:** to advance or to enter a hostile area by proceeding singly or in small dispersed groups ⟨tend rather to ~ to supply lines and rear installations —*Cavalry Jour.*⟩

²infiltrate \"\ *n* **:** something that infiltrates; *specif* **:** a substance that passes into the bodily tissues and forms an abnormal accumulation

in·fil·tra·tion \ˌin(ˌ)filˈtrāshən *also* -ˌfəl-\ *n* **1 :** the act or process of infiltrating ⟨~ of water through a gravel bed⟩ ⟨~ of air into a building⟩ **2 :** something that infiltrates ⟨fatty ~⟩ ⟨anesthetic drug ~⟩ **3 :** a gradual penetration by scattered units ⟨~ of settlers into new territory⟩

infiltration anesthesia *n* **:** anesthesia of an operative site accomplished by injection of anesthetics under the skin

infiltration capacity *n* **:** the rate at which a soil can absorb water

infiltration vein *n* **:** a vein formed in country rock by interstitial deposition from percolating waters — compare IMPREGNATION 2a

in·fil·tra·tive \ˈinfəlˌtrādiv, ənˈfiltrəd-\ *adj* **:** relating to or characterized by infiltration

in·fil·tra·tor \ənˈfilˌtrād.ə(r), ˈinfəl-\ *n* -s **:** one that infiltrates ⟨if the first human agents that come into contact with a given culture . . . are traders, then economic values are the first ~s —P.A.Sorokin⟩

in·fil·tree \ˌinfəlˈtrē, ənˌfilˈtrē\ *n* -s [¹*infiltrate* + *-ee*] **:** one who has entered another country or territory in a manner resembling military infiltration ⟨American policy to provide temporary food and housing to all ~s —Samuel Lubell⟩

in·fil·trom·e·ter \ˌin(ˌ)filˈträməd.ə(r)\ *n* -s [*infiltration* + *-o-* + *-meter*] **:** an apparatus for measuring the rate at which a soil can absorb water

in·fi·ma species \ˈinfəmə-\ *n* [L] **:** the lowest species in a classification or logical division — compare TREE OF PORPHYRY

infin *abbr* infinitive

¹in·fi·nite \ˈinfənə̇t *sometimes* -fəˌnīt *sometimes as opposed to "finite"* (ˈ)inˈfīˌnīt *or* ənˈfīˌnīt; *usu* |d.+V\ *adj* [ME *infinit*, fr. MF or L; MF *infinit*, fr. L *infinitus*, fr. *in-* ¹in- + *finitus* limited, finite — more at FINITE] **1 :** being without limits of any kind **:** subject to no limitation or external determination ⟨philosophy compels faith in real personality, finite and relative in man, ~ and absolute in nature —F.A.Christie⟩ **2 a :** having no end **:** extending indefinitely ⟨speculate and wonder as to the structure of the universe, whether it is bounded or ~ —W.V.Houston⟩ ⟨~ duration⟩ **b :** having innumerable parts **:** capable of endless division or distinction within itself ⟨electrophones capable of ~ gradations of pitch —Robert Domington⟩ **3 :** having no limit in power, capacity, knowledge, or excellence **:** immeasurably or inconceivably great **:** BOUNDLESS ⟨~ mercy⟩ ⟨~ wisdom⟩ ⟨~ patience⟩ ⟨~ discretion⟩ **4 a :** indefinitely large or extensive **:** indefinite in number **:** IMMEASURABLE **b :** VAST, IMMENSE **c :** ENDLESS, INEXHAUSTIBLE ⟨~ ingenuity of man —Mary Webb⟩ **5** *pre-Socratic philosophy* **:** constituting the matrix or an ingredient of formed and determined reality **6** *of a verb form* **:** having neither person, number, nor mood **7 a :** not finite **:** extending or lying beyond any preassigned value however large ⟨the number of positive numbers is ~⟩ **b :** extending to infinity ⟨~ plane surface⟩ ⟨~ branch of a curve⟩ **c :** having the same power as a proper subset of itself **:** capable of being put into a one-to-one correspondence with a subset of itself — used of a mathematical aggregate — **in·fi·nite·ly** *adv* — **in·fi·nite·ness** *n*

²infinite \"\ *n* **:** something that is infinite: **a :** boundless space or duration **:** INFINITY **b :** an incalculable or very great number ⟨an ~ of possibilities⟩ **c :** an infinite quantity or magnitude

infinite canon *n* **:** CIRCULAR CANON 1

infinite integral *n* **:** an improper integral having one or both of its limits infinite

infinite proposition *n* **:** a logical proposition that has an indefinite negative predicate

infinite regress *n* **:** an endless chain of reasoning leading backward by interpolating a third entity between any two entities — compare THIRD MAN

infinite series *n* **:** an endless succession of terms or of factors proceeding according to some mathematical law

¹in·fin·i·tes·i·mal \ˌin,finəˈtesəməl, -tezə- *sometimes* -sm- *or* -zm-\ *n* -s [NL *infinitesimus* infinite in rank (fr. L *infinitus* infinite + *-esimus*, ordinal suffix + E *-al* — more at INFINITE] **1 :** a function that can be made arbitrarily close to zero **2 :** an infinitesimal quantity

²infinitesimal \ˌ=ˌ==ˈ=(=)=\ *adj* **1 :** capable of being made arbitrarily close to zero **2 :** immeasurably or incalculably small **:** very minute — **in·fin·i·tes·i·mal·ly** \-səməlē, -zəmə-ˌli *sometimes* -sməl- *or* -zməl- *or* -səml- *or* -zəml-\ *adv* — **in·fin·i·tes·i·mal·ness** \-səməlnə̇s, -zəm- *sometimes* -sm- *or* -zm-\ *n* -ES

infinitesimal calculus *n* **:** the mathematical methods comprising differential calculus and integral calculus

in·fin·i·tes·i·mal·ism \ˌ=ˌ==ˈ=(=)məˌlizəm\ *n* -s **:** a doctrine that the more a drug is diluted the more potent it becomes

in·fin·i·tes·i·mal·i·ty \-ˌtesəˈmaləd.ē\ *n* -ES **:** the quality or state of being infinitesimal

infinite term *n* **:** an indefinite term in a logical proposition

in·fin·i·ti·val \(ˌ)inˌfinəˈtīvəl, ənˌ-\ *adj* **:** relating to the infinitive — **in·fin·i·tiv·al·ly** \-əlē\ *adv*

¹in·fin·i·tive \ənˈfinəd.iv, -ətiv\ *adj* [LL *infinitivus*, fr. L *infinitus* infinite + *-ivus* -ive — more at INFINITE] **:** formed with the infinitive ⟨~ phrase⟩ — **in·fin·i·tive·ly** \-əvlē, -li\ *adv*

²infinitive \"\ *n* -s **:** an infinite verb form normally identical in English with the first person singular that performs certain functions of a noun and at the same time displays certain characteristics (as association with objects and adverbial modifiers) of a verb and is used with *to* (as in "*to err* is human"; "I asked him *to go*") except with auxiliary and certain other verbs (as in "he can *see*"; "let me *go*"; "no one saw him *leave*")

in·fin·i·tize \ənˈfinəˌtīz\ *vt* -ED/-ING/-S [¹*infinite* + *-ize*] **:** to make infinite **:** make free of finite limitations ⟨man's anxious effort to deny his finitude and to ~ himself by the perverse use of his freedom in pride —Will Herberg⟩

in·fin·i·tude \ənˈfinəˌtüd, -əˌtyüd\ *n* [prob. fr. F, fr. MF, fr. *infinit* infinite] **1 :** the quality or state of being infinite **:** INFINITENESS **2 :** something that is infinite; *esp* **:** a real as distinct from an ideal or theoretical infinity ⟨the ~ surrounding her on every hand —O.E.Rölvaag⟩ **3 :** an infinite number **:** an innumerable quantity

in·fin·i·ty \ənˈfinəd.ē, -ətē, -i\ *n* -ES [ME *infinite*, fr. MF *infinité*, fr. L *infinitat-, infinitas*, fr. *infinitus* infinite + *-itas* -ity] **1 a :** the quality of being infinite **b :** that which is infinite **:** unlimited extent of time, space, or quantity **:** BOUNDLESSNESS ⟨there cannot be more *infinities* than one; for one of them would limit the other —Walter Raleigh⟩ **2 :** unlimited capacity, energy, excellence, or knowledge ⟨~ of God's power⟩ **3 :** an indefinitely great number or amount ⟨~ of stars⟩ **4 a :** a nonexistent limit of a function that can be made to become and remain numerically larger than any preassigned value — symbol ∞ **b :** a nonexistent part of a magnitude that lies beyond any part whose distance from a given reference position is finite — symbol ∞ **c :** a transfinite number **5 :** a distance so great that the rays of light from a point source at that distance may be regarded as parallel

¹in·firm \(ˈ)inˈfərm, ənˈf-, -fə̄m,-fəim\ *adj* [ME *infirme*, fr. L *infirmus, infirmis*, fr. *in-* ¹in- + *firmus* strong, firm — more at FIRM] **1 :** not strong or sound physically **:** of poor or deteriorated vitality esp. as a result of age **:** FEEBLE ⟨~ body⟩ ⟨support of the poor, the insane, and the ~—Calvin Coolidge⟩ **2 :** weak of mind, will, or character **:** FRAIL, IRRESOLUTE, VACILLATING ⟨~ judgment⟩ ⟨~ of purpose: give me the daggers —Shak.⟩ **3 :** not solid or stable **:** INSECURE, PRECARIOUS ⟨rendered this agreeable assumption . . . permanently ~ —Berton Roueché⟩ **syn** see WEAK

²in·firm \ənˈf-\ *vt* -ED/-ING/-S [ME *infirmen*, fr. L *infirmare*, fr. *infirmus* infirm] **1** *obs* **:** to make infirm **:** deprive of strength **:** WEAKEN **2 a :** to make doubtful or challenge the validity of **b :** INVALIDATE ⟨either to confirm or to ~ allegations of fact⟩ — **in·firm·able** \-məbəl\ *adj*

in·fir·ma·rer \ənˈfərmərər\ *n* -s [ME, prob. fr. ML *infirmaria, infirmarium* + ME *-er*] **:** INFIRMARIAN

in·fir·ma·ress \-mərə̇s\ *n* -ES **:** a female infirmarian

in·fir·mar·i·an \ˌinfə(r)ˈma(a)rēən\ *n* -s **:** a person having charge of an infirmary (as in a monastic institution)

in·fir·ma·ry \ənˈfərm(ə)rē, -fə̄m-,-fəim-, -ri\ *n* -ES [ML *infirmarium, infirmaria*, fr. L *infirmus* infirm + *-arium, -aria* -ary] **:** a hospital or place where the infirm or sick are lodged for treatment; *esp* **:** a building or part of a building for the sick or injured members of an institution ⟨convent ~⟩

in·fir·ma·tion \ˌinfə(r)ˈmāshən\ *n* -s [L *infirmation-, infirmatio*, fr. *infirmatus* (past part. of *infirmare* to infirm) + *-ion-, -io* -ion] **:** the process of infirming or making invalid — opposed to *confirmation*

in·fir·mi·ty \ənˈfərməd.ē, -fə̄m-, -fəim-, -ətē, -i\ *n* -ES [ME *infirmite*, fr. L *infirmitas*, fr. *infirmus* infirm + *-itas* -ity — more at INFIRM] **1 :** the quality or state of being infirm **:** FEEBLENESS, FRAILTY **2 a** (1) **:** an unsound, unhealthy, or debilitated state ⟨~ of body⟩ ⟨~ of mind⟩ (2) **:** DISEASE, MALADY ⟨one of the more painful *infirmities* of man⟩ **b :** a defect of personality or weakness of the will **:** FAILING, FOIBLE ⟨a friend should bear his friend's *infirmities* —Shak.⟩

in·firm·ly *adv* **:** in an infirm manner **:** FEEBLY, INSECURELY

in·firm·ness *n* **:** the quality or state of being infirm

¹in·fix \(ˈ)inˈfiks, ən-\ *vt* [L *infixus*, past part. of *infigere* to drive in, fasten in, fr. *in-* ²in- + *figere* to fasten, pierce — more at DIKE] **1 :** to fasten or fix by piercing or thrusting in ⟨and deep within her heart ~ed the wound —John Dryden⟩ **2 :** INSTILL, INCULCATE, IMPRESS ⟨~ an idea in a pupil's mind⟩ **3 :** to insert (a sound or letter) as an infix

²in·fix \ˈinˌfiks\ *n* -ES **:** a derivational or inflectional affix appearing in the body of a word or base rather than at its beginning or end (as Sanskrit *-n-* in *vindami* "I know" as contrasted with *vid* "to know"; English *stand* as contrasted with *stood*) ⟨~es are sometimes inserted in the Hebrew word in order to lend it a different shade of meaning —William Chomsky⟩ — compare PREFIX

in·fix·a·tion \ˌin(ˌ)fikˈsāshən\ *also* **in·fix·ion** \ənˈfikshən\ *n* -s **1 :** the process of infixing **2 :** the state of being infixed

infl *abbr* **1** inflammable **2** inflorescence **3** influence; influenced

in flagrante delicto \ˌin-\ *adv* [modif. of ML *flagrante delicto*] **:** flagrante delicto — sometimes used substantively

in·flame \ənˈflām\ *also* **en·flame** \en-\ *vb* [ME *enflamen, inflamen*, fr. MF *enflamer, enflammer*, fr. L *inflammare*, fr. *in-* ²in- + *flammare* to flame, fr. *flamma* flame — more at FLAME] *vt* **1 :** to set on fire **:** cause to burn, flame, or glow **:** KINDLE **2 :** to excite (as passion or appetite) to an excessive or unnatural action or heat **:** INTENSIFY, ROUSE ⟨*inflamed* mob of religious partisans —Robert Trumbull⟩ **3 a :** to provoke to anger or rage **:** EXASPERATE, IRRITATE, INCENSE, ENRAGE **b :** to cause to redden or grow hot from anger or excitement ⟨events had combined to irritate and then to ~ him —Ngaio Marsh⟩ ⟨face *inflamed* with passion⟩ **4 :** to cause inflammation in (bodily tissue) **:** produce abnormal heat in or swelling of ⟨~ the eyes⟩ ~ *vi* **1 :** to burst into flame **2 :** to become excited or angered **3 :** to become affected with inflammation

inflamed *adj* [fr. past part. of *inflame*] *heraldry* **:** represented as burning or as adorned with tongues of flame

in·flam·er \-mə(r)\ *n* **:** one that inflames

in·flam·ing·ly *adv* **:** in an inflaming manner

in·flam·ma·bil·i·ty \(ˌ)inˌflaməˈbiləd.ē, ən-, -ətē, -i\ *n* **:** the quality or state of being inflammable **:** tendency to ignite readily

¹in·flam·ma·ble \ənˈflaməbəl\ *adj* [F or ML; F, fr. ML *inflammabilis*, fr. L *inflammare* to inflame + *-abilis* -able] **1 :** capable of being easily set on fire and burning violently **:** FLAMMABLE **2 :** easily inflamed, excited, or angered **:** IRASCIBLE ⟨~ temper⟩ — **in·flam·ma·ble·ness** *n* -ES — **in·flam·ma·bly** \-blē, -li\ *adv*

²inflammable \"\ *n* **:** an inflammable substance **:** FLAMMABLE

inflammable air *n, archaic* **:** HYDROGEN

inflammable cinnabar *n* **:** IDRIALITE

in·flam·ma·tion \ˌinfləˈmāshən\ *n* [L *inflammation-, inflammatio*, fr. *inflammatus* (past part. of *inflammare* to inflame) + *-ion-, -io* -ion — more at INFLAME] **1 :** the act of inflaming or the state of being inflamed ⟨impossible to distinguish an ~ from an explosion by the amount of violence produced —*Gaseous Fuels*⟩ ⟨~ of nationalism precipitated the next great war —Hans Kohn⟩ **2 :** a local response to cellular injury (as by infection or trauma) characterized by capillary dilatation, leukocytic infiltration, heat, and commonly pain and serving as a primary mechanism for control of noxious agents and elimination of damaged tissue

in·flam·ma·tive \ənˈflaməd.iv\ *adj* [L *inflammatus* + E *-ive*] **:** INFLAMMATORY

in·flam·ma·to·ri·ly \(ˌ)inˌflaməˈtōrəlē, ən-, -tȯr-, -li\ *adv* **:** in an inflammatory manner **:** so as to inflame

in·flam·ma·to·ry \ənˈflaməˌtōrē, -tȯr-, -ri\ *adj* [L *inflammatus* + E *-ory*] **1 :** tending to inflame or excite the senses **2 :** tending to excite anger, animosity, disorder, or tumult **:** SEDITIOUS ⟨~ speech⟩ **3 :** of, relating to, or marked by inflammation ⟨an ~ response⟩ ⟨an ~ process⟩

¹in·flat·able \ənˈflād.əbəl\ *adj* [²*inflate* + *-able*] **:** capable of being inflated

²inflatable \"\ *n* -s **:** something (as a toy) that can be inflated

¹in·flate \ənˈflāt, *usu* -ād.+V\ *adj* [ME *inflat*, fr. L *inflatus*, past part.] *archaic* **:** INFLATED

²inflate \"\ *vb* -ED/-ING/-S [L *inflatus*, past part. of *inflare*, fr. *in-* ²in- + *flare* to blow — more at BLOW] *vt* **1 :** to swell or distend with air or gas ⟨~ a balloon⟩ — opposed to *deflate* **2 :** to puff up **:** ELATE ⟨~ one with pride⟩ **3 :** to expand or increase abnormally or improperly **:** extend imprudently; *esp* **:** to increase (the volume of money and credit) so that a general rise in the price level occurs ⟨deliberately *inflating* the currency⟩ ~ *vi* **:** to undergo inflation **:** fill with or as if with air **:** DISTEND **syn** see EXPAND

inflated *adj* **1 :** distended with air or gas **2 a :** BOMBASTIC, POMPOUS ⟨~ style⟩ **b :** EXAGGERATED ⟨~ statements are made without anyone being able to check them —G.A.Craig⟩ **3 :** expanded abnormally or unjustifiably in volume ⟨~ currency⟩ or level ⟨~ prices⟩ **4 :** hollow and distended ⟨~ stem⟩ **:** open and swelled out or enlarged ⟨~ perianth⟩

syn INFLATED, FLATULENT, TUMID, and TURGID all mean filled with something insubstantial, as air or gas, or something that causes usu. abnormal swelling or distention. INFLATED implies a blowing up to the point of tautness of surface or empty distention ⟨an *inflated* balloon⟩ or, figuratively, a stretching, expanding, heightening, or puffing up by artificial or empty means ⟨*inflated* rhetoric⟩ ⟨an *inflated* speech⟩ ⟨an *inflated* opinion of oneself⟩ FLATULENT, applying chiefly to persons affected by excessive distention by gas of the stomach or bowels, can be extended to apply to anything that is empty or lacking substance but that gives the transparent impression of fullness or substantiality ⟨enthusiasts who read into him all sorts of *flatulent* bombast —H.L.Mencken⟩ ⟨he was an over-ornate speaker; at his worst he was a purveyor of *flatulent* claptrap —S.H.Adams⟩ TUMID stresses noticeable esp. morbid or abnormal enlargement as by swelling or bloating or, figuratively, an empty but marked pretentiousness ⟨his face looked damp, pale under the tan, and slightly *tumid* —J. G.Cozzens⟩ ⟨the genuine scientist would never employ *tumid* phrases or half-baked simplifications —J.E.Gloag⟩ TURGID is similar to TUMID without suggesting morbidity but often adds the idea of disorder or esp. emotional unrestraint as in the use of bombast, rant, or rhapsody ⟨the book is so *turgid*, so repetitive, so full of nearly meaningless tables —Geoffrey Gorer⟩ ⟨much too much of it dwells on the *turgid* adventures of a man who marries the less attractive of a pair of sisters and indulges a yen for the other —Henry Hewes⟩ ⟨the contrast between the vivid dialogue and the *turgid* narrative passages —David Greene⟩ ⟨a *turgid* speech praising the political boss⟩

in·flat·ed·ly *adv* **:** in an inflated manner

in·flat·ed·ness *n* -ES **:** the quality or state of being inflated **:** POMPOSITY, TURGIDITY

in·fla·tion \ənˈflāshən\ *n* -s [ME *inflacioun*, fr. L *inflation-, inflatio*, fr. *inflatus* + *-ion-, -io* -ion] **1 :** an act of inflating or a state of being inflated: as **a :** DISTENSION **b :** empty pretentiousness **:** POMPOSITY ⟨~ either of language or imagination —Cyril Connolly⟩ **2 :** an increase in the volume of money and credit relative to available goods resulting in a substantial and continuing rise in the general price level — contrasted with *deflation*

in·fla·tion·ary \-shəˌnerē, -ri\ *adj* **:** of, relating to, or productive of inflation ⟨~ signs⟩ ⟨~ policies⟩

inflationary gap *n* **:** an excess of total disposable income over the value of the available supply of goods at a specified price level sufficient to cause an inflation of prices — compare DEFLATIONARY GAP

inflationary spiral *n* **:** a continuous rise in prices that is sustained by the tendency of wage increases and cost increases to react on each other

in·fla·tion·ism \-ˌnizəm\ *n* -s **:** the advocacy of economic inflation

in·fla·tion·ist \-sh(ə)nə̇st\ *n* -s *often attrib* **:** one who favors economic inflation

in·fla·tor *or* **in·flat·er** \ənˈflād.ə(r), -ātə-\ *n* -s **:** one that inflates; *esp* **:** a hand air pump ⟨tire ~⟩

in·fla·tus \ənˈflād.əs\ *n* -ES [L, fr. *inflatus*, past part. of *inflare* to inflate — more at INFLATE] **:** AFFLATUS, INSPIRATION

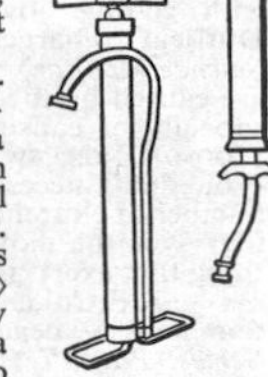

inflators

in·flect \ənˈflekt\ *vb* -ED/-ING/-S [ME *inflecten*, fr. L *inflectere*, fr. *in-* ²in- + *flectere* to bend, turn] *vt* **1 :** to turn from a direct line or course **:** BEND, CURVE ⟨in him . . . snobbery reappeared . . . as the refusal of reality unless it was highly ~ed —V.S. Pritchett⟩ ⟨profound feeling for music has ~ed all his major works —Irving Kolodin⟩ **2 :** to give inflection to (a word) **:** vary (a word) by inflection **:** DECLINE ⟨~ a noun⟩ **:** CONJUGATE ⟨~ a verb⟩ **3 :** to change or vary the pitch of (as the voice or an utterance) **:** MODULATE **4 :** to bend (part of a plant) inward toward the main axis of the part or body ~ *vi* **:** to become modified by inflection ⟨languages in which adjectives ~ like nouns⟩

inflected *adj* **1 :** subjected to or characterized by inflection ⟨~ words⟩ ⟨an ~ language⟩ **2 :** INFLEXED 2 — **in·flect·ed·ness** *n* -ES

in·flect·ible \-təbəl\ *adj* **:** capable of being inflected

in·flec·tion \ən'flekshən\ *n* -S [LL *inflection-, inflectio,* L *inflexion-, inflexio,* fr. *inflectus, inflexus* (past part. of *inflectere* to inflect) + *-ion-, -io* -ion — more at INFLECT] **1 :** the act or result of curving or bending ⟨excel in movements and ~*s* of the hands —Sacheverell Sitwell⟩ **:** BEND, CURVE ⟨enclosed by ~*s* of the river —Anthony Powell⟩ **2 :** change or variation of pitch or loudness **:** modulation of the voice in speaking or singing ⟨questions end on a rising ~⟩ ⟨~*s* of humor, irony, and sentiment which are obvious to a native speaker —Geoffrey Bullough⟩ **3 a :** a modification in pitch or dynamics in a musical line **b :** a change from the monotone in liturgical chanting **4 a :** the variation or change of form that words undergo to mark distinctions of case, gender, number, tense, person, mood, voice, comparison **b :** a form, suffix, or element involved in such variation **c :** ACCIDENCE **5 a :** change of curvature from concave to convex or conversely **b** *or* **inflection point :** the point where such a change takes place

in·flec·tion·al \-shənᵊl, -shnəl\ *adj* **1 :** of, relating to, or characterized by inflection ⟨*-ed* in *played* is an ~ suffix⟩ — distinguished from *derivational* **2** *of a language* **:** characterized by the expression of grammatical relations by means of formal modification through internal change (as in *sing, sang, sung*) or fusional affixation of modifying elements (as in *walk, walked, walking, walks*) — distinguished from *agglutinative* and *isolating* — **in·flec·tion·al·ly** \-ᵊlē, -əlē, li\ *adv*

in·flec·tion·less \-shənləs\ *adj* **:** having no inflections

in·flec·tive \ən'flektiv, -tēv\ *adj* **1 :** capable of, relating to, or tending to inflection **:** DEFLECTING **2 :** INFLECTIONAL ⟨~ language⟩

in·flexed \(')in¦flekst, ən'f-\ *adj* [L *inflexus* (past part. of *inflectere* to inflect) + E *-ed* — more at INFLECT] **1 :** TURNED, BENT **2 :** bent or turned abruptly inward or downward or toward the axis ⟨~ petals of a flower⟩ ⟨~ tentacles⟩

in·flexibility \(¦)in, ən+\ *n* **:** the quality or state of being inflexible **:** UNYIELDINGNESS

in·flexible \(')in, ən+\ *adj* [ME, fr. L *inflexibilis,* fr. *in-* ¹in- + *flexibilis* flexible — more at FLEXIBLE] **1 :** not capable of being bent **:** RIGID **2 :** firm in will or purpose **:** UNYIELDING, INEXORABLE ⟨a man of upright and ~ temper —Joseph Addison⟩ ⟨~ purpose⟩ **3 :** incapable of change **:** UNALTERABLE, IMMUTABLE ⟨arbitrary and ~ rulings of bureaucracy —Edward Shils⟩ **syn** see STIFF

in·flex·i·ble·ness *n* **:** INFLEXIBILITY

in·flexibly \(')in, ən+\ *adv* **:** RIGIDLY, UNALTERABLY, STUBBORNLY, INEXORABLY

in·flex·ion \ən'flekshən\ *chiefly Brit var of* INFLECTION

in·flex·ive \ən'fleksiv\ *adj* [L *inflexus* (past part. of *inflectere* to inflect) + E *-ive*] *chiefly Brit* **:** INFLECTIVE

in·flict \ən'flikt\ *vt* -ED/-ING/-S [L *inflictus,* past part. of *infligere,* fr. *in-* ²in- + *fligere* to strike — more at PROFLIGATE] **1 :** to lay (a blow) on **:** cause (something damaging or painful) to be endured **:** IMPOSE ⟨threaten punishments you do not mean to —Bertrand Russell⟩ ⟨nor cruel and unusual punishments ~*ed* —*U. S. Constitution*⟩ ⟨~ defeat⟩ ⟨~ a beating⟩ **2 :** AFFLICT ⟨miners are still out, and industry . . . is ~*ed* with a kind of creeping paralysis —H.J.Laski⟩

in·flict·able \-təbəl\ *adj* **:** capable of being inflicted ⟨the largest ~ fine for this offense⟩

in·flict·er *or* **in·flic·tor** \-tə(r)\ *n* -S **:** one that inflicts ⟨death with his comrade, the ~ of wounds, roamed the darkened streets —Sean O'Casey⟩

in·flic·tion \ən'flikshən\ *n* -S [MF or LL; MF, fr. LL *infliction-, inflictio,* fr. L *inflictus* + *-ion-, -io* -ion] **1 :** the act of inflicting ⟨if the reader will bear one further ~ of statistics and formal description —Ernest Barker⟩ ⟨~ of damage by an economic association —C.A.Cooke⟩ **2 :** something inflicted ⟨I do not call these people visitors at all . . . they are ~*s* —F.A. Swinnerton⟩

in·flic·tive \-ktiv\ *adj* **:** causing infliction **:** acting as an infliction ⟨*The Raven* . . . delighted the ~ instincts of thousands of reciters for so long —*Times Lit. Supp.*⟩

in·flood \ən+\ *vb* [²in- + *flood*] *vi* **:** to flow in ~ *vt* **:** to overwhelm by flowing in upon ⟨unexpectedly in a gust of wind the scent of a plowed field . . . we are caught up, ~*ed* and informed —Alan Devoe⟩

in·florescence \,in+\ *n* [NL *inflorescentia,* fr. LL *inflores-*

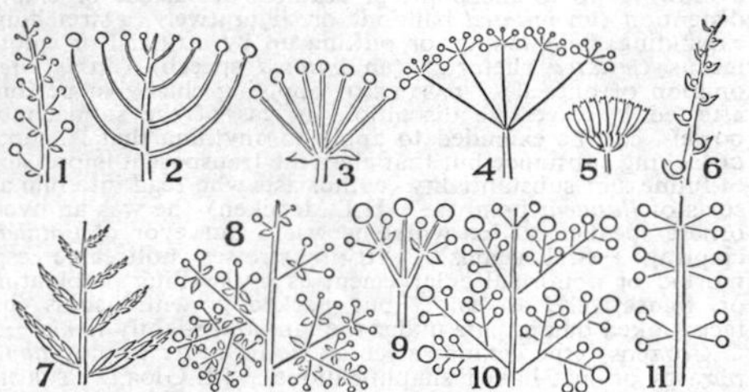

types of inflorescence diagrammatically illustrated: *1* raceme, *2* corymb, *3* umbel, *4* compound umbel, *5* capitulum, *6* spike, *7* compound spike, *8* panicle, *9* cyme, *10* thyrse, *11* verticillaster

cent-, inflorescens (pres. part. of *inflorescere* to begin to bloom, fr. *in-* ²in- + *florescere* to begin to bloom) + *-ia* -y — more at FLORESCENCE] **1 a** (1) **:** the mode of development and arrangement of flowers on an axis (2) **:** a floral axis with its appendages **:** a flower cluster or sometimes a solitary flower **b :** a cluster of reproductive organs on a moss usu. subtended by a bract ⟨many mosses have separate male ~*s*⟩ **2 :** the budding and unfolding of blossoms **:** FLOWERING

in·florescent \¦in+\ *adj* [LL *inflorescent-, inflorescens,* pres. part.] **:** BLOSSOMING, FLOWERING

¹in·flow \(')¦=¦=\ *vi* [²in- + *flow*] **1 :** to flow in **2** *obs, of a celestial body* **:** INFLUENCE

²inflow \'=,=\ *n* **1 :** the act of inflowing **2 :** something that flows in **:** INFLUX ⟨~ of air⟩ ⟨~ of water⟩ ⟨~ of bank deposits⟩ ⟨~ of imports⟩

¹in·flu·ence \'in,flüən(t)s *sometimes* ən'f-\ *n* -S [ME, fr. MF, fr. ML *influentia,* fr. L *influent-, influens,* pres. part. of *influere* to flow in, fr. *in-* ²in- + *fluere* to flow + *-ia* -y — more at FLUID] **1 a :** an ethereal fluid thought to flow from the stars and to affect the actions of men **b :** a supposed emanation of occult power from stars **c** *obs* **:** character or temperament due to such power **2 :** the exercise of a power like the supposed power of the stars **:** an emanation of spiritual or moral force **3** *obs* **:** INFLOW, INFLUX **4 a :** the act, process, or power of producing an effect without apparent exertion of tangible force or direct exercise of command and often without deliberate effort or intent ⟨primitive men thinking that almost everything is significant and can exert ~ of some sort —William James⟩ **b :** corrupt interference with or manipulation of authority for personal gain ⟨~ may have had something to do with getting government money for the hotels —Marcus Duffield⟩ ⟨charges of corruption and ~ peddling —*Christian Science Monitor*⟩ **c :** the exertion of force at a distance ⟨tides are caused by the ~ of the moon and sun⟩ **5 :** the power or capacity of causing an effect in indirect or intangible ways **:** DOMINANCE, SWAY, ASCENDANCY ⟨under the ~ of liquor⟩ ⟨you don't necessarily measure the ~ of a religion by the number of churches it puts up —Green Peyton⟩ ⟨the intoxicating ~ of the mountain air —W.S.Gilbert⟩ **6 :** a person or thing that exerts influence ⟨open water affected by continental ~*s* —R.E.Coker⟩ ⟨Scotch-Irish, who still constitute the dominant ~, began to flow into the settlement —*Amer. Guide Series: Pa.*⟩ **7 :** INDUCTION 4c

syn AUTHORITY, PRESTIGE, WEIGHT, CREDIT: INFLUENCE refers to power exerted over others, often through high position, strength of intellect, force of character, or degree of accomplishment, sometimes exercised unconsciously and felt insensibly, sometimes consciously or calculatedly brought to bear ⟨as provost of the Swedish clergymen he exercised a quickening *influence* over all the Swedish congregations —G. H.Genzmer⟩ ⟨swept aside by the *influence* of the special interests bent on maintaining price levels against deflation —T. W.Arnold⟩ AUTHORITY signifies power resident in a person to command belief, acceptance, or allegiance, often through learning or wisdom ⟨Aristotle's *authority* was so great, and the homocentric system which he had espoused became so enmeshed in literature, that his system had its followers throughout the Middle Ages —G.C.Sellery⟩ ⟨the personal *authority* [of Augustus] which, far more than any legal or constitutional device, was the true secret of his later power —John Buchan⟩ ⟨to face a good orchestra with inward and outward *authority* and assurance —J.N.Burk⟩ PRESTIGE refers to the force of conspicuous excellence or of continued repute as superior, with resultant ability to command deference ⟨the almost magical *prestige* that had belonged to the original humanists —Aldous Huxley⟩ ⟨Napoleon insisted on a strict etiquette. He was right. It was only by keeping up the fiction of grandeur that he could maintain his *prestige* —André Maurois⟩ WEIGHT applies to power over or influence over others, often measurable and undeniable, and sometimes decisive ⟨Mrs. Hawthorne's authoritative air was beginning to have some *weight* with him —Archibald Marshall⟩ ⟨men who take the lead, and whose opinions and wishes have great *weight* with the others —J.G.Frazer⟩ CREDIT applies to ability to influence arising from merit or favorable reputation ⟨his position was distinctly stronger and once more he had shown his ability to handle a delicate situation to the *credit* of his government and himself —W.C.Ford⟩ ⟨the film was a success, with much of the *credit* going to the newcomer —*Current Biog.*⟩ — **under the influence :** in an intoxicated condition ⟨charged with driving *under the influence*⟩

²influence \"\ *vb* -ED/-ING/-S *vt* **1 :** to affect or alter the conduct, thought, or character of by indirect or intangible means **:** SWAY ⟨pilots . . . by listening to passengers who have *influenced* better judgment —*Skyways*⟩ ⟨economic and political factors that ~ decisions by managers of European zones —R.S.Thoman⟩ **2 :** to have an effect on the condition or development of **:** determine partially **:** MODIFY ⟨output was strongly *influenced* by the feelings of the worker about the job —Stuart Chase⟩ ⟨outdoor living has *influenced* the design . . . of furniture —N.C.Brown⟩ **3** *obs* **:** INDUCE, INFUSE ~ *vi, archaic* **:** to exert influence **syn** see AFFECT

in·flu·ence·abil·i·ty \,in,flüənsə'bilǝd·ē *sometimes* ən,f-\ *n* -ES **:** liability to influence

in·flu·ence·able \'=,==səbəl *sometimes* ='==-\ *adj* [¹*influence* + *-able*] **:** liable to be influenced **:** readily subject to influence

influence fuse *n* **:** PROXIMITY FUSE

influence line *n, often cap I* **1 :** LINE OF INFLUENCE **2 :** a graph showing the variation of the longitudinal stress, shear, bending moment, or other effect upon a structural member due to a moving load as a function of the position of that load

influence machine *n* **:** INDUCTION MACHINE

in·flu·enc·er \-sə(r)\ *n* -S **:** one that influences

in·flu·en·cive \'in,flüənsiv\ *adj, archaic* **:** INFLUENTIAL

¹in·flu·ent \'in,flüənt\ *adj* [ME, fr. L *influent-, influens,* pres. part. of *influere* to flow in — more at INFLUENCE] **1 :** flowing in; *esp* **:** contributing water to the zone of saturation and thereby sustaining or raising the water table ⟨~ seepage⟩ **2** *archaic* **:** exercising influence ⟨beneath the ~ heavens —Elizabeth B. Browning⟩

²influent \"\ *n* -S **1 :** a tributary stream **:** AFFLUENT; *also* **:** a stream or part of a stream that contributes water to the zone of saturation underground **2 a :** an animal or rarely a plant that has an important effect on the balance and stability of an ecological community ⟨rabbits and prairie dogs are important ~*s* in some rangelands⟩ **b :** a determining factor in the ecological balance of a human community ⟨location of home in relation to job is an ~ in city growth⟩

in·flu·en·tial \¦in,flü¦enchəl\ *adj* [ML *influentia* influence + E *-al* — more at INFLUENCE] **1 :** exerting or possessing influence **:** POTENT, EFFECTIVE ⟨as ~ as any newspaper in the country —Morley Callaghan⟩ **2 :** having authority or ascendancy **:** IMPORTANT ⟨exert ~ leadership for peace —D.D. Eisenhower⟩ **3** *obs* **:** of the nature of or relating to occult influence — **in·flu·en·tial·ly** \-ch(ə)lē, -li\ *adv*

in·flu·en·za \,in,flü'enzə\ *n* -S [It, influence, epidemic, influenza, fr. ML *influentia* influence; fr. the fact that epidemics were formerly attributed to the influence of the stars — more at INFLUENCE] **1 :** an acute highly contagious infectious virus disease that occurs in endemic, epidemic, or pandemic forms, is characterized by sudden onset, fever, prostration, severe aches and pains, and progressive inflammation of the respiratory mucous membrane, and is frequently complicated by secondary infections (as pneumonia); *broadly* **:** a human respiratory infection of undetermined cause **2 :** any of numerous febrile usu. virus diseases (as shipping fever of horses, swine influenza, infectious laryngotracheitis of poultry) marked by respiratory symptoms, inflammation of mucous membranes, and varying degrees of systemic involvement **3 :** a respiratory disease of dogs and cats that is perhaps identical with human influenza

influenza vaccine *n* **:** a vaccine against influenza; *specif* **:** a mixture of strains of formaldehyde-inactivated influenza virus from chick embryo culture

in·flux \'in,fləks\ *n* [LL *influxus,* fr. L *influxus,* past part. of *influere* to flow in — more at INFLUENCE] **1** *obs* **:** INFLUENCE **2 :** a flowing in **:** INFLOW ⟨~ of light⟩ ⟨~ of air⟩ **3 :** a continuous coming esp. of individuals in large numbers ⟨the city expected an ~ of holiday visitors⟩ **4 :** the mouth or debouchment of a river

in·flux·ion \ən'flǝkshən, 'in,f-\ *n* [LL *influxion-, influxio,* fr. L *influxus* (past part.) + *-ion-, -io* -ion] **:** INFLUX ⟨continual ~*s* of new blood —John Galsworthy⟩

in·fo \'in(,)fō\ *abbr or n* -S information

in·fold \ən'fōld\ *vb* [ME *ynfoldeyn,* fr. *yn-, in-* ²in- + *foldeyn, folden* to fold — more at FOLD] *vt* **:** ENFOLD ~ *vi* **:** to fold inward or toward one another ⟨the neural crests ~ and fuse⟩ ⟨an ~*ed* leaf margin⟩ ⟨~*ing* of the hindgut walls⟩

¹in·form \ən'fȯ(ə)rm, -ō(ə)m\ *vb* [ME *enfourmen, informen,* fr. MF *enformer, enfourmer,* fr. L *informare,* fr. *in-* ²in- + *formare* to form — more at FORM] *vt* **1** *obs* **a :** to give material form to **:** mold or shape physically **b :** to set in order **:** ARRANGE **2 a :** to give character or essence to ⟨to what extent can the practice of science ~, render more significant the objects of common sense —Gail Kennedy⟩ ⟨a piety . . . quietly ~*ing* the outlook of men in politics as elsewhere —W.L. Miller⟩ **b :** to be the formative principle of ⟨eternal objects ~ actual occasions with hierarchic patterns —A.N.Whitehead⟩ ⟨everything that is made from without and by dead rules, and does not spring from within through some spirit ~*ing* it —Oscar Wilde⟩ **c :** to permeate or impregnate so as to become the characteristic quality of **:** ANIMATE, INSPIRE, INFUSE ⟨these poems are ~*ed* with sincerity —Richard Eberhart⟩ ⟨sentimental, Protestant ethos that has always ~*ed* his writing —L.A.Fiedler⟩ **3** *obs* **:** to form (the mind) in respect to character, disposition, or ability **:** TRAIN, DISCIPLINE, INSTRUCT **4** *obs* **:** GUIDE, DIRECT ⟨if old respect hither hath ~*ed* your younger feet —John Milton⟩ **5** *obs* **:** to make known **:** give instruction in (as a doctrine) **6 :** to communicate knowledge to **:** make acquainted **:** TELL, ADVISE, ENLIGHTEN ⟨accused shall enjoy the right . . . to be ~*ed* of the nature and cause of the accusation —*U.S.Constitution*⟩ ⟨obligation as a citizen is to ~ himself . . . regarding the controversial issues —Clifford Houston⟩ ⟨program of ~*ing* the rest of the world about our way of life —H.H.Davis⟩ ~ *vi* **1 :** to give information **:** impart knowledge ⟨in theory news ~*s* while advertising sells —*Banking*⟩ **2 :** to give information or intelligence to a civil authority **:** lay information **:** act as a common informer ⟨I shall not ~ upon you —Oscar Wilde⟩

syn ACQUAINT, APPRISE, ADVISE, NOTIFY, ADVERTISE: These verbs signify to make aware or cognizant (of something). INFORM implies the imparting of knowledge, esp. of facts or events necessary to the understanding of a pertinent matter ⟨to *inform* the students there would be no classes on Saturday⟩ ⟨kept the staff *informed* of Chinese public opinion concerning the American military action there —*Current Biog.*⟩ ACQUAINT usu. lays stress upon less centrally significant matter than INFORM does or suggests a process of introducing to or familiarizing with rather than informing of ⟨these writings were of the nature of travel books, and served . . . to *acquaint* the world with a new country —*Amer. Guide Series: Minn.*⟩ ⟨*acquainting* students with political practices —F.A.Ogg & Harold Zink⟩ To APPRISE someone of something is to communicate something usu. of interest or importance to him ⟨this church, so I was then *apprised,* was founded by St. James the Less —T.G.Henderson⟩ ⟨Tristram's cutting the hazel and writing upon it with his knife in order to *apprise* the queen of his presence —Grace Frank⟩ ⟨to touch him on the sleeve and *apprise* him that I was there —Mary Austin⟩ To ADVISE someone of something is to inform him of something that may make a significant difference to him in an action, policy, or plan; it often suggests a forewarning or counseling ⟨consulted the wine card and *advised* me that the wine I had chosen had no special merit —R.M.Lovett⟩ ⟨I *advised* him strongly of the danger of switching professions without acquiring new professional qualifications —R.G.G.Price⟩ To NOTIFY is to send a notice or make a usu. formal communication generally about something requiring or worthy of attention ⟨the court clerk *notified* the witnesses when to appear⟩ ⟨*notify* a man of his acceptance in a club⟩ To ADVERTISE, rare in current use in this sense, is to inform or notify by way of warning ⟨the translators, good Protestants, were careful to *advertise* the reader that what they offered was Le Clerc's Moreri —*Times Lit. Supp.*⟩

²inform *adj* [MF *informe,* fr. L *informis,* fr. *in-* ¹in- + *forma* form — more at FORM] **1** *obs* **:** lacking regular form **:** SHAPELESS, DEFORMED **2** *obs* **:** lacking created form **:** UNFORMED

in·formal \(')in, ən+\ *adj* [¹*in-* + *formal*] **1 :** not formal **:** conducted or carried out without formal, regularly prescribed, or ceremonious procedure **:** UNOFFICIAL ⟨~ hearing⟩ ⟨~ discussion⟩ ⟨~ contract⟩ ⟨~ inquiries⟩ ⟨~ gathering of friends⟩ **2 :** characteristic of or appropriate to ordinary, casual, or familiar use ⟨~ English⟩ ⟨genial, ~ manner⟩ ⟨~ essay⟩ **3** *obs* **:** DERANGED, MAD ⟨poor ~ women are no more but instruments —Shak.⟩ **4** *of a design* **:** having an asymmetrical composition or arrangement made from unequal shapes and distances ⟨~ balance in a stage set⟩

in·formality \¦in+\ *n* [¹*in-* + *formality*] **1 :** the quality or state of being informal **:** lack of regular, prescribed, or customary form ⟨wayside camps, where the ~ of hardships loosened tongues —Mabel R. Gillis⟩ ⟨everyday speech in all its ~ and ease —R.A.Hall b. 1911⟩ **2 :** an informal act or proceeding ⟨the wedding ceremony was enlivened by several unexpected *informalities*⟩

in·for·ma·lize \ən'fȯ(r)mə,līz\ *vt* [*informal* + *-ize*] **:** to make informal or less formal ⟨college education of the future must . . . be greatly simplified and *informalized* —*Nation*⟩

in·formally \(')in, ən+\ *adv* **:** in an informal manner **:** without ceremony or formality ⟨addressed the gathering ~⟩ ⟨~ dressed in flannels and jacket⟩ **:** UNOFFICIALLY ⟨fast train . . . began to be called, more or less ~, the Cannonball —A.F. Harlow⟩

informal planning *n* **:** architectural planning in which dominant axes and strong visual climaxes are avoided in favor of freer circulation patterns and more subtle dramatic effects

in·for·mant \ən'fȯrmənt, -ō(ə)m-\ *n* -S [L *informant-, informans,* pres. part. of *informare* to inform — more at INFORM] **:** one that informs **:** one who gives information: as **a :** INFORMER **b :** one who supplies cultural or linguistic data in response to interrogation by an investigator ⟨findings . . . based on . . . statements of ~*s* from among both the educated and the uneducated —B.B.Ashcom⟩ ⟨analysis of great civilizations by the use of living ~*s* —Gregory Bateson⟩

in for·ma pau·pe·ris \-¦fȯrmə'pȯpərəs, -'paůp-\ *adj (or adv)* [L, in the form of a pauper] **:** as a poor man **:** relieved of fees and costs in a legal action because of inability to pay ⟨permission was granted to file an appeal *in forma pauperis*⟩

in·for·ma·tion \,infə(r)'māshən\ *n* -S *often attrib* [ME *informacioun,* fr. *enfourmen, informen* to inform + *-acioun* -ation — more at INFORM] **1 a** *obs* **:** an endowing with form **b** *obs* **:** the act of animating or inspiring **c** *obs* **:** TRAINING, DISCIPLINE, INSTRUCTION **d :** the communication or reception of knowledge or intelligence ⟨the function of a public library is ~⟩ ⟨we enclose a price list for your ~⟩ **2 :** something received or obtained through informing: as **a :** knowledge communicated by others or obtained from investigation, study, or instruction **b :** knowledge of a particular event or situation **:** INTELLIGENCE, NEWS, ADVICES ⟨latest ~ from the battle front⟩ ⟨securing ~ about conditions in the upper atmosphere⟩ ⟨~ bureau⟩ **c :** facts or figures ready for communication or use as distinguished from those incorporated in a formally organized branch of knowledge **:** DATA ⟨reliable source of ~⟩ **d :** a signal (as one of the digits in dialing a telephone number) purposely impressed upon the input of a communication system or a calculating machine **3 :** the act of informing against a person or party **4 a :** a formal accusation of a crime made by a prosecuting officer on information brought to his attention as distinguished from an indictment presented by a grand jury **:** COMPLAINT **b :** a pleading by an attorney general or other public officer setting forth a civil case or relief in which some public right of the state is asserted **c :** the document containing the depositions of the witnesses against one accused of crime **5 :** the process by which the form of an object of knowledge is impressed upon the apprehending mind so as to bring about the state of knowing **6 :** a logical quantity belonging to propositions and arguments as well as terms and comprising the sum of the synthetical propositions in which the term, proposition, or argument taken enters as subject or predicate, antecedent or consequent — see QUANTITY 5c **7 :** a numerical quantity that measures the uncertainty in the outcome of an experiment to be performed ⟨when an event occurs whose probability was *p,* the event is said to communicate an amount of ~ log (1/*p*) —W.F.Brown b. 1904⟩ ⟨the amount of ~ is defined, in the simplest cases, to be measured by the logarithm of the number of available choices —C.E. Shannon & Warren Weaver⟩ **syn** see KNOWLEDGE

in·for·ma·tion·al \¦==¦māshənᵊl, -shnəl\ *adj* **:** relating to or giving information **:** INFORMING ⟨~ service of a library⟩

information girl *n* **1 :** a telephone operator who gives information from the central office switchboard **2 :** a clerk at an information desk

information theory *n* **:** a theory that utilizes statistical techniques in dealing with the effect of encoding on the efficiency of processes of signal transmission and of communication between men (as in telecommunication or the printed word) or between men and machines or between machines and machines (as in computing machines)

in·form·a·tive \ən'fȯ(r)məd·iv, -ətiv\ *adj* [¹*inform* + *-ative*] **1** *obs* **:** having power to inform, animate, or vivify **2 :** imparting knowledge **:** INSTRUCTIVE ⟨~ lecture⟩ ⟨~ brochure⟩ **3 :** INFORMATORY — **in·form·a·tive·ly** \-əvlē, -li\ *adv* — **in·form·a·tive·ness** \-ivnəs\ *n*

in·form·ato·ry \-mə,tōrē, -tȯr-, -ri\ *adj* [*information* + *-ory*] **:** INFORMING, INSTRUCTIVE ⟨a witty and ~ book⟩; *specif* **:** devised or intended to convey information ⟨~ bid in contract bridge⟩

informatory double *n* **:** a double made in bridge to convey information to one's partner and to invite a bid from him — called also *takeout double*

informed *adj* [fr. past part. of ¹*inform*] **1 :** having information ⟨an ~ citizenry⟩ ⟨a well-*informed* man⟩ **:** based on possession of information ⟨~ estimate of next year's tax receipts⟩ **2 :** EDUCATED, INTELLIGENT, CULTIVATED ⟨~ taste⟩ ⟨~ opinion⟩ ⟨transition . . . from blind habit to ~ works of art —Ernest Nagel⟩

in·form·er \ən'fȯrmər, -ō(ə)mə(r)\ *n* [ME *enfourmer,* fr. *enfourmen* to inform + *-er* — more at INFORM] **1** *obs* **:** one that informs, animates, or inspires ⟨nature, ~ of the poet's art —Alexander Pope⟩ **2 :** one that informs or imparts knowledge or news **3 :** one that informs against another: **a :** one that informs a magistrate of a violation of law **:** one that lays an information; *esp* **:** one that makes a practice of informing against others for violations of penal laws particularly when the informer may receive as a reward a share of the money penalty imposed — called also *common informer;* compare QUI TAM **b :** one secretly in the service of the police or of a diplomatic agency (as an embassy) that supplies information ⟨a nest of spies and ~*s*⟩

informidable *adj* [[1]in- + *formidable*] *obs* **:** not formidable ⟨foe not ~ —John Milton⟩

informing *adj* [fr. pres. part. of [1]*inform*] **1 :** ANIMATING, INSPIRING ⟨the concrete and the external are . . . the medium through which the ~ spirit is expressed —J.L.Lowes⟩ **2 :** INFORMATIVE, INSTRUCTIVE

in·form·ing·ly *adv* **:** INFORMATIVELY, INSTRUCTIVELY

informs *pres 3d sing of* INFORM

in fo·ro \-ˈfō(ˌ)rō\ *adv* [L, in the forum] **:** before the court **:** within the jurisdiction

in foro con·sci·en·ti·ae \-ˌkänchēˈenchēˌē\ *adv* [L, in the forum of conscience] **:** privately or morally rather than legally ⟨an extrajudicial oath is binding only *in foro conscientiae*⟩

in·for·tu·nate \ənˈfȯ(r)chənət\ *adj* [ME *infortunat*, fr. L *infortunatus*, fr. *in-* [1]in- + *fortunatus* fortunate — more at FORTUNATE] **1** *obs* **:** UNFORTUNATE **2 :** causing or presaging misfortune **:** UNPROPITIOUS

in·for·tune \(ˈ)in¦fȯrchən, ənˈ-\ *n* [ME, fr. MF, fr. L *infortunium*, fr. *in-* [1]in- + *-fortunium* (fr. *fortuna* fortune) — more at FORTUNE] **:** one of the malevolent planets (Saturn, Mars, or sometimes Mercury) in an unfavorable aspect

infortunity *n* -ES [MF *infortunité*, fr. L *infortunitat-*, *infortunitas*, fr. *in-* [1]in- + *fortuna* fortune + *-itat-*, *-itas* -ity] *obs* **:** MISFORTUNE

infos *pl of* INFO

in·fra \ˈinfrə, -n(ˌ)frä, -n(ˌ)frȧ\ *adv* [L] **1 :** UNDER, BELOW **2 :** LATER

infra- *prefix* [L *infra* below, underneath — more at UNDER] **1 a :** below **:** lower in status than — esp. in adjectives formed from adjectives ⟨*infra*human⟩ **b :** after **:** later than ⟨*infra*lapsarian⟩ **2 :** within — esp. in adjectives formed from adjectives ⟨*infra*territorial⟩ **3 :** below in a scale or series — esp. in adjectives formed from adjectives ⟨*infra*red⟩ **4 :** below or beneath (a designated part of the anatomy) — esp. in adjectives formed from adjectives ⟨*infra*costal⟩

in·fra-angelic \¦infrə+\ *adj* [*infra-* + *angelic*] **:** less than angelic **:** HUMAN

in·fra·basal \"+\ *adj* [*infra-* + *basal*] *zool* **:** lying below a basal structure ⟨~ skeletal plate of a crinoid⟩

in·fra·branchial \"+\ *adj* [*infra-* + *branchial*] **:** lying below the gills — used esp. of the ventral part of the pallial chamber in the lamellibranchs

in·fra·central \"+\ *adj* [*infra-* + *central*] *anat* **:** lying below the centrum

in·fra·class \ˈinfrə+,-\ *n* [*infra-* + *class*] **:** a subdivision of a subclass that is more or less exactly equivalent to a superorder

in·fra·clavicle \¦infrə+\ *n* [*infra-* + *clavicle*] **:** a bony element in the shoulder girdle lying below the cleithrum in some ganoid and crossopterygian fishes and supposed to be the true homologue of the clavicle of higher animals

in·fra·clavicular \"+\ *adj* [*infra-* + *clavicular*] **:** relating or belonging to the infraclavicle

in·fra·cos·ta·lis \ˌinfrə(ˌ)käˈstaləs, -tāl-, -täl-\ *n, pl* **infra·costa·les** \-a(ˌ)lēz, -ā(ˌ)lēz, -ä(ˌ)lās\ [NL, fr. *infra-* + L *costa* rib + *-alis* -al — more at COAST] **:** SUBCOSTALIS

in·fract \ənˈfrakt\ *vt* -ED/-ING/-S [L *infractus*, past part. of *infringere* to break, break off, destroy — more at INFRINGE] **:** BREAK, INFRINGE, VIOLATE ⟨~ the Constitution⟩

in·fract·ible \-təbəl\ *adj* [LL *infractus* unbroken (fr. L *in-* [1]in- + *fractus*, past part. of *frangere* to break) + E *-ible* — more at BREAK] **:** INVIOLABLE ⟨a thorough and ~ eight hours devoted to his work in Wall Street —Scott Fitzgerald⟩

in·frac·tion \ənˈfrakshən\ *n* -S [L *infraction-*, *infractio*, fr. *infractus* (past part. of *infringere*) + *-ion-*, *-io* -ion] **1 :** the act of breaking or violating **:** BREACH, VIOLATION, INFRINGEMENT ⟨~ of a treaty⟩ ⟨minor ~*s* of the rules⟩ ⟨~ of code⟩ ⟨~ of discipline⟩ **2 :** an incomplete fracture without displacement of the bone **syn** see BREACH

in·frac·tor \-ktə(r)\ *n* -S [prob. fr. MF *infracteur*, fr. LL *infractor*, fr. L *infractus* (past part. of *infringere*) + *-or*] **:** one that infracts or infringes **:** VIOLATOR, BREAKER

in·fra dig \¦infrə¦dig\ *adj* [modif. of L *infra dignitatem* beneath dignity] **:** being beneath one's dignity **:** UNDIGNIFIED ⟨it was clear . . . that off-season cruising was rather *infra dig* —Richard Gordon⟩ ⟨considered helping with the dishes to be *infra dig*⟩

in·fra·foliar \¦infrə+\ *adj* [*infra-* + *foliar*] **:** situated below the leaves ⟨~ flower clusters⟩

in·fra·glacial \"+\ *adj* [*infra-* + *glacial*] **:** SUBGLACIAL

in·fra·glenoid \"+\ *adj* [*infra-* + *glenoid*] **:** situated below the glenoid cavity of the scapula

infraglenoid tubercle *n* **:** a tubercle on the scapula for the attachment of the long head of the triceps muscle

in·fra·gular \"+\ *adj* [*infra-* + *gular*] **:** SUBESOPHAGEAL

in·fra·human \"+\ *adj* [*infra-* + *human*] **:** less or lower than human ⟨~ attributes⟩; *specif* **:** ANTHROPOID — compare SUPERHUMAN

[1]**in·fra·labial** \"+\ *adj* [*infra-* + *labial*] **:** lying below the lip **:** SUBLABIAL

[2]**infralabial** \"\ *n* **:** a scale or plate bordering the lower jaw on either side of the mental of various reptiles

[1]**in·fra·lap·sar·i·an** \ˌinfrə,lapˈserēən, -sa(a)r-\ *n* -S [*infra-* + L *lapsus* lapse, fall + E *-arian* — more at LAPSE] **:** one that adheres to the doctrine of infralapsarianism — compare SUPRALAPSARIAN

[2]**infralapsarian** \¦==¦===\ *adj* **:** of or relating to the doctrine of infralapsarianism

in·fra·lap·sar·i·an·ism \ˌ==,=ˈ==ə,nizəm\ *n* -S **:** the doctrine that God foresaw and permitted the fall of man and that after the fall he then decreed election as a means of saving some of the human race — compare SUPRALAPSARIANISM

in·fra·linear \¦infrə+\ *adj* [*infra-* + *linear*] **:** placed below the line of writing **:** SUBLINEAR ⟨an ~ system of vocalization for Hebrew⟩

in·fra·littoral \"+\ *adj* [*infra-* + *littoral*] **:** situated to seaward of the region of littoral deposits ⟨~ zone⟩

[1]**in·fra·marginal** \"+\ *adj* [*infra-* + *marginal*] **1 :** situated below a margin **:** SUBMARGINAL ⟨~ convolution of the brain⟩ **2 :** situated below the marginal cell of an insect's wing

[2]**inframarginal** \"\ *n* **:** an inframarginal element

in·fra·natant \"+\ *adj* [*infra-* + *natant*] **:** lying below a supernatant body ⟨unfiltered ~ solution from a growing culture —*Science*⟩

in·fra·neritic \"+\ *adj* [*infra-* + *neritic*] **:** lying at a depth greater than 120 feet below the ocean surface ⟨~ environment of sedimentation⟩ — opposed to *epineritic*

in·frangibility \(ˌ)in, ən+\ *n* **:** INVIOLABILITY ⟨the ~ of the given word is the first rule of politics —H.D.Scott⟩

in·fran·gi·ble \(ˈ)in¦franjəbəl, ənˈf-, -raan-\ *adj* [MF, fr. LL *infrangibilis*, fr. L *in-* [1]in- + *frangere* to break + *-ibilis* -ible — more at BREAK] **1 :** not capable of being broken ⟨~ resolution of character⟩ or separated into parts ⟨~ series⟩ **2 :** not to be infringed or violated ⟨~ law⟩ — **in·fran·gi·ble·ness** *n* — **in·fran·gi·bly** \-blē, -bli\ *adv*

in·fra·orbital \¦infrə+\ *adj* [*infra-* + *orbital*] **:** situated beneath the orbit ⟨~ bone⟩

in·fra·pose \ˌinfrəˈpōz\ *vt* [*infra-* + *-pose* (as in *superpose*)] **:** to place under or beneath — **in·fra·position** \¦infrə+\ *n*

in fra prae·si·dia \ˌinfrəprēˈzidēə\ *adv* [L, under the protection] *of captured property* **:** in safe custody **:** completely under control

[1]**in·fra·red** \¦infrə¦red, -ˌfrä¦-, -ˌfrȧ¦- *sometimes* ¦infə¦r- *by r-dissimilation*\ *adj* [*infra-* + *red*] **1 :** lying outside the visible spectrum at its red end — used of thermal radiation of wavelengths longer than those of visible light **2 :** relating to, producing, or employing infrared radiation ⟨~ therapy⟩ ⟨~ photography⟩ **3 :** sensitive to infrared radiation and capable of photographing in darkness or through haze ⟨~ film⟩

[2]**infrared** \"\ *n* **:** infrared radiation

infrared lamp *n* **:** a high-power incandescent lamp operating at a lower filament temperature than a lamp used for illumination and yielding a large percentage of infrared radiation that is useful for heating purposes

in·fra·roentgen ray \"+...-\ *n* [*infra-* + *roentgen*] **:** GRENZ RAY

in·fra·scap·u·la·ris \ˌinfrə,skapyəˈla(a)rəs\ *n, pl* **infra·scapula·res** \-a(a)(ˌ)rēz\ [NL, fr. *infra-* + *scapula* + *-aris* -ar] **:** the teres minor

In·fra·si·zer \ˈinfrə,sīzə(r)\ *trademark* — used for an apparatus for determining the degree of fineness to which a material (as a mineral or rock) has been ground

in·fra·social \¦infrə+\ *adj* [*infra-* + *social*] *of insects* **:** lacking social organization **:** SOLITARY

in·fra·sonic \"+\ *adj* [*infra-* + *sonic*] **1 :** having a frequency lower than about 16 cycles per second and therefore below the audibility range of the human ear and producing only a fluttering sensation with no sense of pitch — compare SONIC, SUPERSONIC **2 :** utilizing or produced by infrasonic waves or vibrations

in·fra·specific \"+\ *adj* [*infra-* + *specific*] **:** included within a species ⟨~ categories⟩

in·fra·spinal \"+\ *adj* [*infra-* + *spinal*] **:** INFRASPINOUS

in·fra·spi·na·tus \ˌinfrə(ˌ)spīˈnād·əs\ *n, pl* **infraspinati** [NL, fr. *infra-* + L *spina* spine + *-atus* -ate — more at SPINE] **:** a muscle that occupies the chief part of the infraspinous fossa of the scapula and is inserted into the greater tuberosity of the humerus

in·fra·spinous \¦infrə+\ *adj* [*infra-* + *spinous*] **:** lying below a spine; *esp* **:** lying below the spine of the scapula

infraspinous fossa *n* **:** the part of the dorsal surface of the scapula below the spine of the scapula

in·fra·structure \ˈinfrə+,-\ *n* [*infra-* + *structure*] **:** the underlying foundation or basic framework (as of an organization or a system) **:** SUBSTRUCTURE; *esp* **:** the permanent installations required for military purposes

in·fra·temporal \¦infrə+\ *adj* [*infra-* + *temporal*] **:** situated below the temple or temporal bone — used esp. of the lower or more lateral of the two divisions of the temporal fossae of various reptiles

infratemporal fossa *n* **:** a fossa in man and some other vertebrates bounded above by the plane of zygomatic arch, laterally by the ramus of the mandible, and medially by the pterygoid plate, and lodging the masseter and pterygoid muscles and the mandibular nerve

in frau·dem le·gis \-ˈfrōdəm ˈlējəs\ *adv* [L] **:** in circumvention of the rules of law

in·frequency \(ˈ)in, ən+\ *or* **in·frequence** \"+\ *n* [L *infrequentia*, fr. *infrequent-*, *infrequens* infrequent + *-ia* -y] **1** *obs* **:** the quality or state of not being frequented **:** SOLITUDE, ISOLATION **2 :** the state of rarely occurring **:** UNCOMMONNESS, RARENESS ⟨comparative ~ of typhoid fever⟩

in·frequent \"+\ *adj* [L *infrequent-*, *infrequens*, fr. *in-* [1]in- + *frequent-*, *frequens* frequent — more at FREQUENT] **1** *obs* **:** UNFREQUENTED **2 :** seldom happening or occurring **:** RARE, UNCOMMON ⟨far from being ~, the crystalline state is almost universal among solids —K.K.Darrow⟩ **3 :** placed or occurring at considerable distances or intervals **:** OCCASIONAL, SPARSE ⟨~ openings in a wall⟩ — **in·fre·quent·ly** *adv*

in·frig·i·date \ənˈfrijə,dāt\ *vt* -ED/-ING/-S [LL *infrigidatus*, past part. of *infrigidare*, fr. L *in-* [2]in- + LL *frigidare* to make cold, fr. L *frigidus* cold — more at FRIGID] **:** to make cold **:** CHILL

in·fringe \ənˈfrinj\ *vb* -ED/-ING/-S [L *infringere* to break, break off, weaken, destroy, fr. *in-* [2]in- + *-fringere* (fr. *frangere* to break) — more at BREAK] *vt* **1** *obs* **a :** to break down **:** DESTROY **b :** DEFEAT, FRUSTRATE **c :** CONFUTE, REFUTE **d :** IMPAIR, WEAKEN **2 :** to commit a breach of ⟨~ the peace⟩ **:** neglect to fulfill or obey **:** VIOLATE, TRANSGRESS ⟨~ a treaty⟩ ⟨~ an edict⟩ ⟨~ a contract⟩ ⟨~ a patent⟩ ⟨~ a copyright⟩ ⟨both these limits of gradient and curve must be *infringed* to reach the plateau —James Bird⟩ ⟨the statute . . . would ~ fundamental principles —O.W.Holmes †1935⟩ ~ *vi* **:** ENCROACH, TRESPASS — used with *on* or *upon* ⟨where the siesta is no catnap and a ten-o'clock dinner practically ~*s* on tea time —Claudia Cassidy⟩ **syn** see TRESPASS

in·fringe·ment \-jmənt\ *n* -S **1 :** the act of infringing **:** BREACH, VIOLATION, NONFULFILLMENT ⟨~ of a treaty⟩ ⟨~ of the constitution⟩ **2 :** an encroachment or trespass on a right or privilege **:** TRESPASS: **a :** the unlawful manufacture, use, or sale of a patented or copyrighted article, such as constitutes a tort in law **b :** the unlawful use of a trademark or trade name **syn** see BREACH

in·fring·er \-jə(r)\ *n* -S **:** one that infringes ⟨~ of a patent⟩

in·fruc·tes·cence \ˌin,frəkˈtesən(t)s\ *n* [F, fr. *in-* [2]in- + L *fructus* fruit + F *-escence* (as in *inflorescence*) — more at FRUIT] **:** the fruiting stage of an inflorescence

in·fructuous \(ˈ)in, ən+\ *adj* [L *infructuosus*, fr. *in-* [1]in- + *fructuosus* fruitful — more at FRUCTUOUS] **1 :** UNFRUITFUL **2 :** FRUITLESS, UNPROFITABLE — **in·fruc·tu·ous·ly** *adv*

in·fu·la \ˈinfyələ\ *n, pl* **infu·lae** \-ə,lē\ [L; perh. akin to L *redimire* to tie, wreathe, *geminus* twin — more at GEMINATE] **1 :** a fillet of red and white wool worn in ancient Rome as a token of religious consecration or inviolability **2** [ML, fr. L] **a :** one of two lappets that hang from the back of a bishop's miter **b :** a chasuble used principally in France and England from the 11th to the 16th century

infulae

in·fu·mate \ˈinfyə,māt, ənˈfyümət\ *or* **in·fu·mat·ed** \-,mād·əd\ *adj* [*infumate* fr. L *infumatus*, past part. of *infumare* to dry by smoking, fr. *in-* [2]in- + *fumare* to smoke, fr. *fumus* smoke; *infumated* fr. L *infumatus* + E *-ed* — more at FUME] **:** clouded with blackish color ⟨~ insect wing⟩

in·fu·ma·tion \ˌinfyəˈmāshən\ *n* -S [L *infumatus* + E *-ion*] **:** the act or process of drying in smoke

in·fun·dib·u·lar \ˌin(ˌ)fən¦dibyələ(r)\ *adj* [NL *infundibulum* + E *-ar*] **1 :** resembling a funnel **2 a :** of or relating to an infundibulum **b :** INFUNDIBULATE

in·fun·dib·u·la·ta \ˌ=(ˌ)=,dibyəˈlād·ə, -lād·ə\ [NL, fr. *infundibulum* + *-ata*] *syn of* GYMNOLAEMATA

in·fun·dib·u·late \¦=(ˌ)=¦dibyə,lāt, -lət\ *adj* [NL *infundibulum* + E *-ate*] **1 :** having an infundibulum **2 :** INFUNDIBULIFORM

in·fun·dib·u·li·form \-yələ,fȯrm\ *adj* [NL *infundibulum* + *-iform*] **:** having the form of a funnel or cone ⟨~ calyx⟩

in·fun·dib·u·lum \ˌ=(ˌ)=ˈdibyələm\ *n, pl* **infundibu·la** \-lə\ [NL, fr. L, funnel, fr. *infundere* to pour in — more at INFUSE] **:** any of various conical or funnel-shaped organs or parts: as **a :** the hollow conical process of gray matter that is borne on the tuber cinereum and constitutes the stalk of the neurohypophysis by which the pituitary body is continuous with the brain **b :** any of the small spaces having walls beset with air sacs in which the bronchial tubes terminate in the lungs **c :** the enlarged process of the right ventricle from which the pulmonary artery arises **d :** the passage by which the anterior ethmoid cells and the frontal sinuses communicate with the nose **e :** the calyx of a kidney **f :** the abdominal opening of a fallopian tube **g :** a central cavity in the Ctenophora into which the gastric sac leads

[1]**in·fu·ri·ate** \ənˈfyu̇rē,āt, *usu* -ād·+V\ *vt* -ED/-ING/-S [ML *infuriatus*, past part. of *infuriare*, fr. L *in-* [2]in- + *furiare* to madden, fr. *furia* fury — more at FURY] **:** to make furious **:** ENRAGE, MADDEN ⟨his book will . . . ~, enlighten, and rejoice different types of readers —D.W.Brogan⟩

[2]**in·fu·ri·ate** \", -ēət\ *adj* [ML *infuriatus*, past part.] **:** furiously angry **:** INFURIATED ⟨the hunchback weak, but ~, buffeting, biting, and whimpering —Arthur Morrison⟩ — **in·fu·ri·ate·ly** *adv*

in·fu·ri·at·ing·ly *adv* **:** to a maddening degree ⟨his sorely tried and ~ trying wife —Charles Lee⟩ **:** so as to infuriate ⟨~ indifferent⟩

in·fu·ri·a·tion \ən,fyu̇rēˈāshən\ *n* -S **:** the act of infuriating or state of being infuriated

in·fus·cate \ənˈfə,skāt, -,skət\ *or* **in·fus·cat·ed** \-,skād·əd\ *adj* [*infuscate* fr. L *infuscatus*, past part. of *infuscare* to obscure, fr. *in-* [2]in- + *fuscare* to darken, fr. *fuscus* dark brown, blackish; *infuscated* fr. L *infuscatus* + E *-ed* — more at DUSK] **:** OBSCURED ⟨~ minds⟩; *specif* **:** darkened with a brownish tinge ⟨~ wing of an insect⟩ — **in·fus·ca·tion** \ˌin(ˌ)fəˈskāshən\ *n* -S

in·fuse \ənˈfyüz\ *vb* -ED/-ING/-S [ME *infusen*, *enfusen*, fr. MF & L; MF *infuser*, fr. L *infusus*, past part. of *infundere* to pour in, fr. *in-* [2]in- + *fundere* to pour — more at FOUND] *vt* **1** *obs* **:** to pour (a liquid) into something **2 a :** to instill or inculcate a principle or quality in ⟨attributes the fine spirit of the whole project to the self-respect with which men had been *infused* —Dixon Wecter⟩ **b :** INTRODUCE, INSINUATE, SUGGEST ⟨~ an idea⟩ ⟨~ a belief⟩ ⟨*infused* an aviation curriculum into some forty university departments —Phil Gustafson⟩ **3 :** INSPIRE, IMBUE, ANIMATE, FILL ⟨brought together the main ideas . . . and *infused* them with the conception that the universe was the product of a historical development —S.F. Mason⟩ ⟨*infused* only with her passion for her child —Ethel Wilson⟩ **4 :** to steep in water or other fluid without boiling for the purpose of extracting useful qualities **:** DRENCH ⟨~ tea leaves⟩ ~ *vi* **:** to undergo the process of infusion ⟨letting the tea stand a few minutes to ~ —Flora Thompson⟩

syn SUFFUSE, IMBUE, INGRAIN, INOCULATE, LEAVEN: INFUSE implies the introducing into one thing of a second that gives life, vigor, or new significance ⟨*infusing* life into an inanimate body —Mary W. Shelley⟩ ⟨the extraordinary force which Lawrence's imagination *infused* into his prose —*Times Lit. Supp.*⟩ ⟨whose work is for the most part *infused* with the spirit of scientific materialism —L.A.White⟩ ⟨it *infused* into them the feeling that they were not at the mercy of blind economic forces —A.R.Williams⟩ SUFFUSE implies the spreading over or through one thing of a second that gives the first thing an unusual color, aspect, texture, or quality ⟨I felt a large, healthy blush *suffuse* my features —L.P.Smith⟩ ⟨the western sky was *suffused* with the transparent yellow-green of August evenings —Ellen Glasgow⟩ ⟨an exalted feeling of martyrdom well earned *suffused* the exiles —E.J.Simmons⟩ ⟨the novel was *suffused* with a feeling for water and air, with sunlight hot and shifting —Leo Gurko⟩ IMBUE implies the introduction into a person or thing of something that completely permeates ⟨*imbued* so strongly with a sense of duty and obedience —Hanama Tasaki⟩ ⟨*imbued* with a dynamic faith —*Amer. Guide Series: Minn.*⟩ ⟨*imbue* the army with a national spirit —Hajo Holborn⟩ ⟨the mind becomes *imbued* with the scientific method —J.B.Conant⟩ INGRAIN implies a pervading of something with an irremovable dye or something suggesting such a dye ⟨morality *ingrained* in the national character —J.A.Froude⟩ ⟨the principle of serfdom was *ingrained* in medieval society —G.G.Coulton⟩ ⟨her instinctive humility and good manners were too deeply *ingrained*—Helen Howe⟩ ⟨this idea of equality was *ingrained* in the New York cabdriver —D.F.Karaka⟩ INOCULATE, in this extended sense, implies an imbuing of a person with something resembling a disease germ, often suggesting a surreptitious means ⟨those who believe that the great mass of the people are unreasoning beasts that must be controlled by *inoculating* them with myths or fictions —M.R. Cohen⟩ ⟨the democratic leveling had helped to *inoculate* the public with the idea of free schools disassociated from charity —*Amer. Guide Series: Va.*⟩ ⟨third-rate southerners *inoculated* with all the worst traits of the Yankee sharper —H.L.Mencken⟩ LEAVEN implies a transforming of something by introducing into it something else which enlivens, elevates, tempers, or markedly alters the total quality, usu. for the better ⟨*leaven* the dense mass of facts and events with the elastic force of reason —J.H.Newman⟩ ⟨there was need of idealism to *leaven* the materialistic realism of the times —V.L.Parrington⟩ ⟨knowledge . . . must be *leavened* with magnanimity before it becomes wisdom —A.E.Stevenson b. 1900⟩

in·fus·er \-zə(r)\ *n* -S **:** one that infuses; *esp* **:** a device for infusing tea leaves

in·fusibility \¦in+\ *n* **:** the quality or state of being infusible

in·fusible \(ˈ)in, ən+\ *adj* [[1]*in-* + *fusible*] **:** not fusible **:** incapable or very difficult of fusion; *specif, of a mineral* **:** having a melting point higher than the temperature (about 1500°C) of the ordinary blowpipe flame — **in·fu·si·ble·ness** *n* -ES

infusible white precipitate *n* **:** AMMONIATED MERCURY

in·fusion \ənˈfyüzhən\ *n* -S [ME, fr. MF & L; MF, fr. L *infusion-*, *infusio*, fr. *infusus* (past part. of *infundere* to pour in) + *-ion-*, *-io* -ion — more at INFUSE] **1 a :** the act or process of infusing ⟨an ~ of ordinary men and women would lessen the alleged remoteness of the higher civil servants from the life of the people —Ray Lewis & Angus Maude⟩ **b :** something that is infused ⟨horses of this type carry some ~ of . . . Thoroughbred blood —C.F.Rooks⟩ **2 a :** the introducing of a solution (as of glucose or salt) into a vein; *also* **:** the solution so used **b** (1) **:** the steeping or soaking usu. in water of a substance (as a plant drug) in order to extract its virtues (2) **:** the liquid extract obtained by this process **3 :** a watery suspension of decaying organic material ⟨culturing soil amoebas in lettuce ~⟩

in·fu·sion·ism \-zhə,nizəm\ *n* -S **:** the doctrine that the soul is preexistent to the body and is infused into it at conception or birth — compare CREATIONISM, TRADUCIANISM

in·fu·sion·ist \-ˌnəst\ *n* **:** one who adheres to the doctrine of infusionism

infusion process *n* **:** a mashing process in which the whole mash is kept at about 70°C — compare DECOCTION PROCESS

in·fu·sive \ənˈfyüsiv, -üziv\ *adj* **:** INSPIRING, INFLUENCING ⟨the ~ force of Spring on man —James Thomson †1748⟩

in·fu·so·ria \ˌinfyəˈzōrēə, -ˈs|, -ōr-\ *n pl* [NL, fr. neut. pl. of *infusorius*, fr. L *infusus* (past part. of *infundere* to pour in) + *-orius* -ory] **1** *cap* **:** a group of minute organisms typically found in infusions of decaying organic matter: **a** *in early classifications* **:** a heterogeneous group comprising various plant and animal organisms (as bacteria, algae, fungi, protozoans, and small metazoans) **b** *in later classifications* **:** a heterogeneous group of animals comprising protozoans and small metazoans **c** *in early modern classifications* **:** a major division of Protozoa comprising protozoans with differentiated locomotor organelles and including the ciliates **d** *in some recent classifications* **:** a class of Protozoa coextensive with the subphylum Ciliophora **2** *often cap* **:** microscopic animal life — not used technically

in·fu·so·ri·al \¦==¦==ēəl\ *adj* [NL *Infusoria* + E *-al*] **:** relating to, containing, or having Infusoria

infusorial earth *n* **:** KIESELGUHR

[1]**in·fu·so·ri·an** \-ēən\ *adj* [NL *Infusoria* + E *-an*] **:** INFUSORIAL

[2]**infusorian** \"\ *n* -S **:** one of the Infusoria

[1]**in·fu·so·ri·form** \¦==¦==ə,fȯrm\ *adj* [NL *Infusoria* + E *-form*] **:** resembling an infusorian

[2]**infusoriform** \"\ *or* **infusoriform larva** *n* -S **:** the minute ciliated infective larva of the Dicyemida

in·fu·so·ri·gen \ˌ==ˈ==rəjən, -rə,jen\ *n* -S *also* **in·fu·so·ri·gene** \-rə,jēn\ *n* -S [[2]*infusori*form + *-gen*, *-gene*] **:** a reduced individual of certain mesozoans that is formed within the rhombogen and that gives rise to the infusoriform larva

in·fu·so·ri·oid \¦==¦==rē,ȯid\ *adj* [NL *Infusoria* + E *-oid*] **:** like an infusorian

in·fu·so·ri·um \ˌ==ˈ==rēəm\ *n, pl* **infuso·ria** \-ēə\ [NL, back-formation fr. *Infusoria*] **:** INFUSORIAN

in·fu·sory \ənˈfyüzərē, -üsə-\ *n* -ES [NL *Infusoria*] *archaic* **:** INFUSORIAN — usu. used in pl.

ing \ˈiŋ\ *n* -S [ME *enge*, *ynge*, of Scand origin; akin to ON *eng*, *engi* meadow, Norw & Dan *eng;* akin to MLG *enge* meadowland, OS & OHG *angar* meadow, pasture, OE *anga* hook — more at ANGLE] *dial Eng* **:** a low-lying pasture or meadow

[1]**-ing** \iŋ, ēŋ, ən, ēn *after any sound; after* t *(but usu not when* f, k, p, *or* s *precedes) & after* d *(but usu not when* l *or* n *precedes)*, [ə]n; *after* k *(but usu not when* s *precedes) or* g, *sometimes* [ə]ŋ; *after* p, b, *or* v *(the* v *assimilating to* b), *sometimes* [ə]m *as in* ˈräb[ə]m *for "robbing" or* ˈmüb[ə]m *for "moving"; in rapid speech, often* ŋ *or* n *after* ē, ā, ī, *or* ȯi *as in* ˈsāŋ *or* ˈsān *for "saying"; in NewEng often with intrusive* r *preceding when* ȯ *is the last sound in the infinitive form as in* ˈdrȯriŋ *or* ˈdrȯrin *for "drawing"; some have* ŋ *as their only consonant in this suffix & regard any other consonant as inelegant or substandard; some use consonants other than* ŋ *chiefly in informal speech; some use consonants other than* ŋ *for all styles of speech & of these some regard* ŋ *as artificial; for economy of space,* ŋ *is usu the only consonant shown for the suffix -ing in entries in this dictionary*\ *vb suffix or adj suffix* [ME *-inge*, *-ing*, alter. (influenced by *-inge* [3]-ing) of *-inde*, *-ende*, fr. OE *-ende*, fr. *-e-* (vowel historically belonging to the verb stem) + *-nde*, pres. part. suffix — more at -ANT] — used to form the present participle ⟨go*ing*⟩ ⟨sail*ing*⟩ and sometimes to form an adjective resembling a present participle but not derived from a verb ⟨hulk*ing*⟩ ⟨swashbuckl*ing*⟩; regularly accompanied by omission of final postconsonantal *e* of the base word ⟨hop*ing*⟩ ⟨lov*ing*⟩, change of final *ie* of the base word to *y* ⟨ty*ing*⟩, or doubling of the final consonant of the base word immediately after a short stressed vowel ⟨hop*ping*⟩ ⟨plan*ning*⟩

2**-ing** \"\ *n suffix* -s [ME, fr. OE *-ing, -ung* one of a (specified) kind, one belonging to, one descended from; akin to OHG *-ing* one of a (specified) kind, one belonging to, one descended from, ON *-ingr, -ungr*, Goth *-ings* one of a (specified) kind] : one of a (specified) kind ⟨sweet*ing*⟩ ⟨wild*ing*⟩

3**-ing** \"\ *n suffix* -s [ME *-inge, -ing* (in early ME a suffix forming nouns from verbs, in later ME becoming also a gerundial suffix), fr. OE *-ung, -ing*, suffix forming nouns from verbs; akin to OHG *-unga, -ung*, suffix forming nouns from verbs, ON *-ing*, suffix forming nouns from verbs, *-ung*, suffix forming nouns from nouns] **1** : action or process ⟨becom*ing*⟩ ⟨draw*ing*⟩ ⟨runn*ing*⟩ ⟨sleep*ing*⟩ ⟨wash*ing*⟩ : instance of an action or process ⟨a bless*ing*⟩ ⟨a meet*ing*⟩ ⟨my com*ings* and go*ings*⟩ — in nouns formed from any fully inflected verb and functioning either as gerunds capable of being modified by an adverb and capable of having an object if the base verb is transitive ⟨after casually read*ing* the letter twice⟩ or as ordinary nouns ⟨after two casual read*ings* of the letter⟩ **2** : something connected with an action or process: **a** : product, accompaniment, or result of an action or process ⟨an engrav*ing*⟩ ⟨a paint*ing*⟩ — in nouns formed from verbs; often in plural ⟨earn*ings*⟩ ⟨leav*ings*⟩ ⟨shav*ings*⟩ **b** : something used in an action or process ⟨a bed cover*ing*⟩ ⟨the lin*ing* of a coat⟩ — in nouns, esp. collectives ⟨carpet*ing*⟩ ⟨hous*ing*⟩ ⟨rigg*ing*⟩ ⟨shipp*ing*⟩, formed from verbs **3** : action or process connected with (a specified thing) ⟨blackberry*ing*⟩ ⟨capital*ing*⟩ — in nouns formed from nouns **4** : something connected with, consisting of, or used in making (a specified thing) ⟨sack*ing*⟩ ⟨scaffold*ing*⟩ ⟨shirt*ing*⟩ — in nouns, esp. collectives, formed from nouns **5** : something related to (a specified concept) ⟨off*ing*⟩ — in nouns formed from parts of speech other than verbs and nouns; regularly accompanied by omission of final postconsonantal *e* of the base word, change of final *ie* of the base word to *y*, or doubling of the final consonant of the base word immediately after a short stressed vowel

in·ga *in sense 1* ˈiŋgə, *in senses 2 & 3* iŋˈgä *or* ˈiŋgə\ *n* [NL, fr. Pg *ingá* huamuchil, fr. Tupi *ingá, engá*] **1** *cap* : a genus of tropical shrubs and trees (family Leguminosae) having white or red flowers and large pods that contain an edible pulp and yielding an inferior timber of little durability — see GUAMA **2** -s : any plant of the genus *Inga* **3** [Pg *ingá*] -s : CAMACHILE

in·gae·vo·nes \ˌinjəˈvō(ˌ)nēz\ *n pl, usu cap* [L] : a group of Teutonic peoples inhabiting the northern coast of Europe in ancient times

in·gae·von·ic \ˌ=ˈvänik, -ˈvōn-\ *adj, often cap* : of or relating to the Ingaevones

in·ga·lik \ˈiŋgəˌlik\ *n, pl* **ingalik** *or* **ingaliks** *usu cap* **1 a** : an Athapaskan people of the lower Yukon and Kuskokwim river valleys of Alaska **b** : a member of such people **2** : the language of the Ingalik people

1**in·gate** \ˈinˌgāt\ *n* [ME, fr. *in* + *gate* way, street — more at GATE] **1** *dial Eng* : ENTRANCE **2** *obs* **a** : a thing that enters : IMPORT **b** : import duty

2**ingate** \"\ *n* [4*in* + *gate* (channel in a mold)] : a gate through which the metal is poured into a foundry mold

ingather \ˈ=,==\ *vb* [2*in* + *gather*] *vt* : to gather in; *esp* : HARVEST ~ *vi* : to gather together : ASSEMBLE

ingatherer \ˈ=,===\ *n* : one that gathers in : HARVESTER

ingathering \ˈ=,=(=)=\ *n* [4*in* + *gathering*] **1** : the act of gathering : COLLECTION, HARVEST ⟨~ of lenten boxes⟩ ⟨members of the needlework guild turn in their finished garments at the annual ~⟩ **2** : ASSEMBLY ⟨revivalist ~⟩

ing·ber·lach \ˈiŋbərlək\ *n* -s [Yiddish, pl. of *ingberl* piece of ginger candy, dim. of *ingber* ginger, fr. MHG *ingeber, ingewer*, fr. OF *gingebre* — more at GINGER] : a candy made chiefly of ginger and honey

in·geminate \ənˈ+\ *vt* [L *ingeminatus*, past part. of *ingeminare*, fr. *in-* 2in- + *geminare* to geminate — more at GEMINATE] : REDOUBLE, REITERATE **syn** see REPEAT

in·gemination \(ˌ)in, ən+\ *n* : REPETITION, DUPLICATION

ingender *obs var of* ENGENDER

in·gen·er·a·ble \ənˈjen(ə)rəbəl\ *adj* [ME, fr. LL *ingenerabilis*, fr. L *in-* 1in- + *generabilis* generable — more at GENERABLE] : incapable of being engendered or produced : ORIGINAL — **in·gen·er·a·bly** \-blē\ *adv*

1**in·gen·er·ate** \ənˈjenəˌrāt\ *vt* [L *ingeneratus*, past part. of *ingenerare*, fr. *in-* 2in- + *generare* to beget, create — more at GENERATE] : to bring about the generation of : BEGET, CAUSE

2**in·gen·er·ate** \-en(ə)rət\ *adj* [L *ingeneratus*] **1** : INBORN, INNATE **2** *obs* : GENERATED, PRODUCED — **in·gen·er·ate·ly** *adv*

3**in·generate** \(ˈ)inˈjen(ə)rət, ənˈj-\ *adj* [LL *ingeneratus*, fr. L *in-* 1in- + *generatus*, past part. of *generare*] : not generated ⟨God is ~⟩

ingenies *pl of* INGENY

in·ge·nios·i·ty \(ˌ)inˌjēnēˈäsəd·ē, ənˌj-, -jēnˈyä-\ *n* -ES [F *ingéniosité*, fr. *ingénieux* ingenious + *-ité* -ity] : INGENUITY, SKILL, CLEVERNESS

in·ge·nious \ənˈjēnyəs *sometimes* -nēəs\ *adj* [MF *ingenieux*, fr. L *ingeniosus*, fr. *ingenium* natural capacity, natural disposition + *-osus* -ous — more at ENGINE] **1** *obs* : showing or calling for intelligence : marked by mental power ⟨~ studies —Shak.⟩ **2** : marked by especial aptitude at clever discovering, inventing, or contriving ⟨the invention of the knitting frame by another ~ English clergyman —Lewis Mumford⟩ **3** : marked by originality, resourcefulness, and cleverness in conception or execution ⟨the iron safe built into the wall . . . made by an ~ locksmith —Thomas Hardy⟩ **4** [by alter. (influence of L *ingenuus* ingenuous)] *obs* : INGENUOUS **syn** see CLEVER

in·ge·nious·ly *adv* : in an ingenious manner

in·ge·nious·ness *n* -ES : INGENUITY

in·genital \ən+\ *adj* [L *ingenitus* inborn (fr. *in-* 2in- + *genitus*, past part. of *gignere* to beget, bring forth) + E *-al* — more at KIN] : INNATE, INHERENT

1**in·ge·nue** \ˈanjəˌnü, ˈaⁿzhə-, ÷ˈäⁿzhə-, ÷ˈänjə-, ˌ==ˈ=\ *n* -s [F *ingénue*, fr. fem. of *ingénu* ingenuous, fr. L *ingenuus*] **1 a** : an ingenuous unsophisticated girl or young woman : a girl just entering society : DEBUTANTE ⟨suitable dress for an ~⟩; *esp* : a stage part representing a character that is youthful, innocent, appealing, sweet, sympathetic ⟨musical comedy ~⟩ — compare SOUBRETTE **b** : a naive or inexperienced person ⟨this is no time to have a political ~ as secretary of state —H.L.Ickes⟩ **2** : a pale to grayish yellow green that is greener and less strong than water green

2**ingenue** \"\ *adj* : of, related, or appropriate to an ingenue ⟨artless ~ air about her⟩ ⟨~ party dress⟩

in·ge·nu·i·ty \ˌinjəˈn(y)üəd·ē, -ətē, -i\ *n* -ES [L *ingenuitas* ingenuousness, fr. *ingenuus* ingenuous + *-itas* -ity; in sense 2 & 3, influenced in meaning by *ingenious*] **1** *obs* : INGENUOUSNESS, CANDOR **2 a** *obs* : GENIUS, TALENT **b** : the power or quality of ready invention : skill or cleverness in devising or combining ⟨infinite ~ of man . . . in finding new methods of torture for his fellows —Mary Webb⟩ **c** : cleverness or aptness of design or contrivance ⟨despite the ~ of this etymological contention, the origin of the name is still disputed —*Amer. Guide Series: Minn.*⟩ ⟨all the perverted ~ of propaganda —Dean Acheson⟩ **3** : an ingenious device or contrivance ⟨sophistication in the *ingenuities* of language —T.S.Eliot⟩ ⟨explore our stateroom, and scan eagerly the *ingenuities* by which we are to be surrounded for the journey —Frank A. Swinnerton⟩

in·gen·u·ous \ənˈjenyəwəs\ *adj* [L *ingenuus*, fr. *in-* 2in- + *-genuus* (akin to L *gignere* to beget, bring forth) — more at KIN] **1** : FREEBORN ⟨~ Roman subjects⟩ **2** *obs* : of a superior character : NOBLE, HONORABLE ⟨symptoms of an ~ mind rather unfrequent in this age of brass —William Cowper⟩ **3** : marked by lack of reserve, dissimulation, or guile: **a** : showing innocent or childlike simplicity, straightforwardness, frankness ⟨the Earl of Kildare's ~ explanation that he would not have burned a church if he had not thought the bishop was in it —Douglas Bush⟩ **b** : marked by lack of subtle analysis or consideration : SIMPLE, UNWARY, UNAWARE, OPEN ⟨a new invention (the telephone) in which it would seem ~ to believe too soon —Edith Wharton⟩ ⟨at times he was astoundingly ~, and then his dodges would not deceive the dullest —Arnold Bennett⟩ **4** [by alter. (influence of L *ingeniosus* ingenious)] *obs* : INGENIOUS **syn** see NATURAL

in·gen·u·ous·ly *adv* : in an ingenuous manner

in·gen·u·ous·ness *n* -ES : the quality of being ingenuous : absence of guile, reserve, or disguise : CANDOR, SIMPLICITY ⟨his airs of importance were comical in their ~ —Arnold Bennett⟩

ingeny *n* -ES [L *ingenium* natural character, natural disposition — more at ENGINE] *obs* : INTELLIGENCE, GENIUS, INGENUITY

inger \ˈiŋ(g)ə(r)\ *n* -s *cap* : INGRIAN

in·ger·ence \ˈinjərən(t)s, aⁿzhārääⁿs\ *n, pl* **inger·ences** \-rən(t)səz, -rääⁿs\ [F *ingérence*, fr. *ingérer* to intrude (fr. L *ingerere*) + *-ence*] : INTERFERENCE, INTRUSION ⟨~ in the domestic affairs of a neighboring country⟩

inger·man \ˈiŋ(g)ə(r)mən\ *n* -s *cap* : INGRIAN

in·gest \ənˈjest\ *vt* -ED/-ING/-S [L *ingestus*, past part. of *ingerere* to carry in, press upon, fr. *in-* 2in- + *gerere* to bear, wage, cherish — more at CAST] **1** : to take in for digestion (as into the stomach) **2** : to take in : SWALLOW, ABSORB ⟨for a country of forty-seven million, ~*ing* twelve million visitors . . . is a big swallow —Robert Shaplen⟩ ⟨trying to ~ the ideas of philosophers⟩ **syn** see EAT

in·ges·ta \ənˈjestə\ *n pl* [NL, fr. L, neut. pl. of *ingestus*] : food and other materials taken into the body by way of the digestive tract — compare EGESTA

in·ges·tant \-tənt\ *n* -s : something taken into the body by ingestion; *esp* : an allergen so taken

in·gest·ible \-təbəl\ *adj* : capable of being ingested

in·ges·tion \-jes(h)chən\ *n* -s [LL *ingestion-, ingestio* action of pouring in, fr. L *ingestus* + *-ion-, -io* -ion] **1** : the taking of material (as food) into the digestive system **2** : the taking of air, gas, or liquid into an engine

in·ges·tive \-stiv\ *adj* : of or relating to ingestion

in·gine \ənˈjīn\ *n* -s [L *ingenium* natural character, natural disposition — more at ENGINE] *Scot* : GENIUS, INGENUITY

ingiver \ˈ=,==\ *n* [4*in* + *giver*] *Brit* : HANDER-IN

ingiving \ˈ=,==\ *n* [4*in* + *giving* (after *give in*, v.)] : the act of handing in thread to a loom

1**ingle** \ˈiŋ(g)əl\ *n* -s [ScGael *aingeal* light, fire] **1** : FLAME, BLAZE **2** : FIREPLACE **3** : CORNER, ANGLE ⟨cabin . . . with its one large room and small ~*s*, or sleeping closets —H.C. Forman⟩

2**ingle** *n* -s [origin unknown] *obs* : CATAMITE

3**ingle** *vt* -ED/-ING/-S **1** *obs* : FONDLE, CARESS **2** *obs* : CAJOLE, WHEEDLE

ingle cheek *n* [1*ingle*] *chiefly Scot* : FIRESIDE

inglenook \ˈ=,=\ *n* [1*ingle* + *nook*] **1** : CHIMNEY CORNER **2** : a high-backed wooden settle placed close to a fireplace

ingle recess *n* [1*ingle*] : a recessed seating area at a fireplace : INGLENOOK

ingleside \ˈ=,=\ *n* [1*ingle* + *side*] : FIRESIDE

ingliding \ˈ=,==\ *adj* [4*in* + *gliding* (after *glide in*, v.)] *of a diphthong or triphthong* : CENTERING — compare OUTGLIDING

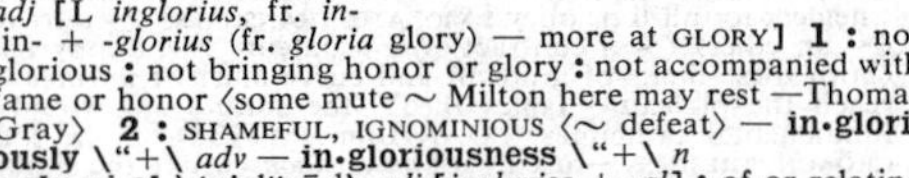

inglenooks 2

in·glorious \(ˈ)in, ən+\ *adj* [L *inglorius*, fr. *in-* 1in- + *-glorius* (fr. *gloria* glory) — more at GLORY] **1** : not glorious : not bringing honor or glory : not accompanied with fame or honor ⟨some mute ~ Milton here may rest —Thomas Gray⟩ **2** : SHAMEFUL, IGNOMINIOUS ⟨~ defeat⟩ — **in·gloriously** \"+\ *adv* — **in·gloriousness** \"+\ *n*

in·glu·vi·al \ənˈglüvēəl\ *adj* [*ingluvies* + *-al*] : of or relating to a crop ⟨~ membrane⟩ ⟨crop-milk is an ~ secretion⟩

in·glu·vi·es \-vēˌēz\ *n, pl* **ingluvies** [L, fr. *in-* 2in- + *-gluvies* (akin to *gluttire* to swallow) — more at GLUTTON] : the crop of a bird or insect

in·glu·vi·itis \(ˌ)inˌglüvēˈīd·əs, ən-\ *or* **in·glu·vi·tis** \ˌinˌglüˈvīd·əs\ *n* -ES [NL, fr. L *ingluvies* + NL *-itis*] : catarrhal inflammation of the crop in fowls

in-goal \ˈ=,=\ *n* [4*in*] : either of the two areas of a rugby field bounded by the goal line, the dead-ball line, and the touch-in-goal lines — see RUGBY illustration

1**ingoing** \ˈ=,==, =ˈ==\ *n* [ME, fr. *in* + *going*] **1** : the act of going in : ENTRANCE **2** *Brit* : a sum paid when taking over a business

2**ingoing** \ˈ=,==\ *adj* [2*in* + *going*] **1** : going in ⟨~ tide⟩ : ENTERING ⟨~ administration⟩ **2** : PENETRATING, THOROUGH ⟨~ mind⟩

in·golds·by car \ˈiŋgəl(d)zbē-\ *n* [fr. *Ingoldsby*, a trademark] : a dump car used to transport certain ores and concentrates

in·got \ˈiŋgət *also* -ˌgät; *usu* |d+V\ *n* -s [ME, prob. modif. (resulting from incorrect division of MF *lingot* as *l'ingot*, understood as containing *l'* the, contr. of *le*, def. art., the, fr. L *ille* that one, that) of MF *lingot* mass of metal cast into a convenient shape — more at LINGOT, LARIAT] **1** : a mold in which metal is cast **2** : a mass of metal cast into a convenient shape for storage or transportation and to be later remelted for casting or finished (as by rolling or forging) — compare PIG

ingot iron *n* : iron containing usu. less than 0.05 percent carbon and similarly small proportions of manganese and other impurities

in-grade \ˈ=,=, =ˈ=\ *adj* [fr. the phrase *in grade*] : occurring within a specified labor grade or rate range or occupational classification ⟨*in-grade* wage increase⟩

ingraft *var of* ENGRAFT

1**in·grain** \ˈinˌgrān, ˈinˈ=\ *vt* -ED/-ING/-S [2*in-* + *grain* (n.)] **1** *obs* : ENGRAIN 1 **2** : to work into the natural texture or mental or moral constitution : infix deeply : SATURATE, IMBUE **syn** see INFUSE

2**in·grain** \ˈ=,=\ *adj* [fr. the phrase (dyed) *in grain*] **1** *obs* : dyed with kermes **2 a** : made of fiber (as wool) that is dyed before being spun into yarn **b** : made of yarn that is dyed before being knitted ⟨~ hose⟩ **3** : of or relating to the formation of a dye or color by chemical reaction on the fiber **4** : thoroughly worked in : INNATE, NATIVE ⟨~ stubbornness of character⟩

3**ingrain** \"\ *n* -s **1** : an article made with ingrain yarns; *specif* : INGRAIN CARPET **2** : innate quality or character

ingrain carpet *n* : a reversible carpet made of ingrain wool and having a similar design with the colors reversed appearing on each side

ingrain dye *or* **ingrain color** *n* : a dye or color formed on the fiber; *esp* : AZOIC DYE — see DYE table I

ingrained \ˈ=,=, =ˈ=\ *adj* [fr. past part. of 1*ingrain*] : worked into the grain or fiber : forming a part of the essence or inmost being : DEEP-SEATED ⟨~ prejudice⟩ — **in·grained·ly** \-ān(ə)dlē, -li\ *adv* — **in·grained·ness** \-ānədnəs, -ān(d)nəs\ *n*

ingrandize *var of* ENGRANDIZE

1**in·grate** \ˈinˌgrāt *sometimes* ənˈg-, *usu* -ād·+V\ *adj* [ME *ingrat*, fr. L *ingratus*, fr. *in-* 1in- + *gratus* pleasing, grateful — more at GRACE] **1 a** *obs* : DISAGREEABLE, UNPLEASANT, UNCONGENIAL **b** *obs* : UNFRIENDLY **2** *archaic* : showing ingratitude : UNGRATEFUL — **in·grate·ly** *adv*

2**ingrate** \"\ *n* -s : an ungrateful person

ingrateful *adj* [1*in-* + *grateful*] *obs* : not grateful

in·gra·ti·ate \ənˈgrāshēˌāt, *usu* -ād·+V\ *vt* -ED/-ING/-S [2*in-* + L *gratia* favor, grace + E *-ate* — more at GRACE] : to commend to favor : find favor or favorable acceptance for : make agreeable to someone ⟨show that Newman's imagery . . . helps to ~ the view that education is a good thing in itself —Geoffrey Tillotson⟩ — usu. used with *with* ⟨where, he flattered himself, his manners would ~ him with the housewives of the district —James Joyce⟩ ⟨with what unwearying politeness he kept on trying to ~ himself with all —R.L. Stevenson⟩

ingratiating *adj* **1** : capable of winning favor : PLEASING ⟨~ smile⟩ ⟨we are prone to respond to art works . . . in terms of their ~ effect —H.E.Clurman⟩ **2** : intended or adopted in order to gain favor : pleasantly persuasive : FLATTERING ⟨her manner is quiet and ~ and a little too agreeable —Gordon Bottomley⟩ ⟨~ manner . . . one does not think compatible with deep spiritual experience —W.B.Yeats⟩ ⟨some of his superiors were even younger than he, but it's possible that they were also more ~ and discreet —L.M.Hughes⟩

in·gra·ti·at·ing·ly *adv* : in an ingratiating manner : PLEASINGLY, FLATTERINGLY

in·gra·ti·a·tion \-ˌgrāshēˈāshən\ *n* -s **1** : the act of ingratiating : process of getting oneself in favor ⟨practice the various arts of ~⟩ **2** : something that ingratiates ⟨American art . . . had no native conviction with which to resist this wealth of ~ —C.D.Maginnis⟩

in·gra·tia·to·ry \-ˈgrāsh(ē)əˌtōrē\ *adj* : tending to ingratiate : INGRATIATING

in·gratitude \(ˈ)in, ən+\ *n* [ME, fr. MF, fr. ML *ingratitudo*, fr. L *in-* 1in- + LL *gratitudo* gratitude — more at GRATITUDE] : lack of gratitude : forgetfulness of or poor return for kindness received : UNGRATEFULNESS ⟨blow, thou winter wind! thou art not so unkind as man's ~ —Shak.⟩

in·gra·ves·cence \ˌingrəˈvesᵊn(t)s\ *n* -s : the state of becoming progressively severe ⟨persistence and ~ of behavior disorders in spite of improved circumstances —Norman Cameron⟩

in·gra·ves·cent \ˌ|=ˈvesᵊnt\ *adj* [L *ingravescent-, ingravescens*, pres. part. of *ingravescere* to become heavier, to become worse, fr. *in-* 2in- + *gravescere* to become heavy, fr. *gravis* heavy, severe — more at GRIEVE] : gradually increasing in severity ⟨~ disease⟩ ⟨~ abnormality of function⟩

in·grav·i·date \ənˈgravəˌdāt\ *vt* -ED/-ING/-S [LL *ingravidatus*, past part. of *ingravidare*, fr. L *in-* 2in- + LL *gravidare* to make pregnant, fr. L *gravidus* pregnant — more at GRAVID] *archaic* : IMPREGNATE

in·gre·di·ence \ənˈgrēdēən(t)s\ *n* -s [in sense 1, alter. of *ingredients*, pl. of 1*ingredient*; in sense 2, fr. L *ingredi* + E *-ence*] **1 a** *archaic* : an ingredient or a mixture of ingredients ⟨later, the gold lost its purity and contained up to ⅕ other ~*s* —H.M.F.Schulman and H.W.Holzer⟩ **b** : the fact of entering as an ingredient ⟨this complete ~ in an occasion, so as to yield . . . fusion of individual essence with other eternal objects —A.N.Whitehead⟩ **2** *obs* : ENTRANCE, INGRESS

1**in·gre·di·ent** \-nt\ *n* -s [ME, fr. L *ingredient-, ingrediens*, pres. part. of *ingredi* to go into, enter, fr. *in-* 2in- + *-gredi* (fr. *gradi* to step, go) — more at GRADE] **1** : something that enters into a compound or is a component part of any combination or mixture : CONSTITUENT ⟨formula which will have just about the same ~*s* as mother's milk —Morris Fishbein⟩ ⟨fashionable books that one must read, because they are ~*s* of the talk of the day —T.L.Peacock⟩ ⟨understanding is one of the most important ~*s* of a successful marriage —Grace Nagel⟩ **2** *obs* : something that moves into or penetrates **syn** see ELEMENT

2**ingredient** \"\ *adj* [L *ingredient-, ingrediens*, pres. part.] **1** *obs* : entering in : PENETRATING **2** : present as or forming an ingredient : COMPONENT ⟨can be used as an ~ product in breads, pies, cakes —*Shareholder*⟩ ⟨when a sequence of words has not yet congealed into phrase, while we can ask whether he knows how to use the ~ words —Gilbert Ryle⟩

in gre·mio \(ˈ)inˈgremēˌō, -rēm-\ *adv* [L, in the bosom, in the lap] : in abeyance

1**in·gress** \ˈinˌgres\ *n* -ES [ME *ingresse*, fr. L *ingressus*, fr. *ingressus*, past part. of *ingredi* to go into, enter — more at INGREDIENT] **1** : the act of entering : ENTRANCE ⟨~ of air into the lungs⟩ ⟨~ of immigrants⟩ ⟨~ of summer tourists⟩ **2** : the power or liberty of entrance or access ⟨~ visa⟩ : means of entering ⟨gate providing ~ to the meadow⟩ **3** : a point in an astrological direction where a significator transits the place of any other planet, the ascendant, or midheaven **4** : an entrance of the moon into the shadow of the earth in an eclipse or of an inferior planet upon the sun's disk in transit or of a satellite or its shadow on a planet : the sun's entrance (as into a sign)

2**in·gress** \(ˈ)in|gres, ənˈg-\ *vi* -ED/-ING/-ES [L *ingressus*, past part.] **1** : to go in : ENTER **2** : to mark an ingress — said of an astrological significator

in·gres·sion \ənˈgreshən\ *n* -s [ME, fr. L *ingression-, ingressio*, fr. *ingressus* (past part.) + *-ion-, -io* -ion] **1** : the action of entering : ENTRANCE **2** : the process whereby potentialities or eternal objects enter into or become complex actual occasions or events ⟨the ~ of an object into an event is the way the character of the event shapes itself in virtue of the being of the object —A.N.Whitehead⟩ **3** : inward migration in gastrulation of large yolk-laden macromeres formed by holoblastic but markedly unequal cleavage

1**in·gres·sive** \(ˈ)in|gresiv, ənˈg-\ *adj* [L *ingressus* (past part.) + E *-ive*] : of or relating to ingress : ENTERING; *specif* : INCHOATIVE ⟨~ aspect⟩ — **in·gres·sive·ness** *n* -ES

2**ingressive** \"\ *n* -s : an ingressive verb

ingri·an \ˈiŋ(g)rēən\ *n* -s *cap* [*Ingria*, district of early Russia on the eastern end of the Gulf of Finland + E *-an*] : a member of a western division of the Finns native to the old Baltic province in which St. Petersburg was built — called also *Inger, Ingerman*

ingross *obs var of* ENGROSS

ingroup \ˈ=,=\ *n, often attrib* [4*in* + *group*] : a social group possessing a sense of solidarity or community of interests as opposed to other social groups — compare OUTGROUP

ingrowing \ˈ=ˈ==\ *adj* [2*in* + *growing* (after *grow in*, v.)] : growing or tending inwards ⟨~ emotions⟩ : developing within confining limits ⟨~ toenail⟩ ⟨French playwriting was ~ and was becoming provincial —Sheldon Cheney⟩

ingrown \ˈ=ˈ=\ *adj* [2*in* + *grown*] **1** : grown in : ENCLOSED; *esp, of a hair or nail* : having the free tip or edge embedded in the flesh **2** : having the direction of growth or activity or interest inward rather than outward : WITHDRAWN, CONTRACTED ⟨the contrast between an outgoing, cultural, vibrant, liberal-aristocratic Athens and an ~, inbred, militaristic, oligarchic Sparta —Norman Cousins⟩ **3** *of a stream* : having enlarged the original course by undercutting the banks of the outer curves — **in·grown·ness** \-nnəs\ *n* -ES

ingrown meander *n* : an incised meander (as of a river) with a steep undercut slope on one side and a gentle slip-off slope on the other side

ingrowth \ˈ=,=\ *n* [4*in* + *growth*] : a growth or development inward ⟨~ of cells⟩; *also* : something that grows inward

ings *pl of* ING

-ings *pl of* -ING

in·guen \ˈiŋgwən, -ˌgwen\ *n, pl* **ingui·na** \-gwənə\ [L] : GROIN

inguin- *or* **inguino-** *comb form* [NL, fr. L *inguin-, inguen*] : inguinal and ⟨*inguino*dynia⟩ ⟨*inguino*scrotal⟩

1**in·gui·nal** \-gwənᵊl\ *adj* [L *inguinalis*, fr. *inguin-, inguen* groin + *-alis* -al — more at ADEN-] **1** : of, relating to, or in the region of the groin **2** : of or relating to either of the lowest lateral regions of the abdomen — compare ABDOMINAL REGION

2**inguinal** \"\ *n* -s : one of the plates on the posterior surface of the bridge of a turtle

inguinal canal *n* : a passage about one and one half inches long that lies parallel to and a half inch above Poupart's ligament: as **a** : a passage in the male through which the testis descends into the scrotum and in which lies the spermatic cord **b** : a passage in the female accommodating the round ligament

inguinal gland *n* : any of the superficial lymphatic glands of the groin made up of two more or less distinct groups of which one is disposed along Poupart's ligament and the other about the saphenous opening

inguinal ligament *n* : POUPART'S LIGAMENT

inguinal ring *n* : ABDOMINAL RING

ingulph *obs var of* ENGULF

in·gurgitate \ən+\ *vb* -ED/-ING/-S [L *ingurgitatus*, past part. of *ingurgitare*, fr. *in-* 2in- + *gurgit-, gurges* whirlpool, abyss — more at VORACIOUS] *vt* **1** : to swallow, devour, or drink greedily or in large quantity : GUZZLE ⟨produces cocktails . . . and ~*s* them absentmindedly without reflection —Aldous Huxley⟩ **2** *obs* : to overload by eating or drinking : CRAM ~ *vi* : GUZZLE, GORMANDIZE, SWILL

in·gurgitation \(ˌ)in, ən+\ *n* [LL *ingurgitation-, ingurgitatio*, fr. L *ingurgitatus* + *-ion-, -io* -ion] : the act of devouring or swallowing ⟨basically Puritan foundations were undermined by the ~ of German transcendentalism —Oskar Seidlin⟩

in·gush \ˈinˌgüsh, =ˈ=\ *n, pl* **ingush** *or* **ingushes** *usu cap* **1** : a Muhammadan people living north of the Caucasian mountains and related to the Chechen **2** : a member of the Ingush people

in·habile \(ˈ)in+\ *adj* [F, fr. L *inhabilis*, fr. *in-* 1in- + *habilis* easily managed, apt, skillful — more at ABLE] *archaic* : not fit or qualified

in·hab·it \ən'habət, *usu* -əd.+V\ *vb* -ED/-ING/-S [ME *enhabiten, inhabiten*, fr. MF & L; MF *enhabiter*, fr. L *inhabitare*, fr. *in-* ²in- + *habitare* to dwell — more at HABIT] *vt* **1** : to occupy as a place of settled residence or habitat : live or dwell in ⟨~*ed* by a rich fauna and flora —W.H.Dowdeswell⟩ ⟨~*ed* a small apartment —Alfred Hayes⟩ **2 a** : to be at home in (a particular sphere of activity or thought) : OCCUPY ⟨endlessly varied characters who ~ the world of medicine —*N.Y.Times*⟩ ⟨the intellectual world we ~ —Cyril Connolly⟩ **b** : to occupy, be present in, or be inside of in any manner or form ⟨the human beings who ~ this tale —Al Newman⟩ ⟨the individual is ~*ed* by multiple wills, persons, or spirits —Weston La Barre⟩ ⟨a sculptural quality that ~*s* many of his most successful prints —Vincent Garofalo⟩ ~ *vi, archaic* : to have residence in a place : DWELL, LIVE

in·hab·it·abil·i·ty \ən,habəd.ə'biləd.ē, -bətə-, -lətē, -i\ *n* : the condition of being inhabitable

¹inhabitable *adj* [ME, fr. MF, fr. L *inhabitabilis*, fr. *in-* ¹in- + *habitabilis* habitable — more at HABITABLE] *obs* : not habitable; *also* : UNINHABITED

²in·hab·it·able \ən'habəd.əbəl, -bətə-\ *adj* [LL *inhabitabilis*, fr. L *inhabitare* + *-abilis* -able] : capable of being inhabited : HABITABLE

in·hab·i·tance \-bəd.ən(t)s, -bətən- *also* -bət°n-\ *n*-S [*inhabit* + *-ance*] : RESIDENCE ⟨grateful for his almost solitary ~ of the city —William Saroyan⟩

in·hab·i·tan·cy \-nsē,-nsi\ *n* **1** : the act of inhabiting or the state of being inhabited : the state, rights, or privileges of one who is an inhabitant : RESIDENCE, OCCUPANCY **2** : the site of the principal office or place of business of a corporation or association; *sometimes* : a fixed place of abode

¹in·hab·i·tant \-nt\ *n* [ME *inhabitaunt*, fr. AF *enhabitant*, fr. MF (pres. part. of *enhabiter*), fr. L *inhabitant-, inhabitans*, pres. part. of *inhabitare* to inhabit] **1** : a person who dwells or resides permanently in a place as distinguished from a transient lodger or visitor ⟨an ~ of a house⟩ ⟨an ~ of a state⟩ — compare CITIZEN, DOMICILE, RESIDENT **2** : one that makes its habitat or is commonly found in a place ⟨with respect to its insect ~*s* —*Am Guide Series: N.H.*⟩ ⟨a normal ~ of the intestines of both man and animals —*Farmer's Weekly* (*So. Africa*)⟩

²inhabitant \"\ *adj* [L *inhabitant-, inhabitans*, pres. part.] *archaic* : RESIDENT, DWELLING

inhabitate *vt* -ED/-ING/-S [L *inhabitatus*, past part.] *archaic* : INHABIT

in·hab·i·ta·tion \ən,habə'tāshən\ *n* [ME *inhabitacioun*, fr. LL *inhabitation-, inhabitatio*, fr. L *inhabitatus* (past part. of *inhabitare* to inhabit) + *-ion-, -io* -ion — more at INHABIT] : the act or an instance of inhabiting : the state of being inhabited ⟨space flight and space ~ —J.N.Leonard⟩

inhabited *adj* : having inhabitants ⟨an ~ area⟩

in·hab·it·er \ən'habəd.ə(r), -ətə-\ *n* -S [ME *enhabiter, inhabiter*, fr. *enhabiten, inhabiten* to inhabit + *-er* — more at INHABIT] *archaic* : one that inhabits

inhabiting *n* -S [ME *enhabiting, inhabiting*, fr. gerund of *enhabiten, inhabiten*] *archaic* : a dwelling place

in·hab·i·tive·ness \-bəd.ivnəs, -bətiv-\ *n* -ES [*inhabit* + *-ive* + *-ness*] : a propensity to remain permanently in the same place or residence ⟨you know my (what the phrenologists call) ~ —J.R.Lowell⟩

in·hab·i·tress \-bə·trəs\ *n* -ES [*inhabiter* + *-ess*] *archaic* : a female inhabitant

¹in·hal·ant \(')in¦hālənt, ən'h-\ *n* -S [¹*inhale* + *-ant* (n. suffix)] : something (as an allergen, an anesthetic vapor, or a medicated nasal spray) that is inhaled

²inhalant \"\ *also* **in·hal·ent** \"\ *adj* [¹*inhale* + *-ant* or *-ent* (adj. suffixes)] **1** : used for inhaling or constituting an inhalant ⟨~ allergens⟩ **2** : INCURRENT ⟨~ pores⟩

in·ha·la·tion \,in(h)ə'lāshən\ *n* -S *often attrib* [¹*inhale* + *-ation*] : the act or an instance of inhaling; *specif* : the action of drawing air into the lungs by means of a complex of essentially reflex actions that involve changes in the diaphragm and in muscles of the abdomen and thorax which cause enlargement of the chest cavity and lungs resulting in production of relatively negative pressure within the lungs so that air flows in until the pressure is restored to equality with that of the atmosphere

in·ha·la·tion·al \¦==¦lāshən°l,-shnəl\ *adj* : by or involving inhalation ⟨~ therapy⟩

in·ha·la·tor \'==,lād.ə(r), -ātə-\ *n* -S [¹*inhale* + *-ator*] : a device designed to provide a suitable mixture of oxygen and carbon dioxide for inhalation and used esp. in conjunction with manual artificial respiration

¹in·hale \ən'hāl, *chiefly before pause or consonant* -āəl\ *vb* -ED/-ING/-S [²*in-* + *-hale* (as in *exhale*)] *vt* **1** : to draw in by breathing ⟨~ air⟩ **2** : to consume or swallow esp. eagerly or greedily ⟨*inhaled* about four meals at once —Ring Lardner⟩ ⟨*inhaling* it from their cupped fingers until their cheeks bulged —R.D.Bowen⟩ ⟨*inhaled* a strong love decoction —Abram Kardiner⟩ ~ *vi* : to breathe in : inhale air, gas, smoke, or other vapor — opposed to *exhale*

²in·hale \", 'in,=\ *n* -S : the act or an instance of inhaling ⟨kept taking deep ~*s* —J.W.Ellison b. 1891⟩

in·hal·er \ən'hālə(r)\ *n* -S **1** : one that inhales **2** : a device by means of which vapors, volatilized remedies, medicinal dusts, or anesthetics can be inhaled — compare INHALATOR **3** : SNIFTER ⟨pouring a liberal amount of brandy into an ~ —Caroline Slade⟩

in·harmonic \¦in+\ *adj* [¹*in-* + *harmonic*] : not harmonic : DISCORDANT

inharmonic theory *n* : a postulate in phonetics: the reinforcing vibrations produced in the superglottic cavities in vowel articulation need not be multiples of the fundamental vocal-cord note — compare FORMANT, HARMONIC THEORY

in·harmonious \¦in+\ *adj* [¹*in-* + *harmonious*] **1** : UNMUSICAL, DISCORDANT ⟨~ sounds⟩ **2** : being not in harmony : CONFLICTING, JARRING, UNCONGENIAL ⟨~ surroundings⟩ — **in·harmoniously** \"+\ *adv* — **in·harmoniousness** \"+\ *n*

in·harmony \(')in, ən+\ *n* [¹*in-* + *harmony*] : lack of harmony : DISCORD

inhaul \'=,=\ *n* [⁴*in* + *haul* (after *haul in*, v.)] : a rope used to draw in a ship's sail (as a spanker on its gaff)

in·haust \ən'hȯst\ *vt* -ED/-ING/-S [²*in-* + *-haust* (as in *exhaust*)] : INHALE, IMBIBE ⟨~*ing* mint juleps —Virginius Dabney⟩

in·hell \ən+\ *vt* [²*in-* + *hell*] *archaic* : to put or fix in hell

in·here \ən'hi(ə)r, -iə\ *vi* -ED/-ING/-S [L *inhaerēre*, fr. *in-* ²in- + *haerēre* to stick, adhere — more at HESITATE] : to be inherent : be a fixed element or attribute : BELONG ⟨thought all virtue *inhered* in the farmer —H.S.Commager⟩ ⟨the excellence *inhering* in the democratic faith —V.L.Parrington⟩

in·her·ence \ən'hirən(t)s, -her-,-hēr-\ *n* -S [ML *inhaerentia*, fr. L *inhaerent-, inhaerens* + *-ia* -y] **1** : the quality, state, or fact of inhering or of being inherent : permanent existence as an attribute ⟨the ~ of multiple meanings and allusions in the particulars of a literary work —B.T.Spencer⟩ **2** : the relation of a quality to a substance or subject ⟨~ rather than existence is said of accidents —James Albertson⟩

in·her·en·cy \-nsē, -nsi\ *n* -ES [ML *inhaerentia*] **1** : INHERENCE **2** : an inherent character or attribute ⟨culture classifications with purely taxonomic *inherencies* —W.Taylor⟩

in·her·ent \-nt\ *adj* [L *inhaerent-, inhaerens*, pres. part. of *inhaerēre*] : structural or involved in the constitution or essential character of something : belonging by nature or settled habit : INTRINSIC, ESSENTIAL ⟨~ rights⟩ ⟨shortcomings ~ in our approach —David Cherin⟩ ⟨an ~ laziness⟩ — **in·her·ent·ly** *adv*

in·her·it \ən'herət, *usu* -əd.+V\ *vb* -ED/-ING/-S [ME *enheriten* to make heir, inherit (influenced in meaning by MF *heriter* & L *hereditare* to inherit), fr. MF *enheriter* to make heir, fr. LL *inhereditare*, fr. L *in-* ²in- + LL *hereditare* to inherit — more at HERITAGE] *vt* **1** : to come into possession of : POSSESS, RECEIVE ⟨power . . . which he ~*s* from the Creator himself —Eric Linklater⟩ **2 a** : to take by descent from an ancestor : take by inheritance : receive as a right or title descendible by law from an ancestor at his decease **b** : to be heir to : SUCCEED ⟨a son ~*s* his father⟩ **3 a** : to receive by genetic transmission : derive or acquire from ancestors ⟨~ a strong constitution⟩ **b** : to have in turn or receive as if from an ancestor ⟨much of the girl's clothing had been ~*ed* from the more fortunate children —Grace Metalious⟩ ⟨~*ed* from antiquity two rather contradictory views of the organic world —S.F.Mason⟩ ~ *vi* : to take or hold a possession, property, estate, or rights by inheritance

in·her·it·abil·i·ty \-,herəd.ə'biləd.ē, -rətə-, -lətē, -i\ *n* : the quality of being inheritable or descendible to heirs

in·her·it·able \-'herəd.əbəl, -rətə-\ *adj* [ME *enheritable*, fr. AF, fr. MF *enheriter* + *-able*] **1 a** : capable of being inherited : TRANSMISSIBLE, DESCENDIBLE ⟨an ~ title⟩ **b** (1) : capable of taking by inheritance (2) : entitled to as a birthright **2** : capable of being transmitted from parent to child ⟨~ qualities⟩ — **in·her·it·able·ness** \-nəs\ *n* -ES — **in·her·it·ably** \-blē,-bli\ *adv*

in·her·i·tage \-'herəd.ij\ *n* [*inherit* + *-age*] *archaic* : INHERITANCE

in·her·i·tance \ən'herəd.ən(t)s, -rətən-,-rət°n-\ *n* -S [ME *enheritaunce*, fr. AF *enheritaunce*, fr. MF *enheriter* + *-ance*] **1 a** : the act of inheriting property: as (1) : the acquisition of real or personal property as heir to another : the perpetual or continuing right which a person and his heirs have to an estate or property (2) *common, feudal, & Scots law* : the acquisition of an ancestor's real estate upon his death by the heir under the Statute of Descent as distinguished from the succession to his personal property by the next of kin under the Statute of Distribution (3) *Roman & Civil law* : the succession upon the death of an owner either by testament or by operation of law by the heir to all the estate, rights, and liabilities of the decedent, the liabilities being restricted to the value of the estate when the heir was given the benefit of inventory **b** : the reception or acquisition of genetic characters or qualities by transmission from parent to offspring **c** : the acquisition of a material or immaterial possession, condition, or trait by transmission from the past or from past generations ⟨resented his children's ~ of slavery from their mothers —Anne K. Gregorie⟩ ⟨hard-won freedoms that are ours by just ~⟩ **2** : something that is or may be inherited: as **a** (1) : something that is derived by an heir from an ancestor or other person or that may be transmitted to an heir by a person (2) *common, feudal, & Scots law* : an estate of inheritance (as a fee simple or a fee tail) **b** : the sum total of genetic characters or qualities transmitted from parent to offspring ⟨on the maternal side his ~ was a happy one⟩ **c** : something material or immaterial that is derived or acquired from the past or from past generations ⟨the random brutality that is the ~ of centuries of blackness —Irving Howe⟩; *esp* : a permanent or valuable possession that is a common heritage or that is received from God or nature ⟨our great ~ of water and land —A.E.Stevenson †1965⟩ ⟨their most precious ~, that thin layer of topsoil —K.D. White⟩ ⟨books are the major channel by which the intellectual ~ is handed down —*New Republic*⟩ **3** *obs* : right of possession : POSSESSION, OWNERSHIP

inheritance tax *n* **1** : an excise tax levied upon the privilege of receiving property as heir or next of kin under the law governing intestate succession, measured by the value of the interest each successor receives, and usu. increased in rate as kinship with the deceased becomes more remote — compare LEGACY TAX **2** : ESTATE TAX

inherited *adj* : constituting something received by inheritance ⟨~ characteristics⟩ ⟨shackled by a mass of ~ conventions — J.L.Lowes⟩ ⟨a city which follows an ~ type of industry — Samuel Van Valkenburg & Ellsworth Huntington⟩ **syn** see INNATE

in·her·i·tor \ən'herəd.ə(r), -rətə-\ *n* [ME *enheritour, enheriter*, fr. *enheriten* to inherit + *-our* or *-er* — more at INHERIT] : one that inherits : HEIR ⟨~*s* of an ancient culture⟩

in·her·i·tress \-rə·trəs\ *also* **in·her·i·trix** \-rə·(,)triks\ *n* -ES [*inheritress* fr. *inheritor* + *-ess*; *inheritrix* fr. *inheritor*, after such pairs as E *mediator: mediatrix*] : a female inheritor

inherits *pres 3d sing of* INHERIT

in·he·sion \ən'hēzhən\ *n* -S [L *inhaesus* (past part. of *inhaerēre* to inhere) + E *-ion* — more at INHERE] : the condition of being inherent in something : INHERENCE

in·hib·it \ən'hibət, *usu* -bəd.+V\ *vb* -ED/-ING/-S [ME *inhibiten*, fr. L *inhibitus*, past part. of *inhibēre*, fr. *in-* ²in- + *-hibēre* (fr. *habēre* to have, hold) — more at GIVE] *vt* **1** : to prohibit from doing something : FORBID, INTERDICT ⟨~*s* the legislature from levying an income tax —*Britannica Bk. of the Yr.*⟩ **2 a** (1) : to repress, restrain, or discourage from free or spontaneous activity esp. through the operation of inner psychological impediments or conflicts or of social and cultural controls ⟨~*ed* from bold speculation by his personal loyalties and interests —V.L.Parrington⟩ ⟨a people long ~*ed* by the prevailing taboos —R.S.Ellery⟩ (2) : to operate against the full development or activity of : check, restrain, or diminish the force, intensity, or vitality of ⟨~*ed* the creative process at its sources —Harry Sylvester⟩ ⟨the heavy tax load that ~*s* investment in capital goods —*Time*⟩ **b** (1) : to reduce or suppress the activity of ⟨many of the iron or copper enzymes are ~*ed* by cyanides —Felix Haurowitz⟩ ⟨lubricating oil ~*ed* against rust, corrosion, and oxidation⟩ (2) : to retard or prevent the formation of ⟨~ rust⟩ (3) : to retard, interfere with, or prevent (a chemical process or reaction) ⟨~ oxidation⟩ ~ *vi* : to cause inhibition ⟨something that entraps and ~*s* —John Portz⟩ **syn** see FORBID, RESTRAIN

in·hib·it·able \-əbəl\ *adj* : capable of being inhibited

inhibited *adj* : being repressed, discouraged, reduced, or retarded: as **a** : characterized by, displaying, or reflecting inhibition ⟨a shy and ~ boy —Alan Harrington⟩ ⟨~ respectability —H.C.Webster⟩ **b** : having its activity reduced or suppressed ⟨~ oils⟩

inhibiting *adj* : tending to inhibit or causing inhibition ⟨an overly strict or ~ discipline —H.V.Gregory⟩

in·hi·bi·tion \,inə'bishən, ,inhə'-, ,in(,)(h)i'-\ *n* -S [ME *inhibicioun*, fr. MF *inhibition*, fr. L *inhibition-, inhibitio*, fr. *inhibitus* + *-ion-, -io* -ion] : the act or an instance of inhibiting or the state of being inhibited: as **a** : the act or an instance of formally forbidding or barring something from being done : PROHIBITION ⟨plain ~*s* to the exercise of that power in a particular way —John Marshall⟩; *also* : something that formally forbids or debars : IMPEDIMENT ⟨the constitutional ~ of his alien birth —F.L.Paxson⟩ **b** (1) : a writ from a higher court (as an ecclesiastical court) staying an inferior judge from further proceedings (2) *Eng eccl law* : a command of an ecclesiastical authority (as a bishop) to a minister not to perform ministerial duties (3) *Scots law* : a personal order prohibiting a party from contracting debts to the prejudice of the rights of others in his heritable property or realty; *also* : an order procured by a husband prohibiting the giving of credit to his wife **c** (1) : a stopping or checking of a bodily action : a restraining of the function of an organ or an agent (as a digestive fluid or enzyme) ⟨~ of the heartbeat by stimulation of the vagus nerve⟩ ⟨~ of plantar reflexes⟩ (2) : interference with or retardation or prevention of a chemical process or activity ⟨~ of a catalyst⟩ ⟨~ of rust⟩ **d** (1) : a desirable restraint or check upon the free or spontaneous instincts or impulses of an individual effected through the operation of the human will guided or directed by the social and cultural forces of the environment ⟨the self-control so developed is called ~ —C.W.Russell⟩ ⟨creating ~*s*, socializing the child, obviously should be one of the goals of a training school —Erwin Schepses⟩ (2) : a neurotic restraint upon a normal or beneficial impulse or activity caused by psychological inner conflicts or by sociocultural forces of the environment ⟨other outspoken neurotic manifestations are general ~*s* such as inability to think, to concentrate —Muriel Ivimey⟩ ⟨~*s*, phobias, compulsions, and other neurotic patterns —*Psychological Abstracts*⟩ (3) : repression of or restraint upon an urge, impulse, or activity of any kind ⟨locked in Puritan ~*s* —H.S.Canby⟩ ⟨obstacles and ~*s* to rural reading —C.M.Wieting⟩ ⟨throwing all her moral teachings and ~*s* overboard —Ruth Park⟩ ⟨laughed without ~ —Jean Stafford⟩

in·hib·i·tive \ən'hibəd.iv, -bətiv\ *adj* : INHIBITORY

in·hib·i·tor *or* **in·hib·it·er** \-bəd.ə(r), -bətə-\ *n* -S : one that inhibits: as **a** (1) : a substance for reducing corrosion or rust formation (as in an antifreeze) (2) : a substance for delaying gum formation (as in gasoline) (3) : ANTIOXIDANT **b** : a substance that interferes with a chemical process or reaction ⟨polymerization ~*s*⟩ : NEGATIVE CATALYST **c** : a substance that reduces the activity of another substance (as an enzyme) — compare ANTIMETABOLITE **d** : a gene that checks the normal effect of another nonallelic gene when both are present

in·hib·i·to·ry \-bə,tōrē, -tȯr-, -ri\ *adj* [ML *inhibitorius*, fr. L *inhibitus* (past part. of *inhibēre* to inhibit) + *-orius* -ory — more at INHIBIT] : of, relating to, or producing inhibition : tending or serving to inhibit : PROHIBITORY ⟨the ~ nervous action⟩ ⟨the ~ action of fluorides —*Americana Annual*⟩

inholding \'=,==\ *n* [⁴*in* + *holding*] : privately owned land inside the boundary of a national park

in home *n* : INSIDE HOME

in·homogeneity \(')in, ən+\ *n* [¹*in-* + *homogeneity*] **1** : lack of homogeneity : the condition of not being homogeneous ⟨the degree of microscopic ~ in an alloy⟩ **2** : a part that is not homogeneous with the larger homogeneous mass in which it is incorporated

in·homogeneous \"+\ *adj* [¹*in-* + *homogeneous*] : not homogeneous : lacking homogeneity — **in·homogeneously** \"+\ *adv*

inhoop *vt* [²*in-* + *hoop* (n.)] *obs* : to enclose in a hoop

in·hospitable \(')in, ən+\ *adj* [¹*in-* + *hospitable*] **1 a** : not hospitable : not disposed to show hospitality ⟨an ~ person⟩ **b** : reflecting or evidencing inhospitality ⟨gave me a brief, ~ look —Louis Auchincloss⟩ **2** : providing no shelter or sustenance : BARREN, DESERT ⟨~ mountain areas⟩ — **in·hospitableness** \"+\ *n* -ES — **in·hospitably** \"+\ *adv*

inhospital *adj* [prob. fr. MF, fr. L *inhospitalis*, fr. *in-* ¹in- + *hospitalis* hospitable — more at HOSPITAL] *obs* : INHOSPITABLE

in·hospitality \(')in, ən+\ *n* [prob. fr. MF *inhospitalité*, fr. L *inhospitalitat-, inhospitalitas*, fr. *inhospitalis* + *-itat-, -itas* -ity] : the quality or state of being inhospitable : a cold or unfriendly reception or treatment of a guest or visitor

in·human \(')in, ən+\ *adj* [MF & L; MF *inhumain*, fr. L *inhumanus*, fr. *in-* ¹in- + *humanus* human — more at HUMAN] **1 a** : lacking the qualities of mercy, pity, kindness, or tenderness : CRUEL, BARBAROUS, SAVAGE ⟨an ~ tyrant⟩ ⟨what ~ rogues there are in the world —A. Conan Doyle⟩ **b** : lacking warmth or geniality : COLD, IMPERSONAL, MECHANICAL ⟨his usual quiet, almost ~ courtesy —F. Tennyson Jesse⟩ **c** : not worthy of or conforming to the needs of human beings ⟨living in conditions that are ~ —*Collier's Yr. Bk.*⟩ ⟨has the world's most ~ subways —*Time*⟩ ⟨one large block which would tend to be ~ and monotonous —*Architect & Building News*⟩ **2 a** : belonging to, resembling, or suggesting a nonhuman species or class of beings ⟨there is something a little ~ about them —Lewis Mumford⟩ ⟨a momentary glimpse . . . of something I didn't understand: something dark and ~ —Kenneth Roberts⟩ **b** : SUPERHUMAN ⟨models of ~ perfection —H.B. Parkes⟩ **syn** see FIERCE

in·humane \(')in, ən+\ *adj* [MF *inhumain* & L *inhumanus*] : not humane : INHUMAN 1 — **in·humanely** \"+\ *adv*

in·humanity \¦in+\ *n* [MF *inhumanité*, fr. L *inhumanitat-, inhumanitas*, fr. *inhumanus* + *-itat-, -itas* -ity] **1** : the quality or state of being cruel or barbarous : CRUELTY ⟨abhorrence of its sickening ~ —G.B.Shaw⟩; *also* : a cruel or barbarous act **2** : absence of warmth or geniality : IMPERSONALITY ⟨a professional ~ toward their job —Nicholas Monsarrat⟩

in·hu·man·ly *adv* : in an inhuman manner

in·hu·man·ness \-n(n)əs\ *n* : the quality or state of being inhuman

in·hu·ma·tion \,inhyü'māshən\ *n* -S [F *inhumation*, fr. *inhumer* to inhume (fr. L *inhumare*) + *-ation*] : BURIAL, INTERMENT

in·hume \ən'hyüm\ *vt* -ED/-ING/-S [prob. fr. F *inhumer*, fr. L *inhumare*, fr. *in-* ²in- + *humus* earth — more at HUMBLE] : to deposit in the earth : BURY, INTER

-i·ni \ə,nī, -rə,ī, 'ē(,)nē, 'ēni, 'ī,nī\ *n pl suffix* [NL, fr. L, masc. pl. of *-inus* -ine] : animals that are or have the form of — in names of higher taxa esp. of tribes and orders ⟨Anacanth*ini*⟩

in·i·ac \'inē,ak\ *also* **in·i·al** \-ēəl\ *adj* [NL *inion* + E *-ac* (as in *iliac*) or *-al*] : relating to the inion

in·im·i·ca·ble \ə'nimәkəbəl\ *adj* [L *inimicus* + E *-able* (as in *amicable*)] : INIMICAL, HOSTILE ⟨~ to the public peace or safety —*U.S. Code*⟩

in·im·i·cal \ə'nimәkəl, -mēk-\ *adj* [LL *inimicalis*, fr. L *inimicus* enemy + *-alis* -al — more at ENEMY] **1 a** : having the disposition or temper of an enemy : viewing with disfavor : HOSTILE ⟨mutually ~ blocs —*Wall Street Jour.*⟩ ⟨~ to that heresy —George Meredith⟩ **b** : reflecting or indicating hostility : UNFRIENDLY ⟨a voice apparently cold and ~ —Arnold Bennett⟩ ⟨under the ~ gaze of his father —Marguerite Steen⟩ **2** : prejudicial in tendency, influence, or effects : HARMFUL, ADVERSE ⟨~ to the interests of the consumer —*Current Biog.*⟩ ⟨~ to the best interests of the company —L.M.Hughes⟩ **syn** see ADVERSE

in·im·i·cal·ly \-mәk(ә)lē, -mēk-, -li\ *adv* : in an inimical manner

in·im·i·cal·ness \-kəlnəs\ *n* -ES : the quality or state of being inimical

in·im·i·ci·tious \ə¦nimə¦sishəs\ *adj* [L *inimicitia* hostility (fr. *inimicus* enemy + *-tia*, suffix used to form abstract nouns) + E *-ous*] *archaic* : INIMICAL

inimicous *adj* [L *inimicus*, fr. *inimicus*, n., enemy] *obs* : INIMICAL

in·im·i·ta·bil·i·ty \(')i,nimәd.ə'biləd.ē, ə,n-, -mətə-, -lətē, -i\ *n* : the quality or state of being inimitable : INIMITABLENESS

in·im·i·ta·ble \(')i¦nimәd.əbəl, ə'n-, -mətə-\ *adj* [MF or L; MF, fr. L *inimitabilis*, fr. *in-* ¹in- + *imitabilis* imitable — more at IMITABLE] : not capable of being imitated : being beyond imitation : MATCHLESS ⟨an ~ style⟩ : not worthy of imitation — **in·im·i·ta·ble·ness** \-nəs\ *n* — **in·im·i·ta·bly** \-blē, -bli\ *adv*

in in·vi·tum \,inən'wē,tüm, -'vīd.əm\ *adv* [L, against an unwilling person] : against a person's will or consent : by force of law irrespective of assent

in·i·o·mi \,inē'ō,mī\ *n pl, cap* [NL, fr. *inion* + *-omi* (fr. Gk *ōmos* shoulder) — more at HUMERUS] : an order of mostly deep-sea teleost fishes lacking fin spines and air bladder and usu. having a dorsal adipose fin and including the lantern fishes, the lizard fishes, and related forms — **in·i·o·mous** \¦==¦ōməs\ *adj*

in·i·on \'inē,än, -ēən\ *n* -S [NL, fr. Gk, back of the head, dim. of *in-, is* sinew, tendon — more at WITHY] : the external occipital protuberance of the skull — see CRANIOMETRY illustration

in·iq·ui·tous \ə'nikwəd.əs, -wətəs\ *adj* [*iniquity* + *-ous*] : characterized by iniquity : UNJUST, WICKED ⟨~ deeds⟩ **syn** see VICIOUS

in·iq·ui·tous·ly *adv* : in an iniquitous manner

in·iq·ui·tous·ness *n* -ES : the quality or state of being iniquitous

in·iq·ui·ty \ə'nikwəd.ē, -wətē, -i\ *n* -ES [ME *iniquite*, fr. MF *iniquité*, fr. L *iniquitat-, iniquitas*, fr. *iniquus* uneven, unjust (fr. *in-* ¹in- + *-iquus*, fr. *aequus* level, equal) + *-itat-, -itas* -ity] **1** : absence of or deviation from just dealing : wrongful conduct : WICKEDNESS ⟨the ~ of bribery⟩ **2** : an iniquitous act or thing : SIN ⟨whose *iniquities* are forgiven —Ps 31:1 (DV)⟩ **3** *Scots law* : INEQUITY, INJUSTICE — used of a decision contrary to law

iniquous *adj* [L *iniquus*] *obs* : INIQUITOUS

in·irritability \(')in, ən+\ *n* : the quality or state of not being irritable

in·irritable \"+\ *adj* [¹*in-* + *irritable*] : not irritable

in·isle \ən+\ *archaic var of* ENISLE

¹ini·tial \ə'nishəl\ *adj* [MF & L; MF, fr. L *initialis*, fr. *initium* beginning (fr. *initus* — past part. of *inire* to go into, begin, fr. *in-* ²in- + *ire* to go — + *-ium*, suffix used to form abstract nouns) + *-alis* -al — more at ISSUE] **1** : of or relating to the beginning : marking the commencement : INCIPIENT, FIRST ⟨~ symptoms of a disease⟩ ⟨this ~ series of outbreaks —Thomas Cadett⟩ **2** : placed or standing at the beginning ⟨the ~ word of a verse⟩ **3** : of that form regularly employed only at the beginning of a word — used of a letter in an alphabet that has two or more positional forms

²initial \"\ *n* -S **1 a** (1) : the first letter of a proper name (2) **initials** *pl* : the initial letters of an individual's name and surname; *also* : the initial letters of the name of an organization, state, or other entity (as U.S.A. for "United States of America" or C.I.O. for "Congress of Industrial Organizations") or of any group of words ⟨the ~*s* "PE" (meaning

"Previous Experience") —*U.S. Code*⟩ **b** (1) **:** a form of an alphabetical letter that regularly is used only at the beginning of a word (2) **:** a large letter beginning a text or a division or paragraph usu. capital and extending over two or more text lines and sometimes ornate and in more than one color **2 :** ANLAGE, PRECURSOR; *specif* **:** a meristematic cell

³**initial** \"\ *vt* **initialed** *or* **initialled**; **initialed** *or* **initialled**; **initialing** *or* **initialling** \-sh(ə)liŋ\ **initials** [²*initial*] **1 :** to affix an initial to ⟨~ a memorandum⟩ **:** to mark (as a handkerchief) with an initial **2 :** to authenticate and approve (as the draft of an international agreement) in a preliminary manner by the affixing of the initials of an authorized representative

initial condition *n* **:** any of a set of starting-point values belonging to or imposed upon the variables in an equation that has one or more arbitrary constants

ini·tial·er \-sh(ə)lə(r)\ *n* -s **:** a person who initials ⟨the ~s of a memorandum⟩

initial letter *n* **:** INITIAL 1b

initial line *n* **:** a ray that is rotated about the vertex to make an angle

ini·tial·ly \-sh(ə)lē, -li\ *adv* [¹*initial* + *-ly*] **:** in the first place **:** at the beginning

initial reserve *n* **:** the terminal reserve for a life-insurance policy as of the close of the preceding year plus the net premium for the current year

initial rhyme *n* **1 :** ALLITERATION **2 :** BEGINNING RHYME

initial series *n, cap I&S* **:** a Maya carved or written dating usu. at the start of a text including the date according to the long count and the date according to the positions reached in the 260-day and 365-day periods

initial side *n* **:** the stationary straight line that contains the point about which another straight line is revolved in forming a trigonometric figure

initial stress *n* **:** stress existing in a structure or mass not subjected to the action of external forces except gravity

¹**ini·ti·ate** \ə'nishē,āt *sometimes* -isē-; *usu* -ād.+V\ *vt* -ED/-ING/-S [L *initiatus,* past part. of *initiare,* fr. *initium* beginning — more at INITIAL] **1 a :** to begin or set going **:** make a beginning of **:** perform or facilitate the first actions, steps, or stages of **:** establish as an institution, custom, or trend ⟨~ a change in fashions⟩ ⟨*initiated* a new road-building program⟩ ⟨~ progressive education⟩ ⟨special powers which actively ~ and actively promote progress —W.H.Mallock⟩ ⟨~ a chain reaction⟩ **b :** to bring about the initial formation of **:** ORIGINATE ⟨polymerization chains so *initiated* —Otto Reinmuth⟩ **c :** to mark the beginning of ⟨the wholesale confiscation of property which *initiated* the Nazi regime —R.H.Jackson⟩ **2 :** to begin the instruction of in some field **:** lead to knowledge of elements or rudiments **:** foster the first steps or beginning progress of **:** aid in becoming familiar or knowing ⟨*initiated* into this tradition by his residence in Italy —Irving Babbitt⟩ ⟨felt that he was finally *initiated* —D.H.Lawrence⟩ **3 :** to receive or induct into membership of a society, club, or group, or into a certain status by or as if by special rites or formalities ⟨*initiated* into a social fraternity⟩ ⟨the club will ~ new members Tuesday⟩ **syn** see BEGIN

²**ini·tiate** \-sh(ē)ə|t, -shē,ā| *sometimes* -sē-; *usu* |d.+V\ *adj* [L *initiatus*] **1 :** initiated or properly admitted (as to an office, secret society, or secret learning) **2** *obs* **:** relating to an initiate ⟨my strange and self-abuse is the ~ fear —Shak.⟩

³**initiate** \"\ *n* -s **1 a :** a person who is undergoing an initiation (as into a secret order) ⟨the relationship between ~s and initiated —*Notes & Queries on Anthropology*⟩ **b :** one who has passed such an initiation or has been properly admitted (as to a fraternal organization) **2 a :** a person who is instructed or adept in some esoteric learning or mode of expression ⟨abstruse and erudite papers intelligible only to the ~ —H.C. Dent⟩ **b :** one who has been previously exposed to some experience **:** one who is at home in some area of experience or activity ⟨the ~ knows that dinner is nearing an end when the rice and tea appear —V.G.Heiser⟩

ini·ti·a·tion \ə,nishē'āshən *sometimes* -isē-\ *n* -s **1 a :** the act or an instance of formally initiating (as into an office, sect, or society) **:** the process of being formally initiated ⟨the practice of anointing with oil . . . became attached to the ~ of a king —*Brit. Book News*⟩ ⟨~ is regarded as a great occasion —A.A.Trouwborst⟩ **b** (1) **:** the rites, ceremonies, ordeals, or instructions with which one is made a member of a sect or society or is invested with a particular function or status ⟨the college fraternity has a scheme of ruthless mock ~s —C.W.Ferguson⟩ (2) **:** the ceremonies and ordeals with which a youth is formally invested with adult status in a primitive community ⟨attended some of the girls' ~, and took part in many functions of native life —Margaret C. Hubbard⟩ **c** (1) **:** the process or an instance of being initiated into some experience or sphere of activity **:** INTRODUCTION ⟨while still in high school, the youth received his ~ into his lifework —*Current Biog.*⟩ ⟨part of the child's ~ into the life of man —George Sampson⟩ ⟨his ~ to venal love is sordid —Henri Peyre⟩ ⟨had already had her ~ into court . . . and is now on probation —Beatrice Griffith⟩ (2) **:** the condition of being initiated or an initiate **:** KNOWLEDGEABLENESS ⟨clear to a reader of any degree of ~ —J.W.Beach⟩ ⟨that dullness which perhaps was due simply to lack of ~ —George Santayana⟩ **2 :** the act, process, or an instance of beginning, setting on foot, or originating **:** the condition of being begun **:** ORIGINATION, BEGINNING ⟨~ of a program to produce and test a vaccine —*Americana Annual*⟩ ⟨does not give them much power of ~ —R.H.Rovere⟩ ⟨the ~ of a leaf⟩

¹**ini·tia·tive** \ə'nishə|d.iv, |tiv *sometimes* -shē,ā| *or* -shēə| *or* -shtiv *or* -shtēv\ *adj* [*initiate* + *-ive*] **:** of or relating to initiation **:** serving to initiate **:** INTRODUCTORY, PRELIMINARY

²**initiative** \"\ *n* -s **1 :** an introductory step or movement **:** an act designed to originate or set on foot (as a process or train of events) ⟨a new Russian ~ must now be anticipated —Frank Gorrell⟩ — often used in the phrase *on one's own initiative* ⟨don't blame me, he acted on his own ~⟩ **2 :** energy or aptitude displayed in initiation esp. of action that pioneers in some field **:** self-reliant enterprise ⟨a man of great ~⟩ ⟨unable to control the product of his ~, science —Norman Kelman⟩ **3 a :** the right or power to introduce a new measure or course of action ⟨the ~ in respect to revenue bills is in the House of Representatives⟩ **b :** a procedure or device which enables a specified number of voters by petition to propose a law and secure its submission to the electorate for approval — compare DIRECT INITIATIVE, INDIRECT INITIATIVE, REFERENDUM

ini·ti·a·tor \ə'nishē,ād.ə(r), -ātə- *sometimes* -isē-\ *n* -s [LL, fr. L *initiatus* (past part. of *initiare* to initiate) + *-or* — more at INITIATE] **:** one that initiates: as **a :** a person who originates or sets on foot some process or movement ⟨a great ~ in art⟩ **b :** DETONATOR c **c :** a substance that initiates a reaction ⟨benzoyl peroxide is used as an ~ in polymerization⟩ — compare CATALYST 1

ini·tia·to·ry \ə'nish(ē)ə,tōrē, -tȯrē, -ri *sometimes* -isēə-\ *adj* [*initiate* + *-ory*] **1 :** constituting an introduction or beginning **:** INTRODUCTORY, OPENING, FIRST ⟨abolished as soon as its ~ horrors were known —J.L.Motley⟩ **2 :** tending or serving to initiate **:** introducing by instruction or by the use and application of symbols or ceremonies **:** ELEMENTARY, RUDIMENTARY ⟨~ rites⟩

inj *abbr* inject; injection

in·ject \ən'jekt\ *vt* -ED/-ING/-S [L *injectus,* past part. of *inicere, injicere,* fr. *in-* ²in- + *-icere, -jicere* (fr. *jacere* to throw) — more at JET] **1 a :** to throw, drive, or force in ⟨~ cold water into a condenser⟩ **b** (1) **:** to force a fluid into (a vessel, cavity, or tissue of man, animal, or plant) for preserving, hardening, or coloring structures (2) **:** to introduce (as by injection or gravity flow) a fluid into (a living body) esp. for the purpose of restoring fluid balance, treating nutritional deficiencies or disease, or relieving pain; *also* **:** to treat (an individual) with injections **c :** INTRUDE **2 :** to introduce as an element or factor in or into some situation or subject ⟨able to ~ both color and humor into this rather formidable subject —C.B.Palmer b. 1910⟩ ⟨~*ed* a disruptive element into the situation —Oscar Handlin⟩ ⟨the twists of raw emotion which she ~s into her portrayal —Roger Manvell⟩

in·ject·able \-təbəl\ *adj* **:** capable of being injected

injected *adj* **1 :** forced in or introduced esp. in the form of a fluid **2 :** CONGESTED 1

in·jec·tion \ən'jekshən\ *n* -s [MF or L; MF, fr. L *injection-, injectio,* fr. *injectus* + *-ion-, -io* -ion] **1 a** (1) **:** the act or an instance of injecting a drug or other substance into the body (2) **:** a solution of a drug, nutrient, or other substance injected (as by catheter or needle) into the tissues, a vein, or a body cavity (3) **:** a solution or suspension of a drug intended for administration under or through the skin or mucous membranes by means of a hypodermic syringe (4) **:** an act or process of injecting vessels or tissues; *also* **:** a specimen prepared by injection — compare CORROSION (5) **:** the state of being injected **:** CONGESTION **b :** the intrusion of molten magma between rocks **c :** the introduction under pressure of one substance (as fuel oil, combustion air, or water spray) into a working space (as a diesel cylinder, a gas-turbine combustor, or a steam desuperheater) **2 :** the act or an instance of introducing some element or factor into a situation or subject ⟨~ into news reports of the editor's political prejudices —Martin Gardner⟩

injection gneiss *n* **:** MIGMATITE

injection molding *n* **:** a method of forming articles of plastic or rubber by heating the molding material until it is able to flow and injecting it into a mold

injection well *n* **:** a well into which gas, air, or water is pumped in order to increase the yield of adjacent wells

in·jec·tor \ən'jektə(r)\ *n* -s **:** one that injects; *specif* **:** a jet pump for injecting feedwater into a boiler or fuel into a combustion chamber

injoint *vt* [²*in-* + *joint* (n.)] *obs* **:** JOIN

in·ju·cun·di·ty \,injü'kəndəd.ē\ *n* -ES [L *injucunditas,* fr. *injucundus* unpleasant, fr. *in-* ¹in- + *jucundus* pleasant — more at JOCUND] *archaic* **:** UNPLEASANTNESS

in·judicial \¦in+\ *adj* [¹*in-* + *judicial*] **:** INJUDICIOUS — **in·judicially** \"+\ *adv*

in·judicious \"+\ *adj* [¹*in-* + *judicious*] **1 :** not judicious **:** lacking in sound judgment **:** INDISCREET ⟨brought by ~ mothers at precisely the most ineligible moments —W.L. Alden⟩ **2 :** not according to sound judgment or discretion **:** UNWISE ⟨an ~ measure⟩ — **in·judiciously** \"+\ *adv* — **in·judiciousness** \"+\ *n*

in·jun \'injən\ *n* -s *cap, often attrib* [alter. of ¹*indian*] **:** AMERICAN INDIAN ⟨he'd tell tales — of *Injuns,* or folks he'd known, or things that was plumb impossible to of happened anywheres —Helen Eustis⟩

in·junct \ən'jəŋ(k)t\ *vt* -ED/-ING/-S [*back-formation* fr. *injunction*] **:** to restrain by injunction

in·junc·tion \ən'jəŋ(k)shən\ *n* -s [MF & LL; MF *injonction,* fr. LL *injunction-, injunctio,* fr. L *injunctus* (past part. of *injungere* to enjoin) + *-ion-, -io* -ion — more at ENJOIN] **1 :** the act or an instance of enjoining **:** an earnest admonition **:** ORDER, PROHIBITION ⟨the Hindu religion has no ~s against birth control —Mildred Gilman⟩ ⟨laid an ~ of secrecy on me⟩ ⟨delivered stern ~s —Gilbert Millstein⟩ ⟨his father's dying ~s⟩ **2 :** an equitable writ granted by a court of equity whereby one is required to do or to refrain from doing a specified act — compare INTERDICT

¹**in·junc·tive** \-ŋ(k)tiv\ *adj* [L *injunctus* + E *-ive*] **1 a :** constituting an order, prohibition, or admonition **:** ENJOINING ⟨this ~ maxim —C.H.Hamburg⟩ **b :** constituting a mood or set of verb forms usu. with imperative, optative, or subjunctive meaning **2 :** of or relating to a legal injunction ⟨~ relief was not available to the state —*New Republic*⟩ ⟨an ~ order⟩

²**injunctive** \"\ *n* -s **:** the injunctive grammatical mood or a verbal form expressing it

in·jur·ant \'injərənt\ *n* -s [*injure* + *-ant*] **:** an injurious agent or substance ⟨some poison gases are lung ~s⟩

in ju·re \(')in'jurē, -'yü-\ *adv* [L] **:** in right, law, or justice **:** in court

in·jure \'injə(r)\ *vt* **injured**; **injured**; **injuring** \-j(ə)riŋ\ **injures** [back-formation fr. ¹*injury*] **1 a :** to do an injustice to **:** WRONG, OFFEND ⟨the *injured* husband sued for divorce⟩ **b :** to harm, impair, or tarnish the standing of (as a reputation or other intangible quality or asset) ⟨~ his authority —H.J. Laski⟩ ⟨~ your prospects —Thomas Hardy⟩ **c :** to give pain to (the sensibilities or feelings) ⟨~ a man's pride⟩ **2 a :** to inflict bodily hurt on ⟨*injured* by a falling brick⟩ **b :** to impair the soundness of ⟨~ your health⟩ **c :** to inflict material damage or loss on ⟨many houses were *injured* by the storm⟩ ⟨this tax will ~ all business⟩

syn HARM, HURT, DAMAGE, IMPAIR, MAR, SPOIL: INJURE implies the doing of an injustice to, or a wronging of, someone, esp. intentionally; it implies also an inflicting upon someone of anything detrimental to looks, health, comfort, success ⟨*injure* a man's reputation by slander⟩ ⟨*injure* a shoulder in a football game⟩ ⟨*injure* a friendship by resentment⟩ HARM stresses the inflicting of pain, suffering, or loss ⟨*harm* a dog by overfeeding it⟩ ⟨bitterness among the elders must not be permitted to *harm* or wound the innocent children of either race —Beverly Smith⟩ ⟨*harm* one's country by careless talk in wartime⟩ HURT implies the inflicting of a wound upon something (as the body, the feelings, or the commonwealth) capable of sustaining an injury ⟨seriously *hurt* in a landing under shore fire⟩ ⟨*hurt* a man's pride by belittling his accomplishments⟩ ⟨*hurt* the state by publicizing its rare and petty political feuds⟩ DAMAGE implies injury resulting in loss of value, completeness, efficiency, function ⟨furniture *damaged* by careless handling by movers⟩ ⟨an eye *damaged* by strain under bad light⟩ ⟨*damage* a motor by overheating it⟩ IMPAIR suggests a making less complete or efficient as by deterioration or diminution ⟨her excitement *impaired* her power of listening —Willa Cather⟩ ⟨beauty *impaired* by age⟩ ⟨labor with the hands or at the desk distorts or *impairs* the body —G.L.Dickinson⟩ ⟨individual rights should not be *impaired* without good reason⟩ MAR implies an injury that makes less perfect ⟨a case of smallpox which *marred* his face for life —*Time*⟩ ⟨his intellect, which was amazingly spotty, *marred* by great gaps —Norman Mailer⟩ ⟨a life of drudgery disfigures the body and *mars* and enervates the soul —G.L. Dickinson⟩ SPOIL in this connection suggests not only impairment or marring but usu. destruction or ruin ⟨they had the long Carroll upper lip that *spoiled* their looks a bit —Mary Deasy⟩ ⟨few streams and lakes which were clear and un*spoiled* by the works of man —Alexander MacDonald⟩ ⟨a great novel *spoiled* by hasty (and lazy) composition —H.J.Laski⟩

in ju·re ces·sio \-¦jurē'ses(h)ē,ō, -¦yürē'kesē,ō\ *n* [L, lit., surrender in law] **:** a procedure in Roman law whereby a defendant formally admits or concedes before the praetor the justice of the plaintiff's claim to specific property and the praetor then adjudges it to belong to the plaintiff

injured *adj* **1 a :** WRONGED, OFFENDED ⟨clearing the reputation of the ~ youth —J.A.Froude⟩ ⟨an air of ~ innocence⟩ ⟨~ vanity⟩ **b :** reflecting or indicating a sense of injury ⟨talking in an ~ way —William Black⟩ ⟨gave her a suspicious, ~ expression —Willa Cather⟩ ⟨relapsed into ~ gloom —Athene Seyler⟩ **2 :** physically damaged or hurt ⟨held up his ~ finger⟩ — **in·jured·ly** *adv*

in·jur·er \-jərə(r), -j(ə)rə\ *n* -s **:** one that injures

in·ju·ria \ən'jürēə, -'yü-\ *n, pl* **injuri·ae** \-jürē,ē, -yürē,ī\ [L, injury] **:** invasion of another's rights **:** actionable wrong **:** INJUSTICE

injuria abs·que dam·no \-¦abz(,)kwē'dam(,)nō, -¦äps(,)kwä'däm(,)nō\ [L, injury without damage] — used in reference to the rule that a wrong that causes no damage will not sustain an action; compare DAMNUM ABSQUE INJURIA

in·ju·ri·ous \ən'jürēəs\ *adj* [ME, fr. MF *injurieux,* fr. L *injuriosus,* fr. *injuria* + *-osus* -ous] **1 :** inflicting or tending to inflict injury **:** HURTFUL, HARMFUL, DETRIMENTAL ⟨inaccurate news stories ~ of national dignity —*Quill*⟩ ⟨routine detection of ~ defects —*Steel*⟩ ⟨~ to health⟩ **2 :** ABUSIVE, OFFENSIVE, DEFAMATORY ⟨speak not ~ words —George Washington⟩ — **in·ju·ri·ous·ly** *adv* — **in·ju·ri·ous·ness** *n* -ES

in·ju·ry \'inj(ə)rē, -ri\ *n* -ES [ME *injurie,* fr. L *injuria,* fr. *injurus, injurius* injurious, unjust, wrong (fr. *in-* ¹in- + *-jurus, -jurius,* fr. *jur-, jus* right, law) + *-ia* -y — more at JUST] **1 a :** an act that damages, harms, or hurts **:** an unjust or undeserved infliction of suffering or harm **:** WRONG ⟨take it as a personal ~ —W.R.Inge⟩ ⟨his tone was one of mingled admiration and ~ —R.H.Davis⟩ ⟨adding insult to ~⟩ **b :** a violation of another's rights for which the law allows an action to recover damages or specific property or both **:** an actionable wrong — distinguished from *harm;* compare TORT **c** *obs* **:** offensive or defamatory speech **:** INSULT **2 :** hurt, damage, or loss sustained ⟨with consequent ~ to morale and efficiency —Adam Yarmolinsky⟩ ⟨*injuries* to health⟩ ⟨without ~ to the concrete —J.R.Dalzell⟩ ⟨suffered severe *injuries* in the accident⟩

syn INJURY, HURT, DAMAGE, HARM, and MISCHIEF mean in common the act or result of inflicting on a person or thing something that causes loss, pain, distress, or impairment. INJURY is the most comprehensive, applying to an act or result involving an impairment or destruction of right, health, freedom, soundness, or loss of something of value ⟨sustain a leg *injury* in a fall⟩ ⟨mental or emotional upset is just as truly an *injury* to the body as a bone fracture, a burn, or a bacterial infection —G.W.Gray b. 1886⟩ ⟨the fundamental skepticism . . . inflicts the most serious *injury* on both science and religion —W.R.Inge⟩ ⟨such change is . . . a great *injury* to the child's independence and freedom from responsibility —Abram Kardiner⟩ HURT applies chiefly to physical injury but in any application it stresses pain or suffering whether injury is involved or not ⟨a would-be fighter . . . that gross, brutal frame was still capable of doing a great deal of *hurt* —Hamilton Basso⟩ ⟨wrongfully withholding from him something which is his due . . . inflicting on him a positive *hurt,* either in the form of direct suffering, or of the privation of some good which he had reasonable ground, either of a physical or of a social kind, for counting upon —J.S.Mill⟩ ⟨leaving forever to the aggressor the choice of time and place and means to cause greatest *hurt* to us at least cost to himself —D.D.Eisenhower⟩ ⟨the dentist's drill may cause quite a *hurt* though it does no injury⟩ DAMAGE applies to injury involving loss, as of property, value, or usefulness ⟨the collision inflicted great *damage* on the car⟩ ⟨realize the immense *damage* his action has done to the good name of America —H.J.Laski⟩ ⟨enough *damage* to a watch so that it no longer keeps accurate time⟩ HARM applies to any evil that injures or may injure ⟨the men were terrified of Yusuf's cruelty, and wanted to retreat out of *harm's* way —C.S. Forester⟩ ⟨a well-founded apprehension of bodily *harm* is sufficient to justify the taking of life —H.W.H.Knott⟩ ⟨a scandal may prove of great *harm* to a man's political career⟩ MISCHIEF is used to avoid the suggestion or image of particular harm or injury, designating generally any misdoing or injury, esp. irresponsible, and stressing the role of an agent, usu. personal ⟨the nearest policeman, who most likely won't turn up until the worst of the *mischief* is done —G.B.Shaw⟩ ⟨he was most violent; if Captain Downing had not been there to restrain him, I vow he'd have done me a *mischief* —Max Peacock⟩ ⟨a fence was defective, and the pigs straying did *mischief* to a trolley car —B.N.Cardozo⟩

²**injury** *vt* -ED/-ING/-ES [ME *injurien,* fr. MF *injurier,* fr. L *injuriari,* fr. *injuria*] *obs* **:** INJURE

injust *adj* [ME *injuste,* fr. MF *injuste,* fr. L *injustus*] *obs* **:** UNJUST

in·justice \(')in, ən+\ *n* [ME, fr. MF, fr. L *injustitia,* fr. *injustus* unjust (fr. *in-* ¹in- + *justus* just) + *-ia* -y — more at JUST] **1 :** absence of justice **:** violation of right or of the rights of another **:** INIQUITY, UNFAIRNESS ⟨flamed out against ~ —John Galsworthy⟩ **2 :** an unjust act or deed **:** WRONG ⟨the ~s that angered him were never genuine —Norman Mailer⟩

¹**ink** \'iŋk\ *n* -s *often attrib* [ME *enke, inke,* fr. OF *enke, enque,* fr. LL *encaustum* ink (orig. the purplish ink used by the late Roman emperors to sign their edicts), fr. neut. of L *encaustus* burned in, painted in encaustic, fr. Gk *enkaustos* — more at ENCAUSTIC] **1 a :** a fluid or viscous material of various colors but commonly black or blue-black that is composed essentially of a pigment or dye in a suitable vehicle and is used for writing and printing — see INDELIBLE INK, PRINTING INK, WRITING INK **b :** a similar solid preparation (as india ink) **2 :** the black protective secretion of a cephalopod

²**ink** \"\ *vt* -ED/-ING/-S **1 :** to cover or smear with ink **:** apply ink to or touch up with ink **2 a :** to go over in ink — usu. used with *in* or *over* **b :** to obliterate with ink — usu. used with *out* ⟨~*ed* out many lines⟩ **c :** to write or draw in ink ⟨~*ed* their crosses to documents they had not the skill to read —G.M.Trevelyan⟩ ⟨pointed out the neatly ~*ed* entry on the bill —Irwin Shaw⟩ **3 a :** to affix one's signature to ⟨the baseball player was offered a raise and readily ~*ed* his contract⟩ **b :** to sign to a contract ⟨~*ed* the players with little difficulty⟩

ink ball *also* **inking ball** *n* **:** a ball-shaped inking pad formerly used by printers

inkberry \'iŋk — *see* BERRY\ *n* **1 :** a holly (*Ilex glabra*) of eastern No. America with evergreen oblong leathery leaves and small black berries — called also *gallberry* **2 :** BOX BRIER **3 :** POKEWEED **4 :** the fruit of an inkberry

ink black *n* **:** the color of dried blue-black ink **:** a dark grayish blue to bluish black — called also *inky black*

inkblot \'ˌ=,=\ *n* **1 :** a blot of ink **2 :** any of several plates showing blots of ink for use in psychological testing

inkblot test *n* **:** RORSCHACH TEST

inkbush \'ˌ=,=\ *n* **:** INKWEED 1

ink cap *n* **:** INKY CAP

ink disease *n* **1 :** a destructive disease of the chestnut in Europe that is caused by a fungus (*Phytophthora cambivora*) and that produces dark cankers and a black exudate on the trunk — called also *black canker* **2 :** a destructive disease of walnuts caused by a fungus (*Phytophthora cryptogea*)

ink·er \'iŋkə(r)\ *n* -s **:** one that inks: as **a :** INKWRITER **b :** a worker who applies ink or stain to goods (as shoe parts or cloth); *specif* **:** a worker who touches up imperfectly dyed cloth or hosiery

inkfish \'ˌ=,=\ *n* **:** CUTTLEFISH, SQUID

ink fountain *n* **:** the mechanism in a printing press that contains the ink and releases it to the rollers

¹**ink·horn** \'iŋk,hȯrn, 'iŋ,kȯrn\ *n* [ME *enkehorn, inkehorn,* fr. *enke, inke* ink + *horn* horn] **:** a small portable bottle of horn or other material for holding ink

²**inkhorn** \"\ *adj* **:** affectedly learned or pedantic ⟨~ terms and crude Latinisms —J.W.H.Atkins⟩

in·kie *or* **in·ky** \'iŋkē, -ki\ *n, pl* **inkies** [by shortening & alter.] *slang* **:** INCANDESCENT LAMP

inkier *comparative of* INKY

inkiest *superlative of* INKY

ink·i·ness \'iŋkēnəs, -kin-\ *n* -ES **:** the quality or state of being inky

ink knife *n* **:** a spatula for mixing printing ink

¹**in·kle** *also* **in·cle** \'iŋkəl\ *vt* -ED/-ING/-S [back-formation fr. *inkling*] *chiefly dial Eng* **:** to have an inkling of ⟨began to ~ what a silly combat weapon it is —E.V.Westrate⟩

²**inkle** *also* **incle** \"\ *n* -s [origin unknown] **:** a colored linen tape or braid woven on a very narrow loom and used for trimming; *also* **:** the thread used

ink·less \'iŋkləs\ *adj* [¹*ink* + *-less*] **:** devoid of ink

in·kling \'iŋkliŋ, -lēŋ, *esp in sense 1* -lən\ *n* -s [ME *yngkiling,* prob. fr. gerund of *inclen* to hint at, indicate; akin to OE *inca* suspicion, doubt, quarrel, OFris *jink* angry, ON *ekki* pain, Lith *ingis* sluggard, OSlav *jędza* illness] **1** *dial chiefly Eng* **a :** a faintly perceptible sound **:** UNDERTONE ⟨could not hear an ~ of his breathing —Elizabeth Enright⟩ **b :** RUMOR **2 a :** a faint or slight suggestion **:** HINT, INTIMATION ⟨there was no path — no ~ even of a track —*New Yorker*⟩ ⟨give only a dim ~ of its native intelligence —H.J.Morgenthau⟩ **b :** a slight knowledge or vague notion ⟨had not the faintest ~ of what it was all about —H.W.Carter⟩ ⟨got his first ~s as to the roles of natural selection —E.H.Colbert⟩

ink·man \'iŋk,man, -,mən\ *n, pl* **inkmen :** a worker who blends inks, powders, or pastes to obtain printing inks of desired colors

ink mushroom *n* **:** INKY CAP

ink plant *n* **1 :** a plant of the genus *Coriaria:* as **a :** a plant (*C. thymifolia*) of tropical America and New Zealand the fruits of which yield a red dye used as ink in Ecuador **b :** a European plant (*C. myrtifolia*) the leaves of which yield a black dye **2 :** POKEWEED

inkpot \'ˌ=,=\ *n* **:** a container for ink

ink print *n* **:** matter printed from inked type as distinguished from embossed matter for reading by the blind

in·kra \iŋ'krä, in'k-\ *n, pl* **inkra** *or* **inkras** *usu cap* **:** GA

inks *pl of* INK, *pres 3d sing of* INK

ink sac *n* **:** an organ in most cephalopods (as the squid) secreting an inky fluid that can be ejected from a duct opening into the terminal part of the rectum

inkshed \'ˌ=,=\ *n* -s [¹*ink* + *-shed* (as in *bloodshed*)] *archaic* **:** profuse use or unnecessary waste of ink in writing ⟨to spare mine own pains and prevent ~ —Andrew Marvell⟩

inkslinger \'ˌ==\ *n* **1 :** WRITER, SCRIBBLER **2 :** a timekeeper in a logging camp

ink spot *n* **:** a plant disease characterized by black blemishes; *specif* **:** a disease of the aspen caused by fungi of the genus *Sclerotinia*

inkstand \'ˌ=\ *n* **:** a small vessel for holding ink into which a pen can be dipped **:** INKWELL; *also* **:** a stand with fittings for holding ink and pens

inkstandish \'ˌ=(ˌ)=\ *n* [¹*ink* + *standish*] *archaic* **:** INKSTAND ⟨desired me to hand him the paper and ~ —Frederick Marryat⟩

inkweed \'ˌ=\ *n* **1 :** any of several western No. American shrubby plants of the genus *Suaeda* used by the Indians for dyeing — called also *inkbush* **2 :** POKEWEED

inkwell \'ˌ=\ *n* **:** a container for writing ink

inkwood \'ˌ=\ *n* **:** a small tree (*Exothea paniculata*) of the family Sapindaceae of Florida and the West Indies having dark-colored wood and purple fruits

inkwell

inkwriter \'ˌ==\ *n* **:** a telegraph receiver in which the message is recorded in ink (as in dots and dashes)

¹**inky** \'iŋkē, -ki\ *adj* -ER/-EST **:** consisting of, using, or resembling ink ⟨the ~ blackness of the ocean —F.G.Kay⟩ **:** soiled with or as if with ink **:** BLACK ⟨~ collars and dirty finger-nails —Angela Thirkell⟩

²**inky** *var of* INKIE

inky black *n* **:** INK BLACK

inky cap *n* **:** a mushroom of the genus *Coprinus* (esp. *C. atramentarius*) having a pileus that melts into an inky fluid after the spores have matured

inlaid \(')=¦=\ *adj* [fr. past part. of ¹*inlay*] **:** set into a surface so as to form a decorative design or decorated with a design so formed; *specif* **:** CHAMPLEVÉ

inlaid binding *n* **:** MOSAIC BINDING

in·laik \'inˌlāk, -lak\ *n* -S [ME (Sc), alter. of ME (Sc) *inlake*, fr. ME *in* + *lake, lak, lac* lack] *Scot* **:** LACK, DEFICIENCY

in–lamb \=ˈ=\ *adj, of ewes* **:** PREGNANT

¹**in·land** \'inˌland, -lənd, -ˌlaa(ə)nd\ *n* [ME, fr. OE, fr. *in* + *land* — more at LAND] **1** *Old Eng & feudal law* **:** the demesne land of the lord of a manor **2 :** the interior part of a country or the part remote from the centers of population ⟨the far ~ of Australia —T.C.Roughley⟩

²**inland** \"\ *adj* **1** *chiefly Brit* **:** confined to a country or state **:** not foreign **:** DOMESTIC, INTERNAL ⟨the consolidated foreign and ~ debt —*Statesman's Yr. Bk.*⟩ ⟨~ revenue⟩ **2 a :** of or relating to the inlands or interior parts of a country **:** lying in the interior **:** INTERIOR ⟨any college town, however ~ and ivory-towered —Nell G. Ahern⟩ **b :** being within the land **:** not bordering on the sea ⟨maritime and ~ provinces⟩ **3 :** limited to the inland or interior or to inland routes ⟨~ transportation⟩ ⟨~ commerce⟩

³**inland** \"\ *adv* **:** into or toward the interior **:** away from the frontier **:** away from the coast ⟨live ~⟩

inland bill *n* **:** a bill of exchange that is or on its face purports to be both drawn and payable within the jurisdiction (as country or state) where it is presented — compare FOREIGN BILL

in·land·er \-də(r)\ *n* -S [¹*inland* + -*er*] **:** one that lives inland

inland marine insurance *n* **:** insurance against loss of or damage to property transported in domestic commerce, instruments of transport and communication, and personal property — compare FLOATER 8, MARINE INSURANCE, OCEAN MARINE INSURANCE

inland water *n* **1 :** any of the waters (as lakes, canals, rivers, watercourses, inlets, and bays) within the territory of a state as contrasted with the open seas or marginal waters bordering another state subject to various sovereign rights of the bordering state — usu. used in pl. **2 :** water of the interior that does not border upon marginal or high seas or is above the rise and fall of the tides — usu. used in pl.; compare MARGINAL SEA, TERRITORIAL SEA, TERRITORIAL WATER

inland waterway *n* **1 :** a navigable river, canal, or sound **2 :** a system of navigable inland bodies of water — usu. used in pl.

in·large \ən+\ *archaic var of* ENLARGE

in·laut \'inˌlau̇t\ *n, pl* **inlau·te** \-au̇d·ə\ *also* **inlauts** [G, fr. *in* (fr. OHG) + *laut* sound, fr. MHG *lūt;* akin to OE *hlūd* loud — more at IN, LOUD] **:** a medial sound or position in a word or syllable — compare ANLAUT, AUSLAUT

in·law \(')in¦lȯ, ən'lȯ\ *vt* -ED/-ING/-S [ME *inlawen*, fr. OE *inlagian*, fr. *in* ²in + -*lagian* (fr. *lagu* law) — more at LAW] *Old Eng law* **:** to clear of outlawry or attainder **:** place under the protection of the law

in–law \'inˌlȯ\ *n, pl* **in–laws** [back-formation fr. *mother-in-law*, etc.] **:** a relative by marriage — usu. used in pl. ⟨how to get along with parents and *in-laws* —Emily H. Mudd⟩

¹**in·lay** \(')in¦lā, ən'lā\ *vt* **inlaid; inlaid; inlaying; inlays** [²*in* + *lay*] **1 a** (1) **:** to set into the body of a surface or ground material ⟨~ arabesques⟩ (2) **:** to pattern or adorn (a surface or ground) by the insertion of other material ⟨~ a panel with contrasting wood⟩ **:** adorn by inlaying ⟨~ wood with mother-of-pearl⟩ (3) **:** to ornament (a leather book cover) by fitting leather or other material into cut-in areas (4) **:** to ornament (a book cover) by affixing printed paper or other decorative material into depressed areas **b** (1) **:** to insert (as a color plate) into a heavier or stouter sheet serving as a mat, frame, or support (2) **:** to provide (a book) with inlaid illustrations **c :** to reinforce (silver-plated ware) at points of wear with an additional coating of silver or piece of silver embedded before electroplating **2 :** to burnish, beat, or fuse (as wire) into an incised cavity in metal, wood, stone, or other material

²**in·lay** \'inˌlā\ *n* -S **1 :** the process or art of inlaying **2 a :** material inlaid or prepared for inlaying; *also* **:** the ornament or pattern formed by inlaying **b** (1) **:** a tooth filling of metal or porcelain shaped to fit a cavity and then cemented into place (2) **:** a piece of tissue (as bone) laid into the site of missing tissue to bridge a defect **3 a :** an allowance (as an extra-wide seam) for clothing alteration **b :** a set-in section on a garment usu. decorative or contrasting

¹**in·lay·er** \(')in¦lāər, ən'l-, -le(ə)r\ *n* -S [¹*inlay* + -*er*] **:** one that inlays

²**in·lay·er** \'inˌl-\ *n* [⁴*in* + *layer*] **:** an inner layer or sheathing

inlay graft *n* **:** a plant graft made by inserting, fastening, and sealing an accurately cut scion in a V-shaped notch in the end of a truncated stock

inlaying *n* -S **1 :** INLAY 1,2a **2 :** the burnishing, beating, or fusing of material (as wire) in an incised cavity in metal, wood, stone, or other material

inleakage \'ˌ==\ *n* [⁴*in* + *leakage*] **:** the quantity that leaks in ⟨an actual ~ of 20,150 cubic feet per hour —*Lumber and its Utilization*⟩

¹**in·let** \'inˌle\|t, -ˌlə\|, *usu* \|d·+V\ *n* -S *often attrib* [⁴*in* + *let*, n. (after *let in*, v.)] **1 :** the act or an instance of letting in **2 a** (1) **:** a bay or recess in the shore of a sea, lake, or river (2) **:** a waterway into a sea, lake, or river **:** CREEK (3) **:** a narrow strip of water running into the land or between islands; *specif* **:** a passage through a barrier island or barrier reef leading to a bay or lagoon ⟨Barnegat *Inlet*⟩ **b :** a place of entrance **:** an opening by which entrance is made **:** ORIFICE ⟨oil ~s⟩ ⟨air ~⟩ ⟨~ and outlet valves⟩ **3 :** something that is let in or inlaid **:** an inserted material **4 :** the upper opening of the cavity of the true pelvis bounded by the brim

²**in·let** \'inˌlet, *usu* -ed·+V\ *vt* **inlet; inlet; inletting; inlets** [²*in* + *let* (v.)] **:** to let in **:** INSERT, INLAY ⟨~ the trigger mechanism down into the stock —*Amer. Rifleman*⟩

in·li·er \'inˌlī(ə)r\ *n* [⁴*in* + -*lier* (as in *outlier*)] **1 :** a mass of rock whose outcrop is wholly surrounded by rock of younger age **2 :** a distinct area or formation that is completely surrounded by another ⟨~s of an older, wilder landscape surrounded by improvement —H.C.Darby⟩; *also* **:** ENCLAVE ⟨abolish the numerous outliers and ~s of territory —R.E. Dickinson⟩

in–line engine \ən'līn, 'inˌl-\ *n* **:** an internal-combustion engine in which the cylinders are arranged in one or more straight lines — compare RADIAL ENGINE

in·list \ən'list\ *archaic var of* ENLIST

in lo·co pa·ren·tis \ən¦lō(ˌ)kōpə'rentəs\ *adv* [L] **:** in the place of a parent ⟨parents or persons standing *in loco parentis* —*U.S.House Bill*⟩

in–lot \'ˌ=\ *n* [⁴*in* + *lot*] **1 :** a lot of land within a larger plot **:** INTERIOR LOT ⟨in a retail district, the corner is more desirable than the *in-lots* —H.E.Hoagland⟩ **2 :** a homestead lot on a townsite granted or sold to an early settler in No. America

in·ly \'inlē, -li\ *adv* [ME *inliche, inly*, fr. OE *inlīce*, fr. *inlīc*, adj., inward, interior, fr. *in*, *inn* in + -*līc* -ly — more at IN] **1 :** INWARDLY, WITHIN ⟨~ excited about her —Vance Palmer⟩ **2 :** INTIMATELY, THOROUGHLY ⟨~ know all wisdom —John Masefield⟩

¹**inlying** \'ˌ==\ *n* -S [⁴*in* + *lying*, gerund of *lie* (after *lie in*, v.)] *chiefly Scot* **:** CONFINEMENT

²**inlying** \"\ *adj* [²*in* + *lying*, pres. part. of *lie*] **:** placed or situated inside or in the interior

inmarriage \'ˌ==\ *n* [⁴*in* + *marriage*] **:** marriage within one's own family, race, or other grouping **:** ENDOGAMY — contrasted with *outmarriage*

inmarry \'ˌ==\ *vi* [²*in* + *marry*] **:** to marry within one's own family, race, profession, or other grouping

¹**in·mate** \'inˌmāt, *usu* -ād·+V\ *n* [⁴*in* + *mate*] **1 a** *obs* **:** LODGER, TENANT **b** *archaic* **:** one who lives in the same house or apartment with another ⟨inquired whether he was a pleasant ~ and a kind neighbor —Harriet Martineau⟩ **2 :** one of a family, community, or other group occupying a single dwelling, home, or other place of residence ⟨rush the enemy settlement when all its ~s are asleep —C.D.Forde⟩ ⟨lifted the door of a pen, stirred up its ~s with his hand —Adrian Bell⟩ ⟨entered the house and seized all its ~s⟩; *esp* **:** a person confined or kept in an institution (as an asylum, prison, or poorhouse)

²**inmate** \"\ *adj, archaic* **:** living in the house of another **:** dwelling with another

inmeats \'ˌ=\ *n pl* [⁴*in* + *meats*] *dial Eng* **:** the inner parts of an animal that are used for food

in me·di·as res \ən¦mādēˌäs'rās, -med-\ *adv* [L, lit., into the midst of things] **:** in or into the heart or substance of a matter; *esp* **:** in or into the middle of a narrative or plot without the formality of an introduction or other preliminary ⟨plunges the reader . . . *in medias res* —J.W.Aldridge⟩

in me·mo·ri·am \ˌinmə'mōrēəm, -'mȯr-, -ēˌam, -ēˌaa(ə)m, -ēˌäm\ *adv* [L] **:** in memory of — used esp. in epitaphs and inscriptions and on floral pieces for the dead

inmesh *var of* ENMESH

in–migrant \'ˌ==\ *n* [⁴*in* + *migrant*] **:** a person who in-migrates

in–migrate \(¦)in+\ *vi* [²*in* + *migrate*] **:** to come to live in a community esp. for work in an expanding industry and often as part of a large-scale movement of workers — compare OUT-MIGRATE — **in–migration** \¦in+\ *n*

in·most \'inˌmōst *also chiefly Brit* -ˌməst\ *adj* [ME *inmast, inmost*, alter. (influenced by *mast, most* most) of *inmest*, fr. OE *innemest*, superl. of *inne*, adv., in, inside, within, fr. *in, inn*, adv., in — more at IN] **:** deepest within **:** farthest from the surface or external part **:** INNERMOST ⟨one's ~ self —J.B.Noss⟩

¹**inn** \'in\ *n* -S *often attrib* [ME *inn, in*, fr. OE *inn* (akin to ON *inni* dwelling, refuge, inn), fr. *inn, in*, adv. — more at IN] **1 a :** a public house for the lodging of travelers for compensation and until capacity is reached **:** HOTEL, HOSTELRY **b :** a place of public entertainment that does not provide lodging **:** TAVERN **2 :** a residence or hostel for students — formerly used of such a residence at a British university and of various houses connected with the study and admission to the practice of law in London — compare INN OF CHANCERY, INN OF COURT

²**inn** \"\ *vi* -ED/-ING/-S [ME *innen, innien*, fr. OE *innian*, fr. *inn*, n.] **:** to lodge, stop, or put up at an inn

inn *abbr* inning

in·nards \'inə(r)dz\ *n pl* [alter. of *inwards*] **1 :** the internal organs of a man or animal ⟨treating their ~ at state expense —Mollie Panter-Downes⟩; *esp* **:** VISCERA ⟨his ~ were rumbling⟩ **2 :** the internal parts or interior of something ⟨churned up from the earth's ~ —*Time*⟩ ⟨the insidious ~ of the women's magazines —Hugh Mulligan⟩; *esp* **:** the internal parts of a structure or mechanism ⟨the iron ~ of a great four-faced clock —*New Yorker*⟩

in·nate \(')i¦nāt, ə'n- *sometimes* (')in¦n-; *usu* -ād· +V\ *adj* [ME *innat*, fr. L *innatus*, past part. of *innasci* to be born, be a native, be naturally suitable, fr. *in-* ²in- + *nasci* to be born — more at NATION] **1 a :** existing in or belonging to some person or other living organism from birth **:** NATIVE, NATURAL ⟨~ vigor⟩ **b :** belonging to the essential nature of something **:** INHERENT ⟨the ~ defect in a plan⟩ **c :** originating in, derived from, or inherent in the mind or the constitution of the intellect rather than derived from experience ⟨~ ideas of God, immortality, right and wrong⟩ — compare A PRIORI, INTUITIVE **2** *obs* **:** formed internally **:** hidden within **:** INTERNAL **3 a :** attached to the apex of the support of a plant (as an anther to the tip of a filament) — compare ADNATE 2 **b :** ENDOGENOUS **c :** immersed or embedded in (as the fruiting bodies in the thallus of a fungus)

syn INBORN, INBRED, CONGENITAL, HEREDITARY, INHERITED: INNATE applies to qualities or characteristics belonging to something as part of its inner essential nature. INNATE designates that which is part of lasting essential character, sometimes present or potential at birth ⟨simple ideas should be kept simple, and their *innate* strength should not be undermined by the use of big words and by periphrases —E.S.McCartney⟩ ⟨because of her ability to sense the *innate* talent of young and untried actors —*Amer. Guide Series: Mich.*⟩ ⟨this stubbornness has been explained as being *innate* in the Germans, as a natural racial cussedness —R.C.Wood⟩ INBORN may describe a natural native distinctive characteristic so deep-seated as to have been born in one, often present at birth ⟨there was in him a rush of *inborn* vitality like an Alpine torrent —Agnes Repplier⟩ ⟨the psychopathic personality is held to be an *inborn* (though not hereditary) deficit and is of the nature of a functional alteration —*Yr. Bk. of Neurology, Psychiatry & Neurosurgery*⟩ INBRED describes that which becomes deeply ingrained into one's nature by early environmental influences without being part of one's nature at birth ⟨those *inbred* sentiments which are . . . the true supporters of all liberal and manly morals—Edmund Burke⟩ ⟨a methodical man, an *inbred* Yankee —W.A.White⟩ CONGENITAL applies to a characteristic present at the birth of a person or inception of a thing or notion, whatever the provenience of that characteristic ⟨the newborn child's chances of survival and healthy development depend in part on his *congenital* equipment —*Times Lit. Supp.*⟩ ⟨yet art for art's sake suffers from a *congenital* disease; it professes to create substance out of form, which is physically impossible —George Santayana⟩ HEREDITARY and INHERITED describe characteristics and conditions not only present at birth but definitely coming from heredity, that is, brought about by transmission from parents and ancestors ⟨an *hereditary* propensity to kill men and eat them. True, he came from a race of cannibals —Herman Melville⟩ ⟨most of us, of course, held fast to the Republican party, for political beliefs were *hereditary*, transmissible in the male line —Ben Riker⟩ ⟨a tendency in the past to confuse *congenital* with *inherited*. It is a commonplace now that conditions present at birth are not necessarily inherited in the biological sense of the word, to quote only congenital syphilis as an example. It is also generally known that many inherited conditions first manifest themselves long after birth —Hans Grüneberg⟩

innated *adj* [L *innatus* + E -*ed*] *obs* **:** INNATE

in·nate·ly *adv* **:** in an innate manner

in·nate·ness *n* -ES **:** the quality or state of being innate

in·nat·ism \ə'nād·ˌizəm\ *n* -S [*innate* + -*ism*] **:** a belief in innate ideas

in·na·tive \(')i(n)¦nād·iv\ *adj* [L *innatus* + E -*ive*] **:** INNATE, NATURAL ⟨some ~ weakness . . . in him who condescends to victory —J.R.Lowell⟩

in·navigable \(')i(n), ə+\ *adj* [L *innavigabilis*, fr. *in-* ¹in- + *navigabilis* navigable — more at NAVIGABLE] **:** not navigable

inned *past of* IN *or of* INN

¹**in·ner** \'inə(r)\ *adj* [ME *inner, inre*, fr. OE *innera, innra*, compar. of *inne* in — more at INMOST] **1 a :** situated farther in ⟨an ~ chamber⟩ ⟨the ~ bark⟩ **b :** near to a center esp. of influence ⟨the ~ circles of the administration⟩ **c :** INTRAMOLECULAR — used esp. of compounds ⟨~ esters⟩ **2 :** of or relating to the mind or spirit or its phenomena ⟨the ~ life of man⟩

syn INWARD, INSIDE, INTERIOR, INTERNAL, INTESTINE, INTESTINAL are often interchangeable. INNER may apply to something far within or near a center; consequently it may apply to something deeply intimate or inaccessible ⟨an *inner* room⟩ ⟨no wish to write anything but a spiritual biography, and outer events only interest me here insofar as they affected my *inner* life —Havelock Ellis⟩ ⟨he had not chosen his course. It had sprung from a necessity of his nature, an *inner* logic that he scarcely questioned —Van Wyck Brooks⟩ INWARD is close in suggestion to INNER; it may apply to direction within ⟨an *inward* curve⟩ ⟨the little houses splashed in the thousands across the countryside sheltered the men turning *inward* in the quest for peace of mind —Oscar Handlin⟩ ⟨that *inward* eye which is the bliss of solitude —William Wordsworth⟩ INSIDE, used often of space relationships, may suggest the restricted, secret, or confidential not shared by those outside ⟨an *inside* room⟩ ⟨*inside* work⟩ ⟨speculating on *inside* information⟩ ⟨even the bare outline was sufficient to gratify the public's craving for the abnormal and the spectacular. But the *inside* story of the catastrophe surpassed even the wildest flights of public fancy —W.H.Wright⟩ INTERIOR may contrast with *exterior* and stress the fact of being within ⟨*interior* decorating⟩ ⟨not to be found in institutionalism, nor in the Scriptures, but in the *interior* life and spirit of man —W.R.Inge⟩ ⟨frightened by an *interior* quietness and by the thought that she had for once in her life stopped thinking —Elizabeth Bowen⟩ INTERNAL, contrasted with *external*, may apply to inner activity, force, development, or effect ⟨interested more in *internal* affairs than foreign⟩ ⟨the slavery which would be imposed upon her by her external enemies and her *internal* traitors —F.D.Roosevelt⟩ ⟨a more general process of *internal* migration that involved both regional shifts and a drift to the cities —Oscar Handlin⟩ INTESTINE and, more rarely, INTESTINAL are occas. used as synonyms for *civil* and *domestic*, in contrast to *foreign*, to describe wars and disturbances ⟨the common people fused, not without considerable *intestine* struggle, to form an Etruscan Latin blend —R.A.Hall b.1911⟩

²**inner** \"\ *n* -S **:** a forward line player in various team sports (as soccer and field hockey) stationed between the left or right wing and the center forward

inner anhydride *n* **:** an anhydride formed by elimination of water from a single molecule

inner bar *n, Eng law* **:** the queen's or king's counsel who are permitted to plead within the bar of the court — compare OUTER BAR

inner barrister *n, Eng law* **:** a barrister ranking lowest among the barristers belonging to an Inn of Court

inner bottom *n* **:** the plating in a ship that is laid over the frames and longitudinals and that with the shell plating forms a double bottom — called also *tank top*

inner cell mass *n* **:** the portion of the blastodermic vesicle of a primate embryo that is destined to become the embryo proper

inner closure *n* **:** the inner of the two ends of the chamber formed by a stop articulation ⟨the bottom of the lungs, the glottis, or the tongue and velum may be the *inner closure*⟩ — compare OUTER CLOSURE

inner–directed \¦==(ˌ)=¦=\ *adj* **:** directed in thought and action by one's own scale of values as opposed to external norms **:** NONCONFORMIST ⟨the American is undergoing a basic change from *inner-directed* to other-directed —H.S.Commager⟩

inner–direction \¦==(ˌ)=¦==\ *n* **:** a sense of direction based on one's own scale of values or standards as opposed to external norms

inner ear *n* **:** the essential part of the vertebrate ear consisting typically of a bony labyrinth in the temporal bone enclosing a fluid-filled membranous labyrinth innervated by the auditory nerve and made up of a vestibular apparatus and three semicircular canals primarily concerned with the labyrinthine sense and a cochlea which is the seat of the actual sound receptor

inner endodermis *n* **:** the endodermal layer separating the stele from the pith (as in a stem where two endodermal layers are present)

inner form *n* **:** a form that prints the side of a sheet on which the second page appears — contrasted with *outer form;* compare SHEET IMPOSITION

inner jib *n* **:** a jib immediately forward of the forestaysail on a ship where several jibs are carried — see SAIL illustration

inner keel *n* [³*keel*] **:** KEELSON

inner light *n, cap I&L* **:** the divine presence in the soul of every man held in Quaker doctrine to give spiritual enlightenment, moral guidance, and religious assurance to all who seek such through faith — called also *Christ Within, Light Within*

¹**in·ner·ly** \'inə(r)lē, -li\ *adv* [ME, fr. *inner* + -*ly* (adv. suffix)] **:** INWARDLY, INLY ⟨a world that was ~ divided —Dorothy Thompson⟩

²**innerly** \"\ *adj* [ME, fr. *inner* + -*ly* (adj. suffix)] **1** *Scot* **:** INWARD, INLYING **2 :** pleasantly familiar and sociable

inner man *n* **1 :** the spiritual or intellectual part of man **2 :** STOMACH ⟨the *inner man* will consume the largest part of your bankroll —T.H.Fielding⟩

inner mission *n* [trans. of G *innere mission*] **:** a movement originating in the 19th century within the Evangelical Church of Germany that sought partly through sisterhoods and lay brotherhoods to serve neglected and unfortunate members of society and that founded Christian lodging houses, Sunday schools, orphanages, and hospitals

innermore \¦==¦=\ *adj* [ME, fr. ¹*inner* + *more*] *now dial Eng* **:** located farther within **:** INNER

¹**in·ner·most** \'==ˌmōst *also chiefly Brit* -ˌməst\ *adj* [ME, fr. *inner* + -*most*] **:** farthest inward **:** INMOST ⟨it is his ~ being that is judged —D.C.Hodges⟩ ⟨the ~ part of the nation —F.D.Roosevelt⟩ — **inner·most·ly** *adv*

²**innermost** \"\ *n* **:** the inmost part **:** inmost being

in·ner·ness *n* -ES **:** the quality or state of being inner **:** inner character ⟨its superior moral sense and its more intense ~ —W.K.Ferguson⟩

inner part *or* **inner voice** *n* **:** a line or part intermediate between the highest and lowest (as the alto or tenor in four-part vocal music)

inner phase *n* **:** DISPERSED PHASE

inner planet *n* **:** one of the four principal planets whose orbits are innermost in the solar system ⟨Mercury, Venus, Earth, and Mars are the *inner planets*⟩

inner post *n* **:** a timber on the forward side of the sternpost to receive the hooding ends of the planking and in square-stern ships to support the transoms

inner product *n* **:** SCALAR PRODUCT

inner proscenium *n* **:** an inner frame (as a wooden framework) built esp. for a stage production to mask lighting equipment or narrow the stage opening or by means of special shape to give a desired design-quality to the production

inner quantum number *n* **:** a vector quantum number denoting the total angular momentum of an atom exclusive of nuclear spin — symbol *J* or *j*

inner salt *n* **:** a salt formed by reaction within the molecule of a compound having both acid and basic properties — compare DIPOLAR ION

inner sanctum *n* **:** SANCTUM

innersole \¦==¦=\ *n* **:** INSOLE

inner speech *n* **:** use of words or word images in thinking without audible or visible speaking

innerspring \'==ˌ=\ *adj* **:** having coil springs inside a padded casing ⟨~ mattress⟩ ⟨~ cushion⟩

inner table *n* **:** either half of a backgammon board as determined by the players but usu. the half nearer the source of light

inner tube *n* **:** an airtight tube of rubber placed inside the casing of a pneumatic tire to hold air under pressure

inner tube, inflated

in·ner·vate \i'nərˌvāt 'i(ˌ)nər-\ *vt* -ED/-ING/-S [²*in-* + *nerve* + -*ate*] **1 :** to supply with nerves **2 :** to arouse or stimulate (a nerve or an organ) to activity

in·ner·va·tion \ˌi(ˌ)nər'vāshən\ *n* [²*in-* + *nerve* + -*ation*] **1 :** the act, process, or an instance of innervating **:** the state of being innervated; *specif* **:** the nervous excitation necessary for the maintenance of the life and functions of the various organs **2 :** the distribution of nerves to or in a part **:** the nerve supply (as of a part or organ) — **in·ner·va·tion·al** \¦=(ˌ)=¦vāshən°l, -shnəl\ *adj*

in·nerve \i+\ *vt* -ED/-ING/-S [²*in-* + *nerve* (n.)] **:** to give nervous energy or power to : give increased energy, force, or courage to : INVIGORATE, STIMULATE

in·ness \ˈinnəs\ *n* -ES [²*in* + *-ness*] : inner nature : INWARDNESS

innholder \ˈ=,==\ *n* [ME *inhalder*, fr. *in, inn* inn + *halder, holder* holder — more at INN, HOLDER] : INNKEEPER

¹inn·ing \ˈiniŋ, -nēŋ\ *pres part of* INN

²in·ning \"\ *n* -S [in sense 1, fr. gerund of ³*in*; in sense 2, fr. ²*in* + *-ing*] **1 a** : the act of taking in, gathering, or enclosing; *specif* : the act of reclaiming land esp. from the sea or a marsh **b innings** *pl* : reclaimed lands **2 a innings** *pl but sing or pl in constr* : a division of a cricket match in which one side continues batting until ten players are retired or the side declares; *also* : the time a player stays as a batsman until he is out, until ten teammates are out, or until his side declares **b** : a team's turn at bat in baseball ending with the third out; *also* : a division consisting of a turn at bat for each team **c** : a division of a contest in other sports (as a turn at serving in badminton, two throws by one player or two throws by each contestant in horseshoes, or a player's turn in croquet) **d** : a chance or turn for action or accomplishment (as to display one's prowess, caliber, or ability) ⟨the factual . . . romance has had its ~ —Parker Tyler⟩ ⟨the young conductor who is currently having his ~*s* —Douglas Watt⟩ ⟨the opposition party now had its ~*s*⟩ ⟨keep silent in order to give the adversary his ~ —Edmond Taylor⟩

innkeeper \ˈ=,==\ *n* : the landlord of an inn

inn·less \ˈinləs\ *adj* : being without an inn

in·no·cence \ˈinəsən(t)s\ *n* -S [ME, fr. MF, fr. L *innocentia*, fr. *innocent-, innocens* innocent + *-ia* -y] **1 a** (1) : freedom from guilt or sin esp. through being unacquainted with evil : purity of heart : BLAMELESSNESS ⟨postulates a state of primitive ~⟩ (2) : CHASTITY ⟨supposed to have not yet lost her ~ —T.B.Macaulay⟩ (3) : the state of being not chargeable for or guilty of a particular crime or offense **b** (1) : freedom from guile or cunning : ARTLESSNESS, SIMPLICITY ⟨the ~ of childhood⟩ (2) : lack of understanding or penetration : SILLINESS, NAÏVETÉ ⟨the ~ . . . to propose remaking the world and human nature —L.O.Coxe⟩ (3) : lack of knowledge : IGNORANCE ⟨written in entire ~ of the Italian language —E.R.Bentley⟩ ⟨full of a chuckling mirth at the ~ of our detractors —Warwick Braithwaite⟩ ⟨~ of the craft of writing —J.W.Aldridge⟩ **2** : one that is innocent; *esp* : an innocent person **3 a** : BLUET 1c(1) **b** : either of two plants: (1) : a small herb (*Collinsia verna*) of the central U.S. (2) : a Californian herb (*C. bicolor*)

in·no·cen·cy \-sənsē, -nsi\ *n* -ES [ME *innocencie*, fr. L *innocentia*] : INNOCENCE; *also* : an innocent action, quality, or thing ⟨associated in my mind with milk and rice and similar *innocencies* of childhood —Elinor Wylie⟩

¹in·no·cent \-sənt\ *n* -S [ME, fr. MF] **1** : an innocent one: as **a** : a person free from or unacquainted with sin; *esp* : a young child **b** *obs* : a person guiltless of a crime charged **c** : a naïve, artless, or unsophisticated person ⟨an ~ and a novice in the ways of the world —Fred Whishaw⟩ **d** : a person who lacks the requisite experience, training, or knowledge : TENDERFOOT ⟨lending a wrench to some ~ who forgot to bring his own —W.L.Worden⟩ **2** [F, short for *herbe de Saint Innocent* Saint Innocent's herb] : BLUET 1c(1) — usu. used in pl.

²innocent \"\ *adj, sometimes* -ER/-EST [ME, fr. MF, adj. & n., fr. L *innocent- innocens*, fr. *in-* ¹in- + *nocent-, nocens* bad, wicked, fr. pres. part. of *nocēre* to harm, hurt — more at NOXIOUS] **1 a** (1) : free from guilt or sin esp. through lack of knowledge of evil : BLAMELESS, PURE, UNTAINTED ⟨an ~ child⟩ (2) : being without evil influence or effect : not arising from evil intention ⟨~ deception⟩ ⟨~ sport⟩ ⟨searching for a hidden motive in even the most ~ conversation —Leonard Wibberley⟩ (3) : reflecting or indicating freedom from guilt or sin : CANDID ⟨a child's trusting ~ eye⟩ ⟨turned on me her ~ gaze⟩ **b** (1) : free from legal guilt or fault ⟨a person ~ of a particular crime⟩ ⟨an ~ agent⟩ : free from an illegality : being without knowledge of circumstances giving notice of a defect in title or of rights existing in third persons ⟨an ~ holder or purchaser for value⟩ : being without intention of evading or circumventing the law (2) : having a lawful character : PERMITTED ⟨a wholly ~ transaction⟩; *specif* : not being contraband ⟨an ~ trade⟩ (3) : lacking or devoid of something : DESTITUTE ⟨~ of any linguistic training —A.F.Hubbell⟩ ⟨her face ~ of cosmetics —Marcia Davenport⟩ ⟨glass still ~ of water and soap —William Faulkner⟩ **2 a** (1) : lacking or reflecting lack of sophistication, guile, or self-consciousness : ARTLESS, INGENUOUS, NAÏVE ⟨a disappointing figure to ~ persons who seek his acquaintance —C.E.Montague⟩ ⟨~ vanity⟩ ⟨what an ~ notion —F.L.Allen⟩ ⟨not ~ . . . but academic and a little self-conscious —Philip Toynbee⟩ (2) : foolishly ignorant or trusting : subject to being duped : SIMPLEMINDED ⟨when it comes to a trade, he is not as ~ as he looks⟩ **b** (1) : not adept in or conversant with something : IGNORANT ⟨almost entirely ~ of Latin —C.L.Wrenn⟩ ⟨the curious but ~ explorer will find himself hopelessly lost —B.R. Redman⟩ (2) : UNSUSPECTING, UNAWARE ⟨perfectly ~ of the confusion he had created —B.R.Haydon⟩ **3** : lacking capacity to injure : INNOCUOUS, HARMLESS ⟨unarmed hands or feet are relatively ~ —Lewis Mumford⟩ ⟨fine ~ weather —John Muir †1914⟩; *specif* : BENIGN 3c ⟨an ~ heart murmur —*Lancet*⟩ — **in·no·cent·ly** *adv* — **in·no·cent·ness** *n* -ES

innocent converter *n* : a person who in good faith believes himself entitled to take and possess a chattel that in fact belongs to another but is nevertheless liable for conversion of the chattel

innocent conveyance *n, early English & American law* : a conveyance of a greater estate than the grantor has that does not produce a forfeiture of an estate in reversion or in remainder

innocent misrepresentation *n* : a representation in good faith reasonably believed true by the one making it but in fact untrue

innocent party *n* : one who has no notice of a fact tainting a litigated transaction with illegality : one not responsible or to blame for a situation which is the basis for relief in court

innocent passage *n* : the right of a foreign ship in grave distress or when overcome by a force majeure to anchor in or stop at a port within the territorial waters of another state without being subject to the general jurisdiction of the latter

innocents' day *n, usu cap I&D* : HOLY INNOCENTS' DAY

in·no·cu·i·ty \,i,nəˈkyüəd·ē\ *n* -ES [prob. fr. F *innocuité*, fr. L *innocuus* + F *-ité* -ity] : the quality or state of being innocuous; *also* : something that is innocuous ⟨conversation will lag and digress politely to *innocuities* —*Plain Talk*⟩

in·noc·u·ous \(ˈ)iˈnäkyəwəs, əˈn-\ *adj* [L *innocuus*, fr. *in-* ¹in- + *-nocuus* (fr. *nocēre* to harm, hurt) — more at NOXIOUS] **1** : producing no ill effect : working no injury : HARMLESS ⟨preliminary tests have proved it to be ~ —*Jour. of Chem. Education*⟩ **2 a** : not likely to arouse animus or give offense : INOFFENSIVE ⟨confined himself to ~ generalities⟩ **b** : not likely to arouse strong feelings : lacking the capacity to excite ⟨elaborate concealment of ~ regions —P.M.Gregory⟩ or move : PALLID, INSIPID, INSIGNIFICANT ⟨a pleasant but ~ suite —Arthur Berger⟩ — **in·noc·u·ous·ly** *adv* — **in·noc·u·ous·ness** *n* -ES

inn of chancery *usu cap I&C* **1** : a house or group of buildings in London formerly used by law students for residence and study but now occupied chiefly by attorneys and solicitors — usu. used with *inn* in pl. **2** : a society occupying an Inn of Chancery — usu. used with *inn* in pl.

inn of court *usu cap I&C* **1** : one of four sets of buildings in London belonging to four societies of students and practicers of the law ⟨Inner Temple, Middle Temple, Lincoln's Inn, and Gray's Inn are the *Inns of Court*⟩ **2** : one of four societies which alone admit to practice at the English bar — usu. used with *inn* in pl.

in·nominable \(ˈ)i(n)ˈnämənəbəl, ə(-\ *adj* [ME, fr. L *innominabilis*, fr. *in-* ¹in- + *nominare* to name + *-abilis* -able — more at NOMINATE] : incapable of being named

in·nominate \(ˈ)iˈnämənət, əˈnä-\ *adj* [LL *innominatus*, fr. L *in-* ¹in- + *nominatus*, past part. of *nominare*] **1 a** : having no name : UNNAMED ⟨there were no fields, as in England, each called by an ancient name; the slender tributaries were often ~ —John Buchan⟩ **b** : having an unknown or unrevealed name : ANONYMOUS ⟨progress . . . made by the accumulated activities of large groups of ~ people —*Times Lit. Supp.*⟩ **2** *Roman & civil law* **a** : of, relating to, or being any of certain classes of contracts that are real but have no special name **b** : of, relating to, or being a commutative contract in any of several categories

innominate artery *n* [trans. of NL *arteria innominata*] : a large artery arising from the arch of the aorta and dividing into the right common carotid and the right subclavian arteries

innominate bone *n* [trans. of NL *os innominatum*] : the large flaring bone that makes a lateral half of the pelvis in mammals and is composed of the ilium, ischium, and pubis which are consolidated into one bone in the adult — called also *hipbone*

innominate vein *n* [trans. of NL *vena innominata*] : a large vein on each side of the lower part of the neck formed by the union of the internal jugular and subclavian veins and in man uniting to form the superior vena cava

in·nom·i·ne \(ˈ)inˈnäməˌnā, -ˌnē, -ˈnōməˌnā\ *n* -S [L *in nomine* (in *in nomine Jesu* in the name of Jesus, the opening words of an introit for which such compositions were orig. written)] : an English polyphonic composition of the 16th and 17th centuries written for an instrumental ensemble (as for viols and keyboard) and using as a cantus firmus a fragment of plainsong from the antiphon for Trinity Sunday

in·no·vant \ˈinəvənt, ˈinōv-\ *adj* [L *innovant-, innovans*, pres. part. of *innovare*] : having innovations (sense 3)

in·no·vate \ˈinəˌvāt, ˈinōv-, *usu* -ād·+V\ *vb* -ED/-ING/-S [L *innovatus*, past part. of *innovare*, fr. *in-* ²in- + *novare* renew, modify, fr. *novus* new — more at NEW] *vt* **1** : to introduce as or as if new ⟨~ a design⟩ **2** *archaic* : to make innovations in : CHANGE ~ *vi* : to introduce novelties : make changes ⟨he is not to ~ at pleasure —B.N.Cardozo⟩

in·no·va·tion \ˌ==ˈvāshən\ *n* -S [prob. fr. MF, fr. LL *innovation-, innovatio*, fr. L *innovatus* + *-ion-, -io* -ion] **1** : the act or an instance of innovating : the introduction of something new ⟨~ as the driving force in practical economic advance —*Times Lit. Supp.*⟩ **2** : something that deviates from established doctrine or practice : something that differs from existing forms : CHANGE, NOVELTY ⟨the technical ~*s* of the agrarian revolution —S.F.Mason⟩ ⟨another ~ is a new straight mile course —*London Calling*⟩ ⟨his most important ~ . . . was the introduction of the seminary method of instruction for advanced students —C.F.Smith⟩ **3 a** : a shoot that arises at or near the apex of the stem of a moss plant usu. after the reproductive organs have completed their development **b** : the formation of such a shoot **4** *Scots law* : an exchange of one obligation for another, the obligor and obligee remaining the same

in·no·va·tion·al \ˌ==ˈvāshənᵊl, -shnəl\ *adj* : of or relating to innovation : tending to innovate ⟨a mind so ~ —John Mason Brown⟩

in·no·va·tive \ˈ==ˌvād·iv\ *adj* : characterized by, tending to, or introducing innovations ⟨~ behavior⟩

in·no·va·tor \-ˌvād·ə(r), -ātə-\ *n* -S [prob. fr. MF *innovateur*, fr. LL *innovator*, fr. L *innovatus* + *-or*] : one that innovates ⟨a theological ~⟩ ⟨~ of a new technique⟩

in·no·va·to·ry \-ˌvəˌtōrē, -ˌvād·ərē\ *adj* : INNOVATIVE

in·noxious \(ˈ)i(n), ə+\ *adj* [L *innoxius*, fr. *in-* ¹in- + *noxius* harmful — more at NOXIOUS] : INNOCUOUS ⟨an ~ substance⟩ — **in·noxiously** \"+\ *adv* — **in·noxiousness** \"+\ *n*

inns *pl of* INN, *pres 3d sing of* INN

inns·bruck \ˈinzˌbrůk, ˈin(t)s,b-\ *adj, usu cap* [fr. *Innsbruck*, Austria] : of or from the city of Innsbruck, Austria : of the kind or style prevalent in Innsbruck

in nu·ce \(ˈ)inˈnü(ˌ)kā\ *adv* [L, in a nut] : in a nutshell ⟨the opening act contains the tragedy *in nuce* —Karl Polanyi⟩

¹in·nu·en·do \ˌinyəˈwen(ˌ)dō\ *adv* [L, by hinting, abl. of *innuendum*, gerund of *innuere* to hint, intimate, fr. *in-* ²in- + *nuere* to nod — more at NUMEN] : in other words : NAMELY — formerly used in legal documents to introduce matter explanatory of the text

²innuendo *also* **inuendo** \"\ *n, pl* **innuendos** *or* **innuendoes** **1** : veiled, oblique, or covert allusion to something not directly named : HINT, INSINUATION ⟨glossy fantasy, stylishness, naughty ~ —*Time*⟩ ⟨a talk punctuated with ~*s* on both sides —J.T.Farrell⟩; *esp* : veiled or equivocal allusion reflecting upon the character, ability, or other trait of the person referred to ⟨try to undermine him by ~ —*Kiplinger Washington Letter*⟩ ⟨how difficult it is to set up a proper defense against ~ —M.S.Watson⟩ ⟨anonymous accusations, rumors, ~*s* —Nathan Schachner⟩ **2** : a parenthetical explanation of the text of a legal document; *esp* : an interpretation in a pleading of expressions alleged to be injurious or libelous

³innuendo *also* **inuendo** \"\ *vb* -ED/-ING/-S [²*innuendo*] *vi* : to make innuendo ~ *vt* : to give effect to by innuendo

in·nu·it *also* **in·u·it** \ˈinyəwət, ˈi,nyüət\ *n, pl* **innuit** *or* **innuits** *also* **inuit** *or* **inuits** *usu cap* [Esk, men, people, Eskimo people, pl. of *innuk, inuk* person, man, Eskimo] **1 a** (1) : the Eskimo people of America as distinguished from the Eskimo people of Asia — compare YUIT (2) : the arctic Eskimo as distinguished from the Aleuts **b** : a member of the Innuit people **2** : the language of the Innuit people

in·nu·mer·a·bil·i·ty \əˌn(y)üm(ə)rəˈbiləd·ē\ *n* -ES [L *innumerabilitas*, fr. *innumerabilis* + *-itas* -ity] : innumerable quality ⟨without any sense of the ~ of the human race —Thornton Wilder⟩

in·nu·mer·a·ble \əˈn(y)üm(ə)rəbəl\ *adj* [ME, fr. L *innumerabilis*, fr. *in-* ¹in- + *numerabilis* numerable — more at NUMERABLE] **1** : too many to be numbered or counted : indefinitely numerous : NUMBERLESS ⟨~ coral reefs and islets —*Americana Annual*⟩ **2** : characterized by vast or countless number ⟨an ~ throng of people⟩ — **in·nu·mer·a·ble·ness** \-nəs\ *n* -ES — **in·nu·mer·a·bly** \-blē, -bli\ *adv*

in·numerous \(ˈ)i(n), ə+\ *adj* [L *innumerus*, fr. *in-* ¹in- + *numerus* number — more at NIMBLE] : NUMBERLESS, INNUMERABLE

in·nutrition \ˌi(n)+\ *n* [¹*in-* + *nutrition*] : lack of nutrition : failure of nourishment

in·nutritious \"+\ *adj* [¹*in-* + *nutritious*] : not nutritious ⟨harsh and ~ fare —*Experiment Station Record*⟩

innyard \ˈ=,=\ *n* : the yard of an inn

ino- — see ³IN-

inobedience *n* [ME, fr. OF & LL; OF, fr. LL *inoboedientia*, fr. *inoboedient-, inoboediens* + L *-ia* -y] *obs* : DISOBEDIENCE

inobedient *adj* [ME, fr. MF & LL; MF, fr. LL *inoboedient-, inoboediens*, fr. L *in-* ¹in- + *oboedient-, oboediens* obedient — more at OBEDIENT] *obs* : DISOBEDIENT

in·obnoxious \ˌin+\ *adj* [¹*in-* + *obnoxious*] : INOFFENSIVE

inobservable *adj* [L *inobservabilis*, fr. *in-* ¹in- + *observabilis* observable — more at OBSERVABLE] *obs* : incapable of being observed

in·observance \ˌin+ *or* **in·observancy** \"+\ *n* [F & L; F *inobservance*, fr. L *inobservantia*, fr. *in-* ¹in- + *observantia* observance — more at OBSERVANCE] **1** : lack of attention : HEEDLESSNESS **2** : failure to observe : NONOBSERVANCE

in·observant \ˌin+\ *adj* [LL *inobservant-, inobservans*, fr. L *in-* ¹in- + *observant-, observans* observant — more at OBSERVANT] : UNOBSERVANT

in·obtrusive \ˌin+\ *adj* [¹*in-* + *obtrusive*] : UNOBTRUSIVE ⟨tried hard to be ~ —L.S.Feuer⟩

in·obvious \(ˈ)in+\ *adj* [¹*in-* + *obvious*] : not obvious

in·occupation \ˌin+\ *n* [¹*in-* + *occupation*] : lack of occupation

ino·cer·a·mus \ˌinōˈserəməs, ˌīn-\ *n, cap* [NL, fr. ³*in-* + Gk *keramos* potter's clay, pottery] : a genus of large filibranchiate bivalve mollusks (suborder Mytilacea) esp. characteristic of the Cretaceous

in·oc·u·la·ble \əˈnäkyələbəl\ *adj* [*inoculate* + *-able*] : susceptible to inoculation : not immune; *also* : transmissible by inoculation

in·oc·u·lant \-lənt\ *n* -S [*inoculate* + *-ant*] : INOCULUM

in·ocular \(ˈ)in, ən+\ *adj* [²*in-* + *ocular*] : inserted in a notch in the corner of the eye ⟨~ antennae⟩

in·oc·u·late \əˈnäkyəˌlāt, *usu* -ād·+V\ *vb* -ED/-ING/-S [ME *inoculaten*, fr. L *inoculare*, fr. *in-* ²in- + *oculus* eye, bud — more at EYE] *vt* **1 a** *archaic* : to insert a bud into or graft (as a tree) by budding **b** : to treat (seeds) with bacteria esp. for the promotion of nitrogen fixation (as in root nodules on legumes) **2 a** (1) : to communicate a disease to (an organism) by inserting its causative agent into the body ⟨12 mice *inoculated* with anthrax⟩ (2) : to introduce microorganisms or viruses onto or into (an organism or substrate) ⟨~ the culture with one loopful of spore suspension⟩ ⟨*inoculated* a rat with bacteria⟩ (3) : to introduce (as microorganisms or immune sera) into or onto a culture medium ⟨~ the spirochetes into blood agar⟩ **b** : SEED 1d **3** : to introduce something into the mind of : IMBUE ⟨*inoculated* them with their own ideas of revolution —Raymond Schuessler⟩ ⟨~ the few who influence the many —*Current Biog.*⟩ ~ *vi* **1** *obs* : to graft by inserting buds **2** : to introduce microorganisms, vaccines, or sera by inoculation **syn** see INFUSE

in·oc·u·la·tion \ə,==ˈlāshən\ *n* -S [L *inoculation-, inoculatio*, fr. *inoculatus* + *-ion-, -io* -ion] : the act, process, or an instance of inoculating: as **a** (1) : the introduction of a microorganism into a suitable medium for its growth ⟨~ of mosaic virus into stocks by aphids⟩; *specif* : the communication of an infective agent (as smallpox virus) to a healthy individual to induce a mild case of disease under optimum conditions and establish lasting immunity (2) : the introduction of a serum or vaccine into a living body to establish immunity to a disease ⟨travelers in the tropics should have typhoid ~*s*⟩ **b** : the introduction of organisms into soil, seed, or water to promote nitrogen fixation or control insect pests or for other purposes **c** : the introduction of a substance into a metallic melt for the purpose of providing additional centers for crystallization **d** : the act or process of imbuing or familiarizing : the fact or an instance of being so imbued or familiarized ⟨getting a weekly or monthly ~ in ways of living and of thinking that were middle-class —F.L.Allen⟩ ⟨~ with alien attitudes and tastes⟩

in·oc·u·la·tive \ə=ˈ==ˌlād·iv\ *adj* : of, relating to, or characterized by inoculation — **in·oc·u·la·tiv·i·ty** \ə,==lə'tivəd·ē\ *n*

in·oc·u·la·tor \-d·ə(r)\ *n* -S [L, one that engrafts, fr. *inoculatus* + *-or*] : one that inoculates

in·oc·u·lum \əˈnäkyələm\ *n, pl* **inocu·la** \-lə\ *or* **inoculums** [NL, fr. L *inoculare*] : material (as spores, bacteria, or contaminated fluids) used in or suitable for use in inoculating or inoculation

ino·des \əˈnō(ˌ)dēz, īˈ-\ *n, cap* [NL, fr. Gk *inōdēs* fibrous, fr. *in-* ³in- + *-ōdēs* -ode] *in some classifications* : a genus of fan palms comprising various arborescent palmettos of the southern U.S., the West Indies, and Mexico that are now usu. included in the genus *Sabal*

inodiate *vt* -ED/-ING/-S [LL *inodiatus*, past part. of *inodiare* — more at ANNOY] *obs* : to make odious or hateful

in·odorous \(ˈ)in, ən+\ *adj* [L *inodorus*, fr. *in-* ¹in- + *odorus* odorous — more at ODOROUS] : emitting no smell : SCENTLESS, ODORLESS

in–off \ˈ=,=\ *n* [fr. the phrase *in off* (*the red ball* or *the white ball*)] : a losing hazard in English billiards

in·offensive \ˌin+\ *adj* [¹*in-* + *offensive*] **1** : causing no harm or injury : UNOFFENDING ⟨an ~ animal⟩ **2 a** : giving no offense or provocation : causing no disturbance : not quarrelsome : PEACEABLE ⟨a quiet, ~ man —Herman Melville⟩ **b** : giving no offense to the senses : not objectionable ⟨a refreshing, ~ . . . stimulant —*Americas*⟩ — **in·of·fen·sive·ly** *adv* — **in·of·fen·sive·ness** *n*

in·official \ˌin+\ *adj* [¹*in-* + *official*] : UNOFFICIAL

in·officious \ˌin+\ *adj* [L *inofficiosus*, fr. *in-* ¹in- + *officiosus* dutiful — more at OFFICIOUS] **1** *obs* : indifferent to obligation or duty **2** : regardless of or contrary to natural duty

inofficious testament *or* **inofficious will** *n* : a will made in violation of natural duty and affection and without just legal cause and depriving children and parents and sometimes others of their legitim of the testator's estate

ino·gen \ˈinəjən, ˈīn-, -ˌjen\ *n* -S [G, fr. *ino-* ³in- + *-gen*] : a hypothetical substance supposed to be continually decomposed and reproduced in the muscles and to serve as an oxygen reserve

in·op·er·a·bil·i·ty \ˌiˌnäp(ə)rəˈbiləd·ē\ *n* : the quality or state of being inoperable

in·operable \(ˈ)in, ən+\ *adj* [prob. fr. F *inopérable*, fr. *in-* ¹in- + *opérable* operable — more at OPERABLE] **1** : not suitable for surgical operation ⟨an advanced and ~ cancer⟩ ⟨a developing cataract still ~⟩ **2** : not operable

in·operative \(ˈ)in, ən+\ *adj* [¹*in-* + *operative*] : not operative or not in operation : not active : producing no effect ⟨the law has become ~⟩ ⟨the quarry has been ~ for some time —L.N.Yedlin⟩ — **inoperativeness** *n*

in·opercular \ˌin+\ *adj* [¹*in-* + *opercular*] : INOPERCULATE

¹in·operculate \ˌin+\ *adj* [¹*in-* + *operculate*] : having no operculum ⟨~ gastropod shells⟩ ⟨~ mosses⟩

²inoperculate \"\ *n* : an inoperculate animal or shell

in·opportune \(ˌ)in, ən+\ *adj* [L *inopportunus*, fr. *in-* ¹in- + *opportunus* opportune — more at OPPORTUNE] : not opportune : UNSEASONABLE, INCONVENIENT ⟨arrive at the most ~ hours —D.R.Murphy⟩ — **in·op·por·tune·ly** \-ünlē\ *adv* — **in·op·por·tune·ness** \-ünnəs\ *n*

in·orb \ən+\ *vt* [²*in-* + *orb* (n.)] : ENSPHERE, ENCIRCLE

in·or·di·na·cy \əˈnȯ(r)dᵊnəsē\ *n* -ES [*inordinate* + *-cy*] *archaic* : the quality, state, or an instance of being inordinate

in·or·di·nance \-ᵊnən(t)s\ *also* **in·or·di·nan·cy** \-nənsē\ *n, pl* **inordinances** *also* **inordinancies** : the quality, state, or an instance of being inordinate

in·ordinary \(ˈ)in, ən+\ *adj* [¹*in-* + *ordinary*] : not ordinary : EXTRAORDINARY

in·or·di·nate \əˈnȯ(r)dᵊnət, *usu* -əd·+V\ *adj* [ME *inordinat*, fr. L *inordinatus*, fr. *in-* ¹in- + *ordinatus*, past part. of *ordinare* to order, arrange — more at ORDAIN] **1** : lacking order : not regulated : DISORDERLY **2** : exceeding in amount, quantity, force, intensity, or scope the ordinary, reasonable, or prescribed limits : EXTRAORDINARY ⟨his ~ desire for approval —Van Wyck Brooks⟩ ⟨~ joviality can atone for an entire lack of ideas —Oscar Wilde⟩ ⟨a book of ~ length⟩ ⟨burns an ~ quantity of gasoline —H.W.Baldwin⟩ **syn** see EXCESSIVE

in·or·di·nate·ly *adv* [ME *inordinatly*, fr. *inordinat* + *-ly*] : in an inordinate manner : to an excessive or unreasonable degree : EXTRAORDINARILY ⟨~ ambitious⟩ ⟨the symphony is ~ long⟩ ⟨~ fond of grasshoppers —C.H.Grandgent⟩

in·or·di·nate·ness *n* -ES : the quality or state of being inordinate : lack of moderation : EXCESS

in·or·di·na·tion \ə,nȯ(r)dᵊnˈāshən\ *n* -S [LL *inordination-, inordinatio*, fr. L *inordinatus* + *-ion-, -io* -ion] *archaic* : INORDINATENESS

¹in·organic \ˌin+(ˌ)ə¦==\ *adj* [¹*in-* + *organic*] **1 a** (1) : being or composed of matter other than plant or animal : MINERAL ⟨the ~ world⟩ (2) : forming or belonging to the inanimate world **b** : being, containing, or relating to a chemical substance or substances not usu. classed as organic ⟨hydrochloric, sulfuric, nitric, and chlorosulfonic acids are called ~ acids —R.E.Kirk⟩ ⟨~ fertilizers⟩ **c** : being in the form of such a substance ⟨~ selenium as in sodium selenite⟩ **2** : not arising from a process of natural or inevitable growth : ARTIFICIAL ⟨an ~ and unnatural lingo never spoken by man —Kenneth Rexroth⟩ : lacking organic structure, character, or vitality ⟨dull ~ things, without individuality or prestige —John Buchan⟩ **3** *of a sound or letter* : lacking an etymological justification — **in·organically** \"+\ *adv*

²inorganic \"\ *n* : an inorganic substance

inorganical *adj* [¹*in-* + *organical*] *obs* : INORGANIC

inorganic chemistry *n* : a branch of chemistry that deals with chemical elements and their compounds excluding hydrocarbons and their derivatives but usu. or often including carbides and other relatively simple carbon compounds esp. some carbon-oxygen and carbon-sulfur compounds (as the oxides of carbon, metallic carbonates, and carbon disulfide) and some carbon-nitrogen compounds (as hydrogen cyanide and metallic cyanides) — compare ORGANIC CHEMISTRY

in·organization \ˌin+\ *n* [¹*in-* + *organization*] : lack of organization

in·organized \(ˈ)in, ən+\ *adj* [¹*in-* + *organized*] : lacking organization

in·ornate \ˌin+(ˌ)ə¦=\ *adj* [L *inornatus*, fr. *in-* ¹in- + *ornatus* adorned — more at ORNATE] : lacking adornment : UNADORNED ⟨the scrupulously ~ clergyman than which nothing could be less liable to suspicion —E.A.Poe⟩

in·osculate \ən+\ *vb* -ED/-ING/-S [²*in-* + *osculate*] : to unite by apposition or contact : unite or join so as to become or make as if one : BLEND ⟨efforts to ~ past and present —R.M. Wendlinger⟩

in·osculation \ən+\n [²in- + osculation] **:** the act, process, or an instance of inosculating; *specif* **:** ANASTOMOSIS
ino·silicate \ˌinō, ˈinō+\ n [³in- + silicate] **:** a class of polymeric silicates in which the silicon-oxygen tetrahedral groups share half of their oxygen atoms so as to form straight chains of indefinite length; *also* **:** a member of this class — called also *metasilicate;* compare CYCLOSILICATE, NESOSILICATE, PHYLLOSILICATE, SOROSILICATE, TECTOSILICATE
ino·sine \ˈinəˌsēn, ˈīn-, -ˌsən\ n -s [ISV *inos-* (fr. Gk *inos*, gen. of *is* sinew, tendon) + *-ine* — more at WITHY] **:** a crystalline nucleoside $C_{10}H_{12}N_4O_5$ formed by partial hydrolysis of inosinic acid or by deamination of adenosine and yielding hypoxanthine and ribose on hydrolysis
ino·sin·ic acid \ˌ≈≈ˈsinik-\ n [part trans. of G *inosinsäure*, fr. *inosin* inosine + *säure* acid] **:** an amorphous nucleotide $C_{10}H_{13}N_4O_8P$ that is found in muscle and is formed by deamination of adenylic acid and that yields hypoxanthine, ribose, and phosphoric acid on hydrolysis
ino·si·tol \əˈnōsəˌtōl, ī'-, -ˌtōl\ n -s [ISV *inosite* inositol (fr. Gk *inos* + ISV *-ite*) + *-ol*] **:** any of nine crystalline stereoisomeric cyclic hexahydroxy alcohols $C_6H_6(OH)_6$; cyclohexane-hexol: as **a :** an optically inactive alcohol that is a component of the vitamin B complex and a lipotropic agent, that occurs widely in plants usu. combined in the form of phytic acid, in microorganisms, and in higher animals and man esp. in vital organs and tissues (as the heart and brain) and often combined in the form of phosphatides, that is obtained chiefly from corn steepwater, and that is used in medicine — called also *i-inositol, meso-inositol, myoinositol* **b :** a sweet dextrorotatory alcohol occurring esp. in the form of its methyl ether pinitol — called also *dextro-inositol* **c :** a sweet levorotatory alcohol occurring esp. in the form of its methyl ether quebrachitol — called also *levo-inositol* **d :** SCYLLITOL
ino·trop·ic \ˌinəˈträpik, ˌīn-\ adj [ISV ³in- + -tropic] **:** influencing muscular contractility — **inot·ro·pism** \əˈnä·trə-ˌpizəm, ī'-\ n -s
in ovo \iˈnō(ˌ)vō\ adv [L] **:** in the egg **:** in embryo
in·oxidizable \(ˈ)in+\ adj [¹in- + oxidizable] **:** not capable of being oxidized
in·paint \ən+\ vt [²in + paint] **:** to repair or restore (a painting) by repainting obliterated areas
in pais \-ˈpā\ adv [pais fr. MF *pais, pays* country — more at PAYSAGE] **:** in the country as distinguished from in court
in pa·ri causa \-ˈpärē-\ adv [LL, in a like case] **:** in a case where all parties stand equal in right according to law
in pari de·lic·to \-dəˈlik(ˌ)tō\ adv [L, in a like offense] **:** in equal fault or wrong — used of parties in a legal case
in pari ma·te·ria \-məˈtirēə\ adv [LL, in a like matter] **:** on the same subject or matter **:** in a similar case ⟨there is virtually nothing of known date *in pari materia* with which it can be compared —*Times Lit. Supp.*⟩
in par·ti·bus in·fi·de·li·um \(ˌ)inˈpärd·əbəˌsinfəˈdālēəm\ *also* **in partibus** adv [ML, lit., in the regions of infidels] **:** in ideologically hostile or unsympathetic surroundings ⟨made himself missionary *in partibus infidelium* for American philosophic naturalism —J.H.Randall⟩
in par·vo \-ˈpär(ˌ)vō\ adv [L] **:** in little **:** in miniature ⟨the reflection, *in parvo*, of the defects of the larger whole —Sonya Forthal⟩
inpatient \ˈ≈ˌ≈≈\ n [⁴in + patient] **:** a patient in a hospital or infirmary who receives lodging and food as well as treatment — distinguished from *outpatient*
in pa·tri·mo·nio \-ˌpa·trəˈmōnēˌō\ adv [L, lit., within inheritance] **:** IN COMMERCIO
inpayment \ˈ≈ˌ≈≈\ n [⁴in + payment] **1 :** the act or an instance of paying in **2 :** a payment to — contrasted with *outpayment*
in pec·to·re \-ˈpektəˌrē\ adv [L, lit., in the breast] **:** in secret ⟨must hold their names *in pectore* —Thomas Barbour⟩
in per·pe·tu·um \-pə(r)ˈpechəwəm\ adv [L] **:** in perpetuity **:** FOREVER ⟨left certain royalties to the home *in perpetuum* —Joseph Wechsberg⟩
in per·so·nam \-pə(r)ˈsōˌnam\ adv (or adj) [L, against a person] **:** against a particular person for the purpose of imposing upon him a personal liability, debt, or obligation to do or not to do a designated act ⟨proceedings and judgments are *in personam* where the court or tribunal has jurisdiction over the defendant and power to enforce obedience against him personally⟩ — compare IN REM
in pet·to \-ˈped·(ˌ)ō\ adv (or adj) [It, lit., in breast; prob. trans. of L *in pectore*] **1 :** in private **:** SECRETLY — used esp. of a cardinal appointed by the pope but not named in consistory **2** [influenced in meaning by E *petty*] **:** in miniature **:** on a small scale ⟨an epic *in petto* —Louis Untermeyer⟩
inphase \ˈ≈ˌ≈\ adj [fr. the phrase *in phase*] **:** being of the same electrical phase
inphase component n **:** the active component of an alternating current in a reactive circuit
in-pig \≈ˈ≈\ adj [fr. the phrase *in pig*] *of a sow* **:** PREGNANT
in-plant \ˈ≈ˌ≈\ adj [fr. the phrase *in plant*] **:** carried on, occurring within, or restricted to the confines of a manufacturing establishment or factory ⟨*in-plant* training programs⟩ ⟨the *in-plant* medical director⟩
in·polygon \ˈin+ˌ-\ n [⁴in + polygon] **:** an inscribed polygon
in·polyhedron \"+ˌ-\ n [⁴in + polyhedron] **:** an inscribed polyhedron

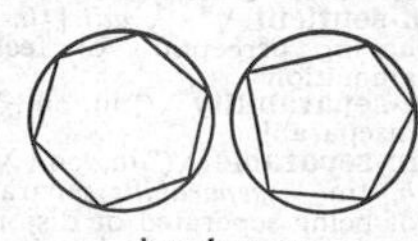
inpolygons

in pos·se \-ˈpäsē\ adv (or adj) [ML] **:** in possibility or capacity **:** not in actuality ⟨contains within itself, *in posse*, implicitly, ideally, the entire logico-dialectical process —Frank Thilly⟩ **:** POTENTIALLY — contrasted with *in esse*
¹inpour \ˈ≈ˌ≈\ n [⁴in + pour (after *pour in*, v.)] **:** a pouring in **:** INRUSH ⟨the ~ of tumultuous Irish immigrants —Helen Sullivan⟩
²in·pour \(ˈ)≈ˈ≈\ vi **:** to pour in ⟨goods and money *inpoured* —J.J.Mallon⟩
inpouring \ˈ≈ˌ≈≈\ n -s [⁴in + pouring (after *pour in*, v.)] **:** INPOUR ⟨viewed the ~ of bedraggled foreigners with alarm —A.D.Graeff⟩
in-print \ˈ≈ˌ≈\ n [fr. the phrase *in print*] **:** a title that is in print
in-process \ən+\ adj [fr. the phrase *in process*] **:** being worked on in manufacture in distinction from raw materials and from finished products
in pro·pria per·so·na \ənˈprōprēəpə(r)ˈsōnə\ adv [L] **:** in one's own person **:** without the assistance of an attorney **:** PERSONALLY
in·put \ˈinˌpu̇t, *usu* -ûd·+V\ *also* **im·put** \ˈim,-\ n [*input* fr. ⁴in + put (after *put in*, v.); *imput* alter. of *input*] **1 :** something that is put in: as **a** *chiefly Scot* **:** a contribution of money **b :** an amount put in ⟨increase the ~ of fertilizer⟩ **c :** power or energy put into a machine or system for storage (as into a storage battery) or for conversion in kind (as into a mechanically driven electric generator or a radio receiver) or conversion of characteristics (as into a transformer or electronic amplifier) usu. with the intent of sizable recovery in the form of output **d :** a component of production (as land, labor, or materials) ⟨~*s* such as seed, twine, ginning fees, and containers —D.G.Johnson⟩ **e :** data or similar information fed into a computer or accounting machine **2 a :** the point at which an input (as of energy, material, or data) is made **b :** the method or equipment used in making an input **3 :** the act, process, or an instance of putting in ⟨requires a continuous ~ of energy both for maintenance and for propagation —G.A.Bartholomew & J.B.Birdsell⟩
input well n **:** INJECTION WELL
in querpo *var of* IN CUERPO
in·quest \ˈinˌkwest\ n [ME *enquest, inquest*, fr. OF *enqueste*, fr. fem. of (assumed) *enquest*, fr. (assumed) VL *inquaestus*, past part. of *inquaerere* to inquire — more at INQUIRE] **1 a :** a judicial or official inquiry or examination esp. before a jury ⟨a coroner's ~⟩ ⟨an ~ to fix damages⟩ **b :** a body of men esp. a jury assembled to hold such an inquiry **c :** the finding of the jury upon such inquiry or the document recording it **2 :** INQUIRY, INVESTIGATION ⟨a two-year ~ into the conduct of the executive —W.E.Binkley⟩ **syn** see INQUIRY
inquest of office : an inquiry made by authority or direction of the proper officer into matters (as escheat of lands) affecting the rights and interests of the crown or of the state
in·quiet \ən+\ vt [ME *inquieten*, fr. MF *inquieter*, fr. L *inquietare*, fr. *inquietus* restless, unquiet, fr. *in-* ¹in- + *quietus* quiet — more at QUIET] *archaic* **:** to disturb the peace of **:** DISQUIET
in·qui·e·ta·tion \(ˌ)inˌkwīəˈtāshən\ n -s [ME, fr. MF, fr. L *inquietation-, inquietatio*, fr. *inquietatus* (past part. of *inquietare*) + *-ion-, -io* -ion] *archaic* **:** DISTURBANCE
in·quietude \(ˈ)in, ən+\ n [ME, fr. MF or LL; MF, fr. LL *inquietudo*, fr. L *inquietus* (fr. *in-* ¹in- + *quietus* quiet) + *-tudo* -tude — more at QUIET] **1 :** disturbed state **:** UNEASINESS, RESTLESSNESS, DISQUIETUDE ⟨the dreadful ~ that comes before a surgical operation —Arnold Bennett⟩ **2 :** a disquieting or anxious thought ⟨occupied by a thousand ~*s* —Sir Walter Scott⟩
¹in·qui·line \ˈinkwəˌlīn, ˈiŋk-, -ˌlən\ n -s [L *inquilinus* tenant, lodger, fr. *in-* ²in- + *-quilinus* (fr. the stem of *colere* to cultivate, dwell) — more at WHEEL] **:** an animal that lives habitually in the nest or abode of some other species (as the burrowing owl in prairie dog colonies or any of several beetles and flies that live with social insects) — **in·qui·lin·ism** \-ˌlə̇ˌnizəm\ n -s — **in·qui·lin·i·ty** \ˌ≈≈ˈlinəd·ē\ n -ES — **in·qui·li·nous** \ˌ≈≈ˈlīnəs\ adj
²inquiline \"\ adj **:** having the character of an inquiline
in·qui·li·no \ˌēŋkēˈlē(ˌ)nō\ n -s [AmerSp, fr. Sp, tenant, lodger, fr. L *inquilinus*] **:** a worker on a Chilean landed estate who is usu. given the use of a small plot of land, implements, seed, and a small wage in return for his labor
in·qui·nate \ˈinkwəˌnāt\ vt -ED/-ING/-S [L *inquinatus*, past part. of *inquinare*, fr. *in-* ²in- + *-quinare* (akin to L *caenum* filth, ordure) — more at OBSCENE] **:** DEFILE, CORRUPT — **in·qui·na·tion** \ˌ≈≈ˈnāshən\ n -s
in·quir·able \ənˈkwīrəbəl\ adj [ME *enquirable*, fr. *enquiren* + *-able*] *archaic* **:** capable of being inquired into **:** subject or liable to inquiry
in·quire *also* **en·quire** \ənˈkwī(ə)r, -īə\ vb -ED/-ING/-S [ME *enquiren, inqueren, inquiren*, alter. (influenced by L *inquirere* to inquire) of *enqueren*, fr. OF *enquerre*, fr. (assumed) VL *inquaerere*, alter. (influenced by L *quaerere* to seek, ask) of L *inquirere*, fr. *in-* ²in- + *-quirere* (fr. *quaerere*)] vt **1 :** to ask about or ask **:** seek to know by asking or questioning ⟨some kindred spirit shall ~ thy fate —Thomas Gray⟩ ⟨*inquired* the way to the station⟩ ⟨*inquired* what the weather was likely to be⟩ **2 a :** to search or search into **:** INVESTIGATE, EXAMINE ⟨failed to ~ the limits of what can be said —Allen Tate⟩ **b** *archaic* **:** to search or ask for — often used with *out* **c** *obs* **:** INTERROGATE, QUESTION ~ vi **1 :** to put a question **:** seek for truth or information by questioning **:** ASK ⟨*inquired* about the horses —*Amer. Guide Series: La.*⟩ **2 :** to make investigation or inquiry **:** engage in study or scrutiny — often used with *into* ⟨their right to ~ into the activities of the teachers⟩ ⟨~ briefly into the effect that comes from the combination of phrases —E.K.Brown⟩ **syn** see ASK — **inquire after :** to ask about the health or well-being of ⟨the parents of the boys he played with always *inquired after* his father and mother —Scott Fitzgerald⟩
in·qui·ren·do \ˌinkwəˈren(ˌ)dō\ n -s [L, by inquiring, ablative of *inquirendum*, gerund of *inquirere* to inquire] **:** an inquiry or an authority to conduct an inquiry
in·quir·er \ənˈkwīrə(r)\ n -s **:** one that inquires **:** QUESTIONER
inquiring adj **1 :** given to inquiry **:** INVESTIGATIVE ⟨an ~ mind⟩ **2 :** appearing to inquire **:** INQUISITIVE ⟨rolled ~ eyes toward my father —Kenneth Roberts⟩ ⟨~ looks⟩ — **in·quir·ing·ly** adv
in·quiry *also* **en·quiry** \ˈinˌkwī(ə)rē, ənˈkwī|, ˈinkwəl, -ri *sometimes* ˈiŋkwəl *or* ˈinˌkwi|\ n -ES [alter. of ME *enquery*, fr. *enqueren* + *-y*] **1 :** the act or an instance of seeking truth, information, or knowledge about something **:** examination into facts or principles **:** RESEARCH, INVESTIGATION ⟨complete freedom of ~⟩ ⟨the scientific method of ~ —C.W.Eliot⟩ ⟨that most modern of *inquiries*, the study of the cosmic rays —K.K.Darrow⟩ ⟨an ~ into the nature of truth⟩; *specif* **:** a formal or official investigation of a matter of public interest by a body (as a legislative committee) with power to compel testimony ⟨witnesses convicted of contempt of congressional *inquiries* —*Current Biog.*⟩ **2 :** the act or an instance of asking for information **:** a request for information **:** QUERY, QUESTION ⟨upon ~, I learned that he was out⟩ ⟨the information desk receives many *inquiries*⟩ ⟨would not answer my ~⟩
syn INQUISITION, INVESTIGATION, INQUEST, PROBE, RESEARCH: INQUIRY is a general term applicable to any quest for truth, knowledge, or information ⟨make *inquiries* about a prospective employee⟩ ⟨they made *inquiries*, and learned that Wild Bill was then in the Mint saloon —S.H.Holbrook⟩ ⟨a letter of *inquiry* to the authorities⟩ ⟨the True, which is the goal of all scientific and all philosophical *inquiry* —W.R.Inge⟩ INQUISITION suggests a sustained search, thorough and often unrelenting, for hidden facts; it may apply to merciless unremitting volleys of questions ⟨an *inquisition* into the bankruptcy proceedings⟩ ⟨the investigating committee subjecting him to a long *inquisition*⟩ INVESTIGATION may apply to a sustained and systematic inquiry, esp. of some specific proceeding ⟨an auditor *investigation* of the reported shortages⟩ ⟨the conduct of men in important areas may often be very legitimately subject to properly conducted Congressional *investigation* —Norman Thomas⟩ ⟨by their bullying tactics, by their having turned needed *investigations* into regrettable *inquisitions* —John Mason Brown⟩ INQUEST, once in more general use as a close synonym for INQUIRY, now usu. applies to an investigation, often by a coroner and his jury, into a cause of death or to a similar investigation into something disastrous or troubling ⟨it turned out on a final *inquest* that the learned lecturer had translated his piece into English —H.J.Laski⟩ ⟨it was decided at the *inquest* that the deceased had committed suicide⟩ ⟨an *inquest* on the fall of Singapore and the sinking of H.M.S. *Repulse* and H.M.S. *Prince of Wales* —*New Yorker*⟩ PROBE, in this sense, may apply to any deep, painstaking inquiry to discover something wrong or improper ⟨a *probe* resulting in the disbarring of several attorneys⟩ ⟨a *probe* into improper tax refunds⟩ RESEARCH applies to careful, prolonged study, esp. to uncover new knowledge ⟨*research* has shown and practice has established the futility of the charge that it was a usurpation when this Court undertook to declare an Act of Congress unconstitutional —O.W.Holmes †1935⟩ ⟨the *researches* . . . in the 17th century into the theory of probabilities greatly advanced the accuracy of calculations —*Encyc. Americana*⟩
inquiry agent n, *Brit* **:** a private detective
in·quis·ite \ənˈkwizə̇t\ vb -ED/-ING/-S [L *inquisitus*, past part. of *inquirere* to inquire — more at INQUIRE] **1 :** to subject to inquisition; inquire into **:** INVESTIGATE, QUESTION ⟨people can stand only a short amount of *inquisiting* —G.P.Wilson⟩ **2** *obs* **:** INQUISITION
¹in·qui·si·tion \ˌinkwəˈzishən\ n -s [ME *inquisicioun*, fr. MF *inquisition*, fr. L *inquisition-, inquisitio*, fr. *inquisitus* (past part. of *inquirere* to inquire) + *-ion-, -io* -ion] **1 :** the act or an instance of inquiring **:** INQUIRY, SEARCH, EXAMINATION, INVESTIGATION ⟨nominated himself for this delicate ~ —S.H. Adams⟩ ⟨proposed a brief ~ into the politics of the place —John Buchan⟩ **2 :** a judicial or official inquiry or examination usu. before a jury (as for ascertaining taxable property or for fixing the guilt of nuisances); *also* **:** the finding of such a jury or the document on which it is recorded **3** [ML *inquisition-, inquisitio*, fr. L] **a** *usu cap* **:** a Roman Catholic ecclesiastical tribunal esp. of medieval times and the early modern period having as its primary objective the discovery, punishment, and prevention of heresy; *specif* **:** an ecclesiastical tribunal set up in Spain under state control in 1478–80 with the object of proceeding against lapsed converts from Judaism, crypto-Jews, and other apostates that was marked by the extreme severity of its proceedings **b :** an official inquiry or investigation conducted with little or no regard for individual rights or characterized by undue harshness, bias, or hostility on the examiner's part ⟨his ~*s* were backed by the authority of the United States government —Elmer Davis⟩ ⟨the whole notion of loyalty ~*s* is a natural characteristic of the police state —*New Republic*⟩ **c :** a severe or searching questioning **:** the ordeal of such a questioning **:** GRILLING ⟨pushed toward the edge by the ~*s* of the psychiatrists —*Time*⟩ ⟨muddling my way . . . through these ~*s* —Adrian Bell⟩ **syn** see INQUIRY
²inquisition \"\ vb -ED/-ING/-S vt **:** to make inquisition or inquiry ~ vt **:** to subject to inquisitional examination
in·qui·si·tion·al \ˌ≈≈ˈzishənᵊl, -shnəl\ adj **:** relating to, characteristic of, or resembling an inquisition ⟨the ~ system that seeks a confession, by physical or moral torture —Janet Flanner⟩ ⟨an ~ tribunal⟩
¹in·quis·i·tive \ənˈkwizəd·iv, -ətˌ|\ adj [ME *inquisitif*, fr. MF, fr. LL *inquisitivus*, fr. L *inquisitus* + *-ivus* -ive] **1 :** given to examination, investigation, or research ⟨be curious, attentive, ~ as to everything —Earl of Chesterfield⟩ **2 a :** disposed to ask questions out of curiosity ⟨if somebody saw a citizen climbing a street sign they might get ~ —Bant Singer⟩; *esp* **:** inordinately or improperly curious about the affairs of another **:** PRYING ⟨I mustn't be ~ and ask questions —W.F.De Morgan⟩ ⟨she was a bit ~, as girls are —Dorothy Sayers⟩ **b :** reflecting or indicating curiosity esp. about the affairs of another ⟨his ~ face beamed with mischief —Dorothy Sayers⟩ ⟨with bright, ~ eyes —Claudia Cassidy⟩ **syn** see CURIOUS
²inquisitive \"\ n -s **:** an inquisitive person ⟨visible to such ~*s* as myself —William Sansom⟩
in·quis·i·tive·ly \|əvlē, -li\ adv **:** in an inquisitive manner
in·quis·i·tive·ness \|ivnə̇s\ n -ES **:** the quality or state of being inquisitive
in·quis·i·tor \ənˈkwizəd·ə(r), -ətə-\ n -s [MF & L; MF *inquisiteur*, fr. L *inquisitor*, fr. *inquisitus* + *-or*] **1 a :** INQUIRER, INVESTIGATOR, QUESTIONER ⟨I am come as an ~ . . . to ask you certain questions —Max Peacock⟩ **b :** a person (as a coroner or sheriff) whose official duty it is to examine and inquire **2** [ML, fr. L] **a :** a member or officer of an Inquisition **b :** a person who conducts an official inquiry or investigation with little or no regard for individual rights or with undue harshness, bias, or severity ⟨bare his entire life and personality to official ~*s* under pain of dismissal —E.A. Mowrer⟩
in·quis·i·to·ri·al \(ˌ)inˌkwizəˈtōrēəl, -ˈtȯr-\ adj **1 a :** of or relating to an ecclesiastical inquisitor **:** having the functions of such an inquisitor ⟨with royal and ~ authorities on the watch for him —G.C.Boyce⟩ **b :** like or typical of an ecclesiastical inquisitor: as (1) **:** heedless of or flouting individual rights in seeking information or enforcing conformity (2) **:** marked by extreme harshness or cruelty ⟨a practical police force with true ~ talents —Waldo Frank⟩ ⟨beyond discovery by the most ~ and powerful methods —J.M.Keynes⟩ **c :** offensively searching or importunate in inquiry **:** PRYING ⟨felt the press ~ to the point of antagonism —*N.Y. Times*⟩ ⟨questioned them in his ~ way —Carleton Beals⟩ **2 :** constituting or relating to a system of criminal procedure in which the judge also acts as prosecutor or in which the proceedings are secretly conducted and the accused must answer questions **3 :** relating to or having the authority to conduct official investigations ⟨the ~ power of the Senate is . . . of the highest importance —Lindsay Rogers⟩ ⟨an ~ agency⟩ — contrasted with *accusatorial* — **in·quis·i·to·ri·al·ly** \-əlē, -li\ adv — **in·quis·i·to·ri·al·ness** n -ES
in·quis·i·tory \ənˈkwizəˌtōrē\ adj [ML *inquisitorius*, fr. *inquisitor*] **:** INQUISITORIAL, SEARCHING ⟨held to a high, persistent, ~ note —Scott Fitzgerald⟩
inquisitous adj [L *inquisitus*, past part.] *obs* **:** INQUISITIVE
in·quis·i·tress \-zə·trə̇s\ n -ES [*inquisitor* + *-ess*] **:** a female inquisitor
inradius \ˈ≈ˌ≈≈≈\ n [⁴in + radius] **:** a radius of an inscribed circle or sphere — opposed to *exradius*
¹in re \-ˈrā, -ˈrē\ *or* **in re·bus** \-ˈrābəs, -ˈrēb-\ adv [*in re* fr. L, in the thing; *in rebus* fr. L, in the things] **1 :** in the individual **:** in the particular existing thing ⟨many metaphysicians hold that universals exist *in re*⟩ — see AVICENNISM; compare REALISM **2 :** in something existing outside the mind **3 :** in the real world
²in re prep [L] **:** in the matter of **:** CONCERNING, RE — often used in the title or name of a case where the proceeding is in rem or quasi in rem and not in personam (as in a matter involving a probate or bankrupt estate, a guardianship, or an application for laying out a public highway) and occasionally in the title or name of an ex parte proceeding (as in an application for a writ of habeas corpus)
in rem \-ˈrem\ adv (or adj) [LL] **:** against or with respect to a thing (as a right, status, or title to property) without reference to the persons involved ⟨the court acted *in rem*⟩ ⟨an *in rem* proceeding⟩ ⟨a judgment *in rem*⟩ — compare IN PERSONAM, QUASI IN REM
in req *abbr* information requested
in re·rum na·tu·ra \-ˈrārəmnəˈtu̇rə, -ˈrēr-\ adv [L] **:** in the nature of things in the world of nature as distinguished from the world of human beings **:** in the realm of material things ⟨they do not signify anything *in rerum natura* —R.F.McRae⟩
¹inring \ˈ≈ˌ≈\ n [⁴in + ring] **:** INWICK
²in·ring \ən+\ vi **:** INWICK
¹inroad \ˈ≈ˌ≈\ n [⁴in + road] **1 :** a sudden hostile incursion or forcible entrance **:** RAID, FORAY ⟨protecting their crops of barley from the ~*s* of sparrows —J.G.Frazer⟩ ⟨their new homes would be reserved to them against future ~*s* by whites —P.W.Gates⟩ **2 :** an advance or penetration esp. at the expense of something or someone **:** a serious encroachment ⟨another sharp ~ on the principle of free speech —*Civil Liberties*⟩ ⟨the ~*s* of the conformist spirit on American literary life —C.J.Rolo⟩ ⟨make ~*s* on the domestic markets of their local competitors —Patrick McMahon⟩ ⟨synthetic materials made deep ~*s* into the use of leather —J.F.W. Anderson⟩
²in·road \ən+\ vb -ED/-ING/-S vt **:** to make an inroad into ~ vi **:** to make inroads
in·roll \ənˈrōl\ *archaic var of* ENROLL
inrooted \ˈ≈ˌ≈≈\ adj [²in + rooted] **:** deeply rooted ⟨the ~ American philosophy of competition —William Best⟩
inrun \ˈ≈ˌ≈\ n [⁴in + run] **:** an inclined trestle down which a ski jumper moves prior to the takeoff
in·rup·tion \ənˈrəpshən\ n -s [by alter.] **:** IRRUPTION
inrush \ˈ≈ˌ≈\ n [⁴in + rush (after *rush in*, v.)] **:** the action or an instance of rushing or pouring in **:** INFLUX ⟨an ~ of cool maritime air —*Farmer's Weekly (So. Africa)*⟩
inrushing \ˈ≈ˌ≈≈\ adj [⁴in + rushing (after *rush in*, v.)] **:** rushing in ⟨the ~ immigrant masses —D.W.Brogan⟩
ins *pl of* IN, *pres 3d sing of* IN
-ins *pl of* -IN
ins *abbr* **1** inscribed **2** inside **3** inspected; inspector **4** insular **5** insulated; insulation **6** insurance
in·salivate \ən+\ vt [²in- + salivate] **:** to mix (food) with saliva by mastication — **in·salivation** \"+\ n
in·salubrious \ˌin+\ adj [L *insalubris*, fr. *in-* ¹in- + *salubris* healthful + E *-ous* — more at SALUBRIOUS] **:** tending to impair health **:** UNWHOLESOME, NOXIOUS ⟨an ~ environment⟩
in·salubrity \ˌin+\ n [F *insalubrité*, fr. MF, fr. *insalubre* insalubrious (fr. L *insalubris*) + *-ité* -ity] **:** unhealthfulness or unwholesomeness esp. of climate
in·salutary \(ˈ)in, ən+\ adj [LL *insalutaris*, fr. L *in-* ¹in- + *salutaris* salutary] **:** not healthful or wholesome ⟨a thoroughly ~ outlook on life⟩
in·san·able \(ˈ)inˌsanəbəl, ənˈs-\ adj [L *insanabilis*, fr. *in-* ¹in- + *sanabilis* curable — more at SANABLE] **:** INCURABLE, IRREMEDIABLE
ins and outs n pl **1 :** physical twists and turns or windings and uncertainties (as of a road) ⟨knows all the *ins and outs* of the short way to the camp⟩ **2 :** characteristic peculiarities or technicalities ⟨had to learn the *ins and outs* of the new plane⟩ **:** RAMIFICATIONS ⟨the *ins and outs* of a mathematical theory⟩
in·sane \(ˈ)inˈsān, ənˈs-\ adj, *sometimes* -ER/-EST [L *insanus*, fr. *in-* ¹in- + *sanus* sane] **1 a** *obs, of the mind* **:** UNSOUND, DISORDERED **b** *of a person* **:** exhibiting unsoundness or disorder of mind **:** affected with insanity **:** MAD; *esp* **:** disordered in mind to such a degree as to be unable to function safely and competently in ordinary human relations — compare PSYCHOTIC **2** *obs* **:** causing insanity **3 :** used by, typical of, or for insane persons ⟨an ~ hospital⟩ ⟨~ ravings⟩ **4 :** utterly foolish or ridiculous **:** lacking any logical or practical basis **:** wildly visionary ⟨a perfectly ~ idea⟩ ⟨such ~ extravagance⟩ ⟨the *insanest* thing you ever saw⟩ — **in·sane·ness** \-ˈānnə̇s\ n
in·sane·ly adv **:** in an insane manner ⟨behaved ~⟩ **:** to an

insane degree : beyond the bounds of reason ⟨~ jealous⟩ : ABSURDLY, RIDICULOUSLY ⟨~ extravagant⟩

insane root *n* **1** : a root believed in medieval times to cause madness in those eating it and usu. identified with either henbane or hemlock **2** : HENBANE 1a

in·san·i·tar·i·ness \(ˈ)in¦sanəˌterēnə̇s, ən's-, -rin-\ *n* -ES : the quality or state of being insanitary

in·sanitary \(ˈ)in, ən+\ *adj* [¹*in-* + *sanitary*] : deficient in sanitation : unclean to such a degree as to be injurious to health : CONTAMINATED, FILTHY, UNHEALTHY ⟨working in ~ surroundings⟩ ⟨~ storage of food⟩

in·sanitation \(ˌ)in, ən+\ *n* [¹*in-* + *sanitation*] : lack of sanitation : careless or dangerous hygienic conditions

in·san·i·ty \ə̇n'sanəd·ē, -ətē, -i\ *n* [L *insanitas*, fr. *insanus* insane + *-itas* -ity] **1 a** : the state of being insane : unsoundness or derangement of the mind usu. occurring as a specific disorder (as schizophrenia or dementia praecox) and usu. excluding such states as mental deficiency, the psychoneuroses, and various character disorders **b** : a mental disorder ⟨dementia praecox is one of the commoner *insanities*⟩ **2** : such unsoundness of mind or lack of understanding as prevents one from having the mental capacity required by law to enter into a particular relationship, status, or transaction or as excuses one from criminal or civil responsibility **3 a** : extreme folly or unreasonableness ⟨the ~ of war⟩ **b** : something utterly foolish or unreasonable ⟨the *insanities* of daily life⟩

syn LUNACY, PSYCHOSIS, MANIA, DEMENTIA: INSANITY, more commonly used in law than in medicine, applies to any mental disorder of such severity as to render the person unfit to manage his own affairs or to enjoy his liberty because of the unreliability of his behavior that makes him a danger to himself and to others. LUNACY, a term legally interchangeable with insanity, popularly implies periodic mental disorder or alternating madness and lucidity. PSYCHOSIS is the technical psychiatric term for any far-reaching and prolonged behavior disorder (as dementia praecox or manic-depressive psychosis). MANIA is a phase of a mental disorder (as manic-depressive psychosis) marked by a mood of sustained and exaggerated elation, emotional expansiveness, overtalkativeness, excessive physical activity, or delusions of greatness, that characterizes any of several psychoses. DEMENTIA is the technical psychiatric term that denotes mental deterioration that is psychogenic in origin (as dementia praecox) or that results from disease that damages the brain substance (as neurosyphilis or arteriosclerosis)

in·sa·tia·bil·i·ty \(ˌ)inˌsāshə¦biləd·ē, ənˌ=ˈ===, -lətē, -i *sometimes* -shēə-\ *n* [prob. fr. F or LL; F *insatiabilité*, fr. MF, fr. LL *insatiabilitas*, fr. L *insatiabilis* insatiable + *-itas* -ity] : the quality or state of being insatiable

in·sa·tia·ble \(ˈ)in¦sāshəbəl, ən's-, *sometimes* -shēə-\ *adj* [ME *insaciable*, *insessiabyll*, fr. MF or L; MF *insaciable*, fr. OF, fr. L *insatiabilis*, fr. *in-* ¹in- + *satiare* to satisfy + *-abilis* -able — more at SATIATE] : incapable of being satisfied or appeased ⟨an ~ desire for knowledge⟩ — **in·sa·tia·ble·ness** *n* -ES

in·sa·tia·bly \-blē,-bli\ *adv* : in an insatiable way : without being satisfied ⟨clawing ~ at the framework of tradition⟩ : in an insatiable degree; *broadly* : EXTREMELY, VERY ⟨~ hungry⟩

in·sa·tiate \(ˈ)in¦sāsh(ē)ə̇t, ən's- *also* **in·sa·ti·at·ed** \-shēˌād·ə̇d\ *adj* [*insatiate* fr. L *insatiatus*, fr. *in-* ¹in- + *satiatus* satiate, satiated; *insatiated* fr. ¹*in-* + *satiated*] : not satiated : not satisfied ⟨~ thirst⟩ ⟨such ~ cruelty⟩ — **in·sa·tiate·ly** *adv* — **in·sa·tiate·ness** *n* -ES

in·satiety \¦in+\ *n* [MF *insacieté*, *insatieté*, fr. L *insatietas*, fr. *in-* ¹in- + *satietas* satiety — more at SATIETY] : lack of satiety; *esp* : unsatisfied desire ⟨clothes they can never hope to own, changes they cannot afford to keep up with — must set up a tremendous store of ~ in the poor and the modest-income groups —P.M.Gregory⟩

insatisfaction *n* [¹*in-* + *satisfaction*] *obs* : DISSATISFACTION

in·saturation \¦in+\ *n* [¹*in-* + *saturation*] : the quality or state of being unsaturated

insc *abbr* inscribed

in·scape \'inzˌkāp, 'in(t)ˌsk-\ *n* [²*in-* + *-scape*] : inward significant character or quality belonging uniquely to objects or events in nature and human experience esp. as perceived by the blended observation and introspection of the poet and in turn embodied in patterns of such specif. poetic elements as imagery, rhythm, rhyme, assonance, sound symbolism, and allusion : INWARDNESS — compare HAECCEITY

insce *abbr* insurance

in·sce·na·tion \ˌinˌsē'nāshən, ˌin(t)sē'-, ˌin(t)sə'-\ *n* -S [²*in-* + *scene* + *-ation*; intended as trans. of G *inszenierung*] : MISE EN SCÈNE

in·science \'insh(ē)ən(t)s, 'in(t)sēə-\ *n* [L *inscientia*, fr. *inscient-*, *insciens* inscient + *-ia*] : lack of knowledge : NESCIENCE

in·scient \-nt\ *adj* [L *inscient-*, *insciens*, fr. *in-* ¹in- + *scient-*, *sciens*, pres. part. of *scire* to know — more at SCIENCE] : exhibiting or based on inscience

in·scrib·able \ə̇nz'krībəbəl, ə̇n'sk-\ *adj* : capable of being inscribed

in·scribe \ə̇nz'krīb, ə̇n'sk-\ *vt* [L *inscribere*, fr. *in-* ²in- + *scribere* to write — more at SCRIBE] **1 a** : to write, engrave, print, or otherwise set down (as characters, symbols, words, or a text) esp. so as to form a lasting or public record **b** : to enter the name of esp. on a list : ENROLL **c** : to write (letters or other characters) in a particular format in cryptology; *esp* : to write (letters or other characters of a plaintext message) according to an agreed-upon route in an agreed-upon geometrical pattern preparatory to transcribing in another manner **2 a** : to write, engrave, print, or otherwise mark characters upon esp. so as to create a lasting or public record **b** : to autograph (a copy of a work of which one is the author) — often used with *to* or *for* ⟨~ one's book to an old friend⟩ **c** : to stamp deeply or impress esp. on the memory **3** : to assign or address (as a work of literature) in a style less formal than that of a dedication **4** : to draw (a figure) within a figure so as to touch in as many places as possible ⟨~ a polygon in a circle⟩ **5** *Brit* : to register the name of the holder of (a stock or other security)

inscribed *adj* [fr. past part. of *inscribe*] **1** : having lines or other markings deeply impressed or having the appearance of written letters (as certain insects) **2** *of a holding of stock or other security, Brit* : having the owner's name entered in a list kept by the issuing company or at a bank authorized to keep it and until recently transferable only by personal attendance of the owner or one entitled to act as his attorney **3** : bearing the author's signature often accompanied by an inscription — used in the book trade of a copy of a book ⟨an ~ copy⟩

¹**in·scrib·er** \-bə(r)\ *n* : one that inscribes

²**in·scrib·er** \'inzˌkrībə(r), 'inˌsk-\ *n* [prob. fr. *in-* (fr. *input*) + *-scriber* (fr. *transcriber*)] : a device for transferring data from a punched tape onto a medium (as magnetic wire) for use in an electronic computer — compare OUTSCRIBER

in·script \'inzˌkript, 'inˌsk-\ *n* [L *inscriptum*, fr. neut. of *inscriptus* (past part.)] : INSCRIPTION

in·scrip·tion \ə̇nz'kripshən, ə̇n'sk-\ *n* [ME *inscripcioun* superscription, heading, fr. L *inscription-*, *inscriptio* act of writing upon, inscription on a monument, title, fr. *inscriptus* (past part. of *inscribere* to inscribe) + *-ion-*, *-io* -ion] **1** : something that is inscribed: as **a** : a text inscribed in order to form a lasting or public record (as on a monument, tablet, pillar, wall) **b** : a brief description of the character, contents, authorship, or occasion of a book or other composition placed at its beginning : TITLE, SUPERSCRIPTION, HEADING **c** (1) : a name and often a message prefixed to a work of literature addressing it to someone in a style or manner less formal than that of a dedication (2) : EPIGRAPH 2 **d** : the wording on a coin, medal, seal, stamp, or currency note : LEGEND **2** *archaic* : a tendinous line intersecting a muscle **3 a** : the act or process of inscribing **b** : the writing of characters in a particular format in cryptology; *esp* : the writing of the characters of a plaintext message along an agreed-upon route in an agreed-upon geometrical pattern before copying them off in another order to make a transposition cipher **c** : the entering of a name on or as if on a list : ENROLLMENT **4** *Brit* **a** : the act of inscribing securities **b inscriptions** *pl* : inscribed securities **5** : the part of a medical prescription that contains the names and quantities of the drugs to be compounded

in·scrip·tion·al \-shənᵊl,-shnəl\ *adj* **1** *archaic* : bearing an inscription **2** : of or relating to an inscription **3** : characteristic of inscriptions ⟨the revival of classical ~ capitals —*Times Lit. Supp.*⟩

in·scrip·tion·less \-shənlə̇s\ *adj* : lacking any inscription ⟨buried beneath an ~ stone⟩

in·scrip·tive \-ptiv\ *adj* [L *inscriptus* (past part. of *inscribere* to inscribe) + E *-ive*] **1** *obs* : INSCRIBED **2** : relating to or constituting an inscription ⟨traced out the ~ lines⟩ — **in·scrip·tive·ly** \-ptə̇vlē\ *adv*

inscroll *var of* ENSCROLL

in·scrutability \(ˌ)inzˌkrüd·ə'biləd·ē, ən-, -nˌsk-, -üt∂-, -lətē, -i\ *n* : the quality or state of being inscrutable

in·scru·ta·ble \(ˈ)inz¦krüd·əbəl, ənz'k-, -n¦sk-, -ütə-\ *adj* [ME, fr. LL *inscrutabilis*, fr. L *in-* ¹in- + LL *scrutabilis* scrutable] **1** : incapable of being investigated and understood ⟨attempting to look into the ~ future⟩ ⟨obeying ancient and ~ laws⟩; *broadly* : not readily comprehensible : MYSTERIOUS ⟨an ~ smile⟩ ⟨many fathers feel that, if they are to maintain their authority, they must be a little distant and ~ —A.C. Benson⟩ **2** : impossible to see or see through physically ⟨an ~ fog⟩ ⟨~ deeps⟩

in·scru·ta·ble·ness *n* -ES : INSCRUTABILITY

in·scru·ta·bly \-blē, -bli\ *adv* : in an inscrutable manner

in·sculp \ə̇nz'kəlp, ə̇n'sk-\ *vt* [ME *insculpen*, fr. L *insculpere*, fr. *in-* ²in- + *sculpere*, *scalpere* to cut, carve — more at SHELF] *archaic* : ENGRAVE, SCULPTURE

in·sculpture \ə̇nz'k-,ə̇n'sk-\ *n* [prob. fr. obs. F, fr. MF, fr. *in-* ²in- + *sculpture*, fr. L *sculptura* sculpture] : CARVING, INSCRIPTION

in·sculptured \ə̇nz'k-,ə̇n'sk-\ *adj* [²*in-* + *sculptured*] : CUT= IN, SCULPTURED ⟨~ epitaphs⟩ ⟨an ~ border⟩

in·seam \'inˌsēm\ *n* [²*in-* + *seam*] : an inner seam: as **a** : the seam from the crotch to the leg bottom of trousers **b** : a seam showing on the inside only used for articles (as gloves) often made with outside seams **c** : a hidden seam in a welt shoe fastening the welt, lining, and shoe upper to the insole

in·seam·er \-mə(r)\ *n* : a worker that sews inseams (as on trouser legs or shoes)

in–season *adj* **1** *of a female mammal* : being in heat **2** : SEASONAL ⟨*in-season* accommodations⟩ ⟨*in-season* fruits⟩

¹**in·sect** \'inˌsekt\ *n* -S [L *insectum*, fr. neut. of *insectus*, past part. of *insecare* to cut into, fr. *in-* ²in- + *secare* to cut; trans. of Gk *entomon* — more at SAW, ENTOMOLOGY] **1 a** : any of numerous small invertebrate animals that are more or less obviously segmented and that include members of the class Insecta and others (as spiders, mites, ticks, centipedes, sowbugs) having superficial resemblance to members of Insecta — not used technically **b** [NL *Insecta*] : a member of the class Insecta (as an ant, bee, fly) **2** *now chiefly substand* : any of various small animals (as an earthworm, coral polyp, turtle) **3** : a small, trivial, or contemptible person

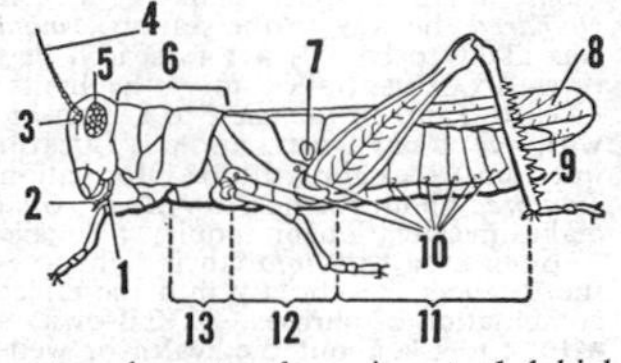

external parts of an insect: *1* labial palpus, *2* maxillary palpus, *3* simple eye, *4* antenna, *5* compound eye, *6* prothorax, *7* tympanum, *8* wing, *9* ovipositor, *10* spiracles, *11* abdomen, *12* metathorax, *13* mesothorax

²**insect** \"\ *adj* **1** : of, relating to, or being insects ⟨~ bites⟩ ⟨~ pests⟩ **2** : used on, for, or against insects ⟨~ pins⟩ ⟨~ powder⟩ ⟨an ~ cabinet⟩ **3** : using or depending on insects ⟨~ feeders⟩ ⟨~ fertilization⟩

in·sec·ta \ə̇n'sektə\ *n pl, cap* [NL, fr. L, pl. of *insectum* insect] **1** *in former classifications* : a large group of segmented animals including (1) many worms and the arthropods, (2) all the arthropods, (3) the true insects, the myriapods, and the arachnids, or (4) the myriapods and the insects **2** : a class of Arthropoda comprising segmented animals that as adults have a well-defined head bearing a single pair of antennae, three pairs of mouthparts, and usu. a pair of compound eyes, a 3-segmented thorax each segment of which bears a pair of legs ventrally with the second and third often bearing also a pair of dorsolateral wings, and an abdomen usu. of 7 to 10 visible segments without true jointed legs but often with the last segments modified or fitted with specialized extensions (as claspers, stings, ovipositors), that breathe air usu. through a ramifying system of tracheae which open externally through spiracles or gills, that exhibit a variety of life cycles often involving complex metamorphosis, and that include the greater part of all living and extinct animals — see PROTURA; compare COLLEMBOLA

¹**in·sec·tan** \(ˈ)in¦sektən, ən's-\ *adj* [NL *Insecta* + E *-an*] : of or relating to the class Insecta

²**insectan** \"\ *adj* [¹*insect* + *-an*] : of or relating to insects

in·sec·tary \¦inˌsektərē, ə̇n's-, 'inˌsekˌterē\ *or* **in·sec·tar·i·um** \ˌ=ˌ='ta(a)rēəm\ *n, pl* **insectaries** \-ēz\ *or* **insectar·ia** \-ēə\ [NL *insectarium*, fr. L *insecta* + *-arium* -ary] : a place for the keeping or rearing of living insects

insect bed *n* : a geologic stratum rich in insect remains

in·sect·ed \(ˈ)in¦sektə̇d, ən's-\ *adj* [L *insectus* (past part. of *insecare* to cut into) + E *-ed*] : cut into : SEGMENTED ⟨the ~ body of a sea anemone⟩

insect flower *n* : PYRETHRUM 2a — usu. used in pl.

insecti- *comb form* [L *insectum*] : insect ⟨*insecti*ferous⟩ ⟨*insecti*fuge⟩

in·sec·ti·ci·dal \ə̇n¦sektə¦sīdᵊl\ *adj* **1** [*insecti-* + *-cidal*] : destroying or controlling insects **2** [*insecticide* + *-al*] : of or relating to an insecticide — **in·sec·ti·ci·dal·ly** \-ᵊlē\ *adv*

¹**in·sec·ti·cide** \ə̇n'sektəˌsīd\ *n* -S [*insecti-* + *-cide* (killing)] : the killing of insects ⟨a carefully controlled mass ~ was going on —*Newsweek*⟩

²**insecticide** \"\ *n* -S [ISV *insecti-* + *-cide* (killer)] : an agent that destroys insects; *broadly* : an agent hostile or repellent to insects — compare LARVICIDE

in·sec·tic·o·lous \¦inˌsek¦tikələs\ *adj* [*insecti-* + *-colous*] : dwelling on the bodies of insects ⟨~ mites⟩

in·sec·ti·fuge \ə̇n'sektəˌfyüj\ *n* -S [*insecti-* + *-fuge*] : an agent that drives away insects usu. without destroying them : an insect repellent

¹**in·sec·tile** \(ˈ)in¦sektᵊl, ən's-, -ˌtīl, -(ˌ)til\ *adj* [L *insectum* + E *-ile*] : like or being an insect : consisting of insects ⟨an ~ mixture for feeding songbirds⟩

²**insectile** \"\ *adj* [¹*in-* + L *sectilis* divided, cut, sectile — more at SECTILE] : not sectile : incapable of being divided

in·sec·tion \ə̇n'sekshən\ *n* [LL *insection-*, *insectio* incision, fr. L *insectus* (past part. of *insecare* to cut into) + *-ion-*, *-io* -ion — more at INSECT] : a notched or segmented part ⟨~*s* of a leaf margin⟩

in·sec·ti·val \¦inˌsek¦tīvəl\ *adj* [¹*insect* + *-ive* + *-al*] : typical of an insect

in·sec·tiv·o·ra \ˌinˌsek'tivərə\ *n pl, cap* [NL, fr. *insecti-* + *-vora*] : an order of mammals comprising the moles, shrews, hedgehogs, and certain related forms that are mostly small, insectivorous, terrestrial or fossorial, and nocturnal — see LIPOTYPHLA, MENOTYPHLA

in·sec·tiv·o·rae \-ˌrē\ *also* **in·sec·tiv·o·ra** \-ˌrə\ [NL, fr. *insecti-* + *-vorae* (fr. L, fem. pl. of *-vorus* -vorous) *or -vora*] *syn of* MICROCHIROPTERA

in·sec·ti·vore \ə̇n'sektəˌvō(ə)r\ *n* -S **1** [NL *Insectivora*] : a mammal of the order Insectivora **2** [F, fr. *insectivore* insectivorous, fr. *insecti-* + *-vore* (fr. L *-vorus* -vorous)] : an insectivorous plant or animal : a carnivore that feeds on insects

in·sec·tiv·o·rous \¦inˌsek¦tiv(ə)rəs\ *adj* [L *insectum* insect + E *-ivorous* (as in *carnivorous*)] : feeding on insects : depending on insects as food

insectivorous plant *n* : a plant that captures and digests insects either passively (as the common pitcher plant or the sundew) or by the movement of certain organs (as the Venus's= flytrap) — compare DROSERACEAE, LENTIBULARIACEAE, SARRACENIACEAE

in·sec·tol·o·gy \ˌinˌsek'täləjē\ *n* -ES [F *insectologie*, fr. *insecte* insect (fr. L *insectum*) + *-o-* + *-logie* -logy — more at INSECT] : ENTOMOLOGY

insect orchis *n* : a twayblade of the genus *Listera*

insect powder *n* : a powder for the extermination of insects; *esp* : PYRETHRUM 2a

in·sec·tu·ous \(ˌ)in¦sekch(əw)əs, ən's-\ *adj* [¹*insect* + *-uous* (as in *contemptuous*)] : involving or full of insects : BUGGY

insect wax *n* : a waxlike substance secreted by an insect; *esp* : CHINESE WAX

in·secure \¦in+\ *adj* [ML *insecurus*, fr. L *in-* ¹in- + *securus* secure] : lacking security: **a** : not confident or sure : UNCERTAIN ⟨feeling somewhat ~ of his reception⟩ **b** : not effectually guarded, protected, or sustained : exposed to danger : UNSAFE ⟨an ~ investment⟩ ⟨property was very ~ during the riots⟩ **c** : not tightly fastened : not firmly fixed in position : SHAKY ⟨the hinge is ~⟩ **d** : not highly stable or well-adjusted : lacking likelihood of permanence or success : UNSTABLE, UNSURE ⟨a marriage ~ from the beginning⟩ ⟨his fortune was increasingly ~⟩ — **in·se·cure·ly** *adv* — **in·se·cure·ness** *n*

in·security \¦in+\ *n* [perh. fr. ML *insecuritas* danger, hazard, fr. L *in-* ¹in- + *securus* secure + *-itas* -ity] : the quality or state of being insecure: as **a** : lack of assurance : APPREHENSIVENESS ⟨a feeling of ~⟩ **b** : lack of safety : HAZARD, RISK ⟨the ~ of his capital⟩ **c** : an insecure condition or circumstance ⟨the minor *insecurities* of life⟩ ⟨noticed the ~ of the lock⟩

inseeing \'=ˌ==\ *adj* [²*in-* + *seeing*, pres. part. of *see*] **1** : having insight **2** : tending to look inward : subjective or egocentric in orientation

in·sel·berg \'in(t)səlˌbərg, 'inzəl-, 'inzəlˌberg\ *n, pl* **inselbergs** \-gz\ *or* **inselber·ge** \-gə\ [G, fr. *insel* island + *berg* mountain] : an isolated mountain partly buried by the debris derived from and overlapping its slopes

in·sem·i·nate \ə̇n'seməˌnāt, *usu* -ād·+V\ *vt* -ED/-ING/-S [L *inseminatus*, past part. of *inseminare*, fr. *in-* ²in- + *seminare* to beget, plant, fr. *semin-*, *semen* seed — more at SEMEN] **1** : to sow or sow in ⟨~ the minds of the young with practical ideals⟩ **2** : to introduce semen into (the female genital tract) by coitus or by other means **syn** see IMPLANT

in·sem·i·na·tion \(ˌ)inˌsemə'nāshən, ən-\ *n* -S : the act or process of inseminating — compare ARTIFICIAL INSEMINATION

in·sem·i·na·tor \=ˈ==ˌnād·ə(r), -ātə-\ *n* -S : one that practices the technique of artificial insemination esp. of cattle

in·sensate \(ˈ)in¦senˌsā|t, ən's-, -n(t)sə̇|, *usu* |d·+V\ *adj* [LL *insensatus*, fr. L *in-* ¹in- + LL *sensatus* gifted with sense, intelligent — more at SENSATE] **1** : having no capacity to perceive : INSENTIENT, INANIMATE ⟨the ~ stones⟩ **2** : lacking or marked by lack of sense or understanding ⟨dull ~ rustics⟩ ⟨~ ignorance⟩ : not based on plan or reason : FOOLISH, FATUOUS ⟨this ~ project⟩ **3 a** : lacking awareness, sensibility, or sensitivity : having no conception of or feeling for ⟨~ to beauty⟩ ⟨~ to his privileges and responsibilities⟩ **b** : lacking humane feeling : UNFEELING; *broadly* : CRUEL, HARSH, BRUTAL ⟨~ destruction⟩ ⟨~ hatred⟩ — **in·sen·sate·ly** *adv* — **in·sen·sate·ness** *n*

in·sense \ə̇n'sen(t)s\ *vt* [ME *ensensen*, fr. MF *ensenser*, fr. OF, fr. *en-* ²in- + *sens* sense, fr. L *sensus* — more at SENSE] *dial Brit* : to give (a person) a sense of the importance or significance of something : impress or imbue firmly with a fact or idea : INSTRUCT, INFORM

in·sensibility \(ˌ)in, ən+\ *n* [LL *insensibilitas*, fr. L *insensibilis* insensible + *-itas* -ity] : the quality or state of being insensible: as **a** : an unconscious or comatose state **b** : lack of physical feeling or sensitivity : an unresponsive or unreactive condition : INSENSITIVITY ⟨marked ~ to cold⟩ ⟨increasing ~ to stimuli⟩ **c** : lack of mental or emotional feeling or response : APATHY ⟨her complete ~ to the honor done her⟩

¹**in·sensible** \(ˈ)in, ən+\ *adj* [ME, fr. MF & L; MF, fr. L *insensibilis*, fr. *in-* ¹in- + *sensibilis* sensible] **1** : incapable or bereft of feeling or sensation: as **a** : not endowed with consciousness : INANIMATE, INSENTIENT ⟨~ earth⟩ **b** : deprived of consciousness : UNCONSCIOUS ⟨to fall ~⟩ **c** : lacking sensory perception : failing to react to stimuli either wholly or to some degree ⟨markedly ~ to pain⟩; *also* : deprived of such perception or ability to react ⟨hands ~ from cold⟩ **2** : incapable of being perceived by the senses or perceptible only with difficulty : IMPERCEPTIBLE; *broadly* : MINUTE, SLIGHT, GRADUAL ⟨~ motion⟩ ⟨~ gradations⟩ **3** *archaic* : lacking sense or intelligence : STUPID, SENSELESS, UNREASONING **4** : devoid or insusceptible of emotion or passion : void of feeling : APATHETIC, INDIFFERENT ⟨~ to fear⟩; *also* : UNAWARE ⟨~ of their danger⟩ **5** : not intelligible : MEANINGLESS — used chiefly in law **6** : devoid of sensitivity : lacking delicacy or refinement — **in·sensibleness** \"+\ *n* — **in·sensibly** \"+\ *adv*

²**insensible** \"\ *n* -S : one that is insensible

in·sensitive \(ˈ)in, ən+\ *adj* [¹*in-* + *sensitive*] : not sensitive: as **a** *obs* : INSENTIENT, INANIMATE **b** : lacking feeling : INSENSIBLE **c** : not physically or chemically sensitive **d** : not morally or mentally sensitive : UNIMPRESSIONABLE — **in·sensitively** \"+\ *adv* — **in·sensitiveness** \"+\ *or* **in·sensitivity** \(ˌ)in, ən+\ *n*

in·sentience \(ˈ)in, ən+\ *n* [fr. *insentient*, after E *sentient: sentience*] : the quality or state of being insentient

in·sentient \"+\ *adj* [¹*in-* + *sentient*] : not sentient : not having perception or feeling : lacking consciousness or animation

in·separability \(ˌ)in, ən+\ *n* : the quality or state of being inseparable

¹**in·separable** \(ˈ)in, ən+\ *adj* [ME, fr. L *inseparabilis*, fr. *in-* ¹in- + *separabilis* separable] **1** : not separable : incapable of being separated or disjoined **2** : invariably attached to a word, stem, or root ⟨*un-* is an ~ prefix⟩ — **in·separableness** \"+\ *n* — **in·separably** \"+\ *adv*

²**inseparable** \"\ *n* -S : one that is inseparable from another — usu. used in pl.

in·separate \(ˈ)in, ən+\ *adj* [LL *inseparatus*, fr. L *in-* ¹in- + *separatus* separate] : not separate : UNITED; *usu* : INSEPARABLE — **in·separately** \"+\ *adv*

in·sequent \(ˈ)in, ən+\ *adj* [¹*in-* + *sequent*] *of the course of a stream* : apparently uncontrolled by the associated rock structure

¹**in·sert** \ə̇n'sər|t, -sə̄|, -səi|, *usu* |d·+V\ *vb* -ED/-ING/-S [L *insertus*, past part. of *inserere*, fr. *in-* ²in- + *serere* to join, bind together — more at SERIES] *vt* **1 a** : to set (something) in : put or thrust in : INTRODUCE ⟨~*ing* the scions in hardy stocks⟩ ⟨~ a key noiselessly in a lock⟩ **b** : to put or introduce into the body of : INTERPOLATE ⟨~*ed* a few words of description⟩ **c** : to set in and make fast (as a piece of fabric) ⟨~ a patch in a pair of torn trousers⟩ ⟨~ a decorative medallion in a tooled leather cover⟩; *esp* : to insert by sewing between two cut edges ⟨~*ing* bands of lace on the front of the blouse⟩ **2** : to attach or fix in a particular position in the course of natural growth — used only in past part. ⟨the meristem is ~*ed* between more or less differentiated tissue regions —Katherine Esau⟩ ~ *vi, of a muscle* : to be in attachment to the part to be moved ⟨retraction is accomplished by two fairly thick bands of retractor muscles which ~ on the lophophore and originate in the body wall —Mary Rogick⟩

²**in·sert** \'inˌs-\ *n* -S : something that is inserted or is for insertion : INSERTION, INSET: as **a** : written or printed material inserted (as a map or plate between the leaves of a book, a circular within the folds of a newspaper, an instruction sheet in a carton of merchandise) **b** : a removable portion of a die or mold **c** : a part of a casting placed in the mold and becoming integral with the metal cast around it **d** : a piece of cloth set into a garment for decoration, ease, and additional fullness

in·sert·able *or* **in·sert·ible** \ə̇n'sərd·əbəl\ *adj* : capable of being inserted

inserted \(ˈ)=ˈ==\ *adj* [fr. past part. of ¹*insert*] : set in : fitted in: as **a** : having the basal part set into another structure ⟨an insect with ~ mouthparts⟩ **b** : attached by natural growth (as a muscle or tendon or the parts of a flower) **c** : not in one piece with the main body and therefore replaceable ⟨an *inserted*-tooth saw⟩ ⟨~ valve seat⟩

in·sert·er \ə̇n'sərd·ə(r)\ *n* -S : one that inserts

in·ser·tion \ə̇n'sərshən, -səsh-, -səish-\ *n* [LL *insertion-*, *insertio*, fr. L *insertus* (past part. of *inserere* to insert) + *-ion-*, *-io* -ion] **1** : the act or process of inserting ⟨the

~ of new ball bearings⟩ **2 :** something that is inserted **:** INSERT: as **a :** the part of a muscle by which it is attached to the part to be moved — distinguished from *origin* **b :** narrow banding (as of lace or embroidery) with finished edges for insertion as ornament between two pieces of fabric **c :** a single appearance of an advertisement (as in a newspaper) **3 :** the mode or place of attachment of an organ or part ⟨the ~ of a muscle⟩ ⟨deep ~ of the petals of a flower⟩ — **in·ser·tion·al** \-shən°l,-shnəl\ *adj*

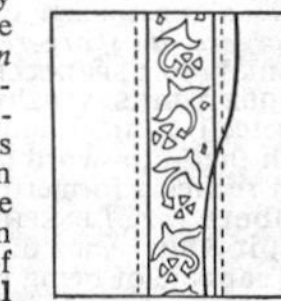
insertion 2b

in·ser·tive \ən'sərd·iv\ *adj* [L *insertivus*, fr. *insertus* (past part.) + *-ivus* -ive] **1** *obs* **:** marked by insertion **:** INSERTED **2 :** tending to insert

in–service \(')in¦==, ən'==\ *adj* **:** going on or continuing while in service ⟨*in-service* training⟩ ⟨*in-service* care of delicate fabrics⟩

in·serviceable \(')in, ən+\ *adj* [¹*in-* + *serviceable*] **:** UNSERVICEABLE

in·ser·vi·ent \ən'sərvēənt\ *adj* [L *inservient-, inserviens*, pres. part. of *inservire* to serve, fr. *in-* ²in- + *servire* to serve — more at SERVE] *archaic* **:** serving or subservient to (as an end or purpose) **:** CONDUCIVE

insession *n* -s [LL *insession-, insessio*, lit., act of sitting in, act of sitting down, fr. L *insessus* (past part. of *insidēre* to sit in, sit on, fr. *in-* ²in- + *sedēre* to sit) + *-ion-*, *-io* -ion — more at SIT] *obs* **:** the act of sitting in a bath; *also* **:** SITZ BATH

in·ses·so·res \,in,se'sōr(,)ēz\ *n pl, cap* [NL, fr. LL, pl. of *insessor* waylayer (lit., one that sits on), fr. L *insessus* (past part.) + *-or*] *in former classifications* **:** an order of birds that have the feet adapted for perching including the Passeres and many others

in·ses·so·ri·al \¦in,se¦sōrēəl\ *adj* **1** [L *insessus* (past part.) + E *-orial*, as in *raptorial*] **:** perching or adapted for perching ⟨~ feet⟩ **2** [NL *Insessores* + E *-ial*] **:** of or relating to the order Insessores

¹**inset** \'=,=\ *n* [⁴*in* + *set* (n.)] **1 a :** a place where something (as water) flows in **:** CHANNEL **b :** a setting in or inflowing (as of a tide) **2 :** something that is inset: as **a :** INSERT a; *esp* **:** one or more separate leaves inserted in a book usu. before binding **b :** a small but not necessarily small-scale graphic representation (as a map or illustration) set within the compass of a larger one **c :** a piece of cloth set into a garment (as for decoration) ⟨a satin skirt with ~*s* of ruffled chiffon⟩ **d :** a part or section of a utensil that fits into an outer part ⟨the ~ of a double boiler⟩ **e** [intended as trans. of G *einsprengling*] **:** PHENOCRYST

²**inset** \", ən'=\ *vt* **inset** *or* **insetted; inset** *or* **insetted; insetting; insets** [²*in-* + *set* (v.)] **1 :** to set in **:** place in as an insert ⟨~ an embroidered panel⟩ **2 :** to provide with an insert ⟨~ a belt with rhinestones⟩

in·set·ter \"+ə(r)\ *n* **:** one that puts in insets (as in a book)

in·severable \(')in, ən+\ *adj* [¹*in-* + *severable*] **:** incapable of being severed **:** INDIVISIBLE **:** impossible to separate — **in·sev·er·ably** \-blē\ *adv*

in·sheathe *also* **in·sheath** \ən+\ *var of* ENSHEATHE

inshining \(')in,==, ən'==\ *n* -s [⁴*in* + *shining*, gerund of *shine*] **:** ILLUMINATION ⟨when the soul feels the divine ~ —H.W. Beecher⟩

¹**inship** *vt* [²*in-* + *ship*] *obs* **:** EMBARK

²**inship** \(')in¦=, ən'=\ *adv* [fr. the phrase *in ship*] **:** on shipboard

inshipment \'in,==\ *n* [⁴*in* + *shipment*] **:** IMPORT — usu. used in pl. ⟨~*s* dropped 4 percent . . . but 8 percent more chicks hatched locally —J.M.Gwin⟩

inshoot \'in,=\ *n* [⁴*in* + *shoot*] **:** a pitched baseball that breaks toward a right-handed batter

¹**inshore** *vt* [²*in-* + *shore* (n.)] *obs* **:** to put on or bring to shore

²**inshore** \(')in¦=, ən'=\ *adj* [fr. the phrase *in shore*] **:** situated or carried on near shore **:** moving toward shore ⟨~ fishing⟩ ⟨an ~ wind⟩

³**inshore** \"\ *adv* [fr. the phrase *in shore*] **:** to or toward shore **:** near shore ⟨drifted ~ during the night⟩

inshore current *n* **:** an ocean current that flows in or to landward of the zone of breaking waves

in·shrine \ən+\ *archaic var of* ENSHRINE

¹**inside** \(')in¦=, ən'=\ *n* [⁴*in* + *side*] **1 :** an inner side or surface: as **a :** the right side of a sword in fencing **b :** the part of a footpath or sidewalk furthest from an adjoining roadway **c :** the concave aspect of a curve **d :** the side of home plate nearer the batter in baseball **2 :** an interior or internal portion or content **:** the part within: as **a :** inward nature, mind, thoughts, or feeling **b :** the inner parts of the body; *usu* **:** VISCERA, ENTRAILS — usu. used in pl. **c :** an inside passenger or seat (as in a stagecoach) **3 :** the middle or principal part of a division of time ⟨the ~ of a week⟩ **4 insides** *pl* **:** the 18 first-quality quires between the outside quires of a ream of writing or drawing paper; *broadly* **:** reams of which all quires or sheets are of first quality — compare OUTSIDE **5 a :** a situation in which information not generally available may be obtained **:** a position of trust and confidence ⟨he was on the ~ in all those deals⟩ ⟨only someone on the ~ could have told⟩ **b** *slang* **:** information not generally available **:** confidential information ⟨has the ~ on what happened at the convention⟩ **6** *or* **inside forward a :** INSIDE LEFT **b :** INSIDE RIGHT

²**inside** \"\ *adj* **1 a :** of, relating to, or being on the inside ⟨an ~ wall⟩ ⟨~ views⟩ **b :** included or enclosed in something ⟨the ~ furnishings⟩ **c :** used inside ⟨~ clothing⟩ **d :** measured from within usu. so as to include the cavity but not the substance ⟨~ diameter⟩ **2 :** employed or working indoors ⟨kept both an ~ man and a gardener⟩ **3 a :** relating or known to a select group **:** coming from an assuredly informed source ⟨~ information⟩ **b :** placed in an organization as an undercover representative of an actually or potentially antagonistic interest ⟨party ~ men in the unions⟩ **4** *of a union* **:** representing the employees of a single employer **syn** see INNER

³**inside** \"\ *prep* **1 a :** within the boundaries of **:** in the interior of ⟨waited ~ the church⟩ ⟨pain originating ~ the muscle⟩ **b :** on the inner side of ⟨place the dot ~ the curve⟩ **2 :** before the end of ⟨answered ~ an hour⟩

⁴**inside** \"\ *adv* **:** on or in the inside **:** INTERNALLY, WITHIN ⟨a house that was spotlessly clean both ~ and outside⟩ ⟨stayed ~ during the storm⟩

inside and out *adv* **:** INSIDE OUT

inside attack *n* **:** a division of a lacrosse team consisting of the inside home, the outside home, and the first attack — compare INSIDE DEFENSE

inside ball *n* **:** baseball play characterized by skillful use of strategy and fine points of technique

inside caliper *n* **:** a caliper for measuring dimensions of a cavity (as the inner diameter of an engine cylinder)

inside clinch *n* **:** a clinch knot in which the seized end of the line is inside the noose — compare OUTSIDE CLINCH

inside defense *n* **:** a division of a lacrosse team consisting of point, cover point, and the first defense — compare INSIDE ATTACK

inside finish *n* **:** the final work in a building necessary for its completion (as the adding of doors, paneled jambs, baseboards) — compare OUTSIDE FINISH

inside form *n* **:** INNER FORM

inside half *n* **:** SCRUM HALF

inside home *n* **:** a lacrosse player whose position is on the right side of the opponent's goal — called also *in home*

inside job *n* **:** an irregular or criminal act perpetrated by or with the connivance of a person occupying a position of trust in respect to the victim of the act ⟨the payroll robbery was an *inside job*⟩; *also* **:** such an act perpetrated by the apparent victim

inside left *n* **:** a forward on a soccer team whose position is between the center forward and the outside left

inside loop *n* **:** ²LOOP 2 f

inside lot *n* **:** INTERIOR LOT

insident *adj* [L *insident-, insidens*, pres. part. of *insidēre* to sit in, sit on — more at INSESSION] *obs* **:** residing in **:** INHERENT

inside of *prep* **:** WITHIN **:** in the compass or on the inner side of ⟨*inside of* the city walls⟩ **:** in no more than ⟨back *inside of* an hour⟩

inside out *adv* **1 :** in such a manner that the inner surface becomes the outer ⟨peeled her gloves off *inside out*⟩ **2 :** THOROUGHLY ⟨knows his material *inside out*⟩

inside–out flower *n* **:** any of several western No. American herbs constituting the genus *Epimedium* of the family Berberidaceae and distinguished by sharply reflexed sepals

inside quire *n* **:** a quire of paper lying between the outside quires

in·sid·er \(')in'sīdə(r), ən-\ *n* -s [¹*inside* + *-er*] **:** a person recognized or accepted as a member of some group, category, or organization: as **a :** a person having access to confidential information because of his position **b :** an officer or a director of a company or a beneficial owner of 10 percent or more of an equity security registered on an exchange ⟨laws regulating the manipulation of a company's securities by ~*s*⟩

inside right *n* **:** a forward on a soccer team whose position is between the center forward and the outside right

inside straight *n* **:** four cards of a poker hand (as 9,8,6,5) that will make a straight if a card of one particular rank is added

inside stuff *n, slang* **:** confidential information

inside track *n* **1 :** the inner side of a curved racecourse **2 :** a position of advantage in competition ⟨the candidate who had the *inside track*⟩

inside turn *n* **:** a normal aircraft turn in which the top surfaces of the aircraft incline toward the inside of the curve

insidiate *vb* -ED/-ING/-S [L *insidiatus*, past part. of *insidiari*, fr. *insidiae* ambush, fr. *insidēre* to sit in — more at INSESSION] *vt, obs* **:** to plot or scheme against **:** lie in wait for **~** *vi, obs* **:** to lie in ambush **:** PLOT, SCHEME — **insidiation** *n* -s *obs* — **insidiator** *n* -s *obs*

in·sid·i·ous \ən'sidēəs *sometimes* -ijəs\ *adj* [L *insidiosus* insidious, cunning, deceitful, fr. *insidiae* ambush + *-osus* -ous] **1 a :** watching for an opportunity to ensnare ⟨an ~ tempter⟩ **:** lying in wait **:** intended to entrap or trick ⟨an ~ plot⟩ **b :** enticing and deleterious ⟨these ~ drugs⟩ **2 a :** acting by imperceptible degrees **:** having a gradual, cumulative, and usu. hidden effect **:** SUBTLE ⟨~ charm⟩ ⟨the ~ pressures of modern life⟩ ⟨an ~ drink⟩ **b** *of a disease* **:** developing so gradually as to be well established before becoming apparent **syn** see SLY

in·sid·i·ous·ly *adv* **:** in an insidious manner **:** GRADUALLY, SLYLY, SECRETIVELY

in·sid·i·ous·ness *n* -ES **:** the quality or state of being insidious

¹**insight** \'in,=\ *n* [ME *insight, insiht*, fr. *in* + *sight, siht* sight — more at SIGHT] **1 :** the power or act of seeing into a situation or into oneself **:** DISCERNMENT, PENETRATION, UNDERSTANDING **2 :** the act or fact of apprehending the inner nature of things or of seeing intuitively **:** clear and immediate understanding ⟨an extraordinary ~ into the complexity of women's emotions —*Current Biog.*⟩ **3** *obs* **:** a physical view **:** INSPECTION, LOOK **4 a :** recognition that one is ill esp. in mind (as in many neuroses but not usu. in typical insanities) **b :** comprehension or awareness of the nature of such illness or of the unconscious forces contributing to the emotional conflict involved **5 :** immediate and clear learning that takes place without recourse to overt trial-and-error behavior

²**insight** \"\ *n* -s [ME *insicht*] *archaic Scot* **:** PERSONAL PROPERTY; *esp* **:** household goods

in·sight·ed \'=,sīd·əd\ *adj* [¹*insight* + *-ed*] **:** endowed with insight

in·sight·ful \'=,sītfəl\ *adj* [¹*insight* + *-ful*] **:** exhibiting or characterized by insight ⟨the chapter . . . is ~ and suggestive of new perspectives —R.C.Angell⟩ — **in·sight·ful·ly** \-fəlē\ *adv*

in·sig·nia \ən'signēə\ *also* **insig·ne** \-(,)nē\ *n, pl* **insignia** *or*

Insignia of the United States Army: *1* General Staff; *2* Adjutant General's Corps; *3* Inspector General; *4* Judge Advocate General's Corps; *5* Quartermaster Corps; *6* Finance Corps; *7* Corps of Engineers; *8* Ordnance Corps; *9* Signal Corps; *10* National Guard Bureau; *11* Military Intelligence Reserve; *12* Infantry; *13* Armor; *14* Artillery; *15* Chemical Corps; *16* Transportation Corps; *17* Dental Corps; *18* Veterinary Corps; *19* Army Security Reserve; *20* Army Nurse Corps; *21* Medical Corps; *22* United States Military Academy; *23* Chaplain, Christian faith; *24* Chaplain, Jewish faith; *25* Medical Service Corps; *26* Aide to a Major General; *27* Warrant Officer; *28* Military Police Corps; *29* Civilian Affairs and Military Government

insignias [*insignia* fr. L, distinctive marks, badges, signs, pl. of *insigne* distinctive mark, badge, sign, fr. neut. of *insignis* marked, distinguished, fr. *in-* ²in- + *signum* mark, sign — more at SIGN] **1 :** a distinguishing mark of authority, office, or honor **:** BADGE, EMBLEM ⟨the *insignia* of royalty⟩ ⟨a collector of *insignias*⟩ **2 :** a typical and characteristic mark or sign by which something is distinguished ⟨the gay *insigne* of the new fighter squadron⟩ ⟨sports letters were originally *insignia* granted for especial competence in a competitive sport⟩

in·significance \¦in+\ *n* [fr. *insignificant*, after E *significant: significance*] **:** the quality or state of being insignificant **:** UNIMPORTANCE ⟨the ~ of the sum involved⟩

in·significancy \"+\ *n* [¹*in-* + *significancy*] **1 :** INSIGNIFICANCE **2 :** an insignificant thing or person

¹**in·significant** \"+\ *adj* [¹*in-* + *significant*] **:** not significant: as **a :** lacking meaning or import **:** MEANINGLESS ⟨forget this ~ quarrel⟩ **b** *obs* **:** INEFFECTIVE, FUTILE **c :** having no importance **:** UNIMPORTANT ⟨our losses were ~⟩ **d :** lacking weight or position (as from character, social standing, influence) **:** CONTEMPTIBLE ⟨this ~ hanger-on⟩ **e :** of little size or importance **:** SMALL ⟨an ~ town⟩ ⟨hard to believe that this ~ insect could be so deadly⟩ — **in·significantly** \"+\ *adv*

²**insignificant** \"\ *n* **:** something that is insignificant

insignificative *adj* [¹*in-* + *significative*] *obs* **:** not significative

in·sig·nis pine \ən'signəs-\ *n* [part trans. of NL *Pinus insignis*] *Austral & New Zeal* **:** MONTEREY PINE

in·simplicity \¦in+\ *n* [¹*in-* + *simplicity*] **:** lack of simplicity; *also* **:** a thing lacking in simplicity

in·sincere \"+\ *adj* [L *insincerus*, fr. *in-* ¹in- + *sincerus* sincere] **:** lacking sincerity or genuineness: **a** *of a person* **:** not being or expressing what one appears to be or express **:** HYPOCRITICAL ⟨a charming but thoroughly ~ woman whose words could never be taken at face value⟩ **b :** not based on reality, fact, or an honest appraisal ⟨an ~ denial⟩ ⟨the ~ and pity-seeking sigh of a spoilt animal —Arnold Bennett⟩ — **in·sincerely** \"+\ *adv*

in·sincerity \"+\ *n* [L *insincerus* insincere + E *-ity*] **1 :** the quality or state of being insincere ⟨the patent ~ of his answer⟩ **2 :** something that is insincere ⟨forgiving her evasions and *insincerities*⟩

in·sin·u·ant \ən'sinyəwənt\ *adj* [L *insinuant-, insinuans*, pres. part. of *insinuare* to insinuate] **:** INSINUATING, INSINUATIVE

in·sin·u·ate \ən'sinyə,wāt, *usu* -ād.+V\ *vb* -ED/-ING/-S [L *insinuatus*, past part. of *insinuare*, fr. *in-* ²in- + *sinuare* to bend, curve, fr. *sinus* curve, fold — more at SINUS] *vt* **1 a :** to introduce (as an idea or point of view) stealthily, slyly, or artfully **:** convey in a subtle, indirect, or covert way **:** instill imperceptibly ⟨cautiously *insinuating* doubts of his guardian's probity into the mind of the boy⟩ ⟨these fears craftily *insinuated* by enemy propaganda⟩ **b :** to impart or communicate with artful indirect wording or oblique reference and without direct or forthright expression **:** HINT, IMPLY ⟨Newman says of a gentleman that . . . he never . . . ~*s* evil which he dare not say out — Sir A. T. Quiller-Couch⟩ **2** [ML *insinuatus*, past part. of *insinuare*, fr. L] *Roman & civil law* **:** to register or file for registration (as a will or a gift) **3 :** to introduce (as oneself) by stealthy, smooth, or artful means ⟨*insinuating* himself into the confidence of the villagers⟩ ⟨gently the cat *insinuated* himself into the snug corner between the chairs⟩; *broadly* **:** to introduce gradually or without fuss and turmoil ⟨as time went on saner ideas *insinuated* themselves into the minds of the members⟩ **4** *obs* **:** to draw or attract (as the mind) to something or to a course by artful or indirect means **5 :** to push, work, or introduce slowly, carefully, or by a roundabout way ⟨cautiously *insinuating* herself into the crowd⟩ ⟨~ a car through traffic⟩ **~** *vi* **1** *archaic* **:** to enter gently, slowly, or imperceptibly **:** CREEP, WIND, FLOW **2** *archaic* **:** to ingratiate oneself **:** obtain access subtly **syn** see SUGGEST

insinuating *adj* **1 :** tending to gradually cause doubt, distrust, or change of outlook ⟨~ remarks⟩ **2 :** winning favor and confidence by imperceptible degrees ⟨these ~ attentions⟩ **:** INGRATIATING **3** *archaic* **:** entering or penetrating slowly or by a roundabout course — **in·sin·u·at·ing·ly** *adv*

in·sin·u·a·tion \ən,sinyə'wāshən\ *n* -s [L *insinuation-, insinuatio*, fr. *insinuatus* (past part.) + *-ion-*, *-io* -ion] **1 :** the act or process of insinuating: as **a :** stealthy or indirect hinting or suggestion **b** [MF & LL; MF, fr. LL *insinuation-, insinuatio*, fr. L] *Roman & civil law* (1) **:** the copying of an act or legal transaction (as a gift) in a public record (2) **:** the first production of a will for probate **c :** the gaining of favor, affection, or influence by gentle or artful means **:** INGRATIATION **d** *archaic* **:** slow or indirect entry or penetration **2 :** something that is insinuated: as **a :** an utterance intended to hint at or imply something subtly, slyly, or indirectly; *esp* **:** one intended to convey something derogatory ⟨his ~*s* about the governor's income⟩ **b** *obs* **:** an ingratiating act or speech

in·sin·u·a·tive \ən'sinyə,wād·|iv, - wə|, |t|, |ēv *also* |əv\ *adj* [L *insinuatus* (past part.) + E *-ive*] **1 :** tending or intended to insinuate **:** INGRATIATING ⟨a timidly ~ look⟩ **2 :** given to, characterized by, or involving insinuation **:** giving hints **:** INSINUATING ⟨an ~ remark⟩ — **in·sin·u·a·tive·ly** \|əvlē, -li\ *adv*

in·sin·u·a·tor \-,wād·ə(r), -ātə-\ *n* -s [LL, warner, fr. L *insinuatus* (past part. of *insinuare* to insinuate) + *-or*] **:** one that insinuates

in·sin·u·a·to·ry \-_wə,tōrē, -tȯrē, -ri\ *adj* [*insinuate* + *-ory*] **:** INSINUATIVE

in·sin·u·en·do \ən,sinyə'wen(,)dō\ *n* -s [blend of *insinuation* and *innuendo*] **:** INSINUATION 2a

¹**in·sip·id** \ən'sipəd\ *adj* [F & LL; F *insipide*, fr. MF, fr. LL *insipidus*, fr. L *in-* ¹in- + LL *sapidus* well-tasted, savory, wise, prudent — more at SAPID] **1 :** lacking taste or savor to such a degree as to be unpleasing or unappetizing to the palate **:** SAVORLESS, TASTELESS ⟨~ overcooked boiled cabbage⟩ **2 :** lacking in qualities that interest, attract, stimulate, or challenge **:** DULL, UNINTERESTING, STALE, COMMONPLACE ⟨which may give occasion to wit and mirth within that circle, but would seem flat and ~ in any other —Earl of Chesterfield⟩ **3 :** cloyingly sentimental or sweet ⟨manages to be appropriately babyish without becoming ~ —Robert Hatch⟩

syn VAPID, FLAT, JEJUNE, INANE, BANAL, WISHY-WASHY: INSIPID indicates a lack of sufficient taste or savor to please, attract, interest, or stimulate; it applies to that which leaves one uninterested or bored ⟨you have so much animation, which is exactly what Miss Andrews wants; for I must confess there is something amazingly *insipid* about her —Jane Austen⟩ ⟨all former delights of turf, mess, hunting field, and gambling-table; all previous loves and courtships . . . were quite *insipid* when compared with the lawful matrimonial pleasures which of late he had enjoyed —W.M.Thackeray⟩ VAPID, often interchangeable with INSIPID, indicates a want of savor, tang, or sparkle likely to please, or liveliness, force, or spirit likely to interest ⟨Sulpicius had a genius for making the most interesting things seem utterly *vapid* and dead —Robert Graves⟩ ⟨his prose is *vapid* and feeble in the essay, and stilted and artificial in the oration —V.L.Parrington⟩ ⟨the *vapid* and silly chatter of ordinary sociability among men and women —J.C.Powys⟩ FLAT is less precisely suggestive of deficiency than the preceding but as strongly condemnatory in indicating want of stimulation, animation, or interest ⟨a thing of frigid conceits worn bare by iteration; of servile borrowings; of artificial sentiment, *flat* as the lees and dregs of wine —J.L.Lowes⟩ ⟨though his men are *flat* his women characters are done with real insight and intuitive understanding —*Times Lit. Supp.*⟩ JEJUNE suggests a meager scantness of substance, a dearth of anything satisfying, nourishing, or strengthening ⟨mere annalists . . . whose work is as colorless as it is *jejune* —J.R.Green⟩ ⟨registration in the universities dwindled as the instruction they offered became increasingly *jejune* and lifeless —S.E.Morison⟩ INANE suggests a vacant emptiness, an utter want of purport, significance, or cogency ⟨the passive, suggestible, mentally monocellular human being whose vast *inane* face is to be met with in all the Broadways and Main Streets of the world, the end product of picture magazines, bad education, mass entertainment, and a vulpine competitive society —Clifton Fadiman⟩ ⟨Blanche's life, begun with who knows what bright hopes and what dreams, might just as well have never been lived. It all seemed useless and *inane* —W.S.Maugham⟩ BANAL indicates complete absence of the freshness that stimulates; it may stress the unrelieved commonplace ⟨the average man, doomed to some *banal* and sordid drudgery all his life long —H.L.Mencken⟩ ⟨the representation of life [in moving pictures] is hollow, stupid, *banal*, childish —J.T.Farrell⟩ WISHY-WASHY may imply weakness through dilution or vacillation ⟨talent is a *wishy-washy* thing unless it is solidly founded on honest hard work — E.G.Coleman⟩

²**insipid** \"\ *n* -s *archaic* **:** one that is insipid

in·si·pid·i·ty \,in(t)sə'pidəd·ē, -ətē, -i\ *n* -ES [F *insipidité*, fr. MF, fr. ML *insipiditas*, fr. LL *insipidus* insipid + L *-itas* -ity] **1 :** the quality or state of being insipid **:** VAPIDITY ⟨the ~ of her thoughts⟩ **2 :** something (as a remark or an idea) that is notably insipid ⟨these *insipidities* of expression⟩

in·sip·id·ly *adv* **:** in an insipid manner **:** so as to be insipid ⟨~ expressed thoughts⟩

in·sip·id·ness *n* -ES **:** INSIPIDITY

in·sip·i·ence \ən'sipēən(t)s\ *n* -s [ME, fr. MF, fr. OF, fr. L *insipientia* folly, fr. *insipient-, insipiens* insipient + *-ia* -y] *archaic* **:** the quality or state of being insipient **:** lack of intelligence

in·sip·i·ent \-nt\ *adj* [MF or L; MF, fr. L *insipient-, insipiens*, fr. *in-* ¹in- + *sapient-, sapiens* wise, fr. pres. part. of *sapere* to taste, have taste — more at SAGE] *archaic* **:** lacking wisdom **:** STUPID, FOOLISH

in·sist \ən'sist\ *vb* -ED/-ING/-S [MF or L; MF *insister*, fr. L *insistere* to stand upon, persist, dwell upon, fr. *in-* ²in- + *sistere* to stand, cause to stand, fr. *stare* to stand — more at STAND] *vi* **1** *archaic* **:** to find support **:** STAND, REST — used with *on* or *upon* **2** *archaic* **:** to continue determinedly or urgently (as in a course of action) : PERSEVERE, PERSIST **3 a** : to take a stand and refuse to give way : hold firmly to something ⟨~*ed* on the accuracy of his account⟩ **b** : to be persistent, urgent, or pressing ⟨~*ed* on going with them⟩ ~ *vt* : to take a firm stand about : persist in a point of view about — used with a clause as object ⟨~*ed* that we come in⟩ ⟨the moderate confederation may ~ that the radicals be ejected from the government⟩ ⟨~ he had done right⟩

in·sis·tence *also* **in·sis·tance** \-tən(t)s\ *n* -s [*insist* + *-ence* or *-ance*] **1** : the act or an instance of insisting ⟨his ~ on coming⟩ **2** : the quality or state of being insistent : PERSISTENCE, URGENCY

in·sis·ten·cy \-tənsē, -si\ *n* -ES : INSISTENCE

¹in·sis·tent \-tənt\ *adj* [L *insistent-, insistens,* pres. part. of *insistere* to insist, stand upon] **1** *archaic* : standing or resting on something **2 a** : insisting or disposed to insist : PERSISTENT, PERSEVERING ⟨~ demands⟩ **b** : compelling attention : obtrusively conspicuous ⟨working in the ~ heat⟩ ⟨~ pounding of waves⟩ ⟨a bold ~ butte⟩ **3** [F *insistant,* pres. part. of *insister* to insist] *of a bird's hind toe* : inserted so far above the base of other toes that only the tip will reach to the ground — opposed to *incumbent* **syn** see PRESSING

²insistent \"\ *n* -s : an insistent person

in·sis·tent·ly *adv* : in an insistent manner

in·sist·er \-tə(r)\ *n* -s : one that insists

in·sist·ing·ly *adv* [fr. *insisting* (pres. part. of *insist*) + *-ly*] : with insistence : INSISTENTLY, URGENTLY

in·sis·tive \ən'sistiv\ *adj* : tending to insist or urge

in·si·tion \in'sishən\ *n* -s [L *insition-, insitio,* fr. *insitus* (past part.) + *-ion-, -io* -ion] **1** *obs* : the act of grafting or a graft **2** : a taking in or adding as if through grafting (as by inoculation)

in·si·ti·tious \¦in(t)sə¦tishəs\ *adj* [L *insiticius,* fr. *insitus,* past part. of *inserere* to engraft, fr. *in-* ²in- + *serere* to plant, sow — more at SOW] : constituting an insertion : INTERPOLATED

in si·tu \(')in'sī(,)tü, -sē(-, -si(-, -)chü\ *adv (or adj)* [L, in position] : in the natural or original position ⟨motion pictures of the heart beating *in situ*⟩ ⟨combines . . . panels with reinforced concrete *in situ* columns —*London Calling*⟩

in·snare \ən+\ *archaic var of* ENSNARE

insoak \'in,=\ *n* [⁴*in* + *soak* (after *soak in,* v.)] : the taking up of free surface water by unsaturated soil

in·sobriety \¦in+\ *n* [¹*in-* + *sobriety*] : lack of sobriety, moderation, or calmness; *esp* : intemperance in drinking

in·sociability \(¦)in, ən+\ *n* : the quality or state of being insociable : lack of sociability

in·sociable \(')in, ən+\ *adj* [L *insociabilis,* fr. *in-* ¹in- + *sociabilis* sociable] **1** *obs* : incapable of being combined **2** : not sociable : not companionable : UNSOCIABLE, TACITURN — **in·sociably** \"+\ *adv*

insocial *adj* [LL *insocialis,* fr. L *in-* ¹in- + *socialis* social] *obs* : UNSOCIABLE — **insocially** *adv, obs*

insofar \¦==¦=\ *adv* : in such measure : to such extent or degree ⟨pledged himself to follow a party line through thick and thin and ~ abandoned his freedom to think —Sidney Hook⟩

insofar as *conj* : in such measure as : to such extent or degree as ⟨we will succeed only *insofar as* we are prepared to sacrifice secondary objectives⟩

insofar that *conj* : in the measure that : to the extent or degree that ⟨cooperated fully *insofar that* many of their projects were jointly conducted⟩

insol *abbr* insoluble

in·so·late \'in(t)(,)sō,lāt, -,sə,-\ *vt* -ED/-ING/ -S [L *insolatus,* past part. of *insolare,* fr. *in-* ²in- + *sol* sun — more at SOLAR] : to place in the sunlight : expose to the sun's rays (as for curing, drying, ripening)

in·so·la·tion \,=(,)='lāshən\ *n* -s [F or L; F, fr. MF, fr. L *insolation-, insolatio,* fr. *insolatus* (past part.) + *-ion-, -io* -ion] **1** : exposure (as of fruits or drugs) to the rays of the sun usu. to induce curing, drying, maturing **2** : SUNSTROKE **3 a** : solar radiation that has been received (as by the earth) **b** : the rate of delivery of all direct solar energy per unit of horizontal surface

insole \'=,=\ *n* [⁴*in* + *sole*] **1** : an inside sole of a shoe **2** : a loose thin strip (as of leather or felt) placed inside a shoe for warmth or ease

insole 2

in·so·lence \'in(t)s(ə)lən(t)s\ *n* -s [ME, fr. L *insolentia,* fr. *insolent-, insolens* insolent + *-ia* -y] **1** : the quality or state of being insolent : HAUGHTINESS, IMPUDENCE : gross disrespect ⟨~ is often an expression of insecurity⟩ **2** : an instance of insolent conduct or treatment : INSULT ⟨unwilling to put up with her petty ~*s*⟩

in·so·len·cy \-lənsē, -si\ *n* -ES **1** : INSOLENCE **2** *obs* : a strange or unusual thing or occurrence

¹in·so·lent \-lənt\ *adj* [ME, fr. L *insolent-, insolens;* akin to L *insolescere* to grow haughty and prob. to L *solēre* to be accustomed, *sodalis* comrade — more at ETHICAL] **1 a** : haughty and contemptuous or brutal in behavior or language : OVERBEARING ⟨how ~ of late he is become —Shak.⟩ **b** : lacking usual or proper respect for rank or position : presumptuously disrespectful or familiar toward equals or superiors : provokingly free or pert ⟨~ street-corner loafers⟩ ⟨I will not tolerate an ~ child⟩ **2** : proceeding from or characterized by insolence ⟨heard out his ~ speech⟩ **3 a** *obs* : exceeding due bounds : EXCESSIVE, EXTRAVAGANT **b** : of such scope as to give an effect of contemptuous self-assurance ⟨the modern world, with its quick material successes and its ~ belief in the boundless possibilities of progress —Bertrand Russell⟩ ⟨mastered the violin with ~ ease⟩ **4** *obs* : not customary : NOVEL, STRANGE, UNUSUAL **syn** see PROUD

²insolent \"\ *n* -s : one who is insolent

in·so·lent·ly *adv* : in an insolent manner : to an insolent degree

in·so·lent·ness *n* -ES : the quality or state of being insolent

in·solidity \¦in+\ *n* [¹*in-* + *solidity*] : lack of solidity : weak flimsy form or quality

in so·li·do \(')in'sälə,dō\ *also* **in so·li·dum** \-,dəm\ *adv (or adj)* [L] : for the whole : involving all — used in civil law of a solidary obligation or contract ⟨an *in solido* obligation⟩ ⟨action may be brought against both the insured and the insurer, jointly and *in solido*⟩; compare JOINT AND SEVERAL

in·solubility \(¦)in, ən+\ *n* [LL *insolubilitas,* fr. L *insolubilis* insoluble + *-itas* -ity] : the quality or state of being insoluble: as **a** : INDISSOLUBILITY **b** (1) : INEXPLICABILITY (2) : something inexplicable

in·solubilization \"+\ *n* : the process of insolubilizing

in·solubilize \(')in, ən+\ *vt* [L *insolubilis* + E *-ize*] : to render insoluble

¹in·soluble \(')in, ən+\ *adj* [alter. (influenced by L *insolubilis*) of ME *insolible,* fr. L *insolubilis,* fr. *in-* ¹in- + *solvere* to free, dissolve + *-bilis* -able — more at SOLVE] : not soluble: as **a** *archaic* : incapable of being loosened : INDISSOLUBLE **b** : having or admitting of no solution or explanation : UNSOLVABLE ⟨an ~ doubt⟩ **c** *obs, of an argument* : UNANSWERABLE, IRREFUTABLE **d** : incapable of being dissolved in a liquid ⟨chalk is ~ in water⟩; *broadly* : soluble only with difficulty or to a slight degree ⟨a very ~ salt, dissolving no more than 1 part in 500,000 of water⟩ — **in·solubleness** \"+\ *n* — **in·solubly** \"+\ *adv*

²insoluble \"\ *n* [alter. (influenced by L *insolubilis,* adj.) of ME *insolible,* fr. *insolible,* adj.] **1** : something (as a problem or difficulty) that cannot be solved **2** : an insoluble substance ⟨the ~*s* in a tanning extract⟩

in·solvability \(¦in, ən+\ *n* : the quality or state of being insolvable

in·solvable \(')in, ən+\ *adj* [¹*in-* + *solvable*] : INSOLUBLE; *esp* : incapable of being solved ⟨an apparently ~ problem⟩ — **in·solv·ably** \-blē,-bli\ *adv*

in·sol·vence \(')in¦sälvən(t)s, ən's-\ *n* -s *archaic* : INSOLVENCY

in·sol·ven·cy \-vənsē, -si\ *n, often attrib* [prob. fr. ML *insolventia,* fr. L *in-* ¹in- + *solvent-, solvens* (pres. part. of *solvere* to pay, free, dissolve) + *-ia* -y] **1** : the fact or state of being insolvent : inability to pay debts **2** : insufficiency (as of an estate) to discharge all enforceable debts

insolvency law *or* **insolvent law** *or* **insolvency statute** *or* **insolvent statute** *n* : a state statute that affords to an insolvent debtor relief from and sometimes full discharge of debts upon his surrender for the benefit of his creditors of all his property not exempt by law and that is suspended when it conflicts with the Federal Bankruptcy Act or covers a field occupied thereby or affects persons or property within the purview of that act

¹in·sol·vent \-vənt\ *adj* [¹*in-* + L *solvent-, solvens* (pres. part.)] **1 a** : unable or having ceased to pay debts as they fall due in the usual course of business; *specif* : having liabilities in excess of a reasonable market value of assets held — compare BANKRUPT **b** : insufficient to pay all debts charged against it ⟨an ~ estate⟩ **c** : IMPOVERISHED, DEFICIENT ⟨these morally ~ teachers⟩ ⟨~ beliefs⟩ **2** : relating to or for the relief of insolvents ⟨~ regulations⟩

²insolvent \"\ *n* : an insolvent debtor

in·som·nia \ən'sämnēə\ *n* -s [L, fr. *insomnis* sleepless (fr. *in-* ¹in- + *somnus* sleep) + *-ia* — more at SOMNOLENT] : prolonged inability to obtain adequate sleep : abnormal wakefulness : SLEEPLESSNESS

¹in·som·ni·ac \-ē,ak\ *n* -s [L *insomnia* + E *-ac* (as in *maniac*)] : a person suffering from insomnia

²insomniac \"\ *adj* **1** : affected with insomnia ⟨an ~ boy⟩ **2 a** : characteristic of or occurring during a period of sleeplessness ⟨~ distress⟩ ⟨these tumbling ~ ideas⟩ **b** : associated with or tending to cause sleeplessness ⟨humid ~ nights⟩ ⟨the ~ flapping of the canvas —S.N.Behrman⟩

in·som·ni·ous \ən'sämnēəs\ *adj* [L *insomniosus,* fr. *insomnia* + *-osus* -ous] : affected with insomnia : SLEEPLESS

in·somnolence *or* **in·somnolency** \(')in, ən+\ *n* [¹*in-* + *somnolence* or *somnolency*] : SLEEPLESSNESS, INSOMNIA

insomuch \¦==¦=\ *adv* [ME *in so muche, in so moche* — more at MUCH] : so much : to such a degree : so — usu. used with *that* or *as* ⟨they made no mistakes at all. *Insomuch* that . . . it is impossible to imagine a more successful outcome —Bernard De Voto⟩

insomuch as *conj* : INASMUCH AS ⟨*insomuch as* news reports have irretrievably blackened our motives⟩

in·sonorous \(¦)in, ən+\ *adj* [¹*in-* + *sonorous*] : lacking resonance

in·sooth \ən'=\ *adv* [ME *in soth, in soothe* — more at SOOTH (n.)] *archaic* : in truth or reality : TRULY, ACCURATELY, FACTUALLY

in·sorb \ən'sȯ(ə)rb\ *vt* -ED/-ING/-S [²*in-* + L *sorbēre* to suck up — more at ABSORB] : to take in : ABSORB

in·sordid \(')in, ən+\ *adj* [¹*in-* + *sordid*] : free from sordidness : GENEROUS

in·sou·ciance \ən'süsēən(t)s, -üshən-, *F* aⁿsüsyäⁿs\ *n* -s [F, fr. *in-* ¹in- + *soucier* to trouble, disturb (fr. L *sollicitare* to disturb, agitate, move) + F *-ance* — more at SOLICIT] : freedom from concern or care : absence of studied attention : an attitude of indifference or unconcern esp. to the impression created (as by one's work, conduct, or comportment) on others ⟨moved on with a sort of elegant ~⟩ ⟨the utter ~ of this financial policy⟩ ⟨the light ~ of these lyrics⟩

in·sou·ciant \-sēənt,-shənt, *F* -syäⁿ\ *adj* [F, fr. *in-* ¹in- + *souciant,* pres. part. of *soucier*] : exhibiting or characterized by insouciance ⟨an ~ manner⟩ ⟨a gay ~ person⟩ — **in·sou·ciant·ly** \-sēəntlē, -shən-, -li\ *adv*

insoul *var of* ENSOUL

insp *abbr* inspector

in·span \(')inz¦pan, ənz'p-, -n¦sp-\ *vb* [Afrik, fr. MD *inspannen,* fr. *in* in (adv.) + *spannen* to stretch, span, hitch up — more at SPAN] *vt, chiefly Africa* : to yoke or harness (draft animals) to a vehicle : hitch draft animals to (a vehicle) ~ *vi, chiefly Africa* : to inspan animals or a vehicle ⟨*inspanned* as soon as we had eaten⟩

inspeak *vt* **inspoke** *or archaic* **inspake**; **inspoken**; **inspeaking**; **inspeaks** [²*in-* + *speak;* prob. trans. of G *einsprechen*] : to instill or infuse by or as if by speaking

¹inspect *n* -s [L *inspectus,* fr .*inspectus,* past part.] *obs* : INSPECTION

²in·spect \ənz'pekt, ən'sp-\ *vb* -ED/-ING/-S [partly fr. L *inspectus,* past part. of *inspicere,* fr. *in-* ²in- + *-spicere* (fr. *specere* to look), & partly fr. L *inspectare,* fr. *inspectus* — more at SPY] *vt* **1** : to view closely and critically (as in order to ascertain quality or state, detect errors, or otherwise appraise) : examine with care : SCRUTINIZE ⟨let us ~ your motives⟩ ⟨~*ed* the herd for ticks⟩ **2** : to view and examine officially (as troops or arms) ~ *vi, archaic* : to look carefully : make an examination (as into a situation) : SEARCH **syn** see SCRUTINIZE

in·spect·able \-təbəl\ *adj* : capable of being inspected or publicly observed

in·spect·ing·ly *adv* : so as to inspect : with an effect of inspecting

in·spec·tion \-kshən\ *n* -s [ME *inspeccioun,* fr. MF *inspection,* fr. L *inspection-, inspectio,* fr. *inspectus* (past part.) + *-ion-, -io* -ion] **1** : the act or process of inspecting : a strict or close examination: as **a** (1) : the physical examination of the injured part of a person suing for damages for personal injury (2) : the examination of articles of commerce to determine their fitness for transportation or sale **b** : official examination to determine and report on the condition of military or naval personnel and matériel **c** : visual observation of the body in the course of a medical examination — compare PALPATION **d** : an investigation of an applicant for insurance **e** : an examination or a survey of a community, of premises, or of an installation by an authorized person (as to determine compliance with regulations or susceptibility to fire or other hazards) **2** : INSIGHT, PERCEPTION — obs. except in the philosophy of A. N. Whitehead

in·spec·tion·al \-shən³l,-shnəl\ *adj* **1** : of or relating to inspection : by means of or involving inspection ⟨~ services⟩ **2** : being or designed to be comprehensible immediately and without study or analysis ⟨an ~ comparison of two languages⟩

inspection arms *n* **1** : a position in the manual of the rifle, carbine, and pistol in which the weapon is held with the chamber open for inspection **2** : the command to take this position

inspection car *n* : a small motorized vehicle with flanged wheels for inspecting railroad track and roadway

inspection car

in·spec·tive \-ktiv\ *adj* [LL *inspectivus,* fr. L *inspectus* (past part.) + *-ivus* -ive] : engaged in or given to inspection : watching or examining closely : visually attentive ⟨an ~ gaze⟩

in·spec·tor \-tə(r)\ *n* -s [L, fr. *inspectus* (past part. of *inspicere* to inspect) + *-or* — more at INSPECT] **1** : one that inspects or makes an inspection; *esp* : a person employed to inspect something (as the work of others, goods imported, the state and hazards of buildings) — often used in combination ⟨customs ~⟩ ⟨fire ~⟩; see MINE INSPECTOR **2** : one that oversees or supervises: as **a** : a police officer in charge of a number of precincts and ranking below a superintendent or deputy superintendent **b** : a person appointed to oversee the conduct of an election (as with respect to the provisions of law and propriety)

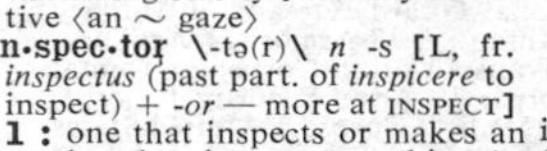

in·spec·tor·ate \-tərət, *usu* -əd·+V\ *n* -s **1** : the office, position, work, or district of an inspector **2** : a body of inspectors

inspector general *n, pl* **inspectors general** [trans. of F *inspecteur général*] : a person that heads an inspectorate : the supervisor of a body of inspectors or a department or system of inspection (as of an army) ⟨the *inspector general* of agriculture⟩; *also* : an officer of a military corps of inspectors that investigates and reports on organizational matters (as discipline, morale, supply, accounts)

in·spec·to·ri·al \¦inz,pek¦tōrēəl, ən-, -n,sp-\ *or* **in·spec·tor·al** \ənz'pekt(ə)rəl, ən'sp-\ *adj* [*inspector* + *-ial* or *-al*] : of, relating to, or involving inspection, an inspector, or an inspector's duties

in·spec·tor·ship \ənz'pektə(r),ship, ən'sp-\ *n* : the status or position of an inspector ⟨obtained his ~ at 35⟩

in·spec·to·scope \ənz'pektə,skōp, ən'sp-\ *n* [fr. *Inspectoscope,* a trademark] : an x-ray device with fluoroscope designed to detect contraband articles (as on the person or in parcels or baggage)

in·spec·tress \-trəs\ *n* -ES [*inspector* + *-ess*] : a female inspector; *esp* : a woman who inspects the work of hotel chambermaids and advises the housekeeper of the need for renovation of rooms and replacement of furniture

in·spec·trix \-ktriks\ *n* -ES [LL, fem. of L *inspector*] : INSPECTRESS

inspersion *n* -s [MF, fr. LL *inspersion-, inspersio,* fr. L *inspersus* (past part. of *inspergere* to sprinkle, fr. *in-* ²in- + *-spergere,* fr. *spargere* to scatter) + *-ion-, -io* -ion — more at SPARK] *obs* : SPRINKLING

in·spex·i·mus \ənz'peksəməs, ən'sp-\ *n* -ES [L, we have inspected] : an English charter or letters patent beginning with the Latin word *inspeximus* in which the grantor confirms and recites a former charter

insphere *var of* ENSPHERE

in·spir·able \ənz'pīrəbəl, ən'sp-\ *adj* [*inspire* + *-able*] **1** : capable of being inspired ⟨while still ~ with a sense of responsibility⟩ **2** : fit for inspiration ⟨barely ~ air⟩

in·spi·rate \'inzpə,rāt *sometimes* -(,)pi,- *or* -,pē,- *or chiefly Brit* -,pī,-; 'in(t)(,)sp-\ *vt* -ED/-ING/-S [L *inspiratus,* past part. of *inspirare* to inspire, breathe into] **1** *archaic* : INSPIRE **2** *phonet* : to articulate during inhalation

in·spi·ra·tion \,=(,)='rāshən\ *n* -s [ME *inspiracioun,* fr. MF or LL; MF *inspiration,* fr. OF, fr. LL *inspiration-, inspiratio,* fr. L *inspiratus* (past part. of *inspirare* to breathe into, inspire) + *-ion-, -io* -ion] **1** : a divine influence or action upon the lives of certain persons that is believed to qualify them to receive and communicate sacred revelation and is interpreted within Christianity as the direct action of the Holy Spirit **2** [MF or LL; MF, fr. LL *inspiration-, inspiratio*] : the act of breathing in; *specif* : the drawing of air into the lungs — opposed to *expiration* **3 a** : the act or power of moving the intellect or emotions : capacity to inspire ⟨the ~ of this lovely scene⟩ **b** : the act of suggesting or influencing opinions or information esp. on a public matter ⟨the ~ of this rumor was traced to a source near the governor⟩ **4 a** : the quality or state of being inspired ⟨an artist whose ~ came from many sources⟩ ⟨found his ~ weakening⟩ **b** : something that is inspired ⟨had a new ~ as he waited⟩ ⟨a scheme that was a pure ~⟩ **5** : someone or something that inspires : an inspiring agent or influence

in·spi·ra·tion·al \,=(,)='rāshən³l, -shnəl\ *adj* **1** : produced by or moved by inspiration ⟨an ~ speaker⟩ **2** : of or relating to inspiration ⟨the ~ element in Scripture⟩ **3** : communicating inspiration ⟨~ talks⟩ — **in·spi·ra·tion·al·ly** \-³l¦ē, -əl¦, ¦i\ *adv*

in·spi·ra·tion·ist \,=(,)='rāsh(ə)nəst\ *n* -s : one who holds a theory of or belief in inspiration esp. of Scripture

in·spi·ra·tive \ənz'pīrəd·iv, ən'sp-; 'inzpə,rād·iv, 'in(t)sp-\ *adj* [L *inspiratus* (past part.) + E *-ive*] : tending to inspire : INSPIRING

in·spi·ra·tor \'inzpə,rād·ə(r), 'in(t)sp-\ *n* -s [LL, fr. L *inspiratus* (past part. of *inspirare* to inspire) + *-or*] **1** : INSPIRER **2** : one that inhales or draws in something: as **a** : INJECTOR **b** : RESPIRATOR

in·spir·a·to·ry \ənz'pīrə,tōrē, ən'sp-, -tȯr-, -ri\ *adj* [L *inspiratus* (past part.) + E *-ory*] : relating to, aiding, used for, or associated with inspiration ⟨~ muscles⟩ ⟨the ~ whoop of whooping cough⟩

in·spire \ənz'pī(ə)r, ən'sp-, -īə\ *vb* -ED/-ING/-S [ME *inspiren, enspiren,* fr. MF & L; MF *inspirer, enspirer,* fr. OF, fr. L *inspirare,* fr. *in-* ²in- + *spirare* to breathe — more at SPIRIT] *vt* **1 a** *archaic* : to breathe or blow into or upon **b** *archaic* : to infuse (as life) by breathing ⟨*inspired* into him an active soul —Wisd Sol 15:11⟩ **c** *obs* : to breathe or blow (as air or vapor) into or upon something **2** : to draw in by breathing : breathe in : INHALE ⟨*inspiring* the crisp fall air⟩ ⟨the baby will ~ the mucus down into its lungs —*Fire Manual (Mass.)*⟩ ⟨be accomplished by increasing the oxygen percentage in the *inspired* air —H.G.Armstrong⟩ — distinguished from *expire* **3 a** : to influence, move, or guide (as to speech or action) through divine or supernatural agency or power ⟨the gods were believed to ~ the oracles⟩ ⟨spoke like a prophet *inspired* from above⟩ **b** : to have an animating, enlivening, or exalting effect upon esp. in a degree or with a result suggestive of the workings of some extraordinary power or influence ⟨had been *inspired* by his mother⟩ ⟨our ability to ~ the plodder —Ellie Tucker⟩ ⟨Milton and Shakespeare ~ the active life of England . . . through exceptional individuals —W.B.Yeats⟩ ⟨books that have *inspired* countless generations⟩ — often used with *with; specif* : to stimulate to creative activity in an art **c** : ENCOURAGE, IMPEL, MOTIVATE — usu. used with *to* ⟨*inspired* them to greater efforts⟩ ⟨a success which *inspired* him to broaden his activities⟩ **d** : AFFECT — usu. used with *with* ⟨experiences that *inspired* him with a yearning for education⟩ ⟨poverty that ~*s* the beholder with pity and disgust⟩ **4 a** : to communicate or impart (as an utterance) to an agent through divine or supernatural power ⟨spoke in words *inspired* by God⟩ **b** : to infuse or introduce into the mind or communicate to the spirit ⟨a steadfastness that *inspired* confidence in his followers⟩ ⟨conduct that ~*s* nothing but disgust⟩ : AROUSE, PROVOKE **5 a** : to bring about : OCCASION, PRODUCE ⟨events that *inspired* a new fashion⟩ ⟨studies that *inspired* several inventions⟩ ⟨hoping that improvement in business would ~ a tax cut⟩ ⟨the attacks *inspired* the passing of stringent food and drug regulations —E.S.Turner⟩ **b** : INCITE, FOMENT ⟨communist-*inspired* riots⟩ **6** : to cause to be said or written by influence and without acknowledgment of actual source or authorship ⟨a rumor that had been *inspired* by interested parties⟩ ~ *vi* **1** : to impart inspiration **2** *obs* : BREATHE, BLOW **3** : to draw in breath : inhale air into the lungs ⟨*inspired* deeply from a small bottle he had taken from his pocket —E.C.Bentley⟩

inspired *adj* [ME *enspired,* fr. past part. of *enspiren* to inspire] **1 a** : moved by or as if by a divine or supernatural influence : affected by divine inspiration ⟨~ prophets⟩ **b** : communicated by divine or supernatural inspiration : having divine authority ⟨the ~ books of the Bible⟩ **2** : breathed in : INHALED **3 a** : suggested by someone in power or in a position to know ⟨~ views⟩ **b** : having received or publishing authoritative views or information ⟨an ~ newspaper⟩ **4** : outstanding or brilliant in a way or to a degree suggestive of divine or supernatural inspiration ⟨an ~ mechanic⟩ ⟨an ~ performance of a concerto⟩ ⟨an ~ answer to an awkward question⟩ — **in·spired·ly** \-īrədlē, -ī(ə)rd-\ *adv*

in·spir·er \-īrə(r)\ *n* -s [alter. (influenced by *-er*) of ME *inspirour,* fr. *inspiren* to inspire + *-our* -or] : one that inspires

inspiring *adj* : that inspires or tends to inspire ⟨~ thoughts⟩ ⟨the music was ~⟩ — **in·spir·ing·ly** *adv*

in·spirit \ənz'p-, ən'sp-\ *also* **en·spirit** \", en-\ *vt* -ED/-ING/-S [²*in-* or ¹*en-* + *spirit* (n.)] **1** : to infuse spirit into : fill with courage, determination, hope, vigor, or exaltation : ANIMATE, HEARTEN ⟨unconquerable jests have ~*ed* men's hearts in long periods of disaster —Agnes Repplier⟩ **2** : to cause to be possessed by a spirit **syn** see ENCOURAGE

in·spir·it·er \"ə(r)\ *n* -s : one that inspirits

inspiriting *adj* : tending or able to inspirit ⟨an ~ letter⟩ — **in·spir·it·ing·ly** *adv*

in·spi·rom·e·ter \,inzpə'rämәd·ə(r), ,inz,pī'-, ,in(t)(,)sp-\ *n* [*inspire* + *-o-* + *-meter*] : an apparatus for measuring air inspired in breathing

¹in·spis·sate \(')inz¦pisāt, ənz'p-, -i,sāt, 'inzpə,sāt, -n(t)(¦)sp-\ *or* **in·spis·sat·ed** \-ād·əd\ *adj* [*inspissate* fr. LL *inspissatus* (past part.); *inspissated* fr. past part. of ²*inspissate*] : thickened in consistency; *broadly* : made thick, heavy, or intense ⟨shed a flood of *inspissated* darkness on a cloud of confusing uncertainties —G.B.Barbour⟩ ⟨*inspissated* class-consciousness —Vincent Sheean⟩

²in·spis·sate \ənz'pi,sāt, 'inzpə,-, -n(t)(')sp-\ *vb* -ED/-ING/-S [LL *inspissatus,* past part. of *inspissare,* fr. L *in-* ²in- + *spissare* to thicken, fr. *spissus* thick; akin to Gk *aspis* shield — more at ASPID-] *vt* : to bring to a heavier consistency : CONDENSE ⟨*inspissating* the serum in the Petri dishes⟩; *broadly* : to make thick, heavy, or intense ⟨parties of school children and factory girls *inspissating* the gloom of the museum atmosphere —Clive Bell⟩ ~ *vi* : to reach or assume a heavier consistency ⟨sap *inspissating* over a fire⟩ — **in·spis·sa·tor** \-ād·ə(r)\ *n* -s

in·spis·sa·tion \,inzpə'sāshən, -(,)pi'-, ,in(t)sp-\ *n* -s [F or ML; F, fr. MF, fr. ML *inspissation-, inspissatio,* fr. LL *inspissatus* (past part.) + L *-ion-, -io* -ion] : the act or process of inspissating or the state of being inspissated

in spite of *prep* [ME] : without being blocked or prevented by the opposing force of : regardless of the adverse effect of : DESPITE, NOTWITHSTANDING ⟨went *in spite of* the rain⟩ ⟨a handsome man *in spite of* his baldness⟩ ⟨plunged ahead *in spite of* all efforts to stop him⟩

inspoke *past of* INSPEAK

inspoken *past part of* INSPEAK

inst *abbr* **1** installment **2** instant; instantaneous **3** institute; institution **4** instruction; instructor **5** instrument; instrumental

in·sta·bil·i·ty \ˌinztə¦=== , ¦in(t)stə-\ *n* [ME *instabilitee*, fr. MF or L; MF *instabilité*, fr. L *instabilitas*, fr. *instabilis* + *-itas* -ity] **:** the quality or state of being unstable: as **a :** lack of physical firmness **:** INSECURITY ⟨the ~ of a building⟩ **b :** lack of determination or uniformity ⟨economic ~⟩ **:** INCONSTANCY ⟨~ of temper⟩ ⟨increasing ~ of cherished institutions⟩; *also* **:** tendency to react violently or explosively ⟨emotional ~⟩ ⟨the extreme ~ of certain chemicals⟩ **c :** an unstable state of the atmosphere that results when the vertical distribution of temperature or moisture is such that an air particle when set in motion will tend to move at increasing speed either upward or downward from its previous position

in·sta·ble \(ˈ)inz¦tābəl, -n¦st-\ *adj* [MF or L; MF, fr. L *instabilis*, fr. *in-* ¹in- + *stabilis* firm, stable — more at STABLE] **:** UNSTABLE

in·stall *also* **in·stal** \ənzˈtȯl, ənˈst-\ *vt* **installed**; **installed**; **installing**; **installs** *also* **instals** [MF *installer*, *instaler*, fr. ML *installare*, fr. L *in-* ²in- + ML *stallum*, *stallus* stall, fr. OHG *stal* place, stall — more at STALL] **1 a :** to place in possession of an office or dignity by seating in a stall or official seat **b :** to place in an office, rank, or order **:** INDUCT ⟨~*ed* the new college president⟩ **2 :** to introduce and establish (oneself or another) in an indicated place, condition, or status ⟨~*ing* himself in the big chair before the fire⟩ ⟨~*ed* his sister as secretary⟩ **3 :** to set up for use or service ⟨the electrician ~*ed* the new fixtures⟩ ⟨had gas heating ~*ed*⟩

in·stal·lant \-lənt\ *n* -s [ML *installant-*, *installans*, pres. part of *installare* to install] **:** one that formally installs another to office

in·stal·la·tion \ˌinztəˈlāshən, ˌin(t)stə-\ *n* -s [F or ML; F, fr. MF, fr. ML *installation-*, *installatio*, fr. *installatus* (past part. of *installare*) + L *-ion-*, *-io* -ion] **1 :** an act of installing or the state of being installed: as **a :** the giving possession of an office, rank, or order with the usual rites or ceremonies **b :** ESTABLISHMENT **c :** the setting up or placing in position for service or use **2 a :** something that is installed for use ⟨admired the new plumbing ~⟩ **b installations** *pl* **:** APPOINTMENTS, FURNISHINGS, EQUIPMENT ⟨the ~*s* were of excellent quality and in very good taste⟩ **3 :** land and improvements installed thereon devoted to military purposes ⟨forts, training camps, and other army ~*s*⟩

in·stall·er \ənzˈtȯlə(r), ənˈst-\ *n* -s **:** one that installs ⟨repairmen and ~*s* of new equipment⟩

installing officer *n* **:** a person that supervises or conducts a formal installing of an officer of an organization

¹**in·stall·ment** *or* **in·stal·ment** \-lmənt\ *n* -s [*install* or *instal* + *-ment*] **1 :** an act of installing or the state of being installed **2** *obs* **:** the seat or place in which one is installed

²**installment** *also* **instalment** \"\ *n* -s [alter. of earlier *estallment*, *estalment* arrangement for payment by installments, prob. fr. MF *estaler* to stop, place, fix (fr. OF, fr. *estal* stop, place, position, fr. OHG *stal* place, stall) + E *-ment* — more at STALL] **1 a :** one of the portions into which a sum of money or a debt is divided for payment at set and usu. regular intervals ⟨the balance may be paid in three equal quarterly ~*s*⟩ **b :** a payment that is part of a sum owed ⟨surprised to get even an ~ on the money he had loaned⟩ **2 a :** one of several parts (as of a publication) presented at intervals **:** FASCICLE **b :** one portion of a story published serially (as in a magazine)

³**installment** *also* **instalment** \"\ *adj* **:** of, relating to, based on, or involving periodic payments of a fixed sum or of a predetermined percentage of a total ⟨~ buying⟩ ⟨~ credit⟩ ⟨~ loan⟩ ⟨an ~ account⟩

installment mortgage *n* **:** a mortgage in which the sum loaned is to be repaid in installments over a period of time

installment plan *n* **:** a plan that involves payment by installments

installment sales insurance *n* **:** insurance that covers the seller's interest in merchandise which is sold on installment terms

installment selling *n* **:** the selling of consumer goods on credit under conditional sales contracts that provide for regular periodic payments after an initial down payment

¹**in·stance** \ˈinztən(t)s, ˈin(t)stə-, ˈinsən-\ *n* -s [ME *instaunce*, fr. MF *instance* act of urging, motive, instant, fr. L *instantia* presence, vehemence in speech, urgency, fr. *instant-*, *instans* (pres. part.) + *-ia* -y — more at INSTANT] **1 a** *archaic* **:** urgent or earnest solicitation **:** urgency or exercise of pressure in either petition or action **b :** INSTIGATION, SUGGESTION, REQUEST ⟨work undertaken at the ~ of the householder⟩ **c** *obs* **:** something that urges **:** an impelling cause or motive **2** [ML *instantia*, trans. of Gk *enstasis*] **a** *archaic* **:** a case or example brought forward in disproof or rebuttal of a generalization **:** EXCEPTION **b :** something that is available or is offered as an illustrative case **:** something cited in proof or as an example ⟨an ~ of true heroism⟩ ⟨carefully documenting each ~ of the use of this diphthong⟩ **c** *obs* **:** TOKEN, SIGN, SYMPTOM **d** *obs* **:** DETAIL, CIRCUMSTANCE **3** [F or LL; F, fr. LL *instantia*, fr. L] **a :** the institution and prosecution of a lawsuit **:** a legal proceeding or process **:** SUIT **b** (1) **:** a demand set forth in a civil law proceeding (2) **:** a specific case referred to as an example (3) **:** a case in an ecclesiastical court that is brought at the request of a party and not upon official request **4 a :** a step, stage, or situation viewed as part of a process or series of events **:** an occasion or period defined by certain events ⟨a well-known writer who prefers, in this ~, to remain anonymous —*Times Lit. Supp.*⟩ ⟨appointments will be made for a three-year period in the first ~⟩ **b :** SUBSTITUTION INSTANCE

syn CASE, ILLUSTRATION, EXAMPLE, SAMPLE, SPECIMEN: INSTANCE and CASE are less specific in meaning and suggestion than the others. The former may be used in reference to any particular person, thing, or situation which may be given to illustrate or explain ⟨the *instance* may be rejected, but the principle abides —B.N.Cardozo⟩ ⟨wanted to work out the problem on a definite *instance* —A.L.Guérard⟩ CASE is now very general in meaning and poor in connotative power; it is used to designate a situation or occurrence showing characteristics to be grouped together and viewed as a configuration or pattern ⟨the *case* of payments made under the head of profits to entrepreneurs, financiers, speculators, and middlemen in various markets —J.A.Hobson⟩ ⟨usually isolated *cases* of deaf and dumb, feebleminded, or otherwise unfortunate children —R.W.Murray⟩ ILLUSTRATION is likely to suggest an instance adduced for the sake of clarifying or demonstrating ⟨the resolution of Washington and his men at Valley Forge is an *illustration* of bravery⟩ EXAMPLE suggests a single item or incident taken as typical or representative ⟨perhaps the best of many American *examples* of the creative artist and thinker . . . in a country and an era dominantly materialistic —H.S.Canby⟩ SAMPLE may indicate a part or a unit of a whole taken more or less at random but still presumed to be typical or representative in showing a general nature, character, or quality ⟨so many happy youths . . . so many divers *samples* from the growth of life's sweet season —William Wordsworth⟩ ⟨the barest *sample* of the riches which the gleaner may gather —B.N.Cardozo⟩ SPECIMEN is close to SAMPLE in its meaning but may suggest scientific or otherwise close analysis ⟨made it my business to examine some *specimens* of the writing —Charles Dickens⟩ SPECIMEN may indicate either the typical or representative example or the merely existent instance ⟨there were a few boomtowns in the Middle West, but the finest *specimens* began to be seen only with the discoveries of gold and silver in the Far West —A.F.Harlow⟩ — **for instance** \fə(r)in- *sometimes* ˈfrin-\ *adv* **:** as an example

²**instance** \"\ *vb* -ED/-ING/-S *vt* **1** *obs* **:** URGE, IMPORTUNE **2 :** to illustrate or demonstrate by an instance ⟨his meaning is well *instanced* in the passage quoted⟩ **3 :** to mention as a case or example **:** CITE ⟨we might ~ the increase in delinquency⟩ ~ *vi* **:** to mention an instance **syn** see MENTION

instance court *n* **:** a branch of a court of admiralty that has jurisdiction over all maritime contracts and torts except prize cases

in·stan·cy \-ənsē, -si\ *n* -ES [L *instantia*] **1 :** URGENCY, INSISTENCE ⟨continued to press his claim with some ~⟩ ⟨the vivid ~ of an involuntary cry —C.E.Montague⟩ **2 :** nearness of approach **:** IMMINENCE ⟨the ~ of peril —*Yale Rev.*⟩ **3 :** immediateness of occurrence or action **:** INSTANTANEOUSNESS ⟨the ~ of their response⟩ ⟨the *instancies* of aviation and television —Mary Madeleva⟩

¹**in·stant** \ˈinztənt, ˈin(t)stə-\ *n* -s [ME, prob. fr. MF, fr. *instant*, adj.] **1 a :** an infinitesimal space of time **:** a point of time ⟨came not an ~ too soon⟩; *esp* **:** a point without temporal duration separating two states each with temporal duration ⟨at the ~ of death⟩ **b :** a point of time present or regarded as present in respect to a particular context **:** MOMENT ⟨the ~ we met⟩ ⟨come here this ~⟩ ⟨the ~ she opened her eyes⟩ **2 :** the present or current month

²**instant** \"\ *adj* [ME, fr. MF or L; MF, fr. L *instant-*, *instans*, fr. pres. part. of *instare* to stand upon, press upon, urge, fr. *in-* ²in- + *stare* to stand — more at STAND] **1 :** INSISTENT, IMPORTUNATE, PRESSING, URGENT ⟨~ in argument⟩ **2 a :** PRESENT, CURRENT ⟨the ~ case being tried⟩ **b :** of or occurring in the present month — abbr. *inst.* ⟨received your letter of the 10th *inst.*⟩; compare PROXIMO, ULTIMO **3 :** closely pressing in respect to time ⟨running an ~ risk of suffocating⟩ **4 :** IMMEDIATE, DIRECT ⟨the ~ dependence of form upon soul —R.W.Emerson⟩ **5 a :** premixed or precooked for easy final preparation ⟨~ cake mix⟩ ⟨~ mashed potatoes⟩ **b :** immediately soluble in water ⟨~ coffee⟩ **syn** see PRESSING

³**instant** \"\ *adv* **:** at once **:** INSTANTLY

in·stan·ta·ne·i·ty \ˌinzˌtantᵊnˈēəd·ē, ənz-, -antəˈnē-, ˌinztəntəˈnē-, -n(ˌ)st-\ *n* -ES [*instantaneous* + *-ity*] **:** the quality or state of being instantaneous

in·stan·ta·neous \ˌinztən¦tānēəs, ¦in(t)stə-, -ānyəs\ *adj* [ML *instantaneus*, fr. L *instant-*, *instans* (pres. part.) + *-aneus* (as in *subterraneus* subterranean)] **1 :** done, occurring, or acting without any perceptible duration of time ⟨~ death⟩ ⟨~ heaters⟩ **2 a :** done without any delay being introduced purposely ⟨~ action⟩ **b** *of a sound recording* **:** capable of being used as soon as recorded **3 :** occurring or present at a particular instant ⟨~ value⟩ ⟨~ velocity⟩ — **in·stan·ta·ne·ous·ly** *adv* — **in·stan·ta·ne·ous·ness** *n* -ES

instantaneous exposure *n* **:** exposure of photographic materials for a short time by an automatic device — compare TIME EXPOSURE

in·stan·ter \ənzˈtantə(r), ənˈsta-\ *adv* [ML, fr. L, earnestly, vehemently, fr. *instant-*, *instans* instant] **:** at once **:** IMMEDIATELY, INSTANTLY

in·stan·tial \(ˈ)inz¦tanchəl, ənzˈt-, -n¦sta-\ *adj* [L *instantia* presence, urgency + E *-al* — more at INSTANCE] **:** of, relating to, constituting, or providing an instance ⟨empirical laws for which there is ~ evidence —Arthur Pap⟩

in·stan·ti·ate \=ˈ=chēˌāt\ *vt* -ED/-ING/-S [L *instantia* presence, urgency + E *-ate*] **:** to represent (an abstraction or universal) by a concrete instance — **in·stan·ti·a·tion** \(ˌ)=ˌ==ˈāshən\ *n* -s

¹**in·stant·ly** *adv* [ME, fr. *instant* (adj.) + *-ly*] **1 :** with urgency or importunity **:** PRESSINGLY **2** *obs* **:** in this or in the most recent moment **:** just now **3 :** without the least delay **:** at once **:** IMMEDIATELY

²**in·stant·ly** \"\ *conj* **:** as soon as **:** IMMEDIATELY, DIRECTLY ⟨recognized her ~ I saw her⟩

in·stant·ness *n* -ES **:** the quality or state of being instant

¹**in·star** \ənzˈt-, ənˈst-\ *also* **en·star** \ən-,en-\ *vt* [²*in-* or ¹*en-* + *star* (n.)] **1** *archaic* **:** to place as a star **:** turn into a star **2 :** to adorn or stud with or as if with stars ⟨a coronet *instarred* with precious stones⟩

²**in·star** \ˈinzˌtär, -nˌst-, -tȧ(r)\ *n* -s [NL, fr. L, figure, form, perh. alter. of *instare* to approach, to be evenly balanced, stand upon — more at INSTANT] **:** a stage in the life of an insect or other arthropod between two successive molts ⟨some insects may have seven or more ~*s*⟩; *also* **:** an individual in a specified instar ⟨collected several third-*instar* larvae⟩

in·state \ənzˈtāt, -nˈstāt, *usu* -ād.+V\ *also* **en·state** \ən-,en-\ *vt* [²*in-* or ¹*en-* + *state* (n.)] **1 :** to set, place, or establish esp. in a rank, office, or status **:** INSTALL ⟨hoped to ~ his sister in her estate⟩ **2** *obs* **a :** INVEST, ENDOW **b :** BESTOW, CONFER

in·state·ment \-mənt\ *n* -s **:** INSTALLATION

in sta·tu nas·cen·di \ənˌstä¦(ˌ)tünəˈsendē, -¦staˌ |(ˌ)chü-, -ˌdī; -¦stä(ˌ)tünäˈskendē\ [L, in the state of being born] **:** in the nascent state ⟨produce the aldehyde *in statu nascendi* —C.D.Hurd⟩ **:** in the course of being formed or developed ⟨if . . . isolation can promote the formation of full species, such species must *in statu nascendi* pass through a phase of less than specific distinction —Fridthjof Økland⟩

in statu quo \-ˈkwō\ [L] **:** in the state in which something is or has been **:** in the former or same state

in·stau·ra·tion \ˌinztȯˈrāshən, ˌinˌst-\ *n* -s [L *instauration-*, *instauratio*, fr. *instauratus* (past part. of *instaurare* to renew, restore) + *-ion-*, *-io* -ion — more at STORE] **1 :** restoration after decay, lapse, or dilapidation **2** *obs* **:** an act of instituting or establishing something

in·stau·ra·tor \ˈ==ˌrād·ə(r)\ *n* -s [LL, fr. L *instauratus* (past part.) + *-or*] **:** one that engages in instauration

in·stead \ənz¦ted, ən¦st-, *more often before "of" than in other positions* + -tid\ *adv* [fr. the phrase *instead of*] **1 :** in the place **:** in lieu **:** as a substitute or equivalent ⟨he came ~⟩ **2 :** as an alternative to something expected or implied **:** in the place of something **:** RATHER ⟨longing ~ for a quiet country life⟩

instead of *prep* [ME *in sted of*] **:** as a substitute for or alternative to ⟨had peanut butter *instead of* jelly⟩ ⟨sent his helper *instead of* coming himself⟩

in·steep \ənzˈtēp, ənˈst-\ *vt* [²*in-* + *steep*] **:** STEEP, SOAK **:** IMBRUE

in·stel·la·tion \ˌinzˌteˈlāshən, ˌinˌste-\ *n* -s [²*in-* + L *stella* star + E *-ation* — more at STAR] **1 :** a setting among the stars **2 :** a turning into a star

in·step \ˈinzˌtep, ˈinˌstep\ *n* [perh. fr. ⁴*in* + *step*] **1 :** the arched middle portion of the human foot next in front of the ankle joint; *esp* **:** the upper surface of this part **2 :** the part of the hind leg of the horse and related animals between the hock and the pastern joint **3 :** the part of a shoe or stocking over the instep **4 :** something (as the slope of a hill) that is felt to resemble the human instep

in·sti·gate \ˈinztəˌgāt, ˈin(t)stə-, *usu* -ād.+V\ *vt* -ED/-ING/-S [L *instigatus*, past part. of *instigare* — more at STICK] **:** to goad or urge forward **:** set on **:** PROVOKE, INCITE ⟨his past experience *instigated* him to boldness⟩ ⟨*instigating* a plot to overthrow the government⟩ **syn** see INCITE

in·sti·gat·ing·ly *adv* **:** in an instigating manner

in·sti·ga·tion \ˌ==ˈgāshən\ *n* -s [ME *instigacioun*, fr. MF or L; MF *instigation*, fr. L *instigation-*, *instigatio*, fr. *instigatus* (past part.) + *-ion-*, *-io* -ion] **1 :** an act of instigating or the state of being instigated **:** INCITEMENT ⟨they agreed at our ~ to confer⟩ ⟨the ~ of the new program⟩ **2 :** something that instigates **:** INCENTIVE ⟨his friends' approval was a real ~ to succeed⟩

in·sti·ga·tive \ˈ==ˌgād·iv\ *adj* [L *instigatus* (past part.) + E *-ive*] **:** tending to instigate

in·sti·ga·tor \-ˌgād·ə(r), -ātə-\ *n* -s [L, fr. *instigatus* (past part.) — *-or*] **:** one that instigates

in·still *also* **in·stil** \ənzˈtil, ənˈstil\ *vt* **instilled**; **instilled**; **instilling**; **instills** *also* **instils** [MF & L; MF *instiller*, fr. L *instillare*, fr. *in-* ²in- + *stillare* to drip, trickle — more at DISTILL] **1 :** to introduce a drop at a time **:** cause to enter drop by drop ⟨~ a few drops of warm olive oil⟩ **2 :** to impart or introduce gradually **:** cause to be taken in little by little ⟨~*ing* a reverence for honest dealings⟩ ⟨~*ed* the teachings of his own faith⟩ **syn** see IMPLANT

in·stil·la·tion \ˌinztəˈlāshən, ˌin(t)stə-\ *n* -s [MF & L; MF, fr. L *instillation-*, *instillatio*, fr. *instillatus* (past part.) + *-ion-*, *-io* -ion] **1 :** an act of instilling **:** introduction by instilling ⟨repeated ~ of penicillin⟩ **2 :** something that is instilled or designed for instillation ⟨an oily ~⟩ ⟨silver ~ for use in the eyes of the newborn⟩

in·still·er \ənzˈtilə(r), ənˈsti-\ *n* -s **:** one that instills

in·still·ment *also* **in·stil·ment** \-lmənt\ *n* -s **:** INSTILLATION 1

¹**in·stinct** \ˈinzˌ(ˌ)tiŋ(k)t, -ˌteŋ-, ˈin(ˌ)stiŋ-\ *n* -s [ME, fr. L *instinctus*, fr. *instinctus* (past part.)] **1** *obs* **:** INSTIGATION, IMPULSE **2 :** a natural or inherent aptitude, tendency, impulse, or capacity ⟨an ~ for the right word⟩ ⟨his ~ toward success⟩ ⟨the religious ~*s* of primitive peoples⟩ **3 a :** complex and specific response on the part of an organism to environmental stimuli that is largely hereditary and unalterable though the pattern of behavior through which it is expressed may be modified by learning, that does not involve reason, and that has as its goal the removal of a somatic tension or excitation **b :** behavior that is mediated by reactions (as reflex arcs) below the conscious level — usu. not used technically

²**in·stinct** \(ˈ)inz¦tiŋ(k)t, ənzˈt-, -n¦sti-\ *adj* [L *instinctus*, past part. of *instinguere* to instigate, incite; akin to L *instigare* to instigate, incite — more at STICK] **1** *obs* **:** implanted by nature **:** INNATE **2** *obs* **:** impelled by an inner or animating or exciting agency **3 :** profoundly imbued **:** FILLED, CHARGED — usu. used postpositively and with *with* ⟨a spirit ~ with human kindness⟩ ⟨~ with patriotism⟩

³**instinct** *vt* -ED/-ING/-S [L *instinctus* (past part.)] **1** *obs* **:** INSTIGATE, IMPEL **2** *obs* **:** to implant as an animating power

in·stinc·tion \ənzˈtiŋ(k)shən, ənˈst-\ *n* -s [obs. E, instigation, inspiration, fr. MF, fr. LL *instinction-*, *instinctio*, fr. L *instinctus* (past part.) + *-ion-*, *-io* -ion] **1** *obs* **:** INSTINCT **2 :** instinctive behavior

in·stinc·tive \(ˈ)inz¦tiŋ(k)tiv, ənˈst-, -)tēv *also* -)təv\ *adj* [¹*instinct* + *-ive*] **:** of, relating to, or constituting instinct **:** derived from or prompted by instinct **:** determined by natural impulse or propensity **:** UNLEARNED, UNREASONED ⟨an ~ dread of mice⟩ ⟨~ behavior⟩ **syn** see SPONTANEOUS

in·stinc·tive·ly \-tə̇vlē, -li\ *adv* **:** in an instinctive manner **:** as a matter of instinct ⟨reached ~ for some support⟩ ⟨~ proud of their traditions⟩

¹**in·stinc·tiv·ist** \=ˈ=tə̇vəst, -tēv-, -təv-\ *n* -s [*instinctive* + *-ist*] **:** one that views society as a manifestation of various instinctive drives; *broadly* **:** one that views human behavior and social adaptation as the resultant of the interplay of various instinctive drives (as for survival) with environmental factors (as group relations)

²**in·stinc·tiv·ist** \(ˈ)=¦===\ *or* **in·stinc·ti·vis·tic** \(¦)=¦=ˈvistik, -tēkˈ\ *adj* **:** based on the predominance of instinct **:** of or relating to instinctivists ⟨~ theories⟩

in·stinc·tu·al \(ˈ)=¦=ch(əw)əl\ *adj* [¹*instinct* + *-ual* (as in *actual*)] **:** of, relating to, or based on instincts ⟨~ behavior⟩ ⟨the ~ society of social insects⟩ — **in·stinc·tu·al·ly** \-)əlē, -li\ *adv*

in·sti·tor \ˈinztəˌtȯ(ə)r, ˈin(t)stə-\ *n* -s [L, fr. *instit-* (perf. stem of *insistere* to occupy a place in, stand upon, persist) + *-or* — more at INSIST] **:** a person (as the manager of a commercial or manufacturing business, a broker, factor, or commission agent) to whom the transaction of some business is committed as agent to such a degree as to bind the principal — used chiefly in Roman and civil law — **in·sti·to·ri·al** \ˌ==ˈtōrēəl\ *adj*

¹**in·sti·tute** \ˈinztəˌtüt, ˈin(t)stə-, -əˌtyüt, *in rapid speech* ˈinzˌt(y)üt *or* ˈin(t)ˌst(y)-; *usu* -üd.+V\ *vt* -ED/-ING/-S [ME *instituten*, fr. L *institutus*, past part. of *instituere*, fr. *in-* ²in- + *-stituere* (fr. *statuere* to stand up, set, place) — more at STATUTE] **1 :** to establish in a particular position or office: as **a :** to invest with spiritual charge of a benefice **:** put (as a pastor) in charge of the care of souls **b :** to appoint as heir under Roman or civil law **2 a :** to originate and get established **:** set up **:** cause to come into existence **:** ORGANIZE ⟨the man that *instituted* these reforms in lexicography⟩ **b :** to set on foot **:** INAUGURATE, INITIATE ⟨*instituting* an investigation of the charges⟩ **3 a** *obs* **:** to ordain or enjoin to be or to be done **b** *archaic* **:** to ground or establish in principles or rudiments **:** INSTRUCT, EDUCATE **syn** see FOUND

²**institute** \"\ *n* -s [L *institutum*, fr. neut. of *institutus* (past part.)] **1** *obs* **:** DESIGN, PLAN, PURPOSE **2** *obs* **:** an act of instituting **3** [MF & L; MF *institut*, fr. L *institutum*] **:** something that is instituted: as **a** (1) **:** an elementary principle **:** a precept or rule recognized as authoritative (2) **institutes** *pl* **:** a collection of such principles and precepts; *esp* **:** a comprehensive summary of legal principles and decisions — compare DIGEST **b** (1) **:** an organization for the promotion of some estimable or learned cause or the welfare of some group ⟨an ~ for the blind⟩ ⟨an ~ for psychical research⟩ (2) **:** an association of persons or organizations that collectively constitute a technical or professional authority in a field of work or study ⟨Horological *Institute* of America⟩ ⟨an ~ of architects⟩ (3) *chiefly Brit* **:** a school or academy esp. for part-time education of workers ⟨teaching in the village ~⟩ (4) **:** an institution for advanced education esp. in science or technology ⟨spent two years at the textile ~⟩ (5) **:** a brief course of instruction or seminars (as for teachers or poultrymen) on business or professional problems **c :** a building or group of buildings occupied by an institute **4** [L *institutus* (past part.)] **a** *Scots law* **:** the person to whom an estate is first given by destination or testament — compare SUBSTITUTE **b** *civil law* **:** an heir appointed by will under a duty to transfer the property to a person designated in the will

in·sti·tut·er \-üd·ə(r)\ *n* -s **:** INSTITUTOR

in·sti·tu·tion \ˌinztəˈtüshən, ˌin(t)stəˈ-, -təˈtyü-, *in rapid speech* inzˈt(y)üsh- *or* in(t)ˈst(y)ü-, *chiefly in substand speech* ˌin(t)səˈ-\ *n* -s [ME *institucioun*, fr. MF & L; MF *institution*, fr. OF, fr. L *institution-*, *institutio* arrangement, custom, instruction, element of instruction, appointment of an heir, fr. *institutus* (past part.) + *-ion-*, *-io* -ion] **1 :** an act or the process of instituting: as **a** [ME *institucioun*, fr. ML *institution-*, *institutio*, fr. L] **:** the investing of a clergyman with the spiritual part of a benefice by which the care of souls is committed to his charge followed in the Church of England by induction **b** (1) **:** the appointment of an heir (2) **:** the appointment of an institute (sense 4a) **c :** ESTABLISHMENT, FOUNDATION, ENACTMENT ⟨the ~ of this custom dates back to the 15th century⟩ **d** *obs* **:** reduction to order or form **:** REGULATION, ORDERING **e** *obs* **:** INSTRUCTION, EDUCATION **f :** the establishment of a sacrament; *usu* **:** the designation, authorization, or ordination by Christ of various signs or ceremonies as sacraments ⟨the words of ~ form part of the eucharistic rite⟩ **2 :** something that serves to instruct (as a textbook or a system of rules or principles) — now usu. restricted to law; compare INSTITUTE 3a **3 :** something that is instituted: as **a** (1) **:** a significant and persistent element (as a practice, a relationship, an organization) in the life of a culture that centers on a fundamental human need, activity, or value, occupies an enduring and cardinal position within a society, and is usu. maintained and stabilized through social regulatory agencies ⟨~ of marriage⟩ ⟨the family is a fundamental social ~⟩ (2) **:** a custom that is usu. widely sanctioned or tolerated and that in some degree contributes to group welfare ⟨the old New England ~ of bundling⟩ ⟨the coffee break has become an ~ in many places⟩ (3) **:** something or someone well established in some customary relationship **:** FIXTURE ⟨the old man was an ~ along the waterfront⟩ ⟨father's Sunday breakfast in bed was a family ~⟩ **b :** an established society or corporation **:** an establishment or foundation esp. of a public character ⟨a literary ~⟩ ⟨the Smithsonian *Institution*⟩ ⟨~*s* of higher learning⟩ **c :** a building or the buildings occupied or used by such organization

in·sti·tu·tion·al \ˌ==¦t(y)üshənᵊl, (ˈ)=¦t(y)ü-, -shnəl\ *adj* **1 :** of, relating to, involving, or constituting an institution ⟨an ~ investor⟩ ⟨~ elements of a political system⟩ ⟨~ care of the blind⟩: as **a :** of or relating to the institution of a sacrament **b** *of advertising* **:** designed to create goodwill and prestige for a company and its products rather than to produce immediate sales of specific products **2 :** provided with or characterized by institutions **:** having or sponsoring institutions esp. of a charitable or educational nature ⟨~ society⟩ — **in·sti·tu·tion·al·ly** \-ᵊlē, -əl|, |i\ *adv*

institutional economics *n pl but sing or pl in constr* **:** a school of economics that emphasizes the importance of nonmarket factors (as social institutions) in influencing economic behavior, economic analysis being subordinated to consideration of sociological factors, history, and institutional development

in·sti·tu·tion·al·ism \ˌ==ˈt(y)üshənᵊlˌizəm, =ˈt(y)ü-, -shnə-, ˌli-\ *n* -s **1 :** adherence to, upholding of, or acceptance of established institutions (as of society or religion) **:** belief in or dependence on that which is sanctified and given authority as an institution ⟨exhibiting an excessive conventionalism and ~ in religion⟩ **2 a :** a policy or theory favoring extended use of public institutions (as for defectives and criminals);

also **:** such use of public institutions ⟨with declining family solidarity ~ became increasingly important in the care of the sick, the unwanted, the aged⟩ **b :** the characteristics (as regimentation, standardization, and impersonality) that are associated with institutional life ⟨there was no ~ about this happy home⟩ **3 a :** the doctrines and teachings of institutional economics **b :** a theory that regards the establishment and maintenance of institutions (as for education, charity, and social activities) as an essential function of a church

in·sti·tu·tion·al·ist \-ᵊləst, -ələ-\ *n* -s **1 :** a writer on or of institutes esp. of the law **2 :** an adherent to, teacher of, or believer in any form of institutionalism **:** a defender of traditional institutions

in·sti·tu·tion·al·iza·tion \-ᵊlə'zāshən, -ᵊl,ī'z-, -ələ'z-, -ə,lī'z-\ *n* -s **1 :** the quality or state of being or becoming institutionalized ⟨a pleasant custom always has a tendency toward ~⟩ **2 :** the action or a result of institutionalizing ⟨the ~ of the insane⟩

in·sti·tu·tion·al·ize \-ᵊl,īz, -ə,līz\ *vt* -ED/-ING/-S *see -ize in Explan Notes* [*institutional* + *-ize*] **1 :** to give the character of an institution to **:** make into or treat like an institution ⟨modern society tends to ~ its burdens⟩; *esp* **:** to incorporate into a system of organized and often highly formalized belief, practice, or acceptance ⟨the Japanese *institutionalized* suicide⟩ ⟨*institutionalized* graft⟩ **2 :** to place in or commit to the care of a specialized institution (as for the insane, alcoholics, epileptics, delinquent youth, or the aged) **3 :** to accustom (a person) so firmly to the care and supervised routine of an institution as to make incapable of managing a life outside

in·sti·tu·tion·ary \¦==¦t(y)üshə,nerē, (')=¦t(y)ü-, -shnərē, -ri\ *adj* **:** of or relating to institution in office ⟨an ~ banquet⟩

in·sti·tu·tion·ize \,==¦t(y)üshə,nīz, ='t(y)-\ [*institution* + *-ize*] *vt* -ED/-ING/-S **:** INSTITUTIONALIZE 1

institutions *pl of* INSTITUTION

in·sti·tu·tive \'==,t(y)üd·iv, '=,t(y)-\ *adj* [L *institutus* (past part. of *instituere* to institute) + E *-ive* — more at INSTITUTE] **1 :** tending to institute **:** concerned with or leading to the institution of something ⟨~ factors⟩ ⟨an ~ meeting⟩ **2** *obs* **:** characterized or formed by institution **:** CONVENTIONAL

in·sti·tu·tor \-üd·ə(r), -ütə-\ *n* -s [L, fr. *institutus* (past part.) + *-or*] **:** one that institutes: as **a :** FOUNDER, ORDAINER, ESTABLISHER ⟨the ~ of this pleasant custom⟩ **b** *archaic* **:** TEACHER, INSTRUCTOR **c :** a Protestant Episcopal bishop or a priest delegated by him who institutes a rector or assistant minister into a parish or church

in·sti·tu·tress \¦==¦t(y)ü-trəs, (')=¦t(y)-\ *also* **in·sti·tu·trix** \-ü-triks\ *n, pl* **institutress·es** \-ü-trəsəz\ *also* **institutrix·es** \-ü-triksəz\ *or* **institutri·ces** \,==¦t(y)ü-trə,sēz, ='t(y)-; ,==(,)t(y)ü-'trī(,)sēz\ [*institutress* fr. *instituter* + *-ess; institutrix* fr. *institutor,* after such pairs as E *director: directrix*] **:** a female institutor

instl *abbr* installation

instmt *abbr* instrument

instn *abbr* **1** institution **2** instruction

in store *adv* (*or adj*) **:** at or from the point where stored with subsequent storage and shipping costs to be paid by the buyer ⟨goods sold *in store*⟩ ⟨payment to be made *in store*⟩ — compare EX STORE, FREE ON BOARD

instore *vt* [ME *instoren,* fr. ML *instaurare,* fr. L, to renew, restore — more at INSTAURATION] *obs* **:** FURNISH, PROVIDE

instr *abbr* **1** instruction; instructor **2** instrument; instrumental

¹instreaming \'inz,t-, 'in,st-\ *adj* [²*in* + *streaming,* pres. part. of *stream* (after *stream in,* v.)] **:** streaming in **:** entering like flowing water

²instreaming \"\ *n* [⁴*in* + *streaming,* gerund of *stream* (after *stream in,* v.)] **:** the action of entering like a stream of water **:** a flowing in ⟨the . . . ~ of beauty and truth —Cecil Sprigge⟩

in·strength·en \ənz't-,ən'st-\ *vt* [²*in-* + *strengthen*] **:** to give an inner strength to **:** strengthen in body or spirit

instrn *abbr* instruction

instroke \'inz,t-,'in,st-\ *n* [⁴*in* + *stroke*] **:** an inward stroke; *specif* **:** a stroke in which the piston in a steam or other engine is moving away from the crankshaft — opposed to *outstroke*

¹instruct *adj* [ME *instructe,* fr. L *instructus* (past part.)] **1** *obs* **:** INSTRUCTED **2** *obs* **:** PROVIDED, EQUIPPED

²in·struct \ənz'trəkt, ən'st-\ *vb* -ED/-ING/-S [ME *instructen,* fr. L *instructus,* past part. of *instruere,* fr. *in-* ²in- + *struere* to build, establish — more at STRUCTURE] *vt* **1 :** to give special knowledge or information to: as **a :** to train in some special field **:** give skill or knowledge in some art or field of specialization **:** educate in respect to a particular subject or area of knowledge ⟨had a tutor to ~ him in English⟩ **b :** to provide with information about something **:** APPRISE ⟨~*ed* us that the toilets were downstairs⟩ ⟨the senses ~ us of most material dangers⟩ **c :** to impart knowledge systematically to ⟨~*ed* three generations of children in the village school⟩ **2 a :** to furnish with directions based on informed or technical awareness of a problem ⟨the judge ~*ed* the jury⟩ **b :** to give an order or command to esp. authoritatively, formally, and with attention to clearness **:** DIRECT ⟨~*s* the eleven companions to await on the hill the outcome of the fight —R.M.Lumiansky⟩ **3 a** *archaic* **:** to put in order **:** PREPARE **b :** to actuate and establish the controls of (an automatic electronic machine) **4** *Scots law* **:** to prove or establish on the basis of evidence **:** PROVE, CONFIRM ~ *vi* **:** to serve as an instructor ⟨~*ed* in the public schools for many years⟩ **syn** see COMMAND, TEACH

instructed *adj* **1 :** EDUCATED, CULTURED ⟨the ~ person is usually tolerant⟩ ⟨planned by an ~ taste⟩ **2 a :** furnished with and restricted in action by specific instructions ⟨sent ~ delegates to the convention⟩ **b :** ordered by informed authority **:** DIRECTED ⟨an ~ verdict⟩ — **in·struct·ed·ly** *adv* — **in·struct·ed·ness** *n* -ES

in·struct·ible \-ktəbəl\ *adj* [L *instructus* (past part.) + E *-ible*] **:** capable of being instructed or taught ⟨~ children⟩ ⟨a very ~ subject⟩

in·struc·tion \-kshən\ *n* -s [ME *instruccioun,* fr. MF&LL; MF *instruction,* fr. LL *instruction-, instructio,* fr. L, act of constructing, act of arranging, fr. *instructus* (past part. of *instruere* to instruct) + *-ion-, -io* -ion — more at INSTRUCT] **1 :** something that instructs or is imparted in order to instruct: as **a :** LESSON, PRECEPT ⟨children should profit from the ~*s* of their elders⟩ **b** *obs* **:** INFORMATION, NEWS, REPORT **c** (1) **:** something given by way of direction or order — usu. used in pl. ⟨gave the maid ~*s* to wait for the grocer⟩ (2) **:** information in the form of an outline of procedures **:** DIRECTIONS — usu. used in pl. ⟨the ~*s* for assembling the model⟩ **2 :** the action, practice, or profession of one that instructs **:** TEACHING ⟨new theories of ~⟩ ⟨engaged in ~ rather than active service⟩ **3 :** the quality or state of being instructed ⟨where ~ is more widely diffused —Havelock Ellis⟩

in·struc·tion·al \-shənᵊl, -shnəl\ *adj* **1 :** relating to, serving for, or promoting instruction **:** EDUCATIONAL ⟨~ methods⟩ ⟨used for ~ purposes⟩ ⟨the director of ~ services⟩ **2 :** containing or conveying instruction or information ⟨an ~ film⟩

instruction card *n* **:** JOB SHEET

in·struc·tive \-ktiv, -tēv *also* -təv\ *adj* [prob. fr. MF *instructif,* fr. L *instructus* (past part.) + MF *-if* -ive] **:** conveying knowledge **:** serving to instruct or inform ⟨experience furnishes very ~ lessons⟩ ⟨such experiences are ~⟩ — **in·struc·tive·ly** \-təvlē, -li\ *adv* — **in·struc·tive·ness** \-tivnəs, -tēv- *also* -təv-\ *n* -ES

in·struc·tor \-ktə(r)\ *n* -s [ME *instructour,* fr. MF or ML; MF *instructeur,* fr. ML *instructor,* fr. L, arranger, preparer, fr. *instructus* (past part. of *instruere* to arrange, prepare, instruct) + *-or*] **:** one that instructs **:** TEACHER ⟨our older brother was our ~ in woodcraft⟩ ⟨an ~ in the local high school⟩; *specif* **:** a teacher in a college or university of a rank below any of the various grades of professor ⟨most colleges recognize the following ascending order of ranks: ~, assistant professor, associate professor, professor⟩

in·struc·to·ri·al \¦=¦=¦tōrēəl\ *adj* **:** of or relating to an instructor ⟨miserable ~ salaries⟩ ⟨~ carelessness⟩

in·struc·tor·ship \ənz'trəktə(r),ship, ən'st-\ *n* **:** the position or status of an instructor ⟨obtained an ~ at the university⟩

in·struc·tress \-ktrəs\ *n* -ES [*instructor* + *-ess*] **:** a female instructor

¹in·stru·ment \'inztrəmənt, 'in(t)strə-\ *n* -s [ME, fr. L *instrumentum,* fr. *instruere* to construct, equip, arrange, instruct + *-mentum* -ment] **1 a :** a means whereby something is achieved, performed, or furthered ⟨the modern university is the ~ for preserving, enlarging, and disseminating our ever-increasing body of knowledge —Harlan Hatcher⟩ **b :** a person or group made use of by another as a means or aid **:** DUPE, TOOL ⟨suspecting . . . that I only wished to make an ~ of him —W.H.Hudson †1922⟩ **2 :** UTENSIL, IMPLEMENT ⟨surgical ~*s*⟩ ⟨~*s* of torture⟩ **3 :** an implement used to produce music esp. as distinguished from the human voice — see PERCUSSION INSTRUMENT, STRINGED INSTRUMENT, WIND INSTRUMENT **4** *obs* **:** an organ of the body **5 a :** a legal document (as a deed, will, bond, lease, agreement, mortgage, note, power of attorney, ticket on carrier, bill of lading, insurance policy, warrant, writ) evidencing legal rights or duties esp. of one party to another **b :** something capable of being presented as evidence to a court for inspection **c :** an act recorded in writing by a notary **:** a notarial act **6 a :** a measuring device for determining the present value of a quantity under observation; *broadly* **:** a device (as for controlling, recording, regulating, computing) that functions on data obtained by such a measuring device **b :** an electrical or mechanical device used in navigating an airplane; *specif* **:** such a device used as the sole means of navigating when there is limited or no visibility **syn** see IMPLEMENT, MEAN — **on instruments :** by means of airplane instruments ⟨flying *on instruments*⟩

²in·stru·ment \-,ment, -,mənt — *see* ²-MENT\ *vt* -ED/-ING/-S **1 :** to address a legal instrument (as a petition) to **2 :** to prepare or score for one or more musical instruments ⟨~ a sonata for orchestra⟩ **:** ORCHESTRATE **3 :** to equip (as a process, machine, or vehicle) with instruments ⟨the whole factory is well ~*ed* —*Farm Chemicals*⟩ ⟨an ~*ed* satellite⟩

¹in·stru·men·tal \¦==¦mentᵊl\ *adj* [ME, fr. ML *instrumentalis,* fr. L *instrumentum* + *-alis* -al] **1 :** serving as a means or intermediary determining or leading to a particular result **:** being an instrument that functions in the promotion of some end or purpose ⟨this novel was ~ in bringing on open conflict⟩ ⟨an ~ act leading to a reward⟩ **2 :** relating to, composed for, or performed on a musical instrument ⟨~ music⟩ ⟨~ ensemble⟩ — compare VOCAL **3 :** of, relating to, or done with an instrument ⟨~ design⟩ ⟨~ navigation⟩ **4 a :** of, relating to, or being a case in grammar expressing means or agency ⟨English shows a surviving trace of the ~ case in *the* of "the more the merrier"⟩ **b :** being a suffixal element that denotes means or agency **5 :** based on or in accordance with instrumentalism — **in·stru·men·tal·ly** \-ᵊlē, -ᵊli\ *adv*

²instrumental \"\ *n* -s **1** *obs* **:** INSTRUMENT, MEANS **2 :** the instrumental case or a word in that case **3 :** a composition played on or for playing on a musical instrument — compare VOCAL

instrumental goods *n pl* **:** PRODUCER GOODS

in·stru·men·tal·ism \,==¦mentᵊl,izəm\ *n* -s [¹*instrumental* + *-ism*] **:** a conception that the significant factor of a thing is its value as an instrument; *specif* **:** the doctrine that ideas are instruments of action and that their usefulness determines their truth

¹in·stru·men·tal·ist \-ᵊləst\ *n* -s [¹*instrumental* + *-ist*] **1 a :** a player of a musical instrument **b :** a composer of instrumental music **2 :** a proponent of instrumentalism

²in·stru·men·tal·ist \¦==¦===\ *adj* **:** advocating instrumentalism **:** INSTRUMENTAL

in·stru·men·tal·i·ty \,==,mən-'taləd-ē, -,men- -, -lətē, -i\ *n* -ES **1 :** the quality or state of being instrumental **:** a condition of serving as an intermediary ⟨the agreement was reached through the ~ of the governor⟩ **2 a :** something by which an end is achieved **:** MEANS ⟨precious metals purified through the ~ of heat⟩ ⟨*instrumentalities* of production⟩ ⟨mechanical *instrumentalities*⟩ **b :** something that serves as an intermediary or agent through which one or more functions of a controlling force are carried out **:** a part, organ, or subsidiary branch esp. of a governing body ⟨the judicial *instrumentalities* of the federal government⟩ ⟨a Chilean government ~ devoted to developing the country's natural resources —*Ethyl News*⟩ **syn** see MEAN

in·stru·men·tal·ize \,=='mentᵊl,īz\ *vt* -ED/-ING/-S **:** to render instrumental **:** DIRECT, ORGANIZE, ADAPT

instrumental theory *n* **:** INSTRUMENTALISM

in·stru·men·tar·i·um \,inztrəmən-'ta(a)rēəm, ,inst-, -,men -\ *n, pl* **instrumentar·ia** \-ēə\ [NL, prob. fr. ML, case for storing papers, cartulary, fr. L *instrumentum* instrument + *-arium*] **:** the equipment needed for a particular surgical, medical, or dental procedure; *also* **:** the professional instruments of a surgeon, physician, or dentist

in·stru·men·ta·ry \¦==¦mentərē, -n·trē\ *adj* **:** of or relating to a legal instrument ⟨an ~ witness⟩

in·stru·men·tate \'inztrəmən-,tāt, 'in(t)strə-\ *vt* -ED/-ING/-S [¹*instrument* + *-ate* (after *orchestrate*)] **:** INSTRUMENT 2

in·stru·men·ta·tion \,===='tāshən, -,men- -\ *n* -s [¹*instrument* + *-ation*] **1 :** a use of or operation with instruments: as **a :** the use of one or more instruments in treating a patient (as in the passing of a cystoscope) **b :** the application of instruments esp. for observation, measurement, or control (as in a manufacturing process or the operation of a machine or vehicle) **2 :** MEANS, AGENCY, INSTRUMENTALITY **3 a** [F, fr. *instrument* (fr. MF, fr. L *instrumentum* instrument) + *-ation*] **:** the arrangement or composition of music for instruments esp. for a band or orchestra — compare ORCHESTRATION **b :** the act or manner of playing musical instruments **c :** the arrangement and distribution of instruments (as in a band or orchestra) **4 a :** a branch of science concerned with the development, manufacture, and utilization of instruments **b :** instruments or the group of instruments employed for a particular purpose (as the control of a machine or recording the data about the function of a vehicle)

in·stru·men·ta·tor \'==man-,tād-ə(r)\ *n* -s [*instrumentate* + *-or*] **:** one that arranges a musical score for performance by a specific group of instruments

instrument board *or* **instrument panel** *n* **:** a panel on which instruments are mounted; *esp* **:** DASHBOARD 2

instrument board

instrumented *past of* INSTRUMENT

instrument flight *n* **:** an airplane flight made on instruments **:** blind flight

instrument flying *n* **:** navigation solely according to information given by instruments within an airplane usu. including radio or radar devices **:** blind flying — contrasted with *contact flying*

instrumenting *pres part of* INSTRUMENT

instrument landing *n* **:** a landing made with no external visibility and solely by means of instruments within an airplane and by ground radio directive devices **:** blind landing

instrument landing system *n* **:** a system for airplane landings in which the pilot is guided by radio beams — abbr. *ILS;* compare GROUND-CONTROLLED APPROACH

in·stru·ment·man \'===,man\ *n, pl* **instrumentmen :** a surveyor who operates a transit, level, or similar instrument

instrument rating *n* **:** a license or rating given to an airplane pilot authorized to do instrument flying

instruments *pl of* INSTRUMENT, *pres 3d sing of* INSTRUMENT

instrument weather *n* **:** weather in which the ground is so invisible from the air that instrument flying is required

instyle *vt* [²*in-* + *style*] *obs* **:** CALL, DENOMINATE

in·suavity \(')in, ən+\ *n* [L *insuavitas,* fr. *insuavis* unpleasant (fr. *in-* ¹in- + *suavis* pleasant) + *-itas* -ity — more at SWEET] **:** lack of suavity **:** BRUSQUENESS

in·subjection \¦in+\ *n* [¹*in-* + *subjection*] **:** lack of subjection **:** a state of disobedience or opposition to authority (as of government)

in·submergible *or* **in·submersible** \"+\ *adj* [*insubmergible* fr. ¹*in-* + *submerge* + *-ible; insubmersible* prob. fr. F, fr. *in-* ¹in- + L *submersus* (past part. of *submergere* to submerge) + F *-ible*] **:** incapable of sinking

in·submissive \"+\ *adj* [¹*in-* + *submissive*] **:** unwilling to submit

¹in·subordinate \"+\ *adj* [¹*in-* + *subordinate*] **:** not subordinate: as **a :** unwilling to submit to authority **:** DISOBEDIENT, MUTINOUS ⟨~ boys⟩ **b :** not holding a lower or inferior position ⟨the bankers of Antwerp placed no limit on their enterprise: economic activity was not subordinate; it had become, from the medieval point of view, ~ —Stringfellow Barr⟩

syn REBELLIOUS, MUTINOUS, SEDITIOUS, FACTIOUS, CONTUMACIOUS: INSUBORDINATE applies to disobedience of orders, infraction of rules, or a generally disaffected attitude toward authority, often in military or other organization similarly constituted ⟨*insubordinate* deckhands confined to the brig⟩ ⟨*insubordinate* native troops feeling that they were being discriminated against⟩ REBELLIOUS may suggest forceful resistance to or insurgence against authority in addition to insubordination and temperamental opposition ⟨*rebellious* mountaineers proposing to set up their own independent republic⟩ ⟨temperamentally *rebellious,* instinctively disliking externally imposed authority —Francis Biddle⟩ MUTINOUS suggests either opposing authority by destroying discipline and order or the forceful overthrow of authority ⟨for more than a year Cortes stayed in the new land, a desolate sandy waste, while the *mutinous* soldiers cursed him —*Amer. Guide Series: Calif.*⟩ ⟨the guards might be overpowered, the palace forced, the king a prisoner in the hands of his *mutinous* subjects —T.B.Macaulay⟩ SEDITIOUS suggests treasonable activities, esp. those designed to weaken or overthrow a government or foster separatist tendencies ⟨*seditious* factionalism went on a rampage and began to wreck our foreign policy —Max Ascoli⟩ ⟨revolutions that were not made in Boston, by Boston gentlemen, were quite certain to be wicked and *seditious* —V.L.Parrington⟩ FACTIOUS suggests an addiction to factions with contentious perversity and irreconcilability threatening central constituted authority ⟨Florence . . . wearing out her soul by *factious* struggles —Margaret Oliphant⟩ ⟨the opposition will be vigilant but not *factious.* We shall not oppose merely for the sake of opposition —Clement Attlee⟩ CONTUMACIOUS indicates persistent, willful, or overt defiance of authority and disobedience, sometimes contemptuous, of authority ⟨a fine was appointed for every failure to obey the bishop's summons; he was empowered to excommunicate *contumacious* persons —F.M.Stenton⟩ ⟨magistrates and populace were incensed at a refusal of customary marks of courtesy and respect for the laws, which in their eyes was purely *contumacious* —W.R.Inge⟩

²insubordinate \"\ *n* **:** an insubordinate person

in·subordinately \¦in+\ *adv* **:** in an insubordinate manner **:** with insubordination

in·subordination \"+\ *n* [prob. fr. F, fr. *in-* ¹in- + *subordination*] **:** the quality or state of being insubordinate **:** defiance of authority **:** MUTINY

in·substantial \"+\ *adj* [prob. fr. F *insubstantiel,* fr. LL *insubstantialis,* fr. *in-* ¹in- + *substantialis* substantial] **:** not substantial: as **a :** lacking substance or reality **:** IMAGINARY, APPARITIONAL ⟨an ~ mirage floating near the horizon⟩ **b :** lacking firmness or solidity of structure **:** FLIMSY, FRAIL ⟨delicate ~ wrists and ankles⟩ — **in·substantiality** \"+\ *n*

in·subvertible \"+\ *adj* [LL *insubvertibilis,* fr. *in-* ¹in- + L *subvertere* to overturn, overthrow + *-ibilis* -ible — more at SUBVERT] **:** incapable of being overthrown or altered in course or orientation ⟨the ~ physical laws⟩

in·success \"+\ *n* [¹*in-* + *success*] **:** lack of success **:** FAILURE

insucken \'=,==\ *adj* [¹*in* + *sucken*] *Scot* **:** situated in or astricted to a sucken

in·sufferable \(')in, ən+\ *adj* [¹*in-* + *sufferable*] **:** incapable of being endured ⟨an ~ injury⟩ **:** intolerable esp. by reason of pompous assurance or assumed superiority ⟨~ self-importance⟩ ⟨a thoroughly ~ child⟩ — **in·sufferableness** \"+\ *n* — **in·sufferably** \"+\ *adv*

in·suf·fi·cience \¦insə¦fishən(t)s\ *n* -s [ME, fr. MF or LL; MF, fr. LL *insufficientia*] **:** INSUFFICIENCY

in·suf·fi·cien·cy \-shənsē, -si\ *n* [LL *insufficientia,* fr. *insufficient-, insufficiens* insufficient + *-ia* -y] **1 :** the quality or state of being insufficient **:** lack of sufficiency: as **a :** lack of mental or moral fitness **:** INABILITY, INCOMPETENCY ⟨the ~ of a man for an office⟩ **b :** lack of adequate supply of something (as force, quality, quantity) **:** INADEQUACY ⟨~ of provisions⟩ **c :** lack of physical power or capacity **:** IMPOTENCE; *specif* **:** inability of an organ or body part to function normally ⟨cardiac ~⟩ ⟨renal ~⟩ **2 :** something insufficient ⟨sadly aware of his own neglects and *insufficiencies*⟩

in·suf·fi·cient \-shənt\ *adj* [ME, fr. MF, fr. LL *insufficient-, insufficiens,* fr. *in-* ¹in- + L *sufficient-, sufficiens* sufficient — more at SUFFICIENT] **:** not sufficient: as **a :** lacking in strength, power, ability, capacity, or skill **:** INCOMPETENT, UNFIT ⟨a person ~ to discharge the duties of an office⟩ **b** *obs* **:** not sufficiently furnished or supplied **:** deficient or lacking in something **c :** inadequate to some implied or designated need, use, or purpose ⟨provisions ~ in quantity⟩ — **in·suf·fi·cient·ly** *adv*

in·suf·flate \'in(t)sə,flāt, ən'sə-\ *vt* -ED/-ING/-S [LL *insufflatus,* past part. of *insufflare,* fr. L *in-* ²in- + *sufflare* to blow, sufflate — more at SUFFLATE] **1 :** to blow or breathe upon or into **:** subject to insufflation ⟨~ a room with insecticide⟩ **2 :** to blow or breathe (something) onto a surface or into a void **:** practice insufflation of ⟨*insufflated* the metallic powder onto the hot surface⟩ ⟨*insufflated* the drug into the depths of the wound⟩

in·suf·fla·tion \,in(t)sə'flāshən\ *n* -s [MF, fr. LL *insufflation-, insufflatio,* fr. *insufflatus* (past part.) + L *-ion-, -io* -ion] **:** an act or the action of breathing or blowing on, into, or in: as **a :** the breathing upon a person or thing in the ritual of various liturgical churches to symbolize (as at baptism) the inspiration of a new spiritual life and the expulsion of evil spirits **b :** the act of blowing (as a gas, powder, or vapor) into a cavity of the body ⟨~ of gas into a fallopian tube to determine its patency⟩

in·suf·fla·tor \'in(t)sə,flād·ə(r), ən'sə-\ *n* -s [*insufflate* + *-or*] **:** a device for insufflating: as **a :** an injector for forcing air into a furnace **b :** a device used in medical insufflation (as of a drug) **c :** a device for blowing the powder used in developing latent fingerprints (as in criminal investigation)

in·su·la \'in(t)s(y)ələ, 'inshə-\ *n, pl* **insu·lae** \-,lē, 'in(t)sə,lī\ **1** [L, lit., island — more at ISLE] **:** an ancient Roman building or a group of buildings standing together forming a block or square and usu. constituting an apartment building **2** [NL, fr. L] **:** ISLAND OF REIL

in·su·lant \'in(t)sələnt *sometimes* 'in(t)syəl- *or* 'inshəl-\ *n* -s [*insulate* + *-ant*] **:** INSULATION

¹in·su·lar \-lə(r)\ *adj* [LL *insularis,* fr. L *insula* island + *-aris* -ar — more at ISLE] **1 a :** of or relating to an island **:** being or having the characteristics of an island **:** dwelling or situated on or forming an island **b** *usu cap* (1) **:** of or relating to Great Britain or to the British isles as distinct from the continent of Europe — compare CONTINENTAL (2) **:** of, relating to, or characteristic of the Insular hand **2 a :** INSULATED, ISOLATED, DETACHED ⟨an ~ building⟩ **b** *of a plant or animal* **:** having a restricted or isolated natural range or habitat **3 a :** of or relating to the people of an island **b :** resulting from isolation or characteristic of isolated people **c :** NARROW, CIRCUMSCRIBED, ILLIBERAL, PREJUDICED **4** [NL *insula* + E *-ar*] **:** of or relating to an island of cells or tissue (as the islets of Langerhans or islands of Reil)

²insular \"\ *n* -s **:** ISLANDER

insular celtic *n, usu cap I&C* **:** the Celtic languages excluding Gaulish

insular hand *or* **insular script** *n, usu cap I* **:** a script characterized by thick initial strokes and heavy shading developed from half uncial under the influence of uncial by Irish scribes about the 5th and 6th centuries A.D. and used in England until the Norman conquest and in Ireland with modifications to the present day

in·su·lar·ism \-lə,rizəm\ *n* -s **:** the quality or state of being insular and esp. of exhibiting narrowness and rigidity of outlook or mind

in·su·lar·i·ty \,=='larəd-ē, -ətē, -i *also* -'ler-\ *n* -ES **1 :** the quality or state of being an island or consisting of islands ⟨the ~ of Great Britain⟩ **2 a :** condition of dwelling on an island or in isolation **b :** narrowness or illiberality of opinion or custom

in·su·lar·ize \'==,lə,rīz\ *vt* -ED/-ING/-S [¹*insular* + *-ize*] **:** to form into or represent as an island

in·su·lar·ly *adv* **1 :** in an insular manner **:** NARROWLY, RIGIDLY ⟨an ~ prejudiced mind⟩ **2 :** throughout an island ⟨~ distributed Philippine plants⟩

¹in·su·lary \'ˌ,lerē\ *n* -ES [prob. modif. (influenced by E *-ary*) of F *insulaire*, fr. *insulaire*, adj., insular, fr. LL *insularis*] *archaic* **:** ISLANDER

²insulary \"\ *adj* [prob. modif. (influenced by E *-ary*) of LL *insularis*] *archaic* **:** INSULAR

¹in·su·late \'in(t)sə,lāt *sometimes* 'in(t)syə- *or* 'inshə-; *usu* -ād·+V\ *vt* -ED/-ING/-S [L *insula* island + E *-ate* — more at ISLE] **1** *archaic* **:** to form an island of **:** isolate by surrounding water **2 a :** to separate or shield (a conductor) from conducting bodies by means of nonconductors so as to prevent transfer of electricity, heat, or sound **b :** to place in a detached situation or in a state of isolation **:** set apart **:** SEGREGATE, ISOLATE ⟨hysterical symptoms quite commonly serve to ~ the patient —Norman Cameron⟩ ⟨*insulating* man from the natural world⟩ **c :** to remove (as specie or a commodity) from the open market **:** STERILIZE ⟨a program designed to ~ the government-held surpluses by using them for special purposes⟩; *also* **:** to stabilize (a market) by such removal

²in·su·late \-,lət, -,lāt\ *adj* [L *insula* island + E *-ate*] **:** set apart **:** ISOLATED

insulating *adj* **:** serving to insulate **:** functioning as insulation ⟨~ material⟩ ⟨an ~ calm⟩

insulating board *or* **insulation board** *n* **:** a board with insulating properties; *esp* **:** a structural or finish material that consists of sheets of lightly compressed vegetable pulp variously finished and is used esp. for its thermal insulating effect resulting from great numbers of minute included air spaces

insulating oil *n* **:** any of various oily liquids (as a hydrocarbon oil) used as insulators and cooling mediums in transformers, switches, or other electrical equipment

insulating varnish *n* **:** varnish used to insulate electrical apparatus (as certain coils or glass fittings)

in·su·la·tion \,ˌˌ'lāshən\ *n* -S **1 a :** an act or action of insulating ⟨work on the ~ of the house⟩ **b :** the quality or state of being insulated ⟨his complete ~ in regard to current events⟩ **:** ISOLATION ⟨~ as a factor in evolution⟩ **2 :** something that insulates; *usu* **:** material that retards the passage of heat, electricity, or sound **:** nonconducting material that is used in insulating

insulation resistance *n* **:** the alternating-current resistance between two electrical conductors or two systems of conductors separated by an insulating material

in·su·la·tive \'ˌˌ,lād·|iv, -āt|, |ēv *also* |əv\ *adj* **:** relating to or constituting insulation ⟨~ value⟩ ⟨an ~ effect⟩

in·su·la·tor \-,lād·ə(r), -ātə-\ *n* -S **1 :** one that insulates; *esp* **:** a worker that applies electrical or thermal insulation **2 a :** a material or body that is a poor conductor of electricity, heat, or sound **b :** a body of electrically nonconducting material for keeping charged conductors from contact with each other or from grounding and often also for supporting them

1 2 3 4 5 6 7 8

insulators 2b: *1, 2* used with antennas; *3* knob, *4* split-knob, *5* cleat, *6, 8* petticoat, *7* standoff

in·su·lin \'in(t)sələn *sometimes* 'in(t)slən *or* 'in(t)syəl- *or* 'inshə-\ *n* -S [NL *insula* + E *-in*] **:** a protein pancreatic hormone secreted by the islets of Langerhans that is essential esp. for the metabolism of carbohydrates, that is obtained commercially in crystalline form usu. from beef or pork pancreas, and that is used in the treatment and control of diabetes mellitus

in·su·lin·ase \-lə,nās, -āz\ *n* -S [*insulin* + *-ase*] **:** an enzyme found esp. in liver that inactivates insulin

in·su·lin·ize \-,nīz\ *vt* -ED/-ING/-S **:** to treat with insulin

insulin shock *n* **:** hypoglycemia associated with the presence of excessive insulin in the system and characterized by progressive development of coma

insulin shock therapy *n* **:** the treatment of mental disorder (as schizophrenia) by insulin in doses sufficient to produce deep coma — compare INSULIN SHOCK

in·sulse \ən'səl(t)s\ *adj* [L *insulsus*, lit., unsalted, fr. *in-* ¹in- + *-sulsus* (fr. *salsus*, past part. of *salere* to salt, fr. *sal* salt) — more at SALT] *archaic* **:** TASTELESS, FLAT, STUPID — **in·sul·si·ty** \-)səd·ē\ *n* -ES

¹in·sult \ən'səlt\ *vb* -ED/-ING/-S [MF or L; MF *insulter*, fr. L *insultare*, lit., to spring upon, leap, fr. *in-* ²in- + *-sultare* (fr. *saltare* to leap) — more at SALTANT] *vi* **1** *archaic* **:** to behave with pride or insolence **:** display arrogance or contempt **:** exult or boast usu. insolently or contemptuously **:** TRIUMPH, VAUNT **2** *obs* **:** to make an attack or assault **~** *vt* **1 a :** to treat with insolence, indignity, or contempt by word or action **:** affront wantonly ⟨his impertinences ~*ed* his sister's guests⟩ **b :** to make little of **:** affect offensively or depreciatively ⟨~*ed* the traditions of the sea by ordering "right" and "left" to be substituted . . . for "starboard" and "port" —Bruce Bliven b.1889⟩ ⟨editorial slovenliness that ~s the reader's mind⟩ **2** *obs* **:** to make an attack on **:** ASSAULT, ASSAIL; *esp* **:** to make a sudden military attack on without the usual preliminaries or formalities **syn** see OFFEND

²in·sult \'in,səlt\ *n* -S [MF or LL; MF *insult*, *insulte*, fr. LL *insultus*, prob. fr. L *in-* ²in- + *-sultus* (fr. *saltus* leap) (prob. influenced by L *insultare* to insult, spring upon); akin to L *salire* to leap — more at SALLY] **1** *archaic* **:** an act of attacking **:** ONSET, ATTACK **2 :** a gross indignity offered to another either by word or act **:** an act or speech of insolence or contempt ⟨his words were a studied ~⟩ ⟨such an offer was an ~ to our intelligence⟩ **3 :** damage or an instance of injury to the body or one of its parts ⟨repeated acute vascular ~s⟩ ⟨any ~ to the constitution of a patient suffering from active tuberculosis —*Jour. Amer. Med. Assoc.*⟩; *also* **:** an agent that produces such an insult ⟨a thermal ~⟩ ⟨damage resulting from malnutritional ~s⟩ **syn** see AFFRONT

in·sult·abil·i·ty \(,)in,səltə'biləd·ē, ən-, -lətē, -i\ *n* -ES **:** capacity for being or readiness to be insulted

in·sult·able \ən'səltəbəl\ *adj* **:** capable of being insulted; *esp* **:** easily insulted **:** OVERSENSITIVE

in·sul·ta·tion \,in,səl'tāshən\ *n* -S [MF, fr. L *insultation-*, *insultatio*, fr. *insultatus* (past part. of *insultare* to insult) + *-ion-*, *-io* -ion] **1** *archaic* **:** an act of insulting **:** contemptuous or insolent treatment **:** scornful exultation **2** *obs* **:** ATTACK, ONSET

insulted *adj* [fr. past part. of ¹*insult*] *chiefly dial* **:** affected with irritation or distaste **:** OFFENDED, ANNOYED

in·sult·er \ən'səltə(r)\ *n* -S **:** one that insults

insulting *adj* **:** containing, characterized by, or constituting insult ⟨~ language⟩ ⟨the ~ agent in a pathologic process⟩ — **in·sult·ing·ly** *adv* — **in·sult·ing·ness** *n* -ES

insultproof \ˌˌ,ˌ\ *adj* **:** not susceptible to insult

in sunder *adv* (*or adj*) [ME, fr. OE *onsundran*, *onsundrum* — more at ASUNDER] *archaic* **:** ASUNDER ⟨breaketh the bow and cutteth the spear *in sunder* —Ps 46:9 (AV)⟩

in·superability \(ˌ)in, ən+\ *n* **:** the quality or state of being insuperable

in·superable \(ˈ)in, ən+\ *adj* [ME, fr. MF & L; MF, fr. L *insuperabilis*, fr. *in-* ¹in- + *superabilis* superable — more at SUPERABLE] **:** incapable of being surmounted: as **a :** incapable of being vanquished **:** INVINCIBLE ⟨these ~ heroes who dared the northern seas⟩ **b :** impossible to overcome ⟨~ difficulties⟩ **c :** incapable of being passed over **:** IMPASSABLE ⟨an ~ barrier⟩ **d :** UNSURPASSABLE — **in·su·per·a·ble·ness** \-nəs\ *n* — **in·su·per·a·bly** \-blē, -bli\ *adv*

in·supportability \ˌin+\ *n* **:** INSUPPORTABLENESS

in·supportable \"+\ *adj* [MF or LL; MF, fr. LL *insupportabilis*, fr. L *in-* ¹in- + *supportare* to carry, convey + *-abilis* -able — more at SUPPORT] **:** impossible to support: as **a :** incapable of being borne **:** UNENDURABLE ⟨~ burdens⟩ ⟨an ~ pain⟩ **b :** incapable of being sustained **:** UNJUSTIFIABLE ⟨~ charges⟩ **c** *obs* **:** IRRESISTIBLE — **in·supportably** \"+\ *adv*

in·supportableness \"+\ *n* -ES **:** the quality or state of being insupportable

in·supposable \"+\ *adj* [¹*in-* + *supposable*] **:** impossible to suppose **:** UNBELIEVABLE

in·suppressible \"+\ *adj* [¹*in-* + *suppress* + *-ible*] **:** impossible to suppress — **in·suppressibly** \"+\ *adv*

in·suppressive \"+\ *adj* [¹*in-* + *suppress* + *-ive*] **:** INSUPPRESSIBLE

in·sur·abil·i·ty \ən,shu̇rə'biləd·ē, -lətē, -i\ *n* -ES **:** the quality or state of being insurable

in·sur·able \ən'shu̇rəbəl\ *adj* [*insure* + *-able*] **:** capable of being or proper to be insured against loss, damage, death (~ property) **:** affording a sufficient ground for insurance

insurable interest *n* **:** an interest (as based on a blood tie or likelihood of financial injury) that is judged to give an insurance applicant a legal right to enforce the insurance contract against the objection that it is a wagering contract contrary to public policy

insurable value *n* **:** the value of property stated in an insurance contract indicating the limit of indemnity that will be paid at the time of loss

in·sur·ance \ən'shu̇r(ə)n(t)s, *chiefly in southern U.S.* 'in,ˌ(ˌ)\ *n* -S *often attrib* [*insure* + *-ance*] **1 a :** the action or process of insuring or the state of being insured usu. against loss or damage by a contingent event (as death, fire, accident, or sickness) **b :** means of insuring against loss or risks ⟨provide ~ against floods⟩ **2 a :** the business of insuring persons or property; *specif* **:** a device for the elimination or reduction of an economic risk common to all members of a large group and employing a system of equitable contributions out of which losses are paid **b :** coverage by contract whereby for a stipulated consideration one party undertakes to indemnify or guarantee another against loss by a specified contingency or peril **c :** the principles and practices of the business of insuring — see ACCIDENT INSURANCE, AUTOMOBILE INSURANCE, BUSINESS INTERRUPTION INSURANCE, CASUALTY INSURANCE, DISABILITY INSURANCE, FIRE INSURANCE, GROUP INSURANCE, HEALTH INSURANCE, LIABILITY INSURANCE, LIFE INSURANCE, MARINE INSURANCE, SOCIAL INSURANCE, UNEMPLOYMENT INSURANCE, WORKMEN'S COMPENSATION INSURANCE; compare ANNUITY, CORPORATE SURETYSHIP, INSURABLE INTEREST, LOSS, MUTUAL, POLICY, PREMIUM, RATE, REINSURANCE, REPRESENTATION, RESERVE, RISK TONTINE, WARRANTY **3 a :** the premium paid for insuring something **b :** the sum for which something is insured

insurance adjuster *n* **:** a person employed by insurer or insured to determine the loss under an insurance policy

insurance agent *n* **:** an agent of an insurer authorized to negotiate contracts of insurance

insurance broker *n* **:** a broker who usu. acts as the agent of the insured in making contracts of insurance but sometimes as the agent of the insurer for some purposes (as payment of the premium) and of the insured for all other purposes

insurance certificate *n* **1 :** a certificate issued by an insurer to a shipper as evidence that a shipment of merchandise is covered under a marine policy **2 :** CERTIFICATE 5

insurance reserve *n* **:** the part of the reserve of an insurance company to be absorbed from the initial reserve in any year in payment of losses — compare INVESTMENT RESERVE

insurance trust *n* **:** an agreement providing for the receipt and distribution of life insurance proceeds by a trustee

in·sur·ant \ən'shu̇r(ə)nt\ *n* -S [*insure* + *-ant*] **:** a person who takes out a policy of insurance; *also* **:** one on whose life a policy of life insurance is taken out

in·sure \ən'shu̇(ə)r, -u̇ə\ *vb* -ED/-ING/-S [ME *insuren*, prob. alter. (influenced by *in-* ²in-) of *assuren* to assure — more at ASSURE] *vt* **1** *obs* **:** to declare to with confidence **:** ASSURE **:** promise solemnly **2 :** to assure against a loss by a contingent event on certain stipulated conditions or at a given rate or premium **:** give, take, or procure an insurance on or for **:** enter into or carry a contract of insurance on — used of either the person who pays the insurance premiums or the society, corporation, or underwriter that undertakes the risk as subject and of the thing to which the risk attaches (as life or property) or the sum secured as object **3 :** ENSURE 3 **~** *vi* **:** to contract to give insurance **:** UNDERWRITE; *also* **:** to procure or effect insurance **syn** see ENSURE

insured *n* -S [fr. *insured*, past part. of *insure*] **:** a person whose life, physical well-being, or property is the subject of insurance **:** the owner of a policy of insurance **:** POLICYHOLDER

insured plan *n* **:** a pension or retirement plan under which contributions are used to purchase life insurance or annuities as a means of funding the benefits promised

in·sur·er \ən'shu̇rə(r)\ *n* -S [*insure* + *-er*] **1 :** one that makes certain or secure **:** one that guarantees ⟨these ~s of peace⟩ **2 :** one that contracts to indemnify another by way of insurance **:** an insurance company or underwriter **3** *archaic* **:** INSURED

¹in·surge \ən+\ *vb* [L *insurgere*, fr. *in-* ¹in- + *surgere* to rise — more at SURGE] *vi* **:** to become insurgent **:** behave insurgently **~** *vt* **:** to make insurgent

²insurge \'in+,-\ *n* [⁴*in* + *surge*] **:** a surging in

in·sur·gence \ən'sərjən(t)s, -səj-,-səij-\ *n* -S [prob. fr. F, fr. *insurgent*, n. (fr. E) + *-ence*] **:** an act or the action of being insurgent **:** UPRISING, INSURRECTION ⟨the recurrent ~ of the lower house⟩

in·sur·gen·cy \-jənsē, -si\ *n* -ES [¹*insurgent* + *-ency*] **1 :** the quality or state of being insurgent; *specif* **:** a condition of revolt against a recognized government that does not reach the proportions of an organized revolutionary government and is not recognized as belligerency **2 :** INSURGENCE

¹in·sur·gent \-nt\ *n* -S [L *insurgent-*, *insurgens*, pres. part. of *insurgere* to rise up, insurge] **1 :** a person who rises in revolt against civil authority or an established government **:** REBEL; *esp* **:** a rebel not recognized as a belligerent — compare RIOT, TREASON **2 :** one that acts contrary to the policies and decisions of his political party

²in·sur·gent \"\ *adj* **1 :** rising in opposition to civil or political authority or against an established government **:** INSUBORDINATE, REBELLIOUS **2 :** surging in ⟨the quick ~ sea⟩ — **in·sur·gent·ly** *adv*

in·sur·ges·cence \,in(t)(,)sər'jes²n(t)s\ *n* -S [¹*insurge* + *-escence*] **:** tendency to make insurrection

insuring clause *n* **:** a clause in an insurance policy that sets out the risk assumed by the insurer or defines the scope of the coverage afforded

in·surmountable \ˌin+\ *adj* [¹*in-* + *surmountable*] **:** incapable of being surmounted, passed over, or overcome **:** INSUPERABLE ⟨~ disadvantages⟩ — **in·surmountableness** \"+\ *n* -ES — **in·surmountably** \"+\ *adv*

in·sur·rect \ˌin(t)sə'rekt\ *vi* [back-formation fr. *insurrection*] **:** to make or engage in insurrection

in·sur·rec·tion \,in(t)sə'rekshən\ *n* -S [ME *insurreccioun*, fr. MF *insurrection*, fr. LL *insurrection-*, *insurrectio*, fr. L *insurrectus* (past part. of *insurgere* to rise against, insurge) + *-ion-*, *-io* -ion — more at INSURGE] **1 :** an act or instance of revolting against civil or political authority or against an established government **2 :** an act or instance of rising up physically **syn** see REBELLION

in·sur·rec·tion·al·ly \-²l|ē, -əl|, |i\ *adv* **:** in respect to insurrection **:** from an insurrectionary point of view

¹in·sur·rec·tion·ary \-shə,nerē, -ri\ *also* **in·sur·rec·tion·al** \ˌˌˌ'rekshən²l, -shnəl\ *adj* [*insurrection* + *-ary* or *-al*] **:** of, relating to, or constituting insurrection **:** given to or tending to induce insurrection **:** REBELLIOUS ⟨~ activity⟩ ⟨~ movements⟩

²insurrectionary \"\ *n* -ES **:** a participant in insurrection **:** INSURGENT

in·sur·rec·tion·ist \,ˌˌ'reksh(ə)nəst\ *n* -S **:** a favorer of or participant in insurrection **:** INSURGENT

in·sur·rec·tion·ize \-shə,nīz\ *vt* -ED/-ING/-S **:** to cause (as a people) to be insurgent **:** make insurrection in (a country)

in·sur·rec·to \,in(t)sə'rek(,)tō\ *n* -S [Sp, fr. L *insurrectus* (past part.)] **:** INSURRECTIONARY, INSURGENT, REBEL

in·susceptibility \ˌin+\ *n* **:** the quality or state of being insusceptible **:** lack of susceptibility

in·susceptible \"+\ *adj* [¹*in-* + *susceptible*] **:** not susceptible **:** incapable of being moved, affected, or impressed ⟨~ of pity⟩ ⟨~ to disease⟩ ⟨~ animals⟩ — **in·susceptibly** \"+\ *adv*

inswarming \'ˌ,ˌˌ\ *adj* [²*in* + *swarming*, pres. part. of *swarm* (after *swarm in*, v.)] **:** entering in or like a swarm

insweeping \'ˌ,ˌˌ\ *adj* [²*in* + *sweeping*, pres. part. of *sweep* (after *sweep in*, v.)] **:** moving sweepingly in

inswinger \'ˌ,ˌˌ\ *n* [²*in* + *swing* (v.) + *-er*] **:** a bowled cricket ball that swerves in the air from off to leg — compare OUTSWINGER

int *abbr* **1** intelligence **2** intercept **3** interest **4** interim **5** interior **6** interjection **7** interleaved **8** intermediate **9** internal **10** international **11** interpreter **12** interval **13** interview **14** intransitive

in·tabulation \ən·+\ *n* [²*in-* + *tabulation*] **:** TABLATURE 1a

in·tact \ən·'takt\ *adj* [ME *intacte*, fr. L *intactus*, fr. *in-* ¹in- + *tactus*, past part. of *tangere* to touch — more at TANGENT] **1 :** untouched esp. by anything that harms or diminishes **:** left complete or entire **:** UNINJURED ⟨obtain your uncle's estate ~ —Kenneth Roberts⟩ ⟨houses largely ~ after some 3500 years —Jacquetta & Christopher Hawkes⟩ ⟨the memory of that night remained ~ —Elinor Wylie⟩ **2** *of a living body or its parts* **:** physically and functionally complete **:** having no relevant component removed or destroyed: **a :** physically virginal **b :** sexually competent **:** UNCASTRATED — used chiefly of a domestic animal — **in·tact·ness** \-k(t)nəs\ *n* -ES

in·ta·gliat·ed \ən·'ta|l,yād·əd, -tä|, |glē,ā-\ *adj* [It *intagliato* (past part. of *intagliare*) + E *-ed*] **:** engraved in or as if in intaglio

¹in·ta·glio \ən·'ta|l(,)yō, -tä|, |glē,ō\ *n* -S *often attrib* [It, fr. *intagliare* to engrave, carve, cut, fr. ML *intaleare*, fr. L *in-* ²in- + LL *taliare* to cut — more at TAILOR] **1 a :** an engraving or incised figure in stone or other hard material; *specif* **:** a figure or design depressed below the surface of the material with the normal elevations of the design hollowed out so that an impression from the design yields an image in relief **b :** the art or process of executing intaglios **c :** a process or method of printing from a face in which the ink-carrying part is sunk that produces raised printing (as in die stamping) or plane printing (as in gravure) — compare LETTERPRESS, PLANOGRAPHY, STENCIL **2 :** something carved in intaglio or stamped so as to resemble an intaglio carving; *esp* **:** a carved gem with the figures or designs carved into a generally flat surface — compare CAMEO **3 :** a countersunk die for producing a figure in relief

²intaglio \"\ *vt* -ED/-ING/-ES **:** to cut or represent in intaglio

intaglio ri·le·va·to \-,rēlə'vä(,)tō\ *or* **intaglio ri·lie·vo** \-rē'lē(,)vō, -rēl'yā(-, -ye(-\ *n* [It, fr. *intaglio* + *rilevato* raised or *rilievo* relief] **:** SUNK RELIEF

intagliotype *n* [¹*intaglio* + *type*] **:** a process for producing from a design drawn on a coated metal plate an intaglio plate for printing; *also* **:** a print from such a plate

intake \'ˌ,ˌ\ *n*, *often attrib* [⁴*in* + *take* (after *take in*, v.)] **1** *dial chiefly Brit* **:** a portion of land taken in or enclosed from a moor, common, or road **:** ENCLOSURE **:** hillside pasture or land reclaimed (as from the sea) **2 a :** an opening through which air, water, steam, or other fluid enters an enclosure ⟨the fuel-mixture ~ of an engine cylinder⟩ ⟨the ~ of an aqueduct⟩ — see JET ENGINE illustration **b :** a main passageway for air in a coal mine **3 a :** the act, process, or an instance of taking in ⟨~ . . . of various life-sustaining material —H.A.Overstreet⟩ ⟨stop the ~ of new clerks —Christopher Strachey⟩ ⟨an ~ of breath⟩ ⟨after the first quick ~ of surprise —Ethel Wilson⟩ ⟨the rate of ~ is an important index —W.F. Mackey⟩; *specif* **:** initial procedures (as interviews) conducted by a social worker, juvenile-court officer, or clinician in considering a client for treatment or service ⟨the role of the ~ worker⟩ ⟨an ~ official⟩ **b** (1) **:** the amount taken in ⟨an adequate ~ of food⟩ ⟨strictly limited my ~ during the day —*Sydney (Australia) Bull.*⟩ (2) **:** energy taken in **:** INPUT (3) **:** the persons taken into a group or organization ⟨half the total ~ were the sons of plebeians —J.W.Saunders⟩ (4) *chiefly Brit* **:** a person taken into a military service **:** RECRUIT ⟨just arrived with a new ~ —Derek Stanford⟩ **4** *Scot* **a :** SWINDLE **b :** SWINDLER

intake stroke *n* **:** the stroke in the cycle of an internal-combustion engine during which the fuel mixture is drawn in before compression

int al *abbr* [L *inter alia*] among other things; [L *inter alios*] among other persons

in·tangibility \(ˌ)in·, ən·+\ *n* **1 :** the quality or state of being intangible ⟨there is a certain ~ about this problem⟩ **2 :** something that is intangible **:** an intangible element ⟨fond of the pretty *intangibilities* of romance —Hugh Miller b. 1891⟩

¹in·tangible \(ˈ)in·, ən·+\ *adj* [F or ML; F, fr. MF, fr. ML *intangibilis*, fr. L *in-* ¹in- + LL *tangibilis* tangible — more at TANGIBLE] **1 :** incapable of being touched or perceived by touch **:** not tangible **:** IMPALPABLE, IMPERCEPTIBLE ⟨that more subtle and ~ thing, the soul —John Buchan⟩ ⟨the ~ constituent of energy —James Jeans⟩ **2 :** incapable of being defined or determined with certainty or precision **:** VAGUE, ELUSIVE ⟨with an ~ feeling of impending disaster —Guy Fowler⟩ ⟨this menace from the North was ~ and evasive —John Buchan⟩ — **in·tangibleness** \"+\ *n* — **in·tangibly** \"+\ *adv*

²intangible \"\ *n* **:** something intangible; *specif* **:** an asset (as goodwill or a patent right) that is not corporeal

intangible assets *n pl* **:** INTANGIBLES

intangible property *n* **:** property having no physical substance apparent to the senses **:** incorporeal property (as choses in action) often evidenced by documents (as stocks, bonds, notes, judgments, franchises) having no intrinsic value or by rights of action, easements, goodwill, trade secrets

in·tar·sia \ən·'tärsēə\ *n* -S [G, prob. modif. (influenced by It *tarsia*) of It *intarsio*, fr. *intarsiare* to inlay, fr. *in-* ²in- + *tarsiare* to inlay, fr. *tarsia* intarsia, fr. Ar *tarṣī*'] **1 :** a mosaic usu. of small pieces of wood which are inserted and glued into hollows of a wooden support that was popular in 15th century Italy for decoration featuring esp. scrolls, arabesques, architectural scenes, and flowers **2 :** the art or process of making such work — **in·tar·si·ate** \-ē,āt, -ēət\ *adj*

in·tar·si·a·tu·ra \ən·,tärsēə'tu̇rə\ *n*, *pl* **intarsiatu·re** \-(,)rā\ [It, fr. *intarsiato* (past part. of *intarsiare*) + *-ura* -ure (fr. L)] **:** INTARSIA

in·tar·sio \-sē,ō\ *n*, *pl* **intar·si** \-(,)sē\ [It] **:** INTARSIA

in·tar·sist \-,səst\ *n* -S [*intarsia* + *-ist*] **:** a person who works in intarsia

intcl *abbr* intercoastal

in·te·ger \'intəjə(r), -tēj-\ *n* -S [L, adj., untouched, entire — more at ENTIRE] **1 :** any of the natural numbers (as 1, 2, 3, 4, 5), the negatives of these numbers, or 0 **2 :** a complete entity ⟨governmental policy is an ~ —Dean Acheson⟩ ⟨they become a whole, an ~, of people who have the same aspirations and hopes —William Faulkner⟩ **syn** see NUMBER

in·te·gra·bil·i·ty \,intəgrə'biləd·ē, -lətē, -i\ *n* -ES **:** the fact or character of being integrable

in·te·gra·ble \'intəgrəbəl\ *adj* [³*integrate* + *-able*] **:** capable of being integrated ⟨a differential equation that is ~⟩ ⟨an ~ function⟩

¹in·te·gral \'intəgrəl *also* in·'tegrəl *or* ÷'in·trəgəl *or* ÷'in·trēgəl\ *adj* [ME, fr. ML *integralis*, fr. L *integr-*, *integer* untouched, entire + *-alis* -al] **1 a :** of, relating to, or serving to form a whole **:** essential to completeness **:** organically joined or linked **:** CONSTITUENT, INHERENT ⟨science has become an ~ part of his cultural environment —C.I.Glicksberg⟩ ⟨an ~ part of the empire⟩ ⟨in great dramas character is always . . . somehow ~ with plot —T.S.Eliot⟩ ⟨political and economic power are ~ one to the other —*Commonweal*⟩ **b** (1) **:** of, being, or relating to a mathematical integer (2) **:** relating to or concerned with mathematical integrals or integration **c :** formed as a unit with another part (as the main part) — often used with *with*; used esp. of a part of a tool or mechanism ⟨the pin is ~ with the pump body —H.F.Blanchard & Ralph Ritchen⟩ ⟨heat transfer through tubes with ~ spiral fins —*Transactions of Amer. Society of Mech. Engineers*⟩ ⟨the steam chest may be an ~ part of the turbine casing or may be bolted to it —B.G.A.Skrotzki & W.A.Vopat⟩ **2 :** composed of constituent parts making a whole **:** COMPOSITE, INTEGRATED ⟨a hospital, a medical school, and a laboratory of science all in one ~ group —V.G.Heiser⟩ **3 :** having nothing omitted or taken away **:** lacking nothing that belongs to it **:** COMPLETE,

ENTIRE, PERFECT ⟨if vocations are declining, it is because ~ Catholic living is declining —J.H.Wilson⟩ — **in·te·gral·ly** \-əlē,-əli\ *adv*

²**integral** *n* -s **1** : an entire thing : TOTALITY, WHOLE **2** *obs* : an integral part : CONSTITUENT, COMPONENT **3** : the result of a mathematical integration either of a function or of an equation

integral calculus *n* [prob. part trans. of NL *calculus integralis*] : a branch of mathematics that deals chiefly with the methods of finding indefinite integrals of functions and the evaluation of definite integrals, calculation (as of lengths of curves, areas, volumes, moments of inertia) by definite integration, mean values of functions, and the solution of certain simple types of differential equations

integral cover *n* : SELF-COVER

integral equation *n* : an equation in which the dependent variable is included at least once under a definite integral sign

integral humanism *n* : a Christian humanism based on Thomistic principles and advocated esp. by Jacques Maritain

in·te·gral·i·ty \ˌintəˈgraləd·ē\ *n* -ES : integral quality or state

integral rational function *n* : POLYNOMIAL

integral tripack *n* : a photographic film or plate consisting of three superposed emulsions each sensitive to a different primary color and coated on a single support — called also *monopack*; compare BIPACK

in·te·grand \ˈintəˌgrand, ˌ==ˈ=\ *n* -s [L *integrandus*, gerundive of *integrare* to integrate] : a mathematical expression to be integrated : the function under the integral sign

¹**in·te·grant** \ˈintə̇grənt, -tēg-\ *adj* [F or L; F *intégrant*, fr. MF, fr. L *integrant-, integrans*, pres. part. of *integrare* to integrate] : INTEGRAL ⟨all these are ~ parts of the republic —Edmund Burke⟩

²**integrant** \"\ *n* -s : an integral part : COMPONENT **syn** see ELEMENT

in·te·graph \-ˌgraf, -ˌrȧf\ *n* [ISV, blend of *integrate* and *-graph*] : an instrument that draws mechanically the graph of an antiderivative of a given mathematical function

¹**in·te·grate** \-ˌgrət, -ˌgrāt\ *adj* [ME *integrat*, fr. L *integratus* (past part.)] : INTEGRATED ⟨we may consider logic . . . as an ~ whole —William Hamilton †1856⟩

²**integrate** \"\ *n* -s : something that is integrated : a complete, organically unified, or perfect entity usu. resulting from a combination of elements : WHOLE ⟨an ~ of images which portray the person at his future best —C.K.Kluckhohn & H.A. Murray⟩ ⟨the cell, the molecule are not aggregates but ~s —H.J.Muller⟩

³**in·te·grate** \ˈintəˌgrāt, *usu* -ād·+V\ *vb* -ED/-ING/-s [L *integratus*, past part. of *integrare*, fr. *integr-, integer* untouched, entire — more at ENTIRE] *vt* **1** *obs* : to make complete : CONSTITUTE ⟨the particular doctrines which ~ Christianity —William Chillingworth⟩ **2** : to form into a more complete, harmonious, or coordinated entity often by the addition or arrangement of parts or elements ⟨that conquest rounded and *integrated* the glorious empire —Thomas De Quincey⟩ ⟨if man is to ~ himself, he must discover his springs of action —P.W.Bridgman⟩ **3** : to combine to form a more complete, harmonious, or coordinated entity: **a** : to unite (as a part or element) with something else ⟨a system of free enterprise carefully *integrated* with teamwork —J.C.Penney⟩ ⟨he who ~s this knowledge with the pattern of culture —David Daiches⟩ **b** : to combine together (as units or elements) ⟨~ the seventeen . . . reports into a few policy statements —E.C.Banfield⟩ ⟨this course . . . is designed to assist him to ~ all of his college experiences —A.C.Eurich⟩ ⟨a customs union that . . . would ~ the economies of the two countries —*Current Biog.*⟩ **c** (1) : to incorporate (as an individual or group) into a larger unit or group ⟨~ the West German divisions into the Atlantic defense system —*New Statesman & Nation*⟩ ⟨the South of that era was never *integrated* into the nation —H.W.Odum⟩ ⟨~ hundreds of thousands of Puerto Rican . . . workers into the organized labor movement —*N.Y. Times*⟩ (2) : to end the segregation of and bring into common and equal membership in society or an organization ⟨attempt to ~ Negroes into the church in a cautious gradual manner —*Jour. of Social Issues*⟩ ⟨moves . . . to ~ Indian children in the public school systems —*Indian Affairs*⟩ **4** : DESEGREGATE ⟨a well-staffed state agency managed . . . to ~ forty formerly segregated school districts —Douglass Cater⟩ **5** : to indicate the whole of : give the sum or total of **6** : to find the integral of (as a function or equation) ~ *vi* : to become integrated ⟨some of the white parishioners . . . were willing to go along with the decision to ~ —*Jour. of Social Issues*⟩ ⟨the show begins to ~ again —Alfred Bester⟩ **syn** see UNIFY

integrated *adj* **1** : characterized by integration: **a** : composed of separate parts united together to form a more complete, harmonious, or coordinated entity ⟨her tightly plotted, admirably ~ novel —John Barkham⟩ ⟨an ~ series of twenty-six dams —*Lamp*⟩ **b** : combining elements usu. taught in separate academic courses or departments ⟨to establish the behavior sciences on an ~ footing —J.W.Bennett⟩ ⟨~ courses⟩ **c** : having in common and equal membership individuals or groups differing in some group characteristic (as race) ⟨Negro units were broken up and reassigned in ~ groups —*New Republic*⟩ ⟨an ~ school⟩ **d** : characterized by psychological integration ⟨an ~ personality⟩ **e** : characterized by close cooperation or partial unity of constituent units ⟨a more closely ~ economic and political system —D.D.Eisenhower⟩ ⟨an ~ Europe⟩ ⟨an ~ military staff⟩ **f** (1) : operating economically as a single coordinated physically interconnected unit or system usu. confined to a specific region ⟨an ~ public utility system⟩ (2) : characterized by possession of sources of supply and continuous control of production and often distribution from raw materials to diversified finished products ⟨an ~ company . . . occupies a favored position as compared with a competitor which is at the mercy of the market —*Financial World*⟩ **g** *of the bar* : characterized by the compulsory membership of all lawyers practicing in a specific area (as a state) ⟨the states having an ~ bar have codes of professional ethics enforceable upon all members —*Jour. of the Amer. Judicature Society*⟩ **h** : characterized by social solidarity, coherency of form and function, and moral or psychological unity among members ⟨its culture is . . . more stable and better ~ —A.L.Kroeber⟩ **2** : incorporated into a group or organization on the basis of common and equal membership despite differing characteristics (as race) ⟨most Indians are ~ with the other residents —W.R.Moore⟩ ⟨Negroes . . . have long been ~ in the police department —Gladwin Hill⟩

integrated logging *n* : a system of logging planned to remove in one cutting all usable timber and to separate the primary products and distribute them to industries where they will bring the highest returns

integrating factor *n* : a factor that renders immediately integrable a differential equation multiplied by it

integrating sphere *n* : a spherical shell used to determine total luminous flux by means of photometric measurement of a spot of light through an aperture in the shell whose white interior produces thorough diffusion of light from a source placed at its center

integrating wattmeter *n* : WATT-HOUR METER

in·te·gra·tion \ˌintəˈgrāshən\ *n* -s [L *integration-, integratio* act of renewing, act of restoring, fr. *integratus* (past part. of *integrare* to renew, integrate) + *-ion-, -io* -ion — more at INTEGRATE] **1** : the act, process, or an instance of integrating : the condition of being formed into a whole by the addition or combination of parts or elements **2 a** : a combination and coordination of separate and diverse elements or units into a more complete or harmonious whole ⟨the automobile is an ~ of a multitude of machine parts —C.C.Furnas⟩ ⟨large-scale ~ of efforts —Oscar Handlin⟩ **b** : a unification and mutual adjustment of diverse groups or elements into a relatively coordinated and harmonious society or culture with a consistent body of normative standards ⟨most urban communities possess some degree of ~ around primary group norms —Kimball Young⟩ ⟨the total ~ of any given culture about its technology —David Bidney⟩ **c** : the organization of teaching matter to interrelate or unify subjects usu. taught in separate academic courses or departments ⟨through ~ it is possible to teach science, health, and safety as part of the regular program —E.J.Goebel⟩ **d** : an arrangement usu. on a hierarchical basis of functions or units of an organization to promote coordination and responsibility ⟨the need for administrative ~ at the county level —C.F.Snider⟩ ⟨an ~ of units previously scattered . . . in departments or otherwise —F.A.Ogg & P.O.Ray⟩ **e** : an incorporation into society or an organization (as a public school) on the basis of common and equal membership of individuals differing in some group characteristic (as race) ⟨ordered ~ of all white and Negro troops in the armed forces —*New Republic*⟩ ⟨the native Polynesian group that strongly objects to ~ with Europeans —*N.Y. Times*⟩ ⟨a positive ~ of the African into the South African community —Margaret Ballinger⟩ **f** (1) : the coordination and correlation of the total processes of perception, interpretation, and reaction ensuring a normal effective life ⟨failure of association and failure of ~ take place among neurotic individuals —R.M.Dorcus & G.W. Shaffer⟩ (2) : a harmonious coordination of the behavior and personality of an individual with his environment ⟨she attempts to enter the world of her fellow teenagers, and after many mistakes she achieves such ~ —Eleanor Scott⟩ **g** : the establishment of close cooperation among or some degree of unification of distinct entities (as countries or groups of countries) esp. in a specific area (as trade or defense) ⟨West European ~ is the first condition for the survival of every country concerned —William Petersen⟩ ⟨the . . . proposal for the economic ~ of Europe into one single market —*Current Biog.*⟩ **h** : the unified control of a number of successive or similar economic esp. industrial processes formerly carried on independently ⟨~ may result in important cost reductions⟩ **3** : the operation of finding a function of which the integrand is the derivative of a function or of solving a differential equation **4** : the sum of the processes by which the developing parts of an organism are formed into a functional and structural whole ⟨at the molecular level of ~ many studies are needed —*Science*⟩

integration by parts : a method of integration by means of the reduction formula $\int udv = uv - \int vdu$

in·te·gra·tion·ist \-sh(ə)nə̇st\ *n* -s : a person that believes in, advocates, or practices integration ⟨opposition to the ~s came from many places in the small southern town⟩

in·te·gra·tive \ˈ==ˌgrād·|iv, -ăt|, |ēv *also* |əv\ *adj* [³*integrate* + *-ive*] **1** : tending to integrate ⟨the ~ action of the nervous system —J.R.Newman⟩ **2** : favoring or implementing integration ⟨the widespread ~ trend of modern science —Weston La Barre⟩ ⟨anthropology's ~ tools —Abraham Edel⟩

in·te·gra·tor \-ād·ə(r), -ātə-\ *n* -s [LL, renewer, restorer, fr. L *integratus* (past part.) + *-or*] : one that integrates ⟨religion has been the supreme ~ of intellectual and emotional experience —H.N.Fairchild⟩; *specif* : a device (as a planimeter or pedometer) that totalizes by mechanical, electromechanical, electronic, or other physical means a multiplicity of variable quantities in a manner comparable to that in which mathematical solutions are arrived at by means of differential equations or integral calculus

integri- *comb form* [L, fr. *integr-, integer* — more at ENTIRE] : whole : entire ⟨*integri*folious⟩ ⟨*integri*palliate⟩

in·teg·ri·ty \ə̇nˈtegrəd·ē, -rətē, -i\ *n* -ES [ME *integrite*, fr. MF & L; MF *integrité*, fr. L *integritat-, integritas*, fr. *integr-, integer* untouched, entire + *-itat-, -itas* -ity] **1 a** : an unimpaired or unmarred condition : entire correspondence with an original condition : SOUNDNESS ⟨personality function depends greatly upon the ~ of brain function —*Diagnostic & Statistical Manual*⟩ ⟨maintenance of the ship's watertight ~ —*Manual of Seamanship*⟩ ⟨designed to assure structural ~ of the aircraft —*Index to Current Tech. Publications*⟩ ⟨the ~ of the national currency is not dependent on its convertibility —*Current Biog.*⟩ **b** : an uncompromising adherence to a code of moral, artistic, or other values : utter sincerity, honesty, and candor : avoidance of deception, expediency, artificiality, or shallowness of any kind ⟨an example of great physical vigor, business ~, and thrift —*Current Biog.*⟩ ⟨a writer of ~ has a duty toward his opinions —C.L.Carmer⟩ ⟨a serious reflection on the intellectual ~ of the accusers —C.R.Davenport⟩ ⟨his ~ told him that this would be at variance with the dramatic truth of his opera —Robert Lawrence⟩ ⟨the ~, the clean drive, and the unforced power that distinguishes the good primitive novel —Frederic Morton⟩ **2** : the quality or state of being complete or undivided : material, spiritual, or aesthetic wholeness : organic unity : ENTIRENESS, COMPLETENESS ⟨the emphasis is always on the ~ and the uniqueness of the finished poem —David Daiches⟩ ⟨has a feeling for the ~ of each separate person —Malcolm Cowley⟩ ⟨seen in its ~ . . . it is a crumbling tower of waste —Charles Dickens⟩ ⟨awareness of the ~ of the British Empire forever —Upton Sinclair⟩ ⟨aesthetic experience is experience in its ~ —John Dewey⟩

in·teg·u·ment \ə̇nˈtegyəmənt\ *n* -s [L *integumentum*, fr. *integere* to cover (fr. *in-* ²in- + *tegere* to cover) + *-mentum* -ment — more at THATCH] **1** : something that covers or encloses : COVERING, ENVELOPE ⟨still encased in a dry brittle ~ that had once been leather —A.B.Chandler⟩ ⟨almost any ~ of a book before the age of cloth, is attractive —R.W.Chapman⟩ **2** : an external coating or investment: as **a** : one of the usu. two envelopes that enclose the nucellus of an ovule, that are often fused, and that sometimes with other parts form the seed coat **b** : an enveloping layer, membrane, or structure (as the skin of a fish or the exoskeleton of an insect)

in·teg·u·men·tal \=ˌ==ˈment³l\ *or* **in·teg·u·men·ta·ry** \-ntərē, -n·trē\ *adj* : of or relating to the integument; *esp* : CUTANEOUS

in·tel·lect \ˈint³lˌekt\ *n* -s [ME, fr. MF or L; MF, fr. L *intellectus*, fr. *intellectus*, past part. of *intellegere, intelligere* to perceive, understand — more at INTELLIGENT] **1 a** : the power or faculty of knowing as distinguished from the power to feel and to will **b** *Aristotelianism* (1) : passive reason (2) : active reason **c** *Scholasticism* : the faculty of penetrating appearances and getting at the substance through abstraction from and elimination of the individual **d** *Thomism* (1) : the receptive faculty of cognition that makes apprehensible the phantasms or intelligible forms — called also *passive intellect, possible intellect, potential intellect* (2) : the aspect of the soul that is immortal and constitutes the active power of thought operating upon the phantasms or intelligible forms — called also *active intellect, agent intellect* **e** : UNDERSTANDING, REASON **2 a** : a person given to reflective thought or reasoning : a person of notable intellect : BRAIN ⟨the outstanding ~ of the whole convention —*Hispanic Amer. Hist. Rev.*⟩ **b** : the totality of intellectual persons ⟨the ~ of the country recognized his superiority⟩ **3 intellects** *pl, now chiefly dial* : WITS, FACULTIES ⟨she wishes I had more ~s —Eden Phillpotts⟩ **syn** see MIND

in·tel·lec·tion \ˌint³lˈekshən\ *n* -s [ME *intelleccioun* intellect, understanding, fr. LL *intellection-, intellectio* synecdoche, lit., understanding, fr. L *intellectus* (past part.) + *-ion-, -io* -ion] **1** : exercise of the intellect : REASONING, COGNITION, APPREHENSION ⟨one of the most sublime acts of ~ of all time —*New Yorker*⟩ **2** : a specific act of the intellect : NOTION, THOUGHT, IDEA ⟨mazy ~s —Alan Devoe⟩

in·tel·lec·tive \|==ˌ|tiv\ *adj* [MF or LL; MF *intellectif*, fr. LL *intellectivus*, fr. L *intellectus* (past part.) + *-ivus* -ive] **1** : relating to, based on, or possessed by the intellect : INTELLECTUAL ⟨those more ~ artificial features which find their expression in refined syntax and style —M.A.Pei⟩ **2** : having intellectual power : INTELLIGENT, RATIONAL, COGNITIVE ⟨awareness of the spiritual ~ soul —Beatrice H. Zedler⟩ — **in·tel·lec·tive·ly** \-tə̇vlē\ *adv*

¹**in·tel·lec·tu·al** \|int³l|ekch(əw)əl, -ksh-\ *adj* [ME, fr. MF & L; MF *intellectuel*, fr. L *intellectualis*, fr. *intellectus* intellect + *-alis* -al] **1 a** : of, belonging to, or relating to the intellect or its use : REFLECTIVE, REASONING ⟨satire is an ~ weapon —Herbert Read⟩ ⟨~ powers⟩ ⟨enabling them to function on the ~ plane —Bruce Bliven b.1889⟩ ⟨began his ~ career as a mathematician —F.S.C.Northrop⟩ — contrasted with *animal* **b** : having its source in or being preeminently guided by the intellect as distinguished from emotion or experience : RATIONAL ⟨has a tremendous ~ sympathy for oppressed people —Green Peyton⟩ ⟨think of such playwrights as coldly ~ —E.R.Bentley⟩ ⟨in no sense an ~ or metaphysical painter —Herbert Read⟩ ⟨the most subtle and ~ edifice ever made by man —Weston La Barre⟩ ⟨disseminated the severe and ~ Florentine style —*Nat'l Gallery of Art*⟩ **c** : calling the intellect into play : requiring use of the intellect ⟨as abstruse and ~ as a chess problem⟩ ⟨there should be a distinction . . . between manual or copying work and ~ work —K.C.Wheare⟩ **2** *obs* : apprehensible by the intellect alone : IMMATERIAL, SPIRITUAL, IDEAL **3 a** *archaic* : endowed with the power to know and reason : INTELLIGENT **b** (1) : devoted to matters of the mind and esp. to the arts and letters : given to study, reflection, and speculation esp. concerning large or abstract issues ⟨sort of the ~ type, but most of the gang are real people —W.H. Whyte⟩ ⟨maintain a person can be ~ and not be intelligent —Jean Stafford⟩ (2) : engaged in activity requiring preeminently the use of the intellect : engaged in mental as distinguished from manual labor; *esp* : engaged in creative literary, artistic, or scientific labor ⟨~ workers should be able to deduct from their income tax the amounts which they must spend for books, documents, research work, and materials in general —*Report: (Canadian) Royal Commission on Nat'l Development*⟩ (3) : reflecting, indicating, or suggesting devotion to matters of the mind : indicating or associated with a studious reflective temper or large mental endowment ⟨had a high ~ forehead —Edmund Wilson⟩ **syn** see MENTAL

²**intellectual** \"\ *n* -s **1** *obs* : INTELLECT, UNDERSTANDING **2 intellectuals** *pl, archaic* : intellectual powers or faculties **3 a** : a person of superior intelligence : a brainy person ⟨an uneducated ~ who had directed his great powers to accumulation and exploitation —S.H.Adams⟩ ⟨an ~ is a person endowed with unusual mental capacity —*Saturday Rev.*⟩ **b** (1) : a person devoted to matters of the mind and esp. to the arts and letters : one given to study, reflection, and speculation esp. concerning large, profound, or abstract issues ⟨afraid to be an ~ — if you wanted to go to art galleries, you were immediately suspect —P.E.Deutschman⟩ ⟨a friendly manner, a quiet voice, and the face of an ~ —William Ridsdale⟩ (2) : a person claiming to belong to an intellectual elite or caste, given to empty theorizing or cerebration, and often inept in the solution of practical problems : EGGHEAD ⟨don't go for the ~ who knows nothing but $2 words —J.P.Whitcomb⟩ ⟨that dreary and narrow creature an ~ —*Manchester Guardian Weekly*⟩ ⟨~ is an ugly word . . . it implies consummate snobbery —Russell Kirk⟩ **c** : a person engaged in activity requiring preeminently the use of the intellect : one engaged in mental as distinguished from manual labor ⟨~s . . . are functioning groups of society, like any of the professionals, such as lawyers, doctors, engineers, professors —F.G.Wilson⟩

intellectual history *n* : a branch of history that deals with the rise and evolution of ideas : history of ideas

in·tel·lec·tu·al·ism \ˌint³lˈekch(əw)əˌlizəm, -ksh-\ *n* -s **1 a** : the viewpoint that knowledge is derived from pure reason : RATIONALISM **b** : the doctrine that the ultimate principle of reality is reason **2 a** : devotion to the exercise of intellect or intellectual pursuits ⟨restore the true ~; that is to say, a love of intellectual things —August Heckscher⟩ **b** : such devotion carried to excess ⟨the unnatural ~ which society inflicts upon the middle class —Ian Watt⟩

¹**in·tel·lec·tu·al·ist** \-ˌlə̇st\ *n* -s [¹*intellectual* + *-ist*] **1** : an adherent of the doctrine of intellectualism **2** : a person given to intellectualism

²**intellectualist** \"\ *adj* : INTELLECTUALISTIC

in·tel·lec·tu·al·is·tic \ˌ==ˌ|=(=)=ˈlistik, -tēk\ *adj* : relating to intellectualism or intellectualists — **in·tel·lec·tu·al·is·ti·cal·ly** \-tə̇k(ə)lē, -tēk-, -li\ *adv*

in·tel·lec·tu·al·i·ty \ˌint³lˌekchəˈwaləd·ē, -ksh-, -lətē, -i\ *n* -ES [LL *intellectualitat-, intellectualitas*, fr. L *intellectualis* intellectual + *-itat-, -itas* -ity] : intellectual power : the quality or state of being intellectual

in·tel·lec·tu·al·i·za·tion \ˌint³lˌekchə(wə)lə̇ˈzāshən, -ksh-, -ˌlīˈz-\ *n* -s : the act, process, or an instance of intellectualizing ⟨opposed to any ~ of art —Herbert Read⟩

in·tel·lec·tu·al·ize \ˌ==ˈ=(=)=ˌlīz\ *vb* -ED/-ING/-S *see -ize in Explan Notes* [¹*intellectual* + *-ize*] *vt* **1** : to give intellectual or rational form or content to : treat or analyze intellectually ⟨tendency to ~ . . . problems —*Current Biog.*⟩ ⟨~s traditional forms like the sonnet and madrigal —Douglas Bush⟩ **2** : to avoid (conscious recognition of the emotional basis of an act or feeling) by substituting a superficially plausible explanation ⟨conflicts that are *intellectualized* —L.E.Hinsie⟩ ~ *vi* : to engage in intellectual discussion : REASON, PHILOSOPHIZE ⟨sat . . . and simply *intellectualized* —Johnny George⟩

in·tel·lec·tu·al·ly \|int³l|ekch(əw)əlē, -ksh-, -kshlē, -li\ *adv* : in an intellectual manner

in·tel·lec·tu·al·ness \ˌint³lˈekch(əw)əlnə̇s, -ksh-\ *n* -ES : the quality or state of being intellectual

intellectual virtue *n, Aristotelianism* : a virtue (as wisdom) concerned with the apprehension of rational principles

¹**in·tel·li·gence** \ə̇nˈteləjən(t)s\ *n* -s *often attrib* [ME, fr. MF, fr. OF, fr. L *intelligentia*, fr. *intelligent-, intelligens* (pres. part.) + *-ia* -y — more at INTELLIGENT] **1 a** (1) : the faculty of understanding : capacity to know or apprehend : INTELLECT, REASON ⟨~, which emerged during the revolutionary cycles of matter as the highest form yet achieved —Hermann Reith⟩ ⟨conceived of history as the expression of a divine ~⟩ (2) *Christian Science* : the basic eternal quality of divine Mind **b** : the available ability as measured by intelligence tests or by other social criteria to use one's existing knowledge to meet new situations and to solve new problems, to learn, to foresee problems, to use symbols or relationships, to create new relationships, to think abstractly : ability to perceive one's environment, to deal with it symbolically, to deal with it effectively, to adjust to it, to work toward a goal : the degree of one's alertness, awareness, or acuity : ability to use with awareness the mechanism of reasoning whether conceived as a unified intellectual factor or as the aggregate of many intellectual factors or abilities, as intuitive or as analytic, as organismic, biological, physiological, psychological, or social in origin and nature **c** : mental acuteness : SAGACITY, SHREWDNESS ⟨did all he was asked to do with ~ and great good humor⟩ **2 a** : an intelligent being; *esp* : an incorporeal spirit : ANGEL ⟨hierarchies of angelic ~s —S.F.Mason⟩ **b** : a person of some intellectual capacity ⟨all those ~s we have agreed to call great —*Times Lit. Supp.*⟩ ⟨the greatest all-round ~ writing in England —P.S.O'Hegarty⟩ **3 a** : the act of understanding : COMPREHENSION, KNOWLEDGE ⟨faith is necessary to the ~ of the Christian mysteries —*Encyc. Americana*⟩ **b** (1) : information communicated : NEWS, NOTICE, ADVICE ⟨more weight is laid upon ~ than on editorials —Horace Greeley⟩ ⟨the joyful ~ that there is hope —Georgina Grahame⟩ ⟨from the engine-room voice tube came ~ of more importance —M.S.Boylan⟩ (2) : interchange of information : COMMUNICATION ⟨accused of maintaining ~ with the enemy⟩ (3) *obs* : a piece of information — usu. used in pl. (4) *archaic* : common understanding or mutual relations : ACQUAINTANCE, INTERCOURSE (5) : evaluated information concerning an enemy or possible enemy or a possible theater of operations and the conclusions drawn therefrom; *also* : the section, agency, or persons engaged in obtaining such information : SECRET SERVICE ⟨investigated me and told me I was qualified for Navy ~ —T.F.Murphy⟩ ⟨an ~ bureau⟩ ⟨available to American and allied ~ organizations —L.W.Doob⟩ **syn** see MIND

²**intelligence** *vt* -ED/-ING/-S *obs* : to bring tidings of (something) or to (someone)

in·tel·li·genced \-jən(t)st\ *adj* [¹*intelligence* + *-ed*] **1** : having mental power : INTELLIGENT **2** : having information : INFORMED

intelligence office *n* : an agency where servants (as domestic help) may be hired ⟨you would know the best real estate and *intelligence offices* —Emily Post⟩

intelligence officer *n* : a staff officer who gathers, evaluates, interprets, and disseminates intelligence and attempts to thwart enemy attempts to gather such information

intelligence quotient *n* : a number held to express the relative intelligence of a person determined by dividing his mental age by his chronological age with chronological years above 14 or sometimes 16 disregarded and then multiplying by 100 to eliminate decimals —abbr. *IQ, I.Q.*

in·tel·li·genc·er \-jənsə(r), -jen(t)s-, ˌ=ˌ==ˈjen-\ *n* -s [¹*intelligence* + *-er*] : one that conveys intelligence or news: as **a** : a secret agent : SPY **b** : a bringer of news : REPORTER ⟨made this wearied ~ sit up and listen —Virgil Thomson⟩ **c** : NEWSPAPER — usu. used as the names of newspapers

intelligence test *n* : any of various tests consisting of standardized questions and tasks designed to determine the mental age of the person examined or his relative capacity to absorb information and solve problems : a test designed to measure capacity to learn apart from actual achievement — compare ACHIEVEMENT TEST, APTITUDE TEST

in·tel·li·gen·cy \-jənsē, -si\ *n* -ES [L *intelligentia* — more at INTELLIGENCE] *archaic* : INTELLIGENCE

¹in·tel·li·gent \-nt\ *adj* [L *intelligent-, intelligens,* pres. part. of *intelligere, intellegere* to perceive, understand, fr. *inter-* + *legere* to choose, select, gather — more at LEGEND] **1 a :** possessing intelligence or intellect : having the power of reflection or reason ⟨assumes the existence of other worlds peopled by ~ beings⟩ **b :** guided or directed by intelligence or intellect : RATIONAL ⟨in the other kind of behavior, often called ~, the animal is able to benefit from its past experience —*New Biology*⟩ **2 a :** having or indicating a high or satisfactory degree of intelligence and mental capacity or powers of perception, consideration, and correct decision : not stupid or foolish ⟨Puritanism presupposed an ~ clergy capable of interpreting Scripture —*Amer. Guide Series: Mass.*⟩ ⟨though she could not read, both her face and conversation were ~ —Willa Cather⟩ **b :** well adapted to its purpose : being the product of intelligence of a high order : revealing or reflecting good judgment or sound and comprehensive thought : WISE, SKILLFUL ⟨an ~ decision⟩ ⟨~ propaganda⟩ ⟨an ~ essay⟩ **3 a :** marked by quick active perception and understanding ⟨an ~ person, looking out of his eyes and hearkening in his ears —R.L.Stevenson⟩ **b** *archaic* : showing or having some special knowledge, skill, or aptitude

syn KNOWING, BRILLIANT, SMART, BRIGHT, QUICK-WITTED, CLEVER, ALERT: INTELLIGENT, limited in connotational range, indicates mental capacity and power, often to a high degree, enabling one to perceive, learn, consider, and judge ⟨what should a mature and *intelligent* nation do in such a crisis? . . . we ought to keep our heads . . . be alert to really serious dangers —Elmer Davis⟩ ⟨it is fairly easy for any *intelligent* mother to know when the baby is hungry —Morris Fishbein⟩ KNOWING may indicate ability to know or possession of special knowledge; it often applies to intimations of special information or sophistication ⟨the *knowing* collectors of records —*Saturday Rev.*⟩ ⟨the two young officers exchanged *knowing* glances —W.M.Thackeray⟩ BRILLIANT indicates uncommon, quick, shining mental keenness, capacity, achievement against difficulty ⟨a shrewd sensible man, only not *brilliant* —George Meredith⟩ ⟨first revealed with bitter and *brilliant* incisiveness the cynical desperation of early postwar adolescents —*Amer. Guide Series: Minn.*⟩ SMART suggests quickness in perceiving, in cannily calculating, or in successful resourcefulness ⟨he was top of the class, and the master said he was the *smartest* lad in the school —D.H.Lawrence⟩ ⟨for hundreds of years the *smartest* businessmen in the world have been coming in to the City of London —D.W.Brogan⟩ SMART may indicate facetious pertness ⟨*smart* retorts are also cherished, especially by the young —L.J.Davidson⟩ BRIGHT indicates a lively alert quickness in learning and understanding ⟨the teachers all knew he was *bright* as brass . . . he took every last one of the prizes —Ellen Glasgow⟩ ⟨foreordained that any *bright* person ought to have seen it coming —*Harper's*⟩ QUICK-WITTED indicates quickness in arising to an occasion, in perceiving and coping with problems or dangers ⟨a *quick-witted* debater hard to entangle or confuse⟩ ⟨making their way through enemy territory under the *quick-witted* leadership of the captain⟩ CLEVER may suggest quick, apt facility at improvising, finding expedients, contriving to cope with problems ⟨*clever* boys and girls like to test their minds on difficulties —Bertrand Russell⟩ ⟨he was a *clever* lawyer . . . and had the jury eating out of his hand —Dorothy Sayers⟩ ALERT indicates a wide-awake care about and concern with any emergent development that might have been unnoticed ⟨*alert* and wary, making off at the first alarm —James Stevenson-Hamilton⟩ ⟨*alert* to this need, Congress authorized five military highways —*Amer. Guide Series: Mich.*⟩ **syn** see in addition MENTAL

²intelligent \"\ *n* -S **1** *obs* : a person who conveys information : SPY **2 :** an intelligent being

in·tel·li·gen·tial \ən¦telə¦jenchəl\ *adj* : of, like, relating to, or having intelligence : exercising or implying understanding ⟨the existential and the ~ elements —Heinrich Zimmer⟩

in·tel·li·gent·ly *adv* : in an intelligent manner ⟨delivered an ~ reasoned summation⟩

in·tel·li·gen·tsia *also* **in·tel·li·gen·tzia** \(,)in,telə'jentsēə, ən,tel- *also* -'jench(ē)ə *or* -'gentsēə\ *n* -S [Russ *intelligentsiya,* fr. L *intelligentia* intelligence — more at INTELLIGENCE] **1 a :** a class of well-educated articulate persons constituting a distinct, recognized, and self-conscious social stratum within a nation and claiming or assuming for itself the guiding role of an intellectual, social, or political vanguard ⟨the basic function of the Encyclopedists and of all later ~s . . . includes both the iconoclastic and the pedagogic, the destructive and the constructive element —Arthur Koestler⟩ ⟨an inferior helot people without any national consciousness, without any ~ —O.D.Tolischus⟩ ⟨it has a restless, unstable, rebellious, and brilliant ~ —R.H.Markham⟩ **b :** a class of persons devoted to matters of the mind and esp. to the arts and letters : a class of persons given to study, reflection, and speculation esp. concerning large, profound, or abstract issues ⟨a café where the local ~ gathered⟩ ⟨a trifling comedy scorned by the ~⟩ **2 :** a class of persons engaged in activity requiring preeminently the use of the intellect : a class of persons engaged in mental as distinguished from manual labor ⟨best opinion in this country accords to professional men and women the status of ~ —M.L.Cooke⟩

in·tel·li·gi·bil·i·ty \(,)=,==jə'bilәd·ē, -lәtē, -i\ *n* -ES **1 :** the quality or state of being intelligible : CLARITY, UNDERSTANDABILITY ⟨the immediate ~ of the prose —Richard Eberhart⟩ **2 :** something that is intelligible

¹in·tel·li·gi·ble \ən'teləjəbəl\ *adj* [ME, fr. L *intelligibilis,* fr. *intelligere* to perceive, understand + *-ibilis* -able — more at INTELLIGENT] **1** *obs* : INTELLIGENT **2 :** capable of being understood or comprehended ⟨an ~ description⟩ ⟨~ pronunciation⟩ **3 a :** apprehensible by the intellect only : purely conceptual ⟨the classical conception, according to which thinking is the inspection of ~ objects —Norman Malcolm⟩ **b :** relating to something that is beyond perception : SUPERSENSIBLE, SUPRASENSUOUS ⟨made the ~ world . . . the starting point of their speculations —Frank Thilly⟩ — **in·tel·li·gi·ble·ness** \-nəs\ *n* -ES — **in·tel·li·gi·bly** \-blē,-bli\ *adv*

²intelligible \"\ *n* -S : an object of the intellect ⟨the intellect's natural capacity for the intuition of ~s —L.J.Thro⟩

intelligible species *n, Thomism* : an object as apprehended through an act of intellectual cognition — contrasted with *sensible species*

in·tem·er·ate \ən'temə,rāt, -,rət\ *adj* [L *intemeratus,* fr. *in-* ¹in- + *temeratus,* past part. of *temerare* to violate, defile, fr. *temere* rashly, by chance — more at TEMERITY] : INVIOLATE, PURE, UNDEFILED

in·temperance \(')in, ən+\ *n* [ME *intemperaunce,* fr. L *intemperantia,* fr. *intemperant-, intemperans* intemperate (fr. *in-* ¹in- + *temperant-, temperans* temperate, fr. pres. part. of *temperare* to temper, regulate) + *-ia* -y — more at TEMPER] **1 :** inclemency or severity esp. of weather **2 a :** excess or lack of moderation in an action ⟨much ~ of statement in the current condemnation of our education —F.N.Robinson⟩ and esp. in satisfying an appetite or passion; *specif* : habitual or excessive drinking of intoxicants **b :** an intemperate act ⟨these daily ~s were disquieting, because men can't talk themselves into permanent rages —*New World*⟩

intemperancy *n* -ES [L *intemperantia*] *obs* : INTEMPERANCE

in·temperate \(')in, ən+\ *adj* [ME *intemperat,* fr. L *intemperatus,* fr. *in-* ¹in- + *temperatus* temperate — more at TEMPERATE] : not temperate: as **a :** immoderate in satisfying an appetite or passion; *specif* : given to excessive use of intoxicating liquors ⟨an ~ drinker⟩ **b :** lacking temperance or moderation : EXCESSIVE, INORDINATE, IMMODERATE, VIOLENT ⟨~ language⟩ ⟨~ zeal⟩ ⟨~ attacks⟩ **c :** not mild : EXTREME, INCLEMENT, SEVERE ⟨~ weather⟩ ⟨an ~ zone⟩ — **in·temper·ate·ly** *adv* — **in·temper·ate·ness** *n*

in·temperature \ən+\ *n* [¹*in-* + *temperature*] *n, archaic* : distempered state : INTEMPERANCE ⟨this season, the ~ of which may last till the middle of May —Tobias Smollett⟩

in·tem·pes·tive \¦in(,)tem¦pestiv\ *adj* [L *intempestivus,* fr. *in-* ¹in- + *tempestivus* tempestive] : UNTIMELY, INOPPORTUNE

in tempo *adv (or adj)* [It] : in time : a tempo — used as a direction in music

in·tem·po·ral \(')in¦temp(ə)rəl, ən·'t-\ *adj* [¹*in-* + *temporal*] : transcending temporal relations : TIMELESS ⟨a cruelly abstract and ~ truth —Claude Vigée⟩ — **in·tem·po·ral·ly** \-rəlē\ *adv*

in·tend \ən·'tend\ *vb* -ED/-ING/-S [alter. (influenced by L *in-* ²in-) of ME *entenden,* fr. OF *entendre,* fr. LL *intendere,* fr. L, to intend, attend, stretch out, extend, fr. *in-* ²in- + *tendere* to stretch, stretch out — more at TEND] *vt* **1 a** *archaic* : to understand or construe in a certain manner : APPREHEND, INTERPRET **b** (1) : SIGNIFY, MEAN ⟨what was ~*ed* by that remark⟩ ⟨by teleology is ~*ed* the purposefulness of nature⟩ (2) : to have in mind : have reference to : refer to ⟨this tavern I think must have been the one ~*ed* . . . in his novel —*Notes & Queries*⟩ **2 a** [ME *intenden, entenden,* fr. MF *entendre,* fr. L *intendere*] (1) : to have in mind as a design or purpose : PLAN ⟨~*s* to do all in his power⟩ ⟨~ not to retrace the march of occupation in detail —Russell Lord⟩ (2) : to have in mind as an object to be gained or achieved ⟨~*s* that general opulence to which it gives occasion —Adam Smith⟩ ⟨~*ed* the advantage of a great number of people —H.E. Scudder⟩ ⟨~*s* only his own advancement⟩ **b :** to design for or destine to a specified purpose or future ⟨the engravings are not ~*ed* for sale —Mary Zimmer⟩ ⟨~*ed* him to be the next president⟩ **3** *archaic* : to proceed on (one's course or way) **4** [ME *intenden, entenden,* fr. MF *entendre*] *archaic* **a :** to direct the mind on : attend to : take care of ⟨~*s* his brother's will —George Chapman⟩ **b :** to direct (the eyes) toward something **5** *obs* : ASSERT, MAINTAIN : PRETEND **6** *archaic* : to stretch out or forth : make tense : EXTEND, STRETCH ~ *vi* **1** [ME *entenden,* fr. MF *entendre*] : to have an aim or end in mind ⟨none of our first plans . . . could be carried out as we ~*ed* —R.L.Stevenson⟩ **2** *archaic* **a** [ME *intenden, entenden,* fr. L *intendere*] : to direct one's course or way : PROCEED **b :** to start or set out : intend to go or set out

syn INTEND, MEAN, DESIGN, PROPOSE, and PURPOSE can mean to have in mind as an end, aim, or function. INTEND implies that the mind is directed to some definite accomplishment or end, often with determination ⟨*intended* 24 books, sketched 14, but left only four —Gilbert Highet⟩ ⟨did not *intend* annexation of Italian land —Hilaire Belloc⟩ or that, in the mind, one conceives a thing as in a particular occupation or function, serving a given purpose, or carrying a particular meaning ⟨the volume was *intended* for reading in the public schools —Agnes Repplier⟩ ⟨was *intended* for the church —L.O. Howard⟩ ⟨the five- and six-year courses are *intended* for pupils likely to proceed to the university —H.C.Dent⟩ ⟨the meaning of the phrase was not what the writers *intended*⟩ MEAN can come close to the sense of INTEND though it carries a weaker implication of determination, often indicating little more than volition or decision ⟨*mean* to pay back a debt⟩ ⟨put something to a use for which it was not *meant*⟩ ⟨*mean* to go to the movies tonight⟩ DESIGN usu. stresses forethought in arriving at an intention, often implying contriving or scheming ⟨*designs* a companion volume in which she will carry further her discussion —Marjorie Nicolson⟩ ⟨plans we had *designed* to put into effect immediately⟩ ⟨putting a machine to uses for which it was not *designed*⟩ ⟨have no protection against *designing* and dishonest people⟩ PROPOSE implies a clear setting forth, in the mind or before others, of one's intention, connoting clear definition or open avowal ⟨*proposed* to live as if the golden age had come again —Van Wyck Brooks⟩ ⟨*proposes* to give a summary of titles at the end of the work —H.O.Taylor⟩ ⟨*proposed* to carry out the preposterous plan —*Lamp*⟩ ⟨the plan turned out better than he had *proposed* at the committee meeting⟩ PURPOSE differs little from PROPOSE except in implying a stronger determination or clearer intent ⟨*purpose* staying there about a month —Mary W. Shelley⟩ ⟨*purpose* to arrange a typical program in this chapter —W.F.Brown b.1903⟩ ⟨*purpose* to write a history of England —T.B.Macaulay⟩

in·tend·ance \ən·'tendən(t)s\ *n* -S [F, fr. MF, fr. *intendant* + *-ance*] **1 :** the care, control, or management of an office, department, or other public business : SUPERINTENDENCE **2 :** an administrative department esp. of an army; *specif* : an army supply service in some countries (as France)

in·tend·an·cy *also* **in·tend·en·cy** \-dənsē, -si\ *n* -ES [*intendancy* prob. fr. F *intendance* + E *-y; intendency* prob. fr. MF *intendance* + E *-ency*] **1 :** the office, function, or employment of an intendant; *also* : a body of intendants **2** *usu* *intendency* [Sp *intendencia,* fr. *intendente*] : a district under an intendant

in·tend·ant \ən·'tendənt\ *n* -S [F, fr. MF, fr. L *intendent-, intendens-,* pres. part. of *intendere* to intend, attend — more at INTEND] : a person who has the charge, direction, or management of some public business: as **a :** an administrator of a French province under the centralized system introduced by Richelieu **b :** an administrative officer next to the governor in Canada under French rule **c :** an official in charge of the colonial treasury sometimes having the governorship of the province in various Spanish and Portuguese colonies **d :** a chief administrative official (as governor of a district or mayor of a city) esp. in some Spanish-American countries

¹intended *adj* [fr. past part. of *intend*] **1 a :** PROPOSED ⟨the first volume of an ~ series⟩; *specif* : BETROTHED, AFFIANCED ⟨his ~ bride⟩ **b :** INTENTIONAL ⟨an ~ insult⟩ **2** *obs* : EXTENDED, STRAINED — **in·tend·ed·ly** *adv* — **in·tend·ed·ness** *n* -ES

²intended *n* -S : an affianced person : BETROTHED ⟨went to the residence of his ~ —D.D.Martin⟩

in·tend·ence \ən·'tendən(t)s\ *n* -S [*intend* + *-ence*] : ATTENDANCE, ATTENTION

in·ten·den·cia \,in(,)ten'den(t)sēə\ *n* -S [Sp, fr. *intendente*] : the house, office, or administrative area of an intendant in a country of Spanish or Portuguese speech

in·ten·den·te \-'dentē\ *n* -S [Sp, fr. F *intendant*] : an intendant in a country of Spanish or Portuguese speech

in·tend·er \ən·'tendə(r)\ *n* -S : a person who intends

intendiment *n* -S [ML *intendimentum* meaning, interpretation, hidden purpose, fr. L *intendere* to intend, attend + *-mentum* -ment — more at INTEND] *obs* : INTENTION; *also* : ATTENTION

intending *adj* : PROSPECTIVE, ASPIRING ⟨the ~ solicitor has a long and expensive training —T.G.Lund⟩ ⟨~ students⟩

in·tend·ment \ən·'ten(d)mənt\ *n* -S [alter. (influenced by E *intend*) of ME *entendement,* fr. MF, OF, fr. *entendre* to intend + *-ment* — more at INTEND] **1 :** INTENTION, DESIGN, PURPOSE ⟨voted for it . . . because its ~s were good —A.J. Beveridge⟩ **2 a :** MEANING, SIGNIFICANCE ⟨acquired further ~ as later men discerned a broader symbolism in them —H.O. Taylor⟩ **b :** the true meaning, understanding, or intention of a law or other legal instrument — compare COMMON INTENDMENT

intends *pres 3d sing of* INTEND

in·ten·er·ate \ən·'tenə,rāt\ *vt* -ED/-ING/-S [²*in-* + L *tener* soft, tender + E *-ate* — more at TENDER] : to make tender or sensitive : SOFTEN ⟨contrives to ~ the granite —R.W.Emerson⟩ — **in·ten·er·a·tion** \ən·,tenə'rāshən\ *n* -S

intens *abbr* intensive

in·ten·sate \ən·'ten,sāt\ *vt* -ED/-ING/-S [*intense* + *-ate*] : INTENSIFY

in·tense \ən·'ten(t)s\ *adj, sometimes* -ER/-EST [ME, fr. MF, fr. L *intensus* stretched, tight, intense, fr. *intensus,* past part. of *intendere* to stretch out, intend] **1 a :** existing in a strained or extreme degree : revealed in the height of its distinctive character ⟨an ~ light⟩ ⟨an expression of ~ anxiety —T.B. Costain⟩ ⟨~ cold⟩ **b** *of color* : very deep ⟨dyed an ~ blue⟩ **c :** having or showing its characteristic trait in extreme degree ⟨an ~ sun shone down⟩ ⟨the moon, ~ and white as the snow —Eudora Welty⟩ ⟨~ bright frosty stars —John Masefield⟩ **d :** extremely marked or pronounced : INTENSIVE ⟨rock alteration is ~, leaving few minerals or rocks in their original condition —*Univ. of Ariz. Record*⟩ ⟨a neurodermatitis with ~ itching and burning of the skin —H.G.Armstrong⟩ **e :** very large : CONSIDERABLE ⟨giving off ~ amounts of radiation —Arthur Charlesby⟩ **2 :** strained or straining in or as if in an extreme effort : done or performed with great zeal, energy, or eagerness : highly concentrated ⟨~ study⟩ ⟨a pursuit of learning *intenser* perhaps than any before or since —Ellery Sedgwick⟩ ⟨listened with ~ attention⟩ **3 a** *obs* : INTENT, BENT, RESOLVED — used with *upon* or *about* **b** (1) : feeling deeply esp. by nature or temperament : exhibiting or reflecting strong feeling or earnestness of purpose ⟨my only love, you are so ~ —Edna S. V. Millay⟩ ⟨so ~ in his moral convictions —G.G.Coulton⟩ ⟨~ in everything he does —*Current Biog.*⟩ ⟨an ~ expression on his face⟩ (2) : charged with artistic emotion or intellectual excitement : possessing the quality of artistic tension ⟨his style is ~, eloquent, personal to himself —H.O.Taylor⟩ ⟨painted his most mature and ~ work —*Americas*⟩ (3) : deeply felt ⟨a man of ~ convictions⟩ — **in·tense·ly** *adv* — **in·tense·ness** *n*

in·ten·si·fi·ca·tion \ən·,ten(t)səfə'kāshən\ *n* -S : the act, process, or an instance of intensifying ⟨an ~ of a process that has already been long at work —Barbara Ward⟩

in·ten·si·fi·er \ən·'ten(t)sə,fī(ə)r\ *n* -S : one that intensifies: as **a :** a device (as a two-part cylinder with rigidly connected pistons of different diameters) for stepping up fluid pressure **b :** a photographic intensifying reagent **c :** a gene that enhances the normal effect of another nonallelic gene when both are present **d :** INTENSIVE ⟨words . . . which have been used emotively as ~s —William Empson⟩

in·ten·si·fy \-,fī\ *vb* -ED/-ING/-S [*intense* + *-ify*] *vt* **1 :** to make intense or more intensive : STRENGTHEN, INCREASE, DEEPEN ⟨are ~*ing* our sales effort —*Wall Street Jour.*⟩ ⟨~ farming on a wide scale —*Farmer's Weekly (So. Africa)*⟩ **2 a :** to increase the density and contrast of (an image on a photographic film or plate) by treating with any of various reagents that act either by producing an additional deposit or by rendering the original deposit more opaque **b :** to make more acute : SHARPEN ⟨~ still more the resultant problems of health and nutrition —R.W.Steel⟩ ~ *vi* **:** to become intense or more intense: as **a :** to grow stronger : INCREASE, DEEPEN ⟨within her own narrowed sphere her sympathies seemed to ~ —*McGill News*⟩ **b :** to grow sharper or more acute ⟨the drought has *intensified* and spread —K.S.Davis⟩ ⟨rivalry among the three departments . . . is ~*ing* —*Newsweek*⟩

syn AGGRAVATE, HEIGHTEN, ENHANCE: INTENSIFY indicates a deepening or strengthening until very noticeable or unusually deep or strong ⟨in the lustrous air all colors were *intensified* —Mary Webb⟩ ⟨the depression of the early thirties *intensified* his dissatisfaction with the capitalist system —Granville Hicks⟩ AGGRAVATE, often used in connection with the unpleasant or evil, applies to an increase in seriousness and demand for attention ⟨the external symptoms of decline have served to *aggravate* long existing internal tensions —J.G. Colton⟩ ⟨the din of its two small rooms *aggravated* by the peripheral racket that came from the kitchen —Jean Stafford⟩ HEIGHTEN may suggest a lifting above the ordinary or accustomed ⟨a painter discards many trivial points of exactness, in order to *heighten* the truthfulness of a few fundamentals —C.E.Montague⟩ ⟨a dramatic incident may *heighten* the popular indignation that leads toward war —Dexter Perkins⟩ ENHANCE suggests a lifting or strengthening above normal, esp. in attractiveness, desirability, or value ⟨the charm of this wild land is *enhanced* by the presence of deer and the famous forest ponies —S.P.B.Mais⟩ ⟨a blue serge suit freshly pressed which *enhanced* the impression he gave of neatness and cleanliness —Henry Miller⟩ ⟨the political prestige of the C.I.O. was *enhanced* by the election —*Collier's Yr. Bk.*⟩

intensifying screen *n* : a fluorescent screen placed usu. on each side of an X-ray photographic film so as to augment the direct effect of the X rays between two such screens

in·ten·sion \ən·'tenchən\ *n* -S [L *intension-, intensio,* fr. *intensus* (past part. of *intendere* to stretch forth) + *-ion-, -io* -ion — more at INTEND] **1** *archaic* : an act of straining, stretching, or bending : TENSION **2 a :** degree or marked degree (as of a quality) : INTENSITY **b :** increase of power or energy : INTENSIFICATION **c :** strong or energetic exercise (as of the mind) : INTENTNESS, DETERMINATION **3 :** CONNOTATION 3 ⟨the ~ of "*triangle*" implies or includes that of "plane figure"⟩ — contrasted with *extension*

in·ten·sion·al \-chən°l, -chnəl\ *adj* : of, relating to, or marked by intension; *specif* : CONNOTATIVE ⟨literature works by ~ means . . . by the manipulation of the informative and affective connotations of words —S.I.Hayakawa⟩ — **in·ten·sion·al·ly** \-°lē, -əlē, -i\ *adv*

in·ten·si·tom·e·ter \ən·,ten(t)sə'tämәd·ə(r)\ *n* [*intensito-* (fr. *intensity*) + *-meter*] : an instrument for measuring the intensity of X rays

in·ten·si·ty \ən·'ten(t)səd·ē, -ətē, -i\ *n* -ES [*intense* + *-ity*] **1 :** the quality or state of being intense: as **a :** extreme or very high degree : extreme strength, force, or energy ⟨the ~ of the sun's rays⟩ ⟨the ~ and accuracy of this fire —S.L.A.Marshall⟩ ⟨strikingly signalizes the ~ of the hope —Bernard De Voto⟩ ⟨rains of unparalleled ~ —W.E.Swinton⟩ **b :** extreme depth of feeling : passionate quality : extreme sensibility ⟨her ~, which would leave no emotion on a normal plane —D.H. Lawrence⟩ ⟨the most striking feature . . . is the ~ of his nature —R.A.Hall b.1911⟩ ⟨instinctively kept to ~, knowing that without passion no art can live —Louise Bogan⟩ **c :** the quality of aesthetic or intellectual emotion or excitement : compactness of artistic statement or expression : artistic tension ⟨lacks the ~ and the profundity that the greatest poetry has —R.A.Hall b.1911⟩ ⟨with ~ the poem may survive anything — even archaic language —J.P.Bishop⟩ ⟨compressed into poetic ~ . . . instead of sprawling forth sloppy, formless, and diffuse —Peter Viereck⟩ ⟨a painting of dramatic ~⟩ ⟨impress their poetry with density and ~, cutting out irrelevancies and long-windedness —Mary M. Colum⟩ **d :** depth of conviction ⟨his voice was hoarse with the ~ of his belief —Irwin Shaw⟩ **e :** strenuousness of effort or application : ENERGY ⟨the campaign was waged with great ~ by both parties⟩ **2 :** the degree or amount of a quality or condition: as **a :** the relative loudness or softness of a tone or a tonal effect **b :** the energy with which air is propelled through the vocal tract in articulating : LOUDNESS **c :** a specified measure of the effect of certain physical agencies expressed as the magnitude of force or energy per unit (as of surface, charge, or mass) — see ELECTRIC INTENSITY, GRAVITATIONAL INTENSITY, LUMINOUS INTENSITY, MAGNETIC INTENSITY, RADIANT INTENSITY, SOUND INTENSITY; compare LUMINOUS-FLUX DENSITY, RADIANT-FLUX DENSITY **d :** SATURATION 4a **e :** a measure of the magnitude of an earthquake **f :** intensive quality : INTENSIVENESS ⟨carried on agriculture with varying degrees of ~ —A.C.Parker⟩ **g :** the vivacity or strength of a sensation ⟨his shame reached a high degree of ~⟩ **h :** cultural vigor esp. of a primitive people as expressed in quantity of cultural content and complexity and interrelations of cultural patterns ⟨a contrast in the . . . ~ of cultural systems —E.H. Spicer⟩ **3 :** an instance of intense quality, condition, or experience ⟨the *intensities,* the moments of feeling and depths of experience that constitute the fundamental part of living —Leon Edel⟩

intensity modulation *n* : modulation in which the brightness of the light displayed on a cathode-ray tube varies with the intensity of the signal

intensity of light : LUMINOUS-FLUX DENSITY

intensity of magnetization : MAGNETIZATION

intensity of radiation : RADIANT-FLUX DENSITY

¹in·ten·sive \(')in¦ten(t)siv, ən·'t-, -sēv *also* -səv\ *adj* [prob. fr. MF *intensif,* fr. ML *intensivus,* fr. L *intensus* intense, stretched + *-ivus* -ive — more at INTENSE] **1** *obs* : INTENSE, VEHEMENT **2 :** of, relating to, or marked by intensity or intensification: as **a :** highly concentrated : ZEALOUS, EAGER, EXHAUSTIVE ⟨~ study⟩ ⟨~ effort⟩ **b :** INTENSIFYING; *esp* : tending to give force or emphasis ⟨an ~ adverb, as *dreadfully* in "it was *dreadfully* cold"⟩ **c** (1) : constituting or relating to a method of cultivation of land designed to increase the productivity of a given area by the expenditure of more capital and labor upon it — opposed to *extensive* (2) : constituting or relating to the method of conducting an industry so as to increase its returns by perfecting its methods and appliances rather than by enlarging its scale **d :** relating to intension **e :** involving the use of large doses or substances having great therapeutic activity **f :** presenting a large and concentrated amount of material to be studied intensely ⟨~ course⟩ ⟨~ training⟩ ⟨~ program⟩ — **in·ten·sive·ly** \-sәvlē, -li\ *adv* — **in·ten·sive·ness** \-sivnəs, -sēv- *also* -səv-\ *n* -ES

²**intensive** \"\ *n* -s **:** an intensive linguistic element (as a word, particle, or prefix)

intensive pronoun *n* **1 :** a pronoun that emphasizes a preceding noun or another pronoun (as *itself* in "borrowing is itself a bad habit") **2 :** a personal pronoun compounded with *-self* and used in apposition with a noun or pronoun or as pronominal adjunct (as *itself* in "the cat looked innocence itself" or *himself* in "he made it himself")

intensive proposition *n* **:** a proposition stating a relation of intension between concepts or one whose meaning is to be understood in intension

¹**in·tent** \ən·ˈtent\ *n* -s [alter. (influenced by L *in-* ²in-) of ME *entent, entente;* ME *entent,* fr. OF, fr. LL *intentus* aim, purpose, intent, fr. L, act of stretching out, fr. *intentus,* past part. of *intendere* to stretch out, intend; ME *entente,* fr. OF, fr. L *intentus* (past part.) — more at INTEND] **1 a** (1) **:** the act, fact, or an instance of intending **:** PURPOSE, DESIGN ⟨suspect him of hostile ~ —S.M.Crothers⟩ ⟨came with ~ to kill⟩ (2) **:** the design or purpose to commit any wrongful or criminal act that is the natural and probable consequence of other voluntary acts or conduct (3) **:** the state of mind or mental attitude with which an act is done **:** VOLITION **b :** an end or object proposed **:** AIM ⟨used his leisure time to good ~⟩ **2 a :** MEANING, PURPORT, IMPORT, SIGNIFICANCE ⟨paraphrase in speech the ~ of the communication —Edward Sapir⟩; *specif* **:** INTENDMENT 2b **b :** the connotation of a term **syn** see INTENTION — **to all intents and purposes** *also* **to all intents** *or* **to all intent and purpose :** in all applications or senses **:** PRACTICALLY, REALLY, VIRTUALLY ⟨the process is *to all intents and purposes* identical with that practiced today —A.C.Morrison⟩

²**intent** \"\ *adj* [L *intentus,* fr. past part. of *intendere* to stretch forth] **1 :** directed with strained or eager attention **:** CONCENTRATED, EARNEST, INTENSE ⟨a gaze so ~ that the girl flushed a little —P.B.Kyne⟩ ⟨his face was ~ as he examined each picture —Lyle Saxon⟩ **2 a** (1) **:** having the mind or attention closely or fixedly directed on something **:** PREOCCUPIED, ENGROSSED ⟨the two men, ~ on their figures, did not notice —Sherwood Anderson⟩ ⟨still too ~ upon his own thoughts —W.M.Thackeray⟩ ⟨so ~ on this fantastic . . . narrative that she had hardly stirred —Walter de la Mare⟩ (2) **:** reflecting or evidencing strained or concentrated attention or preoccupation ⟨her forehead was painfully anxious and ~ as she gave this evidence —Charles Dickens⟩ **b :** having the mind or will concentrated on some end or purpose **:** DETERMINED, RESOLVED, BENT ⟨a selfish interest ~ upon privilege for itself —H.J.Laski⟩ ⟨~ upon making his way in the corporation —Lee Rogow⟩ ⟨the ~ that we should have a week of climbing —E.A.Weeks⟩

in·ten·tion \ən·ˈtenchən\ *n* -s [ME *entencioun, intencioun,* fr. MF & L; MF *entention, intention,* fr. OF, fr. L *intention-, intentio,* lit., act of stretching out, fr. *intentus* (past part.) + *-ion-, -io* -ion] **1 a** (1) **:** an act of intending **:** RESOLVE ⟨announced its ~ to divide its Indian Empire into two dominions —*Current Biog.*⟩ ⟨certainly had no ~ of doing so —Rose Macaulay⟩ (2) **intentions** *pl* **:** purpose with respect to marriage ⟨inquired concerning the young man's ~*s* toward his daughter⟩ (3) **:** a written or printed statement of intention ⟨filed his ~ to run for mayor⟩ **b** (1) **:** the will to administer a sacrament in the form and spirit prescribed by the Roman Catholic Church (2) **:** the will to apply the benefits of a mass or prayers to a particular person or purpose; *also* **:** the person or purpose contemplated **c** (1) *Roman law* **:** the part of a formula in which the plaintiff's claims and the defendant's defenses are stated (2) *old English law* **:** a declaration in a real action **2 :** an intended object **:** AIM, END ⟨complete and final victory was his ~⟩ ⟨his ~ (the intended significance of the poem) . . . and what he actually contrives as a poet to do, conflict —F.R.Leavis⟩ **3 :** the import or meaning of something **:** something that is conveyed or intended to be conveyed to the understanding **:** SIGNIFICANCE ⟨shook his head with a double ~ —James Joyce⟩ **4 a** *archaic* (1) **:** strenuous mental application **:** close attention (2) **:** the act or an instance of straining or tensing (as the eye) **b :** a concept or notion; *esp* **:** a concept considered as the product of attention directed to an object of knowledge — see FIRST INTENTION, SECOND INTENTION **5 :** a process or manner of healing of incised wounds — see FIRST INTENTION, SECOND INTENTION

syn INTENT, PURPOSE, DESIGN, AIM, END, OBJECT, OBJECTIVE, GOAL: INTENTION simply indicates what one proposes to do or accomplish ⟨the main *intention* of the poem has been to make dramatically visible the conflict —Allen Tate⟩ ⟨it was Buchanan's *intention* that his administration should be chiefly characterized by a vigorous foreign policy —C.R.Fish⟩ INTENT may imply more deliberate and clear formulation ⟨to tell a lie, also, with *intent* to deceive was a serious offense —Havelock Ellis⟩ ⟨the clear *intent* of the Taft-Hartley law's provision on secondary boycotts —*Wall Street Jour.*⟩ PURPOSE can apply to what one proposes with resolution and determination ⟨the missionary was here for a *purpose,* and he pressed his point —Willa Cather⟩ ⟨writing her excellent period stories for girls, Elizabeth Howard has a well-defined *purpose* in view —*Current Biog.*⟩ DESIGN may suggest careful ordering, calculating, or scheming ⟨that sense of inherent *design* that characterizes the English or the Russian novel —J.A.Michener⟩ ⟨the TVA is substituting order and *design* for haphazard, unplanned, and unintegrated development —*Amer. Guide Series: Tenn.*⟩ ⟨to keep this strategic peninsula out of the hands of any power which might harbor aggressive *designs* —C.A.Fisher⟩ AIM may imply clear and definite singleness of purpose or intention ⟨the theoretical understanding of the world, which is the *aim* of philosophy —Bertrand Russell⟩ ⟨the next *aim* of the company was to secure the St. Louis and Missouri river trade —Grace L. Nute⟩ END stresses intended effect and may subordinate or contrast with notions of means ⟨the final *end* of government is not to exert restraint but to do good —Rufus Choate⟩ ⟨He knows us and our true *end* is to know Him —J.A.Pike⟩ OBJECT is closely synonymous with END but may be used for more individually determined desires or intentions to accomplish ⟨my *object* all sublime I shall achieve in time — to let the punishment fit the crime —W.S.Gilbert⟩ ⟨the *object* of this society is to elevate the architectural profession as such —*Amer. Institute of Architects*⟩ OBJECTIVE may be used in relation to that which is quite concrete and tangible and immediately attainable ⟨getting the child to want to write is the new-style teacher's first *objective* —John Haverstick⟩ ⟨to fight wars of limited *objective* and to make moderate and reasonable peace settlements —W.H.Chamberlin⟩ GOAL may indicate that which is attained by struggle and endurance of hardship ⟨the achievement of understanding, which is man's highest *goal* —Ida C. Merriam⟩ ⟨could not help thinking that this was my *goal,* that I had been brought to this spot with a purpose, that in this wild and solitary retreat some tremendous adventure was about to befall me —W.H.Hudson †1922⟩

in·ten·tion·al \-chənᵊl, -chnəl\ *adj* [ML *intentionalis,* fr. L *intention-, intentio* intention, attention + *-alis* -al] **1 :** relating to intention or design **:** having an intention ⟨deeply ~ in its message —Fanny Butcher⟩ **2 :** done by intention or design **:** INTENDED, DESIGNED ⟨~ damage⟩ **3 a :** of, relating to, or based on intention (sense 4b) or a particular conception of intention ⟨a simple categorical statement (for example, "Parsifal sought the Holy Grail") is ~ if it uses a substantival expression (in this instance, "the Holy Grail") without implying either that there is or there isn't anything to which the expression truly applies —R.M.Chisholm⟩ **b :** referring or pointing beyond itself ⟨the ~ structure of consciousness —Hannah Arendt⟩ **syn** see VOLUNTARY

intentional fallacy *n* **:** the fallacy that the value or meaning of a work of art (as a poem) may be judged or defined in terms of the artist's intention

in·ten·tion·al·ism \-ᵊl,izəm, -ə,li-\ *n* -s [ISV *intentional* + *-ism*] **:** ACT PSYCHOLOGY

in·ten·tion·al·i·ty \ən·,tenchəˈnaləd·ē\ *n* -ES [ML *intentionalitat-, intentionalitas,* fr. *intentionalis* intentional + L *-itat-, -itas* -ity] **1 :** the quality or state of being intentional; *specif* **:** the characteristic of being conscious of intending an object ⟨three forms of ~ or objective reference, idea, judgment, and desire —Vivian J. McGill⟩

in·ten·tion·al·ly \ən'tenchənᵊlē, -chnəlē, -i\ *adv* **:** in an intentional manner **:** with intention **:** PURPOSELY ⟨~ vague and misleading language⟩

intentional object *n* **:** something whether actually existing or not that the mind thinks about **:** a referent of consciousness — compare PHENOMENOLOGY

intentional pass *n* **:** the act or an instance of deliberately walking a batter in baseball

intentional species *n* **:** mental images or forms produced by sensation and cognition — compare SPECIES

in·ten·tioned \ən·¦tenchənd\ *adj* **:** having intentions of a specified kind ⟨seriously ~ radio work —Leslie Rees⟩ — often used in combination ⟨justify a well-*intentioned* lie —Lucius Garvin⟩

in·ten·tion·less \ən·ˈtenchənləs\ *adj* **:** being without intention

intentions *pl of* INTENTION

intention tremor *n* **:** a slow tremor of the extremities that increases on attempted voluntary movement and is observed in certain diseases (as multiple sclerosis) of the nervous system

in·ten·tive \ən'tentiv\ *adj* [alter. (influenced by L *in-* ²in-) of ME *ententif,* fr. OF, fr. LL *intentivus* intensive, fr. L *intentus* (past part. of *intendere* to intend, attend) + *-ivus* -ive — more at INTEND] **:** ATTENTIVE, INTENT — **in·ten·tive·ly** \-əvlē\ *adv* — **in·ten·tive·ness** \-ivnəs\ *n* -ES

in·tent·ly *adv* **:** in an intent manner

in·tent·ness *n* -ES **:** the quality or state of being intent

intents *pl of* INTENT

in·ter *R* ən·ˈtər, + *vowel* -tər·; *-R* -tə̄, + *suffixal vowel* -tər· *also* -tə̄r, + *vowel in a following word* -tər· *or* -tə̄ *also* -tə̄r\ *vt* **interred; interred; interring; inters** [alter. (influenced by L *in-* ²in-) of ME *enteren,* fr. MF *enterrer,* fr. OF, fr. (assumed) VL *interrare,* fr. *in-* ²in- + L *terra* earth — more at TERRACE] **1 :** to deposit (a dead body) in the earth or in a grave or tomb **:** BURY, INHUME ⟨the good is oft *interred* with their bones —Shak.⟩ **2** *obs* **:** to enclose the dead body of **3** *obs* **:** to put in the ground **:** cover with earth

inter- *prefix* [ME *inter-, entre-, enter-;* ME *inter-,* fr. MF & L; MF, fr. L, fr. *inter;* ME *entre-,* fr. OF, fr. L *inter-;* ME *enter-,* fr. MF & L; MF *entre-,* fr. OF, fr. L *inter-;* akin to OHG *untar* between, among, ON *ithrar,* pl., intestines, OIr *etar, eter* between, among, Gk *enteron* intestine, Skt *antar* between, within, in, and OE *in* — more at IN] **1 :** between, among, in the midst ⟨*inter*mediate⟩ ⟨*inter*polar⟩ ⟨*inter*space⟩ **2 :** mutual, reciprocal ⟨*inter*marry⟩ ⟨*inter*mesh⟩ ⟨*inter*relation⟩ ⟨*inter*twine⟩ **3 :** between or among the parts of ⟨*inter*costal⟩ ⟨*inter*dental⟩ **4 :** carried on between ⟨*inter*collegiate⟩ ⟨*inter*communication⟩ ⟨*inter*national⟩ **5 :** occurring between **:** intervening ⟨*inter*glacial⟩ ⟨*inter*tidal⟩ **6 :** shared by or derived from two or more ⟨*inter*departmental⟩ ⟨*inter*faith⟩ **7 :** between the limits of **:** within ⟨*inter*tropical⟩

inter *abbr* **1** intermediate **2** interrogative

in·ter·academic \¦intə(r)+\ *adj* [*inter-* + *academic*] **:** among or between or common to schools, colleges, or universities ⟨~ exchanges⟩ ⟨~ courtesies⟩

in·ter·acinous \"+\ *also* **in·ter·acinar** \"+\ *adj* [*interacinous* fr. *inter-* + *acinous; interacinar* fr. *interacinous* + *-ar*] **:** situated between or among the acini of a gland

¹**in·ter·act** \ˈintə,(r)akt\ *n* [*inter-* + *act;* intended as trans. of F *entr'acte*] **:** ENTR'ACTE ⟨a mask proper was closely associated with an early Tudor play as an afterpiece rather than as an ~ —E.K.Chambers⟩

²**in·ter·act** \¦==¦=\ *vi* [*inter-* + *act*] **:** to act upon each other **:** have reciprocal effect or influence ⟨required many generations of ~*ing* human beings to make such discoveries and inventions —P.A.Sorokin⟩

in·ter·ac·tant \-ktənt\ *n* -s [²*interact* + *-ant*] **:** one that interacts; *specif* **:** one of two or more substances taking part in a chemical reaction **:** REACTANT

in·ter·ac·tion \¦intə(r)akshən\ *n* **1 :** mutual or reciprocal action or influence ⟨~ of the heart and lungs⟩ ⟨~ of an individual with his social environment⟩ ⟨~ admits causal action between physical events, between mental events, and also between mental and physical events —Vivian J. McGill⟩ **2 :** a measure of how much the effect of one statistical variable upon another is determined by the values of one or more other variables

in·ter·ac·tion·al \-shənᵊl, -shnəl\ *adj* **:** of or relating to interaction or to a theory of interaction ⟨~ ecology⟩ — **interactionally** *adv*

in·ter·ac·tion·ism \-shə,nizəm\ *n* -s **1 :** a theory that mind and body are distinct and interact causally upon one another — compare DOUBLE-ASPECT THEORY, PSYCHOPHYSICAL PARALLELISM **2 :** a theory that derives social processes (conflict, competition, cooperation) from human interaction

in·ter·ac·tion·ist \-ₑnəst\ *n* **:** a proponent of interactionism

in·ter·active \¦intə(r)+\ *adj* [*inter-* + *active*] **1 :** mutually or reciprocally active **2 :** INTERACTIONAL

in·ter·activity \"+\ *n* **:** the fact or process of interacting

in·ter·adaptation \"+\ *n* [*inter-* + *adaptation*] **:** mutual adaptation

¹**in·ter·agency** \"+\ *n* [*inter-* + *agency*] **:** the action or function of an intermediary

²**interagency** \"\ *adj* [*inter-* + *agency* (n.)] **:** involving two or more public or government agencies ⟨~ dispute⟩ ⟨~ committee⟩

in·ter·agent \"+\ *n* [*inter-* + *agent*] **:** an intermediate agent **:** INTERMEDIARY

in·ter alia \¦intə¦(r)ālēə, -lyə\ *adv* [L] **:** among other things ⟨the commission recommended, *inter alia,* that:⟩ ⟨rate of progress will depend upon, *inter alia,* the number of . . . engineers available —L.L.Goodman⟩

inter ali·os \-lē,ōs\ *adv* [L] **:** among other persons

in·ter·allied \¦intə(r)+\ *also* **in·ter·ally** \"+\ *adj* [*inter-* + *allied* (adj.) *or* *ally* (n.)] **:** involving or relating to all or a number of allies ⟨British policy on both German reparations and *Interallied* debts —*Atlantic*⟩ ⟨~ agreement⟩

in·ter·ambulacral \"+\ *adj* [*inter-* + *ambulacral*] **:** situated between ambulacra

in·ter·ambulacrum \"+\ *n* [NL, fr. *inter-* + *ambulacrum*] **:** one of the areas between two ambulacra in an echinoderm

in·ter-american \"+\ *adj, usu cap A* **:** involving or concerning some or all of the nations of No. and So. America ⟨~ affairs⟩ ⟨~ treaties⟩

in·ter·am·ni·an \¦intə¦(r)amnēən\ *adj* [LL *interamnus* interamnian (fr. L *inter-* + *amnis* river) + E *-ian*] **:** situated between or enclosed by rivers

in·ter·animate \¦intə(r)+\ *vt* [*inter-* + *animate*] **:** to animate mutually ⟨love with one another so ~*s* two souls —John Donne⟩

in·ter·animation \"+\ *n* **:** mutual animation

in·ter·articular \"+\ *adj* [*inter-* + *articular*] **:** situated between articulating surfaces ⟨~ cartilage⟩

in·ter·association \"+\ *n* [*inter-* + *association*] **:** mutual association **:** INTERRELATION ⟨~ of sense perceptions⟩

in·ter·astral \"+\ *adj* [*inter-* + *astral*] **:** situated or occurring between or among stars

in·ter·atomic \"+\ *adj* [*inter-* + *atomic*] **:** situated or acting between atoms ⟨~ forces⟩

in·ter·atrial \"+\ *adj* [*inter-* + *atrial*] **:** situated between the atria of the heart ⟨~ septum⟩

in·ter·aural \"+\ *adj* [*inter-* + *aural*] **:** situated between or connecting the ears ⟨~ plane⟩

in·ter·availability \"+\ *n* [*inter-* + *availability*] *Brit* **:** availability mutually extended throughout a specified system or grouping

in·ter·axial \"+\ *also* **in·ter·axal** \"+\ *adj* [NL *interaxis* + *-ial* or *-al*] **:** lying between the axes ⟨~ space in an architectural plan⟩

in·ter·axillary \"+\ *adj* [*inter-* + *axillary*] **:** situated within or between the axils of leaves

in·ter·axis \"+\ *n* [NL, fr. L *inter-* + *axis*] **:** the space between two axes (as of a building plan)

in·ter·balance \"+\ *vt* [*inter-* + *balance*] **:** to balance mutually or reciprocally **:** achieve mutual balance among ⟨intricate *interbalancing* of lead, glass, and stone —M.W.Baldwin⟩

in·ter·banded \"+\ *adj* [*inter-* + *banded*] **:** deposited in alternating layers of different materials ⟨~ quartz and galena⟩

in·ter·bank \"+\ *adj* [*inter-* + *bank* (n.)] **:** involving two or more banks ⟨~ deposits⟩ ⟨~ relations⟩

¹**in·ter·bed** \"+\ *vb* [*inter-* + *bed*] **:** INTERSTRATIFY

²**in·ter·bed** \ˈintə(r),bed\ *n* **:** a typically thin layer of one kind of sedimentary material between layers of another kind

in·ter·behavior \"+\ *n* [*inter-* + *behavior*] **:** interaction between two or more individuals **:** social behavior — **in·ter·behavioral** *adj*

in·ter·bel·la \¦intə(r)¦belə\ *or* **interbel·lum** \-ləm\ *adj* [NL, fr. L *inter* between, among + *bella* (pl. of *bellum* war) or *bellum* — more at INTER-, BELLICOSE] **:** extending or occurring between wars ⟨~ period⟩ ⟨*interbellum* generation of writers⟩

in·ter·blend \¦intə(r)+\ *vb* [*inter-* + *blend*] **:** to blend together **:** INTERMINGLE, COMMINGLE

in·ter·bonding \"+\ *n* [*inter-* + *bonding,* gerund of *bond*] **:** a bonding together ⟨~ of concrete and rock⟩

in·ter·borough \"+\ *adj* [*inter-* + *borough*] **:** relating to, situated in, or operating between two or more boroughs ⟨~ subway system⟩

in·ter·bourse \"+\ *adj* [*inter-* + *bourse* (n.)] **:** issued simultaneously in different countries ⟨~ securities⟩

in·ter·brain \ˈintə(r)+,-\ *n* [*inter-* + *brain*] **:** DIENCEPHALON

in·ter·branch \¦intə(r)+\ *adj* [*inter-* + *branch* (n.)] **:** occurring between branches ⟨~ rivalry in the armed forces⟩

in·ter·breed \"+\ *vb* [*inter-* + *breed*] *vi* **:** to breed together: as **a :** CROSSBREED **b :** to breed within a closed population **:** INBREED ~ *vt* **:** to cause (individuals or groups) to breed together

in·ter·ca·lary \ən·ˈtərkə,lerē, -tə̄k-, -təik-, -ri, ¦intə(r)¦kal(ə)r-\ *adj* [L *intercalarius,* fr. *intercalare* to intercalate + *-arius* -ary; influenced also by L *intercalaris* intercalary, fr. *intercalare* + *-aris* -ar] **1 a** *of a day or month* **:** inserted in a calendar by intercalation **:** INTERCALATED **b** *of a year* **:** containing an intercalary period **2 :** inserted or introduced between the usual or original elements or components **:** INTERPOLATED ⟨~ matter in a text⟩ ⟨~ tissue in a plant⟩ ⟨~ line in a poem⟩

intercalary meristem *n* **:** a meristem developing between regions of mature or permanent tissue (as at the base of the grass leaf) — compare APICAL MERISTEM, LATERAL MERISTEM

in·ter·ca·late \ən·ˈtərkə,lāt, -tə̄k-, -təik-, *usu* -ād·+V\ *vt* -ED/-ING/-S [L *intercalatus,* past part. of *intercalare,* fr. *inter-* + *calare* to call, summon — more at LOW] **1 :** to insert (as a day or month) in a calendar by intercalation **2 :** to insert between or among existing elements **:** INTERPOLATE ⟨~ a vowel into a cluster of consonants⟩ ⟨stories *intercalated* into a narrative⟩ **3 :** to insert (as a sheet of lava) between layers or beds of other rock **:** INTERSTRATIFY — usu. used in the past part.

in·ter·ca·la·tion \=,==ˈlāshən\ *n* -s [MF or L; MF, fr. L *intercalation-, intercalatio,* fr. *intercalatus* (past part.) + *-ion-, -io* -ion] **1 a :** the insertion of one or more days at regular intervals in a calendar in order to bring it into accord with the solar year **b :** a period so inserted **2 a :** the insertion or introduction of something among other existing or original things **b :** something that is so inserted ⟨the poet was reluctant to vary the metrical arrangement of the poem to accommodate an ~ —A.K.Moore⟩ **3 :** the introduction or existence of a bed or layer between other layers or of a particular fossil horizon between fossil zones of different character; *also* **:** an intercalated bed or lenticular deposit ⟨a few lenses of volcanic ash are present as ~*s*⟩

in·tercameral \¦intə(r)+\ *adj* **:** occurring between two chambers of a legislature ⟨~ deadlock⟩

in·ter·capillary \"+\ *adj* [*inter-* + *capillary*] **:** situated between capillaries

¹**in·ter·cardinal** \"+\ *n* [*inter-* + *cardinal*] **:** an intercardinal point of the compass ⟨~*s* are four points from the cardinals and eight points from one another —H.A.Calahan⟩

²**intercardinal** \"\ *adj* **:** lying midway between the cardinal points ⟨~ points of the compass⟩

in·ter·carotid body \"+...-\ *n* [*inter-* + *carotid*] **:** CAROTID BODY

in·ter·carpal \"+\ *adj* [*inter-* + *carpal*] **:** situated between carpal bones

in·ter·cartilaginous ossification \"+...-\ *n* [*inter-* + *cartilaginous*] **:** ENDOCHONDRAL OSSIFICATION

in·ter·caste \"+\ *adj* [*inter-* + *caste* (n.)] **:** existing between or involving two or more castes ⟨~ education⟩ ⟨~ mobility⟩

in·ter·catenated \"+\ *adj* [*inter-* + *catenated,* past part. of *catenate*] **:** chained or linked together ⟨~ ideas⟩

in·ter·cavernous \"+\ *adj* [*inter-* + *cavernous*] **:** situated between and connecting the cavernous sinuses behind and in front of the pituitary body ⟨~ sinus⟩

in·ter·cede \,intə(r)ˈsēd\ *vi* [L *intercedere,* fr. *inter-* + *cedere* to move, go — more at CEDE] **1** *obs* **a :** to get in the way **:** INTERVENE **b :** to come or lie esp. in time or space **2 :** to act between parties with a view to reconciling differences **:** to beg or plead in behalf of another **:** MEDIATE ⟨the Western powers would not ~ in behalf of the people —N.S.Timasheff⟩ ⟨she it was who *interceded* for the old woman with her uncle —Hilaire Belloc⟩

in·ter·ced·er \-də(r)\ *n* **:** one that intercedes

in·ter·cellular \¦intə(r)+\ *adj* [*inter-* + *cellular*] **:** lying between cells ⟨~ space in plant tissue⟩ ⟨~ canals in lumber⟩

intercellular substance *n* **:** MIDDLE LAMELLA

in·ter·cen·sal \"+¦sen(t)səl\ *adj* [*inter-* + *census* + *-al*] **:** occurring between censuses ⟨~ study⟩ ⟨~ figures⟩

in·ter·central \"+\ *adj* [*inter-* + *central*] **1 :** lying or extending between centers ⟨~ nerve fibers⟩ **2** [NL *intercentrum* + E *-al*] **:** of or relating to an intercentrum

in·ter·centrum \"+\ *n* [NL, fr. L *inter-* + *centrum*] **1 :** an element of the vertebral column alternating with the true centra of the vertebrae in several different classes of vertebrates **2 :** HYPOCENTRUM **3 :** one of the ossified intervertebral disks characteristic of certain mammals

¹**in·ter·cept** \¦intə(r)¦sept\ *vt* -ED/-ING/-S [L *interceptus,* past part. of *intercipere,* fr. *inter-* + *-cipere* (fr. *capere* to take, seize) — more at HEAVE] **1 :** to take, seize, or stop by the way or before arrival at the destined place **:** stop or interrupt the progress or course of ⟨~ a letter⟩ ⟨telegram will ~ him at Paris⟩ ⟨~ a forward pass⟩ ⟨~ an attacking bomber⟩ **2** *obs* **:** to stop or prevent from doing something **:** HINDER ⟨who ~*s* me in my expedition —Shak.⟩ **3** *obs* **:** to interrupt communication or connection with ⟨while storms vindictive ~ the shore —Alexander Pope⟩ **4 :** to include (part of a curve, surface, or solid) between two points, curves, or surfaces ⟨the part of a circumference ~*ed* between two radii⟩

²**in·ter·cept** \ˈ==,=\ *n* -s **1 :** a part intercepted; *specif* **:** the part of a coordinate axis included between the origin and the point where a graph crosses the axis **2 :** an interception of a ball passed or thrown by an opponent (as in lacrosse) **3 :** a picked-up code or message (as one sent by radio)

in·ter·cept·er \,==ˈseptə(r)\ *n* -s **:** INTERCEPTOR

in·ter·cep·tion \-pshən\ *n* -s [MF or L; MF, fr. L *interception-, interceptio,* fr. *interceptus* (past part.) + *-ion-, -io* -ion] **1 :** the act of intercepting or state of being intercepted ⟨~ of vital information to and from enemy agents —*All Hands*⟩ ⟨rushing skyward like a fighter going up on an ~ —Terence Horsley⟩ **2 :** an intercepted segment **:** INTERCEPT

in·ter·cep·tive \,==ˈseptiv\ *adj* [¹*intercept* + *-ive*] **:** tending to intercept

in·ter·cep·tor \,==ˈ=tə(r)\ *n* -s [L, fr. *interceptus* (past part.) + *-or*] **:** one that intercepts: as **a :** a device for preventing the entrance of solid matter, grease, or other material into a drain subject to clogging **b :** a light high-speed fast-climbing fighter plane designed for defense against raiding bombers

in·ter·cerebral \¦intə(r)+\ *adj* [*inter-* + *cerebral*] **:** situated between the cerebral hemispheres

in·ter·ces·sion \,intə(r)ˈseshən\ *n* -s [MF or L; MF, fr. L *intercession-, intercessio* intervention, act of becoming surety, interposition of a veto, fr. *intercessus* (past part. of *intercedere* to intervene, become surety) + *-ion-, -io* -ion — more at INTERCEDE] **1 a :** the act of interceding **:** interposition between parties at variance with a view to reconciliation **:** MEDIATION **b :** prayer, petition, or entreaty in favor of another **2** *Roman & civil law* **:** assumption of liability for the debt of another either by substitution or by the addition of a new debtor or surety — compare ADPROMISSION, CUMULATIVE INTERCESSION, EXPROMISSION, FIDEJUSSION

in·ter·ces·sion·al \¦==¦seshənᵊl, -shnəl\ *adj* **:** relating to or characterized by intercession or entreaty

in·ter·ces·sive \¦intə(r)¦sesiv\ *adj* [L *intercessus* (past part.) + E *-ive*] **:** INTERCESSORY

in·ter·ces·sor \=,=ˈsesə(r)\ *n* -s [ME *intercessour,* fr. MF & L; MF *intercesseur,* fr. L *intercessor,* fr. *intercessus* (past part.) + *-or*] **1 :** one who intercedes **:** MEDIATOR **2 :** a bishop who

during a vacancy of the see administers the bishopric till a successor is installed
in·ter·ces·so·ri·al \ˌintə(r)sə¦sōrēəl, -sȯr-\ *adj* : of or belonging to an intercessor
in·ter·ces·so·ry \¦intə(r)¦ses(ə)rē, -ri\ *adj* [ML *intercessorius*, fr. L *intercessus* (past part. of *intercedere* to intercede) + *-orius* -ory — more at INTERCEDE] : relating to or marked by intercession ⟨~ prayer⟩
interchain *vt* [*inter-* + *chain*] *obs* : to link together
[1]**in·ter·change** \ˌintə(r)ˈchānj\ *vb* [alter. (influenced by L *inter-*) of ME *entrechaungen*, fr. MF *entrechangier*, fr. OF, fr. *entre-* inter- + *changier* to change — more at CHANGE] *vt* **1** : to put each of (two things) in the place of the other ⟨~ two tires⟩ **2** : to give and take mutually ⟨~ blows⟩ ⟨~ ideas⟩ ⟨~ goods⟩ **3** *archaic* : to cause to follow alternately : ALTERNATE, VARY ~ *vi* : to change places mutually : take part in an exchange ⟨vowels on each side of the triangle tend to ~ in accordance with certain specific rules —William Chomsky⟩
[2]**in·ter·change** \ˈ==,=\ *n* [alter. (influenced by L *inter-*) of earlier *enterchange*, *enterchaunge*, fr. MF *entrechange*, fr. *entrechangier*, v.] **1** : an act of changing each for the other or one for another : EXCHANGE ⟨~ of currency between nations⟩ ⟨~ of clothing⟩ ⟨~ of segments between chromosomes⟩ **2** : an act of mutually giving and receiving ⟨~ of gifts⟩ ⟨~ of notes⟩ **3** *archaic* : alternate succession : ALTERNATION ⟨sweet ~ of hill and valley —John Milton⟩ **4 a** : a process of moving cars among railroads to provide uninterrupted movement by rail without unloading and reloading **b** : an act of transferring passengers or freight from one carrier to another **5** : a junction of two or more highways by a system of separate levels that permit traffic to pass from one to another without the crossing at grade of traffic streams — compare CLOVERLEAF, GRADE SEPARATION

interchange 5

in·ter·change·abil·i·ty \ˌintə(r)ˌchānjəˈbilədē, -ətē, -i\ *n* : the quality or state of being interchangeable ⟨standardization and ~ of parts has taken place in a series of small steps —A.D.H.Kaplan⟩ ⟨~ of mass and energy, which has become an essential principle in physics —Bertrand Russell⟩
in·ter·change·able \¦==¦chānjəbəl\ *adj* [alter. (influenced by L *inter-*) of ME *entrechaungeable*, *enterchaungable*, fr. MF *entrechangeable*, *entrechangable*, fr. OF, fr. *entrechangier* (v.) + *-able*] **1** : capable of being interchanged **2** *obs* : MUTUAL, RECIPROCAL **3** : following each other in alternate succession : ALTERNATING **4** *obs* : CHANGEABLE, VARIABLE **5** : permitting mutual substitution without loss of function or suitability ⟨same instrument, known in English by the ~ terms virginal and spinet —A.E.Wier⟩ ⟨each car is like every other . . . and parts are so completely standardized that they are ~ —A.M. Sievers⟩ ⟨standard kit consists of . . . four ~ cutting blades —*Steel*⟩ **6** : capable of being exchanged or bartered ⟨~ bond⟩ — **in·ter·change·able·ness** *n* — **in·ter·change·ably** \-blē, -li\ *adv*
interchangeable manufacturing *n* : the making of the parts of machines with such tolerances that any of the parts will properly function in any of the machines
interchangement *n* [alter. (influenced by L *inter-*) of earlier *enterchangement*, fr. F *entrechangement*, fr. MF, fr. OF, fr. *entrechangier* to interchange + *-ment* — more at INTERCHANGE] *obs* : reciprocal exchange ⟨contract . . . strengthened by ~ of your rings —Shak.⟩
interchange point *n* : a location at which freight in transit is transferred from one carrier to another
in·ter·chang·er \ˌ==ˈchānjə(r)\ *n* : one that interchanges; *esp* : HEAT EXCHANGER
interchange track *n* : a track for transfer of freight cars moving in interchange
in·ter·chapter \ˈintə(r)+,-\ *n* [*inter-* + *chapter*] : an intervening or inserted chapter
in·ter·chromomere \¦intə(r)+\ *n* [*inter-* + [2]*chromomere*] : a nongenic area of a chromonema thought to alternate with the genic chromomeres
in·ter·church \"+\ *adj* [*inter-* + *church* (n.)] : common to or shared by many or all churches : emphasizing cooperation and joint action between religious denominations : INTERDENOMINATIONAL ⟨~ movement⟩ ⟨~ aid⟩
intercision *n* -s [L *intercision-*, *intercisio*, fr. *intercisus* (past part. of *intercidere* to cut apart, fr. *inter-* + *-cidere* — fr. *caedere* to cut, strike, beat) + *-ion-*, *-io* -ion — more at CONCISE] **1** *obs* : a cutting off, through, or asunder : INTERRUPTION, INTERSECTION **2** *obs* : a falling off : FAILING
in·ter·citizenship \¦intə(r)+\ *n* [*inter-* + *citizenship*] : citizenship or the right to civic privileges in different bodies politic at the same time ⟨~ in different states of the U.S.⟩
in·ter·city \"+\ *adj* [*inter-* + *city* (n.)] : extending or operating between cities ⟨~ bus⟩ ⟨~ broadcasting network⟩
in·ter·civic \"+\ *adj* [*inter-* + *civic*] : existing or taking place between or among different citizens
in·ter·class \"+\ *adj* [*inter-* + *class* (n.)] : relating to or involving more than one class ⟨~ religious movement⟩ ⟨~ marriage⟩
in·ter·clavicle \"+\ *n* [*inter-* + *clavicle*] : a ventral median membrane bone in front of the sternum and between the clavicles in certain vertebrates (as the monotremes and most reptiles)
in·ter·clavicular \"+\ *adj* [*inter-* + *clavicular*] **1** : situated between the clavicles **2** [fr. *interclavicle*, after E *clavicle*: *clavicular*] : of or relating to the interclavicle
in·ter·club \"+\ *adj* [*inter-* + *club* (n.)] : involving or relating to more than one club ⟨~ yacht race⟩
interclude *vt* -ED/-ING/-S [L *intercludere*, fr. *inter-* + *-cludere* (fr. *claudere* to close) — more at CLOSE] *obs* : to shut off, out, or up : INTERCEPT, CONFINE
in·ter·coastal \"+\ *adj* [*inter-* + *coastal*] : extending or operating between sea coasts ⟨~ steamers running between Atlantic and Pacific ports⟩ ⟨~ railroad traffic⟩
in·ter·coccygeal \"+\ *adj* [*inter-* + *coccygeal*] : lying between the segments of the coccyx
in·ter·college \"+\ *adj* [*inter-* + *college* (n.)] : INTERCOLLEGIATE
in·ter·collegiate \"+\ *adj* [*inter-* + *collegiate*] : characterized by participation or cooperation of two or more colleges or universities : belonging to related colleges ⟨~ athletic competition⟩ — compare EXTRAMURAL
in·ter·col·line \¦intə(r)¦kälən, -ä,līn\ *adj* [*inter-* + L *collis* hill + E *-ine* — more at HILL] : situated between hills
in·ter·colonial \¦intə(r)+\ *adj* [*inter-* + *colonial*] : existing between or among colonies : relating to the intercourse or mutual relations of colonies ⟨~ trade⟩ — **in·ter·colonially** \"+\ *adv*
in·ter·column \"+\ *n* [L *intercolumnium*, fr. *inter-* + *columna* column — more at COLUMN] : the space between two columns
in·ter·columnar \"+\ *also* **in·ter·columnal** \"+\ *adj* [*inter-* + L *columna* column + E *-ar* or *-al*] : existing between pillars ⟨~ space⟩
in·ter·co·lum·ni·a·tion \ˌintə(r)kəˌləmnēˈāshən\ *also* **in·ter·col·um·na·tion** \ˌintə(r),käləmˈnā-\ *n* [L *intercolumnium* intercolumn + E *-ation*] **1 a** : the clear space between the columns of a series **b** : the distance between the centers of a series of columns measured at the bottom of the shaft **2** : the system of spacing the columns of a colonnade measured in terms of the base diameter of the shafts — see AREOSTYLE, ARAEOSYSTYLE, DIASTYLE, EUSTYLE, PYCNOSTYLE, SYSTYLE
in·ter·com \ˈintə(r),käm\ *n* -s [by shortening] : INTERCOMMUNICATION SYSTEM

intercolumniation 2 *a* pycnostyle, *b* systyle, *c* eustyle, *d* diastyle, *e* araeostyle

in·ter·com·mon \ˌintə(r)ˈkämən\ *vi* -ED/-ING/-S [ME *intercomounen*, *entercomenen*, fr. AF *entrecomuner*, fr. OF *entre-* inter- + *comuner* to put in common, share — more at COMMUNE] **1** *obs* : to have dealings or association **2** *obs* : to share with others : participate mutually **3** : to enjoy a right of pasture together
in·ter·com·mon·age \-nij\ *n* : the practice or right of intercommoning
in·ter·communal \¦intə(r)+\ *adj* [*inter-* + *communal*] : existing between communities
in·ter·com·mune \ˌintə(r)kəˈmyün\ *vb* [alter. (influenced by L *inter-*) of ME *entrecomunen*, *entrecommunen*, fr. AF *entrecomuner*, *entrecommuner*] *vi* : to have mutual communion or intercourse by conversation ~ *vt*, *obs* : to deprive of intercourse with other men : OUTLAW
in·ter·communicability \¦intə(r)+\ *n* : the quality of being mutually communicable ⟨~ of human and bovine disease⟩
in·ter·communicable \"+\ *adj* [fr. *intercommunicate*, after E *communicate: communicable*] : capable of being mutually communicated
in·ter·communicate \"+\ *vi* [prob. fr. *inter-* + *communicate*] **1** : to communicate mutually : give and receive information : hold conversation **2** : to afford passage from one to another ⟨*intercommunicating* rooms⟩
in·ter·communication \"+\ *n* [prob. fr. *inter-* + *communication*] : mutual communication ⟨unhampered ~ among the scientists of the world⟩
intercommunication system *n* : a two-way communication system with microphone and loudspeaker at each station for communicating within a limited area (as between offices in the same building or between operating stations on an airplane)
in·ter·communicator \"+\ *n* : an instrument for intercommunication
in·ter·communion \"+\ *n* [*inter-* + *communion*] : open communion between churches or denominations based on official recognition of other bodies and ratified usu. by an agreement between cooperating parties
[1]**in·ter·community** \"+\ *n* [*inter-* + *community*] : the quality of being common to two or more : participation in common ⟨~ of measurements is achieved by the metric system⟩
[2]**intercommunity** \"\ *adj* [*inter-* + *community* (n.)] : existing between two or more communities ⟨~ rivalry⟩
in·ter·company \"+\ *adj* [*inter-* + *company* (n.)] : existing between two or more companies ⟨~ agreements⟩
in·ter·comparable \"+\ *adj* [*inter-* + *comparable*] : capable of being compared
in·ter·compare \"+\ *vt* [*inter-* + *compare*] : to compare (as members of a specified group or their qualities) with one another ⟨to return to the open clusters . . . we can . . . ~ their total luminosities . . . compare them also with the open clusters in our own system —Harlow Shapley⟩
in·ter·comparison \"+\ *n* [*inter-* + *comparison*] : reciprocal or mutual comparison
in·ter·condenser \"+\ *n* [*inter-* + *condenser*] : one of the intermediate stages in a multistage steam-engine condenser
in·ter·confessional \"+\ *adj* [*inter-* + *confessional*] : involving, supported by, or common to groups (as Anglicans and Eastern Orthodox) having different confessions of faith
in·ter·con·nect \¦intə(r)kə¦nekt\ *vt* [*inter-* + *connect*] : to connect mutually or with one another ⟨~*ed* generating stations⟩
in·ter·con·nect·ed·ness \-tədnəs\ *n* : the quality or state of being interconnected : INTERRELATEDNESS ⟨the ~ of the interests of all nations has become so great —H.J.Morgenthau⟩
in·ter·connection \¦intə(r)+\ *n* [*inter-* + *connection*] : connection between two or more : mutual connection ⟨~ of members of an electric power system⟩ ⟨basis of rational belief lies in the ~ of judgments each independently formed —J.H.Muirhead⟩
in·ter·consonantal \"+\ *or* **in·ter·consonantic** \"+\ *adj* [*inter-* + *consonantal*, *consonantic*] : immediately preceded and immediately followed by a consonant
in·ter·continental \"+\ *adj* [*inter-* + *continental*] **1** : existing or extending between or among continents ⟨~ flight⟩ : subsisting or carried on between continents ⟨~ war⟩ **2** : capable of traveling between continents ⟨~ missile⟩ ⟨~ bomber⟩
in·ter·conversion \"+\ *n* [*inter-* + *conversion*] : conversion into one another : mutual conversion ⟨~ of chemical compounds⟩
in·ter·convert \"+\ *vt* [*inter-* + *convert*] : to change each into the other : INTERCHANGE ⟨ordinary and extraordinary rays were ~*ed* when the crystals were placed at right angles —S.F.Mason⟩
in·ter·convertibility \"+\ *n* : the quality of being interconvertible ⟨~ of currencies⟩
in·ter·convertible \"+\ *adj* [*inter-* + *convertible*] : convertible the one into the other : INTERCHANGEABLE ⟨matter and energy are ~⟩ — **in·ter·con·vert·ibly** \-blē, -li\ *adv*
in·ter·cool \¦intə(r)¦kül\ *vt* [back-formation fr. *intercooler*] : to cool (a fluid) in an intercooler
in·ter·cool·er \-lə(r)\ *n* [*inter-* + *cooler*] : a device for cooling a fluid (as air) between successive heat-generating processes (as in a multistage air compressor)
in·ter·corporate \¦intə(r)+\ *adj* [*inter-* + *corporate*] : existing between, involving, or belonging to two or more corporations ⟨~ council⟩ ⟨~ control of stock⟩
in·ter·correlate \"+\ *vt* [*inter-* + *correlate*] : to correlate (members of a group) with each other
in·ter·correlation \"+\ *n* [*inter-* + *correlation*] : correlation between one of the possible pairs in a group of statistical variables and esp. between independent variables
in·ter·cosmic \"+\ *adj* [*inter-* + *cosmic*] : situated between or among the planets or stars ⟨~ dust⟩ — **in·ter·cosmically** \"+\ *adv*
[1]**in·ter·cos·tal** \"+¦käst°l\ *adj* [NL *intercostalis*, fr. L *inter-* + *costa* rib + *-alis* -al — more at COAST] **1 a** : situated between the ribs **b** : of, relating to, or produced by the intercostal muscles **2** : situated between the veins or nerves of a leaf **3** : lying or fitted between the continuous members of a ship's frame ⟨~ plate⟩ ⟨~ keelson⟩ ⟨~ angle iron⟩ — see SHIP illustration — **in·ter·cos·tal·ly** \-°lē, -°li\ *adv*
[2]**intercostal** \"\ *n* : an intercostal part or structure
intercostal artery *n* : any of the arteries supplying or lying in the intercostal spaces and being mostly branches of the aorta
intercostal muscle *n* : any of the short muscles that extend between the ribs filling in most of the intervals between them and serving to move the ribs in respiration
intercostal nerve *n* : one of the anterior divisions of the thoracic nerves that lie in the intercostal spaces
intercostal vein *n* : one of the veins of the intercostal spaces
in·ter·cos·to·brachial nerve \¦intə(r)¦kästō+ . . . -\ *n* [*intercostal* + *-o-* + *brachial*] : the lateral cutaneous branch of the second intercostal nerve that crosses the axilla and supplies the skin of the inner and back part of the upper half of the arm
in·ter·country \¦intə(r)+\ *adj* [*inter-* + *country* (n.)] : INTERNATIONAL
in·ter·course \ˈintər,kō(ə)rs, -kȯ(ə)rs, -tə,kōəs, -tə,kȯ(ə)s\ *n* [ME *intercurse*, prob. modif. (influenced by L *inter-*) of MF *entrecours*, fr. OF, fr. ML *intercursus*, fr. L, intervention, act of running between, fr. *intercursus*, past part. of *intercurrere* to run between, fr. *inter-* + *currere* to run — more at CURRENT] **1** : dealings or connection (as in common affairs, civilities, or business) between persons, organizations, or nations : COMMUNICATION ⟨diffidence . . . renders me inapt for social ~ —Havelock Ellis⟩ ⟨as trade ~ increases between nations —J.A. Hobson⟩ ⟨welcomes extraclass ~ with students and encourages them to think critically —G.H.White⟩ **2** : exchange or interchange esp. of thought and feeling : COMMUNION ⟨sweet ~ of looks and smiles —John Milton⟩ ⟨believed he had direct ~ with the Deity —Ruth Gruber⟩ **3** : physical sexual contact between individuals that involves the genitalia of at least one person ⟨heterosexual ~⟩ ⟨anal ~⟩ ⟨oral ~⟩; *esp* : SEXUAL INTERCOURSE 1 **4** *obs* **a** : alternate succession : ALTERNATION **b** : INTERVENTION, INTERPOSITION **c** : INTERCOMMUNICATION, INTERCONNECTION
in·ter·cranial \¦intə(r)+\ *adj* [*inter-* + *cranial*] : situated or occurring within the cranium
in·ter·create \"+\ *vt* [*inter-* + *create*] : to create jointly with another
in·ter·creedal \"+\ *adj* [*inter-* + *creedal*] : INTERDENOMINATIONAL
in·ter·cres·cence \ˌintə(r)ˈkresən(t)s\ *n* -s [*inter-* + *-crescence* (as in *excrescence*)] : a growing together of tissues
[1]**in·ter·crop** \¦intə(r)+\ *vb* [*inter-* + *crop*] *vt* **1** : to grow a crop in between (another) ⟨*intercropped* their tree fruit . . . with market garden crops —*Biol. Abstracts*⟩ **2** : to use (ground) for a catch crop ~ *vi* : to grow two or more crops simultaneously (as in alternate rows) in the same ground
[2]**in·ter·crop** \ˈintə(r)+,-\ *n* : CATCH CROP ⟨sweet clover ~⟩
[1]**in·ter·cross** \¦intə(r)+\ *vb* [*inter-* + *cross*] *vi* **1** : to cross each other ⟨various shapes and colors . . . ~*ing* without confusion —Earl of Shaftesbury †1713⟩ **2** : CROSS 5 ~ *vt* **1** : to place across each other ⟨framed of iron bars ~*ed*, which formed . . . an immense cage —S.T.Coleridge⟩ **2** : CROSS 9
[2]**in·ter·cross** \ˈintə(r)+,-\ *n* : an instance or a product of crossbreeding
in·ter·crystalline \¦intə(r)+\ *adj* [*inter-* + *crystalline*] : occurring between crystals ⟨~ crack in a metal⟩ — compare TRANSCRYSTALLINE
in·ter·crystallization \"+\ *n* [*inter-* + *crystallization*] : the process of intercrystallizing
in·ter·crystallize \"+\ *vi* [*inter-* + *crystallize*] : to crystallize together at the same time with resulting mutual inclusion so that each component retains through the mass its own crystallographic identity including crystallographic and optical orientation; *sometimes* : to form a solid solution — used of two or more associated minerals
in·ter·cultural \"+\ *adj* [*inter-* + *cultural*] **1** : cultivated between the rows of some other crop **2** : occurring during the growing period ⟨~ tillage⟩ ⟨~ hoeing⟩ **3** : existing between or relating to two or more cultures ⟨~ contact⟩ ⟨~ tension⟩
in·ter·culture \ˈintə(r)+,-\ *n* [*inter-* + *culture*] : INTERCROPPING
in·ter·current \¦intə(r)+\ *adj* [L *intercurrent-*, *intercurrens*, pres. part. of *intercurrere* to run between — more at INTERCOURSE] **1** : running between or among **2 a** *obs* : coming in between or among : lying between **b** : INTERVENING **3** : occurring in the midst of a process : INTERRUPTING ⟨~ sense impressions during a dream⟩ **4** : occurring in and modifying the course of another disease ⟨~ infection⟩ — **in·ter·cur·rent·ly** *adv*
[1]**in·ter·cut** \"+\ *vb* [*inter-* + *cut*] *vt* **1** : to insert a contrasting camera shot into (a take) by cutting ⟨*intercutting* panoramic long shots with closeups of action and expression —*Time*⟩ **2** : to insert (a contrasting camera shot) into a take by cutting ⟨rapidly ~ news shots and animated maps —*New Republic*⟩ ~ *vi* : to alternate contrasting camera shots of the same scene or of different scenes by cutting ⟨*intercutting* for dramatic suspense —Budd Schulberg⟩
[2]**in·ter·cut** \ˈintə(r)+,-\ *n* : an intercut camera shot or film sequence ⟨cartoon sequences to be used as ~*s* when the camera fades out on the principals —T.M.Pryor⟩
in·ter·denominational \¦intə(r)+\ *adj* [*inter-* + *denominational*] : occurring between or among or common to different denominations ⟨~ cooperation between Methodists and Presbyterians⟩
in·ter·denominationalism \"+\ *n* : the principle of fostering intercommunion and cooperative activities among different religious denominations
in·ter·dental \"+\ *adj* [*inter-* + *dental*] **1** : situated or placed between the teeth **2** : formed with the tip of the tongue protruded between the upper and lower front teeth ⟨~ consonants⟩ — **in·ter·dentally** \"+\ *adv*
in·ter·den·tal·i·ty \ˌintə(r)(ˌ)denˈtalədē\ *n* [ISV *interdental* + *-ity*] : interdental articulation: **a** : substitution of the interdental sounds \th\ and \t͟h\ for \s\ and \z\ respectively : LISP **b** : interdental articulation of other alveolars or dentals (as \t\, \d\, \n\, \l\)
in·ter·dentil \ˌintə(r)+\ *n* [*inter-* + *dentil*] : the space between two dentils
in·ter·departmental \"+\ *adj* [*inter-* + *departmental*] : existing, exchanged, or carried on between departments; *esp* : characterized by participation or cooperation of two or more departments of an educational institution ⟨~ major⟩ — **in·ter·departmentally** \"+\ *adv*
in·ter·depend \"+\ *vi* [*inter-* + *depend*] : to depend upon one another
in·ter·dependence \"+\ *n* [*inter-* + *dependence*] : mutual dependence ⟨~ of members of a family⟩ ⟨~ of statistical variables⟩
in·ter·dependency \"+\ *n* [*inter-* + *dependency*] : INTERDEPENDENCE
in·ter·dependent \"+\ *adj* [*inter-* + *dependent*] : mutually dependent — **in·ter·de·pen·dent·ly** *adv*
in·ter·determination \"+\ *n* [*inter-* + *determination*] : cause and effect operating among several factors : multiple causation
in·ter·determined \"+\ *adj* [*inter-* + *determined*, past part. of *determine*] : mutually determined
in·ter·dialect \"+\ *or* **in·ter·dialectal** \"+\ *adj* [*interdialect* fr. *inter-* + *dialect* (n.); *interdialectal* fr. *inter-* + *dialectal*] : existing or occurring between dialects ⟨~ loans⟩ ⟨~ influences⟩
[1]**in·ter·dict** \ˈintə(r),dikt *sometimes* -dīt *or* V -dīd·\ *n* -s [alter. (influenced by L *interdictum*) of ME *entredit*, fr. OF, fr. L *interdictum* prohibition, interdict of a praetor, fr. neut. of *interdictus*, past part. of *interdicere* to interpose, forbid, interdict, fr. *inter* between, among + *dicere* to say — more at INTER-, DICTION] **1** : an ecclesiastical censure of the Roman Catholic Church barring a person or the people of a region from the sacraments, religious services, and Christian burial **2** : a prohibitory decree : PROHIBITION **3 a** *Roman civil law* (1) : an administrative order of the praetor for prevention of encroachments on or wrongs concerning sacred or public property or breaches of the peace (2) : an order issued as a remedy in certain cases (as of disputed possession) forbidding certain things to be done **b** : an order in systems founded on Roman civil law corresponding to the injunction of the English law **c** *civil & Scots law* : one incompetent to manage his affairs by reason of mental weakness, facility, or insanity : one under curatorship as an incompetent : an interdicted person : one under voluntary or judicial interdiction
[2]**in·ter·dict** \¦==¦=\ *vt* -ED/-ING/-S [alter. (influenced by L *interdictum*, n., and *interdictus*, past part.) of ME *entrediten*, prob. fr. OF *entredit*, past part. of *entredire*, fr. L *interdicere*] **1** : to lay under or prohibit by an interdict ⟨~*ed* under heavy penalties the use of the Book of Common Prayer —T.B. Macaulay⟩ **2** : PROHIBIT, DEBAR ⟨~ trade with a foreign nation⟩ **3** : to destroy, cut, or damage by ground or aerial firepower (enemy lines of reinforcement, supply, or communication) in order to stop or hamper enemy movement and to destroy or limit enemy effectiveness **syn** see FORBID
[3]**in·ter·dict** \¦==¦=\ *adj* [ME *interdicte*, fr. L *interdictus*, past part.] *archaic* : INTERDICTED
in·ter·dic·tion \ˌintə(r)ˈdikshən\ *n* [ME (Scot. dial.) *interdiccioun*, fr. L *interdiction-*, *interdictio*, fr. *interdictus* (past part.) + *-ion-*, *-io* -ion] **1** : the act of interdicting or state of being interdicted : INTERDICT, TABOO ⟨in primitive society . . . the same ~ is very frequently laid on the names of common objects —J.G.Frazer⟩ ⟨so little did he comprehend the rigid ~*s* of Montreal society —Walter O'Meara⟩ **2** *civil & Scots law* : a voluntary or judicial restraint placed upon a person suffer-

ing from mental weakness with respect to acts which may affect his estate **3 :** artillery fire or air attack directed on a route or area to deny its use to the enemy ⟨~ bombing⟩ ⟨~ of an airstrip⟩

in·ter·dic·tive \¦==¦diktiv\ *adj* [²*interdict* + *-ive*] **:** INTERDICTORY

in·ter·dic·tor \,==ˈdiktə(r)\ *n* -s [LL, fr. L *interdictus* (past part.) + *-or*] **1 :** one that interdicts **2** *Scots law* **:** a person whose consent is made necessary by a bond of voluntary interdiction to certain acts of the person executing the bond

in·ter·dic·to·ry \¦==¦dikt(ə)rē, -ri\ *adj* [LL *interdictorius*, fr. L *interdictus* (past part. of *interdicere* to interdict) + *-orius* -ory] **:** having the power or effect of interdicting **:** relating or belonging to interdiction **:** PROHIBITORY ⟨~ decree⟩ ⟨coastal road was still under heavy ~ fire —R.E.Lawless⟩

in·ter·dic·tum \,==ˈdiktəm\ *n, pl* **interdic·ta** \-tə\ [L] **:** INTERDICT, INJUNCTION

in·ter·dig·i·tate \,intə(r)ˈdijə,tāt\ *vb* -ED/-ING/-S [*inter-* + L *digitus* finger + *-ate* — more at TOE] *vi* **:** to interlock like the fingers of folded hands **:** INTERFINGER ⟨forests ~ with the grasslands⟩ ~ *vt* **:** INTERSTRATIFY ⟨fluvial and marine sediments form an *interdigitated* succession —Daniel Wirtz & Henning Illies⟩

in·ter·dig·i·ta·tion \,==,==ˈtāshən\ *n* **:** the act of interlocking or the condition of being interlocked or interpenetrated ⟨produce, by ~, alternate strips of warm and cold water —*Encyc. Britannica*⟩

in·ter·dine \¦intə(r)+\ *vi* [*inter-* + *dine*] **:** to join in a common meal ⟨subdivided into subcastes which do not intermarry or ~ —D.G.Mandelbaum⟩

in·ter·disciplinary \"+\ *adj* [*inter-* + *disciplinary*] **:** characterized by participation or cooperation of two or more disciplines or fields of study ⟨an ~ conference⟩ **:** drawing on or contributing to two or more disciplines ⟨~ approach to anthropology⟩

in·ter·district \"+\ *adj* [*inter-* + *district* (n.)] **:** existing between districts ⟨~ athletic contests⟩

in·ter·dome \ˈintə(r)+,-\ *n* [*inter-* + *dome*] **:** an open space between the inner and outer shells of a dome or cupola

in·ter·dotting \"+,-\ *n* -s [*inter-* + *dotting*, gerund of *dot*] **:** dots applied to an area (as of an engraving) for producing a light shading

in·ter·epimeral \¦intə(r)+\ *adj* [*inter-* + *epimeral*] **:** situated between adjacent epimera

¹interess *n* -ES [ME *interesse*] *obs* **:** RIGHT, CONCERN, INTEREST

²interess *vt* -ED/-ING/-ES **1** *obs* **:** INTEREST; *esp* **:** to admit to a right or privilege **2** [MF *interesser*, fr. L *interesse* to be between, differ, concern] *obs* **:** to affect injuriously **:** INJURE

in·ter·es·se \,intəˈresē\ *n* -s [ML] **1 :** a legal interest in property **2 :** interest upon money

in·ter·es·see \¦intərə¦sē\ *n* -s [²*interess* + *-ee*] **:** a party in interest

interesse ter·mi·ni \-ˈtərmə,nī\ *n* [ML, lit., interest of term or end] **:** the right of entry legally conferred by the demise of a leasehold estate before entry is made

¹in·ter·est \ˈin·trəst *also* ˈintərəst *or* ˈintə,rest *or* ˈintərst *sometimes* ˈin·,trest\ *n* -s [ME, prob. alter. of earlier *interesse*, fr. AF & ML; AF *interesse*, fr. ML, legal interest, compensation, interest on money, fr. L, to concern, be of importance, fr. *inter-* + *esse* to be; influenced by MF *interest* damage, loss, compensation for damage, fr. OF, damage, loss, fr. L, it concerns, is of importance, 3d pers. sing. pres. indic. of *interesse* — more at IS] **1 a :** right, title, or legal share in something ⟨what exactly is your ~ in this affair⟩ **:** participation in advantage, profit, and responsibility ⟨half ~ in a hardware business⟩ ⟨offered to buy out his ~ in the company⟩ **:** STAKE, CLAIM **b :** something in which one has a share of ownership or control **:** BUSINESS ⟨has ~s all over the world⟩ **c** *obs* **:** a share in producing a total effect or result **2 a :** the state of being concerned or affected esp. with respect to advantage or well-being **:** GOOD, BENEFIT, PROFIT ⟨engaged a lawyer to look after his ~s⟩ ⟨acting always in his own ~⟩ ⟨each faction made concessions in the common ~⟩ ⟨speed laws passed in the ~ of safety⟩; *specif* **:** SELF-INTEREST ⟨sacrifice of personal ~ by men who believed in the job they were doing —T.W.Arnold⟩ ⟨distinguish fact from fiction . . . ~ from impartiality —Elmer Davis⟩ **b :** something that is the object of desire ⟨natural ~ in seeing his children well educated⟩ **3 a :** the price paid for borrowing money generally expressed as a percentage of the amount borrowed paid in one year ⟨~ on a loan⟩ ⟨~ on a bond⟩ — see COMPOUND INTEREST, SIMPLE INTEREST **b :** the money so paid ⟨~ on certain indebtedness is deductible from taxable income⟩ **c :** the share received by capital from the product of industry as distinguished from rent and profit and wages — see PURE INTEREST **4 :** an excess over and above an exact equivalent ⟨returned the insults with ~⟩ **5 :** the power of influencing ⟨~ with the boss⟩ **6 a :** the persons effectively controlling an enterprise or dominating a field of activity ⟨landed ~⟩ ⟨iron ~⟩ ⟨banking ~⟩ ⟨Protestant ~⟩ **b interests** *pl* **:** the dominating group of owners in a field of business, industry, or finance considered locally, regionally, nationally, or internationally; *sometimes* **:** BIG BUSINESS **7 a :** a feeling that accompanies or causes special attention to some object **:** CURIOSITY, CONCERN ⟨took a lively ~ in the divorce proceedings in court⟩ ⟨lifelong ~ in sports⟩ ⟨~ in arctic exploration⟩ ⟨~ in child welfare⟩ **b :** readiness to attend to and be stirred by a certain class of objects ⟨testing the aptitudes, ~s, emotions of the patient⟩ **c :** something that causes or arouses curiosity or concern ⟨campaign of great intrinsic ~ to military students⟩ ⟨question of great philosophic ~⟩ **8 a** *obs* **:** INJURY **b** *obs* **:** compensation for injury **:** DAMAGES

²interest \"\ *vt* -ED/-ING/-S **1 :** to cause to share or participate ⟨this holding company through which the public is ~*ed* in the Emperor mine —*Sydney (Australia) Bull.*⟩ **2 :** to involve the interest or welfare of **:** AFFECT, CONCERN — used with *in* ⟨~*ed* herself exuberantly in the progress of the political campaign —Robert Grant †1940⟩ ⟨thanked those who had ~*ed* themselves in his behalf⟩ **3 :** to cause or induce to have a share or interest **:** persuade to participate or engage ⟨city authorities began to ~ themselves in the parking problem⟩ ⟨~ a banker in a loan⟩ ⟨can I ~ you in a game of bridge⟩ **4 :** to engage or attract the attention of **:** arouse interest in ⟨would find some picture that ~*ed* him, in an old magazine —Floyd Dell⟩ ⟨offer a market that ought to ~ any businessman —Andrew Boyd⟩

interested *adj* [fr. past part. of ²*interest*] **1 :** having the attention engaged **:** having curiosity or sympathy aroused ⟨~ listeners⟩ ⟨a nice widowed doctor up there who is ~ in her —Hamilton Basso⟩ **2 :** having a share or concern in some affair or project **:** liable to be affected or prejudiced **:** CONCERNED, INVOLVED ⟨in addition to the lender and borrower, the state considers itself an ~ party to these operations —*U.S.Investor*⟩; *esp* **:** having self-interest **:** not disinterested ⟨generosity proceeding from ~ motives⟩ ⟨~ witness⟩ — **in·ter·est·ed·ly** *adv* — **in·ter·est·ed·ness** *n* -ES

in·ter·esterification \¦intə(r)+\ *n* [*inter-* + *esterification*] **:** TRANSESTERIFICATION

interest group *n* **:** a group of persons having a common identifying interest that often provides a basis for action

interesting *adj* [fr. pres. part. of ²*interest*] **1** *obs* **:** of concern **:** IMPORTANT **2 :** engaging the attention **:** capable of arousing interest, curiosity, or emotion ⟨~ news⟩ ⟨~ personality⟩

syn ENGROSSING, ABSORBING, INTRIGUING: INTERESTING may imply a power to provoke attentive interest to an unspecified degree through some such quality as curiosity, sympathy, desire to understand, enthusiasm, or vicarious identification ⟨seemed to me to be increasingly *interesting*; she was acquiring new subtleties, complexities, and comprehensions —Rose Macaulay⟩ ⟨the effect of the moonlight on Netta's face was *interesting*. It was even complicated. It emphasized a certain haggardness, a certain battered, woebegone pitifulness in her —J.C.Powys⟩ ENGROSSING may suggest power to divert attention from other matters and to hold it by challenge, stimulation, provocation ⟨an *engrossing* account of his research problems⟩ ⟨an *engrossing* mystery drama⟩ ⟨the fight with the hooked trout is only one phase of the sport, albeit a very *engrossing* one —Alexander MacDonald⟩ ABSORBING may imply power to hold interest and attention utterly, the person concerned being oblivious to all else ⟨but Maugham's skill as a storyteller is so impelling that one must follow through this *absorbing* tale to its end —R.A.Cordell⟩ ⟨when a woman takes up some *absorbing* pursuit, and finds it and its associations more interesting than her husband's company and conversation and friends —G.B.Shaw⟩ INTRIGUING usu. applies to what attracts attention, esp. by arousing curiosity, puzzling one, archly fascinating, or challenging ingenuity ⟨these *intriguing* beginnings stimulated a great research effort —A.G. N.Flew⟩ ⟨her eyes had a definite slant from some Oriental ancestor, and, with her flaxen hair, gave her face an *intriguing* prettiness —Winifred Bambrick⟩

— **in an interesting condition** *of a woman* **:** PREGNANT

in·ter·est·ing·ly *adv* **:** in an interesting manner ⟨when he ceases to be just ~ neurotic and . . . gets locked up —*Time*⟩

in·ter·est·ing·ness *n* -ES **:** the quality or state of being interesting ⟨others who felt the essential ~ of his writings —*Times Lit. Supp.*⟩

interest lottery *n* **:** a lottery that issues bonds for borrowed money at less than the normal rate of interest and gives chances for prizes as the consideration for the low interest

interest policy *n* **:** an insurance policy which requires insurable interest in the property covered only at the time of loss and not at the inception of the policy

interests *pl of* INTEREST, *pres 3d sing of* INTEREST

in·ter·estuarine \¦intə(r)+\ *adj* [*inter-* + *estuarine*] **:** lying between two estuaries

¹in·ter·face \ˈintə(r)+,-\ *n* [*inter-* + *face*] **1 :** a plane or other surface forming a common boundary of two bodies or spaces ⟨passage of ~s of the diametrically opposed air masses —*Yr. Bk. of General Medicine*⟩ ⟨the ~ between two separate types of oil flowing along a pipeline —*Canadian Banker*⟩ ⟨heat transfer at an air-earth ~ —J.E.Vehrencamp⟩ **2 :** the boundary between two phases in a heterogeneous physical-chemical system ⟨the boundary between . . . two phases is designated as an ~, although the term *surface* is often used with a general meaning which includes all types of interfaces —W.D.Harkins⟩ — compare SURFACE 1

²in·ter·face \¦intə(r)+\ *vt* [*inter-* + *face*] **:** to make (a garment) with an interfacing

in·ter·facial \"+\ *adj* [*inter-* + *face* + *-ial*] **1 :** included between two plane surfaces or faces ⟨an ~ angle⟩ **2** [*interface* + *-ial*] **:** relating to or situated at an interface ⟨~ layer⟩ ⟨~ strength of felt⟩

interfacial tension *n* **:** surface tension at the interface between two liquids

in·ter·facing \ˈintə(r)+,-\ *n* [*inter-* + *facing*] **:** a firm cloth shaped and sewn between the facing and outside of a garment for stiffening and shape retention used esp. in revers, collars, cuffs

in·ter·factional \¦intə(r)+\ *adj* [*inter-* + *factional*] **:** existing between factions ⟨~ disputes⟩

in·ter·faith \"+\ *adj* [*inter-* + *faith* (n.)] **:** occurring between or among people or organizations of different religious faiths or creeds ⟨~ marriage⟩ ⟨~ conference⟩

in·ter·family \"+\ *adj* [*inter-* + *family* (n.)] **:** occurring or existing between families ⟨~ marriage⟩ ⟨~ grafting of plants⟩

in·ter·fascicular \"+\ *adj* [*inter-* + *fascicular*] **:** situated between fascicles ⟨~ tissue⟩

interfascicular cambium *n* **:** cambium located between vascular bundles — compare FASCICULAR CAMBIUM

in·ter·felted \"+\ *adj* [*inter-* + *felted*] **:** pressed closely together ⟨~ fibers⟩ ⟨~ layers of rock⟩

in·ter·fenestral \"+\ *adj* [*inter-* + *fenestral*] **:** situated between windows ⟨~ panel⟩

in·ter·fenestration \,intə(r)+\ *n* [*inter-* + L *fenestratus* (past part. of *fenestrare* to provide with openings or windows) + E *-ion* — more at FENESTRATED] **1 :** width of pier between two windows **2 :** arrangement of windows with relation to the distance between them from axis to axis or from opening to opening

in·ter·fe·rant \,intə(r)ˈfirənt, -fēr-\ *n* -s [*interfere* + *-ant*] **:** the holder of or an applicant for a patent that conflicts with a patent granted earlier

in·ter·fere *R* ¦intə(r)¦fi(ə)r, *-R* -tə¦fiə *or* +V -i(ə)r\ *vi* -ED/-ING/-S [alter. (influenced by L *inter-*) of MF (*s'*)*entreferir* to strike each other, fr. OF, fr. *entre-* inter- + *ferir* to strike, fr. L *ferire* — more at BORE (pierce)] **1 :** to strike one foot against the opposite foot or ankle in walking or running — used esp. of horses **2 :** to come in collision **:** to be in opposition **:** to run at cross-purposes **:** CLASH ⟨*interfering* claims⟩ — used with *with* ⟨carbon dioxide ~s with the liberation of oxygen to the tissues —H.G.Armstrong⟩ **3 :** to enter into or take a part in the concerns of others **:** INTERMEDDLE, INTERPOSE, INTERVENE **4** *obs* **:** to run into another or each other **:** INTERSECT **5 :** to act reciprocally so as to augment, diminish, or otherwise affect one another — used of waves **6 :** to claim substantially the same invention and thus question the priority of invention between the claimants — distinguished from *infringe* **7** *of a football player* **a :** to run ahead of the ballcarrier and provide allowed blocking protection for him **b :** to hinder illegally an attempt of a player to receive a pass or make a fair catch of a punt **syn** see MEDDLE

in·ter·fer·ence \,==ˈfirən(t)s, -fēr-\ *n* -s [*interfere* + *-ence*] **1 :** the act or process of interfering **:** a brushing or kicking of feet or ankles in walking or running **2 :** the act of meddling in or hampering an activity or process ⟨~ in the affairs of another nation⟩ **:** OBSTRUCTION, INHIBITION ⟨cause of our present economic troubles is laid to political ~ with the beneficent workings of private competitive effort for gain —John Dewey⟩ **3 :** the mutual effect on meeting of two wave trains of the same type so that such wave trains of light produce lines, bands, or fringes either alternately light and dark or variously colored and such wave trains of sound produce silence, increased intensity, or beats — compare FRINGE 2e, INTERFERENCE COLORS, INTERFERENCE FIGURE, INTERFERENCE PATTERN, INTERFERENCE SPECTRUM **4 a :** incorrect meshing of gear teeth resulting in contact along other than the proper lines of action **b :** contact so close as to produce deformation and stress **5 :** an instance of interfering with a patent; *also* **:** the proceeding for determining the question of priority involved **6 a :** the act of illegally hampering an opponent (as in football) **b :** the act of protecting a ballcarrier or a passer by blocking would-be tacklers; *also* **:** a player providing this protection **7 :** the inhibiting of coincident crossing over of genes at loci immediately adjacent to a chiasma **8 a :** confusion of received radio signals due to strays or undesired signals **b :** something that produces such confusion **9 :** the disturbing effect exerted by the learning of an act on the performance of a previously learned act with which it is inconsistent **10 :** prevention of typical growth and development of a virus in a suitable host by the presence of another virus in the same host individual — see INTERFERENCE PHENOMENON

interference colors *n pl* **:** colors produced by the strengthening or the weakening of certain wavelengths of a composite beam of light in consequence of interference

interference figure *n* **:** a figure observed with a conoscope when a section of a doubly refracting crystal is in the path traversed by convergent plane-polarized light (as when a centered black cross is superimposed over a black spot at the center of a series of concentric colored rings)

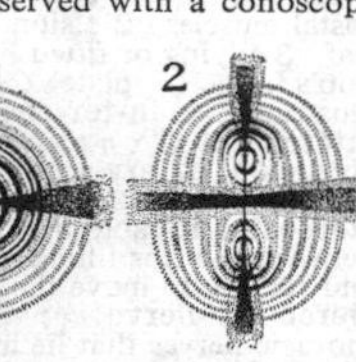

interference figures: *1* produced by a uniaxial crystal; *2* produced by a biaxial crystal when polarizer and analyzer are set at right angles to each other

interference fringe *n* **:** FRINGE 2e

interference pattern *n* **:** an arrangement of fringes or bands (as Newton's rings) due to interference — compare OPTICAL FLAT

interference phenomenon *n* **:** preoccupation of the route of invasion of a pathogenic virus (as by competition for available nutrients) by another virus postulated as the basis of interference — called also *cell-blockade phenomenon*

interference spectrum *n* **:** a spectrum (as in a transparent film) in which the dispersion is due to interference of light

in·ter·fe·ren·tial \¦intə(r)fə¦renchəl\ *adj* [fr. *interference*, after such pairs as E *difference: differential*] **:** of, relating to, or depending on interference (as of light)

in·ter·fer·er *R* ,intə(r)ˈfirər, *-R* -təˈfirə(r\ *n* -s **:** one that interferes

interfering *adj* **:** OBSTRUCTING, MEDDLING ⟨~ old woman⟩ — **in·ter·fer·ing·ly** *adv* — **in·ter·fer·ing·ness** *n* -ES

in·ter·fer·o·gram \,==ˈfirə,gram\ *n* [*interfero*meter + *-gram*] **:** a record made by an interferograph

in·ter·fer·o·graph \-raf, -räf\ *n* [ISV *interfero*meter + *-graph*] **:** an apparatus for making photographic records of optical interference phenomena (as patterns of interference fringes)

in·ter·fer·om·e·ter \,==fəˈräməd·ə(r)\ *n* [ISV *interfero-* (fr. *interfere*) + *-meter*] **:** an instrument for precise determinations of wavelength, spectral fine structure, indices of refraction, and very small linear displacements through the separation of light by means of a system of mirrors and glass plates into two parts that travel unequal optical paths and when reunited consequently interfere with each other — see ACOUSTIC INTERFEROMETER — **in·ter·fer·o·met·ric** \,==¦firə¦me·trik\ *adj* — **in·ter·fer·o·met·ri·cal·ly** \-rək(ə)lē\ *adv* — **in·ter·fer·om·e·try** \,==fəˈrämə·trē\ *n* -ES

in·ter·fertile \¦intə(r)+\ *adj* [*inter-* + *fertile*] **:** capable of interbreeding — **in·ter·fertility** \,intə(r)+\ *n*

in·ter·fibrillar \"+\ *adj* [*inter-* + *fibrillar*] **:** situated between fibrils

in·ter·filamentary \¦intə(r)+\ *adj* [*inter-* + *filamentary*] **:** existing between filaments

in·ter·file \"+\ *vt* [*inter-* + *file*] **:** to file among ⟨~ cards in a catalog⟩

in·ter·finger \,intə(r)+\ *vi* [*inter-* + *finger*] *of rocks* **:** to intergrade through a series of interlocking or overlapping wedge-shaped layers **:** INTERPENETRATE, INTERDIGITATE

in·ter·firm \,intə(r)+\ *adj* [*inter-* + *firm* (n.)] **:** INTERCOMPANY

¹in·ter·flow \"+\ *vi* [*inter-* + *flow*] **1 :** to flow between **2 :** to pass into one another **:** INTERMINGLE

²in·ter·flow \ˈintə(r)+,-\ *n* **:** a flowing into one another **:** INTERMINGLING

in·ter·flu·ence \¦intə(r)¦flüən(t)s, ən·ˈtərfləwən(t)s\ *n* -s [fr. *interfluent*, after such pairs as E *confluent: confluence*] **:** INTERFLOW

in·ter·flu·ent \-nt\ *adj* [L *interfluent-, interfluens*, pres. part. of *interfluere* to flow between, fr. *inter-* + *fluere* to flow — more at FLUID] **:** flowing between or among **:** passing into one another as if by a natural flow **:** INTERMINGLING

in·ter·flu·mi·nal \¦intə(r)¦flümən³l\ *adj* [*inter-* + L *flumin-, flumen* river + E *-al* — more at FLUME] **:** INTERFLUVIAL

in·ter·flu·ous \ən·ˈtərfləwəs\ *adj* [L *interfluus*, fr. *interfluere* to flow between] **:** INTERFLUENT

in·ter·fluve \ˈintə(r),flüv\ *n* -s [*inter-* + L *fluvius* river, stream, fr. *fluere* to flow] **:** the area between adjacent streams flowing in the same direction

in·ter·fluvial \¦intə(r)+\ *adj* [*inter-* + *fluvial*] **:** lying between streams

¹in·ter·fold \"+\ *vt* [*inter-* + *fold*] **:** to fold (paper sheets) together **:** INTERLOCK ⟨~*ing* machine⟩

²interfold \"\ *adj* **:** arranged in interlocking folded sheets ⟨~ paper towels⟩

in·ter·foliar \"+\ *or* **in·ter·foliaceous** \"+\ *adj* [*inter-* + L *folium* leaf + E *-ar* or *-aceous* — more at BLADE] **:** borne between the leaves; *esp* **:** borne between opposite or verticillate leaves ⟨~ stipules in Rubiaceae⟩

in·ter·fo·li·ate \,intə(r)ˈfōlē,āt\ *vt* [*inter-* + L *folium* + E *-ate*] **:** INTERLEAVE

in·ter·fraternity \¦intə(r)+\ *adj* [*inter-* + *fraternity* (n.)] **:** existing or occurring between fraternities ⟨~ dance⟩ ⟨~ council⟩

in·ter·fret \ˈintə(r)+,-\ *n* [*inter-* + *fret* (network)] **:** the interaction between two wind currents of different velocities or directions producing a wave motion of the air often of great amplitude and frequently creating special cloud effects (as mackerel sky or billow clouds)

in·ter·frontal \¦intə(r)+\ *adj* [F, fr. *inter-* + *frontal*] **:** lying between the frontal bones

in·ter·fruitful \"+\ *adj* [*inter-* + *fruitful*] **:** capable of reciprocal cross-pollination ⟨~ strawberry⟩ — **in·ter·fruit·ful·ness** *n*

in·ter·fuel \"+\ *adj* [*inter-* + *fuel* (n.)] **:** existing between fuels ⟨~ competition⟩

in·ter·fuse \,intə(r)ˈfyüz\ *vb* [L *interfusus*, past part. of *interfundere* to pour between, fr. *inter-* + *fundere* to pour — more at FOUND] *vt* **1 :** to combine (one thing and another) as if by scattering or mixing **:** combine intimately as if by fusing or blending **:** INTERMINGLE ⟨curricular designs that would seek to ~ the social sciences and humanities rather than subordinate one to another —Theodore Brameld⟩ **2 :** to pass (one thing or element) into or through others by pouring or spreading **:** INFUSE, DIFFUSE ⟨clustered round the texts, *interfused* with the texts, are all the values discovered in them or added to them by students, critics —Malcolm Cowley⟩ **3 :** to enter widely or deeply into **:** blend with **:** PERVADE, PERMEATE ⟨wit that *interfused* all his writings⟩ ~ *vi* **:** BLEND, FUSE ⟨these patterns, which overlap and ~ —R.B.Heilman⟩

in·ter·fu·sion \-üzhən\ *n* [LL *interfusion-, interfusio* act of flowing between, fr. L *interfusus* (past part.) + *-ion-, -io* -ion] **:** the action or result of interfusing ⟨~ of religion and virtue is not in fact so close as to secure their habitual coexistence —James Martineau⟩ ⟨a national culture is the ~ of many elements⟩ ⟨~ of one color into another⟩

in·ter·galactic \¦intə(r)+\ *adj* [*inter-* + *galactic*] **:** situated or taking place in the vast spaces between galaxies ⟨~ gas⟩

intergatory *n* -ES [by contr.] *obs* **:** INTERROGATORY

in·ter·generic \¦intə(r)+\ *adj* [*inter-* + *generic*] **:** existing or occurring between genera ⟨~ hybridization⟩

in·ter·genic \"+\ *adj* [*inter-* + *genic*] **:** occurring between genes ⟨~ change⟩ ⟨~ interaction⟩

in·ter·ge·no·mal \"+jē¦nōməl\ *adj* [*inter-* + *genome* + *-al*] **:** occurring between genomes ⟨~ pairing⟩

¹in·ter·glacial \"+\ *adj* [ISV *inter-* + *glacial*; orig. formed in G] **:** occurring or formed between glacial epochs ⟨~ climate⟩

²interglacial \"\ *n* -s **:** an age or time of comparatively warm or dry climate between times of glaciation

in·ter·globular \"+\ *adj* [*inter-* + *globular*] **:** situated in the peripheral part of the dentine of teeth ⟨the ramifications of the tubules end in ~ spaces⟩

in·ter·glyph \ˈintə(r)+,-\ *n* [*inter-* + *glyph*] **:** the space between glyphs

in·ter·governmental \¦intə(r)+\ *adj* [*inter-* + *governmental*] **:** between or involving participation by two or more governments or levels of government ⟨~ discussions of commodity stabilization arrangements —Henry Brodie⟩ ⟨an ~ committee⟩

in·ter·gradation \"+\ *n* [*inter-* + *gradation*] **1 :** transition through a series of grades, forms, or kinds that vary (as in evolution) only by consecutive and related differences ⟨may merely represent parallel evolution rather than ~ —Charlotte Avers⟩ **2 :** an intermediate or transitional form **:** a member of a continuously varying series — **in·ter·gradational** \"+\ *adj*

¹in·ter·grade \"+\ *vi* [*inter-* + *grade*] **:** to merge gradually one with another through a continuous series of intermediate forms, kinds, or types

²in·ter·grade \ˈintə(r)+,-\ *n* **:** an intermediate or transitional form

in·ter·graft \¦intə(r)+\ *vi* [*inter-* + *graft*] **:** to be reciprocally capable of being grafted **:** to become united by grafting ⟨most plums ~ freely⟩

in·ter·granular \"+\ *adj* [*inter-* + *granular*] **:** lying or occurring between grains or granules ⟨~ spaces in metamorphic rocks⟩ ⟨~ corrosion of a metal⟩

in·ter·grave \"+\ *vt* [*inter-* + *grave*] **:** to grave or carve between **:** engrave in alternate parts

in·ter·grind \"+\ *vt* [*inter-* + *grind*] **:** to grind together with **:** blend in grinding ⟨resin *interground* with cement⟩

in·ter·group \"+\ *adj* [*inter-* + *group* (n.)] **:** existing or occurring between two or more social groups

in·ter·grow \"+\ *vi* [*inter-* + *grow*] **:** to grow among each other **:** grow intermixed **:** exhibit intergrowth

in·ter·grown \"+\ *adj* **:** characterized by intergrowth ⟨~ knot in timber⟩

in·ter·growth \'intə(r)+,-\ *n* [*inter-* + *growth*] **1 :** a growing between, among, or together; *also* **:** the product of such growth **2 :** growth by intussusception

¹in·ter·hemal \¦intə(r)+\ *adj* [*inter-* + *hemal*] **:** lying between the hemal arches or hemal spines

²interhemal \"\ *n* -s **:** one of the slender elongated bones extending into the flesh of fishes between the hemal spines

in·ter·hemispheric \"+\ *adj* [in sense 1, fr. *inter-* + *hemisphere* + *-ic;* in sense 2, fr. *inter-* + *hemispheric*] **1 :** lying between the cerebral hemispheres **2 :** extending or occurring between hemispheres ⟨~ air flights⟩ ⟨~ warfare⟩

in·ter·house \"+\ *adj* [*inter-* + *house* (n.)] **:** taking place between dormitories, sorority houses, or fraternity houses ⟨an ~ track meet⟩

in·ter·human \"+\ *adj* [*inter-* + *human*] **:** existing or occurring between human beings ⟨~ relations⟩ ⟨~ contagion⟩

¹in·ter·im \'intərəm *also* -ntə,rim *sometimes* -n·trəm\ *n* -s [L, adv., meanwhile, fr. *inter* between — more at INTER-] **1 :** a time intervening **:** MEANTIME, INTERVAL ⟨~ between phases of the battle⟩ ⟨~ between arrival and departure⟩ **2 :** a provisional decision or arrangement; *specif* **:** a compromise attempting to settle controversies between Catholics and Protestants ⟨Ratisbon *Interim*⟩ **syn** see BREAK

²interim \"\ *adv* [L] **:** in the meantime **:** MEANWHILE ⟨had tasted ~ of the life of the sporting gentleman —Adrian Bell⟩

³interim \"\ *adj* **:** belonging to an interim **:** done, made, or occurring for an interim or meantime **:** TEMPORARY, PROVISIONAL ⟨~ committee⟩ ⟨~ government⟩ ⟨~ lease⟩

interim certificate *n* **:** a temporary or preliminary certificate (as of securities)

interim dividend *n* **:** a preliminary distribution of profits by way of a dividend before determining the full dividend to be paid for the year; *also* **:** a dividend declared and paid between regular dividend dates

interim ethics *n* **:** an interpretation of the ethical teachings of Jesus as principles enunciated for governing the conduct of the disciples during the anticipated brief span of time before the coming of the second advent and the passing of the terrestrial world

in·ter·im·is·tic \¦intərə¦mistik\ *adj* [¹*interim* + *-istic*] **:** of or relating to an interim **:** falling in or designed for an interim **:** PROVISIONAL

in·ter·imperial \¦intə(r)+\ *adj* [*inter-* + *imperial*] **:** carried on between or concerning empires or parts of an empire ⟨~ trade⟩

in·ter·industrial \"+\ *or* **in·ter·industry** \"+\ *adj* [*inter-* + *industrial* or *industry* (n.)] **:** existing or occurring between industries ⟨~ transactions⟩ ⟨~ commodity flow⟩ or throughout the parts of an industry ⟨~ wage structure⟩

in·ter·influence \"+\ *vt* [*inter-* + *influence*] **:** to influence reciprocally ⟨dialectic *interinfluencing* —Edward Sapir⟩

in·ter·insular \"+\ *adj* [*inter-* + *insular*] **:** existing or occurring between islands ⟨~ currents⟩

in·ter·insurance \"+\ *n* [*inter-* + *insurance*] **:** RECIPROCAL INSURANCE

in·ter·insurer \"+\ *n* [*inter-* + *insurer*] **:** an underwriter of reciprocal insurance

in·ter·ionic \"+\ *adj* [*inter-* + *ionic*] **:** situated or acting between ions ⟨~ distance⟩ ⟨~ force⟩

¹in·te·ri·or \(')in¦tirēə(r), ən-'t-, -tēr-\ *adj* [MF & L; MF, fr. L, compar. of (assumed) OL *interus* inward, on the inside; akin to L *inter* between, among — more at INTER-] **1 :** being within the limiting surface or boundary ⟨~ communication⟩ **:** INSIDE, INNER — opposed to *exterior* **2 :** remote from the surface, border, or shore **:** situated toward the center of a mass, area, or structure ⟨~ recesses of the castle⟩ **:** INLAND ⟨~ lake⟩ ⟨~ markets⟩ **3 :** belonging to the inner constitution or operation of something or to its private or concealed nature ⟨~ meaning of a poem⟩ **4 :** belonging to mental or spiritual life ⟨~ monologue⟩ **:** not bodily or worldly **syn** see INNER

²interior \"\ *n* -s **1 :** something that is within **:** the internal or inner part of a thing **:** INSIDE ⟨~ of a house⟩ **2 :** the inland part (as of a country, state, kingdom) ⟨deep into the ~ of Australia⟩ **3 :** the inner or spiritual nature **:** inner character **4 :** the internal affairs of a state or nation ⟨Department of the *Interior*⟩ **5 :** a scene or view of the interior of a building ⟨learned to draw ~s⟩ **6 :** an indoor setting or scene in a play or motion picture

interior angle *n* **:** an angle formed between two sides within any rectilinear figure (as a polygon) or between either of two parallel lines and the segment of an intersecting line that lies between them

interior angles: a g h, b g h, g h d, g h c

interior ballistics *n pl but usu sing in constr* **:** a branch of ballistics that deals with the combustion of powder in a gun, the pressure developed, and the motion of the projectile along the bore of the gun — compare EXTERIOR BALLISTICS

interior basin *n* **:** a depression from which no stream flows outward to the sea

interior decorating *n* **:** INTERIOR DESIGN

interior decoration *n* **1 :** INTERIOR DESIGN **2 :** the materials and furnishings of the interior of a building

interior decorator *n* **1 :** INTERIOR DESIGNER **2 a :** one who supplies house furnishings **b :** one who paints or wallpapers building interiors **:** DECORATOR

interior design *n* **:** the art or practice of selecting and organizing the surface coverings, draperies, furniture, and furnishings of an architectural interior

interior designer *n* **:** one who specializes in interior design

interior drainage *n* **:** drainage toward the center of an interior basin rather than to the sea

interior guard *n* **:** a guard maintained within a military installation (as for keeping order, protecting property, guarding prisoners)

in·te·ri·or·i·ty \ən-,tirē'ȯrəd-ē, -tēr-, -'är-, -ətē, -i\ *n* -ES [prob. fr. F or ML; F *intériorité*, fr. ML *interioritat-, interioritas*, fr. L *interior* + *-itat-, -itas* -ity] **:** the quality or state of being interior, internalized, or private — contrasted with *exteriority*

in·te·ri·or·iza·tion \ən-,tirēərə'zāshən, -tēr-, -rī-\ *n* -s **:** the act or process of interiorizing ⟨~ of social values⟩ ⟨~ of the ideals of womanhood —Margaret Cormack⟩

in·te·ri·or·ize \=ˈ=rēə,rīz\ *vt* -ED/-ING/-S *see -ize in Explan Notes* [¹*interior* + *-ize*] **:** to make interior; *esp* **:** to make a part of one's own inner being or mental structure ⟨explanation may lie in women's having *interiorized* cultural notions of feminine inferiority —Helen M. Hacker⟩

interior lines *n pl* **:** lines of operation of an armed force that is operating from a center against converging forces — compare EXTERIOR LINES

interior live oak *n* **:** an evergreen oak (*Quercus wizlizenii*) of western No. America much resembling the coast live oak but occurring chiefly in the foothills of mountain ranges somewhat removed from the coast and forming an important part of the chaparral

interior lot *n* **:** a lot bounded by a street on only one side — called also *inside lot*

in·te·ri·or·ly *adv* **:** on or toward the inside **:** INWARDLY ⟨laughing ~⟩ ⟨grooved ~⟩

interior monologue *n* **:** a usu. extended representation in monologue of a fictional character's sequence of thought and feeling ⟨constant shuttling between *interior monologue* and direct narrative —Dan Wickenden⟩

in·te·ri·or·ness *n* -ES **:** the quality or state of being interior

interior plain *n* **:** a plain remote from the borders of a continent — contrasted with *coastal plain*

interior planet *n* **:** INFERIOR PLANET

interior slope *n* **:** the slope connecting the interior crest with the banquette tread in a fortification

interior spring *n, Brit* **:** an innerspring mattress

in·ter·island \¦intə(r)+\ *adj* [*inter-* + *island* (n.)] **:** existing or operating between islands ⟨~ transport⟩

interj *abbr* interjection

in·ter·ja·cen·cy \,intə(r)'jās°nsē\ *n* -ES **:** the state of being interjacent **:** INTERVENTION

in·ter·ja·cent \¦==¦jās°nt\ *adj* [L *interjacent-, interjacens*, pres. part. of *interjacēre* to lie between, fr. *inter-* + *jacēre* to lie — more at GIST] **:** lying or being between or among others **:** INTERVENING, INTERPOLATED ⟨~ remarks⟩

in·ter·jac·u·late \,intə(r)'jakyə,lāt\ *vt* -ED/-ING/-S [*inter-* + *-jaculate* (as in *ejaculate*)] **:** to ejaculate parenthetically

in·ter·jac·u·la·to·ry \¦==¦jakyələ,tōrē, -tȯr-, -rē\ *adj* [*inter-* + *-jaculatory* (as in *ejaculatory*)] **:** thrown in **:** interspersed parenthetically ⟨~ comment⟩

in·ter·ject \,intə(r)'jekt\ *vb* -ED/-ING/-S [L *interjectus*, past part. of *interjacere, interjicere*, fr. *inter-* + *jacere* to throw — more at JET] *vt* **:** to throw in between or among other things **:** INTERPOSE, INTERPOLATE ⟨~ a statement⟩ ⟨~ a remark⟩ ~ *vi* **1 :** to throw oneself between or among others **:** come between **:** INTERPOSE **2** *obs* **a :** to cross one another **b :** INTERVENE

in·ter·jec·tion \,==ˈjekshən\ *n* -s [ME *interieccioun*, fr. MF & L; MF *interjection*, fr. L *interjection-, interjectio*, fr. *interjectus* (past part.) + *-ion-, -io* -ion] **1 :** the act of interjecting: as **a :** the act of uttering exclamations **:** EXCLAMATION, EJACULATION **b :** the act of putting in between **:** INTERPOSITION ⟨~ of new issues into a debate⟩ ⟨~ of a third party into a quarrel⟩ **2 :** something that is interjected or that interrupts **:** an interposed remark or exclamation ⟨editorial ~s⟩ ⟨topical ~s⟩ **3 a :** an ejaculatory word (as *Heavens! Wonderful!*) or form of speech (as *Alas! eh? ha ha!*) usu. lacking grammatical connection **b :** a cry or inarticulate utterance (as *ouch! phooey! ugh!*) expressing an emotion

in·ter·jec·tion·al \¦==¦jekshən°l, -shnəl\ *adj* **1 :** thrown in between other words **:** PARENTHETICAL ⟨~ remark⟩ **2 :** relating to or of the nature of an interjection **:** consisting of natural and spontaneous exclamations **:** EJACULATORY ⟨~ grunts⟩ — **in·ter·jec·tion·al·ly** \-°lē, -əlē, -i\ *adv*

in·ter·jec·tion·al·ize \,==ˈjekshən°l,īz, -shnə,līz\ *vt* -ED/-ING/-S **:** to make or turn into an interjection

in·ter·jec·tion·ary \¦==¦jekshə,nerē\ *adj* **:** INTERJECTORY, INTERJECTIONAL

interjection point *n* **:** EXCLAMATION POINT

in·ter·jec·tor \¦==¦jektə(r)\ *n* -s **:** one that interjects

in·ter·jec·to·ri·ly \¦==¦jektərəlē\ *adv* **:** in an interjectory manner

in·ter·jec·to·ry \¦==¦jekt(ə)rē, -ri\ *adj* [*interject* + *-ory*] **:** characterized by interjection **:** thrust in between

in·ter·jec·tur·al \¦==¦jekchərəl, -ksh(ə)rəl\ *adj* [L *interjectura* insertion (fr. *interjectus* — past part. — + *-ura* -ure) + E *-al*] **:** INTERJECTIONAL

in·ter·join \¦intə(r)¦jȯin\ *vt* [*inter-* + *join*] **:** to join mutually **:** INTERCONNECT

in·ter·junc·tion \,intə(r)'jəŋkshən\ *n* [L *interjunctus* (past part. of *interjungere* to join together, fr. *inter-* + *jungere* to join, yoke) + E *-ion* — more at YOKE] **:** a joining of two or more things ⟨~ of roads⟩

in·ter·ki·ne·sis \,intə(r)kə'nēsəs, -,kī'-\ *n* [NL, fr. *inter-* + *-kinesis*] **:** the period between any two mitoses of a nucleus (as between the first and second meiotic divisions)

in·ter·ki·net·ic \¦==,=¦ned·ik\ *adj* [fr. NL *interkinesis*, after NL *kinesis*: E *kinetic*] **:** belonging or relating to interkinesis ⟨~ period⟩

in·ter·knit \¦intə(r)+\ *vb* [*inter-* + *knit*] **:** to knit together **:** INTERTWINE, INTERRELATE

in·ter·knot \"+\ *vt* [*inter-* + *knot*] **:** to knot together

¹in·ter·lace \¦intə(r)¦lās\ *vb* [alter. (influenced by L *inter-*) of ME *entrelacen*, fr. MF *entrelacer*, fr. OF *entrelacier*, fr. *entre-* inter- + *lacier* to lace — more at LACE] *vt* **1 :** to unite by or as if by lacing together **:** INTERWEAVE ⟨*interlaced* boughs⟩ ⟨*interlaced* fibers⟩ **2 :** to vary or diversify by alternation, interpolation, or intermixture **:** ALTERNATE, INTERSPERSE, MIX ⟨narrative *interlaced* with anecdotes⟩ ~ *vi* **:** to cross one another as if woven together **:** INTERTWINE, INTERLOCK ⟨*interlacing* letters⟩ ⟨*interlacing* circles⟩

²in·ter·lace \'==,=\ *n* **a :** a form of surface decoration consisting of a number of straps or ribbons so interwoven as to produce a symmetrical design **:** INTERLACEMENT **b :** INTERLACED SCANNING

interlaced *adj* [fr. past part. of ¹*interlace*] **:** INTERLINKED, INTERWOVEN, INTERLOCKED

interlaced scanning *n* **:** television scanning in which each frame is scanned in two successive fields each consisting of all the odd or all the even horizontal lines

in·ter·lace·ment \,==ˈlāsmənt\ *n* -s [alter. (influenced by L *inter-*) of earlier *enterlacement*, fr. F *entrelacement*, fr. MF, fr. OF, fr. *entrelacier* (v.) + *-ment*] **:** the process or result of interlacing **:** a pattern of interlacing elements

in·ter·lac·er \¦==¦lāsə(r)\ *n* **1 :** one that laces shoes during manufacture **2 :** one who makes basketry designs in shoe uppers by cutting slits and weaving in leather strips

in·ter·lac·ery \-s(ə)rē\ *n* [¹*interlace* + *-ery*] **:** interlaced bands, lines, or fibers **:** INTERLACEMENT

interlacing *n* [fr. gerund of ¹*interlace*] **:** INTERLACED SCANNING

interlacing arches *n pl* [fr. pres. part. of ¹*interlace*] **:** usu. circular arches so constructed that their archivolts intersect and seem to be interlaced

interlacing arches

in·ter·lacustrine \¦intə(r)+\ *adj* [*inter-* + *lacustrine*] **:** situated between lakes

in·ter·lamellar \"+\ *adj* [*inter-* + *lamellar*] **:** situated between lamellae

in·ter·lamellation \"+\ *n* [*inter-* + L *lamella* + E *-ation*] **:** a placing in alternate layers

in·ter·laminate \"+\ *vt* [*inter-* + *laminate*] **1 :** to insert between laminae **2 :** to arrange in alternate laminae ⟨*interlaminated* clay and quartz⟩ — **in·ter·lamination** \"+\ *n*

in·ter·language \'intə(r)+,-\ *n* [*inter-* + *language*] **:** language or a language for international communication

in·ter·lap \¦intə(r)+\ *vi* [*inter-* + *lap*] **:** to lap over one another **:** OVERLAP ⟨flew with our wings *interlapping* —*Newsweek*⟩

in·ter·lard \,intə(r)'lärd, -lȧd\ *vt* [alter. (influenced by L *inter-*) of earlier *enterlard*, fr. MF *entrelarder*, fr. OF, fr. *entre-* inter- + *larder* to lard — more at LARD] **1** *obs* **:** to alternate with layers or strips of fat **:** insert lard or bacon in **:** LARD **2 :** to insert between **:** MIX, MINGLE; *esp* **:** to introduce something that is foreign or irrelevant into ⟨~ a conversation with oaths⟩ ⟨~ a text with photographs⟩ ⟨English ~*ed* with Spanish terms⟩

¹in·ter·lay \'intə(r)+,-\ *vt* [*inter-* + *lay*] **:** to provide (as a mounted printing plate) with an interlay

²interlay \"\ *n* **:** something (as a sheet of tissue) placed between a printing plate and its base to make the plate or certain areas a suitable height for proper impression — compare OVERLAY, UNDERLAY

¹in·ter·layer \¦intə(r)+\ *vt* [*inter-* + *layer* (n.)] **:** INTERSTRATIFY, INTERBED

²in·ter·layer \'==+,-\ *n* **:** a layer placed between other layers ⟨plastic ~ in safety glass⟩; *specif* **:** INTERBED

¹in·ter·leaf \¦intə(r)+\ *vt* [*inter-* + *leaf* (n.)] **:** INTERLEAVE

²in·ter·leaf \'==+,-\ *n* **1 :** a usu. blank leaf inserted or fastened between two leaves of a book (as for written notes or for protecting a color plate) **2 :** SLIP SHEET

in·ter·league \¦intə(r)+\ *adj* [*inter-* + *league* (n.)] **:** existing or occurring between leagues ⟨~ trading of players⟩

in·ter·leave \,intə(r)'lēv\ *vt* -ED/-ING/-S [*inter-* + *-leave* (back-formation fr. *leaved*, taken as a past participle)] **1 a :** to equip (as a manifold business form) with an interleaf **b :** SLIP-SHEET **2 :** INTERLAMINATE, INTERSTRATIFY

in·ter·lending \¦intə(r)+\ *adj, Brit* **:** of or relating to interlibrary loan

in·ter·lens \"+\ *adj* [*inter-* + *lens* (n.)] *of a photographic shutter* **:** situated between lens elements

in·ter·library \"+\ *adj* [*inter-* + *library* (n.)] **:** taking place between libraries ⟨~ loan⟩

in·ter·light \"+\ *vt* [*inter-* + *light*] **:** to light intermittently ⟨misery is *interlit* with flashes of pure joyousness —Edmond Taylor⟩

¹in·ter·line \"+\ *vb* [alter. (influenced by L *inter-*) of ME *enterlinen*, fr. ML *interlineare*, fr. L *inter-* + *linea* line — more at LINE] *vt* **1 :** to write or insert between lines already written or printed ⟨*interlined* additions to a manuscript⟩ **:** write or print something between the lines of ⟨~ a page⟩ ⟨~ a book⟩ **2 :** to add an interline to (ruled paper) ~ *vi* **:** to make insertions between written or printed lines

²interline \'intə(r)+,-\ *n* **:** a light often broken line ruled between horizontal lines

³in·ter·line \¦==+\ *vt* [ME *interlinen*, fr. *inter-* + *linen* to line — more at LINE] **:** to provide (as a garment) with an interlining

⁴in·ter·line \"+\ *adj* [*inter-* + *line* (n.)] **:** relating to, involving, or carried by two or more transportation lines ⟨~ traffic⟩ ⟨~ freight⟩ ⟨~ haul⟩ ⟨~ costs⟩

in·ter·lin·e·al \"+¦linēəl\ *adj* [*interlinear* + *-al*] **:** INTERLINEAR — **in·ter·lin·e·al·ly** \-əlē\ *adv*

¹in·ter·linear \"+\ *adj* [ME *interliniare*, fr. ML *interlinearis*, fr. L *inter-* + *linearis* linear — more at LINEAR] **1 :** situated between lines **2 :** inserted between lines already written or printed ⟨~ gloss⟩ ⟨~ corrections⟩ ⟨~ translation⟩ **3 a :** containing insertions between lines ⟨~ manuscript⟩ **b :** written or printed in different languages or texts in alternate lines ⟨~ bible⟩ — **in·ter·lin·e·ar·ly** *adv*

²interlinear \"\ *n* -s **:** a book having interlinear matter; *esp* **:** a school text of a work in a foreign language with interlinear translation

¹in·ter·lin·e·ary \"+¦linē,erē\ *adj* [prob. alter. (influenced by E *-ary*) of ML *interlinearis*] **:** INTERLINEAR

²interlineary \"\ *n* -ES **:** INTERLINEAR ⟨infinite helps of *interlinearies*, breviaries, synopses —John Milton⟩

in·ter·lin·e·ate \,intə(r)'linē,āt\ *vb* -ED/-ING/-S [ML *interlineatus*, past part. of *interlineare* to interline — more at INTERLINE] **:** INTERLINE

in·ter·lin·e·a·tion \,==,==ˈāshən\ *n* [ML *interlineatus* (past part.) + E *-ion*] **1 :** the act of interlining **2 :** something interlined ⟨~s in a later hand⟩ ⟨editorial ~s⟩ ⟨a printed form with typewritten ~s —*N.Y.Times*⟩

in·ter·lin·er \¦==¦līnə(r)\ *n* **1 :** one that interlines **2 :** INTERLINING ⟨~s for arctic and military clothing⟩

in·ter·lin·gua \,intə(r)'liŋgwə\ *n* -s [It, fr. *inter-* + *lingua* language, tongue, fr. L — more at TONGUE] **1 :** INTERLANGUAGE **2** *usu cap* **:** an artificial interlanguage that is based on the linguistic elements common to English and the chief Romance languages and is promoted by the International Auxiliary Language Association

in·ter·lingual \¦intə(r)+\ *adj* [*inter-* + *lingual*] **:** of, relating to, or existing between two or more languages ⟨~ alphabet⟩ ⟨~ dictionary⟩ ⟨~ idiom⟩

in·ter·linguistic \"+\ *adj* [*inter-* + *linguistic*] **1 :** INTERLINGUAL ⟨~ influences⟩ **2 :** of or relating to an interlanguage

in·ter·linguistics \"+\ *n pl but sing in constr* [ISV *inter-* + *linguistics*] **:** the study of interlingual similarities and relationships esp. for the purpose of devising an interlanguage

¹in·ter·lin·ing \"+¦liniŋ\ *n* [ME, fr. gerund of *interlinen*, *enterlinen* to interline — more at INTERLINE] **:** INTERLINEATION

²in·ter·lining \"+\ *n* [*inter-* + *lining*] **1 :** an inner lining (as of a coat or jacket) consisting of a warm or firm fabric shaped and sewn between the ordinary lining and the outside fabric **2 :** any fabric used for making interlinings

¹in·ter·link \"+\ *vt* [*inter-* + *link*] **:** to link together

²interlink \"\ *n* **:** an intermediate or connecting link

in·ter·linkage \"+\ *n* **1 :** the act of interlinking or state of being interlinked **2 :** a system of links ⟨molecular ~⟩

in·ter·lobate \"+\ *adj* [*inter-* + *lobate*] **:** lying between lobes ⟨~ moraines of a retreating glacier⟩

in·ter·lobular \"+\ *adj* [*inter-* + *lobular*] **:** lying between or connecting lobules ⟨~ connective tissue⟩

in·ter·local \"+\ *or* **in·ter·locality** \"+\ *adj* [*inter-* + *local* (adj.) or *locality* (n.)] **:** existing between localities ⟨~ tax differences⟩ — **in·ter·locally** \"+\ *adv*

in·ter·located \"+\ *adj* [*inter-* + *located*, past part. of *locate*] **:** placed between others **:** INTERPOSED

¹in·ter·lock \"+\ *vb* [*inter-* + *lock*] *vi* **:** to engage or interrelate with one another **:** lock into one another **:** interlace firmly ⟨~*ing* fingers⟩ ⟨bolt ~s with its striker⟩ ⟨~*ing* stitches⟩ ~ *vt* **1 :** to lock together **:** unite closely ⟨walls . . . contrived to ~ stone with stone without using an ounce of mortar —John McNulty⟩ **2 :** to connect in such a way that the motion of any part is constrained by another part; *esp* **:** to arrange the connections of (as railroad switches or signals) to ensure successive movement in proper sequence

²in·ter·lock \'intə(r)+,-\ *n* **1 :** the fact or state of being interlocked ⟨~ of corporate directorates⟩ **2 :** an arrangement whereby the operation of one part or mechanism automatically brings about or prevents the operation of another ⟨~ on an elevator door⟩ **3 :** a mechanism for or the act of synchronizing a motion-picture camera and sound-recording devices

³in·ter·lock \¦==+\ *adj* **:** knitted with interlocking stitches by the use of two alternating sets of needles ⟨~ hosiery⟩

interlocked grain *also* **interlocking grain** *n* **:** a wood grain in which the fibers incline in one direction in a number of annual rings and in a reverse direction in succeeding rings

in·ter·lock·er \"+¦läkə(r)\ *n* **:** one that interlocks

interlocking director *n* [fr. pres. part. of ¹*interlock*] **:** one who serves as a director of two or more corporations at one time

interlocking directorate *n* **:** a directorate linked with that of another corporation by interlocking directors so that the businesses managed by them are to some degree under one control

in·ter·loculus \,intə(r)+\ *n* [NL, fr. *inter-* + *loculus*] **:** a space or part between two loculi

in·ter·lo·cu·tion \,intə(r)lō'kyüshən, -lə'-\ *n* [L *interlocution-, interlocutio*, fr. *interlocutus* (past part. of *interloqui* to speak between, fr. *inter-* + *loqui* to speak) + *-ion-, -io* -ion] **1 :** interchange of speech **:** CONVERSATION **2 :** an interruptive utterance **:** INTERRUPTION, INTERPOLATION, PARENTHESIS **3 a** *obs* **:** responsive reading or recital **b** *obs* **:** a speech in reply **:** RESPONSE **c :** mode of intercommunication **4 a** [LL *interlocution-, interlocutio*, fr. L] **:** the making of an interlocutory legal order or decree; *also* **:** the order or decree **b** *Roman law* **:** a constitution of the emperor in the form of an informal expression of the imperial wish

in·ter·loc·u·tor \,intə(r)'läkyəd·ə(r), ¦==\ *n* -s [L *interlocutus* (past part.) + E *-or*] **1 :** one who takes part in dialogue or conversation **2 :** a man in the middle of the line in a minstrel show who questions the end men and acts as leader **3** [ML *interlocutorium*, fr. neut. of *interlocutorius*, adj.] *Scots law* **:** a judgment or order of a court whether interlocutory or finally determining the issues

¹in·ter·loc·u·to·ry \¦==¦läkyə,tōrē, -tȯr-, -rē\ *adj* [*interlocution* + *-ory*] **1 :** consisting of or having the nature of dialogue **:** CONVERSATIONAL ⟨~ observations⟩ **2 :** of or belonging to an interruptive speech or question **:** spoken as an interlocution **3** [ME (Scot. dial.), fr. ML *interlocutorius*, fr. LL *interlocutus* (past part. of *interloqui* to pronounce an interlocutory sentence, fr. L, to speak between) + L *-orius* -ory] *law* **:** not final or definitive **:** made or done during the progress of an action **:** INTERMEDIATE, PROVISIONAL ⟨~ decree in a divorce suit⟩ ⟨~ motion⟩

²in·ter·loc·u·to·ry *n* -ES *obs* **:** an interlocutory decree

in·ter·loc·u·tress *or* **in·ter·loc·u·trice** \,==ˈläkyə·trəs\ *or* **in·ter·loc·u·trix** \-,triks\ *n, pl* **interlocutresses** \-rəsəz\ *or* **interlocutri·ces** \,==,==ˈtrī(,)sēz\ [*interlocutress* fr. *interlocutor* + *-ess*; *interlocutrice* fr. F, fem. of *interlocuteur* interlocutor; *interlocutrix* fr. *interlocutor* + *-trix*] **:** a female interlocutor

in·ter·lope \¦intə(r)¦lōp\ *vb* -ED/-ING/-S [prob. back-formation fr. *interloper*] *vi* **1 :** to encroach on the rights (as in trade) of others **:** trade without a proper license **2 :** INTRUDE, INTERMEDDLE, INTERFERE ~ *vt, obs* **:** INTERCEPT

in·ter·lop·er \'==,lōpə(r), ,==ˈ==\ *n* -s [alter. (influenced by L *inter-*) of earlier *enterloper*, prob. fr. *enter-* inter- + *-loper* (as in *landloper*)] **1 :** one that interlopes **:** an unlawful intruder on a property or sphere of action **2 :** one that interferes or thrusts himself in wrongfully or officiously

in·ter·lot \,intə(r)+\ *vt* [*inter-* + *lot*] **:** to pool (as star lots of wool) into large lots for auction

in·ter·lu·ca·tion \,intə(r)lü'kāshən *also* -)lyü'-\ *n* -s [L *interlucation-, interlucatio* act of pruning, act of thinning, fr. *interlucatus* (past part. of *interlucare* to thin, top, fr. *inter-* + *-lucare* — fr. *luc-, lux* light) + *-ion-, -io* -ion — more at LIGHT] **:** the cutting of trees from a stand so that the remaining trees will grow rapidly

in·ter·lu·cent \ˌintə(r)ˈlüsənt *also* -)lˈyü-\ *adj* [L *interlucent-, interlucens,* pres. part. of *interlucēre* to shine, fr. *inter-* + *lucēre* to shine — more at LIGHT] **:** shining or glowing between or in the midst of other things

[1]**in·ter·lude** \ˈintə(r)ˌlüd *also* -)lˌyüd\ *n* -s [alter. (influenced by L *inter-*) of ME *enterlude,* fr. ML *interludium,* fr. L *inter-* + *ludus* play — more at LUDICROUS] **1 a :** an entertainment of a light or farcical character introduced between the acts of an old mystery or morality play or forming a feature of a festival or fete **b :** one of the farces or comedies derived from these entertainments **2 :** a performance or entertainment between the acts of a play **3 a :** an irrelevant change or happening in a course of events **:** EPISODE ⟨romantic ~⟩ **b :** an intervening or interruptive space of time or such a feature or event **:** INTERVAL ⟨forests with ~*s* of open meadow⟩ ⟨brief ~ of sanity⟩ ⟨~*s* of wit and humor in a tragic story⟩ **4 :** a musical composition inserted between the parts of a musical or dramatic entertainment or religious service; *specif* **:** a short organ piece played between verses of a hymn or psalm

[2]**interlude** \"\ *vi* -ED/-ING/-S **1 :** to perform an interlude **2 :** to occur as an interlude

in·ter·lu·di·al \ˌ==ˈlüdēəl *also* -)lˌyü-\ *adj* **:** of, relating to, or resembling an interlude ⟨~ passage between fugues⟩

in·ter·lu·nar \ˌintə(r)ˈlünə(r) *also* -)lˌyü-\ *also* **in·ter·lu·na·ry** \-nərē\ *adj* [*interlunar* prob. fr. MF *interlunaire,* fr. L *interlunium* interlunation (fr. *inter-* + *luna* moon) + MF *-aire* (fr. L *-aris* -ar); *interlunary* prob. modif. (influenced by E *lunary*) of MF *interlunaire* — more at LUNAR] **:** relating to the interval between old and new moon when the moon is invisible ⟨silent as the moon . . . hid in her vacant ~ cave —John Milton⟩

in·ter·lunation \ˌintə(r)+\ *n* [prob. fr. *inter-* + *lunation*] **1 :** the interlunar period **2 :** a period of darkness or blankness

in·ter·lying \ˌintə(r)+\ *adj* [*inter-* + *lying,* pres. part. of *lie*] **:** lying in between ⟨~ beds of gravel⟩

in·ter·mandibular \ˌintə(r)+\ *adj* [*inter-* + *mandibular*] **1 :** situated between the mandibles **2 :** INTERRAMAL

in·ter·marine \"+\ *adj* [*inter-* + *marine*] **:** carried on between seas or ships on the sea ⟨~ communication⟩

in·ter·marriage \"+\ *n* [*inter-* + *marriage*] **1 :** marriage between members of different racial, social, or religious groups ⟨~ between Negroes and whites⟩ ⟨~ of invaders and the conquered⟩ ⟨Protestant-Catholic ~⟩ **2 a :** INMARRIAGE, ENDOGAMY **b :** INBREEDING

in·ter·marry \"+\ *vi* [*inter-* + *marry*] **1 a :** to marry each other — used of a couple or of one of the contracting parties ⟨statute legitimatizing children whose parents *intermarried* after their birth —Morris Ploscowe⟩ **b :** to marry within a group ⟨the deaf are likely to ~ —H.J.Baker⟩ **2 :** to become connected by marriage between their members **:** give and take mutually in marriage — used of families, castes, social or religious or ethnic groups or of their members ⟨if a peeress by marriage should afterwards ~ with a commoner —T.E.May⟩

in·ter·maxilla \"+\ *n* [NL, fr. *inter-* + *maxilla*] **:** PREMAXILLA

in·ter·maxillar \"+\ *adj* [*inter-* + *maxillar*] **:** INTERMAXILLARY

[1]**in·ter·maxillary** \"+\ *adj* [*inter-* + *maxillary*] **1 :** lying between maxillae; *esp* **:** joining the two maxillary bones ⟨~ suture⟩ **2 :** of or relating to the premaxillae

[2]**intermaxillary** \"\ *n* **:** PREMAXILLA

intermean *n* [*inter-* + *mean*] *obs* **:** something intermediate **:** INTERLUDE

in·ter·meddle \ˌintə(r)+\ *vb* [ME *entermedlen,* fr. MF *entremedler, entremeller, entremesler,* fr. OF, fr. *entre-* inter- + *medler, meller, mesler* to mix — more at MEDDLE] *vt* **1** *obs* **:** INTERMINGLE **2** *obs* **:** INTERPOSE ~ *vi* **:** to meddle with the affairs of others **:** meddle officiously **:** INTERFERE ⟨must know and ~ with mysteries —Mary Webb⟩ ⟨any *intermeddling* with slavery in the federal district —S.E.Morison & H.S.Commager⟩ **syn** see MEDDLE

in·ter·meddler \"+\ *n* **1 :** one who intermeddles ⟨out-of-state ~*s*⟩ **2 a** *obs* **:** INTERMEDIARY **b** *obs* **:** INTERLOPER

in·ter·mede \ˈintə(r)ˌmēd\ *n* -s [F *intermède,* fr. It *intermedio,* fr. LL *intermedium* — more at INTERMEDIUM] **1** *archaic* **:** INTERMEDIUM **2** *or* **in·ter·mède** \aⁿtermed\ **:** INTERMEZZO 1

[1]**intermedia** *pl of* INTERMEDIUM

[2]**in·ter·me·dia** \ˌintə(r)ˈmēdēə\ *n, pl* **intermedi·ae** \-dēˌē\ [NL, fr. L, fem. of *intermedius* intermediate — more at INTERMEDIATE] **:** either member of the middle pair of tail feathers of a bird

in·ter·me·di·a·cy \ˌintə(r)ˈmēdēəsē, -si, *chiefly Brit* -mējəs- *or* -mēdyəs-\ *n* [fr. [2]*intermediate,* after E *immediate: immediacy*] **:** INTERMEDIATENESS

in·ter·me·di·al \ˌintə(r)ˈmēdēəl\ *n* [L *intermedius* + E *-al*] **:** INTERMEDIATE

[1]**in·ter·me·di·ary** \ˌintə(r)ˈmēdēˌerē, -ri, *chiefly Brit* -mējər- *or* -mēdyər-\ *adj* [prob. fr. F *intermédiaire,* fr. L *intermedius* + F *-aire* -ary] **1 :** lying, coming, or done between **:** INTERMEDIATE ⟨~ distribution of perishable products⟩ ⟨importing and other ~ trades⟩ **2 :** acting or capable of acting between others as a mediator ⟨~ agent⟩

[2]**intermediary** \"\ *n* -ES [prob. fr. F *intermédiaire,* fr. *intermédiaire,* adj.] **1 :** one that is intermediate: **a :** MEDIATOR, INTERAGENT, GO-BETWEEN ⟨~ between the people and God⟩ **b :** something that serves as a medium or means **:** mediating agency **2 :** an intermediate form, stage, or product

intermediary host *n* **:** INTERMEDIATE HOST

[1]**in·ter·me·di·ate** \ˌintə(r)ˈmēdēˌāt, *usu* -ād.+V\ *vi* [ML *intermediatus,* past part. of *intermediare,* fr. L *inter-* + LL *mediare* to mediate — more at MEDIATE] **1 :** to come between **:** INTERVENE, INTERPOSE **2 :** to act as intermediate agent **:** MEDIATE

[2]**in·ter·me·di·ate** \ˌintə(r)ˈmēdēət, *chiefly Brit* -mējə- *or* -mēdyə-; *usu* -əd.+V\ *adj* [ML *intermediatus,* fr. L *intermedius* intermediate (fr. *inter-* + *medius* mid, middle) + *-atus* -ate — more at MID] **1 :** lying or being in the middle place or degree **:** between extremes or limits **:** coming or done in between **:** INTERVENING ⟨~ hue⟩ ⟨~ credit⟩ ⟨~ stage of growth⟩ ⟨~ stops on a journey⟩ ⟨~ sizes⟩ **2 a :** of or relating to the period between primary and secondary education usu. comprising the fourth, fifth, and sixth grades **b :** of or relating to the stage between the introductory and advanced stages of a course of study or training ⟨~ French⟩ ⟨~ piano pupil⟩ **c :** taken during the first year after matriculation at a British university other than Oxford or Cambridge ⟨~ examination⟩ ⟨an ~ course⟩ — compare PREVIOUS EXAMINATION, RESPONSION 2b

[3]**intermediate** \"\ *n* -s **1 :** something intermediate **:** a term, member, class, or quality between others of a series **2 :** one that acts between others **:** MEDIATOR, INTERMEDIARY **3 :** an intermediate biological type or form **4 :** a chemical compound formed as an intermediate step between the starting material and the final product (as a dye intermediate) **5 a :** a wool-carding machine that comes between the breaker and the finisher **b :** a machine in cotton manufacture placed between the slubbing billy and the roving frame **6 a :** IDLER WHEEL **b :** the second speed in a vehicle having three forward speeds

[4]**intermediate** \"\ *prep* **:** in the time intervening between — used in law ⟨waste committed ~ the sale and the period when the right to redeem expired —T.M.Cooley⟩

intermediate carrier *n* **:** a transportation line participating in a through movement which neither originates nor terminates the passengers or freight

intermediate disk *n* **:** KRAUSE'S MEMBRANE

intermediate frequency *n* **:** a relatively low frequency to which a signal is converted before demodulation in heterodyne reception — abbr. *i.f.*

intermediate girl scout *n* **:** a member of the Girl Scouts in the age group ranging approximately from 10 through 13 years old

intermediate goods *n pl* **:** PRODUCER GOODS

intermediate host *n* **1 :** a host which is normally used by a parasite in the course of its life cycle and in which it may multiply asexually but not sexually — compare DEFINITIVE HOST **2 :** RESERVOIR 6a; *sometimes* **:** VECTOR 2

in·ter·me·di·ate·ly *adv* **1 :** in an intermediate position **:** between things or times **2 :** to an intermediate degree ⟨~ hot⟩ **3 :** not immediately **:** INDIRECTLY

in·ter·me·di·ate·ness *n* -ES **:** the quality or state of being intermediate

intermediate school *n* **1 :** JUNIOR HIGH SCHOOL **2 :** a school comprising the fourth, fifth, and sixth grades **3 :** a part of the British school system serving children from 12 to 14 years of age — compare JUNIOR SCHOOL, SENIOR SCHOOL

intermediate stock *n* **:** a stock grafted between the basal stock and the scion (as in a double-worked apple tree)

intermediate tissue *n* **:** CONJUNCTIVE TISSUE

intermediate wheatgrass *n* **:** an Asiatic grass (*Agropyron intermedium*) introduced into the rangelands of western U.S. for pasture and fodder use

intermediate wheel *n* **:** an idler wheel in the driving train or the dial train of a timepiece

in·ter·me·di·a·tion \ˌintə(r)ˌmēdēˈāshən\ *n* [ML *intermediatus* (past part.) + E *-ion*] **:** the act of coming between **:** INTERVENTION, MEDIATION

in·ter·me·di·a·tor \-ˈmēdēˌād.ə(r), -ātə-\ *n* [ML *intermediatus* (past part.) + E *-or*] **:** MEDIATOR

in·ter·mediatory \ˌintə(r)+\ *adj* **:** MEDIATORY

in·ter·me·din \ˌintə(r)ˈmēdᵊn\ *n* -s [ISV *intermed-* (fr. NL *pars intermedia*) + *-in*] **:** a hormone secreted by the pars intermedia or the anterior lobe of the pituitary body that induces expansion of chromatophores in various vertebrates

intermedio- *comb form* [L *intermedius*] **:** intermediate and ⟨*intermedio*lateral⟩

in·ter·me·di·um \ˌintə(r)ˈmēdēəm\ *n, pl* **interme·dia** \-dēə\ *or* **intermediums** [LL, fr. L, neut. of *intermedius* intermediate — more at INTERMEDIATE] **1** *obs* **:** an intermediate space or time **:** INTERVAL **2 :** a musical or dance interlude **3 :** an intervening agent **:** INTERMEDIARY, MEDIUM **4 :** a bone or cartilage situated between the radiale and ulnare in the carpus and between the tibiale and fibulare in the tarsus in many vertebrates

in·ter·me·di·us \ˌ==ˈmēdēəs\ *adj* [NL, fr. L, intermediate] **:** tending to be moderately virulent — used esp. of strains of diphtheria bacilli — compare GRAVIS, MITIS

in·ter·mell \ˌ==ˈmel\ *vb* [ME *entremellen, entermellen,* fr. MF *entremeller* — more at INTERMEDDLE] *archaic* **:** INTERMEDDLE, INTERMINGLE

in·ter·member \ˌintə(r)+\ *vb* -ED/-ING/-S [*inter-* + *member* (n.)] **:** to fit into a uniform or harmonious group ⟨storage cupboard which ~*s* with the vertical cabinets —Estelle B. Hunter⟩ ⟨filing sections ~*ed* in a stack⟩

in·ter·membral \"+\ *adj* [*inter-* + *membral*] **:** existing between members — **in·ter·membrally** \"+\ *adv*

intermembral index *n, anthrop* **:** the ratio of the length of the whole arm to the length of the whole leg multiplied by 100

in·ter·membranous \"+\ *adj* [*inter-* + *membranous*] **:** situated or occurring between membranes

intermembranous ossification *n* **:** ossification that takes place in connective tissue without prior development of cartilage — compare ENDOCHONDRAL OSSIFICATION

in·ter·meningeal \"+\ *adj* [*inter-* + *meningeal*] **:** situated or occurring between the meninges ⟨~ hemorrhage⟩

in·ter·menstrual \"+\ *adj* [*inter-* + *menstrual*] **:** occurring between the menses ⟨~ pain⟩

in·ter·ment \ənˈtərmənt, -təm-\ *n* -s [ME *enterment,* fr. MF *enterrement,* fr. OF, fr. *enterrer* to inter + *-ment* — more at INTER] **1 :** the act or ceremony of depositing a dead body in a grave or tomb **:** BURIAL, SEPULTURE, INHUMATION ⟨change from ~ to cremation⟩ **2 :** the act of removing from sight or consideration ⟨decision . . . will result in the ~ of the women's program —Helen Fuller⟩

in·ter·mesenteric \ˌintə(r)+\ *adj* [*inter-* + *mesenteric*] **:** situated between mesenteries

in·ter·mesh \"+\ *vi* [*inter-* + *mesh*] **:** to mesh with one another ⟨~*ing* twin rotors⟩

in·ter·metallic \ˌintə(r)+\ *adj* [*inter-* + *metallic*] **:** composed of two or more metals or of a metal and a nonmetal in an alloy

intermetallic compound *n* **:** an alloy having a characteristic crystal structure and usu. a definite composition not necessarily conforming with the normal rules of valence — often distinguished from *solid solution*

in·ter·mewed \"+\ *adj* [*inter-* + *mewed,* past part. of *mew* (to molt); prob. trans. of MF *entremué*] *of a hawk* **:** having molted once in confinement

in·ter·mez·zo \ˌintə(r)ˈmet(ˌ)sō *sometimes* -ed(ˌ)zō\ *n, pl* **intermez·zi** \-sē, -zē\ *or* **intermezzos** [It, fr. LL *intermedium* — more at INTERMEDIUM] **1 :** a short light sometimes burlesque musical or dramatic piece presented between the acts of serious drama or opera **2 a :** a humorous musical play in the 16th and 17th centuries the acts of which alternated with those of the principal work **b :** a movement coming between the major sections of a symphony or other extended work ⟨as a finale⟩ **c :** a short independent instrumental composition **3 :** DIVERSION, EPISODE, AFFAIR, INTERLUDE ⟨pretty lady who created a domestic ~ —*Newsweek*⟩

in·ter·micellar \ˌintə(r)+\ *adj* [*inter-* + *micellar*] **:** situated between micelles ⟨~ cavities⟩

in·ter·migration \"+\ *n* [*inter-* + *migration*] **:** mutual migration **:** migration in both directions ⟨~ of fauna of neighboring continents⟩

in·ter·mi·na·bil·i·ty \ən‧ˌtərmənəˈbiləd.ē\ *n* -ES **:** ENDLESSNESS

in·ter·mi·na·ble \ən‧ˈtərmənəbəl, -təm-, -təim- *also* -mn-\ *adj* [ME, fr. LL *interminabilis,* fr. L *in-* [1]in- + *terminare* to terminate + *-abilis* -able — more at TERMINATE] **1 :** having no termination **:** wearisomely protracted **:** BOUNDLESS, ENDLESS ⟨~ sermons⟩ ⟨~ debates⟩ ⟨~ forest⟩ — **in·ter·mi·na·ble·ness** *n* -ES — **in·ter·mi·na·bly** \-blē, -li\ *adv*

in·ter·mi·nate \-məˌnāt, -nət\ *adj* [L *interminatus,* fr. *in-* + *terminatus,* past part. of *terminare*] *archaic* **:** having no end or limit

interminated *adj* [[1]*in-* + *terminated*] *obs* **:** LIMITLESS, BOUNDLESS

in·ter·mingle \ˌintə(r)+\ *vb* [*inter-* + *mingle*] **:** to mingle or mix together ⟨*intermingling* different races⟩ ⟨fat and lean *intermingled*⟩

in·ter·ministerial \"+\ *adj* [*inter-* + *ministerial*] **:** existing between ministries ⟨~ commission⟩

in·ter·mis·sion \ˌintə(r)ˈmishən\ *n* -s [L *intermission-, intermissio,* fr. *intermissus* (past part. of *intermittere* to cease, intermit) + *-ion-, -io* -ion] **1 :** the act of intermitting or state of being intermitted **:** INTERRUPTION, BREAK ⟨~ between acts of a play⟩ **2 :** cessation for a time **:** an intervening period of time **:** INTERVAL ⟨work without ~⟩ **3 :** the space of time between two paroxysms of a disease — distinguished from *remission*

in·ter·mis·sive \ˌ==ˈmisiv\ *adj* [L *intermissus* + E *-ive*] **:** INTERMITTENT

in·ter·mit \ˌintə(r)ˈmit, *usu* -id.+V\ *vb* **intermitted; intermitted; intermitting; intermits** [L *intermittere,* fr. *inter-* + *mittere* to send — more at SMITE] *vt* **1 :** to cause to cease for a time or at intervals **:** DISCONTINUE, INTERRUPT, SUSPEND ⟨pray to the gods to ~ the plague —Shak.⟩ ⟨never *intermitted* the custom of dressing for dinner⟩ **2 :** to cause (as a spark) to come and go at intervals ~ *vi* **:** to cease at intervals **:** to be intermittent ⟨a fever that *intermitted* with great regularity⟩ **syn** see DEFER

in·ter·mit·tence \ˌ==ˈmitᵊn(t)s\ *n* -s **1 :** the quality or state of being intermittent **:** periodic cessation or interruption **:** INTERMITTENCY ⟨~ of the pulse⟩ **2 :** periodic recurrence **:** FITFULNESS ⟨violent ~*s* of physical passion —Aldous Huxley⟩

in·ter·mit·ten·cy \-sē, -si\ *n* -ES **:** intermittent character or condition **:** INTERMITTENCE ⟨~ of employment and uncertainty of wages⟩

intermittency effect *n* **:** the photographic effect in which intermittent exposures fail to give the same density as a continuous exposure of the same total energy

in·ter·mit·tent \ˌ==ˈmitᵊnt\ *adj* [L *intermittent-, intermittens,* pres. part. of *intermittere* to intermit — more at INTERMIT] **:** coming and going at intervals **:** not continuous **:** ALTERNATING, RECURRENT, PERIODIC ⟨~ fever⟩ ⟨~ rain⟩ ⟨~ publication⟩ ⟨~ stream⟩ ⟨~ spark⟩ — **in·ter·mit·tent·ly** *adv*

intermittent claudication *n* **:** cramping pain and weakness in the legs esp. the calves on walking that disappears after rest and is usu. associated with inadequate blood supply to the muscles (as in thromboangiitis obliterans, vascular spasm, or arteriosclerosis)

intermittent current *n* **:** an electric current that flows and ceases to flow at regular or irregular intervals but is not reversed

intermittent light *n* **:** a signal or beacon light having equal periods of shining and eclipse — compare FLASHLIGHT, OCCULTING LIGHT

intermittent movement *n* **:** the motion produced by a mechanical device that advances a motion-picture film one or more frames at a time with stationary intervening periods; *also* **:** any such mechanical device

intermittent pulse *n* **:** a pulse that occas. skips a cardiac beat

intermittent sterilization *n* **:** sterilization by heating to boiling several times at intervals of about 24 hours in order that any resistant spores may germinate and be destroyed

in·ter·mit·ter *or* **in·ter·mit·tor** \ˌintə(r)ˈmid.ə(r)\ *n* -s **:** one that intermits; *esp* **:** a device for producing intermittent movement

in·ter·mix \ˌintə(r)+\ *vb* [back-formation fr. earlier *intermixt* intermingled, fr. L *intermixtus,* past part. of *intermiscēre* to intermix, fr. *inter-* + *miscēre* to mix — more at MIX] **:** to mix together **:** INTERMINGLE ⟨coal seams ~*ed* with iron ore⟩

in·ter·mixable \"+\ *adj* **:** capable of being mixed or blended together ⟨~ paint colors⟩

in·ter·mixedly \"+\ *adv* **:** in a mixed manner

in·ter·mixture \"+\ *n* [L *intermixtus* + E *-ure* (as in *mixture*)] **1 a :** the act of mixing together or the state of being mixed together **b :** a mass formed by mixture **:** a mass of ingredients mixed ⟨~ of letters and figures in a cryptogram⟩ **2 :** an additional ingredient **:** ADMIXTURE **3 :** MISCEGENATION

in·ter·modulation \"+\ *n* [ISV *inter-* + *modulation*] **:** the production in an electrical device of currents having frequencies equal to the sums and differences of frequencies supplied to the device or of their harmonics; *also* **:** distortion (as of amplified sound) caused by intermodulation

in·ter·molecular \"+\ *adj* [*inter-* + *molecular*] **:** existing or acting between molecules ⟨~ forces⟩ ⟨~ condensation⟩ — **in·ter·mo·lec·u·lar·ly** *adv*

in·ter·mon·tane \ˌintə(r)ˈmänˌtān\ *or* **in·ter·mont** \-ˈmänt\ *adj* [*intermontane* fr. *inter-* + L *montanus* of a mountain; *intermont* fr. *inter-* + L *mont-, mons* mountain — more at MOUNTAIN] **:** situated between mountains ⟨~ basin⟩

in·ter·morainic \ˌintə(r)+\ *adj* [*inter-* + *morainic*] **:** situated between moraines ⟨~ depression⟩

in·ter·mountain \"+\ *adj* [*inter-* + *mountain*] **:** INTERMONTANE

in·ter·mundane \"+\ *adj* [*inter-* + *mundane*] **:** existing between worlds ⟨~ space⟩

in·ter·mun·di·al \"+ˈməndēəl\ *or* **in·ter·mun·di·an** \-ēən\ *adj* [L *intermundia* + E *-al* or *-an*] **:** INTERMUNDANE

in·ter·mun·di·um \ˌ==ˈməndēəm\ *n, pl* **intermun·dia** \-ēə\ [NL, back-formation fr. L *intermundia,* pl., spaces between worlds, fr. *inter-* + *-mundia* (fr. *mundus* world) — more at MUNDANE] **:** space between worlds

in·ter·mural \ˌintə(r)+\ *adj* [L *intermuralis,* fr. *inter-* + *muralis* of a wall — more at MURAL] **:** lying between walls — **in·ter·murally** \"+\ *adv*

in·ter·muscular \"+\ *adj* [*inter-* + *muscular*] **:** lying between and separating muscles ⟨~ fat⟩

in·ter·mutual \"+\ *adj* [*inter-* + *mutual*] **:** MUTUAL — **in·ter·mutually** *adv* \"+\

[1]**in·tern** *or* **in·terne** \(ˈ)inˌtərn, ənˈt-, -tən,-təin\ *adj* [MF *interne,* fr. L *internus* — more at INTERNAL] *archaic* **:** INTERNAL

[2]**intern** \"\ *vt* -ED/-ING/-S [F *interner,* fr. *interne,* adj.] **1 a :** to confine within prescribed limits esp. during a war ⟨the plane was landed safely and the crew was ~*ed* —T.W.Lawson⟩ **b :** to impound esp. during a war ⟨duty of a neutral to ~ belligerent ships and planes⟩ **2 :** to confine to or as if to a hospital ⟨meddling fools who propose to ~ the dear lady —Norman Douglas⟩

[3]**in·tern** \ˈinˌt-\ *n* -s **:** a person interned **:** INTERNEE

[4]**intern** \"\ *or* **interne** \"\ *n* -s *often attrib* [F *interne,* fr. *interne,* adj.] **1 a :** an advanced student or recent graduate in a professional field (as teaching) who is getting practical experience under the supervision of an experienced worker **b :** one who after completion of an undergraduate medical curriculum serves in residence at a hospital — compare INTERNIST, RESIDENT **2 :** one trained in a profession allied to medicine (as nursing or dentistry) who undergoes a period of practical clinical experience prior to practicing his profession

[5]**intern** \"\ *vi* -ED/-ING/-S **:** to act as an intern

[1]**in·ter·nal** \(ˈ)inˌtərnᵊl, ənˈt-, -tən-, -təin-\ *adj* [L *internus* internal (fr. *inter* between) + E *-al* — more at INTER-] **1 a :** existing or situated within the limits or surface of something **:** INWARD, INTERIOR ⟨~ structure⟩ ⟨~ parts of the body⟩ ⟨~ regions of the earth⟩ ⟨~ mechanism of a toy⟩ ⟨~ funds of a business⟩ — opposed to *external* **b :** situated near the inside of the body ⟨~ layer of abdominal muscle⟩ **:** situated on the side toward the median plane of the body ⟨the ~ surface of the lung⟩ **2 :** capable of being applied through the stomach by being swallowed ⟨~ remedy⟩ ⟨~ stimulant⟩ **3 :** relating to the inner being or consciousness **:** belonging to or existing within the mind **:** SUBJECTIVE ⟨~ monologue⟩ **:** PRIVATE ⟨~ opinion⟩ ⟨~ resentment⟩ ⟨~ sensations⟩ **4 :** originating in or dependent on the thing itself **:** belonging to the mutual relations of the parts of a thing **:** INTRINSIC, INHERENT ⟨~ evidence of forgery in a document⟩ ⟨test a theory for ~ consistency⟩ **5 a :** present or performed within an organism ⟨~ senses⟩ ⟨~ speech⟩ **b :** arising within a sense organ ⟨~ stimulus⟩ **6 :** of or relating to the domestic affairs or administrative functions of a country or state ⟨~ commerce⟩ ⟨~ discord⟩ ⟨~ improvement⟩ ⟨~ debt⟩ **syn** see INNER

[2]**internal** \"\ *n* -s **1 internals** *pl* **:** the internal organs of the body **:** INNARDS **2 a :** an inner or essential quality or property **b** *obs* **:** spiritual nature **:** SOUL

internal angle *n* **:** INTERIOR ANGLE

internal audit *n* **1 :** a usu. continuous examination and verification of books of account conducted by employees of a business — contrasted with *independent audit* **2 :** a review of systems of internal check and internal control of a business

internal auditory meatus *also* **internal acoustic meatus** *n* **:** a short canal in the petrous portion of the temporal bone through which pass the facial, auditory, and glossopalatine nerves

internal ballistics *n pl but usu sing in constr* **:** INTERIOR BALLISTICS

internal black spot *n* **:** a breakdown of garden beets due to boron deficiency and characterized by hard dark necrotic masses of tissue in the root

internal brown spot *or* **internal brown fleck** *n* **:** a nonparasitic disease of the potato that is of unknown cause and is characterized by brown corky spots scattered throughout the interior of the tuber and sometimes by ring-shaped corky surface lesions — called also *corky ring spot*

internal capsule *n* **:** CAPSULE 1b (1)

internal carotid artery *n* **:** the inner branch of the carotid artery supplying the brain, eyes, and other internal structures of the head

internal check *n* **:** an accounting procedure whereby routine entries for transactions are handled by more than one employee in such a manner that the work of one employee is automatically checked against the work of another for detection of errors and irregularities

internal-combustion engine *n* **:** a heat engine in which the combustion that generates the heat takes place inside the engine proper instead of in a furnace — compare DIESEL ENGINE, GAS ENGINE, GASOLINE ENGINE, GAS TURBINE, JET ENGINE, ROCKET ENGINE, EXTERNAL-COMBUSTION ENGINE

internal control *n* **:** a system or plan of accounting and financial organization within a business comprising all the methods and measures necessary for safeguarding its assets, checking the accuracy of its accounting data or otherwise substantiating its financial statements, and policing previously adopted rules, procedures, and policies as to compliance and effectiveness

internal conversion *n* **:** transformation of nuclear gamma-ray energy into electron-emission energy within the atom itself

internal cork *n* **1 :** a virus disease of sweet potatoes characterized principally by the small brown to black corky spots which develop within the roots becoming prominent after harvest and storage **2 :** CORK 5

internal degree *n* **:** a degree granted by a university to a student who has completed the prescribed course in that university — compare EXTERNAL DEGREE

internal energy *n* **:** the total amount of kinetic and potential energy possessed by the molecules of a body and their ultimate parts owing to their relative positions and their motions inside the body and excluding the energy due to the passage of waves through the body and to vibrations of the body

internal environment *n* **:** the fluid medium in which the cells of the body exist

internal friction *n* **:** frictional interaction between adjacent portions in the interior of a substance due to viscous deformation or flow and resulting in the generation of heat

internal gear *n* **:** a gear having teeth on the inside of its circular rim

in·ter·nal·i·ty \ˌin(ˌ)tərˈnaləd·ē\ *n* -ES **:** the quality or state of being internal **:** INTERIORITY

in·ter·nal·iza·tion \ən·ˌtərnᵊlə̇ˈzāshən\ *n* -S **:** the act of internalizing ⟨man's conscience is an ~ of parental . . . authority —Asher Moore⟩

internal gear

in·ter·nal·ize \ən·ˈtərnᵊlˌīz\ *vt* -ED/-ING/-S *see -ize in Explan Notes* [¹*internal* + *-ize*] **:** to make internal **:** give subjective character to **:** INTERIORIZE; *specif* **:** to incorporate (as values, patterns of culture, motives, restraints) within the self as conscious or subconscious guiding principles through learning and socialization — compare INTROJECT

internal law *n* **:** the law of a state regulating its domestic affairs as opposed to that regulating its foreign affairs

in·ter·nal·ly \(ˈ)in¦tərnᵊlē, ən·ˈt-, -tə̄n-, -təin-, -li\ *adv* **1 :** within the termini, enveloping surface, or boundary of a thing **:** within the body **:** beneath the surface **:** INWARDLY **2 :** MENTALLY **:** SPIRITUALLY **3 :** in or in respect to the inner constitution or affairs of something ⟨a doctrine ~ inconsistent⟩

internally fired boiler *n* **:** a boiler whose furnace is wholly or partly surrounded by water — compare EXTERNALLY FIRED BOILER

internal mammary artery *n* **:** a branch of the subclavian artery of each side that runs down along the anterior wall of the thorax and rests against the costal cartilages

internal mammary vein *n* **:** a vein accompanying the internal mammary artery of each side

internal medicine *n* **:** a branch of medicine that deals with the diagnosis and treatment of nonsurgical diseases

internal navigation *n* **:** navigation on inland waterways

in·ter·nal·ness *n* -ES **:** INTERNALITY

internal oblique *n* **:** a sheet of diagonally arranged abdominal muscle lying between the external oblique and transverse layers on either side of the trunk

internal phase *n* **:** DISPERSED PHASE

internal phloem *n* **:** primary phloem internal to the primary xylem and either in contact with it or in discrete strands

internal porch *n* **:** VESTIBULE, LOBBY, NARTHEX 2

internal pressure *n* **:** pressure inside a portion of matter due to attraction between molecules

internal relation *n* **:** a relation that is involved in or essential to the nature of the thing related ⟨logical equivalence of propositions is an *internal relation* —Arthur Pap⟩ — contrasted with *external relation*

internal respiration *n* **:** the exchange of gases (as oxygen and carbon dioxide) between the cells of the body and the blood by way of the fluid bathing the cells — distinguished from *external respiration*

internal revenue tax *n* **:** EXCISE 1b, 1c, 1d

internal rhyme *n* **:** rhyme between a word within a line and another either at the end of the same line or within another line

internal secretion *n* **:** HORMONE

internal student *n* **:** a student studying in the same university from which he expects to receive a degree — compare EXTERNAL STUDENT

internal thread *n* **:** a screw thread on an inner or concave surface (as of a nut that fits on a bolt)

¹in·ter·nasal \¦intə(r)+\ *adj* [*inter-* + *nasal*] **:** situated between the nostrils ⟨~ septum⟩ ⟨~ scale⟩

²internasal \"\ *n* **:** an internasal part; *esp* **:** any of certain scales lying just behind the nostril in snakes

¹in·tern·ation \ˌinˌtərˈnāshən\ *n* -S [F, fr. *interner* to intern + *-ation* — more at INTERN] **:** the act of interning or the state of being interned **:** INTERNMENT

²in·ter·nation \¦intə(r)+\ *n* [*inter-* + *nation*] **:** a population composed of or representing several nationalities

³internation \"\ *adj* [*inter-* + *nation*] **:** existing or occurring between nations ⟨~ rivalry⟩

¹in·ter·na·tion·al *R* ¦intər¦nashənᵊl, -shnəl, -naash-,-naish-, *-R* ¦intə¦na- *sometimes* ¦intᵊn¦a-\ *adj* [*inter-* + *national*] **1 :** existing between or among nations or their citizens **:** relating to the intercourse of nations **:** participated in by two or more nations **:** common to or affecting two or more nations ⟨~ trade⟩ ⟨~ labor union⟩ ⟨~ trade association⟩ **2 :** belonging or relating to an organization or association having members in two or more countries ⟨~ congress⟩ ⟨~ movement⟩ **3 a** *of a unit of measurement* **:** fixed by the mutual agreement of authorized representatives of different countries **b** *of an electrical unit* **:** accepted by the International Conference in London in 1908 and used as a legal unit prior to 1950 ⟨~ coulomb⟩ **4 :** of or relating to the International Code

²international \"\ *n* **1 :** a person having relations with or obligations to more than one nation (as through citizenship in one and permanent residence in another) **2 :** a participant in an international contest **3 :** INTERNATIONAL STOCK **4 a :** a party, organization, or association that transcends national limits; *specif* **:** an international socialist organization **b :** a craft or industrial union with local affiliates in several countries **5 :** a class of racing sailboats that are 33 feet long, sloop-rigged, and of one design; *also* **:** a boat in this class

international auxiliary language *n* **:** INTERLANGUAGE

international candle *n* **:** CANDLE 4a

international carat *n* **:** CARAT 1b

international code *n, usu cap I&C* **:** a marine code adopted by all the leading nations for holding communication at sea by means of 26 flags each standing for a different letter of the Roman alphabet and an additional triangular code flag or answering pennant which are hoisted in various combinations each of which represents according to the code a different word, phrase, or sentence

international copyright *n* **:** copyright secured by treaty between nations

international crime *n* **:** a crime (as piracy, illicit trade in narcotics, slave trading) in violation of international law

international date line *n* **:** DATE LINE

in·ter·na·tio·nale \ˌ=‚=ˌshəˈnal, -näl,-nál\ *n* -S [F, fr. fem. of *international*, adj., fr. E] **:** INTERNATIONAL 4a ⟨a Communist ~⟩

in·ter·na·tion·al·ism *pronunc at* ¹INTERNATIONAL + ˌizəm\ *n* **1 a :** international character, principles, interests, or outlook **b :** international organization, influence, or common participation ⟨friction between governments is . . . reduced by administrative ~ —C.J.Friedrich⟩ **c :** COSMOPOLITANISM ⟨~ in art⟩ **2 :** the doctrine or belief that world peace may be attained by the friendly association of all nations on a basis of equality and without sacrifice of national character for the securing of international justice and for cooperation in all matters of worldwide interest ⟨the alternatives of outright nationalism and outright ~ —*Fortune*⟩ — compare ISOLATIONISM **3 :** the doctrine or belief of an international political association or party ⟨the ~ of the socialists found any barriers of race or nationality repugnant —Oscar Handlin⟩

¹in·ter·na·tion·al·ist \"+ˌəst\ *n* [¹*international* + *-ist*] **1 :** an advocate of internationalism **2 :** a specialist in international law **3 :** a member of a team selected from the country at large to play against the team of another country ⟨tennis ~⟩

²internationalist \"\ *or* **in·ter·na·tion·al·is·tic** \¦=‚=(=)=¦istik, -tēk\ *adj* **:** advocating or influenced by internationalism ⟨~ thought⟩

in·ter·na·tion·al·i·ty \ˌ=‚=ˌshəˈnaləd·ē, -lətē, -i\ *n* **:** the quality or state of being international ⟨~ of the use of scientific language —Otto Neurath⟩

in·ter·na·tion·al·iza·tion \ˌ=‚=(=)=ə̇ˈzāshən, -ˌīˈz-\ *n* **:** an act or process of internationalizing ⟨~ of a waterway⟩

in·ter·na·tion·al·ize \ˌ=‚=ˈ=(=)=ˌīz\ *vt* [¹*international* + *-ize*] **:** to make international in relations, effect, or scope ⟨~ a war⟩ ⟨~ a market⟩; *esp* **:** to place under international control or protection

international language *n* **:** INTERLANGUAGE

international law *n* **:** a body of rules that control or affect the rights of states in their relations with each other and of individuals in their relations to foreign states and with each other when public international factors are involved, that are based in the practice of Great Britain and the U. S. on the customs and usages of civilized nations, treaties, the acts of the executive in international matters, statutes, and judicial decisions esp. including those of international tribunals and in the practice of European continental countries also on the opinions of text writers, and that are generally accepted as binding and enforceable by the participant nations — called also *law of nations*

international legislation *n* **:** the law found in the treaties and international agreements among nations binding the parties thereto but not necessarily being a part of the body of international law binding all nations

in·ter·na·tion·al·ly \¦=‚=¦nashənᵊlē, -shnəlē, -naash-,-naish-, -ᵊli,-əli\ *adv* **:** in an international manner ⟨~ agreed⟩ **:** from an international point of view ⟨~ famous⟩ **:** between different nations or their citizens

international map *n* **:** a map of the world at a scale of one to one million having a uniform set of symbols and conventional signs and printed in modified polyconic projection on sheets each covering an area of 4 degrees latitude by 6 degrees longitude except above the 60th parallel where the longitude covered is 12 degrees on each sheet

international match point *n* **:** a scoring unit used in contract-bridge tournaments played in Europe and based on but not directly proportional to the winning margin of a board

international orange *n* **:** a vivid reddish orange that is redder and much darker than golden poppy and redder, stronger, and much darker than chrome orange

international phonetic alphabet *n, usu cap I, P, & A* **:** IPA

international pitch *n* **1 :** DIAPASON NORMAL **2 :** the tuning standard adopted in 1939 of 440 vibrations per second for A above middle C

international private law *n* **:** CONFLICT OF LAWS

international relations *n pl but sing in constr* **:** a branch of political science concerned with relations between political units of national rank and dealing primarily with foreign policies, the organization and function of governmental agencies concerned with foreign policy, and the factors (as geography and economics) underlying foreign policies

international salute *n* **:** a salute of 21 guns to a national flag

international scientific vocabulary *n, usu cap I&S&V* **:** a part of the vocabulary of the sciences and other specialized studies that consists of words or other linguistic forms current in two or more languages and differing from New Latin in being adapted to the structure of the individual languages in which they appear — abbr. *ISV*

international stock *n* **:** a stock marketable at financial centers outside as well as within the country of issue

international style *n* **1 :** a school of painting showing delicate linearity and decorative treatment of surface popular in Europe during the 14th and early 15th centuries **2 :** functional architectural design employing the latest of building techniques and avoiding traditional or regional influences

international temperature scale *n* **:** a practical temperature scale defining all temperatures above −183° C by specified formulas relating temperatures at one atmosphere pressure to the indications of instruments calibrated at six reproducible fixed points: the boiling point of oxygen (−182.97° C), the ice point (0° C), the steam point (100° C), the boiling point of sulfur (444.6° C), the freezing point of silver (960.8° C), the freezing point of gold (1063° C)

international unit *n* **:** a quantity of a biological (as a vitamin, hormone, antibiotic, antitoxin) or its equivalent based on bioassay that produces a particular biological effect agreed upon internationally

interne *var of* INTERN

in·ter·necine \¦intər¦ne¦ˌsēn, -nē¦, ¦ˌsīn, ¦sᵊn, ¦sə̇n; ¦intərnə̇¦sēn; ən·ˈtərnəˌsēn, -nəsən, -nəˌsīn\ *adj* [L *internecinus*, fr. *internecare* to destroy, kill (fr. *inter-* + *necare* to kill, fr. *nec-*, *nex* violent death) + *-inus* -ine — more at NOXIOUS] **1 a :** marked by great slaughter **:** DEADLY ⟨the alternatives only of ~ war or absolute surrender —W.E.Gladstone⟩ **b :** involving or accompanied by mutual slaughter **:** mutually destructive ⟨zealots who stabbed each other in ~ massacre —F.W.Farrar⟩ **2 :** of, relating to, or involving conflict within a group; *broadly* **:** INTERNAL ⟨absorbed in incurable, rancorous ~ feuds —Barbara Ward⟩ ⟨a bitter ~ struggle among artists —Roger Fry⟩

in·ter·ne·cion \ˌ=‚=ˈneshən, -nēsh-\ *n* -S [L *internecion-, internecio*, fr. *internecare* + *-ion-*, *-io* -ion] **:** mutual destruction **:** MASSACRE

in·ter·necive \¦=‚=¦nesiv, -nēs-; ən·ˈtərnəs-\ *adj* [L *internecivus*, fr. *internecare* + *-ivus* -ive] **:** INTERNECINE

interned *past of* INTERN

in·tern·ee \ˌin·ˌtər¦nē, -tə̄-, -təi-; ən·ˈ=ˌ=\ *n* -S [²*intern* + *-ee*] **:** a person interned

¹in·ter·neural \¦intə(r)+\ *adj* [*inter-* + *neural*] **:** situated between neural arches or neural spines

²interneural \"\ *n* -S **:** one of the spiny bones that extend into the flesh of certain fishes between the neural spines and articulate with the rays of the dorsal fins

in·ter·neuron \"+\ *also* **in·ter·neurone** \"+\ *n* [*inter-* + *neuron, neurone*] **:** an internuncial neuron — **in·ter·neuronal** \"+\ *adj*

interning *pres part of* INTERN

in·ter·nist \ən·ˈtərnəst, -tə̄n-\ *n* -S [*intern-* (fr. *internal medicine*) + *-ist*] **:** a specialist in internal medicine **:** a specialist in the diagnosis and medical treatment of internal diseases

in·tern·ment \ən·ˈtərnmənt, -tə̄n-,-təin-\ *n* -S [F *internement*, fr. *interner* to intern + *-ment* — more at INTERN] **:** the act of interning or the state of being interned ⟨~ of enemy aliens⟩

in·ter·nodal \¦intə(r)+\ *adj* [*inter-* + *nodal*] **:** lying between nodes ⟨~ stem gall⟩ ⟨~ loop of a vibrating string⟩

in·ter·node \ˈintə(r)ˌnōd\ *n* [L *internodium*, fr. *inter-* + *nodus* knot, joint + *-ium* (n. suffix) — more at NET] **:** an interval or part between two nodes **:** SEGMENT

interns *pres 3d sing of* INTERN, *pl of* INTERN

in·tern·ship *also* **in·terne·ship** \ˈin·ˌtərnˌship, -tə̄n-,-təin-\ *n* [⁴*intern, interne* + *-ship*] **1 :** the state or position of being an intern **2 a :** a period of service as an intern **b :** the phase of medical training covered during such service **c :** a training period in actual service as an employee in a technical or business establishment **3 :** a grant enabling a student or recent graduate to serve as an intern

in·ter·nuclear \¦intə(r)+\ *adj* [*inter-* + *nuclear*] **:** situated or extending between nuclei ⟨~ distances in molecules⟩

in·ter·nunce \ˈintə(r)ˌnən(t)s\ *n* -S [L *internuntius, internuncius* — more at INTERNUNCIO] *archaic* **:** INTERNUNCIO

¹in·ter·nun·cial \¦intə(r)¦nən(t)sēəl, -nūn-, ¦sh(ē)əl, ¦ch-\ *adj* [*internuncio* + *-al*] **1 :** of or relating to an internuncio **:** serving as a conveyer of messages **2 :** serving to link sensory and motor neurons — **in·ter·nun·cial·ly** \-əlē\ *adv*

²internuncial \"\ *or* **internuncial neuron** *n* -S **:** a nerve fiber intercalated in the path of a reflex arc in the central nervous system and tending to modify the arc and coordinate it with other bodily activities

in·ter·nun·ci·ary \¦(t)sēˌerē, ¦shē-, ¦chē-; ¦shərē, ¦chə-\ *adj* [*internuncio* + *-ary*] **:** INTERNUNCIAL 1

in·ter·nun·cio \ˌintə(r)ˈnən¦(t)sēˌō, -nün¦, ¦shēˌō, ¦chēˌō\ *n* [It *internunzio*, fr. L *internuntius, internuncius*, fr. *inter-* + *nuntius, nuncius* messenger] **1 :** a messenger between two parties **:** GO-BETWEEN **2 :** a diplomatic papal representative of lower rank than a nuncio **3 :** a minister formerly representing a government (as the Austrian government) at Constantinople

in·ter·nun·ci·us \-ēəs\ *n, pl* **internun·cii** \-ēˌī, -ēˌē\ [L] **:** INTERNUNCIO

in·ter·nuptial \¦intə(r)+\ *adj* [*inter-* + *nuptial*] **1 :** relating to intermarriage **2 :** intervening between married states

in·ter·objective distance \¦intə(r)+ . . . -\ *n* [*inter-* + *objective*] **:** the distance between the pupils of the two eyes

in·ter·oceanic \"+\ *adj* [*inter-* + *oceanic*] **:** existing or extending between oceans ⟨~ communication⟩

in·ter·o·cep·tive \¦intərō¦septiv\ *adj* [*inter-* (as in *interior*) + *-o-* + *-ceptive* (as in *receptive*)] **:** of, relating to, or functioning as an interoceptor — compare EXTEROCEPTIVE, PROPRIOCEPTIVE

in·ter·o·cep·tor \-ptə(r)\ *n* -S [*inter-* (as in *interior*) + *-o-* + *-ceptor* (as in *receptor*)] **:** a receptor (as in the wall of the alimentary tract) responsive to stimuli originating within the body and esp. in the viscera — compare EXTEROCEPTOR

in·ter·ocular \¦intə(r)+\ *adj* [*inter-* + *ocular*] **:** situated between the eyes

in·ter·o·fec·tive \¦intərō¦fektiv\ *adj* [*inter-* (as in *interior*) + *-o-* + *-fective* (as in *effective*)] **:** of, relating to, dependent on, or constituting the autonomic nervous system — distinguished from *exterofective*

in·ter·office \¦intə(r)+\ *adj* [*inter-* + *office*] **:** existing between the offices of an organization ⟨~ memo⟩

in·ter·operation \"+\ *n* [*inter-* + *operation*] **:** reciprocal operation ⟨~ of factors⟩

in·ter·oper·cle \ˌintərōˈpərkəl\ *n* [NL *interoperculum*] **:** the membrane bone between the preopercle and the branchiostegals of a fish

¹in·ter·oper·cu·lar \¦=‚=¦pərkyələ(r)\ *adj* [NL *interoperculum* + E *-ar*] **:** of or relating to an interoperculum

²interopercular \"\ *n* -S **:** INTEROPERCLE

in·ter·oper·cu·lum \ˌ=‚=ˈ=ləm\ *n* [NL, fr. *inter-* + *operculum*] **:** INTEROPERCLE

in·ter·optic \¦intə(r)+\ *adj* [*inter-* + *optic*] **:** lying between the optic lobes

in·ter·orbital \"+\ *adj* [*inter-* + *orbital*] **:** situated or extending between the orbits of the eyes ⟨~ septum⟩ ⟨~ distance⟩

interorbital breadth *n* **:** the distance between the dacrya

in·ter·osculant \"+\ *adj* [*inter-* + *osculant*] *math* **:** osculating with each other **:** INTERSECTING ⟨~ curves⟩

in·ter·osculate \"+\ *vi* [*inter-* + *osculate*] **:** to osculate with each other **:** INTERMIX ⟨*interosculating* blood vessels⟩ — **in·ter·osculation** \"+\ *n*

in·ter·osseous \"+\ *adj* [*inter-* + *osseous*] **:** situated between bones; *esp* **:** lying between the bones of the leg or forearm ⟨~ membrane⟩ ⟨~ artery of the hand⟩ ⟨~ nerve⟩

in·ter·os·se·us \ˌintəˈ(r)äsēəs\ *n, pl* **interos·sei** \-ēˌī\ [NL, fr. *inter-* + L *osseus*, adj., osseous — more at OSSEOUS] **:** any of various small muscles arising from the metacarpals and metatarsals and inserted into the bases of the first phalanges

in·ter·ownership \¦intə(r)+\ *n* [*inter-* + *ownership*] **:** interlocking ownership

in·ter·page \"+\ *vt* [*inter-* + *page*] **:** to insert or put between pages ⟨*interpaged* translation⟩

in·ter·parental \"+\ *adj* [*inter-* + *parental*] **:** existing between parents ⟨~ tension⟩

¹in·ter·parietal \"+\ *adj* [*inter-* + *parietal*] **:** lying between parietal elements; *esp* **:** lying between the parietal bones

²interparietal \"\ *n* **:** an interparietal element (as a bone or scale)

interparietal bone *n* **:** a median triangular bone lying at the junction of the parietal and occipital bones and rarely present in man but conspicuous in various lower mammals — see INCA BONE

in·ter·pa·ri·e·ta·le \ˌintə(r)pəˌrīəˈtālē\ *n* -S [NL, fr. *inter-* + LL *parietale*, neut. of *parietalis* parietal — more at PARIETAL] **:** an interparietal bone or cartilage

in·ter·parliamentary \¦intə(r)+\ *adj* [*inter-* + *parliamentary*] **:** existing among or involving several national legislatures ⟨~ congress⟩

in·ter·paroxysmal \"+\ *adj* [*inter-* + *paroxysmal*] **:** occurring between paroxysms

in·ter·party \"+\ *adj* [*inter-* + *party*] **:** existing between parties ⟨~ cooperation⟩

in·ter·peduncular \"+\ *adj* [*inter-* + *peduncular*] **:** lying between the peduncles of the brain

interpeduncular ganglion *n* **:** a mass of nerve cells lying between the cerebral peduncles in the median plane just dorsal to the pons

in·ter·pel \ˌintə(r)ˈpel\ *vt* **interpelled; interpelled; interpelling; interpels** [MF *interpeller*, fr. L *interpellare* — more at INTERPELLATE] **1** *obs* **:** INTERRUPT **2** *Scots law* **:** PREVENT, PRECLUDE, INTERCEPT

¹in·ter·pel·lant \¦=‚=¦pelənt\ *adj* [L *interpellant-, interpellans*, pres. part. of *interpellare*] **:** INTERRUPTING

²interpellant \"\ *n* -S **:** INTERPELLATOR

in·ter·pel·late \ˌ=‚=ˈpeˌlāt, usu -ād·+V; ən·ˈtərpə-, -tə̄p-, -təip-, *usu* -ād·+V\ *vt* -ED/-ING/-S [L *interpellatus*, past part. of *interpellare*, fr. *inter-* + *-pellare* (fr. *pellere* to drive, beat, push) — more at FELT] **1** *obs* **:** INTERRUPT **2 :** to question formally about a governmental policy or decision

in·ter·pel·la·tion \ˌ=‚=pəˈlāshən; ˌ=‚=ˈlāshən\ *n* -S [L *interpellation-, interpellatio*, fr. *interpellatus* + *-ion-*, *-io* -ion] **1** *obs* **:** an act of interposing **:** INTERCESSION **2 :** INTERRUPTION **3 :** the act of formally bringing into question (as in a European legislature) a ministerial policy or action ⟨~ . . . is the particular method by which the deputies exercise their power of controlling and dismissing cabinets —Ernest Barker⟩ **4** *Scots law* **:** INTERCEPTION, PREVENTION

in·ter·pel·la·tor \ˌ=‚=ˈpelād·ə(r); ˈ=ˌ=ˌlād·ə(r)\ *n* -S [L, fr. *interpellatus* + *-or*] **:** one that interpellates

in·ter·pendent \¦intə(r)+\ *adj* [*inter-* + *pendent*] **1** *archaic* **:** hanging between **:** HESITANT **2** *archaic* **:** INTERDEPENDENT

in·ter·penetrable \"+\ *adj* [*inter-* + *penetrable*] **:** capable of being mutually penetrated ⟨portrays good and evil as ~ and relative —K.O.Myrick⟩

in·ter·penetrant \"+\ *adj* [*inter-* + *penetrant*] **:** mutually penetrating ⟨~ crystals⟩

in·ter·penetrate \"+\ *vb* [*inter-* + *penetrate*] *vt* **:** to penetrate between, within, or throughout **:** penetrate thoroughly **:** PERMEATE ⟨Westerners who *interpenetrated* the East in the nineteenth century —Elmer Davis⟩ **~** *vi* **:** to penetrate mutually ⟨the territories of the two peoples ~ a good deal —C.D. Forde⟩ **syn** see PERMEATE

in·ter·penetration \"+\ *n* [*inter-* + *penetration*] **1 :** thorough penetration **:** PERMEATION **2 :** mutual penetration; *esp* **:** the effect in painting of two or more forms crossing and including shapes in common — compare TRANSPARENCY

in·ter·penetrative \"+\ *adj* [*inter-* + *penetrative*] **:** tending to penetrate mutually ⟨for him realism and mysticism are ~ —B.R.Redman⟩ — **in·ter·penetratively** \"+\ *adv*

in·ter·personal \"+\ *adj* [*inter-* + *personal*] **1 :** existing between persons ⟨~ situation in which speech occurs —Z.S. Harris⟩ **2 :** relating to or involving personal and social relations out of which develop systems of shared expectations, patterns of emotional relatedness, and modes of social adjustment ⟨disrupted ~ relationships —M.J.Pescor⟩ — **in·ter·personally** \"+\ *adv*

in·ter·petaloid \"+\ *adj* [*inter-* + *petaloid*] **:** lying between ambulacral areas ⟨~ spaces on a sea urchin⟩

in·ter·phalangeal \"+\ *adj* [*inter-* + *phalangeal*] **:** existing between phalanges ⟨~ flexion⟩

in·ter·phase \ˈintə(r)ˌ-\ *n* [*inter-* + *phase*] **:** INTERKINESIS — **in·ter·phasic** \¦intə(r)+\ *adj*

in·ter·phone \ˈintə(r)ˌfōn\ *n* [fr. *Interphone*, a trademark] **:** a telephone system (as in an airplane, tank, ship, or office building) for intercommunication between points within a small area

in·ter·piece \-ˌpēs\ *n* [*inter-* + *piece*] **:** INTERLUDE

in·ter·pilaster \ˌintə(r)+\ *n* [*inter-* + *pilaster*] **:** the space between two pilasters

interplace *vt* [*inter-* + *place*] **1** *obs* **:** to place between or among **:** INSERT **2** *obs* **:** to place alternately

in·ter·plait \¦intə(r)+\ *vt* [*inter-* + *plait*] **:** to plait together

in·ter·plane \"+\ *adj* [in sense 1, fr. *inter-* + *plane* (section of an airplane); in sense 2, fr. *inter-* + *plane* (airplane)] **1 :** situated or extending between the upper and lower wing of an airplane ⟨~ strut⟩ **2 :** existing between airplanes ⟨~ communication⟩

in·ter·planetary \"+\ *adj* [*inter-* + *planetary*] **:** existing, carried on, or operating between planets ⟨the density of hydrogen in ~ and interstellar space —*Science*⟩

¹in·ter·plant \"+\ *vt* [*inter-* + *plant* (v.)] **:** to plant (a crop) between plants of another kind **:** set out (young trees) among existing growth

²in·ter·plant \ˈ=‚=ˌ-\ *n* **:** a crop planted between plants of another crop

³in·ter·plant \¦=‚=+\ *adj* [*inter-* + *plant* (n.)] **:** existing between manufacturing plants ⟨~ transfer of material⟩

1in·ter·play \ˈintə(r)+,-\ *n* [*inter-* + *play*] **:** mutual action or influence **:** reciprocal or contrasting action or effect **:** INTERACTION ⟨bureaucratic controls are imposed upon . . . an ~ of private interests —Irving Howe⟩ ⟨~ of character and circumstance —Hallam Tennyson⟩

2in·ter·play \ˌ==+\ *vi* **:** to exert interplay ⟨there enter into imaginative creation three factors which reciprocally ~ —J.L. Lowes⟩

in·ter·plea \ˈintə(r)+,-\ *n* [*inter-* + *plea*] **:** the plea of a defendant disclaiming any interest in the subject matter of a controversy and calling for an interpleader proceeding between the true claimants

in·ter·plead \ˌintə(r)ˈplēd\ *vb* [AF *enterpleder*, fr. *enter-* inter- + *pleder* to plead, fr. OF *plaidier* — more at PLEAD] *vi* **:** to go to trial with each other in order to determine a right on which the action of a third party depends ~ *vt* **:** to bring (two or more claimants) into court in order to compel the litigation of the ownership of a claim ⟨insurance company, not knowing where the payment should go between the three, ~*ed* the claimants —W.H.Atwell⟩

1in·ter·plead·er \-də(r)\ *n* [AF *enterpleder*, fr. *enterpleder*, v.] **:** a proceeding devised to enable a person of whom the same debt, duty, or thing is claimed adversely by two or more parties to compel them to litigate the right or title between themselves and thereby to relieve himself from the suits which they might otherwise bring against him

2interpleader \"\ *n* [*interplead* + *-er*] **:** one that interpleads

in·ter·plical \ˌintə(r)+\ *adj* [*inter-* + *plical*] **:** lying between folds

1in·ter·pluvial \"+\ *adj* [*inter-* + *pluvial*] **:** comparatively dry and occurring between times of greater precipitation ⟨~ age⟩

2interpluvial \"\ *n* -s **:** an interpluvial age or time

in·ter·point \ˈintə(r)+,-\ *n* [*inter-* + *point*] **:** the printing of braille on both sides of the paper in such a way that the points of one side fall between the points of the other side

in·ter·polar \ˌintə(r)+\ *adj* [*inter-* + *polar*] **:** situated or extending between poles ⟨~ field of a magnet⟩ ⟨~ wire⟩

in·ter·po·late \ənˈtərpə,lāt, -tə̄p-, -təip-, *usu* -ād·+V\ *vb* -ED/-ING/-S [L *interpolatus*, past part. of *interpolare* to give a new appearance to, alter, interpolate, fr. *inter-* + *-polare* (fr. *polire* to polish, furbish) — more at POLISH] *vt* **1 a :** to alter or corrupt (as a text) by inserting new or foreign matter; *esp* **:** to change by inserting matter that is new or foreign to the purpose of the author ⟨was both *interpolated* and misunderstood —*Modern Language Notes*⟩ **b :** to insert (words) into a text ⟨*interpolated* editorial comment⟩ **:** put in (a remark) in a conversation **2 :** to insert between other things or parts **:** INTERCALATE ⟨letter which I here ~ as a good example of his style —Osbert Sitwell⟩ ⟨~ a layer of insulating material between ceiling and floor⟩ **3 :** to estimate values of (a function) between two known values ~ *vi* **:** to make insertions — compare EXTRAPOLATE

in·ter·po·lat·er \-ād·ə(r), -ātə-\ *n* -s **:** one that interpolates

in·ter·po·la·tion \=,==ˈlāshən\ *n* -s [L *interpolation-, interpolatio*, fr. *interpolatus* + *-ion-, -io* -ion] **1 :** an act of interpolating or state of being interpolated **:** introduction or insertion of something spurious or foreign **2 :** something that is introduced or inserted **:** INSERTION **3 :** the process of calculating approximate values by interpolating between values already known

in·ter·po·la·tor \=ˈ==,lād·ə(r), -ātə-\ *n* -s [L, fr. *interpolatus* + *-or*] **1 :** INTERPOLATER **2 :** a mechanically rotated clockwork instrument with two cams working in conjunction with a relay to secure the correct telegraphic retransmission of any given number of consecutively repeated dots or dashes

in·ter·pole \ˈintə(r)+,-\ *n* [*inter-* + *pole*] **:** a supplementary pole placed between the regular poles of a direct-current dynamo or motor in order to regulate commutation — called also *commutating pole*

in·ter·political \ˌintə(r)+\ *adj* [*inter-* + *political*] **:** INTERCITY — used of the Greek city-states

in·ter·polymer \"+\ *n* [*inter-* + *polymer*] **:** COPOLYMER

in·ter·polymerization \"+\ *n* **:** COPOLYMERIZATION

in·ter·polymerize \"+\ *vt* [*interpolymer* + *-ize*] **:** COPOLYMERIZE

in·ter·pone \ˌintə(r)ˈpōn\ *vt* -ED/-ING/-S [L *interponere* — more at INTERPOSE] *archaic* **:** INTERPOSE

in·ter·por·tal \ˌ==+ˈpȯrd·ᵊl, -pȯr-\ *adj* [*inter-* + *port* + *-al*] **:** existing between ports of the same country ⟨~ trade⟩

in·ter·pos·al \ˌintə(r)ˈpōzəl\ *n* -s [*interpose* + *-al*] **:** the act of interposing **:** INTERPOSITION, INTERVENTION

in·ter·pose \-ōz\ *vb* [MF *interposer*, modif. (influenced by *poser* to put, place) of L *interponere* (perfect stem *interpos-*), fr. *inter-* + *ponere* to put, place — more at POSE, POSITION] *vt* **1 a :** to place between or in an intermediate position **:** cause to intervene ⟨dense . . . forests ~ an almost impassable barrier —Samuel Van Valkenburg & Ellsworth Huntington⟩ ⟨tending to ~ objects of worship between God and man —W.R.Inge⟩ **b :** to put (oneself) between **:** thrust in **:** INTRUDE ⟨what watchful cares do ~ themselves betwixt your eyes and night? —Shak.⟩ **2 :** to put forth by way of interference or intervention ⟨prevent a decision's being reached by *interposing* a veto⟩ **3 :** to introduce or throw in between the parts of a conversation or argument ⟨interrupted by questions from the class, and listened to whatever we might so ~ —C.I.Lewis⟩ ⟨~ objections⟩ **4 :** to move (a chessman) so as to shield a checked king or a piece that is directly attacked ~ *vi* **1 :** to be or come between ⟨cut through an *interposing* thicket⟩ **2 :** to step in between parties at variance **:** INTERVENE, MEDIATE ⟨listened . . . to their dispute, and at length *interposed* once more on the old man's side —W.H.Hudson †1922⟩ **3 :** to make an interruption or digression ⟨here Adam *interposed* —John Milton⟩

in·ter·pos·er \-zə(r)\ *n* **:** one that interposes

in·ter·pos·ing·ly *adv* **:** so as to interpose

in·ter·po·si·tion \ˌintə(r)pəˈzishən\ *n* [ME *interposicioun*, fr. MF *interposition*, fr. L *interposition-, interpositio*, fr. *interpositus* (past part. of *interponere*) + *-ion-, -io* -ion] **1 :** the act of interposing or the state of being interposed **:** a being, placing, or coming between **:** MEDIATION, INTERVENTION ⟨~ of the state between the federal government and the citizen of the state⟩ **2 :** something that is interposed

interposition growth *n* **:** INTRUSIVE GROWTH

interposure *n* -s *obs* **:** INTERPOSITION

interpr *abbr* interpreter

in·ter·pret \ənˈtərprət, ÷-pət, -tə̄p-, -təip-, *usu* -əd·+V\ *vb* -ED/-ING/-S [ME *interpreten*, fr. MF & L; MF *interpreter*, fr. L *interpretari*, fr. *interpret-, interpres* broker, negotiator, expounder, interpreter, fr. *inter-* + *-pret-, -pres* (prob. akin to L *pretium* value, price) — more at PRICE] *vt* **1 :** to explain or tell the meaning of **:** translate into intelligible or familiar language or terms **:** EXPOUND, ELUCIDATE, TRANSLATE ⟨Emmanuel, which being ~*ed* is, God with us —Mt. 1:23 (AV)⟩ ⟨~ dreams⟩ ⟨can only ~ his conduct as caused by fear⟩ **2 :** to understand and appreciate in the light of individual belief, judgment, interest, or circumstance **:** CONSTRUE ⟨~ a law⟩ ⟨~ a contract⟩ ⟨the gift was naturally ~*ed* as a bribe⟩ ⟨~ the signs of a coming storm⟩ **3 :** to apprehend and represent by means of art **:** show by illustrative representation **:** bring (a score or script) to active realization by performance ⟨an actor ~*s* a role⟩ ⟨~ a song⟩ ~ *vi* **:** to act as an interpreter **:** TRANSLATE

in·ter·pret·abil·i·ty \=,=p(r)əd·əˈbiləd·ē, -)ətə-, -lətē, -i\ *n* -ES **:** the quality or state of being interpretable ⟨~ of signs⟩

in·ter·pret·able \=ˈ=p(r)əd·əbəl, -)ətəb-\ *adj* [LL *interpretabilis*, fr. L *interpretari* + *-abilis* -able] **:** capable of being interpreted or explained ⟨~ as a confession of guilt —P.A. Rollins⟩ — **in·ter·pret·able·ness** *n* -ES — **in·ter·pret·ably** \-blē, -bli\ *adv*

interpretament *n* -s [LL *interpretamentum*, fr. L *interpretari* + *-mentum* -ment] *obs* **:** INTERPRETATION

in·ter·pre·tant \=ˈ=p(r)əd·ənt, -)ətə-\ *n* -s [L *interpretant-, interpretans*, pres. part. of *interpretari*] **1 a :** the disposition or readiness of an interpreter to respond to a sign **b :** a sign or set of signs that interprets another sign **c :** the response or reaction to a sign **2 :** INTERPRETER

in·ter·pre·tate \-ə,tāt\ *vi* -ED/-ING/-S [L *interpretatus*, past part. of *interpretari* to interpret — more at INTERPRET] *archaic* **:** INTERPRET

in·ter·pre·ta·tion \ən,tərprəˈtāshən, ÷-pə-, -tə̄p-, -təip-\ *n* -s [ME *interpretacioun*, fr. MF & L; MF *interpretation*, fr. L *interpretation-, interpretatio*, fr. *interpretatus* + *-ion-, -io* -ion] **1 :** the act or the result of interpreting: as **a :** explanation of what is not immediately plain or explicit ⟨~ of a dream⟩ or unmistakable ⟨~ of a law⟩ ⟨~ of a biblical passage⟩ ⟨~ of an aerial photograph⟩ ⟨~ of symptoms of disease⟩ **b :** translation from one language into another — used of oral translation by interpreters **c :** explanation of actions, events, or statements by pointing out or suggesting inner relationships or motives or by relating particulars to general principles ⟨Marxist ~ of history⟩ ⟨allegorical ~ of a novel⟩ ⟨poetic ~*s* of natural phenomena⟩ **2 :** representation in performance, delivery, or criticism of the thought and mood in a work of art or its producer esp. as penetrated by the personality of the interpreter ⟨~ is a transcendental effort . . . in which the player seeks not to reproduce but to re-create the music the composer wrote —C.M.Smith⟩ ⟨famous for her original ~*s* of several dramatic roles⟩ **3 :** a particular adaptation or application of a method or style or set of principles ⟨the stone house . . . shows a naive and unusual ~ of classical elements —*Amer. Guide Series: Pa.*⟩ ⟨an amusing ~ of the shirt vogue in black cotton —Virginia Pope⟩ **4 :** activity directed toward the enlightenment of the public concerning the significance of the work of a public service or agency; *sometimes* **:** PUBLICITY, PUBLIC RELATIONS ⟨program of ~ developed by a natural-history museum⟩ — **in·ter·pre·ta·tion·al** \=ˌ=ˌ=ˈtāshənᵊl, -shnəl\ *adj*

interpretation clause *n* **:** a clause inserted in a statute or contract declaring the interpretation that is to be put upon certain words

in·ter·pre·ta·tive \ənˈtərp(r)ə,tād·|iv, -tə̄p-,-təip-, |t|, |ēv *also* |əv *sometimes* -)ətə|\ *adj* [*interpret* + *-ative*] **1 :** designed or fitted to interpret **:** EXPLANATORY ⟨~ magazine article⟩ **2 :** according to interpretation ⟨~ distortions in a translation⟩ ⟨~ elasticity of a statute⟩ — **in·ter·pre·ta·tive·ly** \|əvlē, -li\ *adv*

interpretative bigamy *n* **:** BIGAMY 2b

interpretative dance *or* **interpretive dance** *n* **:** a dance depicting a story or a definite emotion rather than following an abstract pattern

in·ter·pret·er \ənˈtərprəd·ə(r), ÷ -pə-, -tə̄p-, -təip-, -ətə-\ *n* -s [alter. (influenced by *-er*) of ME *interpretour*, fr. *interpreten* to interpret + *-our* -or — more at INTERPRET] **1 :** one that interprets, explains, or expounds ⟨early decipherers and ~*s* of hieroglyphic —W.T.Albright⟩ **2 :** one that translates; *esp* **:** a person who translates orally for parties conversing in different tongues **3 :** a machine that prints on punched cards the symbols recorded in them by perforations

in·ter·pret·er·ship \-,ship\ *n* **:** the position of interpreter

in·ter·pre·tive \ənˈtərp(r)əd·|iv, -tə̄p-, -təip-, -)ət|\ *adj* **:** INTERPRETATIVE — **in·ter·pre·tive·ly** \|əvlē, -li\ *adv*

in·ter·pre·tress \ənˈtərp(r)ətrəs\ *also* **in·ter·pret·ess** \-)əd·əs\ *n* -ES **:** a female interpreter

interprets *pres 3d sing of* INTERPRET

in·ter·provincial \ˌintə(r)+\ *adj* [*inter-* + *provincial*] **:** existing between provinces ⟨~ compact⟩

in·ter·proximal \"+\ *also* **in·ter·proximate** \"+\ *adj* [*inter-* + *proximal* or *proximate*] **:** situated between adjacent parts or surfaces; *esp* **:** situated between adjoining teeth ⟨~ space⟩

in·ter·pulmonary \"+\ *adj* [*inter-* + *pulmonary*] **:** situated between the lungs

in·ter·punct \ˈintə(r),pəŋkt\ *n* -s [L *interpunctus*, past part.] **:** INTERPOINT

in·ter·punc·tion \ˌ==ˈpəŋkshən\ *n* -s [L *interpunction-, interpunctio*, fr. *interpunctus* (past part. of *interpungere* to punctuate, interpoint, fr. *inter-* + *pungere* to prick) + *-ion-, -io* -ion — more at PUNGENT] *n* -s **:** PUNCTUATION; *also* **:** PUNCTUATION MARK

in·ter·punctuate \ˌintə(r)+\ *vt* [*inter-* + *punctuate*] **:** PUNCTUATE — **in·ter·punctuation** \"+\ *n*

in·ter·pupillary \"+\ *adj* [*inter-* + *pupillary*] **:** extending between the pupils of the eyes; *also* **:** extending between the centers of a pair of spectacle lenses ⟨~ distance⟩

in·ter·quartile range \"+ . . .-\ *n* [*inter-* + *quartile*] **:** the range of values of the variable in a statistical distribution that lies between the upper and lower quartiles

in·ter·racial \"+\ *or* **in·ter·race** \"+\ *adj* [*inter-* + *racial* or *race*] **1 :** existing between or involving two or more races or members of different races ⟨~ understanding⟩ ⟨an ~ conference⟩ **2 :** of, relating to, or designed for two or more races or members of different races ⟨~ housing⟩

in·ter·radial \"+\ *adj* [*inter-* + *radial*] **:** of or relating to an interradius — **in·ter·radially** \"+\ *adv*

in·ter·ra·di·um \ˌintə(r)ˈrādēəm\ *n, pl* **interra·dia** \-ēə\ [NL, fr. *inter-* + *-radium* (fr. *radius*)] **1 :** one of the areas between radii **2 :** INTERAMBULACRUM

in·ter·radius \ˌintə(r)+\ *n, pl* **interradii** [NL, fr. *inter-* + *radius*] **:** a radius in a coelenterate halfway between two perradii

in·ter·ramal \"+\ *adj* [*inter-* + *ramal*] **:** situated between rami esp. of the lower jaw

in·ter·ramification \"+\ *n* [*inter-* + *ramification*] **:** the union of branches to form a network

in·ter·react \"+\ *vi* [*inter-* + *react*] **:** to react reciprocally — **in·ter·reaction** \"+\ *n*

interred *past of* INTER

in·ter·reef \"+\ *adj* [*inter-* + *reef* (n.)] **:** situated between reefs ⟨~ sedimentation⟩

in·ter·reflection \"+\ *n* [*inter-* + *reflection*] **:** reciprocal reflection ⟨~ of light between surfaces of a lens⟩

in·ter·regional \"+\ *adj* [*inter-* + *regional*] **:** existing between regions ⟨~ zone⟩

in·ter·reg·nal \"+ˈregnᵊl\ *adj* **:** of or relating to an interregnum

in·ter·reg·num \-nəm\ *n, pl* **interregnums** \-mz\ *or* **in·terreg·na** \-nə\ [L, fr. *inter-* + *regnum* dominion — more at REIGN] **1** *obs* **:** reign or tenure of power during a temporary vacancy of a throne or suspension of the ordinary government **2 a :** the time during which a throne is vacant between the death, abdication, or expulsion of a sovereign and the accession of his successor **b :** a period between two regimes of the same form or of different forms of government **3 :** a period during which the normal functions of government or control are suspended **4 a :** a period of freedom from customary authority **b :** a lapse, break, or pause in a continuous series

1in·ter·reign \ˈintə(r),rān\ *n* [MF *interregne*, fr. L *interregnum*] **:** INTERREGNUM

2in·ter·reign \ˌintə(r)+\ *vi* [*inter-* + *reign* (v.)] **:** to reign between other reigns

in·ter·relate \"+\ *vb* [*inter-* + *relate*] *vt* **:** to bring into mutual relation ⟨has not yet learned to ~ his characters —*Saturday Rev.*⟩ ~ *vi* **:** to have mutual relationship ⟨the linguistic system ~*s* with the other systems of the culture —H.L. Smith b.1913⟩

in·ter·related \"+\ *adj* [*inter-* + *related*] **:** having a mutual or reciprocal relation or parallelism **:** CORRELATIVE — **in·ter·re·lat·ed·ly** *adv* — **in·ter·re·lat·ed·ness** *n*

in·ter·relation \"+\ *n* [*inter-* + *relation*] **:** mutual relation **:** INTERRELATEDNESS

in·ter·relationship \"+\ *n* **:** mutual relationship **:** CORRESPONDENCE ⟨~*s* of animal structure and function⟩

in·ter·religious \"+\ *adj* [*inter-* + *religious*] **:** existing between religions ⟨~ goodwill⟩

1in·ter·renal \"+\ *adj* [*inter-* + *renal*] **:** lying between the kidneys

2interrenal \"\ *n* -s **:** INTERRENAL BODY

interrenal body *or* **interrenal gland** *n* **:** a small body of discrete adrenal cortical tissue lying between the kidneys of certain fishes

in·ter·rer \ənˈtərə(r) *also* -tərə(r\ *n* -s **:** one that inters

in·ter·rex \ˈintə(r),reks\ *n, pl* **interre·ges** \ˌ==ˈrē(,)jēz\ [L, fr. *inter-* + *rex* king — more at ROYAL] **:** one who exercises supreme or kingly power during an interregnum **:** a provisional ruler

interring *pres part of* INTER

in·ter·ro·ga·ble \ənˈterəgəbəl, (ˈ)inˌt-\ *adj* [*interrogate* + *-able*] **:** capable of being interrogated

in·ter·ro·gant \ənˈterəgənt\ *n* -s [L *interrogant-, interrogans*, pres. part. of *interrogare*] **:** INTERROGATOR

in·ter·ro·gate \-rə,gāt, *usu* -ād·+V\ *vb* -ED/-ING/-S [L *interrogatus*, past part. of *interrogare*, fr. *inter-* + *rogare* to ask, request — more at RIGHT] *vt* **1 :** to question typically with formality, command, and thoroughness for full information and circumstantial detail ⟨~ a witness⟩ **2** *obs* **:** to ask questions about **3 :** to examine in detail **:** research into the causes, reasons, nature of ⟨modern potters ~ in their laboratories the glazes used in ancient China —C.E.Montague⟩ ~ *vi* **:** to ask questions of someone **:** conduct an examination ⟨frank I will respond as you ~ —Robert Browning⟩ **syn** see ASK

in·ter·ro·gat·ing·ly *adv* **:** QUESTIONINGLY

in·ter·ro·ga·tion \ən,terəˈgāshən\ *n* -s [ME *interrogacioun*, fr. MF *interrogation*, fr. L *interrogation-, interrogatio*, fr. *interrogatus* + *-ion-, -io* -ion] **1 a :** the act of interrogating **b :** a question put **:** INQUIRY **2 a :** a question regarded as a type of sentence or unit of discourse **b :** a questioning with the force of an emphatic affirmation or denial **3 :** QUESTION MARK — **in·ter·ro·ga·tion·al** \=ˌ=ˌ=ˈgāshənᵊl, -shnəl\ *adj*

interrogation point *or* **interrogation mark** *n* **:** QUESTION MARK

1in·ter·rog·a·tive \ˌintəˈrägəd·iv, -ətiv\ *adj* [LL *interrogativus*, fr. L *interrogatus* + *-ivus* -ive] **1 :** having the form or the force of a question ⟨~ sentence⟩ **:** used in a question ⟨~ pronoun⟩ **:** requiring or seeming to require an answer from the hearer or reader ⟨~ inflection in his voice⟩ **2 :** QUESTIONING, INQUISITIVE ⟨had an ~ nose⟩ — **in·ter·rog·a·tive·ly** \-əvlē, -li\ *adv*

2interrogative \"\ *n* -s **1 :** an interrogative utterance **:** QUESTION **2 :** a word (as *who, what, which*) or a particle (as Latin *-ne*) used in asking questions

in·ter·ro·ga·tor \ənˈterə,gād·ə(r), |tə- *sometimes* ,intəˈrägə|\ *n* -s [LL, fr. L *interrogatus* (past part. of *interrogare* to interrogate) + *-or* — more at INTERROGATE] **1 :** one that interrogates **:** QUESTIONER; *specif* **:** one who interrogates prisoners of war ⟨born a German and . . . served as ~ in the American Army —Virginia Peterson⟩ **2 :** a radio transmitter and receiver combined for sending out a signal that triggers a transponder and for receiving and displaying the reply

1in·ter·rog·a·to·ry \ˌintəˈrägə,tōrē, -tȯr-, -ri\ *n* -ES [ML *interrogatorium*, fr. neut. of LL *interrogatorius*] **1 :** a formal question or inquiry; *esp* **:** a question put in writing and required by law to be answered under direction of a court **2 :** a sign or signal denoting interrogation

2interrogatory \ˌ==ˌ==,==\ *adj* [LL *interrogatorius*, fr. L *interrogatus* + *-orius* -ory] **:** containing, expressing, or implying a question **:** INTERROGATIVE ⟨ends most of her remarks with an ~ upward inflection —Dan Wickenden⟩

interrogatory action *n, Roman law* **:** an action in which preliminary issues are tried before litiscontestation

in·ter·ro·gee \ən,terəˈgē\ *n* -s [*interrogate* + *-ee*] **:** someone interrogated

in ter·ro·rem \ˈin,teˈrȯ,rem\ *adv (or adj)* [L, for terror] **:** by way of threat or intimidation ⟨if, after becoming aware of the other party's offense, the injured party could hold it *in terrorem* over his or her head —Edward Jenks⟩

in·ter·rupt \ˌintəˈrəpt\ *vb* -ED/-ING/-S [ME *interrupten*, fr. L *interruptus*, past part. of *interrumpere*, fr. *inter-* + *rumpere* to break — more at REAVE] *vt* **1 :** to stop by breaking in **:** halt, hinder, or interfere with the continuation of (some activity) **:** prevent (one) from proceeding by intrusive or interpolated comment or action ⟨the . . . recovery was ~*ed* by the depression of 1883–85 —F.A.Bradford⟩ ⟨~ a speaker with frequent questions⟩ **2 :** to break or stop the uniformity, continuity, sequence, or course of **:** introduce a difference in ⟨an affair of copious eating and still more copious drinking, ~*ed* by bouts of homemade fun —Aldous Huxley⟩ ⟨the plain narrows and is ~*ed* by broad spurs from the Pennines —L.D.Stamp⟩ **3** *obs* **:** OBSTRUCT, THWART, PREVENT ~ *vi* **:** to break in upon some action or discourse **:** INTERPOLATE; *esp* **:** to break in with questions or remarks while another is speaking ⟨a bad habit of ~*ing*⟩ **syn** see ARREST

interrupted *adj* **1 :** broken in upon **:** DISCONTINUOUS ⟨an ~ stripe⟩ ⟨~ suture⟩ **2 :** not uniform **:** broken in arrangement or symmetry ⟨~ inflorescence⟩ **3 :** consisting of or containing a stop in articulation ⟨\k\ is an ~ consonant⟩ ⟨\dzh\ is an ~ phoneme⟩ **4** *of a map projection* **:** not having continuous outlines **:** split (as along meridians) so as to give better shape and scale for each continent or ocean — **in·ter·rupt·ed·ly** *adv* — **in·ter·rupt·ed·ness** *n* -ES

interrupted cadence *n* **:** DECEPTIVE CADENCE

interrupted continuous waves *n pl* **:** radio waves that are continuous except for periodic interruptions at a materially lower frequency

interrupted current *n* **:** a pulsating electric current produced by opening and closing a continuous-current circuit in a regular manner

interrupted fern *n* **:** an American fern (*Osmunda claytoniana*) with tall erect pinnate fronds and a few pairs of sporogenous pinnae borne at or near the center of the fertile fronds

interrupted key *n, cryptology* **:** an aperiodic keying sequence formed by interrupting a short key at various points and resuming from its beginning each time

interrupted perforation *n* **:** perforation on postage stamps for vending machines or dispensers in which there are unperforated spaces between groups of holes

interrupted screw *n* **:** a screw from which sectors have been removed by longitudinal cuts through the threads so that it can be thrust into a reciprocally machined mating part and locked by only a fraction of a turn

in·ter·rupt·er *also* **in·ter·rup·tor** \ˌintəˈrəptə(r)\ *n* -s **:** one that interrupts: as **a :** a device for periodically and automatically interrupting an electric current **b** *cryptology* **:** a message element or insertion signaling a change of key

in·ter·rupt·ible \ˌ==ˈrəptəbəl\ *adj* **:** capable of being interrupted ⟨~ utility service at reduced rates⟩

in·ter·rup·tion \ˌ==ˈrəpshən\ *n* -s [ME *interrupcioun*, fr. L *interruption-, interruptio*, fr. *interruptus* + *-ion-, -io* -ion] **1 :** an act of interrupting or state of being interrupted **2 :** a breach or break caused by the abrupt intervention of something foreign **3 :** obstruction caused by breaking in upon a course, current, progress, or motion **:** STOP **4 :** temporary cessation **:** INTERMISSION, SUSPENSION **5** *Scots law* **:** an act or proceeding that defeats an adverse title or claim based on prescription by stopping the running of the period of time required for the perfection of the title or claim and starting it running anew **syn** see BREAK

in·ter·rup·tive \ˌ==ˈrəptiv, -tēv *also* -təv\ *also* **in·ter·rup·to·ry** \-tərē\ *adj* [*interrupt* + *-ive* or *-ory*] **:** tending to interrupt — **in·ter·rup·tive·ly** \-təvlē\ *adv*

inters *pres 3d sing of* INTER

1in·ter·scapular \ˌintə(r)+\ *adj* [*inter-* + *scapular*] **:** situated between the shoulder blades **:** of or relating to the region between the shoulders ⟨~ feathers⟩

2interscapular \"\ *n* **:** an interscapular feather

in·ter·scene \ˈintə(r)+,-\ *n* [*inter-* + *scene*] **:** a scene (as in a motion picture) inserted between portions of the main narrative ⟨the passing of time has been done very adroitly by the use of cartoon ~*s* —W.H.Rudkin⟩

in·ter·scholastic \ˌintə(r)+\ *adj* [*inter-* + *scholastic*] **:** characterized by participation or cooperation of two or more secondary schools ⟨has withdrawn from ~ athletics⟩ — compare EXTRAMURAL

in·ter·school \"+\ *adj* [*inter-* + *school*] **:** existing between schools ⟨won first prize in the ~ debating competition⟩ — opposed to *intraschool*

in·ter se \ˈintə(r)ˈsē\ *adv (or adj)* [L] **:** among or between themselves ⟨all species will breed *inter se* —*Farmer's Weekly (So. Africa)*⟩ ⟨relations of the several parts of the empire *inter se* are not subject to international law —*Manchester Guardian Weekly*⟩

in·ter·seamed \ˌintə(r)ˈsēmd\ *adj* [by folk etymology fr. MF *entresemer* to intersperse (fr. *entre-* inter- + *semer* to sow, fr. L *seminare*) + E *-ed* — more at DISSEMINATE] *archaic* **:** INTERSPERSED, SOWN ⟨borders of lilies ~ with roses —Robert Greene⟩

1in·ter·sect \ˌintə(r)ˈsekt\ *vb* -ED/-ING/-S [L *intersectus*, past part. of *intersecare*, fr. *inter-* + *secare* to cut — more at SAW] *vt* **1 :** to pierce or divide by passing through or across (a line or area) **:** CROSS ⟨any two diameters of a circle ~ each other⟩ ⟨canals ~ the city in every direction —*Encyc. Americana*⟩ **2 :** to determine the position of by triangulation ⟨opportunity was taken to ~ some twenty odd peaks —*Geog. Jour.*⟩

3 : to write (as a shorthand stroke) so as to cut across another or be cut across by another ~ *vi* **1** : to meet and cross at a point ⟨~*ing* roads⟩ **2** : to cut into one another so as to share an area in common : OVERLAP ⟨where positive law and morals ~ —Herbert Agar⟩

²**intersect** \ˈ==,=\ *n* -s : a point or curve of intersection

in·ter·sec·tant \ˌ==ˈsektənt\ *adj* : INTERSECTING

intersecting arcade *n* : a Romanesque arcade having interlacing arches

in·ter·sec·tion \ˌ==ˈsekshən, *in sense 3* " *or* ˈ==ˌ==\ *n* -s [L *intersection-, intersectio*, fr. *intersectus* + *-ion-, -io* -ion] **1** : an act, state, or place of intersecting ⟨understand the ~ of visible with invisible worlds —Stephen Spender⟩ **2** : the set of elements common to two or more sets; *esp* : the set of points common to two geometric configurations (as lines, surfaces, or volumes) **3** : a place where two or more highways join or cross; *specif* : an area of potential collision between vehicles traveling on different roadways that cross

¹**in·ter·sec·tion·al** \ˌ==ˈsekshənᵊl, -shnəl\ *adj* [*intersection* + *-al*] : of or relating to an intersection

²**in·ter·sec·tion·al** \"\ *adj* [*inter-* + *sectional*] : existing between sections ⟨~ football game⟩

in·ter·segmental \ˌintə(r)+\ *adj* [*inter-* + *segmental*] : lying between segments; *specif* : lying between the primordial segments of the embryo ⟨~ artery⟩

in·ter·septal \"+\ *adj* [*inter-* + *septal*] : situated between septa ⟨~ space⟩

intersert *vt* -ED/-ING/-S [L *intersertus*, past part. of *interserere*, fr. *inter-* + *serere* to join, bind together — more at SERIES] *obs* : INTERPOLATE, INSERT — **in·ter·ser·tion** *n* -s *obs*

in·ter·sertal \ˌintərˈsərdᵊl\ *adj* [G, fr. L *intersertus* + G *-al* (fr. L *-alis* -al)] *of an igneous rock* : of an ophitic texture in which the interstitial material is glass or a constituent other than augite

in·ter·service \ˌintə(r)+\ *adj* [*inter-* + *service*] : occurring between or relating to two or more of the armed services ⟨~ rivalry⟩

in·ter·sesamoid \"+\ *adj* [*inter-* + *sesamoid*] : situated between sesamoid bones ⟨~ ligament of a horse's fetlock⟩

in·ter·session \ˈintə(r)+,-\ *n* [*inter-* + *session*] : a period between two academic sessions or terms sometimes utilized (as in an adult education program) for brief concentrated courses — **in·ter·sessional** \ˌ==+\ *adj*

in·ter·set \ˌintə(r)+\ *adj* [*inter-* + *set* (past part.)] **1** : set between or among other things **2** : set about ⟨hills ~ with white villas⟩

in·ter·sex \ˈintə(r)+,-\ *n* [ISV *inter-* + *sex*] : an intersexual individual : an intergrade between the sexes

in·ter·sexual \ˌintə(r)+\ *adj* [ISV *inter-* + *sexual*] **1** : existing between sexes ⟨~ hostility⟩ **2** : intermediate in sexual characters between a typical male and a typical female — **in·ter·sexually** \"+\ *adv*

in·ter·sexuality \"+\ *or* **in·ter·sexualism** \"+\ *n* [ISV *inter-* + *sexuality* or *sexualism*] : the quality or state of being intersexual

in·ter·shoot \"+\ *vb* [*inter-* + *shoot*] *vi* : to shoot or flash at intervals ⟨hues . . . ~*ing* and to sight lost and recovered —William Wordsworth⟩ ~ *vt* : to intermingle with : color in streaks ⟨flames ~*ing* the dense smoke⟩

in·ter·social \"+\ *adj* [*inter-* + *social*] : relating to the mutual intercourse or relations of persons in society

in·ter·societal \"+\ *adj* [*inter-* + *societal*] : existing or occurring between societies ⟨~ comparisons of culture⟩

intersole *obs var of* ENTRESOL

in·ter·sow \"+\ *vt* [*inter-* + *sow*] **1** : to sow, scatter, or sprinkle among other things : INTERSPERSE **2** : to intersperse (a planting) with seed of another crop

¹**in·ter·space** \ˈintə(r)+,-\ *n* [*inter-* + *space* (n.); trans. of LL *interspatium*] **1** : intervening space or time : INTERVAL: as **a** : a space between printed letters **b** : an air space in a building **c** : the space between two related body parts whether void or filled by another kind of structure ⟨an ~ between dorsal fins⟩ ⟨the skin of the ~ between the 5th and 6th ribs⟩ **2** : interplanetary or interstellar space

²**in·ter·space** \ˌ==+\ *vt* [*inter-* + *space* (v.)] : to put an interval between (two things) : separate (as the members of a series) by spaces ⟨a line of *interspaced* hyphens⟩

in·ter·spatial \"+\ *adj* [LL *interspatium* (fr. L *inter-* + *spatium* space) + E *-al* — more at SPACE] : of or relating to an interspace — **in·ter·spatially** \"+\ *adv*

in·ter·specific \"+\ *or* **in·ter·species** \"+\ *adj* [*inter-* + *specific* or *species*] : existing between species ⟨~ hybrid⟩

in·ter·sper·sal \ˌintərˈspərsəl\ *n* -s [*intersperse* + *-al*] : INTERSPERSION

in·ter·sperse \ˌintərˈspərs, -təˈspə̄s, -pəis\ *vt* -ED/-ING/-S [L *interspersus* interspersed, fr. *inter-* + *sparsus*, past part. of *spargere* to strew, scatter — more at SPARK] **1** : to scatter or set here and there among things : insert at intervals ⟨~ pictures in a book⟩ **2** : to diversify or adorn with things set or scattered at intervals : place something at intervals in or among ⟨~ a book with pictures⟩

in·ter·spers·ed·ly \-sədlē\ *adv* : in an interspersed manner

in·ter·spersion \ˌintərˈspərzhən, təˈspə̄, -pəi\ *Brit usu & US sometimes* \shən\ *n* -s : the act or fact of interspersing or state of being interspersed: as **a** : the intermingling of kinds of organisms (as species) within an ecological community **b** : the state or degree of intermingling of one kind of organism with others ⟨certain forbs show a high level of ~ in grasslands⟩

in·ter·sphere \ˌintə(r)+\ *vi* [*inter-* + *sphere*] : to fall or come within the spheres or influences of one another

in·ter·spicular \"+\ *adj* [*inter-* + *spicular*] : situated between spicules

in·ter·spinal \"+\ *or* **in·ter·spinous** \"+\ *adj* [*inter-* + *spinal* or *spinous*] : lying between spines; *esp* : lying between the spines of adjacent vertebrae ⟨~ ligament⟩

in·ter·spi·na·lis \ˌintə(r),spīˈnaləs, -nāl-, -nal-\ *n, pl* **inter·spina·les** \-a(,)lēz, -ā(,)lēz, -ä,lās\ [NL, fr. *inter-* + LL *spinalis* spinal — more at SPINAL] : any of various short muscles connecting the spinous processes of contiguous vertebrae

in·ter·sporal \ˌintə(r)+\ *adj* [*inter-* + *sporal*] : situated between spores

in·ter·sprinkle \"+\ *vt* [*inter-* + *sprinkle*] : INTERSPERSE

in·ter·sta·di·al \ˌintə(r)ˈstādēəl\ *n* -s [ISV *inter-* + NL *stadium* + ISV *-al*] : a substage within a glacial stage marking a temporary retreat of the ice

in·ter·stage \ˌintə(r)+\ *adj* [*inter-* + *stage*] : placed between the stages ⟨~ steam turbine⟩ ⟨~ radio amplifier⟩

in·ter·state \"+\ *also* **in·ter·statal** \"+\ *adj* [*inter-* + *state* or *statal*] : relating to the mutual relations of states : existing between or including different states — used esp. of the states of the U.S. and of the states of Australia ⟨~ commerce⟩ ⟨~ highway⟩

interstate extradition *or* **interstate rendition** *n* : extradition from one of the states of the U.S. or one of its territories according to procedure authorized by the U.S. Constitution and by acts of Congress

in·ter·stellar \"+\ *adj* [*inter-* + *stellar*] : located among the stars of the Milky Way or of other galaxies or passing from one star to another ⟨~ space⟩

interstellar line *n* : one of the dark spectral lines of a star or other distant celestial body that is caused by the absorption of atoms and molecules in the intervening interstellar gas and that does not partake of the Doppler shift of the spectral lines produced in the star itself

in·ter·sterile \"+\ *adj* [*inter-* + *sterile*] : characterized by sterility in which pollen of either variety will not fertilize the other : mutually incapable of fertilizing ⟨~ subspecies of a plant⟩

in·ter·sterility \" +\ *n* [*inter-* + *sterility*] : the inability to produce offspring by interbreeding

in·ter·sternite \"+\ *n* [*inter-* + *sternite*] : an intersegmental plate on the undersurface of the insect abdomen

in·ter·stice \ənˈtərstəs, -tə̄s-, -təis-\ *n, pl* **interstic·es** \÷ -stə,sēz, -stəsəz\ [F, fr. LL *interstitium*, fr. L *interstitus* (past part. of *intersistere* to stand still or stop in the middle of something, fr. *inter-* + *sistere* to place, stand) + *-ium* (n. suffix) — more at SOLSTICE] **1** : a space that intervenes between one thing and another : a space between things (as the parts of a body) closely set : CRACK, CREVICE, INTERVAL ⟨~s of a wall⟩ ⟨the ~s of network⟩ **2 a** : an interval of time **b** *interstices pl* : the intervals that the canon law requires between the reception of the various degrees of orders in the Roman Catholic Church

in·ter·sticed \-stəst\ *adj* : provided with interstices : having interstices between : situated at intervals ⟨~ fence palings⟩

in·ter·stimulate \ˌintə(r)+\ *vt* [*inter-* + *stimulate*] : to stimulate reciprocally — **in·ter·stimulation** \"+\ *n*

¹**in·ter·sti·tial** *also* **in·ter·sti·cial** \ˌintə(r)ˈstishəl\ *adj* [*interstitial* fr. LL *interstitium* + E *-al*; *intersticial* alter. (influenced by *interstice*) of *interstitial*] **1** : relating to or situated in the interstices **2** : situated within but not restricted to or characteristic of a particular organ or tissue — used chiefly of isolated cells of uncertain origin and function and of the fibrous tissues that bind together cells and tissues **3** : affecting the interstitial tissues of an organ or part ⟨~ hepatitis⟩ **4** : relating to, characteristic of, or being a solid structure in which usu. smaller atoms or ions of one or more nonmetals occupy holes between larger metal atoms or ions in a crystal lattice ⟨~ carbides . . . in which the small carbon atoms occupy ~ positions in the crystal lattices of the metals—Therald Moeller⟩ — **in·ter·sti·tial·ly** \-shəlē, -li\ *adv*

²**interstitial** \"\ *n* -s : a plant growing in the interstices of an association

interstitial area *n* : a transitional urban area (as between an industrial and residential district) that may be characterized by a degree of cultural isolation and consequent incidence of crime and delinquency

interstitial-cell-stimulating hormone *n* : LUTEINIZING HORMONE

in·ter·sti·tium \ˌ==ˈstishēəm\ *n, pl* **intersti·tia** \-ēə\ [LL — more at INTERSTICE] **1** *obs* : INTERSTICE **2** [NL, fr. LL] : interstitial tissue

in·ter·stock \ˈintə(r)+,-\ *n* : INTERMEDIATE STOCK

in·ter·stratification \ˌintə(r)+\ *n* [*inter-* + *stratification*] : the state of being interstratified

in·ter·stratify \"+\ *vb* [*inter-* + *stratify*] *vt* : to insert between other strata : arrange in alternate strata ⟨lava flow *interstratified* with sedimentary rock⟩ ~ *vi* : to settle in layers between other layers

in·ter·stream \"+\ *adj* [*inter-* + *stream*] : situated between streams ⟨~ divide⟩

in·ter·strial \"+\ *adj* [*inter-* + L *stria* + E *-al*] : situated between striae

in·ter·subjective \"+\ *adj* [*inter-* + *subjective*] **1** : connecting or interrelating two consciousnesses or subjectivities ⟨~ communication⟩ **2** : existing between, accessible to, or capable of being established for two or more subjects : OBJECTIVE ⟨~ reality of the physical world⟩ — **in·ter·subjectively** \"+\ *adv* — **in·ter·subjectivity** \"+\ *n*

in·ter·tangle \"+\ *vt* [*inter-* + *tangle*] : ENTANGLE, INTERTWINE — **in·ter·tanglement** \"+\ *n* -s

in·ter·tentacular \"+\ *adj* [*inter-* + *tentacular*] : situated between tentacles

in·ter·tergal \"+\ *adj* [*inter-* + *tergal*] : situated between tergites

in·ter·tergite \"+\ *n* [*inter-* + *tergite*] : one of the small plates intercalated between the tergites of some insects

in·ter·terminal switching \"+...-\ *n, pl* **interterminal switchings** [*inter-* + *terminal*] : the moving of cars from a point on one railroad line to a point on another when both points are within the switching limits of the same station or industrial switching district — compare INTRATERMINAL SWITCHING

in·ter·territorial \"+\ *adj* [*inter-* + *territorial*] : existing or carried on between territories

in·ter·tessellation \"+\ *n* [*inter-* + *tessellation*] : intricate or complex interrelation comparable to a mosaic design

in·ter·testamental \"+\ *adj* [*inter-* + *testamental*] : of, relating to, or being the period of approximately two centuries between the composition of the last canonical book of the Old Testament and the writing of the books of the New Testament

in·ter·texture \"+\ *n* [*inter-* + *texture*] **1** : the act of interweaving or state of being interwoven **2** : something that is interwoven

in·ter·threaded \"+\ *adj* [*inter-* + *threaded*, past part. of *thread*] : intercrossed by or as if by interwoven threads

in·ter·tidal \"+\ *adj* [*inter-* + *tidal*] : of, relating to, or being the part of the littoral zone that is above low-tide mark ⟨~ faunal elements⟩ — **in·ter·ti·dal·ly** \"+\ *adv*

¹**in·ter·tie** \"+\ *vt* [*inter-* + *tie*] : to connect or fasten mutually ⟨~ power systems⟩

²**in·ter·tie** \ˈintə(r)+,-\ *n* **1** : a horizontal tie other than the sill and plate or other principal ties that secures uprights to one another in a framed work **2** : the act of intertying

in·ter·till \ˌintə(r)+\ *vt* [*inter-* + *till*] **1** : to cultivate between the rows of (a crop) **2** : INTERCROP

in·ter·tillage \"+\ *n* [*inter-* + *tillage*] : cultivation between rows of a crop

in·ter·tissued \"+\ *adj* [*inter-* + *tissue* + *-ed*; trans. of MF *entretissu*] : INTERWOVEN

in·ter·tone \ˈintə(r)+,-\ *n* [*inter-* + *tone*] : a tone of intermediate pitch heard when two other tones of slightly different pitches are sounded simultaneously

in·ter·tongue \"+\ *vi* [*inter-* + *tongue*] : INTERLOCK ⟨beds of dark limestone . . . ~ with the white limestone —C.O.Dunbar⟩

in·ter·tonic \"+\ *adj* [*inter-* + *tonic*] : occurring between stressed syllables (as *-con-* in *uncontested*)

in·ter·trabecular \"+\ *adj* [*inter-* + *trabecular*] : situated between trabeculae

in·ter·trade \"+\ *n* [*inter-* + *trade*] : reciprocal trade

in·ter·traffic \"+\ *n* [*inter-* + *traffic*] : mutual traffic or exchange ⟨a certain amount of legitimate ~ between Russia and the border countries —*Newsweek*⟩ ⟨literary ~ between England and Spain has been sporadic and haphazard —*Times Lit. Supp.*⟩

in·ter·tra·gi·an \ˌintə(r)ˈtrājēən\ *adj* [*inter-* + NL *tragus* + E *-ian*] : situated between the tragus and antitragus ⟨~ canal⟩

in·ter·transversalis \ˌintə(r)+\ *n* [NL, fr. *inter-* + *transversalis*] : any of a series of small muscles connecting the transverse processes of contiguous vertebrae and most highly developed in the neck

in·ter·trappean \"+\ *adj* [*inter-* + ⁵*trap* + *-ean*] : lying between successive basaltic lava flows

in·ter·tribal \"+\ *adj* [*inter-* + *tribal*] : existing or occurring between tribes ⟨~ warfare⟩ : common to or shared by several tribes ⟨~ problems⟩

in·ter·trig·i·nous \ˌintə(r)ˈtrijənəs\ *adj* [L *intertriginosus*, fr. *intertrigin-, intertrigo* + *-osus* -ous] : exhibiting or affected with intertrigo

in·ter·triglyph \ˌintə(r)+\ *n* [*inter-* + *triglyph*] : METOPE

in·ter·tri·go \ˌintə(r)ˈtrī(,)gō\ *n* -s [L, fr. *inter-* + *-trigo* (fr. *terere* to rub) — more at THROW] : inflammation produced by chafing of adjacent areas of skin

in·ter·trochanteric \ˌintə(r)+\ *adj* [*inter-* + *trochanteric*] : being or lying between trochanters

in·ter·tropical \"+\ *also* **in·ter·tropic** \"+\ *adj* [*inter-* + *tropical, tropic*] : situated between or within the tropics : relating to regions within the tropics : TROPICAL

intertropical front *n* : a zone of convergence of trade winds and equatorial winds often marked by heavy rains in tropical regions — compare DOLDRUM 3

in·ter·tropics \"+\ *n pl* : the zones between the tropics of Cancer and Capricorn or any region in them

in·ter·trude \ˌintə(r)ˈtrüd\ *vt* -ED/-ING/-S [LL *intertrudere*, fr. L *inter-* + *trudere* to thrust, push — more at THREAT] : to bring in intrusively : INTERPOLATE

in·ter·tubercular \ˌintə(r)+\ *adj* [*inter-* + *tubercular*] : situated between tubercles

in·ter·tubular \"+\ *adj* [*inter-* + *tubular*] : lying between tubules

in·ter·twine \ˌintə(r)ˈtwīn\ *vb* [*inter-* + *twine*] *vt* : to unite by twining one with another : ENTANGLE, INTERLACE, INTERTWIST ⟨the sex impulse is closely *intertwined* with the life impulse—Susanne K. Langer⟩ ~ *vi* : to twine about one another : become mutually entangled or involved ⟨theological concepts are inevitably *intertwining* —Robert Root⟩ — **in·ter·twine·ment** \-nmənt\ *n* -s

in·ter·twin·ing·ly *adv* : in an intertwining manner

¹**in·ter·twist** \ˌintə(r)+\ *vb* [*inter-* + *twist*] *vt* : to twist together one with another : INTERTWINE ⟨so ~*ed* are our emotions —Roger Fry⟩ ~ *vi* : to twist about one another ⟨~*ing* tendrils⟩

²**in·ter·twist** \ˈ==+,-\ *n* : an act or fact of intertwisting : the state of being intertwisted : TANGLE ⟨peering through an ~ of vines and shrubs⟩

in·ter·university \ˌintə(r)+\ *adj* [*inter-* + *university*] : existing or carried on between universities ⟨~ research⟩

in·ter·urban \"+\ *adj* [*inter-* + *urban*] : going between or connecting cities or towns ⟨~ electric railways⟩ ⟨~ buses⟩

in·ter·val \ˈintə(r)vəl\ *n* -s [ME *intervalle*, fr. MF, fr. L *intervallum* space between ramparts, interval, fr. *inter-* + *vallum* rampart — more at WALL] **1 a** : a space of time between the recurrences of similar conditions or states : PAUSE ⟨~ between coughing spells⟩ ⟨~s of sanity⟩ ⟨~ of thousands of years between glaciations⟩ **b** *Brit* : INTERMISSION **c** : the time between two events or points of time ⟨firing at ~s of ten minutes⟩ ⟨~ between a lightning flash and the following thunder⟩ **d** : a portion of the total time cycle of a traffic signal during which the signal indications do not change **2 a** : a space between things : empty space between objects ⟨posts set up at regular ~s along the road⟩ ⟨buildings placed at wide ~s⟩ **b** (1) : the space between elements in military formation in the direction of width — contrasted with *distance* (2) : the distance between the foremasts of the guides of adjacent units in a compound naval formation **c** : the relative difference in pitch between two simultaneous or successive notes or tones **3** : something that breaks or interrupts a uniform series or surface : an intervening part ⟨grazing land with brief ~s of forest⟩ ⟨the road follows a winding course except for a few straight ~s⟩ **4** *chiefly NewEng* : BOTTOM 6 **5 a** : the totality of numbers belonging to a given set of real numbers **b** : the totality of such numbers between and either including or excluding one or both of two end numbers of the set **c** : the totality of such numbers greater or less than and either including or excluding one of the numbers of the set **d** : a set of points on a line segment that represents one of these totalities **6** : a gap between different qualities or states that may be ideally filled with intervening grades ⟨~ between savagery and culture⟩ ⟨~ between landlord and tenant, master and servant, was less —T.B.Macaulay⟩ **syn** see BREAK

in·ter·vale \-,vāl, -,vəl\ *n* [fr. obs. E *intervale* interval, fr. ME *intervalle*; influenced in meaning by *vale*] *chiefly NewEng* : BOTTOM 6 ⟨~ land⟩

in·ter·valed \ˈintə(r)vəld\ *adj* [*interval* + *-ed*] : having intervals : interrupted at intervals : placed at intervals ⟨march is being made with platoons ~ at two yards —Peter Bowman⟩

in·ter·val·lic \ˌintə(r)ˈvalik\ *adj* [*interval* + *-ic*] : of or relating to an interval ⟨~ relationships of the notes of a melody⟩

in·ter·val·om·e·ter \ˌintə(r)vəˈlämədə(r)\ *n* [*interval* + *-o-* + *-meter*] : a device that operates a control at regular intervals; *specif* : an electrical device that regulates the interval between exposures made with an aerial camera

interval timer *n* : TIMER 1a

in·ter·varietal \ˌintə(r)+\ *adj* [*inter-* + *varietal*] : obtaining between varieties ⟨~ sterility⟩ ⟨~ differences in basal metabolism⟩

in·ter·varsity \"+\ *adj* [*inter-* + *varsity*] *Brit* : INTERUNIVERSITY ⟨~ sports⟩

in·ter·vascular \"+\ *adj* [*inter-* + *vascular*] **1** : lying between or surrounded by blood vessels **2** : situated within a seed vessel or vascular structure

in·ter·vein \"+\ *vt* [*inter-* + *vein*] : to interlace with or as if with veins

in·ter·veinal \"+\ *adj* [*inter-* + *veinal*] : situated or occurring between veins

in·ter·vene \ˌintə(r)ˈvēn\ *vb* -ED/-ING/-S [L *intervenire*, lit., to come between, fr. *inter-* + *venire* to come — more at COME] *vi* **1** : to enter or appear as an irrelevant or extraneous feature or circumstance ⟨business seldom follows any projected course exactly, because unforeseeable developments . . . ~ —*Fortune*⟩ **2** : to occur, fall, or come between points of time or events ⟨an instant *intervened* between the flash and the report⟩ ⟨*intervening* years⟩ **3** : to come in or between by way of hindrance or modification : INTERPOSE ⟨~ to settle a quarrel⟩ ⟨death *intervened* soon after⟩ **4** : to occur or lie between two things ⟨Paris, where the same city lay on both sides of an *intervening* river —*Amer. Guide Series: N. Y. City*⟩ **5 a** : to become a party to an action or other legal proceeding begun by others for the protection of an alleged interest **b** : to interfere usu. by force or threat of force in another nation's domestic affairs in order to protect the lives or property of the nationals of the interfering nation or to further some other purpose deemed vital to its welfare ⟨sending troops overseas to ~ in a civil war⟩ ~ *vt, obs* : to come between : interfere with

in·ter·ven·er *also* **in·ter·ve·nor** \-nə(r)\ *n* -s : one that intervenes

in·ter·ve·nience \ˌ==ˈvēnyən(t)s\ *n* -s : the act or fact of intervening : INTERVENTION

¹**in·ter·ve·nient** \ˌ==ˈvēnyənt\ *adj* [L *intervenient-, interveniens*, pres. part. of *intervenire*] **1** : being or coming in incidentally or extraneously ⟨~ circumstances⟩ **2** : situated or occurring between different points or events : INTERVENING ⟨deep ~ ravines —C.E.Craddock⟩ **3** : INTERMEDIARY

²**intervenient** \"\ *n* -s : one that intervenes

in·ter·ven·tion \ˌ==ˈvenchən\ *n* -s [LL *intervention-, interventio*, fr. L *interventus* (past part. of *intervenire* to intervene) + *-ion-, -io* -ion] **1** : the act or fact of intervening : INTERPOSITION ⟨~ of divine providence⟩ ⟨surgical ~⟩ **2** : interference that may affect the interests of others: as **a** *civil law* : the act of a person who pays commercial paper for honor — called also *payment by intervention* **b** : the act by which a third person in order to protect his own interest interposes and becomes a party to a legal proceeding pending between other parties **c** : the interference of a country in the affairs of another country for the purpose of compelling it to do or forbear doing certain acts or of maintaining or altering the actual condition of its domestic affairs irrespective of its will ⟨spurred Paris and London into armed ~ —T.A.Bailey⟩ — compare MEDIATION — **in·ter·ven·tion·al** \ˌ==ˈvenchənᵊl, -chnəl\ *adj*

in·ter·ven·tion·ism \-chə,nizəm\ *n* -s : the theory or practice of intervening : interference (as by a government) in economic affairs at home or in political affairs of another country — compare ISOLATIONISM, LAISSEZ-FAIRE

in·ter·ven·tion·ist \-,nəst\ *n* -s : one that intervenes or favors intervention

in·ter·ven·tor \-ˈventə(r)\ *n* -s [L, fr. *interventus* (past part. of *intervenire* to intervene) + *-or* — more at INTERVENE] **1** : a person designated by a church to reconcile parties and unite them in the choice of officers **2** : a temporary administrator (as of a province in Central America or So. America) in time of disturbance

¹**in·ter·ventral** \ˌintə(r)+\ *adj* [*inter-* + *ventral*] : of or relating to the posterior pair of primitive ventral structural elements of a typical vertebra

²**interventral** \"\ *n* : an interventral cartilage or ossification

in·ter·ventricular \"+\ *adj* [*inter-* + *ventricular*] : situated between ventricles ⟨~ septa⟩

interventricular foramen \"+. . .-\ *n* : FORAMEN OF MONRO

interversion *n* -s [LL *interversion-, interversio*, fr. L *interversus* (past part. of *intervertere*) + *-ion-, -io* -ion] *obs* : MISAPPROPRIATION, EMBEZZLEMENT

intervert *vt* -ED/-ING/-S [L *intervertere*, lit., to turn aside, fr. *inter-* + *vertere* to turn — more at WORTH] **1** *obs* : to turn to a course or use other than the proper one : MISUSE; *esp* : EMBEZZLE **2** *obs* : CHANGE, INVERT

in·ter·vertebral \ˌintə(r)+\ *adj* [*inter-* + *vertebral*] : situated between vertebrae — **in·ter·vertebrally** \"+\ *adv*

intervertebral disk *n* : one of the tough elastic disks that are interposed between the centra of adjoining vertebrae and that consist of an outer fibrous ring enclosing an inner pulpy nucleus

in·ter·vesicular \"+\ *adj* [*inter-* + *vesicular*] : lying between vesicles

¹**in·ter·view** \ˈintə(r),vyü\ *n* [alter. (influenced by *inter-*) of earlier *enterview*, fr. MF *entrevue*, fr. fem. of *entrevu*, past part. of (*s'*)*entrevoir* to see one another, meet, fr. *entre-* inter- + *voir* to see —more at VIEW] **1 a** *obs* : a mutual sight or view **b** : a meeting face to face : a private conversation; *usu* : a

formal meeting for consultation : CONFERENCE ⟨candidates for the position were called in for ~*s*⟩ **c :** a transient or secret meeting (as of lovers) ⟨the stolen ~*s* of those spring mornings —William Black⟩ **2 a :** a meeting in which a writer or reporter or radio or television commentator obtains information from someone for publication or broadcast **b :** the statement so obtained **c :** a news story reporting or reproducing such a conversation **3 :** a scheduled meeting between a teacher and a student for purposes of instruction or counseling

²interview \"\ *vt* **:** to have an interview with **:** question or converse with esp. in order to obtain information or ascertain personal qualities ⟨~*ing* job applicants⟩ ⟨~ housewives about their color preferences⟩ ⟨~*ing* witnesses in a criminal investigation⟩ ⟨~*ed* the highest government officials and even strangers on buses —J.M.Mead⟩ **~** *vi* **:** to carry on an interview ⟨technique of ~*ing*⟩

in·ter·view·ee \ˌ==ˌvyüˈē\ *n* -s [²*interview* + *-ee*] **:** one that is interviewed ⟨~*s* voted 22 percent for giving food to western Europe —*Newsweek*⟩

in·ter·view·er \ˈ==ˌvyü(ə)r\ *n* **:** one that interviews: *specif* **:** a clerk who does preliminary interviewing of applicants for employment and arranges interviews with the employing officials

in·ter·villous \ˌintə(r)+\ *adj* [*inter-* + *villous*] **:** situated between villi

in·ter·visibility \"+\ *n* **:** the quality or state of being mutually visible

in·ter·visible \"+\ *adj* [*inter-* + *visible*] **:** mutually visible ⟨~ surveying stations⟩

in·ter·visit \"+\ *vi* [alter. (influenced by *inter-*) of F *entrevisiter*, fr. MF, fr. *entre-* + *visiter* to visit — more at VISIT] **:** to exchange visits

in·ter·visitation \"+\ *n* [*inter-* + *visitation*] **:** exchange of visits **:** mutual visiting ⟨classroom ~*s* of schoolteachers⟩

in·ter·vital \"+\ *adj* [*inter-* + *vital*] **:** occurring between two lives

in·ter vi·vos \ˌintə(r)ˈvēˌvōs, -ˈvīˌv-\ *adv* (*or adj*) [L] **:** between living persons **:** from one living person to another ⟨transaction *inter vivos*⟩ ⟨*inter vivos* trust⟩ — compare DONATIO MORTIS CAUSA

in·ter·vo·cal·ic \ˌintə(r)(ˌ)vōˈkalik, -lēk\ *also* **in·ter·vocal** \ˌ==ˈvōkəl\ *adj* [*inter-* + *vocalic* or *vocal*] **:** immediately preceded and immediately followed by a vowel ⟨~ consonant⟩ — **in·ter·vo·cal·i·cal·ly** \ˌ==(ˌ)=ˈ=lək(ə)lē, -lēk-, -li\ *adv*

in·ter·vo·lu·tion \ˌintə(r)vəˈlüshən\ *n* [fr. *intervolve*, after such pairs as E *revolve: revolution*] **:** the state or fact of being intervolved or coiled up

in·ter·volve \ˌintə(r)ˈvälv, -ˈvȯlv\ *vb* -ED/-ING/-S [*inter-* + *-volve* (as in *involve*)] *vt* **:** to involve or roll up one within another ⟨mazes intricate, eccentric, *intervolved* —John Milton⟩ **~** *vi* **:** to twist or coil within one another

in·ter·war \ˌintə(r)+\ *adj* [*inter-* + *war* (n.)] **:** lying between wars ⟨~ years⟩

¹in·ter·weave \"+\ *vb* [*inter-* + *weave*] *vt* **1 :** to weave together ⟨*interweaving* a wool warp with a silk weft⟩ **2 :** to intermingle or blend together ⟨*interweaving* his own insights . . . with letters and memoirs —Phoebe Adams⟩ **~** *vi* **:** INTERTWINE, INTERMINGLE

²in·ter·weave \ˈintə(r)+ˌ-\ *n* **:** the act or result of interweaving ⟨~ of caste and religion . . . is so close that each merges into and is part of the other —Andrew Mellon⟩

in·ter·wed \ˌintə(r)+\ *vi* [*inter-* + *wed*] **:** INTERMARRY

in·ter·wind \"+\ *vb* [*inter-* + *wind*] **:** INTERTWINE, INTERVOLVE

in·ter·word \"+\ *adj* [*inter-* + *word* (n.)] **:** occurring between words ⟨~ juncture⟩

in·ter·work \"+\ *vb* [*inter-* + *work*] *vt* **:** to work into something else **:** INTERWEAVE **~** *vi* **:** to work with or act upon each other **:** INTERACT

in·ter·world \ˈintə(r)+ˌ-\ *n* [*inter-* + *world*] **:** a world existing between other worlds ⟨~*s* of the imagination⟩

in·ter·wo·ven \ˌintə(r)ˈwōvən\ *adj* [fr. past part. of *interweave*] **:** woven together in texture or construction

in·ter·wo·ven·ness \-n(n)əs\ *n* -ES **:** the quality or state of being interwoven **:** close or inseparable connection

in·ter·wreathe \ˌintə(r)+\ *vb* [*inter-* + *wreathe*] **:** INTERTWINE

in·ter·wrought \"+\ *adj* [*inter-* + *wrought*] **:** worked into or through one another **:** complexly associated

in·ter·xylary \"+\ *adj* [*inter-* + *xylem* + *-ary*] **:** existing among xylem elements

in·ter·zonal \"+\ *or* **in·ter·zone** \"+\ *adj* [*inter-* + *zonal* or *zone*] **:** occurring or carried on between zones ⟨~ travel⟩ ⟨~ competition⟩

in·ter·zooecial \"+\ *adj* [*inter-* + *zooecial*] **:** existing between or among zooecia

in·tes·ta·ble \(ˈ)inˈtestəbəl, ənˈt-\ *adj* [LL *intestabilis*, fr. L, execrable, accursed, fr. *in-* ¹in- + *testari* to be a witness, make a will + *-abilis* -able] **1 :** not competent to make a will ⟨an ~ minor⟩ ⟨insane and ~⟩ **2** *obs* **:** incompetent to be a witness

in·tes·ta·cy \ənˈtestəsē, -si\ *n* [¹*intestate* + *-cy*] **:** the quality or state of being or dying intestate

¹in·tes·tate \ənˈteˌstā|t, -ˌstə|, *usu* |d·+V\ *adj* [ME, fr. L *intestatus*, fr. *in-* ¹in- + *testatus*, past part. of *testari* to be a witness, make a will, fr. *testis* witness — more at TESTAMENT] **1 :** having made no valid will ⟨die ~⟩ **2 :** not bequeathed or devised **:** not disposed of by will ⟨an ~ estate⟩ ⟨the administration of ~ property⟩

²intestate \"\ *n* -s **:** one who dies intestate

in·tes·ti·nal \ənˈtestənᵊl, *in rapid speech* -s(ᵊ)nəl; *sometimes chiefly Brit* ˌinˌteˈstīn-\ *adj* [prob. fr. MF, fr. *intestin* + *-al*] **1 a :** of or relating to the intestine ⟨the ~ tube⟩ ⟨~ ferments⟩ **:** affecting the intestine ⟨~ catarrh⟩ **:** taking place in the intestine ⟨~ digestion⟩ **b :** living within the intestine ⟨the ~ flora⟩ ⟨an ~ worm⟩ **2 :** suggesting an intestine: as **a :** being internal or subterranean ⟨the rumbling ~ routes of the subways —Molly L. Bar-David⟩ **b :** intricately circuitous or involute ⟨tangled carvings in gluttonous ~ designs —Peggy Bacon⟩ **syn** see INNER

intestinal calculus *or* **intestinal concretion** *n* **:** DUST BALL

intestinal canal *n* **:** INTESTINE

intestinal flu *n* **:** any of various acute usu. transitory gastrointestinal conditions marked by nausea, vomiting, diarrhea, and griping pains

intestinal fortitude *n* **:** COURAGE, STAMINA, GUTS ⟨the qualities we have discussed — common sense, *intestinal fortitude*, leadership . . . are not the only ones desirable in a second lieutenant —*Infantry Jour.*⟩ ⟨only a man of powerful will and *intestinal fortitude* could have done these things —*Newsweek*⟩

in·tes·ti·nal·ly \-ᵊlē, -əl|, |i\ *adv* **:** in or upon the intestines

¹in·tes·tine \ənˈtestən, *chiefly dial* -ˌstīn\ *adj* [MF or L; MF *intestin*, fr. L *intestinus*, fr. *intus* within — more at ENT-] **1 a :** of or relating to the internal affairs of a state or country — usu. used of something evil or troublesome ⟨an ~ disorder⟩ ⟨an ~ calamity⟩ ⟨~ war⟩ **b :** of or relating to the internal parts of the body **2 :** INWARD ⟨an ~ necessity⟩ **3** *obs* **:** INTERNAL **syn** see INNER

²intestine \"\ *n* -s [MF *intestin*, fr. L *intestinum*, fr. neut. of *intestinus*] **1 :** the tubular portion of the alimentary canal that in the vertebrate lies posterior to the stomach from which it is separated by the pyloric valve and consists typically of a slender but long anterior part made up of duodenum, jejunum, and ileum which function in digestion and assimilation of nutrients and a broader shorter posterior part made up usu. of cecum, colon, and rectum which serve chiefly to extract moisture from the by-products of digestion and evaporate them into feces — often used in pl. ⟨the shot pierced his ~*s* in several places⟩ — see LARGE INTESTINE, SMALL INTESTINE **2 :** the entire alimentary canal esp. when more or less straight and tubular (as in many invertebrates)

in·tes·ti·ni·form \-ˌstənəˌfȯrm\ *adj* [²*intestine* + *-iform*] **:** like an intestine in form

in·tes·ti·no·intestinal \ənˌtestə(ˌ)nō+\ *adj* [²*intestine* + *-o-* + *intestinal*] **:** originating in and acting on the intestine ⟨an ~ reflex⟩

in·tes·ti·no·vesical \"+\ *adj* [²*intestine* + *-o-* + *vesical*] **:** of or relating to the intestine and bladder

in·tex·ine \ˈinˌtekˌsēn, |īn\ *or* **in·tex·tine** \-kˌst|\ *n* -s [*intexine* fr. G, fr. *int-* (fr. L *intus* within) + *exine*; *intextine* alter. (influenced by *extine*) of *intexine*] **:** the inner membrane of the exine when this exists in two layers

intg *abbr* interrogate; interrogator

inthrall *or* **inthral** *vt* **inthralled; inthralled; inthralling; inthralls** *or* **inthrals** [by alter. (influenced by ²*in-*)] **:** ENTHRALL

inthralment *n* -s *archaic* **:** ENTHRALLMENT

inthronization *n* -s [MF or ML; MF *intronisation*, fr. ML *inthronization-*, *inthronizatio*, fr. LL *inthronizatus* (past part. of *inthronizare* to enthrone, modif. — influenced by L *in-* ²in- — of Gk *enthronizein*) + L *-ion-*, *-io* -ion — more at ENTHRONIZE] **:** ENTHRONEMENT, ENTHRONIZATION

¹inthrow \ˈ=ˌ=\ *n* [⁴*in* + *throw* (after *throw in*, v.)] **:** the act or process of throwing soil toward the crop by the cultivating gangs of a row-crop cultivator; *also* **:** the amount of soil thrown

²inthrow \"\ *vt* **:** RIDGE *vt* 2b

intice *archaic var of* ENTICE

in·ti·chi·u·ma \ˌintēchēˈümə\ *n*, *pl* **intichiuma** *usu cap* [native name in central Australia] **:** an Australian magical ceremony having as its object the increase of a clan's totemic species

in·til *or* **in·till** \ənˈtil\ *prep* [ME, fr. ²*in* + *til, till* to — more at TILL] *chiefly Scot* **:** IN, INTO

in·ti·ma \ˈintəmə\ *n*, *pl* **inti·mae** \-ˌmē, -ˌmī\ *or* **intimas** [NL, fr. L, fem. of *intimus* innermost] **1 :** the innermost coat of an organ (as a blood vessel or lymphatic) consisting (as in larger blood vessels) of an endothelial lining backed by a layer of connective tissue and one of elastic tissue **2 :** the innermost coat of a trachea of an insect — **in·ti·mal** \-məl\ *adj*

in·ti·ma·cy \ˈintəməsē, -si\ *n* -ES [²*intimate* + *-cy*] **1 :** the state of being intimate: as **a :** close association or connection ⟨the furnishings suggested at least some ~ with the outside world —C.L.Jones⟩ ⟨in the city you are more free from unwelcome ~ —M.R.Cohen⟩ **b :** close personal relationship esp. marked by affection or love (as in close friendship) ⟨a long ~ with the governor of the state⟩ ⟨long continued ~ with the fields and meadows about him —*Encyc. Americana*⟩ ⟨a common danger had made of these two enemies friends . . . and now that the danger had passed their ~ was done —Jack McLaren⟩ **c :** a relationship marked by depth of knowledge or broadness of information ⟨his ~ with the history of the middle ages⟩ **d :** complete intermixture, compounding, or interweaving ⟨would call for some effort to disentangle a relationship of things marked by such ~⟩ **2 :** the quality or state of being careful and searching in notation of details ⟨an ~ of observation which few scientists can equal —H.S.Canby⟩ **3 a :** a sexual liberty taken ⟨resented the pawing *intimacies* of the man who was driving the car —Erle Stanley Gardner⟩; *specif* **:** sexual intercourse ⟨denied charges of having an affair with a married woman . . . though she said ~ between them had taken place about 25 times —*New York Enquirer*⟩ or an instance of it ⟨indications that she had recently experienced an ~ —R.O.Lawson & S.D.Greene⟩ **b :** an objectionable liberty taken with the person ⟨became embarrassingly familiar with the *intimacies* of fame —Green Peyton⟩ **4 :** the ability of affecting one in a usu. pleasant intimate personal way ⟨music marked by an ~ of expression⟩ **5 :** the state of seeming to be in a close friendly personal relationship — used of inanimate things ⟨the almost cloistered ~ of much of the route —*Amer. Guide Series: Vt.*⟩ **6 :** the capacity for establishing oneself quickly in an intimate personal relationship ⟨only one other man possessing this curious ~ with wild things —Edison Marshall⟩

in·ti·ma·do \ˌintəˈmä(ˌ)dō\ *n* -s [prob. alter. (influenced by Sp *-ado*, as in *renegado*) of ³*intimate*] *archaic* **:** an intimate friend **:** INTIMATE

¹in·ti·mate \ˈintəˌmāt, *usu* -ād·+V\ *vt* -ED/-ING/-S [LL *intimatus*, past part. of *intimare* to make known, fr. L *intimus* innermost, superl. of (assumed) OL *interus* inward, on the inside — more at INTERIOR] **1 :** to give notice of **:** ANNOUNCE, NOTIFY **2 :** to impart or communicate with delicate or indirect wording or covert slight gesture without forthright blunt expression ⟨said that he . . . might not be able to say all that he thought, thus *intimating* to his hearers that they might infer that he meant more —O.W.Holmes †1935⟩ **syn** see SUGGEST

²in·ti·mate \-ˌmət, *usu* -əd·+V\ *adj* [LL *intimatus*, past part. of *intimare* to make known; E *intimate* influenced in meaning by L *intimus* innermost] **1 a :** of or relating to an inner character or essential nature **:** INNERMOST **:** characteristic of the genuine core of something ⟨it is in the purposes he entertains . . . that an individual most completely . . . realizes his ~ selfhood —John Dewey⟩ **b :** belonging to or characterizing the inmost true self **:** indicative of one's deepest nature ⟨his ~ reflections⟩ **2 :** marked by a very close physical, mental, or social association, connection, or contact: as **a :** showing complete intermixture, compounding, fusion **:** thoroughly or closely interconnected, interrelated, interwoven ⟨the ~ relations . . . between economics, politics, and legal principles —V.L.Parrington⟩ ⟨an ~ mixture of rock particles⟩ ⟨an ~ affiliation of house and garden —*Amer. Guide Series: N.Y.*⟩ **b :** showing depth of detailed knowledge and understanding and broadness of information from or as if from long association, near contact, or thorough study and observation ⟨this girl, so ~ with nature —W.H.Hudson †1922⟩ ⟨an ~ knowledge of admiralty law —H.W.H.Knott⟩ **c :** marked by or as if by knowledge of esp. personal details which only an eyewitness or very close confidant might have ⟨of St. Francis and St. Bernard their ~ biographers assure us that . . . they . . . never allowed themselves actual laughter —G.G.Coulton⟩ **d :** marked by or as if by a warmly personal attitude esp. developing through long or close association, by friendliness, unreserved communication, mutual appreciation and interest ⟨pretend that they are in smart society and on ~ terms with people they slander —Oscar Wilde⟩ **:** manifesting warm personal interest ⟨his voice low, ~, full of meaning —Aurelia Levi⟩ **:** arousing a warm personal response ⟨a lyrical and ~ painting⟩ **e :** showing or fostering close personal interests and relations rather than those colder and more distant, formal, or routine **:** suggesting or furthering easy unreserved personal expression, feeling, or relationships through smallness, exclusiveness, limitation, or privacy ⟨an ~ sense of being a member of some mystic brotherhood —W.S.Maugham⟩ ⟨the ~ politics of the eighteenth century were an involved web of human passions —J.H.Plumb⟩ ⟨two plush rooms, one formal, the other cozy and ~ —T.H.Fielding⟩ ⟨an ~ theater that served coffee between its films⟩ ⟨an ~ cocktail lounge⟩; *also* **:** designed or composed chiefly for presentation to a small group ⟨~ opera⟩ ⟨~ music⟩ **f :** marked by or appropriate to very close personal relationships **:** marked by or befitting a relationship of love, warm or ardent liking, deep friendship, or mutual cherishing ⟨always ~ relations between a mother and her young child —Edward Westermarck⟩ ⟨their hand grasp was very ~ and mutually comprehending —Arnold Bennett⟩ **g :** of, relating to, or befitting deeply personal (as emotional, familial, or sexual) matters or matters usu. kept private or discreet ⟨to his intensely aristocratic nature this discussion of his ~ family affairs . . . was most abhorrent —A. Conan Doyle⟩ ⟨clean-minded youth horrifies its elders by facing the ~ facts of life —G.A.Bartlett⟩ **h :** engaged in or marked by sexual relations **:** SEXUAL, MARITAL ⟨ladies were supposed to be without sexual desire . . . in their ~ relations with their husbands they consented graciously —W.E.Woodward⟩ **i :** worn next to the skin ⟨~ underwear⟩ **:** worn in the home ⟨an ~ negligee⟩ **j :** designed or prepared (as by waterproofing) for immediate contact with something to be wrapped ⟨the efficiency of ~ wraps and carton overwraps in preventing corrosion —*Corrosion & Material Protection*⟩ ⟨aluminum foil laminated to paper finds use as an ~ wrapper for a variety of products —N.A.Cooke⟩ **syn** see FAMILIAR

³intimate \"\ *n* -s **:** one who associates or has associated intimately (as with a person or place) ⟨writes as one who . . . has been an ~ of the Parisian scene —R.J.Goldwater⟩ **:** an intimate friend or confidant ⟨counted a banker among his ~*s*⟩ **syn** see FRIEND

in·ti·mate·ly \-ˌmətlē, -li\ *adv* **:** in an intimate manner ⟨the physical and the economic background of poverty are most ~ related —P.E.James⟩ ⟨a city she knows ~ —*Americas*⟩ ⟨every one of which he could have named ~ had he put his memory to it —Kay Boyle⟩ ⟨the author leads his audience easily and ~ —S.W.Reed⟩

in·ti·mate·ness \-ˌmətnəs\ *n* -ES **:** INTIMACY

in·ti·mat·er \-ˌmād·ə(r), -ātə-\ *n* -s [¹*intimate* + *-er*] **:** one that intimates

in·ti·ma·tion \ˌintəˈmāshən\ *n* -s [ME *intimacion*, fr. MF *intimation*, fr. LL *intimation-*, *intimatio*, fr. *intimatus* (past part. of *intimare*) + L *-ion-*, *-io* -ion] **1 :** the act of intimating or the state of being intimated: as **a :** ANNOUNCEMENT, NOTIFICATION **b :** an indirect usu. hinted suggestion or notice ⟨~*s* of immortality —William Wordsworth⟩ ⟨gave only ~ of the fact he was guilty of rudeness⟩ **2 :** something intimated ⟨never learned what his ~ was⟩

in·time \aⁿtēm\ *adj* [F, fr. L *intimus* innermost] **:** INTIMATE

in·tim·i·date \ənˈtiməˌdāt, *usu* -ād·+V\ *vt* -ED/-ING/-S [ML *intimidatus*, past part. of *intimidare*, fr. L *in-* ²in- + *timidus* timid] **:** to make timid or fearful **:** inspire or affect with fear **:** FRIGHTEN ⟨despite his imposing presence and all the grandeur surrounding him, I was not *intimidated* —Polly Adler⟩; *esp* **:** to compel to action or inaction (as by threats) ⟨charged with *intimidating* public officials to get the government to buy machine guns he was selling —*Time*⟩

syn INTIMIDATE, COW, BULLDOZE, BULLY, BROWBEAT agree in meaning to frighten or coerce by frightening means into submission or obedience. INTIMIDATE suggests a display or application (as of force or learning) so as to cause fear or a sense of inferiority and a consequent submission ⟨most of these officials have been badly *intimidated* by the specter of a summons to appear before a Congressional committee —*New Republic*⟩ ⟨many authors and publishers are not merely *intimidated* by the thought of footnotes; they are positively terrified —G.W. Sherburn⟩ COW implies a reduction to a state where the spirit is broken or all courage lost ⟨*cowed* into cooperation through fear of the gangsters —Michael Blundell⟩ ⟨*cowed* the gang with his detective's star —J.T.Farrell⟩ ⟨a ship's company *cowed* to groveling point —John Masefield⟩ BULLDOZE, in its earliest sense signifying to intimidate or coerce by violence, now often can mean to force into line by an application of great force, not necessarily implying though often involving intimidation ⟨a *bulldozed* people, shaking with the ague of the terrorized — W.L.Sullivan⟩ ⟨the sheer strength of his reputation and the force of his will *bulldozing* them into making loans —F.L. Allen⟩ ⟨the highly reputable gentlemen who were *bulldozed* into taking this responsibility have resigned —Robert Moses⟩ BULLY implies intimidation or attempts to intimidate by swaggering overbearing behavior or by the use of unfair force ⟨a mild, long-suffering woman will permit her husband to *bully* her for years, whereas another woman will react violently to the first beating —Jacob Fried⟩ ⟨inevitable that the older boys should become mischievous louts; they *bullied* and tormented and corrupted the younger boys —H.G.Wells⟩ BROWBEAT implies a cowing by scornful contemptuous treatment, esp. intellectual or moral oppression ⟨were *browbeaten* in the hardest and most menial tasks —F.V.W.Mason⟩ ⟨no wish to *browbeat* the reader into accepting my theory of myself or of anything else —George Santayana⟩ ⟨*browbeat* students by a great display of learning⟩

in·tim·i·da·tion \ənˌtiməˈdāshən\ *n* -s [F, fr. MF, fr. *intimider* (fr. ML *intimidare* to intimidate) + *-ation*] **:** the act of intimidating or the state of being intimidated ⟨the voters were kept from the polls by ~⟩ ⟨cringed to see the woman's ~ before her husband's cruelty⟩

in·tim·i·da·tor \ənˈtiməˌdād·ə(r), -ātə-\ *n* -s **:** one that intimidates

in·tim·i·da·to·ry \-ˌdəˌtōrē, *chiefly Brit* =ˌ=ˈdātəri *or* -ā·tri\ *adj* [*intimidate* + *-ory*] **:** tending to intimidate ⟨an ~ array of obstacles —F.S.Mitchell⟩ **:** designed to intimidate ⟨the similarity, in some species, between ~ and courtship displays —E.A. Armstrong⟩

in·ti·mism \ˈintəˌmizəm\ *n* -s [*intimist* + *-ism*] **:** a principle or practice among painters (as in early 20th century France) of selecting as subject matter familiar or intimate scenes or occasions from their own everyday life — compare GENRE

¹in·ti·mist \-ˌməst\ *n* -s *often cap* [F *intimiste*, fr. *intime* intimate + *-iste* -ist] **:** an intimist painter

²intimist \"\ *adj, often cap* **1 :** of, relating to, or practicing intimism **2** *of fiction* **:** dealing chiefly with intimate and private esp. psychological experiences ⟨the peculiarly modern feeling of individual helplessness that the war brought into . . . people's consciousness, and it made sense of that emotion as the ~ novel does not as a rule —Anthony West⟩

in·tim·i·ty \ənˈtiməd·ē\ *n* -ES [F *intimité*, fr. *intime* intimate + *-ité* -ity] *archaic* **:** intimate privacy

in·tinc·tion \ənˈtiŋ(k)shən\ *n* -s [LL *intinction-*, *intinctio* immersion, fr. L *intinctus* (past part. of *intingere* to dip in, fr. *in* ²in- + *tingere* to dip, moisten) + *-ion-*, *-io* -ion — more at TINGE] **:** the administration of the sacrament of Communion by dipping the bread in the wine and giving both together to the communicant

in·tine \ˈinˌtēn, -tīn\ *n* -s [prob. fr. G, fr. L *intus* within, in — more at ENT-] **:** the inner of the two layers forming the wall of a spore (as a pollen grain) — called also *endosporium*; compare EXINE, PERINIUM

intire *archaic var of* ENTIRE

in·ti·sy \ˈintəsē\ *n* -ES [NL (specific epithet of *Euphorbia intisy*)] **:** a spurge (*Euphorbia intisy*) from which rubber-yielding latex is obtained in limited quantities

intitle *archaic var of* ENTITLE

intitulate *vt* -ED/-ING/-S [LL *intitulatus*, past part. of *intitulare*, fr. L *in-* ²in- + *titulus* title] *obs* **:** ENTITLE

in·tit·u·la·tion \ənˌtichəˈlāshən\ *n* -s [MF or ML; MF, fr. ML *intitulation-*, *intitulatio* name, title, fr. LL *intitulatus* (past part. of *initulare*) + L *-ion-*, *-io* -ion] *archaic* **:** the act of giving a title to; *also* **:** the title itself

in·ti·tule \ənˈti(ˌ)chül, -ˌchəl\ *vt* -ED/-ING/-S [MF *intituler*, fr. LL *intitulare*] *Brit* **:** to give a title or designation to — now used chiefly of a legislative act

intl *abbr* international

intmd *abbr* intermediate

intmt *abbr* intermittent

intn *abbr* intention

in·to \ˈintə, -ntü, -n-(ˌ)tü, +V *often* -ntəw\ *prep* [ME, fr. OE *intō*, fr. ²*in* + *tō* to] **1 a —** used as a function word primarily denoting motion so directed as to terminate, if continued, when the position denoted by *in* has been reached and usu. after a verb that carries the idea of motion or a word implying or suggesting motion or passage to indicate a place or thing entered or penetrated or enterable or penetrable by or as if by a movement from the outside to an interior part ⟨came ~ the house⟩ ⟨the river ran ~ the sea⟩ ⟨traveled ~ the next state⟩ ⟨a route ~ the wilderness⟩ ⟨imports ~ this country⟩ ⟨the mountains merge ~ the plain⟩ ⟨brought ~ membership in the club⟩ ⟨off we go ~ the wide blue yonder⟩ but sometimes in constructions in which the idea of motion is carried by the very use of *into* in preference to *in* ⟨among the first ~ the field —*N. Y. Herald Tribune*⟩ ⟨they were ~ their clothes and on deck — H.A.Chippendale⟩ ⟨the child was ~ the cookie jar as soon as no one was looking⟩ ⟨stores them away ~ an inner pocket — A.J.Coutts⟩ ⟨baptized ~ the Catholic Church⟩ **b :** in toward ⟨sailed the boat ~ the pier⟩ ⟨the batter leaned ~ the pitch⟩ ⟨it stood close ~ a fine cottonwood grove —Willa Cather⟩ ⟨keeping well ~ the foot or lower slopes of the scarpside — S.G.Joseph⟩ **2** *chiefly Scot* **:** IN 1a(1) ⟨living ~ his new house⟩ **3 a —** used as a function word indicating a state or condition assumed, brought into being (as by force), or allowed to come about ⟨enter ~ bliss⟩ ⟨drive someone ~ despair⟩ ⟨fall ~ decay⟩ ⟨land brought ~ cultivation⟩ ⟨collapses ~ hysterics and quits —H. F. & Katharine Pringle⟩ **b —** used as a function word that usu. follows words carrying an idea of alteration or suggesting or implying alteration and that indicates a form or condition assumed often with loss of original or essential identity and emergence as something else ⟨came ~ being⟩ ⟨develop ~ a butterfly⟩ ⟨compounds resolved ~ simple substances⟩ ⟨translate a book ~ French⟩ ⟨divide a hospital ~ several wards⟩ ⟨fold a paper ~ four⟩ ⟨the barn was remodeled ~ a garage⟩ ⟨the land was plowed ~ broad ridges and hollows —L.D.Stamp⟩ ⟨the book went ~ edition after edition⟩ ⟨divide the theme ~ a beginning, a middle, and an ending⟩ **4 —** used as a function word to indicate something accepted or acquired (as for possession) ⟨talked himself ~ a good job⟩ ⟨came ~ an inheritance⟩ **5 a** (1) *obs* **:** TO, TOWARD (2) **:** toward and as far as (something considered central) ⟨go ~

town) ⟨go ~ market⟩ **b** : in the direction of ⟨looking ~ the sun⟩ ⟨looked ~ his plate and said nothing⟩ ⟨turned ~ the wind⟩ **c** : up to : as far as ⟨since then — right ~ today — you and I have enjoyed . . . the economic idea of roaring production —Sylvia F. Porter⟩ **d** : AGAINST 2a ⟨run ~ a wall⟩ ⟨fell ~ a fence⟩ ⟨the mixture is run ~ an endless moving wire screen —*Amer. Guide Series: La.*⟩ **6 a** — used as a function word to indicate the dividend in mathematical division ⟨dividing 3 ~ 6 gives 2⟩ **b** *archaic* : BY : together with — used with *multiply* **7** — used as a function word to indicate a set of circumstances, a function, action, or occupation entered upon or taken on ⟨get ~ trouble⟩ ⟨go ~ business⟩ ⟨force ~ compliance⟩ ⟨might be tortured ~ divulging military information —G.A. Craig⟩ **8 a** — used as a function word indicating something in which a literal or figurative insertion or introduction is made or in which there is inclusion ⟨pushed the hose ~ the pipe⟩ ⟨read a new meaning ~ a sentence⟩ ⟨water enters ~ the composition of the human body⟩ ⟨marry ~ an influential family⟩ ⟨introduced a bill ~ the legislature⟩ ⟨play a song ~ a microphone⟩ ⟨soon got ~ the act⟩ **b** — used as a function word to indicate something penetrated by the sight or insight or by an intellectual process (as investigation, reflection, or analysis) ⟨peer ~ the distance⟩ ⟨look ~ the future⟩ ⟨search ~ his motives⟩ ⟨inquire ~ his activities⟩ ⟨insights ~ religion and poetry⟩ ⟨seek to look . . . ~ the hopes and fears of men and women —F.D.Roosevelt⟩ **c** : so as to impress, dent, or force inward ⟨pressed the marble ~ the palm of his hand⟩ ⟨force the grease ~ the bearings⟩ **d** — used as a function word to indicate something slowed or stopped in its course or impeded by interruption ⟨~ the path of a train⟩ ⟨stepped ~ a punch on the jaw⟩ ⟨butt ~ their conversation⟩ **e** : so as to permeate or fill ⟨gases expanding ~ a vacuum —S.F.Mason⟩ **f** : in direct connection or contact with ⟨I am ~ a heavy fish . . . have already taken a twelve-inch bass on the same plug —Paul Brooks⟩ **9** — used as a function word indicating a period of time or an extent of space of which a portion is used or occupied ⟨sang far ~ the night⟩ ⟨went some distance ~ the next month before paying the bill⟩ ⟨stretched ~ the distance⟩ **10** — used as a function word to indicate something contributed to, paid, received in exchange, or dealt with by handling in some way ⟨all the sugar we had went ~ the cake⟩ ⟨his pay check went ~ the rent⟩ ⟨their spare cash went ~ some new furniture⟩ ⟨all their brain power went ~ solving the problem⟩ **11** : so as to include ⟨the company then expanded ~ bakery machines and specialized sewing machines —*Time*⟩

in·to·cos·trin \ˌintəˈkästrən\ *n* -s [fr. *Intocostrin*, a trademark] : an extract of purified curare

in·toed \ˈinˌtōd\ *adj* [²*in* + *toed*] : having the toes turned inward

in·tolerability \(ˌ)in, ən+\ *n* : the quality or state of being intolerable

¹**in·tolerable** \(ˈ)in·, ən·+\ *adj* [ME, fr. L *intolerabilis*, fr. *in-* ¹in- + *tolerabilis* tolerable] **1** : not tolerable : not capable of being borne or endured : UNBEARABLE ⟨~pain⟩ ⟨~ anguish⟩ ⟨an ~ burden⟩ ⟨an almost ~ beauty —Bernard DeVoto⟩ **2** *archaic* : not to be withstood : IRRESISTIBLE **3** : EXTREME, EXCESSIVE ⟨sometimes gives way to an ~ degree of sentimentality over some of his women —C.H.Sykes⟩ ⟨scarcely to have made an impression upon the ~ multitude of volumes which everyone is supposed to have read —Arnold Bennett⟩ ⟨an ~ amount of airless inner space —Lewis Mumford⟩ — **in·tolerableness** \"+\ *n* — **in·tolerably** \"+\ *adv*

²**intolerable** \"\ *adv* : INTOLERABLY

in·tolerance \"+\ *n* [F *intolérance*, fr. L *intolerantia*, fr. *intolerant-*, *intolerans* intolerant + *-ia* -y] **1** : the quality or state of being intolerant: as **a** : the lack of an ability to endure ⟨an ~ of strong light⟩; *specif* : exceptional sensitivity to a drug, food, or other substance ⟨~ to quinine⟩ **b** : ILLIBERALITY, BIGOTRY **2** : an instance of intolerance

in·tolerancy \"+\ *n* [L *intolerantia*] *archaic* : INTOLERANCE

¹**in·tolerant** \"+\ *adj* [F or L; F *intolérant*, fr. L *intolerant-*, *intolerans*, fr. *in-* ¹in- + *tolerant-*, *tolerans* tolerant] **1** : unable to endure ⟨a plant ~ of direct sunlight⟩ ⟨a constitution ~ of excesses⟩ **2 a** : unwilling to endure ⟨~ of all strangers⟩ **b** : unwilling to tolerate a difference of opinion or feeling esp. in religious matters : refusing to allow others the free enjoyment of their opinions or worship : BIGOTED **c** : unwilling to grant equal social, political, or professional rights; *specif* : unwilling to tolerate social equality with one of another racial group — **in·tol·er·ant·ly** *adv*

²**intolerant** \"\ *n* -s : an intolerant person

in·tolerating \(ˈ)in·, ən·+\ *adj* [¹*in-* + *tolerating*, pres. part. of *tolerate*] *archaic* : INTOLERANT

in·toleration \(ˌ)in·, ən·+\ *n* [¹*in-* + *toleration*] : INTOLERANCE

intomb *archaic var of* ENTOMB

in·ton·able \ənˈtōnəbəl\ *adj* : that can be intoned

in·to·na·co \ənˈtänəˌkō, -tōn-\ *n* -s [It, fr. *intonacare* to coat with plaster, fr. (assumed) VL *intunicare*, fr. L *in-* ²in- + *tunica* tunic, coating] : the finishing coat of fine plaster in fresco painting — compare ARRICCIO

in·to·nate \ˈintəˌnāt, ·tō,-, *usu* -ād·+V\ *vt* -ED/-ING/-S [ML *intonatus*, past part. of *intonare*] **1** : INTONE **2** : to sound esp. with a particular intonation : UTTER

in·to·na·tion \ˌ==ˈnāshən\ *n* -s [ML *intonation-*, *intonatio*, fr. *intonatus* (past part. of *intonare*) + L *-ion-*, *-io* -ion] **1** : the act of intoning: **a** (1) : the act of singing the opening phrase of a plainsong, psalm, or canticle (2) : the act of musically reciting usu. in monotone any part of a liturgy **b** (1) : the act of sounding musical tones (as of a scale) (2) : the singing and playing of music according to the aural perception of the prevailing standard of accuracy in pitch **c** : the act of reciting in a singing voice usu. in a monotone **2** : something intoned; *specif* : the opening tones of a Gregorian chant preceding the reciting note usu. sung by the priest alone **3 a** : the manner of singing, playing, or uttering tones ⟨spoke with a foreign ~⟩ ⟨played the piece with a romantic ~⟩ **b** : pitch phenomena in speech; *esp* : such a phenomenon insofar as it makes a syntactical or emotional distinction (as between a declarative and interrogative statement) — **in·to·na·tion·al** \ˌ==ˈnāshənᵊl, -shnəl\ *adj*

intonation pattern *n* : a unit of speech melody in a language or dialect that contributes to the total meaning of an utterance ⟨one's *intonation pattern* in the utterance of *dead* may reveal one's emotional reaction to an announcement of death⟩ ⟨one *intonation pattern* makes *leave* a command, another makes it a question⟩

in·tone \ənˈtōn\ *vb* -ED/-ING/-S [alter. (influenced by ML *intonare*) of earlier *entone*, fr. ME *entonen*, fr. MF *entoner*, fr. ML *intonare*, fr. L *in-* ²in- + *tonus* tone] *vt* **1 a** : to utter in musical or prolonged tones : recite in singing tones or in a monotone ⟨~ the service⟩ ⟨~ the hours of the night⟩ ⟨*intoning* the marriage ceremony with the regular orthodox allowance for nasal recitative —T.L.Peacock⟩ **b** : to sing (as a song) or play (as a sonata) with special attention to the continuity of sound **2** : to sing usu. as a solo or semichorus (the opening phrase of a plainsong, psalm, or canticle) ~ *vi* : to utter something in singing tones or in monotone (as in chanting) — **in·ton·er** \-ōnə(r)\ *n*

in·to·neme \ənˈtōˌnēm\ *n* -s [*intone* + *-eme*] : INTONATION PATTERN

in·tone·ment \-ōnmənt\ *n* -s : the act of intoning or the state of being intoned ⟨the ~ of the service⟩

intoothed \ˈ=ˌ=\ *adj* [²*in* + *toothed*] : having the teeth turned inward

in·tor·sion *or* **in·tor·tion** \ənˈtȯrshən\ *n* -s [LL *intortion-*, *intortio* action of curling, fr. L *intortus* (past part. of *intorquēre* to twist, fr. *in-* ²in- + *torquēre* to twist) + *-ion-*, *-io* -ion — more at TORTURE] : a winding, bending, or twisting around (as of the stem of a plant); *specif* : inward rotation (as of a body part) about an axis or a fixed point — compare EXTORSION

in·tort·ed \-rd·əd\ *adj* [L *intortus* (past part. of *intorquēre*) + E *-ed*] : twisted inward or in and out : TWINED, WREATHED, TANGLED

in to·to \inˈtōd·(ˌ)ō, -tō(ˌ)tō\ *adv* [L, on the whole] : TOTALLY, ENTIRELY, ALTOGETHER ⟨promised to publish the book *in toto*⟩ ⟨accepted the plan *in toto*⟩

intower *vt* [²*in-* + *tower* (n.)] *obs* : to imprison in a tower (as the Tower of London)

intown \ˈ=ˌ=, =ˈ=\ *adj* [¹*in* + *town*] : being in the built-up part of a town ⟨an ~ section of the city⟩

¹**in·tox·i·cant** \ənˈtäksəkənt, -sēk-\ *n* [ML *intoxicant-*, *intoxicans*, pres. part. of *intoxicare*] : something that intoxicates : an intoxicating agent; *esp* : an alcoholic drink ⟨felt he should abstain from the use of ~*s*⟩

²**intoxicant** \"\ *adj* [ML *intoxicant-*, *intoxicans*, pres. part. of *intoxicare*] : INTOXICATING ⟨the drink was warm and ~⟩ ⟨the air comes up from the heights, fine and ~ —Sacheverell Sitwell⟩ — **in·tox·i·cant·ly** *adv*

¹**in·tox·i·cate** \-kə̇t, -ˌkā| *usu* |d·+V\ *adj* [ME *intoxicat*, fr. ML *intoxicatus*, past part. of *intoxicare*] **1** *obs* : POISONED **2** *archaic* : excited or exhilarated beyond self-control by alcoholic drinks or to the point of enthusiasm or frenzy (as by pleasure) or stupefied by a narcotic

²**in·tox·i·cate** \-ˌkāt, *usu* -ād·+V\ *vt* -ED/-ING/-S [ML *intoxicatus*, past part. of *intoxicare*, fr. L *in-* ²in- + *toxicum* poison — more at TOXIC] **1** : POISON **2 a** : to excite or stupefy by alcoholic drinks or a narcotic esp. to the point where physical and mental control is markedly diminished : make drunk : INEBRIATE **b** : to excite to the point of enthusiasm, frenzy, or madness : elate strongly and often excessively ⟨found the idea *intoxicating* and ennobling⟩ ⟨*intoxicated* with dreams of fortune —Van Wyck Brooks⟩ ⟨*intoxicated* by success⟩

intoxicated *adj* **1** : being under the marked influence of an intoxicant : DRUNK, INEBRIATED **2** : emotionally excited, elated, or exhilarated (as by great joy or extreme pleasure) **syn** see DRUNK

in·tox·i·cat·ed·ly \=ˈ==ˌ===, =ˌ==ˈ===\ *adv* : in an intoxicated manner ⟨found herself ~ striving for that careless, exhilarating blitheness —Harriet LaBarre⟩

intoxicating *adj* : producing or fitted to produce intoxication ⟨an ~ beverage⟩ ⟨~ flattery⟩ ⟨~ beauty⟩ — **in·tox·i·cat·ing·ly** \=ˈ==ˌ===, =ˌ==ˈ===\ *adv*

in·tox·i·ca·tion \=ˌ==ˈkāshən\ *n* -s [ML *intoxication-*, *intoxicatio* poisoning, fr. ML *intoxicatus* + L *-ion-*, *-io* -ion] **1** : poisoning or the abnormal state induced by a chemical agent (as a drug, serum, or toxin) ⟨barbiturate ~ may occur as an intractable dermatitis⟩ ⟨lead ~ is a hazard of some occupations⟩ **2 a** : the quality or state of being drunk : INEBRIATION **b** : a strong excitement of mind or feelings (as from joy or pleasure) : an elation that rises to enthusiasm, frenzy, or madness **3** : the act of intoxicating

in·tox·i·ca·tive \=ˈ==ˌkād·iv\ *adj*, *archaic* : of, relating to, or tending to cause intoxication

In·tox·im·e·ter \ˌin‚täkˈsimə̇d·ə(r)\ *trademark* — used for a device used to measure the degree of an individual's intoxication by means of chemical tests of the breath

intpr *abbr* interpreter

intr *abbr* **1** intransitive **2** introduced; introducing; introduction; introductory

in·tra- \in *pronunciations below*, ¦== = ¦in·trə *or* -·(ˌ)trä *or* -·(ˌ)trä\ *prefix* [LL, fr. L *intra* within, fr. (assumed) OL *interus* inward, on the inside — more at INTERIOR] **1 a** : within — esp. in adjectives formed from adjectives ⟨*intra*glacial⟩ ⟨*intra*vaginal⟩ ⟨*intra*cellular⟩ ⟨*intra*-European⟩ ⟨*intra*cosmical⟩ **b** : during — esp. in adjectives formed from adjectives ⟨*intra*natal⟩ ⟨*intra*febrile⟩ ⟨*intra*pyretic⟩ ⟨*intra*vital⟩ **c** : between layers of — esp. in adjectives formed from adjectives ⟨*intra*cutaneous⟩ **d** : underneath — esp. in adjectives formed from adjectives ⟨*intra*dural⟩ **2** : INTRO- ⟨*intra*muscular injection⟩ ⟨*intra*venation⟩ ⟨*intra*cerebral⟩ **3** : internal ⟨*intra*selection⟩

in·tra–abdominal \¦==+\ *adj* [*intra-* + *abdominal*] : being within the abdomen ⟨*intra-abdominal* pressure⟩ or going into the abdomen ⟨an *intra-abdominal* injection⟩ — **in·tra–ab·dominally** \"+\ *adv*

in·tra–atomic \"+\ *adj* [*intra-* + *atomic*] : existing within an atom ⟨the project which led to man's first practical utilization of *intra-atomic* energy —Julian Huxley⟩

in·tra·bi·on·tic \"+(ˈ)bī¦äntik\ *adj* [prob. irreg. fr. *intra-* + Gk *biount-*, *biōn* living + E *-ic* — more at -BIONT] : existing or occurring within an individual

in·tra·cartilaginous \¦==+\ *adj* [*intra-* + *cartilaginous*] *of bone development* : taking place within the substance of the cartilage : ENDOCHONDRAL — compare INTRAMEMBRANOUS

in·tra·cav·i·tar·i·ly \"+¦kavə¦terəlē\ *adv* : in an intracavitary manner

in·tra·cav·i·tary \-ˌterē\ *adj* [*intra-* + *cavity* + *-ary*] : being within or from within a body cavity ⟨~ irradiation of cervical cancer⟩

in·tra·cellular \¦==+\ *adj* [ISV *intra-* + *cellular*] : being or occurring within a body cell or within the body cells : ENDOCELLULAR — **in·tra·cellularly** *adv*

in·tra·cerebral \"+\ *adj* [ISV *intra-* + *cerebral*] : going into the cerebrum ⟨~ inoculation⟩ — **in·tra·cerebrally** \"+\ *adv*

in·tra·cervical \"+\ *adj* [ISV *intra-* + *cervical*] : situated within the cervix of the uterus

in·tra·chordal \"+\ *adj* [*intra-* + *chordal*] : being or occurring within a chord (as the notochord)

in·tra·cisternal \"+\ *also* **in·tra·cistern** \"+\ *adj* [*intracisternal* fr. *intra-* + *cisternal or cistern*] : going into or being or occurring within a cisterna — **in·tra·cis·ter·nal·ly** \"+(ˈ)si¦stərnᵊlē *or* +sə¦-\ *adv*

in·tra·city \¦==+\ *adj* [*intra-* + *city*] : being, occurring, or operating within a particular city ⟨~ buses⟩

in·tra·coastal \"+\ *adj* [*intra-* + *coastal*] : being within and close to the coast or belonging to the inland waters near the coast ⟨an ~ waterway⟩

in·tra·company \"+\ *adj* [*intra-* + *company*] : being or occurring within a company ⟨for the sake of ~ relations —*Current Biog.*⟩

in·tra·continental \"+\ *adj* [*intra-* + *continental*] : being within a particular continent

in·tra·cortical \"+\ *adj* [*intra-* + *cortical*] : being or situated within the cortex

in·tra·cranial \"+\ *adj* [*intra-* + *cranial*] : being or occurring within the cranium ⟨~ pressure⟩ — **in·tra·cra·ni·al·ly** \"+¦krānēəlē\ *adv*

intracranial cast *n* : a cast of the brain cavity in a skull

in·tra·crystalline \¦==+\ *adj* [*intra-* + *crystalline*] : being or occurring within a crystal ⟨an ~ field⟩

in·tractability \(ˌ)in, ən+\ *n* : the quality or state of being intractable

¹**in·tractable** \(ˈ)in, ən+\ *adj* [L *intractabilis*, fr. *in-* ¹in- + *tractabilis* tractable] **1** : not easily governed, managed, or directed : not disposed to be taught, disciplined, or tamed : OBSTINATE, REFRACTORY ⟨an ~ temper⟩ ⟨an ~ child⟩ : unwilling to submit ⟨~ to force⟩ **2** : not easily manipulated or wrought ⟨an ~ metal⟩ **3** : not easily relieved or cured ⟨an ~ pain⟩ ⟨an ~ malady⟩ : not responsive (as to a medicine) ⟨~ to remedies⟩ **syn** see UNRULY

²**intractable** \"\ *n* -s : one that is intractable ⟨most of the group was docile but it did contain its ~*s*⟩

in·tractableness \(ˈ)in, ən+\ *n* : the quality or state of being intractable : STUBBORNNESS, REFRACTORINESS

in·tractably \"+\ *adv* : in an intractable way

in·tra·cutaneous *pronunc at* INTRA- +\ *adj* [ISV *intra-* + *cutaneous*] : INTRADERMAL — **in·tra·cutaneously** \"+\ *adv*

intracutaneous test *n* : a test for immunity or hypersensitivity to a particular antigen made by injecting a minute amount of diluted antigen into the skin — compare PATCH TEST, SCRATCH TEST

in·tra·cytoplasmic \¦==+\ *adj* [ISV *intra-* + *cytoplasmic*] : lying or occurring in cytoplasm (as of a cell) ⟨~ multiplication of sporozoans⟩

in·tra·da \ənˈträdə\ *n* -s [modif. of It *intrata*, *entrata* entrance, introduction, fr. fem. of *intrato*, *entrato*, past part. of *intrare*, *entrare* to enter, fr. L *intrare* — more at ENTER] : a musical introduction or prelude esp. in 16th and 17th century music : ENTRÉE

in·tra·departmental *pronunc at* INTRA- +\ *adj* [*intra-* + *departmental*] : being or occurring within a department ⟨~ rivalry⟩

in·tra·dermal \"+\ *also* **in·tra·dermic** \"+\ *adj* [*intradermal* fr. *intra-* + *dermal*; *intradermic* ISV *intra-* + *dermic*] : being within the skin ⟨an ~ nevus⟩ : being between the layers of the skin ⟨an ~ injection⟩ — **in·tra·der·mal·ly** \"+¦dərməlē\ *also* **in·tra·der·mi·cal·ly** \-mə̇k(ə)lē\ *adv*

in·tra·disciplinary \¦==+\ *adj* [*intra-* + *disciplinary*] : being or occurring within the scope of a scholarly or academic discipline or between the people active in such a discipline

in·tra·district \"+\ *adj* [*intra-* + *district*] : being or occurring within a district ⟨interdistrict and ~ services —D.H.Nucker⟩

intrado *n* -s [modif. of Sp *entrada* entry, income, fr. fem. of *entrado*, past part. of *entrar* to enter, fr. L *intrare* — more at ENTER] *obs* : INCOME

in·tra·dos \ˈin·trəˌdäs, -ˌdōs, -ˌdō; in·ˈträ|ˌdäs, -rä|, |ˌdəs\ *n*, *pl* **intrados** \-ˌdōz\ *or* **intradoses** \-äsə̇z,-ōsə̇z,-əsə̇z\ [F, fr. L *intra* within + F *dos* back — more at INTRA-, DOSSIER] **1** : the interior curve of an arch; *esp* : the inner curved face of the whole body of voussoirs **2** : the inner surface of a vault — compare EXTRADOS

1 intrados 1

in·tra·ductal *pronunc at* INTRA- +\ *adj* [*intra-* + *duct* + *-al*] : being or occurring within a duct ⟨~ pressure⟩

in·tra·dural \"+\ *adj* [ISV *intra-* + *dural*] : being or occurring within the dura mater

in·tra–european \"+\ *adj*, *usu cap E* [*intra-* + *european*] : being or occurring within the boundaries of Europe or between the countries of Europe ⟨*intra-European* political movements⟩

in·tra·fascicular \"+\ *adj* [*intra-* + *fascicular*] : being or occurring within a vascular bundle

in·tra·formational \"+\ *adj* [*intra-* + *formational*] : being or occurring within a geologic formation : originating more or less contemporaneously with the enclosing geologic material — see BRECCIOLA

in·tra·genic \"+\ *adj* [*intra-* + *genic*] : being or occurring within a gene ⟨~ changes⟩

in·tra·glacial \"+\ *adj* [*intra-* + *glacial*] : being or occurring within a glacier or a glacial stage

in·tra·granular \"+\ *adj* [*intra-* + *granular*] : being or occurring within a grain ⟨~ microstructures —*Jour. of Geol.*⟩

in·tra·group \"+\ *also* **in·tra·group·al** \"+¦grüpəl\ *adj* [*intragroup* fr. *intra-* + *group*; *intragroupal* fr. *intra-* + *group* + *-al*] : being or occurring within a single group ⟨increased ~ hostility —J.B.Carroll⟩

in·tra·hepatic \"+\ *adj* [ISV *intra-* + *hepatic*] : being within or originating in the liver — compare EXTRAHEPATIC

intrail *archaic var of* ENTRAIL

in·tra·imperial *pronunc at* INTRA- +\ *adj* [*intra-* + *imperial*] : being, occurring, or carried on within an empire

in·tra·individual \"+\ *adj* [*intra-* + *individual*] : being or occurring within the individual

in·tra–industry *or* **in·tra·industrial** \"+\ *adj* [*intra-* + *industry* or *industrial*] : being or occurring within an industry or between the independent enterprises of an industry

in·tra·island \"+\ *adj* [*intra-* + *island*] : being within or limited to the confines of an island ⟨~ distances are not great —J.H.S.Billmyer⟩ ⟨~ telephone and courier service —John Hersey⟩

in·trait \ˈinˌtrā, ˈtrā, ˈan· -\ *n* [F, fr. *in-* ²in- + *-trait* (as in *extrait* extract, fr. MF, fr. past part. of *extraire* to extract, fr. L *extrahere*) — more at EXTRACT] : one of a class of extracts prepared from plants in which the enzymes are killed before drying

in·tra·lamellar *pronunc at* INTRA- +\ *adj* [*intra-* + *lamellar*] : situated within a lamella — used esp. of the trama in agarics

in·tra·luminal \"+\ *adj* [*intra-* + *luminal*] : being within or arising from within the lumen ⟨~ inflammation of the esophagus⟩

in·tra·marginal \"+\ *adj* [*intra-* + *marginal*] : being, occurring, or operating within a margin

in·tra·matrical \"+\ *adj* [*intra-* + *matrical*] : being or occurring within a matrix — **in·tra·matrically** \"+\ *adv*

in·tra·medullary \"+\ *adj* [ISV *intra-* + *medullary*] : being or lying within a medulla ⟨an ~ tumor of the spinal cord⟩; *esp* : involving use of the marrow space of a bone for support ⟨~ pinning of a fracture of the thigh⟩

in·tra·membranous \"+\ *adj* [*intra-* + *membranous*] *of bone development* : taking place through the ossification of a membrane — compare INTRACARTILAGINOUS

in·tra·mental \"+\ *adj* [*intra-* + *mental*] : INTRAPSYCHIC

in·tra·mercurial *also* **in·tra·mercurian** \"+\ *adj* [*intramercurial* ISV *intra-* + *mercurial*; *intramercurian* fr. *intra-* + *mercurian*] : being within the orbit of the planet Mercury

in·tra·micellar \"+\ *adj* [*intra-* + *micellar*] : being or taking place within a micelle ⟨~ swelling of cellulose by water⟩ — **in·tra·mi·cel·lar·ly** *adv*

in·tra·molecular \¦==+\ *adj* [ISV *intra-* + *molecular*] : situated or occurring within the molecule ⟨~ rearrangement⟩ : formed by reaction between different parts of the same molecule — **in·tra·mo·lec·u·lar·ly** *adv*

intramolecular respiration *n* : the production of carbon dioxide and of organic acids by aerobic organisms or tissues while deprived of atmospheric oxygen

intramolecular salt *n* : INNER SALT

in·tra·montane \¦==+\ *adj* [ISV *intra-* + *montane*] : being within a mountainous region

in·tra·morainic \"+\ *adj* [*intra-* + *morainic*] : being or occurring within the lobate curve of a moraine

in·tra·mundane \"+\ *adj* [*intra-* + *mundane*] : being or occurring within the material world — opposed to *extramundane*

in·tra·mural \"+\ *adj* [*intra-* + *mural*] **1** : being, occurring, or undertaken within the limits usu. of a state, community, organization, or institution (as an academic institution) ⟨the most extensive ~ investigation undertaken in the history of our government —W.H.Hale⟩ ⟨an ~ squabble within the corporation⟩ ⟨the ~ conflicts of four generations of a prolific family —Harrison Smith⟩ ⟨the college's ~ sports program⟩ ⟨~ competition between the departments of the state university⟩ — opposed to *extramural* **2** : being or occurring within the substance of the walls of an organ ⟨~ infarction⟩ ⟨~ circulation⟩ — **in·tra·murally** \"+\ *adv*

in·tra·muscular \"+\ *adj* [ISV *intra-* + *muscular*] : being within a muscle ⟨~ fat⟩ : going into a muscle ⟨~ injection⟩ — **in·tra·muscularly** \"+\ *adv*

in·tra·nasal \"+\ *adj* [*intra-* + *nasal*] : lying within or going into the nasal structures — **in·tra·nasally** \"+\ *adv*

in·tra·natal \"+\ *adj* [*intra-* + *natal*] : occurring chiefly with reference to the child during the act of birth ⟨~ accident⟩ — compare INTRAPARTUM, NEONATAL

in·tra·national \"+\ *adj* [*intra-* + *national*] : being or occurring within a nation ⟨~ movements of the population⟩

intrance *archaic var of* ²ENTRANCE

in·tra·ne·ous \(ˈ)in¦trānēəs, ənˈt-\ *adj* [LL *intraneus*, fr. L *intra* within — more at INTRA-] : being or growing within an area : INTERNAL — opposed to *extraneous*

in·tra·neural *pronunc at* INTRA- +\ *adj* [*intra-* + *neural*] : being or occurring within or going into a nerve or nervous tissue — **in·tra·neurally** \"+\ *adv*

in·tranquil \(ˈ)in·, ən·+\ *adj* [¹*in-* + *tranquil*] : not tranquil : DISTURBED, RESTLESS ⟨an ~ sleep⟩ — **in·tranquillity** \¦in·+\ *n*

in trans *abbr* in transit

intrans *abbr* intransitive

in·transferable \¦in·, (ˈ)in·, ən+\ *adj* [¹*in-* + *transferable*] : incapable of being transferred

in·transgressible \¦in·+\ *adj* [¹*in-* + *transgress* + *-ible*] : that cannot or may not be transgressed

in·tran·si·geance \ənˈtran(t)səjən(t)s, -raan- *also* -ra(a)nzə- *sometimes* ˌinˌtra(a)nˈsij(ē)ən(t)s *or* -ˈzi-\ *also* **in·tran·si·gean·cy** \-nsē,-nsi\ *n*, *pl* **intransigeanc·es** *also* **intransigeancies** [*intransigeance* fr. F, fr. *intransigeant*, after F *-ant*: *-ance*; *intransigeancy* fr. ²*intransigeant* + *-cy*] : INTRANSIGENCE ⟨assume attitudes of bohemian ~ toward society —Philip Rahv⟩

¹**in·tran·si·geant** \-nt\ *n* -s [F (trans. of Sp *intransigente*), fr. *in-* ¹in- + *transigeant*, pres. part. of *transiger* to compromise, fr. L *transigere* to transact] : ¹INTRANSIGENT

²**intransigeant** \"\ *adj* [F (trans. of Sp *intransigente*), fr. *in-* ¹in- + *transigeant*, pres. part. of *transiger*] : ²INTRANSIGENT — **in·tran·si·geant·ly** *adv*

in·tran·si·gence \ən·'tran(t)səjən(t)s, -raan- *also* -ra(a)nzəj-\ *also* **in·tran·si·gen·cy** \-nsē,-nsi\ *n, pl* **intransigenc·es** *also* **intransigencies** [*intransigence* fr. 2*intransigent*, after such pairs as E *abstinent: abstinence; intransigency* fr. 2*intransigent* + *-cy*] : the quality or state of being intransigent ⟨his absolute ~ on any question —*Current History*⟩ ⟨~ in the face of harsh realities —R.J.Slavin⟩ ⟨the desire not . . . to prejudice the integration and defense of the West by ~ on issues —*Current History*⟩

1in·tran·si·gent \-jənt\ *n* -s [Sp *intransigente*, fr. *in-* 1in- + *transigente*, pres. part. of *transigir* to compromise, fr. L *transigere* to transact — more at TRANSACT] : one that is intransigent

2intransigent \"\ *adj* [Sp *intransigente*, fr. *in-* 1in- + *transigente*, pres. part. of *transigir*] **1 a** : refusing to compromise or budge from an often extreme position taken or held : preserving an immovable independence of position or attitude : UNCOMPROMISING ⟨an ~ imperialist who opposed with great force . . . every liberal tendency —R.P.Casey⟩ ⟨felt the man was ~ because of his youth and would modify his views as he grew older⟩ **b** *of two or more* : IRRECONCILABLE ⟨the ~ parties to the dispute⟩ **2** : befitting one that is uncompromising ⟨its previous ~ attitude toward modern art —*Americana Annual*⟩ — **in·tran·si·gent·ly** *adv*

in·tran·si·gent·ism \-nt·,izəm, -n·,ti-\ *n* -s : the quality or state of being intransigent or the policy of an intransigent ⟨the militant ~ of the antislavery forces —A.C.Cole⟩

in-transit \'=·,==, =·'==\ *adj* [fr. the phrase *in transit*] : being in transit ⟨*in-transit* passengers to Europe⟩ : of or relating to something in transit ⟨*in-transit* freight rates⟩

in·transitable \(')in·, ən·+\ *adj* [1*in-* + *transitable*] : not capable of being crossed or passed over ⟨an ~ gorge⟩

1in·transitive \(')in·, ən·+\ *adj* [LL *intransitivus*, fr. L *in-* 1in- + LL *transitivus* transitive] : not transitive: as **a** *archaic* : not transmitted to another : not passing beyond particular limits **b** (1) : not passing over directly to an object ⟨an ~ action⟩ (2) : expressing an action or state as limited to the agent or subject or as ending in itself : not taking a direct object — used of a verb form ⟨the verbs in "the bird flies" and "he runs" are ~⟩; compare 1ABSOLUTE 4d (3) : being a construction containing an intransitive verb form **c** : characterizing a logical relationship between the three statements *x*, *y*, and *z* that occurs when *x* is related to *y* as *y* but not *x* is related to *z* — **in·transitively** \"+\ *adv* — **in·transitiveness** \"+\ *n*

2intransitive \"\ *n* : an intransitive verb form or construction

in·transitivity \(')in·, ən·+\ *n* : the quality or state of being intransitive : INTRANSITIVENESS

in·tran·si·tiv·ize \(')=¦=(=)=,īz\ *vt* -ED/-ING/-S : to make intransitive — **in·tran·si·tiv·iz·er** \-zə(r)\ *n* -S

in tran·si·tu \(')in'tran(t)sə,tü, -ranzə-\ *adv* [L] : during passage from one place to another

in·translatable \(')in·+\ *adj* [1*in-* + *translate* + *-able*] : not translatable

in·transmissibility \"+\ *n* : the quality or state of being intransmissible

in·transmissible \"+\ *adj* [1*in-* + *transmissible*] : not transmissible

in·transmutable \"+\ *adj* [1*in-* + *transmutable*] : not transmutable

in·trant \'in·trənt\ *n* -s [L *intrant-*, *intrans*, pres. part. of *intrare* to enter — more at ENTER] *archaic* : ENTRANT; *esp* : one entering an educational institution or a holy or fraternal order

in·tra·nuclear *pronunc at* INTRA- +\ *adj* [ISV *intra-* + *nuclear*] : being or occurring within or going into a nucleus

in·tra·ocular \"+\ *adj* [ISV *intra-* + *ocular*] : being or occurring within or going into the eyeball

in·tra·oral \"+\ *adj* [*intra-* + *oral*] : being or occurring within the mouth

in·tra·organismal \"+\ *adj* [*intra-* + *organismal*] : situated or originating inside an organism ⟨~ conflicts⟩ ⟨interpretation of ~ processes and relationships — L.A.White⟩

in·tra·organizational \"+\ *adj* [*intra-* + *organizational*] : being or occurring within an organization

in·tra·parietal \"+\ *adj* [*intra-* + *parietal*] **1** : INTRAMURAL 2 **2** : located within the parietal lobe of the cerebrum

in·tra·par·tum \"+¦pärd·əm\ *adj* [NL *intra partum*, lit., during birth, fr. L *intra* during, within + *partum*, accus. of *partus* birth — more at INTRA-, ANTEPARTUM] : occurring chiefly with reference to a mother during the act of birth — compare INTRANATAL

in·tra·party \¦==+\ *adj* [*intra-* + *party*] : being or occurring within the membership or scope of a usu. political party ⟨~ feuding⟩ ⟨~ organization⟩

in·tra·pelvic \"+\ *adj* [*intra-* + *pelvic*] : situated within the pelvis

in·tra·pericardiac \"+\ *adj* [*intra-* + *pericardiac*] : situated within or going into the pericardium ⟨~ injections⟩

in·tra·peritoneal \"+\ *adj* [ISV *intra-* + *peritoneal*] : being within or going into the peritoneal cavity; *also* : going through the peritoneum — **in·tra·peritoneally** \"+\ *adv*

in·tra·petiolar \"+\ *adj* [ISV *intra-* + *petiolar*] **1** : enclosed by the expanded base of the petiole ⟨~ leaf buds in the plane tree⟩ **2** : situated between the petiole and the stem ⟨~ stipules in plants of the family Rubiaceae⟩

in·tra·pial \"+\ *adj* [*intra-* + *pial*] : being or occurring within the pia mater

in·tra·plant \"+\ *adj* [*intra-* + *plant*] : being or occurring within an industrial plant ⟨~ working conditions and policies —*Americana Annual*⟩ ⟨~ disputes⟩

in·tra·psychic *or* **in·tra·psychical** \"+\ *adj* [*intra-* + *psychic* or *psychical*] : being or occurring within the psyche, the mind, or the personality ⟨~ conflicts⟩ ⟨~ processes⟩ — **in·tra·psychically** \"+\ *adv*

in·tra·pulmonary *or* **in·tra·pulmonic** \"+\ *adj* [*intra-* + *pulmonary* or *pulmonic*] : occurring within the lungs ⟨~ pressure⟩

in·tra·school \"+\ *adj* [*intra-* + *school*] : existing within a school ⟨an ~ athletic program⟩ — opposed to *interschool*

in·tra·selection \"+\ *n* [ISV *intra-* + *selection*] : hypothetical competition between structural elements of a tissue or organ resulting in survival of those best suited to a particular function or situation

in·tra·service \"+\ *adj* [*intra-* + *service*] : being or occurring within the armed services ⟨~ rivalry⟩ or within a branch of the armed services ⟨~ advancement⟩

in·tra·shop \"+\ *adj* [*intra-* + *shop*] : being within or confined to a single shop ⟨~ agencies for collective bargaining⟩

in·tra·species \"+\ *adj* [*intra-* + *species*] : INTRASPECIFIC

in·tra·specific \"+\ *adj* [*intra-* + *specific*] : being or occurring within a species or involving the members of one species — **in·tra·specifically** \"+\ *adv*

in·tra·spinal \"+\ *adj* [*intra-* + *spinal*] : being within or going into a spine; *esp* : going into the spinal canal — **in·tra·spinally** \"+\ *adv*

in·tra·state \"+\ *adj* [*intra-* + *state*] : existing within a state ⟨interstate and ~ commerce⟩

in·tra·stelar \"+\ *adj* [*intra-* + *stelar*] : being or occurring within a stele

in·tra·stratal \"+\ *adj* [*intra-* + *stratal*] : being or occurring within strata ⟨~ solution⟩

in·tra·telluric \"+\ *adj* [*intra-* + *telluric*; trans. of G *intratellurisch*] **1** : situated, formed, or occurring deep within the earth — used esp. of a mineral of an igneous rock **2** : of, relating to, or constituting the period or stage of crystallization of igneous rocks prior to eruption

intraterminal switching *n, pl* **intraterminal switchings** : the moving of cars from one place to another on the same railroad line and within the switching limits of one station or industrial switching district — compare INTERTERMINAL SWITCHING

in·tra·thecal \"+\ *adj* [*intra-* + *thecal*] **1 a** : being within a sheath **b** : being or going under the membranes covering the brain or spinal cord ⟨an ~ injection⟩ **2** : being within the theca esp. of a coral — **in·tra·thecally** \"+\ *adv*

in·tra·thoracic \"+\ *adj* [ISV *intra-* + *thoracic*] : being or occurring within the thorax ⟨~ extension of the disease —Cecil Wakeley⟩ ⟨~ pressure⟩

in·tratom·ic \¦in·trə¦tämik\ *adj* [irreg. fr. *intra-* + *atomic*] : INTRA-ATOMIC

in·tra·tracheal *pronunc at* INTRA- +\ *adj* [ISV *intra-* + *tracheal*] : being or occurring within or going into the trachea

in·tra·tropical \"+\ *adj* [*intra-* + *tropical*] : INTERTROPICAL

in·tra·uterine \"+\ *adj* [ISV *intra-* + *uterine*] : being or occurring within the uterus; *esp* : occurring during the part of development that takes place in the uterus

in·tra·vaginal \"+\ *adj* [ISV *intra-* + *vaginal*] **1** : situated within a sheath — used esp. of branches in grasses **2** : being or occurring within or going into the vagina

in·trav·a·sation \(,)in·,travə'sāshən\ *n* -s [prob. fr. *intra-* + *-vasation* (as in *extravasation*)] : the entrance of foreign matter into a vessel of the body

in·tra·venous *pronunc at* INTRA- +\ *adj* [ISV *intra-* + *venous*] : being within or going into or by way of the veins ⟨~ feeding⟩ ⟨an ~ inflammation⟩; *also* : used in intravenous procedures ⟨an ~ needle⟩ ⟨an ~ solution⟩ — **in·tra·venously** \"+\ *adv*

in·tra vi·res \¦in·trə¦vī(,)rēz\ *adv* [NL] *law* : within the powers — opposed to *ultra vires*

in·tra·vital *pronunc at* INTRA- +\ *adj* [ISV *intra-* + *vital*] : INTRAVITAM

in·tra vi·tam \¦in·trə'vī,tam, -trä'wē,täm\ *adv* [NL, during life, fr. L *intra* during, within + *vitam*, accus. of *vita* life — more at INTRA-, VITAL] : during life : while the subject is alive ⟨the symptoms of fatty liver are . . . not sufficient in most cases to make an accurate diagnosis *intra vitam* —O.V.Brumley⟩

in·tra·vi·tam \¦==¦=,=\ *adj* [fr. *intra vitam*, adv.] **1** : performed upon or occurring in a subject that is alive ⟨an ~ diagnosis⟩ ⟨~ blood clotting⟩ **2** *of a stain* : having the property of tinting living cells without killing them

in·tra·vitelline *pronunc at* INTRA- +\ *adj* [*intra-* + *vitelline*] : being or occurring within the yolk of an egg

in·tra·vitreous \"+\ *adj* [*intra-* + *vitreous*] : being or occurring within the vitreous humor

in·tra·xylary \"+\ *adj* [*intra-* + *xyl*em + *-ary*] : situated within the xylem

in–tray \'=·,=\ *n* [4*in* + *tray*] : a shallow wood or metal basket usu. placed on a desk and used for holding incoming material (as letters) or material still to be dealt with — distinguished from *out-tray*

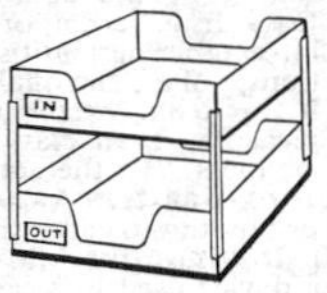

in-tray (top)

in·tra·zonal *pronunc at* INTRA- +\ *adj* [*intra-* + *zonal*] : of or belonging to intrazonal soil or an intrazonal soil

intrazonal soil *n* **1** : a major soil group classified as a category of the highest rank and including soils with more or less well-developed soil characteristics determined by relatively local factors (as the nature of the parent material) that prevail over the normal soil-forming factors of climate and living organisms — compare AZONAL SOIL, ZONAL SOIL **2** : a soil belonging to the intrazonal-soil group

intreat *archaic var of* ENTREAT

intrench *var of* ENTRENCH

in·trep·id \(')in·¦trepəd, ən·'t-\ *adj* [L *intrepidus*, fr. *in-* 1in- + *trepidus* alarmed — more at TREPIDATION] : characterized by resolute fearlessness in meeting dangers or hardships and enduring them with fortitude ⟨an ~ explorer⟩ ⟨an ~ attitude⟩ **syn** see BRAVE

in·tre·pid·i·ty \,in·trə'pidəd·ē, -tre'-, -idətē, -i\ *n* : the quality or state of being intrepid : resolute bravery : VALOR ⟨a girl of immense ~ and she struggled on gallantly —J.C.Powys⟩

in·trep·id·ly *adv* : in an intrepid manner

in·trep·id·ness *n* -ES : INTREPIDITY

in·tri·ca·cy \'in·trəkəsē, -trēk-, -si *sometimes* ən·'trik- *or* 'in·,trik-\ *n* -ES [1*intricate* + *-cy*] **1** : the quality or state of being intricate : complexity or involution in structure or arrangement (as of parts) ⟨these improvements . . . greatly increase the ~ of the mechanisms —Bryan Morgan⟩ ⟨the ~ of his philosophic notions⟩ **2** : something intricate; *esp* : an intricate part, aspect, or relationship ⟨who know and admire the *intricacies* of bullfighting —Murray Sinclair⟩ ⟨with all its *intricacies* of fibers, muscles, and veins —Mary W. Shelley⟩ ⟨involved in the *intricacies* of his own success at law school —Mary Deasy⟩

1in·tri·cate \-kət, *usu* -kəd·+V\ *adj* [ME (Sc), fr. L *intricatus*, past part. of *intricare* to entangle] **1** : having many interwinding, intermeshing, or nicely or complexly interrelating parts, phases, patterns, or elements and being consequently perplexing and hard to grasp in detail, follow through, or execute ⟨a mazy dance in imitation of the ~ windings of the labyrinth —J.G.Frazer⟩ ⟨the wheels, cogs, levers, all the ~ parts of the hay-loading machine —Sherwood Anderson⟩ ⟨~ interlaced diamonds —*Amer. Guide Series: Md.*⟩ **2** : showing an involvement or complexity of various detailed considerations or notions and hence requiring precise analysis : difficult to cope with, resolve, analyze, or solve ⟨the ~ task of reorganizing the economic system on an equitable basis —J.A.Hobson⟩ ⟨our system of civil courts was very ~, and no explanation could be given of it without a long historical preamble —F.W.Maitland⟩ **syn** see COMPLEX

2in·tri·cate \'in·trə,kāt, -trē,-, *usu* -ād·+V\ *vt* -ED/-ING/-S [L *intricatus*, past part. of *intricare* to entangle, fr. *in-* 2in- + *tricae* trifles, impediments, perplexities; perh. akin to L *torquēre* to twist — more at TORTURE] **1 a** *obs* : ENTANGLE, ENSNARE **b** : INTERRELATE, INTERLOCK, INTERMESH ⟨so consistently *intricated* that one rests on another and is involved with what was earlier —Marianne Moore⟩ ⟨a career . . . *intricated* with an epoch —Lucien Price⟩ ⟨pseudopodia, reticulated and *intricated* —*Biol. Abstracts*⟩ **2** *archaic* : to make intricate : COMPLICATE

in·tri·cate·ly *pronunc at* 1INTRICATE +lē *or* li\ *adv* : in an intricate manner ⟨an ~ designed floral pattern⟩ ⟨an ~ abstruse philosophical doctrine⟩

in·tri·cate·ness \"+nəs\ *n* -ES : INTRICACY

in·tri·ca·tion \,in·trə'kāshən, -trē'-\ *n* -s [ME *intricacion*, fr. ML *intrication-*, *intricatio*, fr. L *intricatus* + *-ion-*, *-io* -ion] **1** *obs* : COMPLICATION, COMPLEXITY **2** : INTERRELATION, INTERMESHING

in·tri·gant *or* **in·tri·guant** \¦in·trē¦gänt, ¦an·t-\ *n* -s [F *intrigant*, fr. *intrigant*, adj., that intrigues, fr. It *intrigante*, pres. part. of *intrigare* to intrigue] : one that intrigues : INTRIGUER ⟨talked almost in whispers, like ~*s* —E.P.O'Donnell⟩

in·tri·gante *or* **in·tri·guante** \"\ *n* -s [F *intrigante*, fem. of *intrigant*] : a female intriguer ⟨the most fascinating woman they had ever known, but also . . . an ~ of dark and winding ways —Gertrude Atherton⟩

1in·trigue \ən·'trēg *sometimes* 'in·,t-\ *vb* -ED/-ING/-S [F *intriguer* to puzzle, intrigue, fr. It *intrigare* to intrigue, fr. L *intricare* to entangle] *vt* **1** *archaic* : CHEAT, TRICK **2** : to get, make, or accomplish by intrigue ⟨~ some bill through the senate —Thornton Wilder⟩ ⟨*intrigued* their way through ballrooms and bedrooms —*Time*⟩ ⟨*intrigued* themselves into office —F.M.Ford⟩ **3** *obs* : ENTANGLE, COMPLICATE **4 a** : to arouse the interest, desire, or curiosity of (as by beguiling or baffling) : BEGUILE ⟨a tale that ~*s* the reader⟩ ⟨an *intriguing* smile⟩ ⟨became *intrigued* with sketching children —*Newsweek*⟩ **b** : to engage by intriguing in this way ⟨has become something distinctive enough to ~ our interest —Charlton Laird⟩ ⟨have *intrigued* my attention and tightly gripped my fancy —Paul Ives⟩ ~ *vi* : to carry on an intrigue: as **a** : PLOT, SCHEME ⟨*intrigued* and conspired against him to the end —Hilaire Belloc⟩ **b** : to engage in a clandestine or illicit affair or intimacy

2in·trigue \'in·,trēg, ən·'t-\ *n* -s [F, crafty scheme, plot, love affair, fr. It *intrigo* crafty scheme, fr. *intrigare* to intrigue] **1** *obs* : INTRICACY, COMPLEXITY **2 a** : a covert and involved scheme to accomplish one's end by devious maneuvering and crafty stratagem ⟨the party politicians . . . reverted to their familiar ~*s* and maneuvers —H.G.Wells⟩ ⟨the ~*s* and conspiracies of the middle ages —Edmond Taylor⟩ **b** : a tendency toward or the practice of engaging in such schemes ⟨jealousy and ~ and backbiting, producing a poisonous atmosphere of underground competition —Bertrand Russell⟩ ⟨ambitious, unscrupulous, and cruel, a master of ~ —Victor Seroff⟩ **3** : the plot of a literary or dramatic work esp. marked by an intricacy of design or action or a complex interrelation of events ⟨the play rightly shows greater concern for comic ~ than for human probability —*Time*⟩ **4** : a clandestine affair or intimacy ⟨that hard-to-be-governed passion of youth hurried me frequently into ~*s* with low women —Benjamin Franklin⟩ **syn** see PLOT

in·trigu·er \-gə(r)\ *n* -s : one that intrigues

intriguing \='== *sometimes* '=,==\ *adj* : engaging the interest to a marked degree ⟨one of the most ~ and stimulating characters in modern fiction —Harrison Smith⟩ : FASCINATING ⟨a subject of ~ intricacy⟩ : BEGUILING ⟨a small and ~ young woman⟩ **syn** see INTERESTING

in·trigu·ing·ly *adv* : in an intriguing manner

1in·trin·sic \(')in·¦trinz|ik, ən·'t-, -rin(t)s|, |ēk\ *adj* [MF *intrinsèque* inner, internal, fr. LL *intrinsecus*, fr. L, adv. inwardly, inwards, fr. (assumed) L *intrim* (fr. — assumed — OL *interus* inward, on the inside) + L *-secus* (fr. *sequi* to follow) — more at INTERIOR, SUE] **1** *obs* : PRIVATE, SECRET **2 a** : belonging to the inmost constitution or essential nature of a thing : essential or inherent and not merely apparent, relative, or accidental ⟨form was treated as something ~, as the very essence of the thing in virtue of the metaphysical structure of the universe —John Dewey⟩ ⟨recommend this book for its ~ interest —Daniel George⟩ ⟨~ merit⟩ ⟨a wide gap between ~ feelings and the social expressions of them —H.J.Muller⟩ — opposed to *extrinsic* **b** : originating or due to causes or factors within a body, organ, or part ⟨~ asthma⟩ **c** : being good in itself or irreducible : being desirable or desired for its own sake and without regard to anything else ⟨when anyone says that values are merely matters of opinion or subjective liking, he is speaking only of ~ values —L.W.Beck⟩ **d** : REAL, ACTUAL ⟨a fine big bird, he is . . . but there is no ~ beauty about him —Richard Jefferies⟩ **3** : originating and included wholly within an organ or part — used esp. of certain muscles; opposed to *extrinsic* — **in·trin·si·cal·ly** \|ək(ə)lē, |ēk-, -li\ *adv* — **in·trin·si·cal·ness** \|əkəlnəs, |ēk-\ *n* -ES

2intrinsic *n* -s *obs* : an intrinsic quality

in·trin·si·cal \|əkəl, |ēk-\ *adj* [alter. (influenced by 1*intrinsic*) of earlier *intrinsecal*, fr. LL *intrinsecus* + E *-al*] *archaic* : INTRINSIC

intrinsic factor *n* : a substance produced by normal stomach and intestinal mucosa that facilitates absorption of vitamin B_{12} from the gastrointestinal tract and thereby assists in the development and maturation of red blood cells — compare EXTRINSIC FACTOR

intrinsic fraud *n* : fraud (as by the use of forged documents, false claims, perjured testimony) that misleads a court or jury relying upon it in determining issues and induces the court or jury to find for the party perpetrating the fraud — compare EXTRINSIC FRAUD

in·tro \'in·(,)trō\ *n* -s [short for *introduction*] : a musical introduction in jazz and popular music

intro- *prefix* [ME, fr. MF, fr. L, fr. *intro*, adv., inwardly, to the inside, fr. (assumed) OL *interus* inward, on the inside — more at INTERIOR] **1** : in : into ⟨*intro*jection⟩ **2** : inward : within ⟨*intro*active⟩ ⟨*intro*flex⟩ ⟨*intro*reception⟩ — opposed to *extro-*

in·tro·cep·tive \¦in·trə¦septiv, -rō¦-\ *adj* [*intro-* + *-ceptive* (as in *receptive*)] : capable of receiving within itself

introd *abbr* introduction

in·tro·duce \¦in·trə¦d(y)üs, -rō¦d-, *in rapid speech* ¦in(t)ə(r)¦d-\ *vt* -ED/-ING/-S [ME *introducen* to initiate, instruct, fr. L *introducere* to introduce, fr. *intro-* + *ducere* to lead — more at TOW] **1 a** : to lead, bring, conduct, or usher in esp. for the first time ⟨~ a person into a drawing room⟩ ⟨~ European birds into America⟩ **b** : to cause to take part or be involved by introducing ⟨the fruits of *introducing* party men into municipal affairs —*Sydney (Australia) Bull.*⟩ **2 a** : to bring into play (as in action or thought) ⟨~ abuses into court practices⟩ : bring forward in the course of an action or sequence ⟨~ irrelevancies into the discussion⟩ : add or contribute (as a new element or feature) ⟨~ new business into a play⟩ ⟨*introduced* amendments to the draft extension bill —*Current Biog.*⟩ ⟨*introduced* a new and mutually beneficial element into crop and livestock husbandry —N.C.Wright⟩ **b** : to bring into practice or use : INSTITUTE ⟨~ a new fashion in hats⟩ ⟨the first officer to ~ gunpowder into the French Army —Edmond Taylor⟩ ⟨*introduced* club cars on certain important business expresses —O.S.Nock⟩ ⟨slow to ~ new processes, slow to adopt new inventions —Leo Wolman⟩ **3** *obs* : to cause to exist : bring into being **4** : to lead to or make known by a formal act, announcement, or recommendation: as **a** : to cause to be acquainted : cause to know each other personally ⟨~ two strangers⟩ : make (one person) known to another ⟨~ the boy to her father⟩ **b** : to present formally at court or to society ⟨a party to ~ his daughter to London society⟩ **c** : to present or announce formally or officially or by an official reading ⟨~ a bill to Congress⟩ **d** : to make preliminary explanatory or laudatory remarks about (as a performer or act in a show) ⟨a master of ceremonies . . . to ~ acts on the bill —*Current Biog.*⟩ **e** (1) : to bring (as an actor, singer, or literary character) before the public for the first time (as in a play, a concert, or a novel) ⟨a Hollywood extravaganza *introducing* a young Broadway star⟩ ⟨several excellent mysteries *introducing* a French detective —A.C.Ward⟩ (2) : to bring (a commercial product) to the attention of the public (as by an advertising campaign) **5** : to lead into or preface ⟨*introduces* his study with a detailed description and careful evaluation of the publisher materials used in his report —W.H.Voskuil⟩ : START, BEGIN ⟨~ a subject by a long preface⟩ **6 a** : to put or insert into ⟨~ a catheter into a vein⟩ ⟨some 1800 eggs were *introduced* into a tiny drop of sea water —W.C.Allee⟩ **b** : to put (an atom or group of atoms) into a molecule **7** : to bring to a knowledge of or into intellectual acquaintance with something (as by contact or instruction) ⟨~ readers to the poet's works⟩ — **in·tro·duc·er** \-sə(r)\ *n* -s

in·tro·duce·ment \,=='=mənt\ *n* -s *archaic* : INTRODUCTION

in·tro·duc·ible \¦==¦d(y)üsəbəl\ *adj* : capable of being introduced : fit to be introduced

introduct *vt* -ED/-ING/-S [L *introductus*, past part. of *introducere* to introduce] *obs* : INTRODUCE

in·tro·duc·tion \,in·trə'dəkshən, -rō'd-, *in rapid speech* ,in(t)ə(r)'d-\ *n* -s [ME *introduccion* action of introducing, fr. MF *introduction*, fr. L *introduction-*, *introductio*, fr. *introductus* (past part. of *introducere* to introduce) + *-ion-*, *-io* -ion] **1** : something that introduces: as **a** *obs* (1) : a preliminary step : PREPARATION (2) : initial instruction : a first lesson : instruction in rudiments **b** (1) : a distinguishable part (as of a book or treatise) that provides explanation, information, or comment preparatory or preliminary to the main portion or subject — compare PREFACE, PROEM (2) : a formal or elaborate preliminary treatise esp. introductory to other treatises or to a course or field of study ⟨an ~ to metaphysics⟩ ⟨an ~ to European drama⟩ (3) : a course or a subject matter preparatory to a particular study; *specif*, *cap* : a branch of the study of the Bible that applies the contributions of literary and historical criticism to textual problems (as of date, authorship, place of origin, structure, sources, and purpose) of the books of Scripture **c** : a form esp. polite and conventional used in the introduction of one person to another **d** : a series of chords or a short movement or passage preparing the listener for the main body of a musical composition **e** : an initial anticipatory, explanatory, or promotional statement or set of remarks (as in introducing a speaker, an entertainment, or a commercial product) **2** : the act or process of introducing or the state of being introduced: as **a** : a leading, bringing, conducting, or ushering in or the state of being led, brought, conducted, or ushered in esp. for the first time ⟨responsible for the ~ of aliens into the country⟩ ⟨anticipated his ~ into the dining room⟩ **b** : a causing to take part or be involved ⟨the ~ of crooked politicians into city government⟩ **c** : INSTITUTION ⟨the ~ of new manufacturing processes⟩ ⟨the ~ of a newspaper to cover local events⟩ ⟨the ~ of new rules governing behavior⟩ **d** : a making known or acquainted or a being made known or acquainted ⟨the ~ of the two men to each other⟩ **e** : a formal presentation ⟨the ~ of a young girl to society⟩ ⟨the ~ of a bill into Congress⟩ **f** : a preliminary, preparatory, or initial explaining, talking up, or advertising ⟨an ~ to the subject matter in a preface to a book⟩ ⟨the ~ of an act by a master of ceremonies⟩ ⟨the ~ of a new product on a TV commercial⟩ **g** : a putting in : INSERTION ⟨the ~ of new matter into the recipe⟩ ⟨the ~ of a catheter into a vein⟩ ⟨the ~ into the stomach and esophagus of material which is opaque in appearance under the X ray —Morris Fishbein⟩ **b :** a bringing into play or adding or contributing in the course of an action or sequence or the state of being brought, added, or contributed in this way ⟨the ~ of a spirit of bitterness into the discussion⟩ ⟨the ~ of rude remarks into his report⟩ **3 :** something introduced ⟨resented all new ~s into his old methods of doing things⟩; *specif* **:** an exotic plant (as a new variety of horticultural derivation) or an animal brought into a region where it is not native

in·tro·duc·tive \¦==¦dəktiv, -tēv *also* -təv\ *adj* [fr. *introduction,* after such pairs as E *induction: inductive*] **:** INTRODUCTORY

in·tro·duc·tor \-tə(r)\ *n* -S [LL, fr. L *introductus* (past part. of *introducere* to introduce) + *-or*] *archaic* **:** INTRODUCER

in·tro·duc·to·ri·ly \-kt(ə)rəlē, -li\ *adv* **:** in an introductory manner

in·tro·duc·to·ri·ness \,==ˈ=t(ə)rēnəs, -rin-\ *n* -ES **:** the quality or state of being introductory

in·tro·duc·to·ry \¦==¦=t(ə)rē, -ri\ *adj* [LL *introductorius,* fr. L *introductus* (past part. of *introducere* to introduce) + *-orius* -ory] **:** being or belonging to an introduction or serving to introduce **:** PRELIMINARY, PREFATORY ⟨an ~ section of a book⟩ ⟨an ~ course in mathematics⟩ ⟨remarks ~ to a main speaker⟩

in·tro·flex \¦in·trə¦fleks, -rō¦-\ *vb* -ED/-ING/-ES [*intro-* + *flex*] **:** to flex inward

in·tro·flex·ion *also* **in·tro·flec·tion** \¦==¦flekshən\ *n* [fr. *introflex,* after E *flex: flection*] **:** inward flexion **:** an act or instance of introflexing

in·tro·fy \ˈ==,fī\ *vt* -ED/-ES [modif. (influenced by E *-fy*) of L *introferre* to carry in, fr. *intro-* + *ferre* to carry — more at BEAR] **:** to increase the impregnating power of (as sulfur for wood pulp)

in·tro·gres·sion \,==ˈgreshən\ *n* -S [*intro-* + *-gression* (as in *digression*)] **:** the entry or introduction of a gene from one gene complex into another (as in introgressive hybridization)

in·tro·gres·sive \¦==¦gresiv\ *adj* [fr. *introgression,* after such pairs as E *digression: digressive*] **:** of, belonging to, or marked by introgression

introgressive hybridization *n* **:** the spread of genes of one species into the gene complex of another as a result of hybridization between numerically dissimilar populations in which extensive backcrossing prevents formation of a single stable population

in·troit \ˈin·,trōət, ˈin·,trȯit, ən·ˈtrōət, ən·ˈtrȯit *sometimes* ˈin·trəwət\ *n* -S [MF *introite,* fr. ML *introitus,* fr. L, entrance, fr. *introitus,* past part. of *introire* to go into, enter, fr. *intro-* + *ire* to go — more at ISSUE] **1** *often cap* **:** the first part of the proper of the mass in the Roman rite consisting orig. of the processional psalm but now usu. consisting of an antiphon and verse from one of the psalms followed by the Gloria Patri **2 :** a psalm, anthem, or hymn sung or played at the beginning of the communion service esp. in Anglican churches **3 :** a choral response sung at the beginning of a worship service

in·troi·tal \(ˈ)in¦trōəd·ᵊl, ən·ˈt-, -rōid· -\ *adj* [*introitus* + *-al*] **:** of or relating to an introitus

in·troi·tus \ən·ˈtrōəd·əs, -rōid· -\ *n, pl* **introitus** [NL, fr. L, entrance] **:** the orifice of a body cavity; *esp* **:** the vaginal opening

in·tro·ject \¦in·trə¦jekt, -rō¦-\ *vb* -ED/-ING/-S [back-formation fr. *introjection*] *vt* **1 :** to incorporate or assimilate into oneself subconsciously or unconsciously (attitudes or ideas of others esp. parental figures, or in infantile fancy actual parts or all of another's body) — opposed to *project;* compare INTERNALIZE **2 :** to turn toward oneself (the love felt for another) or against oneself (the hostility felt toward another) ~ *vi* **:** to enter into a situation and play the role either in actuality or in fantasy that the situation suggests or demands

in·tro·jec·tion \,==ˈjekshən\ *n* -S [*intro-* + *-jection* (as in *projection*)] **1 :** a throwing in; *esp* **:** a throwing of oneself into some pursuit or action **2** [ISV *intro-* + *-jection* (as in *projection*); orig. formed as G *introjektion*] **:** a theory that sense perceptions are mental counterparts of the objects perceived **3** [ISV *intro-* + *-jection* (as in *projection*); orig. formed as G *introjektion*] **:** the act or process of introjecting attitudes, ideas, or body parts — opposed to *projection*

in·tro·jec·tive \¦==¦jektiv\ *adj* **:** of, belonging to, marked by, or given to introjection

in·tro·mis·si·ble \¦==¦misəbəl\ *adj* [fr. *intromission,* after such pairs as E *admission: admissible*] **:** capable of intromission

in·tro·mis·sion \,==ˈmishən\ *n* -S [ML *intromission-, intromissio,* fr. *intromissus* (past part. of ML — with reflexive pronoun object — *intromittere*) + L *-ion-, -io* -ion — more at SMITE] **1** *Scots law* **:** an intermeddling with the affairs or effects of another — see LEGAL INTROMISSION, VICIOUS INTROMISSION **2** [F, fr. MF, fr. L *intromissus* (past part. of *intromittere* to send in, let in) + MF *-ion*] **a :** the act of sending, letting, or putting in or the state of being sent, let, or put in **:** INSERTION, ADMISSION; *specif* **:** the introduction of the penis into or its maintenance within the vagina during coitus **b :** the time during which intromission is sustained during coitus

in·tro·mis·sive \¦==¦misiv\ *adj* [fr. *intromission,* after such pairs as E *permission: permissive*] **:** of or belonging to intromission

in·tro·mit \¦==¦mit\ *vb* **intromitted; intromitted; intromitting; intromits** [ME *intromitten,* fr. ML (with reflexive pronoun object) *intromittere* to concern (oneself), meddle, fr. L *intromittere* to send in, let in, fr. *intro-* + *mittere* to send — more at SMITE] *vi, Scots law* **:** to interfere or intermeddle esp. with the effects or goods of another — compare INTROMISSION **1** ~ *vt* [L *intromittere* to send in, let in] **:** to send or put in **:** INSERT, INTRODUCE; *also* **:** to allow to pass **:** ADMIT — **in·tro·mit·ter** \-mid·ə(r)\ *n* -S

in·tro·mit·tent \-mitᵊnt\ *adj* [L *intromittent-, intromittens,* pres. part. of *intromittere* to send in, let in] **:** adapted for or functioning in intromission — used of the copulatory organ of an animal

in·tro·punitive \¦in·trō+\ *adj* [*intro-* + *punitive*] **:** tending to blame or to inflict punishment on the self — opposed to *extrapunitive*

in·trorse \ˈin·,trȯrs, ən·ˈtrō(ə)rs\ *adj* [prob. fr. (assumed) NL *introrsus,* fr. L *introrsus,* adv., inward, contr. of *introversus,* fr. *intro-* + *versus* toward, fr. *versus,* past part. of *vertere* to turn — more at WORTH] **:** facing inward or toward the axis of growth ⟨an ~ anther⟩ **:** having its line of dehiscence toward the gynoecium — compare EXTRORSE — **in·trorse·ly** *adv*

intros *pl of* INTRO

in·tro·spect \¦in·trə¦spekt, -rō¦-\ *vb* -ED/-ING/-S [L *introspectus,* past part. of *introspicere* to look into, fr. *intro-* + *-spicere* (fr. *specere* to look) — more at SPY] *vt* **:** to look within (as one's own mind or psyche) **:** examine (as oneself) with introspection ~ *vi* **:** to engage in or practice introspection — **in·tro·spec·tor** \-ktə(r)\ *n* -S

in·tro·spect·able *or* **in·tro·spect·ible** \-ktəbəl\ *adj* **:** capable of being observed by introspection

in·tro·spec·tion \-kshən\ *n* -S [L *introspectus* + E *-ion*] **:** the examination of one's own thought and feeling **:** a looking into oneself **:** SELF-EXAMINATION; *also* **:** such examination including one's sensory and perceptual experience esp. undertaken under controlled conditions of experiment — opposed to *extrospection* — **in·tro·spec·tion·al** \-shənᵊl,-shnəl\ *adj*

in·tro·spec·tion·ism \-shə,nizəm\ *n* -S **:** a doctrine that psychology must be based essentially on data derived from introspection — compare BEHAVIORISM

¹in·tro·spec·tion·ist \-sh(ə)nəst\ *n* -S **1 :** one esp. given to introspection **2 :** an adherent of introspectionism

²introspectionist \"\ *or* **in·tro·spec·tion·is·tic** \¦==,=shəˈnistik\ *adj* **:** of or relating to introspectionism ⟨a special ~ technique was devised —Ethel Albert⟩

in·tro·spec·tive \¦==¦spektiv,-tēv *also* -təv\ *adj* [*introspect* + *-ive*] **:** of or belonging to introspection **:** employing, marked by, or tending to introspection — opposed to *extrospective* — **in·tro·spec·tive·ly** \-tə̇vlē, -li\ *adv* — **in·tro·spec·tive·ness** \-tivnəs, -tēv- *also* -təv-\ *n* -ES

in·tro·susception \,in·trə, ,in·(,)trō+\ *n* [*intro-* + *susception*] **:** INTUSSUSCEPTION

in·trou·va·ble \aⁿ·trüvabl(ᵊ), -b(lə)\ *adj* [F, fr. *in-* ¹in- + *trouvable* capable of being found, fr. MF, fr. *trouver* to find (prob. fr. — assumed — VL *tropare* to compose) + *-able* — more at TROUBADOUR] **:** impossible to find ⟨pamphlets, all now almost ~ —*Times Lit. Supp.*⟩ — **in·trou·va·bly** \ən·ˈtrüvəblē\ *adv*

in·tro·ver·si·ble \¦in·trə¦vərsəbəl, -rō¦-\ *adj* [*introversion* + *-ible*] **:** capable of being introverted

in·tro·ver·sion \¦in·trə¦vərzhən, -·trō¦-, -vəl, -vəi| *also* |sh-\ *n* -S [*intro-* + *-version* (as in *diversion*)] **1 :** the act of introverting or the state of being introverted ⟨economic ~ —Peter Schmid⟩ ⟨an ~ and not an expansion —D.S.Savage⟩ **2 a :** the act of directing one's attention toward or getting gratification from one's own thoughts and feelings and other intrapsychic experience ⟨neurotic ~ — too much preoccupation with oneself —*Irish Digest*⟩ — opposed to *extroversion* **b :** the state of being wholly or predominantly concerned with and interested in one's own intrapsychic experience **c :** a habitual tendency toward such introversion

in·tro·ver·sive \|siv *also* |ziv\ *adj* [*introversion* + *-ive*] **:** characterized by or given to introversion: **a :** turned in upon itself **:** drawn in or invaginated **b :** tending to turn one's attention to one's own experience **:** notably marked by psychological introversion — opposed to *extroversive;* contrasted with *extratensive* — **in·tro·ver·sive·ly** \|sə̇vlē, |zə̇-\ *adv*

¹in·tro·vert \ˈ==,vər|t, -vəl, -vəi|, ,==ˈ=, *usu* |d·+V\ *vt* -ED/-ING/-S [*intro-* + *-vert* (as in *divert*)] **1 a :** to turn inward or in upon itself: as (1) **:** to bend inward (2) **:** to turn (as the thoughts) introversively **b :** to direct upon oneself ⟨served the purpose of ~*ing* aggressive intentions —Ernst Simmel⟩ **2 :** to draw in or invaginate (one tubular part or organ) within another **3 :** to produce introversion in **:** make an introvert of **:** cause to be introvert

²in·tro·vert \ˈ==,=\ *n* -S **1 :** something that is or can be introverted (as the eyestalks of certain snails or the retractile proboscis of a sipunculid worm) **2 :** one whose personality is characterized by introversion — opposed to *extrovert*

³introvert \"\ *adj* [²*introvert*] **:** of or belonging to psychological introversion **:** characterized by or tending to introversion ⟨~ tendencies⟩ ⟨~ behavior⟩

introverted *adj* [fr. past part. of ¹*introvert*] **1 :** INTROVERSIVE: **a :** turned in upon itself ⟨the ~ Old Kingdom did not carry on extensive intercourse with foreign lands —J.W.Curtis⟩ **b :** marked by introversion ⟨the ~ young man given to odd moods and uncommunicativeness⟩ — opposed to *extroverted* **2** *of a quatrain* **:** having an enclosed rhyme

in·tro·vert·ish \¦==¦=ish\ *adj* [²*introvert* + *-ish*] **:** somewhat introverted

in·tro·ver·tive \¦==¦=iv\ *adj* [¹*introvert* + *-ive*] **:** INTROVERSIVE

in·trude \ən·ˈtrüd\ *vb* -ED/-ING/-S [L *intrudere* to force in, fr. *in-* ²in- + *trudere* to thrust, push — more at THREAT] *vi* **1 :** to thrust oneself in **:** come or go in without invitation, permission, or welcome **:** enter by intrusion **:** ENCROACH, TRESPASS ⟨where none might ~ upon his grief —P.B.Kyne⟩ ⟨manifest no wish to ~ on academic prerogatives —*Saturday Rev.*⟩ ⟨abashed at *intruding* on all these busy people —Jule Mannix⟩ **2** *geol* **:** to enter as if by force ~ *vt* **1 :** to thrust or force in, into, on, or upon esp. without permission, welcome, or fitness ⟨~ political theory into his play⟩ ⟨~ these confidences on you —G.B.Shaw⟩ ⟨didn't want to ~ himself upon her uninvited⟩ ⟨improper to ~ the dog into the houses of other people they were calling on —Joseph Conrad⟩ ⟨the right to ~ its judgment upon questions of policy or morals —O.W.Holmes †1935⟩ **2 :** to settle (a minister) in a parish against the will of the people ⟨ecclesiastical adventurers from the Continent were *intruded* by hundreds into lucrative benefices —T.B.Macaulay⟩ **3** *geol* **:** to cause to enter as if by force

in·trud·er \-də(r)\ *n* -S **:** one that intrudes ⟨the swarming ~s upon the peace of that hill looked like sheep —Kenneth Roberts⟩; *specif* **:** a military aircraft assigned to penetrate alone into enemy territory usu. at night

in·trud·ing·ly *adv* [*intruding* (pres. part. of *intrude*) + *-ly*] **:** in the manner of one that intrudes

in·tru·sion \ən·ˈtrüzhən\ *n* -S [ME *intrusioun* invasion, usurpation, fr. MF *intrusion* act of intruding, fr. ML *intrusion-, intrusio,* fr. L *intrusus* (past part. of *intrudere* to intrude) + *-ion-, -io* -ion] **:** the act of intruding or the state of being intruded: as **a** (1) **:** the entry of a stranger after a particular estate of freehold is determined before the person who holds it in remainder or reversion has taken possession (2) **:** the act of wrongfully entering upon, seizing, or taking possession of the property of another (as in trespassing upon crown lands or in the usurpation of an office) **b :** a trespassing or encroachment **:** an undesirable or unwelcome bringing in or entering ⟨the fire replenished, and the house shut against ~ —Mary Austin⟩ ⟨that other shattering of illusion which comes by way of the ~ of fact —J.L.Lowes⟩ ⟨resented the man's ~ upon his privacy⟩ **c :** a settlement of a minister in a parish against the wishes of the parishioners **d** (1) **:** the forcible entry of molten rock or magma into or between other rock formations; *also* **:** the body of igneous rock resulting from solidification of the intruded magma (2) **:** the plastic injection of masses of salt into overlying rocks; *also* **:** the intruded salt

¹in·tru·sive \(ˈ)in¦trüs|iv, ən·ˈt,-üz|, |ēv *also* |əv\ *adj* [*intrusion* + *-ive*] **1 a :** characterized by intrusion or encroachment ⟨an ~ remark⟩ ⟨far too sensitive to be ~ —Mollie Panter-Downes⟩ ⟨an ~ culture⟩ **b :** showing a tendency to intrusion **:** given to habitual intrusion **:** thrusting one's way into a place, group, or activity where one is not welcome or invited ⟨a loud and ~ individual⟩ **2 a :** thrusting or projecting inward ⟨an ~ arm of the sea⟩ **b :** thrust or forced in: as (1) *of a rock* **:** having been forced while in a plastic or liquid state into cavities or cracks or between layers of other rock — contrasted with *extrusive;* compare ¹BOSS 2, ¹DIKE 3c, SILL (2) **:** PLUTONIC **3** *of an organism* **:** having a range that extends into an area in which it or the group it represents would not be expected to be found **4** *of an archaeological object* **:** lying in a stratum that is not the place of original deposit **5** *of a sound or letter* **:** having nothing that corresponds to it in orthography or etymon ⟨~ \t\ in \ˈmints\ for *mince*⟩ ⟨~ *d* in *thunder*⟩ ⟨~ \r\ in the pronunciation \,indēəˈriŋk\ for *India ink*⟩ **syn** see IMPERTINENT

²intrusive \"\ *n* -S **:** something that is intrusive; *specif* **:** intrusive rock or an intrusive rock

intrusive growth *n* **:** differential growth of the wall of a cell resulting in projection of newly formed parts between adjacent cells or into intercellular spaces — compare GLIDING GROWTH, SYMPLASTIC GROWTH

in·tru·sive·ly \|ə̇vlē, -li\ *adv* **:** in an intrusive manner

in·tru·sive·ness \|ivnəs, |ēv- *also* |əv-\ *n* -ES **:** the quality or state of being intrusive ⟨have lost much of my taste for the special ~ of modern journalism, and it is no longer my opinion that it is necessary for the public to know the whole truth about anybody who has had the misfortune to acquire a little celebrity —Wolcott Gibbs⟩

intrust *var of* ENTRUST

in·tu·bate \ˈin·,t(y)ü,bāt, ən·ˈt-\ *vt* -ED/-ING/-S [²*in-* + *tube* + *-ate*] **:** to treat by intubation **:** perform intubation on

in·tu·ba·tion \,=,=ˈbāshən\ *n* -S [²*in-* + *tube* + *-ation*] **:** the introduction of a tube into a hollow organ (as the trachea or intestine) to keep the latter open or to restore its patency if obstructed

in·tue \ən·ˈt(y)ü\ *vt* [L *intueri*] *archaic* **:** INTUIT

in·tu·ent \(ˈ)in¦t(y)üənt, ən·ˈt(y)ü-, ˈintəwənt, ˈin·tyəw-\ *adj* [L *intuent-, intuens,* pres. part. of *intueri*] *archaic* **:** knowing by intuition

in·tu·it \(ˈ)in¦t(y)üət, ən·ˈt(y)ü-, ˈintəwət, ˈin·tyəw-\ *vb* -ED/-ING/-S [L *intuitus,* past part. of *intueri*] *vt* **:** to know or apprehend directly or by intuition ⟨only through the sensuous can the ideal be ~*ed* —Murray Krieger⟩ ⟨an imaginative artist ~*ing* the motives of men long dead —Howard M. Jones⟩ ~ *vi* **:** to have knowledge directly or by intuition

in·tu·it·able \¦=ˈt(y)üəd·əbəl\ *adj* **:** knowable through intuition

in·tu·i·tion \,in·(,)t(y)üˈishən, ,intəˈwi-, ,in·tyəˈwi-\ *n* -S [ME *intuycion,* fr. LL *intuition-, intuitio,* fr. L *intuitus* (past part. of *intueri* to look at, contemplate, fr. *in-* ²in + *tueri* to look at) + *-ion-, -io* -ion — more at TUITION] **1 a** *obs* **:** the act of looking upon, regarding, examining, or inspecting **b** *archaic* **:** the act of contemplating or considering **:** CONTEMPLATION, CONSIDERATION **c** *obs* **:** a view, regard, or consideration of something as an ulterior goal or acquisition **2 a :** the act or process of coming to direct knowledge or certainty without reasoning or inferring **:** immediate cognizance or conviction without rational thought **:** revelation by insight or innate knowledge **:** immediate apprehension or cognition **b :** knowledge, perception, or conviction gained by intuition ⟨trusting . . . to what are called ~s rather than reasoned conclusions —A.C.Benson⟩ **c :** the power or faculty of attaining to direct knowledge or cognition without rational thought and inference **d** *in Bergsonism* **:** a form of knowing that is akin to instinct or a divining empathy and that gives direct insight into reality as it is in itself and absolutely **e :** quick and ready insight ⟨with one of her quick leaps of ~ she had entered into the other's soul —Edith Wharton⟩ **syn** see REASON

in·tu·i·tion·al \¦=(,)=ˈ(w)ishənᵊl, -shnəl\ *adj* **1 :** of, belonging to, derived from, characterized by, or perceived by intuition **:** INTUITIVE **2 :** of or belonging to intuitionism ⟨an ~ theory⟩ — **in·tu·i·tion·al·ly** \-ᵊlē, -əl|, |i\ *adv*

in·tu·i·tion·al·ism \,=(,)=ˈ(w)ishənᵊl,izəm, -shnə,li-\ *n* -S **:** INTUITIONISM

¹in·tu·i·tion·al·ist \-shənᵊləst, -shnəl-\ *n* -S **:** ¹INTUITIONIST

²in·tu·i·tion·al·ist \¦=(,)=¦=\ *or* **in·tu·i·tion·al·is·tic** \¦==(w)ishənᵊl¦istik, -shnə¦li-\ *adj* **:** ²INTUITIONIST

in·tu·i·tion·ism \,=(,)=ˈ(w)ishə,nizəm\ *n* -S **1 a :** a doctrine that there are self-evident truths intuitively known which form the basis of human knowledge **b :** a doctrine that objects of perception are intuitively known to be real ⟨radical empiricism, naïve realism, and ~ . . . are expressions of an intense longing for reality —Frank Thilly⟩ **2 a :** a doctrine holding that the rightness or wrongness of particular actions or of kinds of actions is immediately intuitable through a special faculty (as the conscience) or that fundamental principles about what is right and wrong can be intuited **b :** a system of ethics that bases its ultimate conceptions on intuitions; *specif* **:** one according to which moral values (as the good) are intuitively apprehended and indefinable or irreducible **3 :** a thesis that mathematics is based upon special intuitions and requires rejection of the law of excluded middle — contrasted with *formalism* and *logicism*

¹in·tu·i·tion·ist \-sh(ə)nəst\ *n* -S **:** an adherent of intuitionism

²in·tu·i·tion·ist \¦=(,)=¦=\ *or* **in·tu·i·tion·is·tic** \-¦(w)ishəˈnistik\ *adj* **1 :** of, belonging to, or based on intuitionism **2 :** advocated by intuitionists

intuition line *n, usu cap I* **:** LINE OF INTUITION

in·tu·i·tive \ən·ˈt(y)üəd·iv, -üət|\ *adj* [ML *intuitivus,* fr. L *intuitus* (past part. of *intueri* to look at, contemplate) + *-ivus* -ive] **1 :** knowing or perceiving by intuition **:** capable of knowing by direct insight or cognition ⟨the ~ faculty⟩ ⟨an ~ power⟩ **2 a :** acquired, known, arrived at, or perceived by intuition ⟨an ~ awareness of another's feelings⟩ ⟨an ~ understanding of the parallelogram of forces —S.F. Mason⟩ ⟨an ~ conviction⟩ **:** known immediately or without the use of inference **:** directly apprehended ⟨~ knowledge⟩ ⟨~ truths⟩ — contrasted with *discursive;* compare INNATE **b :** knowable by intuition **c :** made by intuition or private judgment ⟨the ~ estimates of individuals —H.J.Morgenthau⟩ **3 :** possessing or using intuition or gifted with marked insight ⟨an ~ poet⟩ ⟨an ~ mind⟩ ⟨he was not a systematic critic, but was purely ~ —F.A.Swinnerton⟩ **4 :** ²INTUITIONIST — **in·tu·i·tive·ly** \|ə̇vlē, -li\ *adv* — **in·tu·i·tive·ness** \|ivnəs\ *n* -ES

intuitive reason *n* **:** the faculty of apprehending a priori truths or principles — contrasted with *discursive reason;* compare PURE REASON

in·tu·i·tiv·ism \|i,vizəm\ *n* -S **:** INTUITIONISM 2

¹in·tu·i·tiv·ist \-,vəst\ *n* -S **:** ¹INTUITIONIST

²intuitivist \"\ *adj* **:** ²INTUITIONIST

in·tu·mesce \¦in·(,)t(y)üˈmes\ *vi* -ED/-ING/-S [L *intumescere* to swell, rise, fr. *in-* ²in- + *tumescere* to swell, incho. of *tumēre* to swell — more at THUMB] **:** to enlarge, expand, swell, or bubble up (as from being heated)

in·tu·mes·cence \,==ˈmesᵊn(t)s\ *n* -S [F, fr. L *intumescere* + F *-ence*] **1 a :** an enlarging, swelling, or bubbling up (as under the action of heat) **b :** the state of being swollen **:** marked enlargement **:** INFLATION **2 :** something swollen or enlarged (as a tumor); *specif* **:** an enlargement resembling a knob or pustule and consisting of a group of abnormally enlarged cells appearing on leaves or other plant parts as a result of physiological disturbances

in·tu·mes·cent \¦=(,)=ˈməsᵊnt\ *adj* [L *intumescent-, intumescens,* pres. part. of *intumescere*] **1 :** marked by intumescence **:** swelling, enlarging, or bubbling up **2** *of paint* **:** swelling and charring when exposed to flame and forming an insulating fire-retardant barrier between the flame and the coated material

in-turn \ˈ=,=\ *n* [²*in* + *turn,* after *turn in* v.] **:** a moving curling stone that is rotating clockwise — compare OUT-TURN

inturned \ˈ=¦=\ *adj* [²*in* + *turned,* past part. of *turn*] **:** turned inward ⟨ladies' hose with an ~ knitted welt —W.E.Shinn⟩ **:** INTROVERTED ⟨were somewhat dour and ~ —Oliver La Farge⟩

in·tus·sus·cept \¦intəsəˈsept\ *vb* -ED/-ING/-S [prob. fr. (assumed) NL *intussusceptus,* past part. of (assumed) NL *intussuscipere,* fr. L *intus* within + *suscipere* to take up — more at ENT-, SUSCEPTIBLE] *vt* **:** to cause to turn inward esp. upon itself or to be received in some other thing or part; *esp* **:** to cause (an intestine) to undergo intussusception ⟨the bowel became ~*ed*⟩ ~ *vi* **:** to undergo intussusception ⟨some 3 ft. of the ileum had ~*ed* through the ileocecal valve into the cecum —*Veterinary Record*⟩

in·tus·sus·cep·tion \,===ˈsepshən\ *n* -S [prob. fr. NL *intussusception-, intussusceptio,* prob. fr. (assumed) NL *intussusceptus* + L *-ion-, -io* -ion] **1 :** the reception of one part within another **:** INVAGINATION; *esp* **:** the passing of one portion of the intestine into an adjacent portion producing intestinal obstruction **2 :** the deposition of new particles of formative material among those already embodied in a tissue or structure (as in the growth of living organisms) — usu. distinguished from *accretion* and *apposition*

in·tus·sus·cep·tive \¦===¦septiv\ *adj* **:** of, belonging to, or characterized by intussusception

in·tus·sus·cep·tum \,===ˈseptəm\ *n, pl* **intussuscep·ta** \-tə\ [NL, prob. neut. sing. of (assumed) NL *intussusceptus*] **:** the portion of the intestine that passes into another portion in intussusception

in·tus·sus·cip·i·ens \-səˈsipē,enz, -ēənz\ *n, pl* **intussus·cipien·tes** \-,sipēˈen(,)tēz\ [NL, prob. fr. pres. part. of (assumed) NL *intussuscipere*] **:** the portion of the intestine that receives the intussusceptum in intussusception

intwine *var of* ENTWINE

intwist *var of* ENTWIST

inuendo *var of* INNUENDO

inug·suk \ˈēnəg,sük\ *adj, usu cap* **:** of or relating to a stage of Eskimo culture in west Greenland (A.D. 1200–1400) resulting from contact between Thule Eskimo and medieval Norse cultures

in·u·la \ˈinyələ\ *n* [NL, fr. L, elecampane, modif. of Gk *helenion* — more at HELENIUM] **1** -S **:** the dried roots and rhizomes of elecampane used as an aromatic stimulant and esp. formerly as a remedy in pulmonary diseases **2** *cap* **:** a genus of Old World perennial herbaceous or rarely shrubby plants (family Compositae) having large yellow radiate heads with anthers caudate at base — see ELECAMPANE **3** -S **:** any plant or root of the genus *Inula*

in·u·lase \ˈinyə,lās, -āz\ *also* **in·u·lin·ase** \-yələ,nās, -āz\ *n* -S [*inulase* ISV *inul-* (fr. *inulin*) + *-ase; inulinase* ISV *inulin* + *-ase*] **:** an enzyme obtained esp. from molds (as *Aspergillus niger*) and capable of converting inulin into levulose but without action on starch

in·u·lin \ˈinyələn\ *n* -S [prob. fr. G *inulin,* fr. NL *Inula* genus of plants (family Compositae) + G *-in*] **:** a tasteless white nondigestible polysaccharide that occurs usu. in place of starch in many composite and other plants esp. in the tubers or roots of Jerusalem artichoke, dahlia, or chicory, that on hydrolysis yields levulose, and that is used as a source of levulose and as a diagnostic agent in a test for kidney function

in·um·brate \ˈinəm,brāt, əˈnə-\ *vt* -ED/-ING/-S [L *inumbratus,* past part. of *inumbrare,* fr. *in-* ²in- + *umbrare* to shade, fr. *umbra* shadow — more at UMBRAGE] **:** to put in shadow **:** SHADE

in·unct \əˈnəŋ(k)t\ *vt* -ED/-ING/-S [L *inunctus,* past part. of *inunguere* — more at ANOINT] **:** ANOINT 1

in·unc·tion \əˈnəŋ(k)shən\ *n* -S [ME, fr. L *inunction-, inunctio,* fr. *inunctus* (past part. of *inunguere*) + *-ion-, -io* -ion] **1 :** an act of applying an oil or ointment : ANOINTING; *specif* : the rubbing of an ointment into the skin for therapeutic purposes **2** : OINTMENT, UNGUENT, INUNCTUM

in·unc·tum \-ŋ(k)təm\ *n* -S [NL, fr. L, neut. of *inunctus*, past part. of *inunguere*] : an ointment for rapid absorption usu. containing lanolin as a base

inund *vt* -ED/-ING/-S [L *inundare*] *obs* : INUNDATE

in·un·da·ble \ə̇'nəndəbəl, 'i(,)nənd-\ *adj* [*inundate* + *-able*] : exposed to inundation

in·un·dant \-dənt\ *adj* [L *inundant-*, *inundans*, pres. part. of *inundare*] : FLOODING, INUNDATING

in·un·date \'inən,dāt *sometimes* 'i,nə- *or* ə̇'nə-; *usu* -ād·+V\ *vt* -ED/-ING/-S [L *inundatus*, past part. of *inundare*, fr. *in-* [2]in- + *undare* to rise in waves, fr. *unda* wave — more at WATER] **1 a** : to flood with water : SUBMERGE ⟨rising rivers ~ low-lying farms⟩ ⟨a tidal wave ~*s* the island⟩ **b** : to flood as if with water ⟨red blood *inundated* her face, previously so pale —Thomas Hardy⟩ ⟨I have never felt . . . more *inundated* with frustration —John Mason Brown⟩ **2** : to overwhelm by great numbers or a superfluity of something : SWAMP ⟨was *inundated* by calls, telegrams, and letters —Marya Mannes⟩ ⟨*inundated* the nation with carloads of literature —Estes Kefauver⟩

in·un·da·tion \,i(,)nən'dāshən\ *n* -S [ME *inundacion*, fr. L *inundation-*, *inundatio*, fr. *inundatus* (past part. of *inundare*) + *-ion-*, *-io* -ion] **1** : a rising and spreading of water over land not usu. submerged : FLOOD ⟨the threat of ~ by the sea —Lewis Mumford⟩ ⟨his tears were not drops but a little ~ down his cheeks —Glenway Wescott⟩ ⟨fossil shells give evidence of prehistoric ~*s*⟩ **2** : DELUGE, SWARM ⟨an ~ of telegrams⟩ ⟨an ~ of tourists⟩

in·un·da·tor *pronunc at* INUNDATE +ə(r)\ *n* -S : one that inundates

in·un·da·to·ry \ə̇'nəndə,tōrē, -tȯr-, -ri\ *adj* [*inundate* + *-ory*] : tending to inundate

inu·pik \ə̇'nüpik\ *n* -S *cap* : an Eskimo-Aleut language of arctic America spoken from western Alaska to Greenland

in·urbane \(¦)in, ən+\ *adj* [L *inurbanus*, fr. *in-* [1]in- + *urbanus* of the city, refined — more at URBAN] : lacking in refinement or courtesy — **in·urbanity** \¦in+\ *n*

in·ure \ə̇'n(y)u̇(ə)r, -u̇ə\ *or* **en·ure** \ə̇'-, e'-\ *vb* -ED/-ING/-S [*inure* alter. (influenced by *[2]in-*) of *enure*, fr. ME *enuren*, fr. *[1]en-* + *ure*, n., use, custom — more at URE] *vt* : ACCUSTOM : discipline to accept something : HABITUATE ⟨*inured* to the smell of the stable⟩ ⟨a public . . . that is *inured* to certain ways of seeing and thinking —John Dewey⟩ ⟨being stationed at an arctic base ~*s* a man to cold⟩ ~ *vi* : to come into operation : become operative ⟨we are dealing with a relation . . . that might virtually ~ by usage only —W.E.Gladstone⟩ : ACCRUE ⟨the profits ~ to the benefit of hospitals for crippled children —D.A. Reed⟩; *specif* : to become legally effective ⟨when there is such an identity of interest between the taxpayers that a refund to one will ~ to the benefit of the other . . . the unsatisfied liability may be recovered —W.T.Plumb⟩ **syn** see HARDEN

in·ured \-u̇(ə)rd, -u̇əd\ *adj* [fr. past part. of *inure*] : adapted to existing conditions : accustomed to adverse elements : DISCIPLINED, HARDY ⟨our successors . . . may be graver, more ~ and equable men —V.S.Pritchett⟩ ⟨a peasant . . . lean-faced, dark, wind-*inured* —Robert Lynd⟩ — **in·ured·ness** \-u̇rdnə̇s, -u̇əd-, -u̇rə̇d-\ *n* -ES

in·ure·ment \-u̇(ə)rmənt, -u̇əm-\ *n* -S : the quality or state of being inured

in·urn \ə̇n+\ *vt* -ED/-ING/-S [*[2]in-* + *urn*, n.] : to enclose in or as if in an urn : ENTOMB ⟨the body was cremated and the ashes ~*ed*⟩ ⟨where . . . storied cenotaphs ~ sweet human hopes —R.W.Emerson⟩ — **in·urn·ment** \-mənt\ *n* -S

inusitate *adj* [L *inusitatus*, fr. *in-* [1]in- + *usitatus* usual, customary, fr. past part. of *usitor* to use often, fr. *usus*, past part. of *uti* to use — more at USE] *obs* : UNFAMILIAR

in·us·tion \ə̇'nəschən\ *n* -S [LL *inustion-*, *inustio* branding, fr. L *inustus* (past part. of *inurere* to brand, burn in, fr. *in-* [2]in- + *urere* to burn) + *-ion-*, *-io* -ion — more at EMBER] *archaic* : CAUTERIZATION

in ute·ro \ə̇'n(y)üd·e,rō\ *adv* (*or adj*) [L] : in the uterus : before birth ⟨the infection is apparently acquired *in utero* from a mother with a latent disease —*Yr. Bk. of Pediatrics*⟩

in·utile \(')in, ən+\ *adj* [ME, fr. MF, fr. L *inutilis*, fr. *in-* [1]in- + *utilis* useful — more at UTILE] : of no practical value : USELESS, UNUSABLE ⟨being myth it is ~ —Donald Davidson⟩ ⟨the large proportion of ~ tree volume due to decay —*Ecology*⟩ — **in·utility** \¦in+\ *n*

in utro·que ju·re \,inyü·,trōkwē'ju̇rē, ,inü·,trō(,)kwā'yu̇-\ *adv* [NL, lit., in both laws] : in or under both canon and civil law

in·utterable \(')in, ən+\ *adj* [*[1]in-* + *utterable*] *archaic* : UNUTTERABLE

inv *abbr* **1** [L *invenit*] he designed; he devised; he invented **2** invented; invention; inventor **3** inventory **4** investment **5** invitation **6** invoice

in va·cuo \ə̇n'vakyə,wō\ *adv* [NL] **1** : in a vacuum ⟨this residue may be fractionally distilled *in vacuo* —T.P.Hilditch⟩ **2** : without reference to pertinent facts or materials ⟨the theoretical technique has been evolved *in vacuo* —D.L. Bolinger⟩

in·vad·able \ə̇n'vādəbəl\ *adj* : capable of being invaded

in·vade \ə̇n'vād\ *vb* -ED/-ING/-S [ME *invaden*, fr. L *invadere*, fr. *in-* [2]in- + *vadere* to go — more at WADE] *vt* **1 a** : to enter in a hostile manner : overrun with a view to conquest or plunder ⟨soldiers ~ enemy territory⟩ **b** *obs* : to make a personal attack upon : ASSAULT ⟨what madness could provoke a mortal man to ~ a sleeping god —John Dryden⟩ **2** : to encroach, intrude, or trespass upon : INFRINGE ⟨you can obtain legal counsel to determine if any of your rights have been *invaded* —R.O.Case⟩ ⟨when government ~*s* the traditional area of business —A.L.Nickerson⟩ ⟨during his absence his house was *invaded* and plundered —E.D.Dickinson⟩ ⟨resented these queries as *invading* the family privacy —John Dollard⟩ **3** : to penetrate in the manner of an invader: **a** (1) : to grow over or spread into : PERMEATE ⟨the growing city has *invaded* the surrounding countryside —P.E.James⟩ ⟨the imagery of movement . . . *invaded* secular as well as religious literature —R.W.Southern⟩ ⟨doubts ~ his mind⟩ ⟨an odor of onions ~*s* the room⟩ (2) : to affect injuriously and progressively ⟨gangrene ~*s* healthy tissue⟩ ⟨cholera ~*s* the city⟩ (3) : to push into : enter intrusively ⟨the bow-roofed . . . South Ferry Terminal, its upper deck *invaded* by the el structure —*Amer. Guide Series: N.Y.City*⟩; *specif* : to enter in a molten state ⟨compression . . . forces the granitic part of the crust downward to form a solid root and upward to ~ the thick sediments of the mountain-forming belt as molten rock —W.H.Bucher⟩ **b** : to enter or take possession of : PENETRATE, ENGULF ⟨at midmorning, the sun finally ~*s* the very bottom of the gorge —Lester Womack⟩ ⟨two thousand skiers . . . ~ this alpine region —R.S.Monahan⟩ ⟨layfolk . . . *invaded* ecclesiastical offices and revenues —G.G.Coulton⟩; *specif* : to penetrate steadily by taking up residence in (an area occupied by a population of a different class or ethnic composition) **c** : to raid or take by storm ⟨possums ~ the corn patch⟩ ⟨a young and ambitious small-town girl . . . came to New York to ~ the public-relations field —*Publishers' Weekly*⟩ ~ *vi* : to make an invasion **syn** see TRESPASS

in·vad·er \-də(r)\ *n* -S : one that invades

invading *adj* : of, relating to, or being an invader ⟨~ army⟩ ⟨~ tourists⟩ ⟨~ culture⟩ ⟨~ virus⟩

in·vag·i·nate \ə̇n'vajə̇,nāt, *usu* -ād·+V\ *vb* -ED/-ING/-S [ML *invaginatus*, past part. of *invaginare*, fr. L *in-* [2]in- + *vagina* sheath — more at VAGINA] *vt* **1** : ENCLOSE, SHEATHE ⟨external . . . sex organs of the male, contrasted to the *invaginated* organs of the female —*Yr. Bk. of Neurology, Psychiatry & Neurosurgery*⟩ **2** : to fold in so that an outer becomes an inner surface : INTUSSUSCEPT ⟨~ the sac into the lumen —E.A. Graham⟩ ~ *vi* : to become sheathed or infolded ⟨the sphere of cells then *invaginated* to give a cuplike double-walled gastrula —S.F.Mason⟩

in·vag·i·na·tion \(,)in,vajə'nāshən, ən,v-\ *n* -S **1** : an act or process of invaginating: as **a** : the formation of a gastrula by an infolding of part of the wall of the blastula **b** : intestinal intussusception **2** : an invaginated part

[1]in·val·id \(')in¦valə̇d, ən'v-\ *adj* [L *invalidus* not strong, infirm, weak, inadequate, fr. *in-* [1]in- + *validus* strong — more at VALID] **1 a** : being without foundation in fact or truth : INDEFENSIBLE, UNJUSTIFIED ⟨this argument . . . is ~ on two counts —*Monsanto Mag.*⟩ ⟨now that rockets can escape gravity it is ~ to say that what goes up must come down⟩ **b** : lacking in effectiveness : INADEQUATE, WEAK ⟨acceptance of the new method was a tacit admission that the old technique was ~ and inferior⟩ **2** [ML *invalidus*, fr. L] : being without legal force or effect ⟨declared the wills technically ~ because of some legal flaw —Robert Graves⟩

[2]invalid \"\ *vt* -ED/-ING/-S *archaic* : INVALIDATE

[3]in·va·lid \'invələ̇d, *Brit* ¦invə¦lēd\ *adj* [L & F; F *invalide*, fr. L *invalidus*] **1 a** : suffering from disease or disability : SICKLY, DISABLED ⟨hired a nurse to care for his ~ mother⟩ **b** : of, relating, or suited to one that is sick ⟨~ chair⟩ ⟨the whole family lived on ~ fare, on custards and broths and arrowroot pudding —Jean Stafford⟩ **2** : being in poor condition : WEAKENED, UNSOUND ⟨reminding me that, if my chimney was allowed to stand in that ~ condition, my policy of insurance would be void —Herman Melville⟩

[4]in·va·lid \'invələ̇d; *Brit* 'invə,lēd *also* ,invə'lēd\ *n* -S : one that is sickly or disabled ⟨arranged a bed table for the ~ —Eden Phillpotts⟩ ⟨an exaggeration to assume that France is a chronic economic ~ —Paul Johnson⟩; *specif, archaic* : a member of the armed forces who has become unfit for active duty by illness or injury ⟨his garrison at present consists of a few hundreds of ~*s* —Tobias Smollett⟩

[5]in·va·lid \'invələ̇d, *esp before a syllable-increasing suffix* -,lid; *Brit* ¦invə¦lēd\ *vb* -ED/-ING/-S *vt* **1** : to make sickly or disabled ⟨because of a bone ailment, has been ~*ed* since childhood —*Sat. Eve. Post*⟩ **2** : to classify as sick or disabled and remove from active duty ⟨of the 185 firemen . . . sixty were ~*ed* home because of smoke poisoning, burns, or exhaustion —Joseph Millard⟩; *specif* : to release from military service because of illness or injury ⟨~*ed* out of the Norfolk Yeomanry with rheumatic fever —*Saturday Rev.*⟩ ⟨received three bullets through the body, and was due to be ~*ed* home —Joyce Cary⟩ ~ *vi, archaic* **1** : to become an invalid ⟨cannot conceal from myself that I am ~*ing* —R.W.Sibthorp⟩ **2** : to become released from active duty because of disability ⟨the conscripts . . . ~ at an inexplicable rate —*Spectator*⟩

in·val·i·date \ə̇n'valə,dāt, *usu* -ād·+V\ *vt* [*[1]invalid* + *-ate*] : to weaken or make valueless : DISCREDIT ⟨how far the facts confirm or ~ this proud claim —Aldous Huxley⟩ ⟨deviation from a rule which does not affect any important rights of the alien should not ~ a deportation hearing —*Harvard Law Rev.*⟩ **syn** see NULLIFY

in·val·i·da·tion \(,)in,valə'dāshən, ən,v-\ *n* : the act or process of invalidating or the state of being invalidated

in·va·lid·ish \'invələ̇dish, -,lid-, *Brit* ¦invə¦lēd-\ *adj* : resembling or characteristic of an invalid

in·va·lid·ism \'invələ̇,dizəm, *Brit* ¦invə¦lē,d-\ *n* -S : the quality or state of being an invalid : a usu. chronic condition of disability

in·va·lid·i·ty \¦invə¦lidəd·ē, ¦inva¦-, -idətē, -i\ *n* [MF or ML; MF *invalidité*, fr. ML *invaliditat-*, *invaliditas*, fr. *invalidus* void, without legal force + L *-itat-*, *-itas* -ity] **1** : lack of sound foundation or binding legal force **2** [*[3]invalid* + *-ity*] **a** : incapacity to work because of prolonged illness or disability ⟨insurance for sickness and ~ and for the provision of medical service for the working class —R.V.Sires⟩ **b** : INVALIDISM

in·val·id·ly \(')in¦valə̇dlē, ən'v-, -li\ *adv* : in an invalid manner : ILLEGALLY

in·val·id·ness *n* : the quality or state of being invalid

in·valuable \ə̇n+\ *adj* [*[1]in-* + *value*, v. + *-able*] **1** : of an excellence or worth beyond measure : of incalculable value : PRICELESS ⟨fellow townsmen gave him a standing ovation for his ~ services to the community⟩ ⟨a flair for languages is ~ to the career diplomat⟩ ⟨his firsthand knowledge of the area was ~ to the search party⟩ **2** *archaic* : of no value : WORTHLESS ⟨flattered myself I might not be altogether ~ to your ladyship —George Colman †1836⟩ **syn** see COSTLY

in·valuableness \"+\ *n* : the quality or state of being invaluable

in·valuably \"+\ *adv* : to an invaluable degree : IMMEASURABLY

in·valued \"+\ *adj* [*[1]in-* + *valued* (past part. of *value*, v.)] *archaic* : INVALUABLE ⟨no vulgar price the ~ treasure brought —John Hoole⟩

in·var \'in,vär\ *n* -S [fr. *Invar*, a trademark] : an iron-nickel alloy containing about 36 percent nickel and having a coefficient of linear expansion of approximately 0.000001 inch per inch per degree centigrade at ordinary temperatures

in·variability \(¦)in, ən+\ *n* : the quality or state of being invariable

[1]in·variable \(')in, ən+\ *adj* [prob. fr. F, fr. MF, fr. *in-* [1]in- + *variable*] : CONSISTENT, UNIFORM : showing no deviation : UNCHANGING, UNFAILING ⟨where many words . . . are relatively ~ in meaning from one sentence to another —I.A. Richards⟩ ⟨after dinner . . . retired to the library, according to his ~ habit —Valentine Williams⟩ ⟨was respected for his ~ courtesy and undoubted integrity —H.W.H.Knott⟩ — **in·variableness** \"+\ *n*

[2]invariable \"\ *n* : one that remains constant

in·variably \(')in, ən+\ *adv* : without exception or change : ALWAYS, CONSISTENTLY ⟨those most loved . . . are ~ those who have the capacity for believing in others —W.J.Reilly⟩ ⟨the scene . . . was ~ the room in which I lay —Charles Lamb⟩ ⟨a desire to conduct my life ~ —Arnold Bennett⟩

in·variance \"+\ *n* [*[1]invariant* + *-ance*] : invariability under prescribed or implied conditions

[1]in·variant \"+\ *n* [*[1]in-* + *variant*] : a constant factor : one that does not change; *specif* : a mathematical expression or magnitude that remains unchanged under prescribed or implied conditions

[2]invariant \"\ *adj* [*[1]in-* + *variant*] **1** : CONSTANT, UNCHANGING, UNVARYING, UNIVERSAL ⟨16 subjects were presented, on 4 successive days, with 300 ~ stimuli —*Biol. Abstracts*⟩ ⟨basic human emotions . . . are ~ —H.B.Parkes⟩; *specif* : unaffected by the group of mathematical operations under consideration **2** : having no degree of freedom — used of a physical-chemical system; compare PHASE RULE

invaried *adj* [*[1]in-* + *varied*] *obs* : UNVARIED

in·va·sion \ə̇n'vāzhən\ *n* -S [ME (Sc) *invasioune*, fr. MF *invasion*, fr. LL *invasion-*, *invasio*, fr. L *invasus* (past part. of *invadere* to invade) + *-ion-*, *-io* -ion — more at INVADE] **1 a** : a hostile entrance or armed attack on the property or territory of another for conquest or plunder ⟨the ~ of So. Korea resulted in the first police action by United Nations forces⟩ **b** *obs* : an attack on a person : ASSAULT **2** : an inroad of any kind: as **a** : an entry into or establishment in an area not previously occupied ⟨~ of agricultural Lowland Britain by . . . industries from the Highland Margin —L.D. Stamp⟩ ⟨an ~ of catbrier⟩ ⟨~ of sediments by granite —W.H. Bucher⟩ **b** : the introduction or spread of something hurtful or pernicious ⟨~ of locusts⟩; *specif* : the period during which a pathogen multiplies in and is distributed through the body of a host prior to the development of clinically evident disease ⟨vaccine helps to defeat a virus ~ by promoting the production of antibodies in the bloodstream⟩ **c** : a penetration or occupation by an outside force or agency ⟨tourists . . . making their annual ~ of France —James Pope-Hennessy⟩ ⟨insidious ~*s* of experience into the heart —Mark Schorer⟩ ⟨knew I would not disapprove of this ~ of my place by my young cousin —R.H.Davis⟩; *specif* : the penetration and gradual occupation of an area by a population group of different socioeconomic status or racial or cultural origin than its original inhabitants — compare SUCCESSION **d** : VISIT, TOUR ⟨guest ~*s* by famed choreographers —*Time*⟩ ⟨the enterprising candidate made a two-day ~ of nearby tank towns⟩ **3** : ENCROACHMENT, INTRUSION; *specif* : an encroachment upon a right protected by law affording grounds for an action for damages or some other remedy

in·va·sion·ary \-zhə,nerē, -ri\ *adj* : INVASIVE

invasion currency *or* **invasion money** *n* : paper money issued for use by military forces in an invasion

in·va·sive \ə̇n'vāsiv, -āziv\ *adj* [ME (Sc), fr. MF *invasif*, fr. ML *invasivus*, fr. L *invasus* (past part. of *invadere*) + *-ivus* -ive] **1** *obs* : of, relating to, or characterized by military aggression ⟨shall we . . . make compromise, insinuation, parley, and base truce to arms ~ —Shak.⟩ **2** : tending to spread ⟨for years we have been trying to get rid of ~ bulbs —E.H.M.Cox⟩; *specif* : tending to invade healthy tissue ⟨~ cancer cells⟩ — compare PREINVASIVE **3** *archaic* : tending to encroach on or infringe ⟨~ of tribal rights —H.J.S.Maine⟩

in·va·sive·ness *n* -ES : the quality or state of being invasive; *specif* : the tendency of a pathogenic organism to penetrate into and grow within the host away from the original site of inoculation ⟨~ is a major factor in virulence⟩

in·vecked \(')in¦vekt, ən'v-\ *adj* [modif. (influenced by E *[1]-ed*) of L *invectus*, past part. of *invehere* to carry in, bring in] : INVECTED

in·vec·ta et il·la·ta \ə̇n'vektə,ed·ə̇'läd·ə\ *n pl* [LL, lit., things brought in and things carried in] *Roman & civil & Scots law* : goods of a tenant brought upon the leased premises or goods of others brought there by their consent and for other than temporary use

in·vect·ed \(')in¦vektə̇d, ən'v-\ *adj* [L *invectus* (past part. of *invehere* to carry in, bring in) + E *[1]-ed*] *heraldry* : edged by convex semicircles or arcs : SCALLOPED — compare ENGRAILED

in·vec·tion \-kshən\ *n* -S [L *invection-*, *invectio*, fr. *invectus* (past part. of *invehere* to carry in, bring in) + *-ion-*, *-io* -ion] : an introduction of something from an outside source ⟨an ~ of . . . battle smoke floated among islands of rose-tinted altocumulus —K.M.Dodson⟩

[1]in·vec·tive \ə̇n'vektiv, -tēv *also* -təv\ *adj* [ME *invectiff*, fr. MF *invectif*, fr. LL *invectivus*, fr. L *invectus* (past part. of *invehere*) + *-ivus* -ive] : of, relating to, or characterized by insult or abuse : DENUNCIATORY ⟨a sharp corrective message, suitably ~ —Edith G. Blanchard⟩

[2]invective \"\ *n* -S **1** : an abusive expression or diatribe : a vehement verbal attack ⟨replied with ~*s* fierce and scurrilous —J.A.Froude⟩ ⟨thundering ~ against sin —Ernest Beaglehole⟩ **2** : critical or insulting language : violent abuse : VITUPERATION ⟨as his anger mounted, ridicule and ~ poured from his mouth searing and burning all that they touched —D.L.Cohn⟩ **syn** see ABUSE

in·vec·tive·ly \-tə̇vlē, -li\ *adv, obs* : in an invective manner ⟨thus most ~ he pierceth through the body of our country, swearing —Shak.⟩

in·veigh \ə̇n'vā\ *vb* -ED/-ING/-S [L *invehi* to sail into, attack, inveigh, pass. infin. of *invehere* to carry in, bring in, fr. *in-* [2]in- + *vehere* to carry — more at WAY] *vi* : to protest bitterly or violently : complain vehemently : RAIL — used with *against* ⟨~ against injustice⟩ ⟨~*s* against the arbitrary character of all such unscientific procedures —G.M.Messing⟩ ~ *vt* [L *invehere*] *obs* : INVEIGLE

in·veigh·er \-āə(r)\ *n* -S : one that inveighs

in·vei·gle \ə̇n'vāgəl *also* ə̇n'vēg- *or* ə̇n'vig-\ *vt* **inveigled**; **inveigled**; **inveigling** \-g(ə)liŋ\ **inveigles** [modif. (influenced by E *[2]in-*) of MF *aveugler* to blind, hoodwink, fr. OF *avogler*, fr. *avogle*, *avugle* blind, fr. ML *ab oculis*, fr. L *ab* from + *oculis*, abl. pl. of *oculus* eye — more at OF, EYE] **1** *obs* : DELUDE, MISLEAD, HOODWINK, BEGUILE ⟨your rhetorical flourishes . . . contributed in an high degree to ~ the jury, and bring that noble lord to the scaffold —Robert Atkyns⟩ **2** : to snare by ingenuity or flattery : ENTICE, CAJOLE ⟨used the most subtle means to ~ the author into the office —Edward Bok⟩ ⟨with patience and diplomacy, she can eventually ~ him into marrying her —Nellie Maher⟩ **3** : to acquire by ingenuity or flattery ⟨over gin and water we *inveigled* from him a pack of well-worn cards —Ernest Beaglehole⟩ **syn** see LURE

in·vei·gle·ment \-gəlmənt\ *n* -S : an act, process, or means of inveigling : ENTICEMENT, LURE

in·vei·gler \-g(ə)lə(r)\ *n* -S : one that inveigles

inveil *var of* ENVEIL

in·vent \ə̇n'vent\ *vt* -ED/-ING/-S [ME *inventen*, fr. L *inventus*, past part. of *invenire*, fr. *in-* [2]in- + *venire* to come — more at COME] **1** : to search out or come upon : FIND, DISCOVER ⟨must ~ beds for them —Frederick Way⟩ ⟨this polymer was ~*ed* in England and is an outgrowth of earlier research —Leonard Maner & Harry Wechsler⟩ **2** : to think up or imagine : concoct mentally : FABRICATE ⟨his fund of knowledge seemed inexhaustible, for what he didn't know he ~*ed* —Alvin Redman⟩ ⟨preparing in his mind the harshest response he could ~ —W.F.Davis⟩ **3** : to create or produce for the first time : be the author of : DEVISE, ORIGINATE ⟨he ~*ed* and secured a patent . . . for a rock-boring machine —B.A.Soule⟩ ⟨if the Semitic letters were not derived from Egypt they must have been ~*ed* by the Phoenicians —Edward Clodd⟩ ⟨~*ed* an ingenious kind of ball game —Margaret Bean⟩ ⟨has ~*ed* plenty of good tunes of his own —Sigmund Spaeth⟩ **4** *obs* : FOUND, ESTABLISH, INSTITUTE, INITIATE ⟨festival days in old time were ~*ed* for recreation —John Northbrooke⟩ **syn** see CONTRIVE

in·vent·able *or* **in·vent·ible** \-təbəl\ *adj* : capable of being invented

inventary *n* -ES [LL *inventarium* — more at INVENTORY] *obs* : INVENTORY

in·ven·tion \ə̇n'venchən\ *n* -S [ME *invencioun*, fr. MF *invention*, fr. L *invention-*, *inventio*, fr. *inventus* (past part. of *invenire* to find) + *-ion-*, *-io* -ion] **1** : an act of finding or of finding out : DISCOVERY ⟨~ of the principle of leverage⟩ **2 a** : the power to conceive new ideas and relationships : productive imagination : INVENTIVENESS ⟨old crates and boxes are often more stimulating to a child's ~ than expensive toys⟩ **b** : a faculty for creative selection of theme and imaginative treatment of design or content ⟨the variety and excellence of the classical legacy demonstrate the abundant ~ of the ancient Greeks⟩ ⟨as a teller of tales he had rich ~ and adroit construction —Brander Matthews⟩ **c** : a product of creative imagination or fertile wit ⟨the ~*s*, the devices which serve a novelist best grow . . . out of his necessity —Caroline Gordon⟩ ⟨a cascade of melodic ~ —Harold Sinclair⟩ ⟨those pillars, that stair and varnished roof . . . were among the worst ~*s* of the Gothic revival —W.B.Yeats⟩ **d** : a musical composition or piece imitative in style, usu. short, and usu. written for the piano or other keyboard instrument **3 a** : an act of mental creation or organization : application of knowledge : CONCEPTION, FORMULATION ⟨~ of agreements or compromises —Weston La Barre⟩ ⟨no continuing agency to interpret the party platform after its slapdash ~ every four years —R.L. Strout⟩ ⟨tried a long play of her own ~ —Leslie Rees⟩ **b** : a product of thought or mental synthesis : IDEA, CONCEPT ⟨the idea that the royal family should be a symbol of respectability was an ~ of Queen Victoria —Fritz Stern⟩ ⟨characterized the Supreme Court as the great political ~ of the framers of the Constitution —Felix Frankfurter⟩ ⟨new social ~*s* are made by those who suffer from the current conditions —Ralph Linton⟩; *specif* : a fictitious idea or statement ⟨race theories are . . . a modern ~ to explain such group conflicts —M.R.Cohen⟩ ⟨the whole purpose of the . . . argument being to invalidate the generally accepted romance and prove it an ~ —E.V.Lucas⟩ **4 a** : the creation of something not previously in existence : purposeful experimentation leading to the development of a new device or process : ORIGINATION ⟨necessity is the mother of ~⟩ ⟨machinery of their own ~ —*Amer. Guide Series: Md.*⟩ **b** : an original device or process ⟨writing was a greater ~ than the steam engine —A.N.Whitehead⟩; *specif, U.S. patent law* : a device or process that is not only novel and useful but that reflects creative genius, makes a distinct contribution to and advances science, is recognized by masters of science as such an advance and reveals more than the skill of expert artisans or mechanics in discovering new and useful gadgets or processes of wide commercial application

inventious *adj* [fr. *invention*, after such pairs as E *contention: contentious*] *obs* : INVENTIVE

in·ven·tive \ə̇n'ventiv, -tēv *also* -təv\ *adj* [ME *inventif*, fr. MF, fr. *invention*, after such pairs as MF *action: actif* active] **1** : having the capacity for or being a prolific producer of inventions : CREATIVE, INGENIOUS ⟨an ~ writer⟩ ⟨an ~ composer⟩ ⟨the preposition . . . is a tremendously ~ word —R.M. Weaver⟩ **2** : of, relating to, or characterized by invention ⟨the war gives rise to incidents . . . beyond the ~ power of the human imagination —Maya Deren⟩ ⟨exquisite gold work and ~ ceramics —Angélica Mendoza⟩ ⟨a mechanic of an ~ turn of mind —J.Q.Dealey⟩ — **in·ven·tive·ly** \-tə̇vlē, -li\ *adv*

in·ven·tive·ness \-tivnə̇s, -tēv- *also* -təv-\ *n* -ES : the quality or state of being inventive : INGENUITY, CREATIVITY

in·ven·tor *also* **in·vent·er** \ə̇n'ventə(r)\ *n* -S [*inventor* fr. L, fr. *inventus* (past part. of *invenire*) + *-or*; *inventer* alter. (influenced by E *[2]-er*) of *inventor*] **1** *obs* : one that finds or finds out : DISCOVERER ⟨first ~ of the nervous system —John Freind⟩ **2** : one that conceives by creative imagination ⟨~ of a new ballet⟩ ⟨one must be an ~ to read well —S.P.Sherman⟩ ⟨the next step is to discover what makes a man an ~ rather than a passive culture carrier —Ralph Linton⟩ **3** : one that creates a new device or process : ORIGINATOR ⟨Eli Whitney was the ~ of the cotton gin⟩

in·ven·to·ri·able \'invən-,tōrēəbəl, -tȯr-, ,==ˈ====\ *adj* **1** : capable of being inventoried **2** : includable in an inventory or in its valuation

in·ven·to·ri·al \¦==¦rēəl\ *adj* : of or relating to an inventory — **in·ven·to·ri·al·ly** \-rēəlē\ *adv*

inventorize *vt* -ED/-ING/-S [MF *inventoriser*, fr. *inventoire* inventory (fr. ML *inventorium*) + *-iser* -ize] *archaic* : INVENTORY

¹in·ven·to·ry \'invən-,tōrē, -tȯr-, -ri\ *n* -ES *often attrib* [alter. (influenced by ML *inventorium*) of ME *invitory*, modif. of ML *inventorium*, alter. (influenced by L *-orium* -ory) of LL *inventarium*, fr. L *inventus* (past part. of *invenire* to find) + *-arium* -ary] **1** : an itemized list of current assets: as **a** : a written list or catalog usu. made by a fiduciary under oath of the tangible or intangible property of an individual, organization, or estate describing the items or classes of property so as to be identifiable and usu. placing a valuation thereon **b** (1) : a list or schedule of raw materials, supplies, work in process, and finished goods on hand as of a given date (2) : a list of merchandise held for sale (3) : the aggregate value assigned to an inventory **c** : a survey of natural resources; *specif* : an estimate or enumeration of the wildlife (as game animals) of a region **d** : a questionnaire designed to provide an index of individual interests or personality traits **2** : a detailed study or recapitulation : SURVEY, SUMMARY ⟨offered a brief ~ of the chief inventions of the middle ages —Benjamin Farrington⟩ ⟨the replies . . . provide a nearly complete ~ of the ideas which are afloat among the young people —W.J.Cahnman⟩ ⟨Whitman's verses . . . are often more *inventories* than imaginative projections of America —H.S.Canby⟩ **3 a** : the quantity of goods or materials on hand : STOCK, SUPPLY ⟨adequate *inventories* of washing machines to meet local demand⟩ ⟨it took quite an ~ of heavy tools . . . to do all this —George Woodbury⟩ **b** : a surplus of goods or materials accumulated against future needs : RESERVE ⟨there has piled up a 2000 million dollar ~ of foodstuffs —John Boyd Orr⟩ ⟨industry would purchase for a year in advance what would amount to an ~ of labor —Leland Hazard⟩ **4** : the act or process of taking an inventory ⟨the annual ~ takes two weeks⟩ ⟨depends on a careful and continuing ~ of the entire staff —J.B.Conant⟩ **5** : a comprehensive list of personality traits, personal preferences, attitudes, interests, or abilities used to measure subjective judgments and to evaluate individual characteristics and skills

²inventory \"\ *vb* -ED/-ING/-ES *vt* **1 a** : to make an itemized report or record of : take stock of : CATALOG ⟨~ home troops⟩ ⟨~ waterfowl⟩ ⟨walked in uninvited and *inventoried* the room with one long glance —John Selby⟩; *specif* : to count and list the assets of together with their valuation ⟨~ an estate⟩ **b** : to include in a business inventory **2** : to make a study or recapitulation of : SURVEY, SUMMARIZE ⟨a book of criticism that . . . completely *inventoried* the mind of the age —Rebecca West⟩ ~ *vi* : to have a value by inventory ⟨his estate *inventories* at close to half a million⟩

inventory control *n* : coordination and supervision of the supply, storage, distribution, and recording of materials to maintain quantities adequate for current needs without excessive oversupply or loss

in·ven·tress \ən'ven·trəs\ *n* -ES [*inventor* + *-ess*] : a female inventor

in·ven·trix \-en·triks\ *n* -ES [L, fem. of *inventor* — more at -TRIX] : INVENTRESS

in·veracity \¦in+\ *n* [¹*in-* + *veracity*] **1** : lack of truth : FALSENESS ⟨forced to recognize its inadequacy, its palpable ~ —G.J.Becker⟩ **2** : an intentional falsehood : LIE ⟨the bogus anecdotes of his conversation were not, I am convinced, plain *inveracities*, but things which he had imagined —Christopher Hollis⟩

¹in·ver·ness \¦invə(r)¦nes\ *adj* [fr. *Inverness*, burgh and county in Scotland] **1** : of or from the burgh of Inverness, Scotland : of the kind or style prevalent in Inverness **2** : INVERNESS-SHIRE

²inverness \"\ *n* -ES : a loose belted coat having an often detachable shoulder cape with a close-fitting round collar

inverness-shire \¦invə(r)¦nes(h),shi(ə)r, -iə, -,shə(r)\ *or* **inverness** \¦invə(r)¦nes\ *adj, usu cap I* [fr. *Inverness-shire* or *Inverness*, county in Scotland] : of or from the county of Inverness, Scotland : of the kind or style prevalent in Inverness

¹in·verse \(')in¦vərs, ən'v-, -vəs,-vəis\ *vt* -ED/-ING/-S [L *inversus*, past part. of *invertere*] : INVERT, REVERSE

²in·verse \'=,=, ='=\ *adj* [L *inversus*, past part. of *invertere* to invert — more at INVERT] **1** *archaic* : being upside down : INVERTED ⟨a tower builded on a lake, mocked by its ~ shadow —Thomas Hood †1845⟩ **2** : opposite in nature or relationship : CONTRARY, REVERSED ⟨as high as 70 percent . . . were engaged in repair and conversion work, a condition ~ to prewar operation —*Collier's Yr. Bk.*⟩ ⟨attendance of the students . . . is in ~ ratio to the work in the cornfields —Joaquin Noval⟩ **3 a** : opposite in nature and effect — used of two mathematical operations which when both are performed in succession upon any quantity reproduce that quantity ⟨division is the ~ operation of multiplication⟩ **b** *of a mathematical function* : expressing the same relationship as another function but from the opposite viewpoint

inverness

³inverse \"\ *n* -S **1** : something of a contrary nature or quality : OPPOSITE, REVERSE ⟨had no luck with his experiment so he tried the ~ of this process and got a positive result⟩; *specif* : the opposite color from that of the first card dealt in the winning row in the game of rouge et noir — compare COULEUR 2 **2** : the result of an inversion; *specif* : a proposition which is inferred immediately from another and in which the subject term is the negative of the subject of the given proposition and the predicate term is unchanged ⟨the ~ of "no purposeful effort is entirely wasted" is "some not-purposeful effort is entirely wasted"⟩ — compare CONTRAPOSITION **3** : an inverse function, operation, or point

inverse cosecant *n* : ARC COSECANT

inverse cosine *n* : ARC COSINE

inverse cotangent *n* : ARC COTANGENT

inverse feedback *n* : NEGATIVE FEEDBACK

inverse function *n* : either of two mathematical functions such that each is the inverse of the other

in·verse·ly \(')=¦==\ *adv* : in an inverse order or manner : by inversion

inversely proportional *adj* : having their product constant — used of two variable quantities one of which varies directly as the reciprocal of the other

inverse point *n* : either of two points on a diametral line of a fixed circle or sphere the product of whose distances from the center equals the square of the radius

inverse proportion *n* : the relation between two inversely proportional quantities

inverse ratio *n* : the ratio of the reciprocals of two quantities

inverse secant *n* : ARC SECANT

inverse sine *n* : ARC SINE

inverse spelling *n* : REVERSE SPELLING

inverse-square \¦=,=¦=\ *adj* [fr. the phrase *inverse square*] : according with or relating to the inverse-square law

inverse-square law *n* : a statement in physics: the manner in which a physical quantity (as illumination) varies with the distance from the source is inversely as the square of the distance

inverse tangent *n* : ARC TANGENT

inverse taper *n, of an airfoil* : increase in the chord with distance outboard from the root

inverse-time \¦=,=¦=\ *adj* [fr. the phrase *inverse time*] : done with a purposely delayed action that decreases as the operating force increases — used esp. of electrical relays

inverse trigonometric function *n* : the inverse of any of the six trigonometric functions

inverse voltage *n* : the voltage moving through a rectifier during the reverse half of the alternating-current cycle

in·ver·sion \ən'vər|zhən, -vəī|, -vəi| *also* |shən\ *n* -S [L *inversion-*, *inversio*, fr. *inversus* (past part. of *invertere* to invert) + *-ion-*, *-io* -ion — more at INVERT] **1** : an act or result of turning inside out or upside down : FLEXURE, DOUBLING: as **a** : a folding back of rock strata upon themselves by which their sequence seems reversed **b** : a dislocation of a bodily organ in which it is turned partially or wholly inside out ⟨~ of the uterus⟩ **c** : a condition of being turned inward ⟨~ of the foot⟩ **d** : RETROFLEXION 3 **2** : a reversal of position, order, or relationship: as **a** : the reverse of an established pattern ⟨the structure of an insect . . . is an almost complete ~ of what prevails in a vertebrate animal —A.D.Imms⟩ ⟨so strange an ~ of the paternal and filial relations as this proposition of his son to pay him a hundred pounds —George Eliot⟩ **b** (1) : INVERTED ORDER (2) : ANASTROPHE **c** : a change of cadence by the introduction in a metrical series of a foot in which arsis and thesis have positions symmetrically opposed to the positions they have in the normal esp. adjacent feet of the series : shift of cadence from rising to falling or from falling to rising — compare SUBSTITUTION **d** (1) *of an interval* : a raising of the lower or dropping of the upper tone by an octave (2) *of a triad or seventh chord* : a transposition of the root to some voice other than the bass (3) *of a melody* : a repetition of a phrase or subject (as of a fugue) with each ascending interval inverted into a corresponding descending interval and vice versa (4) *in double counterpoint* : a transposition of an upper and a lower voice part (5) : a transferring of a pedal point from the bass to an upper part **e** *logic* : the operation of immediate inference which gives an inverse proposition — see ³INVERSE 2 **f** (1) : a breaking off of a chromosome section and its subsequent reattachment in reversed position (2) : such a chromosome section **3 a** : a change in the order of the terms of a mathematical proportion effected by inverting each ratio **b** : the operation of inverting or forming the inverse either of a magnitude or of an operation **c** : a change from the order in which elements or parcels of objects are arranged naturally or normally **4** : HOMOSEXUALITY **5 a** : a conversion of a substance showing dextrorotation into one showing levorotation or vice versa ⟨the ~ of sucrose involves hydrolysis of a dextrorotatory material to an equimolar mixture of D-glucose and D-fructose that is levorotatory⟩ **b** : substitution of one of the groups attached to the asymmetric atom of an optically active organic molecule so that an original clockwise arrangement of atoms or groups becomes counterclockwise **c** : a change of a crystalline substance from one polymorphic form into another **6** : a conversion of direct current into alternating current **7** : a reversal of normal atmospheric temperature gradient : increase of temperature of the air with increasing altitude

in·ver·sion·ist \-zh(ə)nəst, -sh-\ *n* -S : one who habitually writes upside down and backward

inversion point *n* **1** : TRANSITION POINT **2** : a point (as on a temperature scale) at which a physical quantity reaches a maximum or minimum or at which it changes algebraic sign

inversion spectrum *n* : a microwave absorption spectrum (as of ammonia vapor) attributed in quantum mechanics to quantized changes in molecular structure from one arrangement to another that is the mirror image of the first

in·ver·sive \(')in¦vərsiv, ən'v-, -rziv\ *adj* [*inversion* + *-ive*] : marked by inversion ⟨~ error⟩ ⟨~ personality⟩

¹in·vert \ən'vər|t, -vəī|, -vəi|, *usu* |d·+V\ *vb* -ED/-ING/-S [L *invertere*, fr. *in-* ²in- + *vertere* to turn — more at WORTH] *vt* **1 a** : to turn inside out or upside down ⟨the magician ~s the bag to show it is empty⟩ ⟨the gardener ~s a bell jar over his rose cutting⟩; *specif* : to print (a part of a stamp or an overprint) upside down **b** : to turn inward ⟨when a foot is ~ed its forepart tends to approach the midline of the body —*Jour. Amer. Med. Assoc.*⟩ **2** : to reverse in position, order, or relationship ⟨both poems ~ the original affective situation, turning despair into success —Malcolm Brown⟩ ⟨in singing the second half of "Ten Little Indians" you ~ the numbers⟩ ⟨the generality concerning molecular weight may not be ~ed, for it is not true that salts with light molecules are invariably salty tasting —F.A.Geldard⟩; *specif* : to subject (a melody) to inversion **3 a** : to subject (sucrose) to inversion **b** : to change (a crystalline compound) from one polymorphous form to another ~ *vi* : to undergo inversion ⟨sucrose ~s⟩ ⟨the quartz starts to ~ to cristobalite —F.H.Norton⟩

²in·vert \'in,v-\ *n* -S : one that is characterized by inversion: as **a** : INVERTED ARCH **b** : the lowest point in the internal cross section of an artificial channel **c** : a stamp having an overprint or some portion of its design inverted **d** : HOMOSEXUAL

³invert \"\ *adj* : subjected to chemical inversion : INVERTED 3 ⟨~ sugar⟩

invert *abbr* invertebrate

in·vert·ase \ən'vərd·,ās, 'in,v-, -āz\ *n* -S [ISV ¹*invert* + *-ase*; prob. orig. formed in F] : an enzyme found in many microorganisms and plants and in animal intestines that is capable of effecting the inversion of sucrose and that is usu. prepared from yeast as a white powder — called also *sucrase*

in·ver·te·bra·cy \ən'vərd·əbrəsē\ *n* -ES [²*invertebrate* + *-cy*] : SPINELESSNESS

in·vertebral \(')in, ən+\ *adj* [¹*in-* + *vertebral*] : INVERTEBRATE

in·vertebrata \(')in, ən+\ *n pl, cap* [NL, fr. neut. pl. of *invertebratus* invertebrate] *in some esp former classifications* : a primary division of the animal kingdom including all except the Vertebrata

¹in·vertebrate \(')in, ən+\ *n* [NL *Invertebrata*] **1** : an animal having no backbone or internal skeleton ⟨in the lower ~s such as coelenterates —W.H.Dowdeswell⟩ **2** : one that is weak or indecisive ⟨its new dangers are the innocuous and the ~ —Sacheverell Sitwell⟩

²invertebrate \"\ *adj* [NL *invertebratus*, fr. L *in-* ¹in- + NL *vertebratus* vertebrate] **1** : lacking a spinal column ⟨~ jellyfish⟩ **2** : lacking in structure or vitality : DISORGANIZED, WEAK ⟨his book is completely ~, breaking sharply in the middle into two books —S.E.Hyman⟩ ⟨moves far beyond the often ~ lyricism . . . into a rhetoric that has intellectual iron —Mark Schorer⟩

inverted *adj* **1 a** : turned upside down or inside out ⟨~ rock strata⟩ ⟨~ lumen of the intestine⟩ ⟨the blood rushed to his head as he zoomed across the field in ~ flight⟩ **b** : inverted in relation to the rest of a stamp — used of parts of a stamp or stamp design ⟨~ center⟩ **c** *heraldry* : having the tip pointing down — used of a wing ⟨an eagle, wings expanded and ~⟩ **d** : RETROFLEX **2** : reversed in position, order, or relationship : contrary to an established pattern ⟨~ spellings⟩ ⟨~ seasons of the southern hemisphere⟩ ⟨much ~ snobbery in the idealization of the English working class —Roy Lewis & Angus Maude⟩; *specif* : based on or characterized by musical inversion ⟨~ melody⟩ **3** : transformed by inversion **4** : HOMOSEXUAL — **in·vert·ed·ly** *adv*

inverted arch *n* : an arch with the crown downward that is much used in foundations, sewers, and tunnels and is often made of solid concrete

inverted comma *n* **1 a** : a type comma reversed so as to produce an upside-down comma at the top of the printed line **b** : the comma so printed that is commonly used singly or in pairs to mark the beginning of a quotation **2** *chiefly Brit* : QUOTATION MARK

inverted engine *n* : an engine whose crankshaft is above the cylinders

inverted interval *n* : a simple musical interval having its lower tone raised or its upper tone lowered an octave

inverted mordent *n* : PRALLTRILLER

inverted order *n* : an arrangement of the elements of a sentence (as subject, predicate) that is the reverse of the usual order and is designed to achieve variety or emphasis (as in "among them were the following" "again she called") or to indicate a question (as in "what does he say") — compare ANASTROPHE

inverted passive *n* : a passive construction in which the subject of the passive verb corresponds to the indirect object of the verb in an active construction (as in "he was awarded a medal by the club")

inverted perspective *n* : REVERSE PERSPECTIVE

inverted pleat *n* : a pleat formed by bringing two folded edges toward or to a center point on the outside of the material to form a box pleat on the inside

inverted-pyramid indention *n* : HALF-DIAMOND INDENTION

inverted siphon *n* : a pipe for conducting water beneath a depressed place

inverted talon *n* : an ogee molding with the convex part at the top

inverted triad *n* : a triad with a tone other than the root in the bass

in·ver·tend \¦in(,)vər¦tend\ *n* -S [L *invertendus*, gerundive of *invertere* to invert — more at INVERT] : a proposition upon which the operation of inversion is performed

inverted pleat

in·vert·er \ən'vərd·ə(r), -vəī|, -vəi|, |tə(r)\ *n* -S **1** : one that inverts **2** : a device for converting direct current into alternating current by mechanical or electronic means

in·vert·ible \|d·əbəl|, |təbəl\ *adj* **1** : capable of being inverted or subjected to inversion **2** : admitting of musical inversion

in·vert·in \ən'vərtᵊn\ *n* -S [ISV ¹*invert* + *-in*] : INVERTASE

inverting *pres part of* INVERT

inverting telescope *n* : a telescope in which the image is seen or photographed upside down usu. because it has no optical erecting system

in·ver·tor \ən'vər|d·ə(r), -vəī|, -vəi|, |tə(r)\ *n* -S [NL (influenced in meaning by L *in* and L *vertere* to turn), irreg. fr. L *invertere* to invert + *-or* — more at ¹IN, WORTH] : a muscle that turns a part (as the foot) inward

inverts *pres 3d sing of* INVERT

invert soap *n* : CATIONIC DETERGENT

invert sugar *n* : a mixture of D-glucose and D-fructose that is sweeter than sucrose, that occurs naturally in fruits and honey, that is usu. made commercially from a solution of cane sugar by hydrolysis (as with acid), and that is used chiefly as a difficultly crystallizable syrup in foods and in medicine

¹in·vest \ən'vest\ *vt* -ED/-ING/-S [ML *investire*, fr. L, to clothe, cover, surround, fr. *in-* ²in- + *vestire* to clothe, fr. *vestis* garment — more at WEAR] **1 a** : to array in the symbols of office or honor : install in an office or honor with customary ceremonies ⟨was ~ed by Queen Elizabeth . . . in a private ceremony —*Springfield (Mass.) Union*⟩ ⟨was ~ed with the George Medal, Britain's highest award for civilian heroism —*Charlottetown (Canada) Guardian*⟩ **b** : to furnish with or make a formal grant (as of power or authority) to : establish officially ⟨by the Constitution of the United States, the president is ~ed with certain important political powers —John Marshall⟩ **c** : to put in possession or control of someone : VEST ⟨provincial life in Tsarist Russia . . . ~ed absolute authority in the head of the family —*London Calling*⟩ **2** [L *investire*] : to envelop or cover completely : SURROUND, COAT ⟨things are ~ed with mystery in the degree that their origins and causes are unknown —Edward Clodd⟩ ⟨could ~ a common murder case with the atmosphere of an Aeschylean drama —Van Wyck Brooks⟩; *specif* : to place (a pattern) in refractory material in the process of investment casting ⟨bell-form bowl, ~ed with a rich turquoise blue glaze —*Parke-Bernet Galleries Catalog*⟩ — see CIRE PERDUE **3** [L *investire*] **a** : CLOTHE, ADORN ⟨brought a light raincoat with which he now ~ed his ample person —John Buchan⟩ ⟨went to the pains of ~ing the production richly, for sets and costumes are fabulous —Louise Mace⟩ **b** *obs* : to put on : DON ⟨cannot find one this girdle to ~ —Edmund Spenser⟩ **4** [MF *investir*, fr. OIt *investire*, fr. L, to surround] : to surround with troops or ships so as to prevent escape or entry : lay siege to ⟨Charleston was never besieged, nor was any serious effort made . . . to ~ it on the land side —O.L.Spaulding⟩ **5** : to endow with some quality or characteristic : INFUSE, ENRICH ⟨talent for ~ing the commonplace with significance —Gerald Bullett⟩ ⟨the realist . . . ~s contemporary events with values that are eventually established as history —Bernard Smith⟩ ⟨the tone of his . . . voice which he tried to ~ with candor and modesty —Bernard De Voto⟩ ⟨swept off his hat with a gesture that ~ed it with plumes —Edna Ferber⟩

²invest \"\ *vb* -ED/-ING/-S [It *investire*, fr. L, to clothe, cover, surround] *vt* **1 a** : to commit (money) for a long period in order to earn a financial return ⟨~ed his savings in stocks, bonds, and real estate⟩ **b** : to place (money) with a view to minimizing risk rather than speculating for large gains at greater hazard **2** : to make use of with particular thought of future benefits or advantages ⟨~ed his savings in a year of study —Norman Foerster⟩ ⟨I am avaricious of time and uneasy if I don't ~ it well —O.W.Holmes †1935⟩ ~ *vi* : to commit funds for future gain or purchase something of intrinsic value : make an investment ⟨anyone who wants to know more before ~ing can write the editor —*Monsanto Mag.*⟩ — often used with *in* ⟨decided to ~ in a first edition as a birthday gift for her husband⟩ ⟨the burghers . . . would not ~ in factories —William Petersen⟩

in·vest·able *also* **in·vest·ible** \-təbəl\ *adj* [²*invest* + *-able*, *-ible*] : available for investment ⟨~ surplus⟩

investient *adj* [L *investient-*, *investiens*, pres. part. of *investire*] *obs* : SURROUNDING, ENVELOPING

in·ves·ti·ga·ble \ən'vestəgəbəl, -tēg-\ *adj* [LL *investigabilis*, fr. L *investigare* to investigate + *-abilis* -able] *archaic* : INVESTIGATABLE

in·ves·ti·gat·able \ən'vestə,gād·əbəl, =,==¦===\ *adj* : capable of being investigated

in·ves·ti·gate \ən'vestə,gāt, *usu* -ād·+V\ *vb* -ED/-ING/-S [L *investigatus*, past part. of *investigare*, fr. *in-* ²in- + *vestigare* to track, trace; akin to L *vestigium* trace, footprint] *vt* : to observe or study closely : inquire into systematically : EXAMINE, SCRUTINIZE ⟨the whole brilliance of this novel lies in the fullness with which it ~s a past —Mark Schorer⟩ ⟨a commission to ~ costs of industrial production —Broadus Mitchell⟩ ⟨synthetic resins *investigated* for possible use in printing inks —H.J.Wolfe⟩ ⟨*investigating* every square cubit of terrain which she might have covered —L.C.Douglas⟩; *specif* : to subject to an official probe ⟨~ a crime⟩ ⟨~ marine casualties⟩ ⟨the F.B.I. ~s every applicant for federal employment⟩ ~ *vi* : to make a systematic examination : STUDY; *specif* : to conduct an official inquiry ⟨the power of Congress to ~ is an implied power in the Constitution —*New Republic*⟩

investigating *adj* : INVESTIGATIVE 2 — **in·ves·ti·gat·ing·ly** \=ˈ==,===, =,=='===\ *adv*

in·ves·ti·ga·tion \ən,vestə'gāshən\ *n* -S [ME *investigacioun*, fr. MF *investigation*, fr. L *investigation-*, *investigatio*, fr. *investigatus* (past part. of *investigare*) + *-ion-*, *-io* -ion] **1** : the action or process of investigating : detailed examination : STUDY, RESEARCH ⟨success of the . . . blend in knitwear has led to active ~ of blends with other fibers —*Amer. Fabrics*⟩ ⟨a strong movement to make American universities centers of scholarly work and scientific ~ —J.B.Conant⟩ **2** : a searching inquiry : EXAMINATION, SURVEY ⟨his doctoral thesis was a penetrating ~ of the causes of race conflict⟩ ⟨carried on energetic ~s of the medicinal flora of Mexico —*Amer. Guide Series: Mich.*⟩; *specif* : an official probe ⟨the first Congressional ~ of loyalty in government —Will Herberg⟩ **syn** see INQUIRY

in·ves·ti·ga·tion·al \=¦=¦gāshənᵊl, -shnəl\ *adj* : INVESTIGATIVE 2

in·ves·ti·ga·tive \=ˈ==,gād·|iv, -āt|, |ēv *also* |əv\ *adj* **1** : characterized by or having a tendency toward investigation ⟨~ scientist⟩ **2** : of or relating to investigation ⟨~ power⟩ ⟨~ technique⟩

in·ves·ti·ga·tor \-,gād·ə(r), -ātə-\ *n* -S [L, fr. *investigatus* (past part. of *investigare*) + *-or*] : one that investigates: as **a** : one that conducts systematic inquiries or experiments : STUDENT, RESEARCHER **b** : an insurance claim adjuster or an underwriter **c** : one who is employed to examine the quality of goods or services of a business, its type of personnel, or the condition of its property — called also *spotter* **d** : one who inquires into the history of an applicant for employment to determine his integrity and loyalty **e** : DETECTIVE

in·ves·ti·ga·to·ry \-ˌgəˌtōrē, -tȯrē, -ri *chiefly Brit* ═¦══-¦gātəri *or* -ā·tri\ *adj* [*investigate* + *-ory*] : INVESTIGATIVE

in·ves·ti·tive \ən'vestəd·iv\ *adj* [ML *investitus* (past part. of *investire* to invest) + E *-ive*] : of, relating to, or having the power of vesting a right

in·ves·ti·ture \-təˌchu̇(ə)r, -ˌchu̇ə, -ˌchə(r), -təˌtu̇-, -tə·ˌtyu̇-\ *n* -S [ME, fr. ML *investitura*, fr. *investitus* (past part. of *investire* to invest) + L *-ura* -ure] **1 a :** the ceremonial conferral of symbols of office or honor ⟨the six newly appointed Master Knights . . . immediately after their ~ with the Cloak and Cross of Malta —*Springfield (Mass.) Catholic Observer*⟩ **b :** an act of ratifying or establishing in office : CONFIRMATION ⟨the ~ of Parliament yesterday was marked by an extreme lack of enthusiasm and applause —Janet Flanner⟩ **c :** LIVERY OF SEIZIN **2 :** an act of infusing or enriching **3 a :** an act of clothing or decorating ⟨to dress the sovereign in a linsey-woolsey garb would . . . be a very unsuitable ~ —R.C.Singleton⟩ **b :** something that covers or adorns ⟨the heavy red damask ~ of the four-poster⟩ ⟨regrettable that the drama does not live up to its rich ~ —*Newsweek*⟩ **4** *archaic* : 2INVESTMENT 2 **5 :** BLOCKADE, SIEGE ⟨the enemy fleet riding to the ~ of Japan —*This World*⟩

1**in·vest·ment** \ən'ves(t)mənt\ *n* -S [1*invest* + *-ment*] **1 a** *archaic* : VESTMENT **b :** an outer layer of any kind : COATING, ENVELOPE: as (1) : an outward habiliment : GUISE ⟨one man asserts his right to grow a beard . . . as the ~ of his motley —*Times Lit. Supp.*⟩ (2) : an external covering of a cell, part, or organism (3) : a layer of heat-resistant material in which a dental appliance (as a bridge or inlay) is cast or in which it is embedded before soldering (4) : refractory material that forms the mold in investment casting **2 :** INVESTITURE 1 ⟨~ with the ring has been an integral part of each coronation —*Literary Digest*⟩ **3 :** BLOCKADE, SIEGE ⟨his proposals for an attack on Montreal . . . and a complete ~ of Quebec by land and sea —J.B.Brebner⟩

2**investment** \"\ *n* -S *often attrib* [2*invest* + *-ment*] **1 a :** an expenditure of money for income or profit or to purchase something of intrinsic value : capital outlay ⟨~ in common stocks⟩ ⟨~ in a diamond brooch⟩ **b :** the sum invested or the property purchased ⟨has a large ~ in a copper mine⟩ ⟨a fine painting is an ~⟩ **2 :** the commitment of funds with a view to minimizing risk and safeguarding capital while earning a return — contrasted with *speculation* **3 :** the commitment of something other than money to a long-term interest or project ⟨the job calls for the ~ of a great deal of hard thinking and planning —D.F.Cavers⟩

investment bank *n* [2*investment*] : an institution that specializes in buying and selling large blocks of securities (as new issues) and in raising funds for capital expansion — **investment banking** *n*

investment banker *n* **1 :** a person employed by an investment bank or engaged in investment banking **2 :** INVESTMENT BANK

investment casting *n* [1*investment*] : casting by the cire-perdue process

investment company *or* **investment trust** *n* [2*investment*] : a company that holds securities of other corporations for investment benefits only — compare HOLDING COMPANY

investment counselor *or* **investment adviser** *n* [2*investment*] : an individual or firm that analyzes and makes recommendations on a client's securities for a fee but does not have physical custody of these securities ⟨*investment counselors* or advisers must register under the Investment Advisers Act of 1940 —J.O.Kamm⟩

investment reserve *n* [2*investment*] : the terminal reserve of an insurance company in any year — compare INSURANCE RESERVE

in·ves·tor \ən'vestə(r)\ *n* -S [1*invest* & 2*invest* + *-or*] : one that invests; *specif* : one that seeks to commit funds for long-term profit with a minimum of risk — contrasted with *speculator*

invests *pres 3d sing of* INVEST

in·ves·ture \ən'ves(h)chə(r)\ *n* -S [1*invest* + *-ure*] *archaic* : INVESTITURE 1

in·vet·er·a·cy \ən'ved·ərəsē, -vetər-,-ve·tr-, -si\ *n* -ES [1*inveterate* + *-cy*] *archaic* **1 :** prejudiced animosity : HOSTILITY **2 :** the quality or state of being obstinate : TENACITY

1**in·vet·er·ate** \-rət, *usu* -rəd·+V\ *adj* [L *inveteratus*, past part. of *inveterare* to make old, to age, fr. *in-* 2in- + *veter-, vetus* old — more at WETHER] **1** *archaic* : obstinately prejudiced or antagonistic : BIASED, HOSTILE ⟨felt ~ against him —Charles Dickens⟩ **2 a :** CONTINUOUS, RECURRENT, CHRONIC ⟨~ bursitis⟩ **b :** deep-rooted or widely accepted : INGRAINED, ESTABLISHED ⟨~ tendency to naturalize foreign words —George Woodcock⟩ ⟨supported by precedent so ~ that the chance of abandonment is small —B.N.Cardozo⟩ ⟨~ and skillful biographer —Marvin Lowenthal⟩ **c :** stubbornly inflexible : ADAMANT, OBSTINATE ⟨~ prejudice⟩ ⟨his ~ demand for the imposition of a severe discipline —C.I.Glicksberg⟩ **d :** long-lasting : PERSISTENT ⟨the ~ smell of ether in a hospital⟩ **3** *obs* : of an advanced age : ANCIENT ⟨rotten wood . . . taken out of an ~ willow tree —John Evelyn⟩ **4 :** fixed by long habit or usage : CONFIRMED, HABITUAL ⟨~ sightseers —Astrid Peters⟩ ⟨an ~ love of alcohol —C.B.Nordhoff & J.N.Hall⟩ ⟨the punishment for ~ idleness was a whipping on the bare back —W.E.Woodward⟩

syn CHRONIC, CONFIRMED, DEEP-ROOTED, DEEP-SEATED: INVETERATE suggests resolute persistence in an idea or attitude making change or moderation impossible or most unlikely ⟨Frenchmen do not crave a master . . . the average Frenchman is probably the world's most *inveterate* individualist —*Christian Century*⟩ ⟨*inveterate* habits of animistic thinking —Lewis Mumford⟩ ⟨the *inveterate* hostility of "creative" writers to criticism —P.E.More⟩ CHRONIC implies long continuation or frequent recurrence of a usu. detrimental condition or trait but lacks the suggestion of determination that may accompany INVETERATE ⟨his *chronic* state of mental restlessness —George Eliot⟩ ⟨envy and rebellion and class resentments are *chronic* moral diseases with us —G.B.Shaw⟩ ⟨the total lack of adequate means of transportation rendered the problem of a grain market a *chronic* difficulty to the frontier farmers —V.L.Parrington⟩ CONFIRMED suggests a pattern that has become fixed by habit or usage ⟨I am a *confirmed* wanderer —Isaac D'Israeli⟩ ⟨a *confirmed* bachelor⟩ ⟨his intense egoism rendered him impatient of all reproof or instruction and . . . he soon became a victim of *confirmed* mannerisms —*Nation*⟩ DEEP-ROOTED and DEEP-SEATED in general refer to qualities so deeply engrained that they have become part of the core of personal character, or to conditions of deep significance and lasting endurance ⟨Lincoln had a *deep-rooted* aversion to slavery⟩ ⟨the *deep-rooted* causes of Indian discontent —*Current History*⟩ ⟨the conviction of Thomas Aquinas, that between true science and true religion there can be no contradiction, is exceedingly *deep-seated* —J.H.Randall⟩ ⟨*deep-seated* sources of cultural antipathy between Asia and the U.S. —M.W.Straight⟩

2**in·vet·er·ate** \-ved·əˌrāt\ *vt* -ED/-ING/-S [L *inveteratus*, past part. of *inveterare*] *archaic* : to establish firmly : root deeply : CONFIRM

in·vet·er·ate·ly \ved·ərətlē, -vetər-,-ve·tr-, -li\ *adv* : in an inveterate manner : PERSISTENTLY

in·vet·er·ate·ness \-ətnəs\ *n* -ES : the quality or state of being inveterate : PERSISTENCE

in·viability \(¦)in, ən+\ *n* : inability to live — used esp. of a genetic constitution that precludes survival ⟨~ of intergeneric hybrids —E.R.Sears⟩

in·viable \(')in, ən+\ *adj* [ISV 1*in-* + *viable*] : incapable of surviving

in·vid·i·ous \ən'vidēəs\ *adj* [L *invidiosus*, fr. *invidia* envy + *-osus* -ose — more at ENVY] **1 :** detrimental to reputation : DEFAMATORY ⟨the ~ implication of the phrase is . . . against those who pursue self-interest through politics —Felix Frankfurter⟩ **2 :** likely to cause discontent or animosity or envy ⟨the four confidential advisers of the crown soon found that their position was embarrassing and ~ —T.B. Macaulay⟩ **3 :** full of envious resentment : JEALOUS ⟨his professional abilities as an officer . . . had to stand ~ scrutiny —J.G.Cozzens⟩ **4 a :** of an unpleasant or objectionable nature : HATEFUL, OBNOXIOUS ⟨~ remarks that were sometimes neither kind nor true —John Hurkan⟩ **b :** causing harm or resentment : INJURIOUS ⟨would be ~ to select for special mention a more or less haphazard list of names —*Survey Graphic*⟩ ⟨far from our purpose to institute any ~ comparisons between these two gifted women —Eugene Field⟩ **syn** see HATEFUL

in·vid·i·ous·ly *adv* : in an invidious manner : ODIOUSLY

in·vid·i·ous·ness *n* -ES : the quality or state of being invidious : ODIOUSNESS

in·vigilancy \(')in, ən+\ *n* -ES [1*in-* + *vigilancy*] *archaic* : lack of vigilance

in·vig·i·late \ən'vijəˌlāt\ *vb* -ED/-ING/-S [L *invigilatus*, past part. of *invigilare*, fr. *in-* 2in- + *vigilare* to watch — more at VIGILANT] *vi* : to keep watch ⟨that invisible power that ~*s* over all things —Henry More⟩; *specif, Brit* : to proctor an examination ~ *vt* : to make watchful

in·vig·i·la·tion \(ˌ)inˌvijə'lāshən, ənˌv-\ *n* -S : an act of surveillance; *specif* : the proctoring of an examination

in·vig·i·la·tor \ən'vijəˌlād·ə(r)\ *n* -S *Brit* : PROCTOR 2b

in·vig·or *or* **in·vig·our** \ən'vigə(r)\ *vt* [alter. (influenced by E 2*in-*) of earlier *envigor*, fr. 1*en-* + *vigor*, n.] *archaic* : INVIGORATE

in·vig·o·rate \ən'vigəˌrāt, *usu* -ād·+V\ *vt* -ED/-ING/-S [prob. fr. 2*in-* + obs. E *vigorate* to invigorate, fr. L *vigoratus*, past part. of *vigorare*, fr. *vigor* — more at VIGOR] : to give life and energy to : ANIMATE ⟨a lotion to ~ the skin⟩ ⟨that puzzling out of new possibilities which ~*s* the imagination —H.A.Overstreet⟩ ⟨an industrial center *invigorated* by defense contracts —R.M.Hodesh⟩ **syn** see STRENGTHEN

invigorating *adj* : having an enlivening effect : BRACING, STIMULATING ⟨~ climate⟩ ⟨thought that he would try these ~ berries since he was inclined to fall asleep during his prayers —Charles Cooper⟩ ⟨his writings are tonic and . . . ~ to those who stand in need of inspiration —R.L.Cook⟩ — **in·vig·o·rat·ing·ly** \═'══ˌ═══, ═ˌ══'═══\ *adv*

in·vig·o·ra·tion \═ˌ══'rāshən\ *n* -S **1 :** the act or process of invigorating ⟨demands for . . . ~ of the Articles were made even before they became effective —Allan Nevins⟩ **2 :** the quality or state of being invigorated ⟨the ~ that derives from . . . the cultural atmosphere of a great city —A.A.Houghton⟩

in·vig·o·ra·tor \═'══ˌrād·ə(r), -ātə-\ *n* -S : one that invigorates

in·vi·nate \ən'vīˌnāt, 'inˌv-\ *vt* -ED/-ING/-S [prob. fr. (assumed) NL *invinatus*, past part. of (assumed) NL *invinare*, fr. L *in-* 2in- + *vinum* wine — more at WINE] : to make present by invination

in·vi·na·tion \ˌinˌvī'nāshən\ *n* -S [F, prob. fr. (assumed) NL *invination-, invinatio*, fr. (assumed) NL *invinatus* + L *-ion-, -io* -ion] : the inclusion of the blood of Christ in the eucharistic wine without change in either substance — compare IMPANATION

in·vin·ci·bil·i·ty \(ˌ)inˌvin(t)sə'biləd·ē, ənˌv-, -lətē, -i\ *n* -ES : the quality or state of being invincible

1**in·vin·ci·ble** \(')in¦vin(t)səbəl, ən'v-\ *adj* [ME, fr. MF, fr. LL *invincibilis*, fr. L *in-* 1in- + *vincibilis* conquerable — more at VINCIBLE] **1 a :** incapable of being vanquished or subjugated : impervious to attack or conquest : UNBEATABLE ⟨~ army⟩ ⟨has been ~ in eight-oared Olympic rowing —*Collier's Yr. Bk.*⟩ **b :** impossible to overcome or subdue : ABSOLUTE, UNSWERVING ⟨the ~ obscurity of his origins —Joseph Conrad⟩ ⟨a resolute, yet not ~, skepticism —A.G.N.Flew⟩ ⟨~ respect for authority⟩ ⟨man's ~ conviction that a sublime soul cannot be imprisoned —W.L.Sullivan⟩ **2 :** beyond an individual's control and so not involving moral responsibility : UNAVOIDABLE — used esp. of lack of knowledge about theological concepts ⟨~ ignorance⟩ — **in·vin·ci·ble·ness** \-nəs\ *n* -ES — **in·vin·ci·bly** \-blē,-bli\ *adv*

2**invincible** \"\ *n* -S : one that is invincible

in·violability \(¦)in, ən+\ *n* : the quality or state of being inviolable

in·violable \(')in, ən+\ *adj* [MF or L; MF, fr. L *inviolabilis*, fr. *in-* 1in- + *violabilis* violable] **1** *obs* : incapable of being broken or destroyed : INDESTRUCTIBLE **2 a :** secure from violation or infringement : INCORRUPTIBLE, SACROSANCT ⟨thinking of conscience as an ~ source of moral certitude —Lucius Garvin⟩ ⟨bound by mores more strict, more rigorous, more ~ than most religious denominations would dare to require —Jessie Bernard⟩ **b :** secure from assault or trespass : UNTOUCHABLE, UNASSAILABLE ⟨the person of the king is ~⟩ ⟨~ frontier⟩ ⟨~ green lawns⟩ — **in·vi·o·la·ble·ness** \-nəs\ *n* — **in·vi·o·la·bly** \-blē, -bli\ *adv*

in·vi·o·la·cy \ən'vīələsē, -si\ *n* -ES [*inviolate* + *-cy*] : the quality or state of being inviolate

in·violate \(')in¦vīələ|t, ən'v- *also* -ˌlā|; *usu* |d·+V\ *also* **in·violated** \-ˌlādəd, -ātəd\ *adj* [ME *inviolat*, fr. L *inviolatus*, fr. *in-* 1in- + *violatus*, past part. of *violare* to violate — more at VIOLATE] **1 a :** free from change or blemish : PURE, UNBROKEN ⟨desired the Italian culture to be ~ and predominant —John Buchan⟩ ⟨cease searching for the perfect shell, the whole ~ form —Anne M. Lindbergh⟩ ⟨while I continue to keep this oath ~ —*Hippocratic Oath*⟩ **b :** free from assault or trespass : UNTOUCHED, INTACT ⟨as he had fallen on the plain, ~ he lay —R.C.Trench⟩ ⟨the . . . first white settlers agreed to keep this ground ~ —*Amer. Guide Series: Conn.*⟩ **2 :** INVIOLABLE 2 ⟨they . . . regarded their hunting zones as their own ~ property —L.S.B.Leakey⟩ ⟨the confidences of this Club are ~ —R.H.Davis⟩ — **in·vi·o·late·ly** *adv* — **in·vi·o·late·ness** *n* -ES

invious *adj* [L *invius*, fr. *in-* 1in- + *via* road — more at VIA] *obs* : lacking roads : TRACKLESS

inviron *obs var of* ENVIRON

in·vir·tu·ate \ən'vərchəˌwāt\ *vt* -ED/-ING/-S [2*in-* + *virtue* + *-ate*] *archaic* : to endow with virtue

in·vis·cate \ən'viˌskāt, 'inˌv-\ *vt* -ED/-ING/-S [LL *inviscatus*, past part. of *inviscare* to snare as with birdlime, fr. L *in-* 2in- + *viscare* to smear with birdlime, fr. *viscum* mistletoe, birdlime — more at VISCID] : to encase in a sticky substance : make viscid — **in·vis·ca·tion** \ˌinˌvi'skāshən\ *n* -S

in·viscid \(')in, ən+\ *adj* [1*in-* + *viscid*] **1 :** not having viscosity ⟨~ fluid⟩ **2 :** relating to the flow of an inviscid body ⟨~ theory⟩

in·visibility \(¦)in, ən+\ *n* [LL *invisibilitat-, invisibilitas*, fr. L *invisibilis* invisible + *-itat-, -itas* -ity] **1 :** the quality or state of being invisible **2 :** something that is invisible

1**in·visible** \(')in, ən+\ *adj* [ME, fr. MF, fr. L *invisibilis*, fr. *in-* 1in- + *visibilis* visible] **1 a :** incapable of being seen through lack of physical substance : not perceptible by vision : INTANGIBLE, UNSEEN ⟨another thriller about an ~ man⟩ ⟨an angel and a high-frequency wave are equally ~ to the mass of mankind —Lewis Mumford⟩; *specif* : not appearing in published financial statements ⟨~ assets and liabilities⟩ **b :** of or relating to service or capital transactions not reflected in statistics of foreign trade ⟨the nation's greatest ~ export, tourism —T.H.Fielding⟩ ⟨a bit of unconscious humor is the listing of movies among ~ imports —George Soule⟩ ⟨Ireland's trade deficit was met by ~ items, including immigrant remittances —Alzada Comstock⟩ **2 :** inaccessible to view : out of sight : HIDDEN ⟨~ hinge⟩ ⟨in stormy weather the seaman's compass takes the place of ~ stars⟩ ⟨the world's largest and finest private or public assemblage of French art . . . is now ~ in the attic of the Hermitage —Janet Flanner⟩ **3 :** of such small size or unobtrusive quality as to be hardly noticeable : IMPERCEPTIBLE, INCONSPICUOUS ⟨~ hair net⟩ ⟨~ plaid⟩ ⟨the translation is almost ~ —Stuart Preston⟩ — **in·visible·ness** \"+\ *n* — **in·visibly** \"+\ *adv*

2**invisible** \"\ *n* : one that is invisible ⟨the ~*s* that lurk in haunted houses⟩ ⟨the present deficit gap . . . must be closed either by greater merchandise exports or larger earnings on ~*s* —J.B.Cohen⟩

invisible church *n* : CHURCH INVISIBLE

invisible government *n* : a government controlled by a person (as a boss) or an agency (as a pressure group) holding no official position and usu. held to be unknown to the public ⟨the interlocking control thus created was an *invisible government* —F.L.Paxson⟩

invisible green *n* **1 :** a very dark green to yellowish green **2 :** a dark bluish green that is greener and duller than average teal green and bluer and slightly less strong than duck green

invisible ink *n* : SECRET INK

in·vi·tant \'invətənt, ən'vītᵊnt\ *n* -S [*invite* + *-ant*] *archaic* : INVITER

1**in·vi·ta·tion** \ˌinvə'tāshən\ *n* -S [MF or L; MF, fr. L *invitation-, invitatio*, fr. *invitatus* (past part. of *invitare* to invite) + *-ion-, -io* -ion] **1 a :** the act of inviting : the requesting of a person's company or participation ⟨I took the ~ to dinner as a dismissal from tea —O.S.J.Gogarty⟩ ⟨joined the expedition at the ~ of the government⟩ **b** (1) : a written or verbal request to be present or participate ⟨address wedding ~*s*⟩ ⟨accept an ~ to membership⟩ (2) : a written or verbal request to do or undertake ⟨an ~ to sing at a benefit concert⟩ ⟨an ~ to assume leadership of a project⟩ (3) *often cap* : a brief exhortation immediately preceding the confession in the communion service of the Anglican and other Protestant churches **c :** SUGGESTION, PROPOSAL ⟨the ~*s* of a master are scarcely to be distinguished from commands —Edward Gibbon⟩ ⟨he refused my ~ to consider the history of Christian intolerance —H.J.Laski⟩ **2 a :** ATTRACTION, STIMULUS, LURE, INCENTIVE ⟨they were forced to move, even though the Sahara desert was no ~ —Emil Lengyel⟩ ⟨good scholarship . . . presents us with evidence which is an ~ to the critical faculty of the reader —T.S.Eliot⟩ **b :** a precipitating factor : INDUCEMENT, CHALLENGE, PROVOCATION ⟨a hatchet painted red was thrown down in a friendly village as an ~ to join in a war —Clark Wissler⟩ ⟨the laws . . . were an ~ to smuggling —Roger Burlingame⟩ ⟨her sultry look was clearly an ~⟩

2**invitation** \¦══¦══\ *also* **in·vi·ta·tion·al** \¦══¦tāshənᵊl, -shnəl\ *adj* : prepared or entered in response to a request or challenge ⟨~ article⟩ ⟨~ exhibit⟩; *specif* : limited to invited participants ⟨~ tournament⟩

1**in·vi·ta·to·ry** \ən'vīd·əˌtōrē\ *adj* [ME, fr. LL *invitatorius*, fr. L *invitatus* (past part. of *invitare*) + *-orius* -ory] : containing an invitation ⟨a brief ~ note⟩ ⟨~ psalm⟩

2**invitatory** \"\ *n* -ES [ME, fr. ML *invitatorium*, fr. LL, neut. of *invitatorius*, adj.] : any of various liturgical forms of invitation used in church services ⟨common *invitatories* are the Venite and Psalm 95⟩

1**in·vite** \ən'vīt, *usu* -īd·+V\ *vb* -ED/-ING/-S [MF or L; MF *inviter*, fr. L *invitare*, prob. fr. *in-* 2in- + *-vitare* (prob. akin to Gk *hiesthai* to hasten, long for) — more at GAIN] *vt* **1 a :** to offer an incentive or inducement to : ENTICE, TEMPT ⟨the book ~*s* interest⟩ ⟨writes about the people and places that ~ his pen —*Atlantic*⟩ ⟨rock-strewn streams ~ the fisherman — *Amer. Guide Series: N.J.*⟩ ⟨virgin spaces of America *invited* colonization —Douglas Bush⟩ ⟨I loaf and ~ my soul —Walt Whitman⟩ **b :** to provide opportunity or occasion for : increase the likelihood of : open the way to ⟨to shrink from responsibility is to ~ social and economic insecurity —H.G. Armstrong⟩ ⟨so long as there is starvation and joblessness in the midst of abundance we are *inviting* the deluge —Ruth Benedict⟩ ⟨lurid emotionalism and tear-jerking nostalgia . . . *inviting* sighs and hisses —Leslie Rees⟩ ⟨wandered slowly along . . . in that wholly relaxed state which always seems to ~ small adventures —William Beebe⟩ **2 a :** to request the presence or participation of : solicit the company of : ASK ⟨~ guests to dinner⟩ ⟨~ educators to a conference⟩ ⟨~ a team to a tournament⟩ ⟨open the door and ~ him in⟩; *esp* : to send a formal invitation to ⟨an affair open only to those who had been *invited*⟩ **b :** to request formally ⟨~ him to be chief executive⟩ ⟨*invited* her to give a talk on flower arrangement⟩ ⟨it is not as yet very clear which . . . are *invited* to consider becoming signatories —I.A.Richards⟩ **c :** to urge politely or indicate a receptiveness to : ENCOURAGE, WELCOME ⟨leaned forward . . . and *invited* me to continue in English —Barbara Henderson⟩ ⟨*inviting* him to put his own motives under examination —Lionel Trilling⟩ ⟨~ bids on a contract⟩ ⟨~*s* oral suggestions from his three clerks —J.P.Frank⟩ ⟨his manner did not ~ approach —H.E.Starr⟩ ~ *vi* : to issue an invitation ⟨he did not ~: he commanded —Max Beerbohm⟩ ⟨the spacious campus . . . ~*s* to the enjoyment of the out-of-doors —*Catalog of Hollins Coll.*⟩

2**in·vite** \'inˌv-\ *n* -S *now chiefly dial* : INVITATION 1 ⟨you sound like you didn't get no ~ to the dance —Richard Bissell⟩

invited *adj* [fr. past part. of 1*invite*] : present or done by invitation ⟨~ guests⟩ ⟨read an ~ paper at the meeting⟩

in·vi·tee \¦inˌvī¦tē, ən¦vī¦tē\ *n* -S [*invite* + *-ee*] : an invited person : GUEST; *specif* : a person (as a customer) present in a place by the express or implied invitation of the occupier in control of that place under circumstances such as impose a duty on the occupier to use reasonable care to protect the safety of such person — compare LICENSEE, TRESPASSER

in·vite·ment \ən'vītmənt\ *n* -S **1** *obs* : INVITATION 1 ⟨would not stand upon ~, but came of himself —George Chapman⟩ **2** *archaic* : INVITATION 2 ⟨unable to resist the delicious ~ to repose —Charles Lamb⟩

in·vit·er *or* **in·vi·tor** \ən'vīd·ə(r), -ītə-\ *n* -S : one that invites

1**inviting** *n* -S [fr. gerund of 1*invite*] *obs* : INVITATION ⟨he hath sent me an earnest ~ —Shak.⟩

2**inviting** *adj* [fr. pres. part. of 1*invite*] **1 :** giving an invitation ⟨the ~ ship would haul the Stars and Stripes to the peak —H.A.Chippendale⟩ **2 :** of an agreeable nature : pleasing to the senses : ATTRACTIVE, TEMPTING ⟨~ climate⟩ ⟨~ prospect⟩ ⟨~ eye⟩ ⟨beautiful binding, ~ type, fine paper —*N.Y. Times Book Rev.*⟩ — **in·vit·ing·ly** *adv* — **in·vit·ing·ness** *n* -ES

in·vi·tress \ən'vī·trəs\ *n* -ES [*inviter* + *-ess*] *archaic* : a female inviter

in vi·tro \(')in'vē·(ˌ)trō\ *adv (or adj)* [NL, lit., in glass] : outside the living body : in a test tube or other artificial environment ⟨*in vitro* cultivation of tissues⟩ — compare IN VIVO

in vi·vo \(')in'vē(ˌ)vō\ *adv (or adj)* [NL, lit., in that which is alive] : in the living body of a plant or animal ⟨*in vivo* synthesis of vitamin D⟩ ⟨microorganisms are not ordinarily destroyed *in vivo* by bacteriostatic drugs —*Jour. Amer. Med. Assoc.*⟩ — compare IN VITRO

in·vo·ca·ble \ən'vōkəbəl, 'invək-\ *adj* [irreg. (influenced by L *invocare* to invoke) fr. *invoke* + *-able*] : capable of being invoked

in·vo·cant \-kənt\ *n* -S [L *invocant-, invocans*, pres. part. of *invocare* to invoke] : one that invokes

in·vo·cate \'invəˌkāt\ *vb* -ED/-ING/-S [L *invocatus*, past part. of *invocare*] *vt, archaic* : INVOKE ⟨still will I ~ his name —John Wesley⟩ ~ *vi* : to make a supplication : PRAY ⟨after that hour to daybreak 'tis held an ungodly thing to ~ —Thomas Herbert⟩

in·vo·ca·tion \ˌinvə'kāshən, -vō'-\ *n* -S [ME *invocacioun*, fr. MF *invocation*, fr. L *invocation-, invocatio*, fr. *invocatus* (past part. of *invocare* to invoke) + *-ion-, -io* -ion] **1 a :** the action or an act of petitioning for help or support : SUPPLICATION, APPEAL ⟨~ to the Muses⟩; *specif, often cap* : a prayer of entreaty that is usu. a call for the divine presence and is offered at the beginning of a meeting or service of worship **b :** a summoning up or calling upon for authority or justification ⟨~ of economic reasons . . . to justify postponement of wage increases —Frank Gorrell⟩ ⟨~ of a celebrated piece of advice attributed to Talleyrand —*Times Lit. Supp.*⟩ **2 a :** an act of conjuring ⟨~ of an ancestral spirit⟩ **b :** a formula for conjuring : INCANTATION ⟨~*s* . . . to bring harm to mother or child —Francis Hackett⟩ **3 a :** a judicial call for papers or evidence from another case — used chiefly in admiralty prize procedure **b :** an act of legal or moral implementation : ENFORCEMENT ⟨~ of treaty provisions⟩ — **in·vo·ca·tion·al** \¦══¦═shənᵊl, -shnəl\ *adj*

in·voca·tive \ən'väkəd·iv; 'invəˌkād·iv, -vōˌ-\ *adj* [LL *invocativus*, fr. L *invocatus* (past part. of *invocare* to invoke) + *-ivus* -ive] : INVOCATORY

in·vo·ca·tor \'invəˌkād·ə(r), -vōˌ-\ *n* -S [LL *invocator*, fr. L *invocatus* (past part. of *invocare* to invoke) + *-or*] : one that invokes

in·voc·a·to·ry \ən'väkəˌtōrē\ *adj* [fr. *invocation*, after such pairs as E *revocation: revocatory*] : of, relating to, or characterized by invocation ⟨~ prayer⟩

1**in·voice** \'inˌvȯis\ *n* -S *often attrib* [modif. of MF *envois*, pl. of *envoi* action of sending, message — more at ENVOY] **1 a :** an itemized statement furnished to a purchaser by a seller and usu. specifying the price of goods or services and the terms of sale : BILL ⟨prices shown on this ~ are net⟩ **b :** a consignment of merchandise ⟨received a large ~ of broomstraw⟩ **c :** a printed form used for detailing charges : BILLHEAD ⟨a picture of the factory appears on the ~⟩ **2 :** BILL OF LADING

2**invoice** \"\ *vb* -ED/-ING/-S *vt* **1 a :** to submit a statement of charges for : BILL ⟨~ desk accessories to the stationery buyer⟩ **b** : to send a consignment of (merchandise) : SHIP ⟨where are the sewing machines *invoiced* me by this steamer —R.H.Davis⟩ **2** : INVENTORY ~ *vi* **1** : to make or render an invoice ⟨please ~ and advise where to pay —*advt*⟩ **2** : to be worth on inventory ⟨his little office would not have *invoiced* more than fifteen hundred dollars —W.A.White⟩

in·voke \ən'vōk\ *vt* -ED/-ING/-S [ME *invoken*, fr. MF *invoquer*, fr. L *invocare*, fr. *in-* [2]in- + *vocare* to call, fr. *voc-*, *vox* voice — more at VOICE] **1 a** : to petition for help or support : call upon for assistance ⟨the gods had to be *invoked* to bring rain —T.E.Sanford⟩ ⟨she would ~ the Travelers' Aid Society, and they would assist her in getting a . . . place to live —Donn Byrne⟩ **b** : to appeal to as furnishing authority or motive : propound as a logical basis ⟨racist doctrines are *invoked* for political ends —Ruth Benedict⟩ ⟨~ the balance-of-payments difficulties to justify . . . import prohibitions —*Economist*⟩ ⟨four theories . . . *invoked* by geographers to explain the origin of the areas —S.A.Cain⟩ ⟨imaginary lesions . . . *invoked* to account for conditions which had a merely psychogenic origin —R.S.Ellery⟩ **2 a** : to call forth by incantation : CONJURE 2 ⟨spokesmen for the two tribes *invoked* the spirits of departed . . . chiefs to tell them they were now as one —*Time*⟩ ⟨~ a plague on all their houses —W.L.Sperry⟩ **b** : to use (a respected name) to imply endorsement by the owner ⟨more misquotations probably have been attributed to Jefferson than to any other American, because many politicians who ~ his name have read him not at all —L.B. Wright⟩ **3 a** : to make an earnest request for : SOLICIT ⟨~ the board's help in getting his old job back —Dixon Wecter⟩ ⟨the student of genetics ~*s* the aid of the physicist and biochemist —J.M.Fogg⟩ **b** : ENTREAT, IMPLORE ⟨~ mercy⟩ ⟨*invoked* their forgiveness⟩ **4 a** : to call for (as papers or other evidence) judicially — used chiefly in admiralty prize procedure **b** : to put into legal effect or call for the observance of : ENFORCE, IMPLEMENT ⟨~ the penalties of the law —Albert Mowbray⟩ ⟨military sanctions may be *invoked* only after economic sanctions have failed —Norman Hill⟩ ⟨*invoked* the veto six times in the dispute —C.D.Fuller⟩ ⟨~ a promise⟩ ⟨unhesitatingly *invoked* the health department's broad powers —Leonard Engel⟩ ⟨because it possesses that right . . . can usually discipline the majority without *invoking* its prerogative —*Foreign Affairs*⟩ **5 a** : to introduce or put into operation : INSTIGATE, EMPLOY ⟨controls alien to . . . peacetime custom will have to be *invoked* —Stacy May⟩ ⟨~ bold visions at a time of unrest —Norman Cousins⟩ ⟨discipline should not be *invoked* . . . without first consulting the union —Earl Brown⟩ ⟨alliteration's artful aid is *invoked* on every page —*Irish Digest*⟩ **b** : to bring about : CAUSE, EXCITE ⟨operations . . . ~ new problems of administration, maintenance and supply —H.H.Arnold & I.C.Eaker⟩ ⟨stabilizing the regime and *invoking* social and patriotic fervor —E.P. Snow⟩

in·vok·er \-kə(r)\ *n* -S : one that invokes

in·volatile \(')in, ən+\ *adj* [[1]*in-* + *volatile*] : not vaporizing or capable of being vaporized — **in·volatility** \(¦)in, ən+\ *n*

in·vol·u·cel \ən'välyə,sel\ *n* -S [NL *involucellum*, dim. of *involucrum*] : a secondary involucre (as in each secondary umbel of a compound umbel) — **in·vol·u·cel·late** \(¦)in-¦välyə¦selət, ən¦v-\ *or* **in·vol·u·cel·lat·ed** \(,)=,=='se,lād·əd\ *adj*

in·vo·lu·cral \¦invə¦lükrəl *also* -vəl¦yü-\ *adj* [prob. fr. (assumed) NL *involucralis*, fr. NL *involucrum* involucre + L *-alis* -al] : of, relating to, or resembling an involucre

in·vo·lu·crate \-krət\ *adj* [prob. fr. (assumed) NL *involucratus*, fr. NL *involucrum* involucre + L *-atus* -ate] : having an involucre

in·vo·lu·cre \'invə,lükə(r) *also* -vəl,yü-\ *n* -S [F, fr. NL *involucrum* involucre] : one or more whorls of bracts situated below and close to a flower, flower cluster, or fruit (in a seed plant): as **a** : a rosette of bracts surrounding a composite flower head (as a daisy) and often resembling a true calyx — see CUPULE 1a **b** : a whorl of bracts subtending the inflorescence in many members of the Umbelliferae

in·vo·lu·cred \-kə(r)d\ *adj* [*involucre* + *-ed*] : INVOLUCRATE

in·vo·lu·cri·form \¦==¦=krə,fȯrm\ *adj* [prob. fr. (assumed) NL *involucriformis*, fr. NL *involucrum* involucre + L *-iformis* -iform] : having the form or appearance of an involucre

in·vo·lu·crum \,=='=krəm\ *n, pl* **involu·cra** \-krə\ [L, fr. *involvere* to wrap, envelop] **1** : a surrounding envelope or sheath ⟨each group has its ~ of space from which it drives any encroaching group —C.S.Coon⟩ **2** [NL, fr. L] : INVOLUCRE **3** [NL, fr. L] : a formation of new bone about a sequestrum (as in osteomyelitis)

involuntarily \(¦)in, ən+\ *adv* : in an involuntary manner

involuntariness \"+\ *n* -ES : the quality or state of being involuntary

involuntary \(')in, ən+\ *adj* [LL *involuntarius*, fr. L *in-* [1]in- + *voluntarius* voluntary] **1 a** : springing from accident or impulse rather than conscious exercise of the will : UNINTENTIONAL, SPONTANEOUS ⟨an ~ inheritance from her rich and backward husband —Nigel Dennis⟩ ⟨concentration became at first effortless, then ~, then necessitous —Charles Morgan⟩ **b** : dictated by authority or circumstance : COMPULSORY ⟨~ servitude⟩ ⟨~ unemployment⟩ **c** *of bankruptcy* : declared upon petition of creditors **2** : not subject to control of the will : independent of volition : REFLEX ⟨~ contraction⟩ ⟨~ weeping⟩

involuntary deposit *n, law* : an accidental or unintentional transference of property to the possession of another without the assent, negligence, or even knowledge of the owner (as of a boat carried onto land by a storm)

involuntary manslaughter *n* : manslaughter resulting from the failure to perform a legal duty expressly required to safeguard human life, or from the commission of an unlawful act not constituting a felony, or from the commission of a lawful act in a negligent or improper manner — compare HOMICIDE, MURDER, VOLUNTARY MANSLAUGHTER

involuntary muscle *n* : muscle governing reflex functions and not under direct voluntary control : SMOOTH MUSCLE

involuntary trust *n* : CONSTRUCTIVE TRUST

[1]**in·vo·lute** \'invə,lüt *also* -vəl,yüt; ,=='=\ *adj* [L *involutus* involved, intricate, fr. past part. of *involvere* to wrap, envelop] **1 a** (1) : curled spirally (2) : having the whorls closely coiled ⟨~ shell⟩ **b** (1) : curled or curved inward (2) : having the edges rolled over the upper surface toward the midrib ⟨an ~ leaf⟩ — compare CONVOLUTE, REVOLUTE **2** : INVOLUTED 3 ⟨the possible moves . . . not only manifold, but ~ —E.A.Poe⟩ **3** : of or relating to an involute ⟨~ curve⟩ ⟨~ gear cutter⟩ — **in·vo·lute·ly** *adv*

[2]**involute** \'==,=\ *n* -S : a curve traced by any point of a perfectly flexible inextensible thread kept taut as it is wound upon or unwound from another curve — compare EVOLUTE

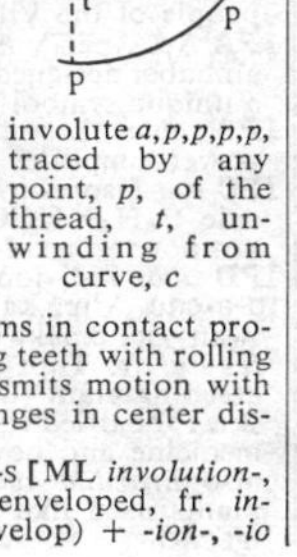

involute *a,p,p,p,p*, traced by any point, *p*, of the thread, *t*, unwinding from curve, *c*

[3]**involute** \¦==¦=\ *vi* -ED/-ING/-S **1** : to curl inward : become involute ⟨the leaf margin ~*s*⟩ **2 a** : to return to a former condition ⟨after pregnancy the uterus ~*s*⟩ **b** : to clear up : DISAPPEAR ⟨the disease ~*s* without desquamation —*Annals of N.Y. Academy of Sciences*⟩

involuted \'==,==, ,=='==\ *adj* [L *involutus* involved, intricate + E *-ed*] **1** : INVOLUTE 1b ⟨~ soil zone⟩ **2** : that has returned to a normal size or condition ⟨~ uterus⟩ **3** : of an involved or complicated nature : ABSTRUSE, INTRICATE ⟨much ~ wordage . . . obscures the fact that the tax law is an issue —Robert Wallace⟩ ⟨a remarkable man, ~, brilliant, and horribly afraid —Charles Neider⟩ — **in·vo·lut·ed·ly** *adv* — **in·vo·lut·ed·ness** *n* -ES

involute tooth *n* : a gear tooth that conforms in contact profile to an involute curve, that engages mating teeth with rolling rather than sliding friction, and that transmits motion with speed practically independent of slight changes in center distance

in·vo·lu·tion \,invə'lüshən *also* -vəl'yü-\ *n* -S [ML *involution-*, *involutio* envelopment, fr. L, something enveloped, fr. *involutus* (past part. of *involvere* to wrap, envelop) + *-ion-*, *-io* -ion] **1 a** : the act or an instance of infolding or entangling : INVOLVEMENT ⟨her subsequent Red ~ was probably from idealistic reaction . . . rather than from Marxist conviction —Wilbur Burton⟩ ⟨some ~*s* of the plot I had quite forgotten —Arnold Bennett⟩; *specif* : an involved grammatical construction usu. characterized by the insertion of clauses between the subject and predicate **b** : the quality or state of being involved : ENVELOPMENT, INTRICACY ⟨his mind . . . is simple; his syntax lacks ~ —Austin Warren⟩ **2** : the act or process of raising a quantity or symbol to any assigned power or affecting it with an assigned exponent — opposed to *evolution* **3 a** : an inward curvature or penetration ⟨~ of a soil deposit⟩ **b** : the formation of a gastrula by ingrowth of cells formed at the dorsal lip **4** : a shrinking or return to a former size ⟨~ of the uterus after pregnancy⟩ **5** : the regressive alterations of a body or its parts that are characteristic of the aging process; *specif* : presenile decline marked by a decrease of bodily vigor and in women by the menopause **6** : a relation of a higher type of reality to a lower type (as mind to matter) upon which it depends

[1]**in·vo·lu·tion·al** \¦invə¦lüshənᵊl, -shnəl *also* -vəl¦yü-\ *adj* [*involution* + *-al*] **1** : of or relating to involutional melancholia ⟨~ depression⟩ **2** : of or relating to the climacterium and its associated bodily and psychic changes ⟨mental hygiene in the ~ time of life⟩

[2]**involutional** \"\ *n* -S : one that suffers from involutional melancholia

involutional melancholia *or* **involutional psychosis** *n* : an agitated depression occurring at the time of the menopause or climacteric and usu. characterized by somatic and nihilistic delusions

involution form *n* : an irregular or atypical bacterium formed under unfavorable conditions (as in old cultures) and variously considered as a degenerating cell or as a specialized reproductive body

in·volve \ən'v¦älv, ¦ȯlv *also* ¦ä(ü)v *or* ¦ȯv\ *vt* -ED/-ING/-S [ME *involven*, fr. L *involvere* to wrap, envelop, fr. *in-* [2]in- + *volvere* to roll — more at VOLUBLE] **1** *archaic* : to enfold or envelop so as to encumber ⟨the number of difficulties in which this question is *involved* —Benjamin Jowett⟩ **2 a** : to draw in as a participant : ENGAGE, EMPLOY ⟨size of operations and . . . numbers of workmen *involved* —G.M.Trevelyan⟩ ⟨an organization . . . heavily *involved* in the nation's defense program —R.J.Cordiner⟩ ⟨kings were constantly *involved* in Continental affairs —G.G.Coulton⟩ ⟨he got *involved* in a lawsuit⟩ **b** : to oblige to become associated (as in an unpleasant situation) : EMBROIL, ENTANGLE, IMPLICATE ⟨led the English . . . to ~ India in the war —D.W.Brogan⟩ ⟨the controversies . . . moved on in all their ugliness to ~ others —John Mason Brown⟩ **c** : to occupy (oneself) absorbingly; *esp* : to commit (oneself) emotionally — usu. used with *in* or *with* ⟨we simply don't see enough of her characters . . . to feel personally *involved* in what they say or feel or do —Dan Wickenden⟩ ⟨she . . . never had the slightest intention of *involving* herself with him —Aurelia Levi⟩ **3 a** *archaic* : to enclose in a covering : WRAP ⟨the embryo is still farther *involved*, in two membranes —Oliver Goldsmith⟩ **b** : to surround as if with a wrapping : ENVELOP, SHROUD ⟨rights and privileges at the root . . . are discovered to be *involved* in doubt —B.N.Cardozo⟩ ⟨*involved* in a howling dancing crowd —Arthur Morrison⟩ **4** : to complicate or make intricate in thought or form **5 a** *archaic* : to wind, coil, or wreathe about : ENTWINE ⟨around me they *involved* a giddy dance —P.B.Shelley⟩ **b** : to relate closely : CONNECT, LINK ⟨the problem is closely *involved* with the management of pastures —Allan Fraser⟩ **6 a** : to have within or as part of itself : CONTAIN, INCLUDE ⟨tragic opera . . . must ~ convincing treatment of an elemental conflict —*Opera News*⟩ ⟨two late-arriving costumes . . . ~ magnificent brocaded coats covering deceptively casual sheaths —Lois Long⟩ ⟨a community program *involving* recreational, cultural, and economic . . . features —*Amer. Guide Series: N.C.*⟩ ⟨this course ~*s* a discussion of the trial rules of evidence —*Loyola Univ. Bulletin*⟩ **b** : to require as a necessary accompaniment : ENTAIL, IMPLY ⟨building their own roads . . . *involved* the construction of over 200 bridges —Joseph Millard⟩ ⟨diseases . . . which ~ long hospitalization —Cecile Starr⟩ ⟨changing those attitudes *involved* a job of mass education —Stanley Frank⟩ ⟨a mission which ~*s* much danger —T.B. Costain⟩ ⟨fusion ~*s* disparate materials . . . arranged so as to work together —*College English*⟩ ⟨insensitiveness ~*s* a meagerness of imagination in human relations —Albert Dasnoy⟩ **c** : to have an effect on : concern directly : AFFECT ⟨biological processes . . . like breathing and digesting, ~ the whole organism —H.J.Muller⟩ ⟨lacerations that ~ muscles or cause severe hemorrhage —H.G.Armstrong⟩ ⟨the problem . . . ~*s* their future —Harrison Smith⟩ ⟨work stoppages . . . *involved* more than 100 thousand workers —*Collier's Yr. Bk.*⟩ ⟨is never really three-dimensional, hence his conflicts do not ~ the reader —Frances Keene⟩ **7** : FILL ⟨a fire building so *involved* with heat, smoke and flame that immediate access to the interior is not possible —W.Y.Kimball⟩ ⟨drawings . . . *involved* with color become either water colors or pastels —Carlyle Burrows⟩ **8** : to engross or occupy fully : ABSORB ⟨*involved* in these imaginings she knew nothing of time —Thomas Hardy⟩ **syn** see INCLUDE

involved *adj* **1** *obs* : COVERT, SECRETIVE, UNDERHAND ⟨plain and direct, not crafty and ~ —Francis Bacon⟩ **2** *obs* : INVOLUTE, TWISTED **3 a** : COMPLICATED, INTRICATE ⟨~ poem⟩ ⟨~ sentence⟩ ⟨the music becomes more ~ —Warwick Braithwaite⟩ ⟨cup with sturdy base and ~ handle —W.E.Cox⟩ **b** : CONFUSED, TANGLED ⟨at his death . . . left his affairs dreadfully ~ —Jane Austen⟩ **4** : AFFECTED, IMPLICATED ⟨far . . . from an ~ understanding of normal human emotions —Robert Bingham⟩ ⟨dealing with . . . the most severely ~ patients —R.J.Thomas⟩ **syn** see COMPLEX

in·volved·ly \-(l)v(ə)dlē\ *adv* : in an involved manner

in·volved·ness \-(l)vədnəs, -(l)v(d)n-\ *n* -ES : INVOLVEMENT

in·volve·ment \-(l)vmənt\ *n* -S **1** : the act or an instance of involving ⟨his ~ of others was inexcusable⟩ ⟨~ is uncalled for because there are no moral and spiritual values at stake —M.W.Straight⟩ ⟨there would be no drama in such a story . . . no ~ of the spectator's own inevitable deep divisions —R.P. Warren⟩ ⟨any action . . . which might be interpreted as ~ in the big power conflict —G.S.Bhargava⟩ **2** : the state or fact of being involved ⟨the fluid senses' ~ in the world —Muriel Rukeyser⟩ ⟨increasing ~ in public life —Herbert Read⟩ ⟨knowledge of . . . diverse peoples, our ~ with them in practical terms and our commitment to them in terms of brotherhood —J.R.Oppenheimer⟩; *specif* : inclusion in a damaged area ⟨rheumatic fever, with or without heart ~ —*Biol. Abstracts*⟩ ⟨the child's face escaped ~ in the injuries —*Springfield (Mass.) Daily News*⟩ **3** : an involved or entangled condition or situation : COMPLEXITY, CONFUSION ⟨further complaints of obscurity, ~ —John Foster⟩

in·volv·er \-(l)və(r)\ *n* -S : one that involves

invt *abbr* **1** [L *invenit*] he designed; he devised; he invented **2** inventory

in·vulnerability \(¦)in, ən+\ *n* : the quality or state of being invulnerable

in·vulnerable \(')in, ən+\ *adj* [L *invulnerabilis*, fr. *in-* [1]in- + *vulnerare* to wound + *-abilis* -able — more at VULNERABLE] **1** : incapable of being wounded, injured, or damaged : immune to physical assault ⟨an armadillo curls up to make himself ~⟩ : IMPREGNABLE ⟨gunners rake the beaches from ~ positions in overhanging cliffs⟩ **2** : immune to or proof against attack : INVINCIBLE, UNASSAILABLE ⟨~ dignity⟩ ⟨though he was now a partner, his position was not ~ —Hamilton Basso⟩ — **in·vulnerably** \"+\ *adv*

in·vulnerableness \"+\ *n* : INVULNERABILITY

inwale \'=,=\ *n* [[4]*in* + *wale*] : a finishing strip of wood fastened inside the frame of an open boat and extending along the top strake to reinforce the gunwale — compare CLAMP 3

[1]**in·wall** \ən+\ *vt* [alter. (influenced by E [2]*in-*) of earlier *enwall*, fr. [1]*en-* + *wall*, n.] : to enclose with or as if with a wall

[2]**in·wall** \'in+,-\ *n* [[4]*in* + *wall*] : an inner wall (as of a blast furnace)

[1]**in·ward** \'inwərd, 'inwəd\ *adj* [ME *inward*, fr. OE *inweard*, *inneweard*, *innanweard;* OE *inweard* akin to MD *inwaert* inward, OHG *inwert*, all fr. a prehistoric WGmc compound whose first constituent is represented by OE *in*, *inn*, adv., in, and whose second constituent is represented by OE *-weard* -ward; OE *inneweard* fr. *inne* within (akin to OHG & ON *inni* within, Goth *inna*, all fr. a prehistoric Gmc word derived from the word represented by OE *in*, *inn*, adv., in) + *-weard* -ward; OE *innanweard* akin to ON *innanverthr* inward, both fr. a prehistoric NGmc-WGmc compound whose first constituent is represented by OE & ON *innan* within, from within, OHG *innan*, *innana* within, Goth *innana* (all fr. a prehistoric Gmc word derived from the word represented by OE *in*, *inn*, adv., in) and whose second constituent is represented by OE *-weard* -ward — more at IN (adv.), -WARD] **1 a** : situated on the inside : INNER, INTERNAL ⟨~ smile⟩ ⟨the whole body moves in response to some ~ rhythm —Ellen Glasgow⟩ **b** : produced from within : MUFFLED ⟨her words were ~ and indistinct —Ann Radcliffe⟩ **2 a** : of or relating to the mind or spirit : MENTAL, SPIRITUAL ⟨~ peace⟩ ⟨the scholar . . . lives an ~ and unmaterial life —P.E.More⟩ ⟨~ struggle of the heroes to find their own truth —Leslie Rees⟩ **b** : of or relating to religious faith : DEVOUT, PIOUS ⟨monks . . . free the soul from corporeality and make it ~ —José Ortega y Gasset⟩ **3 a** : of or relating to close acquaintance : FAMILIAR, INTIMATE ⟨intimate and ~, not outward from the child —R.L.Shayon⟩ ⟨more ~ with the Tudor-Stuart dramatists than any man . . . before or since —T.S.Eliot⟩ **b** *obs* : CONFIDENTIAL, SECRET ⟨what is ~ between us, let it pass —Shak.⟩ **4** *archaic* : of or relating to the homeland : DOMESTIC ⟨the dangers ~ they foresaw would be from the noblemen removed from the Queen's Council —Robert Norton⟩ **5** : directed toward the interior : INGOING ⟨~ slope of radiator grille —*Car Life*⟩ **syn** see INNER

[2]**inward** \"\ *or* **inwards** \"\ *adv* [ME *inward*, *inwardes;* ME *inward* fr. OE *inweard*, fr. *inweard*, adj.; ME *inwardes* fr. *inward* + *-es* (adverbially functioning gen. sing. ending of nouns) — more at INWARD (adj.), -'S] **1 a** : toward the inside : toward the center or interior ⟨the sides of the hole seemed to slope ~ until they met —Gwyn Thomas⟩ ⟨ships . . . that tried to run either ~ or outward through the blockade —C.S. Forester⟩; *specif* : HOMEWARD ⟨~ bound⟩ **b** *obs* : on the inside : INTERNALLY ⟨the maple seldom ~ sound —Edmund Spenser⟩ **2** : toward the inner being : into the mind or spirit ⟨his rich emotions began to turn ~ —H.S.Canby⟩

[3]**inward** \", *in sense 2 usu* 'inə(r)d\ *n* -S [ME, fr. OE *inneweard*, fr. *inneweard*, adj. — more at INWARD (adj.)] **1** : an inner being or nature : ESSENCE, SPIRIT ⟨make thine ~ like unto thine outward —John Payne⟩ — usu. used in pl. ⟨Jefferson puts the ~*s* of the issue in these terms —Archibald MacLeish⟩ **2 a** : an inside or interior part ⟨their forms fled to the dusky ~ of his mysterious box —Ross Lockridge⟩ — often used in pl. ⟨saw him . . . glare down into the mysterious ~*s* of the engine —Wallace Stegner⟩ **b** : INNARDS — usu. used in pl. ⟨the gastroenterologist manages our nervous ~*s* —Greer Williams⟩ **3** *obs* : an intimate friend : CONFIDANT ⟨I was an ~ of his —Shak.⟩

[4]**in·ward** \'in,wȯrd\ *n* [ML *inwarda*, *inguarda*, prob. fr. (assumed) OE *inweard*, fr. OE *in*, *inn*, adv., in + *weard* ward, action of guarding — more at IN (adv.), WARD (n.)] : bodyguard service rendered to a king by his sokemen when he visits their shire

inward dive *n* : a competitive diving category including dives in which the body from a backward standing takeoff position rotates forward around a transverse axis — compare BACK DIVE, FRONT DIVE, REVERSE DIVE, TWIST DIVE

inward light *n, usu cap I&L* : INNER LIGHT

in·ward·ly *adv* [ME, fr. OE *inweardlice* heartily, fervently, fr. *inweardlic* internal, fr. *inweard*, adj., inward + *-lic* -ly] **1** : in the innermost being : MENTALLY, SPIRITUALLY ⟨women's self-possession is an outward thing; ~ they flutter —Joseph Conrad⟩ ⟨read, mark, and ~ digest —C.L.Becker⟩ **2** *obs* : in a complete or private manner : FULLY, INTIMATELY ⟨acquainting me with the state of affairs, more ~ than I knew before —John Milton⟩ **3 a** : on the inside : INTERNALLY ⟨he had bled ~ —Daniel Defoe⟩ **b** : to oneself : INAUDIBLY, SECRETLY ⟨I'd have thought she'd ~ either cursed or spat —Kenneth Roberts⟩ **4** : toward the center or interior ⟨see ~ and represent the world of the imagination —Herbert Read⟩

in·ward·ness *n* -ES [[1]*inward* + *-ness*] **1** : close acquaintance : FAMILIARITY, INTIMACY ⟨read his way into a certain ~ with Chaucer's idiom —John Speirs⟩ **2** : fundamental nature or meaning : ESSENCE, SIGNIFICANCE ⟨apprehending the real ~ of a plowman —C.D.Lewis⟩ ⟨could not grasp the ~ of the text —H.J.Laski⟩ ⟨far from . . . certain as to the true ~ of her violent dismissal —Joseph Conrad⟩ **3** : internal quality or substance ⟨became aware of the ~ of my body, of the blood moving in darkness —R.P.Warren⟩ **4 a** : preoccupation with one's own affairs or attitudes : INTROSPECTION, SUBJECTIVITY ⟨the sensitiveness of James's characters, their seeming ~ —Morris Roberts⟩ ⟨voluntary withdrawal . . . was to mean thereafter an ~ of corporate life —W.L.Sperry⟩ **b** : preoccupation with ethical or ideological values : SPIRITUALITY ⟨Socrates' ~, integrity, and inquisitiveness —H.R.Finch⟩

in·weave \(')in, ən+\ *or* **en·weave** \ən, (')en+\ *vt* [[2]*in-* or [1]*en-* + *weave*, v.] **1 a** : to weave in or together **b** : to decorate by weaving : INSERT, INTERLACE **c** : to mend or patch by reweaving **2** : to incorporate as if by weaving ⟨the vitality of experience which is *inwoven* with their thorniness —J.H. Hanford⟩

[1]**inwick** \'=,=\ *n* [[4]*in* + *wick*, n. (port in curling)] : a shot in curling in which a player's stone is made to carom off the inner edge of an intervening stone so as to knock away from the tee the stone nearest it — compare OUTWICK

[2]**inwick** \"\ *vi* : to make an inwick

inwind *var of* ENWIND

inwit \'=,=\ *n* [ME, fr. *in*, prep. & adv. + *wit*, n.] : inward knowledge : CONSCIENCE, UNDERSTANDING ⟨acting from ~ —Ezra Pound⟩ ⟨spills his yarns with humor and delight or with an ~ of sadness —I.L.Salomon⟩

inwith \'=,=\ *adj (or adv)* [ME, fr. *in*, prep. & adv. + *with*, prep.] *Scot* : INSIDE, BEN

inworn \'=¦=\ *adj* [[2]*in* + *worn*, past part. of *wear* (after *wear in*, v.)] : INGRAINED

in·wound \(')in, ən+\ *adj* [[2]*in* + *wound*, past part. of *wind* (after *wind in*, v.)] : INTERTWINED

in·woven \(')in, ən+\ *or* **en·woven** \ən, (')en+\ *adj* [fr. past part. of *inweave*] **1 a** : INTERWOVEN **b** : ENTWINED **2** : closely associated ⟨~ with the heath in his boyhood —Thomas Hardy⟩

inwrap *var of* ENWRAP

inwreathe *var of* ENWREATHE

in·wrought \(')in, ən+\ *or* **en·wrought** \ən, (')en+\ *adj* [*inwrought* fr. [2]*in* + *wrought*, past part. of *work* (after *work in*, v.); *enwrought* alter. (influenced by [1]*en-*) of *inwrought*] **1 a** : having a decorative element worked or woven in : ORNAMENTED ⟨bonnet . . . ~ with figures —John Milton⟩ **b** *archaic* : WORKED, EMBROIDERED ⟨by beauty's hand ~ —Erasmus Darwin⟩ **2** : worked in as a constituent : INTERWOVEN ⟨~ with the tale are some of the great secrets of philosophy —Marianne Moore⟩

in·ya·la \ən'yälə\ *n, pl* **inyala** [Zulu *inxala*] : NYALA 1

in·yo·ite \'in(,)yō,īt\ *n* -S [*Inyo* county, California, its locality + E *-ite*] : a mineral $Ca_2B_6O_{11}.13H_2O$ consisting of a hydrous calcium borate occurring in colorless monoclinic crystals (hardness 2, sp. gr. 2)

[1]**io** *n* -S [L, interj., fr. Gk *iō*] *obs* : a shout of joy or triumph ⟨rocks, valleys, hills, with splitting ~*s* ring —John Dryden & Nathaniel Lee⟩ — often used interjectionally

[2]**io** \'ē(,)ō\ *n* -S [Hawaiian] : a large hawk (*Buteo solitarius*) that is the only indigenous raptorial bird of Hawaii

IO *abbr* **1** information officer **2** in order **3** inspecting order **4** intelligence officer

Io *symbol* ionium

ioa *var of* IWA

iod *var of* YODH

iod- *or* **iodo-** *comb form* [F *iode* iodine] **1** : iodine ⟨*iod*hydrate⟩ ⟨*iodo*form⟩ **2 a** *now usu iodo-* : containing iodine in place of hydrogen — in names of organic compounds ⟨*iodo*acetophenone⟩ **b** *now usu iodo-* : containing iodine regarded as replacing hydroxyl or oxygen or as coordinated to a central atom — in names of inorganic acids and salts ⟨*iodo*argentate⟩ ⟨*iodo*bismuthate⟩ **c** : containing iodine as iodide sometimes replacing another element or group — in names of minerals and salts occurring as minerals ⟨*iodo*sulfate⟩

iod·amoeba \(ˌ)īˌōd, -ˌäd+\ *n, cap* [NL, fr. *iod-* + *amoeba*] **:** a genus of amoebas commensal in the intestine of man and other mammals and distinguished by uninucleate cysts containing a large glycogen vacuole that stains characteristically with iodine

¹io·date \ˈīə,dāt\ *n* -s [F, fr. *iode* iodine + *-ate*] **:** a salt of iodic acid

²iodate \"\ *vt* -ED/-ING/-S [*iod-* + *-ate*, v. suffix] **:** to impregnate or treat with iodine — **io·da·tion** \ˌīəˈdāshən\ *n* -s

iodhydrin *var of* IODOHYDRIN

iod·ic \(ˈ)īˈädik\ *adj* [F *iodique*, fr. *iode* iodine + *-ique* -ic] **:** of, relating to, or containing iodine — used esp. of compounds in which this element is pentavalent

iodic acid *n* **:** a crystalline oxidizing solid HIO_3 formed by oxidation of iodine (as with fuming nitric acid)

iodic anhydride *n* **:** IODINE PENTOXIDE

io·dide \ˈīə,dīd, -ədəd\ *n* -s [ISV *iod-* + *-ide*] **:** a binary compound of iodine usu. with a more electropositive element or radical **:** a salt or ester of hydriodic acid ⟨potassium ~⟩ ⟨ethyl ~⟩

iodimetry *var of* IODOMETRY

io·di·nate \ˈīədə,nāt\ *vt* -ED/-ING/-S [*iodine* + *-ate*, v. suffix] **:** to treat or cause to combine with iodine or a compound of iodine **:** introduce iodine into (as an organic compound)

iodinated casein *n* **:** an iodine-containing preparation that is made from casein, resembles the thyroid hormone in physiological activity, and is used in animal feeds (as to increase milk production of cows)

io·di·na·tion \ˌīədəˈnāshən\ *n* -s **:** the process of iodinating

io·dine *also* **io·din** \ˈīə,dīn *also* -ədən *or* -dᵊn *or* -,dēn\ *n* -s [F *iode* iodine (fr. Gk *ioeidēs* purple, violet colored, fr. *ion* violet + *-oeidēs* -oid) + E ²*-ine* or *-in* — more at VIOLET] **:** a nonmetallic univalent and polyvalent element belonging to the halogens that is obtained usu. as heavy shining blackish gray crystals subliming to a violet-colored irritating vapor, that occurs naturally only in combination in small quantities esp. in seawater, rocks, soils, and underground brines and in marine plants and animals, that is essential for the normal functioning of the thyroid gland of all vertebrates, that is usu. extracted from the ashes of seaweeds, from Chile saltpeter, or from oil-well brines, and that is used chiefly in medicine (as in antisepsis and in the treatment of cretinism and goiter), photography, and analysis — symbol *I;* see ELEMENT table

iodine bush *n* **:** a shrub (*Allenrolfia occidentalis*) of the family Chenopodiaceae with fleshy jointed stems, leaves resembling scales, and flowers in crowded spikes that grows in moist saline soils in the southwestern U.S. and is used for winter grazing — called also *burroweed, California greasewood, pickleweed*

iodine number *or* **iodine value** *n* **:** a measure of the unsaturation of a substance (as an oil or fat) expressed as the number of grams of iodine or equivalent halogen absorbed by 100 grams of the substance ⟨the *iodine numbers* of linseed oil, olive oil, and coconut oil are approximately 175–201, 77–91, and 8–9.5 respectively⟩

iodine 131 *n* **:** a heavy radioactive isotope of iodine having the mass number 131 and a half-life of 8 days that is produced in the fission of uranium or by bombardment of tellurium with neutrons and that is used esp. in the form of sodium radioiodide in the diagnosis of thyroid disease and the treatment of goiter — symbol I^{131} or ^{131}I; called also *radioiodine*

iodine pentoxide *n* **:** a white crystalline solid I_2O_5 formed by the oxidation of iodine or the dehydration of iodic acid and used to oxidize carbon monoxide quantitatively to carbon dioxide — called also *iodic anhydride*

iodine weed *n* **:** INKWEED 1

io·din·oph·i·lous \ˌīədəˈnäfələs\ *also* **io·din·o·phil** \ˌīəˈdinə,fil\ *or* **io·din·o·phile** \-,fīl\ *or* **io·din·o·phil·ic** \ˌīə,dinəˈfilik\ *adj* [*iodinophilous* fr. *iodine* + *-o-* + *-philous; iodinophil, iodinophile* fr. *iodine* + *-o-* + *-phile, -phil; iodinophilic* prob. fr. *iodinophil* + *-ic*] **:** taking up or coloring readily with iodine — used esp. of various starchy cell inclusions

io·dism \ˈīə,dizəm\ *n* -s [*iod-* + *-ism;* prob. intended as trans. of G *jodkrankheit*] **:** an abnormal local and systemic condition resulting from overdosage with, prolonged use of, or sensitivity to iodine or iodine compounds

io·di·za·tion \ˌīədəˈzāshən, -,dīˈz-\ *n* -s **:** the process of iodizing

io·dize \ˈīə,dīz\ *vt* -ED/-ING/-S [*iod-* + *-ize*] **:** to treat with iodine or an iodide ⟨recommended *iodized* salt as a preventive of thyroid trouble⟩

iodized oil *n* **:** a viscous oily fluid that has an odor like garlic, is made by treating a fatty vegetable oil (as poppy-seed oil) with iodine or hydriodic acid, and is used as a contrast medium in X-ray photography

io·do \īˈō(,)dō, ˈīə,dō\ *adj* [*iod-*] **:** containing iodine — used esp. of organic compounds; compare IOD- 2

iodo- — see IOD-

iodo·acetate \īˌōdō, īˌädō+\ *n* [ISV *iod-* + *acetate*] **:** a salt or ester of iodoacetic acid

iodo·acetic acid \"+ . . . -\ *n* [*iodoacetic* ISV *iod-* + *acetic*] **:** a crystalline acid CH_2ICOOH made by reaction of chloroacetic acid and a metallic iodide and used in biochemical research esp. because of its inhibiting effect on many enzymes (as in glycolysis in muscle extracts)

iodo·behenate \īˌōdə, īˌädə+\ *n* [*iod-* + *behenate*] **:** a salt of iodobehenic acid

iodo·behenic acid \"+. . .-\ *n* [*iodobehenic* ISV *iod-* + *behenic* (in *behenic acid*)] **:** a solid mono-iodo derivative $C_{21}H_{42}ICOOH$ of behenic acid made by reaction of erucic acid and hydriodic acid

iodo·benzene \īˌōdō, īˌädō+\ *n* [ISV *iod-* + *benzene*] **:** a colorless liquid C_6H_5I made usu. from benzene by reaction with iodine and nitric acid — called also *phenyl iodide*

iodo·bromide \"+\ *n* **:** BROMOIODIDE

iodo·bromite \"+\ *n* -s [obs. G *iodobromit* (now *jodobromit*), fr. obs. G *iod-* (now *jod-*) + G *bromit* bromyrite, fr. *brom-* + *-it* -ite] **:** a mineral Ag(Br,Cl,I) consisting of chloride, iodide, and bromide of silver that is isomorphous with cerargyrite and bromyrite

iodo·casein \"+\ *n* **:** IODINATED CASEIN

iodo·chloride \"+\ *n* **:** CHLOROIODIDE

iodo·ethane \īˌōdō, īˌädō+\ *n* **:** ETHYL IODIDE

iodo·form \īˈōdə,fȯrm, īˈäd-\ *n* -s [ISV *iod-* + *-form* (as in *chloroform*)] **:** a yellow crystalline volatile compound CHI_3 that has a penetrating persistent odor, is made usu. by electrolysis of an alkaline solution of a metallic iodide in alcohol or acetone, and is sometimes used as an antiseptic dressing; tri-iodo-methane

iodo·gor·go·ic acid \īˌōdəˌgȯrˈgōik, īˌäd-\ *n* [*iodogorgoic* fr. *iod-* + *gorgo-* (fr. *gorgonin*) + *-ic*] **:** DIIODOTYROSINE

iodo·hy·drin \ī,ōdəˈhīdrən, īˌäd-\ *also* **iod·hy·drin** \ī,ōdˈh-, ī,äd-\ *n* -s [ISV *iod-* + *-hydrin*] **:** any of a class of iodine compounds analogous to the chlorohydrins

iodo·mer·cu·rate \īˌōdəˈmərkyərət, īˌäd-, -,rāt\ *also* **iodo·mer·cu·ri·ate** \-(,)mərˈkyu̇rēət, -ē,āt\ *n* -s [ISV *iod-* + *mercur-* or *mercuri-* + *-ate*] **:** any of a series of complex salts containing iodine and mercury in the anion

iodo·metric \"+\ *adj* [ISV *iodometry* + *-ic*] **:** of, relating to, or by means of iodometry — **iodo·metrically** \"+\ *adv*

io·dom·e·try \ˌīəˈdämə·trē\ *also* **io·dim·e·try** \-dim-\ *n* -ES [*iodometry* ISV *iod-* + *-metry; iodimetry* alter. (influenced by E *-i-*) of *iodometry*] **1 :** the volumetric determination of iodine usu. by titration with a standard solution of sodium thiosulfate using starch as indicator **2 :** a method of quantitative analysis involving the use of a standard solution of iodine or the liberation of iodine from an iodide

io·do·ni·um \ˌīəˈdōnēəm\ *n* -s [ISV *iod-* + *-onium;* orig. formed as G *iodonium*] **:** the univalent cation H_2I^+ derived from hydrogen iodide and known only in disubstituted form

¹iodo·phile \īˈōdə,fīl, īˈäd-\ *or* **iodo·phil·ic** \ˌ=ˌ==ˈfilik\ *adj* [*iodophile* ISV *iod-* + *-phile; iodophilic* fr. *iodophile* + *-ic*] **:** staining in a characteristic manner with iodine — used esp. of starch-containing cells staining blue with iodine

²iodophile \"\ *n* -s **:** an iodophile cell or individual

iodo·phthalein \īˌōdə, īˌädə+\ *n* **:** a symmetrical tetraiodo derivative of phenolphthalein or its soluble blue-violet crystalline disodium salt $C_{19}H_8I_4O(ONa)COONa$ used to render the gall bladder opaque to X rays and to treat typhoid carriers

iodo·protein \"+\ *n* **:** an iodine-containing protein (as iodinated casein) — compare THYROPROTEIN

io·dop·sin \ˌīəˈdäpsən\ *n* -s [*iod-* (fr. Gk *ioeidēs* violet-colored) + *ops-* (fr. Gk *opsis* sight) + *-in* — more at IODINE, -OPSIS] **:** a photosensitive violet pigment in the retinal cones of most animals that is similar to rhodopsin but more labile, that is formed from vitamin A_1, and that is important in daylight vision

iodo·pyr·a·cet \ī,ōdəˈpirə,set, ī,äd-\ *n* -s [*diiodo-pyridone-N-acetic* acid] **:** a salt $C_8H_{19}I_2N_2O_3$ administered intravenously in aqueous solution as a contrast medium for radiography esp. of the urinary tract; the diethanolamine salt of 3,5-diiodo-4-pyridone-*N*-acetic acid — called also *diodone*

iodoso- *comb form* [ISV *iodos-* (fr. *iodous*) + *-o-*] **:** containing the univalent radical —IO consisting of one atom each of iodine and oxygen, esp. replacing hydrogen ⟨*iodoso*benzoic acid $C_6H_4(IO)COOH$⟩

io·do·so·benzene \ˌīəˈdō(,)sō+\ *n* [ISV *iodoso-* + *benzene*] **:** an amorphous solid compound C_6H_5IO that explodes when heated and is formed by treating iodobenzene with chlorine and then with a caustic alkali

iodous \īˈōdəs, īˈäd-, ˈīəd-\ *adj* [ISV *iod-* + *-ous*] **:** relating to or containing iodine and esp. iodine with a valence of three ⟨~ acid HIO_2⟩

iodoxy- *comb form* [ISV *iod-* + *oxy-*] **:** containing the univalent radical —IO_2 of iodic acid, esp. replacing hydrogen ⟨*iodoxy*benzoic acid $C_6H_4(IO_2)COOH$⟩

io·doxy·benzene \ˌīəˈdäksē+\ *n* [*iodoxy-* + *benzene*] **:** a crystalline compound $C_6H_5IO_2$ that explodes when heated and is obtained by gentle oxidation of iodosobenzene

iod·y·rite \īˈädə,rīt\ *n* -s [*iod-* + *argyr-* + *-ite*] **:** a yellowish or greenish hexagonal mineral AgI consisting of native silver iodide usu. occurring in thin plates

io·lite \ˈīə,līt\ *n* -s [G *iolith*, fr. *io-* (fr. Gk *ion* violet) + *-lith* -lite, -lith — more at VIOLET] **:** CORDIERITE

IOM *abbr* interoffice minute

io moth \ˈī(,)ō-\ *n* [NL *io* (specific epithet of *Automeris io*), fr. L *Io*, mythical priestess of Argos who was loved by Zeus, fr. Gk *Iō*] **:** a large yellowish American moth (*Automeris io*) having a large ocellate spot on each hind wing and a larva covered with fascicles of spines that sting like nettles

ion \ˈīən *also* ˈī,än\ *n* -s [Gk, neut. of *iōn*, pres. part. of *ienai* to go — more at ISSUE] **1 :** an atom or group of atoms when combined in a radical or molecule that carries a positive or negative electric charge as a result of having lost or gained one or more electrons and that may exist in solution usu. in combination with molecules of the solvent or out of solution, that may be formed during electrolysis and migrate to the electrode of opposite charge, or that may be formed in a gas and be capable of carrying an electric current through the gas — see ANION, CATION; compare HYDROGEN ION **2 :** a free electron or other charged subatomic particle

-ion *n suffix* -s [ME *-ioun, -ion, -iun*, fr. OF *-ion, -iun*, fr. L *-ion-, -io*] **1 a :** act or process ⟨acidulat*ion*⟩ ⟨rebell*ion*⟩ **b :** result of an act or process ⟨construct*ion*⟩ **2 a :** state or condition ⟨subject*ion*⟩ **b :** thing acted upon or conditioned ⟨ambit*ion*⟩

ion chamber *n* **:** IONIZATION CHAMBER

ion engine *n* **:** a jet engine deriving thrust from a stream of ionized particles

ion exchange *n* **:** a reversible interchange that takes place between ions of like charge and usu. between ions present on an insoluble solid and ions present in a solution surrounding the solid and that may occur naturally or be applied for various purposes — see ANION EXCHANGE, CATION EXCHANGE

ion exchanger *n* **1 :** a solid agent (as a zeolite or a synthetic resin) used in ion exchange — compare ANION EXCHANGER, CATION EXCHANGER **2 :** an apparatus or piece of equipment for effecting ion exchange

ion-exchange resin *n* **:** an insoluble material of high molecular weight that contains either acidic groups for exchanging cations or basic groups for exchanging anions and that may be used in medicine (as for reducing the sodium content of the body or the acidity of the stomach) and in ion exclusion as well as in the usual ion-exchange processes

ion exclusion *n* **:** a process of separating materials in solution by means of an ion-exchange resin that excludes highly ionized particles and takes up slightly ionized particles or particles not ionized

¹io·ni·an \īˈōnēən\ *n* -s *usu cap* [L *ionius*, adj. + E *-an*, n. suffix] **1 :** a native or inhabitant of Ionia; *esp* **:** one of the Greek people descended from an early group of Hellenic invaders of Greece **2 :** a member of a school of philosophers of ancient Greece consisting chiefly of the Milesians but including also the philosophers Heraclitus and Xenophanes

²ionian \(ˈ)=ˈ===\ *adj, usu cap* [L *ionius* Ionian (fr. *Ionia*, ancient district including the south central part of the west coast of Asia Minor and several nearby Aegean islands such as Chios and Samos, fr. Gk *Iōnia*, fr. *Iōn*, n., Ionian + *-ia*) + E *-an*, adj. suffix] **1 a :** of, relating to, or characteristic of Ionia **b :** of, relating to, or characteristic of the people of Ionia **2 :** of or relating to the Ionian group of Greek philosophers ⟨resumed the *Ionian* tradition of scientific research —Benjamin Farrington⟩

ionian mode *n, usu cap I* **1 :** the Greek hypophrygian mode **2 :** an authentic ecclesiastical mode consisting of a pentachord and an upper conjunct tetrachord represented on the white keys of the piano by an ascending diatonic scale from C to C — called also *Ionic mode;* see MODE illustration

¹ion·ic \(ˈ)īˈänik, -nēk\ *adj* [L & MF; MF *ionique*, fr. L *ionicus*, fr. Gk *iōnikos*, fr. *Iōnia* Ionia + *-ikos* -ic] **1** *usu cap* **:** IONIAN **2** *usu cap* **:** belonging to or resembling the Ionic order of architecture that is lighter and more graceful than Doric and is characterized esp. by the spiral volutes of its capital — see CAPITAL illustration **3 :** of, relating to, or consisting of ionics

²ionic \"\ *n* -s **1** *cap* **:** a dialect of ancient Greek used in Ionia that was the vehicle of an important body of literature **2** [LL *ionicus*, fr. L *ionicus*, adj.] **a :** a foot of verse that consists either of (1) two long and two short syllables or (2) two short and two long syllables — called also respectively (1) *major ionic* and (2) *minor ionic* **b :** a verse or meter consisting of ionics

³ionic \"\ *adj* [ISV *ion* + *-ic*] **1 :** of, relating to, existing in the form of, or characterized by ions ⟨~ charge⟩ ⟨~ hydrogen⟩ ⟨~ crystals⟩ **2 :** operated by, utilizing, or taking place by means of ions ⟨~ loudspeaker⟩ ⟨~ conduction⟩

Ionic order: Greek, *A;* Roman, *B*

ionic alphabet *n, usu cap I* [¹*ionic*] **:** a variety of the eastern form of the ancient Greek alphabet having 24 letters in its developed form and officially accepted late in the 5th cent. B.C. at Athens from which its use in time extended throughout the Greek-speaking world

ionic bond *n* [³*ionic*] **:** ELECTROVALENT BOND

ionic displacement *n* [¹*ionic*] **:** the occurrence in iambic meter of a pyrrhic foot followed or sometimes preceded by a spondaic foot that together create an ionic cadence (as in the third and fourth feet in Shakespeare's line "when to the sessions of sweet silent thought" oo|oó|oo|óó|oó)

ion·i·cism \īˈänə,sizəm\ *n* -s *usu cap* [¹*ionic* + *-ism*] **1 :** an Ionic feature; *esp* **:** a characteristic feature of the Ionic dialect — called also *Ionism* **2 :** the quality or state of being Ionic

ion·i·cize \-,sīz\ *vt* -ED/-ING/-S *often cap* [¹*ionic* + *-ize*] **:** to make Ionic

ionic mode *n, usu cap I* **:** IONIAN MODE

ionic valence *n* [³*ionic*] **:** ELECTROVALENCE

io·nism \ˈīə,nizəm\ *n* -s *usu cap* [prob. fr. L *Iones* Ionians (fr. Gk *Iōnes*, pl. of *Iōn* Ionian) + E *-ism*] **:** IONICISM

io·ni·um \īˈōnēəm\ *n* -s [*ion* + *-ium;* so called fr. its ionizing action] **:** a naturally occurring radioactive isotope of thorium having mass 230 — symbol Th^{230} or *Io;* see URANIUM SERIES

ion·iza·tion \ˌīənəˈzāshən, -,nīˈz-\ *n* -s [ISV ²*ionize* + *-ation*] **:** the process of ionizing or the state of being ionized — compare DISSOCIATION

ionization chamber *n* **:** a partially evacuated tube provided with electrodes so that its conductivity due to the ionization of the residual gas reveals the presence of ionizing radiation (as X rays or beta rays)

ionization constant *n* **:** a constant that depends upon the equilibrium between the ions and the molecules that are not ionized in a solution or liquid — symbol *K;* called also *dissociation constant*

ionization current *n* **:** an electric current produced in an ionized gas subjected to an electric field

ionization gauge *n* **:** a low-pressure vacuum gauge in which the pressure is indicated by the ionization current between two specified electrodes at a prescribed voltage

ionization potential *n* **:** the potential difference corresponding to the energy in electron volts that is just sufficient to ionize a gas molecule

¹io·nize \ˈīə,nīz\ *vt* -ED/-ING/-S *often cap* [Gk *iōnizein* to speak Ionic, fr. *Iōn*, n., Ionian + *-izein* -ize] **:** IONICIZE

²ion·ize \"\ *vb* -ED/-ING/-S [ISV *ion* + *-ize*] *vt* **:** to convert wholly or partly into ions ⟨a charged particle . . . ~*s* the air molecules with which it collides —G.W.Gray b. 1886⟩ ⟨*ionized* calcium⟩ ~ *vi* **:** to become converted wholly or partly into ions ⟨a salt ~*s* in water⟩

ion·o·gen \īˈänəjən, -,jen\ *n* -s [ISV *ion* + *-o-* + *-gen*] **1 :** a compound capable of forming ions **:** ELECTROLYTE 2 **2 :** an atom or group capable of being ionized

ion·o·gen·ic \ī,änəˈjenik\ *adj* [*ion* + *-o-* + *-genic*] **:** capable of ionizing

ion·og·ra·phy \ˌīəˈnägrəfē\ *n* -ES [*ion* + *-o-* + *-graphy*] **:** electrochromatography involving the migration of ions (as on wet filter paper)

Io·none \ˈīə,nōn\ *trademark* — used for either of two oily liquid isomeric ketones $C_{13}H_{20}O$ that have a strong violet odor, are found esp. in the essential oil of an Australian shrub (*Boronia megastigma*) but are usu. obtained from citral, and are used esp. in perfumes

ion·o·pho·re·sis \ī,änəfəˈrēsəs\ *n, pl* **ionophore·ses** \-ē,sēz\ [NL, fr. *ion* (fr. E) + *-o-* + *-phoresis*] **:** ELECTROPHORESIS; *esp* **:** the movement of relatively small ions — **ion·o·pho·ret·ic** \ī,änəfəˈred·ik\ *adj*

ion·o·sphere \īˈänə+,-\ *n* [*ion* + *-o-* + *sphere*] **:** the part of the earth's atmosphere beginning at an altitude of about 25 miles and extending outward 250 miles or more, containing free electrically charged particles by means of which radio waves are transmitted to great distances around the earth, and consisting of several regions within which occur one or more layers that vary in height and ionization with time of day, season, and the solar cycle, the gases in this part of the earth's atmosphere being ionized by ultraviolet rays from the sun and to a lesser extent by charged particles from the sun — see D REGION, E REGION, F REGION — **ion·o·spher·ic** \ī,änəˈsfirik, -fer-\ *adj*

io·not·ro·py \ˌīəˈnä·trəpē\ *n* -ES [*ion* + *-o-* + *-tropy*] **:** TAUTOMERISM

ion·oxalis \ˌīən+\ *n, cap* [NL, fr. Gk *ion* violet + NL *Oxalis*] **:** a genus of chiefly tropical American herbs (family Oxalidaceae)

ions *pl of* ION

-ions *pl of* -ION

ionto- *comb form* [NL, fr. Gk *iont-, iōn*, pres. part. of *ienai* to go — more at ISSUE] **:** ion ⟨*ionto*quantimeter⟩ ⟨*ionto*therapy⟩

ion·to·pho·re·sis \ī,äntəfəˈrēsəs\ *n, pl* **iontophore·ses** \-ē,sēz\ [NL, fr. *ionto-* + *-phoresis*] **1 :** ELECTROPHORESIS **2 :** the introduction of drugs through intact skin by the transfer of ions effected by means of the application of a direct electric current — **ion·to·pho·ret·ic** \ī,äntəfəˈred·ik\ *adj*

ion trap *n* **:** a device that prevents the formation of a discolored spot on a television screen by diverting the negative ions from the cathode that would cause it

io·ra \īˈōrə, ēˈō-\ *n* -s [origin unknown] **:** any of several small bright-colored Asiatic songbirds that are related to the bulbuls and that constitute a genus (*Aegithina*)

ios *pl of* IO

io·ta \īˈōd·ə, -ōtə, *in sense 1 sometimes* ēˈō-\ *n* -s [L *iota, jota*, fr. Gk *iōta* — more at JOT] **1 :** the ninth and smallest letter of the Greek alphabet — symbol Ι or ι; see ALPHABET table **2 :** an infinitesimal amount **:** a very small degree **:** JOT ⟨of statesmanship he had not an ~ —S.H.Adams⟩ ⟨he had used a lever . . . nicely, to extract the last ~ of pain —F.V.W.Mason⟩

iota adscript *n* **:** the unpronounced iota of a Greek improper diphthong when written on the line after the long vowel — used in standard printing practice only when the long vowel is a capital

io·ta·cism \-,sizəm\ *n* -s [LL *iotacismus*, fr. Gk *iōtakismos*, fr. *iōta* iota] **:** excessive use of the letter iota or I or a too frequent repetition of its sound; *specif* **:** the use in modern Greek of the sound of iota (Eng. ē in *bē*) in speaking words written with other vowels or diphthongs (as *ē, y, ei, oi*) — compare ITACISM

iota subscript *n* **:** the unpronounced iota of a Greek improper diphthong when written small beneath the preceding long vowel [as ᾳ (*āi*), ῃ (*ēi*), ῳ (*ōi*)]

I O U \ˌī(,)ōˈyü\ *n* -s [fr. the pronunciation of *I owe you*] **:** a paper that has on it the letters IOU and a signature as an acknowledgment of debt, that names a sum of money, and that is sometimes used as the equivalent of a promissory note

-ious *adj suffix* [ME, partly fr. OF *-ious, -ios, -ieus, -ieux*, fr. L *-iosus*, fr. *-i-* (penultimate vowel in nouns such as *religio* religion, *malitia* malice, *species* species, appearance, *spatium* space) + *-osus* -ose, and partly fr. L *-ius* (final portion of the nom. sing. masc. form of adjectives such as *meritorius* that brings in money)] **:** -OUS ⟨edac*ious*⟩

¹io·wa *also* **io·way** \ˈīəwə, -,wā\ *n, pl* **iowa** *or* **iowas** *usu cap* [Dakota *Ayuhwa*, lit., sleepy ones] **1 a :** a Siouan people of Iowa, Minnesota, and Missouri **b :** a member of such people **2 :** a dialect of the Chiwere language

²io·wa \ˈīəwə, ÷ˈīə,wā, *by outsiders sometimes* īˈōə\ *adj, usu cap* [*Iowa*, state in the north central U.S., fr. ¹*iowa*] **:** of or from the state of Iowa ⟨an *Iowa* cornfield⟩ **:** of the kind or style prevalent in Iowa **:** IOWAN

iowa crab *or* **iowa crab apple** *n, usu cap I* [²*iowa*] **:** a wild crab apple (*Malus ioensis*) of the western U.S. with fragrant pink flowers — called also *western crab apple*

¹io·wan \ˈīəwən\ *adj, usu cap* [*Iowa*, state in the north central U.S. + E *-an*, adj. suffix] **1 :** of, relating to, or characteristic of the state of Iowa **2 :** of, relating to, or characteristic of the people of Iowa

²iowan \"\ *n* -s *cap* [*Iowa*, state in the north central U.S. + E *-an*, n. suffix] **1 :** a native or resident of Iowa **2 a :** a substage of the Wisconsin glacial stage **b :** the drift of such substage

IP *abbr* **1** ice point **2** India paper **3** initial point **4** innings pitched **5** installment paid **6** intermediate pressure

ipa \ˈēpə\ *n* -s *usu cap* [AmerSp, of AmerInd origin] **1 :** a people of the Vilela group **2 :** a member of the Ipa people

IPA \ˌī(,)pēˈā\ *n* -s [International Phonetic Alphabet] **:** an alphabet designed to represent each human speech sound with a unique symbol

IPA *abbr* **1** including particular average **2** intermediate power amplifier

IPC *n* -s [*isopropyl N-phenylcarbamate*] **:** a crystalline herbicide $C_6H_5NHCOOCH(CH_3)_2$ that is poisonous to grasses but not to broad-leaved plants; isopropyl carbanilate

IPD *abbr* individual package delivery

ip·e·cac \ˈipə,kak, ˈipē-\ *or* **ipe·cacua·nha** \ˌ==ˌkakyəˈwan(y)ə, ē,pakəˈkwanyə\ *n* -s [*ipecac* short for *ipecacuanha*, fr. Pg, fr. Tupi *ipekaaguéne*] **1 :** a tropical So. American creeping plant (*Cephaelis ipecacuanha*) with drooping flowers **2 a :** the dried rhizome and roots of ipecac formerly used as a medicine and now valued as the source of emetine — called also *Brazilian ipecac* **b :** the dried roots of any of several plants used like ipecac roots — see BASTARD IPECAC, WHITE IPECAC

ipecac spurge *n* **:** a spurge (*Euphorbia ipecacuanhae*) of the eastern U. S. with a root that is emetic and purgative — called also *American white ipecac*

ip·e·cac·u·a·nhic \ˌipəˌkakyəˈwan(y)ik, ¦ipē,-\ *adj* **:** of or relating to ipecac

ipf *abbr* imperfect

iph·i·ge·nia \ˌifəjəˈnīə\ *n, cap* [NL, fr. L *Iphigenia*, daughter of Agamemnon, fr. Gk *Iphigeneia*] **:** a genus of tropical bivalve mollusks related to *Donax*

IPI *abbr* [L *in partibus infidelium*] in the regions of unbelievers

¹ip·id \ˈipəd\ *adj* [NL *Ipidae*] **:** of or relating to the Scolytidae

²ipid \"\ *n* -s [NL *Ipidae*] **:** a member of the Scolytidae

ip·i·dae \ˈipəˌdē\ [NL, fr. *Ip-*, *Ips*, type genus + *-idae*] *syn of* SCOLYTIDAE

ipil \ˈēpəl\ *or* **ifil** \ˈēfəl\ *n* -s [Sp *ipil*, fr. Tag] **1 :** a Philippine and Pacific island tree (*Intsia bijuga*) yielding a valuable brown dye and having a very hard and durable dark wood **2 :** the wood of the ipil

ipil-ipil \ˌēpəˈlēpəl\ *n* -s [Tag *ipil ipil*] **:** a tropical leguminous shrub (*Leucaena glauca*) used esp. in the Philippines as a means of controlling various undesirable grasses in pastures and rangelands

ipin \(ˈ)ē¦pin, -pēn\ *adj, usu cap* [fr. *Ipin*, city in south central China] **:** of or from the city of Ipin, China **:** of the kind or style prevalent in Ipin

ip·i·ti \ˈipəd·ē\ *n* -s [Xhosa & Zulu *i puti*] **:** BLUE DUIKER

ip·i·u·tak \ˌipēˈyüˌtak\ *adj, usu cap* [fr. *Ipiutak*, locality near Point Hope, northwest Alaska, where remains of the culture were discovered] **:** of or relating to an Eskimo culture in western Alaska of about A.D.100–600 characterized by ivory carvings, finely chipped stone implements resembling Siberian artifacts, and villages of semiunderground earth lodges

IPM *abbr, often not cap* inches per minute

ip·o·moea \ˌipəˈmēə\ *n* [NL, fr. Gk *ip-*, *ips* worm + NL *-omoea* (fr. Gk *homoios* like); fr. the twining habit of the plants — more at HOME-] **1** *cap* **:** a genus of herbaceous vines (family Convolvulaceae) having showy campanulate or funnelform flowers with capitate stigmas — see MORNING GLORY, SWEET POTATO **2** *also* **ip·o·mea** \"\ -s **:** a plant or flower of the genus *Ipomoea* **3** *usu* **ipomea** -s **:** the dried root of a scammony (*Ipomoea orizabensis*)

IPP *abbr* India paper proofs

ip·pi·ap·pa \ˌipēˈapə\ *n* -s [by alter.] **:** JIPIJAPA

IPR *abbr, often not cap* inches per revolution

ips \ˈips\ [NL *Ip-*, *Ips*, fr. Gk *ip-*, *ips* woodworm] *syn of* SCOLYTUS

IPS *abbr* **1** *often not cap* inches per second **2** iron pipe size

ip·se dix·it \ˌipsēˈdiksət\ *n, pl* **ipse dixits** [L, lit., he himself said it, trans. of Gk (Dor) *autos epha*; fr. the use of this expression by the Pythagoreans in reference to statements made by Pythagoras himself] **:** an assertion made on authority but not proved **:** DICTUM ⟨has had a good many followers ready to accept his *ipse dixit* —D.W.Hering⟩

ip·se·dix·it·ism \-sədˌizəm\ *n* -s **:** dogmatic assertion or assertiveness ⟨denounces all appeals to a moral faculty as sheer ~ —James Martineau⟩

ip·se·ity \ipˈsēəd·ē\ *n* -ES *sometimes cap* [L *ipse* self, himself + E *-ity*] **:** individual identity **:** SELFHOOD ⟨those heavenly moments . . . when a sense of the divine ~ invades me—L.P. Smith⟩

ip·si·lateral *also* **ip·se·lateral** \¦ipsē, -sə+\ *or* **ip·so·lateral** \-(ˌ)sō+\ *adj* [ISV *ipsi-*, *ipse-*, *ipso-* (fr. L *ipse*) + *lateral*] **:** situated or appearing on or affecting the same side of the body — compare CONTRALATERAL — **ip·si·laterally** \"+\ *adv*

ip·so fac·to \¦ip(ˌ)sōˈfak(ˌ)tō\ *adv* [NL] **:** by the fact or act itself **:** as the result of the mere act or fact **:** by the very nature of the case ⟨does one, *ipso facto*, become a censor when he warns against such censorship —H.C.Gardiner⟩ ⟨training in speech . . . is *ipso facto* training in personality —A.T.Weaver⟩

ipso ju·re \-ˈjürē, -ˈyü-\ *adv* [L] **:** by the law itself **:** by operation of law

ips·wich \ˈip(ˌ)swich, -ˌswēch\ *adj, usu cap* [fr. *Ipswich*, county borough of East Suffolk, England] **:** of or from the county borough of Ipswich, England **:** of the kind or style prevalent in Ipswich

ipswich sparrow *n, usu cap I* [fr. *Ipswich*, town in northeastern Massachusetts where it was observed] **:** a sparrow (*Passerculus princeps*) similar to the Savannah sparrow but larger and paler that breeds on Sable island off the coast of Nova Scotia and migrates south along the Atlantic coast to Georgia

IPT *abbr* indexed, paged, and titled

ipu·ri·ná \ˌēpərēˈnä\ *n, pl* **ipuriná** *or* **ipurinás** *usu cap* **1 a :** an Arawakan people of northwestern Brazil **b :** a member of such people **2 :** the language of the Ipuriná people

ipv *abbr* **1** imperative **2** improve

IPW *abbr* interrogation prisoner of war

IQ \(ˈ)ī¦kyü\ *abbr or n* -s intelligence quotient

IQ *abbr, often not cap* [L *idem quod*] the same as

IQED *abbr* [L *id quod erat demonstrandum*] that which was to be proved

iqui·to \ēˈkēd·(ˌ)ō\ *n, pl* **iquito** *or* **iquitos** *usu cap* [AmerSp] **1 :** a Zaparo people of the upper Amazon **2 :** a member of the Iquito people

ir- — see IN-

IR *abbr* **1** infrared **2** inland revenue; internal revenue **3** intelligence ratio **4** interim report **5** interrogator-responder **6** insoluble residue

Ir *symbol* iridium

ira·cund \ˈīrəˌkənd\ *adj* [L *iracundus*, fr. *ira* anger — more at IRE] *archaic* **:** easily provoked to anger **:** IRASCIBLE

ira·cun·di·ty \ˌīrəˈkəndəd·ē\ *n* -ES *archaic* **:** the quality or state of being iracund **:** ANGER

ira·de \ēˈrädē\ *n* -s [Turk, lit., will, wish, fr. Ar *irādah*] **:** a decree of a Muhammadan ruler

i rail *n, cap I* **:** an I-shaped rail

iran \(ˈ)i¦ran, -raa(ə)n *sometimes* (ˈ)ī¦- *or* (ˈ)ē¦-; (ˈ)i¦rän, (ˈ)ē¦-, -ˈrån\ *adj, usu cap* [fr. *Iran*, country in southwestern Asia] **:** of or from Iran **:** of the kind or style prevalent in Iran **:** IRANIAN, PERSIAN

¹ira·ni \=ˈ=ē, -i\ *n* -s *cap* [Per *īrānī*, fr. *Īrān* Iran] **:** IRANIAN 1

²irani \"\ *adj, usu cap* **:** IRANIAN, PERSIAN

¹ira·ni·an \iˈrānēən, *sometimes* -ran- *or* -raan- *or* -rän- *or* (ˈ)ī¦rā- *or* (ˈ)ī¦ra(a)-\ *adj, usu cap* [*Iran* + E *-ian*] **:** of or relating to Iran or the Iranians or their speech

²iranian \"\ *n* -s *cap* **1 :** a native or inhabitant of Iran — see PERSIAN 1 **2 :** a branch of the Indo-European family of languages that includes Avestan, Old Persian, Median, Scythian, Middle Iranian, and Persian — see INDO-EUROPEAN LANGUAGES table

iran·ic \iˈranik, (ˈ)ī¦r-\ *adj, usu cap* [*Iran* + E *-ic*] **:** IRANIAN

irano- *comb form, usu cap* [*Iran*] **:** Iranian and ⟨*Irano*-British⟩

¹irano-afghan \i¦ra(ˌ)nō, -rä-, -rā-, ī¦ra-, ē¦rā-, ē¦rā-+\ *adj, usu cap I&A* [*Irano-* + *Afghan*] **:** of, relating to, or characteristic of the people that constitute the chief element in the population of the upland territory extending from western Iran to northern India

²irano-afghan \"\ *n, cap I&A* **:** one of the Irano-Afghan people

iraq *also* **irak** \(ˈ)i¦räk, -rak, -råk\ *adj, usu cap* [fr. *Iraq* (*Irak*), country in southwestern Asia] **:** of or from Iraq (*Iraq* oil fields) **:** of the kind or style prevalent in Iraq

¹iraqi *also* **iraki** \=ˈ=ē, -i\ *n* -s *cap* [Ar *ˈirāqīy*, fr. *ˈIrāq* Iraq] **1 :** a native or resident of Iraq **2 :** the dialect of Modern Arabic spoken in Iraq

²iraqi *also* **iraki** \"\ *adj, usu cap* **1 a :** of, relating to, or characteristic of Iraq **b :** of, relating to, or characteristic of the Iraqis **2 :** of, relating to, or characteristic of the Iraqi language

iraq·i·an *also* **irak·i·an** \-ēən\ *n or adj, usu cap* [*Iraq* (*Irak*) + E *-ian*] **:** IRAQI

iras·ci·bil·i·ty \əˌrasəˈbiləd·ē, (ˌ)īˌras-, -raas-, -lətē, -i\ *n* -ES [F *irascibilité*, fr. MF, fr. *irascible* + *-ité* -ity] **:** the quality or state of being irascible **:** proneness to anger **:** IRASCIBLENESS

iras·ci·ble \əˈrasəbəl, (ˈ)ī¦r-, -raas-\ *adj* [MF, fr. LL *irascibilis*, fr. L *irasci* to be angry (fr. *ira* anger) + *-ibilis* -ible — more at IRE] **1 :** marked by hot temper and resentful anger **:** having or showing a disposition to be easily incensed ⟨his proud, ~ individualism that went out of its way to pick a quarrel —V. L.Parrington⟩ ⟨became so ~ that within six months he lost his wife and half of his office staff —Herman Wouk⟩ **2 a :** moved by desire for that which is attained only with difficulty or danger **b :** stirred by combative emotions (as anger, pride, courage, fear) — opposed to *concupiscible*

syn CHOLERIC, SPLENETIC, TESTY, CRANKY, TOUCHY, TECHY, TETCHY: IRASCIBLE stresses a tendency to fiery anger ⟨the *irascible* but kindhearted deity who indulges in copious curses to ease his feelings —M.R.Cohen⟩ CHOLERIC may convey suggestions of impatience and unreasonableness, in addition to indicating hot temper ⟨that fiery formula which has sprung from the lips of so many *choleric* old gentlemen . . . "I shall write to *The Times*" —Max Beerbohm⟩ SPLENETIC may suggest a strong inclination to quick anger coupled with moroseness, sullenness, malice, vindictiveness, or crusty peevishness ⟨a very queer character, by turns *splenetic* and benevolent —*Times Lit. Supp.*⟩ ⟨that *splenetic* temper, which seems to grudge brightness to the flames of hell —W.S.Landor⟩ CROSS is likely to indicate a snappish grumpy irritability ⟨I am determined I will not be *cross;* it is not a little matter that puts me out of temper —Jane Austen⟩ TESTY may indicate quick anger inspiring sharp acid comment and inspired by relatively trivial irritations ⟨he raged . . . he was ever more autocratic, more *testy* —Sinclair Lewis⟩ ⟨the *testy* major was in fume to find no hunter standing waiting —John Masefield⟩ CRANKY may indicate an irritable temper blended with fretfulness or capriciousness ⟨how *cranky* you are . . . don't be so absurd as . . . to act like a child —Anthony Trollope⟩ ⟨she's going to have a kid, and of course women . . . get *cranky* when they're that way —Sinclair Lewis⟩ TOUCHY, TETCHY, and TECHY, the first now being the most common, indicate an over sensitiveness making for irritability, defensiveness, likelihood of taking offense or being hurt ⟨*techy* and impatient of contradiction, sore with wounded pride —W.H.Hazlitt⟩ ⟨a man who had grown too *touchy* to make judicious decisions —*Time*⟩

iras·ci·ble·ness *n* -ES **:** the quality or state of being irascible

iras·ci·bly \-blē, -bli\ *adv* **:** in an irascible manner

irate \(ˈ)ī¦rāt, *usu* -ād·+V\ *adj, sometimes* -ER/-EST [L *iratus*, fr. *ira* anger + *-atus* -ate — more at IRE] **1 :** roused to or given to ire **:** feeling and showing a high degree of anger **:** WRATHFUL, INCENSED ⟨a neighborhood ~ over continued acts of vandalism⟩ ⟨never had enough money to meet his bills, and he was not used to dodging ~ grocers —Sinclair Lewis⟩ ⟨~ against the practice of usury —E.L.Surtz⟩ **2 :** arising from anger ⟨~ words⟩ ⟨an ~ glare⟩ ⟨started to splutter an ~ objection —W.H.Wright⟩ **syn** see ANGRY

irate·ly *adv* **:** in an irate manner **:** ANGRILY

irate·ness *n* -ES **:** the quality or state of being irate

ira·va \iˈrävə\ *n, pl* **irava** *or* **iravas** *cap* [native name in India] **1 :** an untouchable Hindu caste of the Malabar coast region of southwest India **2 :** a member of the Irava caste

ira·ya \iˈrāyə, -rīə\ *n, pl* **iraya** *or* **irayas** *usu cap* [Sp, fr. Iraya, person, human being] **1 a :** a predominantly pagan people inhabiting the mountainous interior of northern Mindoro in the Philippines **b :** a member of such people **2 :** the Austronesian language of the Iraya people

ir·bis \(ˌ)ərˈbēs, irˈ-\ *n, pl* **irbis** *or* **irbises** [Russ, fr. Mongol *irbis* & Kalmuck *irwș*] **:** SNOW LEOPARD

IRBM *abbr or n* -s **:** an intermediate range ballistic missile

IRC *abbr* irregular route carrier

ir drop \(ˈ)ī¦är-\ *n, usu cap I&R* [*I*, symbol for effective current in amperes + *R*, symbol for resistance in ohms] **:** the voltage drop due to energy losses in a resistor

¹ire \ˈī(ə)r, ˈīə\ *n* -s [ME, fr. OF, fr. L *ira;* akin to OE *ofost* haste, zeal, OS *obast* haste, zeal, ON *eisa* to race forward, Gk *hieros* powerful, supernatural, holy, sacred, *inein*, *inan* to empty out, defecate, *oistros* gadfly, frenzy, Skt *iṣṇāti*, *iṣyati* he sets in motion, swings; basic meaning: moving rapidly] **:** ANGER, WRATH ⟨provocation enough to arouse the ~ of a saint⟩ **syn** see ANGER

²ire \"\ *vt* -ED/-ING/-s **:** to provoke to anger **:** arouse ire in ⟨reads a piece in his local newspaper that ~*s* him —Sidney Atkinson⟩ **:** ANGER, IRRITATE

³ire \"\ *n* -s [by shortening] *dial* **:** IRON

ire·ful \ˈī(ə)rfəl, ˈīəf-\ *adj* [ME, fr. *ire* + *-ful*] **1 :** full of ire **:** marked by ire **:** ANGRY, WRATHFUL ⟨an ~ mood⟩ **2 :** given to ire **:** easily angered **:** IRASCIBLE, CHOLERIC ⟨an ill-tempered ~ old man⟩ — **ire·ful·ly** \-fəlē, -li\ *adv* — **ire·ful·ness** *n* -ES

ire·land \ˈī(ə)rlənd, ˈīəl-\ *adj, usu cap* [fr. *Ireland*, one of the British Isles] **1 :** of or from the island of Ireland **:** of the kind or style prevalent in Ireland **:** of the island of Ireland **2 :** of or from the republic of Ireland **:** of the kind or style prevalent in the republic of Ireland

ire·land·er \-ləndə(r), -ˌlan-, -ˌlaan-\ *n* -s *cap* [*Ireland* + E *-er*] **:** a native of Ireland

ireland king of arms *cap I & usu cap K&A* **:** a king of arms for heraldic supervision in Ireland appointed by the king of England and holding an office of which there is record from the reign of Richard II until that of Edward IV — compare ULSTER KING OF ARMS

ire·less \ˈī(ə)rləs, ˈīəl-\ *adj* **:** being without ire — **ire·less·ly** *adv* — **ire·less·ness** *n* -ES

ire·na \īˈrēnə\ *n, cap* [NL, fr. Gk *eirēnē* peace] **:** a genus of birds (family Aegithinidae) consisting of the fairy bluebirds of India

irene \ˈīˌrēn, =ˈ=\ *n* -s [ISV *irone* + *-ene*] **:** a liquid hydrocarbon $(CH_3)_4C_{10}H_8$ derived from naphthalene and obtained by reduction and cyclization of irone with hydriodic acid and phosphorus

irenic *or* **ei·renic** \(ˈ)ī¦renik, -rēn-\ *also* **ireni·cal** \-nəkəl\ *adj* [Gk *eirēnikos*, fr. *eirēnē* peace (prob. of non-IE origin) + *-ikos* -ic, -ical] **:** conducive to or operating toward peace, moderation, harmony, and conciliation and away from contention and partisanship esp. among disputants ⟨~ measures⟩ ⟨~ without being namby-pamby —*Chicago Theol. Seminary Register*⟩ ⟨the viewpoint is ~ and the author seeks to show the best features of each religion and church in turn —N.K. Burger⟩ **syn** see PACIFIC

ireni·cal·ly \-nək(ə)lē\ *adv* **:** in an irenic manner **:** in a way calculated to conciliate or to promote peace

ireni·cism \=ˈ=nəˌsizəm\ *n* -s **:** a social temper or condition or a state of public opinion making for peace

irenicon *var of* EIRENICON

irenics \īˈreniks, -rēn-\ *n pl but usu sing in constr, also* **irenic** \-nik\ **:** irenic theology as distinguished from polemic theology **:** theology concerned with securing Christian unity

ire·si·ne \ˌīrəˈsī(ˌ)nē\ *n* [NL, modif. of Gk *eiresiōnē* branch of olive or laurel wound round with wool and hung with fruits; fr. the woolly calyx] **1** *cap* **:** a genus of tropical American opposite-leaved herbs (family Amaranthaceae) having small spicate or paniculate scarious flowers and often colored foliage — see ACHYRANTHES 2 **2** -s **:** any plant of the genus *Iresine*

ir·gun·ist \irˈgünəst\ *n* -s *usu cap* [NHeb *Irgun* (*Ṣ bai Leumi*), lit., national military organization (fr. *irgun* organization + *ṣbai* military + *leumi* national) + E *-ist*] **:** a member of a militant rightist underground group of Zionists

ir·i·ar·tea \ˌirēˈärd·ēə\ *n, cap* [NL, after Bernardo de *Iriarte* †1814 Span. diplomat and amateur botanist] **:** a small genus of tall pinnate-leaved chiefly Brazilian palms with smooth trunk and crown of leaves supported by long slender prop roots — see STILT PALM

iri·cism \ˈīrəˌsizəm\ *n* -s *usu cap* [¹*Irish* + *-cism* (as in *Scotticism*)] **:** IRISHISM

iri·cize \-ˌsīz\ *vb* -ED/-ING/-s *sometimes cap* [¹*Irish* + *-cize* (as in *scotticize*)] **:** IRISHIZE

irid \ˈīrəd\ *n* -s [NL *Irid-*, *Iris*] **:** a plant of the family Iridaceae

irid- *or* **irido-** *comb form* [L *irid-*, *iris* — more at IRIS] **1 :** rainbow ⟨*iridal*⟩ ⟨*iridescent*⟩ **2** [NL *irid-*, *iris*] **:** iris of the eye ⟨*iridectomy*⟩ ⟨*iridoparalysis*⟩ **:** iris and ⟨*iridocyclitis*⟩ **3** [*iridescent*] **:** iridescent ⟨*iridize*⟩ ⟨*iridocyte*⟩ **4** [NL *Irid-*, *Iris*] **:** the genus Iris ⟨*iridin*⟩ **5** [NL *iridium*] **:** iridium **:** iridium and ⟨*iridosmine*⟩

iri·da·ce·ae \ˌirəˈdāsēˌē, ˌīr-\ *n pl, cap* [NL, fr. *Irid-*, *Iris*, type genus + *-aceae*] **:** a family of perennial herbs (order Liliales) with usu. only basal ensiform leaves and flowers in racemes or panicles that are subtended individually or in clusters by two spathose bracts and have the perianth petaloid and the ovary inferior

iri·da·ceous \¦=ˈ=ˈdāshəs\ *adj* [NL *Iridaceae* + E *-ous*] **1 :** of or relating to the family Iridaceae or esp. the genus *Iris* **2 :** resembling an iris ⟨silvery blue ~ flowers⟩

iri·dal \ˈirədᵊl, ˈīr-\ *adj* [*irid-* + *-al*] **1 :** of or relating to the rainbow **:** IRIDIAN **2 :** of, or relating to the iris of the eye **:** IRIDIC

iri·dec·to·mize \ˌirəˈdektəˌmīz, ˌīr-\ *vt* -ED/-ING/-s **:** to subject to iridectomy

iri·dec·to·my \-mē\ *n* -ES [*irid-* + *-ectomy*] **:** the surgical removal of part of the iris of the eye

irides *pl of* IRIS

ir·i·desce \ˌirə¦des\ *vi* -ED/-ING/-s [back-formation fr. ¹*iridescent*] **:** to be iridescent

ir·i·des·cence \ˌirəˈdesᵊn(t)s\ *n* -s [*irid-* + *-escence*] **1 :** a play of structural colors producing rainbow effects that is exhibited in various bodies as a result of interference in a thin film (as of a soap bubble or mother-of-pearl) or of diffraction of light reflected from a closely ribbed or corrugated surface (as of the plumage of certain birds) and is readily distinguished from the inherent colors of substances by its variation with the angle of incidence of the illumination **2 :** a display or effect suggestive of the play of colors on an iridescent surface in gleaming or glistening or in subtly shifting and changing shades and hues ⟨paled before the ~ of the best of his earlier plays —*Americana Annual*⟩ ⟨a certain ~ of glamor and superiority —Margaret Landon⟩ ⟨no apple tang, no citrous clarity, but the ~ of the papaya, the opaline evanescence of the guava —Waldo Frank⟩ **:** GLITTER, SHEEN, LUSTER, OPALESCENCE

¹ir·i·des·cent \ˌirə¦desᵊnt\ *adj* [*irid-* + *-escent*] **1 :** having iridescence **:** showing colors like those of the rainbow esp. in shifting patterns of hues and shades that vary with a change of light or point of view ⟨a beetle with an ~ back⟩ ⟨as softly ~ as the rays from a jewel —Ellen Glasgow⟩ ⟨smart, lean glass towers with ~ washrooms —Brooks Atkinson⟩ ⟨crunchy, ~, lovely snow —Elaine W. Neal⟩ **:** NACREOUS, OPALESCENT **2 a :** having a gleaming or glittering quality suggestive of the phenomenon of iridescence **:** BRILLIANT, FLASHING ⟨two wickedly witty and ~ novels —*Time*⟩ ⟨a man for whom the map of the present was always ~ with the glories of the past —H.C.Wolfe⟩ ⟨his ~ performance as an art, music, and drama critic —John Mason Brown⟩ **b :** having the constantly shifting fluid character of an iridescence ⟨the life of ~ revery —Edmund Wilson⟩ ⟨that ~ play of meanings —Susanne K. Langer⟩ **3** *of a fabric* **:** CHANGEABLE 4 ⟨curtains of an ~ material, purple in one light, golden brown in another —Howard Moss⟩ ⟨a filmy ~ green carpet —*Amer. Guide Series: Tenn.*⟩

²iridescent \"\ *n* -s **:** an iridescent fabric, trimming, or accessory ⟨the green-blue ~*s* are featured in rayon organdy for a party dress —*Women's Wear Daily*⟩

ir·i·des·cent·ly *adv* **:** in an iridescent manner

irid·i·al \īˈridēəl, əˈr-\ *adj* [*irid-* + *-ial*] **:** of or relating to an iris esp. of the eye **:** IRIDIC

irid·i·an \-ēən\ *adj* [*irid-* + *-ian*] **1 :** of or relating to the iris of the eye **:** IRIDIC **2 a :** resembling a rainbow **b :** having the colors of the rainbow **3 :** containing iridium

irid·ic \(ˈ)ī¦ridik, əˈr-\ *adj* [*irid-* + *-ic*] **1 :** of, relating to, or derived from iridium — used esp. of a compound in which iridium is tetravalent **2 :** of or relating to the iris of the eye ⟨~ grains and a flood of intraocular fluid —*Time*⟩

iri·din \ˈirədᵊn, ˈīr-, -dən\ *n* -s [ISV *irid-* + *-in*] **1 :** a crystalline glucoside $C_{24}H_{26}O_{13}$ occurring esp. in orrisroot **2 :** an oleoresin prepared from the common blue flag for use as a purgative and liver stimulant

irid·io–platinum \ī¦ridē(ˌ)ō, ə¦r-+\ *n* [*iridio-* (fr. NL *iridium*) + *platinum*] **:** a hard alloy of iridium and platinum

irid·i·um \īˈridēəm, əˈr-\ *n* -s *often attrib* [NL, fr. *irid-* + *-ium;* fr. the colorful appearance of some of its solutions] **:** a silver-white hard brittle very heavy chiefly trivalent and tetravalent metallic element of the platinum group that occurs usu. as a native alloy with platinum or with osmium in iridosmine, is resistant to chemical attack at ordinary temperatures, and is used esp. in hardening platinum for alloys suitable for surgical instruments, electrical and other scientific apparatus, jewelry, and the points of gold pens — symbol *Ir;* see ELEMENT table

iri·di·za·tion \ˌirədəˈzāshən, ˌīr-, -ˌdīˈz-\ *n* -s **1 :** the action or process of making iridescent **:** IRISATION **2 :** the action or process of exhibiting iridescence **3 :** a semblance of a halo around a light observed by persons affected with glaucoma

iri·dize \ˈirəˌdīz, ˈīr-\ *vt* -ED/-ING/-s [*irid-* + *-ize*] **:** to make iridescent

irido- — see IRID-

iri·do·choroiditis \¦irə(ˌ)dō, ¦īr-+\ *n* [NL, fr. *irid-* + *choroiditis*] **:** inflammation of the iris and the choroid

iri·do·cyclitis \"+\ *n* [NL, fr. *irid-* + *cyclitis*] **:** inflammation of the iris and the ciliary body

irid·o·cyte \īˈridəˌsīt, əˈr-\ *n* -s [*irid-* + *-cyte*] **:** a cell that occurs esp. in the skin of fishes and reptiles and appears iridescent greenish from included guanine — compare GUANOPHORE

iri·do·do·ne·sis \ˌirə(ˌ)dōdəˈnēsəs, ˌīr-\ *n, pl* **iridodone·ses** \-ēˌsēz\ [NL, fr. *irid-* + Gk *donein* to shake + NL *-sis*] **:** tremulousness of the iris **:** HIPPUS

iri·do·myr·mex \-ˈmərˌmeks\ *n, cap* [NL, fr. *irid-* + GK *myrmēx* ant — more at PISMIRE] **:** a genus containing the Argentine ant

irid·o·phore \īˈridəˌfō(ə)r, əˈr-\ *n* -s [*irid-* + *-phore*] **:** an iridescent chromatophore — compare IRIDOCYTE

iri·dos·mine \ˌirəˈdäzˌmēn, ˌīr-, -ˈmən\ *n* -s [G *iridosmin*, fr. *irid-* + NL *osmium* + G *-in* -ine] **:** a mineral consisting of a native iridium osmium alloy usu. containing some rhodium and platinum and found in tin-white or steel-gray grains isomorphous with siserskite

iri·dos·mi·um \-ˌmēəm\ *n* -s [NL, fr. *irid-* + *osmium*] **:** IRIDOSMINE

irids *pl of* IRID

iring *pres part of* IRE

i ring *n, cap I* **:** a band or hoop secured around the circumference of a metal drum as a reinforcement

¹iris \ˈīrəs\ *n, pl* **iris·es** \-rəsəz\ *or* **iri·des** \ˈirəˌdēz, ˈīr-\ [ME, fr. L, fr. Gk (basic meaning: rainbow) — more at WIRE] **1 :** a prismatic crystal; *esp* **:** a quartz that is iridescent because of internal cracks **2 a :** RAINBOW **b :** a play of colors resembling a rainbow **:** a circle or arch of rainbow hues **3** [NL, fr. Gk] **a :** the opaque muscular contractile diaphragm that is suspended in the aqueous humor in front of the lens of the eye, is perforated by the pupil and is continuous peripherally with the ciliary body, has a deeply pigmented posterior surface which excludes the entrance of light except through the pupil and a variously colored anterior surface in different individuals which determines the color of the eyes — see EYE illustration **b** (1) **:** IRIS DIAPHRAGM; *esp* **:** one used on a motion-picture camera in fading pictures in or out (2) **:** a masking device having a circular opening of which the diameter can be varied

²iris \"\ *n* [NL, fr. L, iris, any of various plants of the family Iridaceae] **1** *cap* **:** the type genus of the family Iridaceae comprising perennial herbaceous plants that develop from rhizomes or bulbs, have linear or sword-shaped mostly basal leaves, erect stalks on which the flowers are borne, and shortlived usu. brightly colored flowers with the three inner perianth segments erect and the three outer spreading or drooping, and include many widely cultivated ornamentals **2** *pl* **irises** *or* **iris** *also* **irides :** any plant or flower of the genus *Iris* — see BEARDED IRIS, BEARDLESS IRIS; DUTCH IRIS, ENGLISH IRIS, GERMAN IRIS, JAPANESE IRIS, SPANISH IRIS **3** *or* **iris blue :** a pale blue to pale purple — called also *endive blue*

³iris \"\ *vt* -ED/-ING/-s **1 :** to make iridescent **:** give the form or appearance of a rainbow to ⟨spray ~*ed* above the falls⟩ **2 :** to operate the iris of a motion-picture camera so as to fade (a picture) — used with *in* or *out*

iris·at·ed \ˈīrəˌsād·əd\ *adj* **:** IRISED, IRIDESCENT ⟨~ crystal beads⟩

iris·ation \ˌīrəˈsāshən\ *n* -s **1 :** the act or process of making iridescent ⟨the ~ of a culture plate by developing bacteria⟩ **2 :** IRIDESCENCE ⟨~*s* in a cloud are evidence that it is composed of water droplets —D.W.Perrie⟩ ⟨in the area of the sun beautiful ~*s* may occur⟩

iris borer *n* **:** a large brown-headed pinkish grub that is the larva of a noctuid moth (*Macronoctua onusta*) and that is destructive to the rhizomes and crowns of various irises

iris diaphragm *n* **:** an adjustable diaphragm of thin opaque plates that can be turned by a ring so as to change the diameter of a central opening usu. to regulate the aperture of a lens (as in a camera or microscope)

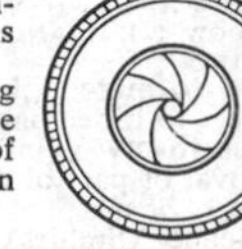
iris diaphragm

irised \ˈīrəst\ *adj* [¹*iris* + *-ed*] **1 :** having or characterized by colors like those of the rainbow **:** IRIDESCENT ⟨the ~ sweep of northern lights⟩ **2 :** having an iris of an indicated kind ⟨pale-*irised* eyes⟩

irises *pl of* IRIS, *pres 3d sing of* IRIS

iris family *n* **:** IRIDACEAE

iris green *n* **:** MALACHITE GREEN 3

¹irish \ˈīrish, -rēsh\ *adj, usu cap* [ME, fr. (assumed) OE *Īrisc*, fr. OE *Īras* Irishmen (of Celt origin; akin to OIr *Ēriu* Ireland) + *-isc* -ish] **1 :** of, relating to, or characteristic of Ireland or its inhabitants **:** produced in or native or peculiar to Ireland **2 a :** being or belonging to the Celtic speech of Ireland **:** IRISH-GAELIC **b** *obs* **:** SCOTTISH-GAELIC

²irish \"\ *n* -ES *see sense 1a* **1** *cap* **a** *pl in constr* **:** natives or inhabitants of Ireland or their immediate descendants esp. when of Celtic speech or culture — compare CELT, GAEL **b** *obs* **:** IRISHMAN, IRISHWOMAN **2** *cap* **:** the Irish language: **a :** the Irish branch of Goidelic **:** the Goidelic speech of the Celts in Ireland **:** IRISH GAELIC — see MIDDLE IRISH, OLD IRISH; INDO-EUROPEAN LANGUAGES table **b** *obs* **:** SCOTTISH GAELIC **c :** English as spoken by the Irish with more or less dialect change and brogue **3** *usu cap, obs* **:** an old game resembling backgammon **4** *usu cap* **a :** IRISH LINEN **b :** IRISH WHISKEY **5** *usu cap* **:** TEMPER, ANGER ⟨don't get your *Irish* up over a little thing like that⟩ **6** *usu cap* **:** a tap-dance step consisting of a shuffle, hop, and step

irish alphabet *n, usu cap I* **:** a modified form of the Latin alphabet used by the ancient Britons and still employed in writing and printing Irish — compare INSULAR HAND

irish blight *n, usu cap I* **:** LATE BLIGHT

irish broom *n, usu cap I* **1 :** a low Iberian shrub (*Cytisus patens*) **2 :** SCOTCH BROOM

irish bull *n, usu cap I* [⁵*bull*] **:** an expression containing apparent congruity but actual incongruity of ideas ⟨"it was hereditary in his family to have no children" is a well-known *Irish bull*⟩

irish chippendale *n, usu cap I&C* **:** ornate carved furniture made prob. in Ireland about the middle of the 18th century and based on Chippendale designs

irish christian brother *n, usu cap I&C&B* **:** BROTHER OF THE CHRISTIAN SCHOOLS

irish coffee *n, usu cap I* **:** a mixed drink consisting of hot sugared coffee liberally laced with Irish whiskey and topped with whipped cream

irish confetti *n, usu cap I* [so called fr. the tradition that Irishmen often throw bricks in a fight] **:** a rock, brick, or fragment of rock or brick

irish crochet *n, usu cap I* **:** a heavy lace of Irish origin that is hand-crocheted or machine-made with rose or leaf designs on a square mesh ground and is used esp. for insertion, edging, and trimming

irish diamond *n, usu cap I* **:** CRYSTAL 2

irish dividend *n, usu cap I* **:** an assessment on stock

irish elk *or* **irish deer** *n, usu cap I* **:** a large extinct Pleistocene deer (*Megaloceros hibernicus*) remains of which are found esp. under the peat of Ireland and England

irish·er \ˈīrishə(r), -rēsh-\ *n* -S *cap* **:** IRISHMAN

irish furze *n, usu cap I* **:** a columnar compact sparse-flowering shrub (*Ulex europaeus strictus*)

irish gaelic *n, cap I&G* **:** the Goidelic speech of the Celts of Ireland esp. as used since the end of the medieval period — compare MIDDLE IRISH, OLD IRISH; see INDO-EUROPEAN LANGUAGES table

irish-gaelic \ˌ==ˈ==\ *adj, usu cap I&G* **:** of, relating to, or characteristic of the Goidelic speech of the Celts of Ireland

irish grazier *n, usu cap I, sometimes cap G* **:** TAMWORTH

irish green *n, often cap I* **:** a deep green

irish harp *n, usu cap I* **:** CLARSACH

irish heath *n, usu cap I* **:** a low evergreen European shrub (*Daboecia cantabrica*) of the family Ericaceae that has slender leaves dark green above and whitish below and small nodding bell-shaped white or sometimes rosy or purplish flowers borne in erect terminal racemes — called also *St.-Dabeoc's-heath*

irish·ism \ˈīriˌshizəm, -rē,-\ *n* -S *usu cap* **1 :** a word, phrase, or mode of expression distinctive of the Irish **2 :** IRISH BULL

irish ivy *n, usu cap 1st I* **:** a European ivy (*Hedera helix hibernica*) that is a variety of English ivy distinguished by larger leaves and fruit

irish·ize \ˈīriˌshīz, -rē,-\ *vt* -ED/-ING/-S *often cap* **:** to make Irish in quality or traits ⟨~ the music⟩

irish juniper *n, usu cap I* **:** a narrow columnar ornamental juniper (*Juniperus communis hibernica*) that is a horticultural variety of the common juniper

irish linen *n, usu cap I* **:** a fine lightweight linen fabric made in Ireland and used esp. for clothing

irish lord *n, usu cap I* **:** any of several sculpins (genus *Hemilepidotus*) of the Bering sea region that are locally important as food fishes

irish·ly *adv, often cap* **:** in the style or way of the Irish

irish mail *n, usu cap I* **:** a 3-wheeled or 4-wheeled toy vehicle activated by a hand lever somewhat on the principle of a manually operated railway handcar

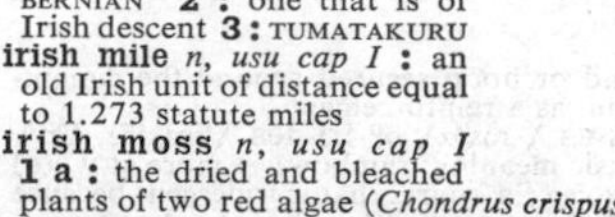
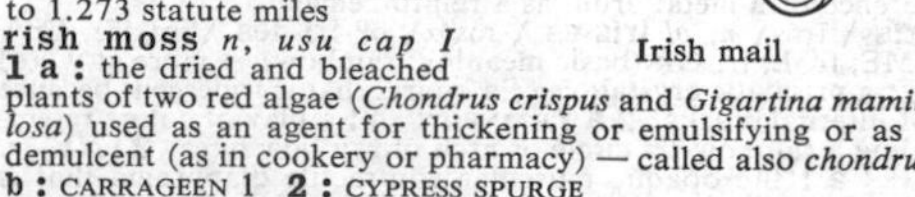
Irish mail

irish·man \ˈ==mən\ *n, pl* **irishmen** *cap* [ME, fr. *Irish* + *man*] **1 :** a native or inhabitant of Ireland **:** HIBERNIAN **2 :** one that is of Irish descent **3 :** TUMATAKURU

irish mile *n, usu cap I* **:** an old Irish unit of distance equal to 1.273 statute miles

irish moss *n, usu cap I* **1 a :** the dried and bleached plants of two red algae (*Chondrus crispus* and *Gigartina mamillosa*) used as an agent for thickening or emulsifying or as a demulcent (as in cookery or pharmacy) — called also *chondrus* **b :** CARRAGEEN 1 **2 :** CYPRESS SPURGE

irish moss extractive *n, usu cap I* **:** CARRAGEENIN

irish·ness *n* -ES *usu cap* **:** the quality or state of being Irish

irish pennant *or* **irish pendant** *n, usu cap I* **:** a loose untidy object about a ship or naval installation; *esp* **:** the end of a line left hanging loose or out of place

irish poplin *n, usu cap I* **:** a fabric with silk warp and worsted filling made orig. in Ireland

irish potato *n, usu cap I* **:** POTATO 2 a (2)

irish·ry \ˈīrishrē, -rēsh-, -ri\ *n* -ES *usu cap* [ME *Irisherie, Irishrie*, fr. *Irish* + *-erie* -ery *or -rie* -ry] **1 :** IRISH 1a **2 a :** Irish quality or character ⟨~ of temperament⟩ **b :** an Irish peculiarity or trait ⟨a deliberate ~⟩

irish setter *n* **1** *usu cap I&S* **:** a breed of bird dogs that are in general comparable to English setters but have a chestnut-brown or mahogany-red coat **2** *usu cap I, often cap S* **:** a dog of the Irish Setter breed

irish snipe *n, usu cap I* **:** an avocet (*Recurvirostra americana*) of No. America

irish stew *n, usu cap I* **:** a stew having as its principal ingredients meat, potatoes, and onions in a thick gravy

irish strawberry *n, usu cap I, Austral* **:** STRAWBERRY TREE

irish system *n, usu cap I* **:** a system of prison management developed for Ireland by Sir Walter Crofton and noted for its mark system and commutation of sentences, classification of prisoners, military discipline, trade and academic training, preparation for free self-control, and release under police supervision

irish terrier *n* **1** *usu cap I&T* **:** a breed of active medium-sized terriers that originated in Ireland and is characterized by a dense close wiry coat of red, golden red, or reddish wheaten **2** *usu cap I & sometimes cap T* **:** a dog of the Irish Terrier breed

irish water spaniel *n* **1** *usu cap I&W&S* **:** a breed of large retrievers developed in Ireland by interbreeding various sporting dogs and the poodle and characterized by a heavy coat of liver-colored curls, a topknot of long curls, and a nearly hairless rattail **2** *usu cap I & sometimes cap W&S* **:** a dog of the Irish Water Spaniel breed

irish whiskey *n, usu cap I* **:** whiskey made in Ireland chiefly of barley

irish wolfhound *n, usu cap I & sometimes cap W* **:** a very large tall hound that in general resembles the deerhound but is much larger and stronger, weighs upward from 90 pounds, and has a shoulder height from 31 inches in the male and 28 inches in the female

irishwoman \ˈ==ˌ==\ *n, pl* **irishwomen** *cap* **:** a woman born in Ireland or of Irish descent

irishy \ˈīrishē, -rēsh-, -shi\ *adj, often cap* **:** suggesting or characteristic of the Irish ⟨~ blue eyes⟩

irish yew *n, usu cap I* **:** a hardy columnar yew (*Taxus baccata stricta*) that has erect branches and dark green foliage and is a horticultural variety of the common Old World yew

iri·sin \ˈīrəsən\ *n* -S [ISV *iris* + *-in*; orig. formed in G] **:** a polysaccharide $(C_6H_{10}O_5)_x$ occurring esp. in the rhizomes of some irises and like inulin yielding levulose on hydrolysis

irising *pres part of* IRIS

iris mauve *n* **:** a grayish yellowish pink that is yellower and slightly less strong than cloud pink

irisroot \ˈ==ˌ=\ *n* **:** ORRISROOT

iris whitefly *n* **:** a whitefly (*Aleyrodes spiraeoides*) that is sometimes a pest on late potatoes in the northwestern U.S.

iri·tis \īˈrīd·əs\ *n* -ES [NL, irreg. fr. *iris* + *-itis*] **:** inflammation of the iris of the eye

¹irk \ˈərk, ˈ3k, ˈəik\ *adj* [ME] *now dial* **:** weary and disgusted

²irk \"\ *vb* -ED/-ING/-S [ME *irken*] *vi, now chiefly Scot* **:** to become tired or wearied esp. to the point of being bored or disgusted or unwilling to do or submit to something ~ *vt* **1** *obs* **:** to be tired of or disgusted with **2 :** to irritate or disgust (as a person) usu. by reason of tiresome or wearying qualities ⟨restrictions that ~*ed* buyers⟩ ⟨it ~*s* me to see such waste⟩ **syn** see ANNOY

³irk \"\ *n* -S **1 :** IRKSOMENESS, TEDIUM ⟨the ~ of a narrow existence⟩ **2 :** a cause or source of annoyance or disgust ⟨the main ~ is the wage level⟩

irk·some \-səm\ *adj* [ME *irksom*, fr. *irken* to irk + *-som* -some] **1** *obs* **:** WEARY, VEXED, DISGUSTED **2 :** tending to irk ⟨an ~ task⟩ **:** IRRITATING, TEDIOUS ⟨such ~ caution⟩ — **irk·some·ly** *adv* — **irk·some·ness** *n* -ES

ir·kutsk \(ˈ)irˈkütsk, ˌər¦-\ *adj, usu cap* [fr. *Irkutsk*, U.S.S.R.] **:** of or from the city of Irkutsk, U.S.S.R. **:** of the kind or style prevalent in Irkutsk

irne *archaic var of* IRON

IRO *abbr* inland revenue officer; internal revenue officer

iro·ha \ˌē(ˌ)rōˈhä, ˌ=ˈ=(ˌ)=\ *also* **iro·fa** \-fä\ *n* -S [Jap, fr. *i* + *ro* + *ha* or *fa*, its first three syllables] **:** the Japanese kana in its popular order in distinction from the scientific arrangement which is based on that of Sanskrit

iro·ko \əˈrō(ˌ)kō\ *n* -S [Yoruba *ìrɔ̀³kò¹*] **1 :** a very large timber tree (*Chlorophora excelsa*) of tropical western Africa with strong durable streaky lustrous light brown to dark brown wood that is extremely resistant to termite attack and often used as a substitute for teak **2 :** the wood of an iroko tree

¹iron \ˈī(ə)rn, ˈīən *sometimes chiefly for the sake of the meter in a line of poetry* ˈīrən\ *n* -S [ME *iren, iron*, fr. OE *īren, īsen, īsern*; akin to OHG *īsan, īsarn* iron, ON *īsarn, jārn*, Goth *eisarn*; all fr. a prehistoric Gmc word prob. of Venetic or Illyrian origin like OIr *īarn* iron, W *haearn*; akin to Venetic *Isaras*, a river; akin to L *ira* anger — more at IRE] **1 a :** a heavy malleable ductile magnetic chiefly bivalent and trivalent metallic element that is silver-white when pure but readily rusts in moist air and is chemically active in other respects (as toward dilute acids), that occurs native in meteorites and combined in most igneous rocks, that is usu. extracted from its ores by smelting with coke and limestone in a blast furnace, that is the most used of metals (as in construction, armaments, tools), and that plays a vital role in biological processes (as in transport of oxygen in the animal body) — symbol *Fe*; see CAST IRON, INGOT IRON, IRON ORE, PIG IRON, STEEL, WROUGHT IRON; ELEMENT table; compare FERRITE **b :** iron in some particular physical or chemical state: as (1) **:** iron chemically combined ⟨~ in the blood⟩ ⟨a tonic of ~ and wine⟩ (2) **:** iron that cannot be hardened by quenching (as wrought iron, pig iron) — distinguished from *steel* ⟨the ~ and steel industry⟩ **2 :** something (as an instrument, appliance, or tool) made of or commonly, customarily, or orig. made of iron: as **a** (1) **:** an iron weapon; *esp* **:** SWORD (2) **:** armed might **:** WEAPONRY (3) *slang* **:** a portable firearm **:** PISTOL **b** (1) **:** something (as chains, handcuffs, shackles) used to bind, confine, or restrain — usu. used in pl. ⟨kept the prisoner in ~*s*⟩ (2) *archaic* **:** BONDS, CAPTIVITY **c :** a branding or cauterizing iron **d irons** *pl, archaic* **:** dies used in striking coins **e :** HARPOON **f :** a heatable device usu. with a flat metal base of some weight that is used to smooth, finish, or press (as cloth) **:** FLATIRON **g :** STIRRUP **h :** SOLDERING IRON **i :** an iron weight with a handle sometimes used in curling instead of the customary stone **j :** the cutter in a tool (as a plane) **k :** one of a series of golf clubs numbered 1 through 9 that have heads of iron or occas. other metal laid back at a progressively greater angle so as to give progressively greater height and less distance to the flight of the ball **3 :** resemblance to iron in some quality (as strength, inflexibility, hardness, durability) ⟨the ~ of that spirit⟩; *also* **:** a quality of exhibiting such resemblance ⟨muscles of ~⟩ **4 :** a unit of measurement equal to one forty-eighth of an inch used in measuring thickness of a shoe sole ⟨a six-*iron* sole⟩ **5 :** MINERAL BROWN **6 :** the iron industry or its production esp. as a market factor ⟨~ has remained steady⟩ — **in irons** *or* **into irons 1** *of a sailing vessel while tacking* **:** having the head to the wind and unable to fill away on either tack **:** incapable of coming about or filling away **2 :** in chains or fetters **:** in confinement — **iron in the fire 1 :** a matter requiring close oversight or attention **:** ENTERPRISE ⟨was a businessman and had other *irons in the fire* —J.D.Beresford⟩ **2 :** a prospective course of action **:** a project not yet realized ⟨got several *irons in the fire* and I'm hoping to land something before very long —W.S.Maugham⟩

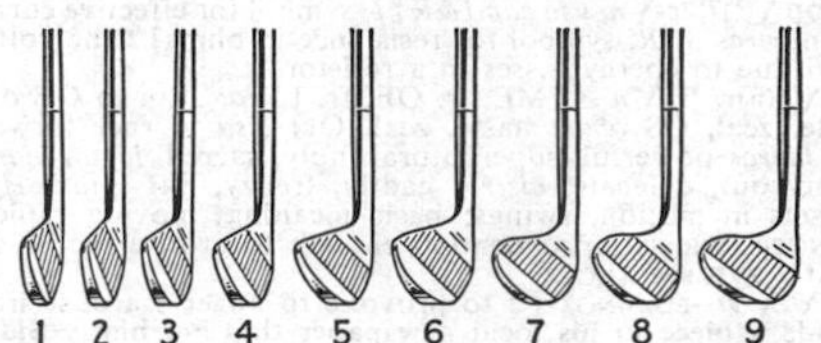

irons 2k: *1* driving iron, *2* midiron, *3* mid-mashie, *4* mashie iron, *5* mashie, *6* mashie niblick, *7* pitcher, *8* pitching niblick, *9* niblick

²iron \"\ *adj* [ME *iren*, fr. OE *īren*, *īsen*, *īsern* (akin to OHG *īsarnīn*, adj., iron, Goth *eisarneins*), fr. *īren*, *īsen*, *īsern*, n.] **1 :** of, relating to, or derived from iron **:** made of or containing iron ⟨an ~ bar⟩; *broadly* **:** made of or consisting of steel or other modified iron **2 :** resembling iron in appearance or color ⟨a grim ~ sky⟩ **3 :** resembling iron in some quality (as hardness, strength, impenetrability, endurance, insensibility): as **a :** having great physical hardness or strength **b :** RUDE, HARD, SEVERE **c :** strong and healthy **:** ROBUST ⟨an ~ constitution⟩ ⟨~ digestions⟩ **d :** INFLEXIBLE, UNRELENTING ⟨~ determination⟩ **e :** holding or binding fast **:** not to be broken ⟨the ~ ties of kinship⟩ **f :** metallic in tone **:** HARSH ⟨an ~ voice⟩ **4** *of a golf shot* **:** played with an iron

³iron \"\ *vb* -ED/-ING/-S [ME *irenen*, fr. *iren*, n.] *vt* **1 :** to furnish, arm, or cover with iron ⟨~*ed* the new wheel⟩ **2 a :** to shackle with irons **:** FETTER, HANDCUFF **b :** to attach or make fast with fittings of iron ⟨~ the toolbox to the truck⟩ **3 a :** to smooth with or as if with an instrument of iron; *esp* **:** to press (as cloth) with a heated flatiron **b :** to remove by ironing — usu. used with an adverb of direction ⟨gently ~*ing* away the wrinkles⟩ **4 :** to take (as a fish) with a gaff or harpoon **5 :** to thin the walls of (a deep-drawn metal article) by reducing the clearance between punch and die ~ *vi* **:** to iron clothes ⟨~*ed all* morning⟩

iron age *n, usu cap I&A* **:** the period of human culture characterized by the smelting of iron and its almost universal use in industry beginning about 1000 B.C. in southern Europe and somewhat earlier in western Asia and Egypt — compare BRONZE AGE, STONE AGE; see HALLSTATT, LA TÈNE

iron alum *n* **1 :** an alum containing iron as the trivalent constituent; *esp* **:** ammonium ferric alum $NH_4Fe(SO_4)_2.12H_2O$ **2** [¹*alum* (aluminum sulfate)] **:** HALOTRICHITE

ironback \ˈ=(ə)ˌ=\ *n* **:** a plate of iron for the back of a fireplace

iron bacteria *n* **:** any of various bacteria of the order Chlamydobacteriales that act upon iron compounds and produce deposits of ocher and bog ore

ironbark \ˈ=(ə)ˌ=\ *n* **1** *or* **ironbark tree :** any of several Australian eucalypts (as *Eucalyptus sideroxylon, E. paniculata, E. siderophloia, E. resinifera*) having hard gray bark and useful timber and in some cases yielding eucalyptus gum **2 :** the extremely heavy hard strong durable wood of an ironbark which is commonly available in large sizes and is extensively used in heavy construction

ironbark acacia *n* **:** an Australian timber tree (*Acacia excelsa*) with very hard dark-grained wood

ironbark box *n* [¹*box*] **:** any of several Australian eucalypts; *esp* **:** a widely distributed stringybark (*Eucalyptus obliqua*)

iron black *n* **:** a powder consisting of precipitated antimony which is used in coating various objects to give them the appearance of polished iron or steel

iron blue *n* **1 :** STEEL GRAY **2 :** any of various strongly colored pigments that range in masstone from reddish blue to jet black and possess good hiding power, that are now usu. made by bringing together solutions of ferrous sulfate, ammonium sulfate, and sodium ferrocyanide and oxidizing the white precipitate formed, that consist of complex compounds regarded as both ferrocyanides and ferricyanides containing positive ions (as ammonium and sodium ions), and that are used chiefly in blueprints, inks, laundry blues, paints and enamels, crayons, and linoleum: as **a :** PRUSSIAN BLUE **b :** TURNBULL'S BLUE

ironbound \ˈ=(ə)¦=\ *adj* [ME *irenbounden*, fr. *iren* iron + *bounden* bound — more at IRON, BOUND] **:** bound with or as if with iron: as **a :** HARSH, RUGGED ⟨an ~ coast⟩ **b :** bound with irons **:** SHACKLED ⟨an ~ prisoner⟩ **c :** RIGID, UNYIELDING, RIGOROUS ⟨~ traditions⟩ ⟨an ~ climate⟩

iron brown *n* **:** MINERAL BROWN

iron buff *n* **:** a fast dye composed of hydrated ferric oxide formed on the fiber by the action of an alkali on an iron salt

iron carbide *n* **:** a binary compound of iron with carbon; *esp* **:** CEMENTITE

iron carbonate *n* **:** a carbonate of iron; *esp* **:** FERROUS CARBONATE

iron carbonyl *n* **:** a compound formed by reaction of metallic iron with carbon monoxide; *esp* **:** the flammable unstable poisonous liquid pentacarbonyl $Fe(CO)_5$ used chiefly in making iron powder and pure iron for use as a catalyst

iron cement *n* **:** a mixture of small cast-iron borings or turnings usu. with ammonium chloride used moist as a cement to make rust joints

iron chink *n* [⁷*chink*; fr. its performance of tasks formerly done by Chinese] **:** a machine for rapidly cleaning and dressing fish (as salmon) at a cannery

iron chloride *n* **:** a chloride of iron: as **a :** FERRIC CHLORIDE **b :** FERROUS CHLORIDE

¹ironclad \ˈ=(ə)¦=\ *adj* [¹*iron* + *clad*] **1 :** sheathed in, protected by, or having an exterior of iron — used esp. of naval vessels **2 a :** RIGOROUS, SEVERE, EXACTING ⟨an ~ oath⟩ ⟨~ controls⟩ **b :** INFLEXIBLE, RIGID ⟨an ~ rule⟩ ⟨~ caste distinctions⟩ **c :** vigorously determined **:** fixed and unshakable ⟨an ~ patriot⟩ ⟨an ~ defense⟩ **3** *of a plant* **:** highly resistant to unfavorable environmental factors (as cold) ⟨only the most ~ roses thrive so far north⟩ ⟨developed several ~ apricots for the North Central states⟩

²ironclad \ˈ=(ə)ˌ=\ *n* -S **1 :** an armored naval vessel **2 :** one (as a knight in armor or a person of precise and rigid morality) that is felt to resemble an armored vessel

iron curtain *n, often cap I&C* [trans. of G *eiserner vorhang* iron fireproof theatrical curtain] **1 :** a political, military, and ideological barrier that cuts off and isolates an area (as of Soviet-controlled territory) preventing free communication and contact with differently oriented areas **2 a :** an intangible barrier against communication of information or ideas; *esp* **:** one that is set up for concealment and bars any opportunity for penetration **b :** a bar to the crossing of a mental or cultural borderline

iron-deficiency anemia *n* **1 :** hypochromic anemia in which deficiency of hemoglobin in the individual red blood cells is the characteristic abnormality — see CHLOROSIS **2 :** HYPOCHROMIC ANEMIA

irone \ˈīˌrōn, =ˈ=\ *n* -S [ISV *iris* + *-one*; orig. formed as G *iron*] **:** any of several oily liquid isomeric ketones $C_{14}H_{22}O$ or a mixture of some of them that have a strong odor of violet and orrisroot, that occur in orris oil, and that are used in perfumes

ironed *past of* IRON

iron·er \ˈī(ə)rnə(r), ˈīən-\ *n* -S **:** one that irons: as **a :** a person who presses or shapes something (as clothes, hats, gloves) with a hand or automatic iron or on a heated form **b :** a machine for ironing fabrics **:** MANGLE

ironfisted \ˈ=(ə)¦==\ *adj* **1 :** STINGY, MEAN, MISERLY **2 :** harsh and ruthless ⟨~ methods⟩

iron-free \ˈ=(ə)¦=\ *adj* **:** containing no iron

iron front *n* **:** a cast-iron facade for a building

iron glance *n* [part trans., part modif. of G *eisenglanz*, fr. *eisen* iron + *glanz* brightness] **:** HEMATITE

iron grass *n* **:** VERNAL SEDGE

iron gray *n* **:** a nearly neutral very slightly greenish dark gray — called also *bat*

iron hand *n* **:** stern or rigorous control

ironhanded \ˈ=(ə)¦==\ *adj* **:** having or acting or governing with a strong or heavy hand **:** INFLEXIBLE, RIGOROUS — **iron·hand·ed·ly** *adv* — **iron·hand·ed·ness** *n* -ES

ironhard \ˈ=(ə)¦=\ *adj* **:** having the hardness of iron **:** very hard or severe ⟨an ~ frost⟩ ⟨an ~ beak⟩

iron hat *n* [ME *iren hat*, fr. *iren* iron + *hat* — more at IRON, HAT] **1 a :** a headpiece of iron or steel used as armor during the middle ages **b** *slang* **:** DERBY 2a **c :** a metal or plastic safety hat **2 :** GOSSAN

ironhead \ˈ=(ə)ˌ=\ *n* **1 a :** WOOD IBIS 1 **b :** AMERICAN GOLDENEYE **2 :** a stupid person

ironheaded \ˈ=(ə)¦==\ *adj* **1 :** furnished or tipped with a head, top, or point of iron **2 :** very hardheaded

ironheads \ˈ=(ə)ˌ=\ *n pl but sing or pl in constr, also* **ironhead** *dial chiefly Eng* **:** KNAPWEED

ironhearted \ˈ=(ə)¦==\ *adj* **:** HARDHEARTED, UNFEELING, CRUEL ⟨an ~ master⟩

iron horse *n* **:** a locomotive engine

iron hydroxide *n* **:** a hydroxide of iron: as **a :** FERRIC HYDROXIDE **b :** FERROUS HYDROXIDE

iron·ic \(ˈ)īˈränik, -nēk *sometimes* əˈr-\ *or* **iron·i·cal** \-nəkəl, -nēk-\ *adj* [LL *ironicus*, fr. Gk *eirōnikos* dissembling, fr. *eirōneia* dissimulation + *-ikos* -ic, -ical — more at IRONY] **1 :** of or relating to irony **:** containing, expressing, or constituting irony ⟨an ~ remark⟩ ⟨it was ~ that he should enter then⟩ **2 :** addicted to the use of irony **:** given to irony ⟨a very ~ man⟩ **3** *obs* **:** DISSEMBLING, PRETENDED **syn** see SARCASTIC

iron·i·cal·ly \-nək(ə)lē, -nēk-, -li\ *adv* **:** in an ironical manner **:** with or so as to constitute irony ⟨~ enough the well-planned scheme failed completely⟩ ⟨answered ~⟩

iron·i·cal·ness \-kəlnəs\ *n* -ES **:** the quality or state of being ironical

ironing *n* -S **1 :** the action or process of smoothing or pressing with or as if with a hot flatiron **2 :** clothes and linens ironed or to be ironed ⟨found the dampened ~ waiting in a basket⟩ ⟨folded and put away the ~⟩

ironing board

ironing board *also* **ironing table** *n* **:** a flat padded cloth-covered surface on which clothes are ironed that was orig. of wood but is now often of ventilated metal, has one end tapered so that garments may be fitted over it, and is usu. equipped with an adjustable support by which it may be held rigid at a convenient working height

iron·ish \ˈī(ə)rnish, ˈīən-, -nēsh\ *adj* **:** resembling or resembling that of iron ⟨an ~ taste⟩

iro·nist \ˈīrənəst\ *n* -S [*irony* + *-ist*] **:** one given to irony **:** a user of irony esp. in the development of a literary work or theme

iro·nize \-,nīz\ *vb* -ED/-ING/-S [*iron*ic + *-ize*] *vt* **:** to make ironic **:** give an appearance or effect of irony to ⟨*ironizing* her account of the meeting⟩ ~ *vi* **:** to use irony **:** speak or behave ironically ⟨why ~ over such trivia⟩

iron-jawed \ˈ=(=)ˌ=\ *adj* **1 :** having a jaw like or of iron ⟨*iron-jawed* pincers⟩ ⟨an *iron-jawed* boxer⟩ **2 :** rigorously determined ⟨an *iron-jawed* disposition⟩

iron law *n* **:** a law or controlling principle that is incontrovertible and inexorable ⟨*iron laws* of historical necessity⟩

iron law of wages [intended as trans. of G *ehernes lohngesetz*, lit., brazen law of wages] **:** a statement in economics: wages naturally tend to fall to the minimum level necessary for subsistence — called also *brazen law of wages*

iron·less \ˈī(ə)rnləs, ˈīən-\ *adj* **:** having no iron ⟨an ~ culture⟩ **:** free from iron ⟨~ diets⟩

ironlike \ˈ=(=)ˌ=\ *adj* **:** resembling iron **:** exhibiting strength or hardness like that of iron ⟨~ determination⟩

iron liquor *n* **:** a black liquid consisting of a solution of crude ferrous acetate $Fe(C_2H_3O_2)_2$ usu. obtained by treating scrap iron with pyroligneous acid and used chiefly as a mordant in dyeing — called also *black liquor*

iron loss *n* **:** the loss of available energy by hysteresis and eddy currents in an electromagnetic apparatus (as a transformer) — compare COPPER LOSS

iron lung *n* **:** a device for artificial respiration in which rhythmic alternations in the air pressure in a chamber surrounding a patient's chest force air into and out of the lungs esp. when the nerves governing the chest muscles fail to function because of poliomyelitis

iron man *in senses 1 & 2* ˈ=(=),man *or* -,maa(ə)n *or* -,mən, *in senses 3,4, & 5* ˈ=(=)ˈman *or* -ˈmaa(ə)n\ *n* **1 :** a maker or manufacturer of iron ⟨*iron men* are uncertain about carloadings⟩; *esp* **:** a worker engaged in the manufacture or processing of iron **2 a :** a railroad worker who handles the rails in tracklaying **b :** a cement worker who weighs out ground iron ore and adds it to slurry or dry-ground rock as it goes into the kiln **c :** a worker who makes iron facsimiles of paper shoe= part models for use in cutting cardboard patterns **3 :** a man of unusual physical endurance ⟨took pride in his mastery of the pitching art, in the reputation he bore as the *iron man* —*Collier's*⟩ **4** *slang* **:** DOLLAR; *esp* **:** a silver dollar **5** *slang* **:** a machine or device that does something formerly performed by hand **:** ROBOT

ironmaster \ˈ=(=),==\ *n* **:** one that conducts or manages the founding or manufacture of iron esp. on a large scale

iron mike *n, slang* **:** an automatic pilot on a ship or airplane

iron minium *n* **:** BERLIN BROWN

iron mold *n* [¹*iron* + *mold*, alter. of *mole* (spot)] **:** a spot (as on cloth) due to staining by rusty iron or by ink

iron–mold \ˈ=(=)ˌ=\ *vt* **:** to stain with iron mold

ironmonger \ˈ=(=),==\ *n* [ME *irenmonger*, fr. *iren* iron + *monger* — more at IRON, MONGER] *Brit* **:** a dealer in iron and hardware

ironmongery \ˈ=(=),=(=)=\ *n* -ES **1** *Brit* **:** HARDWARE **2** *Brit* **:** a hardware store or business **3 :** the craft or technical art of a worker in metals **:** SMITHING ⟨a whole new craft of delicate, precise ~ that had to be developed —A.L.Kroeber⟩

iron-monticellite \ˈ=(=)ˌ==ˈ=,=\ *n* **:** a silicate $CaFeSiO_4$ of iron and calcium that is isomorphous with monticellite

iron mountain *n* **:** a mountain that contains large or economically important amounts of iron ore

iron·ness \ˈī(ə)rnnəs, ˈīənn-\ *n* -ES **:** the quality or state of being iron ⟨an ~ of constitution⟩ ⟨such ~ of will⟩

iron oak *n* **1 :** any of several American oaks (as the blackjack or the common post oak) having notably hard tough durable wood **2 :** a European Turkey oak

iron ore *n* **:** a native compound of iron (as hematite, limonite, magnetite, siderite, goethite, and the bog and clay iron ores) from which the metal may be profitably extracted

iron-ore cement *n* **:** a German cement in which iron ore is substituted for the clay or shale used in making portland cement

iron out *vt* **1 a :** to make smooth or straight ⟨*ironed out* the curves in the highway⟩ ⟨*ironing* the crumpled paper *out*⟩ **b :** to make uniform ⟨*ironing out* irregularities in the wage scale⟩ **2 :** to make tolerable or harmonious by suppression or modification of extremes (as discordant views or aspirations, technical difficulties, or divergent theories) ⟨conferences will *iron out* any conflicts of interest⟩

iron oxide *n* **:** any of several natural or synthetic oxides or hydrated oxides of iron: as **a :** anhydrous or hydrated ferric oxide varying in color from red, brown, or black to orange or yellow depending in part on the degree of hydration and the purity and used esp. as a pigment — compare OCHER, SIENNA **b :** FERROSOFERRIC OXIDE **c :** FERROUS OXIDE **d :** GOETHITE

iron-oxide red *n* **:** a strong brown to reddish brown — called also *agate, Spanish red, tarragona*

iron pan *n* **:** a hard soil layer that is cemented with iron oxides and that usu. consists of sand or sand and gravel

iron pentacarbonyl *n* **:** the iron carbonyl $Fe(CO)_5$

iron pot *n* **:** SCOTER

iron putty *n* **:** an acid-resistant putty prepared from ferric oxide and boiled linseed oil

iron pyrites *or* **iron pyrite** *n* **:** PYRITE 2

iron range *n* **:** any of several highly productive iron-ore districts of the U.S. and Canada in the general vicinity of Lake Superior ⟨the Mesabi *iron range*⟩

iron ration *n* **:** an emergency ration

iron red *n* **1 :** a natural or synthetic red pigment (as Indian red or Venetian red) consisting wholly or in part of iron oxide — compare ROUGE 2a **2 :** any of the colors oxide red; *esp* **:** INDIAN RED — compare IRON-OXIDE RED

irons *pl of* IRON, *pres 3d sing of* IRON

iron safe clause *n* **:** a clause in a fire insurance policy covering merchandise that requires inventory records to be kept in a fireproof safe

iron sand *n* **:** sand rich in iron ore (as that of certain New Zealand coastal areas)

iron scale *n* **:** SCALE 4a(1)

iron scrap *n* **1 :** waste pieces or disused articles of wrought iron suitable for reworking **2 :** cast iron or castings suitable only for remelting

ironshod \ˈ=(=)ˈ=\ *adj* **:** shod, cased, or tipped with iron or steel ⟨~ hooves⟩ ⟨an ~ wheel⟩ ⟨~ barge poles⟩

ironshot \ˈ=(=),=\ *adj, of a mineral* **:** streaked or speckled with iron or an iron ore

ironside \ˈ=(=),=\ *n* **1 :** a man of great strength or bravery **2 a ironsides** *pl, usu cap* **:** any of various bodies of hardy veteran troops **b :** a member of Cromwell's Ironsides cavalry during the English Civil War or of a similar force; *broadly* **:** a hardy veteran puritan soldier **3 ironsides** *pl but sing or pl in constr* **:** an ironclad ship

iron sight *n* **:** a metallic sight for a gun as distinguished from a sight depending on an optical or computing system — compare TELESCOPE SIGHT

iron skull *n, slang* **:** a railway boilermaker

ironsmith \ˈ=(=),=\ *n* [ME *iren smyth*, fr. *iren* iron + *smyth, smith* smith — more at IRON, SMITH] **1 :** IRONWORKER, BLACKSMITH **2 :** any of several East Indian barbets (as *Megalaima oorti faber*) having notes that resemble the sounds made by a blacksmith

iron spinel *n* **:** HERCYNITE

iron stand *n* **:** a raised and usu. ventilated metal stand on which a hot flatiron may be rested when not in use

ironstone \ˈ=(=),=\ *n* **1 :** a hard sedimentary rock rich in iron; *esp* **:** a siderite in a coal region **2 :** IRONSTONE CHINA

ironstone china *n* **:** a hard white stoneware pottery developed in England during the 18th century as a cheaper substitute for bone china and orig. highly decorated but used most extensively as plain white inexpensive tableware throughout much of the 19th century

iron sulfate *n* **:** a sulfate of iron: as **a :** FERRIC SULFATE **b :** FERROUS SULFATE

iron sulfide *n* **:** any of several compounds of iron and sulfur: as **a :** FERROUS SULFIDE **b :** the disulfide FeS_2 occurring in nature as pyrite and marcasite

iron tree *n* **:** a tree of the genus *Metrosideros* (esp. *M. vera*) with notably hard wood

iron-vane meter *n* **:** MOVING-IRON METER

ironware \ˈ=(=),=\ *n* [ME *irenware*, fr. *iren* iron + *ware* — more at IRON, WARE] **:** articles made of iron; *esp* **:** iron household utensils (as cooking vessels or cutlery)

ironweed \ˈ=(=),=\ *n* **:** any of several chiefly weedy plants: as **a :** KNAPWEED **b :** BLUEWEED 1 **c :** BLUE VERVAIN **d** *chiefly Brit* **:** RAGWEED 2 **e :** any of several American plants of the genus *Vernonia*

ironwood \ˈ=(=),=\ *n* **1 :** any of numerous trees and shrubs (as various ebonies, hornbeams, or acacias) with exceptionally tough or hard wood — compare BASTARD IRONWOOD, BLACK IRONWOOD, WHITE IRONWOOD **2 :** the wood of an ironwood

ironwood wattle *n* **:** IRONBARK ACACIA

ironwork \ˈ=(=),=\ *n* [ME *irenwerk*, fr. *iren* iron + *werk* work — more at IRON, WORK] **1 a :** work in iron **:** as beaten, smithed, or dressed iron ⟨did all the ~⟩ ⟨a balcony of lacy ~⟩ **b :** the part of something (as a building, a ship, or a wheel) that is made of iron ⟨the ~ of the carriage was forged locally⟩ **c :** iron articles ⟨dealt in ~⟩ **2 ironworks** *pl but sing or pl in constr* **:** a mill or building where iron or steel is smelted or heavy iron or steel products are made

ironworker \ˈ=(=),==\ *n* **:** a worker in iron: as **a :** a person employed at an ironworks **b :** a shopworker who fabricates structural steel parts **c :** one who builds with structural steel or iron

ironworking \ˈ=(=),==\ *n* **:** the process of fashioning things from iron

ironwort \ˈ=(=),=\ *n* [so called fr. the belief that such mints cure sword wounds] **1 :** any of several shrubby or subshrubby mints that constitute the genus *Sideritis*, often have yellow flowers and whitish woolly stem or leaves, and are chiefly native to the eastern Mediterranean region **2 :** HEMP NETTLE

¹**irony** \ˈī(ə)rnē, ˈīənē, -ni\ *adj* [ME *yrony*, fr. *yron, iren* iron + *-y* — more at IRON] **1 :** made or consisting of iron **:** containing or abounding in iron ⟨~ sands⟩ ⟨~ chains⟩ **2 :** resembling iron in some quality (as taste or hardness) ⟨an ~ flavor⟩

²**iro·ny** \ˈīrənē, -ni *sometimes* ˈīərn-\ *n* -ES [L *ironia*, fr. Gk *eirōneia*, fr. *eirōn* dissembler (perh. fr. *eirein* to say) + *-eia* -y — more at WORD] **1 a :** feigned ignorance designed to confound or provoke an antagonist **:** DISSIMULATION — compare SOCRATIC IRONY **b :** DRAMATIC IRONY **2 a :** humor, ridicule, or light sarcasm that adopts a mode of speech the intended implication of which is the opposite of the literal sense of the words (as when expressions of praise are used where blame is meant) **b :** this mode of expression as a literary style or form ⟨a gift for ~⟩ **c :** an ironic utterance or expression **3 :** a state of affairs or events that is the reverse of what was or was to be expected **:** a result opposite to and as if in mockery of the appropriate result ⟨the ~ of fate⟩ **syn** see WIT

iron yellow *n* **1 :** any of several permanent synthetic yellow to orange pigments (as Mars yellow) consisting wholly or in part of hydrated iron oxide **2 :** MARS YELLOW 2

¹**ir·o·quoi·an** \ˌirəˈkwȯi(y)ən, -ˈwäyən\ *adj, usu cap* [²*Iroquois* + *-an*] **1 :** of, relating to, or characteristic of the language family Iroquoian or one of its members **2 :** of, relating to, or characteristic of the Iroquois

²**iroquoian** \"\ *n* -S *cap* **1 :** a language family of eastern No. America including Cayuga, Cherokee, Conestoga, Erie, Huron, Mohawk, Onondaga, Oneida, Seneca, Tuscarora **2 :** a member of any of the peoples constituting the Iroquois

¹**ir·o·quois** \ˈirə,kwȯi, -wä *sometimes* -wȯiz\ *adj, usu cap* [Fr, adj. & n., fr. Algonquin *Irinakhoiw*, lit., real adders] **1 :** of, relating to, or characteristic of the Iroquois **2 :** of, relating to, or characteristic of the language of the Iroquois

²**iroquois** \"\ *n, pl* **iroquois** \-ȯi(z), -ä(z)\ *usu cap* [F] **1 a :** an Indian people comprising a confederacy of five peoples that consisted orig. of the Cayuga, Mohawk, Oneida, Onondaga, and Seneca of central New York and later included the Tuscarora and fragments of various other peoples **b :** a member of any of such peoples **2 :** any of the languages of the Iroquois

ir·pex \ˈər,peks\ *n, cap* [NL, fr. L *irpex, hirpex* harrow — more at HEARSE] **:** a genus of tooth fungi (family Hydnaceae) that have shelving or resupinate sporophores and include some forms associated with decay of woody plant tissue

irr *abbr* **1** irredeemable **2** irregular

ir·radiance \ə+\ *n* **1** *obs* **:** emission of rays (as of light) **2 :** something (as intellectual or spiritual illumination) that is emitted like rays of light ⟨informed . . . with so splendid a spiritual ~ —J.P.Bishop⟩ **3 :** radiant flux density on a given surface usu. expressed in watts per square centimeter or square meter

ir·radiancy \"+\ *n* **1 :** the quality or state of being irradiant **2 :** IRRADIANCE 3

ir·radiant \"+\ *adj* [L *irradiant-, irradians*, pres. part. of *irradiare*] **:** emitting rays of light **:** serving to or able to illuminate or brighten

¹**ir·radiate** \"+\ *adj* [L *irradiatus*, past part.] **:** made bright with or as if with light **:** ILLUMINATED ⟨a countenance ~ with love⟩

²**ir·radiate** \"+\ *vb* -ED \-ING\-S [L *irradiatus*, past part. of *irradiare*, fr. *in-* ²in- + *radiare* to radiate — more at RADIATE] *vt* **1 a :** to throw rays of light upon **:** shine upon **:** ILLUMINATE, BRIGHTEN ⟨moonlight *irradiating* the placid water⟩ **b :** to enlighten intellectually or spiritually **:** make clear or brilliant ⟨wisdom *irradiated* his counsel⟩ **c :** to affect or treat by radiant heat or other radiant energy; *specif* **:** to treat by exposure to radiation (as of ultraviolet light or radium) **2 :** to send forth like rays of light **:** RADIATE, SHED, DIFFUSE ⟨*irradiating* strength and comfort⟩ ~ *vi* **1** *archaic* **:** to emit rays **:** SHINE **2** *archaic* **:** to issue in rays

irradiated *adj* **1** *of an heraldic figure or device* **:** represented as surrounded with rays of light **2 :** treated, prepared, or altered by exposure to a specific radiation ⟨~ milk⟩ ⟨~ tissues⟩

ir·ra·di·at·ing·ly \ə'==,===, =,==ˈ===\ *adv* **:** so as to irradiate

ir·radiation \(,)i, ə+\ *n* -S [MF, fr. LL *irradiation-, irradiatio*, fr. L *irradiatus* + *-ion-, -io* -ion] **1 a** *archaic* **:** a giving off of rays of light **b :** the emission of radiant energy (as heat) **c :** an emanation, diffusion, or radiation of something from a common center or point of origin or a result of such activity: as (1) **:** the radiation of a physiologically active agent from a point of origin within the body; *esp* **:** the spread of a nervous impulse beyond the usual conduction path (2) *obs* **:** emission of a supposed influence or immaterial fluid from the eyes (3) **:** apparent enlargement of a light or bright object or surface when displayed against a dark background; *esp* **:** the spreading of light by the grains of a photographic emulsion causing the developed image to be larger and more diffuse at the edges than the optical image — called also *diffusion* **2 a** *archaic* **:** a ray of light **b :** mental or spiritual illumination **3 a :** exposure to rays (as ultraviolet light, X rays, or alpha rays) **b :** application of X rays, radium rays, or other radiation (as for therapeutic purposes) **4 :** IRRADIANCE 3

irradiation sickness *n* **:** RADIATION SICKNESS

ir·radiative \ə+\ *adj* **:** tending to irradiate

ir·radiator \ə+\ *n* -S **:** one that irradiates; *esp* **:** an apparatus for applying radiations (as X rays)

ir·rad·i·ca·ble \(ˈ)iˈradəkəbəl, əˈra-, (ˈ)irˈra-, (ˈ)iəˈra-\ *adj* [ML *irradicabilis*, fr. L *in-* ²in- + *radicare* to take root + *-abilis* -able — more at RADICATE] **:** impossible to eradicate **:** DEEP-ROOTED — **ir·rad·i·ca·bly** \-blē\ *adv*

ir·rad·i·cate \əˈradə,kāt\ *vt* -ED/-ING/-S [²*in-* + *radicate*] **:** to root deeply

irrationable *adj* [L *irrationabilis*, fr. *in-* ¹in- + *rationabilis* rationable — more at RATIONABLE] **1** *obs* **:** lacking the power of reason **2** *archaic* **:** UNREASONABLE, UNSUITABLE

¹**ir·rational** \(ˈ)i, ə, (ˈ)ir, (ˈ)iə+\ *adj* [ME *irrationall*, fr. L *irrationalis*, fr. *in-* ¹in- + *rationalis* rational — more at RATIONAL] **:** not rational: as **a** (1) **:** not endowed with reason **:** lacking powers of reasoning or understanding ⟨the lower animals are commonly described as ~⟩ (2) **:** lacking usual or normal mental clarity or coherence ⟨was ~ for several days after the accident⟩ **b :** not governed by or according to reason ⟨~ . . . is a neutral term meaning either what is outside the scope of reason or what has not yet been tested by reason —*Times Lit. Supp.*⟩ **c** *Greek & Latin prosody* (1) *of a syllable* **:** having a quantity other than that required by the meter (2) *of a foot* **:** containing such a syllable (3) *of a meter* **:** containing such feet **d** *of a number* **:** real but not expressible as the quotient of two integers ⟨π and $\sqrt{3}$ are ~ numbers⟩

²**irrational** \"+\ *n* -S **1 :** an irrational being **:** a being not acting according to reason **2 :** an irrational quantity or number **:** SURD

ir·rationalism \"+\ *n* **1 :** a viewpoint or system of belief emphasizing the use of intuition, instinct, feeling, or faith rather than a reliance upon reason or holding that the universe is governed by irrational, volitional, or mysterious forces instead of by reason **2 :** the quality or state of being irrational

¹**ir·rationalist** \"+\ *adj* **:** of, relating to, or advocating irrationalism

²**irrationalist** \"\ *n* **:** a proponent of irrationalism

ir·rationalistic \(ˌ)i, ə, (ˌ)ir, (ˌ)iə+\ *adj* **:** not based on reason **:** ILLOGICAL; *sometimes* **:** IRRATIONALIST

ir·rationality \"+\ *n* [ML or NL *irrationalitas*, fr. L *irrationalis* irrational + *-itas* -ity — more at IRRATIONAL] **1 :** the quality or state of being irrational: as **a :** lack of being endowed with reason **b :** lack of accordance with reason **:** UNREASONABLENESS, FOOLISHNESS **2 :** something that is irrational **:** ABSURDITY **3 :** inequality of dispersion of different colors in refraction spectra (as between crown and flint glass)

ir·rationalize \i, ə, ir, iə+\ *vt* **:** to make irrational

ir·rationally \(ˈ)i, ə, (ˈ)ir, (ˈ)iə+\ *adv* **:** so as to be or appear irrational **:** without or beyond the bounds of reason ⟨~ jealous⟩

ir·rationalness \"+\ *n* **:** the quality or state of being irrational

ir·real \"+\ *adj* [¹*in-* + *real*] **:** not real

ir·reality \ˌi, ˌir, ˌiə+\ *n* [¹*in-* + *reality*] **:** UNREALITY

ir·realizable \(ˌ)i, ə, (ˌ)ir, (ˌ)iə+\ *adj* [¹*in-* + *realizable*] **:** UNREALIZABLE, UNATTAINABLE

ir·rebuttable \ˌi, ˌir, ˌiə+\ *adj* [¹*in-* + *rebut* + *-able*] **:** impossible to rebut **:** not subject to rebuttal ⟨an ~ argument⟩

irrebuttable presumption *n* **:** a presumption that the law does not allow to be rebutted **:** a conclusive presumption

ir·receptive \"+\ *adj* [¹*in-* + *receptive*] **:** UNRECEPTIVE

ir·reciprocal \"+\ *adj* [¹*in-* + *reciprocal*] **:** not reciprocal **:** UNILATERAL ⟨~ permeability⟩

ir·reclaimable \"+\ *adj* [¹*in-* + *reclaim* + *-able*] **:** incapable of being reclaimed ⟨~ swamps⟩; *esp* **:** bad beyond any possibility of redemption ⟨vicious ~ boys⟩ — **ir·reclaimably** \"+\ *adv*

ir·reclaimed \"+\ *adj* [¹*in-* + *reclaimed*] **:** UNRECLAIMED; *esp* **:** not brought under cultivation ⟨~ wasteland⟩

ir·recognition \(ˌ)i, ə, ˌir, ˌiə+\ *n* [¹*in* + *recognition*] **:** failure to recognize **:** absence of recognition

ir·recognizable \(ˌ)i, ə, (ˌ)ir, (ˌ)iə+\ *adj* [¹*in-* + *recognizable*] **:** UNRECOGNIZABLE — **ir·recognizably** \"+\ *adv*

ir·recollection \(ˌ)i, ə, ˌir, ˌiə+\ *n* [¹*in-* + *recollection*] *archaic* **:** failure to recollect **:** FORGETFULNESS

irrecompensable *adj* [MF, fr. *in-* ¹in- + *recompensable* — more at RECOMPENSABLE] *obs* **:** impossible to requite — **irrecompensably** *adv, obs*

ir·reconcilability \(ˌ)i, ə, ˌir, ˌiə+\ *n* **:** the quality or state of being irreconcilable **:** IRRECONCILABLENESS

¹**ir·reconcilable** \(ˌ)i, ə, (ˌ)ir, (ˌ)iə+\ *adj* [¹*in-* + *reconcile* + *-able*] **1 :** impossible to bring into friendly accord or understanding **:** hostile beyond the possibility of reconciliation ⟨~ enemies⟩ ⟨~ factions⟩ **2 :** impossible to make consistent or harmonious ⟨these ~ accounts⟩

²**irreconcilable** \"\ *n* -S **:** one that is irreconcilable; *esp* **:** a member of a group (as a political party) that vigorously opposes compromise or other collaborative techniques

ir·reconcilableness \"+\ *n* **:** the quality or state of being irreconcilable

ir·reconcilably \"+\ *adv* **:** so as to be irreconcilable **:** beyond the possibility of reaching agreement ⟨~ opposed⟩

irreconcile *vt* [¹*in-* + *reconcile*] *obs* **:** to put at variance **:** ESTRANGE

ir·reconciliable \(ˌ)i, ə, (ˌ)ir, (ˌ)iə+\ *adj* [MF, fr. LL *irreconciliabilis*, fr. L *in-* ¹in- + *reconciliare* to reconcile + *-abilis* -able — more at RECONCILE] *archaic* **:** IRRECONCILABLE — **ir·reconciliably** \"+\ *adv, obs*

ir·reconciliation \(ˌ)i, ə, ˌir, ˌiə+\ *n* [¹*in-* + *reconciliation*] **:** lack of reconciliation

ir·recoverable \ˌi, ˌir, ˌiə+\ *adj* [¹*in-* + *recoverable*] **1 :** not capable of being recovered, regained, remedied, or rectified **:** IRREPARABLE ⟨an ~ debt⟩ ⟨suffered an ~ injury⟩ **2** *obs* **:** IRREVOCABLE **3** *archaic* **:** incapable of being restored to health or life — **ir·recoverableness** \"+\ *n*

ir·recoverably \"+\ *adv* **1 :** so as to be irrecoverable **:** beyond any possibility of being recovered, regained, remedied, or rectified ⟨~ lost⟩ ⟨~ ill⟩ ⟨disposed of the evidence finally and ~⟩ **2 :** IRREVOCABLY ⟨determination to commit themselves ~ —J.A.Froude⟩

irrecuperable *adj* [ME, fr. LL *irrecuperabilis*, fr. L *in-* ¹in- + *recuperare* to take back, recover + *-abilis* -able — more at RECOVER] *obs* **:** IRRECOVERABLE — **irrecuperably** *adv, obs*

ir·re·cu·sa·ble \ˌirēˈkyüzəbəl\ *adj* [LL *irrecusabilis*, fr. L *in-* ¹in- + L *recusabilis* capable of being rejected, fr. L *recusare* to reject, refuse + *-abilis* -able — more at RECUSANT] **:** not subject to exception or rejection ⟨an ~ proposition⟩ — **ir·re·cu·sa·bly** \-blē\ *adv*

ir·redeemable \ˌi, ˌir, ˌiə+\ *adj* [¹*in-* + *redeem* + *-able*] **1 :** not redeemable: as **a** (1) *of mortgaged goods* **:** not recoverable on payment of what is due (2) **:** not terminable by payment of the principal — used of a debt or annuity (3) *of a bond with stated maturity* **:** not callable before maturity **b** *of paper money* **:** not convertible into specie at the pleasure of the holder **:** INCONVERTIBLE **2 a :** admitting of no change or release **:** ABSOLUTE, HOPELESS ⟨~ gloom⟩ **b :** insusceptible of redemption or reform **:** utterly and hopelessly bad **:** IRRECLAIMABLE ⟨~ sinners⟩ — **ir·redeemably** \"+\ *adv*

ir·re·den·ta *or* **ir·ri·den·ta** \ˌirəˈdentə\ *n* -S [It *irredenta* (in *Italia irredenta*, lit., unredeemed Italy — used to refer to Italian-speaking areas not incorporated in Italy), fem. of *irredento* unredeemed, fr. *in-* ¹in- (fr. L) + *redento* redeemed, fr. L *redemptus*, past part. of *redimere* to redeem — more at REDEEM] **:** a region related historically or ethnically to one state but politically subject to another ⟨a frontier ~⟩ ⟨treaty inequities that created needless ~s⟩

ir·re·den·tism \-n,tizm\ *n* -S [It. *irredentismo*, the policy of the Italian Irredentists, fr. (*Italia*) *irredenta* + *-ismo* -ism] **:** the principles, policy, or practice of a party or of persons that seek to incorporate within their national boundary territory of which their nation has been deprived or of which the population is ethnically closely related to that of their nation

¹**ir·re·den·tist** \-ntəst\ *n* -S [It *irredentista* one advocating the incorporation of Italia irredenta into Italy, fr. (*Italia*) *irredenta* + *-ista* -ist] **:** an advocate of irredentism

²**irredentist** \ˌ==ˈ==\ *adj* **1 :** of, relating to, or involving irredentists or irredentism ⟨an ~ movement⟩ ⟨~ sentiments⟩ **2 :** living in an irredenta ⟨~ populations⟩ **:** concerning the people of an irredenta ⟨~ problems⟩

ir·reducibility \ˌi, ˌir, ˌiə+\ *n* **:** the quality or state of being irreducible ⟨the ~ of psychological phenomena⟩

ir·reducible \"+\ *adj* [¹*in-* + *reducible*] **1 :** impossible to bring into a desired state, form, or condition ⟨an ~ hernia⟩ **2 a :** impossible to simplify or make easier or clearer ⟨an ~ formula⟩ ⟨an ~ racial or cultural idiosyncrasy —Abram Kardiner⟩ **b :** impossible to make less or smaller ⟨an ~ minimum⟩ — **ir·reducibly** \"+\ *adv*

irreducible equation *n* **:** a mathematical equation equivalent to one formed by equating an irreducible function to zero

irreducible function *n* **:** an integral rational function of a polynomial that cannot be resolved into integral rational factors of lower degree with coefficients in the same number field

ir·re·duc·ti·ble \ˌi(r)rəˈdəktəbəl, ˌiərə-\ *adj* [¹*in-* + *reduct* + *-ible*] **:** IRREDUCIBLE

ir·referable \(ˌ)i, ə, (ˌ)ir, (ˌ)iə+\ *adj* [¹*in-* + *referable*] **:** not referable

ir·reflection *also* **ir·reflexion** \ˌi, ˌir, ˌiə+\ *n* [F *irréflexion*, fr. *in-* 1in- + *réflexion* — more at REFLECTION] **:** lack of mental consideration (as of a project or course of action)

ir·reflective \"+\ *adj* [1*in-* + *reflective*] **:** not based on reflection **:** UNTHINKING, HEEDLESS ⟨an ~ delight⟩ — **ir·reflectively** \"+\ *adv* — **ir·reflectiveness** \"+\ *n*

ir·reflexive \"+\ *adj* [1*in-* + *reflexive*] **1 :** not reflexive **2** *of a logical or mathematical relation* **:** never relating a term to itself — **ir·reflexivity** \(ˈ)i, ə, ˌir, ˌiə\ *n*

ir·reformable \ˌi, ˌir, ˌiə+\ *adj* [1*in-* + *reformable*] **1 :** incapable of being reformed **:** INCORRIGIBLE ⟨an ~ rascal⟩ **2 :** not subject to revision or alteration **:** final or perfect beyond the possibility of improvement ⟨~ dogma⟩ ⟨an ~ judgment⟩

ir·ref·ra·ga·bil·i·ty \(ˌ)i(r)ˌrefrəgəˈbiləd·ē, əˌ-, (ˌ)iəˌ-\ *n* **:** the quality or state of being irrefragable

ir·ref·ra·ga·ble \(ˈ)i(r)ˈrefrəgəbəl, əˈ-, (ˈ)iəˈ-\ *adj* [LL *irrefragabilis*, fr. L *in-* 1in- + *refragari* to resist, oppose (fr. *re-* + *-fragari* — as in *suffragari* to vote for, support) + *-abilis* -able — more at SUFFRAGE] **1 :** impossible to gainsay, deny, or refute ⟨~ arguments⟩ ⟨~ data⟩ ⟨these ~ authorities⟩ **2 :** impossible to break or alter **:** INVIOLABLE, INDESTRUCTIBLE ⟨~ rules⟩ ⟨an ~ cement⟩ — **ir·ref·ra·ga·bly** \-blē\ *adv*

ir·refrangible \ˌi, ˌir, ˌiə+\ *adj* [1*in-* + *refrangible*] **1 :** IRREFRAGABLE 2 **2 :** not capable of being refracted — used of visible light and other radiations

ir·refusable \"+\ *adj* [1*in-* + *refusable*] **:** impossible to refuse

ir·refutability \(ˌ)i, ə, (ˌ)ir, (ˌ)iə+\ *n* **:** the quality or state of being irrefutable

ir·refutable \"+\ *adj* [LL *irrefutabilis*, fr. L *in-* 1in- + LL *refutabilis* refutable — more at REFUTABLE] **:** impossible to refute **:** INCONTROVERTIBLE ⟨an ~ argument⟩ — **ir·refutably** \"+\ *adv*

ir·regardless \ˌi, ˌir, ˌiə+\ *adv* [prob. blend of *irrespective* and *regardless*] *nonstand* **:** REGARDLESS

ir·regenerate \"+\ *adj* [1*in-* + *regenerate*] *archaic* **:** UNREGENERATE

1**ir·regular** \(ˈ)i, ə, (ˈ)ir, (ˈ)iə+\ *adj* [ME *irreguler*, fr. MF, fr. LL *irregularis*, fr. L *in-* 1in- + LL *regularis* regular — more at REGULAR] **1** *of a person* **a** *Roman Catholicism* **:** prevented by an impediment or bar from receiving or exercising clerical orders or offices **b :** behaving without regard to established laws, customs, or moral principles ⟨a wild ~ man in his youth⟩ **c :** not belonging to or not having satisfied the requirements of some particular group or organized body ⟨an ~ physician⟩ **2 a :** failing to accord with what is usual, proper, accepted, or right ⟨~ conduct⟩ **:** contrary to rule or custom ⟨some of his documents were ~⟩ ⟨although it was ~ we accepted the excuse⟩ **b** *of a word or inflection* **:** not conforming to the normal or usual manner of inflection ⟨*sell*, *cast*, *feed* are ~ verbs⟩; *specif* **:** STRONG 16a **c** (1) **:** improper or inadequate because of failure to conform to a prescribed course (2) **:** *of a marriage under Eng or Scots law* **:** celebrated without either proclamation of the banns or publication of intention to marry **:** CLANDESTINE **d :** not belonging to the regular army organization but raised for a special purpose ⟨~ troops are often used as independent commands to harass the enemy⟩ **3 a :** lacking perfect symmetry of form **:** not straight, smooth, even, regular ⟨a rough ~ terrain⟩ ⟨a long ~ coastline⟩ ⟨~ teeth⟩ **b** *of a flower or its parts* **:** lacking uniformity ⟨an ~ corolla⟩; *specif* **:** ZYGOMORPHIC **4 a :** lacking continuity or regularity of occurrence, activity, or function ⟨~ payments⟩ ⟨~ intervals⟩ ⟨an ~ worker⟩ **b** *of a physiological function* **:** failing to occur at regular or normal intervals ⟨~ menstruation⟩ ⟨have your bowels been ~⟩ **c** *of an individual* **:** failing to defecate at such intervals ⟨was constipated and very ~⟩ **d** *of a market* **:** characterized by individual price movements in both directions without establishment of an overall trend ⟨cotton futures were ~⟩

2**irregular** \"\ *n* **:** one that is irregular: as **a :** a soldier (as a guerrilla or partisan) who is not a member of a regular military force — usu. used in pl. **b irregulars** *pl* **:** merchandise that has imperfections or that falls below the manufacturer's usual standard or specifications and is usu. sold unbranded and at a concession in price — compare 2SECOND 4

3**irregular** \"\ *adj* [NL *Irregularia*] **:** EXOCYCLIC

irregular carrier *n* **:** a common carrier that operates without regular schedule or over routes not specified in the certificate or permit

irregular deposit *n* **:** a deposit of money (as for safekeeping) made with the understanding that an equivalent amount but not necessarily the identical money is to be returned to the depositor

ir·regularia \(ˌ)i, ə, ˌir, ˌiə+\ [NL, fr. LL, neut. pl. of *irregularis*] *syn of* EXOCYCLOIDA

ir·regularity \"+\ *n* [ME *irregularite*, fr. OF *irregularité*, fr. ML *irregularitat-*, *irregularitas*, fr. LL *irregularis* irregular + L *-itat-*, *-itas* -ity — more at IRREGULAR] **1 :** the quality or state of being irregular **2 :** something that is irregular; *esp* **:** lack of proper and honest conduct (as in respect to a position of trust) — usu. used in pl. ⟨alleged *irregularities* in the city government⟩ ⟨*irregularities* in his accounts⟩

ir·regularly \(ˈ)i, ə, (ˈ)ir, (ˈ)iə+\ *adv* **:** in an irregular manner **:** at irregular intervals **:** so as to be irregular ⟨came to school very ~⟩

irregular ode *n* **:** an ode characterized by irregularity of verse and stanzaic structure and by lack of correspondence between parts — called also *pseudo-Pindaric ode*

irregular peloria *n* **:** peloria in which symmetry is attained by increase in number of some part — compare REGULAR PELORIA

irregular variable *n* **:** a variable star whose light fluctuations are nonperiodic

1**irregulate** *adj* [ML *irregulatus*, fr. L *in-* 1in- + LL *regulatus*, past part. of *regulare* to regulate — more at REGULATE] *obs* **:** not regulated

2**irregulate** *vt*, *obs* **:** to make irregular **:** DISORDER

ir·regulated \(ˈ)i, ə, (ˈ)ir, (ˈ)iə+\ *adj* [1*in-* + *regulated*] **:** not regulated or controlled ⟨~ moods⟩

ir·relate *or* **ir·related** \ˌi, ˌir, ˌiə+\ *adj* [*irrelate* fr. 1*in-* + L *relatus*, suppletive past part. of *referre* to relate; *irrelated* fr. 1*in-* + *related* — more at RELATE] **:** not related

ir·relation \"+\ *n* [1*in-* + *relation*] **:** UNRELATEDNESS

ir·relative \(ˈ)i, ə, (ˈ)ir, (ˈ)iə+\ *adj* [1*in-* + *relative*] **:** not relative: as **a :** not related or connected **:** lacking mutual relationship ⟨remote and ~ regions —Douglas Carruthers⟩ **b :** not pertinent or relevant ⟨making ~ statements⟩ — **irrelatively** \"+\ *adv*

ir·relevance *or* **ir·relevancy** \"+\ *n*, *pl* **irrelevances** *or* **irrelevancies 1 :** the quality or state of being irrelevant ⟨the ~ of these remarks⟩ **2 :** something irrelevant ⟨a plot full of *irrelevancies* and digressions⟩

ir·relevant \"+\ *adj* [1*in-* + *relevant*] **:** not relevant **:** not applicable or pertinent **:** FOREIGN, EXTRANEOUS ⟨~ allegations⟩ ⟨~ to the matter in hand⟩

ir·relevantly \"+\ *adv* **:** in an irrelevant manner **:** so as to be irrelevant ⟨spoke idly and ~⟩

ir·relievable \ˌi, ˌir, ˌiə+\ *adj* [1*in-* + *relieve* + *-able*] **:** impossible to relieve ⟨~ suffering⟩

ir·religion \"+\ *n* [MF or L; MF, fr. L *irreligion-*, *irreligio*, fr. *in-* 1in- + *religion-*, *religio* religion — more at RELIGION] **1 :** the quality or state of being irreligious **:** lack of religion **:** IMPIETY **2** *obs* **:** a false religion **:** a perverted form of religion

ir·religionist \"+\ *n* **:** a supporter or practicer of irreligion

ir·religiosity \"+\ *n* [LL *irreligiositas*, fr. L *irreligiosus* + *-itas* -ity] **:** the quality or state of being irreligious

ir·religious \"+\ *adj* [L *irreligiosus*, fr. *in-* 1in- + *religiosus* religious — more at RELIGIOUS] **1 :** lacking recognized religious emotions, doctrines, or practices **:** UNGODLY **2 :** of or constituting irreligion **:** PROFANE ⟨~ speech⟩ **3** *obs* **:** relating to, believing in, or practicing a false religion — **irreligiously** \"+\ *adv*

ir·re·me·able \(ˈ)iˌrēmēəbəl, əˈr-, (ˈ)irˌr-, (ˈ)iəˌr-\ *adj* [L *irremeabilis*, fr. *in-* 1in- + *remeare* to go back (fr. *re-* + *meare* to go) + *-abilis* -able — more at PERMEATE] **1 :** offering no possibility of return ⟨an ~ path⟩ **2 :** unable to return to a former place or state **:** IRREVERSIBLE ⟨an ~ stream⟩ ⟨~ tissue degeneration⟩ — **ir·re·me·ably** \-blē\ *adv*

ir·remediable \ˌi, ˌir, ˌiə+\ *adj* [L *irremediabilis*, fr. *in-* 1in- + *remediabilis* remediable — more at REMEDIABLE] **:** impossible to remedy, correct, redress, alter, cure ⟨an ~ error⟩ ⟨~ defects of character⟩ — **ir·remediableness** \"+\ *n* — **ir·remediably** \"+\ *adv*

irremediless *adj* [1*in-* + *remediless*] *obs* **:** REMEDILESS

ir·remissible \ˌi, ˌir, ˌiə+\ *adj* [MF, fr. LL *irremissibilis*, fr. L *in-* 1in- + LL *remissibilis* remissible — more at REMISSIBLE] **:** not remissible: as **a :** impossible to overlook or forgive **:** UNPARDONABLE ⟨~ crimes⟩ **b :** impossible to refrain from or escape **:** OBLIGATORY ⟨~ duties⟩ ⟨an ~ responsibility⟩ — **irremissibly** \"+\ *adv*

ir·remissive \"+\ *adj* [1*in-* + *remissive*] **:** not remissive

ir·removability \"+\ *n* **:** the quality or state of being irremovable

ir·removable \"+\ *adj* [1*in-* + *removable*] **:** not removable: as **a :** impossible to remove or take away **:** not displaceable **b** (1) **:** impossible to remove or dismiss from office or position ⟨an ~ officer⟩ (2) **:** appointed for or granted for life tenure — used of an incumbent of a benefice who cannot be transferred or dismissed except for a grave crime and by canonical process or to a benefice so held **c :** IMMOVABLE, INFLEXIBLE — **irremovably** *adv*

ir·repair \"+\ *n* [1*in-* + *repair*] **:** DISREPAIR

irrepairable *adj* [1*in-* + *repairable*] **:** not capable of being repaired

ir·reparable \(ˌ)i, ə, (ˌ)ir, (ˌ)iə+\ *adj* [ME *irreperable*, fr. MF *irreparable*, fr. L *irreparabilis*, fr. *in-* 1in- + *reparabilis* reparable — more at REPARABLE] **:** not reparable **:** impossible to make good, undo, repair, or remedy **:** IRRETRIEVABLE ⟨an ~ loss⟩ ⟨~ harm⟩ ⟨~ tissue changes⟩

ir·reparableness \"+\ *n* -ES **:** the quality or state of being irreparable

ir·reparably \"+\ *adv* **:** in an irreparable manner or to an irreparable degree

ir·re·pa·tri·a·ble \ˌi(r)rəˌpā·trēəbəl ˌiərə-, -rēˌ-\ *n* -S [1*in-* + *repatriate* + *-able*] **:** a person who cannot be repatriated usu. for political reasons

ir·repealability \ˌi, ˌir, ˌiə+\ *n* **:** the quality or state of being irrepealable

ir·repealable \"+\ *adj* [1*in-* + *repealable*] **:** not capable of being repealed **:** impossible to revoke ⟨~ provisions of the statute⟩

ir·repentance \"+\ *n* [1*in-* + *repentance*] **:** IMPENITENCE

ir·replaceable \"+\ *adj* [1*in-* + *replaceable*] **:** not replaceable — **ir·replaceableness** \"+\ *n* -ES — **ir·replaceably** \"+\ *adv*

ir·repleviable \"+\ *adj* [1*in-* + *replevin* + *-able*] **:** not subject to replevin

ir·replevisable \"+\ *adj* [1*in-* + *replevisable*] **:** IRREPLEVIABLE

ir·reprehensible \(ˌ)i, ə, ˌir, ˌiə+\ *adj* [ME, fr. LL *irreprehensibilis*, fr. L *in-* 1in- + *reprehensus* (past part. of *reprehendere* to reprehend) + *-ibilis* -ible — more at REPREHEND] **:** not reprehensible **:** free from blame or reproach ⟨conduct in all respects ~⟩

ir·representable \"+\ *adj* [1*in-* + *representable*] **:** not representable

ir·repressibility \ˌi, ˌir, ˌiə+\ *n* -ES **:** the quality or state of being irrepressible ⟨his constant ~⟩

1**ir·repressible** \"+\ *adj* [1*in-* + *repress* + *-able*] **:** impossible to repress, restrain, or control ⟨~ joy⟩ ⟨~ conflict⟩ ⟨an ~ chatterbox⟩

2**irrepressible** \"\ *n* -S **:** an irrepressible person

ir·repressibleness \"+\ *n* -ES **:** IRREPRESSIBILITY

ir·repressibly \"+\ *adv* **:** in an irrepressible manner **:** so as to be irrepressible ⟨~ gay⟩

ir·repressive \"+\ *adj* [1*in-* + *repressive*] **:** IRREPRESSIBLE

ir·reproachability \"+\ *n* **:** the quality or state of being irreproachable

ir·reproachable \"+\ *adj* [1*in-* + *reproachable*] **:** not subject to or deserving of reproach **:** BLAMELESS, FAULTLESS, IMPECCABLE ⟨~ manners⟩ ⟨an ~ character⟩

ir·reproachableness \"+\ *n* -ES **:** IRREPROACHABILITY

ir·reproachably \"+\ *adv* **:** so as to be beyond reproach **:** in an irreproachable manner

ir·reproducible \(ˌ)i, ə, ˌir, ˌiə+\ *adj* [1*in-* + *reproducible*] **:** not reproducible **:** impossible to duplicate

ir·reprovable \ˌi, ˌir, ˌiə+\ *adj* [1*in-* + *reprovable*] **1 :** IRREPROACHABLE **2** *obs* **:** INDISPUTABLE

ir·rep·tion \əˈrepshən\ *n* -S [LL *irreption-*, *irreptio*, fr. L *irreptus* (past part. of *irrepere* to creep in, fr. *in-* 2in- + *repere* to creep) + *-ion-*, *-io* -ion — more at REPTILE] **:** an act or instance of entering by stealth or inadvertence ⟨the ~ of pseudo-classical plurals in technical language⟩

ir·rep·ti·tious \ˌiˌrepˌtishəs\ *adj* [L *irreptus* + E *-itious*] **:** marked by or resulting from irreption ⟨an ~ error in transliterating⟩ ⟨~ words in a text⟩

ir·resistance \ˌi, ˌir, ˌiə+\ *n* [1*in-* + *resistance*] **:** lack of resistance **:** SUBMISSIVENESS

ir·resistibility \"+\ *n* **:** the quality or state of being irresistible

1**ir·resistible** *or* **ir·resistable** \"+\ *adj* [1*in-* + *resist* + *-ible*, *-able*] **:** impossible to successfully resist **:** superior to opposition ⟨an ~ attraction⟩

2**irresistible** \"\ *n* -S **:** an irresistible person or thing

ir·resistibleness \"+\ *n* **:** IRRESISTIBILITY

ir·resistibly \"+\ *adv* **:** to an irresistible extent or degree **:** so as to be irresistible

ir·resistless \"+\ *adj* [blend of *irrestible* and *resistless*] *archaic* **:** IRRESISTIBLE

ir·resoluble \(ˌ)i, (ˌ)ir, (ˌ)iə, ə+\ *adj* [L *irresolubilis*, fr. *in-* 1in- + *resolvere* to resolve + *-bilis* -ble — more at RESOLVE] **1** *archaic* **:** incapable of being dissolved or resolved into parts **:** INSOLUBLE **2** *archaic* **:** incapable of being relieved or dispelled **3 :** incapable of being solved **:** impossible to make open, clear, or simple ⟨the question is ~ on the evidence at hand⟩

ir·resolute \(ˈ)i, ə, (ˈ)ir, (ˈ)iə+\ *adj* [1*in-* + *resolute*] **1** *obs* **:** not resolved or solved **:** UNEXPLAINED **2 a :** uncertain how to act or proceed ⟨stood ~ waiting for some inspiration⟩ **b :** lacking strength of purpose or decisiveness of character **:** weak and vacillating ⟨a kindly man but very ~⟩

ir·resolutely \"+\ *adv* **:** in an irresolute manner **:** so as to be or appear irresolute

ir·resoluteness \"+\ *n* **:** the quality or state of being irresolute

ir·resolution \(ˌ)i, ə, ˌir, ˌiə+\ *n* [prob. fr. MF, fr. *in-* 1in- + *resolution* — more at RESOLUTION] **1** *obs* **:** the quality or state of not having formed a decided opinion **:** DOUBT, UNCERTAINTY **2 :** lack of resolution **:** a fluctuation of mind (as in doubt or between hope and fear) **:** INDECISION, VACILLATION

ir·resolvable \ˌi, ˌir, ˌiə+\ *adj* [1*in-* + *resolvable*] **:** incapable of being resolved; *esp* **:** impossible to separate into component parts

ir·resolved \"+\ *adj* [1*in-* + *resolved*] **:** not resolved **:** lacking in certainty, assurance, or decision ⟨a troubled and ~ heart⟩ — **ir·resolvedly** \"+\ *adv*

ir·respective \"+\ *adj* [1*in-* + *respective*] **1** *obs* **:** lacking in respect **:** DISRESPECTFUL **2** *archaic* **:** functioning without or having no regard for persons, conditions, circumstances, or consequences ⟨oversteps in his ~ zeal every decency and every right —S.T.Coleridge⟩

ir·respectively \"+\ *adv*, *obs* **:** in an irrespective manner

irrespective of *also* **irrespectively of** *prep* **:** without respect or regard to **:** independent or regardless of ⟨values his friends *irrespective of* what he may hope to gain from them⟩ ⟨this payment is made *irrespective of* any settlement the court may order⟩

ir·respirable \"+; (ˌ)i, ə, (ˌ)ir, (ˌ)iə+\ *adj* [F, fr. LL *irrespirabilis*, fr. L *in-* 1in + *respirare* to breathe, respire + *-abilis* -able — more at RESPIRE] **:** unfit for breathing ⟨an ~ vapor⟩

ir·responsibility \ˌi, ˌir, ˌiə+\ *n* **:** the quality or state of being irresponsible

1**ir·responsible** \"+\ *adj* [1*in-* + *responsible*] **:** not responsible: as **a :** not required to answer to some higher authority **:** not liable to be called into question **:** subject to no oversight or control ⟨shall the planning be done by some ~ dictatorship or by democratic representatives whose acts are subject to discussion and criticism —M.R.Cohen⟩ ⟨the state is ~ and exempt from all ordinary controls⟩ **b :** not based on sound reasoned considerations ⟨~ optimism⟩ ⟨~ dreams⟩; *esp* **:** uttered without regard to truth, propriety, or fairness ⟨~ gossip⟩ ⟨these ~ charges⟩ **c** (1) **:** lacking a proper or adequate sense of responsibility ⟨~ jacks-in-office⟩ (2) **:** mentally inadequate to bear responsibility in an acceptable or normal manner ⟨the mother . . . was finally declared ~ and of too low intelligence to care for her large brood of children —Eda & Lawrence LeShan⟩ **d :** unprepared or unwilling to meet financial responsibilities ⟨financially ~ drivers⟩

2**irresponsible** \"\ *n* **:** one who is irresponsible

ir·responsibleness \"+\ *n* **:** IRRESPONSIBILITY

ir·responsibly \"+\ *adv* **:** so as to be or appear irresponsible **:** in an irresponsible degree

ir·responsive \"+\ *adj* [1*in-* + *responsive*] **:** not responsive: as **a :** not able, ready, or inclined to respond ⟨the patient was ~ to treatment⟩ ⟨~ to control⟩ **b :** IRRESPONSIBLE a — **irresponsiveness** \"+\ *n*

ir·restrainable \"+\ *adj* [1*in-* + *restrain* + *-able*] **:** UNRESTRAINABLE — **ir·restrainably** \"+\ *adv*

ir·resultive \"+\ *adj* [1*in-* + *result* + *-ive*] **:** lacking result **:** ABORTIVE

ir·resuscitable \"+\ *adj* [1*in-* + *resuscitable*] **:** impossible to restore to life or activity — **ir·resuscitably** \"+\ *adv*

ir·retention \"+\ *n* [1*in-* + *retention*] **:** failure of retention

ir·retentive \"+\ *adj* [1*in-* + *retentive*] **:** lacking ability to retain something ⟨a casual ~ mind⟩ — **ir·retentiveness** \"+\ *n*

ir·reticence \(ˈ)i, ə, (ˈ)ir, (ˈ)iə+\ *n* [1*in-* + *reticence*] **:** something lacking in reticence ⟨the ~*s* that are inseparable from military life⟩

ir·retraceable \ˌi, ˌir, ˌiə+\ *adj* [1*in-* + *retrace* + *-able*] **:** impossible to retrace

ir·retractile \"+\ *adj* [1*in-* + *retractile*] **:** not retractile

ir·retrievability \"+\ *n* **:** the quality or state of being irretrievable

ir·retrievable \"+\ *adj* [1*in-* + *retrieve* + *-able*] **:** not retrievable **:** impossible to recoup, repair, or overcome ⟨an ~ loss⟩ ⟨~ errors in judgment⟩ ⟨~ ruin⟩

ir·retrievableness \"+\ *n* -ES **:** IRRETRIEVABILITY

ir·retrievably \"+\ *adv* **:** so as to be irretrievable **:** to an irretrievable degree or in an irretrievable manner ⟨manuscript ~ lost⟩

ir·rev·e·lant *or* **ir·rev·a·lent** \(ˈ)i(r)ˌrevələnt, əˈr-, (ˈ)iəˌr-\ *adj* [by alter.] *substand* **:** IRRELEVANT

ir·reverence \(ˈ)i, ə, (ˈ)ir, (ˈ)iə+\ *n* -S [ME, fr. L *irreverentia*, fr. *irreverent-*, *irreverens* + *-ia* -y] **1 a :** the quality or state of being irreverent **:** failure to offer due respect to that which is generally reverenced **b :** an irreverent act or utterance ⟨these pert ~*s*⟩ **2 :** condition of being without reverence **:** dishonored or neglected state **:** DISREGARD ⟨treating their elders with complete ~⟩

ir·reverency \"+\ *n* -ES **:** IRREVERENCE 1

ir·reverend \"+\ *adj* [1*in-* + *reverend*] **1 :** not reverend **:** not worthy of reverence **2** *archaic* **:** IRREVERENT — **ir·reverendly** \"+\ *adv*

ir·reverent \"+\ *adj* [L *irreverent-*, *irreverens*, fr. *in-* 1in- + *reverent-*, *reverens* reverent — more at REVERENT] **:** not reverent: as **a :** failing in proper reverence to something entitled to veneration or respect ⟨~ scholars mocking sacred things⟩ **b :** characterized by a lightly pert or exuberant quality or manner ⟨a certain ~ gaiety and ease of manner⟩ — **ir·reverently** \"+\ *adv*

ir·reverential \(ˌ)i, ə, ˌir, ˌiə+\ *adj* [1*in-* + *reverential*] **:** lacking in due respect or reverence **:** IRREVERENT — **ir·reverentially** \"+\ *adv*

ir·reverentialism \"+\ *n* -S **:** the quality or state of being irreverent

ir·reversibility \ˌi, ˌir, ˌiə+\ *n* **:** the quality or state of being irreversible

ir·reversible \"+\ *adj* [1*in-* + *reverse* + *-ible*] **:** incapable of being reversed: as **a :** impossible to recall, repeal, or annul ⟨an ~ decree⟩ **b :** impossible to turn about, back, or upside down ⟨an ~ cover⟩ ⟨~ cushions⟩ **c :** impossible to make run or take place backward ⟨an ~ engine⟩ ⟨~ chemical syntheses⟩ **d** *of a colloid* **:** incapable of undergoing transformation from sol to gel or vice versa **e :** unsymmetrical with respect to constituent elements or terms ⟨an ~ relation⟩ **f** *of a pathological process* **:** of such severity that recovery is impossible ⟨~ shock⟩ ⟨~ anoxic damage to the brain⟩ — **ir·reversibly** \"+\ *adv*

ir·revocability \(ˌ)i, ə, ˌir, ˌiə+\ *n* **:** the quality or state of being irrevocable

ir·revocable \(ˌ)i, ə, (ˌ)ir, (ˌ)iə+\ *adj* [ME, fr. L *irrevocabilis*, fr. *in-* 1in- + *revocabilis* revocable — more at REVOCABLE] **:** incapable of being recalled or revoked **:** past recall **:** UNALTERABLE ⟨an ~ promise⟩ ⟨firm and ~ is my doom —Shak.⟩

ir·revocableness \"+\ *n* **:** IRREVOCABILITY

ir·revocably \"+\ *adv* **:** so as to be irrevocable **:** beyond any possibility of change ⟨~ determined⟩

ir·revoluble \"+\ *adj* [1*in-* + *revoluble*] *archaic* **:** having no finite period of revolution

irridenta *var of* IRREDENTA

ir·ri·ga·ble \ˈirəgəbəl, -rēg-\ *also* **ir·ri·gat·able** \ˈirəˌgād·-əbəl, -ātə-, ˌ==ˈ===\ *adj* [*irrigate* + *-able*] **:** possible to irrigate **:** susceptible of or suitable for irrigation ⟨~ land⟩ — **ir·ri·ga·bly** \ˈirəgəblē, -rēg-, -bli\ *adv*

ir·ri·gate \ˈirəˌgāt, *usu* -ād·+V\ *vb* -ED/-ING/-S [L *irrigatus*, past part. of *irrigare*, fr. *in-* 2in- + *rigare* to water — more at RAIN] *vt* **1 :** WET, MOISTEN ⟨secretions that ~ mucous surfaces⟩: as **a :** to supply (as land or crops) with water by artificial means (as by diverting streams, digging canals, flooding, or spraying) **b :** to apply a continuous stream of liquid to (a part of the body) for a therapeutic purpose **2 :** to refresh or make fertile as if by watering ~ *vi* **1 :** to practice irrigation (as of land) **2** *slang* **:** to drink intoxicating liquor **:** IMBIBE

ir·ri·ga·tion \ˌirəˈgāshən\ *n* -S *often attrib* [L *irrigation-*, *irrigatio*, fr. *irrigatus* + *-ion-*, *-io* -ion] **1 :** the action or process of irrigating: as **a :** the artificial watering of land (as by canals, ditches, pipes, or flooding) to supply moisture for plant growth ⟨~ ditches⟩ ⟨growing crops by ~⟩; *also* **:** a single watering by such means ⟨the berries will need another ~ if it doesn't rain soon⟩ **b :** application of a continuous stream of liquid to a part of the body for a therapeutic purpose ⟨wound ~⟩ **2 :** a refreshing or making fertile as if by watering

ir·ri·ga·tion·al \ˌirəˌgāshənᵊl, -shnəl\ *adj* **:** of or relating to irrigation

irrigation efficiency *n* **:** the ratio between irrigation water actually utilized by growing crops and water diverted from a source (as a stream) in order to supply such irrigation water

ir·ri·ga·tion·ist \ˌirəˈgāsh(ə)nəst\ *n* -S **:** a user or advocate of irrigation esp. in farming

ir·ri·ga·tive \ˈirəˌgād·iv\ *adj* **:** IRRIGATIONAL

ir·ri·ga·tor \-ād·ə(r), -ātə-\ *n* -S **:** one that irrigates: as **a :** an agriculturist who employs irrigation in the growing of crops **b :** a device, apparatus, or system used to irrigate something (as a wound or a crop) **c :** a worker who supervises agricultural irrigation or irrigating equipment

ir·rig·u·ous \əˈrigyəwəs\ *adj* [L *irriguus*, fr. *irrigare* to irrigate — more at IRRIGATE] **1** *archaic* **:** IRRIGATED, MOISTENED; *esp* **:** well-watered **2 :** serving to irrigate or water ⟨slow ~ streams⟩

ir·ri·sion \əˈrizhən\ *n* -S [L *irrision-*, *irrisio*, fr. *irrisus* (past part. of *irridēre* to laugh at, fr. *in-* 2in- + *ridēre* to laugh) + *-ion-*, *-io* -ion — more at RIDICULOUS] **:** a laughing at a person or thing **:** DERISION

1**ir·ri·sor** \əˈrīzər\ [NL, fr. L, mocker, scoffer, fr. *irrisus* + *-or*] *syn of* PHOENICULUS

2**irrisor** \"\ *n* -S **:** a bird of the genus *Phoeniculus* **:** WOOD HOOPOE

ir·ri·sor·i·dae \ˌirəˈsȯrəˌdē, -ˈzȯ-\ [NL, fr. *Irrisor*, type genus + *-idae*] *syn of* PHOENICULIDAE

ir·riso·ry \-īsərē, -īzə-,-izə-\ *adj* [LL *irrisorius*, fr. L *irrisus* (past part. of *irridēre* to laugh at) + *-orius* -ory — more at IRRISION] **:** given to derision **:** DERISIVE

ir·ri·ta·bil·i·ty \ˌirəd·əˈbiləd·ē, -rətəˈ-, -lətē, -i\ *n* -ES [L *irritabilitas*, fr. *irritabilis* + *-itas* -ity] **:** the quality or state of being irritable: as **a :** quick excitability to annoyance, impatience, or anger **:** PETULANCE, FRETFULNESS ⟨~ of temper⟩ ⟨showing increasing ~ as he waited⟩ **b :** abnormal excitability of an organ or part of the body (as the stomach or bladder) **:** heightened responsiveness **c :** the property of protoplasm and of living organisms that permits them to react to environmental changes (as by specific orientation, change of shape, or production or cessation of movement)

ir·ri·ta·ble \'irəd·əbəl, -rətə-\ *adj, sometimes* -ER/-EST [L *irritabilis*, fr. *irritare* to irritate + *-abilis* -able — more at IRRITATE] **:** capable of being irritated: as **a :** likely to become impatient, angry, or disturbed **:** easily exasperated ⟨an ~ disposition⟩ ⟨such ~ neurotic people⟩; *broadly* **:** easily excitable **b :** excessively or unduly sensitive to irritants or stimuli **:** exhibiting abnormal irritability ⟨an ~ colon⟩ **c** *of protoplasm or a living organism* **:** responsive to stimuli

syn FRACTIOUS, PEEVISH, SNAPPISH, WASPISH, PETULANT, PETTISH, HUFFY, HUFFISH, FRETFUL, QUERULOUS: IRRITABLE implies ready, impatient excitability whereby one is angered and exasperated easily ⟨a hot day and the clerk in the store was *irritable* . . . had not slept much the night before and he had a headache —Lyle Saxon⟩ FRACTIOUS may suggest a wilful or truculent unruliness or perverse crossness ⟨those who are spoilt and *fractious*, who must have everything their own way —F.A.Swinnerton⟩ ⟨a wary, querulous, grumbling, vain, testy, self-righteous, honorable man, a defiant and *fractious* servant and a high-handed and mistrustful master —Arthur Schlesinger b.1917⟩ PEEVISH may suggest childish irritability about petty matters ⟨*peevish* because he called her and she did not come, and he threw his bowl of tea on the ground like a willful child —Pearl Buck⟩ ⟨*peevish*, and wrathful, often insolent, and quarrelsome —Charles Kingsley⟩ SNAPPISH may apply to an irritability manifesting itself in sharp, tart, sarcastic objections and rejoinders ⟨a little *snappish* at reflecting how many miles he had to post —Samuel Butler †1902⟩ WASPISH may connote testy, resentful, stinging irascibility ⟨a little *waspish* woman who would have been ahead of me snapped out at a man who seemed to be with her —C.S.Lewis⟩ PETULANT may suggest sulky and capricious dissatisfaction and complaint as though resolved to be displeased ⟨in his youth the spoiled child of Boston, in middle life he was *petulant* and irritable, inclined to sulk when his will was crossed —V.L. Parrington⟩ PETTISH may apply to childish, sulky ill humor of or as if of one slighted ⟨she heard Amy's voice in *pettish* exclamation: "Oh, get out, you!" —Arnold Bennett⟩ HUFFY or HUFFISH may suggest a tending to take undue offense or to have one's arrogant pride hurt and to parade one's blustering irritation ⟨rather *huffy*, and somewhat on the high-and-mighty order with him —Harriet B. Stowe⟩ FRETFUL suggests ill-humored continuing irritability and complaining or whining peevishness ⟨his voice was peevish, almost whining, and there were certain overtones in it which recalled the *fretful* complaining voice —W.H.Wright⟩ QUERULOUS stresses the idea of discontented whining complaining, often childishly futile, resentful, and arising from determined inclination to be displeased ⟨the man himself grew old and *querulous* and hysterical with failure and repeated disappointment and chronic poverty —Aldous Huxley⟩

irritable heart *n* **:** CARDIAC NEUROSIS

ir·ri·ta·ble·ness *n* -ES **:** IRRITABILITY

ir·ri·ta·bly \-blē,-bli\ *adv* **:** in an irritable manner **:** with irritability

ir·ri·ta·ment \'irəd·əmənt, ə'rid· -\ *n* -S [F, fr. L *irritamentum*, fr. *irritare* to irritate, provoke + *-mentum* -ment] *archaic* **:** INCITEMENT, IRRITANT

¹ir·ri·tan·cy \'irəd·ənsē, -rətən-, -si *also* -ət°n-\ *n* -ES [¹*irritant* + *-cy*] *Roman, civil, & Scots law* **:** a making or the quality or state of being made null and void **:** INVALIDATION; *also* **:** IRRITANT CLAUSE

²irritancy \"\ *n* -ES [²*irritant* + *-cy*] **:** the quality or state of being irritating

¹ir·ri·tant \-ənt,-°nt\ *adj* [MF, fr. LL *irritant-, irritans*, pres. part. of *irritare* to invalidate, fr. L *irritus* invalid, fr. *in-* ¹in- + *-ritus* (fr. *ratus* valid, fr. past part. of *reri* to reckon, calculate) — more at REASON] **:** making null and void — compare IRRITANT CLAUSE

²irritant \"\ *adj* [F, fr. MF, fr. L *irritant-, irritans*, pres. part. of *irritare* to irritate, provoke — more at IRRITATE] **:** IRRITATING; *specif* **:** tending to produce irritation or inflammation

³irritant \"\ *n* -S **:** something that irritates or excites; *specif* **:** an agent by which irritation is produced ⟨a chemical ~⟩

irritant clause *n* [¹*irritant*] *Scots law* **:** a clause in an instrument providing that if certain specified events shall take place the instrument shall be void

¹ir·ri·tate \'irə,tāt, *usu* -ād·+V\ *vb* -ED/-ING/-S [L *irritatus*, past part. of *irritare*, fr. ²in- + *-ritare* (perh. akin to L *oriri* to rise) — more at RISE] *vt* **1** *obs* **:** to increase the action of **:** heighten excitement in **:** AGGRAVATE **2 :** to excite impatience, anger, or displeasure in **:** PROVOKE, EXASPERATE, ANNOY ⟨*irritated* by the child's insolence⟩ **3 :** to cause (an organ or tissue) to be irritable **:** produce irritation in ⟨harsh soaps may ~ the skin⟩ ⟨avoid *irritating* the sensitive laryngeal reflexes —*Anesthesia Digest*⟩ **4 :** to produce excitation in (as a nerve) **:** STIMULATE **:** cause (as a muscle) to contract ~ *vi* **:** to cause or induce displeasure or irritation ⟨it's the petty things of life that ~ most⟩ ⟨a soothing lotion for burns that is guaranteed not to ~⟩

syn EXASPERATE, NETTLE, ROIL, RILE, PEEVE, AGGRAVATE, PROVOKE: IRRITATE means to arouse angry annoyance or great displeasure evoking feelings ranging from impatience to rage ⟨it *irritated* him that she peered so into everything that was his, searching him out —D.H.Lawrence⟩ ⟨a Mexican carpenter will *irritate* newcomers beyond endurance by taking a three-hour siesta —Green Peyton⟩ EXASPERATE suggests galling vexation or angry annoyance ⟨her unexplained departure had *exasperated* him —Edith Wharton⟩ NETTLE usu. indicates a stinging pique, sometimes a rankling irritation ⟨a touch of light scorn in her tone *nettled* me —W.J.Locke⟩ ROIL and its variant RILE suggest inducing an angry or resentful state of agitated disturbance ⟨her manner of ignoring him. That *roiled* him inexpressibly —C.S.Forester⟩ ⟨with raucous taunting and ribald remarks to *rile* up the proprietor —W.A.White⟩ PEEVE applies to arousing fretful irritation, sometimes petty or querulous ⟨when she ventured to criticize it, even mildly, he was *peeved* —Louis Auchincloss⟩ AGGRAVATE may apply to repeated action or condition that intensifies anger or irritation ⟨he did not sweat and pray over each card as she must, but he did keep an eye out for reneging and demanded a cut now and then just to *aggravate* her —J.F.Powers⟩ PROVOKE may suggest irritation or anger that excites to action ⟨don't think I am trying to *provoke* you or to make fun of what you have done —Ann Bridge⟩ ⟨a Tory resident who *provoked* local animosities and was charged with high treason —*Amer. Guide Series: Conn.*⟩

²irritate \"\ *vt* [LL *irritatus*, past part. of *irritare* to invalidate — more at IRRITANT] **:** to make null and void **:** DEFEAT

irritated *adj* [fr. past part. of ¹*irritate*] **:** subjected to irritation: as **a :** roused to anger **:** ANNOYED ⟨that tired ~ father⟩ **b :** roughened, reddened, or inflamed by some irritating agent ⟨an ~ skin⟩ ⟨hiding her ~ eyes behind dark glasses⟩ — **ir·ri·tat·ed·ly** \'==,===, ,=='===\ *adv*

irritating *adj* **:** causing displeasure or annoyance **:** PROVOKING — **ir·ri·tat·ing·ly** \'==,===, ,=='===\ *adv*

ir·ri·ta·tion \,irə'tāshən\ *n* -S [MF, fr. L *irritation-, irritatio*, fr. *irritatus* (past part. of *irritare* to irritate, provoke) + *-ion-, -io* -ion — more at IRRITATE] **1 :** an act of irritating or a state of being irritated: as **a :** excitement to activity **:** STIMULATION **b :** excitement of impatience, anger, or passion **:** ANNOYANCE **c :** IRRITABILITY b **2 :** EXCITATION 3; *esp* **:** the act of exciting a muscle to contraction by artificial stimulation

ir·ri·ta·tive \'irə,tād·|iv, -āt|, |ēv *also* |əv\ *adj* [¹*irritate* + *-ive*] **1 :** serving to excite **:** IRRITATING ⟨an ~ agent⟩ **2 :** accompanied with or produced by increased action or irritation ⟨an ~ cough⟩

ir·ri·ta·tor \-ād·ə(r), -ātə-\ *n* -S **:** one that irritates

ir·ri·to·motility \,irə,tō+\ *n* [*irritation* + *-o-* + *motility*] **:** response of plant tissues to external stimuli by means of movements or curvatures

irrogate *vt* -ED/-ING/-S [L *irrogatus*, past part. of *irrogare* to propose against, impose, fr. *in-* ²in- + *rogare* to ask, request — more at RIGHT] *obs Scot* **:** to impose (a penalty) legally — **irrogation** *n* -S *obs*

¹irrorate *vt* -ED/-ING/-S [L *irroratus*, past part. of *irrorare*, fr. *in-* ²in- + *rorare* to moisten, shed moisture, fr. *ror-, ros* dew — more at RORIC] *obs* **:** BEDEW, MOISTEN — **irroration** *n* -S *obs*

²ir·ro·rate \'irə,rāt, ə'rōrət\ *also* **ir·ro·rat·ed** \'irə,rād·əd\ *adj* [*irrorate* fr. L *irroratus*, past part.; *irrorated* fr. L *irroratus* + E *-ed*] **:** covered with little spots **:** SPECKLED ⟨a tawny butterfly with black-*irrorate* wings⟩

ir·rotational \,i, ,ir, ,ia+\ *adj* [¹*in-* + *rotational*] **:** not involving rotation **:** free from vortices ⟨~ flow⟩ ⟨an ~ electrostatic field⟩ — **ir·rotationally** \"+\ *adv*

ir·rubrical \(')i, ə, (')ir, (')ia+\ *adj* [¹*in-* + *rubrical*] **:** not rubrical

ir·ru·ma·tion \,irü'māshən\ *n* -S [L *irrumation-, irrumatio*, fr. *irrumatus* (past part. of *irrumare* to give suck, extend the penis for fellatio, fr. *in-* ²in- + *-rumare*, fr. *ruma, rumis* breast, teat) + *-ion-, -io* -ion] **:** FELLATIO

ir·rupt \ə'rəpt\ *vb* -ED/-ING/-S [L *irruptus*, past part. of *irrumpere*, lit., to break in, fr. ¹*in-* in + *rumpere* to break — more at RUPTURE] *vi* **1 a :** to enter forceably or suddenly **:** appear without warning **:** INTRUDE ⟨the sea had once ~*ed* into the cavern⟩ ⟨the merchants constituted a very tight caste, rarely ~*ing* into social groups either above or below —G.W. Johnson⟩ **b** *of an animal population* **:** to undergo a sudden upsurge in numbers esp. when natural ecological balances and checks are disturbed **2 :** ERUPT 1c ⟨the crowd ~*ed* in a fervor of patriotism —*Time*⟩ ~ *vt* **:** INTRUDE 3 — opposed to *erupt*

ir·rup·ti·ble \(')i(r)¦rəptəbəl, ə'r-, (')iə¦r-\ *adj* **:** UNBREAKABLE

ir·rup·tion \ə'rəpshən\ *n* -S [L *irruption-, irruptio*, fr. *irruptus* + *-ion-, -io* -ion] **:** an act or instance of irrupting: as **a :** a sudden violent or forceable entry **:** a rushing or bursting in ⟨the current ~ of bad manners into everyday life⟩ ⟨an ~ of water through a break in the dike⟩ **b :** a sudden and violent invasion ⟨the ~*s* of the Goths into Italy⟩ **c :** ERUPTION 1 **d :** a sudden sharp increase in the relative numbers of a natural population usu. associated with favorable alteration of the environment

ir·rup·tive \-ptiv\ *adj* **:** irrupting or tending to irrupt ⟨~ forces⟩: as **a :** rushing or bursting in or upon **:** entering forceably or violently ⟨the ~ roar of new engines —J.G. Cozzens⟩ **b** *of an igneous rock* **:** INTRUSIVE **c :** marked by irruption ⟨the ~ stage of rabbit increase⟩ **:** undergoing irruption ⟨the ~ deer herds of the state⟩ — compare CYCLIC — **ir·rup·tive·ly** \-tə̇vlē\ *adv*

IRU *abbr* **1** international radium unit **2** international rat unit

irul \'ē,rül\ *n* -S [Tamil *irul*] **:** ACLE 1,2

iru·la \'irələ\ *n, pl* **irulas** *or* **irula** *usu cap* **:** a primitive Veddoid people inhabiting the Deccan plateau of India and being one of the pre-Dravidian peoples of India

irus·ka \ə'rüskə\ *n* -S [Pawnee, lit., the fire is in me] **:** a dance of a fire-handling sacred male society of the Pawnee Indians that is the precursor of the grass dance

ir·ving·ite \'ərviŋ,īt\ *n* -S *usu cap* [Edward *Irving* †1834 Scot. clergyman + E *-ite*] **:** a member of the Catholic Apostolic Church — often taken to be offensive

¹is [ME (3d pers. sing. pres. indic. and — northern dial. — 1st & 2d pers. sing. pres. indic. and — northern dial. — 1st & 2d & 3d pers. pl. pres. indic. of *been* — suppletive infinitive — to be), fr. OE (3d pers. sing. pres. indic. of *bēon* — suppletive infinitive — to be); akin to OHG *ist* (3d pers. sing. pres. indic. of *sīn* to be), ON *es, er* (3d pers. sing. pres. indic. of *vesa, vera* — suppletive infinitive — to be), Goth *ist* (3d pers. sing. pres. indic. of *wisan* — suppletive infinitive — to be), L *est* (3d pers. sing. pres. indic. of *esse* to be), Gk *esti* (3d pers. sing. pres. indic. of *einai* to be), Skt *asti* is, he is, Hitt *eszi*] *pres 3d sing of* BE, *dial pres 1st & 2d sing of* BE, *substand pres pl of* BE

²is \'iz\ *n* -ES **:** that which is; *specif* **:** that which is factual, empirical, actually the case, or spatiotemporal — contrasted with *ought*

is- *or* **iso-** *comb form* [LL, fr. Gk, fr. *isos* equal] **1 :** equal **:** homogeneous **:** uniform ⟨*is*energic⟩ ⟨*is*acoustic⟩ ⟨*iso*cephaly⟩ ⟨*iso*type⟩ **2** *usu iso-* **a :** isomer of a (specified) compound ⟨*iso*cyanuric acid $C_3(NH)_3O_3$⟩ ⟨*iso*vanillin $CH_3OC_6H_4(OH)$-CHO⟩ **b** (1) **:** of, relating to, or having a branched chain of carbon atoms ⟨*iso*hydrocarbons⟩ ⟨*iso*synthesis⟩ — compare NORMAL 10e (2) **:** having a straight chain of carbon atoms to which one branching methyl group is attached in the position next to one end ⟨*iso*hexyl $(CH_3)_2CHCH_2CH_2CH_2$—⟩ **3** *usu iso-* **:** for or from different individuals of the same species ⟨*iso*antigen⟩ ⟨*iso*antibody⟩

is *abbr* island; isle

IS *abbr* **1** interservice **2** interstate

i's *or* **is** *pl of* I

is·a·be·li·ta \,izəbə'lēd·ə\ *or* **is·a·bel·ite** \-'be,līt\ *n* -S [AmerSp *isabelita*, fr. Sp *Isabelita* (feminine nickname), dim. of *Isabel* (feminine name)] **:** any of various fishes belonging to a genus *Angelichthys* of the family Chaetodontidae; *esp* **:** an angelfish (*A. ciliaris*) colored orange red, sky blue, and golden that is common in the West Indies

is·a·bel·la \,izə'belə\ *also* **is·a·bel** \'izə,bel\ *n* -S *often cap* [MF *isabelle*, fr. *Isabelle* (feminine name)] **:** a moderate yellowish brown to light olive brown that is lighter and stronger than clay drab or medal bronze

isabella grape \;==;==-\ *also* **isabella** *n* -S *usu cap I* [prob. after *Isabella* Gibbs, 19th cent. Am. woman who introduced it into Brooklyn from North Carolina] **:** FOX GRAPE c

isabella moth *n, usu cap I* [NL *isabella* (specific epithet of *Isia isabella*), perh. fr. E *isabella*] **:** a common stout-bodied snuff-colored American arctiid moth (*Isia isabella*) having the hind wings often tinged with orange red

is·a·bel·line \,izə¦belən, -,līn, -,lēn\ *adj* [*isabella* + *-ine*] **:** of the color Isabella

isabelline bear *n* **:** RED BEAR

is·abnormal \¦īs *also* ¦īz+\ *or* **iso·abnormal** \¦ī(,)sō *also* -)zō+\ *n* [*is-* + *abnormal*, adj.] **:** an imaginary line or a line on a chart that connects or marks places on the surface of the earth having equal differences in a given time from the normal temperature of these places or that indicates differences between the calculated and actual temperatures of the different parallels of latitude

is·acoustic \"+\ *adj* [*is-* + *acoustic*] **:** of or relating to equal intensity of sound

is·adelphous \"+\ *adj* [prob. fr. (assumed) NL *isadelphus*, fr. NL *is-* + *-adelphus* -adelphous] **:** having the separate bundles of stamens in a diadelphous flower equal in number

isa·go·ge \'īsə,gōjē, ,=='==\ *n* -S [L, fr. Gk *eisagōgē*, fr. *eisagein* to introduce, fr. *eis* into + *agein* to lead; akin to Gk *en* in — more at IN, AGENT] **:** a scholarly introduction to a branch of study or research — **isa·gog·ic** \¦==¦gäjik\ *or* **isa·gog·i·cal** \-jə̇kəl\ *adj*

isa·gog·ics \,=='gäjiks\ *n pl but usu sing in constr, also* **isa·gog·ic** \-ik\ [*isagoge* + *-ics*] **:** introductory studies; *esp* **:** a branch of theology that is preliminary to actual exegesis and deals with the literary and external history of the Bible

isa·ian \ī'zāən, *chiefly Brit* -zīən\ *or* **isa·ian·ic** \¦=(,)=¦anik\ *adj, usu cap* [*Isaian* fr. *Isaiah*, 8th cent. B.C. major Hebrew prophet + E *-an*, adj. suffix; *isaianic* fr. *Isaiah* + E *-an*, adj. suffix + *-ic*] **:** of, relating to, or having the characteristics of Isaiah or the book of Isaiah ⟨the *Isaianic* character of this prophesy —Robert Gordis⟩ ⟨the somber and threatening, the almost *Isaian*, utterance —Edmund Wilson⟩

is·allobar \(')īs *also* (')īz+\ *n* [ISV *is-* + *all-* + *-bar* (as in *isobar*)] **:** an imaginary line or a line on a chart connecting the places of equal change of atmospheric pressure within a specified time — **is·al·lo·bar·ic** \(¦)ī¦salə¦barik, (¦)ī¦za-, -bar-\ *adj*

is·al·lo·therm \ī'salə,thərm *also* ī'za-\ *n* [ISV *is-* + *all-* + *-therm*] **:** an imaginary line or a line on a chart connecting the places of equal change of temperature within a specified time

is·an·drous \(')ī¦sandrəs *also* (')ī¦za-\ *adj* [*is-* + *-androus*] **:** having the stamens similar and equal in number to the petals

is·an·e·mone \ī'sanə,mōn, ,īsə'nemə(,)nē *also* ī'za- *or* ,īzə-\ *n* [ISV *is-* + *-anemone* (irreg. fr. Gk *anemos* wind) — more at ANIMATE] **:** an isogram of wind speed

is·anom·al \,īsə'näməl *also* ,īzə-\ *n* -S [ISV *is-* + *-anomal* (fr. LL *anomalus* dissimilar) — more at ANOMALOUS] **:** an imaginary line or a line on a chart connecting places that have the same anomalies esp. of temperature or pressure

is·anomalous \¦īs *also* ¦īz+\ *adj* [*isanomal* + *-ous*] **:** relating to an isabnormal or an isanomal

isa·no oil \ə'sä(,)nō-\ *n* [*isano* prob. native name (of the tree *Ongokea klaineana*) in the Congo region of West Africa] **:** an unsaturated fatty oil that is obtained from the kernel of the nuts of a West African tree (*Ongokea klaineana*) of the family Oleoceae, that polymerizes readily, and that is used in coatings

is·an·thous \(')ī¦san(t)thəs *also* -¦za-\ *adj* [NL *isanthus*, fr. *is-* + *-anthus* -anthous] **:** having the flowers regular

is·apostolic \(¦)īs *also* (¦)īz+\ *adj* [LGk *isapostolos* isapostolic (fr. Gk *is-* + *apostolos* apostle) + E *-ic* — more at APOSTLE] **:** equal to or contemporaneous with the apostles — used esp. of bishops consecrated by the apostles

isard *var of* IZARD

isar·ia \ī'sa(a)rēə\ *n, cap* [NL, fr. *is-* + *-aria*] **:** a form genus of imperfect fungi (family Stilbellaceae) that are parasitic on insects and have the conidia borne terminally on slender hyphae that cover the coremiums

isa·rithm \'īsə,rithəm, -th- *also* 'īzə-\ *n* -S [ISV *is-* + *-arithm* (fr. Gk *arithmos* number); orig. formed as G *isarithmus* — more at ARITHM-] **:** a line drawn on a map or chart to connect points having equal numerical values (as of temperature, elevation, or density of population)

isa·tin \'īsətən, -əd·ən\ *n* -S [ISV *isat-* (fr. NL *Isatis*) + *-in*] **:** an orange red crystalline compound $C_8H_5NO_2$ obtained by oxidation of indigo or oxindole or by various syntheses and used as an intermediate for indigoid dyes

isa·tin·ic acid \¦īsə¦tinik-\ *or* **isat·ic acid** \(')ī¦sad·ik-\ *n* [*isatinic* ISV *isatin* + *-ic; isatic* ISV *isatin* + *-ic*] **:** a white solid amino acid $NH_2C_6H_4COCOOH$ obtained by hydrolysis of isatin

-isation — see -IZATION

isa·tis \'īsəd·ə̇s\ *n, cap* [NL, fr. L, woad, fr. Gk — more at WOAD] **:** a large genus of herbs (family Cruciferae) having entire leaves, small yellow flowers, and compressed oblong or orbicular pods — see WOAD

isat·o·gen \ī'sad·əjə̇n, -,jen\ *n* -S [ISV *isatin* + *-o-* + *-gen*] **:** a parent compound $C_8H_5NO_2$ isomeric with isatin and known in the form of various colored derivatives that are made by treating an *ortho*-nitro-phenyl-acetylene with sulfuric acid

isa·to·ic anhydride \¦īsə¦tōik-\ *n* [*isatoic* ISV *isat*in + *-o-* + *-ic*] **:** a high-melting dicarboxylic acid anhydride $C_8H_5NO_3$ made by oxidation of isatin or by reaction of anthranilic acid with phosgene

¹isau·ri·an \ī'sȯrēən\ *n* -S *cap* [*Isauria*, ancient district in south central Asia Minor + E *-an*, n. suffix] **:** a native or inhabitant of Isauria

²isaurian \(')=¦===\ *adj, usu cap* [*Isauria* + E *-an*, adj. suffix] **1 :** of, relating to, or characteristic of Isauria **2 :** of, relating to, or characteristic of the people of Isauria

is·auxesis \¦īs *also* ¦īz+\ *n* [NL, fr. *is-* + *auxesis*] **:** ISOGONY — **is·auxetic** \"+\ *adj*

isa·wa \ə'säwə\ *or* **isa·wi·ya** \,ēsə'wē(y)ə\ *or* **ais·sa·wa** \ī'säwə\ *n pl, usu cap* [Ar *'Isawīyah*, an order of dervishes] **:** members of a Muslim religious brotherhood founded in Morocco about 1500

is·ba *also* **iz·ba** \əz'bä\ *n* -S [Russ *izba*, fr. Old Russian *istŭba* bathing room, prob. of Gmc origin; akin to OHG *stuba* heated room — more at STOVE] **:** a Russian log hut

ISC *abbr* interstate commerce

is·car·i·ot·ic \(¦)iskarē¦äd·ik, ə¦sk-\ *or* **is·car·i·ot·i·cal** \-d·ə̇kəl\ *adj* [Judas *Iscariot*, apostle that betrayed Jesus + E *-ic* or *-ical*] **:** of, relating to, or having the characteristics of Judas Iscariot; *specif* **:** TREACHEROUS

is·che·mia *also* **is·chae·mia** \ə'skēmēə\ *n* -S [NL *ischaemia*, fr. *ischaemus* styptic, stopping blood (fr. Gk *ischaimos*, fr. *ischein* to check, restrain + *haima* blood) + *-ia*; akin to Gk *echein* to have, hold — more at SCHEME, HEM-] **:** localized tissue anemia due to obstruction of the inflow of arterial blood (as by the narrowing of arteries by spasm or disease) ⟨cerebral ~⟩ ⟨renal ~⟩ ⟨myocardial ~⟩ — **is·che·mic** *also* **is·chae·mic** \(')i¦skēmik, ə's-\ *adj*

ischemic contracture *n* **:** shortening and degeneration of a muscle resulting from deficient blood supply

ischi- *or* **ischio-** *comb form* [L *ischi-*, fr. Gk, fr. *ischion* hip joint] **1 :** ischium ⟨*ischi*algia⟩ ⟨*ischio*podite⟩ **2 :** ischial and ⟨*ischio*caudal⟩ **3 :** resembling a hip joint ⟨*ischio*cerite⟩

is·chi·ad·ic \¦iskē¦adik\ *adj* [L *ischiadicus* of pain in the hip, fr. Gk *ischiadikos*, fr. *ischiad-, ischias* sciatica (fr. *ischion* hip joint) + *-ikos* -ic] **:** ISCHIAL

is·chi·al \'iskēəl\ *adj* [prob. fr. (assumed) NL *ischialis*, fr. L *ischi-* + *-alis* -al] **:** of, relating to, or situated near the ischium

is·chi·at·ic \¦iskē¦ad·ik, -atik\ *adj* [LL *ischiaticus* of pain in the hip, alter. (influenced by adjectives ending in *-aticus* such as LL *dramaticus* dramatic) of L *ischiadicus*] **:** ISCHIAL

is·chio·capsular \¦iskē(,)ō+\ *adj* [*ischi-* + *capsular*] **:** of, relating to, or being an accessory ligament of the hip joint passing from the ischium below the acetabulum to blend with the capsular ligament

is·chio·cav·er·no·sus \¦iskē(,)ō,kavə(r)'nōsəs\ *n* -ES [NL, fr. *ischi-* + *-cavernosus* belonging to the corpus cavernosum, fr. L *cavernosus* cavernous] **:** a muscle covering the crus of the penis or clitoris

is·chi·oc·er·ite \,iskē'äsə,rīt\ *n* [*ischi-* + Gk *keras* horn, antenna + E *-ite* — more at HORN] **:** a joint of the antenna of a crustacean

is·chi·op·o·dite \-'äpə,dīt\ *n* [ISV *ischi-* + *-podite*] **:** the third joint from the base of certain limbs of crustaceans (as the thoracic legs of decapods)

is·chio·rectal \¦iskē(,)ō+\ *adj* **:** of, relating to, or adjacent to both ischium and rectum

is·chi·um \'iskēəm\ *n, pl* **is·chia** \-kēə\ [L, hip joint, fr. Gk *ischion*; perh. akin to Skt *sakthi* thigh] **1 :** the dorsal and posterior of the three principal bones composing either half of the pelvis consisting in man of a thick portion, a large rough eminence on which the body rests when sitting, and a forwardly directed ramus which joins that of the pubis **2 :** ISCHIOPODITE

is·chy·o·dus \ə'skīədəs\ *n, cap* [NL, fr. *ischy-* (fr. Gk *ischys* strength) + *-odus*; akin to Gk *echein* to have, hold — more at SCHEME] **:** a genus of Jurassic and Cretaceous chimaeroid fishes of Europe and New Zealand

is·chy·ro·my·i·dae \,iskə̇rō'mīə,dē\ *n pl, cap* [NL, fr. *Ischyromys*, type genus (fr. Gk *ischyros* strong + *mys* mouse) + *-idae*; akin to Gk *echein* to have, hold — more at MOUSE] **:** a family of primitive extinct sciuromorph rodents widely distributed in the northern hemisphere from the Lower Eocene to the Upper Oligocene, distantly related to the mountain beaver, and distinguished by low-crowned generalized cheek teeth

ise *or* **i'se** \(¦)īz\ *usu cap* [contr. of E dial. *I is* I am, fr. E *I* + E dial. *is* — more at IS] *dial* **:** I am

-ise \,īz\ *vb suffix* **:** -IZE — see -IZE in Explan Notes

is·en·trope \'īs°n,trōp, 'īz°n-\ *also* **is·en·trop·ic** \¦==-¦träpik\ *n* -S [*isentrope* ISV prob. back-formation fr. *isentropic*, adj.; *isentropic*, n. fr. *isentropic*, adj.] **:** an isentropic line or surface (as on a meteorological chart or engineering diagram)

is·en·trop·ic \¦==¦träpik, ¦ī,sen·-, ¦ī,zen·-\ *adj* [ISV *is-* + *entropy* + *-ic*] **:** having or indicating constant entropy ⟨the ~ chart, a map of the air unaffected by surface heating and cooling, aids in identifying the air from one map to the next —T.M.Longstreth⟩ **:** taking place without change of entropy ⟨if steam could be expanded in a turbine with no friction or other losses, expansion would be ~ —A.G.Christie⟩ — **is·en·trop·i·cal·ly** \-pə̇k(ə)lē\ *adv*

is·ep·ipte·sis \¦ī,sepə(p)'tēsə̇s, ¦ī,ze-\ *n, pl* **isepipte·ses** \-ē,sēz\ [NL, fr. *is-* + *epi-* + Gk *ptēsis* flight, fr. *petesthai* to fly — more at FEATHER] **:** a line on a map or chart connecting localities reached at one date by different individuals of a species of migratory bird

ises *pl of* IS

is·ethi·o·nate \,ī,se'thīə,nāt, ,ī,ze-\ *n* [ISV *isethion-* (fr. *isethionic*) + *-ate*] **:** a salt or ester of isethionic acid

is·ethionic acid \(¦)īs, (¦)īz+ . . . -\ *n* [*isethionic* ISV *is-* + *ethionic*] **:** a crystalline sulfonic acid $HOC_2H_4SO_3H$ obtained by action of sulfur trioxide on alcohol or ether and used in making surface-active agents

is·fa·han \'isfə,hän, -han, ,=='=\ *adj, usu cap* [fr. *Isfahan*, city in west central Iran] **:** of or from the city of Isfahan, Iran **:** of the kind or style prevalent in Isfahan

ISG *abbr, often not cap* imperial standard gallon

ish \'ish\ *n* -ES [ME (Sc) *ische*, fr. ME *ischen, isshen* to come out, go out, fr. MF *issir* — more at ISSUE] **1** *Scots law* **:** right of exit **:** ISSUE, EXIT ⟨~ and entry⟩ **2** *Scots law* **:** time of expiry (as of a lease) **:** EXPIRY, TERMINATION

-ish \ish, ēsh\ *adj suffix* [ME, fr. OE *-isc;* akin to OHG *-isc, -isk* -ish, ON *-skr,* Goth *-isks* -ish, Gk *-iskos,* dim. n. suffix] **1 :** of or belonging to — chiefly in adjectives indicating nationality or ethnic group ‹Finn*ish*› ‹Gaul*ish*› ‹Turk*ish*› **2 a :** characteristic or typical of ‹boy*ish*› ‹London*ish*› : having the undesirable qualities of ‹amateur*ish*› ‹mul*ish*› **b :** inclined or liable to ‹book*ish*› ‹qualm*ish*› ‹mop*ish*› **c** (1) **:** having a touch or trace of ‹summer*ish*› **:** somewhat ‹purpl*ish*› ‹lat*ish*› (2) **:** having the approximate age of ‹forty*ish*› (3) **:** being or occurring at the approximate time of — esp. in words formed from numerals indicating an hour of the day or night ‹five*ish*› ‹eight*ish*›

ish·er·wood system \ˈishə(r),wu̇d-\ *n, usu cap I* [after Benjamin F. *Isherwood* †1915 Am. naval engineer] **:** a technique of ship construction employing large transverse frames widely spaced and light longitudinal members closely spaced — called also *longitudinal framing*

ishi·ha·ra test \ˌishēˈhärə-\ *n, usu cap I* [after Shinobu *Ishihara* †1963 Jap. ophthalmologist who devised it] **:** a widely used test for the detection of color blindness

ishi·ka·wa·ite \ˌishēˈkäwə,īt\ *n* -s [*Ishikawa* district, north central Honshu, Japan, its locality + E *-ite*] **:** a rare mineral (U, Fe, Y, etc.)(Nb, Ta)O_4 consisting of an oxide of uranium, iron, niobium, tantalum, yttrium, and the rare-earth metals

ish·kash·mi \ishˈkäsh(,)mē\ *n, pl* **ishkashmi** *or* **ishkashmis** *usu cap* **1 :** an Iranian people of the highlands of the southwestern Pamir mountains **2 :** a member of the Ishkashmi people

ish·kyl·dite *or* **ish·kil·dite** \ˈishkəl,dīt\ *n* -s [Russ *ishkil'dit,* fr. *Ishkyldino,* Middle Volga district, U.S.S.R., its locality + Russ *-it* -ite] **:** a mineral $Mg_{15}Si_{11}O_{27}(OH)_{20}$ consisting of a basic silicate of magnesium

ish·ma·el \ˈishmēəl, -(,)mā-\ *n* -s *usu cap* [after *Ishmael* (AV), *Ismael* (DV), son of Abraham by his concubine Hagar; fr. the statement made concerning him in Gen 16:12 (AV) that "his hand will be against every man, and every man's hand against him"] **:** one at odds with or as if with society **:** OUTCAST, OUTLAW, OUTSIDER ‹I am an *Ishmael* by instinct —Samuel Butler †1902› ‹the murder novel, . . . long the *Ishmael* of fiction, shows every sign of rejoining the main fold of literature —Anthony Boucher›

ish·ma·el·ite \-ēə,līt, -āə-\ *n* -s *usu cap* **1 :** a descendant of Ishmael **2 :** ISHMAEL ‹individual animals which as *Ishmaelites* lived a solitary life and ranged alone —P.A.Rollins›

ish·ma·el·it·ish \ˈ=(,)==,līd·ish, ,=(,)==ˈ==\ *adj, usu cap* **:** of, relating to, or having the characteristics of an Ishmaelite ‹the wretched, fearful, *Ishmaelitish* condition of every man against his fellowmen —Hastings Lyon›

isi·ac \ˈisē,ak, ˈizē-,ˈisē-\ *or* **isi·a·cal** \əˈsīəkəl, (ˈ)īˈsī-\ *adj, usu cap* [*isiac* fr. L *isiacus,* fr. Gk *isiakos,* fr. *Isis,* orig. Egyptian goddess of motherhood and the family whose cult spread throughout the Mediterranean world in Hellenistic times; *isiacal* fr. L *isiacus* + E *-al*] **:** of or relating to Isis or the cult of Isis

isi·dae \ˈisə,dē, ˈizə-\ *n pl, cap* [NL, fr. *Isis,* type genus (fr. Gk, orig. Egyptian goddess of motherhood and the family) + *-idae*] **:** a family of gorgonians having an axis composed of alternating horny and calcareous joints

isid·i·if·er·ous \ī¦sidēˈif(ə)rəs\ *or* **isid·i·of·er·ous** \-ēˈäf-\ *adj* [*isidiiferous* fr. *isidium* + *-i-* + *-ferous; isidioferous* fr. *isidium* + *-o-* + *-ferous*] **:** bearing isidia

isid·i·oid \īˈsidē,ȯid\ *adj* [*isidium* + *-oid*] **:** of, relating to, or resembling an isidium

isid·i·ose \-ē,ōs\ *adj* [*isidium* + *-ose*] **:** of or relating to isidia

isid·i·um \īˈsidēəm\ *n, pl* **isid·ia** \-ēə\ [NL, fr. *Isidium,* supposed genus of lichens, irreg. fr. *Isis* genus of gorgonians + Gk *eidos* form; fr. the resemblance of lichens that have isidia to gorgonians — more at IDOL] **:** an outgrowth from the surface of the thallus in certain lichens that resembles a soredium

is·i·do·ri·an *or* **is·i·do·re·an** \¦izə¦dōrēən\ *adj, usu cap* [*Isidore* of Seville †A.D.636 Span. prelate and scholar + E *-an,* adj. suffix] **:** of, relating to, or characteristic of Isidore of Seville

isi·nai *also* **isi·nay** \¦ēsə¦nī\ *n, pl* **isinai** *or* **isinais** *usu cap* **1 a :** a Christianized people of Nueva Vizcaya, Luzon, Philippines **b :** a member of such people **2 :** the Austronesian language of the Isinai people

isin·glass \ˈīzᵊn,glas, ˈīziŋ,g-, -zēŋ-, -laa(ə)s, -lais, -làs\ *n* -ES [prob. by folk etymology (influence of E *glass*) fr. obs. D *huizenblas,* fr. MD *huusblase,* fr. *huus* sturgeon + *blase* bladder; akin to OHG *hūso* beluga and to OHG *blāsan* to blow — more at HUSO, BLAST] **1 :** a semitransparent whitish substance consisting of a very pure form of gelatin orig. prepared from the air bladders of sturgeons from the rivers of western Russia but now largely made from those of sturgeons of other areas or of various other fishes and used chiefly as a clarifying agent and in making jellies and glue — called also *fish gelatin, fish glue* **2 :** mica esp. when in thin transparent sheets **3 :** a colloidal extractive substance (as agar) from various algae

is·lam \isˈläm, izˈläm, -lam, -laa(ə)m, -làm, ˈ=,= *also* ˈizləm *or* ˈisləm\ *n* -s *cap* [Ar *islām* submission (to the will of God), fr. *aslama* to surrender] **1 :** the religious faith of Muslims who profess belief in Allah as the sole deity and in Muhammad as the prophet of Allah ‹*Islam* . . . is the religion of judgment —J.E.Turner› ‹*Islam* was a fellowship —J.C.Archer› **2 a :** the cultural system or civilization erected in history upon the foundations of Islamic religious faith ‹for nine centuries the Turks were the principal champions of *Islam* —Emil Lengyel› ‹the grafting of the spirit of modern nationalism upon the ancient trunk of *Islam* —H.L.Hoskins› **b :** the national political units of the modern world that share the Muslim religion ‹*Islam* is the principal problem of three hundred million people who might be . . . our friends —Mortimer Graves›

is·lam·ic \(ˈ)isˈlämik, (ˈ)iz¦l-, -lam-,-làm-, -mēk\ *adj, usu cap* [F *islamique,* fr. *islam* (fr. Ar *islām*) + *-ique* -ic] **:** of, relating to, or characteristic of Islam ‹*Islamic* traditions› ‹an *Islamic* republic›

is·lam·ics \=ˈ=miks, -mēks\ *n pl but sing in constr, usu cap* **:** the academic study of Islam

is·lam·ism \=ˈ=,mizəm, ˈizlə,mi-, ˈislə,-\ *n* -s *usu cap* **:** the faith, doctrine, or cause of Islam

is·lam·ist \-məst\ *n* -s *usu cap* **1 :** an orthodox Muslim **2 :** a student or scholar of Islamics

is·lam·ite \-,mīt, *usu* -īd·+V\ *n* -s *usu cap* [F, fr. *islam* + *-ite*] **:** MUSLIM

is·lam·it·ic \¦izlə¦mid·ik, ¦isl-, -it|, |ēk\ *adj, usu cap* **:** of, relating to, or characteristic of Islamism **:** MUSLIM

is·lam·iza·tion \,izləməˈzāshən, ,islə-, -,mīˈz-, i,slàməˈ-, i,slaməˈ-, i,slàməˈ-\ *n* -s *usu cap* **:** the act or process of islamizing or being islamized

is·lam·ize \ˈizlə,mīz, ˈislə-, iˈslä,m-, iˈsla,-, iˈslà,-\ *vt* -ED/-ING/-S *often cap* **1 :** to make Islamic in quality, traits, or way of thinking or acting; *esp* **:** to convert to Islamism ‹*Islamizing* the religion of these semibarbarous hordes —P.K. Hitti› **2 :** to bring under the control of Islam

¹is·land \ˈīlənd\ *n* -s *often attrib* [alter. (influenced by E ¹*isle*) of earlier *iland,* fr. ME, fr. OE *īgland;* akin to OFris *eiland* island, ON *eyland;* all fr. a prehistoric NGmc-WGmc compound whose first constituent is represented by OE *īg, īeg* island and whose second constituent is represented by OE *land;* OE *īg, īeg* island akin to OE *ēa* river, OHG *ouwa* land by water, meadow, *aha* river, ON *ey* island, *ā* river, Goth *ahwa* river, L *aqua* water — more at LAND] **1 a :** a tract of land surrounded by water and smaller than a continent **b** *dial* **:** a tract of land cut off on two or more sides by water **:** PENINSULA **2 :** something resembling an island by its isolated, surrounded, or sequestered position: as **a** (1) **:** an elevated piece of land surrounded by swamp or alluvial land ‹thousands were marooned on ~*s* of high ground —*Time*› (2) **:** a piece of woodland surrounded by flat open country **b :** ISLET 2 c — compare ISLAND OF REIL **c** (1) **:** a small isolated space between lines in a fingerprint (2) **:** a lanceolate interruption in a line on the palm held to be a sign in palmistry ‹when the line has an ~ in the center . . . it foretells some trouble —Alice D. Jennings› **d** (1) **:** a showcase, counter, or platform standing apart and approachable on all sides ‹only fast turnover items can be placed on ~*s* —*Printers' Ink*› ‹double built-in cooking top in an ~ arrangement —*Amer. Builder Catalog Directory*› (2) *or* **island platform :** a platform at a railway station that has tracks on each side of it **e** (1) **:** SAFETY ISLAND (2) **:** SAFETY ZONE **f :** a superstructure (as the forecastle, bridge, or poop) on the deck of an aircraft carrier or other ship **3 :** a group or area isolated from its environment by specific characteristics or conditions: as **a :** an isolated ethnological group ‹the Hungarian colony . . . is a picturesque racial ~ —*Amer. Guide Series: Mich.*› ‹there are many cultural ~*s* in the United States —David Riesman› **b :** SPEECH ISLAND

²island \"\ *vt* -ED/-ING/-S **1 :** to make into or as if into an island ‹a clear brown stream . . . ~*ing* a purple and white rock with an amber pool —John Ruskin› **2 :** to dot with or as if with islands ‹a fair expanse of level pasture ~*ed* with groves —William Wordsworth› ‹groups of people ~*ed* upon the dark grass —F.D.Ommanney› **3 :** to place on or as if on an island **:** ISOLATE ‹the great mystery in whose midst we are ~*ed* —Arthur Symons›

island arc *n* **:** an arcuate chain of islands

island carib *n, usu cap I&C* **1 :** an Indian of the Lesser Antilles **2 :** the Arawakan language of the Island Caribs and their modern descendants in British Honduras, Guatemala, and Honduras

island chain *n* **:** a line of islands

island continent *n* **:** an island as large or nearly as large as a continent ‹the *island continent* of Greenland›

is·land·er \ˈīləndə(r)\ *n* -s **:** a native or inhabitant of an island

island–hop \ˈ==,=\ *vi* **:** to go from island to island ‹our *island-hopping,* creek-exploring houseboat life —A.W.Baum›; *esp* **:** to seize island after island in a military offensive ‹instead of *island-hopping,* he suggested that we should employ . . . massive strokes —Joseph Driscoll›

is·land·ish \ˈīləndish\ *adj* **:** of, relating to, or having the characteristics of an island

is·land·less \-n(d)ləs\ *adj* **:** having no islands **:** lacking islands ‹a stretch of ~ ocean fully 500 miles across —F.C.Lincoln›

is·land·man \-n(d)mən\ *n, pl* **islandmen** *now chiefly Irish* **:** ISLANDER ‹comparing them with the *islandmen* who walked up and down as cool and fresh-looking as the sea gulls —J.M. Synge›

island of langerhans *usu cap L* [after Paul *Langerhans* †1888 — more at ISLET OF LANGERHANS] **:** ISLET OF LANGERHANS

island of reil \-ˈrī(ə)l\ *usu cap R* [after Johann C. *Reil* †1813 Ger. physician born in Holland] **:** the central lobe of the cerebral hemisphere that is situated deeply between the lips of the lateral fissure

island of resistance : a strongpoint in a defensive position that is organized for perimeter military defense and normally is capable of mutual support with other similar positions

is·land·ol·o·gy \,īlənˈdäləjē\ *n* -ES **:** a study of islands

island universe *n* **:** a galaxy other than the Milky Way system but not necessarily smaller or less important

is·lay \(ˈ)iz¦lī\ *n* -s [AmerSp] **:** a California wild plum (*Prunus ilicifolia*)

¹isle \ˈīl, *esp before pause or consonant* ˈīəl\ *n* -s [ME *isle, ile,* fr. OF, fr. L *insula,* perh. fr. *in* + *-sula* (akin to L *salum* sea, *sal* salt) — more at IN, SALT] **:** ISLAND; *esp* **:** a small island ‹Australian seas are rich in ~*s* —C.L.Barrett› ‹this 54-acre ~ is an exclusive residential district —*Amer. Guide Series: Minn.*›

²isle \"\ *vt* -ED/-ING/-S **1 :** to make an isle of **2 :** to place on or as if on an isle ‹the faun is *isled* within the spotted wood —Randall Jarrell›

isle·less \ˈī(ə)lləs\ *adj* **:** having no islands

isle·man \ˈī(ə)lmən\ *n, pl* **islemen :** ISLANDER

isle of wight disease \-ˈwīt-\ *usu cap I&W* [*Isle of Wight,* island in the English channel constituting a county of England] **:** a serious European disease of adult honeybees caused by a minute mite (*Acarapis woodi*)

isles·man \ˈī(ə)lzmən\ *n, pl* **islesmen** [*isles* (pl. of ¹*isle*) + *man*] **:** a native or inhabitant of a group of islands (as the Hebrides or Shetland isles)

is·let \ˈīlət, *usu* -əd·+V\ *n* -s [MF *islette,* fr. *isle* + *-ette*] **1 :** a small island **:** ISLE **2 :** something resembling a small island esp. in its isolation or elevation: **a :** ISLAND 2a **b** *chiefly Brit* **:** ISLAND 2c **c :** a small isolated mass of one type of tissue within a different type; *specif* **:** ISLET OF LANGERHANS

is·le·ta \izˈlād·ə\ *n, pl* **isleta** *or* **isletas** *usu cap* [*Isleta,* Indian village and pueblo in central New Mexico occupied by the Isleta people, fr. Sp *isleta* islet, dim. of *isla* island, fr. L *insula*] **1 a :** a Tanoan people of New Mexico **b :** a member of such people **2 :** the language of the Isleta people

is·let·ed \ˈīləd·əd\ *adj* **:** set like an islet or furnished with islets

islet of lang·er·hans \-ˈläŋə(r),hän(t)s, -hänz\ *usu cap L* [after Paul *Langerhans* †1888 Ger. physician] **:** any of the groups of small slightly granular endocrine cells that form anastomosing trabeculae among the tubules and alveoli of the pancreas and secrete the hormone insulin

is·lot \ˈīlət\ *n* -s [F *îlot,* fr. MF *islot,* dim. of *isle*] *archaic* **:** ISLET

ism \ˈizəm\ *n* -s [*-ism*] **:** a distinctive doctrine, cause, system, or theory — often used disparagingly ‹against any ~ that isn't Americanism —J.F.O'Neill› ‹futurism and cubism and all the other ~*s* —J.L.Lowes›

-ism \,izəm\ *n suffix* -s [ME *-isme,* fr. MF & L; MF *-isme,* partly fr. L *-isma* (fr. Gk), & partly fr. L *-ismus,* fr. Gk *-ismos*] **1 a :** act, practice, or process — esp. in nouns corresponding to verbs in *-ize* ‹critic*ism*› ‹hypnot*ism*› ‹plagiar*ism*› **b :** manner of action or behavior characteristic of a (specified) person or thing ‹animal*ism*› ‹Micawber*ism*› **2 a :** state, condition, or property ‹barbarian*ism*› ‹polymorph*ism*› **b :** abnormal state or condition resulting from excess of a (specified) thing ‹alcohol*ism*› ‹morphin*ism*› **c :** abnormal state or condition characterized by resemblance to a (specified) person or thing ‹mongol*ism*› **3 a :** doctrine, theory, or cult ‹Buddh*ism*› ‹Calvin*ism*› ‹Platon*ism*› ‹salvation*ism*› ‹vegetarian*ism*› **b :** adherence to a system or a class of principles ‹neutral*ism*› ‹real*ism*› ‹social*ism*› ‹stoic*ism*› **4 :** characteristic or peculiar feature or trait ‹colloquial*ism*› ‹Latin*ism*› ‹poetic*ism*›

is·ma·el·ism \ˈizmēə,lizəm, -z(,)māə,-\ *n* -s *usu cap* [*Ismael* (DV), *Ishmael* (AV), son of Abraham by his concubine Hagar + E *-ism;* so called fr. a belief that the Arabs are descendants of Ishmael] **:** ISLAMISM

is·ma·ili *or* **is·ma·ʽi·li** \,izmäˈē(,)lē, ,ism-, -məˈē-\ *also* **is·ma·ил·ian** \-ˈlēən\ *n* -s *usu cap* [*Ismaili, Ismaʽili* fr. Ar *Ismaʽīlīy,* fr. *Ismaʽīl* †A.D.760 son of the sixth imam Jafar al-Sadiq and in the opinion of the Ismailis his true successor; *Ismailian* fr. Ar *Ismaʽīlīy* + E *-an*] **:** one of a Shiʽa sect composed of those who recognize the Aga Khan as imam

is·ma·il·ism \-ˈē,lizəm\ *n* -s *usu cap* [*Ismaʽīl* †A.D.760 + E *-ism*] **:** the Ismaili movement or its doctrines

is·ma·il·ite \-ˈē,līt\ *n* -s *usu cap* [*Ismaʽīl* †A.D.760 + E *-ite*] **:** ISMAILI

is·ma·ili·tic \¦izmēə¦lid·ik\ *adj, usu cap* **:** of or relating to the Ismailis

is·me·ne \izˈmē(,)nē\ *n* [NL, fr. L *Ismene,* daughter of Oedipus, fr. Gk *Ismēnē*] **1** *cap, in some classifications* **:** a genus of So. American bulbous perennial herbs that have incurved filaments projecting beyond the margin of the floral cup and are usu. included in the genus *Hemerocallis* **2** -s **:** PERUVIAN DAFFODIL

is·nad \iˈsnäd, izˈn-\ *n* -s [Ar *isnād*] **:** the chain of authorities attesting to the historical authenticity of a particular hadith

is·neg \ˈiz,neg, =ˈ=\ *n, pl* **isneg** *or* **isnegs** *usu cap* [Apayao] **:** APAYAO

is·ness \ˈiznəs\ *n* -ES [¹*is* + *-ness*] **1 a :** the fact that a thing is ‹at the very outset there is no ~ to life —*Yale Rev.*› **b :** the quality or state of elemental or factual existence **2 :** the state of things as they are ‹the economics of the soldier who accepts a rough equation between ~ and oughtness —H.J.Laski› — contrasted with *oughtness*

is·n't \ˈizᵊn(t), *in rapid speech* ˈid|\ [by contr.] **:** is not

iso \ˈī(,)sō\ *adj* [*is-*] **:** ISOMERIC; *esp* **:** having a branched chain ‹~ acids with branching methyl groups› — compare IS- 2

iso- *in pronunciations below,* ¦=(,)= = ¦ī(,)sō *also* ¦ī(,)zō, ¦== = ¦īsō, ¦īsə *also* ¦īzō, ¦īzə\ — see IS-

iso·abnormal *var of* ISABNORMAL

iso·agglutination \"+\ *n* [ISV *is-* + *agglutination*] **:** agglutination of an agglutinogen of one individual by the serum of another of the same species — **iso·agglutinative** \"+\ *adj*

iso·agglutinin \"+\ *n* [ISV *is-* + *agglutinin*] **:** an agglutinin specific for the cells of another individual of the same species

iso·agglutinogen \"+\ *n* [*isoagglutinin* + *-o-* + *-gen*] **:** a substance capable of provoking formation of or reacting with an isoagglutinin

iso·allele \"+\ *n* **:** a member of a pair of alleles each of which produces such a like result as to be indistinguishable by ordinary means

iso·alloxazine \"+\ *n* **:** a yellow solid $C_{10}H_6N_4O_2$ that differs from alloxazine only in the position of one hydrogen atom attached to nitrogen and that is the parent compound of riboflavin and other flavins

iso·amyl \"+\ *n* [ISV *is-* + *amyl*] **1 :** ISOPENTYL **2 :** AMYL 2a

isoamyl acetate *n* **:** the acetic ester $CH_3COOC_5H_{11}$ of amyl alcohol from fusel oil — called also *amyl acetate, banana oil, pear oil;* not used systematically

isoamyl alcohol *n* **1 :** ISOPENTYL ALCOHOL **2 :** AMYL ALCOHOL 2a

iso·amylene \¦=(,)= *at* ISO-+\ *n* [ISV *is-* + *amylene*] **:** a branched-chain amylene; *esp* **:** AMYLENE a

isoamyl nitrite *n* **:** AMYL NITRITE

isoamyl salicylate *n* **:** AMYL SALICYLATE

iso·antibody \¦=(,)= *at* ISO- +\ *n* **:** an antibody against an antigen sometimes present in members of a species that is produced by a member of the species lacking that antigen when exposed to it ‹production of an anti-Rh ~ by an Rh-negative person› — compare RH FACTOR

iso·antigen \"+\ *n* [ISV *is-* + *antigen*] **:** an antigen capable of inducing the production of an isoantibody; *specif* **:** any of several closely similar antigens only one of which may occur in an individual and each of which is capable of inducing the formation of antibodies to any other antigen of its group — **iso·antigenic** \"+\ *adj* — **iso·antigenicity** \"+\ *n*

iso·bar \ˈ== *at* ISO- + ,bär\ *n* [ISV *is-* + *-bar* (fr. Gk *baros* weight) — more at GRIEVE] **1 :** an imaginary line or a line on a map or chart connecting or marking places on the surface of the earth where the height of the barometer reduced to sea level is the same either at a given time or for a certain period **2 a** *also* **iso·bare** \-,ba(a)(ə)r\ **:** one of two or more atoms having practically the same atomic weights but different atomic numbers and hence different chemical properties ‹carbon 14 and ordinary nitrogen 14 are ~*s*› **b :** one of two or more nuclides having the same mass numbers but different atomic numbers — **iso·bar·ism** \-,bä,rizəm, -,ba(a)r,-\ *n* -s

iso·barbaloin \¦=(,)= *at* ISO- +\ *n* **:** a crystalline compound $C_{20}H_{18}O_9$ isomeric with barbaloin and isolated with it from aloin

iso·bar·ic \¦== *at* ISO- + ¦barik\ *adj* [ISV *isobar* + *-ic*] **1 :** showing equal pressure: as **a :** showing points in the atmosphere having equal barometric pressure ‹~ lines› **b :** taking place without change of pressure ‹~ expansion› ‹~ process› **2 :** of, relating to, or having the relationship of an isobar

iso·barometric \¦=(,)=+\ *adj* [ISV *is-* + *barometric*] **:** ISOBARIC

iso·base \ˈ==,bās\ *n* [ISV *is-* + *base*] **:** an imaginary line or a line on a map or chart passing through all points that have been elevated to the same extent since some specified time (as the Glacial epoch)

¹iso·bath \-,bath\ *n* [ISV *is-* + *-bath* (fr. Gk *bathos* depth); akin to Gk *bathys* deep — more at BATHY-] **1 :** an imaginary line or a line on a map or chart that connects all points having the same depth below a water surface (as of an ocean, sea, or lake) **2 :** a line similar to an isobath indicating depth below the earth's surface of an aquifer or geological horizon

²isobath \"\ *or* **iso·bath·ic** \¦==¦bathik\ *adj* [*isobath* ISV *is-* + *-bath* (fr. Gk *bathos* depth); *isobathic* fr. ¹*isobath* + *-ic*] **:** having constant depth

iso·bathy·therm \,==ˈbathə,thərm\ *n* [*is-* + *bathy-* + *-therm*] **:** a line connecting points on the earth's surface where a certain temperature is found at the same depth — **iso·bathy·ther·mal** \¦==¦==¦thərməl\ *or* **iso·bathy·ther·mic** \-mik\ *adj*

iso·bilateral \¦=(,)= *at* ISO- +\ *adj* **:** bilateral with the corresponding opposite parts alike

iso·borneol \¦==+\ *n* [ISV *is-* + *borneol*] **:** a volatile crystalline alcohol $C_{10}H_{17}OH$ stereoisomeric with borneol, synthetically obtainable from alpha-pinene or camphene, and yielding camphor on oxidation

iso·bornyl \"+\ *n* [ISV *is-* + *bornyl*] **:** the univalent radical $C_{10}H_{17}$ derived from isoborneol

iso·bront \ˈ==,bränt\ *also* **iso·bron·ton** \-äntᵊn, ,==ˈ==, ,==ˈbrän,tän\ *n* [*isobront* ISV *is-* + *-bront* (fr. Gk *brontē* thunder); *isobronton* fr. *is-* + *-bronton* (fr. Gk *brontē* thunder) — more at BRONT-] **:** a line on a chart marking the simultaneous development of a thunderstorm at different points on the earth's surface

iso·bryales \¦==+\ *n pl, cap* [NL, fr. *is-* + *Bryales*] **:** a large widely distributed order of Musci comprising mosses that have branched creeping gametophores on which the leaves are so twisted as to appear to be in two rows and usu. pleurocarpous sporophytes with erect capsule and double peristome

iso·butane \"+\ *n* [ISV *is-* + *butane*] **:** a gaseous branched-chain hydrocarbon $(CH_3)_3CH$ usu. accompanying normal butane and used chiefly as an alkylating agent and as a fuel gas; 2-methyl-propane

iso·butene \"+\ *n* [*is-* + *butene*] **:** ISOBUTYLENE — not used systematically

iso·butyl \"+\ *n* [ISV *is-* + *butyl*] **:** the primary alkyl radical $(CH_3)_2CHCH_2$— derived from isobutane

isobutyl alcohol *n* **:** the branched-chain primary butyl alcohol $(CH_3)_2CH_2CH_2OH$ synthetically made usu. from carbon monoxide and hydrogen; 2-methyl-1-propanol

iso·bu·tyl·carbinol \¦==,==+\ *n* [*isobutyl* + *carbinol*] **:** ISOPENTYL ALCOHOL

iso·butylene \¦== *at* ISO- +\ *n* [ISV *is-* + *butylene*] **:** the branched-chain gaseous butylene $(CH_3)_2C{=}CH_2$ obtainable from isobutane by dehydrogenation and used chiefly in making butyl rubber and gasoline components and in alkylating aromatic hydrocarbons — called also *2-methylpropene*

isobutyr- *or* **isobutyro-** *comb form* [ISV, fr. *isobutyric* (in *isobutyric acid*)] **:** related to isobutyric acid ‹*isobutyr*amide› ‹*isobutyro*nitrile›

iso·butyrate \¦== *at* ISO- +\ *n* -s [*isobutyr-* + *-ate*] **:** a salt or ester of isobutyric acid

isobutyric acid \"+ . . . -\ *n* [*isobutyric* ISV *is-* + *butyric*] **:** a colorless liquid acid $(CH_3)_2CHCOOH$ made by the oxidation of isobutyl alcohol and used chiefly in making esters for use as flavoring materials

iso·butyryl \"+\ *n* [ISV *isobutyr-* + *-yl*] **:** the radical $(CH_3)_2CHCO$— of isobutyric acid

iso·caloric \"+\ *adj* **:** having similar caloric value ‹~ diets› — **iso·calorically** \"+\ *adv*

isocandle diagram \ˈ==+, . . . -\ *n* [*isocandle* fr. *is-* + *candle*] **:** a system of isocandle lines for various candlepowers of a source of light

isocandle line *n* **:** a line showing in suitable coordinates all directions in space in which a given source of light has a specified candlepower

iso·car·pic \¦==¦kärpik\ *also* **iso·car·pous** \-pəs\ *adj* [*isocarpic* fr. *is-* + *carpic; isocarpous* fr. *is-* + *-carpous*] **:** having carpels equaling the perianth divisions in number — compare ANISOCARPIC

iso·cellular \¦==+\ *adj* **:** consisting of similar cells

iso·center \ˈ==+,-\ *n* [*is-* + *center*] **:** the point on an aerial photograph intersected by the bisector of the angle between the plumb line and the perpendicular to the photograph

iso·ce·phal·ic \¦=(,)=səˈfalik\ *also* **iso·ceph·a·lous** \¦==ˈsefələs\ *adj* [*is-* + *-cephalic* or *-cephalous*] **:** having the heads of the figures in a composition brought to the same level — used esp. of a bas-relief — **iso·ceph·a·ly** \¦==ˈsefəlē\ *n* -ES

iso·ce·rau·nic \¦=(,)=səˈrȯnik\ *or* **iso·ke·rau·nic** \-kə-\ *adj* [*isoceraunic* fr. *is-* + *ceraun-* + *-ic; isokeraunic* fr. *is-* + *keraun-* (fr. Gk *keraunos* thunderbolt) + *-ic* — more at CERAUN-] **:** showing or having equal frequency or severity or simultaneous occurrence of thunderstorms ‹~ maps›

iso·cer·cal \ˌ⁼⁼ˈsərkəl\ *adj* [*is-* + *-cercal*] **1 :** having symmetrical upper and lower lobes and a gradually tapering vertebral column — used of the tail fin of a fish **2 :** having or relating to an isocercal tail fin — **iso·cer·cy** \ˈ⁼⁼ˌsərsē, -rkē\ *n* -ES

iso·cheim \ˈ⁼⁼ *at* ISO- + ˌkīm\ *n* -S [prob. modif. (influenced by Gk *cheimōn* winter) of F *isochimène*, fr. *is-* + *-chimène* (fr. Gk *cheimainein* to be stormy, be winter); akin to Gk *cheimōn* winter — more at HIBERNATE] **:** a line joining points on the earth's surface having the same mean winter temperature — compare ISOTHERE

iso·chela \ˌ⁼⁼+\ *n* [NL, fr. *is-* + *chela*] **:** a chelate spicule having both ends alike

iso·chor \ˈ⁼⁼ˌkȯ(ə)r\ *also* **iso·chore** \-ˌkō(ə)r\ *n* -S [ISV *is-* + *-chor* (fr. Gk *chōros* place, clear space) — more at CHOR-] **:** a line representing the variation of pressure with temperature when the volume of the substance operated on is constant — **iso·chor·ic** \ˌ⁼⁼ˈkȯrik, -ˈkōr-\ *adj*

iso·chro·mat \ˌ⁼⁼ˈkrōˌmat, ˌ⁼⁼ˈkrō,m-\ *n* -S [*is-* + *-chromat* (fr. Gk *chrōmat-*, *chrōma* color) — more at CHROMATIC] **:** a graph showing intensity as a function of voltage for a given wavelength of the output from an X-ray source

iso·chromatic \ˌ⁼⁼+\ *adj* [ISV *is-* + *chromatic*] **1 a :** of or corresponding to constant color ⟨the ~ variation of refractive index with density for a given wavelength⟩ **b :** connecting points of the same color **c :** coincident with a line of equal stress in a photoelastic stress pattern **2 :** ORTHOCHROMATIC **3** *of cells or tissues* **:** having the same color; *specif* **:** staining similarly with like dyes

iso·chromosome \ˌ⁼⁼+\ *n* **:** a chromosome with identical arms believed to be derived from a telocentric chromosome by fusion of two daughter chromosomes

isoch·ro·nal \(ˈ)īˈsäkrənᵊl\ *adj* [Gk *isochronos* isochronous + E *-al*] **1 :** uniform in time **:** having equal duration **:** recurring at regular intervals **:** ISOCHRONOUS **2** [*isochrone* + *-al*] **:** ISOCHRONIC

iso·chrone \ˈ⁼⁼ *at* ISO- + ˌkrōn\ *n* -S [ISV *is-* + *-chrone* (fr. Gk *chronos* time)] **:** a line on a map or chart connecting points at which an event occurs simultaneously or which represent the same time or time difference (as a line showing the distances that may be reached from a central point in a city in the same length of time)

iso·chron·ic \ˌ⁼⁼ˈkränik, -rōn-\ *adj* [*isochrone* + *-ic*] **1 :** having isochrones ⟨~ map⟩ **2** [ISV *isochron-* (fr. Gk *isochronos* isochronous) + *-ic*] **:** exhibiting isochronism ⟨a muscle and its nerve must be ~ —Alexis Carrel⟩

isochro·nism \īˈsäkrəˌnizəm; ˌīsəˈkrō,n- *also* ˌīzəˈkrō,n-\ *n* -S [F *isochronisme*, fr. Gk *isochronos* isochronous + F *-isme* -ism] **1 a :** the condition or property of having a uniform period of vibration — used of a pendulum or a watch balance **b :** uniformity of rate of operation — used of a timepiece **2 a :** equal duration of units or measures in prosody **b :** emphasis on stable rhythmic units in poetry **3** [*is-* + *chron-* + *-ism*] **:** the condition of having identical chronaxies — used of excitable structures (as motor neurones and muscle fibers)

isoch·ro·nous \(ˈ)īˈsäkrənəs\ *adj* [Gk *isochronos* isochronous (fr. *is-* + *chronos* time) + E *-ous*] **:** equal in duration, interval, or metrical length **:** ISOCHRONAL ⟨the oscillations of a spiral hairspring were ~ —S.F.Mason⟩ ⟨free oscillations of an elastic system were ~ —Adrien Jaquerod⟩ — **isoch·ro·nous·ly** *adv*

isochronous governor *n* **:** a governor that maintains the same speed in the mechanism controlled regardless of the load

iso·citric acid \ˌ⁼⁼ *at* ISO- + . . . -\ *n* **:** a crystalline acid HOOCCH(OH)CH(COOH)CH_2COOH isomeric with citric acid that is found esp. in the leaves of various air plants of the genus *Kalanchoe* and in blackberry juice and is recognized as an intermediate stage in the metabolism of fats and carbohydrates; 2-hydroxy-1,2,3-propane-tricarboxylic acid

iso·cla·site \ˌ⁼⁼ˈklāˌsīt, īˈsäklə,-, -ˌzīt\ *n* [G *isoklas* isoclasite (fr. *is-* + *-klas* -clase) + E *-ite*] **:** a mineral $Ca_2(PO_4)(OH)$.$2H_2O$ consisting of a basic hydrous calcium phosphate occurring in white crystals or columnar forms

[1]**iso·cli·nal** \ˌ⁼⁼ *at* ISO- + ˈklīnᵊl\ *adj* [ISV *is-* + *-clinal*] **:** relating to, having, or indicating equality of inclination or dip: as **a** *also* **isoclinic :** being or relating to an isocline **b :** being or relating to an isoclinic line — **iso·cli·nal·ly** \-ᵊlē\ *adv*

[2]**isoclinal** \"\ *n* -S **:** ISOCLINIC LINE

isoclinal fold *n* **:** an isocline or a fold so closely compressed that it approximates an isocline

iso·cline \ˈ⁼⁼ˌklīn\ *n* -S [*is-* + *-cline*] **:** an anticline or syncline so closely folded that the rock beds of the two sides have the same dip

iso·clin·ic line \ˌ⁼⁼ˈklinik-\ *also* **isoclinic** *n* [*isoclinic* ISV *is-* + *-clinic*] **:** a line on a map or chart joining points on the earth's surface at which a dip needle has the same inclination to the plumb line — compare ACLINIC LINE

iso·colon \ˌ⁼⁼+\ *n* [Gk *isokōlon*, fr. neut. of *isokōlos* of equal members, fr. *is-* + *kōlon* limb, member — more at CALK] **1 :** a period consisting of cola of equal length **2 :** the use of equal cola in immediate succession

iso·con·tae *syn of* ISOKONTAE

iso·cortex \ˈ⁼⁼ *at* ISO- + \ *n* [NL, fr. *is-* + L *cortex* bark — more at CORTEX] **:** NEOPALLIUM

iso·corydine \"+\ *n* **:** a crystalline alkaloid $C_{20}H_{23}NO_4$ isomeric with corydine and occurring with it

isoc·ra·cy \īˈsäkrəsē\ *n* -ES [Gk *isokratia*, fr. *isokratēs* having equal power or equal rights (fr. *is-* + *kratos* strength, power) + *-ia* -y — more at HARD] **:** equality of power or rule; *esp* **:** a system of government in which all have equal political power

iso·cryme \ˈ⁼⁼ *at* ISO + ˌkrīm *or* -ˌkrim\ *n* -S [ISV *is-* + Gk *krymos* frost, icy cold — more at CRUST] **:** an imaginary line or a line on a map or chart connecting points having the same mean temperature for a specified coldest time of the year

isocyan- *or* **isocyano-** *comb form* [ISV, fr. *isocyanic* (in *isocyanic acid*)] **:** containing the univalent group —NC isomeric with cyanogen and present in isocyanides ⟨*isocyano*benzene C_6H_5NC⟩

iso·cyanate \ˌ⁼⁼ *at* ISO- + \ *n* -S [ISV *isocyan-* + *-ate*] **:** a compound containing the univalent radical —NCO consisting of an isocyano group united with oxygen **:** a salt or ester of isocyanic acid ⟨phenyl ~ C_6H_5NCO⟩

iso·cyanic acid \ˌ⁼⁼ + . . . -\ *n* [ISV *is-* + *cyanic acid*] **:** cyanic acid regarded as having the formula HNCO and usu. prepared (as by the reaction of phosgene with the salt of a primary amine) in the form of esters of which some are used in making polyurethans and other resins, plastics, foams, and adhesives

iso·cyanide \"+\ *n* [*is-* + *cyanide*] **:** any of a class of compounds that are isomeric with the normal cyanides, that have the structure RNC, and that are in general colorless volatile poisonous liquids of strong offensive odor ⟨phenyl ~ C_6H_5-NC⟩ — called also *carbylamine*

iso·cyanine \"+\ *n* [ISV *is-* + *cyanine*] **:** any of several simple cyanine dyes in whose structure the carbon atom joining the two quinoline or other heterocyclic rings is attached at different positions in the two rings

iso·cyano \"+\ *adj* [*isocyan-*] **:** relating to or containing the group —NC isomeric with cyanogen — used esp. of organic compounds

iso·cyclic \"+\ *adj* [ISV *is-* + *cyclic*] **:** relating to, characterized by, or being a ring composed of atoms of only one element; *esp* **:** CARBOCYCLIC — distinguished from *heterocyclic*

iso·diametric \"+\ *adj* [ISV *is-* + *diametric*] **1 a :** having equal diameters **b :** having dimensions that are equal in all directions ⟨~ parenchyma cells⟩ **2 :** having lateral axes that are equal ⟨~ crystals⟩

iso·di·a·phere \ˌ⁼⁼ˈdīəˌfi(ə)r\ *n* -S [*is-* + *-diaphere* (fr. Gk *diapherein* to differ, carry across, fr. *dia-* + *pherein* to carry) — more at BEAR] **:** a nuclear species that has the same isotopic number as one or more other nuclear species

iso·dimorphism \ˌ⁼⁼ *at* ISO- + \ *n* [ISV *is-* + *dimorphism*] **:** isomorphism between the two forms of two dimorphous substances (as iron sulfide and cobalt arsenide) in such a way that each form of one is isomorphous with a form of the other — **iso·dimorphous** \"+\ *adj*

iso·dom·ic \ˌ⁼⁼ˈdämik\ *or* **isod·o·mous** \(ˈ)īˈsädəməs\ *adj* [*isodomon* + *-ic* or *-ous*] **:** of or relating to isodomon

isod·o·mon \īˈsädəˌmän, -ˌmən\ *or* **isod·o·mum** \-ˌməm\ *n* -S [L & Gk; L *isodomum*, fr. Gk *isodomon*, neut. of *isodomos* of equal courses, fr. *is-* + *domos* course of masonry, house — more at TIMBER] **:** masonry having blocks of equal length and thickness laid in courses so that each vertical joint of a course comes over the middle of a block just below

iso·dont \ˈ⁼⁼ *at* ISO- + ˌdänt\ *also* **iso·don·tous** \ˌ⁼⁼ˈdäntəs\ *adj* [*isodont* ISV *is-* + *-odont*; *isodontous* prob. fr. F *isodonte* isodont + E *-ous*] **1 :** having the teeth all alike **2** *of a snake* **:** having the maxillary teeth of equal length

iso·dose \ˈ⁼⁼ˌdōs\ *adj* [ISV *is-* + *dose*, n.] **:** of or relating to points or zones in a medium that receive equal doses of radiation ⟨an ~ chart⟩ ⟨the ~ rate lines are in units of roentgens per hour —G.M.Dunning⟩

iso·drin \ˈ⁼⁼ˌdrən\ *n* -S [*is-* + *-drin* (fr. *aldrin*)] **:** a crystalline insecticide $C_{12}H_8Cl_6$ that is a stereoisomer of aldrin and resembles aldrin in properties

iso·durene \ˌ⁼⁼+\ *n* **:** a liquid aromatic hydrocarbon C_6H_2-$(CH_3)_4$ isomeric with durene; 1,2,3,5-tetramethyl-benzene

iso·dynamic \ˌ⁼(ˌ)⁼+\ *adj* [ISV *is-* + *dynamic*] **:** of or relating to equality or uniformity of force

isodynamic line *n* **:** an imaginary line or a line on a map connecting points on the earth's surface at which the horizontal magnetic intensity is the same — called also *isogam*

iso·electric \"+\ *adj* [ISV *is-* + *electric*] **:** having or representing zero difference of electric potential

isoelectric point *n* **:** the point or narrow range on a pH scale at which the concentration of the anionic part of an ampholyte equals that of the cationic part **:** the pH at which the ampholyte will not migrate in an electrical field ⟨the *isoelectric points* of most proteins range from pH values of 4 to 7⟩

iso·electronic \"+\ *adj* [ISV *is-* + *electronic*] **1 :** having the same number of electrons ⟨the fluoride ion, the neon atom, and the sodium ion are ~⟩ — used of atoms or their ions **2 :** having the same number of valency electrons ⟨the carbon dioxide molecule and the cyanate ion are ~⟩ — used of molecules or radicals or ions composed of two or more atoms — **iso·electronically** \"+\ *adv*

iso·eta·les \ˌī⁼(ˌ)⁼əˈtā(ˌ)lēz\ *n pl*, *cap* [NL, fr. *Isoetes* + *-ales*] **:** an order of plants that is assigned to the class Lycopodineae or occas. to the class Filicineae, is known to have existed since the Cenozoic, and comprises *Isoetes* and possibly various extinct genera

iso·etes \īˈsōəˌtēz\ *n* [NL, fr. L, houseleek, fr. Gk, fr. neut. of *isoetēs* equal in years, fr. *is-* + *etos* year — more at WETHER] **1** *cap* **:** a large widely distributed genus (coextensive with the family Isoetaceae) of fern allies comprising the aquatic or marsh-growing quillworts that have a short buried lobed stem from which arises a tuft of quilt-shaped leaves bearing sporangia in their axils — see ISOETALES **2** *pl* **isoetes :** any plant of the genus *Isoetes* **:** QUILLWORT 1

iso·eugenol \ˌ⁼⁼ *at* ISO- + \ *n* [ISV *is-* + *eugenol*, prob. orig. formed in G] **:** an aromatic liquid phenol CH_3CH=C-$HC_6H_3(OCH_3)$OH found esp. in ilang-ilang oil and nutmeg oil, obtained also from eugenol by isomerization with alkali, and used chiefly in perfumes and in the synthesis of vanillin; 4-propenyl-guaiacol

iso·flavone \"+\ *n* [*is-* + *flavone*] **:** a colorless cyrstalline ketone $C_{15}H_{10}O_2$ that occurs as hydroxy derivatives in many plants often in the form of glycosides (as genistin, prunitrin)

iso·flu·ro·phate \ˌ⁼⁼ˈflu̇rəˌfāt\ *n* -S [by shortening] **:** DIISOPROPYL FLUOROPHOSPHATE

iso·gam \ˈ⁼⁼ˌgam\ *n* -S [ISV *is-* + *-gam* (fr. *gamma*)] **:** ISODYNAMIC LINE

iso·gamete \ˌ⁼⁼+\ *n* [ISV *is-* + *gamete*] **:** a gamete showing no differentiation in form or size or behavior from another gamete with which it is capable of uniting to form a zygote — compare HETEROGAMETE — **iso·gametic** \"+\ *adj*

isog·a·mous \(ˈ)īˈsägəməs\ *also* **iso·gam·ic** \ˌ⁼⁼ |*at* ISO- + ˈgamik\ *adj* [*isogamous* prob. fr. (assumed) NL *isogamus*, fr. NL *is-* + *-gamus* -gamous; *isogamic* prob. fr. *is-* + *-gamic*] **1** *of sexual reproduction* **:** characterized by fusion of like individuals or gametes — compare ANISOGAMOUS, HETEROGAMOUS, OOGAMOUS **2 :** having isogamous reproduction ⟨the ~ aquatic forms⟩

isog·a·my \īˈsägəmē\ *n* -ES [ISV *is-* + *-gamy*] **:** isogamous reproduction

iso·gen \ˈ⁼⁼ *at* ISO- + jən, ˌjen\ *n* -S [back-formation fr. *isogenous*] **:** an isogenous structure

iso·ge·ne·ic \ˌ⁼⁼jəˈnēik\ *adj* [by alter. (influenced by *isogeneity*)] **:** ISOGENIC

iso·ge·ne·ity \ˌ⁼⁼jəˈnēədē\ *n* -ES [*is-* + *-geneity* (irreg. — prob. influenced by *heterogeneity* — fr. *gene*)] **:** the quality or state of being isogenic

iso·gen·er·a·tae \ˌ⁼(ˌ)⁼ˌjenəˈräˌtē, -rā,-\ *n pl*, *cap* [NL, fr. *is-* + L *generatae* (fem. pl. of *generatus*, past part. of *generare* to beget) — more at GENERATE] **:** a class of brown algae including those that have two alternating generations similar in vegetative structure and size — compare HETEROGENERATAE

iso·genesis \ˌ⁼⁼+\ *n* [NL, fr. *is-* + L *genesis*] **:** similarity of origin or development

iso·genic \ˌ⁼⁼ˈjenik\ *adj* **:** having the same genic constitution: **a :** HOMOZYGOUS **b :** having all or certain specified genes the same — used of separate individuals

iso·e·nism \īˈsäjəˌnizəm\ *n* -S [*is-* + *gene* + *-ism*] **:** ISOGENEITY

iso·genotypic \ˌ⁼⁼ *at* ISO- + \ *adj* [*is-* + *genotypic*] **:** based on a single genotype — used of two or more generic names

iso·e·nous \(ˈ)īˈsäjənəs\ *adj* [*is-* + *-genous*] **:** having the same origin

iso·geotherm \ˌ⁼⁼ *at* ISO- + \ *n* -S [ISV *is-* + *ge-* + *-therm*] **:** an imaginary line or curved surface beneath the earth's surface through points having the same mean temperature — called also *geoisotherm* — **iso·geothermal** \"+\ *adj* — **iso·geothermic** \"+\ *adj*

iso·gloss \ˈ⁼⁼ˌgläs, -lȯs\ *n* -ES [ISV *is-* + *-gloss* (fr. Gk *glōssa* language, tongue) — more at GLOSS] **1 :** a boundary line between places or regions that differ in a particular linguistic feature ⟨the ~ separating Low German *maken* "to make" from High German *machen*⟩ ⟨dialect boundaries can be established only by means of ~*es* —Hans Kurath⟩ **2 :** a line on a map representing an isogloss — **iso·gloss·al** \ˌ⁼⁼ˈ⁼əl\ *adj*

[1]**iso·gon·ic** \ˌ⁼⁼+ˈgänik\ *also* **isog·o·nal** \(ˈ)īˈsägənᵊl\ *adj* [ISV *is-* + *gon-* (fr. Gk *gōnia* angle) + *-ic* or *-al* — more at -GON] **:** of, relating to, or having equal angles

[2]**isogonic** \"\ *or* **isogonal** \"\ *n* -S **:** ISOGONIC LINE

[3]**isogonic** \"\ *adj* [*is-* + *gon-* + *-ic*] **:** of, relating to, or marked by isogonism or isogony

isogonic line *n* [[1]*isogonic*] **:** an imaginary line or a line on a map joining points on the earth's surface at which magnetic declination is the same — compare ACLINIC LINE, AGONIC LINE

isog·o·nism \īˈsägəˌnizəm\ *n* -S [*is-* + *gon-* + *-ism*] **:** the quality or state of having similar medusae or gonophores — used of hydroids of different genera

isog·o·ny \-ˌnē\ *n* -ES [*is-* + *-gony*] **:** equivalent relative growth of parts in such a way that relative size differences remain constant — compare HETEROGONY

iso·graft \ˈ⁼⁼ *at* ISO- + ,-\ *n* -S [*is-* + *graft*] **:** HOMOGRAFT

iso·gram \ˈ⁼⁼ˌgram\ *n* -S [*is-* + *-gram*] **:** a line on a map or chart along which there is a constant value (as of temperature, pressure, or rainfall)

iso·graph \-ˌgraf, -ráf\ *n* -S [*is-* + *-graph*] **1 :** an instrument consisting of two short straightedges connected by a large circular joint marked with angular degrees that combines the functions of a protractor and a set square **2 :** an electronic calculator for finding both real and imaginary roots of algebraic equations

iso·griv \-ˌgriv\ *n* -S [*is-* + *-griv* (fr. *grivation*)] **:** a line on a map or chart connecting points of equal grivation

isog·y·nous \(ˈ)īˈsäjənəs\ *adj* [ISV *is-* + *-gynous*] **:** ISOCARPIC

iso·gyre \ˈ⁼⁼ *at* ISO- + ,-\ *n* [ISV *is-* + *gyre*] **:** the dark shadow in an interference figure representing the locus of all points that correspond to directions of transmission through the crystal plate in which the state of polarization of the incident rays is unchanged by passage through the plate

iso·haline \ˌ⁼⁼ˈhāˌlēn, -ˈha,-, -ˌlīn\ *or* **iso·hal·sine** \-ˈhalˌsēn, -ˌsīn\ *n* -S [*isohaline* ISV *is-* + *-haline* (fr. Gk *halinos* of salt, fr. *hal-*, *hals* salt + *-inos* -ine); *isohalsine* fr. *is-* + *-halsine* (irreg. fr. Gk *hal-*, *hals* salt) — more at SALT] **:** a line or surface drawn on a map or chart to indicate connecting points of equal salinity in the ocean

iso·hel \ˈ⁼⁼ˌhel\ *n* -S [*is-* + *-hel* (fr. Gk *hēlios* sun) — more at SOLAR] **:** a line drawn on a map or chart connecting places of equal duration of sunshine

iso·hemagglutination \ˌ⁼⁼+\ *n* [*is-* + *hemagglutination*] **:** isoagglutination of red blood cells

iso·hemagglutinin \"+\ *n* [*is-* + *hemagglutinin*] **:** a hemagglutinin causing isoagglutination

iso·hemagglutinogen \"+\ *n* -S [*isohemagglutinin* + *-o-* + *-gen*] **:** an antigen inducing the production of or reacting with specific isohemagglutinins

iso·hemolysin \"+\ *n* [ISV *is-* + *hemolysin*] **:** a hemolysin that causes isohemolysis

iso·hemolysis \"+\ *n* [NL, fr. *is-* + *hemolysis*] **:** the lysis of the red blood cells of one individual of a species by specific antibodies in the serum of another (as in human erythroblastosis fetalis)

iso·hydric \"+\ *adj* [ISV *is-* + *hydr-* + *-ic*] **:** relating to or being solutions of electrolytes having equal concentration of a common ion (as a hydrogen ion) not affecting one another's conductivity on being mixed

iso·hyet \ˌ⁼⁼+ˈhīət\ *also* **iso·hyetal** \ˌ⁼⁼+\ *n* -S [*isohyet* ISV *is-* + *-hyet* (fr. Gk *hyetos* rain); *isohyetal* fr. *isohyetal*, adj. — more at HYET-] **:** an isohyetal line on a map or chart

iso·hyetal \ˌ⁼⁼+\ *adj* [prob. fr. *isohyet* + *-al*] **:** relating to or indicating equal rainfall ⟨~ lines⟩

iso·immunization \ˌ⁼⁼+\ *n* [ISV *is-* + *immunization*] **:** production by an individual of antibodies against constituents of the tissues of others of his own species (as when transfused with blood from one belonging to a different blood group)

iso·ionic point \ˌ⁼⁼+...-\ *n* [*isoionic* ISV *is-* + *ionic*] **:** the hydrogen-ion concentration expressed usu. as the pH value at which the ionization of an amphoteric substance as an acid equals the ionization as a base and becomes identical with the isoelectric point in the absence of foreign inorganic ions

isokeraunic *var of* ISOCERAUNIC

iso·kon·tae \ˌ⁼⁼ˈkän·ˌtē\ *n pl*, *cap* [NL, fr. *is-* + *-kontae* (fr. Gk *kontos* punting pole, fr. *kentein* to prick, goad); fr. the equal length of the flagella — more at CENTER] *in some classifications* **:** a class of green algae comprising forms without motile stages or with flagella of equal length and including most of those now usu. placed in Chlorophyceae — compare HETEROKONTAE

iso·la·bil·i·ty \ˌīsələˈbiləd·ē *also* ˌisə- *sometimes* ˌīzə-\ *n* -ES **:** the quality or state of being isolable

iso·la·ble \ˈ⁼⁼ləbəl\ *also* **iso·lat·able** \ˈ⁼⁼ˌlād·əbəl, -ātə-, ˌ⁼⁼ˈ⁼⁼⁼\ *adj* [*isolable* fr. [1]*isolate* + *-able*; *isolatable* fr. [1]*isolate* + *-able*] **:** capable of being isolated

iso·lant \ˈ⁼⁼lənt\ *n* -S [[1]*isolate* + *-ant*] **:** [3]ISOLATE 4, 5

[1]**iso·late** \ˈīsəˌlāt *also* ˈisə- *sometimes* ˈīzə-; *usu* -ād.+V\ *vb* -ED/-ING/-S [back-formation fr. *isolated*] *vt* **1 a** (1) **:** to set apart from others **:** cause to be detached from others and alone **:** place alone **:** make solitary ⟨a tiny village that had been *isolated* from civilization⟩ (2) **:** to cause to be stranded **:** cut off ⟨*isolated* what was left of the fleeing army⟩ **b :** to keep apart or away from others so as to minimize or wholly reduce any effect on others; *specif* **:** to separate (one with a contagious disease) from others not similarly infected ⟨kept very close track of all carriers and *isolated* them whenever they gave positive results —V.G.Heiser⟩ — compare QUARANTINE **c :** to single out **:** PINPOINT ⟨*isolating* the most important sense of a word⟩ **2 :** to separate (as a chemical compound) from all other substances **:** obtain pure or in a free state **3 :** INSULATE 2a ~ *vi* **:** to cause something to be isolated

[2]**iso·late** \-ˌlāt, -ˌlət, -lət, *usu* |d·+V\ *adj* [prob. fr. [1]*isolate*, after such pairs as *appropriate*, v.: *appropriate*, adj.] **:** ISOLATED

[3]**isolate** \"\ *n* -S **1 :** an isolated factor, function, or process ⟨the smallest human ~ is a culture —J.K.Feibleman⟩ ⟨no one historical epoch and no one cultural ~ can present the permanent features of society —Georgiana Melvin⟩ **2 :** something singled out for observation **:** ABSTRACT 3 ⟨~*s* which could be described . . . as if they completely represented the physical world from which they had been extracted —Lewis Mumford⟩ **3 :** a chemical compound (as geraniol) separated from an essential oil for use in perfumes **4 a :** a spore, single organism, or viable part of an organism that has been isolated (as from diseased tissue, contaminated water, or the air); *often* **:** a pure culture produced from such an isolate **b :** an individual or strain isolated from a natural population (as for the study of a pathogenic fungus or bacterium) **5 :** a relatively homogeneous population separated from related populations by geographic or biologic or social factors or by the intervention of man — compare BIOTYPE, CLONE, ISOLATION 2 **6 :** an individual living in isolation from particular phases of an environment; *esp* **:** an individual socially withdrawn or removed from society through rejection of or incapacity for interpersonal relationships

isolated *adj* [F *isolé* isolated (fr. It *isolato*, fr. *isola* island — fr. L *insula* — + *-ato* -ate) + E *-ate* + *-ed* — more at ISLE] **1 a :** placed alone or apart **:** being alone **:** SOLITARY ⟨could not remain the ~ figure he had been —Sherwood Anderson⟩ **b :** cut or caused to be alone or apart **:** cut off **:** STRANDED ⟨if attacked the ~ pawn can be defended —*New Complete Hoyle*⟩ **2 a :** occurring alone or once **:** UNIQUE ⟨some ~ incident not likely to recur —Dorothy Barclay⟩ **b :** SPORADIC ⟨the reader who has an ~ rather than overall interest —R.S.Browne⟩ ⟨~ instances of ill behavior —Eugene Burr⟩ **3 :** not bonded (as by cement) to an adjacent structure ⟨~ buildings⟩ ⟨an ~ pier⟩ **4 :** separated by more than one single bond in a system of at least two double bonds in a molecule **:** not conjugated ⟨~ double bonds⟩ — **iso·lat·ed·ly** \ˈ⁼⁼ˌ⁼⁼⁼, ˌ⁼⁼ˈ⁼⁼⁼\ *adv*

isolating *adj* [fr. pres. part. of [1]*isolate*] **:** of, relating to, or being a language in which each word typically expresses a distinct idea and in which variations in parts of speech and syntactical relations are determined almost exclusively by the order in which words are joined and by the use of particles so that a sentence typically consists of a string of formally independent words ⟨an ~ language⟩ ⟨the ~ form of speech of the Sino-Tibetan languages⟩ — distinguished from *agglutinative* and *inflectional*; compare ANALYTIC 4

isolating mechanism *n* **:** something (as a geographical, ecological, physiological, anatomical, or psychological barrier) that limits interbreeding between groups and is thereby a major factor in the differentiation of biologic units (as races or species)

iso·la·tion \ˌ⁼⁼ˈlāshən\ *n* -S [F, fr. *isoler* to isolate (fr. *isolé* isolated) + *-ation*] **1 :** the action of isolating or condition of being isolated **2 :** a segregation of a group of organisms from related forms in such a manner as to prevent crossing

isolation booth *n* **:** a small soundproof booth used (as in a television studio) as a small studio within a larger studio

iso·la·tion·ism \-shəˌnizəm\ *n* -S **1 a :** a policy directed toward the isolation of a nation from other nations by a deliberate abstention from alliances and other international political and economic relations ⟨American foreign policy was set on a course of ~ —Dorothy B. Goebel⟩ ⟨a peculiarly hopeless kind of new Asian ~ —H.R.Isaacs⟩ **b :** a disposition or tendency to isolate deliberately an individual or group (as a political party) or a field of endeavor (as education or intellectual activity) from outside and esp. foreign relations or influences ⟨uncontrolled ~ would estrange the party from . . . the leaders of friendly cooperative non-Communist parties —H.A.Steiner⟩ ⟨ivory-tower cultural ~ —Leslie Rees⟩ **2 :** an attitude or conviction favoring adherence to a policy of deliberate isolation ⟨~ can never again dominate America —G.W.Chapman⟩ ⟨the hard core of ~ in the United States has been ethnic and emotional —Samuel Lubell⟩ — compare INTERNATIONALISM, INTERVENTIONISM

[1]**iso·la·tion·ist** \ˌ⁼⁼ˈlāsh(ə)nəst\ *n* -S **:** one that advocates or believes in isolationism ⟨criticism . . . not from ~*s* but from internationalists —*Atlantic*⟩ ⟨anthropological ~*s*⟩

[2]**isolationist** \ˌ⁼⁼ˈ⁼(⁼)⁼\ *adj* **:** of, characterized by, or favoring isolationism ⟨the orthodox believe that much money can be saved, especially of what now goes to foreign aid, by a more ~ foreign policy —Walter Lippmann⟩ ⟨the country was in an overwhelmingly ~ mood —F.L.Allen⟩ ⟨culturally as well as politically ~ —Christian Gauss⟩

iso·la·tive \ˈ⁼⁼ˌlād·|iv, -āt|, |ēv *also* |əv\ *adj* **1** *of a sound change* **:** occurring in isolation **:** not dependent on phonetic environment ⟨OE \stāːn\ *stān* became by ~ change Modern English \stōn*stone*⟩ — compare COMBINATIVE **2 :** ISOLATING

iso·la·tor \-ād·ə(r), -ātə-\ *n* -s **:** one that isolates; *specif* **:** a device that absorbs or prevents the transmission of noise or vibration (as of machinery)

iso·lecithal \¦=(,)= *at* ISO-+\ *adj* [ISV *is-* + *lecithal*] **:** HOMOLECITHAL

iso·lette \ˌīsə¦let *also* ¦is-\ *n* -s [fr. *Isolette*, a trademark] **:** an incubator for premature infants that is designed to provide controlled temperature, humidity, and oxygen supply and to permit feeding and care under aseptic conditions with a minimum of handling

iso·leucine \¦== *at* ISO-+\ *n* [ISV *is-* + *leucine*] **:** a crystalline amino acid $C_2H_5CH(CH_3)CH(NH_2)COOH$ that is isomeric with leucine, that occurs in its dextrorotatory L-form in most dietary proteins but is usu. obtained from the waste from the recovery of sugar from beet molasses, and that like leucine is essential in the nutrition of animals and man; α-amino-β-methyl-valeric acid

iso·line \'==+,līn\ *n* [*is-* + *line*] **:** ISOGRAM

isol·o·gous \(')ī¦säləgəs\ *adj* [ISV *is-* + *-logous* (as in *homologous*)] **:** relating to or being any of two or more closely related chemical compounds in a series whose successive members possess a regular difference in composition other than a difference of one carbon and two hydrogen atoms — sometimes distinguished from *homologous*

iso·logue *or* **iso·log** \'== *at* ISO-+,lȯg *also* ,läg\ *n* -s [ISV, fr. *isologous*, after such pairs as E *analogous: analogue*] **:** a compound isologous with one or more other compounds

[1]**iso·lo·ma** \ˌīsə'lōmə\ [NL, fr. *is-* + Gk *lōma* fringe; akin to Gk *eilein* to wind, roll — more at VOLUBLE] *syn of* KOHLERIA

[2]**isoloma** \"\ *n* -s [NL *Isoloma*] **:** a plant of the genus *Kohleria*

iso·lux \'== *at* ISO-+,ləks\ *n* -ES [*is-* + L *lux* light — more at LIGHT] **:** ISOPHOTE

[1]**iso·magnetic** \¦=(,)= *at* ISO-+\ *adj* [ISV *is-* + *magnetic*] **:** of, relating to, or marked by points of equal magnetic intensity or points of equal value of a component of such intensity ⟨an ~ chart⟩

[2]**isomagnetic** \"\ *n* **:** a line on a map or chart of the earth's surface connecting points of equal magnetic intensity or points of equal value of a component of such intensity

iso·maltose \¦==+\ *n* [ISV *is-* + *maltose*] **:** a syrupy disaccharide $C_{12}H_{22}O_{11}$ isomeric with maltose, present in hydrol (sense 3), and obtainable also from dextran by acid hydrolysis, from glucose by reaction with acids, and from gentiobiose octaacetate by rearrangement

iso·mer \'== *at* ISO-+,mə(r)\ *n* -s [ISV, back-formation fr. *isomeric*; prob. orig. formed in G] **1 :** a compound, radical, or ion isomeric with one or more others **2 :** a nuclide isomeric with one or more others ⟨a metastable ~⟩ — called also *nuclear isomer*

isom·er·ase \ī'sämə,rās, -āz\ *n* -s [ISV *isomer* + *-ase*] **:** any of various enzymes that catalyze isomerization (as of glucose phosphate to fructose phosphate) — compare MUTASE 2

iso·mere \'== *at* ISO-+,mi(ə)r\ *n* -s [*is-* + *-mere*] **:** a corresponding part or segment

iso·mer·ic \¦==¦merik\ *adj* [ISV *isomer-* (fr. Gk *isomerēs* equally divided, fr. *is-* + *meros* part, share) + *-ic* — more at MERIT] **:** of, relating to, or exhibiting isomerism ⟨an and isobutane are ~ compounds⟩ ⟨the thiocyanate and isothiocyanate radicals are ~⟩ — **iso·mer·i·cal·ly** \-rək(ə)lē\ *adv*

isom·er·ide \ī'sämə,rīd\ *n* -s [*isomeric* + *-ide*] **:** ISOMER 1

isom·er·ism \-,rizəm\ *n* -s [ISV *isomeric* + *-ism*] **1 :** the phenomenon exhibited by two or more chemical compounds, radicals, or ions of containing the same numbers of atoms of the same elements in the molecule, radical, or ion and hence having the same molecular formula but differing in the structural arrangement of the atoms and consequently in one or more properties ⟨the ~ of the butyl alcohols⟩ — compare GEOMETRIC ISOMERISM, OPTICAL ISOMERISM, POSITION ISOMERISM, STEREOISOMERISM, TAUTOMERISM **2 :** the phenomenon exhibited by two or more nuclides of having the same mass numbers and the same atomic numbers but of differing in energy state and rate of radioactive decay — called also *nuclear isomerism* **3** [prob. fr. *isomerous* + *-ism*] **:** the condition of having or being made up of corresponding parts or segments; *esp* **:** the condition (as of a plant having the members of each floral whorl equal in number) of having two or more comparable parts made up of identical numbers of similar segments

isom·er·i·za·tion \ī,sämərə'zāshən, -,rī'z-\ *n* -s [ISV *isomer* + *-ization*] **:** the process of isomerizing (as of the straight-chain hydrocarbon butane to the branched-chain hydrocarbon isobutane of higher octane number for gasoline)

isom·er·ize \ī'sämə,rīz\ *vb* -ED/-ING/-S [ISV *isomer* + *-ize*] *vi* **:** to become changed into an isomeric form ~ *vt* **:** to cause to change into an isomeric form

isom·er·ous \(')ī¦sämərəs\ *adj* [ISV *is-* + *-merous*] **:** exhibiting isomerism — opposed to *heteromerous*

isom·ery \ī'sämərē\ *n* -ES [ISV *isomer* + *-y*] **:** ISOMERISM 1

[1]**iso·metric** \¦== *at* ISO-+\ *also* **iso·metrical** \"+\ *adj* [*is-* + *metr-* (fr. Gk *metron* measure) + *-ic* or *-ical* — more at MEASURE] **:** of, relating to, or characterized by equality of measure: as **a :** of, relating to, or having the form of an isometric drawing **b :** EQUIGRANULAR **c :** taking place at constant volume ⟨an ~ change of temperature and pressure⟩ **d** *of muscular contraction* **:** taking place against resistance, without significant shortening of muscle fibers, and with marked increase in muscle tone — compare ISOTONIC **e** *of a stanza or strophe* **:** having lines of equal measure — **iso·metrically** \"+\ *adv*

[2]**isometric** \"\ *n* -s **:** ISOMETRIC LINE

isometric drawing *n* **:** the representation of an object on a single plane (as a sheet of paper) with the object placed as in isometric projection but disregarding the foreshortening of the edges parallel to the three principal axes of the typical rectangular solid, lines parallel to these axes appearing in their true lengths and producing an appearance of distortion

isometric line *n* **1 :** a line (as a contour line) drawn on a map and indicating a true constant value throughout its extent **2 :** a line representing changes of pressure or temperature under conditions of constant volume

isometric projection *n* **:** an axonometric projection in which the three spatial axes of the object are represented as equally inclined to the drawing surface and equal distances along the axes are drawn equal

cube as seen in isometric projection

isometric system *n* **:** a crystal system characterized by three equal axes at right angles (as in the cube and regular octahedron) — see CRYSTAL SYSTEM illustration

iso·me·tro·pia \ˌ=(,)= *at* ISO-+mə'trōpēə\ *n* -s [NL, fr. Gk *isometros* of equal measure (fr. *is-* + *metron*) + NL *-opia*] **:** equality in refraction in the two eyes

iso·morph \'==,mȯrf\ *n* -s [ISV *is-* + *-morph*] **:** something identical with or similar to something else in form or shape or structure: as **a :** one of two or more substances related by isomorphism **b :** an individual or group exhibiting isomorphism **c :** a cipher text pattern recurring with different constituent letters ⟨FXEXRF and PZMZTP are ~s⟩

iso·mor·phic \¦==¦mȯrfik\ *adj* [ISV *is-* + *-morphic*] **:** being of identical or similar form or shape or structure **:** exhibiting isomorphism; *esp* **:** having sporophytic and gametophytic generations alike in shape and size ⟨some algae and fungi are ~⟩ — compare HETEROMORPHIC

iso·mor·phism \¦==¦,fizəm\ *n* -s [ISV *is-* + *-morphism*; prob. orig. formed as G *isomorphismus*] **1 :** the quality or state of being isomorphic: as **a :** similarity in organisms of different ancestry resulting from convergence **b** (1) **:** similarity of crystalline form and structure between substances of similar compositions (as between sulfates of barium $BaSO_4$ and of strontium $SrSO_4$) — sometimes used only of substances that are so closely similar that they can form a more or less continuous series of solid solutions; compare HETEROMORPHISM 2 (2) **:** HOMOEOMORPHISM 1 **2 :** a hypothetical identity of psychological manifestation and brain process

iso·mor·phous \-,fəs\ *adj* [ISV *is-* + *-morphous*] **:** ISOMORPHIC; *esp* **:** isostructural and capable of forming solid solutions together ⟨the ~ components forsterite and fayalite of olivine⟩ ⟨strontium sulfate is ~ with barium sulfate⟩ — used of minerals and other crystalline substances

iso·mor·phy \'==,fē\ *n* -ES [ISV *is-* + *-morphy*] **:** HOMOPLASY

iso·myaria \¦==+\ *n pl, cap* [NL, fr. *is-* + *-myaria*] *in some classifications* **:** a division of Lamellibranchia comprising bivalve mollusks having two adductor muscles of nearly equal size — compare HETEROMYARIA, MONOMYARIA — **iso·my·ar·i·an** \¦=(,)=¦rēən\ *adj*

iso·neph \'==,nef\ *n* -s [ISV *is-* + *-neph* (fr. Gk *nephos* cloud) — more at NEBULA] **:** a line on a map connecting points that have the same average percentage of cloudiness

iso·ni·a·zid \ˌ=='nīəzəd\ *n* -s [*iso*nicotinic acid hydra*zid*e] **:** a crystalline compound $C_5H_4NCONHNH_2$ used orally or intramuscularly in the treatment of tuberculosis often in conjunction with streptomycin or dihydrostreptomycin and para-aminosalicylic acid; isonicotinic acid hydrazide

iso·nicotinic acid \¦==+...-\ *n* [*isonicotinic* ISV *is-* + *nicotinic*] **:** a crystalline acid C_5H_4NCOOH made usu. by oxidation of the corresponding picoline or ethyl-pyridine and used chiefly in making isoniazid; 4-pyridine-carboxylic acid

iso·nic·o·tin·o·yl·hydrazine \ˌ==,nikə,tēnəwəl+\ *or* **iso·nicotinyl·hydrazine** \ˌ==,nikə,tēnᵊl+\ *n* [*isonicotinoylhydrazine* fr. *isonicotin-* (fr. *isonicotinic acid*) + *-o-* + *-yl* + *hydrazine*; *isonicotinylhydrazine* fr. *isonicotin-* (fr. *isonicotinic acid*) + *-yl* + *hydrazine*] **:** ISONIAZID

iso·nip·e·caine \ˌ=='nipə,kān\ *n* -s [prob. fr. *isonipe-* (fr. *isonipecotic acid* isomer of nipecotic acid, fr. *is-* + *nipecotic acid*) + *-caine*] **:** meperidine or its hydrochloride

iso·nitrile \¦==+\ *n* [ISV *is-* + *nitrile*] **:** ISOCYANIDE

iso·ni·tro \ˌīsə¦nī·(,)trō\ *adj* [*isonitro-*] **:** containing the acid bivalent group =NO(OH)

isonitro- *comb form* [*is-* + *nitr-*] **:** containing the acid bivalent group =NO(OH) related to the nitro group ⟨*isonitro*ethane $CH_3CH{=}NO(OH)$⟩ — compare ACI-

iso·ni·tro·so \ˌīsə,nī'trō(,)sō *also* ¦īzə\ *adj* [*isonitroso-*] **:** containing the bivalent hydroxy-imino group =NOH

isonitroso- *comb form* [ISV *is-* + *nitroso-*] **:** containing the bivalent hydroxy-imino group =NOH related to the nitroso group and characteristic of oximes ⟨*isonitroso*acetone $CH_3COCH{=}NOH$⟩

ison·o·my \ī'sänəmē\ *n* -ES [Gk *isonomia*, fr. *isonomos* characterized by equality before the law (fr. *is-* + *nomos* right, law) + *-ia* -y — more at NIMBLE] **:** equality before the law

iso·nuclear \¦== *at* ISO-+\ *adj* [*is-* + *nuclear*] **:** relating to or attached to the same nucleus or ring in the molecule of a chemical compound ⟨an ~ bromo-nitro-naphthalene⟩

iso·octane \¦==+\ *n* [ISV *is-* + *octane*] **:** an octane of branched-chain structure or a mixture of such octanes: as **a :** the flammable liquid hydrocarbon $(CH_3)_2CH(CH_2)_4CH_3$ in whose molecule there is branching only at one end of the chain; 2-methyl-heptane **b :** a flammable liquid hydrocarbon $(CH_3)_2CHCH_2C(CH_3)_3$ made usu. by hydrogenation of diisobutylene and used esp. as a standard in rating motor fuels by their octane number; 2,2,4-trimethyl-pentane — not used technically **c :** HYDROCODIMER — used chiefly commercially

iso·oc·tyl alcohol \¦==+...-\ *n* [*isooctyl* fr. *is-* + *octyl*] **:** an octyl alcohol of branched-chain structure or a mixture of such alcohols; *esp* **:** a mixture of isomeric primary alcohols $C_7H_{15}CH_2OH$ obtained by reaction of heptylenes with carbon monoxide and hydrogen and used esp. in synthesis (as of plasticizers) — not used scientifically

iso·pach \'==,pak\ *n* -s [*is-* + *-pach* (fr. Gk *pachys* thick) — more at PACHY-] **:** an isogram that connects points of equal thickness of a particular geological stratum formation or group of formations

iso·pach·ous \¦==¦pakəs, (')ī¦säpək-\ *adj* **:** of, relating to, or having an isopach ⟨~ contours⟩ ⟨an ~ map⟩

iso·pag \'== *at* ISO-+,pag\ *n* -s [*is-* + *-pag* (fr. Gk *pagos* frost; akin to Gk *pēgnynai* to fasten) — more at PACT] **:** an equiglacial line on a map or chart that connects the points where ice is present for approximately the same number of days in winter

iso·paraffin \¦==+\ *n* [*is-* + *paraffin*] **:** a paraffin hydrocarbon of branched-chain structure — **iso·paraffinic** \"+\ *adj*

iso·pec·tic \¦=='pektik\ *n* -s [*is-* + *pect-* (fr. Gk *pēktos* fixed, frozen, fr. *pēgnynai* to fasten) + *-ic*] **:** an equiglacial line on a map or chart connecting points where ice begins to form at the beginning of winter

iso·pelletierine \¦==+\ *n* [ISV *is-* + *pelletierine*] **:** a liquid alkaloid $C_8H_{15}NO$ from the root bark of pomegranate; 2-acetonyl-piperidine

iso·pentane \"+\ *n* [*is-* + *pentane*] **:** a volatile flammable liquid hydrocarbon $(CH_3)_2CHC_2H_5$ found in petroleum and used in gasoline and as a solvent

iso·pentyl \"+\ *n* [*is-* + *pentyl*] **:** the pentyl radical $(CH_3)_2CHCH_2CH_2$– derived from isopentane; 3-methyl-butyl — called also *isoamyl*

isopentyl alcohol *n* **:** a primary pentyl alcohol $(CH_3)_2CHCH_2CH_2OH$ that has a disagreeable odor and pungent taste and is obtained from fusel oil; 3-methyl-1-butanol — called also *isoamyl alcohol, isobutylcarbinol*

iso·perimetric *also* **iso·perimetrical** \"+\ *adj* [Gk *isoperimetros* isoperimetric (fr. *is-* + *perimetros* perimeter) + E *-ic* or *-ical* — more at PERIMETER] **1 :** of, relating to, or having equal perimeters — used esp. of geometrical figures **2 :** having a constant scale — used of a line on a map

iso·phen·al \¦==¦fēnᵊl\ *adj* [*isophene* + *-al*] **:** of, relating to, or having an isophene

iso·phene \'==,fēn\ *also* **iso·phane** \-,fān\ *n* -s [*isophene* fr. *is-* + *-phene* (fr. Gk *phainein* to show); *isophane* ISV *is-* + *-phane* (fr. Gk *phainein* to show) — more at FANCY] **1 :** a line on a map or chart connecting places within a region at which a particular biological phenomenon (as the flowering of a given plant) occurs at one time **2 :** PHENOCONTOUR

iso·phe·nous \¦==¦fēnəs\ *adj* [*isophene* + *-ous*] **:** having the same phenotype

iso·phone \'==,fōn\ *n* [ISV *is-* + *-phone*] **1 :** a phonetic isogloss (sense 1) **2 :** a phonetic feature shared by some but not all of the speakers of a dialect, language, or group of related languages

iso·pho·ria \ˌ=='fōrēə\ *n* -s [NL, fr. *is-* + *-phoria*] **:** the quality or state of having the visual axes of the two eyes in the same horizontal plane

iso·phorone \¦==+\ *n* [ISV *is-* + *phorone*] **:** a high-boiling liquid ketone $C_9H_{14}O$ made by condensation of acetone and used as a solvent; 3,5,5-trimethyl-2-cyclohexen-one

iso·phote \'==,fōt\ *also* **iso·phot** \-,fät\ *n* -s [ISV *is-* + *-phote*, *-phot* (fr. Gk *phōt-*, *phōs* light) — more at FANCY] **:** a line or surface on a chart forming the locus of points of equal illumination or light intensity from a given source

iso·pho·tic line \¦==¦fōd·ik-\ *n* [*isophotic* fr. *isophote* + *-ic*] **:** ISOPHOTE

iso·phthal·ic acid \¦== *at* ISO-+¦thalik-\ *n* [*isophthalic* ISV *is-* + *phthalic*] **:** a crystalline diacid $C_6H_4(COOH)_2$ isomeric with phthalic acid made usu. by oxidation of *meta*-xylene and used in making synthetic resins and esters for use as plasticizers; *meta*-benzene-dicarboxylic acid

iso·phyl·lia \ˌ=='filēə\ *n, cap* [NL, fr. *is-* + *phyll-* + *-ia*] **:** a genus of madrepores comprising the rose corals

iso·phyl·lous \¦==¦filəs\ *adj* [ISV *is-* + *-phyllous*] **:** having foliage leaves of like form on the same plant or stem — compare ANISOPHYLLOUS

iso·phyl·ly \'==,filē\ *n* -ES [*isophyllous* + *-y*, n. suffix] **:** the quality or state of being isophyllous

iso·pi·es·tic \¦=(,)=,pī¦estik\ *adj* [*is-* + *piest-* (fr. Gk *piestos* compressible, fr. *piezein* to press) + *-ic* — more at PIEZO-] **:** of, relating to, or marked by equal pressure **:** ISOBARIC

iso·plastic graft \¦==+...-\ *n* [*isoplastic* fr. *is-* + *plastic*] **:** HOMOGRAFT

iso·pleth \'==,pleth\ *n* -s [ISV *is-* + *-pleth* (fr. Gk *plēthos* quantity, multitude); akin to Gk *plēthein* to be full — more at FULL] **1 :** an isogram on a graph showing the occurrence or frequency of a phenomenon as a function of two variables — often used of meteorological elements **2 :** a line on a map connecting points at which a given variable has a specified constant value ⟨~s such as isothermal lines or topographic contour lines⟩

iso·pleu·ra \ˌ=='plůrə\ [NL, fr. *is-* + *-pleura*] *syn of* AMPHINEURA

iso·ploid \'==,plȯid\ *adj* [*is-* + *-ploid*] **:** having an even number of genomes in somatic cells

iso·pluvial \¦==+\ *adj* [*is-* + *pluvial*] **:** of, relating to, or marked by equal rainfall ⟨an ~ line⟩

iso·pod \'==,päd\ *n* -s [NL *Isopoda*] **:** one of the Isopoda

isop·o·da \ī'säpədə\ *n pl, cap* [NL, fr. *is-* + *-poda*] **:** a large order of small sessile-eyed malacostracan crustaceans (division Peracarida) that lack a carapace, that have a body usu. depressed with seven free thoracic segments each bearing a pair of similar legs, and that occur in marine, freshwater, or terrestrial habitats or as parasites on invertebrates and fish — compare TANAIDACEA — **isop·o·dan** \(')ī¦säpədən, -əd·ᵊn\ *adj or n* — **isop·o·dous** \-dəs\ *adj*

iso·pod·i·form \ˌīsə¦pädə,fȯrm *also* ¦īzə-\ *adj* [NL *isopodiformis*, fr. *Isopoda* + L *-iformis* -iform] **:** resembling an isopod in form

iso·pogo·nous \¦== *at* ISO- + pə¦gōnəs, ¦pägən-\ *adj* [NL *isopogonus*, fr. *is-* + *-pogonus* (fr. Gk *pōgōn* beard) — more at -POGON] **:** having feathers whose two webs are equal

iso·polity \ˌ==+\ *n* -ES [Gk *isopoliteia*, fr. *isopolitēs* having equal or reciprocal political rights (fr. *is-* + *politēs* citizen) + *-ia* -y — more at POLICE] **:** equality or reciprocity of rights or privileges (as of citizenship) ⟨an agreement between two countries establishing ~ for their citizens⟩

isopoly- *comb form* [ISV *is-* + *poly-*] **:** containing several groups or ions of the same acid-forming element **:** POLY- 2b — in names of complex inorganic acids and their salts ⟨*isopoly*-molybdates⟩ — compare HETEROPOLY-

iso·poly acid \¦==¦pälē-\ *n* [*isopoly* ISV *isopoly-*] **:** any of a large group of complex oxygen-containing acids derived from a single inorganic acid by elimination of water from two or more molecules — distinguished from *heteropoly acid*

iso·por \'==,pō(ə)r\ *n* -s [*is-* + *-por* (fr. Gk *poros* passage, path) — more at FARE] **:** an imaginary line or a line on a map of the earth's surface connecting points of equal annual change in one of the magnetic elements

iso·por·ic \¦==¦pōrik\ *adj* **:** of, relating to, or indicating an isopor

iso·pren·a·line \ˌ=='prenᵊlən, -ᵊl,ēn\ *n* -s [prob. fr. *isopropyl* + adre*naline*] **:** ISOPROTERENOL

iso·prene \'==,prēn\ *n* -s [prob. fr. *is-* + *pr-* (fr. *propyl*) + *-ene*] **:** a flammable liquid diolefin hydrocarbon $CH_2{=}C(CH_3)CH{=}CH_2$ obtained usu. by heating rubber or turpentine (sense 2) or in cracking petroleum and used chiefly in making synthetic rubber; 2-methyl-1,3-butadiene — see POLYISOPRENE, TERPENE

[1]**iso·pre·noid** \¦==¦prē,nȯid\ *adj* [*isoprene* + *-oid*] **:** relating to, containing, or being the branched-chain grouping $(C)_2$-C–C–C of five carbon atoms that is characteristic of isoprene and that recurs in the molecules of many natural compounds (as rubber, terpenes, vitamin A, vitamin E, phytol)

[2]**isoprenoid** \"\ *n* -s **:** an isoprenoid compound

iso·pro·pa·nol \ˌ=='prōpə,nōl, -nȯl\ *n* -s [*is-* + *propane* + *-ol*] **:** ISOPROPYL ALCOHOL — not used systematically

iso·pro·pe·nyl \-ōpənᵊl, -,nil\ *n* [ISV *is-* + *propenyl*] **:** the univalent radical $CH_2{=}C(CH_3)$– isomeric with propenyl ⟨*isopropenyl*-isopropylidene isomerism . . . is typical of many terpenoids —W.S.Ropp⟩

iso·pro·pox·ide \ˌ==,prō'päk,sīd, -,səd\ *n* -s [prob. fr. *is-* + *propox-* (fr. *propoxyl* + *-ide*] **:** a binary compound of the radical $(CH_3)_2CHO$– isomeric with propoxyl; *esp* **:** a base formed from isopropyl alcohol by replacement of the hydroxyl hydrogen with a metal ⟨aluminum ~ $[(CH_3)_2CHO]_3Al$⟩

iso·propyl \¦==+\ *n* [ISV *is-* + *propyl*] **:** the alkyl radical $(CH_3)_2CH$– isomeric with normal propyl

isopropyl alcohol *n* **:** a volatile flammable liquid secondary alcohol $(CH_3)_2CHOH$ made usu. by hydration of propylene by means of sulfuric acid and used as a solvent and rubbing alcohol and as a source of acetone by dehydrogenation; 2-propanol

iso·pro·pyl·arterenol \¦==¦==+\ *n* [*isopropyl* + *arterenol*] **:** ISOPROTERENOL

iso·pro·pyl·ate \ˌ=='prōpə,lāt\ *n* -s [*isopropyl* + *-ate*] **:** ISOPROPOXIDE

isopropyl ether *n* **:** a colorless volatile flammable water-insoluble liquid $[(CH_3)_2CH]_2O$ made from propylene or isopropyl alcohol and used as a solvent

iso·propylidene \¦=(,)=+\ *n* [ISV *is-* + *propylidene*] **:** the bivalent radical $(CH_3)_2C$< isomeric with propylidene — compare ISOPROPENYL

iso·pro·te·re·nol \ˌ==,prōd·ə'rē,nōl, -nōl\ *n* -s [short for *isopropylarterenol*] **:** a crystalline compound $C_{11}H_{17}NO_3$ that is the isopropyl homologue of racemic epinephrine and that is used in the treatment of asthma — called also *isopropylarterenol*

isop·tera \ī'säptərə\ *n pl, cap* [NL, fr. *is-* + *-ptera*] **:** an order of social insects consisting of the termites — **isop·te·rous** \(')=¦=tərəs\ *adj*

iso·pulegol \¦== *at* ISO- +\ *n* [ISV *is-* + *pulegol*] **:** a liquid terpenoid alcohol $C_{10}H_{17}OH$ that has an odor like that of menthol and that is obtained as an intermediate in the synthesis of menthol from citronellol

[1]**iso·pyc·nic** \¦==¦piknik\ *also* **iso·pyc·nal** \-nəl\ *adj* [*is-* + *pycn-* + *-ic* or *-al*] **:** of, relating to, or marked by equal density

[2]**isopycnic** \"\ *or* **isopycnal** \"\ *n* -s **:** a line or surface on a map connecting points of equal density (as of water, air)

iso·quercitrin \¦==+\ *n* [*is-* + *quercitrin*] **:** a pale-yellow crystalline glucoside $C_{21}H_{20}O_{12}$ occurring esp. in cotton flowers and maize and yielding quercetin and glucose on hydrolysis

iso·quinoline \"+\ *n* [ISV *is-* + *quinoline*] **:** a low-melting crystalline or liquid nitrogenous base C_9H_7N that is associated with its isomer quinoline in coal tar and that is the parent structure in many alkaloids (as narcotine, papaverine)

iso·rhythm \'==+,-\ *n* [*is-* + *rhythm*] **:** a single fixed rhythmic pattern typically long and complex that is reiterated throughout the whole of a sung voice part which is usu. the tenor ⟨~ in late medieval motets⟩ — **iso·rhythmic** \¦==+\ *adj*

iso·safrole \¦==+\ *n* [ISV *is-* + *safrole*] **:** a liquid acetal $(CH_2O_2)C_6H_3CH{=}CHCH_3$ that has an odor like that of anise, that is obtained from the essential oils of ilang-ilang and the fruit of Japanese star anise and synthetically from safrole and hot alkali, and that is used chiefly in making piperonal

isos·ce·les \(')ī¦säsə,lēz\ *adj* [LL, fr. Gk *isoskelēs*, fr. *is-* + *skelos* leg — more at CYLINDER] *of a triangle* **:** having two equal sides — see TRIANGLE illustration

isosceles trapezoid *n* **:** a trapezoid with its two nonparallel sides equal

iso·sebacic acid \¦== *at* ISO- + . . . -\ *n* [*isosebacic* fr. *is-* + *sebacic*] **:** a solid mixture of sebacic acid and two isomeric dicarboxylic acids $C_8H_{16}(COOH)_2$ obtainable by reaction of butadiene with sodium, carbon dioxide, and finally hydrogen and useful esp. for making plasticizers and alkyd resins

[1]**iso·seismal** \"+\ *adj* [*is-* + *seismal*] **:** of, relating to, or marked by equal intensity of earthquake shock ⟨an ~ line⟩

[2]**isoseismal** \"\ *n* -s **:** an isoseismal line on a map or chart of the earth's surface connecting points of equal intensity of earthquake shock

iso·seismic \"+\ *adj* [*is-* + *seismic*] **:** ISOSEISMAL

is·osmotic \¦īs *also* ¦īz+\ *adj* [ISV *is-* + *osmotic*] **:** of, relating to, or exhibiting equal osmotic pressure ⟨~ solutions⟩

iso·spon·dyl \¦== *at* ISO -+¦spändᵊl\ *n* -s [NL *Isospondyli*] **:** a fish of the order Isospondyli

iso·spon·dy·li \ˌ=='spändə,lī\ *n pl, cap* [NL, fr. *is-* + *-spondyli*] **:** a large order of teleost fishes that is the most primitive group of teleosts and that includes about 50 living families (as of the herrings and salmons) whose fishes have soft-rayed fins, an air bladder connected with the alimentary canal by a duct, abdominal pelvic fins, the anterior vertebrae unmodified and similar to the others, and usu. a mesocoracoid or precoracoid arch — **iso·spon·dy·lous** \¦==¦dələs\ *adj*

isos·po·ra \ī'säspərə\ *n, cap* [NL, fr. *is-* + *-spora*] **:** a genus of Coccidia closely related to *Eimeria* and including the only species (*I. hominis*) of coccidium known to be parasitic in man

iso·spore \'== *at* ISO- +,-\ *n* [ISV *is-* + *spore*] **1 :** one of the spores produced by a homosporous organism **2 :** a sexual spore exhibiting no sexual dimorphism

iso·spor·ic \¦==¦spōrik\ *adj* [*isospore* + *-ic*] **:** ISOSPOROUS

iso·spor·ous \¦==¦spōrəs, (')ī¦säspərəs\ *adj* [*is-* + *-sporous*] **:** of, relating to, or having isospores

iso·spo·ry \'⸗⸗ *at* ISO- + ˌspōrē; ī'säspərē\ *n* -ES [ISV *is-* + *-spory*] **:** the quality or state of being isosporous

isos·ta·sist \ī'sästəsəst\ *n* -S **:** a specialist in the study of isostasy

isos·ta·sy *also* **isos·ta·cy** \-təsē\ *n* -ES [*isostasy* ISV *is-* + *-stasy* (fr. Gk *-stasia*); *isostacy* alter. (influenced by E *-cy*) of *isostasy* — more at -STASIA] **1 :** the quality or state of being isostatic **2 :** general equilibrium in the earth's crust maintained by a yielding flow of rock material beneath the surface under gravitative stress and by the approximate equality in mass of each unit column of the earth from the surface to a depth of about 70 miles — compare ISOSTATIC COMPENSATION

iso·static \ˌ⸗⸗ *at* ISO- +\ *adj* [ISV *is-* + *static;* orig. formed as F *isostatique*] **1 a :** subjected to equal pressure from every side **b :** being in hydrostatic equilibrium **2 :** relating to or characterized by isostasy

isostatic compensation *n* **:** the deficiency of mass in the earth's crust below sea level that exactly balances the mass above sea level

iso·stemo·nous \ˌ⸗⸗ˌstēmənəs, -stem-\ *adj* [ISV *is-* + *-stemonous*] **:** having stamens equal in number to the perianth divisions

iso·stemo·ny \ˌ⸗⸗'stēmənē, -stem-\ *n* -ES [ISV *isostemon*ous + *-y*] **:** the quality or state of being isostemonous

iso·stere \'⸗⸗ˌsti(ə)r\ *also* **iso·ster** \-ˌste(ə)r\ *n* -S [*is-* + *-stere, -ster* (fr. Gk *stereos* solid) — more at STARE] **1 :** a line on a map or chart connecting points of equal atmospheric density **2** [prob. back-formation fr. *isosteric*] **:** one of two or more substances related by isosterism

iso·ster·ic \ˌ⸗⸗ˌsterik\ *adj* [*is-* + *ster-* (fr. Gk *stereos* solid) + *-ic*] **1 :** of, relating to, or exhibiting isosterism **2 :** of, relating to, or marked by equal atmospheric density

isos·ter·ism \ī'sästəˌrizəm; '⸗⸗ *at* ISO- + ˌstiˌrizəm *or* ˌsteˌr-\ *n* -S [*is-* + *ster-* (fr. Gk *stereos* solid) + *-ism*] **:** the phenomenon of similarity of structure and of resulting similarity of some properties exhibited by two or more molecules or groups or ions containing different atoms though not necessarily the same number of atoms but having the same number of total or valence electrons in the same arrangement (as in carbon monoxide and gaseous nitrogen or in the cyanide and acetylide ions)

iso·structural \ˌ⸗⸗ *at* ISO- +\ *adj* **:** relating to or having a similar crystal structure in that the atoms correspond in position and function although there may not be close chemical relationship **:** ISOTYPIC 2 — used of minerals and other crystalline substances ⟨calcite and sodium nitrate are ∼⟩; compare ISOMORPHOUS

iso·tac \'⸗⸗ˌtak\ *n* -S [*is-* + *-tac* (fr. Gk *takēnai* to melt, be dissolved, pass. aor. infin. of *tēkein* to melt, dissolve) — more at THAW] **:** an equiglacial line on a map or chart connecting points where ice melts at the same time in spring

iso·tach \-ˌtak\ *n* -S [ISV *is-* + *-tach* (fr. Gk *tachys* quick) — more at TACHY-] **:** a line on a map or chart connecting points of equal wind speed

iso·tac·tic \ˌ⸗⸗ˌtaktik\ *adj* [ISV *is-* + *-tactic*] **:** of, relating to, or having a stereochemical regularity of structure in the repeating units of a polymer — compare SYNDYOTACTIC

isote *var of* IZOTE

iso·ther·al \ˌ⸗⸗ *at* ISO- + ˌthirəl\ *adj* [F *isothère* isothere + E *-al*] **:** of, relating to, or marked by the same mean summer temperature ⟨an ∼ line⟩

iso·there \'⸗⸗ˌthi(ə)r\ *n* -S [F *isothère*, fr. *is-* + *-thère* (fr. Gk *theros* summer); akin to Gk *thermos* hot] **:** a line on a map or chart of the earth's surface connecting points having the same mean summer temperature

iso·therm \-ˌthərm\ *n* -S [F *isotherme*, adj., isothermal, fr. *is-* + *-therme* (fr. Gk *thermē* heat, fr. *thermos* hot) — more at WARM] **1 :** a line on a map or chart of the earth's surface connecting points having the same temperature at a given time or the same mean temperature for a given period **2 :** a line on a chart representing changes of volume or pressure under conditions of constant temperature

[1]**iso·ther·mal** \ˌ⸗⸗ˌthərməl\ *adj* [F *isotherme*, adj. + E *-al*] **1 :** of, relating to, or marked by equality of temperature **2 :** of, relating to, or marked by changes of volume or pressure under conditions of constant temperature

[2]**isothermal** \"\ *n* -S **:** ISOTHERM 1

isothermal curve *n* **:** ISOTHERM 2

isothermal line *n* **:** ISOTHERM 1

isothermal region *n* **:** STRATOSPHERE

iso·ther·mic \-mik\ *adj* [ISV *isotherm* + *-ic*] **:** ISOTHERMAL — **iso·ther·mi·cal·ly** \-mək(ə)lē\ *adv*

iso·ther·mo·bath \ˌ⸗⸗'thərməˌbath\ *n* -S [*isotherm* + *-o-* + *-bath* (fr. Gk *bathos* depth); akin to Gk *bathys* deep — more at BATHY-] **:** a line on a diagram of a vertical section of the ocean connecting points of equal temperature

isothiocyan- *or* **isothiocyano-** *comb form* [ISV *is-* + *thiocyan-*] **:** containing the univalent radical —NCS isomeric with the thiocyano radical and present in isothiocyanates ⟨*isothiocyano*amines⟩

iso·thio·cyanate \ˌ⸗⸗ˌthīō+\ *n* -S [ISV *isothiocyan-* + *-ate*] **:** a compound containing the univalent radical —NCS consisting of an isocyano group united with sulfur **:** a salt or ester of isothiocyanic acid — compare MUSTARD OIL 2

isothiocyanato- *comb form* [*isothiocyanate* + *-o-*] **:** ISOTHIOCYAN- — esp. in names of coordination complexes

iso·thiocyanic acid \ˌ⸗⸗ˌthīō+ . . .-\ *n* [*isothiocyanic* ISV *is-* + *thiocyanic*] **:** thiocyanic acid regarded as having the formula HNCS and usu. prepared in the form of esters

iso·tone \'⸗⸗ˌtōn\ *n* -S [*is-* + *-tone* (prob. fr. Gk *tonos* tension, stretching) — more at TONE] **:** one of two or more nuclides having the same number of neutrons

iso·ton·ic \ˌ⸗⸗ˌtänik\ *adj* [ISV *is-* + *tonic*] **1 :** of, relating to, or exhibiting equal tension; *specif, of muscular contraction* **:** taking place in the absence of significant resistance with marked shortening of muscle fibers and without great increase in muscle tone — compare ISOMETRIC **2 :** having the same or equal osmotic pressure **:** ISOSMOTIC — used of solutions ⟨an ∼ salt solution in which blood cells are counted⟩; compare HYPERTONIC, HYPOTONIC — **iso·ton·i·cal·ly** \-nək(ə)lē\ *adv*

iso·tonicity \ˌ⸗⸗ *at* ISO- +\ *n* [*isotonic* + *-ity*] **:** the quality or state of being isotonic

iso·to·nize \'⸗⸗ˌtōˌnīz\ *vt* -ED/-ING/-S [*isoton*ic + *-ize*] **:** to make isotonic

iso·tope \'⸗⸗ˌtōp\ *n* -S [*is-* + *-tope* (fr. Gk *topos* place) — more at TOPIC] **1 a :** one of two or more species of atoms of the same chemical element that have the same atomic number and occupy the same position in the periodic table and that are nearly identical in chemical behavior but differ in atomic mass or mass number and so behave differently in the mass spectrograph, in radioactive transformations, and in physical properties (as diffusibility in the gaseous state) and may be detected and separated by means of these differences ⟨deuterium and tritium are ∼*s* of hydrogen⟩; *esp* **:** one such species of atom or a mixture of such species of atoms prepared for use as a tracer or in medicine — usu. indicated for a specific element by the mass number following the name of the element or written superior to the symbol of the element (as carbon 14, C^{14}, or ^{14}C); compare RADIOISOTOPE **b :** the nucleus of such a species of atom **2 :** NUCLIDE

isotope effect *n* **:** the variation of certain characteristics (as density and spectrum) of an element in accordance with the mass of the isotopes involved

iso·topic \ˌ⸗⸗ˌtäpik, -ˌtōp-\ *adj* [ISV *isotope* + *-ic*] **:** of, relating to, or having the relationship of an isotope — **iso·topi·cal·ly** \-pək(ə)lē\ *adv*

isotopic number *n* **:** the number of neutrons minus the number of protons in an atomic nucleus

iso·to·py \'⸗⸗ˌtōpē, ī'säd·əpē\ *n* -ES [ISV *isotope* + *-y*, n. suffix] **:** the quality or state of being isotopic

isot·ria \ī'sä·trēə\ *n, cap* [NL, fr. *is-* + Gk *tria* three, neut. of *treis* three — more at THREE] **:** a small genus of terrestrial orchids of eastern No. America that are sometimes included in *Pogonia* and that have a nearly terminal whorl of leaves and a usu. solitary greenish yellow flower with long linear sepal — see WHORLED POGONIA

iso·tron \'⸗⸗ *at* ISO- + ·ˌträn\ *n* -S [prob. fr. *iso*tope + *-tron*] **:** an electromagnetic apparatus for separating isotopes introduced as ions from an extended source which group according to their masses under the combined effect of a strong direct field and weak fields that vary at radio frequency

iso·tropic \ˌ⸗⸗·ˌträpik, -rōp-\ *adj* [ISV *is-* + *-tropic;* orig. formed as F *isotropique*] **1 :** exhibiting properties (as velocity of light transmission, conductivity of heat or electricity, compressibility) with the same values when measured along axes in all directions ⟨an ∼ crystal⟩ — compare ANISOTROPIC 1 **2 :** exhibiting equal tendencies to growth in all directions **:** lacking predetermined axes ⟨∼ eggs⟩

isot·ro·pism \ī'sä·trəˌpizəm\ *n* -S [*isotrop*ic + *-ism*] **:** ISOTROPY

isot·ro·pous \(ˈ)⸗ˌ⸗⸗_pəs\ *adj* [*isotrop*ic + *-ous*] **:** ISOTROPIC

isot·ro·py \⸗'⸗⸗pē\ *n* -ES [ISV *isotrop*ic + *-y*, n. suffix] **:** the quality or state of being isotropic

iso·type \'⸗⸗ *at* ISO- +ˌtīp\ *n* [ISV *is-* + *type*] **1 a :** an animal or plant or group common to two or more countries or life regions **b** (1) **:** PARATYPE 1 — usu. used in plant taxonomy (2) **:** a type that is or is considered for technical purposes to be the duplicate of a holotype **2 a :** a conventionalized pictographic symbol (as a drawing or outline or silhouette of a human figure or of a building or of a product) designed to represent (as by repetition or fractionalizing of each symbol or as by scaling each symbol to significantly the same size or to contrasted sizes) a fixed number or quantity of or other unitary fact about the thing symbolized ⟨each ∼ of a soldier in that diagram represents an entire army division⟩ or designed to convey other information ⟨public telephones often have a large ∼ of a bell over the booths as a directional guide to the booths⟩ and typically used in graphic statistical representations (as diagrams, charts) **b :** a graphic statistical representation (as a chart) that utilizes such isotypes

iso·typ·ic \ˌ⸗⸗ˌtipik\ *or* **iso·typ·i·cal** \-pəkəl\ *adj* [*isotype* + *-ic* or *-ical*] **1** *usu isotypical* **:** of or relating to an isotype **2 :** relating to or having a chemical formula analogous to and a crystal structure like that of another specified compound **:** ISOSTRUCTURAL — used of minerals and other crystalline substances ⟨some phosphates and silicates are ∼⟩

iso·urea \ˌ⸗(ˌ)⸗+\ *n* [NL, fr. *is-* + *urea*] **:** PSEUDOUREA

iso·valerate \ˌ⸗(ˌ)⸗+\ *n* -S [ISV *isovaler*ic (in *isovaleric acid*) + *-ate*] **:** a salt or ester of isovaleric acid

iso·valerianic acid \"+ . . . -\ *n* [*isovalerianic* ISV *is-* + *valerianic*] **:** ISOVALERIC ACID

iso·valeric acid \"+ . . . -\ *n* [*isovaleric* ISV *is-* + *valeric*] **:** a liquid acid $(CH_3)_2CHCH_2COOH$ that has a disagreeable odor, that occurs esp. in valerian root in the free state and in some essential oils and marine-animal oils in the form of esters, that is made by oxidation of isopentyl alcohol, and that is used chiefly in making esters for use in flavoring materials; *β*-methyl-butyric acid

iso·valeryl \"+\ *n* -S [ISV *isovaler-* (in *isovaleric acid*) + *-yl*] **:** the radical $(CH_3)_2CHCH_2CO—$ of isovaleric acid

is·oxazole \(ˈ)īs *also* (ˈ)īz+\ *n* [ISV *is-* + *oxazole*] **1 :** a liquid heterocyclic compound C_3H_3NO that is isomeric with oxazole, has a penetrating odor like that of pyridine, and is made by the action of hydroxylamine on propiolaldehyde **2 :** a derivative of isoxazole

iso·zooid \ˌ⸗⸗ *at* ISO- +\ *n* [*is-* + *zooid*] **:** a zooid resembling its parent — opposed to *allozooid*

is·pa·ghul \'ispəˌgül, -ˌgəl\ *n* -S [Per *ispaghōl, aspaghōl*, lit., horse's ear, fr. *asp* horse (fr. MPer) + *ghōl* ear; fr. the shape of the leaf; akin to Skt *aśva* horse — more at EQUINE] **:** an Old World plantain (*Plantago ovata*) with mucilaginous seeds that are used in preparing a beverage

is·pa·han \'ispəˌhän, -han, ˌ⸗⸗'⸗\ *n* -S *often cap* [*Ispahan, Isfahan*, city in west central Iran] **:** a handmade Persian rug that is typically deep red or blue or green with floral or animal patterns in antique design and that is usu. long and narrow

i spy \'ī-\ *n, cap I* [prob. alter. (influenced by E *I*, pron.) of *hy spy*] **:** HIDE-AND-SEEK

[1]**is·ra·el** \'iz|_rēəl *also* 'is| *or* |(ˌ)rāəl *or* |ˌrāl *or* ÷|_rəl *sometimes* |(ˌ)rāˌel *or* |(ˌ)räˌel *or* |ˌrīˌel *or* |(ˌ)råˌel\ *n* -S *cap* [ME, fr. OE, fr. LL, fr. Gk *Israēl*, fr. Heb *Yiśrā'ēl*, lit., let God contend, fr. *sārāh* to fight + *ēl* God] **1 a** (1) **:** the ancient Hebrew people descended from the patriarch Jacob (2) **:** the group of 10 Hebrew tribes anciently inhabiting the northern part of Palestine and constituting a kingdom independent of Judah **b :** the Jewish people of past and present **2 :** a body of individuals (as members of the Jewish or Christian faiths) regarded by itself or others as the actual or spiritual chosen people of God **:** ELECT

[2]**israel** \"\ *adj, usu cap* [*Israel*, independent Jewish state in Palestine, fr. Heb *Yiśrā'ēl*] **:** ISRAELI

[1]**is·rae·li** \iz|'rālē, -li *sometimes* is| *or* ˌ⸗_rēˌā- *or* ˌ⸗|_rəˌā-\ *adj, usu cap* [NHeb *yiśrĕ'ēlī*, fr. Heb, Israelite, Israelitic, fr. *Yiśrā'ēl*] **:** of or from the republic of Israel **:** of the kind or style prevalent in Israel

[2]**israeli** \"\ *n, pl* **israelis** *also* **israeli** *cap* **:** a native or inhabitant of the republic of Israel

israeli hebrew *n, cap I&H* **:** the Hebrew language in colloquial use in present-day Israel

[1]**is·ra·el·ite** *pronunc at* [1]ISRAEL +ˌīt; *usu* -īd·+V\ *n* -S *cap* [ME, fr. LL *Israelita, Israelites*, fr. Gk *Israēlitēs*, fr. *Israēl* Israel + *-itēs* -ite] **1 a** (1) **:** a member of the ancient Hebrew people descended from the patriarch Jacob (2) **:** a member of one of the 10 Hebrew tribes anciently inhabiting the northern part of Palestine — compare SAMARITAN **b :** a member of the Jewish people of past or present **:** JEW **2 :** a member of a body of individuals regarded by itself or others as the actual or spiritual chosen people of God

[2]**israelite** \"\ *also* **is·ra·el·it·ic** \ˌ⸗(ˌ)⸗(⸗)ˌid·ik\ *or* **is·ra·el·it·ish** \-īd·|ish, -īt|, |ēsh\ *adj, usu cap* [[2]*israelite* fr. [1]*israelite; israelitic* fr. LL *israeliticus*, fr. *Israelita, Israelites* + L *-icus* -ic; *israelitish* fr. [1]*israelite* + *-ish*] **:** of or relating to Israel ⟨*Israelite* conquests in Canaan⟩ ⟨*Israelite* prophets⟩

iss *abbr* issue

is·sa \ē'sä, i'-\ *n, pl* **issas** \-sä(z)\ *or* **issa** *usu cap* **1 :** a Hamitic people of the French territory of the Afars and the Issas **2 :** a member of the Issa people

is·sa·char·ite \'isəˌkäˌrīt\ *n* -S *usu cap* [*Issachar*, ninth son of Jacob and ancestor of the tribe (fr. LL, fr. Heb *Yissākhār*) + E *-ite*] **:** a member of the Hebrew tribe of Issachar

is·sei \(ˈ)ēˌsā\ *n, pl* **issei** *also* **isseis** *often cap* [Jap, lit., first generation, fr. *is* first + *sei* generation] **:** a Japanese immigrant to America and esp. to the U. S. — compare NISEI

is·su·able \'ish(y)əwəbəl, 'i(ˌ)shüəb-, *chiefly Brit* 'isyəwəb- *or* 'i(ˌ)syüəb-\ *adj* **1 :** that is of such a kind as to admit issue being taken or joined ⟨an ∼ matter⟩ ⟨∼ terms⟩ **2 :** that is authorized for issuing ⟨∼ goods⟩ ⟨∼ currency⟩ **3 :** that may accrue ⟨∼ profits⟩ — **is·su·ably** \-blē,-bli\ *adv*

issuable plea *n* **:** a plea on the merits on which an adverse party may take issue and go to trial

is·su·ance \-əwən(t)s, -üən-\ *n* -S **1 :** ISSUE 9a, 9b **2 :** ISSUE 2a

is·su·ant \-nt\ *adj* **1** *archaic* **:** coming forth from a specified place or source ⟨∼ from the eternal throne, came like a cloud of light, the bright response —P.J.Bailey⟩ **2** *heraldry* **a :** depicted or shown as coming forth ⟨a panther with flames ∼ from the mouth⟩ **b :** depicted or shown as rising upward (as from the top or bottom line of an ordinary or from another bearing or from the base of an escutcheon) ⟨two sprigs ∼⟩ **c** *of an animal figure* **:** rising upward and having only the upper part visible ⟨a lion rampant ∼ from a fess⟩

[1]**is·sue** \'i(ˌ)shü, 'ish(ˌ)yü, 'i(ˌ)shů, 'ish(ˌ)yů, *before a vowel often* -_sh(y)əw; *chiefly in the southern U. S.* -_sh(y)ə *before a consonant or pause or before a vowel in a following word; chiefly Brit* 'i(ˌ)syü *or* 'i(ˌ)syů *or* 'isyəw\ *n* -S [ME, fr. MF, way out, exit, proceeds, fr. OF *eissue, issue*, fr. fem. of *eissu, issu*, past part. of *eissir, issir* to come out, go out, fr. L *exire* to go out, fr. *ex-* [1]ex- + *ire* to go; akin to Goth *iddja* he went, Gk *ienai* to go, Skt *eti* he goes, and prob. to OE *ēode* he went] **1 issues** *pl* **:** proceeds from a source of revenue (as an estate) ⟨rents, profits, and ∼*s*⟩ **2 a** (1) **:** the action of going out or coming out or flowing out from something **:** OUTGOING, EGRESS, OUTFLOW ⟨the ∼ of water from a broken pipe⟩ ⟨a constant entrance and ∼ of visitors⟩ ⟨the river's place of ∼⟩ (2) **:** the action of coming forth from or as if from something in which one is immersed **:** EMERGENCE ⟨the ∼ of a people from barbarism into a civilized way of life⟩ **b :** the power to go out or come out or flow out from something ⟨potentialities that remain repressed for lack of ∼⟩ **3 a :** a means of going out from something **:** EXIT, OUTLET, VENT ⟨a dark labyrinth that had no ∼⟩ **b :** a place where something goes out from something **:** place of egress ⟨at the northern ∼ of the plaza a beautiful boulevard begins⟩; *specif* **:** the point at which a body of water flows out into another usu. larger body of water ⟨a river whose source and ∼ were unknown⟩ **4 :** OFFSPRING, PROGENY ⟨died without ∼⟩; *specif* **:** one or more persons descended from a common ancestor **5 a :** final outcome **:** RESULT, CONSEQUENCE ⟨no chance at all of a happy ∼ —C.P. Snow⟩ **b** *obs* **:** a final conclusion or decision about something arrived at after consideration **c** *archaic* **:** TERMINATION, END ⟨to hope that his enterprise would have a prosperous ∼ —T. B.Macaulay⟩ **6 a :** a point in question of law or fact; *specif* **:** a single material point of law or fact depending in a suit that is affirmed by one side and denied by the other and that is presented for determination at the conclusion of the pleadings **b** (1) **:** a matter that is in dispute between two or more parties or that is to be disputed by the parties **:** a point of debate or controversy ⟨the ∼ over which of them was to be leader⟩ ⟨seemed to want to make an ∼ of almost everything⟩ (2) **:** a matter not yet finally settled and on the settlement of which something else depends **:** a pregnant unsettled matter **:** vital question ⟨burning ∼*s* of the day⟩ ⟨an ∼ that could make or wreck careers —T.H.White b. 1915⟩ ⟨to judge of each ∼ . . . in the light of fact —Rose Macaulay⟩ **:** PROBLEM ⟨in every genuine metaphysical debate some practical ∼, however conjectural and remote, is involved —William James⟩ **:** a controverted subject or topic ⟨the ∼ of desegregation⟩ **c :** something entailing alternatives between which to choose or decide **:** something involving judgments or decisions ⟨a situation seen in terms of the ∼ it presents —Archibald MacLeish⟩ **d :** the point at which an unsettled matter is ready for a decision **:** the point at which a question is ripe for decision ⟨quickly brought the matter to an ∼⟩ **e :** a means of settling a point of debate or controversy; *specif* **:** a test or trial by means of which a question can be settled — used with *put* ⟨the theory was challenged and finally put to the ∼⟩ **7 a :** a discharge (as of blood) from the body that is caused by disease or other physical disorder or that is produced artificially ⟨had long suffered from an ∼ of blood⟩ **b :** an incision made to produce such a discharge **8 a :** something proceeding or coming forth from a usu. specified source ⟨an ∼ of smoke from a chimney⟩; *esp* **:** something proceeding from a usu. specified source by or as if by flowing out or emanating or emerging from it ⟨hallucinations and other ∼*s* of a disordered imagination⟩ **b** *obs* **:** something done by a specified agent **:** DEED **9 a** (1) **:** the act of officially putting forth or getting out or printing (as new currency or postage stamps) or making available or distributing (as supplies or material) or giving out or granting (as licenses) or proclaiming or promulgating (as a written order or directive) ⟨eagerly awaiting the next ∼ of commemorative stamps⟩ ⟨∼ of supplies by the quartermaster⟩ (2) **:** the act of bringing out (as a new book or a revised edition of a book or a new number of a magazine or a fresh printing of a newspaper) for distribution to or sale or circulation among the public **:** PUBLICATION ⟨∼ of the enlarged edition is awaited with interest⟩ ⟨the many details involved in each day's ∼ of a newspaper⟩ (3) **:** the act of offering securities for sale to investors ⟨a new ∼ of government bonds⟩ (4) *chiefly Brit* **:** CIRCULATION 8a, 8c **b :** the condition or fact of being produced or made available by such action ⟨the book's ∼ at such a time took everyone by surprise⟩ **c :** the thing (as a bank note or a security or an item of supplies or an individual's license or a copy of a book, magazine, newspaper) or the whole quantity of things (as all the postage stamps put forth with a certain design or the whole extent of supplies given out on a certain date or all the copies of a periodical printed for a specific day or month) produced or made available at one time or on a certain date by such action and usu. distinguished (as in date, design, content, nature) from those produced or made available at some other time ⟨waiting for the next ∼ of the magazine⟩ ⟨bought specimens of each new ∼ of stamps⟩ **d** *chiefly Brit* **:** CIRCULATION 8b **10 :** the first delivery of a negotiable instrument complete in form (as a bill or note) to a person who takes it as a holder **syn** see EFFECT — **at issue** *adv* **1 :** in a state of controversy **:** at variance **:** at a point where opposing viewpoints are held **:** in disagreement ⟨for years they remained *at issue* with each other⟩ **2** *also* **in issue :** in the process of being critically discussed or questioned **:** under discussion or in question or in dispute ⟨proceeded to inform them of the point *at issue*⟩

[2]**issue** \"\ *vb* -ED/-ING/-S [ME *issuen*, fr. MF *issu*, past part. of *issir* to come out, go out — more at [1]ISSUE] *vi* **1 a :** to go out or come out or flow out ⟨they *issued* out into the street⟩ ⟨a great sigh of relief *issued* from the ancient lungs —T.B.Costain⟩ ⟨the narrow coastal plain into which the Congo ∼*s* —Tom Marvel⟩ **b :** to come forth from or as if from something in which one is immersed **:** EMERGE ⟨the external acts which . . . ∼ from these precepts —R.W.Southern⟩ **c :** to come to an issue of law or fact in pleading **2 :** ACCRUE ⟨profits *issuing* out of sale of the stock⟩ **3 :** to come forth by way of descent from a specified parent or ancestor **:** become descended **:** be an offspring of a specified parent or ancestor ⟨children that shall ∼ from thee — Isa 39:7 (DV)⟩ **4 a :** to proceed or come forth from a usu. specified source ⟨from the dining room *issued* the sound of two voices —Louis Bromfield⟩ ⟨his enmity *issued* from the old man's fear of a possible young rival —C.S.Forester⟩; *esp* **:** to proceed or come forth from a usu. specified source by or as if by flowing out or emanating or emerging from it ⟨blood *issued* from the cut and trickled down his forehead⟩ **b** (1) **:** to be or have a consequence or final outcome **:** RESULT ⟨social unrest *issuing* in several serious conflicts —C.B.Roden⟩ ⟨any unhappiness that we experience ∼*s* generally from our circumstances —W.F.Hambly⟩ (2) **:** to be of such a kind or to have such a nature as to have or tend toward a specified end or consequence or outcome **:** turn out to have a certain result **:** end up by being something specified ⟨such a theory of ethics ∼*s* in three crucial problems —Iredell Jenkins⟩ ⟨*issuing* in necessary and immutable results —J.H.Newman⟩ **:** EVENTUATE ⟨this change in policy *issued* in a permanent institution — W.R.Inge⟩ **5 a :** to appear or become available through being officially put forth or distributed or granted or proclaimed or promulgated **:** appear through issuance ⟨were astonished at the flood of currency *issuing* each year⟩ **b :** to appear or become available through being brought out for distribution to or sale or circulation among the public **:** appear through publication ⟨no new editions are expected to ∼ from that press⟩ **c :** to go forth by authority ⟨there must be an affidavit made showing reasonable grounds before the warrant can ∼ —Paul Wilson⟩ ∼ *vt* **1 :** to cause to come forth **:** give vent to **:** DISCHARGE, EMIT ⟨a volcano *issuing* smoke and fire⟩ **2** *obs* **:** to bring forth (offspring) **3 a :** to cause to appear or become available by officially putting forth or distributing or granting or proclaiming or promulgating **:** cause to appear through issuance ⟨the government *issued* a new airmail stamp⟩ ⟨*issued* a decree⟩ ⟨*issued* a formal letter to his adherents⟩ ⟨*issued* rifles and rations⟩ **b :** to cause to appear or become available by bringing out for distribution to or sale or circulation among the public **:** PUBLISH ⟨*issued* the book shortly after the author's death⟩ **4 a** *obs* **:** TERMINATE, SETTLE **b** *archaic* **:** to cause to have a specified consequence or final outcome or result **:** cause to end up in something specified **syn** see SPRING

is·sue·less \-üləs, -ůl-,-əl-\ *adj* [ME *issules*, fr. *issu, issue* issue + *-les, -lees* -less — more at [1]ISSUE] **:** being without issue: **a :** having no offspring ⟨died ∼⟩ **b :** producing no result ⟨an ∼ effort⟩ **c :** not maintaining or marked by any stand that would arouse debate or controversy ⟨an ∼ piece of writing⟩

issue of fact : FACT IN ISSUE

issue of law : a question involving primarily the application of principles of law as distinguished from an issue involving primarily the determination of facts in a case **:** a question of law rather than of fact — compare FACT IN ISSUE

issue pea *n* **:** a small globular object (as a dried garden pea or a wooden bead) formerly placed in an abscess or ulcer so as to induce or increase a suppurative discharge

is·su·er \-əwə(r), -üə(r), -ůə(r)\ *n* -S **:** one that issues something (as securities, currency, books)

ist \'ist\ *n, pl* **ists** \'is(t)s\ *n* -S [[1]*-ist*] **:** one that professes or adheres to or specializes in an ism — usu. used disparagingly

[1]**-ist** \əst *sometimes* ˌist\ *n suffix, pl* **-ists** \-s(t)s\ [ME *-iste*, fr. OF & L; OF *-iste*, fr. L *-ista*, fr. Gk *-istēs*, fr. *-is-* (fr. verb

stems in *-izein -ize*) + *-tēs* (suffix forming agent nouns)] **1 a :** one that does **:** one that performs a (specified) action ⟨cycl*ist*⟩ ⟨balloon*ist*⟩ ⟨duell*ist*⟩ **:** one that makes or produces ⟨novel*ist*⟩ ⟨syllog*ist*⟩ **b :** one that plays a (specified) musical instrument ⟨organ*ist*⟩ ⟨violin*ist*⟩ **c :** one that operates a (specified) mechanical instrument or contrivance ⟨telegraph*ist*⟩ **2 a :** one that practices or studies or specializes in a (specified) art or science or particular field of knowledge or particular skill ⟨geolog*ist*⟩ ⟨mytholog*ist*⟩ ⟨algebra*ist*⟩ ⟨ventriloqu*ist*⟩ **b** (1) **:** one that is usu. professionally occupied with or interested in ⟨fashion*ist*⟩ ⟨color*ist*⟩ (2) **:** one that toys with or dabbles in ⟨controvert*ist*⟩ ⟨speculat*ist*⟩ **3 :** one that professes or adheres to or advocates a (specified) doctrine or theory or system or policy or code of behavior or procedure ⟨de*ist*⟩ ⟨social*ist*⟩ ⟨royal*ist*⟩ ⟨hedon*ist*⟩ ⟨pur*ist*⟩ or that supports the doctrine or theory or system or policy or code of behavior or procedure of a (specified) individual ⟨Calvin*ist*⟩ ⟨Darwin*ist*⟩ ⟨Hitler*ist*⟩ — esp. in nouns corresponding to nouns in *-ism* **4 :** one that is marked by ⟨pessim*ist*⟩ ⟨fatal*ist*⟩ — esp. in nouns corresponding to nouns in *-ism*

²-ist \"\ *adj suffix* **:** of, relating to, or characteristic of (something indicated) ⟨dilettant*ist*⟩

is't \(')ist\ [by contr.] *archaic* **:** is it

is·tan·bul \ˌistəm¦bül, -ˌstä¦, -ˌstal, -ˌstaal, -ˌstȧl, ¦n¦b-, -bu̇l *also* ¦ē(ˌ)s-\ *adj, usu cap* [fr. *Istanbul*, city on the European side of the Bosporus in Turkey] **:** of or from the city of Istanbul, Turkey **:** of the kind or style prevalent in Istanbul

¹isth·mi·an \'ismēən\ *n* -s [L *isthmius*, adj., isthmian (fr. Gk *isthmios*, fr. *isthmos* isthmus) + E *-an*, n. suffix] **1 :** a native or inhabitant of an isthmus **2** *usu cap* **:** a native or inhabitant of the Isthmus of Panama

²isthmian \"\ *adj* [L *isthmius*, adj., isthmian + E *-an*, adj. suffix] **:** of, relating to, or situated in or near an isthmus ⟨an ~ route⟩ ⟨an ~ people⟩: as **a** *often cap* **:** of or relating to the Isthmus of Corinth in Greece or the games anciently held there ⟨the *Isthmian* festival⟩ **b** *often cap* **:** of or relating to the Isthmus of Panama connecting the No. American and So. American continents ⟨the *Isthmian* canal⟩

isth·mi·ate \-mēˌāt\ *adj* [NL *isthmiatus*, fr. *isthmi-* (fr. *isthmus*) + L *-atus* -ate] **:** having an isthmus (sense 2)

isth·mic \-mik\ *adj* [L *isthmicus*, fr. Gk *isthmikos*, fr. *isthmos* isthmus + *-ikos* -ic] **1 :** ISTHMIAN **2** *also* **isth·mal** \-məl\ [*isthmus* + *-ic* or *-al*] **:** of, relating to, or taking place in a bodily isthmus ⟨~ ectopic pregnancy⟩

isth·moid \-ˌmȯid\ *adj* [prob. fr. (assumed) NL *isthmoides*, fr. NL *isthm-* (fr. *isthmus*) + L *-oides* -oid] **:** resembling an isthmus

isth·mus \'isməs, *chiefly Brit sometimes* 'istm-\ *n* -ES [L, fr. Gk *isthmos*; perh. akin to ON *eith* isthmus, Gk *ithma* step, motion, *ienai* to go — more at ISSUE] **1 :** a narrow strip of land running through a body of water and connecting two larger land areas (as two continents or a peninsula and the mainland) **2 :** a contracted part or passage connecting two larger structures or cavities: as **a :** an embryonic constriction separating midbrain from hindbrain **b :** the lower portion of the uterine corpus **c :** the fleshy area on the throat of a fish between the gills **d :** a narrow intermediate portion of the pharynx of many nematodes **e :** the constricted connection between the main parts of a desmid

isthmus of the fauces : FAUCES 1

-is·tic \ˈistik, -tēk\ *also* **-is·ti·cal** \-tȯkəl, -tēk-\ *adj suffix* [*-istic* fr. MF & L & Gk; MF *-istique*, fr. L *-isticus*, fr. Gk *-istikos*, fr. *-istēs* -ist + *-ikos* -ic; *-istical* fr. MF *-istique* & L *-isticus* & Gk *-istikos* + E *-al*] **:** of, relating to, or characteristic of ⟨panoist*ic*⟩ — often in adjectives corresponding to nouns in *-ism* or nouns in *-ist* ⟨altru*istic*⟩

is·ti·o·phor·i·dae \ˌistēō'fȯrəˌdē\ *n pl, cap* [NL, fr. *Istiophorus*, type genus + *-idae*] **:** a family of large vigorous marine scombroid fishes comprising important food and sport fishes (as sailfishes, spearfishes, and marlins)

is·ti·oph·o·rus \ˌistē'äfərəs\ *n, cap* [NL, irreg. fr. Gk *histion* sail + NL *-phorus*; akin to Gk *histanai* to cause to stand — more at STAND] **:** a small but widely distributed genus of fishes comprising the sailfishes (sense 1) and being type of the family Istiophoridae

is·tle *also* **ix·tle** \'is(t)lē\ *n* -s [AmerSp *ixtle*, fr. Nahuatl *ichtli*] **:** a fiber obtained from any of various tropical American plants: as **a :** a fiber obtained from the leaves of an epiphytic bromeliad (*Bromelia sylvestris*) **b :** a fiber obtained from any of several Mexican plants of the genus *Agave* (esp. *A. ixtli*) and used esp. for cordage and basketry

¹is·tri·an \'istrēən\ *adj, usu cap* [*Istria* + E *-an*, adj. suffix] **1 :** of, relating to, or characteristic of Istria, a peninsula on the northeast coast of the Adriatic sea **2 :** of, relating to, or characteristic of the people of Istria

²istrian \"\ *n* -s *cap* [*Istria* + E *-an*, n. suffix] **:** a native or inhabitant of Istria

ists *pl of* IST

-ists *pl of* -IST

isu·rus \ī'su̇rəs\ *n, cap* [NL, fr. *is-* + *-urus*] **:** a genus of large voracious sharks that is sometimes made the type of a separate family but usu. included in Lamnidae — see MACKEREL SHARK

ISV *abbr* International Scientific Vocabulary

ISWG *abbr* imperial standard wire gauge

¹it \(ˌ)i|t, ·ət, *usu* |d·+V\ *pron* [ME *it, hit*, fr. OE *hit* — more at HE] **1 a :** that one — used as neuter pronoun of the third person singular that is the subject or direct object or indirect object of a verb or the object of a preposition and usu. used in reference to (1) a lifeless thing ⟨took a quick look at the house and noticed ~ was very old⟩ ⟨saw the corpse and walked over to ~⟩ ⟨~ is now no more —E.H.Collis⟩ or (2) a plant ⟨there is a rosebush near the fence and ~ is now blooming⟩ or (3) an insect ⟨felt a fly land on her neck and squirmed as ~ crawled down⟩ or an animal whose sex is unknown or disregarded ⟨saw the horse break away and watched ~ gallop into the canyon⟩ or (4) an infant or child whose sex is unknown or disregarded ⟨if a child were severely beaten every time ~ sneezed —Bertrand Russell⟩ ⟨heard the baby crying and brought ~ some milk⟩ or (5) a group or classification of individuals or things ⟨the football team is in top form and ~ is sure of victory⟩ ⟨buy a bag of apricots . . . plums and grapes for fifteen cents, wash . . . and eat ~ on our way —Claudia Cassidy⟩ or (6) an abstract noun ⟨beauty is everywhere and ~ is a source of joy⟩ or (7) a word viewed as a word ⟨*machine* is a common word and ~ can be applied to a variety of things⟩ or (8) a phrase or clause ⟨"Go ahead," she said, but he didn't hear ~⟩; sometimes used pleonastically together with a noun as subject of a verb esp. in ballad poetry ⟨our love ~ was stronger by far —E.A.Poe⟩ and in substandard speech ⟨the horse ~ ran away⟩; often used with a present participle like the adjective *its* with a gerund in a way that makes distinction between the two constructions impossible except by arbitrary analysis ⟨wet it before applying to the seal, to prevent ~ sticking —H.S. Kingsford⟩ ⟨there was a doubt about ~ being available —Valentine Heywood⟩; see ITS; compare HE, SHE, THEY **b** (1) **:** that male or female one whose identity is unknown or uncertain — used esp. in indirect or direct questions in reference to one that is usu. not directly indicated (as by pointing) or otherwise clearly specified (as by a qualifying clause or phrase) ⟨don't know who ~ is⟩ ⟨the knocking at the door continued and she finally said "who is ~?"⟩ ⟨someone appeared dimly in the fog and ~ spoke like my brother⟩ (2) **:** that male or female one whose identity is known — sometimes used in the speech of children or usu. disparagingly in the speech of others as a subject or object in reference to any person ⟨just look at my daddy and the big car ~ has⟩ ⟨what a little haughty prude ~ is —W.M.Thackeray⟩ ⟨just listen to ~ talk⟩ **c :** YOU — used in speaking to or as if to a baby ⟨did ~ hurt its little knees and chin⟩ — compare HE 4 **d :** ITSELF — used as indirect or direct object of a verb or as object of a preposition ⟨the plane plunged to earth carrying all its occupants with ~⟩ **2 a** — used as an expletive subject of an impersonal verb that expresses a simple condition or an action without direct or implied reference to an agent in statements or questions about (1) the weather ⟨~ is raining⟩ ⟨~ is getting cold⟩ ⟨is ~ a pretty day —Agnes S. Turnbull⟩ or (2) the time ⟨~ is eleven o'clock⟩ ⟨~ is late⟩ or divisions or points of time (as seasons, holidays, generalized parts of day or night) ⟨~'s only a few months until spring —C.W.Morton⟩ ⟨~ will soon be Christmas⟩ ⟨~ is getting on toward evening⟩ ⟨~ will dawn early tomorrow⟩ or (3) physical or mental conditions ⟨~ hurts when I look at a bright light⟩ ⟨~ makes him sad if he thinks about her too much⟩ or (4) an extent of distance or space ⟨~ is five miles to the next town⟩ **b** — used as an expletive subject in other statements or questions having an undefined subject ⟨if ~ hadn't been for you, I don't know what I would have done⟩ ⟨they have what ~ takes⟩ **3 a** (1) — used as an anticipatory subject of a verb whose logical subject is another word or a phrase or a clause ⟨~ is me⟩ ⟨~ is he who is responsible⟩ ⟨~ is the mayor they like⟩ ⟨~ is well you found out in time⟩ ⟨~ is necessary to repeat the whole thing⟩ ⟨~ is said the danger is great⟩ ⟨~ is a wonderful vacation spot, that town⟩ ⟨~ happened that they were away⟩; often used as subject of a periphrasis to shift emphasis from a logical subject to some other part of a statement ⟨~ was in this city that the treaty was signed⟩ (2) — used as an anticipatory object of a verb whose logical object is another word or a phrase or a clause ⟨I take ~ that there was some kind of rift —Hamilton Basso⟩ ⟨he made ~ clear, that answer of his⟩ ⟨found ~ necessary to continue⟩ ⟨made ~ evident that we needed help⟩ **b** *now chiefly dial* — used with the verb *be* where *there* is now used ⟨are you so proud, so censorious, that ~ is no living with them —Paul Bayne⟩ ⟨~ was an English lady bright, and she would marry a Scottish knight —Sir Walter Scott⟩ ⟨~'s nobody here but me⟩ **c** — used with many transitive verbs as a direct object with little or no meaning and an almost entirely expletive or reinforcing function ⟨really living ~ up⟩ ⟨decided to rough ~ on his vacation⟩ or with many intransitive verbs as an apparent direct object with the same function ⟨footed ~ back to camp⟩ ⟨the satellites were free to go ~ alone —*Newsweek*⟩ or with some words used as nonce verbs as an apparent direct object with the same function ⟨decided that we would . . . hotel ~ —J.K. Jerome⟩ ⟨a man who likes to chef ~ now and then —Gerald Movius⟩ **4 a** (1) **:** a matter discussed or considered or about to be discussed or considered ⟨remembered she had told him about ~⟩ ⟨~ being agreed then —Walter Goodman⟩ (2) **:** a situation referred to either directly or by implication or about to be referred to either directly or by implication ⟨thought ~ was splendid⟩ ⟨doubted ~ would happen⟩ ⟨~ added up to a strangeness for which nothing in the previous frontier culture was a preparation —Bernard DeVoto⟩ (3) **:** a statement or idea or similar object of attention referred to either directly or by implication or about to be referred to either directly or by implication ⟨if you remember these points ~ will help you⟩ **b :** something read (as a passage in a book, words on a sign) ⟨~ tells in the book about the American Revolution⟩ ⟨~ says in the papers he expects to win the election⟩ ⟨a mile back ~ said to take a right turn⟩ or something looked at (as a traffic signal, a directional arrow) ⟨come on, ~ says to go⟩ **5 :** the general state of affairs or circumstances **:** general situation ⟨~ hasn't gone so well today⟩ ⟨came to that remote place to fish, get away from ~ all —Robert Murphy⟩ ⟨remember me, when ~ is well with you —Gen 40:14 (RSV)⟩ **6 a** (1) **:** something that has been done ⟨do ~ some more⟩ or is being done ⟨quit ~⟩ ⟨cut ~ out⟩ or is to be done ⟨go to ~⟩ ⟨he'll do ~ the right way⟩ ⟨decided to make a long weekend of ~ —Rebecca West⟩ (2) **:** some unpleasant or dreaded eventuality ⟨in for ~ now⟩; *specif* **:** punishment or chastisement or retribution ⟨going to catch ~⟩ ⟨put up with his sneers as long as possible and then let him have ~⟩ **b** (1) **:** all that one can desire or experience ⟨claims he's had ~ and that life is now pretty much a bore⟩ (2) **:** all that one can endure or suffer ⟨had a terrible day and swore he'd really had ~⟩ (3) **:** all that one is going to be allowed to have or do ⟨he's had ~ — I'm not going to put up with that nonsense any longer⟩ **c :** all that is required **:** the total extent of something needed or wanted ⟨when you've finished that job, that's ~ and you can go home⟩ ⟨everyone passes by, shakes hands and that's ~ —D.E.Weinland⟩ **d :** an expenditure of effort in attempting to attain an objective **:** STRUGGLE, CONTEST ⟨stick to ~ and you'll win out⟩ **7 :** a way out of a difficulty **:** answer to a problem **:** SOLUTION ⟨I have ~! This is what we'll do⟩ **8 a :** what is important or essential or tenaciously held to or sought after **:** what counts **:** what matters ⟨haven't got a chance and you should realize ~ is all over now⟩; *specif* **:** LIFE ⟨had stopped breathing and I could see ~ was all over⟩ **b** (1) **:** a crucial moment when much is at stake **:** a crisis on whose outcome much or everything depends ⟨an offensive was about to be launched and headquarters felt that this was ~⟩ (2) **:** a point at which the end of life or the end of everything that matters is imminent ⟨this is ~. From now on no power on earth can save the doomed city —F.V.Drake⟩ **9 a :** a quality or group of qualities requisite or desirable for or evidenced in a particular situation ⟨the legislators had ~ on most of the other delegates in convention maneuvering —Bill Hatch⟩ **b :** something that is expected or desired **:** something suitable or satisfactory ⟨that's ~, you're doing fine⟩ **c** (1) **:** something that perfectly or nearly perfectly meets the requirements of a situation **:** the very thing needed or required **:** just the thing wanted ⟨here's a suggestion for a Christmas gift that is really ~⟩ (2) **:** something that is without equal **:** something peerless ⟨stop acting as though you were ~⟩ ⟨she just seems to think she's ~⟩ (3) **:** something beyond which one cannot go **:** the ultimate **:** PINNACLE, ACME ⟨when it comes to graciousness, she's really ~⟩ **10 :** SEXUAL INTERCOURSE ⟨if I wanted to let you touch me I would . . . can't you see I don't want ~ —Morley Callaghan⟩

²it \"\ *adj* [ME *hit*, fr. *hit* (pron.)] *now chiefly dial* **:** ITS

³it \'it, *usu* 'id·+V\ *n* -s [¹*it*] **1 :** the player in a game who performs a key active or passive function (as trying to catch others in a game of tag or to answer questions in a guessing game) essential to the nature of the game **2 :** physical allure esp. when accompanied by personal magnetism and charm **:** SEX APPEAL

-it \ət, əd\ *vb suffix* [ME, alter. of *-ed*] *Scot var of* -ED

it *abbr* item

IT *abbr* **1** immediate transportation **2** immunity test **3** income tax **4** internal thread **5** international tolerance **6** *often not cap* [L *in transitu*] in transit

ita \'ēd·ə\ *n, pl* **ita** *or* **itas** *usu cap* [Tag] **:** AETA

ita·bi·rite \ˌēd·ə'biˌrīt\ *n* -s [*Itabira* (now, Presidente Vargas), town in Minas Gerais state, Brazil) + E *-ite*] **:** a quartzite containing micaceous hematite

ita·cism \'ēd·əˌsizəm\ *n* -s [modif. of Gk *ēta* eta + *-cism* (as in *iotacism*) — more at ETA] **1 :** pronunciation of Greek eta as \ē\ **2 :** IOTACISM

ita·cist \-sə̇st\ *n* -s **:** one that practices or favors itacism — **ita·cis·tic** \¦==¦sistik\ *adj*

it·a·col·u·mite \ˌid·ə'käl(y)əˌmīt\ *n* -s [*Itacolumi*, mountain in Minas Gerais state, Brazil + E *-ite*] **:** a schistose micaceous quartzite that is flexible when split into thin slabs

it·a·con·ate \ˌid·ə'käˌnāt\ *n* -s [*itaconic* (acid) + *-ate*] **:** a salt or ester of itaconic acid

it·a·con·ic acid \¦==¦=nik-\ *n* [ISV, anagram of *aconitic*] **:** a crystalline dicarboxylic acid $HOOCC(=CH_2)CH_2COOH$ obtained by decomposing aconitic acid or usu. by fermentation of sugars with molds of the genus *Aspergillus* and used as a monomer for both vinyl-type polymers and polyesters; methylene-succinic acid

ital- *or* **italo-** *comb form, usu cap* [*Ital-* fr. L *Italus; Italo-* fr. It or L; It, fr. *italo*, fr. L *Italus*] **1 :** Italian ⟨*Ital*american⟩ **2 :** Italian and ⟨*Italo*-Austrian⟩

ital *abbr* italic

¹ital·ian \ə'talyən, *chiefly dial or substand or disparaging* (')ī¦t-\ *n* -s *cap* [ME, fr. L *Italia* Italy (fr. Gk *Italia*) + ME *-an*] **1 a :** a native or inhabitant of Italy **b :** one that is of Italian descent **2 :** the language of the Italians developed from the Vulgar Latin of ancient times

²italian \"\ *adj, usu cap* **1 a :** of, relating to, or characteristic of Italy **b :** of, relating to, or characteristic of Italians **2 :** of, relating to, or characteristic of the Italian language

¹ital·ian·ate \-ˌnāt\ *vt* -ED/-ING/-S [prob. fr. It *italianato*, adj.] **:** ITALIANIZE

²ital·ian·ate \-nə̇t, -ˌnāt\ *adj, usu cap* [It *italianato*, fr. *italiano* Italian (fr. *Italia* Italy — fr. L — + *-ano* — fr. L *-anus* -an) + *-ato* (fr. L *-atus* -ate)] **1 :** ITALIANIZED ⟨an *Italianate* Englishman⟩ **2 :** having an Italian quality **:** marked by Italian characteristics or influence ⟨*Italianate* architecture⟩

italian bee *n, usu cap I* **:** a honeybee predominantly yellowish in color that resembles the Carniolan bee in habits

italian blue *n, often cap I* **:** a vivid greenish blue

italian chestnut *n, usu cap I* **:** SPANISH CHESTNUT

italian clover *n, usu cap I* **:** CRIMSON CLOVER

italian corn salad *n, usu cap I* **:** a southern European succulent plant (*Valerianella eriocarpa*) used as a salad vegetable

italian cypress *n, usu cap I* **:** a Eurasian tree (*Cupressus sempervirens*) with thin gray bark and erect or ascending branches and dark green leaves resembling scales — called also *Mediterranean cypress*

italian earth *n, often cap I* **1 :** RAW SIENNA **2 :** BURNT SIENNA

italian fennel *n, usu cap I* **:** CAROSELLA

italian green *n* **1** *often cap I* **:** TERRE VERTE 2 **2** *usu cap I&G* **:** a sulfur dye — see DYE table I (under *Sulfur Green 11*)

italian greyhound *n, usu cap I* **:** a toy dog of a breed developed by selective breeding from the standard-sized greyhound

italian hand *n, usu cap I* **1 :** a book hand characterized by roundness and a fine sloping line developed about the 12th century A.D. in Italy from the Roman cursive and revived by calligraphers in the early 15th century and used as the model for the first Italian printers and for modern English handwriting — compare ITALIC **2 :** craftiness or subtlety in the conduct of political, business, or personal affairs — usu. used in the phrase *fine Italian hand*

italian honeysuckle *n, usu cap I* **:** ITALIAN WOODBINE

ital·ian·ism \-yəˌnizəm\ *n* -s *usu cap* [prob. fr. MF *italianisme*, fr. OIt *italiano* Italian + MF *-isme* -ism — more at ITALIANATE] **1 a :** a quality or group of qualities distinctive of Italy or the Italian people **b :** a linguistic feature (as a pronunciation or a word or a phrase or an idiom) borrowed from or suggestive of the Italian language **2 a :** specialized interest in or emulation of Italian qualities or achievements **b :** attachment to or furtherance of Italian policies or ideals

ital·ian·ist \-nə̇st\ *n* -s *usu cap* **1 :** a specialist in the study of Italy or the Italian people or the Italian language **2 :** one that is attached to or seeks to further Italian policies or ideals

ital·ian·i·ty \ə̇ˌtalē'anəd·ē, -ˌl'ya-\ *n* -ES *usu cap* **:** the quality or state of being Italian (as in character or allegiance)

ital·ian·iza·tion \ə̇ˌtalyənə̇'zāshən, -ˌnī'z-\ *n* -s *usu cap* **1 :** the action or process of italianizing or of becoming italianized **2 :** something (as a name or word) that has been italianized

ital·ian·ize \ə̇'talyəˌnīz\ *vb* -ED/-ING/-s *often cap, see -ize in Explan Notes* [prob. fr. F *italianiser*, fr. MF, fr. OIt *italiano* Italian + MF *-iser* -ize — more at ITALIANATE] *vi* **:** to act in a fashion regarded as distinctive of Italians; *specif* **:** to follow (as in style or technique) recognized Italian painters ⟨the *italianizing* masters of Antwerp⟩ ~ *vt* **1 :** to make Italian (as in behavior, appearance, culture, style) ⟨foreigners gradually *italianized* by residence in Italy⟩ **:** cause to have Italian characteristics ⟨*italianizing* a style of architecture⟩ **2 :** to change or modify (as a word or expression foreign to Italian) so as to make conform (as in spelling or pronunciation) to characteristics of the Italian language ⟨an *italianized* family name⟩

ital·ian·iz·er \-zə(r)\ *n* -s *often cap* **:** one that italianizes

italian kale *n, usu cap I* **:** SEVEN-TOP TURNIP

italian lake *n, often cap I* **:** YELLOW OCHER 2

ital·ian·ly *adv, usu cap* **:** in an Italian manner

italian millet *n, usu cap I* **:** FOXTAIL MILLET

italian ocher *n, often cap I* **:** RAW SIENNA 2

italian paste *n, usu cap I* **:** ALIMENTARY PASTE

italian pear scale *n, usu cap I* **:** a reddish to purple hard scale (*Epidiaspis piricola*) that is sometimes destructive to various fruit and nut trees in California

italian pink *n, often cap I* **:** DUTCH PINK 2

italian pool *n, usu cap I* **:** pin pool played with four balls

italian poplar *n, usu cap I* **:** LOMBARDY POPLAR

italian roast *n, usu cap I* **:** coffee of an extremely dark roast

italian ryegrass *also* **italian rye** *n, usu cap I* **:** a European grass (*Lolium multiflorum*) much used for hay and in the U.S. also for turf and green-manuring

italians *pl of* ITALIAN

italian sixth *n, usu cap I* **:** an augmented sixth chord consisting of a musical tone with a major third and an augmented sixth above the lowest tone (as A-flat, C, F-sharp)

italian sonnet *n, usu cap I* **:** PETRARCHAN SONNET

italian stone pine *n, usu cap I* **:** STONE PINE 2

italian thistle *n, usu cap I* **:** a hoary thistle (*Carduus pycnocephalus*) native to the Mediterranean region but established as a weed in the southwestern U.S.

italian turnip *or* **italian turnip broccoli** *n, usu cap I* **:** an annual or biennial (*Brassica ruvo*) prob. of European origin but grown elsewhere for its tops and tender flower shoots which are used as greens — called also *broccoli rab*

italian vegetable marrow *n, usu cap I* **:** COCOZELLE

italian vermouth *n, usu cap I* **:** sweet vermouth

italian walnut *n, usu cap I* **:** ENGLISH WALNUT

italian woodbine *n, usu cap I* **:** a Eurasian honeysuckle (*Lonicera caprifolium*) sometimes escaped in America and having the upper leaves connate and the flowers usu. in sessile whorls in the axils

¹ital·ic \ə̇'talik, -lēk *also* (')ī¦t-\ *adj* [L *Italicus* Italian, of Italy, fr. Gk *Italikos*, fr. *Italia* Italy + *-ikos* -ic] **1** *usu cap* **a** [NL *Italica*, fr. L, fem. of *Italicus*] **:** COMPOSITE **a b** *of handwriting* **:** characterized by a sloping angle suggestive of italics ⟨written in a medieval *Italic* script⟩ — compare GOTHIC 3 **c** (1) **:** of, relating to, or characteristic of ancient Italy (2) **:** of, relating to, or characteristic of the peoples of ancient Italy ⟨vanished *Italic* cultures⟩ **d** (1) **:** of, relating to, or characteristic of a branch of the Indo-European language family that includes Latin and other languages (as Oscan, Umbrian) spoken by the peoples of ancient Italy and that also includes the Romance languages (as Italian, French, Spanish) descended from Latin (2) **:** of, relating to, or characteristic of the ancient languages of the Italic branch of the Indo-European language family as contrasted with the modern Romance languages (3) **:** of, relating to, or characteristic of Osco-Umbrian **2** *sometimes cap* **:** of, relating to, produced in, or characteristic of a style of distinctively printed letters or numbers or other characters that slant upward to the right (as in "*these words are italic*") and that are sometimes distinguished from other faces (as some obliques) having about the same degree of slant by the form of the letter *a* and that are typically used to give emphasis to a word or group of words or to refer to words as words or to indicate words or phrases foreign to the language of a context or to refer to titles of long works ⟨beautifully printed ~ letters⟩ ⟨paragraphs beginning with ~ capitals⟩

²italic \"\ *n* -s **1** *sometimes cap* **a :** an italic character **:** italic type ⟨an ~ is used at the beginning of each subdivision⟩ ⟨introduced ~*s* as a device for achieving emphasis⟩ ⟨printed in ~⟩ ⟨a font of ~*s*⟩ **b :** a written letter or number or other character (as in a handwritten or typed manuscript) that is underscored for emphasis or for some other purpose achieved in print by the use of italic type or that is so underscored (as in a handwritten or typed manuscript sent to a printer) to indicate that the matter underscored is to be set in italic type ⟨each ~ is clearly underlined⟩ ⟨writes a delighted "*yes!*" with ~*s* and a mark of exclamation —R.G.F.Robinson⟩ ⟨after the underscored sentence in the manuscript the author writes "~*s* mine"⟩ **c** *usu* **italics** *pl but sometimes sing in constr* **:** exaggerated intonation or some similar oral speech device by which one or more words is heavily and usu. affectedly emphasized or otherwise given sharp prominence ⟨was yapping, her silly voice fraught with ~*s* —Margaret Long⟩ ⟨a woman who has an irritating way of speaking in ~*s* —W.J. Locke⟩ **2** *cap* **a :** a branch of the Indo-European language family that includes Latin and other languages (as Oscan, Umbrian) spoken by the peoples of ancient Italy and that also includes the Romance languages (as Italian, French, Spanish) descended from Latin — see INDO-EUROPEAN LANGUAGES table **b :** the group of ancient languages of this branch as contrasted with the modern Romance languages **c :** OSCO-UMBRIAN

ital·i·cism \-ləˌsizəm\ *n* -s *usu cap* [¹*italic* + *-ism*] **:** ITALIANISM 1b

ital·i·ci·za·tion \ə̇ˌtaləsə̇'zāshən, -ˌsī' *also* ī,-\ *n* [*italicize* + *-ation*] **:** the use of italics or a single underscore in printing or writing

ital·i·cize \-ˌsīz\ *vb* -ED/-ING/-s *see -ize in Explan Notes* [¹*italic* + *-ize*] *vt* **1 a :** to print in italics ⟨the printer *italicized* the whole passage⟩ **b :** to underscore with a single line for emphasis or for some other purpose achieved in print by the use of italic type or so as to indicate that the matter underscored is to be set in italic type ⟨annoyingly *italicizes* sentence after sentence in her notes⟩ **2 :** ACCENTUATE, EMPHASIZE, STRESS: as **a :** to give sharp prominence to (spoken words) usu. affectedly by the use of some oral speech device esp. exaggerated intonation ⟨she was *italicizing* every other word with that deadly, glittering brightness that a woman puts on —George Orwell⟩ ⟨*italicized* words and even phrases surged about in her conversation —Ngaio Marsh⟩ **b :** to bring out strongly or cause to be highlighted **:** play up ⟨decorative features that ~ the building's perfect symmetry⟩ ⟨his scorn for the orthodox language and logic of the law is *italicized* by such wry remarks —Fred Rodell⟩ ⟨serves especially to ~ the principle —N.F.Adkins⟩ ⟨dramatically *italicizes* the movie's theme —*Newsweek*⟩ **c :** to outline sharply **:** bring into sharp relief ⟨the little carmine smudge of her *italicized* lips —Bruce Marshall⟩ ~ *vi* **:** to use italics ⟨has a habit of *italicizing*⟩

¹ital·i·ote \ə'talē,ōt, -ēət\ *also* **ital·i·ot** \-ēət, -ē,ät\ *n* -s *usu cap* [Gk *Italiōtēs*, fr. *Italia* Italy + *-ōtēs* -ote] **:** a Greek inhabitant of ancient Italy

²italiote \"\ *adj, usu cap* **:** of or relating to the Italiotes

italo- — see ITAL-

¹italo·phile \ə'talə,fīl, 'id·ᵊlō,f-\ *also* **italo·phil** \-,fil\ *adj, usu cap* [*Ital-* + *-phile* or *-phil*] **:** friendly to or favoring what is Italian ⟨~ policies⟩

²italophile \"\ *n* -s *usu cap* **:** one that is friendly to or favors what is Italian

it·a·ly \'id·ᵊlē, 'itᵊl-, -li, *in rapid speech* 'itl-\ *adj, usu cap* [fr. *Italy*, country in southern Europe] **:** of or from Italy **:** of the kind or style prevalent in Italy

ita palm *or* **eta palm** \'ēd·ə-\ *n* [of Arawakan origin; akin to Arawak (Guiana) *itē* ita palm, Baniva *itéui*] **:** MIRITI PALM

itas *pl of* ITA

ita·uba \,ēd·ə'übə, ,id-\ *n* -s [Pg *itaúba*, fr. Tupi *itauba*] **1 :** a large South American tree (*Mezilaurus itauba*) of the family Lauraceae that yields a durable russet-brown wood much used in marine and general construction **2 :** the wood of the itauba

¹itch \'ich\ *n* -ES [ME *icche, yicche*, fr. OE *gicce*, fr. *giccan*, v.] **1 a :** a localized or generalized uneasy sensation (as of a crawling, prickling, stinging) in the upper surface of the skin usu. considered to result from mild stimulation of pain receptors and producing a feeling of irritation in the affected area and eliciting an urge to relieve the affected area by scratching **:** ITCHING, PRURITUS ⟨had an ~ and scratched it⟩ **b :** a skin disorder (as a mange) accompanied by such a sensation; *esp* **:** a contagious eruption in man and animals that is marked by this sensation experienced to an intense degree and by surface lesions and that is caused by invasion of the skin by an itch mite (*Sarcoptes scabiei*) that forms minute galleries in the skin and keeps up a constant irritation — usu. used with *the* ⟨has the ~⟩; compare MANGE **2 a** (1) **:** a restless usu. constant often compulsive desire for or hankering after something **:** restless longing **:** uneasy craving ⟨a compelling ~ for money and success —Lee Rogow⟩ ⟨the ~ to travel⟩ ⟨the same restless ~ to be always doing something else —Bertrand Russell⟩ ⟨was uninfected by the ~ of publicity —V.L.Parrington⟩ (2) **:** a restless craving for sensual esp. sexual gratification **:** LUST, PRURIENCE ⟨the ~ of the senses —Bruce Marshall⟩ ⟨with meaty good looks and the gross ~ they often portend —*Time*⟩ ⟨had aroused in him only the vague adolescent ~ of desire which almost any personable woman could satisfy —Aldous Huxley⟩ **b :** a restless usu. constant inclination toward something **:** restless propensity **:** uneasy predisposition or overreadiness ⟨the ~ to justify all conduct on logical grounds —H.J.Muller⟩ ⟨an ~ for activity —Raymond Holden⟩ **3 :** a condition of restless ferment **:** seething agitation **:** STEW ⟨the ~ of aggressive nationalism —Karl Robson⟩ ⟨was in an ~ to be off —Bruce Marshall⟩ ⟨lived in a constant ~ of irritation —Hesketh Pearson⟩

²itch \"\ *vb* -ED/-ING/-ES [ME *ichen, icchen, yicchen*, fr. OE *giccan*; akin to OHG *jucchen* to itch, MD *joken*] *vi* **1 a :** to have a localized or generalized uneasy sensation (as of a crawling, prickling, stinging) in the upper surface of the skin **:** have an itch ⟨seemed to ~ all over⟩ ⟨her arm ~*ed*⟩ **b :** to produce such a sensation ⟨heavy winter underwear that ~*ed*⟩ **2 a :** to have a restless usu. constant often compulsive desire for or hankering after something **:** long restlessly for something **:** crave something uneasily ⟨and ~ to get their hands on a juicy morsel —D.L.Cohn⟩ ⟨were ~*ing* to take immediate action —W.F.Hambly⟩ ⟨~*ed* to see the world⟩ **b :** to have a restless usu. constant inclination toward something **:** have a restless propensity for or uneasy predisposition to something **:** be impatiently eager **:** be overready ⟨killers who ~*ed* to kill again —Hal Burton⟩ **3 :** to be in a restless ferment **:** SEETHE, STEW ⟨~ with one curiosity —Milton Bracker⟩ ⟨~*es* with lechery —J.I.Cope⟩ ~ *vt* **1 :** to cause to have a localized or generalized uneasy sensation (as of a crawling, prickling, stinging) in the upper surface of the skin **:** cause to have an itch ⟨felt it ~ his leg —Joan Williams⟩ ⟨wool socks that ~*ed* his feet⟩ **2 :** IRK, VEX, IRRITATE ⟨had always been amused . . . where the others were ~*ed* —Sinclair Lewis⟩

³itch \"\ *var of* ECHE

itch·i·ly \'ichəlē, -li\ *adv* **:** in an itchy manner **:** NERVOUSLY, RESTLESSLY ⟨holding it ~, as if it were a snake —*Time*⟩

itch·i·ness \-chēnəs, -chin-\ *n* -ES **:** the quality or state of being itchy

¹itching *adj* [fr. pres. part. of ²*itch*] **:** that itches: **a :** having, producing, or marked by an uneasy sensation in the skin ⟨bothered with an ~ back⟩ ⟨an ~ skin eruption⟩ **b** (1) **:** having or marked by a restless desire or craving or longing for something ⟨always glad to cater to her ~ public⟩ (2) **:** restlessly or insatiably seeking after what is novel and different ⟨the time is coming when people will not endure sound teaching, but having ~ ears they will accumulate for themselves teachers to suit their own likings —2 Tim 4:3 (RSV)⟩ (3) **:** restlessly or insatiably seeking after acquisitions esp. money **:** AVARICIOUS ⟨had ~ fingers always ready for a bribe⟩ ⟨an ~ palm⟩ **c :** having or marked by a restless inclination toward or predisposition to something **:** impatiently eager ⟨~ anxiety —G.M.Trevelyan⟩ ⟨an ~ impulse —B.A.Williams⟩; *specif* **:** restlessly disposed to travel about and not to remain long in any one place ⟨born . . . with an ~ foot, he started drifting down through the cattle ranges —W.C.Tuttle⟩ ⟨having had ~ feet in his journalistic days, he had at least six different home towns —Volta Torrey⟩ **d :** being in a restless ferment **:** SEETHING, STEWING ⟨~ adolescents⟩

²itching *n* -s [ME *icchinge, yicching*, fr. gerund of *icchen, yicchen* to itch — more at ITCH] **:** ITCH 1a, 2

itch mite *n* **1 :** any of several minute parasitic mites that burrow into the skin of man and animals and cause itch; *esp* **:** a mite of any of several varieties of a species (*Sarcoptes scabiei*) that causes the itch, is about 1/60 of an inch long, and has a round-ovate body and three-jointed legs and mandibles resembling minute needles **2** *Austral* **:** CHIGGER

itchweed \'⸗,⸗\ *n* **:** a white hellebore (*Veratrum album*) of Europe

itchwood \'⸗,⸗\ *also* **itchwood tree** *n* **:** a tree (*Semecarpus vitiensis*) of the Pacific islands with an irritant milky juice

itchy \'ichē, -chi\ *adj, usu* -ER/-EST **1 :** ITCHING: as **a :** having, affected by, or resembling an itch or the itch ⟨dirty ~ vagabonds⟩ ⟨an ~ disease⟩ **b :** that causes or tends to cause itching ⟨an ~ sweater⟩ ⟨the thermometer leaped in a day from wind-bitten chill to ~ warmth —Sinclair Lewis⟩ **c** (1) **:** filled with restless desire or longing or craving for something ⟨fresh out of high school and ~ for excitement —*Time*⟩ (2) **:** restlessly craving sensual esp. sexual gratification **:** LUSTING, PRURIENT ⟨~ young profligates⟩ **d :** restlessly or compulsively driven toward action **:** impatiently eager ⟨an ~ reformer —W.L.Sullivan⟩ ⟨where some local rifleman shows evidence of an ~ trigger finger —Horace Sutton⟩ **2 :** nervously restless **:** JUMPY, RESTIVE ⟨gets ~ if you're not around⟩

¹-ite \,īt, *usu* ,īd.+V\ *n suffix* -s [ME, fr. OF & L; OF, fr. L *-ita, -ites*, fr. Gk *-itēs* (n. & adj. suffix)] **1 a :** native **:** inhabitant **:** resident ⟨Gotham*ite*⟩ ⟨Brooklyn*ite*⟩ ⟨New Hampshir*ite*⟩ **:** occupant **:** dweller ⟨flat*ite*⟩ ⟨trailer*ite*⟩ **b :** descendant **:** offspring ⟨Adam*ite*⟩ **c** (1) **:** adherent **:** follower **:** supporter ⟨Jacob*ite*⟩ **:** advocate ⟨Darwin*ite*⟩ **:** devotee ⟨Browning*ite*⟩ (2) **:** member of a (specified) group or organization or movement ⟨Puseyite⟩ **2 a** (1) **:** substance produced through some (specified) process ⟨anabol*ite*⟩ ⟨catabol*ite*⟩ (2) **:** commercially manufactured product ⟨ebon*ite*⟩ ⟨lydd*ite*⟩ ⟨vulcan*ite*⟩ **b :** -ITOL — esp. in commercial names ⟨dulc*ite*⟩ **3** [NL *-ites*, fr. L] **:** fossil ⟨corall*ite*⟩ ⟨filic*ite*⟩ **4 :** mineral ⟨erythr*ite*⟩ **:** rock ⟨chromit*ite*⟩ **5** [F, fr. L *-ita, -ites*] **:** segment or constituent part of a body or of a bodily part ⟨som*ite*⟩ ⟨dendr*ite*⟩

²-ite \"\ *n suffix* -s [F, alter. of *-ate* (fr. NL *-atum*) — more at -ATE] **:** salt or ester of an acid with a name ending in *-ous* ⟨nitr*ite*⟩ ⟨sulf*ite*⟩

itea \'id·ēə, 'īd·-\ *n* [NL, fr. Gk, willow — more at WITHY] **1** *cap* **:** a genus of shrubs (family Saxifragaceae) having racemes of small white flowers with linear petals and a 2-valved capsular fruit — see VIRGINIA WILLOW **2** -s **:** any plant of the genus *Itea*

¹item \'īd·əm, 'ītəm, 'ī,tem\ *adv* [ME, fr. L, fr. *ita* thus, prob. after L *id* it, that: *idem* the same — more at ITERATE] **1 :** and in addition **:** LIKEWISE, ALSO — used to introduce and call special attention to a new fact or particular or statement ⟨a length of chain, ~ a hook —Philip Guedalla⟩ **2 a —** used to introduce and call special attention to an initial statement and to each of the new statements that follow that are viewed as forming a related series with the initial statement **b —** used to introduce and call special attention to a single statement that is not viewed as one of a related series **c —** used (1) to introduce and signalize an initial particular or detail and each of the new particulars or details that follow that are viewed as forming a related group with the initial particular or detail or (2) to introduce and signalize each individual thing (as an article of household goods, an article of apparel, an object in an art collection, a book in a library) belonging to an aggregate of individual things that are being listed one after the other in an enumeration (as an inventory or similar list)

²item \'īd·əm, 'ītəm\ *n* -s [MF, fr. *item* (adv.), fr. L] **1 a** *obs* **:** an admonition or warning **b** *now dial* **:** HINT, INTIMATION, INKLING **2 a** (1) **:** an individual particular or detail singled out from a group of related particulars or details ⟨support him down to the ~ —*Time*⟩; *esp* **:** a small or tiny detail ⟨a courteous writer will stop short of rubbing into our minds the last ~ of all that he means —C.E.Montague⟩ (2) **:** a detail of information **:** piece of information ⟨gave names and addresses and other relevant ~*s*⟩ (3) **:** an individualizing or distinguishing mark or part or quality or characteristic ⟨an ~ of his customary appearance —Bernard DeVoto⟩ **:** FEATURE ⟨carefully studied each ~ in the landscape⟩ ⟨more than one ~ in the decorative features of the room was highly original⟩ **:** TRAIT ⟨he was pleased by every unlikeness to things American, by every ~ he could hail as characteristic —H.G.Wells⟩ ⟨inherited ~*s* from both ancestral lines, whether hair color or intelligence —Ruth Benedict⟩ **b** (1) **:** an individual thing (as an article of household goods, an article of apparel, an object in an art collection, a book in a library) singled out from an aggregate of individual things (as those being enumerated in a bill or inventory or similar list) ⟨was charged for three ~*s*⟩ ⟨glanced at each ~ in the list⟩ **:** individual object **:** ARTICLE ⟨cherished ~*s* of Americana —Jerome Weidman⟩ (2) **:** something singled out from a specified or implied category of things of the same kind ⟨bread, meat, and other food ~*s*⟩ ⟨an important ~ of international trade⟩ ⟨various ~*s* of clothing⟩ ⟨thousands of ~*s* of mail⟩ (3) **:** a thing of a particular class or kind as contrasted with a related thing of another class or kind ⟨the real ~ in the series —H.J.Laski⟩ (4) **:** something produced by manufacturing or manual labor or in some other way **:** a piece of goods **:** PRODUCT, COMMODITY ⟨a fast-selling ~⟩ ⟨marketing a variety of ~*s*⟩ ⟨where only a very few ~*s* are sold in bulk —A.S.Igleheart⟩ (5) **:** a check or draft or other financial instrument **c** (1) **:** a film or stage presentation or similar production **:** SHOW ⟨a bright new ~ on Broadway⟩ ⟨had seen this ~ brilliantly danced —Winthrop Sargeant⟩ (2) **:** one of the parts of such a production ⟨the main ~ of the show was to be a program of native dances —Ursula G. Bower⟩ **d** *Brit* **:** a selection of instrumental or sung music **:** musical selection **:** piece of music ⟨before even the first ~ is played listeners are relaxed and receptive —Clifford Lawson-Reece⟩ **3 a :** an object of attention or concern or interest to a specified degree ⟨an ~ of great importance⟩ or in a specified field ⟨an essential ~ for every home⟩ or to a specified individual ⟨excellent pictures add to the value of this book as a shipman's ~ —George Horne b. 1902⟩ ⟨an ~ of historical interest to the collector —Edith Diehl⟩ — compare COLLECTOR'S ITEM **b :** one of usu. two or more points of discussion or consideration **:** TOPIC, SUBJECT, MATTER ⟨there was one more ~ he wanted to speak about⟩ ⟨the index of the book listed all ~*s* covered⟩ ⟨added another ~ to the agenda⟩ **4 a** (1) **:** something that forms a contributory or component part or section of something specified ⟨mentioned a separate ~ of income⟩ ⟨obliteration of religion as an ~ of state policy —Hartzell Spence⟩ (2) **:** one of the elements or circumstances or influences that contributes to producing an indicated result **:** FACTOR ⟨a major ~ of school expense⟩ (3) **:** a subdivision of a cultural trait **:** a particular cultural factor or small group of such factors **b :** something usu. written down that forms part of a larger whole: as (1) **:** one of a series of separate listings (as each of the separate details given in a statement of charges for goods ordered or as each of the separate credits or debits detailed in a book of account) **:** ENTRY (2) **:** a brief line (as a remark, observation, comment) or a paragraph or two having a largely self-contained theme or subject and forming a contributory part of a more extensive piece of writing (as a newspaper column, diary, journal) (3) **:** a brief news bulletin or news report **:** a brief piece of news ⟨one ~ of news reached him after another, each more harassing than the one before —C.S.Forester⟩ (4) **:** a piece of writing (as an article, story, poem) usu. relatively short in length that forms a contributory part of a longer work (as an anthology, reference book, periodical) ⟨contributed a couple of ~*s* to the magazine⟩ (5) **:** a subordinate provision **:** CLAUSE ⟨may also veto ~*s* of proposed legislation and accept the parts of which they approve —A.N.Christensen⟩ **c** (1) **:** a unit of measurement (as a question, statement) in a test or scale (as of mental aptitude) (2) **:** a unit of correlated information (as the data indicated on a business punch card) about an individual person or thing **5 a :** something unspecified **:** an indeterminate thing ⟨her shopping bag was loaded with miscellaneous ~*s* she had bought⟩ **b :** something routine in a group of routine things **:** a run-of-the-mill thing ⟨just one more ~ in a busy day⟩ ⟨is an event, not a mere ~ in the year's publishing list —D.W.Brogan⟩

syn ITEM, DETAIL, and PARTICULAR can signify one of the things, either separate and distinct or considered so, that constitute a whole. ITEM applies chiefly to each thing in a list of things or in a group of things that lend themselves to listing ⟨an *item* in a laundry list⟩ ⟨each *item* of income⟩ ⟨an *item* in an inventory⟩ ⟨the first *item* confronting the mason in the building of footings and foundations for a new building is the excavation —J.R.Dalzell⟩ DETAIL in this connection applies to each separate thing which enters into the building, form, or construction of something as a house, a painting, narrative, or operation ⟨*details* of the building's architecture⟩ ⟨the *details* of modern life which pass daily under our eyes —Matthew Arnold⟩ ⟨the *details* of my employment —Mary W. Shelley⟩ ⟨a painter's fine execution of *details*⟩ PARTICULAR in this connection implies a relationship with any whole and stresses that relationship more than ITEM or DETAIL, emphasizing the smallness, singleness, and concreteness of each item or detail in the whole ⟨we know nothing of their language, and only . . . minor *particulars* of their social customs and religion —R.W. Murray⟩ ⟨the real question is what is the world . . . and that can be revealed only by the study of all nature's *particulars* —William James⟩ ⟨things are necessary or probable in kinds or species not simply as *particulars* —John Dewey⟩

³item \"\ *vt* -ED/-ING/-S **1** *archaic* **:** to figure up **:** COMPUTE, RECKON **2** *archaic* **:** to set down the particular details of **:** make a note or memorandum of

⁴item \"\ *usu cap* — a communications code word for the letter *i*

iteming *n* -s [prob. fr. E dial. *iteming* (taken as pres. part.) trifling, fidgeting, fr. ²*item* + *-ing*] *dial Eng* **:** lack of earnestness **:** FRIVOLITY

item·iza·tion \,īd·əmə'zāshən, ,ītə-, -,mī'z-\ *n* -s **:** the action of itemizing

item·ize \'⸗⸗,mīz\ *vt* -ED/-ING/-S *see -ize in Explan Notes* [²*item* + *-ize*] **1 a** (1) **:** to set down item by item **:** analyze or arrange or present item by item ⟨*itemizing* the cost⟩ ⟨*itemized* all expenses⟩ (2) **:** to specify the separate items of **:** list each item of ⟨*itemized* their contributions to charity⟩ **b :** to make due note of as an item **:** list as an item ⟨must ~ each piece of property —R.B.Gehman⟩ **2 :** to note or state the separate particulars or details of item by item ⟨*itemized* in a glowing eulogy his contribution to science⟩ — **item·iz·er** \-zə(r)\ *n* -s

itemized *adj* **:** arranged or presented with each item listed and detailed ⟨asked for an ~ bill⟩ ⟨an ~ account⟩ **syn** see CIRCUMSTANTIAL

item veto *n* **:** power of an executive (as a governor) to veto separate items of a bill (as an appropriation bill) without vetoing the entire bill

iter \'ī,te(ə)r, 'ī,-\ *n* -s *see sense 2* [L, journey, way, passage, right of way, fr. *ire* to go — more at ISSUE] **1** [ML, fr. L] **:** EYRE **2** *pl* **iti·nera** \ə'tinərə, ī'-\ *or* **iters a :** an ancient Roman road **b** *Roman law* **:** the right to pass over another's land on foot or by horseback — compare ACTUS **3 :** an anatomical passage; *specif* **:** AQUEDUCT OF SYLVIUS

it·er·ance \'id·ərən(t)s, 'itər-\ *n* -s [*iterate* + *-ance* (prob. after *utterance*)] **:** REPETITION, REITERATION, REPETITIOUSNESS, RECURRENCE

it·er·an·cy \-nsē, -nsi\ *n* -ES **:** the quality of being iterant **:** REPETITION, REITERATION, REPETITIOUSNESS, RECURRENCE

it·er·ant \-nt\ *adj* [L *iterant-, iterans*, pres. part. of *iterare*] **:** marked by repetition or reiteration or by repetitiousness or recurrence ⟨~ echoes⟩

it·er·ate \-ə,rāt, *usu* -ād.+V\ *vt* -ED/-ING/-S [L *iteratus*, past part. of *iterare* to iterate, fr. *iterum* again, anew; akin to L *is* he, that, *ita* thus, Skt *itara* the other, *iti* thus] **:** REITERATE ⟨*iterated* his complaint⟩ **syn** see REPEAT

iterated integral *n* **:** an integral of a function of several variables that is evaluated by finding the definite integral with respect to one variable and then the definite integral of the result with respect to the second and so continuing until the desired accuracy is achieved

it·er·a·tion \,⸗⸗'rāshən\ *n* -s [ME *iteracioun*, fr. L *iteration-, iteratio*, fr. *iteratus* (past part.) + *-ion-, -io* -ion] **:** the action of repeating or reiterating **:** REPETITION, REITERATION ⟨constant ~ of the theme of a world out of joint —R.C.Carpenter⟩

¹it·er·a·tive \'⸗⸗,rā|d·|iv, ,rə|, |t|, |ēv *also* |əv\ *adj* [MF *iteratif*, fr. LL *iterativus* frequentative, fr. L *iteratus* (past part.) + *-ivus* -ive] **1 :** marked by or involving repetition or reiteration or repetitiousness or recurrence ⟨~ methods⟩ ⟨~ poetic imagery⟩ **2 :** serving or tending to repeat; *specif, of a verb form or aspect* **:** expressing repetition of an action — compare FREQUENTATIVE, REDUPLICATIVE — **it·er·a·tive·ly** \|əvlē, -li\ *adv* — **it·er·a·tive·ness** \|ivnəs, |ēv- *also* |əv-\ *n* -ES

²iterative \"\ *n* -s **:** a word expressing repetition of an action

¹-i·tes \'īd·(,)ēz, 'ī(,)tēz\ *n suffix, pl* **-ites** [NL — more at ¹-ITE] **:** organism or fossil like (a specified group) or from (an indicated place) — chiefly in generic names usu. of fossils ⟨Agav*ites*⟩ ⟨Malay*ites*⟩

²-ites *pl of* -ITIS

ith·a·gine \'ithə,jīn\ *n* -s [NL *Ithaginis*] **:** BLOOD PHEASANT

ithag·i·nis \ə'thajənəs\ *n, cap* [NL, irreg. fr. Gk *ithagenēs* legitimate, aboriginal] **:** a genus consisting of the blood pheasants

¹ith·er \'ithə(r)\ *dial Brit var of* OTHER

²ither \"\ *dial Brit var of* EITHER

ithu·ri·el's spear \ə'th(y)urēəlz-\ *n, usu cap I* [so called fr. the phrase *Ithuriel with his spear* in *Paradise Lost* (4:810) by John Milton †1674, Eng. poet] **:** GRASSNUT 2

¹ithy·phal·lic \,ithə'falik\ *n* -s [LL *ithyphallicus*, adj.] **1 :** a poem or piece of verse having an ithyphallic meter **2 :** an obscene piece of verse

²ithyphallic \¦⸗⸗¦⸗⸗\ *adj* [LL *ithyphallicus*, fr. Gk *ithyphallikos*, fr. *ithyphallos* phallus + *-ikos* -ic] **1 a :** having a meter typically used in hymns sung at ancient festivals honoring the Greek and Roman god of revelry Bacchus ⟨written in ~ verse⟩; *specif* **:** having the meter of a trochaic dimeter brachycatalectic (–⏑–⏑––) **b** (1) **:** of or relating to festivals anciently celebrated in honor of Bacchus ⟨~ processions⟩ (2) **:** of or relating to the phallus carried in processions held during these festivals **2 a :** having an erect or tumid penis — usu. used of figures in an art representation (as a statue or drawing) ⟨the curious and enigmatical semidisguised human figures are ~ —G.Baldwin Brown⟩ ⟨sketches of ~ bulls⟩ **b** (1) **:** LUSTFUL (2) **:** OBSCENE

ithy·phal·lus \,⸗⸗'faləs\ [NL, fr. Gk *ithyphallos* phallus, erect penis, fr. *ithys* straight + *phallos* penis; akin to Skt *sādhati* he comes to his goal — more at BLOW] *syn of* PHALLUS

-it·ic \¦id·|ik, ¦it|, |ēk\ *adj suffix* [F *-itique*, fr. MF, fr. L *-iticus*, fr. Gk *-itikos*, fr. *-itis* (n. & adj. suffix) + *-ikos* -ic] **:** of, resembling, or marked by — in adjectives formed from nouns usu. ending in *-ite* ⟨dendr*itic*⟩ and *-itis* ⟨bronch*itic*⟩ and sometimes from other nouns ⟨dactyl*itic*⟩

-itides *pl of* -ITIS

itie \'id·ē, 'ī,tī\ *n* -s *usu cap* [by alter. and shortening] **:** ITALIAN — usu. used disparagingly

-ities *pl of* -ITY

itinera *pl of* ITER

itin·er·a·cy \ī'tin(ə)rəsē, -si *also* ə't-\ *n* -ES [²*itinerate* + *-cy*] **:** ITINERANCY

itin·er·an·cy \-rənsē, -si\ *n* -ES **1 a** (1) **:** the action of itinerating ⟨preached to many people in the course of his ~⟩ (2) **:** the condition of being itinerant ⟨the ~ of a medieval minstrel⟩ **b :** a system (as in the Methodist Church) of rotating ministers who itinerate ⟨features of the episcopacy and the ~ —F.S. Mead⟩ **2 a :** official work or duty that involves traveling about from place to place (as in covering a preaching circuit) ⟨returned to the ~ —J.W.Johnston⟩ **b :** a group of persons (as preachers, judges) having such work or duty ⟨a member of the ~⟩

¹itin·er·ant \-rənt\ *adj* [LL *itinerant-, itinerans*, pres. part. of *itinerari* to journey, fr. L *itiner-, iter* journey — more at ITER] **1 :** that travels about from place to place ⟨an ~ agricultural worker⟩ ⟨an ~ theatrical troupe⟩; *esp* **:** that travels about in covering a circuit ⟨an ~ preacher⟩ **2 :** marked by itinerancy ⟨lived an ~ life⟩ ⟨the ~ ministry⟩ **:** given or done or held in the course of traveling about from place to place ⟨~ discourses⟩ ⟨~ teaching⟩ ⟨~ sketching⟩ ⟨~ tent meetings⟩ — **itin·er·ant·ly** *adv*

²itinerant \"\ *n* -s **:** one that travels about from place to place; *esp* **:** one that travels about in covering a circuit

itin·er·ar·i·um \(,)ī,tinə'ra(ə)rēəm, ə,t-\ *n, or* **itinerary** *n, pl* **itineraria** *or* **itinerariums** *or* **itineraries** [ML *itinerarium* (also, account of a journey, itinerary), fr. LL] **:** a prayer given in the Roman Catholic breviary that is used for a person who is about to travel

¹itin·er·ary \ī'tinə,rerē, -,reri *also* ə't- *or* -nərē *or* -nəri\ *n* -ES [ME *itinerarie*, fr. LL *itinerarium*, neut. of *itinerarius* of a journey, itinerary] **1 a** (1) **:** a course of travel **:** route of a journey or tour or trip ⟨an ~ that took them through Canada⟩ (2) **:** an official or royal tour or circuit or visitation **:** PROGRESS ⟨when Queen Elizabeth I made one of her periodical *itineraries* of Kent —Richard Church⟩ **b :** a plan or outline of a prospective route to be followed in the course of traveling or touring **:** sketch of the prospective course of a journey or trip ⟨discussed their ~ before leaving⟩ **2 a :** a travel account **:** record of a journey or tour or trip **:** travel diary ⟨wrote the ~ in the course of the expedition⟩ **b :** a guidebook with information designed for travelers or tourists **:** ROADBOOK ⟨a helpful ~⟩ **3** *archaic* **:** ITINERANT

²itinerary \"\ *adj* [LL *itinerarius*, fr. L *itiner-, iter* journey + *-arius* -ary] **1 :** of or relating to traveling or journeying or touring; *specif* **:** of or relating to routes or roads followed in traveling or journeying or touring ⟨the ~ system developed by the ancient Romans⟩ **2** *archaic* **:** ITINERANT

¹itin·er·ate \ī'tinə,rāt *also* ə't-; *usu* -ād.+V\ *vb* -ED/-ING/-S [LL *itineratus*, past part. of *itinerari* to journey — more at ITINERANT] *vi* **:** to travel about from place to place; *esp* **:** to travel about in covering a circuit ⟨*itinerating* missionaries⟩ ⟨*itinerating* judges⟩ ~ *vt, archaic* **:** to travel through **:** TRAVERSE ⟨~ the country —G.F.Townsend⟩ — **itin·er·a·tion** \(,)ī,tinə'rāshən *also* ə,t-\ *n* -s

²itin·er·ate \-,rət, -,rāt\ *adj* [LL *itineratus* (past part.)] **:** ITINERANT ⟨~ newspapermen —Turner Catledge⟩

-i·tious \ˈishəs\ *adj suffix* [L *-icius, -itius,* adjective suffix added to the base of a noun or past participle] **:** of, relating to, or having the characteristics or properties of (something specified) ⟨excrement*itious*⟩ ⟨cement*itious*⟩

-i·tis \ˈī|d·əs, |təs *sometimes* ˈē|\ *n suffix, pl* **-i·tis·es** \|d·əsəz, |təs-\ *also* **-it·i·des** \ˈid·ə,dēz, ˈitə-\ *sometimes* **-i·tes** \ˈī|d·-(,)ēz, |(,)tēz *sometimes* ˈē|\ [NL, fr. L & Gk; L, fr. Gk, n. & adj. suffix] **1 :** disease usu. inflammatory of a (specified) part or organ **:** inflammation of ⟨laryng*itis*⟩ ⟨bronch*itis*⟩ ⟨appendic*itis*⟩ ⟨neur*itis*⟩ **2** *pl usu -itises* **a** (1) **:** malady arising from (something specified) ⟨too-much-money*itis*⟩ ⟨vacation*itis*⟩ (2) **:** affliction with (something specified) **:** forced endurance or suffering of ⟨television*itis*⟩ — chiefly in nonce formations **b** (1) **:** tendency esp. when excessive to or toward (something specified) **:** marked proneness to ⟨accident*itis*⟩ (2) **:** marked fondness for or obsession with (something specified) **:** weakness for **:** infatuation with ⟨adjectiv*itis*⟩ ⟨jazz*itis*⟩ (3) **:** excessive concern for or promotion or advocacy of or reliance on (something specified) ⟨education*itis*⟩ — chiefly in nonce formations **c :** quality or state of being marked to an often excessive degree by certain typical characteristics of (something specified) ⟨big-business*itis*⟩ — chiefly in nonce formations

it·mo \ˈit(,)mō\ *or* **ik·mo** \ˈik(-\ *n* -s [Tag] **:** BETEL

it·neg \ˈit,neg\ *n, pl* **itneg** *or* **itnegs** *usu cap* [Tinggian] **:** TINGGIAN

-i·tol \ə,tȯl, -tōl\ *n suffix* -s [ISV *-it-* (fr. [1]*-ite*) + *-ol*] **:** polyhydroxy alcohol usu. related to a sugar ⟨mann*itol*⟩ ⟨inos*itol*⟩

ito·na·ma \,ēd·əˈnämə\ *n, pl* **itonama** *or* **itonamas** *usu cap* [AmerSp, of AmerInd origin] **1 a :** a people of northeastern Bolivia **b :** a member of such people **2 :** the language of the Itonama people

it·o·nid·idae \,id·əˈnid·ə,dē\ [NL, fr. *Itonida,* genus of gall midges (prob. fr. L, title of the goddess Minerva, irreg. fr. Gk *Itōnid-, Itōnis,* title of the goddess Athena) + *-idae*] *syn of* CECIDOMYIIDAE

[1]its \(ˌ)its, ˌəts\ *adj* [[1]*it* + *-s* (possessive case ending)] **1 :** of or belonging to it or itself as possessor **:** inherent in it **:** associated or connected with it ⟨going to ~ kennel⟩ ⟨~ weird howl⟩ ⟨did it bump ~ little head⟩ **2 :** of or relating to it or itself as author, doer, giver, or agent **:** effected by it **:** experienced by it as subject **:** that it is capable of ⟨a little child proudly showing the teacher ~ first drawings⟩ ⟨~ remarkable speed⟩ ⟨~ spasmodic reactions⟩ ⟨did ~ very best⟩ **3 :** of or relating to it or itself as object of an action **:** experienced by it as object ⟨this proposal and ~ final enactment into law⟩ ⟨intending ~ betterment⟩ **4 :** that it has to do with or is supposed to possess or to have knowledge of or a share or some special interest in ⟨a dog that knows ~ master⟩ **5 :** that is esp. significant for it **:** that brings it good fortune or prominence — used with *day* or sometimes with other words indicating a division of time ⟨the football team was having ~ day⟩

[2]its \ˈits\ *pron, sing or pl in constr* **:** its one or its ones — used occas. without a following noun as a pronoun equivalent in meaning to the adjective *its* ⟨women take to a thing, any thing, and go deep enough, and they're ~ —A.S.M.Hutchinson⟩ — compare [3]HIS

[3]its \(ˌ)its, ˌəts\ [by alter.] *substand* **:** [1]IT'S

[4]its *pl of* IT

[1]it's \(ˌ)its, ˌəts\ [by contr.] **1 :** it is ⟨*it's* good⟩ **2 :** it has ⟨*it's* been a long time⟩

[2]it's \"\ *adj* [by alter.] *now substand* **:** ITS

it·sel \ətˈsel\ *dial var of* ITSELF

[1]it·self \ət+\ *pron* [ME, fr. OE *hit self,* fr. *hit* it + *self* — more at HE] **1 :** that identical one — compare [1]IT 1a; used (1) reflexively as object of a preposition or direct or indirect object of a verb ⟨the dog will have to look out for ~ while its master is gone⟩ ⟨hurt ~ crossing the street⟩ ⟨watched the cat giving ~ a bath⟩; (2) for emphasis in apposition with *it, which, that, this,* or a noun ⟨it is attractive ~⟩ ⟨which ~ is reason enough⟩ ⟨a bookbinding that ~ is valuable⟩ ⟨this ~ was sufficient excuse⟩ ⟨the letter ~ was missing⟩; (3) for emphasis instead of nonreflexive *it* as object of a preposition or direct or indirect object of a verb ⟨its agility is a source of amusement to its master and is a protection for ~⟩; (4) for emphasis instead of *it* or instead of *it itself* as subject of a verb ⟨never used for any purpose other than what ~ was designed for⟩ or as predicate nominative ⟨an animal is generally concerned for just one thing and that is ~⟩ or in comparisons after *than* or *as* ⟨a dog being chased by an animal smaller than ~⟩; (5) in absolute constructions ⟨~ a splendid specimen of classic art, it is sure to be exhibited throughout the world⟩ **2 :** its normal, healthy, or sane condition ⟨the dog seemed quite ill at first but soon came to ~⟩ **:** its normal, healthy, or sane self ⟨fed the little creature milk and it was soon ~⟩ **3 :** YOURSELF — used in speaking to or as if to a baby ⟨did it hurt ~⟩ — compare [1]IT 1c

[2]itself \"\ *adv* **1** *Irish* **:** in very fact **:** INDEED — used as an intensive usu. at the end of a clause ⟨where is he ~ —J.M. Synge⟩ **2** *Irish* **:** ACTUALLY, EVEN — used as an intensive usu. at the end of a clause ⟨though you are hard on your poor mother ~ —Gerald O'Donovan⟩

it·ty–bit·ty \ˌid·ēˌbid·ē\ *or* **it·sy–bit·sy** \ˌitsēˌbitsē\ *adj* [prob. fr. baby talk for *little bit*] **:** extremely small **:** TINY ⟨an *itty-bitty* piece of cake⟩ — not in formal use

it·u·re·an \,ichəˈrēən\ *n* -s *usu cap* [L *Ituraeus* Iturean (fr. Gk *Ityraios,* adj., of Iturea, country in ancient Palestine) + E *-an*] **:** a native or inhabitant of Iturea, an Arab kingdom in ancient Palestine south of Damascus

itu·ri·te fiber \ˌēd·əˌrēd·ē-\ *n* [origin unknown] **:** the fiber of a So. American herb (*Ischnosiphon obliquus*) of the family Marantaceae

-i·ty \əd·ē, ətē, -i; *when* s, *less often when* r, *precedes, the first vowel is sometimes lost, as in* kəˈpastē *for "capacity"*\ *n suffix* -ES [ME *-ite,* fr. OF or L; OF *-ité,* fr. L *-itat-, -itas,* fr. *-i-* (thematic or, rarely, connective vowel) + *-tat-, -tas* -ty] **:** quality **:** state **:** degree ⟨asinin*ity*⟩ ⟨theatrical*ity*⟩

it·za \ətˈsä\ *n, pl* **itza** *or* **itzas** *usu cap* [Sp *itzá,* of AmerInd origin] **1 a :** a division of the Yucatec people of Petén, Guatemala **b :** a member of such division **2 :** a dialect of Yucatec

IU *abbr* **1** immunizing unit **2** international unit

iu·li·dae \(ī)ˈyülə,dē\ [NL, fr. *Iulus,* type genus + *-idae*] *syn of* JULIDAE

iu·lus \-ləs\ [NL, alter. of *Julus*] *syn of* JULUS

-ium *n suffix* **1** -s [NL, perh. after such words as L *medium*] **a** (1) **:** chemical element ⟨sod*ium*⟩ ⟨uran*ium*⟩ (2) **:** chemical radical ⟨ammon*ium*⟩ **b :** an ion having a positive charge — in names of complex cations (as those derived from an organic base) ⟨imidazol*ium* $[C_3H_4N_2H]^+$⟩ ⟨pyridin*ium*⟩ ⟨nitrosyl*ium* NO^+⟩ — compare -ONIUM **2** *pl* **-iums** *also* **-ia** [NL, fr. L, fr. Gk *-ion* (n. suffix, often of diminutive force)] **:** small one **:** mass — esp. in biological terms ⟨onch*ium*⟩ ⟨pollin*ium*⟩

ius *var of* JUS

IV *abbr* **1** *often not cap* increased value **2** *often not cap* initial velocity **3** intravenous **4** *often not cap* [L *in verbo; in voce*] under the word **5** *often not cap* invoice value **6** iodine value

iva \ˈīvə, ˈēvə\ *n* [NL, fr. *iva* (specific epithet of *Ajuga iva*), prob. fr. F *ive* ground pine, fr. MF, fr. OF *yve,* fr. *if* yew, of Celt origin; fr. its similarity in smell; akin to OHG *īwa* yew — more at YEW] **1** *cap* **:** a small genus of American herbs or shrubs (family Ambrosiaceae) with mostly opposite leaves and small greenish flowers and with the staminate and pistillate both in the same head **2** -s **:** any plant of the genus *Iva* — see MARSH ELDER 2

ivan \ˈīvən *also* ēˈvän\ *n* -s *usu cap* [Russ *Ivan,* proper name, John, fr. ORuss *Ioannŭ,* fr. Gk *Iōannēs* — more at JOHN] **:** RUSSIAN; *esp* **:** a Russian soldier

iva·no·vo \ēˈvänə,vō, -ˌvə\ *adj, usu cap* [fr. *Ivanovo,* city in U.S.S.R.] **:** of or from the city of Ivanovo, U.S.S.R. **:** of the kind or style prevalent in Ivanovo

iva·tan \ˌēvəˌtän\ *n, pl* **ivatan** *or* **ivatans** *usu cap* [native name in the Batan Islands] **1 a :** a people inhabiting the Batan islands of the Philippines **b :** a member of such people **2 :** an Austronesian language of the Ivatan people

[1]-ive \iv, ēv *also* əv\ *adj suffix* [ME *-if, -ive,* fr. MF & L; MF *-if,* fr. L *-ivus;* akin to (assumed) Gk *-eiwos* (whence Gk *-eios* -ive)] **:** that performs or tends toward or serves to accomplish an (indicated) action esp. regularly or lastingly ⟨amus*ive*⟩ ⟨coordinat*ive*⟩

[2]-ive \"\ *n suffix* -s [ME *-if, -ive,* fr. MF & L; MF *-if,* fr. L *-ivus,* adj. suffix] **:** something that performs or tends toward or serves to accomplish an (indicated) action esp. regularly or lastingly ⟨sedat*ive*⟩ ⟨direct*ive*⟩ ⟨correlat*ive*⟩

ivied \ˈīvēd, -vid\ *adj* [[1]*ivy* + *-ed*] **:** covered with ivy ⟨~ walls⟩ ⟨~ ruins⟩

ivies *pl of* IVY

ivin \ˈīvən, ˈiv-\ *n* -s [alter. of earlier *iven,* fr. ME, fr. OE *īfegn, īfig* — more at IVY] *dial Eng* **:** IVY

ivo·ried \ˈīv(ə)rēd, -rid\ *adj* **1** *archaic* **:** made of or covered with ivory **2** *archaic* **:** resembling ivory (as in color, smoothness)

ivo·rine \ˈīvə,rēn, ˌ==ˈ=\ *n* -s *often attrib* [fr. *Ivorine,* a trademark] **:** a substance resembling ivory in color and texture

[1]ivo·ry \ˈīv(ə)rē, -ri\ *n* -ES *see senses 3, 4* [ME *ivor, ivorie,* fr. OF *ivore, ivoire, ivurie,* fr. L *eboreus,* adj., of ivory, fr. *ebor-, ebur* ivory, of Hamitic origin; akin to Egypt *ʾbw* elephant, ivory] **1 a** (1) **:** the hard creamy-white opaque fine-grained elastic modified dentine that composes the tusks of an elephant (2) **:** the dentine of the tusks of large mammals (as narwhals, walruses) other than elephants (3) **:** the dentine of any tooth **b :** a tusk of an elephant or other large mammal **2 a :** creamy whiteness **b** *or* **ivory yellow** *or* **ivory white** (1) **:** a variable color averaging a pale yellow that is darker, slightly redder, and very slightly less strong than cream, paler and slightly redder than straw, and paler and slightly greener than leghorn (2) *of textiles* **:** a yellowish white that is stronger and slightly redder than milk white and redder and slightly less strong than average shell tint **3** *pl* **ivories** *or* **ivory** *slang* **:** TOOTH ⟨fell down and broke one of his *ivories*⟩ ⟨snarled and showed his ~⟩ **4** *pl* **ivories** *or* **ivory :** something made of ivory or of a substance resembling or suggestive of ivory: as **a** *slang* **:** DIE 1a ⟨rattling the ~⟩ ⟨picked up one of the *ivories*⟩ **b :** a carving in ivory ⟨the museum has a remarkable collection of *ivories*⟩ **c** *slang* **:** a pool or billiard ball ⟨watched them shoot the *ivories* around⟩ **d** *slang* **:** one of the keys of a piano keyboard or of the keyboard of a similar instrument (as an accordion) ⟨tickling the *ivories*⟩

[2]ivory \"\ *adj* [ME *iver,* fr. *iver, ivor,* n.] **1 a :** made of ivory **:** consisting of ivory ⟨an ~ figurine⟩ ⟨a tiny ~ box⟩ **b :** resembling or suggestive of ivory **:** having a finish suggestive of the surface of ivory ⟨a fine-grained wood with a highly polished ~ surface⟩ ⟨~ porcelain⟩; *esp* **:** having a creamy whiteness and smoothness suggestive of ivory ⟨admired her ~ arms and shoulders⟩ **c :** of the color ivory **2 :** IVORY-TOWERED ⟨little men in ~ offices, who . . . fear to carry out their instructions in a liberal and imaginative way —Edward Sackville-West⟩

[3]ivory \"\ *dial var of* IVY

ivory–billed woodpecker \ˌ=(=)=ˌ=-\ *or* **ivorybill** \ˈ=(=)=,=\ *n* **:** a nearly extinct large woodpecker (*Campephilus principalis*) having plumage that is glossy black with white along the neck and wings, a large ivory-white bill, and in the male a large scarlet crest

ivory black *n* **1 :** a fine black pigment prepared by calcining ivory scrap **2 :** a bone black usu. of high quality

ivory board *n* **:** a highly finished paperboard coated on both sides

ivory brown *n* **1 :** a brown pigment made by partially carbonizing ivory **2 :** BONE BROWN 2

ivory coast *adj, usu cap I&C* [fr. *Ivory Coast Republic*] **:** of or relating to the Ivory Coast Republic **:** of the kind or style prevalent in the Ivory Coast Republic

ivory coast·er \-ˈkōstə(r)\ *n* -s *cap I&C* [*Ivory Coast,* country in West Africa + E *-er*] **:** a native or inhabitant of the Ivory Coast

ivory coral *n* **:** any of several hard and branching madrepores (family Oculinidae) with widely spaced polyps and firm skeleton

ivory–dome \ˈ=(=)=,=\ *n* **:** BONEHEAD

ivory gull *n* **:** a gull (*Pagophila eburnea*) that is circumpolar in distribution and migrates as far south as New Brunswick and England

ivory–leaves *also* **ivory–leaf** \ˈ=(=)=,=\ *n, pl* **ivory–leaves :** WINTERGREEN 2a

ivory nut *n* **1 :** the nutlike seed of a So. American palm (*Phytelephas macrocarpa*) containing a very hard endosperm — see VEGETABLE IVORY **2 :** APPLENUT

ivory palm *or* **ivory–nut palm** *also* **ivory plant** *n* **:** a palm yielding ivory nuts

ivory plum *n* **1 a :** CREEPING SNOWBERRY **b :** the fruit of creeping snowberry **2 :** WINTERGREEN 2a

ivory shell *n* **:** any of several tropical whelks (family Buccinidae) with ivory-white shells spotted and mottled with orange or brown or red

ivory tint *n* **:** a yellowish gray that is greener and duller than sand and greener and paler than natural

ivory tower *n* [trans. of F *tour d'ivoire;* orig. used by C. A. Sainte-Beuve †1869 Fr. poet & critic with reference to Alfred de Vigny †1863 Fr. poet & novelist] **1 a :** a nonrealistic often escapist or visionary attitude marked by usu. studied aloofness from and lack of concern with practical matters or urgent problems **:** a dreamy impractical attitude divorced from reality and often marked by limited vision or narrow-mindedness ⟨her safe *ivory tower* of aloofness from life —Dorothy C. Fisher⟩ **b :** an often complacently blind preoccupation with what is wholly or nearly wholly speculative or theoretical or abstract or esoteric ⟨the *ivory tower* of speculation —J.L.Liebman⟩ **c :** a state of mental withdrawal from and nonparticipation in practical matters and surrounding activity **:** a retreat from concern with or interest in reality and the world outside the self ⟨living in an *ivory tower*⟩ **2 :** something (as a secluded place or environment or a psychological withdrawal into oneself) that affords a means of retreating from reality and practical issues ⟨viewing college as an *ivory tower*⟩ ⟨she entered the *ivory tower* of her deafness and closed the door —Aldous Huxley⟩ ⟨still seek to preserve an *ivory tower* of intellectual sterility —David Worcester⟩

ivory–tower \ˌ=(=)=ˌ=\ *adj* **1 :** marked by failure or refusal to face or cope with reality and practical matters **:** NONREALISTIC, IMPRACTICAL, DREAMY, ESCAPIST ⟨her thinking is *ivory-tower* —J.F.Dinneen⟩ ⟨were this the only result, the work would indeed have been *ivory-tower* —A.A.Twichell⟩ ⟨the *ivory-tower* point of view of certain academicians and librarians —John Farrar⟩ ⟨*ivory-tower* seclusion of the scholar —Sergius Yakobson⟩ **2 :** preoccupied with what is wholly or nearly wholly speculative or theoretical or abstract or esoteric ⟨*ivory-tower* writers and artists⟩

ivory–towered \ˌ=(=)=ˌ=\ *adj* **1 :** divorced from reality and practical matters **:** living in or surrounded by an ivory tower **:** nurturing an ivory-tower outlook or approach **:** cultivating an ivory-tower method of living or acting ⟨*ivory-towered* esthetic antagonists —Bennett Cerf⟩ ⟨an *ivory-towered* recluse⟩ **2 :** far removed from the outside world and everyday activity **:** REMOTE, SOLITARY, ISOLATED ⟨any college town, however inland and *ivory-towered* —Nell G. Ahern⟩ **:** SHELTERED ⟨an *ivory-towered* home —*Newsweek*⟩

ivory–tower·ish \ˌ=(=)=ˌtau̇(ə)rish\ *adj* **:** rather unrealistic or impractical **:** inclined toward aloofness and preoccupation with what is abstract or esoteric ⟨a young man, naïve, scholarly, somewhat *ivory-towerish* —Clifton Fadiman⟩ ⟨fall between the one extreme of being too superficial and the other of becoming esoteric and therefore *ivory-towerish* —R.J.Leach⟩ — **ivory–tower·ish·ness** *n* -ES

ivory–tower·ism \,=(=)=ˈtau̇(ə),rizəm\ *n* **:** cultivation of or attachment to an ivory-tower attitude or way of living or acting ⟨an *ivory-towerism* that many young Americans reared in a practical tradition view with mistrust —*Newsweek*⟩ ⟨defend contemporary American criticism from preoccupation with aesthetics and *ivory-towerism* —*Amer. Literature*⟩

ivory–tower·ist \-ˌrəst\ *or* **ivory–tower·ite** \-,rīt\ *n* -s **:** one marked by ivory-towerism ⟨ignore the insipidities of the *ivory-towerites* and try to build a new literature —William Small⟩

ivory tree *n* **:** any of several trees of the family Apocynaceae; *esp* **:** an East Indian tree (*Holarrhena antidysenterica*) with hard white wood and a bark formerly much used as a remedy for diarrhea and dysentery

ivorywood \ˈ=(=)=,=\ *n* **:** an Australian timber tree (*Siphonodon australis*) of the family Celastraceae — called also *native guava*

ivory yellow *or* **ivory white** *n* **:** IVORY 2b

ivray *also* **ivraie** \ēvˈrā\ *n* -s [MF *ivraie*] **:** BEARDED DARNEL

iv·ver \ˈivə(r)\ *dial var of* EVER

[1]ivy \ˈīvē, -vi\ *n* -ES [ME, fr. OE *īfig;* akin to OHG *ebahewi, ebah* ivy, and perh. to L *ibex* (lit., climber), Gk *iphyon,* a plant] **1 a :** a widely cultivated ornamental climbing or prostrate or sometimes shrubby vine (*Hedera helix*) native to Europe and Asia that has evergreen leaves and small yellowish flowers and black berries and that clings to upright surfaces (as of walls, rocks, trees) by means of numerous aerial roots having tiny adhering disks — called also *English ivy* **b** (1) **:** MOUNTAIN LAUREL (2) **:** POISON IVY **2 :** a variable color averaging a dark grayish green that is yellower and duller than Persian green and yellower and paler than hemlock green

[2]ivy \"\ *adj* **1 :** ACADEMIC 2, 5 ⟨the situation has grown so acute that it is no longer confined to the ~ towers but creeps out into open public discussion —*Music Educators Jour.*⟩ **2 :** IVY LEAGUE ⟨~ college boys⟩

ivy

ivy–arum \ˌ==ˌ==\ *n* **:** any of various woody vines constituting the genus *Scindapsus* and often cultivated as ornamentals for their glossy often slotted and variegated foliage; *esp* **:** a much-branched tall climber (*S. aureus*) native to the Solomon islands that has large leathery cordate leaves spotted and lined with golden yellow and that climbs by aerial rootlets arising from the nodes — called also *Ceylon creeper*

ivybells \ˈ==,=\ *n, pl* **ivybells :** a slender creeping European bellflower (*Wahlbergia hederacea*) of the family Campanulaceae that has petioled suborbicular to cordate and sometimes obscurely lobed leaves and small pale blue often nodding flowers and that is widely distributed in damp acid peaty areas throughout western Europe

ivyberry \ˈ==- — *see* BERRY\ *n* **:** WINTERGREEN 2a

ivy bindweed *n* **:** BLACK BINDWEED 1

ivy family *n* **:** ARALIACEAE

ivy geranium *also* **ivy–leaved geranium** \ˈ==ˌ=-\ *n* **:** a commonly cultivated trailing So. African plant (*Pelargonium peltatum*) with peltate to nearly orbicular leaves and usu. rosy carmine flowers

ivy gourd *n* **1 :** a tropical Asiatic vine (*Coccinia cordifolia*) of the family Cucurbitaceae with triangular leaves and large white flowers and scarlet fruit **2 :** the fruit of the ivy gourd

ivy green *n* **:** a variable color averaging a grayish olive green that is yellower and slightly darker and stronger than bronze green and yellower and stronger than privet

ivy league *adj, usu cap I&L* **1 a :** belonging to or characteristic of or derived from one or more of a group of long-established eastern U.S. colleges widely regarded as high in scholastic and social prestige ⟨the manager was young, *Ivy League,* and hoping for an early vice-presidency —Jay Wilson⟩ ⟨leaders with *Ivy League* backgrounds —E.J.Kahn⟩ **b :** belonging to an athletic association made up of teams representing these colleges ⟨a couple of *Ivy League* teams⟩ ⟨likely to become an *Ivy League* champion⟩ **2 :** belonging to or characteristic of the students of Ivy League colleges ⟨the *Ivy League* look⟩ ⟨an *Ivy League* suit⟩

ivy leaguer *n, usu cap I&L* **:** a student at or graduate of an Ivy League college

ivy–leaved speedwell \ˌ==ˌ=-\ *also* **ivy speedwell** *n* **:** a speedwell (*Veronica hederaefolia*) having reniform leaves with two or three small lobes on each side of the base

ivy–leaved toadflax *n* **:** KENILWORTH IVY

ivy owl *n* **:** BARN OWL

ivy scale *n* **:** OLEANDER SCALE

ivy–tod \ˈ==,=\ *n* **:** a growth or clump of ivy

ivy tree *n* **1 :** a small often shrubby New Zealand evergreen tree (*Nothopanax arboreum*) of the family Araliaceae having glossy palmate leaves with 3 to 7 leaflets and large doubly compound umbels of small greenish brown flowers; *broadly* **:** any of several other New Zealand trees or shrubs of the genus *Nothopanax* **2** *dial* **:** MOUNTAIN LAUREL

ivy vine *n* **1 :** a woody vine (*Ampelopsis cordata*) of the central U.S. **2 :** VIRGINIA CREEPER

ivyweed \ˈ==,=\ *n* **:** KENILWORTH IVY

ivywood \ˈ==,=\ *n, dial* **:** MOUNTAIN LAUREL

IW *abbr* **1** inside width **2** isotopic weight

iwa *or* **ioa** \ˈēwə\ *n* -s [Hawaiian] **:** FRIGATE BIRD

iwan \ˈē,wän\ *n* -s [origin unknown] **:** a large hall or audience chamber often open on one side and found in Parthian architecture

iwis \ēˈwis, ÷īˈw-\ *adv* [ME, fr. OE *gewis* certain; akin to OHG *giwisso* certainly, ON *vīss* certain, Goth un*wiss* uncertain, unsure, Gk a*īstos* unknown, and the prehistoric root of OE *witan* to know — more at Y-, WIT] *archaic* **:** CERTAINLY, INDEED, TRULY

ix·ia \ˈiksēə\ *n* [NL, fr. Gk *ixos* mistletoe, birdlime + NL *-ia;* akin to L *viscum* mistletoe, birdlime] **1** *cap* **:** a genus of southern African bulbous plants (family Iridaceae) having linear sword-shaped leaves and very showy spikes of mostly pink or purple flowers **2** -s **:** any plant of the genus *Ixia* — called also *corn lily*

ix·i·a·ce·ae \,==ˈāsē,ē\ [NL, fr. *Ixia,* type genus + *-aceae*] *syn of* IRIDACEAE

ixil \ēˈshē(ə)l\ *n, pl* **ixil** \"\ *or* **ixils** \-lz\ *or* **ixi·les** \-shē(,)lās\ *usu cap* **1 a :** an Indian people of central Guatemala **b :** a member of such people **2 :** a Mayan language of the Ixil people

ix·o·des \ikˈsō(,)dēz\ *n, cap* [NL, fr. Gk *ixōdēs* like birdlime, sticky, fr. *ixos* birdlime + *-ōdēs* -ode] **:** a widespread genus (the type of the family Ixodidae) of ticks that suck the blood of man and of many domesticated and wild mammals, transmit diseases of cattle and sheep, and sometimes cause paralysis or other severe reactions

ix·odic \-sädik, -sōd-\ *adj* [NL *Ixodes* + E *-ic*] **:** IXODID

[1]ix·odid \-dəd\ *adj* [NL *Ixodidae*] **:** of, relating to, or caused by ticks of the genus *Ixodes*

[2]ixodid \"\ *n* -s **:** a tick of the genus *Ixodes*

ix·od·i·dae \-sädə,dē\ *n pl, cap* [NL, fr. *Ixodes* + *-idae*] **:** a family of ticks distinguished by the presence of a dorsal chitinous shield — see IXODES

ix·o·doid \ˈiksə,dȯid\ *adj* [NL *Ixodoidea*] **:** of, like, or relating to the Ixodoidea

ix·o·doi·dea \,==ˈdȯidēə\ *n pl, cap* [NL, fr. *Ixodes,* type genus + *-oidea*] **:** a superfamily of Acarina comprising the ticks — compare ARGASIDAE, IXODIDAE

ix·o·ra \ˈiksərə\ *n* [NL, irreg. fr. *Ishvara,* Hindu divinity, fr. Skt *īśvara* ruler, lord] **1** *cap* **:** a large genus of tropical shrubs or small trees (family Rubiaceae) that have leathery evergreen leaves and terminal corymbs of showy salver-shaped flowers and are often cultivated as ornamentals in the warm greenhouse **2** -s **:** any plant of the genus *Ixora*

ixtle *var of* ISTLE

iyar *or* **iy·yar** \ˈē,yär, -ˌyər\ *n* -s *usu cap* [Heb] **:** the 8th month of the civil year or the 2d month of the ecclesiastical year in the Jewish calendar — see MONTH table

iynx \ˈīiŋks, ˈyiŋ-\ *n* -ES [L, fr. Gk] **:** WRYNECK 1

iyo \ˈē(,)(y)ō\ *n* -s [origin unknown] **1 :** African piassava **2 :** a Philippine woody vine (*Tetrastigma harmandii*) of the family Vitaceae having sour but edible fruit

izar \əˈzär\ *n* -s [Hindi *izār,* fr. Ar, veil, covering] **:** a voluminous outer garment of Muslim women that covers the whole body

izard *also* **isard** \ēˈzär(d)\ *n, pl* **izard** \"\ *or* **izards** \-r(z), -rdz\ [F, fr. MF, fr. MF dial. (Gascony) *isart*] **:** a chamois found in the Pyrenees

-ization *also* **-isation** \əˈzāshən *also* ,īˈz-\ *n suffix* -s [*-ize* or *-ise* + *-ation*] **:** action or process ⟨desulfur*ization*⟩ ⟨euchromat*ization*⟩ ⟨con*ization*⟩ **:** state or result ⟨dimer*ization*⟩ ⟨immiser*ization*⟩

izba *var of* ISBA

-ize \,īz *sometimes, as in "baptize",* ˌīz\ *vb suffix* -ED/-ING/-S *see -ize in Explan Notes* [ME *-isen,* fr. OF *-iser,* fr. LL *-izare,* fr. Gk *-izein*] **1 a** (1) **:** to cause to be or become or conform to or be like or resemble (something specified) ⟨system*ize*⟩ ⟨american*ize*⟩ ⟨liquid*ize*⟩ **:** cause to be formed into ⟨union*ize*⟩

⟨diphthongize⟩ (2) : to subject to action by or treatment of (something specified) ⟨criticize⟩ : subject to a (specified) action ⟨plagiarize⟩ (3) : to cause to have or appear to have some (specified) quality ⟨rationalize⟩ : act upon in such a way as to produce a (specified) result in ⟨brutalize⟩ ⟨commercialize⟩ (4) : to impregnate or treat or combine with (something specified) ⟨albuminize⟩ ⟨hydrogenize⟩ (5) : to adapt to (something specified) : modify by means of ⟨avianize⟩ **b** : to make (a specified thing) of : treat like ⟨idolize⟩ ⟨lionize⟩ **c** : to treat in the manner of or according to the method or process of (a specified individual) ⟨bowdlerize⟩ ⟨mesmerize⟩ **2 a** : to become or become like (something specified) ⟨crystallize⟩ **b** : to be productive in or of (something specified) ⟨theorize⟩ : engage in or carry on a (specified) activity ⟨botanize⟩ ⟨philosophize⟩ ⟨attitudinize⟩ ⟨concertize⟩ **c** : to follow after someone or something (specified) : adopt or spread the manner of activity or the outlook or teaching of someone ⟨calvinize⟩

izhevsk \'ē,zhe|fsk, |vzk, |vsk, ⸗'⸗; 'ēzhə̇|\ *adj, usu cap* [fr. *Izhevsk*, city in U.S.S.R.] : of or from the city of Izhevsk, U.S.S.R. : of the kind or style prevalent in Izhevsk

iz·mir \(')iz¦mi(ə)r\ *adj, usu cap* [fr. *İzmir* (formerly Smyrna), Turkey] : of or from the city of Izmir, Turkey : of the kind or style prevalent in Izmir

izod test \'ī,zäd-, 'īzəd-\ *n, usu cap I* [after E. G. *Izod*, 20th cent. Eng. mechanical engineer] : a test of a metal's or plastic's resistance to impact that is made by determining the amount of energy in foot-pounds needed by a swinging hammer to fracture a notched test piece of the material held in a vertical position and supported at its lower end

izo·te *also* **iso·te** \ə̇'zōd·ē\ *n* -s [MexSp, fr. Nahuatl *iczotl*] **1** : any of several Mexican plants of the genus *Yucca; esp* : SPANISH BAYONET **2** : the coarse hard fiber of an izote resembling istle

iz·zard \'izə(r)d\ *n* -s [alter. of earlier *ezod, ezed*, prob. fr. MF *et zède* and Z — more at ZED] *now chiefly dial* : the letter z

iz·zat \'izət\ *n* -s [Hindi *'izzat*, fr. Ar *'izzah* glory] **1** : personal dignity or respect : HONOR ⟨is against my ~ —Rudyard Kipling⟩ **2** : power to command admiration : PRESTIGE ⟨afraid of losing ~⟩

[1]**j** \'jā\ *n, pl* **j's** *or* **js** \'jāz\ *often cap, often attrib* **1 a** : the 10th letter of the English alphabet **b** : an instance of this letter printed, written, or otherwise represented **c** : a speech counterpart of orthographic *j* (as *j* in *jump, ajar*, German *ja*, Spanish *jefe*) **2 a** : a printer's type, a stamp, or some other instrument for reproducing the letter *j* **b** : ONE — see NUMBER table **c** : a unit vector parallel to the y-axis **3** : someone or something arbitrarily or conveniently designated *j* esp. as the 10th in order or class **4** : something having the shape of the letter J

[2]**j** *abbr, often cap* **1** jack **2** January **3** join **4** joule **5** journal; journalism **6** [L *judex*] judge **7** July **8** June **9** junior **10** [L *jus*] law **11** justice **12** juvenile

[3]**j** *symbol, cap* **1** Yahwistic or Judean — used in biblical criticism to designate Yahwistic material esp. from an ancient epic constituting the earliest and a main source of the Hexateuch ⟨the *J* passages in the creation story⟩ ⟨the *J* text⟩ — compare D, E, P **2** *ital* mechanical equivalent of heat **3** *ital* radiant intensity

JA *abbr* **1** joint account **2** joint agent **3** judge advocate

jaag·siek·te *also* **jaag·ziek·te** *or* **jag·siek·te** *or* **jag·ziek·te** \'yäg,sēktə, -,zēk-\ *n* -s [Afrik *jagsiekte*, fr. *jag* hunt + *siekte* sickness] : an apparently infectious disease of sheep that is characterized by proliferation of the pulmonary alveolar epithelium and occlusion of the alveoli and terminal bronchioles and that is usu. held to be caused by an unidentified filterable virus

ja·al goat \'jāəl, 'yäəl\ *n* [Heb *yā'ēl* wild goat] : an ibex (*Capra nubiana*) of the mountains of Ethiopia, Upper Egypt, and Arabia with long slender horns

[1]**jab** \'jab, 'jaa(ə)b\ *vb* **jabbed**; **jabbed**; **jabbing**; **jabs** [alter. of *job* (to strike)] *vt* **1 a** : to pierce with or as if with something sharp : STAB ⟨got *jabbed* in the lower part of his chest, seriously if not fatally —*Westminster Gazette*⟩ **b** : to poke quickly or abruptly : THRUST ⟨*jabbing* the poker among the gray ashes —Rebecca Caudill⟩ **2** : to give a short straight blow to (as a boxing opponent) with the fist ~ *vi* **1** : to make quick or abrupt thrusts with something sharp ⟨*jabbed* around with my spear, knocking off the stalks of dead mulleins —John Moore⟩ ⟨took up his list of dates and *jabbed* at it with a pencil —Dorothy Sayers⟩ **2** : to strike a person with a short straight blow ⟨hooking when he should have *jabbed*, . . . his head sometimes a craning target —*Time*⟩

[2]**jab** \"\ *n* -s : an act of jabbing : a quick or abrupt thrust, stab, or punch; *specif* : a short straight punch in boxing delivered with the leading hand

ja·ba·lí \,häbə'lē\ *or* **ja·va·li** \-ävə-\ *n* -ES [AmerSp *jabalí*, fr. Sp, wild boar, fr. Ar *jabalīy*, short for *khinzīr jabalīy*, fr. *khinzīr* pig + *jabal* mountain] : PECCARY

ja·ba·li·na \,häbə'lēnə\ *or* **jave·li·na** \-ävə-\ *n* -s : PECCARY

jabalpur *usu cap, var of* JUBBULPORE

jab·a·rite \'jabə,rīt\ *n* -s *usu cap* [Ar *jabarīy* (fr. *jabr* power, force) + E *-ite*] : a member of an early school of Muslim determinists who denied that man has freedom of choice and affirmed an absolute predestination fashioned by Allah

[1]**jab·ber** \'jabə(r)\ *vb* **jabbered**; **jabbered**; **jabbering** \-b(ə)riŋ\ **jabbers** [ME *jaberen*, of imit. origin] *vi* : to talk rapidly, indistinctly, or unintelligibly : utter gibberish or nonsense : CHATTER ⟨~*ing* in incomprehensible tongues —F.L. Allen⟩ ⟨kept ~*ing* away —Edita Morris⟩ ~ *vt* : to speak rapidly or indistinctly ⟨~ half a dozen languages —F.L. Lucas⟩

[2]**jabber** \"\ *n* -s : an act of jabbering : rapid, incoherent, or trivial talk with indistinct utterance : GIBBERISH, CHATTER ⟨must we fall into the ~ and babel of discord —Sir Winston Churchill⟩

jab·ber·er \-b(ə)rə(r)\ *n* -s : one that jabbers ⟨sweep the ~*s* out of the way of civilization —G.B.Shaw⟩

jabbering *adj* : tending to or given to jabber : BABBLING ⟨a ~ fool⟩ ⟨was the father of three ~ daughters⟩ — **jab·ber·ing·ly** *adv*

jabbernowl \'jäbə(r),nōl, 'jab-\ *var of* JOBBERNOWL

jab·ber·wocky \'jabə(r),wäkē, -ki\ *also* **jab·ber·wock** \-äk\ *n, pl* **jabberwockies** *also* **jabberwocks** *often attrib* [*jabberwocky* fr. *Jabberwocky*, a nonsense poem in *Through the Looking Glass* by Lewis Carroll (Charles L. Dodgson) †1898 Eng. author and mathematician; *jabberwock* fr. *Jabberwock*, the fabulous monster in the poem *Jabberwocky*] : meaningless speech, writing, or patter : GIBBERISH ⟨bringing the house down with . . . his ~ patter and his energetic clowning —*Life*⟩ ⟨began to babble in ~ —Leo Rosten⟩ ⟨carries on his heated conversations . . . in a sort of *jabberwock* —Arthur Knight⟩

jabbing *adj* [fr. pres. part. of [1]*jab*] : THRUSTING, STABBING ⟨a neat, crisp, ~ bitterness —*Horizon*⟩

[1]**jab·ble** \'jabəl\ *vb* -ED/-ING/-S [imit.] *vt, Brit* : AGITATE, SPLASH ⟨*jabbled* coffee on his saucer —Michael McLaverty⟩ ~ *vi, Brit* : to break in small waves : RIPPLE

[2]**jabble** \"\ *n* -s **1** *Brit* : an agitation on the surface of water : SPLASHING, DASHING, RIPPLING : CHOPPINESS **2** *Brit* : a mental or emotional agitation or turmoil

jabim *usu cap, var of* YABIM

jab·i·ru \¦jabə¦rü\ *n* -s [Pg *jabiru, jabirú*, fr. Tupi & Guarani *jaburú, jabirú*] **1** : a large stork (*Jabiru mycteria*) of tropical America **2 a** : WOOD IBIS 1 **b** : the saddle-billed stork of Africa or a related stork of the genus *Xenorhynchus* of the East Indies and Australia

jab·o·ran·di \,jabə'randē\ *n* -s [Pg *jaborandi, jaborandí*, fr. Tupi *yaborandí*] **1 a** : the dried leaves of a So. American rutaceous shrub (*Pilocarpus jaborandi*) that are a source of pilocarpine — called also *Pernambuco jaborandi* **b** : the dried leaves of a closely related shrub (*P. microphyllus*) that are similarly used — called also *Maranham jaborandi* **2** : the root of a Brazilian plant (*Piper jaborandi*) that is a source of pilocarpine

ja·bot \zha'bō, ja'-, '⸗(,)⸗\ *n* -s [F, crop, jabot, fr. MF, prob. fr. a dial. word akin to OF *gave* throat, crop] **1** : a single or tiered fall of lace, cloth, or both attached to the front of a neckband, worn esp. by men in the 18th century, and still worn by some English counsels **2 a** : a ruffle or pleated frill of cloth, lace, or both attached down the center front of a shirt, blouse, or dress bodice **b** : a similar fall of material in drapery

jabot 2a

ja·bot·i·ca·ba \jə,bäd·ə'käbə\ *n* -s [Pg *jaboticaba, jabuticaba*, fr. Tupi] **1** : a large shrub or small tree (*Myrciaria cauliflora*) of the family Myrtaceae native to Brazil and the West Indies but introduced into the southern U.S. having flowers and fruit borne all along the trunk and main branches and purplish fruit that resembles grapes in appearance and flavor but has tough thick skin and is borne singly or in small clusters **2** : the fruit of the jaboticaba

jabs *pres 3d sing of* JAB, *pl of* JAB

ja·ca \'jäkə\ *n* -s [Pg — more at JACKFRUIT] : JACKFRUIT

ja·cal \hə'käl\ *n, pl* **jaca·les** \-ä(,)lās\ *also* **jacals** [MexSp, fr. Nahuatl *xacalli*, fr. *xamitl* adobe + *calli* house] **1** : a crude house or hut in Mexico and southwestern U.S. with a thatched roof and walls made of upright poles or sticks covered and chinked with mud or clay **2** : the method of construction used in building a jacal

ja·cal·tec \,häkəl'täk\ *or* **ja·cal·te·ca** \-kə\ *n, pl* **jacaltec** *or* **jacaltecs** *or* **jacalteca** *or* **jacaltecas** *usu cap* [Sp *jacalteca*, of AmerInd origin] **1 a** : an Indian people of western Guatemala **b** : a member of such people **2** : a Mayan language of the Jacaltec people

jac·a·mar \'jakə,mär\ *n* -s [F, fr. Tupi *jacamá-ciri*] : any of many picarian birds of the family Galbulidae inhabiting tropical forests from Mexico to Argentina, being usu. brilliant metallic green or bronze above and rufescent below with a white throat, having a long sharp bill, and feeding on insects which they catch on the wing

jac·a·mar·al·cy·on \,jakə,mä'ralsēən\ *n, cap* [NL, fr. F *jacamar* + Gk *alkyōn, halkyōn* kingfisher] : a genus of jacamars having only three toes and including a single Brazilian form (*J. tridactyla*)

jac·a·me·ro·pine \¦jakə¦mirə¦pīn, -,pə̇n\ *adj* [NL *Jacamerops* + E *-ine*] : of or relating to the genus *Jacamerops*

jac·a·me·rops \,⸗⸗'mē,räps\ *n, cap* [NL, irreg. fr. F *jacamar* + NL *-ops*] : a genus of birds comprising the largest of the jacamars which are about 10 inches long

[1]**jac·a·na** \'jakənə\ *n* [modif. of Pg *jaçanã*, fr. Tupi & Guarani] **1** -s : any of several wading birds that chiefly frequent coastal freshwater marshes and ponds in warm regions, that have long slender legs and very long toes by means of which they run about over floating vegetation, a pointed bill with a frontal shield between the eyes, and usu. a sharp spur at the bend of the wing, and that constitute the nearly tropicopolitan family Jacanidae **2** *cap* [NL, fr. Pg *jaçanã*] : the type genus of Jacanidae comprising the New World jacanas

[2]**ja·ca·na** \'häkənə\ *n* -s [AmerSp *jácana, ácana, jacana, acana*, prob. fr. Taino] : a West Indian timber tree (*Pouteria multiflora*) the hard dark wood of which is valued for furniture

ja·can·i·dae \jə'kanə,dē\ *n pl, cap* [NL *Jacana*, type genus + *-idae*] : a small but widely distributed family of birds (suborder Charadrii) that are related to the plovers and sandpipers and comprise the jacanas

[1]**jac·a·ran·da** \¦jakərən¦dä, ,jakə'randə\ *n* -s [Pg *jacarandá*, fr. Tupi *yacarandá*] **1** : any of several Brazilian timber trees (as Brazilian rosewood) with heavy dark wood that resembles rosewood **2** : the wood of a jacaranda

[2]**jac·a·ran·da** \,jakə'randə\ *n* [NL & Pg; NL (the genus), fr. Pg (a tree of this genus)] **1** *cap* : a genus of pinnate-leaved tropical American trees (family Bignoniaceae) with showy blue flowers in panicles **2** -s : a tree of the genus *Jacaranda*

jac·a·re \'jakə,rā, ,⸗⸗'⸗\ *n* -s [Pg, fr. Tupi *jacaré, yacaré*] : CAIMAN

ja·ca·te \hə'kä,tā\ *n* -s [MexSp] : a stout shrub (*Hymenoclea monogyra*) of the family Compositae of the southwestern U.S. and adjacent Mexico, having alternate leaves and heads of greenish flowers and forming dense thickets in sandy arroyos

jacent *adj, obs* [L *jacent-, jacens*, pres. part. of *jacēre* to lie — more at ADJACENT] : RECUMBENT, PRONE

j acid *n, usu cap J* : a crystalline sulfonic acid $NH_2C_{10}H_5$-(OH)SO_3H made by alkaline fusion of a disulfonic acid of beta-naphthylamine and used as an intermediate esp. for direct azo dyes; 6-amino-1-naphthol-3-sulfonic acid

[1]**ja·cinth** \'jāsə̇n(t)th, 'jas-\ *n* -s [ME *iacinct, iacynth*, fr. OF *jacincte, jacinte, jacinthe*, fr. L *hyacinthus*, a precious stone, a flowering plant — more at HYACINTH] : HYACINTH; *sometimes* : a gem more nearly pure orange in color than a hyacinth

[2]**jacinth** \"\ *adj* **1** : being like a jacinth **2 a** *obs* : HYACINTHINE **b** : being of the color jacinthe **c** : TAWNY

ja·cinthe \"\ *n* -s [F *jacinthe*, lit., hyacinth] : a moderate orange that is yellower and stronger than honeydew and yellower and slightly lighter than Persian orange

jac·i·ta·ra palm \¦jasə¦tärə-\ *also* **jacitara** *n* -s [Pg *jacitara*, fr. Tupi] : a Brazilian palm of the genus *Desmoncus* the distal pinnae of whose leaves are represented by retrorse hooks that enable the stem to climb — see TIPITI

[1]**jack** \'jak\ *n* -s *often attrib* [ME *jacke*, fr. *Jacke*, nickname for *Johan* (John)] **1 a** (1) *cap, obs* : a man of the common people; *also* : an impertinent or rude fellow ⟨familiar both with peers and *Jacks* —*Brit. Mag.*⟩ (2) *sometimes cap* : a human being : MAN — used as an intensive in such phrases as *every man jack* ⟨virtually every man ~ —*Time*⟩ or *every jack one* ⟨dead, dead every ~ one of them —W.S.Maugham⟩ (3) *cap, slang* : PAL, BUDDY, GUY — usu. used in address ⟨what they get you for, *Jack* —Thurston Scott⟩ ⟨I love it all, *Jack* —Chandler Brossard⟩ **b** (1) *often cap* : SAILOR — called also *jack-tar* (2) *sometimes cap* : LABORER, SERVANT, ATTENDANT (3) : LUMBERJACK (4) *Austral* : POLICEMAN **c** (1) : a playing card carrying the figure of a servant or soldier and ranking usu. below the queen — called also *knave* (2) [by shortening] : JACKPOT 1a(4) (3) : a player's bet in a lottery that he can name all five numbers that will be drawn **2 a** : a figure usu. of a man that strikes the time on a bell esp. in a turret clock **b** (1) : any of various portable hand-operated machines for lifting heavy weights or otherwise exerting great force by utilizing the principle of the lever, screw, toggle joint, or hydraulic press (2) : a clamp commonly of the screw type for holding work firmly in a desired position (as in a machine) (3) : a usu. triangular wooden brace fastened to the floor by means of a foot iron and a stage screw and hinged to the back of a wall or other scenic unit in a stage set in order to prop it up from behind **c** : a contrivance for turning a spit **d** : an intermediate upright piece of wood at the inner end of each key in any of several keyboard instruments (as a harpsichord or piano) com-

jack 2e(3)

municating its action to the string by means of a quill, a metal tangent, or a hammer **e** (1) **:** a small white target ball at which bowls are rolled in lawn bowling (2) [prob. short for *jackstone*] **:** a small round stone **:** PEBBLE; *esp* **:** one used in the game of jacks (3) **:** a small six-pointed usu. metal object used in the game of jacks (4) **jacks** *pl but sing in constr* **:** a game played with a set of small objects (as stones, bones, or metal pieces, and often a ball) in which the players toss, catch, and move these objects in a variety of figures requiring coordination of hand and eye (5) [by shortening] **:** JACKKNIFE 2 **f :** a bat to close a masonry course **g** (1) *dial Eng* **:** one fourth of a pint; *also* **:** HALF-PINT (2) [by shortening] **:** APPLEJACK ⟨a side of beef and a gallon of ~ to wash it down —G.A.Chamberlain⟩; *also* **:** BRANDY ⟨the stuff tasted like raisin ~ —Gore Vidal⟩ ⟨an extra supply of prune ~ —*Amer. Guide Series: Pa.*⟩ **h** (1) **:** a lever for depressing the sinkers which push the loops down on the needles in a knitting machine (2) **:** a lever that raises a harness esp. on dobby looms (3) **:** CREEL 3 (4) **:** a machine like a fly frame to handle fine cotton roving **i :** a small flag showing nationality flown by a ship usu. on a jack staff at the bowsprit cap or at the bow but elsewhere in making certain signals **j** (1) **:** a bar of iron athwartships at a topgallant masthead to support a royal mast and spread the royal shrouds (2) **:** LAZY JACK 2 **k :** a pan or frame for the fuel of a torch used in hunting or fishing at night; *also* **:** the torch itself **:** JACKLIGHT **l** (1) **:** a receptacle with one or more connections to electric circuits arranged for convenient plugging in of connections to other circuits (2) **:** a female metallic terminal or junction piece by means of which instruments may be quickly inserted in a line or telephone circuits quickly joined at the central office or exchange **m :** SPHALERITE **n** *slang* **:** MONEY ⟨hadn't that much ~ —Nevil Shute⟩ **3 :** something smaller than the usual or typical of its kind — used in combination ⟨~ rafter⟩ ⟨*jackshaft*⟩ **4 a :** any of several fishes: as (1) **:** PIKE, PICKEREL; *esp* **:** a young or small pike (2) **:** WALLEYED PIKE (3) **:** a fish of the family Carangidae; *esp* **:** a crevalle (*Caranx hippos*) (4) **:** a young male fish ⟨a ~ salmon⟩ **b :** the male of various animals esp. of the domestic ass or donkey **c :** any of several birds: as (1) [by shortening] **:** JACKDAW (2) [by shortening] **:** JACKSNIPE **d :** BONE SPAVIN **e** [by shortening] **:** JACKRABBIT **syn** see FLAG

²**jack** \"\ *vb* -ED/-ING/-S *vi* **1 :** to hunt or fish at night with a jacklight; *specif* **:** to hunt game esp. deer illegally at night by shining a spotlight that dazzles and holds immobile **2** *slang chiefly Brit* **:** to give up suddenly or readily — used with *up* ~ *vt* **1 :** to hunt or fish at night with a jacklight **:** kill with the aid of a jacklight ⟨a buck that had been ~*ed* on his own land —*N.Y. Herald Tribune*⟩ **2 a :** to move or lift by or as if by means of a jack — usu. used with *up* ⟨~ up an automobile⟩ ⟨~*ed* up my shorts —Harold Robbins⟩ **b :** RAISE, INCREASE ⟨decided to ~ their fees —*Wall Street Jour.*⟩ — usu. used with *up* ⟨stepped in to ~ up . . . the prices he got —F.L. Allen⟩ **c :** to raise the level or quality of **:** BOLSTER — usu. used with *up* ⟨~*ing* up discipline —R.M.Neal⟩ ⟨has ideas about ~*ing* up audiences —*New Yorker*⟩ ⟨this whole business of ~*ing* up the soul —P.G.Wodehouse⟩ **d :** to take to task **:** call to account **:** reprimand or scold sharply — used with *up* ⟨~*ed* up two or three men of the company —R.P.Reeder⟩ **3 :** to pass (boards) up to a piler on top of a lumber pile

³**jack** \"\ *n* -S [ME *jakke*, fr. MF *jaque, jaques* — more at JACKET] **1 :** a coarse cheap body garment worn for defense during the medieval period; *esp* **:** one made of leather and sometimes lined with metal **2 :** a vessel for holding liquor made orig. of waxed leather and coated on the outside with tar or pitch **:** JUG, TANKARD

⁴**jack** *var of* JACKFRUIT

⁵**jack** *var of* JACK CHEESE

jack-a-dan·dy \ˌjakəˈdandē\ *n, pl* **jack-a-dandies** [¹*jack* + *a* (of) + *dandy*, of unknown origin] **:** a little dandy **:** a little foppish impertinent fellow

¹**jack·al** \ˈjakəl *also* -ˌkȯl\ *n* -S *often attrib* [Turk *çakal*, fr. Per *shagāl, shaghāl*, fr. Skt *sṛgāla, śṛgāla*] **1 a :** any of several wild dogs of the Old World, smaller, usu. more yellowish, and less daring than wolves, sometimes hunting in packs at night but more usu. singly or in pairs, and feeding on carrion and small animals (as poultry); *esp* **:** a common wild dog (*Canis aureus*) of southeastern Europe, southern Asia, and northern Africa **b :** the fur or pelt of this animal **2 a :** a person who tends to the routine needs of or performs menial tasks for another **:** DRUDGE **b :** an individual who for mercenary or self-seeking ends serves or collaborates with another esp. in the commission of base or sordid acts ⟨blackmailed by one of his ~*s* —Edmund Wilson⟩ ⟨denounced these ~ tactics —Stringfellow Barr⟩

²**jac·kal** \həˈkäl\ *n* -S [by alter.] **:** JACAL

jack-a'-lantern *var of* JACK-O'-LANTERN

jackal buzzard *n* **:** a southern African hawk (*Buteo rufofuscus*)

jack·a·legs \ˈjakəˌlegz\ *n pl but sing in constr* [alter. of *jocteleg*] *chiefly Scot* **:** a large clasp knife

jack-a-lent \ˈjakəˌlent\ *n, pl* **jack-a-lents** *usu cap J&L* [¹*jack* + *a* (of) + *Lent*] **1 :** a small stuffed puppet set up to be pelted as a sport in Lent **2 :** a simple or insignificant fellow **:** PUPPET

jack·a·napes \ˈjakəˌnāps\ *n* -ES [ME *Jack Napis, Jac Napes*, nickname for William de la Pole †1450 4th earl and 1st duke of Suffolk] **1 :** MONKEY, APE **2 a :** an impertinent or conceited fellow **:** COXCOMB ⟨beribboned ~ —Frank Yerby⟩ **b :** a pert or mischievous child

jack arch *n* [¹*jack* (something smaller)] **:** a flat arch (as a lintel with a keystone)

jack·a·roo \ˌjakəˈrü\ *var of* JACKEROO

jack·ass \ˈjaˌkas, -kaa(ə)s, -kais *also* -kȧs *in New Eng & Brit esp (in Brit at least) in sense 2*\ *n* [¹*jack* + *ass*] **1 a :** a male ass; *also* **:** DONKEY **b** *Austral* **:** KOOKABURRA **2 :** a stupid person **:** FOOL, DOLT ⟨a conceited ~⟩ **3 :** HAWSE BAG

jackass bark *n* **1 :** a 3-masted ship square-rigged on the foremast, setting square topsails and topgallant sails over a fore-and-aft mainsail, and fore-and-aft rigged on the mizzen **2 :** a 4-masted ship square-rigged on the foremast and mainmast and gaff-rigged on the mizzen and jiggermast **3 :** a sailing ship with three or more masts and a combination of gaffsails and square sails in addition to complete square rig on its foremast

jackass bat *n* **:** a large spotted bat (*Euderma maculata*) occurring in the southwestern U. S. and having enormous ears joined across the forehead by a low band

jackass brig *n* **:** a brig-rigged ship not setting a square mainsail and having a fore-topmast and fore-topgallant mast made of one spar

jackass clover *n* **1 :** CALIFORNIA BUR CLOVER **2 :** a rank-scented annual herb (*Wislizenia refracta*) of the family Capparidaceae that has trifoliolate leaves and long-stalked yellow flowers and is found in the western U. S.

jackass deer *n* **1 :** KOB **2 :** MULE DEER

jack·ass·ery \-sərē\ *n* -ES **:** a piece of stupidity or folly **:** DOLTISHNESS ⟨the most preposterous ~ we ever heard of —Hubert Kay⟩

jackass fish *n* **:** a morwong (*Dactylopagrus macropterus*) of Australia, Tasmania, and New Zealand

jackass hare *or* **jackass rabbit** *n* **:** JACKRABBIT

jackass kingfisher *n* **:** KOOKABURRA

jack·ass·ness *n* -ES **:** the quality or state of being a jackass

jackass penguin *n* **:** a penguin (*Spheniscus demersus*) of western So. America and southern Africa whose note suggests the braying of an ass

jackass rig *n* **:** a rig differing in some particular from the type of rig to which it mainly belongs

jack bean *n* **1 :** a bushy semierect annual tropical American plant of the genus *Canavalia*; *esp* **:** a plant (*C. ensiformis*) having long pods with white seeds and grown esp. for forage — compare SWORD BEAN **2 :** the seed of the jack bean

jackbird \ˈ=,=\ *n* **1 :** a passerine bird (*Callaeas cinerea*) of South Island, New Zealand, resembling the starling **2 :** SADDLEBACK 2d

jack block *n* **:** a block fixed aloft for raising and lowering the topgallant and royal yards of a ship

jackboot \ˈ=,=\ *n* **1 :** a heavy military boot esp. of glossy black leather extending well above the knee and having a wide flaring top and worn esp. during the 17th and 18th centuries **2 :** a military boot without laces that reaches to the calf **3 :** a boot similar in shape to the older military jackboot and worn esp. by fishermen

jackboot 1

jackbooted \ˈ=,==\ *adj* **:** wearing jackboots

jack box *n* **:** a connection box containing one or more jacks into which a piece of electric equipment (as a telephone or loudspeaker) may be plugged

jackboy \ˈ=,=\ *n, archaic* **:** a boy (as a stable-boy) who does menial work

jack-by-the-hedge \ˈ===ˈ=\ *n, usu cap J, dial Eng* **:** GARLIC MUSTARD

jack chain *n* **1 :** a light wire chain whose links are set at right angles to each other resembling a figure eight or having the end of each loop bent round to meet the end of the other loop **2 :** an endless toothed chain for moving logs usu. from the millpond into the sawmill

jack cheese *also* **jack** *n* -S *often cap J* **:** a semisoft whole-milk cheese with high moisture content

jack crevalle *n* **:** a crevalle (*Caranx hippos*)

jack crow *n* **:** a rare West African bird (*Picathartes gymnocephalus*) resembling a crow and having bluish gray back and wings, white underparts, and a bright yellow and black naked head

jack curlew *n* **1 :** WHIMBREL **2 :** HUDSONIAN CURLEW

jackdaw \ˈ=,=\ *n* [¹*jack* + *daw*] **1 :** a common bird (*Corvus monedula*) of Europe and parts of Asia that is closely related to but smaller than the common crow, is glossy black above and dark gray below with silvery gray markings on head and neck, is a clever mimic capable of learning to imitate the human voice, is gregarious in habits usu. nesting in and about buildings, and is readily tamed **2 :** GRACKLE 2; *esp* **:** BOAT-TAILED GRACKLE

jacked *past of* JACK

jack·een \jaˈkēn\ *n* -S [¹*jack* + -*een* (fr. IrGael -*ín*, dim. suffix)] *Irish* **:** an obnoxious self-assertive dude ⟨a jaunty little ~ with a rich brogue —R.B.D.French⟩

jack·er \ˈjakə(r)\ *n* -S **:** one that jacks: as **a :** a person who hunts or fishes at night with a jacklight **b :** a worker who smooths and toughens leather by rolling it under pressure in a rolling jack **c** (1) **:** a sawmill pondman who guides logs into the jack chain that moves them to the log deck of the mill — called also *jackerman, slipman* (2) **:** JACK CHAIN

¹**jack·e·roo** \ˌjakəˈrü\ *n* -S [alter. of *jackaroo*, fr. ¹*jack* + -*aroo* (as in *kangaroo*)] *Austral* **:** a green hand working as an apprentice on a sheep ranch

²**jack·e·roo** \"\ *vi* **jackerooed; jackerooed; jackerooing; jackeroos** *Austral* **:** to work as a jackeroo

¹**jack·et** \ˈjakət, *usu* -əd·+V\ *n* -S *often attrib* [ME *jaket*, fr. MF *jaquet*, dim. of *jaque, jaques* short jacket, pourpoint, jack, fr. *jacques, jacque* peasant, fr. the name *Jacques* James, Jacob] **1 a** (1) **:** a garment like a coat for the upper body usu. having a front opening, collar, lapels, sleeves, and pockets, made in varying lengths from waist to hip, and worn separately or as part of a suit ⟨cardigan ~⟩ ⟨an embroidered pajama ~⟩ (2) *Midland* **:** a man's vest **b :** something worn or fastened around the body but not for use as clothing: as (1) **:** CORK JACKET (2) **:** STRAITJACKET (3) **:** a casing for the upper part of the body usu. made of plaster and serving a supportive, corrective, or restraining purpose **2 a** (1) **:** the natural covering of an animal (as the skin of a snake or fish) (2) **:** the fur or wool of a mammal sometimes together with the skin ⟨a flock with a fine even ~ of wool⟩ (3) **:** a young seal **b :** the skin of a potato — used chiefly of cooked potatoes in the phrase *in their jackets* **3 :** an outer covering or casing: as **a :** a thermally nonconducting cover or lagging (as for a tank, pipe, or engine cylinder); *also* **:** a covering that encloses an intermediate space through which a temperature-controlling fluid may be circulated (as in water-cooling a gasoline-engine cylinder) **b** (1) **:** a cylindrical hollow forging in a built-up gun that is concentric with and shrunk usu. directly upon the tube, extends from the breech usu. to a little forward of the trunnions, and usu. contains the seat for the breechblock or breech plug (2) **:** the tough cold-worked metal casing which forms the outer shell of a built-up bullet and into which lead is swaged to form the complete projectile **c** (1) **:** a cloth covering for a machine roller usu. woven or felted in tubular form (2) **:** a felt cover for a couch roll in a papermaking machine **d :** an easily removable form that supports a foundry mold on all four sides during pouring **e** (1) **:** a wrapper or open envelope for a document (as a letter, dispatch, or the case-history file or personal record of a prisoner, serviceman, or agency client) on which are put directions for its disposition and notations as to its contents, dates of being sent and received, or other details (2) **:** an envelope for enclosing registered mail during delivery from one post office to another **f** (1) **:** a detachable protective wrapper for a book typically consisting of a rectangular sheet of paper elaborately printed with descriptive or promotional material, cut flush at head and foot, and folded around the binding with ends tucked between cover board and free endpaper — called also *book jacket, book wrapper, dust cover, dust jacket, dust wrapper, wrapper* (2) **:** the cover of a paperbound book esp. when folded and tucked under at the fore edge (3) **:** the outside leaves for a booklet, pamphlet, or catalog which is to be stitched or wired through the saddle (4) **:** a paper or paperboard envelope for a phonograph record

²**jacket** \"\ *vt* -ED/-ING/-S **:** to put a jacket on **:** enclose in or with a jacket ⟨reports which had been ~*ed* —C.R.Cooper⟩

jacket crown *n* **:** an artificial crown that is placed over the remains of a natural tooth

jacketed *adj* **1 :** wearing or having a jacket ⟨~ boys on the road⟩ **2 :** enclosed in or by a jacket ⟨~ bullets⟩

jacketing *n* -S **1 a :** fabric used for jackets **b :** JACKET 3a, 3b **2 :** BEATING ⟨gave him an awful ~⟩

jack·field ware \ˈjakˌfēld-\ *n, usu cap J* [fr. *Jackfield*, England] **:** pottery made at Jackfield, Shropshire, England, in the 18th century with a red clay body often decorated in relief and distinguished esp. by its thick black glaze

jackfish \ˈ=,=\ *n* [¹*jack* + *fish*] **:** JACK 4a (1)

jack fishing *n* **1 :** fishing for jacks (as pike) **2 :** fishing with a jacklight

jack-fool \ˈ=ˈ=\ *n, usu cap J* [ME *Jakke fool*] **:** TOMFOOL

jack frost *n, cap J&F* **:** frost or frosty weather personified

jack·fruit \ˈjakˌfrüt\ *or* **jack** *or* **jak** \ˈjak\ *or* **jak·fruit** \ˈjak,-\ *n* -S [*jackfruit, jakfruit* fr. Pg *jaca* jackfruit (fr. Malayalam *cakka*) + E *fruit; jack, jak* fr. Pg *jaca*] **1 :** a large East Indian tree (*Artocarpus heterophyllus*) that is distinguished from the closely related breadfruit by its entire leaves, yields a fine-grained yellow wood, and is widely cultivated in the tropics for its immense fruits which contain an edible but insipid pulp and nutritious seeds that are commonly roasted **2 :** the fruit of the jackfruit **3 :** DURIAN

jackhammer \ˈ=,==\ *n* **1 :** a rock drill of the hammer type usu. held in the hands of the operator **2 :** AIR HAMMER

jack hor·ner pie \ˈjakˈhȯrnər-\ *n, usu cap J&H* [after (*Little*) *Jack Horner*, a nursery-rhyme character depicted as pulling a plum out of a pie] **:** an ornamental pie-shaped container from which favors or toys are extracted often by pulling a ribbon at a party

jack-hunting \ˈ=,==\ *n* **:** hunting with a jacklight

jackies *pl of* JACKY

jack-in-a-bottle \ˈ====\ *n, pl* **jacks-in-a-bottle :** LONG-TAILED TIT

jack-in-a-box \ˈ====\ *n, pl* **jacks-in-a-box 1 :** a tropical East Indian tree (*Hernandia sonora*) which bears a drupe that rattles in the inflated calyx when dry **2** *Brit* **:** CUCKOOPINT

jacking *n* -S **1 :** a process in spinning for giving extra twist or draft or both to the roving often done on a mule **2 :** the practice or act of hunting or fishing with a jacklight ⟨an effort to stop deer ~ —L.S.Marceau⟩

jack-in-office \ˈ==,==\ *n, pl* **jacks-in-office** *sometimes cap J* **:** an insolent fellow in authority ⟨some little *jack-in-office* of a clerk —O.S.J.Gogarty⟩

jack-in-the-box \ˈ====\ *n, pl* **jack-in-the-boxes** *also* **jacks-in-the-box** *sometimes cap J* **1** *obs* **:** SHARPER, CHEAT **2 :** a child's toy consisting of a box out of which a figure springs when the lid is raised **3 :** any of several mechanical contrivances: as **a :** DIFFERENTIAL GEAR **b :** a large wooden screw turning in a nut attached to the cross-piece of a rude press **c :** a lifting jack **:** JACKSCREW **d :** a burglar's tool for opening doors or safes by means of a small but powerful screw **e :** a jim-crow reversing tool **f :** SUN-AND-PLANET MOTION

jack-in-the-box 2

jack-in-the-green \ˈ====\ *n, pl* **jack-in-the-greens** *or* **jacks-in-the-green** *usu cap J&G* **1 :** a man or boy enclosed in a conical framework covered with leaves and boughs to take a prominent part in the May Day games of English chimney sweeps **2 :** an English primrose having sepals resembling leaves

jack-in-the-pulpit \ˈ===ˈ=(ˌ)=\ *n, pl* **jack-in-the-pulpits** *or* **jacks-in-the-pulpit 1 :** any of several plants of the genus *Arisaema*; *esp* **:** an American spring-flowering woodland herb (*A. atrorubens*) with sheathing leaves, an upright club-shaped spadix with open overarching green and purple spathe, and fruit consisting of a mass of bright scarlet berries — see GREEN DRAGON 2 **2 :** TURK'S-CAP LILY b **3 :** LOVE-IN-A-MIST 1 **4 :** a figwort (*Scrophularia californica*) of western No. America with dull red flowers **5 :** PRAIRIE WAKE-ROBIN

jack jumper *n* **:** a sled that consists of one thick runner curved much like a barrel stave to which is attached an upright with a seat having grips on either side of its undersurface and that is used on a slope; *also* **:** a person who rides a jack jumper

jack ketch \ˈjakˈkech\ *n, usu cap J&K* [after *Jack* (John) *Ketch* †1686 Eng. executioner] *Brit* **:** a public executioner; *specif* **:** HANGMAN

¹**jackknife** \ˈ=,=\ *n* [prob. fr. ¹*jack* + *knife*] **1 :** a large strong clasp knife for the pocket **2 :** a large pocketknife **2 :** a dive executed headfirst either forward or backward in which the diver beginning usu. at the highest point of the dive bends from the waist and touches or clasps his ankles while holding his knees unflexed before straightening out to enter the water

jackknife 1

²**jackknife** \"\ *vt* **1 :** to cut with a jackknife **2 :** to double up like a jackknife ⟨willing to ~ himself to get in and out —*Springfield (Mass.) Republican*⟩ **3 :** to cause to jackknife ⟨the tractor and trailer were *jackknifed* by the diesel —*Springfield (Mass.) Union*⟩ ~ *vi* **1 :** to double up like a jackknife ⟨~ on the sofa beside the Christmas tree —D.C.Peattie⟩ **2 :** to turn or rise and form an angle of 90 degrees or less with each other — used esp. of a pair of vehicles one of which is attached to and follows the other (as a tractor and its trailer or two railroad cars)

³**jackknife** \"\ *adj* **:** resembling a jackknife esp. in its manner of opening and closing ⟨a ~ drawbridge⟩ ⟨a ~ door⟩

jackknife clam *n* **:** RAZOR CLAM

jack ladder *n* **1 :** a ship's ladder with wooden rungs and side ropes **2 a :** an inclined plane up which logs are moved from pond to sawmill typically consisting of a V-shaped trough within which an endless chain carries the logs upward **b :** JACK CHAIN

jack lagging *n* **:** rough temporary lagging used in arch centering and brought to the true curve of the intrados to take the weight of the voussoirs

¹**jack·leg** \ˈjaˌkleg, -āg\ *adj* [¹*jack* + -*leg* (as in *blackleg* "sharper")] **1 a :** characterized by lack of skill or training **:** AMATEUR ⟨simplifies the labors of the ~ editor —D.L.Cohn⟩ ⟨a fair ~ carpenter —Stanley Walker⟩ **b :** characterized by unscrupulousness, dishonesty, or lack of professional standards ⟨two ~ lawyers and a cigar-eating judge —F.B.Gipson⟩ **2 :** designed for use as a temporary expedient **:** MAKESHIFT ⟨rigged up a ~ system of landing lights —W.L.White⟩

²**jackleg** \"\ *n* **:** one who is jackleg

Jackleg \"\ *trademark* — used for a support for a rock drill

¹**jacklight** \ˈ=,=\ *n* [¹*jack* + *light*] **:** a torch, lantern, flashlight, or other artificial light used esp. in hunting or fishing at night ⟨spearing fish in the bay with a ~ —Ernest Hemingway⟩

²**jacklight** \"\ *vb* **:** JACK

jack·light·er \"+ə(r)\ *n* **:** a person who hunts or fishes with a jacklight; *esp* **:** one who hunts deer illegally at night with a jacklight

jack line *n* [¹*jack* (something smaller)] **1 :** a small rope or line **2 :** a rod or steel cable connecting a central pumping engine with each of two or more oil wells which it powers

jack mackerel *n* **:** either of two fishes of the genus *Trachurus*: **a :** a California market fish (*T. symmetricus*) that is iridescent green or bluish above and silvery below **b :** a closely related Australian fish (*T. novaezelandiae*)

jack·man \ˈjakmən\ *n, pl* **jackmen 1 :** a textile worker who puts copper printing shells into machines that print cloth **2 :** SCREWMAN **3 :** a repairer of shoes

jack mormon *n, sometimes cap J & usu cap M* **1 :** a non-Mormon living in a Mormon community and sympathetic to or on friendly terms with his neighbors **2 :** a Mormon inactive in the church or not adhering strictly to Mormon tenets **:** a backsliding or nominal Mormon ⟨always paid his tithes — only he had to have his coffee so some called him a *jack Mormon* —*Amer. Guide Series: Ariz.*⟩ ⟨a *jack Mormon*, which means that . . . he no longer pays tithes or holds with the tenet of total abstinence —A.J.Liebling⟩

jacko *var of* JOCKO

jack oak *n* **1 :** BLACKJACK 5 **2 :** an extremely variable oak (*Quercus ellipsoidalis*) of east central No. America having leaves with sharply pointed lobes and ashy gray turbinate to goblet-shaped acorn cups with persistent dull pubescence

jack-of-all-trades \ˌ==ˈ=,=\ *n, pl* **jacks-of-all-trades** *sometimes cap J* **:** a person who can do passable work at various trades **:** a handy or versatile individual ⟨was expected to be a *jack-of-all-trades* —Patricia M. Johnson⟩ ⟨every man would be something of a *jack-of-all-trades* —A.L.Kroeber⟩

jack off *vi* **:** MASTURBATE — usu. considered vulgar

jack-o'-lantern *or* **jack-a-lantern** *also* **jack-o'-lanthorn** \ˈjakə,==\ *or* **jack-with-a-lantern** \ˈ===,==\ *n* **1 a** *obs* **:** a man carrying a lantern **:** a night watchman **b :** IGNIS FATUUS **c :** SAINT ELMO'S FIRE **d :** a lantern made of a pumpkin or other vegetable so prepared as to show in illumination features of a human face **2 :** a large luminescent mushroom (*Clitocybe illudens*)

jack-o'-lantern 1d

jack-over-the-ground \ˈ=ˈ===\ *n, pl* **jacks-over-the-ground :** GROUND IVY 1

jack pike *n* **:** JACK 4a (1)

jack pine *n* **1 :** a slender No. American pine (*Pinus banksiana*) having two stout twisted leaves in each fascicle, one-sided curved cones with spiny-tipped scales, and wood that is used esp. for boxwood and pulpwood **2 :** BRISTLECONE PINE **3 :** LODGEPOLE PINE **4 :** LIMBER PINE

jack-pine sawfly *n* **:** an American sawfly (*Neodiprion pratti banksianae* or *N. banksianae*) having a larva that is a serious defoliator of pine (as jack pine)

jack plane *n* **:** a medium-sized general-purpose bench plane usu. somewhat over a foot in length — see PLANE illustration

jack post *n* **:** either of the posts supporting the crankshaft of a deep-well-boring apparatus

jackpot \ˈ=,=\ *n, often attrib* [¹*jack* (playing card) + *pot*] **1 a** (1) **:** a hand of draw poker in which every player antes in order to increase the gain to the winner and in which no player may open without a pair of jacks or better (2) **:** a game of draw poker in which a pair of jacks or better is required to open — compare ROODLE (3) **jackpots** *pl but sing or pl in constr* **:** draw poker in which every pot is a jackpot (4) **:** an unusually large pot (as in the game of poker) formed by accumulation of stakes from previous play in which no decision was reached **b** (1) **:** a combination on a slot machine which wins for a player a top prize or all the coins in the machine; *also* **:** the sum so won (2) **:** a large fund of money or other impressive reward formed by the accumulation of unwon prizes (as in a quiz contest) ⟨lost TV's biggest ~ so far —*Newsweek*⟩ ⟨the ~ question⟩ (3) : an impressive often unexpected success or reward ⟨lecturing all over the country with an occasional ~ in a friendly town —H.S.Canby⟩ **2 a** : a pool or fund contributed by a number of persons ⟨a ~ which sent the family on their way rejoicing —*Emporia (Kan.) Gazette*⟩ **b** : mail for distant separations for which a postal clerk does not immediately have room in his case and which he masses together in one box or sack for later distribution when space is available **3** *chiefly West* : a tight spot : JAM, SCRAPE ⟨apt to get himself and his friends into a ~ —Ross Santee⟩

jack-pudding \ˈ=ˈ=\ *n, sometimes cap J* : BUFFOON, CLOWN, MERRY-ANDREW

¹jackrabbit \ˈ=,==\ *n* [¹*jack* (jackass) + *rabbit*; fr. its long ears] : any of several large hares (genus *Lepus*) of western No. America having very long ears and long hind legs and living in open country sometimes in such large numbers as to do much injury to forage and crops

²jackrabbit \"\ *vi* -ED/-ING/-S : to make a sudden lurch or jump or a fast start ⟨a car ~*ing* down the street —Paul Jones⟩

jack rafter *n* [¹*jack* (something smaller)] : a short rafter: **a** : one of the shorter rafters used in a hip or valley roof **b** : a secondary roof timber (as a common rafter resting on purlins); *also* : one of the pieces simulating extended rafters under the eaves in some styles of building

jackrod \ˈ=,=\ *n* : JACKSTAY

jack·roll \ˈja,krōl\ *vt* [back-formation fr. *jackroller*] : ROLL 7

jack·roll·er \-lə(r)\ *n* [¹*jack* + *roller*] : one who robs a drunken or sleeping person

jack rope *n* : a rope fastening the foot of a fore-and-aft sail to a boom

jack rose *n* [fr. *jack rose*, a variety of red rose, alter. of *jacqueminot rose* — more at JACQUEMINOT] **1** : a vivid red that is bluer and deeper than apple red or scarlet and bluer and stronger than carmine **2** *usu cap J&R* : a cocktail consisting of lemon juice, apple brandy, and grenadine shaken in ice and strained before serving

jacks *pl of* JACK, *pres 3d sing of* JACK

jack saddle *n* : the saddle of a harness

jack salmon *n* **1** : WALLEYED PIKE **2** *western No. America* : GRILSE; *also* : SILVER SALMON

jackscrew \ˈ=,=\ *n* : a screw-operated jack for lifting or for exerting pressure

jackshaft \ˈ=,=\ *n* [¹*jack* (something smaller) + *shaft*] : COUNTERSHAFT; *specif* : the intermediate driving shaft in an automobile

jack·shay *also* **jack·shea** \ˈjak,shā\ *n* -S [origin unknown] *Austral* : a bushman's quart pot used esp. for boiling water

jacks-in-the-box *pl of* JACK-IN-THE-BOX

jacks-in-the-green *pl of* JACK-IN-THE-GREEN

jacks-in-the-pulpit *pl of* JACK-IN-THE-PULPIT

jackscrew

jacksmelt \ˈ=,=\ *n* [¹*jack* + *smelt*] : a large silversides (*Atherinopsis californiensis*) of the Pacific coast of No. America that sometimes attains a length of 18 inches and is the chief commercial smelt of the California markets

jacksnipe \ˈ=,=\ *n, pl* **jacksnipe** *or* **jacksnipes** [¹*jack* + *snipe*] **1** : a true snipe (*Limnocryptes minima*) of Europe and other parts of the Old World that is smaller and more highly colored than the common snipe **2 a** : PECTORAL SANDPIPER **b** : WILSON'S SNIPE **c** : any of several other snipes

jacks-of-all-trades *pl of* JACK-OF-ALL-TRADES

jack·son \ˈjaksən\ *adj, usu cap* [fr. *Jackson*, Miss.] : of or from Jackson, the capital of Mississippi ⟨*Jackson* merchants⟩ : of the kind or style prevalent in Jackson

jackson cent *n, usu cap J* [after Andrew *Jackson* †1845 7th U. S. president] : HARD-TIMES TOKEN

jackson day *n, usu cap J&D* [after Andrew *Jackson*] : the anniversary on January 8 of the successful defense of New Orleans by General Jackson in 1815 which is a legal holiday in Louisiana and generally observed by Democrats throughout the U. S.

jackson haines \-ˈhānz\ *n, usu cap J&H* [after *Jackson Haines* †1875, Amer. figure skater] : a figure-skating spin executed on the flat of one skate in which the body gradually assumes a low sitting position with the free leg held in front with knee bent and then gradually straightens to an erect position — called also *sit spin*

jack·so·nia \jakˈsōnēə\ *n, cap* [NL, fr. George *Jackson* 19th cent Brit. botanist + NL *-ia*] : a large genus of yellow-flowered Australian shrubs (family Leguminosae) with very variable leaves some of which are like needles and others merely phyllodia

¹jack·so·ni·an \(ˈ)jak¦sōnēən\ *adj, usu cap* [Andrew *Jackson* 7th president of the U. S. (1829–37) + E *-ian*] : of or relating to Andrew Jackson, his views or policies, or his era ⟨stunned by the sheer restlessness of *Jacksonian* America —G.W.Pierson⟩; *esp* : relating to a body of political ideas commonly associated with Andrew Jackson and vigorously championing the right and ability of the common man to participate in politics and administration and opposing the aristocratic principle of government ⟨*Jacksonian* democracy⟩

²jacksonian \"\ *n* -S *usu cap* : a follower of Andrew Jackson : an adherent of Jackson's principles or policies

³jacksonian \"\ *adj, often cap* [*Jacksonian (epilepsy)*] : of or resembling Jacksonian epilepsy

jacksonian epilepsy *n, usu cap J* [John H. *Jackson* †1911 Eng. neurologist + E *-ian*] : symptomatic epilepsy produced by injury to the brain (as by trauma or toxic agents) and manifesting symptoms that vary with the part of the brain injured

jack·son·ism \ˈjaksə,nizəm\ *n* -S, *usu cap* [Andrew *Jackson* + E *-ism*] : Jacksonian political principles and policies ⟨the sophisticated public, which had had too much of *Jacksonism*, was bored by stories of woodsmen and sailors —Van Wyck Brooks⟩

jack·son·ite \-sə,nīt\ *n* -S *usu cap* [Andrew *Jackson* + E *-ite*] : JACKSONIAN

jack·son·ville \ˈjaksən,vil, *esp S* -vəl\ *adj, usu cap* [fr. *Jacksonville*, Fla.] : of or from the city of Jacksonville, Fla. ⟨a *Jacksonville* garden⟩ : of the kind or style prevalent in Jacksonville

jackson vine *n, usu cap J* [fr. the name *Jackson*] : MATRIMONY VINE

jackson white *n, cap J & usu cap W* [prob. after Capt. *Jackson*, Am. slave trader in colonial times] : one of a group of people of mixed Negro, Indian, and white ancestry in the Ramapo mountains of New York and New Jersey

jacks-over-the-ground *pl of* JACK-OVER-THE-GROUND

jack spavin *n* : BONE SPAVIN

jack spool *n* : a large wooden spool on which is wound woolen sliver from a carding machine or woolen yarn for dyeing or warping

jack staff *n* [¹*jack* (flag)] : a staff which is fixed on the bowsprit cap or in the bows of a ship and upon which the jack is hoisted

jackstay \ˈ=,=\ *n* **1 a** : an iron rod, wooden bar, or wire rope stretching along a yard of a ship to which the sails are fastened **b** : a support of wood, iron, or rope running up and down a mast on which the parrel of a yard travels **c** : a reefing rope stretching along the reef band of a square sail from hole to hole **d** : a fixed bar or rope for hanging esp. clothes bags or for securing awning stops (as around a barbette) **2** : a longitudinal rigging provided to maintain the correct distance between the heads of various riggings on an airship

jackstock \ˈ=,=\ *n* [¹*jack* (ass) + *stock*] : male asses

jack·stone \ˈjak,stōn\ *n* [alter. of earlier *chackstone*, alter. of *checkstone*, sing. of *checkstones*] **1** : JACK 2e (4) — usu. used in pl. **2** : JACK 2e (3)

jackstraw \ˈ=,=\ *n* [¹*jack* + *straw*] **1** *obs* : a man without property, worth, or influence **2 a** : one of the pieces used in the game jackstraws **b** **jackstraws** *pl but sing in constr* : a game in which a set of straws or strips (as of bone or wood) are let fall in a heap and each player in turn tries to remove them one at a time with a small instrument and without disturbing the rest of the pile **3** *dial Eng* : any of several small European birds using bedstraw in their nests: as **a** : WHITETHROAT **b** : GARDEN WARBLER **c** : BLACKCAP

jack stringer *n* [¹*jack* (something smaller)] : a bridge stringer placed outside the main stringers

jack-tar \ˈ=ˈ=\ *n, often cap J* : JACK 1b(1)

jack timber *n* [¹*jack* (something smaller)] : a timber (as a rafter, rib, or studding) that from being intercepted is shorter than the others with which it is used

jack tree *n* [⁴*jack*] : JACKFRUIT 1

jack truss *n* [¹*jack* (something smaller)] : a minor truss in a hip roof used where the roof has not its full section

jack wax *n* : a chewy confection made by pouring boiling maple syrup over snow

jack weight *n, archaic* : a weight attached to an endless chain and forming part of a roasting jack

jack-with-a-lantern *var of* JACK-O'-LANTERN

jackwood \ˈ=,=\ *n* [⁴*jack* + *wood*] : the wood of the jackfruit tree

jacky \ˈjakī\ *n* -ES [¹*jack* (quarter pint) + *-y*] *Brit* : GIN ⟨snuff . . . and excellent ~ —W.S.Gilbert⟩

jack yard *n* [¹*jack* (something smaller)] : a spar to extend a fore-and-aft topsail beyond the gaff

jacky winter \ˈjakē-\ *n* [fr. *Jacky*, dim. of *Jack*] : a small brown flycatcher (*Microeca fascinans*) of Australia

ja·cob \ˈjākəb *sometimes* -əp\ *n* -S *cap* [LL, fr. Gk *Iakōb*, fr. Heb *Yaʽăqōbh*, after *Yaʽăqōbh* (Jacob) in the Bible (Gen. 25:20 ff.), the eponymous ancestor of the Israelites] : the ancient Hebrew nation : ISRAEL ⟨yet you did not call upon me, O *Jacob*; but you have been weary of me, O Israel —Isa 43:22 (RSV)⟩

¹jaco·be·an \ˌjakə¦bēən *also* ¦jāk- *sometimes* jəˈkōb-\ *adj, usu cap* [NL *jacobaeus* Jacobean (fr. *Jacobus* —James I — †1625 king of England) + E *-an*] : of or relating to James I of England, his reign, or his times: as **a** : relating to or representing an early 17th century style of architecture that continued the Elizabethan style with freer use of the classical orders **b** : relating to or exemplifying an early 17th century style in furniture influenced by Renaissance models but somewhat simpler and lighter **c** : of, relating to, or typical of writers or literature of the early 17th century ⟨*Jacobean* drama⟩

²jacobean \"\ *n* -S *usu cap* : a Jacobean statesman or writer

³jacobean \"\ *adj, usu cap* [NL *jacobaeus* Jacobean (fr. LL *Jacobus* St. James — in the Bible, Gal 1:19, Jas 1:1, et al. —, fr. Gk *Iakōbos*, fr. Heb *Yaʽăqōbh* Jacob) + E *-an*] : of or relating to the New Testament Epistle of James or to its author

jacobean lily *n, often cap J* [³*Jacobean*] : a Mexican bulbous herb (*Sprekelia formosissima*) of the family Amaryllidaceae cultivated for its handsome bright red solitary flower — called also *Aztec lily*

ja·co·bi·an \jəˈkōbēən, yə-\ *also* **jacobian determinant** *n* -S *usu cap J* [K. G. J. *Jacobi* †1851 Ger. mathematician + E *-an*] : a determinant in which the elements of the first column are the partial derivatives of the first of a set of *n* functions with respect to each of *n* independent variables, those of the second column the partial derivatives of the second function with respect to each independent variable, and so on

jaco·bin \ˈjakəbən *sometimes* ˈjāk- *or* jəˈkōb-\ *n* -S *usu cap* [ME, fr. MF, fr. ML *Jacobinus*, fr. LL *Jacobus* St. James, + L *-inus* -ine; fr. the location of the first Dominican convent in the street of St. James (Rue St.-Jacques) in Paris] **1** : DOMINICAN **2** [F, fr. *Jacobin* Dominican; fr. the group's having been founded in the Dominican convent in Paris in 1789] **a** : a member of an extremist political group advocating equalitarian democracy and famous for its terrorist policies during the French Revolution of 1789 **b** : a political extremist or radical; *esp* : one that advocates the attainment of equalitarian democracy usu. by revolutionary or violent methods ⟨the children of the Boston Federalists grew up under the impression that Democrats, or *Jacobins*, as they were called, were repulsive creatures —C.G.Bowers⟩ **3 a** : a breed of fancy pigeons whose neck feathers are reversed and so form a fluffy hood **b** [F, fr. *Jacobin*, Dominican; fr. the resemblance of the head and neck of such birds to the hood of a Dominican] : a tropical American hummingbird of the genus *Florisuga* (esp. *F. mellivora*)

jaco·bin·ia \ˌjakəˈbinēə, ˌjāk-\ *n* [NL, fr. *Jacobina*, Brazil + NL *-ia*] **1** *cap* : a genus of tropical American herbs and shrubs (family Acanthaceae) having tubular red or orange bilabiate flowers with two stamens **2** -S : any plant of the genus *Jacobinia*

jaco·bin·ic \ˌjakə¦binik, -nēk *sometimes* ¦jāk- *or* **jaco·bin·i·cal** \-nəkəl, -nēk-\ *adj, usu cap* : of or relating to the Jacobins or Jacobinism — **jaco·bin·i·cal·ly** \-nək(ə)lē, -nēk-, -li\ *adv, usu cap*

jaco·bin·ism \ˈ==,bə,nizəm\ *n* -S *usu cap* [F *jacobinisme*, fr. *jacobin* + *-isme* -ism] : the principles and practice of the Jacobins: **a** : the egalitarianism and terrorism of the Jacobins of the French Revolution of 1789 **b** : any violent or revolutionary political extremism ⟨*Jacobinism* . . . means in practice government by a rabble —G.H.Sabine⟩

jaco·bin·ize \-,nīz\ *vt* -ED/-ING/-S *often cap* : to make Jacobinic : convert to Jacobinism

¹jaco·bite \ˈjakə,bīt *also* ˈjāk-; *usu* -īd·+V\ *n* -S *usu cap* **1** [ME, fr. ML *Jacobita*, fr. *Jacobus* Baradaeus (Jacob Baradai) †578 Syrian monk, founder of the Jacobite Church + L *-ita* -ite] : a member of a Syrian monophysite church **2** [ML *Jacobita*, fr. LL *Jacobus* St. James + L *-ita* -ite — more at JACOBIN] : DOMINICAN **3** [*Jacobus* (James II) †1701 king of England + E *-ite*] : a partisan of James II of England or the Stuarts after the revolution of 1688

²jacobite \"\ *adj, usu cap* : of or relating to the Jacobites

jaco·bit·i·cal \¦=¦bid·|əkəl, -it|, |ēk-\ *also* **jaco·bit·ish** \ˈ==,bīd·|ish, -īt|, |ēsh\ *adj, usu cap* [¹*Jacobite* + *-ical* or *-ish*] : of or relating to the Stuart pretenders to the English crown or their adherents

jaco·bit·ism \ˈ==,bīd·,izəm\ *n* -S *usu cap* [¹*Jacobite* + *-ism*] : the cause and activities of the English Jacobites

ja·cobs·ite \ˈjākəb,zīt *sometimes* -kəp,sīt\ *n* -S [F *jakobsite*, fr. *Jakobsberg*, Sweden, its locality + F *-ite*] : a black magnetic isometric mineral $MnFe_2O_4$ consisting of an oxide of manganese and iron and occurring as a member of the magnetite series

jacob's ladder *n, usu cap J* [after *Jacob* (Israel), the eponymous ancestor of the twelve tribes of Israel in the Bible, who in a dream saw a ladder extending from earth to heaven (Gen 28:12), fr. LL, fr. Gk *Iakōb*, fr. Heb *Yaʽăqōbh*] **1 a** : a pinnate-leaved European perennial herb (*Polemonium caeruleum*) with bright blue or white flowers —called also *charity, Greek valerian* **b** : any of several related American herbs (as *P. vanbruntiae*) **2** : CARRION FLOWER 1 **3** : a marine ladder of rope or chain with wooden or iron rungs **4** : an elevator consisting typically of an endless chain and buckets used in lifting coal and other materials

jacob's ladder 3

ja·cob·son's cartilage \ˈjākəbs|ənz-, -kəps|\ *or* **jacobson's turbinal** *n, usu cap J* [after Ludvig L. *Jacobson* †1843 Danish surgeon and anatomist] : a narrow process of cartilage between the vomer and the cartilage of the nasal septum

jacobson's nerve *n, usu cap J* [after L.L.*Jacobson*] : TYMPANIC NERVE 1

jacobson's organ *n, usu cap J* [after L.L.*Jacobson*] : a slender horizontal canal in the nasal mucosa that ends in a blind pouch, has an olfactory function, and is rudimentary in adult man but highly developed in most reptiles

jacob's-rod \ˈ==ˈ=\ *n, pl* **jacob's-rods** *usu cap J* [after *Jacob* in the Bible, who is mentioned as peeling rods of poplar (Gen 30:37)] : an asphodel of the genus *Asphodeline*

jacob's staff *n, usu cap J* [after *Jacob* St. James, symbolized in religious art by a pilgrim's staff — more at JACOBIN] **1** *obs* : a pilgrim's staff **2 a** *obs* : CROSS-STAFF **2** **b** *also* **jacob staff** : a short square rod with a cursor used for measuring heights and distances **c** *also* **jacob staff** : a straight rod or staff pointed and shod with iron at the bottom for insertion in the ground, having a socket joint at the top, and used instead of a tripod for supporting a compass **3** *obs* : a staff with a sword or dagger concealed in it

jacob's-staff \ˈ==ˈ=\ *n, pl* **jacob's-staffs** *usu cap J* [*Jacob's staff* (pilgrim's staff)] **1** : GREAT MULLEIN **2** : a plant of the genus *Fouquieria*

ja·co·bus \jəˈkōbəs\ *n* -ES *usu cap J* [after *Jacobus* (King James I) †1625 king of England, during whose reign unites were coined] : UNITE

jac·o·net \ˈjakə,net, -,nŏt, ,==ˈnet\ *n* -S [modif. of Urdu *jagannāthī*, fr. *Jagannāth* (Puri), India, where such cloth was first made] : a lightweight cotton cloth resembling lawn that is used with or without a semiglaze for clothing and is given a waterproof finish for use in bandages

ja·co·pev·er \,yäkəˈpevə(r)\ *n* -S [Afrik *jakopewer*, prob. irreg. fr. *Jacob Evertsen*, 17th cent. Du. sea captain with bulging eyes and red face] : any of several large-eyed reddish food fishes of southern Africa; *esp* : a common scorpaenid fish (*Sebastichthys capensis*)

ja·cot tool \zhaˈkō, ja-, ˈ=(,)=\ *n, usu cap J* [prob. intended as trans. of F *tour Jacot*, lit., Jacot lathe, prob. fr. the name *Jacot*] : a small hand lathe in which watch pivots are burnished or polished

jac·quard \ˈja,kärd, jəˈk-, -kȧd\ *n* -S *often cap* [after Joseph M. *Jacquard* †1834 French inventor] **1 a** : a loom apparatus or head for weaving figured fabrics that has a mechanism controlled by a chain of variously perforated cards which cause the warp threads to be lifted in the proper sequence for producing figures **b** *or* **jacquard loom** : a loom having a jacquard **2** : a fabric of jacquard weave or jacquard-knitted pattern

jacquard board *n, often cap J* : a tough and very stiff jute board or pressboard used for making jacquard cards

jacquard knitting *n, often cap J* : machine knitting with a jacquard attachment that makes patterns by the use of colored yarns

jacquard weave *n, often cap J* : an intricate variegated weave made on a jacquard loom and used for brocade, tapestry, and damask

jacque·mi·not \ˈjakmə,nō\ *n* -S [*Jacqueminot* or *General Jacqueminot*, a variety of red rose, after Viscount Jean François *Jacqueminot* †1865 French general] : RASPBERRY RED

jacque·rie \zhäˈkrē\ *n* -S *often cap* [F, fr. *jacquerie*, the 1358 peasant revolt in France, fr. MF, fr. *jacques, jacque* peasant + *-erie* -ery — more at JACKET] **1** : a peasants' revolt **2** : the peasant class ⟨stormed and sacked by a famished *Jacquerie* —*Times Lit. Supp.*⟩

jac·tance \ˈjaktən(t)s\ *or* **jac·tan·cy** \-nsē\ *n, pl* **jactances** *or* **jactancies** [MF & L; MF *jactance*, fr. L *jactantia*, fr. *jactant-, jactans* (pres. part. of *jactare* to throw, shake, speak out, boast) + *-ia* -y — more at JET] : vainglorious boasting ⟨~, vanity, peculation to the ruin of 20 years' labor —Ezra Pound⟩

jac·ta·tion \jakˈtāshən\ *n* -S [L *jactation-, jactatio*, fr. *jactatus* (past part. of *jactare*) + *-ion-, -io* -ion] **1** : boastful declaration or display ⟨one of his familiar ~*s* of imperfection —George Saintsbury⟩ **2** [prob. fr. F, fr. L] : a throwing or tossing of the body; *specif* : JACTITATION

jac·ti·tate \ˈjaktə,tāt\ *vi* -ED/-ING/-S [LL *jactitatus*, past part. of *jactitare*, freq. of L *jactare*] : to toss or jerk the body about

jac·ti·ta·tion \,==ˈtāshən\ *n* -S [LL *jactitation-, jactitatio*, fr. *jactitatus* + *-ion-, -io* -ion] **1 a** *archaic* : boastful public assertion or ostentation **b** : false boasting or claim or other false assertion made or repeated to the prejudice of another person: as (1) *or* **jactitation of marriage** : false and actionable pretension that one is married to someone (2) : SLANDER OF TITLE **2** : a tossing to and fro or jerking and twitching of the body or its parts : excessive restlessness esp. in certain psychiatric disorders

ja·cu \jəˈkü\ *n* -S [Pg *jacu, jacú*, fr. Tupi *jacú*] : a So. American guan (esp. *Penelope obscura jacquaçu*)

jacua *var of* JAGUA

jac·u·late \ˈjakyə,lāt\ *vt* -ED/-ING/-S [L *jaculatus*, past part. of *jaculari* — more at EJACULATE] : to throw or hurl forward (as a dart)

jac·u·la·tion \,==ˈlāshən\ *n* -S [L *jaculation-, jaculatio*, fr. *jaculatus* + *-ion-, -io* -ion] : the act of pitching, throwing, or hurling ⟨hills hurled to and fro with ~ dire —John Milton⟩

ja·cun·da \,jäkünˈdä\ *n, pl* **jacunda** *or* **jacundas** *usu cap* [Pg *jacundá*, of AmerInd origin] **1 a** : a Tupian Indian people of northern Brazil **b** : a member of such people **2** : the language of the Jacunda people

jac·u·tin·ga \,jakyəˈtiŋgə\ *n* -S [Pg, fr. Tupi, lit., white jacu] **1** : a So. American guan (*Pipile jacutinga*) **2** [Pg, fr. *Jacutinga*, village in the state of Rio de Janeiro, Brazil, its locality] : a hematitic iron ore that occurs in Brazil and is characterized by thin bedding or lamination

¹jade \ˈjād\ *n* -S [ME] **1** : a broken-down, vicious, or worthless horse : PLUG ⟨struck his armed heels against the panting sides of his poor ~ —Shak.⟩ **2 a** : a low or shrewish woman : WENCH, TERMAGANT ⟨the painted ~ into which inevitably she degenerated —Maurice Valency⟩ **b** : a flirtatious girl : MINX ⟨a laughing ~ of not ungentle mold —J.G.Saxe⟩

²jade \"\ *vt* -ED/-ING/-S **1 a** : to make a jade of (a horse) : wear out by overwork or abuse ⟨when a horse approaches the goal, he does not, unless he is *jaded*, slacken his pace —William Cowper⟩ **b** : to tire by severe or tedious tasks : FATIGUE, FAG ⟨constant repetition of often trivial material ~*s* one's palate —Thomas Heinitz⟩ **2** *obs* : to make ridiculous or expose to scorn ⟨do not now fool myself, to let imagination ~ me —Shak.⟩ ~ *vi* : to become weary : lose heart : FLAG ⟨when I feel my Muse beginning to ~, I retire to the solitary fireside of my study — Robert Burns⟩ **syn** see TIRE

³jade \"\ *n* -S [F, fr. obs. Sp (*piedra de la*) *ijada*, lit., loin stone; Sp *ijada* loin, fr. L *ilia*, pl. of *ilium, ileum* groin, viscera; fr. the belief that jade cures renal colic — more at ILEUM] **1** : a tough compact gemstone that is commonly green but sometimes whitish and takes a high polish: **a** : jade derived from jadeite — called also *imperial jade, true jade* **b** : jade derived from nephrite **2** : JADE GREEN

jaded *adj* [fr. past part. of ²*jade*] **1** : fatigued by overwork or abuse : WORN OUT, EXHAUSTED ⟨come in plenty ~, looking as thin and gaunt as a gutted snowbird —F.B.Gipson⟩ **2** : dulled by surfeit or excess : SATIATED ⟨might pall on ~ appetites —*Americana Annual*⟩ ⟨all the gilded corruption of a ~ and perverted group of men and women —Pamela Taylor⟩ — **jad·ed·ly** *adv* — **jad·ed·ness** *n* -ES

jade gray *n* : a variable color averaging a grayish green that is bluer and duller than average bayberry, bluer, lighter, and stronger than slate green, and yellower and slightly darker than average blue spruce (sense 2a)

jade green *n* **1** : a variable color averaging a light bluish green that is greener and deeper than robin's-egg blue (sense 2), Eton blue, or turquoise (sense 2b) **2** *of textiles* : a variable color averaging a moderate yellowish green that is yellower, lighter, and stronger than tarragon, yellower, lighter, and slightly less strong than malachite green, and yellower and stronger than verdigris

jade·ite \ˈjā,dīt\ *n* -S [F, fr. *jade* + *-ite*] **1** : a monoclinic mineral $NaAlSi_2O_6$ found chiefly in Burma that consists of a sodium aluminum silicate and when cut constitutes a valuable variety of jade **2** : a light green that is bluer and deeper than average mint green and bluer and paler than serpentine

jade plant *n* : any of various plants of the genus *Crassula* (as *C. argentea* and *C. arborescens*)

jadesheen \ˈ=¦=\ *n* : AMERICAN GREEN

jadestone \ˈ=,=\ *n* : ³JADE 1

jad·ish \ˈjādish\ *adj* [¹*jade* + *-ish*] : having the qualities or characteristics of a jade — **jad·ish·ly** *adv* — **jad·ish·ness** *n* -ES

jady \ˈjādē\ *adj, usu* -ER/-EST [¹*jade* + *-y*] : JADISH

jae·ger *also* **ja·ger** \ˈyāgə(r)\ *n* -S [G *jäger*, lit., hunter, fr. OHG *jagari*, fr. *jagōn* to hunt + *-ari* -er — more at YACHT] **1** *or* **jä·ger** \"\ : a German or Austrian rifleman: **a** : one belonging to a military unit composed chiefly of huntsmen using their own weapons **b** : one belonging to a mobile light-infantry unit **2** *or* **jäger a :** HUNTER, HUNTSMAN **b :** an attendant on a person of rank or wealth dressed in hunter's costume **3 :** any of several large and spirited rapacious birds of the family Stercorariidae (as *Stercorarius parasiticus*) that inhabit the northern seas, are usu. blackish brown above and lighter below or chiefly sooty brown or blackish with the bill hooked and cered, are strong flyers, and harass weaker birds until they drop or disgorge their prey — called also *marlinespike;* compare PARASITIC JAEGER, POMARINE JAEGER

¹jag \'jag, -aa(ə)-, -ai-\ *n* -s [ME *jagge*] **1 a :** one of a series of dangling tabs along the edge of a garment used esp. for ornamentation of medieval apparel **:** DAG **b :** a slashed section or slit of a garment revealing an underlying piece of another color used esp. in Renaissance apparel **2** *now dial* **:** SHRED, RAG, TATTER **3** *now dial Eng* **:** a projecting hair or bristle or a hairy or bristly outgrowth (as the awn of oats) **4 :** a sharp projecting part or protuberance **:** TOOTH, BARB **5** *chiefly Scot* **:** PRICK, STAB, JAB **6 :** a piece of metal screwed on the ramrod of a rifle to hold a rag or tow and used for cleaning the barrel **7 :** JAG BOLT

²jag \"\ *vb* **jagged** \-gd\ **jagged** \"; *see* JAGGED *adj*\ **jagging; jags** [ME *jaggen,* fr. *jagge,* n.] *vt* **1** *now dial* **:** STAB, JAB **2 a :** to slash or pink (a garment) with jags **b :** to cut teeth or other indentations into **c :** to make (an edge) ragged by cutting or notching **:** cut unevenly ⟨his hand shook and *jagged* the leaf⟩ ~ *vi* **1 :** PRICK, THRUST ⟨blackest jealousy *jagging* at their hearts —Llewelyn Powys⟩ **2 :** to move in jerks ⟨a blunt tool not only ~*s* and takes longer to cut but . . . will not cut cleanly —Albert Toft⟩ **:** JOG

³jag \"\ *n* -s [origin unknown] **1 a :** a small or part load ⟨a ~ of hay⟩ **b :** a trip for fetching a jag ⟨on the last ~ before dark⟩ **c** *chiefly dial* **:** PORTION, QUANTITY ⟨give the bay mare a ~ of oats⟩ ⟨people bought ~*s* of things they didn't need⟩ **2 a :** a state or feeling of exhilaration or intoxication esp. when induced by liquor **:** an inebriating load (as of liquor) ⟨had a good ~ on when he left the bar⟩ **:** THRILL ⟨takes the stuff because it gives him a ~⟩ **b :** a period of unrestrained indulgence (as in liquor or an emotion) **:** BENDER, SPREE ⟨went on a weekend ~ to forget his troubles⟩ ⟨addicts on marijuana ~*s*⟩ ⟨enjoying a sentimental ~⟩ **:** SPELL ⟨bringing them to tears . . . and ending in a crying ~ himself —Dixon Wecter⟩ **3** *chiefly Scot* **:** a leather bag or pouch

⁴jag \"\ *vt, dial* **:** to convey (a load of something) from one place to another **:** CARRY

JAG *abbr* judge advocate general

ja·ga·tai \ˌjagəˈtī\ *n* -s *usu cap* [fr. *Jagatai,* region in central Asia approximately equivalent to Turkistan, fr. *Jagatai* †1242 Mongol ruler who governed it] **1 :** any of various Eastern Turkic languages: as **a :** UIGHUR 2a **b :** UZBEK 2 **2 :** the Eastern Turkic languages collectively

jag bolt *n* [¹*jag*] **:** an anchor bolt with a barbed flaring shank which resists retraction when leaded into stone or set in concrete — called also *hacked bolt, rag bolt*

jageer *var of* JAGIR

ja·gel·lo \yäˈge(ˌ)lō\ *or* **ja·giel·lo** \yägˈye-\ *n* -s *usu cap* [after Ladislas II (or V) *Jagello* (Pol *Jagiełło*) †1434 grand duke of Lithuania and king of Poland] **:** a member of a dynasty ruling in Lithuania, Poland, Hungary, and Bohemia during the 14th, 15th, and 16th centuries

ja·gel·lo·ni·an \ˌyägəˈlōnēən\ *or* **ja·giel·lo·ni·an** \-gyəˌ-\ *or* **ja·gel·lon** \ˈyägəˌlōn\ *or* **ja·giel·lon** \-gyəˌ-\ *adj, usu cap* **:** of or relating to the Jagellos

¹jager *or* **jäger** *var of* JAEGER

²ja·ger *or* **jae·ger** \ˈyägə(r)\ *n* -s [fr. *Jagers*fontein, town in southwestern Orange Free State, Union of So. Africa, where such diamonds are mined] **:** a high-quality diamond of bluish white grade

jaggar *var of* JUGGER

¹jag·ged \ˈjagəd, -aag-,-aig-\ *adj, often* -ER/-EST [ME, fr. *jagge* jag + *-ed*] **1 :** having a sharply uneven edge or surface **:** marked by jags ⟨the ~ skyline of the city⟩ ⟨a ~ coastline with deep coves and rocky points⟩ ⟨a ~ bolt of lightning⟩ ⟨blasted out great ~ chunks of stone⟩ **2 :** having a harsh or rough quality **:** RAGGED ⟨her voice was ~ with excitement —Sinclair Lewis⟩ **:** RUGGED ⟨some of his ideas, once so ~ and uncompromising, have been smoothed by time —Herbert Kupferberg⟩ **3 :** marked by sharply broken or violently varying movement **:** abruptly irregular ⟨harsh, stubborn harmonies, his ~ rhythms —*Time*⟩

²jagged \-gd\ *adj* [³*jag* + *-ed*] *slang* **:** DRUNK

jag·ged chickweed \-gəd-\ *n* **:** a European herb (*Holosteum umbellatum*) naturalized in eastern No. America and having several white flowers in a long-stalked umbel

jag·ged·ly \-gədlē, -li\ *adv* **:** in a jagged manner

jag·ged·ness \-gədnəs\ *n* -ES **:** the quality or state of being jagged

¹jag·ger \-gə(r)\ *n* -s [²*jag* + *-er*] **1 :** one that jags; *specif* **:** JAGGING WHEEL **2** *chiefly dial* **:** something sharp or prickly: as **a :** BRAMBLE, THORN **b :** a frayed bit of wire on a worn cable

²jagger \"\ *n* -s [³*jag* + *-er*] *dial Brit* **:** one that carries a jag: as **a :** an itinerant peddler **b :** PACKHORSE

³jagger \"\ *n* -s [D *jager,* lit., hunter, fr. MD, fr. *jagen* to hunt + *-er* — more at YACHT] *archaic* **:** a boat accompanying a fishing fleet to supply and empty the boats

jag·gery *also* **jag·ghery** *or* **jag·ga·ry** \ˈjagərē\ *n* -ES [Hindi *jāgrī;* perh. akin to Skt *śarkarā* gravel, grit, sugar — more at SUGAR] **:** an unrefined brown sugar made esp. from palm sap (as in India)

jaggery palm *n* **:** an East Indian palm (*Caryota urens*) having stout-petioled pinnate leaves with wedge-shaped divisions and being a chief source of jaggery — called also *toddy palm*

jagging *pres part of* JAG

jagging wheel *n* [fr. pres. part. of ²*jag*] **:** a wheel with a zigzag or jagged edge for cutting cakes or pastry into ornamental figures

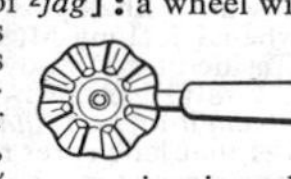
jagging wheel

jag·gy \-gē\ *adj* **jaggier; jaggiest** [¹*jag* + *-y*] **1 :** having or abounding in jags **:** JAGGED, NOTCHED, UNEVEN, ROUGH ⟨~ teeth⟩ **2** *chiefly Scot* **:** PRICKLY

ja·gir *or* **ja·ghir** *or* **ja·geer** *or* **ja·gheer** \jəˈgi(ə)r\ *n* -s [Per *jāgīr,* fr. *jā* place + *-gīr* keeping, holding (fr. *gīriftan* to seize, hold)] **:** a grant of the public revenues of a district in northern India or Pakistan to a person with power to collect and enjoy them and to administer the government in the district; *also* **:** the district so assigned, the revenue from it, or the tenure by which it is held — compare ENAM

ja·gir·dar *also* **ja·ghir·dar** *or* **ja·ghire·dar** *or* **ja·geer·dar** *or* **ja·gheer·dar** \-ˌdär\ *n* -s [Per *jagīrdār,* fr. *jāgīr* + *-dār* holder — more at BHUMIDAR] **:** the holder of a jagir

ja·gla \ˈjäglə\ *n* -s [of Indic origin; akin to Skt *chāgala* goat] **:** SEROW

jag·less \ˈjagləs, -aag-,-aig-\ *adj* [³*jag* + *-less*] **:** having or producing no jag ⟨a stimulating but ~ beverage⟩

jags *pl of* JAG, *pres 3d sing of* JAG

jagsiekte *or* **jagziekte** *var of* JAAGSIEKTE

jag spike *n* [¹*jag*] **:** BOLT

¹ja·gua \ˈhägwə\ *also* **ja·cua** \-äkwə\ *n* -s [Sp *jagua,* fr. Taino *šawa*] **:** GENIPAP

²ja·gua \", ˈyä-\ *n* -s [modif. of Sp *yagua* — more at YAGUA] **:** INAJA

jag·uar \ˈjag|ˌwär, ˈjaig|, |ˌwå(r *also* -gyə| *sometimes* |_wə(r) *or* ÷ -gə|\ *n, pl* **jaguars** *also* **jaguar** [Sp & Pg; Sp *yaguar, jaguar* & Pg *jaguar* fr. Tupi *jaguara* & Guarani *yaguara*] **:** a large powerful cat (*Felis onca*) ranging from Texas to Paraguay but extremely rare in the northern part of its range, having a larger head, heavier body, and shorter thicker legs than the leopard or the cougar, and being of brownish yellow or buff color marked with black spots each of which is surrounded by a somewhat broken ring of smaller ones

jaguar

jag·ua·run·di \ˌjagwəˈrəndē, ˌjaig-, -gyəw-\ *also* **jag·ua·ron·di** \-ˈrän-\ *n* -s [Amer Sp & Pg, fr. Guarani *yaguarundi* & Tupi *jaguarundi*] **:** a slender long-tailed short-legged grayish wildcat (*Felis jaguarondi*) widely distributed from Mexico to Patagonia — see EYRA

ja·güey \häˈgwā\ *n* -s [Amer Sp, fr. Taino] **:** any of several trees of the genus *Ficus; esp* **:** BANYAN

jah \ˈy|ä, ˈj|, |å\ *cap, var of* YAH

ja·hi·li·ya \ˌjähəˈlē(y)ə\ *n, cap* [Ar *jāhilīyah*] **:** the pre-Islamic period in Arabia

jahrzeit *often cap, var of* YAHRZEIT

jahve *or* **jahveh** *cap, var of* YAHWEH

jahvism *or* **jahwism** *cap, var of* YAHWISM

jahvist *or* **jahwist** *usu cap, var of* YAHWIST

jahwe *or* **jahweh** *cap, var of* YAHWEH

jai alai \ˈhī,lī *also* ¦hīə¦lī\ *n, pl* **jai alais** [Sp, fr. Basque, fr. *jai* festival + *alai* merry] **:** a game of Basque origin resembling handball and played (as in Spain and Latin America) on a large walled court by usu. two or four players who use a long curved wicker basket strapped to the right wrist to catch and hurl the ball against the front wall to make it rebound in such a way that the opponent cannot return it before it has bounced more than once — see CESTA, FRONTON, PELOTA

jai alai basket

¹jail \ˈjāl, *esp before pause or consonant* -āəl\ *n* -s [ME *jaiole, jaile,* fr. OF *jaiole,* fr. (assumed) VL *caveola,* dim. of L *cavea* cavity, cage — more at CAGE] **1 :** PRISON **2 :** a building for the confinement of persons held in lawful custody (as for minor offenses or some future judicial proceeding) **:** LOCKUP **3 :** confinement in a jail ⟨kept in ~ until he posted bond⟩ ⟨sentenced to ~ for 30 days⟩

²jail \"\ *vt* -ED/-ING/-S **:** to confine in or as if in a jail **:** lock up **:** IMPRISON

jailbait \ˈ=ˌ=\ *n* **1 :** a temptation to commit an offense for which one can be jailed **2** *slang* **:** a girl under the age of consent with whom unlawful sexual intercourse constitutes statutory rape ⟨knocked up some little ~ —Maritta Wolff⟩

jailbird \ˈ=ˌ=\ *n* **:** a person who is or has been confined in jail; *specif* **:** one jailed long or often

jailbreak \ˈ=ˌ=\ *n* **:** a forcible escape from jail

jail delivery *n* **1 :** the clearing of a jail by bringing the prisoners to trial or by having the legality of their commitments reviewed **2 :** the freeing esp. by force of prisoners in a jail

jail·er *or* **jail·or** \ˈjālə(r)\ *n* -s [ME *jailer,* fr. OF *jaiolier,* fr. *jaiole* + *-ier* -er] **1 :** a keeper of a jail or prison **:** GUARD **2 :** one that restricts another's liberty as if by imprisonment

jail fever *n* **:** TYPHUS 1a

jailhouse \ˈ=ˌ=\ *n* **:** JAIL

jail liberties *or* **jail limits** *n pl* **:** a space or district around a jail which is legally considered as part of the prison and within which a prisoner (as a debtor) is allowed to go at large under a bond of security

¹jain \ˈjīn, ˈjān\ *also* **jai·na** \-nə\ *or* **jain·ist** \-nəst\ *n* -s *usu cap* [*jain* fr. Hindi, fr. Skt *jaina,* fr. *jina* saint, victorious, fr. *jayati* he conquers; *jaina* fr. Skt; *jainist* fr. Hindi *jain* + E *-ist;* akin to Gk *bia* force] **:** an adherent of Jainism

²jain \"\ *or* **jaina** \"\ *also* **jainist** \"\ *adj, usu cap* **:** of or relating to the Jains or Jainism

jain·ism \-ˌnizəm\ *n* -s *usu cap* **:** a religion of India historically traceable to the jina Vardhamana Mahavira of the 6th century B.C. having scriptures, temples, a cultus, and a monastic class and being characterized by the belief that while gods control the realm of time and matter no being higher than an absolutely perfect human soul is necessary for the creation or moral regulation of the universe, and by the personal ideal of the kevalin worked toward through usu. numerous lives in the pursuit of right knowledge, right faith, and right conduct including ahimsa and in veneration of the jinas often involving images — compare DIGAMBARA, SVETAMBARA

jai·pur \ˈjīˌpu̇(ə)r, =ˈ=\ *adj, usu cap* [fr. *Jaipur,* India] **:** of or from the city of Jaipur, India **:** of the kind or style prevalent in Jaipur

jai·puri \ˈjīpə(ˌ)rē, jīˈpu̇rē\ *n, usu cap* [Hindi *jaipurī* fr. Jaipur, fr. Jaipur, city in India] **:** a dialect of Rajasthani

jaj·man \ˈjəjˈmän\ *n, pl* **jaj·mans** \-nz\ *or* **jaj·ma·ni** \-nē\ [Hindi *jajmān,* fr. Skt *yajamāna,* pres part. of *yajati* he sacrifices; akin to Av *yasna* sacrifice] **:** one of a fixed circle of persons in a Hindu caste system whom a member of an occupational group (as a barber) serves as an exclusive and hereditary right

jajoba *var of* JOJOBA

jak *or* **jakfruit** *var of* JACKFRUIT

jakarta *usu cap, var of* DJAKARTA

¹jake \ˈjāk\ *n* -s [fr. *Jake,* nickname for *Jacob*] **:** an uncouth country fellow **:** HICK; *broadly* **:** FELLOW — often used disparagingly

²jake \"\ *adj* [origin unknown] *slang* **:** ALL RIGHT, FINE ⟨it was pretty hot . . . otherwise everything was ~ —Philip Hamburger⟩

³jake \"\ *also* **ja·key** \ˈjākē\ *n, pl* **jakes** *also* **jakeys** [by shortening & alter. fr. *Jamaica (ginger)*] *slang* **:** an alcoholic extract of Jamaica ginger used as a beverage during the prohibition era

jake leg *n* [³*jake*] **:** a paralysis caused by drinking jake or some other strong liquor

jakes \ˈjāks\ *n pl but usu sing in constr* [perh. fr. the F name *Jacques*] **1** *chiefly dial* **:** PRIVY 2 ⟨the fir trees . . . planted to shelter the garden ~ —Llewelyn Powys⟩ **2** *dial Brit* **:** a dirty mess **:** EXCREMENT

ja·khals·bes·sie *also* **jak·kals·bes·sie** *or* **ja·kaals-bes·sie** \ˌjaˌkōlzˈbesē, -ˌkəl-\ *n* -s [Afrik *jakkalsbessie,* fr. *jakkals* jackal + *bessie* berry] **:** an African ebony (*Diospyros mespiliformis*) with evergreen leaves

jako \ˈja(ˌ)kō\ *n* -s [origin unknown] **:** AFRICAN GRAY

jak tree *n* **:** JACKFRUIT 1

ja·kun \jəˈkün\ *n, pl* **jakun** *or* **jakuns** *usu cap* **1 a :** an aboriginal people of the southern part of the Malay peninsula **b :** a member of such people **2 :** the Mon-Khmer language of the Jakun people

jal·ap \ˈjaləp, ˈjäl-\ *n* -s [F & Sp; F *jalop,* fr. Sp *jalapa,* fr. *Jalapa,* town in Mexico] **1** *also* **ja·la·pa** \jəˈläpə, hə'-\ **a :** the dried purgative tuberous root of a Mexican plant (*Exogonium purga*) or the powdered drug prepared from it that contains the resinous glycosides convolvulin and jalapin and is the official jalap — compare JICAMA **b :** the root or derived drug of related plants constituting an inferior source of the jalap resins **2 :** any of various plants yielding jalap

ja·la·pe·ño \ˌhäləˈpān(ˌ)yō\ *n* -s [MexSp] **:** a Mexican pepper

jala·pin \ˈjaləpən, ˈjäl-; jəˈläp-\ *n* -s [*jalap* + *-in*] **:** a cathartic glucosidic constituent of true jalap resin and scammony resin

ja·lee work \ˈjä(ˌ)lē-\ *n* [Hindi *jālī* network, latticework, fr. Skt *jāla* net] **:** carving esp. in marble in the form of a pierced screen **:** LATTICEWORK

ja·leo \həˈlā(ˌ)ō\ *n* -s [Sp, fr. *jalear* to cheer a dancer or singer, fr. *hala,* interj. used to cheer or urge on] **:** a lively Spanish solo dance accompanied by castanets

ja·lopy *also* **jal·lopy** *or* **ja·lop·py** \jəˈläpē, -pi\ *n* -ES [origin unknown] **1** *also* **ja·lop** \-p\ **:** a dilapidated automobile ⟨roaring around in a battered old ~⟩ **2 :** an outdated often mechanically inferior model (as of an airplane)

ja·louse \jəˈlüz\ *vt* -ED/-ING/-S [F *jalouser* to envy, be jealous of, fr. OF, fr. *jalos, jalous, jelous* jealous — more at JEALOUS] **1** *chiefly Scot* **:** SUSPECT, SURMISE ⟨*jaloused* frae your last discourse that ye were perplexed —John Buchan⟩ **2 :** to be jealous of or begrudge jealously ⟨*jaloused* him and planned to do him a harm —Sir Richard Burton⟩

jal·ou·sie \ˈjaləsē, -si *sometimes* ¦==¦sē\ *n* -s [F, lit., jealousy, fr. OF *jalousie, jelousie* — more at JEALOUSY] **1 :** a blind or shutter having horizontal slats that are adjustable or fixed at an angle to admit light and air while excluding sun and rain and to permit looking out from behind them without being visible to the outside **2** *or* **jalousie window :** a window made of adjustable glass louvers that control ventilation

jal·ou·sied \"d\ *adj* **:** equipped with jalousies ⟨a ~ porch⟩ **:** having horizontal slats ⟨~ shutters⟩

jal·pa·ite \ˈjalpəˌīt\ *n* -s [G *jalpait,* fr. *Jalpa,* Zacatecas, Mexico, its locality + G *-it* -ite] **:** a mineral consisting of cupriferous argentite

¹jam *also* **jamb** \ˈjam, -aa(ə)-\ *vb* **jammed** *also* **jambed; jammed** *also* **jambed; jamming** *also* **jambing; jams** *also* **jambs** [perh. of imit. origin] *vt* **1 a :** to press into a close or tight position **:** wedge in ⟨~*s* the piano between the sides of the doorway⟩ **:** fix tightly ⟨~ his hat on his head⟩ ⟨~ his teeth together to stop their chattering⟩ **:** SQUEEZE ⟨~ 50 people into a bus designed for 30⟩ **b** (1) **:** to cause (as some movable part of a machine) to become wedged or fixed so as to be unworkable ⟨a misstroke will ~ the typewriter keys⟩ (2) **:** to make (as a machine) unworkable by such jamming ⟨crashed when a loose nut *jammed* the controls⟩ **c :** to impede or block passage of or along **:** OBSTRUCT ⟨could not get through because traffic was completely *jammed* by the crowd⟩ ⟨the communications channels were *jammed* up with priority messages —Ira Wolfert⟩ **d :** to fill or cause to fill closely or to excess **:** PACK ⟨fans ~ the stadium⟩ ⟨newspaper columns were *jammed* with election propaganda⟩ ⟨~*s* authentic details into his stories⟩ **2 :** to push or apply forcibly **:** force violently ⟨*jammed* himself through the porthole⟩ ⟨*jammed* his spurs into the horse's flanks⟩ ⟨~ the bill through a reluctant legislature by party discipline⟩ ⟨*jamming* political opinions down students' throats —Kenneth Roberts⟩; *specif* **:** to apply (the brakes) suddenly with full force — usu. used with *on* ⟨would ~ the brakes on and throw the passengers forward⟩ **3 :** CRUSH, BRUISE ⟨got his right hand severely *jammed* in the door⟩ **4 :** to bring (a boat) close to the wind so that the upper sails are shaking or laid aback ⟨~ the boat into the wind to avoid collision⟩ **5 a :** to cause interference in (radio or radar signals) **:** make unintelligible (as a radio program or broadcast) by intentionally sending out signals or messages in an interfering manner **b :** to make (as a radio or radar apparatus) ineffective by jamming radio or radar signals or by causing reflection of radar waves from a special device ~ *vi* **1 a :** to become blocked, wedged, or fixed **:** stick fast ⟨an odd cartridge may ~ in the gun⟩ ⟨the line *jammed* and the boat hung useless⟩ **b :** to become unworkable through the jamming of a movable part ⟨the overheated machine *jammed*⟩ **2 :** to force one's way esp. into a restricted space **:** mass together tightly **:** CROWD ⟨continued to ~ into the already crowded hall⟩ ⟨the children *jammed* forward to claim their treats⟩ **3 :** to improvise on a musical instrument with a group **:** take part in a jam session ⟨gathered after hours with their instruments and *jammed* all night⟩ **syn** see PRESS

²jam \"\ *n* -s **1 :** something made closely packed, immovable, or unusable by jamming **:** an instance of jamming ⟨lost the pistol match due to a ~ during the rapid fire⟩; *specif* **:** a crowded mass of people or things causing impedance or blockage ⟨a log ~ in the river⟩ ⟨a flood caused by an ice ~⟩ ⟨delayed an hour by a traffic ~⟩ **2 a :** the quality or state of being jammed **:** STOPPAGE, CONGESTION ⟨the ~ of the legislature caused by the piling up of new bills in the final days⟩ **b :** the pressure or congestion of a crowd of people or things **:** CRUSH ⟨escape from the clangor and ~ of the city streets⟩ **3 :** an involved and embarrassing state of affairs **:** DIFFICULTY, MESS, FIX **:** a tight spot ⟨made him late for his date and got him in a ~ with his girl friend⟩ ⟨can get out of its ~ by finding new foreign markets for its products⟩ **4 :** JAM SESSION **syn** see PREDICAMENT

³jam \"\ *adv* **:** COMPLETELY, CLEAR ⟨filled the jar ~ full⟩ ⟨threw the ball ~ across the field⟩

⁴jam \"\ *n* -s [prob. fr. ¹*jam*] **1 :** a product made by boiling fruit and sugar to a thick consistency without preserving the shape of the fruit ⟨spread raspberry ~ on a slice of bread⟩ **2** *chiefly Brit* **:** something agreeable or easy ⟨this job isn't all ~; it has its headaches⟩ ⟨the test was ~ for him and he finished first⟩ **3** [so called fr. its scent that resembles that of raspberry jam] **:** a shrubby acacia (*Acacia acuminata*) with elongated slender phyllodes and cylindrical axillary spikes of yellow flowers that is an important browse plant in much of Western Australia

⁵jam \"\ *vt* **jammed; jammed; jamming; jams 1 :** to spread with jam ⟨munching *jammed* bread⟩ **2 :** to make into jam ⟨fresh, preserved, or *jammed* fruit⟩

⁶jam \ˈjäm\ *n* -s [Hindi *jām*] **:** the ruler in some northwest Indian states in the region of Cutch, Kathiawar, and the lower Indus

ja·ma *also* **ja·mah** \ˈjämə\ *n* -s [Hindi *jāma,* lit., garment, fr. Per] **:** a long-sleeved cotton coat of at least knee length worn by men in northern India and Pakistan

jamadar *var of* JEMADAR

¹ja·mai·ca \jəˈmākə\ *adj, usu cap* [fr. *Jamaica,* island in the West Indies] **:** of or from the island of Jamaica **:** of the kind or style prevalent in Jamaica **:** JAMAICAN

²jamaica \"\ *n* -s *usu cap* [by shortening] **:** JAMAICA RUM

jamaica apple *n, usu cap J* **1 :** CHERIMOYA **2 :** CUSTARD APPLE

jamaica banana *n, usu cap J* **:** the large yellow commercial banana of the Caribbean region

jamaica bayberry *n, usu cap J* **:** BAYBERRY 1a

jamaica bloodwood *n, usu cap J* **:** FALSE LOGWOOD

jamaica buckthorn *n, usu cap J* **:** CHEROKEE ROSE

jamaica bullace plum *n, usu cap J* **:** GENIP 2

jamaica cherry *n, usu cap J* **1 :** a West Indian fig (*Ficus laevigata*) having globose edible fruits the size of a cherry **2 :** CALABUR TREE

jamaica cucumber *n, usu cap J* **:** GHERKIN

jamaica dogwood *n, usu cap J* **:** a West Indian tree (*Piscidia erythrina*) the narcotic root of which is used as a fish poison in Jamaica

jamaica ginger *n, usu cap J* **1 :** a high grade of ginger grown in Jamaica **2 a :** an alcoholic extract of ginger used as a flavoring essence **b :** the powdered root of ginger used as an infusion in medicine (as in colic or diarrhea)

jamaica honeysuckle *n, usu cap J* **:** a West Indian passionflower (*Passiflora laurifolia*) having fragrant flowers, somewhat astringent leaves, and yellow edible fruit — called also *bell apple, sweet cup, water lemon*

jamaica ironwood *n, usu cap J* **:** a small tropical American tree (*Erythroxylon areolatum*) with yellowish white flowers, red drupes, and hard wood

jamaica mignonette *n, usu cap J, West Indies* **:** HENNA

¹ja·mai·can \jəˈmākən\ *adj, usu cap* [*Jamaica,* island in the West Indies + E *-an*] **:** of or relating to Jamaica

²jamaican \"\ *n* -s *cap* **:** a native or inhabitant of Jamaica

jamaica pepper *n, usu cap J* **:** ALLSPICE

jamaica plum *n, usu cap J* **:** a hog plum (*Spondias mombin*) of the West Indies

jamaica quassia *n, usu cap J* **1 :** BITTERWOOD 1a **2 :** quassia obtained from bitterwood

jamaica rum *n, usu cap J* **:** a heavy-bodied rum made in Jamaica by slow fermentation using dunder and usu. having a pungent bouquet — see GERMAN RUM

jamaica sarsaparilla *n, usu cap J* **1** [so called fr. its once being shipped from Jamaica] **:** SARSAPARILLA 1 **2 :** an inferior sarsaparilla grown in Jamaica

jamaica seal *n, usu cap J* **:** WEST INDIA SEAL

jamaica senna tree *n, usu cap J* **:** a tropical Old World herb (*Cassia obovata*) commonly naturalized in tropical America and having glaucous foliage and bright yellow flowers

jamaica sorrel *n, usu cap J* **:** ROSELLE

jamaica thistle *n, usu cap J* **:** PRICKLY POPPY

jamaica vervain *n, usu cap J* **:** a cosmopolitan tropical weed (*Stachytarpheta anoides jamaicensis*) with oblong leaves and bright blue flowers in slender spikes

jamaica walnut *n, usu cap J* **:** a small Jamaican tree (*Picrodendron baccatum*) with hard heavy strong dark olive to nearly black very bitter waxy wood and a fruit that is a drupe with thin bitter flesh, woody endocarp, and a rugose seed

ja·man \ˈjämən\ *n* -s [Hindi *jāman, jāmun,* fr. Skt *jambula,* fr. *jambu*] **:** JAVA PLUM

¹jamb \ˈjam, -aa(ə)-\ *n* -s [ME *jambe,* fr. MF, lit., leg, fr. LL *gamba, camba* hock (of a horse), leg — more at GAMBOL] **1 :** an upright piece or surface forming the side of an opening (as a doorway, window, fireplace) **2 :** a projecting columnar part (as of a masonry wall) or mass (as of ore) **3 :** LEG, SHANK — used chiefly in heraldry **4** *also* **jambe** \"\ **:** JAMBEAU

²jamb *var of* JAM

jam·ba \'jämbə\ *n* -s [prob. native name in India] : ACLE 1
jam·ba·laya \,jəmbə'līə, -lāyə\ *n* -s [LaF, fr. Prov *jambalaia, jabalaia, jambaraia* stew of rice and fowl] **1** : rice cooked with ham, sausage, chicken, shrimp, or oysters and usu. tomato and seasoned with herbs **2** : a mixture of diverse elements : POTPOURRI
jamb brick *n* : a brick with the corner of one end and side rounded for use on the vertical side of an opening in a brick wall
jam·beau \'jam(,)bō, ⸗'⸗\ *n, pl* **jam·beaux** \-ō(z)\ [ME, fr. (assumed) AF, fr. OF *jambe* leg — more at JAMB] : a piece of medieval plate armor for the leg below the knee : GREAVE — see ARMOR illustration
jam·bee \'jam,bē, ⸗'⸗\ *n* -s [fr. *Jambi* (Djambi), district and town, Sumatra, Indonesia] *archaic* : a walking stick made from East Indian rattans (genus *Calamus*) and popular in the reign of Queen Anne
jam·ber \'jambə(r)\ *n* -s [ME, fr. MF *jambiere*, fr. OF, fr. *jambe* leg] : JAMBEAU
jam·bo \'jam(,)bō\ *or* **jam·bou** *also* **jam·bu** \-)bü\ *n* -s [Hindi *jambū, jambu*, fr. Skt] : ROSE APPLE 1
jam·bok \(')zham¦bäk\ *var of* SJAMBOK
jam·bo·lan \'jambə¦lan\ *or* **jambolan plum** *also* **jam·bo·la·na** \,⸗⸗'länə\ *n* [Pg *jambulão*, fr. Hindi *jambūl*] : JAVA PLUM
jam·bone \'jam,bōn\ *n* [origin unknown] : a lone euchre hand that is played with the bidder's cards exposed on the table
jam·bool *or* **jam·bul** \,jəm'bül\ *n* -s [Hindi *jambūl*, fr. Skt *jambūla*, fr. *jambū, jambu*] **1** : JAVA PLUM **2** : a drug obtained from the bark and seeds of Java plum and formerly believed to be of value in treating diabetes
jamborandi *var of* JABORANDI
jam·bo·ree \,jambə¦rē, ¦jaam-\ *n* -s [origin unknown] **1** : a euchre hand containing the five highest trumps **2** : a noisy or unrestrained carousal or frolic : SPREE ⟨got on a ~ last Tuesday and . . . drank repeatedly at every saloon, insulted every person they encountered, brandished pistols and discharged them —D.D.Martin⟩ **3 a** : a large festive gathering (as of a political party or a league of sports teams) often involving a program of variety entertainment or exhibition performances **b** : a national or international camping assembly of boy scouts — compare CAMPOREE **4** : a long mixed program of entertainment ⟨the summer program also includes Sunday matinees of concerts and fountain play . . . plus four special night ~s featuring fireworks —Janet Flanner⟩
jam·bos \'jam,bäs, -bōs\ *n* [NL, fr. E *jambo*] **1** *cap, in some classifications* : a genus of woody plants (family Myrtaceae) with opposite leathery leaves and panicles or corymbs of showy flowers that includes the Java plum, Malay apple, and rose apple which are usu. placed in the genus *Eugenia* **2** *also* **jam·bo·sa** \jam'bōsə\ *pl* **jambos** *also* **jambosas** [*jambosa* fr. NL *Jambosa*, syn. of *Jambos*] : ROSE APPLE 1
jamb peg *n* : a device used in faceting gems comprising a piece of wood containing a series of holes in which a dop stick can be fixed at varying angles
jambs *pl of* JAMB, *pres 3d sing of* JAMB
jamb shaft *n* : a free or engaged column decorating the jamb of a door opening or window opening (as in medieval architecture) — see ESCONSON
jambstone \'⸗,⸗\ *n* : a stone set vertically at the edge of a window or door opening so that one of its faces forms a jamb or part of a jamb
jamb stove *n* : a stove used in the U. S. in the middle of the 18th century made of five cast-iron plates forming a box and built into a fireplace wall so that the front opens into the fireplace to receive live coals and the back warms an adjoining room
jam cleat *n* [²*jam*] : a cleat with a hinged top for belaying with a single turn of rope and without hitches
james *n* -ES [after *James* I †1625 king of England] *slang* : ¹SOVEREIGN 2
james·ian *also* **james·ean** \'jāmzēən\ *adj, usu cap* **1** [William *James* †1910 Am. philosopher and psychologist + E *-ian* or *-ean*] : of, relating to, or resembling William James or his philosophical or psychological teachings (as pragmatism, radical empiricism) **2** [Henry *James* †1916 Am. writer + E *-ian* or *-ean*] : of, relating to, or resembling Henry James or his writings ⟨a *Jamesian* revival⟩ ⟨has written a *Jamesian* novel of psychological tension⟩

diagram of jamb stove: *1* fireplace room, *2* stove room, *3* end plate, *4* side plate, *5* stove leg, *6* stove hole, *7* flue for stove, *8* chimney of fireplace, *9* lintel beam

james–lange theory \'jāmz'läŋə-\ *n, usu cap J&L* [after William *James* and Carl Georg *Lange* †1900 Dan. physician and psychologist] : a theory in psychology: the affective component of emotion follows rather than precedes the attendant physiological changes
jame·son·ite \'jām(p)sə,nīt, -məs-\ *n* -s [Robert *Jameson* †1854 Scot. mineralogist + E *-ite*] : a gray orthorhombic mineral $Pb_4FeSb_6S_{14}$ consisting of a lead antimony iron sulfide, having a metallic luster, and occurring in fibrous masses
james's powder *or* **james' powder** \'jāmz(əz)-\ *n, usu cap J* [after Robert *James* †1776 Eng. physician] : ANTIMONIAL POWDER
james·town lily \'jāmz,taun\ *n, often cap J* [fr. *Jamestown*, Va.] : JIMSONWEED
jamestown weed *often cap J, var of* JIMSONWEED
jammed *past of* JAM
jam·mer \'jamə(r), -aam-\ *n* -s [¹*jam* + *-er*] : one that jams: as **a** (1) : a vehicular hoist used to load logs by animal or tractor power (2) : one that operates such a jammer **b** : a usu. modulated transmitter that emits a signal that is intended to interfere with or make unintelligible radio or radar signals
jamming *pres part of* JAM
jam·my \'jamē, -aam-, -mi\ *adj* -ER/-EST [⁴*jam* + *-y*] **1** : sticky with jam ⟨fended off the child's ~ hands⟩ **2** *Brit* : DELIGHTFUL, EASY ⟨a way of singing that's just ~⟩
jam nut *n* [²*jam*] : LOCKNUT 1
ja·moke \jə'mōk\ *n* -s [alter. of earlier *jamocha*, blend of *java* and *mocha*] *slang* : COFFEE 1a
jam–pack \'⸗,⸗\ *vt* [¹*jam* + *pack*] : to fill to overflowing : fill by crowding in as much as possible : pack tightly : CRAM ⟨vacationists *jam-packed* the trains⟩ ⟨*jam-packs* his columns with useful information⟩
jam·pan \'jam,pan\ *n* -s [Beng *jhāpān*] : a sedan with two poles used in the hill country of India
jam riveter *n* [²*jam*] : a pneumatic riveting hammer designed for use in a restricted space
jam·ro·sade \,jamrō¦zād\ *n* -s [*jambo* + *rose* + *-ade*] : the fruit of the rose apple
jams *pres 3d sing of* JAM, *pl of* JAM
jam session *n* [²*jam*] : an impromptu performance by a group of jazz musicians typically for the players' own enjoyment and characterized by group improvisation
jam·shed·pur \'jäm,shed,pu̇(ə)r\ *adj, usu cap* [fr. *Jamshedpur*, India] : of or from the city of Jamshedpur, India : of the kind or style prevalent in Jamshedpur
¹jam–up \'⸗,⸗\ *adj* [prob. fr. *jam up*, v.] : very good : FIRST-RATE : BANG-UP ⟨after one course in psychology you turn out to be a whiz-bang, *jam-up* mind reader —J.S.Redding⟩
²jam–up \"\ *n* -s [fr. *jam up*, v.] : ²JAM 1
jam weld *n* [²*jam*] : BUTT WELD
jamwood \'⸗,⸗\ *n* [⁴*jam* + *wood*] : the raspberry-scented wood of the tree used by the aboriginal inhabitants of Australia for spears
JAN *abbr* joint army-navy
ja·nam·bre \hə'näm(,)brā\ *n, pl* **janambre** *or* **janambres** *usu cap* [Sp, of AmerInd origin] **1 a** : an Indian people of northeastern Mexico **b** : a member of such people **2** : the language of the Janambre people, perhaps Coahuiltecan
jan·a·pa \'janəpə\ *also* **jan·a·pan** \-pən\ *n* -s [Tamil *canappu, caṇappai*] : SUNN 2
jan·ders \'jandə(r)z, 'jȯn-,'jän-,'jaan-,'jȧn-\ *dial var of* JAUNDICE

J and WO *abbr* jettison and washing overboard
¹jane \'jān\ *n* -s *usu cap* [ME, prob. modif. of MF *Genes* Genoa, Italy] : a small Genoese coin circulating in England during the 14th and 15th centuries
²jane \"\ *n* -s [fr. the name *Jane*] *slang* : GIRL, WOMAN
jane doe \-'dō\ *n, usu cap J&D* [*Jane* + *Doe* (as in *John Doe*)] : a female party to legal proceedings whose true name is unknown — called also *Mary Major*; compare JOHN DOE
jane·ite *also* **jan·ite** \'jā,nīt\ *n* -s [*Jane* Austen †1817 Eng. novelist + E *-ite*] : an enthusiastic admirer of Jane Austen's writings
janes \'jānz\ *dial var of* JEANS
jan·ga·da \jan'gädə, -aŋ'-\ *n* -s [Pg, fr. Tamil *caṅkaṭam* or Malayalam *caṅṅāṭam*, fr. Skt *saṁghāta* joining of timber, union] : a raft made of logs of light wood with a sail, seat, steering oar, and dagger boards and used by fishermen along the northeast coast of Brazil

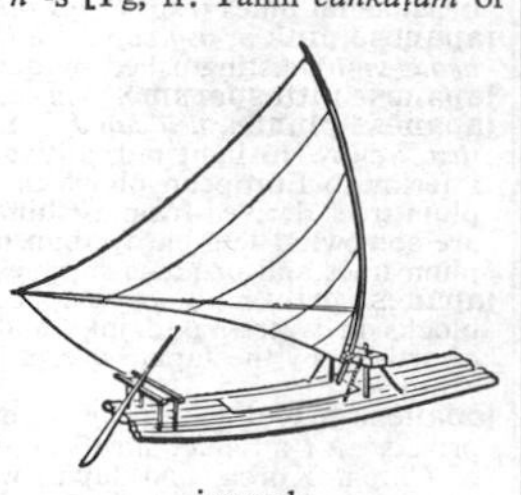
jangada

jangada fiber *n* : the bast fiber from the tibourbou
jan·ga·dei·ro \,jaŋgə'dā(,)rō\ *n* -s [Pg, fr. *jangada* + *-eiro* -er (fr. L *-arius*)] : a Brazilian fisherman who sails a jangada
¹jan·gle \'jaŋgəl, 'jaiŋ-\ *vb* **jangled; jangled; jangling** \-g(ə)liŋ\ **jangles** [ME *janglen*, fr. OF *jangler*, of Gmc origin; akin to MD *jangelen* to grumble, whine, haggle, *janken* to yelp, whine, squeal, G dial. *jangeln* to talk in a whining manner] *vi* **1** *archaic* : to talk idly : BABBLE, CHATTER ⟨some . . . have turned aside unto vain *jangling* —1 Tim 1:6 (AV)⟩ **2** : to quarrel in words : ALTERCATE, WRANGLE ⟨must ~ till at last we fought —A.E.Housman⟩ **3** : to sound harshly or discordantly ⟨the alarm clock *jangled* loudly⟩ ~ *vt* **1** : to utter or sound discordantly or in a babbling or chattering way ⟨the telephone *jangled* a summons⟩ **2 a** : to cause to sound harshly or inharmoniously ⟨~ a bunch of keys⟩ **b** : to excite to tense and discordant irritation ⟨the whimsy that had sometimes *jangled* the nerves of American newsmen —John Lardner⟩
²jangle \"\ *n* -s [ME, fr. MF, fr. OF, fr. *jangler*] **1** : idle talk : CHATTER, BABBLE ⟨his eternal ~ about being the average father of an average American family —Louis Auchincloss⟩ **2** : noisy altercation : CONTENTION, WRANGLING ⟨she hated . . . a shrill squabble of shrews, a degrading ~ between servant and mistress —Jean Stafford⟩ **3** : discordant sound : a confused ringing ⟨music that seemed to be a chaotic ~⟩ ⟨the ~ of sleigh bells⟩ : DISCORD ⟨a haven of calm amid the ~ of modern civilization⟩
jan·gler \-g(ə)lə(r)\ *n* -s [ME, fr. *janglen* + *-er*] : one that jangles
jan·gly \-g(ə)lē, -li\ *adj, sometimes* -ER/-EST [¹*jangle* + *-y*] : marked by jangling ⟨~ costume jewelry⟩ : having a jangling quality ⟨the ~ music of the dance hall piano⟩
jani·ceps \'janə,seps\ *n* -ES [NL, fr. L *Janus*, a two-faced Roman god + *-ceps* headed, fr. *caput* head — more at JANUARY, HEAD] : a double fetal monster joined at thorax and skull and having two equal faces looking in opposite directions
jani·form \-,fȯrm\ *adj* [*Janus* + E *-iform*] : having a face on each of two sides ⟨a coin bearing a ~ head⟩
jan·is·sary *or* **jan·i·zary** \'janə,serē, -,ze-, -ri\ *n* -ES [It *gianizzero*, fr. Turk *yeniçeri*, fr. *yeni* new, inexperienced + *çeri* soldier, military force] **1** *often cap* **a** : a soldier of an elite corps of Turkish troops orig. organized in the 14th century as the sultan's guard, drawn chiefly from subject Christian boys seized in tribute, and continuing as the largest and strongest unit of the army until abolished after revolting in 1826 **b** : a Turkish soldier **2** : a member of a group of loyal or subservient troops, officials, or supporters ⟨a politician with the help of a large following of *janissaries* ready to carry out his personal will⟩ **3** : a West Indian wrasse (*Clepticus parrae*) that is mostly reddish brown with the caudal region green
janissary music *n, often cap J* **1 a** : music of military bands formed on the Turkish model and featuring shrill fifes and loud oboes and drums, cymbals, triangles, and Turkish crescents **b** : orchestral or other music imitating this music or its qualities — called also *Turkish music* **2** : BATTERY 12
¹jan·i·tor \'janəd·ə(r), -nətə-\ *n* -s [L, fr. *janua* door, fr. *janus* arch, gate; perh. akin to Skt *yāna* road, *yāti* he goes, Lith *joti* to ride, L *ire* to go — more at ISSUE] **1** : DOORKEEPER **2** : one that keeps the premises of an apartment, office, or other building clean and free of refuse, tends the heating system, and makes minor repairs
²janitor \"\ *vi* **janitored; janitored; janitoring** \-əriŋ, 'janə·triŋ\ **janitors** : to work as a janitor
jan·i·to·ri·al \¦janə¦tōrēəl, -tȯr-\ *adj* : of or belonging to a janitor : CUSTODIAL ⟨~ duties⟩ ⟨the ~ staff⟩
jan·i·tress \'janə·trəs\ *n* -ES [*janitor* + *-ess*] : a female janitor : CHARWOMAN
jan·i·trix \-nə·(,)triks\ *n* -ES [L, fem. of *janitor*] : JANITRESS
jan·ker \'jaŋkə(r)\ *n* -s [origin unknown] *Scot* : a long pole on two wheels used esp. for hauling logs
jan·kers \'jaŋkə(r)z\ *n pl but sing in constr* [origin unknown] *Brit* : confinement, fatigue duty, or drill imposed as punishment on a member of the armed forces
jan·ko keyboard \'yäŋ(,)kō-\ *n, usu cap J* [after Paul von *Jankó* †1919 Hungarian pianist] : a pianoforte keyboard invented in 1882 consisting of six rows of keys with three digitals to each note, those of each row being at whole-step intervals
jan·mash·ta·mi \,jən'mäshtə,mē\ *n* -s *usu cap* [Skt *janmāṣṭamī*, fr. *janma* birth (fr. *janati* he begets) + *aṣṭama* eighth, fr. *aṣṭā* eight — more at KIN, EIGHT] : a Hindu festival celebrating the birthday of the deified hero Krishna
jann *n* -s [Ar *jānn*] : JINNI
jan·ney coupler \'janē-\ *n, usu cap J* [after Eli H. *Janney* †1912 Am. inventor] : a device for coupling railroad cars and locomotives invented in the early 1880s and employed in principle in the standard automatic coupler of today
¹jan·nock \'janək\ *n* -s [ME *ianock*] *dial Brit* : BANNOCK
²jannock \"\ *adj* [origin unknown] *dial Brit* : straightforward and fair : UPRIGHT, DECENT ⟨to give a lover a chance of a final scene before leaving him . . . was ~ —F.M.Ford⟩
jan·sen·ism \'jan(t)sə,nizəm\ *n* -s *usu cap* [F *jansénisme*, fr. Cornelis *Jansen* (Cornelius Jansenius) †1638 Dutch theologian + F *-isme* -ism] **1** : a theological doctrine condemned by the Roman Catholic Church as heretical that flourished esp. in France in the 17th and 18th centuries maintaining among its principal tenets that freedom of the will (as in accepting or resisting grace) is nonexistent and that the redemption of mankind through the death of Jesus Christ was limited to only a part of mankind and that those not so redeemed are by the positive will of God inescapably condemned to hell **2** : a negative rigoristic moral attitude (as toward sex) associated with adherents of Jansenism : PURITANISM
¹jan·sen·ist \-nəst\ *n* -s *usu cap* [F *janséniste*, fr. C. Jansen + F *-iste* -ist] **1** : an adherent of Jansenism **2** : a member of the Church of Utrecht in Holland originating by schism from the Roman Catholic Church in 1723 and forming part of the Old Catholic Church since 1889
²jansenist \"\ *also* **jan·sen·is·tic** \¦⸗⸗¦nistik\ *adj, usu cap* : of, relating to, or characteristic of the Jansenists or Jansenism
jan·thi·na \'jan(t)thənə\ *n* [NL, fr. L *ianthina*, fem. of *ianthinus* violet-blue, fr. Gk *ianthinos*, fr. *ion* violet + *anthos* flower — more at VIOLET, ANTHOLOGY] **1** *cap* : the type genus of Janthinidae comprising pelagic snails of warm seas that have a thin spiral purple shell, a large head, and protrusible gills **2** -s : any snail of the genus *Janthina*
jan·thi·ni·dae \jan'thinə,dē\ *n pl, cap* [NL, fr. *Janthina*, type genus + *-idae*] : a family of marine snails (suborder Taenioglossa) comprising the violet snails and floating at the surface by means of a raft of air bubbles enclosed in hardened mucus secreted by the foot — see JANTHINA
janty *also* **jantee** *archaic var of* JAUNTY
jan·u·ary \'janyə,werē, -ri *also* ÷'jen-, *dial* -nə,w-\ *n, pl*

januaries *or* **januarys** *usu cap* [ME *Januarie*, fr. L *Januarius*, first month of the ancient Roman year, fr. *Janus*, two-faced god or numen of gates and doors and therefore of beginnings (fr. *janus* arch, gate) + *-arius* -ary — more at JANITOR] : the first month of the Gregorian calendar — abbr. *Jan.*; see MONTH table
janus–faced \'jānə¦sfāst\ *or* **janus** *adj, usu cap J* [after *Janus*, the god or numen] **1** : looking in opposite directions ⟨a *Janus-faced* look at the past and future of our national economy⟩ **2** : having two contrasting aspects ⟨a *Janus-faced* alternation of melodic variations in major and minor throughout the movement⟩ **3** : TWO-FACED, DECEITFUL
janus green *or* **janus green B** *n, usu cap J* : a basic monoazo azine dye made from safranine and dimethylaniline and used chiefly as a biological stain
ja·nus·like \'jānə,slīk\ *adj, usu cap* : looking or acting in opposite or contrasting ways ⟨the *Januslike* quality of Soviet foreign policy created confusion . . . among western statesmen —F.C.Barghoorn⟩
jan·war \'janwər\ *usu cap, Scot var of* JANUARY
jap \'jap\ *n* -s *usu cap, often attrib* [by shortening] : JAPANESE — often used disparagingly
¹ja·pan \jə'pan, -paa(ə)n *also* (')ja¦p-\ *adj* [fr. *Japan*, country consisting of an island chain in the western Pacific off the eastern coast of Asia] **1** *usu cap* : of or from Japan : of the kind or style prevalent in Japan : JAPANESE **2 a** : of, resembling, or characteristic of Japanese lacquered work **b** : coated or treated with japan
²japan \"\ *n* -s [fr. *Japan*, whence it orig. came] **1 a** : a varnish yielding a hard brilliant coating on such surfaces as metal or wood **b** *or* **japan drier** : a varnish that contains a large percentage of resins and driers and that is used as a grinding liquid for paste colors or as a liquid drier for paints **c** *or* **japan black** : a quick-drying black varnish consisting usu. of asphaltum, linseed oil, and thinner that is used for coating metal and that is usu. hardened by baking **2 a** : work varnished and figured in the Japanese manner ⟨the likeness of His Majesty . . . was housed in a circular container of its own, of black ~ —John Godley⟩ **b** : Japanese china or silk
³japan \"\ *vt* **japanned; japanned; japanning; japans** **1** : to cover with a coat of japan or with some other hard brilliant varnish in the manner of the Japanese : LACQUER **2** : to give a high gloss to with varnish supplemented by heating; *specif* : to give a glossy black to (as leather)
japan allspice *n, usu cap J* : a Japanese shrub (*Chimonanthus praecox*) cultivated for its fragrant yellow flowers that blossom before the leaves appear — called also *Japanese allspice*
japan ashberry *n, usu cap J* : an Asiatic evergreen shrub (*Mahonia japonica*) with handsome foliage and yellow flowers
japan bittersweet *n, usu cap J* : JAPANESE BITTERSWEET
japan blue *n, often cap J* : a dark blue that is redder and duller than Peking blue, redder and deeper than Flemish blue, and stronger and slightly redder than Majolica blue (sense 1)
japan camphor *n, usu cap J* : dextrorotatory camphor
japan cedar *n, usu cap J* : JAPANESE CEDAR
japan clover *n, usu cap J* : an annual lespedeza (*Lespedeza striata*) sometimes used as a forage, soil-improving, and pasture crop esp. in the southeastern U.S. — called also *Japanese clover, Jap clover*
¹jap·a·nese \¦japə¦nēz, -ēs, *in rapid speech attributively sometimes* 'jap,n-\ *adj, usu cap* [*Japan* + *-ese*] **1 a** : of, relating to, or characteristic of Japan **b** : of, relating to, or characteristic of the Japanese **2** : of, relating to, or characteristic of the Japanese language
²japanese \"\ *n, cap* **1** *pl* **japanese** : a native or inhabitant of Japan or one of his descendants **2** -s : the language of the Japanese
japanese acid clay *or* **japanese acid earth** *n, usu cap J* : fuller's earth occurring in Japan — called also *Kambara earth*
japanese allspice *n, usu cap J* : JAPAN ALLSPICE
japanese andromeda *n, usu cap J* : a broad-leaved evergreen Asiatic shrub (*Pieris japonica*) with glossy leaves and drooping clusters of whitish flowers that is used as an ornamental — called also *andromeda*
japanese anemone *n, usu cap J* : an Asiatic garden plant (*Anemone nupehensis*) having compound leaves and large showy flowers — called also *Japanese windflower*
japanese angelica tree *n, usu cap J* : a shrub or small tree (*Aralia elata*) having a much-compounded inflorescence with a short main axis and spreading secondary axes
japanese ape *n, usu cap J* : a small brownish ape (*Macaca speciosa*) of Japan that has a naked face and red ischial callosities
japanese apricot *n, usu cap J* : a Japanese ornamental tree (*Prunus mume*) with fragrant white or pink flowers and yellow fruits somewhat smaller than those of the common apricot
japanese arborvitae *n, usu cap J* : a Japanese evergreen tree (*Thuja standishii*) with reddish brown bark, spreading or somewhat upright branches bearing thick compressed branchlets, and leaves that are bright green above with white triangular markings below and that are of two types, those of the main axes terminating in sharp rigid points and those of the lateral branches ending obtusely
japanese artichoke *n, usu cap J* : CHINESE ARTICHOKE
japanese ash *n, usu cap J* **1** : an Asiatic tree (*Fraxinus mandschurica*) having light yellowish wood with a grain resembling that of oak **2** : the wood of Japanese ash used esp. for veneer and joinery — called also *tamo*
japanese aspen *n, usu cap J* : a medium-sized Japanese tree (*Populus sieboldii*) with tomentose twigs and thick leaves
japanese azalea *n, usu cap J* : any of several ornamental azaleas from Japan and China (esp. *Rhododendron japonica*) — compare KURUME AZALEA
japanese banana *n, usu cap J* : an Asiatic banana (*Musa basjoo*) that is cultivated as a foliage plant in Japan
japanese barberry *n, usu cap J* : a compact ornamental Japanese shrub (*Berberis thunbergii*) that has simple spines, entire oblong or spatulate leaves, yellowish flowers either solitary or in small umbels, and bright red persistent berries and that is widespread in cultivation esp. for hedges — compare COMMON BARBERRY
japanese barnyard millet *n, usu cap J* : JAPANESE MILLET
japanese bear *n, usu cap J* : a small black bear (*Ursus japonicus*) of northern Japan that has a small white breast marking
japanese beauty–berry *n, usu cap J* : a Japanese shrub (*Callicarpa japonica*) with long pointed leaves, cymes of pink flowers, and ornamental violet fruit
japanese beech *n, usu cap J* : a beech that is native to Japan and is distinguished from the European beech esp. by its soft light yellowish brown wood
japanese beetle *n, usu cap J* : a small metallic green and brown scarabaeid beetle (*Popillia japonica*) introduced into America from Japan that as a grub feeds on the roots of grasses and decaying vegetation and as an adult eats foliage and fruits and is a serious pest — see MILKY DISEASE
japanese b encephalitis *n, usu cap J&B* : an encephalitis that occurs epidemically in Japan esp. in summer and is caused by an insect-transmitted virus
japanese bitterling *n, usu cap J* : any of several small east Asian cyprinid fishes (genus *Acheilognathus*) characterized by development in the female of a very long ovipositor during the breeding season
japanese bittersweet *n, usu cap J* : an ornamental Asiatic woody vine (*Celastrus articulata*) that has showy orange-yellow fruit with a persistent scarlet aril — called also *Japan bittersweet*
japanese black pine *n, usu cap J* : a large Japanese ornamental tree (*Pinus thunbergii*) having orange-yellow branchlets, leaves three inches or more in length and in bundles of two, and the scales of the cone armed with prickles — called also *black pine*
japanese blue *or* **japanese green** *n, often cap J* : a grayish green that is bluer and deeper than slate green and yellower and duller than average blue spruce (sense 2a)
japanese cane *n, usu cap J* : a sugarcane that usu. has slender stalks and is widely grown for forage
japanese cedar *n, usu cap J* : a large evergreen tree (*Cryptomeria japonica*) grown esp. in Japan and China for its valuable soft wood — called also *Japan cedar*

japanese cherry *n, usu cap J* : JAPANESE FLOWERING CHERRY
japanese chestnut *n, usu cap J* **1** : a Japanese nut tree (*Castanea crenata*) **2** : the fruit of the Japanese chestnut that is larger than the American chestnut but not so sweet
japanese climbing fern *n, usu cap J* : a slender twining fern (*Lygodium japonicum*) with finely divided fronds
japanese clock *n, usu cap J* : a Japanese timepiece indicating six sunrise and six sunset divisions of time whose length varies with the change of seasons
japanese clover *n, usu cap J* : JAPAN CLOVER
japanese cornel *also* **japanese cornel dogwood** *n, usu cap J* : a Japanese dogwood (*Cornus officinalis*) that has scaly bark and is used as an ornamental
[1]**japanese crab** *n, usu cap J* [[1]*crab*] : GIANT CRAB 1
[2]**japanese crab** *or* **japanese crab apple** *n, usu cap J* [[4]*crab*] : SHOWY CRAB APPLE
japanese cypress *n, usu cap J* : any of several Japanese evergreens of the genus *Chamaecyparis; esp* : SUN TREE
japanese deer *n, usu cap J* : a small deer (*Cervus nippon* syn. *C. sika*) of Japan having slightly forked round antlers and a coat that is spotted with white in summer and plain grayish brown in winter — called also *sika*
japanese flood fever *n, usu cap J* : TSUTSUGAMUSHI DISEASE
japanese flowering cherry *n, usu cap J* : any of certain ornamental hybrid cherries developed in Japan chiefly from two species (*Prunus serrulata* and *P. sieboldii*) that bear a profusion of white or pink usu. double and often fragrant flowers followed by small inedible fruit, that have long been admired and revered by the Japanese, and that are now widespread in cultivation in regions of moderate climate — called also *Japanese cherry*
japanese fold *n, usu cap J* : FRENCH FOLD
japanese fowl *n, usu cap J* : one of a Japanese breed of fancy fowls resembling game fowls but having long hackles and tail feathers
japanese gelatin *n, usu cap J* : AGAR 1a
japanese ginger *n, usu cap J* : a commercial ginger root prepared from a Japanese ginger (*Zingiber mioga*) and usu. marketed unscraped and coated with lime
japanese gut *n, usu cap J* : material for fishing leaders made from raw silk fibers bonded with gelatin
japanese hawthorn *n, usu cap J* : an evergreen shrub (*Raphiolepis umbellata*) of China and Japan with glossy dark green leaves and showy white fragrant flowers
japanese hazel *n, usu cap J* : a Japanese shrub (*Corylus sieboldiana*) with edible nuts in a long tubular involucre
japanese hemlock *n, usu cap J* : a Japanese hemlock (*Tsuga diversifolia*) with pubescent branchlets and glossy dark green foliage
japanese herring *n, usu cap J* : a round herring (*Etrumeus micropus*)
japanese holly *n, usu cap J* : a Japanese shrub (*Ilex crenata*) with evergreen, crenate, but not prickly leaves
japanese honeysuckle *n, usu cap J* : an Asiatic twining or trailing honeysuckle (*Lonicera japonica*) that has half-evergreen leaves and fragrant white flowers changing to yellow and that although planted orig. for ornamental purposes has become a troublesome weed in some areas — see HALL'S HONEYSUCKLE
japanese hop *n, usu cap J* : an ornamental climbing vine (*Humulus japonicus*) commonly cultivated for its variegated foliage
japanese horse chestnut *n, usu cap J* : a Japanese tree (*Aesculus turbinata*) sometimes cultivated for its showy, yellowish white, red-spotted flowers
japanese horseradish *n, usu cap J* : WASABI
japanese iris *n, usu cap J* : any of various beardless garden irises that are developed chiefly from two species (*Iris laevigata* and *I. kaempferi*) of eastern Asia and that have ensiform leaves and very large handsome white, blue, reddish purple, or violet flowers with spreading falls and standards
japanese isinglass *n, usu cap J* : AGAR 1a
japanese ivy *n, usu cap J* : BOSTON IVY
japanese kerria *n, usu cap J* : JAPANESE ROSE 1
japanese knot *n, usu cap J* : [3]KNOT c
japanese knotweed *n, usu cap J* : a stout perennial Japanese herb (*Polygonum cuspidatum*) having cordate leaves and panicles of greenish white flowers
japanese lacquer *n, usu cap J* : LACQUER 1b
japanese lacquer tree *n, usu cap J* : JAPANESE VARNISH TREE
japanese lantern *n, usu cap J* : CHINESE LANTERN
japanese lantern plant *n, usu cap J* : CHINESE LANTERN PLANT
japanese larch *n, usu cap J* : a Japanese ornamental tree (*Larix leptolepis*) having leaves with two white bands beneath and each cone scale reflexed at its apex
japanese laurel *n, usu cap J* **1** : an Asiatic dioecious evergreen shrub (*Aucuba japonica*) that has ovate to obtusely acuminate dark green shining leaves often blotched with yellow and that is used as an ornamental — called also *Japan laurel* **2** : JAPANESE RUBBER PLANT
japanese lawn grass *n, usu cap J* : KOREAN LAWN GRASS
japanese leaf *n, usu cap J* : CHINESE EVERGREEN
japanese lilac *n, usu cap J* **1** : a Chinese lilac (*Syringa villosa*) with profuse rose-lilac or whitish late-blooming flowers **2** : JAPANESE TREE LILAC
japanese linden *n, usu cap J* : a Japanese tree (*Tilia japonica*) used as an ornamental
japanese mackerel *n, usu cap J* : a widely distributed mackerel (*Pneumatophorus japonicus*) of the western Pacific — called also *opelu*
japanese maple *n, usu cap J* : a shrub or small tree (*Acer palmatum*) of Japan and Korea that has purple flowers and in most varieties deeply parted green leaves and that is used as an ornamental — called also *full-moon maple*
japanese medlar *n, usu cap J* : LOQUAT
japanese millet *n, usu cap J* : a coarse annual grass with thick appressed purplish inflorescence and awnless spikelets that is considered to be a variety of barnyard grass or a distinct species (*Echinochloa frumentacea*), is cultivated esp. in Japan and southeastern Asia for its edible seeds which resemble millet and for forage, and is an important wildlife food in parts of the U.S. — called also *billion-dollar grass, Japanese barnyard millet, sanwa millet*
japanese mink *n, usu cap J* **1** : an Asiatic weasel (*Mustela sibirica*) **2** *or* **jap mink** : the pale yellowish brown fur of the Japanese mink that is commonly dyed to resemble mink
japanese mint *or* **japanese peppermint** *n, usu cap J* : a Japanese mint (*Mentha arvensis piperascens*) that is a variety of the common mint of Europe
japanese mint oil *or* **japanese peppermint oil** *n, usu cap J* : an essential oil obtained from corn mint and used chiefly as a source of menthol
japanese morning glory *n, usu cap J* : any of certain cultivated morning glories that are derived from an Old World tropical species (*Ipomoea nil*) and are distinguished by a wide color range and by the occurrence of crested, frilled, or double flowers
japanese moss *n, usu cap J* : BABY'S TEARS
japanese mustard *n, usu cap J* : INDIAN MUSTARD
japanese nightingale *n, usu cap J* : an Asiatic hill tit (*Leiothrix lutea*) that is chiefly olivaceous brown with a yellow breast and red bill and feet and that is often kept as a cage bird — called also *Japanese robin*
japanese nutmeg *n, usu cap J* : a Japanese tree (*Torreya nucifera*) with edible seeds
japanese oak *n, usu cap J* : any of several oaks that are native to, grown in, or shipped as timber from Japan: as **a** : an evergreen oak (*Lithocarpus glabra*) closely related to and resembling the tanbark oak of the American Pacific coast **b** : any of several oaks of the genus *Quercus* (esp. *Q. grosseserrata*) with moderately light, fine-grained, even-textured wood
japanese oyster *n, usu cap J* : a large oyster (*Ostrea gigas*) that is native to the coast of Japan and that has been introduced along the Pacific coast of No. America where it is maintained by repeated planting of spat from the natural habitat
japanese pagoda tree *n, usu cap J* : an ornamental Chinese and Japanese tree (*Sophora japonica*) with compound dark green leaves and profuse panicles of yellowish white flowers — called also *Chinese scholartree*
japanese paper *n, usu cap J* : a long-fibered paper made orig. in Japan and often used for printing engravings — called also *Japan paper*
japanese parasol fir *n, usu cap J* : UMBRELLA PINE 1
japanese pear *n, usu cap J* : SAND PEAR 2a
japanese persimmon *n, usu cap J* **1** : an Asiatic persimmon (*Diospyros kaki*) that is prob. native to China but has been developed into numerous horticultural forms esp. in Japan **2** : the fruit of the Japanese persimmon which is usu. larger than native American persimmons
japanese pheasant *n, usu cap J* : a pheasant (*Phasianus colchicus versicolor*)
japanese pine *n, usu cap J* : any of several eastern Asiatic ornamental pines (esp. *Pinus thunbergii* and *P. densiflora*)
japanese pink *n, usu cap J* : a China pink (*Dianthus chinensis heddewigii*) distinguished by dentate or jagged-edged petals
japanese pittosporum *n, usu cap J* : TOBIRA
japanese plum *n, usu cap J* **1** : any of numerous large showy usu. yellow to light red cultivated plums that are sometimes inferior to European plums in flavor **2** : any of numerous plum trees derived from a Chinese tree (*Prunus salicina*) that are somewhat less hardy than most European and American plum trees and produce Japanese plums **3** : LOQUAT
japanese print *n, usu cap J* : a color print executed from wood blocks in water-based inks and developed to a high degree of artistry by the Japanese esp. in the late 18th and early 19th centuries
japanese privet *n, usu cap J* : either of two Asiatic evergreen privets: **a** : an erect shrub or small tree (*Ligustrum lucidum*) of China, Korea, and Japan with glabrous dark green usu. acuminate leaves and flowers in long erect panicles **b** : a somewhat smaller shrub (*L. japonicum*) of Korea and Japan with usu. more obtuse darker green leaves and flowers in looser more lax panicles
japanese quince *n, usu cap J* **1** : LOQUAT **2** : a hardy Chinese shrub (*Chaenomeles lagenaria*) that is distinguished from the common quinces by its scarlet flowers and large stipules and is grown mostly for ornament — called also *Japonica;* compare DWARF JAPANESE QUINCE
japanese radish *n, usu cap J* : DAIKON
japanese raisin tree *n, usu cap J* : a deciduous shrub or small tree (*Hovenia dulcis*) of eastern Asia having a spicy odor, ovate leaves, and reddish edible fruit stalks — called also *honey tree*
japanese red *n, often cap J* : INDIAN RED 2a
japanese red pine *n, usu cap J* : a Japanese ornamental pine (*Pinus densiflora*) that has orange-red bark, yellowish young branches, and minutely serrulate leaves in fascicles of two with the leaf sheaths ending in two long points
japanese river fever *n, usu cap J* : TSUTSUGAMUSHI DISEASE
japanese robin *n, usu cap J* **1** : JAPANESE NIGHTINGALE **2** : a small Japanese bird (*Erithacus akahige*) related to the nightingale
japanese rose *n, usu cap J* **1** : a slender Chinese shrub (*Kerria japonica*) cultivated for its bright yellow often globular flowers — called also *Japan globeflower* **2** : MULTIFLORA ROSE
japanese rubber plant *n, usu cap J* : a succulent shrub (*Crassula argentea*) having very thick shiny green leaves and white or rosy red flowers in close panicles — called also *Japanese laurel*
jap·a·nes·ery \ˌjapəˈnēzərē, -ēsərē\ *n* -ES *sometimes cap* [[1]*Japanese* + *-ery*] : a Japanese ornament : BAUBLE — usu. used in pl. ⟨a shelf full of *japaneseries*⟩
japaneses *pl of* JAPANESE
japanese sago palm *n, usu cap J* : SAGO PALM 2a
japanese sand pear *n, usu cap J* : SAND PEAR 2a
japanese snail *n, usu cap J* : an ovoviviparous freshwater snail (*Viviparus malleatus*) that is native to Japan and is often kept in aquariums where it is a valuable scavenger
japanese snowball *n, usu cap J* **1 a** : a handsome cultivated shrub (*Viburnum plicatum*) with large globose clusters of sterile flowers very similar to those of the guelder rose **b** : the flower cluster of the Japanese snowball **2** *also* **japanese snowbell** : a deciduous shrub or small tree (*Styrax japonica*) having flowers in short glabrous racemes
japanese snowflower *n, usu cap J* : a Japanese shrub (*Deutzia gracilis*) with slender arching branches covered in spring with a profusion of white flowers
japanese spaniel *n, usu cap J* **1** : a toy dog originating in Japan that is bred chiefly as a pet, that differs from the pekingese in its proportions of body and legs, and that is characterized by a silky coat and black and white or red and white coloring **2** : a breed of dogs comprising the Japanese spaniels
japanese spider crab *n, usu cap J* : GIANT CRAB 1
japanese spruce *n, usu cap J* **1** : a Japanese fir (*Abies mariesii*) with densely rusty pubescent twigs **2** : YEDDO SPRUCE
japanese spurge *n, usu cap J* : a low Japanese herb or subshrub (*Pachysandra terminalis*) that has white flowers in terminal spikes and is often used as a ground cover — compare ALLEGHENY SPURGE
japanese star anise *n, usu cap J* : a Japanese evergreen tree (*Illicium anisatum*) with poisonous fruit
japanese storax *n, usu cap J* : JAPANESE SNOWBALL 2
japanese table pine *n, usu cap J* : an umbrella-shaped evergreen shrub (*Pinus densiflora umbraculifera*) grown as an ornamental — called also *Japanese umbrella pine*
japanese tissue *n, usu cap J* : a thin strong lightweight paper orig. handmade in Japan from long native fibers and used for mending tears in book pages and for cleaning lenses
japanese tree lilac *n, usu cap J* : an arborescent lilac (*Syringa amurensis japonica*) of Japan having showy yellowish white flowers — called also *Japanese lilac, Japan tree lilac*
japanese tung oil *or* **japanese wood oil** *n, usu cap J* : a drying oil obtained from a Japanese tung tree (*Aleurites cordata*)
japanese umbrella pine *n, usu cap J* **1** : UMBRELLA PINE 1 **2** : JAPANESE TABLE PINE
japanese varnish tree *n, usu cap J* **1** *or* **japanese sumac** : a Japanese sumac (*Rhus verniciflua*) that resembles the poison sumac and is a source of the natural Japan varnish or Japan lacquer — called also *Japanese lacquer tree* **2** : CHINESE PARASOL TREE
japanese walnut *n, usu cap J* : a valuable Japanese nut tree (*Juglans cordiformis ailanthifolia*) that bears a heart-shaped nut and is used as a walnut stock because of its hardiness — called also *heartnut, Japan walnut*
japanese wax *n, usu cap J* : JAPAN WAX
japanese wax tree *n, usu cap J* : a Japanese sumac (*Rhus succedanea*)
japanese white pine *n, usu cap J* : an evergreen tree (*Pinus parviflora*) used esp. in dwarf form as an ornamental in Japanese gardens
japanese windflower *n, usu cap J* : JAPANESE ANEMONE
japanese wistaria *n, usu cap J* : a Japanese deciduous shrub (*Wisteria floribunda*) that is widely cultivated for ornament and has twining branches and velvety pubescent pods
japanese witch hazel *n, usu cap J* : a Japanese shrub or small tree (*Hamamelis japonica*) that resembles the American witch hazel but bears reddish yellow flowers in midwinter and that is used as an ornamental
japanese wolf *n, usu cap J* : an Asiatic wolf (*Canis hodophylax*)
japanese yellow *n, often cap J* : CHINESE ORANGE 2
japanese yew *n, usu cap J* : a shrubby hardy evergreen (*Taxus cuspidata*) of China and Japan that has lustrous dark green foliage and is cultivated in many horticultural forms
jap·a·nesque \ˌjapəˈnesk, jəˈpaˈ-, ˈjaˈpaˈ-\ *adj, often cap* [*Japan* + *-esque*] : JAPANESY ⟨intensely white and intensely *Japanesque* egrets —William Beebe⟩
jap·a·nesy \ˌjapəˈnēzē, -nēsē\ *adj, usu cap J* [[1]*Japanese* + *-y*] : having or suggesting a Japanese manner or style : resembling what is Japanese ⟨some of the houses had columned verandas and *Japanesy* curved gables —Joseph Wechsberg⟩
japan fox *n, usu cap J* : the pelt of the raccoon dog processed to simulate fox
japan globeflower *n, usu cap J* : JAPANESE ROSE 1
ja·pan·ism \jəˈpaˌnizəm, -paˌ-, *also* jaˈp-\ *n* -s *usu cap* [*Japan* + *-ism*] **1** : a trait or characteristic distinctive of the Japanese or of their civilization or art ⟨modern trend in fine art toward skeletal frameworks . . . can be traced back to the *Japanism* of the 70s —Edgar Kaufmann⟩ **2** : Japanese nationalism ⟨a rising tide of *Japanism* which was soon to overwhelm foreign missionaries —Hugh Byas⟩
jap·a·ni·za·tion \ˌjapənəˈzāshən, -ˌnīˈz-\ *n* -s *often cap* : the act or process of japanizing
jap·a·nize \ˈ==ˌnīz\ *vt* -ED/-ING/-S *often cap* [*Japan* + *-ize*] **1** : to make Japanese: **a** : to cause to acquire traits or characteristics that are or are believed to be distinctively Japanese **b** : to bring into close conformity with Japanese national customs and institutions : change in behavior and attitude to suit the Japanese way of life **2** : to bring (an area) under the political, cultural, or commercial influence of Japan
japan lacquer *n, usu cap J* : JAPAN 1a
japan laurel *n, usu cap J* : JAPANESE LAUREL
japan leather *n, usu cap J* : JAPANNED LEATHER
japan lily *n, usu cap J* : any of several Japanese lilies (as *Lilium auratum, L. japonicum, L. speciosum*)
japan medlar *or* **japan plum** *n, usu cap J* **1** : LOQUAT **2** : JAPANESE PERSIMMON
japanned *past of* JAPAN
japanned leather *n* [fr. past part. of [3]*japan*] : leather having a smooth shiny usu. black surface obtained by coating with japan — compare PATENT LEATHER
japanned peacock *or* **japanned peafowl** *n* [fr. past part. of [3]*japan;* fr. the lustrous quality of the feathers] : a peafowl which is usu. considered a variety of the Indian peacock and in which the wings of the male are largely deep blue
ja·pan·ner \jəˈpanə(r), -paan- *also* jaˈp-\ *n* -s [*Japan* + *-er*] **1** *usu cap, obs* **a** : JAPANESE 1 **b** : a Japanese ship **2** [[3]*japan* + *-er*] : a worker who applies coatings of enamel or varnish in making japanned leather or other japanned articles
japanners' brown *n* : an iron oxide that contains chiefly ferric oxide and is used as a drier for oils esp. in the patent-leather and oilcloth industries
ja·pan·nery \jəˈpanərē *also* jaˈp-\ *n* -ES [[3]*japan* + *-ery*] : a room or other place where leather is japanned
japanning *n* -s [fr. gerund of [3]*japan*] : the process of varnishing with japan; *also* : the material used
japano- *comb form, usu cap* [*Japan* (the country)] : Japanese ⟨*Japanologist*⟩ ⟨*Japanophile*⟩
ja·pan·o·phile \jəˈpanəˌfīl *also* jaˈp-\ *n* -s *usu cap* [*Japano-* + *-phile*] : one who esp. admires and likes Japan or Japanese ways
japan paper *n, usu cap J* : JAPANESE PAPER
japan quince *n, usu cap J* : JAPANESE QUINCE
japan rose *n, usu cap J* **1 a** : any of several Japanese roses (as *Rosa multiflora* and *R. rugosa*) **b** : CAMELLIA 2 **2** : a moderate yellowish pink to orange
japans *pl of* JAPAN, *pres 3d sing of* JAPAN
japan tea *n, usu cap J* : unfermented Japanese tea of a light color
japan tree lilac *n, usu cap J* : JAPANESE TREE LILAC
japan varnish *n, usu cap J* : the natural varnish obtained from the Japanese varnish tree
japan walnut *n, usu cap J* : JAPANESE WALNUT
japan wax *or* **japan tallow** *n, usu cap J* : a yellowish fat obtained from the berries of sumac (as *Rhus verniciflua*) and used chiefly in polishes and textile finishes
japan clover *n, usu cap J* : JAPAN CLOVER
[1]**jape** \ˈjāp\ *vb* -ED/-ING/-S [ME *japen*, perh. fr. MF *japper* to bark at, nag, of imit. origin] *vi* **1** : to say or do something jokingly or mockingly : play tricks : JEER ⟨wondering why you ~ at him⟩ **2** *now chiefly dial* : to have sexual intercourse ~ *vt* : to make mocking fun of : GIBE, TAUNT ⟨*japed* the actors from the balcony⟩
[2]**jape** \"\ *n* -s [ME *jape*, fr. *japen*] : something designed to arouse amusement or laughter: as **a** : an amusing literary or dramatic production ⟨a merry little ~ that was cribbed from a 1940 movie —*Time*⟩ **b** : JOKE, GIBE ⟨volumes of quips, jests, ~*s*, boners, sallies, and bright sayings —Lee Rogow⟩ **c** : a trick played in jest : PRACTICAL JOKE ⟨~*s* and feats of ingenious devilry —Thomas Wood †1950⟩ **syn** see JOKE
jap·er \-pə(r)\ *n* -s [ME, fr. *japen* + *-er*] : one that japes; *esp* : a professional jester
jap·ery \-p(ə)rē\ *n* -ES [ME *japerie*, fr. *japen* + *-erie* -ery] **1** : jesting talk : JOKES ⟨the patterned wheezes and stylized ~ that have stood them in such good stead during nearly two decades of burlesque —Gladwin Hill⟩ **2** : JOKE, JEST ⟨the sort of man who goes in for flippant *japeries* —*Springfield (Mass.) Union*⟩
[1]**ja·phet·ic** \jəˈfed·ik, (ˈ)jāˈf-\ *adj, usu cap* [*Japheth* (Japetus), one of the sons of Noah in the Bible (Gen 5:32 ff.) + E *-ic*] **1** : relating to or derived from Japheth who was a son of Noah — used vaguely as an ethnological epithet for the Caucasians of Europe and some adjacent parts of Asia **2** : of, relating to, or constituting a group of early non-Indo-European languages in Europe and western Asia assumed by some to form one family with the Caucasian languages and including Basque, Etruscan, Minoan, and sometimes Sumerian and Elamite — compare ASIANIC
[2]**japhetic** \"\ *n* -s *cap* **1** : the Japhetic languages **2** : a Japhetic language
jap mink *n, usu cap J* : JAPANESE MINK 2
japonian *n* -s *usu cap* [*Japon* (obs. var. of *Japan*) + E *-ian*] *obs* : JAPANESE
ja·pon·ic \jəˈpänik, jaˈp-\ *adj, usu cap* [*Japon* + E *-ic*] : JAPANESE
ja·pon·i·ca \-nəkə\ *n* -s [NL, fr. fem. of *Japonicus* Japanese, fr. *Japonia* Japan + L *-icus* -ic] **1** : CAMELLIA 2 **2** : JAPANESE QUINCE 2 **3** : CRAPE MYRTLE
jap·o·nism \ˈjapəˌnizəm\ *n* -s *usu cap* [F *japonisme*, fr. *Japon* Japan + F *-isme* -ism] : JAPANISM
japs *pl of* JAP
[1]**ja·pyg·id** \jəˈpijəd\ *adj* [NL *Japygidae*] : of or relating to the family Japygidae
[2]**japygid** \"\ *n* -s : an insect of the family Japygidae
ja·pyg·i·dae \-jəˌdē\ *n pl, cap* [NL, fr. *Japyg-*, *Japyx*, type genus + *-idae*] : a family of soil-inhabiting insects (order Entotrophi) with the anal appendages forcepslike rather than filamentous
ja·pyx \ˈjāpiks\ *n, cap* [NL, prob. after *Japyx*, mythical founder of Japygia, ancient kingdom in southeastern Italy] : the type genus of the family Japygidae
ja·qui·ma \ˈhakəmə\ *n* -s [Sp *jáquima* — more at HACKAMORE] *Southwest* : the headstall of a halter
[1]**jar** \ˈjär, ˈjȧ(r\ *vb* **jarred**; **jarred**; **jarring**; **jars** [prob. of imit. origin] *vi* **1 a** : to make a harsh or discordant sound : GRATE ⟨winced as the iron gate *jarred* against the sidewalk⟩ : RATTLE ⟨an explosion that made the windows ~⟩ **b** : to be out of harmony or in conflict : CLASH — usu. used with *with* ⟨the slapstick tone ~*s* with the underlying seriousness —Leo Marx⟩; *specif* : BICKER ⟨two of the men had been *jarring* at each other . . . — some old feud —Agnes M. Cleaveland⟩ **c** : to have a harshly disagreeable or disconcerting effect ⟨an unexpected pettiness that ~*s*⟩ — often used with *on* or *upon* ⟨resounding harmonies that ~ on unaccustomed ears⟩ ⟨savage expressions that ~ upon the sensitivity of some readers⟩ **2** : to shake or vibrate severely (as from a blow) ⟨bolt had *jarred* loose⟩ ⟨the platform ~*s* as a train rumbles by⟩ ~ *vt* **1** : to cause to jar : affect disagreeably ⟨the din ~*s* her nerves⟩ : shake up ⟨the boat ride will ~ the patient less⟩ : UNSETTLE ⟨the violent opposition *jarred* his resolve⟩ ⟨soldiering had *jarred* men loose from birthplace and habit as nothing else could have done —Dixon Wecter⟩ **2** : to drill (a well) by repeated percussion **3** : to collect or remove (insects) from a plant by jarring or shaking
[2]**jar** \"\ *n* -s **1 a** : a harsh grating sound ⟨the loose floorboard that was lifted with a slight groaning ~ —Arthur Morrison⟩ **b** : a state or manifestation of discord or conflict : CLASH, DISSENSION ⟨except for a ~ in the case of Hyderabad, this revolution has taken place . . . smoothly and peacefully —*White Paper on Indian States*⟩; *esp* : a petty quarrel ⟨heard the loud harsh words of a family ~⟩ **2 a** : a rough shaking (as from a sharp impact) ⟨lenses should be protected from ~*s* and jolts —*Kodak Reference Handbook*⟩ **b** : an unsettling blow (as to the mind or feelings) ⟨gave his nerves the ~ needed to break the habit⟩ ⟨gave a ~ to his composure⟩ **c** : a break or conflict in rhythm, flow, movement, or transition typically rough, abrupt, crude, or disconcerting : an unpleasant discontinuity or incongruity ⟨works persistently, swiftly, without ~ —Sinclair Lewis⟩ **3** : a connecting link between a

well-drill cable and the drilling tool so constructed that when the tool sticks the next upward pull causes a sharp jerk tending to dislodge the tool **syn** see IMPACT

3**jar** \"\ n -s [MF *jarre,* fr. OProv *jarra,* fr. Ar *jarrah* earthen water vessel] **1 :** a rigid container having a wide mouth and often no neck and made typically of earthenware or glass ⟨a ~ that had held jam⟩ ⟨a tobacco ~⟩ ⟨an ornamental cold-cream ~⟩ — compare BOTTLE **2 :** JARFUL ⟨buy pickles by the ~⟩ ⟨enough plums to make a dozen ~s of jelly⟩

jar 1

4**jar** \"\ *vt* **jarred; jarred; jarring; jars :** to put in a jar; *specif* **:** to preserve (as fruit) by canning in glass jars

5**jar** \"\ n -s [alter. of earlier *char* — more at CHARE] *archaic* **:** TURN — used esp. in the phrase *on the jar* ⟨the door was on the ~ and, gently opening it, I entered —Henry Brooke⟩

ja·ra·be \hə'rä(,)bā\ n -s [AmerSp, fr. Sp, syrup, fr. Ar *sharāb* — more at SYRUP] **:** any of several provincial Mexican couple dances (as the hat dance) that have the zapateado as their basic step

ja·ra·gua \,zharə'gwä\ *or* **jaragua grass** n -s [Pg *jaraguá,* fr. Tupi] **:** a tall forage grass (*Hyparrhenia rufa*) native to Brazil but now used elsewhere for hay and forage

1**ja·ra·na** \hə'ränə\ n -s [AmerSp] **1 :** a large Central American manbarklak (*Eschweilera jarana*) with hard heavy durable wood used chiefly for heavy construction **2 :** the salmon pink to reddish brown variegated wood of the jarana

2**jarana** \"\ n -s [AmerSp, fr. Sp, fun, merrymaking, trick, deceit, alter. of *harana, arana* trick, deceit] **1 :** a couple dance of Yucatan that is performed with waltz and zapateado steps **2 :** a stringed instrument of Mexico resembling a ukulele

ja·ra·ra·ca \,zharə'räkə\ n -s [Pg, fr. Tupi *jararaca* & Guarani *yararaca*] **:** any of various So. American pit vipers

ja·ra·ra·cus·su *or* **ja·ra·ra·cu·cu** \,zharə,räkə'sü\ n -s [Pg *jararacuçu, jararacuçú,* fr. Tupi *jararaca wassu* & Guarani *yararaca wassu,* lit., big jararaca] **:** a venomous pit viper (*Bothrops jararacussu*) of Brazil that is related to the fer-de-lance

jar·a·wa \'jarə,wä\ n, pl **jarawa** *or* **jarawas** *usu cap* **1 :** an Andamanese people of So. Andaman Island **2 :** a member of the Jarawa people

jarbird \'=,=\ n [2*jar* + *bird;* fr. the noise it makes with its beak on dead branches] **:** a nuthatch (*Sitta caesia*)

jar·bot \'järbət\ n -s [origin unknown] **:** dilatation of the esophagus in the horse

jar·di·niere *or* **jar·di·nière** \,j|ärd°n|i(ə)r, |ȧd-, -d°n|(y)e(ə)r, -iə,-eə *also* |zh|\ n -s [F *jardinière,* lit., female gardener, fem. of *jardinier* gardener, fr. OF, fr. *jardin* garden (fr. *jart* garden, of Gmc origin; akin to OHG *gart* enclosure) + *-ier* -er — more at YARD] **1 a :** an ornamental stand for plants or flowers **b :** a large round usu. decorative ceramic flowerpot **2 :** a garnish for meat consisting of several vegetables cubed and cooked separately or together

jardiniere 1b

jar·ed·ite \'ja(a)rə,dīt\ n -s *cap* [*Jared,* the eponymous ancestor of the Jaredites according to the *Book of Mormon* (Ether 1:31 ff) + E *-ite*] **:** one of a group of people that according to Mormon belief settled America after the general dispersal accompanying the confusion of tongues at Babel — compare NEPHITE

jarfly \'=,=\ n [2*jar* + *fly;* fr. the harsh whirring noise it produces] **:** CICADA

jar·ful \'=,fu̇l\ n, pl **jar·fuls** *also* **jars·ful** \'jär,fu̇lz, 'jȧ,fu̇lz, -ärz,fu̇l, -äz,fu̇l\ [3*jar* + *-ful*] **:** the quantity held by a jar ⟨mixed several ~s of juice in the bowl⟩

1**jar·gon** \'järgən, 'jäg- *also* -,gän\ n -s [ME *jargoun,* fr. MF *jargon,* prob. of imit. origin] **1 :** chatter or twitter esp. of a bird or animal **2 a :** confused unintelligible language **:** GIBBERISH; *specif* **:** JARGON APHASIA **b :** a strange, outlandish, or barbarous language or dialect ⟨foreign languages were considered rude ~s⟩ **c :** a hybrid language or dialect arising from a mixture of languages that is typically much simplified in vocabulary and grammar (as Pidgin English) and is used for communication between peoples of different speech; *specif, usu cap* **:** CHINOOK JARGON — compare LINGUA FRANCA **3 a :** the technical terminology or characteristic idiom of specialists or workers in a particular activity or area of knowledge; *often* **:** a pretentious or unnecessarily obscure and esoteric terminology **b :** a special vocabulary or idiom fashionable in a particular group or clique **4 :** language vague in meaning and full of circumlocutions and long high-sounding words **syn** see DIALECT

2**jargon** \"\ *vi* -ED/-ING/-S [ME *jargounen,* fr. *jargoun,* n.] **1 :** TWITTER, WARBLE ⟨the birds would begin their early morning ~*ing* —Elizabeth M. Roberts⟩ **2 :** JARGONIZE

jargon aphasia *n* **:** the fluent use of words that bear no relation to the meaning intended

jargon code *n* **:** a full set of code names for use in otherwise plain language communication in order to conceal persons, things, or actions being discussed ⟨in a *jargon code* of Louis XIII, the pope is referred to as "the rose", Rome as "the garden"⟩

jar·gon·ist \'=gənəst\ *or* **jar·gon·eer** \|==|ni(ə)r, -iə\ n -s **:** one that is addicted to jargon

jar·gon·is·tic \|==|nistik, -tēk\ *adj* **:** characterized by the use of jargon **:** phrased in jargon

jar·gon·ize \'==,nīz\ *vb* -ED/-ING/-S *vi* **:** to speak or write jargon ~ *vt* **1 :** to express in jargon **2 :** to make into jargon or into a jargon ⟨developed a *jargonized* form of Dutch in communication with native Africans —Leonard Bloomfield⟩

jar·goon \(')jär|gün, (')jȧ|g- *or* **jar·gon** \-gän\ n -s [F *jargon* — more at ZIRCON] **:** a colorless or pale yellow or smoky zircon

jarhead \'=,=\ n [3*jar* + *head*] *chiefly Midland* **:** MULE; *esp* **:** an army mule

ja·ri·na \zhə'rēnə\ n -s [Pg] **:** IVORY NUT 1

ja·risch-herx·hei·mer reaction \'yärish'herks,hīmər-\ n, *usu cap J&H* [after Adolf *Jarisch* †1902 Austrian dermatologist & Karl *Herxheimer* †1944 Ger. dermatologist] **:** HERXHEIMER REACTION

jark \'järk\ n -s [origin unknown] *archaic* **:** the seal of a counterfeit document

jark·man \-mən\ n, pl **jarkmen** *archaic* **:** a vagabond counterfeiter of documents (as licenses, passes, certificates)

jarl *R* 'yär(ə)l, *-R* 'yȧl\ n -s [ON — more at EARL] **:** a medieval Scandinavian noble ranking immediately below the king — used also of the chiefs of Orkney and Shetland; compare EARL

1**jar·less** \'järləs, 'jȧl-\ *adj* [2*jar* + *-less*] **:** free from jar ⟨a smooth ~ ride⟩

2**jarless** \"\ *adj* [3*jar* + *-less*] **:** not having or requiring jars ⟨the ~ methods of preserving⟩

jarl·ite \'yär,līt\ n -s [C. F. *Jarl,* 20th cent. Danish official in the cryolite industry + E *-ite*] **:** a mineral $NaSr_3Al_3F_{16}$ consisting of an alumino-fluoride of sodium and strontium

jar mill *n* [2*jar*] **:** a small ball mill for pulverizing plastic materials (as paint)

jar·mo·ite \'jär(,)mō,īt\ n -s *usu cap* [*Jarmo,* site of a prehistoric town in northeastern Iraq + E *-ite*] **:** a member of a prehistoric people inhabiting the foothills of southern Kurdistan

ja·rool \jə'rül\ n -s [Hindi *jarūl*] **:** QUEEN'S CRAPE MYRTLE

ja·ro·site \jə'rō,sīt, 'jȧrə,s-\ n -s [G *jarosit,* fr. Barranco *Jaroso,* Almeria, Spain + G *-it* -ite] **:** an ocher-yellow or brown mineral $KFe_3(SO_4)_2(OH)_6$ consisting of basic sulfate of potassium and iron and occurring in minute rhombohedral crystals or in masses — compare AMMONIOJAROSITE, ARGENTOJAROSITE, NATROJAROSITE, PLUMBOJAROSITE

jaro·vi·zation \,yärəvə'zāshən, ,yar-, -,vī'z-\ n -s **:** VERNALIZATION

jaro·vize *or* **iaro·vize** *or* **yaro·vize** \'==,vīz\ *vt* -ED/-ING/-S [Russ *yarovoe* spring grain (fr. *yara* spring) + E *-ize;* akin to Gk *hōra* season — more at HOUR] **:** VERNALIZE

jar-owl \'=,=\ n [2*jar;* fr. the harsh noise it makes] **:** a European goatsucker

jar·rah \'jarə\ n -s [native name in Australia] **1 :** an Australian eucalypt (*Eucalyptus marginata*) with rough bark and ovate leaves **2 :** a red gum (*Eucalyptus rostrata*) **3 :** the wood of jarrah

jarred *past of* JAR

jarring *pres part of* JAR

jar·ring·ly *adv* **:** in a jarring manner ⟨a piano ~ out of tune⟩

jar·ring·ness n -ES **:** the quality or state of being jarring

jars *pres 3d sing of* JAR, *pl of* JAR

jar·vey *also* **jar·vie** \'järvē\ n, pl **jarveys** *also* **jarvies** [fr. *Jarvey,* nickname for *Jarvis*] **1** *chiefly Irish* **:** the driver of a hackney coach or of a jaunting car **2 :** HACKNEY COACH

ja·sey \'jāzē\ n -s [prob. alter. of *jersey*] *Brit* **:** a wig made usu. of worsted

jasi·o·ne \,ja|sē'ō(,)nē, |jā|, |zē-\ n [NL, fr. Gk *iasiōnē* bindweed] *cap* **:** a genus of European herbs (family Campanulaceae) having alternate leaves and blue flowers in a solitary involucrate head — see SHEEP'S-BIT

jasm \'jazəm\ n -s [origin unknown] **:** zest for accomplishment **:** DRIVE, ENERGY ⟨you must have ~ if you want to amount to anything in this world —*Linotype News*⟩

jas·mi·na·ce·ae \,jazmə'nāsē,ē, -asm-\ [NL, fr. *Jasminum,* type genus + *-aceae*] *syn of* OLEACEAE

jas·mine \'jazmən *sometimes* 'jas- *or* 'jaas-\ *or* **jes·sa·mine** \'jes(ə)mən\ *also* **jas·min** *like* JASMINE\ n -s [F *jasmin,* fr. Ar *yāsamīn* (colloq. *yāsmīn*), fr. Per] **1 a** (1) **:** any of numerous usu. limber and often climbing shrubs of temperate and warm regions that constitute the genus *Jasminum* and usu. have extremely fragrant flowers (2) *usu jessamine* **:** a tall-climbing semi-evergreen Asiatic shrub (*J. officinale*) with slender shoots and fragrant white flowers from which a perfume is extracted **b :** any of numerous other plants having sweet-scented flowers — usu. used with preceding qualifier ⟨cape ~⟩ ⟨red ~⟩ **c** *usu jessamine* **:** YELLOW JESSAMINE 2 **d :** MATRIMONY VINE **2 a :** a perfume having an odor like that of jasmine **b :** a constituent of such a perfume consisting of jasmine oil or a formulated preparation with a similar odor **3 :** a light yellow that is greener, lighter, and stronger than average maize, redder, stronger, and slightly lighter than popcorn, and redder and slightly deeper than chrome lemon — compare BUTTER YELLOW

jasmine

jasmine family *n* **:** OLEACEAE

jasmine mango *or* **jasmine tree** *n* **:** FRANGIPANI

jasmine oil *n* **:** a fragrant essential oil obtained from flowers of a jasmine (as *Jasminum officinale* or *J. grandiflorum*) and used in perfumery

jasmine orange *n* **:** ORANGE JESSAMINE

jasmine tea *n* **:** tea scented by being packed with or fired with jasmine flowers — compare SCENTED TEA

jasminewood \'==,=\ n **1 :** the fragrant wood of a tree (*Ochna mauritiana*) of Mauritius **2 :** the tree that yields jasminewood

jasmine yellow *n* **:** BUTTER YELLOW — compare JASMINE 3

jas·mi·num \'jazmənəm, -asm-\ n, *cap* [NL, fr. F *jasmin* jasmine — more at JASMINE] **:** a large genus of tropical chiefly East Indian woody vines or shrubs of the family Oleaceae having mostly pinnate leaves and flowers shaped like salvers

jas·mone \'jaz,mōn, -as,m-\ n -s [ISV *jasmine* + *-one*] **:** a liquid ketone $C_{11}H_{16}O$ that is derived from cyclopentene, has an odor like that of jasmine, is found esp. in jasmine oil, and is used in perfumery

jasp \'jasp\ n -s [ME *jaspe* — more at JASPER] *archaic* **:** JASPER

jas·pa·chate \'jaspə,kāt\ *or* **jasp·ag·ate** \'jas,pagət\ n -s [F & L; F *jaspagate,* fr. L *iaspachates,* fr. Gk *iaspachatēs,* fr. *iaspis* jasper + *achatēs* agate] **:** AGATE JASPER

jas·pé \(')zha|spā, (')ja-\ *adj* [F, fr. past part. of *jasper* to mottle, fr. *jaspe* jasper] **:** resembling jasper in blending of colors **:** clouded in streaks of contrasting colors; *specif* **:** variegated in weaving by the use of warp yarns of differing shades together with single-color filling yarns

1**jas·per** \'jaspə(r), -aas-,-ais- *sometimes* -ås-\ n -s [ME *jaspre, jaspe,* fr. MF *jaspre, jaspe,* fr. L *jaspis,* fr. Gk *iaspis,* of Sem origin; akin to Ar *yashb* jasper, Heb *yāshpheh*] **1 :** an opaque cryptocrystalline quartz of any of several colors (as red, brown, green, yellow) ⟨the wall was built of ~, while the city was pure gold, clear as glass —Rev 21:18 (RSV)⟩; *esp* **:** green chalcedony ⟨one block, pure green as a pistachio nut, there's plenty ~ somewhere in the world —Robert Browning⟩ **2 :** a hard fine-grained ceramic ware containing a high percentage of barium salts and ordinarily stained (as blue or green) with metallic oxides and decorated with sprigged ornamentation **3 :** a blackish green that is bluer than cannon — compare JASPER GREEN

2**jasper** \"\ *adj* **1 :** relating to or composed of jasper **2 :** PEPPER-AND-SALT

3**jasper** \"\ n -s [fr. the name *Jasper*] **:** FELLOW, GUY ⟨aim to stay sober . . . till I work that ~ over —Ross Santee⟩

jasper bar *n* [1*jasper*] **:** 1BAR 8

jas·pered \-pə(r)d\ *adj, archaic* **:** of mottled or variegated color **:** SPECKLED

jasper green *n* **:** a moderate green that is yellower and paler than sea green (sense 1a), bluer and paler than myrtle (sense 3a), and bluer, lighter, and stronger than average laurel green (sense 1) — compare JASPER 3

jas·per·ize \-pə,rīz\ *vt* -ED/-ING/-S **:** to convert into or make to resemble jasper

1**jas·per·oid** \-,rȯid\ *adj* [1*jasper* + *-oid*] **:** resembling jasper

2**jasperoid** \"\ n -S **:** 1JASPER 1

jasper opal *n* **:** a yellow opal resembling jasper

jasper pink *n* **:** a strong yellowish pink that is redder and darker than salmon pink, redder and deeper than melon, and redder than peach red

jasper red *n* **:** a moderate red that is yellower and paler than cerise, claret (sense 3a), average strawberry (sense 2a), or Turkey red and lighter and stronger than pepper red — called also *old coral*

jasper slip *or* **jasper stone** *n* **:** a slip or stone of reddish quartz that is used in polishing watch parts

jas·per·ware \'==,=\ n **:** JASPER 2

jas·pery \-p(ə)rē, -ri\ *adj* **:** of, resembling, or containing jasper

jas·pid·e·an \(')ja|spidēən\ *or* **jas·pid·e·ous** \-ēəs\ *adj* [L *jaspid-, jaspis* jasper + E *-ean, -eous* — more at JASPER] **:** JASPERY

jas·pi·lite *also* **jas·pi·lyte** \'jaspə,līt\ n -s [1*jasper* + *-i-* + *-lite* or *-lyte*] **:** a compact siliceous rock rich in hematite and resembling jasper

jas·pis \'jaspəs\ n -ES [ME, fr. L — more at JASPER] **:** JASPER 1

jas·po·nyx \'jaspə(,)niks, -,späniks\ n -ES [L *iasponyx,* fr. Gk, fr. *iaspis* jasper + *onyx* — more at ONYX] **:** an onyx part or all of whose layers consist of jasper

jasp·opal \'ja,spōpəl\ n [by contr.] **:** JASPER OPAL

jasps *pl of* JASP

jass \'yäs\ n -ES [G dial. (Switzerland)] **1 a :** a two-handed game played with a 36-card or 32-card pack in which points are scored by melding certain combinations and by taking scoring cards in tricks **b :** KLABERJASS **2** *or* **jasz** \"\ **:** the jack of trumps as top card in jass or klaberjass

jas·sach·ni \jə'säkhnē\ n, pl **jassachni** *or* **jassachnis** *usu cap* **1 :** a Buryat people of southern Transbaikalia in Siberia **2 :** a member of the Jassachni people

1**jas·sid** \'jasəd\ *adj* [NL *Jassidae*] **:** of or relating to the Jassidae

2**jassid** \"\ n -s **:** a leafhopper of the family Jassidae; *broadly* **:** LEAFHOPPER

jas·si·dae \'jasə,dē\ n pl, *cap* [NL, fr. *Jassus,* type genus (fr. L *Iassus, Iasus,* ancient town in southwestern Asia Minor, fr. Gk *Iassos, Iasos*) + *-idae*] **:** a family of leafhoppers: **a** *in some classifications* **:** a family coextensive with Cicadellidae **b :** a large cosmopolitan family of small usu. slender leafhoppers that have the ocelli near the margin of the vertex and that include many economically significant pests of cultivated plants some of which (as the beet leafhopper) transmit plant diseases — compare TETTIGELLIDAE

jas·sy \'yäsē\ *adj, usu cap* [fr. *Jassy* (*Iaşi*), Romania] **:** IASI

ja·sus \'jāsəs\ n, *cap* [NL, fr. L *Iasus, Iassus* ancient town] **:** a genus of spiny lobsters including the Cape crawfish

jat \'jät\ n -s *usu cap* [Hindi *jāṭ*] **1 :** an Indo-Aryan people of the Punjab and Uttar Pradesh **2 :** a member of the Jat people

ja·ta·co \hə'tä(,)kō\ n -s [AmerSp] **:** an amaranth (*Amaranthus caudatus*) sometimes used as a food plant in tropical America

ja·ta·ka \'jädəkə\ n -s *usu cap* [Skt *jātaka,* fr. *jāta* born, fr. *janati* he begets — more at KIN] **:** any of some 550 birth stories or narratives of former incarnations of Gautama Buddha collected in Buddhist sacred writings

jat·eo·rhi·za \,jad.ēō'rīzə\ [NL, fr. Gk *iatēr, iatēs* physician + NL *-o-* + *-rhiza*] *syn of* JATRORRHIZA

ja·tha \jə'tä\ n -s [Panjabi *jathā*] **:** an armed band or organized company esp. of Sikhs

jat·ki \'jätkē\ n -s *cap* **:** a dialect of Lahnda

jat·ni \'jätnē\ n -s *usu cap* [Hindi *jāṭnī,* fr. *jāṭ*] **:** a female Jat

JATO \'jād·(,)ō, -ā(,)tō\ *abbr, often not cap* jet-assisted takeoff

ja·to·ba \,zhad·ə'bä\ n -s [Pg *jatobá,* fr. Tupi] **:** COURBARIL

jato unit *n* **:** a unit for assisting the takeoff of an airplane consisting of one or more rocket engines that are usu. discarded after the fuel has been consumed

jat·ro·pha \'ja·trəfə\ n, *cap* [NL, fr. Gk *iatros* physician + *trophē* food, fr. *trephein* to nourish — more at ATROPHY] **:** a widely distributed mainly tropical American genus of herbs, shrubs, and trees (family Euphorbiaceae) usu. having lobed leaves and inconspicuous cymose flowers — see PHYSIC NUT

ja·troph·ic \jə'träfik\ *adj* [NL *Jatropha* + E *-ic*] **:** of or relating to physic nuts

jat·ror·rhi·za \,ja·trə'rīzə\ n, *cap* [NL, fr. *jatro-* (var. of *iatr-*) + *-rhiza*] **:** a genus of woody vines (family Menispermaceae) of eastern Africa and Mauritius having lobed leaves and long loose racemes of flowers — see CALUMBA

jat·ror·rhi·zine \,ja·trə'rī,zēn, -īz°n\ *or* **jat·eo·rhi·zine** \,jad.ēō'r-\ n -s [ISV *jatrorrhiz-, jateorhiz-* (fr. NL *Jatrorrhiza* or *Jateorhiza,* genus name of *Jatrorrhiza palmata* or *Jateorhiza palmata*) + *-ine*] **:** an alkaloid $C_{20}H_{21}NO_5$ that occurs in calumba and is related in structure to berberine

jaud \'jȯd, 'jäd\ *Scot var of* JADE

jau·die \-dī\ n -s [alter. of ME *chaudoun, chaudern* — more at CHAWDRON] **1** *chiefly Scot* **:** edible entrails; *esp* **:** a pig's stomach **2** *chiefly Scot* **:** a pudding made of jaudie

jaug \'jȯg, 'jäg\ *Scot var of* JAG

jauk \'jȯk, 'jäk\ *vi* -ED/-ING/-S [ME (Sc dial.) *jaken*] *Scot* **:** DALLY, DAWDLE

jau·ling·ite \'yau̇liŋ,īt\ n -s [G *jaulingit,* fr. the *Jauling,* Austria + G *-it*] **:** a fossil resin high in oxygen content

jaun \'jän, -ó-, -ȧ-\ n -s [Beng *jān,* fr. Skt *yāna* going, vehicle — more at HINAYANA] **:** a small Calcutta palanquin

1**jaunce** \'jȯn(t)s, -ä-,-ȧ-\ *vi* -ED/-ING/-S [origin unknown] *archaic* **:** PRANCE ⟨spurgalled and tired by *jauncing* Bolingbroke —Shak.⟩

2**jaunce** \"\ n -s *now dial Eng* **:** a tiring jaunt or journey

jaun·der \'jȯndər, 'jän-\ *vi* -ED/-ING/-S [origin unknown] *Scot* **:** PRATTLE, GABBLE

jaun·ders \'jȯndə(r)z, 'jän-,'jan-,'jaan-,'jȧn-\ *dial var of* JAUNDICE

1**jaun·dice** \'jȯndəs, 'jän-,'jȧn- *chiefly dial* 'jan- *or* 'jaan- *or* -də(r)z\ n -s [ME *jaunis, jaundis,* fr. MF *jaunisse,* fr. *jaune* yellow (fr. L *galbinus* yellowish green, fr. *galbus* yellow) + *-isse* -ice] **1 :** yellowish pigmentation of the skin, tissues, and certain body fluids caused by the deposition of bile pigments that follows interference with normal production and discharge of bile (as in certain liver diseases) or excessive breakdown of red blood cells (as after internal hemorrhage or in various hemolytic states) **2 :** a disease or abnormal condition that is characterized by jaundice: as **a :** any of several forms of hepatitis **b :** LEPTOSPIROSIS **c :** TOXEMIC JAUNDICE **3 :** a state or attitude characterized by satiety, distaste, or hostility ⟨looked at me with some ~ in her eye —Kenneth Roberts⟩ **4 :** GRASSERIE

2**jaundice** \"\ *vt* -ED/-ING/-S **:** to affect with envy, hostility, or distaste **:** PREJUDICE ⟨my own experience, as a minor poet, may have *jaundiced* my outlook —T.S.Eliot⟩

jaundice berry *n* [so called fr. its use as a remedy for jaundice] **:** the fruit of a barberry (*Berberis vulgaris*)

jaundiced *adj* **1 a :** yellowed by or as if by jaundice ⟨all looks yellow to the ~ eye —Alexander Pope⟩ **b :** YELLOW ⟨barred windows with ~ borders —John Ruskin⟩ **2 :** exhibiting or affected by envy, distaste, or hostility ⟨long ago looked with a ~ eye on the growth of regimentation —Irwin Edman⟩

jaundice root *n* **:** GOLDENSEAL

jaune bril·lant *also* **jaune bril·liant** \,zhōnbrē|(y)äⁿ\ n, pl **jaunes brillants** \-äⁿ(z)\ [F *jaune brillant,* lit., brilliant yellow] **:** any of several yellow pigments used esp. as artists' colors: as **a :** NAPLES YELLOW 1a **b :** cadmium sulfide either alone or in a mixture (as a cadmium yellow)

1**jaunt** \'jȯnt, -ä-,-ȧ-, *chiefly dial* -a- *or* -aa-\ *vi* -ED/-ING/-S [origin unknown] **1** *archaic* **:** to trudge or trip tediously about ⟨catch my death with ~*ing* up and down —Shak.⟩ **2 :** to make a usu. short journey (as an excursion) for pleasure ⟨~ through orchards and gardens —*Newsweek*⟩

2**jaunt** \"\ n -s **1** *archaic* **:** a difficult or tiring trip or journey ⟨a very long and troublesome ~ —George Washington⟩ **2 :** an excursion undertaken for pleasure ⟨a ~ to the shore or the hills —F.L.Allen⟩

jaun·ti·ly \'jȯnt°lē, 'jän-,'jȧn-, -tə̇l|, |i, *chiefly dial & archaic* 'jan- *or* 'jaan-\ *adv* **:** in a light or carefree manner **:** AIRILY ⟨~ concluded that life was an affliction —Harry Levin⟩

jaun·ti·ness \-tēnəs, -tin-\ n -ES **:** the quality or state of being jaunty **:** SPRIGHTLINESS, UNCONCERN ⟨the synthetic optimism, the false ~ —Bruce Bliven †1977⟩

jaunting car *also* **jaunty car** *n, Irish* **:** a light horse-drawn two-wheeled open vehicle with seats placed lengthwise either face-to-face or back to back — called also *outside car, sidecar*

jaunting car

jaunt·ing·ly *adv* **:** JAUNTILY

1**jaun·ty** \-tē,-ti\ *adj* -ER/-EST [alter. of earlier *jentee,* fr. F *gentil* — more at GENTLE] **1** *archaic* **a :** GENTEEL **b :** FASHIONABLE, STYLISH **2 :** nonchalant or sprightly in manner or appearance **:** AIRY, DEBONAIR, PERKY ⟨a ~ straw hat with a garish band —A.M.Schlesinger b. 1917⟩ ⟨a shrewdly ~ optimist —H.E.Clurman⟩ ⟨such writing jars with its ~ banality —C.C.Abbott⟩

2**jaun·ty** \'jȯnti, 'jȧn-\ n -ES [perh. modif. of F *gendarme* — more at GENDARME] *Brit* **:** the master-at-arms aboard a naval vessel

1**jaup** \'jȯp, 'jäp\ *vb* -ED/-ING/-S [prob. of imit. origin] *chiefly Scot* **:** SPLASH, SPATTER

2**jaup** \"\ n -s *chiefly Scot* **:** a splash or spatter esp. of dirty water

1**java** \'jävə, 'javə, 'jávə\ *adj, usu cap* [fr. *Java,* island in Indonesia] **:** of or from the island of Java **:** of the kind or style prevalent in Java **:** JAVANESE

2**java** \", *in sense 1 usu* 'javə\ n **1** -s *often cap* **:** COFFEE ⟨the boys came down and found me crying into my ~ —John Dos Passos⟩ **2** *usu cap* **a :** a breed of large general-purpose domestic fowls developed in America from oriental stock **b** -s **:** a bird of this breed

java almond *n, usu cap J* **1 :** a large East Indian tree (*Canarium commune*) that has large unequally pinnate leaves and white flowers in clustered terminal panicles followed by ovoid drupaceous fruits and that is a source of elemi **2 :** the rich oily seed of the Java almond used as food and as a source of cooking and illuminating oils but having an integument that causes diarrhea

java bean *n, usu cap J* **:** a strain or race of the sieva bean grown in southeastern Asia but dangerous as a feed because of the presence of a cyanogenetic glucoside in the seeds

java black rot *or* **java dry rot** *n, usu cap J* **:** a storage disease of the sweet potato caused by a fungus (*Diplodia tubericola*) that makes the inside of a root black and brittle

java citronella oil *n, usu cap J* **:** CITRONELLA OIL b

java cotton *n, usu cap J* **:** KAPOK

java grass *n, usu cap J* **:** a grass (*Polytrias praemorsa*) found in the West Indies and cultivated in Panama and in some parts of the U. S. as a lawn grass

java jute *n, usu cap 1st J* **:** KENAF

javali *var of* JABALI

java man *n, usu cap J* **:** either of two prehistoric men of primitive form (*Pithecanthropus erectus* and *P. robustus*) known chiefly from more or less fragmentary skulls found in Trinil, Java — called also *Trinil man*

¹javan \'jävən, 'jav-,'jàv-\ *adj, usu cap* [*Java*, island in Indonesia + E *-an*] **:** JAVANESE

²javan \"\ *n -s cap* **:** a native or inhabitant of Java

¹java·nese \¦javə¦nēz, ¦jäv-, ¦jàv-, -ēs\ *adj, usu cap* [*Java* + *-nese* (as in *Japanese*)] **1 a :** of, relating to, or characteristic of Java **b :** of, relating to, or characteristic of the Javanese **2 :** of, relating to, or characteristic of the Javanese language

²javanese \"\ *n, pl* **javanese** *usu cap* **1 a :** an Indonesian people inhabiting mainly the island of Java **b :** a member of such people **2 :** an Austronesian language of the Javanese people — compare MADURESE, SUNDANESE

javanese skunk *n, usu cap J* **:** TELEDU

javan ox *n, usu cap J* **:** a domesticated banteng of Java

javan peacock *or* **javan peafowl** *n, usu cap J* **:** a peafowl (*Pavo muticus*) of southeastern Asia in which the plumage is predominantly metallic green with ocellations and markings of blue and coppery yellow — compare INDIAN PEACOCK

javan rhinoceros *n, usu cap J* **:** a small one-horned rhinoceros (*Rhinoceros sondaicus*) of Java, Sumatra, and the Indian region west to Calcutta

javan squirrel *n, usu cap J* **:** JELERANG

javan·thro·pus \jə'van(t)thrəpəs; ¦jä,van'thrōpəs, ¦ja,-, ¦jà,-\ *n, cap* [NL, fr. *Java* + *-anthropus*] *in some classifications* **:** a genus of Hominidae comprising the Solo man

java pepper *n, usu cap J* **:** a climbing or somewhat arborescent East Indian pepper (*Piper cubeba*) that is sometimes cultivated for its fruits which are the source of cubeb

java plum *n, usu cap J* **:** a large tree (*Eugenia jambolana*) that is found chiefly in the East Indies and Australia and has strongly astringent seeds and bark used as a drug in India

java skull *n, usu cap J* **:** the skull of Java man

java sparrow *n, usu cap J* **:** a weaverbird (*Padda oryzivora*) that is native to Java, has glaucous gray and black upper parts, pinkish underparts, white cheeks, and large pink bill, resembles a finch, and is a common cage bird

java tea *n, usu cap J* **1 a :** the dried leaves of an East Indian mint (*Orthosiphon stamineus*) from which a powerful diuretic is obtained **b :** the mint that bears such leaves **2 :** any of several black teas grown in Java or resembling those grown there

java teak *n, usu cap J* **:** TEAK 1

ja·vé \'yä(,)vā, 'yà-, -ve\ *cap, var of* YAHWEH

jav·el \'javəl\ *n -s* [ME *javel, javell*] *archaic* **:** a vagabond or worthless fellow

ja·vel green \(')zha¦vel, zhə'¦\ *n, often cap J* [*javel (water)*] **:** a moderate greenish yellow that is greener and duller than citron yellow and greener and deeper than linden green — called also *eau de Javel green*

¹jav·e·lin \'jav(ə)lən\ *n -s* [MF *javeline*, alter. of *javelot*, of Celt origin; akin to W *gaflach* spear, OIr *gabul* forked stick, fork — more at GAFFLE] **1 a :** a light spear cast usu. by hand as a weapon of war or in hunting wild boar and other big game **b** *archaic* **:** a long-shafted combat weapon (as a pike) tipped with metal and used for thrusting **2** *or* **javelin man :** a man armed with a javelin; *esp* **:** a javelin-bearing member of the escort of an English judge **3 a :** a slender shaft of wood not less than 260 centimeters long, tipped with iron or steel, and intended to be thrown for distance as an athletic feat or exercise **b** *or* **javelin throw :** an athletic field event in which a javelin is thrown for distance **4** *or* **javelin formation :** a formation of military airplanes (as bombers) in which the elements fly one behind the other in line though not always at the same altitude

²javelin \"\ *vt* -ED/-ING/-S **1 :** to pierce with or as if with a javelin ⟨lightning ~*s* the hills⟩ **2 :** to throw or hurl like a javelin ⟨pieces of tin and board stuck in the mud where they had been ~*ed* by the heavy explosions —H.D.Skidmore⟩

javelina *var of* JABALINA

javelin bat *n* **:** a large carnivorous spearnose bat (*Phyllostomus hastatus*) of tropical America distinguished by a triangular prolongation of the nose leaf

jav·e·lin·eer \¦jav(ə)lə¦ni(ə)r, -iə\ *n -s* **:** a soldier armed with a javelin

ja·velle water *or* **ja·vel water** \(')zha¦vel, zhə'¦\ *n, usu cap J* [*Javel*, former town now included in Paris, France; trans. of F *eau de Javel, eau de Javelle*] **:** either of two aqueous solutions of hypochlorite used as a disinfectant or a bleaching agent and in photography: **a :** a solution of potassium hypochlorite now little used **b :** a solution of sodium hypochlorite

ja·vell·iza·tion \zhə,velə'zāshən\ *n -s* [*Javelle (water)* + *-ization*] **:** chlorination of water with Javelle water

jav·er \'javə(r)\ *dial var of* JABBER

¹jaw \'jȯ\ *n -s* [ME *jow, jowe, jaw, jawe*, prob. fr. MF *joe, joue* cheek] **1 a :** either of two complex cartilaginous or bony structures in most vertebrates that border the mouth, support the soft parts enclosing it, and usu. bear teeth on their oral margin comprising (1) an upper more or less firmly fused with the skull and (2) a lower hinged, movable, and articulated by a pair of condyles with the temporal bone of either side — called also respectively (1) *upper jaw, maxilla*, (2) *lower jaw, mandible* **b :** the bones, muscles, nerves, and other parts constituting the walls of the mouth and serving to open and close it — usu. used in pl. **c :** any of various organs of invertebrates that perform the function (as the biting or masticating of food) of the vertebrate jaws — compare CHELICERA, MANDIBLE 2, MASTAX **2 :** something resembling the jaw of an animal in form or action: as **a :** one of the sides of a narrow opening (as of a gorge) **b :** either of two or more opposing parts (as of a vise, measuring machine, pair of pliers, stone crusher) movable so as to open and close for holding, grasping, clamping, cutting, or crushing something between them — see VISE illustration **c :** a notched or forked part (as a guide allowing vertical play to a railroad-car axle box) adapted for holding an object in place **d** (1) **:** the inner end of a boom or gaff forked or hollowed so as to partly encircle and move freely on the mast (2) **:** projections from a yard at the slings often connected by the parrel **3 a :** a space lying between or as if between open jaws ⟨escaped from out of the ~*s* of the whale⟩ ⟨close the ~ of the shackle with a bolt⟩ **b :** a position or situation in which one is threatened (as with death) ⟨rode into the ~*s* of danger⟩ **4** *slang* **a :** TALK ⟨no time for ~⟩; *esp* **:** impudent or offensive talk **:** SCOLDING ⟨hold your ~ and be off⟩ ⟨don't have to take any of his ~⟩ **b :** a friendly talk **:** CHAT ⟨looked up his friend and had a good long ~⟩ **5 :** the pitch of a helix formed by a strand of a rope ⟨soft-laid, tarred hemp, 3-stranded with rather long ~ —C.W.T.Layton⟩

²jaw \"\ *vb* -ED/-ING/-S *vt* **1 :** to exercise the jaws upon ⟨~*ed* her bubble gum⟩ **2 :** to scold at ⟨~*ed* him all evening about the accident⟩ **3 :** to talk at tiresomely ⟨~ the customer till his resistance is broken down⟩ ~ *vi* **1 :** to speak abusively or indignantly and at length ⟨left when she began ~*ing* at him⟩ ⟨quit ~*ing* about it⟩ **2 :** to talk at length **:** CHAT, GAB ⟨~*ed* together all day about old times⟩ **syn** see SCOLD

³jaw \"\ *n -s* [origin unknown] *chiefly Scot* **:** WAVE, SPLASH

⁴jaw \"\ *vt* -ED/-ING/-S *chiefly Scot* **:** to throw (liquid) in quantity

ja·wab \jə'wäb, -wȯb\ *n -s* [Hindi *jawāb*, fr. Ar] **:** a building (as the false mosque of the Taj Mahal) erected to correspond to or balance another

jaw·ba·tion \jȯ'bāshən\ *n -s* [alter. (influenced by ¹*jaw*) of *jobation*] *dial Eng* **:** a long tiresome reproof **:** JAWING

jaw bit *n, chiefly Brit* **:** a bar across the jaws of a pedestal underneath an axle box of a railway car

jawbone \'⸗,⸗\ *n* **1 :** JAW 1a; *esp* **:** MANDIBLE **2** *slang* **:** CREDIT, TRUST ⟨got his winter's supplies on ~⟩ ⟨prohibit further ~ at post exchanges —*Newsweek*⟩

jawbreaker \'⸗,⸗⸗\ *n* **1 :** a word difficult to pronounce **2 :** a round hard candy made from sugar syrup **3 :** JAW CRUSHER

jawbreaking \'⸗,⸗⸗\ *adj* **:** difficult to pronounce ⟨a foreign city with a ~ name⟩ — **jaw·break·ing·ly** *adv*

jaw clutch *n* **1 :** DOG CLUTCH **2** *also* **jaw coupling :** CLAW CLUTCH

jaw crusher *n* **:** a machine for crushing rock or ore between two heavy steel jaws

jawed \'jȯd\ *adj* [¹*jaw* + *-ed*] **:** having a specified kind of jaw — usu. used in combination ⟨lean-*jawed*⟩ ⟨lantern-*jawed*⟩

jawfish \'⸗,⸗\ *n* **:** a fish of the percoid family Opisthognathidae comprising tropical marine fishes with a single dorsal fin, a single lateral line, and very large mouth

jawfoot \'⸗,⸗\ *n* **:** MAXILLIPED

jawhole \'⸗,⸗\ *n* [⁴*jaw* + *hole*] *Scot* **:** SEWER, CESSPOOL

jawing *pres part of* JAW

jaw·less \'jȯləs\ *adj* **:** having no jaw

jawless fish *n* **:** any of the primitive vertebrates comprising the superclass Agnatha

jawlike \'⸗,⸗\ *adj* **:** resembling a jaw or pair of jaws in appearance, function, or action

jawline \'⸗,⸗\ *n* **:** the outline of the lower jaw as a facial feature

jaw rope *n* **:** a rope holding the jaws of a gaff to the mast **:** PARREL

jaws *pl of* JAW, *pres 3d sing of* JAW

jaw sealer *n* **:** a machine for sealing flexible package materials by applying pressure with heated bars movable by jaw action

jawsmith \'⸗,⸗\ *n* **:** a professional talker **:** DEMAGOGUE

¹jay \'jā\ *n -s* [ME, fr. MF *jai*, fr. LL *gaius*, prob. fr. the name *Gaius*] **1 a :** a predominantly fawn-colored Old World bird (*Garrulus glandarius*) with a black-and-white crest and wings marked with black, white, and blue **b :** any of numerous typically brightly colored and frequently largely blue birds that with the common Old World jay constitute a subfamily of the family Corvidae, are distinguished from the related crows by smaller size, more arboreal habits, and frequently by possession of an elongated tail and a definite crest, have roving habits, pugnacious ways, and harsh voices, and are often destructive to the eggs and young of other birds — see BLUE JAY, CANADA JAY **2 a :** an impertinent chatterer **b :** a gaudily or flashily dressed person **:** WANTON, DANDY **c :** a person lacking experience (as in city ways) or polish **:** an unsophisticated, countrified, or gullible person **:** GREENHORN, RUBE **3** *or* **jay blue :** a moderate blue that is greener and duller than average copen, redder and slightly duller than azurite blue, redder and duller than Dresden blue, and redder and paler than bluebird

²jay \"\ *adj* -ER/-EST **:** unsophisticated or countrified in character **:** BACKWARD, UNSKILLED, RUSTIC ⟨~*er* than a real hick⟩

³jay \'jā\ *n -s* **:** the letter *j*

jaybird \'⸗,⸗\ *n* **:** JAY 1, 2 ⟨naked as a ~⟩

jaycee \'⸗¦⸗\ *n -s usu cap* [³*jay* + *cee* (letter); fr. the initials of *Junior Chambers* of Commerce, former name of the organization] **:** a member of a major national and international civic organization

jaygee \'⸗¦⸗\ *n -s* [³*jay* + *gee* (the letter); fr. the initials of *junior grade*] **:** LIEUTENANT JUNIOR GRADE

¹jayhawk \'⸗,⸗\ *n* [¹*jay* + *hawk*] **1 :** JAYHAWKER **2 :** a fictitious bird with a large beak used as an emblem in Kansas

²jayhawk \"\ *vt* -ED/-ING/-S **:** to make a predatory attack on **:** RAID

jay·hawk·er \"ə(r)\ *n* **1 a** *often cap* **:** a member of one of the bands of antislavery guerrillas of the Kansas border in raids on Missouri before and during the Civil War **b :** a member of one of the bands of outlaws engaged in raiding in the West following the Civil War **2** *usu cap* **:** KANSAN — used as a nickname

jaypie \'⸗,⸗\ *or* **jaypiet** \'⸗,⸗⸗\ *n* [¹*jay* + *pie, piet*] **1 :** a European jay **2** *dial Eng* **:** MISTLE THRUSH

jay teal *n, dial Eng* **:** a European teal (*Nettion crecca*)

jayvee \'⸗¦⸗\ *n -s* [³*jay* + *vee* (the letter); fr. the initials of *junior varsity*] **1 :** JUNIOR VARSITY **2 :** a member of a junior varsity team — usu. used in pl.

jaywalk \'⸗,⸗\ *vi* [¹*jay* + *walk*] **:** to cross a street carelessly or at an unusual or inappropriate place or in a dangerous or illegal direction so as to be endangered by the traffic — **jaywalker** \'⸗,⸗⸗\ *n*

jaz·er·ant \'jazərənt\ *also* **jaz·er·an** \-n\ *n -s* [ME *jesseraunt*, fr. MF *jaseran, jazerenc*, fr. Ar. *jazā'irī* Algerian, fr. *al-Jazā'ir* Algiers] **1 :** a coat of armor made of small overlapping metal plates usu. mounted on linen or other lining **2 :** armor of the jazerant type

jaz·y·ges \'jazə,jēz, -,gēz\ *n, pl* **jazyges** *usu cap* [L *Jazyges, Iazyges*, fr. Gk *Iazyges*] **1 :** a Sarmatian people orig. occupying the shores of the Black sea **2 :** a member of the Jazyges people

¹jazz \'jaz, -aa(ə)z\ *vb* -ED/-ING/-ES [origin unknown] *vt* **1:** to copulate with — usu. considered vulgar **2 a :** to increase the appeal or excitement of **:** ENLIVEN, POPULARIZE ⟨the newsman who ~*es* a story to sell himself to editor and public —C.K. Streit⟩ — usu. used with *up* ⟨drank bootleg gin to ~ me up —J.D.Hart⟩ **b :** to increase the speed of **:** ACCELERATE ⟨~ the motor⟩ **3 :** to play (music) in the manner of jazz **:** make jazz of ⟨pep up old tunes by ~*ing* them⟩ ~ *vi* **1 :** COPULATE — usu. considered vulgar **2 :** to go seeking pleasure **:** GAD — used with *around* **3 a :** to dance or perform jazz ⟨~*ing* to the music of the band⟩ ⟨a saxophonist who ~*es* at a nightclub⟩ **b :** to dance around in a jazzy manner ⟨chairs and tables . . . ~*ing* crazily to and fro across the cabin —Shevawn Lynam⟩

²jazz \"\ *n* -ES **1 :** COPULATION — usu. considered vulgar **2 a :** American music developed from religious and secular songs (as spirituals, shout songs), blues, ragtime, and other popular music (as brass-band marches) and characterized by improvisation, syncopated rhythms, contrapuntal ensemble playing, special melodic features (as flatted notes, blue notes) peculiar to the individual interpretation of the player, and the introduction of vocal techniques (as portamento) into instrumental performance — see BOP, DIXIELAND; compare SWING **b :** popular dance music influenced by jazz and played (as in the late 1920s) in a loud rhythmic manner **c :** a dance to jazz music with incisive rhythms and often acrobatic and grotesque steps — compare JITTERBUG 1 **3 :** excessively earnest and enthusiastic talk or preoccupation **:** stuffy foolishness **:** HUMBUG ⟨spouted all the scientific ~ at him —Pete Martin⟩

³jazz \"\ *adj* [²*jazz*] **1 :** of, relating to, or having the characteristics of jazz ⟨~ music⟩ ⟨~ fans⟩ **2 :** MOTTLED ⟨the room will be done in ~ colors —Upton Sinclair⟩

jazz ballet *n* **:** a ballet or dance performance in jazz style

jazzbow \'⸗,⸗\ *n* **:** a ready-made bow tie

jazz·i·ly \-zəlē, -li\ *adv* **:** in a jazzy manner

jazz·i·ness \-zēnəs, -zin-\ *n* -ES **:** the quality or state of being jazzy

jazz·ist \-zəst\ *n -s* **:** a lover of jazz

jazz·man \-zmən, -z,man\ *n, pl* **jazzmen :** a performer of jazz

jazzy \-zē, -zi\ *adj* -ER/-EST **1 :** having the character of jazz ⟨loud fast ~ music⟩ **2 :** of an unrestrained, animated, or flashy character ⟨a ~ good-time city⟩ ⟨a ~ Hawaiian shirt⟩

JB *abbr* **1** joint board **2** joint bond **3** junction box

j-bar lift \'⸗,⸗-\ *or* **j-bar** \'⸗,⸗\ *n, cap J* **:** a ski tow consisting of an overhead moving cable carrying a series of suspended bars of J shape on the base of which skiers may half sit and half lean while being pulled uphill

j boat *n, usu cap J* **1 :** a large yacht of the 76-foot rating class **2 :** a small sailboat raced by children

j bolt *n, cap J* **:** a bolt the shape of the letter J with threads usu. only on the longer leg

j-box \'⸗,⸗\ *n, cap J* **:** a container having the form of an upright J through which a textile is passed in a wet finishing process (as bleaching)

jc *abbr* junction

JC *abbr* **1** [L *jurisconsultus*] jurisconsult **2** justice clerk **3** juvenile court

JCB *abbr or n -s* [L *juris canonici baccalaureus*] **:** a bachelor of canon law

JCD *abbr or n -s* [L *juris canonici doctor*] **:** a doctor of canon law

JCL *abbr or n -s* [L *juris canonici licentiatus*] **:** a licentiate in canon law

JC of C *abbr* junior chamber of commerce

JCR *abbr* junior common room

JCS *abbr* joint chiefs of staff

jct *or* **jctn** *abbr* junction

jd *abbr* joined

JD *abbr or n -s* **1** [L *juris doctor*] **:** a doctor of law **2** [L *jurum doctor*] **:** a doctor of laws

JD *abbr* **1** Julian day **2** junior deacon **3** junior dean **4** justice department **5** juvenile delinquent

JEA *abbr* joint export agent

jeal·ous \'jeləs\ *adj* [ME *jelous*, fr. OF *jalos, jalous, jelous*, fr. (assumed) VL *zelosus*, fr. LL *zelus* zeal + L *-osus* -ous — more at ZEAL] **1 a :** intolerant of rivalry or unfaithfulness ⟨shall worship no other god, for the Lord . . . is a ~ God —Exod 34:14 (RSV)⟩ ⟨~ of the slightest interference in household management —Havelock Ellis⟩ **b :** disposed to suspect rivalry or unfaithfulness (as in love) **:** apprehensive of the loss of another's devotion ⟨so ~ she wouldn't let him dance with anyone else⟩ **c :** hostile toward a rival or one believed to enjoy an advantage (as a possession or attainment) **:** ENVIOUS, RESENTFUL ⟨~ because her coat isn't as nice as yours⟩ **2 :** zealous in guarding (as a possession) **:** VIGILANT ⟨his ~ love of privacy and independence —J.W.Beach⟩ **:** SOLICITOUS ⟨students . . . were like sons to him, he was ~ for their welfare —Ellwood Hendrick⟩ **3 :** distrustfully watchful **:** apprehensive of harm or fraud **:** SUSPICIOUS ⟨the ~ caution of New England —Van Wyck Brooks⟩ **syn** see ENVIOUS

jea·louse \jə'lüz\ *vt* -ED/-ING/-S [modif. (influenced by *jealous*) of F *jalouser* to envy, be jealous of — more at JALOUSE] *archaic* **:** SUSPECT, MISTRUST

jeal·ous·ly \'jeləslē, -sli\ *adv* [ME *jelously*, fr. *jelous* jealous + *-ly*] **:** in a jealous manner ⟨a ~ guarded right⟩ ⟨his absorption in a career she ~ hated —Oscar Handlin⟩

jeal·ous·ness *n* -ES [ME *jelousnes*, fr. *jelous* + *-nes* -ness] **:** JEALOUSY

jeal·ou·sy \'jeləsē, -si\ *n* -ES [ME *jelousie*, fr. OF *jalosie, jalousie, jelousie*, fr. *jalos, jalous, jelous* jealous + *-ie* -y — more at JEALOUS] **1 a :** a jealous disposition or state of mind **:** a jealous nature, attitude, or feeling ⟨blinded by ~ to the skill of his fellow workers⟩ ⟨felt a natural ~ toward the winner⟩ **:** hostile rivalry ⟨intense local *jealousies* among existing villages —R.A.Billington⟩ **b** *now dial Brit* **:** SUSPICION, MISTRUST **2 :** zealous vigilance ⟨cherish their official political freedom with fierce ~ —Paul Blanshard⟩ **3** [trans. of F *jalousie*] **:** JALOUSIE

jean \'jēn *chiefly Brit* 'jān\ *n -s* [short for *jean fustian*, fr. ME *Jene, Gene* Genoa, Italy (fr. MF *Genes*) + *fustian*] **1** *also* **jeans** *pl but sing in constr* **:** a durable twilled cotton cloth usu. in solid colors or stripes used esp. for sportswear and work clothes — compare DENIM, ⁹DRILL **2 jeans** *pl* **a :** pants usu. made of jean or denim and worn for work or sports — compare BLUE JEANS **b :** TROUSERS ⟨had to dig into his ~*s* to pay for the rest of the albums —*Down Beat*⟩

jeans 2a

jean·pau·lia \jēn'pȯlēə\ [NL, prob. fr. *Jean Paul* Richter †1825 Ger. author + NL *-ia*] *syn of* BAIERA

jebel *var of* DJEBEL

jeb·u·site \'jebyə,sīt *sometimes* -,zīt *or* 'jēbə-,sīt\ *n -s usu cap* [*Jebus*, ancient city in Palestine (fr. Heb *Yĕbūs*) + E *-ite*] **:** a member of a Canaanite people living in and around the ancient city of Jebus on the site of Jerusalem

jec·o·rin \'jekərən\ *n -s* [ISV *jecor-* (fr. L *jecor-, jecur* liver) + *-in*] **:** a complex lipoidal substance $C_{105}H_{186}N_5O_{46}P_3S$ somewhat resembling lecithin, orig. isolated from liver tissue, and occurring in small quantities in blood and in various tissues

jec·o·rize \'jekə,rīz\ *vt* -ED/-ING/-S [L *jecor-, jecur* liver + E *-ize* — more at HEPATIC] **:** to impart to (fats or oils) some of the properties of cod-liver oil (as by irradiation with ultraviolet light)

jed·burgh cast \'jed,bərə-, -,b(ə)rə-\ *also* **jed·dart cast** \'jedə(r)t-\ *n, usu cap J* [fr. *Jedburgh* or *Jeddart*, town in Roxburgh, Scotland, where in the 17th century a band of marauders was summarily executed] *Scot* **:** a court trial after punishment has been inflicted

jedburgh justice *also* **jeddart justice** *n, usu cap 1st J* **1** *Scot* **:** justice that punishes first and tries afterwards **:** LYNCH LAW **2** *Scot* **:** wholesale punishment or acquittal

jed·ding ax \'jediŋ-\ *n* [*jedding* alter. of *jadding*, pres. part. of *jad* to make a long deep hole in a rock, fr. *jad*, such a hole, of unknown origin] **:** a stonecutter's ax with a flat face and a pointed peen

jee *var of* GEE

jeel \'jē(ə)l\ *n -s* [ME (Sc dial.) *giell*, fr. MF *gel, giel* frost, jelly, fr. L *gelus, gelu* frost — more at COLD] *Scot* **:** JELLY

¹jeep \'jēp\ *n -s* [prob. alter. (influenced by Eugene the *Jeep*, a small fanciful wonder-working animal in the comic strip *Thimble Theatre* by Elzie C. Segar †1938 Am. cartoonist) of *g. p.* (abbr. of *general purpose*)] **1 a** (1) **:** a diminutive multipurpose motor vehicle of 80-inch wheelbase and ¼-ton capacity equipped with four-wheel drive and used by the U. S. Army in World War II — called also *peep* (2) **:** a modified U. S. Army vehicle of this kind having greater horsepower, more comfortable springs, longer wheelbase, increased fuel capacity, and a higher hood **b :** a 1½-ton command car used in the armored divisions of the U. S. Army during World War II **2** *or* **jeep carrier :** ESCORT CARRIER

jeep 1a(1)

²jeep \"\ *vb* -ED/-ING/-S *vi* **:** to travel in a jeep ~ *vt* **:** to convey in a jeep

Jeep \"\ *trademark* — used for a civilian automotive vehicle

jeep·able \-pəbəl\ *adj* [¹*jeep* + *-able*] **:** so rough or narrow as to be impassable to motor vehicles except jeeps ⟨a ~ road⟩

jee·pers \'jēpə(r)z\ *also* **jeepers cree·pers** \'⸗⸗'krēpə(r)z\ *interj* [*jeepers* euphemism for *Jesus*; *jeepers creepers* euphemism for *Jesus Christ*] — used as a mild oath

jeep·ney \'jēpnē\ *n -s* [fr. *jeep* + *jitney*] **:** a Philippine jitney bus converted from a jeep

¹jeer \'ji(ə)r, -iə\ *vb* -ED/-ING/-S [origin unknown] *vi* **:** to speak or cry out with derision or mockery **:** show contempt or scorn in often loud or coarse ridicule or sarcasm ⟨the fellows would ~ at him for knowing a girl —Hugh MacLennan⟩ ⟨~*ed* when he struck out⟩ ~ *vt* **:** DERIDE, MOCK, RIDICULE ⟨~*ed* the umpire's decision⟩ ⟨~*ed* his opponent when he tried to speak⟩ **syn** see SCOFF

²jeer \"\ *n -s* **1 :** a jeering remark or sound **:** TAUNT ⟨the tough kid's ~: "If they're good they're probably phony" —*Time*⟩ **2 :** the quality or state of jeering ⟨knew he was angry, though his voice showed nothing but a gentle ~ —Richard Llewellyn⟩

jeer·er \'jirə(r)\ *n -s* **:** one that jeers

jeer·ing·ly *adv* **:** in a jeering manner

jeers \'ji(ə)rz, -iəz\ *n pl* [ME *jeres*] **:** a combination of tackles for hoisting or lowering the lower yards

jeez *also* **geez** \'jēz\ *interj* [euphemism for *Jesus*] — used as a mild oath

je·fe \'hā(,)fā\ *n -s* [Sp, fr. F *chef* — more at CHIEF] *Southwest* **:** CHIEF, LEADER ⟨labor ~*s* willing to forgive, forget —*Santa Fe New Mexican*⟩

jef·fer·is·ite \'jef(ə)rə,sīt\ *n -s* [William W. *Jefferis* †1906 Am. banker + E *-ite*] **:** a mineral consisting of a vermiculite containing iron, aluminum, and magnesium

jef·fer·son city \'jefə(r)sən-\ *adj, usu cap J&C* [fr. *Jefferson City*, Missouri] **:** of or from Jefferson City, the capital of Missouri ⟨*Jefferson City* schools⟩ **:** of the kind or style prevalent in Jefferson City

jefferson da·vis's birthday \-'dāvəs(əz)-\ *n, usu cap J&D&B* [after *Jefferson Davis* †1889 president of the Confederate States of America] **:** the first Monday in June observed as a holiday in Alabama, Florida, Georgia, Kentucky, and Mississippi

jefferson day *n, usu cap J&D* [after Thomas *Jefferson* †1826 Am. president] **:** April 13 observed as a holiday in Alabama in honor of the birthday of Thomas Jefferson

jef·fer·so·nia \ˌjefə(r)ˈsōnēə, -nyə\ *n, cap* [NL, fr. Thomas *Jefferson* + NL *-ia*] **:** a genus of American and Asiatic herbs (family Berberidaceae) with basal palmately lobed leaves, solitary white flowers, and capsular fruit — see TWINLEAF

¹**jef·fer·so·nian** \ˌ==ˈsōnēən, -nyən\ *adj, usu cap* [Thomas *Jefferson* + E *-ian*] **:** of, associated with, or favoring Thomas Jefferson or Jeffersonianism ⟨the *Jeffersonian* states' rights school —R.G.McCloskey⟩ ⟨the underlying assumptions of *Jeffersonian* democracy —Gerald Stourzh⟩

²**jeffersonian** \"\ *n* -s *usu cap* **:** a follower of Thomas Jefferson **:** an adherent of Jeffersonianism ⟨continuity between the Federalists and the *Jeffersonians* — *Times Lit. Supp.*⟩ ⟨modern *Jeffersonians* . . . believe in government intervention in economic life —Reinhold Niebuhr⟩

jef·fer·so·nian·ism \ˌ==ˈsōnēəˌnizəm, -ōnyəˌn-\ *n* -s *usu cap* **:** the political principles and ideas held by Thomas Jefferson or later associated with his name and centering around a belief in states' rights, a strict construction of the federal Constitution, confidence in the political ability of the common man, and an agrarian as opposed to an industrial or commercial economy

jef·fer·son·ite \ˈjefə(r)səˌnīt\ *n* -s [Thomas *Jefferson* + E *-ite*] **:** a mineral $Ca(Mn,Zn,Fe)Si_2O_6$ consisting of a dark green or greenish black pyroxene

jef·frey pine \ˈjefrē-\ *also* **jef·frey's pine** \-ēz-\ *n, usu cap J* [after John *Jeffrey*, 19th cent. Scot. gardener and botanical explorer] **:** a tall symmetrical pine (*Pinus jeffreyi*) of western No. America that has long blue-green needles in groups of three and elongated cones borne on spreading or somewhat pendulous branches and that is sometimes classified as a variety of the ponderosa pine from which it differs chiefly in lighter color of bark and needles

jeffrey pine beetle *n, usu cap J* **:** a bark beetle (*Dendroctonus ponderosae*) destructive to Jeffrey pine in California

jehad *sometimes cap, var of* JIHAD

je·ho·vah \jəˈhōvə\ *n* -s *cap* [NL, intended as a transliteration of Heb *Yahweh*, the vowel points of Heb *'ădhōnāy* my lord being erroneously substituted for those of *Yahweh;* fr. the fact that in some Heb manuscripts the vowel points of *'ădhōnāy* (used as a euphemism for *Yahweh*) were written under the consonants *yhwh* of *Yahweh* to indicate that *'ădhōnāy* was to be substituted in oral reading for *Yahweh*] **:** ²GOD — a Christian transliteration of the tetragrammaton long assumed by many Christians to be the authentic reproduction of the Hebrew sacred name for God but now recognized to be a late hybrid form never used by the Jews; compare YAHWEH

jehovah god *n, cap J&G* **:** a supreme deity recognized and the only deity worshiped by Jehovah's Witnesses

jehovah's witnesses *n pl, cap J & usu cap W* **:** members of a group that witness by distributing literature and by personal evangelism to beliefs in the theocratic rule of God, the sinfulness of organized religions and governments, and an imminent millennium

je·ho·vism \jəˈhōˌvizəm\ *n* -s *cap* **:** YAHWISM

¹**je·ho·vist** \-vəst\ *n* -s *usu cap* [*Jehovah* + *-ist*] **:** YAHWIST 1

²**jehovist** \"\ *adj, usu cap* **:** YAHWISTIC 1

je·ho·vis·tic \jəˌhōˈvistik, ¦jē¦hō¦v-\ *adj, usu cap* **1 :** of or relating to the religion of Jehovah **2 :** YAHWISTIC

je·hu \ˈjē(ˌ)h(y)ü, ˈjē(ˌ)yü, ˈjā(-\ *n* -s *sometimes cap* [fr. *Jehu* †*ab* 816 B.C. king of Israel who was noted for his furious attacks in a chariot (2 Kings 9:20)] **:** a driver esp. of a cab or coach; *specif* **:** one who drives fast or recklessly ⟨a tattered ~ . . . who took the dune road to Dhaid as though the devil himself were after him —Ralph Hammond-Innes⟩

jeis·tic·cor \ˈjēsti,kȯ(ə)r\ *Scot var of* JUSTAUCORPS

jejun- *or* **jejuno-** *comb form* [*jejunum*] **1 :** jejunum ⟨*jejunectomy*⟩ **2 :** jejunal and ⟨*jejuno*duodenal⟩

je·ju·nal \jəˈjünᵊl, (ˈ)jē¦jü-\ *adj* [*jejun-* + *-al*] **:** of or relating to the jejunum

je·june \jəˈjün, (ˈ)jē¦jün\ *adj* [L *jejunus*] **1** *obs* **:** lacking food **:** HUNGRY **2 :** inadequate to nourish the body or relieve hunger **:** wanting nutritive value ⟨the ~ diets of the very poor⟩ **3 a :** devoid of interest or significance **:** DULL, FLAT, INANE, VAPID ⟨the lectures . . . seemed ~ and platitudinous —John Buchan⟩ ⟨literary history without evaluative criteria becomes ~ and sterile —C.I.Glicksberg⟩ **b :** giving evidence of lack of experience or information ⟨a singularly brief, all too ~, note on the historical events that occasioned the document —*Times Lit. Supp.*⟩ ⟨not appointed because they are qualified in investment or economics, but their comments on such matters need not be ~ —*Economist*⟩ **c :** IMMATURE, JUVENILE, PUERILE ⟨the ~ behavior of an adolescent boy⟩ ⟨~ remarks on world affairs by one who possessed no relevant knowledge⟩
syn see INSIPID

je·june·ly *adv* **:** in a jejune manner

je·june·ness \-ünnəs\ *n* -ES **:** the quality or state of being jejune

je·ju·ni·ty \jəˈjünəd·ē, jēˈjü-\ *n* -ES [L *jejunitas*, fr. *jejunus* jejune + *-itas* -ity] **:** the quality or state of being jejune

je·ju·nos·to·my \jəˌjüˈnästəmē, (ˌ)jēˌjü-\ *n* -ES [ISV *jejun-* + *-stomy*] **1 :** the surgical formation of an opening through the abdominal wall into the jejunum **2 :** the opening made by jejunostomy

je·ju·num \jəˈjünəm, jēˈ-\ *n, pl* **jeju·na** \-nə\ [L (trans. of Gk *nēstis*, fr. *nēstis* fasting), fr. neut. of *jejunus;* fr. the belief that it is empty after death] **:** the first two fifths of the small intestine beyond the duodenum usu. merging almost imperceptibly with the ileum though somewhat larger, thicker-walled, and more vascular and having more numerous circular folds and fewer Peyer's patches

jekyll–and–hyde \ˌjekələn(d)ˈhīd *also* ˈjēk- *or* ˈjāk-\ *adj, usu cap J&H* [after Dr. *Jekyll* and Mr. *Hyde*, the two sides of the split personality of the chief character in *The Strange Case of Dr. Jekyll and Mr. Hyde* (1886) by Robert Louis Stevenson †1894 Scot. writer] **:** of, relating to, or resembling a person who leads a double life or who has two apparently distinct characters one of which is good and the other evil ⟨the hooded bandit was a *Jekyll-and-Hyde* character —M.D. Portman⟩

jelatong *var of* JELUTONG

jel·er·ang \ˈjeləˌraŋ\ *n* -s [origin unknown] **:** a giant squirrel (*Ratufa bicolor*) of Java and southern Asia

jel·ick \ˈyelik\ *n* -s [Turk *yelek*] **:** the bodice or vest of a Turkish woman's dress

¹**jell** \ˈjel\ *vb* -ED/-ING/-S [back-formation fr. *jelly*] *vi* **1 :** to reach the consistency of jelly **:** CONGEAL, SET ⟨the grapes ~*ed* readily⟩ **2 :** to achieve distinctness **:** take shape **:** CRYSTALLIZE, SOLIDIFY ⟨romantic interludes that somehow fail to ~ —Hoffman Birney⟩ ⟨both thought and expression require time to ~ —A.T.Weaver⟩ ⟨long after the public's opinion has ~*ed* —J.W.Irwin⟩ ~ *vt* **:** to give distinctness to **:** cause to take form ⟨it was this discovery which did most to ~ his thought after it had been fluid during two decades —Hunter Mead⟩

²**jell** \"\ *n* -S **:** JELLY

jel·la·ba *or* **djel·la·ba** \jəˈläbə\ *also* **je·lab** \-b\ *n* -s [Ar *jallabah* & *jallāb*, alter. of *jallābīyah*] **:** a full loose garment (as of wool or cotton) with a hood and with sleeves and skirt of varying length orig. worn chiefly in Morocco

jellied gasoline *n* **:** NAPALM

jel·li·fi·ca·tion \ˌjeləfəˈkāshən\ *n* -s **:** the act or process of jellifying or the state of being jellified

jel·li·fy \ˈ==ˌfī\ *vb* -ED/-ING/-ES [¹*jelly* + *-fy*] *vt* **1 :** to make gelatinous **:** JELLY ⟨the red buttery mud is . . . *jellified* —Negley Farson⟩ **2 :** to reduce to slackness or weakness ⟨I turned, all *jellified* at her voice —Eugene Walter⟩ ~ *vi* **:** to become jelly or like jelly ⟨the lazy ear and the ~*ing* mind —*New Republic*⟩

Jell–O \ˈje(ˌ)lō\ *trademark* — used for a gelatin dessert often given the flavor and color of any of various fruits

jelloped *var of* JOLLOPED

¹**jel·ly** \ˈjelē, -li\ *n* -ES [ME *gelly, gellie*, fr. MF *gelee* frost, jelly, fr. fem. of *gelé* (past part. of *geler* to freeze, congeal), fr. L *gelatus*, past part. of *gelare* to freeze, congeal — more at COLD] **1 :** a semitransparent easily melted food preparation having a soft somewhat elastic consistency due to the presence of gelatin, pectin, or a similar substance: as **a :** ³ASPIC **b :** a dessert made usu. by adding gelatin to fruit juices **c :** a fruit product made by boiling sugar and the juice of fruit containing pectin **2 :** a substance resembling jelly esp. in consistency: as **a :** a transparent elastic gel **b :** a semisolid medicated or cosmetic preparation often having a gum base and usu. intended for local application ⟨ephedrine ~⟩ **c :** a jellylike preparation used in electrocardiography to obtain better conduction of electricity ⟨electrode ~⟩ **3 :** a gelatinous blue-green alga of the genus *Nostoc* found on damp ground esp. after a rain **4 :** JELLYFISH **5 :** a gelatin screen used to color or diffuse light (as of a theater spotlight) **6 :** a moral or emotional state felt to resemble jelly; *esp* **:** a state of fear or irresolution ⟨reduced to quivering ~ at the decisive moment⟩ **7 :** a shapeless structureless mass **:** PULP

²**jelly** \"\ *vb* -ED/-ING/-ES *vi* **1 :** to become jelly **:** come to the consistency of jelly **:** SET — compare ²GEL **2 :** to make jelly ⟨will be ~*ing* for days —Elizabeth Janeway⟩ ~ *vt* **:** to bring to the consistency of jelly — compare GELATINIZE

³**jelly** \"\ *adj* [alter. of *jolly*] *Scot* **:** POMPOUS, PROUD

jelly bag *n* **:** a bag typically of cheesecloth or flannel through which the juices for jelly are strained

jelly bean *n* **1 :** a sugar-coated candy bean with a gum or jelly center **2 :** a weak, spineless, or effeminate person ⟨this 50-year-old *jelly bean* —Shelby Foote⟩

jellybread \ˈ==,=\ *n, North* **:** a piece of bread and jelly

jelly doughnut *n* **:** a raised doughnut with jelly filling

jelly end rot *n* **:** a fungous disease of the potato that is caused by fungi of the genera *Fusarium* and *Rhizoctonia* and that produces a soft rot of the stem end of the tubers

jellyfish \ˈ==,=\ *n* **1 a :** any of various usu. marine and free-swimming coelenterates that constitute the sexually reproducing form of hydrozoans and scyphozoans which exhibit alternation of a sexual and an asexual generation and that have a nearly transparent saucer-shaped body with a mouth on the underside which extends by radially situated gastrovascular canals to the margin of the body, extensile marginal tentacles studded with stinging cells, and various sense organs distributed along the margin of the body — called also *sea nettle* **b :** SIPHONOPHORE **c :** CTENOPHORE — not used technically **2 :** a person lacking backbone or firmness ⟨if I should yield to threats . . . I should be a ~ by this time —Elinore M. Herrick⟩

jelly fungus *n* **:** any of various fungi whose appearance or consistency suggests jelly; *specif* **:** any fungus of the order Tremellales

jellyleaf \ˈ==,=\ *n* **:** QUEENSLAND HEMP

jelly lichen *n* **:** a lichen with a gelatinous thallus; *esp* **:** any of numerous lichens having an algal component belonging to the genus *Nostoc*

jellylike \ˈ==,=\ *adj* **:** resembling jelly in appearance or consistency **:** GELATINOUS

jelly of whar·ton \-ˈhwȯrtᵊn *also* -ˈwȯ-\ *usu cap W* [after Thomas *Wharton* †1673 Eng. anatomist] **:** WHARTON'S JELLY

jelly plant *n* **1 :** an Australian edible seaweed (*Eucheuma speciosum*) used in making jelly **2 :** KEI APPLE

jelly powder *n* **:** commercial gelatin mixed with sugar, flavoring, and color for use in making jellied desserts

jelly roll *n* **:** a thin sheet of sponge cake spread with jelly and rolled up while hot

jelly strength *n* **:** the strength of a gel or jelly (as gelatin or glue) expressed often as the weight in grams required to force a plunger into a test sample under specified conditions — called also *gel strength*

jel·u·tong *also* **jel·a·tong** *or* **jel·o·tong** \ˈjeləˌtȯŋ, -täŋ, ˌ==ˈ=\ *n* -s [Malay *jĕlutong*] **1 :** any of several trees constituting a genus (*Dyera*) of the family Apocynaceae **2 :** a glutinous milky juice that is obtained from various jelutongs (esp. *Dyera costulata*), resembles chicle, and is used chiefly in waterproofing, in rubber compounds, and in chewing gum

jem·a·dar \ˈjeməˌdär\ *or* **jam·a·dar** \ˈjəm-\ *n* -s [Hindi *jamaʻdar, jamʻdar* (influenced in meaning by Per *jamāʻat* body of troops), fr. Ar *jamʻ* collections, assemblage + Per *dār* having] **1 :** an officer in the army of India having a rank corresponding to that of lieutenant in the English army **2 :** any of several police or other officials of the government of India

je·mez \ˈhāməs\ *n, pl* **jemez** *usu cap* [Sp *jemez, jemes*, of AmerInd origin] **1 :** a group of Tanoan Amerindian peoples of New Mexico **2 :** a member of a Jemez people

jem·lah goat \ˈjemlə-\ *n, usu cap J* [*jemlah* prob. native name in the Himalayas] **:** TAHR

¹**jem·my** \ˈjemi\ *adj* [alter. (influenced by the nickname *Jemmy*) of *jimp* + *-y*] *now dial Eng* **:** SPRUCE, NEAT, SNAPPY

²**jemmy** \"\ *n* -ES [fr. *Jemmy*, nickname for *James*] **1** *Brit* **:** JIMMY 1 ⟨*jemmies* in action, stealthy footsteps creeping upstairs and down —Rose Macaulay⟩ **2** *Brit* **:** a sheep's head used for food **3** *dial Eng* **:** GREATCOAT

jen \ˈrən\ *n* -s [Chin (Pek) *jen²*] **:** the cardinal Confucian virtue of benevolence to one's fellowmen

je·na glass \ˈyānə-\ *n, usu cap J* [fr. *Jena*, Germany] **:** glass of fine quality esp. suited for chemical and optical ware and other scientific and industrial applications

je ne sais quoi \zhənə,sāˈkwä\ *n* **:** something that cannot be adequately described or expressed

jen·ne·ri·an \(ˈ)jeˈnirēən\ *adj, usu cap* [Edward *Jenner* †1823 Eng. physician + E *-ian*] **:** of or relating to Edward Jenner or the method of Jenner ⟨*Jennerian* vaccination⟩

jen·net \ˈjenət\ *n* -s [ME *genett, jennett*, fr. MF *genet*, fr. Catal *ginet, genet* Zenete (member of a Berber people), mounted soldier, a kind of horse, fr. colloq. Ar *zinēti* (Ar *zanātiy*) of the Zenetes, fr. *Zanātah* the Zenete people] **1** *also* **gen·et** \"\ **:** a small Spanish horse **2** [influenced in meaning by ¹*jenny*] **a :** a female donkey **b :** HINNY

jen·nie harp \ˈjenē-, -ni-\ *n* [*jennie* alter. of ¹*jenny*] **:** the female harp seal

jen·ny \ˈjenē, -ni\ *n* -ES [fr. *Jenny*, nickname fr. the name Jane] **1 a :** a female bird or animal — often used in combination ⟨*jenny* wren⟩ **b :** a female donkey **2 :** SPINNING JENNY **3 :** a traveling crane; *esp* **:** a locomotive crane **4 :** JINNY **5** *or* **jen·nie** \"\ **:** a losing hazard in English billiards made at an acute angle to a long side of the table — see LONG JENNY, SHORT JENNY **6** *or* **jennie** -s *usu cap* [so called fr. its having the designation *JN*] **:** a training airplane used in World War I **7 :** a machine for cleaning grease or paint from surfaces by means of a jet of steam

jenny ass *n* **:** JENNET 2a

jenny cutthroat *n, dial Eng* **:** a whitethroat (*Sylvia communis*)

jenny howlet *n, dial Eng* **:** OWL

jenny lind bed \ˈ==ˈlin(d)-\ *n, usu cap J&L* [after *Jenny* (Johanna Maria) *Lind* †1887 Swed. operatic soprano who successfully toured the U.S. (1850–52)] **:** an American spool bed

jenny wood *n, usu cap J* **:** FREIJO

jenny wren *n* **1 :** WREN **2 :** HERB ROBERT

jen·o·ar \ˈjenəˌwär\ *n* -s [native name in the East Indies] **:** any of several snappers of the Indian ocean; *esp* **:** a snapper (*Lutjanus sebae*) that is a popular food and game fish

jens *pl of* JEN

jeo·fail \ˈjeˌfā(ə)l\ *n* -s [AF *jeo fail, jo faill* I am at fault, I mistake] *archaic* **:** a mistake or oversight in legal pleading or other proceeding or the acknowledgment of such an error

jeop·ard \ˈjepə(r)d\ *vt* -ED/-ING/-S [ME *juparten, jeoparten, jeoparden*, back-formation fr. *jupartie, jeopartie, jeopardie* jeopardy] **:** JEOPARDIZE

jeop·ar·dize \-ˌdīz\ *vt* -ED/-ING/-S [*jeopardy* + *-ize*] **:** to expose to danger (as of imminent loss, defeat, or serious harm) **:** IMPERIL ⟨~ his life⟩ ⟨laws *jeopardizing* freedom of speech⟩ ⟨reforms too long delayed or denied have *jeopardized* peace, undermined democracy and swept away civil and religious liberty —F.D.Roosevelt⟩ **syn** see VENTURE

jeop·ar·dous \-dəs\ *adj* [ME *jupartous, jeopartous*, fr. *jupartie, jeopartie* + *-ous*] **:** marked by risk or danger **:** PERILOUS, HAZARDOUS ⟨takes such ~ episodes philosophically . . . as occupational liabilities —*Natural History*⟩

¹**jeop·ar·dy** \-dē, ˌdi\ *n* -ES [ME *jupartie, jeopartie, jeopardie*, fr. AF *juparti, jeu parti*, fr. OF, alternative, poem treating amorous problems in dialogue form, fr. *ju, jeu* game, play (fr. L *jocus* joke, jest, game) + *parti*, past part. of *partir* to divide — more at JOKE, PART] **1** *obs* **:** PROBLEM, DILEMMA; *also, obs* **:** TRICK **2 :** exposure to or imminence of death, loss, or injury **:** DANGER, HAZARD ⟨place a fortune in ~ by gambling⟩ **3 :** the danger that an accused person is subjected to when duly put upon trial for a criminal offense **syn** see DANGER

²**jeopardy** \"\ *vt* -ED/-ING/-ES **:** JEOPARDIZE, IMPERIL

jeopardy assessment *n* **:** a special assessment under the U.S. income-tax laws levied to collect an alleged deficiency when the taxing officer believes that delay may jeopardize the collection of the claim

je·quir·i·ty \jəˈkwirəd·ē\ *or* **jequirity bean** *n* -ES [Pg *jequiriti, jequiriti*, perh. of Indic origin; akin to Hindi *ratti* ratti — more at RUTTEE] **1 :** the scarlet and black seed of Indian licorice used in India and other tropical regions for beads in rosaries and necklaces and as a standard weight **2 :** INDIAN LICORICE

je·qui·ti·ba \jəˌkēd·əˈbä, zhəˌ-\ *n* -s [Pg *jequitibá*, fr. Tupi] **1 :** a So. American tree (*Cariniana legalis*) that yields a valuable hardwood similar to Colombian mahogany **2 :** the wood of the jequitiba — called also *Brazilian mahogany*

jer·boa \jərˈbōə, jer-\ *n* -s [Ar *yarbūʻ*] **1 :** any of several social nocturnal jumping rodents (family Dipodidae) inhabiting arid parts of the Old World, having long hind legs, long tail, and often large leaflike ears, and being mostly yellowish brown with white underparts and black-tipped tail **2 :** any of various jumping rodents (as a kangaroo rat or a pouched mouse)

jerboa

jerboa kangaroo *n* **:** any of several brush-tailed rat kangaroos (genus *Bettongia*)

jerboa mouse *n* **:** any of various leaping rodents usu. with elongated hind legs (as the sciuromorph pocket mice and kangaroo rats or the myomorph broad-toothed rat)

jerboa pouched mouse *n* **:** any of several small slender leaping marsupials (genus *Antechinomys*) of the central desert of Australia

jerboa rat *n* **:** any of several relatively large Australian rats (family Muridae) with hind legs adapted to leaping (as members of the genus *Conilurus*)

jer·e·me·jev·ite *also* **er·e·me·yev·ite** \ˌ(y)erəˈmā(y)əˌ|vīt, |fīt\ *n* -s [F *jérémêiéwite*, fr. Pavel V. Eremeev (*Jeremeiew*) †1899 Russ. mineralogist + F *-ite* -ite] **:** a mineral $AlBO_3$ consisting of aluminum borate in colorless or yellowish hexagonal crystals (hardness 6.5, sp. gr. 3.28)

jer·e·mi·ad \ˌjerəˈmīəd, -īˌad\ *n* -s [F *jérémiade*, fr. *Jérémie* Jeremiah (fr. LL *Jeremias*) + *-ade* -ad] **:** a lamenting and denunciatory complaint **:** a doleful story **:** a dolorous tirade ⟨a ~ against a civilization that values knowledge above wisdom —Lawrence Durrell⟩

jer·e·mi·ah \-īə\ *n* -s *usu cap* [after *Jeremiah* †*ab*585 B.C. Heb prophet known for his pessimism, fr. LL *Jeremias, Hieremias*, fr. Gk *Hieremias*, fr. Heb *Yirmĕyāh*] **:** a person who complains about the evil, decay, and disaster that he sees about him and who foresees and predicts a calamitous future ⟨*Jeremiahs* lamenting the decline of public morals⟩

jer·e·mi·an·ic \ˌjerəˌmīˈanik\ *also* **jer·e·mi·an** \-ˈmīən\ *adj, usu cap* [*Jeremianic* fr. *Jeremiah* + E *-an* + *-ic; Jeremian* fr. *Jeremiah* + E *-an*] **:** of, relating to, or suggestive of the prophet Jeremiah or the biblical material of Jeremiah ⟨a *Jeremianic* discourse⟩ ⟨a *Jeremianic* tone⟩

je·rez \hāˈrās, -rāth\ *adj, usu cap* [fr. *Jerez*, Spain] **:** of or from the city of Jerez, Spain **:** of the kind or style prevalent in Jerez

jerfalcon *var of* GYRFALCON

jerican *var of* JERRICAN

¹**jerk** \ˈjərk, -ōk, -əik\ *vb* -ED/-ING/-S [prob. alter. of *yerk*] *vt* **1** *obs* **:** to strike with or as if with a whip **2 :** to give a quick and suddenly arrested thrust, push, pull, or twist to ⟨~ a rope⟩ ⟨~ a coat off⟩ ⟨~ out a pistol⟩ **3 :** to throw with a quick motion suddenly arrested ⟨~ money on a table⟩; *specif* **:** to bowl (a cricket ball) illegally (as by bending the arm) **4 :** to utter in an abrupt, snappy, or sharply broken manner ⟨~ out words⟩ **5 :** to prepare and dispense (sodas) ~ *vi* **1 :** to make a sudden spasmodic motion or series of such motions **:** move with a start or starts ⟨fish ~*ing* and tumbling on the deck of a boat⟩ **2 :** to move in short abrupt motions ⟨a cripple ~*ing* along a street⟩ **:** move along with frequent jolts ⟨a train ~*ing* past a station⟩ **3 :** to throw an object with a jerk; *specif* **:** to jerk the ball in bowling in the game of cricket **4** *obs* **:** SNEER
syn SNAP, TWITCH, YANK: JERK indicates sudden, sharp, quick, graceless, forceful movement begun or ended abruptly ⟨thought the train would never start, but at last the whistle blew and the carriages *jerked* forward —G.G.Carter⟩ ⟨*jerked* her head back as if she'd been struck in the face —Dorothy Baker⟩ SNAP may apply to a quite quick action abruptly terminated, as biting or trying to bite sharply or seizing, clutching, snatching, locking, or breaking suddenly ⟨the hounds were fine beasts . . . lank and swift as they bent over the food to *snap* it into their jaws and swallow it quickly —Elizabeth M. Roberts⟩ ⟨the syndicate *snapping* up land as soon as it is for sale⟩ ⟨*snapped* at her because Theophilus did not eat enough —Margaret Deland⟩ TWITCH may indicate quick, sometimes spasmodic, and often light action combining tugging and jerking ⟨shrunken body continued to jerk and quiver, fingers *twitching* at his gray beard —Gerald Beaumont⟩ ⟨one Pan ready to *twitch* the nymph's last garment off —Robert Browning⟩ ⟨put out his hand to *twitch* off a twig as he passed —Willa Cather⟩ YANK indicates quick and heavy tugging and pulling ⟨watches her two-year-old stand passive while another child *yanks* his toy out of his hand —Margaret Mead⟩ ⟨she *yanked* the corset strings viciously —D.B.Chidsey⟩ ⟨by means of long blocks and tackle they set to *yanking* out logs —S.E.White⟩

²**jerk** \"\ *n* -s *often attrib* **1** *obs* **:** a stroke esp. of a whip **:** LASH **2 :** a single quick motion usu. of short duration and length (as a suddenly arrested pull, thrust, push, or jolt) ⟨get up with a ~⟩ **3 a :** jolting, bouncing, or thrusting motions ⟨a rustic dance full of ~ and rhythm⟩ **b :** tendency to produce spasmodic motions ⟨a car with little ~ and noise⟩ **4 a :** an involuntary spasmodic muscular movement due to reflex action; *esp* **:** one induced by an external stimulus — see KNEE JERK **b jerks** *pl* (1) **:** CHOREA (2) **:** involuntary twitchings due to nervous excitement (as in the dancing mania and sometimes in religious revivals) **5** [prob. fr. *jerk* "masturbator", fr. *jerk (off)*] **:** a stupid, foolish, naïve, or unconventional person ⟨these ~*s* . . . who didn't know anything outside their rank and serial number —J.G.Cozzens⟩ ⟨soapbox orators who . . . vary from philosophers to out-and-out ~*s* —Richard Joseph⟩ **6 :** the pushing of a weight from shoulder height to a position overhead **:** the second phase of the clean and jerk in weight lifting

³**jerk** \"\ *vt* -ED/-ING/-S [back-formation fr. ³*jerky*] **:** to cut into long slices or strips and dry in the sun ⟨~ beef⟩ — see CHARQUI

jerked *past of* JERK

jerk·er \-kə(r)\ *n* -s **:** one that jerks

jerk·i·ly \-kəlē, -li\ *adv* **:** in a jerky manner ⟨bowed ~, first to the orchestra, then to the audience —*Time*⟩

¹**jer·kin** \-kən\ *n* -s [origin unknown] **1 :** a close-fitting hip-length jacket made without sleeves or with extended shoulders, being usu. collarless and belted, and in the 16th century doublet over which it was orig. worn **2 :** any of various adaptations of the 16th century jerkin often worn now by both men and women

²**jerkin** \"\ *n* -s [prob. fr. *gerfalcon* + *-kin*] **:** a male gyrfalcon

jerk·i·ness \-kēnəs, -kin-\ *n* -ES **:** the quality or state of being jerky

jerking *pres part of* JERK

jerk·ing·ly *adv* **:** JERKILY

jerkinhead \ˈ==,=\ *n* [prob. alter. (influenced by ¹*jerkin*) of *kirkinhead*] **:** a hipped part of a roof which is hipped only for a part of its height leaving a truncated gable

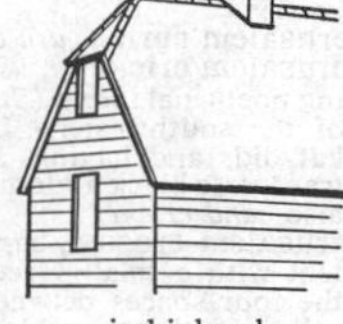

jerkinhead

jerk line *n* **:** a single rein used orig. in the western U.S. that was fastened to the brake handle and ran through the driver's hand to the bit of the lead animal

jerk off *vb* **:** MASTURBATE — usu. considered vulgar

jerk pump *n* **:** a fuel-injection pump in an oil engine which supplies impulsively an accurately metered charge to the nozzle at the time of the opening of the inlet valve

jerks *pres 3d sing of* JERK, *pl of* JERK

jerk·water \'=,==\ *or* **jerk** *adj* [[1]*jerk* + *water;* fr. the fact that rural trains took on water that was carried in buckets from the source of supply] **1 :** insignificant and remote ⟨a ~ town⟩ ⟨a ~ college⟩ **2 :** contemptibly petty, narrow, or trivial : PIDDLING ⟨a ~ carnival act⟩ ⟨a ~ politician⟩

[1]**jerky** \'jərkē, 'jək-,'-jəik-, -ki\ *adj* -ER/-EST [[2]*jerk* + *-y*] **1 a :** moving along with or accompanied by fits and starts : JOLTING ⟨a ~ vehicle⟩ **b :** characterized by abrupt or awkward transitions ⟨a ~ prose style⟩ **2 a :** INANE, FOOLISH ⟨~ adolescents hanging around drugstores⟩ **b :** contemptibly weak or ineffectual ⟨the ~ policies of an ignorant governor⟩

[2]**jerky** \"\ *n* -ES **:** a horse-drawn wagon usu. without springs that is used for carrying passengers

[3]**jer·ky** \"\ *n* -ES [modif. of Sp *charqui* — more at CHARQUI] **:** meat (as beef) that has been jerked

jer·mo·nal \ˌjərmə'näl\ *n* -S [prob. fr. Hindi *jar* cold + *munāl* pheasant] **:** HIMALAYAN SNOW COCK

jer·o·bo·am \ˌjerə'bōəm\ *n* -S *sometimes cap* [after *Jeroboam* I †*ab*912 B.C. king of the northern kingdom of Israel referred to as the "mighty man of valor" (1 Kings 11:28—AV)] **1 :** an oversize wine bottle holding about four quarts ⟨a ~ of champagne⟩ **2** *Brit* **:** CHAMBER POT

je·ro·mi·an \jə'rōmēən\ *adj, usu cap* [St. *Jerome* (Eusebius *Hieronymus*) †420 church father + E *-ian*] **:** of or relating to St. Jerome or his works

jer·ri·can *or* **jerry can** *also* **jeri·can** \'jerē,kan\ *n* [[2]*jerry* + *can*] **:** a 5-gallon fluid container

[1]**jer·ry** \'jerē, -ri\ *n* -ES [fr. *Jerry,* nickname for the names *Jeremy & Jeremiah*] **1** *archaic* **:** the noise that according to custom was made (as by hammering, beating, or rattling) to celebrate the end of someone's term of apprenticeship in the printing trade **2** [by shortening & alter. fr. *jeroboam*] *Brit* **:** CHAMBER POT

[2]**jerry** \"\ *n* -ES *usu cap* [alter. (influenced by [1]*jerry* and the name *Jerry*) of *German*] *chiefly Brit* **:** GERMAN

[3]**jerry** \"\ *adj* -ER/-EST [back-formation fr. *jerry-built*] **:** POOR, SLIPSHOD, MAKESHIFT ⟨~ workmanship⟩

jerry-build \'==,=\ *vb* [back-formation fr. *jerry-built*] *vt* **1 :** to build (as a house) flimsily of materials of poor quality **2 :** to put together, contrive, or devise with insufficient care or planning ⟨attempt to *jerry-build* a military pact —Denis Healey⟩ ⟨*jerry-builds* the English language as if it were the English countryside —Cyril Connolly⟩ **~** *vi* **:** to put up a jerry-built structure **:** do building cheaply and with inferior materials

jerry-builder \'==,==\ *n* **:** one that jerry-builds; *esp* **:** a builder who erects cheap buildings of poor materials and unsubstantial construction esp. on speculation for quick sale

jerry-built \'==,=\ *adj* [*jerry* prob. fr. *Jerry,* nickname for *Jeremy & Jeremiah*] **1 :** built cheaply and unsubstantially of poor or insufficient materials ⟨*jerry-built* wharves⟩ ⟨buying sagging old houses or *jerry-built* new ones —Vera Connolly⟩ ⟨mean-looking little houses, very *jerry-built* —John Morris⟩ ⟨600 acres of *jerry-built* shacks —Emory Ross⟩ ⟨the thin walls of the *jerry-built* house —Virginia Woolf⟩ **2 :** carelessly or hastily put together **:** constructed without due thought or care **:** unsound in planning or execution **:** FLIMSY; *often* **:** constructed or devised at haphazard ⟨*jerry-built* tax legislation —*N.Y. Times*⟩ ⟨the political empire of Rome became more and more *jerry-built* —Weston La Barre⟩ ⟨the movie is a particularly unsatisfying, *jerry-built* affair —Manny Farber⟩

jerry-come-tumble \ˌ==(,)=ˌ==\ *also* **jerry-go-nimble** \ˌ==(,)=ˌ==\ *n* -S *usu cap J* **1** *dial Eng* **:** TUMBLER **2** *dial Eng* **:** CIRCUS

jerry man *n* **:** a wasteman in a mine

jerrymander *var of* GERRYMANDER

[1]**jer·sey** \'jərzē, 'jəz-,'jəiz-, -zi, *dial* 'jārz- *or* 'jäz-\ *adj, usu cap* [fr. *Jersey,* one of the Channel islands] **:** of or from the island of Jersey, Channel islands **:** of the kind or style prevalent in Jersey

[2]**jersey** \"\ *n, often attrib* **1** *also* **jersey cloth** -S **a :** a plain weft-knitted fabric in tubular form made of wool, cotton, nylon, rayon, or silk and used for underwear, dresses, sportswear **b :** TRICOT 1 **2** -S **:** any of various close-fitting usu. circular-knitted garments: as **a :** a man's sleeveless cotton undershirt **b :** a pullover with short or long sleeves worn esp. by children, athletes, or sailors **3 a** *usu cap* **:** a breed of rather small short-horned dairy cattle originating on the island of Jersey in the English channel and now widely distributed, being in color predominantly yellowish brown or fawn although sometimes ranging from silvery gray or pale buff to black with occasional white marking, and being noted for the high fat content of their milk **b** -S *often cap* **:** an animal of the Jersey breed

[3]**jersey** \"\ *adj, usu cap* [fr. (*New*) *Jersey,* fr. *Jersey,* the Channel island] **:** NEW JERSEY

[1]**jer·sey·an** \-zēən, -ziən\ *n* -S *usu cap* [(*New*) *Jersey* + E *-an*] **:** a native or resident of the state of New Jersey

[2]**jerseyan** \"\ *adj, usu cap* **:** of, relating to, or characteristic of New Jersey or New Jerseyites

jersey city *adj, usu cap J&C* [fr. *Jersey City,* New Jersey] **:** of or from Jersey City, N.J. ⟨a *Jersey City* physician⟩ **:** of the kind or style prevalent in Jersey City

jersey cream *n, often cap J* [[2]*Jersey* (cattle)] **:** POLAR BEAR 2

jersey elm *n, usu cap J* [[1]*Jersey*] **:** an elm that is a variety (*Ulmus campestris wheatleyi*) of the English elm with erect branches and broader leaves — called also *Guernsey elm*

jersey giant *n* [[3]*Jersey*] **1** *usu cap J&G* **:** a breed of very large domestic fowls developed in New Jersey by interbreeding large Asiatic fowls with Langshans and being orig. solid black but now having a white variety **2** *usu cap J & often cap G* **:** a bird of the Jersey Giant breed

jer·sey·ite \-zē,īt, -zi,īt\ *n* -S *usu cap* [(*New*) *Jersey* + E *-ite*] **:** a native or resident of the state of New Jersey

jersey justice *n, usu cap 1st J* [[3]*Jersey;* fr. the supposedly more efficient legal system in New Jersey] **:** speedy and effective justice (as in criminal cases)

jersey lightning *n, usu cap J* [[3]*Jersey*] *slang* **:** APPLEJACK

jersey·man \'==mən\ *n, pl* **jerseymen** *usu cap* [*Jersey,* the island + *man*] **1 :** a native or resident of the island of Jersey **2 :** NEW JERSEYITE

jersey pine *n, usu cap J* [[3]*Jersey*] **:** a common open or straggling pine (*Pinus virginiana*) of the eastern U.S. having leaves only an inch or two long

jersey tea *n, usu cap J* [[3]*Jersey*] **1 :** NEW JERSEY TEA **2 :** WINTERGREEN 2a

jert \'jərt\ *chiefly Scot var of* JERK

je·ru·sa·lem \jə'rüs(ə)ləm *also* -üz| *or* |ə,lem\ *adj, usu cap* [fr. *Jerusalem,* Palestine, fr. LL *Jerusalem, Hierusalem,* fr. Gk *Ierousalēm, Hierousalēm,* fr. Heb *Yĕrūshālaim*] **:** of or from Jerusalem, a city of Palestine now divided between the Republic of Israel of which it is the capital and the Hashimite Kingdom of Jordan **:** of the kind or style prevalent in Jerusalem

jerusalem artichoke *n, usu cap J* [*Jerusalem* by folk etymology fr. It *girasole* — more at GIRASOL] **1 :** a perennial American sunflower (*Helianthus tuberosus*) widely cultivated and often occurring as an escape **2 :** the tuber of Jerusalem artichoke used as a vegetable, as a feed for livestock, and as a source of levulose

jerusalem cherry *n, usu cap J* **:** either of two plants of the genus *Solanum* (*S. pseudo-capsicum* or *S. capsicastrum*) cultivated as ornamental house plants for their bright orange to red berries

jerusalem corn *n, usu cap J* **:** DURRA

jerusalem cricket *n, usu cap J* **:** a burrowing nocturnal insect (*Stenopelmatus fuscus*) of the southwestern U.S. related to the katydids and having a large head and transverse black abdominal stripes — called also *sand cricket*

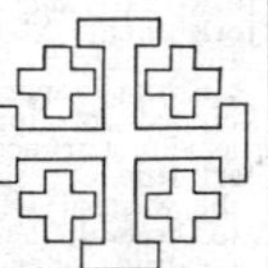

Jerusalem cross

jerusalem cross *n, cap J* **1 :** a cross potent with a small Greek cross in each of the four spaces between the arms **2** [so called fr. the resemblance of the arrangement of the leaves to the shape of the Jerusalem cross] **:** MALTESE CROSS 2

jerusalem haddock *n, usu cap J, West* **:** OPAH

jerusalem oak *n, usu cap J* **1 :** an aromatic oak-leaved goosefoot (*Chenopodium botrys*) **2 :** MEXICAN TEA

jerusalem pea *n, usu cap J* **:** an East Indian perennial bean (*Phaseolus trinervius*) that is closely related to and sometimes considered a variety of the urd bean

jerusalem pine *n, usu cap J* **:** ALEPPO PINE

jerusalem sage *n, usu cap J* **:** any of several plants of the genus *Phlomis* (as *P. fruticosa* or *P. tuberosa*) often cultivated and having dense axillary whorls of purple flowers

jerusalem star *n, usu cap J* **1 :** SALSIFY **2 :** SNOW-IN-SUMMER **3 :** a Eurasian evergreen subshrub (*Hypericum calycinum*) with large showy yellow flowers

jerusalem sunday *n, usu cap J&S* **:** MID-LENT SUNDAY

jerusalem tea *n, usu cap J* **:** MEXICAN TEA

jerusalem thorn *n, usu cap J* **1 :** CHRIST'S-THORN **2 :** a large shrub or shrubby tree (*Parkinsonia aculeata*) that is native to tropical America but naturalized in the southern and southwestern U.S., that has pinnate leaves with small deciduous leaflets, sharp spines, and showy racemose yellow flowers, and that is used for hedging and as emergency food for livestock esp. in dry regions — called also *horsebean* **3 :** CATECHU 2

jer·vine \'jər,vēn, -,vən\ *n* -S [NL *jervina,* fr. Sp *yervina,* perh. fr. *yervo* vetch, chick-pea (fr. L *ervum*) + *-ina* -ine] **:** a crystalline alkaloid $C_{26}H_{39}NO_3$ related in structure to the steroids and found in the rhizomes and roots of white hellebore, American hellebore, and other species of the genus *Veratrum*

jes \'jes\ *n* -ES [prob. native name in West Africa] **:** OTTER SHREW

[1]**jess** *or* **jesse** \'jes\ *n, pl* **jesses** [ME *ges, gesse,* fr. MF *gies, giez,* fr. pl. of *giet, get, jet* throw — more at JET] **:** either of two short straps of leather or other material secured on the legs of a hawk used in falconry and usu. provided with a ring for attaching a swiveled leash

[2]**jess** \"\ *vt* -ED/-ING/-ES **:** to attach jesses to (a hawk)

jesses: *1* ring for leash, *2* swivel, *3* ring for jesses, *4* jesses

jessamine *var of* JASMINE

jes·sa·my \'jesəmē, -mi\ *n* -ES [modif. of *jessamine*] **1** *dial Eng* **:** JASMINE **2** [so called fr. the use of perfume] **:** DANDY, FOP

jes·sant-de-lis *also* **jes·sant-de-lys** \ˌjesᵊn(t)də'lē\ *adj* [*jessant* (prob. alter. of *jacent*) + fleur-*de-lis*] **:** having the upper points of a fleur-de-lis arising from the top of the head and the lower points projecting from the mouth — used of a heraldic leopard's face

jes·se *also* **jes·sie** *or* **jes·sy** \'jesē, -si\ *n, pl* **jesses** *also* **jessies** [prob. after *Jesse,* father of David in the Bible; fr. "And there shall come forth a rod out of the stem of Jesse" (Isa 11:1—AV)] *chiefly dial* **:** a severe scolding or beating ⟨just as soon as I go home I'll give you ~ —Alice Cary⟩

jessed \'jest\ *adj* [[1]*jess* + *-ed*] **:** having on jesses

jes·se tree \'jesē-, -si-\ *or* **jesse** *n* -S *usu cap J* [after *Jesse,* father of David in the Bible] **:** a genealogical tree in which the lineage of Christ is represented in sculpture and decorative art — called also *tree of Jesse*

jesse window *n, usu cap J* [after *Jesse* in the Bible] **:** a decorative window in which a Jesse tree is a principal subject of the design

jes·sur \'jesə(r)\ *n* -S [perh. fr. Beng] **:** RUSSELL'S VIPER

[1]**jest** \'jest\ *n* -S [ME *geste,* fr. OF *geste, jeste,* fr. L *gesta* deeds, fr. neut. pl. of *gestus,* past part. of *gerere* to bear, wage, cherish, accomplish — more at CAST] **1 a** *obs* **:** ACT, DEED, EXPLOIT **b :** an act intended to provoke laughter **:** PRANK ⟨began as a ~ and ended as a tragedy⟩ ⟨signs marking the city limits . . . pranksters carry off and plant in remote spots as a ~ —*Amer. Guide Series: Calif.*⟩ **c :** a ludicrous circumstance or incident ⟨a proper ~, and never heard before, that Suffolk should demand a whole fifteenth for costs and charges —Shak.⟩ **2 a :** a jeering remark **:** GIBE, TAUNT ⟨many a foul ribald ~ at the expense of the prisoner —J.L.Motley⟩ **b :** a witty remark **:** clever quip **:** MOT ⟨the kind of wry ~ that had sent the ancient gods into peals of ironic laughter —T.B. Costain⟩ **3 a :** a frivolous mood or manner — usu. used with *in* ⟨done in ~ and not supposed to be taken seriously⟩ ⟨many a true word is spoken in ~⟩ **b :** GAIETY, MERRIMENT ⟨I knew him, Horatio: a fellow of infinite ~, of excellent fancy —Shak.⟩ **4 :** the butt of a joke **:** LAUGHINGSTOCK ⟨to be the standing ~ of all one's acquaintance —R.B.Sheridan⟩ **syn** see FUN, JOKE

[2]**jest** \"\ *vb* -ED/-ING/-S [ME *gesten* to tell a tale, recite a romance, fr. *geste,* n.] *vi* **1 :** to utter taunts **:** jeer and mock **:** GIBE ⟨mock not nor ~ at anything of importance —George Washington⟩ ⟨~s at scars that never felt a wound —Shak.⟩ **2 :** to speak or act without seriousness or in a frivolous manner ⟨you surely ~, interrupted I; I am a foreigner, and you would abuse my ignorance —Oliver Goldsmith⟩ **3 :** to make a witty remark **:** say something amusing **:** QUIP, JOKE ⟨~ed with her in a low voice —Anne D. Sedgwick⟩ **4** *obs* **:** to make merry ⟨as gentle and as jocund as to ~ go I to fight —Shak.⟩ **~** *vt* **:** to jeer and mock at **:** make fun of **:** RIDICULE, BANTER ⟨~ed his friend for his fondness for horses⟩

jestbook \'=,=\ *n* **:** a book containing jests and jokes — called also *jokebook*

jest·ee \(')je¦stē\ *n* -S **:** a person subjected to jesting

jest·er \'jestə(r)\ *n* -S [alter. of ME *gestour,* fr. *gesten* + *-our* -or] **1** *archaic* **:** a professional teller of gests ⟨harper's strain and ~'s tale went round in vain —Sir Walter Scott⟩ **2 :** FOOL 2a ⟨a court ~⟩ ⟨the world never has believed its ~s even when they knew more than its kings —James Street⟩ **3 :** one given to uttering jests or playing the clown ⟨has played to perfection the role of the world's . . . ~ —*Time*⟩

jest·ing·ly *adv* **:** in a jesting manner

[1]**jesu·it** \'jezh(ə)wət *also* -ez| *or* |wət; *usu* -əd· + V\ *n* -S *usu cap* [NL *Jesuita,* fr. LL *Jesus* + L *-ita* -ite] **1 :** a member of a religious society for men founded by St. Ignatius Loyola in 1534 **2 :** one given to intrigue or equivocation **:** a crafty person **:** CASUIST ⟨one fourth of all power is in these ignorant masses, and they are in the hands of the political *Jesuits* of the South —*No. Amer. Rev.*⟩

[2]**jesuit** \"\ *adj, usu cap* **:** of or relating to the Jesuits or Jesuitism

jesuit berry *n, usu cap J* **:** PARTRIDGEBERRY 1

jesu·it·ed \-(,)wid·əd, -,wəd·-\ *adj, usu cap, archaic* **:** JESUITIC

jesu·it·ic \ˌ==¦wid·ik, -¦wit|, |ēk-\ *or* **jesu·it·i·cal** \|əkəl, |ēk-\ *adj* **1** *usu cap* **:** of or relating to the Jesuits, Jesuitism, or jesuitry **2** *often cap* **:** having qualities thought to resemble those of a Jesuit — usu. used disparagingly ⟨the low cunning and *Jesuitical* trick with which she deludes her husband —S.T. Coleridge⟩ — **jesu·it·i·cal·ly** \|ək(ə)lē, |ēk-, -li\ *adv, often cap*

jesu·it·ism \'== wəd·,izəm, -wə,ti-\ *n* -S **1** *usu cap* **:** the system, doctrine, or practices of Jesuits **2** *often cap* **:** JESUITRY

jesu·it·ize \-əd·,īz, -ə,tīz\ *vb* -ED/-ING/-S *often cap, vi* **:** to act or teach in the actual or ascribed manner of a Jesuit **~** *vt* **:** to indoctrinate with actual or ascribed Jesuit principles — usu. used disparagingly

jesu·it·ry \-ətrē, -ri\ *n* -ES *often cap* **:** principles or practices ascribed to the Jesuits (as the practice of mental reservation, casuistry, and equivocation) — usu. used disparagingly

jesuits' bark *also* **jesuit bark** *n, usu cap J* [so called fr. the fact that it was brought into Europe from the Jesuit missions in So. America] **:** CINCHONA 3

jesuits' drops *n pl, usu cap J* **:** FRIAR'S BALSAM

jesuits' nut *n, usu cap J* **:** WATER CHESTNUT 1

jesuits' tea *also* **jesuit tea** *n, usu cap J* **1 :** MATÉ **2 :** MEXICAN TEA

jesuit style *n, usu cap J* **:** a baroque style of architecture in ecclesiastical buildings of the 16th and 17th centuries

jesuits' water nut *n, usu cap J* **:** WATER CHESTNUT 1

je·sus bug \'jēzəs- *also* -zəz-\ *n, usu cap J* [after *Jesus* Christ; fr. the allusion to his walking on water (Mt 14:25)] **:** WATER STRIDER 1

[1]**jet** \'jet, *usu* -ed· + V\ *n* -S [ME *get, jet,* fr. MF *jaiet, geet, gest,* fr. L *gagates,* fr. Gk *gagatēs,* fr. *Gagas,* river and ancient town in the district of Lycia in southern Asia Minor] **1 :** a very compact velvet-black mineral of the nature of coal that is often used for jewelry **2 :** JET BLACK

[2]**jet** \"\ *adj* [ME *get,* fr. *get, jet,* n.] **1 :** made of jet **2 :** of the color jet

[3]**jet** \"\ *vi* **jetted; jetted; jetting; jets** [ME *jetten,* perh. fr. MF *jeter* to throw, but influenced in meaning by L *jactare* to throw, boast] **1** *obs* **:** to walk with a haughty or pompous air **:** STRUT, SWAGGER ⟨how he ~s under his advanced plumes —Shak.⟩ ⟨when the stage of the world was hung with black they *jetted* up and down like proud tragedians —Thomas Dekker⟩ **2 a** *archaic* **:** to walk along slowly **:** STROLL **b** *obs* **:** to walk in a sprightly manner **:** CAPER, TRIP **3 :** to move about very quickly **:** DART ⟨hoped to see . . . the wingless squirrel ~ from tree to tree —James Montgomery⟩

[4]**jet** \"\ *n* -S *archaic* **:** an artificial way of walking **:** HITCH, SWAGGER ⟨the genteel trip and the agreeable ~ as they are now practiced at the court of France —Eustace Budgell⟩

[5]**jet** \"\ *vb* **jetted; jetted; jetting; jets** [MF *jeter,* lit., to throw, fr. L *jactare* to throw, shake, speak out, boast, fr. *jactus,* past part. of *jacere* to throw; akin to Gk *hienai* to send, Toch A *ya-* to make, do, Hitt *ijami* I make, I do] *vi* **1 a** *obs* **:** INTRUDE, ENCROACH ⟨insulting tyranny begins to ~ upon the innocent and aweless throne —Shak.⟩ **b :** to project or jut prominently ⟨the rock *jetted* out over the deep canyon⟩ **2 :** to spout forth **:** emit a jet **:** GUSH, SPURT ⟨molten material from the bowels of earth ~s up between sedimented water-laid rocks —Russell Lord⟩ ⟨flame and smoke *jetted* from the sides of the five warships —Kenneth Roberts⟩ **~** *vt* **1 :** to make projections on (as a building) **:** cause to project ⟨the second stories of the houses were *jetted,* shadowing the street from the sun⟩ **2** *now dial Eng* **:** to throw (as a ball) with a jerk **3 :** to emit in a stream **:** blow out **:** SPOUT ⟨while I waited . . . the other gun *jetted* smoke —Kenneth Roberts⟩ ⟨*jetted* a powerful stream of water at the burning building⟩ **4 a :** to place (as a pile or caisson) in the ground by means of a jet of water acting at the lower end **b** (1) **:** to bore (as a well) by means of a high-pressure jet of air or water (2) **:** to flush out the drillings from (a well) by means of a jet of water **5 :** to apply an insecticide to (an animal) in small jets under pressure

[6]**jet** \"\ *n* -S [MF, fr. *jeter*] **1 a** (1) **:** a forceful rush of liquid, gas, or vapor through a narrow or restricted opening in spurts or in a continuous flow ⟨trained the powerful ~ of water on the fire⟩ ⟨saw a practical use for these burning ~s of gas escaping from the earth's fissures —Gardiner Symonds⟩ (2) **:** a usu. high-speed stream of fluid that is discharged from a nozzle or orifice in a body and that produces reaction forces tending to propel the body in the direction opposite to that of the discharge — see JET PROPULSION **b :** a nozzle for a jet of gas, water, or other fluid ⟨a garden fountain with more than 200 ~s —F.J.Taylor⟩ **c :** something issuing in or as if in a jet ⟨sometimes the whole story is a ~ of irony —H.M.Reynolds⟩ ⟨talk poured from her in a brilliant ~ —*Time*⟩ **2** *dial Eng* **:** a large ladle **3 :** a projection at the bottom of a piece of foundry type as it comes from the mold that is planed off in finishing — called also *tail, tang* **4 a :** JET AIRPLANE **b :** JET ENGINE

[7]**jet** \"\ *vi* **jetted; jetted; jetting; jets :** to travel by jet airplane ⟨*jetted* to London to see the show —*Newsweek*⟩

[8]**jet** \"\ *n* -S [prob. alter. of *gist*] **:** the main point **:** GIST ⟨but . . . I don't see the ~ of your scheme —R.B.Sheridan⟩

jet airplane *also* **jet plane** *n* **:** an airplane powered by a jet engine that utilizes the surrounding air in the combustion of fuel or by a rocket-type jet engine that carries its fuel and all the oxygen needed for combustion

jetbead \'=,=\ *n* **:** a shrub (*Rhodotypos scandens*) that has black shining fruit and is used as an ornamental

jet black *n* **:** a very dark black

jet coal *n* **:** CANNEL COAL

je·té \zhə'tā\ *n* -S [F, fr. past part. of *jeter* to throw, hurl — more at JET] **:** a sharp leap in ballet with an outward thrust of the working leg — see GRAND JETÉ, TOUR JETÉ

jeté en tour·nant \-,äⁿ,tu̇r'näⁿ\ *n* [F, lit., jeté while turning] **:** TOUR JETÉ

jet engine *also* **jet motor** *n* **:** an engine that produces motion

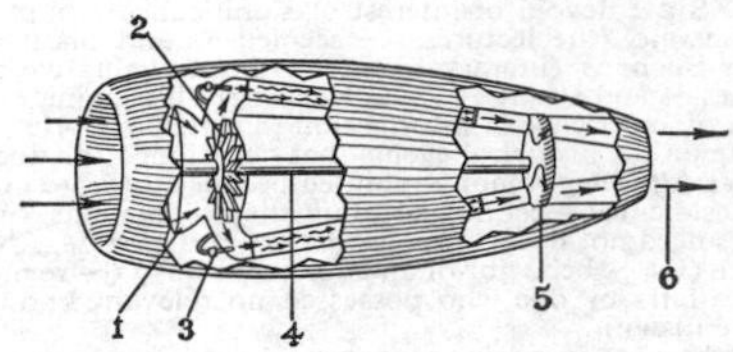

jet engine (simplified cutaway): *1* air intake, *2* impeller or compressor, *3* fuel injection, *4* drive shaft, *5* turbine, *6* exhaust

as a result of the rearward discharge of a jet of fluid; *specif* **:** an airplane engine having one or more exhaust nozzles for discharging rearward a continuous jet or intermittent jets usu. of heated air and exhaust gases to produce forward propulsion — see ROCKET 4

jeth \'jet\ *n* -S *usu cap* [Hindi *Jēṭh,* fr. Skt *Jyaiṣṭha*] **:** a month of the Hindu year — see MONTH table

Jet Liner \'=¦=\ *trademark* — used for a jet-propelled airliner

jet·ness *n* -ES [[2]*jet* + *-ness*] **:** the quality or state of being the color jet black

jeton \'jetᵊn, zhə'tōⁿ\ *or* **jet·ton** \'jetᵊn\ *n, pl* **jetons** *or* **jettons** \-ᵊnz, -tōⁿ(z)\ [F *jeton,* fr. MF, fr. *jeter* to throw, cast up (accounts), calculate — more at JET] **:** [1]COUNTER 1a

jet-pile \'=,=\ *n* **:** a pile placed in position by means of a jet of water under high pressure acting at the toe of the pile to form a space for settling of the pile

jetport \'=,=\ *n* **:** an airport designed esp. for jet planes

jet power *n* **:** power derived from jet engines

jet-propelled \ˌ==¦=\ *adj* **1 :** propelled by one or more jet engines ⟨*jet-propelled* bomb⟩ ⟨*jet-propelled* airplane⟩ **2 :** suggestive of the speed and force of a jet airplane **:** HIGH-POWERED ⟨a good and successful novelist producing his works at *jet-propelled* speed —Antonia White⟩ ⟨she possesses enthusiasm and restless energy, her songs are *jet-propelled* —*Punch*⟩

jet propulsion *n* **:** propulsion of a body by means of a jet of fluid (as in the motion given to an inflated toy balloon when the compressed air is allowed to escape through the neck or the motion given to a rocket by the rearward discharge of a high-speed stream of hot gases produced by the rocket fuel); *specif* **:** propulsion of an airplane by one or more jet engines

jet pump *n* **:** a pump in which a small jet of steam, air, water, or other fluid in rapid motion lifts or otherwise moves by its impulse a large quantity of the fluid with which it mingles

jets *pl of* JET, *pres 3d sing of* JET

jet·sam \'jetsəm\ *n* -S [alter. of [1]*jettison*] **1** *archaic* **:** JETTISON **2 :** the part of a ship, its equipment, or cargo that is cast overboard by the master to lighten the load in time of distress and that sinks or is grounded — distinguished esp. in law from *flotsam* and *lagan* **3 :** FLOTSAM 2

jet·son \'jetsən\ *or* **jet·som** \-səm\ *archaic var of* JETTISON

jet stream *n* **:** a long narrow meandering current of high-speed winds near the tropopause blowing from a generally westerly direction and often exceeding a speed of 250 miles per hour

jet·tage \'jed·ij\ *n* -S [[1]*jetty* + *-age*] **:** dues levied on a ship for the use of a jetty or pier

jet·teau \(,)je¦tō\ *n* -S [modif. of F *jet d'eau*] **:** a jet of water

[1]**jet·ted** \'jed·əd\ *adj* [[1]*jet* + *-ed*] **:** having ornaments of jet

[2]**jetted** \"\ *adj* [fr. past part. of [5]*jet*] *Brit* **:** PIPED, BOUND — used esp. of pockets

[1]**jet·ter** \'jed·ə(r)\ *n* -S [[1]*jet* + *-er*] **:** one that digs jet

[2]**jetter** \"\ *n* -S [[5]*jet* + *-er*] **:** one (as a geyser) that sends out a jet

jet thrust *n* **:** THRUST 3c(2)

jetting *pres part of* JET

[1]**jet·ti·son** \'jed·|əsən, 'jet|, |-əzən\ *n* -S [ME *jetteson,* fr. AF *getteson,* fr. OF *getaison, getaisson* action of throwing, fr. L *jactation-, jactatio* — more at JACTATION] **1** *marine insurance* **:** a voluntary sacrifice of cargo of a ship necessitated by immediately impending danger threatening the general interest —

compare GENERAL AVERAGE **2** : a casting overboard or away (as of an object, a person, an idea) : ABANDONMENT ⟨illustrates more forcibly than any election that has yet taken place the ~ of convictions, of honor, of patriotism —*Saturday Rev.*⟩

2jettison \"\ *vt* -ED/-ING/-S **1** *maritime law* : to make flotsam and jetsam of ⟨deck loads were so heavy that many carriers had to ~ cargo when they got into a stiff blow —D.H.Clark⟩ **2** : to cast off as an encumbrance : get rid of : throw away : ABANDON, DISCARD ⟨if a diver does not know how to control his equipment or to ~ it in an emergency . . . he courts disaster —Byron Porterfield⟩ ⟨the obsolete has been calmly ~*ed*; the translation into the contemporary is complete —J.L.Lowes⟩ ⟨an army too soft to ~ its weaklings is on the way out —*Infantry Jour.*⟩ **3** : to drop (as auxiliary equipment, bombs, cargo, or fuel) from an airplane in flight (as for lightening the load or providing greater safety) ⟨external long-range fuel tanks which can be ~*ed* in combat —Peter Masefield⟩

jet·ti·son·able \-nəbəl\ *adj* : designed for being jettisoned or capable of being easily jettisoned from an airplane ⟨~ fuel tanks⟩

jet·to \ˈje,tō\ *n* -S [It *getto*, fr. *gettare* to throw, fr. L *jactare* — more at JET] : JETTEAU

jetton *var of* JETON

jet·tru \ˈje·(,)trü\ *n* -S *usu cap* : a union of seven Turkish peoples of central Asia formed at the end of the 17th or beginning of the 18th century under one khan

1jet·ty \ˈjed·ē, -etī, ǀi\ *n* -ES [ME *getee, jette*, fr. MF *jetee* action of throwing or thrusting, jetty, fr. fem. of *jeté*, past part. of *jeter* to throw — more at JET] **1 a** : a structure (as a pier or mole of wood or stone) extended into a sea, lake, or river to influence the current or tide or to protect a harbor; *also* : a protecting frame of a pier **b** : a landing wharf or pier often of framed woodwork **2** : a part of a building that projects beyond the rest ⟨one of the most common features of New England colonial architecture was the overhanging second story or ~ as it was called —H.S.Morrison⟩ **3** : a protecting outwork : BASTION, BULWARK **4** *dial Eng* : a narrow passage or raised footpath **syn** see WHARF

2jetty \"\ *vi* -ED/-ING/-ES **1** : PROJECT, JUT — used esp. of a part of a building **2** : to extend like a jetty for a distance into a body of water ⟨the great Municipal Pier which *jetties* out nearly a mile into the lake —*Time*⟩

3jetty \"\ *adj* [**1***jet* + *-y*] : having the color jet black ⟨the sky was of a ~ black, and the stars were brilliantly visible —E.A. Poe⟩ ⟨a wine-red lined cowl which she wore demurely over her ~ hair —Herman Wouk⟩

jetware \ˈ=,=\ *n* : pottery usu. of red clay covered with a jet-black glaze

jeu \ˈzhœ, ǀər(·), ǀə̄, *F* ǀœ\ *n, pl* **jeux** \ǀə(z), ǀərz, ǀər(·), ǀə̄(z), ǀœ\ [F, fr. L *jocus* joke, jest, game — more at JOKE] : GAME

jeu d'es·prit \,=də'sprē\ *n, pl* **jeux d'esprit** [F, lit., play of the mind] : a play or piece of writing displaying cleverness or wit ⟨senseless to ignore as a mistaken *jeu d'esprit* the labor that went into those parodies —Hugh Kenner⟩

jeune fille \,zhə(r)nˈfē, -ə̄n-, *or as F*\ *n, pl* **jeunes filles** \"\ [F] : a young girl

jeune pre·mier \-prəmˈyā\ *n, pl* **jeunes premiers** \-ā(z)\ [F] : the juvenile lead in a play ⟨bowed low . . . as if he were indeed some real *jeune premier* —H.E.Bates⟩

jeu·nesse do·rée \,zhə(r)ˌnesdəˈrā, zhə̄ˈ-, -(,)dō'-, -,dō'-, *or as F*\ *n* [F, gilded youth] : young people of wealth and fashion ⟨one might have taken him for the type of the *jeunesse dorée* of Virginia surrounded with tutors, servants, horses, and dogs —Van Wyck Brooks⟩ ⟨artists are beginning to contest the occupation of that territory with the *jeunesse dorée* —Stuart Preston⟩

1jew \ˈjü\ *n* -S [ME *Gyu, Jewe, Jew*, fr. OF *gyu, jeu, jué, juef*, fr. L *Judaeus*, adj. & n., fr. Gk *Ioudaios*, fr. Heb *Yĕhūdhī*, fr. *Yĕhūdhāh* Judah, Jewish kingdom in southern Palestine, after *Yĕhūdhāh* Judah, 4th son of Jacob and ancestor of the Judahites] **1** *usu cap* **a** : JUDAHITE **b** : ISRAELITE 1 **2** *cap* : a member of the nation existing in Palestine from the 6th century B.C. to the 1st century A.D. within which the elements of Judaism largely developed **3** *cap* : a person belonging to the worldwide group constituting a continuation through descent or conversion of the ancient Jewish people and characterized by a sense of community; *esp* : one whose religion is Judaism — see ASHKENAZI, SEPHARDI **4** *usu cap* : a person believed to drive a hard bargain — usu. taken to be offensive

2jew \"\ *adj, usu cap* : JEWISH — usu. taken to be offensive

3jew \"\ *vt* -ED/-ING/-S *sometimes cap* : to cheat by sharp business practice — usu. taken to be offensive

jewbird \ˈ=,=\ *n* [*jew* + *bird*; fr. its conspicuous beak] : ANI

jewbush \ˈ=,=\ *n* [*jew* + *bush*; prob. fr. the shape of the involucres] : either of two tropical American low shrubs of the genus *Pedilanthus* (*P. tithymaloides* and *P. padifolius*) possessing powerful emetic and drastic properties

jew crow *n* [prob. so called fr. its prominent curved beak] *dial Eng* : CHOUGH

jew down *vt, sometimes cap J* : to induce (a seller) by haggling to lower his price : get (a price or a sum) reduced by haggling — usu. taken to be offensive

1jew·el \ˈjüǀəl, ˈjü| *also* |l, *chiefly Brit* |(,)il\ *n* -S *often attrib* [ME *juel, jowel, jewel*, fr. OF *juel, joel, joiel*, dim. of *ju, jo, jeu* game, play — more at JEOPARDY] **1** *archaic* : an article with intrinsic value usu. used for adornment ⟨here, wear this ~ for me; 'tis my picture —Shak.⟩ **2 a** : a precious stone; *esp* : a stone cut and polished for use as an ornament ⟨they shall fetch thee ~*s* from the deep —Shak.⟩ **b** (1) : one that is highly esteemed or prized ⟨had our prince, ~ of children, seen this hour —Shak.⟩ (2) : something that resembles a jewel ⟨this lake — a ~ nestling amid mountains —H.J.Laski⟩ ⟨presenting the ~ of truth in a pleasing setting —R.A.Hall b.1911⟩ **3 a** : an ornament of precious metal usu. gold or silver, often set with stones or finished with enamel work and now usu. worn as an accessory of dress or as the badge of an order **b** : an article of costume jewelry **4 a** : a bearing for a pivot in a watch or a delicate instrument (as a compass) made of a crystal or a precious stone (as a ruby or sapphire) or of glass **b** : a lining of brass or other soft metal for a bearing (as on a railroad car) **5** : an ornamental boss of colored glass

2jewel \"\ *vt* **jeweled** *or* **jewelled**; **jeweled** *or* **jewelled**; **jeweling** *or* **jewelling**; **jewels 1 a** : to adorn with jewels ⟨you are as well ~*ed* as any of them —Ben Jonson⟩ ⟨the kings go by with ~*ed* crowns —John Masefield⟩ **b** : to equip with jewels ⟨company sells more ~*ed* watches than any other in the U.S. —*Time*⟩ ⟨building precision ~*ed* engines by mass-production methods —*Newsweek*⟩ **c** : to trim with jeweling ⟨lacy white wool . . . heavily ~*ed* with iridescent sequins —*Women's Wear Daily*⟩ **2** : to give beauty or perfection to as if by adorning with jewels ⟨the still swamp water was dark . . . but in open patches it was ~*ed* with reflected stars —Myrtle R. White⟩ ⟨~*ing* all this outer zone of the marsh are the little birds —D.C.Peattie⟩ ⟨a dazzling blaze of ~*ed* words and flashing images —*Times Lit. Supp.*⟩

jewel beetle *n* : any of various usu. brightly colored beetles of the family Buprestidae

jewel block *n* : a block at the extremity of a yard through which the halyard of a studding sail is rove

jewel box *or* **jewel case** *n* **1** : a small chest designed to hold jewelry **2** : something small and exquisite ⟨his house . . . a *jewel box*, quite the most desirable upon the seaside drive —D.C.Peattie⟩

jewel box 1

jewel cloth *n* : a usu. gauzy fabric with sparkling metallic bits sprinkled over its surface that is used chiefly for stage costumes and window displays

jew·el·er *or* **jew·el·ler** \-lə(r)\ *n* -S [ME *jueler, joweler, jeweler*, fr. *juel* jewel + *-er* — more at JEWEL] **1 a** : an artist who designs and makes jewelry — compare GOLDSMITH **b** : one who repairs jewelry **2** : one who deals in precious and costume jewelry, precious stones, watches, and usu. silverware, china, and giftwares **3** : one who specializes in the construction and repair of highly sensitive scientific instruments

jewelers' block insurance *n* : all-risk insurance covering jewelers' stocks including property of others in the custody of the insured

jewelers' putty *n* : PUTTY POWDER

jewelers' rouge *n* : rouge that is of fine quality and fine particle size

jewel fish *n* : a small scarlet and olive African cichlid fish (*Hemichromis bimaculatus*) irregularly speckled with emerald green or sapphire that is sometimes kept in a tropical aquarium

jeweling *or* **jewelling** *n* -S **1** : the act or art of working in or of applying jewels **2** : the ornamentation of pottery with bosses of glass or glaze **3** : an arrangement of real or imitation jewels used as a trimming on a dress

jew·el·lery \-lrī\ *chiefly Brit var of* JEWELRY

jew·el·ry \-lrē,-lri\ *n* -ES [ME *juelrie, jowelrie*, fr. *juel, jowel* jewel + *-rie* -ry] **1** : ornamental pieces (as rings, necklaces, bracelets) made of materials that may or may not be precious (gold, silver, glass, plastic) often set with genuine or imitation gems and worn for personal adornment — see COSTUME JEWELRY **2** : something like jewelry (as in beautifying or adorning) ⟨I wished to see the snow and ice, the divine ~ of winter —John Muir †1914⟩

jewels *pl of* JEWEL, *pres 3d sing of* JEWEL

jewelweed \ˈ=(=),=\ *n* : a plant of the genus *Impatiens* : BALSAM 4: as **a** : a somewhat glaucous annual herb (*I. capensis*) of No. America that occurs from Newfoundland to Alaska and south to Florida chiefly on wet rather acid soil and has extremely variable but typically crimson-spotted orange open flowers and sometimes minute cleistogamous flowers — called also *celandine* **b** : a glaucous annual herb (*I. pallida*) that occurs on wet and usu. calcareous soil in much of eastern and central No. America and has canary yellow to creamy white flowers sometimes spotted with brownish red — called also *snapweed, touch-me-not*

jewelweed family *n* : BALSAMINACEAE

jew·ely *or* **jew·el·ly** *pronunc at* JEWEL + ē *or* i\ *adj* **1** : having or wearing jewels **2** : resembling a jewel : having the brilliance and sparkle of a jewel ⟨the ~ star of life had descended too far —Thomas De Quincy⟩

jew·ess \ˈjüəs\ *n* -ES *usu cap* [ME *Jewesse*, fr. *Gyu, Jewe, Jew* Jew + *-esse* -ess — more at JEW] : a female Jew

jewfish \ˈ=,=\ *n* **1** : any of various large groupers usu. dusky green or blackish, thickheaded, and rough-scaled, with a voracious but sluggish disposition: as **a** : GIANT BASS **b** : SPOTTED JEWFISH **c** : BLACK JEWFISH **2** : any of various other large percoid fishes: as **a** : a western Australian lutjanid (*Glaucosoma hebraicum*) **b** : MULLOWAY

jewing *pres part of* JEW

1jew·ish \ˈjüish, -üēsh\ *adj, usu cap* : of, relating to, or characteristic of a Jew — **jew·ish·ly** *adv, usu cap*

2jewish \"\ *n* -ES *cap* : YIDDISH

jewish calendar *n, usu cap J* : a lunisolar calendar in use among Jewish peoples which is reckoned from the year 3761 B.C., which received its present form from Hillel II about A.D.360, and in which 19 years constitute a metonic cycle — see MONTH table, YEAR table

jew·ish·ness *n* -ES *usu cap* : the quality or state of being Jewish

jewish science *n, cap J&S* : a healing cult adapted from Christian Science to persons with a Jewish background

jew·ism \ˈjü,izəm\ *n* -S *usu cap* **1** : JUDAISM **2** : something characteristic of Jews

jew lizard *n, usu cap J* : an Australian agamid lizard (*Amphibolurus barbatus*)

jew monkey *n, usu cap J* [prob. so called fr. its beard] : any of several sakis and macaques

jew nail *n* : CORRUGATED FASTENER

jew plum *n, usu cap J* : OTAHEITE APPLE

jew·ry \ˈjürē, ˈjürē, -ri\ *n* -ES *usu cap* [ME *Gywerie, Jewerie, Jewrie*, fr. OF *juierie, juiverie*, fr. *gyu, jeu, jué, juif* Jew + *-erie* -ery — more at JEW] **1** : a quarter or district of a city or town inhabited by Jews : GHETTO **2** *archaic* : the land of Judea ⟨let me have a child . . . to whom Herod of *Jewry* may do homage —Shak.⟩ **3 a** : the part of the population of a country that adheres to Judaism ⟨the titular head of Scotch *Jewry* was both a classical scholar and a Hebraist —Maurice Samuel⟩ **b** : the world Jewish community ⟨the recognition of Israel as the focus of Jewish civilization, the cultural center of the world *Jewry* —*Reconstructionist*⟩

jews *pl of* JEW, *pres 3d sing of* JEW

jew's-ear \ˈ=,=\ *n, pl* **jew's-ears** *usu cap J* [intended as trans. of NL *auricula Judae*, lit., ear of Judas, after *Judas* Iscariot, apostle that betrayed Jesus; fr. its resemblance to a human ear and its frequent growth on elder trees, on one of which Judas reputedly hanged himself] : a widely distributed edible fungus (*Auricularia auricula-judae*) growing on decaying wood

jew's harp \ˈjüz *also* ÷ ˈjüs+,-\ *or* **jews' harp** *n, usu cap J* **1** : a small lyre-shaped instrument placed between the teeth and played by twanging an elastic metal tongue whose tone is modified by changing the size and shape of the mouth cavity **2** *also* **jews-harp-plant** \ˈ=,=,=\ : NODDING TRILLIUM **3** : the ring of an anchor

Jew's harp 1

jews' houses *n pl, usu cap J* : the remains of ancient tin-smelting furnaces and miners' houses in Cornwall and Devon

jew's mallow *n, usu cap J* **1** : a stout herb (*Corchorus olitorius*) cultivated in Syria and Egypt as a potherb and in India for its jute fiber **2** : JUTE 1

jew's-stone \ˈ=,=\ *n, pl* **jew's-stones** *usu cap J* [trans. of ML *lapis Judaicus*] **1** : a large fossil clavate spine of a sea urchin **2** : MARCASITE 2

jews'-thorn \ˈ=,=\ *n, usu cap J* [so called fr. the belief that it was used to crown Christ] : CHRIST'S-THORN

jew's trump *n, usu cap J* : JEW'S HARP 1

jew-tongo \ˈ=ˈtäŋ(,)gō\ *n, usu cap J&T* [prob. fr. Jew-Tongo, fr. *jew* (fr. E *Jew*) + *-tongo* (fr. E *tongue*); perh. fr. the existence among its original speakers of former slaves who had been owned by Portuguese Jews] : an English-based creole language of Surinam

jewy \ˈjüē, -üi\ *adj* -ER/-EST *usu cap* : JEWISH — usu. used disparagingly

je·zail \jəˈzī(ə)l, -zā(-\ *n* -S [Per *jazā'il*] : a long heavy Afghan rifle

jez·e·bel \ˈjezə,bel *also* -,bəl\ *n* -S *often cap* [fr. *Jezebel*, 9th cent. B.C. Phoenician princess and wife of Ahab, king of Israel, known for her wicked conduct (1 Kings 16:31 ff)] : an impudent, shameless, or abandoned woman ⟨painted, screaming ~*s* hauled away by the raiding constables —Albert Parry⟩ — **jez·e·bel·ish** \-ish,-ēsh\ *adj, often cap*

jez·ek·ite \ˈjez(h)ə,kīt\ *n* -S [F *ježekite*, fr. Bohuslav *Ježek* 20th cent. Czech mineralogist + F *-ite*] : MORINITE

JG *abbr or n* -S *often not cap* : junior grade : LIEUTENANT JUNIOR GRADE

jhang·ar \ˈjaŋə(r)\ *adj, usu cap* [*Jhang*, district in the Punjab where artifacts were found + E *-ar*] : of or relating to a culture in the Indus valley of about 2000 B.C. characterized by a crude handmade gray or black pottery having incised geometric ornamentation

jhan·si \ˈjän(t)sē\ *adj, usu cap* [fr. *Jhansi*, India] : of or from the city of Jhansi, India : of the kind or style prevalent in Jhansi

jha·ral \ˈjärəl\ *n* -S [Nepali *jhāral*] : TAHR

jheel *or* **jhil** \ˈjē(ə)l\ *n* -S [Hindi *jhīl*] *India* : a pool, marsh, or lake esp. remaining from inundation

JHS *var of* IHS

jhu·kar \ˈjükər, -,kär\ *adj, usu cap* [fr. *Jhukar*, Sind, Pakistan, where artifacts were found] : of or relating to a culture of the Indus valley about 2500 B.C. and later that is known from settlements built upon those of Harappa and is characterized by buildings inferior to Harappa and round crudely decorated seals or seal amulets of pottery

JHVH *or* **JHWH** *var of* YHWH

1jib \ˈjib\ *n* -S [origin unknown] **1** : a triangular sail set upon a stay or its own luff and extending from the head of the foremast or fore-topmast to the bowsprit or the jibboom — see SAIL illustration **2** *dial Eng* : the lower lip or jaw

2jib \"\ *vb* **jibbed; jibbed; jibbing; jibs** *vt* : to cause to swing (as a sail or yard) from one side of a sailing vessel to another (as in tacking) ~ *vi* **1** : to shift across or swing round from one side of a vessel to the other — used of a ship's sail, yard, or boom **2** : to shift or swing in a way resembling jibbing ⟨the value of dollars, francs, and pounds sterling *jibbing* this way and that —*Time*⟩ ⟨black umbrellas milled and *jibbed* everywhere —William Sansom⟩

3jib \"\ *n* -S [prob. by shortening & alter. fr. *gibbet*] : the projecting arm of a crane; *also* : a derrick boom

4jib \"\ *also* **gib** \"\ *vi* **jibbed** *also* **gibbed**; **jibbed** *also* **gibbed**; **jibbing** *also* **gibbing**; **jibs** *also* **gibs** [prob. fr. **2***jib*] **1** : to move restively backward or sidewise : refuse to go; *also* : to stop short or back out : SHY — used of an animal in harness **2 a** : to show hesitation or a tendency to refuse to proceed further or act in a particular way : BALK ⟨he *jibbed* on singing because the women were there —Joseph Furphy⟩ ⟨never *jibbed* at the stiffest climb —Roy Saunders⟩ **b** : to show objection : balk in opposition ⟨it was only the middle classes at which he *jibbed* for he was genuinely devoted to his servants —Eric Keown⟩ ⟨*jibbed* at all grief which could not be brushed aside —Elizabeth Taylor⟩ ⟨we are swallowing monsters that we should have *jibbed* at if they had been offered us by an imaginative and flamboyant traveler —Virginia Woolf⟩ **syn** see DEMUR

5jib \"\ *n* -S : JIBBER

1jibaro *usu cap, var of* JIVARO

2ji·ba·ro *or* **gi·ba·ro** \ˈhēbə,rō\ *n* -S [AmerSp *jíbaro, gíbaro*, prob. fr. *jíbaro* Jivaro] : a Puerto Rican small farmer, rural worker, or laborer esp. of mountainous regions

jib·ba *or* **djib·bah** *also* **jib·bah** \ˈjibə\ *n* -S [Egyptian Ar *jibbah*, var. of Ar *jubbah*] : a long loose cloth outer garment usu. with long sleeves worn esp. by Muslims

1jibber *var of* GIBBER

2jib·ber \ˈjibə(r)\ *n* -S [**4***jib* + *-er*] : one that jibs; *esp* : a balky horse

jib·bings \ˈjibənz, -biŋz\ *n pl* [fr. gerund of Sc *jib* to milk a cow dry (of unknown origin) + *-s*] *Scot* : strippings from a cow

jib·boom \(ˈ)ji(b)ˈbüm\ *n* [**1***jib* + *boom*] : a spar which serves as an extension of the bowsprit and is sometimes itself extended by a flying jibboom — see SHIP illustration

jib crane *n* [**3***jib*] : a crane having a jib

jib door \ˈjib-\ *n* [*jib* of unknown origin] : a door made flush with a wall without dressings or moldings and often disguised by continuing the finishings or decorations of the wall across its surface

1jibe *or* **gybe** \ˈjīb\ *vb* -ED/-ING/-S [perh. modif. (influenced by **1***jib*) of D *gijben, gijpen*] *vi* **1** *of a fore-and-aft sail or its boom* : to shift suddenly and with force from one side to the other when a ship is steered off the wind until the sail fills on the opposite side **2** : to change the course of a vessel so that the sail jibes — compare TACK 1a ~ *vt* : to cause to jibe

2jibe *or* **gybe** \"\ *n* -S : the swing of a sail or its boom in jibing or the turn of a sailboat so that its sail jibes

3jibe \"\ *var of* GIBE

4jibe *also* **gibe** \"\ *vi* -ED/-ING/-S [origin unknown] : to be in accord ⟨his account of the accident ~*s* pretty well with other accounts⟩ ⟨their inferior status did not ~ with democratic ideals —E.N.Palmer⟩ **syn** see AGREE

jibe-o \ˈjī(,)bō, jīˈbō\ *interj* [**1***jibe* + *-o*] — used by the man at the tiller or wheel of a sailboat in warning that the boat is about to jibe

jib guy *n* [**1***jib*] : one of two or more lateral stays running to the head of the jibboom — see SHIP illustration

jibhead \ˈ=,=\ *n* [**1***jib* + *head*] : a small iron bar for stretching the head of a jib when the point of the sail has been cut off

jib-headed \ˈ=ˈ==\ *adj* [**1***jib*] *of a sail* : running up to a point at the head like a jib : TRIANGULAR — compare GAFF-HEADED

jib-header \ˈ=ˈ==\ *n* : a jib-headed topsail

ji·bi \ˈjē(,)bē\ *n* -S [origin unknown] : a small chiefly yellowish green extinct bird (*Hemignathus obscurus ellisianus*) of Oahu

jib iron *n* [**1***jib*] : JIB TRAVELER

jiblet *var of* GIBLET

jib netting *n* [**1***jib*] : a triangular safety netting rigged under a jibboom — see SHIP illustration

ji·boa \jəˈbōə\ *also* **ji·bo·ya** \-ō(y)ə\ *n* -S [Pg *jibóia*, fr. Tupi] : any of several large So. American boas

jib-o-jib \ˈjibə, jib\ *n* -S [**1***jib* + *o* (of) + *jib*] : a small jib set outside of the flying jib

jibs *pl of* JIB, *pres 3d sing of* JIB

jib sheet *n* [**1***jib*] : either of two ropes which lead from the clew of a jib to port and starboard respectively and by which the sail is trimmed

jibstay \ˈ=,=\ *n* [**1***jib* + *stay*] : a stay on which a jib is set

jib topsail *n* [**1***jib*] : a small jib occas. used and set above and outside of all the other jibs

jib traveler *n* [**1***jib*] : an iron ring to which the tack of the jib on some cutters is made fast and which travels on the bowsprit

JIC *abbr* **1** joint industrial council **2** joint intelligence committee

ji·ca·ma \ˈhēkəmə\ *n* -S [MexSp *jícama*, fr. Nahuatl *xicama, xicamatl*] **1** : a tall-climbing Mexican vine (*Exogonium bracteatum*) with showy flowers and a sweet watery root that is sometimes eaten raw or cooked — compare JALAP **2** : YAM BEAN **3** : a small dahlia (*Dahlia coccinea*) with yellow, orange, or scarlet flowers that is sometimes cultivated and is an ancestor of some improved horticultural dahlias

ji·ca·que *or* **xi·ca·que** \hēˈkä(,)kā\ *n, pl* **jicaque** *or* **jicaques** *or* **xicaque** *or* **xicaques** *usu cap* [Sp, fr. Nahuatl *xicaque*, lit., ancient person] **1 a** : an Indian people of northern Honduras **b** : a member of such people **2** : the language of the Jicaque people

ji·ca·que·an \-,keən\ *n* -S *usu cap* : a language family of the Hokan stock in Honduras comprising only the Jicaque language

ji·ca·ra \ˈhēkərə\ *n* -S [MexSp *jícara*, fr. Nahuatl *xicalli*] **1** : CALABASH 2a **2** : a cup or bowl made from the fruit of a calabash tree

ji·ca·ri·lla \,hēkəˈrē(y)ə\ *n, pl* **jicarilla** *or* **jicarillas** *usu cap* [Sp, fr. MexSp, little basket, dim. of *jícara*; fr. the proficiency of the women in basketmaking] **1 a** : an Apache people of the western group ranging through southeastern Colorado, northern New Mexico, and adjacent sections of Kansas, Oklahoma, and Texas **b** : a member of such people **2** : the language of the Jicarilla people

jiff \ˈjif\ *n* -S [by shortening] *slang* : JIFFY

jif·fle \ˈjifəl\ *vi* [origin unknown] *dial Eng* : to move restlessly : FIDGET

jif·fy \ˈjifē, -fi\ *n* -ES [origin unknown] : MOMENT, INSTANT — used chiefly in the phrase *in a jiffy*

1jig \ˈjig\ *n* -S [prob. fr. MF *giguer* to dance, jig, gambol about, frolic, fr. *gigue* fiddle, of Gmc origin; akin to OHG *gīga* fiddle; akin to ON *geiga* to turn aside — more at GIG] **1 a** : any of several lively springy dances in triple rhythm, popular in 16th and 17th century England and Scotland and still commonly danced in Ireland in a way characterized by intricate and dexterous motions of the feet **b** : music to which a jig may be danced **c** : GIGUE 3 **d** : a rapid usu. jerky up-and-down or to-and-fro motion ⟨the ~ of popcorn in a popper⟩ **2** *obs* **a** : a lively usu. jesting or mocking song **b** : a lively or comic act used at the end of a play or as an interlude **3** : TRICK, STRATAGEM, GAME — now used chiefly in the phrase *the jig is up* **4 a** : any of several fishing devices (as a spoon hook) that are jerked up and down or drawn through the water — compare SQUID **b** : a device used to maintain mechanically the correct positional relationship between a piece of work and the tool working on it or between parts of work during their assembly **c** : a device in which crushed ore is concentrated or coal is cleaned in water by a rapid reciprocating vertical motion imparted to the substance either by mechanical means or by a pulsating water column **d** : a machine for dyeing piece goods by passing them at full width through the dye liquor by means of rollers **5** *also* **jigg** \"\ : NEGRO — often taken to be offensive — **in jig time** *adv* : with expeditiousness : RAPIDLY ⟨the tire was whipped off and changed *in jig time* —Dillon Ripley⟩

2jig \"\ *vb* **jigged; jigged; jigging; jigs** [prob. fr. MF *giguer*] *vt* **1** : to dance in the rapid and lively manner of a jig ⟨~ a morris⟩ **2 a** : to give a rapid jerky up-and-down or to-and-fro motion to ⟨*jigged* his feet —Michael McLaverty⟩ ⟨a handful of coins that he rattled by *jigging* his thumb along the table —Saul Bellow⟩ : cause to jig ⟨grabbed a girl and started to ~ her around the yard —C.T.Jackson⟩ **b** : to separate (as ore from gangue or coal from slate) by a rapid up-and-down motion usu. in water **3 :** to catch (a fish) with a jig or by jerking a hook into the body **4 :** to drill (as a well) with a spring pole **5 :** to machine, form, or set in place by means of a jig-controlled tool operation ~ *vi* **1 a :** to dance a jig : execute a lively dance or dance step **b :** to move with a jigging motion or with rapid usu. jerky motions up and down or to and fro ⟨*jigged* furiously up and down to limber his leg muscles —A.J.Liebling⟩ **2 :** to fish with a jig ⟨several men in canoes *jigging* for cod —N.C.McDonald⟩ **3 :** to work with the aid of a jig

³jig \"\ — a communications code word for the letter *j*

jig·a·boo \ˈjigə,bü\ *n* -s [¹*jig* + *-aboo* (as in *bugaboo*)] : NEGRO — often taken to be offensive

jig-a-jig *or* **jig-a-jog** *var of* JIG-JOG

jig·a·ma·ree \ˈjigəmə,rē, ,==ˈ=\ *n* -s [¹*jig* + *-amaree*, of unknown origin] *slang* : something (as a device or contrivance) felt to be too fanciful, difficult, or small in value to designate accurately

jig-back \ˈ=,=\ *adj* [fr. the phrase *jig back*] : having two carriers that alternately ascend and descend — used of an aerial tramway

jig borer *n* [¹*jig*] : a precision machine tool resembling a vertical milling machine, equipped with sensitive adjustments for the table and the position of the cutting tool, and used esp. for locating and drilling or boring holes in jigs

¹jig·ger \ˈjigə(r)\ *n* -s [¹ and ²*jig* + *-er*] **1 :** one that jigs : one that operates a jig: as **a :** one that concentrates ore by jigging — called also *jigman* **b :** one that shakes down the grain into sacks during bagging **c :** the operator of a dyeing jig — called also *jigman, vatman* **2 :** a light tackle usu. consisting of a double and single block and fall : WATCH TACKLE **3 :** ¹JIG 4a **4 a :** a small boat rigged like a yawl **b** *or* **jiggermast** \ˈ==,=\ (1) **:** a small mast stepped in the stern (as in a yawl or ketch) (2) **:** the aftermost mast of a four-masted ship **c :** a sail set on a jiggermast **5 a :** a mechanical contrivance esp. operating with a jerky reciprocating motion: as (1) **:** a machine carrying a revolving mold in which the clay for ceramics is shaped by a profile (2) **:** a machine for slicking or pebbling leather (3) **:** a tool for polishing the upper leather or the edge of a boot sole **b :** something (as a contrivance, device, or gewgaw) too complex, tricky, or trivial to designate accurately : GADGET **6 :** a measure used in mixing drinks and holding usu. one and one half ounces **7 :** JIG 4d **8 :** a cooper's drawknife **9 :** a golf iron with a narrow fairly well lofted face used esp. for approach shots **10 :** a part of a commercial fish trap that impounds the fish **11 :** ¹BRIDGE 3e

jigger 6

²jigger \"\ *vb* **jiggered; jiggered; jiggering** \-g(ə)riŋ\ **jiggers** [freq. of ²*jig*] *vi, of a fish* : to give repeated tugs on a line ~ *vt* **1 :** to jerk up and down : give a series of tugs on **2 :** to alter or rearrange sometimes by manipulating ⟨~*ed* the records to cover up his theft⟩ **3** [¹*jigger*] : to shape with a jigger in ceramics

³jigger \"\ *n* -s [of African origin; akin to Wolof *jiga* insect, Yoruba *ji²ga³* jigger] : CHIGGER

jig·gered \ˈjigə(r)d\ *adj* [origin unknown] : DAMNED — used in mild oaths usu. in the phrase *I'll be jiggered*

jigger flea *n* [³*jigger*] : CHIGOE

jiggering *n* -s [fr. gerund of ²*jigger*] : the process of forming ceramic ware by means of a jigger

jigger·man \ˈjigə(r)mən, -,man\ *n, pl* **jiggermen 1 :** one who forms pottery on a jigger **2 :** one who resurfaces and sharpens large grindstones on a stone-dressing lathe

jigger pump *n* [¹*jigger*] : a pump to force beer into vats

jig·gers \ˈjigə(r)z\ *interj* [origin unknown] — used as a warning esp. that police are coming

jigger saw *n* [by alter.] : JIGSAW

jigger up *vt, slang* : to throw into confusion ⟨won't have the camp arrangements *jiggered up* any more than they are —C.S. Forester⟩ : foul up ⟨the machinery was all *jiggered up*⟩

jiggery-pokery \ˈjigərē¦pōkərē\ *n* -ES [alter. of *joukery-pawkery*] **1** *chiefly Brit* : HUMBUG, NONSENSE **2 :** underhanded dealings, conniving, or manipulations : MONKEY BUSINESS, SKULDUGGERY

jig·get \ˈjigət\ *vi* **jiggeted** *or* **jiggetted; jiggeted** *or* **jiggetted; jiggeting** *or* **jiggetting; jiggets** [²*jig* + *-et* (as in *fidget*)] : to move in a jigging or jerky way : JIG

jig·gety \-gəd·ē\ *adj, sometimes* -ER/-EST : JERKY, UNSTEADY

jigging *pres part of* JIG

jig·gish \ˈjigish, -gēsh\ *adj* : resembling or suitable for a jig or lively movement

¹jig·gle \ˈjigəl\ *vb* **jiggled; jiggled; jiggling** \-g(ə)liŋ\ **jiggles** [freq. of ²*jig*] *vi* : to move with quick little continuous jerks or oscillating motions back and forth or up and down ⟨*jiggling* like a doll on a coiled spring —Raymond Chandler⟩ ~ *vt* : to cause to jiggle ⟨*jiggled* the cup to mix the milk and the coffee —Wirt Williams⟩

²jiggle \"\ *n* -s **1 :** the motion of one that jiggles **2 :** a brief contrived fluctuation in the price of a stock more limited than a pool operation

jig·gly \ˈjig(ə)lē, -li\ *adj, often* -ER/-EST : tending to jiggle : UNSTEADY, JIGGLING ⟨the short leg of a ~ table —*New Yorker*⟩ : marked by a jiggling motion ⟨a ~ ride in a bus⟩

jig grinder *n* [²*jig*] : a precision grinding machine with fine adjustments for work requiring great accuracy (as in the fabrication of jigs and dies)

jiggumbob *n* -s [²*jig* + *-umbob* (of unknown origin)] *obs* : a contrivance or trifle felt to be too fanciful, difficult, or trivial to designate accurately

jig·gy \ˈjigē, -gi\ *adj, often* -ER/-EST : suggesting or having the effect of a jig

¹jig-jog \ˈjig,jäg\ *also* **jig-jig** \-,jig\ *or* **jig-a-jog** \ˈjigə,jäg\ *or* **jig-a-jig** \ˈ==,=\ *vi* [¹*jig* + *jog*] : to move with jigs or jogs : bounce jerkily up and down in proceeding : jolt repeatedly up and down

²jig-jog *also* **jig-jig** *or* **jig-a-jog** *or* **jig-a-jig** \"\ *n* : the movement of something that jig-jogs

³jig-jog *also* **jig-jig** *or* **jig-a-jog** *or* **jig-a-jig** \"\ *adv* : in the manner of one that jig-jogs ⟨trotted *jig-jog* down the road⟩

jig-joggy \ˈjig,jägē\ *adj* : jolting or bouncing jerkily up and down : JOGGING

jig·man \ˈjigmən\ *n, pl* **jigmen** [¹*jig* + *man*] : JIGGER 1a, 1c

jigs *pl of* JIG, *pres 3d sing of* JIG

¹jigsaw \ˈ=,=\ *n* [¹*jig* + *saw*] **1 a :** a machine saw with a narrow vertically reciprocating blade for cutting curved and irregular lines or ornamental patterns in openwork **b :** SCROLL SAW **2 :** JIGSAW PUZZLE ⟨broken up like a ~ loose in its box —Wright Morris⟩ ⟨as the pieces of the ~ are fitted together —*Economist*⟩

²jigsaw \"\ *vt* **1 :** to cut or form by or as if by a jigsaw ⟨coat and skirt ~*ed* out of her deceased father's Sunday suit —Francis & Katharine Drake⟩ **2 :** to arrange or place in an intricate or interlocking way in the manner of the parts of a jigsaw puzzle ⟨giant industrial plants ~*ed* together —Cameron Hawley⟩ ⟨the place was full of planes, tied onto every foot of space —Frank Harvey⟩

jigsaw 1a

³jigsaw \"\ *adj* **1 :** made up of pieces cut by a jigsaw **2 a :** consisting of intricate scrollwork ⟨~ detail around the eaves and windows⟩ ⟨gables decorated with ~ frills —*Amer. Guide Series: Tenn.*⟩ **b :** marked by the use of intricate scrollwork as decoration ⟨ornamental architecture of the ~ period —W.A. White⟩ **c** (1) **:** suggesting intricate scrollwork ⟨its spectacular ~ pattern of islands and inland waterways —W.R.Moore⟩ ⟨driving through its ~ streets —Kamala Markandaya⟩ ⟨transactions . . . of ~ complexity —*Lamp*⟩ (2) **:** suggesting a jigsaw puzzle or its separate pieces ⟨the witness may get history across at last in ~ bits —Mitchell Dawson⟩

jigsaw puzzle *n* : a puzzle made by sawing or cutting a picture into small pieces to be fitted together — called also *picture puzzle*

ji·gua \ˈhēgwə\ *n* -s [AmerSp, fr. Carib] : any of several tropical American trees of the genera *Ocotea* and *Nectandra*

jigue *var of* JIQUI

ji·had *also* **je·had** \jəˈhäd, -had\ *n* -s *sometimes cap* [Ar *jihād*] : a holy war waged on behalf of Islam as a religious duty; *broadly* : a bitter strife or crusade undertaken in the spirit of a holy war

ji·kun·gu \jəˈküŋ(,)gü\ *n* -s [Shambala *zikungu, nkungu*, pl. of *lukungu*] : a tropical African plant (*Telfairia pedata*) of the family Cucurbitaceae cultivated for its edible seeds which also yield an oil

¹jill *often cap, var of* GILL

²jill \ˈjil\ *n* -s [¹*jill*] : a female ferret

jill·et \ˈjilət\ *n* -s [¹*jill* + *-et*] *now Scot* : a vexatiously flirtatious girl : WENCH

¹jil·lion \ˈjilyən\ *n* -s [*j-* + *-illion* (as in *million, billion*)] : an indeterminately large number ⟨any number of spots from one to a ~ —Alfred Bester⟩

²jillion \"\ *adj* : very great many ⟨climbing those stairs a ~ times a day —Jean Stafford⟩

¹jilt \ˈjilt\ *n* -s [alter. of *jillet*] **1** *obs* : an unchaste woman : WHORE **2 a :** a woman who capriciously casts off one previously accepted as a lover **b :** a man who is capricious and irresponsible in love relations ⟨a young ~ who switched from one woman to another every few months⟩

²jilt \"\ *vt* -ED/-ING/-S **1 a :** to cast off or reject (as a lover) capriciously or unfeelingly **b :** to sever close relations with **2** *obs* : DECEIVE, CHEAT

jilt·ee \(ˈ)jil¦tē\ *n* -s : one who has been jilted

jilt·er \ˈjiltə(r)\ *n* -s : one that jilts

jim·ber-jawed \ˈjimbə(r)¦=\ *adj* [prob. alter. of *gimbal* + *jawed*] : having a projecting lower jaw

jimcrack *var of* GIMCRACK

¹jim crow \ˈjimˈkrō\ *n, often cap J&C* [after *Jim Crow*, a stereotype Negro in a song-and-dance act presented by Thomas D. Rice †1860 Am. entertainer that was based on an anonymous song of the early 19th cent. called *Jim Crow*] **1 :** NEGRO — usu. taken to be offensive **2 :** discrimination (as in educational opportunity, social rights, or transportation facilities) against a racial or ethnic group other than white and esp. against the Negro in the southern U.S. by either legal enforcement or traditional sanctions and usu. by restrictive measures designed to prevent intermingling (as of Negroes with whites) on equal terms in public places ⟨the Supreme Court decision outlawing *Jim Crow* in dining cars on interstate trains —*Time*⟩ **3 a :** a machine for bending or straightening rails **b :** a planing machine with a reversing tool that can plane both ways

²jim crow \ˈ=¦=\ *adj, often cap J&C* **1 :** upholding jim crow ⟨gradual relinquishment of *Jim Crow* laws —Raymond Moley⟩ : practicing jim crow ⟨a *jim crow* school⟩ ⟨a *jim crow* town⟩ : marked by jim crow ⟨this *Jim Crow* environment —H.M.Gloster⟩ **2 :** set aside for the use of a racial or ethnic group (as the Negro in the southern U.S.) that is being discriminated against ⟨a *jim crow* railroad car⟩

³jim crow \"\ *vt, often cap J&C* : to subject to jim crow ⟨the exploited and *jim crowed* life of the Negro —Sidney Finkelstein⟩ ⟨many . . . states *jim crow* the Indians —Oliver La Farge⟩

jim crow·ism \ˈ=ˈ=,izəm\ *n, often cap J&C* : racial segregation

¹jim-dandy \ˈjimˈ==\ *n* [*Jim* (nickname for *James*) + *dandy*] : something fine or wonderful of its kind ⟨the bicycle he got as a gift was a *jim-dandy*⟩

²jim-dandy \ˈ=¦==\ *adj* : fine or wonderful of its kind ⟨had a *jim-dandy* voice⟩ ⟨a *jim-dandy* invention⟩

jim dash \ˈ=,=\ *n* [prob. fr. the name *Jim*] : a short printed dash usu. used to separate the decks of a newspaper headline, individual items under one newspaper heading, or separate stories dealing with one event if they follow each other in the same column

jim fish \ˈ=¦=\ *n, usu cap J&F* [*Jim* (nickname for *James*) + *fish*] *SoAfr* : NEGRO — usu. taken to be offensive

jim hill mustard \ˈ=¦hil-\ *n, usu cap J&H* [after *Jim* (James J.) *Hill* †1916 Am. railroad promoter; fr. the growth of the weed along railroad lines J. Hill promoted] : TUMBLE MUSTARD

jim·i·ny *or* **jim·mi·ny** \ˈjimənē, ˈjēm-, -ni\ *interj* [alter. of *gemini*] — used as a mild oath often in the phrases *by jiminy, jiminy crickets, jiminy Christmas*

jim·jams \ˈjim,jamz, -,jaa(ə)mz\ *n pl* [perh. alter. of *delirium tremens*] *slang* : DELIRIUM TREMENS; *also* : a markedly nervous, overwrought, or depressed condition esp. arising from excess or fear ⟨drink so much coffee I get the ~ —*New Yorker*⟩ ⟨attack the January ~ with love and laughter —*Mademoiselle*⟩

jimmer *var of* GIMMER

jim·mies \ˈjimēz, -miz\ *n pl* [alter. of *jimjams*] **1** *slang* **a :** DELIRIUM TREMENS — used with *the* **b :** extreme nervousness or depression **2 :** a fern poisoning of sheep, cattle, and goats marked by seizures of severe trembling often followed by acute respiratory paralysis and death

¹jim·my \ˈjimē, -mi\ *var of* JEMMY

²jimmy \"\ *n* -ES [fr. *Jimmy*, nickname for *James*] **1 :** a short crowbar ⟨the window was pried open with a ~⟩ **2 :** a railroad car for coal **3 :** SPOT 7

³jimmy \"\ *vt* -ED/-ING/-ES : to pry or force open (something fastened) esp. with a jimmy ⟨did he ~ a window or door —T.G.Cooke⟩

jimmyweed \ˈ==,=\ *n* [*jimmies* + *weed*] : RAYLESS GOLDENROD

¹jimp \ˈjimp\ *adj* -ER/-EST [origin unknown] **1** *dial Brit* **a :** slender and trim **b :** neat and spruce **2** *dial Brit* : SCANTY, SKIMPY — **jimp·ly** \-lē\ *adv*

²jimp \"\ *vt* -ED/-ING/-S *dial Brit* : to cut short : SKIMP

³jimp \"\ *adv, dial Brit* : BARELY, SCARCELY

jim·son·weed \ˈjim(p)sən,=\ *or* **james·town weed** \ˈjāmz,taün-\ *or* **jimson** *or* **jimp·son·weed** *also* **jimpson** *n* -s *often cap J* [fr. *Jamestown*, Va.] : an intensely poisonous tall coarse annual weed (*Datura stramonium*) of tropical and perhaps Asiatic origin now naturalized in many parts of the world and having rank-smelling foliage and large white or violet trumpet-shaped flowers that are succeeded by globose prickly fruits—called also *apple of Peru*

jimsonweed

jim·swing·er \ˈjim,swiŋə(r)\ *n* [origin unknown] *South & Midland* : a long-tailed coat

ji·na \ˈjinə\ *n* -s *usu cap* [Skt, saint, victorious — more at JAIN] : one who according to Jainism has conquered temporal and material existence through self-discipline and attained a transcendent and eternal state of bliss; *esp* : one venerated as a tirthankara

jin·dy·wor·o·bak \,jindēˈwörə,bak\ *n* -s [prob. fr. native name in Australia] : one of a group of strongly nationalistic Australians seeking to promote native ideas and traditions esp. in literature

ji·ne·te \hēˈnād·ē\ *n* -s [MexSp, fr. Sp, Zenete, mounted soldier, horseman, one skilled at horsemanship, fr. colloq. Ar *zinētī* of the Zenetes — more at JENNET] : one who trains young horses to the bridle and saddle

jing \ˈjiŋ\ *interj* [short for ¹*jingo*] — a mild oath usu. used in the phrase *by jing*

jing·bang \ˈjiŋ¦baŋ\ *n* -s [origin unknown] *slang* : COMPANY, CROWD — used in the phrase *the whole jingbang*

¹jin·gle \ˈjiŋgəl\ *vb* **jingled; jingled; jingling** \-g(ə)liŋ\ **jingles** [ME *ginglen*, of imit. origin] *vi* **1 :** to make a usu. light sharp continued clinking or varied and mingled tinkling usu. metallic sound ⟨sleigh bells ~⟩ ⟨coins in his pocket *jingled* as he walked⟩ ⟨innumerable pottery bracelets *jingled* up and down upon her arms —Scott Fitzgerald⟩ **2 :** to sound in a way chiefly characterized by continued catchy repetition (as of rhyme, phrase, cadence) — used esp. of verse ~ *vt* : to cause to jingle ⟨*jingled* the coins in his pocket as he talked⟩ ⟨loved to ~ his spurs —Owen Wister⟩ — **jingler** \-g(ə)lə(r)\ *n* -s

²jingle \"\ *n* -s **1 :** a metallic jingling sound ⟨the ~ of the small bells⟩ : a rhythmical cadence ⟨the ~ of the verse as he read it⟩ **2 a :** something that jingles or is designed to jingle ⟨a toy tambourine set about with little ~s⟩ **b** (1) **:** a short verse marked esp. by catchy repetition (as of rhyme, alliterative sounds, cadences) ⟨not so much a poet as a writer of ~s⟩ (2) **:** a short catchy song using such a verse ⟨composing ~s for TV advertising⟩ (3) **:** an incomplete verse used in a contest in which the entrants supply the missing lines **3 :** a two-wheeled covered vehicle used mainly in parts of Ireland and Australia as a public conveyance **4 :** JINGLE SHELL

jingle bell *n* **1 :** a bell mounted on a spring and used to signal the engine room for all speed available **2 a :** CASCABEL **b :** SLEIGH BELL **3 :** a signal bell used on a shop door to announce the entrance of customers

jinglebob \ˈ==,=\ *n* [¹*jingle* + *bob*] : a cattle marking consisting of an ear slashed so that the halves dangle beside the head; *also* : a steer with such a marking

jin·gled \ˈjiŋgəld\ *adj, slang* : mildly drunk

¹jin·gle-jan·gle \ˈjiŋgəl¦jaŋgəl\ *n* -s [redupl. of ²*jingle*] : a jingling and jangling sound ⟨the unpleasant ~ of metallic objects in the trunk of the car⟩

²jinglejangle \"\ *vi* : to make a jinglejangle ⟨~ like goat bells on the Alps —Rose Macaulay⟩

jingle shell *n* : a mollusk of the genus *Anomia* or sometimes of the family Anomiidae having thin flat translucent shell valves that produce sound when dried and shaken together

jingle stick *n* : a usu. toy percussion instrument formed of a stick on which are mounted small metal disks

jin·glet \ˈjiŋglət\ *n* -s [²*jingle* + *-et*] : the ball clapper of a sleigh bell

¹jingling *n* [ME *gingling*, fr. gerund of *ginglen* to jingle — more at JINGLE] **1 :** the act or process of producing a jingle **2 :** JINGLE 1

²jingling *adj* [fr. pres. part. of ¹*jingle*] : making the sound of something that jingles

jingling johnny *n, usu cap 2d J* : PAVILLON CHINOIS

jin·gling·ly *adv* : in a jingling manner

jingling match *n* : an old English game in which blindfolded players try to catch one not blindfolded player who keeps jingling a bell

jin·gly \ˈjiŋg(ə)lē, -li\ *adj, sometimes* -ER/-EST [²*jingle* + *-y*] : having a jingling quality : sounding like a jingle ⟨a ~ sound from a vibrating metallic part⟩ ⟨a ~ verse⟩

¹jin·go \ˈjiŋ(,)gō\ *interj* [prob. euphemism for *Jesus*] — used formerly as an exclamation by conjurers when producing something by sleight of hand; now used as a mild oath usu. in the phrase *by jingo*

²jingo \"\ *n* -ES [fr. *Jingo* supporter of the British belligerent attitude toward Russia in 1878, fr. ¹*jingo*; fr. the fact that the phrase *by jingo* appeared in the refrain of a chauvinistic song sung by the Jingoes] : one characterized by jingoism : a clamorous and belligerent chauvinist ⟨~*es* clamored for war —Ethel Drus⟩

³jingo \"\ *adj* : of or relating to a jingo : marked by jingoism ⟨a ~ nationalism⟩

jin·go·ish \-ish\ *adj* [²*jingo* + *-ish*] : tending to jingoism : marked by jingoism ⟨a ~ statesman⟩

jin·go·ism \-,izəm\ *n* -s [²*jingo* + *-ism*] : clamorous chauvinism or arrogant nationalism esp. marked by a belligerent foreign policy ⟨warfare generates ~ —Barbara Ward⟩ ⟨belligerent ~ and narrow isolationism —J.F.Kennedy⟩

¹jin·go·ist \-,əst\ *n* -s [²*jingo* + *-ist*] : JINGO ⟨the magniloquent parrot cries of the ~ —*Spectator*⟩

²jingoist \"\ *or* **jin·go·is·tic** \¦=(,)=¦istik\ *adj* : JINGO ⟨a ~ slogan advocating war⟩ ⟨*jingoistic* national pride —*New Republic*⟩ — **jin·go·is·ti·cal·ly** \-tək(ə)lē\ *adv*

jingo ring *n* [¹*jingo*] *Scot* : a singing game in which children join hands and dance around one in the center

jinjili *var of* GINGELLY

¹jink \ˈjiŋk\ *n* -s [origin unknown] **1 jinks** \ˈjiŋ(k)s\ *pl* : PRANKS, FROLICS ⟨operettas in which the ~s of a prewar military aristocracy were reclothed in the fashions of 1932 —Christopher Isherwood⟩ ⟨the ~s of a gang of youthful pranksters⟩ **2 :** the act or movement of one that jinks : a dodging away : SLIP

²jink \"\ *vb* -ED/-ING/-S *vi* **1 a :** to move quickly with sudden turns or changes of direction (as in dancing or dodging) ⟨is constantly flying at fast speed, and is forever ~*ing* all over the sky, twisting, turning, weaving, trying to avoid the flak from below —J.S.Childers⟩ **b :** to run away esp. by agile movements ⟨the bear had ~*ed* sideways and vanished into a cave —Christine Weston⟩ ⟨these little white grouse ~ out over the snowy sidings —Richard Perry⟩ **2** *chiefly Scot* : to play tricks and frolic **3 :** to play for five tricks in spoil five after winning three at the risk of losing if unsuccessful the tricks already taken — used with *it* ~ *vt* **1** *chiefly Scot* : to escape by dodging or ducking **2** *chiefly Scot* : to defeat by cheating or trickery

³jink \"\ *n* -s [by *alter.*] *dial Eng* : ³CHINK

⁴jink \"\ *vb* -ED/-ING/-S *dial Eng* : ⁴CHINK ⟨a shunt engine groaned, and ~*ed* the buffers of the freight trucks —Robert Westerby⟩

jin·ker \ˈjiŋkə(r)\ *n* -s [alter. of *janker*] **1** *Austral* : a contrivance like a cart having either two or four wheels and used esp. for log and timber carrying **2** *Austral* : a two-wheeled racing sulky

jin·ket \ˈjiŋkət\ *Scot var of* JUNKET

jinks \ˈjiŋ(k)s\ *n pl but sing in constr* [origin unknown] : CHECKERBERRY

jin·nah cap \ˈjinə-\ *n, usu cap J* [after Mohammed Ali *Jinnah* †1948 Pakistani statesman] : a hat shaped like a fez but made of real or imitation karakul and worn by Pakistani Muslims

jin·ni \jəˈnē, ˈjinē, -ni\ *or* **jinn** *or* **djinn** *or* **djin** \ˈjin\ *also* **djin·ni** *or* **jin·nee** \jəˈnē, ˈjinē, -ni\ *n, pl* **jinn** *or* **jinns** *or* **djinns** *also* **djinn** *or* **djins** [Ar *jinnīy* demon, spirit] **1 :** one of a class of beneficent or malevolent spirits in Islam that inhabit the earth, that are capable of assuming various forms, and that exercise supernatural power **2 :** a supernatural spirit ⟨some ~ of the air made visible for a moment —Osbert Sitwell⟩ ⟨scoffing at the idea of casting out a ~ —Alan Villiers⟩; *esp* : one that takes on human form and serves the one who summons him ⟨magically summoning his private ~ —Hamilton Basso⟩

jin·ny \ˈjinē, -ni\ *n* -ES [alter. of *jenny*] : a block carriage on a crane that sustains pulley blocks hung from an eyebar or crossbar — called also *jenny*

jin·ri·ki·sha *also* **jin·rik·sha** \(j)ənˈrik(,)shō *also* -kə,shō\ *n* -s [Jap, fr. *jin* man + *riki* strength, power + *sha* carriage] : a small light two-wheeled usu. passenger vehicle drawn by one man and orig. used in Japan

jinrikisha

¹jinx \ˈjiŋ(k)s\ *n* -ES [prob. alter of *jynx*; fr. the wryneck's being used in witchcraft] : something that unaccountably foredooms or is felt to foredoom to failure or misfortune : something that is felt to bring bad luck; *esp* : an evil spell or intangible force ⟨felt he had finally broken the ~ that kept him from achieving office⟩

²jinx \"\ *vt* -ED/-ING/-ES **1 :** to foredoom unaccountably to failure or misfortune : bring bad luck upon ⟨the general belief was that his ghost had ~*ed* the ship —James Dugan⟩ ⟨his race and his color have seemed to ~ his personal life —R.G.Hubler⟩ **2 :** to put a stop or end to : make worthless or pointless ⟨~*ed* my story —F.J.Taylor⟩

ji·pi·ja·pa \,hēpēˈhäpə\ *also* **jippi-jappa** \,hip-\ *n* -s [Sp *jipijapa*, fr. *Jipijapa*, Ecuador] **1 :** a Central and So. American plant (*Carludovica palmata*) resembling a palm — called also *toquilla* **2 :** a hat made from fiber from the young leaves of jipijapa

ji·qui \hēˈkē\ *or* **ji·que** \-kā\ *n* -s [AmerSp *jiquí*] **1 :** SABICU **2 :** a Cuban timber tree (*Malpighia obovata*) with hard wood very resistant to moisture

ji·ra·ja·ra \,hirəˈhärə\ *n, pl* **jirajara** *or* **jirajaras** *usu cap* [Sp, of AmerInd origin] **1 a :** a group of peoples of northwestern Venezuela **b :** a member of any of such peoples **2 :** the language of the Jirajara peoples constituting a language family

jird \ˈji(ə)rd\ *n* -s [Berber *agherda, gherda*] : any of several No. African gerbils constituting a genus (*Meriones*) of the Cricetidae

jir·ga *or* **jir·gah** \ˈjərgə, ˈji(ə)r-\ *n* -s [Pashto, prob. of Mongol origin like Per *jarga* circle of men or beasts] : a council of Afghan tribal leaders

jir·kin·et \ˈjərkə̇ˌnet\ *n* -s [alter. of *jerkin* + *-et*] *Scot* **:** a jacket or blouse worn by women

jirt \ˈjərt\ *Scot var of* JERK

jism *or* **gism** \ˈjizəm\ *n* -s [origin unknown] **:** SEMEN — usu. considered vulgar

jit·ney \ˈjitnē, -ni\ *n* -s [origin unknown] **1** *slang* **:** NICKEL 2a **2** [so called fr. the original 5 cent fare] **a :** BUS 1; *esp* **:** a small bus designed to carry paying passengers over a regular route according to a flexible schedule **b :** a small electric truck designed for transporting or towing around a train station, air or bus terminal, or a dock

¹jit·ter \ˈjid·ə(r), -itə-\ *vb* -ED/-ING/-S [origin unknown] *vi* **1 :** to be nervous or act in a nervous way ⟨~*ed* around backstage on the opening night —*Newsweek*⟩; *esp* **:** to experience the jitters ⟨bears his awful responsibility without ~*ing* —*Time*⟩ **2 :** to jog or jig continuously **:** make continuous fast repetitive movements ⟨the wash . . . still ~*ed*, stiff and yellowish on the wire line —Raymond Chandler⟩; *also* **:** to progress in short fast repetitive movements ~ *vt* **:** to cause to jitter; *also* **:** cause to move in jittering movements

²jitter \"\ *n* -s **1 :** the state of mind or the movement of one that jitters **2 jitters** *pl but sing or pl in constr* **:** extreme nervousness **:** a sense of panic — often used with *the* ⟨experienced a bad case of the ~*s* before playing the solo⟩ **3 :** irregular random variation in a signal usu. evidenced by variation in the position of a spot on a radar or television screen

¹jitterbug \ˈ===\ *n* [¹*jitter* + ¹*bug*] **1 :** a dance in which couples two-step, balance, and twirl in standardized patterns or with vigorous acrobatics originating in Harlem in the 1920s and persisting in many variants through the periods of lindy, swing, boogie-woogie, and bop — compare JAZZ 2c **2 a :** one who dances the jitterbug **b :** a devotee of jazz music; *esp* **:** one who sways and gestures in time to jazz music

²jitterbug \"\ *vi* **:** to dance the jitterbug

jit·ter·i·ness \-ərēnə̇s, -rin-\ *n* -ES **:** the quality or state of being jittery

jit·tery \-rē, -ri\ *adj* **1 :** suffering from the jitters ⟨our ~ guards began to question everyone at rifle points —F.E. Fox⟩ ⟨he is tense, ~ — a mass of jangled nerves — his fingers tremble as he lights one cigarette after another —S.N.Behrman⟩ **2 :** marked by jittering movements **:** tending to jitter ⟨warblers . . . are small and ~, and stay hidden in the leaves —J.W. Krutch⟩

jiujitsu *or* **jiujutsu** *var of* JUJITSU

ji·va \ˈjēvə\ *n* -s *sometimes cap* [Skt *jīva* living, alive — more at QUICK] **1** *Hinduism* **a :** the vital energy of life **b :** the individual soul **2** *Jainism* **a :** the individual life monad or separate individual self **b :** the aggregate of all life monads or separate selves **:** LIFE

ji·van·muk·ta \ˌjēvənˈmu̇ktə\ *n* -s [Skt *jīvanmukta*, fr. *jīvan-* (fr. *jīvati* he lives) + *mukta* emancipated, set free, fr. *muñcati* he frees, releases; akin to Skt *jīva* living — more at MUCUS] *Hinduism* **:** one who has attained jivanmukti

ji·van·muk·ti \-(ˌ)tē\ *n* -s [Skt *jīvanmukti*, fr. *jīvan-* + *mukti* release, liberation, fr. *muñcati*] *Hinduism* **:** spiritual release or salvation achieved while still alive — compare MOKSHA

ji·va·ran \ˈhēvərən\ *adj, usu cap* [*Jivaro* + *-an*] **:** JIVAROAN

ji·va·ro \ˈhēvəˌrō\ *or* **ji·ba·ro** \-ēbə-\ *n, pl* **jivaro** *or* **jivaros** *or* **jibaro** *or* **jibaros** *usu cap* [Sp *jíbaro*, of AmerInd origin] **1 a :** a group of peoples of northwestern Peru and southern Ecuador **b :** a member of any of such peoples **2 :** the language of the Jivaro peoples constituting a language family — **ji·va·ro·an** \ˌ==ˈrōən\ *adj, usu cap*

¹jive \ˈjīv\ *n* -s [origin unknown] **1 a** *slang* **:** glib, deceptive, or foolish talk **b :** the jargon of narcotics addicts or of jazz music and nightclub life **c :** a special jargon of difficult or slang terms ⟨a sort of academic ~ interlarded with lengthy and undigested quotations —Dwight MacDonald⟩ **2 :** hot jazz or the jitterbugging sometimes performed to it

²jive \"\ *vb* -ED/-ING/-S *vi* **1** *slang* **:** to talk jive **:** fool around **:** KID **2 a :** to dance to hot jazz; *esp* **:** JITTERBUG **b :** to play hot jazz ~ *vt* **1** *slang* **:** TEASE, KID **2 :** to play (music) hot ⟨small bands *jiving* in cellar clubs⟩

jiz·ya *also* **jiz·yah** \ˈjizyə\ *n* -s [Ar *jizyah*] **:** a capitation tax formerly levied on non-Muslims by the Islamic state

JJ *abbr* **1** judges **2** justices

jl *abbr* journal

JMA *abbr* junior military aviator

JMJ *abbr* Jesus, Mary, Joseph

JMT *abbr* job methods training

jn *abbr* **1** join **2** junction

jna·na \jəˈnänə\ *n* -s [Skt *jñāna*, fr. *jānāti* he knows — more at KNOW] *Hinduism* **:** KNOWLEDGE

jnana–marga \jəˌnänəˈmärgə\ *n* -s [Skt *jñānamārga*, fr. *jñāna* + *mārga* road, way] **:** the Hindu approach to salvation by the way of knowledge developed in the Upanishads and the philosophic systems (as Sankhya, Vedanta, Yoga) and involving mental and ascetic self-discipline often in the companionship of a guru — compare KARMA-MARGA

jnana–yoga \-ˈyōgə\ *n* [Skt *jñānayoga*, fr. *jñāna* + *yoga* — more at YOGA] *Hinduism* **:** spiritual discipline attained by philosophical knowledge

jna·ni \jəˈnä(ˌ)nē\ *n* -s [Skt *jñānī*, fr. *jñāna*] **:** a devotee of jnana-marga

jnc *abbr* junction

JND *abbr* just noticeable difference

jnl *abbr* journal

jnlst *abbr* journalist

jnr *abbr* junior

jnt *abbr* joint

¹jo \ˈjō\ *n* -ES [Sc *jo* joy, alter. of *joy*] *chiefly Scot* **:** SWEETHEART, DEAR — often used in addressing a person ⟨John Anderson, my ~ John —Robert Burns⟩

²jo *var of* JOE

JO *abbr* **1** joint organization **2** junior officer

jo·a·chim·ite \ˈjōəˌkiˌmīt\ *n* -s *usu cap* [*Joachim* of Floris †*ab* 1202 Ital. mystic + E *-ite*] **:** a follower of Joachim of Floris who divided all time into the three ages of the Father, Son, and Holy Spirit of which the second age lasted from A.D. 1 to 1260 and whose doctrine of a spiritual elite destined to convert the world in the third age influenced the Fraticelli

jo·a·chism \ˈjōəˌkizəm\ *n* -s *usu cap* [*Joach*im of Floris + E *-ism*] **:** adherence to the doctrines of the Joachimites

joan \ˈjō(ə)n, ˈjōˈan\ *n* -s *usu cap* [fr. the name *Joan*] **:** a country girl

joannes *var of* JOHANNES

joan silverpin \-ˈ==ˌ=\ *n, usu cap J* [prob. fr. E dial. *Joan's silver pin* article of beauty in a sordid setting; fr. the fact that this showy flower is often found among weeds] **:** any of several poppies; *esp* **:** OPIUM POPPY

joa·quin·ite \wäˈkēˌnīt, wōˈ-\ *n* -s [fr. *Joaquin* ridge, San Benito co., Calif. + E *-ite*] **:** a mineral consisting of a sodium iron titanium silicate and occurring in honey-yellow orthorhombic crystals

jo·ar \jəˈwär\ *var of* JOWAR

¹job \ˈjäb\ *n* -s [perh. fr. obs. E, lump, fr. ME *jobbe*, perh. alter. of *gobbe* — more at GOB] **1 a :** a piece of work ⟨did odd ~*s* for the neighborhood housewives⟩ ⟨gave up the marriage as a bad ~⟩ ⟨the ~ before her, that of phrasing and rephrasing a fugue —Osbert Sitwell⟩ ⟨the bridge was a bigger and longer ~ than the firm expected⟩ **:** PERFORMANCE, ACHIEVEMENT ⟨the new biography is a superb ~⟩ ⟨too lazy to turn out an honest ~⟩; *specif* **:** a small miscellaneous piece of work undertaken on order at a stated rate ⟨have two offset ~*s* to print up today⟩ ⟨the car needed a brake ~⟩ **b :** a quality, product, or result of work ⟨do a better ~ next time⟩ ⟨a more uniform dye ~ is obtained in skeins —H.R.Mauersberger⟩ **c :** an example of a usu. specified type **:** ITEM ⟨at the truck stop were three tractor-trailer ~*s*⟩ ⟨the blonde ~ sitting at the bar⟩ **2 :** something done for private advantage **:** DEAL; *esp* **:** a collusive piece of business ⟨his appointment as judge was a flagrant ~⟩ ⟨suspected the whole incident was a put-up ~⟩ **3** *chiefly Brit* **:** a state or turn of affairs **:** a piece of luck **:** THING — used with *bad* or *good* ⟨it was a good ~ you didn't hit the old man —E.L.Thomas⟩ **4 :** a criminal enterprise; *specif* **:** ROBBERY ⟨the gang that pulled the bank ~⟩ **5 a :** a regular remunerative employment **:** POSITION, SITUATION ⟨got a part-time ~ as a waiter in a café⟩ ⟨holds a key ~ in the government⟩ **b :** a specific duty, role, or function **:** work customarily performed ⟨the stokers' ~ was to feed coal into the furnaces⟩ ⟨the white blood cells . . . have the ~ of fighting infection —Morris Fishbein⟩ ⟨when more light is needed a stronger bulb will do the ~⟩; *specif* **:** an activity or group of related activities contributing to a larger process ⟨divide the manufacturing process into a number of carefully defined ~*s* assigned to individual workers⟩ **6 :** an undertaking requiring unusual exertion **:** EFFORT ⟨the radio whined so loud that it was a ~ to talk through it —Rose Macaulay⟩ **7 :** the object or material on which work is being done ⟨held the ~ with tongs while he hammered it⟩ **8 :** the actual process of doing a piece of work **:** the activity of a job ⟨learned plumbing on the ~ itself⟩ ⟨get on with the ~ of planning the trip⟩ ⟨stuck to the ~ till the tire was off⟩ **9 :** the area used in carrying on a job (as of construction) ⟨lumber stored in piles on the ~⟩ **10 jobs** *pl* **:** defective or slow-selling goods (as publishers' remainders) sold at reduced prices **11** *slang* **:** a thoroughly damaging piece of work **:** a job of destruction or disablement — usu. used in the phrase *do a job on* ⟨the collision really did a ~ on their car⟩ ⟨did a ~ on his rival in the third game, letting him score only one point⟩ **syn** see TASK — **on the job :** attending to one's work ⟨a mechanical servant that is right *on the job* day and night⟩

²job \"\ *vb* **jobbed; jobbed; jobbing; jobs** *vi* **1 a :** to do odd or occasional pieces of work for hire **:** work by the piece ⟨supported himself by *jobbing* in local orchestras⟩ **b :** to do job work **2 a :** to direct or carry on public business so as to secure private advantage or graft **b :** to seek or give a political favor in return for secret influence or graft ⟨a bit of *jobbing* . . . got a grand jury presentment to make a road which served nobody's interest but his own —Samuel Lover⟩ **3 :** to carry on the business of a middleman **:** trade in wholesale lots ⟨his company ~*s* and doesn't sell to the homeowner⟩ ~ *vt* **1 :** to buy and sell (as stock) or let (as a property) for profit **:** SPECULATE **2 :** to hire or let by the job or for a period of service ⟨~ a carriage for the time he would be in the city⟩ **3 :** to make a job of (a matter of public trust or duty) **:** get, deal with, or effect by jobbery **4 :** to do or cause to be done by separate portions or lots **:** SUBLET ⟨~ the city paving to the lowest bidders⟩ **5 :** to do a job on **:** SWINDLE, TRICK ⟨claimed he had been *jobbed* out of the championship⟩ **:** dispose of (as by political intrigue) ⟨assured his election by *jobbing* his political rival⟩

³job \"\ *adj* **1** *Brit* **:** that is for hire by the job or for a given service or period ⟨~ carriage at 2 guineas a day⟩ ⟨a ~ gardener⟩ **2 a :** used in or suitable for job work ⟨~ type⟩ **b :** engaged in job work ⟨~ printer⟩ ⟨~ shop⟩ **c :** done as job work ⟨~ printing⟩ **3 :** of or relating to a job or to employment ⟨guarantee of ~ security⟩ ⟨gloom in the ~ market⟩

⁴job \"\ *vb* **jobbed; jobbed; jobbing; jobs** [ME *jobben*] *vi*, *chiefly dial* **:** JAB ~ *vt* **1** *chiefly dial* **:** JAB **2** *chiefly Austral* **:** to strike or hit esp. with a heavy blow

⁵job \"\ *n* -s **:** a one-handed stroke used in field hockey by a tackler to push the ball away from an opponent's stick

job analysis *n* **:** determination of the precise characteristics of a job or position through detailed observation and critical examination of the sequential activities, facilities required, conditions of work, and the qualifications needed in a worker usu. as a preparatory step toward a job description

job analyst *n* **:** a specialist in job analysis

jo·ba·tion \jōˈbāshən\ *n* -s [*jobe* + *-ation*] *chiefly Brit* **:** a long tedious reproof **:** SCOLDING, LECTURE

job·ber \ˈjäbə(r)\ *n* -s [²*job* + *-er*] **:** one that jobs: as **a** (1) *chiefly Brit* **:** one that buys livestock from farmers and sells to consumers or other dealers ⟨if the ~ comes you can sell the pig —J.M.Synge⟩ (2) **:** STOCKJOBBER (3) **:** WHOLESALER; *specif* **:** a wholesaler in some trades who operates on a small scale or who sells only to retailers and institutions rather than to other wholesale organizations **b** (1) **:** one that works by the job or on job work (2) **:** one that contracts with lumbermen to do one or more parts of a logging operation (3) **:** JOB PRESS

job·ber·nowl \ˈjäbə(r)ˌnōl\ *n* -s [prob. alter. of obs. *jobard* blockhead (fr. ME, fr. MF, fr. *Job*, Old Testament patriarch + MF *-ard*) + *nowl*, alter. of *noll*] *Brit* **:** NUMSKULL, NINCOMPOOP

jobber's drill *n* **:** a straight-shank drill somewhat shorter than the taper-shank drill of the same diameter

jobber's reamer *n* **:** a reamer that may be used either in a machine or when provided with a suitable holder as a hand tool

job·bery \ˈjäb(ə)rē, -ri\ *n* -ES [²*job* + *-ery*] **:** the act or practice of jobbing **:** official corruption **:** political intrigue or graft ⟨all the public posts were filled by ~ —Szyman Askenazy⟩

jobbing *pres part of* JOB

¹job·ble \ˈjäbəl\ *var of* JABBLE

²jobble *n* -s [¹*job* + *-le*] *dial Eng* **:** a small quantity or load

job card *n* **:** a card in a cost-accounting system on which the detailed costs of an order are accumulated **:** COST SHEET

job case *n* **:** any of a class of typecases carrying with some exceptions both capital and lower-case letters — see CALIFORNIA JOB CASE

job classification *n* **:** the grouping of jobs into classes usu. on the basis of type of work or level of pay

job control *n* **:** union influence over the employment practices of an establishment exercised through contract clauses regulating hiring, promotion, transfer, layoff, and discharge and directed toward union security

job description *n* **:** an orderly record of the essential activities involved in the performance of a task that is abstracted from a job analysis and used in classifying and evaluating jobs and in the selection and placement of employees

jobe \ˈjōb\ *vt* -ED/-ING/-S [after *Job*, Old Testament patriarch; fr. the scolding tone of his friends' speeches] *archaic* **:** SCOLD, REPROVE, LECTURE

job evaluation *or* **job rating** *n* **:** systematic qualitative appraisal of each job or position in an establishment either through the assignment of points for job characteristics or through comparison of job factors (as mental effort, experience, and responsibility required) for the purpose of determining the relative position of the job in the job hierarchy and for fixing wage rates

jobholder \ˈ===\ *n* **:** one that has a regular job; *specif* **:** a government employee

job·less \ˈjäbləs\ *adj* **1 :** having no employment **2 :** of or benefiting those who are jobless ⟨~ insurance⟩ — **job·less·ness** *n* -ES

jo block \ˈjō-\ *n, usu cap J* [by contr.] **:** JOHANSSON BLOCK

job lot *n* **1 a :** a miscellaneous collection of goods for sale as a lot usu. to a retailer at a reduced price **b :** a miscellaneous sometimes inferior group ⟨get a *job lot* of deans, dowagers, cabinet ministers, and ambassadors to meet them —W.J.Locke⟩ **2 :** a smaller than normal unit of commodities, goods, or production **3 :** an odd quantity of paper offered for sale at a discount because discontinued or otherwise nonstandard — **in job lots** *adv* **:** in an extensive and often indiscriminate manner **:** WHOLESALE ⟨organizations in elaborate regalia and . . . degrees marketed *in job lots* —C.W.Ferguson⟩

job·mas·ter \ˈjäbˌmastə(r)\ *n* [¹*job* + *master*] *Brit* **:** the keeper of a livery stable

jo·bo \ˈhō(ˌ)bō\ *n* -s [Sp, fr. Taino *hobo*] **1** *West Indies & Mexico* **:** HOG PLUM 1 **2** *West Indies & Mexico* **:** GUMBO-LIMBO 1

job of work *chiefly Brit* **:** JOB 1a ⟨an absence which generally occurred when there was a *job of work* to be done —R.H. Sampson⟩

job order *n* **:** the written authority given a worker or shop to perform certain work

job press *n* **:** PLATEN PRESS; *also* **:** a relatively small press — called also *jobber*

job rotation *n* **:** the assigning of an employee to a variety of tasks in turn to provide diversified experience during training or to counteract boredom

jobs *pl of* JOB, *pres 3d sing of* JOB

job's comforter \ˈjōbz-\ *n, usu cap J* [after *Job*, Old Testament patriarch; fr. the scolding tone of his friends' speeches] **1 :** one that increases (as by tactless or malicious remarks) a person's distress while supposedly comforting him **2 :** FURUNCLE

job sheet *n* **1 :** a page of instruction to aid a worker in performing a task — called also *instruction card* **2 :** JOB CARD

jobsite \ˈ==\ *n* [¹*job* + *site*] **:** JOB 9

job specification *n* **:** a specialized job description designed by emphasizing mental and physical qualifications and special skills required in an operative to facilitate selection and placement of employees

job's tears *n pl, usu cap J* [after *Job*, Old Testament patriarch who wept because of his many afflictions (Job 16:16 ff)] **1 :** hard pearly white seeds often sold as beads or strung in necklaces **2** *sing in constr* **:** an Asiatic grass (*Coix lacryma-jobi*) now widely cultivated in the tropics that produces Job's tears in ornamental and edible varieties — called also *tear grass*

job ticket *n* **1 :** an auxiliary printed form that may accompany a job order to a workshop to be used variously for recording worker's time, identifying material, giving brief instructions as to procedure, routing, tools, and destination **2 :** JOB ORDER

job work *n* **:** commercial printing of orders (as for letterheads, circulars, cards, booklets) — compare BOOKWORK

joc *abbr* **1** jocose **2** jocular

JOC *abbr* joint operations center

joch \ˈyōk\ *n* -s [G, lit., yoke, fr. OHG *joh* — more at YOKE] **:** COL 1

jo·cism \ˈjōˌsizəm\ *n* -s *usu cap* [F *jocisme*, fr. Jeunesse Ouvière Chrétienne (lit., Christian Working Youth), a Catholic youth organization + *-isme* -ism] **:** a Roman Catholic movement among young workers directed toward christianizing the ranks of labor and founded in Belgium during the period 1912–1924 by Canon Joseph Cardijn

¹jo·cist \ˈjōsə̇st\ *n* -s *usu cap* [F *jociste*, fr. Jeunesse Ouvière Chrétienne + *-iste* -ist] **:** a member of the Jocist movement

²jocist \"\ *adj, usu cap* **:** of or relating to Jocism

¹jock \ˈjäk\ *n* -s *often cap* [fr. *Jock*, Sc & Ir nickname for *John*] **1** *Scot & Irish* **:** a country boy **:** LAD **2 :** a soldier in a Scottish regiment

²jock \"\ *n* -s [short for ¹*jockey*] **1 :** JOCKEY 2a ⟨any one of two dozen top ~*s* will get home with the best horse in a race —Eddie Arcaro⟩ **2 :** DISC JOCKEY

³jock \"\ *var of* JOCKSTRAP

jock·er \ˈjäkə(r)\ *n* -s [E slang *jock* penis + *-er* — more at JOCKSTRAP] *slang* **:** a male homosexual

¹jock·ey \ˈjäkē, -ki\ *n, pl* **jockeys** [fr. *Jockey*, Sc nickname for *John*] **1** *Brit* **:** LADDIE, CHAPPIE, FELLOW ⟨a mischievous ~⟩ ⟨a tough old ~ of a colonel⟩ **2 a :** one who rides or drives a horse; *esp* **:** a professional rider in a horse race **b** *archaic* **:** one who handles or deals in horses **:** HORSE TRADER **c :** a person who operates or manipulates an often specified vehicle or other object **:** DRIVER, OPERATOR ⟨a truck ~⟩ ⟨an elevator ~⟩ ⟨a typewriter ~⟩; *specif* **:** one who parks cars or trucks in a storage garage — compare DISC JOCKEY **3 :** a sometimes padded leather flap on a saddle that covers the point of attachment of the stirrup leather or serves as ornament — see STOCK SADDLE illustration **4 :** HARVARD CRIMSON 1

²jockey \"\ *vb* **jockeyed; jockeyed; jockeying; jockeys** *vt* **1 :** to deal shrewdly or fraudulently with **:** get the better of by craft **:** OUTWIT, TRICK, GULL ⟨dozens of unprincipled hucksters at the resort who ~ the unwary for fair⟩ ⟨the newly established method of party horse trading ~*ed* them out of many deputies —Janet Flanner⟩ **2 a :** to ride (a horse) as a jockey ⟨the winning horse was ~*ed* by his son⟩ **b :** to be the driver, pilot, or operator (a vehicle or other mechanism) ⟨~*s* a taxi for a living⟩ **3 a :** to maneuver or manipulate (as a person) by adroit or devious means ⟨proposals for public works were ~*ed* through Parliament by a combination of members —E.H. Collis⟩ ⟨trying to ~ you into some sort of trap —Erle Stanley Gardner⟩ **b :** to change the position of esp. by a series of movements **:** MANIPULATE ⟨~*ed* the camera back and forth till he got just the right angle⟩ **:** MANEUVER ⟨~ the furniture around the living room⟩; *specif* **:** to bring by jockeying ⟨~ a car into a parking space⟩ ⟨flew close to ~ the other plane out of formation⟩ ~ *vi* **1 :** to act as a jockey ⟨~*ed* in races till he was too heavy for the horse⟩ **2 :** to maneuver for advantage ⟨~ for position as the horses race the first lap⟩ ⟨watch the racing fleets . . . ~ for the favoring wind —E.A.Weeks⟩ ⟨behind the scenes ~*ing* . . . to determine the Democratic party's candidate for lieutenant governor —*N.Y.Times*⟩

jockey boot *n* **:** TOP BOOT

jockey cap *n* **:** a lightweight cap with a long visor worn esp. by jockeys

jockey club *n* **:** an association of persons interested in horse racing usu. regulating races in a certain district

jockey cap

jockey coat *n, chiefly Scot* **:** GREATCOAT; *esp* **:** one of broadcloth with wide sleeves

jockey pulley *or* **jockey wheel** *n* **:** IDLER PULLEY

jock·ey·ship \ˈ==ˌship\ *n* **:** the art or practice of jockeying

jockey stick *n* **:** a stick fastened to the hame of the near horse and the bit of the off horse for use in driving with a single rein to prevent crowding

jockey weight *n* **:** a weight that rides on the beam of scales or the lever of a testing machine to provide fine adjustment

jock itch *or* **jockey itch** *n* [³*jock* or *jockey (strap)*] **:** ringworm of the crotch **:** TINEA CRURIS

jocko \ˈjä(ˌ)kō\ *or* **jacko** \ˈja(-\ *n* -s [F *jocko*, of African origin; akin to Efik *id³iok¹* chimpanzee] **1 :** CHIMPANZEE **2 :** MONKEY

jocks *pl of* JOCK

jock·strap \ˈjäkˌstrap\ *also* **jock** *or* **jockey strap** *n* -s [*jockstrap* fr. E slang *jock* penis (short for earlier *jockam*, *jockum*, of unknown origin) + *strap*; *jock* short for *jockstrap*; *jockey strap* alter. of *jockstrap*] **:** a supporter for the genitals worn by men participating in sports or strenuous activities **:** an athletic supporter

jock·te·leg \ˈjäktəˌleg\ *n* -s [origin unknown] *Scot* **:** a large clasp knife

jo·co \ˈjō(ˌ)kō\ *adj* [by shortening] *Scot* **:** JOCOSE

jo·cose \(ˈ)jōˈkōs\ *adj* [L *jocosus*, fr. *jocus* jest, joke + *-osus* -ose — more at JOKE] **1 :** given to jokes and jesting **:** abounding in jokes ⟨felt the preacher was too ~ for his serious position⟩ **2 :** having the character of or containing a joke **:** sportively humorous ⟨made ~ remarks about things the others didn't consider funny at all⟩ **syn** see WITTY

jo·cose·ly *adv* **:** in a jocose manner **:** JOKINGLY

jo·cose·ness *n* -ES **:** JOCOSITY

jo·cos·i·ty \jōˈkäsəd·ē, -ətē, -i\ *n* -ES [L *jocos*us + E *-ity*] **1 :** the quality or state of being jocose ⟨talking with loud ~ —Bruce Marshall⟩ **2 :** a jocose act or saying ⟨a book of . . . sly and devastating *jocosities* —*Amer. Mercury*⟩

jo·co·te \hōˈkō(ˌ)tā\ *n* -s [AmerSp, fr. Nahuatl *xocotl*] **:** MOMBIN

jocote de mi·co \-dāˈmē(ˌ)kō\ *n* [AmerSp, lit., monkey jocote] **:** BARBAS

jo·cu \hōˈkü\ *n* -s [AmerSp (Cuba) *jocú*] **:** DOG SNAPPER

joc·u·lar \ˈjäkyələ(r)\ *adj* [L *jocularis*, fr. *joculus* little jest, little joke, dim. of *jocus* jest, joke + *-aris* -ar — more at JOKE] **1 :** given to or disposed to jesting **:** acting in jest **:** overtly jocose ⟨grew ~ and began to tease the others about their fears⟩ **2 :** said or done in joke **:** of, containing, or of the character of a joke **:** PLAYFUL, MERRY ⟨set the table laughing with his ~ remarks⟩ ⟨the more solemn dances were organized by the chiefs . . . the more ~ ones,however, took place without authority —Irving Rouse⟩ **syn** see WITTY

joc·u·lar·i·ty \ˌjäkyəˈlarəd·ē, -ətē, -i *also* -ler-\ *n* -ES [LL *jocularitas*, fr. L *jocularis* + *-itas* -ity] **1 :** the quality or state of being jocular ⟨a singular display of ~, in which irrelevancy and sheer bad taste are especially conspicuous —N.F.Adkins⟩ **2 :** an instance of being jocular **:** JEST ⟨interspersed . . . were axioms and proverbs and *jocularities* —*New Yorker*⟩

joc·u·lar·ly *adv* **:** in a jocular manner ⟨a subject they had generally avoided or else tried to deal with ~ —Richard Blaker⟩

joc·u·lar·ness *n* -ES **:** JOCULARITY

joc·u·la·tor \ˈjäkyəˌlād·ə(r)\ *n, pl* **joc·u·la·to·res** \ˌjäkyələˈtōr(ˌ)ēz\ *or* **joculators** [ML, fr. L, jester, joker — more at JUGGLER] **:** a wandering entertainer of medieval Europe who for hire practiced the arts of minstrelsy, narration, dancing, juggling, and mime

jo·cum \hōˈküm\ *also* **jo·cu·ma** \-mə\ *n* -s [AmerSp *jocuma*, prob. fr. Taino] **:** MASTIC BULLY

joc·und \ˈjäkənd *sometimes* ˈjōk-\ *adj* [ME *jocound*, *jocund*, fr. LL *jocundus*, alter. (influenced by L *jocus* joke) of L *jucundus* pleasant, fr. *juvare* to help] **:** feeling, exhibiting, or characteristic of mirth or good cheer **:** CHEERFUL, GAY, LIVELY ⟨singing, dancing, and ~ feasting⟩ ⟨a small and ~ blaze upon the hearth —Elinor Wylie⟩ **syn** see MERRY

jo·cun·di·ty \jō'kəndəd·ē, -ətē, -i\ *n* -ES [LL *jocunditas*, fr. *jocundus* + L *-itas* -ity] **1 :** JOCUNDNESS **2 :** a jocund action or speech **:** PLEASANTRY

joc·und·ly *adv* [ME, fr. *jocund* + *-ly*] **:** in a jocund manner

joc·und·ness *n* -ES [ME *jocundnes*, fr. *jocund* + *-nes* -ness] **:** the quality or state of being jocund

jod *var of* YODH

jo-dart·er *or* **joe dart·er** \'jō'därd·ər\ *n* **:** JIM-DANDY

jodel *var of* YODEL

[1]**jodh·pur** \'jädpə(r), 'jōd-, -,pu̇(ə)r, -u̇ə\ *adj, usu cap* [fr. *Jodhpur*, Rajputana, India] **:** of or from the city of Jodhpur, India **:** of the kind or style prevalent in Jodhpur

[2]**jodh·pur** \'jädpə(r) *also* ÷ -dfə-\ *n* -S **1** *also* **jodhpur breeches :** pants for horseback riding cut full through the hips, close-fitting from knee to ankle, and usu. having a strap under the foot — usu. used in pl. **2** *or* **jodhpur boot** *also* **jodhpur shoe :** a short riding boot; *esp* **:** an ankle-high boot fastened with a strap that is buckled at the side — compare CHUKKA

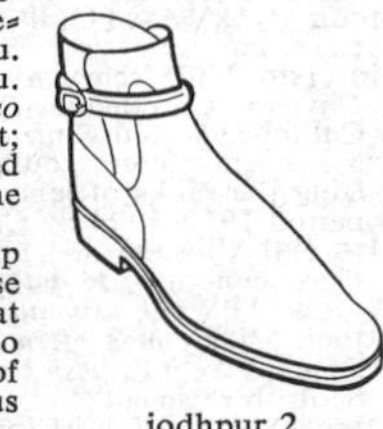

jodhpur 2

jo·do \'jō(,)dō\ *n* -S *usu cap* [Jap *jōdo*] **1 :** PURE LAND **2 :** a Japanese Buddhist sect founded 1175 that promises rebirth in the Pure Land to all those who invoke the name of Amida Buddha and live a righteous life

[1]**joe** \'jō\ *var of* [1]JO

[2]**joe** *or* **jo** \"\ *n, pl* **joes** [short for *johannes*] **:** a gold dobra worth 12,800 reis

[3]**joe** *also* **jo** \"\ *n* -S [prob. alter. of *java*] *slang* **:** COFFEE

[4]**joe** \"\ *n* -S *often cap* [fr. *Joe*, nickname for *Joseph*] **1** — used informally to address a man whose name the speaker does not know **2** *slang* **:** GUY, FELLOW ⟨he's a good ~⟩ ⟨just an average ~⟩ ⟨a couple of ~*s* here who don't play a too crippled game of bridge —Al Hine⟩

joe blow *n, usu cap J&B* [*Joe* + *blow* (prob. arbitrarily chosen to rhyme with *Joe*)] *slang* **:** an ordinary man; *specif* **:** one who is self-important

joebush \'ˌ=ˌ=\ *n* [*joe* (origin unknown) + *bush*] **:** JOEWOOD

joe college *n, usu cap J&C* [*Joe* + *college*] **:** a college boy; *esp* **:** one devoted to amusement

joe doakes \-'dōks\ *n, pl* **joe doakes** *usu cap J&D* [*Joe* + the name *Doakes*] **1 :** an average man **2 :** SO-AND-SO 1

joe mil·ler \-'milə(r)\ *n, usu cap J&M* [fr. *Joe Miller's Jests* book (1739), a collection of jokes by John Mottley †1750 Eng. writer, after *Joe Miller* †1738 Eng. comedian] **1 :** a book of jokes **2 :** JOKE; *esp* **:** a stale joke

joe-pye weed \'jō'pī-\ *n, often cap J&P* [origin unknown] **:** BONESET 1; *esp* **:** either of two tall perennial American herbs (*Eupatorium maculatum* and *E. purpureum*) with stems usu. purplish or blotched with purple, whorled leaves, and terminal clusters of heads of typically purple tubular flowers — see MARSH MILKWEED

joe rocker *n* [origin unknown] **:** GREEN CRAB

joes *pl of* JO

joewood \'ˌ=ˌ=\ *n* [*joe* (origin unknown) + *wood*] **:** a West Indian shrub or small tree (*Jacquinia keyensis*) of the family Theophrastaceae with leathery saponaceous leaves and an extremely hard wood — called also *barbasco*

[1]**jo·ey** \'jōē, -ōi,ōi\ *n* -S [native name in Australia] **1** *Austral* **a :** a baby kangaroo ⟨shot a doe with a ~⟩ **b :** a baby animal **c :** a young child **2** *Austral* **:** ODD-JOBMAN

[2]**joey** \"\ *n* -S *usu cap* [fr. *Joey*, nickname for *Joseph*] **1** [after *Joseph* Hume †1855 Eng. politician who urged the issue of fourpenny pieces] *Brit* **a :** a fourpenny piece **b :** a threepenny piece **2** [after *Joseph* Grimaldi †1837 Eng. pantomimist and clown] **:** a circus clown

[1]**jog** \'jäg *also* 'jȯg\ *vb* **jogged; jogged; jogging; jogs** [prob. alter. of *shog*] *vt* **1 :** to push or shake by prodding (as with the elbow or hand) **:** JOSTLE, NUDGE; *esp* **:** to push or touch in order to give notice, to excite attention, or to warn ⟨*jogged* the reins and the horses started up⟩ ⟨~ you with my elbow when it's time to go⟩ **2 :** to rouse to alertness or action ⟨tied a string on his finger to ~ his memory⟩ **:** REMIND ⟨~ their customers two or three times a year —Paul Friggens⟩ **3 a :** to cause to jog **:** drive (as a horse) at a jog ⟨an exercise boy ... ~*s* the colt around the track —F.A.Wrensch⟩ **b :** to cause (a machine) to operate for an instant ⟨a button permits *jogging* the ... motor to facilitate positioning tools —*Sweet's Catalog Service*⟩ **4 :** to align the edges of (piled sheets of paper) usu. by winding and knocking on or with a flat surface ~ *vi* **1 :** to move up and down or about with a short often heavy motion ⟨walked away quickly, his white-painted holster *jogging* against his hip —Thomas Williams⟩ **2 :** to run or ride at a slow jogging trot ⟨a substitute *jogged* out to the referee⟩ **3 a :** to go at a slow, leisurely, or monotonous pace **:** TRUDGE, PLOD, POKE ⟨a team of oxen *jogged* along ... drawing a vehicle —O.E.Rölvaag⟩ ⟨prefer to ~ along ... in stagecoaches instead of whizzing past in a cloud of dust and cinders —Margaret Deland⟩ ⟨under easy sail the fleet *jogged* along before a moderate trade —S.E.Morison⟩ **b :** to proceed steadily, moderately, and usu. uneventfully ⟨a rebellion crushed, they ~ on as before —George Meredith⟩ ⟨from then on her life *jogged* peacefully along —C.M.L.Beuf⟩

[2]**jog** \"\ *n* -S **1 :** SHAKE, PUSH, JOLT ⟨gave the dispenser a ~ in hopes of jarring the coin loose⟩; *specif* **:** one intended to give notice or awaken attention ⟨gave his sleeping buddy a ~ as the officer approached⟩ ⟨seeing the book there gave his memory a ~⟩ **2 a :** a jogging movement, gait, or trip ⟨getting ... under weigh for a ~ down to the breakwater and beyond to have a look at the weather —Llewellyn Howland⟩ **b :** a slow pace with marked beats — used of a horse

[3]**jog** \"\ *n* -S [prob. alter. of [1]*jag*] **1 :** [1]JAG 4 **2 a :** a short part (as of a line, road, or wall) interrupting the direction of the rest ⟨a window in the ~ facing south⟩ **:** an often right-angled projection, notch, or step ⟨a ~ in the wall enclosing pipes⟩ **b :** the space in the angle of a jog ⟨built shelves in the ~ between chimney and wall⟩ **c :** a brief abrupt change in direction ⟨where the highway makes a ~ around the courthouse square⟩ **3 :** a narrow theatrical flat used in an interior setting (as to form an offset in a wall)

[4]**jog** \"\ *vi* **jogged; jogged; jogging; jogs :** to form or make a jog ⟨the road ~*s* to the right over the hill⟩

jog cart *n* [[1]*jog*] **:** a training sulky that is narrower and has longer shafts than a racing sulky

jog·ger \-gə(r)\ *n* -S [[1]*jog* + *-er*] **:** one that jogs ⟨a memory ~⟩ ⟨a ~ in a sweat suit⟩; *specif* **:** LAYBOY

[1]**jog·gle** \'jägəl\ *vb* **joggled; joggled; joggling** \-g(ə)liŋ\ **joggles** [freq. of [1]*jog*] *vt* **:** to shake slightly **:** push suddenly but slightly so as to cause to shake or totter **:** JOSTLE, JOG ⟨skate up to the muskrat house and ~ it —Pete Barrett⟩ ⟨don't want anything ... that might even ~ your precious status quo —Louis Auchincloss⟩ ~ *vi* **:** to have or go with a shaking or jerking motion **:** shake slightly to and fro or up and down ⟨the faint sounds of fifes *joggling* on backs —Robert De Vries⟩ ⟨when empty, they *joggled* ... violently on their ironshod wheels —Christopher Rand⟩

[2]**joggle** \"\ *n* -S **:** a joggling motion

[3]**joggle** \"\ *n* -S [[3]*jog* + *-le* (dim. suffix)] **1 a :** a notch or tooth in the joining surface of a piece of building material to prevent slipping **b :** a slight step-shaped offset formed into a flat piece of metal (as for providing a flange) **2 :** a dowel for joining two adjacent blocks of masonry **3 :** a joint that is formed by joggles

[4]**joggle** \"\ *vt* **joggled; joggled; joggling; joggles 1 :** to join by means of a joggle so as to prevent sliding apart **2 :** to offset (sheet metal) at a corner or edge for improved fit

joggle beam *n* [[3]*joggle*] **:** a built-up beam or flitch beam secured by joggling

joggle piece *n* [[3]*joggle*] **:** a vertical member in a truss supporting one end of a brace or strut by a shoulder or joggle

joggle plating *n* [[3]*joggle*] **:** plating construction for steel ships in which one edge or both edges of a plate are joggled over the edge of an adjoining one

joggle post *n* [[3]*joggle*] **1 :** JOGGLE PIECE **2 :** a post made of timbers joggled together

jog·gler \-g(ə)lə(r)\ *n* -S [[4]*joggle* + *-er*] **:** an operator of a machine for joggling

jogglework \'ˌ=ˌ=\ *n* [[3]*joggle* + *work*] **:** work (as in masonry) done in joggled courses

joggling board *n* [fr. pres. part. of [1]*joggle*] **:** a board suspended between end supports on which one may joggle for play or exercise **:** SPRINGBOARD

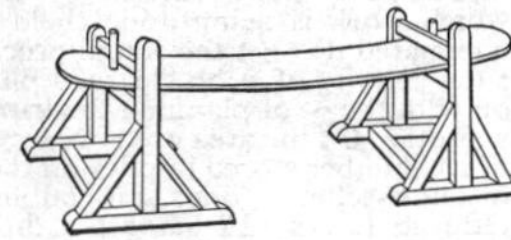

joggling board

jogi *var of* YOGI

jogjakarta *or* **jokyakarta** *usu cap, var of* DJOKJAKARTA

jogs *pl of* JOG, *pres 3d sing of* JOG

jog trot *n* [[2]*jog* + *trot*] **1 :** a slow regular jolting gait **2 :** a routine habit or method persistently adhered to **:** a slow easygoing way or course of action ⟨the sober *jog trot* of domestic bliss—John Galsworthy⟩

jog-trot \'ˌ=ˌ=\ *adj* [*jog trot*] **:** having the character of a jog trot **:** HUMDRUM ⟨the contrast between their violence and our own *jog-trot* existences —Walter de la Mare⟩

jogtrot \"\ *vi* **jogtrotted; jogtrotted; jogtrotting; jogtrots** [*jog trot*] **:** to go at a jog trot ⟨~ all the way home⟩

jo·han·nes *also* **jo·an·nes** \jō'(h)anəs\ *n, pl* **johannes** *also* **joannes** [after *Johannes* or *Joannes* John (or João) V †1750 king of Portugal who first issued such coins and whose name appeared on them] **:** an old Portuguese gold coin first issued in the 18th century and equivalent to 6400 reis — called also *half joe*; compare DOBRA

jo·han·nes·burg \jō'hanəs,bərg, jə'-, -hän-, -nəz,-, -bōg,-bəig *sometimes* yō'-\ *adj, usu cap* [fr. *Johannesburg*, Republic of So. Africa] **:** of or from the city of Johannesburg, Republic of So. Africa **:** of the kind or style prevalent in Johannesburg

jo·han·nes·burg·er \-gə(r)\ *n* -S *cap* [Afrik, fr. *Johannesburg* + Afrik *-er*] **:** a native or inhabitant of Johannesburg, Republic of So. Africa

jo·han·nine \jō'han,īn, (')jō¦hanən\ *adj, usu cap* [*Johannes* (John), one of the twelve apostles of Christ + E *-ine*] **:** of, relating to, or having the characteristics of the Apostle John or the New Testament books whose authorship is ascribed to him

jo·han·nite \jō'ha,nīt\ *n* -S [G *johannit*, fr. Archduke *Johann* (John) of Austria †1859 Austrian general, founder of a museum in Graz, Austria + G *-it* -ite] **:** a mineral $Cu(UO_2)_2(SO_4)(OH)_2.6H_2O$ consisting of a green hydrous basic uranyl copper sulfate that occurs in massive form

jo·hann·sen·ite \jō'han(t)sə,nīt\ *n* -S [Albert *Johannsen* †1950 Am. geologist + E *-ite*] **:** a mineral $CaMnSi_2O_6$ consisting of a silicate of calcium and manganese belonging to the pyroxene group

jo·hans·son block \(')jō,han(t)sən-\ *n, usu cap J* [after C. E. *Johansson*, 20th cent. Swed. engineer] **:** one of a set of gage blocks ground to an accuracy of one hundred-thousandth of an inch or better — called also *Jo block*

john \'jän\ *n* -S [fr. the name *John*, fr. ME *Johan, Jon, John*, fr. LL *Joannes, Johannes*, fr. Gk *Iōannēs*, fr. Heb *Yōḥānān*] **1 a** *often cap* **:** FELLOW, GUY, CHAP ⟨these Wall Street ~*s* can be trimmed —Carl Van Vechten⟩ **b** *usu cap* **:** a Chinese man ⟨the melancholy *Johns* with glazed caps and black pigtails —J.H.Beadle⟩ **c** *usu cap, now chiefly Austral* **:** COP, POLICEMAN ⟨a wild-eyed boy rushed in ... and volunteered to direct the *Johns* to the body —*Sydney (Australia) Bull.*⟩ **2 :** TOILET ⟨have three bathrooms and only two ~*s* —Mary Manning⟩

john a. grindle *n, usu cap J&A&G* [fr. the name *John* + the initial *A.* (prob. fr. a "of") + *grindle*] **:** BOWFIN

john-a-nokes *or* **john-a-noakes** \,jänə'nōks\ *n, usu cap J&N* [alter. of earlier *John at Noke*, fr. the name *John* + *at Noke*, prob. fr. ME *atten ok* at the oak tree] *archaic* **:** a party to legal proceedings whose true name is unknown ⟨as willing to plead for *John-a-Nokes* as for the first noble of the land —Sir Walter Scott⟩ — compare JOHN-A-STILES

john-apple \'ˌ=ˌ=\ *n, usu cap J* [fr. the name *John* + *apple*] *archaic* **:** APPLEJOHN

john-a-stiles *or* **john-a-styles** \,jänə'stī(ə)lz\ *n, usu cap J&S* [alter. of earlier *John at Stile*, fr. the name *John* + *at Stile*, prob. fr. ME *atte stile* at the stile] *archaic* **:** the second party to legal proceedings when the true names of both parties are unknown — compare JOHN-A-NOKES

john barleycorn *n, usu cap J&B* [fr. the name *John* + *barleycorn*] **:** alcoholic liquor personified

johnboat \'ˌ=ˌ=\ *n* [fr. the name *John* + *boat*] **:** a narrow flat-bottomed square-ended boat usu. propelled by a pole or paddle and much used on inland rivers and streams ⟨boys on rafts and in ~*s* —E.W.Smith⟩

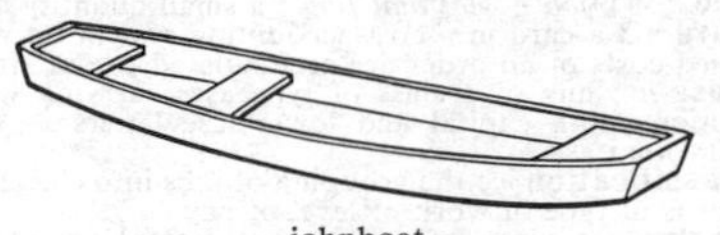

johnboat

john brown *n, usu cap J&B* [fr. the name *John Brown*; prob. trans. of Afrik *Jan Bruin*] **:** a small plump deep-bodied sparid fish (*Gymnocrotaphus curvidens*) of southern Africa that is yellowish to bronzy brown and prized as a sport and food fish

john bull *n, usu cap J&B* [after *John Bull*, a character supposed to typify the English nation in *The History of John Bull*, a satire by John Arbuthnot †1735 Scot. physician and writer] **1 :** the English nation personified **:** the English people ⟨*John Bull* had been weakened by the war —F.A.Magruder⟩ **2 :** a typical or average Englishman ⟨a pipe-smoking *John Bull* astride a bicycle⟩ ⟨he was *John Bull* in a Benedictine robe —Shane Leslie⟩ — **john bull·ish** \-'bu̇lish\ *adj, usu cap J&B* — **john bull·ish·ness** *n, usu cap J&B* — **john bull·ism** \-'bu̇,lizəm\ *n, usu cap J&B*

john chinaman *n, usu cap J&C* [fr. the name *John* + *Chinaman*] **1 :** the Chinese nation personified **:** the Chinese people — usu. taken to be offensive **2 :** a Chinese immigrant; *esp* **:** one living in the U.S. or in Australia — usu. taken to be offensive

john citizen *n, usu cap J&C* [fr. the name *John* + *citizen*] **:** a typical or average citizen **:** JOHN DOE

john crow *n, usu cap J&C* [fr. the name *John* + *crow*] *British West Indies* **:** TURKEY BUZZARD

john doe *n, usu cap J&D* [fr. the name *John Doe*] **1 :** a party to legal proceedings whose true name is unknown; *esp* **:** the first such party when two or more are unknown — compare JOHN STILES, RICHARD MILES, RICHARD ROE **2 :** an anonymous, undistinguished, or average man ⟨brilliant educators and plain *John Does* —K.D.Wells⟩ ⟨the authors of those remarks are now so many *John Does* —Norman Cousins⟩

john dory *n, pl* **john dorys** *usu cap J&D* [fr. the name *John* + *dory* (fish)] **:** a marine fish of the family Zeidae: as **a :** a common European food fish (*Zeus faber*) that is yellow to olive in color and has an oval compressed body, long dorsal spines, and a dark spot on each side **b :** a closely related and possibly identical fish that is sometimes considered a separate species (*Z. capensis*) and is widely distributed in southern seas, being taken often in some quantity off southern Africa, Australia, and New Zealand

john down *n, usu cap J&D* [fr. the name *John* + *down* (feathers)] *Newfoundland* **:** FULMAR 1

joh·ne's bacillus \'yōnəz-\ *n, usu cap J* [after Heinrich A. *Johne* †1910 Ger. bacteriologist] **:** a bacillus (*Mycobacterium paratuberculosis*) that causes Johne's disease

johne's disease *n, usu cap J* [after Heinrich A. *Johne*] **:** a chronic often fatal enteritis of cattle and less commonly of sheep, goats, and horses that is caused by Johne's bacillus and is characterized by persistent diarrhea and gradual emaciation — called also *paratuberculosis*

john-go-to-bed-at-noon \'ˌ=ˌ==ˌ=ˌ=\ *n, usu cap J* [fr. the name *John*] **:** any of several plants whose flowers close about noon; *esp* **:** GOATSBEARD 1

john han·cock \-'han,käk\ *n, usu cap J&H* [after *John Hancock* †1793 Am. statesman; fr. the size and prominence of his signature on the U.S. Declaration of Independence] **:** an autograph signature ⟨put your *John Hancock* on that line —Sinclair Lewis⟩

john henry *n, usu cap J&H* [fr. the name *John Henry*] **:** an autograph signature ⟨would give anything to scratch his *John Henry* off that ... sheet of paper —Richard Hallet⟩

joh·nin \'yōnən\ *n* -S [*john-* (fr. *Johne's bacillus*) + *-in*] **:** a sterile solution of the growth products of Johne's bacillus made in the same manner as tuberculin and used to identify Johne's disease by skin tests, conjunctival reactions, or intravenous injection

john law *n, usu cap J&L* [fr. the name *John* + *law*] **:** a law officer **:** POLICEMAN

john ma·rig·gle \-mə'rigəl\ *n, usu cap J&M* [fr. the name *John* + *mariggle*, of unknown origin] **:** TENPOUNDER 1

john·ny *also* **john·nie** \'jänē, -ni\ *n, pl* **johnnies** [fr. *Johnny*, nickname for *John*] **1** *often cap* **a :** JOHN 1a ⟨one of these gilded *johnnies* who used to sell cars on commission —Dorothy Sayers⟩ **b** *now chiefly Austral* **:** JOHN 1c **2 :** JOHN 2 ⟨wash basins, sinks, and, of course, the ~ —S.S.Rabl⟩ **3 :** a short gown with no collar and with an opening in the back for wear by hospital bed patients ⟨the one string at the back of the neck of the ~ was undone —R.M.Keith⟩

johnnycake \'ˌ=ˌ=ˌ=\ *also* **jon·ny cake** \'jänē,-\ *n* [prob. fr. the name *Johnny* + *cake*] **1 a :** a bread made of white or yellow cornmeal mixed with salt and water or milk and either baked thin in a pan or dropped by spoonfuls onto a hot greased griddle **b :** a bread made of cornmeal, water or milk, and leavening with or without shortening and eggs **2** *Austral* **:** a bread either baked as small cakes in hot ashes or fried

johnny collar \¦ˌ=ˌ=ˌ=\ *n, often cap J* **:** a small round or pointed dress collar that has a front split and that fits close to the neck

johnny-come-lately *also* **johnnie-come-lately** \'ˌ=ˌ=ˌ=ˌ=\ *n, pl* **johnny-come-latelies** *or* **johnny-come-latelys** *also* **johnnies-come-lately** *usu cap J* [fr. the name *Johnny*] **:** a late or recent arrival **:** NEWCOMER ⟨*Johnny-come-latelies* bringing up the rear —*N.Y.Times*⟩ ⟨the *Johnny-come-latelies* climbed the bandwagon —*Chicago Daily News*⟩

johnny cra·paud *or* **johnny cra·peau** \-krà'pō, -'ˌ=(,)ˌ=\ *n, usu cap J&C* [fr. the name *Johnny* + F *crapaud* toad; fr. the reputation of the French for eating frogs — more at CRAPAUD] **1 :** the French people **2 :** FRENCHMAN

johnny darter *n, usu cap J* [fr. the name *Johnny* + *darter*] **:** a small darter (*Boleosoma nigrum*) found in streams of the central U.S.

johnny house *n* [*johnny* + *house*] *chiefly Midland* **:** an outdoor toilet

johnny jump *n, usu cap 1st J* [fr. the name *Johnny* + *jump*, v.; fr. the rapid growth] **:** SHOOTING STAR

johnny-jump-up \'ˌ=ˌ=ˌ=\ *n* -S *usu cap 1st J* [fr. the name *Johnny* + *jump up*, v.; fr. the rapid growth] **1 :** WILD PANSY; *broadly* **:** any of various chiefly small-flowered cultivated pansies **2 :** any of various American violets (as a bird's-foot violet)

johnny-on-the-spot \'ˌ=ˌ=ˌ=ˌ=\ *n, usu cap J* [fr. the name *Johnny* + the phrase *on the spot*] **:** one who is on hand and ready esp. to perform a service or respond to an emergency ⟨luckily he was *Johnny-on-the-spot* ... and was given his highly important post —John Dean⟩

johnny raw *n, usu cap J&R* [fr. the name *Johnny* + *raw*] **:** a raw recruit **:** GREENHORN

johnny reb *n, usu cap J&R* [fr. the name *Johnny* + *reb*] **:** a Confederate soldier in the Civil War

johnny rook *n, usu cap J* [fr. the name *Johnny* + *rook*] **:** a hawk (*Phalcoboenus australis*) of the Falkland islands that is related to the caracaras

johnny smokers *n pl but sing or pl in constr, usu cap J* [fr. the name *Johnny* + *smokers*; fr. the appearance of the feathery styles of the fruit] **:** PRAIRIE SMOKE 1

johnny verde \¦ˌ=¦vərd\ *n, usu cap J* [fr. the name *Johnny* + Sp *verde* green, fr. L *viridis* — more at VERDANT] **:** SAND BASS 1a

john q. public *also* **john q. citizen** *n, usu cap J&Q&P&C* [fr. the name *John* + the initial *Q.* + *public* or *citizen*] **1 :** a member of the public or the community **:** PERSON, CITIZEN ⟨just another *John Q. Citizen* on the road —*Springfield (Mass.) Union*⟩ **2 :** the public or the community personified ⟨Mr. and Mrs. *John Q. Public* suffered no great deprivations —*Domestic Commerce*⟩

johns *pl of* JOHN

john·son bar \'jän(t)sən-\ *n, usu cap J* [fr. the name *Johnson*] **:** the reverse gear lever of a railroad steam locomotive

john·son·ese \,jän(t)sə¦nēz, -ēs\ *n* -S *usu cap* [Samuel *Johnson* †1784 Eng. lexicographer and writer + E *-ese*] **:** a literary style characterized by balanced phraseology and excessively Latinic diction ⟨fell into the pompous rhythm of the later eighteenth century ... into *Johnsonese* —Hastings Lyon⟩

johnson grass *n, usu cap J* [after William *Johnston* †1859 Am. farmer] **:** a tall perennial sorghum (*Sorghum halepense*) that spreads by scaly creeping rhizomes, has been widely introduced as a hay and forage grass, and has become naturalized in many warm regions (as the southern U.S.) where it is a serious pest on cultivated land

[1]**john·so·ni·an** \(')jän¦sōnēən\ *adj, usu cap* [Samuel *Johnson* + E *-ian*] **1 :** of, relating to, or characteristic of Samuel Johnson ⟨a thoroughly *Johnsonian* conception of decorum —Donald Davie⟩ **2 :** of, relating to, or resembling the literary style of Samuel Johnson: as **a :** marked by purity, elevation, and grace ⟨the high style is the style that one thinks of as *Johnsonian* —Lillian De La Torre⟩ **b :** marked by balanced phraseology and excessively Latinic diction ⟨in prolix and *Johnsonian* style —Dinah M. Mulock⟩

[2]**johnsonian** \"\ *n* -S *usu cap* **:** a student, follower, or imitator of Samuel Johnson or his writings

john·so·ni·ana \jän,sōnē'anə, -'änə, -'ānə *also* -'ānə\ *n pl, usu cap* [Samuel *Johnson* + E *-i-* + *-ana*] **:** collected items by, about, or relating to Samuel Johnson

johnson noise *n, usu cap J* [after John B. *Johnson* b1887 Am. physicist] **:** THERMAL NOISE

john stiles \-'stī(ə)lz\ *n, usu cap J&S* [alter. of *john-a-stiles*] **:** a party to legal proceedings whose true name is unknown; *esp* **:** the third such party when three are unknown — compare JOHN DOE, RICHARD MILES, RICHARD ROE

john·ston's organ \'jän(t)stənz-\ *n, usu cap J* [after Christopher *Johnston* †1891 Am. physician] **:** a sense organ in the second antennal segment of insects that responds to movements of the antennal flagellum and serves as a flight-speed indicator

john·strup·ite \'jän,strə,pīt\ *n* -S [G *johnstrupit*, fr. Frederik *Johnstrup* †1894 Danish mineralogist + G *-it* -ite] **:** a mineral approximately $(Ca,Na)_3(Ce,Ti,Zr)Si_2O_8F$ consisting of a complex silicate of cerium and other metals in prismatic crystals (sp. gr. 3.29)

john's-wort \'ˌ=ˌ=\ *n, pl* **john's-worts** *usu cap J* [after St. *John*, one of the twelve apostles of Christ; fr. its having been gathered on the eve of the Feast of St. John (June 24)] **:** SAINT-JOHN'S-WORT

john to·whit \-tü'(h)wit\ *n, usu cap J* [fr. the name *John* + *towhit*, of imit. origin] **:** a West Indian vireo (*Vireo altiloquus*)

john trot *n, usu cap J&T* [fr. the name *John Trot*] **:** a dull man **:** BUMPKIN, BOOR

joie de vi·vre \,zhwädə'vēvr(ᵊ), -vēv(rə)\ *n* [F, lit., joy of living] **:** keen or buoyant enjoyment of life ⟨youthfully innocent *joie de vivre* —John Beaufort⟩

[1]**join** \'jȯin *dial* 'jīn\ *vb* -ED/-ING/-S [ME *joinen*, fr. OF *join-*, *joign-*, stem of *joindre*, fr. L *jungere* — more at YOKE] *vt* **1 a :** to put or bring together and fasten, connect, or relate so as to form a single unit, a whole, or a continuity **:** COMBINE, LINK ⟨~ two blocks of wood with glue⟩ ⟨two moral forces, separate and yet ~*ed*⟩ ⟨~ forces in an effort to stamp out vice⟩ ⟨a bridge ~*ing* the two halves of the city⟩ **b :** to connect (as points) by a line (as a straight line) **c :** ADJOIN ⟨his studio there ~*ed* that of the famous sculptor —J.T.Marshall⟩ **2 :** to put or bring into close contact, association, or relationship **:** ATTACH, UNITE, COUPLE ⟨was later ~*ed* to another battalion⟩ ⟨the agitation of his mind, ~*ed* to the pain of his wound, kept him awake —Francis Parkman⟩ ⟨~*ed* in marriage by a local minister⟩ **3 :** to enter into or engage in (battle) **4 a** (1) **:** to

come into the company of : come into local contact or association with ⟨∼s his wife and three children around the breakfast table —Stuart Chase⟩ ⟨∼ed us for lunch⟩ (2) : to come to ⟨at the next town we ∼ another route⟩ **b** : to connect or associate oneself with: (1) : to participate in : enter into ⟨∼ed the defense of Paris as commander of naval antiaircraft batteries —*Current Biog.*⟩ (2) : to ally oneself with ⟨∼ the government in condemning foreign aggression⟩ (3) : BOARD ⟨∼a vehicle⟩; *esp* : to go aboard (a ship) usu. as a member of the personnel ⟨∼ed the destroyer as executive officer⟩ (4) : to become a member or associate of ⟨∼ a church⟩ ⟨∼ a faculty⟩ ⟨ran away from school to ∼ a traveling tent show —*Current Biog.*⟩ ∼ *vi* **1 a** : to come together so as to be connected or united ⟨English nouns ∼ easily to form compounds⟩ **b** : ADJOIN ⟨at this point the two estates ∼⟩ **2** : to come into close association or relationship: as **a** : to form or enter into an alliance or league ⟨business interests ∼ed to maintain the consolidated system —*Amer. Guide Series: Minn.*⟩ — often used with *up* ⟨the three clubs ∼ed up to improve the town's playground facilities⟩ **b** : to become a member of a group or organization ⟨an ambulance service was organized and I ∼ed in as a stretcher bearer —Nevil Shute⟩ ⟨he is now a Mason but he did not ∼ until last year⟩ ⟨two weeks after he ∼ed up he was sent into the fighting area and saw immediate action⟩ **c** : to enter into or take part in a collective activity ⟨∼ in singing the national anthem⟩ ⟨when there was group dancing . . . they all ∼ed in together —Cabell Phillips⟩

syn CONJOIN, LINK, CONNECT, RELATE, ASSOCIATE, COMBINE, UNITE all signify a bringing or coming together into a more or less close union. RELATE and ASSOCIATE suggest the loosest and most unspecific of unions; LINK, JOIN, CONJOIN, and CONNECT suggest a closer contact to the point of a physical or moral attachment; COMBINE and UNITE suggest a union to the point of some loss of identity or a complete loss of identity of the separate elements. Of the pair RELATE and ASSOCIATE, ASSOCIATE emphasizes the mere fact of the bringing, coming, or being together of two or more persons or things although it suggests by customary implication some kind of unspecified often intangible but compatible or companionable interaction ⟨*associate* with shady characters⟩ ⟨*associate* the sense of hunger and the search for food⟩ ⟨was *associated* with the hospital from 1889 until 1919 —*Amer. Guide Series: Md.*⟩ ⟨the smooth ultralegato style now often *associated* with English music of the period —E.T.Canby⟩ RELATE can signify a bringing or coming together in any number of ways so that the two or more things have some generally only implied physical, moral, or logical bearing on each other ⟨the wing of a bird and the arm of a man are historically *related*⟩ ⟨an interrogation point which *relates* the title closely to the text —G.W.Johnson⟩ ⟨not the least merit of the book is that it *relates* the history of science to other thought currents —F.L.Baumer⟩ ⟨their ability to *relate* what they observe to what they know or have previously observed —Gertrude H. Hildreth⟩ Although they are used to signify a more specific union, LINK, CONNECT, JOIN, and CONJOIN in their nonphysical application may suggest a bringing or coming together as general and unspecified as that implied by RELATE or ASSOCIATE but tend more, esp. in physical application, to signify a junction of some kind, often an inseparable junction as by a chain or by bonding. CONNECT is the most general of these four and suggests a loose attachment, esp. one that preserves the identity of the elements and the evidence of the connection ⟨*connect* the two ends of the pipe⟩ ⟨*connect* the two houses by a path⟩ ⟨the criminal activity has been *connected* with the names of several prominent men⟩ ⟨a number of articles *connected* with her life —*Amer. Guide Series: R.I.*⟩ LINK suggests a slightly closer coupling esp. in the physical application of the word in which is implied inseparability but of still clearly identifiable separate elements ⟨the bridge *linking* the islands of North Hero and Grand Isle —*Amer. Guide Series: Vt.*⟩ ⟨none of the subjects that *linked* us together could be talked about in a bar —Nevil Shute⟩ ⟨eight Anarchists were condemned to death or life imprisonment in a trial that *linked* them to this Haymarket Riot —J.D.Hart⟩ JOIN usu. suggests strongly the idea of physical or moral contact or junction or the making of a continuity of two or more things ⟨apply glue to the edges to be *joined*⟩ ⟨*join* the ends of the wires with solder⟩ ⟨a common purpose *joined* their efforts⟩ CONJOIN usu. emphasizes both the togetherness of a joining and the separateness of the things joined ⟨three *conjoined* quadrangular beakers with a common cover —*Parke-Bernet Galleries Catalog*⟩ ⟨a scientific realism, based on mechanism, is *conjoined* with an unwavering belief in the world of men . . . as being composed of self-determining organisms —A.N.Whitehead⟩ COMBINE and UNITE usu. emphasize the first a mingling and the second a union or integration in which individual identity is lost in a common aim or in the formation of a new product from the mingling or integration. COMBINE stresses a merging by intermixture ⟨*combine* ingredients in making a cake⟩ ⟨*combines* Georgian Colonial and Classical Revival designs —*Amer. Guide Series: Pa.*⟩ ⟨beauty and melody and graceful motion . . . were *combined* in her —W.H.Hudson †1922⟩ UNITE strongly emphasizes the singleness resulting from the junction of persons or elements ⟨*unite* the separated army divisions⟩ ⟨certain chemical elements *unite* to form gases⟩ ⟨*unite* two people in a common purpose⟩ ⟨*unite* a couple in marriage⟩ ⟨a cooperative community in which manual and intellectual labor might be *united* —Allan MacDonald⟩

— **join hands 1** : to clasp or shake hands in token of agreement or affection **2 a** : to make contact : come together ⟨*joined hands* with forces coming from the east⟩ **b** : to join together in an alliance or corporate enterprise or to a common end ⟨the clergy *joined hands* with the laity in maintaining the inherited verse forms —Kemp Malone⟩ — **join out** *or* **join out the odds** *slang* : to engage in the business of procuring : turn pimp — **join the issue** *or* **join issue 1** : to submit a legal issue jointly for decision **2 a** : to accept, fix on, or clearly define a particular issue as the basis of a controversy or other struggle ⟨*the issue* was clearly *joined* —K.S.Latourette⟩ ⟨the Senator did not endorse unfair play, injustice, and indecency, and thus *join the issue* —W.L.Miller⟩ ⟨the minority report was read and *the issue joined* —Walter Goodman⟩ **b** : to take an opposed or contrary position on some question : take issue ⟨it is with his conclusions that we today would *join issue* —K.H. Hartley⟩

²**join** \"\ *n* -S **1** : something that joins : a place or line where joining occurs : JOINT ⟨ensure accurately matching ∼s —W.P. Matthew⟩ ⟨the ∼s between the veins and the arteries, the capillaries —S.F.Mason⟩ ⟨the ∼ of lid and box⟩ **2** : a splice in magnetic recording tape

join·able \-nəbəl\ *adj* : capable of being joined

join·der \'jȯində(r)\ *n* -S [F *joindre* to join — more at JOIN] **1** : act of joining : a putting together : CONJUNCTION ⟨simultaneous production and ∼ of these two pieces at the Argentine Embassy —*Blue Bk. on Argentina*⟩ **2 a** : a joining of parties as plaintiffs or defendants in a suit **b** : acceptance of an issue tendered **c** : a joining of causes of action or defense or of parties in an indictment **d** : a joining of two or more parties in a common transaction

joined *past of* JOIN

¹**join·er** \'jȯinə(r) *dial* 'jīn-\ *n* -S [ME *joinour, joiner*, fr. AF *joignour*, fr. OF *joign-, join-* (stem of *joindre* to join) + AF *-our* -or — more at JOIN] **1** : one that joins: as **a** : a person whose occupation is to construct articles by joining pieces of wood : one who does the woodwork (as doors or stairs) necessary for the finishing of buildings — compare CARPENTER **b** : a worker who stitches together the parts of garments **c** : a worker who prepares sheets of glass for grinding and polishing by arranging them on a plaster-covered table **d** : a worker who inserts sections of stained glass into leads preparatory to their placement in windows **e** : a worker who by hand or by machine shapes the edge of the shank sole of shoes at the joint between the shank and heel — called also *jointer* **f** : a worker who fits and joins the parts of interior furnishings of boats and installs the completed units **g** : a worker who puts rubber articles (as baby pants) through a roller-cutter that joins and trims the edges **2** : JOINTER a(1) **3** : a typically gregarious or civic-minded person who joins many organizations : a person temperamentally given to joining many organizations ⟨the young businessman is not markedly a civic ∼ —W.H.Whyte⟩ ⟨when it comes to clubs and organizations, she is not a ∼ —*Current Biog.*⟩

²**joiner** \"\ *vi* -ED/-ING/-S : to work as a joiner

joiner work *n* : JOINERY

join·ery \'jȯinərē, -ri\ *n* -ES [¹*joiner* + *-y*] **1** : the art or trade of a joiner **2** : work done by a joiner; *also* : things made by a joiner

joining *n* -S [fr. gerund of ¹*join*] **1 a** : the act or an instance of joining one thing to another ⟨an easy ∼ is always possible —L.A.Leslie⟩ **b** : the condition or fact of being joined together : JUNCTURE ⟨apt to name each separate confluence with its own name, since their later ∼s are unknown to him —A.A. Hill⟩ **2 a** : the place or manner of being joined together : JOIN, JOINT ⟨the ∼ is hardly visible⟩ **b** : something that joins two things together **3** : the practice of joining many organizations ⟨used to be the fashion to decry all forms of American ∼ —W.S.Lynch⟩

joins *pres 3d sing of* JOIN, *pl of* JOIN

¹**joint** \'jȯint *dial* 'jīnt-\ *n* -S [ME *joint, jointe*, partly fr. OF *jointe* joint of the body, fr. fem. of *joint*, past part. of *joindre* to join; partly fr. MF *joint* joint (place where two parts meet), fr. past part. of *joindre* — more at JOIN] **1 a** (1) : the point of contact between elements of an animal skeleton (as femur and hipbone) whether movable or rigidly fixed together with the parts (as membranes, tendons, ligaments) that surround and support it ⟨the capsule of the shoulder ∼⟩ ⟨the antennal ∼s of a cockroach⟩ (2) : such a structure regarded as a particular type of mechanism ⟨the ball-and-socket ∼ of the hip⟩ (3) : NODE 4a ⟨the ∼s of a stem of grass⟩ **b** : a part or space included between two articulations, knots, or nodes ⟨the first ∼ of the arm⟩ ⟨a ∼ of cane⟩ **c** : a large piece of meat for roasting **2 a** : a place where two things or parts are joined or united : a union of two or more smooth or even surfaces admitting of a close fitting or junction whether movable or immovable : JUNCTION ⟨a ∼ between two pieces of timber⟩ ⟨a ∼ in a pipe⟩ **b** : a space between the adjacent surfaces of two bodies (as bricks) joined and held together by means of cement, mortar, or other material ⟨a thin ∼⟩ **c** : a fracture or crack in rock not accompanied by dislocation being generally one of many arranged in a systematic pattern, occurring in all firm coherent rocks, and dividing them into blocks **d** : the flexing portion of a cover along either backbone edge of a book; *also* : the groove where the cover hinges — called also *hinge* **e** : the junction of two or more members of a framed structure **f** : a union formed by two abutting rails in a track including the bars, bolts, and other elements necessary to hold the abutting rails together **g** : an area at which two ends, surfaces, or edges are attached (as by adhesive, tape, nails, or staples) **3 a** (1) : a shabby or disreputable place of entertainment or other public house ⟨make a tour of the tough ∼s —W.S.Maugham⟩ ⟨I wouldn't go there; that place is a ∼⟩ (2) : a place (as a nightclub, restaurant, or hotel) open to the public ⟨I'll have you know this is a respectable ∼ —William Grampp⟩ ⟨it depended on the social tone of the ∼ —Scott Fitzgerald⟩ (3) : PLACE, ESTABLISHMENT, DWELLING ⟨there now are buffaloes all over the ∼ —R.M.Yoder⟩ ⟨this is certainly an intellectual ∼ —Sinclair Lewis⟩ ⟨come on over to my ∼⟩ **b** *slang* : a concession stand at a circus or fair **c** *slang* (1) : a marijuana cigarette (2) : a hypodermic needle; *also* : the needle, dropper, and connection used in taking drugs hypodermically — **out of joint 1 a** *of a bone* : having the head slipped from its socket **b** : being out of adjustment or harmony : being at odds : UNSUITABLE, INCONSISTENT ⟨production costs are now entirely *out of joint* with retail prices —Jack Morpurgo⟩ ⟨impractical, romantic, and wholly *out of joint* with their times —W.P.Webb⟩ **2 a** : being in an unsatisfactory or disordered state : UNPROPITIOUS ⟨the times are *out of joint*⟩ **b** : being out of humor : DISGRUNTLED, DISSATISFIED ⟨find themselves a little *out of joint* with the party arrangements —Sir Winston Churchill⟩ ⟨the Ministry are much *out of joint* —Thomas Gray⟩ ⟨must have been many noses put *out of joint* —Alvin Johnson⟩

joints used in masonry: *1* struck; *2* weathered; *3* flush; *4* raked, *5* tooled, concave; *6* tooled, "V"

²**joint** \"\ *adj* [ME, fr. MF, fr. past part. of *joindre* — more at JOIN] **1** : JOINED, UNITED, COMBINED ⟨subjected to the ∼ influences of culture and climate⟩ **2** : common to two or more: as **a** (1) : involving the united activity of two or more : done or produced by two or more working together ⟨issued a ∼ report⟩ ⟨achieved through our ∼ efforts⟩ (2) : constituting an activity, operation, or organization in which elements of more than one armed service participate ⟨the *Joint* Chiefs of Staff⟩ (3) : constituting an action or expression in which two or more governments unite as distinguished from an identic action or expression ⟨a ∼ intervention⟩ ⟨a ∼ note⟩ **b** (1) : shared by or affecting two or more : held or obligating or obligated in common ⟨∼ property⟩ ⟨a ∼ fine⟩ (2) : united in right, status, interest, power, privilege, duty, or obligation (3) : of or relating to the right of survivorship in property held in joint tenancy or by the entirety as distinguished from that held as tenants in common — compare CORREAL, JOINT AND SEVERAL, SEVERAL, SOLIDARITY **3** : united, joined, or sharing with another (as in a right, obligation, status, or activity) : not solitary in interest or action : holding in common with an associate : acting together ⟨∼ heir⟩ ⟨∼ creditor⟩ **4** : of or relating to a joint family

³**joint** \"\ *vb* -ED/-ING/-S [¹*joint*] *vt* **1 a** *obs* : JOIN, UNITE, COMBINE ⟨∼*ing* their force —Shak.⟩ **b** : to unite by a joint : fit together ⟨∼ boards⟩ ⟨her elbows and shoulders are ∼ed wrong —*Irish Digest*⟩ **c** : to provide with a joint : ARTICULATE **d** : to prepare (as a board) for joining by planing the edge to be joined **e** : to file down (saw teeth) to a correct height **2** : to separate the joints of : divide at the joint : cut up into joints ⟨lamb should present little difficulty if thoroughly ∼ed beforehand —Noreen Routledge⟩ ∼ *vi* **1** : to fit as if by joints : coalesce as joints do ⟨the stones ∼ neatly⟩ **2** : to form joints as a stage in growth (as of winter wheat and other small grains)

joint account *n* : a bank or brokerage account owned jointly by two or more persons either of whom may withdraw funds or effect transactions on his signature alone

joint adventure *n* : a partnership or cooperative agreement between two or more persons restricted to a single specific undertaking — called also *joint undertaking*; compare SYNDICATE

joint and several *adj* : constituting or relating to rights which two or more persons entitled thereto may assert either together or separately or to duties and liabilities of two or more persons for which they may be held liable either together or separately (as a note where all makers or any one of them can be held for the full amount) — compare CORREAL, IN SOLIDO, JOINT 2b(3), SEVERAL, SOLIDARITY

joint and survivor annuity *n* : JOINT LIFE AND SURVIVOR ANNUITY

joint annuity *n* : JOINT LIFE ANNUITY

joint assertion *n* : CONJUNCTION 7a

joint author *n* : a person who collaborates with one or more persons in the production of a literary work ⟨*joint authors* of a widely used text⟩

joint bar *n* : a steel member embodying beam strength and stiffness by its structural shape and material and commonly used in pairs to splice rail ends together

joint–bedded \'=,==\ *adj*, *of a quarried stone* : bedded in the wall so that its natural bed is set in a joint — compare FACE-BEDDED

joint chair *n* [¹*joint*] *Brit* : a chair supporting the ends of abutting rails

joint committee *n* : a committee appointed by both houses of a legislature usu. for the purpose of considering joint action or resolving differences between the houses — compare CONFERENCE 3b

joint contributory *adj* : CONTRIBUTORY

joint convention *n* : a meeting together of both branches of the U.S. Congress or of a state legislature

joint denial *n* : the complex proposition asserting that neither of two propositions is true ⟨the *joint denial* "not *p* and not *q*" is true only if *p* and *q* are false⟩ — compare ALTERNATIVE DENIAL

jointed *adj* [ME, fr. *joint, jointe* joint + *-ed*] : having joints : ARTICULATED ⟨a ∼ doll⟩ — often used in combination ⟨loose-jointed⟩ ⟨well-*jointed*⟩

jointed cactus *n* : a cactus of the genus *Opuntia*

jointed charlock *n* : a Eurasian weed (*Raphanus raphanistrum*) closely related to the common radish and having seed pods that are prominently constricted

jointed fern *n* : HORSETAIL 2

joint·ed·ly *adv* : in a jointed manner

joint·ed·ness *n* -ES : the quality or state of being jointed

joint enterprise *n* **1** : JOINT ADVENTURE **2 a** : an undertaking of two or more persons for a common object under circumstances giving each an equal right to control a vehicle or instrumentality and making all chargeable with the negligence of anyone exercising actual control and causing harm to another in actions between the third person and the parties to the enterprise **b** : an undertaking of two or more persons for mutual benefit or pleasure

joint·er \'jȯintə(r)\ *n* -S : one that joints: as **a** (1) : a hand or power planer for smoothing a sawed surface for jointing or mortising (2) : a tool used for filing the points of saw teeth to a uniform height **b** (1) : a bent piece of iron inserted to strengthen joints (2) : a tool for pointing joints (3) : a tool for cutting grooves to indicate joints in freshly laid surfaces of cement **c** : a triangular-shaped edged attachment to a plow beam for covering trash and organic matter in plowing **d** (1) : a worker who joints (as wires, pipes, or scissors blades) (2) : a worker who operates an abrasive saw or wheel for cutting structural stone true for fit in construction (3) : JOINER 1e

jointer b(3)

jointer gauge *n* : an attachment clamped to one side of a bench plane and made adjustable to secure any desired angle between the edge of a board being planed and its face

jointer plane *n* : a woodworker's plane about 2 feet long used for smoothing long surfaces (as the edges of boards in preparation for joining them)

joint evil *or* **joint ill** *n* : NAVEL ILL

joint facility *n* : railway property that two or more carriers jointly own, maintain, or operate by formal agreement

joint family *or* **joint household** *n* : a consanguineal family unit that includes two or more generations of kindred related through either the paternal or maternal line who maintain a common residence and are subject to common social, economic, and religious regulations

joint fir *n* [¹*joint*; fr. the leafless jointed stems] : any of various plants of the family Gnetaceae and esp. of the genera *Gnetum* and *Ephedra* with small scalelike leaves resembling those of some evergreens

joint–fir family *n* : GNETACEAE

joint gap *n* [¹*joint*] : the distance in 64ths of an inch between the ends of contiguous rails measured at a point about ⅝ inch below the top of the rail

joint grass *n* [¹*joint*] **1** : a coarse creeping grass (*Paspalum distichum*) that roots at the joints and is used as fodder and as a soil binder **2** : HORSETAIL 2 **3** : YELLOW BEDSTRAW

jointing *n* -S [fr. gerund of ³*joint*] **1** : the act or process or an instance of making a joint; *also* : the joint thus produced **2** : the process of filling and finishing the joints in masonry with a special caulking material **3** : a condition or structure in rock characterized by the presence of joints

jointing rule *n* : a long straight rule used by bricklayers for securing straight joints and faces

joint·less \'jȯintləs *dial* 'jīnt-\ *adj* : constituting one piece : having no seam or joint

joint life and survivor annuity *n* : an annuity payable as long as any of two or more designated persons shall live

joint life annuity *n* : an annuity payable only until the death of the first of two or more designated persons

joint life insurance *n* : a policy providing for payment of the proceeds upon the first occurrence of death among the persons insured

joint·ly *adv* [ME, fr. *joint* + *-ly*] **1** : in a joint manner: as **a** : TOGETHER, UNITEDLY ⟨activities carried on ∼ with other societies —*Mech. Engineering*⟩ ⟨written ∼ with other scientists —*Current Biog.*⟩ ⟨owned ∼ by several companies⟩; *specif* : so as to be or become liable to a joint obligation **b** : in joint tenancy or in tenancy by the entirety, or with the right of survivorship **2** : in proportion to the product

joint mouse *n* [¹*joint*; fr. the fact that its movement suggests that of a mouse] : a loose fragment (as of cartilage) within a synovial space

joint·ness *n* -ES : the quality or state of being common to two or more persons

joint obligation *n* : an obligation binding each of the obligors to the performance of the entire obligation

joint oil *n* [¹*joint*] : SYNOVIA

joint plant *n* [¹*joint*] : a wandering Jew (*Tradescantia fluminensis*) with green or green and white striped leaves

joint product *n* **1** : a product of joint effort ⟨view this report as truly a *joint product* —C.E.Osgood & T.A.Sebeok⟩ **2** : one of two or more products of substantial importance derived from the same raw material (as gas and coke from coal) — distinguished from *by-product*

joint rate *n* : a rate from a point on one transport carrier to a point on another line made by agreement and published in a concurrent tariff

joint resolution *n* : a resolution passed by both branches of a legislative body; *esp* : one passed by both houses of the U.S. Congress and having the force of law when signed by the president or passed by a two-thirds majority of both houses over the president's veto ⟨a *joint resolution*, requiring mere congressional majorities, has been resorted to when the treaty-making process . . . broke down —F.A.Ogg & P.O.Ray⟩ — compare BILL 3, CONCURRENT RESOLUTION

joint·ress \'jȯin·trəs\ *n* -ES [obs. E *jointer* man who holds a jointure (fr. *jointure* + *-er*) + *-ess*] : a woman who has a legal jointure

joint ring *n* [¹*joint*] *obs* : GEMEL 2

joint runner *n* [¹*joint*] : a piece of asbestos rope with clamps placed around a pipe or tile joint to serve as a dam for the retention of poured molten metal later to be caulked in

joint rust *n* [¹*joint*] : a disease of grasses caused by the cattail fungus and characterized by the development of fungal stromata esp. about the joints of an affected plant — compare CHOKE 5

joints *pl of* JOINT, *pres 3d sing of* JOINT

joint session *or* **joint meeting** *n* : a session of the two houses of a legislature meeting together and acting as one body

joint shingle *n* [¹*joint*] : a short wooden shingle formerly applied by nailing edge to edge instead of overlapping

joint snake *n* [¹*joint*; fr. the deep lateral fold on the body] : GLASS SNAKE

joint splice *n* [¹*joint*] : a reinforce at a joint intended to hold the parts in their true relation

joint stock *n* : stock or capital held in company : capital held as a common stock or fund

joint–stock bank *n* **1** : a bank organized as a joint-stock association **2** : an English or Australian bank whose capital is subscribed by private persons under statutory law as distinguished from a government bank

joint–stock company *n* **1** : a company or association consisting of a number of individuals organized to conduct a business for gain with a joint stock, the shares owned by any member being transferable without the consent of the rest **2** *also* **joint–stock association** : a form of partnership differing from the ordinary form of partnership by the transferability of shares (as in a corporation), by the fact that the death of a stockholder does not dissolve the company, and by the fact that the managing of the company is limited to persons specially authorized — compare CORPORATION, LIMITED LIABILITY

joint stock land bank *n*, *usu cap J&S&L&B* : any of several corporations organized to make mortgage loans direct to farmers and to issue bonds similar to farm loan bonds

joint stool *n* [1*joint*] **:** a stool formed of parts held together by pegged mortise-and-tenon joints **:** a stool made by a joiner

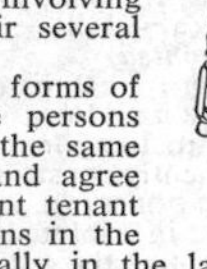
joint stool

joint tariff *n* **:** a schedule of rates agreed upon by two or more carriers involving charges between points on their several lines

joint tenancy *n* **:** one of several forms of tenure in which two or more persons hold in concurrent ownership the same estate in realty or personalty and agree that upon the death of one joint tenant the full title to the estate remains in the surviving joint tenants and finally in the last survivor — compare TENANCY BY THE ENTIRETY, TENANCY IN COMMON

joint tenant *n* **:** one who holds an estate by or in joint tenancy

joint tortfeasor *n* **1 :** one of two or more persons acting in concert in the commission of a tort **2 a :** one of two or more persons who may be joined as defendants in the same single cause of action to recover damage for a tort **b :** one of two or more persons jointly and severally fully responsible for all the damage to a third person caused by their concurring though independent tortious acts **c :** one of two tortfeasors where one is by the policy of the law vicariously liable for the tortious conduct of the other (as where the principal is liable for his agent's conduct or the master for that of his servant)

joint undertaking *or* **joint venture** *n* **:** JOINT ADVENTURE

1join·ture \ˈjȯinchə(r)\ *n* -s [ME, fr. MF, fr. L *junctura*, fr. *junctus* (past part. of *jungere* to join) + *-ura* -ure — more at YOKE] **1 a :** an act of joining **:** the state of being joined **:** UNION ⟨the ~ of two odd names in marriage —E.C.Smith⟩ ⟨the battle seemed on its way to ~ —*Time*⟩ **b :** JOINT, JUNCTURE **2 a** *obs* (1) **:** the joint tenancy of an estate (2) **:** the estate so held **b** (1) **:** an estate settled on a wife to be taken by her in lieu of dower (2) **:** a settlement upon the wife of a freehold estate (as in lands or tenements) for her lifetime at least to take effect upon the decease of the husband and to act as a bar to dower — called also *legal jointure;* compare EQUITABLE DOWER

2jointure \"\ *vt* -ED/-ING/-S **:** to settle a jointure upon

join·tur·ess \-chərəs\ *n* -ES [alter. (influenced by 1*jointure*) of *jointress*] **:** JOINTRESS

joint vein *n* [1*joint*] **:** a small geological vein occupying a joint

joint vetch *n* [1*joint;* fr. the jointed pod] **:** a plant of the genus *Aeschynomene*

joint water *n* [1*joint;* trans. of G *gelenkwasser*] **:** SYNOVIA

jointweed \ˈ=,=\ *n* [1*joint* + *weed*] **:** a plant of the genus *Polygonella; esp* **:** an American herb (*P. articulata*) with jointed almost leafless stems and spikelike racemes of small white flowers

joint wire *n* [1*joint*] **:** hollow wire that is used for joints (as in a watchcase)

jointwood \ˈ=,=\ *n* [1*joint* + *wood*] **:** an East Indian tree (*Cassia nodosa*) with dense showy racemes of pink or red flowers

joint wood berry *n* **:** CRANBERRY BUSH 2

jointworm \ˈ=,=\ *n* [1*joint* + *worm*] **1 :** the larva of any of several small chalcid flies of the family Eurytomidae and genus *Harmolita* which attack the stems of grain and cause swellings like galls usu. at or just above the first joint **2** [so called fr. its jointed appearance] **:** BAMBOO WORM

1joist \ˈjȯist *dial* ˈjīst\ *n* -s [ME *giste, geste,* fr. MF *giste,* fr. (assumed) VL *jacitum,* fr. L *jacēre* to lie + *-itum* (neut. of *-itus,* past participial ending) — more at GIST] **1 a :** any of the small rectangular-sectioned timbers or rolled iron or steel beams ranged parallel from wall to wall in a structure or resting on beams or girders to support the planking, pavement, tiling, or flagging of a floor or the laths or furring strips of a ceiling — see BINDING JOIST, BRIDGING JOIST, CEILING JOIST, TRIMMING JOIST **b :** a similar timber supporting the floor of a bridge or other structure **2 :** a stud or scantling about 3 by 4 inches in section

2joist \"\ *vt* -ED/-ING/-S **:** to furnish with joists

joisting *n* -s [1*joist* + *-ing*] **:** joists esp. when in position supporting a floor

jo·jo·ba \hōˈhōbə, hə'-\ *or* **ja·jo·ba** \hə'-\ *n* [MexSp *jojoba*] **:** a shrub or small tree (*Simmondsia californica*) of the family Buxaceae of southwestern No. America with edible seeds that contain a valuable oil

jo–jotte \jōˈjät\ *n* -s [fr. *Jo-Jotte,* a trademark] **:** a card game based on belotte or klaberjass with some features (as doubling and slam bonuses) of bridge

1joke \ˈjōk\ *n* -s [L *jocus* jest, joke, game; akin to OS *gehan* to say, speak, OHG *gehan, jehan* to say, speak, MW *ieith* language, Toch A & B *yask-* to demand, beg, Skt *yācati* he implores; basic meaning: speaking] **1 a :** something said or done to amuse or provoke laughter **:** something funny or humorous ⟨a tune which can be played backward — a ~ —Edward Sackville-West⟩ ⟨the use of primarily visual ~*s* —*Current Biog.*⟩; *esp* **:** a brief usu. oral narrative designed to provoke laughter and typically having a climactic humorous twist or denouement ⟨had a great fund of off-color ~*s*⟩ **b** (1) **:** the spirit of humor or raillery in which something is said or done ⟨knew they were meant in ~ —James Jones⟩ (2) **:** the humorous or ridiculous element in something ⟨the ~ of it was that the matter was so entirely his own choice —S.E.White⟩ (3) **:** LAUGHTER, RAILLERY, KIDDING — often used in the phrase *take a joke* ⟨the most valuable thing she taught me was to take a ~ —Polly Adler⟩ **c :** PRACTICAL JOKE ⟨mustn't play ~*s* on poor old ladies⟩ **d :** a person or thing that is the object of laughter or ridicule **:** LAUGHINGSTOCK ⟨why, he's the ~ of the whole town⟩ ⟨was still . . . a national ~ —Van Wyck Brooks⟩ **2 a :** something lacking substance, genuineness, or quality **:** something not to be taken seriously **:** a trivial or trifling matter ⟨palaces and haunts . . . in which the state religion is a ~ —Ray Alan⟩ ⟨consider his skiing a ~ —Harold Callender⟩ — often used in negative construction ⟨it is no ~ . . . to encounter week after week a player of settled reputation —Bernard Darwin⟩ **b :** something presenting no difficulty **:** something accomplished with ridiculous ease ⟨that exam was a ~⟩

syn JOKE, JEST, JAPE, QUIP, WITTICISM, WISECRACK, CRACK, GAG can mean, in common, a remark, story, or action intended to evoke laughter. JOKE, when applied to a story or remark, suggests something designed to promote good humor, esp. an anecdote with a humorous twist at the end; when applied to an action, it often signifies a practical joke, usu. suggesting a fooling or deceiving of someone at his expense, generally though not necessarily good humored in intent ⟨everyone knows the old *joke,* that "black horses eat more than white horses", a puzzling condition which is finally cleared up by the statement that "there are more black horses" —W.J.Reilly⟩ ⟨issues had become a hopeless muddle and national politics a biennial *joke* —Dixon Wecter⟩ ⟨a child hiding mother's pocketbook as a *joke*⟩ ⟨the whole tale turns out to be a monstrous *joke,* a deception of matchless cruelty —B.R.Redman⟩ JEST, now literary or affected, in an older sense still connotes raillery or sarcasm but generally today suggests humor that is light and sportive, as banter ⟨continually . . . making a *jest* of his ignorance —J.D.Beresford⟩ ⟨won fame by *jests* at the foibles of his time, but . . . his pen was more playful than caustic —S.T.Williams & J.A.Pollard⟩ JAPE, usu. of literary occurrence, orig. signified an amusing anecdote but today is identical with JEST or JOKE ⟨the merry *japes* of fundamentally irresponsible young men —Edmund Fuller⟩ ⟨the *japes* about sex still strike me as being prurient rather than funny —John McCarten⟩ QUIP suggests a quick, neatly turned, witty remark ⟨full of wise saws and homely illustrations, the epigram, the *quip,* the jest —B.N.Cardozo⟩ ⟨many *quips* at the expense of individuals and their villages —Margaret Mead⟩ ⟨enlivened their reviews with *quips* —W.H. Dunham⟩ WITTICISM is a bookish and WISECRACK or CRACK the more general term for a clever or witty, esp. a biting or sarcastic, remark, generally a retort ⟨all the charming *witticisms* of English lecturers —Eric Sevareid⟩ ⟨a vicious *witticism* at the expense of a political opponent⟩ ⟨merely strolls by, makes a goofy *wisecrack* or screwball suggestion —Hugh Humphrey⟩ ⟨though the gravity of the situation forbade their utterance, I was thinking of at least three priceless *cracks* I could make —P.G.Wodehouse⟩ GAG, orig. in this connection and still signifying an interpolated joke or laugh-provoking piece of business, more generally today applies to any remark, story, or piece of business considered funny, esp. one written into a theatrical, movie, radio, or television script, and sometimes has extended its meaning to signify any trick whether funny or not but usu. one considered foolish ⟨*gags* grown venerable in the service of the music halls —*Times Lit. Supp.*⟩ ⟨the *gag* was not meant to be entirely funny —*Newsweek*⟩ ⟨gave a party the other night and pulled a really constructive *gag* . . . had every guest in the place vaccinated against smallpox —*Hollywood Reporter*⟩ ⟨a frivolous person, given to *gags* and foolishness⟩

2joke \"\ *vb* -ED/-ING/-S [L *jocari,* fr. *jocus*] *vi* **:** to make jokes **:** say or do something as a joke **:** JEST ⟨*joked* about the possibility of . . . lead poisoning due to bullets —Morris Fishbein⟩ ~ *vt* **1 :** to make jokes upon **:** poke fun at **:** KID, BANTER ⟨beginning to ~ him a bit about a nice young lady —Ethel Wilson⟩ **2 :** to obtain by joking ⟨~ a beggar's penny out of you —Robert Lynd⟩

jokebook \ˈ=,=\ *n* **:** JESTBOOK

joke·less \ˈjōkləs\ *adj* **:** lacking jokes

joke·let \-lət\ *n* -s **:** a little joke

jok·er \ˈjōkə(r)\ *n* -s **1 a :** a person given to joking **:** JESTER, HUMORIST, WAG ⟨a ~ with an original turn of mind —*New Yorker*⟩ ⟨one of the town ~*s* put her reluctance to marry down to a hereditary distaste for contracts —Frank O'Connor⟩ **b :** GUY, BLOKE, FELLOW ⟨in walks a ~ very skinny and tall —Garson Kanin⟩ ⟨what a soft bloody job some ~*s* have —David Ballantyne⟩; *sometimes* **:** an insignificant, obnoxious, or incompetent person **:** SLOB ⟨a shame to let a ~ like this win —Harold Robbins⟩ ⟨know just what to do with that ~ —Maxwell Griffith⟩ **2 a :** a small object (as a ball or pea) used in playing thimblerig — called also *little joker* **b** (1) **:** a playing card usu. marked on its face with a picture of a jester and often added to a pack of playing cards as a wild card (as in poker or canasta) or as the highest-ranking card (as in five hundred) (2) **:** a card designated as wild — see BIG JOKER **c** (1) **:** a clause that is ambiguous or apparently immaterial inserted in a legislative bill to make it inoperative or uncertain in some respect without arousing opposition at the time of its passage (2) **:** an unsuspected, misleading, or misunderstood clause, phrase, or word in an agreement, contract, statement, or other document that in effect nullifies or greatly alters its apparent terms or purport (3) **:** something (as an expedient or stratagem) held in reserve to gain one's end or escape from a difficult situation ⟨retained one ~: they could appeal from a Greek legal decision to Roman law —Jaques-Yves Cousteau⟩ (4) **:** a fact, factor, or condition unsuspected or not apparent at first that thwarts or nullifies an apparent advantage ⟨depreciation: the ~ in mechanization —Herrele DeGraff & Ladd Haystead⟩ ⟨the ~ . . . is that we have a pretty persistent and devastating way of getting in the way of ourselves —H.A.Overstreet⟩

joker trap *n* **:** SKEE TRAP

jokes *pl of* JOKE, *pres 3d sing of* JOKE

jokesmith \ˈ=,=\ *n* **:** a joke writer

joke·ster \ˈjōkstə(r)\ *n* -s **:** JOKER

jokey *or* **joky** \ˈjōkē\ *adj, often* **jokier**; *often* **jokiest :** given to joking **:** WAGGISH ⟨a ~ old bird —Sinclair Lewis⟩

jok·ing·ly *adv* **:** in a joking manner

joking relationship *n* **:** an institutionalized relationship of pronounced familiarity between specified relatives widely found among primitive peoples and involving the exchange of frequently sexually colored banter, jocular insults, and the playing of tricks upon one another — compare AVOIDANCE 5

jö·kul \ˈyō,ku̇l\ *also* **jö·kul** \ˈyœ̄,-\ *n* -s [Icel *jökull* icicle, glacier, fr. ON — more at ICICLE] **:** an Icelandic mountain covered with ice and snow **:** an Icelandic snow mountain

jokyakarta *usu cap, var of* DJOKJAKARTA

joll \ˈjäl\ *vi* -ED/-ING/-S [origin unknown] *dial Eng* **:** to move or walk clumsily **:** LURCH

jolley *also* **jollie** *var of* JOLLY

jol·li·er \ˈjälēə(r)\ *n* -s **1 :** a person who jollies, flatters, or banters **2 :** a worker who uses a jolly to make pottery hollow ware **3 :** a worker who operates a rotary pounding machine for flattening the lower edge of the shoe upper where it folds over the insole and smoothing the bottom for attachment of the outsole

jol·li·fi·ca·tion \,jäləfə'kāshən\ *n* -s [1*jolly* + *-fication*] **:** FESTIVITY, MERRYMAKING ⟨a pageant and general ~ will begin at noon —*N.Y. Times*⟩

jol·li·fy \ˈjälə,fī\ *vi* -ED/-ING/-ES [1*jolly* + *-fy*] **:** to make merry **:** CAROUSE

jol·li·ly \-ləlē\ *adv* [ME *jolifly, jolily,* fr. *jolif, joly* + *-ly*] **:** in a jolly manner **:** CHEERFULLY ⟨passing ~ along the street —Laurence Sterne⟩

jol·li·ness \-lēnəs, -lin-\ *n* -ES [ME *jolifnesse, jolynesse,* fr. *jolif, joly* + *-nesse* -ness] **:** the quality or state of being jolly ⟨could not wholly eradicate that inherent English ~ —Roy Lewis & Angus Maude⟩

jol·li·ty \ˈjäləd·ē, -ətē, -i\ *n* -ES [ME *jolifte, jolite,* fr. OF *joliveté, jolifté, jolité,* fr. *jolif, joli* + *-té* -ty] **1 :** the quality or state of being jolly **:** GAIETY, MERRIMENT, CHEER ⟨put on a show of bluff ~ —Irwin Shaw⟩ **2** *Brit* **:** a festive gathering, meeting, or entertainment ⟨the occasion was a ~ of the Bursley Burial Club —Arnold Bennett⟩ **3** *obs* **:** SPLENDOR, MAGNIFICENCE

jol·loped \ˈjäləpt\ *or* **jel·loped** \ˈjel-\ *adj* [obs. E *jollop,* prob. fr. *joll,* var. of *jowl* + *lap*) + *-ed*] *heraldry* **:** WATTLED

1jol·ly \ˈjälē, -li\ *adj* -ER/-EST [ME *jolif, joli,* fr. OF *jolif, joli,* fr. *jol-* (prob. of Scand origin; akin to ON *jōl* Yule, feast) + *-if* -ive — more at YULE] **1 a** (1) **:** full of high spirits **:** GAY, JOYOUS ⟨think no more, lad; laugh, be ~ —A.E. Housman⟩ ⟨seems pretty comfortable and ~ —Rachel Henning⟩ (2) **:** given to conviviality **:** FESTIVE, JOVIAL ⟨a ~ and carefree companion —R.W.Pickford⟩ ⟨~ sportsmen . . . reserved time enough to frolic —*Amer. Guide Series: Mass.*⟩ **b :** attended or marked by mirth or gaiety **:** expressing, suggesting, inspiring, or reflecting a mood of gaiety **:** CHEERFUL, BRIGHT ⟨impressed by his ~ air of success —Arnold Bennett⟩ ⟨the last movement is a ~ rondo —Virgil Thomson⟩ ⟨entirely in the right of it to lead a ~ life —George Eliot⟩ ⟨had a ~ time⟩ ⟨thickets of hawthorn and holly with ~ little streams —S.P.B.Mais⟩ ⟨the countryside has a ~ quality —Rebecca West⟩ **2** *now dial Eng* **a :** gay and attractive in manner and appearance **b :** appearing healthy or in good condition **:** SLEEK, PLUMP, LARGE **3 :** extremely pleasant or agreeable **:** DELIGHTFUL, SPLENDID, BULLY ⟨~ little open carriages —O.S.Nock⟩ ⟨what a ~ new world it is —T.R. Ybarra⟩ ⟨studying the . . . ~ curve of her cheek —Vera Caspary⟩ ⟨why, that's real ~⟩ **syn** see MERRY

2jolly \"\ *adv* **:** VERY, REMARKABLY ⟨did a lot of things that were ~ foolish —R.H.Newman⟩ ⟨hoped it would be a ~ good lesson to them —Dorothy Sayers⟩ — often used as an intensive ⟨they would kindly do as they were ~ well told —John Stockbridge⟩

3jolly \"\ *vb* -ED/-ING/-ES *vi* **:** to engage in good-natured banter or raillery **:** CHAFF, KID ⟨*jollied* and joked with sailors in the street —Dixon Wecter⟩ ~ *vt* **1 :** to put or seek to put in good humor esp. to gain some end **:** COAX, WHEEDLE, INDULGE ⟨~*ing* the illiterate populace along towards the new age —Roland Mathias⟩ ⟨*jollied* my mother by joining her on the sofa —Peter De Vries⟩ ⟨do be good . . . and ~ him along —Robertson Davies⟩ ⟨try to pay for their entertainment by ~*ing* us along —S.E.White⟩ **2 :** to form or shape with a jolly

4jolly \"\ *n* -ES **1** *Brit* **:** MARINE **2** *chiefly Brit* **:** a sociable good time **:** JOLLIFICATION **3** *or* **jol·ley** *also* **jol·lie** \"\ -s **:** a potter's machine like a jigger used for flatware (as plates or saucers) and hollow ware

jol·ly balance \ˈjälē-, ˈyälē-\ *n, usu cap J* [After Philipp von *Jolly* †1884 Ger. physicist] **:** a very delicate spring balance used esp. for the determination of densities by the method of weighing in air and in water

jol·ly boat \ˈjälē-\ *or* **jolly** *n* -ES [origin unknown] **:** a boat of medium size belonging to a ship and used for general rough or small work

jolly rog·er \-ˈräjə(r)\ *n, usu cap J&R* [1*jolly* + *Roger* (the name)] **:** a flag in any of various color combinations bearing one or more emblems of mortality (as a skeleton, a skull and crossbones, or an hourglass) and raised on a pirate ship of the 17th and 18th centuries as a signal that quarter would be given if no resistance were offered but now often believed to have been used by pirates as their ensign; *specif* **:** a black flag bearing a white skull and crossbones — compare BLACK FLAG

Jolly Roger

jolof *usu cap, var of* WOLOF

1jolt \ˈjōlt\ *vb* -ED/-ING/-S [prob. blend of *joll* (obs. var. of 4*jowl*) and obs. *jot* to bump, prob. of imit. origin] *vt* **1 :** to cause to move with a sudden and jerky motion by a push or series of pushes **:** JOUNCE ⟨the lumbering coach ~*ed* its passengers over the miserable road⟩ ⟨~*ed* about by the car's swift turns⟩ **2 a :** to give a sharp knock to so as to dislodge or move ⟨~ it crosswise and lengthwise with a rawhide hammer —H.F.Blanchard & Ralph Ritchen⟩ **b :** to jar in boxing with a quick or hard blow **3 a :** to administer a psychological shock to **:** disturb the composure of ⟨crudely ~*ed* out of that mood —Virginia Woolf⟩ ⟨trying to ~ the world into looking at the future —*New Yorker*⟩ **b :** to shake or interfere with roughly, abruptly, and disconcertingly **:** upset the even tenor or stability of ⟨determination to pursue his own course was ~*ed* badly —F.L. Paxson⟩ ⟨her parents' plans, however, were rudely ~*ed* —Clyde Gilmour⟩ ~ *vi* **1 a** *of a vehicle* **:** to move with a jolt or a series of jolts ⟨the train ~*ed* to a stop —Nathaniel Benchley⟩ ⟨the wagon ~*ed* up the slope —Ellen Glasgow⟩ **b :** to ride or move on foot with a succession of jolts ⟨on into South Carolina they ~*ed* —Dixon Wecter⟩ ⟨my body ~*s* and jars, for I have not got into the trick of drifting slackly down a hillside —Wynford Vaughn-Thomas⟩ ⟨climbed into the tonga and ~*ed* away —John Masters⟩ **2** *slang* **:** to take jolts of narcotics; *esp* **:** to take jolts of heroin ⟨was she still ~*ing* —Wenzell Brown⟩

2jolt \"\ *n* -s **1 a :** an abrupt sharp jerky blow or movement knocking or shaking violently and tending to unsettle or dislodge **:** JOUNCE ⟨well packed for protection against ~*s* in shipment⟩ ⟨received the full ~ from each explosion —L.D. de La Penne & Virgilio Spigai⟩ **b :** a jarring blow in boxing **c** (1) **:** a sudden feeling of shock, surprise, or disappointment caused by some novel or unexpected event or development **:** a psychological blow or shock ⟨that a few men have such far-reaching power gave the people quite a ~ —Paul Wooton⟩ ⟨will give an exciting and much-needed ~ to the complacency of those laymen —J.F.Wharton⟩ ⟨this kind of discussion gives a healthy ~ —David Daiches⟩ ⟨the affair dealt quite a ~ to his pride⟩; *also* **:** an event or development causing such a feeling ⟨his mother's death was quite a ~ to the boy⟩ (2) **:** a damaging but nonphysical blow **:** SETBACK, REVERSE ⟨the . . . argument for evolution had received a severe ~ —R.W.Murray⟩ ⟨had a severe financial ~⟩ **2** *slang* **:** a term in jail **3 a :** a small potent or bracing portion of something **:** SHOT ⟨a reassuring ~ of fresh air —*Atlantic*⟩ ⟨poured a ~ of brandy —Dorothy Baker⟩ ⟨a new perfume that contains a ~ of gardenia —*New Yorker*⟩ **b** *slang* **:** a unit of a narcotic (as heroin) for hypodermic injection ⟨a ~ can be had for a nod and a price —J.B.Clayton⟩ **syn** see IMPACT

jolt·er \ˈjōltə(r)\ *n* -s **:** one that jolts

jolter-head \ˈ=,=\ *also* **jolt-head** \ˈ=,=\ *n* [*jolter-head* alter. of *jolt-head; jolt-head* prob. fr. 2*jolt* + *head*] **1** *archaic* **:** a large or heavy head **2** *now dial chiefly Eng* **:** DUNCE, BOOBY, BLOCKHEAD

jolter-headed \ˈ=,=ˈ==\ *also* **jolt-headed** \ˈ=ˈ==\ *adj* **1** *archaic* **:** having a large or heavy head **2** *now dial chiefly Eng* **:** STUPID, DULL

jolthead porgy \ˈ=,=-\ *also* **jolthead** *n* **:** a large yellow blue-marked porgy (*Calamus bajonado*) of the tropical western Atlantic

jolt·i·ness \ˈjōltēnəs\ *n* -ES **:** the quality or state of being jolty

jolting *adj* **:** tending to jolt **:** attended by or producing jolts ⟨a ~ ride⟩ ⟨a ~ experience⟩ — **jolt·ing·ly** *adv*

jolt·less \ˈjōltləs\ *adj* **:** free from jolts

jolt-wagon \ˈ=,==\ *n, Midland* **:** a farm wagon

jolty \ˈjōltē\ *adj* -ER/-EST **:** causing jolts **:** tending to jolt ⟨a ~ wagon⟩

1jo·nah \ˈjōnə\ *n* -s *usu cap J* [after *Jonah,* Old Testament prophet who by disobeying God's command caused a storm to endanger the ship he was traveling in (Jon 1:4 ff), fr. Heb *Yōnāh*] **:** one believed to bring bad luck or misfortune ⟨perhaps I was the *Jonah* — at least I was the thirteenth man —Arthur Langford⟩ ⟨her left foot was her *Jonah;* nothing had ever happened to her right foot —John Hersey⟩

2jonah \"\ *vt* -ED/-ING/-S *often cap J* **:** to bring bad luck to **:** JINX ⟨ordered the boy on shore again, accusing him of wanting to ~ the whole trip —*Youth's Companion*⟩

jonah crab *n, usu cap J* **:** a large reddish crab (*Cancer borealis*) of the eastern coast of No. America that is sometimes found along rocky shores but is more common in deep water

jon·a·than \ˈjänəthən\ *n* -s *usu cap* [fr. the name *Jonathan;* prob. fr. the frequent use of Old Testament given names among the English colonists in America] **:** AMERICAN; *esp* **:** NEW ENGLANDER ⟨*Jonathans* are antislavery, but not against foreigners —*Chicago Democrat*⟩ — compare BROTHER JONATHAN

jonathan freckle *n, usu cap J* [fr. *Jonathan,* a variety of apple to which the disease is especially destructive, after *Jonathan* Hasbrouck †1846 Am. jurist] **:** a nonparasitic storage disease of apples that produces small circular skin-deep discolorations

jonathan spot *n, usu cap J* [fr. *Jonathan,* a variety of apple to which this disease is especially destructive] **:** a nonparasitic disease of apples that produces circular depressed necrotic areas around the lenticels — called also *spot rot*

jones reductor \ˈjōnz-\ *n, usu cap J* [after Clemens *Jones,* 19th cent. Am. metallurgist] **:** a reductor that consists essentially of a long upright tube filled with granular zinc through which a solution to be reduced (as a ferric salt) is poured

jong \ˈyäŋ\ *n* -s [Afrik, fr. MD *jonge,* fr. *jonc* young; akin to OHG *jung* young — more at YOUNG] *southern Africa* **:** a young man

jon·glery \ˈjäŋglərē\ *n* -ES [F *jonglerie,* fr. MF, alter. of OF *joglerie* — more at JUGGLERY] **:** entertainment provided by a jongleur

jon·gleur \(ˈ)zhōⁿ¦glər(·), ˈjäŋglər\ *n* -s [F, fr. MF, alter. of OF *jogleour* — more at JUGGLER] **1 :** an accompanist for a troubadour in the 12th and 13th centuries **2 :** an itinerant medieval minstrel reciting and singing for hire

jonnock *var of* JANNOCK

jonny cake *var of* JOHNNYCAKE

jon·quil \ˈjän|nkwəl, |ŋk- *sometimes* ˈjə|\ *n* -s [NL & F; NL *junquilia,* fr. F or Sp; F *jonquille,* fr. Sp *junquillo,* dim. of *junco* rush, reed (fr. the appearance of the leaves), fr. L *juncus;* akin to ON *einir* juniper, Sw *en,* L *juniperus* juniper, MIr *ain* reed] **1 a :** a perennial bulbous herb (*Narcissus jonquilla*) native to southern Europe and northern Africa that has long slender leaves resembling those of a rush and is widely cultivated for its yellow or white fragrant clustered flowers which are smaller than those of typical daffodils and have the corona much shortened — compare NARCISSUS 2 **b :** a narcissus or daffodil with a yellow corona — used chiefly in the florist trade **2 a :** DAFFODIL 2 **b :** a light to moderate yellow that is redder and less strong than amber yellow or apricot yellow and redder and stronger than Naples yellow (sense 4a)

jonquil

jon·so·nian \(ˈ)jän¦sōnēən\ *adj, usu cap* [Ben *Jonson* †1637 Eng. dramatist + E *-ian*] **:** of, relating to, or characteristic of Ben Jonson or his works

jon·ty \ˈjȯntē, ˈjän-, -ti\ *Brit var of* 2JAUNTY

1jook *var of* JOUK

²jook \'jůk\ *n* -s [Gullah *juke, joog* disorderly — more at JUKE JOINT] *South* : JUKE JOINT ⟨a ~ from which she was trying to extricate her husband —Marjorie K. Rawlings⟩
jookerie *or* **jookery** *var of* JOUKERY
jook organ *n, South* : JUKEBOX
¹**jor·dan** \'jȯrdᵊn, 'jȯ(ə)d-\ *n* -s [ME (also, a vessel used by physicians and alchemists), prob. fr. the river *Jordan* in Palestine; perh. fr. medieval pilgrims' bringing water from the Jordan back to England] *dial Brit* : CHAMBER POT
²**jordan** \"\, *southern US often* 'jərd- *or* 'jəd- *or* 'jəid-\ *adj, usu cap* [fr. *Jordan*, country in southwestern Asia] : of or from the Hashemite Kingdom of Jordan : of the kind or style prevalent in Jordan : JORDANIAN
³**jordan** \"\ *also* **jordan engine** *or* **jordan refiner** *n* -s *sometimes cap J* [after Joseph *Jordan*, 19th cent. Am. inventor] : a machine for refining paper pulp that consists of a stationary hollow cone having projecting knives on its interior surface and fitting over a rapidly rotating adjustable cone having similar knives on its outside surface
⁴**jordan** \"\ *vt* **jordaned** *also* **jordanned**; **jordaned** *also* **jordanned**; **jordaning** *also* **jordanning** \-dᵊniŋ\ **jordans** : to refine in a jordan
jordan almond *n, usu cap J* [by folk etymology fr. ME *jardin almande*, fr. MF *jardin* garden + ME *almande* almond — more at JARDINIÈRE, ALMOND] **1** : an almond imported from Málaga and used extensively in confectionery **2** : an almond coated with sugar of various colors
jordan chest *n, often cap J* [after Joseph *Jordan*, 19th cent. Am. inventor] : a stock chest that holds paper stock ready to be jordaned
jor·dan curve \(')zhȯ(ə)r¦däⁿ-\ *n, usu cap J* [after Camille *Jordan* †1922 Fr. mathematician] : a closed plane curve (as a circle or an ellipse) that does not intersect itself
¹**jor·da·ni·an** \(')jȯ(r)¦dānēən, -nyən *sometimes* -dan-\ *adj, usu cap* [*Jordan*, country in southwestern Asia + E *-ian*] **1** : of, relating to, or characteristic of Jordan **2** : of, relating to, or characteristic of the people of Jordan
²**jordanian** \"\ *n* -s *cap* : a native or inhabitant of Jordan
jor·dan·ite \'jȯ(r)dᵊn,īt\ *n* -s [G *jordanit*, fr. Dr. *Jordan*, 19th cent. Ger. scientist + G *-it* -ite] : a mineral $Pb_{14}As_7S_{24}$(?) consisting of a lead-gray monoclinic lead arsenic sulfide (sp. gr. 6.39)
jor·danon \'jȯ(r)dᵊn,än\ *n* -s [NL, fr. Alexis *Jordan* †1897 Fr. biologist + Gk *-on* (neuter n. & adj. suffix)] : MICROSPECIES
jordan's law *n, usu cap J* [after David S. *Jordan* †1931 Am. naturalist] : a generalization in evolutionary biology: closely related organisms tend to occupy adjacent rather than identical or distant ranges
jo·ree \jə'rē\ *also* **joree-bird** *n* -s [imit.] *chiefly Midland* : CHEWINK
jo·rist \'jōrəst\ *n* -s [Jan David *Joris* (*Joriszoon*) †1536 Dutch Anabaptist leader + E *-ist*] *usu cap* : DAVIDIST 2
jor·na·da \hȯ(r)'nädə\ *n* -s [Sp, fr. OSp, fr. OProv *jornada*, fr. *jorn* day, fr. LL *diurnum* — more at JOURNEY] *Southwest* : an arduous usu. one-day journey across a stretch of desert ⟨almost perished for lack of water on this grim ~ —R.G.Cleland⟩
jo·ro·ba·do \¦hōrə¦baů\ *n* -s [AmerSp, fr. Sp, humpbacked, fr. *joroba* humpback (fr. OSp *hadruba*, fr. Ar dial. — Spain — *haduba, hudūba*, fr. Ar *hadaba*) + *-ado* -ate (fr. L *-atus*)] : either of two moonfishes (*Vomer setipinnis* and *Selene vomer*)
jo·ro·po \hə'rō(,)pō\ *n* -s [AmerSp] : the national ballroom dance of Venezuela marked by lilting stamping steps in three-quarter time
jor·ram \'yůrəm, 'yōr-\ *n* -s [ScGael *iorram*] *Scot* : a Gaelic boat song
jo·rum \'jōrəm, 'jȯr-\ *n* -s [perh. after *Joram* in the Bible who "brought with him vessels of silver . . . gold, and . . . brass" (2 Sam 8:10 — AV)] **1 a** : a large drinking vessel (as a jug or bowl) ⟨the host smiled . . . and shortly afterwards returned with a steaming ~ —Charles Dickens⟩ **b** : the contents of such a vessel ⟨drinking a ~ of hot whiskey and water —J.E.Agate⟩ **2** : a large quantity ⟨great ~s of ink —Margery Sharp⟩
jo·sef *or* **jo·seph** \'jōzəf\ *or* **jo·sup** \-zəp\ *n* -s [Afrik *josef*, prob. after *Josef* (Joseph), Old Testament patriarch; fr. the brilliant colors of the fish, reminiscent of Joseph's coat of many colors (Gen 37:3 — AV)] : an elephant fish (*Callorynchus capensis*) of southern Africa
jo·se·ite \zhə'zā,īt\ *n* -s [G *joseit*, fr. São *José* do Paraiso, Minas Gerais, Brazil + G *-it* -ite] : a mineral $Bi_3Te(Se,S)$ consisting of a telluride of bismuth that also contains sulfur and selenium
jo·seph \'jōzəf *also* -ōsəf\ *n* -s [prob. after *Joseph*, Old Testament patriarch; fr. his coat of many colors (Gen 37:3 — AV)] : a long cloak; *esp* : an 18th century woman's riding coat buttoning down the front
joseph-and-mary \¦≈≈'≈≈\ *n, usu cap J&M* [after *Joseph* and *Mary*, parents of Jesus; fr. the red and blue flowers that suggested representations of the Holy Family in which Joseph was pictured in red and Mary in blue] *dial Eng* : LUNGWORT 2a
jo·se·phine \'jōzə,fēn *also* -ōsə-\ *n* -s *often cap* [fr. the name *Josephine*] : BLUSH 4a
josephine's-lily *also* **josephine lily** \¦≈≈,≈'≈≈\ *n, pl* **josephine's-lilies** *also* **josephine lilies** *usu cap J* [after *Joséphine* de Beauharnais †1814 empress of France] : a southern African bulbous herb (*Brunsvigia josephinae*) of the family Amaryllidaceae with bright red flowers
jo·se·phin·ite \¦jōzə¦fē,nīt *also* -ōsə-\ *n* -s [*Josephine* co., Oregon + E *-ite*] : a natural alloy of iron and nickel occurring in stream gravel — compare AWARUITE
jo·seph·ite \'jōzə,fīt *also* -ōsə-\ *n* -s *usu cap* **1** [*Joseph* of Volokolamsk, 16th cent. leader in the Russian Orthodox Church + E *-ite*] : a member of a monastic party rising to prominence in the Russian Orthodox Church in the 16th century, adhering to strict forms of ritualism and asceticism, and believing in a close union between church and state — called also *Possessor* **2** [*Joseph* Smith †1914 Mormon leader + E *-ite*] : a member of the Reorganized Church of Jesus Christ of Latter-day Saints
joseph's coat *n, usu cap J* [after *Joseph*, Old Testament patriarch; fr. his coat of many colors (Gen 37:3 — AV)] **1** : a coat of many colors ⟨a country as dappled and patchy as *Joseph's coat* —T.H.Fielding⟩ **2** : any of certain plants with variegated foliage: as **a** : a tampala with red and green variegated leaves grown as an ornamental **b** : COLEUS 2
¹**josh** \'jäsh *also* 'jȯsh\ *vb* -ED/-ING/-ES [origin unknown] *vt* : to make fun of : tease good-naturedly : joke with ⟨whenever they ~ed her, she could laugh at herself as much as they could laugh at her —Edward Kimbrough⟩ ⟨climbed into our bus and ~ed the women schoolteachers —G.P.Musselman⟩ ~ *vi* : to banter lightly : JOKE ⟨~ed with the cameramen and was evidently in fine spirits —*N.Y. Times*⟩
²**josh** \"\ *n* -ES : light and good-humored joking : JEST, JOKE ⟨thoroughly enjoyed all the chatter and ~⟩
josh·er \-shə(r)\ *n* -s : one that joshes ⟨a great little ~ . . . when it comes to kidding —Sinclair Lewis⟩
josh·ua tree \'jä|sh(ə)wə-, ÷|shə,wā- *also* 'jō|\ *also* **joshua** *n* -s *usu cap J* [prob. after *Joshua*, Old Testament patriarch; fr. the grotesquely extended branches, reminiscent of the outstretched arm of Joshua as he pointed with his spear toward the city of Ai (Josh 8:18—AV)] : a branched arborescent yucca (*Yucca brevifolia*) of the southwestern U. S. that has short leaves and clustered greenish white flowers and often grows to a height of 25 feet
jo·si·an·ic \¦jō,sī¦anik, -ōzē-\ *adj, usu cap* [*Josiah* †*ab*608 B.C. king of Judah noted for his reforming spirit + connective *-n-* + E *-ic*] : of or relating to Josiah
jo·sie \'jōzē, -ōsē\ *n* -s [*joseph* + *-ie*] : a fitted outer waist formerly worn by women
jos·kin \'jäskən\ *n* -s [perh. fr. the name *Joseph* + *-kin* (as in *bumpkin*)] : BUMPKIN
¹**joss** \'jäs, 'jȯs\ *n* -ES [pidgin English, fr. Pg *deus* god, fr. L — more at DEITY] : a Chinese idol or cult image
²**joss** \'jäs\ *n* -ES [origin unknown] *dial Eng* : FOREMAN
³**joss** \"\ *vi* -ED/-ING/-ES [prob. short for *jostle*] *dial Eng* : JOSTLE, CROWD
jos·ser \-sə(r)\ *n* -s [origin unknown] *Brit* : FELLOW, CHAP ⟨an absurd old ~ whom her mother made a fool of —G.B.Shaw⟩
joss flower *n* [¹*joss*] : CHINESE SACRED LILY
joss house *n* [¹*joss*] : a Chinese temple or house of idol worship
joss paper *n* [¹*joss*] : gold and silver paper cut to resemble money and burned in front of a joss
joss stick *n* [¹*joss*] : a slender stick of incense burned in front of a joss
¹**jos·tle** \'jäsəl *also* 'jȯs-\ *also* **jus·tle** \'jəs-\ *vb* **jostled** *also* **justled**; **jostled** *also* **justled**; **jostling** *also* **justling** \-s(ə)liŋ\ **jostles** *also* **justles** [*jostle* alter. of *justle*; *justle* freq. of ¹*joust, just*] *vi* **1 a** (1) : to come in contact or into collision : push and shove ⟨all drift and ~ and barge against one another —J.C.Powys⟩ ⟨wanted to get back to the bright lights . . . to ~ with the crowds —Harold Griffin⟩ (2) : to crowd or push or shove another horse in racing ⟨the stewards may disqualify the winner for crossing or *jostling* —Dennis Craig⟩ **b** : to make one's way by pushing and shoving or crowding ⟨men in pearl-buttoned waistcoasts and flared trousers *jostling* round the street market —Osbert Lancaster⟩ **c** : to exist in close proximity : rub elbows ⟨study of the great groups that have *jostled* and migrated around America —Priscilla Robertson⟩ ⟨survivals of barbaric codes of law *jostled* with varying mixtures of Roman law, local custom, and violence —R.W. Southern⟩ **2 a** *obs* : to run atilt in a tournament : JOUST **b** : to vie or struggle in gaining an objective : CONTEND ⟨tribes began to ~ with one another for room —Daniel Defoe⟩ ⟨a novel good enough to ~ with the others in the great stream —Douglas Stewart⟩ ~ *vt* **1 a** (1) : to come in contact or into collision with : push and shove against ⟨*jostled* each other in the dance or at the board —W.M. Thackeray⟩ (2) : to push or shove against (another horse) in racing **b** : to drive or force by or as if by pushing : ELBOW ⟨shrugged his shoulders and *jostled* his way out of the hall —John Buchan⟩ **c** : to stir up : AGITATE, DISTURB ⟨a mind *jostled* once more into uncertainty —Owen Wister⟩ **d** *obs* : to bring into or as if into contact or collision ⟨the churches . . . clash and ~ supremacies with the civil magistrate —John Milton⟩ **e** : to exist in close proximity with : rub elbows with ⟨Europe, where a number of languages ~ each other —D.G. Mandelbaum⟩ ⟨fishing vessels lying close-packed at the moorings, *jostling* each other —Nevil Shute⟩ **2** : to vie or struggle with in attaining an objective : contend with ⟨both men were *jostling* each other for nomination⟩
²**jostle** \"\ *also* **justle** \"\ *n* -s **1** : an encounter that jostles ⟨might glide through . . . life among them without a ~ —Thomas Jefferson⟩ **2 a** : the state of being crowded and jostled together ⟨away from the hustle and the ~ that ought to have been congenial to me —Max Beerbohm⟩ **b** : the act of pushing or shoving in horse racing : INTERFERENCE ⟨the ~ was wholly caused by the fault of some other horse or jockey —Dan Parker⟩
jos·tle·ment \-lmənt\ *n* -s : disturbance by pushing and shoving ⟨bursting in his full-blown way along the pavement, to the ~ of all weaker people —Charles Dickens⟩
jos·tler \-s(ə)lə(r)\ *n* -s : one that jostles
josup *var of* JOSEF
¹**jot** \'jät, *usu* -äd·+V\ *n* -s [L *jota* iota, jot, fr. Gk *iōta*, of Sem origin; akin to Heb *yōdh* yodh] **1** : an instance of iota esp. as the smallest letter of the Greek alphabet — used in translation of the Bible or in allusion to such translation ⟨till heaven and earth pass, one ~ or one tittle shall in no wise pass from the law, till all be fulfilled —Mt 5:18 (AV)⟩ **2** : the least bit : smallest amount : IOTA ⟨he who adds a ~ to such knowledge creates new mind —G.B.Shaw⟩
²**jot** \"\ *vt* **jotted**; **jotted**; **jotting**; **jots** : to write briefly or hurriedly : set down in or as if in the form of a note ⟨wake up six times during the night and ~ another name on the pad —G.S.Perry⟩ — usu. used with *down* ⟨*jotted* down a summary of all their private interviews —Peter Quennell⟩
jo·ta \'hōd·ə, -ō(,)tä\ *n* -s [Sp, prob. fr. OSp *sota* dance, fr. *sotar* to dance, fr. L *saltare* — more at SALTANT] **1** : a Spanish folk dance in ¾ time performed by a man and a woman to intricate castanet and heel rhythms **2** : the music of the jota
jot·ni·an \'jätnēən\ *adj, usu cap* [ON *jötn-, jötunn* giant + E *-ian*; akin to OE *eoten* giant, MLG *etenine* giantess, and perh. to OE *etan* to eat — more at EAT] : of, relating to, or constituting a division of the Precambrian — see GEOLOGIC TIME table
jot·ter \'jäd·ə(r)\ *n* -s **1** : one that jots down memoranda ⟨a great ~ of notes —Jack Alexander⟩ **2** : a memorandum book
jot·ting *n* -s : a brief note : MEMORANDUM ⟨made rapid ~s on chance bits of paper —Walter Pach⟩
jougs \'jügz\ *n pl but sing in constr, also* **joug** \'jüg\ [alter. of earlier *jogis, jougis*, perh. modif. of MF *joug* yoke, fr. L *jugum* — more at YOKE] : an iron collar fastened to a wall or post and used in Scotland as a pillory
jouissance *n* -s [MF, fr. *jouiss-* (stem of *jouir* to enjoy, fr. L *gaudēre* to rejoice) + *-ance* — more at JOY] *obs* : USE, ENJOYMENT; *also* : JOLLITY
¹**jouk** \'jük\ *vb* -ED/-ING/-S [origin unknown] *vi* **1** *dial* **a** : DUCK, DODGE **b** : to evade work **2** *dial* : FAWN, CRINGE **3** *dial* : CHEAT, DECEIVE ~ *vt* **1** *dial* **a** : DUCK, DODGE **b** : to get out of (work) by evasion **2** *dial* : CHEAT, DECEIVE
²**jouk** \"\ *n* -s *chiefly Scot* : SWOOP, SWERVE, JERK
jouk·ery \'jükərī\ *n* -ES *chiefly Scot* : SWINDLING, TRICKERY
joukerypawkery \¦≈≈¦≈≈\ *n* -ES [*joukery* + *pawkery*] *Scot* : JIGGERY-POKERY
joule \'jül, 'jaů(ə)l *sometimes* 'jōl; *the first seems to have been the physicist's own pronunc*\ *n* -s [after James P. *Joule* †1889 Eng. physicist] **1** : the absolute mks unit of work or energy equal to 10^7 ergs or approximately 0.7375 foot-pounds or 0.2390 gram calorie and taken as standard in U. S. **2** : a unit of work or energy that is equal to about 1.00017 absolute joules and that was formerly taken as a standard in U. S. — called also *international joule*
joule effect *n, usu cap J* [after J. P. *Joule*] : production of heat by mechanical work, an electric current, or change in length due to magnetization — compare MAGNETOSTRICTION
joule heat *also* **joulean heat** \'jül|ēən-, 'jaůl| *sometimes* 'jōl|\ *n, usu cap J* [after J. P. *Joule*] : heat resulting from an electric current through a resistance
joule's cycle *n, usu cap J* [after J. P. *Joule*] : BRAYTON CYCLE
joule's equivalent *n, usu cap J* [after J. P. *Joule*] : MECHANICAL EQUIVALENT OF HEAT
joule's law *n, usu cap J* [after J. P. *Joule*] : either of two statements in physics: (1) the rate at which heat is produced by a steady current in any part of an electric circuit is jointly proportional to the resistance and the square of the current (2) the internal energy of an ideal gas depends only upon its temperature irrespective of volume and pressure — compare JOULE-THOMSON EFFECT
joule-thom·son effect \'≈'täm(p)sən-\ *n, usu cap J&T* [after J. P. *Joule* and Sir William *Thomson* (Lord Kelvin) †1907 Brit. physicist] : the change in temperature of a gas on expansion through a porous plug from a high pressure to a lower one under adiabatic conditions, the observation of this change proving among other things that Joule's second law is only approximately true
¹**jounce** \'jaůn(t)s\ *vb* -ED/-ING/-S [ME *jouncen*] *vi* **1** : to fall, drop, or bounce so as to shake **2** : to move or proceed in jounces ⟨the truck *jounced* off across the concrete and the weeds —Josephine Johnson⟩ ⟨*jounced* over a rut —William Attwood⟩ ~ *vt* : to cause to jounce
²**jounce** \"\ *n* -s : a shaking fall or bump : JOLT
jouncy \-sē\ *adj, usu* -ER/-EST : marked by a jouncing motion or effect ⟨innumerable ~ elevator rides —*New Yorker*⟩
jour *abbr* **1** journal; journalism; journalist **2** journey **3** journeyman
¹**jour·nal** \'jərnᵊl, 'jən-, 'jəin-\ *n* -s [ME, fr. MF, fr. *journal*, adj., daily, fr. L *diurnalis*, fr. *diurnus* of the day, daily (fr. *dies* day + *-urnus*, as in *nocturnus* nocturnal) + *-alis* -al — more at DEITY, NOCTURNAL] **1 a** : a usu. daily record of a journey **b** : a record of current transactions usu. kept daily or regularly: as (1) : DAYBOOK 2 (2) : a book of original entry in double-entry bookkeeping either for recording transactions of a particular class (as sales or cash transactions) or for recording transactions not cared for in specialized books **c** : an account of usu. day-to-day events written down regularly or as they occur or presented as if written down in this way **d** : a record of experiences, ideas, or reflections kept regularly for private use **e** : a record of transactions kept by a deliberative body or an assembly; *specif* : the record of daily proceedings of a legislative body kept by the clerk **f** : LOGBOOK, LOG **2** [F, fr. *journal* (record)] **a** : a daily newspaper **b** : a periodical publication esp. dealing with matters of current interest ⟨the editor of a weekly news ~⟩ — often used of official or semiofficial publications of special groups ⟨the *Journal* of the American Medical Association⟩ **3** : the part of a rotating shaft, axle, roll, or spindle that turns in a bearing
²**journal** *adj* [MF — more at ¹JOURNAL] *obs* : DIURNAL
³**journal** *like* JOURNAL\ *vt* -ED/-ING/-S [¹*journal*] **1** : to support on, provide with, or make into a journal : support on a bearing ⟨~ a pulley on a shaft⟩ **2** : to connect by means of a journal ⟨a connecting rod ~*ed* to one end of a walking beam⟩
jour·nal·ary \-ᵊl,erē\ *adj* **1** *obs* : DAILY, DIURNAL **2** : of or belonging to a journal : recorded in or as if in a journal ⟨the ~ form of the novel —A.D.Henderson⟩
journal bearing *n* : BEARING 4c
journal box *n* : a metal housing to support and protect a journal bearing (as on a railroad-car wheel axle)
jour·nal·ese \¦jərnᵊl¦ēz, ¦jən-, ¦jəin-, -ēs\ *n* -s [¹*journal* + *-ese*] **1** : a style of writing held to be characteristic of newspapers **2** : writing marked by simple, informal, and usu. loose sentence structure, the frequent use of clichés, sensationalism in the presentation of material, and superficiality of thought and reasoning
jour·nal·ism \'≈≈,izəm\ *n* -s [F *journalisme*, fr. *journal* (n.) + *-isme* -ism] **1 a** : the collection and editing of material of current interest for presentation through the media of newspapers, magazines, newsreels, radio, or television **b** : the editorial or business management of a newspaper, magazine, or other agency engaged in the collection and dissemination of news **c** : an academic study concerned with the collection and editing of news or the editorial or business management of a news medium **2** : journalistic writing: **a** : writing designed for publication in a newspaper or popular magazine **b** : writing characterized by a direct presentation of facts or description of events without an attempt at interpretation **c** : writing designed to appeal to current popular taste or current public interest **3** : newspapers and magazines **4** : the presentation of events or ideas (as in a painting or play) in a manner regarded as similar to that of journalism
jour·nal·ist \-,əst\ *n* -s [¹*journal* + *-ist*] **1 a** : one engaged in journalism; *esp* : one employed to write or edit the subject matter of a news medium **b** : a writer who aims or is felt to aim chiefly at a mass audience or strives for immediate popular appeal in his writings **c** : an enlisted man (as in the U.S. Navy) who performs public information duties **2** : one who keeps a journal
jour·nal·is·tic \¦≈≈¦istik, -tēk\ *adj* : of, relating to, or having the characteristics of journalism or journalists ⟨the brilliant and amusing example of ~ acumen —*N.Y. Times*⟩ ⟨these ~ illustrations . . . had great aesthetic vitality —Lewis Mumford⟩ ⟨resorted to the ~ device of gingering up the actual records —*New Yorker*⟩; *esp* : marked by literary qualities appropriate to newspapers and popular magazines — **jour·nal·is·ti·cal·ly** \-tək(ə)lē, -tēk-, -li\ *adv*
jour·nal·ize \'≈≈,īz\ *vb* -ED/-ING/-S *see -ize in Explan Notes* [¹*journal* + *-ize*] *vt* : to enter or record in a journal ~ *vi* **1** : to keep a journal in accounting **2** : to keep a personal journal : write down daily or regularly reflections, observations, or ideas — **jour·nal·iz·er** \-zə(r)\ *n* -s
journal voucher *n* : a paper in accounting that authorizes an entry in a journal or a paper that constitutes an authorized entry for direct posting
¹**jour·ney** \'jərnē, 'jən-, 'jəin-, -ni\ *n* -s [ME *jurne, jorne, journey*, fr. OF *jornee, journee*, fr. *jor, jour* day, fr. LL *diurnum*, fr. neut. of L *diurnus* of the day, daily — more at JOURNAL] **1 a** : travel or passage from one place to another : TRIP ⟨a three-day ~⟩ **b** *now chiefly dial* : a day's travel; *also* : the distance traveled during a day **c** *archaic* : a stage of a journey : a portion of a trip undertaken at one time **d** : something suggesting travel or passage from one place to another: as (1) : the course of one's life from birth to death (2) *obs* : the daily course of the sun across the sky (3) : an often extended experience that provides new information or knowledge beyond that which one might normally acquire ⟨a ~ into higher mathematics⟩ ⟨a ~ into the customs of another country⟩ ⟨an inviting and pleasant mental ~ for the reader —Frank Mortimer⟩ ⟨his ~ into faith —Florence Bullock⟩ **2 a** *chiefly dial* : a day's labor or a fixed amount of work as an equivalent **b** : a weight of metal (as 15 pounds troy of gold or 60 pounds troy of silver) that was the supply for one day's minting of coins by hand in the British mint and that made up into coin constitutes the unit out of which one coin is set aside for the trial of the pyx **c** : a cycle of work done in glass manufacturing in converting a quantity of material into glass or glass products **3** *obs* **a** : FIGHT, BATTLE **b** : a military expedition : SIEGE, CAMPAIGN
²**journey** \"\ *vb* **journeyed**; **journeyed**; **journeying**; **journeys** [ME *jorneyen, journeyen*, fr. MF *journoier*, fr. *journee*] *vi* : to go on a journey ⟨spent the summer ~*ing*⟩ : go from home to a distant place ⟨packed his belongings and ~*ed* to another country⟩ : TRAVEL ⟨~ from place to place in search of treasure⟩ ⟨most of us ~ to work by bus, tram, train —Agnes M. Miall⟩ ~ *vt* **1** : to travel over or through : TRAVERSE ⟨~*ed* many a land —Sir Walter Scott⟩ **2** : to separate (coins in the British mint) into journeys
journey-bated *adj, obs* : worn out with journeying
journeycake \'≈≈,≈\ *n* [prob. by folk etymology fr. *johnnycake*] : JOHNNYCAKE
jour·ney·man \'≈≈mən\ *n, pl* **journeymen** *often attrib* [ME, fr. *jurne, journey* + *man*] **1 a** : a worker who has learned a handicraft or trade and is qualified to work at it usu. for another by the day — distinguished from *apprentice* and *master* **b** : an experienced usu. competent or reliable workman in any field usu. as distinguished from one that is brilliant or colorful ⟨a good, reliable ~ of the theatre —*Theatre Arts*⟩ ⟨a good ~ trumpeter —*New Yorker*⟩ ⟨~ work, competent but without much distinction —J.G.Villa⟩ ⟨~'s work too slick and trite to prove itself —K.P.Kempton⟩ ⟨*journeymen* rather than first-rate artists —H.E.Clurman⟩ **2** *archaic* : one hired to work for another : HIRELING **3** : the first rank earned by members of a Camp Fire Girls Horizon Club — compare ARTISAN
journeys accounts *n pl* : the number of days required for travel to a court formerly considered in English law as the fewest within which a new writ could be obtained after the abatement of a previous one
journey weight *n* : a quantity of coins in the British mint
journeywoman \'≈≈,≈≈\ *n, pl* **journeywomen** : a female journeyman
journeywork \'≈≈,≈\ *n* **1 a** : work done by a journeyman esp. by the day **b** : work done for hire **2** : necessary routine and often servile work : HACKWORK
¹**joust** \'jaůst *sometimes* 'jəst *or* 'jüst\ *or* **just** \'jəst\ *n* -s [ME, fr. OF *joste, juste, jouste*, fr. *joster, juster, jouster*] **1 a** : a combat on horseback between two knights with lances esp. in the lists or an enclosed field; *specif* : an often mock combat of this kind as part of a tournament or display : TILT **b jousts** *or* **justs** *pl* : TOURNAMENT **2** : an action resembling that of a man or of men jousting esp. in being personal combat or competition ⟨young people in their ~s with ideas —William Van Til⟩ ⟨the producer's Academy Award-winning ~ against anti-Semitism —*Newsweek*⟩ ⟨the ancient ritual of the ~ from boats, striving to knock each other into the water —Paul Engle⟩
²**joust** \"\ *or* **just** \"\ *vi* -ED/-ING/-S [ME *jousten, justen*, fr. OF *joster, juster, jouster* to gather, unite, joust, fr. (assumed) VL *juxtare*, fr. L *juxta* near, nearby; akin to L *jungere* to join — more at YOKE] **1** : to fight on horseback as a knight or man-at-arms **2 a** : to engage in combat with lances on horseback : engage in a joust : TILT ⟨two knights ~*ing* in the lists⟩ **b** : to participate in an action resembling a joust : engage in personal combat or competition ⟨cars no longer ~*ing* and jostling at the crossings —R.M.Coates⟩ ⟨passenger-car manufacturers ~ like surly giants over the mighty business of making and selling millions of motorcars —A.W.Baum⟩ — **joust·er** *or* **just·er** \-tə(r)\ *n* -s
jousting *also* **justing** *n* -s [ME, fr. the gerund of ME *justen, jousten*] : the action or sport of one that jousts : JOUST, TILT
jousting helmet *or* **jousting helm** *n* : TILTING HELMET
jou·vence blue \(')zhü¦väⁿ(t)s-\ *n* [*jouvence* fr. F, youth (in *fontaine de jouvence* fountain of youth), fr. MF, alter. of

jouvente, fr. L *juventa*, fr. *juvenis* young — more at YOUNG] **:** a moderate bluish green to greenish blue that is deeper than gendarme or cyan blue and duller than parrot blue

jouy print \zhə'wē-, 'zhwē-\ *n, usu cap J* [*Jouy*-en-Josas, France, its original place of manufacture] **:** TOILE DE JOUY

jo·va \'hōvə\ *n, pl* **jova** *or* **jovas** *usu cap* [Sp, of AmerInd origin] **1 :** an important division of the Piman peoples of northeastern Sonora **2 :** a member of the Jova people

jove \'jōv\ *interj, usu cap* [fr. *Jove* (Jupiter), ancient Roman god of the sky, fr. L *Jov-, Juppiter* — more at DEITY] — used typically to express surprise or agreement esp. in the phrase *by Jove*

jove's-beard \'=,=\ *n, pl* **jove's-beards** *usu cap J* **:** JUPITER'S-BEARD

jove's-flower \'=,=\ *n, pl* **jove's-flowers** *usu cap J* **:** CLOVE PINK

jove's-fruit \'=,=\ *n, pl* **jove's-fruits** *usu cap J* **1 :** a spicebush (*Benzoin melissaefolium*) of the southern U.S. **2 :** PERSIMMON

jo·vial \'jōvēəl, -vyəl\ *adj* [MF & LL; MF, fr. LL *jovialis* of the god Jupiter, fr. *Jov-, Juppiter* Jupiter, ancient Roman god of the sky + L *-alis* -al — more at DEITY] **1 a** *obs* **:** JOVIAN **b :** having the nature, disposition, or aspect that according to astrology is determined by Jupiter as natal or ruling planet **2 :** characterized by or showing marked good humor esp. as exhibited in mirth, hilarity, or conviviality **:** JOYFUL, JOLLY ⟨a ~ portly gentleman⟩ ⟨a ~ grin⟩ **syn** see MERRY

jovialist *n* -s **1** *obs* **:** one born under the planet Jupiter **2** *obs* **:** one having a jovial disposition

jo·vi·al·i·ty \,jōvē'alәd·ē, jōv'ya-, -lətē, -i\ *n* -ES **:** the quality or state of being jovial ⟨greeted him with customary ~ —S.E.White⟩ ⟨liked the ~ of the gathering⟩

jo·vial·ize \'jōvēə,līz, -vyə-\ *vb* -ED/-ING/-S *vt, archaic* **:** to make jovial ~ *vi, obs* **:** to act in a jovial way

jo·vial·ly \-əlē, -əli\ *adv* **:** in a jovial manner

jo·vial·ness *n* -ES **:** JOVIALITY

jo·vi·an \'jōvēən\ *adj, usu cap* [L *Jovius* of Jupiter (fr. *Jov-, Juppiter*) + E *-an*] **1 :** of, relating to, or befitting the chief ancient Roman god Jupiter ⟨*Jovian* thunderbolts⟩ ⟨*Jovian* wrath⟩ ⟨the committee's *Jovian* attitude toward justifying its decisions —Paul Moor⟩ ⟨resolved the trouble by *Jovian* fiat —Agnes de Mille⟩ ⟨a *Jovian* detachment from the pressure of events —H.R.Tolley⟩ **2** [L *Jov-, Juppiter*, the planet Jupiter (fr. *Jov-, Juppiter*, the god Jupiter) + E *-ian*] **:** relating to the planet Jupiter ⟨the *Jovian* satellites⟩

jo·vi·cen·tric \,jōvə'sen·trik\ *also* **jo·vi·cen·tri·cal** \-rəkəl\ *adj, usu cap* [L *Jov-, Juppiter*, the planet Jupiter + E *-i-* + *-centric* or *centrical*] **:** centered upon or revolving around the planet Jupiter **:** appearing as viewed from the center of Jupiter — **jo·vi·cen·tri·cal·ly** \-rək(ə)lē\ *adv*

¹jow \'jaů, 'jō\ *vb* -ED/-ING/-S [alter. of ⁴*jowl*] *vt* **1** *dial Brit* **:** to give a blow to **:** STRIKE **2** *dial Brit* **:** to cause (a bell) to ring or toll ~ *vi, dial Brit, of a bell* **:** TOLL, RING

²jow \"\ *n* -s *chiefly Scot* **:** STROKE, KNOCK, TOLL ⟨and every ~ the dead bell gave cried woe to Barbara Allen —*Barbara Allen*⟩

jo·war \jə'wär\ *n* -s [Hindi *joār, jawār*; akin to Skt *yava* barley] *India* **:** DURRA

¹jow·er \'jaů(ə)r\ *vi* -ED/-ING/-S [perh. of imit. origin] *chiefly dial* **:** QUARREL, WRANGLE

²jower \"\ *n* -s *dial* **:** QUARREL, SPAT

¹jowl \'jaů(ə)l *also* 'jōl *sometimes* 'jōl\ *n* -s [alter. (prob. influenced by ¹*jaw*) of ME *chavel, chauel, chawl*, fr. OE *ceafl*; akin to MHG *kivel, kiver* jaw, OS *kaflos*, pl., jaws, ON *kjaptr* jaw, OIr *gop* beak, mouth, Av *zafar-, zafan-* mouth] **1 a :** JAW; *esp* **:** MANDIBLE **b :** one of the lateral halves of the mandible **2 a :** CHEEK 1 **b :** the boneless cheek meat of a hog ⟨a dinner of boiled ~ and black-eyed peas⟩ — see PORK illustration

²jowl \"\ *n* -s [alter. (prob. influenced by ¹*jaw*) of ME *cholle*, prob. fr. OE *ceole* throat — more at GLUTTON] **1 a :** the pendulous part of a double chin **b :** the flesh hanging under the jaw of a fat pig **c :** the dewlap of cattle **d :** the wattle of a fowl **e :** a marked fullness and looseness of the flesh about the lower cheek and jaw usu. associated with aging — usu. used in pl. **2 :** the space and the soft tissues filling it between the branches of the lower jaw of a horse

³jowl \"\ *n* -s [ME *choll, cholle, jol, jolle*] **1** *obs* **:** HEAD 1 **2 :** a cut or dish of fish consisting of the head and usu. adjacent parts

⁴jowl \'jaů(ə)l, 'jōl\ *vb* -ED/-ING/-S [ME *chollen, jollen*, perh. fr. *choll, cholle, jol, jolle* head] *dial* **:** ¹JOW

⁵jowl \"\ *n* -s *dial* **:** ²JOW

jowled \'jaů(ə)ld *also* 'jōld *sometimes* 'jōld\ *adj* [²*jowl* + *-ed*] **:** JOWLY ⟨his big, ~ countenance —W.A.White⟩

jowl·er \-lər\ *n* -s [¹*jowl*, ²*jowl* + *-er*] *chiefly Scot* **:** a dog having extremely large jaws or jowls

jowly \'jaůlē, -li *also* 'jōl- *sometimes* 'jōl-\ *adj, often* -ER/-EST [²*jowl* + *-y*] **:** having marked jowls **:** full and usu. saggy of flesh about the lower cheeks and jaw area ⟨a silver-haired elderly man with a disillusioned ~ face, wrinkled as a leaky balloon —John Dos Passos⟩

jows·er \'jaůzə(r) *sometimes* -aůsə-\ *dial Eng var of* ¹DOWSER

jow·ter \'jaůtə(r)\ *n* -s [origin unknown] *dial Eng* **:** a peddler or hawker esp. of fish

¹joy \'jȯi\ *n* -s [ME *joye, joy*, fr. OF *joie, joye*, fr. L *gaudia*, pl. of *gaudium* joy, fr. *gaudēre* to rejoice; akin to Gk *gēthein* to rejoice, *gauros* proud, MIr *guāire* noble, Toch B *kāw-* to desire, Lith *džiaugiuos* I rejoice] **1 a :** the emotion excited by the acquisition or expectation of good **:** pleasurable feelings or emotions caused by well-being, success, or good fortune or by the prospect of possessing what one loves or desires **:** GLADNESS, DELIGHT **b :** an experience of such emotion **:** ENJOYMENT ⟨the ~ of books —Van Wyck Brooks⟩ **c :** the sign or exhibition of joy **:** GAIETY, JUBILATION, MERRIMENT ⟨after the victory there was great ~ in the town⟩ **d** — used interjectionally as an exclamation of delight esp. in the phrase *oh joy* **2 :** a state of happiness or felicity **:** BLISS **3 a :** a source or cause of joy ⟨motherhood is a ~ rather than a job —Kathleen H. Seib⟩ ⟨found many ~s in . . . rustic life —Ella E. Clark⟩ ⟨this book . . . is a ~ and an instruction —J.A.Michener⟩ ⟨a ~ to look at⟩ **b :** a small endearing or loved child **4** *of a planet* **:** astrological position in a house of agreeable quality or condition **:** an accidental dignity **syn** see PLEASURE

²joy \"\ *vb* -ED/-ING/-S [ME *joyen*, fr. OF *joir, jouir*, fr. L *gaudēre* to rejoice] *vi* **:** to experience or show pleasure or great delight **:** REJOICE, EXULT ⟨a happily married couple ~*ing* in a common ambition —Louise Mace⟩ ⟨could ~ in the purity of tone —W.M.Clark⟩ ~ *vt* **1** *obs* **:** to make joyful or happy **:** DELIGHT, GLADDEN **2** *archaic* **:** ENJOY **3** *obs* **a :** to greet with joy or welcome with honor **b :** CONGRATULATE **4** *obs* **:** to rejoice at

joy·ance \'jȯiən(t)s\ *also* **joy·an·cy** \-nsē\ *n, pl* **joyances** *also* **joyancies** [*joy* + *-ance, -ancy*] **1 :** the action of enjoying oneself **:** FESTIVITY, JUBILATION **2 a :** JOY, PLEASURE, DELIGHT **b** *archaic* **:** ENJOYMENT

¹joyc·ean \'jȯisēən\ *adj, usu cap* [James *Joyce* †1941 Ir. writer + E *-an*] **:** of, relating to, or befitting the writer Joyce or his writings ⟨*Joycean* passages⟩ ⟨*Joycean* stream of consciousness⟩ ⟨*Joycean* bitterness —Ann F. Wolfe⟩

²joycean \"\ *n* -s *usu cap* **1 :** a specialist in the life and writings of James Joyce **2 a :** an imitator of the style or methods of writing of James Joyce **b :** one that is prone to defend Joyce against criticism or that favors Joyce's style or methods

joy·ful \'jȯifəl\ *adj, sometimes* **joyfuller**; *sometimes* **joyfullest** [ME, fr. *joye, joy* + *-ful*] **:** marked by joy: **a :** experiencing pleasure or delight **:** HAPPY, JUBILANT ⟨a mother who is ~ on the return of her lost son⟩ **b :** bringing or causing joy ⟨~ news⟩ **:** inspiring joy ⟨a ~ occasion⟩ **c :** showing joy ⟨a ~ countenance⟩ **syn** see GLAD

joy·ful·ly \-f(ə)lē, -li\ *adv* [ME *joyfully*, fr. *joyful* + *-ly*] **:** in a joyful manner ⟨~ singing Christmas carols⟩

joy·ful·ness \-fəlnəs\ *n* -ES [ME *joyfulnesse*, fr. *joyful* + *-nesse* -ness] **:** JOY

joy girl *n, slang* **:** PROSTITUTE

joyhouse \'=,=\ *n, slang* **:** BROTHEL

joy-juice \'=,=\ *n, slang* **:** an alcoholic liquor

joy·less \'jȯiləs\ *adj* [ME *joyles*, fr. *joy* + *-les* -less] **:** not experiencing joy ⟨a ~ man⟩ **:** not inspiring or causing joy ⟨a ~ occasion⟩ **:** UNENJOYABLE ⟨a ~ trip⟩ ⟨a ~ season⟩ — **joy·less·ly** *adv* — **joy·less·ness** *n* -ES

joy·ous \'jȯiəs\ *adj* [ME, fr. MF *joyeus*, fr. OF *joios*, fr. *joie, joye* joy + *-os* -ous — more at JOY] **:** JOYFUL **syn** see GLAD

joy·ous·ly *adv* **:** JOYFULLY, HAPPILY, MERRILY

joy·ous·ness *n* -ES **:** JOYFULNESS, MERRIMENT, JUBILATION

joy·pop \'jȯi,päp\ *vi, slang* **:** to use drugs only occasionally **:** use drugs as a joypopper

joy·pop·per \-äpə(r)\ *n, slang* **:** an occasional user of drugs **:** a drug user who is not yet totally addicted

¹joyride \'=,=\ *n* [¹*joy* + *ride*] **1 :** a ride (as in car or plane) purely for pleasure **2 a :** a joyride taken esp. in a stolen car without regard for safety or consequences to oneself or others ⟨having stolen an automobile for a ~ —E.D.Radin⟩ **b :** any course of conduct or action marked by a seeking of pleasure with a reckless disregard of cost or consequences ⟨went on a ~, spending his inheritance heedlessly and improvidently⟩

²joyride \"\ *vi* **:** to go on a joyride ⟨after luncheon . . . I could ~ in a plane —C.L.Baldridge⟩ ⟨*joyriding* around in his car all evening⟩ — **joyrider** \'=,==\ *n*

joys *pl of* JOY, *pres 3d sing of* JOY

joy·some \'jȯisəm\ *adj* **:** JOYFUL — **joy·some·ly** *adv*

joy stick *n* [perh. fr. E slang *joy stick* penis; fr. its position between the knees of the aviator] **:** CONTROL STICK

JP *abbr* **1** Japan paper **2** jet-propelled; jet propulsion

JP *abbr or n* -s *often not cap* justice of the peace

JPP *abbr* Japan proof papers

jr *abbr* **1** journal **2** *often cap J* junior **3** juror

JS *abbr* joint support

j's *or* **js** *pl of* J

JSC *abbr* joint-stock company

JSD *abbr or n* -s **:** a doctor of juristic science

j-stick \'=,=\ *n, cap J* **:** J-BAR LIFT

j-stroke \'=,=\ *n, cap J* **:** a canoeing stroke in which the path of the paddle resembles the letter J used by a lone paddler to keep a straight course while paddling on one side of the canoe only

jt *abbr* joint

JTC *abbr* junior training corps

jtly *abbr* jointly

jua·ma·ve \(h)wə'mävē\ *also* **juamave istle** *n* -s [perh. irreg. fr. *Jaumave*, town in eastern Mexico] **:** a high-grade istle derived from a Mexican agave (*Agave funkiana*) and characterized by long pale flexible fibers

jua·ne·ño \(h)wə'nān(,)yō\ *n, pl* **juaneño** *or* **juaneños** *usu cap* [AmerSp, fr. *San Juan Capistrano*, Spanish mission in what is now southwestern California] **1 :** an extinct Shoshonean people of southwestern California speaking a dialect of Luiseño **2 :** a member of the Juaneño people

ju·ang \'jü,äŋ\ *n, pl* **juang** *or* **juangs** *usu cap* **1 a :** a Kol people of Orissa, India **b :** a member of such people **2 :** the Munda language of the Juang people

ju·ar \jə'wär\ *var of* JOWAR

juárez *or* **juarez** *adj, usu cap* **:** CIUDAD JUÁREZ

ju·ba \'jübə\ *n* -s [origin unknown] **1 :** a Haitian dance of African origin having drum and stick accompaniment and performed as a work dance or as a dance for the dead **2 :** a dance of plantation Negroes in the South accompanied by complexly rhythmic hand clapping and slapping of the knees and thighs ⟨the sudden silence after the singing and ~ —R.P. Warren⟩

juba's-brush *or* **juba's-bush** \'jübəz,=\ *n, pl* **juba's-brushes** *or* **juba's-bushes** *usu cap J* [perh. fr. *Juba's*, genitive case of a name *Juba*] **:** an annual weed (*Iresine paniculata*) of the central U.S. and tropical America

ju·bate \'jü,bāt\ *adj* [NL *jubatus*, fr. L, having a mane, fr. *juba* mane + *-atus* -ate; akin to L *jubēre* to command — more at JUSSIVE] **:** fringed with long pendent hairs like a mane

jub·bah *or* **jub·ba** \'jůbə, 'jəbə\ *n* -s [Ar *jubbah*] **:** a long outer garment resembling an open coat, having long sleeves, and formerly worn in Muslim countries esp. by public officials and professional people ⟨arrayed in white cloth robes, a black ~, and a gold sash —John Buchan⟩

jub·bul·pore \'jəbəl,pō(ə)r\ *or* **ja·bal·pur** \'jəbəl,pů(ə)r\ *adj, usu cap* [fr. *Jubbulpore, Jabalpur*, city in Jubbulpore district, Madhya Pradesh, India] **:** of or from the city of Jubbulpore, India **:** of the kind or style prevalent in Jubbulpore

jubbulpore hemp *n, usu cap J* [fr. *Jubbulpore* district, Madhya Pradesh, India, where it is grown] **:** SUNN

ju·be \'yü(,)bā\ *n* -s [F *jubé*, fr. MF, fr. ML *Jube, Domine, benedicere* Deign, O Lord, to bless; prob. fr. the fact that in the medieval church the deacon stood at the rood screen or on the rood loft when pronouncing this benediction before the reading of the Gospel] **1 :** ROOD SCREEN **2 :** the gallery above a rood screen

ju·ber·ous \'jüb(ə)rəs, -bə(r)s\ *adj* [alter. of *dubious*] *South and Midland* **:** doubtful and hesitating **:** DUBIOUS

ju·bi·lance \'jübəlan(t)s\ *n* -s [*jubilant* + *-ance*] **:** the quality or state of being jubilant **:** EXULTATION

ju·bi·lant \-nt\ *adj* [L *jubilant-, jubilans*, pres. part. of *jubilare* to jubilate] **1 :** making noises and demonstrations of joy or triumph ⟨shots fired by ~ cowboys in celebration of frontier legal victories —*Amer. Guide Series: Texas*⟩ **2 :** manifesting or expressing exultation or gladness ⟨~ strings and ceremonious percussion —Irving Kolodin⟩ ⟨the walls . . . were covered with ~ childish drawings —Oliver La Farge⟩ — **ju·bi·lant·ly** *adv*

ju·bi·lar·i·an \'==la(a)rēən\ *n* -s [ML *jubilarius* jubilarian (fr. LL *jubilaeus* jubilee + L *-arius* -ary) + E *-an*, n. suffix] **:** one that celebrates a jubilee commemorating personal service in a state of life or profession; *esp* **:** a religious observing a jubilee

¹ju·bi·late \'==,lāt\ *vi* -ED/-ING/-S [L *jubilatus*, past part. of *jubilare*; akin to MHG *jū, jūch* (exclamation of joy), *jōlen* to yodel, Gk *iygē* shout, howling, Lith *yvas* owl] **:** to utter sounds or make demonstrations of joy and exultation ⟨the war was not officially ended but . . . a war-weary nation *jubilated* —Dixon Wecter⟩

²ju·bi·la·te \,yübə'lä(,)tā, ,jü-\ *n* -s [L, 2d pers. pl. imper. of *jubilare*; fr. the occurrence of this word at the beginning of Ps 99 in the Vulgate (Ps 100 AV and RSV)] **1 :** a song or outburst of joy and gladness ⟨Heaven's grand courts with ~s rang —*Tinsley's Mag.*⟩ **2** [L, 2d pers. pl. imper. of *jubilare*; fr. the occurrence of this word at the beginning of Ps 65 in the Vulgate (Ps 66 AV and RSV), used as the introit for the third Sunday after Easter] *usu cap* **:** the third Sunday after Easter

ju·bi·la·tio \,yübə'lätsē,ō\ *n* -s [L, jubilation] **:** JUBILUS

ju·bi·la·tion \,jübə'lāshən\ *n* -s [ME *jubilacioun*, fr. L *jubilation-, jubilatio*, fr. *jubilatus* (past part. of *jubilare* to jubilate) + *-ion-, -io* -ion] **1 a :** the act of jubilating ⟨we must not rejoice or give way to ~ —Sir Winston Churchill⟩ **b :** the state of being jubilant ⟨he expelled his pent-up ~ in a long whistle —F.G.Slaughter⟩ **2 :** an expression of joy or exultation ⟨the ~s of the garrison were short-lived —C.R.Low⟩

ju·bi·le·an \,jübə'lēən\ *adj* [¹*jubilee* + *-an*] **:** of or relating to a jubilee

¹ju·bi·lee \'jübə,lē, ,==ˈ=\ *n* -s [ME, fr. MF & LL; MF *jubilé*, fr. LL *jubilaeus*, modif. (influenced by L *jubilare* to jubilate) of LGk *iōbēlaios*, fr. Heb *yōbhēl* ram's horn, trumpet, jubilee] **1** *also* **ju·bi·le** \"\ *often cap* **:** a year of emancipation and restoration provided by ancient Hebrew law for celebration every fifty years and held to be characterized by emancipation of Hebrew slaves, restoration of alienated lands to their former owners, and omission of all cultivation of the land — used esp. in the phrase *year of jubilee* ⟨the year of ~ . . . appears to have been calculated but not observed —T.W. Manson⟩ ⟨you shall hallow the fiftieth year . . . it shall be a ~ for you —Lev 25:10 (RSV)⟩ ⟨in this year of ~ ye shall return every man unto his possession —Lev 25:13 (AV)⟩ — compare SABBATICAL YEAR **2 a** (1) **:** a fiftieth anniversary or the completion of fifty years in an office, position, or condition ⟨the Australian florin commemorating the ~ of the constitution of the commonwealth —Lionel Thompson⟩ ⟨the ~ . . . of King George the Third in 1810 —E.J.Shears⟩ (2) **:** a special anniversary or the completion of a significant length of service involving a period other than fifty years — usu. used with qualifying adjective ⟨the seventieth ~ of the reign of the Emperor Francis Joseph —Hans Meyerhoff⟩ ⟨the approach of his thirty-year ~ may have supplied a . . . motive for retirement —W.F.Edgerton⟩ — compare DIAMOND JUBILEE, SILVER JUBILEE **b :** a celebration or commemoration of such an anniversary or of the completion of such a period of service ⟨the sesquicentennial vacation ~ scheduled for this year —*Stamps*⟩ **3 a :** a period of time (as a year) proclaimed by the Roman Catholic pope every 25 years or during a time of rejoicing (as an anniversary) as a time of special solemnity during which a special indulgence may be gained ⟨the first ~ was proclaimed in the year 1300 —Percy Winner⟩ **b** *or* **jubilee indulgence :** a special plenary indulgence granted during a year of jubilee to Roman Catholics who perform certain specified works of repentance and piety usu. including a pilgrimage to Rome ⟨the precise conditions for gaining each ~ are determined by the Roman pontiff —Herbert Thurston⟩ **4** [influenced in meaning by *jubilation*] **:** a state of joy or rejoicing **:** JUBILATION ⟨they . . . only thought of their triumph and abandoned themselves to ~ —W.H.Prescott⟩ **5** [influenced in meaning by *jubilation*] **:** the sound of jubilation **:** joyous shouting ⟨all along the crowded way was ~ and loud huzza —Sir Walter Scott⟩ **6 a :** a period of remission or restitution and sometimes license ⟨moved . . . a general ~ shall be for the debts —*House of Lords Debates*⟩ **b** [influenced in meaning by *jubilation*] **:** a season or occasion of celebration or rejoicing ⟨during the wild ~ of the Restoration —T.B.Macaulay⟩ ⟨we had a big ~ . . . to celebrate our victory —A.F.Harlow⟩ **7** *obs, often cap* **:** a period of fifty years ⟨I have lived among you almost a *Jubilee* —Ephraim Pagitt⟩ **8 :** a Negro folk song characterized by references to a future happy time or a time of deliverance from trials and tribulations ⟨the weary field hollers of the slaves were mingled with merrier elements of the ~s —*N. Y. Times Book Rev.*⟩ — compare HOLLER 3

²jubilee \"\ *adj* **:** FLAMBÉ 2 ⟨cherries ~⟩

ju·bi·lize \'==,līz\ *vi* -ED/-ING/-S [prob. fr. ¹*jubilee* + *-ize*] *archaic* **:** ¹JUBILATE

ju·bi·lus \-ləs\ *n, pl* **jubi·li** \-,lī\ [ML, fr. LL, cry of joy, fr. L *jubilum*, fr. *jubilare* to jubilate] **:** the melisma on the last *a* of *alleluia* from which the sequence of the mass developed — called also *jubilatio*

ju·bus \'jübəs\ *var of* JUBEROUS

juca *var of* YUCA

juck \'jək\ *vi* -ED/-ING/-S [imit.] **:** to make the natural noise of a partridge settling down for the night

juco *abbr* junior college

jud *abbr* **1** judge; judgment **2** judicial; judiciary

judaean *var of* JUDEAN

judaeo- — see JUDEO-

¹ju·dah·ite \'jüdə,īt\ *n* -s *usu cap* [*Judah*, 4th son of Jacob (Gen 29:35), the eponymous ancestor of the Judahites (Josh 15) + E *-ite*] **1 :** a member of the Hebrew tribe of Judah **2 :** a member of the Kingdom of Judah composed of the tribes of Judah and Benjamin

²judahite \"\ *adj, usu cap* **:** of or relating to the tribe or the Kingdom of Judah ⟨a place in *Judahite* territory —N.H. Snaith⟩ ⟨edited to suit a *Judahite* audience —L.A.Weigle⟩

ju·da·ic \(')jü'dāik, -āēk\ *adj, usu cap* [L *judaicus*, fr. Gk *ioudaikos*, fr. *Ioudaios* Jew + *-ikos* -ic — more at JEW] **:** of, relating to, or characteristic of Jews or Judaism ⟨the . . . idea of particularism in *Judaic* thinking —F.S.Nichols⟩

ju·da·i·ca \jü'dāəkə\ *n pl, usu cap* [L, neut. pl. of *judaicus* Judaic] **:** things Jewish; *esp* **:** literary or historical materials relating to Jews or Judaism ⟨a new publication devoted to *Judaica* —W.S. La Sor⟩ ⟨a large collection of *Judaica*

ju·da·i·cal \(')jü'dāəkəl\ *adj, usu cap* [ME *judeicall*, fr. L *judaicus* + ME *-al*] **:** JUDAIC — **ju·da·i·cal·ly** \-k(ə)lē, -li\ *adv*

ju·da·ism \'jüdə,izəm, -dē,i- *sometimes* -(,)dā,i- *or* -,dizəm\ *n* [LL *judaismus*, fr. Gk *ioudaismos*, fr. *Ioudaios* Jew + *-ismos* -ism] **1** *cap* **:** the religion of the Jews characterized by belief in one God and in the mission of Jews to teach the Fatherhood of God as revealed in the Hebrew Scriptures — see CONSERVATIVE JUDAISM, ORTHODOX JUDAISM, RECONSTRUCTIONISM, REFORM JUDAISM **2** *usu cap* **:** the quality or state of being a Jew **:** conformity to Jewish rites, ceremonies, and practices **:** adherence to the religion or culture of the Jews ⟨declared their *Judaism* openly —Cecil Roth⟩ **3** *usu cap* **:** the total complex of cultural, social, and religious beliefs and practices of the Jews **4** *usu cap* **:** the whole body of Jews **:** the Jewish community ⟨losses sustained by *Judaism* . . . by the oppression of Jews in Russia and Rumania —Herbert Loewe⟩

ju·da·ist \'jüdə·əst, -dēə-, -(,)dāə-\ *n* -s *usu cap* [*judaism* + *-ist*] **:** one that believes in or practices Judaism — **ju·da·is·tic** \'=(,)='istik, -tēk\ *adj* — **ju·da·is·ti·cal·ly** \-tək(ə)lē, -tēk-, -li\ *adv*

ju·da·iza·tion \,jüdə|ə'zāshən, ,jüdē|, ,jü(,)dā|, jü,dā|, |,ī'z-\ *n* -s *usu cap* **:** the act or process of judaizing or being judaized

ju·da·ize \'jüdə,īz, -dē,-, -(,)dā,-\ *vb* -ED/-ING/-S *often cap* [LL *judaizare*, fr. Gk *ioudaizein*, fr. *Ioudaios* Jew + *-izein* -ize] *vi* **:** to adopt the customs, beliefs, or character of a Jew **:** become Jewish ⟨they . . . prevailed on the Galatians to *Judaize* so far as to observe the rites of Moses in various instances —Joseph Milner⟩ ~ *vt* **1 :** to imbue with or deeply affect by the doctrines or practices of Judaism ⟨attempts to ~ the Christian Sunday into a sabbath⟩ **2 :** to make Jewish **:** convert to Judaism ⟨descendants of Slav tribes *Judaized* long after the Dispersal —Evelyn Waugh⟩

ju·da·iz·er \-,īzə(r)\ *n* -s *usu cap* **1 :** a Jewish Christian of the apostolic age who attempted to enforce conformity by all Christians to the precepts and practices of Judaism ⟨the *Judaizers* . . . thought that Gentiles, in order to be Christians, should be circumcised —J.W.Hunkin⟩ **2 :** a member of an heretical group arising in the Russian Orthodox Church in the 15th century and favoring an increased emphasis upon the doctrines and rituals of Judaism ⟨the *Judaizers* conducted a campaign of subversive activity within the church —Serge Bolshakoff⟩

¹ju·das \'jüdəs\ *n* -ES *often attrib* [after *Judas* Iscariot, apostle that betrayed Jesus] **1** *usu cap* **:** TRAITOR; *esp* **:** one that betrays under the pretense of friendship ⟨some *Judas* . . . gave the story to the one-party press —G.W. Johnson⟩ **2** *or* **judas window** *also* **judas-hole** *sometimes cap J* **:** a peephole usu. constituted by an aperture resembling a window with a sliding panel and used chiefly for inspection (as in the door of a house or a prison cell) ⟨the guard sprang to reconnoiter through a ~ —*N.Y.Sun*⟩ ⟨peering through the broken ~ in the door of the cell —John Hersey⟩ ⟨after a considerable time a ~ was opened —W.S.Maugham⟩ ⟨the *judas window* of the cell door slammed down —Dickey Chapelle⟩

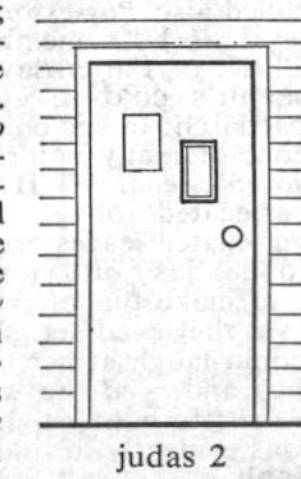
judas 2

²judas \"\ *adj, usu cap* **:** of, relating to, or being an animal used as a decoy or to lead other animals to slaughter ⟨a *Judas* duck⟩ ⟨as sheep are led by a *Judas* goat —James Reach⟩

judas-colored \'==,==\ *adj, usu cap J* [so called fr. a belief that Judas Iscariot was red haired] **:** RED, REDDISH — usu. used of hair ⟨there's treachery in that *Judas-colored* beard —John Dryden⟩

judas-ear \'==,=\ *n, pl* **judas-ears** *usu cap J* [trans. of NL *auricula Judae* — more at JEW'S-EAR] **:** JEW'S-EAR

judas priest *interj, often cap J&P* [euphemism for *Jesus Christ*] — used as a mild oath

judas thorn *n, usu cap J* **:** a Judas tree (*Cercis siliquastrum*)

judas tree *n, usu cap J* [so called fr. a belief that Judas Iscariot hanged himself on a tree of this kind] **:** an often shrubby Eurasian tree (*Cercis siliquastrum*) that has glabrous shoots and rounded deeply cordate leaves and is widely cultivated in mild regions for its abundant purplish rose flowers which appear in early spring; *broadly* **:** a tree or shrub of the genus *Cercis*

jud·cock \'jəd,=\ *n* -s [perh. irreg. fr. *ged* + *cock*] **:** JACKSNIPE

¹jud·der \'jədə(r)\ *vi* -ED/-ING/-S [prob. alter. (prob. influenced by *jar*) of *shudder*] **:** to vibrate with intensity **:** jar strongly ⟨the motors which clattered protestingly to life, backfiring and ~*ing* —J.L.Rhys⟩

²judder \"\ *n* -s **:** the action or sound of juddering ⟨they . . . found some comfort in the ~ of the engines —Audrey Barker⟩

¹ju·de·an *also* **ju·dae·an** \(')jü¦dēən\ *adj, usu cap* [*Judea, Judaea*, southern division of Palestine under Persian, Greek, and Roman rule + E -*an*, adj. suffix] **:** of, relating to, or characteristic of ancient Judea ⟨*Judean* mountains⟩ ⟨the background of *Judaean* history —J.W.Jack⟩

²judean *also* **judaean** \"\ *n* -s *usu cap* [*Judea, Judaea* + E -*an*, n. suffix] **:** an inhabitant of ancient Judea ⟨the Israelites and *Judeans* . . . disclosed no interest in theoretical questions universal in scope —R.H.Pfeiffer⟩

judeo- *also* **judaeo-** *comb form, usu cap* [L *judaeus* Jewish, Jew — more at JEW] **1 :** of or relating to the Jews or Judaism ⟨*Judeo*phobia⟩ **2 :** Jewish and ⟨*Judeo*-Christian⟩ ⟨*Judeo*-Persian⟩

judeo-german \jü¦dā(,)ō, ¦jüdē(,)ō, jü¦dē(,)ō+\ *n, cap J&G* **:** YIDDISH

judeo-spanish \jü¦dā(,)ō, ¦jüdē(,)ō, jü¦dē(,)ō+\ *n, cap J&S* **:** the Romance language of Sephardic Jews in the Balkans, Greece, and Asia Minor

ju·dex \ˈjü,deks\ *n, pl* **judi·ces** \-də,sēz\ [L *judic-, judex*] **1 :** a private person appointed in Roman law to hear and determine a case and corresponding most nearly to a modern referee or arbitrator appointed by the court **2 :** JUDGE

judex or·di·na·ri·us \-,ȯ(r)dᵊnˈa(a)rēəs\ *n, pl* **judices ordina·rii** \-rē,ī\ [ML, lit., regular judge] **:** a judicial magistrate having jurisdiction in his own right as a judge as distinguished from a judex appointed for a particular case

judex pe·da·ne·us \-pəˈdānēəs\ *n, pl* **judices peda·nei** \-ē,ī\ [LL, lit., petty judex] **:** a judex appointed to hear petty causes

¹judge \ˈjəj, *dial* ˈjej\ *vb* -ED/-ING/-S [ME *juggen*, fr. OF *jugier*, fr. L *judicare*, fr. *judic-, judex* judex, judge] *vt* **1 :** to form an authoritative opinion about **:** decide on the merits of ⟨a wall must be *judged* by the way it is built —Paul Potts⟩ ⟨humanity *judged* these authors . . . and found them worthy of enduring fame —Van Wyck Brooks⟩ **2 :** to hear and determine (as a litigated question) or decide in the case of (as a person) in or as if in a court of justice **:** sit in judgment upon **:** TRY ⟨the power of the court to ~ cases in interstate commerce⟩ ⟨*judged* and condemned to death for killing his mother —John Milton⟩ ⟨He shall come to ~ the quick and the dead —*Bk. of Com. Prayer*⟩ **3** *obs* **:** CONDEMN 3a ⟨some whose offenses are pilfering . . . they ~ to be whipped —Francis Bacon⟩ **4 :** to determine or pronounce after inquiry and deliberation **:** CONSIDER ⟨recommend . . . such measures as he shall ~ necessary and expedient —*U.S.Constitution*⟩ ⟨youngsters *judged* delinquent —Dorothy Barclay⟩ **5 :** to exercise paramount civil and military authority over **:** GOVERN, RULE — used of a Hebrew tribal leader in biblical times ⟨and he *judged* Israel in the days of the Philistines twenty years —Judg 15: 20 (RSV)⟩ **6 :** to form an estimate or appraisal of ⟨able to ~ pace to a nicety —*Irish Digest*⟩ ⟨we ~ the distance from remembered comparisons —Weston La Barre⟩ **7 :** to hold as an opinion **:** THINK ⟨I ~ she was right —B.A.Williams⟩ ~ *vi* **1 :** to form an opinion: as **a :** to estimate esp. on the basis of a comparison of facts or ideas ⟨as near as I could ~, we were not twenty yards from the rocks —Frederick Marryat⟩ **b :** to form a conclusion from evidence ⟨when the mind assents to a proposition it ~*s* —J.S. Mill⟩ **c :** to form a critical evaluation — often used with *of* ⟨it is hard to ~ of the general style of the painting from such small portions —O. Elfrida Saunders⟩ **2 :** to hear and determine (as in causes on trial) **:** decide as a judge **:** pronounce judgment ⟨may the Lord ~ between you and me —Gen 16:5 (RSV)⟩ **syn** see INFER

²judge \"\ *n* -s [ME *juge*, fr. MF, fr. L *judic-, judex* judex, judge, fr. *ju-* (fr. *jus* right, law) + *-dic-, -dex* (fr. *dicere* to determine, say) — more at JUST, DICTION] **:** one that judges: **a** (1) **:** a public official invested with authority to hear and determine litigated questions; *esp* **:** the presiding magistrate in a court of justice usu. so named in his commission ⟨the ~ declares the law, the jury finds the facts —Edward Jenks⟩ ⟨European ~*s* are members of a hierarchically organized bureaucracy —C.J.Friedrich⟩ (2) **:** a person who performs one or more functions of such an official (as a justice of the peace or referee) or of any judicial officer — sometimes used as an honorific or courtesy title without much significance ⟨American law early . . . dignified every magistrate by calling him ~ —H.S.Commager⟩ **b** *cap* **:** GOD, CHRIST ⟨the coming of the Lord is at hand . . . behold, the *Judge* is standing at the doors —Jas 5: 8-9 (RSV)⟩ **c** *often cap* **:** a tribal hero exercising paramount civil and military authority over the Hebrews in the biblical period of more than 400 years following the death of Joshua ⟨the Lord raised up ~*s*, who saved them out of the power of those who plundered them —Judg 2:16 (RSV)⟩ **d :** one appointed to decide in a contest or competition (as a trial of skill or speed between two or more parties) **:** UMPIRE ⟨the *Judge* . . . must occupy the judges' box at the time the horses pass the winning post —Dan Parker⟩ ⟨on election day the ~ helps decide disputes at the polls⟩ **e :** one that decides or determines any question, point at issue, or controversy **:** one that gives an authoritative opinion ⟨each house shall be the ~ of the . . . qualifications of its own members —*U.S.Constitution*⟩ ⟨the board shall be the ~ of what constitutes unprofessional conduct —G.B.Cummings⟩ ⟨the best ~ of what his book was about —Ellen Glasgow⟩ **f :** one that has sufficient knowledge or experience to decide on the merits of or to form an authoritative opinion about something (as a question or a work of art) **:** CONNOISSEUR, CRITIC ⟨was an extraordinary ~ of character —C.F.Smith⟩ ⟨a good ~ of poetry —John Dryden⟩

judge advocate *n, pl* **judge advocates :** a legal officer charged with the administration of military justice (as by acting as legal adviser or as prosecutor at a court-martial) and usu. serving on the staff of a military commander ⟨*judge advocates* shall perform their duties under the direction of the Judge Advocate General —*U.S.Code*⟩

judge advocate general *n, pl* **judge advocate generals** *or* **judge advocates general :** the senior legal officer and chief legal adviser in an entire military establishment (as the U.S. Department of Defense or the British army) ⟨the *Judge Advocate General* has ordered the case forwarded to the court for review —J.F.Spindler⟩

judge delegate *n, pl* **judges delegate :** a judge having delegated authority ⟨an extraordinary and rarely constituted court of *judges delegate* —*Nation*⟩ — compare JUDGE ORDINARY

judge lynch *n, usu cap J&L* **:** the lynch law personified ⟨*Judge Lynch* is not the sovereign spirit of America —*Nation*⟩

judge-made \ˈ=ˌ=\ *adj* **:** created by judges or judicial decision — used esp. of law applied or established by the judicial interpretation of statutes so as to extend or restrict their scope

judge ordinary *n, pl* **judges ordinary** [trans. of ML *judex ordinarius*] **1 :** a judge having jurisdiction in his own right ⟨English prelates who were sitting . . . not as *judges ordinary* but as mere delegates of the pope —Frederick Pollock & F.W. Maitland⟩ — compare JUDGE DELEGATE **2 :** a judge having ecclesiastical or probate jurisdiction

judge·ship \ˈjəj,ship\ *n* **:** the jurisdiction or office of a judge ⟨the ~ for the western district of Pennsylvania provided for by the act —*U.S.Code*⟩ ⟨appointed him to a ~ in the circuit court of the United States —W.C.Ford⟩

judg·ess \ˈjəjəs\ *n* -ES **:** a female judge

judg·mat·i·cal \(ˈ)jəj¦madəkəl\ *also* **judg·mat·ic** \-d·ik\ *adj* [prob. irreg. (influenced by such words as *dogmatical, dogmatic*) fr. *judgment* + *-ical* or *-ic*] **:** JUDICIOUS ⟨his ~ introduction to this brief selection . . . of shorter poems —Leonard Bacon⟩ ⟨he . . . is nicely *judgmatic* for a man still in his twenties —E.A.Weeks⟩

judg·mat·i·cal·ly \-d·ək(ə)lē\ *adv* **:** in the manner of a judge **:** GRAVELY ⟨they need to be interpreted ~ —E.L.Bernays⟩

judg·ment *or* **judge·ment** \ˈjəjmənt\ *n* -s [ME *jugement*, fr. OF *jugement*, fr. *jugier* to judge + *-ment* — more at JUDGE] **1 a :** a formal utterance or pronouncing of an authoritative opinion after judging **b :** an opinion so pronounced; *esp* **:** an adverse opinion **:** CENSURE, CRITICISM **2 a** (1) **:** a formal decision or determination given in a cause by a court of law or other tribunal **:** COURT ORDER, SENTENCE — compare DECREE 3b(1), SUMMARY JUDGMENT (2) *Brit* **:** a record or statement of the reasons for a specific judicial decision — compare OPINION **b** (1) **:** an obligation (as a debt) created by decree of a court ⟨collection of . . . automobile ~*s* from uninsured motorists —*Harvard Law Rev.*⟩ — compare ESTOPPEL, QUASI CONTRACT (2) **:** an official certificate evidencing such a decision or decree **c** *archaic* **:** a definitive or authoritative decision usu. pronounced formally as if in a court of justice **3 a** *obs* **:** the action of trying a person or a cause in or as if in a court of justice **:** TRIAL **b** *usu cap* (1) **:** the final judging of mankind by God in which reward or punishment is meted out to each individual according to his deserts — usu. used with *the* ⟨the expected letting loose of . . . anger at the *Judgment* —C.A.Scott⟩ ⟨the dead . . . biding *Judgment*, in its fold have slept —Walter de la Mare⟩ (2) **:** JUDGMENT DAY 1a **4 a :** a divine sentence or decision; *specif* **:** a calamity held to be sent by God as a punishment for wrong committed or as a symbol of divine displeasure **b :** a divine decree **:** a law divinely given ⟨hear, O Israel, the statutes and ~*s* which I speak in your ears this day —Deut 5:1 (AV)⟩ **5** *obs* **:** JUSTICE, RIGHTEOUSNESS ⟨for I the Lord love ~, I hate robbery —Isa 61:8 (AV)⟩ **6 a :** the action of judging **:** the mental or intellectual process of forming an opinion or evaluation by discerning and comparing ⟨the author has sought to exercise some rigor of *judgement* —Ernest Barker⟩ **b :** an opinion or estimate so formed ⟨an economist should form an independent ~ on currency questions —Bertrand Russell⟩ **c** *obs* **:** a religious belief or opinion of a sectarian nature **:** PERSUASION ⟨those of the Presbyterian ~ —Oliver Cromwell⟩ **7 a :** the capacity for judging **:** the power or ability to decide on the basis of evidence ⟨~ is the highest of the human faculties —E.L.Godkin⟩ ⟨some of the sharpest men in argument are notoriously unsound in ~ —O.W.Holmes †1894⟩ ⟨a steadying and composing effect upon their ~ —Matthew Arnold⟩ **b** (1) **:** the exercise of the capacity to judge ⟨in cases where poor ~ was displayed —Harold Koontz & Cyril O'Donnell⟩ ⟨sound professional ~ —*Jour. of Accountancy*⟩ (2) **:** the wise or just exercise of this capacity **:** DISCERNMENT, DISCRETION — used without qualifier ⟨he was not a man of ~ and he allowed personal feeling to influence his action —Hilaire Belloc⟩ ⟨displays . . . tact, clarity, and ~ —*Saturday Rev.*⟩ **8** *obs* **:** one possessing good judgment **:** ²JUDGE f ⟨he's one o' th' soundest ~*s* in Troy . . . and a proper man —Shak.⟩ **9** *logic* **a :** the action of mentally establishing a relation between two or more terms; *esp* **:** the affirmation or denial of a predicate with respect to a subject — compare APPREHENSION **b :** a formal expression embodying such a logical conclusion; *esp* **:** a proposition viewed as a statement of something believed or asserted **10** *philos* **:** the capacity, power, or faculty of judging: as **a** *Scholasticism* **:** the capacity to arrive at a decision about the value of things **b** *Kantianism* (1) **:** the power of relating particular to general terms or concepts — see DETERMINATIVE JUDGMENT, REFLECTIVE JUDGMENT (2) **:** a capacity mediating between reason and the understanding; *broadly* **:** the critical faculty — **judgment not withstanding the verdict** *or* **judgment non ob·stan·te ve·re·dic·to** \-,nänəbˈstantē,verəˈdik(,)tō, -,nōn-\ **:** a legal judgment entered for one party because law and justice require it notwithstanding a verdict of the jury in favor of an opposing party **syn** see SENSE

judg·men·tal \(ˈ)jəj¦mentᵊl\ *adj* **:** of, relating to, or involving judgment ⟨emphasizing the ~ aspect of morality —Sing-nan Fen⟩ ⟨the right to correct ~ errors —H.F.Taggart⟩

judgment book *n* **1 :** a book in which the clerk of a court of record enters judgments **2** *usu cap J&B* **:** the record of all human acts to be opened at the Last Judgment ⟨the leaves of the *Judgment Book* unfold —Bayard Taylor⟩

judgment by default : a judgment entered as a result of the failure of a party to appear or to file a pleading or to perform some other act of an interlocutory nature required by law within the time allowed

judgment cap *n* **:** BLACK CAP

judgment creditor *n* **:** a creditor having a legal right to enforce execution of a judgment for a sum of money ⟨a suit in equity by two *judgment creditors* of an insolvent . . . corporation —*Corporation Jour.*⟩ — compare JUDGMENT DEBTOR

judgment day *n* **1 a** *usu cap J&D* **:** the day of the Last Judgment **:** DOOMSDAY 1 ⟨belief in . . . the *Judgment Day* at the end of the world —E.R.Pike⟩ **b :** a day of final judgment ⟨driven Congress . . . for the sake of a completed record before the *judgment day* of election —F.L.Paxon⟩ **2 :** the day fixed by statute, rule, or custom of a court on which judgments are pronounced or entered upon the court records

judgment debt *n* **:** a legal obligation to pay a debt or damages evidenced by a judgment entered in a court of record and enforceable by execution or other judicial process — compare QUASI CONTRACT

judgment debtor *n* **:** one whose obligation to pay a judgment debt remains unsatisfied ⟨order the appearance of a *judgment debtor* for supplementary examination as to financial ability —F.H.Myers⟩ — compare JUDGMENT CREDITOR

judgment lien *n* **:** a statutory lien usu. upon the real estate of a judgment debtor that becomes effective upon entry of a judgment by a court of record or upon filing notice of the judgment with the appropriate public official

judgment note *n* **:** a promissory note of a kind illegal in some states of the U.S. upon which the holder is enabled to enter judgment and take out execution ex parte in case of default in payment

judgment-proof \ˈ==ˌ=\ *adj* **:** of or being one (as a judgment debtor) from whom nothing can be recovered because he has no property or has fraudulently concealed or removed his property from the jurisdiction of the judgment ⟨an insolvent, *judgment-proof* tort-feasor —R.E.Keeton⟩

judgment rate *n* **:** an insurance rate based on the judgment of the rater instead of on a prescribed schedule

judgment roll *n* **1 :** a parchment roll or a book containing a record of the proceedings and judgment of a case in a court of law ⟨the cost of transcribing the *judgment roll* —*Ward v. Cruse*⟩ **2 :** a roll of papers constituted by a collection of the original records of a judicial proceeding

judgment seat *n, often cap J* **:** the seat of judgment where all are to be tried in the presence of God at the time of the Last Judgment ⟨we must all appear before the *judgment seat* of Christ —2 Cor 5:10 (RSV)⟩

judgment summons *n* **:** a summons issued in an English county court requiring a judgment debtor to appear and show cause why he should not be imprisoned

judgt *abbr* judgment

ju·di·ca·ble \ˈjüdəkəbəl\ *adj* [LL *judicabilis*, fr. L *judicare* to judge + *-abilis* -able — more at JUDGE] **:** capable of being or liable to be judged ⟨a ~ dispute⟩

ju·di·ca·tive \-,kād·iv\ *adj* [ML *judicativus*, fr. L *judicatus* (past part. of *judicare* to judge) + *-ivus* -ive] **:** having the power to judge **:** JUDICIAL ⟨all the ~ authority of the House of Lords —David Hume †1776⟩

ju·di·ca·tor \-,ād·ə(r)\ *n* -s [LL, fr. L *judicatus* (past part. of *judicare*) + *-or*] **:** one that judges or acts as a judge ⟨the authority of its ~*s* called in question —William Robertson †1686⟩

ju·di·ca·to·ry \-kə,tōrē\ *n* -ES [ML *judicatorium* court of law, fr. L *judicatus* (past part. of *judicare*) + *-orium* -ory] **1 :** JUDICIARY 1a ⟨evidence in the Saxon *Judicatory* sometimes consisted in the . . . testimony of the fact itself —Nathaniel Bacon⟩ **2 :** JUDICATURE 2 ⟨the treaties of the U.S. had been . . . put in execution by state *judicatories* —Alexander Hamilton⟩ **3 :** one of the four governing bodies of the Presbyterian Church ⟨the General Assembly is the highest ~ of this Church —*Constitution of the United Presbyterian Church in the U.S.A.*⟩ — compare GENERAL ASSEMBLY, PRESBYTERY, SESSION, SYNOD

ju·di·ca·ture \-kə,chü(ə)r, -kəchər, -,kāchər\ *n* -s [MF, fr. ML *judicatura*, fr. L *judicatus* (past part. of *judicare*) + *-ura* -ure] **1 :** the action of judging **:** the administration of justice (as by courts of law) ⟨~ is nothing else but an interpretation of the laws —Thomas Hobbes⟩ ⟨the Supreme Court of *Judicature* in England⟩ **2 :** a court of justice **:** a legal tribunal ⟨the Court of the Lord Lyon in Scotland is one of the ~*s* of that country —F.J.Grant⟩ **3 :** JUDICIARY 1 ⟨the Lyon Court is a . . . part of the ~ of Scotland —L.G.Pine⟩

judices *pl of* JUDEX

¹ju·di·cial \(ˈ)jü¦dishəl\ *adj* [ME, fr. L *judicialis*, fr. *judicium* judgment (fr. *judic-, judex* judex, judge) + *-alis* -al — more at JUDGE] **1 :** of, relating to, or concerned with a judgment, the function of judging, the administration of justice, or the judiciary ⟨the ~ powers of Congress —W.S.Sayre⟩ ⟨the new ~ code⟩ ⟨a ~ circuit⟩ — compare ADMINISTRATIVE, EXECUTIVE, LEGISLATIVE **2 :** of or relating to judgment concerning the supposed influence of the heavenly bodies on things human ⟨prosecuted . . . for lecturing in ~ astrology —*Times Lit. Supp.*⟩ **3 :** ordered or enforced by a court or other legal tribunal ⟨it could not be the end of the law, whether moral or ~, to license a sin —John Milton⟩ ⟨a ~ sale⟩ — compare CONVENTIONAL **4** *obs* **:** JUDICIOUS ⟨showed himself so ~ and industrious as gave great satisfaction —John Smith †1631⟩ **5 :** of, characterized by, or expressing judgment **:** CRITICAL 1 c ⟨gave a cold, ~ look at his lapel —Claud Cockburn⟩ ⟨a biography . . . appreciative and yet ~ in purpose —Tyler Dennett⟩ **6 :** arising from a judgment of God **:** coming as a divine punishment ⟨a ~ pestilence⟩ **7 :** belonging or appropriate to a judge or the judiciary ⟨with stern ~ frame of mind —W.S.Gilbert⟩ ⟨weight of his ~ wig —Frank Yerby⟩

²judicial *n* -s [ME, fr. *judicial*, adj.] *obs* **:** a law or ordinance that is subject to enforcement by the courts — compare MORAL LAW

judicial act *n* **:** an act involving the exercise of judicial power; *esp* **:** one that determines controversies or questions of right or obligation

judicial administration *n* **1 :** the dispensing of justice according to law esp. through the functioning of a system of courts ⟨the people . . . see the processes of *judicial administration* at close range in thousands of local courts —E.F.Johnson⟩ **2 :** the management of the internal affairs of a system of courts ⟨effective *judicial administration* requires the establishment of businesslike methods —F.M.Vinson⟩

judicial astrology *n* **:** a branch of astrology that professes to foretell the fate and acts of nations and individuals — called also *mundane astrology*

judicial bond *n* **:** COURT BOND ⟨a *judicial bond* given where the law does not require any is not binding —*Hartford Accident & Indemnity Co. v. Abdalla*⟩

judicial combat *n* **:** TRIAL BY BATTLE

judicial committee of the privy council *usu cap J&P & both Cs* **:** a committee of the British Privy Council composed of leading jurists usu. from Great Britain and occasionally from Commonwealth countries that acts as the highest court of appeal from British colonies and from some of the nations of the Commonwealth ⟨appeal to the *Judicial Committee of the Privy Council* still lies from Ceylonese courts —Maurice Duverger⟩

judicial conference *n* **:** a conference composed of judges and sometimes other public officials and leaders of the bar and meeting to study problems and suggest reforms and improvements in the administration of the judicial system in a specific area ⟨each circuit has a *Judicial Conference* of the Circuit —F.M.Vinson⟩

judicial council *n* **:** a governmental agency usu. composed of judges and lawyers and established to study and make recommendations to the legislature on alterations in the laws and in the administration of the courts ⟨*judicial councils* . . . devise ways of simplifying judicial procedure —A.F.Macdonald⟩

judicial discretion *n* **:** the choice among possible decisions exercised by a judge according to the principles of justice and equity in the absence of a specific rule of law governing the case

judicial factor *n* **:** an administrator of an estate appointed under Scots law by the Court of Session — compare RECEIVER

ju·di·ci·al·i·ty \(,)jü,dishēˈaləd·ē\ *n* -ES **:** the quality or state of being judicial ⟨characterized by Olympian ~⟩

judicial legislation *n* **:** laws held to be created by the pronouncements of a judge who departs from a strict interpretation of a law according to the manifest intention of the legislature

ju·di·cial·ly \(ˈ)jü¦dish(ə)lē, -li\ *adv* **:** in a judicial manner

judicial murder *n* **:** death caused by a court sentence held to be legal but unjust ⟨a revolution . . . with no massacres or *judicial murders* of people on the losing side —H.B.Parkes⟩

judicial notice *n* **:** the recognition by a court for the purposes of a case of the existence or truth of certain facts as being self-evident or common knowledge ⟨no evidence is necessary as to any matters of which the court takes *judicial notice* —H.J. Stephen⟩

judicial oath *n* **:** an oath required in the course of judicial proceedings esp. in a court — compare PERJURY

judicial process *n* **:** the series of steps in the course of the administration of justice through the established system of courts ⟨no valid basis within the *judicial process* for pursuing review of my rulings in the case —L.W.Youngdahl⟩

judicial review *n* **1 :** REVIEW 5 ⟨deportation orders shall not become final until the completion of *judicial review* —*Harvard Law Rev.*⟩ **2 :** a constitutional doctrine that gives to a court system and esp. to a supreme court the power to annul legislative or executive acts which the judges declare are contrary to the provisions of the constitution ⟨*judicial review* has . . . been termed America's distinctive contribution to the science of politics —F.A.Ogg & P.O.Ray⟩

judicial separation *n* **:** a separation of husband and wife sanctioned by an order of a court **:** a divorce a mensa et thoro — called also *legal separation*

judicial sequestration *n* **:** a mandate of a Louisiana court directing a sheriff to take possession of property in a dispute to await the order of the court as to who is entitled to possession

judicial township *n* **:** a political division of a county in some western states of the U.S. — compare CIVIL DISTRICT, ELECTION DISTRICT 2

judicial veto *n* **:** the power possessed by a court system and esp. a supreme court to annul legislative and executive acts by declaring them unconstitutional ⟨the explicit assumption . . . that the *judicial veto* is basically undemocratic —*Amer. Polit. Sci. Rev.*⟩

judicial writ *n* **:** a writ issued by a court under its own seal for judicial purposes — compare ORIGINAL WRIT

¹ju·di·ciary \jüˈdishē,erē, -ri *also* -shər-\ *adj* [L *judiciarius*, fr. *judicium* judgment + *-arius* -ary — more at JUDICIAL] **:** of, concerned with, or relating to the judiciary **:** JUDICIAL ⟨the general principle of English ~ law —Edward Jenks⟩ ⟨the appointment of more women to higher ~ positions —*Current Biog.*⟩ ⟨the ~ committee⟩

²judiciary \"\ *n* -ES **1 a :** a system of courts of law in an area (as a nation or state) ⟨the judges are career members of the Italian ~ —Charles Fairman⟩ ⟨the federal ~ is responsible for the trial of cases involving federal laws —W.S.Sayre⟩ **b :** the persons (as the body of judges) constituting this system as an active agency ⟨in England . . . the ~ are recruited primarily from the ranks of practicing barristers —T.G.Lund⟩ **2 :** a branch of government in which judicial power is vested ⟨organization of the government into legislative, *judiciary* and executive —Thomas Jefferson⟩ ⟨the senate committee on the ~⟩ — compare EXECUTIVE 1, LEGISLATIVE

ju·di·cious \(ˈ)jü¦dishəs\ *adj* [MF *judicieux*, fr. L *judicium* judgment + MF *-eux* -ous] **1 :** having or exercising sound judgment ⟨a careful and ~ man —C.H.Lincoln⟩ ⟨this critic is admirably ~ —Milton Rugoff⟩ **2 :** directed or governed by sound usu. dispassionate judgment **:** characterized by discretion ⟨a ~ series of investments —Samuel Butler †1902⟩ ⟨the healthiest trees . . . have had the most ~ pruning —A.S. Igleheart⟩ ⟨compounded by a ~ mixture of ingredients —Malcolm Cowley⟩ **syn** see WISE

ju·di·cious·ly *adv* **:** in a judicious manner **:** with good judgment **:** WISELY ⟨the quality of hay can be . . . improved by ~ fertilizing the fields —*Farmer's Weekly (So. Africa)*⟩ ⟨an occasional word ~ designed to draw out reactions from others —A.T.Weaver⟩

ju·di·cious·ness *n* -ES **:** the quality or state of being judicious **:** sound judgment **:** SAGACITY ⟨~ is . . . apparent in the excellent job of selection —David Riesman⟩

ju·di·ci·um \jüˈdikēəm\ *n, pl* **judi·cia** \-kēə\ [L] **:** JUDGMENT

ju·do \ˈjü(,)dō\ *n* -s [Jap *jūdō*, fr. *jū* weakness, gentleness (fr. Chin — Pek — *jou²* soft, gentle) + *dō* road, art, fr. Chin (Pek) *tao⁴* road, way] **:** a modern refined form of jujitsu utilizing special applications of principles of movement, balance, and leverage

ju·do·ka \ˈjüdō,kä, ,==ˈ=\ *n, pl* **judoka** [Jap *jūdōka*, fr. *jūdō* + *-ka* person] **:** one who participates in judo

ju·do·pho·bia \ˌjüdəˈfōbēə\ *n, usu cap* [prob. fr. *judo-* (alter. of *judeo-*) + *-phobia*] **:** ANTI-SEMITISM

ju·dy \ˈjüdē\ *n* -ES *usu cap* [fr. *Judy*, nickname for the name *Judith*] **:** GIRL ⟨as hep as the average *Judy* about such matters —John & Ward Hawkins⟩

juey \ˈhwā\ *n* -s [AmerSp] *Puerto Rico* **:** GREAT LAND CRAB

¹jug \ˈjəg\ *n* -s [imit.] **:** a sound or note made by a bird (as the nightingale) ⟨the pretty birds do sing, cuckoo, *jug-jug* —Thomas Nash⟩

²jug \"\ *vi* **jugged; jugged; jugging; jugs :** to make the natural sound of a nightingale

³jug \"\ *n* -s [perh. fr. *Jug*, nickname for the name *Joan*] **1 a** *chiefly Brit* **:** a small pitcher usu. used as part of a table service ⟨holding the cream ~ poised above a cup —Frances Towers⟩ **b :** a large deep container usu. of earthenware or glass that has a narrow mouth, is fitted with a handle, and is used to hold liquids — compare BOTTLE **c :** the contents of a jug **2 :** JAIL, PRISON ⟨told them politely to discontinue their operations and get out of town or get thrown in the ~ —Frank Frederick⟩ **3** *slang* **:** BANK

jug 1b

⁴jug \"\ *vb* **jugged; jugged; jugging; jugs** *vt* **1 :** to stew in an earthenware vessel ⟨can ~ a rabbit well enough —Robert Browning⟩ **2 :** to commit to jail **:** IMPRISON ⟨is rudely pinched for stealing . . . and is *jugged* in an English jail —Edmund Gilligan⟩ ~ *vi* **:** to fish usu. for catfish by means of a hook and line attached to a floating jug

⁵jug \"\ *n* -s [fr. *Jug*, nickname for the name *Joan*] *obs* **:** WOMAN ⟨whoops, *Jug*, I love thee —Shak.⟩

⁶jug \"\ *vi* **jugged; jugged; jugging; jugs** [perh. fr. ²*jug*] *of quail or partridge* **:** to nestle or collect in a covey

juga *pl of* JUGUM

¹ju·gal \ˈjügəl\ *adj* [L *jugalis*, lit., of a yoke, fr. *jugum* yoke + *-alis* -al — more at YOKE] **:** MALAR

²jugal \"\ *n* -s **:** a bone lying below the orbit in lower vertebrates and forming part of the cheekbone in some higher forms

jugal lobe *n* [*jugal* fr. *jugum* + *-al*] **:** the modified jugum of a primitive lepidopterous insect

jugal point *also* **ju·ga·le** \jüˈgā(ˌ)lē, -gä(-, -gä(-\ *n* -s [*jugal point* fr. ¹*jugal* + *point*; *jugale* fr. NL, fr. L, neut. of *jugalis* jugal] **:** the point at which lines following the margin of the frontal and temporal processes of the zygomatic bone are joined

ju·ga·tae \jüˈgäd·(ˌ)ē, -ˈgäd·(ˌ)ē\ *n pl, cap* [NL, fr. fem. pl. of *jugatus* jugate] *in some classifications* **:** a division of Lepidoptera that is equivalent to Homoneura and consists of moths having the front wings provided with a jugum

ju·gate \ˈjüˌgāt, -gət\ *also* **ju·gat·ed** \-gād·əd\ *adj* [*jugate* prob. fr. (assumed) NL *jugatus*, fr. NL *jugum* + L *-atus* -ate; *jugated* fr. *jugate* + *-ed* — more at JUGUM] **1 a :** PAIRED **b :** having a jugum **2** [*jugate* fr. L *jugatus*, past part. of *jugare* to join, connect, fr. *jugum* yoke; *jugated* fr. L *jugatus* + E *-ed*] **:** CONJOINED, OVERLAPPING ⟨~ busts on a coin⟩

ju·ga·tion \jüˈgāshən\ *n* -s **:** the quality or state of being jugate

jug–eared \ˈ=ˌ=\ *adj* **:** having protuberant ears

juge d'in·struc·tion \zhüezhdaⁿstrüeksyōⁿ\ *n, pl* **juges d'instruction** \"\ [F, lit., judge of preliminary investigation] *French law* **:** a magistrate for criminal cases to whom complaints are made and who interrogates parties and witnesses, conducts investigations, and formulates charges

ju·gend·stil \ˈyügəntˌshtēl\ *n* -s *usu cap J* [G, lit., style of *Jugend*, fr. *Jugend*, illustrated periodical founded in Munich in 1896 + G *stil* style, fr. MHG, style, stylus, fr. L *stilus* — more at STYLE] **:** a late 19th century and early 20th century German decorative style parallel to art nouveau

ju·ger \ˈjüg(ə)r(ə), ˈyüg, ˈjüj|\ *n, pl* **jugers** \|ə(r)z\ *or* **juge·ra** \ˈyügərə\ [L *jugerum*; akin to MHG *jiuch* morgen, Gk *zeugos* team, yoke (of oxen), L *jugum* yoke] **:** an ancient Roman unit of land area equal to 28,800 square Roman feet or 0.622 acre

jug·ful \ˈjəgˌfu̇l\ *n, pl* **jugfuls** *or* **jugs·ful** \-gˌfu̇lz, -gz,fu̇l\ **1 :** the quantity held by a jug **2 :** GREAT DEAL — used in the phrase *not by a jugful* ⟨haven't seen anything yet — not by a jugful⟩

jugged *past of* JUG

jug·ger *or* **jag·gar** \ˈjəgə(r)\ *n* -s [Hindi *jhagar*] **:** LUGGAR

¹jug·ger·naut \ˈjəgə(r)ˌnȯt, -nȧl, *usu* |d·+V\ *n* -s [Hindi *Jagannāth* lord of the world (i.e. Vishnu, one of the principal Hindu gods), fr. Skt *Jagannātha*, fr. *jagat* world (fr. *jagat* adj., moving, living) + *nātha* lord; fr. a former belief that devotees of Vishnu sometimes allowed themselves to be crushed beneath the wheels of the car on which his image was being drawn in procession; akin to Skt *jigāti* he goes, *gamati* — more at COME] **:** a massive inexorable force or object that advances irresistibly and crushes whatever is in its path ⟨war has always been represented as a ~ —H.L.Matthews⟩ ⟨the tank . . . a formidable ~, is the modern scientific equivalent of the armored knight —G.R.Harrison⟩

²juggernaut \"\ *vt* -ED/-ING/-S **:** to crush under a juggernaut

jugging *pres part of* JUG

jug·gins \ˈjəgənz\ *n* -ES [prob. fr. the name *Juggins*] **:** one easily victimized **:** SIMPLETON ⟨was a clumsy ~ and let the ladder get out of control —Edith C. Rivett⟩

¹jug·gle \ˈjəgəl\ *vb* **juggled; juggled; juggling** \-g(ə)liŋ\ **juggles** [ME *jogelen*, fr. MF *jogler* to joke, sing, fr. L *joculari* to joke, fr. *joculus* little joke, fr. *jocus* joke + *-ulus* — more at JOKE] *vi* **1 :** to perform the tricks of a juggler **:** engage in feats of manual dexterity ⟨the conjurer ~*s* with two oranges —R.L.Stevenson⟩ **2 :** to practice deceit **:** CHEAT, TRICK ⟨never ~*s* or plays tricks with her understanding —Charles Lamb⟩ **3 a :** to engage in manipulation esp. for the purpose of achieving a desired end ⟨the facts were unchangeable — it was useless to ~ with them —O.E.Rölvaag⟩ **b :** to make necessary adjustments **:** JIGGLE ⟨pilot bent to the instrument panel and ~*ed* quickly with his massed controls —Nevil Shute⟩ **4 :** to advance a ball by means of a juggle (as in girls' basketball) ~ *vt* **1 a** (1) **:** to practice deceit or trickery on **:** BEGUILE ⟨is't possible the spells of France should ~ men into such strange mysteries —Shak.⟩ (2) **:** to gain by deceit or trickery — usu. used with *out of* ⟨was simply ~*ing* money out of the pockets of the poor —S.E.Morison & H.S.Commager⟩ **b :** to engage in manipulation with esp. for the purpose of achieving a desired end ⟨~*ed* railroads as though they were letters in a Scrabble game —Bennett Cerf⟩ ⟨could ~ mathematical formulas in such a way as to make the ordinary man dizzy —A.W.Long⟩ **2 a :** to toss in or as if in the manner of a juggler ⟨~*s* nine balls at the same time⟩ ⟨a huge fire would already be ~*ing* its golden coronets in the fireplace —Osbert Sitwell⟩ **b :** to hold or balance insecurely or precariously ⟨tried to catch the ball but only *juggled* it⟩ **c :** to twist and turn **:** jiggle with ⟨~*s* the steering wheel to straighten the car⟩ **3 :** to advance (as a basketball) by means of a juggle

²juggle \"\ *n* -s **1 :** an act or instance of juggling: **a :** a trick of magic **b :** a show of manual dexterity **c :** an act of manipulation esp. for the purpose of achieving a desired end **:** DECEPTION, TRICKERY ⟨quieted by a ~ the apprehension about the size of the public debt —T.B.Macaulay⟩ ⟨a result of their royal father's unscrupulous ~ with the coinage —G.M.Trevelyan⟩ **2 :** the act of advancing a ball by tossing or tapping it into the air and catching it again usu. after taking several steps to gain ground (as in speedball or girls' basketball)

³juggle \"\ *n* -s [perh. alter. of ³*joggle*] **:** a block of timber cut to a specified length

⁴juggle \"\ *dial Eng var of* JOGGLE

jug·gler \ˈjəg(ə)lə(r)\ *n* -s [ME *jogelour*, *joglere*, fr. OE *geogelere*, fr. OF *joglere* joker (accus. *jogleour*), fr. L *joculator*, fr. *joculatus* (past part. of *joculari* to joke) + *-or*] **1 a :** one that performs tricks or acts of magic ⟨one of England's best generals with more tricks up his sleeve than a roving ~ —F.V.W.Mason⟩ **b :** one that is practiced in acts of manual dexterity; *esp* **:** one skilled in keeping several objects in motion in the air at the same time by alternately tossing and catching them **2 :** one that manipulates or deceives esp. for the purpose of achieving a desired end ⟨suave and unscrupulous ~ of words —H.J.Muller⟩

jug·glery \-glərē, -ri\ *n* -ES [ME *jogelrye*, fr. OF *joglerie*, fr. *jogler* to joke, sing + *-erie* -ery] **1 :** the art or practice of a juggler ⟨dances, acts of ~, prayers, and songs are climaxed by the weird fire dance —*Nat'l Geographic*⟩ **2 :** manipulation or trickery often designed to achieve a desired end ⟨the bill merely looks like a rather disingenuous piece of ~ —*Economist*⟩ ⟨the ~ with which . . . he proved whatever he had a mind to —W.S.Maugham⟩

jug–handled \ˈ=ˌ=ˌ=\ *adj* [³*jug*] **:** not properly or fairly proportioned **:** ONE-SIDED ⟨trade between Canada and the U. S. is distinctly *jug-handled* —*Boston Herald*⟩

jughead \ˈ=ˌ=\ *n* **1** *chiefly West & Midland* **a :** MULE **b :** a wild or stubborn horse **2** *chiefly West & Midland* **:** a stupid person **:** LUNKHEAD

ju·glan·da·ce·ae \ˌjüˌglanˈdāsēˌē, -ˌglən-\ *n pl, cap* [NL, fr. *Jugland-*, *Juglans*, type genus + *-aceae*] **:** a family of trees (order Juglandales) that include the walnuts and hickories and are characterized by odd-pinnate leaves, apetalous staminate flowers in catkins, pistillate flowers with a perianth and solitary or few in a cluster, and a drupe with a fibrous or woody epicarp and a nutlike seed — **ju·glan·da·ceous** \ˌ=(ˌ)=ˈdāshəs\ *adj*

ju·glan·da·les \ˌ=(ˌ)=ˈdā(ˌ)lēz\ *n pl, cap* [NL, fr. *Jugland-*, *Juglans* + *-ales*] **:** an order or other group of Dicotyledoneae coextensive with the family Juglandaceae

ju·glans \ˈjüˌglanz\ *n, cap* [NL *Jugland-*, *Juglans*, fr. L *jugland-*, *juglans* walnut, fr. *ju-* (fr. *Juppiter*, god of the sky) + *gland-*, *glans* acorn — more at DEITY, GLAND] **:** a genus (the type of the family Juglandaceae) of walnut trees characterized by the separation of the pith of the branchlets into thin plates and by the indehiscent husk and furrowed shell of the fruit — see BLACK WALNUT, BUTTERNUT, ENGLISH WALNUT

ju·glar \(ˈ)zhüˈglär\ *n* -s *usu cap* [after Joseph C. *Juglar* †1905 Fr. economist] **:** a business cycle of approximately nine years

ju·glone \ˈjüˌglōn\ *n* -s [ISV *jugl-* (fr. NL *Juglans*) + *-one*; orig. formed as G *juglon*] **:** a reddish yellow crystalline compound $C_{10}H_5O_2(OH)$ that is obtained esp. from green shucks of walnuts and is the chief active principle of the brown hair dye from walnuts; 5-hydroxy-1,4-naphthoquinone

jugoslavia *usu cap, var of* YUGOSLAVIA

jug plant *n* **:** a perennial evergreen herb (*Asarum arifolium*) having solitary basal flowers shaped like an urn

jugs *pl of* JUG, *pres 3d sing of* JUG

¹jugu·lar \ˈjəgyələ(r) *sometimes* ˈjüg-, *chiefly in substand speech* ˈjəg(ə)l-\ *adj* [LL *jugularis*, fr. L *jugulum* collarbone, neck, throat; akin to L *jungere* to join — more at YOKE] **1 a :** of or relating to the throat or neck **b :** of or relating to the jugular vein ⟨~ pulsations⟩ **2 a** *of a fish* **:** having the ventral fins located on the throat anterior to the pectorals **b** *of a fin* **:** located on the throat **c :** of or relating to the fishes that have jugular fins

²jugular \"\ *n* -s **1 :** JUGULAR VEIN **2 :** a jugular fish

jugu·la·res \ˌjəgyəˈla(a)(ˌ)rēz, ˌjüg-\ *n pl, cap* [NL, fr. L, pl. of *jugularis* jugular] *in some esp former classifications* **:** an order or other group comprising teleost fishes with the ventral fins well forward on the throat that are now generally included in the order Percomorphi

jugular foramen *n* **:** a large irregular opening from the posterior cranial fossa that is bounded anteriorly by the petrous part of the temporal bone and posteriorly by the jugular notch of the occipital and that transmits the inferior petrosal sinus, the glossopharyngeal, vagus, and accessory nerves, and the internal jugular vein

jugular fossa *n* **:** a depression on the basilar surface of the petrous portion of the temporal bone

jugular ganglion *n* **:** SUPERIOR GANGLION

jugular process *n* **:** a lateral process of the occipital bone near each condyle articulating with the temporal bone

jugular vein *n* **:** any of several veins of each side of the neck: as **a :** a vein in man that collects the blood from the interior of the cranium, the superficial part of the face, and the neck, runs down the neck on the outside of the internal and common carotid arteries, and uniting with the subclavian forms the innominate vein — called also *internal jugular vein* **b :** a smaller and more superficial vein in man that collects most of the blood from the exterior of the cranium and deep parts of the face and opens into the subclavian vein — called also *external jugular vein* **c :** a vein in man that commences near the hyoid bone and joins the terminal part of the external jugular or the subclavian — called also *anterior jugular vein*

jugu·late \ˈjəgyəˌlāt, ˈjüg-\ *vt* -ED/-ING/-S [L *jugulatus*, past part. of *jugulare*, fr. *jugulum* collarbone, neck, throat] **:** to kill esp. by cutting the throat

jugu·lum \-ləm, ˈyügyəl-\ *n, pl* **jugu·la** \-lə\ [NL, fr. L, collarbone, neck, throat] **1 :** the lower throat or the part of the neck just above the breast of a bird **2 :** the jugum of an insect's wing

ju·gum \ˈjügəm, ˈyü-\ *n, pl* **ju·ga** \-gə\ *or* **jugums** [NL, fr. L, yoke — more at YOKE] **1 a :** one of the ridges commonly found on fruits of plants of the family Ammiaceae **b :** a pair of the opposite leaflets of a pinnate leaf **2 :** the most posterior and basal region of an insect's wing that is modified in the primitive Lepidoptera as a backwardly directed basal lobe on the inner margin of the fore wings and that serves to couple the fore and hind wings during flight **3 :** a more or less complicated crossbar linking the two arms of the brachidium of certain brachiopods

ju·gur·thine \jüˈgərthən, -ˌthīn\ *adj, usu cap* [L *jugurthinus*, fr. *Jugurtha* †104 B.C. king of Numidia defeated and captured by the Romans + L *-inus* -ine] **:** of or relating to Jugurtha or his reign ⟨the *Jugurthine* War⟩

¹juice \ˈjüs\ *n* -s [ME *juis*, *jus*, fr. OF *jus* broth, gravy, juice, fr. L; akin to ON *ostr* cheese, Skt *yūṣa* soup, broth] **1 :** the extractable fluid contents of plant cells or plant structures ⟨tomato ~⟩ ⟨lime ~⟩ **2 a :** the extractable fluid contents of animal cells and flesh ⟨press all the ~ from the meat⟩ **b :** the natural fluids of an animal body (as blood, lymph, and secretions) **c :** the liquid or moisture contained in or coming from something ⟨mineral ~*s* in the earth —John Woodward †1728⟩ **3 a :** the inherent quality of a thing **:** inner warmth and vitality **:** ESSENCE ⟨merely as literary productions, they are bursting with authentic human ~*s* —G.W.Johnson⟩ **b :** robust life **:** strength and vigor **:** VITALITY ⟨in the old days there were the pioneers . . . full of ~ and jests —Sinclair Lewis⟩ ⟨dismiss any writing with the ~ of life in it as mere journalism —J.D.Adams⟩ **4 :** a fluid or medium (as electricity, gasoline, oil) that supplies power ⟨ship's scout-bombing groups had traveled just enough farther . . . to leave them short of ~ to get home —Fletcher Pratt⟩

²juice \"\ *vt* -ED/-ING/-S **1 a :** to extract the juice of ⟨*juiced* and canned the tomatoes⟩ **b** *dial* **:** MILK **2 :** to add juice to **:** supply with juice ⟨*juiced* the apple pies⟩

juiced rehearsal *n* **:** a dress rehearsal of a television program in which the mechanical equipment is used as if for the final production

juice·less \ˈjüsləs\ *adj* **1 :** lacking moisture **:** DRY **2 :** lacking interest or stimulation **:** LIFELESS ⟨dull and ~ as only book knowledge can be when it is unrelated to . . . life —John Mason Brown⟩

juice pear *also* **juicy pear** *n* **:** JUNEBERRY

juic·er \ˈjüsə(r)\ *n* -s **1 :** an electrician who arranges the lighting for a stage set (as for a theater or television) **2 :** an appliance with which juice is extracted from fruit or vegetables

juice up *vt* **:** to give life, energy, or spirit to **:** ANIMATE ⟨the show is *juiced up* by its stars —Wendell Brogen⟩ ⟨*juice up* an otherwise dull evening⟩

juic·i·ly \ˈjüsəlē, -li\ *adv* **:** in a juicy manner ⟨"how about a nice thick steak," she said ~ —Thomas Wolfe⟩

juic·i·ness \-sēnəs, -sin-\ *n* -ES **:** the quality or state of being juicy

juicy \ˈjüsē, -si\ *adj* -ER/-EST [ME *jousy*, fr. *jous*, *juis*, *jus* juice + *-y*] **1 :** abounding with juice **:** SUCCULENT ⟨ate red beef and ~ pork —F.V.W.Mason⟩ **2 :** having a high profit potential **:** financially rewarding **:** FAT 3a ⟨found the rewards of business *juicier* than the rewards of politics —Josephine Pinckney⟩ ⟨route over the old Spanish Main is a ~ strip for commercial flying —*Harper's*⟩ **3 a :** RAINY, MOIST, DAMP **b :** wet and sloppy underfoot ⟨sun was shining palely upon . . . roads ~ with black mud —Arnold Bennett⟩ **4 a :** rich in interest **:** COLORFUL, DISTINCTIVE ⟨~ human tradition that produced the masculine brown harmonies of the English pub —Lewis Mumford⟩ **b :** RACY, PIQUANT ⟨the story had all the elements of a ~ scandal —W.A.White⟩ **c :** lusty and full-blown **:** full of vitality ⟨as ripe and ~ a canteen manageress . . . as ever wore frilly crepe de chine —John Metcalf⟩ **d :** VIGOROUS ⟨had the distinct impression . . . that this particular kick had been a ~ one —E.F.Benson⟩

ju·jit·su *or* **ju·jut·su** *or* **jiu·jit·su** *or* **jiu·jut·su** \jüˈjit(ˌ)sü *sometimes* -ˈjət- *or* -ˈjüt-\ *n* -s [Jap *jūjutsu*, fr. *jū* weakness, gentleness (fr. Chin—Pek—*jou²* soft, gentle) + *jutsu* art, fr. Chin (Pek) *shu⁴*] **:** the Japanese art of self-defense without weapons that depends for its efficiency largely upon the principle of making use of an opponent's strength and weight to disable or injure him — see JUDO

ju·ju \ˈjü(ˌ)jü\ *n* -s [of West African origin; akin to Hausa *djudju* fetish, evil spirit] **1 :** a fetish, charm, or amulet of West African tribes ⟨the ~ consisted of a bunch of chicken feathers well soaked in chicken blood and held together by strips of snakeskin —*Time*⟩ **2 :** the magic attributed to or associated with the use of a juju ⟨no one ever would have thought that the old man . . . was in any way connected with ~ —H.L.Ballowe⟩

ju·jube \ˈjüˌjüb\ *n* -s [ME, fr. ML *jujuba*, alter. of L *zizyphum*, fr. Gk *zizyphon*] **1 a :** an edible drupaceous fruit of a tree of the genus *Ziziphus* **:** CHINESE DATE **b** *also* **jujube tree :** a tree that produces jujubes; *broadly* **:** a tree of the genus *Ziziphus* **2 :** a fruit-flavored gumdrop or lozenge

juke \ˈjük, ˈju̇k\ *vi* -ED/-ING/-S [prob. alter. of ¹*jouk*] *chiefly South* **:** to mess around

juke·box \ˈjükˌbäks, *chiefly southern US* ˈju̇k,- *or* ˈjüt,-\ *or* **juke** *n, pl* **jukeboxes** *or* **jukes** [Gullah *juke*, *joog* disorderly, wicked] **:** a cabinet containing an automatic player and numerous phonograph records that are played by inserting a coin in a slot and usu. pushing a button to choose a record

juke joint *n* [Gullah *juke*, *joog* disorderly, wicked (in *juke house* brothel), of West African origin; akin to Wolof *dzug* to lead a disorderly life, Bambara *dzugu* wicked] **:** an establishment having a jukebox; *esp* **:** a small inexpensive establishment for eating, drinking, or dancing to the music of a jukebox

jukes \ˈjüks\ *n, pl* **jukes** \"\ *also* **jukeses** \-ksəz\ *usu cap* [*Jukes*, fictitious name of a family that was the subject of a study of hereditary tendencies to crime, immorality, disease, and poverty by Richard L. Dugdale †1883 Am. sociologist] **:** a stupid person ⟨before the Revolution, more than fifty thousand of England's *Jukes* . . . poured into the colonies —Charles Hamilton⟩ — compare KALLIKAK

ju·lep \ˈjüləp\ *n* -s [ME, fr. MF, fr. Ar *julāb*, fr. Per *gulāb* rose water, julep, fr. *gul* rose + *āb* water — more at ABKAR] **1 :** a drink consisting usu. of sweet syrup, flavoring, and water designed to soothe or stimulate ⟨a very soft well-flavored pleasant saccharine ~ —W.S.Coleman⟩ **2 a :** a tall drink made from gin, rum, or other alcoholic liquor and sometimes flavored with citrus juice ⟨gin ~⟩ ⟨orange ~⟩ **b :** a tall drink consisting of bourbon, sugar, and mint served in a frosted tumbler filled with finely crushed ice — called also *mint julep*

ju·lian \ˈjülyən\ *adj, usu cap* [L *julianus*, fr. Gaius *Julius* Caesar †44 B.C. Roman general and statesman + L *-anus* -an] **:** of, relating to, or characteristic of Julius Caesar

julian calendar *n, usu cap J* **:** a calendar introduced in Rome in 46 B.C. establishing the twelve-month year of 365 days with each fourth year having 366 days, the months each having 31 or 30 days except for February which has 28 or in leap years 29 days — compare GREGORIAN CALENDAR

julian day calendar *n, usu cap J* **:** a system used esp. by astronomers of numbering days consecutively from the arbitrarily selected point of the year 4713 B.C. instead of by cycles of days

julian day number *n, usu cap J* **:** the number of a day in the Julian day calendar (as 2,436,934 for Jan. 1, 1960)

ju·lian·ist \ˈjülyənəst\ *n* -s *usu cap* [*Julian*, 6th cent. bishop of Halicarnassus + E *-ist*] **:** a follower of Julian the Monophysite — compare APHTHARTODOCETAE

julian period *n, usu cap J* [*julian*, adj.] **:** a chronological period of 7980 Julian years that combines the solar and lunar cycles and the Roman indiction cycle and is reckoned from the year 4713 B.C. when the first years of these cycles coincided

julian year *n, usu cap J* **:** the year of exactly 365 days, 6 hours adopted in the Julian calendar

¹ju·lid \ˈjüləd\ *adj* [NL *Julidae*] **:** of or relating to the Julidae

²julid \"\ *n* -s [NL *Julidae*] **:** a millipede of the family Julidae

ju·li·dae \ˈjüləˌdē\ *n pl, cap* [NL, fr. *Julus*, type genus + *-idae*] **:** a family of millipedes (class Diplopoda) having a cylindrical body composed of more than 30 rings and many eyes usu. crowded together in a cluster

ju·lien·ite \ˈjülyəˌnīt\ *n* -s [Flem *juliëniet*, fr. Henry *Julien* †1920 Belg. geologist + Flem *-iet* -ite] **:** a mineral $Na_2Co(SCN)_4.8H_2O$ consisting of a hydrous thiocyanate of sodium and cobalt that occurs in small blue needlelike crystals

¹ju·lienne \ˌjüleˈen, (ˈ)jülˈyen, ˌzhü-, (ˈ)zhü-\ *n* -s [F, prob. fr. the name *Julienne*] **:** a clear soup containing julienne vegetables

²julienne \"\ *adj* **:** cut in long thin strips — used esp. of vegetables and fruit ⟨~ potatoes⟩ ⟨~ peaches⟩ ⟨garnished with ~ carrots⟩

ju·liet \ˈjülyə̇t, ˌjüleˈet *also* ˈjüleə̇ *or* (ˈ)jülˈyet; *usu* |d·+V\ *n* -s [*Juliet*, heroine of Shakespeare's tragedy *Romeo and Juliet* (1594–95)] **:** a woman's slipper with a high front and back and low-cut sides — compare ROMEO

juliet cap *n, usu cap J* **:** a woman's skullcap that is often made of elaborately decorated mesh and used esp. for semiformal and bridal wear

ju·li·ett \ˌjüleˈet\ *usu cap* [prob. irreg. fr. *Juliet*] — a communications code word for the letter *j*

Juliet cap

ju·lio *or* **giu·lio** \ˈjül(ˌ)yō\ *n* -s [It *giulio*, after Pope *Julius* II †1513 (It *Giulio* II)] **:** an Italian silver coin

ju·lius cae·sar cipher \ˌjülyə(s)ˈsēzə(r)-\ *n, usu cap J & 1st C* [after Gaius *Julius Caesar* †44 B.C. Roman general and statesman] **:** a substitution cipher replacing each plaintext letter by one that stands later in the alphabet

jul·lun·dur \ˈjələndə(r)\ *adj, usu cap* [fr. *Jullundur*, city in northwestern India] **:** of or from the city of Jullundur, India **:** of the kind or style prevalent in Jullundur

ju·lus \ˈjüləs\ *n, cap* [NL, fr. Gk *ioulos* catkin, down, wood louse; perh. akin to L *volvere* to roll — more at VOLUBLE] **:** a widely distributed genus of millipedes that is the type of the family Julidae

ju·ly \(ˈ)jüˈlī, jəˈlī, ju̇ˈ-\ *n* -s *usu cap* [ME *julie*, fr. OE *julius*, fr. L, after Gaius *Julius* Caesar †44 B.C. Roman general and statesman who was born in this month] **:** the seventh month of the Gregorian year — see MONTH table

july hound *n, usu cap J* **:** a small chiefly white hound of U. S. origin

ju·ma·da \jəˈmädə\ *n* -s *usu cap* [Ar *jumādā*] **:** one of the two months Jumada I and Jumada II of the Muhammadan year — see MONTH table

ju·ma·no \ˌzhüməˈnō\ *n, pl* **jumano** *or* **jumanos** *usu cap* **1 :** a Uto-Aztecan people of northwestern Chihuahua, Mexico, and prob. a subdivision of the Suma **2 :** a member of the Jumano people

ju·mart \ˈjüˌmärt\ *n* -s [F, fr. Prov *gimerro*, *jamerro*, *chimarro*, fr. OProv *jumerra*, fr. L *chimaera* chimera] **:** a mythical offspring of a bull and a mare or she-ass or of a horse or ass and a cow

¹jum·ble \ˈjəmbəl\ *vb* **jumbled; jumbled; jumbling** \-b(ə)liŋ\ **jumbles** [perh. of imit. origin] *vi* **1 :** to move in a confused or disordered mass **:** move in pell-mell fashion ⟨the soldiers *jumbled* through the door —Robert McLaughlin⟩ **2 a** *archaic* **:** to make discordant sounds **b :** to mingle in a confused or disordered manner **:** form a jumble ⟨entrances and exits tended to ~ —*Time*⟩ **3** *archaic* **:** to travel with jolts ~ *vt* **1 :** to mix in a confused mass **:** put or throw together without order — often used with *up* ⟨~*s* the stories up, giving no indication of when they were written —Edmund Wilson⟩ ⟨*jumbled* up the members of the chorus . . . to suit his pictorial effect —Edward Sackville-West⟩ **2** *archaic* **:** to stir, agitate, or jolt about **:** shake up ⟨a beast . . . whose trot would ~ me —William Cowper⟩

²jumble \"\ *n* -s **1 :** an assemblage of things mingled together without order, coherence, sequence, or plan **:** a confused, amorphous, or disordered mass **:** MEDLEY ⟨picturesque ~*s* of steep roofs, balconies, gables, dormers, and many chimneys —T.E.Tallmadge⟩ ⟨a ~ of fishing craft —Martin

Chisholm⟩ ⟨a thick ~ of technical terms and apparatus —Shirley A. Briggs⟩ ⟨our plans fell into a ~ —Carleton Beals⟩ ⟨an architectural ~⟩ **2** *archaic* **:** an instance of jolting or of being jolted **:** SHOCK, JOLT **3** *Brit* **:** articles for a rummage sale ⟨most of the stuff was very inferior ~ —Nigel Balchin⟩; *also* **:** RUMMAGE SALE ⟨they had a pair at the ~ —H.E.Bates⟩ **syn** see CONFUSION

³jumble *or* **jum·bal** \"\ *n* -s [*jumble* alter. (prob. influenced by ¹*jumble*) of earlier *jumbal*, prob. alter. of obs. *gimbal* finger ring — more at GIMBAL] **:** a small thin sugared cake usu. shaped like a ring

jumbled *adj* **:** lacking order, coherence, sequence, or plan **:** constituting a jumble ⟨a vast ~ waste —Henry Miller⟩ ⟨put his feet on the ~ desk —David Wagoner⟩ ⟨a ~ neighborhood of tenement houses, cheap stores —*New Yorker*⟩ ⟨my ~ memories fall harmoniously into patterns —David Daiches⟩

jum·ble·ment \-lmənt\ *n* -s **:** the act or an instance of jumbling **:** the fact of being jumbled

jumble sale *n*, *Brit* **:** RUMMAGE SALE

jum·bling·ly *adv* **:** in a jumbling manner

jum·bly \-blē\ *adj* **:** JUMBLED, CONFUSED

¹jum·bo \ˈjəm(,)bō\ *n* -s [fr. *Jumbo*, an elephant exhibited by P.T.Barnum] **1 :** a very large or huge specimen of its kind ⟨their size varies from the circumference of a small orange to ~*s* larger than a basketball —Charlotte D. Widrig⟩ **2 a :** a traveling carriage for mounting drills or saws or for transporting excavated material (as in tunnel driving) **b** (1) **:** a main-lead logging block (2) **:** a tongueless double sled used esp. for hauling logs short distances **c** (1) **:** a forestaysail esp. on an American schooner (2) **:** a triangular sail set point downward on the foreyard of a square-rigged ship or a topsail schooner in place of the regular foresail **d :** a record of car movements as posted on oversize sheets of paper maintained in a loose-leaf binder

²jumbo \"\ *adj* **:** being a very large specimen of its kind **:** HUGE ⟨a symphony does not need a ~ orchestra for its performance —Ross Parmenter⟩ ⟨flashed their ~ diamonds —Dawn Powell⟩

jum·bo·ism \-mbō,izəm\ *n* -s **:** admiration for or worship of bigness ⟨too many Americans today are afflicted with ~ —*Springfield (Mass.) Union*⟩

jumbo roll *n* **1 :** the full-width roll of trimmed paper as it comes from the paper machine **2 :** a large roll of paper that is over 10 (or sometimes 12) inches in diameter and is to be used in converting operations

jum·buck \ˈjəm,bək\ *n* [native name in Australia] *Austral* **:** SHEEP

jum·by *or* **jum·bie** \ˈjəmbē\ *n*, *pl* **jumbies** [modif. of Kongo *zumbi* fetish, spirit] *dial* **:** an evil spirit, ghost, or minor demon esp. in Negro belief and folklore

jumby bean *or* **jumby tree** *n* **1 a :** a West Indian necklace tree (*Ormosia monosperma*) **b** *West Indies* **:** the common lead tree (*Leucaena glauca*) **2** *or* **jumby bead :** the seed of a jumby bean

ju·melle \(ˈ)jü¦mel\ *adj* [F, fem. of *jumeau*, fr. MF, fr. OF *jumel*, fr. L *gemellus*, adj. & n., twin, dim. of *geminus* — more at GEMINATE] **:** TWIN, PAIRED — used of objects made or formed in pairs ⟨a ~ window opened upon the little balcony —John Bennett⟩

ju·ment \ˈjümənt\ *n* -s [ME, fr. L *jumentum*; akin to L *jungere* to join — more at YOKE] *archaic* **:** BEAST; *esp* **:** BEAST OF BURDEN

jum·ma \ˈjəmə\ *n* -s [Hindi *jama* collection, amount, fr. Ar *jamaʻ* total, aggregate] *India* **:** ASSESSMENT

jum·na·pa·ri \,jəmnəˈpärē\ *n*, *usu cap* [Hindi] **:** an Indian breed of milch goats

¹jump \ˈjəmp\ *vb* -ED/-ING/-S [prob. akin to Sw *gumpa* to jump, LG *gumpen*] *vi* **1 a** (1) **:** to move or throw itself into or through the air ⟨a pretty stream ~*ing* and twisting down to sea⟩ **:** REAR ⟨the light ~*ed* up —Guy McCrone⟩ (2) **:** to rise and fall agitatedly or abruptly ⟨the formerly placid waters were . . . ~*ing* —Francis Birtles⟩ ⟨the snow ~*ed* in tiny cloud puffs —Victor Canning⟩ **b** (1) **:** to spring free from the ground or some other environing medium by the muscular action of the feet and legs or in some animals the tail **:** project oneself through the air **:** SPRING, LEAP, HOP ⟨a trout will ~ several feet —John Burroughs⟩ ⟨~*ed* on a moving bus⟩ ⟨~*ed* out of bed⟩ ⟨~*ed* down from the tree⟩; *also* **:** to rise to one's feet with a bound or other energetic movement ⟨~*ed* up and vigorously protested the chairman's action⟩ (2) **:** to make a sudden spasmodic movement as a result of surprise or other nervous shock **:** START ⟨~*ed* at his unexpected entry⟩ (3) *in board games* **:** to move over a position occupied by an opponent's man to a vacant one beyond and capture the man (as in checkers) or to so move merely to facilitate progress to one's goal (as in Chinese checkers) (4) **:** to pass over a regular or proper stopping point **:** SKIP ⟨this typewriter ~*s* and needs repairing⟩ (5) *of a published item* **:** to continue from one column or page to another (6) **:** to undergo a vertical or lateral displacement owing to improper alignment of the film on a projector mechanism ⟨images ~ on the screen⟩ (7) **:** to drop from an airborne airplane with a parachute (8) **:** to commence or launch upon a drive, march, expedition, or other enterprise **:** start out **:** BEGIN — used with *off* ⟨the campaign ~*ed* off to a good start⟩ ⟨~*ed* off for the distant mining country⟩; *specif* **:** to start forward in a military attack ⟨at 11:01 a.m. the assault companies ~*ed* off —P.W.Thompson⟩ ⟨the attack ~*ed* off in good weather —*Military Engineer*⟩ (9) **:** to move, obey, or act with energy or alacrity **:** HUSTLE ⟨when he spoke he expected people to ~ —T.O.Thoman⟩ ⟨said he wanted them to ~ to it —Earle Birney⟩ ⟨the first thing the new bureaucrat learns is this: when the phone rings — ~ —*Newsweek*⟩ **2 :** COINCIDE, AGREE, ACCORD — usu. used with *with* ⟨it ~*s* with my humor —Shak.⟩ ⟨that choice ~*s* with the spirit of the age —J.C.Powys⟩ **3 a** (1) **:** to pass or move haphazardly or aimlessly from one thing or state to another **:** shift abruptly ⟨the author ~*s* from region to region —*Geog. Jour.*⟩ ⟨~*ing* from job to job —Albert Deutsch⟩ (2) **:** to change or abandon employment esp. in violation of contract ⟨~*ed* to the Mexican League . . . and drew a five-year ban —*Springfield (Mass.) Daily News*⟩ ⟨~*ed* without notice —Fred Bradna & Hartzell Spence⟩ (3) **:** to rise or climb abruptly from one rank, status, or condition to another often with omission of intermediate stages ⟨~*ed* rapidly from captain through all the grades to colonel —H.H.Arnold & I.C. Eaker⟩ ⟨~*ed* from the Stone Age to the Iron Age without any intervening copper or bronze culture period —R.W.Murray⟩ (4) **:** to increase suddenly and sharply ⟨recruiting began to ~ that very evening —W.G.Shepherd⟩ ⟨population is ~*ing* —W.A.Bridges⟩ (5) **:** to make a jump bid in bridge **b** (1) **:** to make a judgment precipitately or without careful study of one's premises **:** make a mental leap ⟨inclined to ~ from some general observation to the first possible solution —W.J. Reilly⟩ ⟨before you ~ to that happy but unwarranted assumption —S.L.Payne⟩ ⟨no impressionist who ~*s* hastily to conclusions —C.I.Glicksberg⟩ (2) **:** to accept eagerly **:** take quick or immediate advantage — usu. used with *at* ⟨~*ed* at the job⟩ ⟨~*ed* at the chance⟩ (3) **:** to join, enter, or intervene with eagerness or alacrity — usu. used with *in* or *into* ⟨as unhealthy as if . . . the military ~*ed* in, in the recognition that a literate and educated population was important for the quality of future draftees —R.L.Meier & Eugene Rabinowitch⟩ ⟨~*ed* into this . . . business on twenty-four hour notice —F.D.Roosevelt⟩ and in such phrases as *jump aboard* ⟨finally ~*ed* aboard bolshevism —A.M.Rosenthal⟩ and *jump on the bandwagon* ⟨exhibiting a desire to ~ on the bandwagon —M. F.A.Montagu⟩ **4 a :** to attack suddenly or without warning **:** POUNCE — often used with *on* or *upon* ⟨~*ed* upon them without reason —*Pasadena (Calif.) Independent*⟩ **b :** to give a tongue-lashing **:** level severe criticism or censure ⟨~*ed* all over me for it⟩ — often used with *on* or *upon* ⟨people who ~ on modern poetry as obscure —*Time*⟩ or in the phrase *jump down one's throat* ⟨whenever I opened my mouth he ~*s* down my throat —W.S.Gilbert⟩ **5 a :** SWING ⟨the jazz they do blow is interesting and ~*s* —*Metronome Yearbook*⟩ ⟨whole thing ~*s* splendidly —*Jazz Jour.*⟩ **b :** to be very lively **:** bustle with gaiety or activity ⟨the joint was really ~*ing* with kids —Maritta Wolff⟩ ⟨the town was ~*ing* —*Springfield (Mass.) Daily News*⟩ ⟨the place is beginning to ~ already —Chandler Brossard⟩ ⟨Saturday night ~*ed* —Langston Hughes⟩ **~** *vt* **1 a** (1) **:** to pass over or across (a space or object) by or as if by a spring or leap **:** CLEAR ⟨~ a brook⟩ ⟨~ a hurdle⟩ ⟨took eight years before field trials ~*ed* the Atlantic —W.F.Brown b. 1903⟩ ⟨often ~ the border again the same day —*N.Y. Times*⟩ (2) *obs* **:** to expose to danger **:** RISK, HAZARD ⟨~ a body with dangerous physic —Shak.⟩ **b** *in board games* **:** to move over (a man) by jumping **c** (1) **:** to skip over or pass by **:** BYPASS ⟨the transmission of certain characteristics may ~ one or more . . . generations —Henry Wynmalen⟩ ⟨~ electrical connections⟩ (2) **:** to continue (as a newspaper story or article) from one column or page to another (3) **:** ANTICIPATE ⟨~ the green light⟩ ⟨~ the gun⟩ **d** (1) **:** to escape or run away from ⟨couldn't ~ his color —Thurston Scott⟩ (2) **:** to abandon or leave esp. hastily or furtively ⟨~ town without paying their bills —Hamilton Basso⟩ ⟨~*ed* their reservation and were on the warpath —P.A.Rollins⟩ (3) **:** to leave (employment) esp. in violation of contract or other obligation **:** breach (a labor contract) by leaving or taking other employment ⟨draft-age men ~*ing* essential war jobs —*Newsweek*⟩ ⟨wanted to ~ the show —Fred Bradna & Hartzell Spence⟩ ⟨~*ed* ship and settled in the United States —David Dodge⟩ ⟨~*ed* their indentures and bobbed up as journeymen in distant cities —*Newsweek*⟩ ⟨~ contract when tempted by more money —Harriot B. Barbour⟩ (4) **:** to turn off from (one's normal or appointed track or course) ⟨streams that ~*ed* their beds in the flood —*Springfield (Mass.) Union*⟩ ⟨a train ~*ed* the track⟩ (5) **:** to get aboard typically by jumping ⟨~*ed* a freight and rode it to town⟩ ⟨~ a crowded bus —W.J.Finn⟩ **2 a** (1) **:** to attack suddenly or unexpectedly **:** pounce upon ⟨thought he was snooping around and ~*ed* him —Lillian Hellman⟩ ⟨intended to ~ him, sitting or no —Shelby Foote⟩ ⟨suddenly ~*ed* by an enemy patrol party —Ed Cunningham⟩; *specif* **:** to attack (a target) suddenly with military aircraft (2) **:** to scold or criticize severely **:** assail verbally **:** bawl out ⟨that she would never do . . . unless she were ~*ed* into it —F. M.Ford⟩ — often used with *out* ⟨~*ed* the little foreman out —Ross Santee⟩ ⟨went down to ~ the inspector out —F.B. Gipson⟩ **b :** to seize or take possession of in violation of another's rights **:** occupy illegally ⟨~ another man's claim⟩ ⟨~*ing* an assignment for the first time in his life —Michael Foster⟩ **c :** to have coitus with — usu. considered vulgar **3 a** (1) **:** to cause to jump ⟨the wind can ~ those flames one mile or five —Stirling Silliphant⟩ ⟨it ~*s* me out of bed —J.W. Noble⟩ ⟨had to ~ her from the stiles —Jane Austen⟩ (2) **:** to cause (game) to break cover **:** START, FLUSH ⟨~*ed* a mule deer —D.C. Peattie⟩ (3) **:** to come upon suddenly ⟨~*ed* the trail and took cover —H.L.Davis⟩ **b** (1) **:** to elevate in rank esp. by skipping intermediate ranks ⟨one of many junior officers ~*ed* several ranks to fill the void —*Newsweek*⟩ ⟨~*ed* him from instructor to full professor in two years —*Time*⟩ (2) **:** to raise (a bridge partner's bid) by more than one rank (3) **:** to increase esp. swiftly or sharply ⟨~*ed* admission prices from fifty cents to a dollar —F.B.Gipson⟩ **4 :** to bore with a jumper (as in quarrying)

syn JUMP, LEAP, SPRING, BOUND, VAULT, and SALTATE mean, in common, to project oneself upward or through space by or as if by quick muscle action. JUMP, the most general, implies a muscular propelling, or any action resembling a muscular propelling, of the body upward or to a spot other than the one one is in, whether upward, on a level, or below one, or over some obstacle ⟨*jump* with fright⟩ ⟨*jump* three feet across a brook⟩ ⟨*jump* up onto a platform⟩ ⟨*jump* down from the truck⟩ ⟨*jump* over a wall⟩ LEAP, often interchangeable with JUMP, generally suggests a much greater muscular propulsion or a more spectacular result ⟨*leap* a high fence⟩ ⟨*leap* down from a platform⟩ ⟨go *leaping* across a field⟩ SPRING adds to JUMP or LEAP the idea of elasticity, lightness, or grace, stressing more the movement than the going to or over ⟨*spring* up into the air⟩ ⟨*spring* out of a cage⟩ ⟨a deer *springing* across the open field⟩ BOUND, like SPRING, emphasizes the movement but suggests vigor or strength and, often, a consequent forceful speed achieved by fast successive leaps forward ⟨a herd of antelope *bounding* gracefully across the plain⟩ ⟨the speaker, a large vigorous man, came *bounding* down the aisle and up onto the stage⟩ VAULT suggests a leap upward or over something with the aid of the hands laid on an object or with similar assistance ⟨rose to his feet . . . grabbed the sturdy milking stool by one leg, *vaulted* the fence, and plunged into the woods —C.G.D.Roberts⟩ ⟨an acrobat . . . was *vaulting* over chair backs —Margaret Deland⟩ SALTATE implies a jumping or leaping from place to place as in certain ballet movements

— **jump bail :** to abscond while at liberty under bail bonds — **jump over the broomstick** *or* **jump the broom** *dial* **:** to get married ⟨we ought to *jump the broom* —J.H.Stuart⟩ — **jump rope :** to jump over a rope held by its two ends by the jumper or by two other persons and swung around the jumper from head to foot, or back and forth under the feet — **jump the queue** *Brit* **1 :** to go ahead of a waiting line (as at a theater window) ⟨attempt to *jump the queue* is to court disaster —*London Calling*⟩ **2 :** to seek to obtain something in advance of one's turn **:** obtain preferential treatment ⟨*jumping* the allied *queue* and seeking a special arrangement —*Economist*⟩ — **jump the traces 1** *of a horse* **:** to jump over the traces **2 :** to cast off restraint **:** display a rebellious or nonconformist spirit ⟨might *jump the traces* and precipitate a new round of fighting —Lindesay Parrott⟩ ⟨*jumped the traces* more than once —Maurice Ries⟩

²jump *adv*, *obs* **:** EXACTLY, PAT

³jump \ˈjəmp\ *n* -s **1 a** (1) **:** an act of jumping **:** LEAP, SPRING, BOUND ⟨cleared the fence with a running ~⟩ (2) **:** any of several sports competitions featuring a leap, spring, or bound — see BROAD JUMP, HIGH JUMP (3) **:** a space cleared or traversed by a leap (4) **:** an obstacle to be jumped over (as on the course of a steeplechase) simulating natural obstructions met in fox hunting and of varied construction, dimensions, and number **b** (1) **:** a sudden spasmodic movement (as from surprise or other nervous shock) **:** START, TWITCH ⟨gave a ~ as she entered the room⟩ (2) **: jumps** *pl* **:** FIDGETS, WILLIES, NERVOUSNESS ⟨this place fairly gives me the ~*s* —G.K. Chesterton⟩ ⟨just got the ~*s*, I guess —Gore Vidal⟩ **c** *in board games* **:** a move made by jumping **d :** a descent by parachute from an airplane **e :** an act of coitus — usu. considered vulgar **2** *obs* **a :** a critical point or crisis **b :** VENTURE, HAZARD **3 a** (1) **:** a movement made by the tube of a gun before a fired projectile leaves the muzzle (2) **:** a vertical deviation of the path of the trajectory from the line of elevation **b :** an abrupt interruption of level in a piece of brickwork or masonry **c** (1) **:** ⁴BORE (2) **:** BREAKER 3a **d** (1) **:** a sharp or sudden increase ⟨the ~ in the size of the entering freshman class —J. K.Folger⟩ (2) **:** JUMP BID (3) **:** a sudden change **:** a qualitative or quantitative leap **:** an abrupt transition ⟨social progress proceeds by ~*s*⟩ ⟨the ~ from the liquid to the gaseous state⟩ (4) **:** the continuation of a published item (as a newspaper story or article) from one column or page to another; *also* **:** the portion of a published item comprising such a continuation — compare BREAKOVER **e** (1) **:** a quick or short journey esp. by air **:** HOP ⟨reluctant to start a new round of . . . plane ~*s* —*Newsweek*⟩ ⟨a convenient one-night ~ from either St. Louis or Memphis —*Amer. Guide Series: Ark.*⟩ (2) **:** one in a series of moves from one place to another (usually going farther west at each ~ —Dixon Wecter⟩ ⟨kept one ~ ahead of the sheriff⟩ **4 :** an advantage esp. in time **:** START — usu. used in the phrase *get the jump* ⟨might get the ~ on the United States in the development of nuclear power —*N.Y. Times*⟩ ⟨desirous of getting the ~ on the competition —Elmer Davis⟩

syn JUMP, LEAP, SPRING, BOUND, and VAULT signify a single movement achieved by the corresponding action signified by the verb. SALTATION may indicate a sequence or group of such actions **syn** see in addition ¹JUMP

— **on the jump** *adv (or adj)* **:** on the go **:** very busy ⟨kept so much *on the jump* by the motel trade —W.L.Gresham⟩

⁴jump \"\ *adj* [prob. fr. ²*jump*] **1** *obs* **:** EXACT, FITTING, PRECISE **2 :** constituting a jump bid in bridge ⟨~ response⟩ **3 :** SWING ⟨a ~ band⟩

⁵jump \ˈjümp, ˈjəmp\ *n* -s [prob. alter. of *jupe*] **1** *dial Brit* **:** a loose jacket for men **2** *dial Brit* **:** an underbodice worn usu. instead of stays by women — usu. used in pl.

jump·able \ˈjəmpəbəl\ *adj* **:** capable of being jumped

jump ball *n* **:** a method of putting a basketball into play by tossing it in the air between two opponents who jump up and tap it; *also* **:** a ball put into play in this manner

jump bid *n* **:** a bridge bid of more tricks than are necessary in the denomination specified to overcall the preceding bid — called also *jump*

jump boot *n* **:** a boot worn by paratroopers

jump dam *n* **:** a dam designed to prevent the migration of fishes into unsuitable spawning waters

jumped *past of* JUMP

jumped-up \ˈ=,=\ *adj* **:** newly or recently sprung up or arisen ⟨this unconcern for pedigree leads people to suppose that the English lords are a *jumped-up* lot —Nancy Mitford⟩ ⟨the hatred of *jumped-up* genius —Hesketh Pearson⟩

¹jump·er \ˈjəmpə(r)\ *n* -s [¹*jump* + *-er*] **1 :** a person who jumps: as **a** *usu cap* **:** one of a revivalistic sect whose members jump, skip, hop up and down, clap their hands, shout, or otherwise demonstrate an intense spiritual excitation in their meetings — called also *Holy Jumper* **b :** a person who jumps another's claim **c :** a miner who drills with a jumper **d :** a person who quits his employment esp. in violation of contract or other obligation ⟨the special Army camp for drafted job ~*s* —*Newsweek*⟩ **e :** a delivery-route driver's helper **f :** an experienced employee who can help or substitute for one or more of the workers engaged in an industrial process — called also *handyman, utility man* **g :** a person who competes in a jumping event (as the broad jump or a ski jump) **2 a :** a drill or boring tool consisting of a bar which is jumped up and down in the borehole **b :** any of several sleds (as used by boys in coasting or for hauling merchandise over bare ground) **c :** JUMPER SLED **d :** a plowshare specially fitted for rough soil (as by having an upturned colter to cut roots); *also* **:** a plow having a moldboard so attached that it jumps out of the ground when it hits a stump **e :** SWAGE 2b **f :** stones used for leveling courses esp. in random-coursed ashlar **g** (1) **:** a short wire used to close a break or cut out part of a circuit (2) **:** the removable member of a train-line or truck-trailer coupling consisting usu. of two coupling plugs and a connecting cable **h :** HOSE BRIDGE **3 :** any of several jumping animals: as **a :** a saddle horse trained to jump obstacles **b :** SMALLMOUTH BLACK BASS

²jumper \"\ *n* -s *often attrib* [prob. fr. ⁵*jump* + *-er*] **1 a :** a loose blouse, jacket, or smock worn esp. by workmen on the job **b :** a sleeveless dress or a skirt with a bib for women and girls worn usu. with a blouse or sweater **2 a :** a child's one-piece coverall for play or sleeping — usu. used in pl. **b :** a sailor's blouse having long sleeves and a broad square collar tapering to a V neck in front **c** *chiefly Brit* **:** a sweater for women or girls

jumper 1b

jumper sled *n* **:** a log sled having a high crosspiece on which one end of a log is supported while being dragged

jumper stay *n* **:** a stay or tackle set up esp. in heavy weather to prevent a yard or boom from jumping

jump fire *n* **:** a forest fire started some distance ahead of the main front of a larger fire by burning material carried ahead by wind

jump head *n* **:** a headline or heading identifying a jump (sense 3d[4])

jump-hop \ˈ=,=\ *n* **:** a spring from both feet followed by a hop on one foot

jumpier *comparative of* JUMPY

jumpiest *superlative of* JUMPY

jump·i·ness \ˈjəmpēnə̇s, -pin-\ *n* -ES **:** the quality or state of being jumpy **:** NERVOUSNESS ⟨was better able to master his ~ —C.S.Forester⟩

jumping *adj* [fr. pres. part. of ¹*jump*] **1 a :** given to or characterized by making jumps ⟨a ~ animal⟩ **b :** used in making jumps ⟨a ~ pole⟩ **c :** featuring jumps ⟨a ~ race⟩ **2 :** SWING ⟨a ~ band⟩

jumping bean *or* **jumping seed** *n* **:** a seed of any of several Mexican shrubs of the genera *Sebastiania* and *Sapium* of the family Euphorbiaceae that tumbles about because of movements of the contained larva of a small moth (*Carpocapsa saltitans*)

jumping cactus *also* **jumping cholla** *n* **:** CHOLLA

jumping deer *n* **:** MULE DEER

jumping hare *n* [trans. of Afrik *springhaas*, fr. D *springen* to jump + *haas* hare] **:** a sciuromorph rodent (*Pedetes cafer*) of southern and eastern Africa that resembles a kangaroo in form, that is about two feet long, and that is tawny brown in color and of nocturnal and social habits — called also *springhaas*

jumping jack *n* **:** a toy figure of a man jointed and made to jump or dance by means of strings or a sliding stick

jump·ing·ly *adv* **:** in a jumping manner

jumping mouse *n* **:** any of several small hibernating No. American myomorph rodents (family Zapodidae) with long hind legs and tail and no cheek pouches

jumping mullet *n* **:** a very active Australian gray mullet (*Mugil argenteus*) reputed to leap into boats

jumping net *or* **jumping sheet** *n*, *chiefly Brit* **:** LIFE NET

jumping-off place \ˌ==ˈ=-\ *n* **1 a :** a place regarded as marking the farthest limit of civilization **:** a remote or isolated place **b :** the end or edge of the world ⟨seemed suddenly to be at the end of the world, the *jumping-off place* —*Nat'l Geographic*⟩ **2 :** a place from which some enterprise is launched **:** a point of departure ⟨a *jumping-off place* for the conquest of the rest of Europe —P.E.Mosely⟩ ⟨a *jumping-off place* for reflection —Maurice Valency⟩

jumping orchid *n* [so called fr. its habit of suddenly ejecting its pollen masses] **:** an orchid of the genus *Catasetum*

jumping pit *n* **:** the landing area for the high and broad jump and the pole vault events consisting of a pit filled with sawdust or soft loam to cushion the impact

jumping plant louse *n* [*jumping* + *plant louse*] **:** any of numerous plant lice constituting the family Psyllidae

jumping rabbit *n* **:** FIVE-TOED JERBOA

jumping rat *n* **:** any of numerous jumping rodents (as the jerboa, jumping mouse, and kangaroo rat)

jumping shrew *n* **:** ELEPHANT SHREW

jumping spider *n* **:** a spider of the family Salticidae

jumping viper *n* **:** a small rough-skinned stout-bodied pit viper (*Bothrops nummifer*) of Central America and Mexico that slides its body forward when striking thereby considerably increasing its attacking range

jump joint *n* [¹*jump*] **1 :** BUTT JOINT **2 :** a flush joint (as of plank or masonry)

jump line *n* **:** a directional line of print (as "continued on page 7, column 2") at the end of the first part of a divided story or article in a newspaper or periodical or a line (as "continued from page 1") at the continuation

jumpmaster \ˈ=,==\ *n* **:** a person in charge of the jumping (as of parachute troops)

jump-off \ˈ=,=\ *n* -s **1 :** an act of jumping off **:** a place from which to jump off **:** the start of a race or an attack ⟨the *jump-off* was at twelve —Dan Levin⟩ **2 :** an additional round of competition to determine the winner when two or more horses are tied after completion of the first round of jumping

jump page *n* **:** a page on which the continuation of a newspaper article appears

jump pass *n* **:** a pass executed by a player who jumps into the air and releases the ball before landing (as in football and basketball)

jump ring *n* **:** a circle of wire with ends meeting and not welded used as a connecting link in jewelry

jump rope *also* **jumping rope** *n* **:** a rope used in jumping rope — called also *skipping rope*

jumps *pres 3d sing of* JUMP, *pl of* JUMP

jump saw *n* **:** a crosscut circular saw in a sawmill that can be raised or lowered and is used for crosscutting timbers, boards, or slabs

jump scrape *n* **:** an implement resembling a plow that is used to complete ridges or levees for the check system of irrigation

jump seat *n* **1 :** a movable carriage seat **2 :** a folding seat between front and rear seats of a closed passenger automobile

jumpseed \'=,=\ *n* : VIRGINIA KNOTWEED

jump shot *n* **1** : a shot in billiards in which the cue ball is made to jump over an object ball **2** *also* **jump stroke** : a croquet shot made with a downward stroke of the mallet so that the ball jumps over an obstacle **3** : a shot made by a basketball player who jumps into the air and releases the ball with one or both hands at the peak of his jump

jump spark *n* : a spark produced by the jumping of electricity across a gap

jump suit *n* : a uniform worn by paratroopers for jumping

jump turn *n* **1** : a turn in the air executed by a skier who crouches, places the inner pole or both poles near the tip of the lower ski, pulls the knees up, jumps around the pole or poles, and lands in a crouch with the skis edged inward **2** : a turn in the air executed by a dancer who takes off with and lands on both feet

jump weld *n* : a butt weld in which one member is welded at right angles to a relatively larger part

jumpy \'jəmpē, -pi\ *adj* -ER -EST **1** : jumping or inducing to jump ⟨a ~ carriage⟩ : characterized by jumps or sudden variations ⟨the story . . . gets rather jerky and ~ —A.F.W. Plumptre⟩ **2** : NERVOUS, IRRITABLE, JITTERY ⟨if you didn't drink so much, you wouldn't be so ~ —Barnaby Conrad⟩ ⟨~ nerves⟩ ⟨apprehension that bribes will be uncovered . . . makes senators as ~ as they are —R.H.Rovere⟩

jun \'jən\ *n, pl* **jun** [Korean] **1** : a Korean monetary unit equal to 1/100 won — see MONEY table **2** : a coin representing one jun

jun *abbr* junior

junc *abbr* junction

jun·ca·ceae \,jəŋ'kāsē,ē\ *n pl, cap* [NL, fr. *Juncus*, type genus + *-aceae*] : a large widely distributed family of typically tufted herbs (order Liliales) resembling grasses and having a chaffy 6-parted perianth and a capsular fruit — **jun·ca·ceous** \;=;kāshəs\ *adj*

jun·cag·i·na·ce·ae \,jəŋ,kajə'nāsē,ē\ *n pl, cap* [NL, fr. *Juncagin-, Juncago*, type genus (fr. *Juncus*) + *-aceae*] : a family of marsh or bog herbs (order Naiadales) having leaves resembling rushes and small perfect flowers with 3 to 6 stamens and 3 to 6 carpels which separate at maturity

jun·co \'jəŋ(,)kō\ *n* [NL, fr. Sp, a bird, rush — more at JONQUIL] **1 a** *cap* : a genus of small American finches found from the arctic circle to Costa Rica usu. having a pink bill, ashy gray head and back, conspicuous white lateral tail feathers and often reddish brown on the back and sides **b** *pl* **juncos** *or* **juncoes** : any bird of this genus — see CAROLINA JUNCO, SLATE-COLORED JUNCO **2** *pl* **juncos** *or* **juncoes** [AmerSp, fr. Sp, rush] : ALLTHORN

jun·coi·des \,jəŋ'kȯi(,)dēz\ [NL, fr. *Juncus*, genus of marsh plants + L *-oides -oid*] *syn of* LUZULA

¹junc·tion \'jəŋ(k)shən\ *n* -s [L *junction-, junctio*, fr. *junctus* (past part. of *jungere* to join) + *-ion-, -io* -ion — more at YOKE] **1** : the act or an instance of joining or meeting : the state of being joined ⟨a ~ of two armies⟩ ⟨operates a ~ between the French spirit and German ideas and . . . culture —MatthewArnold⟩ **2 a** : a place or point of union or meeting ⟨at the ~ of two . . . fences —Thomas Hardy⟩ **b** *or* **junction point** : a place or point at which carrier lines meet or interchange traffic **c** : an intersection of roads or highways esp. where one of the highways terminates **3** : something that joins: as **a** : JUNCTION BOX **b** : a logical connective **c** : a grammatical unit formed by qualified and qualifying terms (as "the red barn") — compare NEXUS, RANK

²junction \"\ *vb* -ED/-ING/-S : to join at a junction

junc·tion·al \-shənᵊl, -shnəl\ *adj* : relating to junction

junctional nevus *n* : a nevus that develops at the junction of the dermis and epidermis and is potentially cancerous

junction box *n* : a box (as of metal) for enclosing the junction of electric wires and cables

junc·tur·al \'jəŋ(k)chərəl, -)sh(ə)rəl\ *adj* : of or relating to juncture in speech

junc·ture \'jəŋ(k)chə(r), -(k)shə(r)\ *n* -s [ME, fr. L *junctura*, fr. *junctus* (past part. of *jungere* to join) + *-ura* -ure — more at YOKE] **1** : an instance of joining : UNION, JUNCTION ⟨at the ~ of four fields —*Think*⟩ ⟨the ~ of the American Third and Seventh armies —E.K.Lindley & Edward Weintal⟩ ⟨emphasizes the ~ of poetry and music —Gilbert Highet⟩ **2 a** : JOINT, ARTICULATION, CONNECTION, SEAM **b** : the manner of transition between two consecutive speech sounds or between a speech sound and a pause **3** : a point of time; *esp* : one made critical or important by a concurrence of circumstances ⟨at certain ~s in the dancing, the scalps were raised high in the air —G.H.Fathauer⟩ ⟨at this ~ in history⟩

syn PASS, EXIGENCY, EMERGENCY, CONTINGENCY, PINCH, STRAIT (OR STRAITS), CRISIS: these nouns all denote a critical or crucial time or state of affairs, as in the life of a person, an institution, or a country's history. JUNCTURE emphasizes the usu. significant concurrence or convergence of events ⟨we may now be at a vital *juncture* where the ideals of liberalism can best be achieved through separate institutions and not the omnicompetent state —P.W.Kurtz⟩ ⟨occasions when there may be genuine uncertainty as to who should become prime minister. At such a *juncture* it is highly desirable to have someone charged with the duty of inviting a suitable person to form a government —R.M.Dawson⟩ PASS is stronger than JUNCTURE in implying an evil or distressing concurrence or convergence of events or the condition induced by such a concurrence, or, sometimes, a dilemma brought about by it ⟨they did in a desperate *pass* the best they knew —J.J.Mallon⟩ ⟨the frightful *pass* to which destiny had brought her —Arnold Bennett⟩ EXIGENCY emphasizes the pressures brought to bear or the urgency of the demands created by a special situation, esp. a juncture or pass ⟨the *exigencies* of war⟩ ⟨such travel *exigencies* as having to scout around for a room when you're tired and want to hole up for the night —Richard Joseph⟩ ⟨social contacts for a presidential couple are pretty well restricted by official *exigencies* —S.H.Adams⟩ EMERGENCY, implying more of a crucial nature but less necessary difficulty than EXIGENCY, is a sudden, unforeseen juncture or pass calling for immediate action to avoid disaster ⟨a national *emergency*⟩ ⟨aid in helping to meet the *emergency* of a large number of unemployed youths —*Amer. Guide Series: Minn.*⟩ ⟨a great social *emergency*, teenage delinquency —D.W.Maurer & V.H. Vogel⟩ CONTINGENCY is an event or concurrence of events that is fortuitous, only remotely possible, or uncertain of occurrence ⟨sense and ingenuity may be relied upon to cope with special *contingencies* —R.F.Heizer⟩ ⟨the bank had accumulated a surplus . . . which it held against future *contingencies* and risks —*Collier's Yr. Bk.*⟩ PINCH implies pressure or the need for action but without quite the same intensity as EMERGENCY or EXIGENCY ⟨could always in a *pinch* pawn my microscope for three pounds —W.S.Maugham⟩ ⟨ready in a *pinch* to ride roughshod over opposition —William Power⟩ STRAIT, now commonly STRAITS, applies to a troublesome situation from which escape is difficult because of hampering or binding circumstances ⟨a moment of financial *strait* —F.L. Paxson⟩ ⟨her father died and the family was left in dire financial *straits* —*Current Biog.*⟩ ⟨the army's truly desperate *straits* —F.V.W.Mason⟩ CRISIS applies to a juncture or pass whose outcome will make a decisive difference, esp. serving as a turning point as in a life, history, or the course of a disease ⟨her adolescence had passed without the trace of a religious *crisis* —Aldous Huxley⟩

jun·cus \'jəŋkəs\ *n* [NL, fr. L, rush — more at JONQUIL] **1** *cap* : a genus (the type of the family Juncaceae) of chiefly marsh plants of temperate regions that are perennial tufted glabrous herbs with mostly terete or channeled leaves **2** -ES : any plant of the genus *Juncus* — see RUSH

¹jun·dy *or* **jun·die** \'jəndi\ *n, pl* **jundies** [origin unknown] *Scot* : JOSTLE, JOG

²jundy *or* **jundie** \"\ *vb* **jundied; jundied; jundying; jundies** *Scot* : JOSTLE, JOG

¹june \'jün\ *n* -s *usu cap, often attrib* [ME *Junius, Juyn, June;* ME *Junius*, fr. OE & L; OE, fr. L, prob. fr. *Junius*, name of a Roman gens; ME *Juyn, June*, fr. MF & L; MF *juin*, fr. OF, fr. L *Junius;* prob. akin to L *Juno*, ancient Italian goddess] : the 6th month of the Gregorian calendar — see MONTH table

²june \"\ *vb* -ED/-ING/-S [origin unknown] *dial* : to drive briskly

ju·neau \'jü(,)nō\ *adj, usu cap* [fr. *Juneau*, Alaska] : of or from Juneau, the capital of Alaska : of the kind or style prevalent in Juneau

june beetle *or* **june bug** *n, often cap J* : any of numerous rather large leaf-eating scarabaeoid beetles that fly chiefly in late spring and have as larvae white grubs that live in soil and feed chiefly on the roots of grasses and other plants: as **a** : any of various large brown beetles (genus *Phyllophaga*) of eastern No. America **b** : GREEN JUNE BEETLE **c** : any of several European beetles (genus *Phyllopertha*) that are similar in appearance and habits to members of *Phyllophaga* **d** : any of several white-striped beetles (genus *Polyphylla*) of western No. America

june·berry \'jün — *see* BERRY\ *n, usu cap* **1** : any of various No. American trees and shrubs that constitute the genus *Amelanchier* and are sometimes cultivated for their showy white flowers or edible usu. purple or red fruits **2** : the fruit of a Juneberry

junebud \'=,=\ *n, usu cap* : REDBUD

june drop *n, usu cap J* : the falling of young fruit due to improper or incomplete fertilization, disease, or environmental factors at a maximum about June

junefish \'=,=\ *n* : SPOTTED JEWFISH

juneflower \'=,=\ *n, usu cap* : CANADA VIOLET

june grass *n, usu cap J* **1** : KENTUCKY BLUEGRASS **2** : a tufted grass (*Koeleria cristata*) abundant on prairies having narrow leaves and densely flowered terminal panicles like spikes — called also *crested hair grass, prairie June grass*

june pink *n, usu cap J* : SWAMP AZALEA

june·teenth \,jün·'tēn(t)th\ *n* -s *usu cap* [¹*june* + nine*teenth*] : June 19 observed as a general holiday by Negroes in Texas in celebration of the anniversary of the emancipation of slaves in the state

june week *n, usu cap J&W* : graduation week at West Point, Annapolis, and the U.S. Air Force Academy

june yellows *n pl but sing in constr, usu cap J* : a nonparasitic disease of strawberries due to a hereditary factor in some varieties and characterized esp. by yellow and green mottling and streaking of the leaves

jung \'jùŋ\ *n, pl* **jung** *or* **jungs** *usu cap* **1** : an ancient Tatar people of northwest China related to the Hsiung-nu, the Hu, and the Ti **2** : a member of the Jung people

jun·ger·man·nia \,jəŋgə(r)'manēə\ *n, cap* [NL, fr. Ludwig *Jungermann* †1653 Ger. botanist + NL *-ia*] : a formerly recognized genus of liverworts whose members are now included among various genera of the family Jungermanniaceae

jun·ger·man·ni·a·ce·ae \,==,manē'āsē,ē\ *n pl, cap* [NL, fr. *Jungermannia*, type genus + *-aceae*] : a family of liverworts comprising the acrogynous leafy members of the order Jungermanniales or in some esp. former classifications being coextensive with the order — see ACROGYNAE, ANACROGYNAE — **jun·ger·man·ni·a·ceous** \;==;==;āshəs\ *adj*

jun·ger·man·ni·a·les \,==,==ā(,)lēz\ *n pl, cap* [NL, fr. *Jungermannia*, genus of liverworts + *-ales*] : a large and widely distributed order of predominantly tropical liverworts that grow from a definite apical cell, that are characterized by marked diversity of form but with simple primitive tissue organization, and that include the leafy liverworts together with certain lower forms with terrestrial habits and a simple branching thallus or a leafless thalloid shoot — compare ACROGYNAE, ANACROGYNAE; see JUNGERMANNIACEAE

¹jung·i·an \'yùŋēən\ *n* -s *usu cap* [Carl G. *Jung* †1961 Swiss psychologist and psychiatrist + E *-ian*] : an adherent of the psychological doctrines of C. G. Jung

²jungian \"\ *adj, usu cap* **1** : of or relating to C. G. Jung whose psychological doctrines stress the opposition of introversion and extroversion and the concept of mythology and cultural and racial inheritance in the psychology of individuals **2** : of, relating to, or having the characteristics of the psychological doctrines of Jung

¹jun·gle \'jəŋgəl\ *n* -s *often attrib* [Hindi *jaṅgal*, fr. Skt *jāṅgala*] **1** *India* **a** : uncultivated ground **b** : land overgrown (as with brushwood) **2 a** : an impenetrable thicket or tangled mass of tropical vegetation some parts of which can be lived in by native people or wild animals **b** : a tract overgrown with thickets or masses of vegetation **3** : a hobo camp ⟨stays here all the time and runs this ~ —Burl Ives⟩ **4 a** (1) : a confused or chaotic mass or assemblage of objects : TANGLE, JUMBLE ⟨a ~ of gigantic tanks and curiously shaped pipes —*Amer. Guide Series: Ark.*⟩ ⟨an old-fashioned used-car junkyard ~ —N.F.Busch⟩ (2) : something that baffles, perplexes, or frustrates by its tangled, complex, or deviously intricate character : MAZE ⟨a perfect ~ of minute regulations —John Buchan⟩ ⟨a bureaucratic ~ of double-talk and evasions —P.B.Williamson⟩ ⟨difficult . . . to find one's way through the medieval ~ —G.G.Coulton⟩ **b** : a place or scene of ruthless struggle for survival ⟨turned international economy into a ~ —W.L.Clayton⟩ ⟨a tale of teenage gang violence in the concrete ~ —Arthur Gelb⟩

²jungle \"\ *vi* -ED/-ING/-S **1** : to inhabit a jungle ⟨tiny beasts that have *jungled* in that pale forest —John Galsworthy⟩ **2** : to camp in a hobo jungle ⟨*jungled* up with four others beside a creek —Nelson Algren⟩

jungle ballot *n* : BLANKET BALLOT

jungle bear *n* : SLOTH BEAR

jungle cat *n* : a small grayish to tawny Asiatic wildcat (*Felis chaus*) with slightly crested back, somewhat tufted ears, and obscure blotching and striping

jungle cock *n* : a male jungle fowl

jun·gled \-ld\ *adj* [¹*jungle* + *-ed*] : overgrown with jungle

jungle fowl *n* **1** : any of several Asiatic wild birds of the genus *Gallus; esp* : a bird (*G. gallus*) of southeastern Asia from which domestic fowls are believed to have descended **2 a** : an Australian megapode (*Megapodius reinwardtii tumulus*) **b** : any Australian species of the genus *Megapodius*

jungle green *n* : a very dark green

jungle gym *n* [fr. *Junglegym*, a trademark] : a three-dimensional structure of vertical and horizontal bars upon which children can climb and play

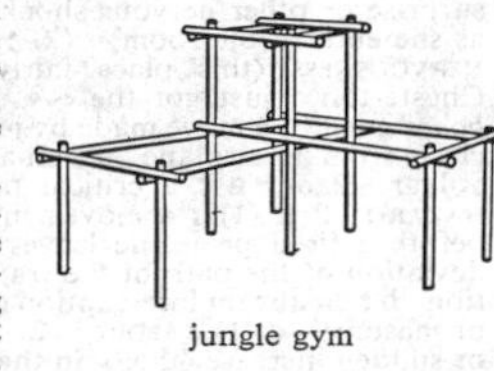

jungle gym

jungle hen *n* : a female jungle fowl

jungle juice *n* : a homemade or improvised alcoholic beverage; *esp* : one concocted by military personnel ⟨apt to be brewing on the ship fifteen different batches of *jungle juice* —T. O.Heggen⟩

jungle mouse *n* : any of several long-snouted often spiny-furred mice of southeastern Asia constituting the genus *Leggada*

jungle rice *n* : SHAMA MILLET

jungle yellow fever *n* : yellow fever endemic in or near forest or jungle areas in Africa and So. America and transmitted by mosquitoes other than members of the genus *Aedes* and esp. by those of the genus *Haemagogus*

¹jun·gli \'jəŋglē\ *n* -s [¹*jungle* + *-i* (as in *Hindi*)] : an inhabitant of an Indian jungle

²jungli *or* **jun·gly** \"\ *adj* **1** : inhabiting an Indian jungle : being or belonging to or characteristic of an inhabitant of such a jungle ⟨the ~ dialect was the only language we heard —S.T.Moyer⟩ **2** *India* : UNCOUTH, UNREFINED ⟨a rude, ~ individual —Alan Moorehead⟩

jun·gly \'jəŋg(ə)lē\ *adj* : of, relating to, or like a jungle ⟨an overgrown ~ garden⟩ ⟨a ~ world of high-pressure pluggers —*Time*⟩

juning *pres part of* JUNE

¹jun·ior \'jünyə(r)\ *n* -s [L, n. & adj.] **1 a** (1) : a person who is younger than another ⟨my ~s were already asleep —Jimmy O'Dea⟩ ⟨told his ~ that theological research was not compatible with longevity —H.J.Laski⟩ (2) *sometimes cap* [LL, fr. L] : a male child : SON ⟨in summer months ~ wears a coat of tan and nothing more —*N.Y. Herald Tribune*⟩ ⟨just as good for mother and the girls as for ~ —S.L.A.Marshall⟩ ⟨~ is improving in his understanding of numbers —Paul Woodring⟩ **b** (1) : a young person; *esp* : JUNIOR MISS ⟨coats and even skirts for teens and ~s —*Springfield (Mass.) Union*⟩ (2) : a clothing size for dresses, coats, and suits usu. for women and girls with slight figures that have youthful designs and little fullness in the bodice **c** : an immature or young animal — used esp. of small and pet stock **2** [ML, fr. L] **a** : a person holding a position of lesser standing in a hierarchy of ranks ⟨executives told their ~s that the day of the order taker was over —F.L.Allen⟩ ⟨the newest ~ on the staff —Albert Christen⟩ ⟨an officer one grade his ~ —Wirt Williams⟩ **b** (1) : a student in his next-to-the-last year before graduating from an educational institution (2) : a student in his third year or having third-year standing at a senior college (3) : a student in his first year at a junior college (4) : a student in his third year at a secondary school (5) : a pupil in a junior school (6) : a member of a church school or Sunday school age-level division that generally includes children of the ages 9 to 11 **3** : a barrister who has not taken silk **4** : a player (as the dealer in piquet) who receives cards later in the deal

²junior \"\ *adj* [L, compar. of *juvenis* young — more at YOUNG] **1 a** : less advanced in age than another : YOUNGER — used chiefly and often cap. to distinguish a son with the same given name as his father; opposed to *senior;* abbr. *Jr* or *jr* **b** (1) : of or relating to youth : YOUTHFUL, YOUNG ⟨some relatively ~ skins are as dry as bone —*Mademoiselle*⟩ (2) : designed for young people esp. of the adolescent age group ⟨a worthwhile ~ novel —Louise S. Bechtel⟩ **c** : of more recent date ⟨only six years ~ to Boston —H.L.Mencken⟩; *specif* : of more recent date and therefore inferior or subordinate as to right of preference ⟨a ~ lien⟩ **d** : ranking below another in point of time of service ⟨the ~ senator from Illinois⟩; *specif* : having less seniority than another ⟨resented having a ~ man get to be an engineer before him⟩ **2 a** [ML, fr. L] : lower in standing or in rank esp. in a hierarchy of ranks ⟨a ~ partner⟩ ⟨made a ~ member —G.A.Wagner⟩ ⟨shifted himself, as ~ officer, to the general's left —J.G.Cozzens⟩ ⟨the task of teaching such courses is customarily assigned to ~ members of the staff —*Times Lit. Supp.*⟩ **b** : associated with another in a secondary or auxiliary role ⟨the ~ author of a methodological study⟩ **c** : duplicating or suggesting on a smaller or diminished scale something typically large or powerful ⟨the ~ hurricane that swept in —Mollie Panter-Downes⟩ ⟨the new store will be a . . . ~ department store —*Retailing Daily*⟩ **3 a** : composed of juniors ⟨the ~ class⟩ **b** : of or relating to juniors, a junior class, or a junior school **c** : of or relating to a church school or Sunday school age-level division of juniors ⟨the ~ curriculum lessons⟩

jun·ior·ate *n* -s **1** : a course of high school or college study for the priesthood, brotherhood, or sisterhood; *specif* : one preparatory to the course in philosophy **2** : a seminary for juniorate training

junior captain *n* : a lieutenant in a fire department

junior church *n* : a program of worship, study, or project work for children carried on in churches during part or all of the adult worship service

junior college *n* **1** : an educational institution of post-high-school rank that offers two years of studies corresponding to the first two years of a senior college and prepares for transfer to such a college **2** : an institution complete in itself that serves the adults of its community by offering technical and vocational studies as well as courses in liberal education — compare COMMUNITY COLLEGE

junior common room *n* : a common room at a British college reserved for the use of undergraduates

junior high school *also* **junior high** *n* : a school organized to facilitate the transition from the elementary school to the high school usu. including the 7th and 8th grades of the elementary school and the 1st year of the high school — contrasted with *senior high school*

ju·nior·i·ty \jün'yȯrəd·ē, -yär-, -ətē, -i\ *n* -ES : the quality, state, or relation of being junior ⟨terms indicating relative rank of seniority or ~ —J.F.Embree & W.L.Thomas⟩

junior leaguer *n, often cap J&L* : a member of a league of young women organized for intelligent participation in civic affairs esp. through direct volunteer service to civic and social organizations and agencies for community betterment

junior levirate *n* : a form of the levirate in which a younger brother (as the next eldest one) marries the widow of the deceased husband

junior library *n, Brit* : a children's library

junior matriculation *n* : a certificate awarded to students who have successfully completed the ordinary course at a Canadian high school — compare SENIOR MATRICULATION

junior miss *n* **1** : an adolescent girl ⟨dresses in sizes for misses and *junior misses* —*N.Y. Times*⟩ **2** : JUNIOR 1b(2)

junior mortgage *n* : a second, third, or later mortgage

junior optime *n* : a man in the optime class at Cambridge University ranking one step below the senior optime and two steps below the wranglers

junior republic *n, usu cap J&R* : a self-governing industrial community for neglected or delinquent children

junior right *n* : the law of descent to the youngest son or in the absence of any issue to the youngest brother formerly existing by Anglo-Saxon custom in parts of England : BOROUGH-ENGLISH — compare PRIMOGENITURE, ULTIMOGENITURE

junior school *n* : a part of the British school system serving children from 7 to 11 years of age — compare INTERMEDIATE SCHOOL, SENIOR SCHOOL

junior seminary *n* : PREPARATORY SEMINARY

junior soldier *n* : a boy or girl between the ages of 7 and 13 who has met the requirements for enrollment as a junior member of the Salvation Army

junior varsity *n* : the members of a varsity squad lacking the experience or class qualification for the first team

junior yearling *n* : an animal of an age between 12 and 18 months on a date of the year specified by rules for livestock exhibits of the season

ju·ni·per \'jünəpə(r)\ *n* -s [ME *junipere, junipur*, fr. L *juniperus* — more at JONQUIL] **1 a** [NL *Juniperus*] : an evergreen shrub or tree of the genus *Juniperus; esp* : one having a prostrate or shrubby habit — see TREE illustration **b** : any of several coniferous trees resembling the juniper: as (1) : a white cedar (*Chamaecyparis thyoides*) (2) : LARCH **c** : RETEM **d** : BOX HUCKLEBERRY **2** : a dark grayish green that is bluer, lighter, and stronger than average ivy, lighter than Persian green, and yellower and lighter than hemlock green

juniper bay *n* [*juniper* + ⁹*bay*] : a swamp in which white cedar (*Chamaecyparis thyoides*) predominates and which often contains sweet bay

juniper berry *n* **1** : the fruit of a plant of the genus *Juniperus* (as the blue berrylike pungent-tasting cone of the common juniper) **2** : BOX HUCKLEBERRY

ju·ni·per·ic acid \;jünə;perik-\ *n* [ISV *juniper-* (fr. NL *Juniperus*, genus that produces it) + *-ic*] : a crystalline hydroxy acid $HOCH_2(CH_2)_{14}COOH$ found in the waxy exudation from several conifers (as *Juniperus sabina*)

juniper oil *or* **juniper-berry oil** *n* : an acrid essential oil obtained from the dried ripe fruit of common juniper and used chiefly in gin flavors and liqueurs and esp. formerly in medicine as a diuretic and stimulant

juniper scale *n* : a tiny dull whitish round scale (*Diaspis carueli*) that feeds on junipers and related trees esp. in ornamental plantings

juniper-tar oil *or* **juniper tar** *n* : CADE OIL

juniper tree *n* **1** : a tree of the genus *Juniperus* **2** : TAMARACK 1a(1)

ju·nip·er·us \jü'nipərəs\ *n, cap* [NL, fr. L, juniper] : a large genus of evergreen shrubs or trees (family Cupressaceae) that have small appressed scale leaves or esp. on juvenile growth acerose leaves, minute solitary terminal flowers, and small cones resembling berries and that include some cultivated as ornamentals and some valued for their timber — see PENCIL CEDAR

juniper webworm *n* : the larva of either of two destructive European tortricid moths (*Phalonia rutilana* and *Dichomeris marginella*) introduced into No. America that devours the foliage of several junipers

¹junk \'jəŋk\ *n* -s *often attrib* [ME *jonke*] **1 a** *obs* : a piece of worn or poor rope or cable **b** : pieces of old cable or old cordage used for making such articles as gaskets, mats, swabs, or oakum **c** *chiefly Brit* : a thick piece or chunk of something : HUNK ⟨a ~ of cold salt mutton —E.O.Schlunke⟩ **d** : hard salted beef supplied to ships **e** : a part of the head of a sperm whale between the case and the white horse containing oil and spermaceti **2 a** (1) **:** old iron, glass, paper, cordage, or other waste that may be treated so as to be used again in some form ⟨one third of the cars . . . are close to ~ in value —*Nation's Business*⟩ ⟨sold the old wreck for ~⟩ (2) **:** secondhand, worn, or discarded articles of any kind having little or no commercial value ⟨furnished the room with ~ obtained from relatives⟩ **b :** a product regarded as shoddy, cheap, or specious **:** something without intrinsic value **:** TRASH; *specif* **:** JUNK JEWELRY ⟨real jewelry, not ~ from Paris —Rose Thurburn⟩ ⟨newest ~ trinkets . . . made for her in Paris —Lois Long⟩ **c :** something devoid of meaning or significance **:** BUNK, HOKUM, NONSENSE ⟨read no more ~ —Nathaniel Benchley⟩ ⟨will have nothing to do with protocol, formalities, and all that ~⟩ **3 :** FISH 5e **4** *slang* **:** NARCOTICS; *esp* **:** HEROIN

²junk \"\ *vt* -ED/-ING/-S **:** to abandon or get rid of as no longer of value or use **:** SCRAP ⟨a dislike to ~ partially depreciated equipment —Harold Koontz & Cyril O'Donnell⟩ ⟨became the first big maker of electric appliances to ~ fair-trade pricing —*Newsweek*⟩ **syn** see DISCARD

³junk \"\ *n* -S [Pg *junco*, fr. Jav *joṅ*] **:** any of various characteristic boats of Chinese and neighboring waters having as common features bluff lines, very high poop and overhanging stem, little or no keel, usu. high pole masts carrying lug sails with battens running entirely across, and a rudder usu. dropping below the keel

junk

junk bottle *n* [¹*junk*] **:** a stout bottle of thick dark-colored glass

¹jun·ker \'yu̇ŋkə(r)\ *n* -S *usu cap, often attrib* [G, fr. OHG *junchērro*, fr. *junc* young + *hērro* lord, master — more at YOUNG, YOUNKER] **1 :** a young German noble **2 :** a member of the Prussian landed aristocracy characterized by extreme militarism, nationalism, and antidemocratic views ⟨the *Junkers*, the hard, ambitious governing class —*Auckland (New Zealand) Weekly News*⟩ ⟨*Junker* influence . . . in the German army —Hajo Halborn⟩

²junk·er \'jəŋkə(r)\ *n* -S [¹*junk* + *-er*] **1** *slang* **:** a narcotics addict **2 :** an automobile of such age and condition as to be ready for scrapping ⟨wanted an old ~ —Gregor Felsen⟩

jun·ker·dom \'yu̇ŋkə(r)dəm\ *n* -S *usu cap* [¹*junker* + *-dom*] **:** the body of Junkers **:** Junker society ⟨lost in the anonymity of Prussian *Junkerdom* —V.L.Albjerg⟩

jun·ker·ism \-kə,rizəm\ *n* -S *usu cap* [¹*junker* + *-ism*] **:** the Junker system of government **:** Junker principles or policies ⟨*Junkerism* has greatly declined in influence —*N.Y. Times*⟩

¹jun·ket \'jəŋkət, 'jəŋ-\ *n* -S [ME *jonket*, *junket*, fr. (assumed) ONF *jonquette* rush basket, dim. of OF *jonchee*, *jonchie*, fr. *jonc* rush, fr. L *juncus* — more at JONQUIL] *dial Brit* **:** BASKET; *esp* **:** one for carrying or catching fish

²jun·ket \'jəŋkət, *usu* -əd·+V\ *n* -S [ME *ioncate*, prob. fr. OIt *giuncata* cream cheese, fr. (assumed) VL *juncata*, fr. L *juncus* rush] **1 a :** a cream cheese or a dish of curds and cream **b :** a dessert of sweetened, flavored milk that is set in a smooth jelly by rennet **c** *obs* **:** a sweet dish, confection, or other delicacy **2 a :** a festive social affair **:** FEAST, BANQUET, PARTY ⟨the farm kitchen frequently was the setting for a country dance or ~ —Marilyn Fenno⟩ **b** (1) **:** a pleasure trip, cruise, or outing ⟨the ~*s* . . . attract hundreds of vacationers —Charles Rawlings⟩ ⟨a high-speed ~ to a tropical port —William McFee⟩ ⟨our first ~ by Italy's railroad system —Claudia Cassidy⟩ (2) **:** a pleasure trip or tour made by an official at public expense ostensibly for purposes of inspection, investigation, or other public business ⟨unnecessary ~*s* by state employees are taking big hunks out of the pockets of . . . taxpayers —*Springfield (Mass.) Union*⟩ ⟨this journey clearly is more than a ~ —W.H.Lawrence⟩ (3) **:** a tour or journey of any kind ⟨the best description of a lecturing ~ ever written —E.A.Weeks⟩ ⟨an agricultural ~ through nine European countries —*Newsweek*⟩ ⟨back from a business ~ through the eastern United States —E.T.Sager⟩

³junket \"\ *vb* -ED/-ING/-S *vi* **1 :** to make an entertainment **:** hold a junket **:** FEAST **2 :** to go on a junket **:** TOUR ⟨~*ed* like contemporary tourists —*N.Y. Herald Tribune*⟩ ~ *vt* **:** ENTERTAIN, FEAST ⟨these cowled academicians ~*ed* and entertained princes —Norman Douglas⟩

jun·ke·teer \,jəŋkə¦ti(ə)r, -iə\ *also* **jun·ket·er** \'jəŋkəd·ə(r)\ *n* -S [³*junket* + *-eer* or *-er*] **:** a person who junkets; *esp* **:** an official who makes a pleasure trip at public expense ostensibly for purposes of inspection or other official business ⟨true ~*s* . . . are a small, potent minority who reflect on every study mission —H.A.Williams⟩

junketing *n* -S **1 :** the act or an instance of junketing ⟨it will be political ~ —L.C.Wilson⟩ **2** *chiefly Brit* **:** FESTIVITY, FEASTING, CELEBRATION ⟨the feasting and ~ went on for days —Harold Albert⟩ ⟨there are to be big ~*s* —*Scots Mag.*⟩

junk·ie \'jəŋkē, -ki\ *n* -S [¹*junk* + *-ie*] **1 :** ²JUNKMAN **2** *or* **junky** -ES \"\ *slang* **:** a narcotics peddler or addict

junk jewelry *n* [¹*junk*] **:** inexpensive costume jewelry

junk mail *n* [¹*junk*] **:** third-class mail (as circulars, leaflets, and other advertising matter) bearing no direct address or not bearing the recipient's name and typically addressed to "occupant", "resident", "householder", or "boxholder"

¹junk·man \'jəŋkmən\ *n, pl* **junkmen** [³*junk* + *man*] **:** a member of the crew of a junk

²junk·man \'jəŋk,man\ *n, pl* **junkmen** [¹*junk* + *man*] **:** a person who deals in resalable junk

junk ring *n* [¹*junk*; fr. its orig. use in confining the hemp packing round the piston of a steam engine] **:** a wide ring around the piston of an internal-combustion engine forming the base for piston rings

junks *pl of* JUNK, *pres 3d sing of* JUNK

junky \'jəŋkē, -ki\ *adj* -ER/-EST [¹*junk* + *-y* (adj. suffix)] **:** having the character of junk **:** constituting junk ⟨a ~ copy of a painting —John Howard⟩

junkyard \'=,=\ *n* [¹*junk* + *yard*] **:** a yard used to keep usu. resalable junk

ju·no·esque \¦jünō¦esk\ *adj, usu cap* [*Juno*, ancient Italian goddess, wife of Jupiter (fr. L) + E *-esque*] **1 :** marked by stately or voluptuous beauty and generous proportions ⟨beautiful in a fine *Junoesque* fashion —Louis Bromfield⟩ ⟨her neck and head are *Junoesque* —P.B.Kyne⟩ **2 :** PLUMP, BUXOM ⟨for the *Junoesque* figure —*Good Housekeeping*⟩ ⟨a *Junoesque* size 40 —*Women's Wear Daily*⟩

¹ju·no·nia \jü'nōnēə\ [NL, fr. LL *Junonia (ales)* peacock (lit., Juno's bird), fr. L *Junonia*, fem. of *Junonius* of Juno, fr. *Junon-, Juno*] *syn of* PRECIS

²junonia \"\ *n* -S [NL, fr. *junonia* (specific epithet of *Scaphella junonia*)] **:** a rare volute mollusk (*Scaphella junonia*) that is creamy white with brown or orange markings, that is much sought by shell collectors, and that is known to occur only in deep water off the coasts of Florida

ju·no's bird \'jü(,)nōz-\ *n, cap J* [trans. of L *Junonis volucris* or LL *Junonia ales*] **:** PEACOCK

junr *abbr* junior

junt \'jənt\ *n* -S [prob. alter. (influenced by *chunk*) of *joint*] *chiefly Scot* **:** large amount **:** CHUNK

jun·ta \'hu̇ntə, 'jən-, 'hən-, 'hün-, 'jün- *also* 'jün- *or* 'zhən- *or* 'un-\ *n* -S [Sp, fr. fem. of *junto* together, joined, fr. L *junctus*, past part. of *jungere* to join — more at YOKE] **1 :** a council or committee for political or governmental purposes ⟨government by ~ is a characteristic feature —L.K.Caldwell⟩ ⟨abetted by the propaganda of exile ~*s* —G.W.Johnson⟩; *esp* **:** a closely knit group of persons composing or dominating a government esp. after a revolutionary seizure of power ⟨a military ~ with the trappings of a constitutional monarchy —E.K.Lindley⟩ ⟨called to account by a revolutionary ~ —Barbara Henderson⟩ ⟨some of the ruling ~*s* in the Arab countries —David Ben-Gurion⟩ **2 :** a closely knit group of persons combined for some common purpose **:** JUNTO ⟨a literary ~⟩

jun·to \'jən(,)tō, -n·(,)tō\ *n* -S [prob. alter. of *junta*] **:** a closely knit group of persons combined for some common purpose and usu. meeting secretly or privately **:** CABAL, FACTION

ju·pa·ti *or* **ju·pa·ty** \'jüpəd·ē\ *or* **jupati palm** *n* -S [Pg *jupati*, fr. Tupi *jupati*, *jubati*] **:** a Brazilian palm (*Raphia taedigera*) attaining an overall height of 70 feet of which not more than 6 or 8 feet represents stem, the remainder consisting of extremely large leathery pinnatisect leaves that are arranged in a terminal crown and rise from long strong stems which are used locally for various structural purposes

jupe \'jüp\ *n* -S [ME *juype*, fr. OF *jupe*, fr. Ar *jubbah*] **1** *chiefly Scot* **:** a man's coat, jacket, or tunic **2** [F] *chiefly Scot* **a :** a man's shirt **b :** a woman's bodice **c :** STAYS — usu. used in pl. **3 :** a woman's skirt

ju·pi·te·ri·an \,jüpə'tirēən\ *n* -S *usu cap* [(*Mount of*) *Jupiter* + E *-ian*] **:** a person that has a well-developed Mount of Jupiter and a long and large finger of Jupiter and that is usu. held by palmists to be characterized by ambition, leadership, and a religious nature ⟨with all his vanity the *Jupiterian* is warm-hearted —W.G.Benham †1944⟩

ju·pi·ter's-beard \'jüpəd·ə(r)z-\ *n, pl* **jupiter's-beards** *cap* [after *Jupiter*, ancient Roman god of the sky, fr. L *Juppiter*; trans. of L *barba Jovis* — more at DEITY] **1 :** HOUSELEEK **2 :** a silvery hairy European shrub (*Anthyllis barba-jovis*) with evergreen foliage and pale yellow flowers **3 :** a fungus (*Hydnum barba-jovis*) **4 :** RED VALERIAN

ju·pon \jü'pän, '=,=\ *n* -S [ME *iopoun*, *iupone*, *iopon*, fr. MF *jupon*, fr. OF *jupe*] **:** a tight-fitting garment like a shirt often padded and quilted and worn under medieval armor; *also* **:** a late medieval jacket similar to the surcoat

jur \'jər\ *vb* **jurred; jurred; jurring; jurs** [imit.] *dial chiefly Eng* **:** PUSH, JAR, BUTT

¹ju·ra \'yu̇rə\ *n pl* [L, pl. of *jur-, jus* law, right] **:** RIGHTS

²ju·ra \'ju̇rə\ *n, cap* [prob. fr. G, after *Jura*, mountain range between France and Switzerland, fr. L] **:** the Jurassic geological period or the rocks belonging to it

ju·ral \'ju̇rəl\ *adj* [L *jur-, jus* law, right + E *-al*] **:** of or relating to law **:** JURISTIC; *also* **:** of or relating to rights or obligations — **ju·ral·ly** \-ə̄lē, -li\ *adv*

ju·ra·ment \'ju̇rəmənt\ *n* -S [L *juramentum*, fr. *jurare* to swear + *-mentum* -ment] *archaic* **:** OATH

ju·ra·men·ta·do \,hu̇rəmən·'tä(,)dō, ,jü-\ *n* -S [Sp, bound by oath] **:** a Muslim Moro who has taken an oath to die while engaged in killing Christians — compare AMOK

ju·ra·men·tum \,ju̇rə'mentəm, ,yü-\ *n, pl* **juramenta** \-tə\ [LL] *Roman, civil, & canon law* **:** OATH

ju·rane \'jü,rān\ *adj, usu cap* [ML *Juranus*, fr. *Jura* mountains + L *-anus* -ane] **1 :** of or relating to the Jura mountains **2 :** of or relating to the medieval duchy of Burgundy

ju·ra·ra \zhə'rärə, ¦zhu̇rə¦rä\ *n* -S [Pg *jurará*, fr. Tupi *jurára*, *yurará*] **:** ARRAU

¹ju·ras·sic \jə'rasik, jü'-, -sēk\ *adj, usu cap* [F *jurassique*, fr. *Jura*, mountain range between France and Switzerland (fr. L) + *-ique* -ic] **:** constituting or relating to the period of the Mesozoic era preceding the Cretaceous and succeeding the Triassic and the corresponding system of rocks — see GEOLOGIC TIME table

²jurassic \"\ *n* -S *usu cap* **:** the Jurassic period or system of rocks

ju·rat \'ju̇,rat\ *n* -S [ME *jurate*, fr. ML *juratus*, fr. L, past part. of *jurare* to swear — more at JURY] **1 :** any of several public officials: as **a :** a municipal officer similar to an alderman in some English towns (as the Cinque Ports) **b :** a magistrate chosen for life in the Channel islands **2 :** a person who has taken an oath; *specif* **:** one in late medieval England sworn to assist the administration of justice (as by giving information about crimes committed in his neighborhood) **3** [short for L *juratum (est)* it has been sworn] **:** a certificate added to an affidavit stating when, before whom, and in British practice where it was made

ju·ra·ta \jə'räd·ə\ *n* -S [ML] **1** *Old Eng law* **:** a jury of 12 men existing at common law and not by statute — compare ASSIZE **2 :** JURAT 3

ju·ra·tion \jə'rāshən\ *n* -S [LL *juration-*, *juratio*, fr. L *juratus* (past part.) + *-ion-*, *-io* -ion] **:** a taking or an administration of an oath

ju·ra·to·ry \'ju̇rə,tōrē\ *adj* [LL *juratorius*, fr. L *juratus* (past part.) + *-orius* -ory] **:** relating to or comprising or expressed in an oath ⟨~ obligation⟩

juratory caution *n* [prob. trans. of F *caution juratoire*, trans. of LL *cautio juratoria*] **1** *Scots law* **:** a security consisting of a sworn inventory and pledge of the goods of the affiant **2** *admiralty law* **:** a suit in forma pauperis

jura-trias \'=¦==\ *n* -ES *usu cap J&T* [²*jura* + *trias*] **:** the Jurassic and Triassic together

jura-triassic \¦=¦=¦=\ *adj, usu cap J&T* **:** of or relating to the Jura-Trias

jure \'ju̇(ə)r\ *vt* -ED/-ING/-S [back-formation fr. *juror*] **:** to make a juror of

ju·rel \hü'rel\ *n* -S [Sp, fr. Sp. dial. *shurel* or Catal *sorell*, fr. LL *saurus* horse mackerel, fr. Gk *sauros* horse mackerel, lizard — more at SAURIA] **:** any of several carangid food fishes of warm seas: as **a :** BLUE RUNNER **b :** a crevalle (*Caranx hippos*)

ju·re ux·o·ris \,jü(,)rē,ok'sōrəs\ *adv* [L] **:** in or by the right of a wife (as in a conveyance by a husband at common law of his wife's estate)

ju·rid·ic \jə'ridik, (')jü¦r-, -dēk\ *adj* [L *juridicus*, fr. *jur-, jus* right, law + *-dicus* (fr. *dicere* to say)] **:** JURIDICAL

ju·rid·i·cal \-dəkəl, -dēk-\ *adj* [L *juridicus* + E *-al*] **1 :** of or relating to the administration of justice or the office of a judge **:** acting or used in the administration of justice **2 :** of or relating to law in general or jurisprudence **:** LEGAL — **ju·rid·i·cal·ly** \-dək(ə)lē, -dēk-, -li\ *adv*

juridical days *n pl* [trans. of L *dies juridici*] **:** days on which courts are open

juridical person *n* **:** JURISTIC PERSON

juried *adj* **:** selected for exhibition by an art jury ⟨a ~ show of fine quality —*Craft Horizons*⟩

juries *pl of* JURY, *pres 3d sing of* JURY

ju·rin's law \'ju̇rənz-\ *n, cap J* [after James *Jurin* †1750 Eng. physician] **:** a law of physics: the height of a capillary column of a liquid at a particular temperature is inversely proportional to the diameter of the tube

ju·ris·con·sult \,ju̇rə'skän,səlt ,ju̇rə'skän's-\ *n* -S [L *jurisconsultus*, fr. *juris* (gen. of *jus* law, right) + *consultus*, past part. of *consulere* to consult] **:** a man learned in law, esp. international and public law

ju·ris·dic·tion \,ju̇rəs'dikshən, -əz', -ə'sti-\ *n* -S [ME *jurisdiccioun*, *jurediccioun*, fr. OF & L; OF *juridiction*, *jurediction*, fr. L *jurisdiction-*, *jurisdictio*, fr. *juris* (gen. of *jus* right, law) + *diction-*, *dictio* act of saying, delivery in public speaking — more at JUST, DICTION] **1 :** the legal power, right, or authority to hear and determine a cause considered either in general or with reference to a particular matter **:** legal power to interpret and administer the law in the premises **2 :** authority of a sovereign power to govern or legislate **:** power or right to exercise authority **:** CONTROL ⟨an American theatrical trade union having ~ over dancers and singers —Anatole Chujoy⟩ ⟨territory subject to the ~ of the U.S. —G.W.Johnson⟩ **3 :** the limits or territory within which any particular power may be exercised **:** sphere of authority ⟨head of one of the world's smallest Masonic ~*s* —*Associated Press*⟩; *specif* **:** an assignment of organizing rights by a national labor federation to a constituent union **syn** see POWER

ju·ris·dic·tion·al \¦==¦dikshənᵊl, -¦sti-, -shnəl\ *adj* **:** of or relating to jurisdiction **:** involving a question of jurisdiction; *specif* **:** involving the right of one of two or more unions to organize and represent the employees of a plant, trade, or industry, the right to exclusive control over certain work, or the territorial limits of such jurisdiction ⟨a ~ dispute⟩ ⟨a ~ strike⟩ — **ju·ris·dic·tion·al·ly** \-ᵊlē, -əlē, -i\ *adv*

ju·ris·dic·tive \-ktiv\ *adj* [*jurisdiction* + *-ive*] **:** of, relating to, or having jurisdiction

ju·ris·prude \'ju̇rə,sprüd\ *n* -S [back-formation (influenced by *prude*) fr. *jurisprudence*] **:** a person who makes ostentatious show of learning in jurisprudence and the philosophy of law or who regards legal doctrine with undue solemnity or veneration ⟨disclaims being a ~ —*New Republic*⟩

ju·ris·pru·dence \,ju̇rə'sprüdᵊn(t)s, ,jür- *also* '==,==\ *n* -S [F & L; F, fr. MF, fr. LL *jurisprudentia*, fr. L *prudentia juris*] **1** *archaic* **:** knowledge of or skill in law **2 a :** a system or body of law **:** a department of law ⟨an exponent of sociological ~⟩ ⟨Roman ~⟩ — compare ANALYTICAL JURISPRUDENCE, FORENSIC MEDICINE **b :** the science or philosophy of law ⟨devoted himself to the study of ~⟩ **c** (1) **:** the course of court decisions as distinguished from legislation and doctrine ⟨a tendency that has become apparent in the ~ of the American courts —Bernard Schwartz⟩ (2) **:** the collected decisions of a court

ju·ris·pru·dent \¦==¦sprüdᵊnt\ *n* -S [LL *jurisprudent-*, *jurisprudens*, fr. L *juris* (gen. of *jus* right, law) + *prudent-*, *prudens* foreseeing, skilled, prudent — more at PRUDENT] **:** a person skilled in jurisprudence **:** JURIST

ju·ris·pru·den·tial \¦ju̇rə(,)sprü¦denchəl\ *adj* [LL *jurisprudentia* + E *-al*] **:** of or relating to jurisprudence — **ju·ris·pru·den·tial·ly** \-ə̄lē\ *adv*

ju·rist \'ju̇rəst, 'jür-\ *n* -S [MF *juriste*, fr. ML *jurista*, fr. L *jur-, jus* law, right + *-ista* -ist — more at JUST] **1 a :** a person who practices law **:** LAWYER **b :** JUDGE ⟨replaced a ~ then under fire —R.G.Spivack⟩ **2 :** a person skilled in the philosophy or science of the law **:** a scholar in the law ⟨19th century philosophical ~*s* —Roscoe Pound⟩

ju·ris·tic \jə'ristik, (')jü¦r-, -tēk\ *adj* **:** of or relating to a jurist or jurisprudence **:** relating to, created by, or recognized in law ⟨~ theory⟩ — **ju·ris·ti·cal·ly** \-tək(ə)lē, -tēk-, -li\ *adv*

juristic act *n* **:** an act of a private individual directed to the origin, termination, or alteration of a right

juristic person *n* **:** a body of persons, a corporation, a partnership, or other legal entity that is recognized by law as the subject of rights and duties — called also *artificial person*, *conventional person*, *fictitious person*

ju·ror \'ju̇rə(r), 'jü- *also* -,rō(ə)r *or* -ō(ə)\ *n* -S [ME *juroure*, *jurrour*, fr. AF *jurour*, fr. OF *jurer* to swear + *-our* -or — more at JURY] **1 a :** one of a number of men sworn to deliver a verdict as a body **:** a member of a jury **b :** a person designated and summoned to serve on a jury **2 :** a person who takes oath of allegiance **3 :** a member of a jury for awarding prizes or determining relative merit at a contest or exhibition

jurr *var of* JUR

jurred *past of* JUR

jurring *pres part of* JUR

jurs *pres 3d sing of* JUR

juruk *usu cap, var of* YURUK

ju·ru·pa·ite \hə'rüpə,īt\ *n* -S [*Jurupa* mts., Riverside co., Calif. + E *-ite*] **:** a hydrous calcium magnesium silicate $(Ca,Mg)_2(Si_2O_5)(OH)_2$

¹ju·ry \'ju̇rē, 'jür-, -ri\ *n* -ES [ME *jure*, *jurie*, fr. AF *juree*, fr. OF *jurer* to swear, fr. L *jurare*, *jurari*, fr. *jur-, jus* law, right — more at JUST] **1 :** a body of men sworn to give a verdict upon some matter submitted to them; *esp* **:** a body of men selected according to law, impaneled, and sworn to inquire into and try any matter of fact and to give their verdict according to the evidence legally produced — compare GRAND JURY, PETIT JURY, TRIAL JURY **2 :** the body of dicasts of ancient Athens **3 a :** a committee for determining relative merit or awarding prizes at an exhibition or competition ⟨two *juries* for its third annual national exhibition —*Americana Annual*⟩ **b :** the director and four judges responsible for officiating at a fencing bout

²jury \"\ *vt* -ED/-ING/-ES **:** to select entries for (an art exhibit) ⟨inviting one man to ~ . . . its quadrennial exhibitions of contemporary American art —Aline B. Saarinen⟩ **:** judge the relative merits of (entries in an art exhibit) ⟨~*ing* the submissions at the invitation of the foundations —G.A.Wagner⟩

³jury \"\ *adj* [origin unknown] **:** improvised for temporary use esp. in an emergency **:** MAKESHIFT ⟨a ~ mast⟩ ⟨a ~ rig⟩ ⟨~ repairs completed, they started again —Will Irwin⟩

jury box *n* **:** the place usu. enclosed by paneling where the jury sits at the trial of a court case

jury chancellor *n, Scots law* **:** the foreman of a jury

jury commission *n* **:** a body of public officers entrusted with the task of ascertaining the names and addresses of persons qualified by law to act as jurors and sometimes of actually selecting by lot a panel of such jurors

jury duty *n* **1 :** the obligation to serve on a jury ⟨clergymen are exempt from *jury duty*⟩ **2 :** service on a jury

ju·ry·less \'==ləs\ *adj* **:** being without a jury

jury list *n* **:** a list of persons qualified to be drawn for jury service, summoned to court to serve as jurors, or sworn to act as jurors in a particular case

ju·ry·man \'==mən\ *n, pl* **jurymen 1 :** a person summoned to a sitting of a court to act as a juror if chosen **2 :** JUROR

jury of the vicinage : a jury formerly drawn from the neighborhood and now drawn from the political subdivision in which the court is held

jury-packing \'==,==\ *n* **:** the practice or an instance of illegally or corruptly influencing a jury by making available for jury service persons known to be biased or partial in a particular case to be tried

jury-rigged \'=¦=¦=\ *adj* [³*jury*] **:** rigged for temporary service

jury room *n* [¹*jury*] **:** the place where a jury in arriving at a verdict deliberates in private

jury strut *n* [³*jury*] **:** an auxiliary strut used as a support for a primary strut

jury wheel *n* [¹*jury*] **:** a revolving device or circular box from which the names of persons to serve as jurymen may be drawn by chance

jurywoman \'==,==\ *n, pl* **jurywomen :** a female member of a jury

¹jus \'jəs\ *or* **ius** \'yüs\ *n, pl* **ju·ra** \'ju̇rə\ *or* **iu·ra** \'yu̇-\ [L — more at JUST] **1 :** LAW **2 :** a legal principle, right, or power

²jus \'zhüs, 'jüs, F 'zhüē\ *n, pl* **jus** [F — more at JUICE] **:** JUICE, GRAVY — compare AU JUS

jus *abbr* justice

jus ab·u·ten·di \-,abyə'tendē, -,dī\ *n* [L, right of abusing] *Roman & civil law* **:** a right to make full use of property even to wasting or destroying it **:** absolute and unlimited ownership with the power of free alienation — compare JUS UTENDI

jus ac·cre·scen·di \-,akrə'sendē, -,dī\ *n* [L, lit., right of increasing] *Roman & civil law* **:** a right of accrual (as the right of survivorship)

jus ad rem \-(')a'drem\ *n* [ML, right to a thing] *civil & canon law* **:** a right to acquire particular property arising out of another's legal duty **:** a jus in personam as distinguished from a jus in rem based on full ownership or possession of particular property **:** an inchoate as distinguished from a perfected right

jus ae·di·li·um \-ē'dilēəm\ *or* **jus ae·di·li·ci·um** \-,ēdə'lis(h)ēəm\ *n* [L, law of the aediles or law of an aedile] *Roman law* **:** the law of the curule aediles set forth in their edicts usu. relating to police and market regulations

jus al·ba·na·gii \-,albə'nājē,ī\ *n* [ML, right of alien confiscation] **:** DROIT D'AUBAINE

jus an·ga·ri·ae \-(,)aŋ'ga(a)rē,ē\ *n* [LL, lit., right of angaria] **:** ANGARY

jus ca·non·i·cum \-kə'nänəkəm\ *n* [ML] **:** CANON LAW

jus ci·vi·le \-sə'vī(,)lē\ *n* [L] **:** CIVIL LAW

jus com·mer·cii \-kə'mərshē,ī\ *n* [L, right of commerce] *Roman & civil law* **:** a right to make contracts, acquire, hold, and transfer property, and have business dealings

jus com·mu·ne \-kə'myü(,)nē\ *n* [L] **1 :** the common law of England **2 :** the common or public law or right as opposed to the jus singulare established for special cases

jus co·nu·bi *or* **jus con·nu·bii** \-kə'n(y)übē,ī\ *n* [L, lit., right of marriage, right of intermarriage] **1 :** CONNUBIUM 2 **2 :** the body of rules and conventions of a people or community governing intermarriage

jus de·li·be·ran·di \-də,libə'randē, -n,dī\ *n* [L, right of deliberating] *Roman & civil law* **:** a right granted to an heir to take a certain time to decide whether to accept the inheritance or not

jus dis·po·nen·di \-,dispə'nendē, -,dī\ *n* [L, right of disposing] **:** a right of disposal as of property **:** power of alienation

jus ec·cle·si·as·ti·cum \-ə,klēzē'astəkəm, -e,k-\ *n* [LL] **:** ECCLESIASTICAL LAW

jus edi·cen·di \-,edə'sendē, -n,dī\ *n* [L, right of decreeing] *Roman law* **:** a right belonging to the curule aediles, praetors, and quaestors and presidents in the provinces of making edicts

jus fru·en·di \-frü'endē, -,dī\ *n* [L, right of enjoying] *Roman & civil law* **:** a right of enjoyment of another's property without destroying its substance

jus gen·ti·um \-'jenchēəm\ *n* [L, law of aliens, law of nations] **1 :** a body of legal rules for the government of aliens subject to Rome and of the intercourse of Roman citizens with aliens **2 :** INTERNATIONAL LAW

jus ho·no·ra·ri·um \-,änə'ra(a)rēəm\ *n* [L, magisterial law] *Roman law* **:** the law established by the edicts of the magis-

trates consisting chiefly of the praetorian law and the law of the curule aediles
ju·si or **hu·si** \'hüsē\ n -s [PhilSp, fr. Tag *husi*] : a fine sheer Philippine fabric for dresses or shirts that is made in plain weave from silk and vegetable fibers
jus in per·so·nam \'j'ə,sinpə(r)'sō,nam\ n [L, right against a person] : a right of legal action against or to enforce a legal duty of a particular person or group of persons — compare JUS IN REM
jus in re \-'rē\ n [ML, lit., right in a thing] : JUS IN REM
jus in rem \-'rem\ n [L, right against a thing] : a right enforceable against anyone in the world interfering with that right founded on some specific relationship, status, or particular property accorded legal protection from interference by anyone (as the right to be free from slander or to enjoy one's property)
jus in·ter gen·tes \-,intə(r)'jen,tēz\ n [L, law among nations] : JUS GENTIUM
jus La·tii \-'lāshē,ī\ n, cap L [L, lit., right of Latium, ancient country of Italy] : the right of a person (as a Latin not a citizen of Rome) who has certain rights of or to Roman citizenship
jus na·tu·rae \-nə'tü(,)rē, -nə'tyü-\ n [L, lit., law of nature] : NATURAL LAW
jus na·tu·ra·le \-,nachə'ra(,)lē, -rā(-, -rä(-\ n [L] : NATURAL LAW
jus per·so·na·rum \-,pərsə'na(a)rəm\ n [L, law of persons] : the law of persons occupying special relations to one another (as parent and child, husband and wife, guardian and ward) or of persons with limited rights (as aliens, minors, slaves, incompetent or insane persons)
jus post·li·mi·ni·i \-,pōstlə'minē,ī\ n [L, right of return to one's threshold] *Roman law* : POSTLIMINIUM
jus pri·mae noc·tis \-,prī(,)mē'näktəs\ n [L, right of first night] **1** : DROIT DU SEIGNEUR **2** : a right granted by the law or custom of a primitive people to some person other than the bridegroom of deflowering the bride
jus pro·pri·e·ta·tis \-p(r)ə,prīə'tād·əs\ n [ML, lit., right of ownership] : a right based on ownership of property irrespective of actual possession
jus pub·li·cum \-'pəbləkəm\ n [L] : public law including in Roman law the criminal and sacred law
jus re·lic·tae \-rə'lik(,)tē\ n [ML, right of a widow] *Scots law* : a widow's right to a share in the free movable estate of her deceased husband to the extent of one third if there are children and otherwise one half
jus re·lic·ti \-,tī\ n [ML, right of a widower] *Scots law* : a widower's right to share in the free movable estate of his deceased wife since 1881 to the extent of one third if there are children and otherwise one half
juss *abbr* jussive
jus san·gui·nis \-'saŋgwənəs\ n [L, right of blood] : a rule that the citizenship of the child is determined by the citizenship of its parents
jus·si·aea \,jəsē'ēə\ n, cap [NL, irreg. fr. Bernard de *Jussieu* †1777 Fr. botanist] : a genus of chiefly tropical aquatic or semiaquatic herbs (family Onagraceae) that are closely related to the evening primroses and have a many-seeded capsule and usu. entire alternate leaves — see PRIMROSE WILLOW
jus·si·ae·an \¦==¦ēən\ or **jus·si·eu·an** \-'yüən\ *also* **jus·si·e·an** \-'ēən\ adj, usu cap [fr. or irreg. fr. Bernard de *Jussieu* †1777 or Antoine Laurent de *Jussieu* †1836 Fr. botanists + E *-an*] : of or relating to the French botanists Bernard de Jussieu or Antoine Laurent de Jussieu ⟨*Jussiaean* classification⟩
jus sin·gu·la·re \-,singyə'la(a)rē\ n [L, individual law, particular law] *Roman & civil law* : a law or right established for special cases as opposed to the jus commune
[1]**jus·sive** \'jəsiv, -sēv *also* səv\ adj [L *jussus* (past part. of *jubēre* to order) + E *-ive*; akin to W *udd* lord, Gk *hysminē* fight, battle, Skt *udyōdhati* it boils up, rages, *yudhyati* he fights] : expressing or having the effect of a command
[2]**jussive** \"\ n -s : a word, form, case, or mood expressing command
jus so·li \'jəs'sō,lī\ n [L, right of the soil] : a rule of the common law that determines the allegiance or citizenship of a child by the place of its birth — compare ALLEGIANCE
[1]**just** *var of* JOUST
[2]**just** \'jəst\ adj *often* -ER/-EST [ME *just, juste*, fr. MF & L; MF *juste*, fr. OF, fr. L *justus*, fr. *jus* right, law, justice, fr. OL *jous*; akin to OIr *huisse, uisse* right, just, Skt *yos* welfare, and perh. to L *jungere* to bind, join; basic meaning: tie, obligation — more at YOKE] **1 a** (1) : having a basis in fact : REASONABLE, WELL-FOUNDED, JUSTIFIED ⟨felt a ~ fear of the consequences of his actions⟩ (2) : conforming to fact or reason : not false : RIGHT, TRUE, ACCURATE ⟨had a very ~ notion of the boy's abilities⟩ ⟨one element in a ~ discrimination —John Dewey⟩ (3) *archaic* : agreeing closely or exactly with a pattern, model, or other original : FAITHFUL **b** *obs* : adapted to some end or purpose : APPROPRIATE, SUITABLE **c** (1) *obs* : regular or exact in operation : CONSTANT, UNIFORM (2) *obs* : being exactly the specified measure, dimension, quantity, or other result of calculation : not approximate but exact (3) : conforming to some standard of correctness : CORRECT, PROPER, FITTING ⟨tended to distort some of the concerto's ~ proportions —Winthrop Sargeant⟩ ⟨react in ~ measure against this naturalism —Irving Babbitt⟩ ⟨combines wit and sentiment in ~ proportions —Douglas Watt⟩ (4) *obs* : EQUAL, EVEN (5) : giving or sounding musical tones at the mathematically exact intervals of their vibration ratios ⟨~ intonation⟩ ⟨~ scale⟩ — compare TEMPERED **d** *archaic* : lacking nothing needed for completeness : COMPLETE, FULL **2 a** : righteous before God **b** (1) : acting or being in conformity with what is morally right or good : RIGHTEOUS, EQUITABLE ⟨a reward directed his way by a ~ providence —W.H.Whyte⟩ ⟨a ~ war⟩ ⟨that is justice, even if it is not ~ —Alan Paton⟩ ⟨his decisions quick and instinctively ~ —Norman Mailer⟩ (2) : MERITED, DESERVED ⟨won him that ~ affection and popularity —F.J.Mather⟩ ⟨received his ~ punishment⟩ **c** : conforming to or consonant with what is legal or lawful : legally right ⟨a ~ title⟩ ⟨~ compensation⟩ ⟨a ~ proceeding⟩ **syn** see FAIR, UPRIGHT
[3]**just** \(¦)jəs(t), (¦)jis(t), (¦)jes(t), *in rapid speech sometimes* (,)dis(t)\ adv [ME, fr. *just*, adj.] **1 a** : EXACTLY, PRECISELY ⟨some indication of ~ how nervous she was —C.B.Flood⟩ ⟨~ the words we often have to look up in a dictionary —G.A. Miller⟩ ⟨capturing . . . ~ the expression of terror which had baffled him —Laurence Binyon⟩ ⟨must always have his meals served ~ so⟩ ⟨has ~ the thing you need⟩ ⟨that's ~ the point in dispute⟩ ⟨you must take me ~ as I am⟩ ⟨an apartment project . . . that cost ~ $20 million —*Wall Street Jour.*⟩ **b** (1) : precisely at the time referred to or implied ⟨was ~ ten when he came in⟩ ⟨not here ~ now⟩ (2) : but a very short time ago : very recently ⟨has ~ been published⟩ ⟨was ~ here⟩ — often used in the phrase *just now* ⟨saw him ~ now⟩ **c** *Brit* : on the point of being — often used with *on* ⟨it was now ~ on eight o'clock —Paul Jennings⟩ **2** *obs* : in a precise or accurate manner : CORRECTLY, ACCURATELY **3 a** : by a very small margin : BARELY ⟨had only ~ time to get back —F.W.Crafts⟩ ⟨could ~ see the very high weathercock of the church —Arnold Bennett⟩ ⟨~ short of the record —*Current Biog.*⟩ ⟨it was ~ over fifty years ago —Alan Devoe⟩ ⟨should be adjusted to ~ clear the dial —W.E.Shinn⟩ ⟨has an entrance ~ within the . . . county line —*Amer. Guide Series: N.Y. City*⟩ **b** : in immediate proximity : IMMEDIATELY, DIRECTLY ⟨lies ~ west of here⟩ ⟨~ across from the campus⟩ ⟨~ down the hall —J.K.Blake⟩ **4 a** : ONLY, MERELY, SIMPLY ⟨~ a note to let you know⟩ ⟨turn it into ~ another automobile —R.C.Ruark⟩ ⟨to them it's ~ a business —*Irish Digest*⟩ ⟨asked for a copy and got it — ~ like that —M.S.Mayer⟩ ⟨there was ~ lots of scenery —J.F.Dobie⟩ ⟨seems incredibly large for ~ the aristocracy —H.P.Becker⟩ ⟨I'm ~ your interpreter —Ernest Hemingway⟩ ⟨I don't think about it; I ~ go —J.J.Godwin⟩ **b** (1) : QUITE, VERY, ABSOLUTELY, REALLY — used as an intensive ⟨that's ~ ducky⟩ ⟨~ had a wonderful time⟩ (2) *chiefly dial* : INDEED, TRULY ⟨I tried a master; but he confused me, ~ —Willa Cather⟩ ⟨couldn't he play the violin, ~ —*Wesfarmers News*⟩ — **just about** adv : ALMOST, APPROXIMATELY ⟨passes *just about* through the middle of the region —P.E.James⟩ ⟨is the work done? *just about*⟩ ⟨shown to *just about* every audience you can name —Cecile Starr⟩ — **just in case** adv : by way of precaution against a possible or anticipated eventuality ⟨surrounded the area *just in case* —*Springfield (Mass.) Union*⟩
just *abbr* justice
just·au·corps \,zhüstə¦kō(ə)r\ or **jus·ti·coat** \'jəstə,kōt\ n, pl **justaucorps** \-r(z)\ or **justicoats** \-ts\ [*justaucorps* fr. F, fr. *juste au corps* close to the body; *justicoat*, alter. (influenced by E *coat*) of *justaucorps*] : a fitted coat or jacket; *specif* : a man's knee-length coat with flaring and stiffened skirts worn in the late 17th and early 18th centuries

justaucorps

juste-mi·lieu \¦zhüstmēl¦yə, -yər(·), -yə̄\ n, pl **juste-milieux** \-yə(z), -yər(·), -yərz, -yə̄(z)\ [F] : the just or golden mean; *esp* : a governmental policy characterized by moderation and compromise
jus·tice \'jəstəs\ n -s *often attrib* [ME *justice, justise*, fr. OE & OF; OE *justise*, fr. OF *justice, justise*, fr. L *justitia*, fr. *justus* just + *-itia* -ice] **1 a** : the maintenance or administration of what is just : impartial adjustment of conflicting claims : the assignment of merited rewards or punishments : just treatment ⟨meting out evenhanded ~⟩ ⟨the natural aspiration for ~ in the human heart —W.A.White⟩ ⟨a splendid example of divine ~ —M.W.Fishwick⟩ ⟨social ~⟩ **b** [ME *justice, justise*, fr. AF & ML; AF *justice*, fr. ML *justitia*, fr. L] : a person duly commissioned to hold courts or to try and decide controversies and administer justice: as (1) : a judge of the Supreme Court of Judicature in England, or formerly of the Court of King's Bench, Common Pleas, or Exchequer (2) : a judge of a common-law court or a superior court of record (3) : a justice of the peace : an inferior magistrate ⟨a police ~⟩ ⟨traffic court ~⟩ **c** (1) : administration of law : the establishment or determination of rights according to the rules of law or equity (2) : infliction of punishment ⟨promises the indulgence of the jury to the husband who has himself executed ~ —H.M.Parshley⟩ **2 a** (1) : the quality or characteristic of being just, impartial, or fair : FAIRNESS, INTEGRITY, HONESTY ⟨possessed a keen sense of honor and ~⟩ ⟨pointed out, with equal ~, that . . . there are good businesses and bad —D.W.Brogan⟩ ⟨"it was nobody's fault . . . ," she added, with scrupulous ~ —Ellen Glasgow⟩ ⟨the same standards used in steel must in ~ be applied to other industries —Mary K. Hammond⟩ (2) : the principle or ideal of just dealing or right action ⟨the courts are not helped as they . . . ought to be in the adaptation of law to ~ —B.N.Cardozo⟩ (3) : conformity to such principle or ideal : RIGHTEOUSNESS ⟨defends the ~ of his cause⟩ **b** (1) *in Platonism* : the condition of harmony existing in a state between its members when each citizen occupies a place in accordance with his merit : the highest of the four cardinal virtues (2) *in Aristotelianism* : the practice of virtue toward others — see COMMUTATIVE JUSTICE, DISTRIBUTIVE JUSTICE, RETRIBUTIVE JUSTICE (3) : that virtue which gives to each his due **c** (1) : the quality of conforming to positive law (2) : the quality of conforming to both positive law and also to divine or natural law **3** : conformity to truth, fact, or reason : CORRECTNESS, RIGHTFULNESS ⟨complained with ~ that English waxes and wanes like the moon —*English Language Arts*⟩ ⟨admitted that there was much ~ in these observations —T.L.Peacock⟩ — **bring to justice** : to cause to be brought before a proper tribunal for trial — **do justice** **1** *obs* : to pledge in drinking **2 a** : to do what is just : administer justice : act justly ⟨longed to *do justice* in the world —*Time*⟩ **b** : to treat fairly or according to merit ⟨to *do* the man *justice*, his writing is brilliant⟩ **c** (1) : to treat or handle adequately or properly ⟨not *doing* full *justice* to his material —Carl Van Doren⟩ ⟨a full schedule may not permit him to *do justice* to his studies —Bates Boyle⟩ ⟨open for experienced salesmen who can *do justice* to America's outstanding line of small leather goods —*Luggage & Leather Goods*⟩ (2) : to consume in a manner showing due appreciation ⟨*do* the food *justice*⟩ ⟨after he likewise had *done* the liquor *justice* —Winston Churchill⟩ **3** : to acquit in a way that is worthy of one's powers ⟨in the concerto he clearly did not *do* himself *justice*⟩
justice clerk n, pl **justice clerks** [ME] : the vice-president of the High Court of Justiciary and the presiding officer of the Outer House of the Court of Session in Scotland — called also *lord justice clerk*
justice court or **justice's court** n : an inferior court not of record having limited criminal or civil jurisdiction, presided over by a justice of the peace, and existing in some states from which appeal usu. may be claimed
justice general n, pl **justices general** [ME] : the former presiding officer of the High Court of Justiciary in Scotland whose duties are now entrusted to the lord president of the Court of Session — called also *lord justice general*
justice in eyre n [ME, trans. of AF *justice en eire*] : an itinerant judge riding the circuit to hold court in the different counties
justice of the peace [ME] : a subordinate magistrate for the conservation of the peace in a specified district with sometimes other incidental administrative and financial powers specified in his commission and with the principal duties of administering summary justice in minor cases, of committing for trial in a superior court on cause shown, and in Great Britain of granting licenses and acting if a county justice as judge at quarter sessions
jus·tic·er \-sə(r)\ n -s [ME *justiser*, fr. MF *justicier*, fr. OF, fr. *justice*] *archaic* : one who maintains or administers justice : JUDGE
jus·tice·ship \-s,ship\ n : the office or dignity of a judge
justice's warrant n : a warrant issued by an inferior magistrate (such as a justice of the peace, alderman, or federal commissioner) as distinguished from a bench warrant issued by a court of record
justiceweed \'==,=\ n : a slender white-flowered herb (*Eupatorium leucolepis*) of the eastern U. S.
jus·ti·cia \,jə'stishēə\ n, cap [NL, fr. James *Justice*, 18th cent. Scot. horticulturist + NL *-ia*] : a genus of perennial herbs or shrubs (family Acanthaceae) growing in water or wet places and having entire leaves and small flowers in long-peduncled axillary spikes or heads — see WATER WILLOW
jus·ti·cia·bil·i·ty \jə,stish(ē)ə'bilədē\ n -ES : the quality of being justiciable
jus·ti·cia·ble \,jə¦stish(ē)əbəl\ adj [F, fr. MF] : capable of being decided by legal principles or by a court of justice : liable to trial in a court of justice ⟨a ~ case⟩
jus·ti·ci·ar \,jə'stishēə(r)\ n -s [ME, fr. (influenced by ME *-ar*) ML *justiciarius, justitiarius*, fr. L *justitia* justice + *-arius* -ary — more at JUSTICE] **1** : a high royal judicial officer in medieval England; *esp* : a justice of one of the superior courts **2** [ML *justiciarius, justitiarius*] : the chief political and judicial officer of the Norman and later kings of England until the 13th century — called also *capital justiciar* **3** : either of two chief judges under early Scotch kings and with jurisdiction north and south respectively of Forth
jus·ti·ci·ar·ship \-(r),ship\ n : the office or dignity of a justiciar
jus·ti·ci·ary \,jə'stishē,erē, -ri\ n -ES [ME *justiciarie*, fr. ML *justiciaria, justitiaria*, fr. L *justitia* justice + *-aria* -ary] **1** : the jurisdiction of a justiciar or of the High Court of Justiciary which consists of original and appellate jurisdiction in serious criminal cases and appellate jurisdiction from sheriff's decisions in civil matters in the small-debts court **2** [ML *justiciarius, justitiarius*] : JUSTICIAR
jus·ti·ci·es \,jə'stishē,ēz\ n, pl **justicies** [ML, lit., you may bring to trial, 2d pers. sing. pres. subj. of *justiciare, justitiare* to bring to trial, fr. L *justitia* justice] *Eng law* : a writ addressed to a sheriff ordering him to do justice in a case (as trespass, vi et armis, or personal action involving not more than 40 shillings) he otherwise could not try
justicoat *var of* JUSTAUCORPS
jus·ti·fi·abil·i·ty \,jəstə,fīə'bilədē, -ətē, -i\ n -ES : the quality of being justifiable
jus·ti·fi·able \'jəstə,fīəbəl, ¦==¦===\ adj [*justify* + *-able*] : capable of being justified : EXCUSABLE, DEFENSIBLE ⟨~ family pride —*Current Biog.*⟩
justifiable homicide n : a homicide (as by accident, by misadventure, in self-defense, in performing a legal duty like quelling a mob or carrying out a death sentence, in preventing a felony involving great bodily harm, or in defense of one's home or members of one's family) justified or excused by law for which no criminal punishment is imposed
jus·ti·fi·able·ness n -ES : the quality or state of being justifiable
jus·ti·fi·ably \-blē, -li\ adv : in a justifiable manner : DEFENSIBLY, EXCUSABLY ⟨~ classified as secret —D.W.Mitchell⟩ ⟨~ expects early action —H.S.Truman⟩
jus·ti·fi·can·dum \,jəstəfə'kandəm\ n, pl **justifican·da** \-də\ [LL, neut. of *justificandus*, gerundive of *justificare* to justify — more at JUSTIFY] : something that is to be justified — compare JUSTIFICANS
jus·ti·fi·cans \,jəstəfə'kanz\ n, pl **justifican·tia** \-nchēə\ [LL, pres. part. of *justificare*] : something (as a principle) that serves to justify
jus·ti·fi·ca·tion \,jəstəfə'kāshən\ n -s [ME *justificacioun*, fr. LL *justification-, justificatio*, fr. *justificatus* (past part. of *justificare* to justify) + *-ion-, -io* -ion] **1 a** : the act, process, or state of being justified by God **b** : the terms under which one is so justified **2 a** (1) : the act or an instance of justifying : VINDICATION, DEFENSE ⟨the ~ of barbarous means by holy ends —H.J.Muller⟩ (2) : the condition of being justified ⟨doubted the historical ~ of the Confiteor . . . in any Lutheran liturgy —S.G.Hefelbower⟩ (3) : something that justifies ⟨finds in it the ~ . . . of his own work —A.P.d'Entrèves⟩ ⟨its only logical ~ would have been swift military success —Hugh Gaitskell⟩ **b** (1) : the showing in court of a sufficient lawful reason why a party charged or accused did or failed to do that for which he is called to answer (2) : something that constitutes such a reason (3) : the justifying of sureties (as on a bail bond) **c** : the act or an instance of verifying or proving ⟨the purpose of ~ is to produce conviction in the hearer —John Ladd⟩ **3** : the process or result of justifying (as a line of type)
jus·ti·fi·ca·tive \'jəstəfə,kād·iv, ,jə'stifə,kād·iv, ¦jəstə¦fikəd·iv\ adj [prob. fr. F *justificatif*, fr. MF, fr. LL *justificatus* (past part.) + MF *-if* -ive] : serving to justify : JUSTIFICATORY
jus·tif·i·ca·to·ry \,jə'stifəkə,tōrē, ¦jəstə¦fikə,-, 'jəstəfəkə,-tōr-, -ri, *esp Brit* ¦jəstifi¦kātəri *or* -ā·tri\ adj [LL *justificatus* (past part.) + E *-ory*] : tending or serving to justify : VINDICATORY
jus·ti·fi·er \'jəstə,fī(ə)r, -īə\ n -s : one that justifies: as **a** : a person who vindicates or absolves **b** : a graver for trimming the walls in enamel work
jus·ti·fy \'jəstə,fī\ vb -ED/-ING/-s [ME *justifien*, fr. MF or LL; MF *justifier*, fr. OF, fr. LL *justificare*, fr. L *justus* just + *-ficare* -fy — more at JUST] vt **1 a** (1) : to prove or show to be just, desirable, warranted, or useful : VINDICATE ⟨science *justifies* itself when it contributes to the desire to know —*Scientific American Reader*⟩ ⟨*justified* to herself his every fault —Ruth Park⟩ ⟨most cats must ~ themselves by catching mice —Charlton Laird⟩ ⟨~ the ways of God to man —John Milton⟩ ⟨undertaking to ~ a single scale of rates for the entire country —*Collier's Yr. Bk.*⟩ ⟨the welcome he received *justified* his visit —A.R.Forde⟩ (2) *obs* : to confirm, maintain, or acknowledge as true, lawful, or legitimate **b** : to prove or show to be valid, sound, or conforming to fact or reason : furnish grounds or evidence for : CONFIRM, SUPPORT, VERIFY ⟨their immediate jubilant reaction has been abundantly *justified* by the sales —Peter Forster⟩ ⟨attempts to ~ his definition of cartography —*Geographical Journal*⟩ ⟨insinuation of personal interest as a determining factor seems to me not *justified* by the facts shown —O.W.Holmes †1935⟩ ⟨*justified* my fondest hopes —D.G.Gerahty⟩ **c** (1) : to show to have had a sufficient legal reason (as that the libel charged is true or that the trespass charged was by license of the possessor) for (an act made the subject of a charge or accusation) (2) : to qualify (oneself) as a surety by taking oath to the ownership of sufficient property **2 a** *archaic* : to execute justice upon : administer justice to **b** *archaic* : to pronounce free from guilt or blame : ABSOLVE ⟨I think — or at least hope — you would have *justified* me —George Meredith⟩ **c** : to judge, regard, or treat as righteous, worthy of salvation, or as freed from the future penalty of sin ⟨God *justifies* with his forgiveness and grace the man who comes to him —Will Herberg⟩ **3 a** : to make level and square the body of (a typefounder's strike) **b** : to set to fit the measure or space closely (as a line of type, matrices, photocomposition, typewriting) or so that all full lines are of equal length and flush right and left (as typewritten matter) **c** : to cause to align evenly at the bottom (as letters of different size) **d** : to adjust to fit and lock up securely (set letterpress matter) ~ vi **1 a** : to show a sufficient lawful reason (as that the plaintiff consented to an act alleged to be a trespass) for an act done or not done **b** : to qualify as bail or surety by taking oath to the ownership of sufficient property ⟨the surety *justified* on the bail bond⟩ **2** : to accept and receive as just or righteous those who respond in wholehearted faith to God as revealed by Jesus Christ ⟨believing with all their being that God *justified* through faith —John Dillenberger & Claude Welch⟩ **3** *printing* **a** : to be capable of or susceptible of justification **b** : to become justified **syn** see EXPLAIN, MAINTAIN
justifying space or **justification space** n : a space that is set by striking the spacebar of a keyboard typesetting machine and that has no predetermined width
justing *var of* JOUSTING
jus·tin·i·a·ni·an or **jus·tin·i·a·ne·an** \,jə¦stinē¦ānēən\ adj, usu cap [*Justinian* fr. *Justinian* I †565 Byzantine emperor (fr. LL *Justinianus*) + E *-ian*; *Justinianean* fr. LL *Justinianeus* of Justinian (fr. *Justinianus* Justinian) + E *-an*] : of or relating to the Byzantine emperor Justinian under whom much of the Western Empire was reconquered and the laws codified in the Justinian Code ⟨the *Justinianean* ordinances on the subject of divorce were revived —B.J.Kidd⟩
justle *var of* JOSTLE
just·ly adv [ME, fr. *just* (adj.) + *-ly*] : in a just manner: as **a** *chiefly dial* : EXACTLY, PRECISELY, QUITE ⟨do not ~ know what your taste in reasons may be —Thomas Gray⟩ **b** : in conformity with law or justice : FAIRLY ⟨treated all his employees ~⟩ **c** : in conformity with fact or reason : CORRECTLY, PROPERLY ⟨~ ranked among the most wonderful efforts of the human hand —H.T.Buckle⟩ ⟨helps them to reason more ~ —M.R.Cohen⟩ **d** : in a manner appropriate to or required by the case : RIGHTLY, FITTINGLY, ACCURATELY ⟨essential that it be well developed and ~ proportioned to the other body measurements —H.G.Armstrong⟩ ⟨expresses quivering nervous strain more ~ than any player we have —*Current Biog.*⟩
just·ness \'jəs(t)nəs\ n -ES [ME *justnesse*, fr. *just* (adj.) + *-nesse* -ness] : the quality or state of being just: as **a** : RIGHTEOUSNESS, UPRIGHTNESS ⟨address as Jehovah a composite idea of authority, fatherhood, ~ —Joseph Macleod⟩ **b** : conformity with truth or reason : VALIDITY, FAIRNESS, SOUNDNESS ⟨the ~ and propriety of their sentiments —William Cowper⟩ **c** : conformity with some standard of aesthetic correctness or propriety : RIGHTNESS, ACCURACY, PRECISION, NICETY ⟨set forth with a ~ and care that proclaimed him a master orchestral artisan —Winthrop Sargeant⟩ ⟨estimating the ~ of the imitation —Irving Babbitt⟩ ⟨impressive in the absolute ~ of its design —R.M.Coates⟩ ⟨which he renders with a memorable ~ and beauty —Edward Sackville-West⟩
just-noticeable difference n : the minimum difference perceptible in any part of a series of sensory qualities ordinarily determined by reference to the corresponding stimulus conditions : the smallest perceptible change in a stimulus situation
just price n [trans. of ML *justum pretium*] **1** : a price conforming to the doctrine developed in antiquity and elaborated in the medieval period that price should in general correspond to the cost of production **2** : a price approved by common estimate, determined by a legal maximum, or conforming to some other standard of rightness or equity
justs *pl of* JUST
just the same adv : even so : NEVERTHELESS ⟨*just the same* I would trust him implicitly⟩
jus uten·di \¦jəsyü'tendē, -,dī\ n [L, right of using] : a personal right or servitude of one gratuitously for the needs of himself and his family and without profit to make use of another's property without consuming it or destroying its substance or capacity for future profit

[1]**jut** \ˈjət, *usu* -əd·+V\ *vb* **jutted; jutted; jutting; juts** [perh. back-formation fr. [1]*jutty*] *vi* **:** to shoot out or forward **:** PROTRUDE ⟨a cigar *jutting* from his teeth —J.A.Michener⟩ ⟨narrow bony shoulders *jutting* from his undershirt —James Jones⟩ ⟨cliffs *jutting* straight up —Peggy Durdin⟩ ⟨hurdles that ~ into the river —Murray Schumach⟩ **~** *vt* **:** to cause to jut ⟨*jutting* out his jaw humorously —Phelim Brady⟩ **syn** see BULGE

[2]**jut** \ˈ"\ *n* -s **:** something that projects or juts **:** PROJECTION ⟨passed behind a ~ of the shore —B.A.Williams⟩

[1]**jute** \ˈjüt, *usu* -üd·+V\ *n* -s *cap* [ME *Jute*, fr. ML *Jutae, Juti*, pl., Jutes, of Gmc origin; akin to OE *Eotas, Eotenas, Iotas* Jutes, ON *Jōtar*] **:** a member of one of the Low German peoples of Jutland of whom some settled in Kent in the 5th century — **jut·ish** \-üd·ish\ *adj, usu cap*

[2]**jute** \ˈ"\ *n* -s *often attrib* [Hindi & Bengali *jūt*, prob. fr. Skt *jūṭa* matted hair] **1 :** the glossy fiber of either of two East Indian plants (*Corchorus olitorius* and *C. capsularis*) used chiefly for sacking, burlap, and the cheaper varieties of twine **2 :** either of the two plants producing this fiber; *also* **:** any other plant of the genus *Corchorus*

jute board *n* **:** a strong plyboard containing no jute fiber but made typically from sulfate and wastepaper pulps and used esp. for shipping containers

jute butts *n pl* **:** fiber from the thick woody butt of the jute stalk used for bagging, twine, paper stock

jute paper *n* **:** a strong paper made largely from jute fiber — compare JUTE BOARD

jutia *var of* HUTIA

jut–jawed \ˈ≈ˌ≈\ *adj* **:** having a jutting jaw ⟨his head was big, *jut-jawed* —Will Henry⟩

[1]**jut·lan·dic** \ˌjətˈlandik\ *adj, usu cap* [*Jutland*, Denmark + E *-ic*] **1 a :** of, relating to, or characteristic of Jutland **b :** of, relating to, or characteristic of the people of Jutland **2 :** of, relating to, or characteristic of the Jutlandic dialect

[2]**jutlandic** \"\ *n* -s *cap* **:** the Danish dialect of Jutland in western Denmark

jutting *adj* **:** PROJECTING, PROTRUDING ⟨the powerful ~ jaw —A.L.Kroeber⟩ — **jut·ting·ly** *adv*

[1]**jut·ty** \ˈjəd·ē\ *vb* -ED/-ING/-ES [ME *jutteyen*] *archaic* **:** to project beyond **:** JUT

[2]**jutty** \"\ *n* -ES [ME *jutte, jutty*, perh. alter. of *jette* jetty] **1** *archaic* **:** PIER, JETTY **2 :** a projecting part of a building ⟨an ugly assortment of *jutties*, ornaments, and blind windows —Joseph Wechsberg⟩

juv *abbr* **1** [L *juvenis*] young **2** juvenile

[1]**ju·ve·nal** \ˈjüvənᵊl\ *n* -s [L *juvenalis*, adj.] *archaic* **:** YOUTH ⟨forever . . . ~s in limb and spirit —*Observer*⟩

[2]**juvenal** \"\ *adj* [L *juvenalis*, fr. *juvenis* young person + *-alis* -al] **:** of, relating to, or being a juvenile ⟨~ bobwhite quail —*Wildlife Rev.*⟩

[3]**juvenal** \"\ *n* -s *usu cap* [after *Juvenal* † *ab* A.D. 140 Roman lawyer and satirist (fr. L D. Junius *Juvenalis*)] **:** a writer resembling or suggestive of the Roman poet Juvenal in his use of biting satire and pungent realism — **ju·ve·na·li·an** \ˌjüvəˈnālēən\ *adj, usu cap*

juvenal plumage *n* [[2]*juvenal*] **:** the plumage of a bird immediately succeeding the natal down

ju·ve·nes·cence \ˌjüvəˈnesᵊn(t)s\ *n* -s [[2]*juvenal* + *-escence*] **:** the state of being youthful or of growing young ⟨if she gave any evidence of ~, he had managed to overlook it —Josephine Pinckney⟩

[1]**ju·ve·nile** \ˈjüvəˌnīl, -ˌnᵊl *sometimes* -(ˌ)nil\ *adj* [F or L; F *juvénile*, fr. L *juvenilis*, fr. *juvenis* young person (fr. *juvenis* young) + *-ilis* -ile — more at YOUNG] **1 a :** of, relating to, or being a juvenile **:** physiologically immature or undeveloped **:** YOUNG ⟨the baby snake varies in color and markings from the ~ —*Farmer's Weekly (So. Africa)*⟩ ⟨his appearance was ~ —Elinor Wylie⟩ ⟨a ~ period that is essentially asexual —W.C.Allee⟩ ⟨gave her a most ~ and engaging look —Edna Ferber⟩ ⟨ten ~ years of my life —F.N.Souza⟩ **b :** being or remaining in a youthful stage of development; *specif* **:** being a plant in which the leaves are assumed to be similar to ancestral adult forms **c :** MAGMATIC ⟨~ waters⟩ **2 a :** of, relating to, characteristic of, or suitable for children or young people ⟨a ~ book⟩ ⟨a ~ phase of love not yet warmed into passion —C.W.Cunnington⟩ ⟨a ~ membership of 82,111 —C.W.Ferguson⟩ **b :** being or relating to an actor who plays a youthful part ⟨played the ~ lead in a new hit⟩ **3 :** reflecting psychological or intellectual immaturity **:** unworthy of an adult **:** CHILDISH ⟨the ~ customs of fraternities —Harold Taylor⟩ ⟨regarded their desperate rebellion as ~ melodrama —Paul Blanshard⟩ ⟨~ behavior⟩ **syn** see YOUTHFUL

[2]**juvenile** \"\ *n* -s **1 a :** a young person **:** CHILD, YOUTH ⟨observed some of the evil effects of factory labor upon ~s —Paul Woodring⟩ ⟨leader of a gang of ~s who stole a car recently —*Springfield (Mass.) Daily News*⟩ **b :** a book for children or young people ⟨a general trade book as well as a ~ —*Publishers' Weekly*⟩ **2 a :** a young individual fundamentally like an adult of its kind except in size and reproductive activity **b :** a bird in juvenal plumage **c :** a 2-year old racehorse **3 :** an actor who plays youthful parts; *sometimes* **:** an actress who plays such parts

juvenile court *n* **:** a court having special jurisdiction over delinquent and dependent children usu. up to the age of 18 and emphasizing in practice clinical and casework techniques with goals of delinquency prevention and rehabilitation of the child rather than punishment

juvenile delinquency *n* **1 :** a status in a juvenile characterized by antisocial behavior (as truancy, waywardness, incorrigibility) that is beyond parental control and therefore subject to legal action **2 :** a violation of the law of the U.S. that is committed by a juvenile and that is not punishable by death or life imprisonment

juvenile delinquent *n* **:** a person adjudged to be a delinquent under an age fixed by law (as 16 or 18 years or 21 years in a few states)

juvenile insurance *n* **:** insurance upon the life of a child usu. issued to a parent who signs the application and pays the early premiums

juvenile officer *n* **:** a police officer charged with the detection, prosecution, and care of juvenile delinquents — compare PROBATION OFFICER

ju·ve·nil·ia \ˌjüvəˈnilēə\ *n pl but sometimes sing in constr* [L, neut. pl. of *juvenilis* juvenile] **1 :** artistic or literary compositions produced in the author's youth and typically marked by immaturity of style, treatment, or thought **:** youthful writing or other artistic work ⟨essentially ~ and are only interesting as such —*Times Lit. Supp.*⟩ ⟨a curious piece of ~ —Milton Crane⟩ ⟨is still ~ — magnificent ~ —Graham Greene⟩ **2 a :** artistic or literary compositions suited to or designed for the young ⟨the crown jewels of ~ —*Saturday Rev.*⟩ **b :** a book, film, or other composition of such character ⟨endow this ~ with what little verisimilitude it has —*Newsweek*⟩

ju·ve·nil·i·ty \ˌjüvəˈniləd·ē, -ətē, -i\ *n* -ES [L *juvenilitat-, juvenilitas*, fr. *juvenilis* juvenile + *-itat-, -itas* -ity] **1 :** youthful condition or manner **2 a :** immaturity of thought or conduct **:** CHILDISHNESS ⟨reveals the fatal ~ . . . beneath the sophisticated surface —D.S.Savage⟩ ⟨the ~ of grown-up people —B.I.Bell⟩ **b :** an instance of such immaturity — usu. used in pl. ⟨pettiness, *juvenilities* —John Adams⟩

ju·via \ˈhüvēə, ˈzhü-\ *n* -s [Sp & Pg, of Arawakan origin; akin to Baniva *iuiya, yuviya* juvia, Baré *yuhiya*] **:** BRAZIL NUT

juxta- *comb form* [L *juxta*, adv. & prep., near, nearby — more at JOUST] **:** situated near ⟨*juxta*-articular⟩ ⟨*juxta*medullary⟩

jux·ta·pose \ˈjəkstəˌpōz *sometimes* ˌ≈≈ˈ≈\ *vt* [prob. fr. E *juxtaposition*, after such pairs as *interposition: interpose*] **:** to place side by side **:** place in juxtaposition ⟨the huts were never closely *juxtaposed* —V.G.Childe⟩ ⟨words perpetually *juxtaposed* in new and sudden combinations —T.S.Eliot⟩ ⟨pain has been . . . *juxtaposed* to pleasure as a form of emotion —F.A.Geldard⟩

juxtaposed *adj* **:** placed side by side **:** being in juxtaposition **syn** see ADJACENT

jux·ta·pos·it \ˌ≈≈ˈpäzət\ *vt* -ED/-ING/-S [L *juxta* near + *positus*, past part. of *ponere* to place — more at POSITION] **:** JUXTAPOSE

jux·ta·po·si·tion \ˌjəkstəpəˈzishən\ *n* -s [L *juxta* near + E *position*] **:** the act or an instance of placing two or more objects in a close spatial or ideal relationship ⟨the proper ~ of rocks, trees —D.C.Buchanan⟩ ⟨the ~ of abstract with concrete, of the homely with the far-fetched —C.D.Lewis⟩; *also* **:** the condition of being so placed ⟨forested mountains and the sea were in ~ —A.L.Kroeber⟩ ⟨the resulting ~ of popular epic and village song —G.F.Jones⟩ — **jux·ta·po·si·tion·al** \ˌ≈≈≈ˈzishənᵊl, -shnəl\ *adj*

JV *abbr* **1** Japanese vellum **2** junior varsity

JVP *abbr* Japanese vellum proofs

JW *abbr* junior warden

jwlr *abbr* jeweler

jyn·gine \ˈjinˌjīn, -njən\ *adj* [NL *Jyng-, Jynx* + E *-ine*] **:** of or relating to the genus *Jynx*

jynx \ˈjiŋ(k)s\ *n* [L *iynx*, fr. Gk] **1** -ES **:** WRYNECK **2** *cap* [NL, fr. L *iynx*] **:** a genus of woodpeckers consisting of the wrynecks

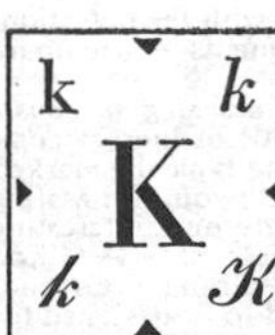

¹k \'kā\ *n, pl* **k's** *or* **ks** \'kāz\ *often cap, often attrib* **1 a :** the 11th letter of the English alphabet **b :** an instance of this letter printed, written, or otherwise represented **c :** a speech counterpart of orthographic *k* (as *k* in *kill, skill, like, joked,* or German *kühn*) **2 :** a printer's type, a stamp, or some other instrument for reproducing the letter *k* **3 :** someone or something arbitrarily or conveniently designated *k* esp. as the 10th or when j is used for the 10th the 11th in order or class **4 :** something having the shape of the letter K **5 :** a unit vector parallel to the z-axis
²k *abbr, often cap* **1** [L *kalendae*] calends **2** karat **3** [*kathode*] cathode **4** keel **5** keg **6** Kelvin **7** key **8** kilo- **9** kilogram **10** king **11** kip **12** kitchen **13** knight **14** knit **15** knot **16** kopeck **17** koruna **18** kran **19** krona **20** krone **21** kroon **22** kurus
³k *symbol* **1** *cap* [NL *kalium*] potassium **2** *often cap* constant **3** [G *konstant*] Boltzmann's constant **4** thermal conductivity **5 a** key — used as a cryptographic subscript ⟨B_p $(D_k) = E_e$ means that D was used as the key letter when B was enciphered into E⟩; see VIGENÈRE CIPHER **b** *cap* a cryptographic numerical keying element or the numerical value of a key letter when the normal alphabet is numbered from 0 to 25 ⟨P + C = K is the Beaufort keying method⟩ **6** *cap* **:** dissociation constant **7** *cap* **:** ionization constant
¹ka *var of* KAY
²ka \'kō, 'kä\ *chiefly Scot var of* CALL
³ka \'kä\ *n* -s [Egypt] **:** the personality double believed in ancient Egypt to be born with an individual and after death to reside in the statue of the deceased in the tomb dependent upon the preservation and nourishment of the body
⁴ka *usu cap, var of* KHA
ka *abbr* [*kathode*] cathode
KA *abbr* king of arms
kaa·ba *or* **ka'·ba** *also* **ka'·bah** *or* **caa·ba** \'käbə, 'kȧbə\ *adj, usu cap* [Ar *ka'bah,* lit., square building, fr. *ka'b* cube] **:** of or relating to the Islamic shrine in Mecca that incorporates a sacred black stone and is the goal of Islamic pilgrimage and the point toward which all Muslims turn in praying — see QIBLA
kaa·ma \'kämə\ *n* -s [Hottentot (Nama dial.) *ǃxamap, Kamab*] **:** HARTEBEEST
kaa·wi yam \'käwē\ *n* [origin unknown] **:** a yam (*Dioscorea aculeata*) of southern Asia and Polynesia with prickly stems and sweet tubers
kab *var of* CAB
ka·babish \kə'babish, -'bäb-\ *n, pl* **kababish** *or* **kababishes** *usu cap* **1 :** a nomadic Arab people in the Anglo-Egyptian Sudan **2 :** a member of the Kababish people
ka·ba·ka \kə'bäkə\ *n* -s [native name in Uganda] **:** the native king of Buganda in Uganda ⟨the Colonial Office a year ago exiled the *Kabaka . . .* of Buganda —*N.Y. Times*⟩
kabala *or* **kabbala** *or* **kabbalah** *often cap, var of* CABALA
kabalassou *var of* CABALASSOU
kabalist *var of* CABALIST
ka·ba·ra·go·ya \kə,bärə'gȯyə\ *n* -s [origin unknown] **:** a large water monitor (*Varanus salvator*) of southeastern Asia, the Malay archipelago, and the Philippines that sometimes reaches a length of seven feet
ka·bar·din \¦kabər¦dēn, ¦käbər-, ¦kä,bär-\ *also* **ka·bard** \kə'bärd\ *n* -s *cap* **1 :** a member of a Circassian people of the Caucasus mountains who comprise over half the population of the Kabardino-Balkarian Autonomous Soviet Socialist Republic and whose religion is Islam **2** *or* **ka·bar·di·an** \kə'bärdēən\ **:** the Caucasic language of the Kabardins — **ka·bar·din·i·an** \¦kabər¦dinēən\ *adj, usu cap*
kabassou *var of* CABASSOU
kab·ba·lah \kə'bälə\ *n* -s [Heb *qabbālāh,* lit., received, fr. *qābēl* to receive] **:** a written certificate issued by a rabbi to a prospective shohet who has passed an examination testing his knowledge of and expertness in shehitah
kabbalist *var of* CABALIST
ka·bel·jou *also* **ka·bel·jau** *or* **ka·bel·jauw** \'käbəl,yaů, 'kab-\ *n* -s [Afrik *kabeljou,* fr. D *kabeljauw* cod] **:** a large South African sciaenid food fish (*Johnius hololepidotus*) having a liver extremely rich in vitamin A that is closely related to and sometimes held identical with the European maigre
kabinda *usu cap, var of* CABINDA
ka·bir·pan·thi \kə,bir'pənˌtē\ *n* -s *usu cap* [Hindi *kabīrpanthī* fr. *Kabīr* †1518 Hindu mystic poet + *panthī* follower] **:** a member of a reform sect of India originating in the 15th century with doctrines based on the teachings of Kabir
ka·bi·stan \¦käbə¦stän, ¦kabə¦stan\ *n* -s *usu cap* [*Kabistan, Kabristan,* locality in southeastern Dagestan, U.S.S.R.] **:** ¹KUBA
ka·bob *also* **ka·bab** *or* **ke·bab** *or* **ke·bob** *or* **ca·bob** \'kä,bäb, kə'bäb; *when "shish" precedes,* kə,bäb\ *n* -s [Per, Hindi, Ar, & Turk; Per & Hindi *kabāb,* fr. Ar, fr. Turk *kebap*] **:** cubes of meat (as lamb) marinated and cooked with onions, tomatoes, or other vegetables esp. on a skewer — usu. used in pl.
kaboodle *var of* CABOODLE
ka·bui \kə'büē\ *n, pl* **kabui** *or* **kabuis** *cap* **1 :** a Naga people of the Naga hills on the Burma-Assam frontier west and northwest of Manipur valley **2 :** a member of the Kabui people
kab·u·kal·li \,kabə'kalē\ *n* -s [native name in British Guiana] **:** CUPIUBA
ka·bu·ki \kə¦bükē, -'bükē, *Jap approximately* 'käbü(,)kē\ *n, usu cap* [Jap, lit., art of singing and dancing] **:** traditional Japanese popular drama with singing and dancing performed in a highly stylized manner
ka·bul \'käbəl, -,bül, -,bül; kə'bül, ka'-, -'bül\ *adj, usu cap* [fr. *Kabul,* city in eastern Afghanistan, capital of Afghanistan] **:** of or from Kabul, the capital of Afghanistan **:** of the kind or style prevalent in Kabul
¹ka·bu·li \'käbə(,)lē; kə'bülē, -'bülē\ *adj, usu cap* [Per *kābulī,* fr. *Kābul* Kabul] **:** of or belonging to Kabul, Afghanistan
²kabuli \"\ *n* -s *cap* **:** a native or resident of Kabul
ka·bu·ri \kə'bürē\ *n* -s [origin unknown] **:** a land crab (*Ucides cordatus*) common in mangrove swamps from the West Indies to southern Brazil
ka·byle *also* **ka·byl** \kə'bī(ə)l, -bē(ə)l\ *n* -s *usu cap* [Ar *qabā'il,* pl. of *qabīlah* tribe] **1 :** a Berber belonging to a Muslim agricultural people of the mountainous coastal area east of Algiers including blond and brunet types and now speaking chiefly Arabic **2 :** the Berber language of the Kabyles
kacha *or* **kachcha** *var of* KUTCHA
ka·cha na·ga \¦kächə¦nägə\ *n, pl* **kacha nagas** *usu cap K&N* **1 :** a group of three allied Naga peoples including the Kabui, the Lyeng, and the Zemi and inhabiting the Naga hills near Manipur **2 :** a member of a Kacha Naga people
kachari *usu cap, var of* CACHARI
kache *usu cap, var of* KHA
kach·e·mak bay \¦kachə,mak¦bā\ *adj, usu cap K&B* [*Kachemak Bay,* locality south of Anchorage, south central Alaska, where remains of the culture were discovered] **:** of or relating to a Pacific Eskimo and Aleutian culture of about A.D. 100–1700 characterized by sealing and by the development of southwest Alaskan types of artifacts and the introduction of foreign traits
¹ka·chin \kə'chin\ *n, pl* **kachin** *or* **kachins** *usu cap* **1 :** CHINGPAW **2 :** the Tibeto-Burman language of the Chingpaw people
²kach·in \'kachən\ *n* -s [perh. alter. of *catechin*] **:** pyrocatechol used as a photographic developer
ka·chi·na *or* **ka·tci·na** *also* **ka·tchi·na** *or* **ca·chi·na** \kə'chēnə\ *n* -s [Hopi *qačina* supernatural] **1 :** one of the deified ancestral spirits believed among the Hopi and other Pueblo Indians to visit the pueblos at intervals (as to bring rain) **2 :** one of the elaborately masked impersonators of the kachinas that dance at agricultural ceremonies **3** *or* **kachina doll :** a doll representing a kachina made from cottonwood root and given to Hopi children by the kachina dancers
k acid *n, cap K* **:** a crystalline sulfonic acid $NH_2C_{10}H_4(OH)(SO_3H)_2$ isomeric with H acid that is used as a dye intermediate; 8-amino-1-naphthol-3,5-disulfonic acid
kackle *var of* KECKLE
ka·da·ga \kə'dägə\ *n, pl* **kadaga** *or* **kadagas** *usu cap* **:** COORG
ka·dai \'kä,dī\ *n* -s *usu cap* **:** a language family of southern China and northern Vietnam held to be related to Thai
ka·dam·ba \kə'dambə\ *n* -s [Skt, of Dravidian origin; akin to Tamil-Malayalam *kaṭampu*] **1 :** an East Indian shade tree (*Anthocephalus cadamba*) of the family Rubiaceae having hard yellowish wood and globose clusters of flowers **2 :** the wood of the kadamba
kadarite *usu cap, var of* QADARITE
ka·da·ya gum \kə'dīə-\ *n* [*kadaya* modif. of Hindi *karāyal* resin] **:** STERCULIA GUM
kad·dish \'kädish\ *n, pl* **kad·di·shim** \kä'dishəm, -(,)-shēm\ *often cap* [Aram *qaddīsh* holy] **1 :** an ancient Jewish prayer in Aramaic recited in several forms by the cantor in the daily ritual of the synagogue and adopted for use on various occasions; *specif* **:** a mourner's prayer recited daily at public services during the first 11 months after the death of a parent or other close relative and on subsequent anniversaries of the death **2 :** the person (as traditionally a son) who recites the mourner's kaddish for the deceased
kadet *var of* ²CADET
kadi *also* **kadhi** *var of* QADI
kadiak bear *usu cap K, var of* KODIAK BEAR
ka·dir *also* **kha·dar** *or* **kha·dir** \'kädə(r)\ *n, pl* **kadir** *or* **kadirs** *usu cap* **:** a primitive jungle-dwelling people somewhat negroid in appearance who are remnants of the pre-Dravidian peoples of India and inhabit the Deccan plateau
ka·do·ha·da·cho \kə,dōhədə'chō\ *n, pl* **kadohadacho** *or* **kadohadachos** *usu cap* [Caddo *Kädohădächo,* lit., real chiefs] **1 :** a Caddoan confederacy of northeastern Texas and southwestern Arkansas including the Cahinnio, Kadohadacho proper, and Upper Natchitoches **2 :** a member of any one of the peoples of the Kadohadacho confederacy
kad·su·ra \'kädsərə, 'käts-\ *n* -s [modif. of Jap *katsura*] **:** KATSURA TREE
ka·du \'kä(,)dü\ *n, pl* **kadu** *or* **kadus** *usu cap* **1 a :** a people inhabiting chiefly the Katha district of Upper Burma east of Manipur, Assam **b :** a member of such people **2 :** the Tibeto-Burman language of the Kadu people
ka·dy *or* **ka·ty** *also* **ca·dy** \'kād¦ē, -āt¦, ¦i\ *or* **cad·dy** \'kad¦\ *n* -ES [perh. alter. of *caddie;* fr. its being worn by boys] **:** a man's hat (as a straw hat or derby)
kae \'kā\ *n* -s [ME (northern dial.) *ka;* akin to MD *ca* jackdaw, OHG *kāa, kā* — more at CHOUGH] *chiefly Scot* **:** JACKDAW
kae·ding petrel \'kādiŋ-\ *or* **kaeding's petrel** *n, usu cap K* [after Henry B. *Kaeding* †1913 Am. mining engineer] **:** a petrel (*Oceanodroma leucorhoa kaedingi*) of the coast and islands of Lower California that is closely related to the Leach's petrel but smaller and with a less forked tail
kaemp·fer·ol \'kempfə,rōl, -rȯl\ *also* **kamp·fer·ol** \'kam-\ *n* -s [Engelbert *Kämpfer* †1716 Ger. physician + ISV *-ol*] **:** a yellow crystalline flavonol coloring matter $C_{15}H_{10}O_6$ found in the free form or in glycosidic combination in many plants
kaf *var of* KAPH
ka·fa *or* **kaf·fa** \'käfə, 'kafə\ *n, pl* **kafa** *or* **kaffa** *usu cap* **1 :** a native or inhabitant of the Kafa region in southwestern Ethiopia **2 :** the Cushitic language of the Kafa
kaf·er·i·ta \,kafə'rēd·ə\ *n* -s [blend of *kaffir* and *feterita*] **:** a hybrid between kafir and feterita
kaf·fa \'käfə, 'kafə\ *n* -s *often cap* [*Kaffa, Kafa,* region and former province in southwestern Ethiopia] **:** a grayish reddish brown that is yellower and lighter than liver and redder and stronger than average taupe brown
kaf·fee·klatsch \'käfə,kläch, -fē,-, -lach\ *n* -ES *often cap* [G, fr. *Kaffee* coffee + *Klatsch* gossip] **:** COFFEE KLATCH
kaf·fir *or* **kaf·ir** \'kafə(r)\ *n* [Ar *kāfir* infidel] **1** *also* **caf·fer** *or* **caf·fre** \"\ *pl* **kaffir** *or* **kaffirs** *or* **kafir** *or* **kafirs a** *usu cap* **:** a member of a group of southern African Bantu-speaking peoples of Ngoni stock **b** *sometimes cap* **:** a South African of negroid ancestry — usu. used disparagingly **2** *also* **caffer** *or* **caffre** -s *sometimes cap* **:** one who is not a Muslim — usu. used disparagingly **3** -s *usu cap* **:** XHOSA — often used disparagingly **4** -s *usu cap* **:** a South African stock (as a land or mining share) traded on the London stock exchange — usu. used in pl. **5** *usu* **kafir** *or* **kafir corn** -s *sometimes cap K* **:** any of various grain sorghums that have stout short-jointed somewhat juicy stalks and erect heads
kaffir bean *n, usu cap K, Africa* **:** COWPEA
kaffir beer *n, usu cap K* **:** a beer prepared by the native population of southern Africa from grain
kaffir boom \-,bōm, -,büm\ *n, often cap K* [part trans. of Afrik *kafferboom,* fr. *Kaffer* Kaffir + *boom* tree, fr. D, fr. MD; akin to OE *bēam* tree — more at BEAM] *Africa* **:** CORAL TREE; *esp* **:** a coral tree (*Erythrina caffra*) with scarlet flowers and light soft wood sometimes used for fence posts or shingles
kaffir bread *n, usu cap K* **1 :** the farinaceous pith of the fruit of a plant of the genus *Encephalartos* (esp. *E. caffer*) used as food in southern Africa **2 :** a plant that bears Kaffir bread
kaffir cat *also* **caffer cat** *or* **caffre cat** *n, usu cap K or 1st C* **:** a widely distributed wildcat (*Felis ocreata,* syn. *F. caffra*) of Africa and Asia Minor that has a tawny striped coat and is regarded as one of the chief ancestors of domesticated cats
kaffir crane *n, usu cap K* **:** a slaty gray crane (*Balearica regulorum*) of southern Africa that has a crown of velvety black plumes
kaffir lily *n, usu cap K* **1 :** CRIMSON FLAG **2 :** a plant of the genus *Clivia; esp* **:** a plant (*C. miniata*) of southern Africa cultivated for its showy flowers
kaffir orange *n, usu cap K* **1 :** an East African tree (*Strychnos spinosa*) having rough bark, grayish green foliage, and dark green round aromatic fruit with hard rind and soft pulp **2 :** the fruit of the Kaffir orange
kaffir piano *n, usu cap K* **:** a marimba of southern Africa
kaffir plum *or* **kaffir date** *n, usu cap K* **1 :** an African tree (*Harpephyllum caffrum*) of the family Anacardiaceae **2 :** the edible fruit of Kaffir plum
kaf·fi·yeh *also* **kef·fi·yeh** \kə'fē(y)ə\ *n* -s [Ar *kūfīyah, kaffīyah* — more at CAFFA] **:** an Arab headdress consisting of a square of cloth folded to form a triangle and bound on the head with an agal
kaf·frar·i·an *also* **caf·frar·i·an** \ka'fra(a)rēən, kə'-\ *adj, usu cap* [*Kaffraria,* region of Cape Province, Union of South Africa + E *-an*] **:** of, relating to, or being the biogeographic province or subregion that includes the Union of South Africa and adjacent areas
kaf·ir \'kafə(r)\ *n, pl* **kafir** *or* **kafirs** *usu cap* [Ar *kāfir* infidel] **1 :** a people of the Hindu Kush in northeastern Afghanistan **2 :** a member of the Kafir people
kafi·ri \'kafərē, kə'firē\ *n* -s *usu cap* **:** the Dard language of the Kafir people
kaftan *var of* CAFTAN
ka·fu·an \kə'füən\ *adj, usu cap* [*Kafu* River, Uganda + E *-an*] **:** of, relating to, or being a Lower Pleistocene culture of Uganda typified by crudely chipped pebble tools
kagaba *usu cap, var of* CÁGABA
ka·go \'kä(,)gō\ *n* -s [Jap] **:** an open palanquin used in Japan
ka·go·shi·ma \¦kägə¦shēmə\ *adj, usu cap* [fr. *Kagoshima,* city on the south coast of Kyushu, Japan] **:** of or from the city of Kagoshima, Japan **:** of the kind or style prevalent in Kagoshima
ka·gu \'kä(,)gü\ *n* -s [native name in New Caledonia] **:** a crested flightless gruiform bird (*Rhynochetos jubatus*) confined to New Caledonia that is slaty gray with orange-red bill and feet and concealed bars of black, white, and rufous on the wings
ka·gu·ra \'kägə(,)rä\ *n* -s [Jap] **:** a stately dance of the Shinto religion that now forms a part of Japanese village festivals
ka·ha \'kä(,)hä, ='=\ *or* **ka·hau** \-,haů, ='=\ *n* -s [native name in Borneo; fr. its cry] **:** PROBOSCIS MONKEY
ka·hal \'kä,häl\ *n* -s [Heb *qāhal* community, gathering] **:** the local governing body of a former European Jewish community administering religious, legal, and communal affairs
ka·ha·la \kə'hälə\ *n* -s [Hawaiian] **:** an amberfish (*Seriola dumerili*) of Hawaiian waters
ka·har \kə'här\ *n* -s [Hindi *kahār*] **:** one of a Hindu caste whose caste occupation is that of a carrier
ka·ha·wai \'kähə,wī\ *n* -s [Maori] **:** AUSTRALIAN SALMON
ka·hi·ka·tea \'kīkə,tēə, 'kak-\ *n* -s [Maori] **:** a New Zealand evergreen tree (*Podocarpus dacrydioides*) valued for its light soft easily worked wood, its resin, and the sweet edible aril surrounding its seed — called also *white pine*
ka·hi·li \kə'hēlē\ *n* -s [Hawaiian] **:** a long pole decorated at one end with a cluster of feather plumes and used as a ceremonial emblem in Hawaii
kahili ginger *n, Hawaii* **:** a butterfly lily (*Hedychium gardnerianum*) that is native to northern India and is cultivated for its long spikes of lemon yellow flowers with bright red stamens
kahn test \'kän-\ *or* **kahn reaction** *or* **kahn** *n* -s *usu cap K* [after Reuben L. *Kahn* b1887 Am. bacteriologist] **:** a serum-precipitation reaction for the diagnosis of syphilis
ka·hu \'kä(,)hü\ *n* -s [Maori] **:** a common harrier (*Circus approximans*) represented by several distinct races in Australasia and the East Indies
ka·hu·na \kə'hünə\ *n* -s [Hawaiian] **1** *Hawaii* **:** a native master of a craft or vocation **2** *Hawaii* **:** a native medicine man **:** a master of Hawaiian religious lore and ceremonial
kahuna ana·ana \ə'nä,nä\ *n, pl* **kahuna anaana** [Hawaiian, fr. *kahuna* + *'anā'anā* black magic] *Hawaii* **:** SORCERER; *esp* **:** one who prays his victims to death
kahuna la·pa·au \-lə'pä,aů\ *n, pl* **kahuna lapaau** [Hawaiian, fr. *kahuna* + *lapa'au* medicinal] *Hawaii* **:** a medical practitioner esp. skilled in herbal medicine
kai \'kī\ *n, pl* **kai** *or* **kais** *usu cap* **1 a :** a people on the Huon gulf, Territory of New Guinea **b :** a member of such people **2 :** the Melanesian language of the Kai people **3 :** KÄTE
kaibal *usu cap, var of* KOIBAL
kai·bar·tha *or* **kai·bart·ta** \kī'bərd·ə, -'bär-\ *n* -s *usu cap* [Beng *kaibartta,* fr. Skt *kaivarta* fisherman] **:** a member of a low caste of Mongoloid origin that is numerous in Assam and Bengal
kaid \'kīd, 'kä,ēd\ *n* -s [Ar *qā'id* leader, commander in chief, fr. *qād* to command] **:** a tribal chief or governor of a district or group of villages in northern Africa
kai·feng \'kī¦fəŋ\ *adj, usu cap* [fr. *Kaifeng,* city in east central China] **:** of or from the city of Kaifeng, China **:** of the kind or style prevalent in Kaifeng
¹kai-kai \'kī,kī\ *n, pl* **kai-kai** [Marquesan; akin to Hawaiian & Samoan *'ai* food, Maori & Tongan *kai*] **1** *or* **kai** *Austral* **:** FOOD **2** *Austral* **:** FEASTING
²kai-kai \"\ *or* **kai** *vt* -ED/-ING/-S *Austral* **:** EAT
kai·ka·ra \kī'kärə\ *n* -s [modif. of Ar *karākīy,* pl. of *kurkīy* demoiselle] **:** DEMOISELLE 2a
kai·ka·wa·ka \'kīkə,wäkə\ *n* -s [Maori] **:** either of two New Zealand evergreen trees of the genus *Libocedrus:* **a :** KAWAKA **b :** MOUNTAIN PINE 3b
kail *var of* KALE
kails \'kālz\ *n pl* [ME *kayles;* akin to MD *kegel* cone, ninepin, OHG *kegil* stake, peg, ON *kaggi* keg — more at KEG] **1** *dial Brit* **:** a set of bone or wooden pins used in playing ninepins **2** *usu sing in constr, dial Brit* **:** a game played with kails
¹kail·yard \'kā(ə)l,=\ *n* [Sc, fr. *kale, kail* + E *yard* — more at KALE] *Scot* **:** KITCHEN GARDEN
²kailyard \"\ *adj, often cap, of a school of writers* **:** characterized by sentimental description of Scottish life and considerable use of Scots dialect ⟨such various aspects of Scottish life as whiskey, deerstalking, salmon fishing, the *Kailyard* school of writers —Janet Adams Smith⟩
kail·yard·er \-də(r)\ *n* -s *often cap* **:** a writer of the kailyard school
kaim \'kām\ *chiefly Scot var of* COMB
kai·ma·kam *also* **qai·ma·qam** *or* **qaim·ma·qam** \¦kīmə¦käm\ *n* -s [Turk *kaymakam,* fr. Ar *qā'im maqām* deputy, fr. *qā'im* standing + *maqām* place] **:** a lieutenant or deputy in the service of the Ottoman Empire
kai·mi clover \'kīmē-\ *n* [origin unknown] **:** a West Indian tick trefoil (*Desmodium canum*) used as a pasture plant esp. in the humid tropics
¹kain *var of* ²CAIN
²kain \'kīn\ *n* -s [Malay] **:** SARONG
kai·nah \'kīnə\ *n, pl* **kainah** *or* **kainahs** *usu cap* [Blackfoot *ah-kai-nah,* lit., many chiefs] **:** BLOOD 9
kainga \'kīŋə\ *n* -s [Maori] **:** a Maori village usu. located on low ground — compare PA
kaingang *cap, var of* CAINGANG
¹ka·ing·in *also* **ca·ing·in** *or* **ca·iñg·in** \kä'ēŋən\ *n* -s [Tag *kaingin*] *Philippines* **:** SWIDDEN ⟨some lonely farmer hewing out a ∼ in the jungle —Wallace Stegner⟩
²kaingin \"\ *adj, Philippines* **:** employing a technique of clearing land by slashing and burning underbrush and trees and plowing the ashes under for fertilizer ⟨well-known ∼ system which has been enormously destructive of valuable timber —A.L.Kroeber⟩
kai·nite \'kī,nīt, 'kā,-\ *also* **kai·nit** \kī'nēt\ *n* -s [G *kainit,* fr. Gk *kainos* new, recent + G *-it* -ite — more at RECENT] **:** a natural salt $KMg(SO_4)Cl.3H_2O$ consisting of a hydrous sulfate and chloride of magnesium and potassium that occurs impure in irregular granular masses, whose color as determined by purity is white, gray, pink, violet, or black, and that is used as a fertilizer and as a source of potassium and magnesium compounds
kai·nos·ite \'kīnə,sīt, 'kän-\ *n* -s [Sw *kainosit,* fr. Gk *kainos* + Sw *-it* -ite] **:** a mineral $Ca_2(Ce,Y)_2(SiO_4)_3CO_3.H_2O$ consisting of hydrous silicate and carbonate of calcium, cerium, and yttrium
kainozoic *var of* CENOZOIC
kai·ros \(')kī¦räs\ *n, pl* **kai·roi** \-rȯi\ [Gk, fitness, opportunity, time; perh. akin to Gk *keirein* to cut — more at SHEAR] **:** a time when conditions are right for the accomplishment of a crucial action **:** the opportune and decisive moment
kais *pl of* KAI
kai·ser \'kīzə(r)\ *n* -s [ME *keiser,* fr. ON *keisari;* akin to OE *cāsere* emperor, OHG *keisur,* Goth *kaisar;* all fr. a prehistoric Gmc word borrowed fr. L *Caesar,* cognomen of Gaius Julius *Caesar* †44 B.C. Roman general and statesman] **:** EMPEROR: as **a :** the head of an ancient or medieval empire (as the Roman Empire or the Holy Roman Empire) **b** [G, fr. OHG *keisur*] **:** the sovereign of Austria from 1804 to 1918 ⟨all the countries over which the Hapsburg ∼s claimed personal lordship —*Century Mag.*⟩ **c** [G, fr. OHG *keisur*] **:** the ruler of Germany from 1871 to 1918 ⟨the appointment of the chancellor of the German Empire by the ∼⟩
kaiser brown *n, often cap K* **:** GINGER 5
kai·ser·dom \-dəm\ *n* -s [prob. trans. of G *kaisertum*] **1 :** the office or authority of a kaiser ⟨opposition to ∼ among many American groups⟩ **2 :** the territory ruled by a kaiser ⟨the most efficient economists of ∼ —*N.Y.Times Mag.*⟩
kai·se·rin \'kīzərən\ *n* -s [G, fem. of *kaiser*] **:** the wife of a kaiser
kai·ser·ism \-,rizəm\ *n* -s *often cap* **:** a political system and practices existing under or symbolized by the rule of the German kaiser ⟨that *Kaiserism* must be repudiated in favor of some new and more liberal political system —F.A.Ogg & Harold Zink⟩ ⟨the . . . absolute political dogmas with which *Kaiserism* is associated —*New Republic*⟩
kai·ser·ship \-zə(r),ship\ *n* **:** the office of kaiser
kai·ta·ka \kī'täkə\ *n* -s [Maori] **:** a mat of fine flax worn as a cloak by the Maoris
kai·thi \'kīd·ē\ *n* -s *usu cap* [Hindi *kaithī, kāyathī* used by the Kayasths, fr. *kāyath* Kayasth, fr. Skt *kāyastha*] **:** an alphabet of Nagari type that is used in writing Bihari and eastern Hindi
kai·val·ya \kī'vəlyə\ *n* -s [Skt, fr. *kevala* exclusively one's own, alone, whole — more at CELIBATE] **:** the final state of Jain and Vedantic salvation characterized as absolute release of one's jiva from all entanglements with ajiva **:** self-directed liberation
kajak *var of* KAYAK
ka·jar \kə'jär, 'kä,j-\ *n, pl* **kajar** *or* **kajars** *usu cap* [Per *Qājār,* of Turk origin] **1 :** a people of northern Iran holding political supremacy through the dynasty ruling Persia from 1794 to 1925 **2 :** a member of the Kajar people
ka·ja·wah \kə'jäwə\ *also* **ke·dja·ve** \kə'-\ *n* -s [Hindi *kajāwa,* fr. Per] **:** a pannier used in pairs on camels and mules esp. in India
ka·ka \'käkə\ *n* -s [Maori] **:** an olive brown New Zealand parrot (*Nestor meridionalis*) that is marked with gray on the

crown and red on the face, neck, abdomen, rump, and underwing coverts and that talks and mimics well in captivity

kaka beak *or* **kaka bill** *n* : an evergreen glory pea (*Clianthus puniceus*) that is a climbing shrub sometimes exceeding 12 feet in height, has brilliant red flowers growing in pendulous axillary racemes and distinguished by the very long pointed keel, and is native to New Zealand but now rare except in cultivation

ka·kap je·ram \ˌkäˌkäpjəˈräm\ *n* [Malay *kakap jĕram*] : a fishing boat of the Malayan east coast

ka·ka·po \ˈkäkəˌpō\ *n* -s [Maori] : a New Zealand parrot (*Strigops habroptilus*) with soft green and brown barred plumage that has well-developed wings but little power of flight, lives in holes or burrows in the ground, and has nocturnal habits — called also *owl parrot*

ka·kar *or* **ka·kur** \ˈkäkə(r)\ *n* -s [Hindi *kākar*] : MUNTJAC 1

kak·a·ral·li *also* **kak·a·rali** *or* **kak·e·ral·li** \ˌkakəˈralē\ *n* -s [native name in British Guiana] **1** *in British Guiana* : SAPUCAIA **2** *in British Guiana* : MANBARKLAK

ka·ka·ri·ki \ˈkäkəˌrēkē\ *or* **ka·ka·wa·ri·ki** \ˈkäkəwə,-\ *n* -s [Maori] **1** : either of two green parakeets of New Zealand: **a** : one (*Cyanorhamphus novae-zelandiae*) having a red crown **b** : one (*Cyanorhamphus auriceps*) having a yellow crown **2** : a small green New Zealand lizard of the genus *Lygosoma*

kak·a·toe \ˌkakəˈtō(ˌ)ē\ *n, cap* [NL, perh. modif. of D *kaketoe* cockatoo — more at COCKATOO] : a genus of moderately large to very large parrots that are widely distributed in the Australasian area, are usu. predominantly white, and include numerous widely known cockatoos (as the pink cockatoo and the sulphur-crested cockatoo)

ka·ka·wa·hie \ˌkäkəwəˈhēˌā\ *n* -s [Hawaiian] : a bright scarlet flower-pecker (*Loxops maculata flammea*) of Molokai Island

ka·ke·mo·no \ˌkäkəˈmō(ˌ)nō, ˌkak-, -mōnə\ *n* -s [Jap] : a picture or writing on silk or paper that is suitable for hanging and that usu. has a roller at its lower edge — compare MAKIMONO

¹ka·ki \ˈkä(ˌ)kē\ *n* -s [Jap] : JAPANESE PERSIMMON

²ka·ki \ˈkäˈkē\ *n* -s [Maori] : a blackish stilt of New Zealand that is usu. considered a color phase of the white-headed stilt but is sometimes assigned to a separate species (*Himantopus novae-zelandiae*)

kak·i·dro·sis \ˌkakəˈdrōsəs\ *n, pl* **kakidro·ses** \-ō,sēz\ [NL, fr. *kak-, cac-* cac- + *-idrosis*] : secretion of sweat of a disagreeable odor

ka·ki·emon \ˌkäkēˈe(ˌ)yāˌmän\ *n* -s *usu cap* [after Sakaida *Kakiemon fl* 1650 Jap. potter] : an enamel-decorated Arita ware

kak·is·toc·ra·cy \ˌkakəˈstäkrəsē\ *n* -ES [Gk *kakistos* (superl. of *kakos* bad) + E *-cracy* — more at CACK] : government by the worst men

kak·kak \ˈkaˌkak\ *n* -s [Chamorro] : a small bittern (*Ixobrychus sinensis*) of Guam

kako- — see CAC-

kak·o·gen·ic \ˌkakəˈjenik\ *adj* [*cac-* + *-genic*] : DYSGENIC

ka·kor·tok·ite \kəˈkō(r)dəˌkīt\ *n* -s [*Kakortok* (Greenland Eskimo name for Julianehaab), Greenland + E *-ite*] : a rock of variable composition occurring in Greenland in black, white, and red sheets — see AGPAITE

ka·ku \ˈkä(ˌ)kü\ *n* -s [Hawaiian] *Hawaii* : GREAT BARRACUDA

kal *abbr* [L *kalendae*] calends

ka·la-azar \ˌkäləəˈzär\ *n* [Hindi *kālā-āzār* black disease, fr. Hindi *kālā* black + Per *āzār* disease] : a severe infectious disease chiefly of eastern and southern Asia that is marked by fever, progressive anemia, leukopenia, and enlargement of the spleen and liver and is caused by a flagellate (*Leishmania donovani*) which is transmitted by the bite of sand flies (genus *Phlebotomus*) and which proliferates in reticuloendothelial cells — called also *visceral leishmaniasis*

ka·lam \kəˈläm\ *n* -s [Ar *kalām* word, speech] : Muslim scholastic theology — compare MUTAKALLIMUN, SHARI'A

Kal·a·mein \ˈkaləˌmīn\ *trademark* — used for sheet metal used esp. on wooden doors to prevent the passage of fire

ka·la·mian \ˌkäləmˈyän\ *n, pl* **kalamian** *or* **kalamians** *usu cap* [native name in northern Sulu Sea] **1** : a Christianized people inhabiting the Calamian islands of the Philippines **2** : a member of the Kalamian people

kalan·choe \ˌkalənˈkōē, kəˈlaŋkə(ˌ)wē\ *n* [NL, perh. fr. Chin (Cant) *kaai laān ts'oi*, a brassica, fr. *kaai* mustard plant + *laān*, an orchid + *ts'oi* vegetables, food] **1** *cap* : a genus of chiefly African and Australian tropical herbs or shrubs (family Crassulaceae) having a four-parted calyx and including numerous forms cultivated as ornamentals **2** -s : any plant of the genus *Kalanchoe*

ka·lan·tas *or* **ca·lan·tas** \ˌkälənˈtäs\ *n* -ES [Tag *kalantas*] : PHILIPPINE CEDAR

kal·a·poo·ia *or* **kal·a·pu·ya** *also* **cal·a·poo·ya** *or* **cal·a·pu·ya** \ˌkaləˈpüyə\ *n, pl* **kalapooia** *or* **kalapooias** *or* **kalapuya** *or* **kalapuyas** *usu cap* **1 a** : an Indian people of the Willamette basin, Oregon **b** : a member of such people **2 a** : a language family of Oregon including Kalapooia and Yoncalla **b** : a language of the Kalapooia family formerly spoken in the Willamette basin, Oregon

kal·a·poo·ian *or* **kal·a·pu·yan** \ˌ==ˈ==yən\ *adj, usu cap* : of or relating to the Kalapooia or their language

ka·la·sie \ˈkäləˌsē\ *n* -s [Dayak (Ngadju dial.) *kalasi*] : a long-tailed monkey of Borneo (*Pygathrix rubicunda*) that has a tuft of long hair on the head

kale *or* **kail** \ˈkāl, *esp before pause or consonant* -āəl\ *n* -s [Sc, fr. ME (northern dial.) *cal, cale*, fr. OE *cāl* — more at COLE] **1 a** : COLE 1 **b** : a very hardy cabbage (*Brassica oleracea acephala*) that has curled often finely cut leaves which do not form a dense head and that is considered by some to be the original form of the cultivated cabbage **c** *Scot* : a plant of the family Cruciferae **2** *Scot* : BROTH, SOUP; *esp* : soup made with kale **3** *chiefly Scot* **a** : FOOD **b** : MEAL **4** *slang* : MONEY ⟨a ritzy neighborhood where everybody had the ~ —J.T.Farrell⟩

kaleege *or* **kaleej** *var of* KALIJ

¹ka·lei·do·scope \kəˈlīdəˌskōp *sometimes* -lēd-\ *n* [Gk *kalos* beautiful + *eidos* form + E *-scope* — more at CALLI-, IDOL] **1** : an instrument that contains loose fragments of colored glass confined between two flat plates and two plane mirrors placed at an angle of 60° so that changes of position exhibit its contents in an endless variety of symmetrical varicolored forms **2** : something resembling a kaleidoscope: as **a** : a variegated changing pattern or scene ⟨the lake a ~ of changing colors —Robert Gibbings⟩ **b** : a succession of changing phases or actions ⟨reduce all experience to a shifting ~ of meaningless incidents —John Dewey⟩ ⟨her day . . . became a ~ of things embarked upon and left for other things —Adrian Bell⟩

²kaleidoscope \"\ *vb* -ED/-ING/-S *vi* : to appear as if in a kaleidoscope ⟨pictures of the lights and the planes spinning and crashing . . . *kaleidoscoped* through his mind —Howard Hunt⟩ ~ *vt* : to view as if in a kaleidoscope ⟨poking . . . fun at our banalities and shortsightednesses as he ~*s* them with the long view of man's cultural achievement —Henry Hewes⟩

ka·lei·do·scop·ic \-ˌ==ˈskäpik, -pēk\ *also* **ka·lei·do·scop·i·cal** \-pəkəl, -pēk-\ *adj* **1** : of, relating to, or formed by a kaleidoscope ⟨gazed raptly at the ~ patterns within the instrument⟩ **2** : having changing tints or variegated color ⟨~ color of the clouds at sunset⟩ **3 a** : constantly changing : rapidly shifting ⟨air was fretted with a ~ network of swifts . . . with swallows, martins, and if late enough, nighthawks —William Beebe⟩ ⟨a year of ~ change, of breathtaking developments crowding so rapidly one upon the other —Allan Taylor⟩ **b** : having infinite variety : possessing many facets ⟨such a being of ~ versatility . . . we call contemptuously a jack-of-all-trades —Havelock Ellis⟩ ⟨shocking inhumanity of the slave trade has been compressed within the pages of this ~ novel with romance and sea adventure —*N.Y. Herald Tribune*⟩ — **ka·lei·do·scop·i·cal·ly** \-pək(ə)lē, -pēk-, -li\ *adv*

ka·le·ma \kəˈlāmə\ *n* -s [Pg] : a violent surf that occurs on the coast of the Guinea region, West Africa

kalendar *var of* CALENDAR — used esp. of ecclesiastical calendars ⟨the Episcopal ~⟩

kalends *var of* CALENDS

kale runt *or* **kale stock** *n* : the stem of kale

kaleyard \ˈ==ˌ=\ *chiefly Scot var of* KAILYARD

kal·gan \(ˈ)kalˈgan, (ˈ)kälˈgän\ *adj, usu cap* [fr. *Kalgan*, city in northern China] : of or from the city of Kalgan, China : of the kind or style prevalent in Kalgan

kalian *var of* CALEAN

kal·i·bo·rite \ˌkaləˈbōrˌīt\ *n* -s [G *kaliborit*, fr. *kali-* (fr. NL *kalium*) + *bor-* + *-it* -ite] : a mineral $KMg_2B_{11}O_{19}.9H_2O$ consisting of a hydrous borate of potassium and magnesium

ka·lic·i·nite \kəˈlisəˌnīt\ *n* -s [G *kalicinit*, fr. F *kalicine* kalicinite (irreg. fr. NL *kalium* + F *-ine*) + G *-it* -ite] : a mineral $KHCO_3$ consisting of an acid carbonate or bicarbonate of potassium

ka·lig·e·nous \kəˈlijənəs, (ˈ)kaˈl-\ *adj* [ISV *kali* alkali (fr. NL) + *-genous*] : forming alkalies — used of the alkali metals

kalij *or* **kaleege** *also* **kaleej** *or* **kal·lege** \ˈkalij, ˈkäl-,ˈkal-, -(ˌ)lēj\ *n, pl* **kalij·es** *or* **kaleeg·es** *also* **kaleej·es** *or* **kalleg·es** [Nepali & Pahari *kālij*] : any of several related crested Indian pheasants (genus *Lophura* or *Gennaeus*) that are related to the Chinese silver pheasant

ka·li·na \kəˈlēnə\ *n, pl* **kalina** *or* **kalinas** *usu cap* [Carib *calina* Caribs, strong men — more at CANNIBAL] : GALIBI

ka·lin·ga *also* **ka·ling·ga** \kəˈliŋgə\ *n, pl* **kalinga** *or* **kalingas** *usu cap* [native name in northern Luzon] **1 a** : any of several peoples inhabiting northern Luzon, Philippines **b** : a member of such people **2** : the Austronesian language of the Kalinga people

ka·li·nin \kəˈlēnən, kəlˈyēnyən\ *adj, usu cap* [fr. *Kalinin*, city in the west central part of European Russia, U.S.S.R.] : of or from the city of Kalinin, U.S.S.R. : of the kind or style prevalent in Kalinin

ka·li·nin·grad \-ˌgrad\ *adj, usu cap* [fr. *Kaliningrad*, city in the western part of European Russia, U.S.S.R.] : of or from the city of Kaliningrad, U.S.S.R. : of the kind or style prevalent in Kaliningrad

kali·nite \ˈkaləˌnīt, ˈkāl-\ *n* -s [*kali-* (fr. NL *kalium*) + connective *-n-* + *-ite*] : a mineral $KAl(SO_4)_2.11H_2O$ consisting of a fibrous and birefringent hydrous sulfate of potassium and aluminum that is distinct from alum in crystallization and water content

kal·i·oph·i·lite \ˌkalēˈäfəˌlīt, ˌkāl-\ *n* -s [G *kaliophilit*, fr. *kalio-* (fr. NL *kalium*) + *-phil* -phile + *-it* -ite] : a colorless mineral $KAlSiO_4$ of volcanic origin consisting of potassium aluminum silicate that occurs in acicular crystals or fine threads (hardness 6, sp. gr. 2.5–2.6)

kal·i·spel \ˌkaləˈspel\ *n, pl* **kalispel** *or* **kalispels** *usu cap* [Kalispel, lit., camas] **1 a** : a Salishan people of northern Idaho and northwestern Montana **b** : a member of such people **2** : a language of the Kalispel and Spokan peoples — called also *Pend d'Oreille*

ka·li·um \ˈkālēəm\ *n* -s [NL, fr. *kali* alkali, potassium (fr. Ar *qily* saltwort) + *-ium*] : POTASSIUM — symbol *K*

ka·li yu·ga \ˌkələˈyügə\ *n, usu cap K&Y* [Skt *kaliyuga*, fr. *kali* ace on a die + *yuga* yoke, age of the world; fr. the fact that the ace is the unluckiest throw in dice games — more at YOKE] : the depraved fourth and final age of a Hindu world cycle : dark age

kalka *usu cap, var of* KHALKHA

kal·kow·skite \kalˈkōfˌskīt\ *n* -s [G *kalkowskyn* (irreg. fr. E. L. *Kalkowsky* †1938 Ger. mineralogist + G *-in* -ine) + E *-ite*] : a mineral $Fe_2Ti_3O_9$(?) consisting of an oxide of iron and titanium and usu. containing small amounts of rare-earth elements, niobium, and tantalum

kalk·vis \ˈkälkˌfis\ *n* -ES [Afrik, fr. *kalk* lime (fr. D, fr. MD *calc*) + *vis* fish, fr. D, fr. MD *visch*; akin to OHG *kalk* lime and to OHG *fisc* fish — more at CHALK, FISH] : a cutlass fish (*Lepidopus caudatus*) of southern Africa

kal·li·kak \ˈkaləˌkak\ *n* -s *usu cap* [*Kallikak*, fictitious name of a family having one branch consisting mainly of intelligent and successful persons and another branch containing a large proportion of mentally deficient and immoral persons that was studied by H. H. Goddard †1957 Am. psychologist, fr. Gk *kalli-* calli- + *kak-* cac-] : a stupid person ⟨rubber masks by means of which an ordinary citizen can transform himself into demon, witch . . . *Kallikak*, bumpkin —Bernard Wolfe⟩ — compare JUKES

kal·li·ma \ˈkaləmə\ *n, cap* [NL, prob. irreg. fr. Gk *kallimos* beautiful, fr. *kallos* beauty — more at CALLI-] : a genus of highly mimetic nymphalid butterflies of southern Asia and the Pacific islands that are often brilliantly colored above but when at rest with wings folded resemble dead leaves in color and markings

kal·li·type \ˈkaləˌtīp\ *n* [ISV *kalli-* (fr. Gk *kalli-* calli-) + *type*] : a contact printing-out photographic process that uses paper sensitized with a ferric salt and silver nitrate and a developer containing borax and Rochelle salt

kal·mia \ˈkalmēə\ *n* [NL, fr. Peter *Kalm* †1779 Swed. botanist + NL *-ia*] **1** *cap* : a genus of No. American evergreen shrubs (family Ericaceae) with oblong to linear leaves and showy flowers that are borne in clusters in the axils of leaves or bracts and have a saucer-shaped basally 10-saccate corolla with an anther resting in each sac — see MOUNTAIN LAUREL, SHEEP LAUREL **2** -s : any plant of the genus *Kalmia*

kal·muck *or* **kal·muk** \ˈkalˌmək, =ˈ=\ *or* **kal·myk** \ˈkal-(ˌ)mik, =ˈ=\ *also* **cal·muck** \ˈkalˌmək, =ˈ=\ *n* -s *usu cap* [Russ *Kalmyk*, fr. Kazan Tatar] **1** : a member of a Buddhist Mongol people orig. of Dzungaria — called also *Eleut* **2** : the Mongolian language of the Kalmucks

ka·lo \ˈkä(ˌ)lō\ *n* -s [Hawaiian] : TARO

ka·lon \kəˈlän, (ˈ)kaˈl-\ *n* -s [Gk, neut. of *kalos* good, beautiful — more at CALLI-] : the ideal of physical and moral beauty esp. as conceived by the philosophers of classical Greece

ka·long \ˈkaˌlōŋ, ˈkäˌl-, kəˈl-, -läŋ\ *n* -s [Jav] : a large fruit bat of the Malay archipelago

kal·op·a·nax \kəˈläpəˌnaks\ *n* -ES [NL, fr. *kalo-* (fr. Gk *kalos* beautiful) + Gk *panax* panacea, fr. *panakēs* all-healing — more at PANACEA] : a showy Japanese tree (*Kalopanax ricinifolium*) of the family Araliaceae that has foliage like that of the castor-oil plant

kal·o·ter·mes \ˌkaləˈtər(ˌ)mēz\ *n, cap* [NL, fr. *kalo-* (fr. Gk *kalos*) + *Termes*] : the type genus of Kalotermitidae comprising many termites that are destructive pests of living trees or of dry timber — see CRYPTOTERMES

¹kal·o·ter·mi·tid *also* **cal·o·ter·mi·tid** \ˌ==ˈ==məd·əd\ *adj* [NL *Kalotermitidae*] : of or relating to the Kalotermitidae

²kalotermitid *also* **calotermitid** \"\ *n* -s [NL *Kalotermitidae*] : a termite of the family Kalotermitidae

kal·o·ter·mit·i·dae \ˌ==(ˌ)tərˈmid·əˌdē\ *n pl, cap* [NL, fr. *Kalotermit-, Kalotermes*, type genus + *-idae*] : a family of primitive termites occurring in most warm regions and including many serious destroyers of wood and growing trees — compare CRYPTOTERMES; see DRY-WOOD TERMITE

ka·lox·y·lon \kəˈläksəˌlän, -lən\ *n, cap* [NL, fr. *kalo-* (fr. Gk *kalos*) + *-xylon*] : a form genus of fossil plants based only on roots

kal·pa \ˈkəlpə\ *n* -s [Skt] : a duration of time in Hinduism covering a complete cosmic cycle from the origination to the destruction of a world system — compare YUGA

kalpak *var of* CALPAC

kal·pis \ˈkalpəs\ *n* -ES [Gk; akin to OIr *cilornn* jar] : a hydria having a rounded shoulder and a small back handle

kal·si·lite \ˈkalsəˌlīt *also* -lts-\ *n* -s [prob. fr. *kalium* + *aluminum* + *silicon* + *-ite*] : a rare mineral $KAlSiO_4$ consisting of aluminosilicate of potassium

kalsomine *var of* CALCIMINE

ka·lua \kəˈlüə\ *adj* [Hawaiian *kālua*, fr. *kālua* to bake in a ground oven] *Hawaii* : baked in an earth oven ⟨~ pig⟩

ka·lum·pang \ˌkäləmˈpäŋ\ *n* -s [Tag *kalumpáng*] *Philippines* : a large tropical Old World tree (*Sterculia foetida*) having foul-smelling blossoms that are followed by red pods enclosing oil-rich and protein-rich seeds sometimes used as food and yielding light soft wood that is sometimes used for carving

ka·lum·pit *also* **ca·lum·pit** \-ˈpēt\ *n* -s [Tag *kalumpit*] : a common Philippine tree (*Terminalia edulis*) that yields a soft wood and dark red fleshy fruits used for preserves

ka·lun·ti \kəˈlüntē\ *n* -s [Taw-Sug] : a lauan (*Shorea kalunti*) with yellow wood

kal·war \(ˌ)kəlˈwō(ə)r\ *n* -s *usu cap* [Hindi *kalvār*, lit., liquor seller, fr. Skt *kalyapāla*, fr. *kalya* liquor + *pāla* guard, keeper] : a member of a Hindu caste engaging in trade

kalymma *var of* CALYMMA

kam *dial var of* ²CAM

ka·ma \ˈkämə\ *n* -s [Skt *kāma* love, wish, desire — more at CHARITY] **1** : enjoyment of the world of the senses constituting one of the ends of man in Hinduism : PLEASURE **2** *in Buddhism & Theosophy* : the human principle of desire — compare KAMARUPA

ka·ma·ai·na \ˌkäməˈīnə\ *n* -s [Hawaiian, fr. *kama* person + *'āina* land] : a longtime resident of Hawaii

ka·ma·chi·le \ˌkäməˈchilē\ *or* **ka·man·chi·le** \ˌkämənˈ-\ *var of* CAMACHILE

kam·a·cite \ˈkaməˌsīt\ *n* -s [obs. G *kamacit* (now *kamazit*), fr. Gk *kamak-, kamax* vine pole, shaft + G *-it* -ite; akin to MHG *hamel* pole, Skt *śamyā* stick, staff] : a mineral consisting of a nickel-iron alloy forming with taenite the mass of most meteoric iron

ka·ma·hi \kəˈmähē\ *n* -s [Maori] : a New Zealand tree (*Weinmannia racemosa*) of the family Cunoniaceae that yields timber and firewood — called also *towai*

ka·ma·la *also* **ka·me·la** *or* **ka·mi·la** \ˈkəmələ\ *n* -s [Skt *kamala*, prob. of Dravidian origin; akin to Kanarese *kōmale, kōval*] **1** : an East Indian tree (*Mallotus philippinensis*) **2** : a reddish cathartic powder from the capsules of the kamala tree that contains rottlerin and is used as an orange dye for silk and wool and as a vermifuge chiefly in veterinary practice

ka·ma·ni \kəˈmänē\ *n* -s [Hawaiian] **1** : MALABAR ALMOND **2** : MASTWOOD

kamansi *var of* CAMANSI

ka·mao \kəˈmäˌō, -mau̇\ *n* -s [Hawaiian *kama'o*] : a bird (*Phaeornis obscura myadestina*) of the family Turdidae found on Kauai Island, Hawaii

ka·mar \kəˈmär\ *n, pl* **kamar** *or* **kamars** *usu cap* **1** : a people of central India now engaged in the practice of plow agriculture **2** : a member of the Kamar people

ka·ma·res *or* **ka·ma·rais** \kəˈmäˌres, -ˌrās\ *n, pl* **kamares** *or* **kamarais** *usu cap* [fr. *Kamares*, cave on the south slope of Mount Ida, Crete, where it was discovered] : a gaily colored Minoan pottery reaching its peak of excellence about 2000 B.C.

ka·mar·e·zite \kəˈmarəˌzīt\ *n* -s [G *kamarezit*, fr. *Kamareza, Kamariza*, near Laurium, Greece + G *-it* -ite] : a mineral $Cu_3(SO_4)(OH)_4.6H_2O$(?) consisting of a hydrous basic copper sulfate

ka·ma·rin·ska·ia \kəˈmärənzkəyə, -mar-, -nsk-\ *n* -s [Russ] : a Russian folk dance that is characterized by acrobatic knee bends, leaps, and leg extensions

ka·ma·ru·pa \ˌkäməˈrüpə\ *n* -s [Skt *kāmarūpa*, fr. *kāma* desire + *rūpa* form] *Theosophy* : the form assumed by the kama after a person's death — compare ASTRAL BODY — **ka·ma·ru·pic** \ˌ==ˈ==pik\ *adj*

¹kamas *or* **kamass** *var of* CAMAS

²kamas *pl of* KAMA

ka·ma·sin \ˈkäməˌsēn, ˌkam-, -sin\ *also* **ka·mass** \ˈkäməs, ˈkam-\ *or* **ka·mas·sian** \kəˈmashən, -asēən\ *or* **ka·mas·sin** *like* KAMASIN\ *n, pl* **kamasin** *or* **kamasins** *usu cap* [*Kamasin, Kamass, Kamassin* fr. Russ *Kamasintsy* (pl.), fr. Kamasin *Kangmāžə*; *Kamassian* prob. fr. *Kamass* + *-ian*] **1 a** : a Samoyed people on the upper Yenisei river, Siberia, who are ethnically largely extinct or absorbed into the Russian culture by intermarriage **b** : a member of such people **2** : the Uralic language of the Kamasin people

ka·mas·si \kəˈmäsē\ *n* -s [Afrik *kamassie*, prob. modif. of Xhosa *kamamasane*] **1** : a tree (*Gonioma kamassi*) of the family Apocynaceae of southern Africa **2** : the hard yellow wood of the kamassi

kam·ba \ˈkämbə\ *n, pl* **kamba** *or* **kambas** *usu cap* **1 a** : a Bantu people of central Kenya **b** : a member of such people **2** : a Bantu language of the Kamba people

kam·bal \ˈkəmbəl\ *n* -s [Hindi, fr. Skt *kambala*] : a coarse woolen blanket or shawl worn in India

kam·ba·la \kəmˈbälə\ *n* -s [Burmese] **1 a** : an East Indian tree (*Sonneratia apetala*) with strong reddish wood **b** : the wood of the kambala **2** : IROKO

kam·ba·ra earth \kəmˈbärə-\ *n, usu cap K* [fr. Kita-*Kambara*, district of Niigata prefecture in Japan] : JAPANESE ACID CLAY

kam·boh \ˈkəmˌbō, ˈkäm-\ *n* -s [Per] : a member of a low caste in the Punjab engaged chiefly in agriculture

kam·cha·dal *also* **kam·cha·dale** \ˌkämchəˈdäl\ *or* **kamcha·dele** \-del, -dē(ə)l\ *n, pl* **kamchadal** *or* **kamchadals** *usu cap* [Russ *Kamchadal* Kamchatkan] **1 a** : a Paleo-Asiatic people of southern Kamchatka who are chiefly hunters and fishers **b** : a member of such people **2** : a Luorawetlan language of the Kamchadal people

¹kam·chat·kan \(ˈ)kamˈchatkən\ *adj, usu cap* [*Kamchatka*, peninsula in the northeastern U.S.S.R. + E *-an*, adj. suffix] : of or relating to the Kamchatka peninsula

²kamchatkan \"\ *n* -s *usu cap* [*Kamchatka* + E *-an*, n. suffix] : KAMCHADAL

kamchatkan sea eagle *n, usu cap K* : an eagle (*Haliaeetus pelagicus*) that has white shoulders, rump, and tail when adult, feeds largely on fish, and is found on the coasts of the western north Pacific — called also *Steller's sea eagle*

¹kame \ˈkām\ *now dial var of* COMB

²kame \"\ *n* -s [Sc, kame, comb, fr. ME (northern dial.) *camb* comb, fr. OE *camb* — more at COMB] : a short ridge, hill, or mound of stratified drift deposited by glacial meltwater — compare ESKER

ka·meel \kəˈmē(ə)l, -ˈmā(-\ *n* -s [Afrik, fr. D, camel, fr. MD *cameel*, fr. L *camelus* — more at CAMEL] *Africa* : GIRAFFE

ka·meel·doorn \-ˌdōrn\ *also* **ka·meel·do·ring bush** \-ˌdōriŋ-\ *or* **ka·meel·thorn** \-ˌthōrn\ *n, pl* **kameeldoorns** *also* **kameelthorns** [*kameeldoorn* fr. obs. Afrik *kameeldoorn* (now *kameeldoring*), fr. Afrik *kameel* + obs. Afrik *doorn* thorn, fr. D, fr. MD *dorn; kameeldoring bush* fr. Afrik *kameeldoring* + E *bush; kameelthorn* part trans. of Afrik *kameeldoring*; akin to OE *thorn* — more at THORN] *Africa* : any of several acacia trees; *esp* : a tall tree (*Acacia giraffae*) on which the giraffe often browses

ka·me·ha·me·ha day \kəˌmāəˈmā(ˌ)hā-\ *n, cap K&D* [after *Kamehameha* I †1819 king of Hawaii] : June 11 observed as a holiday in Hawaii in celebration of the anniversary of the birth of Kamehameha I

kamela *or* **kamila** *var of* KAMALA

ka·me·lau·ki·on \ˌkäməˈlau̇kˌyōn, -au̇kēˌōn\ *n* -s [MGk *kamēlaukion*, alter. (prob. influenced by Gk *kamēlos* camel) of LGk *kamelaukion*] : a tall brimless hat worn by priests and monks in some Eastern rites

kamelaukions

ka·me·rad \ˌkäməˈräät\ *interj* [G, lit., comrade, fr. MF *camarade* companion — more at COMRADE] — used by German soldiers in World War I as a cry of surrender

kame terrace *n* [²*kame*] : a terrace of stratified sand and gravel deposited by streams between a glacier and an adjacent valley wall

ka·mi \ˈkäˈmi\ *n, pl* **kami** [Jap, god] : a sacred power or force; *esp* : one of the Shinto deities including mythological beings, spirits of distinguished men, and forces of nature

ka·mia \kəˈmēə\ *n, pl* **kamia** *or* **kamias** *usu cap* [Kamia *Kamiyai, Kamiyahi*] **1 a** : an Indian people of southeastern California and northwestern Mexico **b** : a member of such people **2** : a Yuman language of the Kamia people

ka·mias \kəmˈyäs\ *n* -ES [Tag *kamyás*] *Philippines* : BILIMBI

ka·mik \ˈkämik\ *n* -s [Esk] : an Eskimo sealskin boot

¹ka·mi·ka·ze \ˌkäməˈkäzē\ *n* -s [Jap, lit., divine wind, fr. *kami* god + *kaze* wind] **1** *often cap* : a member of a Japanese air attack corps assigned to make a suicidal crash on a target (as a ship) **2** : an airplane containing explosives to be flown in a suicide crash on a target

²kamikaze \ˌ==ˈ==\ *adj, sometimes cap* **1** : of, relating to, or resembling that of a kamikaze ⟨extending the ~ way of fighting to whole nations —Norbert Wiener⟩ **2** : SUICIDAL ⟨the city's ~ taxi drivers⟩

kam·lei·ka \kamˈlīkə\ *also* **kam·e·lai·ka** \ˌkaməˈl-\ *n* -s [Esk *kamleika*] : a waterproof pullover shirt made of dried animal intestines and worn in the Aleutians

kam·loops trout \'kam,lüps-\ *also* **kamloops** *n, usu cap K* [fr. *Kamloops*, city in Brit. Columbia] **:** a large black-spotted rainbow trout native chiefly to Lake Pend Oreille, Idaho, and widely introduced in western streams and lakes

käm·mer·er·ite \'kemərə,rīt\ *n* -s [Sw *kämmererit*, fr. A. A. *Kämmerer* 19th cent. scientist in St. Petersburg (Leningrad) + Sw *-it* -ite] **:** a reddish penninite

kampferol *var of* KAEMPFEROL

kam·pi·lan *or* **cam·pi·lan** \käm'pē,län\ *n* -s [Tag *kampilan*] **:** a long straight-edged sheathed cutlass broadening toward the point that is used by the Moro peoples of Mindanao and Sulu

kam·pong *or* **cam·pong** \'käm,pȯŋ, -päŋ, ='=\ *n* -s [Malay *kampong*] **:** a native hamlet or village in a Malay-speaking country

kamp·to·zoa \,kam(p)tə'zōə\ [NL, fr. *kampto-* (fr. Gk *kamptos* flexible) + NL *-zoa* — more at CAMPTO-] *syn of* ENTOPROCTA

ka·muk \kə'mük\ *n, pl* **kamuk** *or* **kamuks** *usu cap* **:** a mountain people of northeast Thailand who practice primitive shifting agriculture and are related to the Kha of Vietnam

ka·mu·ning *or* **ca·mu·ning** \¦kämü¦nēŋ\ *n* -s [Tag *kamuning*] **1 :** a tropical Asiatic tree (*Murraya exotica*) **2 :** the wood of the kamuning noted for its hardness

ka·na \'känə\ *n, pl* **kana** *or* **kanas** *often attrib* [Jap] **1 a :** a Japanese system of syllabic writing dating from the 8th or 9th century A.D. and having characters that can be used exclusively for writing the language but are normally used only for foreign words, for grammatical inflections and function words not represented by kanji, or at the side of kanji to indicate pronunciation **b :** either of the two different but equivalent sets of characters that are used in the kana system and that each have 48 characters increased by the use of two diacritics to 73 — see HIRAGANA, KATAKANA **2 :** a single character belonging to the kana system of writing

kana-a \¦känə¦ä\ *adj, usu cap* [origin unknown] **:** of or relating to a hard thin white to slate gray pottery of the Developmental Pueblo period that is either plain or decorated with black lines

kanaf *also* **kanaff** *var of* KENAF

ka·nai·ma \kə'nīmə\ *n* -s [native name in British Guiana] **:** an evil spirit or a person possessed by an evil spirit believed by Indians of British Guiana and northwestern Brazil to be an avenger

ka·naka \kə'nakə, -nakə; *in Hawaiian, sing & pl are both* "*kanaka*" *but sing is* ='== *& pl is* '=== \ *n* -s *often cap* [Hawaiian, person, human being] **:** POLYNESIAN, MICRONESIAN, MELANESIAN **:** SOUTH SEA ISLANDER

kana-majiri \¦==¦mäjərē\ *n* -s [Jap, fr. *kana* + *majiri* mixture] **:** the standard form of Japanese writing consisting of kanji supplemented by hiragana characters to indicate inflectional endings and function words and to show pronunciation esp. when that would otherwise be doubtful

ka·nam man \kə'nam-\ *n, usu cap K* [fr. *Kanam*, locality on Lake Victoria, Kenya, where the type was discovered] **:** an extinct East African man known from a fragmentary fossil jaw and associated teeth found in early Pleistocene lake beds

kan·a·rese *also* **can·a·rese** \¦kanə¦rēz, -ēs\ *n, pl* **kanarese** *also* **canarese** *usu cap* [*Kanara*, district in southwest India + E *-ese*] **1 a :** a Kannada-speaking people of Mysore, south India **b :** a member of such people **2 :** KANNADA **3 :** the script normally used to write Kannada

ka·na·ri *also* **ca·na·ri** \kə'närē\ *n* -s [Malay *kĕnari*] **:** JAVA ALMOND

ka·nau·ri \kə'naürē\ *or* **ka·na·wa·ri** \-näwərē\ *n* -s *usu cap* **:** a Tibeto-Burman language of Himachal Pradesh, India

ka·na·za·wa \kə'näzəwə\ *adj, usu cap* [fr. *Kanazawa*, city in western Honshu, Japan] **:** of or from the city of Kanazawa, Japan **:** of the kind or style prevalent in Kanazawa

kan·chil \'känchəl\ *n* -s [Malay] **:** any of several small chevrotains of southeastern Asia formerly regarded as constituting several species but now usu. held to be varieties of one (*Tragulus kanchil*)

kan·de·lia \kan'dēlēə, -lyə\ *n, cap* [NL, fr. Malayalam *kandel* tree of the genus *Kandelia* + NL *-ia*] **:** a genus of East Indian trees (family Rhizophoraceae) that are related to and resemble the common mangroves but have laciniate petals and 5-parted or 6-parted calyx

kandh *usu cap, var of* KHOND

[1]**kan·dy·an** \'kandēən\ *adj, usu cap* [*Kandy*, town in central Ceylon, + E *-an*, adj. suffix] **1 :** of, relating to, or characteristic of Kandy, Ceylon **2 :** of, relating to, or characteristic of the people of Kandy

[2]**kandyan** \"\ *n* -s *usu cap* [*Kandy* + E *-an*, n. suffix] **:** a native or resident of Kandy, Ceylon

ka·neel·hart \kə'nā(ə)l,härt\ *n* -s [prob. fr. D, fr. *kaneel* cinnamon (fr. MD *caneel, canele*, fr. MF *cannelle*, fr. ML *canella*) + D *hart* heart, fr. MD *herte, harte*; akin to OE *heorte* heart — more at CANELLA, HEART] **1 :** a tropical tree (*Licania cayenensis*) of Central and So. America **2 :** the very strong wood of kaneelhart

ka·nesh·ite \'käni,shīt\ *n* -s *usu cap* [*Kanesh, Kanish*, ancient city of eastern Asia Minor + E *-ite*] **1 :** an inhabitant of ancient Kanesh in eastern Asia Minor **2** *or* **ka·nish·ite** \"\ **:** the principal dialect of Hittite — called also *Kanesian*

ka·ne·sian \kə'nēzhən\ *or* **ka·ni·sian** \-nizh-\ *adj, usu cap* [irreg. fr. *Kanesh, Kanish* + E *-ian*] **:** of, relating to, or characteristic of the Kaneshites

kang *or* **k'ang** \'käŋ\ *n* -s [Chin (Pek) *k'ang*[4]] **:** a brick platform built across one side or end of a room in a house in northern China or Manchuria, warmed by a fire beneath, and used for sleeping

kan·ga·ny *or* **kan·ga·ni** \kəŋ'gänē\ *n, pl* **kanganies** *or* **kanganis** [Tamil *kaṅkāṇi*, lit., one who sees with the eyes, fr. *kaṇ* eye + *kāṇ* to see] **:** an overseer of labor in Ceylon, India, and Malaya

[1]**kan·ga·roo** \¦kaŋgə¦rü, ¦kaiŋ-\ *n* -s [prob. native name in Queensland, Australia] **1 a :** any of various herbivorous leaping marsupial mammals (family Macropodidae) of Australia, New Guinea, and adjacent islands that have a small head, large ears, long powerful hind legs with the two larger hind toes armed with heavy nails, a long thick tail used as a support and in balancing, and rather small forelegs not used in progression — see MARSUPIALIA, WALLABY **b (1) :** the pelt or fur of the kangaroo **(2) :** leather made from the skin of the kangaroo resembling glazed kid in appearance **2** *Austral* **:** wild young cattle — usu. used in the pl. **3** *Brit* **:** AUSTRALIAN **4 :** KANGAROO CLOSURE ⟨the ~ saves parliamentary time —Derek Walker-Smith⟩

kangaroo

[2]**kangaroo** \"\ *adj* **:** of or relating to a kangaroo court ⟨these ~ qualities of justice that even of the courtroom . . . can make a jungle —Herbert Feinstein⟩

kangaroo acacia *or* **kangaroo thorn** *n* **:** a thorny Australian acacia (*Acacia armata*) often used for hedges

kangaroo apple *n* **1 :** an edible yellow egg-shaped fruit of Australia and New Zealand that has a mealy subacid pulp **2 :** a shrubby or herbaceous perennial plant (*Solanum aviculare*) that is sometimes cultivated in warm regions for its racemes of purple flowers and for the kangaroo apples that it bears

kangaroo bear *n* **:** KOALA

kangaroo beetle *n* **:** any of certain brilliantly colored Old World beetles with thick hind legs constituting the genus *Sagra* that is included in Chrysomelidae or made the type of a separate family

kangaroo closure *n* **:** the restriction of debate to those amendments judged by the presiding officer of a legislative body to be most appropriate ⟨the New Zealand House has not had to adopt . . . the *kangaroo closure* —Walter Nash⟩ — compare GUILLOTINE

kangaroo court *n* **1 :** a mock court in which the principles of law and justice are disregarded or perverted: **a :** one held by vagabonds or by prisoners in a jail or prison camp ⟨*kangaroo courts* . . . are vicious organizations controlled by the most perverted and brutal prisoners —J.V.B.Bennett⟩ ⟨non-Communist prisoners sentenced to death by Red *kangaroo courts* —*Army-Navy-Air Force Jour.*⟩ **b :** one involving comic procedures and ludicrous penalties designed for the amusement of the participants and spectators ⟨*kangaroo courts* — to which anyone not in Western garb can be hauled and fined —Helen Gould⟩ **2 :** a court or a similar body (as a legislative investigating committee) characterized by irresponsible, unauthorized, or irregular status or procedures ⟨in Czechoslovakia . . . *kangaroo courts* have been handing down stiff sentences for "labor sabotage" —C.L.Sulzberger⟩ ⟨two committee jobs which put him . . . in the position of conducting his own *kangaroo court* —*Atlantic*⟩

kangaroo dog *n* **:** an Australian breed of rough-haired dogs that resemble greyhounds and that are used for hunting kangaroos

kangaroo feathers *n pl, Austral* **:** NONSENSE

kangaroo grass *n* **:** any of several grasses of the genus *Themeda*: as **a :** a common perennial forage grass (*Themeda australis*) that is usu. held to occur from Australia across southern Asia and into eastern Africa and that is very closely related to and perhaps a variety of the African rooigras **b :** ULLA GRASS

kangaroo hare *n* **:** HARE WALLABY

kangaroo jerboa *n* **:** RAT KANGAROO

kangaroo mouse *n* **:** any of various small leaping rodents (as dwarf pocket rat, jumping mouse, or pocket mouse)

kangaroo paw *n* **:** an Australian sedgelike spring-flowering herb (*Anigozanthos manglesii*) of the family Amaryllidaceae having the clustered flowers covered with greenish wool except at their red bases — called also *kangaroo's-foot*

kangaroo rat *n* **1 :** RAT KANGAROO **2 :** any of numerous pouched nocturnal burrowing rodents (genus *Dipodomys*) of arid parts of the western U.S.

kangaroo's-foot \,=='=,=\ *or* **kangaroo-foot plant** \,=='=,=-\ *n, pl* **kangaroo's-foots :** KANGAROO PAW

kangaroo vine *or* **kangaroo grape** *n* **:** an Australian woody vine (*Cissus antarctica*) sometimes used as a houseplant

kan·ga·yam \¦kaŋgə¦yäm\ *n* [*Kangayam*, cattle-breeding center in Madras state, southern India] **1** *usu cap* **:** an Indian breed of brown or gray cattle used chiefly for draft **2** *-s often cap* **:** an animal of the Kangayam breed

k'ang hsi \'käŋ'shē\ *adj, usu cap K&H* [after *K'ang-hsi* †1722 Chin. emperor, second of the Ch'ing dynasty] **:** of, relating to, or having the characteristics of Chinese ceramic art or Chinese porcelain wares of the latter half of the 17th century or the first quarter of the 18th century

kang·li \'käŋ'lē\ *also* **kang·la** \-lä\ *n* -s *usu cap* **:** one of the major divisions of the Great Horde

kan·gri \'kəŋ(,)grē\ *n* -s [Hindi *kāṅgṛī*] **:** a small portable earthenware-lined wicker basket used as a warming stove in Kashmir

kangs *pl of* KANG

k'angs *pl of* K'ANG

kan·ho·bal \¦känō¦bäl\ *n* -s *usu cap* **1 a :** an Indian people of western Guatemala **b :** a member of such people **2 :** a Mayan language of the Kanhobal people

ka·nin \'känən\ *n* -s [Tag, fr. *kain* to eat] *Philippines* **:** boiled rice

kanishite *usu cap, var of* KANESHITE

kanisian *usu cap, var of* KANESIAN

kan·je·ra man \'känjərə-\ *n, usu cap K* [fr. *Kanjera*, locality in Kenya where the type was discovered] **:** an extinct East African man known from parts of four thick-walled dolichocephalic skulls found in association with artifacts of Abbevillian type and regarded as a primitive form of *Homo sapiens* possibly belonging to the Middle Pleistocene

kan·ji \'kän(,)jē\ *n, pl* **kanji** *or* **kanjis** [Jap] **1 :** a Japanese system of writing based on the Chinese one and composed principally of characters borrowed or adapted from Chinese — see KANA, KANA-MAJIRI **2 :** a single character belonging to the kanji system of writing

kan·ka·nai \¦käŋkə¦nī\ *n, pl* **kankanai** *or* **kankanais** *usu cap* [native name in northern Luzon] **1 a :** a people inhabiting the southern part of Mountain Province of northern Luzon, Philippines — compare IGOROT **b :** a member of such people **2 :** an Austronesian language of the Kankanai people

kan·krej \'kän,krej\ *n* -es [origin unknown] **:** GUZERAT

kan·na·da \'känədə, 'kan-\ *n* -s *usu cap* [Kanarese *kannaḍa*] **:** the major Dravidian language of Mysore, south India

ka·no \'kä(,)nō\ *adj, usu cap* [fr. *Kano*, city in northern Nigeria] **:** of or from the city of Kano, Nigeria **:** of the kind or style prevalent in Kano

kanon *var of* CANON

ka·no·ne \kə'nōnə\ *n, pl* **kano·nen** \-ōnən\ [G, lit., cannon, fr. It *cannone* — more at CANNON] **:** an expert skier

ka·noon \kä'nün\ *n* -s [Turk *kānun* — more at CANUN] **:** ZITHER

kanpur *usu cap, var of* CAWNPORE

kans \'kän(t)s\ *also* **kans grass** *n, pl* **kans** [Hindi *kās*, fr. Skt *kāśa*] **:** a common Indian grass (*Saccharum spontaneum*) found also in the West Indies that is used for thatching and for forage and in some areas is a troublesome weed — called also *glagah*

kan·sa \'kanzə, -n(t)sə\ *or* **kan·sas** *like* KANSAS\ *n, pl* **kansa** *or* **kansas** *usu cap* [native name in the Kansas river valley] **1 a :** a Siouan people of the Kansas river valley, Kansas **b :** a member of such people **2 :** a dialect of Dhegiha

[1]**kan·san** \'kanzən, 'kaan- *sometimes* -n(t)sən *or* 'kain(t)s-\ *n* -s *cap* [*Kansas*, state in the central U.S. + E *-an*, n. suffix] **:** a native or resident of Kansas

[2]**kansan** \"\ *adj, usu cap* [*Kansas* + E *-an*, adj. suffix] **1 a :** of, relating to, or characteristic of the state of Kansas **b :** of, relating to, or characteristic of the people of Kansas **2 :** of or relating to the second glacial stage during the glacial epoch in No. America

kan·sas \-nzəs *also* -nzəz *sometimes* -n(t)səs *or* -zis *or* -ziz *or* -sis\ *adj, usu cap* [fr. *Kansas*, state in the central U.S., fr. *Kansa, Kansas* (Siouan people)] **:** of or from the state of Kansas ⟨*Kansas* wheatfields⟩ **:** of the kind or style prevalent in Kansas **:** KANSAN

kansas cit·i·an *also* **kansas city·an** \¦=zə(s)¦sid·ēən, -itē- *also* -zəz¦si- *sometimes* -sə(s)¦si-\ *n, cap K&C* **:** a native or resident of Kansas City

kansas city \¦==¦sid·|ē, -it|, |i, *in rapid speech* (')kanz¦si- *or* (')kaan-\ *adj, usu cap K&C* **1** [fr. *Kansas City*, city in western Missouri] **:** of or from Kansas City, Mo. **:** of the kind or style prevalent in Kansas City **2** [fr. *Kansas City*, city in northeastern Kansas] **:** of or from Kansas City, Kans. **:** of the kind or style prevalent in Kansas City

kansas gay-feather *n, usu cap K* **:** a perennial herb (*Liatris pycnostachya*) having spikes of purplish flowers — called also *prairie button snakeroot*

kansas horse plague *n, usu cap K* **:** contagious equine encephalomyelitis

kansas thistle *n, usu cap K* **:** BUFFALO BUR

kan·tar *or* **can·tar** *or* **qan·tar** \kan·'tär, kən-\ *n* -s [Ar *qinṭār*, fr. LGk *kentēnarion* weight of 100 pounds, fr. LL *centenarium, centenarius* — more at CENTENARY] **:** any of various units of weight used in Mediterranean countries (as an Egyptian unit equal to about 99 pounds and a Turkish unit equal to about 124½ pounds)

kan·te·le *also* **kan·te·la** \'käntᵊlə, 'kan-\ *n* -s [Finn *kantele*] **:** a traditional Finnish harp orig. having 5 strings but now having as many as 20 to 30 strings

kan·ten \'kan·,ten\ *n* -s [Jap, lit., cold weather, fr. *kan* midwinter + *ten* sky] **:** AGAR 1a

kantharos *var of* CANTHARUS

[1]**kant·ian** \'kantēən, 'kän- *also* -nchən\ *adj, usu cap* [Immanuel *Kant* †1804 Ger. philosopher + E *-ian*] **1 :** of or relating to the German philosopher Immanuel Kant **2 :** of or relating to Kantianism

[2]**kantian** \"\ *n* -s *usu cap* **:** a follower of Kant or adherent to Kantianism

kant·ian·ism \-,nizəm\ *n* -s *usu cap* **:** the philosophy of Immanuel Kant that endeavors to synthesize the tradition of continental rationalism and British empiricism by holding that phenomenal knowledge is the joint product of percepts given to us through sensations organized under the forms of intuition of space and time and of concepts or categories of the understanding but that reason involves itself in fallacies if it tries to apply to the noumenal the principles of the understanding applicable only to the phenomenal so that the speculative ideas of God, the world, and the self although having heuristic import represent regulative knowledge as distinguished from the constitutive knowledge about the phenomenal at the same time that the ideas of God, freedom, and immortality represent necessary presuppositions for morality — compare CATEGORICAL IMPERATIVE, NOUMENON, PHENOMENON

kan·ti·ara \,kantē'a(a)rə\ *n* -s [origin unknown] **:** a spinose plant (*Carthamus oxycantha*) resembling the safflower that grows in troublesome clumps in Indian grasslands but can be made edible for livestock by beating off the spines

kantikoy *var of* CANTICO

kant·ism \'kant·,izəm, 'kän-\ *n* -s *usu cap* **:** KANTIANISM

kant·ist \-ntəst\ *n* -s *usu cap* **:** KANTIAN

kantuta *var of* CANTUTA

ka·nuck *also* **ka·nuk** \kə'nək\ *cap, var of* CANUCK

ka·nu·ka \'känəkə\ *n* -s [Maori] **:** a shrubby New Zealand tree (*Leptospermum ericoides*) with strong resistant wood that is used for making fences — compare MANUKA

kanun *var of* CANUN

ka·nu·ri \kə'nürē\ *n, pl* **kanuri** *or* **kanuris** *usu cap* **1 a :** a Negro people of the Muslim kingdom of Bornu west of Lake Chad whose history of dominance in that area goes back more than 500 years — compare TIBBU **b :** a member of such people **2 :** the language of the Kanuri people

kan·war \(')kan¦wär\ *n, pl* **kanwar** *or* **kanwars** *usu cap* **1 :** an indigenous people of central India esp. in the Bilaspur district many of whom are large landholders **2 :** a member of the Kanwar people

kan·ya butter \'kanyə-\ *n* [*kanya* perh. modif. of Hausa *ka'³da³nya¹* shea tree] **:** SHEA BUTTER

kanya tree *n* [*kanya* perh. modif. of Hausa *ka'³da³nya¹*] **:** SHEA TREE

kanyaw *var of* CANAO

kan·zu \'kan(,)zü\ *n* -s [Swahili] **:** a long white robe worn by African men (as the Swahili)

kao-chü-li \¦kaůchə¦lē\ *n, pl* **kao-chü-li** *usu cap* **:** a people of probable Tungusic affinities inhabiting the Yalu river region of Korea and Manchuria from the 1st to the 7th centuries A.D.

kaoh·siung \¦kaůshē¦ůŋ, ¦gaů-\ *adj, usu cap* [fr. *Kaohsiung*, city in Formosa, China] **:** of or from the city of Kaohsiung, Formosa, China **:** of the kind or style prevalent in Kaohsiung

kao·liang \¦kaůlē¦äŋ\ *also* **koa·liang** \¦kōl-\ *or* **kow·liang** \¦kaůl-, 'kōl-\ *n* -s [Chin (Pek) *kao*[1] *liang*[2], lit., tall grain, fr. *kao*[1] high, tall + *liang*[2] grain] **1 :** any of various grain sorghums that have slender dry pithy stalks, open erect panicles, and small white or brown seeds and are grown chiefly in China and Manchuria for their grain which is used for food and stalks which are used for fodder, thatching, and fuel **2 :** a spirituous liquor made in China from the juice of kaoliang stalks

ka·olin *also* **ka·oline** \'kāələn, kā'ōl-\ *n* -s [F *kaolin*, fr. *Kao-ling*, hill in Kiangsi province, southeast China, where it was originally obtained] **:** a fine usu. white clay resulting from extreme weathering of aluminous minerals (as feldspar) that contains kaolinite as its principal constituent, that remains white on firing, and that is used chiefly in ceramics and refractories, as an adsorbent, as a filler or extender (as in paper or rubber or pigments), and in medicine — see CHINA CLAY; compare FIRECLAY

ka·olin·ic \¦kāə¦linik\ *adj* [ISV *kaolin* + *-ic*] **:** of, relating to, or resembling kaolin

ka·olin·ite \'kāələ,nīt, kā'ōl-\ *n* -s [*kaolin* + *-ite*] **:** a mineral $Al_2Si_2O_5(OH)_4$ consisting of a hydrous silicate of aluminum that is polymorphous with dickite and nacrite and constitutes the principal mineral in kaolin

ka·olin·it·ic \'kāələ¦nid·ik, kā¦ōl-\ *adj* **:** of, relating to, containing, or resembling kaolinite

ka·olin·iza·tion \,kāələnə'zāshən, ,kāə,lin-, kā,ōlən-, -,nī'z-\ *n* -s [ISV *kaolinize* + *-ation*] **:** the development of kaolin by metasomatism

ka·olin·ize \'kāələ,nīz, kā'ōl-\ *vt* -ED/-ING/-s [ISV *kaolin* + *-ize*] **:** to convert (as feldspar) into kaolin

kaori *var of* KAURI

ka·pa \'käpə\ *n* -s [Hawaiian] *Hawaii* **:** TAPA

ka·pai \kə'pī\ *adj* [Maori] *New Zeal* **:** GOOD

ka·pel·le *also* **ca·pel·le** \kə'pelə\ *n, pl* **kapel·len** *also* **capel·len** \-lən\ *often cap* [G *kapelle*, fr. It *cappella* choir, chapel, fr. ML, chapel — more at CHAPEL] **1 :** the choir or orchestra of a royal or papal chapel **2 :** a musical organization; *esp* **:** ORCHESTRA

ka·pell·meis·ter *also* **ca·pell·meis·ter** \kə'pel,mīstər\ *n, pl* **kapellmeister** *often cap* [G *kapellmeister*, fr. *kapelle* + *meister* master, fr. OHG *meistar*, fr. L *magister* — more at MASTER] **:** the musical director of a kapelle

kapellmeister music *n, often cap K* **:** music of uninspired correctness — usu. used disparagingly

kaph *also* **caph** *or* **kaf** \'käf, 'kȯf\ *n* -s [Heb *kaph*, lit., palm of the hand] **1 :** the 11th letter of the Hebrew alphabet — symbol כ or ך; see ALPHABET table **2 :** a letter of the Phoenician or another Semitic alphabet corresponding to Hebrew kaph

ka·pok *also* **ca·poc** \'kā,päk\ *n* -s [Malay *kapok*] **:** a mass of silky fibers that clothe the seeds of the ceiba tree and are used commercially as a filling for mattresses, cushions, life preservers, and sleeping bags and as insulation — called also *ceiba, Java cotton, silk cotton*

kapok oil *n* **:** a light-yellow semidrying oil obtained from the seeds of the kapok tree and used in foods and in soapmaking

kapok tree *n* **:** SILK-COTTON TREE

ka·po·te \kə'pōd·ə\ *n* -s [Yiddish, fr. F *capote* — more at CAPOTE] **:** a man's long coat of medieval origin worn esp. by Jews of eastern Europe — compare CAPOTE

[1]**kap·pa** \'kapə\ *n* -s [Gk, of Sem origin; akin to Heb *kaph*] **:** the 10th letter of the Greek alphabet — symbol Κ or κ; see ALPHABET table

[2]**kappa** \"\ *n* -s [NL, fr. Gk *kappa*] **:** a cytoplasmic factor in certain paramecia that mediates production of paramecin and thereby makes the medium in which such animals are grown toxic to members of strains not possessing the factor

kap·pa·rah \,käpä'rä, kä'pȯrə\ *n, pl* **kap·pa·roth** *or* **kap·pa·rot** \,käpä'rōt(h), kä'pȯrəs\ [Heb, lit., atonement] **1 :** a symbolic ceremony practiced by some Orthodox Jews on the eve of Yom Kippur in which typically a cock, hen, or coin is swung around the head and offered in atonement or as ransom for one's sins **2 :** SACRIFICE; *specif* **:** something used as a symbolic sacrifice in the kapparah ceremony

kap·pie \'kapē, 'käpē\ *n* -s [Afrik, fr. D *kapje* small cap, dim. of *kap* cap, fr. MD *cappe*, fr. LL *cappa* head covering — more at CAP] *Africa* **:** SUNBONNET ⟨her hair . . . covered by a big black linen ~ which came down over her shoulders —Stuart Cloete⟩

ka·pu \'kä(,)pü\ *n* -s [Hawaiian] *Hawaii* **:** TABOO

ka·pu·ka \'käpəkə\ *n* -s [Maori] **:** a rather small New Zealand broadleaf evergreen tree (*Griselinia littoralis*) sometimes cultivated in warm regions as an ornamental

ka·pur \kə'pů(ə)r\ *or* **ka·por** \-pȯ(ə)r\ *n* -s [Hindi *kapūr*, fr. Skt *karpūra* camphor — more at CAMPHOR] **:** a tree (*Dryobalanops aromatica*) that produces Borneo camphor

ka·put *also* **ka·putt** \kä'půt, kə'-, -püt\ *adj* [G, fr. F *capot* not having made a trick at piquet — more at CAPOT] **1 :** utterly defeated or destroyed **:** FINISHED, DONE FOR, RUINED ⟨after weeks of bombardment the city was ~⟩ **2 :** made useless or unable to function ⟨the TV production masterminds were caught with their cables and cameras ~ —R.L.Shayon⟩ **3 :** hopelessly outmoded or set aside ⟨the notion that reading is ~ each time a mammoth entertainment medium catches hold —Harvey Breit⟩ ⟨all those curls that used to take hours to do are ~ —Ethel Merman⟩

ka·ra·bagh \¦karə¦bä\ *n* -s *usu cap* [fr. *Karabagh*, region in Azerbaidzhan, U.S.S.R.] **:** a small Caucasian rug showing considerable Persian influence in pattern and usu. having magenta, turquoise, and pale green as the prevailing colors

karabiner *var of* CARABINER

ka·ra·chai *also* **ka·ra·tchai** \¦karə¦chī\ *or* **ka·ra·cha·yevt**

\\,==ˈchäyəft\\ *n, pl* **karachai** *or* **karachais** *usu cap* [*Karachai, Karatchai* fr. *Karachai,* region on the northern slope of the western Caucasus mountains, U.S.S.R.; *Karachayevt* fr. Russ *Karachayevtsi* (pl.) Karachai people, fr. *Karachai*] **1 :** a Turkic-speaking people of the Caucasus **2 :** a member of the Karachai people **3 :** the Turkic language of the Karachai people

ka·ra·chi \\kəˈrächē *also* -rache\\ *adj, usu cap* [fr. *Karachi,* Pakistan] **:** of or from the city of Karachi, Pakistan **:** of the kind or style prevalent in Karachi

ka·ra·dagh \\ˈkärəˌdä\\ *n* -S *usu cap* [fr. *Karadagh,* mountain range in Azerbaidzhan province, northwestern Iran] **:** a Persian rug having a bold design and rich coloring

ka·ra·gan·da \\ˌkärəgənˈdä\\ *adj, usu cap* [fr. *Karaganda,* city in the central U.S.S.R.] **:** of or from the city of Karaganda, U.S.S.R. **:** of the kind or style prevalent in Karaganda

kara·ism \\ˈka(a)rəˌizəm\\ *or* **kara·it·ism** \\-rəˌīd-ˌizəm\\ *n* -S *usu cap* [*karaism* fr. *kara-* (fr. LHeb *qĕrāīm* Karaites, fr. Heb *qārā* to read) + *-ism*; *karaitism* fr. *karaite* + *-ism*] **:** a Jewish doctrine originating in Baghdad in the 8th century that rejects rabbinism and talmudism and bases its tenets on interpretation of the Scriptures

karait *var of* KRAIT

kara·ite \\-rəˌīt\\ *n* -S *usu cap* [*kara-* (fr. L Heb *qĕrāīm* Karaites) + *-ite*] **1 :** an adherent of Karaism **2 :** a Turkic dialect spoken by Karaite people from Crimea

karajá *or* **karaya** *usu cap, var of* CARAJÁ

ka·ra·ka \\ˈkärəkə\\ *n* -S [Maori] **:** a New Zealand tree (*Corynocarpus laevigata*) having orange-colored fruit with edible pulp and poisonous seeds that when cooked and dried are also edible and form an important article of native diet

kara·kal·pak *or* **qara·qal·paq** \\ˌkarəkəlˈpak, -rəkälˈ-\\ *n, pl* **karakalpak** *or* **karakalpaks** *or* **qaraqalpaq** *or* **qaraqalpaqs** *usu cap* [Kirghiz, lit., black cap, fr. *kara* black + *kalpak* cap] **1 a :** a Turkic people living near Lake Aral, Central Asia **b :** a member of such people **2 :** the Turkic language of the Karakalpak people

kara kir·ghiz \\ˈkarə(ˌ)kərˈgēz, -arəˌkirˈ-\\ *n, usu cap both Ks* [Kirghiz *Karakyrghyz,* lit., black Kirghiz, fr. *kara* black + *Kyrghyz* Kirghiz] **1 :** a Kirghiz people closely resembling the Mongols and dwelling chiefly in the Tien Shan highlands and the Great Pamir — called also *Black Kirghiz, Burut* **2 :** a member of the Kara Kirghiz people

kar·a·kul *also* **car·a·cul** \\ˈkarəkəl *also* ˈker-\\ *n* [fr. *Karakul,* village in Uzbekistan, U.S.S.R., where the breed originated] **1 a** *usu cap* **:** a breed of hardy slender fat-tailed sheep from Bukhara with coarse wiry brown fur **b** -S *often cap* **:** a sheep of this breed **2** -S **:** the tightly curled glossy black coat of the newborn lamb of the Karakul breed valued as fur — compare ASTRAKHAN, BROADTAIL, PERSIAN LAMB

kar·a·kurt \\ˈkarəˌku̇(ə)rt\\ *n* -S [Turki, fr. *kara* black + *kurt* wolf] **:** a venomous spider (*Latrodectus tredecimguttatus*) of eastern Europe and Siberia — called also *black wolf*

ka·ra·mo·jong \\ˌkarəˈmōˌjäŋ\\ *or* **ka·ra·mo·jo** \\-(ˌ)jō\\ *n, pl* **karamojong** *or* **karamojongs** *or* **karamojo** *or* **karamojos** *usu cap* **1 a :** a pastoral people of northeast Uganda **b :** a member of such people **2 :** a Nilotic language of the Karamojong people

kar·a·mu \\ˈkarəˌmü\\ *n* -S [Maori] **:** a New Zealand shrub or tree of the genus *Coprosma*

ka·ran·da \\kəˈrəndə, -ˌdä\\ *var of* CARAUNDA

ka·ran·ka·wa \\kəˈraŋkəˌwȯ\\ *n, pl* **karankawa** *or* **karankawas** *usu cap* **1 a :** an Indian people of the Gulf coast in Texas **b :** a member of such people **2 :** a language of the Karankawa people **3 :** a language family perhaps related to Coahuiltecan and Tonkawan that comprises the Karankawa language

kar·at *or* **car·at** \\ˈkarət *also* ˈker-\\ *n* -S [prob. fr. MF *carat,* fr. ML *carratus* unit of weight for precious stones — more at CARAT] **:** a unit of fineness for gold equal to 1/24 part of pure gold in an alloy ⟨16-*karat* gold contains 16/24 pure gold⟩ ⟨24-*karat* gold is pure⟩ — abbr. *k* or *kt*

kar·a·tas \\ˈkarəˌtas\\ *n* [NL, fr. Tupi *carautá, caragoatá* karatas] **1** *cap* **:** a genus of tropical American plants (family Bromeliaceae) with the flowers in dense terminal heads **2** -ES **:** any plant of the genus *Karatas* (esp. *K. plumieri*) **3** -ES **:** SILK GRASS 3b

ka·ra·te \\kəˈrätē\\ *n* -S [Jap, lit., empty hand] **:** a Japanese art of self-defense in which kicks and openhanded blows are delivered esp. to vulnerable parts of the body

karatto *var of* KERATTO

karaya *usu cap, var of* CARAJÁ

ka·raya gum *also* **karaya** \\kəˈrīə-\\ *n* -S [*karaya* modif. of Hindi *karāyal* resin] **:** STERCULIA GUM; *esp* **:** a gum derived from an Indian tree (*Sterculia urens*)

[1]**kar·bi** \\ˈkärbē\\ *n* -S [native name in Queensland, Australia] **:** a small stingless wild bee (*Trigona carbonaria*) of Australia that makes a spiral mass of honeycomb

[2]**karbi** \\"\\ *n, pl* **karbi** [Gujarati *kaḍbī*] *India* **:** dried stalks of Indian corn

ka·rel \\kəˈrel, ˈkarəl\\ *n* -S *cap* [back-formation fr. *karelian*] **:** KARELIAN 2

ka·re·la \\ˈkərələ\\ *n* -S [Hindi *karelā,* fr. Skt *kāravella, kāravellaka*] *India* **:** a large balsam apple (*Momordica charantia*) with an elongated warty yellowish to coppery fruit

[1]**ka·re·lian** *also* **ca·re·lian** \\kəˈrēlēən, -lyən\\ *adj, usu cap* [*Karelia,* region in northwestern U.S.S.R. + E *-an,* adj. suffix] **1 :** of, relating to, or characteristic of Karelia, a region of the northwestern U.S.S.R. and the adjoining borders of eastern Finland **2 :** of, relating to, or characteristic of the people of Karelia **3 :** of, relating to, or characteristic of the language of the Karelians

[2]**karelian** *also* **carelian** \\"\\ *n* -S *cap* [*Karelia* + E *-an,* n. suffix] **1 :** a native or inhabitant of Karelia **2 :** the Finno-Ugric language of the Karelian people that is closely related to Finnish and sometimes treated as a dialect of it

ka·ren \\kəˈren\\ *n, pl* **karen** *or* **karens** *usu cap* **1 a :** a group of peoples of eastern and southern Burma **b :** a member of any of such peoples **2 a :** a group of languages spoken by the Karen peoples that is held to be related to the Tibeto-Burman, Thai, or Mon-Khmer language groups **b :** a language of this group

ka·ren·ni \\kəˈrenē\\ *n, pl* **karenni** *or* **karennis** *usu cap* **1 :** one of several Karen peoples of eastern Burma the women of which elongate their necks by heavy coils of brass that thrust the head away from the body **2 :** a member of a Karenni people

ka·rez \\kəˈrez, ˈ==\\ *n, pl* **karez** [Per *kārez*] **1 :** an underground irrigation tunnel bored horizontally into rock slopes in Baluchistan **2 :** a system of irrigation by underground tunnels

kari *var of* KARRI

kar·i·era \\ˌkarēˈerə\\ *n, pl* **kariera** *or* **karieras** *usu cap* **1 :** a people of Western Australia **2 :** a member of the Kariera people

kar·in·gho·ta \\ˌkarənˈgōdə\\ *n* -S [origin unknown] **:** NIEPA 1

kariri *usu cap, var of* CARIRI

kar·i·te *or* **kar·i·ti** \\ˈkarəd-ē\\ *n* -S [F *karité,* of Niger-Congo origin; akin to Wolof *karité* karite] **:** SHEA TREE

karite butter *or* **karite oil** *n* **:** SHEA BUTTER

karl fisch·er reagent \\ˈkärlˈfishər-\\ *n, usu cap K&F* [after *Karl Fischer,* 20th cent. Ger. chemist] **:** a colored solution of pyridine, sulfur dioxide, iodine, and anhydrous methanol that reacts quantitatively with water to form a colorless solution and is used to determine the amount of water in numerous substances

karls·bad salt \\ˈkärlzˌbad-, -l(t)sˌbät-\\ *n, usu cap K* [trans. of G *karlsbader salz,* fr. *Karlsbad* (*Karlovy Vary*), town in western Czechoslovakia renowned for its sulfur springs] **1 :** a mixture of mineral salts including esp. potassium sulfate and sodium sulfate that is obtained from the water of certain springs **2 :** an artificial mixture of potassium sulfate, sodium sulfate, sodium chloride, and sodium bicarbonate

karls·ru·he \\ˈkärlzˌrüə, -l(t)sˌr-\\ *adj, usu cap* [fr. *Karlsruhe,* city in southwest Germany] **:** of or from the city of Karlsruhe, Germany **:** of the kind or style prevalent in Karlsruhe

kar·ma \\ˈkärmə, ˈkar-\\ *n* -S *often cap* [Skt *karman* (nom. *karma*) karma, work, office, fr. *karoti* he does, makes; akin to OIr *cruth* form, Lith *kurti* to build, Skt *kāra* doing, *kr̥ṇoti* he does, makes] **1 :** the force generated by a person's actions that is held in Hinduism and Buddhism to be the motive power for the round of rebirths and deaths endured by him until he has achieved spiritual liberation and freed himself from the effects of such force ⟨release from the ~ of recurrent existences —John Baillie⟩ — compare NIRVANA, SAMSARA **2 :** the sum total of the ethical consequences of a person's good or bad actions comprising thoughts, words, and deeds that is held in Hinduism and Buddhism to determine his specific destiny in his next existence ⟨as our desires shape themselves, so we act and build up our coming fate, our ~ —P.E.More⟩ **3 :** a subtle form of matter held in Jainism to develop in the soul and vitiate its purity, to lengthen the course of individual transmigration, and to postpone the possibility of final salvation ⟨the soul's chief problem . . . of managing to throw off or expel ~ matter from itself —J.B.Noss⟩ — **kar·mic** \\-mik\\ *adj, often cap*

kar·ma·dha·ra·ya \\ˌkərməˈdärəə, -ˈārəyə\\ *n* -S [Skt *karmadhāraya,* fr. *karma-* (fr. *karman*) + *dhāraya* that holds, that maintains; perh. fr. the fact that such words maintain the same function throughout, inasmuch as the syntactic function of the entire compound is the same as the syntactic function of its final constituent would be if used alone; akin to Skt *dhārayati* he holds, carries, keeps — more at FIRM] **:** a class of compound words typically having a noun as second constituent and a descriptive adjective as first constituent (as *bluegrass, blackberry*), a noun as second constituent and an attributive noun as first constituent (as *houseboat*), or an adjective as second constituent and an adverb as first constituent (as *everlasting, widespread*) and having meanings that follow the formula "a *B* that is *A*" for nouns or "*B* in the manner expressed by *A*" for adjectives, where *A* stands for the first constituent and *B* for the second; *also* **:** a compound word belonging to this class

karma-marga \\-ˈmärgə\\ *n* -S [Skt, fr. *karma-* (fr. *karman*) + *mārga* path, fr. *mṛga* deer, gazelle] **:** the strict observation of caste regulations and ritual duties regarded in Hinduism as one path to a happier life in an individual's next incarnation **:** salvation by works — compare BHAKTI-MARGA, JNANA-MARGA

karmatian *or* **karmathian** *usu cap, var of* QARMATIAN

karma-yoga \\ˈ==ˌ==\\ *n* [Skt *karmayoga,* fr. *karma-* (fr. *karman*) + *yoga*] **:** yoga through disinterested service or the selfless performance of duties

kar·mouth *or* **kar·mout** \\(ˈ)kärˈmüt\\ *n* -S [Ar *qarmūṭ*] **:** any of several African siluroid fishes (genera *Clarias* and *Heterobranchus*) that have an accessory breathing organ enabling them to live for a time out of water

karn \\ˈkärn\\ *var of* CAIRN

ka·ro \\ˈkä(ˌ)rō\\ *n* -S [Maori] **:** either of two New Zealand plants of the genus *Pittosporum*: **a :** a shrub or small tree (*P. crassifolium*) with fastigiate branches **b :** an epiphyte (*P. cornifolium*) with whorled leaves

ka·rok \\kəˈräk\\ *n, pl* **karok** *or* **karoks** *usu cap* [Karok *karuk* upstream] **1 a :** an Indian people of the Klamath river valley, California **b :** a member of such people **2 :** the Quoratean language of the Karok people **3 :** QUORATEAN

karolin *var of* CAROLIN

ka·ross \\kəˈräs\\ *n* -ES [Afrik *karos,* perh. alter. of D *kuras* cuirass, fr. MF *curasse, cuirasse* — more at CUIRASS] **:** a simple garment or rug of animal skins usu. used by native tribesmen of southern Africa

kar·pas \\ˈkärˌpäs\\ *n* -ES [Heb *karpās,* fr. Aram *karpas*] **:** a piece of parsley, celery, or lettuce placed on the Passover seder plate as a symbol of spring or hope and dipped in salt water in remembrance of the hyssop and blood of the Passover in Egypt

kar·ree \\kəˈrē, -rā\\ *also* **karree boom** \\-ˌbüm, -ˌbōm\\ *or* **kar·roo·boom** \\-ˈrüˌb-\\ *n* -S [*karree* fr. Afrik, prob. fr. Hottentot *karib*; *karree boom, karrooboom* fr. Afrik *karreeboom,* fr. *karree* + *boom* tree, fr. D, fr. MD; akin to OE *bēam* tree — more at BEAM] **:** a plant of the genus *Rhus* (esp. *R. viminalis*) of southern Africa

kar·ren \\ˈkärən\\ *n* -S [G] **:** a ribbed and fluted rock surface resulting at least in part from differential solution

kar·ri *or* **kari** \\ˈkarē\\ *n* -S [native name in Western Australia] **1 :** a large gum tree (*Eucalyptus diversicolor*) of Western Australia **2 :** the hard durable red wood of karri that constitutes one of the principal commercial timbers of Australia

karri-tree \\ˈkarēˌ\\ *n* [origin unknown] **:** PRINCESS-TREE

kar·roo *or* **ka·roo** \\kəˈrü\\ *n* -S [Afrik *karo,* perh. fr. Hottentot *garo* desert] **:** a dry tableland of southern Africa that often rises in terraces to a considerable elevation

karroo bush *also* **karroo shrub** *n* **1 :** a thorny acacia (*Acacia horrida*) that yields cape gum **2 :** a plant of the genus *Tetragonia* (esp. *T. arbuscula*)

karroo caterpillar *n* **:** the larva of a pyralidid moth (*Loxostege frustralis*) that seriously damages fodder in sheep-farming regions of southern Africa

kar·ru·sel \\ˌkarəˈsel, ˈ==ˌ= *also* ˈker- *or* -zel\\ *n* -S [prob. alter. of *carrousel*] **:** a revolving escapement that is designed to reduce position errors in a watch and is mounted in a carriage similar to that of a tourbillion but differs from it in slower speed of rotation and in having the fourth wheel contained inside the carriage

kar·shu·ni *also* **car·shu·ni** *or* **gar·shu·ni** \\gärˈ-\\ *n* -S *usu cap* [Ar *karshūnīy,* prob. fr. Syr *gershūn* alien, foreign + Ar *-īy* belonging to] **:** Arabic written in Syriac characters esp. as used in the Maronite ritual

karst \\ˈkärst\\ *n* -S [G] **:** a limestone region marked by sinks, abrupt ridges, irregular protuberant rocks, caverns, and underground streams — **karst·ic** \\-tik\\ *adj*

kar·tik \\ˈkard·ik\\ *n* -S *usu cap* [Hindi *kārtik,* fr. Skt *kārttika,* fr. *kṛttikā* Pleiades; perh. akin to Skt *kṛnatti* he spins — more at HURDLE] **:** a month of the Hindu year — see MONTH table

kart·ve·lian \\(ˈ)kärtˈvēlēən, -lyən\\ *also* **karth·li** \\ˈkärtlē\\ *or* **kart·vel** \\ˈkärtˌvel\\ *n* -S *usu cap* **1 :** a member of a group of related peoples of the Caucasus **2 :** the South Caucasic language family including Georgian, Mingrelian, Svanetian, and Laz

ka·ru·na \\ˈkəru̇ˌnä\\ *n* -S [Skt *karuṇā* compassion; perh. akin to OE *hrēowan* to grieve, repent — more at RUE] **:** compassion that is a fundamental quality in the bodhisattva ideal of Mahayana Buddhism

kar·win·skia \\kärˈwinzkēə, -n(t)sk-\\ *n, cap* [NL, fr. Wilhelm *Karwinsky* von Karwin †1855 Ger. traveler + NL *-ia*] **:** a genus of shrubs or small trees (family Rhamnaceae) that are chiefly native to Mexico and the southwestern U.S. and have flowers with small hooded short-clawed petals and fleshy drupes

kary- *or* **karyo-** *also* **cary-** *or* **caryo-** *comb form* [NL, fr. Gk *kary-, karyo-* walnut, nut, kernel, fr. *karyon* — more at CAREEN] **1 :** nucleus of a cell ⟨*karyenchyma*⟩ ⟨*karyokinesis*⟩ — in cytological terms **2 :** nut **:** kernel ⟨*caryopsis*⟩

kary·en·chy·ma \\ˌkarēˈeŋkəmə, -enk-\\ *n* -S [NL, fr. *kary-* + *-enchyma*] **:** KARYOLYMPH

kar·yo·chy·le·ma \\ˌkarē(ˌ)ōˌkīˈlēmə\\ *n* -S [NL, fr. *kary-* + *-chylema* (as in *enchylema*)] **:** KARYOLYMPH

kar·yo·clasic \\ˈ==ˌ=ˈklāsik, -las-\\ *or* **kar·yo·clas·tic** \\-lastik\\ *adj* [*karyoclasic* ISV *karyoclas-* (fr. NL *karyoclasis*) + *-ic*; *karyoclastic* fr. *kary-* + *-clastic*] **:** of or relating to karyoclasis

kar·y·oc·la·sis *or* **kar·y·ok·la·sis** \\ˌkarēˈäkləsəs\\ *n, pl* **karyocla·ses** *or* **karyokla·ses** \\-əˌsēz\\ [NL *karyoclasis,* fr. *kary-* + *-clasis*] **1 :** disintegration of the cell nucleus **2 :** interruption of mitosis (as in colchicine poisoning)

kar·yo·gam·ic \\ˌkarēōˈgamik\\ *adj* **:** of or relating to karyogamy

kar·y·og·a·my \\ˌkarēˈägəmē\\ *n* -ES [ISV *kary-* + *-gamy*] **:** the fusion of cell nuclei (as in fertilization) — compare PLASMOGAMY

kar·yo·kinesis \\ˈkarē(ˌ)ō+\\ *n* [NL, fr. *kary-* + *-kinesis*] **1 :** the nuclear phenomena characteristic of mitosis **2 :** the whole process of mitosis — compare CYTOKINESIS — **kar·yo·kinetic** \\"+\\ *adj*

karyokinetic figure *n* [*karyokinetic* ISV *kary-* + *kinetic*] *biol* **:** ACHROMATIC FIGURE

kar·y·o·log·ic \\ˌkarēəˈläjik\\ *or* **kar·y·o·log·i·cal** \\-jəkəl\\ *adj* **:** of or relating to karyology — **kar·y·o·log·i·cal·ly** \\-jək(ə)lē\\ *adv*

kar·y·ol·o·gy \\ˌkarēˈäləjē\\ *n* -ES [ISV *kary-* + *-logy*] **:** a branch of cytology that deals with the minute anatomy of cell nuclei and esp. the nature and structure of chromosomes

kar·yo·lymph \\ˈkarēō+ˌ-\\ *n* [ISV *kary-* + *lymph*; prob. orig. formed as G *karyolymphe*] **:** the clear homogeneous ground substance of a cell nucleus — called also *enchylema, nuclear sap*; opposed to *karyotin*

kar·y·ol·y·sis \\ˌkarēˈäləsəs\\ *n* [NL, fr. *kary-* + *-lysis*] **:** dissolution of the cell nucleus with loss of its affinity for basic stains sometimes occurring normally but usu. in necrosis — **kar·yo·lyt·ic** \\ˈkarēəˈlid·ik\\ *adj*

kar·y·ol·y·sus \\-ləsəs\\ *n, cap* [NL, fr. *kary-* + *-lysus* (fr. Gk *lyein* to loose, dissolve) — more at LOSE] **:** a genus of haemogregarines parasitic in reptiles

kar·yo·mere \\ˈ===ˌmi(ə)r\\ *n* -S [ISV *kary* + *-mere*] **1 a :** [2]CHROMOMERE **b :** a sperm head **2 :** a swollen vesicular chromosome (as in certain embryonic tissues) — called also *chromosomal vesicle*

kar·y·om·er·ite \\ˌkarēˈäməˌrīt\\ *n* -S [ISV *kary-* + *-mere* + *-ite*; prob. orig. formed as G *karyomerit*] **:** KARYOMERE 2

kar·yo·microsome \\ˈkarē(ˌ)ō+\\ *n* **:** a nuclear microsome

kar·yo·mi·to·ic \\ˈkarēōˌmīˈtōik\\ *or* **kar·yo·mi·tot·ic** \\ˈkarēō+\\ *adj* [*karyomitoic* fr. *karyomitosis* + *-ic*; *karyomitotic* fr. *kary-* + *mitotic*] **:** of or relating to karyomitosis

kar·yo·mitome \\ˈkarēō+\\ *n* [ISV *kary-* + *mitome*] **:** the nuclear reticulum of a cell

kar·yo·mitosis \\"+\\ *n* [NL, fr. *kary-* + *mitosis*] **:** mitotic division of the nucleus of a cell

kar·y·on \\ˈkarēˌän\\ *n* -S [NL, fr. Gk *karyon* nut — more at CAREEN] **:** the nucleus of a cell — **kar·y·on·tic** \\ˈkarēˈäntik\\ *adj*

kar·yo·plasm \\ˈkarēə+ˌ-\\ *also* **kar·yo·plas·ma** \\ˈ===+\\ *n* -S [ISV *kary-* + *-plasm, -plasma*; orig. formed as G *karyoplasma*] **:** NUCLEOPLASM 1 — **kar·yo·plasmic** \\ˈ==(ˌ)=+\\ *or* **kar·y·o·plasmatic** \\"+\\ *adj*

kar·yo·pyk·nosis \\ˈkarē(ˌ)ō+\\ *n* [NL, fr. *kary-* + *pyknosis*] **:** KARYOCLASIS 1 — **kar·yo·pyknotic** \\"+\\ *adj*

kar·y·or·rhec·tic \\ˌkarēəˈrektik\\ *adj* [*kary-* + Gk *rhēktikos* apt to burst, fr. *rhēktos* that can be broken (fr. *rhēgnynai* to break) + *-ikos* -ic] **:** of or relating to karyorrhexis

kar·y·or·rhex·is \\ˌkarēəˈreksəs\\ *n, pl* **karyorrhex·es** \\-kˌsēz\\ [NL, fr. *kary-* + *-rrhexis*] **:** KARYOCLASIS 1

kar·y·os·chi·sis \\ˌkarēˈäskəsəs\\ *n, pl* **karyoschi·ses** \\-əˌsēz\\ [NL, fr. *kary-* + *-schisis*] **:** KARYOCLASIS 1

kar·yo·some \\ˈkarēəˌsōm\\ *n* -S [ISV *kary-* + *-some*; orig. formed as G *karyosom*] **1 :** CHROMOCENTER **2 :** ENDOSOME; *esp* **:** an endosome consisting of a nucleolar mass of heterochromatin as distinguished from one that is a plasmosome

kar·yo·systematic \\ˈkarē(ˌ)ō+\\ *adj* **:** of or relating to karyosystematics

kar·yo·systematics \\"+\\ *n pl but sing in constr* **:** a branch of systematics that seeks to determine natural relationships by the study of karyotypes

kar·yo·the·ca \\ˈkarēō+\\ *n* -S [NL, fr. *kary-* + *-theca*] **:** a nuclear membrane

kar·y·o·tin \\ˌkarēˈōtən, -ˌtin\\ *n* -S [ISV *kary-* + *-tin* (fr. *chromatin*); orig. formed as G *caryotin* (now *karyotin*)] **:** the reticular usu. stainable material of the cell nucleus — opposed to *karyolymph*

kar·yo·type \\-ˌtīp\\ *n* [ISV *kary-* + *type*; prob. orig. formed as F *caryotype*] **1 :** the sum of the specific characteristics of a cell nucleus including chromosome number, form, size, and points of spindle-fiber attachment **2 :** a diagrammatic representation of a physical karyotype — **kar·yo·typ·ic** \\ˈkarēōˈtipik\\ *or* **kar·yo·typ·i·cal** \\-pəkəl\\ *adj*

[1]**kas** *pl of* KA

[2]**kas** \\ˈkäs\\ *n, pl* **kas** [D, fr. MD *casse, cas* chest, box, fr. ONF *casse* — more at CASE] **:** a Dutch cupboard or wardrobe common in the late 17th and the 18th centuries in the New Netherlands colony in America, often paneled, sometimes painted with floral designs, and equipped with two doors, heavy cornices, and usu. a drawer at the bottom

kasbah *or* **kasba** *usu cap, var of* CASBAH

kas·cam·i·ol \\kaˈskamēˌȯl\\ *n* -S [origin unknown] **:** a purple gallinule (*Porphyrula martinicas*) of the West Indies

ka·sha \\ˈkäshə\\ *n* -S [Russ; akin to Pol *kasza* kasha, Lith *košti* to strain] **1 :** a mush made from coarse cracked buckwheat, barley, millet, or wheat **2 :** kasha grain before cooking

Kasha \\ˈkashə\\ *trademark* — used for a soft napped twilled fabric of fine wool and hair having a slight crosswise streaked effect

ka·shan \\kəˈshän\\ *n* -S *usu cap* [fr. *Kashan,* city in central Iran] **1 :** a Persian rug of fine quality, soft color, and fluid floral designs **2 :** a heavy glazed pottery produced in eastern Mediterranean lands during the 16th, 17th, and 18th centuries

[1]**kasher** *var of* KOSHER

[2]**ka·sher** \\käˈshe(ə)r, -eə\\ *or* **ko·sher** \\ˈkōshə(r)\\ *vt* -ED/-ING/-S [*kasher* fr. Heb *kāshēr* to make kosher; *kosher* fr. Yiddish, n., kosher, fr. Heb *kāshēr* kosher, fit, proper] **:** to make (meat or utensils) kosher for use according to Jewish law

kash·gai *also* **khash·gai** \\ˈkashˌgī\\ *n* -S *usu cap* **1 :** a Turkic often nomadic people of southern Iran **2 :** a member of the Kashgai people

ka·shi \\ˈkäshē\\ *n* -S [Ar *qāshīy* belonging to Kashan, fr. *Qāshān* Kashan, city in central Iran] **:** a Persian enameled tile made esp. in the 16th and 17th centuries

ka·shim \\ˈkashəm\\ *n* -S [Esk] **:** an Eskimo house of assembly

kash·mir \\ˈkazhˌmi(ə)r, -aizh-, -iə; -ash-, -aa-, -ai-\\ *var of* CASHMERE

kashmir goat *n, usu cap K* [fr. *Kashmir,* region in the northern part of the Indian subcontinent] **:** an Indian goat raised chiefly for its undercoat of fine soft wool that constitutes the cashmere wool of commerce

kash·miri *or* **cash·miri** \\ˈ=ˈmirē\\ *n, pl* **kashmiris** *or* **kashmiri** *or* **cashmiris** *or* **cashmiri** *usu cap* **1 :** a native or inhabitant of Kashmir **2 :** the Dard language of the Kashmiri people

[1]**kash·mir·ian** \\(ˈ)=ˈmirēən\\ *adj, usu cap* **1 :** of, relating to, or characteristic of Kashmir **2 :** of, relating to, or characteristic of the people of Kashmir

[2]**kashmirian** \\"\\ *n* -S *cap* **:** KASHMIRI

ka·shou·bish \\kəˈshübish\\ *n* -ES *cap* **:** the Kashubian language

kash·ruth *or* **kash·rut** \\käˈshrüt(h), ˈ=ˌ=\\ *also* **kash·rus** \\ˈkäshrəs, -ru̇s\\ *n* -S [*kashruth, kashrut* fr. Heb *kashrūth,* kashrūt, lit., fitness, fr. *kāshēr* kosher, fit, proper; *kashrus* fr. Yiddish, fr. Heb *kashrūth*] **1 :** the state of being kosher according to Jewish religious law ⟨rabbinical approval of the ~ of the new scroll of the Torah⟩ **2 :** the Jewish dietary laws ⟨meals for Orthodox Jews who observe ~⟩ — compare HECHSHER

kashua *var of* CACHUA

ka·shube *or* **ka·shub** \\kəˈshüb\\ *n* -S *usu cap* **1 :** a member of a Slavonic Pomeranian people who live just west of the mouth of the Vistula river **2 :** KASHUBIAN

ka·shu·bi·an \\kəˈshübēən\\ *or* **kasubian** *or* **kas·su·bi·an** *also* **cas·su·bi·an** *or* **ca·su·bi·an** \\kəˈsü-\\ *n* -S *cap* [*Kashube* + E *-ian,* n. suffix] **1 :** KASHUBE 1 **2 :** a West Slavic language closely related to Polish and spoken in the region of Danzig

kasida *var of* QASIDA

kas·ka \\ˈkaskə\\ *n, pl* **kaska** *or* **kaskas** *usu cap* **1 a :** an Athapaskan people of the Liard river valley of the Yukon and British Columbia **b :** a member of such people **2 :** the language of the Kaska people — called also *Nahane*; see MONTAGNARD

kaso·lite \\ˈkasəˌlīt, kəˈsōˌl-\\ *n* -S [*Kasolo,* Katanga, Belgian Congo, its locality + E *-ite*] **:** a mineral $Pb(UO_2)SiO_4H_2O$ consisting of a hydrous uranium lead silicate that occurs in yellow-ocher monoclinic crystals

kas·sel *also* **cas·sel** \\ˈkasəl, ˈkäs-\\ *adj, usu cap* [fr. *Kassel,* city in central Germany] **:** of or from the city of Kassel, Germany **:** of the kind or style prevalent in Kassel

kas·site *or* **cas·site** \\ˈkaˌsīt\\ *n* -S *usu cap* **1 :** a member of a people inhabiting parts of the Iranian plateau south of the Caspian sea and ruling Babylon between 1600 and 1200 B.C. **2 :** the Elamite language of the Kassite people

kas·tu·ra \\kəˈstu̇rə\\ *n* -S [Hindi *kastūrī,* lit., musk, fr. Skt *kastūrikā,* fr. Gk *kastorion* castor, fr. neut. of *kastoreios, kastorios* of a beaver, fr. *kastor-, kastōr* beaver — more at CASTOR] **:** MUSK DEER

kaswa *var of* CACHUA

kat *or* **khat** *or* **qat** *or* **quat** *or* **cat** \\ˈkät\\ *n* -S [Ar *qāt*] **:** a shrub (*Catha edulis*) cultivated by the Arabs for its leaves that act as a stimulant narcotic when chewed or used as a tea — called also *African tea, Arabian tea*

ka·ta \ˈkä(ˌ)tä\ *n* -s [Jap] **:** form practice in judo **:** a set of exercises in judo — compare RANDORI

kata- or **kat-** *prefix* [Gk — more at CATA-] **:** CATA-

katabanian *usu cap, var of* QATABANIAN

ka·tab·a·sis *or* **ca·tab·a·sis** \kəˈtabəsəs\ *n, pl* **kataba·ses** *or* **cataba·ses** \-bəˌsēz\ [Gk *katabasis* descent, fr. *katabainein* to go down, fr. *kata-* cata- + *bainein* to go — more at COME] **1 :** a going or marching down or back **:** RETREAT; *esp* **:** a military retreat ⟨the Russian anabasis and ~ of Napoleon —Thomas DeQuincey⟩ ⟨the tragic and precipitate ~ of the UN troops —H.L.Ickes⟩ **2 :** a troparion sung after the two sides of the choir descend to the middle of the church at the end of each ode of the canon at matins in the Eastern Orthodox Church

kat·a·bat·ic \ˌkad·əˈbad·ik\ *adj* [LGk *katabatikos* of descent, fr. Gk *katabatos* descending (fr. *katabainein* to descend) + *-ikos* -ic] **:** of or relating to the downward motion of air (as in air drainage induced by surface cooling)

kat·a·bel·la \ˌkatəˈbelə\ *n* -s [origin unknown] *dial Brit* **:** HEN HARRIER

katabolism *var of* CATABOLISM

kata·chro·ma·sis *or* **cata·chro·ma·sis** \ˌkad·əˈkrōməsəs\ *n, pl* **katachroma·ses** *or* **catachroma·ses** \-məˌsēz\ [NL, fr. *kata-* or *cata-* + *chrom-* + connective *-a-* + *-sis*] **:** the mitotic nuclear transformations leading to formation of daughter nuclei from the chromosome groups separated in anaphase — compare ANACHROMASIS

katagenesis *var of* CATAGENESIS

ka·ta·ka·na \ˌkäd·əˈkänə\ *n* -s [Jap, fr. *kata* side + *kana*] **:** a set of symbols for writing Japanese kana having characters that are in general squarer and more angular than those of the hiragana

kata·mor·phism *or* **cata·mor·phism** \ˌkad·əˈmȯrˌfizəm\ *n* -s [*kata-* or *cata-* + *-morphism*] **:** the breaking down of rock by chemical or mechanical processes — compare ANAMORPHISM, METAMORPHISM

kata·mor·pho·sis \ˌkad·əˈmȯrfəsəs *sometimes* -ˌmȯrˈfōs-\ *n* [NL, fr. *kata-* + *morphosis*] **:** evolutionary change based on or involving hypomorphosis

ka·ta·na \kəˈtänə\ *n* -s [Jap] **:** a single-edged sword that is the longer of a pair worn by the Japanese samurai

ka·tang \kəˈtäŋ\ *n, pl* **katang** *or* **katangs** *usu cap* **1 :** a Moi people of northern Vietnam **2 :** a member of the Katang people

katastate *var of* CATASTATE

kata·thermometer *or* **cata·thermometer** \ˈ¦kad·ə+\ *n* [*kata-* or *cata-* + *thermometer*] **:** a large-bulbed alcohol thermometer used to measure the cooling effect of particular atmospheric conditions or to measure moderate air velocities by means of the cooling effect

katatonic *var of* CATATONIC

ka·ta·ya·ma \ˌkäd·əˈyämə\ *n, cap* [NL, prob. fr. *Katayama*, town in western Honshu, Japan] **:** a genus of Oriental freshwater snails (family Bulimidae) including important intermediate hosts of a human schistosome (*Schistosoma japonicum*) — see ONCOMELANIA

katcina *or* **katchina** *var of* KACHINA

¹kate \ˈkāt, *usu* -ād·+V\ *n* -s [fr. *Kate*, nickname for the name *Catherine*] **1** *dial Eng* **:** HAWFINCH **2 :** PILEATED WOODPECKER

²kâ·te \ˈkätə\ *n, pl* **kâte** *or* **kâtes** *usu cap* **1 a :** a people of the Huon peninsula of the Territory of New Guinea **b :** a member of such people **2 :** the Papuan language of the Kâte people

kate green·a·way \¦kāt¦grēnəˌwā\ *adj, usu cap K&G* [after *Kate* (Catherine) *Greenaway* †1901 Eng. painter and illustrator of children's books] *of clothing* **:** having a long full skirt, short waist and sleeves, round neck, and usu. a sash and ruffled edges ⟨in her green *Kate Greenaway* pelisse, with the long band of soft beaver running from neck to hem —Victoria Lincoln⟩

ka·tel \ˈkäd·ᵊl\ *n* -s [Afrik, fr. Pg *catel, catre* cot, fr. Tamil-Malayalam *kaṭṭil* bedstead, bier — more at COT] **:** a wooden hammock used in Africa as a bed in a wagon

ka·ter's pendulum \ˈkäd·ə(r)z-\ *n, usu cap K* [after Henry *Kater* †1835 Eng. scientist] **:** a compound pendulum with adjustable knife edges placed respectively at the center of suspension and near the center of oscillation and used to determine acceleration of gravity by means of the period of oscillation

ka·thak \kəˈtäk\ *n* -s [Beng, professional storyteller, fr. Skt *kathaka*, fr. *kathayati* he tells, narrates, fr. *kathā* talk, story, fr. *kathā* how; akin to Skt *ka* who? — more at WHO] **:** an intricate dance of northern India that includes passages of narrative pantomime — compare BHARATA NATYA, KATHAKALI, MANIPURI

ka·tha·ka·li \ˌkäd·əˈkälē\ *n* -s [Malayalam *kathakaḷi* drama, fr. *katha* story (fr. Skt *kathā* talk, fr. *kathā* how) + *kaḷi* play; Skt *kathā* how akin to Skt *ka* who? — more at WHO] **:** a spectacular lyric dance drama of southern India based on Hindu literature and performed with acrobatic energy and highly stylized pantomime — compare BHARATA NATYA, KATHAK, MANIPURI

kat·hal \ˈkətˌhəl\ *n* -s [Hindi *kaṭ-hal*, fr. Skt *kaṇṭakaphala*, fr. *kaṇṭaka* thorn + *phala* fruit] **:** JACKFRUIT 1

ka·tha·re·vu·sa *or* **ka·tha·re·vou·sa** \ˌkäthəˈrevə(ˌ)sə\ *n* -s *cap* [NGk *kathareuousa*, fr. Gk, fem. of *kathareuōn*, pres. part. of *kathareuein* to be pure, fr. *katharos* pure] **:** modern Greek conforming to classic Greek usage and tending to reject non-Greek vocabulary — compare DEMOTIC 3

kath·a·robe \ˈkathəˌrōb\ *n* -s [ISV *katharo-* (fr. Gk *katharos* pure) + *-be* (as in *microbe*)] **:** a katharobic organism

kath·a·robic \¦==¦rōbik, -¦räb-\ *adj* [*katharobe* + *-ic*] **:** living in or being a highly oxygenated medium free from organic matter — compare MESOSAPROBIC, SAPROBIC

kath·a·rom·e·ter \ˌ==ˈrämǝd·ǝ(r)\ *n* [Gk *katharos* pure + E *-meter*] **:** an apparatus for determining the composition of a gas mixture by measuring thermal conductivity

katharsis *var of* CATHARSIS

kathen·o·theism \(ˈ)kat¦henōthēˌizəm, kaˈthe-; (¦)kat¦henō¦th-, ka¦thenō¦th-\ *n* [*katheno-* (fr. Gk *kath' hena* one at a time, fr. *kata* down, according to, by + *hena*, acc. sing. masc. of *heis* one) + *theism* — more at CATA-, SAME] **:** the worship of one god at a time as supreme without denying the existence of other gods and including the tendency to make different gods supreme one after the other — compare HENOTHEISM

kathen·o·the·ist \-ˌəst\ *n* [*kathenotheism* + *-ist*] **:** one whose worship exemplifies kathenotheism

ka·thi·a·wa·ri \ˌkäd·ēəˈwärē\ *n, usu cap* [prob. fr. Hindi or Gujarati *kāṭhiāwāḍī* of Kāṭhiāwāḍ (Kathiawar), peninsula on the western coast of India] **1 :** a breed of small hardy horses of India of partially Arab ancestry **2** -s *often cap* **:** a horse of the Kathiawari breed

ka·this·ma *also* **ca·this·ma** \ˈkāthēzmə\ *n, pl* **kathisma·ta** \käˈthēzmətə\ [MGk *kathisma*, fr. Gk, sinking, settling down, fr. *kathizein* to seat, sit down, fr. *kata-* cata- + *hizein* to seat; akin to Gk *hezesthai* to sit — more at SIT] **:** one of the 20 sections into which the Psalter is divided for liturgical use in the Eastern Orthodox Church

kathodic *var of* CATHODIC

katholikos *var of* CATHOLICOS

¹kati *var of* CATTY

²ka·ti \ˈkäd·ē\ *n, pl* **kati** *or* **katis** *usu cap* **1 :** a Kafir people of easternmost Kafiristan in the Hindu Kush mountains of Afghanistan **2 :** a member of the Kati people

ka·tik \ˈkäd·ik\ *n* -s *cap* [Hindi *kātik*, fr. Skt *kārttika* — more at KARTIK] **:** KARTIK

katin *usu cap, var of* KHATIN

kati·po \ˈkäd·əˌpō, ˈkad-·-\ *n* -s [Maori] **:** a small venomous spider (*Latrodectus hasselti* or *L. scelio*) of eastern Asia, Australia, and New Zealand related to the American black widow and commonly black with a red stripe on the abdomen — see REDBACK SPIDER

kat·man·du \¦katˌman¦dü, -ˌmən- *also* ¦kät,män- *or* ¦kätmən-\ *adj, usu cap* [fr. *Katmandu*, Nepal] **:** of or from Katmandu, the capital of Nepal **:** of the kind or style prevalent in Katmandu

ka·to \ˈkäd·(ˌ)ō\ *n, pl* **kato** *or* **katos** *usu cap* [Pomo, lake] **1 a :** an Athapaskan people of northwestern California **b :** a member of such people **2 :** a language of the Kato and Wailaki peoples

ka·tong lu·ang \ˈkäˌtōŋləˈwäŋ\ *or* **ka·ton luang** \-tōnl-\ *n, pl* **katong luang** *or* **katon luang** *usu cap K&L* [Siamese, lit., savages of the yellow leaf] **1 :** a migratory pygmy people of mountainous regions of Thailand **2 :** a member of the Katong Luang people

ka·ton·kel \kəˈtäŋkəl\ *n* -s [Afrik] **1** *Africa* **:** BARRACUDA 2 **2** *Africa* **:** ATLANTIC BONITO

katoptrite *var of* CATOPTRITE

ka·to·wi·ce \ˌkäd·əˈvētsə\ *adj, usu cap* [fr. *Katowice*, city in southern Poland] **:** of or from the city of Katowice, Poland **:** of the kind or style prevalent in Katowice

kats *pl of* KAT

ka·tsu \ˈkät(ˌ)sü\ *n* -s [Jap] **:** resuscitation of an unconscious judoka

katsup *var of* CATSUP

kat·su·ra tree \ˈkätsərə-\ *also* **katsura** *n* -s [Jap *katsura*] **:** a deciduous tree (*Cercidiphyllum japonicum*) of the order Ranales that has short spurs on its branches, broadly ovate leaves with crenate-serrate margins, and fruit which is a pod enclosing many winged seeds and that is sometimes cultivated as an ornamental esp. for its dark blue-green foliage which turns bright yellow or red in autumn

kat·su·won·i·dae \ˌkatsəˈwänəˌdē\ *n pl, cap* [NL, fr. *Katsuwonus*, type genus (fr. Jap *katsuo* victorfish) + *-idae*] *in some classifications* **:** a family of scombroid fishes comprising the oceanic bonitos and closely related forms and including a type genus (*Katsuwonus*) that is commonly placed in the family Scombridae

ka·tu·ka \ˈkəd·əkə\ *n* -s [perh. fr. Skt *kaṭuka* sharp, bitter, fierce, fr. *kaṭu*, prob. of Dravidian origin; akin to Tamil *kaṭu* to be pungent, ache, Malayalam *kaṭu* pungent, extreme] **:** RUSSELL'S VIPER

ka·tun \ˈkäˌtün\ *n* -s [Maya, fr. *ka* 20 + *tun* year of 360 days] **:** a period of 20 tuns in the Maya calendar — compare BAKTUN, PICTUN

katy *var of* KADY

ka·ty·did *also* **ca·ty·did** \ˈkād·ē¦did, -ät¦, ¦i,- *sometimes* ˌ==ˈ=\ *n* -s [imit.] **1 :** LONG-HORNED GRASSHOPPER; *esp* **:** any of several large green American long-horned grasshoppers that have greatly elongated antennae, a long ovipositor, long hind legs, and stridulating organs on the fore wings of the males with which a loud shrill sound is produced **2 :** a pair of wheels usu. from 7 to 12 feet in diameter used with a heavy axle to transport logs in lumbering

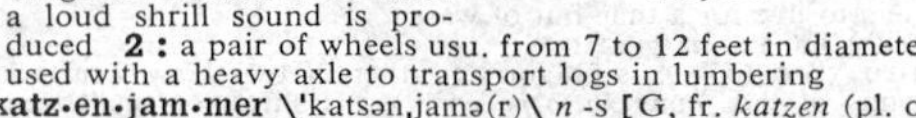

katydid

katz·en·jam·mer \ˈkatsənˌjamə(r)\ *n* -s [G, fr. *katzen* (pl. of *katze* cat, fr. OHG *kazza*) + *jammer* distress, misery, fr. OHG *jāmar*, fr. *jāmar*, adj., sad; akin to OE *geōmor* sad, OS *jāmar* — more at CAT] **1 :** the nausea, headache, and debility that often follow dissipation or drunkenness **:** HANGOVER ⟨asking you what you prescribe for a slight case of ~ —Malcolm Lowry⟩ **2 :** distress, depression, or confusion resembling that caused by a hangover ⟨forgetting the spiritual ~s from which men of culture periodically suffer in new . . . countries —*New Republic*⟩ **3 :** a discordant clamor ⟨during all this ~, divers . . . have been reconnoitering around the craft to learn the identity of its owner —S.J.Perelman⟩

kauch \ˈkäk\ *var of* KIAUGH

kau·mog·ra·pher \kōˈmägrəfə(r)\ *n* -s [Gk *kauma* burning heat (fr. *kaiein* to burn) + E *-o-* + *-grapher* — more at CAUSTIC] **:** a worker who transfers designs, trademarks, or other printed material to cloth articles with a hot iron

kau·nas \ˈkaünəs\ *adj, usu cap* [fr. *Kaunas*, Lithuania] **:** of or from the city of Kaunas, Lithuania **:** of the kind or style prevalent in Kaunas

kau·ri *also* **kau·rie** *or* **kau·ry** *or* **kaw·rie** *or* **kaw·ry** *or* **cow·rie** *or* **kao·ri** \ˈkaürē\ *n, pl* **kauris** *also* **kauries** [Maori *kawri*] **1** *or* **kauri pine :** a tree of the genus *Agathis*; *esp* **:** a tall timber tree (*A. australis*) of New Zealand having fine white straight-grained wood **2 :** the wood of the kauri tree **3** *or* **kauri resin** *or* **kauri gum** *or* **kauri copal :** a light-colored to brown copal from the kauri tree found usu. as a fossil in the ground but also collected by tapping living trees and used chiefly in making varnishes and linoleum

kauri-butanol value *n* **:** a measure of the solvent power of a petroleum thinner for paints and varnishes that is determined as the number of milliliters of the thinner just causing turbidity in a standard solution of a hard kauri in normal butyl alcohol

ka·va *or* **ca·va** \ˈkävə\ *also* **ka·va·ka·va** \¦==¦==\ *n* -s [Tongan & Marquesan *kava*, lit., bitter] **1 a :** an Australasian shrubby pepper (*Piper methysticum*) from whose crushed root an intoxicating beverage is made **b :** the beverage made from kava **2 :** the dried rhizome and roots of the kava shrub formerly used as a diuretic and genitourinary antiseptic

ka·vass \kəˈväs\ *n* -ES [Turk *kavas*, fr. Ar *qawwās* bowman] **1 :** an armed constable or courier in Turkey **2 :** a consular guard in the countries of the eastern Mediterranean

ka·vi·ka \kəˈvēkə\ *n* -s [origin unknown] **:** MALAY APPLE

kavil *var of* CAVEL

ka·vi·ron·do \ˌkävəˈrän(ˌ)dō\ *n, pl* **kavirondo** *or* **kavirondos** *usu cap* **:** BANTU KAVIRONDO

kav·va·nah *or* **kaw·wa·nah** \¦kävə¦nä\ *n, pl* **kav·va·noth** *or* **kav·va·not** *or* **kaw·wa·noth** *or* **kaw·wa·not** \-¦nōt(h), -ōs\ [Heb *kawanāh*, fr. *kawēn* to devote, intend] *Jewish relig* **:** intention to carry out a divine command or precept **:** devotion or fervor in prayer ⟨the women prayed with complete ~⟩

kav·ya \ˈkävyə\ *n* -s [Skt *kāvya*, fr. *kāvya*, adj., poetical] **:** poetic composition in Sanskrit and other Indic languages characterized by decorative elaboration

¹kaw \ˈkȯ\ *n* -s *usu cap* **:** KANSA

²kaw \ˈ"\ *n, pl* **kaw** *or* **kaws** *usu cap* **:** AKHA

ka·wa \kəˈwä\ *n* -s *usu cap* **:** WA

ka·wa·gu·chi \kəˈwägə(ˌ)chē\ *adj, usu cap* [fr. *Kawaguchi*, city in southeastern Honshu, Japan] **:** of or from the city of Kawaguchi, Japan **:** of the kind or style prevalent in Kawaguchi

ka·wai·isu \kəˈwīə(ˌ)sü\ *n, pl* **kawaiisu** *or* **kawaiisus** *usu cap* **1 :** a Shoshonean people of the Tehachapi mountains of southern California **2 :** a member of the Kawaiisu people

ka·wa·ka \kəˈwäkə\ *n* -s [Maori] **:** a New Zealand timber tree (*Libocedrus plumosa*)

¹ka·wa·ka·wa \¦käwə¦käwə\ *or* **kawa** *n* -s [Maori] **1 :** KAVA 1 **2 :** a shrub or small tree (*Piper excelsum*) chiefly of New Zealand that has cordate to ovate aromatic leaves and is held to be sacred by the Maoris

²kawakawa \ˈ"\ *n, pl* **kawakawa** [Hawaiian] *Hawaii* **:** LITTLE TUNA

kaw·chot·ti·ne *also* **kaw·chod·in·ne** \kōˈchädənē\ *n, pl* **kawchottine** *or* **kawchottines** *usu cap* **:** HARE 3

ka·wi \ˈkäwē\ *or* **ka·vi** \-ävē\ *n* -s *usu cap* [Jav *kawi* poem, poetical, fr. Skt *kavi* wise, learned, poet or Skt *kāvya* poetical (fr. *kavi*); prob. akin to Gk *akouein* to hear — more at HEAR] **:** the ancient Austronesian language of Java

¹kay \ˈkā\ *adj* [ME, left] *dial Eng* **:** LEFT, SINISTER

²kay *var of* KEY

³kay *also* **ka** \ˈkā\ *n* -s **1 :** the letter *k* **2 :** something having the shape of the letter K

kaya \ˈkīə, ˈkäyə\ *n* -s [Jap] **:** a Japanese tree (*Torreya nucifera*) with light red bark and yellow lustrous close-grained wood

¹kay·ak *also* **ky·ak** *or* **cay·ak** *or* **ka·jak** \ˈkīˌak *also* -īˌyak\ *n* -s [Esk (Greenland dial.) *qajaq*] **1 :** an Eskimo canoe made of a frame covered usu. with sealskin except for a small opening in the center and propelled by a double-bladed paddle — compare UMIAK **2 :** a portable boat that resembles a kayak and is paddled or sailed widely in the U. S. — compare FALTBOAT

kayak 1

²kayak \ˈ"\ *vi* -ED/-ING/-S **:** to paddle or sail a kayak ⟨I was out ~ing for seal —D.B.Putnam⟩ — **kay·ak·er** \-akə(r)\ *n* -s

kay·an \ˈkīən\ *n, pl* **kayan** *or* **kayans** *usu cap* [native name in northern Borneo] **1 :** a Dayak people of north central Borneo sometimes regarded with the Kenya as a subdivision of the Bahau **2 :** a member of the Kayan people

kayapo *usu cap, var of* CAYAPO

ka·yasth \ˈkäyəst\ *or* **ka·yas·tha** \-stə\ *n* -s *usu cap* [Skt *kāyastha*, prob. fr. *kāya* body, group + *-stha* standing, being in; akin to Skt *cinoti* he gathers, heaps up and to Skt *tiṣṭhati* he stands — more at POET, STAND] **:** a member of a high Hindu caste esp. numerous in Bengal and Uttar Pradesh whose caste occupation is that of clerks, writers, and accountants

kay·en·ta \kīˈ(y)entə\ *adj, usu cap* [fr. *Kayenta*, village in northeastern Arizona, where remains of the culture were found] **:** of or belonging to the northern Arizona branch of the Anasazi culture that provides a record from the period of the earth-lodge villages to the Great Pueblo centers

kayles *var of* KAILS

¹kayo \(ˈ)kā¦ō\ *n* -s [pronunciation of *KO*, abbr. or n.] **:** KNOCKOUT

²kayo \ˈ"\ *vt* **kayoed; kayoed; kayoing; kayoes** *or* **kayos :** to knock out

kayuvava *or* **kayubaba** *usu cap, var of* CAYUVAVA

ka·zak \kəˈzak, -zäk\ *n* -s *usu cap* [Kazak, lit., free person, adventurer, vagabond] **1** *or* **ka·zakh** \ˈ"\ **a :** a Turko-Tatar Muslim people of central Asia **b :** a member of the Kazak people **2** *or* **kazakh** *or* **qa·zaq** \ˈ"\ **:** TURKI **3 :** a bright-colored all-wool Caucasian rug woven by nomads often in sawtooth patterns or highly stylized plant or animal designs **4 :** OXBLOOD

ka·zan \kəˈzan, -zän\ *adj, usu cap* [fr. *Kazan*, city in the eastern part of European Russia, U.S.S.R.] **:** of or from the city of Kazan, U.S.S.R. **:** of the kind or style prevalent in Kazan

kazan tatar *n, usu cap K&T* **1 :** a member of a group of Tatars living in the Tatar Republic, U.S.S.R. **2 :** the Turkic language of the Kazan people

kazarian *usu cap, var of* KHAZAR

kazi *var of* QADI

ka·zoo \kəˈzü\ *also* **ga·zoo** \gə-\ *n* -s [imit.] **:** a device into which a person sings or hums and which consists usu. of an open-ended tube with a membrane-covered side hole ⟨the ~ is that noisemaking toy that comes nowadays in Christmas stockings —Harlan Cleveland⟩ — called also *eunuch flute, mirliton, Tommy talker, zarah*

KB *abbr* **1** King's Bench **2** kitchen and bathroom **3** kite balloon **4** knight bachelor

KBP *abbr* kite balloon pilot

kc *abbr* **1** kilocycle **2** kilocycles per second

KC *abbr* **1** kennel club **2** King's Counsel **3** knight commander

kcal *abbr* kilocalorie; kilogram calorie

k-capture \ˈ¦==¦(ˌ)=-\ *also* **k-electron capture** \¦==¦=(ˌ)=-\ *n, usu cap K* **:** the capture by an atomic nucleus of an electron from an inner energy level or orbit of the extranuclear electrons

Kčs *abbr* [Czech *koruna československá*] koruna

kd *abbr* killed

KD *abbr* **1** kiln-dried **2** knocked down

KDCL *abbr* knocked down, in carloads

KDF *abbr* knocked down flat

KDLCL *abbr* knocked down, in less than carloads

kdm *abbr* kingdom

KE *abbr* kinetic energy

ke- — see KER-

kea \ˈkēə, ˈkēə\ *n* -s [Maori] **:** a large parrot (*Nestor notabilis*) of South Island, New Zealand, that is predominantly green with a very long heavy bill and that is normally insectivorous but sometimes attacks sheep, slashing the back to reach the kidney fat on which it feeds

kea·corn \ˈkāˌkȯrn\ *n* -s [origin unknown] **1** *dial* **:** WINDPIPE **2** *dial* **:** GULLET

keat *var of* KEET

keats·ian \ˈkētsēən\ *adj, usu cap* [John *Keats* †1821 Eng. poet + E *-ian*] **:** of, relating to, or characteristic of the poet Keats or his poetry ⟨the manner of Keats is imitated to excess . . . and there is a similar profusion of *Keatsian* classical allusions —W.H.Gardner⟩

keawe *var of* KIAWE

kebab *or* **kebob** *var of* KABOB

keb·bie \ˈkebi\ *n* -s [prob. alter. of earlier *kibble*, fr. ME *kyble*] *chiefly Scot* **:** a rough hook-headed walking stick

keb·buck *also* **keb·bock** \ˈkebək\ *n* -s [ME (Sc dial.) *cabok*, fr. ScGael *ceapag* (also, piece of sod, barrow wheel)] *dial Brit* **:** a whole cheese

keb·yar \ˈkebˌyär\ *n* -s [Balinese] **:** a Balinese solo dance performed with the upper part of the body from a sitting position with crossed ankles

kechua *usu cap, var of* QUECHUA

kech·u·ma·ran \¦kechəmə¦rän\ *n* -s *usu cap* [*Kechua* + *Aymaran*] **:** a language stock comprising Aymara and Quechua

¹keck \ˈkek\ *vi* -ED/-ING/-S [imit.] **:** to make the sounds of retching

²keck \ˈ"\ *n* -s [back-formation fr. ¹*kex*] *Brit* **:** WILD CHERVIL 1

¹keck·le \ˈkekəl\ *dial var of* CACKLE

²keckle \ˈ"\ *also* **kack·le** \ˈkak-\ *vt* -ED/-ING/-S [origin unknown] **:** to wind with rope to prevent chafing

keck·ling \ˈkek(ə)liŋ\ *n* -s **:** old rope wound around a cable to prevent chafing

keck·sy \ˈkeksi\ *n* -ES [¹*kex* + *-y*] *chiefly dial Eng* **:** KEX

ked \ˈked\ *n* -s [origin unknown] **:** SHEEP KED

ked·dah \ˈkedə, kəˈdä\ *n* -s [Hindi *khedā*] *in India* **:** an enclosure constructed to trap wild elephants

¹kedge \ˈkej\ *adj* [ME *kygge*] *chiefly Scot* **:** BRISK, LIVELY

²kedge \ˈ"\ *vt* -ED/-ING/-S [ME *caggen*] **1 :** to move (a ship) from one position to another by means of a line attached to a kedge dropped at the distance and in the direction desired

³kedge \ˈ"\ *or* **kedge anchor** \ˈ"-\ *also* **kedg·er** \ˈkejə(r)\ *n* -s **:** a small anchor that is used in light work (as kedging)

ked·ger·ee *or* **keg·er·ee** \ˈkejəˌrē, ˌ==ˈ=\ *n* -s [Hindi *khicaṛī*, fr. Skt *khiccā*] **1** *in India* **:** a mixture of rice, beans, lentils, and seasonings sometimes with smoked fish **2 :** cooked flaked fish, rice, hard-boiled eggs, and seasoning heated in cream

kedgy \ˈkejē, -ji\ *chiefly Scot var of* CADGY 1

kedjavé *var of* KAJAWAH

ked·lock \ˈkedˌläk, -ˌlək\ *n* -s [ME *ketelok*, fr. OE *cedelc*] **1 :** CHARLOCK **2 :** WHITE MUSTARD

ke·du·shah \kəˈdüshə\ *n, pl* **kedu·shoth** *or* **kedu·shot** \-ˌshōt(h), -ōs\ *usu cap* [Heb *qĕdhushshāh* holiness] **:** a recital of a prayer in the Jewish ritual introduced into the third benediction of the Amidah and sometimes including the responses

keech \ˈkēch\ *n* -ES [origin unknown] *dial Eng* **:** a fatty lump

¹keek \ˈkēk\ *vi* -ED/-ING/-S [ME *kiken, keken*, prob. fr. MD *kiken* to look; akin to MLG *kīken* to look] *chiefly Scot* **:** PEEP, LOOK ⟨opened the low door and ~ed into the room —Alasdair Carmichael⟩

²keek \ˈ"\ *n* -s *chiefly Scot* **:** PEEP, LOOK ⟨take another ~ at the redcoats —R.L.Stevenson⟩

keekwilee-house \ˈkēkwə(ˌ)lē-\ *n* [Chinook jargon *keekwilee* below, fr. Chinook *gigwalix*] **:** an earth lodge partially below the surface of the ground used by the Indians of the northwest coast of No. America — compare BARRABORA

¹keel \ˈkēl, *esp before pause or consonant* -ēəl\ *vb* -ED/-ING/-S [ME *kelen*, fr. OE *cēlan*, fr. *cōl* cool — more at COOL] *vt* **1** *now dial* **:** COOL; *specif* **:** to keep esp. by stirring or skimming from boiling over ⟨while greasy Joan doth ~ the pot —Shak.⟩ **2** *obs* **:** to make less ardent or violent in feeling ~ *vi* **1** *now dial* **:** ⁴COOL **2** *now dial* **:** to become less ardent or violent in feeling

²keel \ˈ"\ *n* -s [ME *kele*, fr. MD *kiel*; akin to OE *cēol* ship, OS & OHG *kiol*, ON *kjōll* ship, Gk *gaulos* milk pail, kind of ship, OE *cot* small house — more at COT] **1 a** (1) **:** a flat-bottomed ship; *esp* **:** a barge used on the Tyne to carry coal from Newcastle (2) **:** a barge load of coal **b :** a British unit of weight for coal based on the amount one keel can hold now equal to 21.2 long tons **2 :** a long ship of the early Norsemen

³keel \ˈ"\ *n* -s [ME *kele, keole*, fr. ON *kil-, kjǫlr*; akin to MD & MLG *kiel, keel* keel, OE *ceole* throat, beak of a ship — more at GLUTTON] **1 a** (1) **:** a longitudinal timber or series of timbers scarfed together extending from stem to stern along the center of the bottom of a boat, often projecting below the bottom, and constituting the boat's principal timber to which the ribs are attached on each side — compare CENTERBOARD, FALSE KEEL; see SHIP illustration (2) **:** a bar keel or plate keel on a metal ship (3) **:** KEELSON (4) **:** BILGE KEEL **b** (1) **:** BOAT, SHIP (2) **:** a boat or ship having a keel as opposed to one having a centerboard or a flat bottom ⟨the shipyard laid down ten new ~s in a year⟩ **c :** the assembly of members at the bottom of the hull of a semirigid or rigid airship that provides special strength to resist hogging and sagging and serves to distribute the effect of concentrated loads along the hull **2 :** a projection suggesting a keel : RIDGE: as **a :** a biological process forming a ridge : CARINA **b :** a keel molding or the ridge of one

⁴keel \"\ *vb* -ED/-ING/-S *vt* **1 :** to cause to turn or tip to the side away from a vertical plane or over esp. so that the bottom shows : OVERTURN, CAPSIZE — usu. used with *over* or *up* ⟨sailing vessels lying *~ed* over at low tide in the harbors —Richard Joseph⟩ **2 :** to cause to collapse or faint — usu. used with *over* ⟨the continued heat *~ed* over quite a few of the summer visitors⟩ ~ *vi* **1 :** to turn or tip away from a vertical plane or over esp. so that the bottom shows ⟨sailing craft ~ to the lee rail in a spanking breeze —*Amer. Guide Series: Conn.*⟩ : OVERTURN, CAPSIZE — usu. used with *over* or *up* ⟨the yacht swung across wind and *~ed* over⟩ ⟨brakes squealing and slipping on the rails and engines *~ing* over into drifts —Helen Rich⟩ **2 :** to fall in or as if in a faint : SWOON — usu. used with *over* ⟨so tired he *~ed* over onto the bed⟩ ⟨just one drink, and *~ed* right over —George Spanner⟩

⁵keel \"\ *or* **keel disease** *n* -S [⁴*keel*] **:** acute septicemic salmonellosis or paratyphoid of ducklings marked by sudden collapse and death of apparently healthy birds

⁶keel \"\ *n* -S [ME (Sc dial.) *keyle*, prob. fr. ScGael *cīl*] **1** *now chiefly dial* **:** a red ocher used for marking something (as lumber or sheep) : RUDDLE; *also* **:** a mark made with this material (as at the end of a warp of yarn to show whether the weaver has used the full length) **2 :** a colored marking chalk or crayon used by engineers and surveyors

⁷keel \"\ *vt* -ED/-ING/-S *Scot* **:** to mark with keel

keel·age \'kēlij\ *n* -S [³*keel* + *-age*] **:** a toll for a ship entering and anchoring or mooring in a port esp. in Great Britain

keelback \'=,=\ *also* **keelback snake** *n* [³*keel* + *back*] **:** a small aquatic Indian snake (*Natrix piscator*) with strongly keeled dorsal scales

keelbill *or* **keelbird** \'=,=\ *n* [³*keel* + *bill* or *bird*] : ANI

keelblock \'=,=\ *n* [³*keel* + *block*] **:** a block of hard wood used to support the keel of a ship when under construction or when docked

keelboat \'=,=\ *n* [³*keel* + *boat*] **1 :** a shallow covered riverboat with a keel that is usu. rowed, poled, or towed and used for freight **2 :** a yacht or other sailboat having a keel as distinguished from one having a centerboard

keel·boat·man \"mən\ *n, pl* **keelboatmen :** a member of the crew of a keelboat

keel-bully \'=,==\ *n* [²*keel* + *bully*] *Brit* **:** one of the crew of a keel

keeled \'kē(ə)ld\ *adj* [³*keel* + *-ed*] **:** having a carina ⟨~ breastbone⟩ ⟨~ flower⟩

keeled snake *n* **:** a snake with strongly keeled scales; *esp* **:** a venomous Australian elapid (*Tropidechis carinatus*)

¹keel·er \'kēlə(r)\ *n* -S [ME *kelare*, a tub used for cooling liquids, fr. *kelen* to cool + *-are* -er — more at KEEL] *now chiefly dial* **:** a broad shallow tub (as for a liquid or washing something)

²keeler \"\ *n* -S [²*keel* + *-er*] *dial Eng* : KEELMAN

³keeler \"\ *n* -S [³*keel* + *-er*] **:** a boat having a keel; *esp* : KEELBOAT

kee·ler polygraph \"-\ *n, usu cap K* [after Leonarde *Keeler* †1949 Amer. criminologist, its inventor] **:** an instrument for making a graphic record of the changes in blood pressure and pulse and respiration rate of someone being questioned under or as if under suspicion of guilt — called also *lie detector*

keel·haul \'kē(ə)l,hȯl\ *also* **keel·hale** \-hāl, *esp before pause or consonant* -āəl\ *vt* [D *kielhalen*, fr. *kiel* keel (fr. MD) + *halen* to fetch, draw, pull, fr. MD — more at KEEL, HAUL] **1 :** to haul (a person) under the keel of a ship either athwartships or from bow to stern by ropes in punishment (as on a naval vessel) or torture (as by pirates) **2 :** to rebuke with great severity

kee·lie \'kēlē, -li\ *n* -S [imit.] **1** : KESTREL **2** *dial Brit* **:** a street urchin : LOAFER

¹keeling *pres part of* KEEL

²kee·ling \'kēliŋ\ *n* -S [ME *keling*, perh. of Scand origin; akin to Icel *keila* cusk, ON, arm of the sea; akin to OHG *kīl* wedge — more at CHINE] *chiefly Scot* : CODFISH; *esp* **:** a large codfish

kee·li·vine \'kēli,vīn\ *n* -S [origin unknown] *Scot* : PENCIL; *esp* **:** one of black lead

keel·less \'kē(ə)lləs\ *adj* [³*keel* + *-less*] **:** having no keel ⟨a ~ boat⟩

keel line *n* [³*keel* + *line*] **:** the bottom or lowest line of a boat esp. along the keel

keel·man \'kē(ə)lmən\ *n, pl* **keelmen** [²*keel* + *man*] **:** a member of the crew of a keel

keel molding *n* [³*keel*] **:** a brace molding with a central projecting fillet resembling a keel

keels *pres 3d sing of* KEEL, *pl of* KEEL

keel-shaped scraper \'=,=-\ *n* **:** a prehistoric flint scraper consisting of a small core chipped at both ends and sides and resembling the bottom of a boat in shape

keel molding

keel·son *also* **kel·son** \'kelsən, 'kē(ə)l-*also* -lts-\ *n* -S [prob. of Scand origin; akin to Dan & Norw *kjølsvin*, Sw *kölsvin*, Norw dial. *kjølsvill*, prob. fr. *kjøl*, *köl* keel (fr. ON *kölr*) + *svin* pig, fr. ON *svīnn* — more at KEEL, SWINE] **:** a longitudinal structure in the framing of a ship to contribute stiffness, prevent local deformations, and distribute over a considerable length the effect of concentrated loads: **a :** a structure of timbers in a wooden ship parallel with and above the keel and fastened to it by long bolts passing through the floor timbers **b :** a deep continuous structure of plates and bars in a metal ship usu. in the form of a strong I beam secured at its ends to the stem and the sternpost and connected at its upper and lower edges to the reverse frames and keel plates respectively — called also *middle-line keelson*, *vertical keel*; see BILGE KEELSON, SIDE KEELSON; SHIP illustration

kee·lung \'kē,lu̇ŋ\ *adj, usu cap* [fr. *Keelung*, Formosa] **:** of or from the city of Keelung, Formosa, China **:** of the kind or style prevalent in Keelung

kee·mun \'kā,mu̇n, 'kē,mən\ *n* -S *usu cap* [fr. *Keemun* (Ch'imen) district in Anhwei province, China] : CONGOU

¹keen \'kēn\ *adj* -ER/-EST [ME *kene* wise, bold, brave, sharp, fr. OE *cēne* wise, bold, brave; akin to OHG *kuoni* bold, strong, MD *coene* bold, brave, ON *kœnn* wise, skillful, clever, OE *cnāwan* to know — more at KNOW] **1 a :** having a fine edge or point : SHARP ⟨a ~ blade⟩ ⟨a ~ sword⟩ **b :** affecting one as if by cutting **:** causing great distress to the mind or sensibilities ⟨~ sarcasm⟩ ⟨a ~ sense of guilt⟩ **c** (1) **:** affecting the senses or creating physical discomfort as if by cutting : PENETRATING, PIERCING ⟨a ~ wind⟩ ⟨~, cold winters —Edith Hamilton⟩ : STINGING ⟨a ~ slap⟩ : SHRILL ⟨a high ~ sound⟩ (2) **:** sharp or pungent to the sense ⟨a ~ scent⟩ **2 a :** characterized by intense interest, feeling, or desire **:** showing a quick and ardent responsiveness : EAGER, ENTHUSIASTIC ⟨a ~ swimmer⟩ ⟨fiery and dominant natures, eager to conquer, ~ to impress —A.C.Benson⟩ ⟨~ to go on a picnic⟩ ⟨both of them were ~ on skiing⟩ ⟨very ~ about the girl⟩; *also* **:** giving evidence of such qualities ⟨the features lean and ~ from restless intellectual energy —J.A.Froude⟩ **b** *of emotion or feeling* : INTENSE, GREAT ⟨a ~ desire to be in the forefront of activity⟩ ⟨the ~ delight in the chase —F.W.Maitland⟩ ⟨a ~ personal interest in the boy⟩ ⟨the ~ dread of the gods —M.R.Cohen⟩ **3 a :** acute or quick and penetrating (as in mental power) ⟨a ~ mind⟩ ⟨~ in their bargain —H.E.Scudder⟩ **:** intellectually sharp or incisive ⟨a ~ wit⟩ ⟨~ questions⟩ : ASTUTE ⟨~ businessmen —Gilbert Highet⟩; *also* **:** giving evidence of astuteness or the play of alert or carefully calculating minds ⟨~ competition⟩ ⟨debate was not as ~ as it might have been —Winston Churchill⟩ **b :** extremely sensitive in perception or in perceiving distinctions ⟨a ~ eyesight⟩ ⟨a ~ sense of smell⟩ **c :** marked by fine and extremely precise distinctions ⟨~ refinements of logic⟩ **4** *of ice in curling* **:** hard and clear **5** *Brit, of a price* **:** favorable to the purchaser : LOW ⟨outfits for all ranks and services at very ~ prices —*Nautical Mag.*⟩ **6** *slang* : WONDERFUL, DESIRABLE — a generalized expression of approval **syn** see EAGER, SHARP

²keen \"\ *adv* [ME *kene*, fr. *kene*, adj.] : KEENLY ⟨businessmen ~ set on practical affairs —J.W.Beach⟩

³keen \"\ *vt* -ED/-ING/-S [¹*keen*] **:** to put a sharp edge on : SHARPEN ⟨the cutting edge of the knife is first *~ed* up —J.V.A.Long⟩ ⟨~ the razor —Christopher Morley⟩

⁴keen \"\ *vb* -ED/-ING/-S [IrGael *caoinim* (I) lament, fr. OIr *coīnim*] *vi* **1 a :** to wail or bewail with a keen ⟨*~ed* like a squaw bereft —Minnie H. Moody⟩ **b :** to make a sound suggesting a keen ⟨the soft *~ing* of the screech owls —A.W. Derleth⟩ ⟨the night was rent by *~ing* sirens —*Time*⟩ ⟨the *~ing* in the aerials rose to a witches' chorus —T.H.Raddall⟩ ⟨violins *~ed* in the shadows —Albert Hubbell⟩ **2 :** to lament, mourn, or complain loudly ~ *vt* **:** to utter by keening ⟨*~ed* our sorrow —*Punch*⟩

⁵keen \"\ *n* -S [IrGael *caoine*] **1 a :** a lamentation or dirge for the dead uttered in a loud wailing voice **b :** a rhythmic recounting of the life and character of a dead person or an exhortation to vengeance for his death — compare CORONACH **2 :** a lamentation or cry of grief

keen·er \-nə(r)\ *n* -S [⁴*keen* + *-er*] **:** one that keens; *esp* **:** a professional usu. female mourner at a wake or funeral

keene's cement \'kēnz-\ *n, usu cap K* [after Richard W. *Keene*, 19th cent. Eng. inventor] **:** a hard-finish gypsum plaster to which alum has been added and which is used chiefly as a gauging plaster in lime mortar for walls (as of hospitals, stores, railroad stations) where an unusually tough and durable plaster is required

¹keening *adj* [fr. pres. part. of ⁴*keen*] **:** having the quality of or suggesting a keen ⟨the . . . cicada and his ~ cry —K.F. Weaver⟩ ⟨a long ~ scream like a rabbit caught in a gin trap —Hartley Howard⟩

²keening *n* -S [fr. gerund of ⁴*keen*] **1 :** the act of keening ⟨mourning . . . is celebrated by self-laceration, the destruction of property, and daily ~ —William Lipkind⟩ ⟨~ was not confined to the period of death —Alfred Métraux⟩ ⟨the ~ of bagpipes —Lyn Harrington⟩ **2 :** ⁵KEEN ⟨never had heard a ~ —Mary Deasy⟩

keen·ly *adv* [ME *kenely* boldly, bravely, sharply, fr. *kene* wise, bold, brave, sharp + *-ly* — more at KEEN] **:** in a keen manner ⟨stared at him ~ —Nevil Shute⟩ ⟨~ aware of the evils of the society —H.R.G.Greaves⟩ ⟨cleverly construed and ~ written —*Time*⟩

keen·ness \'kēnnəs\ *n* -ES [¹*keen* + *-ness*] **:** the quality or state of being keen ⟨exhibited a ~ of judgment unusual in one his age⟩ ⟨the ~ of his desire to succeed⟩

keen-scented \'=;==\ *adj* **:** having a keen sense of smell ⟨a *keen-scented* hound⟩

¹keep \'kēp\ *vb* **kept** \'kept\ **kept; keeping; keeps** [ME *kepen* to observe, heed, seek, seize, keep, fr. OE *cēpan* to observe, heed, seek, seize; akin to OE *capian* to look, OS *kapōn*, OHG *chapfēn* to look, ON *kōpa* to stare, and perh. to Russ *zabota* care, worry] *vt* **1 a :** to observe or fulfill (something prescribed or obligatory) **:** adhere to or not swerve from or violate (as a faith) **:** practice or perform as a duty **:** not neglect **:** be faithful to (as a promise): as (1) **:** to notice with due, approved, or customary actions and feelings **:** act fittingly in relation to by refraining from anything inappropriate or unsuitable ⟨*~ing* a Sabbath day by ceasing from all work —H.G.Cowan⟩ (2) **:** to conform to in habits or conduct (as by regular attendance to or the performance of appropriate duties) or adjust one's schedule of activities to include ⟨~ chapel⟩ ⟨~ early hours⟩ (3) **:** to act (as in playing an instrument, singing, marching) in accord with (as a preestablished time, tempo, or rhythm) ⟨asked the musicians to ~ time with the metronome⟩ ⟨could not ~ the tricky rhythm of the Latin-American dance⟩ **b :** to reside at a British university long enough to complete the requirements of (a term); *esp* **:** to eat a sufficient number of dinners in hall at the Inns of Court to make (a term) count for the purpose of being called to the bar **2 :** PRESERVE, MAINTAIN: as **a :** to watch over and defend esp. from danger, harm, or loss ⟨prayed God to ~ and help his family⟩ ⟨anxious to ~ his son from illness and accident⟩ ⟨his sanguine nature *kept* him from worry⟩ **b** (1) **:** to have the care of **:** be responsible for : TEND ⟨the shepherd boy *kept* sheep on the moors at night⟩ ⟨*kept* a garden for his parents⟩ ⟨was paid to ~ the furnace⟩ (2) **:** to support by providing with a home, food, clothing, or other requisites of existence ⟨the foster parents *kept* the child for a year until his real parents could be found⟩ (3) **:** to maintain in a good, fitting, or orderly condition ⟨objected to *~ing* the house⟩ ⟨a meticulously *kept* orchard⟩ (4) **:** to maintain habitually by undertaking the expense of ⟨what sort of table do they ~ —Jane Austen⟩ **c :** to continue to maintain **:** not cease from or intermit ⟨~ silence⟩ ⟨~ guard over the child⟩ **d** (1) **:** to cause to remain in a given place, situation, or condition **:** maintain unchanged **:** hold or preserve in a particular state ⟨~ valuables under lock and key⟩ ⟨*kept* all perishable food cold⟩ ⟨~ a person waiting⟩ — often used with a following prepositional phrase or adverb indicating place or direction ⟨*kept* the boys away from the house⟩ ⟨*kept* the top of the box down with weights⟩ ⟨*kept* the dog in the house⟩ ⟨*kept* the children in⟩ ⟨*kept* the cat out⟩ ⟨~ the birds off the antenna⟩ (2) **:** to preserve (food) in an unspoiled condition ⟨~ meat by packing it in ice⟩ ⟨~ potatoes in storage in a cool cellar⟩ **e** (1) **:** to have or retain in one's service or in an established position or relationship ⟨~ a maid and a butler⟩ ⟨~s two assistants⟩ — often used with *on* ⟨*kept* the cook on until she could find a new employer⟩ (2) **:** to possess (as a domestic animal) usu. for certain services or advantages ⟨~s a horse⟩ ⟨~s several head of cattle⟩ (3) **:** to maintain in exchange for sexual favors ⟨never married but *kept* a mistress for several years⟩ ⟨found the woman was *~ing* a man several years her junior⟩ (4) **:** to control totally the policy, principles, and ideas of (as a newspaper) by one's money or economic power ⟨a *kept* press⟩ **f** (1) **:** to maintain a record in (as of daily occurrences or transactions) ⟨~ a journal⟩ ⟨~ books for a business firm⟩ (2) **:** to enter (as an account or record) in a book **g :** to have customarily in stock for sale ⟨bought the best sherry the store *kept*⟩ **3 a :** to restrain from departure or removal **:** not let go of : HOLD, DETAIN ⟨~ him as a prisoner for a week⟩ ⟨*kept* the children after school for disobedience⟩ ⟨nothing to ~ me in the hot city⟩ **b :** to hold back : RESTRAIN, PREVENT ⟨tried to ~ him from going out at night⟩ ⟨nothing *kept* him from going through with it⟩ **c :** SAVE, RESERVE, STORE ⟨asked the grocer to ~ a good cut of beef for her each week⟩ ⟨*kept* the hardest questions until the end of the examination⟩ **d :** to refrain from communicating, revealing, or betraying **:** not divulge ⟨~ a secret⟩ ⟨~ his counsel⟩ **4 a :** to retain or continue to have in one's possession or power esp. by conscious or purposive policy ⟨were able to conquer the island but were unable to ~ it⟩ ⟨found the money and figured he could ~ it⟩ ⟨the court decided the couple could ~ the child⟩ **b :** WITHHOLD ⟨*kept* most of his inheritance from him⟩ ⟨*kept* the sad news from the parents⟩ **c :** to have in control **:** not lose ⟨~ one's temper⟩ **5 :** to keep to ⟨ill and ~s her room —Jane Austen⟩ ⟨with a cold that has left her weak, so that she has *kept* the house for over a fortnight —O.W.Holmes †1935⟩ **6 a :** to continue in (as a course) **:** not deviate from ⟨~ the path rather than strike off through the woods⟩ ⟨~ the center of the road⟩ **b :** to stay or remain on or in usu. against opposition ⟨~ your seat⟩ ⟨~ the saddle despite the bucking of the horse⟩ ⟨~ the field under fire⟩ ⟨*kept* his ground even though attacked again and again⟩ **7 a :** CONDUCT, MANAGE ⟨~ a meeting⟩ **:** carry on ⟨~ a business⟩ ⟨the chairman was not there to ~ the yearly assembly⟩ ⟨*kept* a small tearoom⟩ **b** *archaic* **:** to keep up **c :** to make out or manage in respect to the welfare of (oneself) ⟨how have you been *~ing* yourself⟩ **8 :** to associate with (company) ⟨concerned about the company she was *~ing*⟩ **9** *dial Eng* **:** to frighten or scare away (birds) ~ *vi* **1** *now Brit* : LIVE, LODGE ⟨could not find where the man *kept* in town⟩ **2 a :** to maintain a course, direction, or progress **:** persevere in going ⟨~ along the main route for 10 miles⟩ ⟨*kept* to the south all day⟩ **b :** to continue usu. without interruption a particular action ⟨the fire *kept* burning all night⟩ ⟨~ smiling⟩ — often used with *on* ⟨*kept* on talking until he was told to stop⟩ **c :** to persist resolutely or stubbornly in a practice or a course of action often in spite of opposition or warning **:** continue firmly or obstinately ⟨~s asking us to go swimming⟩ — often used with *on* ⟨*kept* on drinking after the doctor told him to stop⟩ **3 a :** to stay or remain (as in a particular place or condition) ⟨~ in the house if it rains⟩ ⟨the wind *kept* to the east⟩ ⟨~ in a happy frame of mind⟩ ⟨~ out of the way⟩ ⟨~ in touch with friends⟩ ⟨*kept* warm with blankets and hot soup⟩ ⟨*kept* clean by washing daily⟩ **b :** to be in regard to health ⟨how are you *~ing*⟩ **c :** to keep up ⟨was unable to ~ with the older boys on the hike⟩ ⟨it follows the herring schools and sometimes ~s with them for days —F.G.Kay⟩ **4 :** ABSTAIN, REFRAIN ⟨couldn't ~ from talking⟩ **5 a :** to remain in good condition **:** not go bad or deteriorate ⟨the food will ~ for a long time under refrigeration⟩ ⟨knowledge does not ~ any better than fish —A.N.Whitehead⟩ **b :** to remain undivulged ⟨knew the secret would ~ if he told nobody⟩ **c :** to call for no immediate action ⟨the matter will ~ until morning when we can see a lawyer⟩ **6 :** to be or remain in session ⟨school ~s five days a week⟩ **7 :** to keep wicket

syn KEEP, KEEP (*back*), KEEP (*out*), RETAIN, DETAIN, WITHHOLD, RESERVE, HOLD, and HOLD (*back*) can mean, in common, not to relinquish one's possession, custody, or control. KEEP is the most general term, carrying the common meaning ⟨*keep* one's car for another year⟩ ⟨*keep* one's balance⟩ ⟨*keep* one's right to vote⟩ KEEP (*back*) is interchangeable with any of the remaining terms ⟨*keep back* a part of an employee's pay⟩ ⟨*keep back* a person who wants to rush out into a storm⟩ ⟨*keep back* some tickets for a friend⟩ KEEP (*out*) applies to the keeping of some portion of a whole ⟨*keep out* a part of a week's pay for emergencies⟩ RETAIN implies continued keeping esp. against a threatened taking or loss ⟨*retain* one's possessions even in war⟩ ⟨*retain* one's sanity⟩ ⟨*retain* control of a company⟩ DETAIN implies a delay in letting go from one's control ⟨*detain* a man suspected of a crime⟩ ⟨*detain* a ship in quarantine⟩ WITHHOLD implies a delay in letting go or a refusal to give or let go ⟨*withhold* information⟩ ⟨*withhold* payments on a house⟩ ⟨*withhold* one's help⟩ RESERVE implies either a keeping in store or withholding from present use esp. for some future or special need or purpose ⟨*reserve* a certain percentage for emergencies⟩ ⟨*reserve* a space in a house for a playroom⟩ ⟨*reserve* seats at an opera⟩ HOLD and HOLD (*back*) are often used in place of WITHHOLD or KEEP (*back*) and sometimes in place of DETAIN or RESERVE when restraint in letting go is implied ⟨*hold* a portion of a week's pay as a fine⟩ ⟨*hold* a person suspected of a crime⟩ ⟨*hold back* some tickets that are on sale as a favor to a friend⟩ ⟨*hold* one's condemnation until a later date⟩ ⟨*hold back* one's judgment until all the evidence has been considered⟩

syn OBSERVE, CELEBRATE, SOLEMNIZE, COMMEMORATE: KEEP, along with others in this set, can mean the noticing or honoring of a day or occasion fittingly or duly. KEEP is rather mild in its implications and may suggest merely a customary or wonted notice without anything untoward or inappropriate; it implies opposition to *break* ⟨his build was all compact, for force, well-knit . . . he *kept* no Lent to make him meager —John Masefield⟩ OBSERVE may indicate a heightened solemnity, attention to correct details, and a proper attitude ⟨knowing that the usual ritual would have to be *observed* —T. B.Costain⟩ ⟨New Hampshire *observes* one holiday not possessed by any other state —*Amer. Guide Series: N.H.*⟩ In today's English and esp. in nonreligious contexts CELEBRATE is likely to suggest notice of an occasion by festivity or indulgence ⟨*celebrate* New Year's Eve⟩ ⟨*celebrating* a friend's good fortune⟩ ⟨many parties *celebrating* a football victory⟩ SOLEMNIZE is likely to carry a contrasting suggestion, that of grave dignity or splendid ceremony ⟨mysterious rites were *solemnized*, and . . . of those terrific idols some received such dismal service —William Wordsworth⟩ ⟨this blessed day ever . . . shall be kept festival: to *solemnize* this day the glorious sun stays in his course —Shak.⟩ COMMEMORATE stresses the idea of remembrance and suggests observance or ceremony, or a symbol or monument designed to ensure against forgetfulness and oblivion ⟨the first time it had ever been rung to *commemorate* the death of a monarch —*New Yorker*⟩ ⟨their six children all died in early youth, and the Bradleys determined to *commemorate* them by founding an educational institution —Marie A. Kasten⟩

— **keep an eye on :** to watch carefully although not continuously ⟨*keep an eye on* the pot so it doesn't boil over⟩ ⟨*keep an eye on* the children while I'm away⟩ — **keep at :** to persevere or persist in doing or concerning oneself with — **keep bach** *slang* **:** to live as a bachelor; *esp* **:** to keep house in the absence of one's wife — **keep cases 1 :** to be in charge of the casebox **2 :** to keep a watch on **:** keep tabs on — **keep company :** to go together as frequent companions or in courtship ⟨after marriage they could look back with pleasure on the time they were *keeping company*⟩ — **keep (one) company :** to stay or travel with (one) to provide companionship — **keep cut** *obs* **:** to keep one's distance **:** act warily — **keep face :** to retain one's poise or equanimity esp. under circumstances that would tend to destroy it — **keep faith :** to observe and live up to one's moral commitments (to something) **:** show steady loyalty — often used with *with* ⟨*keep faith* with one's religion⟩ ⟨*keep faith* with one's children⟩ — **keep hands off :** to refrain from interfering ⟨requested that the government *keep hands off* in the internal affairs of other countries⟩ — **keep house 1 :** to occupy or maintain a separate house or establishment as opposed to living with parents or relatives or boarding out ⟨~s is married and *keeping house*⟩ **2** *Brit* **:** to remain secluded at home to evade creditors — **keep in mind** *Scot* **:** to keep in mind : REMEMBER — **keep one's end up** *or* **keep up one's end 1 :** to do one's fair share in an enterprise involving two and often more people or participants ⟨could *keep his end up* in a conversation on almost any subject⟩ **2 :** to preserve one's wicket by defensive play — used of a batsman in cricket — **keep one's feet :** to stay upright **:** keep one's balance — **keep one's hand in :** to keep in practice ⟨tried to *keep his hand in* at tennis by playing a little at least once a week⟩ — **keep pace :** to keep up ⟨had no trouble *keeping pace* with the faster runners⟩ ⟨did not wish to *keep pace* with the neighbors in social life⟩ — **keep standing :** to hold intact (as set type) — **keep step :** to keep in step ⟨*keep step* with the other marchers⟩ ⟨*keep step* with the times and turn it to your sales advantage —*Women's Wear Daily*⟩ — **keep the field :** to continue a campaign — **keep the peace :** to avoid or prevent a breach of the peace or any crime likely to result in such a breach — **keep to 1 a :** to confine oneself to **:** remain in **:** not leave ⟨*kept to* the house during his convalescence⟩ ⟨*kept to* the main roads in his travels⟩ **b :** to limit oneself to (as a particular kind of diet) **2 :** to abide by ⟨*keep to* the rules of the game⟩ **:** conform to ⟨*keep to* the hour decided on —Agnes M. Miall⟩ **:** not deviate from ⟨*keep to* the point⟩ — **keep to oneself 1 :** to keep secret ⟨knew what the facts were but *kept* them *to himself*⟩ ⟨*kept* their knowledge . . . *to themselves* and made no attempt to spread it —Sean MacCormac⟩ **2 :** to remain solitary or apart from other people **:** avoid social relations ⟨a shy girl who *kept* pretty much *to herself*⟩ — **keep wicket :** to play as wicketkeeper in cricket

²keep \"\ *n* -S [ME *kep*, *keep*, fr. *kepen* to keep — more at KEEP] **1** *archaic* : HEED, NOTICE — usu. used in the phrases *give keep*, *take keep* **2 :** the act of keeping or the state of being kept: as **a** *archaic* : CUSTODY, GUARD, CHARGE **b** : MAINTENANCE **3 :** one that keeps or protects: as **a :** STRONGHOLD, FORTRESS, CASTLE; *specif* **:** the strongest and securest part of a medieval castle often used as a place of residence esp. during a siege **b** : KEEPER ⟨has been made the ~ of an anticritical defensive system —F.R.Leavis⟩ **c** : PRISON, JAIL **d :** a cap or other mechanical device for retaining anything in place; *specif* **:** a light iron casting resting on the hanger at the bottom of a locomotive axle box to keep the lubricating pad in position **4 a :** the means or provisions by which one is kept ⟨the horse was hardly worth its ~⟩ **b** *Brit* **:** pasture for grazing or the grass in such pasture **c :** a conditioning tonic or regimen for game cocks **5 keeps** *pl but sing in constr* **:** a game of marbles played for keeps **6 :** a football play in which the quarterback fakes a pass but keeps the ball and runs with it **syn** see LIVING — **for keeps** *adv* **1 a :** with the provision that one keep what he has won ⟨the two men were playing the game *for keeps*⟩ **b :** with deadly seriousness **:** with the firm intention of winning or overcoming if at all possible ⟨found out that his rival was not fooling but competing with him *for keeps*⟩ **2 :** with the intention of remaining in a particular state or relationship for good : PERMANENTLY ⟨after his experience in foreign countries he came home *for keeps*⟩

3 : with finality **:** with the result of ending the matter ⟨stole their crown jewels . . . and *for keeps* —Ethel M. Thornbury⟩ ⟨plugged *for keeps* in a gun duel with a desperado —John McCarten⟩

keep·able \-pəbəl\ *adj* **:** capable of being kept for some time without deterioration ⟨some foods are ~ under refrigeration⟩

keep away *vi* **:** to sail less close to the wind ~ *vt* **:** to cause (a sailing ship) to keep away

keep back *vt* **1 :** RESTRAIN ⟨had a hard time *keeping* her *back*⟩ ⟨*kept* the man *back* from committing the crime⟩ **:** hold back **:** RETARD ⟨*kept* the completion of the plan *back* by a year⟩ **2 a :** to refrain from giving **:** WITHHOLD ⟨*kept* a portion of his pay *back*⟩ **b :** to refrain from divulging ⟨*kept* the information *back* until he was paid for it⟩ **c :** RESERVE, SAVE ⟨*kept* rare items *back* for customers who would pay the best prices⟩ ~ *vi* **:** to refrain from approaching or advancing near (as to something dangerous) ⟨asked the children to *keep back* while the fireworks were exploding⟩ **syn** see KEEP

keep down *vt* **1 a :** to hold in subjection **:** SUPPRESS ⟨had trouble *keeping* the insurgents *down*⟩ **b :** to keep in control ⟨*kept* the horse *down* with the curb⟩ **c :** LIMIT, RESTRICT ⟨tried to *keep* expenses *down*⟩ **d :** to prevent from growing, advancing, or succeeding ⟨can't *keep* a good man *down*⟩ **2 :** to prevent from regurgitating or vomiting ⟨felt sick but succeeded in *keeping* his dinner *down*⟩ **3 :** to set or leave set in lowercase in printing

¹keep·er \-pə(r)\ *n* -S [ME *keper*, fr. *kepen* to keep + *-er* — more at KEEP] **1 :** one that keeps something (as by watching over, guarding, maintaining, supporting, restraining): as **a :** GUARDIAN, PROTECTOR ⟨am I my brother's ~ —Gen 4:9 (RSV)⟩ **b :** one that conforms to or abides by (as a custom, rite, or law) ⟨a ~ of the Lord's commandments⟩ **:** one that fulfills (as a promise or pledge) **c :** one that has charge of (as a prison, prisoners, inmates of an institution, the grounds or buildings of an estate, animals in a zoo); *specif* **:** GAMEKEEPER **d :** one that owns, maintains, or carries on (as a boarding house, castle, store) **e :** GUARD **f** *obs* **:** one that keeps a mistress **g :** one whose vocation or avocation is the care of (as bees) **h :** WICKETKEEPER **i :** CURATOR ⟨a ~ of manuscripts in a library⟩ **j :** one whose job is to keep something in good or satisfactory condition ⟨a boat ~⟩ ⟨a greenhouse ~⟩ **k :** an armature that preserves the intensity of magnetization of a permanent magnet **2 :** a device that keeps something in position: as **a :** LATCH **b :** the strike of a lock **c :** GUARD RING **d :** LOCKNUT **e :** a loop of string tied in the eye of a bowstring to keep it in place when the bow is unbraced **f :** the keep in a locomotive axle box **g :** a leather loop on a rifle sling for holding the sling tight on the arm when firing with the sling **3 :** a fruit or vegetable that keeps well **4 :** a fish large enough to be legally caught

²keeper \"\ *vt* -ED/-ING/-S *Brit* **:** to maintain (a game preserve) under the care of a keeper ⟨marsh . . . strictly ~*ed* and alive with fowl —*Country Life*⟩

keep·er·ing \-p(ə)riŋ\ *n* -S *Brit* **:** the occupation or work of a keeper (as a gamekeeper)

keeper of the broad seal *obs* **:** KEEPER OF THE GREAT SEAL

keeper of the great seal *or* **keeper of the seal :** a high officer of state in England and Scotland who has custody of the great seal **:** LORD CHANCELLOR

keeper of the privy purse : PRIVY PURSE 2

keeper of the privy seal [ME *keper of the prive seale*] **1 :** LORD PRIVY SEAL **2 :** an officer in Scotland and Cornwall analogous to the English lord privy seal

keep·er·ship \ˈkēpə(r),ship\ *n* **:** the office or position of keeper

keep in *vt* **1 a :** to keep from expressing **:** hold back ⟨*kept* his feelings *in* until he nearly burst⟩ ⟨was unable to *keep* the secret *in*⟩ **b :** to detain in the school after regular school hours as a punishment ⟨*kept* the children *in* for disobedience⟩ **2** *archaic* **:** to keep (a fire) burning ~ *vi* **1** *of a fire* **:** to keep burning **2 :** to stay on good or favorable terms ⟨anxious to *keep in* with the boss⟩

¹keeping *n* -S [ME *keping*, fr. gerund of *kepen* to keep — more at KEEP] **1 :** the act of one that keeps: as **a :** CUSTODY, GUARD, MAINTENANCE ⟨left the small child in the woman's ~⟩ ⟨the ~ of the lighthouse⟩ **b :** the observance of a rule, obligation, or rite **c :** a reserving or preserving for future use **d** *obs* **:** the maintaining of a mistress **2 a :** the means by which something is kept **:** KEEP, SUPPORT, PROVISION, FEED ⟨provided good ~ for the cattle⟩ **b :** the state of being kept or the condition in which something is kept ⟨the house is in good ~⟩ **3 :** CONFORMITY, CONGRUITY, HARMONY, CONSISTENCY — usu. used in the phrases *in keeping* or *out of keeping* ⟨behavior in ~ with the solemnity of the occasion⟩ ⟨simplicity and restraint is in admirable ~ with the earnest purpose of the pioneers —*Amer. Guide Series: Minn.*⟩ ⟨a doctrine so out of ~ with the facts of Japanese life —Kazuo Kawai⟩

²keeping *adj* [ME *keping*, fr. pres. part. of *kepen* to keep] **:** of or relating to something that remains unspoiled over a period of time ⟨apples with good ~ quality⟩

keeping room *n, dial* **:** a family living room

keep off *vt* **1 :** to keep away **:** keep back ⟨had a hard time *keeping* the children *off* when he brought out the pony⟩ **2 :** to ward off **:** AVERT ⟨a charm to *keep off* disease and misfortune⟩ ~ *vi* **:** to keep back ⟨asked the spectators to *keep off* because the animal was unpredictable⟩

keep out *vt* **:** to keep back **:** WITHHOLD ⟨*kept* a portion of every employee's paycheck *out*⟩; *also* **:** RESERVE, SAVE ⟨*kept* some of the best cuts of meat *out* for a good customer⟩ **syn** see KEEP

keeps *pres 3d sing of* KEEP, *pl of* KEEP

keep·sake \ˈkēp,sāk\ *n* [¹*keep* + *-sake* (as in *namesake*)] **1 :** something kept or given to be kept as a memento (as of a friend or a happy occasion) **2 :** GIFTBOOK 2 **3 :** a giftbook made up for a particular group or occasion and serving as a specimen of fine printing

keep under *vt* **:** to hold in subjection ⟨*kept* the conquered people *under* for 50 years⟩

keep up *vt* **1 :** to go on with **:** persevere in **:** continue usu. with persistence ⟨*kept* the talk *up* until midnight⟩ ⟨*kept* his criminal activity *up* until he was caught⟩ ⟨*kept up* their correspondence⟩ **:** MAINTAIN, SUSTAIN ⟨*kept up* a front for Mama, who was not to be worried —Andrea Parke⟩ ⟨*kept* their standards *up*⟩ **2 :** to prevent from diminishing or deteriorating **:** keep in good condition ⟨worked every day to *keep* the garden *up*⟩ ⟨*kept* his credit *up* by paying his bills regularly⟩ **3** *archaic* **:** to keep confined or penned up ~ *vi* **1 :** to stay even (as in acts of strength, endurance, or speed) ⟨although he was small he could *keep up* with the larger boys in sports⟩ **:** stay along (as in thoughts or studies) ⟨able to *keep up* with his class in school⟩ **2 :** to keep adequately informed — used with *on* or *with* ⟨*kept up* with the affairs of the office⟩ ⟨*keep up* on international relations⟩ **3 :** to continue without interruption **:** maintain a particular course, condition, or series of actions ⟨the rain *kept up* all night⟩ **4 :** to match one's neighbors or contemporaries in accomplishment or in the acquisition of material goods **:** be in fashion — usu. used with *with* ⟨*keeping up* with the professors —*Yale Rev.*⟩ ⟨farm folk seem to place less emphasis than city folk upon competitive consumption, or spending to *keep up* with the Joneses —Day Monroe⟩

keesh *var of* KISH

kees·hond \ˈkās,hȯnd, -hȯn-, -nt\ *n* [D, prob. fr. *Kees* (nickname for *Cornelis* Cornelius) + *hond* dog, fr. MD; akin to OHG *hunt* dog — more at HOUND] **1** *usu cap* **:** a Dutch breed of compact medium-sized gray dogs that have a dense heavy coat and a foxy head **2** *pl* **keeshonds** *or* **kees·hon·den** \-ndən\ *often cap* **:** a dog of the Keeshond breed

keest \ˈkēst\ *n* -S [D, kernel, pit, marrow, fr. MD *keest, keeste*] *Scot* **:** inner vital substance **:** MARROW ⟨cold to the ~⟩

keester *var of* KEISTER

keet *or* **keat** \ˈkēt\ *n* -S [imit.] **:** GUINEA FOWL; *esp* **:** a young guinea fowl

keeve *or* **kieve** \ˈkēv\ *n* -S [ME *kive, keve*, fr. OE *cȳf*, prob. borrowed in prehistoric times fr. (assumed) VL *cupia*, fr. L *cupa* tub, vat — more at HIVE] **1 :** a tub or vat esp. for liquids (as a bleaching kier or dolly tub) **2** *Brit* **:** a rock basin hollowed out by water

kee·wa·tin \(ˈ)kē¦wāt°n\ *adj, usu cap* [fr. *Keewatin* district, Northwest Territories, Canada] **:** of or relating to a division of the Archeozoic — see GEOLOGIC TIME table

kef \ˈkef, ˈkēf, ˈkāf\ *or* **kif** \ˈkif\ *n* -S [colloq. Ar *kēf* (*kayf*) enjoyment, pleasure] **1 :** a state of dreamy tranquillity **:** LANGUOR **2 :** a smoking material (as hashish) that produces kef ⟨basks there . . . smoking . . . his ~ —Hendrik de Leeuw⟩

kef·fel \ˈkefəl\ *n* -S [W *ceffyl* horse, fr. L *caballus* horse, nag — more at CAVALCADE] *dial Brit* **:** a usu. old or worthless horse **:** NAG

keffiyeh *var of* KAFFIYEH

ke·fir *also* **ke·phir** \keˈfi(ə)r, kəˈf-, ˈkefər\ *n* -S [Russ *kefir*, fr. a native name in the Caucasus] **:** a slightly effervescent acidulous beverage of low alcoholic content made chiefly in southern Russia of cow's milk that is fermented by means of kefir grains

kefir grain *n* **:** a small mass resembling a tiny cauliflower, occurring in kefir, containing casein and other milk solids together with the yeasts and lactobacilli that cause the characteristic kefir fermentation, and serving as a starter to induce this fermentation when introduced into fresh milk

keg \ˈkeg, -ā-, ÷ -a-, ÷ -ai-\ *n* -S [alter. of earlier *cag*, fr. ME *kag*, of Scand origin; akin to ON *kaggi*, *-kaggr* keg, cask, Sw & Dan *kagge*; prob. akin to OHG *kegil* stake, peg, MD *kegge* wedge, Sw dial. *kage* tree stump, and perh. to Lith *žāgaras* dry twig; basic meaning: branch, stake] **1 :** a small cask or barrel having a capacity of 30 gallons or less **2 :** the contents of a keg

kegeree *var of* KEDGEREE

ke·gler *also* **kegel·er** *or* **kegel·ler** \ˈkeg(ə)lə(r), ˈkāg-\ *n* -S [G *kegler*, fr. *kegeln* to bowl (fr. *kegel* bowling pin, cone, fr. OHG *kegil* stake, peg) + *-er* — more at KEG] **:** ¹BOWLER

keg·ling *also* **kegel·ing** *or* **kegel·ling** \-g(ə)liŋ\ *n* -S [G *kegeln* to bowl + E *-ing*] **:** BOWLING

keg·meg \ˈkeg,meg\ *var of* CAGMAG

ke·gon \ˈkā,gän, -gōn\ *n, usu cap* [Jap, fr. *ke* lotus + *gon* dignity] **:** a sect of Japanese Buddhism originating in the 8th century and teaching the unreality of phenomenal antitheses and the ultimate unity of all reality in and through the Buddha

ke·hil·lah *or* **ke·hi·la** \kəˈhilə\ *n, pl* **kehil·loth** *or* **kehil·lot** \-,lōt(h), -ōs\ [Heb *qĕhillāh* assembly, community] **:** the Jewish community of a city organized for the administration of charities and communal work

ke·hoe·ite \ˈkē(,)hō,īt\ *n* -S [Henry *Kehoe*, 19th cent. Am. mineralogist + E *-ite*] **:** a mineral $Al_8(Zn,Ca)_3(PO_4)_6(OH)_{12}$-$21H_2O(?)$ consisting of a massive basic hydrous calcium aluminum zinc phosphate (sp. gr. 2.3)

kei apple \ˈkā-, ˈkī-, ˈkəi-\ *n, usu cap K* [fr. Great *Kei* river, Cape Province, Union of South Africa] **1 :** the edible fruit of a southern African shrub (*Dovyalis caffra*) of the family Flacourtiaceae that is shaped like a small apple and is used for pickles and preserves **2 :** the shrub that bears the Kei apple

keik \ˈkēk\ *var of* KEEK

kei·ki \ˈkākē\ *n* -S [Hawaiian] **1** *Hawaii* **:** CHILD **2** *Hawaii* **:** an immature plant

keist \ˈkāst\ *Scot var of* CAST

keis·ter \ˈkēstə(r), ˈkīs-\ *or* **kees·ter** \ˈkēs-\ *n* -S [origin unknown] **1 :** SATCHEL, SUITCASE; *specif* **:** one carried by an itinerant peddler **2** *slang* **:** BUTTOCKS ⟨they . . . get paid all those thousands — to sit on their ~*s* —Rod Nordland⟩

keit·loa \ˈkītləwə, ˈkāt-, ˌ=ˈlōə\ *n* -S [Sechuana *kgetlwa, khetlwa*] **:** a black rhinoceros that has a posterior horn which equals or exceeds the anterior in length and that has been considered to constitute a distinct species

kek·chi *or* **quek·chi** \ˈkek(,)chē\ *n, pl* **kekchi** *or* **kekchis** *or* **quekchi** *or* **quekchis** *usu cap* **1 a :** an Indian people of north central Guatemala **b :** a member of such people **2 :** the Mayan language of the Kekchi people

ke·ku·lé formula \ˈkākə,lā-\ *n, usu cap K* [after Friedrich August *Kekulé* von Stradonitz †1896 Ger. chemist] **:** a structural formula for an organic compound that depicts each valence bond as a short line; *esp* **:** the hexagonal ring formula for benzene — see BENZENE RING illustration

ke·ku·ne oil *or* **ke·ku·na oil** \kəˈkünə-\ *n* [prob. native name in Ceylon] **:** CANDLENUT OIL

ke·la·bit \kəˈläbət\ *n, pl* **kelabit** *or* **kelabits** *usu cap* [native name in Sarawak] **1 :** a Dayak people of northern Sarawak **2 :** a member of the Kelabit people

kelb-el-bahr \ˌkel,belˈbär\ *n* -S [Ar *kalb al-baḥr*, lit., the dog of the sea (river, Nile)] **:** any of several large formidable characin fishes of the Nile and rivers and lakes of tropical Africa that constitute the genus *Hydrocyon*, reach a length of about three feet, have strong teeth, and in form resemble a salmon

keld \ˈkeld\ *n* -S [prob. of Scand origin; akin to ON *kelda* spring, marshy place, prob. fr. *kaldr* cold — more at COLD] **1** *dial Eng* **:** SPRING, FOUNTAIN **2** *dial Eng* **:** the still part of a body of water

kel·e·be \ˈkelə(,)bē\ *n* -S [Gk *kelebē*, prob. of non-IE origin] **:** an ovoid krater having handles that drop almost vertically to the shoulder from horizontal extensions on the rim

kelebe

k electron *n, usu cap K* **:** an electron in the K-shell

k-electron capture *usu cap K, var of* K-CAPTURE

ke·lep \kəˈlep\ *n* -S [Kekchi *kelép*] **:** a Central American stinging ant (*Ectatomma tuberculatum*) that lives in small colonies in the ground esp. near clearings

kell \ˈkel\ *n* -S [ME (northern dial.) *kelle*, alter. of *calle* — more at CAUL] *dial Brit* **:** CAUL; *specif* **:** a net cap worn by women

kelleg *or* **kellock** *var of* KILLICK

kellin *var of* KHELLIN

kel·li·on \keˈlē,än, -ē,ōn\ *n, pl* **kel·lia** \-ēə, -ē(,)ä\ [LGk, lit., little cell, fr. L *cella* cell + Gk *-ion* (dim. suffix) — more at CELL] **:** a small religious house of the Eastern Church occupied by not more than three monks and three lay brothers

kel·logg oak \ˈke,lȯg-, -,läg-, -,lag-\ *or* **kellogg's oak** *n, usu cap K* [after Albert *Kellogg* †1887 Am. botanist] **:** CALIFORNIA BLACK OAK

kel·lup·weed \ˈkeləp,=\ *n* [*kellup* (alter. of *kelp*) + *weed*] **:** OXEYE 1d

¹kel·ly \ˈkelē, -li\ *n* -ES [prob. by folk etymology (influence of the name *Kelly*) fr. *callow*] **:** the topsoil removed in order to secure clay for brickmaking

²kelly \"\ *vt* -ED/-ING/-ES **:** to cover (as a molding floor for bricks) with kelly

³kelly \"\ *or* **kel·lie** \"\ *var of* KILLIE

⁴kelly *n, pl* **kellies** *or* **kellys** [prob. fr. the name *Kelly*] **:** a man's stiff hat (as a derby or a flat-topped straw hat) ⟨only the dudes wore straw *kellies* —*New Yorker*⟩

⁵kelly \"\ *or* **kelly green** *n, often cap K* [fr. the common Irish name *Kelly*; fr. green's being a traditional Irish color] **:** a variable color averaging a strong yellowish green that is greener and duller than cyprus green and greener, stronger, and slightly lighter than emerald (sense 2b) ⟨comes in red, ~, white, or black —*Women's Wear Daily*⟩

⁶kelly \"\ *n* -S [prob. alter. of E dial. *kelp*, of unknown origin] *Austral* **:** CROW ⟨gave the ~*s* a rare blessing and left them to their feast —*Sydney (Australia) Bull.*⟩

⁷kelly \"\ *also* **kelly joint** *n* -S [prob. fr. the name *Kelly*] **:** GRIEF STEM

kelly pool *n, usu cap K* **:** a pool game in which each player draws a number and while playing on the object balls in numerical order aims to pocket the ball having his number on it and thereby win the game but if his ball is pocketed by another player he loses his chance of winning and continues to play with the aim of pocketing the balls of other players

kelm·scott \ˈke(l)mzkət, ˈkeüm-, -m(p)sk-; -mz,kät, -m(p)-,sk-\ *adj, usu cap* [fr. the *Kelmscott* Press, publishing firm in Hammersmith, England, fr. *Kelmscott*, England, home of William Morris †1896 Eng. poet and artist, its founder] **:** produced by the Kelmscott Press ⟨*Kelmscott* books⟩ ⟨the *Kelmscott* Chaucer⟩

ke·loid *also* **che·loid** \ˈkē,lȯid\ *n* -S [F *kiloïde, chéloïde*, fr. Gk *chēlē* claw + F *-oïde* -oid] **:** a thick scar resulting from excessive growth of fibrous tissue and occurring esp. after burns or radiation injury — **ke·loi·dal** \(ˈ)kē¦lȯid°l\ *adj*

kelp \ˈkelp, ˈkeüp\ *n* -S [ME *culp*] **1 a :** any of various large brown seaweeds of the orders Laminariales and Fucales — see GIANT KELP **b :** a mass or growth of large seaweeds; *esp* **:** a mass of those burned for the ashes **2** *also* **kelp ash :** the ashes of seaweed used formerly as a source of alkali and now as a source of iodine

kelp bass *n* **:** a dusky sea bass (*Paralabrax clathratus*) that is blotched with darker brown or gray above and silvery or yellowish below, is common in kelp beds along the California coast, and is an esteemed sport fish

kelp crab *n* **:** any of several spider crabs common among algae and eelgrass along the Pacific coast of No. America: as **a :** the common kelp crab (*Pugettia producta* syn. *Epialtus productus*) **b :** GRACEFUL KELP CRAB **c :** SHEEP CRAB

kelp·er \-pə(r)\ *n* -S **:** one that gathers or prepares kelp

kelpfish \ˈ=,=\ *n* **:** any of various fishes inhabiting kelp beds: as **a :** a large variably colored blenny (*Heterostichus rostratus*) found among kelp or eelgrass along the California coast or another member of the family Clinidae **b :** any of several brilliantly colored percoid fishes of the family Odacidae found along the coasts of Australia and New Zealand — called also *rock whiting*

kelp fly \ˈ=,=\ *n* **:** any of various rather large flattened two-winged flies that constitute the family Coelopidae and have larvae that feed on kelp

kelp goose *n* **:** a goose (*Chloephaga hybrida*) of littoral habits found in the Falkland islands and adjacent So. America

kelp greenling *n* **:** GREENLING 1a(2)

kelp gull *n* **:** a black-backed gull (*Larus dominicanus*) of the southern hemisphere

kelp hen *n* **:** a weka of South Island of New Zealand that feeds on marine animals and prob. represents a dark phase of a species (*Gallirallus australis*) though sometimes considered a separate species (*G. brachypterus*)

¹kel·pie *also* **kel·py** \ˈkelpē, ˈkeüp-\ *n, pl* **kelpies** [perh. fr. ScGael *cailpeach, calpach, colpach* heifer, steer, colt] **:** a water spirit usu. equine in form that is held esp. in Scottish folklore to delight in or bring about the drowning of travelers ⟨the hidden lair of . . . the ~*s* and the spirits of the night —Raymond Foxall⟩

²kelpie \"\ *n* -S [after *Kelpie*, an early specimen] **:** an Australian sheep dog of a breed developed in the 19th century in New South Wales by crossing the dingo with various British sheep dogs

kelp pigeon *n* **:** a sheathbill (*Chionis alba*) having a pinkish or yellowish black-tipped bill and occurring from the Falkland islands south to parts of Antarctica

kelp plover *n* **:** DOWITCHER

kelp raft *n* **:** a mass of floating kelp

kelpwort \ˈ=,=\ *n* **:** GLASSWORT 2

kelpy \ˈkelpē, ˈkeüp-\ *adj, sometimes* -ER/-EST [*kelp* + *-y*] **:** abounding in or characterized by kelp

kel·sey locust \ˈkelsē- *also* -ltsē-\ *n, usu cap K* [after Harlan P. *Kelsey* *b*1872 Am. horticulturist] **:** an American shrub (*Robinia kelseyi*) having rose or purple flowers, glabrous branches, and glandular hispid pods

kelson *var of* KEELSON

¹kelt \ˈkelt\ *n* -S [ME (northern dial.), prob. fr. ScGael *cealt*] **:** a salmon or sea trout that is weak and emaciated after spawning

²kelt \"\ *n* -S [ScGael *cealt*] *dial Brit* **:** homespun frieze cloth usu. of black wool with a mixture of white

³kelt \"\ *cap, var of* CELT

¹kelter *var of* KILTER

²kel·ter \ˈkeltər\ *vi* -ED/-ING/-S [origin unknown] *chiefly Scot* **:** to move restlessly **:** UNDULATE

³kel·ter \ˈkəltə(r)\ *n* -S [origin unknown] **1** *dial Eng* **:** property of any kind; *esp* **:** MONEY **2 :** RUBBISH, TRASH

keltic *usu cap, var of* CELTIC

kel·ty \ˈkeltī\ *n* -ES [origin unknown] *Scot* **:** an additional glass of liquor forced upon a reluctant drinker

kel·vin \ˈkelvən\ *adj, usu cap* [after William Thomson, Lord *Kelvin* †1907 Brit. physicist] **:** relating to, conforming to, or having a thermometric scale on which the unit of measurement equals the Celsius degree and according to which absolute zero is 0 K, the equivalent of —273.15°C, and water freezes at 273.15 K and boils at 373.15 K

kelvin balance *n, usu cap K* [after Lord *Kelvin*] **:** a device for comparing the force produced by an electric current flowing through fixed and movable coils and the force of gravity

kelvin's law *n, usu cap K* [after Lord *Kelvin*] **:** a statement in electrical economics: the most economical cross-section area for an electric conductor is that for which the cost of energy lost in a given period equals the interest for the same period of the capital involved

ke·mal·ism \kəˈmä,lizəm\ *n* -S *usu cap* [*Kemal* Atatürk (Mustafa Kemal) †1938 Turkish general and statesman + E *-ism*] **:** the political, economic, and social principles advocated by Kemal Atatürk and designed to create a modern republican secular Turkish state out of a portion of the Ottoman empire

¹ke·mal·ist \-ləst\ *n* -S *usu cap* [*Kemal* Atatürk + E *-ist*] **:** a follower of Kemal Atatürk **:** an adherent of Kemalism ⟨the economic policies of the *Kemalists*⟩

²kemalist \"\ *adj, usu cap* **:** of, relating to, or having the characteristics of Kemalism or Kemalists ⟨the modern *Kemalist* pattern of revolution —*Atlantic*⟩ ⟨the Ottoman empire collapsed and *Kemalist* Turkey was born — Necmeddin Sadak⟩

ke·man·cha \kəˈmänchə\ *n* -S [Ar *kamanjah*, fr. Per] **:** an Arabian violin that has usu. a single string and a gourd resonator and is held vertically when played

¹kemb \ˈkem\ *vt* **kembed** \-md\ *or* **kempt** \-m(p)t\ **kembed** *or* **kempt; kembing; kembs** [ME *kemben*, fr. OE *cemban*; akin to OS *kembian* to comb, OHG *kemben, chempen*, ON *kemba*; denominatives fr. the root of E ¹*comb*] *dial* **:** COMB

²kemb \"\ *n* -S *dial* **:** COMB

ke·me·ro·vo \ˈkemə,rō(,)vō\ *adj, usu cap* [fr. *Kemerovo*, U.S.S.R.] **:** of or from the city of Kemerovo, U.S.S.R. **:** of the kind or style prevalent in Kemerovo

ke·mi·ri nut \kəˈmirē-\ *also* **kemiri** *n* -S [Jav *kĕmiri*] **:** CANDLENUT 1

¹kemp \ˈkemp\ *n* -S [ME *kempe*, fr. OE *cempa*; akin to OS *kempio* warrior, OHG *kempho*, ON *kappi*; all fr. a prehistoric WGmc-NGmc word derived fr. a word meaning "combat", "battle"; akin to OE *camp, comp* combat, battle, OHG *kamph* combat, battle, ON *kapp* contest, zeal; all borrowed fr. L *campus* plain, field, battlefield — more at CAMP] **1 a** *dial Brit* **:** a strong and worthy warrior or athlete **:** CHAMPION **b** *dial Eng* **:** an impetuous rogue **2** *dial Brit* **:** a competition or contest esp. among reapers in a harvest field

²kemp \"\ *vi* -ED/-ING/-S [ME *kempen*, prob. fr. *kempe*, n.] *chiefly Scot* **:** to contend or compete for championship esp. in a reaping contest

³kemp \"\ *n* -S [ME *kempe* coarse hair, of Scand origin; akin to ON *kampr* mustache; akin to OE *cenep* mustache, OFris *kenep* mustache, MD *canef*been cheekbone, and perh. to ON *knefill* pole, stake — more at KNAVE] **:** a coarse dead fiber esp. of wool or mohair that is usu. short, wavy, and white, has little affinity for dye, and is used in mixed wools (as in carpets or for novelty effects)

kem·pas \ˈkem,pas\ *n* -ES [Malay *kĕmpas*] **1 :** a leguminous Malayan tree (*Koompassia malaccensis*) with very hard heavy strong wood **2 :** the wood of the kempas

kemp·ite \ˈkem,pīt\ *n* -S [James F. *Kemp* †1926 Am. geologist + E *-ite*] **:** a mineral $Mn_2(OH)_3Cl$ consisting of a basic manganese oxychloride occurring in small emerald green orthorhombic crystals

kem·ple \ˈkempəl\ *n* -S [alter. of earlier *kimple*, of Scand origin; akin to ON *-kimbull* bundle, Icel *kimbill* small bundle, small haystack, Norw dial. *kimbel* bundle of grass] **:** a Scotch unit of measure for straw varying around 400 pounds

kemp's loggerhead *or* **kemp's turtle** \ˈkemps-\ *n, usu cap K* [fr. the name *Kemp*] **:** RIDLEY

kempt \ˈkem(p)t\ *adj* [ME, fr. past part. of *kemben* to comb — more at KEMB] **:** neatly kept **:** TRIM ⟨lips . . . unsmiling above the faintly grizzled and elegantly ~ —Jean Stafford⟩

kempy \ˈkempē\ *adj, sometimes* -ER/-EST [³*kemp* + *-y*] **:** containing or resembling kemp ⟨a lean hairy animal . . . whose ~ wool brings only the lowest market prices —C.A.Amsden⟩

¹ken \ˈken\ *vb* **kenned** *also* **kend** \-nd\ *or* **kent** \-nt\ **kenned** *also* **kend** *or* **kent; kenning; kens** [ME *kennen*; partly fr. OE *cennan* to make known, declare, acknowledge; partly fr. ON *kenna* to perceive, know; both akin to OHG *kennen* to make known, Goth *kannjan*; causatives fr. the root of OE *cunnan* to know — more at CAN] *vt* **1** *archaic* **:** to have sight of : SEE ⟨as far as I could ~ thy chalky cliffs, . . . I stood upon the hatches in the storm —Shak.⟩ **2** *now dial* : to recognize by or as if by sight : DISCERN ⟨*kenned* in the beautiful lady the child of his friend —S.T.Coleridge⟩ **3** *now chiefly Scot* **a** : to have acquaintance with ⟨have *kend* every wench in the Halidome of St. Mary's —Sir Walter Scott⟩ **b** : to have knowledge of ⟨it was getting dark, and they didn't ~ the ground like us —John Buchan⟩ **c** : to have awareness or understanding of ⟨do ye ~ what ye're saying, man? —William Black⟩ **4** *Scots law* : to admit to ownership of heritable property ~ *vi* **1** *now chiefly Scot* : to have knowledge : KNOW ⟨it was his father then ye *kent* of —Sir Walter Scott⟩ **2** *obs* : to have the power of sight ⟨spaces distant from them as far as a man may ~ —Marchamont Needham⟩

²ken \"\ *n* -s **1** *obs* : the distance that bounds the range of ordinary vision esp. at sea ⟨are safely come within a ~ of Dover —John Lyly⟩ **2 a** : the range of vision ⟨then felt I like some watcher of the skies when a new planet swims into his ~ —John Keats⟩ **b** : the sight or view esp. of a place or person ⟨'tis double death to drown in ~ of shore —Shak.⟩ **c** : the power or exercise of vision ⟨searched with fixed ~ to know what place it was wherein I stood —H.F.Cary⟩ **3** : the range of recognition, comprehension, perception, understanding, or knowledge ⟨abstract words that are beyond the ~ of young children —Lois M. Rettie⟩ ⟨all knowledge and experience come within the historian's ~ —W.G.Carleton⟩ **syn** see RANGE

³ken \"\ *n* -s [prob. short for *kennel*] : HOUSE; *esp* : a rowdy resort for thieves and beggars ⟨has fishwives and boozing ~*s* enough to supply all of America —Kenneth Roberts⟩

⁴ken \"\ *n* -s [Jap, lit., fist] : a Japanese game of forfeits

ken- *or* **keno-** *comb form* [Gk, fr. *kenos;* akin to Arm *sin* empty, vain] : empty ⟨*kenotron*⟩

ke·naf *also* **ka·naf** *or* **ka·naff** \kəˈnaf\ *n* -s [Per] **1** : a valuable fiber plant (*Hibiscus cannabinus*) of the East Indies now widespread in cultivation **2** : the fiber of kenaf used for cordage and canvas manufacture — called also *ambari, bastard jute, Bombay hemp, deccan hemp, Java jute*

kench \ˈkench\ *n* -ES [origin unknown] : a bin or enclosure in which fish or skins are salted

ken·dal green \ˈkendᵊl-\ *also* **kendal** *n* -s *usu cap K* [ME, fr. *Kendal,* borough of Westmorland, England] : a green woolen cloth resembling homespun or tweed

kendal sneck bent *n, usu cap K* [prob. fr. *Kendal,* England] : a fishhook of wide squarish and curved pattern — see FISHHOOK illustration

ken·dle \ˈken(d)ᵊl\ *dial var of* KINDLE

kend·na \ˈken(d)nə\ [*kend* (past of ¹*ken*) + *na*] *chiefly Scot* : did not know

ken·do \ˈken(,)dō\ *n* -s [Jap *kendō*] : a Japanese sport of fencing with staves

ken·dyr *or* **ken·dir** \(ˈ)kenˈdi(ə)r\ *n* -s [Russ & Turk; Russ *kendyr',* fr. Turk *kendir*] **1** : a strong bast fiber that resembles Indian hemp and is used in Asia as cordage and as a substitute for cotton and hemp **2** : an Old World dogbane (*Apocynum venetum*) cultivated chiefly in Asiatic Russia for the kendyr that it produces

ken·il·worth ivy \ˈkenᵊl,wərth-\ *n, usu cap K* [fr. *Kenilworth* Castle, Warwickshire, Eng.] : a delicate trailing Old World plant (*Cymbalaria muralis*) of the family Scrophulariaceae with palmately lobed and veined leaves and small pale violet flowers with a yellow palate

ke·nite \ˈkē,nīt\ *n* -s *usu cap* : a member of an ancient people of southern Palestine related to the Amalekites

ken·na \ˈken(n)ə\ [¹*ken* + *na*] *chiefly Scot* : do not know

kenned \ˈkend\ *adj* [ME *kend,* fr. past part. of *kennen* to know — more at KEN] *chiefly Scot* : WELL-KNOWN, FAMILIAR ⟨wearying terribly for the sight of a ~ face —John Buchan⟩

ken·ne·dya \kəˈnēdēə, ˈkenə,dēə\ *n, cap* [NL, after Lewis *Kennedy* †1818, Eng. nurseryman] : a genus of Australian woody vines (family Leguminosae) bearing showy red or purplish flowers whose corolla has a long keel

¹ken·nel \ˈkenᵊl\ *n* -s [ME *kenel,* fr. (assumed) ONF *kenil,* fr. (assumed) VL *canile* (whence OF *chenil* kennel, F dial. *cani*), fr. L *canis* dog — more at HOUND] **1 a (1)** : a house for a dog or pack of hounds **(2)** : an establishment for the breeding or boarding of dogs — usu. used in pl. **b** : a house or other dwelling place regarded as unfit for human residence **2 a** : a pack of dogs or other animals **b** : a group of persons ⟨literary agent who has a ~ of eccentric clients —Martin Levin⟩ **3** : a bed or den of an animal (as a fox or otter) **4** : GABLE 2b

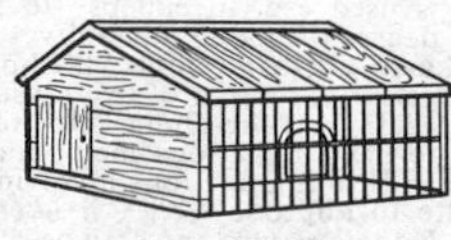

kennel 1a(1)

²kennel \"\ *vb* **kenneled** *or* **kennelled; kenneled** *or* **kennelled; kenneling** *or* **kennelling; kennels** *vi* **1** : to take shelter or lie in a kennel ⟨the fox ~*s* on the hillside⟩ **2** : to lodge in a dwelling place regarded as unfit for human residence ⟨the dull sodden faces of the man and woman who ~*ed* there —E.P.Roe⟩ ~ *vt* **1 a** : to put or keep in a kennel ⟨~ your hound for he has been well whipped —J.H.Wheelwright⟩ ⟨the apple trees under which the dogs were ~*ed* —Eve Langley⟩ **b** : to provide with a dwelling place regarded as unfit for human residence ⟨that quarter of the town where they are ~*ed* is . . . inhabited by strangers —Richard Steele⟩ **2** : to provide or seek lodging or shelter for esp. in a secluded place ⟨writers and painters . . . ~*ing* themselves in the depths of the country —*Times Lit. Supp.*⟩ **3** : to keep within bounds or under control : CONFINE, RESTRAIN ⟨indulge our enthusiasms while keeping our angers and envies ~*ed* —Brand Blanshard⟩ ⟨constantly striving to keep his quickly roused temper ~*ed*⟩

³kennel \"\ *n* -s [alter. of ²*cannel*] : a gutter in a street ⟨streets were ill-paved and . . . sloped down on both sides to the ~*s* —G.M.Trevelyan⟩

kennel club *n* : an association of dog fanciers concerned esp. with advancing the interests of one or more breeds of dogs usu. by establishing standards, providing competitions, or recording pedigrees

ken·nel·ly–heav·i·side layer \ˈkenᵊlē'heve,sīd-\ *n, usu cap K&H* [after Arthur W. *Kennelly* †1939 Am. electrical engineer and Oliver *Heaviside* †1925 Eng. physicist, its discoverers] : IONOSPHERE

kennelmaid \ˈ⸗⸗,⸗\ *n* : a woman who takes care of kennels

ken·nel·man \ˈkenᵊlmən\ *n, pl* **kennelmen** : one who takes care of kennels

ken·ner·ly's salmon \ˈkenərl|ēz-, -R -nəl| *or* -nᵊl|\ *n, usu cap K* [fr. the name *Kennerly*] : KOKANEE

ken·ni·cott's willow warbler \ˈkenəkəts-, -ə,käts-\ *n, usu cap K* [fr. the name *Kennicott*] : a warbler (*Acanthopneuste borealis kennicotti*) that breeds in Alaska

¹ken·ning \ˈkeniŋ\ *n* -s [ME, fr. gerund of *kennen* to ken — more at KEN] **1** *obs* : range of sight : VIEW **2** *chiefly Scot* **a** : COGNITION, RECOGNITION **b** : a perceptible but small amount : LITTLE ⟨his father was . . . a ~ on the wrong side of the law —R.L.Stevenson⟩

²kenning \"\ *n* -s [ON, fr. *kenna* to perceive, know, name, name with a kenning + *-ing* — more at KEN] : a metaphorical compound word or phrase used esp. in Old English and Old Norse poetry ⟨Germanic verse . . . laid main stress upon the trope known as ~; the ocean is the "whale's bath", the "foaming fields", the "sea-street" —F.B.Gummere⟩

kenningwort \ˈ⸗⸗,⸗\ *n* [¹*kenning* + *wort*] : CELANDINE 1

ken·ny method *or* **ken·ny treatment** \ˈkenē-\ *n, usu cap K* [after Elizabeth *Kenny* †1952 Australian nurse, its developer] : a method of treating poliomyelitis consisting of application of hot fomentations to relax spasmodic contraction of affected muscles, reeducation through guided passive movement of the separate muscles with reestablishment of the patient's awareness of them, and guided active coordination

ke·no \ˈkē(,)nō\ *n* -s [modif. of F *quine* set of five winning numbers in a lottery, fr. OF *quines,* pl., throw at dice where each die shows 5, fr. L *quini* five each, fr. *quinque* five — more at FIVE] : a game resembling lotto in which numbers printed on pellets taken from a keno goose are announced to the players who cover the same numbers on cards and in which five numbers covered in the same horizontal row win for the player — see BINGO

keno- — see KEN-

keno goose *n* : a flexible sack with a narrow neck that releases one numbered pellet at a time for use in playing keno — called also *goose*

ke·no·sis \kəˈnōsəs, kēˈ-\ *n* -ES [LGk *kenōsis,* fr. Gk, evacuation, action of emptying, fr. *kenoun* to purge, empty (fr. *kenos* empty) + *-sis* — more at KEN-] **1** : the act of Christ in emptying himself of the form of God, taking the form of a servant, and humbling himself to the extent of suffering death **2** : the act of voluntarily giving up personal rights and ambitions and accepting suffering as a follower of Christ

ke·not·ic \-ˈnäd·|ik, -ät|, |ēk\ *adj* [Gk *kenōtikos* purgative, emptying, fr. (assumed) Gk *kenōtos* (verbal of Gk *kenoun*) + Gk *-ikos* -ic] : of, affirming, or marked by kenosis ⟨~ theories of the Incarnation that stem from Philippians 2:7⟩ ⟨a ~ Christology⟩ ⟨the ~ character of Russian Christianity⟩

ke·not·i·cism \|ə,sizəm\ *n* -s : the doctrine of or belief in the kenosis of Christ

ke·not·i·cist \-,səst\ *n* -s : an advocate or adherent of kenoticism

ken·o·tron \ˈkenə-,trän\ *n* -s [*ken-* + *-tron*] : a high-vacuum diode used as a rectifier in appliances (as X-ray equipment and electrostatic precipitators) where high voltage and low current are required

kens *pres 3d sing of* KEN, *pl of* KEN

ken·sing·ton \ˈkenziŋtən, -n(t)siŋ-\ *n* -s [fr. the name *Kensington*] *dial* : a covered-dish supper

ken·speck·le \ˈkenz,pekəl, -n,sp-\ *or* **ken·speck** \-pek\ *adj* [prob. of Scand origin; akin to Norw *kjennspak* quick at recognizing, fr. *kjenne* to know, recognize (fr. ON *kenna*) + *spak* wise, gentle, tractable, fr. ON *spakr* — more at KEN] *chiefly Scot* : having a distinctive appearance : CONSPICUOUS

¹kent *past of* KEN

²kent \ˈkent\ *adj, usu cap* [fr. *Kent* county, England] : of or from the county of Kent, England : of the kind or style prevalent in Kent : KENTISH

³kent \"\ *n* -s [alter. of *quant*] *chiefly Scot* : STAFF, POLE: as **a** : a shepherd's staff **b** : a punting pole with a flange near the end

⁴kent \"\ *vb* -ED/-ING/-S *vi, chiefly Scot* : to push or propel a boat with a kent ~ *vt, chiefly Scot* : to push or propel with a kent

kent bugle *n, usu cap K* [prob. after Edward Augustus †1820 1st duke of Kent, Eng. soldier] : KEY BUGLE

ken·tia \ˈkentēə\ *n* [NL, fr. William *Kent* †*ab* 1828 Dutch gardener and traveler in the Orient + NL *-ia*] **1** *cap* : a genus of pinnate-leaved palms that are natives of Australia and the East Indies and have spadices with angled branchlets and flowers with six stamens **2** -s : any of several palms formerly assigned to the genus *Kentia:* as **a** : either of two feather palms (*Howea forsteriana* and *H. belmoriana*) from Lord Howe Island that are extensively cultivated for their ornamental foliage **b** : UMBRELLA PALM 1

kent·i·cism \ˈkentə,sizəm\ *n* -s *usu cap* [*Kent* county + *-icism* (as in *Anglicism*)] : a word or phrase peculiar to the Kentish dialect

kent·ish \ˈkentish\ *adj, usu cap* [ME, fr. OE *Centisc,* fr. *Cent* Kent + OE *-isc* -ish] **1** : of, relating to, or characteristic of the county of Kent, England **2** : of, relating to, or characteristic of the people of Kent

kentish glory *n, usu cap K* : an orange-brown moth (*Endromis versicolor*) with black-and-white markings that is common in parts of England and whose larva feeds on birch

kent·ish·man \-shmən\ *n, pl* **kentishmen** *cap* : a native or inhabitant of Kent

kentish nightingale *n, usu cap K, dial Eng* : BLACKCAP 2a

kentish plover *n, usu cap K* : a widely distributed ring plover (*Charadrius alexandrinus*) that sometimes breeds on the east coast of England

ken·tle \ˈkentᵊl\ *n* -s [by alter.] : QUINTAL

kent·ledge \ˈkent,lej\ *n* -s [origin unknown] : pig iron or scrap metal used as ballast

ken·tro·gon \ˈkentrə,gän\ *n* -s [Gk *kentron* sharp point, center of a circle + E *-gon* — more at CENTER] : a larva of a parasitic barnacle (order Rhizocephala)

ken·tro·lite \ˈkentrə,līt\ *n* -s [G *kentrolith,* fr. Gk *kentron* sharp point + G *-lith* -lite] : a dark reddish brown mineral $Pb_2Mn_2Si_2O_9$ consisting of a lead manganese silicate

¹ken·tuck \kənˈtək, (ˈ)kenˈ|t-, (ˈ)kän'|t-\ *adj, usu cap* [fr. *Kentucky,* the state] *dial* : KENTUCKIAN

²kentuck \"\ *n* -s *cap, dial* : KENTUCKIAN

¹ken·tuck·i·an \kənˈtəkēən, -təkiən *sometimes* ken-·\ *adj, usu cap* [*Kentucky* + E *-an*] **1** : of, relating to, or characteristic of Kentucky **2** : of, relating to, or characteristic of the people of Kentucky

²kentuckian \"\ *n* -s *cap* : a native or resident of Kentucky

ken·tucky \-təkē, -ki\ *adj, usu cap* [*Kentucky,* state in the U. S., prob. of Iroquoian origin; akin to Iroquois *kenta* level, prairie] : of or from the state of Kentucky : of the kind or style prevalent in Kentucky : KENTUCKIAN

kentucky bass *or* **kentucky black bass** *n, usu cap K* : SPOTTED BLACK BASS

kentucky bluegrass *also* **kentucky blue** *n, usu cap K* : a valuable pasture and meadow grass (*Poa pratensis*) that has tall stalks and slender bright green leaves, is one of the chief constituents in mixtures of seed for lawns, and is found in both Europe and America where it reaches its finest development in the central U.S. — called also *bluegrass, June grass, meadow grass, smooth meadow grass*

kentucky cardinal *n, usu cap K* : ²CARDINAL 5

kentucky coffee tree *n, usu cap K* : a tall No. American tree (*Gymnocladus dioica*) of the family Leguminosae with bipinnate leaves and large woody brown pods whose seeds have been used as a substitute for coffee — called also *bonduc*

kentucky flat *n, usu cap K* : ARK 2b

kentucky green *n, often cap K* : a dark yellowish green that is yellower and less strong than holly green (sense 1), lighter and stronger than deep chrome green, yellower and darker than golf green, and yellower, lighter, and stronger than average hunter green

kentucky jean *n, usu cap K* **1** : a homemade jean woven with a cotton warp and a wool weft **2** : a garment of Kentucky jean

kentucky rifle *n, usu cap K* : a long-barreled flintlock of relatively small caliber developed in the early 18th century in Pennsylvania and extensively used on the American frontier

kentucky warbler *n, usu cap K* : a warbler (*Oporornis formosus*) of the eastern U.S. that is olive green above and yellow below and has the head marked with black

kentucky windage *n, usu cap K* [*Kentucky* (*rifle*)] : a windage correction made by aiming a firearm to the right or left of the target rather than by adjustment of the sights

¹ken·ya \ˈkenyə *also* ˈkēn-\ *adj, usu cap* [fr. *Kenya,* country in eastern Africa] : of or from Kenya : of the kind or style prevalent in Kenya : KENYAN

²ken·ya *or* **ken·yah** \ˈkenyə\ *n, pl* **kenya** *or* **kenyas** *or* **kenyah** *or* **kenyahs** *usu cap* [native name in northern Borneo] **1** : a Dayak people of north central Borneo sometimes held with the Kayan to constitute a subdivision of the Bahau **2** : a member of the Kenya people

¹ken·yan \ˈkenyən *also* ˈkēn-\ *adj, usu cap* [*Kenya* + E *-an*] **1** : of, relating to, or characteristic of Kenya **2** : of, relating to, or characteristic of the people of Kenya

²kenyan \"\ *n* -s *cap* : a native or inhabitant of Kenya

¹kep \ˈkep\ *vt* **kepped** \-pt\ **kep·pen** \-pən\ *or* **kip·pen** \ˈkipən\ **kepping; keps** [ME *keppen,* alter. of *kepen* to observe, heed, seek, seize, keep — more at KEEP] **1** *dial Brit* : to intercept and hinder ⟨~ him on his way home⟩ **2** *dial Brit* : to make a catch of : serve as a catch for

²kep \"\ *n* -s *dial Brit* : CATCH, HAUL

keph·a·lin \ˈkefələn\ *var of* CEPHALIN

kephir *var of* KEFIR

kepi \ˈkāpē, ˈkepē\ *n* -s [F *képi,* fr. G dial. (Switzerland) *käppi,* dim. of *kappe* cap, fr. OHG *kappa* cloak, cape, fr. LL *cappa* head covering, cloak — more at CAP] : a military cap having a close-fitting band, a round flat top sloping toward the front, and a visor ⟨the forage cap was the American version of the French ~ —W.F.Harris⟩

kep·le·ri·an \(ˈ)keˈplirēən\ *adj, usu cap* [Johannes *Kepler* †1630 Ger. astronomer + E *-ian*] **1** : of or relating to the astronomer Kepler **2** : being in accord with Kepler's laws

keplerian telescope *n, usu cap K* : a refracting telescope usu. used in astronomical observations including a positive objective lens and a positive eyepiece and giving an inverted image and a relatively wide field of view

kep·ler's law \ˈkeplə(r)z-\ *n, usu cap K* [after Johannes *Kepler*] **1** : a statement in astronomy: the orbit of each planet is an ellipse that has the sun at one focus **2** : a statement in astronomy: the radius vector from the sun to each planet generates equal orbital areas in equal times **3** : a statement in astronomy: the ratio of the square of the revolution period to the cube of the orbital major axis is the same for all the planets

kept *past of* KEEP

ker- *also* **ke-** *prefix* [imit.] — used in onomatopoeic or echoic forms imitating the noise of a falling object ⟨*ker*plop⟩

ker·a·lan \ˈkerələn\ *n* -s *cap* [*Kerala* state, India + E *-an*] : a native or inhabitant of Kerala state, southern India

ke·ra·na *or* **ker·ra·na** \kəˈränə\ *n* -s [modif. of Per *karranāī,* fr. *nāī* reed, reed pipe] : a long Persian trumpet

ker·a·sin \ˈkerəsən\ *n* -s [ISV *keras-* (prob. fr. Gk *keras* horn) + *-in* — more at HORN] : a cerebroside $C_{48}H_{93}NO_8$ that occurs esp. in Gaucher's disease and that yields lignoceric acid on hydrolysis

kerat- *or* **kerato-** — see CERAT-

ker·a·ter·pe·ton \,kerəˈtərpə,tän\ *n, cap* [NL, fr. *kerat-* + Gk *herpeton* creeping thing, snake] : a genus of broad-headed extinct amphibians similar to salamanders found in the Carboniferous of Ohio and Ireland

ker·a·tin \ˈkerəd·ən, -ətᵊn\ *also* **ceratin** \ˈse-\ *n* -s [ISV *kerat-, cerat-* + *-in*] : any of various sulfur-containing fibrous proteins that form the chemical basis of epidermal tissues (as horn, hair, wool, nails, feathers), that are insoluble in most solvents and unlike collagen and other proteins are typically not digested by enzymes of the gastrointestinal tract, and that produce elastic properties of fibers — compare PSEUDOKERATIN

ker·a·tin·i·za·tion \,kerəd·ənəˈzāshən\ *n* -s [ISV *keratinize* + *-ation*] : conversion into keratin or keratinous tissue

ker·a·tin·ize \ˈ⸗⸗ᵊn,īz\ *vb* -ED/-ING/-S [ISV *keratin* + *-ize*] *vt* : to make keratinous ⟨tissues *keratinized* by friction⟩ ~ *vi* : to become keratinous or converted into keratin ⟨a *keratinizing* scar⟩

ke·rat·i·no·phil·ic \kəˌratᵊnōˈfilik\ *adj* [*keratin* + *-o-* + *-philic*] : showing strong affinity for hair, skin, feathers, horns, and other keratinized material — used chiefly of fungi capable of growing on such materials

ke·rat·i·nous \kəˈratᵊnəs\ *adj* [Gk *keratinos,* fr. *kerat-, keras* horn — more at HORN] : HORNY

ker·a·ti·tis \,kerəˈtīd·əs\ *n* -ES [NL, fr. *kerat-* + *-itis*] : inflammation of the cornea of the eye characterized by burning or smarting, blurring of vision, and sensitiveness to light and caused by infectious or noninfectious agents — compare KERATOCONJUNCTIVITIS

ker·a·to·conjunctivitis \ˈ,kerəd·ō+\ *or* **cer·a·to·conjunc·tivitis** \ˈ,serəd·ō+\ *n* [NL, fr. *kerat-,* or *cerat-* + *conjunctivitis*] : combined inflammation of the cornea and conjunctiva: **a** : a virus disease of man often epidemic and marked by pain, redness, and swelling with tenderness of adjacent lymph nodes and profuse watery discharge from the eyes — called also *pinkeye* **b** : a highly contagious rickettsial disease of cattle marked by inflammation of the conjunctiva and cornea and infective discharge from eyes and nose

ker·a·to·der·ma \,kerəd·ōˈdərmə\ *n* [NL, fr. *kerat-* + *-derma*] : a horny condition of the skin

ker·a·to·gen·ic \ˈ⸗⸗⸗ˈjenik\ *adj* [*kerat-* + *-genic*] : capable of inducing proliferation of epidermal tissues

ker·a·tog·e·nous \,kerəˈtäjənəs\ *adj* [*kerat-* + *-genous*] : producing horn or horny tissue

ker·a·toid \ˈkerə,tȯid\ *adj* [ISV *kerat-* + *-oid*] : HORNY

ker·a·toi·dea \,kerəˈtȯidēə\ [NL, fr. *kerat-* + *-oidea*] *syn of* KERATOSA

Ker·a·tol \ˈkerə,tȯl, -tōl\ *trademark* — used for a pyroxylin-coated waterproof material used esp. in bookbinding

ker·a·tol·y·sis \,kerəˈtäləsəs\ *n* [NL, fr. ISV *keratin* + NL *-o-* + *-lysis*] **1** : the process of breaking down or dissolving keratin **2** [NL, fr. *kerat-* + *-lysis*] : a skin disease marked by peeling of the horny layer of the epidermis

¹ker·a·to·lyt·ic \,kerəd·ōˈlid·ik\ *adj* [ISV *kerat-* + *-lytic*] : relating to or causing keratolysis

²keratolytic \"\ *n* -s : a keratolytic agent (as salicylic acid)

ker·a·to·ma·la·cia \,kerəd·ōməˈlās(h)ēə\ *n* -s [NL, fr. *kerat-* + *-malacia*] : a softening and ulceration of the cornea of the eye resulting from severe systemic deficiency of vitamin A — compare XEROPHTHALMIA

ker·a·to·phyre \ˈkerəd·ō,fī(ə)r\ *n* -s [ISV *kerat-* + *-phyre;* orig. formed as G *keratophyr*] **1** : any of various rocks resembling hornfels **2** : a compact porphyritic rock with anorthoclase as its prevailing feldspar and with or without quartz

ker·a·to·plas·ty \ˈ-,plastē\ *n* -ES [ISV *kerat-* + *-plasty*] : plastic surgery on the cornea; *esp* : corneal grafting

ker·a·to·sa \,kerəˈtōsə, -ōzə\ *n pl, cap* [NL, fr. *kerat-* + L *-osa* (neut. pl. of *-osus* -ous)] : an order of Demospongiae comprising the horny sponges with a spongin skeleton and without spicules and including the commercially important family Spongiidae

ker·a·tose \ˈkerə,tōs\ *or* **cer·a·tose** \ˈse-\ *adj* [NL *Keratosa*] : of or relating to the Keratosa

ker·a·to·sis \,kerəˈtōsəs\ *n, pl* **kerato·ses** \-ō,sēz\ [NL, fr. *kerat-* + *-osis*] **1** : a disease of the skin marked by overgrowth of horny tissue **2** : an area of the skin affected by keratosis

ker·a·tot·ic \ˈ⸗⸗ˈtäd·ik\ *adj* [fr. NL *keratosis,* after such pairs as NL *hypnosis:* E *hypnotic*] : of or relating to keratosis : affected by keratosis

ke·rat·to *also* **ka·rat·to** \kəˈrad·(,)ō\ *n* -s [prob. fr. native name in the West Indies] **1** : any of several West Indian agaves (esp. *Agave keratto*) **2** : the fiber from keratto

ke·rau·lo·phon \kəˈrȯlə,fän\ *also* **ke·rau·lo·phone** \-fōn\ *n* -s [*keraulophon* fr. G, fr. E *keraulophone; keraulophone* fr. Gk *keras* horn + *aulos* reed instrument like an oboe + E *-phone* — more at HORN, ALVEOLUS] : a labial pipe-organ stop of 8-foot pitch having metal pipes

kerauno- *comb form* [Gk — more at CERAUN-] : thunder

ke·rau·no·graph \kəˈrȯnə,graf, -räf\ *n* [ISV *kerauno-* + *-graph*] **1** : a figure impressed by lightning upon a body or material **2** : CERAUNOGRAPH — **ke·rau·no·graph·ic** \ˈ⸗⸗ˈgrafik\ *adj* — **ker·au·nog·ra·phy** \,kerȯˈnägrəfē\ *n* -ES

kerb \ˈkərb\ *n* -s [by alter.] *Brit* : CURB 5 g, 6

ker·bau \ˈkər,bau\ *n* -s [Malay] *in Malaysia* : WATER BUFFALO; *esp* : a usu. black wide-horned variety of Siamese origin used chiefly in rice cultivation

¹kerch \ˈkərch\ *n* -ES [ME *kerche,* short for *kerchef*] : KERCHIEF 1a

²kerch \ˈkerch\ *adj, usu cap* [fr. *Kerch,* Crimea, U.S.S.R.] : of or from the city of Kerch, U.S.S.R. : of the kind or style prevalent in Kerch

ker·cher \ˈkəchə(r\ *n* -s [ME *keverchef, kercher,* modif. of MF *cuevrechief, cuerchief*] *dial Eng* : HANDKERCHIEF

¹ker·chief \ˈkərchəf, ˈkəch-,ˈkəich-, -,chēf\ *n, pl* **kerchiefs** *also* **ker·chieves** \|fs, |vz; *see pl at* HANDKERCHIEF\ [ME *courchef, kerchef, coverchief,* fr. OF *cuevrechief, couvrechef, cuerchief,* fr. *covrir* to cover + *chief,* chef head — more at COVER, CHIEF] **1 a** : a square of cloth worn usu. folded by women as a head covering **b** : a similar cloth worn about the neck or shoulders **2** : HANDKERCHIEF 1

kerchief 1a

²kerchief \"\ *vt* -ED/-ING/-S : to put a kerchief over ⟨~*ed* her hair before going out into the rain⟩

ker·chief·like \ˈ-f,līk\ *adj* : resembling a kerchief

¹ker·choo \kəˈchü\ *n* -s [imit.] : the characteristic sound of a person sneezing

²kerchoo *vi* -ED/-ING/-S : to make a kerchoo

ke·re *or* **qe·re** \kəˈrē\ *also* **qe·ri** \ˈkrē\ *n* -s [Heb *qĕrī* imper. of *qārā'* to read] : a reading that in the traditional

Jewish mode of reading the Hebrew Bible is substituted for one actually standing in the consonantal text with the consonants of the word or phrase to be read being usu. given in the margin and the vowel points if the text is vocalized being inserted in the text — called also *keri;* compare KETHIB

ke·rek \kə'rek\ *n, pl* **kerek** *or* **kereks** *usu cap* **1 a :** a people constituting a small branch of the Kamchadal-Koryak ethnic group **b :** a member of such people **2 :** the language of the Kerek containing elements of Eskimo

kere per·pe·tu·um \-pə(r)'pechəwəm\ *n* [NL, lit., perpetual kere] **:** a kere which is always substituted for a particular word in the Hebrew Bible and whose consonants are not written in the margin but are supplied by the reader from memory

ke·res \'kä,räs\ *n, pl* **keres** *usu cap* **1 a :** a Pueblo people of New Mexico including the Acoma, Cochiti, Laguna, San Felipe, Santa Ana, Santo Domingo, and Sia **b :** a member of the Keres people **2 :** the language of the Keres people constituting the Keresan family

ker·e·san \'kerəsən\ *n, pl* **keresan** *usu cap* **:** a language family consisting of Keres only and having no close relationship to any other language group

ke·re·wa \kə'räwə\ *n, pl* **kerewa** *or* **kerewas** *usu cap* **1 a :** a Papuan people on the Gulf of Papua **b :** a member of such people **2 :** the language of the Kerewa people

¹kerf \'kərf, 'kə̄f\ *n* -s [ME *kirf, kerf* (also, action of cutting), fr. OE *cyrf* action of cutting, something cut off; akin to MHG *kerbe, kerp* notch, OE *ceorfan* to carve — more at CARVE] **1 a :** a slit or notch made in cutting usu. by a saw or cutting torch **b :** the width of cut that a saw or cutting torch makes in wood or other material **2 :** GROOVE 2a(4) **3 :** a deep narrow cut in a face of coal (as to facilitate mining or to remove clay or dirt seams)

²kerf \"\ *vt* -ED/-ING/-S **:** to make a kerf in esp. by sawing; *specif* **:** to cut (as a beam) transversely along the underside in order to permit bending

kerf graft *n* **:** a graft similar to a cleft graft except that the cut in the stock is made with a saw

ker·flop \kə(r)'fläp\ *adv* [*ker-* + *flop*] **:** with or as if with a flop

ker·fuf·fle \kə(r)'fəfəl\ *n* -s [alter. of *carfuffle*] **:** STIR

ker·gue·len cabbage \'kərgələn-, ¦kergə¦len-\ *n, usu cap K* [fr. *Kerguelen* island in the southern Indian ocean] **:** an herb (*Pringlea antiscorbutica*) of the family Cruciferae of the island of Kerguelen that is unique in its family in being wind-pollinated

ke·ri *or* **qe·ri** \kə'rē\ *also* **k'ri** *or* **kri** *or* **q'ri** *or* **qri** \'krē\ *n* -s [Heb *qerī* — more at KERE] **:** KERE

ke·ri·ah \kē'rēə\ *n, pl* **keri·oth** *or* **keri·ot** \-ē,ōt(h), -ōs\ [Heb *qerī'āh*] **:** the traditional act or ceremony among Jews of rending one's garment at the funeral of a near relative as a symbol of mourning

ke·ri·on \'kirē,än\ *n* -s [NL, fr. Gk *kērion* honeycomb — more at CERION] **:** inflammatory ringworm of the hair follicles of the beard and scalp usu. accompanied by secondary bacterial infection and marked by spongy swelling and the exudation of sticky pus from the hair follicles

keri perpetuum *n* [NL, lit., perpetual keri] **:** KERE PERPETUUM

ker·lock \'kəlak\ *dial Eng var of* CHARLOCK

kerman *usu cap, var of* KIRMAN

ker·man·ji \kə(r)'mänjē\ *n* -s *cap* [Kurdish] **1 :** the western dialect of the Kurdish language spoken in the region of eastern Turkey **2 :** the Kurdish language

¹ker·man·shah \¦kermən¦shä, kər'män,-\ *adj, usu cap* [fr. *Kermanshah,* Iran] **:** of or from the city of Kermanshah, Iran **:** of the kind or style prevalent in Kermanshah

²kermanshah *usu cap, var of* KIRMANSHAH

³kermanshah \"\ *n* -s *often cap* **:** COCONUT 4

ker·mes \'kər(,)mēz, -məs; kər'mes; *in sense 1b* 'kər(,)mēz\ *n* [F *kermès,* fr. Ar *qirmiz* — more at CRIMSON] **1 a** *pl* **kermes :** the dried bodies of the females of various scales (genus *Kermes*) that are found on the kermes oak of the Mediterranean region, are round and about the size of a pea, and constitute the oldest dyestuff known producing a red color resembling but much inferior to that of cochineal **b** *cap* [NL, fr. F *kermès* or E *kermes*] **:** a genus (the type of the family Kermesidae) of scales comprising those that form kermes and various related No. American and Australian scales **2** *pl* **kermes :** KERMES MINERAL **3** *or* **kermes scarlet** *pl* **kermes :** a somewhat variable color averaging scarlet

ker·mes·ite \'kərmē,zīt, -mə,sīt; kər'me,sīt\ *n* -s [F *kermésite,* fr. *kermès* + *-ite*] **:** a mineral Sb_2S_2O consisting of antimony oxysulfide occurring usu. as tufts of cherry-red capillary crystals and resulting from the alteration of stibnite

kermes mineral *also* **kermes** *n* **:** a soft brown-red powder consisting essentially of antimony trisulfide and antimony trioxide and used formerly as an alterative, diaphoretic, and emetic

kermes oak *also* **kermes** *n* **:** a dwarf often shrubby evergreen oak (*Quercus coccinea*) of the Mediterranean region that is the host of the kermes insect and has a bark rich in tannin

ker·mis \'kərməs, 'ke(ə)rm-\ *or* **ker·mess** \", kər'mes\ *or* **kir·mess** \kər'mes\ *n* -ES [D *kermis,* fr. MD *kercmisse, kermisse,* fr. *kerke, kerc* church + *misse* mass, church festival] **1 :** a local outdoor festival of the Low Countries orig. held annually on the feast day of the local patron saint **2 :** an entertainment and fair usu. given for the purpose of raising money

¹kern \'kərn, 'kə̄n\ *vb* -ED/-ING/-S [ME *curnen, kernen,* fr. (assumed) OE *cyrnen,* fr. OE *corn* — more at CORN] *vi, dial Eng* **:** to form kernels ⟨good weather for the grain to ~⟩ ~ *vt, dial Eng* **:** to form or set (as a crop of fruit) ⟨trees that had ~*ed* their best crop in years⟩

²kern \"\ *n* -s *dial Eng* **:** KERNEL, GRAIN ⟨~ of corn⟩ ⟨~*s* of sand⟩

³kern \"\ *also* **kerne** \", 'ke(ə)rn, 'keən\ *n* -s [ME *kerne,* fr. MIr *cethern* band of soldiers, fr. *cath* battle, fr. OIr; akin to Gaulish *catu-* battle, W *cad,* OE *heatho-,* OHG *hadu-,* ON *hǫth-* battle, Skt *śatru* enemy] **1 :** a foot soldier; *esp* **:** a light-armed soldier of medieval Ireland or Scotland ⟨those rough rugheaded ~*s* —Shak.⟩ — compare GALLOWGLASS **2 :** a rude or boorish countryman esp. from Scotland or Ireland

⁴kern \'kərn, 'kə̄n\ *chiefly dial var of* KIRN

⁵kern \", 'kəin\ *n* -s [modif. of F *carne* corner, projecting angle, fr. F dial. (Picardy & Normandy), fr. L *cardin-, cardo* hinge — more at CARDINAL] **1 :** a part of the face of a typecast letter that projects beyond the body (as the upper or lower extremity of *f* or the tail of *Q*) **2 :** a corresponding part of a printed letter

⁶kern \"\ *vb* -ED/-ING/-S *vt* **1 :** to form with a kern (as a letter) **2 :** to smooth (type) about the kern ~ *vi* **:** to become kerned — used of a letter or some part of a letter

⁷kern \"\ *n* -s [G, core, kernel, nucleus, fr. OHG *kerno;* akin to ON *kjarni* kernel, core, OE *corn*] **:** NUCLEUS 2l

¹ker·nel \'kərnᵊl, 'kə̄n-,'kəin-\ *n* -s [ME *curnel, kirnel, kernel,* fr. OE *cyrnel,* dim. of *corn* grain, seed — more at CORN] **1** *chiefly dial* **:** a fruit seed **2 :** the inner portion of a seed within the integuments — usu. used of edible seeds and of the contents of the endocarp in nuts, drupes, and similar fruits ⟨peach ~⟩ ⟨as brown in hue as hazelnuts, and sweeter than the ~*s* —Shak.⟩ **3 :** a whole grain or seed of a cereal ⟨~ of corn⟩ ⟨wheat and barley ~*s*⟩ **4** *chiefly dial* **a :** a hard swelling under the surface of the skin **b :** a small gland or body resembling a gland **5 :** a central or essential part: as **a :** the gist of a concept or idea ⟨a ~ of recognizable truth . . . which commands respect —*Wall Street Jour.*⟩ ⟨the ~ of this argument is made out to be a mere matter of logic —O.P.Wood⟩ ⟨recent tendency to regard myth, ritual, and magic as the ~ instead of the husk of religion —W.R.Inge⟩ **b :** the core of a structure or organization ⟨its position as a world power and the ~ of a great empire —Vera M. Dean⟩ **6 :** ¹CORE 1t

²kernel \"\ *vb* **kerneled** *or* **kernelled; kerneled** *or* **kernelled; kerneling** *or* **kernelling; kernels** [ME *kyrnellen,* fr. *curnel, kirnel, kernel,* n.] *vi* **:** to form or produce kernels **:** ripen into kernels ~ *vt* **:** to envelop or enclose as a kernel ⟨great artist ~*ed* in the . . . man of the world —Osbert Sitwell⟩

³kernel \"\ *vt* **kerneled** *or* **kernelled; kerneled** *or* **kernelled; kerneling** *or* **kernelling; kernels** [ME *kernelen,* fr. MF *querneler, kerneler,* var. of *creneler* — more at CRENEL] **:** CRENELLATE

ker·neled *or* **ker·nelled** \-ᵊld\ *adj* [¹*kernel* + *-ed*] **:** having a kernel ⟨farms in this section produce a red ~ corn —*Amer. Guide Series: Pa.*⟩

ker·nel·late \'kərnᵊl,āt\ *vt* -ED/-ING/-S [ML *kernellatus,* past part. of *kernellare,* fr. ME *kernelen*] **:** CRENELLATE

ker·nel·ly \'kərnᵊlē\ *adj* [¹*kernel* + *-y*] **1 :** having kernels or many kernels **2 :** resembling kernels

kernel smut *n* **:** COVERED SMUT

kernel spot *n* **:** a disease of the pecan kernel caused by a fungus (*Coniothyrium caryogenum*) and characterized by irregularly roundish dull brown spots

ker·nic·ter·us \kə(r)'niktərəs\ *n* -ES [NL, fr. G *kern* core, kernel, nucleus + NL *icterus* — more at KERN] **:** a condition marked by the deposit of bile pigments in the nuclei of the brain and spinal cord and by degeneration of nerve cells that occurs usu. in infants as a part of the syndrome of erythroblastosis fetalis

ker·nig sign \'kernig-\ *or* **kernig's sign** *n, usu cap K* [after Vladimir *Kernig* †1917 Russ. physician] **:** an indication usu. present in meningitis that consists of pain and resistance on attempting to extend the leg at the knee with the thigh flexed at the hip

kerning *pres part of* KERN

kern·ite \'kər,nīt\ *n* -s [fr. *Kern* co., Calif. + E *-ite*] **:** a mineral $Na_2B_4O_7.4H_2O$ that consists of a hydrous sodium borate occurring in colorless to white crystals and cleavage masses and that is an important source of borax — called also *rasorite*

ker·nos \'kər,näs\ *n, pl* **ker·noi** \-nȯi\ [Gk] **:** an ancient Greek vessel consisting of several small cups joined on a pottery ring or attached to the rim of a vase

kernos in cross section

kern river indian \'kərn-\ *n, usu cap K&R&I* [fr. the *Kern river,* in California] **:** an Indian of the Tübatulabal or a related people living on the Kern river in California

kern river trout *n, usu cap K&R* [fr. the *Kern river* in California] **:** a variety of rainbow trout occurring only in the Kern river in California

kerns *pres 3d sing of* KERN, *pl of* KERN

ker·o·gen \'kerəjən, -,jen\ *n* -s [Gk *kēros* wax + E *-gen* — more at CEREUS] **:** bituminous material occurring esp. in oil shale and yielding oil when heated — **ke·rog·e·nous** \kə'räjənəs\ *adj*

ker·o·sene *or* **ker·o·sine** \'kerə,sēn, 'kar-, ,==\'=\ *n* -s [*kerosene* fr. Gk *kēros* wax + E *-ene* (as in *camphene*); *kerosine* alter. of *kerosene;* fr. the use of paraffin in its manufacture — more at CEREUS] **:** a flammable hydrocarbon oil that is less volatile than gasoline, that is usu. obtained by distillation of petroleum, and that is used for burning in lamps and heaters or furnaces, as a fuel or fuel component for jet engines, and as a solvent or thinner (as in insecticide emulsions or paints) — see LAMP illustration

ker·plunk \kə(r)'pləŋk\ *adv* [imit.] **:** with a loud dull sound **:** with a thud ⟨a coconut which fell ~ at his feet⟩

kerrana *var of* KERANA

kerr cell \'kär-, 'kər-\ *n, usu cap K* [after John *Kerr* †1907 Scot. physicist] **:** a cell that contains electrodes immersed in nitrobenzene or other liquid, that exhibits double refraction in a high degree and with short time lag, and that is used in devices where the intensity of light is to be changed rapidly in accordance with the voltage applied to the electrodes (as in the recording of sound tracks for motion pictures) — compare KERR EFFECT 1

kerr effect *n, usu cap K* [after John *Kerr*] **1 :** the production of double refraction in various dielectrics when placed in a strong electric field **2 :** the rotation of the plane of polarization when plane-polarized light is reflected from the end of a magnet

¹ker·ria \'kerēə\ *n* [NL, fr. William *Kerr* †1814 Eng. gardener + NL *-ia*] **1** *cap* **:** a genus of Chinese shrubs (family Rosaceae) with solitary yellow often double flowers **2** -s **:** any shrub of the genus *Kerria*

²kerria \"\ *n, cap* [NL, fr. Robert *Kerr* †1813 Eng. scientific writer + NL *-ia*] **:** a genus of aquatic New World oligochaete worms

ker·rie \'kerē\ *n* -s **:** KNOBKERRIE

ker·ril \'kerəl\ *n* -s [native name in India] **:** a sea snake (*Kerilia jerdoni*) of the Asiatic coast from the Persian gulf to Japan

¹kerry \'kerē, -ri\ *adj, usu cap* [fr. County *Kerry,* Ireland] **:** of or from County Kerry, Ireland **:** of the kind or style prevalent in County Kerry

²kerry \"\ *n* **1** *usu cap* **:** an Irish breed of small hardy long-lived black cattle noted for their milk **2** -ES *often cap* **:** an animal of the Kerry breed

kerry blue terrier *n* **1** *usu cap K & B & T* **:** an Irish breed of medium-sized terriers of uncertain ancestry that has a long head, a deep chest, and a silky coat of blue of any shade, stands about 18 inches high, and weighs from 30 to 38 pounds **2** *usu cap K* **:** a dog of the Kerry Blue Terrier breed

kerry hill *n, usu cap K&H* [fr. *Kerry Hill* in Kerry, town in Wales] **:** a breed of hardy English mutton-type sheep

kers \'kərs, 'kärs\ *dial var of* CRESS

ker·sen·neh \kə(r)'senə\ *also* **ker·san·né** \-sanā\ *n* -s [Ar *kirsannah*] **:** ERS

¹ker·sey \'kərzē, 'kə̄z-, -zi\ *n, pl* **kerseys** *also* **kersies** [ME, fr. *Kersey,* village in Suffolk, Eng.] **1 a :** a coarse ribbed woolen cloth for hose and work clothes woven first in medieval England **b :** a heavy wool or wool and cotton fabric made in plain or twill weave with a smooth surface and used esp. for uniforms and coats **2 :** a garment of kersey

²kersey \"\ *adj* **1 :** made of kersey **2** *obs* **:** HOMESPUN

ker·sey·mere \'==,mi(ə)r, -iə\ *n* -s [alter. (influenced by ¹*kersey*) of *cassimere*] **:** a fine woolen fabric with a close nap made in fancy twill weaves

ker·u·ing \'kerəwiŋ\ *n* -s [Malay *kĕruing*] **:** APITONG

ke·ryg·ma \kə'rigmə, kē'-\ *also* **ke·rug·ma** \-rəg-\ *n, pl* **kerygma·ta** *also* **kerugma·ta** \-məd·ə\ [Gk *kērygma,* fr. *kēryssein* to proclaim, preach] **1 :** the preaching or proclamation of the Christian gospel esp. in the form found in the primitive Christian church **2 :** the original Christian gospel preached by the apostles

ker·yg·mat·ic \¦kerig¦mad·ik\ *adj* [Gk *kērygmat-, kērygma* + E *-ic*] **:** of, relating to, or based upon the kerygma

ker·yl \'kerəl\ *n* -s [*kerosine* + *-yl*] **:** a mixture of alkyl radicals that is derived from kerosine specially purified for making sulfonated anionic detergents and that consists chiefly of one or more radicals ranging in size from decyl to tetradecyl or hexadecyl ⟨condensation of ~ chloride with benzene yields keryl-benzene⟩

ke·rys·tic \kə'ristik, kē'-\ *adj* [fr. (assumed) Gk *kērystos* (verbal of Gk *kēryssein* to preach) + E *-ic*] **:** HOMILETIC

ke·sar \'kāzə(r)\ *archaic var of* KAISER

kest \'kest\ *dial Brit var of* CAST

kes·trel \'kestrəl\ *n* -s [ME *castrel,* fr. MF *cresserele, crecerelle, quercelle,* fr. *crecelle, cresselle* rattle, fr. (assumed) VL *crepicella,* alter. (influenced by L *crepare* to crack, rattle) of L *crepitacillum,* fr. *crepitare* to rattle, crackle — more at CREPITATE] **:** a common small European falcon (*Falco tinnunculus*) that is noted for its habit of hovering in the air against a wind, is about a foot long, and is bluish gray above in the male and reddish brown in the female; *broadly* **:** any of various related small Old World falcons — compare SPARROW HAWK

¹ket \'ket\ *n, pl* **ket** [ME, flesh, meat, of Scand origin; akin to ON *kjǫt* flesh, meat, OSw *köt, kiot, kiöt;* perh. akin to Skt *guda* bowel, rectum — more at COT] **1** *dial Brit* **a :** CARRION **b :** FILTH, RUBBISH **2** *dial Brit* **:** a good-for-nothing person

²ket \"\ *n, pl* **ket** [prob. alter. of ³*cot*] *Scot* **:** a fleece of wool

³ket \"\ *n, pl* **ket** *or* **kets** *cap* **1 a :** a people of the middle Yenisei region of Siberia that constitutes the only western Paleo-Asiatic group **b :** a member of such people **2 :** the Yeniseian language of the Ket people

ket- *or* **keto-** *comb form* [ISV, fr. *ketone*] **1** *usu* **keto- a :** containing the ketone group ⟨*keto*hexose⟩ — in names of classes of compounds; compare ALD- 1 **b :** containing a ketone group regarded as formed by replacement of two hydrogen atoms in a methylene group by oxygen — in names of specific organic compounds ⟨*keto*propionic acid⟩; compare OX- **c** *usu ital* **:** containing an unmodified ketone group — in names of open-chain ketonic forms of specific sugars ⟨*keto*-D-fructose⟩; compare ALDEHYDO- 1 **2 :** related to a ketone ⟨*ket*oxime⟩ — compare ALD- 2

ke·ta \'kēd·ə\ *n* -s [Russ] **:** DOG SALMON 1

ke·tal \'kē,tal\ *n* -s [*ket-* + *-al*] **:** an acetal derived from a ketone

ket·a·pang \'ked·ə,paŋ\ *n* -s [Malay *kĕtapang*] **:** a low-grade variety of gutta

ke·ta·zine \'kēd·ə,zēn, -,zən\ *n* [ISV *ket-* + *azine*] **:** an azine $R_2C{=}NN{=}CR_2$ formed from a ketone

ketch \'kech\ *n* -ES [alter. of earlier *catch,* fr. ME *cache,* prob. fr. *cacchen* to chase, catch — more at CATCH] **:** a fore-and-aft-rigged boat similar to a yawl but having a larger mizzen and having the mizzenmast stepped farther forward typically of the rudderhead or of the after end of the waterline

ketch

ketchup *var of* CATSUP

ket·e·lee·ria \,ked·ᵊl'irēə\ *n, cap* [NL, fr. J.B.*Keteleer,* 19th cent. Belgian gardener + NL *-ia*] **:** a genus of Asiatic conifers (family Pinaceae) that resemble firs and have persistent cone scales and keeled upper leaf surfaces

ket·em·bil·la \,ked·əm'bilə\ *or* **kit·am·bil·la** \,kid-·\ *n* -s [Singhalese *kätämbilla*] **1 :** a hairy purple acid tropical fruit that is used esp. for preserves and is closely related to the kei apple **2 :** a small shrubby tree (*Dovyalis hebecarpa*) of the family Flacourtiaceae that is native to Ceylon and is cultivated in various tropical areas for the ketembillas it bears

ke·tene \'kē,tēn\ *n* -s [ISV *ket-* + *-ene;* orig. formed as G *keten*] **:** a colorless poisonous gaseous compound $CH_2{=}C{=}O$ of penetrating odor that is made by pyrolysis of acetic acid or acetone and used as an acetylating agent (as in making acetic anhydride from acetic acid or acetic esters from alcohols); *also* **:** any of various derivatives of this compound — see DIKETENE

ke·thib *or* **ke·thibh** *also* **ke·thiv** *or* **ke·tib** *or* **k'thib** *or* **kthib** *or* **k'thibh** *or* **kthibh** \kə't(h)ēv\ *n* -s [Heb *kĕthībh,* fr. Aram, written] **:** a reading in the consonantal text of the Hebrew Bible for which in traditional Jewish practice there is substituted a different reading whose consonants are usu. given in the margin — compare KERE

kethubah *var of* KETUBAH

ke·ti·mine \'kēd·ə,mēn, -,mən\ *n* [ISV *ket-* + *imine*] **:** a Schiff base of the general formula $R_2C{=}NH$ or $R_2C{=}NR'$ formed by condensation of a ketone with ammonia or a primary amine

ke·to \'kēd·(,)ō, -ē(,)tō\ *adj* [*ket-*] **:** of or relating to a ketone **:** being or containing the ketone group — compare OXO

keto- — see KET-

keto acid *n* **:** a compound that is both a ketone and an acid ⟨acetoacetic acid is a beta *keto acid*⟩

ke·to·bem·i·done \,kēd·ō'bemə,dōn\ *n* -s [*ket-* + *carb*ethoxy + *methyl* + *-id* + *-one*] **:** a narcotic ketone $C_{15}H_{21}NO_2$ related chemically to meperidine

ke·to-enol tautomerism \'kēd·ō+ . . . -\ *n* [*ket-* + *enol*] **:** tautomerism in which the keto and enol forms of a compound (as ethyl acetoacetate) are in equilibrium

ke·to·gen·e·sis \,kēd·ō+\ *n* [NL, fr. *ket-* + L *genesis*] **:** the production of ketone bodies (as in diabetes and other conditions of impaired metabolism)

ke·to·genic \,kēd·ə¦jenik\ *adj* [ISV *ket-* + *-genic*] **:** producing ketone bodies

ketogenic diet *n* **:** a diet that supplies a large amount of fat and minimal amounts of carbohydrate and protein and that is used esp. in epilepsy to produce a ketosis and alter the degree of bodily alkalinity

ke·to·glutaric acid \¦kēd·ō+(,)=¦== . . . -\ *n* [ISV *ket-* + *glutaric*] **:** either of two crystalline keto derivatives of glutaric acid; *esp* **:** the alpha keto isomer $HOOCCH_2CH_2COCOOH$ formed in various metabolic processes (as the Krebs cycle and transaminations involving glutamic acid)

ke·to·heptose \"+\ *n* [*ket-* + *heptose*] **:** a heptose of a ketonic nature **:** HEPTULOSE

ke·to·hexose \"+\ *n* [ISV *ket-* + *hexose*] **:** a hexose (as fructose or sorbose) of a ketonic nature **:** HEXULOSE

ke·tol \'kē,tōl, -tȯl\ *n* -s [ISV *ket-* + *-ol*] **:** a compound (as an acyloin) that is both a ketone and an alcohol **:** HYDROXY KETONE

ke·tol·y·sis \kē'täləsəs\ *n* [NL, fr. *ket-* + *-lysis*] **:** the decomposition of ketones

ke·to·lyt·ic \¦kēd·ə¦lid·ik\ *adj* [ISV *ket-* + *-lytic*] **:** of, relating to, or characterized by ketolysis

ke·tone \'kē,tōn\ *n* -s [G *keton,* alter. of *azeton* acetone — more at ACETONE] **:** any of a class of organic compounds (as acetone) that are characterized by a carbonyl group attached to two carbon atoms usu. contained in hydrocarbon radicals (as in the general formula RCOR) or in a single bivalent radical and that are similar to aldehydes but are less reactive

ketone body *n* **:** any of the three compounds acetoacetic acid, acetone, and beta-hydroxybutyric acid recognized as products of fatty-acid catabolism and found in the blood and urine in abnormal amounts in diabetes mellitus and other conditions of impaired metabolism — called also *acetone body*

ketone group *n* **:** the characteristic group of ketones consisting of carbonyl attached to two carbon atoms

ke·to·ne·mia *or* **ke·to·nae·mia** \,kēd·ə'nēmēə\ *n* -s [NL, fr. ISV *ketone* + NL *-emia, -aemia*] **1 :** a condition marked by an abnormal increase of ketone bodies in the circulating blood **2 :** KETOSIS 2 — **ke·to·ne·mic** \¦==¦nēmik\ *adj*

ke·ton·ic \kē'tänik\ *adj* [ISV *ketone* + *-ic*] **:** relating to, containing, or derived from a ketone

ke·ton·imine \¦kē,tōn+\ *n* [ISV *ketone* + *imine*] **:** KETIMINE — used esp. of dyes

ke·to·nize \'kē,tō,nīz\ *vb* -ED/-ING/-S [*ketone* + *-ize*] *vt* **:** to convert into a ketone ~ *vi* **:** to become converted into a ketone

ke·ton·uria \,kēd·ə'n(y)u̇rēə\ *n* -s [NL, fr. ISV *ketone* + NL *-uria*] **:** the presence in man and domestic animals of excess ketone bodies in the urine (as in diabetes mellitus, starvation acidosis, or other conditions involving reduced or disturbed carbohydrate metabolism)

ke·tose \'kē,tōs\ *n* -s [ISV *ket-* + *-ose*] **:** a sugar (as fructose or sorbose) containing one ketone group per molecule — contrasted with *aldose;* see MONOSACCHARIDE

ke·to·side \'kēd·ə,sīd\ *n* -s [*ket-* + glycoside] **:** a glycoside that on hydrolysis yields a ketose

ke·to·sis \kē'tōsəs\ *n, pl* **keto·ses** \-ō,sēz\ [NL, fr. *ket-* + *-osis*] **1 :** an abnormal increase of ketone bodies in the body in conditions of reduced or disturbed carbohydrate metabolism (as in uncontrolled diabetes mellitus) **2 :** a nutritional disease of cattle and sometimes sheep, goats, or swine that is marked by reduction of blood sugar and the presence of ketone bodies in the blood, tissues, milk, and urine, that is associated with digestive and nervous disturbances, that usu. results from long-continued feeding of coarse rations low in available sugar or from liver inefficiency associated with vitamin A deficiency, and that is esp. likely to occur in heavy milkers shortly after parturition — compare MILK FEVER 2a

ke·to·steroid \¦kēd·ō+\ *n* [ISV *ket-* + *steroid*] **:** a steroid (as androsterone, cortisone, or estrone) containing a ketone group ⟨excretion of 17-*ketosteroids* in the urine⟩

ke·tot·ic \kē'täd·ik\ *adj* [fr. NL *ketosis,* after such pairs as NL *hypnosis:* E *hypnotic*] **:** of or relating to ketosis **:** affected with ketosis

ke·tox·ime \kē'täk,sēm\ *n* [ISV *ket-* + *oxime*] **:** an oxime of a ketone

ket·tle \'ked·ᵊl, \tᵊl, ÷ 'kil; *some who have* ¦ki\ *in "teakettle" and/or "kettle of fish" have* ¦ke\ *in other contexts*\ *n* -s [ME *ketel,* fr. ON *ketill;* akin to OE *cietel* kettle, OHG *kezzil,* Goth *katilē* (gen. pl.); all fr. a prehistoric Gmc word borrowed fr. L *catillus* small bowl, dish, dim. of *catinus* bowl, pot; perh. akin to Gk *kotylē* cup, small vessel] **1 a** (1) **:** a metallic vessel in which liquids or semifluid masses are boiled; *esp* **:** TEAKETTLE (2) **:** a cooking utensil with a bail handle **b :** a quantity cooked in a kettle at one time ⟨could eat a whole ~ of stew⟩ **2 a** *obs* **:** KETTLEDRUM 1 ⟨let the ~ to the trumpet speak —Shak.⟩ **b :** the metallic bowl of a kettledrum across which the parchment head is stretched **3 a :** POTHOLE **b :** a steep-sided hollow without surface drainage esp. in a deposit of glacial drift and often containing a lake or swamp **4** *North* **:** a shallow metal pail ⟨dinner ~⟩

kettle base *adj* **:** ²BOMBÉ

kettle–bottomed \ˈ≈≈ˌ≈≈\ *adj, of a ship* **:** having a flat hull

kettledrum \ˈ≈≈ˌ≈\ *n* **1 :** a percussion instrument that consists of a hollow brass or copper hemisphere with a parchment head the tension of which can be changed by hand screws or foot pedal to vary the pitch, that is played with a pair of sticks with large padded heads, and that is used in pairs, threes, or fours of different sizes in both orchestra and concert band — see TIMPANI **2** *obs* **:** KETTLEDRUMMER **3 :** an informal party at which light refreshments are usu. served

kettledrum 1

ket·tle·drum·mer \"ə(r)\ *n* **:** one that plays the kettledrums

kettle front *adj* **:** ²BOMBÉ

ket·tle·man \ˈ≈≈mən\ *n, pl* **kettlemen :** an industrial worker who melts, cooks, or dyes substances in a heated container: as **a :** a brewery worker who makes the wort that is the basis for beer **b :** one who refines impure lead to secure a commercial grade **c :** one who cooks the ingredients of paints, varnishes, or oils **d :** BURNER MAN

kettle of fish *see* KETTLE\ **1 :** a bad state of affairs **:** MESS, PREDICAMENT ⟨here's a pretty how-de-do, here's a pretty *kettle of fish* —W.S.Gilbert⟩ **2 :** a thing to be considered or reckoned with **:** MATTER, AFFAIR ⟨books and discs . . . were two very different *kettles of fish* —Roland Gelatt⟩ ⟨a far different *kettle of fish* from the fictionalized life stories of Hollywood —Lee Rogow⟩

ket·tler \ˈke\|d·ᵊlə(r), \|t(ᵊ)lə-, ÷ˈki\|\ *n* -s **:** a textile worker who prepares gums for use in mixing printing colors

ket·tle stitch \ˈked·ᵊl-, -etᵊl-\ *n* [part trans. of G *kettelstich,* fr. *kettel* small chain (dim. of *kette* chain, fr. OHG *ketina,* fr. L *catena*) + *stich* stitch — more at CHAIN] *bookbinding* **:** a knot formed in the sewing thread at the ends of the sections to hold them together — called also *catch stitch*

ke·tu·bah *or* **ke·thu·bah** \ˌke,t(h)üˈvä, kəˈsüvə\ *n, pl* **ketu·both** *or* **ketu·bot** \-,t(h)üˈvōt(h), -ˈsü,v-, -ōs\ *or* **ketubahs** *or* **kethuboth** *or* **kethubot** *or* **kethubahs** [Heb *kĕthūbhāh* document] **:** a formal Jewish marriage contract that provides for a money settlement payable to the wife in the event of divorce or at the husband's death

ke·tu·pa \kəˈtüpə\ *n* [NL, prob. fr. Malay *kĕtupok* fish owl] **1** *cap* **:** a genus of large chiefly tropical owls that is closely related to *Bubo* and contains various fish owls **2** -s **:** FISH OWL

ke·tyl \ˈkēd·ᵊl\ *n* -s [*ket-* + *-yl*] **:** any of a class of unstable compounds made by treating ketones with a metal (as sodium)

keuper \ˈkȯipə(r)\ *adj, usu cap* [G] **:** of or relating to the upper division of the German Trias — see GEOLOGIC TIME table

keur·boom \ˈkər,büm\ *also* **keur** \ˈkər\ *n* -s [Afrik *keurboom,* fr. *keur* choice + *boom* tree] **:** a pinnate-leaved shrub (*Virgilia capensis*) of southern Africa having purple flowers and being of the family Leguminosae

keV *abbr* kilo-electron volt

ke·va·lin \ˈkävələn\ *n* -s [Skt, fr. *kevala* alone, pure, absolute — more at CELIBATE] *Jainism* **:** one who is set free from matter **:** a liberated soul

keva·zin·go \ˌkevəˈziŋ(ˌ)gō, ˌkäv-\ *also* **ke·wa·sin·go** \ˌkäwəˈsi-, -əˈzi-\ *or* **ke·wa·sin·ga** \-ŋgə\ *n* -s [native name in western Africa] **1 :** any of various African bubingas of the genus *Copaifera* **2 :** the wood of a kevazingo used esp. for decorative veneers

¹kev·el \ˈkevəl\ *or* **cav·el** \ˈkav-\ *n* -s [ME *kevile* pin, hasp, peg, fr. ONF *keville,* fr. L *clavicula* small key — more at CLAVICLE] **:** a strong timber, bollard, or cleat (as a cross timber in a bollard or a timber bolted across two stanchions)

²kev·el \ˈkevəl\ *n* -s [of Scand origin; akin to ON *kefli* stick of wood, *kafli* cut-off piece, Norw *kavle, kjevle* piece of wood, roller; akin to OFris *kavelia* to cast lots, MD *kavele* piece of wood for casting lots, Lith *žabas* branch, bunch of twigs] **:** CUDGEL, STAFF

³kevel \"\ *n* -s [ME *kevell*] **:** a hammer for roughly shaping or breaking stone

ke·wee·naw·an \ˌkēwēˈnȯən\ *adj, usu cap* [*Keweenaw* Point, Mich. + E *-an*] **:** of or relating to a division of the Proterozoic see GEOLOGIC TIME table

Kewpie \"\ *trademark* — used for a small chubby doll with a topknot of hair

kew weed \ˈkyü-\ *n* [prob. fr. *Kew* Gardens (Royal Botanic Gardens), London, Eng.] **:** FRENCHWEED 2

¹kex \ˈkeks\ *n* -ES [ME] *dial chiefly Eng* **:** the dry stalk of various hollow-stemmed plants (as cow parsnip)

²kex \"\ *adj, dial Eng* **:** resembling kex **:** dry and hollow

³kex \"\ *n* -ES [Maya] **:** a Maya therapeutic rite in which an ailing person pledges an offering of food to the force or agency of his illness in return for his health

¹key \ˈkē\ *n* -s *often attrib* [ME *key, kay, keye,* fr. OE *cǣg, cǣge, cǣga;* akin to OFris *kēi, kāi* key, MLG *keie, keige* spear, and perh. to OHG *kīl* wedge — more at CHINE] **1 a :** an instrument usu. of metal so designed that it may be inserted in a lock in order to operate the bolt or catch **b :** a tool with a shaft that fits into printers' quoins and is rotated to tighten or loosen them **c :** a small metal piece with a slot in one end used to roll up a strip of metal (as on a can of sardines) or to roll up the body of a collapsible metal tube (as a tube of toothpaste) **2 :** something that affords or prevents entrance, possession, or control **3 a :** something that serves to reveal or solve a problem, difficulty, or mystery ⟨the ~ to a riddle⟩ **b :** a simplified version that accompanies something as a clue to its explanation (as an outline map, a word-for-word translation, a book containing solutions to problems); *specif* **:** a list of words or phrases giving the value of symbols (as a pronunciation alphabet) **c :** an arrangement of the salient characters of a group of plants or animals or of species or genera for the purpose of determining the names and taxonomic relationships of unidentified members of a group **d :** the matter used to key an advertisement **e :** a map legend **4 keys** *pl* **:** spiritual authority in a Christian religion ⟨power of the ~s⟩; *specif* **:** the power or jurisdiction of the presidency in the Mormon Church **5 :** a tool or device used to transfer, wind, or otherwise move usu. in order to secure or tighten: as **a** (1) **:** COTTER PIN (2) **:** COTTER **b :** a keystone in an arch **c :** a wedge used to make a dovetail joint **d :** a wedge between two feathers to break a stone **e :** the last board laid in a floor **f :** a tapered block driven into a recess in a scarf joint between two timbers so as to draw them more firmly together **g :** a small wooden wedge that is forced into the dovetail joint at a corner of a stretcher frame of a painting in order to tighten the canvas **h :** a wedge used to split a tenon in a mortise or the upper end of a tool handle (as a hammer or ax) for the purpose of tightening **i :** any of the metal U-shaped devices used to secure the bands or cords in position in a bookbinder's sewing press **j :** a strip of wood inserted in a timber across the grain to prevent casting **k :** a small usu. metal parallel-sided piece that is flat or tapered on top and that is used for securing a part (as a pulley, crank, or hub) **6 a :** one of the levers (as a digital or pedal) of a keyboard musical instrument that actuates the mechanism and produces the tones **b :** a lever by which a vent is opened or closed in the side of a woodwind instrument (as a clarinet or bassoon) or a valve or piston is controlled in a brass instrument (as a French horn or trumpet) **c :** a depressible digital that serves as one unit of a keyboard and that works usu. by lever action to set in motion a character (as in a typewriter) or an escapement (as in some typesetting machines) **d :** KEYBUTTON **7 :** SAMARA **8 a :** a leading, prominent, or critical individual or principle ⟨a ~ actor⟩ ⟨the ~ features of a new car⟩ **b :** a component of a liquid mixture that is being separated by fractional distillation ⟨the least volatile of these components is the heavy ~ and the most volatile is the light ~ —E.G.Scheibel⟩ **9** [trans. of ML *clavis*] **a** *obs* **:** the lowest note or keynote of a scale **b** (1) **:** a system of seven tones based on their relationship to a keynote or tonic; *specif* **:** the tonality of a scale (2) **:** the total harmonic and melodic relations of such a system **10 a :** characteristic style, tone, or intensity of thought, feeling, or action **b :** the tone or pitch of a voice ⟨speaking in a plaintive ~⟩ **c :** the pervading tone and intensity of color (as in a painting) **d :** the predominant tone of a photograph with respect to its lightness or darkness — compare HIGH-KEY, LOW-KEY **11 :** a decoration or charm resembling a key **12 a** (1) **:** plastering forced between laths to hold the rest in place (2) **:** the hold that plaster has on a wall (3) **:** the roughness of a wall that causes plaster to adhere to it **b :** a hollow in a brick or tile to hold mortar **c :** the rough surface on the wrong side of a veneer to hold the glue **13 a :** a metallic lever for rapidly and easily opening and closing the circuit of telegraphic-station equipment **b :** a small switch for opening or closing an electric circuit **14 :** a projecting portion used to prevent movement at a construction joint (as of a floor, wall, pavement, footing, dam) into the adjacent section **15** *or* **keymove** \ˈ≈ˌ≈\ **:** the first move in the solution of a chess problem or combination **16 a :** the control of a cryptographic process (as a code book, grille, cipher alphabet, or set of alphabets) **b :** the enciphering or deciphering instructions for a cryptogram: as (1) **:** the settings of a ciphering machine (2) **:** the column sequence of a transposition (3) **:** KEYING SEQUENCE (4) **:** KEY WORD (5) **:** KEY LETTER (6) **:** an element in a keying sequence — see PERIODIC KEY, PERIOD KEY, RUNNING KEY, SPECIFIC KEY, VIGENÈRE CIPHER **17 :** KEYHOLE 4

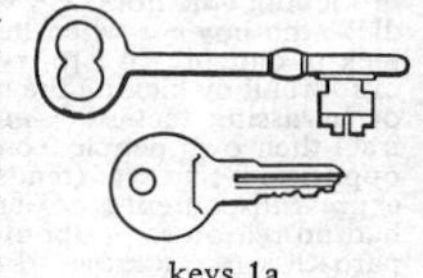
keys 1a

²key \"\ *vb* -ED/-ING/-s [ME *keyen,* fr. *key, kay, keye,* n.] *vt* **1 :** to lock with or as if with a key **:** FASTEN: as **a :** to secure by a key (as a hammerhead to a handle, a pulley on a shaft, plaster to lathing) **b :** to finish off (an arch) by inserting a keystone **c :** to expand and tighten (as a canvas stretcher on a painting) with keys **2 a :** to fix or determine the musical key of **b :** to regulate the musical pitch of ⟨~ the strings⟩ **c :** to control (a process) in cryptography ⟨in ~*ed* columnar transposition the column sequence is controlled by a key word⟩ — compare KEYING SEQUENCE **3 :** to apply color to (as a painting) in a particular key **4 :** HARMONIZE, ATTUNE ⟨remarks ~*ed* to a situation⟩ **5 :** to transmit by means of a telegraph key **6 :** to identify (a biological specimen) by means of a key **7 :** to insert in (an advertisement) some direction or other matter intended to identify answers **:** apply a symbol to (an advertisement) by means of which identification is effected **8 :** to produce or cause nervous tension in — used with *up* ⟨~*ed* up over the prospect of an operation⟩ **9 :** KEYBOARD ~ *vi* **:** to use a key: as **a :** to permit of identification by means of a key — often used with *out* ⟨the specimen ~*s* out to a genus of common starfish⟩ **b :** to operate a telegraph key

³key \"\ *archaic var of* QUAY

⁴key \"\ *also* **kay** *like* ¹CAY\ *n* -s [modif. (influenced by ³*key*) of Sp *cayo,* fr. Lucayo *cayo*] **:** a low island or reef; *specif* **:** one of the coral islets off the southern coast of Florida

key·age \ˈkēij\ *archaic var of* QUAYAGE

keyaki *var of* KIAKI

ke·yau·wee \kəˈyaù(ˌ)wē\ *n, pl* **keyauwee** *or* **keyauwees** *usu cap* **1 :** an extinct people of northern No. Carolina presumed to have been Siouan **2 :** a member of the Keyauwee people

keybank \ˈ≈ˌ≈\ *n* **:** a rectangular set of keys comprising one of the removable setting-key units of a Monotype keyboard

key bargain *n* **:** the terms of a collective agreement that set a precedent for other companies or industries

key bed *n, geol* **:** a distinctive stratum or group of strata that serves to facilitate correlation in field mapping or subsurface studies **:** the horizon or bed on which elevations are taken or to which elevations are referred in making a structure contour map — called also *key horizon*

key bit *n* **:** the projection on a key for operating a tumbler lock

key block *n, chiefly Brit* **:** KEY PLATE

¹keyboard \ˈ≈ˌ≈\ *n, often attrib* [¹*key* + *board*] **1 a :** a bank of keys on which the performer on a musical instrument (as a piano) plays and which consists of a double row of seven white and five raised black keys to the octave **b :** one of several such banks constituting a set **:** MANUAL **c :** a set of manuals **2 :** an assemblage of systematically arranged keys by which a machine (as a typewriter) is operated **3 :** a board on which keys for locks (as of hotel rooms) are hung

part of the keyboard of a piano

²keyboard \"\ *vb* -ED/-ING/-s *vi* **:** to operate a machine (as for typesetting) by means of a keyboard ~ *vt* **:** to capture, set, or input (as data or text) by means of a keyboard ⟨the computer is instructed . . . by ~*ing* the directions into its terminal —*Tech. News Bull.*⟩ — **keyboarder** *n*

keyboard paper *n* **:** a continuous roll of paper for use as a ribbon for a Monotype machine

key bolt *n* **:** a bolt secured at one end by a key or cotter

key brick *n* **:** a brick made so that each narrow side is inclined at the same angle toward the end of the brick

key bugle *n* **:** a bugle having six keys and a chromatic range of about two octaves

key·button \ˈ≈ˌ≈≈\ *n* **:** any of the small buttons or knobs depressed by the fingers in operating a keyboard machine

key chord *n, music* **:** a tonic triad

key–cold \ˈ≈ˈ≈\ *adj, now dial Brit* **:** cold as a metal key **:** devoid of the warmth of life: as **a :** cold in death **b :** apathetic and indifferent

key deer *n, usu cap K* [⁴*key*] **:** a nearly extinct race of very small white-tailed deer native to the Florida keys

key desk *n* **:** CONSOLE 3a

key drawing \ˈ≈ˌ≈≈\ *n* **:** an outline drawing that indicates position of printed matter or that serves as a guide for color separation

keyed \ˈkēd\ *adj* [partly fr. ¹*key* + *-ed;* partly fr. past part. of ²*key*] **1 :** furnished with keys ⟨a ~ instrument⟩ **2 :** reinforced by a key or keystone ⟨a ~ arch⟩ **3 :** set to a key (as a tune) **4 :** ADJUSTED, ATTUNED, FITTED ⟨~ to the present situation⟩ ⟨every thought ~ to the reaction of the strangers —Agnes S. Turnbull⟩

keyed bugle *n* **:** KEY BUGLE

keyed horn *n* **:** BASS HORN

key·er \ˈkēə(r)\ *n* -s **:** a device (as a mechanical key or vacuum tube) that turns an electronic circuit on or off

key form *n* **:** the form that is run first of a set of forms used to print work in two or more colors

key fossil *n* **:** INDEX FOSSIL

key fruit *n* [so called fr. its growing in bunches suggesting a hanging bunch of keys] **:** SAMARA

key harp *n* **:** a keyboard musical instrument having tuning forks as vibrators

¹keyhole \ˈ≈ˌ≈\ *n* [¹*key* + *hole*] **1 :** a hole or aperture (as in a door or lock) for receiving a key **2 a :** a hole or groove in beams intended to be joined together to receive the key that fastens them **b :** a slot for a key or cotter **3 :** a hole made by a bullet that has keyholed **4 :** the free-throw area in basketball

²keyhole \"\ *vi* [¹*keyhole;* fr. the shape of the hole made by the bullet] *of a bullet* **:** to strike a target when (as from tumbling or ricocheting) the long axis of the bullet is not in the same line as the line of flight

³keyhole \"\ *adj* [¹*keyhole*] **1 :** revealingly intimate **:** INSIDE ⟨a ~ report⟩ ⟨a ~ view of private lives⟩ ⟨intimate, almost ~ narrative portrait —*New Yorker*⟩ **2 :** intent on revealing intimate details ⟨continual nursing of demagogic power in the hands of a few ~ columnists —Erwin Canham⟩

keyhole limpet *n* [so called fr. the perforation at the apex of its shell] **:** a limpet of the genus *Fissurella*

keyhole neckline *n* **:** a neckline in the shape of a keyhole

keyhole saw *n* **:** a saw used for cutting short-radius curves that is similar to a compass saw but usu. has a narrower blade and finer teeth — see PISTOL GRIP illustration

keyhole urchin *n* **:** a flat sea urchin of the order Exocycloida with long narrow apertures occurring near the margin of the test

keyhole neckline

key horizon *n* **:** KEY BED

key industry *n* **:** an industry (as the production of machine tools or chemicals) whose output is essential to the successful operation of many other industries

¹key·ing \ˈkēiŋ -ē·ēŋ\ *n* -s [¹*key* + *-ing* (n. suffix)] **:** the process of turning an electronic circuit off or on either manually or automatically ⟨such ~ represents the simplest possible form of modulation, and is applicable to all kinds of oscillators —W.A.Edson⟩

²keying \"\ *adj* **:** possessing the ability to turn an electronic circuit off or on ⟨a ~ device⟩

keying by *n* [fr. the gerund of *key by,* v.] **:** the action of clearing an automatic stop in an emergency and permitting a train to pass a signal set at danger

keying sequence *n* [fr. pres. part. of ²*key*] **:** a sequence of numbers or letters that enciphers or deciphers a polyalphabetic substitution cipher letter by letter

key job *n* **1 :** a critical or vital job **2 :** a job that can be evaluated accurately and then used as representative of other similar jobs

key·less \ˈkēləs\ *adj* [¹*key* + *-less*] **:** lacking or not requiring a key

keyless watch *n, Brit* **:** STEM-WINDER

key letter \ˈ≈ˌ≈≈\ *n* **:** a letter (as a letter of a repeated key word) functioning as an element in a cryptographic keying sequence

key light *n* **:** the main light illuminating a subject in photography

key line *n* **:** a line (as at the foot of a printed page) listing and explaining symbols used

keylock \ˈ≈ˌ≈\ *n* **1 :** a lock opened by a key **2 :** a wrestling hold in which a contestant uses both arms to lock an opponent's arm in a bent position

key·man \ˈkē,man, -maa(ə)n\ *n, pl* **keymen :** a person doing work of vital importance (as in a business organization) ⟨within ministry and cabinet alike, the prime minister is the ~ —F.A.Ogg & Harold Zink⟩

keyman insurance *n* **:** insurance upon the life of a valuable employee naming the employing firm as beneficiary — compare BUSINESS LIFE INSURANCE

key money *n* **1** *Brit* **:** a payment required of a tenant esp. of an apartment on taking possession of the key **2 :** a bribe paid by a prospective tenant in order to obtain housing ⟨the *key money* for an average studio in Paris is in the neighborhood of one thousand dollars —Paul Bowles⟩

keymove *var of* KEY

¹keynes·i·an \ˈkānzēən\ *adj, usu cap* [John M. *Keynes* †1946 Eng. economist + E *-ian*] **:** of or relating to Keynesianism

²keynesian \"\ *n* -s *usu cap* **:** an adherent or advocate of Keynesianism

keynes·i·an·ism \-ēə,nizəm\ *n* -s *usu cap* **:** the economic theories and programs ascribed to John Maynard Keynes and his followers; *specif* **:** the advocacy of monetary and fiscal programs by government to increase employment

¹keynote \ˈ≈ˌ≈, *in sense 1 sometimes* ˈ≈ˈ≈\ *n* [¹*key* + *note*] **1 :** the first and harmonically fundamental tone of a scale **:** TONIC **2 :** the fundamental or leading fact or idea **:** the prevailing tone ⟨this simple statement may be taken as the . . . ~ of the whole system —C.H.Driver⟩ ⟨sadness is the ~ of this little collection —*Books Abroad*⟩

²keynote \ˈ≈ˌ≈\ *vt* **1 :** to set a keynote in ⟨the mood of compassion that ~*s* most of her writing —Ann F. Wolfe⟩ ⟨~ the overall color scheme . . . with a romantic mural —*N.Y. Herald Tribune*⟩ **2 a :** to deliver the keynote address at ⟨~ a Midwest farm political rally —*Wall Street Jour.*⟩ **b :** to declare in or as if in a keynote address ⟨"we want peace . . .," the secretary *keynoted* —*Newsweek*⟩

keynote address *or* **keynote speech** *n* **:** an address (as at a political convention) intended to present the issues of primary interest to the assembly but often concentrated upon arousing unity and enthusiasm ⟨the *keynote address* . . . is a highly emotional performance —D.D.McKean⟩ ⟨highlighting the convention's opening day is tonight's *keynote speech* —*TV Guide*⟩

key·not·er \ˈkē,nōd·ə(r), -ōtə-\ *n* **:** one that sets the keynote; *esp* **:** one that delivers a keynote speech ⟨to serve as temporary chairman and ~ of the Republican national convention —*Current Biog.*⟩

keynote speaker *n* **:** KEYNOTER

key of art **:** ALEMBROTH

key of life **:** ANKH

key pad *n* **:** a pad on a key of a wind instrument (as a flute or clarinet) making the hole leakproof

key pattern *n* **:** a Greek fret first found in the Geometric period and used throughout the classical era

key pipe *n* **:** a tubular opening in a lock for the shank of the key

key plate *n* **1 :** the part of a stove top in which the lids are placed **2 :** a protective usu. metal plate surrounding a keyhole **3 :** a plate that prints the central design on a bicolor postage stamp — compare DUTY PLATE **4 :** one of a set of color-printing plates that contains greater detail than the others and that is often the black plate

key plug *n* **:** the part of a lock into which the key is inserted

¹keypunch \ˈ≈ˌ≈\ *n* **:** a machine actuated by a keyboard and used to cut holes or notches in punch cards

²keypunch *vt* **:** to cut holes or notches in (a punch card) with a keypunch — **keypuncher** \ˈ≈ˌ≈≈\ *n*

keys *pl of* KEY, *pres 3d sing of* KEY

key seat *n* **:** a bed or groove in a mechanical part to receive a key

keyseat \ˈ≈ˌ≈\ *vt* [*key seat*] **:** to supply (as a mechanical part) with a key seat ⟨a ~*ed* shaft⟩

key·seat·er \ˈkē,sēd·ə(r)\ *n* **1 :** a machine for keyseating machine parts **2 :** one that operates a keyseating machine

key–sequence \ˈ≈ˌ≈≈\ *n* **:** KEYING SEQUENCE

key signature *n* **:** one or more sharps or flats placed immediately after the clef to designate the musical scale to be understood on the staff that in turn establishes the tonality

keyslot \ˈ≈ˌ≈\ *n* **:** a keyway esp. in a shaft

keysmith \ˈ≈ˌ≈\ *n* **1 :** a person who makes or repairs keys **2 :** an operator of a key-duplicating machine

key station *n* **:** a broadcasting station at which a network program originates

¹keystone \ˈ≈ˌ≈\ *n* [¹*key* + *stone*] **1 :** the wedge-shaped piece at the crown of an arch; *esp* **:** such a piece inserted last and locking the other pieces in place **2 :** something analogous to the keystone of an arch in position or function **:** a part or force on which associated things depend for support ⟨the ~ of his faith⟩ ⟨~ of a system of defense⟩: as **a :** crushed stone of small size used in bituminous bound roads to fill the voids of the large aggregate — compare COVER STONE **b :** a bondstone in masonry **c** *or* **keystone sack :** second base in baseball

keystone 1

²keystone \"\ *vt* **:** to support by means of a keystone

keystone effect *n* **:** a type of distortion in a television picture whereby a square pattern appears larger at the top than at the bottom

key·ston·er \ˈkē,stōnə(r)\ *n, usu cap* [*Keystone State,* nickname for Pennsylvania (fr. its central position among the original 13 states) + *-er*] **:** PENNSYLVANIAN 1 — used as a nickname

Key·tain·er \ˈkē,tānə(r)\ *trademark* — used for a small usu. leather case for carrying keys (as in the pocket)

key·trumpet *n* **:** a trumpet with side holes covered with keys that control its pitch

key turner *n, obs* : TURNKEY
key-type \ˈ=,=\ *n* : a single design used on the stamps of different colonies of a country
key valve *n* : a valve designed to be operated by a removable key to prevent unauthorized operation
keyway \ˈ=,=\ *n* **1** : a groove or channel for a key (as in a shaft or the hub of a pulley) : KEY SEAT **2** : the aperture for the key in a lock having a flat metal key **3** : a groove or channel for a key in a construction joint (as in a floor or wall) or underneath a retaining wall or dam
key word *n* : a word that is a key : **a** : a word exemplifying the meaning or value of a letter or symbol (as *then* in the statement "*th-* as in *then*") **b** : a word used as a cipher key: as (1) : a word that governs a transposition procedure (2) : a word from which a mixed alphabet is derived (3) : a word repeated to form a keying sequence
kg *abbr* **1** keg **2** kilogram **3** king
KGC *abbr* **1** knight grand commander **2** knight grand cross
kgm *abbr* **1** kilogram **2** kilogram-meter
KGPS *abbr, usu not cap* kilograms per second
k-gun \ˈ=,=\ *n, usu cap K* [¹*k*] : a naval depth-charge projector
kha *or* **ka** \ˈkä\ *also* **ka·che** \ˈkä(,)chā\ *n, pl* **kha** *or* **khas** *or* **ka** *or* **kas** *usu cap* **1 a** : a people of Nepal of mixed Mongoloid and Indo-Aryan blood **b** : a member of such people **2 a** : an agrarian aboriginal people of Laos **b** : a member of such people
kha·ba·rovsk \kəˈbärəfsk, -rəvzk\ *adj, usu cap* [fr. *Khabarovsk*, U.S.S.R.] : of or from the city of Khabarovsk, U.S.S.R. : of the kind or style prevalent in Khabarovsk
khadar *or* **khadir** *var of* KADIR
khad·dar \ˈkädə(r)\ *also* **kha·di** \ˈkädē\ *n* -s [Hindi *khādar, khādī*] : homespun cotton cloth worn by adherents of the movement for autonomy in India instead of the mill-made foreign product — compare SWADESHI, SWARAJ
kha·gan \kä'(g)än\ *also* **kha·kan** \-ˈ(k)än\ *n* -s [Turk *kağan*] : KHAN
khair \ˈkī(ə)r\ *n* -s [Hindi, fr. Skt *khadira*] : CATECHU 2
¹**khaki** *also* **khakee** \ˈka\|kē, ˈkä\|, ˈkȧ\|, \|ki, *Canadian often* ˈkär\|\ *n* -s [Hindi *khākī* dusty, dust-colored, fr. *khāk* dust, fr. Per] **1 a** : a khaki-colored cloth; *esp* : a durable cotton or woolen cloth used for military uniforms **b** : a garment of khaki-colored cloth; *esp* : a military uniform — usu. used in pl. ⟨covered with mud to the eyes, in old ~*s* —F.M.Ford⟩ **2** : a light yellowish brown that is yellower and duller than walnut brown, yellower and less strong than cinnamon, and duller and slightly yellower than manila or fallow
²**khaki** *also* **khakee** \"\ *adj* : of the color khaki — used esp. of cloth
khaki bush *also* **khaki·bos** \-ˌbüs, -ˌbȯs\ *n* [*khakibos* fr. Afrik, fr. *khaki* + *bos* bush] *chiefly Africa* : AFRICAN MARIGOLD
khaki camp·bell \-ˈkam(b)əl, -aambəl\ *n* [after Mrs. Adale *Campbell*, 19th cent. Brit. duck breeder] **1** *usu cap K&C* : an English breed of small brownish upright ducks noted for their extensive production of large white eggs **2** -s *often cap K&C* : a bird of the Khaki Campbell breed
khaki election *n* : an election held during or shortly after a war in the expectation that the party in power will benefit from war enthusiasm
khaki weed *n, chiefly Austral* : CHAFF-FLOWER
khak·sar \(ˈ)käkˈsär\ *n* -s *usu cap* [Hindi *khāksār*, fr. Per *khāksār* humble, prob. fr. *khāk* dust + *-sār* like] : a member of a militant Muslim nationalist movement of India
kha·lal \kəˈläl\ *adj* [Ar *khalāl*] : of, relating to, or constituting the second of four recognized stages in the ripening of a date in which it reaches its full size and changes from green to red or yellow or a combination of the two colors — compare KIMRI, RUTAB, TAMAR
kha·lat *or* **khi·lat** \kəˈlat\ *n* -s [Hindi *khalʻat, khilʻat*, fr. Ar *khilʻah*] : a robe presented by a person of rank and worn as a mark of distinction in India
kha·lif \kəˈlēf\ *or* **kha·li·fa** \kəˈlēfə\ *var of* CALIPH
khal·kha *also* **khal·ka** *or* **kal·ka** \ˈkalkə\ *n* -s *usu cap* **1** : a member of a Mongol people inhabiting all but the western part of Outer Mongolia **2** : the language of the Khalkha people used as the official language of the Mongolian People's Republic
khal·sa \ˈkäl(t)sə\ *n* -s [Hindi *khāliṣa, khālsa* pure, genuine, fr. Per, fr. Ar *khāliṣah*] **1** : the exchequer of an Indian state **2** *usu cap* : a militant theocracy arising in the late 17th century and continuing today as one of the significant divisions of the Sikhs — compare NANAKPANTHI
kham·bu \ˈkäm(,)bü\ *also* **kham·ba** \-bə\ *n, pl* **khambu** *or* **khambus** *also* **khamba** *or* **khambas** *usu cap* **1** : a Tibetan Mongoloid people of the southern slopes of the Himalayas **2** : a member of the Khambu people
kha·mir \kəˈmi(ə)r\ *n* -s *usu cap* : a dialect of the Cushitic language Agau
kham·sin *also* **kham·seen** *or* **cham·sin** \kamˈsēn\ *n* -s [Ar (*rīḥ al-*) *khamsīn* the wind of the fifty (days between Easter and Pentecost)] : a hot southerly Egyptian wind coming from the Sahara usu. in the spring and often carrying fine particles of sand ⟨the ~ . . . has been known to take paint off cars and force fine sand into camera shutters —G.E.Edgerton⟩ — compare SIROCCO
kham·ti \ˈkäm(p)tē\ *n, pl* **khamti** *or* **khamtis** *usu cap* **1 a** : a Tai people of northeastern Assam and Burma related to the Thais **b** : a member of such people **2** : a Thai language of the Khamti people
¹**khan** \ˈkän, -a-, -aa(ə)-, -ȧ-\ *also* **cham** \ˈkam, -aa(ə)-\ *n* -s [ME *caan*, fr. MF, of Turkic origin; akin to Jagatai *khān*, Turk *han* prince, khan] **1** : a medieval sovereign of China and ruler over the Turkish, Tatar, and Mongol tribes ⟨at the critical moment . . . the great ~ died —Sir Winston Churchill⟩ **2** : a local chieftain or man of rank esp. in Afghanistan, Iran, and some areas of central Asia — used sometimes as a title of respect
²**khan** \"\ *n* -s [Ar *khān*, fr. Per] : a caravansary or rest house in some Asian countries ⟨huge ~*s* . . . still receive shipments of goods that wind into Aleppo by camel train —*N.Y.Times*⟩
khan·ate \-ˌnāt, -ˌnət\ *n* -s *sometimes cap* [¹*khan* + *-ate*] : the dominion or jurisdiction of a khan ⟨the capital of a semi-independent ~ —E.D.Laborde⟩
khan·jar \ˈkanˌjär\ *or* **han·djar** \ˈha-\ *n* -s [Ar *khanjar*] : a short curved dagger of Muslim countries ⟨the broad silver-sheathed ~*s* — the mark of authority in the northern deserts —Ralph Hammond-Innes⟩
khan·kah \ˈkäŋkə\ *n* -s [Hindi *khānaqāh*, fr. Per *khāna* house + *gāh* place] : a dervish monastery
khan·sa·mah *or* **khan·sa·ma** \ˌkänsəˈmä, känˈsämə\ *n* -s [Hindi *khānsāmān*, fr. Per, fr. *khān* lord + *sāmān* stores] : a male servant in India: **a** : HOUSE STEWARD **b** : BUTLER **c** : COOK
khan·ty \ˈkäntē\ *n* -ES *usu cap* : OSTYAK
kha·num *or* **ha·num** \ˈhänəm, ˈkä-, =ˈnəm, =ˈnüm\ *n* -s [Per & Turk; Per *khānum*, fr. Turk *hanım*, fem. of *han* prince, sovereign, khan] : a woman of rank or position esp. in Turkey and Iran
kha·pra beetle \ˈkäprə, ˈka\ *n* [Hindi *khaprā*, lit., destroyer, fr. Skt *kṣapayati* he destroys; akin to Skt *kṣiṇoti* he destroys — more at PHTHISIS] : a dermestid beetle (*Trogoderma granarium*) native to the Indian subcontinent and now a serious pest of stored grain in most parts of the world
kha·ria \ˈkärēə\ *n* -s *usu cap* **1** : a member of a people of western Bengal **2** : the Munda language of the Kharia people
kha·rif \kəˈrēf\ *adj* [Hindi *kharīf*, fr. Ar *kharīf* gathered, autumn, autumnal crop, fr. *kharafa* to gather] : of, relating to, or constituting India's autumn and lesser crop that consists chiefly of pearl millet, durra, and maize and that is sown in June just before the monsoon rains and is harvested from August on — compare RABI
kha·ri·jite \ˈkärəˌjīt\ *n* -s *usu cap* [Ar *khārijī* one that departs, dissenter + E *-ite*] : a member of a Muslim secessionist sect establishing a radically democratic and puritanical reform community in the 7th century
khar·kov \ˈkär,kȯf, -rkəl, \|v\ *adj, usu cap* [fr. *Kharkov*, U.S.S.R.] : of or from the city of Kharkov, U.S.S.R. : of the kind or style prevalent in Kharkov
¹**kha·rosh·thi** \kəˈrōshtē\ *n* -s *usu cap* [Skt *kharoṣṭī*] : a cursive script of Aramaic origin used in northwestern India, Afghanistan, and Turkistan from about 300 B.C. to at least the middle of the 5th century A.D.
²**kharoshthi** \"\ *adj, usu cap* : of, relating to, or written in the script Kharoshthi
khar·toum \(ˈ)kärˈtüm\ *adj, usu cap* [fr. *Khartoum*, Sudan] : of or from Khartoum, capital of the Sudan : of the kind or style prevailing in Khartoum
khar·toum·er *also* **khar·tum·er** \=ˈ=ə(r)\ *n* -s *cap* [*Khartoum*, Sudan + E *-er*] : a native or inhabitant of Khartoum; *specif* : one of an organized Arab slaving company of the 19th century
khar·war \(,)kərˈwär\ *n, pl* **kharwar** *or* **kharwars** *usu cap* [Santali *kharwār*] **1** : a Bengal people speaking a Munda language **2** : a member of the Kharwar people
khashgai *usu cap, var of* KASHGAI
kha·si \ˈkäsē\ *or* **kha·sia** \-ēə\ *n* -s *usu cap* **1** : a member of any of several Mongoloid peoples of the Khasi and Jaintia hills of Assam **2** : the Mon-Khmer language of the Khasi people
khas-kura \kä'skůrə\ *n* -s *usu cap* : an Indic dialect of Nepal
khat *var of* KAT
kha·tin *or* **ka·tin** \kəˈtin\ *n, pl* **khatin** *or* **khatins** *or* **katin** *or* **katins** *usu cap* : ⁴TIN
kha·tri \ˈkə·trē\ *n* -s [Hindi *khatrī, khattrī*, fr. Skt *kṣatriya* — more at KSHATRIYA] : a member of a Hindu caste employed in trade who claim Kshatriya origin
khatti *usu cap, var of* HATTI
kha·tun \(ˈ)käˈtün\ *n* -s [Hindi *khātūn*, fr. Per *khānum*] : a woman of rank or position in Muslim countries
kha·wa·rij \kəˈwärij\ *n pl, usu cap* [Ar *khawārij*, pl. of *khārijī* one that departs, dissenter] : KHARIJITES
khaya \ˈkīə, ˈkāə\ *n* [NL, fr. Wolof *khaye* khaya tree] **1** *cap* : a genus of African timber trees (family Meliaceae) with wood closely resembling mahogany **2** -s : any tree of the genus *Khaya*
kha·zar *also* **kho·zar** *or* **cha·zar** \kəˈzär\ *or* **ka·za·ri·an** \-rēən\ *n, pl* **khazar** *or* **khazars** *usu cap* **1** : a Tatar people existing as a nation in the Caucasus and southeastern Russia from about the end of the 2d century A.D. to the end of the 11th century **2** : a member of the Khazar people
khe·dive \kəˈdēv, ke'-\ *n* -s [F *khédive*, fr. Turk *hidiv*, fr. Per *khidīw* prince] : the ruler of Egypt from 1867 to 1914 governing as a semi-independent viceroy of the sultan of Turkey
khe·di·vi·al \-vēəl\ *also* **khe·div·al** \-vəl\ *adj, often cap* : of or relating to a khedive ⟨a bribe to some ~ minister —A.J. Liebling⟩ ⟨a *Khedival* decree —Salma Bishlawy⟩
khe·di·vi·ate \-vēət, -vē,āt\ *also* **khe·div·ate** \-vət, -,vāt\ *n* -s *often cap* : the government or dominion of a khedive
khel·la \ˈkelə\ *n* -s [Ar *akhillah*] : a bishop's-weed (*Ammi visnaga*)
khel·lin *also* **kel·lin** \ˈkelən\ *n* -s [*khella* + *-in*] : a crystalline compound $C_{14}H_{12}O_5$ obtained from the fruit of khella and used as an antispasmodic in asthma and a coronary vasodilator in angina pectoris
kher·wa·ri \kə(r)ˈwärē\ *n* -s *usu cap* : any of a group of closely related Munda languages including Ho, Mundari, and Santali
khe·sa·ri \kəˈsärē\ *or* **khesari gram** *n* -s [Hindi *khesārī, khisārī, kisārī*] *India* : GRASS PEA
kheth *var of* HETH
khid·mat·gar *or* **khid·mut·gar** \ˈkidmətˌgär\ *or* **khit·mat·gar** *or* **khit·mut·gar** \ˈkitm-\ *n* -s [Hindi *khidmatgār*, fr. Ar *khidmah* service + Per *-gār* (suffix denoting possession or agency)] *India* : a male waiter
khi·la·fat \ˈkiləˌfat, kəˈläfət\ *n* -s [Turk *hilâfet*, fr. Ar *khilāfah* caliphate] : the chief spiritual authority of Islam as exercised by the Turkish sultans
khilat *var of* KHALAT
khirghiz *usu cap, var of* KIRGHIZ
khi·tan *or* **ki·tan** \kēˈtän\ *also* **chi-dan** *or* **chi-tan** \ˈchēˈdän\ *n, pl* **khitan** *or* **khitans** *or* **kitan** *or* **kitans** *usu cap* **1** : a conquering Tatar people maintaining hegemony of northern China in the Liao dynasty from the 10th to the 12th centuries **2** : a member of the Khitan people
khlyst \ˈklist\ *n, pl* **khlys·ty** \kliˈstē\ *or* **khlysts** *usu cap* [Russ, lit., whip, prob. of imit. origin] : a member of a secret Russian Christian sect that originated in the 17th century or earlier, taught that God becomes incarnate in many Christs through their suffering, and followed ascetic and ecstatic practices
khmer *or* **kmer** \kəˈme(ə)r\ *n, pl* **khmer** *or* **khmers** *or* **kmer** *or* **kmers** *usu cap* **1 a** : an aboriginal people of Cambodia noted for their architectural achievements ⟨the mighty *Khmer* empire . . . ruled most of Indo-China and bequeathed the matchless jungle temple of Angkor Wat to posterity —*Time*⟩ **b** : a member of such people **2** : a Mon-Khmer language of the Khmer people that is the official language of Cambodia — **khmeri·an** \-merēən, -mir-\ *adj, usu cap*
khmu \kəˈmü\ *n, pl* **khmu** *or* **khmus** *usu cap* **1** : the most numerous group of the Kha people of northern Laos **2** : a member of the Khmu people
khoa \kəˈwä\ *n* -s [Hindi *khoā*] : a semidehydrated whole milk product of India
khoi·san \ˈkȯi,sän\ *n* -s *usu cap* **1** : a group of African peoples speaking Khoisan languages **2** : a subfamily of African languages comprising Hottentot and the several languages known as Bushman and related to Sandawe and Hatsa with which it forms the Macro-Khoisan family
kho·ja *or* **kho·jah** \ˈkōjə\ *n* -s [Turk & Per; Turk *hoca*, fr. Per *khwāja*] **1** *also* **ho·dja** \ˈhō-\ **a** : a member of any of various classes (as wealthy merchants) in Muslim lands — used as a title of respect **b** : a Muhammadan teacher **2** *cap* [Hindi *khoja*, fr. Per *khwāja*] *India* : a member of an Ismaili sect surviving as a subsect of the ancient Assassins
kho·ka·ni \kōˈkänē\ *n, pl* **khokani** *or* **khokanis** *usu cap* **1** : a Durani people of Afghanistan **2** : a member of the Khokani people
khond *or* **kandh** \ˈkänd\ *n, pl* **khond** *or* **khonds** *or* **kandh** *or* **kandhs** *usu cap* **1** : any of several Dravidian peoples of Orissa, India **2** : a member of a Khond people
khon·di \-dē\ *n* -s *usu cap* : KUI
khor \ˈkō(ə)r\ *n* -s [Ar *khawr*] : WATERCOURSE, RAVINE
kho·ras·san \ˌkōrəˈsän\ *also* **khu·ra·san** \ˌkůr-\ *n, pl* **khorassan** *or* **khorassans** *usu cap* [fr. *Khorassan* or *Khurasan*, province of Iran] : a Persian rug or carpet often of Herat or animal pattern and vivid coloring
kho·shot \ˈkōˌshät\ *n, pl* **khoshot** *or* **khoshots** *usu cap* **1** : a Kalmuck people converted to Lamaism in the early 17th century **2** : a member of the Khoshot people
kho·ta·na \kōˈtänə\ *n, pl* **khotana** *or* **khotanas** *usu cap* : KOYUKON
kho·ta·nese *n, pl* **kho·ta·nese** \ˌkōtᵊnˈēz, -ēs\ *usu cap* [*Khotan*, region in Turkistan, central Asia + E *-ese*] : an Iranian language of central Asia found in documents from the eighth century to the tenth century
kho·war \ˈkōˌwär\ *n* -s *usu cap* : a Dard language of Chitral, northwest Pakistan
khozar *usu cap, var of* KHAZAR
khud \ˈkəd\ *n* -s [Hindi *khad*] *India* : RAVINE, PRECIPICE
khun·nong \kůˈnȯŋ, -näŋ\ *n, pl* **khunnong** *or* **khunnongs** *usu cap* **1** : a Tibeto-Burman people occupying the upper tributary region of the Irrawaddy river and dwelling in communal houses **2** : a member of the Khunnong people
khus·khus \ˈkəskəs\ *or* **khuskhus grass** *also* **khus** \ˈkəs\ *or* **kus·kus** *or* **cus·cus** \ˈkəskəs\ *n* -ES [Per & Hindi *khaskhas*] : an aromatic grass (*Andropogon zizanoides*) whose esp. fragrant roots yield an oil used in perfumery and are also made into mats in tropical India — called also *vetiver*
khut·bah *or* **khut·ba** \ˈkůtbə\ *n* -s [Ar *khuṭbah*] : a pulpit address of prescribed form that is read in mosques on Fridays at noon prayer and contains an acknowledgment of the sovereignty of the reigning prince
¹**khwa·raz·mi·an** \kwəˈrazmēən, kwäˈ-\ *adj, usu cap* [*Khwarazm*, province of ancient Persia + E *-ian*] **1** : of or relating to Khwarazm **2** : of or relating to the Khwarazmian people
²**khwarazmian** \"\ *or* **khwa·rez·mi·an** \-rez-\ *or* **khwa·riz·mi·an** \-riz-\ *n* -s *usu cap* **1** : an Uzbek people **2** : a member of the Khwarazmian people
kHz *abbr* kilohertz
ki *var of* TI
ki *abbr* **1** kilocycle **2** king **3** kitchen
KIA *abbr* killed in action
ki·aat \kēˈät\ *n* -s [Afrik, prob. fr. native name in southern Africa] : a tree (*Pterocarpus angolensis*) of southern Africa having heavy strong durable wood that is used for furniture, joinery, and flooring
ki·a·boo·ca *or* **ki·a·boo·ka** *or* **ky·a·boo·ka** *also* **kya-bouka** \ˌkīəˈbükə\ *n* -s [origin unknown] : AMBOYNA 1
ki·aki *or* **ke·ya·ki** \kēˈ(y)äkē\ *n* -s [Jap *kiaki*] : a Japanese timber tree (*Zelkova serrata*) with fine hard wood
kia·mu·sze \jēˈämə,sə(r), -sə\ *adj, usu cap* [fr. *Kiamusze*, Manchuria] : of or from the city of Kiamusze, Manchuria : of the kind or style prevalent in Kiamusze
ki·ang *also* **ky·ang** *or* **ki·yang** \kēˈ(y)äŋ\ *n, pl* **kiangs** *also* **kiang** [Tibetan *kyaṅ* (written *rkyaṅ*)] : an Asiatic wild ass (*Equus hemionus*) typically having reddish back and sides, white underparts, muzzle, and legs, and a dusky stripe along the spine and occurring in many local races most of which have at various times been considered separate species
kia ora \ˌkēəˈōrə\ *interj* [Maori *kia ora*, lit., be well] — used as a salutation or toast in Australia and New Zealand
kiaugh \ˈkyäk\ *n* -s [prob. fr. ScGael *cabhag* hurry, troubles] *Scot* : TROUBLE, ANXIETY, STIR
ki·a·we *or* **ke·a·we** \kēˈäwā\ *n* -s [Hawaiian *kiawe*] : any of several mesquites introduced into and to some extent naturalized in Hawaii
kib·be *also* **kib·beh** \ˈkibə\ *n* -s [Ar *kubbah*] : ground lamb and wheat baked as a cake
¹**kib·ble** \ˈkibəl\ *n* -s [G *kübel* tub, bucket, fr. OHG *-chubilī*, modif. of (assumed) VL *cupia* — more at KEEVE] *Brit* : a hoisting bucket used in mining
²**kibble** \"\ *vt* **kibbled; kibbled; kibbling** \-b(ə)liŋ\ **kibbles** [origin unknown] : to grind coarsely ⟨*kibbled* dog biscuit⟩ ⟨*kibbled* grain⟩
³**kibble** \"\ *n* -s : coarsely ground meal or grain
kib·butz \kiˈbůts, -üts\ *n, pl* **kib·but·zim** \(,)kiˌbůtˈsēm, -büt-\ [NHeb *qibbūṣ*, fr. Heb, gathering] : a collective farm or settlement in Israel cooperatively owned and managed by the members and organized on a communal basis ⟨the ~ is one of four main types of agricultural settlement —John Hersey⟩ ⟨in each ~ the . . . living arrangements are centralized with a common dining hall and children's quarters —Joan Comay⟩
kib·butz·nik \kiˈbůtsnik, -büt-\ *n* -s [Yiddish *kibutsnik*, fr. *kibuts* kibbutz (fr. NHeb *qibbūṣ*) + *-nik* (n. suffix denoting a person engaged in or connected with — something specified —, fr. Pol & Russ)] : a member of a kibbutz
¹**kibe** \ˈkīb\ *n* -s [ME *kybe*] : a chap or crack in the flesh caused by cold : an ulcerated chilblain esp. on the heel ⟨the clouted shoe of the peasant galls the ~ of the courtier —Sir Walter Scott⟩
²**kibe** \"\ *vt* -ED/-ING/-S : to affect with kibes ⟨make me as angry as a *kibed* heel —T.B.Costain⟩
ki·bei \(ˈ)kēˈbā\ *n, pl* **kibei** *also* **kibeis** *often cap* [Jap] : a son or daughter of issei parents who is born in America and esp. in the U.S. and educated largely in Japan — distinguished from *nisei*; compare SANSEI
ki·bit·ka \kəˈbitkə\ *n* -s [Russ, of Turkic origin; akin to Kazan Tatar *kibit* booth, stall, tent, Uighur *käbit*] **1** : a Kirghiz circular tent of latticework and felt **2** : a Russian covered vehicle on wheels or runners
kibitz \ˈkibəts *also* kəˈbits\ *vb* -ED/-ING/-ES [Yiddish *kibitsen*, fr. G *kiebitzen*, fr. *kiebitz* pewit, busybody, fr. MHG *gibitz* pewit, of imit. origin] *vi* : to act as a kibitzer ⟨observation which amounts, if not to democratic control, at least to democratic ~*ing* —Elmer Davis⟩ ⟨an awful thing to ~ on a man and his wife, and hear what they really talk about —J.M.Cain⟩ ~ *vt* : to observe as a kibitzer: **a** : to be a kibitzer at ⟨~*ing* a Pullman card game —Bob Broeg⟩ **b** : to watch the performance of as a kibitzer ⟨~*ed* him at poker —Theodore Sturgeon⟩
kibitz·er \-sə(r)\ *n* -s [Yiddish *kibitser*, fr. *kibitsen* + *-er*] : an outsider or nonparticipant who looks on and may offer unwanted advice or comment esp. at a card game ⟨contract bridge has achieved a following both of ~*s* and players probably never surpassed in the history of any nonathletic game —*N.Y. World-Telegram*⟩ ⟨nothing can be more of a trial at the scene of an illness or an accident than a ~ —Robert Rice⟩
kibla *or* **kiblah** *var of* QIBLA
¹**ki·bosh** *also* **ky·bosh** \ˈkī,bäsh, kəˈbäsh\ *n* -ES [origin unknown] : something that serves as a check or stop — used chiefly in the phrase *to put the kibosh on* ⟨the directive puts the ~ on one of the few potentially valuable efforts that the United States has been making in the field of psychological warfare —R.H.Rovere⟩ ⟨might even be able to put the ~ on the plan before it was put into operation⟩
²**kibosh** \"\ *vt* -ED/-ING/-ES : BLOCK, FRUSTRATE ⟨a limited . . . budget ~*ed* the architects' first proposal —*Architectural Forum*⟩
ki·chai \ˈkē,chī\ *n, pl* **kichai** *or* **kichais** *usu cap* **1** : a Caddo people of north-central Texas **2** : a member of the Kichai people
kich·el \ˈkikəl\ *n, pl* **kich·lach** \-kləḵ\ *or* **kichel** [Yiddish *kikhel* small cake, dim. of *kukhen* cake, fr. OHG *kuocho* — more at CAKE] : a semisweet baked product made of eggs, flour, and sugar usu. rolled and cut in diamond shape and baked until puffed
kichua *usu cap, var of* QUECHUA
¹**kick** \ˈkik\ *vb* -ED/-ING/-S [ME *kiken*] *vi* **1 a** (1) : to thrust out the foot or feet with force : strike out with the foot or feet (as in defense or bad temper or in effecting a swimming stroke); *esp* : to give impetus to something with a usu. fast blow with the foot (2) : THRUST, DRIVE ⟨the bomber's engines ~ with a 350,000-pound thrust⟩ **b** : to have a habit of kicking ⟨the horse ~*s* when men approach him with a saddle⟩ ⟨the boy ~*s* when he gets into fights⟩ **c** : to execute a kick in dancing **d** : to try to score or gain ground in a game of football by kicking the ball **e** : to engage in small annoying or harassing tactics ⟨~*ing* at neighboring countries to distract their own people from internal problems⟩ **2 a** : to show opposition : REBEL ⟨tends to ~ against authority⟩ **b** : to express discontent : COMPLAIN ⟨had studied very little and so had no reason to ~ about low grades⟩ **3** *slang* : DIE — compare KICK IN, KICK OFF **4** *of a firearm* : to recoil when fired — often used with *back* **5 a** *of a cricket pitch* : to cause a bowled ball to rebound erratically **b** *of a bowled ball in cricket* : to rebound erratically — often used with *up* **6** : to function with vitality and energy ⟨still alive and ~*ing* at 75 years⟩ ⟨continue to flourish and . . . wax fat and ~ —*Dock Leaves*⟩ **7 a** : to move or go erratically or jerkily as if being kicked ⟨an engine that ~*ed* a good deal when it was started in cold weather⟩ ⟨the jumping jack ~*ed* about on the floor until it ran down⟩ **b** : to move from one to another of or stay or rest in various successive places as circumstance or whim dictates ⟨an old chair that ~*ed* around the house for years⟩ ⟨during winters ~*ed* about Florida and other warm areas⟩ ~ *vt* **1 a** : to strike, thrust, or hit with the foot usu. with force **b** : to strike usu. suddenly with force as if kicking **c** : to impel or drive as if by kicking; *specif* : to cause (a railroad car) to be carried by momentum to a particular track position by uncoupling while still moving **d** : to cause (a racehorse or racing car) to show a sudden burst of speed ⟨~*ed* his car into the lead —*Newsweek*⟩ **2** : to score (a goal or point) by kicking the ball in a game of football **3** *chiefly dial* : to refuse (a person) after an invitation or an offer of marriage : JILT ⟨took to drink after being ~*ed* in favor of a rival⟩ **4** *slang* : to heap reproaches upon (oneself) ⟨~*ed* himself every time he thought of the lost opportunity⟩ **5** : RAISE 17a **6** *slang* : to free oneself of or break (a drug habit) **syn** see OBJECT — **kick against the pricks** : to feel or show usu. pointless opposition to or resentment of an often necessary authority one is subject to — **kick downstairs** : to kick out : EJECT — **kick one's heels** : to wait or pass the time aimlessly or futilely — **kick over the traces** : to cast off restraint : become insubordinate : throw off authority or control — **kick the beam 1** : to be extremely lightly weighted **2** : to become or be of extremely small value ⟨the prices of building plots *kicked the beam* —Marguerite Steen⟩ — **kick the bucket** *slang* : DIE — **kick up one's heels 1 a** : to show sudden extreme delight or energy inspired by such delight **b** : to have a lively time ⟨had no time to take a holiday and *kick up my heels* when I came back from the war —Rebecca West⟩ **2** *slang* : DIE
²**kick** \"\ *n* -s **1 a** : an act of kicking : a blow or sudden force-

ful thrust with the foot and esp. the toe ⟨felt the ~ so strongly that a pain shot up his leg⟩; *specif* **:** a sudden propelling (as of a ball) with a blow of the foot esp. in football — see DROP-KICK, FREE KICK, PLACE-KICK **b :** a forceful thrust or sudden drive ⟨the engine drove the car ahead in a series of ~*s*⟩ **c :** a vigorous elevation of a leg (as in dancing) ⟨a high ~ and then a pirouette⟩ **d :** the power to kick **:** degree of force in kicking **e :** a rhythmic often forceful motion of the legs used alone or in conjunction with arm movements to propel a swimmer through the water **f :** a burst of speed or the ability to exhibit a burst of speed in racing esp. as unleashed in the last part of a race **2** *slang Brit* **:** SIXPENCE **3** *archaic slang* **:** the latest fashion or style **4 a :** a sudden forceful jolt, jerk, jog, or thrust suggesting a kick ⟨felt the sudden ~ of the drill in his hand as the power was turned on⟩ ⟨a noticeable upward ~ in the barograph trace —G.H.T.Kimble⟩; *specif* **:** the recoil of a gun **b :** an electrical impulse or the deflection on a meter that records it **c :** a single automatic operation of a business machine **5** *slang* **:** DISMISSAL, DISCHARGE; *specif* **:** a dishonorable discharge from the armed forces ⟨the maximum penalty is . . . a year and a ~ —F.B.Wiener⟩ — compare ³BOOT 8b **6** *slang* **:** POCKET, POCKETBOOK ⟨without a dime in his ~ for a cup of coffee⟩ **7** *chiefly Brit* **:** KICKER 1b ⟨not a powerful ~, he is very accurate —Len Smith⟩ **8 :** an indentation at the bottom of a molded glass bottle to lessen its holding capacity **9** *chiefly Brit* **:** a projection on a stock board or brick mold for forming a frog in the brick; *also* **:** the frog so formed **10 a :** a feeling of opposition or objection ⟨had a ~ against the new schedule⟩ **b :** an expression of opposition or objection ⟨heard all sorts of ~*s* against the administration⟩ **c :** the grounds for objection ⟨trying to find out what the ~ was⟩ **11 a :** a quick and forcible effect suggestive of a kick: as (1) **:** the effect or force of an explosive when exploded ⟨the high-test gasoline had quite a ~⟩ (2) **:** a marked physical effect (as of stimulation by alcohol) ⟨got a quick ~ out of drinking⟩; *also* **:** ability to produce such an effect ⟨a drink with no ~ in it⟩ **b** (1) **:** a feeling of pleasure or of marked enjoyment **:** THRILL ⟨get a ~ out of that music⟩ (2) **:** a source of such pleasure ⟨the play had a dramatic ~ that made it very successful⟩ **c kicks** *pl, slang* **:** PLEASURE, THRILLS, FUN ⟨playing for ~*s*, not money⟩ **d** *slang* **:** way of getting one's pleasure or livelihood **:** manner or style of behaving or performing ⟨the band is on a Dixieland ~⟩ ⟨went on a mystery-reading ~ —*Time*⟩ **12 :** a sudden and striking surprise, revelation, or turn of events **:** TWIST ⟨the novel ended with an ironical ~⟩ **13** *slang* **:** RAISE ⟨a demand for a salary ~ —Pete Martin⟩ — **kick in the pants :** a humbling setback — **kick in the teeth :** a sudden usu. violent often contemptuous setback ⟨the pleased delegation . . . got a delayed *kick in the teeth* —*Time*⟩

kick·able \-kəbəl\ *adj* **:** capable of being kicked **:** fit or deserving to be kicked

kick·a·poo \'kikə,pü\ *n, pl* **kickapoo** *or* **kickapoos** *usu cap* [Kickapoo *kiwĕgapawa*, lit., he stands about] **1 a :** an Indian people orig. of Wisconsin but now living in Oklahoma and Chihuahua, Mexico **b :** a member of such people **2 :** a dialect of Fox

kick around *vt* **1 a :** to treat in an inconsiderate or high-handed fashion ⟨business was so good he felt he could *kick* the customers *around* a little⟩ ⟨*kicks* his children *around* a good deal⟩ ⟨men and women who are so frequently *kicked around*, abused, misunderstood, and unappreciated —William Benton⟩ **b** *slang* **:** to treat in a casual, unsystematic, or experimental way ⟨*kicked* the music *around* for a while, trying it out⟩ **2** *slang* **:** to consider, examine, or discuss (as an idea) from all angles usu. by random suggestion or discussion ⟨*kicked* the notion *around* for an hour or so to see if it might be feasible⟩ ~ *vi* **:** to work in a hit-or-miss fashion or wherever work offers itself ⟨*kicked around* in stock companies —R.F.Shepard⟩

kick back *vi* **1 :** to recoil upon one usu. in an unexpected way ⟨his accusations *kicked back* and he found himself in jail⟩ **2 :** to pay a kickback ⟨forced to *kick back* out of every paycheck⟩ ~ *vt* **1 :** to restore (something stolen) to the owner **2 :** to give back (money) as a kickback ⟨asked to *kick* a dollar *back* each week⟩

kickback \'ˌ=,=\ *n* -s [*kick back*] **1 :** the action or the effect of kicking back: as **a** (1) **:** the starting backward of an internal-combustion engine while being cranked (2) **:** the backward thrust of a piece of work being fed into a machine (as a circular saw) — called also *backkick* **b :** a strong esp. unfavorable reaction ⟨was unable to take the medicine because of a marked ~⟩ — called also *backkick* **2 :** REFUND: as **a :** a percentage payment exacted as a condition for granting assistance by one in a position to open up or control a source of income or gain ⟨appointees paid a ~ to the ward boss out of each paycheck⟩ **b :** a usu. secret rebate of part of a purchase price by the seller to the buyer or to the one who directed or influenced the purchaser to buy from such seller **c :** a rebate given to a seller (as an automobile dealer) by a finance company that purchases the buyer's promissory note or installment paper **3 :** high voltage produced (as in a radio transmitting set) by the sudden interruption of current in a low-voltage circuit — called also *backkick* **4 :** KICKBOARD 1

kickball \'=,=\ *n* **:** a children's game that resembles baseball and is played with an inflated ball which is kicked instead of batted

kickboard \'=,=\ *n* **1 :** one of two high boards on either side of the pit end of a bowling alley that separate adjacent alleys and keep flying pins in the right alley **2 :** a buoyant rectangular board grasped with the hands by a swimmer while developing kicking techniques — called also *flutterboard*

kickdown \'=,=\ *n* -s [fr. *kick down*, v.] **:** a change to lower gear in an automotive vehicle; *also* **:** the manually operated or automatic device for making such a change

kicked *past of* KICK

kick·er \'kikə(r)\ *n* -s **1 :** one that kicks: as **a :** an animal having the habit of kicking **b :** a member of a football team who makes or is designated to make dropkicks, place-kicks, or punts **c :** a person who protests, complains, or grumbles esp. habitually **d :** a sawmill device for throwing logs from the conveyor trough onto the log deck **e :** a mechanical part that gives a sharp push to some object (as for feeding or ejecting work from a machine) **f :** a device for opening a stove door or other object by pressure applied with the foot **g :** a ball (as in cricket and tennis) that rebounds erratically or high **h :** WILD-OAT KICKER **i :** a small internal-combustion engine in a boat; *also* **:** a boat driven by such an engine **j :** an aircrewman who releases or propels out of a cargo airplane bundles to be parachuted to a drop zone on the ground **2 :** TEDDER **3 :** a protective covering for the toes and instep of a goalkeeper in field hockey usu. made of canvas or soft leather with a padding of felt or sponge rubber **4 :** an unmatched card retained with a pair or three of a kind when drawing cards in draw poker **5 :** a machine for softening skins in tanning **6 :** a line of newspaper type set above a headline usu. in a different typeface and intended to provoke interest in, editorialize about, or provide orientation for the matter in the copy it heads **7 :** KICK 12

kickier *comparative of* KICKY

kickiest *superlative of* KICKY

kick in *vt, slang* **:** CONTRIBUTE ⟨asked to *kick* a dollar *in* for a present for the boss⟩ ~ *vi* **1** *slang* **:** DIE ⟨*kicked in* at the ripe old age of 90⟩ **2** *slang* **:** to make a contribution ⟨an unknown contributor *kicked in* with $1000⟩

kick–in \'=,=\ *n* -s [fr. *kick in*, v.] **:** a free kick in soccer used to put the ball in play after it has gone out of bounds over a sideline

kicking *pres part of* KICK

kicking–colt \'=,=\ *n* **:** JEWELWEED a

kicking–horses \'=,==\ *n pl but usu sing in constr* **:** JEWELWEED a

kick·ish \'kikish\ *adj, now dial Eng* **:** IRRITABLE, CANTANKEROUS

kick off *vi* **1 :** to start or restart the play in football by a place-kick from a point close to or at the center of the field **2 :** to begin proceedings or undertake the initial move or action ⟨the entertainers *kicked off* with a fast song and dance⟩ **3** *slang* **:** DIE ⟨worth a cool million when he *kicked off*⟩ ~ *vt* **:** to start or signalize the beginning of (a concerted effort) ⟨*kick* the drive for funds *off* with a nationwide broadcast⟩

kickoff \'=,=\ *n* -s [*kick off*] **1 :** the act of kicking off: as **a :** a kick that puts the ball into play in a football or soccer game **b :** COMMENCEMENT ⟨makes no bones about it being the ~ for his big bid for the Democratic Presidential nod —*Newsweek*⟩ ⟨is also hoping to round up some of its oldest living customers for this ~ party —Bennett Cerf⟩ **2 :** a device (as a power-operated lever) for casting work off a machine table out of a cavity in a die

kick out *vi* **1 :** to kick the ball deliberately over a touchline (as when stalling for time) in a soccer game **2 :** to take a free kick after a touchback or safety in a game of football ~ *vt* **:** to turn out, dismiss, or eject usu. forcefully or summarily ⟨tried to keep the lad in his employ but finally had to *kick* him *out*⟩ ⟨when he entered the house he was *kicked out* immediately⟩ ⟨suggested *kicking* all enemy aliens *out*⟩

kickout \'=,=\ *n* -s [*kick out*] **:** the act of kicking out or of kicking something out

kick over *vi* **:** to begin to fire — used of an internal-combustion engine ⟨after a moment of cranking the motor *kicked over*⟩ ~ *vt* **:** to cause (an internal-combustion engine) to turn over and usu. begin to fire ⟨could not *kick* the motor *over*⟩

kickpipe \'=,=\ *n* **:** a short section of pipe to protect an electric cable from mechanical damage where it emerges from a floor or deck

kickplate \'=,=\ *n* **:** a protective plate (as of metal or plastic) applied to the bottom of a door or cabinet or to the riser of a step to prevent marring of the finish by shoe marks

kick pleat *n* **:** a short inverted pleat used to give breadth (as at the bottom of a skirt for ease in walking or at the bottom of a slipcover for ease in fitting the band around corners)

kicks *pres 3d sing of* KICK, *pl of* KICK

kick·shaw \'kik,shȯ\ *n* -s [by folk etymology fr. F *quelque chose* something, anything] **1** *or* **kickshaws** *pl but usu sing in constr* **a :** a fancy dish in cookery **:** TIDBIT, DELICACY **b :** something elegant but trifling **:** TRIFLE, TOY **2** *archaic* **:** a fantastic person

kick·sies \'kiksiz\ *n pl* [*kicks* trousers (fr. pl. of ²*kick*) + *-ie* + *-s*] *slang Brit* **:** TROUSERS, PANTS

kick–sled \'=,=\ *n* **:** a sled popular in Scandinavia that consists usu. of a low seat on runners and that is propelled usu. by one holding the back of the seat, standing on a runner with one foot, and pushing with the other

kicksorter \'=,==\ *n* **:** a device that sorts and records electrical pulses of given intensities (as pulses from an ionization chamber)

kickstand \'=,=\ *n* **:** a device for holding up a bicycle or motorcycle when not in use consisting of a metal bar or rod that is attached by a swivel device to the frame and may be kicked to a vertical position as a prop

kick starter *or* **kick start** *n* **:** a motor starter (as on a motorcycle) that is activated by a thrust of the foot usu. assisted by the body weight

kick through *vi* **1** *slang* **:** to kick in **2** *slang* **:** to make a confession ⟨*kick through* and tell me what it is —Erle Stanley Gardner⟩

kick turn *n* **:** a standing half turn in skiing made by raising one ski so that it is nearly vertical to the ground, turning the ski outward and downward so that it is brought down pointed backward, and bringing the other ski around parallel to it

kick up *vt* **1 :** to cause to rise or be propelled upward forcefully ⟨the tires *kicked* little stones *up*⟩ ⟨clouds of dust *kicked up* by passing cars⟩ **2 a :** RAISE ⟨signal the auctioneer quietly and *kick* the bid *up* another thousand —Grant Cannon⟩ **b :** to stir up **:** PROVOKE ⟨*kicked* a row *up* over nothing⟩ ⟨*kick up* a fuss⟩ ~ *vi* **1 :** to give evidence of disorder ⟨felt his stomach start to *kick up*⟩ **2 :** to become insubordinate **:** act in a protesting or unexpectedly independent way ⟨when the New Woman began *kicking up* on the American scene in the middle of the 19th century —Lois Long⟩

kickup \'=,=\ *n* -s [*kick up*] **1 :** a noisy quarrel **:** DISTURBANCE, ROW **2 a :** KICK 1c **b :** a method in speedball of converting a ground ball to an aerial ball by means of the foot **3 :** KICK 8 **4 :** an upward bend made in the frame of a motor vehicle to clear the rear axle

kick wheel *n* **:** a potter's wheel worked by a foot pedal or by kicking a heavy disk at the foot of the vertical shaft

kickx·ia \'kiksēə\ *n, cap* [NL, fr. Jean *Kickx* †1831 and his son Jean *Kickx* †1864 Belgian botanists + NL *-ia*] **:** a small genus of Old World creeping pubescent herbs (family Scrophulariaceae) having pinnately veined oval leaves and flowers with a prominent palate — see CANCERWORT

kicky \'kikē\ *adj* -ER/-EST **1** *chiefly dial* **:** SASSY, CONTRARY **2 :** likely to kick

¹**kid** \'kid\ *n* -s [ME *kide*, of Scand origin; akin to ON *kith* kid, OSw *kidh;* akin to OHG *kizzī* kid; prob., like MIr *cit* sheep, Alb *qith* young male goat, fr. a cry to goats and sheep to return to the fold] **1 a** (1) **:** a young goat usu. under one year old (2) **:** a young individual of various related animals (as many antelopes and some deer) **b :** a young individual of various other animals ⟨a sea-otter ~⟩ **2 a :** the flesh, fur, or skin of a kid **b :** something made of kid: as (1) **:** KIDSKIN (2) **:** KID LEATHER (3) **:** KID GLOVE **3 :** CHILD, YOUNGSTER ⟨took the ~*s* to the playground⟩ ⟨a ~ of eighteen —Dan Cushman⟩ ⟨grade-school ~*s*⟩ **4** *slang* **:** a young person marked by proficiency or expertness ⟨quite some ~ when it comes to staying in the public eye⟩

²**kid** \"\ *vi* **kidded; kidded; kidding; kids** [ME *kidden*, fr. *kide*, n.] **:** to bring forth young — used of a goat or an antelope

³**kid** \"\ *adj* [¹*kid*] **1 :** of, relating to, or made of kid **2 :** YOUNGER — used in the phrases *kid brother* and *kid sister*

⁴**kid** \"\ *vb* **kidded; kidded; kidding; kids** [prob. fr. ¹*kid*] *vt* **1 :** DECEIVE, FOOL **2 :** to make fun of usu. good-humoredly and often by innocent deception ⟨used to ~ him then about his intellectual face —G.W.Brace⟩ ⟨a medicine-show barker *kidding* the crowd⟩ ⟨any nation that could ~ its own foibles was . . . new and pleasant —*Time*⟩ ⟨*kidded* him into thinking the police were inquiring about him⟩ ~ *vi* **1 :** to make fun of someone or something **2 a :** JOKE **b :** to indulge in good-humored fooling or horseplay — often used with *around* — **kid·der** \-də(r)\ *n* -s

⁵**kid** \"\ *n* -s [ME *kidde, kid*] *dial Eng* **:** a bundle of heath and twigs **:** FAGOT

⁶**kid** \"\ *vt* **kidded; kidded; kidding; kids :** to bind (fagots) in bundles

⁷**kid** \"\ *vi* **kidded; kidded; kidding; kids** [prob. alter. of earlier *cod*, fr. ¹*cod*] *dial Eng* **:** to form pods — used of a legume

⁸**kid** \"\ *n* -s [prob. alter. of ¹*cod*] *dial Eng* **:** the seed pod of a legume

⁹**kid** \"\ *n* -s [prob. alter. of ¹*kit*] **:** a small wooden tub; *esp* **:** a sailor's mess tub

kidcote \'=,=\ *n* [prob. fr. ¹*kid* (young goat) + *cote* (shed for animals); fr. the use of any available shed in small towns to house lawbreakers] *archaic* **:** JAIL

kid·der·min·ster \'kidə(r),minztə(r), -n(t)st-\ *or* **kidderminster carpet** *n* -s *usu cap* [fr. *Kidderminster*, borough in Worcester county, England] **:** ingrain carpet — called also *Scotch carpet*

kid·di·er \'kidēə(r)\ *also* **kid·der** \-də(r)\ *n* -s [origin unknown] *dial Eng* **:** a huckster esp. of agricultural produce

kid·ding·ly *adv* **:** in the manner of one that is kidding

kid·dish \'kidish, -dēsh\ *adj* **:** CHILDISH ⟨beginning to come along as well with her ~ admirers —W.C.Williams⟩ — **kid·dish·ly** *adv* — **kid·dish·ness** *n* -ES

¹**kid·dle** \'kidᵊl\ *n* -s [ME *kydle*, fr. ONF *quidel*, fr. MLG *kiedel*] **:** a barrier that extends across a river and that is designed to deflect the water and river fish through an opening across which a fishnet may be stretched

²**kiddle** \"\ *dial Eng var of* CUDDLE

kid·do \'ki(,)dō\ *n, pl* **kiddos** *or* **kiddoes** [¹*kid* + *-o*] — used as a familiar form of address ⟨don't worry about me, ~ —Max Arnold⟩ ⟨this means war, and ~, you're right in the middle —H.L.Spinner⟩

kid·dush \'ki(,)düsh, -,dəsh; kə'düsh\ *n* -ES [Heb *qiddūsh* sanctification] **:** a Jewish ceremony that proclaims the holiness of the incoming Sabbath or festival and that consists of a benediction pronounced customarily before the evening meal over a cup of wine or two loaves of white Sabbath bread ⟨hurried home in time for ~ on Friday evening⟩

kiddush ha·shem \-hə'shām\ *n* [Heb *qiddūsh hashshēm* sanctification of the name (of God)] **:** a religious or moral act according to Jewish religion that causes others to reverence God **:** religious martyrdom — compare HILLUL HASHEM

kid·du·shin \kə'düshən, ,=='shēn\ *n* -s [Aram *qiddūshīn*, pl. of Heb *qiddūsh*] **:** a betrothal ceremony preceding the Jewish marriage ceremony

kid·dy *or* **kid·die** \'kidē, -di\ *n, pl* **kiddies** [¹*kid* + *-y*, *-ie*] **:** a small child

kid finish *n* **:** a bookbinding finish of paper or boards resembling the surface of undressed kid leather

kid glove *n* **:** a dress glove made of kidskin or of some leather that resembles kidskin — **with kid gloves** *adv* **:** with special consideration **:** in a tactful manner ⟨never threatened to abuse or discriminate against him, instead treated him *with kid gloves* —*Time*⟩

kid–glove \'=,=\ *adj* [*kid glove*] **1** *or* **kid–gloved** \'=;=\ **a :** marked by a calculated fastidiousness and delicacy esp. in the avoidance of the rough or the uncouth in talk or action **b :** marked by extreme considerateness, care, and gentleness (as in handling) ⟨would no longer expect *kid-glove* treatment for their monarchist activities —*New Internat'l Yr. Bk.*⟩ ⟨I never thought I'd have a situation that called for such *kid-gloved* treatment —Francis Towle⟩ **2** *of a citrus fruit* **:** having an easily removable skin

kid–glove orange *n* **:** MANDARIN 4b(1)

kid leather *n* **1 :** soft pliable leather made from either goatskin or kidskin and used for shoes, gloves, garments, and handbags **2 :** a chrome tanned grain glove leather made from goatskin or lambskin

kid·let \'kidlət\ *n* -s [¹*kid* + *-let*] *slang* **:** KIDDY

¹**kid·nap** \'kid,nap\ *vt* **kidnapped** *or* **kidnaped; kidnapped** *or* **kidnaped; kidnapping** *or* **kidnaping; kidnaps** [prob. back-formation fr. *kidnapper*] **1** *obs* **:** to carry off to enforced labor esp. in the British colonies in America **2 a :** to carry (an unwilling person) away by unlawful force or fraud or to seize and detain for the purpose of so carrying away — compare ABDUCTION 2 **b :** to seize and carry or take away often wrongly ⟨*kidnapped* the children for the afternoon⟩ ⟨quite a business *kidnapping* pet dogs and watching the "Lost" columns for reward notices —T.W.Duncan⟩ ⟨*kidnapping* a sizable coastwise steamer —*Nat'l Geographic*⟩

²**kidnap** \"\ *adj* **:** of, relating to, or being a kidnapping ⟨a ~ plot⟩ ⟨the ~ car⟩

kid·nap·per *or* **kid·nap·er** \-pə(r)\ *n* -s [¹*kid* (child) + obs. *napper* thief, fr. *nap* (to seize) + *-er*] **:** one that kidnaps; *esp* **:** one that abducts a child for ransom

kidnapping *or* **kidnaping** *n* -s [fr. gerund of ¹*kidnap*] **:** the act or an instance of stealing, abducting, or carrying away a person by force or fraud often with a demand for ransom

kid·ney \'kidnē, -ni\ *n* -s *often attrib* [ME *kidenei, kidney*, fr. *kiden-, kidn-* (origin unknown) + *ei, ey* egg, fr. OE *ǣg* — more at EGG] **1 a :** one of a pair of vertebrate organs situated in the body cavity near the spinal column that serve to excrete urea, uric acid, and other waste products of metabolism, that in man are bean-shaped organs about 4½ inches long lying behind the peritoneum of the posterior part of the abdomen and embedded in a mass of fatty tissue, and that consist chiefly of nephrons by which urine is secreted, collected, and finally discharged into the pelvis of the kidney whence it is conveyed by the ureter to the bladder to be periodically discharged — compare MESONEPHROS, METANEPHROS, PRONEPHROS **b :** any of various more or less complex excretory organs of invertebrate animals — see GREEN GLAND; compare NEPHRIDIUM **2 :** sort or kind esp. as regards persuasion, disposition, or temperament ⟨a nice helpful guy, of a different ~ entirely from the ubiquitous Secret Police functionaries —Paula Lecler⟩ **3 :** a kidney-shaped aggregate of ore **syn** see TYPE

kidney bean *n* **1 :** the seed of any cultivated bean derived from the common species (*Phaseolus vulgaris*); *esp* **:** any of certain rather large dark red kidney-shaped beans **2 :** a plant producing kidney beans

kidney chop *n* **:** a loin chop (as of lamb or veal) containing a kidney whole or in part — see VEAL illustration

kidney corpuscle *n* **:** MALPIGHIAN CORPUSCLE

kidney cotton *n* [so called fr. the shape of the mass in which the seeds are found] **1 :** a shrub or small tree (*Gossypium brasiliense*) yielding a long-staple cotton **2 :** the fiber obtained from kidney cotton

kidney desk *n* **:** a desk that is kidney-shaped in top and horizontal section

kidney ore *n* [so called fr. its occurrence in kidney-shaped masses] **:** a mineral consisting of a variety of hematite

kidney desk

kidneyroot \'==,=\ *n* [so called fr. the belief that such plants cure kidney diseases] **1 :** JOE-PYE WEED **2 :** COYOTE BRUSH

kidney–shaped \'==,=\ *adj* **:** shaped like a kidney **:** RENIFORM

kidney stone *n* **1 :** a kidney-shaped pebble **2 :** RENAL CALCULUS

kidney table *n* **:** a usu. small side table with a kidney-shaped top

kidney vetch *n* **:** a perennial Eurasian herb (*Anthyllis vulneraria*) having heads of red or yellow flowers and formerly used as a remedy for renal disorders

kidney worm *n* **:** any of several nematode worms parasitic in the kidneys: as **a :** GIANT KIDNEY WORM **b :** a common and destructive black-and-white worm (*Stephanurus dentatus*) that is related to the gapeworm but attains a length of two inches and is parasitic in the kidneys, lungs, and other viscera of the hog in warm regions — called also *lardworm*

kidneywort \'==,=\ *n* [so called fr. the use of such plants to cure kidney diseases] **1 :** NAVELWORT 1 **2 :** STAR SAXIFRAGE **3 :** COYOTE BRUSH

kids *pl of* KID, *pres 3d sing of* KID

kidskin \'=,=\ *n* [¹*kid* + *skin*] **1 :** the skin of a young goat **2 :** KID LEATHER

kid stuff *n* **1 :** something befitting or appropriate only to children ⟨realized that all that saluting and about-facing was *kid stuff* —T.W.Duncan⟩ **2 :** something extremely simple or easy ⟨convinced him that running for the town council would be *kid stuff*⟩

kie·kie \'kēā,kēā, 'kē,kē, 'kī,kī\ *n* -s [Maori] **:** a New Zealand climbing shrub (*Freycinetia banksii*) with edible berries

kiel \'kēl, *esp before pause or consonant* -ēəl\ *adj, usu cap* [fr. *Kiel*, Germany] **:** of or from the city of Kiel, Germany **:** of the kind or style prevalent in Kiel

kiel·ba·sa \kil'bäsə, k(y)el-, kēl-\ *n, pl* **kielbasas** \-səz\ *also* **kielba·sy** \-sē\ [Pol *kiełbasa* sausage; akin to Russ *kolbasa* sausage, Czech & Slovenian *klobasa*] **:** uncooked smoked sausage

kier \'ki(ə)r\ *n* -s [prob. of Scand origin; akin to ON *ker* tub, vessel, Norw dial. *kjer;* akin to OHG *char* vessel, bowl, Goth *kas* vessel] **:** a large metal vat in which fibers, yarns, and fabrics are boiled off, bleached, or dyed

kier–boil \'=,=\ *vt* **:** to scour (as cotton) by boiling in a kier usu. with an alkaline solution

kier·ing \'kiriŋ\ *n* -s **:** the process of treating in a kier

¹**kier·ke·gaard·ian** \¦kirkə¦gärdēən, ¦kyerkə¦gōrēən\ *adj, usu cap* [Sören Aabye *Kierkegaard* †1855 Danish philosopher + E *-ian*] **:** of or relating to the Danish philosopher Kierkegaard or his existentialist philosophy ⟨discourage the growth of a *Kierkegaardian* cult —James Collins⟩ — compare CHRISTIAN EXISTENTIALISM

²**kierkegaardian** \"\ *n* -s *usu cap* **:** a follower of Kierkegaard **:** an adherent of Kierkegaardian philosophy

kier·man \'kirmən\ *n, pl* **kiermen :** one who works at a kier

kie·sel·guhr *or* **kie·sel·gur** \'kēzəl,gü(ə)r, -,ü̇ə\ *n* -s [G *kieselgur*, fr. *kiesel* pebble, flint + *guhr, gur* guhr] **:** loose or porous diatomite — compare TRIPOLI

kie·ser·ite \'kēzə,rīt\ *n* -s [G *kieserit*, fr. Dietrich G. *Kieser* †1862 Ger. physician + G *-it* -ite] **:** a mineral $MgSO_4H_2O$ that consists of hydrous magnesium sulfate and is white when pure

ki·ev \'kē,(y)e|f, -eyə|, |v\ *adj, usu cap* [fr. *Kiev*, U.S.S.R.] **:** of or from the city of Kiev, U.S.S.R. **:** of the kind or style prevalent in Kiev

¹ki·ev·an \'kē,(y)efən, -evən\ *adj, usu cap* [*Kiev*, U.S.S.R. + E *-an*] **:** of or relating to Kiev, U.S.S.R.; *esp* **:** of the 11th and 12th centuries of Kiev's supremacy ⟨*Kievan* Russia⟩

²kievan \"\ *n* -s *cap* **:** a native or inhabitant of Kiev, U.S.S.R.

kieve *var of* KEEVE

kif *var of* KEF

Ki·ja·fa \kē'(y)afə, -)äfə\ *trademark* — used for a wine made from the juice and flavored with the pits of a small black Danish cherry

ki·kar \'kēkə(r), 'kik-\ *n* -s [Hindi *kīkar*] **:** GUM ARABIC TREE

kike \'kīk\ *n* -s [prob. alter. of *kiki*, redupl. of *-ki*, common ending of names of Jews who lived in Slavic countries] **:** JEW — usu. taken to be offensive

ki·ke·pa \kē'kāpə\ *n* -s [Hawaiian] **:** a tapa or sarong worn by Hawaiian women with the top under one arm and over the shoulder of the opposite arm

ki·kon·go \kē'käŋ(,)gō\ *n, usu cap* **:** KONGO

ki·ku \'kē(,)kü\ *n* -s [Jap] **:** CHRYSANTHEMUM 1

kiku·mon \'kikə,män, 'kēk-\ *n* -s [Jap, fr. *kiku* + *mon* badge, crest] **:** CHRYSANTHEMUM 3

ki·ku·yu \kə'kü(,)yü, kē'-\ *n, pl* **kikuyu** *or* **kikuyus** *usu cap* **1 a :** a Bantu-speaking agricultural negroid people of Kenya **b :** a member of such people **2 :** a Bantu language of the Kikuyu people

kikuyu grass *n, often cap K* **:** a southern African forage grass (*Pennisetum clandestinum*) introduced into Australia and So. America

kil *abbr* **1** kilderkin **2** kilogram **3** kilometer

kild *abbr* kilderkin

kil·dare \(')kil¦da(a)|(ə)r, -de|, |ə\ *adj, usu cap* [fr. County *Kildare*, Ireland] **:** of or from County Kildare, Ireland **:** of the kind or style prevalent in County Kildare

kildare green *n, often cap K* **:** a moderate yellow green that is greener, lighter, and stronger than average moss green, yellower and lighter than average pea green, and yellower and paler than apple green (sense 1)

kil·dee \'kildē\ *dial var of* KILLDEER

kildeer *var of* KILLDEER

kil·der·kin \'kildə(r)kən\ *n* -s [ME *kinderkin, kilderkin*, fr. MD *kindekijn, kinnekijn*, fr. ML *quintale* quintal + MD *-kijn* (dim. suffix) — more at QUINTAL, -KIN] **1 :** a cask about half the size of a common barrel and sometimes smaller **2 :** an English unit of capacity equal to ½ barrel or 18 imperial gallons

kiley *var of* KYLIE

kil·hig \'kil,hig\ *or* **kil·lig** \'kilig\ *n* -s [origin unknown] **:** a short thick pole used in logging to direct the fall of a tree

ki·lim \kē'lēm\ *n* -s [Turk, fr. Per *kilīm*] **:** a pileless tapestry-woven carpet, mat, or spread made in Turkey, Kurdistan, the Caucasus, Iran, and western Turkestan

ki·li·wa \kə'lēwə\ *or* **ki·li·wi** \-wē\ *n, pl* **kiliwa** *or* **kiliwas** *or* **kiliwi** *or* **kiliwis** *usu cap* **1 a :** an Indian people of northern Lower California, Mexico **b :** a member of such people **2 :** a Yuman language of the Kiliwa people

kil·ken·ny \(')kil¦kenē, -ni\ *adj, usu cap* [fr. County *Kilkenny*, Ireland] **:** of or from County Kilkenny, Ireland **:** of the kind or style prevalent in County Kilkenny

¹kill \'kil\ *vb* **killed** \-ld\ *or chiefly dial* **kilt** \-lt\ **killed** *or chiefly dial* **kilt; killing; kills** [ME *cullen, killen* to strike, beat, kill; perh. akin to OE *cwellan* to kill — more at QUELL] *vt* **1 a :** to deprive of life **:** put to death **:** cause the death of ⟨~*ed* by enemy fire⟩ ⟨this poison ~*s* rats⟩ ⟨the accident ~*ed* six people⟩; *also* **:** to terminate suddenly the life processes of (as in preparing tissue for fixing and microscopic examination) **b :** to destroy as if by killing ⟨~*s* whatever core of human decency he ever had in him —Aldous Huxley⟩ ⟨an industry ~*ed* by competition⟩ ⟨an unfavorable report would . . . ~ any chance of getting a license —*Wall Street Jour.*⟩ **c :** to slaughter (as a hog) for food **:** convert a food animal into (as pork) by slaughtering **d** (1) **:** to shatter (a clay target) by hitting in skeet shooting (2) *of a ship* **:** SINK ⟨~*ed* ships and . . . wounded ships staggering away from battle —Ira Wolfert⟩ **e :** to subvert completely the plans and hopes of **:** outwit with the result of putting in a hopeless position ⟨the calamitous failure of his plan ~*ed* him more than if he had lost all his money⟩ **2 a :** to put an end to esp. abruptly **:** cause to cease **:** stop esp. with finality ⟨knew he could not ~ the evil in the world⟩ ⟨~ the enterprise by denying it the money necessary to proceed⟩ ⟨the censors ~*ed* the play after its first week⟩ ⟨~*ed* the engine and got out of the car⟩ ⟨a snack to ~ her hunger⟩ ⟨the fire-*killing* power of the chemical⟩ **b :** to get rid of **:** ELIMINATE ⟨~ foam in pulp in paper mills⟩ **c :** DEFEAT, VETO ⟨the bill was ~*ed* on the first vote⟩ ⟨asked for a transfer but his petition was ~*ed*⟩ **d** (1) **:** to take out or omit or mark for omission (something published as in a newspaper or presented as on a stage) **:** mark for deletion (something designed for publication or presentation) ⟨~*ed* a good part of the article for political reasons⟩ ⟨~*ed* the story as it was written for the late edition⟩ ⟨~*ed* the second act and substituted a new one after the second week⟩; *also* **:** to order (as set type) to be destroyed or distributed (2) **:** to stop the use of (as a stage prop or broadcast microphone) or the functioning of (as a stage light) **3 a :** to destroy the vital or active or essential quality of ⟨~ a disease with antibiotics⟩ ⟨~*ed* the pain with drugs⟩ ⟨the heat ~*ed* the yeast⟩ ⟨believed that to explain a joke is to ~ it⟩ **b :** NEUTRALIZE ⟨threw an alkali in the solution to ~ the acid⟩ **c :** to deprive of the power to germinate ⟨~ the seed⟩ **d :** to do damage or injury to (as flour) by overheating **e :** SPOIL, RUIN ⟨the addition of the wrong color totally ~*ed* the portrait⟩ **f** (1) **:** to injure or hurt severely **:** cause extreme pain to ⟨my feet are ~*ing* me⟩ (2) *chiefly Irish* **:** to knock unconscious ⟨got ~*ed* in a fight and didn't come to until morning⟩ **g :** to tire or exhaust esp. almost to the point of collapse ⟨the heat and the heavy work ~*ed* him and he had to lie down for a while⟩ ⟨no use ~*ing* ourselves getting to the train —J.P. Marquand⟩ **h :** to lessen or impede markedly ⟨the frantic maneuver ~*ed* her speed —Joseph Millard⟩ **i :** to impress a cancellation mark upon (a stamp) ⟨the stamp was ~*ed* with a blue grid —E.R.Guilford⟩ **4 a :** to make a markedly favorable impression on **:** affect strongly ⟨on her first stage appearance she ~*ed* the audience⟩ **b** *slang* **:** to impress as hilariously funny or ridiculous ⟨his jokes ~*ed* me⟩ **5 :** to occupy oneself in some convenient way merely to pass (time or a unit of time) **:** fill in (time or a unit of time) ⟨ways in which to ~ an hour until train time⟩ ⟨~ an entire afternoon over a pot of tea —Lin Yutang⟩; *also* **:** to provide or serve as a convenient occupation or distraction to help pass (time or a unit of time) ⟨reading ~*ed* a good deal of time during the trip⟩ **6 a :** to treat in such a manner as to destroy undesirable properties and so make suitable for further treatment or for a specific purpose ⟨~ soap stock by boiling with alkali⟩ ⟨~ fur by means of chemicals in preparation for dyeing⟩ **b :** to cause (molten steel) to become quiet and free from bubbling by adding a strong deoxidizing agent (as aluminum) that combines with oxygen and minimizes reaction between oxygen and carbon during solidification **c :** KNOT 5 **d :** DE-ENERGIZE ⟨~ a live electrical circuit⟩ **e :** to reduce the strength of (plaster of paris) by mixing with an excess of water **7 :** to break or burn (an object in a mortuary rite of a nonliterate culture) for the purpose of separating from the material substance the spirit which may then accompany and serve the spirit of a recently deceased person **8 :** to play (a return shot) so hard in a racket game that one's opponent cannot make return — compare SMASH **9 a :** to consume (as an alcoholic beverage) totally ⟨~*ed* his drink and held out the glass —W.L.Gresham⟩ **b :** to consume the total contents of (as a bottle of liquor) ⟨~*ed* two bottles of wine over dinner⟩ ~ *vi* **1 a :** to perform the act of killing something **:** commit murder or slaughter **b :** to make an irresistible impression ⟨dressed to ~⟩ **c :** to produce exhaustion or fatigue ⟨a ~*ing* occupation⟩ **2 :** to undergo killing or slaughter — usu. used of a food animal

syn KILL, SLAY, MURDER, ASSASSINATE, DISPATCH, EXECUTE all mean, in common, to put to death. KILL merely states the fact ⟨*kill* a rabbit⟩ ⟨a man *killed* by a twenty-foot fall⟩ ⟨the drought *killed* most of the vegetation⟩ ⟨*kill* a proposal⟩ SLAY in being a more literary word implies a force and wantonness and a generally more dramatic action ⟨the law which forbade the sinful *slaying* of a cat —Agnes Repplier⟩ ⟨his hoary tales of how Dion O'Banion was *slain* in his flower shop —Herman Kogan⟩ ⟨in 1258 the terrible conqueror Hulagu swept over Baghdad and *slew* the Caliph with 80,000 of the faithful —*Times Lit. Supp.*⟩ MURDER implies motive and usu. premeditation in a criminal human act ⟨*murder* a wealthy man for his money⟩ ⟨the fear which drove Rome to *murder* Carthage and Corinth and her own character as well —Herbert Agar⟩ ⟨that theory is *murdered* by the brutal fact that there are many among the older generation who will not believe —G.W. Johnson⟩ ASSASSINATE implies the killing of a person by stealth or treachery, esp. of a person in governmental or political power ⟨*assassinate* a monarch⟩ DISPATCH in this connection stresses speed and directness in murdering or otherwise putting to death and is usu. used intentionally to avoid the violent or odious connotations of the other terms ⟨eight to twelve otters were *dispatched* before the main herd dispersed —*Nature Mag.*⟩ ⟨one of his first tasks was to *dispatch* a sick and dying horse with a sledgehammer —*Times Lit. Supp.*⟩ ⟨then reached up, caught Wright by the coat, drew him down on to him, and at one stab *dispatched* him —*Amer. Guide Series: La.*⟩ EXECUTE is the term used for putting to death one condemned to death by a legal or quasi-legal process ⟨*execute* a man convicted of murder⟩ ⟨the mob summarily *executed* the horse thief⟩

²kill \"\ *n* -s **1 a :** KILLING 1 ⟨an animal moving in for the ~⟩ ⟨indicted a man for a ~ in the downtown section of the city⟩ **b :** an act of hunting with the intent of killing for food ⟨an animal on a ~⟩ **c** (1) **:** the death or killing (as of weeds) by weed killers, insecticides, or other lethal preparations (2) **:** the ability to kill **:** a killing force (as of a weed killer) ⟨the residual ~ of DDT⟩ **2 :** something killed: as **a :** an animal or bird shot in a hunt; *collectively* **:** the animals or birds shot in a hunt, during a season, or in a particular period of time ⟨the annual ~ of cock pheasants is estimated at 750,000 —*Amer. Guide Series: Mich.*⟩ **b :** an enemy airplane shot down or otherwise destroyed by military action while in flight ⟨a group captain's determination to get maximum ~*s* at his fighter station —*Sydney (Australia) Bull.*⟩; *also* **:** an enemy submarine or ship destroyed **c :** something to be destroyed (as by gunfire) ⟨guide missiles to the ~ —J.J. Haggerty⟩ **d :** copy that has been omitted or marked for omission from a publication (as a newspaper) **e :** a return shot in a racket game that has been driven so hard that one's opponent cannot handle it **3 :** an order or instruction to kill (as set type matter or a news story) **4 :** KILLING 3 **5 :** an animal used as bait in big-game hunting — **on the kill 1** *of an animal* **:** having the intention of killing (as for food) **2 :** intending to stop at almost nothing to achieve one's end ⟨politicians *on the kill* in an election year⟩

³kill \"\ *n* -s *often cap* [D *kil*, fr. MD *kille*; akin to East Fris. *kille* watercourse, ON *kill* small bay, arm of the sea, and perh. to OHG *kil* wedge — more at CHINE] **:** CHANNEL, CREEK, RIVER, STREAM — used chiefly in place names in Delaware and the state of New York (as Catskill mountains)

kill·able \'kiləbəl\ *adj* **:** capable of being killed esp. legally **:** fit to kill

¹kil·lar·ney \kə'lärnē, -lån-, -ni\ *adj, usu cap* [fr. *Killarney* mountains, Ontario, Canada] **:** of, relating to, or constituting mountain-making movements near the end of the Proterozoic era — see GEOLOGIC TIME table

²killarney \"\ *or* **killarney green** *n* -s *often cap K* [fr. *Killarney*, district in County Kerry, Ireland] **:** a moderate yellowish green to green that is stronger than Gretna green

kil·las \'kiləs\ *n* -ES [Corn *kyllas*] *Cornwall* **:** argillaceous slate

kill back *vt* **:** to kill (a tree or shrub) at the top ⟨low temperature *killed* the tree *back*⟩ ⟨the tops of all the garden shrubs were *killed back* by the storm⟩

kill-courtesy *n, obs* **:** BOOR

kill-cow \'ˌ=ˌ=\ *n* **1** *now dial* **:** a man of real or fancied importance **:** PERSONAGE **2** *now dial* **:** a serious or consequential matter

kill·crop \'kil,kräp\ *n* [LG *kilkrop*] **:** a voracious infant **:** a fairy changeling

kill·dee \'kildē\ *dial var of* KILLDEER

kill·deer *or* **kil·deer** \'kil,di(ə)r, -iə\ *n, pl* **killdeers** *or* **killdeer** *or* **kildeers** *or* **kildeer** [imit.] **:** a plover (*Charadrius vociferus* syn. *Oxyechus vociferus*) found throughout temperate No. America and in southern areas in migration to So. America, being about 10 inches long, grayish brown above, ferruginous in the rump, and white below and with two black bands on the breast and neck, and having a much-repeated cry that is plaintive and penetrating

kill-devil \'=ˌ=\ *n* **1** *dial* **:** West Indian rum **2 :** liquor that is cheap or poor in quality

killed *past of* KILL

kil·le·fer *also* **kil·li·fer** \'kiləfə(r)\ *n* -s [fr. the name *Killefer*] **:** a tractor-drawn agricultural machine that is used for deep tillage and loosening of the subsoil and consists essentially of one or more wheel-mounted pointed horizontal knives or chisels

kill·er \'kilə(r)\ *n* -s *often attrib* [¹*kill* + *-er*] **1 :** one that kills: **a :** MURDERER; *esp* **:** a homicidal criminal or maniac **b :** SLAUGHTERER; *also* **:** one who buys animals for slaughter ⟨~*s* took a big share of the choice of low prime yearlings —*Chicago Daily Drovers Jour.*⟩ **c :** an effective bait in fishing **d :** something that has a forceful and usu. violent impact ⟨a backhand stroke that was a ~⟩ ⟨his punch was a ~⟩ **e** *slang* **:** one who gives an admirable or irresistible personal or sartorial impression ⟨she was no ~ on looks —Garson Kanin⟩ **2 :** an animal to be killed for food or other use **3** *or* **killer whale :** a fierce carnivorous gregarious whale (*Orcinus orca* syn. *Orca orca*) 20 to 30 feet long that is black with yellowish white areas on sides and underparts, has a high dorsal fin, powerful tail, and sharp strong teeth, and preys on large fishes, seals, and even in groups on the larger whales **4 :** a postal canceling stamp; *also* **:** a cancellation mark on a postage stamp

killer 4

killer bar *n* **:** a bar or line on a postmarking stamp or in the postmark it produces

killer boat *also* **killer ship** *n* **:** one of the small fast boats accompanying a factory ship in whaling and responsible for the pursuit and capture of a whale

killer-diller \¦kilə(r)¦dilə(r)\ *n* -s [redupl. of *killer*] *slang* **:** something highly and usu. factitiously sensational of its kind ⟨plot hocus-pocus and *killer-diller* battles between good and evil —Jean Garrigue⟩ ⟨*killer-diller* love scenes —C.J.Rolo⟩

killer plant *n* **:** an East African plant (*Adenia sinensis*) of the family Passifloraceae that contains a highly poisonous alkaloid — called also *modecca flower*

kil·lick \'kilik\ *also* **kel·leg** \'keləg\ *or* **kel·lock** \'kelək\ *or* **kil·lock** \'kilək\ *n* -s [origin unknown] **1 :** ANCHOR; *esp* **:** a small anchor **2 :** a jury anchor formed by a stone usu. bound within sticks of wood

killickinnic *or* **killikinick** *or* **killickinnick** *var of* KINNIKINNICK

kil·lie *also* **kil·ly** \'kilē\ *or* **kel·ly** *or* **kel·lie** \'kelē\ *n, pl* **killies** *or* **kellies** [*kill* + *-ie, -y*] **:** KILLIFISH

kil·li·fish \'kilē,fish, -li,-\ *n* [*killie* + *fish*] **1 :** any of numerous small oviparous fishes of the family Cyprinodontidae which are usu. striped or barred with black, which are much used as bait and in mosquito control, and some of which live equally well in fresh and brackish water or even in the sea — see GUDGEON, MAYFISH, MUMMICHOG **2 :** TOPMINNOW 1

killig *var of* KILHIG

¹kill·ing \'kiliŋ, -lēŋ\ *n* -s [ME, fr. gerund of *killen* to strike, kill — more at KILL] **1 :** the act of one that kills; *esp* **:** MURDER, HOMICIDE **2 :** KILL 2a **3 :** a sudden notable success esp. in stock speculation or business ⟨a ~ he made in railway securities —Robert Shaplen⟩

²killing \"\ *adj* [fr. pres. part. of ¹*kill*] **1 :** having the effect of killing: as **a :** producing death **:** FATAL, DEADLY ⟨a ~ disease⟩ ⟨a ~ drink⟩ **b :** having a markedly deleterious or painful effect or impact extremely difficult to endure ⟨the strain of concentration was ~, so he gave up⟩; *also* **:** calling for great strength, stamina, or endurance ⟨a ~ pace⟩ **c :** having an irresistible and notable effect ⟨a ~ humor⟩ ⟨a ~ dress⟩ **2 :** arousing the desire to kill ⟨as ~ a hatred between them as though they were two jungle beasts —Jean Stafford⟩

killing bottle *n* **:** a bottle containing a poisonous vapor (as cyanide) for killing insects to be preserved as specimens

killing frost *n* **:** a frost low enough in temperature to kill most exposed garden vegetation and fruit buds

kill·ing·ly *adv* **:** in a killing manner

kil·lin·ite \'kilə,nīt\ *n* -s [*Killiney*, bay and village, County Dublin, Ireland + E *-ite*] **:** a mineral consisting of a variety of pinite

killjoy \'=ˌ=\ *n* [¹*kill* + *joy*] **:** one that inspires gloom or counteracts joy or high spirits **:** one that tends to pessimism or a depressing solemnness esp. among people that are happy or optimistic **:** one that dispirits ⟨professional ~*s* whose chief fear it is that people . . . might get some fun out of life —T.P.Whitney⟩

kill-kid \'=ˌ=\ *n* [¹*kill* + *kid* (young goat); fr. the poisonous foliage] **:** SHEEP LAUREL

kill off *vt* **1 :** to destroy in large numbers or totally ⟨the flood of hunters *killed* the buffalo *off* rapidly until only a few were left⟩ ⟨the flowers were *killed off* by the first frost⟩ ⟨the lack of enthusiasm *killed* the project *off* quickly⟩ **2 :** to get rid of **:** ELIMINATE ⟨the low prices they asked *killed* their competition *off*⟩

kil·lo·gie \kə'lōgi\ *n* -s [perh. irreg. fr. Sc *kill* kiln, fr. ME, alter. of *kilne* — more at KILN] *chiefly Scot* **:** the sheltered space before a kiln fire

kill out *vt* **:** to complete the curing of (tobacco) by exposing to high temperature to dry out the stem and stop further chemical change

kills *pres 3d sing of* KILL, *pl of* KILL

kill-time \'=ˌ=\ *n* **:** an occupation that serves to kill time

kill-wart \'=ˌ=\ *or* **killwort** \'=ˌ=\ *n* [*kill-wart* fr. ¹*kill* + *wart*; fr. its use to remove warts; *killwort* by folk etymology fr. *kill-wart*] **:** CELANDINE 1

killy fish *n* **:** KILLIFISH

kil·ly hawk \'kilē-\ *n* [*killy* of imit. origin] **:** SPARROW HAWK 2

kil·mar·nock willow \(')kil¦märnək-\ *n, usu cap K* [fr. *Kilmarnock*, burgh in Ayr county, Scotland] **:** a small Old World willow that is a variety (*Salix caprea pendula*) of the great sallow with crooked pendulous branches

¹kiln \'kil(n)\ *n* -s *often attrib* [ME *kilne*, fr. OE *cyln, cylen*, fr. L *culina* kitchen, fr. *coquere* to cook — more at COOK] **:** an oven, furnace, or heated enclosure used for processing a substance by burning, firing, or drying: as **a :** LIMEKILN **b :** BRICKKILN **c :** an oven with a heat-resistant lining used to fire ceramics **d :** a room or shed through which warm air is circulated for the removal of moisture (as from grain, lumber, or tobacco) — compare KILN EVAPORATOR

²kiln \"\ *vt* -ED/-ING/-S **:** to burn, fire, or dry in a kiln

kiln-dried \'=¦=\ *adj* **:** dried or cured in a kiln ⟨*kiln-dried* lumber⟩

kiln-dry \'=,=\ *vt* **:** to dry (wood) in a kiln **:** season artificially

kiln evaporator *n* **:** a room with a slatted floor through which heat is circulated for drying fruit

kilneye \'=,=\ *or* **kilnhole** \'=,=\ *n* **:** the mouth of a kiln; *specif* **:** an opening in a limekiln for removal of the lime

kiln·man \'=mən\ *n, pl* **kilnmen :** one who loads or fires a kiln or controls the drying or baking done therein

kiln-run \'=,=\ *adj* **:** as taken from the kiln **:** not sorted as to quality ⟨*kiln-run* brick⟩

kiln scum *n* **:** WHITEWASH 3

¹ki·lo \'kē(,)lō, 'ki(-\ *n* -s **1 a** [by shortening] **:** KILOGRAM **b :** KILOWARE **2** [by shortening] **:** KILOMETER

²kilo \"\ *usu cap* — a communications code word for the letter *k*

kilo- *comb form* [F, modif. of Gk *chilioi* — more at MILE] **:** thousand — chiefly in names of units in the metric system ⟨*kilo*ampere⟩ ⟨*kilo*gauss⟩ ⟨*kilo*joule⟩

kilo·calorie \'kilō+,-\ *n* [ISV *kilo-* + *calorie*] **:** CALORIE b(1)

kilo·cy·cle \'kilə,sīkəl\ *n* [ISV *kilo-* + *cycle*] **:** one thousand cycles; *esp* **:** one thousand cycles per second — used as a unit of radio frequency ⟨broadcasting on a frequency of 1250 ~*s*⟩; abbr. *kc*

kilo·gram *or* **kilo·gramme** \-,gram, -raa(ə)m\ *n* [F *kilogramme*, fr. *kilo-* + *gramme* gram — more at GRAM] **1 :** the basic metric unit of mass and weight equal to the mass of a platinum-iridium cylinder kept at the International Bureau of Weights and Measures near Paris and nearly equal to 1000 cubic centimeters of water at the temperature of its maximum density — see METRIC SYSTEM table; abbr. *kg* **2 :** a unit of force equal to the weight of a kilogram under standard gravity

kilogram calorie *n* **:** CALORIE b(1)

kilogram-meter \'==,=¦==\ *n* **:** the mks gravitational unit of work and energy equal to the work done by a kilogram force acting through a distance of one meter in the direction of the force **:** about 7.235 foot-pounds

kilo·hertz \'kilə +,-\ *n* [ISV *kilo-* + *hertz*] **:** a unit of frequency equal to one thousand hertz — abbr. *kHz*

kilo·liter \'kilə+,-\ *n* [F *kilolitre*, fr. *kilo-* + *litre* liter — more at LITER] **:** a metric unit of capacity equal to 1000 liters — see METRIC SYSTEM table; abbr. *kl*

kilome·ter \÷kə'läməd·ə(r), |tə- *also* 'kilə,mē|\ *n* [F *kilomètre*, fr. *kilo-* + *mètre* meter — more at METER] **:** a metric unit of length equal to 1000 meters — see METRIC SYSTEM table; abbr. *km*

kilo·parsec \'kilə+\ *n* **:** one thousand parsecs

kilo·ton \'kilə,tən\ *n* [*kilo-* + *ton*] **1 :** one thousand tons **2 :** an explosive force equivalent to that of one thousand tons of TNT — used esp. in reference to an atom or hydrogen bomb — abbr. *kt*

kil·o·var \-,vär\ *n* -s [*kilo*volt + *a*mpere + *r*eactive] **:** the part of a kilovolt-ampere contributed by reactance

kilo·volt \'kilə,vōlt\ *n* [ISV *kilo-* + *volt*] **:** a unit of electromotive force equal to one thousand volts — abbr. *kv*

kilo·volt·age \-tij\ *n* **:** potential difference expressed in kilovolts

kilovolt-ampere \'==,=¦=,=\ *n* **:** a unit of apparent power in an electric circuit equal to 1000 volt-amperes

kilo·ware \'kilə+,-\ *n* [*kilo* + *ware*] **1 :** packaged mixtures of unsorted postage stamps accumulated esp. by European post offices largely from parcel tags and sold by the kilogram **2 :** a package of unsorted stamps usu. sealed by the government to indicate that the mixture is as orig. assembled by the post office

kilo·watt \'kilə,wät, *usu* -äd.+V\ *n* [ISV *kilo-* + *watt*] **:** a unit of power equal to 1000 watts or about 1.34 horsepower — abbr. *kw*

kilowatt-hour \'==,=¦=\ *n* **:** a unit of work or energy equal to that expended in one hour at a steady rate of one kilowatt or to 3.6×10^6 joules

kilp \'kilp\ *dial Eng var of* KELP

kil·roy \'kil,rȯi\ *n* -s *usu cap* [after *Kilroy*, mythical soldier of World War II whose name was inscribed in unlikely places all over the world by Amer. soldiers] **:** an inveterate traveler ⟨like the roamers *Kilroy* and Ulysses —Peter Viereck⟩; *esp* **:** a transient soldier ⟨of all the *Kilroys* of history who have passed through here . . . it was Napoleon who best summed up the strategic importance of Malta —J.P.O'Donnell⟩

¹kilt \'kilt\ *vb* -ED/-ING/-S [ME *kilten*, of Scand origin; akin to Dan *kilte* (*op*) to gather up (as a skirt), Sw dial. *kilta* (*sej*) to gather up one's skirts, ON *kjalta* fold made by a gathered skirt, OSw *kilta* lap, and perh. to Goth *kilthei* womb — more at CHILD] *vt* **1** *now chiefly dial* **:** to gather up or tuck in (as a skirt) for protection or freedom of action **2** *archaic* **:** to truss up **:** HANG ⟨brought the country to order by ~*ing* thieves and banditti with strings —Sir Walter Scott⟩ **3 :** to equip with a kilt ⟨insists that nominees prove Scottish relationship or extraction, or they don't get ~*ed* —*Sat. Eve. Post*⟩ ~ *vi* **:** to move nimbly

²kilt \"\ *n* -s **1 :** a pleated wraparound skirt usu. of tartan reaching from the waist to the knees worn by men and boys in Scotland and esp. by Scottish regiments in the British armies **2 :** something that resembles a Scottish kilt; *esp* **:** a short plaid skirt for women or girls

³kilt *chiefly dial past of* KILL

¹kilt·ed \'kiltəd\ *adj* [fr. past part. of ¹*kilt*] **1 :** gathered in or tucked up ⟨clam diggers with ~ skirts⟩ **2 :** gathered in vertical pleats **:** KNIFE-PLEATED ⟨yoke of ~ nylon⟩

²kilted \"\ *adj* [²*kilt* + *-ed*] **:** wearing a kilt ⟨a tall ~ Highlander⟩ ⟨~ regiment⟩

kil·ter \'kiltə(r)\ *also* **kel·ter** \'kel-\ *n* -S [origin unknown] **1 a :** good working condition **:** ORDER, ADJUSTMENT — usu. used in the phrase *out of kilter* ⟨the car wouldn't go because the engine was out of ~⟩ ⟨his nerves are out of ~ —James Hilton⟩ **b :** BALANCE, ALIGNMENT ⟨unexpected expenses threw the budget out of ~⟩ ⟨a truck rammed the house and pushed it out of ~⟩ **2 :** 4SKEET

kilt·ie \'kiltē, -ti\ *n* -S [2*kilt* + *-ie*] **1** *or* **kilty** \"\ -ES *often cap* **:** one who wears a kilt; *specif* **:** a member of a Highland regiment **2 a :** a shoe with a long slashed tongue that folds over the instep to cover the lacing **b :** SHAWL TONGUE

kiltie 2a

kim·ber·ley \'kimbə(r)lē\ *n* -S *often cap* [fr. *Kimberley*, town in northern Cape Province, Union of So. Africa] **:** a commercial grade of white diamond ranking below Wesselton

kimberley horse disease *n, usu cap K* [fr. *Kimberley*, district of Western Australia] **:** WALKABOUT DISEASE

kim·ber·lin \'kimbələn\ *n* -S [prob. alter. of ME *kymeling, comling* — more at COMELING] *dial Eng* **:** NEWCOMER, STRANGER

kim·ber·lite \'kimbə(r),līt\ *n* -S [*Kimberley*, Union of So. Africa + E *-ite*] **:** an agglomerate biotite-peridotite that occurs in pipes in southern Africa and less extensively in Kentucky and that is weathered yellow at the surface, is blue farther down, and often contains diamonds — called also *blue earth, blue ground, blue stuff*

kim·bun·du \kim'bün(,)dü\ *n, usu cap* **:** a Bantu language of northern Angola — called also *Mbundu*

kim·chi *also* **kim·ch'i** *or* **kim·chee** \'kimchē\ *n* -S [Korean] **:** a vegetable pickle seasoned with garlic, red pepper, and ginger that is the national dish of Korea

kim·mer \'kimər\ *var of* CUMMER

kim·me·ri·an \kə'mirēən, -mēr-\ *usu cap, var of* CIMMERIAN

kim·nel \'kimnᵊl\ *n* -S [ME *kymelyn, kymnelle*, prob. fr. OE *cumb*, a liquid measure — more at COOMB] *now dial Eng* **:** a large wooden tub for brewing, kneading, and salting meat

ki·mo·no \kə'mōnə *sometimes* -ō(,)nō\ *or* **ki·mo·na** \-ōnə\ *n* -S [Jap *kimono* clothes] **1 :** a loose wraparound robe with wide sleeves and a broad sash traditionally worn by Japanese men and women ⟨a neat waiting maid in striped ~ —*Outlook*⟩ **2 :** a loose dressing gown copied from the Japanese robe and worn chiefly by women and babies — **ki·mo·noed** \-nəd, -nōd\ *or* **ki·mo·naed** \-nəd\ *adj*

kimono 2

kimono sleeve *n* **:** a sleeve cut in one piece with the bodice

kim·ri \'kimrē\ *adj* [Ar] **:** of, relating to, or constituting the first of four recognized stages in the ripening of a date in which it makes its most rapid growth and remains green — compare KHALAL, RUTAB, TAMAR

kim·squit \'kimzkwət, -im(p)skw-\ *n, pl* **kimsquit** *or* **kimsquits** *usu cap* **1 :** a Bellacoola people of Dean Inlet on the Kimsquit river, British Columbia **2 :** a member of the Kimsquit people

1kin \'kin\ *n, pl* **kin** *see sense 1a* [ME, fr. OE *cyn*; akin to OHG *kind* child, *chunni* family, race, ON *kyn*, Goth *kuni* family, race, L *genus* kind, race, *gignere* to beget, Gk *genea* birth, race, family, *genos* race, kin, kind, *gignesthai* to be born, Skt *janati* he begets, *jana* person] **1 a** *pl* **kins :** a group of persons of common ancestry **:** CLAN, STOCK ⟨chiefs of the ~*s* —P.A.Sorokin⟩ **b** *archaic* **:** LINEAGE, EXTRACTION, BIRTH ⟨some one perhaps of gentle ~ —Edmund Spenser⟩ **2 a :** one's immediate family **:** RELATIVES, KINDRED ⟨an outcast among . . . the ~ of his father —Ruth Benedict⟩ **b :** a blood relation **:** KINSMAN ⟨he wasn't any ~ to you —Jean Stafford⟩ — compare CONSANGUINITY **3** *obs* **:** the quality or state of being related **:** KINSHIP ⟨without a crime, except his ~ to me —John Dryden⟩ **4 a :** a related group **:** similar kind **:** ILK ⟨the positivists and their ~ —W.V.Quine⟩ **b :** one having community of interest or close affinity with another ⟨abstraction and generalization have always been recognized as close ~ —John Dewey⟩ — **of kin :** closely related **:** AKIN ⟨he was *of kin* to the . . . prizefighter —*Times Lit. Supp.*⟩

2kin \"\ *adj* **:** of the same nature or family **:** having affinity **:** KINDRED, RELATED ⟨Germany . . . is the ~ land of these people of Pennsylvania —G.P.Musselman⟩

3kin \'kīn\ *chiefly Scot var of* KIND

4kin \'kin\ *n* -S [ME *kyne, kynne*, alter. of *chin, chine* crack, fissure, chasm — more at CHINE] *dial Eng* **:** CRACK, CREVICE; *specif* **:** a chap in the skin

5kin \'kin\ *n, pl* **kin** [Jap] **:** CATTY

6kin \"\ *n* -S [Chin (Pek) *ch'in²*] **:** an ancient Chinese musical instrument resembling a zither and having from 5 to 25 silk strings — compare KOTO

7kin \'jin\ *n* -S *usu cap* [Chin (Pek) *Chin¹*] **1 :** a Tatar people founding an 11th century dynasty in China and being ancestral to the Manchus **2 :** a member of the Kin people

kin- *or* **kine-** *or* **kino-** *or* **cin-** *or* **cino-** *comb form* [Gk *kinēma* motion — more at CINEMATOGRAPH] **:** motion **:** action ⟨*kinesthesia*⟩ ⟨*kinoplasm*⟩ ⟨*kineplasty*⟩

-kin \kən\ *also* **-kins** \-nz\ *n suffix, pl* **-kins** [*-kin* fr. ME, fr. MD *-kin, -ken, -kijn*; akin to OS *-kīn*, dim. suffix, OHG *-chīn*; *-kins* fr. ME, suffix used to form surnames (as *Jenkins*), fr. *-kin* + *-s*, patronymic suffix (as in *Roberts*)] **:** little ⟨*catkin*⟩ ⟨*babykins*⟩

kinaesthesia *or* **kinaesthesis** *var of* KINESTHESIA

ki·nah *also* **qi·nah** \kē'nä\ *n, pl* **ki·noth** *or* **ki·not** *also* **qi·noth** *or* **qi·not** \-nōt(h)\ [Heb *qīnāh* dirge, lamentation] **1 :** a Hebrew elegy chanted traditionally on the Ninth of Ab **2 :** a dirge or lament esp. as sung by Jewish professional mourning women

kinah meter *n* **:** a Hebrew poetic meter typically having the line divided into two stichs with three stresses in the first stich and two stresses in the second

ki·nase \'kī,nās, 'ki,-\ *n* -S [ISV *kinetic* + *-ase*; orig. formed in G] **1 :** a substance (as enterokinase) that converts a zymogen into an enzyme — compare COENZYME **2 :** any of various enzymes (as hexokinases) that promote phosphorylation processes ⟨adenylic ~ or myosine catalyzes the transfer of phosphate groups among the adenosine phosphates⟩ — compare PHOSPHORYLASE

kin·car·dine·shire \kən'kärdᵊn,shi(ə)r, kin'-, -,shər\ *or* **kincardine** *adj, usu cap* [fr. *Kincardineshire* or *Kincardine* county, Scotland] **:** of or from the county of Kincardine, Scotland **:** of the kind or style prevalent in Kincardine

kinch \'kinch\ *n* -ES [alter. of 3*kink*] *chiefly Scot* **:** a noose or loop in a rope

kin·chin \'kinchən\ *n* -S [G *kindchen*, dim. of *kind* child, fr. OHG — more at KIN] *slang* **:** CHILD ⟨~*s* . . . sent on errands by their mothers —Charles Dickens⟩

kin·cob *also* **kin·kob** *or* **kin·khab** \'kin,käb, -iŋ,-\ *n* -S [Hindi *kimkhāb, kamkhwāb*, fr. Per] **:** an Indian brocade usu. of gold or silver or both

1kind \'kīnd\ *n* -S [ME *kind, kinde*, fr. OE *cynd, gecynd*; akin to OE *cyn* kin — more at KIN] **1 a** *archaic* **:** a universal order or inherent tendency in nature ⟨God holds us by laws of ~ —Nathaniel Fairfax⟩ ⟨lovers wanting sight shall follow ~ —Thomas Watson †1592⟩; *specif* **:** natural disposition **b :** a natural grouping without taxonomic connotations **:** SPECIES ⟨people . . . cut off by the desert or the frozen north from communication with their ~ —Ellen Glasgow⟩ ⟨the ways that mud turtles had found best for their ~ —J.W.Krutch⟩ ⟨search for the real essences of natural ~*s* —Stuart Hampshire⟩ **c** *archaic* **:** FAMILY, LINEAGE ⟨of a gentle ~ and noble stock —Shak.⟩ **d** *archaic* **:** a related grouping **:** SECT ⟨poets ever were a careless ~ —William Collins †1759⟩ **2 a** *archaic* **:** STYLE, ASPECT, MANNER, WISE ⟨mirthful . . . but in a stately ~ —Alfred Tennyson⟩ ⟨in no ~ desirous that his majesty should be under any obligation —Thomas Hale⟩ **b** *South & Midland* **:** WAY — used with superlative ⟨he's heartburning the worst ~ over that little gal —*Amer. Guide Series: Tenn.*⟩ ⟨he's goin' to coax his father the hardest ~ —W.D.Howells⟩ **3 a** *obs* **:** SEX ⟨ask . . . what inquest made her dissemble her disguised ~ —Edmund Spenser⟩ **b** *archaic* **:** innate character **:** INSTINCT ⟨though fickle she prove, a woman has't by ~ —Robert Burns⟩ **c :** fundamental nature or quality **:** ESSENCE ⟨problems of social science differ from problems of individual behavior in degree . . . not in ~ —Edward Sapir⟩ **4 a :** a group united by common traits or interests **:** CATEGORY, CLASS ⟨examples of ~*s* of steel are: crucible, Bessemer, basic open-hearth —S.E.Rusinoff⟩ ⟨colonial houses . . . perfect of their ~ —R.W.Hatch⟩ ⟨there are ~*s* of madness which are really forms of inspiration —R.M.Weaver⟩ ⟨the ~ is satire —*Times Lit. Supp.*⟩ ⟨turned to Washington . . . to find companionship among his own ~ —Allen Johnson⟩ ⟨the people I have in mind are the ~ who assume most of the responsibility for unpaid . . . civic duties —J.W.Hoffman⟩ — sometimes used as a zero plural with a preceding *these* or *those* and a following *of* ⟨these ~ of sensational statements —Sir Winston Churchill⟩ **b** (1) **:** a specific variety **:** TYPE, BRAND ⟨one ~ of uniform for all . . . troops —L.H. Smith⟩ ⟨the ~ of analysis followed —W.D.Preston⟩ ⟨what ~ of car do you drive⟩ — often used in the phrase *kind of a* ⟨some ~ of a house is the first requirement of civilized man —L.F.Salzman⟩ ⟨what ~ of an organization —H.E.Gaston⟩ ⟨consider the ~ of a community in which they have faith —Eric Goldman⟩ ⟨that ~ of a girl —Hamilton Basso⟩ (2) **:** a recognized or desirable variety ⟨novel which won all ~*s* of praise —*Saturday Rev.*⟩ ⟨can be more ~*s* of a fool in a short time —W.C.Tuttle⟩ ⟨didn't figure that was any ~ of a life —H.S.Chippendale⟩ **c :** a doubtful or barely admissible member of a specified category — used with *of* and the indefinite article ⟨gave a ~ of snort —John Dos Passos⟩ ⟨the whole universe . . . turned a ~ of gray —H.A.Chippendale⟩ ⟨it's ~ of a vacation —W.H.Whyte⟩ ⟨~ of a blend of humor and pathos⟩ **d :** the same rank — used of playing cards ⟨four of a ~⟩ **5** *Christian relig* **:** either of the elements bread or wine used in the Eucharist ⟨Communion is given in one ~ only in Germany —C.B.Moss⟩ **6 a :** goods or commodities as distinguished from money ⟨economic measures providing aid in ~ rather than in cash —Frank Lorimer⟩ **b :** the equivalent of what has been offered or received ⟨reply in ~⟩ ⟨it hadn't seemed such a terrible thing to hurt him until she was paid back in ~ —William Heuman⟩ **7 :** AMOUNT — used in the phrase *that kind of money* ⟨he's got to be good to pull down that ~ of money —Richard Llewellyn⟩ **syn** see TYPE

2kind \"\ *adj* -ER/-EST [ME *kinde, kind*, fr. OE *gecynde*, fr. *cynd, gecynd*, n.] **1** *obs* **:** consistent with nature **:** NATURAL, FITTING ⟨is but ~ for a cock's head to breed a comb —Stephen Gosson⟩ **2** *now dial* **:** of a good variety or in thriving condition — used of crops ⟨graft . . . ~ fruits upon thorns —John Hales⟩ ⟨the cultivation having been perfect, the barley crop will be ~ —S.C.Scrivener⟩ **3** *now chiefly dial* **a :** of an affectionate nature **:** FOND, INTIMATE ⟨reserve your ~ looks and language for private hours —Jonathan Swift⟩ **b :** GRATEFUL ⟨should declare himself . . . ~ for all those benefits —*Homilies*⟩ **4 a :** of a sympathetic nature **:** FRIENDLY, OBLIGING ⟨was always ~ to the boy —A. Conan Doyle⟩ ⟨everyone is so friendly and ~ —A.J.McConnell⟩ **b :** of a forbearing nature **:** governed by consideration and compassion **:** GENTLE, LENIENT ⟨naturally you are ~ to pets —*Boy Scout Handbook*⟩ ⟨generally was ~ in his judgment of me —O.W.Holmes †1935⟩ **c :** arising from or characterized by sympathy or forbearance ⟨a ~ act⟩ **5** *now chiefly dial* **a :** of a pleasant nature **:** AGREEABLE ⟨the soft green . . . countryside is so ~ to your eyes —Richard Joseph⟩ **b :** soft and yielding to the touch ⟨the wool was . . . ~ to handle —*Westralian Farmers Co-op. Gazette*⟩

syn KIND, KINDLY, BENIGN, and BENIGNANT can mean, in common, having or manifesting a nature that is gentle, considerate, and inclined to benevolent or beneficent actions. KIND and KINDLY, often interchangeable, both suggest gentleness, humaneness, and a sympathetic interest in the welfare of others, KIND applying more often to the disposition to sympathy and helpfulness, KINDLY stressing more the expression of a sympathetic, helpful nature, mood, or impulse ⟨a *kind* person with a *kindly* interest in the problems of others⟩ ⟨a person *kind* to animals⟩ ⟨the *kindly* attentions of an elderly stranger⟩ ⟨the critics were by no means *kind* to the play —J.K.Newnham⟩ ⟨felt *kindly* and protective and superior —Christopher Isherwood⟩ BENIGN and BENIGNANT stress mildness and mercifulness and apply more often to the acts, utterances, or policies, gracious or patronizing, of a superior rather than an equal ⟨a *benign* master⟩ ⟨the *benign* rule of a benevolent despot⟩ ⟨the transformation of a *benign* personality into a belligerent one —Lewis Mumford⟩ ⟨looked up into his *benignant* face, as if she had come thither for his pardon and paternal affection —Nathaniel Hawthorne⟩ ⟨heaven was divinely merciful, infinitely *benignant*. It spared him, pardoned his weakness —Virginia Woolf⟩

3kind \"\ *adv, now dial* **:** KINDLY ⟨how ~ he puts it —Charles Dickens⟩

4kind *vt* -ED/-ING/-S [prob. fr. 1*kind*] *obs* **:** BEGET

kind *abbr* kindergarten

kin·dal \'kindᵊl\ *n* -S [native name in India] **1 :** an Indian tree (*Terminalia paniculata*) with hard gray or grayish-brown wood that resembles black walnut **2 :** the wood of the kindal tree

kinder *comparative of* KIND

kin·der·be·weijs *also* **kin·der·be·wys** \,kində(r)bə'vīs\ *n* -ES [D *kinderbewijs*, fr. *kinder* (pl. of *kind* child) + *bewijs* proof] *Roman Dutch law* **:** a deed by a surviving spouse certifying and securing the amounts due to minor children out of the estate of a deceased

1kin·der·gar·ten *R* 'kində(r),gär|tᵊn, |dᵊn, *-R* -də,gä|\ *n* -S [G, fr. *kinder* (pl. of *kind* child) + *garten* garden] **1 :** a school or division of a school below the first grade usu. serving pupils of the 4 to 6 age group and fostering their natural growth and social development through constructive play with blocks, clay, crayons and by group games, songs, and exercise **2 :** the room or building in which a kindergarten is housed

2kindergarten \"\ *adj* **1 :** of or relating to a kindergarten ⟨teaching at the ~ level⟩ **2 :** of or relating to an elementary level or initial phase ⟨a ~ lecture on the meaning of nationhood —Robert Trumbull⟩ ⟨have as yet only reached the ~ stage in learning how to manage our complex economic problems —A.H.Hansen⟩

kin·der·gart·ner *also* **kin·der·gar·ten·er** \|t(ᵊ)nə(r), |d(ᵊ)n-\ *n* -S [G *kindergärtner*, fr. *kindergarten* + *-er*] **1 :** a child attending kindergarten or of kindergarten age ⟨~*s* and first graders⟩ ⟨pajamas and robes for toddlers and ~*s* —*Parents Mag.*⟩ **2 :** a teacher at the kindergarten level ⟨~, experienced, summer camp —*N.Y.Times*⟩

kin·der·hook \'kində(r),hůk\ *or* **kin·der·hook·ian** \¦==-'hůkēən\ *adj, usu cap* [fr. *Kinderhook*, Pike county, Ill.] **:** of or relating to the lowest formational division of the Mississippian series in the Mississippi valley or the epoch of its deposition — see GEOLOGIC TIME table

kindest *superlative of* KIND

kindhearted \'==¦==\ *adj* **:** having a sympathetic nature **:** HUMANE, COMPASSIONATE ⟨a ~ landlord — ever anxious to ameliorate the condition of the poor —Anthony Trollope⟩ — **kind·heart·ed·ly** *adv*

kind·heart·ed·ness *n* -ES **:** the quality or state of being kindhearted

1kin·dle \'kindᵊl, *rapid* -nᵊl\ *vb* **kindled; kindled; kindling** \-(ᵊ)liŋ\ **kindles** [ME *kindlen*, fr. ON *kynda* to kindle + ME *-len* -le; akin to MHG *künten, künden* to kindle, OHG *cuntesal* fire] *vt* **1 :** to start (a fire) burning **:** LIGHT, IGNITE ⟨~ a fire with a match⟩ **2 a :** to awaken or intensify to awareness ⟨armies cannot be raised . . . unless the rage of the people is first *kindled* by lies and name-calling —Kenneth Roberts⟩ ⟨these two delightful . . . handbooks should ~ a child's imagination —Muna Lee⟩ **b :** to stir up **:** AROUSE, INSPIRE ⟨his enthusiasm ~*s* his comrades⟩ ⟨hopes that . . . *kindled* close to half of France —Janet Flanner⟩ **c :** to bring into being **:** INSTITUTE ⟨the Good Neighbor policy . . . which was *kindled* by Sumner Welles —A.C.Wilgus⟩ **3 :** to cause to glow **:** ILLUMINATE ⟨animation *kindling* his pale face —A.J.Cronin⟩ ⟨*kindling* with color the pale lichens —Thomas Vance⟩ ~ *vi* **1 a :** to start a fire ⟨some fire to ~ with —Stith Thompson⟩ **b :** to begin to burn **:** catch fire ⟨dry leaves ~ at the touch of flame⟩ **2 a :** to flare up **:** gather intensity ⟨their mutual resentment again *kindled* —Edward Gibbon⟩ **b :** to grow warm or animated **:** become stirred emotionally ⟨no boy will fail to ~ to the struggles of his California youth —Ethna Sheehan⟩ **3 :** to sparkle or become illuminated as if with fire **:** GLOW ⟨light *kindled* in the liquor —Frances G. Patton⟩ ⟨could see her eyes widen, ~ and flinch —John Fountain⟩

2kindle \"\ *n* -S [ME, prob. fr. *kinde, kind*, n., kind + *-le* — more at KIND] *now dial* **:** the young of an animal **:** LITTER ⟨a ~ of kittens⟩ — **in kindle :** PREGNANT — used chiefly of a rabbit

3kindle \"\ *vb* **kindled; kindled; kindling; kindles** [ME *kindlen*, prob. fr. *kindle*, n.] *vt* **:** to give birth to **:** BEAR ⟨one of our does *kindled* a single rabbit —*Amer. Small Stock Farmer*⟩ ~ *vi* **:** to bring forth young ⟨bred one of the Angora does to ~ about the time I would be making the move —*Standard Rabbit Jour.*⟩ — now used chiefly of a rabbit

kindle-coal *or* **kindle-fire** *n* ['1*kindle*] *obs* **:** one that stirs up strife ⟨Satan is the great *kindle-coal* —William Gurnall⟩

kin·dler \'kind(ᵊ)lə(r), *rapid* -n(ᵊ)l-\ *n* -S [ME, fr. *kindlen* + *-er*] **1 :** one that kindles **2 :** KINDLING 2

kind·less \'kīndləs, *rapid* -nl-\ *adj* ['*kind* + *-less*] **1** *obs* **:** INHUMAN ⟨remorseless, treacherous, lecherous, ~ villain —Shak.⟩ **2 :** DISAGREEABLE, UNSYMPATHETIC, UNCONGENIAL ⟨no thought less kindly — toward even thee that are ~ —A.C. Swinburne⟩ ⟨the unreturned of ~ land and sea —Walter de la Mare⟩ — **kind·less·ly** *adv*

kind·li·ness \'kīndlēnəs, -lin-, *rapid* -nl-\ *n* -ES [ME *kindlinesse*, fr. *kindly* + *-nesse* -ness] **1 :** the quality or state of being kindly **:** FRIENDLINESS, BENEVOLENCE **2 :** the quality or state of being agreeable or manageable **:** PLEASANTNESS, TRACTABILITY ⟨~ of climate⟩ ⟨~ of feel . . . makes esparto papers preeminent for their printing qualities —F.H.Norris⟩ ⟨steel of the future will be very different in ~ of working —William Metcalf⟩

1kin·dling \'kindliŋ, -lēŋ, *rapid* -nl-\ *n* -S [ME, fr. gerund of *kindlen* to kindle (ignite) — more at 1KINDLE] **1 a :** an act or instance of igniting ⟨the ~ of a bonfire⟩ **b :** an act or instance of exciting or causing to glow ⟨a ~ of enthusiasm⟩ ⟨looking at the sunset, watching the ~ of the clouds —Susan Ertz⟩ **2 :** easily combustible material of a convenient size for starting a fire ⟨crumpled paper makes good ~ for the stove⟩ ⟨a famous old covered bridge that was carried away and crushed to ~ . . . in the spring flood —*Amer. Guide Series: Conn.*⟩

2kindling \"\ *n* -S [ME, fr. gerund of *kindlen* (to give birth) — more at 3KINDLE] **:** an act of giving birth — used chiefly of a rabbit

kindling temperature *or* **kindling point** *n* **:** IGNITION TEMPERATURE

kindling wood *n* **:** wood of a size or kind to kindle readily — called also *fat pine, lightwood, pine, pitch pine, rich-pine*

1kind·ly \'kīndlē, -li, *rapid* -nl-\ *adj* -ER/-EST [ME, fr. OE *cyndelic, gecyndelic*, fr. *cynd, gecynd* kind + *-līc* -ly — more at KIND] **1 a** *obs* **:** consistent with nature **:** NATURAL, APPROPRIATE ⟨the earth shall sooner leave her ~ skill to bring forth fruit —Edmund Spenser⟩ **b** *archaic* **:** related by birth or blood **:** HEREDITARY, LEGITIMATE ⟨their ~ possessions which . . . their predecessors and they had kept —John Spalding⟩ ⟨he must be a genuine or ~ son —W.E.Hearn⟩ **2 :** of an agreeable or beneficial nature **:** PLEASANT, FAVORABLE ⟨~ climate⟩ ⟨the soil is ~ to my feet —K.M.Dodson⟩ ⟨a ~ half century —Sinclair Lewis⟩ ⟨two of these periods . . . were most ~ toward his profession of architect —*Times Lit. Supp.*⟩ **3 :** KIND 2 **4 a :** of a sympathetic or generous nature **:** FRIENDLY, BENEVOLENT ⟨was greatly pleased and for that day . . . more ~ with her —Pearl Buck⟩ ⟨benefited greatly from their charity and ~ interest in him —Raymond Holden⟩ ⟨homespun, ~, shrewd men whose strength resided in their neighborliness —Norman Cousins⟩ **b :** expressive of a sympathetic nature ⟨~ look⟩ ⟨~ eye⟩ **5 :** SEA-KINDLY **syn** see KIND

2kindly \"\ *adv, sometimes* -ER/-EST [ME, fr. OE *cyndelice, gecyndelice*, fr. *cyndelic, gecyndelic*, adj.] **1 a :** in the normal way **:** NATURALLY ⟨old wounds which had healed ~ —*Amer. Mercury*⟩ **b :** in a natural way **:** READILY, SPONTANEOUSLY ⟨nearing the three furlongs he . . . was galloping ~ —*Sydney (Australia) Sunday Telegraph*⟩ — often used with *take to* ⟨a wild, fleet-footed people, who did not take ~ to restraint —R.A.Billington⟩ ⟨unadorned styles which some audiences take to more ~ than to . . . polished grace —Robert Bendiner⟩ **2 a :** in a kind manner **:** SYMPATHETICALLY, GENEROUSLY ⟨treats his horse ~ and never uses spurs⟩ ⟨the foundation is not looking ~ upon requests for grants⟩ **b :** in an appreciative manner **:** as a gesture of good will ⟨takes criticism ~⟩ ⟨would take it ~ if you would put in a good word for the boy⟩ **c :** in a gracious or considerate manner **:** COURTEOUSLY, OBLIGINGLY ⟨the party which I was ~ invited to join —Anthony Trollope⟩ ⟨the encipherer had ~ divided the words of his message off with commas —Fletcher Pratt⟩ ⟨~ fill out the attached questionnaire⟩ **3** *chiefly South* **:** in a way **:** RATHER ⟨going up the hollow was ~ like going up a big green tunnel —J.H.Stuart⟩

kindly tenant *n, Scots law, obs* **:** a tenant favored with a low or easy rent because his landlord wanted to favor him or believed him a descendant of an original possessor of the land

kind·ness \'kīnnəs *also* -ndnəs\ *n* -ES [ME *kindenesse*, fr. *kinde, kind* + *-nesse* -ness] **1 :** an act or instance of being kind **:** FAVOR ⟨a well-established lawyer did a great ~ in taking into his office this young man —Ruth P. Randall⟩ **2 a :** the quality or state of being kind **:** SYMPATHY, CLEMENCY ⟨man's supreme manifestation of the spirit is ~ —Albert Schweitzer⟩ ⟨cooler air . . . enwrapped him in its ~ —Joseph Whitehill⟩ **b** *archaic* **:** a feeling of fondness **:** AFFECTION, LOVE ⟨a lady for whom he had once entertained a sneaking ~ —Washington Irving⟩

kind of \'kīndə(v), -dē,-di,-dər\ *adv* **:** to a moderate degree or extent **:** RATHER, PARTLY ⟨I *kind of* like you all the same —Robert Westerby⟩ ⟨the wind *kind of* slowed up after while —Vance Randolph⟩

1kin·dred \'kindrəd\ *n, pl* **kindred** *see sense 1a* [ME *kinrede, kindrede*, fr. 1*kin* + *-rede* (fr. OE *rǣden* condition, rule, estimation, fr. *rǣdan* to advise, rule, guess, read) — more at READ] **1 a** *pl* **kindreds :** a natural grouping **:** PEOPLE, POPULATION ⟨every ~, every tribe on this terrestrial ball —Edward Perronet⟩ ⟨among the winter-scourged ~*s* —C.G.D.Roberts⟩ **b** (1) **:** a group of related individuals **:** FAMILY, CLAN ⟨the ~ has an organic quality; what happens to the individual member is felt by the whole group —A.D.Rees⟩ (2) **:** RELATIVES ⟨if his ~ still remain to him —Alexis de Tocqueville⟩ **c :** a genealogical group **:** LINEAGE ⟨study the incidence of cancer among members of a ~⟩ **2** *archaic* **a :** relationship by blood or marriage **:** KINSHIP ⟨a secret match . . . raised him to ~ with the throne —J.R.Green⟩ **b :** possession of similar qualities **:** AFFINITY ⟨thy ~ with the great of old — Alfred Tennyson⟩

2kindred \"\ *adj* **1 a :** of an allied nature **:** SIMILAR ⟨pamphlets of a ~ sort —G.C.Sellery⟩ ⟨an auditorium for concerts, lectures, and ~ events⟩ **b :** having common qualities or stemming from the same source **:** CONGENIAL, RELATED ⟨~ spirit⟩ ⟨~ arts of music, painting and letters —Elinor Wylie⟩ ⟨~ Germanic languages⟩ ⟨sound waves . . . penetrate to the listener's inner ear and there set up ~ vibrations —Charlton Laird⟩ **2** *archaic* **a :** of the same ancestry **:** COGNATE ⟨countries . . . already occupied by their ~ tribes —Edward Gibbon⟩ **b :** of, relating to, or done by a kinsman ⟨what ~ crime . . . am I decreed to expiate —Tobias Smollett⟩

kin·dred·less \-ədləs\ *adj* **:** not having kindred

kin·dred·ness *n* -ES **:** the quality or state of being related **:** KINSHIP

kin·dred·ship \-əd,ship\ *n* **:** KINSHIP

kinds *pl of* KIND, *pres 3d sing of* KIND

1kine \'kīn\ *archaic pl of* COW

2kine \'kinē\ *var of* CINE

3kine \"\ *n* -S [by shortening] **:** KINESCOPE

kine- — see KIN-

ki·ne·ma \'kinəmə\ *var of* CINEMA

kinema red *n* **:** GOYA

1kin·e·mat·ic \¦kinə¦mad·|ik, ¦kīn-, -at|, |ēk\ *also* **kin·e·mat·i·cal** \|əkəl, |ēk-\ *adj* [back-formation fr. *kinematics*] **1 :** of or relating to kinematics or the motions of bodies **2 :** of or relating to mechanical elements having relative motion — compare PAIR 2a(8) — **kin·e·mat·i·cal·ly** \|ək(ə)lē, |ēk-, -li\ *adv*

2kinematic \"\ *var of* CINEMATIC

kin·e·mat·ics \|iks, |ēks\ *also* **cin·e·mat·ics** \'sin-\ *n pl but sing in constr* [modif. (influenced by Gk *kinēmat-, kinēma* motion) of F *cinématique*, fr. Gk *kinēmat-, kinēma* + F *-ique* -ics — more at CINEMATOGRAPH] **:** a branch of dynamics that deals with aspects of motion (as acceleration and velocity) apart from considerations of mass and force

kinematic viscosity *n* : COEFFICIENT OF KINEMATIC VISCOSITY

kin·e·mat·o·graph \ˌkinəˈmadəˌgraf, ˌkīn-, -atə-, -ˌrȧf\ *var of* CINEMATOGRAPH

kin·e·ma·tog·ra·phy \ˌkinəməˈtägrəfē, ˌkīn-, -fi\ *var of* CINEMATOGRAPHY

kin·e·plas·ty \ˈkinəˌplastē, ˈkīn-\ *var of* CINEPLASTY

kinepox \ˈ=ˌ=\ *n* [¹*kine* + *pox*] : COWPOX

kin·e·sal·gia \ˌkinəˈsalj(ē)ə, ˌkīn-\ *n* -S [NL, fr. *kinesis* + *-algia*] : pain occurring in conjunction with muscle action

¹kin·e·scope \ˈkinəˌskōp\ *n* [fr. *Kinescope*, a trademark] **1** : a cathode-ray tube having at one end a screen of luminescent material on which are produced visible images (as television pictures or oscillograph curves) **2** : a motion picture made from a kinescope image

²kinescope \"\ *vt* **kinescoped**; **kinescoped**; **kinescoping**; **kinescopes** : to make a kinescope of (a television program)

kinesi- *or* **kinesio-** *comb form* [Gk *kinēsi-*, fr. *kinēsis* motion — more at KINESIS] : movement : motion ⟨*kinesi*meter⟩ ⟨*kinesi*ology⟩

-ki·ne·sia \kəˈnēzh(ē)ə, ˌkīˈ-\ *or* **-ci·ne·sia** \səˈ-, ˌsīˈ-\ *n comb form* -S [NL, fr. Gk *-kinēsia*, fr. *kinēsis*] : movement : motion ⟨hyper*kinesia*⟩ ⟨para*kinesia*⟩

ki·ne·si·at·rics \kəˌnēsēˈa·triks, kī,-, -ēzē-\ *n pl but sing in constr* [ISV *kinesi-* + *-iatrics*] : KINESITHERAPY

ki·ne·sic \kəˈnēs|ik (ˌ)kī¦n-, -ēz|\ *adj* [Gk *kinēsis* + E *-ic*] : of or relating to kinesics ⟨~ investigation⟩ — **ki·ne·si·cal·ly** \|ək(ə)lē\ *adv*

ki·ne·sics \kəˈnēsiks, kīˈ-, -ēzi-\ *n pl but sing in constr* [Gk *kinēsis* + E *-ics*] : a systematic study of nonlinguistic body motion (as blushes, shrugs, waves) in its relation to communication ⟨man did not become truly human until he developed spoken language but one might guess that for millennia ~ was the . . . mode of communication —Stuart Chase⟩

kin·e·sim·e·ter \ˌkinəˈsimədə(r), ˌkīn-\ *also* **ki·ne·si·om·e·ter** \kəˌnēsēˈämə-, kī,-, -ēzē-\ *n* [*kinesi-* + *-meter*] : an instrument for measuring bodily movements

ki·ne·si·o·log·ic \kə¦nēsēə¦läjik, kī¦n-, -ēzē-\ *or* **ki·ne·si·o·log·i·cal** \-jəkəl\ *adj* : of, relating to, or involving the methods of kinesiology

ki·ne·si·ol·o·gy \=ˌnēsēˈäləjē, -ēzē-\ *n* -ES [*kinesi-* + *-logy*] **1** : study of the principles of mechanics and anatomy in relation to human movement ⟨~ of corrective exercise⟩ ⟨~ of the ethnic dance⟩ **2** : KINESITHERAPY

ki·ne·sis \kəˈnēsəs, kīˈ-\ *or* **ci·ne·sis** \səˈ-, sīˈ-\ *n, pl* **kineses** *or* **cineses** \-ēˌsēz\ [NL, fr. Gk *kinēsis* motion, fr. *kinein* to move + *-sis*; akin to L *ciēre* to move — more at CITE] **1** : physical movement including quantitative, qualitative, and positional change **2** : movement that is induced by stimulation (as by light) and is not specifically orienting — compare TAXIS

-ki·ne·sis \kəˈnēsəs, ˌkīˈ-\ *n comb form, pl* **-kineses** [NL, fr. Gk *kinēsis*] **1** : activation ⟨chemo*kinesis*⟩ ⟨photo*kinesis*⟩ **2** : division ⟨karyo*kinesis*⟩

ki·ne·si·therapy \kə¦nēsē, kī¦nēsē+\ *n* [ISV *kinesi-* + *therapy*] : the therapeutic and corrective application of passive and active movements (as by massage) and of exercise

kin·es·the·sia \ˌkinəsˈthēzh(ē)ə *sometimes* ˌkīn-\ *or* **kin·es·the·sis** \-ˈthēsəs\ *also* **kin·aes·the·sia** *or* **kin·aes·the·sis** \ˌkinəs- *sometimes* ˌkīn-\ *n, pl* **kinesthesias** *or* **kinestheses** [NL, fr. *kin-* + *esthesia or esthesis*] **1** : a sense mediated by end organs that lie in the muscles, tendons, and joints and are stimulated by bodily movements and tensions : MUSCLE SENSE **2** : the sensory experience derived from the muscle sense

kin·es·thet·ic *also* **kin·aes·thet·ic** \¦==ˈthed·|ik, -et|, |ēk\ *adj* [fr. NL *kinesthesia*, after such pairs as NL *anesthesia*: E *anesthetic*] : of or relating to bodily reaction or motor memory ⟨get ~ pleasure from watching skaters waltz⟩ ⟨seldom had a ~ image of the first weight at the moment of lifting . . . the second —R.S.Woodworth⟩ — **kin·es·thet·i·cal·ly** *also* **kin·aes·thet·i·cal·ly** \|ək(ə)lē, |ēk-, -li\ *adv*

kinet- *or* **kineto-** *also* **cinet-** *or* **cineto-** *comb form* [Gk *kinētos* moving — more at KINETIC] : movement : motion ⟨*kineto*genic⟩

ki·net·ic \kəˈned·|ik, (ˈ)kī¦n-, -et|, |ēk\ *adj* [Gk *kinētikos* of motion, fr. *kinētos* moving (fr. *kinein* to move) + *-ikos* -ic — more at KINESIS] **1** : relating to kinetics or to the motion of material bodies and the forces and energy associated therewith **2 a** : of or relating to motion : ACTIVE, LIVELY ⟨modern dance has been called ~ pantomime⟩ ⟨a ~ world with mobility . . . as its keynote —F.D.Graham⟩ **b** : supplying motive force : ENERGIZING, DYNAMIC ⟨jumped to attention . . . upon the ~ arrival of the master —S.N.Behrman⟩ ⟨a ~ artist . . . inflames the passions of readers —*Saturday Rev.*⟩ ⟨a ~, creative force —*N.Y.Times*⟩ ⟨the complex civilization of which Rome was the ~ center —H.O.Taylor⟩ **3** : of or relating to kinesis ⟨~ occupational therapy⟩ ⟨response to light may be ~ —V.B. Wigglesworth⟩ **4** : KINESTHETIC ⟨in the concert hall . . . listening to actual musical sound enriched by the ~ force of human participation —Goddard Lieberson⟩

ki·net·i·cal·ly \|ək(ə)lē\ *adv* : in a kinetic manner

kinetic energy *n* : energy (sense 5) that is associated with motion

kinetic friction *n* : SLIDING FRICTION

kinetic potential *n* : the difference between the kinetic energy and the potential energy of a dynamic system expressed as a function of the position coordinates and their time derivatives — called also *Lagrangian function*

ki·netics \kəˈned·|iks, kīˈ-, -et|, |ēks\ *n pl but sing or pl in constr* **1** : a branch of dynamics that deals with the effects of forces upon the motions of material bodies **2 a** : a branch of physical science that deals with the rate of change in a physical or chemical system; *specif* : REACTION KINETICS **b** : the rate of change or reaction in such a system **c** : the mechanism by which a physical or chemical change is effected ⟨the ~ of the acid-catalyzed reaction between organic acids and alcohols —C.E.Leyes⟩

kinetic theory *n* : a theory in physics: the minute particles of a substance are in vigorous motion on the assumptions that (1) the particles of a gas move in straight lines with high average velocity, continually encounter one another and thus change their individual velocities and directions, and cause pressure by their impact against the walls of a container and that (2) the temperature of a substance increases with an increase in either the average kinetic energy of the particles or the average potential energy of separation (as in fusion) of the particles or in both when heat is added — called also respectively (1) *kinetic theory of gases*, (2) *kinetic theory of heat*

ki·ne·to·chore \kəˈnēd·əˌkō(ə)r, kīˈ-, -nel, |t|, |ō,-, -kȯ(ə)r\ *n* -S [*kinet-* + Gk *chōros* place — more at CHOR-] : CENTROMERE

ki·ne·to·gen·e·sis \=¦==ˈjenəsəs\ *n* [NL, fr. *kinet-* + L *genesis*] : evolution of animal structures presumed to be due to animal movements — **ki·ne·to·ge·net·ic** \=¦==jə¦ned·ik\ *adj* — **ki·ne·to·ge·net·i·cal·ly** \-d·ək(ə)lē\ *adv*

ki·ne·to·graph \=ˈ==ˌgraf, -ˌrȧf\ *n* [*kinet-* + *-graph*] : an apparatus for taking a series of photographs of moving objects for examination with the kinetoscope — **ki·ne·to·graph·ic** \=¦==¦grafik\ *adj*

ki·ne·to·ne·ma \=¦==ˈnēmə\ *n, pl* **kinetonema·ta** \-məd·ə\ [NL, fr. *kinet-* + *-nema*] : a modified portion of chromonema associated with the centromere

ki·ne·to·nucleus \=¦==+\ *n* [NL, fr. *kinet-* + *nucleus*] : a kinetoplast formerly thought to be a secondary nucleus exclusively concerned with motor activities — compare TROPHONUCLEUS

ki·ne·to·phone \=ˈ==ˌfōn\ *n* [*kinet-* + *-phone*] : a machine combining a kinetoscope and a phonograph synchronized so as to produce the illusion of motion in a scene with accompanying sounds

ki·ne·to·phonograph \=¦==+\ *n* [*kinet-* + *phonograph*] : KINETOPHONE

ki·ne·to·plast \=ˈ==ˌplast\ *also* **ci·ne·to·plast** \səˈ-, sīˈ-\ *n* -S [ISV *kinet-* + *-plast*] : a complex cell structure made up of basal granules, associated fibrils, and related bodies found in association with the base of certain flagella and undulating membranes and regarded as actively concerned with the motility of these structures

Ki·ne·to·scope \kəˈ==ˌskōp, kīˈ-\ *trademark* — used for a device for viewing through a magnifying lens a sequence of pictures of a changing scene on an endless band of film moved continuously over a light source and a rapidly rotating shutter that creates an illusion of motion

kin·e·to·sis \ˌkinəˈtōsəs, ˌkīn-\ *n, pl* **kineto·ses** \-ōˌsēz\ [NL, fr. *kinet-* + *-osis*] : MOTION SICKNESS

kin·folk \ˈkinˌfōk\ *also* **kins·folk** \-nz,-\ *n pl* [*kinfolk* alter. of *kinsfolk*; *kinsfolk* fr. ME *kynsefolke*, fr. *kynse*, *kinnes* (gen. of ¹*kin*) + *folke*, *folk* folk] : RELATIVES

¹king \ˈkiŋ\ *n* -S *except sense 13a, often attrib* [ME, fr. OE *kyning*, *cyning*; akin to OS & OHG *kuning*, *kunig* king, ON *konungr*; all fr. a prehistoric WGmc-NGmc compound whose first constituent is represented by E ¹*kin*, and whose second constituent is represented by E *-ing* (n. suffix)] **1 a** : a male monarch who reigns over a major territorial unit : the ruler of a kingdom ⟨~*s* were makers of the laws —James I⟩ ⟨distinguish between the ~ and the crown —C.H.McIlwain⟩ ⟨in . . . Britain the sovereign is not the *King* but the King-in-Parliament —W.H.Wickwar⟩ **b** : the paramount or an esp. important chief (as the head of an Indian or African tribe) ⟨occupied by Shingess, ~ of the Delawares —A.S.Withers⟩ **2** *cap* : GOD, CHRIST 1 ⟨to worship the *King*, the Lord of hosts —Zech 14:16 (RSV)⟩ ⟨that the *King* of glory may come in —Ps 24:7 (RSV)⟩ **3** : one that holds a supreme or preeminent position in a particular sphere or class; *esp* : a chief among competitors ⟨the cattle ~*s* rode up from the south —Alan Moorehead⟩ ⟨even if no longer ~, cotton remains the chief cash crop —Howell Walker⟩ ⟨this ~ of books —*Brit. Bk. Centre*⟩ ⟨their ~*s* of steel and oil and chemicals —*Nation*⟩ **4** *obs* : QUEEN BEE **5** : the principal piece in a set of chessmen that may move ordinarily one square in any direction and has the power of capture but is obliged never to enter or remain in exposure to capture **6** : a playing card marked with a stylized figure of a king and usu. the initial letter K **7** : one that occupies a position like that of or plays the part of a male monarch — often used in real or mock titles ⟨*King* of Arms of the Order of the Garter —A.L.Wagner⟩ ⟨a decorated float carrying the *King* of Misrule —*Springfield (Mass.) Daily News*⟩ ⟨in all the school games he was the ~ —Robert Graves⟩ ⟨~ of the club's annual hobby show —*Springfield (Mass.) Union*⟩ ⟨public opinion is ~ —L.W.Doob⟩ **8** : any of a class of fuller's teasels **9** : a checker that as a result of reaching an opponent's king row has been crowned and given the power of moving backward as well as forward **10** : the second officer in a Royal Arch chapter of Masons **11** : a sexually mature male termite **12** : KING SALMON ⟨fisherman who come . . . to catch the ~*s* —R.L.Haig-Brown⟩ **13 a** *usu cap* : an American breed of large vigorous utility pigeons developed to produce large numbers of squabs that weigh about one pound at four weeks of age **b** *often cap* : any pigeon of the King breed ⟨not bred so extensively as the white *King* —Rudolph Seiden⟩ **14** : a king-size cigarette

²king \"\ *vb* -ED/-ING/-S [ME *kingen*, fr. *king*, n.] *vi* : to act the king : RULE — usu. used with *it* ⟨in our . . . country science ~*s* it over the realm of intellectual discourse —Clifton Fadiman⟩ ~ *vt* **1** : to cause to be a king ⟨then am I ~*ed* again —Shak.⟩ **2** *archaic* : GOVERN ⟨England . . . is so idly ~*ed* —Shak.⟩

³king \"\ *usu cap* — a communications code word for the letter *k*

king al·fred's candle \-ˈalfrədz-\ *n, usu cap K&A* [after *Alfred* the Great †901 king of the West Saxons in England; fr. the belief that he developed such a device] : an early time-telling device consisting of a candle marked off in time bands to show the passage of time by the amount the candle burns down

king at arms *often cap K&A* : KING OF ARMS — not in official use

king auk *n* **1** : GREAT AUK **2** : DOVEKIE 2

king ball *n* : a red or black ball that is placed on a white spot in front of the holes on a bagatelle board and that must be struck by one of the other balls before a score can be made

kingbird \ˈ=ˌ=\ *n, often cap* : any of various American tyrant flycatchers — see ARKANSAS KINGBIRD, CASSIN'S KINGBIRD, EASTERN KINGBIRD, GRAY KINGBIRD

king blossom *n* : the large central flower in a cluster of apple flowers on the fruiting spur

kingbolt \ˈ=ˌ=\ *n* **1** : a vertical bolt by which the forward axle and wheels of a vehicle or the trucks of a railroad car are connected with the other parts **2** : an iron tie rod used in place of a king post in the construction of a roof

king carp *n* : MIRROR CARP

king charles's head \-ˈchärlz(əz)-\ *n, usu cap K&C* [after *Charles* I †1649 king of England, who was beheaded; fr. the habit of Mr. Dick, character in *David Copperfield*, novel by Charles Dickens †1870 Eng. novelist, of introducing the subject of King Charles's head into all discussions] : OBSESSION 3 ⟨that *King Charles's head* of modern America, the menace of Communism —*Times Lit. Supp.*⟩

king charles spaniel \-lz-\ *n, usu cap K&C* [after *Charles* II †1685 king of England, who was fond of such dogs] : a dog of a black and tan variety of the English toy spaniel

king closer *n* : a closer bigger than half a brick; *specif* : a brick with one corner cut away making the header at that end half the width of the brick — compare QUEEN CLOSER

king cobra *n* : a large and very venomous elapid snake (*Naja hannah*) found from India to southern China and the Philippines and attaining a length of 12 feet or more — called also *hamadryad*

king conch *n* : a large conch (*Strombus gigas*) with a pink outer shell often used in cameo cutting; *also* : any of certain other large conchs or helmet shells — compare QUEEN CONCH

king crab *n* **1** : any of several closely related large marine arthropods of eastern No. America and eastern Asia constituting the only surviving members of the order Xiphosura and class Merostomata and having a broad crescentic cephalothorax with a pair of large compound eyes and two simple eyes on the upper surface and six pairs of legs arising from the lower surface about the centrally placed mouth, a small abdomen articulated to the cephalothorax with its segments fused into a single piece, swimming appendages to which the flat leaflike gills are attached, and a long stiff movably articulated caudal spine; *esp* : an arthropod (*Limulus polyphemus* syn. *Xiphosurus polyphemus*) found on sandy and muddy bottoms on the coasts of No. America from Maine to Mexico and the West Indies that attains a length of nearly two feet — called also *horseshoe crab* **2 a** : a large European spider crab (*Maia squinado*) **b** : a large scarlet anomuran crab (*Lopholithodes mandtii*) of shallow water from California to Alaska **c** : the largest of the edible crabs (*Paralithodes camtschaticus*) often measuring five feet from claw tip to claw tip, weighing up to 15 pounds, and widely distributed in the No. Pacific

kingcraft \ˈ=ˌ=\ *n* **1** : the art of governing as a king; *esp* : the use of clever tactics or cunning in exercising the functions of kingship ⟨a sort of correspondence course in ~ —Dorothy M. Stuart⟩ **2** : the craft or profession of a king ⟨to abolish ~, priestcraft, caste, monopoly —Walt Whitman⟩

king crow *n* : BLACK DRONGO

kingcup \ˈ=ˌ=\ *also* **kingcob** \ˈ=ˌ=\ *n* **1** : any of various common buttercups (as *Ranunculus bulbosus*, *R. acris*, or *R. repens*) **2** : a marsh marigold (*Caltha palustris*)

king devil *n* : any of various European hawkweeds (esp. *Hieracium praealtum*) that have been introduced into and are locally troublesome weeds in the northeastern U.S.

king·dom \ˈkiŋdəm\ *n* -S [ME, fr. OE *cyningdōm*, fr. *cyning* king + *-dōm* -dom — more at KING] **1** *obs* : KINGSHIP **2 a** : a major territorial unit subject to a monarchical form of government usu. headed by a king or queen : the realm of a king ⟨inclusion of additional provinces in the Italian ~⟩ ⟨when plantations were like small ~*s* —William Beebe⟩ ⟨travels through the ~*s* of Europe⟩ — compare EMPIRE 1a, PRINCIPALITY **3** : a politically organized community (as a nation or state) having a monarchical form of government usu. headed by a king ⟨the new Christian ~*s* found themselves at war with the Barbary —C.S.Forester⟩ ⟨decreed Spain a ~ (without a king) —S.G.Rich⟩ **4** *often cap* **a** : the eternal kingship or sovereignty of God ⟨Jesus, to whom the authority of the ~ is delegated, heals sickness —R.H.Strachan⟩ **b** : the spiritual realm over which God reigns as king : HEAVEN ⟨all I now have is what my Father is keeping . . . for us in His ~ —*Voice of Prophecy News*⟩ **c** : the fulfillment on earth of God's will esp. in complete perfection ⟨the time is fulfilled, and the ~ of God is at hand —Mk 1:14 (RSV)⟩ **d** : the invisible society of human beings in which God is held to be obeyed ⟨members of the ~ were to strive to be examples of the life which God deemed ideal for men —K.S.Latourette⟩ **5** : a realm or region in which something is dominant ⟨the rise of a ~ of wheat in the Old Northwest —W.O.Lynch⟩ ⟨in the untroubled ~ of reason —Bertrand Russell⟩ ⟨a cattle ~⟩ **6** : one of the three primary divisions into which natural objects are commonly classified — see ANIMAL KINGDOM, MINERAL KINGDOM, PLANT KINGDOM **7** : an area or sphere in which one exercises authority like a king ⟨his gambling ~ —Dean Jennings⟩ ⟨busy . . . increasing the size and ornamentations of our personal ~*s* —*Saturday Rev.*⟩ **8** : a hostel for men or for women that provides living quarters at low cost to members of a religious movement among Negroes in the U.S. known as Father Divine's Peace Mission Movement ⟨with Father Divine . . . at a meeting in one of his ~*s* —M.L.Bach⟩

kingdom come *n* [fr. the phrase *Thy kingdom come* in the *Lord's Prayer*] : the next world : HEAVEN ⟨the guns that would blow everyone to *kingdom come* —Meridel Le Sueur⟩

king·domed \ˈkiŋdəmd\ *adj* **1** : ROYAL ⟨~ Achilles in commotion rages —Shak.⟩ **2** : consisting of more than one kingdom — often used in combination ⟨a multi*kingdomed* confederation⟩

kingdom hall *n, usu cap K&H* : a local Jehovah's Witnesses meeting place where religious services are held

kingdomtide \ˈ==ˌ=\ *n, often cap* : a season of the church year preceding Advent and observed by some Christians as a time for emphasizing the message of the kingdom of God

king eagle *n* : IMPERIAL EAGLE

kinged *past of* KING

king eider *or* **king duck** *n* : a circumpolar eider duck (*Somateria spectabilis*) having very large lateral gibbous processes at the base of the bill

king-emperor \ˈ=ˈ=(=)=\ *n* : a king who is also ruler of an empire; *specif* : the British monarch in his onetime capacity as emperor of India ⟨the darling of the Saxon *king-emperors* —F.H.Cramer⟩ ⟨the . . . *king-emperor* of one fourth of the world —*Literary Digest*⟩

king fern *n* : ROYAL FERN

kingfish \ˈ=ˌ=\ *n* **1 a** : any of several marine croakers of the family Sciaenidae: as (1) : a whiting (*Menticirrhus saxatilis*) of the No. American Atlantic coast (2) : a small silvery California food fish (*Genyonemus lineatus*) — called also *chenfish* (3) : MULLOWAY **b** : any of various scombroid fishes; *esp* : CERO **c** : any of various marine percoid fishes esp. of the family Carangidae (as an amberfish) **2** : an undisputed master in an area or group : COCK OF THE WALK ⟨the ~ in the gem trade in the whole Persian gulf —*Amarillo (Texas) Sunday News-Globe*⟩ ⟨the ~ of San Antonio's underworld —*Survey Graphic*⟩

king·fish·er \ˈkiŋˌfishə(r)\ *n* : any of numerous nonpasserine birds constituting the family Alcedinidae that are usu. crested and bright-colored with a rather short tail, long stout sharp bill, and weak syndactyl feet — see ALCEDO, BELTED KINGFISHER, DACELO, KOOKABURRA

kingfisher daisy *n* : a densely hairy annual herb (*Felicia bergeriana*) of the family Compositae found in southern Africa that is used as an ornamental and has bright blue ray flowers and a yellow disk

king hair *n* : GUARD HAIR

king har·ry \-ˈhari\ *n, usu cap K&H* [after one of the *King Henrys* of England; so called fr. its conspicuous crown] *dial Eng* : GOLDFINCH

kinghead \ˈ=ˌ=\ *n* : GREAT RAGWEED

king·hood \ˈkiŋˌhu̇d\ *n* [ME, fr. *king* + *-hood*] : KINGSHIP

kinghunter \ˈ=ˌ==\ *n* : KOOKABURRA

king-in-council \ˈ==ˈ==\ *n, pl* **kings-in-council** *often cap K &C* : the British monarch acting with the advice and consent of the privy council usu. as a formal means of giving legal effect to cabinet decisions ⟨executive decisions are reached by the *king-in-council*⟩

kinging *pres part of* KING

king-in-parliament \ˈ==ˈ===\ *n, pl* **kings-in-parliament** *often cap K&P* : the collective legal entity composed of the British monarch and the two houses of parliament acting together that constitutes the supreme legislative authority of the United Kingdom ⟨the lawmaking function is vested in the *king-in-Parliament* —F.A.Ogg & Harold Zink⟩

king-killer \ˈ=ˌ==\ *n* : REGICIDE

king·klip \ˈkiŋˌklip\ *n* -S [short for *kingklipfish*, fr. *king* + *klipfish*; trans. of Afrik *koningklipvis*] : a mottled cusk eel of southern Africa (*Genypterus capensis*) that attains a length of five feet and is highly esteemed as food ⟨~ liver is of a delicacy and flavor unsurpassed by even chicken liver —J.L.B.Smith⟩

king·less \ˈkiŋləs\ *adj* [ME *kingles*, fr. *king* + *-les* -less] : lacking a king ⟨a ~ people —Lord Byron⟩

king·let \-ət\ *n* -S **1** : a weak or petty king; *esp* : one that rules over a small territory ⟨four eastern ~*s* receiving investiture at the hands of the emperor —*Century Mag.*⟩ **2** : any of several very small birds of the genus *Regulus* that resemble the warblers but have some of the habits of titmice — see GOLDCREST, GOLDEN-CRESTED KINGLET, GOLDEN-CROWNED KINGLET, RUBY-CROWNED KINGLET

king·li·ness \ˈkiŋlēnəs\ *n* -ES : the quality or state of being kingly

king·ling \-liŋ\ *n* -S [¹*king* + *-ling*] : a little or petty king ⟨Germany has had more kings, ~*s*, and knights —*American*⟩

king lory *n* : KING PARROT

¹king·ly \ˈkiŋlē, -li\ *adj* -ER/-EST [ME *kingly*, fr. *king* + *-ly*] **1** : having the status of king or royal rank ⟨before the murder of her ~ guest —William Stephenson⟩ **2** : of, suitable for, or usu. associated with a king ⟨symbolizing ~ power and justice —*N.Y.Herald Tribune*⟩ ⟨veneration of the ~ office —Charles Beadle⟩ ⟨venison was considered a ~ food —G.B.Saul⟩ ⟨a mere soldier, with few ~ qualities —J.R.Green⟩ **3** : having the character, qualities, or attributes of or usu. associated with a king ⟨a ~, i.e. self-ruling people —K.R.Popper⟩ **4** : characterized by having a king as ruler or as head of the state : MONARCHICAL ⟨the ~ form of government —Connop Thirlwall⟩

²kingly \"\ *adv, often* -ER/-EST : in a kingly manner ⟨and heard him ~ speak —Alfred Tennyson⟩

king mackerel *n* : a cero (*Scomberomorus cavalla*) esp. noted as a sport fish

kingmaker \ˈ=ˌ==\ *n* : one that uses his power and influence to cause another to become a king; *esp* : one that exerts great influence over the selection of candidates for political office ⟨that great ~ Warwick —Samuel Daniel⟩ ⟨the chief financiers of some campaigns have been persons of great wealth, with no . . . ax to grind save the desire to be ~*s* —V.O.Key⟩

king monkey *n* : a guereza (*Colobus polykomus*) of Sierra Leone having a white forehead suggesting a crown

king mullet *n* : YELLOW GOATFISH

king nut *or* **king nut hickory** *n* : BIG SHELLBARK

king of arms *often cap K&A* [ME *king of armes*] : an officer of arms of the highest rank : a principal herald — called also *king at arms*

king of beasts [ME *king of bestes*] : LION

king of birds : EAGLE

king of heralds : a principal herald in medieval Europe

king of kings [ME *king of kinges*] : a monarch having other monarchs under him: as **a** : an earthly sovereign ⟨this forthright declaration by the *king of kings* . . . forms a fitting conclusion to the long story of Justinian's wars —P.N.Ure⟩ **b** *cap 1st K, often 2d K* : GOD, CHRIST 1 ⟨the blessed and only Sovereign, the *King of kings* and Lord of lords —1 Tim 6:15 (RSV)⟩ ⟨the deity is treated as the *King of Kings* —D.S. Sarma⟩

king of the anteaters : a So. American antbird (*Grallaria varia* syn. *G. rex*)

king-of-the-herrings \ˈ===ˈ==\ *n* : OARFISH

king of the mackerels : either of two large pelagic fishes of the family Molidae: **a** : a fish (*Ranzania truncata*) of the Atlantic ocean **b** : a fish (*Ranzania makua*) of the Pacific ocean

king of the mullets **1** : a European bass (*Labrax lupus*) **2** : CARDINAL FISH

king-of-the-salmon \ˈ===ˈ==\ *n* : a dealfish (*Trachypterus rex-salmonorum*) of the northern Pacific ocean

king of the vultures : KING VULTURE
king orange *n* **1** : a citrus tree that produces a moderate sized fruit with a rich savory pulp enclosed in a thick deep orange-yellow to orange tuberculated rind and that may be a variety of the mandarin or a hybrid possibly between this and the sweet orange **2** : the fruit of the king orange
king ortolan *n* **1** : KING RAIL **2** : FLORIDA GALLINULE
king parrot *n* : any of various Australian birds (genus *Alisterus*) of the family Psittacidae; *esp* : an Australian parrot (*A. scapulatus*) about 16 inches long that is chiefly bright scarlet on the head and underparts and green above
king penguin *n* : a large penguin (*Aptenodytes patagonica*) of the Falklands and Kerguelen
kingpin \ˈ=,=\ *n* **1** : any of several bowling pins: as **a** : HEADPIN **b** : the number 5 pin **2** : one that holds a chief or most prominent place in a group or undertaking ⟨~ of the great steel industry —F.L.Allen⟩ ⟨sought by the government . . . as the ~ of dope peddlers —*Associated Press*⟩ ⟨recognized ~ in the tailor-made car field —*Ethyl News*⟩ **3 a** : KINGBOLT 1 **b** : KNUCKLE PIN **4** : one that holds together a complex system or arrangement ⟨the . . . chancellor is fully aware of the fact that he is the ~ of the constitutional setup —C.J.Friedrich & H.J. Spiro⟩

king penguin

king plank *n* : the center plank of a wooden deck
king post *n* **1** : a vertical member connecting the apex of a triangular truss (as of a roof) with the base — called also *crown post;* see ROOF illustration **2** : a short strong tubular mast that supports the cargo boom of a shipboard derrick — called also *derrick post, samson post*

1 king post

king-post truss *n* : a truss having a vertical central strut
king quail *n, Austral* : PAINTED QUAIL b
king rail *n* : a rather large long-billed No. American rail (*Rallus elegans*) having plumage streaked above with black and tawny olive and a rufous or cinnamon-red breast when in full plumage
king rod *n* : KINGBOLT 2
king row *n* **1** : a row of four playing squares on the edge of a checkerboard nearest each player **2** : the men on a king row at the start of a game of checkers ⟨to keep a *king row* intact⟩
king rummy *n* : a card game of the contract rummy group
kings *pl of* KING, *pres 3d sing of* KING
king salmon *n* : a large usu. red-fleshed salmon (*Oncorhynchus tshawytscha*) of the northern Pacific ocean that attains an average weight of about 20 pounds but is reported to sometimes exceed 100 pounds and is of great commercial importance — called also *black salmon, Chinook salmon, quinnat salmon*
king's beadsman *n* : BEADSMAN 2b
king's bench *n, usu cap K&B* [ME *kyngesbenche*] : COURT OF KING'S BENCH
king's birthday *n, usu cap K&B* : the legal holiday on which the British monarch's birthday is publicly celebrated in the United Kingdom and many other parts of the Commonwealth and Empire
king's blue *n* **1** : a light to moderate blue that is greener and less strong than bluet **2** : SMALT 2 **3** : COBALT BLUE 1a
king's books *n pl* : the crown taxation list of ecclesiastical benefices and preferments in England
king's champion *n, usu cap K&C* : one who formerly at the coronation of the sovereign of England declared his readiness to defend the sovereign's title to the crown against any challenger
king's color *n, often cap K&C* **1** : a union jack carried on the right of the regimental color by most British regiments **2** : a white ensign bearing the royal cipher used on ceremonial occasions by the Royal Navy
king's counsel *n, usu cap K&C* **1** : a group of barristers of preeminence selected upon nomination of the lord chancellor to serve as counsel to the British crown and as such entitled to certain honorary privileges (as the wearing of a silk gown) **2** : a member of this group of barristers ⟨the first woman attorney to win the high legal distinction of being a *King's Counsel* —P.J.Noel-Baker⟩
king's english *n, usu cap K&E* **1** : standard, pure, or correct English speech or usage ⟨can think as speedily in classic Greek as . . . in the *King's English* —*Saturday Rev.*⟩ **2** : English speech used by educated persons in southern England ⟨separating the *King's English* from the American language —M.A. Pei⟩
king's evidence *n, usu cap K* : one who gives evidence for the crown in British criminal proceedings ⟨willingness to turn *King's evidence*⟩ — compare STATE'S EVIDENCE
king's evil *n, often cap K&E* [ME *kinges evil;* fr. the belief that it could be healed by the touch of a king] : SCROFULA
king's-fern \ˈ=,=\ *n, pl* **king's-ferns** : ROYAL FERN
king's friends *n pl, often cap K&F* : members of the British parliament supporting the attempts of George III to increase the personal power of the monarch ⟨the *King's Friends* . . . were in the main recruited from the ranks of the Tories —Sidney Low & F.S.Pulling⟩
king's-fruit \ˈ=,=\ *n, pl* **king's-fruits** : MANGOSTEEN
king's grith *n* : KING'S PEACE 1
king·ship \ˈkiŋ,ship\ *n* **1** : the office of king ⟨the traditional attributes of ~ —D.W.S.Lidderdale⟩ ⟨~ . . . has always been a symbol of national unity —Ernest Barker⟩ **2** : the quality or state of being a king : MAJESTY ⟨the king is thus divested of his ~ and . . . becomes merely a corpse —J.G.Frazer⟩ **3** : government by a king : a monarchical form of government headed by a king ⟨the medieval theory of ~ —G.H.Sabine⟩ ⟨whose contribution to the cause of ~ was less . . . enduring —Hector Bolitho⟩
king-size \ˈ=,=\ *or* **king-sized** \ˈ=ˈ=\ *adj* **1** : longer than the regular or standard size — used of a cigarette ⟨about the length of a *king-sized* cigarette —*Scientific Monthly*⟩ **2** : much larger in size than is usual for a particular class of things : OVERSIZE ⟨regular or *king-size* portions —*N.Y.Times*⟩ ⟨a *king-size* cocktail⟩ ⟨*king-size* bed six by seven feet⟩ **3** : exceeding others of the kind in some conspicuous quality : EXTRAORDINARY ⟨a *king-size* hobby —Barbara Lenox⟩ ⟨a *king-size* movie⟩ ⟨a *king-size* lightning storm⟩
king's man *n* **1** : an adherent of the king; *esp* : a supporter of the British cause during the American Revolution ⟨neither *king's man* nor rebel —*Sat. Eve. Post*⟩ **2** : a customhouse officer
king's mark *n, usu cap K* : an official mark consisting of a leopard's or lion's head crowned that is used as part of a hallmark
king snake *n* : any of numerous brightly marked colubrid snakes (genus *Lampropeltis*) of the southern and central U.S. that are voracious consumers of rodents — called also *milk snake*
king snapper *n* [so called fr. the markings on the young which suggest the mark the British Board of Ordance places upon government stores] : GOVERNMENT BREAM
king sora *n* : FLORIDA GALLINULE
king's paprika *n* [trans. of G *königspaprika*] : Hungarian paprika that is made from whole peppers including seeds and stalks
king's peace *n, sometimes cap K&P* [ME *kynges pees*] **1** : the special protection secured by the monarch in Anglo-Saxon and medieval England to particular persons (as members of the royal household) or places (as the king's highway) and occas. to specific periods of time (as coronation days) ⟨the *king's peace* was to abide in his assembly and . . . extend to the members in coming to it and returning from it —T.E.May⟩ **2** : the general peace for the protection of persons and property secured in medieval times to large areas and later to the entire royal domain by the law administered by authority of the British monarch ⟨the *king's peace* had . . . grown from an occasional privilege into a common right —Frederick Pollock⟩
king spoke *n* : the spoke of the steering wheel of a ship that is upright when the rudder is fore and aft and is usu. distinguished by a Turk's head
king's proctor *n, usu cap K&P* : an officer of the judiciary in England who may intervene in actions for divorce chiefly to prevent collusive proceedings
king's purple *n* : ROYAL PURPLE 2
king's ransom *n* : a very large sum of money ⟨a rare book sometimes sells for a *king's ransom* —R.D.Altick⟩
king's regulations *n pl, usu cap K&R* : regulations for the British armed forces issued by the crown
king's remembrancer *n, usu cap K&R* : an officer of the British judiciary who is responsible for the collection of debts due to the monarch
king's scholar *n, usu cap K&S* : a student in an English school or college who is supported by a foundation created by or under the auspices of a king ⟨a *King's Scholar* at Cambridge⟩
king's scout *n, usu cap K&S* : a boy scout who has achieved the highest rating in British scouting by earning ten proficiency badges including four from a required list
king's shilling *n* : a shilling whose acceptance by a recruit from a recruiting officer constituted until 1879 a binding enlistment in the British army ⟨he's taken the *king's shilling*⟩
king's silver *n, usu cap K* : POST-FINE
king's spear *n, Brit* : JACOB'S-ROD
kings·ton \ˈkiŋztən, -ŋ(k)st-\ *adj, usu cap* [fr. *Kingston,* Jamaica] : of or from Kingston, the capital of Jamaica : of the kind or style prevalent in Kingston
kingston valve *n, usu cap K* [prob. fr. the F. C. *Kingston* Co., Los Angeles, Calif.] : a conical valve opening outward from a ship and closed by the underwater pressure of the sea that is used esp. on a ballast tank of a submarine
king's x *interj, usu cap K&X* [prob. short for *king's excuse*] — used as a cry in children's games to claim exemption from being tagged or caught or to call for a time out ⟨how they make haste to cry with fingers crossed *King's X* — no fairs to use it any more —Robert Frost⟩
king's yellow *n* **1** : arsenic trisulfide used as a pigment **2** : ORPIMENT 2
king tody *n* : ROYAL FLYCATCHER
king truss *n* : a truss framed with a king post
king turtle *n* : a large No. American soft-shelled turtle (*Amyda spinifera*)
king vulture *n* : a large vulture (*Sarcoramphus papa*) ranging from Mexico to Paraguay that is creamy white in color with wings, rump, and tail black and the caruncul ate head and the neck colored scarlet, yellow, orange, and blue
king·wa·na \kiŋˈwänə\ *n, pl* **kingwana** *or* **kingwanas** *usu cap* : a dialect of Swahili widely used in the eastern Congo as a trade language
king whiting *n* : a whiting (*Menticirrhus americanus*) of the east coast of No. America from Maryland to Texas
king wil·liam pine \-ˈwilyəm-\ *n, usu cap K&W* [after *William* IV †1837 king of England] : a Tasmanian tree (*Athrotaxis selaginoides*) of the family Taxodiaceae with sharp-pointed leaves that curve inward and overlap loosely
kingwood \ˈ=,=\ *n* **1** : the wood of any of various trees esp. of the genus *Dalbergia; specif* : a handsome Brazilian wood from a tree (*D. cearensis*) of Ceará **2** : a tree that yields kingwood **3** : GONCALO ALVES 2
¹kink \ˈkiŋk\ *vi* -ED/-ING/-S [ME *kinken* — more at CHINK] *dial* : to be seized with a kink : gasp convulsively (as in laughing or coughing)
²kink \"\ *n* -S *dial* : a fit or paroxysm of coughing or laughter ⟨the sister was in ~s of laughter —Donagh MacDonagh⟩
³kink \"\ *n* -S [D; akin to MLG *kinke* kink — more at CONGER] **1 a** : a short and often tight twist or curl caused by a doubling or winding of something (as a rope or hair) upon itself ⟨looped hose should be changed . . . to reverse folds and prevent ~s —G.E. Stecher⟩ **b** : a bend in something (as a line) otherwise straight : INDENTATION, PROJECTION ⟨a dozen curly streets with ~s in them —Thomas Wood †1950⟩ ⟨a ~ in a line on a graph⟩ **c** : a buckling of a railroad track due to longitudinal movement of the rails by creeping or expanding **2 a** : a twist or turn in a person's nature or disposition : a mental or physical peculiarity : ECCENTRICITY, QUIRK ⟨the ~ in his psychology which made him such a menace to society —P.G.Wodehouse⟩ ⟨a suspicious contempt for the intellectual life . . . is a ~ in the American character —J.J.Wright⟩ **b** : an odd notion : WHIM ⟨got a ~ in her head that diamonds she must have —Julian Hawthorne⟩ **3** : a clever and often unusual idea or method of doing something ⟨every ~ . . . time-saver, or quality-improvement suggestion entered in the contest —*Textile Industries*⟩ ⟨cost-cutting shop ~s —*U.S. Daily*⟩ **4** : a cramp or stiffness in some part of the body : CRICK ⟨taking the ~s out of his legs —Sinclair Lewis⟩ **5 a** : an imperfection (as in design or construction) that is likely to cause difficulties in the operation of something ⟨to spot the ~s . . . that get into an airplane as a result of faulty design —G.W.Gray b.1886⟩ ⟨number of ~s . . . to be ironed out of the system —Cecile Starr⟩ **b** : a particular type of imperfection in a crystal that is important in the theoretical study of plastic deformation

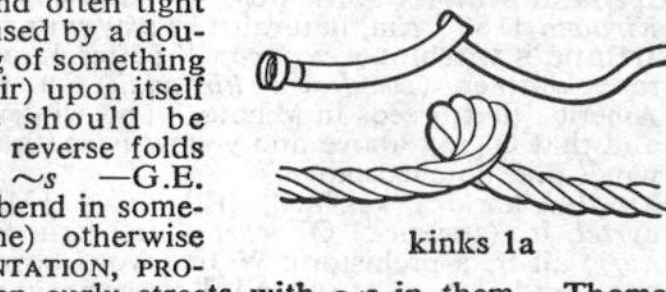
kinks 1a

⁴kink \"\ *vb* -ED/-ING/-S *vi* : to wind into or form a kink : become tightly twisted at one or more points ⟨vinyl hose . . . will not ~ —*Monsanto Mag.*⟩ ~ *vt* : to cause to form a kink : make a kink in ⟨the sinkers are projected forward to ~ the yarn around the needles —*Full-Fashioned Knitting Machine Primer*⟩
kin·kaid·er \kinˈkādə(r)\ *n* -S *usu cap* [Moses P. *Kinkaid* †1922 Am. congressman + E *-er*] : a settler on free land in Nebraska under terms of the Kinkaid Act in 1904 which allowed each bona fide settler 640 acres upon payment of a filing fee of 14 dollars ⟨the place *Kinkaiders* make their home and prairie chickens freely roam —Carl Sandburg⟩
kin·ka·jou \ˈkiŋkə,jü\ *n* -S [F, of Algonquian origin; akin to Ojibwa *qwingwâage* wolverine — more at QUICKHATCH] : a nocturnal arboreal carnivorous mammal (*Potos caudivolvulus* syn. *Cercoleptes caudivolvulus*) of the family Procyonidae inhabiting Mexico and Central and So. America that is about three feet long with a slender body, long prehensile tail, large lustrous eyes, and soft woolly yellowish brown fur
kinkcough \ˈ=,=\ *n* [¹*kink* + *cough*] : WHOOPING COUGH
kink·er \ˈkiŋkə(r)\ *n* -S [prob. fr. ⁴*kink* + *-er*] : an acrobat or other performer in a circus
kinkhab *var of* KINCOB
kink·host \ˈkiŋk,hōst\ *n* [ME (northern dial.), fr. *kinken* to gasp + *host* cough — more at CHINK, HOAST] *archaic Scot* : WHOOPING COUGH
kin·kle \ˈkiŋkəl\ *n* -S [³*kink* + *-le*] : a little kink ⟨to shake the ~s out o' back an' legs —J.R.Lowell⟩
kin·kled \-ld\ *adj* : having kinkles : KINKY ⟨~ hair⟩
kinkob *var of* KINCOB
kinks *pl of* KINK, *pres 3d sing of* KINK
kinky \ˈkiŋkē, -ki\ *adj* -ER/-EST **1** : having or full of kinks : closely twisted or curled ⟨the Negro in Africa has short tight ~ hair —Weston La Barre⟩ **2** : LIVELY, SPIRITED ⟨fresh and ~ horses —Will James⟩ **3** : CROOKED 2 ⟨professional calligraphic swindler and ~ penman —*Graphic Arts Monthly*⟩
kin·less \ˈkinləs\ *adj* : having no relatives ⟨left for friendless and ~ souls —E.B.Tylor⟩
kin·nery \ˈkin(ə)rē\ *n* [¹*kin* + *-ery*] *South & Midland* : KINFOLK, RELATIVES
kin·ni·kin·nick *also* **kin·ni·ki·nic** *or* **kin·ni·ki·nick** *or* **kin·ni·kin·nic** *or* **kin·ni·kin·nik** \ˌkinəkəˈnik\ *or* **kil·lic·kin·nic** *or* **kil·li·ki·nick** *or* **kil·lic·kin·nick** \ˌkiləkˈ-\ *n* -S [of Algonquian origin; akin to Natick *kinukkinuk* mixture, Ojibwa *kinikinige* he mixes by hand] **1** : a mixture of the dried leaves and bark of certain plants (as sumac leaves and the inner bark of a dogwood, esp. the silky cornel) and sometimes tobacco smoked by the Indians and pioneers in the Ohio valley and the region of the Great Lakes **2** : a plant used in kinnikinnick: as **a** : BEARBERRY **b** : SILKY CORNEL **c** : RED OSIER **d** : either of two sumacs (*Rhus virens* and *R. microphylla*) chiefly of the southwestern U.S. and Mexico
kin·nle \ˈkin°l\ *Scot var of* ²KINDLE
kin·nor \kēˈnō(ə)r\ *n* -S [Heb *kinnōr*] : an ancient Jewish lyre
¹ki·no \ˈkē(,)nō\ *also* **kino gum** *n* -S [of African origin; akin to Mandingo *keno, kano* African kino] **1** : any of several dark red to black tannin-containing dried juices or extracts obtained from various tropical trees: as **a** : the dried juice obtained usu. from the trunk of an East Indian tree (*Pterocarpus marsupium*) as brown or black fragments and used as an astringent in diarrhea — called also *East India kino, Malabar kino* **b** : BUTEA GUM **c** : EUCALYPTUS GUM **2** : a tree that produces kino (esp. *Pterocarpus marsupium*)
²kino \"\ *n* -S [G, short for *kinematograph,* fr. F *cinématographe* — more at CINEMATOGRAPH] : a motion-picture theater in Europe ⟨fond of going to the ~ —Truman Capote⟩
kino- — see KIN-
kin·o·mere \ˈkinə,mi(ə)r, ˈkīn-, -nō,-\ *n* -S [*kin-* + *-mere*] : CENTROMERE
kin·o·plasm \-,plazəm\ *also* **kin·o·plas·ma** \,==ˈplazmə\ *n* [ISV *kin-* + *-plasm, -plasma;* orig. formed as G *kinoplasma*] : an active protoplasmic component held to form filaments and mobile structures (as cilia or spindle fibers) — opposed to *trophoplasm*
kin·o·rhynch \ˈ==,riŋk\ *n* -S [NL *Kinorhyncha*] : a worm of the class Kinorhyncha
kin·o·rhyn·cha \,==ˈriŋkə\ *n pl, cap* [NL, fr. *kin-* + *-rhyncha* (fr. Gk *rhynchos* snout, proboscis)] : a class of Aschelminthes comprising minute marine worms of uncertain systematic position having certain resemblances to arthropods and annelids but prob. more closely related to the nematodes — see ECHINODERES
kin·o·ster·ni·dae \,==ˈstə(r)nə,dē\ *n pl, cap* [NL, fr. *Kinosternon,* type genus + *-idae*] : a small family of No. American freshwater turtles comprising the mud turtles
kin·o·ster·non \-)nən\ *n, cap* [NL, fr. *kin-* + Gk *sternon* breast — more at STERNUM] : a genus (the type of the family Kinosternidae) of No. American freshwater turtles distinguished by fully hinged plastral lobes capable of completely closing the shell
kinot *or* **kinoth** *pl of* KINAH
kin·ross-shire \kinˈrȯs(h),shi(ə)r, -,shər\ *or* **kin·ross** \kinˈrȯs\ *adj, usu cap K* [fr. *Kinross-shire* or *Kinross* county, Scotland] : of or from the county of Kinross, Scotland : of the kind or style prevalent in Kinross
kins *pl of* KIN
-kins — see -KIN
kinsfolk *var of* KINFOLK
kin·sha·sa \kinˈshäsə\ *adj, usu cap* [fr. *Kinshasa* (formerly *Léopoldville*), capital of Congo] : of or from Kinshasa : of the kind or style prevalent in Kinshasa
kin·ship \ˈkin,ship\ *n* [¹*kin* + *-ship*] : the quality or state of being kin: as **a** : personal relationship by blood and sometimes by marriage ⟨her ~ with no less than twelve sovereigns —A.P. Stanley⟩ **b** : relationship by descent from a common ancestor or membership in a common group (as a clan) ⟨the Negroes . . . were already conscious of ~ with other men similarly marked throughout the world —Oscar Handlin⟩ ⟨the instinctive British feelings of ~ and common freedom —Barbara Ward⟩ ⟨a ~ of man with other animals —Weston La Barre⟩ **c** : the socially recognized relationship between people in a culture who are or are held to be biologically related or who are given the status of relatives by ritual **d** : a likeness in character or qualities : possession of common features ⟨its mineral waters . . . carry startling ~ to seawater —Helen A. Levin⟩ ⟨in . . . his character studies critics have found a ~ with the early Flemish masters —*Amer. Guide Series: Mich.*⟩ **e** : a community of interest; *esp* : a sense of oneness ⟨acquiescence when negation seems to question our ~ with the crowd —B.N.Cardozo⟩ ⟨a sense of professional ~ —Douglas Bush⟩ **f** : a close connection between things that resembles a blood relationship ⟨anthropology's ~ with the humanities⟩
kinship system *n* : the system of social relationships connecting people in a culture who are or are held to be related and defining and regulating their reciprocal obligations ⟨*kinship systems* vary in different forms of social organization —Thomas Gladwin⟩
kins·man \ˈkinzmən\ *n, pl* **kinsmen** [ME *kinnesman,* fr. *kinnes* (gen. of ¹*kin*) + *man*] : a man of the same race or family : one related by blood or sometimes by marriage : RELATION, RELATIVE ⟨Polynesians, distant *kinsmen* of the New Zealand Maori —Ernest Beaglehole⟩ ⟨a very great . . . American whom I am proud to call my ~ —A.E.Stevenson †1965⟩
kins·man·ship \-ən,ship\ *n* : KINSHIP
kins·people \ˈkinz+,-\ *n, pl* **kinspeople** : RELATIVES ⟨reach their sick ~ in Germany —B.J.Hendrick⟩
kins·woman \"+,-\ *n, pl* **kinswomen** [ME *kinneswoman,* fr. *kinnes* (gen. of ¹*kin*) + *woman*] : a female relative ⟨the murdered prince had married a ~ of the earl —E.A.Freeman⟩
kin·tra \ˈkin·trə\ *Scot var of* COUNTRY
kin·try \-ri\ *Scot var of* COUNTRY
ki·nu·ra \kəˈnu̇rə\ *n* -S [prob. irreg. fr. Gk *kinyra,* a kind of lyre, fr. Heb *kinnōr*] : a small-scaled reed-organ pipe of thin nasal tone that is used in theater pipe organs for comic effects
ki·o·ea \,kēōˈāə\ *n* -S [Hawaiian] : BRISTLE-THIGHED CURLEW
ki·o·ko \kēˈō(,)kō\ *n, pl* **kioko** *or* **kiokos** *usu cap* : CHOKWE 1
ki·o·re \kēˈōrē\ *n* -S [Maori] : the native rat (*Rattus exulan*) of New Zealand now wholly or nearly replaced by the introduced Norwegian and black rats
ki·osk *also* **ki·osque** \ˈkē,äsk *sometimes* =ˈ= *or* ˈkī,äsk\ *n* -S [Turk *kösk,* fr. Per *kūshk* portico, palace] **1** : an open summerhouse or pavilion often having a roof supported by pillars and usu. built in gardens and parks ⟨~s on the heights above the Bosporus —*Manchester Guardian Weekly*⟩ **2** [F *kiosque,* fr. Turk *kösk*] : a structure resembling or felt to resemble a kiosk: as **a** : an outdoor newsstand ⟨the bountiful supply of newspapers displayed on every ~ —I.F.Fraser⟩ **b** : a structure housing the entrance to a subway **c** *chiefly Brit* : a stand or booth at which merchandise is sold or information is provided ⟨bought tea and buns at the station ~ —Lionel Shapiro⟩ ⟨the ticket ~ closed —T.W.Duncan⟩ ⟨a little information ~ —*Irish Digest*⟩ **d** : TELEPHONE BOOTH ⟨the red telephone ~s . . . at the side of the road —Richard Joseph⟩ **e** : a structure used as a receptacle or as housing for machinery ⟨transformer ~s for the distribution of electricity —*World*⟩

kiosk 1

ki·o·wa \ˈkīə,wä, -,wā, -əwə\ *n, pl* **kiowa** *or* **kiowas** *usu cap* [Kiowa *Gá-i-gwŭ, Kâ-i-gwŭ,* lit., principal people] **1 a** : a Tanoan people in adjoining parts of Oklahoma, Kansas, Colorado, New Mexico, and Texas **b** : a member of such people **2** : the language of the Kiowa people
kiowa apache *n, usu cap K&A* **1 a** : an Athapascan people associated with the Kiowa **b** : a member of such people **2** : the language of the Kiowa Apache people
¹kip \ˈkip\ *n* -S [obs. D, bundle of hides, bundle of flax, fr. MD; akin to MLG *kip* bundle of hides, bunch of fish, ON *kippi* bundle, sheaf] **1** : a set or bundle of undressed hides of young or small animals (as calves, lambs, colts) **2** : one of the undressed hides in a kip; *specif* : a skin coming from a bovine animal in size between a calf and a matured animal and weighing from 16 to 25 pounds in green salted condition
²kip \"\ *n* -S [origin unknown] *dial Eng* : the common tern
³kip \"\ *n* -S [perh. fr. Dan *kippe* cheap tavern] **1** : BED ⟨ready for the ~ after this screwball day —K.M.Dodson⟩ ⟨was in ~ —Richard Llewellyn⟩ **2** : SLEEP ⟨get some ~ —Paul Scott⟩
⁴kip \"\ *vi* **kipped; kipped; kipping; kips** : to lie in bed : SLEEP ⟨a ragged blanket to ~ in by nights —Richard Dehan⟩ — sometimes used with *down* ⟨you can ~ down . . . and get a bit of sleep —Edith Sitwell⟩
⁵kip \"\ *n* -S [G *kippe* edge, seesaw, arm of a balance, kip, fr. LG, point, edge, fr. L *cippus* stake, post — more at CEPE] **1 a** : a gymnastic feat that is executed when hanging by the hands from a piece of apparatus and consists of moving from

a position in which the legs are above the head to one with the head above the feet by flexing the hips and swinging the legs forward and upward above the head, then arching the back and thrusting with the chest and forcibly kicking the legs downward to raise the body — called also *upstart* **b :** a similar movement executed from a cross seat on the parallel bars by dropping backward with straight arms into position **2 :** a synchronized swimming stunt in which from a back layout position both knees are drawn to the chest and the trunk is submerged backward to a head down vertical position followed by extension of the legs and complete submersion of the body

6**kip** \"\ *vi* **kipped; kipped; kipping; kips :** to perform a kip in gymnastics or swimming

7**kip** \"\ *n* -s [*kilo* + *pound*] **:** a unit of weight equal to 1000 pounds used to express deadweight load

8**kip** \"\ *n* -s [origin unknown] **:** a small piece of wood from which the pennies are tossed in the Australian game of two-up

9**kip** \"\ *n* -s [Siamese] **:** the basic monetary unit of Laos from 1955 divided into 100 at — see MONEY table

kip·chak \kip'chäk\ *n* -s *usu cap* [Russ, fr. Jagatai] **1 a :** one of the ancient Turkic peoples of the Golden Horde related to the Uighurs and Kirghiz **b :** a member of the Kipchak people **2 :** the Turkic language of the Kipchak people

kipe \'kīp\ *n* -s [ME, fr. OE *cȳpa, cȳpe;* akin to MLG *kīpe* basket, Norw dial. *kaup* wooden vessel, OE *cot* (hut) — more at COT] *dial Eng* **:** a large basket used usu. for a measure

kip·fel \'kipfəl\ *n* -s [G, dim. of *kipf* wagon post, kipfel, fr. OHG *kipfa, chipf* wagon post, fr. L *cippus* post — more at CEPE] **:** a crescent-shaped cookie or roll

kip·ling·ese \,kipliŋ'ēz, -ēs\ *n* -s *usu cap* [Rudyard *Kipling* †1936 Eng. poet and novelist + E *-ese*] **:** the literary style of Rudyard Kipling ⟨write a chanty in *Kiplingese* —*Dial*⟩

kip·ling·esque \,==¦esk\ *adj, usu cap* [Rudyard *Kipling* + E *-esque*] **1 :** of, resembling, or having the characteristics of the literary style of Rudyard Kipling ⟨the poems . . . were direct, *Kiplingesque* —Gertrude Stein⟩ **2 :** characterized by an attitude of superiority over and a responsibility for nonwhite peoples often associated with the writings of Rudyard Kipling ⟨a *Kiplingesque* condescension toward China —F.J.Brown & J.S.Roucek⟩

kip·page \'kipij\ *n* -s [modif. of F *équipage* (as in *être en piteux équipage* to be in a sorry plight) — more at EQUIPAGE] *Scot* **:** an excited or irritated state **:** COMMOTION, CONFUSION ⟨dinna pit yoursell into a ~ —Sir Walter Scott⟩

kip·peen \ki'pēn\ *n* -s [IrGael *cipín*] *chiefly Irish* **:** a short thin stick **:** SWITCH

kippen *past part of* KEP

1**kip·per** \'kipə(r)\ *n* -s [ME *kypre,* fr. OE *cypera,* prob. fr. *coper* copper; fr. the color — more at COPPER] **1 :** a male salmon or sea trout during or after the spawning season **2 :** a kippered herring or salmon

2**kipper** \"\ *vt* -ED/-ING/-S **:** to cure by splitting, cleaning, salting, and smoking

3**kipper** \"\ *adj* [origin unknown] *dial* **:** CHIPPER

4**kipper** \"\ *n* -s [native name in Australia] **:** a young Australian aborigine who has passed through the initiatory rite

kip·per·er \-pərə(r)\ *n* -s **:** one that kippers fish

kipp generator \'kip-\ *n, usu cap K* [after Petrus Jacobus *Kipp* †1864 Du. druggist and chemist] **:** a glass laboratory apparatus for generating a gas (as hydrogen sulfide by the action of an acid on ferrous sulfide)

Kipp generator

kipping *pres part of* KIP

kips *pl of* KIP, *pres 3d sing of* KIP

kip·si·gis \'kipsēgəs\ *or* **kip·si·kis** \-ēkəs\ *n, pl* **kipsigis** *or* **kipsikis** *usu cap* **1 a :** a predominantly pastoral people of west-central Kenya **b :** a member of such people **2 :** NANDI

kipskin \'=,=\ *n* [1*kip* + *skin*] **:** 1KIP 2

ki·pu·ka \kē'pükə\ *n* -s [Hawaiian] **:** an area of older land ranging in size from a few square feet to several square miles surrounded by later lava flows ⟨~s result from either topographic irregularities or the viscosity of the lava —H.T.Stearns & G.A.Macdonald⟩

kip-up *n* -s [fr. *kip up,* v.] **:** a kip executed from a supine position on the mat in tumbling

ki·ran·ti \kē'räntē\ *n* -s *usu cap* **:** a group of Tibeto-Burman dialects centering in eastern Nepal

kir·by \'kərbē\ *or* **kirby hook** *n* -s [fr. the name *Kirby*] **:** a fishhook of evenly curved pattern — see FISHHOOK illustration

kirch·hoff's law \'kirk,hōfs-\ *n, usu cap K* [after Gustav R. *Kirchhoff* †1887 Ger. physicist] **1 :** a statement in physics: in an electric network the algebraic sum of the currents in all the branches that meet at any point is zero **2 :** a statement in physics: if any closed circuit is chosen from the branches of an electric network, the algebraic sum of the products formed by multiplying the resistance of each branch by the current in that branch is equal to the algebraic sum of the electromotive forces in the several branches forming the circuit **3 :** a statement in physics: the ratio of the emissive power to the absorptivity is the same for all bodies at the same temperature and equals the emissive power of a black body at that temperature

kir·ghiz *or* **kir·ghis** *or* **kir·giz** *or* **khir·ghiz** \kir'gēz, kiə'-\ *n, pl* **kirghiz** *or* **kirghizes** *or* **kirghese** *or* **kirgheses** *or* **kirghis** *or* **kirghises** *or* **kirgiz** *or* **kirgizes** *or* **khirghiz** *or* **khirghizes** *usu cap* [Kirghiz *Kyrghyz*] **1 a :** a widespread people of Turkic speech and Mongolian race prob. with some Caucasian intermixture inhabiting chiefly the Central Asian steppes and related to the steppe-dwelling Kazak — see KARA-KIRGHIZ **b :** a member of the Kirghiz people **2 :** the Turkic language of the Kirghiz

ki·ri \'kērē\ *n* -s [Jap] **1 :** a paulownia (*Paulownia tomentosa*) **2 :** the light soft straight-grained pale brown wood of the kiri that is easily worked and very resistant to shrinking and swelling and that is used in Japan esp. as a base for lacquer work and in lining fine cabinetry

ki·ril·li·tsa \kə'rilətsə\ *n* -s *usu cap* [Russ, fr. *Kirill* (Cyril) — more at CYRILLIC] **:** CYRILLIC ALPHABET

kiri·mon \'kirə,män, 'kērē,m-\ *n* -s [Jap, fr. *kiri* + *mon* badge, crest] **:** one of the two imperial badges of Japan consisting of three leaves of the paulownia surmounted by three budding stems — compare CHRYSANTHEMUM 3

kirimon

ki·rin \'kē'rin\ *adj, usu cap* [fr. *Kirin,* Manchuria] **:** of or from the city of Kirin, Manchuria **:** of the kind or style prevalent in Kirin

ki·ri·ri \¦kērē¦rē\ *n* -s *usu cap, var of* CARIRI

ki·ri·wi·na \,kērē'vēnə\ *n, pl* **kiriwina** *or* **kiriwinas** *usu cap* **:** an Austronesian language of the Trobriand islands

1**kirk** *also* **kurk** \'ki(ə)rk, 'kərk, 'kiək, 'kōk\ *n* -s *often attrib* [ME (northern dial.) *kirke, kirk,* fr. ON *kirkja,* fr. OE *cirice* — more at CHURCH] **1** *chiefly Scot* **:** CHURCH ⟨bells in the city ~s —*Christian Century*⟩ ⟨coming to the ~ this morning —Guy McCrone⟩ **2** *usu cap* **:** the Church of Scotland as distinguished from the Church of England or the Episcopal Church in Scotland — usu. used with *the* ⟨the essential autonomy of the *Kirk* —J.Y.Evans⟩

2**kirk** \"\ *vt* **kirked** \-kt\ *or* **kirk·it** \-kət\ **kirked** *or* **kirkit; kirking; kirks** [ME (Sc dial.) *kirken,* fr. *kirke, kirk,* n.] **1** *chiefly Scot* **:** CHURCH **2** *Scot* **:** to take (a bride or couple) to church for the first time after the wedding ceremony ⟨I'm to be married the morn and *kirkit* on Sunday —Sir Walter Scott⟩

kirk·cud·bright·shire \,kər'kübri,shi(ə)r, -,shər\ *or* **kirk·cud·bright** \,='=bri\ *adj, usu cap* [fr. *Kirkcudbrightshire* or *Kirkcudbright* county, Scotland] **:** of or from the county of Kirkcudbright, Scotland **:** of the kind or style prevalent in Kirkcudbright

kirk·er \'kərkər\ *n* -s *usu cap* [1*kirk* + *-er*] **:** a member or adherent of the Church of Scotland — see AULD KIRKER, FREE KIRKER

kirk·in·head \'kərkən,hed\ *n* [perh. irreg. fr. 1*kirk* + *head*] **:** JERKINHEAD

kirk keeper *n, Scot* **:** one that attends a kirk regularly

kirk·man \'kirkmən, 'kər-\ *n, pl* **kirkmen** [ME (northern dial.), fr. *kirk* + *man*] **1** *chiefly Scot* **:** CHURCHMAN **2 :** a member or adherent of the Church of Scotland

kirk·shot \'kərk,shät\ *n* [alter. of OE *ciricsceat* — more at CHURCHSCOT] **:** CHURCHSCOT

kirk·town \'kərk, taůn\ *also* **kirk·ton** \-,tən\ *n* [ME (Sc dial.) *kirktoun,* fr. *kirke, kirk* + *toun* town — more at TOWN] **1 :** the hamlet in the immediate neighborhood of the parish church in country parishes of Scotland **2 :** GLEBE 2a

kirk·yard \'kirk,yärd, 'kərk-\ *n* [ME (northern dial.) *kirkyard,* fr. *kirk* + *yard*] *chiefly Scot* **:** CHURCHYARD

kir·man \kir'män\ *or* **ker·man** \kər-, ker-\ *n* -s *usu cap* [fr. *Kirman* or *Kerman* province, Iran] **:** a Persian carpet or rug characterized by elaborate fluid designs and soft colors ⟨a *Kirman* is the only Persian carpet that looks feminine —Rumer Godden⟩

kir·man·shah \¦kirmən¦shä, kər'män,shä\ *or* **ker·man·shah** \¦kermən¦-, kər'män,-\ *n* -s *usu cap* **:** KIRMAN

kirmess *var of* KERMIS

1**kirn** \'kirn, 'kərn\ *n* -s [ME (northern dial.) *kirne,* fr. ON *kirna;* akin to ON *kjarni* churn — more at CHURN] *chiefly Scot* **:** CHURN

2**kirn** \"\ *vb* -ED/-ING/-S *chiefly Scot* **:** CHURN

3**kirn** \"\ *n* -s [perh. of Scand origin; akin to ON *korn* grain — more at CORN] **1** *chiefly Scot* **:** HARVEST HOME 2 ⟨the good old custom of the ~ —J.G.Lockhart⟩ **2** *chiefly Scot* **:** the last handful or sheaf reaped at the harvest — called also *mell*

kirn baby *or* **kirn doll** *or* **kirn maiden** *n* [3*kirn*] **:** HARVEST DOLL

ki·rom·bo \kə'räm(,)bō\ *also* **ki·roum·ba** \-raůmbə\ *n* -s [Malagasy *kiròmbo*] **:** a crested conspicuously colored coraciiform bird (*Leptosomus discolor*) of Madagascar related to the rollers

ki·rov \'kērəf\ *adj, usu cap* [fr. *Kirov,* U.S.S.R.] **:** of or from the city of Kirov, U.S.S.R. **:** of the kind or style prevalent in Kirov

ki·rov·ite \'kērə,vīt\ *n* -s [Russ *kirovit,* fr. Sergei M. *Kirov* †1934 Russ. revolutionary leader + Russ *-it* -ite] **:** a mineral $Fe,MgSO_4 7H_2O$ consisting of a hydrous sulfate of iron and magnesium isomorphous with melanterite and pisanite

ki·ro·vo·grad \kə'rōvə,grad\ *adj, usu cap* [fr. *Kirovograd,* U.S.S.R.] **:** of or from the city of Kirovograd, U.S.S.R. **:** of the kind or style prevalent in Kirovograd

kir·pan \kir'pän, kər-\ *n* -s [Panjabi & Hindi *kirpān,* fr. Skt *kṛpāṇa* sword — more at HARVEST] **:** the sacred dagger of the Sikhs ⟨the right of every Sikh . . . to wear a ~ —J.C.Archer⟩

kirsch \'kirsh, -iəsh\ *also* **kirsch·was·ser** \'k-,sh,väsə(r)\ *n, pl* **kirsches** *also* **kirschwassers** [*kirsch* fr. G, short for *kirschwasser; kirschwasser* fr. G, fr. *kirsche* cherry + *wasser* water] **:** a dry colorless brandy made in the Black Forest region of Germany, in Alsace, France, and in Switzerland that is distilled from the fermented juice of the black morello cherry and has a bitter almond flavor derived from the ground cherry pits placed in the juice prior to distillation

kirsch·ner value \'kirshnər-\ *n, usu cap K* [fr. the name *Kirschner*] **:** a value similar to a Reichert value that indicates the content in a fat of the water-soluble fatty acids (as butyric acid) having soluble silver salts

kir·se·baer \'kirsə,ba(a)(ə)r\ *n* -s [Dan *kirsebær,* short for *kirsebærbrændevin,* fr. *kirsebær* cherry + *brændevin* brandy] **:** a Danish cherry liqueur

kir·sen \'kərsᵊn\ *now dial var of* 2CHRISTEN

kirt·land's owl \'kərtlən(d)z-\ *n, usu cap K* [after Jared P. *Kirtland* †1877 Am. naturalist] **:** SAW-WHET OWL

kirtland's warbler *n, usu cap K* [after Jared P. *Kirtland*] **:** a rare warbler (*Dendroica kirtlandii*) of northeastern No. America that breeds in Michigan and winters in the Bahamas and that is gray above and yellow beneath with long pointed wings and notched tail

1**kir·tle** \'kər|dᵊl, 'kə|, 'kəi|, |tᵊl\ *n* -s [ME *kirtel,* fr. OE *cyrtel,* fr. (assumed) OE *curt* short; akin to OS *kurt,* OHG *kurz;* all fr. a prehistoric WGmc word borrowed fr. L *curtus* shortened — more at SHEAR] **1 :** a garment resembling a tunic or coat usu. reaching to the knees and worn by men often as the principal body garment until the 16th century **2 :** a long gown or dress worn during the middle ages by women usu. beneath a cloak and also in modern times as part of coronation robes ⟨wearing her . . . ~ of blue —H.W.Longfellow⟩

2**kirtle** \"\ *vt* -ED/-ING/-S **:** to cover or enwrap (as in a kirtle) ⟨the wild Albanian *kirtled* to his knee —Lord Byron⟩

kirve \'kərv\ *vi* -ED/-ING/-S [prob. alter. of *carve*] **:** to undercut coal in a mine

ki·saeng *also* **ki·sang** \'kē,saŋ\ *n, pl* **kisaengs** *or* **kisaeng** [Korean *kisaeng*] **:** a Korean professional singing and dancing girl

ki·san \kē'sän\ *n* -s [Hindi *kisān,* fr. Skt *kṛṣāṇa* one who plows, fr. *karṣati* he plows] **:** a small farmer or agricultural worker in India **:** PEASANT

1**kish** \'kish\ *n* -ES [IrGael *cis,* fr. MIr *cess*] **:** a large square wicker basket used in Ireland for carrying peat

2**kish** \"\ *also* **keesh** \'kēsh\ *n* -ES [prob. modif. of G *kies* gravel, pyrites, fr. MHG *kis;* akin to OHG *kisil* pebble — more at CHISEL] **:** graphite that separates on slow cooling of molten cast iron or pig iron rich in carbon

kish·en *or* **kish·on** \'kishən\ *n, pl* **kishen** *or* **kishon** [Manx *kishan*] **:** a Manx unit of capacity equal to 1.03 U.S. pecks or 1 British peck

kish·i·nev \'kishə,nef\ *adj, usu cap* [fr. *Kishinev,* U.S.S.R.] **:** of or from the city of Kishinev, U.S.S.R. **:** of the kind or style prevalent in Kishinev

kish·ke \'kishkə\ *n* -s [Yiddish, gut, sausage, of Slav origin; akin to Pol *kiszka* gut, sausage, Ukrainian *kyška,* Russ *kishka* gut; akin to Gk *kysthos* vulva — more at HOARD] **:** beef or fowl casing stuffed with a savory filling (as of matzoth flour, chicken fat, and onion) and roasted **:** stuffed derma

ki·si \'kēsē\ *n* -s [Hopi] **:** a bower of interwoven branches used for keeping snakes before a Hopi snake dance

kis·ka·dee \'kiskə(,)dē\ *n* -s [imit.] **:** DERBY FLYCATCHER

kis kilim \'kēs-\ *n, often cap both Ks* [fr. *Kis Kilim,* a kind of carpet, fr. Turk *kızkilim,* fr. *kız* girl + *kilim*] **:** RUSSIAN CALF

kis·lev *or* **chis·lev** \'kisləf\ *n* -s *usu cap* [Heb *Kislēw*] **:** the 3d month of the civil year or the 9th month of the ecclesiastical year in the Jewish calendar — see MONTH table

kis·met \'kiz,met, -,mət\ *also* **kis·mat** \-,mət\ *n* -s *often cap* [Turk *kısmet,* fr. Ar *qismah* portion, lot] **:** FATE 1, 2a

1**kiss** \'kis\ *vb* **kissed** *also archaic* **kist** \'kist\ **kissed** *also archaic* **kist; kissing; kisses** [ME *kissen,* fr. OE *cyssan;* akin to OHG *kussen* to kiss, ON *kyssa,* Goth *kukjan;* denominatives fr. the root of OE *coss* kiss, OHG *kus, kuss,* ON *koss;* prob. akin (with phonological conservation due to the imit. nature of the word) to Gk *kynein* to kiss, Hitt *kuwassanzi* they kiss, Skt *cūṣati* he sucks] *vt* **1 a :** to touch or press with the lips (as in affection, greeting, reverence) **:** salute or caress with the lips ⟨~*ed* his wife on the mouth and the baby on the cheek⟩ ⟨~ the foot of the image⟩ **b :** to kiss with a smack ⟨~*ed* her loudly⟩ ⟨~ the children good-night⟩ **2 :** to put or effect by kissing ⟨~ away her tears⟩ **3 a :** to touch gently as if fondly or caressingly ⟨a soft wind that ~*es* the flowers⟩ **b :** to touch or hit lightly; *specif* **:** to contact (another billiard ball) lightly ~ *vi* **1 :** to make or give salutation with the lips **:** to salute or caress one another with the lips ⟨~ and be friends⟩ **2 :** to come in contact, touch, or collide gently **:** REBOUND ⟨the cue ball ~*es* from the red ball⟩ **3** *of duodenal ulcers* **:** to be directly opposite or lie against one another — **kiss good-bye 1 :** to take one's leave of **:** LEAVE ⟨*kissing* the old dump *good-bye* tonight —J.T.Farrell⟩ **2 :** to resign oneself to the loss of **:** part with ⟨whenever you have a ship ashore you can *kiss* a million bucks *good-bye* —J.W. Noble⟩ — **kiss hands :** to touch the hand of a sovereign or superior with the lips as a ceremonial sign of homage or submission (as on meeting or parting) ⟨was sent for by the king and *kissed hands* as prime minister⟩ — **kiss my foot** — used to express contempt (as in denying a request) — **kiss one's hand :** to kiss one's own hand with a motion toward another person in sign of affection — **kiss the book :** to touch with the lips the Bible, New Testament, or Gospels in taking an oath — **kiss the ground :** to prostrate oneself as a sign of homage — **kiss the rod :** to accept punishment or correction submissively

2**kiss** \"\ *n* -ES [ME, alter. (influenced by *kissen,* v.) of *cos,* fr. OE *coss* — more at 1KISS] **1 :** the act of kissing **:** a salute or caress with the lips **:** SMACK **2 a :** a gentle touch or contact **b :** the light contact or interference of one billiard ball with another — called also *kiss-off* **3 a :** a meringue sometimes with shredded coconut or other material added **b :** a bite-size piece of candy often wrapped in paper or foil ⟨chocolate ~⟩

kiss·abil·i·ty \,kisə'bilədē\ *n* **:** the quality or state of being kissable

kiss·able \'kisəbəl\ *adj* **:** so attractive as to invite kissing ⟨a ~ mouth⟩ — **kiss·able·ness** *n* -ES — **kiss·ably** \-blē\ *adv*

kis·sar \'kisə(r)\ *n* -s [colloq. Ar *qīsār* (Ar *qīthār*)] **:** a five-stringed lyre of northern Africa and Ethiopia

kiss-curl \'=,=\ *n* **:** a loose curl falling across the forehead or along the cheek

kiss·er \'kisə(r)\ *n* -s **1 :** one that kisses **2** *slang* **:** MOUTH ⟨a poke in the ~⟩ **3** *slang* **:** FACE ⟨threw the money in his ~⟩

kis·si \'kisē\ *n, pl* **kissi** *or* **kissis** *usu cap* **1 a :** an agricultural people of French Guinea, Liberia, and Sierra Leone **b :** a member of such people **2 :** a West-Atlantic language of the Kissi people

kiss impression *n* **:** impression (as of paper against an inked printing surface) that is extremely light

kissing bug *n* **:** CONENOSE

kissing cousin *or* **kissing kin** *n* **:** a cousin or other collateral relative whom one knows just well enough to kiss more or less formally upon occasional meeting ⟨distantly related but not *kissing cousins*⟩

kissing dance *n* **:** a social couple dance culminating in a kiss

kissing gate *n, dial Eng* **:** a gate swinging in a V-shaped enclosure that allows only one person to pass at a time

kiss·ing·ly *adv* **:** in a lightly touching manner

kiss-in-the-ring \'=‚=‚=\ *n* **:** drop the handkerchief in which the pursuing player may kiss the player he catches

kiss-me \'=,=\ *n* -s **:** any of various plants: as **a :** WILD PANSY **b :** LONDON PRIDE 1 **c :** HERB ROBERT

kiss-me-at-the-gate \'====‚'=\ *n* **:** a fragrant Chinese honeysuckle (*Lonicera fragrantissima*) grown in the southern U.S. for ornament

kiss-me-over-the-garden-gate \'==,===‚'=\ *n* **:** any of various plants: as **a :** PRINCE'S-FEATHER 2 **b :** ACHIMENES 2

kiss-me-quick \'==,=\ *n* -s **:** a small bonnet worn off the face esp. in the latter half of the 19th century

kiss of death [so called fr. the betraying kiss with which Judas pointed out Jesus in the garden of Gethsemane (Mark 14: 44–45)] **:** an act or association ultimately causing ruin ⟨track bucks baseball but this need not be the automatic *kiss of death* —Tommy O'Brien⟩ ⟨for an American to offer . . . friendship meant the *kiss of death* — for the Russian —Gouverneur Paulding⟩

kiss off *vt* **:** DISMISS ⟨*kisses* the other performers *off* as mere amateurs⟩

kiss-off \'=,=\ *n* -s [*kiss off*] **1 :** KISS 2b **2 a :** an event marking the end (as of a relationship) **b :** an act of dismissal

kiss of peace : a religious ceremonial kiss symbolizing fraternal unity and originating in the early church

kiss spot *n* **:** a spot appearing on vegetable-tanned leather caused by contact with another hide in tanning

1**kist** *archaic past of* KISS

2**kist** \'kist\ *n* -s [ME *kiste,* fr. ON *kista* — more at CHEST] *chiefly dial* **:** any of various chests: as **a :** a clothes or linen trunk **b :** COFFIN

3**kist** \"\ *var of* CIST

4**kist** \"\ *n* -s [Ar *qist*] *India* **:** an installment (as of land revenue) or the time for paying it

kist·vaen \'kist,vīn\ *n* -s [modif. of W *cistfaen,* fr. *cist* chest + *faen,* mutated form of *maen* stone] **:** 1CIST 1

kis·wa *or* **kis·wah** \'ki,swä\ *n* -s [Ar *kiswah*] **:** a black cloth covering the Kaaba

1**kit** \'kit, *usu* -id·+V\ *n* -s [ME *kitt, kyt,* prob. fr. MD *kitte, kit* jug, vessel] **1 a** *dial Brit* **:** a wooden tub or small barrel (as for butter, milk, water, fish) **b :** a round shipping container of wood or metal usu. having tapered sides, a solid bottom on the larger end, and a closure at or in the smaller end and holding about five gallons **2 a** (1) **:** a collection of equipment and often supplies typically carried in a box or bag **:** an outfit of necessary implements, effects, or materials ⟨a plumber's ~⟩ ⟨a first-aid ~⟩ (2) **:** a container (as a bag, box, or folder) for such a collection ⟨essential medical supplies in a clear plastic ~⟩ ⟨a big green ~ bulging with leaflets⟩ **b** *chiefly Brit* **:** an outfit of clothing and accouterments **:** UNIFORM, REGALIA ⟨troops in full battle ~ —Hal Lehrman⟩ ⟨the first game is won by players wearing their own ~ —Denzil Batchelor⟩ **:** DRESS, WEAR ⟨dressed in riding ~, a sleeveless brown silk shirt, breeches, and high boots —Eve Langley⟩ **c** *chiefly Brit* **:** EQUIPMENT, GEAR ⟨run over to my billet and get some overnight ~ —Lionel Shapiro⟩ **d :** a commercially packaged set of parts (as of a scale model, boat, or automobile accessory) usu. ready to assemble and often accompanied by finishing materials and tools **e :** a collection of printed material giving information or instruction on one subject and assembled (as in a folder) for distribution ⟨a free ~ which includes just about everything a prospective visitor should know about the state —*Springfield (Mass.) Republican*⟩ ⟨sent instruction ~s to every high school so youngsters can learn how to make out income-tax returns —*Newsweek*⟩ **3** *or* **kit and biling** *or* **kit and boodle** *or* **kit and caboodle :** a group of persons or things **:** LOT — used with *whole* ⟨sent the whole *kit and caboodle* of them home⟩ **4** *dial Eng* **:** BASKET; *esp* **:** one used for fish **5 :** a group of pigeons trained to fly together

2**kit** \"\ *vt* **kitted; kitted; kitting; kits** *chiefly Brit* **:** EQUIP, OUTFIT — often used with *up* ⟨enlisted in the Navy and went . . to be *kitted* up —A.P.Herbert⟩

3**kit** \"\ *n* -s [origin unknown] **:** a small violin formerly used by dancing masters

4**kit** *also* **kitt** \"\ *n* -s [short for *kitten*] **1 :** KITTEN 1 **2 a :** a young immature or much undersized individual of one of the smaller fur-bearing animals ⟨fox ~⟩ **b :** the skin or pelt of such an animal

5**kit** \"\ *vi* **kitted; kitted; kitting; kits :** to give birth to kits

ki·tab \kē'täb\ *n* -s [Ar *kitāb* book] *Islam* **:** a book esp. of sacred scripture and usu. of the scripture of the Jews, Christians, Zoroastrians, or Muslims

ki·ta·bi \-bē\ *n* -s [Ar *kitābī,* fr. *kitāb*] *Islam* **:** one who believes in a book of sacred scripture and with whom a Muslim may marry in what is deemed a lawful marriage

kit·a·mat *or* **kit·i·mat** \,kid·ə'mat\ *n, pl* **kitamat** *or* **kitamats** *or* **kitimat** *or* **kitimats** *usu cap* **1 :** a Wakashan people of Douglas Channel, British Columbia **2 :** a member of the Kitamat people

kitambilla *var of* KETEMBILLA

kitan *usu cap, var of* KHITAN

ki·ta·ne·muk \kə'tanə,mək\ *n, pl* **kitanemuk** *or* **kitanemuks** *usu cap* **1 :** a Shoshonean people living between the Tehachapi mountains and the Mojave desert, Calif. **2 :** a member of the Kitanemuk people

ki·tar *or* **kit·tar** \kə'tär\ *n* -s [Ar *qītār, qīthār* — more at GUITAR] **:** an Arabian guitar

kit bag *n* **1 :** KNAPSACK **2 :** a rectangular usu. leather traveling bag with sides that come together and fasten at the top or open to the full width of the bag and with two straps that wrap around the bag to secure it

kit bag 2

kit boat *n* **:** precut parts of a boat that can be assembled by the purchaser into a complete boat

kit-cat *or* **kit-kat** \'kit,kat\ *n* [after *Kit* (*Christopher*) *Cat* or *Catling,* 18th cent. Eng. keeper of the tavern where the club originally met] **1** *usu cap K&C or both Ks* **:** a member of an early 18th century London club of Whig politicians and men of letters **2** [prob. so called fr. the portraits hung in a dining room of the Kit-cat club whose low ceiling made the smaller size necessary] : a portrait of less than half length but including the hands ⟨some thirty major portraits hanging on the walls, besides *kit-cats*, heads, sketches . . . and all the lesser oddities of a collection many years in the making —Clemence Dane⟩

¹kitch·en \'kichən\ *n* -s [ME *kichene, kichen,* fr. OE *cycene;* akin to OHG *chuhhina* kitchen, MLG *kökene,* MD *cokene, cökene;* all fr. a prehistoric WGmc word borrowed fr. LL *coquina,* fr. L, fem. of *coquinus* of cooking, fr. *coquere* to cook + *-inus* -ine — more at COOK] **1 a :** a room or some other space (as a wall area or separate building) with facilities for cooking : a place for preparing meals ⟨living room, dining room, and the ~⟩ ⟨a soup ~ where the starving villagers were fed⟩ ⟨a mobile ~ for soldiers in the field⟩ **b :** the personnel that prepares, cooks, and serves food ⟨send orders to the ~⟩ ⟨the ~ sent up a meal⟩ **c :** a combination of kitchen fixtures including cabinets and often stove, refrigerator, and sink marketed as a unit and installed as built-in equipment **2** *now chiefly Scot* **:** food from the kitchen; *specif* **:** food eaten as a side dish with other food **3 a :** any of a series of compartments in which sublimed arsenic fumes from a furnace for treating arsenical ore and baghouse dust are condensed **b :** the laboratory of a reverberatory furnace

²kitchen \"\ *adj* **1 :** of, relating to, or of a kind suitable for use in a kitchen ⟨mop the ~ floor⟩ ⟨~ clock⟩ ⟨a ~ stove⟩ **2 :** that works in a kitchen ⟨a ~ maid⟩ **3 :** used as a kitchen ⟨soldiers bringing supplies to the ~ tent⟩ **4 a :** constituting or having the characteristics of a pidgin language that is used largely for communication between servants and their employers when the two groups are not native speakers of the same language **b :** constituting or having the characteristics of a language as spoken by uneducated speakers ⟨want official acceptance of their language — a sort of ~ Dutch —Serge Fliegers⟩

³kitchen \"\ *vt* -ED/-ING/-S **1** *obs* **:** to furnish food to : entertain with kitchen fare **2** *chiefly Scot* **a :** to make palatable : SEASON **b :** to serve (food) as kitchen

Kitchen Bouquet *trademark* — used for bouquet garni

kitchen cabinet *n* **1 :** a cupboard with drawers and shelves designed to hold within easy reach utensils and materials used in preparing food **2 :** an unofficial and informal group of advisers to the head of a government who are held to have more influence with him than his official cabinet ⟨certain of our Presidents have turned to *kitchen Cabinets* to aid them —*Fortune*⟩

kitchen dresser *n, Brit* : KITCHEN CABINET 1

kitch·en·er \-ch(ə)nə(r)\ *n* -s [¹*kitchen* + *-er*] **1 :** the person in charge of a monastery kitchen **2** *Brit* **:** a cooking range

kitch·en·ette *also* **kitch·en·et** \,kichə'net, *usu* -ed·+V\ *n* -s [¹*kitchen* + *-ette*] **:** a very small compactly arranged room or an alcove containing cooking facilities

kitchen garden *n* **:** a household garden in which vegetables and often fruits and herbs are cultivated ⟨a flower garden on one side and a *kitchen garden* at the back⟩

kitchen kaffir *n, usu cap both Ks* [²*kitchen*] **:** a pidgin language based on Xhosa, Afrikaans, and English and sometimes used in communication between Europeans and Africans in So. Africa

kitchen match *n* **:** a wooden splint match that can be lighted by any friction surface

kitchen midden *n* [trans. of Dan *kökkenmödding*] **:** a refuse heap; *specif* **:** a mound (as a Neolithic shell heap) marking the site of a primitive human habitation ⟨army engineers, excavating for a mess hall . . . dig unexpectedly into the refuse heap of a prehistoric *kitchen midden* —Corey Ford⟩

kitchen police *n* **1 :** enlisted men detailed to assist the cooks in an army mess **2 :** the work of kitchen police — abbr. *K.P.*

kitchen rose *n* **:** CINNAMON ROSE

kitchen stuff *n* **1 :** food for cooking : kitchen requisites (as vegetables) **2 :** kitchen refuse or waste; *esp* **:** fat collected from pots and pans

kitchenware \'==,=\ *n* **:** hardware (as cutlery and cooking utensils) for kitchen use

kitch·ie \'kichi\ *Scot var of* KITCHEN

kitch·in \'kichən\ *n* -s *usu cap* [after Joseph A. *Kitchin b*1910 Amer. political scientist] **:** a business cycle formed by a recession of about three and a half years during a prosperity phase ⟨the *Kitchins* can be best observed, for all countries, on the chart of rates of changes —J.A.Schumpeter⟩

¹kite \'kīt, *usu* -īd·+V\ *n* -s [ME, fr. OE *cӯta;* akin to MHG *kūze* owl, ON *kӯta* to quarrel, Gk *goan* to lament, Lith *gausti* to sound, drone — more at COMELY] **1 :** any of various usu. rather small hawks of the family Accipitridae that have long narrow wings, a deeply forked tail, a weak bill, and feet adapted for taking such prey as insects and small reptiles, that feed also on offal, and that are noted for graceful sustained flight; *specif* **:** a common comparatively large European scavenger (*Milvus milvus*) with chiefly reddish brown plumage — compare BLACK KITE, BLACK-SHOULDERED KITE, SWALLOW-TAILED KITE, WHITE-TAILED KITE

kite 3

2 : a person that preys on others **3 :** a contrivance consisting of a surface of a light material stretched over a light often diamond-shaped framework, often provided with a balancing tail, and intended to be flown in the air at the end of a long string — see BOX KITE **4 a :** ACCOMMODATION BILL **b :** a check drawn against uncollected funds in a bank account **c :** a check that has been fraudulently raised before cashing **5 kites** *pl* **:** the lightest and usu. the loftiest sails (as skysails, spinnakers) ordinarily carried only in a light breeze — called also *flying kites* **6 :** something suggested or tried in order to see how people react : a tentative proposal or venture : TRIAL BALLOON, FEELER ⟨published what has all the appearance of being a ~ for his whole project —Peter Ure⟩ **7 a :** a drag to be towed under water at any depth up to about 40 fathoms that on striking bottom is upset and rises to the surface — called also *sentry* **b :** a device (as a heavy wooden platform) attached to a submerged line towed by a mine sweeper or between two vessels to make the line tow at a predetermined depth for clearing mined areas **8 a :** a heavier-than-air aircraft which is without propelling means other than the towline pull and whose support is derived from the force of the wind moving past its surfaces **b** *slang Brit* **:** AIRPLANE **9 :** a step cut for a gem having a diamond shape and eight quadrilateral facets **10 :** a letter smuggled past prison censorship

²kite \"\ *vb* -ED/-ING/-S *vi* **1 :** to get money or credit by a kite; *specif* **:** to create a false bank balance by manipulating deposit accounts **2 :** to go in a rapid, carefree, or flighty manner: **a :** to run or move very fast ⟨that dog went *kiting* down the street traveling all of 20 knots —Kenneth Roberts⟩ **b :** GALLIVANT ⟨would ~ off to the movies just about dish-washing time⟩ ⟨used to ~ around with the other kids in the evening⟩ **c :** to rise rapidly : SOAR ⟨tin prices *kited* in world markets . . . to another record high —*Wall Street Jour.*⟩ **d :** to leave suddenly : DECAMP ⟨walked out on me . . . took the boys and *kited* —Vance Bourjaily⟩ **3 :** to fly a hawk-shaped paper kite over the haunts of game birds (as grouse) to frighten them into lying close ~ *vt* **1 :** to cause to soar; *specif* **:** to inflate (as a price) in amount ⟨war-risk insurance has *kited* shipping costs skyward —*Time*⟩ **2 :** to use (a kite) to get money or credit ⟨had *kited* the worthless draft on innocent victims —M.H.Hunt⟩; *specif* **:** to raise the amount of (a check) by fraud before cashing it ⟨a $27.50 check could be *kited* to $327.50 —*Newsweek*⟩

kite balloon *n* **:** an elongated captive balloon with lobes that keep it headed into the wind for increased lift — abbr. *KB*

kite eagle *n* **:** a nearly black East Indian eagle (*Ictinaëtus malayensis*) having a short crest and a very large claw on the inner toe

kite falcon *n* **:** CUCKOO FALCON

kiteflying \'=,==\ *n* **:** the issuing of political news in such form that it may later be disavowed

kit·er \'kīd·ə(r)\ *n* -s **:** one that kites

kite-shaped \'=,=\ *adj, of a shield* **:** having a bowed top, long straight sides, and a pointed bottom

kite track *n* **:** a racetrack with only one turn and with the stretches converging to a point

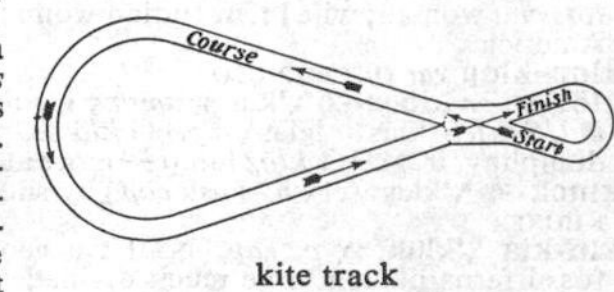

kite track

kit fox *n* [⁴*kit*] **1 a :** a small fox (*Vulpes velox*) of the plains of western No. America **b :** a related species (*V. macrotis*) of the southwestern U.S. **2 :** the fur or pelt of the kit fox

kith \'kith\ *n* -s [ME *kiththe, kith,* fr. OE *cӯththu, cӯthth,* fr. *cūth* known — more at COUTH] **1 :** familiar friends, neighbors, fellow countrymen, or acquaintances **2 :** KINDRED **3 :** a culturally homogeneous social group tending to be endogamous

kith and kin *n pl* [ME] **1 :** friends and kindred **2 :** KINDRED, RELATIONS

kith·a·ra \'kithərə, ki'thärə\ *var of* CITHARA

kithe *or* **kythe** \'kīth\ *vb* -ED/-ING/-S [ME *kithen, kythen,* fr. OE *cӯthan,* fr. *cūth* known — more at UNCOUTH] *vt, chiefly Scot* **:** to make known : MANIFEST, DECLARE ~ *vi, chiefly Scot* **:** to become known or manifest : APPEAR

kitimat *usu cap, var of* KITAMAT

kit-kat *var of* KIT-CAT

kit·ke·hah·ki \'kitkə,häkē\ *n, pl* **kitkehahki** *or* **kitkehahkis** *usu cap* **1 :** a people of the Pawnee confederacy **2 :** a member of the Kitkehahki people

kit·ksan \,kitkə'san\ *n, pl* **kitksan** *or* **kitksans** *usu cap* [Tsimshian, lit., people of the Skeena river] **1 a :** a division of the Tsimshian people in the upper Skeena river valley, British Columbia **b :** a member of such people **2 :** a dialect of Tsimshian

kit·ling \'kitlən\ *n* -s [ME, fr. ON *ketlingr,* fr. *katt-, kötte* cat + *-lingr* -ling — more at CAT] *dial Brit* **:** KITTEN

kit·man \'kitmən, -,man\ *n, pl* **kitmen** [¹*kit* + *man*] **:** an automobile-factory stock clerk who assembles matched hardware for each car

kitmutgar *var of* KHIDMATGAR

ki·tol \'kē,tōl, -tōl\ *n* -s [irreg. fr. Gk *kētos* sea monster, whale + E *-ol*] **:** a crystalline alcohol $C_{40}H_{58}(OH)_2$ obtainable esp. from whale-liver oil and capable of yielding vitamin A (as by heating)

kitool *var of* KITTUL

kits *pl of* KIT, *pres 3d sing of* KIT

kitsch \'kich\ *n* -ES [G, fr. *kitschen* to slap (a work of art) together, fr. G dial., to scrape up mud from the street] **:** artistic or literary material held to be of low quality, often produced to appeal to popular taste, and marked esp. by sentimentalism, sensationalism, and slickness ⟨the traditional gap . . . between ~ and literature —William Phillips b.1907⟩

kitt *var of* KIT

kittar *var of* KITAR

kitted *past of* KIT

kit·tel \'kid·ᵊl\ *n, pl* **kittel** [Yiddish *kitel,* fr. MHG *kitel, kietel* cotton or hempen outer garment, prob. fr. Ar *quṭn* cotton] **:** a white cotton or linen robe worn by Orthodox Jews on Rosh Hashana and Yom Kippur and at the Passover Seder and also used as a burial shroud

¹kit·ten \'kitᵊn\ *n* -s [ME *kitoun,* modif. (influenced by *kitling*) of (assumed) ONF *caton* (whence F dial. — Normandy — *caton*), dim. of ONF *cat,* fr. LL *cattus* — more at CAT] **1 a** (1) **:** a young cat (2) **:** a cat less than nine months old — used esp. in relation to competitive showing **b :** an immature individual of various other small mammals ⟨hamster ~⟩ ⟨rabbit ~⟩ **2 :** ⁴KIT 2b **3** *chiefly dial* **:** one of the rolls of dust that collect under furniture — usu. used in pl.

²kitten \"\ *vb* -ED/-ING/-S [ME *kytnen* fr. *kitoun,* n.] *vi* **:** to give birth to kittens : LITTER ~ *vt* **:** to give birth to ⟨that's what I've been called since I was ~*ed* —*Irish Statesman*⟩

kittenball \'==,=\ *n* **:** SOFTBALL

kitten-breeches \'==,==\ *n pl but sing or pl in constr* [so called fr. the shape of the blossoms] **:** DUTCHMAN'S-BREECHES

kit·ten·ish \'kit(ᵊ)nish, -nēsh\ *adj* **1 :** resembling or like that of a kitten **2 :** marked by coy or affected playfulness ⟨she was fat and over forty, but still ~ —*Farmer's Weekly* (So. Africa)⟩ — **kit·ten·ish·ly** *adv* — **kit·ten·ish·ness** *n* -ES

kit·ten·less \'kitᵊnləs\ *adj* **:** having no kitten ⟨a ~ cat⟩

kit·ter·een \,kid·ə'rēn\ *n* -s [origin unknown] **:** a two-wheeled one-horse carriage with a movable top

kitting *pres part of* KIT

kit·ti·wake \'kid·ē,wāk\ *n* -s [imit.] **:** any of various gulls of the genus *Rissa* having the hind toe short or rudimentary; *esp* **:** ATLANTIC KITTIWAKE

¹kit·tle \'kid·ᵊl, 'kitᵊl\ *vt* -ED/-ING/-S [ME (northern dial.) *kytyllen,* prob. fr. ON *kitla* — more at TICKLE] **1** *chiefly Scot* **:** TICKLE **2** *chiefly Scot* **:** ENLIVEN, TITILLATE **3** *chiefly Scot* **:** to flatter and please **4** *chiefly Scot* **:** to keep guessing : PERPLEX

²kittle \"\ *adj* -ER/-EST **1** *chiefly Scot* **a :** easily excited : TOUCHY, SKITTISH, FIDGETY **b :** QUICK, APT ⟨she's ~ of her hands —George Meriton⟩ **c :** VARIABLE, CAPRICIOUS ⟨Fortune will play ~ tricks —John Barr⟩ **d :** nicely balanced : DELICATE **2** *chiefly Scot* **:** hard or risky to deal with or do : TICKLISH ⟨to paint an angel's ~ work —Robert Burns⟩ ⟨it's a ~ thing to keep the likes o' him waitin' —S.R.Crockett⟩

³kittle \"\ *vi* -ED/-ING/-S [prob. of Scand origin; akin to Norw dial. *kjetla* to kitten, fr. *kjetling* kitten, fr. ON *ketlingr* — more at KITLING] **1** *chiefly Scot* **:** KITTEN **2** *chiefly Scot* **:** GENERATE, ARISE

kittle cattle *n, pl* **kittle cattle** *usu pl in constr* [²*kittle*] *chiefly dial* **:** a group of people that are difficult to manage and inclined to be capricious ⟨*kittle cattle* who do rather unpredictable things —*Country Life*⟩

kit·tling \'kitlən\ *var of* KITLING

kit·tlish \'kitlish\ *also* **kit·tly** \-li\ *adj* [¹*kittle* + *-ish* or *-y*] *chiefly Scot* **:** TICKLISH, KITTLE

kitt·litz's murrelet \'kitləts(əz)-\ *n, usu cap K* [after Baron Friedrich von *Kittlitz* †1874 Ger. officer, ornithologist, and traveler] **:** a murrelet (*Brachyramphus brevirostre*) having buff spots and ranging from Japan and Kamchatka to Alaska

kit·tly-benders \'kitlē+,-\ *n pl* [*kittly* (perh. fr. ¹*kittle* + *-y*) + *benders,* pl. of *bender*] **:** thin bending ice; *also* **:** the act of running over such ice

kit·tul *also* **kit·tool** *or* **ki·tul** \kə'tül\ *n* -s [Sinhalese *kitul, hitul,* fr. Skt *hintāla*] **1 a :** a brownish black fiber resembling horsehair yielded by the leafstalks of the Asiatic jaggery palm and used chiefly in making brushes for polishing linens and cottons and for brushing velvets — called also *black fiber* **b :** JAGGERY PALM **2 a :** a fiber derived from the gomuti palm resembling kittul **b :** GOMUTI PALM

¹kit·ty \'kid·ē, -itī, |i\ *n* -ES [fr. *Kitty,* nickname for *Catherine*] **1** *also* **kittie** \"\ -s *chiefly Scot* **:** a girl of easy virtue : WENCH **2 :** KITTY WREN

²kitty \"\ *n* -ES [⁴*kit* + *-y*] **:** CAT 1a; *esp* **:** KITTEN

³kitty \"\ *n* -ES [¹*kit* + *-y*] **1 :** a small bowl or other receptacle **2 a** (1) **:** a fund in a poker game accumulated by taking one or two chips from each large pot and used (as to pay expenses or buy refreshments) for the players (2) **:** a pool that belongs to all players in a game but that participates in the scoring or settlement of certain hands as though it were a player opposed to the bidder **b :** a sum of money or collection of goods usu. accumulated by occasional small contributions and often administered by or for the contributors : POOL, FUND ⟨enough in the ~ to make the trip —E.K.Gann⟩ ⟨a campaign ~ raised by oil and utility companies —*Time*⟩ ⟨the ground crew's ~ of cigarettes —Saul Levitt⟩ **c :** the widow in skat, pinochle, and other games — called also *blind* **3 :** JACK 2e(1)

⁴kitty \"\ *n* -ES [prob. alter. of *kidcote*] *dial chiefly Eng* **:** JAIL

⁵kitty \"\ *n* -ES [by shortening & alter.] **:** KITTIWAKE

kitty-corner *or* **kitty-cornered** *var of* CATERCORNER

kitty wren *n* [fr. the name *Kitty*] **:** the small European wren of the genus *Troglodytes* (*T. troglodytes*)

ki·tu·na·han \kə'tünəhən\ *n* -s *usu cap* **:** a language family of southwestern Canada and northwestern U.S. comprising Kutenai

ki·va \'kēvə\ *n* -s [Hopi] **:** a Pueblo Indian structure used as a ceremonial, council, work, and lounging room for men that is usu. round and is at least partly underground with entrance and lighting usu. from the roof and that includes a fireplace, altar space, and sipapu

¹kiv·er \'kivə(r)\ *n* -s [ME *kevere,* alter. of *keve, kive* keeve — more at KEEVE] *dial Eng* **:** a shallow vessel or wooden tub

²kiver \"\ *dial var of* COVER

ki·wai \kē'wäē\ *n, pl* **kiwai** *or* **kiwais** *usu cap* **1 a :** a Papuan people inhabiting islands at the mouth of the Fly River, Territory of Papua **b :** a member of such people **2 :** the language of the Kiwai people

ki·wa·ni·an \kə'wänēən\ *n* -s *usu cap* [*Kiwanis* (*club*) + E *-an*] **:** a member of one of the major service clubs

ki·wi \'kē(,)wē\ *n* -s [Maori, of imit. origin] **1** *also* **kiwi-kiwi** \'=(,)=:=(,)=\ **:** a flightless New Zealand bird of the genus *Apteryx* that is about the size of a domestic chicken, has very rudimentary wings, stout legs, a long straight or slightly curved bill with nostrils near the tip, and hairlike plumage of various shades of gray and brown, nests in burrows, and lays eggs as large as one fourth its weight which are incubated by the male **2** *usu cap* **:** NEW ZEALANDER — used as a nickname

kiwi

kiyang *var of* KIANG

¹ki-yi \(')kī'yī\ *interj* [origin unknown] — used to express exultation

²ki-yi \"\ *vi* **ki-yied; ki-yied; ki-yiing; ki-yis** [imit.] **:** YELP ⟨a . . . dog ran *ki-yiing* past us —Klondy Nelson & Corey Ford⟩

³ki-yi \"\ *n* -s **1 :** a bark or yelp (as of a dog) **2 :** DOG

⁴ki-yi \"\ *n* -s [origin unknown] *in the U.S. Navy* **:** a small brush for scrubbing clothing or canvas

ki-yi \'kē(,)yē\ *n* -s [origin unknown] **:** a small chub (*Leucichthys kiyi*) abundant in deep water in the Great Lakes

ki·zil \kə'zil\ *n, pl* **kizil** *or* **kizils** *usu cap* **1 :** a Russianized Mongolo-Tatar people around Achinsk, central Siberia **2 :** a member of the Kizil people

kiz·il·bash \,kizəl'bäsh\ *n, pl* **kizilbash** *or* **kizilbashes** *usu cap* [Turk *kızılbaş,* fr. *kızıl* red + *baş* head] **1 :** a Persianized Turk of a class devoted to business and professional pursuits in Afghanistan; *also* **:** a member of a community of Turkish or mixed-race colonists in Asia Minor **2 :** a community of Kurdish Turks in eastern Turkey who are Christians and whose women refuse to veil their faces **3 :** a nomadic people in the plains around Ankara, Karahisar, and Tokat professing the Muslim religion but practicing ancient pagan rites

kj *abbr* kilojoule

kjel·dahl \'kel,däl\ *adj, usu cap* [after Johan G. C. T. *Kjeldahl* †1900 Dan. chemist] **:** of, relating to, or being a method for determining the amount of nitrogen (as in an organic substance) by digesting a sample with boiling concentrated sulfuric acid and other reagents, adding an excess of alkali, distilling, collecting the ammonia expelled, and determining the ammonia by titration ⟨~ analysis⟩ ⟨~ apparatus⟩

kjeldahl flask *n, usu cap K* [after Johan G. C. T. *Kjeldahl*] **:** a round-bottomed usu. long-necked glass flask for use in digesting the sample in the Kjeldahl method

kjel·dahl·iza·tion \,kel,däləˈzāshən\ *n* -s *sometimes cap* **:** the process of kjeldahlizing

kjel·dahl·ize \'kel,dä,līz\ *vt* -ED/-ING/-S *sometimes cap* [*Kjeldahl* (*method*) + *-ize*] **:** to subject to the Kjeldahl method or a modification of this method

kl *abbr* kiloliter

klab \'kläb\ *n* -s [by shortening] **:** KLABERJASS

kla·ber·jass \'kläbə(r),yäs\ *n* [G] **:** a two-handed game played with 32 cards in which a player scores by holding a higher sequence than his opponent, by holding both the king and queen of trumps, by taking the last trick, and by taking scoring cards in tricks — called also *clabber, clob, clobber, jass, klab, klob*

Kjeldahl flask

klallam *usu cap, var of* CLALLAM

kla·man·tan *or* **kle·man·tan** \klə'män·,tän\ *n, pl* **klamantan** *or* **klamantans** *or* **klemantan** *or* **klemantans** *usu cap* [native name in Borneo; akin to Indonesian *Kalimantan* Borneo] **1 :** any of numerous Dayak peoples living in western, central, and northern Borneo **2 :** a member of any of the Klamantan peoples

klam·ath \'klaməth\ *n, pl* **klamath** *or* **klamaths** *usu cap* **1 a :** a Lutuamian people of southeastern Oregon and northern California **b :** a member of such people **2 :** a language of the Klamath people

klamath weed *n, usu cap K* [fr. *Klamath* river, Oregon and California] **:** a cosmopolitan yellow-flowered perennial St.-John's-wort (*Hypericum perforatum*) common in fields and waste places and useful for wildlife but a noxious weed when established in rangelands

klan \'klan, -aa(ə)n\ *n* -s *usu cap* [fr. (*Ku Klux*) *Klan,* a secret organization — more at KU KLUX] **1 :** an organization of Ku Kluxers **2 :** a subordinate unit of the Ku Kluxers' organization

klan·ism \'kla,nizəm, -laa,n-\ *n* -s *usu cap* **:** the beliefs or practices of Ku Kluxers

klans·man \'klanzmən, -laanz-\ *n, pl* **klansmen** *usu cap* **:** KU KLUXER

klap·match *or* **clap·match** \'klap,mach\ *n* [by folk etymology fr. D *klapmuts* cap with earflaps, hooded seal, fr. *klap, klep* brim, earflap + *muts* cap] **:** a female seal

klap·roth·ite \'kläprə,thīt\ *or* **klap·roth·o·lite** \klä'prōthə,līt\ *n* -s [*klaprothite* fr. G *klaprothit,* fr. Martin H. *Klaproth* †1817 German chemist + G *-it* -ite; *klaprotholite* alter. of *klaprothite*] **:** a steel-gray mineral $Cu_6Bi_4S_9$ consisting of a sulfide of copper and bismuth

klatch *or* **klatsch** \'klach, -ä-\ *n* -ES [G *klatsch* gossip, action of gossiping, fr. *klatschen* to gossip, of imit. origin] **:** a gathering characterized by informal conversation ⟨you meet him at a literary cocktail ~ —Victor Riesel⟩

klav·ern \'klavə(r)n\ *n* -s [blend of *klan* and *cavern*] **1 :** a meeting place of Ku Kluxers ⟨sallies forth to the ~ and there dons his resplendent robe —Stetson Kennedy⟩ **2 :** a local unit of the Ku Kluxers' organization

kla·vier \klə'vi(ə)r, kla'-, -iə\ *n* -s [G, fr. F *clavier* — more at CLAVIER] **:** CLAVIER 2

kla·vier·stück \-,shtik, *G* klä'vēr,shtʏk\ *n* [G, fr. *klavier* piano + *stück* piece] **:** a piano piece

Klax·on \'klaksən\ *trademark* — used for an electrically operated horn or warning signal

klea·gle \'klēgəl\ *n* -s *often cap* [*klan* + *eagle*] **:** a high-ranking officer in the hierarchy of the Ku Kluxers' organization

kle·bels·berg·ite \'klabəlz,bər,gīt\ *n* -s [Hung *klebelsbergit,* fr. Kuno *Klebelsberg* †1932 Hung. statesman + Hung *-it -ite*] **:** a mineral consisting of a basic antimony sulfate found in the interstices between crystals in columnar aggregates of stibnite

kleb·si·el·la \,klebzē'elə, -epsē-\ *n* [NL, fr. Edwin *Klebs* †1913 Ger. pathologist + NL *-i-* + *-ella*] **1** *cap* **:** a genus of plump nonmotile gram-negative frequently encapsulated bacterial rods (family Enterobacteriaceae) commonly held to comprise a single variable species — see PNEUMOBACILLUS **2** -s **:** an organism of the genus *Klebsiella*

klebs-löff·ler bacillus \'kläps|'leflə(r)-, 'klebz|\ *n, usu cap K&L* [after Edwin *Klebs* and Friedrich A. J. *Löffler* †1915 Ger. bacteriologist] **:** a bacterium (*Corynebacterium diphtheriae*) that causes human diphtheria

kleene·boc \'klīn(ə),bäk, -lān-\ *n* -s [Afrik *kleinbok,* fr. *klein* small + *bok* male antelope] **:** ROYAL ANTELOPE

Klee·nex \'klē,neks\ *trademark* — used for a cleansing tissue

klein bottle \'klīn-\ *n, usu cap K* [after Felix *Klein* †1925 Ger. mathematician and inventor] **:** a surface that is closed in such a way that it is possible to pass from a point on one side to the corresponding point on the opposite side without passing through the surface and that is formed by passing the nar-

Klein bottle

row end of a tapered tube through the side of the tube and flaring this end out to join the other end

klein·ite \'klī,nīt\ *n* -s [G *kleinit*, fr. Karl *Klein* †1907 Ger. mineralogist + G *-it* -ite] **:** a mineral approximately $Hg_{12}(NH_4)_6SO_4Cl_6(OH)_3O_3$ consisting of a basic oxide, sulfate, and chloride of mercury and ammonium

kleist·ian jar \'klīstēən-\ *n, usu cap K* [Ewald J. von *Kleist* †1748 Ger. scientist and dean of the cathedral of Kamin, Pomerania, one of its discoverers] **:** LEYDEN JAR

klemantan *usu cap, var of* KLAMANTAN

klen·du·sic \(')klen¦d(y)üsik\ *also* **klen·du·sive** \-siv\ *adj* [*klendusity* + *-ic* or *-ive*] **:** characterized by klendusity

klen·du·si·ty \ˌ=ˈsəd-ē\ *n* -ES [irreg. fr. Gk *kleidoun* to lock up (fr. *kleid-, kleis* key) + *endysis* entry, act of putting on + E *-ity* — more at CLOSE, ENDYSIS] **:** the tendency of a plant or variety to escape infection as a result of having some property (as a thick cuticle or hairy surface) that prevents or hinders inoculation **:** disease-escaping ability

klepht *or* **clepht** \'kleft\ *n* -s *often cap* [NGk *klephtēs*, lit., robber, fr. Gk *kleptēs* robber, fr. *kleptein* to steal] **:** a Greek belonging to one of several independent armed sometimes brigandish communities formed after the Turkish conquest of Greece — **kleph·tic** \-tik\ *adj, usu cap*

klept- *or* **klepto-** *comb form* [Gk, fr. *kleptein* to steal; akin to Goth *hlifan* to steal, L *clepere* to steal, OPruss *auklipts* concealed] **:** stealing **:** theft ⟨*kleptistic*⟩ ⟨*kleptomania*⟩

klep·to·ma·nia *or* **clep·to·ma·nia** \ˌkleptəˈmānēə, -nyə\ *n* [NL, fr. *klept-* + LL *mania*] **:** a persistent neurotic impulse to steal esp. without economic motive in which the object stolen is usu. believed to have symbolic significance to the kleptomaniac

¹klep·to·ma·ni·ac *or* **clep·to·ma·ni·ac** \-nē,ak\ *n* [*klept-* + *maniac*] **:** a person evidencing kleptomania

²kleptomaniac *or* **cleptomaniac** \ˌ==¦==,=\ *adj* **:** of, relating to, or having the characteristics of kleptomania or a kleptomaniac

k-level \'=,==\ *n, usu cap K* **:** the energy level of an electron in a K-shell

klez·mer \'klezmər\ *n, pl* **klez·mo·rim** \klezˈmȯrəm\ *or* **klezmers** [Yiddish, modif. of Heb *kĕlēy zemer* musical instruments] **:** a Jewish instrumentalist; *specif* **:** a member of a band of folk musicians in eastern Europe hired to play at Jewish weddings and gatherings

klick·i·tat *also* **klik·i·tat** \'klikə,tat\ *n, pl* **klickitat** *or* **klickitats** *usu cap* [Chinook, lit., beyond (the Cascade mountains)] **1 a :** a Shahaptian people of southern Washington **b :** a member of such people **2 :** a language of the Klickitat people

klieg eyes *or* **kleig eyes** \'klēg-\ *n pl, sometimes cap K* [*klieg (light)* or *kleig (light)*] **:** a condition marked by conjunctivitis and watering of the eyes resulting from excessive exposure to intense light

klieg light *or* **kleig light** *n, sometimes cap K* [after John H. *Kliegl* †1959 & his brother Anton T. *Kliegl* †1927 Amer. lighting experts born in Germany] **:** a carbon arc lamp used in taking motion pictures

kline reaction *or* **kline test** \'klīn-\ *n, usu cap K* [after Benjamin S. *Kline* b1886 Amer. pathologist] **:** a rapid precipitation test for the diagnosis of syphilis

kling \'kliŋ\ *n* -s *usu cap* [Malay *kĕling*] **:** a Dravidian prob. of Tamil origin of the seaports of southeastern Asia and Malaysia

klink *var of* CLINK

kli·no·kinesis \¦klī(,)nō+\ *n* [NL, fr. Gk *klinein* to lean, slope + NL *-o-* + *kinesis* — more at LEAN] **:** movement that is induced by stimulation and that involves essentially random alteration of direction

kli·no·kinetic \"+\ *adj* [Gk *klinein* + E *-o-* + *kinetic*] **:** of or relating to klinokinesis

klinostat *n* -s [G, fr. *klino-* clin- + *-stat*] **:** CLINOSTAT

kli·no·taxis \¦klīnə+\ *n* [NL, fr. Gk *klinein* + NL *-o-* + *-taxis*] **:** directional orientation involving turning toward a stimulus

klip·bok \'klip,bäk\ *n* -s [Afrik, fr. *klip* cliff, rock + *bok* male antelope] **:** KLIPSPRINGER

klip·das·sie \'klip,däsē\ *or* **klip·das** \-äs\ *n, pl* **klipdassies** *or* **klipdases** [Afrik, fr. *klip* + *dassie* or *das*] **:** a hyrax (*Procavia capensis*) of southern Africa

klip·fish *or* **clip·fish** \'klip,fish\ *n* [in sense 1, part trans. of Dan *klipfisk*, Norw *klippfisk* & G *klippfisch*; Dan & Norw, prob. fr. G, fr. *klippe* rock near the sea, cliff + *fisch* fish; in sense 2, part trans. of Afrik *klipvis*, fr. *klip* rock, stone (fr. MD *klippe*) + *vis* fish; akin to OE *clif* cliff — more at CLIFF] **1 :** a fish (as cod) split open, salted, and dried **2 :** a fish of the family Clinidae **:** KELPFISH

klip·haas \'klip,häs\ *n* -ES [Afrik, fr. *klip* + *haas* hare] **:** ROCK HARE

¹klip·pe \'klipə\ *n* -s [G, fr. Sw *klippa* to cut, shear, clip, fr. ON] **:** a coin with a square or lozenge-shaped flan (as in 17th century German necessity money)

²klippe \"\ *or* **klip** \'klip\ *n, pl* **klip·pen** \-pən\ *or* **klips** [G *klippe* cliff, crag, rock near the sea, fr. MHG, fr. MLG; akin to OE *clif* cliff — more at CLIFF] **:** an outlying isolated remnant of an overthrust rock mass owing its isolation to erosion **:** OUTLIER

klip·salamander \'klip,==,==\ *n* [Afrik, fr. *klip* + *salamander*] **:** a spiny girdle-tailed lizard (*Cordylus cordylus*) that is widely distributed in rocky uplands of southern Africa and that exhibits black and yellowish or reddish color phases; *broadly* **:** GIRDLETAILED LIZARD

klip·spring·er \'klip,spriŋə(r)\ *n* [Afrik, fr. *klip* + *springer* springer, leaper] **:** a small antelope (*Oreotragus oreotragus*) that is somewhat like the chamois in habits and is found from Cape Colony to Somaliland — called also *klipbok*

klis·mos \'kliz,mäs, -,məs\ *n* -ES [Gk, fr. *klinein* to lean, recline — more at LEAN] **:** a chair of Greek design having a concavely curved back rail and curved legs

klis·ter \'klistə(r)\ *n* -s [Norw, lit., paste, fr. MLG *klīster*; akin to OE *clǣg* clay — more at CLAY] **:** a soft wax used on skis esp. for corn snow or crust

klm *abbr* kilometer

klob \'kläb\ *n* -s [by shortening and alter.] **:** KLABERJASS

klock·mann·ite \'kläkmə,nīt\ *n* -s [G *klockmannit*, fr. Friedrich *Klockmann* †1937 Ger. mineralogist + G *-it* -ite] **:** a mineral CuSe consisting of a selenide of copper found in tarnished blue-black granular aggregates

klomp \'klämp\ *n, pl* **klom·pen** \-pən\ [D *klomp* lump, wooden shoe, fr. MD *clompe* clod, block; akin to LG *klump* lump, clump — more at CLUMP] **:** a wooden shoe worn in the Low countries

klomp

klompen dance *n* [part trans. of D *klompendans*, fr. *klomp* + *dans* dance] **:** a Dutch folk dance performed in wooden shoes

klon·dike \'klän,dīk\ *n* -s *usu cap* [fr. *Klondike*, region in Yukon territory, Canada, where a gold rush took place (1897-99)] **1 :** a source of valuable material or wealth ⟨every new road a *Klondike* to the country through which it passes —Cy Warman⟩ ⟨Yiddish represents a potential *Klondike* of barely tapped resources for Germanic and Slavic specialists —H.H. Paper⟩ **2 :** solitaire in which 28 cards are laid out in 7 piles consisting respectively of 1 to 7 cards with the top card of each pile face up and the remaining cards of the pack built in descending sequence of alternate colors as the player goes once through the rest of the pack one card at a time with the object of removing aces from the tableau as they become available and of building on them up to kings — called also *Canfield*

klon·dik·er \-kə(r)\ *n* -s *usu cap* [*Klondike* region + E *-er*] **:** an inhabitant of the Klondike region of northwestern Canada; *esp* **:** one who prospects for gold

klong \'klȯŋ, -ä-\ *n* -s [native name in Thailand] **:** a canal in Thailand used for transportation and drainage ⟨the pond . . . narrowed into a ~ that rimmed the far width of the compound —Kathryn Grondahl⟩

kloof \'klüf, *Afrik* 'klüȯf\ *n* -s [Afrik, fr. MD *clove* cleft, crevice; akin to OHG *klobo* forked stick, fetter, OS *klobo* shackle for the foot, ON *klofi* cleft, OHG *klioban* to split — more at CLEAVE (split)] *Africa* **:** a deep glen **:** GORGE, RAVINE ⟨the narrow ~s of the echoing hills —Stuart Cloete⟩

klootch·man \'klüchmən\ *also* **klooch** \-ch\ *n, pl* **klootchmen** *also* **klooches** [Chinook Jargon *klootshman*, fr. Nootka *łotssma* woman; wife] **:** an Indian woman of northwestern No. America

klop-klop *var of* CLOP-CLOP

klös·se *or* **kloes·se** \'klāsə, *among speakers of German descent in US often* 'klās *or* 'glās\ *n pl* [G *klösse*, pl. of *kloss* lump, clod, dumpling, fr. MHG *klōz* lump — more at CLOUT] **:** DUMPLINGS

kluck·er \'kləkə(r)\ *n* -s *usu cap* [by shortening & alter.] **:** KU KLUXER

klu·kia \'klükēə\ *n, cap* [NL] **:** a genus of early Mesozoic fossil ferns having large much divided fronds and sporangia arranged in spikes (as in ferns of the genus *Schizaea*)

klunk *var of* CLUNK

klux \'kləks\ *vt* -ED/-ING/-ES *often cap* [by shortening] **:** KU-KLUX

klux·er \'kləksə(r)\ *n* -s *usu cap* [by shortening] **:** KU KLUXER

klux·ery \-sərē\ *n* -ES *usu cap* [short for *Ku-Kluxery*] **:** KLANISM

klux·ism \-,sizəm\ *n* -s *usu cap* [short for *Ku-Kluxism*] **:** KLANISM

Kly·don·o·graph \klīˈdänə,graf, -rȧf\ *trademark* — used for an instrument that makes a photographic record of electric surges in power lines

klys·tron \'klīsträn\ *n* -s [fr. *Klystron*, a trademark] **:** an electron tube in which bunching of electrons is produced by subjecting them to acceleration and deceleration by high potential across a gap and which is used for the generation and amplification of ultrahigh-frequency current (as in radar)

km *abbr* **1** kilometer **2** kingdom

kmer *usu cap, var of* KHMER

KMPS *abbr, often not cap* kilometers per second

kmw *abbr* kilomegawatt

kmwh *abbr* kilomegawatt-hour

kn *abbr* knot

¹knack \'nak\ *n* -s [ME *knak, knakke*] **1 a :** a task or chore requiring adroitness and dexterity **b :** a clever way of doing something **c :** TRICK, SCHEME, STRATAGEM **2 a :** a special ready capacity that is hard to analyze or teach for dexterous adroit performance esp. of the unusual, technical, or difficult ⟨the ~ of writing unforgettable, irresistible melodies —Roland Gelatt⟩ **b :** TRAIT, TENDENCY, INCLINATION; *esp* **:** one strictly individual and difficult to explain or analyze ⟨these rents in the interior of the earth had a ~ of enlarging themselves —Norman Douglas⟩ **3 a** *archaic* **:** an ingenious device **:** a cleverly made contrivance; *broadly* **:** TOY, TRINKET, KNICKKNACK **b** *obs* **:** a dainty article of food **:** DELICACY **c** *obs* **:** an ingenious literary device **:** CONCEIT **syn** see GIFT

²knack \"\ *n* -s [ME *knak*, of imit. origin like MHG *knacken* to make a cracking noise, OE *cnocian* to knock — more at KNOCK] **:** a sharp sound (as of the snapping of a finger)

³knack \"\ *vb* -ED/-ING/-s *vt, dial Brit* **:** to strike together so as to make a sharp snapping noise ~ *vi, now dial* **:** to make a sharp abrupt snapping noise **:** CRACK

knack·a·way \'nakə,wā, 'näk-\ *also* **knock·a·way** \'näk-\ *n* [by folk etymology fr. MexSp *anacua* — more at ANAQUA] **:** ANAQUA

knäck·e·bröd \(kə)ˈnekə,brə(r)d, -bərd,-brəd,-bred\ *n* -s [Sw, fr. *knäcka* to break + *bröd* bread] **:** a very crisp and brittle unleavened rye bread made in large flat circular pieces often with a hole in the center

¹knack·er \'nakə(r)\ *n* -s [³*knack* + *-er*] **:** something (as a castanet) used to make a sharp sound or noise; *esp* **:** one of two pieces of bone or wood held loosely between the fingers and struck together by moving the hand — usu. used in pl.

²knacker \"\ *n* -s [prob. fr. E dial. *knacker, nacker* harness-maker, saddle maker, prob. of Scand origin; akin to Icel *hnakkur* saddle; akin to ON *hnakki, hnakkr* back of the neck — more at NECK] **1** *also* **knacker·man** \-mən\ *Brit* **:** one that buys worn-out domestic animals or their carcasses and disposes of the products for other purposes than use as human food (as for animal food or fertilizer) ⟨Jones will sell you to the ~, who will cut your throat and boil you down for the foxhounds —George Orwell⟩ **2** *Brit* **:** one that buys up old structures (as buildings or ships) for their constituent materials **3** *dial Eng* **:** an old worn-out domestic animal (as a horse)

knack·ery \'nakəri\ *n* -ES [²*knacker* + *-y*] *Brit* **:** the place of business of a knacker **:** RENDERING PLANT

knack·wurst *or* **knock·wurst** \'näk,=\ *n* -s [G *knackwurst*, fr. *knacken* to make a cracking noise (fr. MHG) + *wurst* sausage — more at KNACK, BRATWURST] **:** a sausage that is shorter and thicker than a frankfurter and more heavily seasoned

knacky \'nakē\ *adj* -ER/-EST [¹*knack* + *-y*] *chiefly dial* **:** HANDY, INGENIOUS, CLEVER

knag \'nag\ *n* -s [ME *knagge, knagg*; akin to MLG *knagge* knot in wood, pin, peg, Sw *knagg* knot in wood, lump, Norw *knagg, knagge* pin, peg, handle, and perh. to OE *cnotta* knot — more at KNOT] **1 a** *obs* **:** a short projection or spur esp. from a tree trunk or branch **b** *archaic* **:** a wooden peg for hanging things on **2** *obs* **:** a prong of an antler

knagged *adj* [ME, fr. *knagge, knagg* + *-ed*] *obs* **:** KNAGGY

knag·gy \'nagē\ *adj* -ER/-EST **:** full of or covered with gnarled knotty protuberances **:** CRAGGY, RUGGED, ROUGH ⟨the old dark ~ skull —Isak Dinesen⟩

knai·del \kəˈnādəl, 'knā-\ *n, pl* **knai·dlach** \-dləḵ\ [Yiddish *kneydel*, fr. MHG *knödel* — more at KNÖDEL] **:** DUMPLING 1a

¹knap \'nap\ *n* -s [ME *knap*, fr. OE *cnæpp*; akin to OFris *knapp* button, MLG, hill, heel of a shoe, ON *knappr* button, OE *cnotta* knot — more at KNOT] *chiefly dial* **:** a top or crest of a hill **:** SUMMIT; *also* **:** a small hill or knoll

²knap *also* **nap** \"\ *n* -s [ME, of imit. origin] **:** a sharp or abrupt blow **:** RAP, KNOCK

³knap \"\ *vb* **knapped**; **knapped**; **knapping**; **knaps** [ME *knappen*, of imit. origin like MD *cnappen* to make a snapping noise, LG *knappen*] *vt* **1** *dial Brit* **:** to strike a sharp crisp blow to or with ⟨*knapped* his knuckles against the gatepost⟩ **:** RAP **2** *also* **nap :** to break with a quick jerk or blow; *esp* **:** to break up or dress (as flints) **3** *chiefly dial Brit* **:** to bite sharply or eagerly at **:** SNAP, CROP ⟨sheep *knapping* the new flush⟩ **4** *dial Brit* **:** to speak or utter brightly or affectedly **:** CHATTER ~ *vi* **1** *chiefly dial Brit* **:** to bite sharply or eagerly **2** *dial Brit* **:** to chatter smartly **:** BABBLE

knap·per *also* **nap·per** \-pə(r)\ *n* -s [³*knap* + *-er*] **:** one that knaps; *esp* **:** one that dresses flints or other stone by knapping

knap·ping hammer *also* **nap·ping hammer** \'napiŋ-\ *n* **:** a hammer having a medium-weight head with two slightly convex faces used for knapping stone

¹knap·sack \'nap,sak\ *n* [LG *knappsack* or D *knapzak*, fr. LG & D *knappen* to make a snapping noise, bite into, eat + LG *sack* (fr. MLG *sak*) & D *zak* bag, sack, fr. MD *sac* — more at KNAP, SACK] **1 :** a bag or case often of canvas supported on the back by a strap over each shoulder and used esp. for carrying supplies while on a march **2** *or* **knapsack tank :** a container equipped with pressurizing and spraying devices, carried on the back, and used to transport materials (as insecticides or fire-extinguishing chemicals) to the point of application

knapsack 1

²knapsack \"\ *vb* -ED/-ING/-S *vt* **:** to equip with a knapsack ⟨~*ed* travelers⟩ ~ *vi* **:** to travel on foot dependent for supplies on the contents of a knapsack

knapsack sprayer *or* **knapsack pump** *n* **:** a spraying apparatus consisting of a knapsack tank together with pressurizing device, line, and sprayer nozzle, used chiefly in fire control and in spraying fungicides or insecticides

knapscull *also* **knapscap** *n* [ME *knapescall*] *obs Scot* **:** HELMET

knap·weed \'nap,=\ *n* [ME *knopwed*, fr. *knop* + *wed, weed* weed — more at KNOP, WEED] **:** any of various plants of the genus *Centaurea*; *esp* **:** a weedy perennial (*C. nigra*) that is native to Europe but widely naturalized and that has tough wiry stems and knobby heads of purple flowers

knarl *archaic var of* GNARL

knar·ry \'närē\ *also* **knarred** \-rd\ *adj* [*knarry* fr. ME, fr. *knarre* + *-y*; *knarred* fr. *knar* + *-ed*] **:** KNOTTY, GNARLED

knat *or* **knatte** *archaic var of* GNAT

knaur \'nȯ(ə)r\ *or* **knar** \'när\ *n* -s [ME *knarre* rough stone, knot in wood — more at KNUR] **:** a knot or burl on wood

knau·tia \'naủd-ēə\ [NL, fr. Christian *Knaut* †1716 Ger. physician + NL *-ia*] *syn of* SCABIOSA

¹knave \'nāv\ *n* -s [ME (also, boy), fr. OE *cnafa* boy, male servant; akin to OHG *knabo* boy, OHG *knebil* piece of wood used in fastenings, ON *knefill* stick, pole, and prob. to OE *cnotta* knot — more at KNOT] **1** *archaic* **a :** a serving boy **b :** a male servant or menial **c :** a man of humble birth or position **2 :** a tricky deceitful fellow **:** an unscrupulous person **:** ROGUE, RASCAL **3 :** JACK 1 c (1) **syn** see VILLAIN

²knave \"\ *vb* -ED/-ING/-S *vt* **1** *obs* **:** to give the name of knave to **2** *obs* **:** to make a knave of (as oneself) ~ *vi, archaic* **:** to behave knavishly

knave bairn *n* [ME *knavebarn*, fr. *knave* + *barn* child — more at BAIRN] *chiefly Scot* **:** a male child

knav·ery \'nāv(ə)rē, -ri\ *n* -ES **1 a :** the practices of a knave **:** petty villainy **:** knavish action **:** FRAUD, TRICKERY, RASCALITY **b :** a roguish or mischievous trick **:** a rascally scheme — usu. used in pl. **2** *obs* **:** tricks of dress **:** quaint ornaments **:** TRINKETRY **3** *obs* **:** mischievous sportiveness **:** roguish mischief

knave·ship \'nāv,ship\ *n* **1 :** the condition of being a knave **:** the personality of a knave **2** *Scots law* **:** a small customary due formerly paid in meal to the miller's servant at a thirlage mill in return for grinding a quantity of grain

knav·ess \'nāvə̇s\ *n* -ES **:** a female knave

knav·ish \-vish, -vēsh\ *adj* [ME *knavyssh*, fr. *knave* + *-yssh, -ish* -ish] **:** having the characteristics of or appropriate to a knave: **a** *obs* **:** MISCHIEVOUS, ROGUISH ⟨a ~ lad, thus to make poor females mad —Shak.⟩ **b :** DISHONEST, FRAUDULENT ⟨~ booksellers put forth volumes of trash —T.B.Macaulay⟩

knav·ish·ly *adv* **:** in a knavish manner

knav·ish·ness *n* -ES **:** the quality or state of being knavish **:** KNAVERY

knaw \'nȯ, 'nä\ *dial Brit var of* KNOW

knaw·el \'nȯ(ə)l\ *n* -s [modif. of G *knäuel, knauel*, lit., ball of yarn, fr. MHG *kniuwel*, alter. of *kliuwel*, dim. of *kliuwe* ball of yarn, fr. OHG *kliuwa* — more at CLEW] **:** a low spreading Old World annual weed (*Scleranthus annuus*) with inconspicuous greenish flowers that is now widely distributed in No. America; *also* **:** any of several other weedy plants of this genus

knead \'nēd\ *vb* -ED/-ING/-S [ME *kneden*, fr. OE *cnedan*; akin to OS *knedan* to knead, OHG *knetan*, ON *knotha* to knead, OSlav *gnesti* to press, OPruss *gnode* trough for kneading bread, OE *cnotta* knot — more at KNOT] *vt* **1 a :** to work and press into a mass with or as if with the hands ⟨~*ing* clay to perfect smoothness⟩ **b :** to mix (as the materials of bread) into a well-blended whole by or as if by repeatedly drawing out and pressing together **c :** to make (as bread) by such a process **2 :** to manipulate or work on with or as if with a kneading motion ⟨~*ed* the shoulder muscles to relieve the stiffness⟩ **:** alter or affect with or as if with repeated small pressures ⟨gradually ~*ing* the idea into shape⟩ **3 :** to make kneading movements with ⟨~*ing* her fists into her waist —J.S. Redding⟩ ~ *vi* **:** to make kneading movements **:** perform the action of kneading with or as if with the hands ⟨a kitten ~*ing* on the bed⟩ ⟨~*ed* away at the cheeks —Constance Foley⟩

knead·able \-dəbəl\ *adj* **:** suitable for kneading; *esp* **:** having the proper texture for kneading with the hands ⟨flour that produces an excellent ~ dough⟩

kneaded eraser *also* **kneaded rubber** *n* **:** a soft pliable eraser of unvulcanized rubber used esp. to remove graphite or charcoal marks from drawing paper

knead·er \'nēdə(r)\ *n* -s **:** one that kneads

knead·ing·ly *adv* **:** in the manner of one that kneads **:** with a kneading movement ⟨pressed her fingers ~ against the cushion⟩

kneading table *n* **:** DOUGH TRAY

knead·man \'nēdmən\ *n, pl* **kneadmen :** a worker that tends a machine which kneads flour paste for macaroni products

kne·bel·ite \'nābə,līt\ *n* -s [G *knebelit*, fr. Karl Ludwig von *Knebel* †1834 Ger. translator + G *-it* -ite] **:** a variously colored mineral $(Fe,Mn)_2SiO_4$ consisting of iron manganese silicate and occurring esp. in Sweden (sp. gr. 4.1)

¹knee \'nē\ *n* -s *often attrib* [ME *kne, knee*, fr. OE *cnēow, cnēo*; akin to OHG *kneo* knee, ON *knē*, Goth *kniu*, L *genu*, Gk *gony*, Skt *jānu*] **1 a** (1) **:** a joint of the ginglymus type in the middle part of the human leg that is the articulation between the femur, tibia, and patella (2) **:** the part of the leg that includes this joint ⟨scrubbing the floor on hands and ~s⟩ **b :** the corresponding joint in the hind limb of a quadrupedal vertebrate formed by the femur above and the tibia or tibia and fibula below **2 a :** a bending of the knee (as in respect or courtesy) ⟨a man of parts well able to make a good ~⟩ **b :** a blow with the bent knee — usu. used with *the* ⟨got the ~ in the face as he tried to get up⟩ **3 :** something felt to resemble the human knee esp. in its angular bent form: as **a** (1) **:** a crook in a tree branch (2) **:** a piece of timber naturally or artificially bent for use in supporting structures coming together at an angle (as the framing and deck beams of a ship) (3) **:** a piece of metal of similar form and corresponding function **b** *archaic* **:** an angular joint in a grass **c :** a rounded or somewhat conical process arising from the roots of a few swamp-growing trees (as the bald cypress and tupelo gum) and projecting above the surrounding water — compare BUTTRESS ROOT **d :** the part of a cabriole furniture leg that curves outward immediately below the junction of leg and frame **e :** a vertical curve in a stair handrail that is convex on top — compare RAMP **f :** the part of the head block of a sawmill that is attached to the dogs holding a log **g :** the part of a composing stick which is attached and at right angles to the back rim and with which the measure is set **h :** an abrupt change in direction in a curve (as on a graph); *esp* **:** one approaching a right angle in shape **4 :** any of several bodily parts that are structurally or functionally comparable to the human knee: as **a :** the carpal joint of the forelimb of a quadrupedal vertebrate corresponding to the wrist in man — see HORSE illustration **b** (1) **:** the tarsal joint of a bird corresponding to the ankle of man (2) **:** the corresponding joint of a quadrupedal mammal — not used technically **c :** the joint between the femur and tibia of an insect **5 :** the part of a garment that covers the knee — **on one's knees :** in a state of serious or irremediable defeat or failure ⟨a great nation economically *on its knees*⟩ — **on the knees of the gods** [trans. of Gk *theōn en gounasi*] **:** beyond human control or knowledge — **over in the knees :** KNEE-SPRUNG — **to one's knees :** into a state of submission or defeat ⟨forced *to his knees* by competition⟩

²knee \"\ *vb* **kneed**; **kneed**; **kneeing**; **knees** [ME *knewen*, fr. OE *cnēowian*, fr. *cnēow, cnēo* knee] *vi* **1** *obs* **:** to bend the knee **:** bow low **:** KNEEL **2 :** to bend like a knee — often used with *over* ⟨heavy-headed grain may lodge or ~ over⟩ ~ *vt* **1** *archaic* **:** to bend the knee to in supplication or deference **2 :** to go over or traverse on the knees ⟨painfully ~*ing* his way up the stairs⟩ **3 a :** to strike or touch with the knee ⟨*kneed* his opponent repeatedly⟩ **b :** to move or cause to move with the knee ⟨*kneed* the door open⟩ **c :** to press the flanks of (a saddle horse) with the knees in alerting or encouraging **4 :** to repair or replace the knee of (as a garment) **5 :** to cut the knee of so as to disable ⟨~ a steer⟩ **6 :** to secure by a knee ⟨transoms must be *kneed* to the horn timber —Edwin Monk⟩

knee action *n* **:** a front-wheel suspension (as of an automobile) permitting independent vertical movement of each front wheel

knee baby *n, dial* **:** a baby barely able to walk ⟨a *knee baby* and a lap baby⟩

knee bend *n* **:** an exercise performed by dropping from an upright to a squatting position and resuming an upright position without aid of the hands

kneeboard \'=,=\ *n* **:** a low wall surrounding a riding ring

knee bone *n* **:** PATELLA

knee boot *n* **1 :** a cover for a knee or for the knees: **a :** a carriage boot for protecting the knees from rain or splatter **b :** a protective boot of padded leather used on the knees of a horse that tends to overreach or strike himself in the knee **2 :** a boot reaching to the knee ⟨wading in *knee boots*⟩

knee brace *n* **:** a bracing member of a structure that is placed diagonally from one to another of two adjoining principal members

knee breeches *n pl* **:** BREECHES

kneebrush \'=,=\ *n* **1 :** a tuft or brush of hair on the knees of some antelopes and other animals **2 :** POLLEN BRUSH

knee buckle *n* **:** a buckle used to fasten knee breeches at or just below the knee
kneecap \ˈ=,=\ *n* **1 :** PATELLA **2 :** a protective cover for the knee
knee colter *n* **:** a knee-shaped colter
knee–crooking \ˈ=,==\ *adj* **:** OBSEQUIOUS, FAWNING
kneed \ˈnēd\ *adj* [¹*knee* + *-ed*] **1 :** having a knee or knees ⟨a graceful ~ table⟩ — often used in combination ⟨a knobby-*kneed* boy⟩ **2 :** having a bend or angle like that of the bent human knee **:** GENICULATE ⟨steep ~ gables⟩
knee–deep \ˈ=ˈ=\ *adj* [ME *kne-depe,* fr. *kne, knee* knee + *depe, deop* deep — more at KNEE, DEEP] **1 :** rising to the knees **:** KNEE-HIGH ⟨*knee-deep* snow⟩ **2 a :** sunk to the knees ⟨men *knee-deep* in water⟩ **b :** deeply engaged or occupied **:** OVERWHELMED ⟨*knee-deep* in turmoil⟩ ⟨*knee-deep* in war⟩
knee drill *n* **:** a special Salvation Army service at which most of the time is spent on the knees in prayer
knee drop *n* **:** a fundamental trampoline stunt in which the performer drops to his knees on the bed and then rebounds to a standing position
knee–halter \ˈ=,==\ *vt* **:** to restrain (a horse) by passing a line from the halter or bridle to the knee of a foreleg so as to permit grazing but prevent free or fast movement
knee–high \ˈ=ˈ=\ *adj* **:** rising or reaching upward to the knees ⟨*knee-high* stockings⟩
knee–high blackberry *n* **:** SAND BLACKBERRY
kneehole \ˈ=,=\ *n* **:** an open space (as under a desk) for the knees
kneehole desk *n* **:** a flat-topped desk having a kneehole with flanking tiers of drawers
kneeing *pres part of* KNEE
knee jerk *n* **:** an involuntary forward jerk or kick induced by a light blow or sudden strain upon the patellar tendon of the knee that causes a reflex contraction of the quadriceps muscle

kneehole desk

knee joint *n* **1 :** KNEE 1a(1) **2 :** TOGGLE JOINT
knee–jointed \ˈ=ˈ==\ *adj* **1 :** GENICULATE, KNEED **2 :** having jointed knees ⟨a *knee-jointed* doll⟩
¹**kneel** \ˈnēl, *esp before pause or consonant* -ēəl\ *vi* **knelt** \ˈnelt\ *or* **kneeled** \ˈnē(ə)ld\ **knelt** *or* **kneeled; kneeling; kneels** [ME *knelen,* fr. OE *cnēowlian;* akin to MLG *knēlen,* MD *cnielen;* denominatives fr. the root of E ¹*knee*] **1 :** to bend the knee **:** fall or rest on the knees ⟨*knelt* to drink from the spring⟩ — sometimes used with *down* ⟨*kneeling* down to pray⟩ **2** *of a rifleman* **a :** to assume a position formerly used in extended-order infantry drill in which the individual while half-faced to the right kneels on the right knee, rests the left forearm across the left thigh, and grasps a rifle in the position of order arms with the right hand above the lower band **b :** to support oneself on the knees while or for the purpose of firing a rifle
²**kneel** \"\ *n* -s **:** an act or instance of kneeling
kneel·er \ˈnēlə(r)\ *n* -s [ME *knelere,* fr. *knelen* to kneel + *-ere* -er] **1 :** one that kneels (as in worship) **2 :** something (as a cushion, stool, board) to kneel on **3 a :** a stone cut to provide a change of direction in masonry **b :** a stone so cut as to support and retain the coping of the slope of a gable
knee·let \ˈnēlət\ *n* -s [¹*knee* + *-let*] **:** a protective covering for the knee
¹**kneeling** *n* -s [ME *kneling,* fr. gerund of *knelen* to kneel — more at KNEEL] **1 :** the act of one that kneels **:** GENUFLECTION **2 :** a place or space for kneeling (as in a church)
²**kneeling** *adj* **:** suitable for use in kneeling ⟨a ~ cushion⟩ **:** designed to be used while kneeling ⟨~ desks⟩
kneel·ing·ly *adv* **:** in or from a kneeling position
knee mortar *n* **:** a light grenade discharger used by the Japanese during World War II
knee of head : an arrangement of timbers outside the stem and below the bowsprit that forms an overhanging bow in a wooden ship
kneepad \ˈ=,=\ *n* **:** a protective pad for the knee sometimes attached to a garment
kneepan \ˈ=,=\ *n* [ME *knepanne,* fr. *kne* knee + *panne* pan — more at KNEE, PAN] **1 :** PATELLA **2 :** a concavity at the distal end of the femur of an insect
knee plate *n* **1 :** a broad steel plate covering the thigh and projecting on each side and used chiefly in body armor for tilting **2 :** a plate for connecting a beam or girder to the frame of a ship
knee rafter *n* **:** a diagonal brace between a principal rafter and a tie beam
knee roll *n* **:** a padded margin sometimes introduced on the forepart of the skirt of an English saddle to keep a rider's leg from slipping forward
knee roof *n* **:** CURB ROOF
knees *pl of* KNEE, *pres 3d sing of* KNEE
knee·sie \ˈnēzē\ *n* -s [*knees* (pl. of ¹*knee*) + *-ie*] *slang* **:** an action of flirting or becoming friendly or intimate ⟨played ~*s* under the table —Lane Foster⟩
knee–sprung \ˈ=,=\ *adj, of a horse* **:** having the knees bent when they should normally be straight; *esp* **:** having the knees protruding too far forward — compare BUCK KNEE
kneestone \ˈ=,=\ *n* **:** a kneeler for a gable slope
knee strap *n* **1 :** a strap to hold a shoe on a cobbler's knee **2 :** an iron strap or facing for a knee timber
knee–tied \ˈ=,=\ *adj, of a horse* **:** having a poor conformation in the front legs with the anteroposterior diameter of the leg just below the knee too narrow
knee timber *n* **1 :** timber with natural knees or angles in it **2 :** a piece of timber with a knee or angle in it
knee tool *n* **:** a knee-shaped tool holder; *usu* **:** a turret-lathe or screw-machine tool holder that supports tools for simultaneous turning and internal-cutting operations
knee wall *n* **:** a partition for supporting roof rafters when the span is great or for forming a side wall (as of a second-story room) under a pitched roof
kneif·fia \ˈnīfēə\ *n, cap* [NL, fr. F. G. *Kneiff* †1832 Ger. physician and botanist + NL *-ia*] *in some classifications* **:** a genus of No. American day-blooming herbs (family Onagraceae) having stamens of unequal length and a 4-angled ovary and often included in *Oenothera* — compare SUNDROPS
kneipp·ism \ˈnī,pizəm\ *also* **kneipp's cure** \ˈnīps-\ *or* **kneipp cure** *n, usu cap K* [*Kneippism* fr. Sebastian *Kneipp* †1897 Ger. priest who developed it + E *-ism; Kneipp's cure* or *Kneipp cure* after S. Kneipp, trans. of G *Kneippsche kur* or *Kneipp-kur*] **:** treatment of disease by forms of hydrotherapy (as walking barefoot in morning dew)
¹**knell** \ˈnel\ *vb* -ED/-ING/-S [ME *knillen, knellen,* fr. OE *cnyllan;* akin to MHG *erknellen* to resound, toll, MHG *knüllen* to strike, beat, ON *knylla,* and prob. to OE *cnotta* knot — more at KNOT] *vt* **1** *obs* **:** to ring (a bell) with slow solemnity **:** TOLL **2 :** to summon by or as if by a knell **3 :** to announce or proclaim by or as if by a knell ⟨the bell buoy ~*s* your hour —Marguerite J. Adams⟩ ~ *vi* **1 a** *of a bell* **:** RING; *esp* **:** to toll at a death, funeral, or disaster **b :** to sound a knell **2 a :** to give forth a sound like a knell ⟨the owl at its ~*ing* —Dylan Thomas⟩ **b :** to sound a warning or have a sound or import of evil omen
²**knell** \"\ *n* -s [ME *cnul, knel,* fr. OE *cnyll,* fr. *cnyllan,* v.] **1 :** a stroke or sound of a bell (as when tolled at a funeral or at the death of a person) **:** a death signal or passing bell **2 :** a warning of or a sound indicating the passing away of something ⟨this decision sounded the ~ of our hopes⟩
knelt *past of* KNEEL
kne·mi·do·kop·tes \,nēmədōˈkäp(,)tēz\ *n, cap* [NL, fr. Gk *knēmid-, knēmis* greave, legging + NL *-o-* + *-koptes* (fr. Gk *koptein* to smite, cut off); akin to Gk *knēmē* shinbone — more at CAPON, HAM] **:** a genus of itch mites attacking birds — see DEPLUMING MITE, SCALY-LEG MITE; compare SCALY LEG — **kne·mi·do·kop·tic** \ˈ;==;=ˈ=tik\ *adj*
knet *dial past of* KNIT
knettle *var of* NETTLE
knew *past or dial past part of* KNOW

knez \kəˈnez\ *n, pl* **knezes** *also* **knezi** [of Slav origin; akin to Serbo-Croatian *knez* prince, Russ *knyaz',* OSlav *kŭnędzĭ,* of Gmc origin; akin to OHG *kuning* king — more at KING] **:** a Slavic prince or duke
knib \ˈnib\ *n* -s [by alter.] **:** NIB 6a, 6b
knicht *archaic var of* KNIGHT
knick \ˈnik\ *n* -s [*knick*point] **:** NICK 6
knick·er \-kə(r)\ *n* -s *often attrib* [short for *knickerbocker*] **1 knickers** *pl* **:** KNICKERBOCKERS **2 knickers** *pl* **:** pants for women or girls: as **a :** bloomers with fullness gathered on a band at the knee **b** *chiefly Brit* **:** UNDERPANTS **c :** sport or leisure pants similar in design to knickerbockers
knick·er·bock·er *R* ˈnikə(r),bäkər, *-R* ˈnikə,bäkə(r\ *n* -s *often attrib* [after Diedrich *Knickerbocker,* pretended author of *History of New York* (1809), by Washington Irving †1859 Am. author] **1** *usu cap* **:** a descendant of the old Dutch settlers of New York; *broadly* **:** NEW YORKER **2 a :** loose-fitting knee-length pants gathered at the knee on a band for sports and informal wear by men and boys — usu. used in pl. ⟨~*s* for golfing⟩ ⟨wearing a ~ suit⟩ **b :** KNICKER 2c **3 :** a wool and cotton clothing fabric resembling tweed and made from nubby yarns with flecks of color

knickerbockers 2a

knick·er·bock·ered \-äkə(r)d\ *adj* **:** wearing knickerbockers
knick·ered \ˈnikə(r)d\ *adj* **:** wearing knickers
knick·knack \ˈnik,nak\ *n* [redupl. of *knack*] **1** *obs* **:** a petty trick or artifice **2** *or* **nick·nack** *or* **nic·nac :** a small or trivial article (as of furniture or dress) intended rather for ornament than for use; *esp* **:** a small functionless souvenir
knick·knack·ato·ry \-ə,tōrē\ *n* -ES [*knickknack* + *-atory* (as in *conservatory*)] *archaic* **:** a repository or collection of knickknacks
knick·knack·ery \-ak(ə)rē\ *n* -ES **:** a knickknack or knickknacks
knick·knacky \-akē\ *adj* **1 :** devoted to, characterized by, or concerned with knickknacks ⟨a cluttered ~ room⟩ ⟨such a ~ taste⟩ **2 :** FINICAL, TRIFLING, TRIVIAL
knickline \ˈ=,=\ *n* **:** a line formed by the point or angle of a nick in a slope (as of a hill)
knickpoint \ˈnik,=\ *n* [part transl. of G *knickpunkt,* fr. *knicken* to bend + *punkt* point] **:** a place in a stream bed where a nick occurs
¹**knife** \ˈnīf\ *n, pl* **knives** \-īvz\ [ME *knif,* fr. OE *cnīf,* prob. fr. ON *knīfr;* akin to MLG *knīf* knife, MD *cnijf,* OE *cnotta* knot — more at KNOT] **1 a :** a simple instrument used for cutting consisting of a sharp-edged usu. steel blade provided with a handle **b :** a weapon consisting of or resembling a knife **c :** a culinary utensil consisting of a knife usu. with blade of silver or steel and a handle of metal, ceramic, bone, or pearl ⟨dinner *knives*⟩ ⟨dainty fruit *knives*⟩ **d :** a sharp cutting blade or tool in a machine (as a band saw, a wood-planing machine, or a mowing machine) **e :** any of various instruments used in surgery primarily to sever tissues whether having the form of a conventional knife or scalpel or cutting by other means (as electric or radio-frequency currents); *also* **:** SURGERY — used with *the* ⟨finally decided to submit to the ~⟩ ⟨was under the ~ for several hours⟩ **2 :** MUMBLETY-PEG **3 :** the shape of an envelope flap as produced by the knife on the cutting machine ⟨the size, ~, and watermark of a stamped envelope⟩
²**knife** \"\ *vb* -ED/-ING/-S *vt* **1 :** to use a knife on: as **a :** to stab, slash, or wound with a knife **b :** to prune with a knife **2 a :** to cut or mark with a knife: as (1) **:** to shape or cut out (as shoe uppers) with a knife (2) **:** to trim (as shoe soles) with a knife **b :** to spread (as paint) with a knife **3 :** to try to defeat by underhand means (as a political candidate of one's own party) **:** to work secretly against (one justified in expecting support) **:** UNDERMINE ⟨aiding today those he knows will ~ him tomorrow⟩ **4 a :** to move like a knife in ⟨birds *knifing* the autumn sky⟩ **b :** to impart an action like that of a knife to ⟨*knifed* his hand against his opponent's neck⟩ ~ *vi* **:** to progress or cut a way with or as if with the blade of a knife ⟨the cruiser *knifed* through heavy seas⟩ ⟨a hot sun *knifing* down through the haze⟩ ⟨*knifed* rapidly along the bone⟩
knife and fork *n* **1** *Brit* **:** one that eats **:** TRENCHERMAN ⟨a good *knife and fork*⟩ **2 a knives and forks** *pl* (1) **:** paired and solitary cones of the common club moss (*Lycopodium clavatum*) (2) **:** a club moss that bears knives and forks **b :** a key fruit of the sycamore maple — usu. used in pl.
knife bar *n* **:** CUTTER BAR
knife bayonet *n* **:** a bayonet with considerable breadth of blade and a handle that enables it to be used as a knife, dagger, or entrenching tool
knifeboard \ˈ=,=\ *n* **1 :** a board on which knives are cleaned or polished **2** *Brit* **:** a seat on the roof of an old-fashioned omnibus
knife box *also* **knife case :** a receptacle for knives and other table cutlery: as **a :** an often ornate wooden container with sloping top used esp. during the 18th century in pairs for the storage of knives and spoons **b :** an open usu. handled tray or rack for the storage of table cutlery
knife–boy \ˈ=,=\ *n, Brit* **:** an underservant occupied primarily with the care of knives and general odd jobs about a large household
knife–edge \ˈ=ˈ=\ *n* **:** a sharp narrow edge or margin like that of a knife: as **a :** a sharp wedge of steel or other hard material used as a fulcrum or axis of motion for a lever arm or beam in a machine or instrument of precision (as a scale, testing machine, pendulum) to minimize friction **b :** a narrow ridge (as of rock, ice, or sand) **c :** GIRDLE d
knife–edged \ˈ=,=\ *adj* **:** having an edge like a knife; *usu* **:** extremely sharp or precise ⟨*knife-edged* pleats⟩ ⟨a *knife-edged* wit⟩
knife file *n* **:** a tapered file with a triangular cross section suggesting that of a knife blade
knife fish *n* **:** any of several fishes sometimes kept in the tropical aquarium; *esp* **:** a small brownish green fish (*Gymnotus carapo*) from So. America related to the electric eel but lacking electric organs
knife·ful \ˈnīf,fu̇l\ *n, pl* **knives·ful** *or* **knife·fuls** \-īvz,fu̇l, -īf,fu̇lz\ **:** the quantity a knife will hold or convey
knife grinder *n* **1 :** one that grinds knives: as **a :** an itinerant tradesman who sharpens knives or other edged tools **b :** a device (as a grindstone or emery wheel) used for grinding or sharpening knives or other edged tools **2 :** a European nightjar (*Caprimulgus europaeus*)
knife–handle \ˈ=,==\ *n* **:** RAZOR CLAM
knife hook *n, obs* **:** SICKLE 1a
knife key *n* **:** a compass key having a knife at one end
knife lanyard *n* **:** LANYARD 3a
knife·less \ˈnīfləs\ *adj* **:** lacking a knife
knifelike \ˈ=,=\ *adj* **:** resembling or suggesting a knife: **a :** having a sharp edge or ridge ⟨a ~ ridge of land⟩ ⟨a narrow ~ profile⟩ **b :** keen and incisive ⟨icy ~ reasoning⟩ **c :** sharp and penetrating **:** PIERCING ⟨~ pains⟩ ⟨a ~ cold⟩
knife·man \ˈnīfmən\ *n, pl* **knifemen :** a man that uses or works on or works with knives (as a knife fighter or a knife grinder)
knife money *n* **:** ancient Chinese bronze money having the shape of knives
knife pleat *n* **:** one of a series of narrow sharply pressed pleats all turned in one direction
knif·er \ˈnīfə(r)\ *n* -s **:** one that knifes; *esp* **:** a person who stabs or slashes another with a knife
knife rest *n* **1 :** CHEVAL-DE-FRISE **2 :** a support on which a carving knife may be rested on the dining table when not in use
knif·er·man \ˈnīfə(r)mən\ *n, pl* **knifermen :** a slaughterhouse worker who severs hog heads and lets them hang by a thin strip of meat to expose neck glands for government inspection
knifes *pres 3d sing of* KNIFE
knifesmith \ˈ=,=\ *n* **:** a maker of knives **:** CUTLER
knife stone *n* **:** HONE 1; *esp* **:** a fine-grained whetstone for setting and finishing an edge

knife switch *n* **:** an electric switch in which contact is made by pushing one or more flat metal blades between the jaws of spring clips

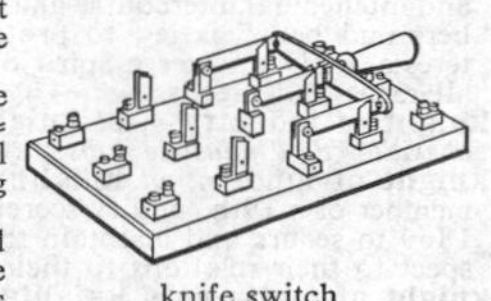
knife switch

knife tool *n* **:** a tool suggestive of a knife: as **a :** a knife-shaped graver **b :** a small wheel used in seal engraving for cutting fine lines
knife urn *n* **:** an urn-shaped knife box popular in the late 18th and early 19th centuries
knifeway \ˈ=,=\ *n* **:** a long tapering usu. hardened straight bar (as a V bar)
knif·fin system \ˈnifən-\ *n, usu cap K* [after Wm. *Kniffin,* 19th cent. Am. horticulturist] **:** a system or method of training grapevines whereby a trunk is carried to the upper of two braced supporting wires along which the annually renewed fruiting canes are tied and from which the bearing branches are allowed to hang down
knifing *pres part of* KNIFE
¹**knight** \ˈnīt, *usu* -īd.+V\ *n* -s [ME, boy, youth, knight, fr. OE *cniht, cneoht* boy, youth, military follower; akin to OS & OHG *kneht* boy, youth, military follower, OE *cnotta* knot — more at KNOT] **1 a** (1) **:** a mounted man-at-arms of the European feudal period serving a king or other superior usu. in return for a tenure of land; *esp* **:** a man ceremonially inducted by a feudal superior into special military rank commonly immediately below that of baron usu. available only after completing regular periods of service as page and squire — compare DUB *vt* 1a (2) **:** a man upon whom a corresponding dignity has been conferred by a sovereign in recognition of personal merit (3) **:** a member of an order of knighthood or of chivalry ⟨a *Knight* of the Garter⟩ (4) **:** a member of a social or fraternal order ⟨*Knights* of Labor⟩; *also* **:** a member of such an order holding a particular degree or rank that is officially so designated ⟨members, acolytes, and ~*s* of the Inner Tabernacle⟩ **b** (1) **:** a person of ancient history or mythology of a rank equivalent to that of knight — often used to translate Latin *miles* (2) **:** EQUES **c :** KNIGHT OF THE SHIRE **d :** a man who devotes himself to a lady as her attendant or champion **e :** a man associated in his personal or professional character with something specified (as an implement, tool, place, material) — often used in trade or craft nicknames ⟨those petty rascals often called ~*s* of the bridewell⟩ ⟨a ~ of the quill earning a pittance by his writings⟩ **2 a :** a chess piece that may cross occupied squares and that has an L-shaped move of three squares of which two are in a horizontal or vertical row and one is perpendicular to the row **b :** a face card ranking between the queen and the jack in many European packs of playing cards **3 :** a small bitt with sheaves through which the running rigging of a ship is passed

knight 2a

²**knight** \"\ *vt* -ED/-ING/-S [ME *knighten,* fr. *knight,* n.] **:** to make a knight of **:** induct into the state or an order of knighthood **:** DUB
knight·age \-īd·ij\ *n* -s **1 :** knights or a body of knights ⟨the king and all his ~⟩ **2 :** a register and account of knights ⟨the several ~*s* and peerages that register men of nobility and note⟩ **3 :** KNIGHTHOOD ⟨hardy service may win a commoner ~⟩
knight bachelor *n, pl* **knights bachelors** *also* **knights bachelor :** a knight belonging to the most ancient but the lowest order of English knights and not a member of an order of chivalry — see KNIGHT BANNERET
knight banneret *n, pl* **knights bannerets** *also* **knights banneret** [ME] **:** a knight of an ancient English order of knighthood that was commonly conferred as a reward for valor on the field of battle and that entitled the holder to bear a banner rather than the pennon of a knight bachelor
knight baronet *n, pl* **knights baronets :** BARONET
knight commander *n, pl* **knights commanders :** a member of the second class in an honorary order (as the Order of the Bath) with more than one class of membership ranking below a knight grand cross and above a companion
knight–companion \ˈ=ˈ==\ *n, pl* **knights–companions** *also* **knight–companions :** a knight belonging to an order of knighthood having only one class ⟨the Order of the Garter . . . consists of the sovereign and twenty-five *knights-companions* —Valentine Heywood⟩
knight–errant \ˈ=ˈ==\ *n, pl* **knights–errant** [ME *knight erraunt*] **:** a wandering knight; *esp* **:** one traveling at random in search of adventures in which to exhibit military skill, prowess, and generosity
knight–errantry \ˈ=ˈ===\ *n, pl* **knight–errantries 1 a :** the character or actions of a knight-errant **:** the practice of wandering in quest of adventures **b :** quixotic conduct **:** a quixotic or romantic adventure or scheme **2 :** KNIGHTS-ERRANT
knight·ess \ˈnīdəs\ *n* -ES **1** *obs* **:** a woman filling the role of a knight either as a fighter or as a member of an order of chivalric import **:** female knight **2 :** the wife of a knight
knight·ful·ly \ˈnītfəlē\ *adv* **:** in the manner of a knight **:** BRAVELY, CHIVALROUSLY
knight grand commander *n, pl* **knights grand commanders :** a member of an honorary order (as the Star of India) that admits other than Christians to membership corresponding in rank to a knight grand cross
knight grand cross *n, pl* **knights grand cross :** a member of the highest class in an honorary order (as the Bath) with more than one class of membership — see KNIGHT COMMANDER
knighthead \ˈ=,=\ *n* [so called fr. its having been carved to represent knights] **1 :** one of two timbers rising in the bows of a wooden ship just within the stem with one on each side of the bowsprit — called also *bollard timber* **2 :** a triangular bulkhead just abaft the cutwater with a hole through which the bowsprit of a ship passes
knight·hood \ˈnīt,hu̇d\ *n* [ME *knighthod,* fr. *knight* + *-hod* -hood] **1 :** the rank, dignity, condition, profession, or vocation of a knight or of knights as a class ⟨won a ~ for his devotion to civic reform⟩ ⟨~ was at one time both a social obligation and a symbol of maturity⟩ **2 :** the character of a knight **:** qualities befitting a knight or knights as a class **:** KNIGHTLINESS, CHIVALRY **3 a :** knights as a class ⟨the early ~ held a place distinct from the great lords on the one hand and the mass peasantry on the other⟩ **b :** a body of knights ⟨the legendary ~ of King Arthur⟩
knighthood–errant \ˈ=,=ˈ==\ *n* **:** KNIGHTS-ERRANT
knight hospitaler *n, pl* **knights hospitalers** *usu cap K&H* **:** HOSPITALER
knight·ia \ˈnīd·ēə\ *n, cap* [NL, fr. Thomas A. *Knight* †1838 Eng. plant physiologist + NL *-ia*] **:** a small genus of Australasian trees or shrubs (family Proteaceae) with alternate leathery leaves, showy racemose flowers, and follicular fruit — see REWA-REWA
knightless *adj, obs* **:** unbecoming a knight **:** UNCHIVALROUS
knight·li·hood \ˈnītlē,hu̇d\ *n* **:** KNIGHTLINESS
knightlike \ˈ=,=\ *adj* [ME *knightlik,* fr. *knight* + *-lik* -like] **:** KNIGHTLY 1
knight·li·ness \ˈnītlēnəs\ *n* -ES **:** the quality or state of being knightly; *broadly* **:** chivalrous courtesy or gracious kindness ⟨a natural ~ characterized all his relations with others⟩
knight·ling \ˈnītliŋ\ *n* -s **:** a knight of little worth or importance **:** petty knight
¹**knight·ly** \ˈnītlē, -li\ *adj* [ME, fr. *knight* + *-ly*] **1 a :** of or relating to a knight **b :** befitting a knight **:** CHIVALROUS **2 :** consisting or made up of knights
²**knightly** \"\ *adv* [ME, fr. *knightly,* adj.] **:** in a manner becoming a knight
knight marshal *n, pl* **knights marshals 1 :** a former military officer analogous to the modern quartermaster **2 :** a onetime officer of the British royal household who had judicial cognizance of transgressions committed in the royal household or verge and of contracts to which a member of the king's household was a party
knight of columbus *n, pl* **knights of columbus** *usu cap K&C* [after Christopher *Columbus* — more at COLUMBUS] **:** a member of a fraternal and benevolent society of Roman Catholic

men founded at New Haven, Conn., in 1882 to promote social and intellectual intercourse among its members, to aid its members and beneficiaries, to protect and promote Catholic interests, and to foster a spirit of fraternity among citizens of all races and creeds

knight of industry *n, pl* **knights of industry** [trans. of F *chevalier de l'industrie*] *obs* **:** SWINDLER

knight of labor *n, pl* **knights of labor** *usu cap K&L* **:** a member of a 19th century secret labor organization formed in 1869 to secure and maintain the rights of workingmen in respect to their relations to their employers

knight of malta *n, pl* **knights of malta** *usu cap K&M* [fr. *Malta*, island in the Mediterranean, the seat of the order from 1530–1798] **:** HOSPITALER

knight of pyth·i·as \-'pithēəs\ *n, pl* **knights of pythias** *usu cap K&P* [after *Pythias*, 4th cent. B.C. Pythagorean philosopher whose devotion to his friend Damon is legendary] **:** a member of a secret fraternal order founded at Washington, D.C., in 1864 for social and charitable purposes

knight of rhodes \-'rōdz\ *n, pl* **knights of rhodes** *usu cap K&R* [fr. *Rhodes*, city and island in the Aegean sea, former seat of the order] **:** HOSPITALER

knight of st. john of jerusalem *n, pl* **knights of st. john of jerusalem** *usu cap K&S & both Js* [after *St. John of Jerusalem* (John the Baptist), cousin of Jesus] **:** HOSPITALER

knight of the carpet *also* **knight of the chamber** *n, pl* **knights of the carpet** **1 :** a knight who is knighted in formal ceremony (as kneeling in a royal audience chamber) as distinguished from one knighted informally on the field of battle — compare CARPET KNIGHT **2 :** a recipient of knighthood for service or distinction other than military

knight of the golden circle *n, pl* **knights of the golden circle** *usu cap K&G&C* **:** a member of a former American secret organization formed about 1855 to promote the interests of the South and the slavery cause

knight of the maccabees *n, pl* **knights of the maccabees** *usu cap K&M* [after *Maccabees*, 2d & 1st cent. B.C. Jewish family in Palestine] **:** a member of a secret beneficiary society formed in Ontario in 1878 and introduced into the U. S. in 1881 and having a ritual based on characteristics of the ancient Maccabean family

knight of the pestle *n, pl* **knights of the pestle :** APOTHECARY

knight of the post *n, pl* **knights of the post :** a professional false witness of 15th to 17th century England

knight of the road *n, pl* **knights of the road** **1** *obs* **:** HIGHWAYMAN **2 :** TRAVELING SALESMAN **3 :** TRAMP

knight of the round table *n, pl* **knights of the round table** *usu cap K&R&T* **:** a knight belonging to the legendary order instituted by King Arthur

knight of the shire *n, pl* **knights of the shire** [ME] **1 :** a knight selected by the freeholders to represent a shire in the House of Commons esp. in medieval times ⟨the *knight of the shire* was the connecting link between the baron and the shopkeeper —T.B.Macaulay⟩ **2 :** a parliamentary representative from a shire or county as distinguished from a representative of a city or a borough ⟨the number of *knights of the shire* was increased to 159 —T.E.May⟩

knight of the sword *n, pl* **knights of the sword** *usu cap K&S* **:** a member of a German religious order of knights founded in 1202 by Bishop Albert of Riga in Livonia to convert the heathen Estonians and Livonians and appropriate their lands, confirmed by the pope in 1204, and merged into the Teutonic Order in 1237

knight of the temple *n, pl* **knights of the temple** *usu cap K&T* **:** TEMPLAR 1

knights *pl of* KNIGHT, *pres 3d sing of* KNIGHT

knight service *also* **knight's service** *n* [ME *knightes service*] **1 :** the military service by rendering which a knight held his lands; *also* **:** the tenure of lands held on condition of performing military service **2 :** service such as a knight can or should render; *broadly* **:** good or valuable service

knight's fee *n* [ME *knightes fee*] **:** the amount of land the holding of which imposed the obligation of knight service, being sometimes a hide or less and sometimes six or more hides

knight's–spur \'=,=\ *n, pl* **knight's–spurs :** LARKSPUR 1a

knight's–star \'=,=\ *or* **knight's–star lily** *n, pl* **knight's–stars** *or* **knight's–star lilies :** BARBADOS LILY

knight's tour *n* **:** a chess problem in which a knight makes a circuit of the board touching each square once

knight templar *n, pl* **knights templars** *or* **knights templar** *also* **knight templars** *usu cap K&T* **1** TEMPLAR 1 **2 :** a member of the Knights Templars, an order of Freemasonry conferring three degrees in the York rite — compare CHIVALRIC RITE

kniph·o·fia \nip'hōfēə, nī'fō-\ *n* [NL, fr. Johan H. *Kniphof* †1763 Ger. botanist + NL *-ia*] **1** *cap* **:** a genus of showy African herbs (family Liliaceae) having clumps of long radical leaves and tall scapes of red or yellow drooping flowers with reflexed perianths **2** -s **:** a plant of the genus *Kniphofia* — called also *tritoma*

knish \kə'nish\ *n* -ES [Yiddish, fr. Russ *knish, knysh*, a kind of cake; akin to Ukrainian *knyš*, Pol *knysz*] **:** a round or square of rich baking-powder dough folded over a savory meat or cheese filling and baked or fried

knis·te·neaux \kə,nistə'nō\ *n pl but sing in constr, usu cap* [modif. of F *Christenaux* — more at CREE] **:** CREE

¹knit \'nit, *usu* -id·+V\ *vb* **knit** *or* **knitted** *or dial* **knet** \'net, *usu* -ed·+V\ **knit** *or* **knitted** *or dial* **knet; knitting; knits** [ME *knitten*, fr. OE *cnyttan*; akin to MLG *knütten* to knit, knot together; denominatives fr. the root of E ¹*knot*] *vt* **1** *now chiefly dial* **:** to make fast or join with knots **:** tie together **:** form into a knot or into knots **2 :** to cause to unite in a functional whole as if by knitting or knotting: as **a :** to link firmly or closely (as by interlocking, intertwining, or intertying) ⟨*knitted* her hands until the knuckles blanched⟩ **:** CONJOIN, CEMENT, CONSOLIDATE ⟨~ the timbers into a sturdy frame⟩ **b :** to cause to grow together ⟨time and rest will ~ the fractured bone⟩ **c :** to bind by immaterial (as social or legal) ties ⟨~ together by common interests⟩ **d :** to draw together **:** contract into wrinkles ⟨*knitting* his brow in thought⟩ **3 a :** to form (as a fabric or a garment) by the interlacing of a yarn or yarns in a series of connected loops by means of hand or machine needles ⟨*knitting* socks to match the sweater⟩ **b :** to form or bring into being (some immaterial tie) ⟨a new philosophy that *knitted* a new understanding between the classes⟩ ~ *vi* **1 :** to make knitted fabrics or objects **:** do knitting ⟨some women ~, others sew⟩ **2 :** to unite into a functional whole as if by being knitted or knotted: as **a :** to become compact **:** CONSOLIDATE **b :** to grow together ⟨fractures in old bones ~ slowly⟩ **c :** to become drawn together **:** contract into wrinkles **3** *now dial Brit* **a** (1) *of fruit* **:** SET (2) *of a plant* **:** to grow or set fruit **b** *of bees* **:** SWARM **4** *obs* **:** EFFERVESCE, FOAM

²knit \"\ *n* -S *often attrib* **1 a :** knitting or style of knitting **b :** knitted material **c :** KNIT STITCH **2 :** a contraction or wrinkling up (as of the brow)

knitback \'=,=\ *n* [so called fr. its use to heal broken bones] **:** a coarse branching hairy comfrey (*Symphytum officinale*) sometimes cultivated for its white, yellowish, purple, or rose flowers

knitch \'nich, kə'n-\ *n* -ES [ME *knytche, knucche*, fr. OE *gecnycc* bond; akin to MLG *knocke* bundle, MHG *knock* back of the neck, *knoche* bone — more at KNUCKLE] *dial Eng* **:** BUNDLE, FAGOT

knit goods *n pl* **1 :** knitted fabrics; *esp* **:** fabrics made on a knitting machine and used for underwear, hosiery, and other clothing **2 :** articles made from such fabrics **:** knitted garments

knit stitch *n* **:** a basic knitting stitch usu. made with the yarn at the back of the work by inserting the right needle into the front part of a loop on the left needle, catching the yarn from the left side with the point of the right needle, and bringing it through the first loop to form a new loop — compare PURL STITCH

knit·ted \'nid·əd, -itəd\ *adj* **:** made or characterized by knitting ⟨~ garments⟩ — often used in combination ⟨hand-*knitted* woolens⟩

knit·ter \'nid·ə(r), -itə-\ *n* -S [ME, fr. *knitten* to knit + *-er* — more at KNIT] **1 :** a person that knits by hand or operates a knitting machine **2 :** a machine for making knit goods (as hose, jersey, sweaters)

knit·ting \'nid·|iŋ, -it|, |ēŋ\ *n* -S [ME, fr. gerund of *knitten* to knit] **1 :** the action or method of one that knits by hand or machine; *also* **:** the action of a machine that knits **2 :** work in progress or products made by a person or machine that knits **3 :** the occupation of operating a machine that knits **4** *obs* **:** FASTENING; *esp* **:** KNOT — **stick to one's knitting** *or* **tend to one's knitting** *also* **mind one's knitting :** to mind one's business **:** avoid interfering in or involving oneself with the affairs of others

knitting machine *n* **:** a machine for mechanically knitting fabrics (as jersey or tricot) and articles of wear (as sweaters or hosiery) — see CIRCULAR-KNIT, FLAT-KNIT

knitting needle *n* **1 :** one of two or more slender rods with one or both ends pointed or a flexible rod with both ends pointed used for hand knitting and made usu. of metal, bone, or plastic — see NEEDLE illustration **2 :** a spring needle or a latch needle used for machine knitting

knitting pin *n* **:** a single-pointed needle for hand knitting

knittle *var of* NETTLE

knit up *vt* **1 a :** to tie up **:** SECURE, UNITE **b :** to make or repair by knitting ⟨*knit up* several pairs of Christmas mittens⟩ ⟨*knit* a torn sleeve *up*⟩ **2 :** to bring to an end **:** CONCLUDE ⟨to *knit* these remarks *up* briefly⟩

knitwear \'=,=\ *n* **:** knitted clothing including hosiery, underwear, and outerwear

knive \'nīv\ *vb* -ED/-ING/-S [fr. ¹*knife*, after such pairs as E *wife: wive*] **:** KNIFE

knives *pl of* KNIFE

knives and forks *pl of* KNIFE AND FORK

knivesful *pl of* KNIFEFUL

¹knob *also* **nob** \'näb\ *n* -S [ME *knobbe*; akin to MLG *knubbe*, *knobbe* knot on a tree, knob, Norw *knubb* block, ME *knoppe*, *knopp* bud, knob — more at KNOP] **1 a** (1) **:** a relatively small usu. rounded mass typically projecting from the surface or extremity of something **:** a usu. rounded projection or protuberance or protrusion ⟨a heavy club with ~s at one end⟩ ⟨his nose ends in a puggy ~ —N.M.Clark⟩ ⟨a skull having a couple of peculiar ~s⟩ (2) *archaic* **:** a small rather hard swelling (as a bump, pimple, pustule) on the surface of the skin (3) **:** a twisted knot or hard excrescence or protuberance esp. of wood **:** GNARL ⟨~s in the trunk of a tree⟩ (4) **:** a tiny ball, loop, or tuft (as of thread or hair) formed by twisting or coiling or otherwise tightly drawing together one or more strands; *specif* **:** KNOP c ⟨little ~s of wool or cotton in different colors —Mary Thomas⟩ (5) **:** ³BUN 2 ⟨dark hair drawn into a tight little ~ on the neck —Flora Thompson⟩ **b** (1) **:** a small rounded mass of often carved ornamental work (as a boss at the intersection of the ribs in a vaulting) topping or capping a larger piece of work or serving as a contrastive detail (2) **:** a small globular usu. ornamental body typically at the top or other extremity of something (as at the top or end of a finial or on the hilt of a sword or at the front and top of a saddlebow) **:** POMMEL (3) **:** FINIAL **c** (1) **:** a usu. rounded projection by which something can be grasped or otherwise manipulated or moved ⟨a metal bar with a ~ at one end⟩; *specif* **:** a usu. rounded handle (as of a drawer or door) ⟨a door with a heavy ~ of wrought metal⟩ (2) **:** a usu. rounded projection or a disk or dial typically having a guide mark or series of guide marks around the edge and capable of being turned or pulled or pushed so as to actuate or otherwise operate or control something (as a radio or television set) ⟨he reached to turn on the radio but she pushed his hand from the ~ almost angrily —E.K.Gann⟩ ⟨an expert at knocking ~s off safes —Paul McClung⟩ ⟨turns a control ~ on the instrument panel —T.W.Rodes⟩ **d :** a spool-shaped porcelain insulator for supporting electric wires — see INSULATOR illustration **2 a** (1) **:** a usu. rounded land prominence (as a knoll, hillock, hill, small mountain) with usu. steep sides; *esp* **:** an isolated prominent rounded hill (2) **knobs** *pl* **:** an area marked by a group of such prominences ⟨a rifleman from the east Kentucky ~s —I.S.Cobb⟩ **b** (1) **:** a usu. tapering upward projection from the summit of a hill or mountain **:** PEAK ⟨bare crags and ~s —W.M.Davis⟩ (2) **:** something (as a boulder or group of boulders or a stony area) projecting from the summit or sides of a hill or mountain ⟨erosion wore down the mountains, exposing ~s of harder granite —*Amer. Guide Series: Minn.*⟩ ⟨patches of ragged grass and ~s of boulders —Dixon Wecter⟩ **3** *chiefly Brit* **:** a small lump of something **:** a small piece ⟨a scraggly looking salad and a few ~s of cheese —Dawn Powell⟩ ⟨a ~ of coal⟩; *esp* **:** a small cube ⟨a ~ of sugar⟩ ⟨dropped a ~ of ice into the glass⟩ **4** *archaic* **:** HEAD ⟨a diminutive head like the ~ of a mannikin —George Santayana⟩ — **with knobs on** *adv* **:** in an esp. eminent manner **:** to an esp. notable degree ⟨anglophile though the first three pictures were, the new one is more so *with knobs on* —*Newsweek*⟩ ⟨whatever problem a town can have . . . we have it — *with knobs on* —Sam Pollock⟩

²knob *also* **nob** \"\ *vt* **knobbed; knobbed; knobbing; knobs** **1 :** to cause to have knobs **:** form knobs upon ⟨*knobbing* a sheet of metal⟩ **2 :** to provide with a knob ⟨wrought-iron gates, *knobbed* on either side with stone balls —Edmund Wilson⟩

knob and tube wiring *n* **:** open electric-wiring work in which the wires are supported on knobs or cleats and encased in tubes where they pass through beams or partitions

knobbed \'näb(ə)d\ *adj* [ME, fr. *knobbe* knob + *-ed*] **1 :** having a knob or knobs ⟨a ~ stick⟩; *specif* **:** ending in a knob ⟨a pole ~ at each extremity⟩ **2 :** covered with knobs **:** KNOBBY ⟨a ~ tree trunk⟩

knobbed crab *n* **:** a spiny spider crab (*Mithrax caribbaeus*) of the West Indies and the northern coast of So. America

knobbed goose *n* **:** CHINESE GOOSE 2

knobbed wrack *n* **:** a common brown alga (*Ascophyllum nodosum*) of northern oceans

knob·ber \'näbə(r\ *n* -S [¹*knob* + *-er*] *Brit* **:** a two-year-old male deer

knob·bi·ly \'näbəlē\ *adv* **:** in such a way as to form protuberances ⟨her ~ corseted bulk —Marcia Davenport⟩

knob·bi·ness \-bēnəs\ *n* -ES **:** the quality or state of being knobby

knob·bish \-bish\ *adj* **:** rather knobby ⟨skinny as a rail, and kind of ~ at the joints —Helen Eustis⟩

knob·ble \'näbəl\ *n* -S [ME *knoble*, fr. *knob* + *-le* (dim. suffix)] **:** a little knob or lump

knob·bled \-ld\ *adj* **:** KNOBBLY

knob·bly *or* **nob·bly** \'näblē, -li\ *adj, often* -ER/-EST [¹*knob* + *-ly*] **:** KNOBBY; *esp* **:** having or covered with very small knobs ⟨a ~ pane of translucent glass⟩

¹knob·by \'näbē, -bi\ *adj, usu* **knobbier**; *usu* **knobbiest** [¹*knob* + *-y*] **1 a :** having knobs **:** having several or many knobs **:** covered with knobs: as (1) **:** having protuberances, projections, or protrusions ⟨~ bones⟩ ⟨~ knees⟩ ⟨~ knuckles⟩ **:** BUMPY ⟨grinned toothlessly and extended a ~ hand —Dorothy Sayers⟩ (2) **:** having usu. rounded land prominences **:** HILLY ⟨~ farmland⟩ **b :** shaped like or suggestive of a knob ⟨little ~ noses —Joseph Conrad⟩ **2 a :** involving difficulties **:** PERPLEXING, INTRICATE, KNOTTY ⟨some of the ~ problems of publishing —Harvey Breit⟩ **b :** resisting compromise or evasion or unequivocal solution **:** stubbornly unyielding **:** HARD, OBSTINATE ⟨prefer to turn away from the ~ facts of life —*Time*⟩

²knobby \"\ *var of* NOBBY

knob celery *n* **:** CELERIAC

knob·cone pine \'=,=-\ *n* **:** a pine (*Pinus attenuata*) native to the Pacific coast of the U.S. with a prominent knob on each scale of the cone

knob grass *n* **:** HORSE BALM 1

knob·ker·rie *also* **knob·ker·ry** \'näb,kerē\ *n, pl* **knobkerries** [modif. (influenced by ¹*knob*) of Afrik *knopkierie*, fr. *knop* knob, bud (fr. MD *cnoppe*) + *kierie* stick, club, fr. Hottentot *kïrri* — more at KNOP] **:** a rather short wooden club with a heavy round knob at one end that may be thrown as a missile or used in close attack and that is used esp. by aborigines of southern Africa

knob-ker-rie

knob lock *n* **:** a door lock with a spring bolt operated by a knob and a dead bolt operated by a key

knobs *pl of* KNOB, *pres 3d sing of* KNOB

knobstick \'=,=\ *n* **1 :** a stick, cane, or club with a rounded knob at its head; *specif* **:** KNOBKERRIE **2** *Brit* **:** STRIKEBREAKER, SCAB

knob·thorn *also* **knob·thorne** \'näb,thō(ə)rn\ *n* -S **:** an acacia (*Acacia nigrescens*) of southern Africa having a bark often dotted with thorn-tipped knobs

knobweed \'=,=\ *n* **1 :** KNAPWEED **2 :** HORSE BALM 1

knobwood \'=,=\ *n* **1 :** a tree (*Zanthoxylum capense*) of southern Africa with compound leaves and greenish paniculate flowers **2 :** the wood of the knobwood

¹knock \'näk\ *vb* -ED/-ING/-S [ME *knoken, knokken*, fr. OE *cnocian, cnucian*; akin to MHG *knochen* to press, ON *knoka* to hit, beat; all of imit. origin] *vi* **1 :** to strike upon the surface of something (as a door) with a short sharp fairly heavy blow (as with the knuckles) esp. so as to indicate one's desire to gain admittance (as into a room) or otherwise to attract attention **:** RAP ⟨~*ed* on the green painted door and it was opened almost at once —Louis Bromfield⟩ ⟨stood there ~*ing* on the gate⟩ ⟨~*ed* on the table before beginning to speak⟩ **2 :** to collide fairly heavily or jarringly with something **:** strike against or bump into something ⟨~*ed* into one person after another in the crowd⟩ ⟨his ~*ing* knees belied the bluster of his talk —W.F.Hambly⟩ **3 a :** to stir about or move along briskly, usu. noisily, and often clumsily or haphazardly **:** BUSTLE ⟨heard him ~*ing* round in the kitchen —Lucy M. Montgomery⟩ ⟨went ~*ing* rapidly down the road⟩ ⟨~*ing* along at a reasonable rate —Dillon Anderson⟩ **b :** to go or move about in an irregular, haphazard, or aimless way **:** travel about in a careless or indifferent manner and often with no particular objective **:** WANDER, ROAM, ROVE — usu. used with *about, around* ⟨~*ing* idly up and down the country⟩ ⟨decided to ~ around the world awhile⟩ ⟨~*ed* about the mountains for a couple of weeks⟩ ⟨spent a couple of hours ~*ing* around town⟩ **c** (1) **:** to lead an irregular life often in straitened difficult circumstances **:** live like a vagrant — used with *about, around* ⟨content to ~ about the world in a more or less disreputable way —R.W.Southern⟩ ⟨goes ~*ing* about the roads day and night —W.B.Yeats⟩ (2) **:** to exist in a condition of complete or nearly complete inaction, idleness, or neglect **:** pass the time inactively or idly **:** hang around **:** LOITER, DAWDLE — used with *about, around* ⟨used to ~ around that neighborhood⟩ ⟨would you have my pictures ~*ing* about some art dealer's place —Louis Bromfield⟩ **4 a :** to make a rattling, thumping, or pounding noise (as of loose connecting rods or loose bearings or other parts in a machine that strike against each other or another surface or as of improperly timed or uneven combustion in an internal-combustion engine) ⟨heard the motor ~*ing*⟩ **b :** to undergo detonation (sense 2) ⟨an engine fuel that ~*s*⟩ **5 :** to speak ill of something esp. in a petty way **:** find fault with or criticize something adversely and often captiously ⟨malcontents who were perpetually ~*ing*⟩ **6 :** to end the play in a card game (as gin rummy) and call for a comparison of hands ⟨at this point the player may ~⟩ ~ *vt* **1 a** (1) **:** to deal a short sharp fairly heavy blow to **:** strike sharply **:** deal a jarring blow to **:** HIT, RAP, BUFFET ⟨~*ed* him on the chin⟩ ⟨~*s* it about more than any rough road will ever do —Hardiman Scott⟩ (2) **:** to get rid of or as if by dealing a stunning blow to **:** knock out **:** knock on the head ⟨he can ~ the worry if he takes a Scotch and soda —Ernest Hemingway⟩ ⟨an effective remedy for ~*ing* colds⟩ (3) **:** to affect in an indicated way by or as if by striking sharply, beating, battering, hammering, or pounding ⟨would ~ any road to pieces —Tom Wintringham⟩ ⟨~*ed* it apart⟩ (4) **:** to produce or make by so striking or battering ⟨~*ed* a hole in the wall⟩ ⟨a workroom composed of two or three servants' bedrooms ~*ed* into one —C.D.Lewis⟩ **b** (1) **:** to set forcibly into sudden movement ⟨kept ~*ing* the croquet ball along with her mallet⟩ or send flying ⟨swung hard with his bat and ~*ed* the baseball over the fence⟩ or drive in an indicated direction ⟨~*ed* the book away from his face⟩ or to, into, or onto an indicated thing, place, or position by a short sharp blow, thrust, or stroke or a series of such blows or thrusts ⟨~*ed* a nail up into the ceiling⟩ **:** give a sudden impetus to by driving with a short sharp blow **:** impel or propel suddenly and swiftly (2) **:** to drive out by so striking **:** force out or expel by or as if by a blow ⟨was ~*ing* the dust out of his clothes —Henry Baerlein⟩ ⟨threatened to ~ his brains out⟩ ⟨will ~ such notions out of your head —T.B.Costain⟩ ⟨can ~ all the interest out of it —H.L.Davis⟩ (3) **:** to drive forcibly off or down by or as if by so striking **:** cause to be so removed ⟨~*ed* the head off the statue⟩ ⟨~*ed* a considerable sum off the price⟩ (4) *of a dog* **:** to drive (game birds) from cover **:** FLUSH ⟨moved in and ~*ed* the birds —*Amer. Field*⟩ **c :** SHAKE, UPSET, BOTHER, DISTURB ⟨never gives up the idea that he can win, and nothing can ~ him —D.W.Maurer⟩ **d** *chiefly Brit* (1) **:** to knock out (sense 2a) ⟨struck him under the right eye with her clenched fist and ~*ed* him —Sigerson Clifford⟩ (2) **:** to make a strong impression on **:** produce a strong effect in; *esp* **:** to move to admiration or applause ⟨nothing ~*s* a country audience like a hornpipe —J.K.Jerome⟩ **2 :** to cause to collide fairly heavily or jarringly with something **:** cause to strike against, run into, or bump into something ⟨~*ed* two oil drums against each other —Vicki Baum⟩ ⟨didn't look where they were going and ~*ed* their heads together⟩ **3 :** to speak ill of esp. in a petty way **:** find fault with or criticize adversely and often captiously ⟨can satirize the manners and morals of our times and even ~ the government —Lee Rogow⟩ ⟨instructions were to keep smiling, ~ nobody —S.H.Adams⟩ **4 :** to obtain by or as if by striking or beating ⟨a young man who can ~ some fun out of life —A.J.Cronin⟩ — **knock cold :** to knock out (sense 2a) ⟨ran his head into the wall and was *knocked cold*⟩ — **knock dead :** to move strongly esp. to admiration or applause **:** knock over ⟨a comedian who really *knocks* them *dead*⟩ — **knock for a goal :** to knock for a loop — **knock for a loop** **1 a :** to overcome utterly **:** completely vanquish **:** ROUT ⟨*knocked* his opponent *for a loop*⟩ **b :** to make short work of **:** get rid of or demolish ⟨*knocked* his faith in human nature *for a loop*⟩ **2 :** to make speechless **:** cause to be at a complete loss **:** OVERWHELM, BEWILDER, AMAZE, DUMBFOUND ⟨the news *knocked* them *for a loop*⟩ — **knock into a cocked hat** **1 a :** to utterly demolish **:** RUIN ⟨*knocked* all our plans *into a cocked hat*⟩ ⟨threatened to *knock* the industry *into a cocked hat*⟩ **b :** to prove to be false **:** utterly disprove ⟨a theory that was finally *knocked into a cocked hat*⟩ **2 :** to surpass eminently **:** excel by far ⟨something that'll *knock* all the other achievements of man *into a cocked hat* —John Galsworthy⟩ — **knock on the head** *or* **knock in the head** **1 :** to stun or kill by a blow on the head ⟨had been *knocked on the head* some dark night —R.L.Stevenson⟩ **2 :** to check (a plan, project, procedure) effectively or put an end to **:** SQUELCH, SQUASH ⟨has *knocked* this rumor *in the head* —*U.S. News & World Report*⟩ — **knock out of the box :** to cause (an opposing pitcher) to retire from a baseball game by hitting pitched balls with marked effectiveness — **knock spots off** *or* **knock the spots off** *also* **knock spots out of :** to surpass eminently **:** excel by far ⟨she *knocks spots off* anybody I've seen in London —J.B.Priestley⟩ — **knock together :** to make or assemble esp. hurriedly or in a makeshift way ⟨*knocked together* his own desk and bookcase⟩

²knock \"\ *n* -S [ME *knokke, knok*, fr. *knokken, knoken*, v.] **1 a :** a short sharp fairly heavy blow **:** RAP ⟨a loud ~ on the door⟩ **b** (1) **:** a blow of misfortune or hard treatment ⟨the school of hard ~*s* had given him a tenacious grasp on reality —Dixon Wecter⟩ ⟨some of the disappointments and hard ~*s* life has dealt —A.B.Herr⟩ ⟨takes the ~*s* of the world —M.N. Todd⟩ (2) **:** something that checks, interrupts, or reverses good conditions or progress **:** SETBACK, REVERSAL, UPSET ⟨appeared to receive a damaging ~ from the events —Mollie Panter-Downes⟩ **2 a :** a rattling, thumping, or pounding noise (as of loose connecting rods in a machine or as of uneven combustion in an internal-combustion engine) ⟨was worried by the ~ in his car⟩ **b :** DETONATION 2 ⟨a motor fuel that is not subject to ~⟩ **3 :** a piece of often petty faultfinding or of adverse and often captious criticism ⟨likes praise but can't stand the ~*s*⟩ ⟨can take the ~*s*, not worrying what people say —Stella Molony⟩ **4 :** an innings in cricket ⟨won the toss and decided to take first ~⟩

knock about *or* **knock around** *vt* **1 :** to cause to move irregularly and abruptly from one point to another by or as if by repeated blows **:** JOLT, JAR ⟨the crowd pushed and shoved and the two boys got *knocked about*⟩ **2 :** to treat roughly or subject to difficulties and hardship **:** mistreat physically or mentally ⟨has been pretty badly *knocked around* during his life⟩ ⟨come into life with large preconceived ideas and are *knocked about* in consequence —Lionel Trilling⟩

¹knockabout \'⸗,⸗\ *adj* [*knock about*] **1 :** designed or suitable for rough or casual informal use ⟨~ clothing⟩ ⟨a ~ travel valise⟩ **2 a :** noisy and rough **:** boisterously violent ⟨was especially fond of ~ games⟩ ⟨~ diversions⟩ **b :** marked by, given to, or skilled at boisterously funny antics and farce and often extravagant burlesque or slapstick ⟨a ~ film comedy⟩ ⟨a ~ vaudeville act⟩ ⟨~ comedians in baggy pants —*Time*⟩ **3 :** marked by or given to irregular, haphazard, or aimless wandering about **:** traveling about carelessly or like a vagrant **:** ROAMING ⟨are afraid the place is full of ~ single men —O.E. Rölvaag⟩

²knockabout \"\ *n* -s [partly fr. ¹*knockabout;* partly fr. *knock about*] **1 a** (1) **:** a performer of knockabout comedy ⟨a couple of vaudeville ~s⟩ (2) **:** a performance or instance of knockabout comedy ⟨a grave ceremony that gradually turned into hilarious ~⟩ **b :** boisterous farcical humor of the kind found in knockabout comedy ⟨the rehearsal scene was good ~ —Leslie Rees⟩ **2 a** *Austral* **:** a handyman on a sheep station **b :** one that wanders about or travels in an irregular, haphazard, or aimless way **:** WANDERER, VAGRANT ⟨a man without family, a ~ —D.C.Peattie⟩ **3 :** a sloop with a simplified rig marked by absence of bowsprit and topmast and by having a single headsail on the forestay **4 :** something designed or suitable for rough or casual informal use: as **a :** an article of clothing (as a coat, hat) designed or suitable for such use **b :** an unpretentious vehicle esp. designed or suitable for short trips or other casual informal use ⟨a secondhand car that will serve as a ~⟩ ⟨was now in a one-cylinder ~ which in every way lived up to its name —William Beebe⟩

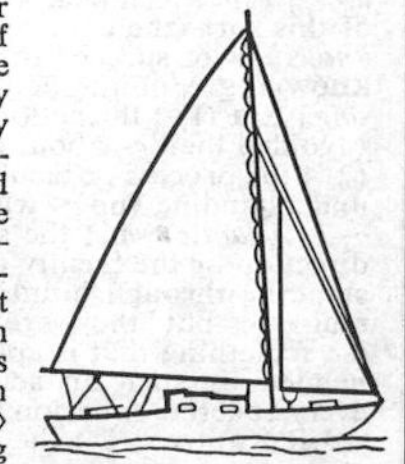

knockabout 3

knockaway *var of* KNACKAWAY

knock back *vt, chiefly Brit* **:** SWALLOW; *specif* **:** to toss down (an alcoholic beverage) ⟨smelt of the brandy they had just been *knocking back* —Bruce Marshall⟩

knock-back \'⸗,⸗\ *n* -s [fr. *knock back,* v.] *Austral* **:** REBUFF, REFUSAL ⟨he's had a *knock-back* from his old man —John Morrison⟩

knock down *vt* **1 a** (1) **:** to strike to the ground or lay low with or as if with a short sharp blow **:** FELL, PROSTRATE ⟨hit him on the chin and *knocked* him *down*⟩ (2) **:** to lower in degree **:** tone down **:** put down ⟨needs to have his self-esteem *knocked down*⟩ **:** HUMBLE, HUMILIATE ⟨try not to frustrate him or *knock down* his cap —*Education Digest*⟩ **b :** to hit with or as if with a projectile or other missile and cause to fall **:** shoot down ⟨thinking of ways to *knock* planes *down* from the skies —J.P. Baxter b.1893⟩ **:** bring down by a shot **:** POT ⟨*knocking down* game birds⟩ **c** (1) **:** to dispose of effectively **:** put out of the way **:** get rid of **:** ELIMINATE, QUASH ⟨each objection had been *knocked down* —*Times Lit. Supp.*⟩ (2) *Austral* **:** to spend (money) with abandon ⟨*knock down* their checks there —George Farwell⟩ **d :** to check or abate (flames or heat) at the edges of a blazing area **e :** to cause (a vessel) to heel over or list heavily or beyond recovery ⟨lets the wind blow on both sides of the sail . . . and the boat cannot be *knocked down* —Peter Heaton⟩ **2 :** to dispose of to or as if to a bidder at an auction sale ⟨*knocked* the clock *down* for a trifling sum⟩ **3 :** to take apart (something assembled) typically for convenience of moving, packing, storing, or shipping **:** DISASSEMBLE ⟨*knocked* the table *down* before boxing it⟩ **4 a** *slang* (1) **:** to appropriate dishonestly **:** STEAL ⟨*knocked down* plenty of the cash without getting caught⟩ (2) **:** ROB ⟨*knocked down* a bank⟩ **b :** to receive as income or salary **:** make by earning **:** EARN, DRAW, GET ⟨positions where they were able to *knock down* good money —*Infantry Jour.*⟩ ⟨were *knocking down* close to $150,000 a year —*Newsweek*⟩ **5 :** to hammer out the round and joints of (a book to be rebound) after removal of the cover; *also* **:** to flatten out the frayed ends of (cords or bands) after lacing in **6 :** to make a reduction in (an amount) **:** REDUCE, LOWER ⟨*knocked* the price *down* a dollar or two⟩ **7 :** LOWERCASE ⟨*knocking down* an initial letter that had been printed as a capital⟩ **~** *vi* **1 :** to be adaptable to being knocked down ⟨a portable device that easily *knocks down*⟩ **2** *of wind or a body of water* **:** to become tranquil **:** SUBSIDE ⟨the sea was *knocking down* steadily —R.F.Mirvish⟩

¹knockdown \'⸗,⸗\ *n* -s [*knock down*] **1 a** (1) **:** the action of knocking down ⟨a general ~ of prices —*Newsweek*⟩ (2) **:** the condition of being knocked down; *specif* **:** the condition of a ship (as a sailboat) that is heeling over, listing heavily, or beyond recovery from the impact of wind or water **b** (1) **:** a temporary or permanent disordered state that is produced in an insect by an insecticide or other control agent and that is marked by cessation of the insect's normal activity and often followed by the insect's death (2) **:** the degree to which an insecticide or other control agent successfully incapacitates or kills insects (3) **:** the percentage of a test group of insects that is successfully incapacitated or killed by an insecticide or other control agent — compare KILL 1c **2 a :** a blow that knocks down ⟨watched for the first ~ in the fight⟩ **b :** an overwhelming or crushing blow (as of misfortune) **:** a severe setback ⟨it was a bad ~ for both of us —Lucien Price⟩ **3 :** something (as a piece of furniture) that can easily be assembled or disassembled **4** *slang* **:** an introduction to a person ⟨give a guy a ~ to your girl friends —Jerome Weidman⟩

²knockdown \"\ *adj* [partly fr. *knock down;* partly fr. ¹*knockdown*] **1 a :** that knocks down or is capable of knocking down ⟨a ~ jab to the jaw⟩ **:** having such force or strength as to strike down **:** PROSTRATING, INCAPACITATING ⟨his schemes have met a ~ blow —Amy Lowell⟩ ⟨the ~ power of an insecticide⟩ **b** (1) **:** that cannot be successfully opposed **:** OVERWHELMING, OVERPOWERING ⟨a bewildering assortment of ~ arguments —J.W.Krutch⟩ ⟨would provide an almost ~ proof —A.G.N.Flew⟩ **:** CRUSHING ⟨a ~ defeat⟩ (2) **:** pushing hindrances or objections relentlessly aside by sheer force or drive **:** BULLDOZING ⟨his ~ style of polemics —W.E.Woodward⟩ **:** bluntly assured **:** CATEGORICAL ⟨he had his ~ answer for anyone who questioned his qualifications —Van Wyck Brooks⟩ **c :** KNOCK-DOWN-AND-DRAG-OUT ⟨can explode any moment into a ~ fight —*Newsweek*⟩ **2 a :** that can easily be put together or taken apart (as for convenience of storing or shipping) **:** made up of parts that are readily assembled or disassembled ⟨a ~ piece of furniture⟩ **b :** KNOCKED-DOWN **3 a :** lowest possible **:** MINIMUM ⟨the auctioneer set the ~ bid at $5.00⟩ **b :** extremely low ⟨can make the trip at ~ cost⟩ **:** REDUCED ⟨bought supplies at ~ prices⟩

¹knock-down-and-drag-out \'⸗,⸗⸗'⸗,⸗\ *or* **knock-down, drag-out** \'⸗,⸗'⸗,⸗\ *adj* [*knock down* + *and* + *drag out,* v.] **:** marked by extreme violence or bitterness and by the giving of no quarter **:** carried to the last extremity ⟨a *knock-down-and-drag-out* fight⟩ ⟨*knock-down-and-drag-out* political debates⟩ ⟨one of the toughest *knock-down, drag-out* little battles ever fought —*Infantry Jour.*⟩

²knock-down-and-drag-out \"\ *n* -s **:** a knock-down-and-drag-out fight or controversy ⟨are both spoiling for a real *knock-down-and-drag-out* on this issue —*New Republic*⟩

knocked *past of* KNOCK

knocked-down \'⸗'⸗\ *adj* [fr. past part. of *knock down*] **:** not assembled or only partly assembled **:** consisting of parts that can be assembled ⟨prefabricated *knocked-down* buildings⟩ — abbr. *K.D.*

knock·er \'näkə(r)\ *n* -s [ME *knokker,* fr. *knokken* to knock + *-er* — more at KNOCK] **1 :** one that knocks: as **a :** a usu. ornamental fixture attached to the outer surface of a door and consisting typically of a metal plate to which a metal ring or bar or hammer is hinged that may be raised and lowered with sharp force against the surface of the plate or door so as to produce a rapping noise designed to indicate one's desire to gain admittance **b** *dial Eng* **:** a spirit or goblin believed to dwell in mines and to show by knocking where ore is **c :** a faultfinder or a person given to adverse often captious criticism ⟨when I see a ~ and a troublemaker I let him know what I think of him —L.B.Salomon⟩ **d** (1) **:** a slaughterhouse worker who stuns cattle with a sledgehammer before they are killed (2) **:** one that knocks ripe fruit (as prunes, olives, nuts) from trees typically with a rubber mallet and a pole (3) **:** CAKE PULLER **2 :** BREAST — often considered vulgar **3 :** TESTIS — often considered vulgar **4** *slang* **:** FELLOW ⟨that fish is a big ~⟩ **:** GUY ⟨hit the dirty ~ right in the jaw⟩ — **up to the knocker** *slang Brit* **1 :** up to par ⟨didn't feel *up to the knocker*⟩ **2 :** up to the fullest or best possible extent or degree ⟨was prepared *up to the knocker*⟩

knocker 1a

knocker-off \'⸗⸗'⸗\ *n, pl* **knockers-off** *or* **knocker-offs** [*knock off* + *-er*] **1 :** a worker who knocks temporary hoops from barrels by hand or by machine after heads and permanent hoops have been placed **2 :** a worker who uses a chisel to break apart castings and remove sprues from molded and cast articles

knocking *pres part of* KNOCK

knocking over *n, pl* **knockings over** *or* **knocking overs** [fr. gerund of *knock over*] **:** the action of a knitting machine device that pushes the newly formed loops off the needles

knocking shop *n* [fr. gerund of *knock* "to copulate with", fr. ¹*knock*] *slang Brit* **:** BROTHEL

knock-knee \'⸗,⸗\ *n* **:** a condition in which the legs curve inward at the knees as a result of disease or unphysiologic stresses on the bones ⟨afflicted with *knock-knee*⟩

knock-kneed \'⸗'⸗\ *adj* **1 :** having knock-knee ⟨an emaciated *knock-kneed* child⟩ **2 a :** functioning or moving awkwardly or jerkily or laboriously ⟨a *knock-kneed* mind⟩ ⟨*knock-kneed* lines of verse⟩ **:** LIMPING, LAME, INEPT, WEAK ⟨a *knock-kneed* excuse⟩ **b :** devoid of smoothness and grace **:** CLUMSY, GAUCHE ⟨a *knock-kneed* collection of provincial practitioners —*Times Lit. Supp.*⟩ ⟨a *knock-kneed* vase in the foreground —H.L.Mencken⟩

knock-knees \'⸗,⸗\ *n pl* **:** knees that approach each other or knock together because of knock-knee ⟨developed *knock-knees* at an early age⟩

knock·less \'näkləs\ *adj* **:** having or producing no knock ⟨a ~ motor fuel⟩ **:** devoid of knocks ⟨the easy sheltered ~ unshocked life —*Forum*⟩

knock-me-down \'⸗⸗,⸗\ *adj* **:** that overpowers or overwhelms **:** BULLDOZING ⟨*knock-me-down* Johnsonian pragmatism —George Saintsbury⟩ ⟨a *knock-me-down* doctrine —Joseph Conrad⟩

knockmeter \'⸗,⸗⸗\ *n* **:** an instrument that measures the intensity of knock (sense 2)

knock off *vi* **1 :** to discontinue doing something; *specif* **:** to cease from work or some other occupation ⟨*knocks off* for several days and lolls about in pajamas —E.P.Snow⟩ **2** *slang* **:** DIE **~** *vt* **1 a :** to do esp. in a hurried or routine way **:** take care of **:** get through with **:** attend to **:** DISPATCH ⟨*knocking off* routine duties with very little thought⟩ **b :** to produce esp. roughly or hastily **:** turn out hurriedly ⟨*knocks off* one book after another⟩ **2 a** (1) **:** to discontinue (work or some other occupation) **:** leave off ⟨arranged that they should *knock off* work at five —Nevil Shute⟩ **:** desist from **:** STOP, QUIT (2) **:** to cause to leave off from (work or some other indicated occupation) **:** DISMISS ⟨the foreman *knocked off* the workers for lunch⟩ ⟨told them he was tired of their talking and that he wished they would *knock it off*⟩ **b :** to dispense with **:** pass over **:** SKIP ⟨hoped that the usual inspection would be *knocked off*⟩ **3 :** DEDUCT ⟨*knocked off* 20 cents to make the price more attractive⟩ **4 a :** to take into custody **:** SEIZE, ARREST, NAB ⟨had enough sense not to get *knocked off* by the police —Richard Llewellyn⟩ **b :** RAID ⟨*knocked off* a gambling joint⟩ **5 a :** KILL, MURDER ⟨*knocked off* two men, purely on mercenary grounds —Lewis Baker⟩ **b :** OVERCOME, DESTROY ⟨*knocked off* each center of rebellion⟩ **c :** to get rid of **:** ELIMINATE ⟨*knocked off* every objection⟩ ⟨usually has to *knock off* only one or two opponents —W.S.Carlson⟩ **d :** to dispose of to or as if to a bidder at an auction sale **:** knock down **6 a** *slang* (1) **:** STEAL ⟨*knocked off* a few trinkets in the store⟩ (2) **:** ROB ⟨*knocked off* a couple of banks⟩ **b :** RECEIVE, GET, OBTAIN ⟨*knocks off* a Nobel prize —Ethel Merman⟩ **7 :** to swallow down **:** toss off **:** finish off ⟨ordered a schooner of beer and *knocked it off* with unaffected enthusiasm —A.J. Liebling⟩

knock-off \'⸗,⸗\ *n, pl* **knock-offs** [*knock off*] **1 :** the action of knocking off; *esp* **:** the automatic coming to a halt of a machine or of a part of a machine through the action of a device actuated when the functioning of the machine becomes faulty **2 :** a cam or other device designed to safeguard a machine or part of a machine from continuing to function when operation becomes faulty **3 :** the time set for leaving off from work or from some other occupation ⟨finished the greater part of the job long before *knock-off*⟩

knock on *vt* **:** to knock onward **:** knock forward; *specif* **:** to knock (the ball in rugby) forward in the direction of the opponents' dead-ball line with the hand or arm

¹knock-on \'⸗,⸗\ *n, pl* **knock-ons** [*knock on*] **:** the action of knocking on

²knock-on \"\ *adj* [*knock on*] **:** produced or projected as a result of the collision of an energetic particle (as a neutron or fission fragment) from outside an atom with an elementary particle inside ⟨a *knock-on* shower of particles⟩ ⟨a *knock-on* atom⟩ ⟨a *knock-on* electron⟩

knock out *vt* **1 a :** to produce esp. roughly or hastily **:** turn out hurriedly ⟨in that same month he *knocked out* eleven novelettes —*Time*⟩ **b :** to get through with **:** take care of esp. in a hurried or routine way **:** attend to **:** DISPATCH ⟨quickly *knocked out* the few things that had to be looked after⟩ **2 a** (1) **:** to fell (a boxing opponent) by hitting esp. on the chin and making unconscious or otherwise unable to rise or continue within a specified time ⟨*knocked* him *out* in the first round⟩ (2) **:** to make unconscious or to stupefy esp. by hitting on the head ⟨the flowerpot hit him on the head and *knocked* him *out*⟩ **b** (1) **:** to make the further use of impossible without replacement or repair **:** put out of commission **:** make inoperative ⟨telephone communications had been *knocked out*⟩ **:** DEMOLISH, DESTROY ⟨*knocking out* the bridges and an ammunition dump —Lee Rogow⟩ ⟨*knocked out* twelve transport aircraft —*Time*⟩ (2) **:** to put an effective end to **:** get rid of **:** ELIMINATE, CRUSH, SQUASH, SQUELCH ⟨*knocked out* commercial gambling —A.E.Stevenson †1965⟩ **3 a :** to make (as oneself) exhausted **:** tire out **:** wear out ⟨*knocked* themselves *out* with excessive work⟩ **b :** to exert (as oneself) to the breaking point or beyond endurance **:** exert to the utmost **:** drive to the point of exhaustion ⟨*knocking* myself *out* to get top grades —W.H.Whyte⟩ ⟨*knocked* ourselves *out* preparing for the grand opening —Polly Adler⟩ **4 :** to strike (the inverted bowl of a pipe of tobacco) on something or with something so as to cause burning or burned tobacco to fall out ⟨*knocked* his pipe *out* before refilling it⟩ **5 :** to knock out of the box ⟨the pitcher was *knocked out* in the fifth inning⟩

¹knockout \'⸗,⸗\ *n* -s [*knock out*] **1** *Brit* **:** an auction or sale or similar transaction at which a combination (as of bidders) illegitimately forces out other potential competitors and arranges by prior agreement to have one member of the combination secure at a set price the thing being offered so as later to profitably dispose of the thing (as by reauctioning) **2 a** (1) **:** the act of knocking out or the condition of being knocked out (2) **:** a blow or attack that knocks out ⟨won the fight by a ~⟩ ⟨an attempted early ~ by the enemy —R.W. Stokley⟩ **b** (1) **:** termination of a bout in boxing that occurs when an opponent is knocked out (2) **:** TECHNICAL KNOCKOUT **3 :** something sensationally striking or attractive **:** something altogether out of the ordinary or superlatively excellent ⟨she combines looks with poise and is a ~ at any party⟩ ⟨a hilarious book that is a real ~⟩ ⟨has produced a new film that is a ~⟩ **4 a :** something (as a set of pins in a die) that can be loosened or forced out typically to release or force out something else (as work in a punch or die) **b** (1) **:** a partially punched-out or cutout piece esp. in metal or plastic designed to be forced out when an opening is required; *esp* **:** such a partially punched piece in the side of a junction box (2) **:** the hole produced when such a piece is forced out

²knockout \"\ *adj* [partly fr. *knock out;* partly fr. ¹*knockout*] **1 a :** that knocks out: as (1) **:** that makes unconscious or stupefies ⟨delivered a ~ blow to the head⟩ ⟨mixed a ~ drink⟩ (2) **:** that incapacitates or puts out of commission or demolishes or destroys ⟨planned a ~ offensive against the enemy⟩ ⟨a ~ air attack⟩ (3) **:** that eliminates from competition ⟨only three teams were left in the running after the preliminary ~ matches⟩ **b :** that can be loosened or forced out ⟨removal of hot work from a press by means of ~ pins in the die⟩ or that is equipped with pieces that can be loosened or forced out ⟨metal file cases that are punched with ~ holes⟩ **2 :** sensationally striking or attractive or unusual or excellent ⟨wore a ~ dress⟩ ⟨ideas for a ~ gift⟩

knockout drops *n pl* **:** drops of a solution of a drug (as chloral hydrate) put into a drink and designed to make the drinker unconscious or stupefied

knock over *vt* **1 a** (1) **:** FELL, PROSTRATE **:** knock down ⟨*knocked* him *over* with one blow⟩ (2) **:** to upset badly **:** greatly disturb **:** OVERWHELM ⟨was *knocked over* by the news⟩ **b :** to get rid of **:** dispose of **:** ELIMINATE ⟨*knocked over* every difficulty⟩ **c :** to get through with **:** finish up with **:** DISPATCH ⟨*knocked over* a book a day —R.L.Taylor⟩ **2 a :** STEAL; *esp* **:** HIJACK ⟨*knocks over* a truckload of merchandise —J.B. Martin⟩ **b :** ROB ⟨*knocking over* a jewelry store —John McCarten⟩ **3 :** to receive as income or salary ⟨*knocks over* a good sum each year⟩ **4 :** to move strongly esp. to admiration or applause ⟨which for really brilliant suddenness of perception *knocks* one *over* completely —H.J.Laski⟩

knockover \'⸗,⸗⸗\ *n* -s [*knock over*] **:** the act of knocking over **:** the condition of being knocked over

knock poker *n* **:** a card game in which each player holds five cards and attempts to build a good poker hand but draws and discards as in rummy and may end the play by knocking

knock rummy *n* **:** rummy played by two to six players in which the winner is the player with the lowest count in unmatched cards and in which a player may end the play by knocking

knocks *pres 3d sing of* KNOCK, *pl of* KNOCK

knock under *vi, archaic* **:** to admit defeat **:** give in **:** give up **:** YIELD ⟨why should we *knock under* and go with the stream —H.D.Thoreau⟩

knock up *vt* **1 a** (1) **:** to arrange or devise esp. hurriedly or with little thought ⟨decided to *knock up* a tennis match⟩ **:** prepare quickly or without much care ⟨*knock up* a meal for us —Irwin Shaw⟩ (2) **:** to strike up casually ⟨*knocked up* an acquaintance with a few people⟩ **b :** to knock together ⟨two small wooden buildings, casually *knocked up* —Josephine Pinckney⟩ **c :** to practice informally with (as a tennis ball, shuttlecock) in warming up before a match (as in tennis, badminton, squash) **2** *Brit* **:** ROUSE, SUMMON; *specif* **:** to cause (as by knocking at the door) to awaken or rise from sleep or rest **3 a :** to make exhausted **:** knock out ⟨hurried too fast and it *knocked* me *up* —G.M.Hopkins⟩ **b** (1) **:** to put out of top condition **:** cause to deteriorate ⟨too much food and idleness had *knocked* them *up*⟩ (2) **:** to bring to an end **:** DESTROY ⟨unfair competition had *knocked up* the once flourishing business⟩ **c :** WOUND, HURT ⟨got pretty badly *knocked up*⟩ ⟨if I'm killed over there — that isn't likely, I'm more of the damned sort that gets *knocked up* —Ellen Glasgow⟩ **4 a :** to run up (as a score) **:** MAKE, ACHIEVE ⟨*knocking up* a good score⟩ **b** *Brit* **:** to receive as income or salary **:** EARN, GET **5** *slang* **:** to make pregnant ⟨no girls get married around here till they're *knocked up* —Ernest Hemingway⟩ **6 :** to make uneasy **:** DISTURB, BOTHER ⟨felt rather *knocked up* by the news⟩ **7 a** *Brit* **:** to knock down (sense 5) **b :** JOG 4 **~** *vi* **1 :** to become totally exhausted or otherwise unfit **:** break down ⟨a few of the beasts had *knocked up* and had to be abandoned —I.L. Idriess⟩ **2 :** to chance upon or meet up with something indicated — used with *against* ⟨*knocked up* against formidable difficulties⟩ ⟨happened to *knock up* against an old friend⟩ **3 :** to practice informally (as by volleying) in warming up before a match (as in tennis, badminton, squash)

knockup \'⸗,⸗\ *n* -s [*knock up*] **:** informal practice (as by volleying) in warming up before a match

knockwurst *var of* KNACKWURST

knod·den \'nädᵊn, kə'n-\ *adj* [fr. obs. past part. of *knead*] *dial Eng* **:** KNEADED

knö·del *or* **knoe·del** \kə'nōdᵊl\ *n, pl* **knödel** *or* **knödels** *or* **knoedel** *or* **knoedels** [G *knödel,* fr. MHG, dim. of *knode* knot, fr. OHG *knodo* — more at KNOT] **:** DUMPLING

knoe·ve·na·gel reaction \kə'nə(r)və,nägəl-, kə'nōv-\ *or* **knoevenagel condensation** *n, usu cap K* [after Emil *Knoevenagel* †1921 Ger. chemist] **:** an aldol-type condensation catalyzed by amines that takes place between an aldehyde or ketone and a compound containing an active methylene group (as in esters of acetoacetic acid, malonic acid, or cyanoacetic acid)

¹knoll \'nōl\ *n* -s [ME *knol,* fr. OE *cnoll;* akin to MHG *knolle* clod, lump, tuber, ON *knollr* mountaintop, OE *cnotta* knot — more at KNOT] **1 a** *now dial Eng* **:** the top of a hill **b** (1) **:** a usu. small rounded submerged elevation rising from the floor of a body of water; *esp* **:** the upper part or top of such an elevation (2) **:** a usu. rounded submerged projection of a shoal, reef, bank, or bar **2 :** a usu. small rounded land eminence **:** MOUND, HILLOCK

²knoll \"\ *n* -s [ME, prob. alter. of *knel* — more at KNELL] *archaic* **:** KNELL

³knoll \"\ *vb* -ED/-ING/-S [ME *knollen,* prob. alter. of *knellen* — more at KNELL] *archaic* **:** KNELL

knolly \-lē\ *adj* **:** marked by knolls ⟨a ~ section of the country⟩

knoop hardness \'nüp-\ *n, usu cap K* [after F. *Knoop,* 20th cent. Am. chemist] **:** the relative hardness of a material (as a metal) that is determined by the depth to which the bluntly pointed diamond pyramid of a hardness tester is made to penetrate it

knop \'näp\ *n* -s [ME *knoppe, knop,* fr. OE *-cnoppa;* akin to MLG *knuppe, knoppe* bud, MD *cnoppe* knob, bud, OHG *knopf* knot, bud, knob, ON *knyfill* short horn, OIr *gnobh* knot in wood, OE *cnotta* knot — more at KNOT] **:** a usu. ornamental knob: as **a :** a small rounded or angular ornamental enlargement or protuberance that is usu. at the mid or upper part of the stem of a vessel (as a chalice, goblet) or at the same part of the shank or shaft of some other object (as a candlestick, andiron) and that usu. serves as an aid in grasping or holding **b :** KNOB 1b **c :** a tiny ball, loop, or tuft of a fiber (as wool, silk, cotton) that is formed in or on a yarn, thread, or cloth and that is often of a color varying from that of the yarn, thread, or cloth or from that of other balls, loops, or tufts formed in or on the yarn, thread, or cloth

knop·ite \'nä,pīt\ *n* -s [G *knopit,* fr. Adolf *Knop* †1893 Ger. mineralogist + G *-it* -ite] **:** perovskite containing cerium

knopped \'näpt\ *adj* [ME, fr. *knoppe* + *-ed*] **:** having one or more knops ⟨a glass bowl with a ~ stem⟩ ⟨~ yarn⟩

knop·per \'näpə(r)\ *n* -s [G; akin to OHG *knopf* knot, bud, knob] **:** a gall that is formed by a gall wasp on the leaves and immature acorns of various oaks and that is used in tanning and dyeing

knop·pie spider \'näpē-\ *n* [Afrik *knoppie,* dim. of *knop* knob, bud — more at KNOBKERRIE] **:** either of two venomous spiders (*Latrodectus geometricus* and *L. indistinctus*) of southern Africa that are closely related to the American black widow

knop's solution \'näps-, kə'nōps-\ *n, usu cap K* [after J. A. L. W. *Knop* †1891 Ger. chemist] **:** a nutrient solution used in growth experiments with higher plants and containing definite proportions of calcium nitrate, potassium nitrate, magnesium sulfate, monobasic potassium phosphate, and potassium chloride dissolved in water

knop yarn *n* **:** a ply yarn with knops that is often made by twisting one ply faster than another

knorhaan *also* **knoorhaan** *var of* KORHAAN

knor·ria \'nórēə, 'när-\ *n, cap* [NL, fr. Georg W. *Knorr* †1761 Ger. collector of petrified objects + NL *-ia*] **:** a form genus based on fossil stems of Carboniferous age that are intermediate in structure between those typical of the Lepidodendraceae and the Sigillariaceae

knosp \'näsp\ *n* -s [G *knospe,* lit., bud; akin to OHG *knopf* knot, bud, knob — more at KNOP] *archaic* **:** KNOP

knos·si·an *also* **cnos·si·an** \(kə)'näsēən, *chiefly Brit* -nōs-\ *adj, usu cap* [*Knossos* or *Cnossus,* city in ancient Crete (fr. Gk *Knōssos*) + E *-ian*] **:** of, relating to, or characteristic of the city of Knossos

[1]**knot** \'nät, *usu* -äd·+V\ *n* -s [ME *knotte, knot*, fr. OE *cnotta;* akin to OHG *knoto & knodo* knot, ON *knūtr* knot, *knūta* top of a bone, knuckle, Lith *gniùsti* to press, *gniùtulas* bale, paper, lump; basic meaning: to press together; something clumped together] **1 a** (1) **:** an intertwining, looping, bending, hitching, folding, gathering together, or tangling of one or more parts of a pliant relatively slender length of something in such a way as to produce a tying together, fastening, binding, or connecting of the length on, to, or with itself, another length, or some other thing ‹a cord with ~s in it› ‹one rope was attached to another by a loose ~› (2) **:** the interlacement or other disposition or arrangement or formation produced in a length by such manipulation ‹wondered how to undo the ~› (3) **:** a specific localized point or mass produced in a length by such manipulation; *esp* **:** a lump or knob or some other relatively tight mass produced in a length by such manipulation ‹made heavy ~s in the rope every five feet› (4) **:** a bow or rosette or cockade or epaulet or some other ornamental arrangement of a material (as ribbon) produced by such manipulation ‹wore a faded red worsted ~, the emblem of his rank, on his left shoulder —F.V.W.Mason› (5) **:** a length of hair rolled or coiled or twisted into a usu. tight mass on the head **:** BUN ‹with iron-gray hair in a ~ on top of her head —Marcia Davenport› **b :** something perplexingly intricate or involved or difficult **:** a problem or complication that cannot be easily solved ‹a matter full of legal ~s› **c :** something that ties or binds together **:** a bond of union ‹the two nations renewed the ~ between them —R.W.Van Alstyne›; *esp* **:** the bond of marriage ‹hoped to loose the ~ by divorce› **d :** the central point or heart of something **:** the hard center **:** NUB, CORE, ESSENCE ‹confront the ~ of meaning—*Western Rev.*› ‹the very ~ and center of my being —R.L.Stevenson›; *esp* **:** the heart of something complicated or problematical ‹the very ~ of the difficulty —W.E.Gladstone› **2 a** (1) **:** a usu. firm or hard lump or swelling or protuberance in or on a part of an animal body or bone or process ‹a ~ in a gland› ‹a pendulous fold of flesh full of ~s› ‹a bone with two or three ~s› ‹a ~ at the end of the animal's horn›; *esp* **:** an often contorted lump or swelling or protuberance in a muscle ‹strained at the oars until the muscles of their arms stood out in ~s› (2) **:** a puckering or furrowing or wrinkling of the lower central area of the forehead typically occurring in deep concentration or as an indication of displeasure ‹went over it slowly with the ~ between his brows —Vincent McHugh› (3) **:** a tight constriction or the sensation of such a constriction ‹music that dissolved the ~s in their minds —Van Wyck Brooks› ‹his throat caught in a dry ~, his head felt leaden —Marcia Davenport› ‹moving slowly, as in a dream, his stomach in a ~ —Gregor Felsen› (4) **:** a constricted or contorted mass **:** a tight bundle ‹I was tired and tense, my nerves were in ~s —Polly Adler› **b :** a lump or swelling or protuberance in or on a part of a plant: as (1) **:** the node of a grass (2) **:** a protuberance or an excrescence on a stem or branch or root; *esp* **:** a hard irregular lump formed at the point where a branch grows out of the trunk of a tree ‹the first American settlers employed . . . pine ~s, which were dipped in pitch and burned with a bright but smoky flame —A.L.Powell› (3) *chiefly dial Brit* **:** BUD, BLOOM — used esp. in the phrase *in the knot* ‹now the hawthorn is coming in the ~› **c :** a relatively small concreted mass that may occur in rocks or in precious stones or in glass or in similar objects or substances and that is typically harder than the surrounding material or that otherwise differs (as in the direction of its grain) from the surrounding material **d :** a cross section of the hard lump on a tree trunk from which a branch grows out and which appears in a board as a rounded usu. cross-grained area that may fall out and leave an irregular hole **e :** a fungous disease of trees marked by the development of abnormal excrescences **3 a :** an ornamental usu. carved or hammered knob, boss, or stud **b :** an ornamental often functional mass (as a corbel or similar member or as the capital of a column) used in architecture and consisting typically of carved or sculptured foliage **4** *now dial Brit* **:** a hill or similar land eminence of moderate height; *esp* **:** a rocky hill of moderate height **5 a :** a small group of persons closely clustered together ‹~s of people talking and arguing on street corners —S.V.Benét› ‹a chatty little ~ at the back of PTA meetings —Bice Clemow› **b :** CLUMP ‹a ~ of palm trees› **:** BUNCH ‹a ~ of drooping dandelions› **6** *now chiefly dial* **:** KNOT GARDEN **7 :** a measured length of yarn, thread, or cord **8 a** (1) **:** one of the lengths marked off on a log line each of which is 47 feet 3 inches in extent and has the same relation to one nautical mile as 28 seconds has to one hour so that the number of such divisions running out from the log reel within a 28-second interval will indicate that the identical number of nautical miles will be covered within one hour by the ship if it maintains the same speed (2) **:** the point marking the dividing line between each such length **b :** one nautical mile per hour — used as a unit of measurement in expressing the rate of speed of seagoing ships and of airplanes and in expressing the relative strength of water currents and the degree of intensity of air currents ‹a ship that logs 10 ~s› ‹a plane traveling 450 ~s› ‹a 30-*knot* wind›; abbr. *kn., kt., k.* **c :** one nautical mile ‹the ship reached a speed of 12 ~s an hour› — not used technically **9 :** an elevated land region formed by the juncture of several mountain regions **10 :** a space curve that is closed

[2]**knot** \"\ *vb* **knotted; knotted; knotting; knots** [ME *knotten*] *vt* **1 a** (1) **:** to tie, fasten, bind, or connect with a knot **:** do up or secure with a knot ‹*knotted* his clothes into a tight bundle› (2) **:** to tie into a knot **:** form into a knot ‹*knotted* the shoelace and couldn't untie it› **b** (1) **:** to make a knot in or cause to be full of knots ‹broad soft neckties, which he *knotted* in large loose bows —Laura Krey› ‹*knotted* the rope every five feet› (2) **:** to make (lace, net, or other fancywork) by twisting and looping thread into knots to form designs **2 a** (1) **:** to unite closely or bind firmly together **:** cause to be closely joined or associated ‹the ties of blood that were *knotted* into all the relationships of communal life —Oscar Handlin› (2) **:** to group closely together ‹their horses were *knotted* about an instructor —Hugh MacLennan› (3) **:** to pull together ‹official and private problems ~ the plot into an intriguing pattern —Fanny Butcher› **b :** to cause to be joined in a confused or tangled way **:** ENTANGLE ‹ligatures, i.e. combinations in which two or more letters are *knotted* together and lose their original shape —E.H.Minns› ‹creepers of many kinds . . . *knotting* the undergrowth into impenetrable thickets —C.D. Forde› **3 :** to cause (the forehead or brows) to become knitted ‹saw him ~ and unknot his eyebrows —Donn Byrne› **4 :** to make (the score of an athletic contest or other competition) even **:** tie up **:** EQUALIZE ‹slammed in a 30-footer to ~ it again at 3 all —John Drebinger› **5 :** to cover the knots of (wood) with a conditioning preparation (as shellac) before painting ~ *vi* **1 a :** to form knots **:** become knotted ‹wet cords tend to ~› ‹took a long drink, the raw alcohol *knotting* and burning in his chest —Irwin Shaw› ‹the men bent forward, grunting deep in their lungs, their belly muscles *knotting* with the pull of the oars —Frank Yerby› — often used with *up* ‹the tendons of his legs began to ~ up —Andrew Hamilton› **b :** to form a constricted or contorted mass **:** form lumps ‹planets . . . were formed by a process of shriveling and *knotting* —Waldemar Kaempffert› **2 :** to become gathered together into a small group **:** cluster together ‹commandomen, who roamed here and there, *knotting* into groups for the exchange of experiences —John Brophy› **3 :** to make lace, net, or other fancywork by twisting and looping thread into knots to form designs

[3]**knot** \"\ *n* -s **:** any of several sandpipers (genus *Calidris*) that breed in the Arctic and winter in temperate or warm parts of the New and Old World: as **a :** a stocky gregarious Old World bird (*C. canutus*) whose plumage in the breeding season is chestnut and black above and that has a russet head and russet underparts **b :** a similar American bird that forms a subspecies (*C. canutus rufus*) and that is predominantly gray and spotted with black and ruddy brown above and that has a pale brown head and pale brown underparts **c :** a bird (*C. tenuirostris*) that is grayish brown to dark brown above with white underparts and white bars on the wings and tail and that breeds in northeastern Asia and winters southward to Australia — called also *great knot, Japanese knot*

knot bindweed *n* **:** BLACK BINDWEED 1

knot garden *n* **1 :** an elaborately designed garden esp. of flowers or herbs **2 :** a piece of ground marked by shrubbery or small trees arranged in an intricately formal pattern and typically trimmed into ornamental and often bizarre shapes **:** TOPIARY

knotgrass \'ˌ,ˌ\ *n* **1 :** a common cosmopolitan weed (*Polygonum aviculare*) with jointed stems, prominent sheathing stipules, and minute flowers **2 :** any of several grasses (as fiorin oat grass) with geniculate stems; *esp* **:** JOINT GRASS 1

knothead \'ˌ,ˌ\ *n* **:** a dull-witted blunderer **:** DUMBBELL, SIMPLETON

knothole \'ˌ,ˌ\ *n* **:** a hole in a board or tree trunk where a knot or branch has come out

knot·less \'nätləs\ *adj* **:** devoid of knots

knotroot \'ˌ,ˌ\ *n* **1 :** CHINESE ARTICHOKE **2 :** HORSE BALM 1

knotroot grass *n* **:** a No. American grass (*Muhlenbergia mexicana*) used as a soil binder and as hay

knots *pl of* KNOT, *pres 3d sing of* KNOT

knot sawyer *n* **:** one who saws defective parts from lumber

knot·ted \'näd·əd, -ätəd\ *adj* [ME, fr. *knotte, knot* knot + -*ed*] **:** KNOTTY; *esp* **:** twisted or contorted and marked by swollen joints ‹had been wringing nothing but a scanty living from the soil with their gnarled and ~ hands —C.A. & Mary Beard›

knot·ter \-äd·ə(r), -ätə-\ *n* -s **1 :** one that makes knots: as **a :** a worker who makes nets by hand **b :** a device that knots threads **2 :** one that removes knots: as **a :** a device used in papermaking by which lumps are removed from paper pulp **b :** LIMBER

knotter bill *or* **knotter hook** *n* **:** KNOTTING BILL

knot·ti·ly \-äd·əlē\ *adv* **:** in a knotty manner ‹a ~ involved problem›

knot·ti·ness \-äd·ēnəs, -ät\, |in-\ *n* -ES **:** the quality or state of being knotty ‹bewildered by the ~ of the legal points involved›

knotting *n* -s **1 :** fancywork produced by twisting and looping thread into knots to form designs **2 :** a conditioning preparation (as shellac) used to cover the knots of wood before painting

knotting bill *or* **knotting hook** *n* **:** a metal hook with a blunt point on which is formed the knot that secures a quantity of grain gathered up by a grain binder

knot·ty \'näd·ē, -ät|, |i\ *adj, usu* -ER/-EST [ME *knotty*, fr. *knotte, knot* knot + -*y* — more at KNOT] **:** marked by or full of knots: as **a :** full of difficulties or complications **:** hard to solve or understand **:** INVOLVED, PUZZLING, INTRICATE ‹the ~ problems of a complex society —V.L.Parrington› ‹~ points of international law —Lisle Bell› **b :** tied in or with knots ‹a ~ rope› **c** (1) **:** twisted or contorted and marked by protuberances **:** GNARLED ‹ancient ~ trees› **:** BUMPY, KNOBBY ‹her old ~ hands› (2) **:** having many hard irregular lumps at the points where branches grow out ‹cut down a ~ tree trunk› (3) **:** showing cross sections of such lumps or having knotholes ‹~ pieces of lumber› **d :** marked by or indicative of robustness or ruggedness **:** WIRY, TOUGH ‹a sinewy ~ strength —Jack London› **syn** see COMPLEX

knotty brake *n* **:** MALE FERN

knotty gut *n* **:** NODULAR DISEASE

knotty guts *n pl* **1** *sing or pl in constr* **:** NODULAR DISEASE **2 :** intestines affected with nodular disease

knotty pine *n* **1 :** LODGEPOLE PINE **2 :** pine wood marked by an esp. decorative distribution of knots when finished for use unpainted esp. on walls or ceilings

knotty rhatany *n* **:** PERUVIAN RHATANY

knotweed \'ˌ,ˌ\ *n* **:** any of several plants of the genus *Polygonum; esp* **:** KNOTGRASS 1

knotweed spurge *n* **:** SEASIDE SPURGE

[1]**knout** \'naùt, 'nüt\ *n* -s [Russ *knut*, of Scand origin; akin to ON *knūtr* knot — more at KNOT] **:** a flogging whip with a lash of leather thongs twisted with wire used for punishing criminals

[2]**knout** \"\ *vt* -ED/-ING/-S **:** to flog with a knout

[1]**know** \'nō\ *vb* **knew** \'n(y)ü\ *or dial* **knowed** \'nōd\ **known** \'nōn *sometimes* -ōən\ *also dial* **knowed; knowing; knows** [ME *knowen, knawen*, fr. OE *cnāwan;* akin to OHG *bichnāan* to recognize, ON *knā* I can, L *gnoscere, noscere* to become acquainted with, come to know, Gk *gignōskein* to come to know, perceive, OSlav *znati* to know, Skt *jānāti* he knows] *vt* **1 a** (1) **:** to apprehend immediately with the mind or with the senses **:** perceive directly **:** have direct unambiguous cognition of ‹taught that one could come to ~ objective truth› (2) **:** to have perception, cognition, or understanding of esp. to an extensive or complete extent ‹learning to ~ one's mind —Virgil Thomson› ‹insisted on the importance of ~*ing* oneself› (3) **:** to recognize the quality of **:** see clearly the character of **:** DISCERN ‹*knew* him for what he was› ‹~s him as honest and reliable› (4) **:** to recognize in a specific capacity ‹one glance and they ~ him as the one destined to lead them› **b** (1) **:** to apprehend as being the same as something previously apprehended **:** recognize as being an object of perception identical with a previous object of perception **:** recognize as familiar ‹*knew* her father as soon as she saw him› ‹said they would ~ that face anywhere› (2) **:** to have acquaintance or familiarity with through experience or acquisition of information or hearsay ‹*knew* no such restraints —Hugh Seton-Watson› ‹*knew* the law fairly well› ‹~s foreign languages›; *specif* **:** to have personal acquaintance with (a person) ‹whom he had learned to ~ and love —Allen Johnson› ‹recognizes many people by sight but doesn't ~ them all› (3) **:** to have experience of ‹the region has *known* a steadily increasing . . . number of visitors —S.H.Holbrook› ‹*knew* great delight› ‹did not ~ happiness with the woman he married —Ruth P. Randall› **c :** to apprehend as being distinct from something previously apprehended **:** recognize as being an object of perception distinct from a previous object of perception **:** recognize as distinct **:** DISTINGUISH ‹barely able to ~ one thing from another› **2 a :** to have cognizance, consciousness, or awareness of **:** have within the mind as something apprehended, learned, or understood ‹*knew* they could never have what city folks had —M.W.Straight› ‹~s that this is quite true› ‹*knew* many would not believe him› ‹didn't ~ who she was or where she was going› ‹was *known* to be a friend of hers› **b :** to have a practical understanding of or a distinct skill in through instruction, study, practice, or experience ‹~s how to write vividly —William Clerk› ‹~s the fundamentals perfectly› **3 :** to apprehend with certitude as true, factual, sure, or valid **:** perceive or have within the mind's grasp with clarity and the conviction of certainty **:** have certitude about and clear comprehension of ‹~ what they want and intend to get it› ‹*knew* the solution to almost any problem› **4** *archaic* **:** to have sexual intercourse with ~ *vi* **1 a :** to have perception or cognition or understanding of something esp. to an extensive or complete extent ‹you ~ better› ‹people who ~ will not waste their time that way› ‹we want to ~, we will not be content with a fairy tale of love —L.O.Coxe› **b :** to have cognizance, consciousness, or awareness of something **:** be aware of the existence or fact of something ‹*knew* of her but had not yet met her› ‹*knew* about what had happened› **2 :** to have information **:** have acquaintance with facts ‹*knew* differently and therefore refused the offer› **3 :** to have something within the mind's grasp with certitude and clarity ‹do you ~, or is that only your opinion› — **know one's onions :** to know one's stuff — **know one's stuff :** to be thoroughly proficient or highly skilled in a field of activity or an area of knowledge **:** know the ropes ‹can rely on her completely because she really *knows her stuff*› — **know the ropes :** to have experience and understanding of the details, methods, and procedures involved in accomplishing or furthering something esp. without unnecessary delay ‹*knew the ropes* and soon had everything organized smoothly› — **not know from nothing** *slang* **:** to know nothing about something **:** be completely ignorant ‹don't *know from nothing* —Erskine Caldwell›

[2]**know** \"\ *n* -s **:** the fact of knowing **:** KNOWLEDGE ‹the inside ~ of a journalist —Douglass Cater› — **in the know** *adv (or adj)* **:** in possession of confidential or otherwise relatively limited or exclusive knowledge, information, or awareness ‹the sense of importance which comes from a feeling that one is *in the know* —Stanley Walker› ‹*in-the-know* intellectuals›

know·abil·i·ty \ˌnōə'biləd·ē\ *n* **:** capability of being known ‹the question of the ~ of the external world —*Humanist*›

know·able \'nōəbəl\ *adj* **:** capable of being known ‹the philosophical proposition that the external physical world and all its laws are fully ~ —*Atlantic*› — **know·able·ness** *n* -ES

know-all *var of* KNOW-IT-ALL

knowe *or* **know** \'nō, 'naù\ *chiefly Scot var of* KNOLL

knowed *past of* KNOW

know·er \'nōə(r)\ *n* -s [ME, fr. *knowen* to know + -*er* — more at KNOW] **:** one that knows

know-how \'ˌ,ˌ\ *n* -s [fr. the phrase *know how*] **:** practical knowledge of how to do or accomplish something with smoothness and efficiency **:** ability to get something done with a minimum of wasted effort **:** accumulated practical skill or expertness ‹business *know-how*› ‹needed the *know-how* of a good carpenter› ‹salesmanship *know-how*› ‹the *know-how* involved in producing a play› ‹developed his bowling *know-how*›; *esp* **:** technical knowledge, ability, skill, or expertness of this sort ‹the company needed to use all its ingenuity and *know-how* to succeed in laying the oil lines›

[1]**know·ing** \'nōiŋ, -ōēŋ\ *n* -s [ME, fr. *knowen* to know + -*ing*] **1 a** (1) **:** the action or fact of knowing or understanding ‹avoided their ~ about this› ‹her ~ was a source of comfort› (2) **:** the process or faculty of getting to know or of arriving at understanding ‹no ~ what may happen› ‹a power beyond his ~ —*Atlantic*› **b :** the action of knowing by intuition or indirection or the faculty of getting to know or arrive at understanding through intuition or indirection ‹the ~s of art are real . . . but they are not utterly reliable —H.J.Muller› **c :** something that is apprehended or capable of being apprehended by such an action, process, or faculty ‹underlying every concrete situation he sees the fusion of ~s and the known —J.R.Kantor› **2 :** the condition or fact of possessing understanding or information or of being aware of something ‹in private, in secret ~ —N.L.Rothman›

[2]**knowing** \"\ *adj, sometimes* -ER/-EST [ME, fr. pres. part. of *knowen* to know] **1 a :** having or reflecting knowledge, information, or insight **:** marked by understanding and intelligence **:** well-informed and marked by a ready capacity for further learning **:** KNOWLEDGEABLE ‹a ~ student› ‹a ~ instructor› **b** (1) **:** having or reflecting the keen awareness and insight and power of discernment typical of the specialist or expert **:** highly perceptive esp. in a specialized or exclusive field ‹a ~ collector of rare books› ‹has done an excellent and ~ job in selecting the material for this book —J.C. Smith› (2) **:** having or reflecting distinct skill ‹~ brushwork on ceiling and doors —Claudia Cassidy› **c** (1) **:** that indicates or is marked by awareness of and careful conformity to what is chic and currently in style **:** SMART ‹a ~ selection of gloves and accessories› (2) **:** marked by sophistication or snobbishness ‹a distasteful air of pretentious smartness, of being altogether too ~ —Herbert Read› **2 a** (1) **:** shrewd and keenly alert **:** QUICK-WITTED, ASTUTE ‹a ~ handling of the business deal› **:** WIDE-AWAKE ‹any ~ person could have seen what was going on› (2) **:** WORLDLY-WISE ‹produces ~ chuckles —E.R.Bentley› ‹perhaps a bit too ~ and sensuous —Robert Lawrence› **b :** that reflects or is designed to indicate possession of confidential, secret, or otherwise exclusive inside knowledge or information ‹poised her fork and gave her guest a ~ look —Louis Bromfield› ‹a ~ wink› ‹maintain a discreet and ~ silence on the subject —Harry Gordon› **:** that indicates an awareness or insight not generally shared ‹the two young officers exchanged ~ glances —W.M.Thackeray› **3 a :** that knows, is capable of knowing, or is the means of knowing **:** COGNITIVE ‹in full possession of the ordinary ~ faculties› **b** *archaic* **:** COGNIZANT ‹~ to and familiar with the whole circumstances —George Catlin› **4 :** that is done with awareness or deliberateness **:** that is intentional ‹indiscriminate classification of innocent with ~ activity —*Civil Liberties*› **syn** see INTELLIGENT

know·ing·ly *adv* [ME, fr. *knowing* + -*ly*] **:** in a knowing manner ‹smiled ~›; *esp* **:** with awareness, deliberateness, or intention ‹had never ~ hurt him —Max Peacock›

know·ing·ness *n* -ES **:** the quality or state of being knowing ‹the brisk ~ of a competent journalist —C.J.Rolo›

[1]**know-it-all** \'ˌˌ,ˌ\ *also* **know-all** \'ˌ,ˌ\ *n, pl* **know-it-alls** *also* **know-alls :** one that rashly and annoyingly claims to know or acts as if knowing all about everything or nearly everything **:** one to whom nothing new can apparently be told or who views any advice or suggestion from others as of little or no value or as something that had already been considered and acted on or rejected ‹loud cocky *know-it-alls*› ‹a humbling enigma for the *know-alls* —D.B.W.Lewis›

[2]**know-it-all** \"\ *also* **know-all** \"\ *adj* [[1]*know-it-all, know-all*] **:** of, relating to, or having the characteristics of a know-it-all ‹a *know-it-all* attitude› ‹a *know-all* manner› ‹should not be so *know-it-all* about what the Almighty was up to —Gretchen Finletter›

knowledgable *var of* KNOWLEDGEABLE

[1]**knowl·edge** \'nälij, -lēj,-ləj, *Brit sometimes* 'nōl-\ *vt* -ED/-ING/-S [ME *knawlechen, knowlechen*, irreg. fr. *knowen, knawen* to know — more at KNOW] **1** *obs* **:** to recognize as being something indicated **:** admit the status, claims, or authority of **:** ACKNOWLEDGE **2** *obs* **:** to recognize, admit, or confess the fact or truth of

[2]**knowledge** \"\ *n* -s [ME *knawlage, knowlage, knawlege, knowlege*, fr. *knawlechen, knowlechen*, v.] **1** *obs* **a :** ACKNOWLEDGMENT **b :** COGNIZANCE **2 :** the fact or condition of knowing **a** (1) **:** the fact or condition of knowing something with a considerable degree of familiarity gained through experience of or contact or association with the individual or thing so known ‹a thorough ~ of life and its problems› ‹has a fair ~ of the people of that country› ‹a remarkable ~ of human nature› (2) **:** acquaintance with or theoretical or practical understanding of some branch of science, art, learning, or other area involving study, research, or practice and the acquisition of skills ‹~ of advanced mathematics› ‹has little ~ of the techniques of drawing and painting› ‹a ~ of foreign languages› **b** (1) **:** the fact or condition of being cognizant, conscious, or aware of something ‹was elated by ~ of their success› ‹the ~ that it was really important› ‹his ~ of what she had had to endure› (2) **:** the particular existent range of one's information or acquaintance with facts **:** the scope of one's awareness **:** extent of one's understanding ‹said that to the best of his ~ the matter had not yet been attended to› **c :** the fact or condition of apprehending truth, fact, or reality immediately with the mind or senses **:** PERCEPTION, COGNITION ‹intellectual ~› ‹the nature of ~› **:** COMPREHENSION, UNDERSTANDING ‹intuitive ~› ‹proceeding from the lower to the higher degrees of ~› **d :** the fact or condition of possessing within mental grasp through instruction, study, research, or experience one or more truths, facts, principles, or other objects of perception **:** the fact or condition of having information or of being learned or erudite ‹a man of great ~› ‹always seeking after more and more ~› **3** *archaic* **:** CARNAL KNOWLEDGE **4 a :** the sum total of what is known **:** the whole body of truth, fact, information, principles, or other objects of cognition acquired by mankind ‹adding to the vast store of ~› ‹all branches of ~› **b** *archaic* **:** a branch of learning **:** ART, SCIENCE

syn KNOWLEDGE, SCIENCE, LEARNING, ERUDITION, SCHOLARSHIP, INFORMATION, and LORE agree in signifying what is or can be known. KNOWLEDGE applies to any body of known facts or to any body of ideas inferred from such facts or accepted as truths on good grounds ‹a *knowledge* of languages› ‹a *knowledge* of the habits of snakes› ‹a *knowledge* of modern chemistry› ‹to benefit by the accumulated *knowledge* of centuries› SCIENCE still sometimes interchanges with KNOWLEDGE but commonly applies to a body of systematized knowledge comprising facts carefully gathered and general truths carefully inferred from them, often underlying a practice, usu. connoting exactness, and often denoting knowledge of unquestionable certainty ‹must bear in mind that geographic discovery also is *science*, and it was a scientific theory that impelled the venture of Columbus —I.M.Price› ‹the defense of nations had become a *science* and a calling —T.B.Macaulay› ‹the *science* of administration —A.S.Link› ‹the art of feeding preceded the *science* of nutrition by many centuries —F.B. Hadley› ‹the diagnosis of disease is no longer primarily guesswork but rather a *science*› LEARNING applies to knowledge gained by study, often long and careful and sometimes connoting comprehensiveness and profundity ‹to expose children to as much *learning* as possible› ‹a full, rich, human book, packed with information lightly dispensed and fortified with *learning* easily worn —Honor Tracy⟩ ⟨a man of great and profound *learning* but little common sense⟩ ERUDITION usu. stresses wide, profound, or recondite learning, sometimes suggesting pedantry ⟨often flabbergast their elders with their *erudition* — a scholarly but lively sense of words, a sound background in history and economics, the ability to translate or even to speak two or three foreign languages —Stanley Walker⟩ ⟨all the encyclopedic *erudition* of the middle ages —J.L.Lowes⟩ ⟨balancing an immense load of *erudition* upon a precarious foundation of fact —*Times Lit. Supp.*⟩ SCHOLARSHIP implies the learning, careful mastery of detail, esp. of a given field, and the critical acumen characteristic of a good scholar ⟨the immense and rapidly expanding *scholarship* not only in psychology but in history, sociology, and anthropology as well, which illuminates the study of the family —Lynn White⟩ ⟨unusually equipped in both scientific and classical *scholarship* in addition to his command of his own field, a brilliant and powerful lecturer —E.S.Bates⟩ ⟨his learning and general *scholarship* were universally recognized, and in his special sphere of law he had no peer in this country —T.D. Bacon⟩ INFORMATION generally applies to knowledge, commonly accepted as true, of a factual kind usu. gathered from others or from books ⟨this book, packed with *information* of the life and movements of big game —*Times Lit. Supp.*⟩ ⟨to seek *information* about a man from friends and credit records⟩ ⟨a book of *information* about early river boats⟩ LORE suggests special, often arcane, knowledge, usu. of a traditional, anecdotal character and of a particular subject ⟨fairy *lore*⟩ ⟨one of the most bizarre occurrences in railroad *lore* —Bennett Cerf⟩ ⟨bird *lore*⟩ ⟨taught the *lore* of medicinal herbs —*Amer. Guide Series: La.*⟩

knowl·edge·abil·i·ty *also* **knowl·edg·abil·i·ty** \\,==ə'biləd·ē, -lətē, -i\\ *n* **:** the quality or state of being knowledgeable

knowl·edge·able *also* **knowl·edg·able** \\'==əbəl\\ *adj* [[2]*knowledge* + *-able*] **1 a :** marked by or indicating intelligence or knowledge **:** mentally alert and well-informed **:** KNOWING ⟨~ about the technique of painting —Herbert Read⟩ ⟨the keenest and most ~ questions —Norman Cousins⟩ ⟨limousines with ~ chauffeur-guides —*advt*⟩ **b :** marked by a keen sense of discernment **:** marked by notable ability to evaluate and discriminate **:** highly perceptive **:** having awareness and insight ⟨a ~ critic⟩ ⟨sparse but ~ comments —*Newsweek*⟩ **2 a :** marked by an open receptive mind **:** not narrow-minded or otherwise intellectually cramped **:** not provincial in outlook **:** BROAD-MINDED, LIBERAL ⟨addressed himself to a ~ audience that he knew would not be shocked⟩ **b :** responsive and alive to intellectual or cultural stimulation ⟨an eager, ~ group of students⟩ **3 :** marked by deliberateness or awareness **:** INTENTIONAL, CONSCIOUS ⟨an intolerably ~ affectation —Eric Partridge⟩ ⟨not influenced by his ~ prejudices —A.C.Gimson⟩ — **knowl·edge·able·ness** *also* **knowl·edg·able·ness** *n* -ES — **knowl·edge·ably** *also* **knowl·edg·ably** \\-blē, -bli\\ *adv*

knowl·edged \\-jd\\ *adj* [[2]*knowledge* + *-ed*] **:** marked by or equipped with knowledge ⟨trained — at least in his own fashion — and ~ in our ways —S.E.White⟩

knowl·edge·less \\-jləs\\ *adj* **:** devoid of knowledge **:** IGNORANT ⟨naked and ~ —Carl Sandburg⟩

knowledges *pres 3d sing of* KNOWLEDGE, *pl of* KNOWLEDGE

knowledging *pres part of* KNOWLEDGE

[1]known \\'nōn *sometimes* -ōən\\ *adj* [ME *knowen, knawen,* fr. past part. of *knowen, knawen* to know — more at KNOW] **:** that is apprehended or perceived by the mind or senses **:** that has become a part of knowledge ⟨a ~ truth that no one denies⟩ **:** familiar through knowledge or experience ⟨beyond the limits of the ~ world —A.C.Whitehead⟩; *esp* **:** generally recognized ⟨a ~ authority in this matter⟩

[2]known \\"\\ *n* -S **1 :** something known **:** something familiar or recognized; *specif* **:** a substance of known composition — used esp. in chemical analysis ⟨chemical determinations performed on ~*s* —A.A.Benedetti-Pichler⟩ **2 :** a letter (as in a^2+2ab) or some other symbol (as π) used in a mathematical equation to represent a known number or quantity

[1]know-noth·ing \\'nō,nəthiŋ, -thēŋ\\ *adj* **1 :** extremely ignorant ⟨a *know-nothing* blunderer⟩ **2** *often cap K&N* **:** of, relating to, or characterized by know-nothingism ⟨the *Know-Nothing* party . . . proposed the political proscription of Roman Catholics —W.L.Sperry⟩ ⟨the *know-nothing* anti-intellectualism that parades . . . as anti-Communism —Stringfellow Barr⟩

[2]know-nothing \\"\\ *n, pl* **know-nothings 1 :** one that knows little or nothing **:** IGNORAMUS **2** *usu cap K&N* [so called fr. the fact that some members of the organization replied "I don't know" to any questions that were asked them about it] **:** a member of a 19th century short-lived secret American political organization prominent in the decade before the Civil War and hostile to the political influence of recent immigrants and Roman Catholics **3 :** AGNOSTIC **4 :** an exponent or adherent of 20th century political know-nothingism ⟨counting on the *know-nothings* . . . to exploit the present atmosphere of uncertainty and insecurity —Norman Cousins⟩ ⟨assaults upon intellectuals by political *know-nothings* —Richard Robbins⟩

know-noth·ing·ism \\-ŋ,izəm\\ *n* -S **1** *usu cap K&N* **:** the principles and policies of the 19th century Know-Nothings **2 :** the fact or condition of knowing nothing or of desiring to know nothing or the conviction that nothing can be known with certitude esp. in religion or morality ⟨an ethical *know-nothingism* in which there is no longer any certainty . . . as to what is and what is not evil —F.B.Millett⟩ **3** *sometimes cap K&N* **:** a political attitude or philosophy of the mid-twentieth century characterized chiefly by anti-intellectualism and exaggerated patriotism and by fear of foreign and subversive influences ⟨fighting the battle inside the government against the forces of hysteria and *know-nothingism* —Reed Harris⟩

knows *pres 3d sing of* KNOW, *pl of* KNOW

know-what \\'=,=\\ *n, pl* **know-whats** [fr. the phrase *know what*] **:** clear recognition of the objective of a selected course of action ⟨the know-why and the *know-what* which businessmen find necessary for all persons in administrative or executive positions —C.E.Henson⟩

know-why \\'=,=\\ *n, pl* **know-whys** [fr. the phrase *know why*] **:** understanding of the reasons underlying something (as a course of action) ⟨our frontier past and our industrialized present both incline us toward a preoccupation with technique, with know-how rather than *know-why* —Dwight Macdonald⟩

knox·ville \\ näks,vil *esp S* -vəl\\ *adj, usu cap* [fr. *Knoxville,* Tenn.] **:** of or from the city of Knoxville, Tenn. ⟨a *Knoxville* industry⟩ **:** of the kind or style prevalent in Knoxville

knox·vil·lite \\-vi,līt, -və,-\\ *n* -S [*Knoxville,* town in Napa county, Calif. + E *-ite*] **:** MAGNESIOCOPIAPITE

knt *abbr* knight

knub \\'nəb\\ *n* -S [prob. fr. LG *knubbe,* fr. MLG *knubbe, knobbe,* knot on a tree, knob — more at KNOB] **1 a** *dial* **:** KNOB **b :** NUB 4 **2** *or* **knubs** *pl but sing or pl in constr* **:** FRISON

knubbly *var of* NUBBLY

knubby *var of* NUBBY

[1]knuck·le \\'nəkəl\\ *n* -S [ME *knokel;* akin to MLG *knökel* knuckle, MHG *knöchel, knüchel;* diminutives fr. the root of MLG *knoke* bone, MLG *knoche;* akin to OE *cnycled* bent, ON *knykill* small knot, OE *cnotta* knot — more at KNOT] **1 a** (1) **:** the joint where the ends of two bones meet or articulate (2) **:** the tarsal or carpal joint and the parts including the flesh immediately above or below in a quadruped (as a pig) used for food **:** the knee or hock joint and adjoining parts of a quadruped; *often* **:** the shank of a quadruped used as food (3) **:** the shoulder joint of a whale **b** (1) **:** a rounded prominence formed by bending a joint where two bones meet or articulate; *esp* **:** one of the prominences formed at each of the joints and bases of the fingers of the human hand when the hand is shut or when the fingers are clenched (2) **:** a projection at the carpal or tarsal joints of a quadruped **2 :** something that protrudes like a knuckle, that is shaped like a knuckle, or that is otherwise suggestive of a knuckle: as **a :** a sharply flexed loop of intestines incarcerated in a hernia **b** (1) **:** one of the joining parts of a hinge through which a pin or rivet passes (2) **:** KNUCKLE JOINT (3) **:** the rotating piece used for the coupling device in various forms of automatic car couplings (as the rotating hook of a railroad-car coupler designed to hook up with the coupler of another car) **c** (1) **:** the meeting of two surfaces at a sharp angle (as in a roof or as in the timbers of a ship) (2) **:** the outer part of a sharply angled jetty, a breakwater, or other construction at or along a shore **d :** a small, decorative, carved, or rolled terminal part esp. on a piece of furniture (as at the end of one of the arms of a chair) **e :** a chunk or knob of rock ⟨their bodies calloused by ~*s* of falling rock —Robert Payne⟩ **f :** a point or support on which something pivots or turns **:** pivotal point ⟨the ship used the end of the pier as a ~ for swinging around⟩ **3 knuckles** *pl but sing or pl in constr* **:** BRASS KNUCKLES — **near the knuckle 1 :** near the permitted, accepted, or tolerable limit of what can be said or done: as **a :** verging on the border line between decency and indecency ⟨jokes that were embarrassingly *near the knuckle*⟩ **b :** verging on what is offensive or injurious to one's sensibilities ⟨accusations too *near the knuckle* for them to ignore⟩ **2 :** near to what is of greatest importance, interest, or concern ⟨the real reasons for doing this are, perhaps, *nearer the knuckle* than they think —John Holloway⟩

[2]knuckle \\"\\ *vb* **knuckled; knuckled; knuckling** \\-k(ə)liŋ\\ **knuckles** *vi* **1 :** to knuckle under ⟨*knuckled* to no pressure groups —*Newsweek*⟩ **2 :** to project or protrude like a knuckle **3 :** to be affected with cocked ankles — usu. used of a horse or of an affected fetlock joint and often with *over* ⟨~*s* over badly on the off hind leg⟩ ⟨the fetlocks of colts may ~ for some time after birth without permanent harm⟩ ~ *vt* **1 :** to strike ⟨the seaman *knuckled* his forehead and wheeled around —Clark Russell⟩ or press or rub with the knuckles ⟨shook himself and rose, *knuckling* his eyes —Lawrence Durrell⟩ ⟨he *knuckled* his hair and he frowned —Thurston Scott⟩ **2 :** to shoot (a marble) from between the knuckle of the thumb and the bent forefinger **3 :** to form a bend or a knuckle joint in (as steel plates or wire fencing)

knuckle ball *n* **:** a baseball pitch made by gripping the ball with the knuckles or fingernails of the index and second and sometimes third fingers pressed against the top of the ball and thrown usu. with little speed or spin so as to give it a typically erratic course

knuck·le·ball·er \\'nəkəl,bȯlə(r)\\ *n* -S **:** a baseball pitcher that specializes in pitching knuckle balls

knucklebone \\'==,=\\ *n* [ME *knokylle bone,* fr. *knokylle, knokel* knuckle + *bone, bon* bone] **1 a :** one of the bones forming a knuckle of a human finger **b :** a long bone with a knobbed end (as a femur or humerus); *also* **:** the knob of such a bone — now used only of animals **2 a :** the tetrahedral metacarpal or metatarsal bone of a sheep; *esp* **:** such a bone marked on its surfaces and used in ancient times in gaming and divination usu. through being tossed like one of a pair of dice **b knucklebones** *pl but sing in constr* **:** a game played with such marked bones or with small metal objects resembling such bones; *esp* **:** JACKS

knuck·led \\'nəkəld\\ *adj* **:** having knuckles

knuckle down *vi* **1 :** to place the knuckles on the ground preparatory to shooting a marble ⟨*knuckled down* and shot for the center hole⟩ **2 :** to apply oneself with seriousness or concentration **:** apply oneself earnestly ⟨let's have no more nonsense and *knuckle down* to business⟩ **3 :** to knuckle under

knuck·le-dust \\'nəkəl,dəst\\ *vt* [back-formation fr. *knuckle-duster*] **:** to strike with the fist; *specif* **:** to strike with brass knuckles

knuck·le-dust·er \\-tə(r)\\ *n* -S **1 :** BRASS KNUCKLES **2 :** one that specializes in or is given to attacking with the fists; *specif* **:** one that uses brass knuckles

knucklehead \\'==,=\\ *n* **:** a stupid blunderer **:** DUMBBELL — **knuckleheaded** \\¦==¦==\\ *adj*

knuckle joint *n* **:** a hinge joint in which a projection with an eye on one piece enters a jaw between two corresponding projections with eyes on another piece and is retained by a pin or rivet

knuckle joint

knuckle-kneed \\¦==¦=\\ *adj* **:** having projecting or bulging knees

knuckle line *n* **:** the line of meeting of two surfaces of a ship at an angle

knuckle man *or* **knuckle boy** *n* **:** a mine-car clipper who works at the top of a haulage slope attaching and detaching mine cars to and from cables and coupling trains of cars

knuckle pin *n* **:** a pin or rivet connecting the two parts of a knuckle joint

knuckle post *n* **:** the vertical post of an automobile steering knuckle on which the knuckle is pivoted

knuckle press *or* **knuckle-joint press** *n* **:** a punch press using a toggle joint **:** TOGGLE-JOINT PRESS

knuck·ler \\'nək(ə)lə(r)\\ *n* -S **1 a :** a marble that a player knuckles **b :** KNUCKLE BALL **2 :** a hydraulic-press operator who shapes steel parts for use in shipbuilding

knuckles *pl of* KNUCKLE, *pres 3d sing of* KNUCKLE

knuck·le·some \\'nəkəlsəm\\ *adj* **:** KNUCKLY

knuckle under *vi* **:** to admit defeat **:** give in **:** give up **:** YIELD, SUBMIT ⟨if it hadn't been for her pride, she'd have *knuckled under* and gone back home —Jane Woodfin⟩

knuckling *n* -S [fr. gerund of [2]*knuckle*] **:** COCKED ANKLES

knuck·ly \\'nək(ə)lē\\ *adj, often* -ER/-EST **:** having bony protuberances; *specif* **:** having prominent knuckles ⟨~ fingers⟩

knucks \\'nəks\\ *n pl* [alter. of *knuckles,* pl. of [1]*knuckle*] **1** *sing in constr* **:** a game of marbles at the end of which the winner has the option of shooting a marble at the opponent's knuckles held on the ground **2** *sing or pl in constr* **:** BRASS KNUCKLES

knull·ing \\'nəliŋ\\ *n* -S [by alter.] **:** KNURLING

knur \\'nər(·)\\ *n* -S [ME *knorre;* akin to ME *knarre* rough stone, knot in wood; akin to MHG & MLG *knorre* burl, knot, OHG *chniurig* knotty, solid, Norw *knart, knort* knot, burl, OE *cnotta* knot — more at KNOT] **1 :** a hard excrescence (as on a tree trunk or stone) **:** GNARL **2** *dial Brit* **:** a usu. wooden ball (as used in the game of knur and spell)

knur and spell *n* **:** a game played in northern England that resembles trapball

[1]knurl \\'nərl, *esp before pause or consonant* 'nər·əl; 'nə̄l, 'nəil\\ *n* -S [prob. blend of *knur* and *gnarl*] **1 a** (1) **:** a small protuberance, excrescence, or knob (2) **:** a small ridge or bead; *esp* **:** one of a series of small ridges or beads used on a usu. metal surface (as of a thumbscrew) as a means of ensuring a firm grip or as a decorative feature **b :** a contorted knot in wood **2 a** *chiefly Scot* **:** a short thickset person; *esp* **:** DWARF **b** *Scot* **:** a tangled mass (as of hair) **:** SNARL **3 :** a tool for knurling

[2]knurl \\"\\ *vt* -ED/-ING/-S **:** to provide (as a thumbscrew) with small ridges or beading (as for ensuring a firm grip) **:** make knurls on **:** MILL

knurled *adj* **1 :** GNARLED ⟨the ~ swollen knuckles of his other hand —Norman Mailer⟩ **2 :** provided with knurls ⟨a ~ thumbscrew⟩

knurling *n* -S **1 a :** the making of knurls **b :** the ridges on knurled work **:** knurled work **2 a :** a breaking up of a rounded molding as if for a bead and reel but usu. with more elaboration **b :** molding so treated

knurly \\-ərlē, -ə̄l-,-əil-, -li\\ *adj, often* -ER/-EST [[1]*knurl* + *-y*] **1 :** GNARLY **2 :** DWARFISH

knurry *adj* [*knur* + *-y*] *obs* **:** KNURLY

knut \\(kə)'nət\\ *n* -S [prob. alter. of [1]*nut*] **:** a fop of the late 19th or early 20th century

knys·na boxwood \\(kə)'niznə-\\ *or* **knysna** *n* -S [fr. *Knysna,* Union of So. Africa] **:** EAST LONDON BOXWOOD

ko \\'kō, 'gō\\ *n* -S *usu cap* [Chin (Pek) *ko*[1] elder brother] **:** a Chinese porcelain produced in the 12th century and distinguished by its dark clay and fine crackle

[1]KO \\(')kā¦ō\\ *abbr or n, pl* **KO's** \\-ōz\\ *sometimes not cap* **:** KNOCKOUT

[2]KO \\"\\ *vt* **KO'd** \\-ōd\\ **KO'd; KO'ing; KO's** *sometimes not cap* **:** to knock out

KO *abbr* keep off

koa \\'kōə\\ *n* -S [Hawaiian] **1 :** a Hawaiian timber tree (*Acacia koa*) with light gray bark, crescent-shaped leaves, and white flowers in small round heads **2 :** the fine-grained red wood of the koa now used esp. for furniture

ko·ae \\kō'ä,ā\\ *n* -S [Hawaiian] *Hawaii* **:** TROPIC BIRD

koa finch *n* **:** any of several Hawaiian birds of the genera *Pseudonestor* and *Psittirostra* (family Drepaniidae) that resemble the finches

koa ha·o·le \\-hä'ō(,)lā\\ *n* [Hawaiian] **:** LEAD TREE

ko·ala *also* **koala bear** *or* **co·ala** \\kō'älə, kə'wä-\\ *n* -S [*koala* native name in Australia] **1 :** a sluggish Australian arboreal marsupial (*Phascolarctos cinereus*) that is about two feet long and has large hairy ears, thick ashy gray fur, and sharp claws and that feeds on eucalyptus leaves — called also *kangaroo bear, native bear* **2 :** the pelt of the koala

ko·a·li \\kō'älē, kə'wä-\\ *n* -S [Hawaiian] **:** any of several tropical morning glories of the genus *Ipomoea* (as *I. tuberculata* or *I. insularis*) used in Hawaii as cordage

koaliang *var of* KAOLIANG

ko·an \\'kō,än\\ *n, pl* **koans** *or* **koan** [Jap *kōan,* lit., public plan, fr. *kō* public + *an* proposal, plan] **:** a paradox used in Zen Buddhism as an instrument of meditation in training monks to despair of an ultimate dependence upon reason and to force them into sudden intuitive enlightenment

ko·asa·ti \\,kōə'säd·ē\\ *n, pl* **koasati** *or* **koasatis** *usu cap* **1 a :** a Muskogean people of northern Alabama **b :** a member of such people **2 :** the language of the Koasati people

[1]kob \\'käb, 'kōb\\ *also* **ko·ba** \\'kōbə\\ *n, pl* **kob** *or* **kobs** [of Niger-Congo origin; akin to Wolof *koba* roan antelope, Fulani *kōba*] **:** any of various African antelopes (genus *Adenota*) related to the waterbucks

[2]kob \\'käb\\ *n* -S [by shortening & alter.] **:** KABELJOU

ko·ban \\'kō,bän\\ *also* **co·bang** *or* **ko·bang** \\-bäŋ\\ *n* -S [Jap *koban,* fr. *ko* small + *ban* size, format] **:** an oval Japanese gold coin of widely varying value issued from the 17th century to the 19th century

ko·be \\'kōbē\\ *adj, usu cap* [fr. *Kobe,* city in western Honshu, Japan] **:** of or from the city of Kobe, Japan **:** of the kind or style prevalent in Kobe

ko·bell·ite \\'kōbə,līt\\ *n* -S [Sw *kobellit,* fr. Franz von *Kobell* †1882 Ger. mineralogist and poet + Sw *-it* -ite] **:** a mineral $Pb_2(Bi,Sb)_2S_5$ consisting of a blackish gray sulfide of antimony, bismuth, and lead

ko·bird *also* **kow·bird** \\'kō,=\\ *n* [*ko-, kow-* (prob. imit.) + *bird*] **:** YELLOW-BILLED CUCKOO

ko·bold \\'kō,bȯld, -bōld\\ *n* -S [G — more at COBALT] **1 :** a gnome held esp. in German folklore to inhabit underground places ⟨looked like ~*s* from some magic mine —Rudyard Kipling⟩ **2 :** a domestic spirit often held in Germanic folklore to be mischievous

ko·bus \\'kōbəs\\ *n, cap* [NL, fr. E [1]*kob*] **:** a genus of antelopes containing the typical waterbucks

koch \\'kōch\\ *n, pl* **koches** *usu cap* **:** a member of a hinduized Mongoloid people of Assam

ko·chi \\'kōchē\\ *adj, usu cap* [fr. *Kochi,* city on south coast of Shikoku, Japan] **:** of or from the city of Kochi, Japan **:** of the kind or style prevalent in Kochi

ko·chia \\'kōkēə\\ *n* [NL, fr. W. D. J. *Koch* †1849 Ger. botanist + NL *-ia*] **1** *cap* **:** a genus of herbs (family Chenopodiaceae) having a turbinate perianth and broadly winged fruit — see SUMMER CYPRESS **2** -S **:** a plant of the genus *Kochia*

koch phenomenon \\'kȯk-, 'kȯk-,'kōk-,'käk-\\ *n, usu cap K* [after Robert *Koch* †1910 Ger. bacteriologist] **:** the response of a tuberculous animal to reinfection with tubercle bacilli marked by necrotic lesions that develop rapidly and heal quickly and caused by hypersensitivity to products of the tubercle bacillus

koch's bacillus *or* **koch bacillus** *n, usu cap K* **:** a bacillus (*Mycobacterium tuberculosis*) that causes human tuberculosis

koch's postulates *also* **koch's laws** *n pl, usu cap K* **:** a statement of the steps required to establish a microorganism as the cause of a disease: (1) it must be found in all cases of the disease; (2) it must be isolated from the host and grown in pure culture; (3) it must reproduce the original disease when introduced into a susceptible host; (4) it must be found present in the experimental host so infected

koch-weeks bacillus \\-'wēks-\\ *n, usu cap K&W* [after Robert *Koch* †1910 and John E. *Weeks* †1949 Am. ophthalmologist, who discovered it independently] **:** a bacterium of the genus *Hemophilus* associated with human conjunctivitis

KO'd *past of* KO

ko·da·gu \\'kōdə,gü\\ *n, pl* **kodagu** *or* **kodagus** *usu cap* **1 a :** an aboriginal people of the mountainous region of Coorg in southern India **b :** a member of such people **2 :** the Dravidian language of the Kodagu people

ko·dak \\'kō,dak\\ *vb* -ED/-ING/-S [*Kodak*] *vi* **:** to take photographs with a Kodak camera ~ *vt* **:** to take a photograph of with a Kodak camera

Kodak \\"\\ *trademark* — used for a small hand camera

ko·da millet *also* **koda** \\'kōdə\\ *or* **ko·dra** \\-drə\\ *n* -S [*koda, kodra* fr. Panjabi *kodā, kodrā,* fr. Skt *kodrava*] **:** DITCH MILLET

ko·di·ak bear \\'kōdē,ak\\ *also* **ka·diak bear** \\kəd'yak-, -yäk\\ *or* **kodiak** *n* -S *usu cap K* [fr. *Kodiak* Island, southern Alaska, its habitat] **:** a brown bear (*Ursus middendorffi*) of Alaska that is larger and has shorter thicker claws than the grizzly and feeds largely on salmon

kod·kod \\'kōd,kōd\\ *n* -S [perh. native name in Chile or Argentina] **:** PAMPAS CAT

koe·ber·lin·ia \\,kōbə(r)'linēə\\ *n, cap* [NL, fr. C. L. *Köberlin,* 19th cent. Ger. clergyman and amateur botanist + NL *-ia*] **:** a monotypic genus of nearly leafless thorny shrubs of dry parts of the southwestern U.S. and adjacent Mexico that bear racemes of small white flowers and tend to form dense thickets and that are placed in the family Capparidaceae or sometimes isolated in a separate family

koech·lin·ite \\'keklə,nīt\\ *n* -S [Rudolf *Koechlin* †1939 Austrian mineralogist + E *-ite*] **:** a mineral Bi_2MoO_6 consisting of a bismuth molybdate

ko·el *or* **ko·il** \\'kōəl, 'kȯi(ə)l\\ *n* -S [Hindi *koel, koil,* fr. Skt *kokila* — more at CUCKOO] **:** any of several cuckoos (genus *Eudynamys*) of India, the East Indies, and Australia — called also *long-tailed cuckoo*

koel·lia \\'kelēə\\ [NL, fr. Johann L. C. *Kölle* †1797 Ger. physician and botanist + NL *-ia*] *syn of* PYCNANTHEMUM

koel·reu·te·ria \\,kel,rȯi'tirēə, -rü'-\\ *n* [NL, fr. Josef G. *Kölreuter* †1806 Ger. botanist + NL *-ia*] **1** *cap* **:** a small genus of Asiatic trees (family Sapindaceae) distinguished by large terminal panicles of flowers and inflated papery capsular fruit — see GOLDENRAIN TREE **2** *-s* **:** any tree of the genus *Koelreuteria*

koe·nen·ite \\'kānə,nīt\\ *n* -S [G *koenenit,* fr. Adolf von *Koenen* †1915 Ger. geologist + G *-it* -ite] **:** a mineral $Mg_5Al_2(OH)_{12}Cl_4$ consisting of a basic chloride of aluminum and magnesium

koenigsberg *usu cap, var of* KÖNIGSBERG

koe·pang·er \\'kü,päŋə(r)\\ *n* -S *usu cap* [*Koepang, Kupang,* city at the southwestern end of Timor + E *-er*] **:** a native or inhabitant of the city of Kupang on the Indonesian island of Timor

ko·e·ri *or* **ko·i·ri** \\'kōərē\\ *n, pl* **koeri** *or* **koeris** *or* **koiri** *or* **koiris** *usu cap* **1 :** an agricultural Aryo-Dravidian people of northeastern Hindustan **2 :** a member of the Koeri people

koet·tig·ite *or* **köt·tig·ite** \\'ked·i,gīt\\ *n* -S [Otto *Köttig,* 19th cent. Ger. chemist + E *-ite*] **:** a mineral $Zn_3(AsO_4)_2.8H_2O$ consisting of a hydrous arsenate of zinc

koettstorfer value *usu cap K, var of* KÖTTSTORFER VALUE

koft·ga·ri \\'kȯftgə(,)rē\\ *n* -S [Hindi *koftgarī,* fr. Per *kōftgarī,* fr. *kōftgar* maker of koftgari, fr. *kōft* blow, beating + *-gar* doing; akin to Skt *kāra* doing — more at KARMA] **:** Indian damascene work in which steel is inlaid with gold

ko·fu \\'kō(,)fü\\ *adj, usu cap* [fr. *Kofu,* city in south central Honshu, Japan] **:** of or from the city of Kofu, Japan **:** of the kind or style prevalent in Kofu

ko·gas·in \\kō'gasən, 'kō,g-\\ *n* -S [G, fr. *ko-* (fr. *koks* coke, irreg. fr. E *coke*) + *gas* (fr. NL) + *-in* (fr. *benzin* benzine, gasoline)] **:** a liquid mixture of saturated and unsaturated aliphatic hydrocarbons made by reaction of carbon monoxide and hydrogen in the Fischer-Tropsch process

ko·gia \\'kōjēə\\ *n, cap* [NL] **:** a genus of whales consisting of the pygmy sperm whales

kogon *var of* COGON

ko·he·ko·he \\¦kōē¦kōē\\ *n* -S [Maori] **:** a New Zealand tree (*Dysoxylum spectabile*) of the family Neliaceae whose wood is used for furniture and interior finish

ko-hemp \\'kō,=\\ *n* [Chin *ko*[2] kudzu + E *hemp*] **1 :** KUDZU **2 :** a fiber of the kudzu vine

kohen *n, pl* **kohanim** *also* **kohens** *usu cap, var of* COHEN

koh-i-noor \\'kōə,nu̇(ə)r\\ *n, pl* **koh-i-noors** *often cap* [fr. *Koh-i-noor,* famous diamond that became part of the British crown jewels after the annexation of Punjab by Great Britain in 1849, fr. Per *Kōh-i-nūr,* lit., mountain of light] **:** something that is or is felt to be the best of its kind; *esp* **:** a usu. large and valuable diamond ⟨a young Spaniard with a *Koh-i-noor* of a diamond on his finger and pearls the size of camphor balls in his shirt front —W.J.Locke⟩

ko·hi·sta·ni \ˌkō(h)əˈstänē, -tanē\ *n* -s *usu cap* **1 a :** a Himalayan people of northern Pakistan **b :** a member of such people **2 :** a Dard language of the Kohistani people

¹kohl \ˈkōl\ *also* **co·hol** \ˈkōəl\ *or* **ko·hol** \ˈkōəl\ *n* -s [Ar *kuḥl*] **:** a preparation (as of antimony or soot mixed with other ingredients) used esp. in Arabia and Egypt to darken the edges of the eyelids

²kohl *usu cap, var of* KOL

koh·le·ria \kōˈlirēə\ *n, cap* [NL, fr. Michael *Kohler*, 19th cent. Swiss naturalist + NL *-ia*] **:** a genus of rhizomatous often shrubby tropical American herbs (family Gesneriaceae) that are widely cultivated for their soft velvety foliage and showy often scarlet flowers with four or five stamens and partly inferior ovary

kohl·rabi \kōlˈrabē, -räbē, ˈ=ˌ==\ *n, pl* **kohlrabies** [G, modif. (influenced by G *kohl* cabbage) of It *cavoli rape*, pl. of *cavolo rapa* kohlrabi, fr. *cavolo* cabbage (fr. L *caulis*) + *rapa* turnip, fr. L — more at HOLE, RAPE] **1 a :** any of a race of cabbages having an edible stem that becomes greatly enlarged, fleshy, and turnip-shaped **b :** any plant of the kohlrabi type **2 :** BROMATIUM

kohlrabi

kohl·rausch flask \ˈkōlˌrau̇sh-\ *n, usu cap K* [after Rudolf H. A. *Kohlrausch* †1858 Ger. physicist] **:** a volumetric flask that has an enlarged neck and usu. holds 100 or 200 milliliters

kohlrausch's law *n, usu cap K* [after Friedrich W. G. *Kohlrausch* †1910 Ger. physicist] **:** a statement in physical chemistry: the migration of an ion at infinite dilution is dependent on the nature of the solvent and on the potential gradient but not on the other ions present

kohs blocks *n pl, usu cap K* [after Samuel C. *Kohs* b1890 Am. psychologist] **:** a set of small variously colored blocks that are used to form test patterns in psychodiagnostic examination

ko·hua \kōˈhüə\ *n* -s [Maori] **:** a Maori earth oven

ko·hua·na \kōˈwänə\ *n, pl* **kohuana** *or* **kohuanas** *usu cap* **1 :** a Yuman people of the Colorado river valley in Arizona, California, and Mexico **2 :** a member of the Kohuana people

koi \ˈkȯi\ *n* -s [Jap] **:** CARP 1a

koi·a·ri \kȯiˈ(y)ärē\ *n, pl* **koiari** *or* **koiaris** *usu cap* **1 a :** a Papuan people inhabiting Papua **b :** a member of such people **2 :** the language of the Koiari people

koi·bal \(ˈ)kȯiˈbäl\ *also* **kai·bal** \(ˈ)kī;-\ *n, pl* **koibal** *or* **koibals** *usu cap* **1 :** a tatarized Samoyed people of the East Siberian region **2 :** a member of the Koibal people

koil *var of* KOEL

koil·onych·ia \ˌkȯilōˈnikēə\ *n* -s [NL, fr. Gk *koilos* hollow + NL *-onychia* — more at CAVE] **:** abnormal thinness and concavity of fingernails occurring esp. in hypochromic anemias — called also *spoon nail*

koi·lo·rach·ic *or* **koi·lor·rhach·ic** \ˌkȯilōˈrakik, -ləˈ-\ *adj* [*koilo-* (fr. Gk *koilos* hollow) + *rach-, rrhach-* (fr. Gk *rhachis* spine) + *-ic* — more at RACHI-] **:** having the lumbar region of the spinal column concave ventrally

koi·me·sis \ˈkēməsəs\ *n* -ES [MGk *koimēsis*, fr. Gk, sleep, sleep of death, fr. *koiman* to put to sleep — more at CEMETERY] **:** a feast in the Eastern Orthodox Church commemorating the death and the corporeal assumption of the Virgin Mary now celebrated on August 15

koi·ne \(ˈ)kȯiˈnē, ˈkȯiˌnē\ *n* -s [Gk *koinē*, fr. fem. of *koinos* common — more at CO-] **1** *usu cap* **:** the Greek language commonly spoken and written by the Greek-speaking population of eastern Mediterranean countries in the Hellenistic and Roman periods **2 :** a dialect or language of a region, country, or people that has become the common or standard language of a larger area and of other peoples — compare LINGUA FRANCA

KO'ing *pres part of* KO

koi·non \kȯiˈnän\ *n* -s [Gk, neut. of *koinos* common] **:** the common element in an apo koinou construction

koi·no·nia \ˌkȯinəˈnēə, ˌkenə-\ *n* -s [Gk *koinōnia* communion, association, partnership, fr. *koinos* common] **1 :** the Christian fellowship or body of believers **2 :** intimate spiritual communion and participative sharing in a common religious commitment and spiritual community ⟨the ~ of the disciples with each other and with their Lord⟩

koiri *usu cap, var of* KOERI

koi·ro·pot·a·mus \ˌkȯirōˈpädəməs\ *n, cap* [NL, irreg. fr. Gk *choiros* pig + *potamos* river; akin to Gk *piptein* to fall — more at -CHOERUS, FEATHER] **:** a genus of wild hogs comprising the African river hogs

ko·ji \ˈkōjē\ *n* -s [Jap *kōji*] **1 :** a yeast or other starter prepared in Japan from rice inoculated with the spores of a mold (*Aspergillus oryzae*) and permitted to develop a mycelium **2 :** an enzyme preparation from koji that is similar to diastase from malt

ko·jic acid \ˈkōjik-\ *n* [*kojic* fr. *koji* + *-ic*] **:** a crystalline water-soluble phenolic-type toxic antibiotic $HOC_5H_2O_2CH_2OH$ derived from gamma-pyrone and made by fermentation (as of glucose with molds of the genus *Aspergillus*)

ko·ka·ko \kōˈkäˌ(ˌ)kō\ *n* -s [Maori] *New Zeal* **:** WATTLE CROW

ko·kam \kōˈkäm\ *n* -s [Malay *kukang, kongkang*] **:** LORIS 1b

ko·ka·ma \kōˈkämə\ *n* -s [Tswana *kukama*] **:** GEMSBOK

ko·kan \ˈkōkən\ *n* -s [Hindi] **:** an East Indian timber tree (*Duabanga sonneratioides*) of the family Sonneratiaceae

ko·kan·ee \kōˈkanē\ *also* **kokanee salmon** *n* -s [prob. fr. *Kokanee* creek, southeastern British Columbia] **:** a small landlocked sockeye salmon that rarely reaches a pound in weight but that is an important food fish in certain inland waters

ko·ker·boom \ˈkōkə(r)ˌbüm, -bōm\ *n* [Afrik, fr. D *koker* quiver, sheath (fr. MD *coker*) + *boom* tree, fr. MD; akin to OE *cocer* quiver and to OE *bēam* tree — more at COCKER, BEAM] **:** QUIVER TREE

ko·kil \ˈkōkəl\ *or* **ko·ki·la** \-kələ\ *n* -s [Skt *kokila* — more at CUCKOO] **:** a koel (*Eudynamys scolopacea honorata*) of India

ko·klas *or* **ko·klass** \ˈkōkləs\ *n* -ES [native name in Nepal] **:** PUKRAS

¹ko·ko \ˈkō(ˌ)kō\ *n* -s [prob. of Niger-Congo origin; akin to Twi *kɔ̄kɔ* koko] **1 :** any of several araceous plants including the taro that are cultivated in tropical western Africa for their starchy edible roots **2** *also* **kok·ko** \ˈkä(ˌ)kō\ [origin unknown] **:** LEBBEK

²koko \"\ *n* -s [Maori] **:** TUI

³koko \"\ *n, pl* **koko** *or* **kokos** *usu cap* **1 :** a group of numerous aboriginal peoples of northern Queensland **2 :** a member of any of the Koko peoples

ko·koon \kəˈkün\ *n* -s [Tswana *kgokoñ*] **:** BRINDLED GNU

ko·koo·na \kəˈkünə\ *n* [NL, fr. Singhalese *kokuṅ* kokoona] **1** *cap* **:** a genus of East Indian trees (family Celastraceae) having flowers with a 3-celled ovary and producing 3-angled fruit **2** -s **:** any tree of the genus *Kokoona*

ko·ko·pu \ˈkōkəˌpü\ *n* -s [Maori] **:** any of various New Zealand fishes of the genus *Galaxias* that resemble the trout — compare GALAXIIDAE

ko·ko·wai \ˈkōkəˌwī\ *n* -s [Maori] **1 :** red ocher used in New Zealand as a pigment esp. on woodwork **2 :** the earth from which kokowai is obtained

kokra \ˈkōkrə, ˈkäk-\ *also* **kokra wood** *n* -s [origin unknown] **1 :** COCOWOOD 1 **2 :** COCUSWOOD

kok-saghyz *or* **kok-sagyz** \ˌkōksəˈgēz, ˈkäk-, -giz\ *n* -ES [Russ *kok-sagyz*, fr. Turki *kok-sagiz*, fr. *kok* root + *sagiz* rubber, gum] **:** a perennial dandelion (*Taraxacum koksaghyz*) native to the Kazakh republic of Russia that has fleshier leaves and more numerous flower heads than the common dandelion of No. America and Europe and is cultivated for its fleshy roots which have a high rubber content — called also *Russian dandelion*

kok·ta·ite \ˈkäktəˌīt\ *n* -s [Czech *koktait*, fr. Jaroslav *Kokta*, 20th cent. Czechoslovak mineralogist + Czech *-it* -ite] **:** a mineral $(NH_4)_2Ca(SO_4)_2.H_2O$ consisting of a hydrous sulfate of calcium and ammonium

ko·ku \ˈkō(ˌ)kü\ *n, pl* **koku** [Jap] **:** any of three Japanese units of capacity: **a :** a unit for dry measure equal to 5.12 bushels **b :** a unit for liquid measure equal to 47.65 gallons **c :** a unit for vessels equal to 10 cubic feet

ko·kum butter \ˈkōkəm-\ *also* **kokum** *or* **co·cum** \ˈkō-\ *n* -s [*kokum, cocum*, fr. Marathi *kokam, kokamb* mangosteen] **:** a semisolid fat or liquid oil obtained from the seeds of a small East Indian tree (*Garcinia indica*) and used in India for food — called also *Goa butter*

ko·ku·ra \ˈkōkərə, kōˈkürə\ *adj, usu cap* [fr. *Kokura*, city in northern Kyushu, Japan] **:** of or from the city of Kokura, Japan **:** of the kind or style prevalent in Kokura

kol *or* **kohl** \ˈkōl\ *n, pl* **kol** *or* **kols** *or* **kohl** *or* **kohls** *usu cap* **1 :** a people of Bengal and Chota Nagpur, India **2 :** a member of such people

kola *var of* COLA

ko·lac·ky \kəˈläch(k)ē\ *or* **ko·lach** \ˈkōˌläch\ *also* **ko·la·ce** \kəˈläche\ *or* **ko·latch** \ˈkōˌläch\ *n, pl* **kolacky** *or* **kolaches** [Czech *koláč*; akin to Russ *kolach* kolacky, Bulg *kolač* kolacky, OSlav *kolo* wheel — more at WHEEL] **:** a bun made of rich sweet yeast-leavened dough filled with jam or fruit pulp

ko·lam \kəˈläm\ *n, pl* **kolam** *or* **kolams** *usu cap* **1 :** a people of the Gond ethnic group in central India **2 :** a member of the Kolam people

ko·la·mi \kəˈlämē\ *n* -s **:** the Dravidian language of the Kolam people

ko·la nut *also* **kola** *or* **co·la nut** \ˈkōlə-\ *n* -s [²*cola* + *nut*] **:** the bitter caffeine-containing seed of a kola tree that is approximately the size of a chestnut and is chewed as a condiment and stimulant — see ²COLA 2a

ko·lar gold fields \ˈkōˌlär-\ *adj, usu cap K&G&F* [fr. *Kolar Gold Fields*, city in southern India] **:** of or from the city of Kolar Gold Fields, India **:** of the kind or style prevalent in Kolar Gold Fields

ko·lar·i·an *also* **co·lar·i·an** \kōˈla(a)rēən\ *n* -s *usu cap* [prob. fr. *Kolar*, town in southern India + E *-ian*] **:** KOL

kola tree *or* **cola tree** *n* [²*cola* + *tree*] **:** a tree of the genus *Cola* (esp. *C. nitida*) native to tropical Africa but now cultivated in tropical America and Asia — see KOLA NUT

ko·lat·tam \kōˈläd·əm\ *n* -s [Tamil *kōl* stick + *āṭṭam* dance] **:** a folk dance of southern India accompanied by the striking together of sticks

kol·beck·ite \ˈkōlˌbeˌkīt\ *n* -s [G *kolbeckit*, fr. Friedrich *Kolbeck* †1943 Ger. mineralogist + G *-it* -ite] **:** a mineral consisting of a hydrous silicate and phosphate of beryllium, aluminum, and calcium

kol·be reaction \ˈkōlbə-\ *or* **kolbe synthesis** *n, usu cap K* [after A. W. Hermann *Kolbe* †1884 Ger. organic chemist] **1 :** the synthesis of a hydrocarbon (as ethane) by the electrolysis of a salt (as sodium acetate) **2 :** the synthesis of salicylic acid by heating a mixture of sodium phenoxide and carbon dioxide under pressure at 180° to 200°C

kolbe-schmitt reaction *or* **kolbe-schmitt synthesis** \-ˈshmit-\ *n, usu cap K & 1st S* [after A. W. Hermann *Kolbe* †1884 and Rudolf *Schmitt* †1898 Ger. chemist] **:** a modified Kolbe reaction for synthesizing salicylic acid and other phenolic acids at temperatures of from 130° to 140°C

ko·lea \kōˈlāə\ *n* -s [Hawaiian] *Hawaii* **:** a golden plover (*Pluvialis dominica fulva*) that commonly passes through Hawaii in its migratory flights

ko·lek \ˈkōˌlek\ *n* -s [Malay] **:** a Malayan canoe often rigged with a rectangular sail

ko·lel \kōˈlāl\ *n, pl* **ko·le·lim** \kōˈlāləm, -ālem\ *also* **kolels** [NHeb *kōlēl*, fr. Heb *kālal* to comprise, include] **:** a community or congregation of Jewish settlers in Palestine receiving financial support from the halukkah fund

kole·ro·ga \ˌkōləˈrōgə, ˌkäl-\ *n* -s [Kannada *koḷerōga*, fr. *koḷe* rot + Skt *roga* disease] **:** a disease of an areca palm (*Areca catechu*) caused by a fungus (*Phytophthora arecae*)

kol·ha·pur \ˈkōləˌpu̇(ə)r\ *adj, usu cap* [fr. *Kolhapur*, city in western India] **:** of or from the city of Kolhapur, India **:** of the kind or style prevalent in Kolhapur

ko·li \ˈkōlē\ *n, pl* **koli** *or* **kolis** *usu cap* **1 :** a low-caste people of Bombay, Mysore, Andhra Pradesh, Madhya Pradesh, Rajasthan, and the Punjab, India **2 :** a member of the Koli people

ko·lin·sky \kəˈlinzkē, -n(t)skē\ *n* -ES [Russ *kolinskiĭ* of Kola, fr. *Kola*, town and peninsula in northwestern U.S.S.R.] **1** *or* **kolinski** \"\ **a :** any of several Asiatic minks (esp. *Mustela sibirica*) **b :** the fur or pelt of any of these minks — called also *red sable, Tatar sable* **2 :** LEAFMOLD

kol·khoz *also* **kol·koz** *or* **kol·khos** \(ˌ)kəlˈkȯz, kōl-, ˌkäl-, -ȯs\ *n, pl* **kolkho·zy** \-ȯzē\ *or* **kolkhozes** [Russ *kolkhoz*, short for *kollektivnoe khozyaĭstvo* collective farm, fr. *kollektivnoe* (neut. of *kollektivnyĭ* collective) + *khozyaĭstvo* household, economy, farm] **1 :** a collective farm of the U.S.S.R. **2 :** a system of collectivized agriculture based on the kolkhoz and developed or enforced esp. among satellite countries

kol·khoz·nik \-ȯznik\ *n, pl* **kolkhozni·ki** \-nəkē\ *or* **kolkhozniks** [Russ, fr. *kolkhoz* + *-nik* (suffix indicating a person)] **:** a member of a kolkhoz

kolk·witz·ia \kōlˈkwitsēə, käl-\ *n* [NL, fr. Richard *Kolkwitz* b1873 Ger. biologist + NL *-ia*] **1** *cap* **:** a genus of Chinese shrubs of the family Caprifoliaceae having short-stipuled leaves and tubular flowers succeeded by ovoid bristly achenes **2** -s **:** any plant of the genus *Kolkwitzia*; *esp* **:** BEAUTY BUSH

kol·ler·gang \ˈkälə(r)ˌgaŋ\ *n* [G, fr. *kollern* to roll + *gang* motion, course, route, fr. OHG, act of going — more at GANG] **:** EDGE RUNNER 2

kolm \ˈkō(l)m\ *n* -s [Sw] **:** a Swedish shale exceptionally high in uranium oxide U_3O_8

kol·mer \ˈkōlmə(r)\ *or* **kolmer reaction** *or* **kolmer test** *n* -s *usu cap K* [after John A. *Kolmer* b1886 Am. pathologist] **:** a complement fixation test for the diagnosis of syphilis

kol ni·dre \ˈkōlˈni(ˌ)drā, kōl-, -ˌdrē, -ˌdrə, ˌ=ˌniˈdrā\ *n, usu cap K&N* [Aram *kol nidhrē* all the vows; fr. the opening phrase of the prayer] **1 :** the recital of an Aramaic prayer in the synagogue on the eve of Yom Kippur asking for annulment of vows to God and forgiveness of transgressions **2 :** a traditional melody to which the words of Kol Nidre are sung or chanted

ko·lo \ˈkō(ˌ)lō\ *n* -s [Serbo-Croatian, fr. OSlav, wheel — more at WHEEL] **:** a central European folk dance in which dancers form a circle and progress slowly to right and left while one or more soloists perform elaborate steps in the center

ko·loa ma·pu \kōˌlōəˈmä(ˌ)pü\ *n* [Hawaiian, fr. *koloa* duck + *mapu* floating] *Hawaii* **:** PINTAIL 1a

koloa mo·ha \-ˈmō(ˌ)hä\ *n* [Hawaiian, fr. *koloa* duck + *moha* shining] *Hawaii* **:** SHOVELER 2

kols *pl of* KOL

kol·skite \ˈkōlzˌkīt, -lˌsk-\ *n* -s [Russ *kolskit*, perh. fr. *Kolskiĭ Poluostrov* Kola Peninsula, northwestern U.S.S.R. + Russ *-it* -ite] **:** a mineral $Mg_5Si_4O_{13}.4H_2O$(?) consisting of a serpentine

kol·son *or* **kol·sun** \ˈkōlsən\ *n* -s [native name in India] **:** DHOLE

ko·lusch·an \kōˈləshən, -lüsh-\ *n* -s *usu cap* [perh. irreg. fr. Aleut *kalukaq* wooden utensil, trough; fr. the trough-shaped labrets worn by Tlingit women] **:** TLINGIT 3

ko·mat·ik \kōˈmad·ik\ *n* -s [Esk (Labrador dial.)] **:** an Eskimo sledge with wooden runners and crossbars lashed with rawhide

komatik

kom·bu \ˈkäm(ˌ)bü\ *n* -s [Jap, kombu, kelp, tangle] **:** a food prepared esp. in Japan from various broad-fronded kelps of the family Laminariaceae

ko·mi \ˈkōmē\ *n, pl* **komi** *or* **komis** *cap* [Zyrian] **1 a :** a people of north central U.S.S.R. — called also *Zyrian* **b :** a member of such people **2 :** ZYRIAN

kom·i·nu·ter \ˈkäməˌn(y)üd·ə(r)\ *n* -s [G, fr. L *comminutus* (past part. of *comminuere* to crush, pulverize) + G *-er*, fr. OHG *-āri* — more at COMMINUTE, -ER] **:** a ball mill used in grinding raw materials or clinker in the manufacture of portland cement

ko·mi·tad·ji *or* **co·mi·tad·ji** *also* **ko·mi·ta·ji** \ˌkōməˈtäjē, ˌkäm-\ *n* -s [Turk *komitacı* rebel, member of a secret revolutionary society, fr. *komita* revolutionary committee, secret society] **:** a member of a guerrilla band in Macedonia or the Balkan countries

kom·man·da·tu·ra \kəˌmandəˈtu̇rə\ *also* **kom·man·dan·tur** \ˌkämənˌdanˈtu̇(ə)r\ *or* **kom·man·dan·tu·ra** \ˌkämənˌdanˈtu̇rə\ *n* -s *usu cap* [*kommandatura, kommandantura* prob. modif. of G *kommandantur* command post, fr. *kommandant* commandant (fr. F *commandant*) + *-ur* -ure; *kommandantur* fr. G, command post] **:** a military government headquarters; *esp* **:** a Russian or interallied headquarters in a European city subsequent to World War II

kommers *often cap, var of* COMMERS

kom·me·tje *or* **co·mi·tje** \ˈkäməchē\ *n* -s [obs. Afrik (now *kommetjie*), lit., mug, cup, fr. D, dim. of *kom* basin, bowl, fr. MD *com, comme*; akin to MHG *kumpf* bowl — more at COOMB] **:** a small depression common in parts of the African veld

kom·mos *or* **com·mos** \kəˈmäs, käˈ-; ˈkäˌmäs, -ˌməs\ *n* -ES [Gk *kommos* kommos, beating of the breast, fr. *koptein* to beat, smite — more at CAPON] **:** a lament in Greek tragedy sung in parts alternating between chief actor and chorus

ko·mo·do dragon \kəˈmō(ˌ)dō-\ *or* **komodo lizard** *n, usu cap K* [fr. *Komodo* Island, Indonesia] **:** a dull brown or black monitor lizard (*Varanus komodoensis*) of Komodo and adjacent small islands lying east of Java that attains a length of 10 feet, weighs up to 300 pounds, and feeds largely on eggs but occas. on animals as large as wild pigs or small deer

ko·mon·dor \ˈkämənˌdȯ(ə)r\ *n* [Hung] **1** *usu cap* **:** a Hungarian breed of large powerful shaggy-coated white dogs with black nose and dark brown eyes that are used as guard dogs and as herd dogs **2** *pl* **komondors** \-rz\ *also* **komondo·rock** *or* **komondo·rok** \-dərək\ *often cap* **:** a dog of the Komondor breed

kom·so·mol *or* **com·so·mol** \ˌkäm(p)səˈmȯl\ *also* **con·so·mol** \ˌkän(t)s-\ *n* -s *usu cap* [Russ *komsomol*, short for *Kommunisticheskiĭ Soyuz Molodezhi* Communist Union of Youth, fr. *kommunisticheskiĭ* communist + *soyuz* union + *molodezhi*, gen. of *molodezh'* youth] **:** a member of a Russian Communist youth organization with members between the ages of 16 and 23 years

ko·na \ˈkōnə\ *or* **kona storm** *n* -s [Hawaiian *kona*] **:** a storm of southerly or southwesterly winds and heavy rains in Hawaii

ko·nak \kōˈnäk\ *n* -s [Turk] **:** a large house in Turkey; *esp* **:** one used as an official residence ⟨we went to visit the big white ~ . . . which I loved so dearly —Selma Ekrem⟩

konakri *or* **konakry** *usu cap, var of* CONAKRY

ko·nar·i·ot \kəˈna(a)rēˌōt, -ēät\ *or* **ko·nar·i·ote** \-ēˌōt, -ēət\ *n* -s *usu cap* [perh. irreg. fr. *Konya*, city and district in southwest central Turkey] **:** a Turk orig. from the Konya district of Asia Minor now settled in Macedonia

kond *or* **kondh** *usu cap, var of* KHOND

kon·de \ˈkänˌdā\ *n, pl* **konde** *or* **kondes** *usu cap* **1 a :** a Bantu people of Nyasaland **b :** a member of such people **2 a :** a Bantu people of Tanganyika **b :** a member of such people **3 :** a Bantu language of either of the Konde peoples

kon·di·to·rei \ˌkändətōˈrī\ *n* -s *often cap* [G, fr. *konditor* confectioner (blend of earlier *kanditor* confectioner — fr. *kandieren* to candy, fr. F *candir* or It *candire*, both fr. Ar *qandī* candied — and *kondieren* to preserve, fr. L *condire*) + *-ei* -y, fr. MHG *-īe*, fr. OF *-ie* — more at CANDY, CONDITE] **:** a shop selling confectionery or pastry

kon·dra·ti·eff \kənˈdrād·ēˌef\ *n* -s *usu cap* [after Nikolai D. *Kondratev* b1892 Russ. economist] **:** a business cycle with a periodicity of between 50 and 60 years

kon·fyt \kənˈfīt\ *n* -s [Afrik *konfyt*, fr. D *konfijt*, fr. MD *confijt*, fr. MF *confit* — more at COMFIT] *chiefly Africa* **:** PRESERVES

kon·go \ˈkän(ˌ)gō\ *n, pl* **kongo** *or* **kongos** *usu cap* **1 a :** a Bantu people of the lower Congo river **b :** a member of such people **2 :** a Bantu language of the Kongo people used as a trade language in the western Congo and adjacent parts of western equatorial Africa and Angola — compare TSHILUBA

kon·go·ni *also* **con·go·ni** \känˈgōnē\ *n, pl* **kongoni** [Swahili] **:** a hartebeest (*Alcelaphus cokei*) of East Africa

kongs·berg·ite \ˈkäŋzˌ(ˌ)bərˌgīt\ *n* -s [F, fr. *Kongsberg*, town in southern Norway + F *-ite*] **:** a mineral consisting of a native silver mercury amalgam

ko·nia *or* **ko·ni·eh** \ˈkōnēə\ *n* -s *usu cap* [fr. *Konia, Konya*, district in southwest central Turkey] **:** a Turkish rug woven usu. in soft shades of red, blue, and yellow

kö·nigs·berg *or* **ko·nigs·berg** *or* **koe·nigs·berg** \ˈkānigzˌbərg, ˈkə(r)n-, ˈkən-, ˈkœniks̩berk\ *adj, usu cap* [fr. *Königsberg* (now *Kaliningrad*), city in the former province of East Prussia, Germany] **:** of or from Königsberg **:** of the kind or style prevalent in Königsberg

ko·nim·e·ter \kōˈnimәd·ə(r)\ *also* **co·ni·om·e·ter** \ˌkōnēˈämәd·ə(r)\ *n* [*koni-* or *conio-* (fr. Gk *konia* dust) + *-meter* — more at INCINERATE] **:** a device for estimating the dust content of air (as in a mine or a cement mill)

ko·ninck·ite \ˈkōniŋˌkīt, -nən,k-\ *n* -s [F *koninckite*, fr. L. G. de *Koninck* †1887 Belg. geologist + F *-ite*] **:** a mineral $FePO_4.3H_2O$ consisting of hydrous ferric phosphate in yellow aggregates of radiated structure

ko·nini \kəˈninē, -ˈnēnē\ *n* -s [Maori] **:** a tree fuchsia (*Fuchsia excorticata*) of New Zealand that often attains a height of 40 feet and that has pendulous showy flowers — called also *native fuchsia*

ko·nio·cortex \ˌkōnē(ˌ)ō+\ *n* [*konio-* (fr. Gk *konia* dust) + *cortex*] **:** granular-appearing cerebral cortex esp. characteristic of sensory areas

ko·ni·ol·o·gy *also* **co·ni·ol·o·gy** \ˌkōnēˈäləjē\ *n* -ES [*konio-, conio-* (fr. Gk *konia* dust) + *-logy*] **:** a science that deals with atmospheric dust and its effects on plant and animal life

kon·jak \ˈkänˌjak\ *n* -s [Jap *konjaku*] **:** a large aroid (*Amorphophallus rivieri*) grown in Japan for its large tuberous corms used for making flour

konk *var of* CONK

kon·ka·ni \ˈkäŋkə(ˌ)nē, ˈkōŋ-\ *n* -s *usu cap* [Marathi *Koṅkaṇī*, fr. *Koṅkaṇ* Konkan, coast region of western India where it is spoken] **:** an Indic language of the west coast of India sometimes considered a dialect of Marathi

konk·er tree \ˈkäŋ(k)ə(r)-, ˈkōŋ(k)-\ *n* [¹*conker* + *tree*] **:** HORSE CHESTNUT 1a

ko·no \ˈkō(ˌ)nō\ *n, pl* **kono** *or* **konos** *usu cap* **1 a :** a peasant people of Sierra Leone **b :** a member of such people **2 :** a Mande language of the Kono people closely related to Vai

ko·no·hi·ki \ˌkōnəˈhēkē\ *n* -s [Hawaiian] **1 :** a headman of a Hawaiian land division who also controls fishing rights in adjacent waters **2 :** a Hawaiian land division with its accompanying fishing rights

kon·seal \ˈkänˌsē(ə)l\ *n* [fr. *Konseals*, a trademark] **:** CACHET 3

-kont \ˌkänt\ *n comb form* -s [ISV, fr. Gk *kontos* pole, fr. *kentein* to prick — more at CENTER] **:** flagellum of a cell

kon·ta·kion *or* **con·ta·kion** \kənˈtäkyōn\ *n, pl* **konta·kia** *or* **conta·kia** \-yä\ [MGk *kontakion*, lit., scroll, prob. dim. of LGk *kontak-, kontax* pole, fr. Gk *kontos*] **:** a short hymn in the Eastern Orthodox Church in praise of a saint

kon·yak \ˈkänˌyak\ *n, pl* **konyak** *or* **konyaks** *usu cap* **1 a :** a people of the Assam-Burma frontier area **b :** a member of such people **2 :** the Tibeto-Burman language of the Konyak people

kon·ze \ˈkänzə\ *n* -s [Konde *nkonzhe*] **:** an African hartebeest (*Alcelaphus lichtensteini*) of the Zambesi and Nyasa regions

koo·doo *or* **ku·du** *also* **kou·dou** \ˈkü(ˌ)dü\ *n* -s [Afrik *koedoe*, prob. fr. Xhosa *iqudu, iquda*] **:** a large African antelope (*Strepsiceros strepsiceros* syn. *kudo*) that has large annulated spirally twisted horns and is grayish brown with vertical white stripes on the sides — compare LESSER KOODOO

koofah *var of* GUFA

kook·a·bur·ra \ˈku̇kəˌbərə\ *n* -s [native name in Australia] **:** a kingfisher (*Dacelo gigas*) of Australia that is about the size of a crow, has a call resembling loud laughter, and feeds in part on reptiles — called also *kinghunter, laughing jackass*

koo·le·tah \ˈküləˌtä\ *n* -s [Esk (Greenland dial.)] **:** an Eskimo coat made of caribou skin

koo·li·man \ˈküləˌman, -ˌmən\ *var of* COOLAMON

koo·lo·kam·ba \ˌküləˈkambə, -käm-\ *n* -s [native name on the Gabon river, Gabon, equatorial Africa] **:** a dark-faced West African chimpanzee sometimes regarded as a separate species (*Pan koolokamba*)

koom·bar \'kümbə(r)\ *n* -s [Tamil *kumiḻ*] : an East Indian timber tree (*Gmelina arborea*) used esp. for building foundations and for boat decks

koom·kie \'kümkē\ *or* **koon·kie** \-üŋkē\ *n* -s [Hindi *kumakī* helper, fr. Per] : a trained usu. female elephant used in India to decoy and train wild male elephants

koorajong *var of* KURRAJONG

koorhaan *var of* KORHAAN

koor·ka \'kůrkə\ *n* -s [origin unknown] : a coleus (*Coleus parviflorus*) native to Africa but cultivated widely in India for its edible tubers

kootch *var of* COOCH

koo·tcha \'küchə\ *or* **koo·tchar** \-chə(r)\ *n* -s [native name in Australia] : a small stingless wild Australian honeybee of the genus *Trigona*

kootenai *usu cap, var of* KUTENAI

kope \'kōp\ *chiefly Midland var of* ³COOP

ko·peck *or* **ko·pek** *also* **co·peck** \'kō,pek\ *n* -s [Russ *kopeĭka*, fr. *kop'e* lance; fr. the fact that the Czar was orig. depicted on the coin with a lance in his hand; akin to Russ *kopat'* to dig, hollow, Gk *koptein* to smite, cut off — more at CAPON] **1** : a Russian unit of monetary value equal to $1/100$ of a ruble — see MONEY table **2** : a coin orig. of base silver representing one kopeck

koph *var of* QOPH

ko·pi \'kōpē\ *n* -s [Moriori] *New Zeal* : KARAKA

kop·je *or* **kop·pie** \'käpē\ *n* -s [Afrik *koppie* kopje, cup, fr. D *kopje* small head, cup, fr. MD *cop, coppe* — more at CUP] : a small hill found esp. on the African veld sometimes reaching 100 feet above the surrounding country and often covered with scrub

kop·lik's spots \'käpliks-\ *also* **koplik spots** *n pl, usu cap K* [after Henry *Koplik* †1927 Am. pediatrician] : small bluish white dots surrounded by a reddish zone that appear on the mucous membrane of the cheeks and lips before the appearance of the skin eruption in a case of measles

kop·pa \'käpə\ *n* -s [Gk, of Sem origin; akin to Heb *qōph* qoph] : a letter of the early Greek alphabet replaced by kappa in the eastern Greek alphabet except for use as a numeral with the value 90 but retained in the western Greek alphabet and ultimately becoming the Latin letter *Q*

kop·pel·flö·te \'käpəl,flād·ə, -flədə, *G* 'kɔpəl,flœtə\ *n* -s [G, fr. *koppel* tie, connection (fr. MHG *koppel, kuppel*, fr. OF *cople, couple* pair, bond) + *flöte* flute, fr. MHG *vloite*, fr. OF *flaute, fleute* — more at COUPLE, FLUTE] : an open flute stop in a pipe organ having a neutral tone and serving as a basis upon which to erect tonal pyramids of mutation ranks

kopp·ite \'kä,pīt\ *n* -s [G *koppit*, fr. Hermann F. M. *Kopp* †1892 Ger. chemist + G *-it* -ite] : a mineral consisting of a pyrochlore containing cerium, iron, and potassium

kopt *cap, var of* COPT

kor *also* **cor** *or* **core** \'kō(ə)r, 'kȯ(ə)r\ *n* -s [Heb *kōr*] : an ancient Hebrew and Phoenician unit of measure of capacity identical with the homer but used in later Old Testament times only in liquid measurement

ko·ra \'kōrə\ *n* -s [origin unknown] : WATER COCK

ko·rah·ite \'kōrə,īt\ *n* -s *usu cap* [*Korah*, great-grandson of Levi (Exod 6:21 [AV]) + E *-ite*] : a descendant of the biblical Levite Korah who founded a line of prominent temple musicians

ko·rai period \'kōr,ī-\ *n, usu cap K* [*Korai, Koryu*, dynasty ruling Korea from about A.D. 918 to 1392] : the historical and stylistic period from about A.D. 918 to 1392 in Korea

korait *var of* KRAIT

ko·ra·kan \'kōrə,kän\ *or* **ku·rak·kan** \'kůrə,kän\ *n* -s [Tamil *kuṟakkaṉ*, fr. Sinhalese *kurakkan* ragi] : RAGI

ko·ran *or* **qur·'an** *or* **qu·ran** *or* **qo·ran** \kə'ran, (')kō;r-, (')kȯ;r-, (')ků;r-, -rän, -raa(ə)n, -rän *sometimes* 'kōran *or* 'kōrən\ *n* -s *usu cap* [Ar *qur'ān*, fr. *qara'a* to read, recite] : the book composed of writings accepted by Muslims as revelations made to Muhammad by Allah and as the divinely authorized basis for the religious, social, civil, commercial, military, and legal regulations of the Islamic world

ko·ra·na \kə'ränə\ *n, pl* **korana** *or* **koranas** *usu cap* **1 a** : any of a group of racially mixed Hottentot peoples orig. from the area along the Orange, Vaal, and Modder rivers in southern Africa **b** : a member of any of such peoples **2** : a dialect of Hottentot spoken by the Korana peoples

ko·ran·ic *or* **qur·'an·ic** \kə'ranik, kō-, kȯ'-, ků'-, -rän-, -raan-, -rän-\ *adj, usu cap* : of, relating to, or prescribed by the Muslim sacred scriptures contained in the Koran ⟨they come to be able to sip alcoholic drinks without *Koranic* scandal — Hal Lehrman⟩

ko·ra·ri \'kōrə,rē\ *n* -s [Maori] : NEW ZEALAND FLAX

korban *var of* CORBAN

kor·dax *or* **cor·dax** \'kȯ(ə)r,daks\ *n* -ES [L *cordax*, fr. Gk *kordax*; akin to Gk *kradan* to shake, brandish — more at CARDINAL] **1** : a phallic dance by nude horned figures in the Dionysian orgies of ancient Greece **2** : a lewd coarse dance derived from the Dionysian kordax and incorporated into Greek and Latin comedy **3** : any of various lively Renaissance court dances

kor·do·fan gum \'kȯrdə,fan-\ *n, usu cap K* [fr. *Kordofan* province, Republic of the Sudan] : a superior gum arabic from the Kordofan district of the Republic of the Sudan

kor·do·fan·ian \,kȯrdə'fanēən\ *n, cap* [*Kordofan* province, Republic of the Sudan + E *-ian*] : a small group of languages spoken in the Kordofan district of the Republic of the Sudan apparently constituting a language family

ko·rea \kə'rēə, *in rapid speech* 'krēə, *chiefly southern US* (')kō;rēə\ *adj, usu cap* [fr. *Korea*, country in eastern Asia] : of or from Korea : of the kind or style prevalent in Korea : KOREAN

¹ko·re·an *also* **co·re·an** \-ēən\ *adj, usu cap* [*Korea* + E *-an*, adj. suffix] **1 a** : of, relating to, or characteristic of Korea **b** : of, relating to, or characteristic of the Koreans **2** : of, relating to, or characteristic of the Korean language

²korean *also* **corean** \"\ *n* -s *cap* [*Korea* + E *-an*, n. suffix] **1** : a native or inhabitant of Korea **2** : the language of the Korean people now usu. written in the Hankul alphabet

korean box *or* **korean boxwood** *n, usu cap K* : a compact slow-growing notably hardy box (*Buxus microphylla koreana*) with conspicuously winged branches and obovate leaves ¼ to ½ inch long

korean lawn grass *n, usu cap K* : an Asiatic grass (*Zoisia japonica*) used in China and Japan and more recently in America as a lawn grass — called also *Japanese lawn grass*

korean lespedeza *n, usu cap K* : a much-branched annual lespedeza (*Lespedeza stipulacea*) that is native to Korea but is widely cultivated for hay and forage esp. in regions of hot dry climate

korean pine *n, usu cap K* : a pine (*Pinus koraiensis*) of eastern Asia having reddish gray bark and differing from Swiss pine in having longer leaves with the margins toothed to the apex and cones four to six inches long

koreanspice viburnum \=¦==¦=-\ *n, usu cap K* : a much-branched spreading deciduous spring-flowering shrub (*Viburnum carlesii*) having both its young branchlets and its inflorescence tomentose and having clove-scented flowers with a cylindrical corolla tube

korean velvet grass *n, usu cap K* : MASCARENE GRASS

koreish *usu cap, var of* QURAISH

ko·resh·an \kō'reshən\ *adj, usu cap* [Heb *Kōresh* Cyrus (after *Cyrus* R. Teed †1908 Am. physician who founded Koreshanity) + E *-an*, adj. suffix] : of or relating to Koreshanity

ko·resh·an·i·ty \,kō,re'shanəd·ē\ *n* -ES *usu cap* [*koreshan* + *-ity*] : the doctrines and beliefs of a communal religious society founded in 1886 by Cyrus R. Teed to reestablish church and state upon a basis of divine fellowship

kor·haan \'kō(ə)r,hän\ *or* **knor·haan** *also* **knoor·haan** \'nō-\ *or* **koor·haan** \'kō-\ *n, pl* **korhaan** *or* **korhaans** *or* **knorhaan** *or* **knorhaans** [*korhaan, koorhaan* fr. Afrik *korhaan*, fr. D, black grouse, fr. *korren* to coo (fr. MD *curren*, prob. of imit. origin) + *haan* cock, rooster, fr. MD *hane; knorhaan, knoorhaan* fr. Afrik *knorhaan*, fr. D, black grouse, alter. (influenced by *knorren* to grumble, fr. MD *cnorren*, prob. of imit. origin) of *korhaan;* akin to OE *hana* rooster — more at CHANT] **1** : any of several African bustards **2** *usu knoorhaan* [so called fr. the sound they make when taken out of the water] **a** : any of several gurnards of southern Africa **b** : a large grunt (*Pomadasys operculare*) of the Indian ocean that is a food and game fish in southern Africa

koriak *usu cap, var of* KORYAK

ko·ri bustard \'kōrē-\ *n* [*kori* fr. a native name in southern Africa] : GOM-PAAUW

ko·ri·ma·ko \,kōrə'mä(,)kō\ *n* -s [Maori] : a New Zealand bellbird (*Anthornis melanura*)

ko·rin \'kōrən\ *n* -s [origin unknown] : a gazelle (*Gazella rufifrons*) of Senegambia, West Africa

Ko·ri·na \kə'rēnə\ *trademark* — used for limba wood

kor·ku \'kȯ(ə)r(,)kü\ *n, pl* **korku** *or* **korkus** *usu cap* **1 a** : a people inhabiting the forested hills of southern Madhya Pradesh, India **b** : a member of such people **2** : the Munda language of the Korku people

kor·nel·ite \'kȯ(r)nᵊl,īt\ *n* -s [Hung *kornelit*, fr. *Kornel* Hlavacsek, 19th cent. person otherwise unidentified + Hung *-it* -ite] : a mineral $Fe_2(SO_4)_3.7H_2O$ consisting of a ferric sulfate heptahydrate

kor·ne·rup·ine \,kȯ(r)nə'rü,pēn, -,pən\ *n* -s [Dan *kornerupin*, fr. A. N. *Kornerup*, 19th cent. Dan. geologist + Dan *-in* -ine] : a mineral $(Mg,Fe,Al)_{20}(Si,B)_9O_{43}$ consisting of a magnesium aluminum iron borosilicate resembling sillimanite in appearance

ko·ro \'kō(,)rō\ *n* -s [Jap *kōro*, fr. *kō* incense + *ro* hearth, furnace] : a squat broad-mouthed usu. covered jar (as of bronze, pottery, or jade) used mostly as an incense burner

ko·roa \kə'rōə\ *n, pl* **koroa** *or* **koroas** *usu cap* **1** : a Tunican people of the Yazoo and Mississippi river valleys, Mississippi **2** : a member of the Koroa people

kor·o·mi·ko \,kōrə'mē(,)kō\ *also* **kor·o·mi·ka** \-ēkə\ *n* -s [Maori] **1** : any of several shrubs of the genus *Veronica* (esp. *V. salicifolia* and *V. parviflora*) **2** : a drug obtained from a koromiko plant

ko·ro·na \'kōrə,nō\ *n, pl* **korona** *or* **koronas** [Hung, lit., crown, fr. L *corona* — more at CROWN] **1** : the basic monetary unit of Hungary 1892–1925 **2** : a silver coin representing one korona

Kor·o·seal \'kōrə,sē(ə)l\ *trademark* — used for a thermoplastic composition of polyvinyl chloride that is rubberlike and resistant to oil, sunlight, and flame and is used esp. in insulation, tank linings, gaskets, and coatings for textiles and paper

kor·ri·gan \'kȯrə,gän\ *n* -s [Bret, fem. of *korrig* gnome, dim. of *korr* dwarf] : a long-haired nocturnal often malevolent Breton fairy sorceress

kor·ri·gum \'kärəgəm\ *n* -s [modif. of Kanuri *kargum*] : a reddish fawn antelope (*Damaliscus korrigum*) of western Africa with black markings

kors *pl of* KOR

kor·sa·koff's psychosis *or* **korsakoff's syndrome** *also* **kor·sa·kow's psychosis** *or* **kor·sa·kow's syndrome** \'kȯ(r)sə,kȯfs-, -,kȯvz-\ *n, usu cap K* [after Sergei *Korsakov* †1900 Russ. psychiatrist] : an abnormal mental condition that is usu. a sequel of chronic alcoholism, is often associated with polyneuritis, and is characterized by an irregular memory loss for which the patient attempts to compensate through confabulation

ko·ru·na \'kȯrə,nä\ *n, pl* **ko·run** \-,rün\ *or* **ko·ru·ny** \-,rənē\ *also* **korunas** \-,rə,näz\ [Czech, lit., crown, fr. L *corona*] **1** : the basic monetary unit of Czechoslovakia — see MONEY table **2** : a coin representing one koruna

kor·wa \'kȯ(ə)rwə\ *n, pl* **korwa** *or* **korwas** *usu cap* **1 a** : a people of the western Chota Nagpur region of southwestern Bihar, India, apparently related to the Mundas **b** : a member of such people **2** : the Munda language of the Korwa people

kor·yak *or* **kor·iak** \'kȯ(ə)rē,yak\ *n, pl* **koryak** *or* **koryaks** *or* **koriak** *or* **koriaks** *usu cap* **1 a** : an Americanoid people of northeastern Siberia **b** : a member of such people **2** : the Luorawetlan language of the Koryak people

KO's *pl of* KO, *pres 3d sing of* KO

ko·sam \'kō,sam\ *n* -s [origin unknown] : a small evergreen shrub (*Brucea amarissima*) of the family Simaroubaceae that is widely distributed in open country in much of southeastern Asia and in northern Australia, is noted for the bitterness of all its parts, and has various uses esp. in local medicine — see KOSAM SEED

kosam seed *n* : the very bitter fruit of the kosam sometimes used in the treatment of various diarrheas and dysenteries

ko·share \kō'sha(ə)r\ *n, pl* **koshare** *or* **koshares** *often cap* [Keres] **1** : a Pueblo Indian clown society representing ancestral spirits in ceremonies invoking rain and fertility **2** : a member of the koshare

¹ko·sher \'kōshə(r)\ *or* **ka·sher** \kä'she(ə)r, -eə\ *adj* [Yiddish *kosher*, fr. Heb *kāshēr* fit, proper] **1** : sanctioned by Jewish law : ritually fit, clean, or prepared for use according to Jewish law ⟨∼ meat⟩ ⟨a ∼ scroll of the law⟩ **2** : selling, serving, or using food that is ritually fit according to Jewish law ⟨a ∼ restaurant⟩ ⟨she keeps a ∼ house⟩ **3** : GENUINE, LEGITIMATE, PROPER ⟨a strong minority feeling that Piltdown was not a very ∼ specimen —*New Yorker*⟩ ⟨tried to stop me from withdrawing the money, sensing that something was not ∼, but I wouldn't listen —Polly Adler⟩ ⟨the rifle report that followed shortly after seemed perfectly ∼ at the time; after all, they do fire guns at army bases —Frederic Ramsey⟩

²kosher *var of* KASHER

kosher hide *n* : the hide of an animal slaughtered in accordance with rabbinical law by crosswise cutting of the throat — called also *cutthroat*

ko·sin \'kōsᵊn\ *n* -s [ISV *kos-* (fr. ¹*koso*) + *-in*] : a yellowish brown amorphous anthelmintic powder containing all of the constituents of brayera — called also *brayerin*

kosmos *var of* COSMOS

¹ko·so \'kō(,)sō\ *or* **kos·so** \'kä(-\ *or* **kous·so** \'kü(-\ *n* -s [prob. fr. Galla *kosso*] : BRAYERA

²koso \'kō(,)sō\ *n, pl* **koso** *or* **kosos** *usu cap* **1** : a Shoshonean people of southeastern California **2** : a member of the Koso people

kos·suth hat \(')kä¦süth-, (')kō¦süth-, 'kō,shüt-\ *n* [after Lajos *Kossuth* †1894 Hung. patriot and statesman] : a hat with a flat-topped crown and rolled brim

kossuth hat

kos·te·letz·kya \,kästə'letskēə\ *n, cap* [NL, fr. V. F. *Kosteletzky* †1887 Bohemian botanist] : a small genus of herbs of the family Malvaceae that are native chiefly to the southern U.S. and tropical America and that differ from the mallows in having a single ovule in each cell of the ovary

ko·stro·ma \,kästrə'mä\ *adj, usu cap* [fr. *Kostroma*, city in north central part of European Russia, U.S.S.R.] : of or from the city of Kostroma, U.S.S.R. : of the kind or style prevalent in Kostroma

kot \'kät, 'kȯt\ *n, pl* **kot** *or* **kots** *usu cap* **1 a** : an extinct people once living along the Agul river tributary of the Yenisei river in Siberia **b** : a member of the Kot people **2** : the Yeniseian language of the Kot people

¹ko·ta \'kōd·ə\ *or* **ko·tar** \'kō,tär\ *n, pl* **kota** *or* **kotas** *or* **kotar** *or* **kotars** *usu cap* **1 a** : an artisan and buffalo-herding people of the Nilgiri hills of southwestern India **b** : a member of such people **2** : the Dravidian language of the Kota people

²kota \"\ *n, pl* **kota** *or* **kotas** *usu cap* **1** : a Bantu-speaking people of the interior of French Equatorial Africa noted in recent times for the quality of their carving esp. of wooden religious masks **2** : a member of the Kota people

ko·thor·nos \'käthər,näs, kō'thȯrnəs\ *n* -ES [Gk] : COTHURNUS 1

ko·to \'kōd·(,)ō\ *n* -s [Jap] : a long Japanese zither having 13 silk strings — compare ⁶KIN

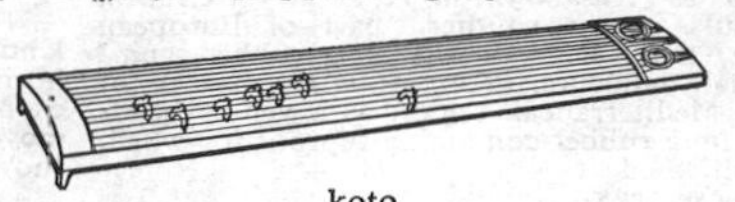

koto

ko·to·ite \'kōd·ə,wīt\ *n* -s [G *kotoit*, fr. Bundjiro *Koto* †1935 Jap. geologist and petrographer + G *-it* -ite] : a mineral $Mg_3(BO_3)_2$ consisting of a borate of magnesium

ko·to·ko \kə'tō(,)kō\ *n, pl* **kotoko** *or* **kotokos** *usu cap* **1** : a people of the lower Shari-Logone basin in the environs of Lake Chad **2** : a member of the Kotoko people

kotow *var of* KOWTOW

ko·tschu·be·ite \kə'chübē,īt\ *n* -s [F *kotchoubeïte*, fr. P. A. V. *Kochubey*, 19th cent. Russ. count + F *-ite*] : a rose-red mineral consisting of a chrome-bearing clinochlore

köttigite *var of* KOETTIGITE

kötts·torf·er value *or* **koetts·torf·er value** \'ket,stȯrfər-\ *n, usu cap K* [prob. fr. the name *Köttstorfer, Koettstorfer*] : SAPONIFICATION VALUE

ko·tu·ku \'kōd·ə,kü\ *n* -s [Maori] *NewZeal* : GREAT WHITE HERON 1

kot·wal *or* **cot·wal** \'kōt,wäl\ *n* -s [Hindi *kotwāl*, fr. Per] : a chief police officer or town magistrate in India

kot·wa·lee \'kōt,wälē\ *n* -s [Hindi *kotwālī*, fr. Per, fr. *kotwāl*] : a police station in India

kotyliform *var of* COTYLIFORM

kou \'kaů\ *n* -s [Hawaiian] *Hawaii* : a tree (*Cordia subcordata*) of the Pacific islands whose wood is used for making household utensils

koudou *var of* KOODOO

koulan *var of* KULAN

kou·miss *or* **ku·miss** *or* **ku·mys** *or* **ku·myss** \kü'mis, 'kümə̇s\ *n* -ES [Russ *kumys*, fr. Kazan Tatar & Kirghiz *kumyz*] : a fermented beverage made orig. by the nomadic peoples of central Asia from mare's milk and now also from cow's milk elsewhere — compare LEBEN

kou·prey \'kü(,)prā\ *also* **kou·proh** \-rō\ *n* -s [native name in Cambodia] : a blackish brown short-haired forest ox (*Bibos sauveli or Novibos sauveli*) of Cambodia that attains a large size, that has a long tail, large dewlap, and spreading recurved horns like those of the yak, and that may be an ancestor of the zebus

kourbash *var of* KURBASH

kou·ros \'kü,rōs\ *n, pl* **kou·roi** \-rōi\ [Gk *koros, kouros* boy — more at CRESCENT] : a sculptured figure of a Greek youth (as an athlete) of which many examples dating from classical antiquity are extant

¹kouse *also* **kous** \'kaů(ə)s\ *n, pl* **kous·es** [by alter.] : COUS

²kouse *also* **kous** \'kaůs\ *n, pl* **kous·es** [origin unknown] : PEARL MILLET

kouskous *var of* COUSCOUS

kousso *var of* KOSO

kousso flower *n* [*kousso* prob. fr. Galla *kosso* brayera] : BRAYERA

kov·no \'kȯv(,)nō, -,nə\ *adj, usu cap* [fr. *Kovno* (*Kaunas*), Lithuania] : KAUNAS

kowbird *var of* KOBIRD

ko·whai \'kō,wī\ *n* -s [Maori] : a shrub or small tree (*Sophora tetraptera*) of Australasia and Chile that yields a hard strong wood

kowliang *var of* KAOLIANG

¹kow·tow *or* **ko·tow** \(')kaů¦taů *sometimes* kō'taů\ *n* -s [Chin (Pek) *k'o¹ t'ou²*, fr. *k'o¹* to strike, bump + *t'ou²* head] : an act of kowtowing

²kowtow *or* **kotow** \"\ *vi* -ED/-ING/-S **1** : to kneel and touch the forehead to the ground (as in old Chinese custom) in token of homage, worship, or deep respect ⟨everyone should ∼ to the abbot, even the chief, but no one receives the abbot's kowtow —Ju-K'ang T'ien⟩ **2** : to show obsequious deference : FAWN ⟨you'll never find a Swiss ∼*ing* or bootlicking —T.H. Fielding⟩ ⟨a brilliant scholar . . . ∼*ed* to the regime and became an empty, self-hating shell of a man —*Time*⟩

ko·yem·shi \kō'yem(,)shē\ *n, pl* **koyemshi** *or* **koyemshis** *often cap* [Zuñi] : a Zuñi Indian clown society whose members wear the mask of the mudhead and are credited with curing illness by their dancing and clowning **2** : a member of the koyemshi

ko·yu·kon \kō'yü,kän\ *n, pl* **koyukon** *or* **koyukons** *usu cap* **1 a** : an Athapaskan people of the Yukon river valley of west central Alaska **b** : a member of such people **2** : the language of the Koyukon people — called also *Khotana, Ten'a*

ko·zhi·kode \'kōzhə,kōd\ *adj, usu cap* [fr. *Kozhikode* (*Calicut*), India] : CALICUT

ko·zo \'kō(,)zō\ *n* -s [Jap *kōzo*] : PAPER MULBERRY

KP *abbr or n* -s kitchen police

KP *abbr* **1** king post **2** King's Proctor **3** knotty pine

kpel·le \kə'pelə\ *n, pl* **kpelle** *or* **kpelles** *usu cap* **1 a** : a people of central Liberia **b** : a member of the Kpelle people **2** : a Mande language of the Kpelle people

KPH *abbr* kilometers per hour

kr *abbr* **1** kiloroentgen **2** kran **3** kreuzer **4** krona **5** krone **6** kroon

Kr *symbol* krypton

kra \'krä\ *n* -s [Malay *kera*] : CRAB-EATING MACAQUE

¹kraal \'kröl, -ä-\ *n* -s [Afrik, fr. Pg *curral* pen for cattle, enclosure, fr. (assumed) VL *currale* enclosure for vehicles — more at CORRAL] **1 a** : a village of southern African natives (as Hottentots or Kaffirs) **b** : the organized social unit that the kraal represents : the native village community **2 a** : a single hut or group of huts in which natives in southern Africa live **b** : an enclosure for domestic animals in southern Africa **c** : an elephant corral in Sri Lanka, India, or Thailand **d** [D, fr. Pg *curral*] : an enclosure for keeping turtles, lobsters, or sponges alive in shallow water — called also *manyatta*

²kraal \"\ *vt* -ED/-ING/-S : to pen in a kraal

krae·pe·lin·i·an \¦krepə¦linēən *also* -rap-\ *adj, usu cap* [Emil *Kraepelin* †1926, Ger. psychiatrist + E *-ian*] : of or relating to Emil Kraepelin or to his system of psychiatric classification

kraft \'kraft, -aa(ə)-, -ai-, -á-\ *n* -s *often attrib* [G, lit., strength, fr. OHG — more at CRAVE] : a strong paper (as most brown wrapping and bag papers) or board made from sulfate pulp ⟨∼ paper⟩ ⟨∼ process⟩ ⟨∼ liner⟩

krait *or* **ko·rait** *also* **ka·rait** \'krīt, kə'r-\ *n* -s [Hindi *karait*] : any of several brightly banded unaggressive but extremely venomous nocturnal elapid snakes of the genus *Bungarus* that are native to eastern Asia and adjacent islands and frequent cultivated land and human habitations and feed esp. on other snakes

kra·ken \'kräkən\ *n* -s [Norw dial., the kraken, fr. Norw dial. *krake* kraken + Norw *-n* (suffixed definite article)] : a fabulous Scandinavian sea monster perhaps imagined on the basis of chance sightings of giant squids

krakow *usu cap, var of* CRACOW

kra·ko·wi·ak \krə'kōvē,ak\ *n* -s [Pol, fr. *Krakow, Cracow*, city and department in southern Poland] : a Polish usu. group folk dance that combines elements of the ancient round, the more recent square, and the modern polka ⟨tread out bouncing ∼ measures to the accompaniment of flute, fiddle, and accordion —H.M.Robinson⟩

¹kra·ma \'krämə\ *n* -s [Gk, mixture, mixed wine, fr. *kerannynai* to mix — more at CRATER] : the mingled and consecrated wine and water into which the consecrated bread is broken at the Eucharist in the Eastern Orthodox Church

²krama \"\ *or* **kro·mo** \'krō(,)mō\ *n* -s *usu cap* [Jav *krama*] : the form of Javanese used in speaking to or in the presence of social superiors

kra·me·ria \krə'mirēə\ *n* [NL, fr. J. G. H. and W. H. *Kramer*, 18th cent. Ger. botanists + NL *-ia*] **1** *cap* : a genus of shrubs that are usu. placed in the family Leguminosae but have sometimes been included among the Polygalaceae or isolated in a monotypic family, that have flowers with irregular petals and a one-celled ovary which are followed by indehiscent prickly fruits, and that in some cases have astringent roots which are sometimes used in pharmacy and tanning **2** -s : the dried roots of certain plants of the genus *Krameria* — see RHATANY — **kra·me·ri·a·ceous** \=¦==¦āshəs\ *adj*

kran \'krän\ *n* -s [Per *qrān*] **1** : the basic monetary unit of Persia from 1826 to 1932 **2** : a silver coin representing one kran

krang *var of* KRENG

krantz *also* **krans** \'kran(t)s, -ä-\ *n* -ES [Afrik *krans*, lit., wreath, fr. D, fr. MD *crans* — more at CRANCE] : a sheer cliff or precipice in southern Africa ⟨crawled forward and looked over the edge of the ∼ —Stuart Cloete⟩

krantz·ite \'kran(t),sīt\ *n* -s [G *krantzit*, fr. A. *Krantz*, 19th cent. Ger. mineralogist + G *-it* -ite] **:** a fossil resin similar to amber

krap·fen \'kräpfən\ *n, pl* **krap·fen** [G *krapfen*, fr. OHG *krāpfo* hook, fritter — more at CRAVE] **:** BISMARCK

kra·pi·na man \'kräpənə-\ *n, usu cap K* [*Krapina*, locality in northern Croatia, Yugoslavia] **:** an early broad-headed Neanderthal man known from several fragmentary skeletons found associated with Mousterian artifacts in a rock shelter in northern Croatia

kra·sis \'kräsəs\ *n, pl* **kra·seis** \-ā(,)sēs\ [Gk, mixing, combination, fr. *kerannynai* to mix — more at CRATER] **:** the act or practice of mingling water with wine in the Eastern Orthodox Eucharist **:** MIXED CHALICE — compare KRAMA

kras·no·dar \'kraznə,där, ,==ˈ=\ *adj, usu cap* [fr. *Krasnodar*, city in southern part of European Russia, U.S.S.R.] **:** of or from the city of Krasnodar, U.S.S.R. **:** of the kind or style prevalent in Krasnodar

kras·no·yarsk \'kraznə,yärsk, ,==ˈ=\ *adj, usu cap* [fr. *Krasnoyarsk*, city in west central Siberia, U.S.S.R.] **:** of or from the city of Krasnoyarsk, U.S.S.R. **:** of the kind or style prevalent in Krasnoyarsk

kra·ter *or* **cra·ter** \'krād·ər, krä'tā(ə)r\ *n* -s [Gk *kratēr* mixing bowl, krater — more at CRATER] **:** a vessel of Greek and Roman antiquity resembling an amphora but having a larger body and a wide mouth and used for mixing wine and water — compare KELEBE

kraters

k ration *n, usu cap K* [after A.B.*Keys* b1904 Am. physiologist] **:** a lightweight packaged ration of emergency foods developed for U.S. armed forces in World War II

kratoch·vil·ite \krə'tächvə,līt, 'krad·ək,vi,l-\ *n* -s [ISV *kratochvil*- (prob. fr. Josef *Kratochvil* †1958 Czechoslovak petrographer) + *-ite*] **:** FLUORENE

krat·o·gen \'krad·əjən, -,jen\ *n* -s [G, fr. *krato*- (fr. Gk *kratos* mastery, strength) + *-gen* — more at HARD] **:** a region that has remained undisturbed while an adjacent area has been affected by mountain-making movements — compare OROGEN — **krat·o·gen·ic** \;=='jenik\ *adj*

kra·ton \'krā,tän, -ra,t-\ *n* -s [ISV, perh. alter. of *kratogen*] **:** KRATOGEN

krau·rite \'krò,rīt\ *n* -s [G *kraurit*, fr. Gk *krauros* brittle + G *-it* -ite] **:** DUFRENITE

krau·ro·sis \krò'rōsəs\ *n, pl* **krauro·ses** \-ō,sēz\ [NL, fr. Gk *krauros* brittle + NL *-osis*] **:** atrophy and shriveling of the skin or mucous membrane esp. of the vulva where it is often a precancerous lesion — **krau·rot·ic** \(')=;räd·ik\ *adj*

¹krau·sen \'kròiz°n\ *vt* -ED/-ING/-S [G *kräusen* to add herbs to brewing beer, fr. *krausen, kräusen* to curl back from the edge (said of foam), curl, fr. MHG *krūsen* to curl, fr. *krūs* curly — more at CURL] **:** to add strong newly fermenting wort to (beer) to produce natural carbonation — compare GYLE

²krausen \"\ *n* -s **:** fermenting wort

krau·se's corpuscle \'kraüzəz-\ *n, usu cap K* [after Wilhelm *Krause* †1910 Ger. anatomist] **:** any of various rounded sensory end organs occurring in mucous membranes (as of the conjunctiva or genitals)

krause's end-bulb *n, usu cap K* **:** KRAUSE'S CORPUSCLE

krause's membrane *n, usu cap K* **:** one of the isotropic cross bands in a striated muscle fiber that consists of disks of sarcoplasm linking the individual fibrils

kraus·ite \'krau̇,sīt\ *n* -s [Edward Henry *Kraus* †1973 Am. mineralogist + E *-ite*] **:** a mineral $KFe(SO_4)_2.H_2O$ consisting of a hydrous sulfate of potassium and iron

kraut \'krau̇t, *usu* -au̇d·+V\ *n* -s [G, sauerkraut, cabbage, plant, herb, fr. OHG *krūt* herb, cabbage — more at SAUERKRAUT] **1 a :** SAUERKRAUT **b :** turnips cured in the same way as cabbage kraut **2** *often cap* **:** a German soldier or civilian — usu. used disparagingly ⟨one of the . . . techniques of annoying the ~ today is to whistle at him —*Atlantic*⟩

kraut grass \'krau̇t,=\ *also* **kraut weed** \-au̇t-,=\ *n* [prob. alter. (influenced by *kraut*) of *crowd grass, crowdweed*] **:** CHARLOCK

krebs cycle \'krebz-\ *n, usu cap K* [after H. A. *Krebs* †1981 Eng. biochemist] **:** a cyclic sequence of reactions occurring in the living organism (as in muscle tissue) and forming a phase of the metabolic function in which acetic acid or acetyl equivalent is oxidized through a series of intermediate acids to carbon dioxide and water and thus provides energy for storage in the form of energy-rich phosphate bonds (as in adenosine triphosphate) that can make it available for use in other vital processes (as muscular work) — called also *citric acid cycle, tricarboxylic acid cycle*

kreef \'krāf\ *n* -s [Afrik, fr. D *kreeft* lobster, crayfish, fr. MD *creeft*; akin to OHG *krebiz* crab — more at CRAB] **:** CAPE CRAWFISH

kre·feld \'krā,felt, -ld\ *adj, usu cap* [fr. *Krefeld*, Germany] **:** of or from the city of Krefeld, Germany **:** of the kind or style prevalent in Krefeld

kreis \'krīs\ *n, pl* **krei·se** \-īzə\ [G, lit., circle, fr. OHG *kreiz*; akin to MLG *kreit*, *krēt* circle, *krit* enclosed combat area — more at KULTURKREIS] **:** a unit of local government in Germany corresponding to a county

kreit·to·nite \'krīt°n-,īt, -rāt-\ *n* -s [G *kreittonit*, fr. Gk *kreittōn* stronger (compar. of *kratys* strong) + G *-it* -ite — more at HARD] **:** a black gahnite

kremers·ite \'kremər,zīt, 'krām-\ *n* -s [G *kremersit*, after P. *Kremers*, 19th cent. Ger. chemist who described it + G *-it* -ite] **:** a volcanic mineral product $[(NH_4),K]_2FeCl_5.H_2O$ consisting of a hydrous chloride of potassium, ammonium, and iron that occurs in red octahedrons

¹krem·lin \'kremlən\ *n* -s [earlier *cremelena, cremelina*, prob. modif. of obs. G *kremelin*, modif. of Russ *kreml'*] **1 :** the citadel or fortress of a Russian city or town ⟨the ensembles of the fortified monasteries and ~s —Arthur Voyce⟩ **2** *usu cap* [fr. the *Kremlin*, citadel of Moscow now serving as the governing center of the U.S.S.R.] **a :** a governing center or executive stronghold usu. regarded as secretive and impenetrable ⟨there are many *Kremlins* outside Russia, whose secrets, too, are guarded —Irwin Edman⟩ ⟨some of the permanent secretaries and undersecretaries live in an invisible *Kremlin* —*Economist*⟩ **b :** the supreme governing oligarchy of Soviet Russia ⟨on both sides of the Iron Curtain the battle between *Kremlin* and Vatican continues —C.L.Sulzberger⟩

²kremlin \"\ *adj, usu cap* **:** of or relating to the Kremlin esp. as symbolizing the central government of the U.S.S.R. or its policies ⟨*Kremlin* leaders⟩

krem·lin·ism \-,nizəm\ *n* -s *usu cap* **:** the policies and practices characteristic of the Soviet Russian government ⟨*Kremlinism* threatens the security and even the physical existence of mankind by keeping alive the global anarchy —H.D.Lasswell⟩

krem·nitz white *or* **crem·nitz white** \'kremnəts-\ *n, usu cap K&C* [fr. *Kremnitz, Kremnica*, east central Czechoslovakia] **:** a white lead suitable esp. for use in inks and as an artist's color — called also *Krems white*

krems white *or* **crems white** \'kremz-, -m(p)s-\ *n, usu cap K&C* [perh. fr. *Krems*, city in Austria] **:** KREMNITZ WHITE

kreng \'kreŋ\ *or* **krang** *or* **crang** \'kraŋ\ *n* -s [D *kreng*, fr. MD *crenge* carrion, carcass; perh. akin to OE *cringan* to yield, fall in battle, die — more at CRINGE] **:** the carcass of a whale after removal of the blubber and baleen

kreng·ing hook \'kreŋiŋ-\ *or* **crang·ing hook** \'kraŋiŋ-\ *n* [*krenging, cranging* fr. *kreng, crang* + *-ing*] **:** a hook for holding the blubber of a whale while cutting it away

kren·ner·ite \'krenə,rīt\ *n* -s [G *krennerit*, fr. J. S. *Krenner* †1920 Hung. mineralogist + G *-it* -ite] **:** a mineral $AuTe_2$ consisting of a gold telluride

kreo- — see CRE-

krep·lach *or* **krep·lech** *or* **crep·lich** \'kreplək\ *n, pl* **kreplach** *or* **kreplech** *or* **creplich** [Yiddish *kreplech*, pl. of *krepel*, fr. (assumed) MHG dial. *krepel* (whence G dial. *kräppel* fritter), dim. of MHG dial. *krape, krāpe* fritter; akin to OHG *krāpfo* hook, fritter — more at CRAVE] **:** triangular pockets of noodle dough filled with chopped meat or cheese, boiled, and eaten with soup or as a side dish

kreu·zer *also* **kreut·zer** *or* **creut·zer** \'krȯitsə(r)\ *n* -s [G *kreuzer*, fr. MHG *kriuzer* (trans. of ML *denarius cruciatus, cruciger*, fr. the cross marking them), fr. *kriuze* cross, fr. OHG *krūzi*, fr. L *cruc-, crux* — more at RIDGE] **:** a small coin of silver and later of copper used in Austria, Germany, and Hungary from the 13th to the mid-19th centuries

krex \'kreks, 'gr-\ *vi* -ED/-ING/-S [prob. fr. PaG *greckse* to grunt, ail, fr. G *krächzen* to croak, fr. *krachen* to crack, crash, roar, fr. OHG *krahhōn* to crack — more at CRACK] *dial* **:** GRUMBLE, COMPLAIN ⟨always something to ~ about⟩

k'ri *or* **kri** *var of* KERI

krib·er·gite \'kribər,gīt\ *n* -s [Sw *kribergit*, prob. irreg. fr. *Kristineberg* mine, Västerbotten province, northern Sweden, its locality + Sw *-it* -ite] **:** a mineral approximately $Al_{16}(PO_4)_8(SO_4)_3(OH)_{18}.10H_2O$ consisting of a hydrous basic sulfate and phosphate of aluminum

kri·der's hawk \'krīdə(r)z-\ *n, usu cap K* [fr. the name *Krider*] **:** a hawk of the central U.S. that is a variety (*Buteo jamaicensis kriderii*) of the red-tailed hawk and has the underparts almost pure white

krieg·spiel \'krēgz,pē(ə)l, -ēg,sp-, -ēk,shp-\ *n* [G *kriegsspiel*, fr. *krieg* war + *spiel* game] **1 :** a game in which blocks, pins, and flags representing contending forces and guns are moved about according to rules based on war conditions **2 :** chess in which neither player sees the other's board but is given some information as to the opponent's moves by a referee who keeps track of all moves on a third board

krie·ker \'krēkə(r)\ *n* -s [perh. fr. D *krieken* to chirp, peep (of imit. origin) + E *-er*] **:** PECTORAL SANDPIPER

krig·ia \'krigēə\ *n* [NL, fr. David *Krig*, 18th cent. Am. plant collector + NL *-ia*] **1** *cap* **:** a genus of small branched yellow-flowered No. American herbs that are related to the chicories but resemble dandelions and have a pappus of both bristles and chaff and short achenes **2** -s **:** any plant of the genus *Krigia* — called also *dwarf dandelion*

krill \'kril\ *n* -s [Norw *kril* young fry of fish] **:** planktonic crustaceans and larvae of the order Euphausiacea that constitute the principle food of whalebone whales which feed by straining krill-containing water through their plates of baleen

krim·mer *also* **crim·mer** \'krimə(r)\ *n* -s [G *krimmer*, fr. *Krim* Crimea, peninsula in the southern part of European Russia, U.S.S.R.] **1 :** a gray fur resembling astrakhan or Persian lamb that is made from the pelts of young lambs of the Crimean peninsula region — compare BROADTAIL, KARAKUL **2 :** a pile fabric resembling krimmer fur

krim-saghyz *var of* KRYM-SAGHYZ

kris *or* **kriss** *also* **creese** \'krēs *sometimes* 'kris\ *n, pl* **krises** *or* **krisses** [Malay *kĕris*] **:** a Malay or Indonesian dagger often with two scalloped cutting edges and ridged serpentine blade ⟨the ~ of a noble or high-class family is a sacred possession —Virginia A. Oakes⟩

kris

kris dance *n* **:** a Balinese trance dance in which the dancer attacks himself with a kris

krish·na·ism \'krishnə,izəm\ *n* -s *usu cap* [*Krishna*, eighth avatar of Vishnu, one of the principal Hindu gods + E *-ism*] **:** a widespread form of Hindu worship addressed to Krishna as eighth avatar of Vishnu

kri·ta yu·ga \,krid·ə'yügə\ *n, usu cap K&Y* [Skt *kṛtayuga*, fr. *kṛta* best throw at dice (that of the four) + *yuga* yoke, age of the world — more at YOKE] **:** the first and best age of a Hindu world cycle

kri·voi rog \;krī,vȯi;rōg, kri;vȯi;rȯk\ *adj, usu cap K&R* [fr. *Krivoi Rog*, city in southeast central Ukraine, U.S.S.R.] **:** of or from the city of Krivoi Rog, U.S.S.R. **:** of the kind or style prevalent in Krivoi Rog

kroehn·kite *or* **kröhn·kite** \'kreŋ,kīt\ *n* -s [modif. of Sp *krönnkite*, fr. B. *Kröhnke*, 19th cent. Ger. mineralogist + Sp *-ite*] **:** a mineral $Na_2Cu(SO_4)_2.2H_2O$ consisting of an azure-blue hydrous copper sodium sulfate that occurs massive

krom·draai ape-man \'kräm,drī-\ *also* **kromdraai man** *n, usu cap K* [*Kromdraai*, town in Transvaal, So. Africa, site of the finds] **:** an australopithecine (*Paranthropus robustus* or *Australopithecus robustus*) known from skull and skeletal fragments from southern Africa and distinguished by an extraordinarily massive jaw — compare SWARTKRANZ APE-MAN

kro·mes·ki *or* **kro·mes·ky** *also* **cro·mes·ki** *or* **cro·mes·qui** \krō'meskē\ *n, pl* **kromeskis** *or* **kromeskies** [modif. of Russ *kromochki*, pl. of *kromochka* slice of bread, dim. of *kroma* slice of bread] **:** a croquette wrapped in bacon, dipped in batter, and fried

krom·nek disease \'kräm,nek-\ *n* [Afrik *kromnek*, fr. *krom* crooked (fr. D, fr. MD *crom, cromb*) + *nek* neck, fr. D, fr. MD *necke* nape of the neck; akin to OE *crumb* crooked and to OE *hnecca* neck — more at CRUMP, NECK] *in southern Africa* **:** TOMATO STREAK

kromo *usu cap, var of* KRAMA

kro·mo·gram \'krōmə,gram\ *n* [alter. of *chromogram*] **:** the set of three photographic positives used in a chromoscope — called also *chromogram*

¹kro·na \'krōnə\ *n, pl* **kro·nur** \-nə(r)\ [Icel *krōna*, lit., crown, fr. ON *krūna, krōna*, fr. MLG *krūne, krōne*, prob. fr. OF *corone, corune* — more at CROWN] **1 :** the basic monetary unit of Iceland — see MONEY table **2 :** a coin representing one krona

²kro·na \", 'krünə\ *n, pl* **kro·nor** \-,nȯ(ə)r\ [Sw, lit., crown, fr. OSw *krūna, krōna*, fr. MLG *krūne, krōne*] **1 :** the basic monetary unit of Sweden — see MONEY table **2 :** a coin representing one krona

¹kro·ne \'krōnə\ *n, pl* **kro·nen** \-nən\ [G, lit., crown, fr. OHG *corōna*, fr. L *corona* — more at CROWN] **1 :** the basic monetary unit of Austria from 1892 to 1925 **2 :** a coin representing one krone

²krone \"\ *n, pl* **kro·ner** \-nə(r)\ [Dan, lit., crown, fr. ODan *krūne, krōne*, fr. MLG] **1 a :** the basic monetary unit of Denmark — see MONEY table **b :** a coin representing one Danish krone **2 a :** the basic monetary unit of Norway — see MONEY table **b :** a coin representing one Norwegian krone

kroo \'krü\ *or* **kroo·boy** \-,bȯi\ *n, pl* **kroo** *or* **krooboys** *usu cap* [*Kroo* alter. of *Kru*] **:** KRU 1b

kroon \'krün\ *n, pl* **kroo·ni** \-nē\ *or* **kroons** [Estonian *kron*, fr. G *krone*] **1 :** the basic monetary unit of Estonia from 1928 to 1940 **2 :** a coin or note representing one kroon

kru \'krü\ *n, pl* **kru** *or* **krus** *usu cap* **1 a :** an indigenous Negro people of Liberia skilled as boatmen **b :** a member of the Kru people — called also *Kruman* **2 :** a Kwa language of the Kru people **3 :** a language group containing Kru, Bassa, and Grebo

kru·bi \'krübē\ *n* -s [prob. native name in Sumatra] **:** a tropical East Indian aroid (*Amorphophallus titanum*) having a spathe that resembles the corolla of a morning glory and attains a diameter of several feet

kru·ken·berg tumor \'krükən,bərg-\ *n, usu cap K* [after Friedrich E. *Krukenberg* b1871 Ger. pathologist] **:** a metastatic ovarian tumor of mucin-producing epithelial cells usu. derived from a primary gastrointestinal tumor

kru·man *or* **kroo·man** \'krümən\ *n, pl* **krumen** *or* **kroomen** *usu cap* **:** KRU 1b

krumm·holz \'krům,hōlts\ *n, pl* **krummholz** *usu cap* [G, fr. *krumm* crooked (fr. OHG *krumb, krump*) + *holz* wood, fr. OHG — more at CRUMP, HOLT] **:** stunted forest characteristic of most alpine regions — called also *elfinwood*

krumm·horn *also* **krum·horn** \-,hȯrn\ *n* [G *krummhorn* — more at CROMORNE] **1 :** a Renaissance reed wind instrument with a curved tube — called also *cromorne* **2 :** CROMORNA

krummhorn with cap removed to show reed

krym-saghyz *or* **krim-saghyz** \;krimsə;gēz, -giz\ *n* -ES [Russ *krym-sagyz*, fr. *Krym* Crimea, peninsula in the southern part of European Russia, U.S.S.R. + Turki *sagiz* rubber, gum] **:** a small dandelion (*Taraxacum megalorrhizon*) of the Mediterranean region with yellow heads and a long rubber-containing taproot for which it is cultivated

kryo- — see CRY-

kry·o·gen yellow G \'krīōjən-, -,jen-\ *n, usu cap K&Y* [*kryogen* perh. fr. *cry-* + *-gen*] **:** a sulfur dye — see DYE table I (under *Sulfur Yellow 3*)

kryokonite *var of* CRYOCONITE

kryolite *var of* CRYOLITE

krypt- *or* **krypto-** — see CRYPT-

kryp·ton \'krip,tän, -,tən\ *n* -s [Gk, neut. of *kryptos* hidden — more at CRYPT] **:** a colorless inert gaseous element that occurs in air to the extent of about one part per million by volume and in gases from thermal springs and other natural gases, that is obtained by separating from liquid air, and that is used in electric lamps (as small quartz lamps for extremely brilliant illumination) — symbol *Kr*; see ELEMENT table

k's *or* **ks** *pl of* K

KS *abbr* **1** keep standing **2** king's scholar

KSF *abbr, often not cap* kips per square foot

ksha·tri·ya *also* **kshat·tri·ya** *or* **ksat·ri·ya** \(kə)'sha·trē(y)ə, (kə)'shə-, 'ksh- *sometimes* 'ch-\ *n* -s *usu cap* [Skt *kṣatriya*, fr. *kṣatra* dominion, fr. *kṣayati* he possesses, rules — more at CHECK] **1 :** a twice-born Hindu of the second ancient varna assigned by classical law to a governing or military occupation **2 :** a twice-born Hindu belonging to one of a large group of modern upper castes traditionally derived from the ancient Kshatriya varna — compare BRAHMAN, SUDRA, VAISYA

k-shell \'=,=\ *n, usu cap K* **:** the innermost shell of electrons surrounding an atomic nucleus and constituting the lowest available energy level for the electrons — compare L-SHELL, M-SHELL

k star *n, usu cap K* **:** a star of spectral type K — see SPECTRAL TYPE table

kt *abbr* **1** karat **2** kiloton **3** knight **4** knot

k'thib *or* **kthib** *or* **k'thibh** *or* **kthibh** *var of* KETHIB

KTL *abbr, often not cap* [Gk *kai ta loipa*] et cetera

k truss *n, usu cap K* **:** a building truss in which the vertical member and two oblique members in each panel form a K

kua·la lum·pur \'kwälə'lüm,pů(ə)r, 'kwəl-, -'ləm-\ *adj, usu cap K&L* [fr. *Kuala Lumpur*, Federation of Malaya] **:** of or from Kuala Lumpur, capital of the Federation of Malaya **:** of the kind or style prevalent in Kuala Lumpur

kuan \'gwän, 'kw-\ *n* -s *usu cap* [Chin (Pek) *kuan¹* official] **1 :** a type of Chinese pottery of the Sung period in the 12th century **2 :** imperial porcelain made at Ching-tê-chên

kuan hua \'gwän'(h)wä\ *n, usu cap K&H* [Chin (Pek) *kuan¹ hua⁴*, fr. *kuan¹* official + *hua⁴* speech, language] **:** MANDARIN

¹ku·ba \'kübə\ *n* -s *usu cap* [fr. *Kuba*, town in northeast Azerbaidzhan, U.S.S.R.] **:** an eastern Caucasian carpet of coarse but firm weave resembling the Shirvan in design — called also *Kabistan*

²ku·ba \'kübə\ *n, pl* **kuba** *or* **kubas** *usu cap* **1 :** a Bantu-speaking people of the central Congo **2 :** a member of the Kuba people

ku·ba·chi \kü'bächē\ *n, pl* **kubachi** *or* **kubachis** *usu cap* **1 :** a Caucasian people of Dagestan **2 :** a member of the Kubachi people

ku·bong \'kü,bȯŋ, -bäŋ\ *n, pl* **kubong** [Malay] **:** FLYING LEMUR

ku·bu \'kü(,)bü\ *n, pl* **kubu** *or* **kubus** *usu cap* [native name in Sumatra] **1 :** an Indonesian Veddoid people of Sumatra **2 :** a member of the Kubu people

ku·che·an \(')kü;chēən\ *n* -s *cap* [*Kuche, Kucha*, town and oasis in west central Sinkiang, China + E *-an*] **:** TOCHARIAN B

ku·chen \'kükən, 'kük-\ *n, pl* **kuchen** [G, cake, fr. OHG *kuocho, chuohho* — more at CAKE] **:** any of several varieties of coffee cake typically made from sweet yeast dough and variously shaped, flavored, and frosted

ku·dize \'k(y)ü,dīz\ *vt* -ED/-ING/-S [*kudos* + *-ize*] **:** grant honors to **:** PRAISE

ku·dos \-,däs, -,dōs\ *n, pl* **ku·dos** \-,dōz\ [Gk *kydos*; akin to OSlav *čudo* wonder, Gk *akouein* to hear — more at HEAR] **1 :** fame and renown resulting from an act or achievement **:** PRESTIGE ⟨occupations linked to inferior castes in Africa and India bring no ~ to their practitioners, no matter how skilled the craftsman —E.A.Hoebel⟩ ⟨the curate's undaunted demeanor . . . was generally supposed to have terrified the burglars into flight and much ~ accrued to him thereby —Kenneth Grahame⟩ **2 :** praise given for achievement **:** ACCOLADE 3c ⟨a masterly study of primitive versus industrial society . . . with the ~ going to the pagan man —Betty Kirk⟩ ⟨they will compel new respect and admiration far beyond the ~ civilization finds itself obliged to pay —*Collier's*⟩

kudu *var of* KOODOO

ku·dzu \'ku̇d(,)zü\ *also* **kudzu vine** *n* -s [Jap *kuzu*] **:** a prostrate vine (*Pueraria thunbergiana*) of China and Japan that is used widely for hay and forage and for erosion control and soil improvement and that has tuberous edible roots and stems which yield a fiber — see KO-HEMP

kue *also* **ku** \'kyü\ *n* -s **:** the letter *q*

kufa *var of* GUFA

¹ku·fic *also* **cu·fic** \'k(y)üfik\ *adj, usu cap* [*Al Kufa*, town in south central Iraq + E *-ic*] **1 :** of, relating to, or characteristic of Al Kufa, a city of Mesopotamia or of its inhabitants **2 :** constituting, belonging to, characteristic of, or written in the Arabic script Kufic

²kufic *also* **cufic** \"\ *n, usu cap* **1 :** a highly angular form of the Arabic alphabet orig. used at Al Kufa esp. for costly copies of the Koran **2 :** any angular variety of the Arabic alphabet — compare NESKHI

ku·gel \'kügəl\ *n* -s [Yiddish, lit., ball, fr. MHG *kugel, kugele* — more at CUDGEL] **:** a baked pudding (as of potatoes, noodles, bread, or cabbage) served as a side dish or dessert

ku·gel·hof \-,hōf\ *n* -s [modif. of G *gugelhupf, gugelhopf* — more at GUGELHUPF] **:** GUGELHUPF

ku·hio day \kü'hēo-, ;==ˈ=-\ *n, usu cap K&D* [after Prince Jonah *Kuhio* Kalanianaole †1922 Hawaiian delegate to the U.S. Congress] **:** March 26 that is observed as a holiday in Hawaii to commemorate the birthday of Prince Jonah Kuhio Kalanianaole

kuh·lia \'külēə, -lyə\ *n, cap* [NL, fr. Heinrich *Kuhl* †1821 Ger. naturalist + NL *-ia*] **:** the type genus of Kuhliidae — see AHOLEHOLE

kuh·li·idae \kü'līə,dē\ *n pl, cap* [NL, fr. *Kuhlia*, type genus + *-idae*] **:** a family of small Indo-Pacific marine and freshwater percoid fishes — see KUHLIA

kuh·nia \'k(y)ünēə\ *n, cap* [NL, fr. Adam *Kuhn* †1817 Am. physician and botanist + NL *-ia*] **:** a genus of No. American perennial herbs (family Compositae) with alternate resinous leaves and heads of cream-colored tubular flowers

kui \'küē\ *n, pl* **kui** *or* **kuis** *usu cap* **1 a :** a people of southeastern Thailand and adjacent Cambodia who are brachycephalic and of short stature **b :** a people of the Shan states **c :** a Dravidian people of central India **2 :** the Dravidian language of the Kui people of India

kui·by·shev \'kwēbə,shef, 'küēb-, -ev\ *adj, usu cap* [fr. *Kuibyshev*, city in the eastern part of European Russia, U.S.S.R.] **:** of or from the city of Kuibyshev, U.S.S.R. **:** of the kind or style prevalent in Kuibyshev

ku·itsh \kü'ēch\ *n, pl* **kuitsh** *or* **kuitshes** *usu cap* **1 a :** an Indian people of the Pacific coast in Oregon **b :** a member of such people **2 :** a dialect of Siuslaw

ku·ja·wi·ak \kü'yävē,ak\ *n* -s [Pol, fr. *Kujawy*, region in north central Poland] **:** a Polish couple dance resembling a waltz with lilting arm and body movements

kuke \'kyük\ *n* -s *usu cap* [by alter.] **:** KIKUYU

ku·ki \'kükē\ *n, pl* **kuki** *or* **kukis** *usu cap* **1 a :** any of numerous hill peoples in southern Assam, India **b :** a member of a Kuki people **2 :** a language of a Kuki people

kuki-chin \'kükē'chin\ *n* -s *usu cap K&C* **:** a group of Tibeto-Burman languages spoken by the Kuki and Chin peoples

ku-klux \'k(y)ü,kləks, *often* ÷ 'klü- *by assimilation to the* kl *of* "Klux" & "Klan"\ *vt* -ED/-ING/-ES *often cap both Ks* [fr. *Ku-Klux, Ku-Klux Klan*, secret organization originating in the southern U.S. after the Civil War and advocating maintenance of white supremacy by violent methods] **:** to maltreat or terrorize in a way thought to be typical of Ku Kluxers ⟨*ku-kluxed* him by shooting him with bird shot —R.H.Collins⟩

ku klux·er \-əksə(r)\ *n, pl* **ku kluxers** *usu cap both Ks* **1** *also* **ku klux** *pl* **ku kluxes :** a member of a secret society advocating white supremacy and often using violent methods to intimidate Negroes in the South in the period following the Civil War **2 :** a member of a secret fraternal group achieving prominence in many parts of the U.S. in the second decade of the 20th century and believed to confine its membership to

native Protestant whites ⟨wilder than the . . . stories about Catholics which are afloat among our own *Ku Kluxers* —*New Republic*⟩
ku klux·ism \-ək,sizəm\ *also* **ku klux·ery** \-əksərē\ *n*, *usu cap both Ks* **:** the principles and practices of Ku Kluxers ⟨the bitterness of the days of reconstruction and *Ku Kluxism* —*Amer. Missionary*⟩ ⟨the spirit of *Ku Kluxism* . . . among the older American elements —Samuel Lubell⟩
kuk·ri *also* **kuk·eri** \'kük(ə)rē\ *n* -s [Hindi *kukṛī*] **:** a curved short sword with a broad blade used principally by the Gurkhas of India
kukri
kuk·su \'kük(,)sü\ *adj*, *usu cap* [origin unknown] **:** of or relating to an Indian religious cult or its rites practiced in the southern Sacramento valley of California
ku·ku \'kü(,)kü\ *n* -s [Maori] **:** a New Zealand fruit dove (*Hemiphaga novae-seelandiae*) that is locally important as a game bird — called also *kukupa*
ku·kui \kü'küē\ *n* -s [Hawaiian] **:** CANDLENUT 2
kukui oil *n* **:** CANDLENUT OIL
ku·ku·ku·ku \,kükə'kü(,)kü\ *n*, *pl* **kukukuku** *or* **kukukukus** *usu cap* **1 :** a people inhabiting parts of Morabe and Papua in eastern New Guinea **2 :** a member of the Kukukuku people
ku·ku·pa \'kükəpə\ *n* -s [Maori] **:** KUKU
ku·la \'külə\ *n*, *pl* **kula** [of Melanesian origin] **:** a Melanesian interisland system of exchange in which prestige items (as necklaces and arm shells) are ceremoniously exchanged with a concomitant trade in useful goods — compare EXCHANGE 1b
ku·lah \(')kü¦lä\ *n* -s *usu cap* [fr. *Kula*, town in western Turkey in Asia] **:** a Turkish rug that is often a prayer rug and that uses the Ghiordes knot
ku·lak \(')kü¦lak, -¦läk *also* (')kyü¦lak\ *n*, *pl* **kulaks** \-ks\ *also* **kula·ki** \-'lakē, -'läkē\ [Russ, lit., fist, of Turkic origin; akin to Turk *kol* arm] **1 :** a prosperous or wealthy peasant farmer in 19th century Russia often associated with gaining profit from renting land, usury, or acting as a middleman in the sale of the products of other farmers **2 :** a farmer characterized by Communists as having excessive wealth usu. by possession of more than a minimal amount of property and ability to hire laborers or sometimes merely by unwillingness to join a collective farm and as a result denounced as an oppressor of less fortunate farmers and subjected to severe penalties (as heavy fines and confiscation of property) ⟨a large proportion of the ~s of the twenties were liquidated —L.K.Soth⟩
ku·la·man \'külə,män\ *n*, *pl* **kulaman** *or* **kulamans** *usu cap* [native name in southern Mindanao] **1 a :** a people inhabiting southern Mindanao, Philippines **b :** a member of such people **2 :** an Austronesian language of the Kulaman people
ku·lan *or* **kou·lan** \'kü,län\ *n* -s [Kirghiz *kulan*] **:** the wild ass of the Kirghiz steppe that is prob. a variety of the kiang
ku·la·na·pan \kü'länəpən\ *n* -s *usu cap* **:** a language family of the Hokan stock comprising several languages all known as Pomo
kula ring *n* **1 :** KULA **2 :** the circle of Melanesian islands participating in the kula exchange
kul·li \'kəlē\ *adj*, *usu cap* [fr. *Kulli*, locality in southern Baluchistan, Pakistan, site of the finds] **:** of or relating to a prehistoric culture of southern Baluchistan characterized by polychrome vases and small objects modeled in clay (as figurines of women and animals, bird whistles, carts)
kul·tur \kül'tü(ə)r\ *n* -s *often cap* [G, fr. L *cultura* culture — more at CULTURE] **1 :** CULTURE 5b ⟨the dwindling survivors of New England *Kultur* —H.L.Mencken⟩ ⟨our ~ should have its own characteristics —*Irish Statesman*⟩ **2 :** culture chiefly of late 19th century Germans that is a state of civilization characterized by an emphasis on practical efficiency rather than on humanitarian refinements and subordination of the individual to a highly organized state **3 :** culture that is an ideal state of civilization unique to Germany chiefly to militant German expansionists during the Nazi and late Hohenzollern periods usu. to emphasize an alleged superiority of German material and political development over the cultures of other nations and peoples ⟨the ethnocentric doctrine of Germanic *Kultur* . . . utilized for political purposes to justify cultural and political absolutism —David Bidney⟩ ⟨German textbooks were fine-combed for the propaganda of *Kultur* —*Amer. Mercury*⟩
kul·tur·kampf \-,käm(p)f\ *n* -s *usu cap* [G, fr. *kultur* + *kampf* conflict, struggle, fr. OHG *kamph* combat — more at KEMP] **:** conflict between civil government and religious authorities esp. over control of education and church appointments ⟨the *Kulturkampf* . . . frets the life of practically every continental nation —*Christian Century*⟩ ⟨planning a protracted *Kulturkampf* against the Church —*Time*⟩
kul·tur·kreis \-,krīs\ *n*, *pl* **kulturkrei·se** \-īzə\ *usu cap* [G, fr. *kultur* + *kreis* area, circle, fr. OHG *kreiz* circular line, encirclement, district; akin to MLG *kreit*, *krēt* circle, enclosed dueling space, OHG *krizzōn* to scratch in (as letters), *krazzōn* to scratch — more at SCRATCH] **:** a culture complex developing in successive epochs from its center of origin and becoming diffused over large areas of the world ⟨the horse-raising peoples in the primary herding *Kulturkreise* —Lawrence Krader⟩ ⟨the concept of the *Kulturkreise* developed by the Vienna school of ethnology⟩
ku·ma·mo·to \,küma¦mōd·(,)ō\ *adj*, *usu cap* [fr. *Kumamoto*, city in western Kyushu, Japan] **:** of or from the city of Kumamoto, Japan **:** of the kind or style prevalent in Kumamoto
kuman *usu cap*, *var of* CUMAN
ku·ma·ra \'kümərə\ *n* -s [Maori] *New Zealand* **:** SWEET POTATO
ku·ma·ra·hou \,---'haů\ *n* -s [Maori] *New Zealand* **:** any of several native woody plants: as **a :** a branching shrub (*Pomaderris elliptica*) with leaves lustrous above and whitish tomentose below and cymes of fragrant pale yellow flowers **b :** a small sometimes shrubby tree (*Quintinia serrata*) that is more or less covered with whitish scales and has shining leathery serrated leaves and cymes of pale lilac flowers
ku·ma·so \kü'mä(,)sō\ *n*, *pl* **kumaso** *or* **kumasos** *usu cap* **:** an indigenous Caucasoid people of Japan formerly inhabiting Kyushu — compare AINU
kumbh me·la \'kůmmə,lä\ *n*, *usu cap K&M* [Hindi *kumbh melā* festival in the sign of the zodiac Aquarius, fr. Skt *kumbha* pot, Aquarius + *melā* assembly — more at HUMP, MILITATE] **:** a Hindu festival occurring once every 12 years in one of four sacred sites where bathing for purification of sin is considered esp. efficacious
kum·bi \'kůmbē\ *n* -s [origin unknown] *India* **:** the silky fiber of the white silk cotton tree
kum·buk \'kům,bůk\ *n* -s [origin unknown] **:** ARJUN
kum·har \(')kům¦här\ *n* -s *usu cap* [Hindi *kumhār*, fr. Skt *kumbhakāra*, fr. *kumbha* pot + *kāra* maker; akin to Skt *karoti* he does, makes — more at HUMP, KARMA] **:** a member of a potter caste of India
kumiss *or* **kumys** *or* **kumyss** *var of* KOUMISS
kum·kum \'kům,kům\ *n* -s [Hindi *kuṅkum*, fr. Skt *kuṅkuma* saffron, perh. of Sem origin; akin to Heb *karkōm* saffron, crocus — more at CROCUS] **1 :** red turmeric powder used for making the distinctive Hindu mark on the forehead **2 :** the mark on the forehead made with kumkum
küm·mel \'kiməl\ *n* -s [G, lit., caraway seed, fr. OHG *kumil*, *kumīn* cumin — more at CUMIN] **:** a colorless aromatic liqueur flavored principally with caraway seeds
kumni *usu cap*, *var of* KURMI
kum·quat *also* **cum·quat** \'kəm,kwät\ *n* -s [Chin (Cant) *kam kwat*, fr. *kam* gold + *kwat* orange] **1 a :** any of several small yellow to orange citrus fruits with sweet spongy rind and somewhat acid pulp that are used chiefly candied or in preserves **b :** a tree or shrub of the genus *Fortunella* that bears kumquats: as (1) **:** a Chinese tree (*F. margarita*) that is widely cultivated in warm regions and that bears ovoid orange-colored kumquats (2) **:** a tree (*F. japonica*) that is known only in cultivation and that bears spherical golden yellow kumquats **2** *Austral* **:** DESERT LEMON
ku·myk *also* **ku·mik** \(')kü¦mik\ *or* **ku·muk** \-¦mək\ *n* -s *usu cap* **1 a :** a Turkish people of the Caucasus **b :** a member of such people **2 :** the Turkic language of the Kumyk people
ku·nai \'kü,nī\ *n* -s [native name in eastern New Guinea] *New Guinea* **:** COGON
ku·na·ma \kü'nämə\ *n* -s *usu cap* **1 :** a language spoken in northern Ethiopia **2 :** a branch of the Chari-Nile language family containing only the Kunama language
kunbi *usu cap*, *var of* KURMI
kundt tube \'kůnt-\ *n*, *usu cap K* [after August *Kundt* †1894 Ger. physicist] **:** an acoustically resonating horizontal glass tube in which the standing-wave nodes are exhibited by the distribution of a fine powder and that is used to measure the velocity of sound in gases
kung *usu cap*, *var of* QUNG
kun·gu cake \'kůŋ(,)gü\ *n* [*kungu* fr. Nyanja *nkungu* kungu fly] **:** a food made by the natives about Lake Nyasa consisting of compressed cakes of kungu flies
kungu fly *n* **:** any of certain small mayflies (genus *Caenis*) and midges (genus *Corethra*) that breed on Lake Nyasa — see KUNGU CAKE
kun·kur *or* **kun·kar** \'kəŋkə(r)\ *also* **con·ker** \'käŋ-\ *n* -s [Hindi *kaṅkar*, fr. Skt *karkara*] **:** a limestone used esp. in India for making lime and building roads
kunst·lied \'kůnzt,lēt, -n(t)st-\ *n* -s [G, fr. *kunst* art (fr. OHG, skill, knowledge) + *lied* song, fr. OHG *liod*; OHG *kunst* akin to OFris *kunst* knowledge, MD *const*, *cunst*, OS *kunst*, all fr. a prehistoric derivative of the verb represented by OHG *kunnan* to know, be able — more at CAN, LAUD] **:** ART SONG
kunz·ite \'kůnt,sīt\ *n* -s [George F. *Kunz* †1932 Am. gem expert + E *-ite*] **:** a variety of spodumene that occurs in beautiful pinkish lilac crystals and is used as a gem
kuo-yü \'gwō'yüe\ *n* -s *usu cap* [Chin (Pek) *kuo²* *yü³*, lit., national language, fr. *kuo²* nation + *yü³* language] **:** a form of Mandarin taught in the schools and used in government
kupf·fer cell \'kůpfə(r)-\ *also* **kupf·fer's cell** *n*, *usu cap K* [after Karl Wilhelm von *Kupffer* †1903 Ger. anatomist] **:** a fixed histiocyte of the walls of the liver sinusoids that is stellate with large oval nucleus and the cytoplasm commonly packed with fragments resulting from phagocytic action
kupf·fer·ite \-fə,rīt\ *n* -s [ISV *kupffer-* (fr. Adolph T. *Kupffer* †1865 Russ. physicist) + *-ite*] **:** a green aluminous variety of amphibole
ku·phar \'küfə(r)\ *n* -s [Ar *quffah* basket] **:** GUFA
ku·ping tael \¦gü,piŋ-\ *n* [Chin (Pek) *k'u⁴* *p'ing²* treasury scale for silver (fr. *k'u⁴* treasury + *p'ing²* level, standard weight) + E *tael*] **:** the tael used for reckoning taxes and dues other than customs
kup·per \'kəpə(r)\ *n* -s [perh. fr. Sindhi *kapar*] **:** SAW-SCALED VIPER
ku·ra clover \kə'rä-, 'kůrə-\ *n*, *usu cap K* [perh. fr. *Kura*, river in Georgia and Azerbaidzhan, U.S.S.R.] **:** a perennial clover (*Trifolium ambiguum*) native to the Caucasus and Romania and introduced into America — called also *honey clover*, *pellett clover*
kurakkan *var of* KORAKAN
kur·bash *or* **kour·bash** *or* **cour·bash** *or* **cur·bash** \'ků(ə)r-,bash, -'-\ *n* -ES [Turk *kırbaç*] **:** a lash or whip of hide used as an instrument of punishment
kur·chee bark *or* **kur·chi bark** \'kůrchē-\ *n* [*kurchee*, *kurchi* perh. of Indic origin; akin to Skt *kūrca* beard, bunch, bundle of grass — more at QUILT] **:** a Tellicherry bark from a tree (*Holarrhena antidysenterica*) of the family Apocynaceae that contains conessine and other alkaloids
kurd \'ků(ə)rd, 'kərd\ *n* -s *usu cap* **1 :** one of a numerous pastoral and agricultural people inhabiting a large mountainous plateau region in adjoining parts of Turkey, Iran, Iraq, and Syria and in the Armenian and Azerbaidzhan sectors of the Soviet Caucasus **2 :** KURDISH
¹kurd·ish \-dish\ *adj*, *usu cap* **1 :** of, relating to, or characteristic of the region inhabited by the Kurds **2 :** of, relating to, or characteristic of the Kurds or their language
²kurdish \"\ *n* -ES *usu cap* **:** the Iranian language of the Kurds
kur·di·stan \¦kůrdə¦stan, ¦kər-; ¦kůrdə¦stän\ *n* -s *usu cap* [fr. *Kurdistan*, region inhabited by Kurds in Turkey in Asia, Iraq, and Iran] **:** one of the several varieties of rugs woven by the Kurds whose best examples are noted for fine colors and durability
ku·re \'k(y)ůrē, 'kü(,)rā\ *adj*, *usu cap* [fr. *Kure*, city in southwest Honshu, Japan] **:** of or from the city of Kure, Japan **:** of the kind or style prevalent in Kure
kur·gan \(')kü(ə)r¦gän\ *n* -s [Russ, of Turkic origin; akin to Turk *kurgan* fortress, castle] **:** a burial mound of eastern Europe or Siberia
ku·rie plot \'kyůrē-\ *n*, *usu cap K* [after F. N. D. *Kurie* *b*1907 Am. physicist] **:** a graphic means of comparing theoretical and observed momentum distributions in continuous beta-ray spectra
¹ku·ril·ian \k(y)ü'rilēən, -rēl-\ *adj*, *usu cap* [*Kuril* islands, group of islands south of Kamchatka belonging to the U.S.S.R. + E *-ian*, adj. suffix] **1 :** of, relating to, or characteristic of the Kuril islands **2 :** of, relating to, or characteristic of the people of the Kuril islands
²kurilian \"\ *n* -s *cap* [*Kuril* islands + E *-ian*, n. suffix] **:** a native or inhabitant of the Kuril islands
kurios *usu cap*, *var of* KYRIOS
kurk *var of* KIRK
kur·ku \'ků(ə)r(,)kü\ *n*, *pl* **kurku** *or* **kurkus** *usu cap* **:** KORKU
kur·mi \'kůrmē\ *also* **kum·ni** \'kůmnē\ *or* **kun·bi** \'kůmbē, -ůnbē\ *n* -s *usu cap* [Hindi *Kurmī*] **:** a member of an important agricultural caste distributed throughout India with the exception of the extreme south
kur·nai \'ků(ə)r,nī\ *n*, *pl* **kurnai** *or* **kurnais** *usu cap* **1 a :** a people of the southeastern coast of Australia living in permanent villages **b :** a member of such people **2 :** the language of the Kurnai people
kur·na·kov·ite \kůr'näkə,vīt\ *n* -s [Russ *kurnakovit*, fr. N. S. *Kurnakov* †1941 Russ. mineralogist + Russ *-it* -ite] **:** a mineral $Mg_2B_6O_{11}.13H_2O$ consisting of hydrous borate of magnesium
kur·ra·jong \'kərə,jöŋ, -jäŋ\ *also* **koo·ra·jong** \'kůr-\ *or* **cur·ra·jong** \'kər-\ *n* -s [native name in Australia] **:** any of certain Australian shrubs or trees esp. of the family Sterculiaceae that have strong tough bast fibers used by the aborigines for making cordage, nets, and matting **:** BOTTLE TREE: as **a :** FLAME TREE a(1) **b :** a widely distributed eastern Australian tree (*Brachychiton populneum*) with soft light attractively grained wood sometimes used for interior finish, flowers whitish without and red and yellow within, and foliage that is an important emergency food for cattle — compare GREEN KURRAJONG
kurrajong leaf roller *n* **:** the destructive larva of an Australian pyralidid moth (*Sylepta clytalis*) feeding on kurrajong foliage
kur·rol's salt \'kər¦ölz-, 'kůr¦\ *n*, *usu cap K* [perh. fr. the name *Kurrol*] **:** an insoluble sodium metaphosphate or potassium metaphosphate; *esp* **:** a fibrous crystalline sodium metaphosphate $NaPO_3$ IV formed by seeding a melt at 550° C
kursk \'ků(ə)rsk\ *adj*, *usu cap* [fr. *Kursk*, city in central part of European Russia, U.S.S.R.] **:** of or from the city of Kursk, U.S.S.R. **:** of the kind or style prevalent in Kursk
kur·to·rach·ic \¦kərd·ə¦rakik\ *adj* [*kurto-* (irreg. fr. Gk *kyrtos* bulging, convex) + *rach-* (fr. Gk *rhachis* spine) + *-ic* — more at CYRT-] **:** having the lumbar region of the spinal column concave dorsally
kur·to·sis \,kər'tōsəs\ *n* -ES [Gk *kyrtōsis* convexity, fr. *kyrtos* convex + *-ōsis* -osis] **:** the state or quality of peakedness or flatness of the graphic representation of a statistical distribution
ku·ru·ba \kə'rübə\ *n*, *pl* **kuruba** *or* **kurubas** *usu cap* **:** a member of a pastoral people in Mysore and other parts of southern India
ku·rukh \'kůrək\ *n*, *pl* **kurukh** *or* **kurukhs** *usu cap* **1 a :** a primitive people of central India who antedate the Dravidians in India — called also *Oraon* **b :** a member of such people **2 :** the Dravidian language of the Kurukh people
ku·ru·ma \'kürəmə\ *n* -s [Jap] **:** JINRIKISHA
ku·rum·ba \kə'rümbə\ *n*, *pl* **kurumba** *or* **kurumbas** *usu cap* **1 :** a member of a jungle people living on the slopes of the Nilgiri hills of southern India who are remnants of the oldest pre-Dravidian population of the Deccan **2 :** a member of a shepherd caste of southern India who are known for a variety of blanket that they weave
ku·ru·me azalea \'kürə,mā-\ *n*, *often cap K* [fr. *Kurume*, city in northern Kyushu, Japan] **:** any of certain garden azaleas of variable hardiness with white, pink, rose, scarlet, or lavender flowers originating in Japan chiefly by selection from or hybridization of a native Japanese azalea (*Rhododendron obtusum*) with hairy shoots and evergreen or deciduous leaves
ku·rus \kə'rüsh\ *n*, *pl* **kurus** [Turk *kuruş*] **:** a Turkish piaster equal to $^1/_{100}$ lira — see MONEY table
kur·vey \kə(r)'vā\ *vi* **kurveyed**; **kurveyed**; **kurveying**; **kurveys** [Afrik *karwei*, prob. fr. D *karweien* to do odd jobs, fr. *karwei* job, task, fr. MD *corweye* corvée, fr. MF *corvee* — more at CORVÉE] **:** to carry goods about in an ox wagon in southern Africa
kur·vey·or \-āə(r)\ *n* -s [modif. (influenced by E *-or*) of Afrik *karweier*, fr. *karwei* to kurvey + *-er* (fr. D, akin to OE *-ere* -er)] **:** a traveling trader in southern Africa who carries goods about in a large ox wagon
kus *pl of* KU
ku·sa *also* **ku·sha** \'kü(,)s(h)ä\ *n* -s [Hindi *kusā*, fr. Skt *kuśa*] **1 :** a grass (*Eragrostis cynosuroides*) of India used in Hindu ceremonies — called also *darbha* **2 :** KANS
ku·sai·an \(')kü¦sīən\ *n* -s *cap* [*Kusaie*, island in the eastern Caroline islands + E *-an*, n. suffix] **:** a Micronesian native or inhabitant of Kusaie in the eastern Caroline islands
ku·sam \'kü,sam\ *n* -s [origin unknown] **:** a tree (*Schleichera oleosa*) of the family Sapindaceae that grows in dry forests of southeastern Asia, has pinnate leaves, apetalous flowers, and dry fruits surrounded by pulpy arils and that yields a hard heavy reddish brown timber and from its seeds an oil that is used locally for cooking, illumination, and medicine — see MACASSAR OIL
ku·san \'küsᵊn\ *n*, *pl* **kusan** *or* **kusans** *usu cap* **1 a :** an Indian people of Oregon **b :** a member of such people **2 :** a language family in western Oregon including Coos
ku·shan \'kü,shän\ *n*, *pl* **kushan** *or* **kushans** *usu cap* **:** a Saka people invading India from central Asia, formerly having a ruling house with control extending over northwest India, much of present-day west Pakistan, and the Ganges valley to Benares, and eventually becoming absorbed as Kshatriyas or Sudras
ku·si·man·se \,küsə'man(t)sə\ *or* **ku·si·man·sel** \-səl\ *n* -s [prob. native name in Liberia] **:** a small dark brown burrowing carnivorous mammal that is a native of West Africa and related to the mongoose
¹kuskus *var of* KHUSKHUS
²kus·kus \'kü,sküs\ *var of* COUSCOUS
kuss·maul breathing \'kü,smaül-\ *or* **kussmaul respiration** *n*, *usu cap K* [after Adolf *Kussmaul* †1902 Ger. physician] **:** abnormally slow deep respiration characteristic of air hunger and occurring esp. in acidotic states
kus·ti \'kü(,)stē, -'-\ *n* -s [Per *kustī*, *kushtī*, fr. *kusht* waist, side, fr. MPer *kust*, *kustak*] **:** the sacred cord or girdle worn by Parsis as a mark of their faith — compare SACRED SHIRT
ku·su \'kü(,)sü\ *n* -s [origin unknown] **:** any of several African striped mice
ku·sum \kə'süm\ *n* -s [Hindi, fr. Skt *kusumbha*] *India* **:** SAFFLOWER
kutch *var of* CUTCH
kutcha *or* **ka·cha** *or* **kach·cha** \'kəchə\ *adj* [Hindi *kaccā*] **:** being in a crude or raw state **:** MAKESHIFT, UNFINISHED ⟨where they cannot get a pukka railway, they take a ~ one —Lord Elgin⟩
ku·tchin \kü'chin\ *n*, *pl* **kutchin** *or* **kutchins** *usu cap* **1 a :** an Athapaskan people of the Yukon and Mackenzie river valleys, Alaska and northwestern Canada **b :** a member of such people **2 :** a language of the Kutchin people — called also *Loucheux*
ku·te·nai *or* **ku·te·nay** *also* **koo·te·nai** \'küt'n,ā, -t(,)nā, -tnē\ *n*, *pl* **kutenai** *or* **kutenais** *or* **kutenay** *or* **kutenays** *usu cap* **1 a :** a people of the Rocky mountains on both sides of the U.S.–Canada boundary **b :** a member of such people **2 :** the Kitunahan language of the Kutenai people
ku·ti·ra gum *also* **ku·tee·ra gum** \kə'tirə-\ *n* [Hindi *katīrā*] **:** any of several sterculia gums
kut·na·ho·rite \,kətnə'hör,īt, ,kůt-\ *n* -s [G *kutnahorit*, fr. *Kutná Hora*, western Czechoslovakia, its locality + G *-it* -ite] **:** a mineral $Ca(Mn,Mg,Fe)CO_3$ that consists of a carbonate of calcium, manganese, magnesium, and iron and that is isomorphous with either dolomite or calcite
kut·tar \kə'tär\ *n* -s [Hindi *kaṭār*, fr. Skt (prob. Prakrit) *kaṭṭāra*, fr. Skt *kartati* he cuts — more at SHEAR] **:** a short dagger used in India with a handle consisting of two parallel bars joined by a crosspiece that is gripped with the hand

kuttar

ku·vasz \'kü,väs, 'kü,-\ *n* [Hung, fr. Turk *kavas* armed constable, guard, doorkeeper, fr. Ar *qawwās* bowman] **1** *usu cap* **:** a long-established Hungarian breed of tall and light-footed but sturdy white dogs **2** *pl* **ku·va·szok** \-vä,sök\ *often cap* **:** any dog of the Kuvasz breed used for centuries as guard and hunting dogs
ku·wait \kə'wāt\ *adj*, *usu cap* [fr. *Kuwait*, country on the Persian gulf] **:** of or from the country of Kuwait **:** of the kind or style prevalent in Kuwait
¹ku·wai·ti \-wād·ē\ *adj*, *usu cap* [Ar *kuwaytīy*, fr. *Kuwayt* Kuwait] **1 :** of, relating to, or characteristic of Kuwait, a country on the Persian gulf **2 :** of, relating to, or characteristic of the people of Kuwait
²kuwaiti \"\ *n* -s *cap* **:** a native or inhabitant of Kuwait
ku·yo·non \'küyō,nän\ *n*, *pl* **kuyonon** *or* **kuyononons** *usu cap* [Kuyonon, fr. *Kuyo* Cuyo, island in the central Philippines + Kuyonon *-non* people, language] **1 a :** a Christianized people inhabiting Cuyo and eastern Palawan islands and parts of other islands in the northern Sulu sea **b :** a member of such people **2 :** an Austronesian language of the Kuyonon people
kv *abbr* kilovolt
kva *abbr* kilovolt-ampere
kvah *abbr* kilovolt-ampere-hour
kvar *abbr* kilovar
kvarh *abbr* kilovar-hour
kvass *also* **kvas** \kə'väs, 'kfäs\ *or* **quass** *or* **quas** \", 'kwäs\ *n* -ES [Russ *kvas*; akin to OSlav *kvasŭ* sour drink — more at CHEESE] **:** a weak homemade beer of Eastern European countries (as Russia) made by pouring warm water over a mixture of cereals and allowing it to ferment
kvu·tzah *or* **kvu·tza** \kə,vüt'sä, -'-\ *n*, *pl* **kvu·tzoth** *or* **kvu·tzot** \-sōt(h), -sōs\ *also* **kvutzahs** *or* **kvutzas** [NHeb *qəbhūṣāh* (pl. *qəbhūṣōth*), fr. Heb, group, gathering] **:** a Jewish communal and cooperative farm or settlement in Israel that is usu. smaller than a kibbutz and established on state-owned land
kw *abbr* kilowatt
kwa \'kwä\ *n*, *pl* **kwa** *usu cap* **:** a branch of the Niger-Congo language family that contains the Akan languages and Agni, Ga, Fon, Ewe, Yoruba, Ibo, Edo, and Nupe, and less certainly Kru, Bassa, and Grebo and that is spoken along the coast and a short distance inland from Liberia to Nigeria
kwa·ki·utl \¦kwäkē¦(y)üdᵊl, (')kwä¦k(y)ü-\ *n*, *pl* **kwakiutl** *or* **kwakiutls** *usu cap* **1 a :** a Wakashan people on both shores of Queen Charlotte Sound and on northern Vancouver Island **b :** a member of such people **2 :** the language of the Kwakiutl people
kwal·hi·o·qua \,kwäl(h)ē'ōkwə\ *n*, *pl* **kwalhioqua** *or* **kwalhioquas** *usu cap* **1 :** an Athapaskan people of southwestern Washington **2 :** a member of the Kwalhioqua people
kwang·ju \'gwaŋ¦jü, 'kw-\ *adj*, *usu cap* [fr. *Kwangju*, Korea] **:** of or from the city of Kwangju, Korea **:** of the kind or style prevalent in Kwangju
kwang·tung ware \'gwäŋ¦dùŋ-, 'kw-, -¦tùŋ-\ *n*, *usu cap K* [fr. *Kwangtung*, province in southeast China] **:** a Chinese porcelanous stoneware that possibly originated in Sung times varying from almost white to dark brown or red and usu. having a variegated glaze
kwapa *usu cap*, *var of* QUAPAW
kwa·shi·or·kor \¦kwäshē¦örkər, -ē,ör¦kō(ə)r\ *n* -s [native name in Ghana] **:** severe malnutrition in infants and children that is characterized by failure to grow and develop, changes in the pigmentation of the skin and hair, edema, fatty degeneration of the liver, anemia, and apathy and is caused by a diet excessively high in carbohydrate and extremely low in protein

kwa·tu·ma \kwä'tümə\ *n* -s [native name in southern Africa] **:** any of several moray eels (genus *Lycodontis*) of southern Africa

kwa·zo·ku \'kwäzō,kü, kwä'zō(,)kü\ *n, pl* **kwazoku** [Jap] **:** the class of nobility of both civil and feudal origin in the Japanese social scale — compare HEIMIN, SHIZOKU

kweek \'kwāk\ *n* -s [Afrik, fr. D, couch grass; akin to OE *cwice* couch grass — more at QUITCH] **1** *southern Africa* **:** a grass of the genus *Cynodon* **2** *also* **kweekgrass** \'=,=\ *southern Africa* **:** COUCH GRASS 1a

kwei·lin \'gwā¦lin, 'kw-\ *adj, usu cap* [fr. *Kweilin*, city in southeast China] **:** of or from the city of Kweilin, China **:** of the kind or style prevalent in Kweilin

kwei·yang \'gwā¦yäŋ, 'kw-\ *adj, usu cap* [fr. *Kweiyang*, city in southern China] **:** of or from the city of Kweiyang, China **:** of the kind or style prevalent in Kweiyang

kwe·ni \'kwānē\ *n, pl* **kweni** *or* **kwenis** *usu cap* **:** GURO

kwe·ri *also* **kwiri** \'kwirē\ *n* -s *usu cap* **:** a people of the southern British Cameroons

kwh *abbr* kilowatt-hour

kwo·ma \'kwōmə\ *n, pl* **kwoma** *or* **kwomas** *usu cap* **1 a :** a Papuan people of the Sepik district, Territory of New Guinea **b :** a member of such people **2 :** the language of the Kwoma

kyabooka *also* **kya-bouka** *var of* KIABOOCA

ky·ack \'kī,ak *also* -ī,yak\ *n* -s [origin unknown] **:** a packsack to be swung on either side of a packsaddle

kyah \kē'(y)ä\ *n* -s [Beng] **:** an Indian partridge (*Francolinus gularis*) having a strong spur

kyak *var of* KAYAK

kyang *var of* KIANG

kyanite *var of* CYANITE

ky·a·nize \'kīə,nīz\ *vt* -ED/-ING/-S [fr. John H. *Kyan* †1850 Eng. inventor + E *-ize*] **:** to preserve (wood) by steeping in a solution of corrosive sublimate

kyat \kē'(y)ät\ *n* -s [Burmese] **1 :** the basic monetary unit of Burma established in 1952 — see MONEY table **2 :** a coin representing one kyat

kyathos *var of* CYATHUS

kybosh *var of* KIBOSH

kye \'kī\ *n pl* [ME *ky*, fr. OE *cȳ* — more at COW] *now dial* **:** KINE

kyle \'kī(ə)l\ *n* -s [ScGael *caol*, fr. *caol* narrow; akin to OIr *cōil*, *cōel* narrow, Latvian *kaîls* naked, bald] *Scot* **:** CHANNEL, SOUND, STRAIT ⟨at the widening mouth of the ~ —David Innes⟩

ky·lie *or* **ki·ley** \'kīlē\ *n, pl* **kylies** *or* **kileys** [native name in Australia] **:** an Australian boomerang having one side flat and the other convex

ky·lin \'kē'lin\ *n* -s [modif. of Chin (Pek) *ch'i²* *lin²*, fr. *ch'i²* male kylin + *lin²* female kylin] **:** a unicorn of Chinese myth depicted with the tail of an ox and the legs and body of a deer — see FÊNG HUANG

ky·lix \'kīliks, 'kil-\ *or* **cy·lix** \'sīl-,'sil-\ *n, pl* **kyl·i·kes** \'kilə,kēz\ *or* **cyl·i·ces** \'sil-\ [Gk *kylix;* akin to Gk *kalyx* calyx — more at CHALICE] **:** a drinking cup that has two looped handles on a shallow bowl set upon a slender center foot

kylix

ky·loe \'kī(,)lō\ *n* -s *usu cap* [origin unknown] **:** WEST HIGHLAND

kym- *or* **kymo-** — see CYM-

ky·mat·i·on \kī'mad·ē,än, kə'-\ *var of* CYMATIUM

kym·ba·lon \'kimbə,län\ *n* -s [Gk — more at CYMBAL] **:** CYMBAL 1a

ky·mo·gram \'kīmə,gram\ *n* [ISV *cym-* + *-gram*] **:** a record made by a kymograph

ky·mo·graph \-raf,-ráf\ *or* **cy·mo·graph** \'sī-\ *n* [ISV *cym-* + *-graph*] **1 :** a recording device including an electric motor or clockwork that drives a usu. slowly revolving drum which carries a roll of plain or smoked paper and also having an arrangement for tracing on the paper by means of a stylus a graphic record of motion or pressure (as of the organs of speech, blood pressure, or respiration) often in relation to particular intervals of time **2 :** a device for recording on a moving X-ray film the motion of an organ (as the heart) by means of a series of still images — **ky·mo·graph·ic** \¦==-¦grafik\ *adj*

ky·mog·ra·phy \kī'mägrəfē\ *n* -ES [ISV *cym-* + *-graphy*] **:** the making of kymographic records

kymric *usu cap, var of* CYMRIC

kyn·uren·ic acid \¦ki|nyə¦renik-, ¦kī|\ *n* [*kynurenic* ISV *kyn-* (fr. Gk *kyn-*, *kyōn* dog) + *-uren-* (irreg. fr. Gk *ouron* urine) + *-ic* — more at HOUND, URINE] **:** a crystalline acid $C_9H_5N(OH)COOH$ occurring in the urine of dogs and other animals as one of the normal products of tryptophan metabolism

kyn·uren·ine \,=='re,nēn, -,nən\ *n* -s [ISV *kynuren-* (fr. *kynurenic*) + *-ine*] **:** an amino acid $NH_2C_6H_4COCH_2CH(NH_2)COOH$ occurring in the urine of various animals as one of the normal products of tryptophan metabolism and capable of forming kynurenic acid and other products; 3-anthranoyl-alanine

ky·oo·dle \(')kī¦(y)üdᵊl\ *vi* **kyoodled**; **kyoodled**; **kyoodling** \-d(ᵊ)liŋ\ **kyoodles** [imit.] **:** to make loud useless noises **:** HOLLER, YAP ⟨the dogs waved their tails happily and sought out a rabbit and went *kyoodling* after it —John Steinbeck⟩ ⟨quit listening to all this *kyoodling* from behind the fence —Sinclair Lewis⟩

kyo·to \kē'(y)ōd·(,)ō, -ō(,)tō *sometimes* 'kyō-\ *adj, usu cap* [fr. *Kyoto*, city in west central Honshu, Japan] **:** of or from the city of Kyoto, Japan **:** of the kind or style prevalent in Kyoto

ky·pho·scoliosis \¦kī(,)fō+\ *n, pl* **kyphoscolioses** [NL, fr. *kypho-* (fr. *kyphosis*) + *scoliosis*] **:** backward and lateral curvature of the spine

ky·pho·scoliotic \"+\ *adj* [fr. NL *kyphoscoliosis*, after such pairs as NL *hypnosis:* E *hypnotic*] **:** of, relating to, or marked by kyphoscoliosis

ky·phos·i·dae \kī'fäsə,dē\ *n pl, cap* [NL, fr. *Kyphosus*, type genus + *-idae*] **:** a family of chiefly tropical percoid shore fishes resembling bass and including a number of important herbivorous food fishes — see KYPHOSUS, RUDDERFISH

ky·pho·sis \kī'fōsəs\ *n, pl* **kypho·ses** \-ō,sēz\ [NL, fr. Gk *kyphōsis*, fr. *kyphos* humpbacked, bent + *-ōsis* -osis — more at CYPHELLA] **1 :** abnormal backward curvature of the spine — opposed to *lordosis* **2 :** the state of one who is affected with kyphosis — **ky·phot·ic** \(')=¦fäd·ik\ *adj*

ky·pho·sus \kī'fōsəs\ *n, cap* [NL, fr. Gk *kyphos* + L *-osus* -ose] **:** a genus that includes the Bermuda chub and is the type of the family Kyphosidae

kyr·i·a·le \,kirē'ä(,)lā\ *also* **kyr·i·al** \'kirēəl\ *n* -s *usu cap* [NL *kyriale*, fr. *kyrie* + ML *-ale* (as in *missale* missal)] **:** a liturgical book containing the text and plainsong notation of the parts of the ordinary of the mass (as the Kyrie, Sanctus, Agnus Dei) that are sung by the congregation

ky·rie elei·son \¦kirē,āə'lā(ə),sän, -lāsᵊn,-lāəsən, *in rapid speech* ,kirēə'l-\ *or* **kyrie** \'kirē,ā\ *n, pl* **kyrie eleisons** *or* **kyries** *often cap K&E* [*kyrie eleison* fr. LL, fr. Gk *Kyrie eleēson* Lord, have mercy; *kyrie* fr. NL, fr. LL *kyrie eleison*] **1 :** a petitionary invocation (as in the ordinary of the mass and in the breviary) addressed to the Trinity and beginning with the words "kyrie eleison" **2 :** either of two Anglican liturgical responses beginning with the words "Lord, have mercy upon us": **a :** one accompanying the decalogue **b :** one following the summary of the Law

kyr·i·elle \¦kirē¦el\ *n, pl* **kyrielle** [F, fr. OF *kyriele*, lit., kyrie eleison, fr. LL *kyrie eleison*] **:** a French verse form in short usu. octosyllabic rhyming couplets often paired in quatrains and characterized by a refrain which is sometimes a single word or sometimes the full second line of the couplet or fourth line of the quatrain

ky·ri·os \'kirē,äs\ *also* **ku·ri·os** \'kůr-\ *n, pl* **kyri·oi** \-ē,ȯi\ *or* **kyrios·es** \-ē,äsəz\ *also* **kuri·oi** *or* **kurios·es** *usu cap* [Gk *kyrios* lord, master, fr. *kyros* power, might — more at CURIOLOGIC] **:** LORD ⟨early Christians confessed Jesus Christ as their ~ instead of the emperor⟩

kyte \'kīt\ *n* -s [prob. fr. LG *küt* bowel; akin to MD *cuy* calf of the leg, *cuut* fish roe, MLG *kūt* calf of the leg, fish roe, G dial. (Bavarian) *kütz* part of the entrails, Skt *guda* bowel — more at COT] *chiefly Scot* **:** STOMACH, BELLY ⟨sit down and fill your ~ —R.L.Stevenson⟩

kythe *var of* KITHE

kyu·rin \kyə'rēn\ *n, pl* **kyurin** *or* **kyurins** *usu cap* **:** a member of a Lezghian people of the Caucasus mountains

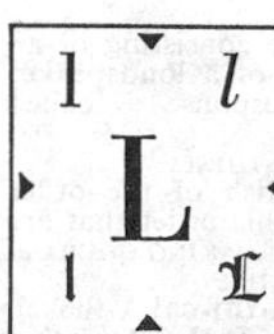

¹l \ˈel\ *n, pl* **l's** *or* **ls** *often cap, often attrib* **1 a :** the 12th letter of the English alphabet **b :** an instance of this letter printed, written, or otherwise represented **c :** a speech counterpart of orthographic *l* (as clear *l* in *lean* or Polish *lipa,* dark *l* in *cool* and Polish *łapa*) **2 :** 50 — see NUMBER table **3 :** a printer's type, a stamp, or some other instrument for reproducing the letter *l* **4 :** someone or something arbitrarily or conveniently designated *l* esp. as the 11th or when j is used for the 10th the 12th in order or class **5 :** something having the shape of the capital letter L: as **a :** ²ELL 2 **b :** ²ELL 3 **6 :** ELEVATED RAILROAD ⟨riding on the *L*⟩ ⟨an *L* train⟩

²l *abbr, often cap* **1** lady **2** lake **3** lambert **4** land **5** landing **6** landplane **7** large **8** lat **9** late **10** Latin **11** latitude **12** launch **13** law **14** leaf **15** league **16** learner **17** leather **18** leave **19** left **20** legitimate **21** lempira **22** length **23** letter **24** leu **25** lev **26** lewisite **27** [L *lex*] law **28** liaison **29** [L *liber*] book **30** Liberal **31** [L *libra*] pound **32** licentiate **33** lift **34** light **35** lightning **36** line **37** liner **38** link **39** liquid **40** lira **41** lit **42** liter **43** [L *loco*] in the place; [L *locus*] place **44** lodge **45** long **46** longitude **47** lord **48** lost **49** low **50** lumen

³l *symbol, cap* **1** *ital* inductance **2** *ital* kinetic potential

l- \in sense 1 ˌlē(ˌ)vō or ˌel, in sense 2 ˌel\ *prefix* [ISV, fr. *lev-*] **1 :** levorotatory — usu. printed in italic ⟨*l*-tartaric acid⟩; compare LEV- **2 :** having a similar configuration at a selected carbon atom in an optically active molecule to the configuration of levorotatory glyceraldehyde — usu. printed as a small capital ⟨L-fructose⟩

¹la \ˈlä\ *n* -s [ME, fr. ML, fr. L *labii* lip's, a word sung to this note in a medieval hymn to St. John the Baptist] **1 :** the sixth tone of the diatonic scale in solmization **2 :** the tone A in the fixed-do system

²la \ˈlō, ˈlä\ *interj* [ME (northern dial.), fr. OE *lā*] **1** *now chiefly dial* — used for emphasis ⟨indeed, ~, 'tis a noble child —Shak.⟩ ⟨~! Yes, I've heard tell about that old mortar —*Ford Times*⟩ **2** *now chiefly dial* — used to express surprise ⟨~ . . . how very smirking —Charles Dickens⟩

³la \ˈlä\ *adj, usu cap* [F, fem. of *le,* def. art., the, fr. L *ille* that one, that — more at LARIAT]: THE — used with the family name of a woman ⟨shrugged elaborately — a crib . . . from *La* Dietrich —Nicholas Monsarrat⟩

la *abbr* last

LA *abbr* **1** landing account **2** law agent **3** leading aircraftsman **4** legislative assembly **5** letter of authority **6** library association **7** lighter than air **8** lightning arrester **9** local agent **10** local authority **11** low altitude

La *symbol* lanthanum

LAA *abbr* light antiaircraft

laad \ˈläd\ *Scot var of* LAD

¹laa·ger \ˈlägə(r)\ *n* -s [obs. Afrik *lager* (now, *laer*), fr. G, camp, couch, lair, fr. OHG *legar* couch, lair — more at LAIR] **1** *Africa* **:** CAMP; *esp* **:** a travelers' encampment protected by a circle of wagons **2 :** a military encampment or defensive position protected by a ring of armored vehicles

²laager \ˈ"\ *vi* -ED/-ING/-S **:** to form or camp in a laager **:** ENCAMP

laag·te \ˈläktə\ *n* -s [Afrik, fr. *laag* low; akin to ON *lāgr* low — more at LOW] *Africa* **:** a usu. relatively wide and level valley in the veld

laap *var of* LERP

laa·ven,nīt \ˈlävə,nīt\ *also* **lav·en·ite** \ˈlav-\ *n* -s [Norw *låvenit,* fr. *Låven,* island in the Langesund fiord, Norway + Norw *-it* -ite] **:** a mineral consisting of a complex silicate of zirconium, calcium, manganese, and sometimes other elements occurring in prismatic crystals

¹lab \ˈlab, -aa(ə)b\ *n* -s [ME *labbe,* fr. *labben* to blab] *archaic* **:** ¹BLAB 1

²lab \ˈ"\ *n* -s [by shortening] **:** LABORATORY

lab *abbr* labor

lab·a·dism \ˈlabə,dizəm\ *n* -s *usu cap* [F *labadisme,* fr. Jean de *Labadie* †1674 Fr. religious reformer + F *-isme* -ism] **:** the doctrines and practices of Labadists

¹lab·a·dist \-ˌdəst\ *n* -s *usu cap* [Jean de *Labadie* †1674 + E *-ist*] **:** a member of a communistic sect of radical Pietists of the 17th and 18th centuries emphasizing spiritual rebirth and the inner illumination of the Holy Spirit as religious necessities

²labadist \ˈ"\ *adj, usu cap* **:** of or relating to Labadists or to their doctrines and practices

la bamba \lä-\ *n* -s *often cap L&B* [AmerSp, the bamba] **:** BAMBA

la·ban system \ˈläbən-\ *n, usu cap L* [after Rudolf *Laban* †1958 Swiss dancing instructor] **:** a method of recording bodily movement (as in a dance) on a staff by means of direction and other symbols that can be aligned with musical accompaniment — see ICOSAHEDRON

la·ba·ria \ləˈbärēə\ *also* **la·bar·ri** \-rē\ *or* **la·bar·ria** *or* **la·ba·rea** \-rēə\ *n* -s [AmerSp *labaria*] **:** a So. American venomous snake variously identified as a coral snake or any of several pit vipers

la·bar·raque's solution \ˌlabəˈrak(s)-\ *n, usu cap L* [after Antoine G. *Labarraque* †1850 Fr. chemist and pharmacist] **:** JAVELLE WATER b

lab·a·rum \ˈlabərəm\ *n* -s [LL] **1 :** an imperial standard of the later Roman emperors resembling the vexillum; *esp* **:** the standard adopted by Constantine after his conversion to Christianity consisting of a purple silk banner hanging from a crosspiece on a pike and surmounted by a golden crown bearing the chi-rho **2 :** any symbolical standard or banner

lab·ba \ˈlabə\ *n* -s [of Arawakan origin; akin to Arawak *labba* paca] **:** PACA

lab·ber \ˈlabə(r)\ *vb* -ED/-ING/-S [perh. of imit. origin] *dial Eng* **:** SPLASH, WET

lab·da·num \ˈlabdənəm\ *or* **lad·a·num** \-adᵊn-\ *n* -s [ML *lapdanum,* fr. L *ladanum, ledanum,* fr. Gk *ladanon, lēdanon,* fr. *lēdon* rockrose, of Sem origin] **:** a soft blackish brown to greenish oleoresin that is obtained from various rockroses (as *Cistus ladanum, C. creticus*), has a fragrant odor and bitter taste, and is used in perfumes esp. as a fixative

-labe \ˌlāb *sometimes* ˌlab *or* ˌlaa(ə)b\ *n comb form* -s [ME, fr. MF, fr. ML *-labium,* fr. LGk *-labion,* dim. of Gk *-labos* (fr. *lambanein* to take) — more at LEMMA] **:** instrument **:** implement ⟨cosmolabe⟩

lab·e·fac·tion \ˌlabəˈfakshən\ *n* -s [LL *labefaction-, labefactio,* fr. L *labefactus* (past part. of *labefacere* to cause to totter, shake, fr. *labare* to totter + *facere* to make) + *-ion-, -io* -ion] **:** a weakening or impairment esp. of moral principles or civil order **:** DOWNFALL, OVERTHROW

¹la·bel \ˈlābəl\ *n* -s *often attrib* [ME fr. MF, fr. OF *label* ribbon, fringe, label in heraldry, prob. of Gmc origin; akin to OHG *lappa* flap, lappet — more at LAP] **1** *archaic* **:** a narrow piece (as of cloth) **:** STRIP, RIBBON, LAPPET; *specif* **:** one attached to a document to hold an appended seal **2** *obs* **:** a rider or appendix orig. appended to a document on an attached strip **3 :** a heraldic charge consisting of a narrow bar with usu. three pendants and used esp. as a cadency mark to distinguish an eldest or only son during his father's life — called also *file* **4 :** a representation (as in medieval art) of a band or scroll containing an inscription **5 a :** a slip (as of paper, parchment, cloth, leather, metal) that is inscribed and affixed to something for identification, direction, or description **:** TAG, STICKER ⟨write your name on the ~ and tie it to the basket⟩ ⟨books with gilt-lettered red morocco ~s⟩ **b :** written, printed, or graphic matter attached to or accompanying an article or inscribed on its container or wrapper identifying the contents or giving other appropriate information (as the destination of a parcel, the use of a medicine, the title of a book) ⟨read the ~ on the bottle⟩ **c :** a descriptive, classifying, or identifying word or phrase: as (1) **:** EPITHET ⟨the term stream of consciousness . . . is already established as a literary ~ —Robert Humphrey⟩ ⟨acquired the ~ of "playboy" which seemed to stick —Brian Crozier⟩ ⟨hanging the subversive ~ on their own liberal clergy —Ralph Winnett⟩ (2) **:** a word or phrase used with but not as part of a dictionary definition usu. in abbreviated form and distinctive type to provide information (as grammatical function or area or level of usage) about the word defined ⟨the ~ *obsolete* is abbreviated *obs*⟩ (3) **:** a newspaper headline merely identifying the subject matter of an article rather than summarizing action **6 :** a projecting molding by the sides and over the top of an opening; *specif* **:** a dripstone of square form characteristic of late Gothic work in England **7 :** an adhesive stamp: **a :** POSTAGE STAMP **b :** a stamp issued for some purpose (as revenue, notification of postage due) other than postage **8 :** PANEL 3f(3) **9 :** a labeled atom in a molecule **10 a** (1) **:** a brand of commercial recordings issued under a usu. trademarked name ⟨there are now available to record buyers more than 10,000 different ~s —Joel Turner⟩ ⟨from the Decca group we have, on the parent ~, Liszt's "Faust" Symphony —Thomas Heinitz⟩ (2) **:** one of the commercial recordings so issued ⟨issue . . . compositions first on classical ~s and then as "pops" singles —*Current Biog.*⟩ **b :** a company issuing commercial recordings under one or more brand names ⟨spent practically their entire recording careers with one ~ —J.S.Wilson b. 1913⟩ ⟨most of the recordings made by these jazzmen were for small ~s —Bill Simon⟩

²label \ˈ"\ *vt* **labeled** *or* **labelled; labeled** *or* **labelled; labeling** *or* **labelling** \-b(ə)liŋ\ **labels 1 :** to give a label to: **a :** to affix a label to **:** mark with a label ⟨~ a bottle⟩ **b :** to describe or designate with a label ⟨subdivides his discussions . . . by sections ~*ed* with numerals and letters —Robert Halsband⟩ ⟨many girls ~*ed* "bad" turned out to be . . . mentally ill —Marjorie Rittwagen⟩ **2 a :** to distinguish (an element or atom) by using a radioactive isotope or an isotope of unusual mass for tracing through chemical reactions or biological processes ⟨the distribution of ~*ed* phosphorus [radiophosphorus] in a moth larva —E.O.Lawrence⟩ **b :** to distinguish (as a compound or molecule) esp. by introducing a labeled atom ⟨glycine ~*ed* with carbon 14 in the carboxyl group⟩

label clause *or* **labels clause** *n* **:** a clause in marine insurance limiting the liability of the assurer when only labels, capsules, or wrappers are damaged to the cost of reconditioning to an amount not exceeding the insured value of the goods

la·bel·er *or* **la·bel·ler** \-b(ə)lə(r)\ *n* -s **:** one that labels; *esp* **:** one who labels (as a product) by hand or by machine

la·bel·late \ləˈbe,lāt\ *adj* [NL *labellum* + E *-ate*] **:** having a labellum

la·bel·loid \-lȯid\ *adj* [NL *labellum* + E *-oid*] **:** resembling a labellum

la·bel·lum \ləˈbeləm\ *n, pl* **labella** \-lə\ [NL, fr. L, small lip, dim. of *labrum* lip — more at LIP] **1 :** the median membrane of the corolla of an orchid often differing markedly from the other two petals in shape and size, occasionally spurred, and while morphologically inner becoming by torsion of the ovary the outer or lower member **2 a :** a prolongation of the labrum of various beetles and true bugs that covers the basal part of the rostrum **b :** either of a pair of sensitive fleshy lobes in two-winged flies that terminate the proboscis sheath and consist of the expanded end of the elongated labium

labels *pl of* LABEL, *pres 3d sing of* LABEL

label stop *n* **:** a finishing boss at either end of a label, sill, or sill course

-labes *pl of* -LABE

labia *pl of* LABIUM

¹la·bi·al \ˈlābēəl\ *adj* [ML *labialis,* fr. L *labium* lip + *-alis* -al — more at LIP] **1 :** of or relating to the lips or labia ⟨a ~ gland⟩ ⟨a ~ scale⟩ **2 :** giving its tones from impact of an air current on a lip or liplike edge ⟨a ~ instrument like the flute⟩ **3 :** produced with the participation of one or both lips — used of consonants (as \f\, \v\, \p\, \b\) and of rounded vowels (as \ü\) and semivowels (as \w\) — compare BILABIAL, LABIODENTAL

²labial \ˈ"\ *n* -s **1 :** FLUE PIPE **2 :** a labial consonant **3 :** one of the small scales that border the lips of most snakes and many other reptiles

labial gland *n* **1 :** one of the small tubular mucous and serous glands lying beneath the mucous membrane of the lips **2 :** one of the glands opening at the base of the labium of insects usu. functioning as salivary glands but in some groups producing silk or some other substance

la·bi·al·i·ty \ˌlābēˈaləd·ē\ *n* -ES **:** the quality or state of being labial

la·bi·al·iza·tion \ˌlābēələˈzāshən\ *n* -s [¹*labial* + *-ization*] **:** the action or result of labializing **:** ROUNDING

la·bi·al·ize \ˈlābēə,līz\ *vt* -ED/-ING/-S [¹*labial* + *-ize*] **:** to make labial: **a :** ROUND 1c(2) **b :** to replace with a sound that is labial ⟨in Spanish *auto,* from Latin *actus,* a velar stop has been *labialized*⟩

la·bi·al·ly \ˈlābēəlē, -li\ *adv* **:** in a labial manner **:** with or by means of the lips

labial palp *n* **:** a palp of a bivalve mollusk

labial palpus *n* [part trans. of NL *palpus labialis*] **:** either of the jointed appendages on the front of the mentum of an insect — see INSECT illustration

labial stop *n* **:** a pipe-organ stop composed of labial pipes

labial teeth *n pl* **:** the incisor and canine teeth

la·bia ma·jo·ra \ˈlābēəməˈjōrə, -jȯrə\ *n pl* [NL, lit., larger lips] **:** the outer fatty folds bounding the vulva

labia mi·no·ra \-məˈnōrə, -nȯrə\ *n pl* [NL, lit., smaller lips] **:** the inner highly vascular largely connective-tissue folds bounding the vulva

la·bi·a·tae \ˌlābēˈā,tē\ *n pl* [NL, fr. fem. pl. of *labiatus* labiate] *cap* **:** a family of mostly aromatic herbs, shrubs, or rarely trees (order Polemoniales) distinguished esp. by the four-lobed ovary which becomes four one-seeded nutlets in fruit — see MINT

¹la·bi·ate \ˈlābēət, -ē,āt, *usu* -d·+V\ *adj* [NL *labiatus,* fr. L *labium* lip + *-atus* -ate — more at LIP] **1 :** having lips **:** LIPPED: **a :** having the limb of a tubular corolla or calyx divided into two unequal parts projecting one over the other like the lips of a mouth (as in the snapdragon, sage, catnip) **b** *anat* **:** having thickened fleshy margins **2 :** belonging to the Labiatae

²la·bi·ate \ˈlābē,āt\ *n* -s [NL *Labiatae*] **:** a plant of the Labiatae

labiate bear *n* [prob. trans. of NL *Ursus labiatus;* fr. its prominent lips] **:** SLOTH BEAR

la·bi·at·ed \ˈlābē,ād·əd\ *adj* **:** LABIATE

lab·i·dog·na·tha \ˌlabəˈdägnəthə\ [NL, fr. Gk *labid-, labis* handle, forceps + NL *-gnatha*] *syn of* ARANEAE VERAE

la·bi·el·la \ˌlabēˈelə\ *n, pl* **labiel·lae** \-e(ˌ)lē\ [NL, dim. of L *labium* lip] **:** HYPOPHARYNX

la·bile \ˈlābəl, ˈlā,bīl *also* -,bel\ *adj* [ME *labyl,* fr. MF *labile,* fr. LL *labilis* fleeting, transient, apt to slip, fr. L *labi* to slip, fall + *-ilis* -ile — more at SLEEP] **1** *obs* **:** prone to slip, err, or lapse **2** [F, fr. MF] **:** characterized by a ready tendency toward or capability for change **:** CHANGEABLE, UNSTABLE ⟨an emotionally ~ patient⟩ **:** ADAPTABLE ⟨has so ~ a face that some of her scenes . . . rock with emotion —Manny Farber⟩ **3 :** readily or continually undergoing chemical or physical or biological change or breakdown (as in the presence of a specified factor) ⟨heat-*labile* and heat-stable antigens⟩ ⟨the germinative plasma of the eggs is ~, producing under the influence of various conditions of nourishment different results —Auguste Lameere⟩ ⟨~ diabetes⟩ **:** fluctuating widely ⟨~ blood pressure in hypertensives⟩: as **a :** readily undergoing cleavage or molecular rearrangement or other chemical modification ⟨one of the chlorine atoms is readily removed as hydrogen chloride and is termed ~ or hydrolyzable chlorine —H.L.Haller & Ruth L. Busbey⟩ ⟨acid-*labile* phosphate⟩ — compare UNSTABLE **b :** characterized by shifting interchange (as of component material) without alteration in kind ⟨~ equilibrium of a fluid⟩ **c** *psychol* **:** tending to discharge rather than to retain affect **d** *geol* **:** unstable mechanically or chemically ⟨stable and ~ minerals⟩ ⟨a ~ stratum⟩

la·bil·i·ty \ləˈbiləd·ē\ *n* -ES **:** the quality or state of being labile ⟨believe that a fall in population level . . . might enhance evolutionary ~ —N.E.Collias & C.H.Southwick⟩

la·bi·li·za·tion \ˌlābələˈzāshən\ *n* -s **:** the action or process of labilizing

la·bi·lize \ˈlābə,līz\ *vt* -ED/-ING/-S [*labile* + *-ize*] **:** to render labile (as in chemical structure)

labio- *comb form* [L *labium* lip — more at LIP] **1 :** the lips ⟨*labio*graph⟩ ⟨*labio*plasty⟩ **2 :** labial and ⟨*labio*nasal⟩ ⟨*labio*velar⟩

¹la·bio·dental \ˌlābē(ˌ)ō+\ *adj* [*labio-* + *dental*] **:** produced with the participation of lip and teeth or lips and teeth (as the lower lip and the upper front teeth) ⟨the ~ fricative \f\ and \v\⟩ **:** DENTILABIAL — compare BILABIAL, DENTAL, LABIAL

²labiodental \ˈ"\ *n* **:** a labiodental sound

¹la·bio·nasal \ˈ"+\ *adj* [ISV *labio-* + *nasal*] **:** both labial and nasal — used of the sound \m\

²labionasal \ˈ"\ *n* **:** the sound \m\

¹la·bio·velar \ˈ"+\ *adj* [ISV *labio-* + *velar*] **:** both labial and velar ⟨the ~ sound \w\⟩

²labiovelar \ˈ"\ *n* **:** a labiovelar sound

la·bio·ve·lar·iza·tion \ˌlābēō,vēlərəˈzāshən\ *n* -s **:** the action or result of labiovelarizing

la·bio·ve·lar·ize \ˌ===ˈvēlə,rīz\ *vt* [¹*labiovelar* + *-ize*] **:** to make labiovelar

la·bite \ˈlä,bīt\ *n* -s [ISV *lab-* (fr. *Laba* river, the Caucasus, U.S.S.R.) + *-ite;* orig. formed as Russ *labit*] **:** a mineral $MgSi_3O_6(OH)_2.H_2O$ consisting of hydrous basic silicate of magnesium

la·bi·um \ˈlābēəm\ *n, pl* **labia** \-ēə\ [NL, fr. L, lip — more at LIP] **1 :** any of the folds at the margin of the vulva — compare LABIA MAJORA, LABIA MINORA **2 a :** the lower lip of a labiate corolla — compare GALEA **b :** the liplike lower margin of the foveola in plants of the genus *Isoetes* **3 a :** the lower lip of an insect that is formed by the second pair of maxillae united in the middle line and variously modified in different insects but consists typically of a submentum, mentum, and ligula and bears two labial palpi **b :** the coalescent pedipalpi of some mites **c :** a liplike part of a neuropodium in a polychaete worm **d :** the metastoma of a crustacean **e :** the columellar part of the aperture of a gastropod shell **f :** the movable sclerite forming the ventral wall of the head of a spider

lab·lab \ˈla,blab\ *n* -s [Ar *lablāb*] **:** any of several vines of the genus *Dolichos* or related genera; *specif* **:** HYACINTH BEAN

lab-lab \ˈ"\ *n* -s [Tag, lit., quagmire, marsh] *Philippines* **:** a mass of microscopic algae chiefly of the Myxophyceae found on the mud in fishponds and used as food by the fry

¹la·bor \ˈlābə(r)\ *n* -s *see -or in Explan Notes* [ME *labour, labor,* fr. OF, fr. L *labor* drudgery, hardship, work; prob. akin to L *labi* to slip, slide — more at SLEEP] **1 a :** TOIL, WORK: (1) **:** expenditure of physical or mental effort esp. when fatiguing, difficult, or compulsory ⟨with ~ I excavated a pit —W.H. Hudson †1922⟩ ⟨with enormous ~s he made himself into a popular writer —Carl van Doren⟩ ⟨sentenced to six months at hard ~⟩ (2) **:** human activity that produces the goods or provides the services in demand in an economy **:** the services performed by workers for wages as distinguished from those rendered by entrepreneurs for profits ⟨each entrepreneur is eager to buy all the kinds of specific ~ he needs —Ludwig Von Mises⟩ **b** (1) **:** the physical activities involved in parturition consisting essentially of a prolonged series of involuntary contractions of the uterine musculature together with both reflex and voluntary contractions of the abdominal wall ⟨drugs that induce ~⟩ ⟨the record of her previous pregnancies and ~s⟩ ⟨went into ~ after a fall⟩ (2) **:** the period of time during which such labor takes place ⟨a 12-hour ~⟩ **c :** heavy pitching and rolling of a ship under way **2 :** an act or process requiring labor **:** TASK ⟨translation is a ~ that must be done afresh for each succeeding age —J.C.Swaim⟩ **3 :** a product of labor ⟨muddy waters had swept inland . . . submerging in one implacable tide the ~ of years —William Beebe⟩ ⟨inspecting his completed ~s with a critical eye⟩ **4 a :** an economic group comprising those who do manual labor or work for wages ⟨the native ~ is a floating population —*Geog. Jour.*⟩ **:** workingmen as an economic or political force ⟨~ has the right to assemble, to bargain collectively, and to strike —Curtis Bok⟩ ⟨win the vote of ~ in the coming elections⟩ **b :** workers employed in an establishment or available for employment **:** hired help ⟨the injection of ourselves and all our ~ against bubonic plague —*Think*⟩ **:** MANPOWER ⟨a plentiful supply of cheap ~ from across the border⟩ **c :** the organizations or officials (as unions or union leadership) representing groups of workers **:** organized labor ⟨those in ~ who advocate profit sharing by employees⟩ ⟨a conference between ~ and management⟩ **5** *usu* **labour** *usu cap* **a :** the Labour party of the United Kingdom ⟨when *Labour* is in a position to form a government, the sovereign . . . calls the leader as prime minister —R.T.McKenzie⟩ **b :** the Labour party in another nation of the British Commonwealth (as Australia or New Zealand) ⟨*Labour* won its first signal political triumph in the New South Wales elections —Alexander Brady⟩ **syn** see WORK

²labor \ˈ"\ *vb* **labored; labored; laboring** \-b(ə)riŋ\ **labors** *see -or in Explan Notes* [ME *labouren, laboren,* fr. MF *labourer,* fr. OF *laborer, labourer,* fr. L *laborare* to suffer, toil, work, fr. *labor,* n.] *vi* **1 :** to exert one's powers of body or mind esp. with painful or strenuous effort **:** to perform labor **:** WORK, STRIVE ⟨~*ed* to pull their wagons along the slushy road —F.V.W.Mason⟩ ⟨when a writer ~s long over a single passage⟩ ⟨began to ~ on the creation of a treaty system —D.J.Dallin⟩ ⟨~*ed* as a miner⟩ ⟨~s for the restoration of normal conditions⟩ **2 :** to move with great effort (as against opposition or under a burden) ⟨the boat ~*ed* upriver —Sherwood Anderson⟩ ⟨the ponderous woman ~*ed* puffingly up one flight of stairs —J.B. Benefield⟩ ⟨I had ~*ed* through the *Prometheus* with a Greek dictionary —H.J.Laski⟩ **3 :** to be in or enter into labor in the bearing of a child or young **4 :** to suffer from some disadvantage or distress — usu. used with *under* ⟨~*ed* under the handicap of arthritis⟩ ⟨~ under a delusion⟩ **5** *of a ship* **:** to pitch or roll heavily ⟨~*ed* heavily in a chopping sea —J.L. Motley⟩ ~ *vt* **1** *dial Brit* **:** TILL, CULTIVATE ⟨the cultivated area . . . is ~*ed* by some 65,000 farmers —J.M.Mogey⟩ **2 :** BURDEN, TIRE, DISTRESS ⟨the details . . . are endless and I won't ~ you with them —Horace Sutton⟩ **:** make laborious ⟨anxiety . . . troubled and ~*ed* her mature work —Sara H. Hay⟩ **3** *archaic* **a :** to spend labor on or produce by labor ⟨anvils ~*ed* by the Cyclops' hands —John Dryden⟩ **b :** to strive to effect or achieve **:** work for ⟨earnestly . . . ~*ed* that reunion —Edmund Burke⟩ **4 :** to treat or work out in often laborious detail **:** develop fully **:** ELABORATE ⟨no need to ~ the obvious —Bernard DeVoto⟩ **5** *obs* **:** to use one's influence or favor with or for **:** URGE ⟨the Devil . . . ~s all he can to bring them into the same pit —Robert Burton⟩ **6 :** to cause to labor ⟨poets ~*ing* their wits on tasks like these —Gilbert Highet⟩ **7** *obs* **:** BEAT, POUND, RUB ⟨take the white of an egg and ~ the same —*Book of St. Albans*⟩ ⟨the ass . . . if he be ~*ed* with a cudgel —Richard Carew⟩ **8** *obs* **:** to bring by labor or endeavor to a specified position or state ⟨~*ed* him out of his house —Robert Crowley⟩

³labor \ˈ"\ *adj, see -or in Explan Notes* [¹*labor*] **1 a :** of or relating to labor ⟨~ costs⟩ ⟨an ample ~ supply⟩ ⟨~ legislation⟩ **b :** of, representing the views or interests of, or dominated by organized labor ⟨~ political activity⟩ ⟨editorials in the ~ press⟩ ⟨a ~ leader⟩ ⟨districts that are traditionally liberal and ~ —*NewRepublic*⟩ **c :** affecting labor and management ⟨a ~ contract⟩ **2** *usu cap* **:** of, relating to, or constituted by a political party that claims to represent the interests of working men and women or that is characterized by a membership in which organized labor groups predominate: as **a :** of, relating to, or constituted by one of several minor political parties usu. having a brief period of activity in the U.S. during the late 19th and 20th centuries — usu. used in combination ⟨the Farmer-*Labor* party of Minnesota⟩ ⟨the American *Labor* party in New York state . . . constituted an important political bloc —H.S.Gilbertson⟩ **b** *usu* **labour** (1) **:** of, relating to, or constituted by a major political party of the United Kingdom in the 20th century associated with socialistic policies (as the nationalization of basic industries) and characterized by an organization in which trade unions are predominant ⟨election of a *Labour* candidate to the London County Council⟩ ⟨a *Labour* majority in the House of Commons⟩ (2) **:** of, relating to, or constituted by a political party in another nation of the British Commonwealth that is usu. similar in membership to the Labour party of the United Kingdom ⟨the power of the *Labour* caucus in Australia⟩ ⟨New Zealand's first *Labour* government⟩

⁴la·bor \laˈbō(ə)r, -bȯ(ə)r\ *n* -s [MexSp, fr. Sp, farming, tilling, work, fr. L, work] **:** an old Texas unit of land area equal to about 177 acres

lab·o·ra·to·ri·al \ˌlab(ə)rəˈtōrēəl, -tȯr-\ *adj* **:** of, utilizing, or resembling a laboratory — **lab·o·ra·to·ri·al·ly** \-ēəlē\ *adv*

lab·o·ra·to·ri·an \ˌ=(=)=ˈrēən\ *n* -s **:** a laboratory worker

[1]**lab·o·ra·to·ry** \ˈlabrə,tōrē, -tȯr-, -ri *sometimes* ˈlabər-, *chiefly in substand speech by r-dissimilation* ˈlabə,t-, *chiefly Brit* ləˈbärə·tri *or* -ärətəri\ *n* -ES [ML *laboratorium*, fr. L *laboratus* (past part. of *laborare* to labor) + *-orium* -ory — more at LABOR] **1 a :** a place devoted to experimental study in any branch of natural science or to the application of scientific principles in testing and analysis or in the preparation usu. on a small scale of drugs, chemicals, explosives, or other products or substances ⟨a chemical ~⟩ ⟨a biological ~⟩ ⟨a rolling crime ~⟩ ⟨the weather research plane, a powerful flying ~ —Walter Hayward⟩ **b :** a place equipped for or an organized activity involving experimentation or observation in a field of study (as child development) or practice in a skill (as reading) ⟨was equipped with a psychology ~⟩ ⟨composition ~ . . . for students requiring special help in English fundamentals —*King College Bull.*⟩ **c :** a period in an academic schedule set aside for laboratory work ⟨a course with two lectures and one ~ a week⟩ **2 a :** something resembling a laboratory in carrying on a process of production or testing ⟨the ~ of the mind⟩ ⟨the ~ of ongoing human experience —L.A.Weigle⟩ **b :** an environment that provides opportunity for systematic observation, experimentation, or practice ⟨a settlement house serving as a sociological ~⟩ ⟨the new nation of Israel, a social ~⟩ **3 :** the hearth of a reverberatory furnace

[2]**laboratory** \"\ *adj* **1 :** of, working, used, or done in a laboratory ⟨get ~ approval for the new appliance⟩ ⟨a ~ assistant in accounting⟩ ⟨a ~ manual⟩ ⟨perform ~ experiments⟩ **2 :** befitting, suggestive of, or resembling that of a laboratory ⟨insisted on . . . ~ conditions in an election —*N.Y. Times*⟩ ⟨a cheap liquor . . . had a fierce ~ flavor —Norman Lewis⟩ ⟨a kind of ~ method in fiction —Robert Humphrey⟩ **3 :** of or involving observation or experimentation or practice for educational purposes ⟨a ~ period⟩ ⟨a ~ course⟩

laboratory school *n* **:** a school operated by a college or university and used esp. for student teaching and the demonstration of classroom practices

labor bank *n* **:** a bank owned and operated by a labor union

labor camp *n* **1 :** a penal colony (as in the U.S.S.R.) where forced labor is performed **2 :** living facilities (as in the western U.S.) for migratory labor

labor court *n* **:** a governmental agency established to adjudicate a management-labor dispute not resolved by the parties involved or any dispute over contract interpretation; *also* **:** a similar agency empowered only to subject disputants to compulsory investigation

labor day *n* **1** *usu cap L&D* **:** a day set aside for special recognition of the workingman: as **a :** the first Monday in September, observed in the U.S. and Canada as a legal holiday **b :** May 1 in many countries **2** [trans. of Russ *trudoden*, fr. *trud* labor + *den* day] **:** a Soviet unit of labor crediting a collective-farm worker with more or less than his actual working time according to his skill and productivity

labored *adj* [fr. past part. of [2]*labor*] **:** produced or performed with labor ⟨breathing of the men . . . seemed immensely loud and ~ —Irwin Shaw⟩ **:** bearing marks of labor and effort **:** elaborately wrought **:** not easy or natural ⟨a ~ signature that would seem to indicate only the most rudimentary kind of schooling —Hamilton Basso⟩ ⟨the cumbersome paraphernalia of expression which make his poetry so ~ and artificial —M.R. Adams⟩ — **la·bored·ly** *adv* — **la·bored·ness** *n* -ES

la·bor·er \ˈlābərə(r)\ *n* -S [ME *laborer, labourer*, fr. MF *laboureur*, fr. OF *laboreor*, fr. *laborer* to labor + *-eor* -or — more at LABOR] **1 :** one that labors; *specif* **:** a person who does unskilled physical work for wages sometimes as assistant to a skilled artisan ⟨a bricklayer's ~⟩ **2** *archaic* **:** WORKER 3

labor exchange *n* **1 :** an exchange for direct transfer of products according to the amount of labor expended in making them without the intervention of money **2 a :** EMPLOYMENT AGENCY **b** *chiefly Brit* **:** EMPLOYMENT EXCHANGE

labor force *n* **1 :** a body of employed workers (as of a corporation or in an industry) at a particular place or period of time **2 :** the total number of employable workers ⟨a national *labor force*⟩; *specif* **:** the number of persons in the U.S. at least 14 years of age who are actually employed or are seeking employment

labor grade *n* **:** one of a series of wage groupings of the jobs within a plant or company that are considered of approximately equal worth on the basis of job evaluation

labor income *n* **:** the annual income of a farmer after business expenses and an interest charge for capital invested are subtracted ⟨to compare *labor income* with city salaries, the value of house rent and the products used must be added —H.E. Botsford⟩

laboring *pres part of* LABOR

la·bor·ing·ly *adv* **:** in a laboring manner **:** LABORIOUSLY

laboring oar *n* [fr. *laboring*, pres. part. of [2]*labor*] **:** a part or task requiring greater effort than others ⟨the officer who pulls the *laboring oar* in the club's activities⟩

la·bo·ri·ous \ləˈbōrēəs, -bȯr-\ *adj* [ME, fr. MF or L; MF *laborieux*, fr. L *laboriosus*, fr. *labor* + *-iosus* -ious] **1 :** devoted to labor **:** INDUSTRIOUS, HARDWORKING, DILIGENT ⟨as men of research . . . they are magnificently ~ and accurate —Aldous Huxley⟩ **2 :** involving or characterized by hard or toilsome effort or by detailed elaboration **:** LABORED ⟨months of ~ research⟩ ⟨slow and ~ transportation⟩ ⟨~ and futile negotiations⟩ ⟨several ~, overlong, painfully "arty" stories —William Peden⟩ ⟨picturesque scenery painted with ~ literalism —*Amer. Guide Series: Pa.*⟩ **3** *chiefly Brit* **:** doing unskilled labor **:** LABORING ⟨cottages for the ~ and industrious part of the community —G.E.Fussell⟩ — **la·bo·ri·ous·ly** *adv* — **la·bo·ri·ous·ness** *n* -ES

la·bor·ism \ˈlābə,rizəm\ *n* -S **1** *usu cap* **a :** the principles and policies of the Labour party **b :** the Labour party or its members **2 :** a system characterized by policies and attitudes favoring a predominance of labor and its interests in economics and politics ⟨~ and not . . . imperialism is the policy of the latest stage of capitalism —J.A.Schumpeter⟩

la·bor·is·tic \ˌlābəˈristik\ *adj* [[1]*labor* + *-istic*] **:** characterized by policies or attitudes favorable to labor ⟨this chamber . . . turned out to be so much more Fascist than ~ —H.R.Spencer⟩ ⟨a ~ society⟩

la·bor·ite \ˈ==,rīt, *usu* -īd·+V\ *n* -S **1 :** a member of a group favoring the interests of labor ⟨one of those radical ~s who shunned association with any but wage earners —*Public*⟩ **2** *usu cap* **a :** a member of a political party that claims to be devoted chiefly to the interests of labor ⟨Illinois *Laborites* . . . demand 44-hour week —*N.Y. Times*⟩ **b** *usu* **labourite :** a member of the British Labour party ⟨Liberal, *Laborite* and Conservative are all maneuvering for position —*So. Atlantic Quarterly*⟩ ⟨the British *Labourites* look forward to an industrial democracy —J.H.Randall⟩

la·bor·less \ˈlābə(r)ləs\ *adj* **:** involving or doing no labor **:** EASY, IDLE

labor market *n* **1 :** the institutions and processes through which employment and wages are determined ⟨groups excluded from the *labor market*⟩ **2 :** the factors affecting the supply of and demand for labor ⟨a *labor market* favorable to employers⟩ **3 :** the area within which workers compete for jobs and employers compete for workers ⟨draw workers from a large *labor market*⟩

labor movement *n* **1 :** an organized effort on the part of workers to improve their economic and social status by united action through the medium of labor unions **2 :** the activities of labor unions to further the cause of organized labor

labor of love : a labor voluntarily undertaken or performed without consideration of any benefit or reward

labor organization *n* **:** an organization, agency, or representative committee in which employees participate for the purpose of engaging in collective bargaining with employers

labor relations *n pl* **:** relations between management and labor esp. as involved in collective bargaining and maintenance of contract

labors *pl of* LABOR, *pres 3d sing of* LABOR

laborsaving \ˈ==,==\ *adj* **1 :** adapted to supersede or diminish labor ⟨~ devices⟩ ⟨a ~ plan of work⟩ **2** *printing* **a :** ready cut or cast in multiples of a standard size (as the pica) — used of a rule, slug, or furniture **b :** having mortised ends — used of metal furniture

labor skate *n, slang* **:** a member of a labor union

la·bor·some \ˈlābə(r)səm\ *adj* [[1]*labor* + *-some*] **:** LABORIOUS 2 — **la·bor·some·ly** *adv*

labor spy *n* **:** an agent of an employer hired to report on union activities **:** STOOL PIGEON

labor theory of value : a theory of value holding that the quantity of labor in a product regulates its value and utilized by Marx to claim for labor the sole rightful claim to production

labor union *n* **:** a labor organization created for the purpose of advancing (as by collective bargaining) its members' interests (as in respect to wages and working conditions) — compare CRAFT UNION; see INDUSTRIAL UNION

la·bou·chère \ˌlabüˈsher\ *n* -S *usu cap* [prob. after Henry du Pré *Labouchère* †1912 Eng. journalist and political leader] **:** a system of betting on roulette, faro, and other games whereby the bettor takes a column of consecutive numbers consistent with the amount he is willing to risk and bets the sum of the top and bottom numbers, canceling the numbers involved in any bet won and adding to the series the amount of each bet lost

la·boul·be·nia \lə,bülˈbēnēə, ˌla,b-, ˌlä,b-\ *n, usu cap* [NL, fr. Jean J. A. *Laboulbène* †1898 Fr. physician and entomologist + NL *-ia*] **:** the type genus of the family Laboulbeniaceae

la·boul·be·ni·a·ce·ae \(ˌ)=,=,bēnēˈāsē,ē\ *n pl, cap* [NL, fr. *Laboulbenia*, type genus + *-aceae*] **:** a family of minute fungi (order Laboulbeniales) living as parasites upon insects and having a thallus consisting of only a few cells and a spermatial type of sexual reproduction resembling that of the red algae — **la·boul·be·ni·a·ceous** \ˈ=;=;=ˈāshəs, ˈ=,=;=-\ *adj*

la·boul·be·ni·a·les \=,=ˈ=ˈā(ˌ)lēz\ *n pl, cap* [NL, fr. *Laboulbenia* + *-ales*] **:** an order of euascomycetous fungi coextensive with the family Laboulbeniaceae

labour *Brit var of* LABOR

la·bour·din *or* **la·bour·dine** \ləˈbü(ə)rdᵊn, -r,dēn\ *n* -S *cap* [prob. fr. F, fr. *Labourd*, department of Basses Pyrénées, France] **:** a dialect of Basque spoken largely in the extreme west of the Department of Basses Pyrénées in France

labouring *n* -S [fr. *labouring, laboring*, gerund of *labour, labor*] *Scot* **:** FARM

la·bour·ist \ˈlābərəst\ *n* -S *usu cap* **:** LABORITE 2

labourite *usu cap, var of* LABORITE

[1]**lab·ra·dor** \ˈlabrə,dȯ(ə)r, -ȯ(ə)\ *adj, usu cap* [fr. *Labrador*, peninsula, Newfoundland and Quebec provinces in Canada] **:** of or from Labrador **:** of the kind or style prevalent in Labrador **:** LABRADOREAN

[2]**labrador** \"\ *n* -S **1** *or* **labrador blue** *often cap L* **:** a dark grayish to blackish blue **2** *usu cap* **:** LABRADOR RETRIEVER

labrador duck *n, usu cap L* **:** an extinct black-and-white sea duck (*Camptorhynchus labradorius*) related to the eiders

[1]**lab·ra·dor·e·an** *or* **lab·ra·dor·i·an** \ˈ==ˈdȯrēən\ *adj, usu cap* [*Labrador*, peninsula, Canada + E *-an*] **1 :** of or relating to Labrador **2 :** of or forming the continental ice sheets of the Pleistocene epoch whose centers were located east or southeast of Hudson Bay

[2]**labradorean** *or* **labradorian** \"\ *n* -S *cap* **:** a native or inhabitant of Labrador

lab·ra·dor·es·cence \ˌ==,dȯˈresᵊn(t)s\ *n* -S [*labradorite* + *-escence* (as in *fluorescence*)] **:** a play of colors or colored reflections exhibited esp. by labradorite and caused by internal structures that selectively reflect only certain colors

lab·ra·dor·ite \ˈ==,dȯ,rīt\ *n* -S [*Labrador*, peninsula, Canada, its locality + E *-ite*] **:** a mineral consisting of a plagioclase feldspar in which the ratio of albite to anorthite lies between 5:5 and 3:7 and which commonly shows a beautiful play of gray, blue, green, and other colors and is hence much used for ornamental purposes — **lab·ra·dor·it·ic** \ˈ==,dȯˈrid·ik\ *adj*

labrador jay *n, usu cap L* **:** a Canada jay of northeastern Canada that is usu. considered to be a distinct race

labrador pine *n, usu cap L* **:** JACK PINE 1

labrador retriever *n, usu cap L* **:** a retriever largely developed in England from stock originating in Newfoundland and characterized by a short dense hard unwaved usu. black coat, notable breadth of head, chest, and rib cage, and superior ability as a retriever of both waterfowl and upland game

labrador spar *or* **labrador stone** *n, usu cap L* **:** LABRADORITE

labrador tea *n, usu cap L* **:** either of two shrubs of the genus *Ledum*: **a :** a low-growing evergreen (*L. groenlandicum*) of eastern No. America having white or creamy bell-shaped flowers and leaves clothed beneath with rusty hairs and sometimes used for making a tea **b :** a related Rocky mountain shrub (*L. glandulosum*)

la·bral \ˈlābrəl\ *adj* [NL *labrum* + E *-al*] **:** of or relating to a labrum

la·bret \ˈlā,bret\ *n* -S [L *labrum* lip + E *-et*] **:** an ornament (as of wood, shell, or stone) worn by some primitive peoples in a perforation of the lip

[1]**labrid** \ˈlābrəd, ˈlab-\ *adj* [NL *Labridae*] **:** of or relating to the family Labridae

[2]**labrid** \"\ *n* -S **:** a fish of the family Labridae

lab·ri·dae \ˈlabrə,dē\ *n pl, cap* [NL, fr. *Labrus*, type genus + *-idae*] **:** a large and important family of percoid fishes having the palate toothless, the anterior teeth of the jaws separate and usu. strong, and the lower pharyngeals completely united into one bone with conical or tubercular teeth — see WRASSE

[1]**la·broid** \ˈlā,brȯid, ˈla,b-\ *adj* [NL *Labrus* + E *-oid*] **:** related to or resembling fishes of the family Labridae

[2]**labroid** \"\ *n* -S **:** a labroid fish

la·brum \ˈlābrəm, ˈlab-\ *n* -S [NL, fr. L, lip, edge — more at LIP] **1 :** the upper or anterior lip of insects and crustaceans and other arthropods consisting of a single median piece or flap immediately in front of or above the mandibles **2 :** the external margin of a gastropod shell **3 :** the labium of an arachnid

la·brus \ˈlābrəs\ *n, cap* [NL, fr. L *labrus, labros*, a fish] **:** the type genus of the family Labridae

la·brus·ca \ləˈbrəskə\ *adj, often cap* [NL, fr. *labrusca* (specific epithet of *Vitis labrusca*) fr. L, wild vine] **:** of, relating to, or derived from an American fox grape (*Vitis labrusca*) that has been important in the development of hardy cultivated grapes ⟨several new ~ hybrids⟩ ⟨a hardy ~ grape⟩

la·brys \ˈlābrəs, ˈlab-\ *n* -ES [Gk, prob. of Carian origin] **:** an ancient Cretan sacred double ax

labs *pl of* LAB

la·bur·num \ləˈbərnəm, -bə̄n-\ *n* [NL, fr. L, laburnum, bean trefoil] **1** *cap* **:** a small genus of Eurasian poisonous shrubs and trees (family Leguminosae) having trifoliolate leaves and pendulous racemes of bright yellow flowers **2** -S **:** any plant of the genus *Laburnum*; *esp* **:** an ornamental tree (*L. anagyroides*) often cultivated for Easter decoration — called also *bean trefoil, golden chain, golden rain* **3** -S [L] **:** any of several similar plants of related genera (as *Cytisus*)

lab·y·rinth \ˈlabə,rin(t)th, -,rən-\ *n, pl* **labyrinths** \-n(t)s, -n(t)ths\ [alter. (influenced by L *labyrinthus*) of ME *laborintus*, fr. L *labyrinthus*, fr. Gk *labyrinthos*, prob. of Carian origin; akin to Gk *labrys* double ax] **1 a :** a structure full of intricate passageways that make it difficult to find the way from the interior to the entrance or from the entrance to the center ⟨the ~ constructed by Daedalus for Minos, king of Crete, in which the Minotaur was confined⟩ **b :** a maze in a park or garden formed by paths separated by high thick hedges **2 a :** something often bewilderingly involved or tortuous in structure, arrangement, or character **:** a complex that baffles exploration ⟨a ~ of swamps and shifting channels —P.E.James⟩ ⟨the ~ of a great novel —E.K.Brown⟩ **b :** a situation or state (as of mind) from which it is difficult to extricate oneself ⟨a ~ of despair⟩ ⟨sank into the blissful ~ of a dream —Earle Birney⟩ **c :** INTRICACY, PERPLEXITY — usu. used in pl. ⟨sustain the reader through the analytical ~s —Hunter Mead⟩ ⟨guided them through the ~s of city life —Paul Blanshard⟩ **3 a :** the internal ear or its bony or membranous part — see BONY LABYRINTH, MEMBRANOUS LABYRINTH **b :** the portions of the cortex of the kidney consisting of tortuous uriniferous tubules **c :** a body structure (as the accessory respiratory organ of a labyrinth fish) made up of a maze of cavities and canals **4 :** an intricate sometimes symbolic pattern; *specif* **:** such a pattern inlaid in the pavement of a medieval church **5 a :** a device consisting of an arrangement (as a succession of grooves and collars, grooves and rings, tortuous passageways) usu. for the purpose of offering resistance to fluid flow (as to prevent leakage, promote condensation, separate component elements according to specific gravities) **b :** an enclosure consisting of an undulatory passage connected to the rear of a loudspeaker and providing improved low-frequency response — called also *acoustical labyrinth*

lab·y·rin·thal \ˈ==ˈrin(t)thəl\ *adj* **:** LABYRINTHINE

labyrinth fish *n* [NL *Labyrinthici*] **:** a fish of the order Labyrinthici; *esp* **:** any of various fish of this order that are often kept in the tropical aquarium — see CROAKING GOURAMI

lab·y·rin·thi·an \-thēən\ *adj* **:** LABYRINTHINE

lab·y·rin·thic \-thik, -thēk\ *also* **lab·y·rin·thi·cal** \-thəkəl, -thēk-\ *adj* [*labyrinthic* fr. LL *labyrinthicus*, fr. L *labyrinthus* labyrinth + *-icus* -ic; *labyrinthical* fr. LL *labyrinthicus* + E *-al*] **:** LABYRINTHINE — **lab·y·rin·thi·cal·ly** \-thək(ə)lē\ *adv*

lab·y·rin·thi·ci \ˌ==ˈrin(t)thə,sī\ *n pl, cap* [NL, fr. pl. of LL *labyrinthicus* of a labyrinth, labyrinthine] *in former classifications* **:** an order of freshwater and brackish water fishes chiefly of southeastern Asia that are now usu. included among the Percomorphi and that are adapted to meet unfavorable conditions by a labyrinthine outpocketing of the gill chamber permitting them to take oxygen from the air as well as from water — compare ANABAS, LABYRINTH FISH

lab·y·rin·thine \ˈ==ˈrin(t)thən, -),thēn, -thīn\ *adj* [*labyrinth* + *-ine*] **1 :** of, like, or like that of a labyrinth **:** marked by extreme intricacy or ramification ⟨a ~ network of tortuous footways —R.T.Hopkins⟩ ⟨a ~ bureaucracy⟩ **:** INVOLVED ⟨sprawling ~ sentences —A.L.Scott⟩ **:** CIRCUITOUS ⟨got his way by ~ maneuvering⟩ **2 :** of, relating to, affecting, or originating in the internal ear ⟨~ deafness⟩ ⟨~ function⟩ **3** [NL *Labyrinthici* + E *-ine*] **:** belonging to or characteristic of the Labyrinthici

labyrinthine sense *n* **:** a complex sense concerned with the perception of bodily position and motion, mediated by end organs in the vestibular apparatus and the semicircular canals, and stimulated by alterations in the pull of gravity and by head movements — compare VESTIBULAR SENSE

labyrinthine tooth *n* **:** a tooth characteristic of the Labyrinthodontia having the dentin enfolded into complex patterns and ridges

lab·y·rin·thi·tis \ˌlabərənˈthīd·əs\ *n* -ES [NL, fr. E *labyrinth* + NL *-itis*] **:** inflammation of a labyrinth (as of the internal ear)

[1]**lab·y·rin·tho·dont** \ˈlabəˈrin(t)thə,dänt\ *adj* [NL *Labyrinthodontia*] **1 :** of or relating to the Labyrinthodontia **2 :** having labyrinthine teeth

[2]**labyrinthodont** \"\ *n* -S **:** an amphibian of the group Labyrinthodontia

lab·y·rin·tho·don·ta \ˌ==,==ˈdäntə\ [NL, fr. Gk *labyrinthos* labyrinth + NL *-odonta*] *syn of* LABYRINTHODONTIA

lab·y·rin·tho·don·tia \-änch(ē)ə\ *n pl, cap* [NL, fr. Gk *labyrinthos* labyrinth + NL *-odontia* — more at LABYRINTH] **1 :** a superorder of Amphibia comprising extinct amphibians of the Devonian, Upper Paleozoic, and Triassic that are extremely variable in form and size but typically resemble rather heavy-bodied salamanders or crocodiles, that have the centra of the vertebrae ossified from blocks or arches of cartilage, a completely roofed bony skull, and usu. labyrinthine teeth, that are known chiefly from fragmentary remains, and that are considered to be the earliest true tetrapods and in some respects to bridge the gap between the crossopterygians and the most primitive reptiles **2** *in some classifications* **:** a subdivision of Stegocephalia that comprises forms with labyrinthine teeth and is nearly equivalent to Temnospondyli — **lab·y·rin·tho·don·tid** \ˌ==,==ˈdäntəd\ *adj or n* — **lab·y·rin·tho·don·toid** \-än,tȯid\ *adj*

lab·y·rin·thu·la \ˌ==ˈrin(t)thələ\ *n, cap* [NL, dim. of L *labyrinthus* labyrinth] **:** a genus of rhizopods parasitic in aquatic plants, the individuals forming pseudoplasmodia by anastomosis of filar pseudopodia but encysting independently and sometimes passing through transient flagellate stages — see LABYRINTHULALES

lab·y·rin·thu·la·les \ˌ==,==ˈlā(ˌ)lēz\ *n pl, cap* [NL, fr. *Labyrinthula* + *-ales*] **:** an obscure order of Myxomycetes comprising *Labyrinthula* and a few related parasites of aquatic plants when these are considered plants rather than protozoans

[1]**lac** *also* **lack** \ˈlak\ *n* -S [Per *lak* & Hindi *lākh*, fr. Skt *lākṣā*] **1 :** a resinous substance secreted by the lac insect and used chiefly in the form of shellac — see SEED LAC, STICK LAC **2 :** any of various plant or animal substances that yield hard coatings resembling lac and shellac

[2]**lac** *var of* LAKH

LAC *abbr* leading aircraftsman

la·can·don \ˌläkänˈdōn\ *n, pl* **lacandon** \"\ *or* **lacando·nes** \-ō,nās\ *usu cap* [MexSp, of AmerInd origin] **1 a :** an Indian people of Yucatan and Chiapas, Mexico **b :** a member of such people **2 :** a dialect of Yucatec

lac·ca \ˈlakə\ *n* -S [NL & It; NL, prob. fr. It, fr. ML, fr. Ar *lakk*, fr. Per *lak* — more at LAC] **:** LAC

lac·case \ˈla,kās\ *n* -S [ISV *lacc-* (prob. fr. NL *lacca*) + *-ase*; orig. formed in F] **:** a blue copper-containing oxidase occurring esp. in the sap of lacquer trees and having an ability to produce lacquer from the sap and induce oxidation of certain polyhydroxy phenols (as urushiol)

lac·cate \ˈla,kāt\ *adj* [NL *lacca* + E *-ate*] **:** having a varnished or lacquered appearance ⟨a bracket fungus with shining ~ surface⟩

lac·ci·fer \ˈlaksəfə(r)\ *n, cap* [NL, fr. *lacca* + *-i-* + *-fer*] **:** a genus (the type of the family Lacciferidae) that comprises the commercially important lac insects

lac·col \ˈla,kȯl, -kōl\ *n* -S [ISV *lacc-* (fr. NL *lacca*) + *-ol*] **:** a crystalline phenol $C_{17}H_{31}C_6H_3(OH)_2$ occurring in the sap of lacquer trees

lac·co·lith \ˈlakə,lith\ *also* **lac·co·lite** \-līt\ *n* -S [Gk *lakkos* cistern, pit + E *-lith* or *-lite*] **:** a mass of igneous rock intruded between sedimentary beds and producing a domic bulging of the overlying strata — **lac·co·lith·ic** \ˈ==ˈlithik\ *also* **lac·co·lit·ic** \-id·ik\ *adj*

lac dye *n* **:** a scarlet dye like cochineal used formerly in dyeing and pigment making and obtained from stick lac by extraction with alkali — see [4]LAKE 1a(1)

[1]**lace** \ˈlās\ *n* -S [ME *las, lace*, fr. OF *laz*, fr. L *laqueus* snare — more at DELIGHT] **1** *obs* **:** SNARE, NET **2 :** a cord or string used for drawing together two edges (as of a garment, a shoe, a machine belt) **3 :** an ornamental braid for trimming men's hats, coats, or uniforms ⟨gold ~⟩ ⟨silver ~⟩ **4 a :** a fine openwork fabric with a ground of mesh or net on which patterns may be worked at the same time as the ground or applied later and which is made of thread by looping, twisting, or knotting either by hand with a needle or bobbin or by machinery — see BOBBIN LACE, NEEDLEPOINT **b :** a similar fabric made by crocheting, tatting, darning, embroidering, weaving, or knitting — see HAIRPIN LACE, LIMERICK LACE **5** *obs* **:** a dash of spirits added (as to coffee)

[2]**lace** \"\ *vb* -ED/-ING/-S [ME *lacen*, fr. OF *lacier*, fr. L *laqueare* to ensnare, fr. *laqueus*] *vt* **1 :** to draw together the edges of by or as if by means of a lace passed through eyelet holes **:** TIE — often used with *up* ⟨*laced* up their shoes⟩ **2 :** to twine, draw, or pass as a lace **:** THREAD, INTERTWINE, EMBROIDER **3 :** to confine or compress by tightening laces esp. of a corset ⟨the old custom of *lacing* children in whalebone bodices⟩ ⟨*laced* her waist out of vanity⟩ **4 :** to adorn or trim with or as if with lace or decorative braid ⟨cloth *laced* with silver⟩ ⟨the landscape . . . was *laced* with countless creeks —D.C.Peattie⟩ **5 a :** BEAT, LASH, THRASH ⟨~ my quivering palm —Charlotte Brontë⟩ ⟨*laced* the bushes with bullets —*Springfield (Mass.) Daily News*⟩ **b :** BEST, DEFEAT ⟨*laced* his opponent in a hard-fought game⟩ ⟨was *laced* in the primaries⟩ **6 a :** to add a dash of an alcoholic liquor to (a food or beverage) ⟨*laced* his coffee with rum —Hugh Cave⟩ ⟨lobster Newburg *laced* with sherry —*Publishers' Weekly*⟩ **b :** to add savor, zest, or spice to **:** LIVEN ⟨the book *laced* with irreverent and therefore readable notes on the involvements of English history —*Saturday Rev.*⟩ **7 :** to throw or drive (a ball) hard and usu. in a straight line ⟨*laced* his ball straight down the middle of the fairway⟩ ⟨*laced* his second homer of the game into the stands⟩ **8** *in bookbinding* **:** to draw the tapes or sewing cords through (the boards of the cover) — usu. used with *in* **~** *vi* **1 :** to compress or confine the waist (as with a corset) **2 :** to admit of lacing or tying ⟨covered with a tarpaulin that *laced* up the middle⟩ **3 :** to make a physical or verbal attack — usu. used with *into* ⟨I had a riding whip with me and . . . I

rushed at the fellow and fairly *laced* into him —Robert Graves⟩ ⟨reviewers *laced* into the play —*Time*⟩

lacebark \'=,=\ *or* **lacebark tree** *n* [¹*lace* + *bark*] **1 :** a West Indian tree (*Lagetta lintearia*) **2 :** an Australian Kurrajong (*Sterculia acerifolia*) with interlaced bast fibers **3 :** RIBBON TREE **4 :** RIBBONWOOD 1

lacebark pine *n* **:** a Chinese tree (*Pinus bungeana*) that is often shrubby in cultivation and has flaky bark that becomes chalky-white, leaves in clusters of three, and cone scales with a recurved umbo resembling a spine

lace bryozoan *or* **lace coral** *n* **:** a member of the family Fenestellidae

lace bug *n* **:** any of the small bugs that constitute the large hemipterous family Tingidae, that have bodies and wings covered with a lacy network of raised lines, and that include many that suck plant juices and are serious pests

lace-curtain \'=,==\ *adj* **:** having social or economic standing **:** FASHIONABLE — often used to imply ostentation or pushing parvenu traits; compare SHANTY ⟨stickin' up his nose and actin' like he was highbrow, *lace-curtain* Irish —J.T.Farrell⟩ ⟨full of fine writing and *lace-curtain* English —Malcolm Cowley⟩

laced *adj* [fr. past part. of ²*lace*] **1 a :** tied or fastened with a lace **b :** trimmed or decorated with lace **2 a :** streaked with color — used esp. of a flower **b :** edged with a band of color differing from the body color — used of a bird's feather

¹**lac·e·dae·mo·ni·an** *also* **lac·e·de·mo·ni·an** \ˌlasədə-ˈmōnēən, -dē,-, -nyən\ *adj, usu cap* [L *lacedaemonius* Lacedaemonian (fr. Gk *lakedaimonios*, fr. *Lakedaimōn* Lacedaemon, Sparta, ancient city of Greece) + E *-an*] **1 :** of or relating to Lacedaemon **:** SPARTAN **2 :** LACONIC

²**lacedaemonian** \"\ *n* -s *usu cap* **:** SPARTAN

laced mutton *n* [fr. *laced*, past part. of ²*lace*] *obs* **:** PROSTITUTE

lace fern *n* **:** any of several American ferns of the genus *Cheilanthes* with finely dissected bipinnate fronds

lace flower *n* **1 :** WILD CARROT **2 :** a Rocky mountain herb (*Tiarella unifoliata*) **3 :** BLUE LACE FLOWER

lace fly *n* **:** LACEWING

lace glass *n* **:** glass having patterns resembling lace

lace grass *n* **:** a slender grass (*Eragrostis capillaris*) of the eastern U.S. with a large panicle on branches that resemble hairs

laceleaf \'=,=\ *n* **:** LATTICE PLANT

lace·less \'lāsləs\ *adj* **:** lacking lace

lacelike \'=,=\ *adj* **:** resembling lace **:** LACY ⟨~ branches —Elizabeth A. Martin⟩

lace lizard *n* **:** either of two large monitors (*Varanus varius* and *V. giganteus*) of Australia

lace paper *n* **:** a strong clean paper suitable for perforation with an openwork design in imitation of lace

lace pillow *n* **:** PILLOW 3

lace plant *n* **1 :** LATTICE PLANT **2 :** ARTILLERY PLANT

lacepod \'=,=\ *n* **:** FRINGEPOD

lac·er \'lāsə(r)\ *n* -s **:** one that laces (as shoes or footballs during manufacture or book covers during binding)

lac·er·a·bil·i·ty \ˌlasərəˈbiləd·ē\ *n* **:** the quality or state of being vulnerable to laceration

lac·er·a·ble \'lasərəbəl\ *adj* [LL *lacerabilis*, fr. L *lacerare* to lacerate + *-abilis* -able] **:** capable of being lacerated

¹**lac·er·ate** \'lasə,rāt, *usu* -ād·+V\ *adj* [L *laceratus*, past part.] **:** LACERATED

²**lacerate** \"\ *vt* -ED/-ING/-S [L *laceratus*, past part. of *lacerare* to tear, prob. fr. *lacer* mangled; akin to Gk *lakis* rent] **1 :** to tear or rend roughly **:** wound jaggedly ⟨my feet *lacerated* and swollen —Herbert Passin⟩ ⟨oil smears trail on the blue water from her *lacerated* flank as a torpedo strikes home —H.W. Baldwin⟩ ⟨*lacerated* by rocks —Claud Cockburn⟩ ⟨enlarge and ~ the heart —Sacheverell Sitwell⟩ **2 :** to cause sharp mental or emotional pain to **:** PIERCE, HARROW, TORMENT ⟨Puritan susceptibilities had been *lacerated* —Arnold Bennett⟩ ⟨delighted in *lacerating* frauds and crackpots —Richard Maney⟩ — **lac·er·a·tive** \-ˌrād·iv, -rəd-\ *adj*

lacerated *adj* **1 a :** torn jaggedly **:** RENT **b :** HARROWED, TORTURED ⟨may well conceal ~ pity —Pier-Maria Pasinetti⟩ **2 :** having the margin or apex deeply and irregularly cut or incised

lac·er·a·tion \ˌlasəˈrāshən\ *n* -s [MF, fr. L *laceration-, laceratio*, fr. *laceratus* (past part.) + *-ion-, -io* -ion] **1 :** the act of lacerating **2 :** a breach or wound made by lacerating

la·cer·ta \lə'sərd·ə\ *n, cap* [NL, fr. L, lizard — more at LEG] **:** a genus (the type of the family Lacertidae) of lizards formerly including nearly all known lizards but now restricted to certain typical Old World forms — see GREEN LIZARD, SAND LIZARD

la·cer·tae \-d·(ˌ)ē\ *n pl, cap* [NL, fr. pl. of L *lacerta* lizard] **:** a division of Lacertilia comprising the typical lizards as distinguished from the chameleons and geckos

la·cer·tian \lə'sərsh(ē)ən\ *adj or n* [L *lacerta* lizard + E *-ian*] **:** LACERTILIAN

¹**la·cer·tid** \lə'sərd·əd\ *adj* [NL *Lacertidae*] **:** of or relating to the genus *Lacerta* or family Lacertidae

²**lacertid** \"\ *n* -s **:** a lacertid lizard

la·cer·ti·dae \-d·əˌdē\ *n pl, cap* [NL, fr. *Lacerta*, type genus + *-idae*] **:** a large Old World family of terrestrial zoophagous lizards with well-developed limbs, pleurodont dentition, and deeply notched tongue

la·cer·ti·form \-ˌfȯrm\ *adj* [prob. fr. F *lacertiforme*, fr. L *lacerta* lizard + F *-iforme* -iform] **:** having the form or structure of a typical lizard

lac·er·til·ia \ˌlasə(r)'tilēə\ *n pl, cap* [NL *Lacerta* + *-ilia* (as in NL *Reptilia*)] **:** a division of Reptilia (usu. a suborder of Squamata) comprising the true lizards, chameleons, geckos, and various related limbless forms all related closely to the snakes in structure and of origin no earlier apparently than the Jurassic and typically distinguished by a tapering tail, well-developed pentadactyl limbs, a scaly or tuberculated skin, and movable eyelids — compare GILA MONSTER

¹**lac·er·til·i·an** \ˌ==ˈtilēən\ *adj* [NL *Lacertilia* + E *-an*] **:** of or relating to the Lacertilia or to a lizard

²**lacertilian** \"\ *n* -s **:** one of the Lacertilia **:** LIZARD

la·cer·ti·loid \lə'sərd·əˌlȯid\ *adj* [NL *Lacertilia* + E *-oid*] **:** like or relating to the Lacertilia

lac·er·tine \'lasə(r)ˌtīn, -ˌtən\ *adj* [L *lacerta* lizard + E *-ine*] **1 :** resembling a lizard **:** LACERTILIAN **2 :** adorned with interlacings suggestive of lizard forms

la·cer·toid \lə'sərˌtȯid\ *adj* [L *lacerta* lizard + E *-oid* — more at LEG] **:** resembling a lizard

la·cer·tus fi·bro·sus \lə'sərd·əsfī'brōsəs\ *n* [NL, lit., fibrous forearm] **:** an aponeurotic expansion from the medial border of the biceps tendon to the fascia of the ulnar side of the forearm

lac·ery \'lās(ə)rē\ *n* -ES **:** a lacy appearance or pattern ⟨~ of impermanent girders —Frank Clune⟩ ⟨the ~ of intertwined trees —Nora Waln⟩

laces *pl of* LACE, *pres 3d sing of* LACE

lace stitch *n* **:** a loose open stitch used in the lighter parts of a design

lacewing \'=,=\ *also* **lacewing fly** *or* **lacewinged fly** \'=,=-\ *n* **:** any of various neuropterous insects of *Chrysopa, Hemerobius,* and related genera having delicate lacelike wing venation, long antennae, and brilliant eyes and producing larvae useful in destroying aphids and other small insects — see APHIS LION

lacewood \'=,=\ *n* **1 :** LACEBARK 2 **2 :** SYCAMORE 3b — used esp. of the quartersawed wood **3 :** SILK OAK

lacework \'=,=\ *n* **:** forms consisting of or resembling lace ⟨the sculptured sections of the church facades seem to be covered with delicate ~ —Sirarpie Der Nersessian⟩

lacey *var of* LACY

lach·e·na·lia \ˌlashəˈnālēə\ *n* [NL, fr. W. de *Lachenal* †1800 Swiss botanist + NL *-ia*] **1** *cap* **:** a genus of bulbous plants (family Liliaceae) of southern Africa with ingulate basal leaves and tubular red and yellow flowers **2** -s **:** any plant of the genus *Lachenalia* — see CAPE COWSLIP, LEOPARD LILY

lach·es \'lachəz, 'lāch-, 'lash-\ *n, pl* **laches** \"\ [ME *lachesse*, fr. MF *laschesse*, fr. OF *lasche* lax, indolent, fr. *laschier* to loose, fr. LL *laxicare* to become shaky, fr. L *laxare* to loosen — more at LAXATE] **1 :** slackness or carelessness toward duty or opportunity **:** NEGLIGENCE, REMISSNESS ⟨not to be saved by the most liberal allowance of trisyllabic feet, for libertine accentuation, and for other ~ of the kind —George Saintsbury⟩ **2 a** *in equity* **:** neglect to do a thing at the proper time **:** undue delay in asserting a right or claiming a privilege — compare STATUTE OF LIMITATIONS **b :** culpable negligence

lach·e·sis \'lakəsəs\ *n, cap* [NL, fr. Gk, Lachesis, one of the three Fates, disposer of lots, fr. *lachein*, 2d aoristic infinitive of *lanchanein* to obtain by lot] **:** a genus of American pit vipers comprising the bushmaster and related snakes that are sometimes included in the genus *Trimeresurus*

lach·nan·thes \lak'nan(t)(ˌ)thēz\ *n, cap* [NL, fr. Gk *lachnos, lachnē* soft woolly hair + NL *-anthes*; akin to OSlav *vlasŭ* hair; fr. the woolly flowers] **:** a genus of No. American herbs (family Haemodoraceae) having leaves both clustered at the base and scattered on the stem and loosely woolly flowers in a compound cyme — see REDROOT

lach·no·ster·na \ˌlaknō'stərnə\ [NL, fr. Gk *lachnos, lachnē* soft woolly hair + *sternon* breast, chest — more at STERNUM] *syn of* PHYLLOPHAGA

lachrymable *adj* [L *lacrimabilis*, fr. *lacrima*, tear + *-abilis* -able — more at TEAR (of the eye)] *obs* **:** LAMENTABLE, TEARFUL

lach·ry·ma chris·ti *or* **lac·ri·ma chris·ti** \ˌlakrəmə'kri(ˌ)stē, -ˌstī\ *n, pl* **lachry·mae christi** *or* **lacri·mae christi** \-(ˌ)mē-'kri(ˌ)stē, -ˌstī; -ˌmī'kri(ˌ)stē\ *usu cap L&C* [ML, Christ's tear, fr. L *lacrima Christi*] **:** a still Italian wine produced from grapes grown near Vesuvius that is white, red, or rosé and sweet or dry

lach·ry·mal *or* **lac·ri·mal** \'lakrəməl\ *adj* [MF or ML; MF *lacrymal*, fr. ML *lacrimalis*, fr. L *lacrima* tear + *-alis* -al] **1** *usu lacrimal* **:** of, relating to, or situated near the organs that produce tears **2 :** marked by tears **:** LACHRYMOSE ⟨a ~ farewell⟩ **3 :** of or relating to tears ⟨~ effusions⟩

lachrymation *var of* LACRIMATION

lachrymator *var of* LACRIMATOR

lachrymatory *var of* LACRIMATORY

lach·ry·mist \'lakrəməst\ *n* -s [L *lacrima, lacruma* tear + E *-ist*] *archaic* **:** one given to weeping

lach·ry·mose \'lakrəˌmōs\ *adj* [L *lacrimosus*, fr. *lacrima* tear + *-osus* -ose — more at TEAR (of the eye)] **1 :** given to tears or weeping **:** suffused with tears **:** TEARFUL **2 :** fit to bring tears or induce mournfulness **:** DISMAL, MELANCHOLY ⟨their songs were sentimental and ~, full of dying heroes and parted lovers —Bernard DeVoto⟩ — **lach·ry·mose·ly** *adv* — **lach·ry·mos·i·ty** \ˌ==ˈmäsəd·ē\ *n* -ES

lachs·schin·ken \'läks(h)ˌshiŋkən\ *n, pl* **lachsschinken** *or* **lachsschinkens** [G, lit., salmon ham, fr. *lachs* salmon + *schinken* ham; prob. fr. its color and appearance] **:** a boned double loin of pork that is rolled, mild-cured, slightly smoked, and pressed into a casing

1 acid *n, usu cap L* **:** a crystalline acid $HOC_{10}H_6SO_3H$ used as an intermediate for azo dyes; 1-naphthol-5-sulfonic acid

lacier *comparative of* LACY

laciest *superlative of* LACY

lac·i·ly \'lāsəlē\ *adv* **:** in a lacy fashion or manner

lac·i·ness \-sēnəs\ *n* -ES **:** the quality or state of being lacy

lac·ing \'lāsiŋ, -sēŋ\ *n* -s [ME *lacinge*, gerund of *lacen* to lace — more at LACE] **1 :** the action of one that laces (as by tying, tightening, beating) **2 a :** a fastening lace for clothing ⟨shoe ~⟩ ⟨corset ~⟩ **b :** ornamental braid or trimming for uniforms or clothing **c :** a thong of thin leather or a series of metal clips used to join the ends of a machine-driving belt **3 :** a marginal band of color contrasting with the chief color (as on the ear of a rabbit or on a feather) **4 a :** a dash of alcoholic liquor in a food or beverage ⟨coffee with a ~ of whiskey⟩ **b :** a trace or sprinkling that enlivens or adds spice or savor ⟨sprinkles the whole sound track with a ~ of simpering snorts —Goodman Ace⟩ ⟨the committee was made up of old Bostonians with a ~ of others —Francis Russell⟩ **5 a** *or* **lacing line :** a rope or line laced through eyelets along the edge of a sail or awning to attach it to a boom, gaff, or yard **b :** a knee timber fitted behind a ship's figurehead **6 :** BATTERING, TROUNCING ⟨gave the marble thief a quick but thorough ~ —*Argosy*⟩ ⟨what kind of a ~ will the taxpayers take —B.M.Bowie⟩

lacing course *n* **:** a course usu. of brick built into a wall constructed of stone or other irregularly shaped material to bond and level it

la·cin·ia \lə'sinēə\ *n, pl* **lacini·ae** \-ēˌē\ *or* **lacinias** [NL, fr. L, lappet, flap; akin to L *lacer* mangled — more at LACERATE] **1 :** a narrow incised segment in a leaf or similar structure **2 a :** the inner process of the stipes of an insect's maxilla and esp. of its first maxilla **b :** a slender fleshy process on the head of a fish

la·cin·i·ate \lə'sinēˌāt\ *or* **la·cin·i·at·ed** \-ād·əd\ *adj* [L *lacinia* lappet, flap + E *-ate* or *-ated* (fr. *-ate* + *-ed*)] **:** bordered with a fringe **:** cut into deep irregular usu. pointed lobes **:** narrowly incised with divisions coarser than fimbriate — used of a plant or animal part

la·cin·i·a·tion \ˌ===ˈāshən\ *n* -s [NL *lacinia* + E *-ation*] **1 :** LACINIA **2 :** the quality or state of being laciniate

la·cin·i·ose \lə'sinēˌōs\ *adj* [L *laciniosus*, fr. *lacinia* lappet, flap + *-osus* -ose] **:** LACINIATE, FRINGED

lac insect *n* **:** a scale (*Laccifer lacca*) of southeast Asia that produces lac; *broadly* **:** any of various related scales

la·cin·u·la \lə'sinyələ\ *n, pl* **lacinu·lae** \-yəˌlē\ *or* **lacinulas** [NL, dim. of L *lacinia* lappet, flap] **:** a small lacinia — **la·cin·u·late** \-yəˌlāt\ *adj* — **la·cin·u·lose** \-ˌlōs\ *adj*

la·cis \'lāsəs\ *n* -ES [F, fr. MF, fr. OF, fr. *lacier* to lace — more at LACE] **:** NETWORK, NET; *specif* **:** a square-meshed lace with darned patterns

¹**lack** \'lak, *chiefly southern US dial* 'līk\ *vb* -ED/-ING/-S [ME *laken*, fr. MD, to be lacking, to blame; akin to MD *lac* lack, fault] *vi* **1 :** to be wanting or missing **:** FAIL ⟨nothing is ~*ing* but the will⟩ ⟨space ~*s* for a linguistic analysis —Eric Partridge⟩ ⟨the sense of distance ~*s*; a ridge nearby can be a far-off mountain range —Paul Bowles⟩ **2 :** to want supply or satisfaction **:** be short ⟨enjoined the tapster to see to it that no one ~*ed* for his thirst —Arnold Bennett⟩ ⟨such language is comparatively ~*ing* in responsibility —R.M.Weaver⟩ ~ *vt* **1 :** to be void or destitute of **:** be without or deficient in ⟨what . . . the church ~*s* is democracy —Leo Pfeffer⟩ ⟨~*ed* the ability to become a great singer —W.J.Reilly⟩ ⟨this statement, like all simple statements, ~*s* detail —Charlton Laird⟩ ⟨her voice may be flexible enough, but ~*s* the requisite strength —Lafcadio Hearn⟩ **2** *obs* **:** to feel the absence of **:** MISS ⟨you're loved, sir. They that least lend it you shall ~ you first —Shak.⟩ **3 :** to stand in need of **:** REQUIRE, WANT — used formerly in the vendor's cry *what do you lack?*

syn LACK, WANT, NEED, and REQUIRE can imply the absence of something, esp. essential or to be desired. LACK implies such an absence, esp. due to shortage of supply ⟨blankets were made of sage bark cords when rabbit skins were *lacking* —C.D.Forde⟩ ⟨a delicacy of design that larger houses often *lack* —*Amer. Guide Series: N.H.*⟩ ⟨many languages *lack* grammatical person entirely —Weston La Barre⟩ WANT in this application stresses a deplorable lack or adds to LACK the idea of pressing desire or urgent necessity ⟨an age *wanting* in moral grandeur —Matthew Arnold⟩ ⟨an American truck that *wanted* only a few repairs —Richard Llewellyn⟩ ⟨poverty-stricken and *wanting* even the necessities of existence⟩ NEED is used more commonly than WANT in this context to stress necessity ⟨what the business and industrial world most *need* and seek —R.W.McEwen⟩ ⟨assist an increasing number of American families in finding the things they *need* and want —*Annual Report J. C. Penney Corp.*⟩ ⟨both of these bridges are badly *needed* —*Americana Annual*⟩ ⟨it only *needed* that the letter should be correctly addressed —H.E.Scudder⟩ ⟨*need* food and clothing⟩ REQUIRE, similar to if not stronger than NEED in implying necessity, can also suggest the importunity of urgent desire or craving ⟨he found his studies too easy to *require* serious attention —E.S.Bates⟩ ⟨so ill as to *require* constant attendance⟩ ⟨the continuing deficit *requires* either higher rates or a sales tax —*New Republic*⟩ ⟨the reactor *requires* radically new metals to withstand great heats —Tris Coffin⟩

²**lack** \"\ *n* -s [ME *lac*, fr. MD, lack, fault; akin to MLG *lak* lack, error, ON *lakr* lacking, defective, OFris *lec* damage, ON *leka* to leak — more at LEAK] **1 :** the fact or state of being wanting or deficient **:** inadequate or missing supply or provision **:** DEFICIENCY, FAILURE, WANT ⟨explain the comparative ~ of simian fossils —R.W.Murray⟩ ⟨~ of true insight into human passion —A.T.Quiller-Couch⟩ **2 :** that which is lacking **:** the thing needed ⟨green forage is a ~ of desert regions⟩ **syn** see ABSENCE

³**lack** *var of* LAC

lack·a·dai·si·cal \ˌlakəˌdāzəkəl, ˌēk- *sometimes* -ˌās\ *adj* [by folk etymology fr. *lackaday* + *-ical*] **:** lacking life, spirit, or zest **:** devoid of energy or purpose **:** IDLE, VACUOUS ⟨communism is in deadly earnest, whereas the so-called "free world" is ~ —J.F.Dulles⟩ ⟨a mere ~, spiritless young man-about-town —P.G.Wodehouse⟩ **syn** see LANGUID

lack·a·dai·si·cal·ly \-k(ə)lē, -li\ *adv* **:** in a lackadaisical manner

¹**lack·a·dai·sy** \'lakəˌdāzē\ *n* -ES [by folk etymology fr. *lackaday*] **:** INDIFFERENCE, LASSITUDE

²**lackadaisy** \"\ *interj, archaic* — used to express sorrow or regret

lack·a·day \'lakəˌdā\ *interj* [by alter. and shortening fr. *alack the day*] *archaic* — used to express sorrow or regret

lacker *var of* LACQUER

¹**lack·ey** *or* **lac·quey** \'lakē, -ki\ *n* -s [MF *laquais*, perh. fr. Catal *lacayo, alacayo*] **1 :** a liveried retainer **:** FLUNKY, FOOTMAN ⟨there was jumping of ~*s*, a slamming of car doors, a glare of headlights —Winifred Bambrick⟩ **2 :** a servile follower **:** HANGER-ON, TOADY ⟨join him in refusing to be ~*s* of an appointive official —M.W.Straight⟩ ⟨continued to caricature him as a ~ of capitalism —*Time*⟩

²**lackey** *or* **lacquey** \"\ *vb* -ED/-ING/-S *vi, obs* **:** to play the lackey **:** dance attendance **:** TOADY ~ *vt* **:** to wait upon **:** serve obsequiously **:** ATTEND ⟨a thousand liveried angels ~ her —John Milton⟩ ⟨stop ~*ing* and valeting the spirit of the age —W.L.Sullivan⟩

lackey moth *also* **lackey** *n* -s [so called fr. the resemblance of the caterpillar's coat to a footman's livery] **:** a European moth (*Malacosoma neustria*) with a larva that is a tent caterpillar sometimes injurious to orchard trees and other woody plants

lacking *prep* [fr. *lacking*, pres. part. of ¹*lack*] **:** WANTING

¹**lackland** \'=,=\ *n* [¹*lack* + *land*] **:** a person owning no land

²**lackland** \"\ *adj* **:** owning no land **:** LANDLESS, PROPERTYLESS ⟨~ adventurers are honored above men of honest birth —T.B. Costain⟩

¹**lackluster** \'=,==\ *adj* [¹*lack* + *luster* (n.)] **:** lacking in sheen, radiance, or vitality **:** DULL, UNINSPIRED ⟨looked into space with ~ eyes —Bram Stoker⟩ ⟨the town has ~ dirt streets and plenty of stray dogs —W.A. Krauss⟩ ⟨eager new recruits too often are beaten down to the hangdog, ~ average —Bennett Cerf⟩

²**lackluster** \"\ *n* **:** absence or want of luster ⟨attempts to justify the ~ of psychoanalytic biography —R.M.Wendlinger⟩

lackmoid *var of* LACMOID

lacks *pres 3d sing of* LACK, *pl of* LACK

¹**lackwit** \'=,=\ *n* [¹*lack* + *wit*] **:** a dull or witless person **:** BLOCKHEAD, FOOL ⟨appealed strongly to the throng of ~*s* —H.L.Wilson⟩ ⟨the ~*s* who repeat these snappy sayings scarcely comprehend the distinction —*Springfield (Mass.) Union*⟩

²**lackwit** \"\ *adj* **:** lacking intelligence ⟨saddled with a ~ assistant —*Time*⟩

lac lake *n* [¹*lac*] **:** INDIAN LAKE

lac·moid *also* **lack·moid** \'lakˌmȯid\ *n* -s [*lacmoid*, ISV *lacm-* (fr. *lacmus*) + *-oid*; prob. orig. formed as G *lakmoid; lackmoid*, alter. of *lacmoid*] **:** a violet-blue dye resembling litmus that is made by the action of nitrites on resorcinol and is used as an indicator in titration

lac·mus *or* **lak·mus** \'lakməs\ *n* -ES [D *lakmoes*, fr. MD *leecmōs*, fr. *lēken* to drip (akin to OE *leccan* to moisten) + *mōs* green vegetables, mushy foods; akin to OE, OS, OFris *mōs* food, OHG *muos*, OE *mete* food — more at LEAK, MEAT] **:** LITMUS

¹**la·co·ni·an** \lə'kōnēən\ *adj, usu cap* [L *Laconia*, region of ancient Greece (fr. Gk *Lakōn*, n. & adj., Laconian) + E *-an*] **1 :** of, relating to, or characteristic of Laconia, a region of ancient Greece **2 :** of, relating to, or characteristic of the people of Laconia

²**laconian** \"\ *n* -s *cap* **:** a native or inhabitant of Laconia

¹**la·con·ic** \lə'känik, -nēk\ *adj* [L *Laconicus*, fr. Gk *Lakōnikos*, fr. *Lakōn* Laconian + *-ikos* -ic] **1** *archaic, usu cap* **:** of or relating to Laconia or the Laconians **:** SPARTAN **2 a :** speaking or writing with Spartan brevity **:** CURT, TERSE, UNDEMONSTRATIVE ⟨~, these Indians —Weston La Barre⟩ ⟨an antiseptic romance between Jones and a ~ young widow —Martin Levin⟩ **b :** spoken, written, or expressed briefly or sententiously **:** PITHY ⟨the tone of the commentary ~ and masculine —*Times Lit. Supp.*⟩ ⟨a ~ derby-hatted interlude that stops the show —Henry Hewes⟩ **syn** see CONCISE

²**laconic** \"\ *n* -s **1** *obs* **:** a laconic person **2 a :** curt or concise expression **b laconics** *pl* **:** concise sentences

laconical *adj* [L *Laconicus* + E *-al*] *archaic* **:** LACONIC

la·con·i·cal·ly \-nək(ə)lē, -nēk-, -li\ *adv* **:** in a laconic manner

la·con·i·cism \lə'känəˌsizəm\ *n* -s [¹*laconic* + *-ism*] **:** LACONISM ⟨one of the most heroic ~*s* of all literature —D.C. Smith⟩

la·con·i·cum \lə'känəkəm\ *n, pl* **laconi·ca** \-əkə\ [L, fr. neut. of *Laconicus* Laconic] **:** the sweating room of an ancient Roman bath

lac·o·nism \'lakəˌnizəm\ *n* -s [MF & Gk; MF *laconisme*, fr. Gk *lakōnismos* imitation of Lacedaemonian manners, esp. in terseness of expression, fr. *lakōnizein* to speak laconically, laconize] **1 :** brevity or terseness of expression ⟨the provocative ~ of the newspaper headline, which conceals meaning almost as often as it expresses it —B.R.Redman⟩ **2 :** a laconic expression

lac·o·nize \'lakəˌnīz\ *vb* -ED/-ING/-S [Gk *lakōnizein*, fr. *Lakōn* Laconian + *-izein* -ize] *vi* **:** to incline to the Spartan cause or manner ~ *vt* **:** to subject to Spartan rule

la co·ru·na \ˌläkə'rün(y)ə\ *or* **la co·ru·ña** \-ünyə\ *adj, usu. cap L&C* [fr. *La Coruña*, Spain] **:** of or from the city of La Coruna, Spain **:** of the kind or style prevalent in La Coruna

lac·o·so·mat·i·dae \ˌlakōsə'madəˌdē\ *n pl, cap* [NL, fr. *Lacosomat-, Lacosoma*, genus of moths (fr. Gk *lakkos* pit, tank, pond + *sōmat-, sōma* body) + *-idae*] *syn of* MIMALLONIDAE

¹**lac·quer** *also* **lack·er** \'lakə(r)\ *n* -s [*lacquer*, alter. (prob. influenced by F *laque* lac) of earlier *lacker*, fr. obs. *leckar, laker, lacre* lac, fr. OPg *lacra, lacre, lácar*, variants of *laca*, fr. Ar *lakk* — more at LACCA] **1 a :** a spirit varnish (as shellac) often colored and used esp. for coating brass and other metals to heighten their luster or prevent tarnishing **b :** any of various tough durable natural varnishes; *esp* **:** a varnish obtained by tapping the Japanese varnish tree — called also *Chinese lacquer, Japanese lacquer;* compare BURMESE LACQUER **c :** any of various clear or colored synthetic liquid organic coatings that typically dry to form a film by evaporation of a volatile constituent and are used for many industrial purposes; *esp* **:** a coating in which a cellulose derivative (as cellulose nitrate) serves to form such a film with or without a natural or synthetic resin (as an alkyd) ⟨automotive ~*s* are sprayed on⟩ — compare ENAMEL 3, VARNISH 1a **d :** a highly glazed finish for fabrics usu. applied in patterns on a plain ground **e :** a resinous coating applied to flat sheet metal or formed metal cans and usu. dried by baking **2** *or* **lacquer ware :** a decorative article made of wood coated with Japanese or other Oriental lacquer and often inlaid with ivory or metal; *collectively* **:** such articles or ware **3** *or* **lacquer red :** a variable color averaging a dark reddish orange that is redder, stronger, and slightly lighter than ocher red and redder, stronger, and slightly lighter than burnt sienna **4 a :** a dressing (as an alcoholic solution of a gum or resin) for the hair usu. applied by spraying and intended to keep the hair smooth and in place **b :** NAIL POLISH

²**lacquer** *also* **lacker** \"\ *vt* -ED/-ING/-S **1 :** to coat with lacquer **:** VARNISH **2 :** to give a smooth finish or appearance to **:** to make glossy **:** POLISH ⟨wound up with a virtuosity that ~*ed* over any rough patches that had been laid bare in the White Paper —B.A.Young⟩ ⟨does not . . . ~ the phrase as did some of the accusers —Jerome Mellquist⟩

lacquer disc *n* **:** a phonograph record made usu. from a nitrocellulose lacquer

lacquered *adj* **:** coated with or as if with lacquer **:** GLOSSY, POLISHED, VARNISHED

lac·quer·er \-kərə(r)\ *n* -s **:** one that lacquers

lacquer film *n* **:** a lamination of lacquer, rubber cement, and waxed paper used for stencils in a silk-screen process

lacquering *n* -s **1 :** the application of lacquer **2 :** a lacquer finish

lacquer man *n* **:** one who mixes and tints lacquer paints

lacquer tree *or* **lacquer plant** *n* **:** a tree yielding lacquer or

Japan wax; *specif* : JAPANESE VARNISH TREE — compare VARNISH TREE
lacquerwork \'ˌ=,=\ *n* : LACQUER 2
lacquey *var of* LACKEY
lacrima christi *usu cap L&C, var of* LACHRYMA CHRISTI
lac·ri·mal *var of* LACHRYMAL
lacrimal bone *n* : a small thin bone making up part of the front inner wall of each orbit and giving passage to the lacrimal duct
lacrimal canal *n* **1** : LACRIMAL DUCT 1 **2** : the bony passage lodging the nasolacrimal duct
lacrimal caruncle *n* : a small reddish follicular elevation at the medial angle of the eye
lacrimal duct *n* **1** : a short canal leading from a minute orifice on a small elevation at the medial angle of each eyelid **2** : any of several small ducts leading from the lacrimal gland to the lateral angle of the eye
lac·ri·ma·le \ˌlakrə'ma(ˌ)lē, -mā(-, -mä(-\ *n* -s [NL, fr. neut. sing. of ML *lacrimalis* lachrymal — more at LACHRYMAL] : the point where the posterior edge of the lacrimal bone intersects the fronto-lacrimal suture
lacrimal gland *n* : an acinous gland that is about the size and shape of an almond and secretes tears
lacrimal sac *n* : a dilatation resembling a pouch that is located within the medial canthus of the eye, receives tears from the two lacrimal ducts (sense 1), and transmits them to the nasolacrimal duct
lacrimal sinus *n* : TEARPIT
la·cri·man·do \ˌläkrə'män(ˌ)dō, ˌlak-\ *adj (or adv)* [It, lit., weeping, lamenting, fr. L *lacrimandus*, gerundive of *lacrimare* to weep, shed tears] : DOLOROSO, LAMENTING, PLAINTIVE — used as a direction in music
lac·ri·ma·tion *also* **lach·ry·ma·tion** \ˌlakrə'māshən\ *n* -s [L *lacrimation-, lacrimatio*, fr. *lacrimatus* (past part. of *lacrimare* to weep) + *-ion-, -io* -ion] : the secretion of tears : WEEPING; *specif* : abnormal or excessive secretion of tears due to local or systemic disease
lac·ri·ma·tor *or* **lach·ry·ma·tor** \'==,mād·ə(r)\ *n* -s [*lacrimation* or *lachrymation* + *-or*] : a tear-producing substance (as chloroacetophenone) : TEAR GAS
[1]**lac·ri·ma·to·ry** *or* **lach·ry·ma·tory** \'lakrəmə,tōrē, -tȯr-, -ri\ *n* -ES [prob. fr. ML *lachrymatorium*, fr. neut. of *lachrymatorius*, adj., lacrimatory] : a vase found in ancient Roman tombs and formerly regarded as meant for the tears of mourners but now believed to have been a perfume bottle — called also *tear bottle*
[2]**lacrimatory** *or* **lachrymatory** \"\ *adj* [ML & LL; ML *lachrymatorius*, fr. LL *lacrimatorius*, fr. L *lacrimatus* (past part. of *lacrimare* to shed tears, weep, fr. *lacrima* tear) + *-orius* -ory — more at TEAR (of the eye)] **1** : of, relating to, or prompting tears **2** : meant to contain tears
lac·ri·mi·form \'lakrəmə,fȯrm\ *adj* [L *lacrima* tear + E *-iform*] : shaped like a teardrop
lac·ri·moid \'lakrə,mȯid\ *adj* [L *lacrima* tear + E *-oid*] : resembling a teardrop
la·cri·mo·so \ˌläkrə'mō(ˌ)sō, ˌlak-\ *adj (or adv)* [It, lit., tearful, lachrymose, fr. L *lacrimosus* — more at LACHRYMOSE] : marked by a plaintive style — used as a direction in music
la·croix·ite \lə'krwä,zīt\ *n* -s [F, fr. F. A. Alfred *Lacroix* †1948 Fr. mineralogist + F *-ite*] : a mineral approximately $Na(Ca,Mn)AlPO_4(OH)_3$ that consists of a basic phosphate of aluminum, calcium, manganese, and sodium often containing fluorine and that occurs in pale yellowish green crystals (hardness 4.1)
la·crosse \lə'krȯs *also* -räs\ *n* -s *often attrib* [CanF *la crosse*, lit., the crosier, the hooked stick] : a game originating among the No. American Indians that is played on a turfed field by 2 teams of 10 players each of whom uses a long-handled stick with which the ball is caught, carried, and thrown with the object being to throw the ball into the opponents' goal — compare CROSSE

lacrosse stick

lacrosse stick *n* : CROSSE
lacs *pl of* LAC
lact- *or* **lacti-** *or* **lacto-** *comb form* [*lact-* fr. F&L; F, fr. L, fr. *lact-, lac*; *lacti-* fr. F & LL; F, fr. LL, fr. L *lact-, lac*; *lacto-* fr. *lact-* + *-o-* — more at GALAXY] **1** : milk ⟨*lact*albumin⟩ ⟨*lacto*meter⟩ ⟨*lacti*genic⟩ **2 a** : lactate and ⟨*lacto*phosphate⟩ **b** : lactic acid ⟨*lact*amide⟩ ⟨*lacto*nitrite⟩ **c** : lactose ⟨*lacti*tol⟩ ⟨*lacto*bionic acid⟩
lac·ta·gogue \'laktə,gäg *sometimes* -gȯg\ *n* -s [*lact-* + *-agogue*] : GALACTAGOGUE
lact·al·bu·min \ˌlak,tal'byümən, -ü,min *sometimes* lak'talbyə-\ *n* -s [ISV *lact-* + *albumin*] : an albumin that is similar to serum albumin and is obtained from the whey of milk; *esp* : a protein fraction from whey including beta-lactoglobulin used in foods and in preparing protein hydrolysates
lac·tam \'lak,tam, =ˈ=\ *n* -s [ISV *lact*one + *am*ide; orig. formed in G] : any of a class of inner amides of amino carboxylic acids formed by the loss of a molecule of water from the amino and carboxyl groups and characterized by the carbonyl-imido grouping —CONH— in a ring — compare LACTIM, LACTONE, SULTAM
lac·ta·ri·us \lak'ta(a)rēəs, -ter-, -tār-\ *n*, *cap* [NL, fr. L, milky] : a large genus of white-spored agarics (family Agaricaceae) that exude a white or colored milky juice when cut or broken and that include an edible species (*L. deliciosus*) and some poisonous ones
lac·ta·ry \'laktərē\ *adj* [L *lactarius*, fr. *lact-* + *-arius* -ary] *archaic* : of or relating to milk : yielding a white milky juice
lac·tase \'lak,tās, -āz\ *n* -s [ISV *lact-* + *-ase*] : an enzyme that hydrolyzes lactose and other beta-galactosides and occurs esp. in the intestines of young mammals and in yeasts
[1]**lac·tate** \-āt, *usu* -ād·+V\ *n* -s [*lact-* + *-ate*] : a salt or ester of lactic acid
[2]**lactate** \"\ *vi* -ED/-ING/-S [L *lactatus*, past part. of *lactare* to suckle, secrete milk, fr. *lact-, lac* milk] : to secrete milk
lac·ta·tion \lak'tāshən\ *n* -s [prob. fr. F, fr. LL *lactation-, lactatio* suckling, fr. L *lactatus* (past part.) + *-ion-, -io* -ion] **1** : the secretion and yielding of milk by the mammary gland **2** : one complete period of lactation extending from about the time of parturition to weaning — **lac·ta·tion·al** \(ˈ)lak¦tāshənᵊl, -shnəl\ *adj* — **lac·ta·tion·al·ly** \-ᵊlē, -əlē, |i\ *adv*
lactation tetany *n* : MILK FEVER 1
[1]**lac·te·al** \'laktēəl\ *adj* [L *lacteus* of milk (fr. *lact-, lac* milk) + E *-al* — more at GALAXY] **1** : relating to, consisting of, producing, or resembling milk ⟨~ fluid⟩ ⟨~ organs⟩ **2 a** : conveying or containing a milky fluid (as chyle) ⟨a ~ channel⟩ **b** : of or relating to the lacteals ⟨impaired ~ function⟩
[2]**lacteal** \"\ *n* -s : one of the lymphatic vessels arising from the lymphatic radicles of the villi of the small intestine and conveying chyle from the intestine through the mesenteric glands to the thoracic duct
lacteal gland *n* : a lymph gland situated upon a lacteal vessel
lac·te·nin \'laktənən\ *n* -s [perh. fr. *lact-* + nitrogen + *-in*] : a nitrogenous substance present in milk that inhibits bacterial growth
lac·te·ous \'laktēəs\ *adj* [L *lacteus* of milk, milky, fr. *lact-, lac* milk] **1** *archaic* : MILKY, WHITE **2** : LACTEAL
lactescence *n* -s [L *lactescere* to turn to milk + E *-ence*] **1** : MILKINESS **2** : a copious flow of milky sap
lac·tes·cent \(ˈ)lak¦tesᵊnt\ *adj* [L *lactescent-, lactescens*, pres. part. of *lactescere* to turn to milk, incho. of *lactēre* to be milky, fr. *lact-, lac* milk] **1** : becoming or appearing milky **2 a** : secreting milk **b** : yielding a milky juice — used of a plant
lacti- — see LACT-
lac·tic \'laktik, -tēk\ *adj* [F *lactique*, fr. *lact-* + *-ique* -ic] **1** : of or relating to milk : obtained from sour milk or whey **2** : involving the production of lactic acid ⟨~ fermentation⟩
lactic acid *n* [part trans. of F *acide lactique*] : a hygroscopic usu. syrupy alpha-hydroxy acid $CH_3CH(OH)COOH$ that readily undergoes self-esterification when heated and is known in three optically isomeric forms: (1) the dextrorotatory L-form present normally in blood and muscle tissue as a product of the metabolism of glucose and glycogen; (2) the levorotatory D-form obtained by biological fermentation of sucrose; and (3) the racemic DL-form present in sour milk, beer, sauerkraut, pickles, and other food products and made usu. by bacterial fermentation (as of whey, molasses, raw sugar, or starch hydrolysates) but also synthetically, and used chiefly in foods and beverages, in medicine, in tanning and dyeing, and in making esters for use as solvents and plasticizers — called also respectively (1) *dextro-lactic acid or sarcolactic acid*, (2) *levo-lactic acid*, (3) *dl-lactic acid or ordinary lactic acid*; compare HYDRACRYLIC ACID
lactic acid bacterium *or* **lactic bacterium** *n* : any of various bacteria chiefly of the genera *Lactobacillus* and *Streptococcus* that produce predominantly lactic fermentation on suitable media and some of which are used in the commercial production of lactic acid and as cheese and butter starters
lactic casein *n* : acid casein precipitated from milk by lactic acid
lactic fermentation *n* : fermentation in which lactic acid is produced from carbohydrate materials (as lactose in whey) by the action of any of various organisms but esp. the lactic acid bacteria
lac·tide \'lak,tīd, -təd\ *n* -s [ISV *lact-* + anhyd*ride*; prob. orig. formed in F] **1** : a crystalline dilactone $C_6H_8O_4$ formed from two molecules of lactic acid by self-esterification **2** : a dilactone formed from an alpha-hydroxy acid other than lactic acid
lac·tif·er·ous \(ˈ)lak¦tif(ə)rəs\ *adj* [F or LL; F *lactifère* lactiferous, fr. LL *lactifer* (fr. *lacti-* — fr. L *lact-, lac* milk — + L *-fer* — adj. comb. form) + E *-ous* — more at GALAXY, -FER] **1** : secreting or conveying milk **2 a** : yielding a milky juice **b** : LATICIFEROUS — **lac·tif·er·ous·ness** *n* -ES
lac·tif·ic \-fik\ *also* **lac·tif·i·cal** \-fəkəl\ *adj* [*lactific* fr. F *lactifique*, fr. *lacti-* lact- + *-fique* -fic; *lactifical* fr. F *lactifique* + E *-al*] : producing milk
lac·ti·fy \'laktə,fī\ *vt* -ED/-ING/-ES [*lact-* + *-fy*] : to transform by lactic fermentation
lac·tim \'lak,tim, =ˈ=\ *n* -s [ISV *lact*one + *im*ide; orig. formed in G] : any of a class of hydroxy imides tautomeric with lactams and characterized by the enolic grouping —C(OH)=N—
lac·ti·tol \'laktə,tōl, -tōl\ *n* -s [*lact-* + *-itol*] : a crystalline alcohol $C_{12}H_{24}O_{11}$ obtained by hydrogenation of lactose
lac·tiv·o·rous \(ˈ)lak¦tiv(ə)rəs\ *adj* [*lact-* + *-vorous*] : feeding on milk
lacto- — see LACT-
lac·to·bac·il·la·ce·ae \ˌlaktō,basə'lāsē,ē\ *n pl*, *cap* [NL, fr. *Lactobacillus*, type genus + *-aceae*] : a large family of rod-shaped or spherical gram-negative usu. microaerophilic and nonmotile bacteria that require carbohydrates for growth, fermenting them chiefly to lactic acid, and include the lactic acid bacteria as well as important pathogens — see DIPLOCOCCUS, LACTOBACILLUS, STREPTOCOCCUS
lac·to·bacillus \¦lak(ˌ)tō+\ *n* [NL, fr. *lact-* + *Bacillus*, genus of bacteria] **1** *cap* : a genus of gram-positive nonmotile lactic-acid-forming bacteria (family Lactobacillaceae) including various commercially important lactic acid bacteria **2** *pl* **lactobacilli** : any bacterium of the genus *Lactobacillus*
lactobacillus ca·sei factor \-'kāsē,ī-\ *n, cap L* [NL *Lactobacillus casei* (lit., *Lactobacillus* of cheese), species of *Lactobacillus* that produces it] : folic acid or a higher conjugated pteroylglutamic acid
lac·to·bac·te·ri·a·ce·ae \ˌlaktō(ˌ)bak,tirē'āsē,ē\ [NL, irreg. fr. *Lactobacter*, syn. of *Lactobacillus* (fr. *lact-* + *-bacter*) + *-aceae*] *syn of* LACTOBACILLACEAE
lac·to·bi·on·ic acid \¦laktō(ˌ)bī¦änik-\ *n* [ISV *lactobio*se lactose (fr. *lact-* + *biose*) + *-onic*] : a syrupy acid $C_{11}H_{21}O_{10}$-COOH obtained by oxidation of lactose
lac·to·chrome \'laktə,krōm\ *n* [*lact-* + *-chrome*] : RIBOFLAVIN
lac·to·flavin \¦lak(ˌ)tō+\ *n* [ISV *lact-* + *flavin*] : RIBOFLAVIN
lac·to·gen \'laktəjən, -,jen\ *n* -s [*lact-* + *-gen*] : LACTOGENIC HORMONE
lac·to·genesis \¦lak(ˌ)tō+\ *n* [NL, fr. *lact-* + *genesis*] : initiation of lactation
lac·to·gen·ic \¦laktə¦jenik\ *adj* [*lact-* + *-genic*] : inducing lactation
lactogenic hormone *n* : a crystalline protein of the anterior lobe of the pituitary gland that induces lactation, maintains the corpora lutea in a functioning state in mammals, and stimulates the crop gland in birds — called also *luteotrophin, prolactin*
lac·to·globulin \¦lak(ˌ)tō+\ *n* [ISV *lact-* + *globulin*; prob. orig. formed in Sw] : a crystalline protein fraction that is obtained from the whey of milk and is soluble in half-saturated ammonium sulfate solution but insoluble in pure water — called also *beta-lactoglobulin*; compare LACTALBUMIN
lac·tom·e·ter \lak'tämәd·ə(r)\ *n* [*lact-* + *meter*] : a hydrometer for determining the specific gravity of milk
lac·tone \'lak,tōn\ *n* -s [ISV *lact-* + *-one*] : any of a class of inner esters of hydroxy carboxylic acids formed typically by the loss of a molecule of water from the hydroxyl and carboxyl groups of the acids, characterized by the carbonyl-oxy grouping —OCO— in a ring, and classed according to the position of the hydroxyl group in the parent acid ⟨gamma-*lactones* from gamma-hydroxy acids contain five-membered rings and delta-*lactones* from delta-hydroxy acids contain 6-membered rings⟩ — compare SULTONE — **lac·ton·ic** \(ˈ)lak¦tänik\ *adj*
lac·to·nitrile \¦lak(ˌ)tō+\ *n* [ISV *lact-* + *nitrile*] : a liquid $CH_3CH(OH)CN$ made by addition of hydrogen cyanide to acetaldehyde and used in making esters of lactic acid; acetaldehyde cyanohydrin
lac·to·ni·za·tion \ˌlaktōnə'zāshən\ *n* -s : the process of lactonizing
lac·to·nize \'laktō,nīz\ *vb* -ED/-ING/-S [*lactone* + *-ize*] *vt* : to convert into a lactone ~ *vi* : to become converted into a lactone
lac·to·phosphate \¦lak(ˌ)tō+\ *n* [*lact-* + *phosphate*] : a mixture of a lactate and a phosphate ⟨calcium ~⟩
lac·to·prene \'laktə,prēn\ *n* -s [*lact-* + *isoprene*] : any of several synthetic rubbers that are polymers or copolymers of an acrylic ester (as ethyl acrylate) and are characterized by good resistance to flexing and good resistance to hydrocarbon oils, oxygen and ozone, weather, and heat but not to low temperatures
lac·tose \'lak,tōs\ *n* -s [ISV *lact-* + *-ose*; prob. orig. formed in F] : a slightly sweet dextrorotatory reducing disaccharide sugar $C_{12}H_{22}O_{11}$ that is present in milk, that is less soluble in water than glucose or sucrose, that on hydrolysis yields glucose and galactose and on fermentation by various organisms yields esp. lactic acid (as in the souring of milk), that is usu. obtained from whey by evaporation as hard crystals of the alpha form containing a molecule of water, and that is used chiefly in foods, medicines, and culture media (as for the manufacture of penicillin); 4-β-galactosyl-glucose
lac·to·side \'laktə,sīd\ *n* -s [*lactose* + *-ide*] : a glycoside that yields lactose on hydrolysis
lac·tos·uria \ˌlaktō's(h)ùrēə, -ōs'yù-\ *n* -s [NL, fr. ISV *lactose* + NL *-uria*] : the presence of lactose in the urine
lac·to·vegetarian \¦lak(ˌ)tō+\ *adj* [*lact-* + *vegetarian*] : of or relating to a diet of milk, vegetables, fruits, grains, and nuts and sometimes eggs
lac·to·yl \'laktə,wil\ *or* **lac·tyl** \'lak,til\ *n* -s [ISV *lact-* + *-oyl* or *-yl*] : the radical $CH_3CH(OH)CO$— of lactic acid
lac tree *n* [[1]lac] : LACQUER TREE
lac·tu·ca \lak'tükə, -k'tyü-\ *n*, *cap* [NL, fr. L, lettuce — more at LETTUCE] : a genus of widely distributed milky-juiced herbs (family Compositae) having a beaked achene and soft white multiseriate pappus — see LETTUCE, PRICKLY LETTUCE
lac·tu·car·i·um \ˌlaktə'ka(a)rēəm, -'ker-, -'kār-\ *n* -s [NL, fr. *Lactuca*, genus that produces it + L *-arium*] : the dried milky juice of a prickly lettuce (*Lactuca virosa*) resembling opium in physical properties and formerly used as a sedative
la·cu·na \lə'k(y)ünə\ *n*, *pl* **lacu·nae** \-k(y)ü(ˌ)nē, -kü,nī\ *or* **lacunas** \-k(y)ünəz\ [L, pit, cleft, pool — more at LAGOON] **1** : a blank space : a missing part : GAP, HOLE; *also* : DEFECT, FLAW ⟨the *lacunae* in substantive information —P.M.Hauser⟩ ⟨with a cultured man there is no gap or ~ between his opinions and his life —J.C.Powys⟩ **2** [NL, fr. L] **a** : one of the follicles in the mucous membrane of the urethra **b** : one of the minute cavities in bone or cartilage occupied by the cells **c** (1) : one of the small pits on the surface of some of the lichens (2) : a gap in the protoxylem resulting from breakdown of protoxylem elements during elongation of a root or shoot — called also *carinal canal* (3) : a depressed space or pit on the outer surface of a pollen grain **d** : one of the spaces among the tissues of lower animals that serve in place of vessels for the circulation of the body fluids **3** [NL, fr. L] *cap* : a large cosmopolitan genus of chinks that is the type of the family Lacunidae but was often formerly included in Littorinidae **syn** see BREAK
la·cu·nal \-k(y)ünᵊl\ *or* **la·cu·nar** \-nə(r)\ *adj* [*lacuna* + *-al* or *-ar*] : LACUNARY
la·cu·nar \"\ *n*, *pl* **lacunars** \-nə(r)z\ *or* **lac·u·nar·ia** \ˌlakyə'na(a)rēə\ [L, fr. *lacuna* pit] **1** *pl* *lacunars* : a vault or ceiling constructed with recessed panels **2** *pl* *lacunaria* : a recessed panel forming part of a regularly patterned ceiling, vault, or soffit : COFFER
lacu·nary \'lakyə,nerē, lə'k(y)ünərē\ *adj* [*lacuna* + *-ary*] : of, relating to, or including lacunae
lacu·nate \lə'k(y)ü,nāt, 'lakyə,n-\ *adj* [NL *lacuna* + E *-ate*] : LACUNARY
la·cune \lə'k(y)ün\ *n* -s [F or L; F *lacune*, fr. L *lacuna* pit, cleft, pool — more at LAGOON] : LACUNA
la·cu·ni·dae \-nə,dē\ *n pl*, *cap* [NL, fr. *Lacuna*, type genus + *-idae*] : a cosmopolitan family of marine gastropods (suborder Taenioglossa) that comprise the chinks and are characterized by a conical umbilicate shell with a slit leading to the umbilicus
lac·u·nome \'lakyə,nōm\ *n* -s [It *lacunoma*, fr. NL *lacuna* + *-oma*] : a system of lacunar spaces sometimes demonstrable in some animal cells and suggested to be comparable to the vacuolar apparatus of the typical plant cell
la·cu·nule \lə'k(y)ü,nyül\ *n* -s [*lacuna* + *-ule*] : a small lacuna
la·cu·nu·lose \-)ünyə,lōs\ *adj* [*lacunule* + *-ule* + *-ose*] : having minute lacunae
la·cus·tral \lə'kəstrəl\ *adj* [*lacustr*ine + *-al*] : LACUSTRINE
[1]**la·cus·tri·an** \-rēən\ *adj* [*lacustr*ine + *-an*] : LACUSTRINE
[2]**lacustrian** \"\ *n* -s : LAKE DWELLER
la·cus·trine \-rən\ *adj* [prob. fr. F or It *lacustre* lacustrine (fr. L *lacus* lake; prob. influenced by L *paluster*, *palustris* marshy) + E *-ine* — more at LAKE] **1** : of, relating to, or formed in lakes ⟨~ waters⟩ ⟨~ deposits⟩ **2** : growing or living in lakes ⟨a ~ flora⟩ ⟨~ fishes⟩ **3** : of or relating to dwellings built on piles in lakes esp. in prehistoric central Europe, Scotland, and Ireland
LACW *abbr* leading aircraftswoman
lac wax *n* : SHELLAC WAX
lacy *or* **lacey** \'lāsē, -si\ *adj* **lac·i·er**; **lac·i·est** : resembling, exhibiting, or consisting of lace : LACELIKE ⟨a ~ lady from the past with a passion for the future —*Newsweek*⟩ ⟨ended with ~, upper-register piano notes —Whitney Balliett⟩ ⟨you start out . . . to look at the ~ iron balconies and the old houses —R.M.Hodesh⟩
lad \'lad, -aa(ə)d\ *n* -s [ME *ladde*] **1 a** *obs* : a male attendant : MANSERVANT **b** *obs* : a man of low station : VARLET, KNAVE **c** *Brit* : a stableboy in a racing stable : GROOM **2 a** : a male person of any age between early boyhood and maturity : BOY, YOUTH, STRIPLING ⟨a young country ~⟩ ⟨a ~ not yet twenty⟩ ⟨all the local ~s and lasses⟩ **b** : a male child : SON ⟨~s, less often girls, are named after nephews or nieces —J.G.Frazer⟩ **3** : MAN, FELLOW, CHAP — often used familiarly or in affection or admiration ⟨here's luck, ~⟩ ⟨a great ~ with the ladies⟩ ⟨a couple of likely ~s for a brawl⟩ **4** : SWEETHEART ⟨have ye seen aught of my bonnie ~⟩
la·da·khi *also* **la·da·ki** \lə'däkē\ *n*, *pl* **ladakhi** *or* **ladakhis** *also* **ladaki** *or* **ladakis** *usu cap* **1** : a native or inhabitant of Ladakh, a region of eastern Kashmir **2** : a Tibetan dialect of Ladakh
la·dang \'lä,däŋ\ *n* -s [D, fr. Malay] : a milpa in tropical Asia
ladanum *var of* LABDANUM
[1]**lad·der** \'ladə(r)\ *n* -s *often attrib* [ME, fr. OE *hlǣder*, *hlǣder*; akin to MD *lēder* ladder, OHG *leitara* ladder, ON *hlith* swinging gate, Goth *hleithra* hut, tent, and to OE *hlinian, hleonian* to lean — more at LEAN (incline)] **1 a** : a usu. portable structure for use in climbing up or down that consists commonly of two parallel sidepieces of wood, metal, or rope joined at short intervals by a series of crosspieces that serve as rests for the feet — see AERIAL LADDER, EXTENSION LADDER, STEPLADDER **b** *obs* : the steps leading to a gallows **c** : a set of vertical or inclined steps on a ship : ship's stairway — see ACCOMMODATION LADDER; compare COMPANIONWAY **2** : a means of rising or climbing : that by which one attains to a higher position or status ⟨the only ~ is education in a technical school —Roger Burlingame⟩ ⟨~s used by the unscrupulously ambitious —T.H.Eliot⟩ ⟨the societal organizations and the institutions that serve . . . as social ~s —*Social Forces*⟩ ⟨the pathetic conviction that learning alone was the ~ to political power —Roy Lewis & Angus Maude⟩ — compare STEPPING-STONE **3** : something that resembles or suggests a ladder in form or use: as **a** *chiefly Brit* : RUN 12a **b** : FISH LADDER **c** : CONVEYER 2a(6) **d** : a series of cross straps attached to the backs of venetian-blind tapes to support the slats **e** : BACKBONE 5, LADDER TRACK **f** : a succession of gunfire salvos fired with uniform differences in range to determine the proper range for achieving hits **g** : a cultivating implement of India resembling a harrow **4** : a series of usu. ascending steps or stages : a scheme of comparative rank or order : SCALE ⟨trying to better his position on the social ~⟩ ⟨ranked objectively in a ~ of economic desirability —*Jour. of Accountancy*⟩ ⟨a toehold on the academic ~ —Lynn White⟩ ⟨slipped down the power ~ —C.L.Sulzberger⟩ ⟨a world whose standards appear to be at the bottom of the ~ —P.M.Mazur⟩ **5 a** : LADDER COMPANY **b** : LADDER TRUCK

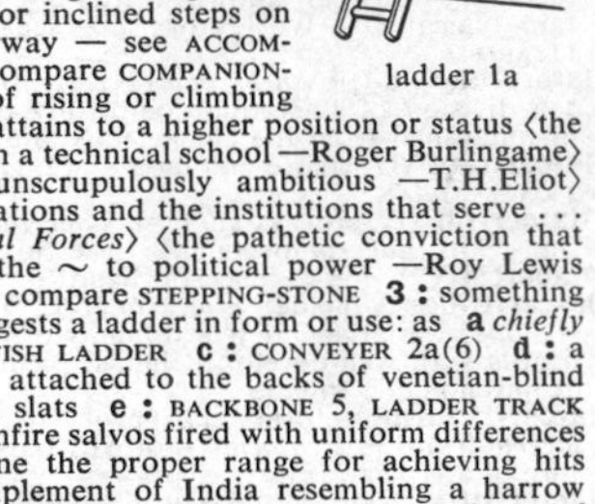
ladder 1a

[2]**ladder** \"\ *vb* **laddered**; **laddered**; **laddering** \-d(ə)riŋ\ **ladders** *vt* **1** : to provide with ladders : scale by means of a ladder ⟨~ a building⟩ **2** : to provide with a fish ladder ⟨~ a falls⟩ **3** *chiefly Brit* : to cause or develop a ladder in ⟨~ a stocking⟩ **4** *India* : to work (land) with a ladder : HARROW **5** : to mark transversely as if with rungs of a ladder : BAR, STRIPE ⟨slant rays ~*ed* the lofty shade —D.C.Peattie⟩ ~ *vi* **1** *chiefly Brit* : to develop a ladder : RUN ⟨stockings which ~*ed* the first time they were worn⟩ **2** : to rise like or as if on the successive rungs of a ladder ⟨dusty leaves ~*ing* up a goldenrod stem —W.O.Mitchell⟩ ⟨~*ing* up the bestseller list —*Time*⟩
ladder-back \'=,=\ *adj, of furniture* : having a back consisting of two upright posts connected by horizontal slats : LADDER-BACKED ⟨a *ladder-back* chair⟩
ladder-backed \'==¦=\ *adj* : having a back resembling a ladder; *esp* : having barred markings on the back that are suggestive of the rungs of a ladder ⟨*ladder-backed* woodpeckers⟩
ladder chain *n* : a chain resembling a ladder in shape
ladder company *n* : a fire department unit comprising the firemen to operate a ladder truck
laddered *adj* **1** : provided with a ladder ⟨a ~ loft⟩ **2** : that has developed a ladder ⟨a ~ stocking⟩
ladder fire *n* : a method of adjusting artillery or mortar fire by firing in rapid succession three rounds with the same deflection but at different ranges
laddering *n* -s : ladders or material for ladders
ladder jack *n* : a bracket for supporting a platform or scaffold from a ladder
lad·der·less \'lad·ə(r)ləs\ *adj* **1** : having no ladder ⟨a ~ loft⟩ **2** *chiefly Brit* : free from ladders : resistant to laddering ⟨~ stockings⟩
ladderlike \'==,=\ *adj* : resembling a ladder (as in form or appearance or in being graduated or progressive) : SCALAR, SCALARIFORM
lad·der·man \'ladə(r)mən, -,man\ *n*, *pl* **laddermen** : a member of a ladder company
ladders *pl of* LADDER, *pres 3d sing of* LADDER
ladder shell *n* : a prominently ribbed spiral marine shell of *Epitonium* or related genera : WENTLETRAP
ladder snake *n* : a southern European rat snake (*Elaphe scalaris*) with ladderlike markings on back and sides

ladder tape *n* **:** a tape support for a venetian blind that consists of two long strips of a woven or plastic fabric joined at intervals by narrow cross strips on which the slats of the blind rest

ladder tournament *n* **:** a tournament in which the names of all contestants are drawn and arranged one above the other on a posted list and in which each entrant is entitled to challenge one of the two contestants directly above him and if victorious to assume his opponent's place in the ranking

ladder track *n* **:** a main track connecting successive body tracks in a railroad yard **:** BACKBONE 5

ladder truck *n* **:** a piece of mobile fire apparatus carrying ladders and usu. other fire-fighting and rescue equipment

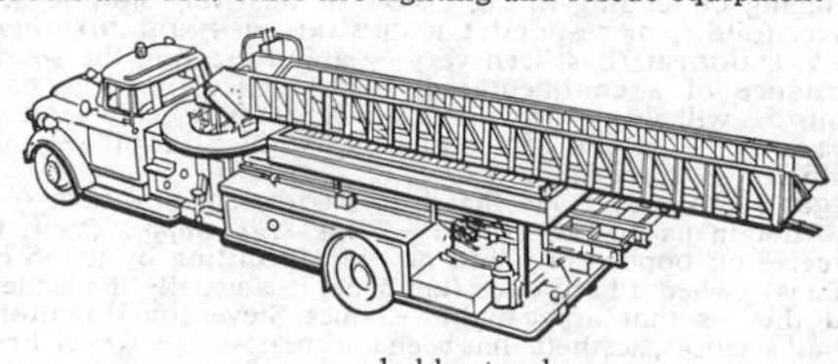

ladder truck

ladderway \'==,=\ *n* **:** a series of ladders for passage up or down in a mine; *also* **:** a compartment in which ladders are used

lad·dery \'lad(ə)rē\ *adj* **:** resembling a ladder

lad·die \'ladē, -di\ *n* -s [dim. of *lad*] **:** a young lad

lad·dish \'ladish\ *adj* **:** resembling or belonging to a lad **:** BOYISH, IMMATURE, YOUTHFUL — **lad·dish·ness** *n* -ES

¹lade \'lād\ *vb* **laded; lad·ed** \-dəd\ *or in vt sense 1* **lad·en** \-dᵊn\ **lading; lades** [ME *laden*, fr. OE *hladan*, *ladan* to heap, load, draw water; akin to OHG *hladan* to load, ON *hlatha*, Goth *afhlathan* to load, OSlav *klasti* to load, place] *vt* **1 a :** to put a load or burden on or in **:** furnish with freight or cargo **:** LOAD ⟨~ a vessel⟩ ⟨*laded* their asses with the corn —Gen 42:26 (AV)⟩ ⟨the lighter a ship is *laden* the greater will be the effects of an uneven trim —*Manual of Seamanship*⟩ ⟨countless ore-*laden* motor trucks —Tom Marvel⟩ **b :** to put or place as a load or burden esp. for shipment or carriage **:** take aboard **:** PACK, SHIP, STOW ⟨*lading* tea and silks from Canton —F.R.Dulles⟩ ⟨exclude from the protection of their policies cargo *laden* on deck —W.D.Winter⟩ ⟨bring to town their produce, *laden* in wagons —*Amer. Guide Series: Pa.*⟩ **c :** to load heavily: (1) **:** to provide or supply abundantly or to repleteness **:** CHARGE, CRAM, FILL ⟨their breasts were *laden* with decorations and medals —F.J.Mather⟩ ⟨packed with annotations and statistics and *laden* with footnotes —*Times Lit. Supp.*⟩ ⟨let the air with joy be *laden* —W.S.Gilbert⟩ ⟨silt-*laden* soil —R.A.Billington⟩ ⟨the suspense-*laden* room —Cortland Fitzsimmons⟩ (2) **:** to weigh down **:** weigh upon heavily **:** BURDEN, OPPRESS ⟨weak and heavy *laden* —Joseph Scriven⟩ ⟨*laden* with the deep, nostalgic morbidness of youth —Walter O'Meara⟩ ⟨three misery-*laden* men —Albert Deutsch⟩ **2 :** to lift or throw (a liquid) in or out with or as if with a ladle or dipper **:** DIP, DRAW, LADLE ⟨*laded* several dippers of water into a basin⟩ ⟨*laded* metal⟩ ⟨the molten glass is *laded* from the pot to the forming table⟩ ~ *vi* **1 :** to take on cargo **:** LOAD **2 :** to take up or convey a liquid by dipping **syn** see BURDEN

²lade *now dial var of* LOAD

³lade \'lād\ *n* -s [ME, fr. OE *lād* course, way — more at LODE] **1** *chiefly Scot* **:** MILLRACE **2 a :** the mouth of a river **b :** WATERCOURSE

¹lad·en \'lādᵊn\ *vt* **ladened; ladened; ladening** \-d(ᵊ)niŋ\ **ladens** [¹*lade* + -*en*] **:** LADE ⟨heavily ~*ed* with equipment —Isabel M. Lewis⟩

²laden *adj* [fr. *laden*, past part. of ¹*lade*] **:** BURDENED, CHARGED, LOADED ⟨leading a ~ mule —Arthur Loveridge⟩ ⟨a ~ silence . . . prevailed —Osbert Sitwell⟩ ⟨a ~ heart⟩

la·den·burg flask \'lādᵊn,bərg-\ *n, usu cap L* [after Albert *Ladenburg* †1911 Ger. chemist] **:** a distilling flask with bulbed neck

lad·er \'lādə(r)\ *n* -s **:** one that lades

lad·hood \'lad,hu̇d\ *n* **:** BOYHOOD

¹la-di-da *also* **la-de-da** *or* **la-di-dah** \ˌlädēˌdä\ *vi* -ED/-ING/-S [perh. alter. of *lardy-dardy*, adj.] **:** to speak or act in a la-di-da manner **:** behave in an affectedly refined or elegant manner

²la-di-da *also* **la-de-da** *or* **la-di-dah** \"\ *or* **lah-di-dah** \"\ *n* -s **1 :** a person who affects gentility or elegance **:** a pretentious imitator of cultivated speech or manners **2 :** behavior characteristic of a la-di-da **:** affected gentility or gentility so exaggerated as to seem affected **:** GENTEELNESS; *esp* **:** an exaggeratedly genteel accent or a mincing prissiness of expression ⟨with your car and your *la-di-da* and Honorable and all the rest of it —Nigel Balchin⟩ ⟨the soldier's blasphemy takes the curse off the aesthete's *la-di-da* —J.W.Beach⟩

³la-di-da *also* **la-de-da** *or* **la-di-dah** *or* **lah-di-dah** \"\ *adj* **1 :** characteristic of a la-di-da **:** affectedly refined or polished **:** exaggeratedly upper-class in speech and manners **:** GENTEEL ⟨with their gentlemen's voices and *la-di-da* manners —C.S.Forester⟩ ⟨the exotic and inscrutable Chinese . . . is no more true to life than the *la-di-da* Englishman —Owen Lattimore⟩ ⟨complaints against the *la-de-da* pronunciation of some of their hirelings —H.L.Mencken⟩ **2 a :** HIGHFALUTIN, PRETENTIOUS ⟨collecting and drinking wine . . . a dandy hobby, if the vocabulary weren't so *la-di-da* —Clifton Fadiman⟩ **b :** MINCING, SISSIFIED ⟨a *la-di-da* book about men's clothes —G.T.Hellman⟩ **3 :** characteristic of the world of fashion and wealth **:** ELEGANT, HIGH-TONED, STYLISH ⟨the *la-di-da* doings of high society —J.P.O'Donnell⟩ **:** EXTRAVAGANT, LAVISH ⟨*la-de-da* parties and glamour girls —*Time*⟩

ladies *pl of* LADY

ladies aid *n, usu cap L&A* **:** a local organization of churchwomen for the purpose of assisting financially the church to which they belong — compare AID 3c

ladies auxiliary *n, usu cap L&A* **:** an organization of women that is auxiliary usu. to a men's fraternal or social organization — compare AUXILIARY 9

ladies chain *n, often cap L&C* **:** a square-dance figure in which the women give their right hands to each other as they cross over to the opposite men who take their left hands and swing them as they arrive

ladies' cloth *var of* LADY'S CLOTH

ladies' day *n, often cap L&D* **:** a day on which women receive a special privilege (as attendance as guests at a meeting of a men's club or free admission to a baseball game)

ladies'-delight *var of* LADY'S-DELIGHT

ladies'-eardrop *var of* LADY'S-EARDROP

ladies' ladder *var of* LADY'S LADDER

ladies' man *also* **lady's man** *n* **:** a man who shows a marked fondness for the company of women or is very gallant in his attentions to women

ladies'-pocket *var of* LADY'S-POCKET

ladies' room *n* **:** a women's lavatory esp. in a public or semipublic building or establishment (as a theater or restaurant)

ladies' slipper *var of* LADY'S SLIPPER

la·dies'-streamer \ˈlādē(z)+,-\ *n* [by folk etymology fr. NL *Lagerstroemia*, genus name] **:** CRAPE MYRTLE

ladies'-tobacco *also* **lady's-tobacco** \ˌ===ˌ==\ *n* **:** a plant of the genus *Antennaria*

ladies' tresses *also* **lady's tresses** *or* **lady's traces** \ˌ==ˌ==\ *n pl but sing or pl in constr* **:** an orchid of the genus *Spiranthes*

la·di·fy *or* **la·dy·fy** \'lādə,fī, -dē,-\ *vt* -ED/-ING/-ES **1 :** to make a lady of **:** treat as a lady **:** call by the title *Lady* **2 :** to make ladylike; *esp* **:** to make suitable for a lady ⟨manners that had been carefully *ladified*⟩ ⟨*ladified* copies of a man's best briars —*advt*⟩

la·dik \lä'dēk\ *n* -s *usu cap* [fr. *Ladik*, village in Turkey] **:** a rug of fine texture woven in and near Ladik in central Anatolia

la·din \lə'dēn\ *n* -s *cap* [Rhaeto-Romanic, fr. L *Latinum* Latin — more at LATIN (n.)] **1 :** ROMANSH **2 :** one speaking Romansh as a mother tongue

la·di·na \lə'dēnə\ *n* -s *often cap* [AmerSp, fem. of *ladino*] **:** a female ladino

lading *n* -s [fr. *lading*, gerund of ¹*lade*] **1 a :** LOADING 1a **b :** an act of bailing, dipping, or ladling **2 :** something that lades **:** a load or something that makes up a load (as the contents of a shipment) **:** CARGO, FREIGHT, BURDEN

¹la·di·no \lə'dē(,)nō\ *n* -s [Sp, fr. *ladino*, adj., cunning, learned, lit., Latin, fr. L *latinus* Latin — more at LATIN (adj.)] **1** *cap* **:** JUDEO-SPANISH **2** *often cap* [AmerSp, fr. Sp *ladino*, adj.] **a :** a westernized Spanish-speaking Latin American who is not of pure Spanish extraction; *esp* **:** MESTIZO **b :** a Central American of mixed or pure Spanish descent who does not belong to an Indian community **3** [AmerSp, fr. Sp *ladino*, adj.] *Southwest* **:** a cunningly vicious horse or steer **4** *cap* **:** a Judeo-Spanish-speaking Jew of the Balkan or Mediterranean countries; *also* **:** SPAGNUOLO

²la·di·no \lə'dī(,)nō, -dē(,)nō, -dīnə\ *or* **ladino clover** *n* -s *often cap L* [perh. irreg. fr. *Lodi*, commune of Italy + It -*ino*, adj. suffix] **:** a large nutritious rapidly growing clover that is a horticultural variety of white clover reaching two to four times the size of common white clover and widely planted for hay, ensilage, and grazing and as a cover crop

¹lad·kin \'ladkən\ *n* -s **:** a little lad

²ladkin \"\ *n* -s [origin unknown] **:** a glazier's tool for opening cames

¹la·dle \'lādᵊl\ *n* -s [ME *ladel*, fr. OE *hlædel*, fr. *hladan* to lade — more at LADE] **1 :** a deep-bowled long-handled spoon used esp. for dipping up and conveying liquids **2 :** an instrument or device resembling a ladle in form or function: as **a :** a vessel with a pouring lip or nozzle for conveying liquid metal from a furnace to another apparatus for further treatment or to a mold for casting **b** (1) **:** a copper scoop attached to a staff and used with muzzle-loading cannon to withdraw the projectile and charge from a loaded piece (2) **:** a ring with handles used for carrying spherical shot **c :** a long-handled box for taking up collections in church

ladle 1

²ladle \"\ *vt* **ladled; ladled; ladling** \-d(ᵊ)liŋ\ **ladles :** to take up and convey in a ladle **:** dip with or as if with a ladle ⟨*ladled* a bowl of stew for himself —A.B.Mayse⟩ ⟨*ladled* the fish into the weir boat —Mary H. Varse⟩ ⟨information-*ladling* college professors —H.A.Overstreet⟩

la·dle·ful \'lādᵊl,fu̇l\ *n* -s [ME *ladel-ful*, fr. *ladel* ladle + -*ful*] **:** the quantity held by a ladle

ladle in *vt* **:** to put in with or as if with a ladle **:** INSERT ⟨*ladled in* a few such scriptural phrases —Mark Twain⟩

ladle out *vt* **:** to dish out **:** FURNISH, GIVE, PROVIDE ⟨*ladle out* two bowls of porridge —Margaret Kennedy⟩ ⟨*ladle* it *out* slowly⟩ ⟨a more dynamic socialism than the one being officially *ladled out* —Mollie Panter-Downes⟩ ⟨charm is sometimes *ladled out* in too much profusion —C.H.Sykes⟩

la·dler \'lād(ᵊ)lə(r)\ *n* -s **:** one that ladles

ladle up *vt* **:** to serve with or as if with a ladle ⟨lustily singing out for someone to *ladle* him *up* —Herman Melville⟩

lad o' parts \,ladə'pärts, -per-\ *Scot* **:** a clever or talented fellow **:** MAN OF PARTS

ladp *abbr* ladyship

la·drone *or* **la·dron** *in sense 1* 'lādrən *or* 'ladrən, *in sense 2* lə'drōn\ *n, pl* **ladrones** *or* **ladrons** [prob. fr. MF *ladron* thief, robber, fr. L *latron-, latro*] **1** *usu* **ladrone**, *chiefly Scot* **:** BLACKGUARD, ROGUE **2** *usu* **ladron** [Sp *ladrón*, fr. L *latron-, latro*] *Southwest* **:** THIEF, ROBBER

lads *pl of* LAD

lad's-love \'=,=\ *n* **:** BOY'S-LOVE

¹la·dy \'lādē, -di\ *n* -ES *often attrib* [ME *lady*, *lavedi*, *lafdi*, fr. OE *hlǣfdige*, fr. *hlāf* bread + -*dige* (fr. root of a prehistoric verb meaning to knead); akin to OE *dǣge* maid, kneader of bread — more at LOAF, DAIRY] **1** *obs* **:** a mistress of servants **:** a woman who looks after the domestic affairs of a family **:** female head of a household **2 a :** a woman having proprietary rights, rule, or authority **:** a woman to whom obedience or homage is owed as a ruler or feudal superior — usu. used chiefly in the phrase *lady of the manor;* compare LORD 1 **b** (1) **:** a woman receiving the particular homage of a knight (2) **:** a woman who is the object of a lover's devotion **:** LADYLOVE, MISTRESS, SWEETHEART **3 a :** a woman of good family or of a superior social position ⟨inclined to remind you that she was a ~ by birth —W.S.Maugham⟩ ⟨begins as a narrative with a warm and vigorous picture of the decline of the ~ . . . into the woman —H.S.Canby⟩ ⟨the airs of a ~⟩ ⟨once a ~ could not be a stenographer or a shopgirl —Katharine F. Gerould⟩ — compare GENTLEMAN 1b; used also of a woman in a courteous mode of reference ⟨show this ~ to a seat⟩ ⟨the *ladies'* singles championship⟩ or usu. in the pl. of address ⟨that will be all, *ladies*⟩ ⟨*ladies* and gentlemen⟩ **b :** a woman of refinement and gentle manners **:** a woman whose conduct conforms to a certain standard of propriety or correct behavior **:** well-bred woman ⟨with a *lady's* respect for tranquillity she forbore to discuss these troubles —Frances G. Patton⟩ ⟨no woman with a bosom could be quite a ~ in his eyes —Hugh MacLennan⟩ ⟨a ~ . . . quiet, reserved, gracious, continent . . . gentle, and a woman —W.D.Steele⟩ — compare GENTLEMAN 1c **c :** a woman irrespective of social status or personal qualities **:** FEMALE ⟨a ~ doctor⟩ ⟨a char*lady*⟩ ⟨a two-headed boy and a bearded ~⟩ ⟨~ novelists⟩ ⟨the iceman, the blackberry ~, and the poor blind man with the brooms —Eudora Welty⟩ ⟨noticed the cold eye of the ~ behind the bar —Margery Allingham⟩ ⟨as fit as a ~ sharpshooter —Ethel Merman⟩ **4 :** WIFE ⟨the president and his ~⟩ ⟨his daughter was now a general's ~ —John De Meyer⟩ ⟨fashionable doctors and their *ladies* —Gene Baro⟩ **5** — used as a title prefixed to the names of various supernatural beings and personified abstractions ⟨*Lady* Venus⟩ ⟨*Lady* Luck⟩; compare DAME 1c **6 a :** any of various titled women in Great Britain — used as a courtesy title for the daughter of a duke, marquess, or earl ⟨*Lady* Philippa Stewart, daughter of the fourteenth Duke of Norfolk⟩ and for the wife of a younger son of a duke or marquess ⟨*Lady* Randolph Churchill, wife of a younger son of the Duke of Marlborough⟩ and as a mode of reference for a marchioness, countess, viscountess, or baroness ⟨the Marchioness of Lothian, addressed as *Lady* Lothian⟩ and for the wife of a baronet or knight ⟨Sir William and *Lady* Craigie⟩ **b :** a female member of certain orders of knighthood or chivalry ⟨Her Majesty is *Lady* of the Most Noble Order of the Garter —*Burke's Peerage*⟩ ⟨appointed by Pope Pius as a ~ of the grand cross of the Equestrian Order of the Holy Sepulchre —*Springfield (Mass.) Union*⟩ — compare DAME 1g **7 a** *obs* **:** the queen in a set of chess men **b** *slang* **:** a queen in a deck of playing cards **8** [so called fr. the fancied resemblance to the outline of a seated woman's figure] **:** the triturating apparatus in the stomach of a lobster **9 :** a gunner's mate in charge of the lady's hole on a man-of-war **10 a :** a female animal ⟨one was a ~, her swimmerets . . . covered with black eggs —Robert Hunter⟩ ⟨a ~ goat⟩ ⟨the male trout are handsome, the ~ trout pretty and available —*Ford Times*⟩ **b :** a female harlequin duck — compare LORD-AND-LADY **11 ladies** *pl but sing in constr, chiefly Brit* **:** LADIES' ROOM ⟨slipped into the *ladies* to powder her nose⟩

²lady \"\ *vb* -ED/-ING/-ES *vt, obs* **:** to make a lady of or to make ladylike ~ *vi* **:** to play the lady — used with *it* ⟨~*ing* it over her former friends⟩

lady altar *n, usu cap L* **:** an altar dedicated in honor of the Virgin Mary

lady am·herst's pheasant \-'am(,)ərs(t)s-\ *n, usu cap L&A* [after Sarah E. *Lady Amherst* †1876 Brit. amateur naturalist] **:** a pheasant (*Chrysolophus amherstiae*) native to western China and Tibet and having a green crown, red crest, and black-barred white cape and a white breast and abdomen

lady baltimore cake *n, usu cap L&B* [prob. after *Lady Baltimore*, wife of Lord Baltimore †1632 — more at BALTIMORE] **:** a usu. white butter cake with boiled frosting and a filling of chopped raisins, figs, and nuts — compare LORD BALTIMORE CAKE

lady beetle *n* **:** LADYBUG

ladybird \'==,=\ *n* **1** *also* **ladybird beetle :** LADYBUG **2 :** PINTAIL 1 **3 :** SWEETHEART

lady bountiful *n, pl* **lady bountifuls** *or* **ladies bountiful**, *often cap L&B* [after *Lady Bountiful*, character in *The Beaux' Stratagem* (1707), play by George Farquhar †1707 British dramatist born in Ireland] **:** a woman notable for or conspicuous in her benevolences

lady bracken *or* **lady brake** *n* [¹*lady*] **:** a common brake (*Pteridium aquilinum*)

ladybug \'==,=\ *n* [after Our *Lady*, the Virgin Mary] **:** any of the small more or less hemispherical often brightly colored beetles that constitute the family Coccinellidae, are distributed throughout temperate and tropical regions, and with the exception of a few herbivorous forms feed in both larval and adult stages upon small insects and the eggs of larger ones — see VEDALIA

lady chair *n* **1 :** a seat formed by the interlocked hands and wrists of two persons **2 :** an upholstered chair without arms or with very low only slightly projecting arms

lady chapel *n, usu cap L & often cap C* [ME (*oure*) *lady chapell*, fr. *oure lady* Our Lady, the Virgin Mary + *chapell* chapel] **:** a chapel dedicated to the Virgin Mary, containing a Lady altar, and located usu. in a cathedral or parish church but sometimes in a separate building

lady court *n* **:** a court held by a lady of a manor

lady crab *n* **1 :** a brightly spotted swimming crab (*Ovalipes ocellatus*) that is very common on the sandy shores of the Atlantic coast of the U.S. **2 :** a crab (*Portunus puber*) of the English coasts that is closely related and similar to the American lady crab

lady cracker *n* **:** a diminutive firecracker

lady day *n, usu cap L&D* [ME (*oure*) *lady day*, fr. *oure lady* Our Lady, the Virgin Mary + *day*] **:** a feast of the Virgin Mary; *specif* **:** ANNUNCIATION DAY

lady fern *n* **:** a widely distributed fern (*Athyrium filix-femina*) with slender bipinnate fronds showing considerable variation in form; *broadly* **:** any fern of the genus *Athyrium* — usu. used with a qualifying term

ladyfinger \'==,==\ *n* **1 a :** LADY'S-FINGER **b ladyfingers** *pl but sing or pl in constr* **:** a foxglove (*Digitalis purpurea*) **2 :** a small finger-shaped sponge cake **3 :** any of several small-fruited bananas **4 :** a large elongated dessert grape of European origin and superior flavor

ladyfish \'==,=\ *n* **:** any of several marine fishes: as **a :** a bonefish (*Albula vulpes*) **b :** a crimson and gold wrasse (*Bodianus rufus*) of Florida and the West Indies and south to Brazil — called also *Spanish hogfish* **c :** TENPOUNDER

lady friend *n* **1 :** a female friend ⟨no other relatives . . . no *lady friend* with whom you could stay —William Black⟩ ⟨less a secretary than an intimate *lady friend* —H.J.Laski⟩ **2 :** a man's female companion ⟨soldiers, and bankers, and their wives and *lady friends* —*New Yorker*⟩ ⟨spending the day at the beach with his *lady friend*⟩ **3 :** the female partner in an intimate esp. an illicit relationship **:** LOVER, MISTRESS

ladyfy *var of* LADIFY

lady-help \'=='=\ *n, Brit* **:** a woman who performs domestic duties at a usu. low wage in consideration of recognition as the social equal of her employer

la·dy·hood \'lādē,hu̇d\ *n* **1 :** the state of being a lady **:** quality or nature of a lady ⟨the changing status of woman from ~ to the position of political citizen —Amy Loveman⟩ **2 :** LADIES ⟨representative of the ~ of her day⟩

ladying *pres part of* LADY

lady-in-waiting \'===='==\ *n, pl* **ladies-in-waiting :** a lady of a queen's or a princess's household appointed to wait upon or attend her

la·dy·ish \'lādēish\ *adj* **:** somewhat like a lady; *esp* **:** having or showing undesirable ladylike characteristics — **la·dy·ish·ly** *adv* — **la·dy·ish·ness** *n* -ES

lady-killer \'==,==\ *n* **:** a man who captivates women or who has the reputation of being fascinating to women

lady-killing \'==,==\ *n* **:** the activities or arts of a lady-killer

la·dy·kin \'lādēkən\ *n* -s [¹*lady* + -*kin*] **:** a little lady — sometimes used as an endearment

la·dy·kind \-ē,kīnd\ *n* [¹*lady* + -*kind* (as in *womankind*)] **:** LADIES — compare WOMANKIND

la·dy·less \-ēləs\ *adj* **:** lacking ladies **:** not accompanied by a lady

ladylike \'==,=\ *adj* **1 :** resembling a lady in appearance or manners **:** WELL-BRED ⟨editorials urging our girls to be ~ —Virgil Henry⟩ ⟨one establishment may appeal to the conservative ~ type —Lois Long⟩ **2 :** becoming or suitable to a lady **:** marked by conformity to a lady's standards ⟨in a ~ manner she was sick —Sinclair Lewis⟩ ⟨bought her something ~ to put on her back —Eudora Welty⟩ **3 :** foolishly or weakly like a woman: **a :** feeling or showing too much concern about elegance or propriety ⟨~ embarrassment at not being the wife of a real doctor —Lewis Vogler⟩ **b :** lacking in strength, force, or virility **:** WEAK, SOFT, YIELDING ⟨the average puncher was womanly though Heaven knows he was in no wise ~ —P.A.Rollins⟩ **syn** see FEMALE

la·dy·like·ness *n* -ES **:** the quality or state of being ladylike ⟨Spanish fans, the acme of ~ —*New Yorker*⟩

ladylove \'==,=, ,=='=\ *n* **:** SWEETHEART, MISTRESS

lady mass *n, usu cap L & often cap M* [orig. ME *masse of our Lady*] **:** a mass said in honor of the Virgin Mary

lady mayoress *n* **:** a lord mayor's wife

lady of loretto *usu cap both Ls* **:** LORETTO NUN

lady of pleasure : PROSTITUTE

lady of the bedchamber : one of the ladies of noble family holding the official position of personal attendant on a British queen or princess

lady of the evening : PROSTITUTE

lady of the house : a mistress of a dwelling **:** HOUSEWIFE — used with *the* ⟨is the *lady of the house* at home⟩

lady-of-the-night \'===='=\ *n* **:** a West Indian shrub (*Brunfelsia americana*) with fragrant showy yellowish white flowers

lady palm *n* **:** an Asiatic fan palm of the genus *Rhapis* with clustered slender reedy stems

lady paramount *n, pl* **ladies paramount 1 :** the official in charge of the women's division of an archery tournament **2 :** the chief official of a women's archery tournament

lady pea *n* **:** COWPEA

lady's bedstraw *n* [fr. earlier *our lady's bedstraw*, after *Our Lady*, the Virgin Mary] **:** YELLOW BEDSTRAW

lady's bower *n* **:** a traveler's-joy (*Clematis vitalba*)

lady's chair *n* **:** LADY CHAIR 1

lady's cloth *or* **ladies' cloth** *n* **:** a closely woven lightweight woolen cloth of fine quality for women's wear

lady's-comb \ˌ=ˌ=\ *n, pl* **lady's-combs** [intended as trans. of L *pecten Veneris*, lit., Venus' comb] **:** a European herb (*Scandix pectenveneris*) with slender pointed fruits

lady's-delight *or* **ladies'-delight** \ˌ=ˌ=\ *n, pl* **lady's-delights** *or* **ladies'-delights :** WILD PANSY

lady's-eardrop *or* **ladies'-eardrop** \ˌ=ˌ=,=\ *n, pl* **lady's-eardrops** *or* **ladies'-eardrops** *but sing or pl in constr* **1 :** any of several plants of the genus *Fuchsia* (esp. *F. coccinea*) **2 :** SPOTTED JEWELWEED **3 :** BLEEDING HEART

lady's-finger \ˌ=ˌ==\ *n, pl* **lady's-fingers :** any of various plants with finger-shaped parts: as **a :** any of several legumes (as kidney vetch or bird's-foot trefoil) **b** *dial Eng* **:** CUCKOOPINT **c :** OKRA

lady's-glove \ˌ=ˌ=\ *n, pl* **lady's-gloves 1 :** FOXGLOVE **2** *dial Eng* **a :** FLEAWORT **b :** BIRD'S-FOOT TREFOIL 1a

lady's gown *n, Scots law* **:** a present made by a purchaser of real estate to the wife of the grantor on her renouncing her life interest in the property sold

lady's-grass \ˌ=ˌ=\ *n, pl* **lady's-grasses** *Austral* **:** a crab grass (*Digitaria sanguinalis*)

la·dy·ship \'lādē,ship, -di,-\ *n* [ME *ladishipe*, *lafdischipe*, fr. *ladi*, *lafdi* lady + -*shippe*, -*schipe* -ship] **1 :** the condition of being a lady **:** rank of lady **2** *often cap* **:** the personality of a woman having the rank or title of Lady — used in a mode of reference ⟨her *Ladyship*⟩ or of address ⟨your *Ladyship*⟩

lady's hole *n* **:** a place in an old-time man-of-war for keeping gunner's small stores

lady's-laces \ˌ=ˌ==\ *n, pl* **lady's-laces 1 :** REED CANARY GRASS **2 :** RIBBON GRASS

lady's ladder *or* **ladies' ladder** *n* **:** shrouds in which the ratlines are placed unusually close together

lady's-lint \ˌ=ˌ=\ *n, pl* **lady's-lints :** GREATER STITCHWORT

lady's maid *n* **:** a woman servant who cares for a lady's clothes and assists her in making her toilet

lady's-maid \'==,=\ *vb* [*lady's maid*] **:** to serve or attend as a lady's maid **:** MAID

lady's man *var of* LADIES' MAN
lady's-mantle \ˈ==ˌ==\ *n, pl* **lady's-mantles** [after *Our Lady*, the Virgin Mary] : any of several plants of the genus *Alchemilla; esp* : a common European herb (*A. xanthochlora*) having stems and petioles densely covered with spreading hairs
lady's-nightcap \ˈ==ˌ=ˌ=\ *n, pl* **lady's-nightcaps 1** : WOOD ANEMONE b **2** : HEDGE BINDWEED **3** : a Canterbury bell (*Campanula medium*)
lady's-paintbrush \ˈ==ˌ=ˌ=\ *n, pl* **lady's-paintbrushes** : ORANGE HAWKWEED
lady's-pocket \ˈ==ˌ==\ *also* **ladies' pocket** *n, pl* **lady's-pockets** *also* **ladies' pockets** : SPOTTED JEWELWEED
lady's-purse \ˈ==ˌ=\ *n, pl* **lady's-purses** : SHEPHERD'S PURSE
lady's slipper *or* **lady-slipper** *also* **ladies' slipper** \ˈlādē(z)-ˌ==\ *n* **1** : any of several No. American temperate-zone orchids esp. of the genus *Cypripedium* having flowers whose shape suggests a slipper **2** : GARDEN BALSAM **3** *dial Eng* : BIRD'S-FOOT TREFOIL 1a **4** *usu pl* : GARDEN COLUMBINE

lady's slipper

lady's-smock \ˈlādē(z)ˌ=\ *also* **lady smock** *n, pl* **lady's-smocks** *also* **lady smocks 1** : any of several plants of the genus *Cardamine; esp* : CUCKOOFLOWER **2** *dial Eng* : HEDGE BINDWEED **3** : a California toothwort (*Dentaria integrifolia*)
lady's-sorrel \ˈ==ˌ==\ *n, pl* **lady's-sorrels** : YELLOW WOOD SORREL
lady's-thimble \ˈ==ˌ==\ *n, pl* **lady's-thimbles 1** : HAREBELL 1 **2** : FOXGLOVE 1
lady's thumb *n* : a common widely distributed erect branched weedy annual herb (*Polygonum persicaria*) with purplish stems, racemes of small pink flowers, and large lanceolate leaves often with a blackish blotch suggesting a thumbprint
lady's-tobacco *var of* LADIES'-TOBACCO
lady's tresses *or* **lady's traces** *var of* LADIES' TRESSES
lady's woman *n* : LADY'S MAID
lady tulip *n* : a Eurasian tulip (*Tulipa clusiana*) with smooth glabrous stems and small flowers that are blotched at the base — called also *candlestick tulip*
lady washington geranium *n, usu cap L&W* [after Martha *Washington* †1802, wife of George Washington †1799 and first lady of the White House] : MARTHA WASHINGTON GERANIUM
lady wrack *n* : BLADDER WRACK
lae·lap·ti·dae \lēˈlaptəˌdē\ *n pl, cap* [NL, irreg. fr. *Laelap-*, *Laelaps*, type genus (fr. L, name of a dog, fr. Gk *lailap-, lailaps* hurricane) + *-idae*] : a family of mites living as ectoparasites on animals
lae·lia \ˈlēlēə\ *n* [NL, perh. fr. Caius *Laelius fl* 2d cent. B.C. Roman statesman + NL *-ia*] **1** *cap* : a genus of Central and So. American orchids having solitary or racemose variously colored flowers with a 3-lobed labellum and pseudobulbs bearing one or two oblong leaves **2** *-s* : any plant of the genus *Laelia*
laelia pink *n, often cap L* : a dark purplish pink to light grayish purplish red
laemmergeyer *var of* LAMMERGEIER
lae·mo·dip·o·da \ˌlēməˈdipədə\ *n pl, cap* [NL, fr. *laemo-* (fr. Gk *laimos* throat, gullet) + *-ipoda* (fr. Gk *dipod-, dipous* having two feet) — more at GYMNOLAEMATA, DIPODOMYS] *in some classifications* : a division of Amphipoda comprising crustaceans (as the whale lice and members of the genus *Caprella*) in which the abdomen is small and rudimentary and the legs are often reduced to five pairs
laender *pl of* LAND
laen·nec's cirrhosis \(ˈ)lā|ˈnek(s)-, (ˈ)le|, ˌlā,ä|\ *n, usu cap L* [after René T. H. *Laënnec* †1826 French physician] : hepatic cirrhosis in which increased connective tissue spreads out from the portal spaces compressing and distorting the lobules, causing impairment of liver function, and ultimately producing the typical hobnail liver
lae·o·trop·ic \ˌlēəˈträpik\ *or* **lae·ot·ro·pous** \lēˈä·trəpəs\ *or* **lei·o·trop·ic** \ˌlīə·ˈträpik\ *adj* [*laeotropic* or *laeotropous* fr. Gk *laios* left + E *-tropic* or *-tropous; leiotropic* irreg. fr. Gk *laios* left + E *-tropic* — more at LEV-] : turning to the left : SINISTRAL — used esp. of various shells, of spiral cleavage patterns, or of the movement of volvox colonies
lae·sio enor·mis \ˈlēshēˌōēˈnȯrməs\ *or* **laesio ultra di·mi·di·um** \-dəˈmidēəm\ *or* **laesio ultra du·plum** \-ˈd(y)üpləm\ *n* [*laesio enormis*, LL, lit., enormous injury; *laesio ultra dimidium*, L, injury over half; *laesio ultra duplum*, L, injury over double] *Roman & civil law* : the injury that is suffered by a vendor who has sold something for less than half its value or in some civil-law systems by a purchaser who has bought something at more than double its price and that in most cases gives the right of rescinding the sale
laet \ˈlat\ *n* -s [OE *læt*; perh. akin to OE *lǣtan* to let] : one of a class composed chiefly of freedmen with a status between tribesmen and slaves in ancient Kent
lae·ta·re sunday \lāˈtärē-, -(ˌ)rā-\ *n, usu cap L&S* [L *laetare* rejoice, 2d pers. sing. pres. imper. pass. of *laetare* to make glad; fr. the fact that *laetare* is the opening word of the introit for that day] : the fourth Sunday in Lent
laetation *n* -s [LL *laetatus* (past part. of *laetare* to fertilize, manure, fr. L, to make glad, fr. *laetus* glad, fertile) + E *-ion* — more at LARD] *obs* : MANURE
lae·tic \ˈlēd·ik\ *adj* [LL *laeticus* — more at LIEGE] : of or relating to a class of non-Roman cultivators of the soil during the later Roman empire who paid tribute for the lands which they occupied
laev- *or* **laevo-** — see LEV-
lae·vi·gra·da \ˌlēvəˈgrādə\ [NL, neut. pl., fr. *laevi-* (prob. irreg. fr. L *levis* light) + *-grada* (fr. L *gradi* to walk, step)] *syn of* PYCNOGONIDA
laevo *var of* LEVO
la·farge cement \ləˈfärzh-, -rj-\ *n* [fr. *Lafarge*, a trademark] : a nonstaining cement composed of plaster of paris, lime, and marble dust and used in mortar for setting marble and limestone
la·fay·ette \ˌläfēˈet, ˌlaf-\ *n* -s [after Marquis de *Lafayette* †1834 French statesman] **1** : a butterfish (*Poronotus triacanthus*) **2** : a spot (*Leiostomus xanthurus*)
la flèche \ləˈflesh\ *n, usu cap L&F* [fr. *La Flèche*, commune, Sarthe dept., France] : a domestic fowl of a French breed that is greenish black with a large V-shaped comb
la france pink *n, often cap L&F* [so called fr. *La France*, a variety of rose] : a moderate pink that is yellower and darker than arbutus pink and bluer and deeper than hydrangea pink — called also *debutante pink*
laft \ˈlaft\ *Scot var of* ¹LOFT
¹**lag** \ˈlag, -aa(ə)g, -aig\ *vb* **lagged; lagged; lagging; lags** [prob of Scand origin; akin to Norw *lagga* to go slowly] *vi* **1** : to stay or fall behind : fail to keep up : **a** (1) : to move slowly : hang back : LINGER, LOITER ⟨as he neared the old home, his steps *lagged* —L.C.Douglas⟩ ⟨*lagged* behind intent on my collecting —David Fairchild⟩ ⟨*lagging* a step or two behind in embarrassment —Harold Sinclair⟩ ⟨at no time in my life have seconds *lagged* so much —T.B.Bruff⟩ ⟨business continued to ~ —*Wall Street Jour.*⟩ (2) : DELAY, PROCRASTINATE ⟨will let applicants ~ a bit in providing this information —*Wall Street Jour.*⟩ **b** : to move, function, or develop with comparative slowness: (1) : to be slow or become retarded esp. by comparison with something closely associated or related — usu. used with *behind* ⟨accomplishment *lagging* behind purpose⟩ ⟨rents *lagged* far behind prices —W.P.Webb⟩ ⟨new hospital construction continues to ~ behind the need —D.D. Eisenhower⟩ ⟨through inattention, she *lagged* behind at school —Elizabeth Taylor⟩ (2) : to become retarded in attaining maximum value or development ⟨the current ~s behind the voltage⟩ ⟨insulin of the modified protamine type has relatively quick action, for it ~s two hours only —*Yr. Bk. of Endocrinology*⟩ **c** : to slacken or weaken little by little : FLAG ⟨interest in the fascinating drama of French politics never *lagged* —C.G.Bowers⟩ ⟨that concern with books and reading has never *lagged* —Ruth Gagliardo⟩ **2 a** : to shoot a taw or toss a jack toward a line marked on the ground to determine the order of play in ringer or jacks **b** : to cause a cue ball to rebound from the foot cushion of a billiard table so as to stop as near as possible to the head cushion or sometimes the head string (as for determining order of play) : STRING **c** : to throw coins or counters to decide possession by relative closeness to a fixed mark ⟨gambling with Bryan and McKinley buttons, *lagging* at a line —C.L.Baldridge⟩ ~ *vt* **1** *obs* : to cause to lag : RETARD **2** : to lag behind ⟨a circuit in which the current ~s the voltage —A.E.Fitzgerald⟩ ⟨the one that reaches a particular point in a cycle last is said to ~ the other —N.M.Cooke & John Markus⟩ **3** : to pitch or shoot (as a coin, counter, marble) at a mark ⟨beer corks *lagged*, in lieu of pennies, along the sidewalk cracks —Nelson Algren⟩ ⟨~ aggies —P.D. Boles⟩ **syn** see DELAY
²**lag** \ˈ"\ *n* -s **1** : one that lags : one that is last ⟨the ~ of all the flock —Alexander Pope⟩ **2 lags** *pl, obs* : DREGS, LEES ⟨the lags of the people —Shak.⟩ **3** *obs* : the lowest class ⟨the common ~ of people —Shak.⟩ **4 a** : the action or the condition of lagging : a falling or staying behind ⟨a region marked in the recent past by relative conservatism, inertia, and ~ —Hylan Lewis⟩ ⟨a series of spurts and ~s —*Times Lit. Supp.*⟩ ⟨this work must go forward without ~ —D.D.Eisenhower⟩ ⟨a definite ~ had come in business and industry —W.A.White⟩ ⟨a considerable ~ of the blood pressure curve behind the G curve —H.G.Armstrong⟩ **b** : comparative slowness or retardation (as in movement, operation, development) ⟨the social and political ~ that makes the world go on operating in terms of old antagonisms —*Saturday Rev.*⟩ ⟨adjustments for price ~ —*Collier's Yr. Bk.*⟩ ⟨this apparent ~ behind American practice —O.S.Nock⟩ ⟨their intellectual ~ in comparison with the rest of Europe —S.H.Cross⟩ **c** : a falling behind or retardation of one phenomenon with respect to another phenomenon to which it is closely related; *esp* : delay of a physical effect behind its cause or of the response of an indicating instrument behind the changed condition it registers ⟨the ~ of sound in some opera houses —Warwick Braithwaite⟩ ⟨the ~ of an alternating current in an inductive circuit behind the impressed voltage⟩ ⟨~ of strain behind stress in an imperfectly elastic material under varying stress⟩ ⟨because they have no ~ and indicate an error as it occurs, the horizon and gyro are a tremendous aid in flying the airplane more easily and precisely —H.L.Redfield⟩ **d** (1) : an amount of lag or the time during which lagging continues : degree or length of retardation or delay ⟨the ~ between the present and the latest reasonably accurate figures may be four or five years —E.W.Miller⟩ ⟨during this ~ the government should provide help —H.S.Truman⟩ ⟨in Scotland the ~ was a longer one —Ian Finlay⟩ ⟨made up more than two thirds of the ~ behind whites with which they came North —A.L.Kroeber⟩ (2) : a space or period of time esp. between related events or phenomena : INTERVAL ⟨the ~ between composition and publication is not a uniform one —*Nation*⟩ ⟨in the ~ between basketball season and baseball —Norman Mailer⟩ ⟨in the ~s of silence which fell over the shouts —Lawrence Durrell⟩ **5** : the action of lagging for opening shot (as in ringer or billiards)
³**lag** \ˈ"\ *adj* **1** : LAST, HINDMOST — used chiefly in the phrase *lag end* ⟨the *lag* end of my life —Shak.⟩ **2** *chiefly dial* : coming tardily after or behind : BELATED, LATE
⁴**lag** \ˈ"\ *vt* **lagged; lagged; lagging; lags** [origin unknown] **1** *obs* : STEAL **2** *slang* **a** : to transport for crime or send to penal servitude; *broadly* : to send to jail : IMPRISON ⟨the first big-timers to be *lagged* for using the mails —D.W.Maurer⟩ **b** *slang chiefly Brit* : ARREST, APPREHEND ⟨don't kindle a fire, unless you want to get *lagged* —Joseph Furphy⟩
⁵**lag** \ˈlag\ *n* -s [⁴*lag*] **1 a** *slang chiefly Brit* : a person transported for crime or sent to penal servitude : one who is serving or has served a term in prison : CONVICT, JAILBIRD ⟨the typical young ~ —*Times Lit. Supp.*⟩ **b** *Austral* : EX-CONVICT; *esp* : a convict immigrant to Australia ⟨impossible for him not to know that his father was a ~ —Rex Ingamells⟩ **2** *slang chiefly Brit* : a term of transportation or penal servitude : jail sentence : STRETCH
⁶**lag** \ˈlag, -aa(ə)g, -aig\ *n* -s [prob. of Scand origin; akin to ON *lǫgg* rim of a barrel, Sw *lagg* stave] **1** : a barrel stave **2 a** : a wooden stave or slat forming part of a covering for a cylindrical object (as a boiler or a carding-machine cylinder) **b** : a strip of any of various materials (as felt or asbestos) used in making a covering or casing esp. for a cylindrical structure **3** : a bearing strip in an arch or vault centering **4** *textile manuf* **a** : a wooden link in a pattern chain **b** : a large pin in the revolving cylinder of a picker
⁷**lag** \ˈ"\ *vt* **lagged; lagged; lagging; lags 1** : to cover or provide with lags or lagging (as for protection against wear or thermal insulation) **2** : to fasten with lag screws ⟨~ a machine to a bench⟩
lag- *or* **lago-** *comb form* [NL, fr. L, fr. Gk *lagō-*, fr. *lagōs*] : hare ⟨*lago*phthalmos⟩ ⟨*lago*pous⟩
lag·an \ˈlagən\ *also* **lag·end** \-nd\ *or* **lag·on** \-n\ *or* **li·gan** *or* **li·gen** \ˈlīgən\ *or* **lo·gan** \ˈlōg-\ *n* -s [MF *lagan, lagand*, or ML *laganum* debris washed up from the sea, the right to possess such debris, prob. of Gmc origin; akin to ON *lǫg* law — more at LAW] : goods thrown into the sea with a buoy attached in order that they may be found again — distinguished esp. in law from *flotsam* and *jetsam*
lag bolt *n* [⁶*lag*] : LAG SCREW
lag-bolt \ˈ=ˌ=\ *vt* [*lag bolt*] : LAG-SCREW
lag b'omer *or* **lag be-omer** *or* **lag ba-omer** \ˈläg'bōmə(r), -gbəˈō-\ *n, usu cap L&O* [Heb, 33d in omer] : a Jewish holiday falling on the 33d day of the omer and commemorating the heroism of Bar Cocheba and Akiba — see OMER 2b
la·gen \ˈlägən\ *n* -s [L *lagena* large flask] : an obsolete unit of capacity for liquids
la·ge·na \ləˈjēnə\ *n* [L, large flask, fr. Gk *lagynos*] **1** *pl* **lagenas** \-nəz\ *or* **lage·nae** \-ē(ˌ)nē\ : FLASK, BOTTLE **2** *pl* **lagenae** [NL, fr. L, large flask] : the terminal part of the cochlea; *esp* : a knob-shaped appendage of the sacculus of a bird or reptile corresponding to the cochlea of a fish or amphibian **3** *cap* [NL, fr. L, large flask] : a genus of Foraminifera having a single-chambered often flask-shaped test
lag·e·na·ri·a \ˌlajəˈna(a)rēə\ *n, cap* [NL, fr. L *lagena* large flask + NL *-aria*] : a genus of herbaceous vines (family Cucurbitaceae) characterized by more or less bottle-shaped fruit and having as its only species the bottle gourd
lag·e·nid·i·a·ce·ae \ˌlajəˌnidēˈāsēˌē\ *n pl, cap* [NL, fr. *Lagenidium*, type genus (fr. L *lagena* large flask + NL *-idium*) + *-aceae*] : a family of freshwater aquatic fungi (order Lagenidiales) having zoospores that are formed in a vesicle or that complete their development in a vesicle
lag·e·nid·i·a·les \-ˌē(ˌ)ˈālēz\ *n pl, cap* [NL, fr. *Lagenidium* + *-ales*] : an order of chiefly aquatic fungi (subclass Oomycetes) that are mostly parasitic in algae and water molds and that have a simple or somewhat branched holocarpic thallus
la·ge·ni·form \ləˈjēnəˌfȯrm\ *adj* [L *lagena* large flask + E *-iform*] : shaped like a flask : dilated below and tapering to a slender neck above
lag·e·noph·o·ra \ˌlajəˈnäf(ə)rə\ *n, cap* [NL, fr. *lageno-* (fr. Gk *lagēnos, lagynos* large flask) + *-phora*] : a small genus of composite herbs of New Zealand and Australia that have small solitary flower heads with white or light blue ray flowers and yellow disk flowers and that differ from members of the genus *Bellis* by possession of terminally beaked achenes
lag·e·nos·to·ma \-ˈästəmə\ *n, cap* [NL, fr. *lageno-* (fr. Gk *lagēnos* flask) + *-stoma*] : a form genus of Carboniferous seed ferns based on fossil seeds
¹**la·ger** \ˈlägə(r), ˈlág-\ *or* **lager beer** *n* -s [*lager*, short for *lager beer*, part trans. of G *lagerbier* beer made for storage, fr. *lager* camp, couch, lair (fr. OHG *legar* couch, bed) + *bier* beer (fr. OHG *bior*) — more at LAIR, BEER] : a beer brewed by bottom fermentation and stored in refrigerated cellars for clarification and maturing and usu. dry, light in color, and well carbonated
²**lager** \ˈ"\ *vt* -ED/-ING/-S : to store (beer) during a period of aging often accompanied by a secondary fermentation
³**lager** *var of* LAAGER
la·ger·stroe·mia \ˌlägə(r)ˈstrēmēə, ˌläg-, ˌlag-\ *n, cap* [NL, fr. Magnus *Lagerstroem* †1759 Swedish naturalist and merchant + NL *-ia*] : a genus of shrubs (family Lythraceae) of tropical Asia and Africa with usu. showy paniculate flowers and capsular fruits with winged seeds — see CRAPE MYRTLE
la·get·ta \ləˈjed·ə\ *n, cap* [NL, fr. AmerSp *lageto* lagetto] : a genus of West Indian shrubs or small trees (family Thymelaeaceae) with large alternate leaves and spicate or racemose white flowers
la·get·to \ləˈged·(ˌ)ō\ *n* -s [AmerSp *lageto*] *Jamaica* : LACEBARK
lag fault *n* [¹*lag*] : a minor low-angle thrust fault resulting within an overthrust mass from one part of the mass being thrust farther than an adjacent higher or lower part
lag·gar \ˈlagə(r)\ *n* -s [Hindi] : LUGGAR; *esp* : a female luggar
¹**lag·gard** \ˈlagə(r)d, ˈlaag-, ˈlaig-\ *adj* [¹*lag* + *-ard* (n. suffix)] : lagging or tending to lag : slow or relatively slow to act, move, follow, or respond : BACKWARD, BEHINDHAND, DILATORY, SLUGGISH ⟨has been very ~ about erecting the sound substance of a continental defense —R.E.Lapp⟩ ⟨~ payments . . . will always be with us —T.A.Sumberg⟩ ⟨the ~ speed of sound —C.G.Burke⟩ ⟨entering, with ~ foot —Hugh Walpole⟩ **syn** see SLOW
²**laggard** \ˈ"\ *n* -s : one that lags : LOITERER, LINGERER ⟨~s who detain us on our course —*Times Lit. Supp.*⟩ ⟨swift to perceive an opportunity and no ~ in profiting by it —S.H. Adams⟩ ⟨when a herd does stampede, it is usually the leaders and the ~s that are caught —James Stevenson-Hamilton⟩ ⟨of all sciences, aesthetic has been the greatest ~ —Roger Fry⟩
¹**lag·gard·ly** \-lē,-li\ *adv* : in a laggard manner ⟨Mercury, setting ~ in the west —William Beebe⟩
²**laggardly** \ˈ"\ *adj* : being laggard or a laggard ⟨choked on a ~ crumb —Monica Stirling⟩ ⟨the ~ employer . . . should learn to take advantage of government assistance —*Manchester Guardian Weekly*⟩
lag·gard·ness *n* -ES : the quality or state of being laggard ⟨the long ~ of social legislation —R.E.Montgomery⟩
lagged *adj* [fr. past part. of ¹*lag*] : affected by lagging : showing or reflecting a lag (as in time) : DELAYED, RETARDED, TARDY ⟨the influence of disposable income is partially ~ —E.C. Bratt⟩
¹**lag·ger** \ˈlagə(r), -aag-, -aig-\ *n* -s [¹*lag* + *-er*] : one that lags or falls behind : LAGGARD, LOITERER
²**lagger** *vi* -ED/-ING/-S *obs* : LAG, LOITER
³**lag·ger** \ˈlagə(r\ *n* -s [⁴*lag* + *-er*] *slang chiefly Brit* : CONVICT, EX-CONVICT
⁴**lag·ger** \ˈlagə(r), -aag-, -aig-\ *n* -s [⁷*lag* + *-er*] : one that covers or provides with lags or lagging
lag·gin *or* **lag·gen** \ˈlagən\ *n* -s [prob. of Scand origin; akin to ON *lǫgg* rim of a barrel] *chiefly Scot* : the staves of a hooped vessel (as a barrel or cask) esp. at their bottom — usu. used in pl.
¹**lag·ging** \ˈlagiŋ\ *n* -s [fr. *lagging*, gerund of ⁴*lag*] *slang chiefly Brit* : a term or sentence of imprisonment, transportation, or penal servitude
²**lag·ging** \ˈ", -aag-, -aig-\ *n* -s [⁶*lag* + *-ing*] : a lag or material used for making lags: as **a** : material applied for thermal insulation esp. around a cylindrical object ⟨during cold weather, the oil tank and the oil lines may be covered with asbestos padding, called ~, to keep the oil warm during flight —B.A.Shields⟩ **b** : poles or planking erected to prevent cave-ins in earthwork (as in a mine or tunnel) **c** : wooden strips for transferring to the centering form the weight of an arch under construction **d** : a detachable protective surface (as on a pulley or a drum)
lag·ging·ly *adv* [fr. *lagging*, pres. part. of ¹*lag* + *-ly*] : in a lagging manner : LOITERINGLY, TARDILY
lag gravel *n* [²*lag*] **1** : residual gravel remaining on a surface after finer materials have been removed by winds **2** : gravel rolled or dragged along a stream bed at a slower rate than the finer particles of sediment
la·gid·i·um \ləˈjidēəm\ *n, cap* [NL, fr. Gk *lagidion*, dim. of *lagōs* hare] : a genus of histricomorph rodents (family Chinchillidae) comprising the mountain vizcachas
laglast \ˈ=ˌ=\ *n* : one that lags or lingers to the last ⟨~ stragglers⟩
lag line *n* [¹*lag*] : a line toward which players lag (as in marbles)
-lag·nia \ˈlagnēə, ˈlaig-\ *n comb form* -s [NL, fr. Gk *lagneia*] : lust ⟨copro*lagnia*⟩
la·gniappe \ˈlan,yap, =ˈ=\ *n* -s [AmerF (Louisiana), fr. AmerSp *la ñapa* the lagniappe, fr. Sp *la* the (fem. of *el*, def. art., the) + AmerSp *ñapa, yapa* lagniappe, fr. Quechua *yápa* addition — more at LARIAT] **1 a** *chiefly Louisiana* : a small gift given a customer by a merchant at the time of a purchase ⟨a sack of lemon drops for ~ with the groceries⟩ ⟨giving her half a yard extra for ~ —Lyle Saxon⟩ **b** : something given or obtained gratuitously or by way of bonus or good measure ⟨the . . . beautiful widow from whom he first accepts a reward of five thousand dollars, and later her love as a sort of ~ —Neal Cross⟩ **2** : a gratuity of any kind : TIP
-lag·ny \ˌlagnē, -ni\ *n comb form* -ES [ISV, fr. NL *-lagnia*] : -LAGNIA
lago- — see LAG-
la·goa san·ta man \ləˈgōəˈsantə-\ *n, usu cap L&S* [fr. *Lagoa Santa*, city in Brazil, near where the remains were found] : an extinct So. American man with a markedly long, narrow, and high-vaulted cranium known from skeletal remains found in Brazilian caves and orig. regarded as an extremely primitive human type but now usu. held to be a product of inbreeding of the original Mongoloid American stock
lag·o·chi·las·ca·ris \ˌlagōkīˈlaskərəs\ *n, cap* [NL, fr. *lag-* + *chil-* + *Ascaris*] : a genus of nematode worms believed to be normally parasitic in the intestine of the clouded leopard but in a few instances encountered as a subcutaneous parasite of man in Trinidad and Dutch Guiana
lag of the tide : the interval by which the time of high or low water falls behind the mean time in the 2d and 4th quarters of the moon — opposed to *priming of the tide*
lag·o·morph \ˈlagəˌmȯrf\ *n* -s [NL *Lagomorpha*] : an animal of the order Lagomorpha : HARE, RABBIT, PIKA
lag·o·mor·pha \ˌ==ˈmȯrfə\ *n pl, cap* [NL, fr. *lag-* + *-morpha*] : an order of Eutheria comprising gnawing mammals (as the rabbits, hares, and pikas) that resemble the rodents but have two pairs of upper incisors one behind the other, being formerly regarded as rodents, and then constituting a suborder (Duplicidentata) of Rodentia — **lag·o·mor·phic** \ˌ==ˈmȯrfik\ *adj* — **lag·o·mor·phous** \-fəs\ *adj*
lag·o·my·i·dae \ˌlagəˈmīəˌdē\ [NL, fr. *Lagomys* (syn. of *Ochotona*) (fr. *lag-* + *-mys*) + *-idae*] *syn of* OCHOTONIDAE
lagon *var of* LAGAN
¹**la·goon** *also* **la·gune** \ləˈgün\ *n* -s *often attrib* [F & It; F *lagune*, fr. It *laguna*, fr. L *lacuna* pit, pool, pond, fr. *lacus* lake — more at LAKE] **1 a** : a shallow sound, channel, pond, or lake near or communicating with the sea ⟨~s of Venice⟩ ⟨the ~ of a coral island⟩ — see ATOLL **b** : a shallow freshwater pond or lake usu. near or communicating with a larger lake or a river ⟨long freshwater ~s yellow with lagoon flowers —Willa Cather⟩ ⟨riverbed ~s —*Amer. Guide Series: Ark.*⟩ **2** [It *lagone*, aug. of *lago*, fr. L *lacus*] : a pool esp. in a basin formed by a hot spring **3** : a shallow artificial pond for the natural oxidation of sewage and ultimate drying of the sludge
²**lagoon** \ˈ"\ *vt* -ED/-ING/-S : to subject (sewage) to natural oxidation and drying in a lagoon
la·goon·al \-nᵊl\ *adj* : of or relating to a lagoon ⟨~ and basinal areas —*Jour. of Geol.*⟩ ⟨a ~ sedimentary origin is indicated —A.M.Bateman⟩
la·goon·side \-nˌsīd\ *n* : the land bordering on a lagoon
lag·oph·thal·mos *or* **lag·oph·thal·mus** \ˌlaˌgäfˈthalməs\ *n* -ES [NL, fr. L & Gk; L *lagophthalmos* person afflicted with lagophthalmos, fr. Gk *lagōphthalmos*, adj., hare-eyed, unable to close the eye, fr. *lagōs* hare + *ophthalmos* eye] : pathological incomplete closure of the eyelids : inability to close the eyelids fully
la·go·pous \ləˈgōpəs\ *adj* [Gk *lagōpous* ptarmigan, a plant (lit., rough-footed like a hare)] : having hairy rhizomes suggestive of the foot of a hare
la·go·pus \ˈ"\ *n, cap* [NL, fr. L, ptarmigan, a plant, fr. Gk *lagōpous*, fr. *lagōs* hare + *pous* foot] : a genus of northern game birds (family Tetraonidae) comprising the ptarmigans and the red grouse
lag·or·ches·tes \ˌlaˌgȯ(r)ˈkeˌstēz\ *n, cap* [NL, fr. *lag-* + Gk *orchēstēs* dancer, fr. *orcheisthai* to dance — more at ORCHESTRA] : a genus consisting of the hare wallabies

la·gos \ˈlāˌgäs\ *adj, usu cap* [fr. *Lagos*, city in Nigeria] **:** of or from Lagos, the capital of Nigeria **:** of the kind or style prevalent in Lagos

lagos ebony *n, usu cap L* [fr. *Lagos*, former province of Nigeria] **:** a West African timber tree (*Diospyros dendo*) with hard black heartwood

lagos rubber *n, usu cap L* [fr. *Lagos*, former province of Nigeria] **:** high-grade rubber yielded in moderate quantity by a tropical African tree (*Funtumia elastica*) sometimes cultivated prior to the general cultivation of Brazilian rubber trees

la·gos·to·mus \ləˈgästəməs\ *n, cap* [NL, fr. *lag-* + *-stomus*] **:** a genus of hystricomorph rodents (family Chinchillidae) comprising the plains vizcacha

lag·o·thrix \ˈlagəˌthriks\ *n, cap* [NL, fr. *lag-* + *-thrix*] **:** a genus consisting of the woolly monkeys

la·gran·gi·an function \ləˈgranjēən-\ *n, usu cap L* [Joseph L. Lagrange †1813 Italian-born geometer and astronomer in France + E *-ian*] **:** KINETIC POTENTIAL

lag·ri·man·do \ˌlägrəˈmän(ˌ)dō, ˌlag-\ *adj (or adv)* [It, lit., weeping, lamenting, fr. L *lacrimandus*, gerundive of *lacrimare* to weep, shed tears — more at LACRIMATORY] **:** LACRIMANDO

lag·ri·mo·so \-mō(ˌ)sō\ *adj (or adv)* [It, lit., tearful, lachrymose, fr. L *lacrimosus* — more at LACHRYMOSE] **:** LACRIMOSO

la grippe \ləˈgrip, läˈ-\ *n* [F, the grippe] **:** GRIPPE

lags *pl of* LAG, *pres 3d sing of* LAG

lag screw *n* [⁶*lag*; fr. its original use in securing lags to drums or cylinders] **:** a screw having a wrench head and woodscrew threads terminating in a point — called also *lag bolt*

lag screw

lag-screw \ˈ=ˌ=\ *vt* [*lag screw*] **:** to fasten or join with a lag screw

lag·ting *or* **lag·thing** \ˈlägˌtiŋ\ *n* -S *often cap* [Norw *lagting*, fr. *lag* company, society (fr. ON, layer, due place, *lög*, pl., law) + *ting* parliament, thing (fr. ON *thing*) — more at LAW, THING] **:** a Scandinavian legislative body: **a :** the upper section of the Norwegian parliament **b :** the legislature of the Faeroe islands

¹**la·gu·na** \ləˈgünə\ *n* -S [Sp, fr. L *lacuna* — more at LAGOON] **:** LAGOON, LAKE, POND ⟨salt lakes and ~s within the tropics almost always have foul bottom waters —W.C.Krumbein & R.M.Garrels⟩

²**laguna** \"\ *n, pl* **laguna** *or* **lagunas** *usu cap* [Sp, pond, lagoon; fr. the lagoon near the site of the tribe's pueblo] **1 a :** a Keres pueblo people of New Mexico **b :** a member of such people **2 :** the language of the Laguna people

lagune *var of* LAGOON

la·gu·ne·ro \ˌlägüˈnā(ˌ)rō\ *n, pl* **lagunero** *or* **laguneros** *usu cap* [MexSp, fr. Sp *lagunero*, adj., of a lagoon, fr. *laguna* lagoon] **1 :** an extinct Uto-Aztecan people or group of peoples of northern Mexico **2 :** a member of a Lagunero people

la·gu·rus \ləˈgyu̇rəs\ *n, cap* [NL, fr. *lag-* + *-urus*] **:** a genus of European grasses with the spikelets in woolly heads — see HARE'S-TAIL GRASS

la·hai·na disease \ləˈhīnə-\ *n, usu cap L* [fr. *Lahaina*, district and city in Maui, Hawaii] **:** a fungal root disease of sugar cane

la·har \ˈläˌhär\ *n* -S [Jav] **:** a mudflow containing much volcanic debris

lah-di-dah *var of* LA-DI-DA

lahn·da \ˈländə\ *n* -S *cap* **:** an Indic language of West Punjab

la·hore \ləˈhō(ə)r, -hȯ(ə)r\ *adj, usu cap* [fr. *Lahore*, city in Pakistan] **:** of or from the city of Lahore, Pakistan **:** of the kind or style prevalent in Lahore

la·hu \ˈläˌhü\ *n, pl* **lahu** *or* **lahus** *usu cap* **1 a :** a widespread group of peoples inhabiting the hilly region between the Salween and Mekong rivers in northern Thailand, Laos, southern Yunnan, and the Shan States of Burma **b :** a member of any of such peoples **2 :** the Tibeto-Burman language of the Lahu people

la·hu·li \ˈlähəˌlē\ *n, pl* **lahuli** *or* **lahulis** *cap* **1 :** a native or inhabitant of Lahul, northern Kashmir **2 :** the Tibetan dialect of the Lahuli

¹**lai** \ˈlā\ *n* -S [F, fr. OF — more at LAY] **1 :** a medieval type of short tale in French literature that is usu. in octosyllabic verse and deals with subjects of Celtic origin often connected with Arthur or the Round Table **2 :** a medieval type of lyric poem revived in the 17th century and composed in unsymmetrical couplets each sung to its own melody

²**lai** \ˈlī\ *n, pl* **lai** *or* **lais** *usu cap* **1 a :** a Mongoloid people of the Chin Hills in Burma **b :** a member of such people **2 :** the Tibeto-Burman language of the Lai people

la·ic \ˈlāik\ *n* -S [LL *laicus*, adj. & n., fr. LGk *laikos*, fr. Gk, of the people, fr. *laos* people + *-ikos* -ic] **:** a member of the laity **:** LAYMAN ⟨the book has a place . . . not in the cloisters but among the ~s —G.W.Johnson⟩

la·i·cal \-ə̇kəl\ *also* **la·ic** \ˈ=ik\ *adj* [*laical* fr. LL *laicalis*, fr. *laicus* + L *-alis* -al; *laic* fr. LL *laicus*] **:** of or relating to a layman or the laity ⟨taking off his collar, which till now he has worn in clerical fashion . . . and setting it in *laical* position —Rebecca West⟩ — **la·i·cal·ly** \-ək(ə)lē\ *adv*

laich \ˈläk\ *Scot var of* LOW

la·i·cism \ˈlāəˌsizəm\ *n* -S [*laic* + *-ism*] **:** the nonclerical control or administration of a political system or a social function

la·ic·i·ty \lāˈisəd·ē\ *n* -ES [F *laïcité*, fr. LL *laicus* + F *-ité* -ity] **:** control or influence by the laity

la·i·ci·za·tion \ˌlāəsə̇ˈzāshən, -ˌsīˈ-\ *n* -S **:** the process or act of laicizing

la·i·cize \ˈlāəˌsīz\ *vt* -ED/-ING/-S [*laic* + *-ize*] **:** to make lay **:** put under the direction of or throw open to laymen ⟨resisting efforts of the state to ~ education —*New Republic*⟩

¹**laid** \ˈläd\ *Scot var of* LOAD

²**laid** \"\ *adj* [fr. past part. of ¹*lay*] **1** *of paper* **:** watermarked with laid lines — compare WOVE **2** *of embroidery* **:** made by couching

laid fabric *n* **:** a fabric lacking weft threads and having the warp threads bonded together by rubber latex or other binding material

laid line *n* **:** any of the closely spaced parallel lines in laid paper made by laid wires

laid·ly \ˈlādlī\ *chiefly Scot var of* LOATHLY

laid wire *n* **:** any of the wires on the surface of a dandy roll running parallel with its axis

laigh \ˈläk\ *Scot var of* LOW

laik \ˈläk\ *Scot var of* LACK

lain *past part of* LIE

lainch \ˈlänch\ *chiefly Scot var of* LAUNCH

laine \ˈlān\ *n* -S [F, fr. L *lana* wool — more at WOOL] **:** woolen cloth **:** WOOL

¹**lair** \ˈla(a)(ə)r, ˈle|, |ə, *Scot* ˈlār\ *n* -S [ME *lair*, *leir*, fr. OE *leger*; akin to OHG *legar* bed, act of lying, cohabitation, ON *legr* grave, cohabitation, Goth *ligrs* bed; derivative fr. the root of E ¹*lie*] **1** *Scot* **:** a burial lot in a graveyard **2 a** *dial Brit* **:** a resting or sleeping place **:** BED ⟨upon a ~ composed of straw with a blanket stretched over it —Sir Walter Scott⟩ **b** *dial Brit* **:** a place where pastured livestock lie or rest **c** *Brit* **:** a pen or shed for cattle on the way to market or kept for slaughtering **3 a :** the bed or living place of a wild animal **:** DEN **b :** something that resembles the den of an animal: as (1) **:** a hidden base of operations ⟨the sinking of a boat by the . . . pirates to cut off approach to their ~ —*Amer. Guide Series: La.*⟩ ⟨believed to be at least one of the chief ~s from which the zeppelins sallied forth to the attack —*Times Hist. of the War*⟩ (2) **:** a secret place **:** HIDEAWAY ⟨got up from her ~ among the strawberries and wandered across the meadow —John Buchan⟩ ⟨the children followed the grown-ups into the house, and retiring to their ~ under the sewing machine studied the new personage from safety —Oliver La Farge⟩

²**lair** \"\ *vi* -ED/-ING/-S **:** to make or go to a lair **:** REST ⟨where shall we today for from now we follow new trails —Rudyard Kipling⟩ ⟨carnivores of the late Wisconsin period undoubtedly ~*ed* . . . intermittently with human occupation —F.C.Hibben⟩

³**lair** \"\ *n* -S [Sc, fr. ME (northern dial.) *lar* learning, fr. OE *lār* lore — more at LORE] *chiefly Scot* **:** LORE; *esp* **:** knowledge acquired through instruction

⁴**lair** \"\ *n* -S [ME, fr. ON *leir* loam, clay; akin to ON *līm* lime — more at LIME] *chiefly Scot* **:** MIRE, MUD

⁵**lair** \"\ *vb* -ED/-ING/-S *vt*, *chiefly Scot* **:** to cause to sink in the mire ⟨watery flows in which sheep and cattle sometimes ~ themselves —William McIlwraith⟩ ~ *vi*, *chiefly Scot* **:** WALLOW

laird \ˈla(a)(ə)rd, ˈle|, |əd, *Scot* ˈlärd\ *n* -S [ME (northern dial.) *lard*, *laverd* lord — more at LORD] *Scot* **:** a landed proprietor; *esp* **:** the owner of a small estate

laird·ship \-ˌship\ *n* [*laird* + *-ship*] **:** the estate belonging to a laird

lairstone \ˈ=ˌ=\ *n* [¹*lair* + *stone*] *Scot* **:** GRAVESTONE

lais *pl of* LAI

laisse \ˈles, ˈläs\ *n* -S [F, fr. OF, lit., string, leash — more at LEASH] **:** the irregular strophe of Old French poetry; *esp* **:** a strophe of the chansons de geste

¹**laissez-faire** *also* **laisser-faire** \ˌle|(ˌ)sā|fa(a)|(ə)r, ˌlā|, -fe|, |ə *also* |(ˌ)zā|f- *sometimes* |sē|f- *or* |si|f- *or* |zē|f- *or* |zi|f-\ *adj* [*laissez-faire* fr. F *laissez faire* let (people) do (as they choose) (motto of 18th cent. Fr. economists who protested excessive government regulation of industry); *laisser-faire* fr. F *laisser faire* to let (people) do (as they choose)] **:** of, adhering to, or favoring the doctrine or practice of laissez-faire ⟨in economic philosophy the High Victorians were mainly *laissez-faire* —*Saturday Rev.*⟩ ⟨economic liberalism of the *laissez-faire* type —Frank Thilly⟩ ⟨the social disorganization and *laisser-faire* purposelessness . . . present in the cultural life of these young people —Ernest & Pearl Beaglehole⟩

²**laissez-faire** *also* **laisser-faire** \"\ *n* -S **1 :** a doctrine opposing governmental interference (as by regulation or subsidy) in economic affairs beyond the minimum necessary for the maintenance of peace and property rights ⟨the reaction against free trade and *laissez-faire* —*Atlantic*⟩ ⟨few people . . . hold that *laisser-faire* could solve the economic problems of the British community —*Economist*⟩ ⟨a central position between *laissez-faire* and a planned economy —J.S.Schapiro⟩ — compare FREE ENTERPRISE, MERCANTILISM, PLANNED ECONOMY **2 :** a philosophy or practice characterized by a usu. deliberate abstention from direction or planning **:** a policy of noninterference esp. with individual freedom of choice and action ⟨a poverty that proclaimed *laissez-faire* in ethics —Francis Hackett⟩ ⟨the unhampered elective system which is merely the pedagogical form of . . . *laisser-faire* —P.E.More⟩ ⟨a policy of *laissez-faire* towards the artists —*Times Lit Supp.*⟩ — compare MANAGERIALISM

laissez-faire·ism \|(ə)ˌrizəm\ *n* -S **:** the doctrine of laissez-faire ⟨the classic statement of the judicial version of *laissez-faireism* —E.S.Corwin⟩

laissez-passer \-ˌpaˈsā, -ˌpȧˈ-, -ˌpäˈ-\ *n* -S [F, fr. *laissez passer* let (someone) pass] **:** PERMIT, PASS ⟨thought a *laissez-passer* rendered him immune to search —John Gunther⟩ ⟨a new *laissez-passer* to the frontiers of the universe —Ritchie Calder⟩ ⟨agreements to enable officials . . . to use the United Nations *laissez-passer* for official travel —*New Internat'l Yr. Bk.*⟩

lait \ˈlāt\ *vb* -ED/-ING/-S [ME *laiten*, fr. ON *leita*, causative fr. the root of ON *līta* to look — more at LITMUS] *vt*, *dial Eng* **:** to search for ~ *vi*, *dial Eng* **:** SEARCH

lai·tance \ˈlātᵊn(t)s\ *n* -S [F, fr. *lait* milk (fr. L *lact-*, *lac*) + *-ance* — more at GALAXY] **:** an accumulation of fine particles on the surface of freshly placed concrete occurring when there is an upward movement of water through the concrete due to the presence of too much mixing water, to excessive tamping, or to vibration of the concrete

¹**laith** \ˈlāth\ *Brit var of* LATHE

²**laith** \ˈlāth\ *Scot var of* LOATH

³**laith** \ˈlāth\ *Scot var of* LOATHE

la·i·ty \ˈlāəd·ē, -ətē, -i\ *n* -ES [⁵*lay* + *-ty*] **1 :** the great body of the people of a religious faith as distinguished from its clergy **2 :** the great body of the people as distinguished from those of a particular profession (as medicine or law) or those specially skilled ⟨writers who can interpret this wholeness, both to their colleagues and the ~ —P.B.Sears⟩

lak·a·toi \ˌlakəˈtȯi\ *n* -S [Papuan] **:** a dugout double canoe used by natives of Australasia

¹**lake** \ˈlāk\ *n* -S *often attrib* [in sense 1, fr. ME *lak*, fr. OE *lacu* stream, pool; akin to OHG *lahha* puddle, MLG & MD *lake* puddle, stagnant pool, ON *lækr* brook, OE *leccan* to moisten; in sense 2, fr. ME *lac*, *lak*, *lake*, partly fr. OE *lacu*; partly fr. OF *lac* lake, pond, fr. L *lacus* basin, pond, lake; akin to OE & OS *lagu* sea, water, ON *lögr* sea, water, OIr *loch* lake, pond, Gk *lakkos* pond, cistern, reservoir, OSlav *loky* pool, cistern — more at LEAK] **1** *dial Eng* **:** a small stream or channel **:** BROOK, RIVULET **2 a :** a considerable inland body of standing water, an expanded part of a river, a reservoir formed by a dam, or a lake basin intermittently or formerly covered by water — see LAGOON 1, POND **b :** a pool of other liquid (as lava, oil, or pitch) **c :** something resembling a lake ⟨surrounded by a rosy ~ of azaleas —*Christian Science Monitor*⟩

²**lake** \"\ *n* -S [ME *leyk*, *laik*, fr. ON *leikr* play; akin to OE *lāc* warlike activity, play, booty, OHG *leih* play, melody, song, Goth *laiks* dance, ON *leika* to play — more at ³LAKE] *dial Eng* **:** AMUSEMENT

³**lake** \"\ *vi* -ED/-ING/-S [ME *leyken*, *laiken*, fr. ON *leika* to play, deceive, dance; akin to OE *lācan* to leap, spring, fight, MHG *leichen* to hop, make a fool of, Goth *laikan* to hop, jump, OIr *loig* calf, Gk *elelizein* to cause to vibrate, to quiver, Skt *rejate* he trembles] *dial Eng* **:** to amuse oneself **:** PLAY, FROLIC ⟨a toy for the baby to ~ with⟩

⁴**lake** \"\ *n* -S [F *laque* lac, lake, fr. MF, fr. OProv *laca*, fr. Ar *lakk*, fr. Per *lak* — more at LAC] **1 a** (1) **:** a purplish red pigment prepared from lac dye or cochineal by precipitation of the coloring matter with a metallic compound (2) **:** the color of this lake **b :** any of a large group of organic pigments that are usu. bright in color and more or less translucent when in the form of an oil paint, that are composed essentially of a soluble dye rendered insoluble by adsorption on or chemical combination with an inorganic carrier, and that were first prepared from natural dyes (as madder) and later from alizarin but are now usu. prepared from many types of synthetic dyes by precipitation (as with a soluble alkaline earth metal salt or a phosphotungstate or a molybdotungstate or tannin) on a carrier (as hydrated alumina) — called also *color lake*; see DYE table I (under *Organic pigments*); compare MORDANT 1, TONER **2 :** a transparent or semitransparent appearance produced by the use of lakes or resembling that produced by lakes **3 :** CARMINE 2

⁵**lake** \"\ *vb* -ED/-ING/-S *vi*, *of blood* **:** to alter so that the hemoglobin is dissolved in the plasma ~ *vt* **:** to cause (blood) to lake

lake ball *n* **:** a compact rounded mass of organic material sometimes formed in sediment on a lake bottom

lake basin *n* **1 :** the depression occupied by a lake **2 :** the area from which drainage reaches a lake

lake bass *n* **:** LARGEMOUTH BLACK BASS

lake bed *n* **:** LAKE BASIN 1

lake bordeaux B *n, usu cap L&B* [⁴*lake*] **:** an organic pigment — see DYE table I (under *Pigment Red 63*)

lake cress *n* **:** an aquatic herb (*Armoracia aquatica*) of the mustard family of No. America with submersed or prostrate stems

lake duck *n* **1 :** LESSER SCAUP **2 :** MALLARD

lake dweller *n* **:** one that lives in a lake dwelling

lake dwelling *n* **:** a dwelling built on piles in a lake; *specif* **:** one built in prehistoric times

lake fly *n* **1 :** any of numerous midges of the genus *Chironomus* and related genera **2 :** MAYFLY

lakefront \ˈ=ˌ=\ *n* **:** land that usu. is developed, has buildings, and fronts on a lake ⟨a row of neat summer cottages on the ~⟩

lakehead \ˈ=ˌ=\ *n* **:** the part of a lake most distant from its outlet

lake herring *n* **:** a cisco (*Leucichthys artedi*) found from Lake Memphremagog to Lake Superior and northward and important as a commercial food fish; *broadly* **:** CISCO

lake indian *n, usu cap L&I* **:** SENIJEXTEE

lake lamprey *n* **:** SEA LAMPREY

lakeland \ˈ=ˌland, -ˌlənd\ *n* **:** a region that has many lakes

lakeland terrier *n* [fr. *Lakeland* (Lake district), mountainous region in northwestern England where the breed was developed] **1** *usu cap L* **:** an English breed of rather small harsh-coated straight-legged terriers **2** *sometimes cap L* **:** a dog of the Lakeland terrier breed

lake lawyer *n* **:** LAWYER 2b

lake·let \ˈlāklə̇t\ *n* -S **:** a little lake ⟨a luxuriant sunken garden surrounding a ~ —Aubrey Drury⟩

la·ken·vel·der \ˈläkənˌveldə(r)\ *n* [modif. of G *Lakenfelder*] **1** *usu cap* **:** a German breed of strikingly marked black-and-white domestic fowls somewhat resembling leghorns **2** -S *sometimes cap* **:** a bird of the Lakenvelder breed

lake perch *n* **:** YELLOW PERCH

lake pickerel *n* **1 :** ⁴PIKE 1a **2 :** CHAIN PICKEREL

lake pitch *n* **:** a soft Trinidad asphalt rich in bituminous matter and soluble in petroleum spirit — compare LAND PITCH

lak·er \ˈlākə(r)\ *n* -S [¹*lake* + *-er*] **:** one associated with a lake or lakes: as **a :** a visitor to a lake; *esp* **:** a visitor to the Lake district in England **b** *usu cap* [*Lake (school)*, a group of 19th cent. Eng. poets (fr. *Lake* district, region in northwestern England) + E *-er*] **:** a poet of the Lake School **c :** a fish living in or taken from a lake; *esp* **:** LAKE TROUT **d** (1) **:** a person familiar with sailing on a lake; *esp* **:** a sailor on a Great Lakes ship (2) **:** a boat for lake navigation; *esp* **:** a ship esp. designed as to draft, beam, length, or structure to operate on the Great Lakes and associated canals **e** *North* **:** an expert at fishing on a lake

lake red *n, usu cap L&R* [⁴*lake*] **:** any of several organic pigments — see DYE table I (under *Pigment Red 50* and *53*)

lakes *pl of* LAKE, *pres 3d sing of* LAKE

lake salmon *n* **1 :** LANDLOCKED SALMON **2 :** LAKE TROUT b

lake sheepshead *n* **:** FRESHWATER DRUM

lakeshore \ˈ=ˌ=\ *n* **:** the land adjacent to or bordering a lake; *esp* **:** the beach of a lake ⟨on the ~ fishing boats bumped their prows —Rumer Godden⟩

lake shore disease *n, north* **:** pine of cattle

lake shrimp *n* **:** a common commercial saltwater shrimp (*Penaeus setiferus*)

lakeside \ˈ=ˌ=\ *n* **:** LAKESHORE ⟨in this little graveyard by the ~ —Amy Lowell⟩

lake sturgeon *n* **:** a sturgeon (*Acipenser fulvescens*) of the Great Lakes and Mississippi river that becomes four to six feet long and is now rare over much of its former range

lake trout *n* **:** any of various trout and salmon found in lakes: as **a :** any of several European trouts that are varieties of the brown trout **b :** a large dark No. American char (*Salvelinus namaycush*) that is highly variable in skin and flesh color, sometimes exceeds 50 pounds in weight, and is an important commercial food fish in northern lakes — called also *namaycush*, *salmon trout*, *togue*

lake village *n* **:** a group of lake dwellings

lake·ward \ˈlākwə(r)d\ *adj* **:** directed toward a lake ⟨wall of high buildings aligned along the ~ side of the city —A.J. Liebling⟩

lake water cress *n* **:** LAKE CRESS

lakeweed \ˈ=ˌ=\ *n* **:** WATER PEPPER

lake whitefish *or* **lake whiting** *n* **:** a large predominantly pale green whitefish (*Coregonus clupeaformis*) that is a superior food and sport fish esp. of the Great Lakes

¹**lakh** *also* **lac** \ˈläk, ˈlak\ *n* -S [Hindi *lākh*, fr. Skt *lakṣa*, lit., mark, sign] **1** *India* **:** one hundred thousand ⟨a population of 20 ~s⟩ ⟨50 ~s of rupees⟩ **2** *India* **:** a great number ⟨we need ~s of schools . . . for our illiteracy is disgraceful —J.A. Michener⟩

²**lakh** \"\ *adj, India* **:** hundred thousand ⟨10 ~ rupees⟩

³**lakh** \"\ *n, pl* **lakh** *or* **lakhs** *usu cap* **1 :** a member of a division of the Lezghians in central Dagestan **2 :** the North Caucasic language of the Lakh people

la·kher \ˈläkə(r)\ *n, pl* **lakher** *or* **lakhers** *usu cap* **:** a member of a head-hunting people of southern Assam and western Burma who are predominantly agricultural

lakh·mid \ˈlakmə̇d\ *n* -S *cap* [*Lakhm*, great-great-grandfather of ʻAmr ibn-ʻAdi, 3d cent. A.D. founder of the dynasty + E *-id*] **:** a northeastern Arabian dynasty strongly allied with Persia at the rise of Islam

la·kie \ˈlākē\ *or* **lakie tide** *n* -S [prob. fr. ¹*lake* + *-ie*] **:** a temporary retrograde movement of the tide observed in the Firth of Forth

lak·in \ˈlākə̇n\ *or* **lak·ing** \-kə̇n,-kiŋ\ *n* -S [of Scand origin; akin to ON *leika* toy, doll, fr. *leika* to play — more at LAKE] *dial Brit* **:** TOY, PLAYTHING

laking *pres part of* LAKE

lak·ish \ˈlākish\ *adj, often cap L* [*Lake (school)* + E *-ish* — more at LAKER] **:** of, relating to, or in the style of the Lake School of poetry ⟨did not accuse him of the *Lakish* fault of mysticism —J.R.Derby⟩

lak·ist \-kə̇st\ *n* -S *often cap* [*Lake (school)* + E *-ist*] **:** one of the poets of the Lake School or one of their adherents

lak·miut \ˈlakˌmyüt, -ˌmē,(y)üt\ *n, pl* **lakmiut** *or* **lakmiuts** *usu cap* **1 :** a Kalapooian people formerly on Lakmiut river, Oregon **2 :** a member of the Lakmiut people

lakmus *var of* LACMUS

la·ko·ta \ləˈkōd·ə\ *n, pl* **lakota** *or* **lakotas** *usu cap* **:** DAKOTA

laky \ˈlākē\ *adj* -ER/-EST [⁴*lake* + *-y*] **:** of, relating to, or resembling lake; *specif, of blood* **:** LAKED

la·lang \ˈläˌläŋ\ *also* **lalang grass** *or* **lal·lang grass** \"+,-\ *n* -S [Malay *lalang*] **1** *Malaya* **:** COGON **2 :** savannah lands of eastern Asia characterized by the presence of cogon

la·la·pa·loo·za *or* **lal·la·pa·loo·za** *or* **lol·la·pa·loo·sa** \ˌläləpəˈlüzə\ *n* -S [origin unknown] *slang* **:** something superior or unusual **:** an outstanding example ⟨a filing system for keeping track of things that is . . . a ~ —H.R.Medina⟩

la·li \ˈlälē\ *n* -S [Fijian, Tongan, & Samoan] **:** a large drum made of a hollowed log and used in ceremonies and to summon to church and meetings in Western Polynesia and Fiji

-la·lia \ˈlālēə\ *n comb form* -S [NL, fr. Gk *lalia* chatter, prattle, fr. *lalein* to chat, talk (prob. of imit. origin like G *lallen* to babble, stammer, L *lallare* to sing a lullaby) + *-ia* -y] **:** speech disorder (of a specified type esp. relating to the articulation of speech sounds) ⟨brady*lalia*⟩ ⟨rhino*lalia*⟩ — compare -PHASIA, -PHEMIA, -PHONY 2

La·lique *trademark* — used for an elaborate French art glass typically made by a combination of pressing, blowing, frosting, and cutting

lal·lan \ˈlalən\ *or* **lal·land** \-n(d)\ *Scot var of* LOWLAND

lal·lans \-nz\ *n, pl* **lallans** *or* **lallanses** *usu cap* **:** LOWLAND SCOTS

lal·la·tion \laˈlāshən\ *n* -S [L *lallare* to sing a lullaby + E *-tion* — more at -LALIA] **1 :** infantile utterance whether in infants or in older speakers (as by retardation or mimicry) **2 :** a defective articulation of the letter *l*, the substitution of \l\ for another sound, or the substitution of another sound for \l\ — compare LAMBDACISM

Lal·ly \ˈlalē\ *trademark* — used for a concrete-filled cylindrical steel structural column

lal·ly·gag *or* **lol·ly·gag** \ˈlälēˌgag, -gaa(ə)g, -gaig\ *vi* **lallygagged** *or* **lollygagged**; **lallygagged** *or* **lollygagged**; **lallygagging** *or* **lollygagging**; **lallygags** *or* **lollygags** [origin unknown] **1** *dial* **:** to fool around **:** LOITER, DAWDLE ⟨*lollygagging* around on some shore station —Maxwell Griffith⟩ **2** *dial* **:** to neck esp. in public **:** SMOOCH **3 :** to chatter incessantly

la·lo \ˈlä(ˌ)lō\ *n* -S [origin unknown] **:** a shoot that arises when the tip is removed from a sugarcane culm

lalo- *comb form* [NL, fr. Gk *lalos* talkative, prattling, fr. *lalein* to chat, talk — more at -LALIA] **:** speech **:** the speech organs

la·lop·a·thy \laˈläpəthē\ *n* -ES [ISV *lalo-* + *-pathy*] **:** a disorder of speech

lal·o·ple·gia \ˌlaləˈplēj(ē)ə\ *n* -S [NL, fr. *lalo-* + *-plegia*] **:** paralysis of the muscles involved in speech

-la·ly \ˌlalē, ˌlalē, -li\ *n comb form* -ES [NL *-lalia*] **:** -LALIA

¹**lam** \ˈlam, ˈlaa(ə)m\ *vb* **lammed**; **lammed**; **lamming**; **lams** [of Scand origin; akin to ON *lemja* to thrash, flog, beat; akin to OE *lemman* to lame, OHG *lemmen*; causative denominatives fr. the root of E ¹*lame*] *vt* **:** to beat soundly **:** THRASH, STRIKE, WHACK ~ *vi* **1 :** STRIKE, THRASH — usu. used with *into* or *out* ⟨*lammed* out wildly at them⟩ **2 :** to flee hastily **:** beat it **:** SCRAM ⟨let's ~ out of here⟩

²**lam** \"\ *n* -S **:** FLIGHT — used in the phrase *on the lam* ⟨to hide a former lover, now on the ~ from Dartmoor —Robert Hatch⟩ ⟨that so-and-so of a promoter had taken it on the ~ —Irene Kuhn⟩

³**lam** \"\ *also* **lamm** \"\ *n* -S [F *lame* lamina, blade, lam — more at LAME] **:** any of the lower levers connected by cords

between harnesses and treadles in various looms to enable the weaver to bring down several harnesses with one foot

lam *abbr* laminated

1la·ma \'lämə, 'lȧmə\ *n* -s [Tibetan *blama*] **:** a priest or monk of Tibetan Buddhism

2lama \"\ *n* [NL, fr. F, llama, fr. Sp *llama* — more at LLAMA] **1** *cap* **:** a genus of mammals (family Camelidae) that includes the llama, alpaca, guanaco, and other living and extinct So. American mountain ruminants with heavy woolly coats **2** -s **:** a dark grayish yellowish brown that is stronger and slightly yellower and lighter than seal, slightly redder and lighter than sepia brown, lighter and stronger than otter brown, and very slightly redder and deeper than bison — called also *elk, goose*

la·ma·ism \-mə,izəm\ *n* -s *usu cap* [1*lama* + *-ism*] **:** a form of Mahayana Buddhism that is found esp. in Tibet and is notable for the variety and elaboration of its ritual practices and the complexity of its hierarchical organization

la·ma·ist \-məəst\ *n* -s *usu cap, often attrib* **:** an adherent of Lamaism — **la·ma·is·tic** \ˌ≈≈'istik\ *adj, usu cap*

la·man·ite \'lāmə,nīt\ *n* -s *usu cap* [*Laman*, eponymous ancestor of the Lamanites in the *Book of Mormon* (Jacob 3:5) + E *-ite*] *Mormonism* **:** a member of a people descended from Laman, a son of the Jewish prophet Lehi, and identified as the ancestors of the American Indians — compare NEPHITE

la·man·tin \lə'mant°n\ *n* -s [F, alter. (resulting from incorrect division) of *la manati* the manatee, fr. *la* the + *manati* manatee, fr. Sp *manati* — more at MANATEE] **:** MANATEE

la·marck·ian \lə'märkēən\ *adj, usu cap* [J. B. de Monet *Lamarck* †1829 Fr. botanist and biologist + E *-ian*] **:** of or relating to Lamarckism

la·marck·ian·ism \-ēə,nizəm\ *n* -s *usu cap* **:** LAMARCKISM

la·marck·ism \-är,kizəm\ *n* -s *usu cap* [J. B. de Monet *Lamarck*, its formulator + E *-ism*] **:** a theory of organic evolution asserting that environmental changes cause structural changes in animals and plants esp. by inducing new or increased use of organs or parts resulting in adaptive modification or greater development and similarly cause disuse and eventual atrophy of other parts and that such changes are transmitted to offspring — compare DARWINISM, EVOLUTION 5 b, NEO-LAMARCKISM

la·ma·sery \'lämə,serē, 'lam-\ *n* -ES [F *lamaserie*, fr. *lama* + *-serie* (fr. Per *sarāī* palace, large house) — more at CARAVANSARY] **:** a monastery of lamas

1lamb \'lam, 'laa(ə)m\ *n* -s *often attrib* [ME, fr. OE; akin to OHG, ON, Goth *lamb*, OHG *elaho* elk — more at ELK] **1 a :** a young sheep esp. less than one year old or with no permanent teeth developed **b :** the young of various other animals; *esp* **:** those of some of the smaller antelopes **2** *cap* **a :** LAMB OF GOD **b** *Eastern Church* **:** the Eucharistic Host cut from a holy loaf of the oblation and consecrated **3 a :** a person innocent, gentle, or weak as a lamb ⟨I didn't need to lie, for he took it like a ~ —John Buchan⟩ **b :** DEAR, PET ⟨you're a ~, but it isn't fair —Dorothy Sayers⟩ **c :** a person easily cheated or deceived **:** DUPE; *esp* **:** an inexperienced trader (as in securities) who is readily fleeced ⟨the ~s of every college faculty are subject to the temptation of finance—R.M.Lovett⟩ **4 a :** the flesh of a lamb used as food **b :** LAMBSKIN **5 :** a fierce cruel person **:** RUFFIAN — **in lamb :** PREGNANT — used of a ewe

lamb 4 a: *A* wholesale cuts: *1* leg, *2* loin, *3* rack, *4* breast, *5* shank, *6* shoulder; *B* retail cuts: *a* leg; *b* sirloin chops and roast; *c* loin chops and rolled loin roast; *d* patties and chopped roast; *e* rib chops and crown roast; *f* riblets, stew, and stuffed or rolled breast; *g* square-cut shoulder roast, cushion roast, Saratoga chops, rolled shoulder, boneless shoulder chops; *h* neck slices; *i* shanks; *k* blade chops; *m* arm chops

2lamb \"\ *vb* -ED/-ING/-S *vi* **:** to bring forth a lamb ~ *vt* **1 :** to bring forth (a lamb) **2 :** to tend (ewes) at lambing time **3 :** to put lambs to graze on (as a field) — often used with *down*

1lam·ba \'lambə, 'läm-\ *n* -s [Malagasy] **:** a large wrap resembling a shawl that is worn by natives of Madagascar and is made of various fabrics in solid colors or patterns

2lamba \"\ *n, pl* **lamba** *or* **lambas** *usu cap* **1 a :** a Bantu people of northern Rhodesia **b :** a member of the Lamba people **2 :** a Bantu language of the Lamba people

lambale \'≈,≈\ *n* -s [1*lamb* + *ale*] **:** a feast formerly held in England at the time of shearing lambs about Whitsuntide

lam·baste *or* **lam·bast** \(')lam¦bāst, (')laam-, -baa(ə)st, -baist, -bȧst\ *vt* -ED/-ING/-S [prob. fr. 1*lam* + *baste* (to beat)] **1 :** to assault violently **:** BEAT, POUND, WHIP ⟨nothing pleased him so much as to get a big logging chain . . . and go at a budmash mate and ~ the evil spirits out of him —*McClure's*⟩ ⟨give a thorough *lambasting* to the Japanese in the First Battle of the Philippines —P.J.Searles⟩ **2 :** to administer a verbal or written thrashing to **:** tear into **:** EXCORIATE ⟨has been much *lambasted* for his ideas —*Ebony*⟩ ⟨approves in principle every major administration policy and ~s certain details —J.H. Crider⟩ ⟨politicians who shout and fear, point with pride, and ~ with abandon —Read Bain⟩

lamb·da \'lamdə, 'lam-\ *n* -s [Gk *labda, lambda*, of Sem origin; akin to Heb *lāmedh* lamedh] **1 :** the 11th letter of the Greek alphabet — symbol Λ or λ; see ALPHABET table **2** [back-formation fr. *lambdoid*] **:** the point of junction of the sagittal and lambdoid sutures of the skull — see CRANIOMETRY illustration **3 :** one thousandth of a cubic centimeter

lamb·da·cism \-də,sizəm\ *n* -s [LL *labdacismus*, fr. Gk *labdakismos*, fr. *labda, lambda* lambda + connective *-k-* + *-ismos -ism*] **1 :** excessive use of the letter *l* or the sound \l\ (as in alliteration) **2 :** defective articulation of \l\ or substitution of other sounds for it **3 :** substitution of \l\ for another sound (as \r\ when a Chinese says \'chelē\ for English *cherry*) — compare LALLATION

lambda point *n* **:** the temperature of approximately 2.19°K at which the transition from helium I to helium II takes place — often printed with Greek lambda (*λ-point*)

lamb·doid \'≈,dȯid\ *or* **lamb·doi·dal** \(')≈¦dȯid°l\ *adj* [*lambdoid* fr. F *lambdoïde*, fr. MF, fr. Gk *labdoeidēs, lambdoeidēs*, lit., lambda-shaped, fr. *labda, lambda* + *-oeidēs* -oid; *lambdoidal* fr. F *lambdoïde* + E *-al*] **:** of or relating to a suture that connects the occipital and parietal bones

lam·ben·cy \'lambənsē, 'laam-, -si\ *n* -ES [*lambent* + *-cy*] **:** the quality or state of being lambent **:** something that is lambent

lam·bent \-nt\ *adj* [L *lambent-, lambens*, pres. part. of *lambere* to lick — more at LAP] **1 :** playing lightly on or over a surface **:** gliding over **:** WAVERING, FLICKERING ⟨a fire of resinous wood . . . began to crackle and throw ~ shadows about the brass andirons —Hervey Allen⟩ **2 :** softly bright or radiant ⟨her eyes are ~ with love —Francis Yeats-Brown⟩ **3 :** light and brilliant ⟨the play of the author's ~ wit reminds one of the effect of sunshine on rippling water —B.R.Redman⟩ ⟨the coda . . . is brisk and ~ —Vernon Young⟩ **syn** see BRIGHT

lam·bent·ly *adv* **:** in a lambent manner

lamb·er \'lamə(r), 'laam-\ *n* -s [2*lamb* + *-er*] **1 :** a person who tends ewes at lambing time **2 :** a ewe that is lambing

lam·bert \'lambə(r)t, 'laam-\ *n* -s [after Johann H. *Lambert* †1777 Ger. physicist] **:** the cgs unit of brightness equal to the brightness of a perfectly diffusing surface that radiates or reflects one lumen per square centimeter

lambert conformal conic projection *or* **lambert conformal projection** *n, usu cap L* [after J. H. *Lambert*] **:** a conformal conic map projection with straight-line meridians that meet at a common center beyond the limits of the map and with parallels of which two are standard that are arcs of circles intersecting the meridians at right angles

lambert pine *n, usu cap L* [after Aylmer B. *Lambert* †1842 Eng. botanist] **:** SUGAR PINE

lambert's blue *n, often cap L* [after J. H. *Lambert*] **:** AZURITE BLUE

lambert's law *n, usu cap L* [after J. H. *Lambert*, its formulator] **:** either of two laws in physics: **a :** COSINE LAW **b :** the negative logarithm of the transmittance of a layer of substance is proportional to the thickness of the layer, the constant of proportionality for natural logarithms being the absorption coefficient — called also *Bouguer's law*

lam·beth conference \'lambəth-, -,beth-\ *n, usu cap L* [fr. *Lambeth* palace, London, residence of the archbishop of Canterbury] **:** a conference of the bishops of the worldwide Anglican communion called usu. about every 10 years by the archbishop of Canterbury to consult but not to legislate for the constituent churches

lambeth delft *n, usu cap L&D* [fr. *Lambeth*, metropolitan borough, London] **:** English glazed earthenware of the 17th century — compare FAIENCE

lambeth walk *n, usu cap L&W* [fr. *Lambeth Walk* (1937), song by Douglas Furber †1961 Brit. author and Noel Gay †1954 Brit. musician, fr. *Lambeth Walk*, a street in London, England] **:** a jaunty ballroom dance combining a strutting march with figures resembling those of a square dance

lamb·ie \'lamē, 'laam-, -mi\ *n* -s [1*lamb* + *-ie*] **:** LAMB — used as an endearment

lambing *pres part of* LAMB

lambing paralysis *n* **:** PREGNANCY DISEASE

lambing sickness *n* **:** milk fever in sheep

lam·bis \'lambəs\ *n, cap* [NL] **:** a genus of conchs (family Strombidae) comprising the scorpion shells of shallow waters of the tropical eastern hemisphere

lambitive *adj* [L *lambitus* (past part. of *lambere* to lick) + E *-ive* — more at LAP] *obs* **:** taken by licking with the tongue — used of medicines

lambkill \'≈,≈\ *n* -s [1*lamb* + *kill* (v.); fr. their poisonous effect on grazing sheep] **1 :** SHEEP LAUREL **2 :** STAGGERBUSH

lamb·kin \-,kən\ *n* -s [1*lamb* + *-kin*] **1 :** a little lamb **2 :** INNOCENT, CHILD — used as an endearment

lam·blia \'lamblēə\ [NL, fr. Wilhelm Dusan *Lambl* †1895 Austrian physician + NL *-ia*] *syn of* GIARDIA

lam·bli·a·sis \lam'blīəsəs\ *n* [NL *Lamblia* + *-iasis*] **:** GIARDIASIS

lamblike \'≈,≈\ *adj* **:** resembling a lamb**:** GENTLE, MEEK

lamb·ling \'lamlȯŋ\ *n* -s [1*lamb* + *-ling*] **:** LAMBKIN

lamb mint *n* **1 :** SPEARMINT **2 :** PEPPERMINT

lamb of god *cap L&G* [ME] **:** a figurative representation of Christ

lamb plant *n* [so called fr. its shaggy appearance] **:** SCYTHIAN LAMB

lam·bre·quin \'lambə(r)kən, -brək-\ *n* -s [F, fr. MF *lampequin, lambequin*, fr. (assumed) MD *lamperkijn*, dim. of *lampers, lamper*, a kind of fine glossy crape, veil made of this material; prob. akin to MD *lamfeter* hood for a hunting bird] **1 :** a scarf usu. with slashed edges used to cover a knight's helmet as protection from sun and rain **2 a :** MANTLING 1 **b :** a short decorative drapery for a shelf edge or for the top of a window casing **:** VALANCE **c :** a scalloped color pattern used esp. at the edge of porcelain tableware

lambs *pl of* LAMB, *pres 3d sing of* LAMB

lamb's-cress \'≈,≈\ *n, pl* **lamb's-cresses :** a bitter cress (*Cardamine hirsuta*)

lambsdown \'≈,≈\ *n* [*lamb's* (gen. of 1*lamb*) + *down*] **:** a knitted fabric that is usu. made with a cotton back and a heavily napped woolen face and used esp. for children's clothes and blankets

lamb's ears *n pl but usu sing in constr* **:** a perennial hedge nettle (*Stachys olympica*) densely covered with whitish silky wool — called also *woolly hedge nettle*

lamb's-foot *n, pl* **lamb's-foots :** a common plantain (*Plantago major*)

lambskin \'≈,≈\ *n* [ME *lambeskin* fr. *lamb* + *skin*] **1 a :** a lamb's skin or a small fine-grade sheepskin or the leather made from either **b :** such a skin dressed with the wool on and used esp. for winter clothing **2 :** a cotton or wool cloth made to imitate lamb's wool; *esp* **:** a cotton with a satin-weave face and a napped back **3 :** a white leather apron worn as a badge by a Freemason

lamb's-lettuce \'≈¦≈≈\ *n, pl* **lamb's-lettuces :** CORN SALAD

lamb's-mint \'≈,≈\ *n, pl* **lamb's-mints :** LAMB MINT

lamb's-quarters \'≈,≈≈\ *n pl but sing or pl in constr, also* **lamb's-quarter** \'≈,≈≈\ **1 :** a common weedy goosefoot (*Chenopodium album*) with glaucous foliage that is sometimes used as a potherb and has been introduced from Europe into No. America **2 :** any of several oraches; *esp* **:** GARDEN ORACHE

lamb's-tongue \'≈,≈\ *n, pl* **lamb's-tongues 1 a :** HOARY PLANTAIN 1 **b :** LAMB'S-QUARTERS 1 **c :** an American dogtooth violet **2 a :** a molding having a tapering tongue-shaped section or half such a section **b :** an ovolo and fillet worked alternately along the edge of a board

lamb succory *n* **:** a small European herb (*Arnoseris minima*) of the family Compositae with leaves in a basal rosette and small yellow flower heads — called also *dwarf nipplewort*

lamb's wool *n* **1 a :** the soft elastic wool shorn from lambs seven or eight months old **b :** the superior woolen woven from lamb's wool **2 :** a sugared and spiced hot ale beverage containing the pulp of roasted apples

lamb's-wool sponge \'≈,≈-\ *n* **:** WOOL SPONGE

lamb tail *n* **:** a stout perennial weedy herb (*Trichinium exaltatum*) of the family Amaranthaceae that is common in Australia

lam·dan \läm'dän, 'lämdən\ *also* **lam·den** \'lämdən\ *n, pl* **lam·da·nim** \,lämˌdä'nēm; läm'dänəm, -dȯn-, -(,)nēm\ [*lamdan* fr. Heb *lamdān*, lit., one who has learned, fr. *lāmadh* to learn; *lamden* fr. Yiddish, fr. Heb *lamdān*] **:** a man learned in Jewish law **:** a Talmudic scholar

1lame \'lām\ *adj, usu* -ER/-EST [ME, fr. OE *lama*; akin to OS & OHG *lam* lame, crippled, ON *lami* lame, MW *llyveithin* weak, Lith *limti* to break down, and perh. to Gk *nōlemes* untiringly] **1 a :** physically disabled; *also* **:** having a part and esp. a limb so disabled as to impair freedom of movement **b :** halting in movement **:** LIMPING **2 :** lacking needful parts **:** ill composed **:** WEAK, INARTICULATE, HALTING ⟨put up some story to the rector — it must have been a pretty ~ one —Dorothy Sayers⟩ ⟨a broken leg is not so bad as a ~ intellect —Irving Bacheller⟩ ⟨machines, at their best, are ~ counterfeits of living organisms —Lewis Mumford⟩

2lame \"\ *vt* -ED/-ING/-S [ME *lamen*, fr. *lame*, adj.] **1 :** to make lame **:** CRIPPLE ⟨was *lamed* for life, and could never ride horseback again —Willa Cather⟩ **2 :** to make impotent or vain **:** DISABLE, FRUSTRATE, HAMSTRING, MAIM, NULLIFY, UNDERCUT ⟨*lamed* the productive and recuperative capacities of Europe generally —G.F.Kennan⟩ ⟨that would ~ your power of bargaining with him —G.B.Shaw⟩ ⟨schools *lamed* by losses of staff —C.E.Montague⟩

3lame \"\ *chiefly Scot var of* LOAM

4lame \"\ *n* -s [MF, fr. L *lamina*] **1 :** a thin plate (as of metal) **:** LAMINA **2 lames** *pl* **:** small overlapping steel plates joined to slide on one another and form a piece of medieval armor

5la·mé \(')la¦mā, (')lä¦-, lə'-\ *n* -s [F, fr. *lamé*, adj., worked with silver or gold thread, fr. *lame* lame, silver or gold thread + *-é* (fr. L *-atus* -ate)] **:** a brocaded clothing fabric sometimes in plain weave made from any of various fibers combined with tinsel filling threads often gold or silver which form the pattern or the ground

lame-brain \'≈,≈\ *n* **:** a dull-witted or erratic person **:** CRACKPOT, DOLT, NUMSKULL ⟨a reception desk outside the city room on most papers to keep out the *lame-brains* —John McNulty⟩

la·medh *or* **la·med** \'lä,med\ *n* -s [Heb *lāmedh*, lit., oxgoad] **1 :** the 12th letter of the Hebrew alphabet — symbol ל; see ALPHABET table **2 :** a letter of the Phoenician or some other Semitic alphabets corresponding to Hebrew lamedh

lame duck *n* **1 :** a person unable to meet financial obligations — used esp. of a speculator on an exchange **2 :** an elected officer or group (as a legislature) continuing to hold political office during a usu. brief interim between defeat for reelection and the inauguration of a successor ⟨the president nominated for the Interstate Commerce Commission a *lame duck* —E.W. Carter & C.C.Rohlfing⟩ ⟨the 20th amendment abolished the *lame-duck* sessions of Congress⟩ **3 :** one that falls behind in ability or performance sometimes because of injury or deprivation **:** NE'ER-DO-WELL, STRAGGLER, VICTIM, WEAK SISTER ⟨*lame ducks* and neglected possibilities —George Santayana⟩ ⟨*lame ducks* and half-talents . . . used to be granted solo appearances —*New Republic*⟩ ⟨she always has to have a *lame duck* to look after —Louis Auchincloss⟩

lam·el \'lamәl\ *n* -s [in sense 1, fr. L *lamella*; in sense 2, fr. NL *lamella*] **1 :** a thin plate **2 :** LAMELLA 2

lamell- *or* **lamelli-** *comb form* [NL, fr. *lamella*] **:** lamella ⟨*lamellose*⟩ ⟨*lamelli*ferous⟩ ⟨*lamelli*form⟩

la·mel·la \lə'melə\ *n, pl* **lamel·lae** \-,lē, -,lī\ *also* **lamellas** [NL, fr. L, small metal plate, dim. of *lamina* thin plate] **1 :** an organ, process, or part resembling a plate: as **a :** one of the thin plates composing the gills of a bivalve mollusk — see BRACHIOPOD illustration **b :** one of the bony concentric layers surrounding the Haversian canals in bone **c :** a gill in fungi of the order Agaricales **2 :** a small medicated disk prepared from gelatin and glycerin for use esp. in the eyes ⟨*lamellae* of atropine⟩

lamel·lar \lə'melə(r), 'laməl-\ *adj* [*lamell-* + *-ar*] **:** composed of or arranged in lamellae **:** LAMELLATE — **lamel·lar·ly** *adv*

la·mel·la·ri·idae \lə,melə'rīə,dē\ *n pl, cap* [NL, fr. *Lamellaria*, type genus (fr. *lamell-* + *-aria*) + *-idae*] **:** a family of marine gastropod mollusks (suborder Taenioglossa) having a delicate shell which is often completely enclosed within the mantle

lamel·late \'laməlәt, lə'mel-, -,lāt\ *adj* [NL *lamellatus*, fr. *lamell-* + L *-atus -ate*] **1 :** composed of or furnished with lamellae **2 :** LAMELLIFORM — **lam·el·late·ly** *adv*

lamel·lat·ed \,lād·əd\ *adj* [*lamell-* + *-ate* + *-ed*] **:** LAMELLATE

lam·el·la·tion \,lamə'lāshən\ *n* -s [*lamell-* + *-ation*] **1 :** formation or division into lamellae **2 :** LAMELLA

lamelli- — see LAMELL-

1la·mel·li·branch \lə'melə,braŋk\ *adj* [NL *Lamellibranchia*] **:** of or relating to the Lamellibranchia

2lamellibranch \"\ *n* -s **:** one of the Lamellibranchia **:** a bivalve mollusk

la·mel·li·bran·chia \≈,≈≈'braŋkēə\ *n pl, cap* [NL, fr. *lamell-* + *-branchia*] **:** a class of Mollusca including the clams, oysters, and mussels, having the body bilaterally symmetrical, compressed, and more or less completely enclosed within the mantle that secretes a bivalved shell whose right and left parts are connected by a hinge over the animal's back, having no distinct head, usu. two lamelliform gills on each side of the body, and the ventral region differentiated in most of the forms into a muscular plowshare or tongue-shaped foot by means of which the animal burrows or moves about, and having the posterior margins of the mantle lobes drawn out in the burrowing species into tubes through which water passes into and out of the mantle cavity — **la·mel·li·bran·chi·ate** \≈¦≈≈¦braŋkēət, -ē,āt\ *adj or n*

la·mel·li·bran·chi·a·ta \≈,≈≈,braŋkē'äd·ə, -'ād·ə\ [NL, fr. *lamell-* + *-branchiata*] *syn of* LAMELLIBRANCHIA

1la·mel·li·corn \≈'≈≈,kȯrn\ *adj* [NL *Lamellicornia*] **1 a** *of an antenna* **:** having the form characteristic of the Lamellicornia **b** *of an insect* **:** having lamellicorn antennae **2 :** of or relating to the Lamellicornia

2lamellicorn \"\ *n* -s **:** a lamellicorn beetle

la·mel·li·cor·nia \≈,≈≈'kȯrnēə\ *n pl* [NL, fr. *lamell-* + L *-cornia*, neut. pl. of *-cornis* -corn] *cap* **:** a superfamily or other group of beetles that are distinguished by 5-jointed tarsi and by having three or more of the terminal segments of the antennae expanded into flattened plates which give the antennae a club-shaped appearance and that include the stag beetles, dung beetles, leaf beetles, and related forms — see SCARABAEOIDEA

la·mel·li·form \≈'≈≈,fȯrm\ *adj* [*lamell-* + *-form*] **:** having the form of a thin plate

la·mel·li·rostral \≈¦≈≈+\ *adj* [*lamell-* + *rostral*] **:** having a bill with transverse toothlike ridges inside the edges ⟨ducks and other ~ birds⟩

la·mel·li·ros·tres \≈,≈≈'rä(,)strēz\ *n pl, cap* [NL, fr. *lamell-* + *-rostres* (fr. L *rostrum* beak) — more at ROSTRUM] *in some classifications* **:** a group of birds including the ducks, geese, swans, mergansers, and usu. the flamingos and having transverse ridges like teeth just inside the edges of the bill — compare ANSERES

la·mel·loid \lə'me,lȯid, 'lamə,-\ *adj* [*lamell-* + *-oid*] **:** resembling a lamella

la·mel·lose \-,lōs\ *adj* [*lamell-* + *-ose*] **:** LAMELLATE — **lam·el·los·i·ty** \,lamə'läsəd·ē\ *n* -ES

la·mel·lule \lə'mel(,)yül\ *n* -s [L *lamellula* small metal plate, dim. of *lamella* small metal plate — more at LAMELLA] **:** a small lamella

lame·ly *adv* **:** in a lame manner **:** in the manner of one who is lame

lamen *var of* LAMIN

lame·ness *n* -ES **:** the quality or state of being lame

1la·ment \lə'ment *sometimes* la'-\ *vb* -ED/-ING/-S [MF & L; MF *lamenter*, fr. L *lamentari*, fr. *lamentum*] *vi* **:** to mourn vocally **:** sorrow aloud **:** WAIL, WEEP ⟨the millions ~*ed*; for ages they had sorrowed —Virginia Woolf⟩ ⟨nightingales ~ without ceasing —L.P.Smith⟩ ~ *vt* **1 :** to express sorrow for **:** BEWAIL, MOURN ⟨must regret the imprudence, ~ the result —Jane Austen⟩ ⟨katydids were ~*ing* fall's approach —E.W. Smith⟩ ⟨~*ed* that this particular piano should be so seldom played on —W.F.De Morgan⟩ **2** *archaic* **:** to express sorrow for (oneself) **syn** see DEPLORE

2lament \"\ *n* -s [MF or L; MF, fr. L *lamentum*; akin to ON *lō* sandpiper, *lōmr* loon, Goth *lailōun* they reviled, L *latrare* to bark, Gk *lēros* trash, nonsense, delirium, Arm *lam* I weep, Skt *rāyati* he barks] **1 :** a crying out in grief **:** COMPLAINT, SORROWING, WAILING ⟨let reason govern thy ~ —Shak.⟩ ⟨the ~ of the professionals who disapproved —E.O.Hauser⟩ **2 :** a lament crystallized in song or in literary form **:** DIRGE, ELEGY ⟨bagpipes skirled, . . . playing at first a ~ for him —Raymond Daniell⟩ ⟨the dance band . . . was wailing a . . . ~ —Raymond Chandler⟩ ⟨learned a lot of blues songs and ~s —James Jones⟩

la·men·ta·bi·le \,lämən-'täbə,lā\ *adv (or adj)* [It, fr. L *lamentabilis* lamentable] **:** SADLY, PLAINTIVELY — used as a direction in music

lam·en·ta·ble \'laməntəbəl *also* ÷lə'men-\ *adj* [ME, fr. MF & L; MF, fr. L *lamentabilis*, fr. *lamentari* to lament + *-abilis* -able] **1 :** to be regretted or lamented **:** DEPLORABLE, PITIABLE ⟨a ~ breakdown in transport organization —Philip Gibbs⟩ ⟨that afternoon, so untouched by premonition, was yet full of ~ fate —Osbert Sitwell⟩ **2 :** expressing grief **:** DOLEFUL, MOURNFUL, SORROWFUL ⟨a faint and ~ cry —Walter de la Mare⟩ ⟨made her ~ complaint —H.O.Taylor⟩ — **lam·en·ta·ble·ness** \-bəlnəs\ *n* -ES — **lam·en·ta·bly** \-blē, -bli\ *adv*

lam·en·ta·tion \,lamən-'tāshən *sometimes* ,men-\ *n* -s [ME *lamentacioun*, fr. MF & L; MF *lamentation*, fr. L *lamentation-, lamentatio*, fr. *lamentatus* (past part. of *lamentari* to lament) + *-ion-, -io* -ion — more at LAMENT] **:** the act of lamenting or bewailing **:** vocal expression of sorrow **:** COMPLAINT ⟨such a scene of frenzy and ~ as Rome had rarely witnessed —John Buchan⟩ ⟨great consternation and ~ among business people when the bank rate goes up —G.B.Shaw⟩

lamented *adj* **:** mourned for ⟨the imprint of our wise and ~ friend —A.E.Stevenson b1900⟩ — **la·ment·ed·ly** *adv*

la·ment·er \lə'mentə(r)\ *n* -s **:** one that laments

la·men·to·so \,lämən'tō(')sō, ,lam-, -)zō\ *adv (or adj)* [It, fr. LL *lamentosus*, fr. L *lamentum* lament + *-osus* -ous] **:** PLAINTIVELY, SADLY — used as a direction in music

lamer *comparative of* LAME

lames *pres 3d sing of* LAME, *pl of* LAME

lamés *pl of* LAME

lame sickness *n* [trans. of Afrik *lamsiekte*] **:** LAMSIEKTE

lamest *superlative of* LAME

la·met \lä'met\ *n, pl* **lamet** *or* **lamets** *usu cap* **:** KHA

lam·e·ter \'lāmətər\ *n* -s [irreg. fr. 1*lame*] *now Scot* **:** a lame person **:** CRIPPLE

la·mia \'lāmēə\ *n, pl* **lamias** \-ēəz\ *or* **lami·ae** \-ē,ē\ [ME, fr. L, fr. Gk, devouring monster — more at LEMUR] **:** WITCH, SHE-DEMON, VAMPIRE ⟨a ~ with a British accent —Carlo Baker⟩

la·mi·a·ce·ae \,lāmē'āsē,ē\ [NL, fr. *Lamium* + *-aceae* — more at LAMIUM] *syn of* LABIATAE

la·mi·a·ceous \¦≈≈¦āshəs\ *adj* [NL *Lamiaceae* + E *-ous*] **:** LABIATE 2

la·mi·idae \lə'mīə,dē\ *n pl, cap* [NL, fr. *Lamia*, type genus (fr. Gk *lamia* devouring monster) + *-idae*] **:** a family of beetles closely related to and often included among the Cerambycidae — see OBEREA

lam·in \'lamən\ *n* -s [L & NL *lamina*] **1 :** LAMINA **2 :** an astrologer's charm consisting of a thin metal plate

lamin- *or* **lamini-** *or* **lamino-** *comb form* [*lamina*] **:** lamina ⟨*laminar*⟩ ⟨*laminiferous*⟩

lam·i·na \'lamənə\ *n, pl* **lami·nae** \-,nē, -,nī\ *or* **laminas** [in sense 1, fr. L; in other senses, NL, fr. L] **1 :** a thin plate or scale **:** FLAKE, LAYER **2 a :** the part of the neural arch of a vertebra extending from the pedicle to the median line **b** (1) **:** the blade or expanded part of a foliage leaf — distinguished from *petiole* (2) **:** a foliose expansion (as of the thallus in an alga) **c :** one of the narrow thin parallel plates of soft vascular sensitive tissue that cover the pododerm of the walls of an animal's hoof and fit between corresponding horny laminae on the inside of the wall of the hoof — called also *sensitive lamina* **3 a :** a minor layer of a stratified rock usu. separable and produced by intermittent deposit **b :** a thin layer between cleavage planes in slate or schist **4 :** a plane section of a body having infinitesimal thickness

lamina cri·bro·sa \-kri'brōsə\ *n, pl* **laminae cribro·sae** \-,sē, -,sī\ [NL, lit., cribrose lamina] **:** any of several anatomical structures having the form of a perforated plate: as **a :** the cribriform plate of the ethmoid bone **b :** the part of the scleroid coat of the eye penetrated by the fibers of the optic nerve **c :** a perforated plate that closes the internal auditory meatus

lam·i·na·gram *or* **lam·i·no·gram** \'lamənə,gram\ *n* [NL *lamina* or E *lamin-* + *-gram*] **:** a roentgenogram of a layer of the body made by means of a laminagraph

lam·i·na·graph *or* **lam·i·no·graph** \-,raf, -,räf\ *n* [NL *lamina* or E *lamin-* + *-graph*] **:** an X-ray machine that makes roentgenography of body tissue possible at any desired depth — **lam·i·na·graph·ic** *or* **lam·i·no·graph·ic** \;==;grafik\ *adj* — **lam·i·nag·ra·phy** \,=='nagrəfē\ *or* **lam·i·nog·ra·phy** \-'näg-\ *n* -ES

lam·i·nal \'lamən°l\ *adj* [*lamin-* + *-al*] **1 :** LAMINAR **2 :** produced with the participation of the front upper surface of the tongue (as \sh\, \zh\, \ch\, \j\, \y\)

lamina pro·pria \-'prōprēə\ *n, pl* **laminae propri·ae** \-rē,ē, -rē,ī\ [NL, lit., one's own lamina] **:** a highly vascular layer of connective tissue under the basement membrane lining a layer of epithelium

lam·i·nar \'lamənə(r)\ *adj* [*lamin-* + *-ar*] **1 :** arranged in, consisting of, or like laminae ⟨cut felt parts exhibit no tendency to separate into layers, despite the ~ formation of the batt from which the material was fabricated —*Story of Felt*⟩ **2 :** of, relating to, or being a streamline flow ⟨the ~ motion of a fluid about a sphere —J.K.Vennard⟩

laminar flow *n* **:** streamline flow in a viscous fluid near a solid boundary — contrasted with *turbulent flow*

lam·i·nar·ia \,lamə'na(a)rēə\ *n* [NL, fr. *lamin-* + *-aria*] **1** *cap* **:** the type genus of the family Laminariaceae comprising chiefly perennial kelps with an unbranched cylindrical or flattened stipe and a smooth or convoluted blade that is either simple or deeply incised into segments **2** -s **:** any kelp of the genus *Laminaria; broadly* **:** any kelp of the order Laminariales — **lam·i·nar·i·oid** \;==;==,ōid\ *adj*

lam·i·nar·i·a·ce·ae \,==,==ē'āsē,ē\ *n pl, cap* [NL, fr. *Laminaria*, type genus + *-aceae*] **:** a large family of kelps (order Laminariales) that includes many large kelps chiefly of northern waters and in some classifications is considered coextensive with the order — **lam·i·nar·i·a·ceous** \;==;==;āshəs\ *adj*

lam·i·nar·i·a·les \,==,=='ā(,)lēz\ *n pl, cap* [NL, fr. *Laminaria* + *-ales*] **:** an order of marine brown algae that include many economically important kelps, are largely restricted to cold or polar seas, are distinguished by a complex and often very large sporophyte which is usu. differentiated into well-defined holdfast, stipe, and blade, and have microscopic gametophytes

lam·i·nar·i·an \;==;na(a)rēən\ *adj* [NL *Laminaria* + E *-an*] **:** of, relating to, or characterized by the presence of kelps of the genus *Laminaria*

lam·i·nar·in \,=='na(a)rən\ *n* -s [ISV *laminar-* (fr. NL *Laminaria*) + *-in*] **:** a polysaccharide found in various brown algae that like starch yields only glucose on hydrolysis but differs from starch in molecular structure and properties

lam·i·narite \'lamənə,rīt, ,=='na(a),r-\ *n* -s [NL *Laminaria* + E *-ite*] **:** a fossil plant that is supposedly a seaweed related to the kelps of the genus *Laminaria*

lam·i·nary \'lamə,nerē\ *adj* [*lamin-* + *-ary*] **:** LAMINAR

¹lam·i·nate \-,nāt, *usu* -ād.+V\ *vb* -ED/-ING/-s [*lamina* + *-ate* (v. suffix)] *vt* **1 :** to roll or compress (as metal or plastic) into a thin plate **2 :** to separate into laminae **3 a :** to make by uniting superposed layers of one or more materials (as by means of an adhesive or bolts) — compare LAMINATED GLASS, LAMINATED PLASTIC, LAMINATED WOOD **b :** to unite (superposed layers of material) by an adhesive or other means ⟨asphalt is used to ~ sheets of paper —*Science*⟩ ⟨polyethylene film has been *laminated* to paper for waterproof bags —*Chem. & Engineering News*⟩ ~ *vi* **:** to divide into laminae

²lam·i·nate \-,nə̇t, -,nāt, *usu* |d.+V\ *adj* [*lamina* + *-ate* (adj. suffix)] **1 :** consisting of a lamina or laminae **:** LAMINATED **2 :** bearing or covered with laminae

³laminate \"\ *n* -s [¹*laminate*] **:** a product made by laminating; *specif* **:** LAMINATED PLASTIC

lam·i·nat·ed \-,nād.əd, -ātəd\ *adj* [*lamina* + *-ate* + *-ed*] **1 :** LAMINATE 1 ⟨shale is ~ clay —*Chem. Industries*⟩ ⟨chocolate cake ~ in very fine layers with a light creamy paste between —Edmund Wilson⟩ **2** [fr. past part. of ¹*laminate*] **:** made by laminating **:** composed of layers of firmly united material ⟨glued ~ arches are ideal for many kinds of buildings —*Architectural Record*⟩

laminated glass *n* **:** plate consisting of two or more sheets of glass with plastic sheeting bonded between to resist shattering — called also *safety glass, shatterproof glass*

laminated plastic *n* **:** a plastic made of superposed layers of paper, wood, or fabric bonded or impregnated with resin and compressed under heat

laminated spring *n* **:** LEAF SPRING

laminated wood *n* **:** layers of wood glued or otherwise united with the grains parallel to form boards or timbers — compare PLYWOOD

lam·i·na·tion \,lamə'nāshən\ *n* -s **1 a :** the process of laminating **b :** the quality or state of being laminated **c :** a laminated structure **d :** LAMINA — compare STRATIFICATION **2 :** a crack parallel to the principal surfaces of sheet metal **3** *or* **la·mi·na·tion** \,lāmē'āshən\ **:** a single stratum of a stratified ecological community

lam·i·na·tor \'lamə,nād.ə(r), -ātə-\ *n* -s **:** one that laminates; *esp* **:** one that makes a laminated plastic

lam·in·board \'lamən,=\ *n* [*lamin-* + *board*] **:** a veneered wood consisting of a core of parallel sheets cemented together and faced with plies with the grain of the latter usu. at right angles to that of the core

lam·i·nec·to·my \,lamə'nektəmē\ *n* -ES [ISV *lamin-* + *-ectomy*] **:** surgical removal of the posterior arch of a vertebra

laming *pres part of* LAME

lamini- — see LAMIN-

lam·i·ni·plantar \;lamənə+\ *adj* [*lamin-* + *plantar*] **:** having a side of the tarsus covered with a single horny plate which meets that of the other side in a ridge behind (as in most singing birds except the larks) — opposed to *scutelliplantar* — **lam·i·ni·plantation** \,===+\ *n* -s

lam·i·ni·tis \,lamə'nīd.əs\ *n* -ES [NL, fr. *lamin-* + *-itis*] **:** inflammation of a lamina esp. of a horse's foot that is accompanied by heat, pain, and lameness and is caused by overexertion on hard footing or more often is secondary to some other condition (as digestive disturbances due to overeating) **:** ³FOUNDER 1

lamino- — see LAMIN-

laminogram *var of* LAMINAGRAM

laminograph *var of* LAMINAGRAPH

lam·i·nose \'lamə,nōs\ *adj* [*lamin-* + *-ose*] **:** LAMINATE

lam·i·no·si·op·tes \,==(,)nō,sī'äp(,)tēz\ *n, cap* [NL, fr. *lamin-* + *-sioptes* (prob. fr. Gk *siōpan* to keep quiet, be still)] **:** a genus of oval sarcoptoid mites that live subcutaneously in birds (as poultry) and apparently cause the host no damage

lam·i·nous \'lamənəs\ *adj* [*lamin-* + *-ous*] **:** LAMINATE

lam·ish \'lāmish\ *adj* [¹*lame* + *-ish*] **:** somewhat lame

lamister *var of* LAMSTER

lam·i·ter *var of* LAMETER

la·mi·um \'lāmēəm\ *n, cap* [NL, fr. L, dead nettle, fr. (assumed) Gk *lamion*, dim. of *lamia* monster — more at LEMUR] **:** a genus of Old World herbs (family Labiatae) having cordate dentate leaves and showy galeate flowers with basal style and 3-sided nutlets — see DEAD NETTLE, HENBIT

lamm *var of* LAM

¹lam·mas \'laməs\ *n* -ES [ME *Lammasse, Lammesse*, fr. OE *hlāfmæsse*, fr. *hlāf* bread, loaf + *mæsse* mass; fr. the fact that formerly loaves made from the first ripe grain were consecrated on this day — more at LOAF, MASS] **1** *or* **lammas day** *usu cap L & D* **:** the first day of August **2** *or* **lam·mas·tide** \-mə,stīd\ *usu cap* **:** the time of year around Lammas day

²lammas \"\ *vi* [¹*lammas* (influenced in meaning by ¹*lam*)] *dial Eng* **:** to go or depart esp. in a hurry

lammas lands *or* **lammas meadows** *n pl, usu cap 1st L* [so called fr. their becoming common on Lammas day] *Eng law* **:** lands or meadows held in severalty during the crop-raising period but subject to rights of common at other times (as for pasturage)

lammas shoot *n, often cap L* **:** a young leafy shoot produced usu. in late summer by a woody plant (as an oak) from a bud that would normally open the following spring

lammed *past of* LAM

lam·mer \'lamər\ *n* -s [ME (northern dial.) *lambre, laumbre*, fr. MF *l'ambre* the amber, fr. *l', le* the + *ambre* amber, ambergris — more at AMBER] *chiefly Scot* **:** AMBER

lam·mer·gei·er *or* **lam·mer·gey·er** *also* **lam·mer·geir** *or* **laem·mer·gei·er** \'lamə(r),gī(ə)r, 'lem-\ *n* -s [G *lämmergeier*, fr. *lämmer* (pl. of *lamm* lamb, fr. OHG *lamb*) + *geier* vulture, fr. OHG *gīr* — more at LAMB, GIER-EAGLE] **:** the largest European bird of prey (*Gypaetus barbatus aureus*) indigenous to mountain regions from the Pyrenees to northern China, having a length of about 3½ feet and often a wingspread of nearly 10 feet, and resembling both the eagles and the vultures — called also *bearded vulture*

lamming *pres part of* LAM

lam·na \'lamnə\ *n, cap* [NL, fr. Gk, a shark, prob. alter. of *lamia* devouring monster (or, a shark) — more at LEMUR] **:** the type genus of the family Lamnidae comprising the porbeagle and a few related forms

lam·ni·dae \-nə,dē\ *n pl, cap* [NL, fr. *Lamna*, type genus + *-idae*] **:** a family of large fierce pelagic sharks including the porbeagle and related forms — see MACKEREL SHARK — **lamnoid** \-,nȯid\ *adj or n*

la·mo·na \lə'mōnə\ *n* [prob. fr. *Lamona*, Wash.] **1** *usu cap* **:** an American breed of white, short-legged domestic fowls **2** -s *often cap* **:** any bird of the Lamona breed

¹lamp \'lamp, -aa(ə)-, -ai-\ *n* -s [ME *lampe, lamp*, fr. OF *lampe*, fr. L *lampas*, fr. Gk, torch, lamp, fr. *lampein* to give light, shine; akin to OIr *lassaim* I flame, OPruss *lopis*, Hitt *lap-* to glow, be hot, ON *leiptr* lightning] **1 a :** a light-giving device: as (1) **:** a device with an oil reservoir and a wick that gives light as it burns (2) **:** a glass bulb enclosing a filament that glows because of its resistance to electric current (3) **:** any of various other devices that produce artificial light ⟨gas ~⟩ ⟨acetylene ~⟩ ⟨fluorescent ~⟩ **b :** a source of natural light (as the sun, the moon, or a star) ⟨the ~s of heaven⟩ **c :** any of various devices for the application of heat: as (1) **:** an apparatus for drying foundry molds during their fabrication (2) **:** a therapeutic heat lamp **2 :** a source of intellectual, moral, or spiritual illumination ⟨thy word is a ~ to my feet and a light to my path —Ps 119:105 (RSV)⟩ ⟨wanted them to be ~s unto themselves —Emma Hawkridge⟩ **3 :** EYE ⟨my wasting ~s —Shak.⟩ ⟨turned her hot ~s on me —R.P.Warren⟩ — **of the lamp** *adv (or adj)* **:** of laborious study or excogitation **:** of strain or effort **:** without spontaneity, inspiration, or reality ⟨refined or artificial, smelling a little *of the lamp* —B.N.Cardozo⟩ ⟨a theory born *of the lamp* —Russell Lord⟩

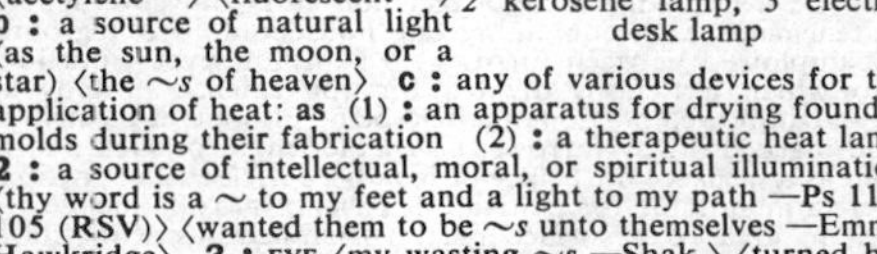

lamps 1a: *1* ancient oil lamp, *2* kerosene lamp, *3* electric desk lamp

²lamp \"\ *vb* -ED/-ING/-s *vt* **1** *archaic* **:** to furnish with lamps **2 :** to light or brighten by or as if by lamps ⟨scattered lights ~*ing* the rush and roll of the abyss —Robert Browning⟩ **3** *slang* **:** to look at **:** EYE, SEE ⟨I've ~*ed* two dicks — had their eye on us all day —Elmer Davis⟩ ⟨for the love of Patrick Henry, ~ that! —*Cosmopolitan*⟩ ~ *vi* **:** to shine as or like a lamp ⟨the Spirit-Seven companioning God's throne they ~ before —Robert Browning⟩

³lamp \"\ *vi* -ED/-ING/-s [prob. of imit. origin] *chiefly Scot* **:** to walk quickly taking long strides

lam·pad \'lam,pad\ *n* -s [L *lampad-, lampas* — more at LAMP] **:** LAMP, CANDLESTICK — used of the seven lamps of fire in Rev 4:5 ⟨till wheeling round the throne the ~s seven (the mystic words of heaven) permissive signal make —S.T.Coleridge⟩

lam·pa·dite \'lampə,dīt\ *n* -s [F, fr. Wilhelm A. *Lampadius* †1842 Ger. chemist + F *-ite*] **:** a bog manganese containing copper and often cobalt oxides

lam·pa·ra \'lampərə\ *or* **lampara net** *n* -s [prob. fr. Sp *lámpara*, lit., lamp, fr. OSp *lámpada*, fr. L *lampad-, lampas* — more at LAMP] **:** a fishing net that somewhat resembles a purse seine and is used esp. for taking bait fishes

¹lam·pas \'lampəs\ *n* -ES [ME *lawmpas*, a kind of glossy crape, fr. MD *lampers* — more at LAMBREQUIN] **:** a brocaded fabric of silk and rayon or cotton having jacquard-woven designs in two or more colors and used chiefly for upholstery

²lampas \", -pəz\ *n* -ES [MF, fr. OF] **:** a congestion of the mucous membrane of the hard palate just posterior to the incisor teeth of the horse due to irritation and bruising from harsh coarse feeds

lam·pat·ia \lam'pad.ēə\ *n* -s [Nepali *lāmpatiyā*, fr. *lām* long (fr. Skt *lamba* pendent, long, fr. *lambate* it hangs down) + *pāt* leaf, fr. Skt *pattra* wing, feather, leaf; akin to Skt *patati* he flies, falls — more at FEATHER, LIMP] **:** KOKAN

¹lampblack \'=,=\ *n* [¹*lamp* + *black*] **1 :** a fine bulky black soot deposited (as from the flame of a smoking oil lamp) in incomplete combustion of carbonaceous materials; *esp* **:** a soot obtained by burning liquid hydrocarbons (as creosote oil or petroleum fuel oils) that is characterized by a duller less intense black than channel black and other carbon blacks, by a bluish undertone, and by a content of varying amounts of oily matter in addition to carbon and that is used chiefly as a pigment (as in paints, enamels, printing inks, and concrete) and as a source of carbon for electric brushes — usu. distinguished from *carbon black* **2 :** a nearly neutral slightly bluish black that is darker and slightly greener than Quaker blue

²lampblack \"\ *vt* **:** to cover, coat, or smear with lampblack **:** blacken with lampblack ⟨~*ed* platinum —Agnes M. Clerke⟩

lampbrush chromosome \'=,=-\ *n* [trans. of G *lampenbürstenchromosom*] **:** a greatly enlarged pachytene chromosome having apparently filamentous granular loops extending from the chromomeres that is esp. characteristic of certain animal oocytes

lam·per \'lampə(r)\ *vi* -ED/-ING/-s [³*lamp* + *-er*] *dial Eng* **:** to walk or go heavily

lam·per eel \'lampə(r)ē(ə)l\ *n* [*lamper* alter. of *lamprey*] **1** *or* **lamper** -s **:** LAMPREY **2 :** CONGO SNAKE

lam·pern \'lampə(r)n\ *n* -s [ME *lamproun, lampurn*, fr. MF *lamprion, lampreon*, dim. of *lampreie* lamprey — more at LAMPREY] **:** a European river lamprey (*Lampetra fluviatilis*)

lam·pers \'lampə(r)z\ *n* -ES [by alter.] **:** ²LAMPAS

lamp furnace *n, obs* **:** a furnace heated by a lamp

lamp holder *n* **:** an electric lamp socket

lamphole \'=,=\ *n* **:** a vertical pipe or shaft between manholes into which a light may be lowered for inspecting a sewer

lamphouse \'=,=\ *n* **:** a light housing on an instrument (as a motion-picture projector, photographic enlarger, microscope)

lamping *adj* [fr. pres. part. of ²*lamp*] *archaic* **:** SHINING, FLASHING

lam·pi·on \'lampēən\ *n* -s [F, fr. It *lampione*, aug. of *lampa* lamp, fr. F *lampe* — more at LAMP] *archaic* **:** a small lamp (as a pot of oil with a wick) formerly used at illuminations

lamp-iron \'=,=(=)\ *n* **:** a projecting iron rod from which to hang a lamp

lamp·ist \'lampə̇st\ *n* -s [F *lampiste*, fr. *lampe* lamp + *-iste* -ist] **:** a maker or tender of lamps

lamp·ist·ry \-trē\ *n* -ES [F *lampisterie*, fr. *lampiste* + *-erie* -ery] **:** the work of a lampist

lamp·less \'lampləs\ *adj* **:** lacking lamps **:** DARKENED, UNLIGHTED

lamp·let \-plə̇t\ *n* -s **:** a small lamp

lamplight \'=,=\ *n* **:** the light of a lamp ⟨the ~ seemed to brighten —Willa Cather⟩

lamplighter \'=,==\ *n* **1 :** one that lights a lamp: as **a :** a person who lights streetlights **b :** a spill of paper or wood for lighting lamps **2 :** any of certain fishes of the genus *Pomoxis; esp* **:** WHITE CRAPPIE

lamplit \'=,=\ *adj* **:** lighted by a lamp ⟨solitude had come again . . . and the ~ paper —Virginia Woolf⟩

lamp·man \'lampmən\ *n, pl* **lampmen :** a workman who takes care of lamps (as in a mine or on a railway)

lamp oil *n* **1 :** oil for use in lamps **2** *chiefly Midland* **:** KEROSINE

lam·pong \'läm,pȯŋ\ *n, pl* **lampong** *or* **lampongs** *usu cap* [Malay] **1 a :** an Indonesian people inhabiting southern Sumatra **b :** a member of such people **2 :** the Austronesian language of the Lampong people

¹lam·poon \(')lam¦pün, (')laam-\ *n* -s [F *lampon*, prob. fr. *lampons!* let us guzzle! (a frequent refrain in 17th cent. French satirical poems), 1st pers. pl. imperative of *lamper* to guzzle, fr. MF, of imit. origin] **1 :** a polemic satire usu. directed against an individual ⟨had written a "scurrilous ~" in Latin verse about him —Douglas Stewart⟩ ⟨corridors hung with colored ~s of English barristers —Louis Auchincloss⟩ — compare PASQUINADE **2 :** a light mocking satire ⟨the old farces and later musical ~s —G.J.Nathan⟩

²lampoon \"\ *vt* -ED/-ING/-s **:** to make the subject of a lampoon **:** RIDICULE, SATIRIZE ⟨apart from her singing satires, she also ~s piano styles —Clyde Gilmour⟩ ⟨was viciously ~*ed* by the cartoonists —*Newsweek*⟩ ⟨the aristocracy he had ~*ed* mercilessly for many years rose to his defense —*Current Biog.*⟩

lam·poon·er \-nə(r)\ *n* -s **:** a maker of lampoons

lam·poon·ery \-ə'pün(ə)rē, -ri\ *n* -ES **:** the satire of a lampooner

lam·poon·ist \-nə̇st\ *n* -s **:** LAMPOONER

lamppost \'=,=\ *n* **:** a post supporting a usu. outdoor lamp or lantern (as a streetlight)

lam·prey \'lamprē\ *or* **lamprey eel** *n* -s [ME, fr. OF *lampreie, lamproie*, fr. ML *lampreda*, alter. of LL *naupreda, naupride*, prob. fr. Gaulish] **:** any of various freshwater and saltwater vertebrates that constitute the order Hyperoartia, are widely distributed in temperate and subarctic regions, and resemble eels but have a large circular jawless suctorial mouth with numerous small conical teeth in a cuplike cavity and one to three larger ones on the palate, a single nostril consisting of a blind sac, seven gill pouches opening internally into a canal lying below and communicating with the esophagus just behind the mouth, and small eggs which produce toothless eyeless ammocoetes larvae — see PETROMYZON, SEA LAMPREY

lam·prid·i·dae \lam'pridə,dē\ *n pl, cap* [NL, fr. *Lamprid-*, *Lampris*, type genus (fr. Gk *lampros* bright) + *-idae*] **:** a family of fishes (order Allotriognathi) comprising a single genus and including solely the opah

lampro- *comb form* [NL, fr. Gk, fr. *lampros* bright, fr. *lampein* to give light, shine — more at LAMP] **:** bright ⟨*lamprophyre*⟩

lam·pro·pel·tis \,lamprə'peltə̇s\ *n, cap* [NL, fr. *lampro-* + *-peltis* (fr. Gk *peltē* small shield) — more at PELTA] **:** a genus of American colubrid snakes comprising the king snakes

lam·pro·phyl·lite \-'fi,līt\ *n* -s [*lampro-* + *phyll-* + *-ite*] **:** a rare mineral $Na_2SrTiSi_2O_8$ consisting of a silicate of titanium, strontium, and sodium

lam·pro·phyre \'lamprə,fī(ə)r\ *n* -s [ISV *lampro-* + *-phyre*; orig. formed as G *lamprophyr*] **:** any of a series of dark rocks of basaltic habit that resemble trap, occur usu. in narrow dikes, and sometimes contain glittering plates of biotite — **lam·pro·phyric** \,==;firik, -fīr-\ *adj*

lamps *pl of* LAMP, *pres 3d sing of* LAMP

lampshade \'=,=\ *n* **:** a shade arranged to soften or direct lamplight

lamp shell *n* **:** a brachiopod shell esp. of the genus *Terebratula* or a related genus

lamp·si·lis \'lampsələs\ *n, cap* [NL, alter. of *Lasmacampsilis*, prob. fr. *lasma-* (intended as latinization of F *lame* lamina) + Gk *kampsis* action of bending (fr. *kamptein* to bend, fr. *kampē* bend, turning) + L *-ilis* (adj. ending) — more at CAMP] **:** a genus of No. American freshwater mussels including the yellowback and the pocketbook

lampstand \'=,=\ *n* **:** a pillar, tripod, or stand for supporting or holding a lamp

lampwick \'=,=\ *n* **1 :** a wick or wicking for a lamp **2 :** a European mint (*Phlomis lychnitis*)

lampworker \'=,==\ *n* **:** a glassblower who fashions objects (as vials, radio tubes, artistic novelties) by lampworking

lampworking \'=,==\ *n* **:** the process of fashioning objects from glass tubing and cane softened to workability over the flame of a small lamp — compare GLASSBLOWING

¹lam·py·rid \'lampərə̇d\ *adj* [NL *Lampyridae*] **:** of or relating to the Lampyridae

²lampyrid \"\ *n* -s **:** a beetle or firefly of the family Lampyridae

lam·pyr·i·dae \lam'pirə,dē\ *n pl, cap* [NL, fr. *Lampyris*, type genus + *-idae*] **:** a family of beetles of medium or small size having usu. an elongate form and rather soft wing covers which do not clasp the sides of the abdomen and including many nocturnal species with luminous organs as well as some species with wingless females — see CANTHARIDAE, GLOWWORM

lam·py·ris \'lampərə̇s\ *n, cap* [NL, fr. L, glowworm, fr. Gk, fr. *lampein* to shine — more at LAMP] **:** a genus (the type of the family Lampyridae) including common European fireflies

lams *pl of* LAM, *pres 3d sing of* LAM

lam·siek·te \'lam,sēktə, 'läm-\ *or* **lam·ziek·te** \-,zē-\ *n* -s [Afrik *lamsiekte*, fr. *lam* lame, (fr. MD) + *siekte* disease, sickness, fr. MD, fr. *siek* ill, sick; akin to OHG *lam* lame and to OHG *sioh* sick, ill — more at LAME, SICK] *Africa* **:** botulism of phosphorus-deficient cattle due to ingestion of bones and carrion containing clostridial toxins

lam·ster \'lamztə(r), -m(p)st-\ *or* **lam·is·ter** \-məstə(r)\ *n* -s [²*lam* + *-ster* or *-ister* (as in *barrister*)] **:** FUGITIVE; *esp* **:** one fleeing or hiding from the police ⟨fled to Canada, fought extradition, and has remained a ~ ever since —D.W.Maurer⟩ ⟨most people here are *lamisters* . . . away from home because they didn't have it good enough —A.J.Liebling⟩

la·mut \lə'müt\ *n, pl* **lamut** *or* **lamuts** *usu cap* **1 a :** a Tungus maritime people dwelling about the Sea of Okhotsk **b :** a member of such people **2 :** the Tungusic language of the Lamut people

län \'len\ *n, pl* **län** *or* **läns** [Sw, fr. OSw *læn* fee, fief, fr. MLG *lēn*; akin to ON *lān* loan — more at LOAN] **:** an administrative district, province, or county from which members of the First Chamber of the Swedish parliament are elected on a proportional basis

lan- *or* **lani-** *or* **lano-** *comb form* [L *lan-, lani-*, fr. *lana* — more at WOOL] **:** wool ⟨*lanolin*⟩ ⟨*lanthionine*⟩ ⟨*laniferous*⟩ ⟨*lanostero*l⟩

LAN *abbr* local apparent noon

lan·ac \'la,nak\ *n* -s [*laminar air navigation and anticollision*] **:** a system of radar navigation that enables an airplane to avoid collisions and to fly at desired altitudes before landing

la·nai \lə'nī, -nä,ē\ *n* -s [Hawaiian] **:** a living room open in part to the outdoors **:** an outdoor space used as a living room **:** a lounging terrace **:** PORCH, VERANDA

la·nao \lə'naů\ *n, pl* **lanao** *or* **lanaos** *usu cap* **:** MARANAO

la·nar·kia \lə'närkēə\ *n, cap* [NL, fr. *Lanark* county, Scotland, its locality + NL *-ia*] **:** a genus of fossil ostracoderms from Silurian beds having the body covered with small pointed hollow spines

lan·ark·ite \'lanə(r),kīt\ *n* -s [F, fr. *Lanark* county, Scotland + F *-ite*] **:** a mineral Pb_2OSO_4 consisting of a basic lead sulfate occurring massive or in monoclinic crystals

lan·ark·shire \'lanə(r)k,shi(ə)r, -,shiə, -,shə(r)\ *or* **lanark** *adj, usu cap* [fr. *Lanarkshire* or *Lanark* county, Scotland] **:** of or from the county of Lanark, Scotland **:** of the kind or style prevalent in Lanark

lan·as \'lanəs\ *or* **lanas disease** *n* -ES [Jav, soft, melted] **:** BLACK SHANK

la·nate \'lā,nāt\ *also* **la·nat·ed** \-nād·əd\ *adj* [L *lanatus*, fr. *lana* wool + *-atus* -ate, -ated — more at WOOL] **:** covered with fine hair or hairlike filaments **:** WOOLLY

la·nat·o·side \lə'nad·ə,sīd\ *n* -s [NL *lanata* (specific epithet of *Digitalis lanata*, fr. L, fem. of *lanatus* woolly) + E *-oside*] **:** any of three poisonous crystalline cardiac steroid glycosides occurring in the leaves of a foxglove (*Digitalis lanata*): **a :** the glycoside $C_{49}H_{76}O_{19}$ yielding digitoxin, glucose, and acetic acid on hydrolysis — called also *lanatoside A* **b :** the glycoside $C_{49}H_{76}O_{20}$ yielding gitoxin, glucose, and acetic acid on hydrolysis — called also *lanatoside B* **c :** the bitter glycoside $C_{49}H_{76}O_{20}$ yielding digoxin, glucose, and acetic acid on hydrolysis and used similarly to digitalis — called also *lanatoside C*

¹lan·ca·shire \'laŋkə,shi(ə)r, 'laiŋ-, -,shiə, -,shə(r)\ *adj, usu cap* [fr. *Lancashire*, England] **:** of or from Lancashire, England **:** of the kind or style prevalent in Lancashire

²lancashire \"\ *or* **lancashire cheese** *n* -s *usu cap L* **:** a white moist cheese of loose friable texture from finely cut curds of different ages

lancashire wrestling *n, usu cap L* **:** a British style of wrestling whose object is to bring the opponent to the mat from a prescribed standing position

lan·cas·ter \'laŋkəstə(r), 'laiŋ-; 'lan,ka(i)s-, 'laan,kaas-, 'laŋ-,ka(a)s-, 'laiŋ,kais-\ *adj, usu cap* **1** [fr. *Lancaster* borough, England] **:** of or from the municipal borough of Lancaster, England **:** of the kind or style prevalent in Lancaster **2** [fr. *Lancaster* county, England] **:** LANCASHIRE

lan·cas·te·ri·an \ˌ;ₛka(a)ˈstirēən, -ˌkaiˌ-, -ˌkəˌ-, -tēr-\ *or* **lan·cas·tri·an** \(ˈ)ₛˈka(a)strēən, -ˌkais-\ *adj, usu cap* [Joseph *Lancaster* †1838 Eng. educationist + E *-ian*] **:** of or relating to a monitorial system of instruction in which advanced pupils in a school teach pupils below them

¹lancastrian \"\ *adj, usu cap* [fr. House of *Lancaster*, English royal family, after John of Gaunt, duke of *Lancaster* †1399 + E *-ian*] **:** of or relating to the English royal house of Lancaster

²lancastrian \"\ *n* -s *usu cap* **:** a member or supporter of the English royal house of Lancaster that derived from the fourth son of the Plantagenet King Edward III and included Henry IV, Henry V, and Henry VI — compare YORKIST

³lancastrian \"\ *adj, usu cap* [*Lancaster* county & *Lancaster* borough, England + E *-ian*] **:** of or relating to Lancashire or Lancaster

⁴lancastrian \"\ *n* -s, *cap* **:** a native or inhabitant of Lancashire or Lancaster

¹lance \'lan(t)s, -aa(ə)-, -ai-, -à-\ *n* -s [ME *launce*, fr. OF *lance*, fr. L *lancea*] **1 :** a weapon of war consisting of a long shaft with a sharp steel head and carried by mounted knights or light cavalry **2 a :** LANCET 2 **b :** a spear with a sharp point and keen cutting edges used by whalers; *also* **:** a similar implement for spearing fish **c :** a small implement used in the Eastern Orthodox Church to cut particles from loaves of altar bread **d :** a pointed blade or tooth in a router or other tool for cutting the grain along or around the path of the tool **3 a :** a medieval military unit comprising a knight and his retinue **b :** a soldier armed with a lance **:** LANCER **4** *obs* **a :** shoot of a tree **5 :** a small iron rod that suspends the core of a foundry mold in casting a shell **6 :** one of the small paper cases filled with combustible composition used esp. for marking the outlines of a fireworks set piece **7 :** OXYGEN LANCE

²lance \"\ *vb* -ED/-ING/-S [ME *launcen*, fr. MF *lancier, lancer*, fr. LL *lanceare* to handle a lance, pierce with a lance, fr. L *lancea* lance] *vt* **1 :** to pierce with a lance or similar weapon **2 :** to open with or as if with a lancet **:** to make an incision in or into ⟨~ a boil⟩ ⟨~ a vein⟩ **3 :** LAUNCH, HURL, FLING ⟨signal lamps *lanced* spreading cones —Wirt Williams⟩ ⟨~ himself short and straight, lower the muleta so the bull would follow it, and . . . put the sword in —Ernest Hemingway⟩ **~** *vi* **:** to move forward by or as if by cutting one's way ⟨bombers would buzz overhead and ~ toward shore —Norman Mailer⟩ ⟨tanks *lanced* on into the German bulge —*Time*⟩

³lance *var of* LAUNCE

lance bucket *n* **:** a socket attached to a saddle for holding the butt of a cavalry lance

lance corporal *n* [*lance* (as in *lancepesade*) + *corporal*] **1 :** a private appointed to perform temporarily the duties of a corporal **:** an acting corporal **2 :** a marine enlistee just below the lowest noncommissioned officer and above a private first class

lanced \-n(t)st, -nsəd\ *adj* [¹*lance* + *-ed*] **:** shaped and pointed like a lance ⟨~ foliage⟩

lance·field group \-n(t),sfēld-\ *also* **lancefield's group** *or* **lancefield grouping** *n, usu cap L* [after Rebecca *Lancefield* b1895 Am. bacteriologist] **:** one of the serologically distinguishable groups (as group A, group B) into which streptococci can be divided

lance·gay \-n(t)s,gā\ *n* -s [ME *launcegay*, fr. MF *lancegaie*, fr. *lance* + *-gaie* (as in *archegaie, azagaie*, a kind of lance) — more at ASSEGAI] **:** a medieval lance or throwing spear

lance head \'ₛ,ₛ\ *or* **lance-headed snake** \'ₛ,ₛₛ-\ *n* [trans. of F *fer-de-lance*] **:** FER-DE-LANCE

lance-jack \'ₛ,ₛ\ *n* [*lance* (as in *lancepesade*) + *jack*] *chiefly Brit* **:** LANCE CORPORAL

lance-knight \'ₛ,ₛ\ *n* [intended as trans. of G *lanzknecht*, by folk etymology (influence of *lanze* lance) fr. *landsknecht* — more at LANSQUENET] **:** LANSQUENET 1

lance·let \-n(t)slət\ *n* -s [¹*lance* + *-let*] **1** *obs* **:** LANCET **2 :** any of certain small elongate translucent marine animals that constitute *Branchiostoma* and related genera making up the Cephalochorda and that become from half an inch to four inches long and are found burrowing in the sand in shallow waters on the coasts of warm and warm-temperate seas in many parts of the world — see AMPHIOXUS

lancelike \'ₛ,ₛ\ *adj* **:** slender and pointed like a lance

lance-linear \'ₛ'ₛₛ\ *adj* **:** narrowly lanceolate

lance·man \-n(t)smən\ *n, pl* **lancemen :** a soldier armed with a lance or pike

lance-oblong \'ₛ'ₛ,ₛ\ *adj* **:** oblong and lanceolate ⟨*lance-oblong* leaf⟩

lan·ce·o·lar \'lan(t)sēələ(r), lan'sē-\ *adj* [L *lanceola* (dim. of *lancea* lance) + E *-ar*] **:** LANCEOLATE

lan·ce·o·late \-lət, -,lāt\ *also* **lan·ce·o·lat·ed** \-,lād·əd\ *adj* [*lanceolate* fr. LL *lanceolatus*, fr. L *lanceola* + *-atus* -ate; *lanceolated* fr. LL *lanceolatus* + E *-ed*] **:** shaped like a lance head **:** tapering to a point at the apex and sometimes at the base ⟨~ leaf⟩ ⟨~ prism⟩ — **lan·ce·o·late·ly** *adv*

lancepesade *n* -s [MF & OIt; MF *lancepessade*, fr. OIt *lancia spezzata* battle-trained or seasoned soldier, select soldier, lit., broken lance, fr. *lancia* lance (fr. L *lancea*) + *spezzata*, fem. of *spezzato*, past part. of *spezzare* to break into pieces, fr. *s-* dis- (fr. L *dis-*) + *pezza* piece, fr. ML *petia* — more at PIECE] *obs* **:** LANCE CORPORAL

lancepod \'ₛ,ₛ\ *n* **:** an Australian leguminous plant of the genus *Lonchocarpus*; *esp* **:** BLOODY BARK

lanc·er \'lan(t)sə(r), -aan-,-ain-,-àn-\ *n* -s [MF *lancier*, fr. *lance* + *-ier* -er — more at LANCE] **1 :** one who carries a lance; *specif* **:** a light cavalry soldier armed with a lance ⟨the 16th (Queen's) *Lancers*⟩ **2 lancers** *pl but sing in constr* [F *lancier*, fr. MF] **a :** a set of five quadrilles each in a different meter **b :** the music for the lancers

lances *pl of* LANX *or of* LANCE, *pres 3d sing of* LANCE

lance sergeant *n* **:** a corporal appointed to perform temporarily the duties of a sergeant **:** acting sergeant

lance snake *n* **:** FER-DE-LANCE

lan·cet \'lan(t)sət, -aan-,-ain-,-àn-\ *n* -s [ME *lancette*, fr. MF, dim. of *lance*] **1** *obs* **a :** LANCE **b :** DART, JAVELIN **2 :** a sharp-pointed and commonly two-edged surgical instrument of various forms used to make small incisions (as in a vein or a boil) **3 a** (1) **:** LANCET WINDOW (2) **:** a single light in a traceried window having the shape of a lancet window **b :** LANCET ARCH **4 :** an iron bar for tapping a melting furnace

lancet arch *n* **:** an acutely pointed arch — see ARCH illustration

lancet architecture *n* **:** the early Gothic in England

lan·cet·ed \-sǝd·əd\ *adj* **:** having a lancet arch or lancet windows

lancet fish *n* **1 :** any of several large voracious deep-sea fishes of the genus *Alepisaurus* (as *A. ferox*) having long pointed teeth and a long high dorsal fin **2 :** SURGEONFISH

lancet fluke *n* **:** a small liver fluke (*Dicrocoelium dendriticum* or *D. lanceolatum*) widely distributed in sheep and cattle and rarely occurring in man

lancet window *n* **:** a high narrow window with an acutely pointed head and without tracery

lancewood \'ₛ,ₛ\ *n* **1 :** tough elastic wood of various trees that is used esp. for carriage shafts, archery bows, fishing rods, and cabinetwork **2 :** a tropical American tree (*Oxandra lanceolata*) of the family Annonaceae that furnishes most of the lancewood of commerce

lancet window

lanch \'lanch, -aa(ə)-,-ai-,-à-\ *dial var of* LANCE

lan·cha \'lanchə\ *or* **lan·chara** \lan-'chärə, -charə\ *n* -s [*lancha* fr. Sp or Pg; Sp, fr. Pg, fr. Malay *lancharan*, fr. *lanchar* effortless speed; *lanchara* fr. Pg, fr. Malay *lancharan*] **:** a light sailing ship largely used for trading in the East Indian archipelago and the Philippines

lan·chow \'lan¦jō\ *adj, usu cap* [fr. *Lanchow*, China] **:** of or from the city of Lanchow, China **:** of the kind or style prevalent in Lanchow

lan·ci·form \'lan(t)sə,fȯrm\ *adj* [ISV ¹*lance* + *-iform*] **:** shaped like a lance or lancet ⟨~ window⟩

lan·ci·nate \-sə,nāt\ *vb* -ED/-ING/-S [L *lancinatus*, past part. of *lancinare* to lacerate; akin to *lacer* mangled — more at LACERATE] **:** PIERCE, STAB, LACERATE — **lan·ci·na·tion** \ˌₛₛ'nāshən\ *n* -s

lancing *pres part of* LANCE

¹land \'land, -aa(ə)nd\ *when a consonant follows without pause the d is sometimes lost, as in -nz for "lands" and -n,slīd for "landslide"\ n* -s *often attrib* [ME *land, lond*, fr. OE *land, lond*; akin to OHG *lant* land, ON & Goth *land*, OIr *land* open space, area, OPruss *lindan* (acc.) valley, ORuss *lyadina* weed, underbrush] **1 :** the solid part of the surface of the earth in contrast to the water of oceans and seas ⟨sailing out of sight of ~⟩ ⟨a narrow isthmus connecting two great ~ masses⟩ ⟨~ animals⟩ ⟨~ birds⟩ ⟨travel by ~⟩ or to the air ⟨air bombing prepared for the advance of ~ forces⟩ ⟨attacked by ~, sea, and air⟩ **2 a :** a portion (as a country, estate, farm, or tract) of the earth's solid surface considered by itself or as belonging to an individual or a people ⟨out of the ~ of Egypt⟩ ⟨people of faraway ~s⟩ **b :** the people of a country ⟨the ~ rose in rebellion⟩ **c :** REALM, DOMAIN ⟨no longer in the ~ of the living⟩ ⟨a ~ of dreams⟩ **d :** the country as distinguished from the town; *esp* **:** farming country ⟨the independent farmer and his family are leaving the ~ —Eric Sevareid⟩ ⟨the only one of his family to take to the ~⟩ **3 a :** ground or soil in respect to its situation, nature, or quality ⟨wet ~⟩ ⟨good ~⟩ ⟨mountain ~⟩ ⟨stubble ~⟩ **b** *obs* **:** FLOOR, GROUND **c :** the natural environment and its attributes within which production takes place **:** the surface of the earth and all its natural resources **4 a :** ground owned privately or publicly **:** landed property ⟨a house with ten acres of ~⟩ ⟨to divide ~s among heirs⟩ **b** *law* **:** any ground, soil, or earth whatsoever regarded as the subject of ownership (as meadows, pastures, woods) and everything annexed to it whether by nature (as trees, water) or by man (as buildings, fences) extending indefinitely vertically upwards and downwards **c :** an interest or estate in land; *broadly* **:** TENEMENT, HEREDITAMENT — compare REAL ESTATE **d** *Scot* **:** a building having a common entry but several flats or tenements each containing one household **5 a :** ground left unplowed between furrows **b :** any of several portions into which a field is divided for convenience in plowing **c :** the unplowed portion of a field being plowed **d :** a strip of land marked off by furrows; *also* **:** the length of such a strip used as a measure of surface or length **e** *Africa* **:** the portions of a farm suitable for cultivation **:** FIELD, PATCH ⟨mealie ~⟩ **6 :** an area of a surface partly machined (as with holes, indentations, furrows, or grooves) that is left without such machining: as **a :** the level part of a millstone between two furrows **b :** the surface of the bore of a rifle between consecutive grooves **c :** the metal between the flutes of a twist drill **d :** the uncut surface between two adjacent grooves of a phonograph record **7 :** the lap of the strakes in a clinker-built boat or of plates in a steel ship — called also *landing*

²land \"\ *vb* -ED/-ING/-S *vt* **1 :** to set or put on shore from a ship or other watercraft after a voyage or water trip **:** DISEMBARK, DEBARK ⟨I'll undertake to ~ them on our coast —Shak.⟩ **2 a :** to set down after conveying ⟨the cab ~*ed* him at the station⟩ **b :** to cause to reach or come to rest in a particular place, position, or condition ⟨his recklessness ~*ed* him in trouble⟩ ⟨unable to ~ a solid punch in the early rounds⟩ ⟨~*ed* the quoit near the stake⟩ **c :** to bring (an airplane) to a landing **3 a :** to catch and bring to shore or into a boat ⟨~ a fish⟩ **b :** to win, gain, capture, or secure usu. as the result of artful effort or competition ⟨~ a job⟩ ⟨salesman ~*ed* the order⟩ ⟨a treaty ~*ed* after long parleys⟩ ⟨~ a racing prize⟩ ⟨~ a husband⟩ **c** *Brit* **:** to put in difficulties **:** EMBARRASS ⟨committee found itself ~*ed* with a witness whose tactics baffled and embarrassed it —*New Statesman & Nation*⟩ **~** *vi* **1 a :** to go ashore from a ship or boat; DISEMBARK **b** *of a ship or boat* **:** to touch at a place on shore **:** come to shore **2 a :** to come to the end of a course or to a stage in a journey **:** come to rest **:** ARRIVE ⟨late that night we ~*ed* at a motel⟩ — often used with *up* ⟨more likely ~ up in the desert —Greville Texidor⟩ **b :** to strike or meet the ground (as after a fall, leap, flight) ⟨~*ed* in a heap at the bottom of the stairs⟩ ⟨the ball must ~ inside the lines of the service court⟩ ⟨fell off the porch and ~*ed* on his head⟩ **c** *of an airplane* **:** to alight on the ground, the water, or other surface — **land on :** to come down on **:** criticize or scold sharply ⟨came in late for dinner and the whole family ~*ed on* him⟩

³land \"\ *or* **lands** \-dz\ *interj* [euphemism fr. *Lord, Lord's*] — used to express surprise or wonder ⟨~ sakes, why did you do that⟩ ⟨~ knows where he went⟩

⁴land \'länt\ *n, pl* **län·der** *or* **laen·der** \'lendə(r)\ [G, land, country, province, fr. OHG *lant* land — more at ¹LAND] **:** a unit of local government in Germany corresponding to a state

land agent *n* **1** *Brit* **:** one who manages the lands of an estate **2 a :** an official administering public lands **b :** a broker acting in the claiming or purchase of public or private land (as by settlers)

land·art \'landərt\ *Scot var of* LANDWARD

lan·dau \'lan,daù *also* -dō *sometimes* -dō\ *n* -s [fr. *Landau*, Bavaria, Germany, where it was first manufactured] **:** a four-wheeled covered carriage with a top divided into two sections the back section of which can be let down or thrown back while the front section can be removed or left stationary; *also* **:** a closed automobile body with provision for opening or folding the rear quarter

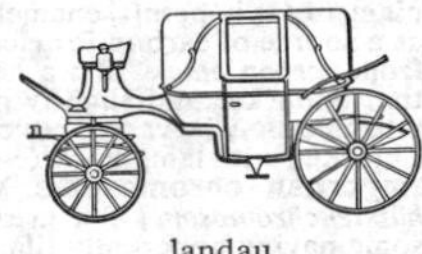

landau

lan·dau·let *also* **lan·dau·lette** \ˌlandə'let\ *n* -s [*landaulet* fr. *landau* + *-let*; *landaulette* alter. (influenced by *-ette*) of *landaulet*] **1 :** a small landau **:** a coupé with a folding top **2 :** an automobile body with an open driver's seat and an enclosed rear section having one cross seat and a collapsible roof

land bank *n* **1 :** a bank issuing its currency upon real property **2 :** a bank (as the Federal Land Bank) that invests in farm mortgages and issues its own bonds to secure funds for the purpose

land battleship *or* **land cruiser** *n* **:** ¹TANK 3

landblink \'ₛ,ₛ\ *n* [¹*land* + *blink* (as in *iceblink*)] **:** a glow that is yellower than iceblink and that is seen in arctic regions over snow-covered land

land·book \'lan(d),bu̇k\ *or* **land·boc** \-bäk\ *n* -s [landbook trans. of OE *landbōc*; *landboc* fr. OE *landbōc*, fr. *land* + *bōc* book — more at LAND, BOOK] **:** an early English charter granting land

land-bred \'ₛ'ₛ\ *adj* **:** not seafaring

land breeze *n* **:** a breeze blowing usu. at night toward the sea from the more rapidly cooling land

land bridge *n* **:** a strip of land connecting two landmasses (as two continents or a continent and an island)

land broker *n, Brit* **:** a real-estate broker

land caltrop *n* **:** a common tropical weed (*Tribulus terrestris*) with yellow flowers and spiny fruit

land certificate *n* **1 :** a document issued by a government evidencing the official registration of the record of a title to real property **2 :** a preliminary or intermediate document issued by a government evidencing that the grantee named therein will become entitled to a patent or grant of specified land upon fulfilling named conditions

land court *n* **:** a court having jurisdiction over registration of title to land and matters incidental thereto

land crab *n* **1 :** any of certain crabs chiefly of the family Gecarinidae of the coasts of warm countries that live mostly upon land and breed in the sea and that include many forms (as *Gecarinus ruricola*) that attain considerable size and are eaten by man **2** *Austral* **:** a burrowing crawfish (*Eugaeus fossor*)

land crake *n, Brit* **:** CORNCRAKE

land cress *n* **1 :** WINTER CRESS **2 :** BITTER CRESS 1 **3** *NewZeal* **:** an annual swine cress (*Coronopus didymus*) having trailing stems and causing taint of milk in cows

land crocodile *n* **:** MONITOR 3

L and D *abbr* **1** loans and discounts **2** loss and damage

land dayak *n, usu cap L&D* [perh. by folk etymology fr. *Landak*, a subdivision of the Land Dayak, in western Borneo] **1 :** a Dayak people inhabiting western Borneo **2 :** a member of the Land Dayak people

land diameter *n* [¹*land* (surface of a rifle bore)] **:** the diameter of a rifled firearm measured between diametrically opposite lands — compare CALIBER 1a

land drake *n, Brit* **:** CORNCRAKE

land·drost \'lan(d),drȯst\ *also* **land·trost** \-,tr-\ *n* -s [Afrik *landdros* (formerly spelled *landdrost*), fr. *land* land, country (fr. MD) + *drost* sheriff; akin to OHG *lant* land — more at LAND, DROSTDY] **:** a Boer magistrate in a rural district of South Africa prior to the establishment of British administration ⟨the special court . . . of three ~s with a jury —Manfred Nathan⟩

lande \'läⁿd\ *n* -s [F — more at LAUND] **1 :** an infertile moor **2 landes** *pl* **:** sandy barrens bordering the sea in southwestern France

land·ed \'landəd, -aan-\ *adj* [in sense 1, fr. ME *londed, landed*, fr. *land, lond* land + *-ed*; in sense 2, fr. past part. of ²*land*] **1 :** having an estate in land ⟨~ gentry⟩ ⟨~ interest⟩ **:** consisting in land or real estate or its possession **:** derived from land ⟨~ estate⟩ **2 :** DELIVERED ⟨~ cost of merchandise⟩

¹land·er \'landə(r), -aan-\ *n* -s [²*land* + *-er*] **1 :** a worker stationed at one of the levels of a mine shaft to unload rock from the bucket or cage and load drilling and blasting supplies to be lowered to the crew **2 :** a quarry worker who guides and steadies blocks of stone as they are hoisted from the quarry and loaded on trucks or railroad cars

²länder *pl of* LAND

land·ert \'landərt\ *Scot var of* LANDWARD

lan·des·ite \'landə,sīt\ *n* -s [Kenneth K. *Landes* b1899 Am. geologist + E *-ite*] **:** a mineral $Fe_6Mn_{20}(PO_4)_{16}.27H_2O(?)$ consisting of a rare hydrous ferromanganese phosphate occurring as a brown alteration crust on reddingite

landfall \'ₛ,ₛ\ *n* **1 a :** a sighting of land when at sea; *esp* **:** the first sight of land after a voyage ⟨time of ~ is the most interesting period in the voyage for the navigator —Benjamin Dutton⟩ ⟨run your easting down and make your ~ —Alan Villiers⟩ **b :** the first sight of land after a water crossing by airplane **c :** a shore sighted from a ship at sea or an airplane over water ⟨saw the bright island ~s blooming under a sunny sky —David Dodge⟩ **2 :** an approach to or landing on a shore ⟨if the weather be thick, hesitate to attempt a dangerous ~ until the weather clears —G.W.Mixter⟩ **3 :** LANDSLIDE

landfang *n* [¹*land* + *fang* (catching)] *obs* **:** firm holding ground for an anchor

landfast \'ₛ,ₛ\ *adj* **:** fast on the shore ⟨~ ice⟩

landfill \'ₛ,ₛ\ *n* **:** disposal of trash and garbage by burying it under layers of earth in low ground

landflood \'ₛ,ₛ\ *n* [ME *londflod*, fr. *lond* land + *flod* flood — more at LAND, FLOOD] **:** an overflowing of land by inland water

landfolk \'ₛ,ₛ\ *n, archaic* **:** the people of a country

land force *n* **:** a military force serving on land as distinguished from naval or air forces

landform \'ₛ,ₛ\ *n* **:** a feature of the earth's surface due to natural causes ⟨plains, plateaus, and mountain ranges are major ~s⟩ ⟨hills, canyons, sea cliffs, alluvial fans, moraines, eskers, and dunes are among the innumerable minor ~s⟩

land-gav·el *or* **land·gaf·ol** \'lan(d),gavəl\ *n* -s [ME & OE; ME *londgavel, landgavel*, fr. OE *landgafol, londgafol*, fr. *land, lond* land + *gafol* gavel — more at GAVEL] **:** land rent in early England

land girl *n, Brit* **:** a woman farm worker doing work to replace a man absent in military service

land-grabber \'ₛ,ₛₛ\ *n* **:** one that seizes land illegally, unfairly, or selfishly: as **a :** one who secures public land by misrepresentation or fraud **b** *Ireland* **:** one who takes the holding of an evicted tenant

land-grant college \'ₛ,ₛ-\ *or* **land-grant university** *n* **:** one of certain institutions for higher education receiving federal aid under the Morrill acts of 1862 and 1890

land-grant deduction *n* **:** a deduction in freight and passenger rates formerly received by the federal government on its traffic over a railroad in consideration of land grants

land-grant road *n* **:** a railroad that under federal Land Grant acts was aided in construction by grants of land

land·grave \'lan(d),grāv\ *n* -s [modif. of G *landgraf*, fr. MHG *lantgrāve*, fr. *lant* land, country, province (fr. OHG, land) + *grāve* count — more at LAND, BURGRAVE] **1 :** a German count having a certain territorial jurisdiction — compare BURGRAVE **2 :** a county nobleman in the Carolina colony ranking just below the proprietary

land·grave·ship \-v,ship\ *n* **:** LANDGRAVIATE

land·gra·vess \-vəs\ *n* -ES [*landgrave* + *-ess*] **:** LANDGRAVINE

land·gra·vi·ate \lan(d)'grāvē,āt, 'ₛ,ₛvē,āt, -ēət\ *n* -s [MF *landgraviat*, fr. ML *landgraviatus*, *landgravius* landgrave (fr. MHG *lantgrāve*) + MF *-at* (fr. L *-atus* -ate)] **:** the office, jurisdiction, or authority of a landgrave

land·gra·vine \'lan(d)grə,vēn\ *n* -s [modif. of G *landgräfin*, fr. MHG *lantgrævinne*, fr. *lantgrāve* + *-inne* (fem. suffix)] **:** the wife of a landgrave or a woman holding the rank and position of a landgrave

landholder \'ₛ,ₛₛ\ *n* **:** a holder or owner of land

landholding \'ₛ,ₛₛ\ *n* **1 :** the state or fact of holding or owning land **2 :** property in land

land-horse \'ₛ,ₛ\ *n* **:** the horse on a plow's land side

landing *n* -s **1 a :** a going or bringing on or to shore or land **b :** an act of alighting or falling on the earth or other surface ⟨airplane ~⟩ ⟨forced ~⟩ **2 a :** a place for landing and taking on passengers and cargo **b :** a place or platform where logs are collected preparatory to further transportation by water or land **3 :** a level part of a staircase at the end of a flight of stairs or connecting one flight with another **4 :** a place usu. the bank where the ore is discharged from a mine **5 :** LAND 7

landing angle *n* **:** the angle of attack of the main supporting surfaces of an airplane at the instant of touching the ground in a three-point landing

landing beam *n* **:** a radio beam projected from a landing field to indicate to the pilot of an airplane his height above the ground and the proper path for a landing approach

landing circle *n* **:** a roughly circular course flown by an airplane just prior to landing esp. on a carrier

landing craft *n* **:** any of numerous naval craft specially designed for putting ashore troops and equipment esp. in amphibious beach assault

landing field *n* **:** an area of land prepared for the landing and takeoff of airplanes

landing flap *n* **:** a flap that is mounted on the undersurface near the trailing edge of an airplane wing and that when lowered increases both the drag and the lift and thus permits landing at lower speed

landing force *n* **1 :** LANDING PARTY **2 :** the army or marine component of an amphibious attack force

landing gear *n* **1 :** the understructure that absorbs the landing shock and supports the weight of an aircraft when in contact with the land or water **2 :** a retractable support for the forward end of a semitrailer when parked without the tractor unit

landing light *n* **:** a floodlight mounted usu. in the wing edge of an airplane for night landings
landing man *n* **:** a worker who bunches logs at a landing
landing mat *n* **:** a mat of metal mesh or interlocking pierced steel planking used for making quickly assembled all-weather airplane runways
landing net *n* **1 :** a dip net used in fishing to take the captured fish from the water **2 :** a rope net dropped from the deck of a transport to enable troops to descend to landing craft

landing net 1

landing party *n* **:** a detachment of a ship's company organized for emergency or ceremonial duty ashore
landing ship *n* **:** any of numerous ocean-going naval vessels designed for amphibious landings
landing signal officer *n* **:** an officer who assists pilots in landing aboard an aircraft carrier — abbr. *LSO*
landing stage *n* **:** a usu. floating and anchored platform at the end of a pier or wharf for the landing and embarking of passengers and freight; *sometimes* **:** PIER, DOCK
landing strake *n* **:** the line of planking or plating second below the gunwale of a ship
landing strip *n* **:** AIRSTRIP
landing surveyor *n* **:** a British customs officer who appoints and oversees the landwaiters
landing T *or* **landing tee** *n* **:** WIND TEE
landing waiter *n* **:** LANDWAITER
landjumper \ˈ=,==\ *n* [¹*land* + *jumper*] **:** one that unlawfully takes possession of land either owned by or in the possession of another
landlady \ˈ=,==\ *n* **1 :** a woman who owns real estate which she rents or leases to others **2 :** a woman who owns or manages an inn, rooming house, or boardinghouse **3** *Scot* **:** the mistress of a private house **:** HOSTESS
land law *n* **:** law relating to property in land
land lead *n* **:** a passage of water through an ice field
land league *n* **1 :** a league used as a land unit equal to three statute miles — compare MARINE LEAGUE **2 :** ¹LEAGUE 2
land leech *n* **:** any of various bloodsucking leeches chiefly of moist tropical regions that live on land and are often troublesome to man and other animals; *esp* **:** a leech of the gnathobdellid genus *Haemadipsa*
länd·ler \ˈlentlə(r)\ *n, pl* **ländler** *or* **ländlers** [G, fr. G dial. *Landl* upper Austria, where it originated + G *-er* (fr. OHG *-āri*)] **1 :** an Austrian couple dance of rural origin in triple time that was a precursor of the waltz but slower and performed with stamping somewhat dragging steps **2 :** music for the ländler
land·less \ˈlandləs *rapid* -nl-\ *adj* **1 :** having no property or estate in land ⟨~ peasantry⟩ **2 :** containing no land ⟨~ seas⟩ — **land·less·ness** *n* -ES
landlike \ˈ=,=\ *adj* **:** resembling land ⟨crimson cloud that ~ slept along the deep —Alfred Tennyson⟩
landline \ˈ=,=\ *n* **1 :** a line of transportation or of communication (as by telegraph) on land **2 :** the boundary between land and water or sky ⟨sun came up too: it broke clear of the ~ —Shelby Foote⟩
¹**land·lock** \ˈlan(d),läk\ *n* [prob. back-formation fr. *landlocked*] **:** a landlocked state or place
²**landlock** \ˈ"\ *vt* [back-formation fr. *landlocked*] **:** to cause to be landlocked **:** enclose within land
land·locked \ˈ=,=\ *adj* [¹*land* + *locked*] **1 :** enclosed or nearly enclosed by land ⟨~ harbor⟩ ⟨~ country⟩ **2 :** confined to fresh water by or as if by some barrier — used of fish that ordinarily seek the sea after spawning
landlocked salmon *n* **1 :** a landlocked phase that is sometimes regarded as a distinct variety (*Salmo salar sebago*) or a separate species (*S. sebago*) of the salmon of the Atlantic and is native to lakes of eastern No. America from New Hampshire to New Brunswick — called also *Sebago salmon* **2 :** LAKE TROUT
landlooker \ˈ=,==\ *n* **:** CRUISER 4a
land·loper *or* **land·loup·er** \ˈlan(d),lōpə(r), -lōp-, -lüp-\ *n* -S [D *landloper*, fr. MD, fr. *land* + *loper* runner, fr. *lopen* to run + *-er;* akin to OHG *lant* land and to OHG *loufan* to run — more at LAND, LEAP] **1 :** VAGABOND, VAGRANT **2** *obs* **:** LANDLUBBER
land·lord \ˈlan(d),lȯrd, -aan-, -lō(ə)d\ *n* [ME, fr. ¹*land* + *lord*] **1 :** one who lets land to another **:** the owner or holder of land or houses which he leases or rents to another — compare LESSOR ⟨*landlord*-ridden countryside⟩ **2 :** the master of an inn or lodging house ⟨my companion fetched out the jolly ~ —Joseph Addison⟩ **3** *Scot* **:** a host in a private house
land·lord·ism \-ȯr,dizəm\ *n* **1 :** the state of being a landlord **:** characteristics of a landlord in action, opinions, or speech **2 :** the relations of landlords to tenants esp. as to leased agricultural lands **:** the system or doctrine of the ownership of the soil being vested in one who leases it to the cultivators ⟨evils of absentee ~⟩
land·lord·ly \-ȯrdlē\ *adj* **:** of, relating to, or characteristic of a landlord ⟨~ manner⟩ ⟨~ rights⟩
land·lord·ry \-drē\ *n* -ES **:** landlords as a group or class
land·lord·ship \-d,ship\ *n* **:** the condition or position of a landlord
land·lub·ber \ˈlan(d),ləbə(r), -aan-\ *n* [¹*land* + *lubber*] **1 :** one who passes his life on land **:** LANDSMAN **2 :** one who is unacquainted with the sea or unskilled in seamanship — **land·lub·ber·ish** \-bərish\ *adj* — **land·lub·ber·ly** \-rlē\ *adj*
land·lub·bing \-biŋ\ *adj* [*landlubber* + *-ing*] **:** living as a landlubber **:** LANDLUBBERLY
land·man \ˈlan(d)mən, -,man\ *n, pl* **landmen 1** *obs* **:** one of a particular or specified country **2** *archaic* **:** FARMER, RUSTIC, COUNTRYMAN **3 :** LANDSMAN 2 **4 :** LEASEMAN 1
landmark \ˈ=,=\ *n* **1 :** a mark for designating the boundary of land **:** a fixed object (as a monument of any sort, a river, marked tree, stone, ditch) by which the limits of a farm, a town, or other portion of territory may be known and preserved **2 a :** a conspicuous object on land that serves as a guide to navigation at sea **b :** a natural object or man-made structure that marks a course or characterizes a locality ⟨the Armory remains — a solid fortlike ~ of weathered brick —*Amer. Guide Series: Minn.*⟩ ⟨a huge crooked tree was so prominent a ~ for early French voyageurs — *Amer. Guide Series: Mich.*⟩ **c** (1) **:** an anatomical structure used as a point of orientation in locating other structures (as in surgical procedures) (2) *anthrop* **:** a point on the body or skeleton from which measurements are taken **3 :** an event, achievement, characteristic, or modification that marks a turning point or a stage ⟨forty years after its composition the essay stands as a ~ in American criticism —Lionel Trilling⟩ ⟨a ~ in the shift of American values —W.H.Whyte⟩ **4 :** a traditional guiding precept or principle ⟨the young are abandoning old ~s⟩
landmark baptist \ˈ=,=-\ *or* **landmarker** \ˈ=,==\ *n, usu cap L&B* [so called fr. the stress laid on what this sect regards as the landmarks of Baptist Christianity] **:** a Baptist of the strictly denominational American Baptist Association which originated in Texas and Arkansas in 1905 and took its present name in 1924
landmass \ˈ=,=\ *n* **:** a large area of land
land measure *n* **:** a unit or series of units of area (as square rod, acre) used esp. in measuring land
land–mere *n* -S *obs* **:** BOUNDARY
land mine *n* **1 :** a mine that is placed on or just below the surface of the ground and is usu. designed to be exploded by the weight of vehicles or troops passing over it **2 :** AERIAL MINE 2
land·oc·ra·cy \lanˈdäkrəsē\ *n* -ES [¹*land* + *-o-* + *-cracy*] **:** a class gaining prominence or power through the possession of land
land office *n* **:** a government office in which the entries upon and sales of public land are registered and other business respecting the public lands is transacted
land–office business *n* **:** extensive and rapid business **:** rush of sales or transactions ⟨travel agencies had done a *land-office business* —*Time*⟩
land of nod *usu cap N* [fr. the *Land of Nod* in the Bible (Gen 4:16); influenced in meaning by ¹*nod;* fr. the nodding in drowsiness] **:** the state of sleep ⟨a friendly fat toad . . . who had lately taken himself off to the *land of Nod* under the rough bank fringing my lawn —David Gunston⟩
land of the leal *usu cap both Ls, Scot* **:** HEAVEN
lan·dol·phia \lanˈdälfēə, -dōl-\ *n* [NL, fr. J. F. *Landolphe* †1825 Fr. ship captain + NL *-ia*] **1** *cap* **:** a genus of Old World tropical woody vines (family Apocynaceae) having large yellow or white cymose flowers with narrow lobes succeeded by large berrylike fruits — see CONGO RUBBER **2** -S **:** any plant of the genus *Landolphia*
landolphia rubber *n* **:** CONGO RUBBER
landolt ring *n, usu cap L* [after Edmond *Landolt* †1926 Fr. ophthalmologist] **:** one of a series of incomplete rings or circles used in studying visual discrimination or acuity
land otter *n* **:** any of various otters of *Lutra* and related genera that are primarily terrestrial in contrast to the sea otter
land·own·er \ˈlan,dōnə(r), -aan-,-\ *n* **:** an owner of land
land·own·er·ship \-(r),ship\ *n* **:** ownership of land ⟨remnants of feudal ~ —J.P.Warbury⟩
landowning \ˈ=,==\ *adj* **:** having property in land ⟨~ nobility⟩ **:** relating to landowners ⟨~ interests⟩
land pike *n* **1 :** HELLBENDER 1 **2 :** RAZORBACK 2
land pirate *n* **1** *obs* **:** a literary pirate **2 :** one who robs on land: as **a :** HIGHWAYMAN **b :** LAND SHARK **3 :** LAND-GRABBER a
land pitch *n* **:** a hard Trinidad asphalt — compare LAKE PITCH
landplane \ˈ=,=\ *n* [¹*land* + *airplane*] **:** an airplane designed to land on and take off from land
land plaster *n* **:** gypsum or gypsiferous rock ground fine for use as a fertilizer and for correcting a puddled soil condition caused by the presence of sodium and potassium carbonates
land–poor \ˈ=¦=\ *adj* **:** pecuniarily embarrassed through owning much unprofitable or encumbered land ⟨a thousand acres and we couldn't afford to buy a cow. Do you know what it means to be *land-poor* —Ellen Glasgow⟩
land power *n* **1 :** military strength **2 :** a nation having great military strength — compare SEA POWER
L and R *abbr* lake and rail
land·race \ˈlan,drās\ *n* [Dan, fr. *land* land, country + *race*] **1** *usu cap* **:** any of several locally developed breeds or races of swine of northern Europe; *esp* **:** a Danish breed of long-bodied white bacon-type swine — called also *Danish Landrace* **2** *often cap* -S **:** any animal of a Landrace breed
land rail *n* **1 :** CORNCRAKE **2 :** an Australasian rail (*Rallus philippensis*)
landraker *n, obs* **:** FOOTPAD, HIGHWAYMAN, TRAMP
landreeve \ˈ=,=\ *n* **:** a subordinate officer on an extensive estate who acts as the steward's assistant
land reform *n* **:** legislative or other measures for effecting a more equitable distribution of agricultural land esp. by dividing large estates into small holdings
landright \ˈ=,=\ *n* [OE *landriht* (akin to OHG *lantreht* law of the land, OS *landreht*, OFris *landriucht*), fr. *land, lond* land + *riht* right — more at LAND, RIGHT] **:** right or obligation connected with occupation of or property in land
lan·dry's paralysis \ˈlandrēz-\ *n, usu cap L* [after Jean Baptiste *Landry* †1865 Fr. physician] **:** motor paralysis beginning in the legs and rapidly extending to the trunk and arms and finally to the muscles of respiration **:** acute ascending paralysis
¹**lands** *pl of* LAND, *pres 3d sing of* LAND
²**lands** *var of* LAND
¹**land·scape** \ˈlanz,kāp, -aan-, -n(d),sk-\ *n, often attrib* [D *landschap*, fr. MD *landscap* region, tract of land (akin to OE *landscipe* region, OHG *lantscaf*, ON *landskapr*), fr. *land* + *-scap* -ship; akin to OHG *lant* land and to OHG *-scaf* -ship — more at LAND, -SHIP] **1 a :** a picture representing a view of natural scenery (as fields, hills, forests, water) ⟨~ painting⟩ — compare MARINE 5; SEASCAPE **b :** the art of depicting such scenery **2 a :** the surface of the earth **:** the landforms of a region in the aggregate esp. as produced or modified by geologic forces ⟨most ~s are complex rather than simple —Leland Horberg⟩ ⟨glacial ~s⟩ ⟨lunar ~⟩ **b :** a portion of land or territory that the eye can comprehend in a single view including all the objects so seen ⟨plans for altering the ~⟩ ⟨~ engineering⟩ **3 a** *obs* **:** VISTA, PROSPECT **b** *obs* **:** a faint sketch **:** ADUMBRATION **4** *obs* **:** EPITOME, COMPENDIUM
²**landscape** \ˈ"\ *vb* -ED/-ING/-S *vt* **:** to make a landscape of **:** to improve by landscape architecture or gardening ~ *vi* **:** to engage in landscape gardening
landscape architect *n* **:** one whose profession is the arrangement of land for human use and enjoyment involving the placement of structures, vehicular and pedestrian circulation, plantings, and relationships with adjacent areas
landscape architecture *n* **:** the planning and design of landscape by a landscape architect
landscape engineer *n* **:** one who is concerned with the problems of engineering in the field of landscape architecture
landscape gardener *n* **:** one who is skilled in landscape gardening
landscape gardening *n* **:** the development and decorative planting of gardens and grounds
landscape management *n* **:** the care and maintenance of landscape or ornamental plantings
landscape marble *n* **:** a close-grained limestone with dark dendritic markings suggesting natural scenery
landscape mirror *n* **:** CLAUDE LORRAINE GLASS
landscape panel *n* **:** a wooden panel so placed that the grain runs horizontally
land·scap·er \-pə(r)\ *n* -S **:** LANDSCAPE GARDENER
land·scap·ist \-pəst\ *n* -S **:** a painter of landscapes
land scrip *n* **:** a certificate entitling the holder to obtain a certain portion of the public land either by entry or the payment of a portion of the price
land seal *n* **:** HARBOR SEAL
land·seer newfoundland \ˈlan(d),si(ə)r-\ *or* **landseer** *n* -S *usu cap L&N* [after Sir Edwin H. *Landseer* †1873 Eng. animal painter] **:** a black-and-white Newfoundland dog
land's end *n* **:** the extreme point of a country or region
land settlement *n, India* **:** the act of arranging the terms and incidence of the land tax in specific areas
land·shard \ˈlan(d)shə(r)d\ *n* [¹*land* + *shard*] *dial Eng* **:** a strip of unplowed land between two pieces of plowed land
land shark *n* **1 :** a swindler of sailors on shore **2 :** LAND-GRABBER a
landship \ˈ=,=\ *n* **1 :** a large transport wagon **:** COVERED WAGON **2 :** TANK 3
landside \ˈ=,=\ *n* **1 :** the side of something near water that is turned toward the land **2** *obs* **:** SHORE **3 :** the side of a furrow next to the land in plowing **4 :** a sidepiece opposite the plow moldboard sometimes forming a V with the share edge (as in a bar share) or consisting of a revolving disk wheel that guides the plow and receives the side pressure when the furrow is turned — see PLOW illustration
land·skip \ˈlanz,kip, -n(d),sk-\ *archaic var of* LANDSCAPE
lands·knecht \ˈläntskə,nekt\ *n* -S [G — more at LANSQUENET] **:** LANSQUENET
land–slater \ˈ=,==\ *n* **:** WOOD LOUSE 1
landsleit [Yiddish *landslayt* compatriots (suppletive pl. of *landsman*), fr. MHG *lantsliute* alter. of *lantliute* natives, compatriots, fr. *lant* land (fr. OHG) + *liute* people, fr. OHG *liuti*, pl. of *liut* person, people — more at LAND, LIBERAL] *pl of* LANDSMAN
¹**landslide** \ˈ=,=\ *n* [¹*land* + *slide*] **1 :** the rapid downward movement under the influence of gravity of a mass of rock, earth, or artificial fill on a slope; *also* **:** the mass that moves or has moved down **2 :** a great majority of votes for one side; *esp* **:** a one-sided election
²**landslide** \ˈ"\ *vi* **1 :** to produce a landslide **2 :** to win an election by a heavy majority
landslip \ˈ=,=\ *n* **:** LANDSLIDE 1
lands·mål *or* **lands·maal** \ˈlän(t)smȯl\ *n* -S *often cap* [Norw *landsmål* (formerly spelled *landsmaal*), fr. *land* country, land + *mål* speech] **:** a literary form of Norwegian based on the spoken dialects of Norway that dates from a grammar and dictionary by Ivar Aasen about 1850 and was designed as a national language distinct from that of Denmark — called also *New Norse;* compare RIKSMÅL
¹**lands·man** \ˈlan(d)zmən\ *n, pl* **landsmen** [*land's* (gen. of ¹*land*) + *man*] **1 :** a fellow countryman **2 :** one who lives on the land; *esp* **:** one who knows little or nothing of the sea **3 a** *obs* **:** a sailor on his first voyage **b :** a sailor who has had little experience and is rated below an ordinary seaman
²**lands·man** \ˈläntsmən\ *n, pl* **lands·leit** \-t,slīt\ [Yiddish, compatriot, fr. MHG *lantsman*, alter. of *lantman*, fr. OHG, fr. *lant* land + *man* — more at LAND, MAN] **:** a fellow Jew orig. from the same town or section esp. of eastern Europe ⟨friendly advice to a newly arrived ~⟩
lands·man·shaft \ˈläntsmən,shäft\ *n, pl* **landsmanshaf·ten** \-ftən\ [Yiddish, fr. G *landsmannschaft* association of compatriots, fr. *landsmann* compatriot (fr. MHG *lantsman*) + *-schaft* (fr. OHG *scaf-* ship)] **:** a Jewish association of landsleit organized esp. for social and philanthropic purposes
land snail *n* **:** a terrestrial gastropod usu. belonging to the pulmonate suborder Stylommatophora
landspout \ˈ=,=\ *n* **:** a phenomenon like a waterspout but occurring over land — compare TORNADO, WHIRLWIND
land station *n* **:** a radio transmitting station on land for communicating with mobile stations — compare AERONAUTICAL STATION
land steward *n* **:** a person who acts for another in management of land
land·sturm \ˈlänt,shtu̇rm\ *n* -S [G, orig., call to arms rendered by storm-warning bells, fr. *land* land (fr. OHG *lant*) + *sturm* storm (fr. OHG) — more at LAND, STORM] **1 :** a calling out of the militia **:** a general levy in time of war **2 :** MILITIA, HOME RESERVES
land–taxer \ˈ=,==\ *n* **:** an advocate of land taxes
land–tax parish *n* **:** a district in Great Britain separately assessed for the land tax
land tie *n* **:** a tie rod or chain used to connect a retaining wall, an outside flight of steps, or other structure to an anchor plate embedded in the earth behind it
land tortoise *or* **land turtle** *n* **:** any of various tortoises (family Testudinidae) that are usu. slow and clumsy in their movements and habitually live on dry land
land trash *n* **:** broken ice near shore
landtrost *var of* LANDDROST
land trust *n* **:** an unincorporated association for holding real estate by putting the title in one or more trustees for the benefit of the members
land up *vt* **:** to fill, surround, cover, or block with earth ⟨a channel that had been partly *landed up*⟩
land urchin *n* **:** HEDGEHOG
land·vogt \ˈlänt,fōkt\ *n* -S [G, fr. *land* land, province, country (fr. OHG *lant* land) + *vogt* bailiff, fr. OHG *fogat*, fr. ML *vocatus* legal representative — more at LAND, FOUD] **:** the governor of a German royal province or district
landwaiter \ˈ=,==\ *n* **:** a customs officer in England who takes account of imports for purposes of taxation and watches over and certifies to the observance of the prescribed form in the shipping of exports
¹**land·ward** \ˈlandwə(r)d, -aan-\ *also* **land·wards** \-)dz\ *adv* [*landward* fr. ME, fr. *land* + *-ward; landwards* fr. *landward* + *-s*] **:** toward the land — **to landward** *adv* **:** toward land **:** toward or on the landside
²**land·ward** \ˈlandərd\ *adj* **1** *Scot* **:** relating to or indicating the country **:** RURAL ⟨a decrease in the ~ population⟩ ⟨*landward*-bred⟩ **2** *also* **land·wards :** lying or being toward the land **:** being on the side toward the land ⟨on the ~ side Oslo is encircled by hills —Frederick Arnold⟩
land warrant *n* **:** a transferable certificate from the land office authorizing a person to assume possession of a specified quantity of public land
landwash \ˈ=,=\ *n* **1 :** the line of high tide **2 :** the wash of the sea on the shore
landway \ˈ=,=\ *n* **:** a path, road, or route on land ⟨seaways and ~s would continue to fulfil vital functions —William Walton⟩ ⟨upwarping of continents creates ~s over which terrestrial plants and animals may migrate —F.E.Clements & R.W.Cheney⟩
land·wehr \ˈlänt,vā(ə)r\ *n* -S [G, fr. MHG *lantwer* forces called for defense of the land, fr. OHG *lantweri* defense of the land, fr. *lant* land + *weri* defense — more at LAND, WEIR] **:** the part of the organized national armed forces (as in the former German and Austrian empires, Japan, Switzerland) that has completed the required service with the colors and constitutes the second line of defense
land wheel *n* **:** the wheel of a sulky plow which travels on the unplowed land
land·whin \ˈland,hwin, -n,dw-\ *n* -S *dial Eng* **:** RESTHARROW
land wind *n* **:** LAND BREEZE
landwire \ˈ=,=\ *n* **:** an electric service or communication line strung over the ground
landworker \ˈ=,==\ *n* **:** FARMHAND
landwrack *or* **landwreck** *n, obs* **:** destruction of something on land **:** RUIN, DEVASTATION
land yard *n, dial Eng* **:** a measure of length equal to a rod or a little more
¹**lane** \ˈlān\ *n* -S [ME, fr. OE *lane, lanu;* akin to OFris *lâne* lane, MD *lane* lane, ON *lön* row of houses, and perh. to Gk *elan* to drive — more at ELASTIC] **1 a :** a narrow passageway between fences or hedges that is not traveled as a highroad **b :** an alley between buildings **c :** a narrow way among trees, rocks, or other objects ⟨~ between rows of machines in a factory⟩ ⟨traffic ~ of a department store⟩ **2 :** a narrow passageway or track ⟨a ~ between lines of men⟩ **3 a** *or* **lane route :** a route across an ocean between specified degrees of latitude or longitude in which all steamers traveling in the same direction are supposed to keep in order to avoid collisions **b :** a channel of water in a floe or field of ice **c :** a strip of roadway adequate to accommodate a single line of vehicles **d :** AIR LANE **e :** any of several parallel courses marked out on a running track, rowing course, or swimming tank in which a competitor must stay during a race **f :** a bowling alley
²**lane** \ˈ"\ *vb* -ED/-ING/-S *vi* **:** to form a lane ⟨long sash of bloodred sun *laning* to the ship⟩ **:** separate into lanes ⟨*laning* of flowing liquids⟩ ~ *vt* **:** to make into lanes ⟨the road has been four-*laned*⟩
³**lane** \ˈ"\ *Scot var of* LONE
lane·ly \ˈlānlī\ *Scot var of* LONELY
lane snapper \ˈlān-\ *n* [prob. fr. the name *Lane*] **:** a small snapper (*Lutjanus synagris*) found from Florida to northern Brazil
lane·some \ˈlān(t)səm\ *Scot var of* LONESOME
la·ne·te \ˌlanəˈtē\ *n* -S [Tag *laniti*] **:** any of several Philippine trees or their wood: **a :** a valuable timber tree (*Wrightia laniti* of the family Apocynaceae) with soft wood that is used for carving and for musical instruments **b :** a tree (*Allaeanthus luzonicus*) of the family Moraceae having leaves and flowers that are cooked for food
laneway \ˈ=,=\ *n* [¹*lane* + *way*] *Brit* **:** LANE
¹**lang** \ˈlaŋ\ *now chiefly dial var of* LONG
²**lang** \", -ä-\ *n* -S [native name in India] **:** GRASS PEA
lang *abbr* language
lan·ga·ha \ˈlaŋˈgä(,)hä\ *n* -S [origin unknown] **:** a brownish red opisthoglyphous snake (*Langaha nasuta*) of Madagascar
lang·ban·ite \ˈlȯŋbə,nīt\ *n* -S [Sw *långbanit*, fr. *Långban*, Värmland, Sweden, its locality + Sw *-it* -ite] **:** a hexagonal mineral $(Mn,Sb,Ca,Fe,Mg)_9(SiO_4)$(?) occurring in iron-black prismatic crystals consisting of a manganese, iron, and antimony silicate and oxide (hardness 6.5; sp. gr. 4.92)
lang·bein·ite \ˈläŋ,bī,nīt\ *n* -S [G *langbeinit*, fr. A. *Langbein*, 19th cent. Ger. chemist + G *-it* -ite] **:** a mineral $K_2Mg_2(SO_4)_3$ much used in the fertilizer industry consisting of potassium magnesium double sulfate in colorless isometric crystals
lang·hans' layer \ˈläŋ,hänz-, -n(t)s\ *n, usu cap 1st L* [after Theodor *Langhans* †1915 Ger. pathologist] **:** CYTOTROPHOBLAST
lang·ite \ˈlaŋ,īt\ *n* -S [Victor von *Lang* †1921 Austrian physicist + E *-ite*] **:** a mineral $Cu_4(SO_4)(OH)_6.H_2O$ (?) composed of a basic hydrous sulfate of copper
lang·lauf \ˈläŋ,lau̇f\ *n* -S [G, fr. *lang* long (fr. OHG) + *lauf* race, run, running, fr. OHG *hlouf* — more at LONG, LEAP] **:** cross-country running or racing on skis — compare DAUERLAUF
lang·lau·fer \-,lau̇fə(r)\ *n, pl* **langlaufer** *or* **langlaufers** [G, fr. *lang* + *läufer* runner, racer, fr. MHG *loufære, löufære,*

fr. *loufen* to run (fr. OHG *hlouffan*) + *-ære* -er — more at LEAP] **:** a cross-country skier

lang lay \'laŋ-\ *n* [prob. fr. ¹*lang*] **:** a lay of a wire rope in which the wires in each strand are twisted in the same direction as the strands in the rope

lang·ley \'laŋlē\ *n* -s [after Samuel P. *Langley* †1906 Am. astronomer] **:** a unit of solar radiation equivalent to one gram calorie per square centimeter of irradiated surface

lan·go \'läŋ(,)gō\ *n, pl* **lango** *or* **langos** *usu cap* **1 a :** one of a group of Negro peoples in Uganda speaking dialects of a distinct language **b :** a member of such people **2 :** a Nilotic language of the Lango people

lan·go·bard \'laŋgə,bärd\ *n* -s *cap* [L *Langobardi*, pl. — more at LOMBARD] **:** LOMBARD 1

¹**lan·go·bar·dic** \¦==¦bärdik\ *adj, usu cap* [L *Langobardi* + E *-ic*] **:** of or relating to the Lombards

²**langobardic** \"\ *or* **lan·go·bar·di·an** \-dēən\ *n* -s *cap* **:** the West Germanic language of the Lombard people

langoon *n* -s [fr. *Langon*, town in southwestern France, its locality] *obs* **:** a French white wine

lan·goo·ty \,laŋ'güd·ē\ *n* -ES [Hindi *lāgoṭī*] **:** a piece of cloth hanging in front from a waistband worn by lower-class people in India

lan·gos·ta \laŋ'gästə\ *n* -s [AmerSp, fr. Sp, locust, European lobster, fr. (assumed) VL *lacusta*, alter. of L *locusta* — more at LOCUST] **:** a So. or Central American spiny lobster of the genus *Panulirus*

lan·gouste \(')läⁿ'güst\ *n* -s [F, fr. MF, fr. OProv *langosta*, fr. (assumed) VL *lacusta*] **:** SPINY LOBSTER; *esp* **:** the common European lobster (*Palinurus vulgaris*)

lan·grage \'laŋgrij\ *also* **lan·grel** \-rəl\ *n* -s [origin unknown] **:** shot formerly used in naval warfare for tearing sails and rigging and consisting of bolts, nails, and other pieces of iron fastened together or enclosed in a canister

lang·sat \'läŋ,sät\ *or* **lang·set** \-set\ *n* -s [Malay *langsat*] **:** LANSEH

langs·dorf·fia \(')laŋz¦dó(r)fēə\ *n, cap* [NL, fr. G. H. von *Langsdorff* †1852 Ger. physician + NL *-ia*] **:** a genus of parasitic fleshy yellow herbs (family Balanophoraceae) with purplish scales and yellow flowers

lang·shan \'laŋ,shan\ *n* [fr. *Langshan*, locality near Shanghai, China] **1** *usu cap* **:** an Asiatic breed of large single-combed domestic usu. black or white fowls resembling the Cochins but with longer neck, tail, and legs **2** -s *often cap* **:** any bird of the Langshan breed

lang·spiel *also* **lang·spil** \'laŋz,pē(ə)l, -ŋ(k),sp-\ *n* -s [Norw *langspil, langspel*, fr. *lang* long (fr. ON *langr*) + *spil, spel* play, fr. MLG *spil;* akin to OHG *spil* play — more at LONG, SPIEL] **:** a harp formerly played in the Shetland islands and Iceland

¹**lang syne** \(')laŋ'zīn, (')laiŋ-, -'sīn\ *adv* (*or adj*) [ME (Sc) *lang sine*, fr. *lang* long + *sine, syne* since — more at LONG, SYNE] *chiefly Scot* **:** at a distant time in the past

²**lang syne** \"\ *n, chiefly Scot* **:** times past **:** old times ⟨old men sat . . . and talked politics, racing, or *lang syne* —Ruth Park⟩

¹**lan·guage** \'laŋgwij, 'laiŋ-, -wēj *sometimes* -ŋw-\ *n* -s *often attrib* [ME *langage, language*, fr. OF, fr. *langue* tongue, language (fr. L *lingua*) + *-age* — more at TONGUE] **1 :** the words, their pronunciation, and the methods of combining them used and understood by a considerable community and established by long usage ⟨French ~⟩ ⟨Bantu group of ~*s*⟩ ⟨classical Latin is a dead ~⟩ ⟨~ barrier between two countries⟩ **2 a :** audible, articulate, meaningful sound as produced by the action of the vocal organs **b :** a systematic means of communicating ideas or feelings by the use of conventionalized signs, sounds, gestures, or marks having understood meanings ⟨finger ~⟩ ⟨~ of flowers⟩ ⟨~ of painting⟩ ⟨mathematics is a universally understood ~⟩ **c :** an artificially constructed primarily formal system of signs and symbols (as symbolic logic) including rules for the formation of admissible expressions and for their transformation — compare METALANGUAGE, OBJECT LANGUAGE, PHYSICAL LANGUAGE, SENSE-DATUM LANGUAGE, THING-LANGUAGE **d :** the means by which animals communicate or are thought to communicate with each other ⟨~ of the birds⟩ ⟨dog ~⟩ **3 a :** the faculty of verbal expression and the use of words in human intercourse ⟨~ exists only when it is listened to as well as spoken —John Dewey⟩ **:** significant communication **b** *archaic* **:** the faculty of speech; *esp* **:** ability to speak a foreign tongue **4 :** a special manner of use of expression: as **a :** form or manner of verbal expression ⟨elegant ~⟩ **:** characteristic mode of expression of an individual speaker or writer **:** STYLE ⟨figurative ~⟩ **b :** the vocabulary and phraseology belonging to an art or department of knowledge ⟨legal ~⟩ ⟨~ of chemistry⟩ ⟨~ of diplomacy⟩ ⟨a deep-voiced six-footer who talks the farmer's ~ —*Time*⟩ **c :** abusive epithets **:** PROFANITY ⟨shouldn't of blamed the fellers if they'd cut loose with some ~ —Ring Lardner⟩ **5** *obs* **:** TALK; *esp* **:** CENSURE, ABUSE ⟨safely venture to hold ~ —T.B.Macaulay⟩ **6 a** *archaic* **:** a people or nation as distinguished by its speech ⟨all the people, the nations, and the ~, fell down and worshiped the golden image —Dan 3: 7(AV)⟩ **b :** a national division of an international order ⟨~ of Aragon of the Hospitalers⟩

syn TONGUE, SPEECH, IDIOM, DIALECT: LANGUAGE is likely to indicate a more general and established and less specific and individual means of communication ⟨English and French are *languages*, that is to say they are systems of habits of speech, exactly like Eskimo or Hottentot or any other *language* —R.A.Hall b. 1911⟩ ⟨the noble *language* of Milton and Burke would have remained a rustic dialect, without a literature, a fixed grammar, or a fixed orthography —T.B.Macaulay⟩ TONGUE may suggest a more specific and narrowed concept than LANGUAGE ⟨a common language was the ancestor of both of these *tongues* [English and German] —*Publ's Mod. Lang. Assoc. of Amer.*⟩ SPEECH may call attention to the spoken rather than the written communication ⟨they argued, corresponded, delivered speeches, made jokes, and wrote satires in Latin. It was not a dead language but a living *speech* —Gilbert Highet⟩ IDIOM may suggest the more individual, specific, peculiar, and different from the general ⟨the French-English *idiom* of Louisiana as Mr. Cable presents it; the Negro-English idiom of the upper South as Mr. Harris presents it —A.J.Nock⟩ ⟨returning to the *idiom* of the Icelandic saga and to the metric of Langland —C.D.Lewis⟩ DIALECT may refer to a variant of a language, esp. one restricted to a limited area and one not entirely unintelligible to speakers of the language of which it is a phase ⟨the situation with regard to the American Indian languages, with many tribes speaking apparently unrelated languages which are in turn subdivided into *dialects*, is extremely complex —Thomas Pyles⟩ ⟨this language was once a *dialect* developed from a language which may be reconstructed from the historic tongues, and which is conventionally termed Proto-Teutonic —L. H.Gray⟩. In general literary use these terms are often interchangeable ⟨from her early years she must have treasured up those pithy bits of local *speech*, of native *idiom*, which enrich and enliven her pages. The *language* her people speak to each other is a native *tongue* —Willa Cather⟩

²**language** \"\ *vt* -ED/-ING/-S *dial* **:** to express in language

³**language** \"\ *n* -s [by folk etymology fr. *languet*] **:** LANGUET 2a

language arts *n pl* **:** the subjects (as reading, spelling, literature, composition, debate, dramatics) taught in elementary and secondary schools that aim at developing the learner's comprehension of written and oral language as well as his use of it for communication and expression

languaged \-jd; *stressed* \¦==\ *adj* [ME *langaged*, fr. *langage* language + ¹*-ed*] **1 :** skilled in language **:** learned in languages **:** having a language **:** using a specified kind of speech — used usu. with a qualifying word ⟨well-*languaged* man⟩ **2 :** expressed in language ⟨beautifully ~ sermons⟩

lan·guage·less *pronunc at* ¹LANGUAGE + ləs\ *adj* **:** having no language

langue \'läⁿg\ *n* -s [F — more at LANGUAGE] **1 :** LANGUAGE 6b **2 :** language that is a system of elements or a set of habits common to a community of speakers — contrasted with *parole*

langued \'laŋd\ *adj* [MF *langue* + E *-ed*] *heraldry* **:** having the tongue visible and of a specified tincture ⟨lion armed and ~ gules⟩

langue de boeuf \¦läŋdə¦bə(r)f, -bəf\ *n, pl* **langues de boeuf** \"\ [ME *lange de boef*, fr. MF *langue de bœuf*, lit., ox tongue] **:** a pike with a blade very wide at the head and tapering rapidly to a point used esp. in the 15th century; *also* **:** a short sword or dagger of this shape

langue d'oc *or* **langue·doc** \läŋ'dök, läⁿgdök\ *n* [F, fr. OF, lit., language of *oc;* fr. the use of the word *oc* for "yes" in contrast to the use of the word *oïl* for "yes" in northern France] **:** PROVENÇAL

¹**langue·do·cian** \¦laŋ(g)(w)ə¦dōshən, (')laŋ¦d-\ *adj, usu cap* [*Languedoc*, region in south central France + E *-ian*] **:** of or relating to Languedoc

²**languedocian** \"\ *n* -s *cap* **1 :** a native or inhabitant of Languedoc **2** [F *langue d'oc* + E *-ian*] **:** the Provençal dialect

langue d'oïl \läŋ'dói(ə)l; läⁿgdöil, -döēl,-döy\ *n* [F, fr. OF, lit., language of *oïl;* fr. the use of the word *oïl* for "yes" in contrast to the use of the word *oc* for "yes" in Provençal] **:** FRENCH 1

lan·gues·cent \(')laŋ¦gwesᵊnt\ *adj* [L *languescent-, languescens*, pres. part. of *languescere* to become faint, incho. of *languēre* to be faint — more at SLACK] **:** becoming languid or fatigued

lan·guet *also* **lan·guette** \'laŋgwət, (')laŋ¦gwet\ *n* -s [ME *languet, languette*, fr. MF *languete, languette*, dim. of *langue* tongue — more at LANGUAGE] **1 :** something resembling the tongue in form or function: as **a :** LATCHET 2 **b :** a part of a sword hilt that overlaps the scabbard **c :** a tongue of land **2 a :** the inner tongue or flat plate opposite the mouth of an organ flue pipe — called also *languid* **b :** the tongue of a harmonium or organ reed **c :** the finger key of a wind instrument **d :** the tongue of a harpsichord jack **3 :** one of the small pointed processes on the median line of the branchial sac of certain ascidians

¹**lan·guid** \'laŋgwəd, 'laiŋ-\ *adj* [MF *languide*, fr. L *languidus*, fr. *languēre* to languish, be languid — more at SLACK] **1 :** drooping or flagging from or as if from exhaustion **:** lacking vigor **:** WEAK ⟨arms too ~ with happiness to embrace him —John Galsworthy⟩ **2 :** sluggish in character or disposition **:** DULL, LISTLESS ⟨~ enjoyment of the daydream —Nathaniel Hawthorne⟩ ⟨stretched out a ~ hand —Dorothy Sayers⟩ **3 :** lacking force or vividness **:** SLOW ⟨heard . . . in a moment of exhausted or ~ interest —A.T.Quiller-Couch⟩ ⟨contrast between his huge bulk and his ~, almost effeminate, demeanor —Robert Hichens⟩

syn LANGUISHING, LANGUOROUS, LACKADAISICAL, LISTLESS, SPIRITLESS, ENERVATED: LANGUID may indicate an inability or indisposition to exert or concern oneself owing to weakness, malaise, or ennui ⟨she turned and walked from the room with *languid* deliberate steps; her air was curiously apathetic, and she moved as though she were intolerably weary —Elinor Wylie⟩ ⟨struck by something *languid* and inelastic in her attitude, and wondered if the deadly monotony of their lives had laid its weight on her also —Edith Wharton⟩ LANGUISHING may suggest delicate indolence, often accompanying boredom or futilely wistful pensiveness ⟨the pair had completely lost their pallid looks and *languishing* manners; they were as bright-eyed and agile as the hares —Elinor Wylie⟩ LANGUOROUS may suggest the debilitated languidness characteristic of soft, delicate living, effete shrinking from exertion, and indulgence in emotionalism and sentimentality or an atmosphere compatible with such languidness ⟨reclining on the couch reading a novel in *languorous* ease⟩ LACKADAISICAL suggests an indifferent or apathetic and inattentive attitude militating against exertion and for futile, halfhearted performance ⟨had the gift of instilling a corresponding vigor into all his *lackadaisical* black soldiers, who at first sight seemed to be hopelessly addicted to lolling under a bush, and inflexibly determined to do nothing —Kenneth Roberts⟩ LISTLESS suggests combined lack of sustained interest and appearance of languor, esp. as brought about by ennui, boredom, or illness ⟨was struck by her *listless* attitude: she sat there as if she had nothing else to do —Edith Wharton⟩ ⟨struck with the *listless*, slovenly behavior of these men; there was nothing of the national vivacity in their movements; nothing of the quick precision perceptible on the deck of a thoroughly disciplined armed vessel —Herman Melville⟩ SPIRITLESS applies to utter lack of fire, animation, or force ⟨for once she did not greet him with flowery excitement but with a noncommittal "Hello". She seemed *spiritless* —Sinclair Lewis⟩ ⟨dominated the starving, *spiritless* wretches under him with savage enjoyment —F.V.W.Mason⟩ ENERVATED implies a tiring out, exhausting, and sapping, often by luxury or sloth ⟨the *enervated* and sickly habits of the literary class —R.W.Emerson⟩ ⟨*enervated* by licentiousness, ruined by prodigality and enslaved by sycophants —T.B.Macaulay⟩

²**languid** \"\ *n* -s [by alter.] **:** LANGUET 2a

lan·guid·ly *adv* **:** a languid manner

lan·guid·ness *n* -ES **:** the quality or state of being languid

¹**lan·guish** \'laŋgwish, 'laiŋ-, -wēsh, *esp in pres part* -wəsh\ *vi* -ED/-ING/-ES [ME *languishen, languissen*, fr. MF *languiss-*, stem of *languir*, fr. (assumed) VL *languire*, fr. L *languēre*] **1 :** to become languid **:** lose strength or animation **:** be or become dull, feeble, or spiritless **:** lose force or vividness ⟨conversation ~*ed*⟩ **:** FADE ⟨plants ~ in the drought⟩ **2 :** to be or live in a state of lessened or lessening strength or vitality **:** DROOP ⟨~*ing* spirits⟩ **:** pine with longing ⟨~ for years in prison⟩ **:** suffer neglect ⟨contract . . . has ~*ed* in committee ever since —*Newsweek*⟩ **3 :** to assume an expression of weariness or tender grief or emotion appealing for sympathy ⟨~*ed* at him through screwed-up eyes —Edith Wharton⟩

²**languish** \"\ *n* -ES [ME, fr. *languishen*, v.] *archaic* **1 :** the act or state of languishing ⟨one desperate grief cures with another's ~ —Shak.⟩ **2 :** a languishing tender look or expression ⟨the warm, dark ~ of her eyes —J.G.Whittier⟩

lan·guish·er \-shə(r)\ *n* -s **:** one that languishes

lan·guish·ing *adj* [ME, fr. pres. part. of *languishen* to languish] **1 a :** losing health and strength ⟨could not rouse him from his ~ state⟩ **b :** LINGERING ⟨~ illness⟩ **2 :** expressing longing, desire, or tender sentiment ⟨exchanged ~ glances⟩ **syn** see LANGUID

lan·guish·ing·ly *adv* **:** in a languishing manner ⟨drooped her eyelids ~⟩

lan·guish·ment \-shmənt\ *n* -s [MF *languissement*, fr. *languiss-* + *-ment*] **1** *archaic* **:** the act or state of languishing **:** ILLNESS, WEAKNESS, SADNESS, LASSITUDE **2** *archaic* **:** tenderness of look or bearing **:** amorous pensiveness

lan·guor \'laŋ(g)ə(r), 'laiŋ-\ *n* -s [ME *langour, langor*, fr. OF, fr. L *languor*, fr. *languēre* to feel faint, languish — more at SLACK] **1** *obs* **:** enfeebling disease **:** SUFFERING **2 :** a state of the body or mind caused by exhaustion or disease and characterized by a languid feeling **:** LASSITUDE ⟨~ of convalescence⟩ **3 :** listless indolence **:** DREAMINESS ⟨certain ~ in the air hinted at an early summer —James Purdy⟩ **4 :** DULLNESS, SLUGGISHNESS **:** lack of vigor **:** STAGNATION ⟨from ~ she passed to the lightest vivacity —Elinor Wylie⟩

lan·guor·ous \-ŋ(g)(ə)rəs\ *adj* [MF *langoureux*, fr. *langour* + *-eux* -ous] **1** *obs* **:** GRIEVOUS, SORROWFUL **2 :** producing or tending to produce languor ⟨~ climate⟩ **:** characterized by languor ⟨haunting ~ verse —*Times Lit. Supp.*⟩ **syn** see LANGUID

lan·guor·ous·ly *adv* **:** in a languorous manner ⟨sprawling ~ on a sofa⟩

lan·gur *also* **lun·goor** \,ləŋ'gü(ə)r\ *n* -s [Hindi *lāgūr*, prob. fr. Skt *lāṅgūlin* having a (long) tail] **:** any of various Asiatic long-tailed monkeys that with the proboscis monkey and the African guerezas constitute a family (Colobidae) and are of slender build, usu. gray or brownish gray in color, and have bushy eyebrows and a chin tuft

lani- — see LAN-

laniard *var of* LANYARD

lani·ar·i·us \,lānē'a(a)rēəs, ,lan-\ *n, cap* [NL, fr. L, butcher, fr. *laniarius* of a butcher] **:** a genus of African shrikes comprising the boubous

lani·ary \'==,erē\ *adj* [L *laniarius* of a butcher, fr. *lanius* butcher (prob. of Etruscan origin like L *lanista*) + *-arius* -ary] *of teeth* **:** adapted for tearing **:** CANINE

lani·ate \-ē,āt\ *vt* -ED/-ING/-S [L *laniatus*, past part. of *laniare* to rend, prob. fr. *lanius* butcher] **:** to tear in pieces

la·ni·idae \lə'nīə,dē\ *n pl, cap* [NL, fr. *Lanius*, type genus + *-idae*] **:** a family of dentirostral oscine birds consisting of the true shrikes and various related birds

laning *pres part of* LANE

la·nis·ta \lə'nistə\ *n, pl* **lanis·tae** \-,stē, -,stī\ [L, of Etruscan origin] **:** a trainer of gladiators in ancient Rome

la·ni·us \'lānēəs\ *n, cap* [NL, fr. L, butcher] **:** a genus consisting of the typical shrikes

lank \'laŋk, -aiŋk\ *adj* -ER/-EST [fr. (assumed) ME *lank*, fr. OE *hlanc;* akin to OHG *hlanca* loin, flank, ON *hlykkr* bend, noose, L *clingere* to girdle, OSlav *klęčati* to kneel; basic meaning: bending] **1 :** slender and thin **:** not well filled out **:** not plump ⟨meager and ~ with fasting grown —Jonathan Swift⟩ ⟨~ cattle⟩ **:** SCANTY, MEAGRE ⟨~ grass⟩ **2** *archaic* **:** LANGUID, DROOPING ⟨reared her ~ head —John Milton⟩ **3** *of hair* **:** hanging straight and limp without spring or curl **syn** see LEAN

lank·i·ly \-kəlē, -li\ *adv* **:** in a lanky manner **:** so as to suggest lankiness

lank·i·ness \-kēnəs, -kin-\ *n* -ES **:** the quality or state of being lanky

lank·ish \-kish,-kēsh\ *adj* **:** somewhat lank

lank·ly *adv* **:** in a lank manner **:** LIMPLY

lank·ness *n* -ES **:** the quality or state of being lank

lanky \'laŋkē, -aiŋ-, -ki\ *adj* -ER/-EST **:** tall, spare, and usu. loose-jointed **:** BONY, RAWBONED ⟨that tall, blond, ~ girl who had followed him about everywhere —Louis Auchincloss⟩ **syn** see LEAN

lan·ner \'lanə(r)\ *n* -s [ME *laner*, fr. MF *lanier*, short for *faucon lanier*, fr. OF, fr. *faucon* falcon + *lanier* cowardly, fr. *lanier* woolworker, coward, fr. L *lanarius* woolworker, fr. *lana* wool + *-arius* -ary — more at WOOL] **:** a falcon (*Falco biarmicus feldeggii*) of southern Europe or a member of a related variety in southwestern Asia or Africa that resembles the American prairie falcon; *specif* **:** the female of one of these falcons

lan·ner·et \¦lanə¦ret\ *n* -s [ME *lanerette, lanret*, fr. MF *laneret*, dim. of *lanier* lanner] **:** a male lanner

lano- — see LAN-

lan·o·ceric acid \¦lanə¦sil·rik-, -se|\ *n* [ISV *lan-* + *cer-* + *-ic*] **:** a crystalline dihydroxy acid $(HO)_2C_{29}H_{57}COOH$ found as an ester in wool grease

lan·o·lat·ed \'lanᵊl,ād·əd\ *adj* [*lanolin* + *-ate* + *-ed*] **:** containing lanolin ⟨~ hand cream⟩ ⟨~ soap⟩

lan·o·lin \'lanᵊlən\ *also* **lan·o·line** \", -ᵊl,ēn\ *n* -s [ISV *lan-* + *-ol* + *-in, -ine;* orig. formed as G *lanolin*] **:** wool grease refined for use chiefly in ointments and cosmetics: **a :** a yellowish sticky unctuous mass absorbable by the skin and containing incorporated water — called also *hydrous wool fat* **b :** a similar brownish yellow anhydrous mass — called also *anhydrous lanolin, refined wool fat*

lan·o·lize \-ᵊl,īz\ *vt* -ED/-ING/-S [*lanolin* + *-ize*] **:** to add lanolin or lanolin derivatives to (as soap)

la·nose \'lā,nōs\ *adj* [L *lanosus*, fr. *lana* wool + *-osus* -ose — more at LANATE, WOOLLY — **la·nos·i·ty** \lā'näsəd·ē, lə'-\ *n* -ES

la·nos·ter·ol \lə'nästə,rōl, -rōl\ *n* -s [*lan-* + *sterol*] **:** a crystalline tetracyclic alcohol $C_{30}H_{49}OH$ that occurs in wool grease and yeast and may be regarded as a triterpenoid sterol

läns *pl of* LÄN

Lans·downe \'lanz,daůn\ *trademark* — used for a fine lightweight dress fabric in twill weave with a silk or rayon warp and a worsted or cotton filling

lan·seh *also* **lan·sa** \'lan(t)sə\ *or* **lan·sat** \-sət\ *n* -s [of Indonesian origin; akin to Malay *langsat* lanseh] **1 :** the edible yellow berry of an East Indian tree (*Lansium domesticum*) of the family Meliaceae **2 :** the tree that bears the lanseh

lans·ford·ite \'lan(t)sfə(r)‚dīt, -anzf-\ *n* -s [G *lansfordit*, fr. *Lansford*, Pa., its locality + G *-it* -ite] **:** a mineral $MgCO_3 \cdot 5H_2O$ composed of a hydrous basic carbonate of magnesium like paraffin when first taken out of the ground but altering to nesquehonite on exposure

lan·sing \'lan(t)siŋ, 'laan-,'lain-, -sēŋ\ *adj, usu cap* [fr. *Lansing*, Mich.] **:** of or from Lansing, the capital of Michigan **:** of the kind or style prevalent in Lansing ⟨a *Lansing* product⟩

lansing virus *also* **lansing strain** *n, usu cap L* **:** a strain of the virus causing poliomyelitis that is pathogenic for monkeys and rodents and has been extensively used in study of the disease

lanson *var of* LANZON

lans·que·net \'lan(t)skə‚net, -anzk-, -kə¦nā\ *n* -s [F, modif. of G *landsknecht*, fr. MHG *landsknecht*, fr. *lands* (gen. of *lant* land, country, province, fr. OHG) + *kneht* boy, youth, foot soldier, fr. OHG, boy, youth, military follower — more at LAND, KNIGHT] **1 :** a German foot soldier in foreign service in the 15th, 16th, and 17th centuries **:** a mercenary foot soldier **2 :** a card game similar to faro played in central Europe since the 15th century or before

lant \'lant\ *n* -s [back-formation fr. *lants* (taken as pl.), alter. of *launce, lance*] **:** SAND LAUNCE

lan·ta·ka *or* **lan·ta·ca** \¦län¦tä¦kä\ *n* -s [Tag *lantakà*] **:** a Philippine piece of artillery like a culverin

lan·ta·na \lan'tānə\ *n* [NL, fr. ML or NL, viburnum, fr. It dial. (Switzerland and northern Italy)] **1** *cap* **:** a genus of tropical sometimes half-climbing shrubs (family Verbenaceae) having umbellate heads of small bright-colored flowers and juicy drupaceous fruit — see RED SAGE **2** -s **:** any plant of the genus *Lantana*

lanterloo *n* [F *lanturelu, lanturlu* piffle — more at LOO] *obs* **:** LOO

¹**lan·tern** *R* 'lantərn, 'laan-,'lain-, *-R* -tən *also* -tᵊn\ *n* -s *often attrib* [ME *lanterne*, fr. MF, fr. L *lanterna*, fr. Gk *lamptēr* stand for holding a torch, lantern, fr. *lampein* to give light, shine — more at LAMP] **1 :** a protective enclosure for a light with transparent openings and often a supporting frame or carrying handle **:** a portable lamp **2 :** a giver of light ⟨~ of science⟩ **3 a** *obs* **:** LIGHTHOUSE **b :** the chamber in a lighthouse that contains the light **c :** a structure with glazed or open sides raised above an opening in a roof to light or ventilate the interior space below **:** MONITOR 5 **d :** a small tower or cupola or one stage of a cupola **4 a :** a foundry lamp **b :** CORE BARREL **c :** LANTERN PINION **5 :** ARISTOTLE'S LANTERN **6 :** PROJECTOR 2b

lanterns 1: *1* barn, *2* bull's-eye

²**lantern** \"\ *vt* -ED/-ING/-S **1 :** to furnish with a lantern ⟨~ a lighthouse⟩ ⟨~ a fishing boat⟩ **:** light the way of with a lantern **2** [F *lanterner*, fr. *lanterne* lantern, street lamp] **:** to put to death by hanging to a street lamppost

lantern clock *n* **1 :** a clock designed to be mounted in a wall and having its driving weights together with their supporting cords and the greater part of the pendulum outside of the case **2 :** a brass pendulum or foliot shelf clock of the 17th century whose chief features are a dome formed by a bell and open fretwork connecting the bell and dial

lantern fish *n* **1 :** any of numerous small mostly deep-sea fishes constituting the family Myctophidae that have a large mouth and large eyes and usu. numerous luminous spots or glands upon the body **2 :** a fish of the order Iniomi

lantern flounder *n* **:** ²MEGRIM a

lantern fly *n* **:** any of certain usu. large and brightly colored insects that are chiefly of the genera *Laternaria* and *Fulgora* of the family Fulgoridae and that have the front of the head prolonged into a large hollow vesicle formerly supposed to be luminous; *broadly* **:** an insect of the superfamily Fulgoroidea

lantern gurnard *n* **:** a European gurnard (*Trigla obscura*) having a brilliant silvery band along the sides

lantern jaw *n* **1 :** an undershot jaw **2 lantern jaws** *pl* **:** long thin jaws

lantern-jawed \¦==¦=\ *adj* **:** having a lantern jaw

lanternleaf \'==,=\ *n* [alter. of *Lenten leaf*] **:** CREEPING CROWFOOT

lantern light *n* **1 :** a transparent pane in a lantern **2 :** a skylight raised above the roof level

lan·tern·man \'==,man, -,mən\ *n, pl* **lanternmen :** a man who carries a lantern; *specif* **:** NIGHTMAN 1

lantern pinion *n* **:** a gear pinion having cylindrical bars instead of teeth inserted at their ends in two parallel disks — called also *trundle*

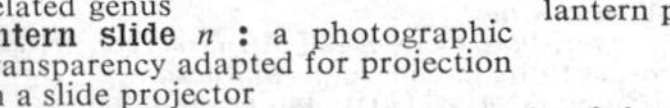
lantern pinion and spur gear

lantern ring *n* **:** a packing ring for shaft or piston-rod glands having a cross section resembling the letter H

lantern shell *n* **:** a translucent marine bivalve shell of *Laternula* or a related genus

lantern slide *n* **:** a photographic transparency adapted for projection in a slide projector

lantern sprat *n* **:** the common sprat when infested with a phosphorescent lernaean parasite (*Lerneonema monilaris*)

lan·tha·na \ˈlan(t)thənə\ *n* -s [NL, fr. *lanthanum* + *-a*] **:** lanthanum oxide La_2O_3 obtained as a white powder

lan·tha·nide \-thəˌnīd, -ˌnəd\ *n* -s [ISV *lanthan-* (fr. NL *lanthanum*) + *-ide*] **:** a chemical element of the lanthanide series — called also *lanthanon*; symbol *Ln*

lanthanide contraction *n* **:** the decrease in size (as of radii of atoms or ions or of atomic volumes) with increasing atomic number of the metals of the lanthanide series

lanthanide series *n* **:** the group of rare-earth metals often including lanthanum and sometimes yttrium — compare PERIODIC TABLE

lan·tha·nite \-ˌnīt\ *n* -s [G *lanthanit*, fr. NL *lanthanum* + G *-it* -ite] **:** a mineral $(La,Ce)_2(CO_3)_3.8H_2O$ composed of hydrous lanthanum carbonate occurring in white crystals or earthy

lan·tha·non \-ˌnän, -ˌnən\ *n* -s [NL, alter. of *lantha*] **:** LANTHANIDE

lan·tha·no·tus \ˌ==ˈnōd·əs\ *n, cap* [NL, fr. Gk *lanthanein* to escape notice + *ōt-, ous* ear — more at LATENT, EAR] **:** a genus of stout-bodied pleurodont lizards including a single species (*L. borneensis*) of Borneo

lan·tha·num \ˈlan(t)thənəm\ *n* -s [NL, fr. Gk *lanthanein* to escape notice] **:** a white soft malleable trivalent metallic element that tarnishes readily in moist air and forms colorless compounds, that occurs in rare-earth minerals and is usu. included in the rare-earth group, and that is one of the major components of misch metal — symbol *La*; see ELEMENT table

lan·thi·o·nine \lanˈthīəˌnēn, -ˌnən\ *n* -s [*lan-* + *thion-* + *-ine*] **:** an amino acid $S[CH_2CH(NH_2)COOH]_2$ obtained esp. by the action of alkali on wool, hair, or cystine

lan·tho·pine \ˈlan(t)thəˌpēn, -ˌpən\ *n* -s [ISV *lanth-* (fr. Gk *lanthanein*) + *opium* + *-ine*; orig. formed as G *lanthopin*] **:** a crystalline alkaloid $C_{23}H_{25}NO_4$ found in opium

lant·horn \ˈlantˌhȯrn, -ō(ə)n, *or like* LANTERN\ *n* -s [by folk-etymology (influence of ¹*horn*, of which the sides were formerly made) fr. *lantern*] *chiefly Brit* **:** LANTERN

lants *pl of* LANT

lantskip *obs var of* LANDSCAPE

lan·tum \ˈlantəm\ *n* -s [origin unknown] **:** a large hurdy-gurdy

la·nu·gi·nous \ləˈn(y)üjənəs\ *also* **la·nu·gi·nose** \-jəˌnōs\ *adj* [L *lanuginosus*, fr. *lanugin-, lanugo* + *-osus* -ous, -ose] **:** covered with down or fine soft hair **:** DOWNY — **la·nu·gi·nous·ness** *n* -ES

la·nu·go \ləˈn(y)ü(ˌ)gō\ *n* -s [L, down — more at WOOL] **:** a dense cottony or downy growth; *specif* **:** the soft woolly hair that covers the human fetus and that of some other mammals; *also* **:** hair of this type persisting after birth; DOWN

la·nu·vi·an \ləˈn(y)üvēən\ *n* -s *cap* [*Lanuvium*, city in ancient Latium, Italy + E *-an*] **:** the language of ancient Lanuvium that was closely related to Latin

lanx \ˈlaŋ(k)s, -ä-\ *n, pl* **lan·ces** \ˈlanˌsēz, ˈläŋˌkās\ [L — more at BALANCE] **:** an ancient Roman platter usu. of metal

lan·yard *also* **lan·iard** \ˈlanyə(r)d\ *n* -s [ME *lanyer*, fr. MF *laniere*, fr. OF *lasniere* strap, thong, noose, prob. modif. (influenced by *laz* snare, noose) of a word of Gmc origin; akin to OHG *nestila*, *nestilo* bow, band, shoelace, OS *nestila* string, hair band, OE *net* — more at LACE, NET] **1** *obs* **:** THONG, STRAP **2 a :** a piece of rope or line for fastening something in ships; *esp* **:** one of the pieces passing through deadeyes and used to extend shrouds or stays **b :** a line for raising and lowering flags and pennants **3 a :** a cord worn around the neck by sailors to which is usu. attached a knife — called also *knife lanyard* **b :** a cord worn by members of a military unit cited for distinction as a symbol of the unit citation **c :** a strong cord worn about the neck or shoulder and attached to a pistol **4 :** a strong cord with a hook at one end used in firing cannon

lanyard knot *n* **:** STOPPER KNOT

lan·zon \länˈzōn, -ˈsōn\ *or* **lanson** \-ˈsōn\ *n, pl* **lanzo·nes** \-näs\ *or* **lanso·nes** \-näs\ [PhilSp *lanzón, lansón*] **:** LANSEH

¹**lao** \ˈlau̇\ *n, pl* **lao** *or* **laos** *cap* **1 a :** a Buddhist people living in Laos and adjacent parts of northeastern Thailand and constituting an important branch of the Tai race **b :** a member of such people **2 :** the Thai language of the Lao people

²**lao** \"\ *also* **lao·tian** \(ˈ)lāˈōshən, ˈlau̇shən\ *adj, usu cap* [*Laotian* fr. ¹*Lao* + connective *-t-* + E *-ian*] **:** of or relating to the Lao people

la·oc·o·on \lāˈäkəˌwän\ *n* -s *often cap* [after *Laocoon*, ancient Greek priest of Apollo (fr. Gk *Laokoōn*) who is portrayed in a 1st cent. B.C. sculpture in a heroic struggle against two giant serpents] **:** one that struggles heroically with crushing or baffling difficulties ⟨a man engaged in a *Laocoon* struggle with his imagination —Robert Lynd⟩ ⟨gives the impression of being . . . forced into ~ attitudes —Graham Greene⟩

lao·dah *also* **low·dah** \ˈlau̇ˈdä\ *n* -s [Chin (Pek) *lao³ ta⁴*, fr. *lao³* old + *ta⁴* great] **:** the skipper of a Chinese craft

¹**la·od·i·ce·an** \(ˌ)lāˌädəˈsēən\ *adj, usu cap* [*Laodicea*, ancient city in Asia Minor (fr. L, fr. Gk *Laodikeia*) + E *-an*] **1 :** of or relating to ancient Laodicea, a city of Asia Minor and site of an early Christian church **2 :** lukewarm or indifferent in religion or politics

²**laodicean** \"\ *n* -s *usu cap* **1 :** a native or inhabitant of ancient Laodicea; *esp* **:** a member of the Laodicean church **2 :** one that is lukewarm or indifferent

la·od·i·ce·an·ism \(ˌ)=ˌ===ˈsēəˌnizəm\ *n* -s *usu cap* **:** indifference in religion or politics

laoighis \ˈlāsh, ˈlēsh\ *adj, usu cap* [fr. *Laoighis* county, Ireland] **:** of or from County Laoighis, Ireland **:** of the kind or style prevalent in County Laoighis

laos \ˈlau̇s, ˈlāˌäs *sometimes* ˈlāōs, *chiefly Brit* ˈlau̇z\ *adj, usu cap* [fr. *Laos*, kingdom in Indochina] **:** of or from the kingdom of Laos **:** of the kind or style prevalent in Laos

lao·tian \lāˈōshən, ˈlau̇shən\ *n* -s *cap* [¹*Lao* + connective *-t-* + E *-ian*] **:** one of the Lao people

¹**lap** \ˈlap\ *n* -s [ME *lappe*, fr. OE *læppa*; akin to OFris *lappa* flap, OS *lappo* lappet, OHG *lappa* flap, lappet, ON *leppr* rag, L *labi* to glide, slide — more at SLEEP] **1 a :** a loose panel or free-hanging flap esp. of a garment — called also *lappet* **b** *archaic* **:** the skirt of a coat or dress ⟨with the ~ of my coat cast over my face —Sir Walter Scott⟩ **c :** the front edges of a jacket or coat that come together in a double layer when closed **2 a** *obs* **:** a loose or pendent bodily organ (as a lobe of the liver or the lungs) **b :** a pendent protrusion of the body — usu. used in combination ⟨ear*lap*⟩ ⟨dew*lap*⟩ **3 a** (1) **:** the clothing that lies on the knees, thighs, and lower part of the trunk when one sits down (2) **:** the front part of the lower trunk and thighs of a seated person ⟨sit on grandpa's ~⟩ **b :** an environment of nurture ⟨reared in the ~ of luxury⟩ **c :** a concave surface resembling that of a lap ⟨a green lake sparkling in the ~ of a pine-clad mountain —C.B.Davis⟩ **4** *obs* **a :** a fold of a garment used as a repository; *specif* **:** a chest fold (as of a toga) used as a pocket **b :** BOSOM ⟨brought back again into the ~ of the Romish Church —Edward Bowles⟩ **5 :** responsible custody **:** CHARGE, CONTROL ⟨going to drop the whole thing in your ~ —Hamilton Basso⟩ ⟨the outcome of this experiment is in the ~ of the gods⟩ ⟨the gold of Asia Minor was poured into the ~ of the pre-Hellenes —Edward Clodd⟩

²**lap** \"\ *vb* **lapped**; **lapped**; **lapping**; **laps** [ME *lappen*, fr. *lappe*, n.] *vt* **1 a** (1) **:** to fold over or around something **:** WIND ⟨~ a bandage around the wrist⟩ (2) **:** to enclose in a cover or binding **:** WRAP ⟨~ the wrist in a bandage⟩ **b :** to envelop entirely **:** SURROUND, SWATHE ⟨life flowed smoothly on *lapping* him in a changeless amber vacuum —A.J.Shirren⟩ ⟨no pains had been spared . . . to ~ them in tasteful and simple luxury —Lucius Beebe⟩ **2 :** to fold over esp. into layers: as **a :** to convert (cotton, wool, flax, or other fiber) into a lap **b** (1) **:** to fold (paper pulp) into a lap (2) **:** to fold (paper) for packaging by laying one set of sheets halfway along another set and rolling each overlapping end over each overlapped end **3 :** to hold protectively in or as if in the lap **:** CUDDLE, NESTLE ⟨legs that were intended to . . . ~ her children —A.R.Foff⟩ ⟨hills . . . fruitful valleys *lapped* in them —Thomas Carlyle⟩ **4 a :** to place over or next to so as to partially or wholly cover **:** OVERLAP ⟨~ shingles in laying a roof⟩ **b :** to unite (as beams or timbers) so as to preserve the same breadth and depth throughout — compare ⁴SCARF 1 **5 a :** to dimension, smooth, or polish (as a metal surface or body) to a high degree of refinement or accuracy with a lap or loose abrasive material ⟨*lapping* is an abrading process for refining the surface finish and geometrical accuracy of flat, cylindrical, and spherical surfaces —K.B.Lewis⟩ ⟨bearing surfaces are ground, *lapped*, and honed to a precision mirror finish —Joseph Heitner⟩ **b :** to work two surfaces together with or without abrasives until a very close fit is produced — often used with *in* ⟨the valve is hand *lapped* in its seat with very light pressure and just for long enough to be sure valve is perfectly tight in its seat —H.F.Blanchard & Ralph Ritchen⟩ **6 a :** to lead (an opponent) by one or more circuits of a racecourse ⟨the champion *lapped* him at the mile⟩ **b :** to complete the circuit of ⟨*lapped* the course in 3 minutes 8 seconds —*N.Y. Herald Tribune*⟩ ~ *vi* **1 :** FOLD, WIND ⟨crowds . . . *lapped* around the corner —*Time*⟩ **2 a :** to project beyond or spread over ⟨long enough to ~ 1″ over the toepiece —*Amer. Girl*⟩ ⟨ranchrias *lapped* a few miles over the eastern bank of the Sacramento —Julian Dana⟩ **b :** to lie partly over or alongside of something or of one another ⟨formation flying so tight that the wings ~⟩ ⟨the edges of the coat ~ deeply⟩ **c :** to use newly received funds to cover up a previous shortage **:** KITE **3 :** to traverse a course ⟨the experimental racer *lapped* at unprecedented speed⟩

³**lap** \"\ *n* -s *often attrib* **1 a :** the amount by which one object overlaps or projects beyond another: as (1) **:** the distance one course of shingle or slate roofing extends over the second one below (2) **:** the part that overlaps to form a seam or joint (as the beveled ends joining sections of an endless belt) (3) **:** the distance that a steam-engine slide valve in its middle position has to move to begin to open the steam or exhaust port (4) **:** the distance one steel plate overlaps another (as in the shell plating of a ship) — compare LAPSTRAKE **b :** the part of an object that overlaps another ⟨the front ~ of a winter coat should be at least six inches wide⟩ **2 :** a smoothing and polishing tool commonly in the form of a piece of wood, leather, felt, or soft metal used with or without an embedded abrasive **3 :** a doubling or layering of a flexible substance: as **a :** a fleecy sheet or layer of combed fibers (as of cotton, wool, or flax) usu. wrapped on a cylinder and ready to be spun **b :** a sheet of wet paper pulp from a wet machine folded into convenient size for handling and shipping **c :** a surface defect in steel or glass caused by the folding over on itself of a part of the molten material and the failure of the surfaces to unite **d :** a defect in veneering resulting from misplacement of the sheets of veneer so that one overlaps the other rather than forming a smooth butt joint **4 a :** one circuit around a racecourse **b :** one round of play (as in a game of mancala) **c :** one segment of a larger unit (as in a journey or time cycle) ⟨the next thousand-mile ~ of our journey —Wendell Willkie⟩ ⟨it was the last ~ of term —Mavis Gallant⟩ ⟨the last ~ of a long all-day operation —John Muggeridge⟩ **d :** one complete turn (as of a rope around a drum) **5 :** points won in excess of the number necessary to win a card game and applied to the score of the next game

⁴**lap** \"\ *vb* **lapped**; **lapped**; **lapping**; **laps** [ME *lapen*, *lappen*, fr. OE *lapian*; akin to OHG *laffan* to lick, Icel *lepja* to lap, L *lambere* to lick, Gk *laphyssein* to devour, gulp down, Arm *lap'el* to lick] *vi* **1 :** to scoop up food or drink with the tip of the tongue ⟨uncover, dogs, and ~ —Shak.⟩ **2 a :** to make a gentle intermittent splashing sound ⟨waves *lapped* at their feet —Laura Krey⟩ ⟨the *lapping* of the quiet water —Mary Webb⟩ **b :** to move in little waves **:** WASH ⟨when the last wavelet of some old receding ocean *lapped* over them —C.E.W. Bean⟩ ⟨a changing crowd *lapped* up against the front of the garage —Scott Fitzgerald⟩ ~ *vt* **1 :** to scoop up (food or drink) with the tongue ⟨held her kitten to ~ milk —Anne D. Sedgwick⟩ — often used with *up* **2 :** to flow or splash against in little waves ⟨the foundations of the city's buildings have been *lapped* by tides for centuries and many have been badly eroded —Arnaldo Cortesi⟩

⁵**lap** \"\ *n* -s [ME *lappe* taste, fr. *lapen*, *lappen*, v.] **1 a :** an act of lapping ⟨the cat took a ~ or two at the saucer⟩ **b :** as much as can be carried to the mouth by one scoop of the tongue **:** LICK, TASTE ⟨saw a pink tongue shoot out . . . and have a ~ of her soup —*Newsweek*⟩ **2 a :** a thin or weak beverage or food ⟨hounds should be fed . . . some light broth or ~ in the morning —F.M.Ware⟩ **b** *obs* **:** LIQUOR **3 :** a gentle splashing sound ⟨the hollow ~ of the sea at the foot of the cliff —G.G.Carter⟩

⁶**lap** \"\ *now chiefly dial past of* LEAP

⁷**lap** \"\ *n, pl* **lap** *or* **laps** [alter. of *lop*] **:** a treetop left in the woods after logging **:** ¹LOP

la·pa·cho \ləˈpä(ˌ)chō\ *n* -s [Sp, of AmerInd (prob. Argentine) origin] **:** any of several tropical American timber trees of the genera *Tabebuia* and *Tecoma*

la·pa·chol \ləˈpäˌchōl, -chōl\ *n* -s [ISV *lapach-* (fr. *lapacho*) + *-ol*; orig. formed in F] **:** a yellow crystalline coloring matter $C_{15}H_{14}O_3$ derived from alpha-naphthoquinone and found in the grain of lapacho and similar woods

la·pac·tic \ləˈpaktik\ *adj* [Gk *lapaktikos*, fr. (assumed) Gk *lapaktos* (verbal of Gk *lapassein* to empty) + Gk *-ikos* -ic; akin to Gk *leptos* thin, weak — more at LEPER] **:** CATHARTIC, LAXATIVE

lap·a·ge·ria \ˌlapəˈjirēə\ *n* [NL, fr. Marie Joséphine Rose Tascher de *la Pagerie* (maiden name of Joséphine de Beauharnais) †1814 wife of Napoleon Bonaparte + NL *-ia*] **1** *cap* **:** a genus of Chilean vines (family Liliaceae) having trumpet-shaped flowers — see CHILE-BELLS **2** -s **:** any plant of the genus *Lapageria*

lap·an \ˈlapən\ *n* -s [prob. alter. of *lapin*] **:** the meat of a castrated rabbit

lap·a·rot·o·my \ˌlapəˈräd·əmē\ *n* -ES [ISV *laparo-* (fr. Gk *lapara* flank, fr. *laparos* slack, loose) + *-tomy*; akin to Gk *leptos* thin, weak] **:** surgical section of the abdominal wall (as for diagnosis or further surgery)

la paz \ləˈpaz, -paa(ə)z; -päz, -pȧ|, |s\ *adj, usu cap L&P* [fr. *La Paz*, city in western Bolivia, capital of Bolivia] **:** of or from La Paz, the administrative capital of Bolivia **:** of the kind or style prevalent in La Paz

lapboard \ˈ=ˌ=\ *n* **:** a board used on the lap as a substitute for a table or desk ⟨wrote his first drafts in longhand on a ~⟩ ⟨commuters playing cards on a ~⟩

lap child *or* **lap baby** *n, South & Midland* **:** a baby not yet able to walk

lap dissolve *n* [³*lap*] **:** DISSOLVE

lapdog \ˈ=ˌ=\ *n* **:** a small pet dog suitable for holding in the lap

lap dovetail *n* **:** a dovetail joint in which the recesses in one piece are cut only part way through so that part of the thickness of one board overlaps the end of the other

la·pel \ləˈpel *sometimes* laˈ-\ *n* -s [¹*lap* + *-el*] **:** a turned-back facing usu. wide and pointed at the top and tapering to nothing at the bottom that is usu. one of a pair along the front edges of a jacket, dress, or coat and extends from the collar or neckline to or toward the waistline

la·pel·er \-lə(r)\ *n* -s **:** one that makes or sews lapels

la·pelled \-ld\ *adj* **1 :** having lapels **2 :** turned back as lapels

lap·ey·rou·sia \ˌlapəˈrüz(h)ēə\ *n* [NL, irreg. fr. Jean François de Galaup de *La Pérouse* †1788 Fr. sailor and explorer + NL *-ia*] **1** *cap* **:** a genus of southern African bulbous herbs (family Iridaceae) having blue or red flowers with a slender perianth tube and stamens inserted on the throat **2** -s **:** any plant of the genus *Lapeyrousia*

lap·ful \ˈlapˌfu̇l\ *n* -s **:** as much as the lap can contain

la·phyg·ma \ləˈfigmə\ [NL, fr. Gk, greedy attack, fr. *laphyssein* to devour, gulp down — more at LAP] *syn of* SPODOPTERA

lap·i·dar·i·an \ˌlapəˈda(a)rēən\ *adj* [L *lapidarius* of stone + E *-an*] **1 :** of, relating to, or inscribed on stone ⟨a ~ record⟩ **2 :** LAPIDARY 2 ⟨ornate ~ phrases —*New Republic*⟩

lap·i·da·rist \ˈ==dərəst, -ˌder-\ *n* -s [prob. fr. ¹*lapidary* + *-ist*] **:** LAPIDARY 2

¹**lap·i·dary** \-ˌderē, -ri\ *n* -ES [ME *lapidarie*, fr. L *lapidarius*, fr. *lapidarius*, adj.] **1 a :** a cutter, polisher, or engraver of precious stones other than diamonds **b :** the art of cutting gems ⟨an evening course in ~ —*Minerals Yearbook*⟩ **2 :** a connoisseur of precious stones and the art of cutting them ⟨the ~ is often called upon to ascertain the nature of rough gem minerals —F.J.Sperisen⟩

²**lapidary** \"\ *adj* [L *lapidarius* of stone, fr. *lapid-, lapis* stone + *-arius* -ary; akin to Gk *lepas* crag] **1 a :** LAPIDARIAN 1 ⟨his face is lean, leathery, but not ~ —Harvey Breit⟩ **b :** of or relating to precious stones or the art of cutting them ⟨the ring is of no ~ value — Lord Byron⟩ **2 :** having the elegance and precision associated with inscriptions on stone ⟨his poetry . . . alternates between the ample elegiac and the ~ epigram — Charles Weir⟩ ⟨the more ~ and terse this subject the better it is suited for symphonic elaboration —P.H.Lang⟩

lap·i·date \-ˌdāt\ *vt* -ED/-ING/-S [L *lapidatus*, past part. of *lapidare* to stone, fr. *lapid-, lapis* stone] *archaic* **:** to pelt or kill with stones

lap·i·da·tion \ˌ==ˈdāshən\ *n* -s [L *lapidation-, lapidatio* action of stoning, fr. *lapidatus* + *-ion-, -io* -ion] **1 :** the penalty of stoning to death ⟨adultery . . . would be punished by ~ —Sir Richard Burton⟩ **2 :** an act of pelting with stones

la·pid·e·ous \ləˈpidēəs\ *adj* [L *lapideus*, fr. *lapid-, lapis* stone + *-eus* -eous] **:** of the nature of stone **:** STONY

lap·i·des·cent \ˌlapəˈdesᵊnt\ *adj* [L *lapidescent-, lapidescens*, pres. part. of *lapidescere* to petrify, fr. *lapid-, lapis* stone] *archaic* **:** tending to petrify **:** PETRIFYING

lap·i·dic·o·lous \ˌ==ˈdikələs\ *adj* [ISV *lapidi-* (fr. L *lapid-, lapis*) + *-colous*] **:** living under a stone — used esp. of an insect

lap·i·dif·ic \-ˈdifik\ *also* **lap·i·dif·i·cal** \-fəkəl\ *adj* [*lapidific* prob. fr. (assumed) NL *lapidificus*, fr. L *lapidi-* (fr. *lapid-, lapis*) + *-ficus* -fic; *lapidifical* prob. fr. (assumed) NL *lapidificus* + E *-al*] *archaic* **:** LAPIDESCENT

la·pid·i·fi·ca·tion \ləˌpidəfəˈkāshən\ *n* -s [prob. fr. (assumed) NL *lapidification-, lapidificatio*, fr. ML *lapidificatus* (past part. of *lapidificare*) + L *-ion-, -io* -ion] **:** the act or process of lapidifying **:** FOSSILIZATION, PETRIFACTION

la·pid·i·fy \ˈ===ˌfī\ *vb* **lapidified**; **lapidified**; **lapidifying**; **lapidifies** [F *lapidifier*, fr. ML *lapidificare*, fr. L *lapidi-* (fr. *lapid-, lapis*) + *-ficare* -fy] *archaic* **:** to convert into stone or stony material **:** PETRIFY

lap·i·dist \ˈlapədəst\ *n* -s [L *lapid-, lapis* stone + E *-ist*] **:** LAPIDARY 1a, 2

la·pies \ləˈpēz\ *n pl* [modif. of F dial. (Swiss) *lapiaz*, *lapiez*, fr. (assumed) VL *lapida* stone, alter. of L *lapid-, lapis*] **:** grooves and ridges formed on a rock surface by solution of limestone

la·pil·lo \ləˈpi(ˌ)lō\ *n* -s [It, fr. L *lapillus*] **:** lava in the form of lapilli

la·pil·lus \-ˌləs\ *n, pl* **lapil·li** \-ˌlī, -(ˌ)lē\ [L, small stone, dim. of *lapis* stone] **1 :** a stony or glassy fragment of lava ¼ to 1½ inches in diameter thrown out in a volcanic eruption **:** volcanic cinder — usu. used in pl. ⟨showers of ashes and *lapilli* —Norman Douglas⟩ **2 :** OTOLITH

lap·in \ˈlapən\ *n* -s [F, rabbit, perh. of Iberian origin; akin to the source of L *lepus* hare] **:** RABBIT; *specif* **:** a castrated male rabbit

lap·in·ized *also* **lap·in·ised** \ˈlapəˌnīzd\ *adj* [*lapin* + *-ize*, *-ise* + *-ed*] **:** attenuated by passage through rabbits ⟨a ~ virus⟩

lapis la·zu·li \ˌlapəˈslazə(ˌ)lē, ˌlap-, -azh- *also* -əˌlī *or* ˌlapəˈsläzə(ˌ)lē\ *also* **lapis** *n* [ME, fr. ML, fr. L *lapis* stone + ML *lazuli*, gen. of *lazulum* lapis lazuli, fr. Ar *lāzaward* — more at AZURE] **1 :** a semiprecious stone usu. of a rich azure blue color that is essentially a lazurite but contains hauynite, sodalite, and other minerals, occurs usu. in small rounded masses frequently showing spangles of iron pyrites, and is probably the sapphire of the ancients **2 :** LAPIS LAZULI BLUE

lapis lazuli blue *n* **:** a moderate blue that is redder and duller than average copen and redder and deeper than azurite blue, dresden blue, or pompadour

lapis lazuli ware *n* **:** blue Wedgwood pebbleware veined with gold

lap joint *n* **:** a joint made by overlapping two ends or edges and fastening them together — compare BUTT JOINT — **lap-jointed** \ˈ=ˌ==\ *adj*

la·place's equation \ləˈpläˌsəz-, -plaˌ\ *n, usu cap L* [after Pierre Simon de *Laplace* †1827 Fr. astronomer and mathematician] **:** the equation $\frac{\partial^2 u}{\partial x^2}+\frac{\partial^2 u}{\partial y^2}+\frac{\partial^2 u}{\partial z^2}=0$ often written $\nabla^2 u=0$ in which x,y, and z are the rectangular Cartesian coordinates of a point in space and u is a function of those coordinates

laplace station *n, usu cap L* **:** a geodetic station at which coincident triangulation and astronomic longitude and azimuth determinations are made

la·plac·ian \ləˈpläsēən, -las-; -läshən\ *or* **laplacian operator** *n* -s *usu cap L* [Pierre Simon de *Laplace* †1827 + E *-ian*] **:** the differential operator ∇^2 that yields the left member of Laplace's equation

lap·land \ˈlapˌland, -lənd\ *adj, usu cap* [fr. *Lapland*, region of northern Norway, northern Sweden, northern Finland, and the northwestern U.S.S.R.] **:** of or from Lapland **:** of the kind or style prevalent in Lapland

lapland cornel *n, usu cap L* **:** a low herblike cornel (*Cornus suecica*) found in northern regions of Eurasia and No. America and having dark violet flowers

lap·land·er \-də(r)\ *n, cap* **:** LAPP

lapland longspur *n, usu cap 1st L* **:** a longspur (*Calcarius lapponicus*) native to Europe and Asia but found also in No. America

lapland pine *n, usu cap L* **:** a Scotch pine (*Pinus sylvestris lapponica*) of narrow pyramidal habit

lapland rosebay *or* **lapland rhododendron** *n, usu cap L* **:** a dwarf shrub (*Rhododendron lapponicum*) of the mountainous region of eastern No. America having scurfy branches, thick scurfy leaves, and purple flowers and forming extensive depressed mats esp. in arctic and subarctic regions

lap-lap \ˈlaˌplap\ *n* -s [origin unknown] **:** a loincloth worn by So. Pacific islanders

la pla·ta \ləˈpläd·ə\ *adj, usu cap L&P* [fr. *La Plata*, city in eastern Argentina] **:** of or from the city of La Plata, Argentina **:** of the kind or style prevalent in La Plata

lap-love \ˈ=ˌ=\ *n* **:** FIELD BINDWEED

lap man *n* **:** a worker who removes pulp sheets from wet-machine press rolls and folds them into laps

lapo-lapo \ˌläpōˈläˌpō\ *or* **la·pu·la·pu** \ˌläpüˈlä(ˌ)pü\ *n* -s [Tag *lapulapo*] **:** any of certain Philippine groupers; *esp* **:** a grouper (*Cephalopholis argus*) related to the coney and brilliantly marked with iridescent blue

la·por·tea \ləˈpȯrd·ēə\ *n, cap* [NL, fr. *Laporte*, 19th cent. person otherwise unidentified] **:** a genus of perennial chiefly tropical stinging herbs or trees (family Urticaceae) having large serrate leaves and axillary stipules — see AUSTRALIAN NETTLE TREE, WOODNETTLE

lapp \ˈlap\ *n* -s *cap* [Sw] **1 :** a member of a people of northern Scandinavia, Finland, and the Kola peninsula of northern Russia who are typically nomadic herders of reindeer, fishermen, and hunters of sea mammals **:** LAPLANDER **2 a :** any one of the closely related Finno-Ugric languages spoken by the Lapps **b :** the Lapp languages taken as a group

¹**lap·pa** \ˈlapə\ [NL, fr. L, burr] *syn of* ARCTIUM

²**lappa** \"\ *n* -s [NL *Lappa*] **:** the root of the great bur used as a diuretic and alterative

lappa clover *n* [*lappa* prob. modif. of NL *lappaceum* (specific epithet of *Trifolium lappaceum*), fr. L, neut. of *lappaceus* burrlike, fr. *lappa* burr + *-aceus* -aceous] **:** a Eurasian clover (*Trifolium lappaceum*) with lavender-rose colored flowers that is grown as a forage and hay crop in some parts of the U.S.

lap·page \ˈlapij\ *n* -s **:** the amount by which one surface overlaps another

lapped *past of* LAP

lapped seam *var of* LAP SEAM

¹**lap·per** \ˈlapə(r)\ *n* -s [⁴*lap* + *-er*] **:** one that laps food or drink with the tongue

²**lapper** \"\ *n* -s [²*lap* + *-er*] **1 a :** one that wraps or folds **b :** one that converts fiber into laps **2 a :** one that dimensions,

smooths, or polishes with a lap **b :** ³LAP 2 **c :** a textile worker who handles laps

³**lapper** \"\ *vb* -ED/-ING/-S [alter. of ¹*lopper*] *chiefly Scot* **:** COAGULATE, CLOT, CURDLE — used esp. of milk

lap·pet \'lapət\ *n* -S [¹*lap* + -*et*] **1 a :** ¹LAP 1a **b** (1) **:** a fold or flap on headgear ⟨simple cap with upturned ~ —George Eliot⟩; *specif* **:** one of a pair of streamers on a woman's headdress usu. hanging down on either side of the face (2) **:** INFULA **c :** LAPEL **2 a** *archaic* **:** ¹LAP 2 **b :** a lateral extension of the shell of the living chamber of an ammonoid cephalopod **3 :** a flat overlapping or free-hanging piece (as a roofing tile or a keyhole guard) **4 :** LAPPET MOTH **5 a :** a loom attachment consisting of one or more needlebars with pendent needles carrying a series of floating warp threads to be introduced into the body of the fabric **b :** a lightweight patterned material (as dotted swiss) woven with the aid of a lappet attachment and used chiefly for curtains and dresses

lappet caterpillar *n* **:** the stout more or less flattened hairy larva of a lappet moth

lap·pet·ed \'lapəd·əd\ *adj* **:** having lappets — used esp. of headgear

lappet loom *n* **:** a loom for lappet weaving

lappet moth *n* [so called fr. the small lobes at the sides of the body of the larva] **:** any of several stout-bodied medium-sized hairy moths of the family Lasiocampidae — see LAPPET CATERPILLAR

lappet weaving *n* **:** machine embroidery by the use of a lappet attachment — see LAPPET 5a

lap·pic \'lapik\ *adj, usu cap* **:** of or relating to Lapland or the Lapps

lapping *n* -S [ME *lappinge*, gerund of *lappen* to lap, wrap] **1 :** WRAPPING, BINDING; *specif* **:** the protective wrapping of the middle of a bowstring **2 :** OVERLAPPING; *specif* **:** a covering of a current cash shortage by deferring the deposit of funds received until a later date

¹**lapp·ish** \'lapish\ *adj, usu cap* [*lapp* + -*ish*] **:** LAPPIC

²**lappish** *n, pl* **lappish** *usu cap* **:** LAPP

lap plate *n* [³*lap*] **:** a strap for a butt joint

lap·pu·la \'lapyələ\ *n, cap* [NL, fr. L *lappa* burr + -*ula*] **:** a large genus of rough-pubescent herbs (family Boraginaceae) found in temperate regions having small flowers in terminal racemes and nutlets armed with barbed prickles — see STICKSEED

lap–rivet \'=,=\ *vt* **:** to rivet together (plates) with the ends or edges overlapping

lap robe *n* **:** a covering (as a blanket) for the legs, lap, and feet esp. of a passenger in a car or carriage — compare BUFFALO ROBE

laps *pl of* LAP, *pres 3d sing of* LAP

laps·able *or* **laps·ible** \'lapsəbəl\ *adj* **:** liable to lapse

lap·sa·na \'lapsənə\ *n, cap* [NL, fr. L, charlock, fr. Gk *lapsanē*, *lampsanē*] **:** a genus of Old World herbs (family Compositae) having pinnatifid leaves and yellow-rayed flower heads — see NIPPLEWORT

lap·sang sou·chong \;lap,saŋ'sü,ch|ȯŋ, -ü,sh|, -ü,j|, |äŋ\ *n, usu cap L* **:** a fine grade of souchong with a characteristic smoky flavor

¹**lapse** \'laps\ *n* -S [L *lapsus* fault, error, fall, slide, fr. *lapsus*, past part. of *labi* to glide, slide — more at SLEEP] **1 a :** an accidental mistake in fact or departure from an accepted norm **:** trivial fault **:** SLIP, ERROR ⟨~ of memory⟩ ⟨~ of taste⟩ ⟨the performances show this great pianist at the height of his powers, whatever rhythmical or technical ~*s* they may contain —Edward Sackville-West⟩ **b :** a temporary deviation ⟨~ from consciousness⟩ ⟨~ from respectability⟩ ⟨writes well, despite occasional ~*s* into polysyllabic humor —*Geog. Jour.*⟩ **2 a :** FALL; *specif* **:** a decrease of temperature, pressure, or value of other meteorological element as the height increases — see LAPSE RATE **b :** LOSS, LOWERING, DECLINE, DROP ⟨a sudden ~ of confidence —Josephine Johnson⟩ ⟨~ in the supply of college graduates during the war years —M.L. Kastens⟩ ⟨~ from grace⟩ **3 a** (1) **:** the termination or failure of a right or privilege through neglect to exercise it within some limit of time or through failure of some contingency — compare EXPIRY (2) **:** *Eng eccl law* **:** the transfer of the right to present or collate a rector to a vacant benefice from one having the first right and neglecting to exercise it to one having a secondary right (3) **:** termination of coverage (as by life insurance) for nonpayment of premiums **b :** an interruption or discontinuance ⟨~ of a custom⟩ ⟨resumed dividends after a ~ during the depression —P.J. O'Brien⟩ ⟨masters narrative ~*s* with great skill —C.C.Rister⟩ **4 a :** a yielding to temptation or inclination **:** transitory disregard of moral principles **:** FOLLY ⟨his laxity of conduct, his moral ~*s* —S.H.Adams⟩ **b :** an abandonment of religious faith or principles **:** APOSTASY, BACKSLIDE ⟨prior to Adam's ~ —R.W.Murray⟩ **5 a** *archaic* **:** a continuous flow or gentle downward glide (as of water) ⟨down comes the stream, a ~ of living amethyst —Thomas Aird⟩ **b :** a continuous passage or an elapsed period of time **:** COURSE, INTERVAL ⟨a transaction involving a considerable ~ of time because the shares could not be sold until the state debt was paid —W.P.Webb⟩ ⟨except for a ~ of two years when he studied abroad, he has taught continuously since graduation⟩ **syn** see ERROR

²**lapse** \"\ *vb* -ED/-ING/-S *vi* **1 a :** to fall into error or folly **:** depart from an accepted standard ⟨~*s* into addiction again at the first temptation —*Time*⟩ ⟨purchases . . . where his discrimination *lapsed* —Basil Taylor⟩; *specif* **:** BACKSLIDE ⟨in their view Constantinople had *lapsed* into heresy —R.M. French⟩ **b :** to sink or slip involuntarily **:** SUBSIDE, RELAPSE ⟨murmurs good morning . . . and ~*s* into silence —Gertrude Samuels⟩ ⟨some *lapsed* into reading and others into sleep —Earle Birney⟩ ⟨why does starry-eyed youth ~ into flabby middle-aged vacuity —Douglas Bush⟩ ⟨the moment his attention is relaxed . . . he will ~ into bad Shakespearean verse —T.S.Eliot⟩ **2 :** to go out of existence **:** fall into decay or disuse **:** DISAPPEAR, TERMINATE ⟨the nest-building impulse . . . ~*s* when the eggs are laid —E.A.Armstrong⟩ ⟨could think of no rejoinder . . . and our conversation *lapsed* —Maurice Cranston⟩ ⟨a relationship may be allowed to ~, but it can never be dissolved —G.M.Foster⟩ ⟨this series of experiments seems to have *lapsed* around 1910 —Frank Denman⟩ **3 :** to fall or pass from one proprietor to another or from the original destination by the omission, negligence, or failure of some one (as a patron or legatee) ⟨a legacy ~*s* when it fails to vest⟩ ⟨an insurance policy ~*s* with forfeiture of value from nonpayment of a premium when due⟩ **4 a** *of time* **:** to run its course **:** PASS ⟨the whole fund might be lost . . . by the *lapsing* of the time allowed —A.D.White⟩ **b :** to glide past ⟨saw the washed pavement *lapsing* beneath my feet —L.P.Smith⟩ **c :** to glide gently along ⟨lolled with their lovers by *lapsing* brooks —W.H.Auden⟩ ⟨barges *lapsing* on its tranquil tide —C.C.Clarke⟩ ~ *vt* **1** *obs* **:** LOSE, FORFEIT ⟨a vestry cannot ~ their right of presentation —William Byrd⟩ **2 :** to make ineffective by failing to meet the requirements of **:** let slip **:** NULLIFY ⟨*lapsed* his policy⟩ ⟨the high percentage of patients *lapsing* therapy —*Jour. Amer. Med. Assoc.*⟩

lap seam *also* **lapped seam** *n* **:** a seam in which the edges overlap; *esp* **:** a seam in leather or cloth made by extending a cut or folded edge over a cut edge to the width of the seam allowance and stitching in place

¹**lapsed** *adj* [fr. past part. of ²*lapse*] **1 :** surrendered or nullified because of failure to meet stipulated obligations **:** FORFEITED, VOID ⟨dispose of the realm as a ~ fief —G.C.Sellery⟩ ⟨the widow gets no insurance because of a ~ policy⟩ **2 :** guilty of error or defection **:** FALLEN; *specif* **:** APOSTATE ⟨the deliberately ~ Catholic cannot be such without mortal sin —D.J.Corrigan⟩ **3 :** dropped out of sight or use **:** VANISHED ⟨now in the moonlight, and now ~ in shade —Lord Byron⟩ ⟨the ~ custom of an annual dinner —*John Bull*⟩

²**lapsed** *n pl* **:** early Christians deserting the faith because of persecution ⟨in Rome the bishop . . . was prepared to permit the restoration of the ~ —K.S.Latourette⟩

laps·er \'lapsə(r)\ *n* -S **:** one that lapses

lapse rate *n* **:** the rate of change of any meteorological element with increase of height; *specif* **:** the rate of decrease of temperature with increase of height — called also *vertical gradient*

lap shaver *n* [¹*lap* + *shaver*; fr. the former practice of holding the leather on a board in the lap while shaving it] **:** a machine for shaving leather to a specified thickness

lap siding *n* [³*lap*] **1 :** building siding consisting of beveled boards wider and longer than clapboards — compare DROP SIDING **2 :** an arrangement of two railroad sidings at a station in such a way that the turnout of one overlaps that of the other

lap stick *n* [*lap* prob. short for ²*lapidary*] **:** DOP STICK

lapstone \'=,=\ *n* **:** a stone or iron plate which is held in the lap and on which a shoemaker hammers leather

¹**lapstrake** *also* **lapstreak** \'=,=\ *adj* [³*lap* + *strake* or *streak*] **1 :** having overlapping strakes **:** CLINKER-BUILT — usu. used of a boat ⟨~ dinghy⟩ **2 :** characterized by the lapping of each strake on the outside of the one beneath it ⟨~ construction⟩

²**lapstrake** *also* **lapstreak** \"\ *n* **:** a boat of lapstrake construction

lapstraked *also* **lapstreaked** \'=,=\ *adj* [³*lap* + *strake* or *streak* + -*ed*] **:** LAPSTRAKE

lap·strak·er *also* **lap·streak·er** \-kə(r)\ *n* -S [¹*lapstrake*, *lapstreak* + -*er*] **:** LAPSTRAKE

lap·sus \'lapsəs\ *n, pl* **lapsus** [L — more at LAPSE] **:** ¹LAPSE 1a

lap table *n* **:** LAPBOARD

lapulapu *var of* LAPO-LAPO

lap up *vt* **1 :** to respond to enthusiastically or accept eagerly ⟨she simply *lapped up* admiration —Helen Howe⟩ ⟨readiness to *lap up* the latest sensation —Herbert Brucker⟩ **2 :** DRINK ⟨sat there . . . *lapping up* the wonderful Japanese beer —J.A. Michener⟩

la·pu·tan \lə'pyütᵊn\ *adj, usu cap* [*Laputa*, imaginary flying island in Swift's *Gulliver's Travels* whose inhabitants engage in a great variety of impractical projects + E -*an*] **:** ABSURD, VISIONARY

lap–weld \'=;=\ *vt* [³*lap* + *weld*, v.] **:** to join by welding along overlapping edges or seams

lap weld \'=,=\ *n* [fr. *lap-weld*] **:** a joint made by lap-welding

lap winding *n* **:** a drum winding for generator and motor armatures in which each coil or set of windings overlaps the next so that there are as many armature paths as there are field-magnet poles

lap·wing \'la,pwiŋ\ *n* [ME *lapwinge*, by folk etymology (influence of ME *winge* wing) fr. *lappewinke*, by folk etymology (influence of ME *lappen* to lap, wrap) fr. OE *hlēapewince*; akin to OE *hlēapan* to leap and to OE *wincian* to wink, blink, *wancol* unsteady, wavering — more at LEAP, WINK] **1 :** an abundant crested plover (*Vanellus vanellus* syn. *V. cristatus*) of Europe, Asia, and northern Africa with upperparts and crest bronzy green, throat and breast black, and sides of the head and neck and most of the underparts white that is noted for its slow irregular flapping flight and its shrill wailing cry **2 :** any of several related plovers

lapwing gull *n* **:** a black-headed gull (*Larus ridibundus*)

laq·ue·ar \'lakwēər, -ē,är\ *n, pl* **laquear·ia** \,lakwē'a(a)rēə\ [L; akin to L *lacus* lake, basin — more at LAKE] **:** COFFER 4a

laque·us \'lakwēəs, 'lak-\ *n, pl* **laquei** \-ē,ī, -ē,ē\ [L, noose, snare — more at DELIGHT] **:** LEMNISCUS 2

lar \'lär\ *n* [L — more at LARVA] **1** *pl* **lares** \'lā,rēz, 'la(a)(,)rēz, 'lä,rās\ *often cap* **:** a tutelary god or spirit of the ancient Romans associated with a particular locality (as a field or the home) sometimes conceived as a beneficent ancestral spirit or as the equivalent for the dead of the genius of the living **2** *also* **lar gibbon** -S [NL (specific epithet of *Hylobates lar*), fr. L] **:** a Malayan gibbon (*Hylobates lar*) with white hands and feet

lar·a·mide \'larə,mīd, -,məd\ *adj, usu cap* [irreg. fr. *Laramie* mountains, southeastern Wyoming and northern Colorado] **:** of or relating to the mountain-making movements near the opening of the Cenozoic era — see GEOLOGIC TIME table

lar·a·mie \-,mē\ *adj, usu cap* [fr. *Laramie*, county in Wyoming] **:** of, relating to, or constituting a division of the American Upper Cretaceous — see GEOLOGIC TIME table

la·rar·i·um \lə'ra(a)rēəm\ *n, pl* **larar·ia** \-ēə\ [LL, fr. L *lar* + -*arium*] **:** the shrine of the lares in an ancient Roman home

larb \'lärb\ *n* -S [origin unknown] **:** a bearberry (*Arctostaphylos uva-ursi*)

¹**lar·board** \'lärbərd, 'lābəd\ *n* [alter. (influenced by *starboard*) of ME *ladeborde*, *latheborde*, *latebord*, perh. fr. *laden* to load + *bord* ship's side — more at LADE, BOARD] **:** the left-hand side of a ship to one on board facing toward the bow **:** PORT — opposed to *starboard*

²**larboard** \"\ *adj* **:** PORT ⟨the ~ side of a ship⟩

lar·bo·lins *also* **lar·bow·lines** \-bələ̇nz\ *n pl* [perh. irreg. fr. ¹*larboard* + -*lings*, pl. of -*ling*, n. suffix] *archaic* **:** PORT WATCH

lar·ce·ner \'lärs(ᵊ)nə(r), 'lās-\ *n* -S [*larceny* + -*er*] **:** LARCENIST

lar·ce·nist \-nəst\ *n* -S [*larceny* + -*ist*] **:** one who commits larceny

lar·ce·nous \-nəs\ *adj* [*larceny* + -*ous*] **1 :** having the character of or constituting larceny ⟨a ~ act⟩ **2 :** committing larceny **:** THIEVISH ⟨~ rascals⟩ — **lar·ce·nous·ly** *adv*

lar·ce·ny \-nē, -ni\ *n* -ES [ME, fr. MF *larcin* theft (fr. L *latrocinium* robbery, fr. *latron-*, *latro* mercenary soldier, brigand) + ME -*y*, -*ie* -y — more at LATRON] **1** *common law* **:** the unlawful taking and carrying away of personal property without the consent of its lawful possessor whereby every part of the property stolen is removed however slightly from its former position and is at least momentarily in the complete possession of the thief and with intent to steal or to deprive the rightful owner of his property permanently — compare EMBEZZLEMENT; see AGGRAVATED LARCENY, GRAND LARCENY, PETTY LARCENY, SIMPLE LARCENY **2 :** any of various statutory offenses whereby property is obtained by embezzlement, trick, false pretenses, fraud, breach of trust, or theft

larch \'lärch, 'lāch\ *n* -ES [prob. fr. G *lärche*, fr. MHG *larche*, *lerche*, fr. (assumed) OHG *larihha*, *lericha*, fr. L *laric-*, *larix*] **1 a :** a tree of the genus *Larix* — see EUROPEAN LARCH, TAMARACK **b :** any of several other trees of the family Pinaceae: as (1) **:** NOBLE FIR (2) **:** AMABILIS FIR (3) **:** CORSICAN PINE (4) **:** GOLDEN LARCH **2 :** the wood of a larch esp. belonging to the genera *Larix* or *Abies*

larch agaric *n* **:** AGARIC 3

larch canker *n* **:** a destructive disease of the larch and to a lesser extent of fir and pine caused by an ascomycetous fungus (*Dasyscypha willkommii*) that produces flattened depressed cankers on the twigs and branches

larch casebearer *n* **:** a casebearer that is the larva of a minute moth (*Coleophora laricella*), that lives in a case made of a hollowed silk-lined leaf, and that mines in the leaves of larches sometimes causing severe defoliation

larch·en \'lärchən, 'lāch-\ *adj* **:** being a larch **:** made up of larches ⟨a ~ wood⟩

larch fir *n* **:** lumber consisting of a mixture of Douglas fir and western larch

larch pine *n* **:** CORSICAN PINE

larch sawfly *n* **:** a very destructive red-and-black sawfly (*Pristiphora erichsonii*) of No. America and Europe whose whitish larva often defoliates the larch

larch turpentine *n* **:** VENICE TURPENTINE

¹**lard** \'lärd, 'lād\ *vt* -ED/-ING/-S [ME *larden*, fr. MF *larder*, fr. OF, fr. *lart*, *lard*, n.] **1 a :** to insert fattening into (lean meat) before cooking; *broadly* **:** to dress (meat) for cooking by inserting or covering with something (as strips of fat) ⟨~*ing* a boned chicken⟩ ⟨a hare ~*ed* with truffles⟩ **b :** to cover or soil with grease ⟨age-blackened time-*larded* beams⟩ **2 :** to mix or garnish with something esp. by way of improvement, decorative finish, or show **:** BEDECK, STREW, INTERLARD ⟨speeches ~*ed* with compliments⟩ **3** *obs* **:** to make rich with or as if with fat **:** ENRICH

²**lard** \"\ *n* -S [ME, fr. MF, fr. OF *lart*, *lard*, fr. L *lardum*, *laridum*; akin to L *laetus* glad, *largus* abundant, generous, Gk *larinos* fat] **1** *archaic* **:** fatty tissue of the hog **:** fat pork **2 :** a soft white solid or semisolid fat obtained by rendering fatty tissue of the hog — see LEAF LARD

lar·da·ce·in \lär'dāsēən, lā'd-\ *n* -S [ISV *lardaceous* + -*in*] **:** ²AMYLOID 3

lar·da·ceous \(')=;dāshəs\ *adj* [prob. fr. (assumed) NL *lardaceus*, fr. L *lardum* fat pork + -*aceus* -aceous] **1 :** resembling lard ⟨a ~ mass⟩ **2 :** AMYLOID 2 ⟨~ degeneration⟩

lar·der \'lärdər, 'lādə(r\ *n* -S [ME, fr. MF *lardier*, fr. OF, fr. *lart*, *lard* + -*ier*, n. suffix denoting a place (fr. L -*arium*)] **1 a :** a place (as a pantry) where meat and other foodstuffs are stored **b :** a store of food **:** food in stock or available **2** *Brit* **:** a collection of unwanted animals (as various predators) killed by a gamekeeper and hung up to act in the manner of a scarecrow

larder beetle *n* **:** a dark brown or nearly black beetle (*Dermestes lardarius*) that is about ¼ inch long and has a bristly larva which feeds on dried animal products (as meats, skins, feathers)

lar·de·rel·lite \,lärdə'rel,īt\ *n* -S [F. de Larderel †1925 Ital. mineowner + E -*ite*] **:** a mineral $(NH_4)_2B_{10}O_{16}.5H_2O(?)$ consisting of a hydrous ammonium borate and occurring as a white crystalline powder

lar·der·er \'lärdərər, 'lādərə(r\ *n* -S [ME *larderere*, fr. *larder* + -*ere* -er] *archaic* **:** one in charge of a larder

lar·di·ner \-d(ᵊ)nə(r)\ *n* -S [ME, larder, larderer, fr. AF, larderer, irreg. fr. OF *lardier* larder] **1 :** LARDER 1a **2** *archaic* **:** LARDERER, STEWARD

larding needle *n* **:** a large needle with a hollow split end that is used for inserting lardoons into meat

lar·di·zab·a·la·ce·ae \,lärdə,zabə'lāsē,ē\ *n pl, cap* [NL, fr. *Lardizabala*, type genus (fr. Miguel *Lardizábal* y Uribe, 18th cent. Mex. statesman) + -*aceae*] **:** a family of chiefly woody vines (order Ranales) with leaves usu. digitate and baccate fruit — **lar·di·zab·a·la·ceous** \;=;=;=;=;lāshəs\ *adj*

lard oil *n* **:** an oil consisting chiefly of olein that is expressed from lard and used esp. as a lubricant, cutting oil, or illuminant

lar·doon \(')lär¦dün, (')lā¦d-\ *also* **lar·don** \'=,dän\ *n* -S [F *lardon* piece of fat pork, fr. OF, fr. *lart*, *lard*] **:** a strip of material (as of salt pork) for insertion into meat in larding

lardry *n* -ES [MF *larderie*, fr. *lard* (fr. OF *lart*, *lard*) + -*erie* -ery] *obs* **:** LARDER 1a

lard stearin *n* **:** the solid residue left after the expression of lard oil

lard stone *n* **:** STEATITE

lard type *n* **:** a type of hog adapted to converting feed (as corn) into fat — compare MEAT TYPE

lardworm \'=,=\ *n* **:** KIDNEY WORM

lardy \'lärdē, 'lādē, -di\ *adj* -ER/-EST [²*lard* + -*y*] **1 :** containing or resembling lard **:** of the character or consistency of lard ⟨a white ~ skin⟩ ⟨a heavy ~ cake⟩ **2 :** fat or tending to become fat esp. to excess ⟨~ hogs⟩

lardy–dardy \¦lärdē¦därdē, ¦lādē¦dādē, -di...di\ *adj* [imit. (of an affected manner of speech)] *slang* **:** languidly and affectedly dandyish — compare LA-DI-DA

lares *pl of* LAR

lares and penates *n pl* **:** one's most valued personal or household effects ⟨those *lares and penates* which a householder, driven from his city home, cannot bring himself to leave behind —Jerome Weidman⟩

lar·ga·men·te \,lärgə'mentē\ *adv (or adj)* [It, slowly, broadly fr. *largo* slow, broad, fr. L *largus* abundant, generous] **:** with slowness and breadth — used as a direction in music

lar·gan·do \lär'gän(,)dō\ *adj (or adv)* [It, making slow, widening, verbal of *largare* to make slow, widen, fr. LL, to widen, loosen, fr. L *largus* abundant, generous] **:** ALLARGANDO

¹**large** \'lärj, 'lāj\ *adj* -ER/-EST [ME, fr. OF, fr. L *largus* abundant, generous — more at LARD] **1** *obs* **:** liberal in giving or expending **:** GENEROUS, PRODIGAL, LAVISH **2** *obs* **a :** ample in quantity **:** ABUNDANT **b :** ample in extent **:** ROOMY, CAPACIOUS **c :** ample in breadth **:** BROAD, WIDE **d** *of a measure or period* **:** completely fulfilled **:** being as great as or greater than called for **3 :** having more than usual power, capacity, range, or scope **:** COMPREHENSIVE ⟨~ liberty⟩ ⟨a ~ treatment of a subject⟩ ⟨a ~ sympathy⟩ ⟨having a ~ discretion in settling such subjects⟩ ⟨taking the ~ view⟩ **4 a :** exceeding most other things of like kind in bulk, capacity, quantity, superficial dimensions, or number of constituent units **:** of considerable magnitude **:** BIG — opposed to *small* ⟨a ~ horse⟩ ⟨a ~ expenditure⟩; usu. replaced by *great* in qualifying linear dimensions ⟨a ~ mountain of great height⟩ **b :** dealing in great numbers or quantities **:** extensive in scope ⟨a ~ importer⟩ ⟨problems of ~ businesses⟩ **c** (1) **:** GREAT 1c (2) *of a taxon* **:** including more than an average number of kinds of plants or animals ⟨a ~ family represented by over 200 species in No. America alone⟩ **5 a** *obs, of language or expression* **:** marked by or tending toward vulgarity **:** COARSE, GROSS, IMPROPER **b** *obs* **:** easy and unrestrained in conduct **:** LAX, UNINHIBITED **c** *archaic* **:** involving few restrictions **:** permitting considerable liberty (as of action or conscience) **6** *archaic* **a** *of an utterance* **:** full and lengthy **:** copious in words **:** PROLIX **b** *of a person* **:** tending to be frequent, lengthy, or diffuse in writing or speech **:** given to prolixity **7** *of a wind* **:** blowing from a desirable direction with respect to a ship's course **:** FAVORABLE **8 :** POMPOUS, EXTRAVAGANT, BOASTFUL ⟨~ talk⟩

²**large** \"\ *adv* [ME, fr. *large*, adj.] **1** *obs* **:** AMPLY, FULLY, LIBERALLY, FREELY **2 a :** with the wind abaft the beam ⟨a ship sailing ~⟩ **b :** at a distance **:** wide of something (as a course, the shore, a mark) **3 :** POMPOUSLY, EXTRAVAGANTLY, BOASTFULLY ⟨talks ~ but works not at all⟩

³**large** \"\ *n* -S [ME, fr. *large*, adj.] **1** *obs* **:** LIBERALITY, GENEROSITY, BOUNTY **2 :** LIBERTY, FREEDOM — now used only in the phrase *at large* **3 :** a size of paperboard 24 inches by 19 inches **4 :** the longest note in mensural notation, equal to two longs in imperfect time or three in perfect time — called also *double long*, *maxim* — **at large** *adv* **1 :** without restraint or confinement ⟨cattle grazing *at large*⟩ ⟨remained *at large* after conviction pending an appeal to the higher court⟩ **2 :** to the full extent **:** at length **:** fully and often diffusely ⟨discussed the matter *at large*⟩ **3** *archaic* **:** without final settlement, completing, or perfecting **4 a :** in a general or indefinite way **:** without precise limits ⟨arrangements made *at large*⟩ **b :** without particular aim or plan **:** at random **5** *obs* **:** so as to be or spread over a large area **6 :** as a whole **:** in general without regard to particularities ⟨society *at large* suffers from crime as sharply as the individual victim⟩ **7 :** by or as the representative of the whole of an area having political subdivisions rather than a particular district or other subdivision ⟨a member elected *at large*⟩ — **at–large :** chosen by or representing the whole of an area (as a state or a city) having political subdivisions rather than a particular district or other subdivision — usu. used in combination with a preceding noun ⟨in the Republican convention each state has four delegates-*at-large* —W.S.Sayre⟩ ⟨a congressman-*at-large*⟩ — **in large** *or* **in the large** *adv* **:** on a large scale **:** in general

⁴**large** \"\ *vi* -ED/-ING/-S [¹*large*] *of a wind* **:** to shift so as to blow abaft the beam

large–billed water thrush \'=,=-\ *n* **:** LOUISIANA WATER THRUSH

large black *n, usu cap L&B* **1 :** a British breed of black lop-eared bacon-type swine **2 :** an animal of the Large Black breed

large bond *n* **:** a bond having a par value of over $1000 — compare BABY BOND

large brown bat *n* **:** BIG BROWN BAT

large buckeye *n* **:** SWEET BUCKEYE

large calorie *n* **:** CALORIE b(1)

large cane *n* **:** GIANT CANE

large–cone pine *also* **large–coned pine** \'=,=-\ *n* **:** COULTER PINE

large coralroot *n* **:** a widely distributed and highly variable No. American coralroot (*Corallorhiza maculata*) that grows in dry woodlands and usu. has a whitish perianth spotted with red or purple

large crabgrass *n* **:** a common annual crabgrass (*Digitaria sanguinalis*) that is native to Europe but a naturalized weed in much of No. America

large cranberry *n* **:** AMERICAN CRANBERRY

large crested tern *n* **:** an Oriental tern (*Thalasseus bergii*) with a black cap produced into a prominent crest

large–eyed \'=¦=\ *adj* **1 :** having large eyes ⟨a *large-eyed* shrimp⟩ or a large eye ⟨*large-eyed* darning needles⟩ **2 a :** having the eyes wide open in or as if in interest, curiosity, or amazement ⟨gave a shy *large-eyed* glance⟩ **b :** of a kind or degree to make the eyes open wide ⟨waiting in *large-eyed* wonder⟩

large–flowered bellwort \'=,=-\ *n* **:** a slender woodland herb (*Uvularia grandiflora*) of eastern No. America with perfoliate leaves and lemon-yellow bell-shaped flowers

large–flowered dogwood *n* **:** a tall arborescent dogwood (*Cornus nuttallii*) of upland areas of the Pacific coast having the flower cluster subtended by long white or rosy bracts up to three inches long

large–flowered everlasting *n* **:** PEARLY EVERLASTING

large-flowered wake-robin *n* : GREAT WHITE TRILLIUM
large-handed \ˈ¦=ˌ=\ *adj* **1** *obs* : GRASPING, RAPACIOUS **2** : OPENHANDED, LIBERAL
largehearted \ˈ¦=ˌ=\ *adj* : having a generous disposition : SYMPATHETIC, CHARITABLE, KINDLY ⟨a ~ humane person —H.E.Starr⟩
large intestine *n* : the posterior division of the vertebrate intestine being wider and shorter than the small intestine, typically divided into cecum, colon, and rectum, and concerned esp. with the dehydration of digestive residues into feces
largeish *var of* LARGISH
large knot *n* : a sound knot in lumber that is not less than 1½ inches in diameter
large-leaved aster \ˈ=ˌ=-\ *n* : a common No. American woodland herb (*Aster macrophyllus*) with large cordate basal leaves and lavender or violet flowers
large-leaved magnolia *or* **large-leaved cucumber tree** *n* : a large spreading shrub or medium-sized tree (*Magnolia macrophylla*) of the southern U.S. with long oblong silky leaves and large white purple-centered flowers
large·ly *adv* [ME, fr. ¹*large* + *-ly*, adv. suffix] : in a large manner: as **a** : to a large extent : EXTENSIVELY, ABUNDANTLY **b** : in a general or wide sense : on a large scale : GENERALLY, COMPREHENSIVELY **c** : POMPOUSLY **d** *obs* : at length : FULLY, FREELY, LOOSELY, WIDELY
large-minded \ˈ¦=ˌ=\ *adj* : liberal in ideas : characterized by breadth of view : not narrow in mind or outlook ⟨*large-minded* men, thinkers as well as statesmen —James Bryce⟩
large mononuclear leukocyte *n* : MONOCYTE
largemouth black bass \ˈ=ˌ=-\ *also* **largemouthed black bass** *or* **largemouth bass** *or* **largemouthed bass** *or* **largemouth** *n* : a wide-ranging and rather large black bass (*Micropterus salmoides*) chiefly of warm sluggish waters that is blackish green above and lighter or whitish below with the angle of the jaw falling behind the eye — compare SMALLMOUTH BLACK BASS
large-mouthed bowel worm *n* : BOWEL WORM
larg·en \ˈlärjən, ˈlȧj-\ *vb* -ED/-ING/-S *archaic* : ENLARGE
large·ness *n* -ES [ME *largenesse* magnitude, liberality, fr. ¹*large* + *-nesse* -ness] : the quality or state of being large: as **a** : large size : MAGNITUDE, BULK, BIGNESS, EXTENSIVENESS **b** : large scope or range : COMPREHENSIVENESS, BREADTH **c** : LIBERALITY **d** *obs* : DIFFUSENESS, PROLIXITY **e** : POMPOUSNESS
large order *n* : something difficult to attain or accomplish ⟨got the planting done without outside help; a *large order* for three boys in their early teens⟩
large paper edition *n* : an edition of a book printed with wider margins and often better quality paper and binding than the regular edition : a deluxe edition
large pole *n* : a forest tree with a diameter of from 8 to 12 inches
large post *n* : a size of paper 16½ inches by 21 inches
larger *comparative of* LARGE
larger duckweed *n* : GREAT DUCKWEED
larges *pres 3d sing of* LARGE
large-scale \ˈ¦=ˌ=\ *adj* [fr. the phrase *large scale*] : large in comparison with others of the same general class: as **a** : involving great numbers or quantities : having wide scope or extensive proportions ⟨a *large-scale* attack on polio⟩ ⟨*large-scale* preparations for war⟩ **b** *of a map* : having a scale (as one inch to a mile) that permits the plotting of much detail with comparatively great exactness — compare SMALL-SCALE
large-souled \ˈ¦=ˌ=\ *adj* : LARGEHEARTED
lar·gess *or* **lar·gesse** \lärˈjes, lȧˈ-, ˈ=ˌ=\ *n, pl* **largess·es** [ME *largesse*, fr. OF *largece, largesse*, fr. *large* generous — more at LARGE] **1** *obs* : LIBERALITY, GENEROSITY **2** : liberal giving or assistance esp. when accompanied by condescension from a superior to an inferior or from one of higher rank or status to one of lower ⟨nor can we make other people like us by a one-sided ~ —S.F.Bemis⟩ ⟨obtained his post through his old teacher's ~⟩ **3** : something given: as **a** : a free gift usu. given in connection with some auspicious event ⟨there was given after the coronation a ~ to every man of a silver penny and a measure of wheat⟩ or traditional occasion ⟨coins for the harvest home ~⟩ **b** : gratuities given (as for service) esp. when excessive or ostentatious : large tips ⟨scattering ~ at every stopping place⟩ **c** : aid, support, or other valuables received as or as if as a gift or through the benevolence of another ⟨dependent for her livelihood on the ~ of a moody lover —Jean Stafford⟩ ⟨living on government ~⟩ **4** : an innate quality (as of mind or spirit) ⟨from some ~ of feeling —Nancy Cardozo⟩ ⟨a writer of imaginative ~ —Irving Howe⟩ ⟨his generosity of spirit, an absolutely natural ~ —Harvey Breit⟩ **5** *obs* : LIBERTY, FREEDOM, LEAVE
largest *superlative of* LARGE
large-toothed aspen *or* **large tooth aspen** \ˈ=ˌ=-\ *n* : a No. American tree (*Populus grandidentata*) with coarse-toothed leaves and soft wood
large tupelo *n* : TUPELO GUM
large twayblade *n* : an orchid (*Liparis liliifolia*) of eastern No. America with lustrous elliptical to nearly ovate leaves, angled scape, and terminal raceme of 5 to 40 purple and green or wholly green flowers
large water grass *n* : DALLIS GRASS
large white *n* **1** *usu cap L&W* **a** : a British breed of large long-bodied white bacon-type swine **b** : an animal of the Large White breed — see YORKSHIRE 1 **2** : CABBAGE BUTTERFLY b
large yellow ladyslipper *n* : a lady's slipper (*Cypripedium calceolus pubescens*) of mesophytic woodlands of eastern and central No. America that has slightly fragrant greenish yellow and often purple-marked flowers
¹**lar·ghet·to** \lärˈged·(ˌ)ō\ *adv* (*or adj*) [It, somewhat slow, fr. *largo* slow, broad] : in a somewhat slow manner — used as a direction in music
²**larghetto** \ˈ"\ *n* -S : a larghetto movement
lar·ghis·si·mo \-ˈgēsəˌmō, -ˈgis-\ *adv* (*or adj*) [It, very slow, very broad, fr. L *largissimus* very abundant, most abundant, superl. of *largus*] : in as slow a manner as possible — used as a direction in music
lar gibbon *n* : LAR 2
larging *pres part of* LARGE
larg·ish *also* **large·ish** \ˈlärjish, ˈlȧj-, -jēsh\ *adj* : rather large
lar·gi·tion \lärˈjishən\ *n* -S [L *largition-, largitio*, fr. *largitus* (past part. of *largiri* to lavish, bestow, fr. *largus* abundant, generous) + *-ion-, -io* -ion] **1** *obs* : bestowal of largess **2** : GIFT, GRATUITY — **lar·gi·tion·al** \(ˈ)¦=ˈjishənᵊl, -shnəl\ *adj*
¹**lar·go** \ˈlär(ˌ)gō, ˈlȧ(-\ *adv* (*or adj*) [It, slow, broad, fr. L *largus* abundant, generous — more at LARD] : in a very slow and broad manner — used as a direction in music
²**largo** \ˈ"\ *n* -S [It, fr. *largo*, adj.] : a largo movement
la·ri \ˈlāˌrī\ *n pl, cap* [NL, fr. LL, pl. of *larus* gull — more at LARUS] : a suborder of Charadriiformes that includes the gulls, terns, jaegers, and skimmers
¹**lar·i·at** \ˈlarēət *also* ˈler-, *usu* -əd·+V\ *n* -S [AmerSp *la reata* the lasso, fr. Sp *la* the (fem. of *el*, def. art., the, fr. L *ille* that one, that, alter. — influenced by L *is* he — of *ollus*) + AmerSp *reata* lasso, fr. Sp, rope used to keep animals in single file, fr. *reatar* to tie in single file, tie again, fr. *re-* (fr. L) + *atar* to tie, fasten, fr. L *aptare* to put on, fit, fr. *aptus* fit, suitable; L *ollus* akin to L *uls* beyond — more at ALL, ITERATE, APT] : a long light but strong rope usu. of hemp or strips of hide used with a running noose for catching livestock or with or without the noose for picketing grazing animals — compare LASSO
²**lar·i·at** \-ēə|t, -ē,a|, *usu* |d·+V\ *vt* -ED/-ING/-S *West* : to secure, catch, or equip with a lariat ⟨~*ed* saddles⟩
lariat loop *n* : a small circular loop which is formed at one end of a lariat by knotting and through which the other end of the lariat is passed when preparing a running noose or lasso
lar·ick \ˈlarik\ *n* -S [L *laric-, larix*] *chiefly Scot* : LARCH
lar·id \ˈlarəd\ *n* -S [NL *Laridae*] : a bird of the family Laridae
lar·i·dae \-rəˌdē\ *n pl, cap* [NL, fr. *Larus*, type genus + *-idae*] : a family (suborder Lari) including the gulls and terns and sometimes the jaegers — compare STERCORARIIDAE
la·ri·go \ˈlarəˌgō\ *n* -S [perh. modif. of Sp *látigo* latigo] : a ring at each end of the cinch of a western saddle through which the latigos pass
lar·i·got \ˈlarəˌgō\ *n* -S [F] **1** : FLAGEOLET 1 **2** : NINETEENTH 3b
la·ri·idae \ləˈrīəˌdē\ [NL, fr. *Laria* (a prior but largely disused equivalent of *Bruchus*) (prob. fr. L *lar* + NL *-ia*) + *-idae* — more at LARVA] *syn of* BRUCHIDAE
la·rin \ˈlärən\ *or* **la·ri** *also* **lar·ree** \ˈlärē\ *n* -S [Per *lārī*] : a piece of silver wire doubled over and sometimes twisted into the form of a fishhook that was formerly used as money in parts of Asia
lar·ine \ˈla(a)rˌīn, -ˌrən\ *adj* [NL *Larinae* subfamily containing the gulls, fr. *Larus*, type genus + *-inae*] : of or relating to gulls esp. as distinguished from terns
la·rith·mic \ləˈrithmik, -th-\ *adj* [back-formation fr. *larithmics*] : of or relating to larithmics
la·rith·mics \-ks\ *n pl but sing in constr* [Gk *laos* people + *arithmos* number + E *-ics* — more at ARITHMO-] : the scientific study of the quantitative aspects of population
lar·ix \ˈla(a)rəks\ *n* [NL, fr. L, larch] **1** *cap* : a genus of trees (family Pinaceae) that are widely distributed in the north temperate zone and have deciduous foliage in clusters of acicular leaves of different lengths on short lateral spurs or scattered singly on the terminal shoots, solitary staminate flowers, and persistent cone scales — compare PSEUDOLARIX **2** -ES : a tree of the genus *Larix*
¹**lark** \ˈlärk, ˈlȧk\ *n* -S [ME *larke*, fr. OE *lāwerce*; akin to OHG *lērihha* lark, ON *lævirki*] **1** : any of numerous singing birds of the family Alaudidae mostly of Europe, Asia, and northern Africa; *esp* : SKYLARK 1 — compare HORNED LARK **2** : any of various usu. ground-living birds of families other than Alaudidae — usu. used in combination ⟨meadow*lark*⟩ ⟨tit*lark*⟩ **3** : a grayish yellow that is duller than chamois, redder and slightly darker than crash, and redder and slightly less strong than old ivory **4 a** : POET ⟨my fellow ~*s* —Vachel Lindsay⟩ **b** : SINGER
²**lark** \ˈ"\ *vi* -ED/-ING/-S : to catch or hunt larks ⟨~*ing* with birdlime⟩
³**lark** \ˈ"\ *vb* -ED/-ING/-S [prob. alter. of ³*lake*] *vi* **1** : to behave sportively or mischievously : engage in harmless pranks : FROLIC ⟨~*ing* all day in the hills⟩ ⟨boys ~*ing* about after school⟩ **2** : to ride across country or over obstacles ~ *vt* : to make sport of : TEASE
⁴**lark** \ˈ"\ *n* -S **1 a** : a merry adventure : FROLIC, ROMP : a bit of harmless amusing mischief : PRANK **b** : something not taken or intended to be taken very seriously ⟨if an officer comes . . . to make inspection he is usually on a ~ —T.R. Fisher⟩ **2** *slang Brit* : a course of action or way of life
lark bunting *n* : a large finch (*Calamospiza melanocorys*) of the plains of the western U.S. that has the male black with a large white wing patch
lark-colored \ˈ=¦=ˌ=\ *adj* : of a sandy brown like that of the European larks
¹**lark·er** \ˈlärkər, ˈlȧkə(r\ *n* -S [¹*lark* + *-er*] : a catcher of larks
²**larker** \ˈ"\ *n* -S [³*lark* + *-er*] : one that engages in a lark or in larking
lark finch *n* : LARK SPARROW
lark-heel *in sense 1* ˈ=ˌ=, *in sense 2* ˈ=¦=\ *or* **lark's-heel** \ˈ=ˌ=\ *n, pl* **lark-heels** *or* **lark's-heels** **1** : LARKSPUR **2** : a long heel sometimes seen in Negroes
lark-heeled \ˈ=¦=\ *adj, of a bird* : having the claw of the hind toe long and straight ⟨a *lark-heeled* cuckoo⟩
lark·i·ness \ˈlärkēnəs, ˈlȧk-, -kin-\ *n* -ES [*larky* + *-ness*] : light-hearted gaiety : SPORTIVENESS
larking *adj* [fr. pres. part. of ³*lark*] : dashing and gay : GIDDY, FROLICSOME — **lark·ing·ly** *adv*
lark·ish \ˈlärkish, ˈlȧk-, -kēsh\ *adj* [⁴*lark* + *-ish*] : gaily mischievous : FROLICSOME ⟨a ~ mood⟩ — **lark·ish·ly** *adv* — **lark·ish·ness** *n* -ES
lark plover *n* : SEED SNIPE
lark's-claw \ˈ=ˌ=\ *n, pl* **lark's-claws** [*lark's* (gen. of ¹*lark*) + *claw*] : LARKSPUR
lark's head *n* [*lark's* (gen. of ¹*lark*) + *head*] : a hitch made by passing the bight of a line through a ring or around an object and then passing the two ends through the bight

lark's head

lark·some \ˈlärksəm, ˈlȧk-\ *adj* [⁴*lark* + *-some*] : marked by or inclined toward sportive or mischievous behavior : FROLICSOME, PLAYFUL ⟨the melodrama had not been produced for ~ purposes —*London Daily News*⟩ ⟨a moderately ~ fellow —E.J.Kahn⟩
lark sparrow *n* : a sparrow (*Chondestes grammacus*) that is abundant in the Mississippi valley, is streaked above and white below with the head varied with black, grayish white, and chestnut, and is represented in the western U.S. by a paler bird which forms a distinct subspecies (*C. grammacus strigatus*)
larkspur \ˈ=ˌ=\ *n* [¹*lark* + *spur*; fr. the shape of the calyx] **1 a** : a plant of the genus *Delphinium*; *esp* : a cultivated annual plant of this genus — compare DELPHINIUM 2 **b** : the dried ripe seeds of a European larkspur (*Delphinium ajacis*) from which an acetic tincture is sometimes prepared for use against ectoparasites (as lice) **2** : a moderate greenish blue that is bluer and paler than average peacock and greener and slightly deeper than Brittany

larkspur

larky \ˈlärkē, ˈlȧkē, -ki\ *adj* -ER/-EST [⁴*lark* + *-y*] : ready for a lark : giddy and frolicsome : SPORTIVE
lar·mier \ˈlärmē,ā, -m,yā\ *n* -S [F, fr. MF, fr. *larme* tear] : DRIP 4
lar·mor frequency \ˈlär,mȯ(ə)r-\ *n, usu cap L* [after Sir Joseph *Larmor* †1942 Brit. mathematician] : the frequency of Larmor precession
larmor precession *n, usu cap L* : the precession of a particle having magnetic moment (as an atom when spinning in a magnetic field)
larmor's theorem *n, usu cap L* **1** : a statement in physics: the only sensible effect of a magnetic field upon the motions of atomic electrons is the Larmor precession **2** : a statement in physics: in an enclosure traversed by thermal radiation uniformly in all directions the radiation pressure is equal to one third of the radiant energy per unit volume
lar·moy·ant \(ˈ)lär¦mȯiənt *or as F*\ *adj* [F, pres. part. of *larmoyer* to be tearful, snivel, fr. OF *larmoier* to weep, shed tears, fr. *larme* tear, fr. L *lacrima* — more at TEAR] : LACHRYMOSE
lar·nau·di·an \(ˈ)lär¦nōdēən\ *adj, usu cap* [*Larnaud*, locality in Jura mountains, eastern France + E *-ian*] : of, relating to, or being a late bronze age period in Europe
lar·nax \ˈlär,naks\ *n, pl* **larna·kes** \-nə,kēz\ [Gk, perh. alter. of (assumed) Gk *narnax* (whence LGk *narnax* chest); akin to OE *nearu* narrow — more at NARROW] : a chest usu. of terra cotta and often ornamented that was used in ancient Greece esp. as a sepulchral chest
larn·ite \ˈlär,nīt\ *n* -S [*Larne*, city in northern Ireland, its locality + E *-ite*] : a mineral β-Ca_2SiO_4 consisting of the unstable beta form of calcium silicate
lar·oid \ˈla(a)r,ȯid\ *adj* [NL *Larus* + E *-oid*] : resembling or relating to gulls : like or like that of members of the genus *Larus*
laron *n* -S [MF *larron*, fr. L *latron-, latro* mercenary soldier, brigand — more at LATRON] *obs* : ROBBER
lar·over \ˈla,rōvə(r)\ *var of* ¹LAYOVER
lar·rea \ləˈrēə, -rāə\ *n* [NL, fr. J. A. H. de *Larrea*, 18th cent. Span. patron of science] **1** *cap* : a small genus of American xerophytic shrubs (family Zygophyllaceae) including the creosote bush **2** -S : a shrub of the genus *Larrea*
larree *var of* LARIN
lar·ri·dae \ˈlarə,dē\ *n pl, cap* [NL, fr. *Larra*, type genus + *-idae*] : a family of stocky medium-sized large-eyed digger wasps that nest in sandy soil
lar·ri·gan \ˈlarəgən\ *n* -S [origin unknown] : an oil-tanned moccasin with legs that is used esp. by lumbermen and trappers
¹**lar·ri·kin** \ˈlarəkən\ *n* -S [origin unknown] *chiefly Austral* : a noisy disorderly fellow : HOODLUM, ROWDY
²**larrikin** \ˈ"\ *adj, chiefly Austral* : BOISTEROUS, ROWDY, DISORDERLY
lar·ri·kin·ism \-kə,nizəm\ *n* -S *chiefly Austral* : larrikin behavior
¹**lar·rup** \ˈlarəp *also* ˈler-\ *vb* -ED/-ING/-S [perh. imit.] *vt* **1** *dial* : to flog soundly : BEAT, WHIP **2** *dial* : to defeat decisively ⟨~*ed* the senator in the farm counties⟩ ~ *vi, dial* : to slouch or move in a heavy awkward fashion : progress in a noisy bumbling manner
²**larrup** \ˈ"\ *n* -S *dial* : BLOW : something (as a switch) for dealing blows
larruping *adv* (*or adj*) [fr. pres. part. of ¹*larrup*] *dial* : in a way or of a kind to beat others : of notable quality or size : VERY ⟨~ good baked ham⟩
¹**lar·ry** \ˈlarē\ *n* -ES [perh. fr. *Larry*, nickname for the name *Lawrence*] **1** : a long-handled hoe usu. with a perforated blade that is used esp. for mixing mortar **2** : thin sloppy mortar : GROUT
²**larry** \ˈ"\ *vt* -ED/-ING/-ES : to fill in with grout sometimes with bricks or spalls in it : GROUT
³**larry** \ˈ"\ *n* -ES [prob. alter. of ¹*lurry*] *dial Eng* : CONFUSION, EXCITEMENT, NOISE
⁴**larry** \ˈ"\ *n* -ES [alter. of *lorry*] **1** : a small usu. motor-driven car with a drop bottom used for hauling slate or rock from the tipple to the dump of a mine **2** : a hand-pushed or motor-driven car with a hopper that is used for weighing or measuring and distributing bulk materials and is suspended between overhead tracks or carried on rails — called also *weigh larry*
lar·ry·man *also* **lar·ri·man** \ˈlarēmən\ *n, pl* **larrymen** *also* **larrimen** [⁴*larry* + *man*] : an operator of a larry
lars *pl of* LAR
lar·sen·ite \ˈlärsᵊn,īt\ *n* -S [Esper S. *Larsen* *b*1879 Am. geologist + E *-ite*] : a mineral $PbZnSiO_4$ consisting of a lead and zinc silicate occurring at Franklin, N.J., in colorless orthorhombic prisms
lar·um \ˈla(a)rəm, -er-, -är-, -ȧr-\ *n* -S [short for *alarum*] : ALARM
lar·us \ˈla(a)rəs\ *n, cap* [NL, fr. LL, gull, fr. Gk *laros*; perh. akin to L *lamentum* lament — more at LAMENT] : a large cosmopolitan genus of gulls comprising many of the better-known gulls and being the type of the family Laridae — see BONAPARTE'S GULL, GLAUCOUS GULL, HERRING GULL, LAUGHING GULL
lar·va \ˈlärvə, ˈlȧvə\ *n, pl* **lar·vae** \-(ˌ)vē, -ˌvī\ *also* **larvas** [L, evil spirit, specter, mask; akin to L *lar* tutelary god, lar and perh. to L *lascivus* wanton — more at LUST] **1 a** *obs* : a disembodied spirit : GHOST **b** : an ancient Roman specter or apparition; *esp* : a malevolent spirit **c** : a supernatural monster — used chiefly in medieval occultism **2** [NL, fr. L] **a** : the immature, wingless, and often vermiform feeding form that hatches from the egg of a holometabolous insect, increases in size, undergoes other minor changes while passing through several molts, and is finally transformed into a pupa or chrysalis from which the adult ultimately emerges — see CATERPILLAR, GRUB, MAGGOT **b** : NYMPH 3 **c** : the early form of any animal that at birth or hatching is fundamentally unlike its parent and must pass through more or less of a metamorphosis before assuming the adult characters — used of later states than *embryo*
lar·va·cea \lärˈvāshēə\ *n pl, cap* [NL, fr. *larva* + *-acea*] : an order of small free-swimming pelagic tunicates constituting *Appendicularia* and related genera, having a permanent caudal appendage supported by a notochord, being usu. hermaphroditic, and lacking a metamorphosis
larvacide *var of* LARVICIDE
lar·vae·vo·rid \lärˈvēvərəd\ *adj or n* [NL *Larvaevoridae*] : TACHINID
lar·vae·vor·i·dae \ˌlärvəˈvȯrə,dē\ [NL, fr. *Larvaevora* (a prior but largely disused equivalent of *Tachina*) (fr. NL *larvae* — pl. of *larva* — + *-vora*) + *-idae*] *syn of* TACHINIDAE
lar·val \ˈlärvəl, ˈlȧv-\ *adj* [L *larvalis*, fr. *larva* + *-alis* -al] **1** : of or relating to a spectral larva **2** [NL *larvalis*, fr. *larva* + L *-alis* -al] **a** : of, relating to, typical of, or being an animal larva ⟨the ~ eye⟩ ⟨~ crayfishes⟩ **b** : immature of its kind ⟨~ societies⟩ ⟨~ hopes and fears⟩
lar·va·lia \lärˈvālēə\ [NL, fr. neut. pl. of *larvalis* larval] *syn of* LARVACEA
larva mi·grans \-ˈmī,granz\ *n, pl* **larvae migran·tes** \-ˌmīˈgran,tēz\ [NL, lit., migrating larva] : CREEPING ERUPTION
larva of de·sor \-dəˈzō(ə)r, -ˈdȧ,z-\ *usu cap D* [prob. fr. the name *Desor*] : a pilidium (as of certain nemerteans) that is modified for creeping
lar·var·i·um \lärˈva(a)rēəm\ *n, pl* **larvar·ia** \-ēə\ *also* **larvariums** [NL, fr. *larva* + *-arium*] **1** : a nest or shelter made and occupied by the larvae of some insects **2** : a container for the rearing of insect larvae
lar·vate \ˈlär,vāt\ *or* **lar·vat·ed** \-ˌād·əd\ *adj* [*larvate* fr. NL *larvatus*, fr. L *larva* mask + *-atus* -ate; *larvated* prob. fr. L *larva* mask + E *-ate* + *-ed*] : covered or concealed by or as if by a mask
larve \ˈlärv\ *n* -S [F, fr. L *larva*] *archaic* : LARVA
larvi- *comb form* [NL, fr. *larva*] : larva : larval ⟨*larvi*colous⟩ ⟨*larvi*form⟩ *larvi*gerous⟩
lar·vi·cid·al \ˌ¦lärvə¦sīdᵊl\ *adj* : of, relating to, or being a larvicide
¹**lar·vi·cide** *also* **lar·va·cide** \ˈlärvə,sīd\ *n* -S [*larvi-* or *larva* + *-cide*] : an insecticide or other pesticide used for killing larvae — compare ADULTICIDE
²**lar·vi·cide** \ˈ"\ *vt* -ED/-ING/-S : to treat with a larvicide ⟨effects of DDT mosquito *larviciding* on wildlife —*Public Health Reports*⟩
lar·vic·o·lous \(ˈ)lär¦vikələs\ *adj* [*larvi-* + *-colous*] : living in the body of a larva — used esp. of a parasitoid insect
lar·vik·ite \ˈlärvi,kīt\ *or* **laur·vik·ite** \ˈlaů(ə)rv-\ *n* -S [G *larvikit*, fr. *Larvik*, Norway, its locality + G *-it* -ite] : an alkali-syenite rock composed chiefly of cryptoperthite or anorthoclase in rhombic crystals and widely used as an ornamental building stone
lar·vip·a·rous \(ˈ)lär¦vipərəs\ *adj* [prob. fr. (assumed) NL *larviparus*, fr. NL *larvi-* + L *-parus* -parous] : bearing and bringing forth young that are larvae — used esp. of specialized two-winged flies and some mollusks; compare OVIPAROUS, VIVIPAROUS
lar·vi·phag·ic \ˌ¦lärvə¦fajik\ *adj* [*larvi-* + *-phagic* (fr. *-phagy* + *-ic*)] : LARVIVOROUS
lar·vi·pos·it \ˈlärvə,päzət, ˌ==ˈ==\ *vi* -ED/-ING/-S [*larvi-* + *posit*] : to deposit living larvae instead of eggs — compare OVIPOSIT
lar·vi·po·si·tion \ˌlärvəpəˈzishən\ *n* : the act of larvipositing
lar·viv·o·rous \(ˈ)lär¦vivərəs\ *adj* [prob. fr. (assumed) NL *larvivorus*, fr. NL *larvi-* + L *-vorus* -vorous] : feeding upon larvae esp. of insects ⟨~ fishes⟩
lar·vule \ˈlär(ˌ)vyül\ *n* -S [*larva* + *-ule*] : the earliest larval stage of an ephemerid insect in which the respiratory, circulatory, and nerve systems do not appear to be developed
laryng- *or* **laryngo-** *comb form* [NL *laryng-* & LL *laryngo-*, fr. Gk *laryng-, laryngo-*, fr. *laryng-, larynx*] **1** : larynx ⟨*laryn*gopathy⟩ ⟨*laryng*itis⟩ **2 a** : laryngeal and ⟨*laryngo*pharyngeal⟩ **b** : of the larynx ⟨*laryngo*vestibulitis⟩
¹**la·ryn·ge·al** \ləˈrinj(ē)əl, ¦larən¦jēəl\ *adj* [NL *laryngeus* laryngeal (fr. *laryng-* + L *-eus* -eous) + E *-al*] **1** : of, relating to, or used on the larynx ⟨~ forceps⟩ **2** *also* **la·ryn·gal** \ləˈriŋgəl\ [*laryngal* ISV *laryng-* + *-al*] *phonetics* : produced by or with constriction of the larynx ⟨~ articulation of sounds⟩ — **la·ryn·ge·al·ly** \ləˈrinj(ē)əlē, ¦larən¦jēəlē, -li\ *adv*
²**laryngeal** \ˈ"\ *n* -S **1** : a laryngeal part (as a nerve or artery) **2** *also* **laryngal** **a** : a laryngeal sound **b** : any of a set of several (as three or four) phonemes reconstructed for Proto-Indo-European chiefly on indirect evidence
laryngeal artery *n* : either of two arteries supplying blood to the larynx: **a** : an artery derived from the inferior thyroid artery — called also *inferior laryngeal artery* **b** : an artery derived from the superior thyroid artery — called also *superior laryngeal artery*
la·ryn·ge·al·ization \ləˌrinj(ē)ələˈzāshən, ˌlarən,jēə-, -ˌlīˈz-\ *n* -S : articulation with laryngeal modification
la·ryn·ge·al·ize \ləˈrinj(ē)ə,līz, ¦larən¦jēə-\ *vt* -ED/-ING/-S : to articulate (as a vowel) with laryngeal modification

laryngeal nerve *n* **:** either of two branches of the vagus nerve supplying the larynx

laryngeal pouch *also* **laryngeal sac** *or* **laryngeal saccule** *n* **:** a saccular expansion of the lateral wall cavity of the larynx between the true and false vocal cords that is greatly developed in certain monkeys (as the orang)

la·ryn·ge·at·ing \lə'rinjē,ād·iŋ\ *n* -s [*larynge-* (as in *laryngeal*) + *-ate* + *-ing*] **:** contraction and relaxation of laryngeal musculature unaccompanied by phonation **:** subvocal speech

lar·yn·gec·to·mee \,larən'jektə'mē\ *n* -s [*laryngectomy* + *-ee*] **:** a person who has undergone laryngectomy

lar·yn·gec·to·mize \,=='==,mīz\ *vt* -ED/-ING/-S [*laryngectomy* + *-ize*] **:** to subject (a person) to laryngectomy

lar·yn·gec·to·my \-,mē\ *n* -ES [NL *laryngectomia*, fr. *laryng-* + *-ectomia* -ectomy] **:** surgical removal of all or part of the larynx

la·ryn·gic \lə'rinjik\ *adj* [NL *laryngicus*, fr. *laryng-* + L *-icus* -ic] **:** LARYNGEAL

lar·yn·gis·mus \,larən'jizməs\ *n, pl* **laryngis·mi** \-,mī\ [NL, fr. *laryng-* + L *-ismus* -ism] **:** LARYNGOSPASM

laryngismus stri·du·lus \-'strijələs\ *n, pl* **laryngismi stridu·li** \-,lī\ [NL, lit., stridulous laryngismus] **:** a sudden spasm of the larynx that occurs in children and esp. in rickets and is marked by difficult breathing with prolonged noisy inspiration — compare LARYNGOSPASM

¹lar·yn·git·ic \;==;jid·ik\ *adj* [*laryngitis* + *-ic*] **:** of, relating to, or characteristic of laryngitis **:** affected with laryngitis

²laryngitic *n* -s **:** an individual suffering from laryngitis

lar·yn·gi·tis \,larən'jīd·əs, -ītəs *also* ,ler-\ *n, pl* **laryngit·i·des** \-jid·ə,dēz, -jitə-\ [NL, fr. *laryng-* + *-itis*] **:** inflammation of the larynx

laryngo- — see LARYNG-

la·ryn·go·fissure \lə'riŋgō+\ *n* [ISV *laryng-* + *fissure*] **:** surgical opening of the larynx by an incision through the thyroid cartilage esp. for the removal of a tumor

la·ryn·go·log·i·cal \lə,riŋgə'läjəkəl\ *or* **la·ryn·go·log·ic** \-jik\ *adj* [*laryngological* fr. *laryngology* + *-ical*; *laryngologic* ISV *laryngology* + *-ic*] **:** of or relating to laryngology

lar·yn·gol·o·gist \,larən'gäləjəst\ *n* -s [ISV *laryngology* + *-ist*] **:** a physician specializing in laryngology

lar·yn·gol·o·gy \-jē\ *n* -ES [ISV *laryng-* + *-logy*] **:** a branch of medical science dealing with the study and treatment of diseases of the larynx and nasopharynx

la·ryn·go·pharyngeal \lə'riŋgō+\ *adj* **:** of or common to both larynx and pharynx

la·ryn·go·pharynx \=';==+\ *n* [NL, fr. *laryng-* + *pharynx*] **:** the lower part of the pharynx lying behind or adjacent to the larynx — compare NASOPHARYNX

la·ryn·go·phone \='=gə,fōn\ *n* [ISV *laryng-* + *-phone*] **:** a communication-system transmitter in which the vibration-receiving diaphragm is strapped to the throat over the larynx from which it receives speech vibrations directly

la·ryn·go·scope \-,skōp\ *n* [ISV *laryng-* + *-scope*] **:** an instrument or apparatus for examining the interior of the larynx — **la·ryn·go·scop·ic** \=;=;=skäpik\ *or* **la·ryn·go·scop·i·cal** \-pəkəl\ *adj* — **la·ryn·go·scop·i·cal·ly** \-ək(ə)lē\ *adv* — **lar·yn·gos·co·py** \,larən'gäskəpē\ *n* -ES

la·ryn·go·spasm \lə'riŋgə+,-\ *n* [ISV *laryng-* + *spasm*] **:** spasmodic closure of the larynx — compare LARYNGISMUS STRIDULUS

la·ryn·go·tracheal \=;=(,)gō+\ *adj* [ISV *laryng-* + *tracheal*] **:** of or common to the larynx and trachea

la·ryn·go·tracheitis \"+\ *n* [NL, fr. *laryng-* + *trache-* + *-itis*] **:** inflammation of both larynx and trachea — see INFECTIOUS LARYNGOTRACHEITIS

la·ryn·go·tracheobronchitis \"+\ *n* [NL, fr. *laryng-* + *trache-* + *bronch-* + *-itis*] **:** inflammation of the larynx, trachea, and bronchi; *specif* **:** an acute severe infection of these parts marked by swelling of the tissues and excessive secretion of mucus leading to more or less complete obstruction of the respiratory passages

lar·ynx \'lariŋ(k)s, -rēn- *also* 'ler-, *substand* 'lärniks *or* 'lān- *or* -nēks\ *n, pl* **la·ryn·ges** \lə'rin(,)jēz\ *also* **larynxes** [NL *laryng-*, *larynx*, fr. Gk; prob. akin to MHG *slurken* to swallow, Sw dial. *slurka* to lap up, L *lurco* glutton] **:** the modified upper part of the respiratory passage of air-breathing vertebrates bounded above by the glottis and continuous below with the trachea and having a complex cartilaginous or bony skeleton capable of limited motion through the action of associated muscles and in man, most other mammals, and a few lower forms a set of elastic vocal cords that play a major role in sound production and speech — compare SYRINX

las *pl of* LA

la·sa·gna \lə'zänyə, lä'-\ *or* **la·sa·gne** \", -(,)yā\ *n, pl* **lasa·gne** \-(,)yā\ [*lasagna* fr. It, fr. (assumed) VL *lasania*, fr. L *lasanum* cooking pot, fr. Gk *lasana* (pl.) trivet, *lasanon* (sing.) chamber pot; *lasagne* fr. It, pl. of *lasagna*; perh. akin to Skt *radhyati* he cooks] **1 :** broad flat noodles **2 :** lasagna baked and served usu. with a tomato, cheese, and meat sauce

las·car \'laskə(r)\ *also* **lash·kar** \-shk-\ *n* -s [Hindi *lashkar* army, fr. Per, fr. Ar *al-'askar* the army; E *lascar*, *lashkar* influenced in meaning by Hindi *lashkarī* soldier, sailor, fr. *lashkar*] **1 :** an East Indian sailor **2 :** an East Indian army servant **3 :** an East Indian native artilleryman of a low grade in the British Army

las·cive \lə'sēv\ *adj* [F *lascif*, fr. L *lascivus*] **:** LASCIVIOUS ⟨licentious violet and ~ rose —Wallace Stevens⟩

las·civ·i·ous \lə'sivēəs, la'-\ *adj* [L *lascivia* wantonness (fr. *lascivus* wanton + *-ia* -y) + E *-ous* — more at LUST] **1 :** inclined to lechery **:** LEWD, LUSTFUL ⟨flaunted the adulteries of ~ women —H.O.Taylor⟩ **2 :** tending to arouse sexual desire **:** LIBIDINOUS, SALACIOUS ⟨suggestive, even ~ poses —*Amer. Bk. Publishers Council*⟩ ⟨pleasant, ~ verses —*Times Lit. Supp.*⟩ — **las·civ·i·ous·ly** *adv* — **las·civ·i·ous·ness** *n* -ES

la·ser \'lāzə(r)\ *n* -s [*light amplification by stimulated emission of radiation*] **:** a device that utilizes the natural oscillations of atoms for amplifying or generating electromagnetic waves in the region of the spectrum from the ultraviolet to the far-infrared including the visible region

las·er·piti·um \,lasə(r)'pishēəm, ,lazə-, -pid·ē-\ *n, cap* [NL, alter. of L *lasserpicium*, a plant] **:** an Old World genus of perennial herbs (family Umbelliferae) with compound umbels of flowers and 8-winged fruits

¹lash \'lash, -aa(ə)-,-ai-\ *vb* -ED/-ING/-ES [ME *lashen* to throw quickly, strike with a lash, move violently, prob. partly of imit. origin and partly fr. *lashe*, n.] *vi* **1 a :** to move violently or suddenly **:** DASH, RUSH, FLY ⟨~*ed* out eastward with the agility for which he was dreaded —Emil Lengyel⟩ ⟨~ through the brilliant sunlight of a wide arena —P.B.Martin⟩ **b** *of a horse* **:** KICK — used with *out* ⟨~*ed* out . . . at the cursing men behind us —Kenneth Roberts⟩ **c :** BEAT, POUR ⟨the rain ~*ed* against the windowpanes —J.C.Powys⟩ ⟨hail ~*ed* down mercilessly⟩ **2 a :** to strike with or as if with a whip ⟨~*ing* about him with a stout staff⟩ ⟨it had ~*ed* across a human skull —Helen Nielsen⟩ ⟨the final plunge of a wave ~*es* against the opposing land —P.S.Welch⟩ ⟨~*ed* back at the enemy —S.E. Morison & H.S.Commager⟩ **b :** to make a sudden darting, sinuous, or striking movement like the lash of a whip ⟨the snake ~*ed* and curled —William Beebe⟩ **3 :** to make a verbal assault or riposte **:** engage in biting criticism or censure ⟨~*ing* at the bullet-headed commander —J.A.Michener⟩ ⟨uses . . . newspaper ads to ~ back —*Printers' Ink*⟩ — usu. used with *out* ⟨the author ~*es* out at Fascism —J.L.LaMonte⟩ ⟨~*ed* out on the rare occasions when he was aroused —Green Peyton⟩ **4** *now chiefly dial Brit* **:** to spend money recklessly — usu. used with *out* ~ *vt* **1 a** (1) **:** to throw quickly or impetuously **:** FLING, DASH ⟨the frightened mare ~*ed* up her heels⟩ (2) **:** to move violently ⟨the kitten . . . ~*ed* its angry tail —Ethel Wilson⟩ ⟨~*ed* her feather fan to and fro —Elizabeth Bowen⟩ **b :** POUR, EMIT — usu. used with *out* ⟨~ out some 34,000,000 copies of newspapers a week —*English Digest*⟩ **2 a** (1) **:** to strike with a lash **:** WHIP, SCOURGE ⟨penitents ~*ing* themselves till the blood came⟩ (2) **:** to strike forcibly and quickly esp. in a succession of blows **:** beat upon ⟨the whale ~*ed* the sea⟩ ⟨light ~*ed* my eyes —Wirt Williams⟩ ⟨rain ~*es* the windows⟩ ⟨the wind ~*ed* the waves into destructive fury⟩ **b** (1) **:** to assail or castigate with nonphysical means ⟨the jealousy, the hatred, the terror which ~ our souls —A.L.Guérard⟩; *esp* **:** to assail with stinging, biting, or satirical words ⟨~*ed* the vices of the time⟩ (2) **:** to goad, incite, or excite to some action or into some state **:** DRIVE ⟨~*es* him into murder —G.B.Shaw⟩ ⟨~*ed* itself into a passion against Spain —Dexter Perkins⟩ ⟨easy to ~ them into fury —J.A.Froude⟩ (3) **:** to cause to lash ⟨a rising wind was ~*ing* the rain against the windows —Val Mulkerus⟩ **3** *dial chiefly Brit* **:** to spend recklessly **:** THROW ⟨prepared to ~ the money around —Edward Sheehy⟩

²lash \"\ *n* -ES [ME *lashe*, prob. fr. *lashen*, v., to throw quickly, move violently] **1 a** (1) **:** a stroke with a whip or with anything slender, pliant, and tough ⟨received ten ~*es*⟩ (2) **:** the flexible part of a whip; *specif* **:** the piece (as of whipcord) forming its end ⟨twenty feet long from butt to ~ —H.L. Davis⟩ (3) **:** something used for whipping **:** WHIP ⟨used the ~ on kids who trespassed on his property —Ronald Sercombe⟩ (4) **:** punishment by flogging ⟨provides fines, jail terms, and the ~ for any incitement to violation —H.S.Warner⟩ **b :** a sudden swinging blow **:** a sweeping stroke ⟨felt the ~ of his hand on her cheek⟩ **c :** a pelting driving onslaught (as of wind or rain) ⟨has to stand up to the ~ of a north wind —*Monsanto Mag.*⟩ ⟨the bitter ~ of the rain —T.B.Costain⟩ **2 :** a sharp or stinging blow of a nonphysical kind ⟨under the ~ of competition —C.F.Wittke⟩ ⟨the ~ of public opinion —Robert Trumbull⟩ ⟨give him another ~ with my tongue —Michael McLaverty⟩ **3 :** EYELASH **4 :** a cord or group of strings for lifting simultaneously certain warp yarns to form a figure in weaving **5 :** BACKLASH 1b

³lash \"\ *vt* -ED/-ING/-ES [ME *lasschen* to lace, fr. MF *lachier*, *lacier* — more at LACE] **:** to bind with a rope, cord, thong, or chain so as to fasten ⟨~ something to a spar⟩ ⟨~ a pack⟩ — **lash a hammock :** to roll a hammock up usu. lengthwise with the bedding inside and bind it

lash cleat *n* [³*lash* + *cleat*] **:** a small metal hook screwed into the frame of a theatrical flat for attaching a lash line

lashed \'lasht, -aa(ə)-,-ai-\ *adj* [²*lash* + *-ed*] **:** having eyelashes usu. of a specified kind — used chiefly in combination ⟨that long-*lashed* teen-age floozy —James Stern⟩

lash·er \'lashə(r), -aash-,-aish-\ *n* -s **1 :** one that lashes or whips **2** *dial chiefly Eng* **a :** the water rushing through a weir **b :** WEIR **c :** a pool receiving the water from a weir

la·shi \'läshē\ *n, pl* **lashi** *or* **lashis** *usu cap* **1 :** a people of Tibeto-Burman affiliations related to the Lisu and inhabiting the frontier region between northern Yunnan and Burma **2 :** a member of the Lashi people

lashing *n* -s [fr. gerund of ³*lash*] **:** something (as a rope, wire, or chain) used for binding, wrapping, or fastening

lash·ing·ly *adv* [*lashing* (pres. part. of ¹*lash*) + *-ly*] **:** in a lashing manner

lash·ings \'lashiŋz, -aash-,-aish-, -shēnz,-shənz\ *also* **lash·ins** \-shənz\ *n pl* [fr. *lashings*, pl. of *lashing*, gerund of ¹*lash*] *chiefly Brit* **:** a great plenty **:** ABUNDANCE ⟨a porcelain bath with ~ of hot water —Agatha Christie⟩ ⟨~ of chocolate and other light snacks —D.L.Busk⟩

lash·kar \'ləshkə(r), 'lash-\ *adj, usu cap* [fr. *Lashkar*, city in north central India] **:** of or from the city of Lashkar, India **:** of the kind or style prevalent in Lashkar

lash·less \'lashləs, -aash-,-aish-\ *adj* **:** having no eyelashes

lash line *n* [³*lash* + *line*] **:** a light rope usu. of sash cord used for fastening flats together in setting up stage scenery

lash·orn \'la,shȯrn\ *n* -s [origin unknown] *Midland* **:** FRASER FIR

lash rope *n, chiefly West* **:** a rope used for lashing a pack (as on a packsaddle)

lash-up \'=,=\ *n* [fr. the phrase *lash up*, fr. ³*lash* + *up*] **1 :** something improvised esp. in an emergency **:** MAKESHIFT, CONTRAPTION, CONTRIVANCE ⟨crammed with an ingenious time-bomb *lash-up*—*Time*⟩ **2 :** SETUP, OUTFIT ⟨sounded as if he knew the *lash-up* well enough —Nard Jones⟩ ⟨man, Lieutenant, you got a real *lash-up* here —Gordon Webber⟩

la·si·o·cam·pa \,lāzēō'kampə, ,lāsē-\ *n, cap* [NL, fr. *lasio-* (fr. Gk *lasios* shaggy) + *-campa*; akin to Gk *lēnos* wool — more at WOOL] **:** the type genus of the family Lasiocampidae

¹la·si·o·cam·pid \,==='=pəd\ *adj* [NL *Lasiocampidae*] **:** of or relating to the Lasiocampidae

²lasiocampid \"\ *n* -s **:** a moth of the family Lasiocampidae

la·si·o·cam·pi·dae \,==='=pə,dē\ *n, pl, cap* [NL, fr. *Lasiocampa*, type genus + *-idae*] **:** a family of moths including the tent caterpillars, eggars, and lappet moths and being of medium size, stout-bodied and usu. tan or grayish, with pectinate antennae in both sexes

la·si·o·rhi·nus \,==='rīnəs\ *n, cap* [NL, fr. *lasio-* (fr. Gk *lasios* shaggy) + *-rhinus* — more at WOOL] **:** a genus containing solely the hairy-nosed wombat

lasi·urus \,=='yürəs\ *n, cap* [NL, fr. Gk *lasios* shaggy + NL *-urus*] **:** a genus of bats (family Vespertilionidae) including the red bat — compare NYCTERIS

la·si·us \'lās(h)ēəs\ *n, cap* [NL, fr. Gk *lasios* shaggy] **:** a genus of ants containing some of the brown and black ants of No. America and Europe that form large colonies nesting in the ground

¹lask \'lask\ *n* -s [perh. alter. of ⁴*lax*] *now dial Eng* **:** DIARRHEA

²lask \"\ *vi* -ED/-ING/-S [origin unknown] *archaic* **:** to sail with wind abeam or on the quarter

las·ket \'laskət\ *n* -s [perh. alter. (influenced by ¹*gasket*) of ¹*latchet*] **:** LATCHING

las pal·mas \lä'spälməs\ *adj, usu cap L&P* [fr. *Las Palmas*, Canary islands, Spain] **:** of or from the city of Las Palmas in the Canary islands, Spain **:** of the kind or style prevalent in Las Palmas

las·pey·re·sia \,laspə'rēzh(ē)ə\ *n, cap* [NL, prob. fr. Jacob H. *Laspeyres* fl1805 Ger. zoologist + NL *-ia*] **:** a genus of olethreutid moths containing many pests (as the pea moth)

la spe·zia \lä'spetsēə\ *adj, usu cap L&S* [fr. *La Spezia*, seaport in northwest Italy] **:** of or from the city of La Spezia, Italy **:** of the kind or style prevalent in La Spezia

las·pring \'laspriŋ\ *n, pl* **laspring** *or* **lasprings** [alter. of earlier *last-spring*, by folk etymology (influence of ²*last* and *spring*, n.) fr. earlier *lakspynke*, fr. ¹*lax* + *pink* (salmon parr)] *dial Brit* **:** a young salmon

lasque \'lask\ *n* -s [perh. fr. Per *lashk* bit, piece] **:** a flat thin diamond usu. cut from an inferior stone and used esp. in Hindu work

lass \'las, -aa(ə)-,-ai-\ *n* -ES [ME *las*, *lasce*] **1 a :** young woman **:** GIRL ⟨the story of a small French ~ —*New Yorker*⟩ **b :** SWEETHEART ⟨the young hero of the story . . . and his ~ —Mary Ross⟩ **2** *chiefly Scot* **:** MAIDSERVANT

las·sie \'lasē, -aas-,-ais-, -si\ *n* -s [*lass* + *-ie*] **:** LASS, GIRL

las·sik \'lasik\ *n, pl* **lassik** *or* **lassiks** *usu cap* **1 :** an Athapaskan people of northwestern California **2 :** a member of the Lassik people

las·si·tude \'lasə,tüd, -aas-, -ə-,tyüd\ *n* -s [MF, fr. L *lassitudo*, fr. *lassus* weary — more at LET] **1 :** a condition of weariness or debility **:** FATIGUE ⟨when the walk is over, ~ recommends rest —William Cowper⟩ ⟨chronic ~ typically accompanies this disease⟩ **2 :** a condition of listlessness or indifference **:** LANGUOR ⟨surrendered to an overpowering ~, an extreme desire simply to sit and dream —Alan Moorehead⟩ ⟨succumbed to the ~ that pervades most of our prisons —Frank O'Leary⟩ ⟨sunk in an indifference and ~ —John Galsworthy⟩

lasslorn \'=,=\ *adj* **:** forsaken by one's sweetheart ⟨broom groves, whose shadow the dismissed bachelor loves, being ~ — Shak.⟩

¹las·so \'la(,)sō, 'laa-, ='sü, '=(,)sü\ *also* **las·soo** \='sü, '=-(,)sü\ *n, pl* **lassos** *or* **lassoes** *also* **lassoos** [Sp *lazo*, fr. L *laqueus* noose, snare — more at DELIGHT] **:** a rope or long thong of leather with a running noose that is used esp. for catching horses and cattle — compare LARIAT

²lasso \"\ *also* **lassoo** \"\ *vt* -ED/-ING/-ES **:** to catch with or as if with a lasso

lasso

lasso cell *n* **:** ADHESIVE CELL

las·sock \'lasək\ *n* -s [*lass* + *-ock*] *Scot* **:** a little girl **:** LASSIE

las·so·er *pronunc at* LASSO +ə(r)\ *n* -s **:** one that lassoes ⟨most skillful ~ —*Arctic*⟩

lass-rope \'las,=\ *n* [*lass-* (fr. ¹*lasso*) + *rope*] **:** LARIAT

las·sú \'lä(,)shü\ *n* -s [Hung] **:** the slow introductory section of a csardas or Hungarian rhapsody — contrasted with *friss*

¹last \'last, -aa(ə)-,-ai-,-á-\ *vb* -ED/-ING/-S [ME *lasten*, fr. OE *lǣstan* to last, follow, perform; akin to OHG *leisten* to perform, Goth *laistjan* to follow; denominative fr. the root of OE *lāst* footprint — more at ⁶LAST] *vi* **1 :** to continue in time **:** go on ⟨the meeting ~*ed* till late in the evening⟩ ⟨winter ~*s* from December to March —*Amer. Guide Series: Nev.*⟩ **2 a** (1) **:** to continue in pristine, fresh, or unimpaired condition **:** go on or remain without loss of quality or effectiveness **:** SURVIVE, ENDURE ⟨that paint job will ~ a long time⟩ ⟨it is a book that will ~ —K.S.Latourette⟩ (2) **:** to continue to be available ⟨half price while they ~⟩ **b :** to manage to continue (as in a particular status, position, course of action) **:** stick it out **:** hold out ⟨once I ~*ed* without them for seven weeks — Monica Sheridan⟩ ⟨he won't ~; he'll quit before the week's out⟩ **c :** to continue to live ⟨he will not ~ very much longer — James Dennis⟩ ⟨couldn't have ~*ed* . . . five minutes —Lyle Saxon⟩ ~ *vt* **1 :** to continue in existence or action as long as or longer than **:** SUSTAIN, SURVIVE, ENDURE ⟨if, of course, he ~*ed* the war —Wirt Williams⟩ — often used with *out* ⟨cattle which could ~ out the drives —S.E.Fletcher⟩ ⟨could not ~ out the apprenticeship —Whitcomb Crichton⟩ **2 :** to suffice for the needs of ⟨on these two courses is golf to ~ you a lifetime — Judson Philips⟩ **syn** see CONTINUE

²last \"\ *adj* [ME *last*, *latst*, fr. OE *latost*; akin to OHG *lezzisto* last, ON *latastr* slowest; superl. of the adjective represented by OE *læt* late, slow — more at LATE] **1 a :** being, occurring, or coming after all others in time, place, or order of succession **:** following all the rest ⟨the ~ one out will please shut the door⟩ ⟨the ~ two days of the month⟩ ⟨was saying some ~ word to her —Scott Fitzgerald⟩ — sometimes used with an ordinal number to indicate position before the extreme end of a series ⟨the second ~ paragraph on the page⟩ **b :** being the only remaining ⟨the ~ stronghold of Atlantic salmon in the United States —Pete Barrett⟩ **2 :** of or relating to the terminal stage or point (as of life) **:** FINAL ⟨buried with impressive ~ rites⟩ ⟨comforted his ~ hours⟩; *specif* **:** administered to one dying — used of the sacraments of penance, viaticum, and extreme unction **3 :** next before the present **:** most recent **:** LATEST ⟨~ week⟩ ⟨his ~ book⟩ **4 a** (1) **:** lowest in rank or degree ⟨dead ~ in the five-paper Chicago field —*Newsweek*⟩ (2) **:** lowest in quality **:** WORST ⟨thieving is the ~ crime —Augusta Gregory⟩ **b :** farthest of all from a specified quality or condition **:** most unlikely ⟨all good men, and the ~ to condone any form of vice —Norman Douglas⟩ **5 a :** CONCLUSIVE, DEFINITIVE ⟨the ~ explanation of all rational belief in concrete matters —Father Zeno⟩ **b :** highest in degree **:** EXTREME, UTMOST, SUPREME ⟨exposed to the ~ term of contempt — Malcolm Cowley⟩ ⟨the ~ enduringness is reserved . . . for those odd chaps who discover things like the Pythagorean theorem —Clifton Fadiman⟩ **c :** SINGLE — used as an intensive ⟨every ~ square inch of good land —James Reach⟩ ⟨every ~ thing was the best of its kind —Frances G. Patton⟩

syn LATEST, CONCLUDING, FINAL, TERMINAL, ULTIMATE, EVENTUAL: LAST designates that which comes at the end of a series; it may imply that no more will follow or it may simply indicate that which has most recently occurred or been in existence ⟨the *last* page of the book⟩ ⟨the *last* days of his life⟩ ⟨his *last* book was successful and he is planning another⟩ ⟨that's my *last* duchess painted on the wall —Robert Browning⟩ LATEST, superlative of *late*, is often used in preference to LAST to indicate the most recent in situations in which *late* is unlikely to mean tardy or delayed ⟨his *latest* book⟩ ⟨the *latest* news⟩ ⟨the *latest* fashion in dresses⟩ CONCLUDING describes that which brings something to a conclusion ⟨repeating his main points in his *concluding* remarks⟩ FINAL emphasizes definite, decisive closing or ending of a series or process ⟨a *final* examination⟩ ⟨a *final* decree of divorce⟩ ⟨while sacrifices accepted as *final* emerged as nothing more than rehearsals for greater sacrifices to come —M.W.Straight⟩ ⟨judgment that is *final*, that settles a matter —John Dewey⟩ TERMINAL may indicate a limit or stopping point or mark beyond which a thing does not continue ⟨a soldier on *terminal* leave⟩ ⟨the *terminal* r of bar and car⟩ ⟨a disease in its *terminal* stages⟩ ULTIMATE describes a last element, stage, or event that is the outcome of a long process, often the most remote or the most important development ⟨the earth's refrigeration and the *ultimate* collapse of our solar system — L.P.Smith⟩ ⟨the word came into English from French but its *ultimate* source is Arabic⟩ ⟨control or occupation by Nazi forces of any islands of the Atlantic would jeopardize the immediate safety of portions of North and South America, and of the island possessions of the United States, and the *ultimate* safety of the continental United States itself —F.D.Roosevelt⟩ EVENTUAL while lacking implications of finality in sequence, indicates inevitability or probability of future occurrence even if after a very long period, or the actual fact of occurrence often after a very long period ⟨the belief that science shows man to be only an accident and an incident in a cosmic order that is moving toward *eventual* lifeless rest —C.C.Walcutt⟩ ⟨the *eventual* emergence of a science of grammar had been prepared for by generations of curious inquiry and practical endeavor —Benjamin Farrington⟩

— **on one's last legs :** at or near the end of one's resources **:** on the verge of failure, exhaustion, or ruin ⟨the old car was *on its last legs*⟩

³last \"\ *adv* [ME, fr. OE *latost*; akin to OHG *lazzōst*, adv., last; adverb fr. the superlative adjective represented by OE *latost*, adj. — more at ²LAST] **1 :** after all others in time, place, or succession **:** at the end ⟨~ came the foot soldiers and supply trains⟩ ⟨ranks ~ in my estimation⟩ **2 :** on the most recent occasion **:** most lately ⟨saw him ~ in New York⟩ **3 :** in conclusion **:** FINALLY ⟨~, I wish to consider the economic outlook⟩

⁴last \"\ *n* -s [ME *last*, *laste*, fr. *last*, *latst*, adj. — more at ²LAST] **:** something that is last: as **a :** the end of life **:** time of dying ⟨her pen was busy to the ~ —F.L.Pattee⟩ **b :** the last-mentioned person or thing ⟨these ~ could be scattered in case of a threatened air raid —Elmer Davis⟩ **c :** a last look, pronouncement, or other action ⟨looked his ~ on the old homestead⟩ ⟨I've spoken my ~ on that subject⟩ **d :** the last part **:** CONCLUSION, END ⟨would not hear the ~ of his story⟩ ⟨fought gamely to the ~⟩ ⟨remained in enemy hands until the very ~ —C.E.Black & E.C.Helmreich⟩ ⟨came home the ~ of March⟩ **e :** final appearance or mention ⟨hated to see the ~ of her —Ellen Glasgow⟩ ⟨knew he would never hear the ~ of that mistake⟩ **f :** one that ranks lowest ⟨would inevitably come in an inglorious ~ —Osbert Lancaster⟩ **g :** the final one ⟨the ~ of the tests was held today⟩ **h :** the score awarded for winning the final trick in certain card games (as pinochle) — **at last** *or* **at long last** *adv* **:** at the end of a certain period **:** after delay **:** FINALLY ⟨*at long last* returned to America — Dixon Wecter⟩ ⟨*at last* you've come home⟩

⁵last \"\ *n* -s [ME, unit of weight, load, fr. OE *hlæst* load; akin to MD *last* load, OHG *hlast*; derivative fr. the root of OE *hladan* to load — more at LADE] **:** any of several greatly varying units of weight, capacity, or quantity: as **a :** a unit of weight equal to about 4000 pounds **b :** an English unit of capacity for grain equal to 10 quarters or 80 bushels **c :** a unit of quantity for herring equal to 13,200, 10,000, or 20,000 fish

⁶last \"\ *n* -s [ME *laste*, fr. OE *lǣste*, fr. *lāst* footprint; akin to OHG *leist* shoemaker's last, ON *leistr* sock, Goth *laists* footprint, L *lira* furrow, track — more at LEARN] **:** a wooden or metal form which is shaped like the human foot and over which a shoe is shaped or repaired

three-way last

⁷last \"\ *vb* -ED/-ING/-S *vt* **:** to shape with a last **:** fasten or fit to a last ⟨~ a shoe⟩ ~ *vi* **:** to perform the operation of shaping with a last

last·age \-tij\ *n* -s [ME *lestage* tax levied on traders at fairs or markets, ballast of a ship, fr. MF *lastage*, *lestage* ballast of a ship, lastage, fr. *laster* to ballast (fr. OFris *hlesta* to load & MD *lasten* to load; akin to each other and both descended fr. a prehistoric denominative fr. the root of OE *hlæst* load) + *-age*] **:** a port duty for the privilege of loading a ship

last clear chance *n* **:** a doctrine in English and American law of negligence: contributory negligence of the plaintiff will not bar his action if the defendant had a clear chance of avoiding inflicting injury had he exercised due care

last day *n, often cap L&D* **:** JUDGMENT DAY 1a

last ditch *n* [²*last* + *ditch*] **:** a place of final defense **:** the last resort ⟨the journals of opinion are about the *last ditch* for the individualist —H.L.Smith b. 1906⟩ ⟨likely to fight acculturation to the *last ditch* —Ralph Linton⟩

last–ditch \ˈ⸗ˈ⸗\ *adj* [*last ditch*] **1 :** fought or conducted from the last ditch **:** waged with desperation and uncompromising spirit ⟨a *last-ditch* fight to block ratification —Leo Egan⟩ ⟨*last-ditch* resistance⟩ **2 :** made in a final effort to avert disaster ⟨it was a *last-ditch* gamble —Noel Houston⟩ ⟨a *last-ditch* effort to pare expenses —T.M.Pryor⟩

last–ditch·er \ˈ⸗ˈdichə(r)\ *n* [*last ditch* + *-er*] **:** a person ready to fight to the end **:** an irreconcilable combatant

lasted *past of* LAST

last·er \ˈlastə(r), -aas-, -ais-, -äs-\ *n* -S [⁶*last* + *-er*] **1 :** a workman who stretches shoe uppers around lasts **:** an operator of a lasting machine **2 :** a tool for stretching leather on a last

Las·tex \ˈla,steks\ *trademark* — used for an elastic yarn consisting of a core of latex thread wound with threads of cotton, rayon, nylon, or silk and used to give a one-way or two-way stretch to fabrics and garments

last gospel *n, often cap L&G* **:** the liturgical gospel usu. John 1:1–14 recited by the celebrant following the close of the Mass in Roman Catholic churches, of the Divine Liturgy in Armenian churches, and of the Holy Communion service in many Episcopal churches

last hand *n, obs* **:** the finishing touches **:** the final polish

last heir *n* **:** the person (as a lord or the sovereign) to whom in English law lands escheat for want of an heir

last in, first out *adj* **:** being or relating to a method of valuing inventories by which items from the last lot received are assumed to be used or sold first and all requisitions are priced at the cost per item of the lot last stocked — compare FIRST IN, FIRST OUT

¹**last·ing** \ˈlastiŋ, -aas-,-ais-, -äs-, -tēŋ\ *adj* [ME, alter. of *lastende*, pres. part. of *lasten* to last] **:** existing or continuing a long while **:** ENDURING, DURABLE, ABIDING ⟨left a ~ mark on foreign policy —Blair Bolles⟩ ⟨a book of ~ significance⟩ — **last·ing·ly** *adv* — **last·ing·ness** *n* -ES

²**lasting** \"\ *n* -S [ME, gerund of *lasten* to last] **1** *archaic* **:** CONTINUANCE, DURATION **:** durable quality; *specif* **:** long life ⟨one of the great precepts of health and ~ —Francis Bacon⟩ **2** [¹*lasting*] **:** a sturdy cotton or worsted cloth in twill or satin weave made in narrow widths for use esp. in the shoe and luggage trades

last judgment *n, usu cap L&J* [ME *last juggement*, fr. ²*last* + *juggement* judgment] **:** the final judgment of mankind before God at the end of the world ⟨a moral perfection which will secure their acceptance at the *Last Judgment* —C.H.Dodd⟩ ⟨Muhammad's . . . doctrine of the *Last Judgment* —H.A.R. Gibb⟩

last·ly *adv* [ME *lestely*, fr. *leste*, *last* last + *-ly*] **:** in the last place **:** in conclusion **:** at the end ⟨~, we try to develop in them a realization —K.G.Marten⟩

last mile *n* **:** the walk of a condemned person to the place of execution ⟨like the shaving of the head before the *last mile* —Saul Levitt⟩

last minute *n* [²*last* + *minute*] **:** the moment or interval of time just before some usu. climactic, decisive, or disastrous event or development ⟨help came to the garrison at the *last minute*⟩

last–minute \ˈ⸗ˈ⸗⸗\ *adj* [*last minute*] **:** made or occurring at the last minute ⟨*last-minute* plans for preventing the war —T.B.Costain⟩ ⟨*last-minute* amendments⟩

last name *n* **:** SURNAME 2a — contrasted with *first name*

last·ness \-s(t)nəs\ *n* -ES **:** the condition of being last

last post *n* **:** a bugle call in the British Army equivalent to taps

lasts *pres 3d sing of* LAST, *pl of* LAST

last straw *n* **:** the last of a series (as of events, indignities, or burdens) that brings one beyond the ultimate point of endurance and causes a defeat, downfall, or breakdown ⟨that remark was the *last straw*⟩

last supper *n, usu cap L&S* **:** a representation usu. in painting (as that of Leonardo da Vinci in Milan) of the supper partaken of by Christ and his disciples on the night of his betrayal

last word *n* **1 :** the final remark in a controversy or other verbal exchange ⟨always manages to get in the *last word*⟩ **2 a :** power, right, or act of final decision **:** final judgment or say ⟨the *last word* lies with Asia and Africa —A.J.Toynbee⟩ ⟨under our proposal the civilians have the *last word* in everything —A.H.Vandenberg †1951⟩ **b :** authoritative statement or treatment **:** definitive work ⟨surely be the *last word* on the subject for many years⟩ **3 :** one that is the most advanced, up-to-date, or currently fashionable exemplar of its kind **:** ACME ⟨a character who was the *last word* in exquisite vice —Daniel George⟩ ⟨the *last word* in fireproof construction —G.F.T.Ryall⟩ ⟨absolutely the *last word* in schools —*Newsweek*⟩

lasty \ˈlastē\ *adj* [¹*last* + *-y*] *chiefly dial* **:** DURABLE, LASTING

la·sya \ˈläsyə, -sēə\ *n* -S [Skt *lāsya*, fr. *lāsayati* she dances; akin to Skt *lasati* he plays — more at LUST] **:** the lyric and feminine dance type of India — contrasted with *tandava*

¹**lat** \ˈlat\ *dial var of* LET

²**lat** \ˈlät\ *n* -S [Hindi *lāṭ*, *lāṭh*, alter. (influenced by Skt *lakuṭa*, *laguḍa* stick, club) of Skt *yaṣṭi* pillar, stick, club] **:** a separate column or pillar in some Buddhist buildings in India corresponding to the Greek stela but usu. larger

³**lat** \ˈlät\ *n, pl* **lats** \-ts\ *or* **la·ti** \ˈlä(,)tē\ [Latvian *lats*, fr. *Latvija* Latvia] **1 :** the basic unit of monetary value of Latvia from 1922 to 1940 **2 :** a coin representing one lat

lat *abbr* **1** latent **2** lateral **3** latitude

LAT *abbr* local apparent time

la·tah \ˈläd·ə\ *n* -S [Malay] **:** a neurotic condition marked by automatic obedience, echolalia, and echopraxia observed esp. among Malays

lat·a·kia \,lad·əˈkēə\ *n* -S [fr. *Latakia*, seaport in Syria] **:** a superior aromatic Turkish smoking tobacco

la·tania \ləˈtānēə, -tan-\ *n, cap* [NL, fr. F *latanier* + NL *-ia*] **:** a small genus of fan palms of the Mascarene islands and the adjacent coast — see CHINESE FAN PALM

latania scale *n* **:** a widespread scale (*Aspidiotus lataniae*) esp. damaging to avocado and to greenhouse plants

la·ta·nier \ləˈtan(,)yā\ *n* -S [F, prob. fr. Island Carib *alátani*] **1 :** any of various fan palms of the southern U.S. and the Caribbean region **2 :** the leaf of a latanier used in craftwork (as basketry)

la·tax \ˈlā,taks\ [NL, fr. Gk, a water quadruped, prob. the beaver; prob. akin to Gk *latax* last remnant of a cup of wine — more at LATEX] *syn of* ENHYDRA

¹**latch** \ˈlach\ *vb* -ED/-ING/-ES [ME *lachen*, *lacchen*, fr. OE *læccan*; akin to Gk *lambanein*, *lazesthai* to take, grasp] *vi* **1 a** (1) **:** to lay hold esp. with the hands or arms **:** GRASP, SEIZE, GRAPPLE ⟨searching for crevices to ~ upon —Norman Mailer⟩ — usu. used with *on* or *onto* ⟨tractors ~ on to remains of derrick and drilling tools —*Irish Digest*⟩ ⟨~*ed* onto a . . . pass —*New Yorker*⟩ (2) **:** to gain or come into possession **:** get hold — usu. used with *on* or *onto* ⟨had ~*ed* on to 444,000 shares —*Newsweek*⟩ ⟨can I ~ on to some of your dough —C.O.Gorham⟩ ⟨knew that he had ~*ed* on to a good thing —Philip Hamburger⟩ (3) **:** to keep firm possession or grasp **:** HOLD — usu. used with *on* or *onto* ⟨you ought to know enough to ~ onto your gear —John Hersey⟩ **b :** to gain understanding or comprehension **:** TUMBLE — usu. used with *on* ⟨slow to . . . in ~*ing* on to the notion that her husband's work is important —John McCarten⟩ **c :** to associate oneself closely or intimately **:** attach oneself — used with *on* or *onto* ⟨I'd think he'd ~ onto a girl like that —W.C.Fridley⟩ ⟨nobody's ~*ing* onto me —Saul Levitt⟩ ⟨~*ed* onto this racket right under his nose —Harold Robbins⟩ **2** *dial Eng* **:** ALIGHT ~ *vt, dial Brit* **:** CATCH, GET, RECEIVE

²**latch** \"\ *n* -ES [ME *lache*, *lacche*, fr. *lachen*, *lacchen*, v.] **1 :** a device that holds something in place by entering a notch or cavity; *specif* **:** the catch which holds a door or gate when closed even if not bolted **2** *now dial Eng* **:** a loop or noose that fastens or holds **:** SNARE **3 :** the hinged piece of a knitting-machine needle that holds the engaged loop in position while the needle is penetrating another loop

³**latch** \"\ *vb* -ED/-ING/-ES *vt* **:** to catch or fasten by means of a latch ⟨~ the door⟩ ~ *vi* **:** to latch itself **:** shut so that the latch catches ⟨will the door ~⟩

⁴**latch** \"\ *var of* ¹LETCH

latch bolt *n* [²*latch*] **:** a bevel-headed self-acting spring bolt

¹**latch·et** \ˈlachət\ *n* -S [ME *lachet*, fr. MF *lachet*, *lacet* shoestring, string for lacing up a garment, fr. *laz* noose, snare (fr. L *laqueus*) + *-et* — more at DELIGHT] **1** *obs* **:** THONG, LOOP **2 :** a narrow strap, thong, or lace esp. of leather by which a shoe or sandal is fastened upon the foot

²**latchet** \"\ *n* -S [origin unknown] *Austral* **:** a flying gurnard or a closely related fish

latching *n* -S [fr. gerund of ¹*latch*] **:** an eye formed on the headrope of a bonnet by which it is attached to the foot of a sail — called also *lasket*; usu. used in pl.

latchkey \ˈ⸗,⸗\ *n* **1 :** a key used to lift or pull back a latch of a door **2 :** a front door key

latch needle *n* **:** a fine steel needle for machine knitting that has a butt at one end and at the other a short hook closed by a latch — see KNITTING NEEDLE

latch pin *n* [²*latch*] *Midland* **:** SAFETY PIN

latchstring \ˈ⸗,⸗\ *n* **:** a string on a latch that may be left hanging outside the door to permit the raising of the latch from the outside or drawn inside to prevent intrusion

latd *abbr* latitude

¹**late** \ˈlāt, *usu* -ād·+V\ *adj* **lat·er** \ˈlād·ə(r), -ātə-\ **lat·est** \-ād·əst, -ātə-\ [ME, late, slow, fr. OE *læt*; akin to OFris *let* late, OS *lat* lazy, OHG *laz* slow, ON *latr* slow, lazy, Goth *lats* lazy, OE *lǣtan* to let, allow, leave, cause — more at LET] **1** *now dial* **a :** SLOW, SLUGGISH **b :** TEDIOUS **2 a** (1) **:** coming or doing after the due, usual, or proper time **:** not early ⟨the train is ~⟩ ⟨spring is very ~ this year⟩ ⟨there were only a few ~ customers left —Vicki Baum⟩ ⟨~ fruits⟩ ⟨sells a million copies to a large and ~ audience —J.D.Hart⟩ (2) **:** of, relating to, or given or imposed because of tardiness ⟨kept on receiving ~ marks⟩ ⟨had to pay a ~ penalty⟩ **b** (1) **:** of or relating to an advanced stage in point of time or development **:** ADVANCED ⟨the decline of trade under the ~ empire —D.W. McConnell⟩ ⟨few men have remained good fellows till so ~ an age —Robert Lynd⟩; *specif* **:** far advanced toward the close of the day or night ⟨keeps very ~ hours⟩ (2) **:** coming or occurring at an advanced stage (as of life or a period) ⟨rich old man captured . . . in a ~ marriage —William Howell⟩ ⟨the comparatively ~ peopling of the Plains —Edward Sapir⟩ **c :** continuing or doing until an advanced hour ⟨looking in on one of the ~ nightclubs —Erle Stanley Gardner⟩ ⟨a ~ sleeper⟩ **3 a :** living not long ago but not now **:** comparatively recently deceased **b :** being something or holding some position or relationship recently but not now ⟨memorial week will be observed at his ~ home —*Springfield (Mass.) Daily News*⟩ ⟨formal peace between the ~ belligerents —*Foreign Policy Bull.*⟩ ⟨do not love any of their ~ enemies —*Dublin Sunday Independent*⟩ **c :** made, appearing, or happening just previous to the present time **:** RECENT ⟨many ~ students of society —Roger Burlingame⟩ ⟨missions which have been performed in ~ combat —H.H.Arnold & I.C.Eaker⟩ **syn** see LAST, TARDY

²**late** \"\ *adv* -ER/-EST [ME, fr. OE, fr. *læt*, adj.] **1 a :** after the usual or proper time or the time appointed **:** after delay ⟨came to work⟩ **b :** at or to a distant or advanced point in time **:** far into the night, day, week, or other period ⟨don't sit up ~⟩ ⟨the decision was reached ~ in 1951⟩ ⟨I'll see you *later* on⟩ **2 :** not long ago **:** LATELY, RECENTLY ⟨a socialite, ~ of London and now of New York⟩ — **of late** *adv* **:** LATELY, RECENTLY ⟨have not seen him *of late*⟩ ⟨*of late* he has not been able to make his rounds⟩

late blight *n* **:** a blight of plants in which symptoms appear late in the growing season: as **a :** a disease of solanaceous plants and esp. of the potato and tomato caused by a fungus (*Phytophthora infestans*) and characterized by decay of leaves, stems, and in the potato also of tubers **b :** a leaf spot disease of celery caused by a fungus (*Septoria apii* or *S. apii-graveolentis*) — see CELERY BLIGHT

late·bra \ˈlad·əbrə; ləˈtēbrə, -teb-\ *n* -S [NL, fr. L, hiding place, fr. *latēre* to lie hidden] **:** a flask-shaped mass of white yolk extending from the blastodisc of a bird's egg to the center of the yellow yolk

latecomer \ˈ⸗,⸗⸗\ *n* **:** one that arrives late **:** a recent arrival ⟨a ~ in the struggle —Galbraith Welch⟩ ⟨a comparative ~ into jazz music —Deems Taylor⟩

late cut *n* **:** a cut made at a ball in cricket when it is near the batsman's wicket

lat·ed \ˈlād·əd\ *adj* [¹*late* + *-ed*] **:** BELATED

late egyptian *n, cap L&E* **1 :** DEMOTIC EGYPTIAN **2 :** NEW EGYPTIAN

¹**la·teen** \ləˈtēn, laˈ-\ *adj* [F *latine* (in the term *voile latine* lateen sail), fr. MF (in *voile latine*), fem. of *latin*, lit., Latin, fr. L *latinus* — more at LATIN] **:** being or relating to a rig used esp. on the north coast of Africa and in adjacent waters and characterized by a triangular sail extended by a long spar that is slung to a usu. low mast

²**lateen** \"\ *n* -S **1** *also* **la·teen·er** \-nə(r)\ **:** a lateen-rigged ship **2 :** a lateen sail

late greek *n, cap L&G* **:** the Greek language as used in the 3d to 6th centuries

late latin *n, cap both Ls* **:** the Latin language as used by the early church fathers through the 6th century and by other writers from the 3d to the 6th centuries inclusive

lateen 2

late·ly *adv* [ME, fr. ¹*late* + *-ly*] **:** not long ago **:** RECENTLY ⟨died as ~ as September of last year⟩ ⟨have not seen many of them ~⟩

late–magmatic \ˈ⸗,⸗ˈ⸗⸗\ *adj* **:** relating to rocks or minerals that crystallize during the later stages of the cooling period of a magma ⟨*late-magmatic* reactions⟩

lat·en \ˈlātᵊn\ *vb* **latened; latened; latening** \-t(ᵊ)niŋ\ **latens :** to make or become late ⟨time is ~*ing*⟩

la·ten·cy \ˈlātᵊnsē, -si\ *n* -ES [¹*latent* + *-cy*] **1 a :** the quality or state of being latent **:** dormant condition ⟨sprung from ~ into expression —H.B.Alexander⟩ **b :** something that is latent ⟨writers who know how to evoke these *latencies* —E.C.Lindeman⟩ **2 :** the state or period of living and developing in a host without producing symptoms — used of an infective agent or disease **3** *or* **latency period :** a stage of personality development variously explained as cultural or biological in origin which extends from about the age of five to the beginning of puberty and during which sexual urges often appear to lie dormant ⟨children in ~ —G.S.Blum⟩ **4 :** REACTION TIME ⟨the ~ of the reflex wink . . . is notably short —R.S.Woodworth⟩

la tène \läˈten, -tän\ *adj, usu cap L&T* [fr. *La Tène*, shallows at the east end of Lake of Neuchâtel, Switzerland, site of discovery of Iron-Age remains] **:** of or relating to the later period of the Iron Age in Europe assumed to date from 500 B.C. to A.D. 1 — compare HALLSTATT

late·ness *n* -ES [ME *latnesse*, fr. OE *lætnes* slowness, fr. *læt* late, slow + *-nes* -ness — more at LATE] **:** the quality or state of being late ⟨the ~ of his arrival⟩ ⟨the ~ of the season⟩

la·ten·si·fi·ca·tion \lā,ten(t)səfəˈkāshən\ *n* -S [blend of ¹*latent* and *intensification*] *photog* **:** intensification of a latent photographic image by chemical treatment or prolonged uniform exposure to light of low intensity after the initial exposure

la·ten·si·fy \⸗ˈ⸗⸗,fī\ *vt* -ED/-ING/-S [fr. *latensification*, after E *intensification*: *intensify*] **:** to subject to latensification

¹**la·tent** \ˈlātᵊnt\ *adj* [L *latent-*, *latens*, pres. part. of *latēre* to lie hidden; akin to OHG *luog* den, lair, ON *lōmr* deceit, Gk *lanthanein* to escape notice, OSlav *lajati* to lie in wait for] **1 a :** existing in hidden, dormant, or repressed form but usu. capable of being evoked, expressed, or brought to light **:** existing in posse **:** not manifest **:** POTENTIAL ⟨the perennial vitality ~ in tradition —J.L.Lowes⟩ ⟨the heat ~ in firewood —Laurence Binyon⟩ ⟨a small fraction of his ~ capacities —Quincy Howe⟩ ⟨in the first innovations the germs of all subsequent improvements were ~ —Henry Orenstein⟩ ⟨his sinister qualities, formerly ~, quickened into life —Thomas Hardy⟩ ⟨all the ~ brutality, degradation and stupidity of a small American mining or industrial town —H.F.West⟩ ⟨the ~ meaning of dreams —G.S.Blum⟩ ⟨the vast resources said to be ~ in the desert —*Atlantic*⟩ **b :** present or capable of living or developing in a host without producing visible symptoms of disease ⟨some of the lily mosaics may survive for years as ~ viruses in insusceptible strains⟩ ⟨a ~ virus of the red raspberry that is highly destructive to blackcaps⟩ ⟨a ~ infection⟩ **c** *of a fingerprint* **:** obtained at the scene of a crime and usu. scarcely visible but capable of being developed for study ⟨use a reading glass or common magnifying glass to search for ~ prints —D.K.Fitch⟩ **2 :** CONCEALED, DISGUISED

syn DORMANT, QUIESCENT, POTENTIAL, ABEYANT, and IN ABEYANCE: LATENT applies to that which is submerged and not clearly apparent or certainly present to any but a most searching examination but may emerge and develop with effect and significance ⟨the heat *latent* in coal —G.B.Shaw⟩ ⟨a *latent* tenderness which breaks out at last in the story of Griseldis —J.R.Green⟩ ⟨the *latent* uneasiness in Darnay's mind was roused to vigorous life by this letter —Charles Dickens⟩ ⟨the theological passage of arms, which brought out all her *latent* antagonism to the prejudiced young pietist —Israel Zangwill⟩ DORMANT indicates that which is quite inactive, as though sleeping, but which may be awakened later into significant activity or effect ⟨though this strength pervaded every action of his, it seemed but the advertisement of a greater strength that lurked within, that lay *dormant* and no more than stirred from time to time, but which might arouse, at any moment, terrible and compelling —Jack London⟩ ⟨that haunting fear of being drowned in a confined space which lies *dormant* in the mind of most seamen —F.W.Crofts⟩ ⟨the purchasing power of workers newly employed revived demands *dormant* for many years and stimulated a gigantic outpouring of goods —Oscar Handlin⟩ QUIESCENT stresses the fact of inactivity at the time in question, without necessary implications of causes or of past or future activity ⟨a flare-up in the now *quiescent* struggle between the two Chinas —*New Republic*⟩ ⟨somewhat *quiescent* during the winter, the city takes on a new tempo with the coming of summer —*Amer. Guide Series: Mich.*⟩ ⟨simple insects, which we shall have to call collembolas, were difficult to capture. They leaped with agility many times their own length, and when *quiescent* looked like bits of fungus —William Beebe⟩ POTENTIAL applies to that which does not at the time under consideration have being, essence, character, or effect as indicated but which is likely in time to have that being or effect ⟨thousands of people in rural districts who constitute a *potential* labor supply for new factories —*Amer. Guide Series: Va.*⟩ ⟨yet such figures can be misleading in that they indicate *potential* rather than actual strength —D.W.Mitchell⟩ ⟨if narcotic addiction is to be eliminated, the *potential* addicts must be reached before they are exposed —D.W.Maurer & V.H.Vogel⟩ ABEYANT and the more common IN ABEYANCE indicate the fact of current inactivity, of not being used, implemented, caused, or allowed to function at the time under consideration ⟨a lurking and *abeyant* fear —Edith Wharton⟩ ⟨until all danger of counter-revolution should have been removed, personal rights and liberties would have to be kept strictly *in abeyance* —F.A.Ogg & Harold Zink⟩ ⟨the union has put its strike threat *in abeyance* and evidently will stay on the job as long as government possession lasts —*N.Y.Times*⟩

²**latent** \"\ *n* -S **:** a latent fingerprint ⟨compared the prints with those of the ~*s* —Erle Stanley Gardner⟩

latent ambiguity *n* **:** an uncertainty which does not appear upon the face of a legal instrument but arises from evidence aliunde **:** an uncertainty not involved in words themselves but arising from outside matters — opposed to *patent ambiguity*

latent bud *n* **:** a bud often concealed that may remain dormant indefinitely but under certain conditions develops into a shoot

latent content *n* **:** the underlying meaning of a dream exposed by interpretation of the dreamwork

latent defect *n* **:** an unknown defect (as in a title to real property) not discoverable by such inspection or test as the law reasonably requires under all the circumstances

latent heat *n* **:** thermal energy absorbed or evolved in a process (as fusion or vaporization) other than change of temperature — compare SENSIBLE HEAT

latent image *n* **:** an invisible image produced by an effect of light on matter (as silver halide or halides) which can be rendered visible by the subsequent process of photographic development

latent learning *n* **:** learning that occurs prior to the introduction and acquisition of a reward

la·tent·ly *adv* **:** in a latent manner

latent mosaic *n* **:** a latent virus disease that produces a mottling or mosaic

latent period *n* **1 :** LATENCY 2 **2 :** REACTION TIME; *specif* **:** the time interval between establishment of excitation and the beginning of identifiable reaction in an effector organ — called also *true latent period*

latent strabismus *n* **:** a tendency to squint controllable by muscular effort

latent virus disease *n* **:** a moderately virulent but highly infective virus disease esp. common in potatoes that often show no visible external symptoms although the yield is significantly reduced

later *comparative of* LATE

later- *or* **lateri-** *or* **latero-** *comb form* [L *later-*, fr. *later-*, *latus*] **1 :** side ⟨*laterad*⟩ **:** sidewise ⟨*laterigrade*⟩ **2 :** lateral and ⟨*latero*-anterior⟩

-la·ter \lad·ə(r), lətə-\ *n comb form* -S [alter. of ME *-latrer*, fr. MF *-latre* -later (fr. LL *-latres*, fr. Gk *-latrēs*) + ME *-er*; akin to Gk *latron* pay, hire — more at LATHE] **:** one who worships or shows fanatical devotion ⟨biblio*later*⟩

lat·er·ad \ˈlad·ə,rad\ *adv* [*later-* + *-ad*] *anat* **:** toward the side

¹**lat·er·al** \ˈlad·ərəl, -atərəl, -a·trəl\ *adj* [L *lateralis*, fr. *later-*, *latus* side + *-alis* -al; prob. akin to L *latus* wide — more at LATITUDE] **1 a :** of or relating to the side **:** situated on, directed toward, or coming from the side ⟨the ~ branches of a tree⟩ ⟨a ~ view⟩ **b** *obs* (1) **:** being, acting, or moving side by side (2) *of winds* **:** blowing from the same general direction **c :** being to the right or left of a true course ⟨~ deviation⟩ **2 a** (1) *of a body part* **:** lying at or extending toward the right or left side **:** lying away from the median axis of the body ⟨the lungs are ~ to the heart⟩ (2) **:** being a body part so situated ⟨the ~ branch of the axillary artery⟩ **b** *bot* **:** relating to, characteristic of, or borne upon the side of any organ or of the axis ⟨a ~ bud⟩ — compare BASILAR, MEDIAN, TERMINAL **c** (1) **:** situated to one side of and parallel to a main vein or mine working ⟨a ~ vein or drift⟩ (2) **:** being or relating to any horizontal underground workings as contrasted with shafts, raises, and winzes ⟨~ development⟩ **3 :** having or characterized by a stocky thickset body-build and a short broad face ⟨babies of the ~ type⟩ — opposed to *linear* **4 :** produced with the tongue forming an occlusion at some point along its longitudinally middle line but with an opening at one or both sides ⟨\l\and \lʸ\ are ~⟩

²**lateral** \"\ *n* -S **:** something having a lateral situation, growth, or extension: as **a :** a side ditch or conduit (as in an irrigation, drainage, sewer, gas, or water system) — compare MAIN **b :** a side branch from an electrical wiring or conduit system **c :** a drift to one side of and parallel to a main drift or haulage way **d :** a lateral pass in football **e :** a lateral tooth, scale, or other body part **f :** a lateral sound

³**lateral** \"\ *vb* -ED/-ING/-S [²*lateral*] *vi* **:** to throw a lateral pass ~ *vt* **:** to throw laterally

lateral column *n* **:** the column of the spinal cord between the dorsal and ventral roots of the spinal nerves

lateral conjugation *n* **:** sexual union between neighboring cells of the same filament of an alga — compare SCALARIFORM CONJUGATION

lateral–cut \ˈ⸗(⸗)⸗ˈ⸗\ *adj, of a phonograph record* **:** having the undulations cut by a stylus vibrating parallel to the record face

lateral disc *n* **:** a disc record produced by lateral recording

lateral ethmoid *n* **:** ECTETHMOID

lateral fin *n* **:** one of the paired fins of a fish

lateral fissure *n* **:** a deep fissure of the lateral aspect of each cerebral hemisphere that divides the temporal from the parietal and frontal lobes

lat·er·al·i·ty \,lad·əˈralәd·ē\ *n* -ES **:** preference in use of homologous parts on one lateral half of the body over those on the other **:** dominance in function of one of a pair of lateral homologous parts ⟨studies of the ~ of individuals in the performance of different tasks —K.C.Garrison⟩

lat·er·al·i·za·tion \,lad·ərələˈzāshən, ,la·trəl-, -,līˈz-\ *n* -S **:** the action or an instance of lateralizing

lat·er·al·ize \ˈ⸗(⸗)⸗,līz\ *vt* -ED/-ING/-S **:** to direct to or localize on one side **:** make lateral

lateral lemniscus *n* **:** a band of nerve fibers passing between the cochlear nuclei and the inferior colliculus and thalamus

lateral line *n* **1 a :** a longitudinal line along each side of the body of most fishes that is usu. distinguished by modified and often differently colored scales and marks the position and orifices of the lateral line organ **b :** a narrow longitudinal tract in either side of the body wall of various oligochaete worms that is made up of the cell bodies of the circular muscle layer — see FISH illustration **2 :** LATERAL LINE ORGAN 1

lateral line organ *n* **1 :** a system of epithelial mucus-secreting tubes in the sides of most fishes, supplied at intervals with sensory endings and considered to be responsive to low frequency vibrations **2 :** one of the sensory end organs of the lateral line organ

lat·er·al·ly \'lad·ərəlē, 'latərə-, 'la·trə-, -li\ *adv* **:** by, to, or from the side **:** SIDEWAYS ⟨will work its way often for many miles, upward or ~ —*Oil*⟩

lateral meristem *n* **:** a meristem (as the cambium and cork cambium) that is arranged parallel to the sides of an organ and that is responsible for increase in diameter of the organ — compare APICAL MERISTEM, INTERCALARY MERISTEM

lateral moraine *n* **:** a moraine deposited by a glacier at its side

lat·er·al·most *pronunc at* 1LATERAL + ,mōst\ *adj* [1*lateral* + *-most*] **:** farthest to the side

lateral pass *n* **:** a pass in football thrown parallel to the line of scrimmage or obliquely to the rear

lateral planation *n* **:** the reduction of the land in interstream areas to a plane by the lateral erosion of streams

lateral plate *n* **:** an unsegmented sheet of mesoderm on each side of the vertebrate embryo from which develops the coelom and its linings

lateral recording *n* **1 :** a recording process in which the cutting stylus produces a groove that remains constant in depth but undulates from side to side in accordance with the sound being recorded **2 :** a disc record produced by lateral recording

lateral sinus *n* **:** TRANSVERSE SINUS

lateral tooth *n* **:** a tooth situated before or behind the middle of the hinge in a bivalve shell — compare CARDINAL TOOTH

lateral vein *n* **:** either of a pair of large veins running in the lateral body walls of elasmobranchs and various other low vertebrates and opening in front into the ducts of Cuvier

lateral ventricle *n* **:** the internal cavity of each cerebral hemisphere consisting in man of a central body and three cornua, an anterior curving forward and outward, a posterior curving backward and inward, and an inferior curving downward

later·an \'lā·trən, 'letərən\ *Scot var of* LECTERN

later–day \'==,=\ *adj* **:** LATTER-DAY ⟨in *later-day* tenements, constructional details vary —J.J.McCarthy⟩ ⟨burst upon the outraged *later-day* Victorians like verbal bombshells —J.G. Fletcher⟩

lateri- — see LATER-

1lat·eri·grade \'lad·ərə,grād\ *adj* [ISV *lateri-* + *-grade*] **:** running sidewise or characterized by such running ⟨~ locomotion⟩

2laterigrade \"\ *n* -s **:** a laterigrade animal (as a crab spider of the family Thomisidae)

lat·er·ite \'lad·ə,rīt\ *n* -s [L *later* brick, tile + E *-ite; prob.* akin to L *latus* wide — more at LATITUDE] **1 :** a residual product of rock decay that is red in color and has a high content in the oxides of iron and hydroxide of aluminum and a low proportion of silica **2 a :** a zonal group of red soils developed in hot humid climates that show intense weathering and chemical change and leaching away of bases and silica leaving aluminum and iron hydroxides **b :** a crusted soil of this group or a horizon in such soil developed through restricted drainage; *esp* **:** a mottled quarriable clay which hardens on exposure to air — **lat·er·it·ic** \'==¦rid·ik\ *adj*

lat·er·i·tious *or* **lat·er·i·ceous** \¦lad·ə¦rishəs\ *adj* [L *latericius, lateritius* made of brick, fr. *later* brick + *-icius, -itius* -itious] **:** BRICK-RED **:** resembling brick **:** of the color of red brick

lat·er·i·za·tion \,lad·ərə'zāshən, -,rī'z-\ *n* -s [*laterite* + *-ization*] **:** the process of conversion of rock to laterite

lat·er·nar·ia \,lad·ə(r)'na(a)rēə\ *n, cap* [NL, fr. LL *laterna* lantern (alter. of L *lanterna*) + NL *-aria* — more at LANTERN] **:** a large genus of lantern flies

la·ter·nu·la \lə'tərnyələ\ *n, cap* [NL, fr. LL *laterna* + L *-ula*] **:** a genus of marine bivalve mollusks (suborder Anatinacea) comprising the lantern shells

latero- — see LATER-

la·tes \'lā,tēz\ *n, cap* [NL, irreg. fr. Gk *latos* Nile perch] **:** a genus of large percoid fishes of fresh and brackish water including the Nile perch and the begti

1lat·est \'lād·əst, -ātə-\ *adj* [fr. superl. of 1*late*] *archaic* **:** LAST ⟨my ~ breath was spent in blessing her —Alfred Tennyson⟩ — **at latest** *or* **at the latest** *adv* **:** at a time not later than specified ⟨be there by 10 *at the latest*⟩

2latest \"\ *n* -s **:** the most recent or currently fashionable style **:** the most recent development ⟨a display of the very ~ in spring outfits⟩ ⟨the ~ in fire-fighting equipment⟩

late·wake \'lāt·,wāk\ *dial Brit var of* LYKEWAKE

lateward *adv (or adj)* [ME, fr. 1*late* + *-ward*] *obs* **:** LATE, BACKWARD

latewood \'=,=\ *n* **:** SUMMERWOOD

1la·tex \'lā,teks\ *n, pl* **lat·i·ces** \'lad·ə,sēz, 'lād·-\ *or* **latexes** *often attrib* [NL *latic-, latex,* fr. L, fluid, prob. fr. Gk *latag-, latax* last remnant of a cup of wine; akin to OHG *letto* clay, ON *lethja* mud, W *llaid*] **1 :** a milky usu. white fluid of variable composition that is usu. made up of various gum resins, fats, or waxes and often a complex mixture of other substances frequently including poisonous compounds, that is found in or produced by cells of plants esp. of the Asclepiadaceae but also of the Apocynaceae, Sapotaceae, Euphorbiaceae, Papaveraceae, Moraceae, and Compositae, and that yields rubber, gutta-percha, chicle, and balata as its chief commercial products ⟨~ pillows⟩ ⟨~ foundation garments⟩ — see RUBBER **2 :** any of various emulsions in water of a synthetic rubber or plastic obtained by polymerization and used chiefly in paint and other coatings (as for paper) and adhesives ⟨GR-S ~⟩

2latex \"\ *vt* -ED/-ING/-ES **:** to treat (as a textile material) with a latex

latex foam *or* **latex foam rubber** *n* **:** FOAM RUBBER

la·tex·osis \,lā,tek'sōsəs\ *n* -ES [NL, fr. *latex* + *-osis*] **:** abnormal exudation of latex (as in certain diseases of various latex-producing plants)

latex paint *n* **:** a paint whose binder consists of a latex that is usu. a synthetic resin polymerized in water phase — compare EMULSION PAINT

1lath \'lath, -aa(ə)-,-à-\ *n, pl* **laths** \-t͟hz,-ths\ *also* **lath** *often attrib* [ME *lat, latte, lath, lathe,* fr. OE *lætt;* akin to MD *lat, latte* lath, OHG & ON *latta* lath, W *llath* yard (measure of length)] **1 a :** a thin narrow strip of wood used (as by nailing to rafters, ceiling joists, studding) in making a groundwork (as for slates, tiles, plaster) or in constructing a light framework (as a trellis) **b :** a building material in sheets (as expanded or otherwise perforated metal, stiffened wire cloth, gypsum) used as a base for plaster **c :** a small angle iron used to support the covering of an iron roof **d :** a quantity of laths **:** LATHING ⟨built with ~ and plaster⟩ **e :** a thin narrow strip of wood used for any purpose **f :** FOREPOLE **2 a :** someone or something that is long, thin, and narrow ⟨a ~ like you, to hoist a hulk like me —W.W.Gibson⟩ **b :** TOBACCO STICK **c :** a thin or narrow and usu. small aggregate of rock or mineral ⟨the biotite is in ~s ranging up to several millimeters in length —*Jour. of Geol.*⟩

2lath \"\ *vt* -ED/-ING/-S **:** to cover or line with laths

lath brick *n* **:** a long slender brick used esp. in making the floor on which malt is placed in the drying kiln — compare PAMENT

1lathe \'lāt͟h\ *vt* [ME *lathen* to invite, fr. OE *lathian* — more at LURE] *archaic* **:** to invite esp. to a wedding or funeral

2lathe \"\ *n* -s [ME, fr. OE *lǣth;* akin to ON *lāth* landed property, OE *unlǣd,* unlǣde poor, miserable, Goth *unleds* poor, Gk *latron* pay, hire, Skt *rāti* generous] **:** one of the administrative divisions each containing several hundreds into which Kent, England, is divided

3lathe \"\ *n* -s [ME, fr. ON *hlatha;* akin to ON *hlatha* to load — more at LADE] *now dial Brit* **:** GRANARY, BARN

4lathe \"\ *n* -s [prob. fr. ME *lath* supporting stand, prob. of Scand origin; akin to Dan *-lad* supporting structure (as in *drejelad* lathe, *savelad* saw bench), Norw dial. *la, lad* small wall, pile, Sw dial. *lad* folding table, lay of a loom; akin to ON *hlatha* to load] **1 :** a machine in which work is rotated about a horizontal axis and shaped by a fixed cutting, boring, or drilling tool while being held in a chuck, faceplate, or mandrel or between centers in headstock and tailstock **2 :** 7LAY 1

5lathe \"\ *vt* -ED/-ING/-S **:** to cut or shape with a lathe

lathe·man \'lāt͟hmən\ *n, pl* **lathemen :** a lathe operator

1lath·er \'lat͟hə(r)\ *sometimes chiefly Brit* 'lāt͟h-\ *n* -s [fr. (assumed) ME *lather,* fr. OE *lēathor;* akin to ON *lauthr* froth, OE *lēah* lye — more at LYE] **1 a :** a foam or froth consisting of extremely small bubbles formed when soap or some other detergent is agitated with or in water **b :** foam or froth from profuse sweating (as on a horse) **:** a condition of sweating profusely ⟨worked himself into a ~⟩ **2 :** a highly agitated or overwrought state **:** DITHER ⟨in a ~ of nervous apprehension —Walter O'Meara⟩ ⟨why is she in such a ~ to get money —J.B.Benefield⟩ ⟨in a ~ of hurry to get everything finished at once —G.W.Brace⟩

2lather \"\ *vb* **lathered; lathered; lathering** \-t͟h(ə)riŋ\ **lathers** [ME *latheren,* alter. (influenced by — assumed — ME *lather,* n.) of *letheren, litheren,* fr. OE *lethran, lӯthran;* akin to ON *leythra* to wash; denominative fr. the root of OE *lēathor,* n.] *vt* **1 :** to spread lather over ⟨~ the face⟩ **2 :** to beat severely **:** FLOG ⟨will ~ your hide —*Ballad Book*⟩ **3 :** EXCITE, AGITATE — usu. used with *up* ⟨used to ~ up the floor clerk to the point of frenzy —*Sat. Eve. Post*⟩ ~ *vi* **:** to form a lather or a froth like lather ⟨good soap ~s profusely and quickly —*Danceland*⟩

3lath·er \'lathə(r), -aath-, -àth-\ *n* -s [2*lath* + *-er*] **:** a person who makes laths or puts up laths as a base for plaster or fireproofing material

4lath·er \'lāt͟hə(r)\ *n* -s [5*lathe* + *-er*] **:** a person who works a lathe

lath·er·er \'lat͟hərə(r), -āt͟h-\ *n* -s **:** one that lathers

latherwort \'==,=\ *n* **:** SOAPWORT

lath·ery \'lat͟h(ə)rē, -āt͟h-, -ri\ *adj* [1*lather* + *-y*] **:** covered with or as if with lather

lathes *pl of* LATHE, *pres 3d sing of* LATHE

lathework *n* **:** machine engraving; *specif* **:** the part of the design of a stamp or currency note that is engraved by machine

lathhouse \'=,=\ *n* **:** a structure made chiefly of laths or slats spaced so as to reduce excessive sunlight while permitting moderate air circulation and used for growing plants that require some shade and protection from strong winds

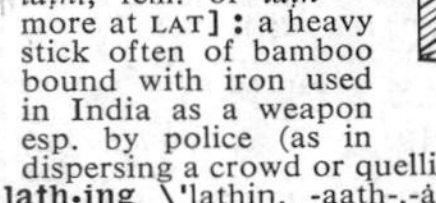

lathhouse

la·thi *also* **la·thee** \'lä(,)tē\ *n* -s [Hindi *lāṭhī,* fem. of *lāṭh* — more at LAT] **:** a heavy stick often of bamboo bound with iron used in India as a weapon esp. by police (as in dispersing a crowd or quelling a riot)

lath·ing \'lathiŋ, -aath-, -àth-, -thēŋ\ *n* -s [fr. gerund of 2*lath*] **1 :** the action or process of placing laths **2 :** a quantity or an installation of laths **:** LATHS

lathing hatchet *n* **:** a hatchet for trimming and nailing laths having a long thin blade and a head that is crosshatched with grooves

lathing nail *n* **:** LATH NAIL

lath nail *n* [ME *lathnail,* fr. 1*lath* + *nail*] **:** a slender nail for fastening laths

lath·raea \la'thrēə\ *n, cap* [NL, fr. Gk *lathraios* secret; akin to Gk *lanthanein* to escape notice — more at LATENT] **:** a genus of parasitic plants (family Orobanchaceae) having scaly leaves, small flowers, and explosively splitting capsules

lath·ri·di·idae \,lathrə'dīə,dē\ *n pl, cap* [NL, fr. *Lathridius,* type genus (fr. Gk *lathridios* secret) + *-idae;* fr. the small size of beetles belonging to this genus; akin to Gk *lanthanein*] **:** a family of small widely distributed light brown to dark brown beetles that have the wings fringed with short hair and feed chiefly on fungi

laths *pl of* LATH, *pres 3d sing of* LATH

lath screen *n* **:** a screen made chiefly of laths or slats spaced so as to reduce excessive sunlight while permitting moderate air circulation that is frequently placed over hotbeds or cold frames to provide some shade and protection from strong winds

lathy \'lathē, -aath-,-àth-, -thi\ *adj* -ER/-EST [1*lath* + *-y*] **:** being like a lath **:** long and slender **:** THIN ⟨a tall, thin, and ~ man —John Shandon⟩

lathyarn \'=,=\ *n* **:** a single tarred or untarred yarn put up in stranded form or with many ends

lath·y·rism \'lathə,rizəm\ *n* -s [ISV *lathyr-* (fr. NL *Lathyrus*) + *-ism*] **:** poisoning produced by the use as food of the seeds of certain plants of the genus *Lathyrus* and characterized by spastic paralysis of the legs

lath·y·rus \-rəs\ *n* [NL, fr. Gk *lathyros* chickling — more at LENTIL] **1** *cap* **:** a genus of plants (family Leguminosae) including many peas and vetchlings and differing from mem bers of the genus *Pisum* in having the style not sulcate — see EVERLASTING PEA, SWEET PEA **2** -ES **:** any plant of the genus *Lathyrus*

1lati *pl of* LAT

2la·ti \'lād·ē\ *n* -s *usu cap* **:** a language spoken by a small group of hill people on the Vietnam-China border that was formerly held to constitute an independent language family but is now assigned to the Kadai group

lati- *comb form* [ME, fr. L, fr. *latus* — more at LATITUDE] **:** wide **:** broad ⟨*lati*rostral⟩

latices *pl of* LATEX

lat·i·cif·er·ous \¦lad·ə¦sif(ə)rəs\ *adj* [ISV *latici-* (fr. NL *latic-, latex* latex) + *-ferous*] **:** containing, bearing, or secreting latex

la·ti·fon·do \,läd·ə'fōn(,)dō\ *n, pl* **latifon·di** \-(,)dē\ [It, fr. L *latifundium*] **:** a latifundium in modern Italy

lat·i·fun·di·ary \,lad·ə'fəndē,erē\ *adj* [*latifundium* + *-ary*] **:** of or relating to the system of landownership through latifundia

la·ti·fun·dio \,läd·ə'fündē,ō, -fün-\ *n* -s [Sp, fr. L *latifundium*] **:** a latifundium in Spain or Latin America

la·ti·fun·dis·mo \,==,=='diz(,)mō\ *n* -s [AmerSp, fr. Sp *latifundio* + *-ismo* -ism] **:** the system of great landed estates in Latin America

la·ti·fun·dis·ta \-istə\ *n* -s [AmerSp, fr. Sp *latifundio* + *-ista* -ist] **:** the owner of a latifundio

lat·i·fun·di·um \,lad·ə'fəndēəm\ *n, pl* **latifun·dia** \-ēə\ [L, fr. *lati-* + *-fundium* (fr. *fundus* piece of landed property, bottom) — more at BOTTOM] **:** a great landed estate (as in ancient Italy or in eastern Europe before World War I) often held by an absentee owner and typically employing servile or semiservile labor and primitive agricultural techniques ⟨changed a region of *latifundia* into one of peasant proprietors —David Mitrany⟩

la·ti·go \'läd·ə,gō, 'lad-·\ *n, pl* **latigos** *also* **latigoes** [Sp *látigo*] *chiefly West* **:** a long strap on a saddletree to tighten and fasten the cinch

latigo leather *n* **:** a cattlehide leather tanned with a combination of alum and gambier and used esp. for halters, cinches, and saddle strings

latigo strap *n, chiefly West* **:** LATIGO

lat·i·me·ria \,lad·ə'mirēə\ *n* [NL, fr. Marjorie E. D. Courtenay-*Latimer* *b*1907 So. African museum director + NL *-ia*] **1** *cap* **:** a genus of living coelacanth fishes that is the type of the family Latimeriidae **2** -s **:** any fish of the genus *Latimeria*

lat·i·me·ri·idae \,==,mə'rīə,dē\ *n pl, cap* [NL, fr. *Latimeria,* type genus + *-idae*] **:** a family of living deep-sea coelacanth fishes currently known only from the southern African genus *Latimeria* and the Malagasy genus *Malania* and having their nearest relatives among fishes that became extinct in the Mesozoic

1lat·in \'latᵊn *also* -ad·ən *or* -atən\ *adj, usu cap* [ME, fr. OE, fr. L *Latinus,* fr. *Latium,* ancient country of Italy having Rome as its principal city from the 5th century B.C. + L *-inus* -ine] **1 :** of or relating to Latium or the Latins (sense 2) ⟨the *Latin* language⟩ **2 a :** of, relating to, or composed in Latin ⟨*Latin* grammar⟩ ⟨the *Latin* idiom⟩ **b :** ROMANCE ⟨the modern *Latin* tongues⟩ **3 :** of or relating to that portion of the Christian church that employs the Latin rite in its services **4 a :** of or relating to the peoples, nationalities, or countries whose chief or official languages are Romance ⟨the sister *Latin* nations have drawn closer —Thomas Okey⟩; *specif* **:** LATIN-AMERICAN ⟨make increasing amounts of U. S. dollar exchange available to the *Latin* countries —R.J. Alexander⟩ **b :** relating to the collective psychology or temper held to be characteristic of such peoples ⟨lively, one-legged . . . , very *Latin* in temperament —Rosemary Benét⟩ ⟨a way that is characteristically *Latin* —M.S.Dworkin⟩ ⟨in him they see a *Latin* disdain —W.L.Sullivan⟩ ⟨don't think I'm being complicated and *Latin* —Louis Bromfield⟩ **5 :** of, relating to, or characteristic of the Latin alphabet

2latin \"\ *n* -s *cap* [in sense 1, fr. ME, fr. OE, fr. L *Latinum,* fr. *latinum,* neut. of *latinus,* adj.; in other senses, fr. ME, user of the Latin language, fr. L *Latinus,* n., inhabitant of Latium, fr. *latinus,* adj.] **1 :** the Italic language of ancient Latium and of Rome and until modern times the dominant language of school, church, and state in western Europe **2 :** a member of the people of ancient Latium **3 :** a member of that portion of the Christian church that employs the Latin rite in its services **4 :** a member of one of the Latin peoples ⟨though a Latin, he disliked the French —Brand Blanshard⟩; *specif* **:** LATIN AMERICAN ⟨grouping of *Latins* on one side and North Americans on the other —S.P.Brewer⟩ **5 :** the Latin alphabet

3latin \"\ *vt* -ED/-ING/-S *often cap* **:** to translate into Latin

latin alphabet *n, usu cap L* **:** an alphabet that was adapted from the early form of the Etruscan alphabet for writing Latin, that had orig. 20 or 21 letters but in the classical Latin period 23 and from the Medieval Latin period 26, and that has also come to be used often with minor modifications for writing numerous other languages including English so that it is now the most extensively used of all the world's alphabets — called also *Roman alphabet*

latin–american \¦===¦===\ *adj, usu cap L&A* [fr. *Latin America,* those parts of America colonized by the Spanish and Portuguese + E *-an,* adj. suffix] **:** of or relating to the countries of No., Central, and So. America excluding French Canada whose chief or official languages are Romance languages

latin american *n, cap L&A* [fr. *Latin America* + E *-an,* n. suffix] **:** a native or inhabitant of Latin America

lat·in·ate \'latᵊn,āt\ *adj, often cap* **:** of, relating to, resembling, or derived from Latin ⟨a preference for *Latinate* terms —R.M. Weaver⟩ ⟨attempted to make English grammar less *Latinate* —J.H.Sledd & G.J.Kolb⟩ ⟨the prose of the opening chapters is somewhat stiff and ~ —Richard Church⟩

latin cross *n, usu cap L* **1 :** a figure of a cross having a long upright shaft and a shorter crossbar traversing it above the middle **2 :** CRUX IMMISSA 1

Latin cross 1

lat·in·er \'latᵊnə(r)\ *n* -s *usu cap* **:** a Latin scholar

latin grammar school *or* **latin school** *n, usu cap L* [*latin grammar school* fr. *latin grammar* (fr. 1*latin* + *grammar*) + *school; latin school* fr. 2*latin* + *school*] **:** GRAMMAR SCHOOL 1a

la·tin·i·an \la'tinēən, lə'-\ *n* -s *usu cap* **:** a division of the Italic languages that is commonly restricted to the ancient languages Latin, Lanuvian, and Faliscan, but is occas. used to include the modern Romance languages — see INDO-EUROPEAN LANGUAGES table

la·tin·ic \la'tinik, lə'-\ *adj, usu cap* **:** relating or related to the Latin language or the Latin peoples

lat·in·ism \'latᵊn,izəm\ *n* -s *usu cap* [ML *latinismus,* fr. L *latinus* Latin + *-ismus* -ism — more at LATIN] **1 a :** a word, phrase, or inflection characteristic of Latin; *esp* **:** one appearing in the context of another language **b :** a word, phrase, grammatical construction, or inflection derived from or imitative of Latin **c :** a mode of speech or writing imitative or suggestive of Latin models **2 :** Latin quality, character, or mode of thought ⟨the self-assertive *Latinism* of the French ruling classes —Emil Lengyel⟩

lat·in·ist \-tᵊnəst\ *n* -s *usu cap* [ML *latinista,* fr. L *latinus* Latin + *-ista* -ist] **1 :** a person esp. skilled or informed in the Latin language or classical Latin literature or civilization **:** a specialist in the Latin language and culture **2 :** one who favors or propagates the Latin language or introduces Latin elements into another language

la·tin·i·ty \la'tinəd·ē, lə'-\ *n* -ES *often cap* [L *latinitat-, latinitas,* fr. *latinus* Latin + *-itat-, -itas* -ity] **1 a :** manner of speaking or writing Latin **:** LATIN ⟨the eccentric ~ of which he was master —F.M.Stenton⟩ **b :** knowledge of Latin ⟨today's youth has no *Latinity* —S.H.Adams⟩ **2 :** Latin quality, character, or traits **:** LATINISM ⟨the conflict between ~ and teutonism —Brewton Berry⟩ **3 :** the status or right of a person having the jus Latii

lat·in·ization \,latᵊnə'zāshən, -ᵊn,ī'z-\ *n* -s *sometimes cap* **:** the act, process, result, or an instance of latinizing ⟨this ~ of English —Frederick Bodmer⟩

lat·in·ize \'latᵊn,īz\ *vb* -ED/-ING/-s *often cap* [LL *latinizare,* fr. L *latinus* Latin + *-izare* -ize] *vt* **1 a** *obs* **:** to translate into Latin **b :** to give a Latin form to (a word or phrase of another language) ⟨*latinized* Greek words⟩ **c :** to make latinate esp. by the use of Latin loan words ⟨the diction may be plain or heavily *latinized* —Douglas Bush⟩ **d :** ROMANIZE 2a **2 :** to make Latin or Italian in doctrine, ideas, or traits; *specif* **:** to cause to resemble the Roman Catholic Church ⟨~ the Church of England⟩ ~ *vi* **1 :** to use Latinisms in writing or speech **2 :** to come under the influence of the Romans or of the Roman Catholic Church

la·ti·no \la'tē(,)nō, lə'-\ *n* -s *often cap* [AmerSp, fr. Sp *latino,* adj., Latin, fr. L *latinus*] **:** LATIN AMERICAN

latin right *n, cap L* **:** JUS LATII

latin rite *n, cap L* **1 :** forms of Christian worship and liturgy utilizing Latin in their expression and employed predominantly in the Roman Catholic Church of the West **2 :** the part of the Roman Catholic Church that employs Latin liturgies

latin square *n, often cap L* **:** one of a set of square arrays resembling determinants in which no element occurs twice in the same column or row and by means of which statistical investigations may be planned and carried out

lat·in·xua \'latᵊn,(h)wä\ *n* -s *usu cap* [irreg. fr. 1*latin*] **:** a system for romanization of the Chinese language utilizing an alphabet of 28 romanized characters based on Chinese phonetic principles

lation *n* -s [L *lation-, latio* action of bringing or proposing, fr. *latus* (used as past part. of *ferre* to carry) + *-ion-, -io* -ion — more at TOLERATE] *obs* **:** LOCOMOTION

lati·plantar \¦lad·ə+\ *adj* [*lati-* + *plantar*] **:** having the hinder part of the tarsus rounded ⟨~ birds⟩ — opposed to *acutiplantar*

lati·rostral *also* **lati·rostrate** \"+\ *adj* [*lati-* + *rostral* or *rostrate*] **:** having a broad beak

lat·i·rus \'lad·ərəs\ *n, cap* [NL, perh. modif. of Gk *lathyros* chickling — more at LENTIL] **:** a genus of band shells having a prolongation of the margin of the aperture resembling a horn

latis *pl of* LATI

lat·ish \'lād·|ish, -āt|, |ēsh\ *adj (or adv)* **:** somewhat late ⟨it was ~ when we showed up —A.B.Guthrie⟩ ⟨I get up ~ —O.W.Holmes †1935⟩

la·tis·si·mus dor·si \lə,tisəməs'dȯ(ə)r,sī\ *n, pl* **latissi·mi dorsi** \-,mī'd-\ [NL, lit., broadest (muscle) of the back] **:** a broad flat superficial muscle of the lower part of the back that draws the arm backward and downward and rotates it inward

la·tite \'lā,tīt\ *n* -s [*Latium,* Italy + E *-ite* — more at LATIN] **:** a lava intermediate between andesite and trachyte that is the extrusive equivalent of monzonite

lat·i·tude \'lad·ə,tüd, -atə-, -ə-,tyüd\ *n* -s [ME, fr. L *latitudin-, latitudo,* fr. *latus* wide + *-tudin-, -tudo* -tude; akin to OSlav *postĭlati* to spread, Arm *lain* wide] **1 a** *archaic* **:** extent or distance from side to side **:** BREADTH **b (1) :** angular distance from some specified circle or plane of reference; *specif* **:** angular distance north or south from the earth's equator measured through 90 degrees with the length of a degree varying from 68.704 statute miles at the equator to 69.407 at the poles because of the flattened figure of the earth — compare

ASTRONOMICAL LATITUDE, CELESTIAL LATITUDE, GALACTIC LATITUDE, GEOMAGNETIC LATITUDE (2) **:** a region or locality as marked by its latitude — usu. used in pl. ⟨silences them earlier than the sun of our ~*s* —Richard Semon⟩ **c** (1) **:** the projection on the meridian of a given course in a plane survey equal to the length of the course multiplied by the cosine of its bearing (2) **:** the distance of a point in a survey from a specified east-west line of reference **2 a** *archaic* (1) **:** EXTENT, AMPLITUDE ⟨indulged himself in the utmost possible ~ of sail —T.L.Peacock⟩ (2) **:** SCOPE, RANGE **b** (1) **:** the range of exposures within which a film or plate will produce a negative or positive of satisfactory quality (2) **:** the permissible variation from the recommended development time without noticeable change of image contrast **3 :** freedom of action or decision esp. in selecting from a variety of courses or opinions **:** permitted or tolerated range or variety of action or opinion ⟨in foreign affairs alone he allowed himself a certain ~ —John Buchan⟩ ⟨took action to restrict the ~ of the chairman in determining the course of the committee's action —*N.Y. Times*⟩ ⟨allow him greater ~ in expressing his opinions —*Current Biog.*⟩

latitude effect *n* **:** the variation of any physical quantity with latitude; *specif* **:** an increase of cosmic-ray intensity with magnetic latitude esp. at high altitudes

lat·i·tu·di·nal \ˌ==ˈtüd(ᵊ)nəl, -ˈtyü-\ *adj* [L *latitudin-, latitudo* latitude + E *-al*] **:** of or relating to latitude and esp. to geographical latitude **:** in the direction of latitude — **lat·i·tu·di·nal·ly** \-d(ᵊ)nəlē, -li\ *adv*

¹lat·i·tu·di·nar·i·an \ˌ==ˌtüdᵊnˈerēən, ˌ==ˌtyü-, -ᵊnˈa(a)r-, -ᵊnˈär-\ *n* -S [L *latitudin-, latitudo* latitude + E *-arian* (as in *trinitarian*)] **1 :** a person who is broad and liberal in his standards of belief and conduct **:** one who displays freedom in thinking esp. in religious matters **2** *often cap* **:** a member of the Church of England who favors freedom and difference of opinion respecting government, worship, or doctrine within the church

²latitudinarian \"\ *adj* **:** not insisting on strict conformity to a particular standard, norm, or formula **:** TOLERANT ⟨eligible under the ~ policy of admissions —C.W.Ferguson⟩; *specif* **:** tolerant of variations in opinion or doctrine ⟨~ theology⟩

lat·i·tu·di·nar·i·an·ism \ˌ==ˌ==ˈ===ˌnizəm\ *n* -S **:** a latitudinarian system or condition **:** latitudinarian beliefs or doctrines ⟨a broad, liberal ~ in theology —F.S.Mead⟩

lat·i·tu·di·nous \ˌ==ˈtüdᵊnəs, ˌ==ˈtyü-\ *adj* [L *latitudin-, latitudo* + E *-ous*] **:** having latitude or breadth esp. of thought or interpretation

la·tium \ˈlāsh(ē)əm, ˈläd·ē,üm, -d·ēəm\ *n* -S *usu cap* [LL, fr. *Latium*, Italy — more at LATIN] **:** JUS LATII

¹la·tive \ˈlād·iv\ *adj* [L *latus* (used as past part. of *ferre* to carry) + E *-ive* — more at TOLERATE] **:** being or relating to a grammatical case that denotes motion as far as or up to ⟨a ~ suffix⟩

²lative \"\ *n* -S **:** the lative case or a word in it

lat·ke \ˈlätkə\ *n, pl* **lat·kes** \-əs, -əz\ [Yiddish, fr. Russ *latka*, a pastry, prob. fr. (assumed) obs. Russ *oladka*, dim. of ORuss *oladiya* flat cake of leavened wheat dough, prob. fr. (assumed) MGk *eladion* oil cake, fr. Gk *elaion* olive oil, fr. *elaia* olive — more at OLIVE] **:** GRIDDLE CAKE; *esp* **:** one made from grated raw potato

lat·o·sol \ˈlad·əˌsäl, -sȯl\ *n* -S *sometimes cap* [*lato-* (irreg. fr. L *later* brick) + *-sol* (as in *podsol*, var. of *podzol*) — more at LATERITE] **:** leached red and yellow tropical soils — usu. used in pl. ⟨true *Latosols* . . . are found only in the tropics —F.E.Bear⟩ — **lat·o·sol·ic** \ˌ==ˈ=ik\ *adj, sometimes cap*

la·trant \ˈlā·trənt\ *adj* [L *latrant-, latrans*, pres. part. of *latrare* to bark — more at LAMENT] *archaic* **:** BARKING, SNARLING, COMPLAINING

la·tra·tion \lə·ˈtrāshən\ *n* -S [L *latratus* (past part. of *latrare* to bark) + E *-ion*] *archaic* **:** the act or an instance of barking

la·tria \lə·ˈtrīə\ *n* -S [ML, fr. LL, service, worship, fr. Gk *latreia*; akin to Gk *latron* pay, hire — more at LATHE] *Roman Catholicism* **:** the supreme homage that is given to God alone — distinguished from *dulia* and *hyperdulia*

lat·ri·dae \ˈla·trəˌdē\ [NL, fr. *Latris*, type genus + *-idae*] *syn of* LATRIDIDAE

la·trid·i·dae \lə·ˈtridəˌdē\ *n pl, cap* [NL, fr. *Latrid-, Latris*, type genus (irreg. fr. Gk *latris* maidservant) + *-idae*; akin to Gk *latron* pay, hire] **:** a small family of marine percoid fishes of Australia and New Zealand known as trumpeters

la·trine \lə·ˈtrēn\ *n* -S [F (usually in pl. *latrines*), fr. L *latrina*, contr. of *lavatrina*, fr. *lavere* to wash — more at LYE] **:** a receptacle (as a pit in the earth or a water closet) for use in defecation and urination or a room (as in a barracks or hospital) or enclosure (as in a camp) containing such a receptacle **:** TOILET

latrine fly *n* **:** a small housefly (*Fannia scalaris*) that breeds in excrement and excreta and causes myiasis in man

lat·ro·dec·tism \ˌla·trəˈdekˌtizəm\ *n* -S [ISV *latrodect-* (fr. NL *Latrodectus*) + *-ism*] **:** poisoning due to the bite of a spider of the genus *Latrodectus*

lat·ro·dec·tus \-ktəs\ *n, cap* [NL] **:** a genus of nearly cosmopolitan arachnomorph spiders (family Theridiidae) that include all the well-known venomous spiders, that are of medium size and dark or black in color and often marked with red, and that have a large globular usu. glossy abdomen and long and wiry legs

la·tron \ˈlā·trən\ *n* -S [L *latron-, latro* mercenary soldier, brigand; akin to Gk *latron* pay, hire — more at LATHE] *archaic* **:** BRIGAND

-la·try \lə·trē, -ri\ *n comb form* -ES [ME *-latrie*, fr. OF, fr. LL *-latria*, fr. Gk *latreia* service, worship; akin to Gk *latron* pay, hire] **:** worship of or fanatical devotion to a (specified) object ⟨helio*latry*⟩

lats *pl of* LAT

lat·ten *or* **lat·tin** \ˈlatᵊn\ *n* -S [ME *latoun, laton*, fr. MF *laton, leton*, fr. OProv, fr. Ar *lāṭūn*, of Turkic origin; akin to Turk *altın* gold] **1 :** an alloy of or resembling brass hammered into thin sheets formerly much used for church utensils — called also *black latten* **2 a :** iron plate covered with tin **:** sheet tin **b** (1) **:** metal in thin sheets ⟨gold ~⟩ (2) **lattens** *pl* **:** metal sheets between 1⁄64 and a little less than 1⁄32 of an inch in thickness

lat·ter \ˈlad·ə(r), -atə-\ *adj* [ME, fr. OE *lætra* slower; akin to MHG *lazzer* slower, ON *latari*; compar. of the adjective represented by OE *læt* late, slow — more at LATE] **1 a :** belonging to a subsequent time or period **:** coming after something else **:** LATER ⟨the ~ stages of a process⟩ ⟨promises to deal with ~ events in a second volume⟩ ⟨how spiritless, how fallen upon meager ~ days —D.C.Peattie⟩ **b** (1) **:** belonging or relating to the end (as of life or the world) **:** LAST, FINAL ⟨in his ~ years threw his printing press into the sea —Mabel Dolmetsch⟩ ⟨remind worshipers of . . . their own ~ end —G.G.Coulton⟩ ⟨proclaimed these were the ~ days, with God's judgment drawing nigh⟩ (2) **:** belonging to the second half of the two divisions of a period ⟨indicates composition in the ~ months of 1813 —K.N.Cameron⟩; *specif* **:** SECOND ⟨during the ~ half of the nineteenth century —F.L.Allen⟩ **c :** RECENT, PRESENT ⟨the human race in these ~ days —G.M.Trevelyan⟩ **2 :** being the last named of two or more mentioned or understood things ⟨the novel . . . grows out of the epic as a reaction against the ~ —Leon Livingstone⟩ ⟨the drum, the rattle, and the flute, the ~ reserved wholly for love songs —*Amer. Guide Series: Minn.*⟩

latter-day \ˌ==ˈ=\ *adj* **1 :** of a later or subsequent time or period ⟨these *latter-day* prospectors were unsuccessful —*Amer. Guide Series: Wash.*⟩ **2 :** of present or recent times ⟨considers most amusingly the *latter-day* state of eastern potentates —*Times Lit. Supp.*⟩ ⟨the complex modern documents of *latter-day* corporation finance —T.J.Grayson⟩

latter-day saint *n, usu cap L&S, often cap D* **:** a member of a religious body that traces its origin back to Joseph Smith who in 1830 announced that he had discovered buried golden tablets and translated their hieroglyphics into the Book of Mormon considered by his followers as a new revelation from God equal with but not supplanting the Bible **:** MORMON

latter lammas *n, usu cap 2d L* [so called ironically fr. the fact that there is only one Lammas in a year] **:** a day that will never come

lat·ter·ly *adv* **1 :** at a subsequent time **:** LATER ⟨had been a salesman . . . and ~ a guide to anglers and hunters —Margaret K.Zieman⟩ ⟨had a school and, ~ at any rate, a Roman Catholic chapel —D.B.Forrester⟩ **2 :** of late **:** RECENTLY ⟨~, they have given to it more than its due place —J.G.Edwards⟩ ⟨buys food and drink . . . and, ~, quite a lot of beer —John Hyslop⟩

lattermath \ˈ==ˌ=\ *n* [*latter* + *math* (mowing)] *now dial Eng* **:** AFTERMATH

¹lat·tice \ˈlad·əs, -atəs\ *n* -S *often attrib* [ME *latis*, fr. MF *lattis*, fr. *latte* lath, fr. OF, prob. of Gmc origin; akin to OHG *latta* lath — more at LATH] **1 a :** a framework or structure of wood or metal made by crossing laths or other thin strips so as to form a network ⟨the ~ of a window⟩ **b :** a window, door, or gate having a lattice **c :** a representation or imitation of a lattice **d :** a lattice used as the sign of an alehouse **2 a :** a system of small intersecting diagonal or zigzag bars or angles that rigidly connect two parallel parts of a structural member **b :** a rectangle cut up into equal small rectangles by parallels to the sides **c :** a regular geometrical arrangement of points or objects over an area or in space: as (1) **:** SPACE LATTICE (2) **:** a geometrical arrangement of fissionable material in a nuclear reactor **3 :** something resembling a lattice as **a** (1) **:** narrow strips of pastry laid over a pie in lattice fashion (2) **:** potato slices perforated in cutting to resemble latticework ⟨~ potatoes⟩ **b :** a decorative openwork (as of interwoven strips of leather on a shoe) **c :** a vestigial sieve plate with indefinite outlines and perforations minute or lacking

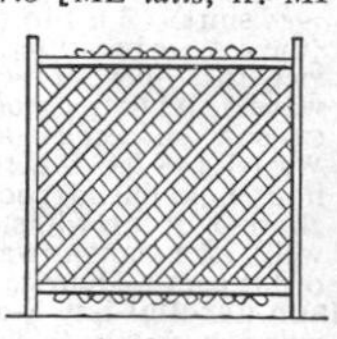
lattice 1a

²lattice \"\ *vt* -ED/-ING/-S [ME *lattizen*, fr. *latis* lattice] **1 :** to make a lattice of **:** give the appearance of a lattice to ⟨neatly arranged in strips that *latticed* his baldness —Pearl Kazin⟩ **2 :** to close or enclose (as an opening) with or as if with latticework ⟨~ a window⟩

lattice bar *n* **:** one of the diagonal connecting bars in a lattice (sense 2a)

lattice constant *n* **:** one of the geometrical constants of a crystal lattice: as **a :** the distance between identical points at two of the corners of the unit cell **b :** the angle between two edges of the cell

lat·ticed \-st\ *adj* **1 :** furnished with a lattice or latticework ⟨the huge, ~ iron door —Donn Byrne⟩ ⟨from the ~ shelves looked down an imposing array of eighteenth-century quartos —John Buchan⟩ **2 :** marked or arranged so as to represent or suggest a lattice; *specif* **:** CLATHRATE ⟨a ~ leaf⟩

lattice girder *or* **lattice beam** *or* **lattice frame** *n* **:** a girder with top and bottom flanges connected by a latticework web

latticelike \ˈ==ˌ=\ *adj* **:** like or resembling a lattice

lattice plant *or* **latticeleaf** \ˈ==ˌ=\ *n* [so called fr. the veined, skeletonized leaves] **:** a plant of the genus *Aponogeton*; *esp* **:** a plant (*A. fenestralis*) of Madagascar

lattice shell *n* **:** an oval shell (family Cancellariidae) with short spire and moderately large aperture

lattice truss *n* **:** a truss having its upper and lower chords so connected by diagonal members as to resemble latticework

latticewise \ˈ==ˌ=\ *adv* **:** in the manner of a lattice

latticework \ˈ==ˌ=\ *n* [ME *latise werk*, fr. *latise, latis* lattice + *werk* work] **1 :** a lattice or work made of lattices **:** an assemblage of lattices

latticing *n* -S **:** LATTICE, LATTICEWORK ⟨the ~ of a lattice girder⟩

lat·ti·ci·nio \ˌlad·əˈchēn(ˌ)yō\ *n, pl* **latti·ci·ni** \-ē(ˌ)nē\ [It, dairy product, cheese, butter, fr. LL *lacticinium*, fr. L *lact-, lac* milk — more at GALAXY] **:** a glass or glassware containing milk-white canes or threads and made principally in Murano near Venice

lattin *var of* LATTEN

latuka *usu cap, var of* LOTUKO

la·tus rec·tum \ˌlad·əsˈrektəm, ˌläd-, ˌlād-\ *n* [NL, lit., straight side] **:** the chord of a conic section through a focus and parallel to a directrix

lat·via \ˈlatvēə\ *adj, usu cap* [fr. *Latvia*, country in northern Europe] **:** of or from Latvia **:** of the kind or style prevalent in Latvia **:** LATVIAN

¹lat·vi·an \-ēən\ *adj, usu cap* [*Latvia* + E *-an*, adj. suffix] **:** of or relating to Latvia, the country of the Letts on the Baltic

²latvian \"\ *n* -S *cap* [*Latvia* + E *-an*, n. suffix] **1 :** a native or inhabitant of Latvia **2 :** the Baltic language of the Latvian people

la·uan \lə'wän\ *n* -S [Tag *lawaan*] **:** any of various Philippine timbers (as from trees of the genera *Shorea* and *Parashorea*) that are light yellow to reddish brown or brown, moderately close-grained, and rather stringy, and of moderate strength and durability, and that include some which enter commerce as Philippine mahogany

laub·mann·ite \ˈlau̇bməˌnīt\ *n* -S [Heinrich *Laubmann*, 20th cent. Ger. mineralogist + E *-ite*] **:** a mineral $Fe_3Fe_6(PO_4)_4(OH)_{12}$ consisting of a basic phosphate of ferrous and ferric iron

lauch \ˈläk\ *Scot var of* LAUGH

¹laud \ˈlȯd\ *n* -S [ME *laudes* (pl.), fr. MF or ML; MF *laudes* (pl.), fr. ML *laudes* (pl.), fr L, pl. of *laud-, laus* praise; akin to OE *lēoth* song, OHG *liod* song, ON *ljōth* stanza, Goth *liuthon* to sing praises] **1 lauds** *pl but sing or pl in constr, often cap* **:** a religious service that constitutes the second or with matins the first of the canonical hours and that is usu. sung at dawn in monastic houses **2** [ME *laude* (influenced in meaning by L *laud-, laus* praise), fr. *laudes* (pl.)] **:** public acclaim **:** PRAISE ⟨his chief employment being the ~ of his dead love —W.H.Dixon⟩ — now used chiefly in hymns ⟨all glory, ~ and honor to Thee —J.M.Neale⟩ **3 :** a hymn of praise

²laud \"\ *vt* -ED/-ING/-S [L *laudare*, fr. *laud-, laus* praise] **:** to sing the praises of **:** ACCLAIM, EXTOL ⟨we ~ and magnify Thy glorious name —*Bk. of Com. Prayer*⟩ ⟨editors and publishers are to be ~*ed* for their accomplishment —J.A.Mourant⟩

³la·ud \läˈüd\ *n* -S [Sp *laúd*, fr. OSp *alaút*, fr. Ar *al-ʽūd* the wood, fr. *al* the + *ʽūd* wood] **1 :** LUTE **2 :** CITTERN

laud·abil·i·ty \ˌlȯdəˈbiləd·ē, -lətē, -i\ *n* [LL *laudabilitat-, laudabilitas*, fr. L *laudabilis* laudable + *-itat-, -itas* -ity] **:** the quality or state of being worthy of praise **:** PRAISEWORTHINESS

laud·able \ˈlȯdəbəl\ *adj* [ME, fr. L *laudabilis*, fr. *laudare* to laud, praise + *-abilis* -able] **1 :** worthy of praise **:** COMMENDABLE ⟨showed ~ courtesy in the face of provocation⟩ ⟨originality, a ~ characteristic in any textbook —L.L.Snyder⟩ **2** *archaic* **:** of a normal or salutary nature **:** HEALTHY — **laud·ably** \-blē, -bli\ *adv*

laud·able·ness *n* -ES **:** LAUDABILITY

laudable pus *n* **:** pus discharged freely (as from a wound) and formerly supposed to facilitate the elimination of unhealthy humors from the injured body

lau·dan·i·dine \lȯˈdanəˌdēn, -anədən\ *n* -S [ISV *laudanine* + *-idine*] **:** a crystalline levorotatory alkaloid $C_{20}H_{25}NO_4$ obtained from opium or by resolution of laudanine into its optically active forms; *levo*-laudanine

lau·da·nine \ˈlȯdᵊnˌēn, -ᵊnən\ *n* -S [ISV *laudanum* + *-ine*; orig. formed as G *laudanin*] **:** a poisonous crystalline optically inactive alkaloid $C_{20}H_{25}NO_4$ obtained from opium

lau·dan·o·sine \lȯˈdanəˌsēn, -ˌsən\ *n* -S [G *laudanosin*, irreg. fr. *laudanin* laudanine] **:** a poisonous crystalline alkaloid $C_{21}H_{27}NO_4$ obtained from opium; the methyl ether of dextrorotatory laudanine

lau·da·num \ˈlȯdᵊnəm\ *n* -S [NL] **1** *obs* **:** any of various opium preparations orig. obtained from alchemists **2 :** a tincture of opium

lau·da·tion \lȯˈdāshən\ *n* -S [ME *laudacion*, fr. L *laudation-, laudatio*, fr. *laudatus* (past part. of *laudare* to laud, praise) + *-ion-, -io* -ion] **:** an act or instance of praising **:** EULOGY

lau·da·tive \ˈlȯdəd·iv\ *adj* [L *laudativus*, fr. *laudatus* + *-ivus* -ive] **:** LAUDATORY

lau·da·tor \ˈlȯˌdād·ər, ˌ=ˈ==, lau̇ˈdä,tȯ(ə)r\ *n* -S [L, fr. *laudatus* + *-or*] **:** one that lauds or eulogizes

lau·da·to·ri·ly \ˈlȯdəˌtōrəlē, -tȯr-, -li\ *adv* **:** in a laudatory manner

lau·da·to·ry \ˈlȯdəˌtōrē, -tȯr-, -ri\ *adj* [LL *laudatorius*, fr. L *laudatus* + *-orius* -ory] **:** of, relating to, or containing praise **:** COMMENDATORY, EULOGISTIC

¹laud·ian *also* **laud·ean** \ˈlȯdēən\ *adj, usu cap* [William *Laud* †1645 Eng. prelate, archbishop of Canterbury + E *-ian* or *-ean*] **:** of, relating to, characteristic of, or supporting Archbishop Laud in his repudiation of Roman Catholicism, affirmation of the continuity of the Church of England with the primitive church, and support of the divine right of kings and bishops

²laud·ian \"\ *n* -S *usu cap* **:** a supporter of Archbishop Laud or his doctrines

laud·ian·ism \-ˌnizəm\ *n* -S *usu cap* **:** the principles and practices established by Archbishop Laud and his supporters

laud·num bunches \ˈlȯdnəm-\ *n pl but usu sing in constr, usu cap L&B* [origin unknown] **1 :** a morris dance with corner figures, leaps, and capers **2 :** the music for Laudnum Bunches

lauds *pl of* LAUD, *pres 3d sing of* LAUD

laue·gram \ˈlau̇əˌgram\ *n, usu cap* [Max von *Laue* b1879 Ger. physicist + E *-gram*] **:** LAUE PATTERN

laue pattern \ˈlau̇ə-\ *or* **laue photograph** *n, usu cap L* **:** a photographic record of the diffraction pattern formed when a beam of X rays passes through a thin crystal plate

laue spot *n, usu cap L* **:** a spot corresponding to maximum X ray intensity in the Laue pattern of a crystal

¹laugh \ˈlaf, -aa(ə)-, -ai-, -á-, -ä-\ *vb* -ED/-ING/-S [ME *laughen*, fr. OE *hliehhan, hlehhan, hlæhan*; akin to OHG *lachēn* to laugh, ON *hlæja*, Goth *hlahjan* to laugh, OE *hlōwan* to moo — more at LOW] *vi* **1 a :** to give audible expression to an emotion (as mirth, joy, derision, embarrassment, or fright) by the expulsion of air from the lungs resulting in sounds ranging from an explosive guffaw to a muffled titter and usu. accompanied by movements of the mouth or facial muscles and a lighting up of the eyes ⟨~*ing* loudly at a funny clown⟩ ⟨others . . . read for the sake of sarcastically ~*ing* —Aldous Huxley⟩ **b :** to find amusement or pleasure in something **:** enjoy oneself ⟨~ at the memory of an embarrassing encounter⟩ **c :** to become amused or derisive ⟨her eyes ~*ed*⟩ ⟨he was ~*ing* I knew though his face was . . . grave —George Meredith⟩ — often used with *at* ⟨a very skeptical public ~*ed* at our early efforts —Graenum Berger⟩ **2 a :** to produce the sound or appearance of laughter ⟨~*ing* voice⟩ ⟨~*ing* brook⟩ ⟨a cypress tree that ~*ed* with all its leaves —Ruth Tomalin⟩ **b :** to be of a kind that inspires joy ⟨the blue sky of Autumn ~*s* above —Amy Lowell⟩ ~ *vt* **1 :** to bring to a specified state by laughing ⟨eat and drink . . . and ~ themselves fat —John Trapp⟩ ⟨this book ~*s* the littlest child into . . . manners —*N. Y. Herald Tribune*⟩ ⟨~*ed* aside academic rules —C.V. Woodward⟩ ⟨~ him to scorn⟩ ⟨~*ed* away the popular taste for bombast —Van Wyck Brooks⟩ ⟨a less able speaker would have been ~*ed* off the stage —J.D.Hicks⟩ **2 :** to utter laughingly ⟨~*s* her consent⟩ — **laugh in one's sleeve** *or* **laugh up one's sleeve** *also* **laugh in one's beard :** to become inwardly elated **:** congratulate oneself secretly (as on having successfully played a trick on someone) — **laugh on the wrong side of one's mouth :** CRY — **laugh out of court :** to eliminate from serious consideration by ridicule ⟨their flimsy arguments are *laughed out of court* —V.L.Parrington⟩ ⟨they went far towards *laughing* him *out of court* —J.F.Dobie⟩

²laugh \"\ *n* -S **1 a :** an act or instance of laughing ⟨the appealing look passed into a smile and the smile into a ~ —Thomas Hughes⟩ ⟨the ~, however wry, goes deeper and hurts more than the snarl —Dudley Fitts⟩ ⟨the longest pause . . . followed by the longest ~ ever heard on radio —Goodman Ace⟩ **b** *archaic* **:** a disposition to laughter **:** HILARITY ⟨full of ~, and must give it some vent —John Crowne⟩ **c :** something that resembles a laugh ⟨rejoiced to see the first ~ of the fire —Leigh Hunt⟩ ⟨heard the ~ of a loon⟩ **2 a :** a cause for derision or merriment **:** JOKE, ADVANTAGE ⟨the ~ of the twenties was my confident insistence that I would defeat Jack Dempsey —Gene Tunney⟩ ⟨a book with a ~ on page one —Bennett Cerf⟩ ⟨had the ~ on him then —David Fairchild⟩ ⟨rack their poor brains to get the ~ of us —George Meredith⟩ **b :** an expression of scorn or mockery **:** JEER ⟨he failed to make good and they gave him the ~⟩ ⟨even in the most straitlaced societies the ~ was against the husband —Edith Wharton⟩ **3 laughs** *pl* **:** a means of entertainment **:** DIVERSION, SPORT ⟨girl mobsters beating up other girls simply for ~*s* —*Newsweek*⟩ ⟨when others might ridicule or overplay it for ~*s*, he can write breezily of a zealous nun —John Farrelly⟩

laugh·able \-fəbəl\ *adj* **:** giving rise to mirth or derision **:** COMICAL, ABSURD ⟨antique finery, which would have been ~ on another woman —W.H.Hudson †1922⟩

syn RISIBLE, FUNNY, DROLL, COMICAL, COMIC, FARCICAL, RIDICULOUS, LUDICROUS: LAUGHABLE is a general term describing that which intentionally or unintentionally occasions laughter either benign or derisive ⟨considered it a *laughable* affair, and was continually bobbing his head out the galley door to make jocose remarks —Jack London⟩ ⟨the lower classes aped the rigid decorum of their "betters" with *laughable* results —Harrison Smith⟩ RISIBLE is a close synonym for LAUGHABLE, also lacking special connotation ⟨has some *risible* material that she delivers well —*New Yorker*⟩ FUNNY describes that which occasions laughter esp. through obvious peculiarity or absurdity ⟨where a *funny* little happy-go-lucky, native-managed railway runs to Jodhpore —Rudyard Kipling⟩ ⟨children thought he was a very *funny* old Chinaman, as children always think anything old and strange is *funny* —John Steinbeck⟩ DROLL indicates laughable qualities arising from either odd quaintness or arch waggishness ⟨a serious child with a *droll* adult expression⟩ ⟨are apt to take on a *droll* sly humor, especially those "tall tales" of exaggeration —*Amer. Guide Series: N. C.*⟩ COMICAL describes that which elicits spontaneous hilarity ⟨the abrupt transition of her features from assured pride to ludicrous astonishment and alarm was *comical* enough to have sent into wild uncharitable laughter any creature less humane —Arnold Bennett⟩ ⟨gave his figure a *comical* air of having been loosely and inaccurately strung together from a selection of stuffed bags of cloth —Leslie Charteris⟩ COMIC is sometimes a close synonym of COMICAL but may differ from it in applying to that which calls for a degree of reflection and occasions more thoughtful mirth ⟨people laugh at absurdities that are very far from being *comic* —Joseph Conrad⟩ FARCICAL applies to that which is so extravagant or extreme as to provoke laughter or derision ⟨the cases described in the preceding pages are mainly *farcical* in their extravagance —Aldous Huxley⟩ ⟨almost *farcical* to suppose that Henry, as a Norman prince, could not talk his own language to his Norman bride —William Empson⟩ RIDICULOUS describes that which is derided as vain or inappropriate ⟨to be always harping on nationality is to convert what should be a recognition of natural conditions into a *ridiculous* pride in one's own oddities —George Santayana⟩ ⟨formed a humorous compound consisting of 168 letters, a thing that would be *ridiculous* rather than funny in English —E.S.McCartney⟩ LUDICROUS indicates that which is so absurd or preposterous that it excites both laughter and scorn ⟨enacted a scene as *ludicrous* as it was pitiable —Charles Kingsley⟩ ⟨had friendships, one after another, so violent as to be often *ludicrous* —Hilaire Belloc⟩

laugh·able·ness *n* -ES **:** the quality or state of being laughable

laugh·ably \-fəblē, -li\ *adv* **:** in a laughable manner ⟨the plane itself looks almost ~ archaic —*Irish Digest*⟩

laugh·er \-f(ə)r\ *n* -S [ME, fr. *laughen* to laugh + *-er*] **:** one that laughs

¹laughing *n* -S [ME, gerund of *laughen* to laugh] **:** the act or process of emitting a laugh ⟨a sound of ~ came from down the corridor⟩ ⟨~ exercises the diaphragm as well as the risorius⟩

²laughing *adj* [in sense 1, fr. gerund of ¹*laugh*; in sense 2, fr. pres. part. of ¹*laugh*] **1 :** LAUGHABLE ⟨this is no ~ matter⟩ **2 :** expressing or seeming to express mirth or good humor **:** MERRY, JOCULAR ⟨~ girl⟩ ⟨~ mood⟩ ⟨along for an ouzel's nest along . . . a ~ stream —D.C.Peattie⟩ — **laugh·ing·ly** *adv*

laughing bird *n* [*laughing* fr. pres. part. of ¹*laugh*] *dial Eng* **:** GREEN WOODPECKER

laughing falcon *n* **:** a So. American falcon (*Herpetotheres cachinnans*)

laughing frog *n* **:** an edible European frog (*Rana ridibunda*)

laughing gas *n* [*laughing* fr. gerund of ¹*laugh*] **:** NITROUS OXIDE

laughing goose *n* [*laughing* fr. pres. part. of ¹*laugh*] **:** WHITE-FRONTED GOOSE

laughing gull *n* **1 :** a black-headed gull (*Larus ridibundus*) **2 :** an American gull (*Larus atricilla*)
laughing hyena *n* **:** SPOTTED HYENA
laughing jackass *n* **1 :** KOOKABURRA **2 :** LAUGHING OWL **3 :** an orchid (*Arethusa bulbosa*)
laughing muscle *n* [*laughing* fr. gerund of ¹*laugh*] **:** RISORIUS
laughing owl *n* [*laughing* fr. pres. part. of ¹*laugh*] **:** a reddish-brown owl (*Sceloglaux albifacies*) of New Zealand that is almost extinct
laughingstock \'==,=\ *n* [*laughing* (fr. gerund of ¹*laugh*) + *stock*] **:** an object of ridicule **:** BUTT ⟨his ineptitude with a power mower made him the ~ of the neighborhood⟩
laughing thrush *n* [*laughing* fr. pres. part. of ¹*laugh*] **:** any of several Asiatic singing birds; *esp* **:** a bird of the genus *Garrulax* often kept as a cage bird
laugh off *vt* **:** to minimize by treating as amusingly or absurdly trivial ⟨officials *laugh off* these reports as nonsense —L.E. Davies⟩ ⟨you can't *laugh off* a royal commission —Alan Villiers⟩
laughs *pres 3d sing of* LAUGH, *pl of* LAUGH
laugh·some \'=səm\ *adj, archaic* **:** provocative of or addicted to laughter **:** MERRY
¹**laugh·ter** \'laftə(r), -aaf-,-aif-,-àf-,-äf-\ *n* -s [ME, fr. OE *hleahtor;* akin to OHG *lahtar* laughter, ON *hlātr;* derivative fr. the root of OE *hliehhan* to laugh — more at LAUGH] **1 a :** a sound of or as if of laughing ⟨~ rippled through the room⟩ ⟨after the scream came hideous ~⟩ ⟨the glowing gully rang with a kookaburra's ~ —Rex Ingamells⟩ ⟨there is ~ in its waters —Robert Gibbings⟩ **b :** an inclination to laugh **:** EXUBERANCE, AMUSEMENT ⟨the ~ in him has turned the scale —Walter Lippmann⟩ ⟨the capacity for civilized enjoyment, for leisure and ~ —Bertrand Russell⟩ **2 :** ²LAUGH 1a ⟨the three ~s broke forth together —Dorothy M. Richardson⟩ **3** *archaic* **:** a cause of merriment ⟨would be argument for a week, ~ for a month —Shak.⟩
²**laugh·ter** \'laftə(r), 'lätə-, 'lōtə-\ *n* -s [of Scand origin; akin to ON *lāttr* place where animals lay their young; akin to ON *leggja* to lay — more at LAY] *dial Brit* **:** a clutch of eggs
laugh·ter·less \'laftə(r)ləs, -aaf-,-aif-,-àf-,-äf-\ *adj* **:** of a grim or mirthless nature **:** SERIOUS
lau·ha·la \lau̇'hälə, *attrib* (')=¦==\ *n* -s [Hawaiian, fr. *lau* leaf + *hala* pandanus] **1 :** TEXTILE SCREW PINE **2 a :** dried pandanus leaves used as a material for weaving ⟨a handbag of ~⟩ **b :** a Polynesian mat woven of dried pandanus leaves
lau·ia \lau̇'ēə\ *n* -s [Hawaiian] *Hawaii* **:** PARROT FISH
lau·lau \'lau̇,lau̇\ *n* -s [Hawaiian] *Hawaii* **:** meat and fish (as pork and salmon) wrapped in leaves (as taro or ti) and baked or steamed
lau·mont·ite *also* **lau·mon·ite** *or* **lo·mon·ite** \lō'män(t·),īt\ *n* -s [*laumontite, laumonite* alter. of *lomonite,* irreg. fr. F. P. N. G. de *Laumont* †1834 Fr. mineralogist + E *-ite*] **:** a white monoclinic mineral $CaAl_2Si_4O_{12}.4H_2O$ consisting of a hydrous calcium and aluminum silicate and having a vitreous luster that upon exposure to the air loses water, becomes opaque, and crumbles
launce *also* **lance** \'lȯn(t)s, -ä-, -a-, -aa(ə)-, -ai-, -à-\ *n* -s [prob. fr. ¹*lance*] **:** SAND LAUNCE
¹**launch** \'lȯnch, -ä-, -à-, *dial* -a-, -aa(ə)-, -ai-\ *vb* -ED/-ING/-ES [ME *launchen,* fr. ONF *lancher,* fr. LL *lanceare* to handle a lance, pierce with a lance — more at LANCE] *vt* **1 a :** to dart or throw forward ⟨~*ed* a looping right to the jaw⟩ ⟨suddenly ~*ed* himself from between his guards . . . and vanished into the rocks and heather, still handcuffed —Philip Rooney⟩ **b :** to throw or propel with force **:** FLING, SHOOT ⟨finding another stone, I raised and was about to ~ it —W.H.Hudson †1922⟩ ⟨~ an arrow at a target⟩; *specif* **:** to release or catapult (a self-propelling object) from a ramp, rack, or other device ⟨~ a torpedo⟩ ⟨~ a carrier plane⟩ ⟨~ a rocket⟩ ⟨~ a satellite⟩ **c :** COMMENCE ⟨~ a hostile action⟩ **:** commit (as troops) to battle ⟨~*ed* his cavalry against them —Tom Wintringham⟩ **d :** to direct (as abuse or criticism) against ⟨~*ed* a determined attack on academic criticism —C.I.Glicksberg⟩ ⟨~*ed* a fresh anathema against him —R.W.Southern⟩ ⟨~*ed a* . . . protest against the political power of the well-to-do —J.D.Hicks⟩ **2** *obs* **:** LANCE 1, 2 **3 a :** to put or cause to slide into the water **:** set afloat ⟨~ a canoe⟩ ⟨~ a battleship⟩ ⟨~ a lifeboat⟩ **b** (1) **:** to give (a person) a start ⟨~ a daughter in society⟩ ⟨~ a son in business⟩ ⟨~*ed* their peoples on the path of war and conquest —Sir Winston Churchill⟩ (2) **:** EMBARK ⟨she ~*ed* herself on her nursing career⟩ ⟨his massive task begins and he ~*es* himself upon it —Ira Wolfert⟩ ⟨he was now well ~*ed* on a speech of his own —Waldo Frank⟩ ⟨pipeline companies now are ~*ed* on a . . . construction and expansion program —*Trends*⟩ **c** (1) **:** to originate or set in motion **:** put into operation **:** INITIATE, INTRODUCE ⟨~ an enterprise⟩ ⟨~ a program⟩ ⟨~ a fund drive⟩ ⟨~ a new product⟩ (2) **:** to get off to a good start **:** gain public acceptance for ⟨a literary dinner to ~ the book —*Newsweek*⟩ **d :** to cast forth or send out ⟨~*ed* himself upon the intellectual currents of the age —H.O.Taylor⟩ ⟨~ a first-class minstrel company on the road —C.F. Wittke⟩ ⟨a young pair ~*ed* their first invitations in the third person —Edith Wharton⟩ **4** *obs* **:** to hoist (as a yard) or push out (as capstan bars) — used of equipment on sailing ships ~ *vi* **1 a :** to spring forward **:** take off ⟨a junco had ~*ed* off a chinquapin twig —W.V.T.Clark⟩ ⟨the catapult snagged and the plane overturned before it could ~⟩ **b** (1) **:** to throw oneself energetically **:** PLUNGE ⟨~ into a brilliant harangue⟩ ⟨~*ed* into a vigorously rhythmic, sharply accentuated playing of the . . . prelude —Irving Kolodin⟩ (2) **:** to speak out critically **:** LASH ⟨listened . . . politely for ten minutes and then ~*ed* out —H.J.Laski⟩ **2 a** *archaic* **:** to slide down the ways **:** become launched ⟨the *Resolution* now in the dock ~*es* on Tuesday —*London Gazette*⟩ **b :** to set out **:** GO ⟨one of the party . . . had ~*ed* off by himself —*Appalachia*⟩ **c :** to make a start **:** COMMENCE ⟨had ~*ed* on his hour of study —Hallam Tennyson⟩ ⟨~ upon the production of films —Jean Begeman⟩; *specif* **:** to go into business
²**launch** \"\ *n* -ES [ME *launche,* fr. *launchen,* v.] **:** LAUNCHING ⟨may hold up a ~ for days —H.H.Martin⟩ ⟨after ~ it could shift targets —Clay Blair⟩
³**launch** \"\ *n* -ES [Sp or Pg; Sp *lancha,* fr. Pg, fr. Malay *lancharan,* fr. *lanchar* effortless speed] **1** *archaic* **:** a large often sloop-rigged ship's boat of relatively shallow draft designed to carry men and stores and often fitted with a light gun in the bow **2 :** a small open or half-decked motorboat used commercially or as a pleasure craft in harbors and coastal waters
launch·able \-chəbəl\ *adj* **:** capable of being launched
launch·er \-chə(r)\ *n* -s **:** one that launches: as **a :** a device for firing a grenade from a rifle **b :** a device for launching a rocket or rocket shell; *specif* **:** ROCKET LAUNCHER **c :** CATAPULT
launching *n* -s **1 a :** an act or instance of initiating (as a program or enterprise) ⟨a major project . . . is the ~ of a series of books of poetry —F.W.Boardman⟩ ⟨the ~ of . . . Nashville's third television station —*Retailing Daily*⟩ **b :** an act or instance of public introduction **:** PRESENTATION ⟨a coming-out ball and other social ~*s* —*Irish Digest*⟩ ⟨ideas emerge not only from Paris ~*s* but also New York designers' concepts —*Women's Wear Daily*⟩ **2 a :** the act or process of placing a boat in the water **b :** WAY 13a **c :** a ceremony accompanying the launching of a ship **3 :** the act or process of releasing a self-propelled object from a ramp, rack, or other device ⟨the pads may get more of a workout for satellite ~*s* —*Newsweek*⟩
launching pad *n* **:** a nonflammable platform from which a rocket or guided missile can be launched
launching ways \'==,=\ *or* **launchways** \'=,=\ *n pl but sing or pl in constr* **:** WAY 13a
launch·man \-chmən\ *n, pl* **launchmen :** an operator of a motor launch
laund \'lȯnd\ *n* -s [ME *launde,* fr. MF *lande* heath, of Celt origin; akin to OIr *land* open space — more at LAND] *archaic* **:** an open usu. grassy area among trees **:** GLADE ⟨through this ~ anon the deer will come —Shak.⟩
¹**laun·der** \'lȯndə(r), 'län-,'lán-, *dial* 'lan- *or* 'laan-\ *n* -s [ME *lander, launder* launderer, laundress, alter. of *lavender,* fr. MF *lavandier* (masc.) male launderer, *lavandiere* (fem.) laundress, fr. ML *lavandarius* (masc.) male launderer, *lavandaria* (fem.) laundress, fr. L *lavandus* that needs to be washed (gerundive of *lavare* to wash) + *-arius, -aria* -ary — more at LYE] **:** a conduit or trough for water and other liquids: as **a :** a box conduit conveying middlings or tailings suspended in water in ore dressing **b :** a refractory trough conveying molten metal **c :** a usu. movable wooden trough into which water is run or pumped while engineering construction work is carried on
²**launder** \"\ *vb* **laundered; laundered; laundering** \-d(ə)riŋ\ **launders** [obs. *launder* launderer, laundress, fr. ME *lander, launder*] *vt* **1 a :** to wash (as clothes) in water ⟨nylon shorts are easy to ~⟩ ⟨his only towel and he had ~*ed* it himself —Katharine N. Burt⟩ **b :** to wash and iron ⟨put on a freshly ~*ed* shirt⟩ **2 a :** to remove dirt or impurities from **:** CLEANSE ⟨the cat ~*s* her kittens with her tongue⟩ ⟨a dust-collecting device for ~*ing* air⟩ ⟨~ greasy tools with supersonic sound waves⟩ **b :** to free from flaws or objectionable matter **:** PURIFY, CENSOR ⟨succeeded pretty well in ~*ing* the grammar —H.R. Warfel⟩ ~ *vi* **1 a :** to wash or wash and iron clothing or household linens ⟨cooks, cleans, ~*s,* and does other household chores⟩ **b :** to withstand washing and ironing ⟨this fabric ~*s* well⟩ **2 :** SLUICE ⟨water . . . which his colleague has ~*ed* out of his ears —Maurice Collis⟩
laun·der·abil·i·ty \-d(ə)rə'bilәd·ē\ *n* **:** the quality or state of being washable ⟨~ is a major factor in choosing a summer dress⟩
laun·der·able \'=d(ə)rəbəl\ *adj* **:** capable of being washed
laun·der·er \-dərə(r)\ *n* -s [ME, fr. ME *lander, launder* launderer, laundress + *-er*] **:** one that launders
laun·der·ette \¦=də¦ret\ *n* -s [fr. *Launderette,* a service mark] **:** a commercial establishment in which automatic washing machines are installed for the use of individual customers
laundering *n* -s **:** the act or process of washing or cleansing ⟨cotton dresses, faded from many ~*s* —Hamilton Basso⟩ ⟨the coal undergoes another ~ as it passes over screens for final sizing —*Amer. Guide Series: Pa.*⟩
launder man *n* [¹*launder*] **:** a worker who cleans and repairs launders
Laun·der-Om·e·ter \,==ˈrämәd·ə(r)\ *trademark* — used for a machine with rotating containers for testing the colorfastness of dyed cloth to washing solutions or the efficiency of washing solutions in cleansing soiled cloth
laun·dress \'=drəs\ *n* -ES [obs. E *launder* launderer, laundress (fr. ME *lander, launder*) + E *-ess*] **:** a woman who does household laundry
Laun·dro·mat \'=drə,mat\ *service mark* — used for a self-service laundry
laun·dry \'lȯndrē, 'län-,'lán-, -dri, *dial* 'lan-,'laan-\ *n* -ES *often attrib* [obs. E *launder* launderer, laundress + E *-y*] **1 a** *obs* **:** LAUNDERING **b :** a collection of clothes or household linens to be laundered ⟨a truck picks up the ~ once a week⟩ **2 a :** a room or area set aside for doing the family wash **b :** a commercial establishment where laundering is done
laundry·man \-mən, -,man\ *n, pl* **laundrymen 1 :** one who works at laundering (as in a commercial laundry, home, factory, camp, or institution) **2 :** an institutional or industrial worker who prepares soiled articles for delivery to the laundry and checks and takes care of them upon their return **3 :** the driver of a laundry truck
laundry soap *n* **:** soap (as rosin soap) for the laundry
laundry tray *or* **laundry tub** *n* **:** a fixed tub (as of slate, earthenware, soapstone, enameled iron, or porcelain) with running water and drainpipe for washing clothes and other household linens — called also *set tub*

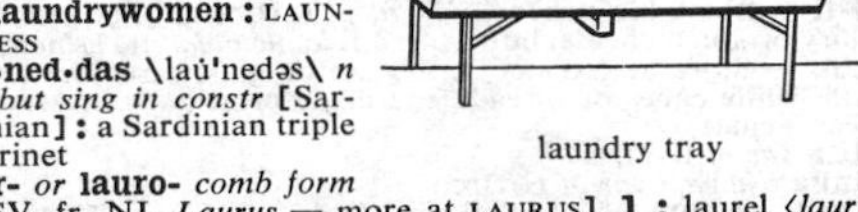
laundry tray

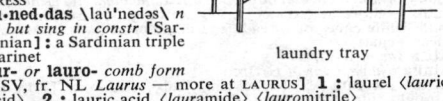

laundrywoman \'==,==\ *n, pl* **laundrywomen :** LAUNDRESS
lau·ned·das \lau̇'nedəs\ *n pl but sing in constr* [Sardinian] **:** a Sardinian triple clarinet
laur- *or* **lauro-** *comb form* [ISV, fr. NL *Laurus* — more at LAURUS] **1 :** laurel ⟨*lauric* acid⟩ **2 :** lauric acid ⟨*lauramide*⟩ ⟨*lauromitrile*⟩
lau·ra \'lävrə\ *n* -s [LGk, fr. Gk, lane, alley; akin to OIr *līe* stone, Gk *laas* stone, Alb *lerë* rock, rockfall] **:** a monastery of the Eastern Church orig. consisting of a number of monks living a communal life yet inhabiting separate cells grouped around a church
lau·ra·ce·ae \lȯ'rāsē,ē\ *n pl, cap* [NL, fr. *Laurus,* type genus + *-aceae*] **:** a family of shrubs and trees (order Ranales) having flowering with definite stamens in several series of three, more or less united sepals, no petals, and a single pistil — **lau·ra·ceous** \(')lȯ¦rāshəs\ *adj*
laur·aldehyde \(')lȯr, (')lär+\ *n* **:** a fragrant crystalline compound $C_{11}H_{23}CHO$ found in some essential oils (as from needles of the silver fir of Europe) and used in perfumes
lau·rate \'lȯ,rāt, 'lä,-\ *n* -s [ISV *laur-* + *-ate*] **:** a salt or ester of lauric acid
¹**lau·re·ate** \'lȯrēət,'lär-, *usu* -əd.+V\ *adj* [ME *laureat,* fr. L *laureatus* crowned with laurel, fr. *laurea* laurel wreath (fr. fem. of *laureus* of laurel, fr. *laurus* laurel + *-eus* -eous) + *-atus* -ate — more at LAUREL] **1 a :** of an excellence esp. in poetry worthy of the laurel wreath **b :** of or relating to a prizewinner ⟨at the ~ concert Sunday night —*N. Y. Times*⟩ ⟨~ pension⟩ ⟨Nobel ~ geneticist —*Newsweek*⟩ **2** *archaic* **:** of, relating to, or resembling laurel ⟨to grace by youthful brow the ~ wreath . . . she brings —Thomas Gray⟩ **3 :** crowned or decked with laurel ⟨~ head of Caesar⟩ ⟨strew the ~ hearse —John Milton⟩
²**laureate** \"\ *n* -s **1 :** a recipient of an honor or award for outstanding achievement in an art or science ⟨Nobel ~ in physics⟩; *specif* **:** POET LAUREATE ⟨~ John Masefield's special ode —*College English*⟩ **2 :** one that praises **:** EULOGIST ⟨the ~ of a dying society —Martin Turnell⟩ ⟨dry and amusing ~ of Cape Cod —Carl Van Doren⟩
³**lau·re·ate** \-ē,āt, *usu* -ād.+V\ *vt* -ED/-ING/-S **1 :** to crown with or as if with a laurel wreath as a mark of honor or achievement; *specif* **:** to confer a European university degree upon ⟨privileges which made the member of one university a citizen of all others . . . whether he was *laureated* in Paris or Bologna —J.H.Burton⟩ **2 :** to appoint to the office of poet laureate
laureated *adj* **:** LAUREATE 3
lau·re·ate·ship \-rēət,ship\ *n* **:** the office of poet laureate
lau·re·a·tion \,lȯrē'āshən, ,lär-\ *n* -s [³*laureate* + *-ion*] **1 :** an act of crowning with or as if with laurel as a mark of honor or achievement **2** *archaic* **:** the conferring of an academic degree ⟨the right of ~ conceded to the University of Vienna by Maximilian I —William Hamilton †1856⟩
¹**lau·rel** \'lȯrəl, 'lär-\ *n* -s [ME *lorel, lorer, laurer,* fr. OF *lorier,* fr. *lor* laurel, fr. L *laurus* — more at DAPHNE] **1 a :** a tree or shrub of the genus *Laurus; specif* **:** a tree (*Laurus nobilis*) bearing foliage used by the ancient Greeks to crown victors in the Pythian games — called also *bay, bay laurel, bay tree* **b :** the leaves of the laurel that yield a fragrant oil — compare BAY LEAF **2 a :** a branch or wreath of laurel awarded as a token of victory or preeminence **b** (1) **:** a recognition of superior achievement **:** mark of public esteem **:** HONOR ⟨added one more ~ to his growing collection today when he was voted the . . . most valuable player —*Springfield (Mass.) Union*⟩ — usu. used in pl. ⟨his technique . . . sufficed to win him such ~*s* as few architects have enjoyed —C.H.Whitaker⟩ (2) **laurels** *pl but sing or pl in constr* **:** CHAMPIONSHIP, REPUTATION ⟨won the regional ~*s* and went on to the finals⟩ ⟨after winning the title he decided to rest on his ~*s* and retire from the ring⟩ ⟨enthusiastic critical acclaim for the newcomer is forcing older actors to look to their ~*s*⟩ **3 a :** a British gold coin bearing a laureate head of a monarch **:** UNITE **b :** a unit of value corresponding to one of these coins ⟨a half-*laurel*⟩ **4 :** a tree or shrub that resembles the laurel: as **a :** CHERRY LAUREL **b :** SPURGE LAUREL **c :** any of several plants of the heath family: as (1) **:** MOUNTAIN LAUREL (2) **:** BIG LAUREL **d :** MADRONA **e :** CALIFORNIA LAUREL **f :** any of several tropical American trees of the genera *Cordia, Sebesten,* and *Magnolia* **g :** OLEANDER **h :** any of several New Zealand and Australian evergreen trees of the genera *Cryptocarya, Pittosporum, Corynocarpus,* and *Likea* **5 :** a variable color averaging a dark grayish green that is bluer than average ivy, bluer and duller than Persian green, and yellower and paler than hemlock green — compare LAUREL GREEN

European laurel

²**laurel** \"\ *vt* **laureled** *or* **laurelled; laureled** *or* **laurelled; laureling** *or* **laurelling; laurels :** to deck or crown with or as if with laurel
laurel bay *n* [ME *lorel baye,* fr. *lorel* laurel + *baye* bay] **1** *obs* **:** the laurel berry **2 :** LAUREL 1a **3 :** EVERGREEN MAGNOLIA
laurel camphor *n* **:** dextrorotatory camphor
laurel cherry *n* **:** CHERRY LAUREL 2
laureled *or* **laurelled** *adj* **1 :** crowned or decked with laurel **:** LAUREATE **2 :** recognized publicly for excellence or achievement **:** PRAISED, HONORED
laurel family *n* **:** LAURACEAE
laurel green *n* **1 :** a variable color averaging a moderate green that is yellower and duller than sea green (sense 1a) and bluer and less strong than myrtle (sense 3a) **2 :** a light olive
laurel-leaved willow \'==,=-\ *n* **:** BAY WILLOW 1
laurel magnolia *n* **:** EVERGREEN MAGNOLIA
laurel oak *n* **1 :** either of two American oaks with glossy leaves resembling those of the European laurel: **a :** a large oak (*Quercus laurifolia*) of the southeastern U.S. with a rather smooth dark brown bark, nearly evergreen leaves, and a small acorn with a shallow cup — called also *pin oak* **b :** SHINGLE OAK 1 **2 :** a moderate reddish brown that is yellower than roan and yellower and slightly lighter and stronger than mahogany — called also *acajou*
laurel pink *n* **:** a deep pink to moderate red that is bluer and less strong than rose dorée or watermelon
laurel sumac *n* **:** an aromatic Californian shrub (*Rhus laurina*) having paniculate flowers and whitish fruit
laurel-tree \'==,=\ *n* [ME *lorel tre* laurel, fr. *lorel* laurel + *tre, tree* tree] **:** RED BAY
laurelwood \'==,=\ *n* **:** DAGAME
lau·ren·cia \lȯ'ren(t)sēə, -nchə\ *n, cap* [NL, fr. M. de la *Laurencie,* 19th cent. Fr. naturalist + NL *-ia*] **:** a genus of mostly flattened leathery red algae (family Rhodomelaceae) — see PEPPER DULSE
lau·ren·tian \lȯ'rench(ē)ən\ *adj, usu cap* [L *Laurentius* Lawrence (in sense 1 representing the St. Lawrence river, southern Quebec and southeast Ontario, Canada, and in sense 2 representing D. H. Lawrence †1930 Eng. novelist) + E *-an*] **1 a :** of, relating to, or near the St. Lawrence river ⟨*Laurentian* hills⟩ **b :** of or relating to mountain-making movements of the Archeozoic era — see GEOLOGIC TIME table **2 :** of or relating to D. H. Lawrence
lau·ren·tide \'lȯrən,tīd, 'lär-\ *adj, usu cap* [irreg. fr. L *Laurentius* Lawrence (representing the St. Lawrence river)] **:** of or relating to the region of the St. Lawrence river
laurent's acid \-ä"z-\ *n, usu cap L* [after Auguste *Laurent* †1853 Fr. chemist] **:** a crystalline naphthylaminesulfonic acid $H_2NC_{10}H_6SO_3H$ made by sulfonating alpha-naphthylamine and used as an intermediate for azo dyes; 5-amino-1-naphthalenesulfonic acid
lau·rer's canal \'lau̇(r)ərz-, 'lau̇rəz-\ *n, usu cap L* [after Johann Friedrich *Laurer* †1873 Ger. pharmacologist] **:** a muscular duct in some trematode worms that arises from the oviduct between the ovary and the vitalleine duct and passes to the dorsal surface
lau·ric acid \'lȯ|rik-, 'lä|\ *n* [*lauric* ISV *laur-* + *-ic*] **:** a crystalline fatty acid $CH_3(CH_2)_{10}COOH$ occurring in the form of its glycerol esters in the berries of the European laurel (*Laurus nobilis*) and esp. in coconut oil and palm-kernel oil and used often as obtained from coconut oil in mixtures with other fatty acids in making chiefly metallic soaps, esters, and lauryl alcohol
lau·rin \'lȯrən, 'lär-\ *n* -s [ISV *laur-* + *-in*] **:** a glycerol ester of lauric acid; *esp* **:** TRILAURIN
lau·ri·nox·y·lon \,lȯrə'näksə,län, ,lär-\ *n* -s [NL, fr. *laurino-* (fr. L *laurinus* of laurel, fr. *laurus* laurel + *-inus* -ine) + *-xylon*] **:** a fossil dicotyledonous wood resembling that of the existing genus *Laurus*
lau·ri·on·ite \'lȯrēə,nīt, 'lärē-, 'lävrē-\ *n* -s [G *laurionit,* fr. *Laurion,* Greece, its locality + G *-it* -ite] **:** a basic lead chloride $Pb(OH)Cl$ found in prismatic crystals at Laurion, Greece
lau·rite \'lȯ,rīt, 'lä,-\ *n* -s [G *laurit,* prob. fr. the name *Laura* + G *-it* -ite] **:** a mineral RuS_2 consisting of an iron-black ruthenium sulfide often containing osmium and found in minute crystals or grains
lau·rit·sen electroscope \'lau̇|rətsən-, 'lȯ|, 'lä|\ *n, usu cap L* [after Charles C. *Lauritsen* †1968 and Thomas *Lauritsen* *b*1915 Am. physicists born in Denmark, who designed it] **:** an electroscope in which the sensitive element is a quartz fiber used in precise measurements of ionizing radiation
lauro- — see LAUR-
lau·ro·cer·a·sus \,lȯrō'serəsəs, ,lär-\ *n, cap* [NL, fr. *laur-* + L *cerasus* cherry tree — more at CHERRY] *in some classifications* **:** a genus of trees and shrubs that occur in warm or tropical regions, that include the European cherry laurel and related plants with alternate usu. evergreen leaves and pentamerous white flowers in racemes, and that are now commonly included in the genus *Prunus*
lau·ro·yl \'lȯrə,wil, 'lär-\ *or* **lau·ryl** \-rəl\ *n* -s [ISV *laur-* + *-yl*] **:** the radical $CH_3(CH_2)_{10}CO—$ of lauric acid
lau·rus \'lȯrəs, 'lär-\ *n, cap* [NL, fr. L, laurel — more at DAPHNE] **:** a genus of trees (family Lauraceae) having alternate entire leaves and small tetramerous involucrate flowers succeeded by fruits that are ovoid berries — see ¹LAUREL 1a
lau·rus·tine \'lȯrə,stīn, 'lär-, -tēn\ *n* -s [NL *laurustinus,* fr. L *laurus* laurel + *tinus* a plant, prob. the laurustine; prob. akin to OE *thīnan* to become moist, OSlav *tina* mud, OE *thawian* to thaw — more at THAW] **:** a European shrub (*Viburnum tinus*) widely cultivated for its evergreen leaves and white or pink fragrant flowers
lau·rus·ti·nus *or* **lau·res·ti·nus** \,==ˈstīnəs, -tēn-\ *n* -ES [NL] **:** LAURUSTINE
laur·vik·ite \'lau̇rvi,kīt\ *var of* LARVIKITE
lau·ryl \'lȯrəl, 'lär-\ *n* -s [ISV *laur-* + *-yl*] **1 :** normal dodecyl **2 :** a mixture of alkyl radicals derived from commercial lauryl alcohol — compare SODIUM LAURYL SULFATE
lauryl alcohol *n* **1 :** a crystalline compound $CH_3(CH_2)_{10}CH_2OH$ made by reduction of ethyl laurate; normal dodecyl alcohol **2 :** a liquid mixture containing lauryl alcohol and other alcohols that is produced commercially by reduction of coconut oil, the fatty acids from coconut oil, or their esters and is used esp. in making anionic detergents
lau·sanne \lō'zän, -zan\ *adj, usu cap* [fr. *Lausanne* Switzerland] **:** of or from the city of Lausanne, Switzerland **:** of the kind or style prevalent in Lausanne
lau·sen·ite \'lȯsᵊn,īt, 'lau̇zᵊn-\ *n* -s [Carl *Lausen,* 20th cent. Am. mining engineer + E *-ite*] **:** a mineral $Fe_2(SO_4)_3.6H_2O$ consisting of a hydrous ferric sulfate — called also *rogersite*
lau·ta·rite \'lau̇d·ə,rīt\ *n* -s [G *lautarit,* fr. Oficina *Lautaro,* Chile, its locality + G *-it* -ite] **:** a mineral $Ca(IO_3)_2$ consisting of calcium iodate and occurring in prismatic crystals
¹**lau·ter** \'lau̇d·ər\ *adj* [G, clear, pure, fr. OHG *hlūtar* pure — more at CLYSTER] **1 :** CLEAR ⟨~ mash⟩ **2 :** CLARIFIED ⟨~ beer⟩
²**lauter** \"\ *vt* -ED/-ING/-S **:** to treat (mash) in a lauter tub **:** FILTER
lauter tub *or* **lauter tun** *n* **:** a large tank containing a slotted or perforated false bottom for filtering the clear liquid wort from the residual grain in the mash in brewing
lau·tite \'lau̇,tīt\ *n* -s [G *lautit,* fr. *Lauta,* Germany, its locality + G *-it* -ite] **:** a mineral $CuAsS$ consisting of a sulfide and arsenide of copper probably related to arsenopyrite
laut·ver·schie·bung \'lau̇tfer,shē(,)bu̇ŋ\ *n, pl* **lautverschie·bung·en** \-ŋən\ [G, fr. *laut* sound + *verschiebung* shift] **:** CONSONANT SHIFT
lav *abbr or n* -s lavatory

la·va \'läv·ə, 'lav·, 'lȧv·\ *n* -s *often attrib* [It, fr. It dial. (Naples), lava, torrent of floodwater, fr. L *labes* fall; akin to L *labi* to glide, slide — more at SLEEP] **1 a :** fluid rock that issues from a volcano or from a fissure in the earth's surface, that consists of mineral matter dissolved in mineral matter at high temperatures, and that is more fluid when at higher temperatures and when basic rather than acid — compare MAGMA **b :** any of several solid materials (as obsidian, pumice) resulting from the cooling of lava under different conditions ⟨black ~s⟩ ⟨a ~ bed⟩ ⟨~ plateaus of vast dimensions —O.D.Von Engeln⟩ **2 :** a nearly neutral slightly brownish black that is lighter than African

la·va·bo \lə'vä(,)bō, *chiefly Brit* -vā(-\ *n* -s [L, I shall wash, 1st pers. sing. fut. indic. of *lavare* to wash — more at LYE] **1** *often cap* **a :** a ceremonial cleansing in certain Christian churches in which the celebrant liturgically washes his hands after touching the Host in the offertory and repeats in the Roman rite Psalms 25:6 (DV) beginning *Lavabo* **b :** a basin used in this ceremonial washing **2 a :** a washbasin and a tank with a spigot that are both fastened to a wall **b :** a decorative wall basin and water container that is sometimes used for flowers

lava cone *n* **:** a volcanic cone composed predominantly of lava flows

lava flow *n* **:** a stream or sheet of molten or solidified lava

1**la·vage** \lə'väzh, -vȧzh\ *n* -s [F, action of washing, fr. MF, fr. *laver* to wash (fr. L *lavare*) + *-age*] **:** WASHING; *esp* **:** the therapeutic washing out of an organ

2**lavage** \"\ *vt* -ED/-ING/-S **:** to wash (a lesion) or wash out (an organ) therapeutically

la·va·la·va \¦lävə¦lävə\ *n* [Samoan, clothing] **:** a rectangular cloth worn like a kilt or skirt by men, women, and children in Polynesia and esp. in Samoa that is now usu. of a bright cotton print often with white or yellow floral designs on a red or blue background

lava·liere *or* **lava·lier** *also* **laval·liere** \¦lavə¦li(ə)r, ¦läv-\ *n* -s [F *lavallière* necktie with a large bow, prob. fr. Françoise Louise de la Baume Le Blanc, Duchesse de *La Vallière* †1710 mistress of Louis XIV] **1 :** a pendant ornament on a fine chain that is worn as a necklace **2 :** something suggesting a lavaliere (as a spot of white on the neck of a cat)

la·van·din \lə'vandən\ *n* -s [perh. fr. F, irreg. fr. NL *Lavandula*] **:** a hybrid lavender (*Lavandula hybrida*) cultivated for its essential oil esp. in France

lavandin oil *n* **:** a fragrant yellowish essential oil obtained from the flowers of lavandin and used in soaps and perfumes

la·van·du·la \lə'vanjələ\ *n, cap* [NL, fr. ML *lavandula, lavendula* marjoram, lavender — more at LAVENDER] **:** a genus of Eurasian herbs or shrubs (family Labiatae) having small spicate flowers with a tubular 5-toothed calyx — see LAVENDER

la·van·du·lol \-,lōl, -,lȯl\ *n* -s [ISV *lavandul-* (fr. NL *Lavandula*) + *-ol*] **:** a liquid terpenoid alcohol $C_{10}H_{17}OH$ occurring in lavender oil from France

la·van·ga \lə'vaŋgə\ *n* -s [modif. of Skt *lavaṅgalatā*, fr. *lavaṅga* clove tree + *latā* creeper] **:** a spiny woody vine (*Luvunga scandens*) of the family Rutaceae that is native to southeastern Asia and is used as a stock for citrus grafts

lav·a·ret \¦lavə¦ret, '==,rət\ *n* -s [F, fr. LL *levaricinus*] **:** a central European whitefish (*Coregonus lavaretus*) found in mountain lakes

la·vash \'lä,väsh\ *n* -ES [Arm] **:** a large thin crisp unleavened wafer with a rough surface from air bubbles

lava soil *n* **:** soil derived from lava ⟨rich *lava soils* —W.G.East⟩

lava·te·ra \,lävə'tirə, lə'vädərə\ *n, cap* [NL, fr. J. R. Lavater, 17th cent. Swiss physician and naturalist] **:** a genus of herbs, shrubs, and trees (family Malvaceae) with large flowers subtended by an involucre of 6 to 10 bractlets

la·va·tion \lā'vāshən, lə'-\ *n* -s [L *lavation-, lavatio*, fr. *lavatus* (past part. of *lavare* to wash) + *-ion-, -io* -ion] **:** WASHING, CLEANSING, LAVAGE — **la·va·tion·al** \-shən°l, -shnəl\ *adj*

lav·a·to·ri·al \¦lavə¦tōrēəl, -tȯr-\ *adj* **:** LAVATORY

1**lav·a·to·ry** \'lavə,tōre, -tȯr-, -ri\ *n* -ES [ME *lavatorie*, fr. ML *lavatorium*, fr. L *lavatus* (past part. of *lavare* to wash) + *-orium*] **1 :** a basin or other vessel for washing: as **a :** PISCINA **b :** a water basin in a sacristy **2 :** a ritual washing of the hands by a celebrant of the Eucharist **:** LAVABO 1a **3 :** a place for washing: as **a :** a room with conveniences for washing the hands and face and usu. with one or more toilets **b :** a fixed bowl or basin with running water and drainpipe for washing the hands and face **c :** a place, trough, or tub in which bodies are washed before burial **4 :** WATER CLOSET, TOILET

wall-hung lavatory 3b

2**lavatory** \"\ *adj* **:** of, related to, or characteristic of washing

1**lave** \'lāv\ *n* -s [ME (northern dial.), fr. OE *lāf*; akin to OHG *leiba* remainder, ON *leifar* (pl.) remnants, Goth *laiba* remnant; derivative fr. the root of OE *belīfan* to remain, be left over — more at LEAVE] *now dial* **:** something that is left or remains **:** RESIDUE, REMAINDER ⟨he aye did as the ~ did —J.G.Lockhart⟩

2**lave** \"\ *vb* -ED/-ING/-S [ME *laven*, fr. OE *lafian*; akin to MD *laven* to refresh, soak, OHG *labōn* to refresh, wash; all fr. a prehistoric WGmc word borrowed fr. L *lavare* to wash — more at LYE] *vt* **1 :** to wash or flow along or against **:** WASH, BATHE ⟨*laved* her injured foot in the cold stream —W.H.Hudson †1922⟩ ⟨baptism is performed by *laving* the candidate's head —George Stimpson⟩ ⟨all stuffed into a whole long loaf of bread and *laved* generously with oil —R.B.Gehman⟩ **2 :** POUR **3** *obs* **:** to dip or scoop up or out (as with a ladle) **:** LADE, BAIL ~ *vi, archaic* **:** to wash oneself **:** BATHE ⟨in her chaste current oft the goddess ~s —Alexander Pope⟩

3**lave** \"\ *dial var of* LEAVE

la·veer \lə'vi(ə)r\ *vi* [D *laveren*, fr. MD *laveren, loveren*, fr. MF *louvier*, fr. *lof* side of a ship toward the wind — more at LUFF] *archaic* **:** to beat against the wind in sailing **:** TACK

lavement *n* -s [F, fr. OF, action of washing, fr. *laver* to wash (fr. L *lavare*) + *-ment*] *obs* **:** ENEMA, LAVAGE

1**lav·en·der** \'lavəndə(r)\ *n* -s [ME *lavendre*, fr. AF, fr. ML *lavandula, lavendula, livendula* marjoram, lavender, perh. irreg. fr. L *lividus* livid — more at LIVID] **1 a :** a Mediterranean mint (*Lavandula officinalis*) that is widely cultivated for its narrow aromatic leaves and spikes of lilac-purple flowers which are dried and used in sachets — called also *English lavender*; see LAVENDER OIL **b :** any of several other plants of the genus *Lavandula* used similarly to English lavender but often considered inferior — see SPIKE LAVENDER **2 :** a variable color averaging a pale purple that is bluer and deeper than wistaria (sense 2a), flossflower blue, or mauvette and bluer, darker, and slightly stronger than phlox pink

2**lavender** \"\ *vt* **lavendered; lavendered; lavendering** \-d(ə)riŋ\ **lavenders :** to sprinkle or perfume with lavender

lavender blue *n* **:** a light to brilliant purplish blue

lavender cotton *n* **:** a branching shrub (*Santolina chamaecyparissus*) of the Mediterranean region with strong-scented foliage

lavender gray *n* **:** a light bluish gray that is darker and slightly redder than sky gray or chicory

lavender mist *n* **:** a pale purple that is paler than average lavender, bluer and duller than wistaria (sense 2a), and bluer, stronger, and slightly lighter than flossflower blue

lavender oil *n* **:** a colorless to yellowish aromatic essential oil obtained from the flowers of several species of lavender (as *Lavandula officinalis* in France) and used chiefly as a perfume and also in medicine as a stimulant

lavender thrift *n* **:** SEA LAVENDER 1

lavender water *n* **:** a perfume consisting primarily of an alcoholic solution of lavender oil

la·ven·du·la \lə'venjələ\ *syn of* LAVANDULA

lave net *n* [perh. fr. 2*lave* + *net*] **:** a fishnet used in shallow estuaries in Great Britain

lavenite *var of* LAAVENITE

la ven·ta \lə'ventə\ *adj, usu cap L&V* [fr. *La Venta*, village in southeastern Mexico, site of the finds] **:** of or relating to a culture of southeastern Mexico of about 500 B.C. to A.D. 600 characterized by huge stone realistic figures and carved jade figurines and ornaments

1**la·ver** \'lāvə(r)\ *n* -s [ME, alter. (influenced by *-er*) of *lavour*, fr. MF *lavoir, lavouer*, prob. fr. ML *lavatorium* — more at LAVATORY] **1** *archaic* **:** a vessel, tub, or cistern for washing **:** BASIN 1a **2** *archaic* **:** something that cleanses physically or spiritually ⟨with ~s pure and cleansing herbs wash off the clotted gore —John Milton⟩ ⟨Christ's ~ hath refreshing power —John Keble⟩ **3 a :** a large brazen vessel near the Mosaic tabernacle and in Solomon's temple where priests washed their hands and feet **b :** one of several vessels in Solomon's temple in which the offerings for burnt sacrifices were washed **4** *archaic* **:** the basin of a fountain

2**laver** \"\ *n* -s [NL, fr. L, a water plant] **1 :** any of several seaweeds: as **a :** RED LAVER **b :** SEA LETTUCE **2 :** AMANORI

lav·er·a·nia \,lavə'rānyə\ *n, cap* [NL, fr. Charles L. A. *Laveran* †1922 Fr. physician + NL *-ia*] *in some classifications* **:** a genus of malaria parasites (family Plasmodiidae) that is now usu. included in the genus *Plasmodium*

lav·er·ock *or* **lav·rock** \'lav(ə)rək\ *n* [ME *laverok*, fr. OE *lāwerce* — more at LARK] *chiefly Scot* **:** LARK

laverwort \'==,=\ *n* [2*laver* + *wort*] **:** 2LAVER

la·vette \la'vet\ *n* -s [prob. fr. *lavatory* + *-ette*] **:** LAVATORY 3a

1**lav·ish** \'lavish, -vēsh\ *n* -ES [ME *lavas*, fr. MF *lavasse, lavache* downpour of rain, fr. *laver* to wash, fr. L *lavare* — more at LYE] *now dial* **:** an unstinted outpouring **:** ABUNDANCE, PROFUSION ⟨he'll maybe see trouble and a ~ of it too —Elizabeth M. Roberts⟩

2**lavish** \"\ *adj, sometimes* -ER/-EST [ME *lavas*, fr. *lavas*, n.] **1 :** expending or bestowing profusely **:** PRODIGAL ⟨the war redistributed national wealth with a ~ and careless hand —Allan Nevins & H.S.Commager⟩ ⟨peculiarly ~ of endearments to his second son —D.H.Lawrence⟩ ⟨remarkably ~ with invective —H.J.Muller⟩ **2 a** *archaic* **:** unrestrained in speech **:** EFFUSIVE ⟨the ~ tongue shall honest truths impart —George Crabbe †1832⟩ **b** *obs* **:** unrestrained in conduct or disposition **:** IMPETUOUS, WILD ⟨when rage and hot blood are his counselors, when means and ~ manners meet together —Shak.⟩ **3 :** expended or produced in abundance **:** characterized by profusion or excess **:** UNSTINTED ⟨a country in which there is ~ consumption and no production —G.B.Shaw⟩ ⟨the ~ attentions of his mother —George Meredith⟩ ⟨bearing a sandwich board on which his name was inscribed in ~ capitals —Max Beerbohm⟩ **syn** see PROFUSE

3**lavish** \", *chiefly in pres part* -vəsh\ *vt* -ED/-ING/-ES **:** to expend or bestow with profusion **:** use with prodigality **:** SQUANDER ⟨the princes of the Renascence ~*ed* upon private luxury . . . enormous amounts of money —Lewis Mumford⟩ ⟨~*ed* his great talents on paltry themes —C.H.Sykes⟩

lav·ish·ly \-vəshlē, -vēsh-, -li\ *adv* **:** in a lavish manner ⟨both volumes are ~ illustrated —S.E.Morison⟩ ⟨the candidates found their halting utterances ~ reported —John Buchan⟩

lav·ish·ment \-vishmənt, -vēsh-\ *n* -s **:** the action of lavishing

lav·ish·ness *n* -ES **1 :** a lavish quality **:** ABUNDANCE ⟨marveling at the ~ of the green world about him —Ferdinand Moltke-Hansen⟩ **2 :** a lavish manner or propensity **:** EXTRAVAGANCE, PRODIGALITY ⟨granted with special ~ to the medical profession —Richard Watts⟩

la·vol·ta \lə'vōltə, -väl-\ *n* -s [It *la volta* the lavolta, the turn, fr. *la* the (fem. of *il*, def. art., the, fr. L *ille* that one, that) + *volta* lavolta, turn, fr. *voltare* to turn, fr. (assumed) VL *volvitare*, freq. of L *volvere* to roll — more at LARIAT, VOLUBLE] **:** an early French couple dance characterized by pivoting and making high springs or bounds

lav·ro·vite *or* **lav·roff·ite** \'lavrə,vīt, -rə,fīt\ *n* -s [Russ *lavrovit*, fr. N. von *Lavrov*, 19th cent. Russ. scientist + Russ *-it* -ite] **:** a mineral consisting of a pyroxene colored green by vanadium

lavs *pl of* LAV

1**law** \'lȯ\ *n* -s [ME (northern dial.), fr. OE *hlāw, hlǣw*; akin to OHG *hlēo* grave mound, Goth *hlaiw* tomb, L *clivus* hill, *-clinare* to incline — more at LEAN] *dial Brit* **:** a conical hill or mound — usu. used in place names ⟨Berwick ~⟩

2**law** \"\ *n* -s *often attrib* [ME *lawe*, fr. OE *lagu*, of Scand origin; akin to ON *lǫg* law, pl. of *lag* layer, due place, order; akin to OE *orlæg* fate, OS *gilagu*, OHG *urlag* fate, ON *liggja* to lie — more at LIE] **1 a** (1) **:** a binding custom or practice of a community **:** a rule or mode of conduct or action that is prescribed or formally recognized as binding by a supreme controlling authority or is made obligatory by a sanction (as an edict, decree, rescript, order, ordinance, statute, resolution, rule, judicial decision, or usage) made, recognized, or enforced by the controlling authority (2) **:** the whole body of such customs, practices, or rules constituting the organic rule prescribing the nature and conditions of existence of a state or other organized community (3) **:** COMMON LAW 1,2 — see MARTIAL LAW, MILITARY LAW, PRIVATE LAW, PUBLIC LAW, ROMAN LAW **b** (1) **:** the control or regulation brought about by the existence or enforcement of such law ⟨preserved ~ and order in the town⟩ (2) **:** the action of laws considered as a means of redressing wrongs **:** trial or remedial justice under or by the laws of the land **:** judicial remedy; *also* **:** court action **:** LITIGATION ⟨developed the habit of going to ~ for the slightest provocation —H.A.Overstreet⟩ (3) **:** a law enforcement agent or agency ⟨when he found that goods had been stolen he called in the ~⟩ ⟨put out a guard to watch for the ~ while they robbed the store⟩ **c** (1) **:** a rule, order, or injunction that it is advisable or obligatory to follow or observe ⟨a ~ of self-preservation⟩ (2) **:** a rule or custom of conduct ⟨taking a walk every evening was one of his personal ~s⟩ **d :** something consonant or compatible with established law or enforceable by such law ⟨the decrees were judged not to be ~ and so were rescinded⟩ **e :** CONTROL, AUTHORITY ⟨the child submits to no ~⟩ **f :** a rule or generalization (esp. of established law) as opposed to a fact ⟨a question of ~, not a question of fact⟩ **2** *usu cap* **a :** divine teaching or instruction; *esp* **:** a divine commandment or a revelation of the will of God **b :** the whole body of God's commandments or revelations **:** the will of God **c** *obs* **:** a religion or religious system **d :** a religious dispensation **3 :** a rule of construction or procedure (as in art, a craft, or games) conforming to the conditions of success **:** PRINCIPLE ⟨the ~s of poetry⟩ ⟨the ~s of architecture⟩ ⟨a ~ of courtesy⟩ **4 :** a rule of right living or good conduct esp. when conceived as having the sanction of God's will, of conscience or the moral nature, or of natural justice **:** MORAL LAW **5 a :** the whole body of laws relating to one subject or emanating from one source usu. including the writings on them and the judicial proceedings under them ⟨insurance ~⟩ ⟨criminal ~⟩ ⟨probate ~⟩ — compare ADJECTIVE LAW, CIVIL LAW, COMMERCIAL LAW, DECISIONAL LAW, EQUITY, LAW MERCHANT, STATUTORY LAW, SUBSTANTIVE LAW **b :** a rule or a body of rules or prescriptions for conduct to be observed in a particular place or under particular circumstances ⟨the ~ of the house⟩ **6 a :** the legal profession — usu. used with *the* **b :** law as a department of knowledge **:** legal science **:** JURISPRUDENCE **c :** legal learning or knowledge ⟨a man with much history and letters but little ~⟩ **7** *obs* **:** MERCY, INDULGENCE **8 :** an allowance of time or distance given to a weaker competitor in sports or to a hare or fox before the hounds are released in hunting **9 a :** a statement of an order or relation of phenomena that so far as is known is invariable under the given conditions ⟨a ~ of thermodynamics⟩ ⟨the ~s of chemistry⟩ — often used in combination with the name of the discoverer of the order or relation ⟨Boyle's ~⟩ ⟨Gresham's ~⟩ **b :** a relation proved or assumed to be true between or among mathematical expressions **c :** the observed regularity of nature

syn RULE, CANON, PRECEPT, REGULATION, ORDINANCE: each of these terms indicates a principle governing action or procedure. LAW implies issuance and imposition of that principle as binding and obligatory by an ultimate sovereign authority ⟨the *laws* of our federal government⟩ In physical sciences LAW suggests a principle or assertion formulated on the basis of conclusive evidence or tests and presumably universally valid ⟨when this formula first dawned on the mind of Newton, it was a scientific conjecture; when it was tested and proved to conform to facts, it became an accepted scientific *law* —P.E.More⟩ LAW may refer to that which is unwritten or uncodified but universally accepted ⟨the common *law* of England⟩ RULE, often interchangeable with LAW in ordinary uses, may be used in more personal, individual, or specific situations with somewhat less inexorability and power implied ⟨so many handsome girls are unmarried, and so many of the other sort wedded, that there is no possibility of establishing a *rule* —W.M. Thackeray⟩ ⟨ritual is not easy compliance with usage; it is strict compliance with detailed and punctilious *rule* —W.G. Sumner⟩ ⟨the *rules* of stud poker are drawn up to accord with the laws of chance⟩ CANON in nonreligious use may suggest a principle of treatment or judgment in intellectual and creative activities that is generally accepted as a valid guide or test ⟨the Aristotelian *canon* that the "nature" of a thing must be sought in its completed development, its final form —W.R.Inge⟩ ⟨prefer the particular to the general, the definite to the vague — as a *canon* of rhetoric —A.T.Quiller-Couch⟩ More than other words in this group PRECEPT is likely to suggest something that is advisory and nonobligatory ⟨the Old Bailey, at that date, was a choice illustration of the *precept* that "whatever is right" —Charles Dickens⟩ ⟨the one child to whom the "spare-the-rod" *precept* did not apply —Margaret Deland⟩ REGULATION suggests directives for a detail of procedure or conduct applying within an organization and established with executive or administrative authority ⟨regular scholarships are awarded in accordance with the following *regulations* set up by the Committee on Scholarships —*Official Register of Harvard Univ.*⟩ ⟨a colonel not on flying status was by *regulation* ineligible for most Air Force commands —J.G.Cozzens⟩ ORDINANCE suggests an obligatory order, direction, or injunction governing some detail of conduct and issued and enforced by a limited and not sovereign agency, for instance a municipal government or a county or shire governing board ⟨an *ordinance* about parking on Main Street⟩ ⟨the new *ordinance* about delinquent property taxes⟩ **syn** see in addition PRINCIPLE

— **have the law on :** to institute legal proceedings against

3**law** \"\ *vb* -ED/-ING/-S [ME *lawen*, fr. *lawe*, n.] *vi* **:** to go to law ~ *vt* **1** *chiefly dial* **:** to sue or prosecute at law ⟨I won't go to the sheriff and I won't ~ you; I'll shoot you —Luke Short⟩ **2 :** to mutilate (an animal) so as to prevent mischief **:** EXPEDITATE

4**law** \"\ *now dial var of* LOW

5**law** \"\ *interj* [partly alter. of 2*la*, partly euphemism for *Lord*] *now dial* — used esp. to express surprise

la·wa \'lä(,)wä\ *n, pl* **lawa** *or* **lawas** *usu cap* **1 a :** the Wa of the Shan plateau in Burma **b :** a member of such people **2 a :** one of two related ethnic groups of Mon-Khmer-speaking people of Thailand that live near Chiengmai and the Korat plateau respectively **b :** a people of Thailand living in the Kanburi province **c :** a member of one of these three peoples

law-abiding \'==,==\ *adj* **:** abiding by or obedient to the law — **law-abid·ing·ness** *n* -ES

law agent *n, Scots law* **:** LAWYER, SOLICITOR

law binding *n* **:** a plain book binding made in light brown calf, sheep, or buckram with leather backbone and used on lawbooks

lawbook \'=,=\ *n* **:** a book containing or dealing with laws, legal subjects, or cases adjudicated

law-borrow \'=,bä(,)rō\ *or* **law-burrow** \'=,bə(,)rō\ *n* [ME (Sc) *law borow*, fr. ME *law, lawe* law + *borow, borwe* something deposited as security, pledge — more at LAW, BORROW] *Scots law* **:** a cautionary or security measure designed to keep the peace; *also* **:** the process necessary to put such a measure into effect — usu. used in pl.

lawbreaker \'=,==\ *n* [ME *lawbreker*, fr. *law, lawe* law + *breker* breaker] **:** one who violates the law

lawbreaking \'=,==\ *n* **:** the act of violating the law

law buckram *n* **:** BUCKRAM 2a

law calf *n* **:** a fine grade of light brown calfskin for binding lawbooks

law clerk *n* **:** a student of law or a lawyer studying law or working under the supervision of a lawyer or judge in order to learn law or gain experience, often for little or no pay

lawcourt \'=,=\ *n* **:** 1COURT 3; *esp* **:** COURT OF LAW

law day *n* [ME *lawe day*, fr. *lawe* law + *day*] **1** *obs* **:** a day in which a court is or is to be in session; *also* **:** the session of such a court **2 :** a day named in a bond or mortgage for the payment of the money secured by it

law french *n, cap F* **:** the form of Anglo-French used in England in judicial proceedings, pleadings, and lawbooks from medieval times to the 17th century

law·ful \'lȯfəl\ *adj* [ME *laweful*, fr. *lawe* law + *-ful*] **1 a :** conformable to law **:** allowed or permitted by law **:** enforceable in a court of law **:** LEGITIMATE **b :** constituted, authorized, or established by law **:** RIGHTFUL ⟨the ~ owner⟩ ⟨a ~ day to hold court⟩ **2 :** LAW-ABIDING ⟨made his appeal to all ~ citizens against the criminals⟩

syn LAWFUL, LEGAL, LEGITIMATE, and LICIT can mean, in common, sanctioned by law. LAWFUL implies law of any kind and often comes close to PERMISSIBLE ⟨a *lawful* king⟩ ⟨a *lawful* husband⟩ ⟨found that there is nothing fortuitous about color mixtures but, on the contrary, that they are entirely regular and *lawful* in operation —F.A.Geldard⟩ ⟨the behavior of organisms is plainly *lawful*, the business of science is still to determine how they arrive —H.J.Muller⟩ ⟨that was the only sense in which ambition was *lawful* for a Christian: ambition for the work and not for self —Bruce Marshall⟩ ⟨the time has come when, if ever, it is *lawful* for me to doubt as it is imperative for you to affirm —O.W.Holmes †1935⟩ LEGAL usu. implies the law of the statute books or the courts, often applying more to what is not contrary to that law than to what is allowable by the terms of it ⟨a *legal* resident of the state⟩ ⟨*legal* ownership of property⟩ ⟨*legal* control of crime⟩ ⟨*legal* dishonesty in business⟩ LEGITIMATE now implies not only recognition by law but acceptance by custom, tradition, the rules of inference, a sense of fitness or rightness, or standards of authenticity ⟨the difference between crooked dealing and *legitimate* profiting⟩ ⟨in the light of the parallels which I have adduced the hypothesis appears *legitimate*, if not probable —J.G.Frazer⟩ ⟨a short novel of what might be called *legitimate* adventure —E.L.Acken⟩ ⟨both toy and *legitimate* wooden shoes are manufactured —Loyal Durand⟩ ⟨*legitimate* to claim that much of our truly wonderful prodigality of talent is due to the work of gifted teachers —J.A.Michener⟩ ⟨this *legitimate* contrast to be made between China and western Europe —E.R.Hughes⟩ ⟨the problem of selling books is met through the industry's most *legitimate* channels, namely the bookstores —A. A. Van Duym⟩ LICIT usu. implies strict conformity to law in the way something (esp. what is specifically regulated by law) is performed, executed, or carried on ⟨the state is given its right to determine what is *licit* and illicit for property owners in the use of their possessions —*Commonweal*⟩ ⟨extremely difficult to disentangle truth from falsehood, and far more reliance must be placed on personal and private sources of information than would be *licit* if these barriers did not exist —E.S.Skillin⟩ ⟨the biggest dealer in ivory, both *licit* and illicit, in the town —Stuart Cloete⟩ ⟨a wife's *licit* love⟩

lawful age *n* **:** the age specified by law for entering into a particular relationship or engaging in a particular transaction; *specif* **:** the age at which one normally attains to full legal rights and responsibilities

law·ful·ly \-f(ə)lē, -li\ *adv* [ME *lawefully*, fr. *laweful* + *-ly*] **:** in a lawful manner

lawful money *n* [ME *laweful moneye*, fr. *laweful* + *moneye* money] **1 a :** any money whether coin or currency that may by the laws of a country be circulated as a medium of exchange — compare LEGAL TENDER **b :** any money recognized in a community as a medium of exchange **2 :** money (as bank reserves) designated as acceptable for a particular purpose

law·ful·ness \-fəlnəs\ *n* -ES [ME *lahfulnesse*, fr. *lahful, laweful* lawful + *-nesse* -ness] **:** the quality or state of being lawful **:** LEGALITY

lawful rate *n* **:** a rate for interstate or intrastate traffic established and published in accord with the laws, rules, and regulations prescribed by interstate and state commissions — called also *legal rate*

lawgiver \'=,==\ *n* [ME *lawe givere*, fr. *lawe* law + *givere* giver] **:** one that makes, enacts, or transmits a law or system of laws ⟨the scientific ~s —Douglas Bush⟩; *esp* **:** LEGISLATOR a ⟨the prophet was both teacher and ~⟩

law-hand \'=,=\ *n* **:** a special style of handwriting used in engrossing old legal documents in England

1**law·ing** \'lȯiŋ\ *n* -s [ME, gerund of *lawen* to go to law — more at LAW] **1 :** LITIGATION **2** *obs* **:** EXPEDITATION

2**lawing** \"\ *n* -s [obs. Sc *law* charge to be paid (fr. ME — northern dial. — *lagh*, fr. ON *lag* market price, tax, layer, due place, order) + E *-ing* — more at LAW] *chiefly Scot* **:** a bill for food or drink (as at a tavern) ⟨paid my ~ —*Kinmont Willie*⟩

lawk \'lȯk\ *or* **lawks** \-ks\ *interj* [euphemism for *Lord*] *dial Brit* — used to express surprise

law lamb *n* **:** a grade of light-brown sheepskin made from the younger and finer-grained skins and used on lawbooks

law latin *n, cap 2d L* **:** the Low Latin containing latinized English and old French words that is used in English law

law·less \'lȯləs\ *adj* [ME *lawelees,* fr. *lawe* law + *-lees* -less] **1 a :** being without law **:** having no laws **:** not regulated by law ⟨the ~ desert⟩ ⟨thought is anarchic and ~ —Bertrand Russell⟩ **b :** not based on law ⟨the ~ dictates of the conqueror⟩ **2** *archaic* **:** exempt from the operation of law **3 a :** not restrained or controlled by consideration for a law (as of morality or decency) **:** UNRULY, DISORDERLY ⟨the frontier . . . produced a ~ class of Indian traders —H.E.Davis⟩ **b :** ILLEGAL ⟨engaging in ~ activity until the police finally caught him⟩ — **law·less·ly** *adv* — **law·less·ness** *n* -ES

lawlike \'=,=\ *adj* **:** being like the law (as in methods, principles, or terminology)

law list *n* **:** a publication compiling the names and addresses of those engaged in the practice of law and information of interest to the law profession often including the courts, court calendars, lawyers engaged in specialized fields (as admiralty or patent law), public officers, stenographers, handwriting experts, private investigators, or abstracts of law **:** a legal directory

law lord *n* **:** a member of the British House of Lords who by appointment as a lord of appeal in ordinary or as lord chancellor or by possession of eminent legal experience usu. obtained by having held high judicial office is qualified to participate in the proceedings of the House as a court of last resort ⟨no appeal can be decided by the House unless at least three *law lords* . . . are present at the hearing —Edward Jenks⟩

lawmaker \'=,==\ *n* [ME *lawe maker,* fr. *lawe* law + *maker, makere* maker] **:** one that makes laws **:** LEGISLATOR, LAWGIVER ⟨several bills . . . held over from the last session will be considered by the ~*s* —*Publishers' Weekly*⟩ ⟨the wise man and ~ of Athens —J.A.Macy⟩

law·man \'lȯmən\ *n, pl* **lawmen** [trans. of OE *lageman,* fr. *lage-* (fr. *lagu* law) + *man*] **1 :** an hereditary official acting chiefly as a doomster in boroughs of medieval England formerly under Danish rule ⟨the *lawmen* of Lincoln were holders of heritable franchises —F.W.Maitland⟩ **2** [[2]*law* + *man*] **:** a law enforcement officer (as a sheriff or policeman) ⟨the killing of a ~ is not taken lightly in the Texas border country —Caddo Cameron⟩

law merchant *n, pl* **laws merchant** [ME *lawe marchaund* (trans. of ML *lex mercatoria*), fr. *lawe* law + *marchaund, marchant,* adj., merchant] **1 :** the legal rules formerly applied to cases arising in commercial transactions esp. by the courts of piepoudre, the staple courts, and merchant's courts **2 :** COMMERCIAL LAW

[1]**lawn** \'lȯn, 'län\ *n* -S [ME, fr. *Laon,* town in northern France] **1 :** a sheer plainwoven cotton or linen fabric that is given various finishes (as semicrisp) when used for clothing **2** [so called fr. the use of the fabric lawn for the sleeves of an Anglican bishop's official dress] **:** the office or dignity of a bishop **3 a :** a lawn or silk sieve **b :** a brass or copper sieve of fine texture

[2]**lawn** \"\ *vt* -ED/-ING/-S **:** to screen (as pigment) through a lawn or silk screen

[3]**lawn** \"\ *n* -S *often attrib* [alter. of *laund*] **1** *archaic* **a :** an open space between woods **:** GLADE **b :** a level stretch on a mountainside **2 :** ground covered with grass and not tilled; *esp* **:** ground covered with fine grass kept closely mowed esp. in front of or about a house or as part of a garden or park

[4]**lawn** \"\ *vt* -ED/-ING/-S **:** to make into or like a lawn

lawn billiards *n pl but usu sing in constr* **:** TROCO

lawn bowling *n* **:** a game played on a closely cropped green with wooden balls which are rolled as close as possible to a jack — called also *bowls, bowling on the green*

lawn chair *n* **:** any usu. reclining chair used or designed to be used for sitting or reclining comfortably outdoors esp. on lawns or in garden areas

lawn finish *n* **:** a finish on paper similar to linen finish

lawn green *n* **:** a moderate yellow green that is greener, lighter, and stronger than average moss green, yellower and deeper than average pea green, yellower and darker than apple green (sense 1), and yellower, lighter, and stronger than spinach green

lawnleaf \'=,=\ *n, pl* **lawnleaves :** DICHONDRA 2

lawn mixture *n* **:** a mixture of grass seeds of various types intended primarily for making lawns

lawn mower *n* **:** a hand-operated or power-operated machine for cutting grass on lawns

lawn mower

lawn mowings *n pl* **:** clippings from a lawn that has been mowed sometimes used for mulching purposes or added to a compost pile

lawn party *n* **1 :** a social party held on a lawn or in a garden **:** GARDEN PARTY **2 :** an outdoor carnival or fete that usu. features games and amusements (as pony rides or fortune-telling) and booths for the selling of food or drinks or chances on prizes and that is held for the raising of money usu. for a church or some civic purpose

lawn pennywort *n* **:** a tufted and creeping Asiatic herb (*Hydrocotyle rotundifolia*) that has round cordate leaves and that is adventive in lawns in the eastern U. S.

lawn plant *n* **:** a So. American herb (*Lippia canescens*) prostrate and rooting at the nodes and commonly grown in drier parts of California as a substitute for lawn grasses

lawn sleeves *n pl but sing or pl in constr* **:** the episcopal office **:** BISHOP

lawn tennis *n* **:** TENNIS; *specif* **:** tennis played on a grass court — distinguished from *court tennis*

[1]**lawny** \'lȯnē, 'länē, -ni\ *adj* [[1]*lawn* + *-y*] **:** made of, wearing, or resembling lawn

[2]**lawny** \"\ *adj* [[3]*lawn* + *-y*] **:** having or resembling a grass lawn

law of absorption : a theorem in logic: to affirm that either some proposition is true or else that that proposition and some other proposition are both true is equivalent to affirming the first proposition

law of acceleration : a generalization in biology: the order of development of a structure or organ is directly related to its importance to the organism

law of action and reaction : LAW OF MOTION 3

law of areas *or* **law of equal areas :** KEPLER'S LAW 2

law of averages : BERNOULLI'S THEOREM 1

law of boyle and mar·i·otte \-,marē'ät\ *usu cap B & M* [after Robert *Boyle* †1691 Brit. physicist and Edme *Mariotte* †1684 Fr. physicist who independently discovered it] **:** BOYLE'S LAW

law of causation *or* **law of causality :** a principle in philosophy: every change in nature is produced by some cause

law of combining volumes : GAY-LUSSAC'S LAW

law of conservation of energy : CONSERVATION OF ENERGY

law of conservation of mass : CONSERVATION OF MASS

law of conservation of momentum : CONSERVATION OF MOMENTUM

law of constant angles : a law in crystallography: the angles between the various faces of a crystal remain unchanged throughout its growth

law of constant proportion : LAW OF DEFINITE PROPORTIONS

law of constant return : a statement in economics: an increase of the scale of production in an industry gives a proportionate increase of return or the increase in area of land cultivated requires a proportionate increase in outlay for labor or materials

law of continuity : a principle in philosophy: there is no break in nature and nothing passes from one state to another without passing through all the intermediate states

law of contradiction : a principle in logic: a thing cannot at the same time both be and not be of a specified kind (as a table and not a table) or in a specified manner (as red or not red)

law of cosines 1 : a law in trigonometry: the square of a side of a plane triangle equals the sum of the squares of the remaining sides minus twice the product of those sides and the cosine of the angle between them **2 :** a law in trigonometry: the cosine of an arc of a spherical triangle equals the product of the cosines of the remaining arcs plus the product of the sines of those arcs and the cosine of the angle between them

law of definite proportions : a statement in chemistry: every definite compound always contains the same elements in the same proportions by weight

law of demand : a statement in economics: the quantity of an economic good purchased will vary inversely with its price — compare INFERIOR GOOD

law of diminishing returns : a principle in economics: at any given stage of technological advance an increase in productive factors (as labor or capital) applied beyond a certain point fails to bring about a proportional increase in production

law of diminishing utility : a principle in social science: as one acquires successive units of a good, the intensity of desire for additional units declines

law of dominance : MENDEL'S LAW 3

law of dulong and petit *usu cap D & P* **:** DULONG AND PETIT'S LAW

law of effect : a statement in psychology: in trial-and-error learning satisfying or successful behavior is repeated whereas unsatisfying or unsuccessful behavior is not

law of error : the equation of the normal probability curve to which the accidental errors associated with an extended series of observations tend to conform — called also *normal law of error*

law of excluded middle : a principle in logic: if one of two contradictory statements is denied the other must be affirmed

law of exponents : one of a set of rules in algebra: exponents of numbers are added when the numbers are multiplied, subtracted when the numbers are divided, and multiplied when raised by still another exponent: $a^m \times a^n = a^{m+n}$; $a^m \div a^n = a^{m-n}$; $(a^m)^n = a^{mn}$

law of fechner *usu cap F* **:** WEBER-FECHNER LAW

law office *n* **:** an office maintained by a lawyer or a firm of lawyers for the practice of law

law officer *n* **:** a public official employed to administer or advise in legal matters: **a** *or* **law officer of the crown** *usu cap C* **:** the attorney general or the solicitor general of England ⟨the opinions of the *law officers of the Crown* . . . are not usually laid before Parliament —T.E.May⟩ **b :** an official of a general court-martial in the U.S. armed forces who may not vote but is charged with advising the members of the court on matters of law and who is appointed from the Judge Advocate General's Corps or from the bar of a federal court or the highest court of a state

law of frontality : the convention of frontality (as in Egyptian art)

law of gravitation : a statement in physics: any particle in the universe attracts any other particle with a force that is proportional to the product of the masses of the two particles and inversely proportional to the square of the distance between them

law of guld·berg and waa·ge \-'gu̇l,bergən'vägə\ *usu cap G&W* [after Cato M. *Guldberg* †1902 Norw. chemist and mathematician and Peter *Waage* †1900 Norw. chemist, its formulators] **:** LAW OF MASS ACTION

law of identity : one of three principles in logic: **1 :** a statement (as "a house is a house") in which the subject and predicate are the same is true **2 :** the copula in an identity affirms an existent of which the identity is true **3 :** a statement of an identity is the expression of an abstract relation of identity symbolized by a term (as *A* in "A is A") that apparently refers in its separate instances to the subject and predicate respectively

law of independent assortment : MENDEL'S LAW 2

law of inertia : LAW OF MOTION 1

law of large numbers : a law in statistics: the probability that the mean of a random sample differs from the mean of the population from which the sample is drawn by more than a given amount approaches zero as the size of the sample approaches infinity

law of mass action : a statement in chemistry: the rate of a chemical reaction is directly proportional to the molecular concentrations of the reacting substances

law of motion 1 : a statement in dynamics: a body at rest remains at rest and a body in motion remains in uniform motion in a straight line unless acted upon by an external force — called also *Newton's first law of motion* **2 :** a statement in dynamics: the acceleration of a body is directly proportional to the applied force and is in the direction of the straight line in which the force acts — called also *Newton's second law of motion* **3 :** a statement in dynamics: for every force there is an equal and opposite force or reaction — called also *Newton's third law of motion*

law of multiple proportions : a statement in chemistry: when two elements combine in more than one proportion to form two or more compounds the weights of one element that combine with a given weight of the other element are in the ratios of small whole numbers

law of nations [trans. of L *jus gentium*] **1 :** JUS GENTIUM **2 :** INTERNATIONAL LAW

law of nature 1 : a natural instinct or a natural relation of human beings or other animals due to native character or condition **2 :** a generalized statement of natural processes; *specif* **:** one of the chief generalizations of science variously conceived as imposed upon nature by the Creator, as representing an intrinsic orderliness of nature or the necessary conformity of phenomena to reason and understanding, or as the observed regular coincidences of phenomena which are ultimate data for our knowledge **3 :** NATURAL LAW

law of parsimony 1 : economy of assumption in reasoning **2 :** economy of pain or effort in seeking pleasure or gain

law of partial pressures : a statement in physics: the component of the total pressure contributed by each ingredient in a mixture of gases or vapors is equal to the pressure that it would exert if alone in the same enclosure — called also *Dalton's law*

law of priority : a principle in taxonomy: the first properly published name of a species or genus takes precedence over any subsequently published — compare NOMENCLATURE, NOMEN CONSERVANDUM

law of recapitulation : RECAPITULATION THEORY

law of reflection : a statement in optics: when light falls upon a plane surface it is so reflected that the angle of reflection is equal to the angle of incidence and that the incident ray, reflected ray, and normal ray all lie in the plane of incidence

law of refraction : a law in physics: in the refraction of radiation at the interface between two isotropic media the incident ray and the corresponding refracted ray are coplanar with the refracting surface at the point of incidence and the ratio of the sine of the angle of incidence to the sine of the angle of refraction is equal to the refractive index

law of segregation : MENDEL'S LAW 1

law of signs 1 : a rule in algebra: the product or the quotient of two numbers of like sign is positive **2 :** a rule in algebra: the product or the quotient of two numbers of unlike sign is negative

law of sines 1 : a law in trigonometry: the ratio of each side of a plane triangle to the sine of the opposite angle is the same for all three sides and angles **2 :** a law in trigonometry: the ratio of the sine of each arc of a spherical triangle to the sine of the opposite angle is the same for all three arcs and angles

law of sufficient reason : a principle in logic: for everything that is there is a reason why it should be as it is rather than otherwise

law of superposition : a law in geology: where there has been no subsequent disturbance sedimentary strata were deposited in ascending order with younger beds successively overlying older beds

law of supply and demand : a statement in economics: the competitive price that clears the market for a commodity is determined through the interaction of offers and demands

law of tangents : a law in plane trigonometry: in any plane triangle the tangent of one half the difference of any two angles is to the tangent of one half their sum as the difference of the sides opposite the respective angles is to the sum of those sides

law of the flag : the law of the sovereign state under whose protection a ship is registered and whose flag the ship flies

law of the jungle : a code that dictates survival by any means possible and that is presumed to be in effect among animals in their natural state or people unrestrained by any established law or civilized personal or civic control; *also* **:** activity following this code

law of the minimum : a law in physiology: when a process is conditioned by several factors its rate is limited by the factor present in the minimum

law of thermodynamics 1 : a law in physics: CONSERVATION OF ENERGY — called also *first law of thermodynamics* **2 :** a law in physics: mechanical work can be derived from the heat in a body only when the body is able to communicate with another at a lower temperature or all actual spontaneous processes result in an increase of total entropy — called also *second law of thermodynamics* **3 :** a law in physics: at the absolute zero of temperature the entropy of any pure crystalline substance is zero and its derivative with respect to temperature is zero — called also *third law of thermodynamics*

law of the staple : the law merchant as administered in the staple courts

law of thought : any of several principles in logic: **a :** LAW OF CONTRADICTION **b :** LAW OF EXCLUDED MIDDLE **c :** LAW OF IDENTITY

law of ti·ti·us \-'tētsēəs\ *usu cap T* [after J. D. *Titius* †1796 Ger. mathematician] **:** BODE'S LAW

law of transposition : a principle in logic: transposition yields a valid inference

law of von baer *usu cap B* **:** VON BAER'S LAW

law of war : the code that governs or one of the rules that govern the rights and duties of belligerents in international war chiefly affecting prisoners, spies, traitors, private property, blockades, and rights of capture

law of weber-fechner *usu cap W&F* **:** WEBER-FECHNER LAW

law proper *n, pl* **laws proper :** POSITIVE LAW

law·rence's goldfinch \'lȯrənsəz-, 'lär-\ *n, usu cap L* [after George N. *Lawrence* †1895 Am. ornithologist] **:** a goldfinch (*Spinus lawrencei*) of southern California and northern Mexico having yellow lower parts and greenish yellow upper parts

law·ren·cian *or* **law·ren·tian** \(')lȯ¦renchən, (')lä¦-\ *adj, usu cap* [*lawrencian* fr. D. H. *Lawrence* †1930 Eng. novelist + E *-ian; lawrentian* alter. (influenced by *laurentian*) of *lawrencian*] **:** of, relating to, or befitting the writings of D. H. Lawrence ⟨has an affair with a *Lawrencian* foreman who has been dismissed from his employment —*Times Lit. Supp.*⟩

law·renc·ite \'lȯrən,sīt, 'lär-\ *n* -S [F, fr. J. *Lawrence* Smith †1883 Am. chemist and mineralogist + F *-ite*] **:** a mineral consisting of ferrous chloride often found in meteoric iron

laws *pl of* LAW, *pres 3d sing of* LAW

law sakes *or* **law sakes alive** *interj* [euphemism for *for the Lord's sake*] *dial* — used to express surprise or protest

law sheep *n* **:** a fine grade of light-brown sheepskin made from the outside of the skins and commonly used in binding lawbooks

law skiver *n* **:** a sheepskin skiver tanned to imitate law sheep

laws of planetary motion : KEPLER'S LAWS

law·son \'lȯsᵊn\ *adj, usu cap* [after Thomas W. *Lawson* †1925 Am. financier for whom furniture of this kind was designed] **:** being of or belonging to an overstuffed furniture design marked by square seat cushions, short squarish back rests, and high square or roll arms ⟨a *Lawson* sofa⟩ ⟨furniture built on *Lawson* lines⟩

law·sone \'lȯ,sōn\ *n* -S [*laws-* (fr. NL *Lawsonia*) + *-one*] **:** a yellow crystalline dye $C_{10}H_5O_2(OH)$ obtained esp. from leaves of Egyptian henna; 2-hydroxy-1,4-naphthoquinone

law·so·nia \lȯ'sōnēə\ *n, cap* [NL, fr. Isaac *Lawson* †1747 Scot. naturalist + NL *-ia*] **:** a genus of tropical Old World shrubs (family Lythraceae) having tetramerous flowers and a four-celled capsular fruit — see HENNA

law·so·ni·ana \(,)lȯ,sōnē'anə, -'änə, -'ānə\ *n* -S [NL (specific epithet of *Chamaecyparis lawsoniana*), fem. of *lawsonianus* of Lawson, fr. Peter *Lawson*, 19th cent. Scot. nurseryman who introduced the species into cultivation + L *-ianus* -ian] **:** PORT ORFORD CEDAR

law·son·ite \'lȯsᵊn,īt\ *n* -S [Andrew C. *Lawson* †1952 Am. geologist + E *-ite*] **:** a pale or grayish blue mineral $CaAl_2Si_2O_6(OH)_4$ in prismatic orthorhombic crystals consisting of hydrous calcium aluminum silicate

lawson's cypress *or* **lawson cypress** *n, usu cap L* [After Peter *Lawson*, 19th cent Scot. nurseryman] *chiefly Brit* **:** PORT ORFORD CEDAR

law stationer *n* **:** one that deals in paper, forms, and other stationer's supplies used by lawyers and that in Great Britain and Ireland also makes fair or engrossed copies of legal instruments

lawsuit \'=,=\ *n* **:** a suit in law **:** a case before a court **:** any of various technical legal proceedings (as an action, prosecution)

law·sy *or* **law·zy** \'lōzē\ *interj* [euphemism for *Lordy*] *dial* — used to express surprise, astonishment, or strength of feeling

lawter *n* -S [of Scand origin; akin to ON *lāttr* place where animals lay their young — more at LAUGHTER] *dial Eng* **:** [2]LAUGHTER

law-way \'=,=\ *n* **:** a custom or tradition that acts practically as a law esp. among a people

law-worthy \'=,==\ *adj* **:** entitled to or coming within the benefits or rules of law or legal procedure

law·yer \'lȯyə(r), 'lȯiə-\ *n* -S [ME *lawyere,* fr. *lawe* law + *-ere, -iere* -er] **1 :** a specialist in or a practitioner of law **:** one (as an attorney, counselor, solicitor, barrister, or advocate) whose profession is to conduct lawsuits for clients or to advise as to the prosecution or defense of lawsuits or as to legal rights and obligations in other matters **2 a :** BOWFIN **b :** the New World burbot **c :** GRAY SNAPPER **3 a** *dial Eng* **:** a bramble or the thorny stem of a brier **b :** any of various trailing brambles of New Zealand (esp. *Rubus australis*) that scramble over other growth, can be held in position by backward-pointing hooks, and sometimes attain a basal thickness of 5 to 6 inches **4 :** BLACK-NECKED STILT

lawyer bush *or* **lawyer cane** *n* **:** LAWYER 3b

law·yer·ess \-ərəs\ *n* -ES **:** a female lawyer

law·yer·ing \-riŋ\ *n* -S **:** following the profession or performing the functions of a lawyer — often used disparagingly

lawyerlike \'==,=\ *adj* **:** resembling or befitting a lawyer ⟨~ speech⟩

law·yer·ly \-lē, -li\ *adj* **:** LAWYERLIKE

lawyer palm *n* **:** an Australian climbing palm (*Calamus australis*) with slender prickly stems and pinnate leaves

lawyer vine *n* **1 :** LAWYER 3b **2 :** LAWYER PALM

[1]**lax** \'laks\ *n* -ES [partly fr. Norw *laks,* fr. ON *lax;* partly fr. Sc (also obs. E) *lax,* fr. ME, fr. OE *leax;* OE *leax* akin to OHG *lahs* salmon, ON *lax,* Russ *losos'* salmon, Toch B *laks* fish] **:** SALMON

[2]**lax** \'laks\ *vt* -ED/-ING/-ES [ME *laxen,* fr. L *laxare,* fr. *laxus*] **:** RELAX, LOOSEN ⟨~*ed* its hold in death —G.M.Trevelyan⟩

[3]**lax** \"\ *adj* -ER/-EST [ME, fr. L *laxus* slack, loose, spacious — more at SLACK] **1 a** *of the bowels* **:** LOOSE, OPEN **b :** having the bowels open **2 :** not strict or stringent ⟨~ discipline⟩ ⟨~ laws⟩ **3 a :** not tense, firm, or rigid **:** SLACK, RELAXED ⟨took his ~ hand in hers —David Walden⟩ ⟨a ~ tone of voice⟩; *also* **:** EASYGOING, CARELESS ⟨a man of ~ habits⟩ **b :** having an open or loose texture ⟨a ~ fiber⟩ ⟨a ~ soil⟩ **c :** not close together **:** SCATTERED ⟨a ~ flower cluster⟩ **4** *of a speech sound* **:** produced with the muscles involved in a relatively relaxed state ⟨the vowels \i\ and \u̇\ in contrast with the vowels \ē\ and \ü\ are ~⟩ — compare TENSE

syn see NEGLIGENT

[4]**lax** \"\ *n* -ES *now chiefly dial* **:** looseness of the bowels **:** DIARRHEA

lax·ate \'lak,sāt\ *vt* -ED/-ING/-S [L *laxatus,* past part. of *laxare,* fr. *laxus* slack, loose, spacious] *obs* **:** LOOSEN, RELAX

lax·a·tion \lak'sāshən\ *n* -S [ME *laxacion,* fr. L *laxation-, laxatio,* fr. *laxatus* + *-ion-, -io* -ion] **1 :** the act of loosening or relaxing or the state of being loosened or relaxed **2 :** a bowel movement

[1]lax·a·tive \ˈlaksəd·|iv, -ət|\ *adj* [ME *laxatif,* fr. ML *laxativus,* fr. L *laxatus* + *-ivus* -ive] **1 :** having a tendency to loosen or relax; *specif* **:** producing bowel movements and relieving constipation **2 a** *archaic* **:** subject to looseness or free movement — used of the bowels **b :** subject to or marked by looseness of the bowels ⟨obese and ~ robins —Christopher Morley⟩ ⟨on silage alone animals are liable to become too ~ —*Successful Farming*⟩ **3 :** running freely **:** LOOSE, UNRESTRAINED ⟨a ~ tongue⟩ — **lax·a·tive·ly** \|əvlē, -li\ *adv* — **lax·a·tive·ness** \|ivnəs\ *n* -ES

[2]laxative \"\ *n* -S [ME *laxatif,* fr. *laxatif,* adj.] **:** a laxative drug **:** a mild cathartic

lax·ism \ˈlak,sizəm\ *n* -S [prob. fr. (assumed) NL *laxismus,* fr. L *laxus* slack, loose + *-ismus* -ism] **:** a viewpoint in the probabilistic controversy that in a conflict between liberty and law a slightly probable argument for liberty suffices to furnish a basis for action — compare PROBABILISM 2

lax·ist \-səst\ *n* -S [prob. fr. (assumed) NL *laxista,* fr. L *laxus* + *-ista* -ist] **:** a believer in laxism

lax·i·ty \-səd·ē, -sətē, -i\ *n* -ES [L *laxitat-, laxitas* spaciousness, fr. *laxus* slack, loose, spacious + *-itat-, -itas* -ity] **:** the quality or state of being lax: as **a :** LOOSENESS ⟨a certain ~ of bowels⟩ **b :** lack of tenseness ⟨a ~ in his grip⟩ **:** lack of strictness ⟨a ~ in discipline⟩ **c :** looseness of structure or texture ⟨a ~ in the weave of the cloth⟩ **d :** CARELESSNESS ⟨~ in handling participles —E.S.McCartney⟩

lax·ly *adv* **:** in a lax manner

lax·ness *n* -ES **:** the quality or state of being lax

[1]lay \ˈlā\ *vb* **laid** \ˈlād\ **laid; laying; lays** [ME *leyen, leggen,* fr. OE *lecgan;* akin to OHG *leggen* to lay, ON *leggja,* Goth *lagjan;* causative fr. the root of OE *licgan* to lie — more at LIE] *vt* **1 :** to bring down with force **:** beat down **:** strike prostrate ⟨a blow from a swinging club *laid* him in the dust⟩ ⟨wheat *laid* flat by the wind and rain⟩ **2 a :** to put or set down **:** place so as to lie flat **:** place carefully or gently ⟨*laid* a comforting hand on his shoulder⟩ ⟨*laid* her hat on the table⟩ **b :** to place (as in bed) for rest or sleep; *esp* **:** BURY **c :** to copulate with — not often in formal use **d :** to cause (as land) to disappear below the horizon or to seem lower and lower by moving away — opposed to *raise* **3 a :** to produce and deposit (an egg) **b :** to set (as a mine) in the ground or in water **c :** to drop (a bomb) or spread (a smoke screen) from an airplane **4** *obs* **:** to put down (as in writing, in rhyme, in Latin) **:** COUCH **5 :** to cause to be still **:** CALM, ALLAY ⟨manufacture an oil especially to ~ waves —H.A.Calahan⟩ ⟨~ the dust⟩ ⟨chased the clouds . . . and *laid* the winds —John Milton⟩; *esp* **:** to cause (a ghost or spirit) to return to the grave or lower world **6 a :** to deposit as a wager **:** BET; *also* **:** to bet on ⟨~ the favorite⟩ **b** *obs* **:** PLEDGE, MORTGAGE **7** *dial Eng* **:** to assist in childbirth **:** DELIVER **8 :** to press down smooth and even ⟨brushing to ~ the nap⟩ ⟨warp slashing ~s the surface fibers of the yarn, making it more compact, smoother, and stronger —*Encyc. of Chem. Technol.*⟩ **9 :** LAYER **10 a** *obs* **:** to impose a tax on **:** ASSESS **b** *obs* **:** to deal a blow to **11 a** *obs* **:** to set a watch or ambush on (a place) **b** *obs* **:** to quarter (as soldiers) upon **12 a :** to dispose over or along a surface ⟨~ a pavement⟩ ⟨~ an ocean cable⟩ or a prepared position ⟨~ a railroad track⟩ ⟨~ a sewer⟩ ⟨~ pipe to a spring⟩ **b :** to spread on a surface ⟨~ plaster⟩ ⟨~ paint⟩ **c :** to place (as brick, stone, or tile) in a wall or a pier **d :** to put (strands) in place and twist to form a rope, hawser, or cable; *also* **:** to make (as a rope, cable, cordage, yarn) by so doing — often used with *up* **13 :** to set in order for a meal ⟨~ the table⟩ ⟨places were *laid* for three people⟩ **14 a :** IMPOSE — sometimes used with *down* **b :** to place (new type) in a case — compare DISTRIBUTE **15 a :** to impose as a duty, burden, or punishment ⟨~ a tax on land⟩ ⟨his father *laid* an injunction upon him never to reveal the secret⟩ **b :** INFLICT ⟨~ blows⟩ **c :** to put or cast as a burden of reproach ⟨found someone to ~ the blame on⟩ **d :** to advance as an accusation **:** CHARGE, IMPUTE ⟨the disaster was *laid* to faulty inspection⟩ ⟨guilt for the murder was *laid* at his door despite strenuous denials⟩ **16 :** to place (something immaterial) on something ⟨~s stress on correct grammar⟩ ⟨*laid* special stress on cleanliness⟩ **17 :** to prepare the outlines or details of **:** CONTRIVE ⟨when they . . . slay for passion's sake, they ~ no elaborate schemes —Dorothy Sayers⟩ ⟨deep-*laid* plot⟩ ⟨must somehow form part of the pattern, or ~ the design of the book —F.A.Swinnerton⟩ **18 :** to put in place **:** put to **:** APPLY ⟨*laid* the watch to his ear⟩ ⟨~ siege to a town⟩: as **a :** to put in position for action or operation ⟨~ a fire in the fireplace⟩ ⟨~ glass for grinding⟩ ⟨dogs were *laid* on the scent⟩ ⟨the ship was *laid* alongside the pier⟩ ⟨thought it all out before ~*ing* pen to paper⟩ **b :** to adjust (a fieldpiece or machine gun) with the proper direction and elevation to obtain the desired trajectory **19 :** ANNEX, APPROPRIATE ⟨woe unto them that . . . ~ field to field —Isa 5:8 (AV)⟩ **20 :** to cause to lie in a (specified) condition ⟨so mad I'd like to ~ his head open with a liquor bottle —Earl Hamner⟩ ⟨~ waste the land⟩ ⟨employees . . . whose behavior ~s them open to blackmail —Elmer Davis⟩ ⟨seem to have *laid* the writers under certain inhibitions —V.L.Parrington⟩ **21 a :** to present for consideration **:** put forward **:** ASSERT, STATE, ALLEGE ⟨~ claim to an estate⟩ ⟨*laid* an information against the Kitchen Committee . . . for selling liquor without a license —A.P.Herbert⟩ **b :** to submit for examination and judgment ⟨*laid* his case before the commission⟩ **22 :** to place fictitiously ⟨scene is *laid* in wartime London⟩ **23 :** to line up **:** ASSEMBLE ⟨~ aft on the quarterdeck all the liberty party⟩ ~ *vi* **1 :** to produce and deposit eggs **2** *nonstand* **:** [1]LIE **3 a :** WAGER, BET **b :** to assert strongly **:** PREDICT, DECLARE **4** *dial* **:** to await an opportunity **:** PLAN, PREPARE, SCHEME ⟨~*ing* for a chance to escape⟩ **5 a :** to apply oneself vigorously ⟨*laid* to his oars⟩ **b** *naut* **:** GO, COME; *esp* **:** to place oneself in a specified position ⟨~ aloft⟩ ⟨~ forward⟩ **6** *chiefly Midland, of the wind* **:** to decrease in force **:** SUBSIDE **syn** see SET — **lay aboard :** to place a ship close alongside of (a ship) for fighting or for boarding — **lay a course** *or* **lay one's course 1 :** to sail toward the point intended without tacking **2 :** to sail in a certain direction **:** HEAD — **lay a finger on :** to touch or meddle with however lightly **:** do the least violence to — **lay an egg 1 :** to fail to get a favorable response (as from an audience) **:** fall flat **:** FIZZLE **2** *slang* **:** to drop a bomb — **lay at** *now chiefly dial* **:** ATTACK, ASSAIL — **lay bare :** UNCOVER, REVEAL, DISCLOSE, EXPOSE ⟨searches out and *lays bare* every insincerity of liberal professions —V.L.Parrington⟩ — **lay by the heels 1 :** to seize and imprison **:** CAPTURE **2 :** to cause the downfall of **:** bring down **:** OVERTAKE ⟨Romanticism . . . proceeded to hold the field till it was *laid by the heels* by naturalism —Edmund Wilson⟩ — **lay eyes on :** to catch sight of **:** SEE — **lay for :** to lie in wait for **:** prepare to capture or attack **:** AMBUSH — **lay hands on 1 :** to get hold of **:** SEIZE, OBTAIN **2 :** to commit violence upon **:** handle roughly; *also* **:** to kill (oneself) ⟨feared that in his despair he might *lay hands on* himself⟩ **3 :** to ordain or bless by imposition of hands — **lay hold of :** to take hold of **:** GRASP, SEIZE ⟨*lay hold of* that rope and pull⟩ ⟨ideas difficult to *lay hold of*⟩ — **lay into :** to pitch into **:** ATTACK — **lay it on :** to do something with vigor or lavishness or extravagance: as **a :** to charge exorbitantly **b :** to be unduly severe (as in a reprimand) **c :** to exaggerate or flatter grossly — **lay one's account** *archaic* **:** EXPECT, ANTICIPATE — used with *with, on,* or *for* — **lay oneself out :** to take pains **:** try earnestly **:** do one's best ⟨*laid themselves out* to make their guest comfortable⟩ — **lay one's finger on :** to discover and point out with accuracy — **lay on the line 1 :** to advance or put up (a sum of money) in full ⟨the option was about to expire, and a million dollars had to be *laid on the line* —Marquis James⟩ **2 :** to make (as an offer or a statement) without reservations or conditions ⟨the court *laid* the proposition *on the line* that the due process clause protected freedom of speech —C.P.Curtis⟩ — **lay on the table 1 :** to remove (a parliamentary motion) from consideration indefinitely **2** *or* **lay upon the table** *Brit* **:** to put (as legislation) on the agenda — **lay on the wood :** to bat forcefully in cricket — contrasted with *sit on the splice* — **lay wait :** to lie in wait **:** AMBUSH

[2]lay \"\ *n* -S **1 :** something that lies or is laid or as if laid: as **a :** LAYER, STRATUM **b** *obs* **:** WAGER **c** *obs* **:** CHANCE, HAZARD **d** *dial Eng* **:** TAX; *esp* **:** a pecuniary tax levied by local authority **2 :** a place to lie or lodge **:** COVERT, LAIR **3 a :** line of action **:** PLAN, TACK **b :** line of business or work **:** OCCUPATION **4 a :** terms of sale or employment **:** PRICE ⟨he sold his farm at a good ~⟩ **b :** a share of the profit of a venture (as on a whaling or fishing vessel) paid wholly or partly in lieu of wages **c :** employment on shares **5 a :** a strip or layer of leather or felt laid upon or beneath another in a harness or saddle **b :** a layer or thickness of cloth; *esp* **:** a layered pile of cloth on which patterns are laid out by cutters in the garment trade **6 a :** the amount of advance of any point in a rope strand for one complete turn **b :** the nature of a fiber rope as determined by the amount of twist put into the rope, the angle of the strands in the rope, and the angle of the threads in the strands — see HARD LAY, LONG LAY, MEDIUM LAY, ORDINARY LAY, SOFT LAY **c :** the direction in which the components of a rope or cable are laid **7 :** the way in which a thing lies or is laid in relation to something else **:** position or arrangement of parts: as **a :** topographical features and situation ⟨the houses . . . took form from the ~ of the land to which they were fastened —Isa Glenn⟩ **b :** the manner in which parts of garment patterns are laid out on the cloth for cutting **c :** the direction of tool or abrasive marks on a machined surface **8 a :** the position of a sheet to be printed relative to the printing surface **b :** the plan or scheme of arrangement of the type in a case or of the keyboard of a typesetting machine **c :** the arrangement of imposed pages on the stone or of printed pages in the signature; *also* **:** a plan showing such arrangement — called also *laydown* **d :** a guide or gage to which a sheet is laid when being fed into a printing press **9 :** the plowshare of a moldboard plow **10 a :** the state of one that lays eggs **:** the capacity to lay eggs ⟨a hen just coming into ~⟩ ⟨in full ~⟩ **b :** the act of laying an egg ⟨time of ~⟩ **11 :** a partner in sexual intercourse — usu. considered vulgar

[3]lay \"\ *past of* LIE

[4]lay \"\ *n* -S [ME, fr. OF *lai,* perh. of Scand origin; akin to ON *lag* tune, meter, layer, due place, order — more at LAW] **1 :** a simple narrative poem **:** BALLAD **2 :** MELODY **:** a melody fragment **:** SONG ⟨birds chanting their cheerful ~s⟩

[5]lay \"\ *adj* [ME, fr. OF *lai,* fr. LL *laicus,* fr. Gk *laikos* of the people, fr. *laos* people + *-ikos* -ic] **1 :** belonging or relating to those not in holy orders **:** not of the clergy **:** not clerical **:** not ecclesiastical ⟨politics and commerce had gradually become dominant with crusaders, and the conduct of the enterprises became more completely ~ —H.O.Taylor⟩ ⟨the Vatican not interested in supporting either the ~ republicanism of France —*Times Lit. Supp.*⟩ **2 :** of or relating to members of a religious house that are occupied chiefly with domestic or manual work — distinguished from *choir* ⟨~ brothers⟩ ⟨~ sisters⟩ **3 :** not of or from a particular profession **:** not having special training or knowledge **:** UNPROFESSIONAL **:** COMMON, ORDINARY ⟨~ public⟩ ⟨~ citizen⟩ ⟨like so many other ~ writers with little actual building experience —S.H.Van Gelder⟩ ⟨~ opinion⟩ ⟨~ vocabulary⟩ **syn** see PROFANE

[6]lay \"\ *dial Brit var of* [1]LEA

[7]lay \"\ *n* -S [alter. of [4]*lathe*] **1 :** a section of a loom that oscillates and carries the reed, shuttle boxes, and batten during the process of beating up; *specif* **:** the batten of a loom that beats up the newly laid filling **2** *Scot* **:** [4]LATHE 1

lay abbot *n* **:** a layman holding title to an abbey and its revenues

lay about *vi* **1 :** to strike in all directions **:** hit out at random **2 :** to take steps in preparation **:** seek means **:** go about

la·ya·ná \ˌlīəˈnä, ˌlīə-\ *n, pl* **layaná** *or* **layanás** *usu cap* [Sp, of AmerInd origin] **1 :** an Arawakan people living opposite the mouth of the Apa river in Paraguay **2 :** a member of the Layaná people

lay analyst *n* **:** a psychoanalyst who is not a physician

lay aside *vt* [ME *leyen aside,* fr. *leyen* to lay + *aside*] **1 :** to put out of use or consideration **:** DISCARD, ABANDON, SHELVE ⟨plans for a new school have been *laid aside*⟩ ⟨time to *lay* old prejudices *aside* and grudges⟩ ⟨*laid aside* his pose of indifference⟩ **2 :** to set aside for special or future use **:** RESERVE, SAVE ⟨able to *lay* a few dollars *aside* each week⟩

lay away *vt* [ME *leyen away,* fr. *leyen* to lay + *away*] **1 :** to lay aside **2 :** to store for preservation or future use **3 :** to spread (hides) flat in tanning liquor **4 :** BURY, INTER **5 a :** to put (specified cards) in the crib in cribbage **b :** to bury (specified cards or cards worth a specified number of points) in pinochle ⟨*lay* two kings *away*⟩ ⟨*laid away* 18 points⟩

layaway \ˈ=,=,=\ *n* -S [*lay away*] **1 :** the liquor or pit of liquor in which hides are laid away in tanning **2 :** an article of merchandise reserved for future delivery to a customer who pays a deposit and agrees to complete payment when the article is called for at a later date

layback \ˈ=,=\ *n* -S [fr. the phrase *lay back*] **1 :** a combination of a receding nose and undershot jaw in certain animals (as a bulldog) **2 :** a rock-climbing maneuver in which a climber maintains his balance in a nearly horizontal position by pulling strongly against an underhold or sidehold **3 :** the backward inclination of an oarsman's body at the completion of the power phase of a stroke

lay baptism *n* **:** baptism administered by a member of the laity usu. under the stress of necessity (as because of the unavailability of a clergyman)

lay bone *n* [[1]*lay*] **:** either of the pubic bones of a hen

layboy \ˈ=,=\ *n* [[1]*lay* + *boy;* prob. fr. the fact that this work was formerly done by a boy] **:** a device that stacks and jogs into even piles sheets of pulp or paper received from cutters, ruling machines, paper machines, and printing presses — called also *jogger*

lay by *vt* **1 :** to lay aside **:** put away **:** DISCARD **2 :** to store for future use **:** SAVE **3 a** *South & Midland* **:** to cultivate (as corn) for the last time **b :** to store (a crop) after harvesting **4 :** to lay to (a ship) ~ *vi* **:** to lay to **:** hold in the wind **:** PAUSE

lay-by \ˈ=,=\ *n* -S [*lay by*] **1 :** a portion of a stream or canal widened so that boats may lie up or pass each other **2 :** a siding for empty cars (as at a mine) **3** *Brit* **:** a branch from or a widening of a road to permit vehicles to stop without obstructing traffic **4 :** LAYAWAY 2

lay chalice *n* **:** communion for the laity under the species of wine as well as of bread

lay clerk *n* **:** a member of a choir in an Anglican cathedral or collegiate church

lay communion *n* **:** the state of being in communion with the church as a layman; *specif* **:** the condition of Roman Catholic clerics reduced to lay status

lay cord *n* [[1]*lay*] **:** the loop of cord around the crossbar of a bookbinder's hand-sewing frame to which the sewing cord is fastened

lay corporation *n* **:** a corporation composed of laymen and organized for other than spiritual purposes — contrasted with *ecclesiastical corporation*

lay day *n* [prob. fr. [1]*lay*] **1 :** one of the days allowed by the charter party for loading or unloading a vessel — compare DEMURRAGE **2 :** a day of delay in port

lay deacon *n* **:** one in deacon's orders who engages in secular occupations

lay down *vt* **1 :** to put aside or give up (something borne) **:** SURRENDER ⟨called on them to *lay* their arms *down*⟩ ⟨*laid down* his kingly power⟩ **2** *obs* **:** to put down as a wager, stake, or payment **3 a :** to construct or put in place the foundation or main framework or features of ⟨inherited tendencies . . . do not operate as they do in birds or ants to *lay down* inexorably his whole way of life —Ruth Benedict⟩ **b :** ESTABLISH, PRESCRIBE ⟨*lays down* common codes for reporting so that all countries understand each other's messages —J.M.Stagg⟩ ⟨scale *laid down* for a map⟩ **c :** to assert or command dogmatically **:** expound or state positively ⟨*lay down* the law⟩ ⟨it may be *laid down* as a maxim, that wherever a great deal can be made by the use of money —Adam Smith⟩ **d :** to lay off (sense 1) **4 :** to plant or sow (a field) with a crop; *also* **:** to plant (a crop) ⟨had already *laid* his melons *down*⟩ **5** *archaic* **:** to cause (a ship) to lie on the side — used of the wind or sea **6** *archaic* **:** to lay embroidery on **7 a :** to store or put in a supply of (as wine) in a cellar **b :** to pack for aging ⟨*lay down* sauerkraut⟩ or preservation ⟨*lay down* eggs in waterglass⟩ **8 :** to deliver (merchandise) at a specified destination **9 a :** MELD **b :** to lead or play (a card) in bridge ~ *vi* **1 :** to lie down **2 :** to meld as many matched sets as one has in rummy

lay-down \ˈ=,=\ *adj* [*lay down*] *of a collar* **:** turned over

laydown \"\ *n* -S [*lay down*] **1 :** the arrangement of piles of book sections in sequence preparatory to gathering — called also *layout* **2 :** LAY 8c **3 :** a declarer's hand in bridge that is so easily able to fulfill his contract that he might or does expose it and claim the required number of tricks

lay elder *n* [[5]*lay*] **:** [3]ELDER 4b

[1]lay·er \ˈlā(ə)r, ˈle(ə)r, ˈleə\ *n* -S [ME *leyer, legger,* fr. *leyen, leggen* to lay + *-er*] **1 :** one that lays: as **a** *obs* **:** MASON **b :** one whose work is laying something — usu. used in combination ⟨brick*layer*⟩ **c :** a hen that lays or is kept to lay eggs **d :** one who lays odds **:** BOOKMAKER **e :** a machine for twisting strands in making rope **f :** a workman who removes sheets of handmade paper from the felts after pressing — called also *layerman, layman* **g :** a member of a gun crew who lays the gun **2 a :** one thickness, course, or fold laid or lying over or under another ⟨~ of bricks⟩ ⟨~ of plaster⟩ ⟨~ of paint⟩ ⟨~ of veneer⟩ ⟨several ~s of clothing⟩ ⟨~s of an onion⟩ ⟨upper ~s of the atmosphere⟩ **b :** STRATUM, BED ⟨~ of clay⟩ ⟨~ of sandstone⟩ ⟨fill the dish with alternate ~s of potatoes and cheese⟩ **c :** HORIZON 2 **d :** any of several strata of plant forms in an ecological association ⟨a moss ~ in a bog⟩ **3 a :** a branch or shoot of a plant treated to induce rooting while still attached to the parent plant (as by mounding with soil or by bending over and covering often intermittently with soil) — compare STOOL **b :** a plant prepared by layering **4 a** *dial Eng* **:** a field in which a grass and a grain crop are planted together with the grass crop growing up after the grain is harvested **b** *archaic* **:** earth suitable for cultivation **:** SOIL **c :** LEA 2b **5** *obs* **:** an artificial oyster bed **6 :** a pit of strong tanning liquor into which hides are put on coming from the handler

[2]layer \"\ *vb* -ED/-ING/-S *vt* **1 :** to propagate (a plant) by means of layers — see AIR LAYERING, MARCOTTAGE ~ *vi* **1 :** to separate into layers ⟨mists ~*ed* thick about him —Stewart Toland⟩ **2** *of a plant* **:** to multiply by layering; *esp* **:** to form roots where a stem comes in contact with the ground ⟨many brambles spread by ~*ing* under natural conditions⟩

lay·er·age \-ərij, -eər-\ *n* -S **:** the practice or art of layering plants

layer board *n* **:** a board support for lead roof gutters

layer cake *n* **:** a fancy cake that is in layers held together by a sweet filling and that is usu. covered with frosting

lay·ered \ˌlā(ə)r)d, ˌle(ə)rd, ˌleəd\ *adj* [[1]*layer* + *-ed*] **:** having layers **:** arranged in or divided into layers **:** covered in layers ⟨the earth's crust is ~⟩ ⟨a many-*layered* social structure⟩ ⟨~ relief map in eight colors⟩

layering *n* -S [fr. gerund of [2]*layer*] **:** the shading or coloring of the areas between contour lines of a map in a manner suggestive of progressive change for emphasizing or clarifying differences in elevation

lay·er·man \-ə(r)mən, -eə(-\ *n, pl* **layermen** [[1]*layer* + *man*] **:** LAYER 1f

layer of langhans *usu cap 2d L* [after Theodor *Langhans* †1915 Ger. pathologist] **:** CYTOTROPHOBLAST

layer-on \ˈ=(=)ˈ=\ *n, pl* **layers-on** [*lay on* + *-er*] *Brit* **:** a worker who feeds a printing press by hand

layer-out \ˈ=(=)ˈ=\ *n, pl* **layers-out** [*lay out* + *-er*] **:** one that lays out: as **a :** one who prepares a body for burial **b :** one who lays out articles for sorting or drying **c :** one whose work is the laying out of patterns on materials for cutting

layer's cramp *n* **:** lameness or leg weakness of poultry in heavy lay possibly due to nerve injury or to calcium deficiency

layer-up \ˈ=(=)ˈ=\ *n, pl* **layers-up** [*lay up* + *-er*] **:** one that lays up: as **a :** a worker who arranges strips or folds of material (as cloth) **b :** a worker who glues sheets of veneer to make plywood

lay·ette \(ˈ)lā¦et\ *n* -S [F, fr. MF, small box, small drawer, fr. *laye* box, drawer (fr. MD *laeye, lade* box) + *-ette;* MD *laeye, lade* akin to MHG *lade* box, ON *hlatha* barn — more at LATHE (barn)] **1 :** a complete outfit of clothing and equipment for a newborn infant **2 :** a special web spun by some spiders for the use of the newly hatched spiderlings

lay fee *n* [ME, fr. [5]*lay* + *fee*] **:** a fee in land held on condition of the rendering of secular as opposed to religious services — compare FRANKALMOIGN, PETER'S PENCE

lay figure *n* [*lay* (fr. [2]*layman*) + *figure*] **1 :** a jointed model of the human body that may be put in any attitude and that is used by artists as a model for showing the disposition of drapery — compare DUMMY **2 :** one who serves the will of others without independent volition **:** a person or fictitious character of no marked individuality **:** PUPPET, DUMMY

layfolk \ˈ=,=\ *n, pl in constr* [ME, fr. [5]*lay* + *folk*] **:** ordinary people **:** LAYMEN ⟨decreed that no ~ should possess books of scripture —G.G.Coulton⟩

lay·ia \ˈlā(y)ə\ *n, cap* [NL, fr. George T. *Lay,* 19th cent. Eng. botanist + NL *-ia*] **:** a genus of mostly Californian annual herbs (family Compositae) having showy heads of yellow or white ray flowers — see TIDYTIPS

lay in *vt* **1 :** to store up **:** lay by ⟨*lay in* an ample supply of groceries⟩ **2** *archaic* **:** to assert as a claim **3 a :** to paint in roughly subject to finishing, elaboration, or addition **b :** to put (masses of color) on a canvas ⟨helped him to *lay* the background blues and browns *in*⟩ **4 a :** to heel in (a plant) **b :** [4]TRAIN 2 **5** *Brit* **:** to shut down or discontinue working (a colliery or coal pit)

laying *pres part of* LAY

laying duck *n* **:** EIDER 1

laying on of hands 1 : a form used in consecrating to office, in the rite of confirmation, and in blessing persons and consisting in placing the hands upon the head of the person on whom the divine blessing is invoked **2 :** a Mormon rite used in conferring the Holy Ghost upon one baptized and performed only by a member of the Melchizedek priesthood **3 :** the application of a spiritual healer's hands to the patient's body

laying press *n* **:** LYING PRESS

laying top *n* **:** a conical grooved wooden block placed between the strands in laying a rope

laylight \ˈ=,=\ *n* [[1]*lay*] **:** a glazed panel usu. set flush with the ceiling for admitting natural or artificial light

lay·lock \ˈlālək, -ā,läk\ *dial var of* LILAC

lay lord *n* **:** a British peer who is not a law lord

lay low *vt* **1 :** to bring or strike to earth **:** FELL ⟨hurricane winds are likely to *lay low* the balloon⟩ **2 :** to knock out of a fight or out of action ⟨flu had *laid* him *low*⟩ **3 :** KILL ⟨*laid low* six or seven jackdaws —Ian Niall⟩ ~ *vi* **:** to lie low

[1]lay·man \ˈlāmən\ *n, pl* **lay·men** \-mən *sometimes* -,men\ [ME *lay man,* fr. [5]*lay* + *man*] **1 :** one of the laity as distinguished from the clergy **2 :** one not belonging to some particular profession or not expert in some branch of knowledge or art

[2]layman \"\ *n* [D *leeman, ledeman,* fr. *lee-, lede-* (fr. *lid* limb, part of the body, fr. MD *lit, let*) + *man,* fr. MD — more at LITH, MAN] *obs* **:** LAY FIGURE

[3]layman \"\ *n, pl* **laymen** [[1]*lay* + *man*] **:** LAYER 1f

layne \ˈlān\ *vb* -ED/-ING/-S [ME *laynen,* fr. ON *leyna* to conceal; akin to OE *lȳgnan* to deny, OHG *lougnen,* Goth *laugnjan* to deny, ON *ljūga* to lie, tell a lie — more at LIE] *vt, chiefly Scot* **:** to hold back, conceal, or disguise (information) ~ *vi, chiefly Scot* **:** to refrain from telling something

lay off *vt* **1 :** to mark or measure off; *specif* **:** to draw on the mold-loft floor to full dimensions the lines or outlines of (a ship and its members) **2 :** to steer (a ship) away from the shore or from a pier or another ship **3 a** *of a bookmaker* **:** to place all or part of (a bet accepted) with another bookmaker in order to reduce the risk **b :** to subscribe to or cause subscriptions to be made to (a new issue of securities offered to a corporation's stockholders) so as to reduce the liability of the issue's underwriters **4 :** to distribute (a coat of paint) evenly **5** *Midland* **:** PLAN, INTEND ⟨*laid off* to go to town the next day⟩ **6 a :** to halt or suspend operation of (as a mill or factory) **b :** to cease to employ (a worker) usu. temporarily because of slack in production and without prejudice to the worker — usu. distinguished from *fire* **7 :** to add (a card or cards) in rummy to sets already melded **8 a :** to refrain or cease from pursuing or annoying **:** let alone ⟨if you'll *lay off* me I'll promise not to do it again⟩ **b :** AVOID, SHUN, QUIT ⟨advised to *lay off* smoking and alcohol⟩ ~ *vi* **1 :** to lie off **2 a :** to stop work ⟨time to *lay off*⟩ **b :** to take time off or a rest from working ⟨*lays off* a couple of days each month⟩ or activity ⟨weekends he just likes to *lay off*⟩

lay·off \'=,=\ *n* -s [*lay off*] **1 a :** the act of laying off an employee or a work force **b :** OFF-SEASON, SHUTDOWN **2 a :** a period of being away from or out of work **b :** a period of being out of an activity or competition ⟨champion was badly out of condition from a long ~⟩

lay of the land : the disposition of circumstances which one is considering ⟨wanted to know more about the *lay of the land* before investing⟩

lay on *vt* **1 :** to apply to or spread on a surface ⟨*lay* a coat of paint *on*⟩ ⟨*lay on* liniment to soothe his lameness⟩ **2 :** to take on or gain (as flesh, fat) ⟨*laid* 10 pounds *on* in a month⟩ **3** *Brit* **a :** to provide for the supply of (as water, gas, electricity) ⟨a 3-room flat with gas and hot water *laid on*⟩ **b :** to provide or make arrangements for (as a convenience, entertainment, or service) ⟨stage shows and open-air dancing all *laid on* —Richard Huson⟩ **4 a :** to feed (sheets) into a printing press **b :** to place (a form) on the bed of a press ~ *vi* **:** ATTACK, BEAT ⟨seized a club and began to *lay on* for dear life⟩

lay out *vt* **1 :** to extend or stretch out at length: as **a :** to prepare (a corpse) for burial **b :** to knock flat or unconscious ⟨can *lay* him *out* in the first round⟩ **2 a :** to plan in detail **:** map out ⟨*lay out* an election campaign⟩ ⟨the work for tomorrow is all *laid out*⟩ **b :** to make an arrangement of (copy, illustration) for printing **c :** to set (book sections) in the right order for gathering **3 :** to mark (work) for drilling, machining, filing to specified contour and dimensions **4 :** ARRANGE, DESIGN ⟨walks, flower beds, and lawn were *laid out* in a formal pattern⟩ **5 :** DISPLAY, EXHIBIT **6** *Midland* **:** PROPOSE, PLAN, INTEND ⟨was *laying out* to look for another job⟩ **7 :** to make an expenditure of (a sum of money) **:** SPEND ~ *vi South & Midland* **:** to absent oneself (as from school) without permission

lay·out \'=,=\ *n* -s [*lay out*] **1 a :** the act or process of laying out or planning in detail **b :** the plan or design or arrangement of something that is laid out: as (1) **:** a plan or design to show the arrangement and general appearance of something to be produced or reproduced graphically (as by printing or photography) ⟨an artist's ~ of an advertisement⟩ ⟨a typographer's ~ of a projected book⟩ (2) **:** arrangement of matter to be reproduced; *esp* **:** the placement of negatives preparatory to plate making (as for offset or gravure printing) (3) **:** the position of men, machines, and materials within a manufacturing plant in relation to the flow of goods in process of manufacture **2 :** something that is laid out: as **a :** an area usu. of green cloth marked to indicate spaces on which may be placed bets on various contingencies (as in roulette) **b :** cards dealt (as in solitaire) into a prescribed pattern on which plays may be made **:** TABLEAU **c :** something displayed **:** SPREAD ⟨the dinner was a fine ~⟩ **d :** ESTABLISHMENT, PLACE ⟨lives in an elaborate ~ including swimming pool, private golf course, tennis court, acres of woods⟩ **3 :** LAYDOWN **4 :** a set or collection of tools or apparatus ⟨miner's ~⟩ ⟨opium ~⟩ **b** *chiefly South & West* **:** OUTFIT, GANG **5 :** a body position used in diving, swimming, and gymnastics in which the trunk is extended, the head is back, the back is arched, and the arms are extended sideways — compare [11]PIKE, TUCK

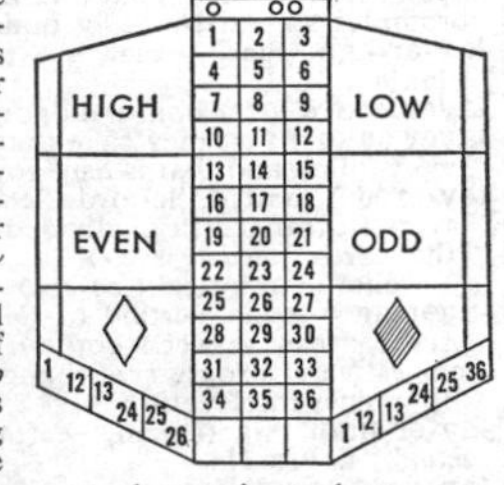

layout in roulette

layout man *n* **1 :** one who plans the layout of material to be printed or reproduced **2 :** a worker who marks out patterns on metal, stone, glass, textiles, or other material in preparation for such subsequent operations as cutting, bending, punching: as **a :** one who outlines on stock lumber the shape of furniture or other parts **b :** one who marks guide lines on metal parts to indicate material to be removed in machining **c :** one who uses a guiding design to prepare settings for stones on models of jewelry **d :** one who indicates by chalk lines the way in which steel plates are to be cut for use in ship or locomotive building — called also *duplicator*

lay over *vt* **1 :** POSTPONE ⟨voted to *lay* the measure *over* until the following meeting⟩ **2** *dial* **:** EXCEL, SURPASS ⟨it *lays over* anything else of the kind⟩ ~ *vi* **:** to lie over

[1]**layover** \'=,==\ *n* -s [origin unknown] *dial* **:** something whose identity is intentionally concealed — used typically in the phrase *layovers to catch meddlers* as an evasive answer to a question from a child

[2]**layover** \"\ *n* -s [*lay over*] **:** a stay or wait for a period in a place **:** STOPOVER ⟨~ between trains⟩

lay preacher *n* **:** an unordained preacher

lay race *n* **:** the part of a lay on which the shuttle travels in weaving — called also *shuttle race*

lay reader *n* **:** a layman authorized by a bishop to read parts of the public service in an Anglican or Protestant Episcopal church

lay rector *n* **:** a layman who receives the tithes of a parish or in whom the rectory is vested

lays *pres 3d sing of* LAY, *pl of* LAY

lay·san albatross \'lī,sän-\ *n, usu cap L* [fr. *Laysan*, islet in Leeward Islands, Hawaii] **:** an albatross (*Diomedea immutabilis*) that is white with dark back and wings and is found on Laysan and adjacent islands of the Pacific ocean

lay sermon *n* **:** an address or essay on moral and religious questions by a layman

layshaft \'=,=\ *n* [prob. fr. [1]*lay*] **:** COUNTERSHAFT 2

laystall \'=,=\ *n, Brit* **:** a place where rubbish and dung are deposited

lay to *vt* [ME *leyen to*, fr. *leyen* to lay + *to*] **:** to bring (a ship) into the wind and hold stationary except for drifting ~ *vi* **1 :** to lie to **2 :** to apply or exert oneself ⟨told to get a shovel and *lay to* with the others⟩ **3 :** to deal blows **:** strike out ⟨*laying to* right and left with a club⟩

lay underwriter *n* **:** an underwriter of life or accident or health insurance who is without medical training

lay up *vt* **1 :** to save or put by for future use **:** store up **:** lay away **:** HOARD, ACCUMULATE, SAVE ⟨*lay* not *up* for yourselves treasures upon earth —Mt. 6:19 (AV)⟩ **2 a** *obs* **:** IMPRISON **b :** to disable or confine with illness or injury ⟨*laid up* with a bad knee⟩ **3 :** to take (as a ship) out of active service ⟨when you *lay* the yacht *up* it is best to remove the motor —Peter Heaton⟩ **4 a :** to leave (a field) in a specified condition ⟨*laid up* for pasture⟩ **b :** to reserve (a field) for a crop **5 a :** to set (as stones, bricks) one on top of another (as in a wall) **b :** to construct (as a wall) by laying bricks or stones ⟨the front was *laid up* in ashlar⟩ **c :** to spread (cloth) in a pile of many layers — compare LAY 5b **d :** to assemble (layers of veneer or cores) after application of the glue or adhesive in preparation for pressing and bonding plywood **6 :** to drive (a horse) in a heat of a trotting race so as neither to win nor to be distanced **7 :** to form (a hot rivet that is in position) by striking several hard blows ~ *vi* **1 :** to lie up **2 :** to shape the course of a ship ⟨time to *lay up* for home⟩

lay-up \'=,=\ *n* -s [*lay up*] **1 :** the action of laying up or the condition of being laid up: as **a :** the condition (as of a ship) of being set aside out of active service **b :** an assembly of layers of veneer or cores for pressing **c :** a jumping one-hand shot in basketball made off the backboard from close under the basket

lay vicar *n* **:** CLERK VICAR

laywoman \'=,==\ *n, pl* **laywomen :** a woman who is unordained and thus a member of the laity in distinction from the clergy

laz \'läz\ *or* **la·ze** \-zə\ *or* **la·zi** \-zē\ *n, pl* **laz** *or* **lazes** *or* **laze** *or* **lazi** *or* **lazis** *usu cap* **1 a :** a Muslim Kartvelian Sunnite people of Caucasia found on both sides of the Turkish-Soviet frontier **b :** a member of such people **2 :** the south Caucasic language of the Laz people

lazar \'lazə(r), 'lāz-\ *n* -s [ME, fr. ML *lazarus*, fr. LL *Lazarus*, beggar with sores mentioned in Lk 16:20] **:** a person afflicted with a repulsive disease; *specif* **:** LEPER

laz·a·ret·to \,lazə'red·(,)ō\ *or* **laz·a·ret** *also* **laz·a·rette** \,lazə'ret\ *n* -s [It dial. (Venetian) *lazareto*, alter. (influenced by It *lazzaro* leper, fr. ML *lazarus*) of *nazareto*, fr. *Santa Maria di Nazaret*, church in Venice that maintained a well-known hospital] **1** *usu lazaretto* **:** a hospital for contagious diseases **2 :** a building or a ship used for detention in quarantine **3** *usu lazaret* **:** a space in a ship between decks used as a storeroom

lazar house *n* **:** LAZARETTO 1; *esp* **:** a hospital for lepers

Laz·a·rist \'lazərəst\ *n* -s *usu cap* [College of St. *Lazare*, Paris, occupied by the Vincentians from 1632 to 1792 + E *-ist*] **:** VINCENTIAN 1

lazarlike \'==,=\ *adj* **:** full of sores **:** LEPROUS

Laz·a·rus \'laz(ə)rəs\ *n* -ES *often cap* [ML] **:** a diseased esp. leprous beggar **:** LAZAR

[1]**laze** \'lāz\ *vb* -ED/-ING/-S [back-formation fr. [1]*lazy*] *vi* **:** to act or lie lazily ⟨*lazing* in the sun⟩ **:** LAZY, IDLE ~ *vt* **:** to pass (as time) in idleness or relaxation ⟨~ away whole days⟩

[2]**laze** \"\ *n* -s **:** the act or state of lazing ⟨a long ~ at the beach⟩ **:** IDLENESS, LAZINESS, RELAXATION

la·zi·ly \'lāzəlē, -li\ *adv* **:** in a lazy manner ⟨drifting ~ downstream in the peaceful atmosphere⟩

la·zi·ness \-zēnəs, -zin-\ *n* -ES **:** the quality or state of being lazy

la·zule \'la(,)zhül\ *n* -s [ML *lazulum* — more at LAPIS LAZULI] **:** LAPIS LAZULI

lazuli *n* -s [by shortening] **:** LAPIS LAZULI

lazuli bunting *or* **lazuli finch** *n* **:** a finch (*Passerina amoena*) of the western U.S. having the head, neck, and upper parts blue, buff on the breast, and a white belly

laz·u·line \'lazə,lēn, 'lazhə-, -,līn\ *adj* [*lazuli* + *-ine*] **:** of the color of lapis lazuli

laz·u·lite \-,līt\ *n* -s [G *lazulith*, fr. *lazu-* (fr. ML *lazulum*) + *-lith*] **:** an azure-blue mineral $(Mg,Fe)Al_2(PO_4)_2(OH)_2$ occurring in small masses or in monoclinic crystals, consisting of hydrous phosphate of aluminum, iron, and magnesium, and isomorphous with scorzalite (hardness 5–6, sp. gr. 3.06–3.12) — **laz·u·lit·ic** \'==¦lid·ik\ *adj*

laz·u·rite \-,rīt\ *n* -s [G *lasurit*, fr. ML *lazur* lapis lazuli (fr. Ar *lāzaward*) + G *-it* -ite — more at AZURE] **:** a mineral $(Na,Ca)_8(Al,Si)_{12}O_{24}(S,SO_4)$ occurring as the chief constituent of lapis lazuli, isomorphous with sodalite, and composed of a sodium silicate containing sulfur

[1]**la·zy** \'lāzē, -zi\ *adj* -ER/-EST [perh. fr. MLG *lasich* feeble, faint; akin to MHG *erleswen* to become weak, ON *lasinn* dilapidated, Goth *lasiws* weak, Bulg *loš* bad] **1 a :** disliking physical or mental exertion **:** not energetic or vigorous **:** INDOLENT, INACTIVE ⟨having to deal with a ~ slut, might feel strongly tempted to take up the nearest broomstick —G.B. Shaw⟩ ⟨gifted but ~ artist⟩ **b :** encouraging or causing inactivity or indolence ⟨~ summer day⟩ ⟨~ weather⟩ ⟨~ chair⟩ **c :** marked by lack of activity ⟨spent a ~ weekend at home⟩ ⟨~ expedient⟩ **2 :** moving slowly and without or as if without energy **:** SLUGGISH ⟨~ river⟩ ⟨spoke with a ~ articulation⟩ **3 :** not firmly erect **:** DROOPING, LAX ⟨~ corn⟩ ⟨a rabbit with ~ ears⟩ ⟨habitually ~ posture⟩ **4** *of a letter or number* **:** placed on its side ⟨~ E livestock brand⟩ ⟨~ 2 on a bank note⟩ — see BRAND illustration

syn LAZY, INDOLENT, SLOTHFUL, and FAINEANT can all signify not easily aroused to responsible, purposeful activity. LAZY stresses an aversion to work and a habitual tendency to idleness ⟨we were too *lazy* . . . We passed our indolent days leaving everything to somebody else —H.G.Wells⟩ ⟨the lion is by nature so essentially *lazy* that he will never do more hunting than he feels to be necessary —James Stevenson-Hamilton⟩ ⟨even when the heat is not extreme, a sudden rise may make us uncomfortable and *lazy*, as often occurs in the spring —Ellsworth Huntington⟩ INDOLENT implies a constitutional love of ease and inactivity or dislike of purposeful activity ⟨an *indolent* son sleeping away his life⟩ ⟨he was an *indolent* man, who lived only to eat, drink, and play at cards —Jane Austen⟩ ⟨life is more leisured without being essentially *indolent* —*Amer. Guide Series: Va.*⟩ SLOTHFUL suggests temperamental inactivity or slowness when action or speed is called for ⟨he would use political means to jog a *slothful* conscience and marshal its forces —V.L.Parrington⟩ ⟨waiting for the hostler's *slothful* boy to bring out the horses —*Amer. Guide Series: Va.*⟩ FAINEANT, now infrequent, implies a disposition to do nothing even under urgency ⟨in a typical statement of the *faineant* judicial philosophy he sometimes espouses, [he] refused to put judgment on so slender a foundation —E.V.Rostov⟩ ⟨to avoid all issues by electing a *faineant* mayor and city council⟩

[2]**lazy** \"\ *vb* -ED/-ING/-ES **:** to move or lie lazily **:** LAZE

lazyback \'==,=\ *n* **:** a backrest attached to a carriage seat

lazybed \'==,=\ *n* **1** *chiefly Brit* **:** a small plot of land tilled by hand on rocky ground **2** *chiefly Brit* **:** a plot of potatoes or other crop not tilled but covered with soil, leaves, or sawdust

lazybird \'==,=\ *n* **:** COWBIRD

lazy board *n* **:** a projecting seat for the driver placed on the left side of a freight wagon within reach of the brake

lazybones \'==,=\ *n pl but sing or pl in constr* **:** a lazy person

lazy crab *n* **:** a large sedentary crab (*Parthenope horrida*) of the East and West Indies having long heavy chelipeds and rough and spiny shell

lazy daisy stitch *n* **:** an embroidery stitch formed by an elongated loop held down at the free end by a small stitch

lazy daisy stitch

lazy eight *n* **:** an aerial maneuver in which a plane by gradual climbing, banking, and turning traces an imaginary figure eight on its side

lazy guy *n* **:** a guy for steadying the boom of a fore-and-aft sail

la·zy·ish \'lāzēish, -ziish\ *adj* **:** somewhat lazy

lazy jack *n* **1 :** a device that compensates for expansion and contraction (as in a pipe line) consisting of two linked bell cranks pivoted at the vertices of their complementary angles **2 :** an often forked line reaching from the masthead or the topping lift on each side of a fore-and-aft sail to about the middle of the boom to confine the sail when it is lowered — usu. used in pl.

lazy painter *n* **:** a long painter led from well forward of a boom to a boat riding to one of the guess-warps of that boom to permit hauling the boat up to a ladder

lazy-shark \'==,=\ *n, Africa* **:** CAT SHARK 1

lazy squaw stitch *n* **:** a stitch used in coiled basketwork consisting essentially of loops alternately encircling one and two coils

lazy strap *n* **:** a looped strap attached to the breeching of a harness through which the traces are passed to prevent sagging

lazy su·san \,==+'süzᵊn\ *n, usu cap S* [[1]*lazy* + *Susan* (the name)] **1 :** MUFFIN STAND **2 :** a revolving tray placed on a dining table for serving food, condiments, relishes; *broadly* **:** any similar revolving device (as for storage shelves or display racks)

lazy susan 2

lazy tongs *n pl* **:** a series of jointed and pivoted bars capable of great extension used orig. for picking up something at a distance; *broadly* **:** any of various devices adjustable in similar manner

laz·za·ro·ne \,lazə'rōnē, ,lädzə-\ *n, pl* **lazzaro·ni** \-nē\ [It, aug. of *lazzaro* beggar, leper, fr. ML *lazarus* — more at LAZAR] **:** one of the homeless idlers of Naples who live by chance work or begging

laz·zo \'läd(,)zō\ *n, pl* **laz·zi** \-(,)zē\ [It, perh. fr. Sp *lazo* lasso, noose, snare, fr. L *laqueus* noose, snare — more at DELIGHT] **:** a piece of interpolated comic business or dialogue in the commedia dell'arte — compare BURLA

lb [L *libra*] *abbr* pound

LB *abbr* **1** landing barge **2** left on base **3** leg bye **4** letter box **5** light bomber **6** local board

LBF *abbr* lactobacillus bulgaricus factor

LBP *abbr* length between perpendiculars

lbr *abbr* **1** labor **2** lumber

LC *abbr* **1** label clause **2** lance corporal **3** landing craft **4** law courts **5** left center **6** letter of credit **7** level crossing **8** lightly canceled **9** line of communication **10** *often not cap* [L *loco citato*] in the place cited **11** lord chamberlain **12** lord chancellor **13** *often not cap* lower case

l casei factor *n, cap L* [*l* initial of *lactobacillus*] **:** LACTOBACILLUS CASEI FACTOR

l c classification *n, usu cap L & 1st C* **:** LIBRARY OF CONGRESS CLASSIFICATION

LCD *abbr* least common denominator; lowest common denominator

lce *abbr* lance

LCJ *abbr* lord chief justice

lcl *abbr* local

LCL *abbr* less-than-carload; less-than-carload lot

LCM *abbr* least common multiple; lowest common multiple

LCT *abbr* local civil time

ld *abbr* **1** land **2** lead **3** limited **4** load **5** lord

LD *abbr* **1** [L *laus Deo*] praise be to God **2** left defense **3** lethal dose **4** line of departure **5** line of duty **6** local delivery **7** long delay **8** long distance

LDC *abbr* lower dead center

ldg *abbr* **1** landing **2** leading **3** loading **4** lodging

LDO *abbr* limited duty officer

ldp *abbr* **1** ladyship **2** lordship

ldr *abbr* leader

ldry *abbr* laundry

LDS *abbr* **1** Latter-day Saints **2** [L *laus Deo semper*] praise to God always

-le \əl, ᵊl\ *vb suffix* **-led; -led; -ling** \(ə)liŋ, (ᵊ)l-\ **-les** [ME *-len*, fr. OE *-lian*; akin to OHG *-ilōn*, *-alōn*, verb suffixes indicating repeated action] — indicating repeated action or movement esp. of a trifling or small-scale character ⟨prattle⟩ ⟨wriggle⟩ ⟨hobble⟩

le *abbr* lease

LE *abbr* **1** labor exchange **2** leading edge **3** left end **4** low efficiency **5** low explosive **6** lupus erythematosus

[1]**lea** *or* **ley** \'lē, 'lā\ *n* -s [ME *lee*, *leye*, fr. OE *lēah*; akin to OHG *lōh* thicket of shrubs, L *lucus* grove, Skt *loka* open space, world, L *lux* light — more at LIGHT] **1 :** GRASSLAND, PASTURE ⟨the lowing herd winds slowly o'er the ~ —Thomas Gray⟩ **2** *usu ley* [ME *leye*, fr. *leye*, adj.] **a :** arable land sown to grasses or clover for hay or grazing and usu. plowed and planted with other crops after two or more years **b :** a crop of grass or clover raised on cultivated land — called also *layer*

[2]**lea** \'lē\ *adj* [ME *leye*, fr. OE *lǣg-* (in *lǣghrycg* lea rig); akin to OE *licgan* to lie — more at LIE] **:** lying under grass **:** FALLOW, UNPLOWED

[3]**lea** \"\ *n* -s [ME *lee*, perh. back-formation fr. *lees* unit of measure of thread, leash (taken as a plural) — more at LEASH] **1 :** a unit of 300 yards used in counting linen yarns — compare COUNT 8 a **2 :** a unit of 120 yards of a yarn used for testing

[4]**lea** \", 'lā\ *n* -s [ME *ley*, fr. ON *lē*; akin to MLG *lē* sickle, OE *losian* to get lost, perish — more at LOSE] *dial Eng* **:** SCYTHE

[5]**lea** \'lē\ *chiefly Scot var of* LEAVE

lea *abbr* **1** league **2** leather **3** leave

LEA *abbr* local education authority

[1]**leach** *var of* LEECH

[2]**leach** \'lēch\ *n* -ES [in sense 1, prob. alter. of [1]*letch*; in other senses, fr. [3]*leach*] **1 a :** a perforated vessel to hold wood ashes through which water is passed to extract the lye **b :** a pit or tub in which ooze is made by steeping tanbark in water **2 a :** LEACHATE **b :** the saturated brine that is drained from the salt or left in the pan when the salt is drawn out **3 :** the process or an instance of leaching ⟨is about 60°F. for the last ~ —R.N.Shreve⟩

[3]**leach** \"\ *vb* -ED/-ING/-ES *vt* **1 a :** to subject to the action of percolating water or other liquid in order to separate the soluble components **:** LIXIVIATE ⟨~ an ore⟩ — compare EXTRACT 1e **b :** to dissolve out by the action of a percolating liquid — often used with *out* ⟨~ out alkali from ashes⟩; compare EXTRACT 1d **c** (1) **:** to remove nutritive or harmful elements from (soil) by percolation ⟨soil ~*ed* of its salts by torrential rains⟩ (2) **:** to remove (nutritive or harmful elements) from soil by percolation — often used with *out* ⟨~*ed* out the beneficial nutrients —*Harper's*⟩ ⟨~*ing* excess salt out of the soil —D.W.Israelsen⟩ **2 :** to draw out or remove as if by percolation ⟨the evil . . . is ~*ed* out of him —I.L.Salomon⟩ **:** draw out or remove something from as if by percolation ⟨the teeth of women during pregnancy are not ~*ed* of their lime salts —F.L.Hise⟩ ~ *vi* **:** to pass out or through by percolation ⟨will not ~ out of the wood with rainwater —*Monsanto Mag.*⟩

leach·abil·i·ty \,lēchə'biləd·ē\ *n* **:** the quality or state of being leachable ⟨experiments on the ~ of salts —*Experiment Station Record*⟩

leach·able \'lēchəbəl\ *adj* **:** capable of being leached

leach·ate \'lē,chāt\ *n* -s **:** the liquid that has percolated through soil or other medium **:** a solution obtained by leaching

leach·er \'lēchə(r)\ *n* -s **:** one that leaches: as **a :** a worker who makes tanning liquor by leaching — called also *leachman* **b :** a worker who leaches minerals from crushed ore **c :** a worker who leaches soda ash from black ash

leach house *n* **:** the part of a tannery where leaching is performed

leaching *n* -s **1 a :** the process or an instance of separating the soluble components from some material by percolation **b :** the process of extracting tannin by boiling ground-up bark or other vegetable tanning material in water **c :** the process or an instance of removing nutritive or harmful elements from soil by percolation **2 :** a product of leaching ⟨swamp water, colored by the ~*s* of gum, cypress, maple, and juniper —*Amer. Guide Series: N.C.*⟩

leach·man \'lēchmən\ *n, pl* **leachmen :** LEACHER

leach's petrel \'lēchəz-\ *or* **leach petrel** *n, usu cap L* [after William E. Leach †1836 Eng. naturalist] **:** a petrel (*Oceanodroma leucorhoa*) distinguished from the storm petrel by its larger size, forked tail, longer wings, andestinctive bounding flight

leachy \'lēchē\ *adj* -ER/-EST [[3]*leach* + *-y*] **:** permitting liquids to pass by percolation **:** not capable of retaining water **:** POROUS, PERVIOUS ⟨a ~ soil⟩

[1]**lead** \'lēd\ *vb* **led** \'led\ **led** \'led\ **leading** \'lēdiŋ, -dēŋ\ **leads** \'lēdz\ [ME *leden*, fr. OE *lǣdan*; akin to OHG *leiten* to lead, ON *leitha*; causative fr. the root of OE *lithan* to go, OHG *līdan* to go, pass, ON *lītha*, Goth *-leithan*; akin to Av *raēθ-* to die, Toch A *lit-* to go away] *vt* **1 a :** to cause to go with oneself **:** take or bring with use of duress ⟨*led* the condemned man to the scaffold⟩ ⟨*led* them captives to a distant land⟩ **b** *dial Brit* (1) **:** to convey (stone, coal, or other materials) in a vehicle (2) **:** to convey (a crop) from the field (as to a place of storage) **2 a** (1) **:** to guide on a way **:** show the way to a place esp. by going with or in advance of ⟨*led* the officers to his hiding place⟩ ⟨can a blind man ~ a blind man —Lk 6: 39 (RSV)⟩ — often used in the phrase *lead the way* ⟨he *led* the way and we followed⟩ (2) **:** to serve as a passage for **:** conduct to some place or in some direction ⟨a road ~*ing* the traveler to the heart of the city⟩ (3) **:** to guide by indicating the way **:** mark out or show the way to ⟨*led* through the fog by the distant lights of the city⟩ (4) **:** to direct or draw the gaze or attention of ⟨we are *led* on from page to page —R.S.Hillyer⟩ ⟨a straight line . . . can ~ the eye in two directions only —C.W.H.Johnson⟩ **b :** to guide or conduct with the hand or by means of some physical contact or connection ⟨a third native . . . to ~ your pony —James Stevenson-Hamilton⟩ **c** (1) **:** to guide or constrain in its passage or course ⟨a rope is *led* around the curve⟩ (2) **:** to conduct or serve as the way or channel for ⟨pipes . . . *led* the water into canals —G.W. Murray⟩ **3 a :** to go through (life or some other period of time) **:** PASS, LIVE ⟨there he *led* a very peaceful existence⟩ ⟨*led* one of the most dramatic careers of criminal history —Anne Brooks⟩ **b :** to cause (another person) to pass a life of a particular kind ⟨she *led* him a dog's life⟩ ⟨such a life as that man *led* me⟩ **4 a** (1) **:** to go with usu. at the head and direct the operations of (an armed force or other expedition) ⟨*led* a cavalry group in a raid behind enemy lines⟩ ⟨*led* a safari into little-known territory⟩ (2) **:** to march in front of **:** go at the head of ⟨a tall drum major *led* the band⟩ — often used in the phrases *lead the way* ⟨*led* the way in the adoption of social legislation⟩ and *lead the van* ⟨*led* the van in solving problems susceptible of certain knowledge —G.C.Sellery⟩ (3) **:** to have the first place in ⟨~*s* the world in the production of steel⟩ ⟨*led* the league for the most double plays —*Current Biog.*⟩ (4) **:** to have a margin of advantage or superiority over ⟨*led* his closest

opponent by 200 votes〉 **b** (1) **:** to take a principal or directing part in **:** have charge or direction of 〈*led* a successful campaign to suspend import duties —*Current Biog.*〉 〈*led* the minority party in the senate〉 (2) **:** to guide by performance of one's own part 〈*led* the congregation in prayers〉 〈*led* the audience in singing the national anthem〉 (3) **:** DIRECT, CONDUCT 〈*led* the orchestra in a poor performance of the overture〉 (4) **:** to guide or direct in a course of study, discussion, or similar group activity 〈~ a Sunday-school class〉 〈~ a discussion group in foreign affairs〉 **c :** to suggest to (a witness) the answer desired by putting leading questions 〈counsel is ~*ing* this witness, putting the words in her mouth —Erle Stanley Gardner〉 **5 a** (1) **:** to bring by reasoning, cogency, or other influence to some conclusion or condition 〈a heart-shaped Venetian map . . . *led* him to the happy belief that the land he discovered was in eastern Asia —Tad Szulc〉 〈reflection *led* him to a better understanding of the problem〉 (2) **:** to prevail upon **:** CAUSE, INDUCE 〈situations which can ~ an inquiring mind to engage in aesthetic thought —Hunter Mead〉 〈this reasoning ~*s* him to propose the creation of a new profession —*Jour. of Accountancy*〉 **b :** ENTICE, ALLURE 〈*led* him into evil courses〉 〈*led* him astray〉 **6 :** to play as the first card or suit of a game, round, or trick 〈going to ~ trumps〉 **7 a :** to aim a weapon in front of (a moving object) 〈~ a duck〉 〈~ an airplane〉 **b :** to pass a ball ahead of (an intended receiver) so that it can be received on the run **c :** to be in advance of in phase 〈in a capacitative circuit the current may ~ the voltage〉 **8 :** to direct (a blow) at an opponent in boxing **~** *vi* **1 a** (1) **:** to guide or conduct someone or something along a way 〈you ~ and we'll follow〉 (2) **:** to guide or direct someone in reference to action or opinion 〈follow the truth of scholarship wherever it may ~ —*New School for Social Research Bull.*〉 〈that sort of project . . . ~*s* on to new fields of endeavor —B.G.Gallagher〉 **b** (1) **:** to serve as a passage 〈flagstone walks ~ to the gateway —*Amer. Guide Series: La.*〉 〈a narrow covered bridge ~*s* across the . . . river —*Amer. Guide Series: Vt.*〉 〈short lanes that ~ to the water —C.R.Sumner〉 (2) **:** to have a specified terminus, course, or direction **:** RUN 〈a long valley ~*ing* up into the heart of the main range —E.E.Shipton〉 〈swampy canals ~ on either side to vast bayous —Tom Marvel〉 〈does the road ~ uphill all the way —O.W.Holmes †1935〉 〈rang by means of a thick yellow rope which *led* down from the belfry —Grace Metalious〉 〈the line ~*s* as if the whale were ahead of the boat when in reality he is right under it —M.A.Chippendale〉 (3) **:** to serve as an entrance, channel, or connection 〈ran to the door that *led* to the kitchen —Kenneth Roberts〉 〈his eyes on the glass window ~*ing* into the reception room —Jane Woodfin〉 **2 a :** to be first or foremost in some respect 〈this state ~*s* in wealth and population〉 〈the incumbents were ~*ing* in all races〉 **b** (1) **:** to begin or open a passage or course of action 〈*led* with "What a superb literal translation" —Bennett Cerf〉 — usu. used with *off* 〈*led* off for the southern opponents of the measure —*Current Biog.*〉 〈will ~ off with a Christmas story —Richard Bissell〉 〈*led* off at bat for the home team〉 (2) **:** to play the first card of a trick, round, or game (3) **:** to direct the first of a series of blows at an opponent in boxing **3 :** to tend toward a definite result **:** EVENTUATE — used with *to* 〈his plan need not ~ to fresh delays —Kenneth Fairfax〉 〈~*s* to overgrazing and the destruction of vegetation —W.B.Fisher〉 〈study ~*ing* to a bachelor of arts degree〉 **syn** see GUIDE — **lead by the nose :** to cause to obey or follow meekly or submissively 〈*leads* her husband *by the nose*〉 — **lead into :** to lead so as to permit the last play to the trick to be made from (a specified hand, high card, or combination of cards) — **lead one a dance :** to subject one to irksome or exasperating experiences **:** put off or thwart one by delays or time-consuming artifices 〈*led* her *boy friend a* fine *dance*〉 — **lead one a merry chase :** to cause one extreme difficulty by speed or evasive tactics 〈*led* his *pursuers a merry chase* over hill and dale〉 — **lead one up the garden path** *also* **lead one up the garden** *Brit* **:** to pull the wool over one's eyes **:** DECEIVE, MISLEAD 〈so you *led us up the garden path* . . . you cooked up a beautiful story —William Sansom〉 — **lead through :** to lead so as to force a play from (a specified player, high card, or combination of cards) before one or more other players play to the table — **lead toward :** to lead so as to force one or more opponents to play before (a specified player, high card, or combination of cards)

[2]**lead** \ˈlēd\ *n* -s [ME *lede* action of leading, guidance, fr. *leden*, v. — more at [1]LEAD] **1 a** (1) **:** position at the front **:** VAN 〈the bowmen were in the ~〉 〈took the ~ on the dark winding road〉 (2) **:** INITIATIVE 〈took the ~ in fighting the measure〉 (3) **:** the act or privilege of playing first in a card game, round, or trick 〈your partner has the ~〉; *also* **:** the card, suit, or piece so played 〈his ~ was the ace〉 (4) **:** the condition of being first to bet voluntarily in a round of a poker game **b** (1) **:** an act of directing or guiding **:** LEADERSHIP 〈look to the president for a unifying ~ —D.W.Brogan〉 (2) **:** EXAMPLE, PRECEDENT 〈followed the ~ of the majority leader in voting〉 **c** (1) **:** the condition or position of having a margin of advantage or superiority **:** the condition of being ahead 〈this country has the ~ over all rivals in steel production〉 〈took the ~ in the race from the first〉 (2) **:** the measure or margin of such advantage or superiority 〈enjoys a good ~ over all competitors〉 〈a ~ of a boat's length〉 **2 :** one that leads or acts as a guide: as **a :** an artificial waterway (as to a mill) **b** (1) **:** the announcement by one voice part of a musical theme to be repeated by the other parts (2) **:** a mark in a canon serving as a cue for the entrance of other parts (3) **:** the first place in change ringing **c :** the player who throws the jack and bowls first in lawn bowling or who throws the first stone in curling **d** (1) **:** LODE (2) **:** an auriferous gravel deposit in an old river bed; *esp* **:** one buried under lava **e :** a channel of water through a field or floe of ice; *esp* **:** one that is wider than a lane **f :** something serving as an indication, tip, or clue 〈may turn up a ~ —Hamilton Basso〉 〈provides ~*s* for further research in Africa —W.R.Bascom〉 **g :** a role for a leading man or leading woman; *also* **:** one who plays such a role **h :** LEASH **i :** a length of net, supported on stakes, placed to guide fish into the pot of a pound net **j** *forestry* **:** a block or series of blocks or rollers attached to a stationary object to guide the cable by which logs are dragged **k** (1) **:** the first summary or introductory section of a news story varying in length from a sentence to several paragraphs 〈reporters would spend hours . . . polishing up ~*s* —C.B.Jones〉 (2) **:** a news story that is of chief importance in an edition of a newspaper and that is usu. given the most prominent display (3) **:** the first and presumably most significant item in a news broadcast **l :** the first of a series of blows delivered by one or both boxers **m :** LEADER 1a(1) **n :** a pattern of movement of a horse at a canter or gallop in which one or the other of the front feet consistently strikes the ground first **o** *Brit* **:** LEADER 1m **p :** the leading or top part in a section of a jazz band 〈one man who blew almost all the ~ —*Metronome*〉; *also* **:** the man who plays that part **3 a** (1) **:** the distance measured along a straight railroad track from the point of switch to the point of frog in a turnout (2) **:** a piece of track leading from a switch to a frog (3) **:** an extended track connecting either end of a yard with the main track (4) **:** the distance from the point where material is excavated to that where it is deposited in roadbed construction **b :** the distance of haul **c** (1) **:** a flexible or solid insulated conductor connected to or leading out from an electrical device (2) **:** the angle between the line joining the brushes of a continuous-current dynamo and the plane perpendicular to the undisturbed magnetic field between the poles (3) **:** the advance of the current phase in an alternating circuit beyond that of the electromotive force producing it **d** (1) **:** the width of port opening at the end of the stroke of a steam engine (2) **:** the distance measured in length of piston stroke or the corresponding angular displacement of the crank of the piston from the end of the compression stroke when ignition takes place in an internal-combustion engine **e** (1) **:** the course of a rope from end to end (2) **:** a line of fire hose extended toward a fire **f** (1) **:** the amount of axial advance of any point in the thread for a complete turn (as of a screw or worm) (2) *usu* **leed :** such rate of advance in the helical rifling of a gun barrel **g :** the distance one leads a moving target **h :** the distance from the start of one climb to the next belay point in mountaineering **i :** a position taken by a base runner off the base in the direction of the next base

[3]**lead** \ˈlēd\ *adj* **1 :** acting as a leader **:** going in front **:** LEADING, LEAD-OFF 〈the ~ mule〉 〈now it was the ~ cruiser's turn to leave the formation —J.A.Michener〉 〈the ~ article in this month's issue〉 **2 :** given prominent display as of first importance 〈a ~ headline〉 〈a ~ editorial〉

[4]**lead** \ˈled\ *n* -s [ME *leed*, fr. OE *lēad*; akin to MD *lood* lead, MHG *lōt*, MIr *luaide*] **1 a :** a heavy soft malleable ductile plastic but inelastic bivalent or tetravalent metallic element that is bluish white when freshly cut but tarnishes readily in moist air to dull gray, that occurs mostly in combination (as in galena and cerussite) and usu. is extracted from its ores by smelting and refined by removal esp. of copper, silver, zinc, and bismuth, and that is used often in the form of alloys chiefly in pipes, sheaths for cables, acid-resistant linings, plates for lead-lead acid cells, solder, type metal, and shields against radioactivity and in making pigments and chemicals — symbol *Pb*; see ACTINIUM SERIES, ELEMENT table, LEAD POISONING, THORIUM SERIES, URANIUM SERIES **b :** a trait or quality suggestive of some attribute of lead; *specif* **:** SLUGGISHNESS 〈perk up and get the ~ out of their heels —Frederick Way〉 **2 a** *dial Eng* **:** a milk pan made of or lined with lead **b :** a plummet or mass of lead (as used in sounding at sea) — see SOUNDING LEAD **c leads** *pl, Brit* **:** a lead roof usu. flat **d leads** *pl* **:** lead framing for a pane (as in a window of lattice-work or stained glass) **e :** a thin strip of metal usu. lead but sometimes brass ranging from ½ to 3 points in thickness, less than type high, and used to separate lines of type; *often* **:** a 2-point lead — compare THICK LEAD, THIN LEAD, REGLET, SLUG **f :** a lead or tin socket to hold one or more needles in a knitting machine by the shanks **3 a :** GRAPHITE 1 **b :** a thin cylinder or stick of marking substance (as graphite) in or for a pencil **c :** WHITE LEAD **4 :** BULLETS, PROJECTILES 〈let fall half a ton of ~ over our lines —P.C.Mitchell〉 〈moved out to Oklahoma when ~ was still law —Whitney Balliett〉 **5 :** a nearly neutral, slightly reddish dark gray that is lighter and slightly bluer than grebe — called also *squirrel* **6 :** TETRAETHYL LEAD

[5]**lead** \ˈled\ *vb* -ED/-ING/-S [ME *leden, leeden*, fr. *leed*, n. — more at [4]LEAD] *vt* **1 a :** to cover or line the inside of with lead **:** clog with lead (as the grooves of a rifle with continuous firing) **b :** to weight with a piece of lead **:** attach lead to **2 a :** to fix (window glass) in position with leads **b :** to secure with melted lead (as a bolt or railing into stonework) — often used with *in* **3 :** to smooth (as the bore of a gun) with a lead lap **4 :** to place leads or other spacing material between the lines of (type matter); *also* **:** to add spacing between the lines of (as printed or photocomposed matter) — often used with *out* **5 :** to treat or mix with lead or a lead compound 〈~*ed* zinc〉 〈~*ed* gasoline〉 **~** *vi* **1 :** to take soundings with the lead **2 :** to become coated or clogged with lead 〈a gun barrel may ~〉

[6]**lead** \ˈled\ *adj* [[4]*lead*] **1 :** relating to or made of lead **:** containing lead 〈~ bullets〉 〈~ pipes〉 〈a ~ mine〉 **2 :** containing lead oxide 〈a ~ glaze〉

lead acetate \ˈled-\ *n* **:** an acetate of lead: as **a :** the poisonous efflorescent soluble crystalline normal salt $Pb(C_2H_3O_2)_2 \cdot 3H_2O$ that has a slightly sweet taste, that is usu. made by reaction of lead monoxide with acetic acid, and that is used chiefly as a mordant in dyeing and printing, as a drier in paint, in the manufacture of other lead salts, and in medicine esp. formerly as an astringent — called also *sugar of lead* **b :** LEAD SUBACETATE **c :** LEAD TETRAACETATE

lead angle \ˈlēd-\ *n* [[2]*lead*] **:** the angle between the tangent to a helix or screw thread and the plane perpendicular to the helical axis

lead arsenate \ˈled-\ *n* **:** an arsenate of lead: as **a :** a crystalline acid salt $PbHAsO_4$ made usu. by reaction of lead monoxide with arsenic pentoxide and used as an insecticide; di-lead orthoarsenate — called also *acid lead arsenate, standard lead arsenate* **b :** a mixture of basic orthoarsenates of lead used as an insecticide esp. on sensitive plants — called also *basic lead arsenate*

lead ash *or* **lead ashes** \ˈled-\ *n* **:** LITHARGE 1

lead azide \ˈled-\ *n* **:** a crystalline explosive compound $Pb(N_3)_2$ made by reaction of sodium azide with lead acetate or lead nitrate and used as a detonating agent

leadback \ˈled,=\ *n* [[4]*lead*] **:** a red-backed sandpiper (*Erolia alpina pacifica*)

lead back \(ˈ)lēd¦=\ *vt* **:** to lead (a card) from a suit that one's partner led originally

lead bullion \ˈled-\ *n* **:** impure lead containing gold and silver

lead-burn \ˈled,=\ *vt* [back-formation fr. *lead burner*] **:** to join (two pieces of lead) by fusion (as in plumbing or roofing or joining storage-battery cells)

lead burner \ˈled-\ *n* [[4]*lead* + *burner*] **:** a worker who welds by lead-burning

lead cable borer \ˈled-\ *n* **:** a western bostrychid beetle (*Scobicia declivis*) that normally bores into hardwood but often damages telephone cables and liquor casks

lead carbonate \ˈled-\ *n* **:** a carbonate of lead: as **a :** the poisonous insoluble normal salt $PbCO_3$ occurring naturally as the mineral cerussite and obtained synthetically as a white crystalline powder **b :** a poisonous basic salt $Pb_3(OH)_2(CO_3)_2$ occurring naturally as the mineral hydrocerussite and obtained synthetically as a component of white lead (sense a)

lead-chamber process \ˈled-\ *n* **:** CHAMBER PROCESS 1

lead chloride \ˈled-\ *n* **:** a chloride of lead; *esp* **:** the poisonous dichloride $PbCl_2$ occurring naturally as the mineral cotunnite and obtained synthetically as insoluble white crystals

lead chromate \ˈled-\ *n* **:** a chromate of lead: as **a :** the poisonous normal salt $PbCrO_4$ that occurs naturally as the mineral crocoite, that is obtained synthetically as a yellow crystalline powder by precipitation from a solution of a lead compound and sodium chromate or sodium dichromate, and that is used as a pigment either alone or in admixture with other compounds **:** CHROME YELLOW **b :** a poisonous basic salt Pb_2OCrO_4 or a mixture of chromates containing it that is used as a reddish yellow to orange to red pigment — compare CHROME ORANGE, CHROME RED

lead colic \ˈled-\ *n* **:** intestinal colic associated with obstinate constipation due to chronic lead poisoning — called also *painter's colic*

lead-collision course \¦lēd-\ *n* **:** an interception course designed for radar-equipped rocket-armed interceptors in which an airplane closes on the target airplane on a straight-line heading which if pursued would end in collision, the rockets being fired automatically to arrive at the point of collision ahead of the interceptor — compare PURSUIT CURVE

lead-colored bush tit \ˈled,=-\ *n* **:** a bush tit (*Psaltriparus minimus plumbeus*) of the arid interior of No. America from Wyoming to western Texas

lead curve \ˈlēd-\ *n* [[2]*lead*] **:** the curve in the turnout interposed between the heel of a railroad switch and the frog

lead dioxide \ˈled-\ *n* **:** a poisonous compound PbO_2 that occurs naturally as the mineral plattnerite but is usu. obtained as an insoluble brown crystalline powder by oxidation (as by electrolysis) of lead monoxide or lead salts and that forms the active material of the positive plates of lead-lead acid cells and as an oxidizing agent in the dye and chemical industries

[1]**lead·en** \ˈledᵊn\ *adj* [ME *leden*, fr. OE *lēaden*, fr. *lēad* lead + *-en*] **1 a :** made of lead 〈a ~ box〉 **b** (1) **:** of the color lead (2) **:** of the color lead gray (3) **:** dull gray **:** DUN 〈a ~ sky〉 〈of a dull ~ paleness —Anthony Trollope〉 **2 a :** lacking value or quality **:** POOR, MEAN 〈his golden tact and ~ taste —H.M.Reichard〉 **b** (1) **:** oppressively heavy 〈all their equipment had become ~ —Norman Mailer〉 〈his body seemed a trifle less ~ —John Buchan〉 **:** OPPRESSIVE 〈a ~ silence fell —Jean Stafford〉 (2) **:** DRAGGING, SLUGGISH 〈had a lot of power and a lot of ~ feet —Ty Cobb〉 **c** (1) **:** DULL, EXPRESSIONLESS, INERT 〈the heavy ~ eyes turn on you —R.W. Emerson〉 〈its hero is a ~ bore —*New Yorker*〉 (2) **:** lacking spirit, animation, or sparkle **:** HEAVY-FOOTED, FLAT 〈giving the music a ~ character —Arthur Berger〉 〈their ironies are ~ —Charles Lee〉 〈there's a rather ~ first act —*Springfield (Mass.) Union*〉 〈this version . . . is full of fine shots of India . . . but the picture itself is ~ —John McCarten〉 — **lead·en·ly** *adv* — **lead·en·ness** \-ᵊn(n)əs\ *n* -ES

[2]**leaden** \ˈ"\ *vt* -ED/-ING/-S **:** to make like lead 〈the dead palace floors had ~*ed* his feet —William Sansom〉 〈a brain ~*ed* with fear〉

leaden flycatcher *n* **:** a small flycatcher (*Myiagra rubecula*) of Australia and New Guinea

lead·er \ˈlēdə(r)\ *n* -S [ME *leder, ledere*, fr. *leden* to lead + *-er, -ere* -er] **1 :** something that leads: as **a** (1) **:** a primary or terminal shoot of a plant (as a main branch of an apple tree or the terminal shoot of a spruce tree) (2) **:** the upper portion of the primary axis of a tree esp. when extending beyond the rest of the head and forming the apex **b :** a remark or question intended or likely to bring a response esp. of a particular kind **:** a leading remark or question 〈did not respond to his tactful ~〉 **c :** TENDON, SINEW 〈the ~*s* in his wrists moved like baling wire —Dillon Anderson〉 **d :** the principal wheel in machinery; *also* **:** a part to guide exactly the motion of another piece **e leaders** *pl* (1) **:** dots or hyphens (as in a table or index) to lead the eye horizontally across a space to the right word or number (2) **:** a piece of type faced with a row of dots or hyphens **f** *chiefly Brit* **:** a newspaper editorial **g :** a branch or small vein leading to a larger one in a mine **h :** a thin paper tube containing quick match to cause rapid ignition (as of fireworks) **i** (1) **:** a net, fence, or wall for leading fish into a pound, weir, or trap (2) **:** a short length of material (as silkworm gut, wire, or heavy line) used to attach the end of a fishline to a lure or hook **j :** a pipe for conducting water or other fluid to some particular place (as a rainwater pipe from a roof to a cistern or the ground or a hot-air pipe in a heating system for a building) **k :** an article of value offered at an attractive special low price to stimulate business — compare LOSS LEADER **l :** LEAD 3a(2) **m :** a short length of blank film attached to each end of a filmstrip or of a reel of motion-picture film for threading into a film mechanism **n :** a length of yarn, rope, or cloth left threaded in a machine (as a textile machine) to act as a guide for new material attached to it **o** *or* **leader stroke :** an electrical discharge that precedes the main discharge and ionizes the path through which the main discharge surges (as in a lightning stroke) **p :** something that ranks first or has a margin of advantage or precedence over others 〈the ~*s* among major communicable diseases〉 〈steel and utilities were the ~*s* in today's stock market〉 **2 :** a person or animal that leads: as **a :** GUIDE, CONDUCTOR 〈acted as our ~ on the hazardous climb〉 **b** (1) **:** a person who directs and usu. accompanies an armed force **:** COMMANDER, CAPTAIN 〈captains of war, and ~*s* of their armies —John Locke〉 (2) **:** a person who by force of example, talents, or qualities of leadership plays a directing role, wields commanding influence, or has a following in any sphere of activity or thought 〈the great religious ~*s* of mankind〉 〈a ~ in the reform movement〉 〈summoned a conference of business ~*s*〉 **c** (1) **:** the principal officer of a British political party who usu. exercises authority over both the parliamentary party and the national party organization 〈while the party remains in opposition the ~ of the Parliamentary Labour Party has nothing like the authority granted by the Conservative Party to its ~ —R.T.McKenzie〉 (2) **:** a member often chosen by caucus of his party to exercise general direction of or management of a particular phase of party activities in a legislative body — usu. used with a qualifier — compare FLOOR LEADER, LEADER OF THE OPPOSITION, MAJORITY LEADER, MINORITY LEADER (3) **:** such a member exercising primary authority over the business of the whole legislative body when his party constitutes a majority in the house — usu. used in phrases including the name of the legislative body 〈responsible to the prime minister as ~ of the House —T.E.May〉 〈~ of the House of Lords〉 〈the ~ of the Executive Council . . . in New Zealand —Walter Nash〉 (4) **:** one that exercises paramount but to some degree responsible authority over a state or local party organization 〈the ~ is seldom the titular head of the party organization —H.R.Penniman〉 〈the ~ of the Connecticut Democratic party〉 — compare [5]BOSS 3a (5) **:** the principal member of the party elite in a totalitarian system (as fascism or naziism) endowed by official ideology with a heroic or mystical character, exercising state power with a minimum of formal constitutional restraints, and characterized by extreme use of nationalist demagogy and claims to be above narrow class or group interests 〈the ~ manipulates the people as an artist molds clay —G.H.Sabine〉 **d** (1) **:** CONDUCTOR 6 (2) **:** the leading performer of a musical ensemble 〈the concertmaster is the ~ of the violin section〉 **e :** the front or foremost person in a file or advancing body **f :** the first player in any of various games **g** (1) **:** a horse placed in advance of others (as either of a forward pair of horses or the front horse of a tandem team) (2) *Midland* **:** LEAD HORSE **h :** a person who directs a class in the Methodist Church **i :** the counsel in an English legal proceeding who is entitled to precedence over his associates or is entitled to manage a case **j** (1) **:** an adult immediately responsible for the guidance of a Girl Scout troop (2) **:** a woman who guides the activities of blue birds — compare ADVISER, GUARDIAN **k :** a skilled employee who supervises one or more groups of workers **:** STRAW BOSS, FOREMAN

leader head *n* **:** a box usu. of metal placed at the top of a leader to collect roof water

lead·er·less \-(r)ləs\ *adj* **:** being without a leader

lead·er·man \-(r)mən\ *n, pl* **leadermen :** a subforeman in a shipyard

leader of the opposition : the principal member of the opposition party in a British legislative body who is given the status of a salaried government official and an important role in organizing the business of the house 〈one of the ministers will open the debate and he will . . . be followed by the *leader of the opposition* —Eric Taylor〉

leader pin *n* **:** GUIDE PIN

lead·er·ship \ˈlēdə(r),ship\ *n* **1 :** the office or position of a leader 〈forced from the ~ by younger men —*Collier's Yr. Bk.*〉 〈could not have maintained that ~ without her reputation for fair play —Lewis Galantiere〉 〈assumed ~ of the opposition〉 **2 a :** the quality of a leader **:** capacity to lead 〈could not fail to perceive that there was no ~ in him —S.H. Adams〉 〈~ is that ingredient of personality which causes men to follow —H.S.Gilbertson〉 〈only a few people possess the quality of ~ —J.A.Schumpeter〉 **b :** the act or an instance of leading 〈the essence of ~ is the successful resolution of problems —Dean Acheson〉 〈true ~ . . . is enlightenment and exhortation —Max Eastman〉 〈fought bravely under his ~〉 〈~ molds individuals into a team —Harold Koontz & Cyril O'Donnell〉 **c :** a group of persons who lead 〈a ~ is one of the major functional divisions to be found in all groups —H.D.Lasswell & Abraham Kaplan〉 〈the party ~ ignored the dispute —Frank Tollman〉 〈recruit youth ~ in the conduct of recreation activity —*Springfield (Mass.) Union*〉

leader tape *n* **:** a nonmagnetic tape of paper or plastic used in magnetic recording at the beginning or end of a reel or as a marking for the beginning of a selection within the tape

lead glance \ˈled-\ *n* [trans. of G *bleiglanz*] **:** GALENA

lead glass \ˈled-\ *n* **:** glass containing a high proportion of lead oxide and having a relatively high refractive index and high dispersion value

lead grass \ˈled-\ *n* [[4]*lead* + *grass*; prob. fr. its weight] **:** GLASSWORT

lead gray \ˈled-\ *n* **1 :** a brownish gray **2 :** a light grayish olive

lead·hill·ite \ˈled,hi,līt\ *n* -S [F, fr. *Leadhills*, Lanarkshire, Scotland + F *-ite*] **:** a monoclinic mineral $Pb_4(SO_4)(CO_3)_2(OH)_2$ of a yellowish or greenish white color consisting of basic sulfate and carbonate of lead

lead horse \ˈlēd-\ *n, dial* **:** the horse on the left side in a team of two — called also *leader*

leadier *comparative of* LEADY

leadiest *superlative of* LEADY

[1]**lead-in** \ˈlē,din\ *n, pl* **lead-ins** [fr. *lead in*, v.] **:** something that leads into something else: as **a :** the part of a radio antenna that runs from the larger or main elevated portion to the transmitting or receiving set **b :** something that opens or introduces **:** something that gradually leads the eye or attention from one thing to another 〈with a front-cover portrait serving as a *lead-in* to a five-page article —*Publishers' Weekly*〉 〈a *lead-in* which can attract people who don't agree with you —P.P.Van Riper〉; *specif* **:** that part of a radio program or a radio broadcaster's talk which leads into the commercial 〈tuneful program *lead-ins* —*Advertising Age*〉

²lead-in \"\ *adj* **:** that leads in — used esp. of an electrical conductor ⟨a *lead-in* wire⟩; see INCANDESCENT LAMP illustration

¹leading \'lēdiŋ, -dēŋ\ *n* -s [ME *leding*, fr. gerund of *leden* to lead, conduct] **1 a :** the act or an instance of conducting from one place to another ⟨proposed a ~ of the excess water to arid lands⟩ **b** (1) **:** the act or an instance of commanding or directing **:** COMMAND, LEADERSHIP ⟨entrusted the ~ of the army to the earl⟩ (2) *archaic* **:** ability to lead or command **:** AUTHORITY ⟨men of great ~ and property in the state⟩ **2 :** capacity to enlighten **:** GUIDANCE, ENLIGHTENMENT — usu. used in the phrase *men of light and leading* ⟨commissioned six men of light and ~ to settle the . . . question —Ernest Weekley⟩

²leading \'lē-\ *adj* [fr. pres. part. of ¹*lead*] **1 a :** preceding others in order of march or other movement **:** coming first ⟨the ~ boat was destroyed before it had a chance to fire⟩ **b :** ranking first or among the first in regard to influence, importance, or popularity ⟨a ~ topic of conversation⟩ ⟨the ~ ski center in this area⟩ ⟨among the ~ infectious diseases⟩ ⟨a ~ item in all the stores⟩ ⟨played a ~ part in the settlement of the colony⟩ **c :** exercising leadership in some area **:** according or meriting prominence as a leader ⟨a ~ citizen of the town⟩ ⟨a ~ exponent of the dance⟩ ⟨married into one of the ~ pastoral families —E.H.Collis⟩ ⟨a ~ literary critic⟩ **d :** GUIDING, DIRECTING ⟨a ~ thread in American foreign policy⟩ ⟨what are his ~ motives⟩ **e :** given prominent or most prominent display ⟨the ~ story in this morning's paper⟩ ⟨a ~ editorial⟩ **2 :** being in advance during normal rotation or motion — used esp. of an edge or side of a mechanical part **3 :** ranking immediately below a petty or noncommissioned officer in the British armed forces ⟨~ seaman⟩ ⟨~ signalman⟩ ⟨~ aircraftsman⟩ **syn** see CHIEF

³leading \'lediŋ, -dēŋ\ *n* -s [ME *leeding* action of covering or lining with lead, fr. gerund of *leden*, *leeden* to lead, cover or line with lead] **:** a covering or framework of lead **:** LEADWORK ⟨the ~ of a Tudor window⟩

leading article \'lē-\ *n* **1** *chiefly Brit* **:** EDITORIAL — compare LEADER 1f **2 :** the article given the most significant position or most prominent display in a periodical

leading case \'lē-\ *n* **:** a case so well reasoned and important in the rules of law determined and in the principles declared that it becomes well known and is frequently cited by courts and lawyers as not only settling the points of law ruled upon, but as of assistance in resolving new questions of law

leading edge \'lē-\ *n* **1 :** the foremost edge of an airfoil or propeller blade **2 :** the forward edge of a part on a vehicle or of something that itself moves ⟨the *leading edge* of an automobile hood⟩ ⟨the *leading edge* of an air mass⟩

leading lady \'lē-\ *n* **:** an actress who plays the leading feminine role in a play or movie

leading light \'lē-\ *n* **1 :** a light that serves as a navigational guide (as in entering or leaving port) **2 :** a prominent and influential member (as of a community or church)

leading load \'lē-\ *n* **:** CONDENSIVE LOAD

lead·ing·ly \'lē-\ *adv* **:** in a leading manner

leading man \'lē-\ *n* **:** an actor who plays the leading male role in a play or movie

leading mark \'lē-\ *n* **:** a conspicuous object (as a prominent landmark easily seen from seaward) that serves as a navigational guide (as in entering or leaving port)

leading motive \'lē-\ *n* [trans. of G *leitmotiv*] **:** a dominant motive in or leading to action; *specif* **:** a musical leitmotiv

leading question \'lē-\ *n* **:** a question so framed as to guide the person questioned in making his reply **:** LEADER

leading rein \'lē-\ *n* **:** the use of an opened-out rein in such a way as to direct the horse's head and neck to the left or right

lead-in groove \'lē,din-\ *n* **:** a blank spiral groove extending from the outer edge of a disc to the beginning of recording and having a distance of pitch that is much greater than normal

leading stone \'lē-\ *n* **:** LODESTONE

leading strings \'lē-\ *n pl* **1 :** strings by which children are sometimes supported when beginning to walk **2 :** a state of dependence or tutelage **:** GUIDANCE ⟨*leading strings* had been so willingly accepted that they were scarcely felt —E.M. Forster⟩ — usu. used in the phrase *in leading strings* ⟨no longer in *leading strings* to his wife or his wife's father —Francis Hackett⟩ ⟨passed his whole adolescence in his mother's *leading strings* —Van Wyck Brooks⟩

leading tone *or* **leading note** \'lē-\ *n* **:** the seventh musical degree of a major or minor scale — called also *subtonic*

leading-tone seventh *or* **leading seventh** \'lē-\ *n* **:** a musical seventh chord composed of the seventh, second, fourth, and sixth notes or tones of the major scale — compare TRIAD; see SEVENTH CHORD illustration

leading truck \'lē-\ *n* **:** a swiveling frame mounted on two or four wheels under the front of a locomotive to guide it around curves and help carry the weight

leading wheel \'lē-\ *n* **:** a wheel situated before the driving wheels of a locomotive

leading wind \'lē-\ *n* **:** a free or fair wind

lead-lead acid cell \'led;led-\ *n* **:** a storage cell in which the positive plate is lead dioxide, the negative plate is spongy lead, and the electrolyte is dilute sulfuric acid

lead·less \'ledləs\ *adj* **1 :** being without lead **2 :** not using lead — used of a printing process (as photocomposition)

¹**lead line** \'led-\ *n* [ME *leede lyne*, fr. *leede*, *leed* lead + *lyne*, *line* line] **1 a :** SOUNDING LINE **b** *usu* **leadline :** the lower line of a gillnet having lead or other weights at intervals to keep the bottom of the net submerged — compare CORKLINE **2 :** a dark line along the gums due to deposition of lead sulfide (as in chronic exposure to lead compounds or fumes)

²**lead line** \'lēd,=\ *n* [²*lead* + *line*] **1 :** a wire rope with an eye at each end used to anchor the snatch block in setting a lead in logging **2 :** a line for leading a horse usu. for excercise

¹**lead·man** \'ledmən, -,man\ *n*, *pl* **leadmen** [⁴*lead*] **:** SOUNDER, ¹LEADSMAN

²**lead·man** \'lēdmən, -,man\ *n*, *pl* **leadmen** [²*lead*] **:** LEADER 2k

lead monoxide \'led-\ *n* **:** a poisonous compound PbO that is obtained usu. in different yellow to brownish red forms by heating lead moderately in air and that is used chiefly in making plates for lead-lead acid cells, in compounding rubber, in glass, glazes, and vitreous enamels, and in the manufacture of other lead compounds — see LITHARGE, MASSICOT

lead nitrate \'led-\ *n* **:** a poisonous soluble crystalline salt $Pb(NO_3)_2$ obtained by reaction of lead or a lead compound with nitric acid and used chiefly in making other lead salts and in fireworks; *also* **:** any of several closely related basic salts

lead ocher \'led-\ *n* **:** MASSICOT 2

lead off \(')lē,dȯf, -däf\ *vt* **:** to make a start on **:** OPEN ⟨*led off* his comments by describing details of the attack —*N.Y. Times*⟩ ⟨able to *lead off* another offensive —H.L.Merillat⟩

leadoff \'lē,d-\ *n* -s [*lead off*] **1 :** a beginning or leading action; *specif* **:** a hit made in offense in boxing **2 :** a player who leads off; *esp* **:** the player who heads the batting order or bats first in an inning in baseball

lead-off \'=,=\ *adj* [*lead off*] **:** leading off **:** STARTING, OPENING ⟨a *lead-off* batter⟩ ⟨my *lead-off* proposal —Inez Robb⟩ ⟨the *lead-off* essay —Clifton Fadiman⟩

lead oleate \'led-\ *n* **:** a poisonous white powder or yellowish pasty mass made usu. by precipitation from solutions of a lead salt and a commercial sodium oleate and used chiefly as an additive to lubricants and as the base for a medicinal plaster or a molding wax — compare DIACHYLON

lead on \(')lē,dȯn, -dän\ *vt* **:** to entice or induce to proceed in a course esp. when unwise or mistaken ⟨a more or less ignorant girl is *led on* by her irresponsible lover —H.M. Parshley⟩ ⟨*led* me *on* to think that he loved me⟩

lead-out groove \'lē,daut-\ *n* [*lead-out* fr. the phrase *lead out*] **:** a blank spiral groove of coarse pitch extending from the end of a recording inward to the locked or eccentric groove near the disc center

lead-over groove \'lē,dōvə(r)-\ *n* [*lead-over* fr. the phrase *lead over*] **:** a coarse-pitch groove joining recordings of short duration to carry the pickup stylus from one recording to the next on the record

lead oxide \'led-\ *n* **:** a binary compound of lead and oxygen; *esp* **:** LEAD MONOXIDE — compare LEAD DIOXIDE, MINIUM, RED LEAD

lead palsy \'led-\ *n* **:** localized paralysis caused by lead poisoning esp. of the extensor muscles of the forearm leading to wristdrop

lead pencil \'led-\ *n* **:** a pencil of which the marking material is graphite

lead peroxide \'led-\ *n* **:** LEAD DIOXIDE — not used systematically

lead-pipe cinch \'led,=-\ *also* **lead-pipe** *n* [*lead-pipe* fr. the phrase *lead pipe* pipe made of lead, fr. ME *lede pype*, fr. *lede*, *leed* lead + *pype*, *pipe* pipe] *slang* **:** something very easy or certain ⟨ought to be a *lead-pipe cinch* to find —*Big Detective Cases*⟩ ⟨if it wasn't him it was you and that's a *lead-pipe cinch* —Nelson Algren⟩

leadplant \'led,=\ *n* **:** any of several American shrubs of the genus *Amorpha*; *esp* **:** a shrub (*A. canescens*) of the western U.S. having hoary pinnate leaves and dull-colored racemose flowers and in some opinions indicating the presence of lead ore

lead poisoning \'led-\ *n* **:** chronic intoxication produced by the absorption of lead into the system and characterized by anemia with stippling of red cells, severe colicky pains, a blue lead line on the gums, and local muscular paralysis (as wrist=drop) — called also *plumbism*, *saturnism*

leads *pres 3d sing of* LEAD, *pl of* LEAD

lead screw \'lēd-\ *n* **:** the screw that moves the tool carriage of a lathe when cutting threads — compare FEED SCREW

lead sheet \'lēd-\ *n* **:** the manuscript of a song consisting of the melody, words, and indication of the basic harmony written in simple form

lead silicate \'led-\ *n* **:** any of various salts (as the normal monosilicate $PbSiO_3$) made by reaction of lead monoxide or a lead salt with silica or a silicate and used chiefly in glass and ceramics and as pigments (as in compounding rubber) — see WHITE LEAD c

¹**leads·man** \'ledzmən\ *n*, *pl* **leadsmen** [*lead's* (gen. of ⁴*lead*) + *man*] **:** a man who uses a sounding lead to determine depth of water

²**leads·man** \'lēdzmən\ *n*, *pl* **leadsmen** [*lead's* (gen. of ²*lead*) + *man*] **:** ²LEAD 2c

lead soap \'led-\ *n* **:** any of various lead salts of higher carboxylic acids (as fatty acids) esp. for use as a drier in paints and varnishes or as an additive to lubricants

lead spar \'led-\ *n* **:** CERUSSITE

lead subacetate \'led-\ *n* **:** a poisonous basic salt $Pb(C_2H_3O_2)_2.PbO$ used esp. in solution (as in Goulard's extract); basic lead acetate

lead sulfate \'led-\ *n* **:** a sulfate of lead: as **a :** the poisonous normal sulfate $PbSO_4$ occurring native as anglesite and obtained synthetically as a white crystalline powder **b :** any of several basic salts (as the monobasic sulfate Pb_2OSO_4 occurring naturally as lanarkite) or a mixture containing one or more of these used as a pigment — compare ²BLUE LEAD 2, WHITE LEAD b

lead sulfide \'led-\ *n* **:** a compound PbS occurring naturally as the mineral galena and obtained synthetically as a black precipitate when solutions of lead salts are exposed to hydrogen sulfide

lead-swinger \'led,swiŋə(r)\ *n* [⁴*lead* + *swinger* (one that swings); perh. fr. the belief of some sailors that the leadsman's job is an easy one] *chiefly Austral* **:** SHIRKER, SLACKER; *esp* **:** MALINGERER ⟨the sick and the lame, the halt and the *lead-swinger* —I.L.Idriess⟩

lead tetraacetate \'led-\ *n* **:** a poisonous crystalline compound $Pb(C_2H_3O_2)_4$ made usu. by reaction of red lead with glacial acetic acid and used as an oxidizing agent esp. in organic synthesis

lead tetraethyl \'led-\ *n* **:** TETRAETHYL LEAD

lead time \'lēd-\ *n* **1 :** the time interval between the conception or designing of a product and its actual production and use **2 :** the time interval between the placing of an order and delivery

lead track \'lēd-\ *n* **:** ²LEAD 3a(3)

lead tree \'led-\ *n* **1 :** lead crystallized in arborescent forms from a solution of some lead salt (as by suspending a strip of zinc in lead acetate) **2 :** a plant of the genus *Leucaena*; *esp* **:** a low scrubby tree (*Leucaena glauca*) prob. native to tropical America but now pantropical in distribution and often cultivated as a ground cover, for windrows or hedging, and as forage for cattle and sheep though reputedly toxic to horses and swine

lead up \(')lē¦dəp\ *vt*, *obs* **:** to lead off (a dance) ~ *vi* **1 :** to prepare the way **:** constitute the antecedents or preliminaries — used with *to* ⟨the series of events which *led up* to the former's dismissal —*Current Biog.*⟩ ⟨the first 60 pages of this book *lead up* to the revolution of 1911 —*Times Lit. Supp.*⟩ **2 :** to make a gradual or indirect approach to a topic — used with *to* ⟨would she let her have the dress? Perhaps she should have *led up* to it —Stuart Cloete⟩

lead-up \'lē,dəp\ *n* [*lead up*] **:** something that leads up to or prepares the way for something else ⟨the race will serve as a *lead-up* to the classic —*Sydney (Australia) Bull.*⟩

lead water \'led-\ *n* **:** Goulard's extract diluted with water

leadwood \'led,=\ *n* **1 :** LEATHERWOOD 1a **2 :** an African tree or shrub (*Combretum imberbe*) with pale gray bark and small pale green leaves

lead wool \'led-\ *n* **:** lead in the form of fine shreds or shavings used for calking pipe joints

leadwork \'led,=\ *n* **1 :** something made of lead **2 :** work that is done with lead

leadwort \'led,=\ *n* **1 :** a plant of the family Plumbaginaceae esp. of the genus *Plumbago*; *specif* **:** a plant (*P. europaea*) with lead-blue flowers **2 :** LEADPLANT

leady \'ledē, -di\ *adj* -ER/-EST [ME *leedy*, fr. *leed* lead + -*y*] **:** containing or resembling lead

¹**leaf** \'lēf\ *n*, *pl* **leaves** \'lēvz\ [ME *leef*, fr. OE *lēaf*; akin to OHG *loub* leaf, foliage, ON *lauf*, Goth *laufs* leaf, foliage, L *liber* inner bark of a tree, pith of papyrus, book, Gk *lypē* grief, pain, Skt *lumpati* he injures, robs, Russ *lupit'* to peel, *lub* bast; basic meaning: to peel] **1 a** (1) **:** a lateral outgrowth from a stem that constitutes part of the foliage of a plant and functions primarily in food manufacture by photosynthesis, that arises in regular succession from the growing point, that consists typically of a flattened green blade which is joined to the stem by a petiole often with a pair of stipules at its base, which in cross section exhibits an outer covering of epidermal cells penetrated by stomata usu. more numerous on the lower surface, which has one or more layers of palisade cells beneath the upper epidermis and between these and the lower epidermis a mass of spongy parenchyma cells, both palisade and spongy tissue being ramified by a network of veins, and that is distinguished from a leaflet, cladophyll, or phylloclade by the presence of a bud at the juncture of petiole and stem and from a phyllode by differentiation into blade and petiole (2) **:** any of various modified leaves (as a bract, sepal, petal, or scale) that are primarily engaged in functions other than food manufacture; *esp* **:** FLORAL LEAF (3) **:** PETAL ⟨a candied rose ~⟩ **b** (1) **:** the leaves of trees or plants **:** FOLIAGE (2) **:** the leaves of any plant as an article of commerce; *specif* **:** the leaves of the tea plant **c** (1) **:** tobacco leaves; *also* **:** the leaf form of tobacco ⟨Connecticut seed ~⟩ (2) **:** raw unmanufactured tobacco (3) **:** the whole leaf **:** unstemmed tobacco (4) **:** a grade of tobacco leaves consisting of those of the best quality — distinguished from *seconds* and *lugs* **2 :** something resembling or suggestive of a leaf: as **a :** a part of a book or folded sheet containing two pages, one on each side; *also* **:** the written or printed matter on it **b** (1) **:** a side, division, or part (as of window shutters, folding doors, hydraulic gates) that slides or is hinged (2) **:** the movable parts of a table top whether hinged or separate (as in an extension table) (3) **:** one of the moving portions of a drawbridge (4) **:** LEAF SIGHT (5) **:** either flap of a hinge **c** *now chiefly dial* **:** one of the layers of fat about the kidneys of a hog; *also* **:** a similar layer of fat in other animals **d** (1) **:** a thin sheet or plate of any natural or artificial substance **:** LAMINA ⟨the *leaves* of a gill⟩ (2) **:** metal in thin layers usu. thinner than foil ⟨silver ~⟩ **e :** an ornament (as on a capital) shaped like a leaf **f** (1) **:** a tooth of a pinion (as of a gear pinion) (2) **:** one of the cylindrical pieces serving as the teeth of a lantern pinion (3) **:** one of the plates of a leaf spring **g** *dial Brit* **:** a hat brim **h :** a thin section of a filter consisting of a frame or wire screen covered by a filter medium (as cloth) — called also *filter leaf* **i :** a loop of a leaf-shaped curve **j :** HARNESS 4 **k :** isinglass dried in the form of a leaf **l :** a foundry molder's leaf-shaped trowel or tool — **in leaf :** in or with foliage ⟨lush pasture and woods *in leaf* —Thomas Wood †1950⟩

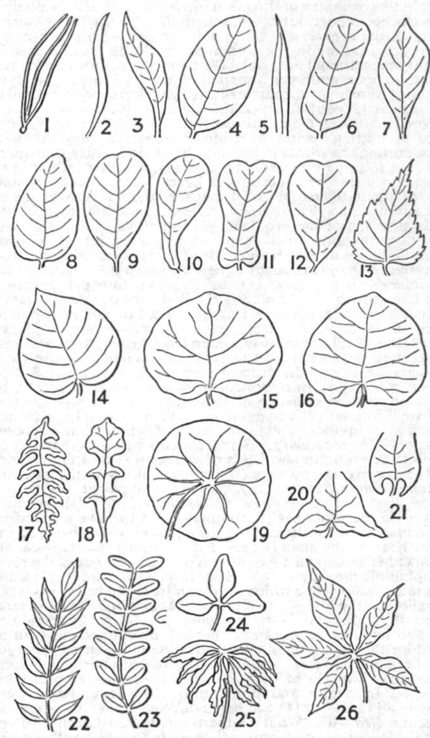

forms of leaves: *1* acerate; *2* linear; *3* lanceolate; *4* elliptic; *5* ensiform; *6* oblong; *7* oblanceolate, with acuminate tip; *8* ovate in form, with acute tip; *9* obovate; *10* spatulate; *11* pandurate; *12* cuneate; *13* deltoid; *14* cordate; *15* reniform; *16* orbiculate; *17* runcinate; *18* lyrate; *19* peltate; *20* hastate; *21* sagittate; *22* odd-pinnate; *23* abruptly pinnate; *24* palmate (trifoliolate) *25* palmate (pedate in form with margin incised) *26* palmate (quinquefoliolate)

²**leaf** \"\ *vb* -ED/-ING/-S *vi* **1 :** to shoot out or produce leaves **:** LEAVE ⟨chestnuts which were just ~*ing* in the spring sun —M.E.Bates⟩ — often used with *out* ⟨a fern just ~*ing* out —W.V.T.Clark⟩ **2** *of metallic powder in enamel or paint* **:** to assume an overlapping arrangement like that of fish scales on a painted or coated surface **3 :** to turn over the pages — often used with *through* ⟨~*s* through the old newspaper files —Francis Russell⟩ ⟨~*ing* through the fifteen letters that had come from her —Norman Mailer⟩ ~ *vt* **:** to turn over esp. one by one ⟨~*ed* the pages —Louis Vaczek⟩ ⟨~*ed* his notes a final time —Kathryn Grondahl⟩ **:** turn over the pages of ⟨~*ing* a new novel⟩

³**leaf** \"\ *adj* **1 :** of, relating to, or in the form of a leaf ⟨~ fiber⟩ **2 :** LEAVED — used in combination ⟨clover-*leaf*⟩ ⟨cut-*leaf*⟩

leaf·age \'lēfij, -fēj\ *n* -s **1 a :** a quantity of leaves **:** LEAVES ⟨much ~ was also found in the nests —*Ecology*⟩ **b :** the leaves of plants as produced in nature **:** FOLIAGE ⟨the deep ~ of a garden —Anne D. Sedgwick⟩ ⟨crouched amongst the ~ watching them —W.H.Hudson †1922⟩ ⟨maples in ~ full —Mary Austin⟩ **2 :** the representation of foliage esp. for ornamental purposes ⟨all four legs of the table show scrolls and ~ —*Antiques*⟩

leaf and square *n* **:** a small plasterer's tool for modeling and ornamental work consisting of a handle with a leaf-shaped blade at one end and a rectangular blade at the other

leaf and square

leaf-and-tongue *or* **leaf-and-dart** \¦==¦=\ *n* **:** an ornamental pattern of alternating leaves and narrow tongues or darts

leaf beet *n* **:** SPINACH BEET

leaf beetle *n* **:** a beetle of the family Chrysomelidae

leafbird \'=,=\ *n* **:** GREEN BULBUL

leaf bite *n* **:** a disease of the coconut palm esp. in Jamaica caused by an imperfect fungus (*Thielaviopsis paradoxa*)

leaf blight *n* **:** a plant disease characterized by a general browning, death of foliage, and falling of leaves: **a :** FIRE BLIGHT 1 **b :** LEAF CAST

leaf blister *n* **:** any of several diseases caused by leaf-curl fungi of the genus *Taphrina*: as **a :** a disease of the pear caused by a fungus (*T. bullata*) **b :** a disease of the oak caused by a fungus (*T. coerulescens*)

leaf-blister sawfly *n* **:** a sawfly (*Phylacteophaga eucalypti*) whose larvae damage eucalyptus foliage in Australia

leaf blotch *n* **:** a plant disease esp. of fungous origin producing irregular dead or discolored areas in the leaves and distinguished from leaf spot mainly by the more indistinct or diffuse margins

leaf-book \'=,=\ *n* **:** CODEX 2

leafboy \'=,=\ *n* **:** a person who supplies the stringers with tobacco leaves from the baskets in which they are brought from the field in harvesting primed tobacco

leaf bud *n* **1 :** a bud that develops into a leafy shoot and does not produce flowers — compare FLOWER BUD, MIXED BUD **2 :** a grayish yellowish brown that is darker than deer, slightly darker than acorn, and slightly yellower than olive wood

leaf-bud cutting *n* **:** a cutting consisting of a segment of current season's growth with a leaf, axillary bud, and a small section of stem used in the propagation of various plants — called also *leaf mallet cutting*

leaf bug *n* **:** any of various bugs esp. of the families Tingidae and Miridae; *specif* **:** FOUR-LINED PLANT BUG

leaf bundle *n* **:** LEAF TRACE

leaf butterfly *n* **:** any of various butterflies that mimic leaves; *esp* **:** those constituting the nymphalid genus *Kallima* found in southern Asia and the East Indies

leaf case moth *n* **:** a bagworm (*Hyalarcta hübneri*) that damages leaves and fruit in Australia

leaf cast *n* **:** any of several diseases of conifers (as that caused by fungi of the order Hysteriales) producing a falling of the needles

leaf chafer *n* **:** a scarabaeid beetle that feeds as an adult on foliage of various plants

leaf climber *n* **:** a climbing plant that supports itself by means of its leaves which either have petioles (as in the clematis) that twist round the support or develop tendrils (as in the pea)

leaf-climbing \'=¦==\ *adj* **:** supporting itself by means of its leaves ⟨a *leaf-climbing* plant⟩

leaf crumpler *n* **:** any of several small American moths or their caterpillars that form a nest by crumpling and fastening leaves together in clusters; *esp* **:** a moth (*Acrobasis indigenella*) of the family Pyralidae that feeds on the apple and related trees

leafcup \'=,=\ *n* **:** either of two tall coarse weedy No. American perennial composite herbs (*Polymnia uvedalia* and *P. canadensis*) that are strongly scented and have large thin opposite leaves and panicled corymbs of pale yellow or whitish flower heads

leaf curl *n* **:** a plant disease characterized by curling of leaves: as **a :** a disease of peaches caused by a fungus (*Taphrina deformans*) **b :** LEAF ROLL **c :** a virus disease of raspberries — called also *raspberry curl* **d :** EARLY BLIGHT a

leaf–cushion \'=,=\ *n* **:** the remnant of the thickened leaf base remaining after abscission in some extinct plants and in various conifers (as members of the genus *Picea*)

leaf cutter *n* **1 :** LEAF-CUTTING ANT **2** *or* **leaf–cutter bee :** LEAF-CUTTING BEE

leaf cutting *n* [[1]*leaf* + *cutting*, n.] **:** a cutting consisting of a leaf instead of a shoot commonly used in propagating a plant (as begonia, gloxinia, African violet) — see SECTIONAL LEAF CUTTING

leaf–cutting ant \'=,==-\ *n* [*leaf-cutting* fr. [1]*leaf* + *cutting*, pres. part. of *cut*] **:** any of several chiefly tropical American ants of the genus *Atta* that cut and carry off the leaves of plants which they use in culturing various fungi for food

leaf–cutting bee *n* **:** any of various wild bees of the genus *Megachile* that cut rounded and oval pieces from the edges of leaves or petals to use in building their nests

leaf disease *n* **1 :** a disease localized in the foliage **2 :** a coffee disease caused by a rust fungus (*Hemileia vastatrix*) — called also *coffee disease*

leaf drop *n* **:** a premature falling of leaves (as the blighting and drooping of leaves associated with various virus diseases of the potato) — compare LEAF FALL

leaf–drop streak *n* **:** a phase of rugose mosaic developing soon after infection and characterized by necrotic streaks on the stem and underside of the veins of some of the leaves and by falling of the leaves from the lowest upward

leaf–eating ladybird \'=,==-\ *n* **:** an Australian coccinellid beetle (*Epilachna 28-punctata*) whose larvae and adults damage potatoes and other plants

leafed \'lēft\ *adj* **:** having leaves **:** having leaves of a specified character or number — used chiefly in combination ⟨broad=leafed⟩ ⟨three-leafed⟩

leaf·er \'lēfə(r)\ *n* -s **:** a bindery worker who inserts leaves or sheets

leaf·ery \'lēf(ə)rē\ *n* -ES **:** LEAFAGE

leaf fall *n* **1 :** the natural separation and dropping of the leaf at the end of the growing season and over a short period in deciduous plants or intermittently throughout the year in coniferous trees — compare ABSCISSION **2 :** fallen leaves on the forest floor

leaf fat *n* **:** the fat that lines the abdominal cavity and encloses the kidneys of a hog and that is used in the manufacture of leaf lard and neutral lard

leaf feeding *n* **:** the application of nutrients to the foliage of plants

leaf fish *n* [so called fr. its resemblance to a floating dead leaf] **:** a small brown nandid fish (*Monocirrhus polyacanthus*) of tropical So. American freshwaters

leaf folder *n* **:** any of several moths whose larvae make shelter cases by folding the leaves of plants

leaf–footed \'=,==\ *adj* **:** having leaflike expansions on the appendages **:** PHYLLOPODOUS

leaf–footed bug *also* **leaf–foot bug** *n* **:** a large sap-sucking bug of the genus *Leptoglossus* having leaflike expansions on its legs: as **a :** a bug (*L. oppositus*) injurious to cucumber, melon, and squash **b :** a bug (*L. phyllopus*) very injurious to orange, peach, pear, and other fruit

leaf gap *n* **:** a gap that surrounds a leaf trace

leafgirl \'=,=\ *n* **:** a girl or woman performing the work of a leafboy

leaf gold *n* **:** GOLD LEAF

leaf green *n* **1 :** CHLOROPHYLL **2 :** a variable color averaging a moderate yellow green that is greener, lighter, and stronger than average moss green, greener and deeper than average pea green, and greener and duller than apple green (sense 1) — compare FOLIAGE GREEN

leafhopper \'=,==\ *n* **:** any of numerous small leaping homopterous insects constituting a family Cicadellidae that suck the juices of plants and on account of their abundance do considerable damage esp. to grass and fruit trees — see GRAPE LEAFHOPPER

leafier *comparative of* LEAFY

leafiest *superlative of* LEAFY

leaf·i·ness \'lēfēnəs, -fin-\ *n* -ES **1 :** FOLIAGE ⟨in these bits of ~ a few birds find grateful homes —John Muir †1914⟩ **2 a :** the extent to which a plant is provided with leaves **b :** the extent to which a cured legume hay has retained its leaves

leafing *pres part of* LEAF

leaf insect *n* **:** any of several insects of the family Phylliidae (order Orthoptera) in which the wings and expansions upon the legs resemble leaves in color and form and which are common in southern Asia and the East Indies

leaf·it \'lēfət\ *n* -s [irreg. fr. [1]*leaf*] *archaic* **:** LEAFLET 1

leaf lard *n* **:** lard made from leaf fat into the highest quality lard

leaf·less \'lēfləs\ *adj* **:** being without leaves ⟨a ~ tree⟩ — **leaf·less·ness** *n* -ES

leaf·let \'lēflət, *usu* -əd·+V\ *n* -s **1 a :** one of the divisions of a compound leaf **b :** a small or young foliage leaf **2 :** a leaflike organ or part; *esp* **:** the thin projecting part of the valve of a blood vessel **3 a :** a single sheet of paper unfolded or folded but not trimmed at the folds and bearing print (as an advertisement or instructions) on one or both sides **b :** a sheet of small pages folded but not stitched

leaf lettuce *n* **:** any of various cultivated lettuces that constitute a distinct variety (*Lactuca sativa crispa*) and are distinguished by leaves having curled, crisped, or incised margins and forming a loose rosette which does not develop into a compact head — compare HEAD LETTUCE

leaf lichen *n* **:** a foliaceous lichen

leaflike \'=,=\ *adj* **:** resembling a leaf in structure or function **:** having a broad flat thin form ⟨~ gills⟩

leaf louse *n* **:** APHID

leaf mallet cutting *n* **:** LEAF-BUD CUTTING

leaf manna *n* **:** LERP

leaf meal *n* **:** the dried and ground product of young leafy alfalfa plants used as a supplement in feeding livestock and poultry

leaf metal *n* **:** metal (as gold, silver, or tin) in thin leaves

leaf miner *n* **:** any of various small insects that in the larval stages burrow in and eat the parenchyma of leaves and mostly belong to the lepidopterous superfamily Tineoidea and the dipterous group Acalyptratae

leaf–mining \'=,==\ *adj* **:** being or living as a leaf miner ⟨*leaf-mining* beetles⟩

leaf mold *n* **1** *or* **leaf soil :** a compost or layer composed chiefly of decayed vegetable matter (as fallen leaves) — compare HUMUS **2 :** a mold or mildew of foliage

leafmold \'=,=\ *n* [*leaf mold*] **:** a dark brown that is lighter than art brown — called also *kolinsky*, *weathered oak*

leaf monkey *n* **:** any of several oriental langurs (genus *Presbytis*) — compare BANDED LEAF MONKEY, CRESTED LEAF MONKEY

leaf mosaic *n* **1 :** the arrangement of foliage in most plants (as in the common ivy) in such a pattern as to expose the maximum number of leaves to the direct rays of the sun with little loss of intervening space **2 :** MOSAIC 7

leaf mustard *n* **:** INDIAN MUSTARD

leaf–nosed \'=,=\ *adj* **:** having a leaflike membrane or plate on the nose — used esp. of bats of the families Phyllostomatidae, Rhinolophidae, and Hipposideridae

leaf–nosed snake *n* **:** any of several small pale yellowish dark-blotched colubrid snakes (genus *Phyllorhynchus*) widely distributed at lower altitudes in southwestern No. America and having the rostral plate greatly expanded

leaf of life : AIR PLANT 2

leaf plant *n* **1 :** FOLIAGE PLANT **2 :** AIR PLANT 2

leaf–raker \'=,==\ *n* **:** a person who engages in leaf-raking

leaf–raking \'=,==\ *n* **:** work or a work project designed to relieve the plight of unemployed persons by providing them with gainful employment but having little or no intrinsic value ⟨we shall never again have to resort to *leaf-raking* as a way of making work for people —Henry Wallace⟩

leaf red *n* **:** CARTHAMUS RED

leaf roll *n* **1 a :** any of various plant diseases characterized by an upward rolling of the leaf margins **b :** a virus disease of the potato characterized by an upward rolling of the leaf margins, smaller tubers, and netlike necrotic areas in the phloem **2 :** potato mosaic that is characterized by a rolling upward or inward of the leaf margins

leaf roller *n* **:** the larva of an insect (as a tortricid moth) that makes a nest by rolling up plant leaves

leaf rosette *n* **:** ROSETTE 5

leaf rust *n* **:** a rust disease of plants and esp. of cereal grasses (as wheat or rye) primarily affecting the leaves

leafs *pres 3d sing of* LEAF

leaf scald *n* **1 :** LEAF SCORCH a **2 :** a vascular disease of sugarcane caused by a bacterium (*Bacterium albilineans*) characterized by creamy or grayish streaking and later withering of the leaves

leaf scorch *n* **:** an abnormal condition of foliage characterized by a burned or scorched appearance of the tissues: as **a :** a nonparasitic disease of the apple and other fruits in which there is a marginal burning of the leaves **b :** a purplish red scorch of strawberry leaves caused by a fungus (*Diplocarpon earliana*) **c :** a disease of the cherry caused by a fungus (*Gnomonia erythrostoma*)

leaf sewer *n* **:** a moth (family Tortricidae) or its caterpillar that makes a nest by rolling up a leaf and fastening the edges together with silk as if sewn

leaf–shaped \'=,=\ *adj* **:** shaped like a leaf

leaf sheath *n* **1 :** SHEATH 2b **2 :** OCREA

leaf sight *n* **:** a hinged sight on a firearm that can be raised or folded down

leaf spine *n* **:** a spine (as of the barberry) developed from a leaf instead of from a branch

leaf spot *n* **1 :** a discolored area on a leaf caused by parasitic organisms or environmental factors; *esp* **:** one having a more or less sharp line of demarcation between it and healthy tissue — compare BLOTCH, MOSAIC **2 :** a disease characterized by discolored often circular spots on the leaves — compare ANGULAR LEAF SPOT, LEAF BLOTCH

leaf spring *n* **:** a spring made of superposed strips, plates, or leaves

leafstalk \'=,=\ *n* **:** PETIOLE

leaf stripe *n* **:** any of several diseases of plants causing striped discolorations on the leaves (as virus diseases of sugarcane or barley stripe)

leaf supply *n* **:** the one or more vascular bundles connecting the leaf with the vascular system of the branch or stem — compare TRACE

leaf–tailed gecko \'=,=-\ *n* **:** an Australian desert lizard (*Phyllurus platurus*) having a broad flat tail

leaf tendril *n* **:** a tendril developed from a part of a leaf (as of the pea)

leaftier *also* **leaftyer** *n* **:** a moth larva that lives in a folded leaf held together by silk strands

leaf tobacco *n* **:** LEAF 1c(2), 1c(3)

leaf trace *n* **:** a trace associated with a leaf — compare BRANCH TRACE

leafwood \'=,=\ *n*, *Brit* **:** HARDWOOD

leafwork \'=,=\ *n* **:** ornamental work resembling leaves

leafworm \'=,=\ *n* [ME *lefe-worm*, fr. OE *lēafwyrm*, fr. *lēaf* leaf + *wyrm* worm] **:** a moth larva that feeds on leaves — compare COTTON LEAFWORM

leafy \'lēfē, -fi\ *adj* -ER/-EST [[1]*leaf* + *-y*] **1 a :** furnished with or abounding in leaves **:** clothed with leaves ⟨the ~ forest⟩ ⟨the ~ month of June —S.T.Coleridge⟩ **b :** having broad=bladed leaves **:** BROAD-LEAVED ⟨mosses, grasses, and ~ plants⟩; *specif* **:** consisting chiefly of leaves ⟨a ~ vegetable⟩ **2 :** made or consisting of leaves ⟨a ~ bed —Lord Byron⟩ **3 :** resembling a leaf; *specif* **:** LAMINATE ⟨a ~ layer⟩

leafy liverwort *n* **:** a liverwort of the order Jungermanniales with a leafy gametophyte that has one ventral and two dorsal rows of leaves on the stem and is usu. epiphytic — called also *scale moss*

leafy spurge *n* **:** a tall perennial European herb (*Euphorbia esula*) naturalized and troublesome as a weed in the northern U. S. and Canada and having persistent rootstocks and linear to narrowly oblong leaves

leag \'lēg\ *n* -s [origin unknown] **:** a kelp (*Laminaria cloustoni*)

[1]**league** \'lēg *sometimes* 'lig\ *n* -s [ME *lege*, fr. LL *leuga*, *leuca*, of Gaulish origin; akin to the source of OE *lēowe* league] **1 :** any of various units of distance from about 2.4 to 4.6 statute miles; *esp* **:** an English unit of about three miles — see LAND LEAGUE, MARINE LEAGUE **2 :** any of various units of land area equal to a square league (as an old Spanish unit equal to 4439 acres or 1796 hectares used in the old California surveys and an old Texas unit equal to 4428.4 acres or 1792.1 hectares)

[2]**league** \"\ *n* -s [ME (Sc) *ligg*, fr. MF *ligue*, fr. OIt *liga*, fr. *ligare* to bind, fr. L — more at LIGATURE] **1 a :** an agreement or covenant made between two or more nations, heads of state, or other political entities to achieve cooperatively a desired end ⟨~*s* are commonly made for mutual defense —Thomas Hobbes⟩ ⟨the ~ is between states of unequal quality —Sir Walter Scott⟩ **b :** an association or combination of nations or other political entities formed by such an agreement or covenant ⟨the economic and social work of the *League* of Nations —Mary E. Bradshaw⟩ ⟨the Political Committee of the Arab *League* —H.L.Hoskins⟩ ⟨Plymouth, Massachusetts Bay, Connecticut, and New Haven united in a ~ of friendship —W.S.Sayre⟩ — compare ALLIANCE, CONFEDERATION, ENTENTE **c :** an association of persons or groups united by common interests or for the achievement of common ends ⟨the organization of ~*s* for bowling and softball —Robert Hazel⟩ ⟨playwrights and musicians organize themselves into ~*s* of authors, composers, and performers —Thomas Munro⟩; *specif* **:** an association of baseball clubs — see MAJOR LEAGUE, MINOR LEAGUE **d :** an informal and often tentative compact or alliance — usu. used in the phrase *in league* ⟨privately in ~ with some particularly unsavory crooks —John Brooks⟩ ⟨entirely in ~ with her mother to embarrass me —Lloyd Alexander⟩ **2 :** a class or category of a particular quality or rank ⟨a bit out of your ~, though —Hugh Cave⟩ ⟨my sons are not in the same ~ with me when it comes to building a campfire —Hodding Carter⟩ ⟨don't make me laugh, I'm not in your ~ —Robert De Vries⟩ ⟨had no idea your folks were in that sort of ~ —Louis Auchincloss⟩

[3]**league** \"\ *vb* -ED/-ING/-S **:** to unite in a league **:** combine for mutual support ⟨we four were *leagued* together by a tacit treaty —C.E.Montague⟩

[1]**lea·guer** \-gə(r)\ *n* -s [D *leger* camp, siege, couch, lair, fr. MD; akin to OHG *legar* act of lying, bed — more at LAIR] **1 a :** a military camp: as (1) **:** the camp of a besieging army (2) **:** LAAGER **b :** SIEGE ⟨the ~ of Leningrad was broken —R.C.K.Ensor⟩ **2** *archaic* **:** a resident ambassador or agent

[2]**lea·guer** \"\ *vb* **leaguered; leaguered; leaguering** \-g(ə)riŋ\ **leaguers** *vi* **:** ENCAMP; *specif* **:** to form a laager ⟨at no time did a squadron ~ forward of the local infantry —J.C.Gorman⟩ **~** *vt* **:** BESIEGE, BELEAGUER ⟨the tide of war beats high around the ~*ed* walls —J.J.Roche⟩

[3]**leagu·er** \"\ *n* -s [[2]*league* + *-er*] **:** a member of a league — usu. used with a qualifier indicating membership in a particular league ⟨12 million youth ~*s* —Kuo-Chan Chao⟩

[4]**lea·guer** \"\ *n* -s [D *ligger*, *legger* tun, fr. *liggen* to lie (akin to OE *licgan* to lie) & *leggen* to lay (akin to OE *lecgan* to lay) + *-er* (akin to OE *-ere* -er) — more at LIE, LAY, -ER] **:** an old Dutch unit of liquid capacity equal to about 128 imperial gallons (153.7 U. S. gallons or 5.82 hectoliters) still in use (as in the Union of So. Africa)

[1]**leak** \'lēk\ *vb* -ED/-ING/-S [ME *leken*, fr. ON *leka* to drip, leak; akin to OE *leccan* to moisten, OHG *lecchen* cracked by heat, leaky, OIr *legaim* I melt, dissolve, Arm *lič* swamp] *vi* **1 a :** to enter or escape through a hole, crevice, or other opening usu. by a fault or mistake ⟨the possibility of oil or exhaust fumes ~*ing* in —H.G.Armstrong⟩ ⟨if the granary be not tight, the grain will ~ out —C.H.Grandgent⟩ **b :** to let a substance (as water or gas) or light in or out through a hole, crevice, or other opening ⟨a camera bellows may ~⟩ ⟨the boat ~*s*⟩ ⟨the gas tank ~*s*⟩ **2 :** URINATE **3 :** to become known despite efforts at concealment **:** become public information **:** get out ⟨it's top secret, not a word can ~ for forty-eight hours —Louis Vaczek⟩ ⟨how it had been done would ~ across in time —Frank Ritchie⟩ — often used with *out* ⟨news of the discoveries ~*ed* out —*Amer. Guide Series: Nev.*⟩ **~** *vt* **1 a :** to permit to enter or escape through a leak ⟨camera bellows which . . . ~ light —*Eastman Kodak Monthly Abstract Bull.*⟩ ⟨hot in the train, the windows ~*ed* cinders —Lionel Trilling⟩ ⟨the little granary ~*ed* wheat —C.T.Jackson⟩ **b :** to cause to be issued as if by a leak **:** give off ⟨exquisite mosaics ~*ed* the sour stench —L.C.Douglas⟩ ⟨July night ~*ed* heat —J.T.Farrell⟩ ⟨phonographs ~*ed* . . . symphonies and string quartets —Winthrop Sargeant⟩ **2 :** to give out or pass on (as secret information) surreptitiously ⟨~*ed* information which resulted in some people making quick profits —*Springfield (Mass.) Union*⟩ ⟨~ important news to friendly newspapers⟩

[2]**leak** \"\ *n* -s [ME *leke*, prob. fr. ON *leki*; akin to ON *leka* to leak] **1 a :** a crack, crevice, fissure, or hole that usu. by mistake admits or lets escape (as water or light) ⟨the ship sprang a ~⟩ ⟨a camera bellows may have a light ~⟩ **b :** something that permits the admission or escape of something else usu. with prejudicial effect ⟨even the tightest precautions have some ~*s* —*Time*⟩ ⟨errors in change and pilfering are common ~*s* in the grocery business⟩ **c :** a loss of electricity or of electric current sometimes due to faulty insulation; *also* **:** the point or the path at which such loss occurs **2 :** the act, process, or an instance of leaking ⟨in the sun the outward ~ of energy is carried by radiation —Fred Hoyle⟩ ⟨through the process of premeditated ~*s*, the press may tell all —*New Republic*⟩ **3 :** a soft watery rot of fruits or vegetables caused by various fungi (as *Rhizopus stolonifer* or *Pythium debaryanum*) **4 :** an act of urinating — usu. used with *take* ⟨stopped to take a ~ —Saul Bellow⟩; not often in polite use

[3]**leak** *adj* [prob. of Scand origin; akin to ON *lekr* leaky; akin to ON *leka* to leak] *obs* **:** LEAKY

leak·age \'lēkij, -kēj\ *n* -s **1 a :** the act, process, or an instance of leaking ⟨fear of ~ of military understandings —F.W.D. Deakin⟩ ⟨such defects cause ~ of cement paste —J.R.Dalzell⟩ ⟨~ of body fluids from a surgical wound⟩ **b** (1) **:** loss of electricity due to a leak (2) *or* **leakage flux :** magnetic flux that does not follow a useful path (as between the pole pieces of a dynamo without passing through the armature) **2 :** an allowance of a certain rate percent for loss by leaking **3 :** something or the amount that issues or is lost through a leak ⟨in the grocery business . . . a ~ of about one percent is fairly common —Kenneth Ives⟩

leakage inductance *n* **:** the part of the inductance of a circuit that corresponds to the leakage flux

leakage reactance *n* **:** the part of the reactance of a circuit that corresponds to the leakage flux

leak·er \'lēkə(r)\ *n* -s **:** one that leaks: as **a :** a poultry egg with a cracked shell and broken membrane **b :** a leaky receptacle for canned goods

leak·i·ness \-kēnəs, -kin-\ *n* -ES **:** the condition of being leaky

leak·less \-kləs\ *adj* **:** being without a leak

leak·man \-kmən\ *n*, *pl* **leakmen :** a worker who looks for and repairs leaks in filled whiskey barrels

leakproof \'=,=\ *adj* **:** proof against leakage ⟨a ~ roof⟩

leaky \'lēkē, -ki\ *adj* -ER/-EST [[2]*leak* + *-y*] **1 a :** permitting water or other fluid (as blood) to leak in or out ⟨a ~ roof⟩ ⟨a ~ heart valve⟩ **b :** exuding large drops of water — used of butter **2** *archaic* **:** given to blabbing **:** not closemouthed

[1]**leal** \'lē(ə)l\ *adj* [ME *lel*, *leel*, fr. OF *leel*, *leal*, *leial*, fr. L *legalis* legal, of or relating to law — more at LEGAL] **1** *chiefly Scot* **:** LOYAL, TRUE ⟨~ to the core of her intrepid Scottish heart —Harry Lauder⟩ **2** *Scot* **:** free from error, inaccuracy, or falsehood **syn** see FAITHFUL

[2]**leal** \"\ *adv* [ME *lel*, *leel*, fr. *lel*, *leel*, adj.] *Scot* **:** in a leal manner

leal·ly \-ē(ə)lē, -li\ *adv* [ME *lelly*, fr. *lel*, *leel*, adj. + *-ly*] *Scot* **:** in a leal manner

[1]**leam** \'lēm\ *n* -s [ME *leme*, fr. OE *lēoma*; akin to OS *liomo* gleam, radiance, ON *ljōmi* radiance, OE *lēoht* light — more at LIGHT] *chiefly Scot* **:** a gleam of light **:** RADIANCE

[2]**leam** \"\ *vi* -ED/-ING/-S [ME *lemen*, fr. *leme*, n.] *chiefly Scot* **:** to shine forth **:** GLEAM

[3]**leam** \"\ *n* -s [origin unknown] *dial Eng* **:** a drain in a fen

[4]**leam** \"\ *vt* -ED/-ING/-S [origin unknown] *dial Brit* **:** to take (nuts) from the husks

leam·er \-mə(r)\ *n* -s [[4]*leam* + *-er*] *dial Brit* **:** a nut fully ripe and ready to fall from the husk

[1]**lean** \'lēn\ *vb* **leaned** \'lēnd, *chiefly Brit* 'lent\ *or chiefly Brit* **leant** \'lent\ **leaned** *or chiefly Brit* **leant; leaning; leans** [ME *lenen*, fr. OE *hleonian*, *hlinian*; akin to OS *hlinōn* to lean, OHG *hlinēn* to lean, L *clinare* to bend, incline, Gk *klinein* to lean, Skt *śrayate* he leans on] *vi* **1 a :** to incline, deviate, or bend from a vertical position ⟨~*ed* forward to get a better look⟩ **:** be in an inclining position ⟨this fence ~*s* badly⟩ **b :** to incline or bend so as to receive support **:** cast one's weight by inclining or bearing down to one side ⟨~ on me as we walk⟩ ⟨~*ed* on his staff⟩ **c :** to put the weight of one's body into a stroke ⟨~*ed* into another inviting pitch —*N.Y. Times*⟩ **2** *now chiefly Scot* **:** to sit or lie down — usu. used with *down* **3 :** to rest, rely, or draw for support or inspiration — used with *on* or *upon* ⟨preferring not to ~ on his father in building a career —*Current Biog.*⟩ ⟨this room not only ~*s* on the past but improves on it —Edgar Kaufmann⟩ ⟨~*s* heavily upon certain modern clichés —R.D.Altick⟩ ⟨eastern Brazilians ~ more heavily on the sweet potato —R.H. Lowie⟩ **4 :** to incline in opinion, taste, or desire ⟨~*ed* toward a teaching career —*Current Biog.*⟩ ⟨~ to the belief that there was foul play —S.H.Adams⟩ ⟨~*s* toward the native dishes —A.L.Himbert⟩ **~** *vt* **1 :** to cause to lean **:** INCLINE, REST ⟨~*ed* her head upon her arm —Pearl Buck⟩ ⟨~ the board against the wall⟩ **2** *now chiefly Scot* **:** to seat or lay (oneself) — usu. used with *down* — **lean over backward :** to go to the opposite extreme in order to offset a tendency ⟨*leaning over backward* to offend no one —H.L.Smith b. 1913⟩ ⟨*leaned over backward* . . . to avoid the appearance of favoritism —*Nation*⟩

[2]**lean** \"\ *n* -s **:** the act or an instance of leaning **:** SLOPE, INCLINATION ⟨the ~ of a sail⟩ ⟨the wall has a decided ~⟩ ⟨body ~ is apparent only on the sharpest of curves —Walt Woron⟩

[3]**lean** \"\ *adj* -ER/-EST [ME *leene*, *lene*, fr. OE *hlǣne*] **1 a :** lacking flesh **:** not plump **:** THIN, LANK ⟨a ~ body⟩ ⟨a ~ man⟩ ⟨~ cattle⟩ **b :** having little fat or free from fat **:** chiefly or wholly of muscle ⟨eats only ~ meat⟩ **2 :** lacking richness, sufficiency, or productiveness: as **a :** lacking nutritive quality **:** MEAN, MEAGER ⟨supped on ~ fare⟩ **b :** POOR, SCANTY ⟨ample profits will produce better goods and services than ~ profits —*Report of Amer. Tel & Tel. Co.*⟩ ⟨~ material resources⟩ ⟨~ tax collections —*N.Y.Times*⟩ **c :** attended or characterized by privation, hardship, or scarcity ⟨a ~ life, that of a college professor —A.W.Long⟩ ⟨important as a source of food after a ~ winter —F.C.Lincoln⟩ ⟨came upon ~ days —Anatole Chujoy⟩ **d :** UNPRODUCTIVE, INFERTILE ⟨never ceased to love the ~ red soil —Josephine Y. Case⟩ ⟨attempts to make ~ soils yield —*Amer. Guide Series: Mich.*⟩ **e :** scantily furnished or provided **:** DEFICIENT ⟨a paper that was slim in size and ~ on news —W.A.Swanberg⟩ ⟨this year, so ~ in its new plays —John Mason Brown⟩ **f** *printing* (1) **:** not susceptible of fast and easy setting and hence unprofitable as piecework — contrasted with *phat* (2) **:** THIN, SLENDER ⟨type with a ~ face⟩ ⟨a ~ stroke in a letter⟩ **3 :** deficient in some essential or important quality or ingredient: as **a** *of clay* **:** deficient in plasticity **b** *of coal* **:** deficient in volatile matter **c** *of lime* **:** containing impurities and not slaking freely **d** (1) *of ore* **:** containing little valuable mineral (2) *of an alloy* **:** DILUTE **e :** low in combustible component — used esp. of fuel mixtures for internal-combustion engines; opposed to *rich* ⟨if the gasoline-air mixture is too ~ (too much air) excess air passes out the exhaust —Irving Frazee⟩ **f :** deficient in cementing material — used esp. of concrete and mortars **4 :** characterized by an artistically effective economy of style or expression **:** not lush **:** not verbose ⟨an orchestral suite . . . is ~, supple and sure —*New Yorker*⟩ ⟨~, compact writing that implies as much as it states —Stanley Cooperman⟩ ⟨his diction . . . is ~, his imagery precise —Herbert Read⟩ ⟨retold in ~ and forthright prose —*Word Study*⟩

syn SPARE, LANK, LANKY, GAUNT, RAWBONED, ANGULAR, SKINNY, SCRAWNY: LEAN stresses lack of fat and of rounded contours ⟨a *lean* face with prominent cheekbones⟩ ⟨described as *lean* and wiry . . . six feet tall and weighs 170 pounds —*Current Biog.*⟩ SPARE may suggest an easy sinewy frame resulting from lack of excess ⟨his *spare,* not unsolid, but unobtrusive figure —John Galsworthy⟩ ⟨the *spare,* alert, and jaunty figure that one often finds in army men —Thomas Wolfe⟩ LANK may suggest tallness as well as leanness, sometimes suggesting the wiry strength of an economical build, sometimes connoting the effects of wasting away ⟨the hounds were fine beasts, they seemed *lank* and swift —Elizabeth M. Roberts⟩ ⟨meager and *lank* with fasting grown, and nothing left but skin and bone —Jonathan Swift⟩ LANKY may suggest a leanness accompanied by loose-jointed articulation or by callow awkwardness ⟨Lincoln, an awkward, *lanky* giant —Allan Nevins & H.S.Commager⟩ ⟨very tall and *lanky,* all wrists and ankles —Margaret Deland⟩ GAUNT may suggest a bony haggard leanness resulting from continued strain and undernourishment ⟨this one with the passing of the years had grown lean and *gaunt* and the rocklike bones of her face stood forth and her eyes were sunken —Pearl Buck⟩ ⟨always a very lean boy, but now he is looking positively *gaunt* —Compton Mackenzie⟩ RAWBONED describes persons not noticeably fat but stresses large often ungainly build ⟨a long, gawky, *rawboned* Yorkshireman —Rudyard Kipling⟩ ⟨tall, lean, stooping, *rawboned,* with coarse features —V.L.Parrington⟩ ANGULAR applies to leanness accompanied by a degree of graceless stiffness ⟨*angular* face and straight hair rather unattractive —Dorothy Sayers⟩ ⟨the thin, *angular* woman, with her haughty eye and her acrid mouth —Lytton Strachey⟩ SKINNY may suggest noticeable thinness resulting from inadequate food and suggesting lack of vitality ⟨the *skinniest* human being I ever saw. He had not enough flesh on his bones to make a decent-sized chicken —Robert Lynd⟩ SCRAWNY is closely synonymous with SKINNY but may suggest an underlying toughness ⟨*scrawny* kid, all legs and arms —Agatha Christie⟩ ⟨they were *scrawny* and underfed and "pinched their guts" with their belts for lack of food —*Amer. Guide Series: Tenn.*⟩

⁴lean \"\ *vt* -ED/-ING/-S [ME *lenen,* fr. OE *hlǣnian,* fr. *hlǣne,* adj.] **1 :** to make lean ⟨~*ed* down for travel —A.B.Guthrie⟩ ⟨~*ed* out by his illness —*Time*⟩; *specif* **:** to make (a fuel mixture) lean — often used with *out* **2 :** to cut the lean from (whale blubber)

⁵lean \"\ *n* -S [ME *lene,* fr. *leene, lene,* adj.] **:** the part of flesh which consists principally of muscle without the fat **:** lean meat

lean·er \-nə(r)\ *n* -S [¹*lean* + *-er*] **:** one that leans; *specif* **:** HOBBER

lean·ing \-niŋ, -nēŋ\ *n* -S [ME *leninge,* fr. OE *hlinung, hlining,* fr. *hleonian, hlinian* to lean + *-ung, -ing* -ing] **1 :** the act or an instance of deviating from a vertical position **:** SLOPE ⟨detected a certain list or ~ of the tower⟩ **2 :** INCLINATION ⟨had a strong ~ toward law⟩ ⟨a reformer with radical ~*s* —Martin Gardner⟩

syn PROPENSITY, PROCLIVITY, PENCHANT, FLAIR: LEANING suggests a liking or attraction likely to influence although often not decisive about an eventual choice, policy, or course ⟨in spite of their antirationalistic *leanings,* the mystics of the twelfth and thirteenth centuries remained true to the established doctrines —Frank Thilly⟩ ⟨an able comedy actor with a *leaning* towards farce —E.H.Collis⟩ PROPENSITY may apply to an innate or deeply engrained longing or attraction making a certain course of action highly probable ⟨only precariously civilized and within us there is the *propensity,* persistent as the force of gravity, to revert under stress and strain, under neglect or temptation, to our first natures —Walter Lippman⟩ PROCLIVITY may apply to a strong inclination, sometimes notably individual, often to one indulged or manifested ⟨her free speech, her Continental ideas, and her *proclivity* for championing new causes even when she did not know much about them —Willa Cather⟩ ⟨despite her *proclivity* for gossip she was reticent upon family affairs —A.J.Cronin⟩ PENCHANT may indicate a decided taste for, special ability at, or strong proclivity for ⟨Americans, though in years now well in the past, had shown a *penchant* for tinkering with the money supply —J.K. Galbraith⟩ ⟨the psychiatrist does not deny that the child who rebels against his father is in many significant ways different from the same individual as a middle-aged adult who has a *penchant* for subversive theories —Edward Sapir⟩ FLAIR may refer to an instinctive ability or perception joined with innate power of discernment; it may also be a synonym for *aptitude, talent,* or *knack* ⟨good, although not quite tops, at his job until about a year before. Then something had happened to his judgment — his *flair* —Frances & Richard Lockridge⟩ ⟨as an ordinary clergyman he showed a great *flair* for organizing and the true ministry —George Bellairs⟩

leaning tower *n* [*leaning* fr. pres. part. of ¹*lean*] **:** any of many towers which are out of the true vertical and have a visible slant (as that of Pisa, Italy, which is 16½ feet out of the perpendicular in a height of 179 feet)

leanly *adv* **:** in a lean manner

lean·ness \ˈlēnnəs\ *n* -ES [ME *lenenes,* fr. OE *hlǣnnes,* fr. *hlǣne* lean + *-nes* -ness] **:** the quality or state of being lean

leans *pres 3d sing of* LEAN, *pl of* LEAN

leant \ˈlent\ *chiefly Brit past of* LEAN

¹lean-to \ˈlēn,tü\ *n* -S [ME *lenetoo,* fr. *lenen* to lean + *too, to* to] **1 :** a wing or extension of a building having a single-pitched roof typically built against and supported by the wall of a higher structure with a double-pitch or complete roof; *specif, NewEng* **:** a section of a barn often so constructed and used to house cows **2 :** a rough shelter formed by a sloping roof (as of boughs) supported typically by two uprights (as posts or trees)

lean-to 1

²lean-to \"\ *adj* **:** having only one slope or pitch — used of a roof

lea oak \ˈlē-\ *or* **lea's oak** *n, usu cap L* [after Thomas G. *Lea* †1844 Am. botanist] **:** a hybrid American oak (*Quercus leana*) regarded as a cross between the shingle oak (*Q. imbricaria*) and the black oak (*Q. velutina*)

¹leap \ˈlēp, *dial or sometimes with reference to manege in Brit speech* ˈlep\ *vb* **leaped** *also* **leapt** \ˈlept, *chiefly Brit* ˈlept\ **leaped** *also* **leapt; leaping; leaps** [ME *lepen* to run, jump, leap, fr. OE *hlēapan;* akin to MD *lopen* to run, OHG *hlouffan* to run, ON *hlaupa* to jump, leap, Goth us*hlaupan* to jump up] *vi* **1 :** to run hastily or with a leaping gait **:** RUSH, BOUND ⟨~*ed* home to greet his father⟩ ⟨~*ed* into the fray⟩ **2 a** (1) **:** to spring free from the ground or some other supporting surface by the muscular action of the feet and legs or in some animals the tail **:** project oneself through the air **:** HOP, VAULT ⟨~*ed* high into the air⟩ ⟨~ over a fence⟩ ⟨~ down from a wall⟩ ⟨a fish ~*ed* out of the water⟩ ⟨~*ed* on a moving bus⟩ ⟨~*ed* on his horse and rode off⟩ (2) *chiefly Scot* **:** to dance in skipping or bounding movements (3) **:** to spring high from one foot to the other in dancing (4) **:** to rise or throw itself into or through the air **:** move precipitately or violently ⟨guns on the hillocks ~*ed* as they bellowed —Kenneth Roberts⟩ ⟨the great rocket ~*ed* skyward⟩ ⟨a tongue of flame ~*ed* down the stairway —Frank Yerby⟩ ⟨a sparkling waterfall ~*s* from a cliff —*Amer. Guide Series: Oregon*⟩ (5) **:** to rise to one's feet with a bound or other energetic movement ⟨~*ed* up and asked the chairman some pointed questions⟩ **b :** to beat high **:** THROB ⟨my heart would have ~*ed* at sight of him —Kenneth Roberts⟩ **3 a :** to pass abruptly or without transition (as from one state or topic to another) ⟨the states of Latin America have ~*ed* . . . from the ox-drawn cart to the airplane —Vera M. Dean⟩ ⟨made his face ~ into a sudden grimacing life —Bruce Mason⟩ ⟨~ irreverently from one trifling matter to another —H.A.Overstreet⟩ **b :** to increase suddenly and sharply ⟨costs on a job ~ entirely out of proportion —P.J.Adam⟩ **c :** to act or move precipitately or without careful thought or study (as in making judgments) ⟨~ to conclusions⟩ **d :** to join, enter, or intervene with eagerness or alacrity ⟨~*ed* to his absent friend's defense⟩ ⟨~*ed* into the discussion⟩ **e :** to take quick or immediate advantage **:** accept eagerly — usu. used with *at* ⟨~*ed* at the chance⟩ ~ *vt* **1 a :** to pass over by a leap ⟨~ a wall⟩ ⟨~ a ditch⟩ **b :** to pass over as if by a leap ⟨a mind that seemed to have ~*ed* the usual transitional stages —*Amer. Guide Series: Vt.*⟩ **2 :** to copulate with **:** COVER, SERVE — used of a male animal (as a stallion) **3 :** to cause to leap ⟨~ a horse across a ditch⟩ **syn** see JUMP

²leap \"\ *n* -S [ME *leep,* fr. OE *hlȳp;* akin to OE *hlēapan* to run, jump, leap] **1 a** (1) **:** an act of leaping **:** SPRING, BOUND (2) **:** a spring high into the air from one foot to the other in dancing **b** (1) **:** a place that is or must be leaped over or one leaped from ⟨took the ~ with great ease⟩ (2) **:** the distance covered by a leap ⟨a ~ of 10 feet⟩ (3) **:** a place in a waterfall where fish can shoot up in ascending the stream (4) **:** the sudden descent of a river to a lower level ⟨five clear ~*s* with intervening cascades —Arthur Holmes⟩ **c** (1) **:** an act of covering a female animal (2) *obs* **:** an act of coitus **2 a** (1) **:** a sudden passage, transition, or change (as from one state to another) ⟨made an abrupt and difficult ~ from a Latin classroom to an editorial desk —E.S.McCartney⟩ ⟨knowledge took a great ~ forward —Stuart Chase⟩ (2) **:** a choice exercised in the area of ultimate concerns **:** an existential decision ⟨a ~ of faith⟩ **b :** a skip in successive musical notes or tones **c :** a sharp or sudden increase ⟨a ~ of over 117 percent —Rex Lardner⟩ — **by leaps and bounds :** with extraordinary rapidity ⟨population is increasing *by leaps and bounds*⟩ **syn** see JUMP

³leap \"\ *n* -S [ME *leep* basket, fr. OE *lēap;* akin to ON *laupr* basket, OE *lēaf* leaf — more at LEAF] **1** *dial Eng* **:** a basket or box used esp. for chaff or seed **2** *dial Eng* **:** WEEL

leap day *n* **:** February 29, the intercalary day in the Gregorian calendar; *broadly* **:** an intercalary day in any calendar

leap·er \-pə(r)\ *n* -S [ME *lepere* one that leaps, one that runs, fr. OE *hlēapere* dancer, courier, fr. *hlēapan* to run, jump, leap + *-ere* -er] **:** one that leaps; *specif* **:** a circus performer who does acrobatic jumps

¹leapfrog \ˈ=,=\ *n* [¹*leap* + *frog*] **1 :** a game in which one player bends down on all fours and another places his hands on the first player's shoulders or back and leaps over him **2 :** an act of leapfrogging ⟨aerial assaults, perhaps followed by new amphibious ~*s* —*Time*⟩

²leapfrog \"\ *vb* **leapfrogged; leapfrogged; leapfrogging; leapfrogs** *vi* **:** to leap or progress in or as if in the game of leapfrog: as **a :** to move from one locality to another in one or more jumps ⟨the vast majority came to our shores and then *leapfrogged* West —G.W.Pierson⟩ ⟨*leapfrogging* from city to city, lecturing —Bernard Kalb⟩ ⟨people *leapfrogged* from one suburban rim to the other⟩ **b :** to pass or go ahead of each other in turn ⟨giant trucks and midget cars *leapfrogging* along a highway⟩ ~ *vt* **1 :** to go ahead of (each other) in turn **:** leapfrog over ⟨packaging improvements and sales have been *leapfrogging* each other —*Modern Packaging*⟩ ⟨arranged to fish alternate pools, *leapfrogging* each other —Nevil Shute⟩ ⟨teams of scientists ~ each other, spurting ahead of the column to set up their instruments —*Time*⟩; *specif* **:** to advance (two military units or parts of two military units) by keeping one unit in action while moving the other unit past or through it to a position farther in front **2 :** to evade (an obstacle) by or as if by a bypass or jump ⟨demonstrated its ability to ~ defense pacts and unfriendly borders —John Bird⟩ — **leapfrogging** *n* -S

¹leap·ing \ˈlēpiŋ, -pēŋ\ *n* -S [ME *leping,* fr. OE *hlēaping* dancing, fr. *hlēapan* + *-ung* -ing] **:** an act of one that leaps ⟨~ is usually done with a springboard that catapults the performer high into the air⟩

²leaping \"\ *adj* [ME *lepinge,* alter. (influenced by *-ing,* suffix forming gerunds) of OE *hlēapende,* fr. pres. part. of *hlēapan* to run, jump, leap] **1 :** marked by or using leaps ⟨a ~ gait⟩ ⟨~ animals⟩ **2 :** used for leaps ⟨a ~ board⟩ — **leapingly** *adv*

leaping tuna *n* **:** BLUEFIN TUNA

leaping weir *n* **:** a weir before an aqueduct or sewer intake to cause flood water to overshoot the opening

leaps *pres 3d sing of* LEAP, *pl of* LEAP

leapt *past of* LEAP

leap year *n* [ME *lepe yere,* fr. *lepe, leep* leap, jump + *yere, yeer* year] **1 :** one of the years in the Gregorian calendar containing the intercalary day February 29 **:** a Gregorian year of 366 days —see YEAR table **2 :** an intercalary year in any calendar

leap-year day *n* **:** LEAP DAY

¹lear \ˈli(ə)r, -iə\ *vt* -ED/-ING/-S [ME *leren, leeren,* fr. OE *lǣran;* akin to OHG *lēren* to teach, ON *læra,* Goth *laisjan* to teach, OE *leornian* to learn] **1** *archaic* **:** to give instruction to **:** TEACH **2** *archaic* **:** LEARN

²lear \ˈlēr\ *n* -S [ME *lere,* fr. *leren, leeren* to teach] *Scot* **:** LORE; *esp* **:** knowledge gained through instruction

³lear \ˈli(ə)r\ *n* -S [ME *layour, lyer,* fr. MF *lieure* thickening for sauce, tie, bond, fr. LL *ligatura* tie, bond — more at LIGATURE] *archaic* **:** a thick sauce or gravy **:** a thickening for sauce or soups

⁴lear \"\ *var of* ⁶LEER

⁵lear *var of* LEHR

lea rig *n* [fr. (assumed) ME (northern dial.) *leye rig,* fr. OE *lǣghrycg,* fr. *lǣg-* fallow + *hrycg* back, ridge — more at LEA (fallow), RIDGE] *Scot* **:** a grassy ridge or piece of land **:** a ridge left unplowed in a cultivated field

learn \ˈlərn, ˈlən, ˈləin *dial* ˈlärn *or* -ˈlan\ *vb* **learned** \-nd,-nt, *Brit usu* -nt\ *also* **learnt** \-nt\ **learned** *also* **learnt; learning; learns** [ME *lernen,* fr. OE *leornian;* akin to OHG *lirnēn, lernēn* to learn, *-leisa* track, L *lira* furrow, track, Russ *lekha* garden bed, furrow; basic meaning: furrow, track] *vt* **1 a :** to gain knowledge or understanding of or skill in by study, instruction, or experience **:** receive instruction in ⟨~ a language⟩ ⟨~ arithmetic⟩ ⟨~ a trade⟩ ⟨~ dancing⟩ ⟨a law which must . . . be *learnt,* but can never be taught —Havelock Ellis⟩ ⟨only just *learnt* how to enjoy life —Joyce Cary⟩ **b :** to develop an ability to or readiness for by practice, training, or repeated experience — usu. used with an infinitive ⟨~ to read⟩ **c :** to become aware **:** REALIZE ⟨he had ~*ed* that in order to do what he wanted in writing he would have to publish himself —H.S.Canby⟩ **d :** to acquire (as a skill or habit or a modification of an existing habit) through experience, practice, or exercise ⟨we ~ our responses —W.H.Kilpatrick⟩ **e :** to commit to memory **:** MEMORIZE **2 a** *now chiefly substand* **:** TEACH ⟨send the Sirocco ten times a year . . . to ~ us to be toads —F.M.Ford⟩ ⟨had to ~ myself just about . . . everything —Harold Sinclair⟩ ⟨that will ~ you to keep out of mischief⟩ ⟨I'll ~ you to have done with misspellings —Augusta Gregory⟩ **b** *obs* **:** to inform (a person) of something **3 :** to find out **:** ASCERTAIN, HEAR ⟨I ~ that he will arrive shortly⟩ ⟨what have you ~*ed* about this matter⟩ ~ *vi* **:** to acquire knowledge or skill **:** make progress in acquiring instruction or skill **:** receive instruction ⟨~*ed* fast and well when he put his mind to it⟩ ⟨evidently went to school to play, not to ~⟩ **syn** see DISCOVER

learn·able \-nəbəl\ *adj* **:** capable of being learned ⟨it is a ~ thing —Edmond Taylor⟩

learned *in sense* **a** -nəd *sometimes* -nd, *in sense* **b** -nd *or* -nt\ *adj* [ME *lerned* instructed, educated, fr. past part. of *lernen* to learn] **:** of or relating to learning: as **a** (1) **:** possessing or characterized by academic learning **:** ERUDITE ⟨a ~ periodical⟩ ⟨the dean was a ~ man, and loved long Latin words —W.M. Thackeray⟩ (2) **:** associated with or dedicated to learning ⟨such ~ languages as Latin and Greek⟩ ⟨a ~ society⟩ (3) **:** well informed, skilled, or practiced in a specific field ⟨both are ~ in Horace —E.T.Booth⟩ ⟨experience had made my eye ~ in the valuing of motion —Thomas De Quincey⟩ **b :** acquired by the learning process ⟨~ skills⟩ ⟨~ responses⟩ — **learned·ly** *adv* — **learned·ness** *n* -ES

learned profession *n* **:** one of the three professions, theology, law, and medicine, traditionally associated with extensive learning or erudition; *broadly* **:** any profession in the preparation for or practice of which academic learning is held to play an important part

learn·er \ˈlərnər; ˈlənə(r, ˈləin-\ *n* -S [ME *lerner,* fr. OE *leornere,* fr. *leornian* to learn + *-ere* -er] **:** one that learns **:** STUDENT, APPRENTICE **:** a beginner in some field ⟨a slow ~⟩ ⟨a foreign ~ of English —A.S.Hornby⟩; *specif* **:** an employee being taught and trained to perform a task or fill a position requiring a degree of skill and experience through instruction that is usu. informal and of indefinite duration as distinguished from that of an apprentice

learn·ing \-niŋ, -nēŋ\ *n* -S *often attrib* [ME *lerning,* fr. OE *leornung,* fr. *leornian* to learn + *-ung* -ing] **1 a** (1) **:** the act or experience of one that learns ⟨the ~ of a trade⟩ ⟨gives . . . evidence of trial-and-error ~ in paramecia —W.N.Kellogg⟩ ⟨~ may be regarded as a property of all living organisms —R. C.Noble⟩ ⟨~ experiences⟩ (2) **:** the process of acquisition and extinction of modifications in existing knowledge, skills, habits, or action tendencies in a motivated organism through experience, practice, or exercise — compare MATURATION **b** (1) **:** something that is learned or taught ⟨increasing the practical value of the ~*s* —H.R.Douglass⟩ ⟨the film does provide ~*s* —Catherine M. Adler⟩; *specif* **:** a subject that is taught in school ⟨emphasize the mastery of essential ~*s* —M. B.Smith⟩ (2) *obs* **:** ACQUIREMENT **2 a :** knowledge or skill acquired by instruction or study **:** ERUDITION ⟨book ~⟩ ⟨a man of good education and ~ —Jonathan Swift⟩ ⟨obtuseness in perception can never be made good by any amount of ~ —John Dewey⟩ **b :** knowledge accumulated and handed down by generations of scholars **:** CULTURE ⟨~ is a sacred deposit from the experience of ages —William Hazlitt⟩ ⟨Assyrian ~ of the seventh century B.C. is well represented —H.J.J.Winter⟩ **3** *dial* **:** formal education **:** SCHOOLING **syn** see KNOWLEDGE

learns *pres 3d sing of* LEARN

learnt *past of* LEARN

lears *pres 3d sing of* LEAR, *pl of* LEAR

leary *var of* LEERY

leas·able \ˈlēsəbəl\ *adj* **:** capable of being leased

¹lease *or* **leaze** \ˈlēz\ *vb* -ED/-ING/-S [ME *lesen,* fr. OE *lesan* to gather, glean; akin to OHG *lesan* to gather, select, ON *lesa* to gather, pick, Goth *lisan* to gather, Lith *lesti* to peck up] *vi, now dial Eng* **:** to glean grain ~ *vt, dial Eng* **:** to separate (as impurities from grain) by picking

²lease \"\ *n* -S [ME *leese, lese,* fr. OE *lǣs* open pasture (gen., dat., & acc. *lǣse, lǣswe*); perh. akin to ON *lāth* landed property — more at LATHE] *dial* **:** an open pasture or common

³lease \ˈlēs\ *n* -S [ME *les,* fr. AF, fr. *lesser,* v.] **1 :** a contract by which one conveys lands, tenements, or hereditaments for life, for a term of years, or at will or for any less interest than that of the lessor, usu. for a specified rent or compensation; *also* **:** the act of such conveyance, the instrument by which it is made, or the term for which it is made — distinguished from *license* **2 :** a piece of land or property that is leased **3 :** a continuance or opportunity of continuance esp. in vigorous existence or action usu. because of some favoring change or development **:** HOLD, TERM — often used in the phrase *lease on life* or *lease of life* ⟨criticism took on a new ~ on life —C.I. Glicksberg⟩ ⟨with the development of civilian air commerce it took on a new ~ of life —*Current Biog.*⟩ ⟨if the election yields a majority prepared to support them, the ministry is given a new ~ on life —F.A.Ogg & Harold Zink⟩ ⟨the Scottish forwards seemed to have got a new ~ of life —John Buchan⟩

⁴lease \"\ *vb* -ED/-ING/-S [AF *lesser,* fr. OF *laissier, lessier* to let loose, let go, leave, fr. L *laxare* to loosen, fr. *laxus* slack, loose, spacious — more at SLACK] *vt* **1 :** to grant or convey to another by lease **:** LET ⟨*leased* his house for the summer⟩ **2 :** to hold under a lease ⟨a tenant ~*s* his land from the owner⟩ ~ *vi* **1 :** to take a lease of **:** to be under lease or be subject to lease ⟨this property ~*s* at a monthly rental of $100⟩ **2 :** to lease a property ⟨fitted to limn the genus summer renter, having *leased* to a few invaders himself —*N. Y. Times Mag.*⟩

⁵lease \"\ *n* -S [perh. alter. of ¹*leash*] **1 :** a system of crossing warp threads with cords or rods alternately over and under one end or in groups to keep them in position during beaming and weaving **2 :** LASH 4

⁶lease \"\ *vt* -ED/-ING/-S **:** to make a lease in (yarn or thread)

lease and release *n* **1 :** a nearly obsolete common-law mode of conveyance of freehold estates by means of a lease vesting a leasehold estate in the lessee upon actual entry and a subsequent release of the reversion to the lessee, thus vesting the fee in the lessee without livery of seisin **2 :** a nearly obsolete mode of conveyance under the Statute of Uses by means of a bargain and sale for a leasehold interest conventionally for a year, which under the statute vested the leasehold estate without entry, with a subsequent release vesting the fee in the lessee without entry or livery of seisin

leaseback \ˈ=,=\ *n* [fr. the phrase *lease back*] **:** the sale of property to a financial or eleemosynary institution that leases it to the vendor for a period of years at a rental that will give a return and amortize the investment — called also *sale-and-leaseback*

leasehold \ˈ=,=\ *n, often attrib* **1 :** a tenure by lease **2 :** land held by lease; *specif* **:** land held as personalty under a lease for years

leaseholder \ˈ=,==\ *n* **:** one having a leasehold

leasehold insurance *n* **:** insurance against loss to a lessee because of cancellation of a lease as a result of fire or other specified peril

leasehold mortgage *n* **:** a mortgage under which a leasehold interest in property secures a debt or obligation

lease hound *n* **:** LEASEMAN 1

¹lease-lend \ˈ=ˈ=\ *n, often attrib* [⁴*lease* + *lend,* v.] **:** LEND-LEASE

²lease-lend \"\ *vt* **:** LEND-LEASE

lease·less \ˈlēsləs\ *adj* **:** not having a lease

lease·man \ˈlēsmən\ *n, pl* **leasemen 1 :** a person in the petroleum industry who negotiates with landowners for land options, oil-drilling leases, and royalties and with producers for the pooling of production in a field — called also *landman, lease hound, leaser* **2 :** a person who contacts property owners to lease sites for the erection of advertising billboards

lease picker *n* [⁵*lease*] **:** ²LEASER

¹leas·er \-sə(r)\ *n* -S [⁴*lease* + *-er*] **:** LEASEMAN 1

²leaser *n* -S [⁵*lease* + *-er*] **:** a textile worker who forms a lease

lease rod *or* **lease stick** *n* **:** one of the usu. two rods that form and keep the lease orderly during separation of the warp threads

lease system *n* **:** a system of hiring out prisoners at a fixed rate per day to a contractor

¹leash \ˈlēsh\ *n* -ES [ME *lees, lese, leshe,* fr. OF *laisse,* fr. *laissier* to let loose — more at LEASE] **1 a** (1) **:** a thong, cord, or chain attached to an animal's collar or harness or to a hawk's jess and held in the hand for the purpose of leading, checking, or controlling the bird or animal or fastened to an object to secure or tether it ⟨a puppy on a ~⟩ — often used in the phrase *in leash* or *on leash;* called also *lead* (2) **:** such an article used for leading or restraining a small child (as on a walk) **b :** CONTROL, RESTRAINT, CHECK ⟨keep the reader under a guiding ~ —Robert Humphrey⟩ — usu. used in the phrase *in leash* ⟨the plan had been devised to keep floods in ~ —*Amer. Guide Series: Texas*⟩ ⟨the same quivering emotion held in tight ~ —R.C.Carpenter⟩ **2 a :** a set of three animals (as greyhounds, foxes, bucks, or hares) **:** a brace and a half ⟨a ~ of Russian wolfhounds —*Nat'l Geographic*⟩ **b :** any set of three individuals ⟨a ~ of stalwart sons —Green Peyton⟩ **3 a :** LASH 4 **b :** ⁵LEASE 1

²leash \"\ *vt* -ED/-ING/-ES **1 :** to tie together or hold with a leash **2 :** CONTROL, RESTRAIN ⟨exhausted by the effort of keeping his emotions ~*ed* —W.B.Marsh⟩

leas·ing \ˈlēzən, -ziŋ\ *n* -S [ME *lesing,* fr. OE *lēasung,* fr. *lēasian* to tell a lie (fr. *lēas* devoid, false) + *-ung* -ing — more at -LESS] *now chiefly Scot* **:** the act of lying **:** FALSEHOOD

lea's oak *usu cap L, var of* LEA OAK

lea·sow \ˈlezə\ *n* -S [ME *lesow, leswe,* fr. OE *lǣs* open pasture (gen., dat., & acc. *lǣse, lǣswe*) — more at LEASE] *dial Brit* **:** rough pasture land

¹least \ˈlēst\ *adj* [ME *leest,* fr. OE *lǣst;* akin to OFris *lērest* least; superl. corresponding to the compar. represented by OE *lǣssa* less, smaller — more at LESS] **1 :** lowest in importance or position ⟨the ~ of my worries⟩ ⟨anyone who preached its abrogation would be ~ in the Kingdom of Heaven —M.R.Cohen⟩ **2 a :** smallest in size or degree ⟨the ~ finger of his left hand appeared to have suffered a slight sprain —Elinor Wylie⟩ **b** *now dial* **:** being the smallest or youngest child — often used in the phrase *least one* or *least un* ⟨one of the ~ uns at home gets took down —M.E.Sheppard⟩ ⟨too busy . . . to show affection for any but the ~ one —Charlie M. Simon⟩ **c :** being a member of a kind distinguished by diminutive size — used in plant or animal names **d :** smallest possible **:** SLIGHTEST ⟨the ~ noise would startle her⟩ ⟨negotiates his way with trust and the ~ violence —Robert Francis⟩ ⟨treasures every ~ indication that she may be softer than her sister —E.K.Brown⟩ ⟨the ~ means shall be used to achieve the greatest end —Robert Richman⟩ ⟨believed that the ~ government was the best government —Irving Stone⟩

²least \"\ *n* -S [ME *leest,* fr. OE *lǣst,* fr. *lǣst,* adj.] **1 :** something that is least **:** something of the lowest or slightest possible value, importance, or scope ⟨that's the ~ of my worries⟩ ⟨the ~ that may be said⟩ ⟨at his ~ . . . he is diverting —Robert Phelps⟩ ⟨the ~ it can then do is to lend a hand —W.H.Whyte⟩ **2 :** a game in skat in which the object is to win as few points as possible with jacks trumps and with a base value of 10 points and which is played when no player bids voluntarily — **at least** or **at the least** *adv* **1 :** at the lowest estimate **:** as the minimum ⟨*at least* once a year . . . my wife and I drive up into New England —Budd Schulberg⟩ **2 :** in any case **:** at any rate ⟨unknown to the outside world, *at least* until recently —N.D.Palmer & S.C.Leng⟩ — **in the least** *adv* **:** in the least degree or manner ⟨not *in the least* unfriendly⟩

³least \"\ *adv* [ME *leest*, fr. *leest*, adj.] **:** in the smallest or lowest degree ⟨the ~ important of his reasons⟩ ⟨may grant a divorce to the party ~ in fault —Morris Ploscowe⟩ ⟨the Federal government acts best when it acts ~ —Max Ascoli⟩

least bittern *n* **:** a small American bittern (*Ixobrychus exilis*) that is largely black above with chestnut or yellowish brown sides fading to white below

least common denominator *n* **:** LOWEST COMMON DENOMINATOR

least common multiple *n* **:** LOWEST COMMON MULTIPLE

least flycatcher *n* **:** a small plainly colored flycatcher (*Empidonax minimus*) common in eastern No. America

least sandpiper *n* **:** the smallest American sandpiper (*Erolia minutilla*) — compare STINT

least squares *n pl* **:** a statistical method of fitting a line or plane to a set of observational points in such a way that the sum of the squares of the distances of the points from the line or plane is a minimum ⟨a straight line was fitted to the data by means of *least squares* —*Jour. of Research*⟩ ⟨a *least squares* fit of the best straight line to the points of Fig. 1 yields a slope —*Physical Rev.*⟩

least tern *n* **:** a very small tern of temperate No. America and Middle America that is usu. considered to constitute a race (*Sterna albifrons antillarum*) of the little tern

least·ways \'lēs,twāz\ *adv* [¹*least* + *-ways*] *dial* **:** at least ⟨~ I'm the only one working there regular —Harold Sinclair⟩

least weasel *n* **:** a small weasel (*Mustela rixosa*) having a short tail without a black tip that is found from Alaska to the Alleghenies and is the smallest American weasel

least·wise \-wīz\ *adv* [¹*least* + *-wise*] **:** at least ⟨or ~ that the robbers be made to answer for it —George Eliot⟩

leat \'lēt\ *n* -s [perh. fr. (assumed) ME *leet*, fr. OE *gelǣt* road junction, conduit; akin to OHG *gilāz* road junction; both fr. a prehistoric WGmc compound consisting of a prefix represented by OE *ge-* (perfective, associative, and collective prefix) and a final constituent derived fr. the root of OE *lǣtan* to let, leave, allow — more at CO-, LET] *dial Eng* **:** an artificial water trench esp. leading to or from a mill

¹leath·er \'leth̲ə(r)\ *n* -s [ME *lether*, fr. OE *lether-*; akin to OHG *leder* leather, ON *lethr-*, OIr *lethar*] **1 a :** the skin of an animal or some part of such skin tanned, tawed, or otherwise dressed for use to render it resistant to putrefaction and relatively soft and flexible when dry **b :** dressed hides ⟨a dealer in ~⟩ **2 a :** SKIN; *specif* **:** a person's skin ⟨fell and scraped a bit of ~ off⟩ **b :** the pendulous part of the ear of a dog (as a hound) — see DOG illustration **3 :** something wholly or partly made of leather: as **a** (1) **:** STRAP (2) *chiefly Irish* **:** a strap used to discipline schoolchildren ⟨hit the front desk a ferocious crack with the ~ —James Plunkett⟩ **b :** a pump washer ⟨that pump leaks at the ~s —Joseph Whitehill⟩ **c :** STIRRUP LEATHER ⟨riding as the Boers always did, with long ~s —Stuart Cloete⟩ **d leathers** *pl* **:** leggings or breeches made of leather ⟨a number of members of the Quality, on shining horses, their ~s creaking beautifully —F.M.Ford⟩ **e :** any of various balls used in games: as (1) **:** CRICKET BALL (2) **:** FOOTBALL (3) **:** BASEBALL **f :** the tip of a billiard cue **g :** the leather-covered part of an oar that engages the oarlock **h :** POCKETBOOK, PURSE, WALLET ⟨maybe you can get his ~; I couldn't —J.F.Fishman⟩ **4 :** a brownish orange that is yellower, stronger, and slightly lighter than spice or gold pheasant and paler and slightly yellower than feuille morte — called also *adust, oriolé, tan*

²leather \"\ *vt* -ED/-ING/-S [ME *letheren*, fr. *lether*, n.] **1 a :** to apply or supply leather to **:** bind or cover with leather **:** form into leather **b :** to form a surface like leather on (a skin or pelt) esp. by treading **2 :** to beat with a strap **:** THRASH ⟨before I ~ the answers out of you —B.T.Cleeve⟩

³leather \"\ *adj* [¹*leather*] **:** relating to, made of, or resembling leather ⟨a ~ jacket⟩

leatherback \'==,=\ *n* **1 :** the largest existing sea turtle (*Dermochelys coriacea*) distinguished by its flexible carapace composed of a mosaic of small bones embedded in a thick leathery skin, occurring in all warm seas but most commonly in the Atlantic, measuring up to nine feet, and weighing over a thousand pounds **2** *dial* **:** a soft-shelled turtle of the family Trionychidae

leatherbark \'==,=\ *n* **:** a tree of the genus *Dirca* or the genus *Thymelaea*

leatherboard \'==,=\ *n* **:** an artificial leather made by a pulping and compressing process typically from scrap leather or fibrous materials (as waste paper and wood pulp)

leather breeches *n pl, chiefly Midland* **:** green beans dried and cooked in the pod

leather brown *n* **:** a moderate brown that is lighter, stronger, and slightly yellower than bay, lighter and stronger than auburn, redder, lighter, and stronger than chestnut brown, and slightly darker than marron glacé

leather brown 5RT *n, usu cap L&B* **:** a basic dye — see DYE table I (under *Basic Brown 2*)

leather carp *n* **:** a scaleless variety of the carp (sense 1) developed under domestication

leathercloth \'==,=\ *n* **:** a cloth usu. of cotton or plastic made to imitate leather by various coating, embossing, and finishing processes

leathercoat \'==,=\ *n* **:** a russet apple

Leath·er·ette \,leth̲ə'ret\ *trademark* — used for a product that is colored, finished, and embossed in imitation of leather grains and qualities and is used esp. in bookbinding and in the manufacture of various fancy articles

leather fern *n* **1 :** TEN-DAY FERN **2 :** GOLDEN FERN

leatherfish \'==,=\ *n* [so called fr. the leathery skin] **:** any of various filefishes

leatherflower \'==,=\ *n* **1 :** any of several plants of the genus *Clematis; esp* **:** a plant (*C. viorna*) of the southeastern U.S. having large reddish purple bell-shaped flowers with leathery recurved sepals **2 :** the flower of leatherflower

leather-hard \'==,=\ *adj, of clayware* **:** partly dry and hard enough for tooling

leatherhead \'==,=\ *n* **1 :** BLOCKHEAD, DUNCE **2** *Austral* **:** FRIARBIRD **3** [so called fr. the practice of wearing a leather cap] **:** a 19th century watchman or policeman esp. in New York City

leather-headed \'==,==\ *adj* **:** STUPID, SLOW-WITTED

leath·er·ine \,leth̲ə'rēn\ *n* -s [¹*leather* + *-ine*, n. suffix] **:** an artificial or imitation leather

leathering *n* -s [fr. gerund of ²*leather*] **1 :** the act or an instance of forming, applying, or furnishing with leather **2 :** a covering or furnishing of leather **3 :** a process of inserting narrow strips of leather or cloth into long-haired pelts (as fox) to improve appearance and reduce bulkiness of garments

leath·er·ize \'leth̲ə,rīz\ *vt* -ED/-ING/-S **:** to convert into leather **:** treat so as to resemble leather

leatherjacket \'==,==\ *n* **1 a :** a filefish (family Monacanthidae) **b** *also* **leather jack :** any of several fishes (genus *Oligoplites*) of the family Carangidae having the scales reduced and embedded in the skin; *esp* **:** a common fish (*O. saurus*) of both coasts of tropical America **2 :** any of several Australian trees with very tough close smooth bark; *esp* **:** COACHWOOD 1a **3** *Austral* **:** a johnnycake pan-fried or baked in hot ashes

leather lake *n* **:** FEUILLE MORTE

leatherleaf \'==,=\ *n* **1 :** a north temperate bog shrub (*Chamaedaphne calyculata*) of the family Ericaceae with evergreen coriaceous leaves and small white cylindrical flowers **2 :** LEATHERFLOWER **3 :** a stiff leathery-leaved fern (*Polypodium scouleri*) with ovate fronds parted to the midrib

leather-lunged \'==,=\ *adj* **:** having an inordinately loud voice or tending to speak in an inordinately loud manner ⟨only the *leather-lunged* representatives could make themselves heard by their colleagues —Harold Zink⟩

leather mouse *n* **:** ³BAT 1

leath·ern \'leth̲ə(r)n\ *adj* [ME *letherne*, fr. OE *lethern*, *lethren*, fr. *lether* leather + *-en*, adj. suffix] **1 :** made of leather **:** consisting of leather ⟨a ~ purse⟩ **2 :** like or suggestive of leather ⟨the ~ wings of a bat⟩

leatherneck \'==,=\ *n, often cap* [so called fr. the leather neckband that was formerly part of the marine uniform] **:** MARINE

Leath·er·oid \'leth̲ə,rȯid\ *trademark* — used for an artificial leather consisting of chemically treated paper combined with rubber and sandarac

leather paper *n* **:** an imitation leather made from properly colored paper embossed with a leather grain and sometimes varnished

leatherroot \'==,=\ *n* **:** a stout Californian purple-flowered herb (*Psoralea macrostachya*) with tough roots used as fiber by the Indians

leather rot *n* **:** a firm rot of strawberries caused by fungi of the genus *Phytophthora*

leathers *pl of* LEATHER, *pres 3d sing of* LEATHER

leather star *n* **:** a common brightly colored starfish (*Dermasterias imbricata*) of the western coast of No. America distinguished by a thick leathery membrane covering the surface of the body

leather turtle *n* **:** LEATHERBACK

leatherware \'==,=\ *n* **:** goods made of leather

leatherwing \'==,=\ *or* **leather-winged bat** *n* **:** ³BAT 1

leather-winged \'==,=\ *adj* **:** having wings like leather

leatherwood \'==,=\ *n* **1 a** *also* **leatherwood bush :** a small tree or shrub (*Dirca palustris*) with tough pliant stems and small yellow flowers — called also *moosewood* **b :** a tree (*Cyrilla racemiflora*) of the southeastern U.S. and So. America **2 a :** COACHWOOD 1 **b** (1) **:** a gum-yielding tree (*Eucryphia billardieri*) of Tasmania (2) **:** the red wood of such a tree

leatherwood fern *n* **:** EVERGREEN WOOD FERN 1

leatherwork \'==,=\ *n* **:** work in leather **:** something made of leather

leatherworker \'==,==\ *n* **:** a person who works in leather: as **a :** a worker who cuts, skives, sews, and otherwise prepares leather trim for automobiles **b :** a maker of the leather parts of surgical appliances **c :** a worker who makes and repairs gun slings, straps, and similar articles

leatherworking \'==,==\ *n* **:** the process or occupation of making things from leather

leath·ery \'leth̲(ə)rē, -ri\ *adj* [¹*leather* + *-y*] **:** of or resembling leather in appearance or consistency **:** TOUGH ⟨showing his ~ calluses —James Still⟩ ⟨the ~ old solicitor —Christopher Morley⟩ ⟨those ~ weeds, so hard to kill —Cyril Connolly⟩ ⟨her husband's dark, ~ library —Louis Auchincloss⟩

leathery turtle *n* **:** LEATHERBACK 1

lea·the·sia \lē'thēzh(ē)ə\ *n, cap* [NL, prob. fr. the name *Leathes* + NL *-ia*] **:** a genus of brown algae of the family Corynophlaeaceae having a globose generally hollow convoluted and gelatinous thallus made up of radiating threads

leath·wake \'lēth,wāk\ *adj* [ME *lithwayke*, fr. OE *lithewāc*, *leothuwāc*, fr. *lith* limb, part of the body + *wāc* weak, pliant — more at LITH, WEAK] *dial Eng* **:** capable of being flexed **:** SUPPLE

¹leave \'lēv\ *vb* **left** \'left\ **left; leaving; leaves** [ME *leven*, fr. OE *lǣfan*; akin to OHG *verleiben* to leave, ON *leifa*, Goth *bilaibjan*; causative fr. the root of OE *belīfan* to remain, be left over, OHG *bilīban*; akin to L *lippus* blear-eyed, dripping, Gk *lipos* fat, lard, Skt *limpati* he smears; basic meaning: to smear with fat, make sticky] *vt* **1 a :** BEQUEATH, DEVISE ⟨*left* a fortune to his wife⟩ ⟨was *left* a substantial legacy⟩ **b** (1) **:** to have remaining after one's death or extinction ⟨*left* a widow and two children⟩ ⟨*left* many water color sketches that . . . have won for him a significant place —*Amer. Guide Series: Minn.*⟩ ⟨prehistoric peoples *left* behind material witnesses to their cultures —Brewton Berry⟩ (2) **:** to cause to remain as a trace, vestige, or effect upon removal or cessation ⟨*left* a large stain on the tablecloth⟩ ⟨a wound that would probably ~ a scar⟩ ⟨these cheerful trees would ~ a sorry gap . . . if they were to disappear —Tom Marvel⟩ (3) **:** to cause to be or remain in some specified condition ⟨the educational system under English rule *left* the Irish-speaking people illiterate in their native tongue —David Greene⟩ ⟨the incident *left* him furious⟩ ⟨the war *left* Rome exhausted —W.K.Ferguson⟩ ⟨his rhetoric ~s me cold⟩ ⟨*left* me in the dark as to his true intentions⟩ ⟨a plan that would ~ younger members of the staff out in the cold⟩ ⟨*left* me holding the bag⟩ **2 a** (1) **:** to permit to remain undisturbed or in the same position ⟨~ the door open⟩ ⟨cut down the infected trees, but *left* the sound ones⟩ ⟨took cash and jewelry, but *left* the stock certificates⟩ **:** permit to remain unoccupied ⟨~ room in the car for your little sister⟩ (2) **:** to refrain from or omit doing, including, or dealing with ⟨*leaving* aside for the moment matters of political strategy —Y.G.Krishnamurti⟩ ⟨much was *left* undone⟩ ⟨*left* out many points of interest⟩; *also* **:** to fail to include or take along ⟨the poor kid always gets *left* at home⟩ — often used with *out* ⟨she's always *left* out when it comes to a date or a party⟩ (3) **:** to have as a remainder in a mathematical operation ⟨4 from 7 ~s 3⟩ (4) **:** to have as a remainder after consuming or utilizing ⟨did away with the whole pie, *leaving* nothing for me⟩ ⟨only one ton of coal is *left*⟩ — often used with *over* ⟨give what is *left* over to the dog⟩ ⟨too hungry to ~ anything over⟩ (5) **:** to allow to remain in the possession of after taking a part away ⟨how much does that ~ you⟩ **:** YIELD ⟨the price . . . which ~s him this profit —Adam Smith⟩ (6) **:** to fall short of being satisfactory by (an indicated amount) — used chiefly in the phrase *leave much to be desired* or *leave something to be desired* ⟨his playing ~s much to be desired⟩ **b** (1) **:** to let be without interference **:** permit to remain subject to another's action, control, or consideration **:** COMMIT, REFER ⟨~ it to you to decide —A.A.Hill⟩ ⟨unwilling to ~ it at that —*Time*⟩ ⟨it is well to ~ much to the reader's imagination —C.E. Montague⟩ ⟨the rest being *left* to the judgment of God —Irwin Shaw⟩ (2) **:** to refrain from interfering with the control, action, or destiny of ⟨~ them to work without hampering interference —*Irish Digest*⟩ ⟨was *left* to shift for himself⟩ ⟨~ him to do it himself —M.C.A.Henniker⟩ (3) *substand* **:** LET ⟨~ him go⟩ ⟨~ him be⟩ ⟨~ him have it⟩ ⟨~ loose of the rope⟩ ⟨~ him through⟩ **3 a** (1) **:** to take leave of or withdraw oneself from whether temporarily or permanently **:** go away or depart from ⟨*left* school at an early age⟩ ⟨~ the room this minute⟩ ⟨the cold did not ~ him for weeks⟩ ⟨it was clear their zest had *left* them —T.B.Costain⟩ (2) **:** to branch off **:** diverge from ⟨the road now ~s the river valley and enters the hill country⟩ (3) **:** to arrive at the position of the last exterior contact with ⟨the moon ~s the earth's shadow in a lunar eclipse⟩ **b :** to put, place, deposit, or deliver before or in the process of departing or withdrawing ⟨the caller *left* his card⟩ ⟨~ your hat in the hall⟩ ⟨the bus *left* me off at the corner⟩ **4 a :** DESERT, ABANDON, FORSAKE ⟨her husband *left* her and she is considering a divorce⟩ **b :** to terminate association with **:** quit the service of ⟨*left* the company in May⟩ ⟨has a job waiting when he ~s the army⟩ **5 a** (1) **:** to give up the practice or use of or a devotion or addiction to ⟨the opium eater who cannot ~ his drug —Thomas Wolfe⟩ (2) **:** to abandon as a field of interest or activity ⟨thinking of *leaving* business for research⟩ ⟨*left* her austere tales of rural New England to write a romance of the swashbuckling seventeenth century —Carl Van Doren⟩ **b :** CEASE, DESIST, STOP ⟨the ground was green with celandine, that had just *left* blowing —Mary Webb⟩ ~ *vi* **1** *obs* **a :** CEASE, STOP **b :** to break off (as in a narrative) **:** leave off **2 :** to set out **:** DEPART ⟨time to ~ for the station⟩ ⟨*left* for the office at eight sharp⟩ — **leave alone 1 :** to leave in solitude ⟨afraid that she would be *left alone* —Carson McCullers⟩ **2 :** to refrain from touching or disturbing ⟨*leave* that paper *alone*⟩ **3 :** to refrain from using or having to do with ⟨*leave* the beer *alone* tonight —A.P.Gaskell⟩ ⟨housewives can presumably take their soap operas or *leave* them *alone* —M.C.Faught⟩ **syn** see GO, LET, RELINQUISH, WILL

²leave \", *dial & in Brit armed services* -ēf\ *n* -s *often attrib* [ME *leve*, fr. OE *lēaf*; akin to MHG *loube* permission, OE *alȳfan* to allow — more at BELIEVE] **1 a** (1) **:** permission to do something ⟨asked ~ to read a short statement⟩ ⟨absent by ~ of the Senate on official business —*Congressional Record*⟩ ⟨came without ~ to shoot on the estate —H.E.Scudder⟩ ⟨applied for ~ to inspect it —G.B.Shaw⟩ (2) **:** LIBERTY, LICENSE — used chiefly in the phrase *take leave* ⟨the subscribers take ~ respectfully to inform the public —*Amer. Guide Series: La.*⟩ **b** (1) **:** an authorized absence or vacation from duty or employment usu. with pay ⟨canceled all ~s⟩ ⟨collected his ~ pay⟩ ⟨most Federal employees earn annual ~, for vacation and other purposes —*Federal Jobs Outside Continental U.S.*⟩; *also* **:** the extent, duration, or period of such allowed absence ⟨still have 2 days' ~ coming to me⟩ — often used in the phrase *on leave* ⟨a professor on sabbatical ~⟩ ⟨on ~ from his law firm for government service⟩ ⟨had left orders that he was not to be bothered while on ~⟩ (2) **:** authorized absence or vacation from military duty usu. charged to the accumulated leave to which a person is entitled under provisions of law — compare FURLOUGH, LIBERTY (3) **:** authorized absence from an institution (as a school or hospital) ⟨at home on ~ from a state hospital —*Springfield (Mass.) Daily News*⟩ ⟨~ privileges are not extended to freshmen⟩ (4) **:** LEAVE OF ABSENCE ⟨at once agreed to give the necessary ~ —F.W.Crofts⟩ ⟨don't know if I can get ~ for that long a time⟩ **2 a :** an act of leaving the presence or company of a person or of departing from a place typically with some expression of regard or farewell — usu. used in the phrase *take leave* ⟨took very courteous ~ of the ladies⟩ ⟨took his ~ about nine⟩ ⟨reluctantly took our ~ of that pleasant town⟩ **b :** an act or experience of separation or alienation — usu. used in the phrase *take leave* ⟨have you taken ~ of your senses⟩ ⟨let us take ~ of that subject and turn to another⟩ **3** [¹*leave*] **a :** the position of billiard balls after a shot is completed **b :** the pins left standing after a bowler has rolled the first ball

³leave \"\ *vi* -ED/-ING/-S [ME *leven*, fr. *leef* leaf] **:** to send out leaves **:** LEAF — often used with *out* ⟨the black locust ~s out later than the other shade trees —Brooks Atkinson⟩

⁴leave \"\ *chiefly dial var of* LIEF

leave and license *n* **:** a plea in defense in an action of trespass that sets up the permission of the plaintiff

leaved \'lēvd\ *adj* [ME *leved*, fr. *leef* leaf + *-ed*] **1 :** having or displaying leaves ⟨a ~ branch⟩ **2 :** having leaves of a specified character or number — usu. used in combination ⟨the palmate-*leaved* horse chestnut⟩ ⟨four-*leaved* clover⟩

leave in *vt* **:** to pass a bid or double made in bridge by one's partner or rarely opponent

leavelooker \'=,==\ *n* [prob. fr. ²*leave* "license" + *looker*] **:** a municipal inspector of markets in an English town (as in Lancashire)

¹leav·en \'levən\ *n* -s [ME *levain*, fr. MF, fr. (assumed) VL *levamen*, fr. L *levare* to raise — more at LEVER] **1 a :** a substance (as yeast) acting or used to produce fermentation in dough or a liquid; *esp* **:** SOURDOUGH **b :** a material (as sour milk and soda or baking powder) used to produce a gas that lightens dough or batter while it is baking; *also* **:** a gas so produced (as carbon dioxide, air, or steam) **2 :** LEAVENING ⟨a few really funny stories by way of ~ —Geoffrey Boumphrey⟩ ⟨without the ~ of popular education, a landlocked region was not apt to make much progress —S.E.Morison & H.S.Commager⟩

²leaven \"\ *vt* **leavened; leavened; leavening** \-v(ə)niŋ\ **leavens** [ME *levainen*, fr. *levain*, n.] **1 a :** to cause (as dough) to ferment **b :** to make light by aerating (as with carbon dioxide by the action of yeast or baking powder) **:** RAISE 11b ⟨practically all breads, rolls, and some products like coffee cake are yeast-*leavened;* crackers, biscuits, pretzels, cookies, and the major portion of cakes are chemically ~*ed* —Oscar Skovholt⟩ **2 :** to mingle or permeate with some modifying, alleviating, or vivifying element ⟨serious poetry ~*ed* with wit —Sara H. Hay⟩ ⟨a large fund of shrewd ability ~*ed* by charm —*Current Biog.*⟩ ⟨his bitterness is ~*ed* by a mischievous humor —N.R.Nash⟩ **syn** see INFUSE

leavening *n* -s [fr. gerund of ²*leaven*] **1 :** a leavening agent **:** LEAVEN **2 :** a trait or element that modifies, alleviates, or vivifies ⟨with a Welsh and French ~ in her mother's background —*Current Biog.*⟩ ⟨a ~ of genuine tourists —Rex MacGall⟩

leav·en·less \-vənləs\ *adj* **:** having no leaven

leave of absence 1 : permission to be absent from duty or employment ⟨obtained a *leave of absence* from the university —*Current Biog.*⟩ **2 :** LEAVE ⟨on an informal *leave of absence* from the First National Bank —Jean Boley⟩

leave off *vt* **1 :** to desist from **:** break off **:** STOP ⟨*left off* thinking about himself at all —L.C.Douglas⟩ ⟨*leave off* work at five⟩ ⟨is reluctant to *leave off* arguing⟩ **2 :** to stop wearing or using **:** omit to put in the usual position ⟨warm enough to *leave* his overcoat *off*⟩ **3 :** to abandon the use of **:** give up ⟨I have *left off* all other medicines —*Farmer's Weekly (So. Africa)*⟩ ~ *vi* **:** to make an end **:** break off **:** STOP ⟨the rain . . . finally *left off* at noon —H.E.Bates⟩ ⟨starts . . . where most writers *leave off* —Burke Wilkinson⟩

leave out *vi* **1** *chiefly South & Midland* **:** to go away **:** set out **:** LEAVE ⟨*left out* in a buggy⟩ **2** *dial* **:** to end for the day ⟨school *leaves out* at four o'clock⟩

leave over *vt, Brit* **:** to cause to remain unconsumed or undone till a future time ⟨*leave* this pie *over* for tomorrow⟩ ⟨*left* the job *over* until the next week⟩

leav·er \'lēvə(r)\ *n* -s **:** one that leaves ⟨high school ~s aged from 16 to 18 —L.R.McColvin⟩

lea·ver·wood \'lēvə(r),wu̇d, 'lev-\ *n* [by alter.] **:** LEATHERWOOD 1 a

leaves *pl of* LEAF *or of* LEAVE, *pres 3d sing of* LEAVE

leave-taking \'=,==\ *n* [ME *leve-taking*, fr. *leve* leave + *taking*, gerund of *taken* to take] **:** a taking of leave **:** ADIEU, DEPARTURE, FAREWELL

leav·ing \'lēviŋ, -vēŋ\ *n* -s [ME *leving*, fr. gerund of *leven* to leave] **:** something left **:** REMNANT, RELIC, RESIDUE — usu. used in pl. ⟨the ~s of meals —*Times Lit. Supp.*⟩

leaving certificate *n* [*leaving* fr. gerund of ¹*leave*] *Brit* **:** SCHOOL CERTIFICATE

leavy \'lēvē\ *adj* -ER/-EST [ME *levy*, fr. *leef* leaf + *-y*] *archaic* **:** LEAFY

leaze *var of* LEASE

le·bach·ia \lə'bäkēə, -bak-\ *n, cap* [NL, fr. *Lebach*, town in northern France + NL *-ia*] **:** a genus of Paleozoic fossil conifers differing mainly from other conifers in having hairs on the leaves

¹leb·a·nese \,lebə'nēz, -ēs\ *adj, usu cap* [*Lebanon*, country in southwestern Asia + E *-ese*] **1 :** of, relating to, or characteristic of Lebanon **2 :** of, relating to, or characteristic of the people of Lebanon

²lebanese \"\ *n, pl* **lebanese** *cap* **:** a native or inhabitant of Lebanon

leb·a·non \'lebənən *sometimes* -bə,nän\ *adj, usu cap* [fr. *Lebanon*, country in southwestern Asia] **:** of or from the republic of Lebanon **:** of the kind or style prevalent in Lebanon **:** LEBANESE

lebanon cedar *n, usu cap L* [fr. *Lebanon*, mountain range in Palestine — more at CEDAR OF LEBANON] **:** CEDAR OF LEBANON

leb·bek \'le,bek\ *n* -s [origin unknown] **1** *or* **lebbek tree :** an Old World tropical leguminous tree (*Albizzia lebbeck*) that has large leaves with 4 to 8 pinnae and 10 to 18 oblong or obovate nearly sessile leaflets and greenish yellow flowers in globose axillary heads followed by long lustrous seed pods which clatter in the wind, that is widely planted in warm regions as a shade and ornamental tree, and that yields a valuable mottled coarse-grained wood somewhat resembling mahogany —called also *koko, siris, woman's tongue tree* **2 :** the wood of the lebbek — called also *East Indian walnut*

leb·en *also* **leb·an** \'lebən\ *n* -s [Ar *laban*] **:** a liquid or semisolid food made from curdled milk by the peoples of the Levant and No. Africa — compare KOUMISS, YOGURT

le·bens·raum \'lābənz,rau̇m\ *n* -s *often cap* [G, lit., living space, fr. *leben* life, living + *raum* space] **1 :** territory that is held to be necessary for the existence or the economic self-sufficiency of a state ⟨lands . . . earmarked by the Nazis as part of their ~ —H.C.Wolfe⟩ **2 :** space required (as by a community, institution, organism, individual) for life, growth, or activity ⟨the library is badly in need of new ~ —Hollis W. Piatt⟩

le·ber·wurst \'lābər,vu̇rst\ *n* -s [G, fr. *leber* liver (fr. OHG *lebra*) + *wurst* sausage — more at LIVER, BRATWURST] **:** LIVER SAUSAGE

leb·haft \'lāp,häft\ *adj* [G, lively, fr. MHG *lebehaft* alive, fr. *leben* to live (fr. OHG *lebēn*) + *-haft* (adj. suffix) — more at LIVE] **:** VIVACE, LIVELY — used as a direction in music

le·bis·tes \lə'bi(,)stēz\ *n, cap* [NL, fr. Gk *lebias*, a small fish + *-istēs* -ist] : a genus of So. American topminnows that includes the guppy

leb·ku·chen \'lāp,kükən\ *n, pl* **lebkuchen** [G, fr. MHG *lebekuoche*, fr. *lebe* loaf (akin to MHG *leib* loaf, fr. OHG *leib, hleib*) + *kuoche* cake, fr. OHG *kuocho, chuohho* — more at LOAF, CAKE] : a Christmas cookie usu. made with honey, brown sugar, almonds, candied fruit peel, and spices

le·blanc process \lə'blaⁿ-, -äŋk-\ *n, usu cap L* [after Nicolas *Leblanc* †1806 French chemist] : a process formerly used for manufacturing soda by treating salt with sulfuric acid, heating the resulting sodium sulfate with limestone and coal, and extracting with water the soluble sodium carbonate from the dark-colored mass formed; *also* : a similar process for manufacturing potash

le·bran·cho \lə'brän(,)kō, -än(-\ *n* -s [AmerSp] : a common mullet (*Mugil liza*) of the Caribbean area and south to Brazil — called also *blueback mullet*

le·ca·ni·um \lə'kānēəm\ *n* [NL, fr. Gk *lekanion* small dish or pan, dim. of *lekanē* basin, dish, pan — more at LEKANE] **1** *cap* : a genus of naked soft-bodied somewhat hemispherical scales **2** -s : any insect of the genus *Lecanium* — called also *tortoise scale;* see PEACH SCALE

lec·a·no·man·cy \'lekənō,man(t)sē\ *n* -ES [Gk *lekanomanteia*, fr. *lekanē* basin + *-manteia* -mancy] : divination by inspection of water in a basin

lec·a·no·ra \,lekə'nōrə, -nȯrə\ *n* [NL, fr. Gk *lekanē* basin + *hōra* beauty, grace; fr. the form and color of the apothecium] **1** *cap* : a genus (the type of the family Lecanoraceae) of crustaceous lichens that have apothecia in which the disk is surrounded by a pale margin and that are sometimes used for dyeing or for food — see ARCHIL, MANNA LICHEN **2** -s : any lichen of the genus *Lecanora* — **lec·a·no·ra·ceous** \,lekə(,)nō¦rāshəs, -nȯ¦-\ *adj* — **lec·a·no·rine** \,lekə'nō,rīn, -nȯ|,|rēn\ *adj* — **lec·a·no·roid** \|,rȯid\ *adj*

lec·a·no·ra·les \,lekə(,)nō'rā(,)lēz, -nȯ'-\ *n pl, cap* [NL, fr. *Lecanora* + *-ales*] *in some classifications* : an order comprising all the lichens that produce apothecia

lec·a·no·ric acid \,lekə¦nōrik-, -nȯrik-\ *n* [ISV *lecanor-* (fr. NL *Lecanora*) + *-ic*] : a crystalline phenolic acid $C_{15}H_{12}O_5$-COOH obtained from lichens

lech \'lek\ *n* -s [W *llech* slab, slate; akin to Bret *liac'h* stone monument, OIr *lie* stone (gen. *liac*)] : a prehistoric monumental stone; *specif* : the capstone of a cromlech

le·cha·te·lier·ite \lə,shäd·ᵊl'i,rīt\ *n* -s [F *lechateliérite*, fr. Henry-Louis *Le Châtelier* †1936 Fr. chemist + E *-ite*] : a mineral SiO_2 consisting of a vitreous or glassy silica formed naturally by the melting of quartz sand as a result of lightning or occas. the heat of impact of meteorites

le cha·te·lier's law *or* **le chatelier's principle** \lə'shäd·ᵊl,yāz-\ *n, usu cap 1st L & C* [after Henry-Louis *Le Châtelier*] : a statement in physics and chemistry: if the equilibrium of a system is disturbed by a change in one or more of the determining factors (as temperature, pressure, or concentration) the system tends to adjust itself to a new equilibrium by counteracting as far as possible the effect of the change

lechayim *or* **lechayyim** *var of* LEHAYIM

lech·ea \'lekēə\ *n, cap* [NL, fr. Johan *Leche* †1764 Sw. botanist] : a genus of herbs or subshrubs (family Cistaceae) having much-branched stems and minute purplish or greenish trimerous flowers — see PINWEED

¹**lech·er** \'lechə(r)\ *n* -s [ME *lechour*, fr. OF *lecheor*, fr. *lechier* to lick, live in debauchery or gluttony (of Gmc origin; akin to OHG *leckōn* to lick) + *-eor* -or — more at LICK] : a man who engages in lechery

²**lecher** \"\ *vi* -ED/-ING/-S [ME *lecheren*, fr. *lechour*, n.] : to practice lechery ⟨something better to do than drink and ~ —Agnes Repplier⟩

lech·er·ous \-ch(ə)rəs\ *adj* [ME, fr. MF *lechereus*, fr. OF, fr. *lecheor* + *-eus* -ous] **1** : given to lechery ⟨a ~ and self-indulgent good-for-nothing —Thomas Halton⟩ **2** : of, suggesting, or having the characteristics of a lecher ⟨well calculated to raise a ~ gleam in the . . . eye —R.S.Lanier⟩ **3** : arousing lust : sexually provocative ⟨a young girl came on with a ~ fandango —G.A.Wagner⟩ — **lech·er·ous·ly** *adv* — **lech·er·ous·ness** *n* -ES

lech·er wires \'lekə(r)-\ *n pl, usu cap L* [after Ernst *Lecher* †1926 Austrian physicist] : a pair of parallel wires so adjusted in length that the frequency of an electromagnetic wave may be determined from the position of the nodes and loops of the standing electromagnetic waves formed along the wires

lech·ery \'lech(ə)rē, -ri\ *n* -ES [ME *lecherie*, fr. OF, fr. *lechier* to lick, live in debauchery or gluttony + *-erie* -ery — more at LECHER] **1** : inordinate indulgence in sexual activity : LEWDNESS, LASCIVIOUSNESS ⟨a horrific sex prudishness which dissolved into an enervating ~ —*Times Lit. Supp.*⟩ **2** : an act of lechery ⟨his tasteless *lecheries* —*N.Y. Herald Tribune*⟩

le·cho·sa \lā'chōsə\ *or* **le·cho·za** \-ōzə\ *n* -s [Sp *lechosa*, fr. fem. of *lechoso* milky, fr. *leche* milk (fr. L *lact-, lac*) + *-oso* -ous (fr. L *-osus*) — more at GALAXY] : PAPAYA

lech·ri·o·dont \'lekrēō,dänt\ *adj* [fr. Gk *lechrios* slanting + E *-odont*] *of a salamander* : having palatal teeth only in anteriorly diverging or transverse rows on the posterior end of the vomers

lech·ri·o·don·ta \,≈≈≈'däntə\ *n pl, cap* [NL, fr. Gk *lechrios* slanting + NL *-odonta*] *in some classifications* : a primary division of Caudata comprising salamanders that are lechriodont

lech·u·gui·lla *also* **lech·e·gui·lla** \,lechə'gē(y)ə\ *n* -s [MexSp, fr. Sp, wild lettuce, dim. of *lechuga* lettuce, fr. L *lactuca* — more at LETTUCE] : any of several Mexican agaves (as *Agave lecheguilla*) yielding istle fiber

lechuguilla fever *also* **lechuguilla poisoning** *n* : a serious intoxication occurring in sheep and goats in the southwestern U.S. as a result of their feeding on a lechuguilla (*Agave lecheguilla*) and involving necrosis of the liver and kidney accompanied by jaundice and in light-skinned animals photosensitization and dermatitis

le·chwe \'lēchwē\ *also* **li·chi** \-chē\ *n* -s [of Bantu origin; akin to Sesuto *letsa* lechwe] : an African antelope (*Onotragus leche*) that is somewhat smaller than the related waterbuck and is chiefly fulvous with white belly and blackish legs

le·cid·ea \lə'sidēə\ *n, cap* [NL, fr. Gk *lekid-, lekis*, dim. of *lekos* dish — more at BALANCE] : a large genus (the type of the family Lecideaceae) of crustose lichens found on rocks and tree trunks and distinguished by the usu. dark hypothecium — **le·cid·e·a·ceous** \lə¦sidē¦āshəs\ *adj* — **le·cid·e·i·form** \lə'sidēə,fȯrm\ *adj* — **le·cid·e·ine** \-ēən\ *adj* — **le·cid·i·oid** \-ē,ȯid\ *adj*

lecith- *or* **lecitho-** *comb form* [ISV, fr. Gk *lekith-, lekitho-* fr. *lekithos*, prob. of non-IE origin] : yolk of an egg ⟨*lecithin*⟩ ⟨*lecitho*protein⟩

lec·i·thal \'lesəthəl\ *also* **lec·i·thic** \-thik, -thēk\ *adj* [*lecith-* + *-al* or *-ic*] : having a yolk — often used in combination ⟨homo*lecithal*⟩ ⟨telo*lecithal*⟩ — **lec·i·thal·i·ty** \,≈≈'thaləd·ē\ *n* -ES

lec·i·thin \'lesəthən\ *n* -s [ISV *lecith-* + *-in*] **1** : any of several waxy hygroscopic phosphatides that are widely distributed in animals and plants (as in nervous tissue), that form colloidal solutions in water and have emulsifying, wetting, and antioxidant properties, and that are choline esters of phosphatidic acids yielding on complete hydrolysis two fatty acid molecules and one molecule each of glycerol, phosphoric acid, and choline **2** : a commercially produced mixture of phosphatides containing lecithin: as **a** : a yellow to brown waxy solid obtained from egg yolk and used chiefly in medicine — called also *ovolecithin* **b** : a brown unbleached to light yellow bleached plastic to fluid substance that is obtained in the manufacture of soybean oil and usu. contains oil and other components as well as phosphatides and that is used in foods (as margarine, chocolate, bakery products) and animal feeds, in pharmaceutical and cosmetic products, in paints and printing inks, and in gasoline, lubricating oils, and other petroleum products as an additive — called also *commercial lecithin, soybean lecithin*

lec·i·thin·ase \-thə,nās, -āz\ *n* -s [ISV *lecithin* + *-ase*] : any of four enzymes that hydrolyze lecithins or cephalins by attacking different ester linkages: as **a** : a crystallizable enzyme that is found esp. in many venoms and that accelerates the removal of only one of the two fatty acid units in a molecule — called also *lecithinase A, phospholipase A;* compare LYSOLECITHIN **b** : an enzyme that is found in various plant and animal extracts and in bacteria and that accelerates the removal of the remaining fatty acid unit — called also *lecithinase B, phospholipase B*

lec·i·tho·pro·tein \¦lesə(,)thō+\ *n* [*lecith-* + *protein*] : any of a class of compounds of lecithin or other phosphatide with protein

leck \'lek\ *n* -s [origin unknown] *dial Brit* : a hard clay subsoil

le·clan·ché cell \lə¦klä¹n¦shā-\ *n, usu cap L* [after Georges *Leclanché* †1882 French chemist] : a zinc-carbon primary cell whose exciting liquid is a solution of sal ammoniac

le·conte's sparrow \lə'känt(s)-\ *n, usu cap L* [after John L. *Le Conte* †1883 Am. entomologist] : a small streaked buffy and brown sparrow (*Passerherbulus caudacutus*) of the grasslands of the west-central U.S. and Canada

le·cont·ite \lə'känt·,īt\ *n* -s [John L. *Le Conte* + E *-ite*] : a mineral $Na(NH_4,K)SO_4·2H_2O$ consisting of a hydrous sodium potassium ammonium sulfate found in bat guano

le·cros·ia \lə'krōsēə\ *n, cap* [NL, fr. *Le Cros*, town in southeastern France + NL *-ia*] : a genus of fossil coniferous woody plants of the Carboniferous and Permian periods characterized by isolated erect ovoid female cones that consist of numerous sessile narrow scales each of which bears two winged seeds

lect *abbr* **1** lector **2** lecture, lecturer

lec·tern \'lektə(r)n, -,tərn, -,tən, -,tə̇in\ *n* -s [ME *lectorne, lectrun*, alter. (influenced by ML *lectorinum, lectrinum* lectern) of *lettorne, letrune*, fr. MF *letrun, letrin*, fr. ML *lectorinum, lectrinum*, fr. LL *lector* + L *-inum* (neut. of *-inus* -ine) — more at LECTOR] **1 a** : a reading desk in a church on which the Bible is placed and from which scripture lessons are read during public worship **b** : a singing desk used in the choir of a church **2** : a desk or stand with a sloping top and usu. a ledge at the bottom of the slope designed to support a book or script in a convenient position for a reader standing before it ⟨was always standing restlessly at his ~ when his classes assembled —James Thurber⟩ ⟨spoke from an ornate ~⟩

lectern 1a

lec·tin \'lektən\ *n* -s [L *lectus* (past part. of *legere* to gather, select) + E *-in*] : a substance that is not known to be an antibody but that combines specifically with an antigen and produces phenomena resembling immunological reactions

lec·tion \'lekshən\ *n* -s [LL *lection-, lectio* — more at LESSON] **1** : a lesson or selection from sacred writings read in a church service **2** [NL *lection-, lectio*, fr. L] : a variant reading in a copy or edition of a text ⟨are offended by the obtrusion of the new ~s into the text —Thomas De Quincey⟩

lec·tion·ary \'lekshə,nerē, -ri\ *n* -ES [ML *lectionarium*, fr. LL *lection-, lectio* lection + *-arium* -ary] **1** : a book of lections for use in a church service **2** : a list of lections for use in a church service

lec·ti·ster·ni·um \,lektə'stərnēəm\ *n, pl* **lectisterniums** \-ēəmz\ *or* **lectister·nia** \-ēə\ [L, fr. *lectus* couch + *-i-* + *-sternium* (fr. *sternere* to spread) — more at LIE, STREW] : a religious rite of ancient Greece and Rome marked by the placing of images of gods on couches and the spreading of food before them

lec·tor \'lektə(r), -k,tȯ(ə)r, -ȯ(ə)\ *n* -s [LL, fr. L, one that reads, fr. *lectus* (past part. of *legere* to read) + *-or*] **1** : one whose chief duty is to read the lessons in a church service; *specif* : one ordained in the second lowest office of the minor orders in the Roman Catholic Church **2** [ML, fr. L] : a public lecturer at a college or university

lec·tor·ate \'lekt(ə)rət, -tə,rāt\ *or* **lec·tor·ship** \'lektər,ship, -k,tȯr,-\ *n* -s *often cap* [LL *lectoratus*, fr. *lector* lector + L *-atus* -ate] : the office or order of lector

lec·to·type \'lektə,tīp\ *n* [Gk *lektos* picked, chosen (fr. *legein* to gather, choose) + E *type*] : a specimen chosen as type of a species or subspecies if the author of the classification fails to designate a type

¹**lec·ture** \'lekchə(r), -kshə(r)\ *n* -s *often attrib* [ME, fr. MF, fr. L *lectura*, fr. *lectus* (past part. of *legere* to gather, select, read) + *-ura* -ure — more at LEGEND] **1** *archaic* **a** (1) : the act of reading : PERUSAL ⟨that face whose ~ shows what perfect beauty is —Philip Sidney⟩ (2) : something read or perused ⟨would limit . . . the Latin ~s to selected plays —Catherine Macaulay⟩ **b** (1) : the act of reading aloud ⟨her tongue faltered: the ~ flowed unevenly —Charlotte Brontë⟩ (2) : something read aloud ⟨then came a ~ out of some pious writer —Daniel Rock⟩ **2 a** : a discourse given before an audience esp. for instruction ⟨resources for growth . . . in books, exhibits, conferences, ~s —Gertrude H. Hildreth⟩ ⟨~ hall⟩ **b** *archaic* : a course of lectures usu. given regularly in accordance with the terms of their foundation : LECTURESHIP **3 a** : an instructional discourse given by a member of a college or university faculty ⟨are still using ~s to pass out information —Lynn White⟩ ⟨the ~ method⟩ ⟨a ~ course⟩ **b** : a college or university class; *esp* : one at which a lecture is given ⟨students . . . carrying only one subject or a short series of ~s —L.L.Bethel⟩ **c** *obs* : a private lesson ⟨attends every morning to give him a ~ upon speaking —Samuel Foote⟩ **4** *obs* : an instructive example ⟨heaven means to make one half of the species a moral ~ to the other —Edward Young⟩ **5** : a severe or formal reproof : REPRIMAND, SCOLDING ⟨was giving the rest of the family a sharp-tongued ~ —Eve Langley⟩

²**lecture** \"\ *vb* **lectured; lectured; lecturing** \-kchəriŋ, -ksh(ə)riŋ\ **lectures** *vi* : to deliver a lecture or a course of lectures ⟨found time to ~ at various colleges —J.C.Archer⟩ ~ *vt* **1** : to deliver a lecture to ⟨*lecturing* a group of tourists —Jack Goodman⟩ **2** : to reprove severely or formally : REBUKE, REPRIMAND ⟨she's always *lecturing* me —S.N.Behrman⟩ ⟨was mildly *lectured* for his part in the escapade⟩

lecture bottle *n* : a narrow metal cylinder about a foot long for holding a compressed gas (as hydrogen sulfide)

lec·tur·ee \¦lekchə¦rē, -kshə-\ *n* -s : one who listens to or receives a lecture ⟨lecturers who exercised their wits at the expense of the ~s —Vincent Sheean⟩

lec·tur·er \'≈≈rə(r)\ *n* -s **1** : one that lectures; *specif* : one giving a lecture course in a college or university ⟨the best ~ on the campus⟩ **2** : a clergyman in the Church of England holding an ancient teaching and preaching office ⟨to church, where our ~ made a sorry silly sermon —Samuel Pepys⟩ **3 a** : a member of the faculty of a British college or university who ranks below a professor **b** : a member of a college or university faculty having a temporary or part-time appointment

lec·ture·ship \'lekchə(r),ship, -kshə-\ *n* **1** : the office or position of lecturer; *esp* : the position of lecturer in a college or university **2 a** : a course of lectures **b** : a foundation supporting a lecture or course of lectures

lec·tur·ette \,lekchə¦ret, -ksh-\ *n* -s : a short lecture

lec·y·thi·da·ce·ae \,lesəthə'dāsē,ē\ *n pl, cap* [NL, fr. *Lecythid-, Lecythis*, type genus + *-aceae*] : a family of large tropical trees (order Myrtales) having alternate leaves and large fruit with a woody epicarp — **lec·y·thi·da·ceous** \¦≈≈≈'dāshəs\ *adj*

lec·y·this \'lesəthəs\ *n, cap* [NL, fr. LL *lecythus*] : a genus (the type of the family Lecythidaceae) of very large So. American trees distinguished by the woody operculate capsular fruit — see SAPUCAIA; compare MONKEY POT

lec·y·thoid \-sə,thȯid\ *adj* [*lecythus* + *-oid*] : resembling a lecythus

lec·y·thus \'lesəthəs\ *or* **lek·y·thos** \'lekə,thäs\ *also* **lek·y·thus** \-kəthəs\ *n, pl* **lecy·thi** \-sə,thī\ *or* **leky·thoi** \-kə,thȯi\ [LL & Gk; LL *lecythus*, fr. Gk *lēkythos*, prob. of non-IE origin] : a cylindrical or round and squat vase used by the ancient Greeks for oils and ointments

lecythus

led *past of* LEAD

-led *past of* -LE

led *abbr* ledger

led captain *n* : an obsequious follower : SYCOPHANT, TOADY ⟨and a rich lad at school or college has his followers, tuft-hunters, *led captains* —W.M.Thackeray⟩

le·de·bur·ite \'lādə,bu̇,rīt\ *n* -s [G *ledeburit*, fr. Adolf *Ledebur* †1906 Ger. metallurgist + G *-it* -ite] : the cementite-austenite eutectic structure in iron-carbon alloys or commercial cast iron

le·der·ho·sen \'lādə(r),hōzᵊn\ *n pl* [G, fr. MHG *lederhose*, fr. *leder* leather + *hose* leg covering, trousers] : knee-length leather trousers worn esp. in Bavaria

led farm *n, chiefly Scot* : a farm owned and managed by a nonresident farmer

¹**ledge** \'lej\ *n* -s [ME *legge*, prob. fr. *leggen* to lay — more at LAY] **1** : a raised or projecting edge or molding added to protect or check: as **a** : a bar forming the top of a gate **b** : a strip making the raised edge of a shelf, tray, or printer's galley **c** : the side of a rabbet against which a door or window closes **d** : CHAIR RAIL **e** : BATTEN, CLEAT **2** : a narrow shelf forming the top or projecting from the side of a wall or other vertical structure ⟨~s high on two walls served as plate racks⟩ **3** : RIDGE, REEF; *esp* : one under water near the shore **4 a** : a narrow horizontal shelf formed in a rock wall or declivity **b** : rock solid enough to form a ledge : BEDROCK **5** : an architectural stringcourse, molding, or fillet **6** : an ingate for a mold **7** : a mass of rock that constitutes a valuable mineral deposit : LODE, VEIN **8 a** : an athwartships timber supporting the deck of a wooden ship from beneath **b** : COAMING

²**ledge** \"\ *vb* -ED/-ING/-S *vi* : to form a ledge ~ *vt* : to form as or supply with ledges : place on or as if on a ledge

ledged \-jd\ *adj* : having ledges

ledge·less \-jləs\ *adj* : having no ledge

ledge·man \-jmən\ *n, pl* **ledgemen** : BREAKER 4e

¹**ledg·er** \'lejə(r)\ *n* -s [ME *legger*, prob. fr. *leggen* to lay + *-er* — more at LAY] **1 a** *obs* : a book of permanent record : REGISTER **b** : a book containing accounts to which debits and credits resulting from business transactions are posted from books of original entry **2** : a memorial stone slab laid flat over a grave ⟨buried . . . under a black marble ~ close to the North wall —J.L.Chester⟩ **3** : a horizontal timber that is secured to the uprights of scaffolding during building construction and supports the putlogs **4** *archaic* : a resident ambassador, agent, or commissioner **5** *or* **leg·er** \"\ **a** : LEDGER BAIT **b** : LEDGER LINE **c** : LEDGER TACKLE **6** *dial Brit* : a narrow wooden strip used to secure thatch to a roof

²**ledger** \"\ *vi* -ED/-ING/-S : to fish with ledger tackle

³**ledger** *adj, obs* : lying or remaining in a place : RESIDENT, STATIONARY

ledger bait *n* : fishing bait rigged so that the bait lies on the bottom below the sinker

ledger bark *n* [after Charles *Ledger*, 19th cent. Eng. botanist in Peru] : the chief commercial cinchona bark derived from cultivated Javanese cinchonas and notably rich in quinine

ledger blade *n* : a stationary blade in a machine for shearing cloth

ledger board *n* **1** : a horizontal board forming the top rail of a simple fence or the handrail of a balustrade **2** : a flooring board in scaffolding **3** : RIBBON 2b

ledger line *n* **1** : a fishing line arranged so that the lead and bait rest upon the bottom **2** *also* **leger line** : a short line added above or below the staff to extend its range in musical notation

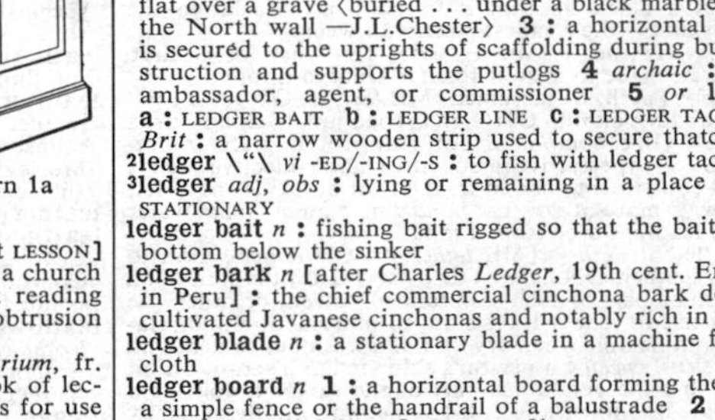

ledger lines 2

ledger paper *n* : a strong durable medium to heavy writing paper with good erasing quality used in business ledgers and record books

ledger plate *n* **1** : the shearing base over which a section of a reciprocating sickle or mower knife slides in cutting with an agricultural binder, reaper, or mower **2** : LEDGER STRIP

ledger score *n* : BACK SCORE 2

ledger strip *n* : a narrow strip of lumber nailed to the side of a girder and flush with its bottom edge to help support floor or ceiling joists notched to accommodate it — called also *ledger plate*

ledger tackle *n* : fishing tackle arranged so that the lead and bait rest upon the bottom

ledg·ing \'lejiŋ, -jēŋ\ *n* -s : a ledged structure or group of ledges : LEDGE

ledg·ment *or* **ledge·ment** \-jmənt\ *n* -s [ME *legement*, fr. *legge* ledge + *-ment* — more at LEDGE] : a horizontal suite of moldings (as the base moldings of a building)

ledgy \-jē\ *adj* -ER/-EST : abounding in ledges : consisting of a ledge or reef ⟨fields are ~ in places —E.B.White⟩

le·dol \'lē,dȯl, -dōl\ *n* -s [ISV *led-* (fr. NL *Ledum*) + *-ol*] : a crystalline sesquiterpenoid alcohol $C_{15}H_{25}OH$ occurring in the oil from the leaves and flowering tops of the marsh tea and in other essential oils

le·duc effect \lə'dük-\ *n, usu cap L* [after Sylvestre Anatole *Leduc*, 20th cent. French physicist] : RIGHI-LEDUC EFFECT

le·dum \'lēdəm\ *n* [NL, fr. Gk *lēdon* rockrose — more at LABDANUM] **1** *cap* : a genus of shrubs (family Ericaceae) of cold regions having a deciduous corolla of separate petals and a septicidal capsule — see LABRADOR TEA, MARSH TEA **2** -s : any plant of the genus *Ledum*

ledum camphor *n* : LEDOL

¹**lee** \'lē\ *n* -s [ME *le, lee*, fr. OE *hlēo, hlēow;* akin to OFris *hlī* protection, shelter, OS *hleo*, ON *hlē* protection, shelter, lee side, *hlȳr* lukewarm, OHG *lāo* lukewarm, Goth *hlija* hut, tent, L *calēre* to be warm, W *clyd* warm, cozy, Skt *śarad* autumn; basic meaning: warm] **1** : protecting shelter ⟨find a place . . . where we could get a little ~ provided we anchored close enough to the shore —Peter Heaton⟩ ⟨had squatted in the ~ of a rock —Farley Mowat⟩ ⟨worked in the ~ of the great, but did great things himself —*Times Lit. Supp.*⟩ **2** : the side (as of a ship or mountain) that is sheltered from the wind and provides shelter from it ⟨the smaller vessels clung to the ~ of some high mangrove island —Marjory S. Douglas⟩ ⟨a tramp snoring under the ~ of a haystack —Nicholas Monsarrat⟩ — **by the lee** *adv* : with the sails brought aback by falling off when running free

²**lee** \"\ *adj* **1** : of or relating to the side sheltered from the wind — opposed to *weather* ⟨the rocky point . . . was in sight, broad on the ~ bow —Frederick Marryat⟩ **2 a** : located on the side away from which an advancing glacier moves ⟨~ slope⟩ — opposed to *stoss* **b** : located on the side away from which the prevailing wind blows — used of a hillside or a knob of rock

³**lee** \"\ *n* -s [ME *lie*, fr. MF, fr. ML *lia*, prob. of Celt origin; akin to OIr *lige* bed, Gaulish *legasit* he laid, W *llaid* mud — more at LIE] : the settlings of liquor (as wine) during fermentation and aging : DREGS, SEDIMENT — now used only in pl. ⟨the wine of life is drawn and the mere ~s . . . left —Shak.⟩ ⟨broken men, bond servants, "gaolbirds," the ~s and settlings of the old world —V.L.Parrington⟩

lee·an·gle *also* **li·an·gle** \'lē,aŋgəl\ *n* -s [native name in Australia] : a heavy weapon of the Australian aborigines with a sharp-pointed end about nine inches long bent at right angles to the shank

leeboard \'≈,≈\ *n* : either of the wood or metal planes attached outside the hull of a sailing ship or sailboat to prevent leeway

lee–bow \'≈,≈\ *vt* : to get (a tide or current) on a sailing ship's lee bow to offset a leeward course caused by the wind

¹**leech** \'lēch\ *n* -ES [ME *leche*, fr. OE *lǣce;* akin to OHG *lāhhi* physician, ON *lǣknir*, Goth *lekeis* physician, and perh. to Gk *legein* to gather, choose, speak — more at LEGEND] **1 a** *archaic* : PHYSICIAN, SURGEON ⟨make each prescribe to other as each other's ~ —Shak.⟩ ⟨presents herself as a ~ able to cure the disease —Mary D. Anderson⟩ **b** *now dial Brit* : VETERINARIAN **2** [so called fr. its former use by physicians for bleeding patients] **a** : any of numerous carnivorous or bloodsucking annelid worms constituting the class Hirudinea, having typically a flattened segmented body of lanceolate outline that is broader near the posterior end and has externally well-marked annulations which are far more numerous than the true segments, a sucker at each end of the body, a mouth within the anterior sucker, and a large stomach with capacious pouches at the sides, being hermaphroditic usu. with direct development, and occurring chiefly in fresh water although a few are marine and some tropical forms are terrestrial — see GNATHOBDELLIDA, PHARYNGOBDELLIDA, RHYNCHOBDELLIDA

b : an insect larva superficially resembling a leech 3 : a hanger-on who seeks advantage or gain : PARASITE ⟨the shark is there and the shark's prey; the spendthrift and the ~ that sucks him —William Cowper⟩ ⟨~es . . . hateful parasites feeding upon the blood of artists —Robertson Davies⟩ **syn** see PARASITE

2**leech** \"\ vb -ED/-ING/-ES [ME *lechen*, fr. *leche*, n.] *vt* **1 a** : to treat as a physician : CURE, HEAL ⟨cobra poison none may ~ —Rudyard Kipling⟩ **b** : to bleed by the use of leeches **2** : to fasten onto as a leech : feed on the blood or substance of : DRAIN, EXHAUST ⟨bankers who had always ~*ed* them white —D.A.Munro⟩ ~ *vi* : to attach oneself in or as if in the manner of a leech ⟨she would ~ on to him and drain the life out of him —W.L.Gresham⟩

3**leech** *or* **leach** \"\ *n* -ES [ME *lek, leche, lyche*, fr. MLG *līk* rope to which the sail is fastened; akin to MHG *geleich* joint, limb — more at LIGATURE] **1** : either vertical edge of a square sail — see SAIL illustration **2** : the after edge of a fore-and-aft sail

leechcraft \'ˌ=,=\ *n* [ME *lechecraft*, fr. OE *lǣcecræft*, fr. *lǣce* physician + *cræft* craft — more at LEECH, CRAFT] : the art of healing : medical knowledge and skill

leech·dom \'lēchdəm\ *n* -S [ME *lechedom*, fr. OE *lǣcedōm*, fr. *lǣce* + *-dōm* -dom] *archaic* : MEDICINE

leecheater \'ˌ=,==\ *n* **1** : CROCODILE BIRD **2** : SPUR-WINGED PLOVER

leechee *var of* LITCHI

leeches *n pl* [fr. pl. of 1*leech* (worm); fr. the appearance of the blisters] *dial* : summer sores of the horse or mule

leech line *n* [3*leech*] : a line attached to the middle of the leech of a sail and used to haul the leech up to the yard

leech rope *n* [3*leech*] : the part of the boltrope that is sewed to the leech of a sail

1**leed** \'lēd\ *n* -S [ME *lede, leden*, fr. OE *Læden, Leden* Latin, language, fr. (assumed) VL *Ladinus*, fr. L *Latinus* — more at LATIN] **1** *now Scot* : spoken or written language : SPEECH **2** *Scot* : SONG, TUNE

2**leed** *var of* LEAD

leeds \'lēdz\ *adj, usu cap* [fr. *Leeds*, England] : of or from the city of Leeds, Yorkshire, England : of the kind or style prevalent in Leeds

lee-enfield rifle \'lē'en,fēld-\ *n, usu cap L&E* [James P. *Lee* †1904 American inventor born in Scotland + *Enfield*, town near London, Eng.] : a short repeating British military rifle fed from a magazine and fitted with a knife bayonet

lee·fang *or* **lee·fange** \'lē,faŋ\ *n* -S [1*lee* + *fang*] *Brit* : TRAVELER 3b

lee·ful \'lēfəl\ *adj* [ME *leveful*, fr. *leve* leave + *-ful* — more at LEAVE] *archaic* : LAWFUL, LICIT

lee gauge *n* : a position to leeward of another ship — used in the phrase *to have the lee gauge of;* compare WEATHER GAUGE

leeg·te \'lēktə\ *n* -S [Afrik, emptiness, valley, fr. *leeg* empty, fr. MD *lēdich* free, idle, empty] : LAAGTE

lee helm *n* : a helm kept somewhat alee to offset a sailing ship's tendency in some conditions to fall away from the wind to leeward ⟨the ship carries a *lee helm*⟩

leek \'lēk\ *n* -S [ME *lek, leek*, fr. OE *lēac* leek, onion, garlic; akin to OS *lōk* leek, OHG *louh*, ON *laukr* leek, garlic, and perh. to Gk *lygizein* to bend — more at LOCK] **1 a** : a biennial herb (*Allium porrum*) that is closely related to the garlic and onion, is known only in cultivation but believed to be derived from a wild Eurasian plant (*A. ampeloprasum*), and is commonly grown as an annual for its mildly pungent succulent linear leaves and esp. its thick cylindrical stalk consisting of blanched leafstalks and small simple bulb **b** : any of several alliums usu. with slender cylindrical bulbs — usu. used in combination ⟨sand ~⟩; see WILD LEEK **2** *or* **leek green a** : RESEDA 2a **b** : a moderate yellow green that is greener and duller than average moss green, yellower and duller than average pea green or apple green (sense 1), and yellower and less strong than spinach green — called also *porret, prasine* **3** : GREEN LEEK

leek moth *n* : a small European moth (*Acrolepia assectella*) having a larva that burrows in and feeds on the developing leaves of leeks and some related plants

lee·lane \'lē,lān\ *adj* [*lee* (prob. alter. of 1*lief*) + *lane* (lone)] *Scot* : all alone — used with a possessive pronoun

lee·lang \'lē,laŋ\ *adj* [*lee-* (prob. alter. of 2*lief*) + *lang* (long)] *Scot* : LIVELONG

1**leem** \'lēm\ *var of* LEAM

2**leem** \"\ *Scot var of* 1LOOM

1**leep** \'lēp\ *vt* -ED/-ING/-S [prob. of Scand origin; akin to ON *hleypa* to cause to leap, curdle, Norw *løpe, løypa* to curdle, boil or fry gently, Icel. *hleypa* to curdle, put in boiling water for a short time, fry gently; causatives fr. the root of ON *hlaupa* to leap — more at LEAP] *dial Brit* : BOIL, SCALD

2**leep** \"\ *vt* -ED/-ING/-S [Hindi *lipnā*] *India* : to plaster (as a wall) with cow dung

1**leer** *n* -S [ME *ler, lere* cheek, face, aspect, fr. OE *hlēor* cheek, face; akin to OS *hleor* cheek, MD *lier, liere*, ON *hlȳr* cheek, *hlust* ear — more at LISTEN] *obs* : COMPLEXION, ASPECT, COUNTENANCE

2**leer** \'li(ə)r, 'li(ə)\ *vb* -ED/-ING/-S [prob. fr. obs. *leer* cheek, fr. ME *ler, lere*] *vi* **1** : to cast a sidelong glance : give a lascivious, knowing, or malicious look : FLEER ⟨~*ed* like the face of a trollop worn out by the passage of men and time —T.H.Raddall⟩ ⟨poured the drink, added water, and looked again at the judge, ~*ing* with a kind of comic cunning —R.P. Warren⟩ **2** *obs* : to move furtively : SLINK, SNEAK ⟨~*ed* away on the other side, as one ashamed of what he had done —John Bunyan⟩ ~ *vt* **1** : to glance with or turn (the eye) **2** : to seduce with the eye

3**leer** \"\ *n* -S : a sly, sinister, or immodest glance : a knowing or wanton look ⟨she gives the ~ of invitation —Shak.⟩ ⟨the sordid furtive ~ of the profit seeker —A.L.Guérard⟩

4**leer** \"\ *adj, archaic* : looking slyly, wantonly, or knowingly

5**leer** \"\ *adj* [ME *lere*, fr. OE *gelǣr*; akin to OS & OHG *lāri* empty; prob. derivatives fr. the stem of OE *lesan* to gather, glean — more at LEASE] **1** : EMPTY, UNLADEN **2** *dial Eng* : weak from hunger : HUNGRY

6**leer** \'lēə(r)\ *n* -S [ME *leere*, prob. fr. OE *līra* fleshy part of the body — more at LEG] *now dial Brit* : FLANK, LOIN

7**leer** *var of* LEHR

leer·fish \'lir,fish\ *also* **leer·vis** \-,vis\ *n* [*leerfish* part trans. of Afrik *leervis*, fr. *leer* leather + *vis* fish; *leervis* fr. Afrik] : a leading carangid game fish (*Hypacanthus amia*) of the west coast of Africa that is bluish gray, vigorous, and often 6 feet in length — called also *garrick*

leer·i·ly \'lirəlē\ *adv* : in a leery manner

leer·i·ness \-rēnəs\ *n* -ES : WARINESS

leering *adj* : LEWD, SLY, MALICIOUS ⟨a fine ~ gusto —Wolcott Gibbs⟩ ⟨an uneasy ~ quality . . . that I find in dubious taste —Dudley Fitts⟩ ⟨she had run in fear of him, his evil ~ eye —Amy Lowell⟩ — **leer·ing·ly** *adv*

leerman *var of* LEHRMAN

leer·ness \'lirnəs\ *n* -ES [ME *lerenesse*, fr. OE *lǣrnes*, fr. *gelǣr* empty + *-nes* -ness] : EMPTINESS

leer·sia \'lirzēə\ *n, cap* [NL, fr. Johann D. *Leers* †1774 Ger. botanist + NL *-ia*] : a genus of perennial chiefly swamp grasses having flat roughish leaves and one-flowered spikelets — see RICE CUT-GRASS, WHITE GRAMA

1**leery** \'lēri\ *adj* [5*leer* + *-y*] *dial Eng* : 5LEER

2**leery** \'lirē, -ri\ *adj* -ER/-EST [4*leer* + *-y*] **1** *archaic* : ALERT, KNOWING, WIDE-AWAKE **2** : exhibiting suspicion or doubt : DISTRUSTFUL, WARY — usu. used with *of* ⟨the local woodpeckers . . . are ~ of any sort of enclosure —*New Yorker*⟩ ⟨bookmakers were beginning to get ~ of taking his bets —Robert Rice⟩ ⟨liberalism has been singularly ~ of defining its own theoretical principles —Max Ascoli⟩

lees *pl of* LEE

lee's birthday \'lēz-\ *n, usu cap L&B* [after Robert E. *Lee* †1870 Am. soldier, commander in chief of the Confederate armies] : January 19 observed as a legal holiday in 10 southern states

leese *vb* [ME *lesen*, fr. OE *lēosan* — more at LOSE] *vt, obs* : LOSE ~ *vi, obs* : to be a loser

lee shore *n* **1 a** : a shore lying off a ship's leeward side and constituting a severe danger in storm ⟨a dangerous *lee shore* —F.D.Ommanney⟩ **b** : a source of peril or cause of ruin ⟨dramatizes our present course as a drift toward the *lee shore* of totalitarianism —C.E.Ayres⟩ **2** *obs* : a shore offering shelter from storm

1**lee·some** \'lēsəm\ *adj* [ME *lefsum*, fr. *lef* dear + *-sum* -some — more at LIEF] *Scot* : PLEASANT, DELIGHTFUL

2**leesome** \"\ *adj* [ME *lefsum*, fr. *leve* leave + *-sum* -some — more at LEAVE] *Scot* : LAWFUL, JUST

1**leet** *n* -S [fr. (assumed) ME, fr. OE *gelǣte*, fr. *lǣtan* to let — more at LET] *obs* : a place where roads meet or cross : INTERSECTION

2**leet** \'lēt\ *n* -S [ME *lete*, fr. AF *lete* or ML *leta*] **1** : COURT LEET **2** : the jurisdictional district of a court leet

3**leet** \"\ *n* -S [ME (Sc) *lite*] *chiefly Scot* : a list of candidates

4**leet** \'lēt\ *n* -S [origin unknown] *dial Brit* : STACK, PILE

5**leet** \"\ *dial Eng var of* LIGHT

1**leeve** \'lēv\ *chiefly dial var of* LIEF

2**leeve** \"\ *dial Brit var of* 1LIVE

1**lee·ward** \'lüə(r)d (*usual nautical pronunc*), 'lēwə-\ *adj* [1*lee* + *-ward*] : situated away from the wind : DOWNWIND ⟨~ side of the house —Hamlin Garland⟩ — opposed to *windward*

2**leeward** \"\ *n* -S : the lee side ⟨advisable to try to sail to ~ of your objective —H.A.Calahan⟩ — opposed to *windward*

lee·ward·ly \-dlē\ *adj* : tending to fall off to leeward or to make leeway — opposed to *weatherly*

lee·ward·most \-d,mōst *also chiefly Brit* -dməst\ *adj, archaic* : most leeward

leeward tide *also* **lee tide** *n* : a tide running onshore or offshore while the wind blows in the same direction and thus creating danger for small craft

leeway \'ˌ=,=\ *n* [1*lee* + *way*] **1 a** : off-course lateral movement of a ship when under way caused by wind or current **b** : DRIFT ANGLE 2 **2** : the measure of discrepancy between fact and standard : degree of deviation from a criterion or goal : margin of shortcoming in performance ⟨men had to catch up on a dreadful ~ of ignorance —A.T.Quiller-Couch⟩ **3 a** : allowable variation : TOLERANCE ⟨there can be little ~ in the size of the explosive charge —*Science Yr. Bk.*⟩ **b** : degree of freedom of action or permitted discretion : room for choice ⟨a professor of English . . . can generally enjoy more intellectual ~ than a professor of sociology —Irving Howe⟩ **c** : margin of safety ⟨an hour's ~ to catch the plane⟩ ⟨maintains a capital reserve to provide financial ~⟩ **syn** see ROOM

lee wheel *n* : the share in steering done by one or more assistants to a ship's helmsman — compare WEATHER WHEEL

lef·se \'lefsə\ *n, pl* **lef·sen** \-sən\ *or* **lefses** [Norw, fr. *lev, leiv* pancake, slice of bread, fr. ON *hleifr* loaf — more at LOAF] : a large thin potato pancake served buttered and folded

1**left** \'left\ *adj, sometimes* -ER/-EST [ME *luft, lift, left*, fr. OE *left, lyft-* (as in *lyftādl* palsy) weak; akin to MD *lucht, luft, loft* left, MLG *lucht*] **1 a** : of or relating to the hand that in most persons is weaker, to the side of the body on which it is, or to the parts of that side of the body ⟨combat men who looked at a man's ~ chest before they looked at his face —C.H.Norcross⟩ **b** : located on an observer's left or directed as his left hand would point ⟨outflanked the army's ~ wing⟩ ⟨the ~ fork of the road looked the more inviting of the two⟩ **2** *often cap* : of, adhering to, or constituted by the left esp. in politics ⟨this ~ government with a cabinet of moderate liberals —F.A.Magruder⟩ ⟨the Communists and their political ally, the *Left* Socialists —C.A.L.Rich⟩ ⟨fashionable . . . among many ~ intellectuals —Philip O'Connor⟩ ⟨the ~ religious movements . . . animated by the social gospel —G.A.Almond⟩ ⟨untiring representative of the ~*est* of left-wingers —*Glasgow Herald*⟩ ⟨in some respects they are going still ~*er* —A.A. Berle⟩ — **over the left shoulder** *or* **over the left** : not at all — used as an aside to indicate negation of what is said

2**left** \"\ *n* -S [ME *luft, lift, left*, fr. *luft, lift, left*, adj.] **1 a** : the left hand ⟨lashed out with his ~ —Gregor Felsen⟩ **b** : the location or direction lying on the left side of one's body ⟨passed a house on his ~⟩ **c** : the part (as the wing of an army) that is on the left side of an observer facing in the direction it faces **d** : the member of a pair situated or used on the left side **2 a** : LEFT FIELD **b** : a boxer's blow with the left fist ⟨broke through the American's defense repeatedly with jolts and spearing ~*s* —P.J.Cunningham⟩ **3** *often cap* **a** : the part of a legislative chamber located to the left of the presiding officer and usu. occupied in continental European and other countries having a similar political pattern by members professing a more radical position on political issues than other members ⟨loud applause in the center and on certain benches of the ~ —D.W.S.Lidderdale⟩ ⟨in the other European countries . . . the ~ is occupied by the Communists and Socialists —Enzo Di Cocco⟩ — compare CENTER 3c, RIGHT **b** : the members of a legislative body occupying the left as a result of their political views ⟨members of the Chamber of Deputies . . . became tense; the *Left* became vociferous —A.W.Macmahon & W.R.Dittmar⟩ **4** *usu cap* **a** : individuals or groups professing views usu. characterized by opposition to and a desire to alter (as by reform or revolution) the established order esp. in politics and usu. advocating change in the name of the greater freedom or well-being of the common man ⟨the tradition of liberalism, democracy, and socialism belongs to the democratic *Left* —Simon Paynter⟩ ⟨the totalitarianism of the *Left* —Howard Rushmore⟩ ⟨his position in the literary *Left* —Paul Potts⟩ ⟨his contempt for the Right is exceeded only by his contempt for the *Left* —Bergen Evans⟩ — compare RIGHT **b** : the symbolic position occupied by persons professing such views : a radical as distinguished from a conservative position ⟨the clericalist threat from the Right drove the earlier governments of the Third Republic . . . further to the radical *Left* —*Times Lit. Supp.*⟩ ⟨after an interval of twenty or thirty years the *Left* of one period becomes the Right of the next —Barbara & Robert North⟩

3**left** \"\ *adv* [ME *luft, lift, left*, fr. *luft, lift, left*, adj.] : on or to the left ⟨questing neither ~ nor right —Rudyard Kipling⟩ ⟨as right-center governments continued to ignore reform, the people moved ~ —*New Republic*⟩

4**left** *past of* LEAVE

1**left-bank** \'ˌ=ˌ=\ *adj, often cap L&B* [fr. the *Left Bank* (of the Seine river), the bohemian district of Paris, France; trans. of F *Rive Gauche*] : of, relating to, or situated in the bohemian district of Paris

2**left-bank** \"\ *vb* [fr. the phrase *left bank*] *vt* : to bank (an airplane) to the left ~ *vi* : to bank to the left (as an airplane or a bird in flight)

left bower *n* : the jack of the other suit of the same color as the trump suit (as in euchre and five hundred)

left-center \'ˌ=ˌ==\ *n, often cap L&C* [trans. of F *centre gauche*] : a political group or an organized party belonging to the Center but closely associated with the Left in policies and practice ⟨in Denmark . . . the Liberals represented the Right-Center and the Radicals the *Left-Center* —Barbara & Robert North⟩ — compare RIGHT-CENTER

left face *n* [fr. the imper. phrase *left, face*] : the act of turning 90 degrees to the left from the halted position of attention as a military maneuver — often used as a command; compare ABOUT-FACE, RIGHT FACE

left field *n* **1** : the part of the baseball outfield to the left facing from the plate **2** : the station of the player defending left field — see BASEBALL illustration

left fielder *n* : one who plays left field

left-footed \'ˌ=ˌ==\ *adj* **1** : stronger or more adept with the left foot ⟨a *left-footed* player for the left wing, and vice-versa —C.W.Alcock⟩ **2** : AWKWARD, CLUMSY, WEAK ⟨the new version sounds *left-footed* and pathetic —J.M.Conly⟩ — **left-footed·ness** *n*

left-hand \'ˌ=ˌ=\ *adj* [ME *lefthand*, fr. the phrase *left hand*] **1** : situated on the left : nearer the left hand than the right ⟨decided to try the *left-hand* house⟩ **2** : using or being performed with the left hand : LEFT-HANDED ⟨made a *left-hand* pitch⟩ **3 a** *of a door* : opening to the left away from one **b** *of a hinge* : fitting or designed to fit a left-hand or left-hand reverse bevel door **c** *of a lock* (1) : fitting or designed to fit on a left-hand or left-hand reverse bevel door or on a right-hand reverse bevel door if both sides of the lock operate (2) : throwing or designed to throw left **4 a** *of a turning tool* : designed to cut to the left **b** *of a thread chaser* : designed to cut a left-hand screw thread **c** *of a milling cutter* : designed to rotate clockwise **5 a** : DEVIOUS, INDIRECT, OBLIQUE ⟨his statement was verified in a *left-hand* way —Earl Brown⟩ **b** : CLUMSY **c** : SINISTER **6 a** : MORGANATIC **b** : of, relating to, united in, or born of an illicit liaison : ILLEGITIMATE ⟨never acknowledged his *left-hand* family⟩ **7** *of a rope* : LEFT-LAID **8 a** : of or relating to a division of non-Brahmanical castes in southern India formerly subjected to social and ceremonial disabilities **b** : of or relating to a division of Shaktism marked by secret orgiastic rites

1**left-handed** \'ˌ=ˌ==\ *adj* [ME *left handed*, fr. *left hand* + *-ed*] **1** : having the left hand more apt or usable than the right : preferring the left hand : SOUTHPAW ⟨a brilliant *left-handed* pitcher⟩ **2 a** : marked by clumsiness or ineptitude : AWKWARD **b** : exhibiting deviousness or indirection : OBLIQUE, UNINTENDED ⟨New England contributed to freedom of conscience only by the *left-handed* method of making martyrs to that cause —G.W.Johnson⟩ **c** *obs* : given to malevolent scheming or contriving : SINISTER, UNDERHAND **3** : marked by uncertain or ambiguous intent : BACKHANDED, DUBIOUS, DOUBLE-EDGED ⟨is not very grateful for this support, which it considers a *left-handed* compliment —J.A.C.F.Auer⟩ ⟨did the industry a *left-handed* favor —*Steelways*⟩ **4** *archaic* : portending ill : INAUSPICIOUS **5 a** : of, relating to, or born of a morganatic marriage **b** : of or relating to an illicit or informal liaison : ILLEGITIMATE ⟨though only four marriages between Frenchmen and Indians were recorded, *left-handed* marriages are known to have been frequent —*William & Mary Quarterly*⟩ **6** : LEFT-HAND 4 **7 a** : having a crystal structure that has a mirror-image relationship to another enantiomorphous structure regarded as right-handed in which the same compound can crystallize ⟨*left-handed* quartz⟩ **b** : having crystal faces that result from and may be used to characterize such a structure **c** : LEVOROTATORY **8** *of a rope* : LEFT-LAID **9** : SINISTRAL ⟨*left-handed* whelks⟩ — **left-hand·ed·ly** *adv* — **left-hand·ed·ness** *n* -ES

2**left-handed** \"\ *adv* : with the left hand : in a left-handed manner : LEFT-HANDEDLY ⟨pitched *left-handed*⟩

left-handed rope *or* **left-hand rope** *n* **1** : a left-laid rope in which the strands are formed of yarns with right-handed twist — called also *back-handed rope;* compare RIGHT-HANDED ROPE **2** : any left-laid rope

left-hand·er \'left'handə(r), -aan-\ *n* **1** : a left-handed person : SOUTHPAW ⟨young *left-hander* who tossed two shutouts —*N.Y. Times*⟩ **2** : a blow struck with the left hand ⟨started in with a fine *left-hander* on his right eye —O.Henry⟩

left-hand lady *n* : CORNER LADY

left-hand reverse bevel *adj, of a cupboard or closet door* : opening to the left toward one

left-hand rule *n* : a rule in electricity: if the thumb and first two fingers of the left hand are arranged at right angles to each other on a conductor and the hand oriented so that the first finger points in the direction of the magnetic field and the middle finger in the direction of the electric current then the thumb will point in the direction of the force on the conductor

left-hand screw thread *n* : a screw thread whose helix moves upward when the screw is inserted vertically from above in a fixed mating thread and turned clockwise

left heart *n* : the left auricle and ventricle : the half of the heart containing oxygenated blood

left·ish \'leftish, -tēsh\ *adj* : showing leftist tendencies ⟨highbrow ~ periodical —Isaac Deutscher⟩ ⟨a ~ congressman⟩

left·ism \'lef,tizəm\ *n* -S *sometimes cap* **1** : the principles and views of the Left; *also* : the movement embodying these principles ⟨the real danger is not liberalism or ~ —*New Republic*⟩ ⟨~, British style, played an important part in the freedom movement —Christopher Rand⟩ **2** : advocacy of or adherence to the doctrines of the Left ⟨a swing from the right of the Popular Front to a ~ —James Burnham⟩ ⟨charges and taints of ~ —Lawrence Stessin⟩

1**left·ist** \'leftəst\ *n* -S *often cap* [2*left* + *-ist*] **1** : a member of a group (as a political party) belonging to the Left ⟨the United Front of *Leftists* . . . obtained 25 seats —*Amer. Scholar*⟩ ⟨~*s*, encouraged by their success in Sunday's general election —*N.Y. Herald-Tribune*⟩ **2** : one that believes in or advocates principles associated with the Left : RADICAL ⟨contrary to the opinion of romanticists and ~*s* —L.L.Sharkey⟩ ⟨many . . . unaffiliated ~*s* were at one time Communists or Communist sympathizers —Granville Hicks⟩

2**leftist** \"\ *adj, often cap* **1** : of, relating to, or favoring the Left or a group belonging to the Left ⟨the *Leftist* ticket . . . would be certain of 238 of the 473 seats —*N.Y. Herald-Tribune*⟩ ⟨~ elements . . . have taken a leading part in the nationalist movements —A.H.McDonald⟩ **2** : favoring, characterized by, or based upon the principles of the Left ⟨the ~ . . . movement of this generation —Lillian Symes⟩ ⟨the present ~ attitude of the . . . administration —M.K.Hart⟩

left-laid \'ˌ=ˌ=\ *adj, of rope* : formed of strands twisted to the left of an observer viewing them lengthwise

left-luggage office \'ˌ=ˌ==ˌ==\ *n, Brit* : CHECKROOM

left·ments \'leftmənts\ *n pl* [4*left* + *-ment* + *-s*] : LEFTOVERS, REMAINDERS, RESIDUE

left-most \'left,mōst\ *adj* : farthest on the left

left-off \'ˌ=ˌ=\ *adj* [fr. the past part. of *leave off*] : laid aside : CAST-OFF ⟨all sent Christmas and birthday presents and parcels of *left-off* clothing —Flora Thompson⟩

1**leftover** \'ˌ=,==\ *adj* [fr. the past part. of *leave over*] : remaining as unused residue ⟨put the Thermos bottles back in, and the *leftover* lobster and things —B.A.Williams⟩ ⟨spring has been like *leftover* winter here —Janet Flanner⟩

2**leftover** \"\ *n* -S **1** : an unused or unconsumed residue: as **a** : fragments of food remaining from a meal ⟨made supper from the ~*s* from dinner —J.B.Benefield⟩ ⟨poetry in full retreat . . . all literature living on sufferance, feeding on ~*s* —H.J.Muller⟩ **b** : a dish prepared from leftovers ⟨a pretty appetizing morsel when incorporated with other ingredients for a ~ —Nancy Dixon⟩ **c** : SURPLUS ⟨bedding, cooking equipment and similar supplies presumably can be drawn from the army's ~*s* —R.A.H.Thompson⟩ **2** : an anachronistic survival : VESTIGE ⟨the forelimbs of the heavy vertical reptiles seem . . . to have become useless ~*s* —Weston LaBarre⟩ ⟨an aristocratic ~ in modern government—Mollie Panter-Downes⟩

left rudder *n* : a position of a ship's rudder that will turn the ship to the left — often used as a command

left shoulder arms *n* [fr. the imper. phrase *left shoulder, arms*] : a position in the manual of arms in which the rifle is held in the left hand with the barrel resting against the left shoulder and the muzzle inclined to the rear — often used as a command; compare RIGHT SHOULDER ARMS

1**left stage** *n* [1*left* + *stage*] : the half of a theatrical stage to the left of an actor facing the audience

2**left stage** *adv* (*or adj*) : toward or on the half of a theatrical stage to the left of an actor facing the audience ⟨enters *left stage*⟩ ⟨quite ignored the whole *left stage* fiasco⟩ — compare DOWNSTAGE, RIGHT STAGE, UPSTAGE

left·ward \'leftwərd\ *or* **left·wards** \-dz\ *adv* (*or adj*) [ME *leftward*, fr. *left* + *-ward*] : toward or on the left ⟨veered ~ and so missed the stalled car⟩ ⟨prevent any more legislation with a ~ tinge —*New Republic*⟩ — **left·ward·ly** *adv*

left wing *n* **1** : the division of a group (as a political party) that believes in or advocates leftist principles and practices ⟨the right wing and the *left wing* of his own party —R.L.Strout⟩ ⟨the leader of Labour's radical *left wing* —*N.Y. Times*⟩ ⟨the *left wing* in the needle trades —*Nation*⟩ — compare RIGHT WING **2** : LEFT 4a ⟨in the estimation of the *left wing* of American politics —*Nation*⟩

left-wing \'left'twiŋ\ *adj* [*left wing*] : of, adhering to, or favoring the Left ⟨the history of English *left-wing* political thought —*Brit. Book News*⟩ ⟨the bulk of the *left-wing* intelligentsia—George Orwell⟩ ⟨a veteran pro-Commie . . . leader of the *left-wing* camarilla —Victor Riesel⟩

left-wing·er \-ŋə(r)\ *n* -S **1** : a member of a left wing ⟨the Labor *left-wingers* claim the walkout as a victory for themselves —*Irish Statesman*⟩ **2** : LEFTIST ⟨nearly all English *left-wingers*, from Laborites to Anarchists —George Orwell⟩

lefty \'leftē, -ti\ *n* -ES **1** : LEFT-HANDER **2** : a political leftist

1**leg** \'leg, 'lāg\ *n* -S *often attrib* [ME *leg, legge*, fr. ON *leggr* leg, bone; akin to OE *līra* fleshy part of the body, ON *lær* thigh, L *lacertus* muscles, upper arm, *lacerta* lizard, Gk *lax* with the foot, Skt *ṛkṣalā* foot joint of a hoofed animal] **1** : one of the appendages of an animal that are used chiefly in supporting the body and in moving from point to point esp. by walking: as **a** (1) : one of the paired limbs of a vertebrate so used ⟨bipeds like man have two ~*s;* quadrupeds have four⟩

— compare ARM, WING (2) : the part of such a limb between

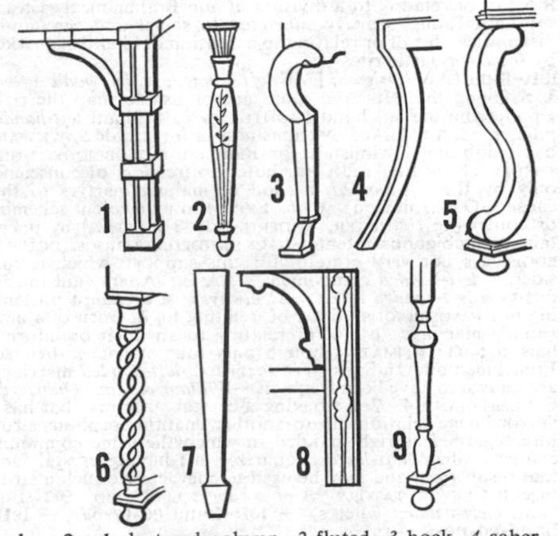

legs 2c: *1* clustered column, *2* fluted, *3* hock, *4* saber, *5* scroll, *6* spiral, *7* taper, *8* truss, *9* turned

the knee and the foot — distinguished from *thigh* **b :** one of the paired jointed segmental appendages of an arthropod; *esp* **:** one of the rather generalized appendages used in walking or crawling ⟨a typical abdominal ~ of a caterpillar consists of three parts —R.E.Snodgrass⟩ **2 :** something resembling an animal leg in form or use: as **a** (1) **:** a pole or bar serving as a support (as in a tripod) or as a prop or shore (as to a ship or building) ⟨the four ~*s* of each tower rest in large porcelain insulators —*Scientific American*⟩ (2) **:** something resembling or held to resemble such a support ⟨the third ~ upholding this tripod of international economic cooperation —Paul Bareau⟩ **b :** a contrivance or representation made to resemble or function esp. as a human leg ⟨the unfortunate man wore a wooden ~⟩ **c :** a support of a piece of furniture ⟨a chair ~⟩ ⟨the table's single pedestal . . . branched into four ~*s* —Adrian Bell⟩ **d :** a branch of a forked or jointed object (as an instrument) ⟨the ~*s* of a pair of compasses⟩ **e :** a section of rope in a knot or a bridle ⟨the ~*s* of a bowline⟩ ⟨the towing stresses will be divided between the two ~*s* of the bridle —*Manual of Seamanship*⟩ **f :** a part of a structure ⟨a starting ~ on the north side of a T-maze —*Psychological Abstracts*⟩ **g :** the part of a plant stem between the base and the point from which branches arise ⟨the bush should have a 6 to 9 in. ~, free from growth —J.H.Watt⟩ **3 :** a cut of meat: **a :** the back half of a hindquarter of lamb, mutton, or veal — compare HAM; see LAMB illustration **b :** the drumstick of a fowl **4 a :** the part of an article of clothing that covers the leg ⟨the ~*s* of trousers⟩ ⟨the ~ of a stocking⟩ **b :** the part of the upper of a boot that extends above the ankle **5 :** a bow made by drawing one leg back and bending the other **:** OBEISANCE, SCRAPE — used chiefly in the phrase *to make a leg* ⟨they . . . stood up and made a ~ respectfully in the direction of the Governor —Frank Yerby⟩ **6 :** either side of a triangle as distinguished from the base or hypotenuse **7** *Brit* **:** BLACKLEG 2 ⟨he was a horse chanter; he's a ~ now —Charles Dickens⟩ **8** *or* **leg up :** BOOST — often used in the phrase *to give a leg up* ⟨gave me my first ~ to literary standing —W.A.White⟩ ⟨the opportunity to give his profession a ~ *up* —R.E.Garis⟩ ⟨where . . . candidates need a ~ *up* toward election —L.C.Wilson⟩ **9 a :** the portion of the on side of a cricket field that lies behind the batsman and between the boundary and the extended line of the popping crease ⟨trying to force a ball to ~ —Ray Robinson⟩ **b :** a fielding position on this side in cricket; *also* **:** a player fielding in this position — see LONG LEG, SHORT LEG, SQUARE LEG; CRICKET illustration **c :** guard covering the leg stump in cricket **10 a :** the course and distance sailed by a boat on a single tack ⟨on the windward ~ —H.A.Calahan⟩ ⟨turn about on the next ~ of her zigzag course to windward —N.D.Ford⟩ **b** (1) **:** a straight-line portion of a flight pattern or air route ⟨the pilot . . . flies a crosswind ~ of half a mile —Joseph Bryan & P.G.Reed⟩ ⟨turned onto the base ~, just before landing —*Skyways*⟩ (2) **:** BEAM 2e(2) **c :** a portion of an entire trip or distance **:** STAGE ⟨another ~ of his continental journey —*Publishers' Weekly*⟩ ⟨on the homeward ~ of her . . . around-the-world tour —Anna Einarson⟩ **d :** the portion of the total distance or course that each member of a relay team must complete ⟨swam his ~ of the relay in 56 seconds flat —*N.Y. Times*⟩ **11 :** the case containing the vertical part of the belt that carries the buckets in a grain elevator **12 :** either of the two inclined sides of an anticlinal deposit **13 a :** one of several (as three) events or games necessary to be won to decide a competition ⟨gained a ~ on the trophy⟩ ⟨his horse won the first two ~*s* of the triple crown⟩ **b :** either half of a double entry in betting (as the daily double) **14 :** one of the two projecting parts of a structural-metal angle **15 a :** a branch electrical circuit **b :** a phase of a polyphase system **16 :** a branch or lateral circuit connecting a communications instrument with the main line **17 :** a road radiating from an intersection of which it forms a part ⟨location of . . . service stations in the ~*s* of interchanges —*Globe and Mail*⟩ **18 :** one of a pair of strips of material (as drapery) usu. hung parallel to the proscenium arch to mask the extreme offstage sides of a set **19 :** one link of several stations in a communications network **20 :** DIVISION 2 ⟨one ~ of the deal violates the exchange control regulations —R.F.Mikesell⟩ — **a leg to stand on :** SUPFORT; *esp* **:** a basis for one's position in a controversy — usu. used in the negative ⟨would not have *a leg to stand on* in his defiance —A.L.Hammond⟩ ⟨he had no legal *legs to stand on* —*Spectator*⟩ — **on one's last legs :** near death, extinction, or defeat ⟨looking like he was *on his last legs* —J.T.Farrell⟩ ⟨evident to any impartial observer that colonialism in Asia was *on its last legs* —*Yale Rev.*⟩ — **on one's legs** *or* **upon one's legs :** on one's feet ⟨*upon his legs*, in the House of Commons —John Almon⟩

[2]leg \"\ *vb* **legged; legged; legging; legs** *vi* **1 :** to use the legs in walking; *esp* **:** walk fast **:** RUN ⟨he . . . *legged* after him —Elgar Dolson⟩ — often used with *it* ⟨I *legged* it out to the barn —*New Yorker*⟩ **2 :** to bestir oneself for someone or something ⟨three . . . Congressmen *legged* for moving the Supreme Court —Julien Hyer⟩ **3 :** to propel a boat through a canal tunnel by moving the feet against the top or sides ⟨we've the tunnel to ~ through —C.S.Forester⟩ ~ *vt* **:** to propel (a boat) through a canal tunnel by means of the legs

leg *abbr* **1** legal **2** legate; legation **3** legato **4** legend **5** legislation; legislative; legislature **6** [L *legit*] he reads; [L *legunt*] they read

[1]leg·a·cy \ˈlegəsē, -si\ *n* -ES [ME *legacie*, fr. MF or ML; MF *legacie*, fr. ML *legatia* office or jurisdiction of a legate, fr. L *legatus* (past part. of *legare* to send as a deputy, bequeath) + *-ia* -y — more at LEGATE] **1** *obs* **a :** the office, dignity, or function of a legate **b :** the business committed to a legate **:** COMMISSION 3 ⟨he came and told his ~ —George Chapman⟩ **2 :** a gift by will esp. of money or other personal property **:** BEQUEST 2 — compare CUMULATIVE 2b, DEMONSTRATIVE LEGACY, [2]DEVISE, GENERAL LEGACY, MODAL, RESIDUARY LEGACY, SPECIFIC LEGACY **3 a :** something received (as from an ancestor or predecessor) resembling or suggestive of a gift by will ⟨their chief intellectual ~ to posterity —Norman Douglas⟩ ⟨men whose main ~ to us was a simple, direct . . . style —D.J.Lloyd⟩ ⟨she has left her granddaughter a rich ~ of expert knowledge —Alice Winchester⟩ **b :** something coming from the past (as from an age, event, or policy) ⟨a beautiful ~ from the age of Enlightenment —F.J.Mather⟩ ⟨one . . . ~ of the Roman domination of Europe —Harvey Graham⟩ ⟨military intervention . . . continued as a ~ of the dollar diplomacy —R.M.Lovett⟩ **4 :** a candidate for membership in an organization (as a fraternity) who is given special status because he is related to a member

[2]legacy \"\ *vt* -ED/-ING/-ES *archaic* **:** to give as a legacy

legacy by damnation *or* **legacy per dam·na·ti·o·nem** \-ˌdamˌnāshēˈōˌnem\ *n, pl* **legacies by damnation** *or* **legacies per damnationem** [*legacy by damnation* trans. of L *legatum per damnationem; legacy per damnationem* part trans. of L *legatum per damnationem*] **:** a form in Roman law for declaring a legacy in which the heir is ordered to pay money or deliver property to the legatee in any event or pay its value

legacy duty *n, chiefly Brit* **:** LEGACY TAX

legacy hunter *n* **:** one that is attentive to old and rich persons in the hope of obtaining a legacy

legacy tax *n* **:** a tax levied on the privilege of passing title by will to property, esp. personal property — compare DEATH TAX, ESTATE TAX, INHERITANCE TAX

[1]le·gal \ˈlēgəl *sometimes* ˈlig-\ *adj* [ME, fr. MF, fr. L *legalis* of or relating to law, fr. *leg-*, *lex* law (prob. orig. meaning a collection) + *-alis* -al; prob. akin to L *legere* to gather, select — more at LEGEND] **1 a :** according with the Mosaic law **b :** of, relating to, or based on the doctrine of salvation through works rather than by grace **2 :** of or relating to law ⟨may request . . . an advisory opinion on any ~ question —*U.N. Charter*⟩ ⟨the question of control was a ~ one which should not have been submitted to the jury —D.N.Edelstein⟩ ⟨~ textbooks⟩ **3 a :** deriving authority from law **:** founded upon law **:** de jure ⟨a ~ government⟩ ⟨the duly constituted and ~ successors of the ancien régime⟩ — compare LEGITIMATE, POLITICAL **b :** having a formal status derived from or as if from law often without a basis in actual fact **:** TITULAR ⟨an artificial ~ difference —F.D.Roosevelt⟩ **c :** established by law; *esp* **:** STATUTORY ⟨the ~ test of mental capacity —K.C. Masteller⟩ **4 :** conforming to or permitted by law or established rules (as of a game) **:** according to the principles of law **:** conforming to the procedures and methods prescribed by law ⟨an enterprise which is not only ~ for positivists but positively enjoined by their creed —W.P.Alston⟩ ⟨their action was made regular and ~ —J.R.Green⟩ — compare CONSTITUTIONAL **5 :** recognized or made effective by a court of law as distinguished from a court of equity **:** existing or valid in law as distinguished from equity — compare EQUITABLE 2 **6 :** of, relating to, or having the characteristics of the profession of law or of one of its members ⟨a bottle . . . that some ~ friend had sent him —J.G.Cozzens⟩ ⟨stood in ~ gravity —Hamlin Garland⟩ ⟨surprised to hear it from a ~ gentleman —Ellen Wilkinson⟩ **7 a :** created by the constructions of the law ⟨passed her life in a kind of ~ childhood —Charles Dickens⟩ ⟨a ~ fiction⟩ **b :** recognized as such by law ⟨as a ~ woman . . . she could presumably marry —Norman Ober⟩ **8 :** arising by operation of law as distinguished from that which arises by agreement or act of the parties ⟨a ~ hypothec⟩ — compare CONVENTIONAL 1a **syn** see LAWFUL

[2]legal \"\ *n* -S **1 :** a requirement or right established by law; *esp* **:** LEGAL REVERSION **2 :** a paid advertisement in a newspaper consisting of matter required by law or ordinance to be made public **3** *or* **legal investment :** a class of securities in which trustees, savings banks, and other investors regulated by law may legally invest

legal age *n* **:** LAWFUL AGE

legal aid society *or* **legal aid association** *n* **:** an organization affording counsel and representation in court to litigants unable to pay a lawyer

legal buckram *n* **:** [1]BUCKRAM 2b

legal cap *n* [*cap* fr. *-cap* (as in *foolscap*)] **:** a white writing paper for legal use that is usu. 8½ inches wide and 13 or 14 inches long and is often ruled ⟨some . . . use *legal cap* with margins ruled in red —Eva L. Connelly & T.P.Moroney⟩

legal capacity *n* **:** the capability and power under law of a person to occupy a particular status or relationship with another or to engage in a particular undertaking or transaction ⟨by giving the organization *legal capacity* —*Internat'l Court of Justice/Advisory Opinion*⟩ ⟨the *legal capacity* to sue⟩

legal chemistry *n* **:** FORENSIC CHEMISTRY

legal duty *n* **:** an obligation arising out of contract or law — compare LEGAL RIGHT 3

le·gal·ese \ˌlēgəˈlēz, -ēs *sometimes* ˌlig-\ *n* -S **:** the specialized language of the legal profession that is usu. wordy and complicated and often unintelligible to an outsider ⟨befogged far beyond the ordinary achievements of military ~ —Bernard DeVoto⟩

legal estoppel *n* **:** COMMON-LAW ESTOPPEL

legal fiction *n* **:** FICTION 4

legal foreclosure *n* **:** a method of foreclosure used in some states of the U.S. that is carried out by proceedings at law (as by writ of entry or of ejectment or of scire facias) rather than in equity and bars the equity of redemption

legal fraud *n* **:** constructive or equitable fraud for which a court of equity and sometimes a court of law will grant a remedy

legal heir *n* **:** HEIR AT LAW

legal holiday *n* **:** a holiday established by legal authority and characterized by legal restrictions on work and transaction of official business

legal intromission *n, Scots law* **:** intromission undertaken upon grounds recognized in law as sufficient — compare VICIOUS INTROMISSION

le·ga·lis ho·mo \ləˌgäləsˈhō(ˌ)mō\ *n, pl* **lega·les ho·mi·nes** \-ä(ˌ)lāsˈhȯməˌnās\ [ML, lit., legal man] **:** one possessing full legal capacity under Old English law and not debarred of any of his rights in court (as to make oath, testify, and serve as a juror) by outlawry, excommunication, infamy, or disqualification **:** one within the protection of the law **:** one standing rectus in curia

le·gal·ism \ˈlēgəˌlizəm *sometimes* ˈlig-\ *n* -S **1 :** the principles and practices characterizing the theological doctrine of strict conformity to a code of deeds and observances (as the Mosaic law) as a means of justification ⟨the first great battle which the Church had to fight was with Jewish ~ —R.C.Trench⟩ ⟨the worship of the Bible with its attending moralism, ~, and obscurantism —*Saturday Rev.*⟩ **2 a :** an often excessive reliance on legal principles and practices esp. as interpreted literally **:** an adherence to the letter as distinguished from the spirit of the law **:** an emphasis on the importance of formulated rules (as for governing conduct) ⟨a revolt against formalism and ~ . . . inspired by American pragmatic philosophy —T.I. Cook⟩ ⟨the best that can be said for ritualistic ~ is that it improves conduct —Aldous Huxley⟩ **b :** a legal term or rule often having little or no meaning in actual practice ⟨sterile ~*s* developed . . . to make war respectable —R.H.Jackson⟩ **3** *usu cap* **:** the philosophy of the Chinese Legalists ⟨the contrast between Confucianism and *Legalism* —*Times Lit. Supp.*⟩

le·gal·ist \-ləst\ *n* -S **1 :** one that believes in or advocates theological legalism **2 :** one that views things from a legal standpoint; *esp* **:** one that places primary and often excessive emphasis on legal principles as interpreted literally or on the formal structure of governmental institutions ⟨he condemns . . . the ~ who divorces international law from politics —R.N. Swift⟩ **3** *usu cap* **:** one of a group of thinkers flourishing in China during the 3d and 4th centuries B.C. and greatly influencing Chinese ethical and political philosophy by an advocacy of government on the basis of a fixed body of laws as distinguished from the Confucian ideal of government by moral example ⟨the authoritarianism of the *Legalists* —*Times Lit. Supp.*⟩

le·gal·is·tic \ˌlēgəˈlistik, -tēk *sometimes* ˌlig-\ *adj* **:** characterized by legalism ⟨the American tendency to approach foreign policy in moralistic and ~ fashion —W.G.Carleton⟩ ⟨a ~ religion⟩ ⟨no amount of ~ argument can becloud this issue —F.D.Roosevelt⟩ — **le·gal·is·ti·cal·ly** \-tək(ə)lē, -tēk-, -li\ *adv*

le·gal·i·ty \ləˈgaləd·ē, lēˈ-, -ətē, -i\ *n* -ES [ME *legalite*, fr. MF & ML; MF *legalité*, fr. ML *legalitat-*, *legalitas*, fr. L *legalis* legal + *-itat-*, *-itas* -ity — more at LEGAL] **1 :** attachment to or observance of law; *esp* **:** conformity to or reliance upon the letter of theological law **2 :** the quality or state of being legal **:** LAWFULNESS ⟨Supreme Court . . . upheld the ~ of such contributions —J.A.Morris b. 1904⟩ ⟨a supreme court to rule on the ~ of legislation —*Collier's Yr. Bk.*⟩ **3 legalities** *pl* **:** obligations imposed by law ⟨entrenched and protected by *legalities* —Agnes Repplier⟩

le·gal·iza·tion \ˌlēgələˈzāshən -līˈz- *sometimes* ˌlig-\ *n* -S **:** the act of legalizing **:** the state of being or having been legalized ⟨the ~ of the employment of the navy in enforcing the laws of trade —*Edinburgh Rev.*⟩ ⟨~ of a document to be submitted in evidence⟩

le·gal·ize \ˈlēgəˌlīz *sometimes* ˈlig-\ *vt* -ED/-ING/-S *see -ize in Explan Notes* [[1]*legal* + *-ize*] **1 a :** to make legal **:** give legal validity or sanction to ⟨~ an act which without those instructions would have been a plain trespass —John Marshall⟩ ⟨the state was one of the first to ~ prizefighting —*Amer. Guide Series: La.*⟩ ⟨the . . . act ~*s* hardships which it was never the intention of Parliament to create —*Fortnightly Rev.*⟩ **b :** to authenticate a document or a signature thereon so that it may be admissible in evidence ⟨these documents should be notarized . . . and then *legalized* at the nearest consulate —Manuel Perez⟩ **2 :** to interpret or apply in a legalistic spirit ⟨you persist to ~ the gospel —J.W.Fletcher⟩

legal jointure *n* **:** JOINTURE 2b

le·gal·ly \-gəlē, -li\ *adv* **1 :** in a legal manner **:** in accordance with the law **:** LAWFULLY ⟨dissolution of a ~ valid marriage —Edward Jenks⟩ **2 :** from the point of view of law ⟨legal science can only cognize ~ —William Ebenstein⟩ ⟨~ she had no claim to the estate⟩

legal man *or* **legal person** *n* [trans. of ML *legalis homo*] **:** LEGALIS HOMO

legal medicine *n* **:** FORENSIC MEDICINE

legal memory *n* **:** the minimum period of time usu. prescribed by statute for a custom existing for that time to have the force of law or for conduct continued for that time to be the foundation of a legal right or title not otherwise provable — compare PRESCRIPTION, TIME IMMEMORIAL

legal name *n* **1 a :** the designation of a person recognized by the law as correct and sufficient and constituting under common law one given name followed by the family name and in modern times requiring or permitting one or more middle given names or initials in abbreviation thereof and upon the marriage of a female the substitution of her husband's family name for her maiden or former family name **b :** the designation of a firm or corporation similarly recognized by law **2 :** a name by which a person, firm, or corporation is actually known in a community and which discloses true identity recognized as sufficient in legal matters or proceedings

legal officer *n* **:** a military officer engaged chiefly in legal duties — see JUDGE ADVOCATE, JUDGE ADVOCATE GENERAL

legal rate *n* **:** LAWFUL RATE

legal representative *n* **:** a personal representative having legal status: **a :** one that represents another (as a deceased or incompetent person) **:** one that succeeds to the interest in property of a person living or corporate — compare ADMINISTRATOR, ASSIGNEE, CURATOR, EXECUTOR, GUARDIAN, HEIR, LEGATEE, RECEIVER, TRUSTEE IN BANKRUPTCY; DISTRIBUTION 1d **b :** an agent having legal status; *esp* **:** one acting under a power of attorney

legal reserve *n* **:** the minimum amount as determined by government standards of the deposits held by a bank or of the assets of a life insurance company required by law to be kept as reserves

legal residence *n* **1 :** the permanent fixed place of abode at a specific address to which one intends to return despite temporary absences or residence elsewhere **:** a domiciliary house or habitation where one intends to dwell indefinitely despite temporary absences **2 :** a domicile that may or may not constitute an actual place of abode at a specific address **3 :** DOMICILE 2c

legal reversion *n* **:** the period of time allowed by Scots law for a debtor to redeem his heritable property from a debt adjudged against it — called also *legal*

legal right *n* **1 a :** a claim recognized and delimited by law for the purpose of securing it **b :** the interest in a claim which is recognized by and protected by sanctions of law imposed by a state, which enables one to possess property or to engage in some transaction or course of conduct or to compel some other person to so engage or to refrain from some course of conduct under certain circumstances, and for the infringement of which claim the state provides a remedy in its courts of justice **2 :** the aggregate of the capacities, powers, liberties, and privileges by which a claim is secured **3 :** a capacity of asserting a legally recognized claim — compare LEGAL DUTY **4 :** a right cognizable in a common-law court as distinguished from a court having jurisdiction in equity

legals *pl of* LEGAL

legal secretary *n* **:** a government official in several British colonies performing the functions of an attorney general ⟨the governor shall appoint a person to be *legal secretary* —*Ceylon Constitution*⟩

legal separation *n* **:** JUDICIAL SEPARATION — not used technically

legal–size \ˈ=,=ˌ=\ *or* **legal–sized** \ˌ=,=ˌ=\ *adj* **1 :** of a size conforming to standards set by law ⟨the river is stocked with *legal-size* trout —E.W.Smith⟩ **2 :** of a size commonly used in the work of the legal profession ⟨a *legal-size* filing cabinet⟩ ⟨*legal-sized* paper⟩

legal tender *n* **1 :** the act of tendering in the performance of a contract or satisfaction of a claim the payment or service which the law prescribes or permits and at such time and place as the law prescribes or permits **2 :** currency in such amounts and denominations as the law authorizes a debtor to tender and requires a creditor to receive in payment of money obligations — compare LAWFUL MONEY

legal term *n* **:** either Whitsunday or Martinmas fixed by Scots law for the payment of semiannual rent or interest as distinguished from a conventional day agreed upon for such payment

legal weight *n* **:** the weight of goods and interior wrapping but not including the weight of the container — used esp. in foreign trade

leg·an·tine \ˈlegəntən, -n·ˌtīn\ *adj* [prob. fr. L *legant-*, *legans* (pres. part. of *legare* to send with a commission or charge, send as a deputy) + E *-ine*] **:** LEGATINE ⟨exercise his ~ functions —William Robertson †1686⟩

leg art *n* **:** CHEESECAKE 2 ⟨a lush display of . . . *leg art* —*Time*⟩

[1]leg·a·tary \ˈlegəˌterē\ *n* -ES [L *legatarius*, fr. *legatus* (past part. of *legare* to bequeath) + *-arius* -ary] *archaic* **:** LEGATEE ⟨the benevolence of the testator towards the ~ —George Wythe⟩

[2]legatary \"\ *adj* **:** of or relating to a legacy

[1]leg·ate \ˈlegət, *usu* -əd·+V\ *n* -S [ME, fr. OE *legat*, fr. OF & L; OF *legat*, fr. L *legatus* ambassador, deputy, provincial governor, fr. *legatus*, past part. of *legare* to send with a commission or charge, bequeath, fr. *leg-*, *lex* law — more at LEGAL] **1 a :** an ecclesiastic representing the Roman Catholic pope and invested with the authority of the Holy See ⟨among the ~*s* sent by the pope —M.W.Baldwin⟩ ⟨the papal ~*s* . . . joined with the council and the representatives of the three other patriarchs —K.S.Latourette⟩ — compare APOSTOLIC DELEGATE, NUNCIO **b :** the governor of a province in the Papal States **2 :** an emissary usu. having official status (as an ambassador, delegate, or envoy) **3 a :** a deputy of a Roman general or of the governor of a Roman province **b :** a provincial governor of the Roman Empire

[2]le·gate \ləˈgāt\ *vt* -ED/-ING/-S [L *legatus*, past part.] **:** BEQUEATH 1 **syn** see WILL

legate a la·te·re \-ˌäˈläd·əˌrā\ *n* [part trans. of ML *legatus a latere*, lit., legate from the side] **:** a confidential papal legate of the highest degree who is appointed esp. for a particular mission and not as a permanent representative abroad — distinguished from *nuncio*

leg·a·tee \ˌlegəˈtē\ *n* -S [[2]*legate* + *-ee*] **:** one to whom a legacy is bequeathed or to whom a devise is given ⟨the Florida decree was binding . . . on the ~ of the plaintiff —H.S.Drinker⟩ ⟨the working class . . . is the ~ of racist attitudes —W.R.Goldschmidt⟩

leg·ate·ship \ˈlegətˌship\ *n* **:** the dignity and office of a legate

leg·a·tine \ˈlegəˌtēn, -ˌtīn, -ˌtən\ *adj* [ML *legatinus*, fr. L *legatus* legate + *-inus* -ine] **:** of, headed by, or enacted under the authority of a legate ⟨the pope would send a ~ commission to England —F.M.Stenton⟩ ⟨a ~ constitution⟩

le·ga·tion \ləˈgāshən, lēˈ-\ *n* -S [ME *legacioun*, fr. MF & L; MF *legation*, fr. L *legation-*, *legatio*, fr. *legatus* (past part. of *legare* to send with a commission or charge, depute) + *-ion-*, *-io*

-ion — more at LEGATE] **1 a :** the sending forth of a legate or a diplomatic representative **b :** the charge or business entrusted to such an envoy : MISSION **2 :** a body of deputies sent on a mission; *specif* **:** a diplomatic mission in a foreign country headed by a minister ⟨air attachés on the staffs of our embassies and ~*s* —F.A.Ogg & P.O.Ray⟩ **3 :** LEGATESHIP **4 :** the official residence and office of a diplomatic minister at the seat of a foreign government ⟨troops occupied the premises of the American ~ —G.H.Stuart⟩

leg·a·tive \'legəd·iv\ *adj* [LL *legativus*, fr. L *legatus* (past part. of *legare* to depute) + *-ivus* -ive] **:** LEGATINE

¹le·ga·to \lə'gä(,)tō, lā'-\ *adv (or adj)* [It, lit., tied, bound, fr. past part. of *legare* to bind, tie, fr. L *ligare* — more at LIGATURE] **1 :** in a manner that is smooth and connected between successive tones — often used as a direction in music **2 :** in a smooth and continuous manner **:** without abrupt break in movement — often used as a direction in dancing

²legato \"\ *n* -s **:** a smooth and connected manner of performance (as of a musical instrument); *also* **:** a passage of music so performed

leg·a·tor \lə'gād·ə(r)\ *n* -s [L, fr. *legatus* (past part. of *legare* to bequeath) + *-or* — more at LEGATE] **:** one who bequeaths a legacy **:** TESTATOR

leg bail *n* **:** FLIGHT **:** escape by flight — **give leg bail** *or* **take leg bail :** to run away **:** ESCAPE

leg band *n* **:** an identification tag on the leg of a bird (as a fowl or pigeon)

leg·bar \'leg,bär\ *n, usu cap* [Leghorn + *barred* rock] **:** a breed of autosexing domestic fowls developed by crossing brown leghorns with barred rocks

leg before wicket *adj* **:** having with any part of the person except the hand illegally stopped a bowled ball that would otherwise have hit the wicket ⟨to be out, *leg before wicket*⟩ ⟨to be clearly *leg before wicket*⟩ — used of a batsman in cricket

leg boot *n* **:** a laceless and strapless boot with the leg often extending almost to the knee

leg-break \'=,=\ *n* **:** a bowled ball in cricket that breaks from the leg side to the off side

leg bye *n* **:** a bye in cricket made on a bowled ball that glances off some part of the batsman's person other than his hand

leg drop *n* **:** a scenery drop from which the center portion has been cut to produce two legs with a space between

¹leg·end \'lejənd\ *n* -s [ME *legende*, fr. MF & ML; MF *legende*, fr. ML *legenda*, fr. L *legendus*, gerundive of *legere* to gather, select, read; akin to Gk *legein* to collect, gather, choose, speak, *logos* word, reason, speech, account, Alb *mb-leth* I collect] **1 a :** the story of the life of a saint **b :** a collection of such stories **c :** ACCOUNT, HISTORY ⟨those rambling letters . . . are naught else than a ~ of the cumbersome life and various fortunes of a cadet —James Howell⟩ **2 a :** LECTIONARY 1 **b :** PASSIONAL **3 a :** a story coming down from the past; *esp* **:** one handed down from early times by tradition and popularly regarded as historical although not entirely verifiable ⟨all the well-known families had their grotesque or tragic or romantic ~*s* —W.B.Yeats⟩ ⟨~*s* regarding buried treasure . . . are as numerous as they are improbable —Thomas Barbour⟩ ⟨steeped himself in the ~*s* of the river —Saxe Commins⟩ **b :** the total body of such stories and traditions; *esp* **:** the collective stories and traditions of a particular group (as a people or clan) ⟨a place in American ~⟩ ⟨local ~ perpetuates the tale —*Amer. Guide Series: Oregon*⟩ ⟨lives on in ~⟩ **c :** a popular myth usu. of current or recent origin ⟨the ~*s* they weave offer valuable clues to their nature —Julian Towster⟩ ⟨creation of a ~ about a movie star by the publicity department⟩ **d :** one around whom such stories and traditions have grown up **:** one having a special status as a result of possessing or being held to possess extraordinary qualities that are usu. partly real and partly mythical ⟨a ~ at forty-seven, as he has been for some years —Ward Morehouse⟩ ⟨had already had a resounding public career and . . . become a ~ in his own time —Vincent Sheean⟩ **e :** the subject of a legend ⟨some cartoons . . . are good enough to become ~ —Gerald Gottlieb⟩ ⟨big bonuses in prosperous times are ~ —*Newsweek*⟩ **4 a :** the wording (as an inscription, motto, or title) on an object ⟨a brass placard bore the ~ —Erle Stanley Gardner⟩ ⟨cancellation with the three-line ~ —*Stamps*⟩ ⟨the ~*s* on both sides of the coins —J.F.Lhotka⟩ ⟨on one side of the glass entrance is a ~ twenty feet in height —R.G.Young⟩ **b :** CAPTION 4b **c :** an explanatory list of the symbols appearing on a map or chart **d :** a statement on the label of a drug product indicating that federal law prohibits the druggist from dispensing it except on the prescription of a physician **syn** see MYTH

²legend \"\ *vt* -ED/-ING/-S **:** to inscribe (as a map or illustration) with a legend

le·gen·da \lə'jendə\ *n pl* [ML, lit., things to be read, fr. L *legenda*, neut. pl. of *legendus*, gerundive of *legere* to read, gather] **:** stories and other writings (as from a passional) to be read usu. for edification

leg·end·ar·i·ly \'lejən,derəlē\ *adv* **:** by legend **:** in a legendary manner ⟨~ successful personality —*N. Y. Herald Tribune*⟩

¹leg·end·ary \-,derē, -ri\ *n* -ES [ML *legendarius* collection of saints' lives, fr. *legenda* legend + L *-arius* -ary — more at LEGEND] **1 :** a book containing a collection of legends; *esp* **:** one devoted to stories of the lives of saints ⟨ordered as a sign of repentance to write a ~ of good women —H.S.Bennett⟩ **2 :** a writer of legends ⟨the ancient . . . historians and more modern *legendaries* —John Spencer⟩

²legendary \"\ *adj* **:** of, relating to, or having the characteristics of legend or a legend **:** according to legend ⟨the ~ cry of the arctic trailblazers —Horace Sutton⟩ ⟨all that ~ and Talmudic lore which has become so familiar to us —J.R. Green⟩ ⟨~ history reported in the next generation —J.A. Froude⟩ **syn** see FICTITIOUS

leg·end·ist \-ndəst\ *n* -S **:** a writer of legends

leg·end·ize \-n,dīz\ *vt* -ED/-ING/-S **:** to endow (as a person) with a legend ⟨to be *legendized* as the father of the world's most remarkable group of brothers and sisters —J.N.Moody⟩

leg·end·ry \-ndrē\ *n* -ES **:** LEGENDS ⟨its heritage of romantic ~ —Aubrey Drury⟩ ⟨his place in American ~ —C.L.Carmer⟩

leger *var of* LEDGER

leg·er·de·main \,lejə(r)də'mān\ *n* -S [ME *lygarde-de-mayne*, *lechardemane*, fr. MF *leger de main* light of hand] **1 a :** SLEIGHT OF HAND **b :** the practice of magic or trickery usu. involving sleight of hand **2 :** an artful deception or display of trickery held to resemble sleight of hand ⟨a remarkable piece of diplomatic ~ —Anthony West⟩

le·ger·i·ty \lə'jerəd·ē\ *n* -ES [MF *legereté*, fr. OF, lightness, fr. *leger*, *legier* light in weight (fr. — assumed — VL *leviarius*, fr. L *levis*) + *-té* -ty — more at LIGHT (in weight)] **:** a mental or physical agility and quickness **:** NIMBLENESS ⟨the ~ of the French mind made the . . . visitor quick to comprehend his desire for solitude —Elinor Wylie⟩

leges *pl of* LEX

leg·ga·da \'legədə\ *n, cap* [NL] **:** a genus of murid rodents that comprises the jungle mice and is sometimes regarded as a subgenus of *Mus*

legged \'legəd *or* 'lāg-, *Brit usu* -gd\ *adj* [ME, fr. *leg* (n.) + *-ed*] **:** having legs ⟨a ~ table⟩ **:** having such or so many legs ⟨hairy-*legged*⟩ ⟨one-*legged*⟩ **:** so shaped in the legs ⟨bow*legged*⟩

leg·ger \'legə(r)\ *n* -S **1 :** one who legs a canal barge through a tunnel **2 a :** a machine for knitting the legs of hosiery — compare FOOTER **b :** an operator of this machine **3 :** LEGMAN **4** [by shortening] **:** BOOTLEGGER **5 :** a butcher in a slaughter-house or packing plant who works on the legs of carcasses

leg·gie·ra·men·te \lə,jerə'men·(,)tā\ *adv (or adj)* [It, lit., lightly, fr. *leggiero*, adj.] **:** in a light, delicate, and brisk style — used as a direction in music

leg·gie·ro \-e(,)rō, -i(,)-\ *adv (or adj)* [It, fr. OF *legier* light in weight — more at LEGERITY] **:** LIGHTLY, GRACEFULLY — used as a direction in music

leg·gi·ness \-gēnəs, -gin-\ *n* -ES **:** the quality or state of being leggy

leggings for a child

leg·ging *or* **leg·gin** \'legən, -giŋ, -gēn\ *n* -S [¹*leg* + *-ing*] **:** a covering for the leg usu. of leather or cloth: **a :** a covering made in various lengths and worn for protection (as by children, industrial workers, and sportsmen) ⟨shoes topped with soft leather ~*s* —Jean & Franc Shor⟩ — usu. used in pl. **b :** GAITER **c :** PUTTEE ⟨the man in the field . . . in his field jacket and *leggins* —*Infantry Jour.*⟩ — **d leggings** *pl* **:** ²CHAPS

leg·ginged *also* **leg·gined** \-nd,-ŋd\ *adj* **:** clad in leggings ⟨white-*legginged* soldiers⟩

leg glance *n* **:** a glance that deflects a cricket ball to the leg side

leg guard *n* **:** PAD 1a (3)

leg·gy \ lege, -gi\ *adj* -ER/-EST **1 :** having conspicuous legs: as **a :** having disproportionately long legs esp. as a result of immature or faulty development ⟨a long, thin, ~, gawky boy —A.J.Beveridge⟩ ⟨using ~ . . . high-withered animals for cavalry horses —C.F.Rooks⟩ **b :** having long, well-formed, and attractive legs ⟨a girl in a red outfit . . . , lithe and ~ and of course attractive —*Commonweal*⟩ **c** (1) **:** SPINDLY — used of a plant or seedling ⟨the plants will become ~ and straggly —Helen M. Fox⟩ (2) **:** having few or no lower branches ⟨beneath old ~ shrubs —*Nature Mag.*⟩ **2 :** characterized by a display of legs ⟨~ photography⟩

leg-harness \'=,=\ *n* [ME *legharneis*] **:** armor for the legs ⟨armed with . . . *leg-harness*, sword, spear, and dagger —P.F. Tytler⟩

leg hit *n* **:** a hit that sends a cricket ball to leg

¹leg·horn \'leg,hȯrn, -e,gȯ-, -ō(ə)n, 'legə(r)n; *with reference to fowls* 'legə(r)n *is usual in US &* le'gȯ(ə)n *or* lə'g- *in Brit*\ *adj, usu cap* [fr. *Leghorn*, Italy] **:** of or from the city of Leghorn, Italy **:** of the kind or style prevalent in Leghorn

²leghorn \"\ *n* [fr. *Leghorn*, Italy, its place of exportation] **1 -s a :** a fine plaited straw made from an Italian wheat that is usu. cut green and bleached ⟨a terrific hat of natural ~ —Lois Long⟩ **b :** a hat or bonnet of this straw ⟨had they new hats or last year's ~*s* —*Atlantic*⟩ **2 a** *usu cap* **:** a Mediterranean breed of rather small hardy nonbroody domestic fowls having smooth yellow legs, white ear lobes, and rose or single combs, laying numbers of white eggs of good size, and occurring in several color varieties — see WHITE LEGHORN **b** -S *often cap* **:** any bird of this breed **3** -S **:** a pale yellow that is deeper and slightly redder than ivory, redder and deeper than cream, and redder and less strong than straw yellow

leg·i·bil·i·ty \,lejə'biləd·ē, -ətē, -i\ *n* -ES **:** the quality or state of being legible ⟨the influence of typeface on the ~ of print —Helen A. Webster & M.A.Tinker⟩

leg·i·ble \'lejəbəl\ *adj* [ME *legibille*, fr. LL *legibilis*, fr. L *legere* to read + *-ibilis* -able — more at LEGEND] **1 :** capable of being read or deciphered **:** distinct to the eye **:** PLAIN ⟨a handsome, supremely ~ type —Bruce Bliven b.1916⟩ ⟨small but ~ gold watches —*New Yorker*⟩ ⟨a used stamp . . . with a light but ~ cancellation —H.M.Ellis⟩ **2 :** capable of being discovered or understood by apparent marks or indications ⟨murder sweltered in his heart and was ~ upon his face —Thomas Wolfe⟩ — **leg·i·bly** \-blē, -li\ *adv*

le·gion \'lējən\ *n* -S [ME *legiun*, *legioun*, fr. OF *legiun*, *legion*, fr. L *legion-*, *legio*, fr. *legere* to levy, gather, read + *-ion-*, *-io* -ion] **1 :** the principal unit of the Roman army comprising at first 3000 but later 5000 to 6000 foot soldiers with a complement of cavalry ⟨withdrawal of the Roman ~*s* from Britain⟩ ⟨Caesar's ~*s*⟩ — compare COHORT **2 :** a large military force; *esp* **:** ARMY 1a ⟨the French Foreign *Legion*⟩ ⟨the Arab *Legion*⟩ **3 :** a very large number (as of persons or things) **:** HOST, MULTITUDE ⟨won him . . . a ~ of devoted followers —Irving Kolodin⟩ ⟨the growing ~ of nature lovers —A.F.Gustafson⟩ ⟨the tales which have made him a legendary character are ~ —Laura Gilpin⟩ **4 :** a now uncommon taxonomic category of varying rank sometimes corresponding to a superfamily and sometimes to a class **5 :** a national association of ex-servicemen ⟨the American *Legion* has championed a universal draft plan —C.W.Ferguson⟩ ⟨delegates from the various branches of the British *Legion* —*Whitaker's Almanack*⟩

¹le·gion·ary \-jə,nerē, -ri\ *adj* [L *legionarius*, fr. *legion-*, *legio* legion + *-arius* -ary] **:** of, relating to, or constituting a legion ⟨accompanied by three or four ~ soldiers —A.C.Whitehead⟩ ⟨a ~ camp⟩ ⟨~ forces⟩

²legionary \"\ *n* -ES **:** LEGIONNAIRE

legionary ant *n* **:** ARMY ANT; *specif* **:** any of several predatory ants of *Eciton* and related genera chiefly of tropical America that build no permanent nests and travel in large colonies

le·gioned \-jənd\ *adj* **:** formed in legions ⟨like ~ soldiers —John Keats⟩

le·gion·naire \,lējə'na(a)(ə)r, -nel, |ə\ *n* -S *often cap* [F *légionnaire*, fr. MF, fr. *legion* + *-aire* -ary] **:** a member of a legion ⟨Arab *Legionnaires* with their red scarves —Horace Sutton⟩ ⟨the American doughboy who probably still regales his fellow ~*s* . . . with provoking tales —*Nation*⟩

leg-iron \'=,=\ *n* **:** a shackle for the leg ⟨no . . . handcuffs, shackles, or *leg-irons* could hold him —Walter Gibson⟩

leg·is·late \'lejə,slāt, *usu* -ād-+V\ *vb* -ED/-ING/-S [back-formation fr. *legislator*] *vi* **:** to perform the function of legislation **:** make or enact laws ⟨whether Congress has a right to investigate in fields where the Constitution forbids it to ~ —Elmer Davis⟩ ⟨allowed to ~ for themselves —J.A.Froude⟩ ~ *vt* **:** to cause, create, or bring about by legislation ⟨morality cannot be *legislated* —B.G.Gallagher⟩ ⟨proceed to ~ a better world into being —Lloyd Harrington⟩ ⟨*legislated* some of its own members into seats in a new legislature —R.M.Dawson⟩

leg·is·la·tion \,lejə'slāshən\ *n* -S [L *legis latio*, *legis latio* legal bill, action of proposing a law, fr. *legis* (gen. of *lex* law) + *lation-*, *latio* action of proposing — more at LEGAL, LATION] **1 :** the action of legislating **:** the making or giving of laws (as by an individual or an organized body); *specif* **:** the exercise of the power and function of making rules (as laws, ordinances, edicts) having the force of authority by virtue of their promulgation by an official organ of a state or other organization ⟨the major function of Congress is ~ —W.S.Sayre⟩ ⟨the regulation of these various . . . interests forms the principal task of modern ~ —James Madison⟩ — compare FIRST READING, REPORT STAGE, SECOND READING, THIRD READING **2 :** the enactments of a legislator or a legislative body ⟨one of the most progressive passages in German ~ —*Social Service Rev.*⟩ ⟨the ~ passed . . . by the California State Board of Education —N.P. Sacks⟩ ⟨rent-control ~ was . . . extended for another year —*Collier's Yr. Bk.*⟩ **3 :** a matter of business (as a bill or nomination) for or under consideration by a legislative body ⟨he has the power to introduce ~⟩ ⟨this proposed ~⟩

¹leg·is·la·tive \'lejə,slād·iv, |t|, |ēv *also* -slə|\ *adj* [*legislator* + *-ive*] **1 :** having the power or performing the function of legislating ⟨the ~ power may not rule by arbitrary decrees —J.H.Hallowell⟩ ⟨a national constitutional convention is clearly a ~ body —M.O.Hudson⟩ — compare ADMINISTRATIVE, EXECUTIVE, JUDICIAL **2 a :** of or relating to a legislature ⟨~ committees⟩ ⟨~ clerk⟩ ⟨~ act⟩ **:** composed of members of a legislature ⟨~ cabinet⟩ ⟨~ caucus⟩ ⟨a presession ~ conference⟩ **b :** created by a legislature esp. as distinguished from an executive or judicial body ⟨~ budget⟩ ⟨~ justice⟩ **c :** designed to assist a legislature or its members ⟨~ reference bureau⟩ ⟨~ research agency⟩ **3 :** of, concerned with, or created by legislation ⟨~ advocate⟩ ⟨~ courts⟩ ⟨~ home rule⟩

²legislative \"\ *n* -S **1** *obs* **:** the power and function of legislating **2 :** the body or department exercising the power and function of legislating **:** LEGISLATURE 1 ⟨the ~ cannot transfer the power of making laws to any other hands —John Locke⟩ ⟨having both the executive and the ~ of the same party —Ellen D. Ellis⟩ — compare ADMINISTRATION, EXECUTIVE, JUDICIARY

legislative agent *n* **:** LOBBYIST — compare LEGISLATIVE COUNSEL

legislative assembly *n, often cap L&A* **1 :** a bicameral legislature in an American state or territory ⟨election to the *legislative assembly* in Montana or Oregon⟩ ⟨in Puerto Rico . . . a daily record of its proceedings shall be published by the *Legislative Assembly* —G.K.Lewis⟩ **2 :** the lower house of a bicameral legislature; *esp* **:** one in a state or province of a nation that is a member of the British Commonwealth ⟨depriving the . . . government in South Australia of its absolute majority of the floor of the *Legislative Assembly* —*Australian Weekly Rev.*⟩ ⟨elected members of the *Legislative Assemblies* of the Indian States⟩ **3 :** a unicameral legislature ⟨the membership of the East African Central *Legislative Assembly* —*United Kingdom Dependencies*⟩; *esp* **:** one in a Canadian province ⟨the *Legislative Assembly* in Alberta⟩

legislative council *n, often cap L&C* **1 :** the upper house of a bicameral legislature: **a :** one in a British colony whose members usu. are chosen by the governor of the colony ⟨property requirements for members of the Cape Colony's *Legislative Council*⟩ ⟨the Assembly and the *Legislative Council* constitute the legislature of Bermuda⟩ **b :** the upper house of the New Zealand Parliament abolished in 1950 ⟨constitutional documents pertaining to the New Zealand *Legislative Council* —H.J.Benda⟩ **c :** one in a state or province of a nation that is a member of the British Commonwealth ⟨the *Legislative Council* of Quebec is composed of twenty-four members —R.M.Dawson⟩ ⟨in New South Wales the Labour Party twice came close to abolishing the *Legislative Council* —J.D.B.Miller⟩ **2 :** a unicameral legislature in a British colony containing the governor, official members appointed by the governor, and usu. unofficial members appointed or elected to represent the people ⟨*legislative councils* on the usual crown colony model —W.E.Simnett⟩ ⟨the normal type of colonial legislature in the modern dependent empire . . . is the *legislative council* —Martin Wight⟩ **3 :** the unicameral legislature of a territory of the U.S. ⟨the expenses of the *legislative council* of the territory of Michigan —*Niles' Register*⟩ ⟨the Virgin islands . . . are composed of two municipalities, each having a *legislative council* —W.S.Sayre⟩ **4 :** a permanent committee usu. composed of several members chosen from both houses that meets between sessions of a state legislature to study state problems and plan a legislative program ⟨the median size of *legislative councils* . . . is around 18 members —H.W.Davey⟩

legislative counsel *n* **:** LOBBYIST; *specif* **:** one that appears before a committee holding hearings on proposed legislation

legislative day *n* **:** a day during which a legislature is in session **:** a period of time that commences with the opening of a daily session and ends with adjournment for that day and that may often last more than one calendar day

leg·is·la·tive·ly \|əvlē\ *adv* **:** in a legislative manner **:** by legislation ⟨it was only ~ that the Lords could have to deal with this matter —*Annual Register*⟩

leg·is·la·tor \'lejə,slād·ə(r), -ātə- *sometimes* ¦==¦slād·,ȯ(ə)r *or* -ā,tȯ- *or* -ō(ə)r\ *n* -S [L *legis lator*, lit., proposer of law, fr. *legis* (gen. of *lex* law) + *lator* proposer, bearer, fr. *latus* (suppletive past part. of *ferre* to carry, propose) + *-or* — more at LEGAL, TOLERATE, BEAR (to carry)] **:** one that makes laws esp. for a political unit (as a nation or state): **a :** an individual or an organized group that enacts a fundamental law (as a constitution) ⟨every form of government . . . is created by the ordinance of the ~ —C.H.McIlwain⟩ **b :** one that makes or helps to make laws and other enactments of policy as distinguished from a fundamental law ⟨the president often is termed our chief ~ —F.A.Ogg & P.O.Ray⟩ **c :** a member of a legislative body ⟨while ~*s* themselves . . . originate a certain number of bills, even more come from outside —F.A.Ogg & P.O.Ray⟩

leg·is·la·to·ri·al \,lejəslə'tōrēəl, -tȯr-\ *adj* **:** LEGISLATIVE

leg·is·la·tor·ship \'==,slād·ə(r),ship, -ātə-\ *n* **:** the position of legislator

leg·is·la·tress \',lejə'slā·trəs\ *also* **leg·is·la·trix** \-ā·triks\ *n, pl* **legislatresses** \-rəsəz\ *also* **legislatrixes** \-ksəz\ *or* **legislatri·ces** \,==='slā·trə,sēz, -slə·'trī(,)sēz\ [*legislatress* fr. *legislator* + *-ess*; *legislatrix* fr. *legislator*, after such pairs as E *executor: executrix*] **:** a woman who makes laws **:** a female member of a legislative body

leg·is·la·ture \'lejə,slāchə(r) *sometimes* ,=='=\ *n* -S [*legislator* + *-ure*] **1 :** a body of persons having the power to legislate; *specif* **:** an organized body having the authority to make laws for a political unit and often exercising other functions (as control of the administration) ⟨the ~ in every state except Nebraska is a bicameral . . . body —F.A.Ogg & P.O.Ray⟩ ⟨the imperial parliament is historically the supreme ~ of the king's dominions —Martin Wight⟩ — compare ASSEMBLY 1a, CONGRESS 3, PARLIAMENT, SENATE **2** *obs* **:** the exercise of the power or function of legislating **:** LEGISLATION 1 ⟨inconvenient to have both the ~ and the execution in the same hands —Gilbert Burnet⟩

le·gist \'lējəst\ *n* -S [MF *legiste*, fr. ML *legista*, fr. L *leg-*, *lex* law + *-ista* -ist] **1 :** a specialist in law or a branch of law; *esp* **:** one learned in Roman or civil law ⟨the ~*s* elaborated their ideas of the royal rights with the aid of the Roman law —G.C.Sellery⟩ **2 :** a medieval law student **3** *usu cap* **:** one of a group of Chinese philosophers emphasizing penal law as the principal means of social control ⟨the *Legists* urged the full rigor of military despotism —C.P.Fitzgerald⟩ — compare CONFUCIAN

¹le·git \lə'jit, lē'-, *usu* -id·+V\ *n* -S [by shortening] *slang* **:** legitimate drama or theater

²legit \"\ *adj, slang* **:** LEGITIMATE ⟨an almost forgotten Broadway ~ house —*Variety*⟩ ⟨rehearse as though for the ~ stage —Hal March⟩ ⟨a few ~ playwrights —F.N.Karmatz⟩ ⟨a racket boy with a lot of ~ business —Harold Robbins⟩

leg·i·tim \'lejə,tim\ *n* -S [F *légitime*, fr. MF, fr. ML *legitima*, fr. L, fem. of *legitimus* legitimate] **:** the portion of an estate usu. including both real and personal property reserved to the children and sometimes other heirs upon the death of the father under Roman, civil, and Scots law — compare DEAD'S PART, REASONABLE PART

le·git·i·ma·cy \lə'jid·əməsē, lē'-, -itəm-, -si\ *n* -ES **:** the quality or state of being legitimate: as **a :** the legal status of kinship between a child and its natural parent usu. resulting from conception and birth in lawful wedlock and entitling the child to support by and the right to bear the surname of its lawful father together with the unrestricted right of inheritance and the maximum protection of the law — compare BASTARDY, ILLEGITIMACY **b** (1) **:** the possession of title or status as a result of acquisition by means that are or are held to be according to law and custom ⟨old-established governments do not need to produce certificates of ~ —Aldous Huxley⟩ ⟨acceptance by almost everybody . . . of the ~ of their rulers' authority —D.W.Brogan⟩ (2) **:** the right to rule possessed by a monarch as a result of strict adherence to the hereditary principle ⟨the Stuart belief in ~ —G.H.Sabine⟩ **c :** a conformity to recognized principles or accepted rules and standards ⟨the ~ of a large majority of the world's postal paper —H.M.Ellis⟩ ⟨~ of personal success —Kenneth de Courcy⟩

¹le·git·i·mate \-mət, *usu* -əd·+V\ *adj* [ML *legitimatus*, past part. of *legitimare* to legitimate, fr. L *legitimus* legitimate, fr. *leg-*, *lex* law — more at LEGAL] **1 :** lawfully begotten **:** born in wedlock **:** having full filial rights and obligations by birth ⟨a ~ child⟩ **2 :** GENUINE ⟨the ~ work of an artist⟩ ⟨many of them had ~ grievances against him —W.A.Swanberg⟩ **3 a** (1) **:** accordant with law or with established legal forms and requirements ⟨a ~ government⟩ ⟨pharmacies, hospitals, and other ~ storage places for narcotics —D.W.Maurer & V.H. Vogel⟩ (2) **:** LAW-ABIDING ⟨the ~ citizen⟩ ⟨it does not occur to the successful racketeer that he is not respectable; he is simply not ~ —D.W.Maurer⟩ **b :** ruling by or based upon the strict principle of hereditary right ⟨a ~ king⟩ ⟨a ~ monarchy⟩ **4 a :** conforming to recognized principles or accepted rules and standards ⟨~ advertising expenditure for the national advertiser —L.H.Bristol⟩ ⟨Australian notions of ~ conduct on the cricket field —D.W.Brogan⟩ **b** *of a taxon* **:** published validly and in strict accordance with the rules of the relevant international code — compare VALID **5 :** following in logical sequence **:** REASONABLE ⟨a ~ result⟩ ⟨a ~ inference⟩ ⟨from this it would be ~ to conclude —B.P.Babkin⟩ **6 a :** of, relating to, or comprising a category of plays acted by live professional actors that does not include revues, burlesque, and many forms of musical comedy ⟨costs far more to produce a musical than . . . a standard ~ play —F.M.Whiting⟩ ⟨the ~ drama⟩ **b :** producing or performing in such plays ⟨does not feel that television has hurt the ~ theatre as yet —Clarissa Start⟩ ⟨a ~ actor⟩ **syn** see LAWFUL

²le·git·i·mate \-ə,māt, *usu* -ād·+V\ *vt* -ED/-ING/-S [ML *legitimatus* (past part.)] **:** to make lawful or legal: **a** (1) **:** to give legal status or authorization to ⟨was *legitimated* by at most 58.7 percent of the voters —Kurt Glaser⟩ ⟨even to ~ vice —John Milton⟩ (2) **:** to show or affirm to be justified ⟨the untestable absolutes by which so much . . . human suffering is perennially *legitimated* —Charles Frankel⟩ **b :** to put (a bastard) in the position or state of a legitimate child before the law by legal means (as the subsequent marriage of the parents) ⟨the principle that marriage of parents should ~ prior-born children —Morris Ploscowe⟩ — compare ADOPT 1

³**le·git·i·mate** \-,mət\ *n* -s [¹*legitimate*] **1 :** one having a legitimate status ⟨~*s* and natural children —*Dublin Univ. Mag.*⟩ **2 :** legitimate drama or theater — usu. used with *the*

le·git·i·mate·ly *adv* **:** in a legitimate manner **:** according to law or rules **:** LEGALLY, PROPERLY ⟨in a position to see, quite ~, what appeared to be an official dispatch —Elmer Davis⟩ ⟨an obscure region on which curiosity is ~ focused —*Geog. Jour.*⟩

le·git·i·mate·ness *n* -ES **:** the quality or state of being legitimate

le·git·i·ma·tion \lə,jid·ə'māshən\ *n* -s [ME *legitimacioun*, fr. MF or ML; MF *legitimation*, fr. ML *legitimation-, legitimatio*, fr. *legitimatus* (past part. of *legitimare* to legitimate) + L *-ion-, -io* -ion] **1 :** the act or process of making legitimate ⟨English domestic law allowed ~ by subsequent marriage —J.H.C.Morris⟩ ⟨the ~ of money⟩ **2** *obs* **:** LEGITIMACY a

le·git·i·ma·tize \lə'jid·əmə,tīz, lē'-, -itəm-\ *vt* -ED/-ING/-s **:** LEGITIMATE ⟨American law has adopted a concept . . . that the intermarriage of parents ~*s* children —Morris Ploscowe⟩ ⟨the approbation of the men ~*s* the government —James Mackintosh⟩

legitime *adj* [ME, fr. MF, fr. L *legitimus* — more at LEGITIMATE] *obs* **:** LEGITIMATE

le·git·i·mism \lə'jid·ə,mizəm\ *n* -s *often cap* [F *légitimisme*, fr. *légitime* legitimate + *-isme* -ism] **:** adherence to the principles of political legitimacy or to a person claiming or holding authority based upon such principles ⟨international principles such as nonintervention, neutrality, and ~ —Bruce Bliven b.1889⟩ ⟨*Legitimism* has always been strong in Spain —*Blackwood's*⟩

¹**le·git·i·mist** \-,məst\ *n* -s *often cap* [F *légitimiste*, fr. *légitime* legitimate + *-iste* -ist] **:** one that believes in or supports political legitimacy: as **a :** a supporter of the elder branch of the Bourbon dynasty to the crown of France — compare ORLEANIST **b :** one that supports the Alid claim of hereditary authority based on descent from Muhammad

²**legitimist** \"\ *adj* **:** of, belonging to, or supporting political legitimacy ⟨a ~ party⟩ ⟨a ~ movement⟩

le·git·i·mize \-ə,mīz\ *vt* -ED/-ING/-s *see -ize in Explan Notes* **:** LEGITIMATE ⟨she wouldn't marry and ~ the child —Marcia Davenport⟩ ⟨national patriotism *legitimized* war between nations —J.S.Schapiro⟩

legits *pl of* LEGIT

leg·len *or* **leg·lin** \'leglən\ *n* -s [perh. fr. MD *legelkijn, lagelijn* small flask, dim. of *lagel, lagele, legel, legele* flask, cask, fr. L *lagena* large flask — more at LAGENA] *Scot* **:** a milk pail ⟨the lady . . . came forth to see her maidens pass to the herds with their ~*s* —Sir Walter Scott⟩

leg·less \'legləs\ *adj* **:** having no legs

leg·let \-lət\ *n* -s [¹*leg* + *-let*] **:** an ornamental band or ring for the leg ⟨these armlets and ~*s* were . . . worn for superstitious reasons —Rafael Karsten⟩

leglike \'=,=\ *adj* **:** like a leg esp. in action or function

leg·man \'=,man, -aa(ə)n\ *n, pl* **legmen 1 a :** a newspaperman who chiefly gathers information and sends in reports from the scene of an occurrence or from a special locale — compare BEAT MAN, REWRITE MAN **b :** REPORTER; *esp* **:** one that goes after his own information **2 :** one that assists another by gathering information or running errands and often performing subordinate administrative tasks ⟨~ for a movie columnist⟩

leg-of-mutton *or* **leg-o'-mutton** \,==(,)==\ *adj* **:** having the general shape or outline of a leg of mutton; *esp* **:** having a full upper arm and a fitted lower arm and wrist — used of the sleeve of a woman's garment

leg-of-mutton rig *n* **:** BERMUDA RIG

leg-of-mutton sail *n* **:** a triangular sail with its apex at the masthead

le·gong \'lā,gäŋ\ *n* -s *often cap* [Balinese] **:** a delicate and graceful Balinese drama dance that is performed by two young girls in sumptuous costumes

leg-pull \'=,=\ *n* [back-formation fr. *leg-pulling*] **:** a deception or hoax usu. of a humorous character ⟨always full of jokes and *leg-pulls* —David Garnett⟩ ⟨the . . . anecdote near the end of the memoir sounds like a final *leg-pull* —Hugh Kenner⟩

leg-puller \'=,==\ *n* **:** one that practices leg-pulls ⟨listen to the . . . redoubtable *leg-pullers* spouting their reminiscences of the wide and wonderful —*John O'London's Weekly*⟩

leg-pulling \'=,==\ *n* -s [fr. the phrase *pull one's leg*] **:** the action of one that practices leg-pulls or an instance of such action ⟨fishermen's yarns and mutual *leg-pulling* —Sam Pollock⟩ ⟨never could stand criticism or *leg-pulling* —Paul Scott⟩

le·grand·ite \lə'gran,dīt\ *n* -s [*Legrand*, name of a 20th cent. Belgian mine manager who collected the specimen + E *-ite*] **:** a mineral $Zn_{14}(OH)(AsO_4)_9 \cdot 12H_2O$ consisting of a hydrous basic arsenate of zinc

legroom \'=,=\ *n* **:** space in which to extend the legs while seated ⟨more ~ per passenger⟩ ⟨the right ~ for every driver —*Newsweek*⟩

legs *pl of* LEG, *pres 3d sing of* LEG

leg show *n* **:** a theatrical performance featuring a display of their legs by the female performers — compare BURLESQUE 3, STRIPTEASE

leg spin *n* **:** a spin imparted to a bowled cricket ball that tends to cause it to break from the leg side to the off side

leg stump *n* **:** the outside stump near the batsman in cricket — compare MIDDLE STUMP, OFF STUMP

leg theory *n* **:** a technique in cricket in which a concentration of fielders is placed on the leg side and the bowling aimed generally at the leg stump to tempt the batsman to make leg hits — compare BODY-LINE, OFF THEORY

le·guan *or* **le·guaan** \lə'gwän\ *n* -s [prob. fr. D, fr. F *l'iguane* the iguana, fr. *le* the + *iguane* iguana, fr. Sp *iguana*] **:** a large lizard ⟨the ~ had the tortoise gripped in its jaws —W.H. Archer⟩

leg·u·a·tia \,legyü'āsh(ē)ə\ *n, cap* [NL, fr. François *Leguat* †1735 French Huguenot traveler + NL *-ia*] **:** a genus of fossil birds including an extinct rail (*L. gigantea*) found in the Mascarene islands

leg·u·le·ian \,legyə'lēən\ *n* -s [L *leguleius* pettifogger (fr. *leg-, lex* law) + E *-an* — more at LEGAL] **:** PETTIFOGGER ⟨some silly ~*s* . . . argue unawares against their own clients —Joseph Washington⟩

leg·ume \'le,gyüm, lə'g-, le'-, *in sense 1b* lā'gēm\ *n, pl* **legumes** \-ümz,-ēmz\ [F *légume*, fr. MF, fr. L *legumen*, fr. *legere* to gather — more at LEGEND] **1 a :** the fruit or seed of a leguminous plant (as peas or beans) used for food **b :** a vegetable used for food — used chiefly in menus **2 a :** leguminous plant; *esp* **:** one grown as a forage or green-manure crop (as clover, alfalfa) **3 :** a dry dehiscent one-celled fruit developed from a simple superior ovary and usu. dehiscing into two valves with the seeds attached to the ventral suture **:** POD — compare FRUIT 1d, LOMENT; see FRUIT illustration

legume inoculation *n* **:** the inoculation of legume seeds with a specific culture of bacteria that multiply in the roots of a legume plant forming nodules where the bacteria fix atmospheric nitrogen for the nutrition of the plant

le·gu·me·lin \lə'gyüməlin\ *n* -s [*legume* + *-el* + *-in*] **:** an albumin obtained from the pea and other leguminous seeds

le·gu·men \lə'gyümən\ *n, pl* **legumi·na** \-mənə\ *or* **legumens** [L] **:** LEGUME

le·gu·min \"\ *n* -s [F *légumine*, fr. *légume* + *-ine* -in] **:** a globulin found as a characteristic constituent of the seeds of leguminous plants

le·gu·mi·no·sae \lə,gyümə'nō(,)sē\ *n pl, cap* [NL, fr. fem. pl. of *leguminosus* leguminous] **:** a very large family of dicotyledonous plants (order Rosales) that includes herbs, shrubs, trees, and climbers usu. with highly irregular flowers, with a fruit which is a legume or loment, and commonly with root nodules containing nitrogen-fixing bacteria and that is divided into several subfamilies which in many classifications are considered separate families

le·gu·mi·nous \lə'gyümənəs, le'-\ *adj* [NL *leguminosus*, fr. L *legumin-* legumen + *-osus* -ous] **1 :** of, resembling, or consisting of peas or other legumes **2 :** of or relating to the Leguminosae

¹**leg up** *n* **:** LEG 8

²**leg up** *vt* **:** CONDITION 3 e ⟨a colt . . . properly hardened and *legged up* —F.A.Wrensch⟩

legwork \'=,=\ *n* **:** work or activity involving a preponderance of physical movement and esp. of walking from place to place: **a :** the work of a legman **b :** detailed investigation (as of a crime) **c :** the practical administration of a scheme or enterprise as distinguished from its planning

le havre *or* **havre** \lə'häv, -hàv, -vr(ᵊ), ÷-härv\ *adj, usu cap L&H* [fr. *Le Havre*, France] **:** of or from the city of Le Havre, France **:** of the kind or style prevalent in Le Havre

le·ha·yim *or* **le·cha·yim** *or* **le·hay·yim** *or* **le·chay·yim** \lə'kāyəm, -,yēm\ *n* -s [Heb *leḥayim*, lit., to life] **:** a traditional Jewish toast — often used interjectionally ⟨raised his glass and said "*lehayim!*"⟩

le·hi·ite \'lē,hī,īt\ *n* -s [*Lehi*, Utah, its locality + E *-ite*] **:** a mineral $(Na,K)_2Ca_5Al_8(PO_4)_8(OH)_{12} \cdot 6H_2O(?)$ consisting of a hydrous basic phosphate of calcium and aluminum

leh·mann love grass \'lāmən-, 'lē\ *or* **lehmann's love grass** *n, usu cap L* [prob. fr. the name *Lehmann*] **:** an African drought-resistant grass (*Eragrostis lehmanniana*) grown esp. in arid sections of western No. America as a hay and forage crop and for erosion control

lehr *also* **leer** *or* **lear** \'li(ə)r,'le(ə)r, 'lāər\ *n* -s [G *lehr, leer* model, pattern, measuring instrument, fr. MHG *lēre* model, measure] **:** a long oven in which glassware is annealed as it travels through on a continuous belt

lehr·man *also* **leer·man** \-mən\ *n, pl* **lehrmen** *also* **leermen :** one that works at a lehr

le·hua \lā'hüə\ *n* -s [Hawaiian] **1 :** a common very showy tree (*Metrosideros villosa*) of the Pacific islands having bright red corymbose flowers and a hard wood **2 :** the blossom of the lehua

¹**lei** \'lā(ē), -(i)\ *n* -s [Hawaiian] **:** a wreath, garland, or necklace of flowers, leaves, shells, or other materials that is a symbol of affection in Polynesia

lei

²**lei** *pl of* LEU

¹**leib·niz·ian** *also* **leib·nitz·ian** \līp'nitsēən -īb'-\ *n* -s *usu cap* [Gottfried Wilhelm von *Leibniz* †1716 Ger. philosopher and mathematician + E *-ian*] **:** a follower of Leibniz or an adherent of Leibnizianism

²**leibnizian** *also* **leibnitzian** \(')=';===\ *adj, usu cap* **:** of or relating to Gottfried Wilhelm von Leibniz or his philosophy

leib·niz·ian·ism \='==ə,nizəm\ *n* -s *usu cap* **:** the philosophy of Leibniz and his followers distinguished by (1) its monadism (2) its theory of pre-established harmony (3) the viewpoint that this is the best of all possible worlds because God has chosen it out of an infinity of possible worlds for that reason and apparent evil is not a positive reality but a mere privation and (4) its proposals for a universal calculus of reasoning and scientific language, presaging symbolic logic — compare OPTIMISM 1a

¹**leices·ter** \'lestə(r)\ *adj, usu cap* **1** [fr. *Leicester*, city in England] **:** of or from the city of Leicester, England **:** of the kind or style prevalent in Leicester **2** [fr. *Leicester*, former county in England] **:** LEICESTERSHIRE

²**leicester** \"\ *n, usu cap* [fr. *Leicester*, former county in England; fr. its being orig. bred there] **:** a breed of white-faced long-wool mutton-type sheep originating in England but now widely kept and having white fleece that is finer than that of most long-wool sheep

³**leicester** \"\ *or* **leicester cheese** *n* -s *usu cap L* **:** a hard cheese made of whole cow's milk resembling cheddar and Cheshire cheese

leicester red *n, usu cap L* **:** a variety of heavy pressed brick

leices·ter·shire \'lestər,shi(ə)r, -,shər; -tə,shiə, -,shə\ *adj, usu cap* [fr. *Leicestershire* county in England] **:** of or from the county of Leicestershire, England **:** of the kind or style prevalent in Leicestershire

leich·hardt's pine *also* **leichhardt's tree** \'lī,kä|rts-, 'līk,hä|\ *n, usu cap L* [prob. after F. W. Ludwig Leichhardt †1848 Ger. explorer in Australia] **:** a low-growing Australian and East Indian tree (*Sarcocephalus cordatus*) of the family Rubiaceae that has light gray-brown wood with a spongy grain and globular heads of bright yellow flowers

lei day *n, usu cap L&D* **:** May Day in Hawaii celebrated with pageants and prizes for the most beautiful or distinctive leis

leif·ite \'lē,fīt, 'lā,-\ *n* -s [ISV *leif-* (fr. *Leif* Ericson *fl*1000 Norse mariner and adventurer) + *-ite*] **:** a mineral $Na_2AlSi_4O_{10}F$ consisting of a rare fluoride and silicate of sodium and aluminum and found in Narsarsuak, Greenland

leigh·ton·ite \'lātᵊn,īt\ *n* -s [Tomás Rafael *Leighton* b1894 Chilean civil and mining engineer + E *-ite*] **:** a mineral $K_2Ca_2Cu(SO_4)_4 \cdot 2H_2O$ consisting of a hydrous sulfate of copper, calcium, and potassium

lein·ster \'lenztə(r), -n(t)st-\ *adj, usu cap* [fr. *Leinster*, province of Ireland] **:** of or from the province of Leinster, Ireland **:** of the kind or style prevalent in Leinster

leio- *or* **lio-** *comb form* [NL, fr. Gk *leio-*, fr. *leios* — more at LIME] **:** smooth ⟨*leio*cephalous⟩ ⟨*leio*phyllous⟩ ⟨*leio*dermia⟩

lei·o·lo·pis·ma \,līəlō'pizmə\ *n, cap* [NL, fr. *leio-* + MGk *lopisma* peel, fr. Gk *lopos*] **:** a large genus of skinks having limbs more or less reduced or even absent

leio·myoma \,==+\ *n, pl* **leiomyomas** *or* **leiomyomata** [NL, fr. *leio-* + *myoma*] **:** a tumor consisting of smooth muscle fibers — **leio·myomatous** \"+\ *adj*

lei·o·my·o·sarcoma \,līō,mīō+\ *n* [NL, blend of *leiomyoma* and *sarcoma*] **:** a sarcoma composed in part of smooth muscle cells some of which are of embryonic form

lei·o·thrix \'līō,thriks\ *n, cap* [NL, fr. *leio-* + *-thrix*] **:** a genus of hill tits (family Timaliidae) comprising the mesia and the Japanese nightingale

lei·ot·ri·chi \lī'ä·trə,kī\ *also* **leiotri·ches** \-,kēz\ *n pl, usu cap* [NL, pl., fr. *leio-* + *-trichi*] **:** a division of mankind comprising peoples having straight smooth hair

lei·ot·ri·chous \(')lī;ä·trəkəs\ *adj* [NL *leiotrichi* + E *-ous*] *anthrop* **:** having straight smooth hair — **lei·ot·ri·chy** \='==kē\ *n* -ES

leiotropic *var of* LAEOTROPIC

lei·poa \lī'pōə\ *n* [NL, fr. Gk *leipein* to leave + *ōion* egg; fr. the fact that it deserts its eggs] **1** *cap* **:** a genus of Australian mound-building megapodes with black, white, brown, and gray ocellated plumage that are about two feet long, have a short crest, and comprise a single species (*L. ocellata*) **2** -s **:** any bird of the genus *Leipoa*

leip·zig \'līpsi|g, -sē|\ *also* **leip·zic** \|k\ *adj, usu cap* [fr. *Leipzig*, Germany] **:** of or from the city of Leipzig, Germany **:** of the kind or style prevalent in Leipzig

leipzig yellow *n, usu cap L* **:** a chrome yellow pigment

leir \'lēr\ *n* [alter. of ³*lair*] *Scot* **:** LEARNING 2a

leis *pl of* LEI

leish·man·ia \lēsh'manēə, lish-, -'mān-\ *n* [NL, fr. Sir William B. *Leishman* †1926 Brit. medical officer + NL *-ia*] **1** *cap* **:** a genus of flagellates (family Trypanosomatidae) parasitic in the tissues of vertebrates, probably transmitted by insects in a manner comparable to trypanosomes, and occurring parasitically as a minute ovoid or spherical nonflagellated body with a definite kinetoplast and usu. an intracellular axoneme but in culture and presumably in the invertebrate host assuming the form typical of a leptomonas—see KALA-AZAR, ORIENTAL SORE **2** -s **:** any organism of the genus *Leishmania*; *also* **:** any member of the family Trypanosomatidae when showing the typical intracellular leishmanial form — **leish·mani·al** \=='==əl\ *adj*

leish·ma·ni·a·sis \,=,mə'nīəsəs\ *also* **leish·man·i·o·sis** \(,)=,manē'ōsəs, -,mān-\ *n, pl* **leishmania·ses** \-ə,sēz\ *or* **leishmanio·ses** \-ō,sēz\ [NL, fr. *Leishmania* + *-iasis* or *-osis*] **:** infection with or disease caused by protozoans of the genus *Leishmania* — compare KALA-AZAR; see ORIENTAL SORE

leish·man·ic \(')=manik\ *adj* [NL *Leishmania* + E *-ic*] **:** LEISHMANIAL

leish·man·i·form \lēsh'manə,fȯrm, lish-\ *adj* [NL *Leishmania* + E *-form*] **:** resembling a leishmania

leish·mani·oid \='manē,ȯid, -'mān-\ *adj* [NL *Leishmania* + E *-oid*] **:** like or resembling a leishmania

¹**leis·ter** \'lēstə(r), 'lis-\ *n* -s [of Scand origin; akin to ON *ljōstr* leister, Norw *ljoster*, Dan *lyster* leister, ON *ljōsta* to strike, stab, MIr *loss* tail, end, W *llost* spear, ON *lauss* loose — more at -LESS] **:** a spear armed with three or more barbed prongs for catching fish

²**leister** \"\ *vt* -ED/-ING/-s **:** to spear with a leister

leis·ter·er \-tərə(r)\ *n* -s **:** one who catches fish with a leister

lei·sur·able \'lēzh(ə)rəbəl *also* 'lezh- *sometimes* 'lāzh-\ *adj* **1 :** proceeding deliberately without haste **:** LEISURELY ⟨walked at a ~ pace along the road⟩ **2 :** free from a need for haste ⟨a book written in ~ hours⟩

¹**lei·sure** \'lēzhə(r) *also* 'lezh- *sometimes* 'lāzh-\ *n* -s [ME *leiser, leisere, laiser*, fr. OF *leisir*, fr. *leisir*, v., to be permitted, fr. L *licēre* — more at LICENSE] **1 a :** freedom or spare time provided by the cessation of activities: as (1) **:** free time as a result of temporary exemption from work or duties ⟨did not know how to occupy his ~⟩ ⟨worked harder, for their ~ was doubled and they arrived fresh at the factory —Eric Keown⟩ ⟨~ has been gained by a vast number of people who until recently had been merely beasts of burden —H.W.Van Loon⟩ (2) **:** time at one's command that is free of engagements or responsibilities ⟨increase of ~, diminution of hustle are the ends to be sought —Bertrand Russell⟩ **b :** a period of unemployed time — often used in pl. ⟨possessed sufficient literary quality to tempt my rare ~*s* —H.J.Kaplan⟩ **2 a :** apparent effortlessness **:** EASE, LEISURELINESS ⟨its distinction and its charm lie in the ~ and grace of its style —Sara H. Hay⟩ **b** *obs* **:** calm deliberation **:** judicious care ⟨much ~ and accurateness were used in filling the tube —Henry Power⟩ **3 a :** opportunity provided by free time ⟨the settlers . . . had neither ~ nor impulse for a conscious art —*Amer. Guide Series: Minn.*⟩ ⟨the intellect should have ~ to refresh itself at the fountainhead —S.M.Crothers⟩ **b :** the duration of such opportunity **:** time left ⟨the authority of the government . . . for whose sanction there was no ~ to wait —James Mill⟩ — **at leisure** *or* **at one's leisure :** in one's own time **:** at one's convenience ⟨should live long enough to carry out my extensive plan *at leisure* —Havelock Ellis⟩ ⟨hope she won't repent *at her leisure* —Margaret Deland⟩ — **by leisure** *obs* **:** in a leisurely manner **:** SLOWLY ⟨I'll trust *by leisure* him that mocks me once; thee never —Shak.⟩ **syn** see REST

²**leisure** \"\ *adj* **1 :** UNOCCUPIED, UNEMPLOYED, LEISURED ⟨now he writes in his ~ hours —W.J.Reilly⟩ ⟨something that sounds like an enchanted picture, a picture of life as it ought to be for the ~ classes —J.J.Chapman⟩ **2** *of clothing* **:** suitable for leisure and informal occasions **:** CASUAL

lei·sured \-zhə(r)d\ *adj* **:** having leisure **:** characterized by leisureliness ⟨even the artist and the sculptor were not regarded . . . as ~ men —Ida Craven⟩ ⟨life is more ~ without being essentially indolent —*Amer. Guide Series: Va.*⟩ ⟨world had grown too large . . . for the constitution which a small ~ landowning class had created —J.H.Plumb⟩

lei·sure·ful \-zhə(r)fəl\ *adj* [ME *leiserful*, fr. *leiser* leisure + *-ful*] *archaic* **:** having leisure **:** LEISURELY

lei·sure·less \-ə(r)ləs\ *adj* **:** having no leisure

lei·sure·li·ness \-lēnəs, -lin-\ *n* -ES **:** the quality or state of being leisurely ⟨elegance, urbanity, a quill-pen ~ . . . are not much valued in our day —Louis Kronenberger⟩ ⟨broad streets, an almost southern ~, and fewer tall buildings than are seen in most cities —*Amer. Guide Series: Ind.*⟩

¹**lei·sure·ly** \-lē,-li\ *adv* [ME *laiserly*, fr. *laiser* leisure + *-ly*] **:** without haste **:** DELIBERATELY, SLOWLY ⟨in order to write the book I would have to visit America, travel ~, have money in my pocket —Henry Miller⟩ ⟨others shove in, at first ~ and then more and more like schoolboys —G.W.Stonier⟩

²**leisurely** \"\ *adj* **:** characterized by leisure **:** taking abundant time **:** showing deliberation ⟨this book . . . has the ~ flow of recollection and anecdote —Crane Brinton⟩ ⟨rivers that for the most part pursue a long and ~ course to the sea —Ellen Semple⟩ **syn** see SLOW

lei·sure·ness *n* -ES **:** LEISURELINESS

leisure-time \';=;=\ *adj* **:** taking place during time not used for gainful employment ⟨the *leisure-time* problems of the Filipino immigrant are legion —F.J.Brown & J.S.Roucek⟩

leitch's blue \'lēchəz-\ *n, often cap L* [prob. fr. the name *Leitch*] **1 :** CYANINE BLUE 1a **2 :** CYANINE BLUE 2

leith·ner's blue \'lītnə(r)z-\ *n, usu cap L* [perh. modif. and part trans. of G *leidener blau* Leyden blue] **1 :** COBALT BLUE 2 **2 :** COBALT BLUE 1a

leit·mo·tiv *or* **leit·mo·tif** \'līt,mō,tēf\ *n* -s [G *leitmotiv*, fr. *leit-* leading (fr. *leiten* to lead, fr. OHG) + *motiv* motive fr. F *motif* — more at LEAD] **1 a :** a marked melodic phrase or figure in Wagnerian music drama expressive of or associated with a certain idea, person, or situation and accompanying its reappearance **b :** a similar principle of construction in other music **2 :** something resembling a musical leitmotiv (as a word or phrase, an emotion, an idea) that is repeated again and again **:** a dominant recurring theme ⟨faith in the saving grace of art has been the ~ of the entire autobiography—C.J. Rolo⟩ ⟨the word "again" has become the ~ of German life —Norbert Mühlen⟩ ⟨a competent designer instinctively chooses a theme or ~ for a given structure, and allows it to influence all his choice of form and line —W.D.Teague⟩

leit·ne·ria \līt'nirēə\ *n, cap* [NL, fr. Edward F. *Leitner*, 19th cent. Am. botanist + NL *-ia*] **:** a genus (coextensive with the family Leitneriaceae) including solely the corkwood (*L. floridana*) and being commonly isolated in a distinct order near Myricales

lei·trim \'lē·trəm\ *adj, usu cap* [fr. *Leitrim*, county in Ireland] **:** of or from county Leitrim, Ireland **:** of the kind or style prevalent in county Leitrim

leix \'lāsh, 'lēsh\ *adj, usu cap* [fr. *Leix*, county in Ireland] **:** LAOIGHIS

¹**lek** \'lek\ *n, pl* **lekë** \'lekə\ *or* **leks** *also* **lek** [Alb] **1 :** an Albanian monetary unit formerly equal to ⅕ Albanian franc, established as the basic unit in 1947 — see MONEY table **2 :** a coin representing one lek

²**lek** \"\ *n* -s [prob. fr. Sw, play, game, sport, fr. ON *leikr* — more at LAKE (amusement)] **:** a site to which birds (as grouse) regularly resort for purposes of sexual display and courtship

lek·ach \'lekək\ *n* -s [Yiddish, perh. fr. Aram *lĕkhakh* to mix thoroughly] **:** a leavened honey cake

le·kai salmon \lə'kī-\ *n* [origin unknown] **:** DOG SALMON 1

lek·a·ne \'lekə(,)nē\ *n, pl* **leka·nai** \-,nī\ [Gk *lekanē*, fr. *lekos* dish, pot — more at BALANCE] **1 :** a basin-shaped vessel or large bowl of ancient Greece **2 :** a late form of painted vase of southern Italy resembling a stamnos but provided with upright handles and often with a cover of elaborate form

lekin *var of* LIKIN

lekythos *also* **lekythus** *var of* LECYTHUS

l electron *n, cap L* **:** an electron in the L-shell of energy in an atom

lel·wel \'lel,wel\ *n* -s [origin unknown] **:** a large rufous Sudanese antelope (*Alcelaphus lelwel*)

le·mair·eo·cereus \lə,merēō+\ *n, cap* [NL, fr. Charles *Lemaire* †1871 Fr. horticulturist + NL *-o-* + *Cereus*] **:** a genus of tropical American cacti usu. of tall branching habit with stout spines, funnel-shaped flowers, and globular or ovoid often edible fruit — see CHICHIPE

leman \'lemən, 'lēm-\ *n* -s [ME *leman, lemman, lefman, leofmon*, fr. *lef, leof* lief, dear + *man, mon* man — more at LIEF, MAN] **1** *obs* **:** a sweetheart or lover of either sex **2** *archaic* **:** one who is loved illicitly; *esp* **:** MISTRESS

le·man·ea \lə'manēə\ *n, cap* [NL, fr. M. *Leman*, 18th. cent. Fr. botanist] **:** a genus of dull gray or greenish red algae (order Nemalionales) whose filaments form solid or hollow cylinders in tufts in swift waters

leman·ry \'lemənrē, 'lēm-\ *n* -ES [ME, fr. *leman* + *-ry*] *archaic* **:** unlawful love

le mans \lə'mäⁿ\ *adj, usu cap L&M* [fr. *Le Mans*, France] **:** of or from the city of Le Mans, France **:** of the kind or style prevalent in Le Mans

leme *var of* ¹LEAM

le·mel \'leməl\ *n* -s [alter. of earlier *limall, limmell*, fr. ME *lemaille, limail*, fr. MF *limaille*, fr. OF, fr. *limer* to file, fr. L *limare* — more at LIMATION] **:** metal filings

¹**lem·ma** \'lemə\ *n, pl* **lemmas** \-məz\ *or* **lemma·ta** \-məd·ə\ [L, fr. Gk *lēmma* thing received or taken, assumption, fr. root of *lambanein* to receive, take, grasp — more at LATCH] **1 a :** a preliminary or auxiliary proposition or theorem demonstrated or accepted for immediate use in a demonstration of some other proposition **b** (1) **:** the premise of a syllogism in early Greek logic (2) **:** a major premise of the Stoics **2 :** the argu-

ment or theme of a composition prefixed as a title or introduction; *also* : the heading or theme of a comment or note **3** : a word or phrase glossed in a glossary

²lemma \"\ *n* -s [Gk, rind, husk, fr. *lepein* to peel — more at LEPER] : the lower of the two bracts enclosing the flower in the spikelet of grasses — called also *flowering glume*; see WILD OAT illustration

lem·mer \'lemə(r)\ *n* -s [origin unknown] : one that butchers whales — compare FLENSER

lem·ming \-miŋ\ *n* -s [Norw *lemming, lemende, lomund*, fr. ON *lōmundr* (assumed fr. acc. pl. *lōmundi*); akin to ON *lōmr* guillemot, *lō* curlew, Goth *lailoun* they derided, L *latrare* to bark — more at LAMENT] : any of several small rodents of circumpolar distribution belonging to the genera *Lemmus* and *Dicrostonyx*, being four or five inches long with a very short tail, furry feet, and small ears, usu. colored tawny yellowish varied with black and reddish, and best known for the recurrent mass migrations of a European form (*L. lemmus*) which often continue into the sea where vast numbers are drowned

lemming mouse *n* **1** : any of several small rodents of the genus *Synaptomys* that are confined to northern No. America and resemble the voles (genus *Microtus*) but have a very short tail and peculiar teeth — see BOG LEMMING **2** : any of a number of No. American voles (genus *Phenacomys*) related to the muskrat

lemmo- *comb form* [Gk *lemma* rind, husk + E *-o-*] : neurilemma ⟨*lemmo*blastic⟩ ⟨*lemmo*cyte⟩

lem·mus \'leməs\ *n, cap* [NL, fr. *lemmus* lemming, fr. Norw *lemming*] : a genus of myomorph rodents consisting of the typical lemmings

lem·na \'lemnə\ *n, cap* [NL, fr. Gk, a water plant] : a genus (the type of the family Lemnaceae) of very small aquatic herbs having simple fronds with a single root

lem·na·ce·ae \lem'nāsē,ē\ *n pl, cap* [NL, fr. *Lemna*, type genus + *-aceae*] : a family of aquatic plants (order Arales) consisting of a single flat or thickened frond bearing a root or roots below and one or two naked flowers on the upper surface — see DUCKWEED — **lem·na·ceous** \(')lem¦nāshəs\ *adj*

lem·nad \'lem,nad\ *n* -s [NL *Lemna* + E *-ad*] : DUCKWEED

¹lem·ni·an \'lemnēən\ *adj, usu cap* [L *Lemnius* Lemnian (fr. Gk *Lēmnios*, fr. *Lēmnos* Lemnos, island in the Aegean Sea) + E *-an*] : of or relating to the Greek island of Lemnos

²lemnian \"\ *n* -s *cap* : a native or inhabitant of Lemnos

lemnian bole *or* **lemnian earth** *n, usu cap L* : a gray to yellow or red clay obtained from Lemnos and used formerly in medicine as an adsorbent and protective

lem·nis·cate \lem'niskət\ *n* -s [NL *lemniscata*, fr. fem. of L *lemniscatus* with hanging ribbons, fr. *lemniscus* pendent ribbon (fr. Gk *lēmniskos*) + *-atus* -ate] *math* : the locus of the foot of the perpendicular from the center of a conic on its tangent

lem·nis·cus \-iskəs\ *n, pl* **lemnis·ci** \-i,sī, -i,skē\ [NL, fr. L, ribbon] **1** : a form ÷ of the obelus **2** : a band of fibers; *specif* : a band of nerve fibers of the second neurons in the sensory path terminating in the thalamus — called also *fillet, laqueus*; compare LATERAL LEMNISCUS, MEDIAL LEMNISCUS **3** : either of two club-shaped organs hanging into the body cavity from the base of the proboscis in the Acanthocephala

¹lem·on \'lemən\ *n* -s [ME *lymon*, fr. MF *limon*, fr. ML *limon-, limo*, fr. Ar *laymūn*] **1 a** (1) : an acid fruit that is botanically a syncarpous polycarpellary many-seeded pale yellow berry of oblong form usu. with a nipple at the apex and a yellow rind that contains the fragrant lemon oil and is often candied or preserved — compare ⁶LIME (2) : the stout thorny tree (*Citrus limon*) that bears this fruit — see CITRON **b** : any of numerous trees and shrubs of families other than Rutaceae having fruit similar to the lemon — used with a qualifying word **2 a** : LEMON YELLOW **b** : CHLOR **3** : something (as a float for a ring buoy) shaped like a lemon **4** : something or someone that proves to be unsatisfactory or undesirable : DUD, FAILURE ⟨it is quite possible that one manufacturer . . . may find that he has created an all-around ~ —*Atlantic Bull.*⟩ ⟨being stuck with a ~ on the dance floor —William Irish⟩

²lemon \"\ *adj* **1** : containing lemon : having the flavor or scent of lemon ⟨~ tea⟩ ⟨~ bitters⟩ ⟨sipping a ~ drink⟩ **2** : of the color lemon yellow (sense 1) ⟨the winter afternoons glowed with a hazy ~ light —Carson McCullers⟩

lem·on·ade \¦lemə¦nād\ *n* -s [F *limonade*, fr. *limon* lemon (fr. MF *lymon*) + *-ade*] : a beverage of sweetened lemon juice mixed with plain or carbonated water

lemonade berry *n* : an evergreen shrub or small tree (*Rhus integrifolia*) of southern California with simple obtuse leaves, white or pinkish flowers in dense panicles, and dark red glandular hairy fruit — called also *sourberry*

lemonade bush *or* **lemonade sumach** *or* **lemon bush** *n* : SQUAWBUSH 2

lemonado *n* -s [Sp *limonada*] *obs* : LEMONADE

lemon balm *n* : a bushy perennial Old World mint (*Melissa officinalis*) often cultivated for its fragrant lemon-flavored leaves — called also *garden balm, sweet balm*

lemon chrome *n* **1 a** : a pale chrome yellow pigment **b** : barium chromate used as a pigment **2** : a brilliant yellow that is redder and deeper than butter yellow or jasmine yellow

lemon chrome yellow *n* : LIGHT CHROME YELLOW

lemon cucumber *n* : MANGO MELON

lemon curd *n* : lemon juice and rind, sugar, butter, and eggs cooked together until thick and used as a spread or tart filling

lemon dab *n* : SMEAR DAB

lemonfish \'==,=\ *n, South* : COBIA

lemon geranium *n* : a common garden pelargonium (*Pelargonium limoneum*) having lemon-scented foliage

lemongrass \'==,=\ *n* : any of several grasses of the genus *Cymbopogon*: as **a** : a grass (*C. citratus*) of robust habit that has a large compound inflorescence and is cultivated in tropical regions (as the West Indies) as a source of lemongrass oil **b** : a similar East Indian grass (*C. flexuosus*) that is also a source of lemongrass oil **c** : CITRONELLA 2

lemongrass oil *n* : a yellow to reddish brown essential oil that has an odor of lemon or verbena, is obtained esp. from either of two lemongrasses (*Cymbopogon citratus* or *C. flexuosus*), and is used chiefly as a perfume (as in soap) and as a source of the aldehyde citral

lem·on·ish \'lemənish\ *adj* : somewhat resembling a lemon

lemonlike \'==,=\ *adj* : resembling or suggestive of lemon

lemon lily *n* : a day lily (*Hemerocallis flava*) with lemon yellow flowers

lemon mint *n* : an annual horsemint (*Monarda citriodora*) with densely pubescent foliar bracts

lemon oil *n* : a fragrant yellow essential oil obtained from the peel of lemons usu. by expression and used chiefly as a flavoring agent and in perfumes

lemon scab *n* : citrus scab of the lemon

lemon–scent \'==,=\ *n* : LEMONWEED 2

lemon–scented gum \'==,==-\ *n* : a fragrant-leaved ornamental spotted gum (*Eucalyptus maculata citriodora*)

lemon shark *n* : a moderate-sized shark (*Negaprion brevirostris*) of the warm Atlantic that is yellowish brown to gray above with yellow or greenish sides and is sought for its hide and oily liver but in some areas is feared as a man-eater

lemon sole *n* : a small European sole (*Solea lascaris*); *broadly* : any of several other flatfishes (as a Georges Bank flounder or megrim)

lemon thyme *n* : a lemon-scented wild thyme (*Thymus serpyllum vulgaris*)

lemon verbena *n* : a small shrub (*Lippia citriodora*) of Chile and Argentina that has narrow verticillate lemon-scented leaves and is used in gardens

lemon vine *n* : BARBADOS GOOSEBERRY 1

lemon walnut *n* : BUTTERNUT 1a

lemonweed \'==,=\ *n* **1** : SEA MAT **2** : any of several lemon-scented composite herbs of the genus *Pectis* in the southwestern U.S.

lemonwood \'==,=\ *n* **1** *in New Zealand* : TARATA **2** : a southern African evergreen tree (*Psychotria capensis*) with hard tough elastic wood used for making bows **3** : DAGAME

lem·ony \'lemənē\ *adj* : suggestive of lemon : LEMON ⟨all the more palatable for the ~ taste —Christopher Morley⟩ ⟨we had cold fried chicken and . . . ~ iced tea —Jean Stafford⟩

lemon yellow *n* **1 a** : a variable color averaging a brilliant greenish yellow **b** : a brilliant yellow — called also *Cassel yellow, Chinese yellow* **2** : a pigment of the color lemon yellow: as **a** : a preparation of barium chromate often mixed with zinc chromate **b** : a preparation of lead chromate with lead carbonate

le·mo·si \,lemə'zē, -ə'sē\ *or* **li·mo·si** \,lim-\ *n* -s *usu cap* [Catal *llemosi*, prob. fr. (assumed) VL *lemovicensis* of the Lemovices, fr. L *Lemovices*, a Gallic people inhabiting what is now the region of Limousin in west central France] **1** : the langue d'oc in the Iberian peninsula **2** : the written literary speech in the Catalan region between the 13th and 16th centuries that is held by the Catalans to be different from Provençal

lem·o·vi·ces \,lemə'vī(,)sēz\ *n pl, usu cap* [L] : an ancient Gallic people occupying what became the French province of Limousin

lem·pi·ra \lem'pirə\ *n* -s [AmerSp, after *Lempira*, Indian chief who opposed the Spanish conquest] **1** : the basic monetary unit of Honduras — see MONEY table **2** : a coin or note representing one lempira

le·mur \'lēmə(r) *sometimes* -,myů(ə)r *or* -ůə\ *n* [NL, fr. L *lemures*, pl., nocturnal spirits, ghosts; fr. its nocturnal habits; akin to Gk *lamia* devouring monster, *lamyros* gluttonous, Latvian *lamāt* to rail at, *lamatas* mousetrap; basic meaning: open jaws] **1** *cap* : the type genus of Lemuridae **2** -s : any of numerous arboreal chiefly nocturnal mammals formerly widespread but now largely confined to Madagascar that are related to the monkeys but are usu. regarded as constituting the distinct superfamily Lemuroidea and that resemble monkeys in general form and habits but usu. have a muzzle like a fox, large eyes, very soft woolly fur, and a tail which is sometimes rudimentary but usu. long and furry and never prehensile — see AYE-AYE, LORIS, POTTO, TARSIER

lemur 2

lem·u·res \'lemyə,rēz\ *n pl* [L] : hostile spirits of the unburied dead exorcised from homes in religious observances of early Rome — compare LAR, MANES

¹le·mu·ri·an \lə'myůrēən\ *adj* [NL *Lemur* + E *-ian*] : lemuroid

²lemurian \"\ *adj, usu cap* [*Lemuria*, hypothetical former continent in the Indian ocean supposed to be now represented chiefly by Madagascar (fr. NL *Lemur*) + E *-an*] : MALAGASY

¹lem·u·rid \'lemyərəd, -,rid, 'lēmə-\ *adj* [NL *Lemuridae*] : of or relating to the Lemuridae

²lemurid \"\ *n* -s : a lemur of the family Lemuridae

le·mu·ri·dae \lə'myůrə,dē\ *n pl, cap* [NL, fr. *Lemur*, type genus + *-idae*] : a family comprising the typical lemurs

le·mu·ri·form \lə'myůrə,fórm\ *adj* [NL *Lemur* + E *-iform*] : of, relating to, or resembling lemurs

le·mu·ri·for·mes \lə,myůrə'fór,mēz\ *n pl, cap* [NL, fr. *Lemur* + *-iformes*] *in some classifications* : a division of Lemuroidea comprising the typical lemurs, the aye-aye, and sometimes the tree shrews

lem·u·rine \'lemyə,rīn, 'lēmə-\ *adj* [NL *Lemur* + E *-ine*] : LEMUROID

¹lem·u·roid \-,róid\ *adj* [NL *Lemuroidea*] : of, relating to, or resembling the lemurs or the Lemuroidea

²lemuroid \"\ *n* -s [NL *Lemuroidea*] : one of the Lemuroidea

lem·u·roi·dea \,==='róidēə\ *n pl, cap* [NL, fr. *Lemur* + *-oidea*] **1** *in some classifications* : a suborder of Primates including lemurs, lorises, tarsiers, and living and extinct related mammals **2** : a superfamily or other division of Primates comprising the typical lemurs

lenape \lə'näpē, lə'napē, 'lenə(,)pē, lə'nap, lə'näp\ *n, pl* **lenape** *or* **lenapes** *usu cap* [Delaware, lit., person, Indian] : ¹DELAWARE

le·nard rays \'lā,närt-, lə'närd-\ *n pl, usu cap L* [after Philipp *Lenard* †1947 Ger. physicist] : a mixture of cathode rays that have emerged from a vacuum tube into the outside space through a window consisting of a piece of thin metal foil and rays emitted by the foil as a result of the incidence of the cathode rays

len·ca \'leŋkə\ *n, pl* **lenca** *or* **lencas** *usu cap* [Sp, of Amerind origin] **1 a** : an Indian people of central Honduras and Salvador **b** : a member of such people **2** : the Lencan language of the Lenca people

len·can \-kən\ *n* -s *usu cap* : a language family of uncertain relationships comprising the Lenca language

¹lend \'lend\ *vb* **lent** \-nt\ **lent**; **lending**; **lends** [ME *lenden*, alter. (influenced by past *lende*, after such pairs as ME *sende* sent: *senden* to send) of *lenen*, fr. OE *lǣnan*, fr. *lǣn* loan — more at LOAN] *vt* **1 a** : to give into another's keeping for temporary use on condition that the borrower return the same or its equivalent ⟨the purser has kindly *lent* us excellent binoculars —W.R.Benet⟩ ⟨some 46 works *lent* by museums and private collectors —*Harvard Foundation Newsletter*⟩ **b** : to let out (money) for temporary use on condition that it be repaid with interest at an agreed time ⟨it is sometimes said that the capitalists who *lent* the government the money for the war deserve the hire of it —G.B.Shaw⟩ ⟨commercial banks were obliged . . . to reduce their investments in securities in order to ~ more in advances to customers —*World Economic Survey*⟩ **c** : to place (a subordinate) at the disposal of another for temporary service ⟨he was *lent* by the army to the Institute of Inter-American Affairs as a specialist —*N.Y. Times*⟩ — compare ¹LOAN 2b **2 a** : to give the assistance or support of : ADD, AFFORD, FURNISH, PROVIDE, SUPPLY ⟨his teaching . . . had *lent* to Oxford thought much of its early originality and distinction —G.G.Coulton⟩ ⟨contributed much to the development of the cog railroad . . . ~*ing* his mechanical ability to the problems encountered —*Amer. Guide Series: N.H.*⟩ **b** : to devote the use or effort of (as a part of the body or a faculty of the mind) ⟨the young king seemed to ~ a willing ear —George Eliot⟩ ⟨~ a hand to those in charge of these schools —J.B.Conant⟩ ⟨*lent* eager attention to these hopeful projections⟩ ⟨~*s* a courteous arm to woman or child⟩ **c** : to adapt or apply (oneself or itself) : ACCOMMODATE, OFFER ⟨the peoples *lent* themselves to the nearest leader in their quest for salvation as a group —Francis Hackett⟩ ⟨a buggy exhibit did not ~ itself to much exciting variation —Ben Riker⟩ ⟨hypotheses which ~ themselves to the straining of facts in their support —Edward Clodd⟩ **3** *dial chiefly Brit* : to deal or deliver (a blow) to someone ~ *vi* : to make a loan

²lend \"\ *n* -s *dial* : temporary possession and use by a borrower : LOAN ⟨the ~ of her brass fender —Mary Lavin⟩

lend·able \-dəbəl\ *adj* : available for lending ⟨will tend to further reduce the supply of ~ funds —L.H.Olsen⟩

lend·er \-də(r)\ *n* -s [ME *lendare*, alter. (influenced by ME *lenden* to lend) of *lenere*, fr. OE *lǣnere*, fr. *lǣnan* to lend + *-ere* -er] : one that lends

lending *n* -s [ME *lendinge*, alter. (influenced by ME *lenden* to lend) of *lenninge, leninge*, gerund of *lenen* to lend — more at LEND] **1** : a giving or letting out for temporary use **2** : something lent

lending library *n* **1** : RENTAL LIBRARY **2** *chiefly Brit* **a** : the lending department of a public library **b** : PUBLIC LIBRARY

¹lend–lease \'=¦=\ *n* [after the title of the U.S. *Lend-Lease* Act (1941)] : the transfer of goods and services to an ally to aid in a common cause (as the winning of a war) with payment being made by a return of the original items or their use in the common cause or by a similar transfer of other goods and services ⟨*lend-lease* . . . will stand forth as the most unselfish and unsordid financial act of any country —Sir Winston Churchill⟩ ⟨the two-way *lend-lease* in ideas —*New Republic*⟩

²lend–lease \"\ *vt* : to provide by means of lend-lease ⟨have returned most of the naval craft *lend-leased* them during the war —*Christian Science Monitor*⟩

len·du \'len(,)dü\ *n, pl* **lendu** *or* **lendus** *usu cap* **1 a** : a people of Uganda **b** : a member of such people **2** : a central Sudanic language of the Lendu people

lenes *pl of* LENIS

leng·en·bach·ite \'leŋən,bä,kīt\ *n* -s [*Lengenbach*, Switzerland, its locality + E *-ite*] : a mineral $Pb_6(Ag,Cu)_2As_4S_{13}$ consisting of a sulfide of lead, silver, copper, and arsenic

length \'leŋ(k)th, 'len(t)th\ *n, pl* **lengths** \-ths, 'leŋks\ [ME *lengthe*, fr. OE *lengthu* (akin to OFris *lengethe* length, MD *lengede, lengde*, ON *lengd*), fr. *lang, long* long + *-thu* -th — more at LONG] **1 a** : the longer of the 2 straight-line dimensions of a surface or plane or the longest of the 3 straight-line dimensions of a solid : extent from end to end — distinguished from *width* ⟨the island was three miles in ~⟩ **b** : a distance or dimension expressed in units of linear measure ⟨a ~ of 10 inches⟩ **c** : the quality or state of being long — opposed to *shortness* ⟨weariness and boredom exaggerated the ~ of the journey⟩ **d** : WAVELENGTH **2 a** : duration or extent in time ⟨doesn't seem to prove much, considering the ~*s* of the lives of both women —Elizabeth Bishop⟩ ⟨stood weaving on his feet for the ~ of a long breath —F.B. Gipson⟩ ⟨finally the ~ of the high school was standardized . . . at four years —T.H. Briggs⟩ **b** (1) : relative duration of a sound (as a vowel or syllable in speech or prosody or a note in music) (2) : protracted duration or stress of a sound in speech, prosody, or music ⟨the long *a* gives the word *sale* its ~⟩ **c** *archaic* : prolixity or excess in expression ⟨there is such ~ in grief —Shak.⟩ **3 a** : distance or extent in space ⟨it would be hard, even in New England, to match Main Street for its ~ of 18th century square houses —Elizabeth Coatsworth⟩ ⟨appeared dimly white round a distant bend of the dusty road, a weary ~ behind —Haldane Macfall⟩ **b** (1) : the measure of something taken as a unit of distance ⟨darted across the highway scarcely two car ~*s* ahead of me⟩ ⟨kept most of his acquaintances at arm's ~⟩ (2) : the length of a competitor (as a horse or boat) taken as a unit in stating the margin of a lead or of victory in a race ⟨he led by three ~*s* at the top of the stretch⟩ (3) : the fully extended body ⟨stretched her ~ lazily on the warm earth⟩ ⟨took a hard right on the jaw and measured his ~ on the floor⟩ **4 a** *chiefly Scot* : an indicated or specified distance ⟨I'll go with you the ~ to the hall⟩ **b** : the degree, limit, or extreme to which a course of action or a line of thought or discussion is carried ⟨tended to carry his policy of masterly inactivity to dangerous ~*s* —Harvey Graham⟩ ⟨even went the ~ of reading the play . . . to ascertain what it was all about —G.B.Shaw⟩ ⟨here we see the foolish ~*s* to which human malevolence will go —Norman Douglas⟩ **5 a** : a long expanse or stretch ⟨brushed her ~*s* of lustrous hair⟩ ⟨large ~*s* of seas and shores between my father and my mother lay —Shak.⟩ **b** : a piece constituting or usable as part of a whole or of a connected series : SEGMENT, SECTION ⟨steel bars are furnished in standard shapes and sizes, in both coils and straight ~*s* —*advt*⟩ ⟨short ~*s* of film with both ends spliced together to permit continuous repetition —W.F. Mackey⟩ **6 a** : FLUIDITY **b** : ability to yield a fluid mixture — compare OIL LENGTH **7** *archaic* : a 42-line portion of an actor's part **8** : the volume of wort drawn from a quantity of malt during brewing **9** : the holding of more than a player's proportionate share of the cards of one suit in a card game (as four or more at bridge) ⟨he had ~ in trumps⟩ **10 a** : the distance an esp. well pitched ball in cricket travels before hitting the ground ⟨bowled a good ~⟩ ⟨pitched the ball a fraction short of a ~ —Ray Robinson⟩ **b** : the distance to be shot in archery **11** : the vertical dimension of an article of clothing esp. with reference to the part of the body it reaches or its height above the floor ⟨stockings are made in three ~*s*⟩ ⟨evening dresses in short and long ~*s*⟩ ⟨knee-*length* pants⟩ ⟨a hip-*length* jacket⟩ ⟨a floor-*length* gown⟩ — **at length** *adv* **1** : COMPREHENSIVELY, FULLY ⟨an important clash of principles which have to be debated *at length* —*London Calling*⟩ **2** : at last : FINALLY ⟨events looked forward to with trepidation, when *at length* they occur, often fall flat —George Santayana⟩

length–breadth index *n* : CRANIAL INDEX

length·en \-thən\ *vb* **lengthened**; **lengthened**; **lengthening** \-th(ə)niŋ\ **lengthens** *vt* **1** : to extend in length : make longer : ELONGATE, PROLONG, PROTRACT ⟨~*ed* their skirts halfway to their shoe tops —Mary Austin⟩ ⟨overhauls and renewals which would undoubtedly have ~*ed* her life —F.W. Crofts⟩ **2 a** *obs* : to eke out (provisions) : STRETCH **b** : to increase by diluting ⟨standing by the counter ~*ing* out a short supply of wine —Charles Dickens⟩ ~ *vi* : to grow longer ⟨fall ~*ed* out into winter —Laura Krey⟩ ⟨faces ~*ed* as the news became more certain⟩ **syn** see EXTEND

length·en·er \-th(ə)nə(r)\ *n* -s : one that lengthens

length·ful \-thfəl\ *adj* [*length* + *-ful*] *archaic* : LONG

length–height index *n* **1** : the ratio of the auricular height of the head to its length **2** : the ratio of the distance between basion and bregma on the skull to its length

length·i·ly \-thəlē, -li\ *adv* : in a lengthy or prolix manner

length·i·ness \-thēnəs, -thin-\ *n* -ES : the quality or state of being lengthy : PROLIXITY

length·ways \-th,wāz\ *adv* : LENGTHWISE

¹lengthwise \'=,=\ *adv* [*length* + *-wise*] : in the direction of the length : LONGITUDINALLY ⟨opened his newspaper, folded it ~ —Nathaniel Benchley⟩

²lengthwise \"\ *adj* : moving, placed, or directed on or toward the long axis ⟨tiers of planks had been fashioned into ~ seats —Agnes M. Cleaveland⟩

lengthy \-thē, -thi\ *adj* -ER/-EST **1 a** : protracted excessively or tediously : OVERLONG — used of written or spoken expression ⟨~ and histrionic discussions —*N.Y. Times*⟩ **b** : unduly copious : PROLIX — used of a speaker or writer ⟨must not be ~⟩ **2** : EXTENDED, LONG ⟨no very ~ journey was involved —Allan Fraser⟩ ⟨twirled his ~ key chain —Don Davis⟩ ⟨a ~ debate⟩

len·gua \'leŋgwə\ *n, pl* **lengua** *or* **lenguas** *usu cap* [Sp, lit., tongue, fr. L *lingua*; fr. its custom of wearing labrets — more at TONGUE] **1 a** : a group of Amerind peoples of Gran Chaco, Paraguay, including the Macá and Mascoi **b** : a member of any such people **2** : a language of a Lengua people

le·nien·cy \'lēnēənsē, 'lēnyən-, -si *sometimes* 'len-\ *or* **le·nience** \-ən(t)s\ *n, pl* **leniencies** *or* **leniences** : a lenient disposition or practice : MERCY ⟨had the ~ of the unprincipled —Francis Hackett⟩

le·nient \-ənt\ *adj* [L *lenient-, leniens*, pres. part. of *lenire* to soften, fr. *lenis* soft, mild; akin to Latvian *lēns* mild, slow, lazy, OSlav *lěnŭ* — more at LET (to permit)] **1** *archaic* : relieving pain (as a medicine) or stress (as soothing influence) : ASSUASIVE, EMOLLIENT **2** : of mild and tolerant disposition or effect : INDULGENT, MERCIFUL ⟨strict legality was mitigated by his ~ understanding⟩ ⟨contiguous states were attracting capital and enterprise through ~ laws —Broadus Mitchell⟩ **syn** see FORBEARING, SOFT

le·nient·ly *adv* : in a lenient manner

len·i·fy \'lenə,fī, 'lēn-\ *vt* -ED/-ING/-ES [MF or LL; MF *lenifier*, fr. LL *lenificare*, fr. L *lenis* soft, mild + *-ficare* -fy] *archaic* : ALLEVIATE, ASSUAGE, MITIGATE, SOFTEN

leni–lenape *or* **lenni–lenape** \¦lenē *pronunc at* LENAPE\ *n, usu cap both Ls* [Delaware, lit., real person, fr. *leni, lenni* real + *lenape* person, Indian] : ¹DELAWARE

len·in·grad \'lenən,grad, -raa(ə)d\ *adj, usu cap* [fr. *Leningrad*, U.S.S.R.] : of or from the city of Leningrad, U.S.S.R. : of the kind or style prevalent in Leningrad

len·in·grad·er \-də(r)\ *n* -s *cap* [*Leningrad*, U.S.S.R. + E *-er*] : a native or resident of Leningrad

len·in·ism \'lenə,nizəm\ *n* -s *usu cap* [*Lenin* (real name, Vladimir Ilich Ulyanov) †1924 Russ. Communist leader + E *-ism*] : the political, economic, and social principles and policies advocated by Lenin; *esp* : the theory and practice of communism developed by or associated with Lenin ⟨the application of the principles of *Leninism* to an entirely new situation —D.J.Dallin⟩ ⟨appreciate *Leninism* as an organizational technique —B.I.Schwartz⟩ ⟨the . . . development of Marxism through *Leninism* and Stalinism —Francis Conklin⟩ — compare BOLSHEVISM, MARXISM, MARXISM-LENINISM, STALINISM

¹len·in·ist \'lenənəst\ *n* -s *usu cap* [*Lenin* + E *-ist*] : a follower of Lenin : an adherent of Leninism ⟨our party has always been a party of *Leninists* —*Russian Information & Rev.*⟩ ⟨a *Leninist* . . . on the question of power —Lucjan Blit⟩

²leninist \"\ *adj, usu cap* : of, relating to, or having the characteristics of Leninism or Leninists ⟨the *Leninist* form of communism —*Brit. Book News*⟩ ⟨backing a party with *Leninist* organization —M.F.Lindsay⟩

len·in·ite \'lenə,nīt\ *adj or n, usu cap* [*Lenin* + E *-ite*] : LENINIST

¹le·nis \'lēnəs, 'lān-\ *adj* [NL, fr. LL, smooth (of breathing, as in LL *spiritus lenis*), fr. L, soft, smooth, mild — more at LENIENT] *of one of two homorganic consonants* : produced with more lax articulation and weaker expiration — opposed to *fortis* ⟨\d\ in *doe* is ~, \t\ in *toe* is fortis⟩

²lenis \"\ *n, pl* **le·nes** \'lē(,)nēz, 'lā(,)nās\ [NL, fr. LL, adj., smooth] **1** : a lenis consonant **2** : SMOOTH BREATHING

le·nite \lə'nīt, lē'-\ vb -ED/-ING/-S [back-formation fr. *lenition*] vt : to transform by lenition ~ vi : to undergo lenition

le·nit·ic \-'nid·ik\ adj [L *lenitas* mildness + E *-ic*] : LENTIC

le·ni·tion \-'nishən\ n -S [L *lenitus* (past. part. of *lenire* to soften) + E *-ion*; intended as trans. of G *lenierung*] 1 : the change from fortis to lenis articulation 2 : the replacement of a consonant in a Celtic language by a phonetically related consonant requiring less energy of articulation (as voiceless \k\ by voiced \g\ or stopped \k\ by continuant \k\)

¹len·i·tive \'lenəd·iv\ adj [MF *lenitif*, fr. ML *lenitivus*, fr. L *lenitus* (past part. of *lenire* to soften, alleviate) + *-ivus* -ive — more at LENIENT] 1 : alleviating pain or acrimony : ASSUASIVE, MITIGATING, SOOTHING ⟨this is not a ~ novel —John Barkham⟩ 2 *obs* : of mild or lenient disposition : GENTLE

²lenitive \"\ n -S 1 *archaic* : a soothing medicine or application 2 : a means of mitigation or alleviation : PALLIATIVE ⟨the gentle ~ of sleep —Elinor Wylie⟩

len·i·ty \-nəd·ē\ n -ES [L *lenitat-, lenitas*, fr. *lenis* soft, mild + *-itat-, -itas* -ity] : the quality or state of being lenient : MILDNESS, GENTLENESS, LENIENCY **syn** see MERCY

len·ni·lite \'lenᵊl,īt\ n -S [*Lenni* Mills, Pa., its locality + E *-lite*] : a mineral consisting of a vermiculite

len·no·ace·ae \,lenə'wāsē,ē\ n pl, cap [NL, fr. *Lennoa*, type genus + *-aceae*] : a family of fleshy parasitic herbs (order Ericales) that are natives of California and Mexico and that lack green foliage, have small flowers in a head or compact thyrse and 5 to 10 stamens, and produce a 2-celled capsular fruit — **len·no·aceous** \,lenə¦wāshəs\ adj

len·now \'le(,)nō\ adj [origin unknown] *dial chiefly Eng* : LIMP

le·no \'lē(,)nō\ n -S [perh. fr. F *linon* linen fabric, lawn, fr. MF *lin* flax, linen, fr. L *linum* — more at LINEN] 1 *also* **leno weave** : an open weave in which pairs of warp yarns cross one another and thereby lock the filling yarn in position 2 : a fabric made with a leno weave; *esp* : MARQUISETTE

¹lens \'lenz\ n, pl **lenses** *except sense 6* [NL, fr. L, lentil (plant); fr. its shape — more at LENTIL] 1 a *also* **lense** \"\ : a piece of glass or other transparent substance that has two opposite regular surfaces either both curved or one curved and the other plane and that is commonly used in an optical instrument (as a camera, microscope, eyeglasses) to form an image by focusing rays of light — see CONVERGING LENS, DIVERGING LENS; CAMERA illustration b : a combination of two or more simple lenses — see OPTICAL SYSTEM c : a piece of plane colorless glass or colored or polarizing glass used (as in safety goggles or sunglasses) to protect the eye from dust or glare 2 : a device for directing or focusing radiation other than light (as sound waves, radio microwaves, electrons) ⟨a revolutionary metal ~ capable of focusing radio waves —*Mech. Engineering*⟩ 3 : a medium that focuses or clarifies ⟨this artist . . . is the ~ through which the 16th century can be examined microscopically and understood —F.H.Taylor⟩ 4 *also* **lense** : something shaped like a double-convex optical lens: as a : LENTIL 2 ⟨a ~ of ore⟩ ⟨a ~ of sandstone⟩ b : a deposit of archaeological material (as ashes or shells) that has a lens-shaped cross section on excavation 5 *also* **lense** : a highly transparent biconvex lens-shaped or nearly spherical body in the eye that focuses light rays entering the eye typically onto the retina, in the vertebrate lying immediately behind the pupil and being made up of slender curved rod-shaped ectodermal cells in concentric lamellae surrounded by a tenuous mesoblastic capsule and through a peripheral suspensory ligament continuous with the ciliary muscle contraction of which relaxes the ligament allowing the lens to become more spherical and thereby altering its focal length — compare ACCOMMODATION; see EYE illustration 6 *cap* [NL, fr. L, lentil] : a genus of small erect or partly climbing herbs with pinnate leaves, small inconspicuous whitish flowers, and small flattened pods — see LENTIL

1 2 3 4 5 6

lens 1a: *1* plano-convex, *2* biconvex, *3* converging meniscus, *4* plano-concave, *5* biconcave, *6* diverging meniscus

²lens \"\ vb -ED/-ING/-ES vi : to deposit or form a geologic lens ~ vt : to take a picture of : PHOTOGRAPH; *esp* : to make a motion picture of

³lens \"\ [NL, fr. L, lentil] *syn of* ENTADA

len·sat·ic compass \(')len¦zad·ik-\ n [¹*lens* + *-atic* (as in *quadratic*)] : a magnetic compass having a magnifying lens for reading the compass scale

lens board n : a removable panel support for a camera lens usu. equipped with iris diaphragm and shutter mounted in the lens barrel

lens cell n : a cell whose function is assumed to be light sensitivity that is found in the epidermis of leaves and other organs

lensed \'lenzd\ adj [¹*lens* + *-ed*] : provided with a lens

lens hood n : a shade for excluding stray light from a camera lens

lens·less \'lenzləs\ adj : having no lens

lenslike \'=,=\ adj : having the shape or function of a lens

lens louse n, pl **lens lice** : a person overeager to get into a news photograph or one who seeks undue prominence before a television or motion picture camera

lens·man \-zmən\ n, pl **lensmen** : PHOTOGRAPHER, CAMERAMAN ⟨it was common to see a Leatherneck ~ wield a .45 automatic pistol in one hand and a 16 mm. camera in the other —Sam Jaffe⟩

lens mount n : the housing containing the components of a lens

lens paper or **lens tissue** n : a soft nonabrasive lintless tissue paper used for wiping and wrapping lenses

lens placode n : an ectodermal placode from which the lens of the embryonic eye develops

lens turret n : a device that can be rotated to allow the user of a photographic or television camera his choice of two or more lenses of different focal length

¹lent *past of* LEND

²lent \'lent\ n -S *usu cap* [ME *lente, lenten, leinte* springtime, Lent, fr. OE *lengten, længten, lencten;* akin to OS *lentin* spring, MD *lente, lenten, lentin*, OHG *lengizin, lenzin;* all fr. a prehistoric WGmc compound whose constituents are represented respectively by E *long* and Goth *-tein-* in *sinteins* daily; akin to Skt *dina* day, L *dies* — more at DEITY] 1 a : a period of penitence and fasting observed on the 40 weekdays from Ash Wednesday to Easter in the Roman Catholic and some other churches of Western Christianity : QUADRAGESIMA b : a somewhat longer Lent observed in Eastern Orthodox churches — compare XEROPHAGY 2 : a period of fasting ordained by any religion

³lent \"\ n -S [ME *lente*, fr. *lent*, past part. of *lenden* to lend — more at LEND] *dial Brit* : LOAN

⁴lent \"\ adj [ME *lente*, fr. MF *lent*, fr. OF, fr. L *lentus* slow, calm, flexible — more at LITHE] 1 *obs* : SLOW — used esp. of a fever or a fire 2 *archaic* : LENTO

len·ta·men·te \,lentə'men·(,)tā\ adv (or adj) [It, lit., slowly, fr. *lento*, adj., slow, fr. L *lentus*] : SLOWLY — used as a direction in music

len·tan·do \len·'tän(,)dō\ adv (or adj) [It, lit., becoming slower, fr. L *lentandus*, gerundive of *lentare* to lengthen in time, make flexible, fr. *lentus* slow, flexible] : in a retarding manner — used as a direction in music

lent corn or **lent grain** n, *usu cap L* [²*lent*] *dial Eng* : grain sown in Lent

lent·en \'lentᵊn, -ntən\ adj, *often cap* [ME *lenten, leinten*, fr. OE *lengten, læncten, lencten* of spring, Lenten, fr. *lencten, lengten* Lent, springtime — more at LENT] 1 : of or relating to Lent 2 : suitable to Lent : suggestive of fasting or abstinence : MEAGER, SOMBER, SPARE ⟨a somewhat rigorous and *Lenten* manner in which to pass the happy festival of Easter —Elinor Wylie⟩ 3 : MEATLESS ⟨~ soup⟩

lenten lily n, *usu cap 1st L* : DAFFODIL

lenten pie n, *usu cap L* : meatless pie

len·tib·u·lar·i·a·ce·ae \,len·,tibyə,la(a)rē'āsē,ē\ n pl, cap [NL, fr. *Lentibularia*, type genus (prob. irreg. fr. L *lent-, lens* lentil + *tubulus* small tube, dim. of *tubus* tube) + *-aceae* — more at LENTIL, TUBE] : a family of insectivorous aquatic or bog herbs (order Polemoniales) having irregular flowers and capsular fruits — see BLADDERWORT, PINGUICULA, UTRICULARIA — **len·tib·u·lar·i·a·ceous** \(¦)=¦==,==¦āshəs\ adj

len·tic \'lentik\ adj [L *lentus* slow, calm, sluggish + E *-ic*] : of, relating to, or living in still waters (as lakes, ponds, swamps) — compare LOTIC

len·ti·cel \'lentə,sel\ n -S [NL *lenticella*, lit., small lentil, dim. of *lent-, lens* lentil] : a pore that is common in the stems of woody plants, is usu. opposite a stoma, is composed chiefly of loosely packed unsuberized cells produced by a phellogen, and is the path of exchange of gases between the atmosphere and the stem tissues

len·ti·cel·late \¦lentə¦selət\ adj [NL *lenticellatus*, fr. *lenticella* lenticel + L *-atus* -ate] : having or producing lenticels

len·ti·cle \'lentəkəl\ n -S [L *lenticula* lentil (plant, seed)] : a geological lens of moderate extent : LENTIL

len·tic·u·la \len·'tikyələ\ n, pl **lenticulas** \-ləz\ or **lentic·u·lae** \-,lē\ [L, freckly eruption, freckles, lentil, dim. of *lent-, lens* lentil — more at LENTIL] 1 *med* : FRECKLE 2 [NL, dim. of *lent-, lens* lens] : a small optical lens

len·tic·u·lar \(')=¦==lə(r)\ adj [L *lenticularis*, fr. *lenticula* lentil + *-aris* -ar] 1 : like a lentil in size or form : having the shape of a double-convex lens ⟨a ~ cloud⟩ ⟨a ~ truss⟩ 2 : of or relating to a lens 3 : of, relating to, mediated by, or indicating the lenticular nucleus 4 *photog* a : LENTICULATED ⟨~ film⟩ b : utilizing lenticules ⟨a ~ photographic process⟩ — **len·tic·u·lar·ly** adv

lenticular ganglion n : CILIARY GANGLION

len·tic·u·lar·is \(,)len·,tikyə'la(a)rəs\ adj [L, lenticular] : shaped like a lens — used of clouds

lenticular nucleus n : the larger and external nucleus of the corpus striatum including the outer reddish putamen and two inner pale yellow globular masses constituting the globus pallidus

¹len·tic·u·late \(')=¦=lət, -,lāt\ adj [LL *lenticulatus* like a lentil in form, fr. L *lenticula* lentil + *-atus* -ate] : having lenticels

²len·tic·u·late \-,lāt\ vt -ED/-ING/-S [*lenticule* + *-ate*] *photog* : to provide with lenticules (as by embossing, molding, or coating) ⟨*lenticulated* film⟩

len·tic·u·la·tion \(,)=,==¦lāshən\ n -S 1 : the process of lenticulating 2 : LENTICULE 3

len·ti·cule \'lentə,kyül\ n -S [L *lenticula*] 1 *med* : FRECKLE 2 [influenced in meaning by NL *lent-, lens*] : a small geological lentil 3 [influenced in meaning by NL *lent-, lens*] : any of the minute lenses produced (as by embossing) on the base side of a photographic film, serving to record elements of two or more photographic images, and used in stereoscopic or color photography

len·ti·form \-,fȯrm\ adj [L *lent-, lens* lentil + E *-iform*] : LENTICULAR

len·tig·i·nous \(')len·,tijənəs\ *also* **len·tig·i·nose** \-,nōs\ adj [L *lentiginosus*, fr. *lentigin-, lentigo* lentigo + *-osus* -ous] : of or relating to lentigo : FRECKLED

len·ti·go \len·'tī(,)gō, -tē(-\ n, pl **len·tig·i·nes** \-tijə,nēz\ [L, fr. *lent-, lens* lentil] 1 : a small melanotic spot in the skin, the pigmentation being unrelated to exposure to sunlight and the lesion potentially malignant; *esp* : NEVUS — compare FRECKLE 2 : FRECKLE

len·til \'lentᵊl\ n -S [ME, fr. OF *lentille*, fr. L *lenticula*, dim. of *lent-, lens;* akin to Gk *lathyros* chickling, *lathyris* caper spurge] 1 a : a widely cultivated Eurasian annual plant (*Lens culinaris*) grown for its flattened seeds that are cooked like peas or beans and are also ground into meal and for its leafy stalks that are used as fodder b : the seed of the lentil 2 : a thin-edged geological stratum of limited extent enclosed by strata of different material

len·tile \'lentᵊl\ *archaic var of* LENTIL

lentil tare n : SLENDER VETCH

len·tisc or **len·tisk** \'len·,tisk, ='=\ n -S [ME *lentisk*, fr. L *lentiscus*] : LENTISCUS

len·tis·cus \len·'tiskəs\ n, pl **lentiscus·es** \-iskəsəz\ or **lentis·ci** \-i,sī, -i(,)skē\ [L] 1 : MASTIC TREE 2 : a preparation of mastic leaves

len·tis·si·mo \len·'tisə,mō\ adv (or adj) [It, lit., very slow, fr. L *lentissimus*, superl. of *lentus* slow] : in a very slow manner — used as a direction in music

len·ti·tude \'lentə,tüd, -ə-,tyüd\ n -S [F or L; F, fr. L *lentitudo*, fr. *lentus* flexible, slow + *-tudo* -tude — more at LITHE] *archaic* : SLOWNESS, SLUGGISHNESS

lent lily or **lent rose** n, *usu cap Lent* [²*lent*] 1 *dial chiefly Eng* : DAFFODIL 2 : MADONNA LILY

len·to \'len·(,)tō\ adv (or adj) [It, adv., fr. *lento*, adj., slow, fr. L *lentus*] : in a slow manner — used as a direction in music

¹len·toid \'len·,tȯid\ adj [NL *lent-, lens* lens + E *-oid*] : shaped like a lens ⟨a ~ gem⟩ ⟨~ bodies in the retina⟩

²lentoid \"\ n -S : a lens-shaped structure

len·tor \'len·,tȯ(ə)r\ n -S [L, fr. *lentus* sticky, flexible, slow + *-or*] 1 *archaic* : VISCIDITY — used of the blood 2 *archaic* : SLOWNESS

len·zi·tes \'lenzə,tēz\ n, cap [NL, fr. H. O. *Lenz* 19th cent. Ger. botanist + L *-ites* -ite] : a genus of bracket fungi (family Polyporaceae) having the hymenium of frequently interconnected plates resembling gills and including a fungus (*L. sepiaria*) that causes a dry rot of timber

lenz's law \'len(t)səz-, -nzəz-\ n, *usu cap 1st L* [after H. F. E. *Lenz* †1865 Ger. physicist, its formulator] : a law in physics: the electromotive force due to electromagnetic induction tends to produce a current in such direction that the reaction of the current with the inducing flux opposes whatever change is responsible for the induction

leo \'lē(,)ō\ n -S *usu cap* [L, lit., lion — more at LION] : the fifth sign of the zodiac — see SIGN table, ZODIAC illustration

le·od·i·ce \lē'ädə(,)sē\ n, cap [NL, prob. irreg. fr. Gk *Laodikē* Laodice, a proper name] : a genus (the type of the family Leodicidae) of polychaete worms that includes the largest known polychaetes

¹le·od·i·cid \-sə̇d, -,sid\ adj [NL *Leodicidae*] : of or relating to the Leodicidae

²leodicid \"\ n -S : a worm of the family Leodicidae

le·o·dic·i·dae \,lēə'disə,dē\ n pl, cap [NL, fr. *Leodice*, type genus + *-idae*] : a family of polychaete worms related to the Nereidae

le·o·nar·desque \,lēō¦när¦desk\ adj, *usu cap* [*Leonardo* da Vinci †1519 Florentine painter, sculptor, architect, engineer, and scientist + E *-esque*] : of, relating to, or suggesting Leonardo or the subjects or style of his paintings

le·o·nar·di·an \¦lēō¦närdēən\ adj, *usu cap* [*Leonard* Mountain, Brewster co., Tex. + E *-ian*] : of or relating to a subdivision of the Permian following the Wolfcamp and preceding the Guadalupian —see GEOLOGIC TIME table

le·on·ci·to \,lēən'sē(,)tō\ n -S [Sp *león* lion (fr. L *leon-, leo*) + *-cito* (dim. suffix)] : LION MONKEY

le·o·nese \,lēō¦nēz, ¦lēə-, -ēs\ n, pl **leonese** *cap* [Sp *leonés*, fr. *León*, region and ancient kingdom of Spain + Sp *-és* (adj. & n. suffix), fr. (assumed) VL *-esis* — more at -ESE] 1 : a native of León 2 : the Spanish dialect spoken in León

le·on·har·dite \,lēən'här,dīt\ n -S [G *leonhardit*, fr. Karl C. von *Leonhard* †1862 Ger. mineralogist + G *-it* -ite] : a laumontite altered by loss of water

¹le·o·nine \'lēə,nīn, -,nən\ adj [ME, fr. L *leoninus*, fr. *leon-, leo* lion + *-inus* -ine — more at LION] 1 : resembling or suggesting that of a lion ⟨a ~ head and shoulders —Albert Spalding⟩ ⟨evoked the ~ rage of the master —F.J.Mather⟩ 2 : of or relating to a lion

²leonine \"\ adj, *usu cap* [ML *Leoninus*, fr. *Leon-, Leo* Pope *Leo* IV †855 + L *-inus* -ine] : of or relating to Pope Leo IV ⟨thenceforth known as the *Leonine* city, it contained St. Peter's —M.W.Baldwin⟩

³leonine \"\ adj, *usu cap* [NL *Leoninus*, fr. *Leon-, Leo* Pope *Leo* XIII †1903 + L *-inus* -ine] : of or relating to Pope Leo XIII ⟨the translation . . . is from the Latin of the *Leonine* edition —W.L.Farrell⟩

leonine partnership n [trans. of L *leonina societas*] : a partnership in which one partner is made liable for the losses but is not entitled to share in the profits and which is usu. regarded as not legally permissible

leonine rhyme n [prob. trans. of F *rime léonine*, fr. MF] : internal rhyme used in leonine verse

le·o·nines \'lēə,nīnz, -,nənz\ n pl : LEONINE VERSE

leonine verse n [prob. fr. F *léonin*, fr. MF, fr. OF] 1 : Latin verse in which the last word in the line rhymes with the word just before the middle caesura (as in "gloria factorum temere conceditus horum") 2 : English verse in which the end of the line rhymes with a sound occurring near the middle of the line (as in Tennyson's "the long light shakes across the lakes")

le·o·nite \'lēə,nīt\ n -S [G *leonit*, fr. *Leo* Strippelmann 19th cent. Ger. director of salt works + connective *-n-* + G *-it* -ite] : a mineral $K_2Mg(SO_4)_2.4H_2O$ consisting of a hydrous magnesium potassium sulfate occurring in monoclinic crystals

le·o·no·tis \,==¦nōd·əs\ n, cap [NL, fr. Gk *leōn* lion + *ōt-, ous* ear — more at LION, EAR] : a small genus of tropical herbs or low shrubs (family Labiatae) of southern Africa with whorls of showy very irregular red, yellow, or white flowers — see DAGGA 2

le·on·ti·a·sis \,lēən·tīəsə̇s\ n, pl **leontia·ses** \-ə,sēz\ [NL, fr. Gk *leontiasis* early stage of elephantiasis, fr. *leont-, leōn* lion + *-iasis*] 1 : leprosy affecting the flesh of the face and giving it a leonine appearance 2 *or* **leontiasis ossea** : an overgrowth of the bones in the head producing enlargement and distortion of the face

le·on·to·ce·bus \lē,äntə'sēbəs\ n, cap [NL, fr. Gk *leont-, leōn* lion + NL *Cebus*] : a genus of So. American marmosets comprising the tamarins

le·on·to·don \lē'äntə,dän\ n, cap [NL, fr. Gk *leont-, leōn* lion + NL *-odon*] : a genus of Old World weedy herbs (family Compositae) having pinnatifid leaves, solitary heads of mostly yellow ray flowers, and achenes with a plumose pappus — see FALL DANDELION

le·on·to·po·di·um \=,=='pōdēəm\ n, cap [NL, fr. L *leontopodion*, a plant, lion's-foot, fr. Gk, fr. *leont-, leōn* lion + *-podion* -podium] : a small genus of herbs (family Compositae) that are natives of mountainous regions of Eurasia and So. America and have small discoid flower heads much exceeded by the white woolly black-tipped bracts

le·o·nu·rus \,lēə'n(y)urəs\ n, cap [NL, fr. Gk *leōn* lion + NL *-urus*] : a genus of stout Old World herbs (family Labiatae) having cut-lobed leaves, close whorls of axillary flowers and angled nutlets — see MOTHERWORT

leop·ard \'lepə(r)d\ n -S *often attrib* [ME *leupard, leopard, lepard*, fr. OF *lepart, leupart, liepart*, fr. LL *leopardus*, fr. Gk *leōn* lion + *pardos* pard — more at LION, PARD] 1 a : a large strong cat (*Felis pardus*) of southern Asia and Africa that is usu. tawny or buff with black spots arranged in broken rings or rosettes, is somewhat arboreal, and often lies in ambush for its prey that consists of most animals small or weak enough for it to overcome — called also *panther* b : any of several other cats closely resembling a leopard — usu. used with a qualifying word ⟨hunting ~⟩ 2 a (1) : a heraldic representation of a lion passant guardant (2) : a heraldic representation of a lion guardant b : a heraldic representation of a leopard 3 : a leopard that is a symbol of unchangeableness ⟨can the Ethiopian change his skin or the ~ his spots? —Jer 13:23 (RSV)⟩ 4 : the fur or pelt of a leopard

leopard 1a

leopard cat n 1 : a small spotted cat (*Felis bengalensis*) of southern Asia and Malaysia 2 : OCELOT

leop·ard·ess \'lepə(r)də̇s\ n -ES : a female leopard

leopard flower n : BLACKBERRY LILY

leopard frog n 1 : a common American frog (*Rana pipiens*) that is bright green with large black white-margined blotches on the back 2 : a frog (*Rana sphenocephala*) of the southeastern U. S. similar to the leopard frog

leop·ard·ine \'lepə(r),dēn\ n -S [*leopard* + *-ine*] : rabbit fur processed to simulate leopard

leopard lily n 1 : a Californian lily (*Lilium pardalinum*) with mottled orange flowers 2 : a plant (*Lachenalia pendula*) of southern Africa with spotted flowers 3 : a plant of the genus *Sansevieria* 4 : BLACKBERRY LILY

leopard lizard n : a large blotched and barred iguanid lizard (*Crotaphytus wislizenii* syn. *Gambelia wislizenii*) of Mexico and the western U. S.

leopard man n, pl **leopard men** : a member of a West African native secret society that practices clawing its victims to death for ritual or cannibalistic purposes

leopard moth n : a large European moth (*Zeuzera pyrina*) that has white wings thickly spotted with black, bores in fruit and shade trees in its larval stage, and is now abundant in eastern No. America

leopard of england *usu cap E* : LION OF ENGLAND

leopard plant n : an herb (*Ligularia kaempferi*) native to Japan; *esp* : the ornamental form of the leopard plant (*L. k. aureomaculata*)

leopard's-bane \'==,=\ n, pl **leopard's-banes** 1 *also* **leopardbane** \'==,=\ : a plant of the genus *Doronicum* 2 : a perennial herb (*Arnica cucanlis*) with a glandular stem and sessile or short-based leaves 3 : HERB PARIS

leopard seal n : a spotted antarctic seal (*Hydrurga leptonyx*) occas. encountered on the south coasts of Australia and New Zealand — called also *sea leopard*

leopard's face n, pl **leopard's faces** or **leopards' faces** : a heraldic representation of the head of a leopard affronté without any of the neck showing — compare LION'S FACE

leopard shark n : any of several sharks more or less mottled or blotched with black on a lighter ground: as a : a small widely distributed Pacific cat shark (*Triakis semifasciata*) of commercial importance as a food fish in California b : TIGER SHARK c : a sluggish mollusk-eating Indo-Pacific shark (*Stegostoma fasciatum*)

leopard's head n, pl **leopard's heads** or **leopards' heads** 1 : LEOPARD'S FACE 2 a : a heraldic representation of the head and neck of a leopard affronté b : a heraldic representation of the head and neck of a leopard in profile

leopard-skin chief \'==,=-\ n : a mediator or arbitrator who settles disputes and feuds among the Nuer

leopard snake n : a widely distributed European spotted colubrid snake (*Elaphe situla*) closely related and similar in habits to the American corn snake

leopard squirrel n : THIRTEEN-LINED GROUND SQUIRREL

leopard tortoise n : a large black yellow-spotted African land tortoise (*Geochelone pardalis*) often attaining a shell length of 20 inches and weighing more than 50 pounds

leopard tree n : an Australian tree (*Flindersia maculosa*) whose bark splits off in irregular pieces thereby giving the trunk a spotted appearance — called also *leopardwood*

leopardwood \'==,=\ n 1 a : LETTERWOOD b : a tree yielding such wood 2 a : leopard tree wood b : LEOPARD TREE

le·o·pol·din·ia \,lēə,pōl'dinēə\ n, cap [NL, fr. Maria *Leopoldina* †1826 wife of Dom Pedro I of Brazil + NL *-ia*] : a small genus of very large pinnate-leaved palms mostly confined to the Amazon valley including some (as *L. piassaba*) that yield a piassava fiber

le·o·pold·ite \'==,dīt\ n -S [G *leopoldit*, fr. *Leopoldshall*, town in Germany (now part of Stassfurt), its locality + G *-it* -ite] : SYLVITE

lé·o·pold·ville \'lēə,pōl(d),vil\ adj, *usu cap* [fr. *Léopoldville*, Congo] : of or from Léopoldville, capital of Congo : of the kind or style prevalent in Léopoldville

le·o·tard \'lēə,tärd\ n -S [after Jules *Léotard*, 19th cent. Fr. aerial gymnast] 1 : a close-fitting garment for the torso that sometimes has long sleeves, a high neck, or ankle-length legs and that is worn for practice or performance by dancers, acrobats, and aerialists — often used in pl. 2 : TIGHTS — often used in pl.

leotard 1

¹lep·a·did \'lepəd·ə̇d, -,did\ adj [NL *Lepadidae*] : of or relating to the Lepadidae

²lepadid \"\ n -S : a barnacle of the family Lepadidae

le·pad·i·dae \lə'padə,dē\ n pl, cap [NL, fr. *Lepad-, Lepas,* type genus + *-idae*] **:** a family of goose barnacles typified by the genus *Lepas*

lepas \ˈlepəs, ˈlēˌpas\ *n, cap* [NL, fr. L, limpet, fr. Gk] **:** a widely distributed genus (the type of the family Lepadidae) of goose barnacles

lep·cha \ˈlepchə\ *n, pl* **lepcha** *or* **lepchas** *usu cap* **1 a :** a Mongoloid people of Sikkim, India **b :** a member of such people **2 :** the Tibeto-Burman language of the Lepcha people

lep·er \ˈlepə(r)\ *n* -s [ME, fr. ME *leper, lepre* leprosy, fr. OF *lepre, liepre,* fr. LL *lepra* (L *leprae,* pl.), fr. Gk *lepra,* fr. *lepein* to peel; akin to OE *lǣfer* rush, reed, *lōf* fillet, band, OHG *leber* rush, L *lepidus* agreeable, charming, nice, Russ *lepen'* small piece, *lepest* tatter, petal, *lapot'* bast shoe] **1 :** a person affected with leprosy **2 :** a person shunned for moral or social reasons ⟨to be an artist is to be a moral ~, an economic misfit, a social liability —Henry Miller⟩ ⟨afraid to join the society of the pious . . . I looked upon myself as a ~ —Robert Nesbit⟩

le·pe·ro \ˈlepəˌrō\ *n* -s [AmerSp *lépero*] **:** a Mexican of low social and economic standing ⟨half-naked ~*s* who roamed the streets and begged —T.E.Sanford⟩

leper's squint *or* **leper window** *n* **:** a small window in the exterior wall of some medieval churches through which lepers are believed to have viewed the service being conducted at the altar

lep·id \ˈlepəd\ *adj* [L *lepidus*] *archaic* **:** evoking amusement or pleasure **:** WITTY ⟨as for the joyous and ~ consul, he jokes upon neutral flags and frauds —Sydney Smith⟩ ⟨~ fables —*Edinburgh Rev.*⟩

lepid- *or* **lepido-** *comb form* [NL, fr. Gk, fr. *lepid-, lepis,* fr. *lepein* to peel] **:** flake **:** scale ⟨*Lepidoptera*⟩

lep·i·dine \ˈlepəˌdēn, -ˌdən\ *n* -s [NL *Lepidium* + E *-ine*] **:** an oily nitrogenous base $C_{10}H_9N$ found in coal tar and obtained esp. by the distillation of cinchonine; 4-METHYL-QUINOLINE

le·pid·i·um \ləˈpidēəm\ *n, cap* [NL, fr. L, a plant, dittander, pepperwort, fr. Gk *lepidion,* dim. of *lepid-, lepis* scale, flake] **:** a genus of herbs of the family Cruciferae having a rounded fruit with a notch or depression at its summit — see CANARY GRASS 2, GARDEN CRESS

lep·i·do·blas·tic \ˌlepədōˈblastik\ *adj* [ISV *lepid-* + *-blastic;* orig. formed as G *lepidoblastisch*] **:** relating to a texture in a metamorphic rock corresponding to the scaly texture of an igneous rock

lep·i·do·car·pa·ce·ae \ˌ===ˌkärˈpāsēˌē\ *n pl, cap* [NL, fr. *Lepidocarpon,* type genus + *-aceae*] *in some classifications* **:** a family of plants that is coextensive with the genus *Lepidocarpon* and comprises plants believed to have been arborescent lycopsids with male and female fructifications on separate plants or in separate cones

lep·i·do·car·pon \ˌ===ˈkärˌpän\ *n, cap* [NL, fr. *lepid-* + *-carpon* (fr. Gk *karpos* fruit) — more at HARVEST] **:** a form genus of Carboniferous fossil lycopsid plants (order Lepidodendrales) known from strobili with heterosporous megasporangia containing a single mature seedlike megaspore and three abortive megaspores that is sometimes considered to be on the ancestral line of true seed plants

lep·i·do·cro·cite \-ˈkrōˌsīt\ *n* -s [G *lepidokrokit,* fr. *lepid-* + Gk *krokē* thread + G *-it* -ite] **:** a ruby red to reddish brown mineral FeO(OH) consisting of an iron oxide hydroxide that is an important constituent of some iron ores and often occurs with goethite

lep·i·do·den·dra·ce·ae \-ˌdenˈdrāsēˌē\ *n pl, cap* [NL, fr. *Lepidodendron,* type genus + *-aceae*] **:** a family of fossil pteridophytic plants (order Lepidodendrales) that are characterized by conspicuous spirally arranged leaf scars on the trunk

lep·i·do·den·dra·les \-ˌdenˈdrā(ˌ)lēz\ *n pl, cap* [NL, fr. *Lepidodendron* + *-ales*] **:** an order of arborescent fossil plants (class Lycopodineae) arising during the Lower Devonian, being a conspicuous floral element throughout the Carboniferous, and being characterized by dichotomous branching both in the formation of the crown and of the thick spreading rootlike supports — see LEPIDODENDRACEAE

lep·i·do·den·drid \-ˈdendrəd\ *n* -s [NL *Lepidodendron* + E *-id*] **:** a plant or fossil of *Lepidodendron* or a related genus

lep·i·do·den·droid \ˌ===ˈ=ˌdrȯid\ *adj* [NL *Lepidodendron* + E *-oid*] **:** resembling or related to the lepidodendrids

lep·i·do·den·dron \-ˈ=drən\ *n, cap* [NL, fr. *lepid-* + *-dendron*] **1 :** a genus (the type of the family Lepidodendraceae) of fossil trees having closely set slender or subulate leaves and resembling modern club mosses in their fructification — see LEPIDOSTROBUS **2** -s **:** any tree of the genus *Lepidodendron*

lep·i·do·i·dei \ˌlepəˈdȯidēˌī\ *n pl, cap* [NL, fr. *lepid-* + *-oidei*] *in some classifications* **:** a group of extinct ganoid fishes

le·pid·o·lite \ləˈpidᵊlˌīt, ˈlepədōˌlīt\ *n* -s [G *lepidolith,* fr. *lepid-* + *-lith*] **:** a mineral of somewhat variable composition typically $K(Li, Al)_3(Si, Al)_4O_{10}(F, OH)_2$ that consists of a mica containing lithium and usu. occurs in rose-colored masses made up of small scales

lep·i·do·mel·ane \ˌlepədōˈmeˌlān\ *n* -s [G *lepidomelan,* fr. *lepid-* + *-melane*] **:** a mineral $K_2(Fe, Mg)_{4-6}(Si, Al, Fe)_8O_{20}(OH)_4$ consisting of a mica that is a biotite containing ferric iron

lep·i·do·phloi·os \-ˈflȯiˌäs\ *n, cap* [NL, fr. *lepid-* + Gk *phloios* bark — more at PHLOEM] **:** a form genus of fossil plants of the family Lepidodendraceae consisting of stems with overlapping or imbricated scars

lep·i·do·phyl·lous \ˌ===ˈfiləs\ *adj* [*lepid-* + *-phyllous*] **:** having scaly leaves

lep·i·do·phyl·lum \ˌ===ˈfiləm\ *n, cap* [NL, fr. *lepid-* + *-phyllum*] **:** a form genus of lepidodendroid fossils based on leaves or parts of leaves that is now recognized to be part of *Lepidodendron*

lep·i·do·phyte \ˈ===ˌfīt\ *n* -s [ISV *lepid-* + *-phyte*] **:** a Paleozoic fern — **lep·i·do·phyt·ic** \ˌ===ˈfid·ik\ *adj*

lep·i·dop·ter \ˌlepəˈdäptə(r), ˈ==ˌ==\ *n* -s [NL *Lepidoptera*] **:** an insect of the order Lepidoptera

lep·i·dop·tera \ˌ==ˈt(ə)rə\ *n pl, cap* [NL, fr. *lepid-* + *-ptera*] **:** a large order of insects comprising the butterflies and moths whose adult forms have four broad or lanceolate wings usu. covered with minute overlapping often brightly colored scales, have a long tubular proboscis composed of the maxillae and usu. capable of being coiled spirally between the labial palpi, have mandibles wanting or very rudimentary, and feed chiefly on the nectar of flowers, whose caterpillar larvae have well-developed mandibles, feed chiefly on leaves to which they frequently do great damage, and undergo a complete metamorphosis, and whose pupae in the more advanced families are completely obtected and are frequently enclosed in a cocoon composed partly of silk secreted by glands opening on the larval labium — **lep·i·dop·te·ral** \ˌ==ˈ=t(ə)rəl\ *adj* — **lep·i·dop·te·ran** \-rən\ *n or adj* — **lep·i·dop·te·rid** \-rəd\ *n* -s

lep·i·dop·ter·ist \ˌ==ˈ=tərəst\ *n* -s [NL *Lepidoptera* + E *-ist*] **:** a specialist in lepidopterology

lep·i·dop·te·ro·log·i·cal \ˌ==ˌ=tərəˈläjəkəl\ *adj* **:** of or relating to lepidopterology

lep·i·dop·ter·ol·o·gist \ˌ==ˌ=təˈräləjəst\ *n* -s **:** LEPIDOPTERIST

lep·i·dop·ter·ol·o·gy \-jē\ *n* -ES [ISV *lepidopter-* (fr. NL *Lepidoptera*) + *-o-* + *-logy*] **:** a branch of entomology dealing with the Lepidoptera

lep·i·dop·te·ron \ˌ==ˈ=t(ə)rər, -təˌrän\ *n, pl* **lepidoptera** \-t(ə)rə\ [NL, sing. of *Lepidoptera*] **:** an insect of the order Lepidoptera

lep·i·dop·ter·ous \ˌ==ˈ=t(ə)rəs\ *adj* [NL *Lepidoptera* + E *-ous*] **:** of, relating to, or having the characteristics of the Lepidoptera

lep·i·dos·a·phes \ˌlepəˈdäsəˌfēz\ *n, cap* [NL, fr. *lepid-* + Gk *saphēs* clear, distinct] **:** a genus of destructive armored scales including the oystershell scale

[1]**lep·i·do·sau·ria** \ˌlepədōˈsȯrēə\ *n pl, cap* [NL, fr. *lepid-* + *-sauria*] **:** a subclass of fossil and recent reptiles first appearing in the early Permian, comprising reptiles with two temporal openings and a scaly skin, and including modern lizards, snakes, and tuataras — **lep·i·do·sau·ri·an** \ˌ===ˈ=rēən\ *adj or n*

[2]**lepidosauria** \"\ [NL, fr. *lepid-* + *-sauria*] *syn of* SQUAMATA

lep·i·do·siren \ˌ===+\ *n* [NL, fr. *lepid-* + *Siren*] **1** *cap* **:** a genus of eel-shaped dipnoan fishes containing a single species (*Lepidosiren paradoxa*) inhabiting the swamps of the Amazon and La Plata rivers and their tributaries and with the related *Protopterus* constituting a family (Lepidosirenidae) **2** -s **:** any fish of the genus *Lepidosiren* or of the family Lepidosirenidae — **lep·i·do·sirenoid** \ˌ===+\ *adj or n*

lep·i·do·sis \ˌlepəˈdōsəs\ *n, pl* **lepido·ses** \-ōˌsēz\ [NL, fr. *lepid-* + *-osis*] **1 :** a scaly skin disease (as ichthyosis) **2 :** the arrangement and character of the scales or shields of an animal

lep·i·do·some \ˈlepədəˌsōm, ləˈpid-\ *n* -s [ISV *lepid-* + *-some,* orig. formed as F *lépidosome*] **:** GOLGI BODY

lep·i·do·sper·ma \ˌlepədōˈspərmə\ *n, cap* [NL, fr. *lepid-* + *-sperma*] **:** a large genus of sedges of the family Cyperaceae having imbricated subdistichous floral scales — see SWORD SEDGE

lep·i·do·sper·mae \-ˌmē\ *n pl, cap* [NL, fr. *lepid-* + *-spermae*] *in some classifications* **:** a class of fossil pteridosperms resembling lepidodendrons but bearing seeds instead of megaspores

lep·i·dos·tei \ˌlepəˈdästēˌī\ *n pl, cap* [NL, fr. *lepid-* + *-ostei* (pl. of *-osteus*)] *in some classifications* **:** a group or order of ganoid fishes that includes the Lepisosteidae and several related extinct families now usu. divided between the orders Cycloganoidei, Halecostomi, and Ginglymodi and that has numerous representatives in the Mesozoic and constitutes the dominant type of fish in the Jurassic

lep·i·do·ste·idae \ˌlepədōˈstēəˌdē\ [NL *Lepidosteus* + *-idae*] *syn of* LEPISOSTEIDAE

lep·i·dos·te·us \-ˈdästēəs\ [NL, fr. *lepid-* + *-osteus*] *syn of* LEPISOSTEUS

lep·i·dos·tro·bus \-ˈdästrəbəs\ *n* -ES [NL, fr. *lepid-* + Gk *strobos* act of whirling round — more at STROPHE] **:** a fossil composed of a large cluster of spirally arranged imbricated sporophylls and described orig. as belonging to a form genus of the same name but now believed to represent the fructification of a plant of the genus *Lepidodendron*

lep·i·dote \ˈlepəˌdōt\ *adj* [Gk *lepidōtos* scaly, fr. *lepid-, lepis* scale — more at LEPID-] **:** covered with scurf or scurfy scales ⟨~ rhododendrons⟩

lep·i·do·tes \ˌ==ˈdō(ˌ)ēz\ *n, cap* [NL, fr. Gk *lepidōtos* scaly] **:** a widely distributed genus of Mesozoic fishes of the order Cycloganoidei

lep·i·do·trich·i·um \ˌlepədōˈtrikēəm\ *n, pl* **lepidotrich·ia** \-ēə\ [NL, fr. *lepid-* + *trich-* + *-ium*] **:** one of the elongated jointed rays in the fins of certain bony fishes representing highly modified rows of scales

lep·i·do·tus \ˌ==ˈdōd·əs\ [NL, fr. Gk *lepidōtos* scaly] *syn of* LEPIDOTES

lep·i·du·rus \-ˈd(y)u̇rəs\ *n, cap* [NL, fr. *lepid-* + *-urus*] **:** a genus of phyllopod crustaceans of the family Triopidae including a species (*L. couesi*) common in western No. America

lepi·lemur \ˈlepə+\ *n, cap* [NL, fr. L *lepidus* pleasing, agreeable + NL *Lemur* — more at LEPER] **:** a small genus of rare and little-known lemurs — see SPORTIVE LEMUR

lep·i·o·ta \ˌlepēˈōd·ə\ *n* [NL, fr. Gk *lepion* thin rind, scurf, dim. of *lepos* rind, husk, scale, fr. *lepein* to peel — more at LEPER] **1** *cap* **:** a genus of white-spored agarics having a prominent annulus and a flat expanded pileus and including several edible mushrooms (as *L. procera*) and others (as *L. morgani*) regarded as poisonous **2** -s **:** any fungus of the genus *Lepiota* — called also *parasol mushroom*

-le·pis \ləpəs\ *n comb form* [NL, fr. Gk *lepis* — more at LEPID-] **:** flake **:** scale — in generic names ⟨Bothrio*lepis*⟩ ⟨Osteo*lepis*⟩

le·pis·ma \ləˈpizmə\ *n, cap* [NL, fr. Gk, peel, fr. *lepizein* to peel, fr. *lepos* rind, scale + *-izein* -ize] **:** a genus (the type of the family Lepismatidae) of primitively wingless insects of the order Thysanura having a long flat body covered with shining scales and terminated by three long jointed styles — see SILVERFISH; compare FIREBRAT — **le·pis·mid** \-məd\ *n* -s

[1]**lep·i·sos·te·id** \ˌlepəˈsästēəd\ *adj* [NL *Lepisosteidae*] **:** of or relating to the Lepisosteidae

[2]**lepisosteid** \"\ *n* -s **:** a fish of the family Lepisosteidae

lep·i·sos·te·idae \ˌ==ˌsäˈstēəˌdē\ *n pl, cap* [NL, fr. *Lepisosteus,* type genus + *-idae*] **:** a family of freshwater ganoid fishes comprising the genus *Lepisosteus*

lep·i·sos·te·us \-ˈsästēəs\ *n, cap* [NL, fr. Gk *lepis* scale + *-osteus*] **:** a genus of ganoid fishes comprising the American freshwater gars

lepo- *comb form* [prob. fr. NL, fr. Gk *lepos* — more at LEPIOTA] **:** husk **:** rind **:** scale ⟨*lepo*cyte⟩ ⟨*lepo*thrix⟩

le·po·mis \ləˈpōməs\ *n, cap* [NL, fr. Gk *lepis* scale, flake + *-pomis* (fr. *pōma* lid, cover, operculum); akin to Gk *poimēn* herdsman, shepherd, *pōy* herd, flock — more at LEPID-, FUR] **:** a genus of No. American freshwater sunfishes (family Centrarchidae) that includes the bluegill and several closely related panfishes

[1]**lep·o·rid** \ˈlepərəd, -ˌrid\ *adj* [NL *Leporidae*] **:** of or relating to the Leporidae

[2]**leporid** \"\ *n* -s **:** a mammal of the family Leporidae

le·por·i·dae \ləˈpȯrəˌdē\ *n pl, cap* [NL, fr. *Lepor-, Lepus,* type genus + *-idae*] **:** a family consisting of the hares and rabbits and with the pikas constituting the order Lagomorpha

lep·o·ride \ˈlepərəd, -ˌrid, -ˌrīd, -ˌrēd\ *n* -s [F *léporide,* fr. L *lepor-, lepus* hare — more at LAPIN] **:** BELGIAN HARE — used esp. by those who consider the Belgian hare to be a hybrid between the European rabbit and hare

lepori·form \ˈlepərəˌfȯrm, ləˈpȯr-\ *adj* [L *lepor-, lepus* hare + E *-iform*] **:** resembling a hare in form

lep·o·ril·lus \ˌlepəˈriləs\ *n, cap* [NL, dim. of L *lepor-, lepus* hare] **:** a genus of large gregarious blunt-nosed Australian rats that build community houses of sticks, grasses, and debris

[1]**lep·o·rine** \ˈlepəˌrīn, -ˌrən\ *adj* [L *leporinus,* fr. *lepor-, lepus* hare + *-inus* -ine] **:** of, relating to, or resembling a hare

[2]**leporine** \"\ *n* -s **:** LEPORIDE

lep·o·spon·dyl \ˌlepəˈspändᵊl, ˈ==ˌ==\ *n* [NL *Lepospondyli*] **:** an amphibian of the order, subclass, or other division Lepospondyli

lep·o·spon·dy·li \ˌ==ˈspändəˌlī\ *n pl, cap* [NL, fr. *lepo-* + *-spondyli*] **:** a taxonomic category comprising amphibians in which the centra of the vertebrae develop directly as bone without an intermediate cartilaginous stage: as **a :** an order or other division comprising the extinct Aistopoda, Microsauria, and Nectridia **b :** a subclass of Amphibia comprising the above groups together with the Caudata and Gymnophiona

lep·o·spon·dy·lous \ˌ==ˈ=dələs\ *adj* [*lepo-* + *spondylous*] **1 :** having vertebrae enclosing the notochord each of which consists of a cylinder of bone shaped like an hourglass in longitudinal section — used esp. of some extinct stegocephalian amphibians **2** [NL *Lepospondyli* + E *-ous*] **:** of or relating to the Lepospondyli **3 :** having the vertebral centra develop directly as bone

lep·o·thrix \ˈlepəˌthriks\ *n, pl* **lepothrixes** \-ksəz\ *also* **le·pot·ri·ches** \ləˈpä·trəˌkēz\ [NL, fr. *lepo-* + *-thrix*] **:** TRICHOMYCOSIS

lep·per \ˈlepə(r)\ *n* -s [*lep* + *-er*] **:** a horse skilled in jumping **:** JUMPER

lep·py \ˈlepē\ *n* -ES [origin unknown] *chiefly West* **:** a motherless calf **:** DOGIE

lep·ra \ˈleprə\ *n* -s [LL, leprosy — more at LEPER] **1** *archaic* **:** any of various skin diseases **2 :** LEPROSY

lepra reaction *n* **:** one of the acute episodes of chills and fever, malaise, and skin eruption occurring in the chronic course of leprosy

lep·re·chaun *also* **lep·re·caun** *or* **lep·re·haun** \ˈleprəˌkȯn, -ˌkän, -ˌän *sometimes* -ˌkən *or* -ˌkən\ *n* -s [IrGael *leipreachān, luprachān,* fr. MIr *lūchorpān,* fr. *lū* small + *corpān,* dim. of *corp* body, fr. L *corpus* — more at MIDRIFF] **:** a mischievous elf of Irish folklore usu. conceived as a shoemaker and believed to reveal the hiding place of treasure if caught

lep·rid \ˈleprəd\ *n* -s [ISV *lepr-* (fr. LL *lepra* leprosy) + *-id*] **:** a skin lesion characteristic of neural leprosy

lep·roid \ˈleˌprȯid\ *adj* [LL *lepra* leprosy + E *-oid*] **:** resembling leprosy

lep·rol·o·gist \leˈpräləjəst\ *n* -s **:** a specialist in leprology

lep·rol·o·gy \-jē\ *n* -ES [LL *lepra* leprosy + E *-o-* + *-logy*] **:** the study of leprosy and its treatment

lep·ro·ma \leˈprōmə\ *n, pl* **lepromas** \-məz\ *or* **leproma·ta** \-məd·ə\ [NL, fr. LL *lepra* leprosy + NL *-oma*] **:** a nodular lesion of leprosy

lep·ro·ma·tous \(ˈ)leˈprämədəs, -rōm-\ *adj* [NL *lepromat-, leproma* + E *-ous*] **1 :** characterized by the formation or presence of lepromas ⟨~ leprosy⟩ **2 :** relating to or exhibiting nodular leprosy ⟨cases of the ~ type⟩ ⟨a higher ~ rate⟩

lep·ro·min \leˈprōmən\ *n* -s [NL *leproma* + E *-in*] **:** an extract of human leprous tissue used in a skin test for leprosy infection

lep·ro·sar·i·um \ˌleprəˈsa(a)rēəm, -ser-, -sär- *sometimes* -sär-\ *n, pl* **leprosariums** *or* **leprosar·ia** \-ēə\ [ML, fr. LL *leprosus* leprous + L *-arium*] **:** a hospital for lepers

lep·rose \ˈleˌprōs\ *adj* [LL *leprosus* leprous] **:** SCURFY, SCALY

lep·ro·sery \ˈleprəˌserē, -eri\ *n* -ES [F *léproserie,* fr. L *leprosus* leprous + F *-erie* -ery] **:** LEPROSARIUM

le·pro·sis \ləˈprōsəs\ *n* -ES [NL, fr. LL *lepra* leprosy + NL *-osis*] **:** a disease of the sweet orange of undetermined cause that is characterized by the spotting of smooth bark and fruits and by the scaling of the bark on the larger limbs and sometimes on the trunk — called also *nailhead rust, scaly bark;* compare PSOROSIS

lep·ro·sy \ˈleprəsē, -si\ *n* -ES [*leprous* + *-y*] **1 :** a chronic disease caused by infection with an acid-fast bacillus (*Mycobacterium leprae*) and characterized by the formation of nodules on the surface of the body and esp. on the face or by the appearance of tuberculoid macules on the skin that enlarge and spread and are accompanied by loss of sensation followed sooner or later in both types by involvement of nerves with eventual paralysis, wasting of muscle, and production of deformities and mutilations **2 :** an ideological or moral influence that is felt to deteriorate sound principles or moral values ⟨cannot think of a single collective organization today . . . untainted by the ~ of nihilism —Ignazio Silone⟩ ⟨even moral ~ can be cured by divine grace —*Time*⟩ ⟨this badness is not radical . . . this ~ cannot destroy man's original grandeur —Jacques Maritain⟩

lep·rot·ic \(ˈ)leˈpräd·ik\ *adj* [*leprosy* + *-otic*] **:** of, caused by, or infected with leprosy ⟨~ lesions⟩

lep·rous \ˈleprəs\ *adj* [ME *leprous, leprus, lepros,* fr. LL *leprosus,* fr. *lepra* leprosy + L *-osus* -ous — more at LEPER] **1 a :** infected with leprosy **b :** of, relating to, or associated with leprosy or a leper ⟨~ neuritis⟩ **2 a :** resembling or suggestive of leprosy or a leper ⟨plates and superstructure were ~ with rust —N.R.Raine⟩ ⟨a morally ~ character with a lust for power —Sidney Hook⟩ **b :** LEPROSE — **lep·rous·ly** *adv* — **lep·rous·ness** *n* -ES

lepry *n* -ES [ME *leprie,* fr. *lepre* leprosy + *-ie* -y — more at LEPER] *obs* **:** LEPROSY

-lep·sy \ˌlepsē, -si\ *also* **-lep·sia** \ˈlepsēə\ *or* **-lep·sis** \-lepsəs\ *n comb form, pl* **-lepsies** \-sēz, -siz\ *also* **-lepsias** \-sēəz\ *or* **-lep·ses** \-(ˌ)sēz\ [*-lepsy* fr. MF *-lepsie,* fr. LL *-lepsia,* fr. Gk *-lēpsia,* fr. *lēpsis* act of taking hold or receiving, seizure (fr. *lēptos,* verbal of *lambanein* to take, seize) + *-ia* -y; *-lepsia,* NL, fr. LL & Gk; LL, fr. Gk *-lēpsia; -lepsis,* L, fr. Gk *-lēpsis,* fr. *lēpsis* — more at LATCH] **:** taking **:** seizure ⟨epi*lepsy*⟩ ⟨andro*lepsia*⟩

lept- *or* **lepto-** *comb form* [*lept-,* NL, fr. Gk *leptos,* lit., peeled, husked, fr. *lepein* to peel; *lepto-* fr. Gk, fr. *leptos* — more at LEPER] **:** small **:** weak **:** thin **:** fine ⟨*Lept*andra⟩ ⟨*lepto*logy⟩ ⟨*lepto*rrhine⟩

lepta *pl of* LEPTON

[1]**lep·tan·dra** \lepˈtandrə\ [NL, fr. *lept-* + *-andra*] *syn of* VERONICASTRUM

[2]**leptandra** \"\ *n* -s *often cap* [NL *Leptandra,* genus name of *Leptandra virginica*] **:** CULVER'S ROOT

lep·ta·zol \ˈleptəˌzōl, -ˌzōl\ *n* -s [prob. fr. *lept-* + *az-* + *-ol*] **:** PENTYLENETETRAZOL

lep·tene \ˈlepˌtēn\ *also* **lep·ten·ic** \(ˈ)lepˈtenik\ *adj* [*leptene* fr. G *lepten,* fr. *lept-* + *-en* (as in G *euryen* euryene); *leptenic* fr. *leptene* + *-ic* — more at EURYENE] **:** having a high, a narrow, or a high narrow forehead with an upper facial index of 55 to 60 on the skull and of 53 to 57 on the living

lep·te·ny \ˈleptənē\ *n* -ES **:** the quality or state of being leptene

lep·ti·no·tar·sa \ˌleptənōˈtärsə\ *n, cap* [NL, fr. *lept-* + *-ino-* (fr. *-inus* -ine) + *-tarsa* (fr. *tarsus*)] **:** a genus of beetles of the family Chrysomelidae containing the Colorado potato beetle

lep·tite \ˈlepˌtīt\ *n* -s [ISV *lept-* + *-ite*] **:** a mineral consisting of a fine-grained leucocratic metamorphic rock that is composed essentially of quartz and feldspar sometimes along with dark minerals

lep·to·bos \ˈleptə+ˌ-\ *n, usu cap* [NL, fr. *lept-* + *Bos*] **:** an extinct polled bovine held to be an ancestor of domestic cattle

lep·to·car·dia \ˌleptəˈkärdēə\ [NL, fr. *lept-* + *-cardia*] *syn of* LEPTOCARDII

lep·to·car·dii \-dēˌī\ *n pl, cap* [NL, fr. *lept-* + *-cardii* (fr. Gk *kardia* heart) — more at HEART] *in some classifications* **:** a class coextensive with Cephalochorda and often considered the lowest division of Vertebrata

lep·to·ceph·a·lid \-ˈsefələd\ *n* -s [NL *leptocephalus* + E *-id*] **:** LEPTOCEPHALUS 2a

lep·to·ceph·a·lous \ˌ==ˈsefələs\ *also* **lep·to·ce·phal·ic** \-səˈfalik\ *adj* [NL *leptocephalus* + E *-ous* or *-ic*] **1 :** of, relating to, or having the characteristics of a leptocephalus **2** [*leptocephaly* + *-ous* or *-ic*] **:** characterized by or exhibiting leptocephaly

lep·to·ceph·a·lus \ˌ==ˈsefələs\ *n* [NL, fr. *lept-* + *-cephalus*] **1** *cap, in some esp. former classifications* **:** a genus (the type of the family Leptocephalidae) of small pelagic fishes comprising the leptocephali when these are not larvae of other fishes **2** *pl* **lep·to·ceph·a·li** \-ˌlī\ **a :** a small-headed transparent ribbonlike pelagic first larva of various eels that lives three years in the open sea before migrating to coastal waters and gradually transforming into an elver **b :** any of various similar larvae of fishes other than eels **3** *pl* **leptocephali** [NL, fr. *lept-* + *-cephalus*] **a :** LEPTOCEPHALY **b :** an individual with leptocephaly

lep·to·ceph·a·ly \-lē\ *also* **lep·to·ce·pha·lia** \-səˈfālyə\ *n, pl* **leptocephalies** *also* **leptocephalias** [NL *leptocephalia,* fr. *lept-* + *cephal-* + *-ia* -y] **:** abnormal narrowness and tallness of the skull

lep·to·cer·cal \ˌ==ˈsərkəl\ *adj* [*lept-* + *-cercal*] **1 :** tapering off to a long slender point — used of the tail of a fish (as a sting ray) **2 :** having a leptocercal tail

lep·to·chlorite \ˌ==+\ *n* [ISV *lept-* + *chlorite;* prob. orig. formed as G *leptochlorit*] **:** a mineral consisting of any of several chlorites of indistinct crystallization — opposed to *orthochlorite*

lep·to·clase \ˈleptəˌklās, -āz\ *n* -s [ISV *lept-* + *-clase;* prob. orig. formed in F] **:** a minute crack or fracture in rock

[1]**lep·to·dac·tyl** \ˌ==ˈdaktᵊl\ *adj* [NL *leptodactylus,* fr. *lept-* + *-dactylus* (fr. Gk *-daktylos* -dactylous)] **:** LEPTODACTYLOUS

[2]**leptodactyl** \"\ *n* **:** a bird or other animal having slender toes

lep·to·dac·tyl·id \ˌ==ˈ=tələd\ *adj* [NL *Leptodactylidae*] **:** of or relating to the Leptodactylidae

lep·to·dac·tyl·i·dae \-ˌdakˈtiləˌdē\ *n pl, cap* [NL, fr. *Leptodactylus,* type genus + *-idae*] *in some classifications* **:** a family of toothed toads that is more or less coextensive with Bufonidae

lep·to·dac·ty·lous \ˌ==ˈdaktələs\ *adj* [*lept-* + *-dactylous*] **:** having slender toes ⟨~ birds⟩

lep·to·dac·ty·lus \ˌ==ˈdaktələs\ *n, cap* [NL, fr. *lept-* + *-dactylus* (fr. Gk *daktylos* finger, toe)] **:** a genus of toothed toads that is usu. placed in the family Bufonidae and that comprises the So. American bullfrogs and related forms

lep·to·der·mous \ˌ==ˈdərməs\ *also* **lep·to·der·ma·tous** \-məd·əs\ *adj* [*lept-* + *-dermous* (as in *pachydermous*) or *-dermatous*] **:** having a thin skin — used esp. of the theca of a moss

lep·tod·o·ra \lepˈtädərə\ *n, cap* [NL, fr. *lept-* + Gk *dora* hide, fr. *derein* to skin, flay — more at TEAR (rend)] **:** a genus (the type of the family Leptodoridae) of freshwater entomostracans of the order Cladocera

lep·to·form \ˈleptəˌfȯrm\ *n* [*lept-* + *form*] **:** a plant rust having a telial stage that is not preceded by a resting stage — compare MICROFORM

lep·to·kur·tic \ˌ==ˈkərd·ik\ *adj* [*lept-* + Gk *kyrtos* bulging, convex, curved + E *-ic;* akin to L *curvus* bent, curved — more at CROWN] **1** *of a frequency distribution curve* **:** being more peaked than the corresponding normal distribution curve **2** *of*

a frequency distribution **:** being more concentrated about the mean than the corresponding normal distribution
lep·to·kur·to·sis \ˌ==ˌkər'tōsəs\ *n* [NL, fr. E *leptokurtic* + NL *-osis*] **:** the condition of being leptokurtic
lep·to·lep·i·dae \ˌ==ˈlepəˌdē\ *n pl, cap* [NL, fr. *Leptolepis*, type genus + *-idae*] **:** a family of primitive clupeoid fishes of the Upper Lias and Lower Cretaceous
lep·tol·e·pis \lep'täləpəs\ *n, cap* [NL, fr. *lept-* + *-lepis*] **:** a genus (the type of the family Leptolepidae) of primitive clupeoid fishes that includes numerous small thin-scaled fishes with the tail nearly homocercal
lep·to·li·na \ˌleptə'līnə, -lēnə\ *also* **leptoli·nae** \-lī,nē, -lē,nī\ [NL] *syn of* HYDROIDA
lep·tol·o·gy \lep'täləjē\ *or* **lep·to·nol·o·gy** \ˌleptə'näləjē\ *n* -ES [*leptology* fr. *lept-* + *-logy; leptonology* fr. Gk *lepton* (neut. of *leptos* small, fine) + E *-o-* + *-logy* — more at LEPT-] **:** CRYSTALLOGRAPHY
lep·to·mat·ic \ˌleptə'mad·ik\ *adj* [*leptome* + *-atic* (after such pairs as E *symptom: symptomatic*)] **:** of or relating to the leptome
lep·tome \'lep,tōm\ *also* **lep·tom** \-täm\ *n* -S [G *leptom*, fr. *lept-* + *-om* -ome] **1 :** a part of the mestome that conducts food materials **2 :** a somewhat rudimentary phloem in cryptogams
lep·to·medusae \ˌlep(ˌ)tō+\ *n pl, cap* [NL, fr. *lept-* + *medusae* (pl. of *medusa*)] **:** a suborder of the order Hydroida or in some classifications a separate order of Hydrozoa comprising coelenterates in which the hydranths and the productive zooids are protected by a theca, the medusae bear gonads on the radial canals, and the lithocysts when present are of ectodermal origin — **lep·to·medusan** \"+\ *adj or n*
lep·to·meningeal \ˌlep(ˌ)tō+\ *adj* [NL *leptomeninges* + E *-al*] **:** of or involving the leptomeninges ⟨~ infection⟩
lep·to·meninges \"+\ *n pl* [NL, fr. *lept-* + *meninges*] **:** the pia mater and the arachnoid
lep·to·meningitis \"+\ *n* [NL, fr. *lept-* + *meningitis*] **:** inflammation of the pia mater and the arachnoid membrane
lep·tom·er·yx \lep'täməriks\ *n, cap* [NL, fr. *lept-* + *-meryx*] **:** a genus of small Oligocene ruminants of western No. America distantly related to the recent chevrotains
lep·to·mi·ta·les \ˌlep(ˌ)tō,mī'tā(ˌ)lēz\ *n pl, cap* [NL, fr. *Leptomitus*, genus of water molds (fr. Gk *leptomitos* of fine threads, fr. *lepto-* lept- + *mitos* thread) + *-ales*] **:** an order of water molds (subclass Oomycetes) resembling the Saprolegniales but forming branching chains because of regular constrictions of the hyphae
[1]**lep·tom·o·nad** \lep'täməˌnad\ *adj* [NL *Leptomonad-*, *Leptomonas*] **:** of or relating to the genus *Leptomonas*
[2]**leptomonad** \"\ *n* **:** LEPTOMONAS 2
lep·tom·o·nas \-ˌnəs\ *n* [NL, fr. *lept-* + *-monas*] **1** *cap* **:** a genus of flagellates of the family Trypanosomatidae that are parasites esp. of the digestive tract of insects and that occur as elongated flagellates with anterior flagellum and no undulating membrane but also pass through stages indistinguishable from intracellular crithidias and leishmanias **2** -ES **a :** any flagellate of the genus *Leptomonas* **b :** a flagellate of the family Trypanosomatidae when exhibiting a typical leptomonad form
[1]**lep·ton** \lep'tȯn\ *n, pl* **lep·ta** \-tä\ [Gk, fr. neut. of *leptos* small — more at LEPT-] **1 :** a small bronze coin of ancient Greece **2 :** a small bronze Judaean coin minted until the middle of the 1st century A.D. **3** [NGk, fr. Gk] **a :** a unit of value of modern Greece equal to $\frac{1}{100}$ of a drachma — see MONEY table **b :** a coin representing such a lepton
[2]**lep·ton** \'lep,tän, -tən\ *n* [NL, fr. Gk, neut. of *leptos* small, fine] **1** *cap* **:** a genus of minute bivalve mollusks (suborder Submytilacea) with round flat thin shells **2** -S **:** any mollusk of the genus *Lepton*
[3]**lepton** \"\ *n* -S [*lept-* + *-on*] **:** any of a family of particles (as electrons, muons, and neutrinos) that have one-half quantum unit of spin, obey Fermi-Dirac statistics, and experience no strong interactions
lep·to·necrosis \ˌlep(ˌ)tō+\ *n* [NL, fr. E *leptome* + NL *necrosis*] **:** a necrosis of the phloem tissues
lep·to·ne·ma \ˌleptə'nēmə\ *n* -S [NL, fr. *lept-* + *-nema*] **:** a chromatin thread or chromosome at leptotene **:** a meiotic chromosome before the beginning of synapsis — compare PACHYNEMA
lep·to·phis \'leptəfəs\ *n, cap* [NL, fr. *lept-* + *-ophis*] **:** a genus of slender harmless tree snakes of Central and So. America
lep·to·pro·sopic \ˌ==prə¦säpik, -säp-\ *also* **lep·to·pro·sopous** \-sōpəs\ *adj* [G *leptoprosop* leptoprosopic (fr. *lepto-* lept- + Gk *prosōpon* face) + E *-ic* or *-ous* — more at PROSOP-] **:** having a long, a narrow, or a long narrow face with a facial index of 88 to 93 on the living and of 90 to 95 on the skull
lep·to·proso·py \ˌ==ˈpräsəpē, -ˌprə'sōpē\ *n* -ES **:** the quality or state of being leptoprosopic
lep·top·ti·los \lep'täptəlәs\ *n, cap* [NL, fr. *lept-* + Gk *-ptilos* -feathered, -winged (fr. *ptilon* down, feather)] **:** a genus of storks consisting of the adjutant birds and marabous
lep·tor·rhine *also* **lep·to·rhine** \'leptə,rīn\ *or* **lep·tor·rhin·i·an** \ˌ==¦rinēən\ *or* **lep·tor·rhin·ic** \-¦rinik\ *adj* [*leptorrhine & leptorhine* prob. fr. F *leptorrhin*, fr. *lepto-* lept- + *-rrhin* -rrhine; *leptorrhinian* fr. F *leptorrhinien*, fr. *lepto-* lept- + *-rrhin* -rrhine + *-ien* -ian; *leptorrhinic* fr. *leptorrhine* + *-ic*] **:** having a long narrow nose with a nasal index of less than 47 on the skull or of less than 70 on the living
lep·tor·rhi·ny \'leptə,rīnē\ *n* -ES **:** the quality or state of being leptorrhine
[1]**lep·to·some** \-ˌsōm\ *also* **lep·to·so·mat·ic** \ˌ==ˌsō¦mad·ik\ *or* **lep·to·som·ic** \-¦sōmik\ *adj* [*leptosome* fr. G *leptosom*, fr. *lepto-* lept- + *-som* (fr. Gk *sōma* body); *leptosomatic* fr. *leptosome* + *-atic* (after E *somatic*); *leptosomic* fr. *leptosome* + *-ic* — more at -SOME (body)] **:** ASTHENIC 2, ECTOMORPHIC — opposed to *eurysome*
[2]**lep·to·some** \'leptə,sōm\ *also* **lep·to·som** \-säm\ *n* -S [G *leptosom*, n. & adj.] **:** an ectomorphic individual
lep·to·sper·mone \ˌ==ˈspər,mōn\ *n* -S [NL *Leptospermum* + E *-one*] **:** a pale yellow viscous oily ketone $C_{15}H_{22}O_4$ occurring in the essential oils from various plants of the genus *Leptospermum*
lep·to·sper·mum \-ˌməm\ *n, cap* [NL, fr. *lept-* + *-spermum*] **:** a genus of Australasian shrubs or small trees of the family Myrtaceae having small rigid alternate leaves and white flowers — see TEA TREE
lep·to·sphae·ria \-'sfirēə\ *n, cap* [NL, fr. *lept-* + Gk *sphaira* sphere + NL *-ia* — more at SPHERE] **:** a genus of ascomycetous fungi that is commonly placed in the family Sphaeriaceae, is characterized by the production of dark ascospores with five or more septa, and includes saprophytes and a few fungi that are associated with leaf spots or rots of economic plants
lep·to·spi·ra \-'spīrə\ *n* [NL, fr. *lept-* + L *spira* coil, twist — more at SPIRE (spiral, curl)] **1** *cap* **:** a genus of extremely slender aerobic spirochetes (family Treponemataceae) free-living or parasitic in mammals that includes a number of important pathogens (as *L. icterohaemorrhagiae* of Weil's disease or *L. canicola* of canicola fever) **2** *pl* **leptospira** \"\ *also* **leptospiras** \-rəz\ *or* **leptospi·rae** \-ˌrē\ **:** any spirochete of the genus *Leptospira*
lep·to·spi·ral \ˌ==¦==rəl\ *adj* [NL *leptospira* + E *-al*] **:** of, due to, or involving leptospira ⟨~ infection⟩ ⟨~ disease⟩
leptospiral jaundice *n* **:** WEIL'S DISEASE
lep·to·spi·ro·sis \ˌ==ˌspī'rōsəs\ *n, pl* **leptospiro·ses** \-ˌsēz\ [NL, fr. *Leptospira* + *-osis*] **:** any of several diseases of man and domestic animals (as cattle and dogs) caused by infection with spirochetes of the genus *Leptospira* — see STUTTGART DISEASE, WEIL'S DISEASE; compare CANICOLA FEVER
lep·to·spo·ran·gi·a·tae \ˌlep(ˌ)tōspəˌranjē'ā,tī, -'ä,tī\ *n pl, cap* [NL, fr. fem. pl. of *leptosporangiatus*, adj.] *in some classifications* **:** a group comprising all the orders of ferns in which sporangium formation is leptosporangiate — compare EUSPORANGIATAE
lep·to·spo·ran·gi·ate \¦(=)=spə¦ranjēət, -ē,āt\ *adj* [NL *leptosporangiatus*, fr. *lept-* + *sporangium* + L *-atus* -ate] **:** having each sporangium formed from a single epidermal cell ⟨~ ferns⟩ — opposed to EUSPORANGIATE
lep·to·staph·y·line \¦leptə¦stafə,līn, -ˌlən\ *adj* [*lept-* + Gk *staphylē* uvula + E *-ine*] **:** having a palate which is narrow and high with a palatal index of less than 80 on the skull
lep·to·staph·y·li·ny \ˌ==¦==ˌlīnē\ *n* -ES [ISV *leptostaphyline* + *-y*] **:** the quality or state of being leptostaphyline

lep·tos·tra·ca \lep'tästrəkə\ *n pl, cap* [NL, fr. *lept-* + *-ostraca*] **:** a division of Malacostraca including the Phyllocarida, the Nebaliacea, and various fossil forms that are regarded as intermediate between the typical malacostracans and the lower crustaceans although classed among the former — see NEBALIA — **lep·tos·tra·can** \(')=¦=kən\ *adj & n* — **lep·tos·tra·cous** \(')=¦==kəs\ *adj*
lep·to·stro·ma·ta·ce·ae \ˌleptəˌstrōmə'tāsē,ē\ *n pl, cap* [NL, fr. *Leptostromat-*, *Leptostroma*, type genus (fr. *lept-* + *stroma*) + *-aceae*] **:** a family of imperfect fungi of the order Sphaeropsidales having more or less dimidiate shield-shaped black pycnidia
lep·to·tene \'leptə,tēn\ *n* -S [ISV *lept-* + *-tene*; orig. formed as F *leptotène*] **:** a stage of the meiotic prophase immediately preceding synapsis in which the chromosomes appear as fine discrete threads — compare PACHYTENE — **lep·to·tenic** \¦==¦tēnik, -¦ten-\ *adj*
lep·to·thermal \¦leptə+\ *adj* [*lept-* + *thermal*] **:** of or relating to a portion of the hydrothermal sequence of ore deposits that lies between mesothermal and epithermal
lep·to·thrix \'==ˌthriks\ *n* [NL, fr. *lept-* + *-thrix*] **1** *cap* **:** a genus of sheathed filamentous bacteria (family Chlamydobacteriaceae) that are unbranched or exhibit false branching, that multiply by division or by motile swarmers, and that have the sheath encrusted with ferric hydroxide — see LEPTOTRICHIA **2** *pl* **lep·to·trich·ia** \ˌ==ˈtrikēə\ *also* **lep·tot·ri·ches** \lep'tä·trə,kēz\ **:** a bacterium of the genus *Leptothrix*
lep·to·trich·ia \ˌ==ˈtrikēə\ *n, cap* [NL, fr. *Leptotrich-*, *Leptothrix* + *-ia*] **:** a genus of long filamentous typically oral bacteria that are often placed among the actinomycetes but have sometimes been included in the genus *Leptothrix*, or divided among several other genera
lep·to·typhlops \¦leptə+\ *n, cap* [NL, fr. *lept-* + *Typhlops*, genus of snakes — more at TYPHLOPIDAE] **:** a genus (the type of the family Leptotyphlopidae) of small burrowing vermiform snakes of Africa, southwestern Asia, and the warmer parts of America
lep·tus \'leptəs\ *n* [NL, fr. Gk *leptos* small, thin — more at LEPT-] **1** *pl* **leptuses** \-təsəz\ *also* **lep·ti** \-ˌtī, -(ˌ)tē\ *often cap* **:** any of several 6-legged larval mites — often used as if a generic name; compare CYSTICERCUS 1 **2** *cap* **:** a genus of predaceous mites (family Erythraeidae) that are parasitic as larvae on insects
lepus \'lepəs, 'lēp-\ *n, cap* [NL, fr. L, hare — more at LAPIN] **:** a genus (the type of the family Leporidae) comprising the typical hares
lere \'lēr\ *vb* [ME *leeren, leren*, fr. OE *lǣran* to teach; akin to OS *lērian* to teach, OHG *lēren*, Goth *laisjan*; causative fr. the root of E *lore*] *archaic Scot* **:** LEARN
ler·naea \ˌlər'nēə\ *n, cap* [NL, fr. L, fem. of *Lernaeus* Lernaean] **:** a genus (the type of the family Lernaeidae) of copepod crustaceans that in some stages are parasitic usu. externally on fishes — **ler·nae·i·form** \-ēə,fȯrm\ *or* **ler·nae·oid** \-ē,ȯid\ *adj*
[1]**ler·nae·an** *also* **ler·ne·an** \ˌlər'nēən\ *adj* [L *Lernaeus* of Lerna near ancient Argos (fr. Gk *Lernaios*, fr. *Lernē* Lerna) + E *-an*] **1** *usu cap* **:** of or relating to Lerna, a lake or swamp near Argos **2** [NL *Lernaea* + E *-an*] **:** of or relating to the genus *Lernaea*
[2]**lernaean** \"\ *n* -S **:** a crustacean of the genus *Lernaea*
le·rot \(')lā¦rō\ *n* -S [F *lérot*, fr. MF, fr. *loir*, fr. L *glir-*, *glis* dormouse] **:** any of several dormice of a genus (*Eliomys*) of southern Europe and northern Africa
lerp \'lərp\ *also* **laap** \'läp\ *n* -S [native name in Australia, lit., sweet] **:** a sweet waxy secretion found in Australia and Tasmania on the leaves of eucalyptus trees that is produced as a protection by the young of jumping plant lice of *Spondyliaspis* and related genera and is eaten by aborigines
lerp insect *n* **:** JUMPING PLANT LOUSE
ler·ret \'lerət\ *n* -S [origin unknown] **:** an open boat with two sails and 2, 4, or 6 oars that is used in the English channel
ler·wa \'lərwə\ *n, cap* [NL, fr. Nepali *larwā* snow partridge; akin to Skt *laṭvā, laṭvākā, laḍvākā*, a bird] **:** a genus constituted by the snow partridge
-les *pres 3d sing of* -LE
LES *abbr* local excitatory state
[1]**les·bi·an** \'lezbēən\ *adj, often cap* [L *Lesbius* of Lesbos (fr. Gk *Lesbios*, fr. *Lesbos*, island in the Aegean Sea) + E *-an*] **1 :** of or relating to Lesbos (now Mytilene) **2** [so called fr. the reputed sensuality of the Lesbian people and literature] **:** highly sensual **:** EROTIC ⟨~ novels⟩ **3** [so called fr. the reputed homosexual band associated with Sappho *fl* ab 600 B.C. Greek lyric poet of Lesbos] **:** of or relating to homosexual relations between females
[2]**lesbian** \"\ *n* -S *often cap* **1 :** an Aeolic dialect of ancient Greek used in Lesbos **2 :** a female homosexual
les·bi·an·ism \-ˌnizəm\ *n* -S **:** lesbian love **:** SAPPHISM
les·che \'le(ˌ)skē\ *n* -S [Gk *leschē*; akin to Gk *lechos* bed — more at LIE] **:** a social gathering place of classical antiquity
lese majesty *or* **lèse ma·jes·té** \'lēz'majəstē, -ti\ *n, pl* **lese majesties** *or* **lèse majestés** [*lese majesty* part trans. of MF *lese majesté, leze majesté*, fr. L *laesa majestas*, lit., injured majesty; *lèse majesté* fr. F, fr. MF] **1 a** (1) **:** a crime (as high treason) committed against a sovereign power ⟨people convicted of *lèse majesté* —*Hartford (Conn.) Courant*⟩ (2) **:** an offense violating the dignity of a ruler as the representative of a sovereign power ⟨as *lèse majesté* against Stalin surpass all other crimes —Georg Mann⟩ **b :** a detraction from the dignity or importance of a constituted authority ⟨*lèse majesté* toward the Church —*New Yorker*⟩ ⟨time has so mellowed Strachey's *lèse majesté* that his biography has been accepted . . . as a human portrait of the great Queen —*Time*⟩ ⟨to belittle the Hong Kong and Shanghai Bank has always been almost *lèse majesté* here —Christopher Rand⟩ **2 :** an affront to position or authority **:** INDIGNITY, OUTRAGE ⟨some varlet put a parking ticket on the . . . car, which is *lèse majesté*, and the whole town had to prostrate itself —Claudia Cassidy⟩ ⟨any criticism of it is . . . *lese majesty* —Hunter Mead⟩
lesghian *usu cap, var of* LEZGHIAN
le·sion \'lēzhən\ *n* -S [ME *lesioun*, fr. MF *lesion*, fr. OF, fr. LL *laesion-, laesio*, fr. L, verbal attack, fr. *laesus* (past part. of *laedere* to injure, hurt) + *-ion-, -io* -ion] **1 a :** INJURY, IMPAIRMENT, FLAW ⟨looking for . . . ~*s*, for bubbles in the gutta-percha —*London Times*⟩ ⟨crime . . . has become the symptom of a radical ~ in the stamina of humanity —M.D.Zabel⟩ **b :** an abnormal change in structure of an organ or part due to injury or disease; *esp* **:** one that is circumscribed and well defined **2** *civil & Scots law* **:** loss from another's failure to fulfill a contract **:** injury arising from failure to receive the full equivalent of what was bargained for in a commutative contract **syn** see WOUND
les·ke·ace·ae \ˌleskē'āsē,ē\ *n pl, cap* [NL, fr. *Leskea*, type genus (fr. Nathaniel G. *Leske* †1786 Ger. naturalist) + *-aceae*] **:** a family of pleurocarpous mosses (order Hypnobryales) that grow on trees and rocks, are typified by the genus *Leskea*, and are characterized by papillose, rounded, or rhomboid leaves and mostly erect capsules — **les·ke·aceous** \ˌ==¦āshəs\ *adj*
les·leya \'leslēə, 'lezl-, ˌ==ˈ=\ *n, cap* [NL, fr. J. P. *Lesley* †1903 Am. geologist] **:** a genus of fossil plants of Carboniferous age and uncertain affinities that resemble ferns
les·ley·ite \'leslē,īt, -ezl-\ *n* -S [John *Lesley*, Jr., 19th cent. Am. on whose farm it was found + E *-ite*] **:** a mineral approximately $K_2Al_8\frac{2}{3}Si_4O_{20}(OH)_4$ consisting of a brittle mica that is related to margarite but contains potassium
le·so·tho \lə'sō(ˌ)tō\ *adj, usu cap* [fr. *Lesotho*, country in southern Africa] **:** of or from the country of Lesotho **:** of the kind or style prevalent in Lesotho
les·pe·de·za \ˌlespə'dēzə\ *n* [NL, irreg. (by misreading of the surname) fr. V. M. de *Zespedes fl*1785 Span. governor of East Florida] **1** *cap* **:** a genus of herbaceous or shrubby plants (family Leguminosae) having exstipulate leaves, often both apetalous fertile and papilionaceous sterile flowers, and one-jointed one-seeded pods covered by the calyx, some members of which are widely used for forage, soil improvement, and esp. hay in the southern U.S. — see BICOLOR LESPEDEZA, KOREAN LESPEDEZA, SERICEA LESPEDEZA **2** -S **:** any plant of the genus *Lespedeza*
les·que·rel·la \ˌleskə'relə, ˌlāk-\ *n, cap* [NL, fr. Leo *Lesquereux* †1889 Swiss paleobotanist in U.S. + NL *-ella*] **:** a genus of low annual or perennial American herbs (family Cruciferae) having stellate pubescence, simple leaves, yellow racemose flowers, and inflated pods — see BLADDERPOD

[1]**less** \'les\ *adj* **less·er** \'lesə(r)\ **least** \'lēst\ [ME *lasse, las, less, lesse*, partly fr. OE *lǣs*, adv. & n. and partly fr. *lǣssa*, adj.; akin to OS & OFris *lēs* less, MHG *lin* tepid, faint, OHG *bilinnan* to cease, ON *linr* soft, gentle, weak, *linna* to cease, *læ* fraud, treason, bane, Goth *aflinnan* to go away, MIr *lēine* shirt, *lian* soft, Gk *liazesthai* to bend, recoil, sink, *limos* hunger, *liaros* warm, soft, gentle, Lith *liesas* thin] **1 :** of a more limited number **:** FEWER ⟨~ operating miles of railway track —*N.Y. Times*⟩ ⟨~ than two years later —C.S.Forester⟩ ⟨the subcommittee shall consist of not ~ than three nor more than five members⟩ ⟨the more watch officers, the ~ watches —Wirt Williams⟩ ⟨~ family ties than a wild thing in the woods —H.L. Mencken⟩ **2 a :** of humbler rank **:** LOWLIER ⟨no ~ a person than Winston Churchill —A.A.Hill⟩ **b** *obs* **:** of a lower quality **:** INFERIOR ⟨hope to joy is little ~ in joy than hope enjoyed —Shak.⟩ **3** *archaic* **:** younger or of diminished magnitude **:** MINOR ⟨Dr. Franklin the ~ —T.B.Macaulay⟩ ⟨the tyrant of ~ Asia —Josuah Sylvester⟩ ⟨barons . . . upward we call the greater nobility, the others beneath them the ~ nobility —John Selden⟩ **4 a :** of reduced size, extent, or degree **:** SMALLER, SLIGHTER ⟨the much ~ subordination of the individual to the social community than of the cell or organ to the animal body —Julian Huxley⟩ **b :** more limited in quantity or amount ⟨after 1764 Adams devoted even ~ time than formerly to making a living —C.L.Becker⟩
[2]**less** \"\ *adv* [ME *lesse, lasse, less*, fr. OE *lǣs*] **1 :** to a lesser extent or degree ⟨doubtful cases . . . are bound to come up in regard to the ~ investigated languages —A.L.Kroeber⟩ ⟨was ~ angry than perplexed —Jean Stafford⟩ ⟨coccinellids . . . were common during April and May and ~ so in June —*Jour. of Economic Entomology*⟩ ⟨the more they were exposed to the campaign . . . the ~ voters changed their positions —R.M. Goldman⟩ ⟨Italian is no ~ a mother tongue for her than English —Irving Kolodin⟩ **2 :** more emphatically not ⟨they were not attacking the churches, still ~ religion as such —Elmer Davis⟩ — **less than** *adv* **:** by no means **:** far from **:** not at all ⟨the road . . . was something *less than* smooth —M.W.Fishwick⟩ ⟨America's friends abroad would be *less than* candid if they did not report the fact —Barbara Ward⟩
[3]**less** \"\ *prep* [ME *las, lesse*, fr. OE *lǣs*, prep., adv., & n.] **1 :** diminished by **:** with the subtraction of **:** MINUS ⟨the weight so found, ~ the weight of the sieve, shall be considered to be the drained weight —*Definitions & Standards for Food*⟩ **2 :** with the exception of **:** EXCLUDING ⟨appeared originally, ~ some stitchwork, in the *New Yorker* —John Lardner⟩
[4]**less** \"\ *n, pl* **less** [ME *lesse, lasse*, fr. OE *lǣsse* (fr. *lǣssa*, adj.), *lǣs*] **1 a :** a smaller portion or quantity ⟨no ~ than 97 million dollars has been added —J.B.Conant⟩ ⟨the radio towers were askew and ~ of them protruded above the snow —*Geog. School Bull.*⟩ **b :** something not as consequential or elaborate ⟨people have been sent to Siberia for ~ —*Time*⟩ ⟨hewed to the current architectural concept that "~ is more"⟩ **2 :** something inferior to that with which it is compared ⟨of two evils choose the ~⟩ **3** *obs* **:** one that is of inferior rank ⟨nemesis . . . doth raze the great and raise the ~ —Samuel Daniel⟩
[5]**less** \"\ *pron* [ME *lesse, lasse*, pron. & adj., fr. OE *lǣsse* (fr. *lǣssa*, adj.)] **1 :** something smaller or below average ⟨can not honorably do ~⟩ **2** *pl in constr* **:** fewer persons or things ⟨~ were available than he had hoped⟩
[6]**less** \"\ *conj* [ME, fr. earlier *lasse than, lesse than*, fr. *lasse, lesse* (adv.) + *than*] *now dial* **:** UNLESS
-less \ləs\ *adj suffix* [ME *-les, -lesse*, fr. OE *-lēas*, fr. *lēas* devoid, false; akin to OS *lōs* loose, false, MD *los* loose, OHG *lōs*, ON *lauss* loose, Goth *laus* empty, OE *losian* to get lost, perish — more at LOSE] **1 :** destitute of **:** not having **:** free from ⟨wit*less*⟩ ⟨child*less*⟩ ⟨father*less*⟩ ⟨doubt*less*⟩ **2 :** beyond the range of — in adjectives formed from nouns of action ⟨count*less*⟩ **3 :** unable or lacking power to be acted on or to act (in a specified way) — in adjectives formed from verbs ⟨resist*less*⟩ ⟨daunt*less*⟩ ⟨quench*less*⟩ ⟨tire*less*⟩ ⟨fade*less*⟩ ⟨cease*less*⟩
less and less *adv (or adj)* **:** to a progressively smaller size or extent ⟨watched his figure grow *less and less* in the dim grey light —O.E.Rölvaag⟩ ⟨a world that . . . has been *less and less* governed by reason —Lewis Mumford⟩
lesse *obs var of* LESS
les·see \(')le¦sē\ *n* -S [ME, fr. AF, fr. *lessé*, past part. of *lesser* to lease — more at LEASE (let)] **1 :** one taking possession of real estate under a lease, esp. a written lease **:** a tenant of a leasehold estate **2 :** a bailee under bailment agreement providing a rental for personal property
[1]**less·en** \'lesᵊn\ *vb* **lessened**; **lessened**; **lessening** \-s(ᵊ)niŋ\ **lessens** [ME *lessenen*, fr. *lesse*, adj., less + *-nen* -en] *vi* **1 :** to shrink in size, number, or degree **:** DECREASE ⟨as transportation improves, distances seem to ~⟩ ⟨with the tightening of border restrictions, the stream of refugees ~*s*⟩ ⟨the medicine begins to take effect and symptoms ~⟩ ⟨attacks on academic freedom seem to have ~*ed* —F.M.Hechinger⟩ **2** *archaic* **:** to become smaller to the perception as distance increases ⟨the white sail is ~*ing* from thy view —Robert Southey⟩ ⟨distant warblings ~ on my ear —Thomas Gray⟩ **~** *vt* **1 :** to reduce in size, extent, or degree **:** make smaller ⟨~*s* the chain length of the cellulose —G.S.Hotte⟩ ⟨~ the gap between income and outgo —E.B. George⟩ ⟨the use of chlordane ~*s* beetle damage⟩ ⟨grammatical errors . . . ~ the respect of the reader —Milton Hall⟩ ⟨international conferences help to ~ tensions between nations⟩ **2 a** *archaic* **:** MINIMIZE, MITIGATE, DISPARAGE ⟨not that I endeavor to ~ . . . my offense —John Milton⟩ ⟨far from wishing to ~ the merit of this . . . benevolent action —Junius⟩ **b** *obs* **:** to lower in status or dignity **:** DEGRADE ⟨the making of new lords ~*s* all the rest —John Selden⟩ **syn** see DECREASE
[2]**lessen** \"\ *conj* [contr. of *less than*, fr. ME *lesse than* — more at LESS (conj.)] *dial* **:** UNLESS
lessening *n* -S [ME, fr. gerund of *lessenen* to lessen] **:** REDUCTION, DIMINUTION ⟨~ or complete elimination of government controls —*Annual Report Continental Steel Corp.*⟩ ⟨a marked ~ of redness and swelling —*Better Homes & Gardens*⟩
[1]**less·er** \'lesə(r)\ *adj* [ME *lasser, lesser*, comp. of *lasse, less*, less] **1 :** of less size, quality, or significance **:** SMALLER **:** INFERIOR ⟨~ rivers⟩ ⟨~ men⟩ ⟨~ works⟩ **2** *in plant or animal names* **:** of a size less than that of similar forms
[2]**lesser** \"\ *adv* **:** [2]LESS 1 ⟨never a man in Christendom can ~ hide his love . . . than he —Shak.⟩ — now used chiefly with an adjective to form the comparative ⟨works of *lesser*-known composers —*Music Lovers' Encyc.*⟩
lesser adjutant *n* **:** an Asiatic stork (*Leptoptilus javanicus*)
lesser alcaic *n, usu cap A* **:** an Alcaic with four iambic feet
lesser archilochian *n, usu cap A* **:** ARCHILOCHIAN b
lesser asclepiad *n, usu cap A* **:** ASCLEPIAD
lesser bindweed *n* **:** FIELD BINDWEED
lesser black-backed gull *n* **:** a European black-backed gull (*Larus fuscus graellsi*)
lesser broomrape *n* **:** CLOVER BROOMRAPE
lesser bulb fly *n* **:** a small syrphid fly (*Eumerus tuberculatus*) having a grayish to yellowish larva that bores in and destroys the bulbs of various plants (as narcissus, onion, iris)
lesser butcher-bird *n, Eng* **:** BEARDED TIT
lesser celandine *n* **:** a perennial herb (*Ranunculus ficaria*) that is native to Europe but naturalized locally in many areas, has more or less heart-shaped leaves, yellow flowers resembling buttercups, and tuberous roots which have been used as a poultice for the relief of piles — called also *pilewort*
lesser centaury *n* **:** a common European glabrous annual centaury (*Centaurium minus*) with flowers in dense cymes
lesser chimpanzee *n* **:** a small chimpanzee (*Pan paniscus* or *Pan satyrus paniscus*) found locally south of the Congo river in Zaire
lesser civet *n* **:** RASSE
lesser clover leaf weevil *n* **:** a small green to blue-green weevil (*Hypera nigrirostris*) with a shiny black head and beak and a larva that feeds in the developing head of clover
lesser cornstalk borer *n* **:** a crambid moth (*Elasmopalpus lignosellus*) with a slender greenish larva that burrows in the stalk of Indian corn and various other plants near the ground level and is esp. destructive in warmer parts of the New World
lesser covert *n* **:** one of the last of the secondary coverts of a bird

lesser crested tern *n* **:** a large Oriental tern (*Thalasseus bengalensis*)
lesser curlew *n* **:** WHIMBREL
lesser curvature *n* **:** the short border of the stomach primitively ventral but in man turned to the right
lesser duckweed *n* **:** an Old World duckweed (*Lemna minor*) that is widely naturalized in No. America
lesser emerald bird of paradise : a bird of paradise (*Paradisea minor*) with brilliant plumes formerly used on hats
lesser finner *n* **:** LESSER RORQUAL
lesser grain borer *n* **:** a small cosmopolitan bostrychid beetle (*Rhizopertha dominica*) that is a serious pest of stored grain
lesser housefly *n* **:** a fly (*Fannia canicularis*) that is smaller than the housefly — called also *little housefly*
lesser koodoo *n* **:** an antelope (*Strepsiceros imberbis*) of Somaliland that is similar to but smaller than the koodoo
lesser omentum *n* **:** an omentum connecting the liver and stomach and supporting the hepatic vessels
lesser peach tree borer *n* **:** a borer that is the larva of a clearwing moth (*Synanthedon pictipes*) that usu. attacks the forks and crotches of peach trees and other stone-fruit trees esp. in the southern U.S.
lesser rorqual *n* **:** the smallest finback (*Balaenoptera acutorostrata*)
lesser scaup *or* **lesser scaup duck** *n* **:** a common No. American diving duck (*Aythya affinis*) similar to the greater scaup but smaller and with the black head glossed with purple rather than green — called also *lake duck*
lesser snipe *n* **:** a jacksnipe (*Limnocryptes minima*)
lesser snow goose *n* **:** a snow goose of the subspecies (*Chen caerulescens caerulescens*) found along the Pacific flyways — called also *Alaska goose, white brant*
lesser socratic *n, usu cap S* **:** SOCRATIC 2
lesser spearwort *n* **:** either of two creeping species of *Ranunculus:* **a :** an English spearwort (*R. flammula*) — called also *banewort* **b :** a spearwort of the U.S. (*R. pusillus*)
lesser stomach worm *n* **:** a small threadlike nematode worm (*Ostertagia ostertagi*) often present in immense numbers in the pyloric part of a sheep's stomach
lesser yellowlegs *n pl but sing or pl in constr* **:** a yellowlegs (*Totanus flavipes* or *Tringa flavipes*) that is about 11 inches long including the bill, is streaked brownish gray on the head, neck, breast, and upperparts, has white on the belly, and is barred on the sides and the tail — compare GREATER YELLOWLEGS
les·ses \'lesəz\ *n pl* [ME, fr. MF, fr. *lesser, lessier* to leave — more at LEASE] *archaic* **:** the dung of a beast of prey
les·est \'lesəst\ *adj* [superl. of [1]*less*] *now dial* **:** LEAST
les·sing·ite \'lesiŋ,īt\ *n* -s [Russ *lessingit*, fr. Frantz Yulievich Levinson-*Lessing*, 20th cent. Russ. professor + Russ *-it* -ite] **:** a mineral $Ca_2Ce_4Si_3O_{13}(OH)_2$(?) consisting of a silicate of calcium and cerium
less·ness *n* -ES **:** the quality or state of being less **:** INFERIORITY
[1]**les·son** \'lesᵊn\ *n* -s [ME *lessoun*, fr. OF *leçon, lecon* lesson, reading, fr. LL *lection-, lectio*, fr. L, act of reading, fr. *lectus* (past part. of *legere* to read) + *-ion-, io* -ion — more at LEGEND] **1 :** a portion of Scripture read for instruction as part of a worship service ⟨here endeth the first ~⟩ **2 a :** a piece of instruction **:** TEACHING ⟨the ~ intended by an author —G.B. Shaw⟩ ⟨the second of the great ~*s* of Quakerism . . . respect for the individual —H.S.Canby⟩; *specif* **:** a reading or exercise assigned to a pupil as part of his schoolwork ⟨get out your books and study your ~*s*⟩ ⟨~*s* to be got and recited —H.C. McKown⟩ **b :** a fact, principle, or technique learned or to be learned by study or experience ⟨many revealing ~*s* of past experience have been overlooked —Bruce Payne⟩ ⟨the ~*s* of the flood also emphasize . . . that the landward side of the banks needs protection —J.A.Steers⟩ ⟨teach a horse his ~*s* —Ephraim Chambers⟩ **3 a :** one of the segments into which a course of instruction is divided ⟨this textbook presents the material in 20 ~*s*⟩; *specif* **:** a period of formal instruction devoted to a single subject and usu. lasting no more than an hour ⟨music ~⟩ ⟨French ~⟩ ⟨finished her ~*s* with the governess —Audrey Barker⟩ **b :** an object or event from which knowledge may be derived **:** instructive example ⟨the ~ of Coventry should be accepted by . . . every American city that is at all vulnerable to enemy air raids —*Training Manual for Auxiliary Firemen*⟩ ⟨he stands, a ~ to us in integrity —C.D.Lewis⟩; *specif* **:** a rebuke or punishment intended to forestall the repetition of an offense ⟨sent the culprit to the office and let the principal give him a ~⟩ **4 a** *obs* **:** an instrumental piece or set of pieces esp. for a keyboard instrument — compare SUITE 2b **b :** an exercise or study serving to advance musical knowledge or proficiency
[2]**lesson** \"\ *vt* **lessoned; lessoned; lessoning** \-s(ᵊ)niŋ\ **lessons 1 :** to give a lesson to **:** INSTRUCT ⟨~*ed* his contemporaries in the platitudes —Clement Wood⟩ ⟨I look at it, I talk to it, I ~ it and plead —Don Marquis⟩ **2 :** LECTURE, REBUKE, PUNISH ⟨I'll ~ you, you madman —Mary Johnston⟩ ⟨the ~*ing* of a naughty Christian Europe —James Binder⟩
les·so·nia \le'sōnēə\ *n, cap* [NL, fr. R. P. *Lesson* †1849 Fr. naval pharmacist + NL *-ia*] **:** a genus (the type of the family Lessoniaceae) of large brown algae (order Laminariales) that resemble full-grown palm trees and occur chiefly in offshore waters of the southern Pacific
les·sor \'le,sȯ(ə)r, -ó(ə), ·'·\ *n* -s [ME *lessour*, fr. AF, fr. *lesser* to lease + *-our* -or — more at LEASE (let)] **1 :** one that surrenders possession of real estate under a lease (as a written lease) **:** a grantor of a leasehold estate **2 :** a bailor under a bailment agreement providing a rental for personal property
less–than–carload *adj* **:** insufficient in weight to fill a freight car and therefore not qualifying for a carload rate — abbr. *LCL*
less–than–truckload *adj* **:** insufficient in weight to make a minimum truckload — abbr. *LTL*
[1]**lest** \'lest\ *conj* [ME *lest the, leste, lest*, fr. OE *thȳ lǣs the*, fr. *thȳ* (instrumental of *thæt* this, that, which) + *lǣs*, adj., less + *the*, relative particle — more at THAT, LESS] **1 :** for fear that **:** so that (one) should not ⟨prefer a man who acts decisively . . . rather than one who hesitates ~ he be guilty of imprudence —C.B.Kelland⟩ **2 :** THAT — used after an expression denoting fear to introduce the cause of apprehension ⟨live in daily apprehension ~ the wholesome sons and daughters whom they commit to a college return to them as brazen fools —W.L. Sullivan⟩
[2]**lest** \"\ *archaic var of* LEAST
les·to·bi·o·sis \,lestō,bī'ōsəs\ *n, pl* **lestobio·ses** \-ō,sēz\ [NL, fr. Gk *lēistēs* robber + NL *-biosis;* akin to L *lucrum* gain, profit — more at LUCRE] **:** cleptobiosis in which covert thievery replaces aggressive plundering
les·to·bi·ot·ic \¦··,bī¦äd·ik\ *adj* [fr. NL *lestobiosis*, after such pairs as NL *hypnosis:* E *hypnotic*] **:** of, relating to, or marked by lestobiosis
les·to·don \'lestə,dän\ *n* [NL, fr. Gk *lēistēs* robber + NL *-odon*] **:** a genus of large So. American Pleistocene ground sloths
le·su \'lā(,)sü\ *n, pl* **lesu** *or* **lesus** *usu cap* **1 a :** a people inhabiting New Ireland **b :** a member of such people **2 :** the Austronesian language of the Lesu people
[1]**let** \'let, *usu* -ed·+V\ *vt* **letted; letted** *or* **let; letting; lets** [ME *letten*, fr. OE *lettan* to delay, hinder; akin to OS *lettian* to hinder, MD *letten* to hinder, OHG *lezzen* to delay, hurt, ON *letja* to hold back, Goth *latjan;* causative-denominatives fr. the stem of E *late*] *archaic* **:** HINDER, IMPEDE, PREVENT ⟨by Heaven! I'll make a ghost of him that ~*s* me —Shak.⟩ ⟨mine ancient wound is hardly whole and ~*s* me from the saddle —Alfred Tennyson⟩
[2]**let** \"\ *n* -s [ME *lette, lett, let*, fr. *letten* to let (hinder)] **1 :** something that prevents or impedes **:** OBSTRUCTION ⟨free to inquire without ~ or hindrance —B.G.Gallagher⟩ ⟨the task of a socialist movement to challenge without ~ the moral values of society —Lloyd Harrington⟩ ⟨perennials reseeding themselves without outside meddling help or ~ —William Faulkner⟩ **2 :** a stroke, point, or service esp. in racket and net games that does not count and must be replayed
[3]**let** \"; *in rapid speech the* t *may be lost before "me" & "'s"*\ *vb* **let; let; letting; lets** [ME *leten, læten*, fr. OE *lǣtan;* akin to OFris *lēta* to let, permit, OS *lātan*, MD *laten*, OHG *lāzzan*, ON *lāta*, Goth *letan* to let, permit, Gk *lēdein* to be tired, L *lassus* weary, tired, *lenis* soft, mild, Lith *leisti* to let; basic meaning: to let go] *vt* **1 :** MAKE, CAUSE ⟨the king . . . ~ me know that when and if that story was told he would do the telling himself —John Barkham⟩ ⟨doctor, ~ me know the worst⟩ ⟨he ~ it be known that he might consider parting with his Stradivarius⟩ **2 a** *chiefly Brit* **:** RENT, LEASE ⟨she ~ him the rooms at once —Margaret Kennedy⟩ ⟨~ the premises⟩ ⟨the island is now ~ as grazings —A.A.MacGregor⟩ — often used with *off* or *out* ⟨working part of their land themselves and *letting* off the rest —Alfons Dopsch⟩ ⟨small holdings which were ~ out on long leases by the crown —Alan Edwards⟩ **b :** to award or assign esp. after asking for bids or proposals ⟨bids are opened before the contract is ~ —T.W. Arnold⟩ ⟨another contract for some 300 miles will be ~ —*Wall Street Jour.*⟩ ⟨~ one's timber rights⟩ — often used with *out* ⟨work was ~ out to be done in the homes —*Amer. Guide Series: N.H.*⟩ **3 a** *chiefly dial* **:** to allow to remain **:** leave behind ⟨I'll give him my commission, to ~ him there a month —Shak.⟩ **b** *obs* **:** to surrender completely **:** RELINQUISH ⟨to her mother Nature all her care she ~*s* —Edmund Spenser⟩ **4 a :** to give opportunity to or fail to prevent ⟨jagged holes . . . ~ him see the mountains —Paul Bartlett⟩ ⟨throw them together . . . and ~ dialogue and incident evolve —Richard Garnett †1906⟩ ⟨live and ~ live⟩ ⟨very particular not to ~ his beasts stray —F.D.Smith & Barbara Wilcox⟩ ⟨~*s* himself be pushed around —Margaret Mead⟩ **b** (1) — used in the imperative to introduce a request or proposal ⟨~ us pray⟩ ⟨~ not the reader be frightened away by a first impression —William Barrett⟩ ⟨at the outset, ~ it be acknowledged —D.C.Buchanan⟩ ⟨~ sleeping dogs lie⟩ (2) — used esp. in Ireland as an intensive auxiliary to form the second person imperative ⟨~ you go along with her, stranger —J.M.Synge⟩ **c** — used imperatively as an auxiliary to express a warning ⟨~ one drama hit the air waves with this dialogue . . . and the wires will be clogged by protests —Jessamyn West⟩ ⟨~ him set foot on my property and I'll have him arrested⟩ ⟨just ~ him try⟩ **5 :** to free from confinement **:** RELEASE, SPILL ⟨consult you about *letting* the water from the great pond —E.G.Bulwer-Lytton⟩ ⟨received no American aid . . . so he must attempt to prolong the emotion *letting* —*New Republic*⟩ ⟨fight until their blood is all ~ —Winston Churchill⟩ — used with *off* or *out* ⟨got mad and ~ off steam by kicking the dog⟩ ⟨~ out a scream⟩ **6 :** to facilitate the passage of by eliminating a restraint **:** allow to go **:** permit to enter, pass, or leave ⟨he ~ the lid back down slowly —W.F.Davis⟩ ⟨the pickets would not ~ them through⟩ ⟨who ~ the cat in⟩ ⟨the warden ~*s* the prisoner out⟩ ⟨~*s* the car into high gear —F.L.Allen⟩ ⟨~*s* the slack out⟩ ⟨~ himself quietly out the bedroom window⟩ ⟨~ herself down light and easy, for that chair . . . was frail —Dorothy C. Fisher⟩ **7 :** to deliver on attestation **:** ADMIT ⟨~ to bail⟩ **8** *obs* **:** to refrain or abstain from ⟨did not ~ to praise the clear unmatched red and white —Shak.⟩ ~ *vi* **1** *chiefly Brit* **:** to become rented or leased ⟨the flat ~*s* for £35 a month⟩ **2 :** to become awarded to a contractor ⟨blueprints of . . . projects advertised for *letting* —*U.S.Code*⟩

syn LET, ALLOW, PERMIT, SUFFER, LEAVE mean to refrain from preventing. LET is less formal than PERMIT or ALLOW ⟨*let* him go⟩ ⟨wanted to go but his parents would not *let* him⟩ and besides signifying, at one extreme, a positive giving of permission can, at the other, signify failure to prevent because of negligence, inability, or inaction ⟨to *let* the cold in by forgetting to close a door⟩ ⟨tremble so that he *let* the plate fall from his hands⟩ ⟨countries that *let* themselves become dependent on the labor of other countries —G.B.Shaw⟩ ALLOW and PERMIT both imply more strongly than the comparable use of LET the power or authority to prohibit or prevent or to refrain from prohibiting or preventing. ALLOW usu. implies a forbearing to prohibit; PERMIT implies a more express willing or acquiescing ⟨nothing is *permitted*, everything is *allowed*⟩ ⟨under absentee ownership the machinery was *allowed* to become obsolescent —*Amer. Guide Series: N.H.*⟩ ⟨*allow* a child to go out without his overcoat⟩ ⟨would have liked to have begun the study of art, but family finances did not *permit* this —*Current Biog.*⟩ ⟨*permits* his cattle to graze on the new pasture in such numbers that the feed is quickly used up —P.E.James⟩ SUFFER is often but rather bookishly interchangeable with ALLOW in its narrowest sense ⟨*suffer* little children to come unto me —Lk 18:16 (AV)⟩ but more usu. implies indifference or reluctance ⟨would the state *suffer* its foundation to be destroyed —Henry Adams⟩ ⟨*suffered* herself to be led to the tiny enclosure —S.E. White⟩ LEAVE when used in this sense implies strongly a noninterference ⟨*leave* them to determine their own fates⟩ ⟨the parents *left* the children free to come and go as they pleased⟩ ⟨his principle was to choose competent lieutenants, and then to *leave* them to work without hampering interference —*Irish Digest*⟩

— **let alone 1 :** to say nothing of **:** not to mention ⟨but does he have the boldness, *let alone* the skill, of his own convictions —*New Republic*⟩ ⟨no provision for the health of servants, *let alone* for their comfort —O.S.J.Gogarty⟩ **2 a :** to refrain from interfering with **:** leave undisturbed ⟨in the spring or summer, *let* nests *alone* —*Boy Scout Handbook*⟩ ⟨the government . . . promised to *let* them *alone* in part of the Everglades —Marjory S. Douglas⟩ ⟨could not *let* well enough *alone* —L.O.Coxe⟩ — often used as an imperative ⟨*let it alone;* you'll break it⟩ **b :** to leave to oneself ⟨the red-faced boy wanted nothing so much as to be *let alone*⟩ ⟨her mother told her to *let* the frightened kitten *alone*⟩ **3 :** to exclude from consideration ⟨the . . . party is inclined to *let* nationalization pretty well *alone* —Alzada Comstock⟩ — **let be :** to let alone **:** leave untouched — **let fly 1 :** to hurl with force **:** THROW, SHOOT ⟨warriors *let fly* their spears —Tom Marvel⟩ ⟨*let fly* two torpedoes —E.L.Beach⟩ **2 :** to release suddenly (the sheets of a sail) so as to spill wind **3 a :** to hurl an object (as a projectile) ⟨*let fly* with a tremendous pass —G.S.Halas⟩ ⟨infuriated householders have been known to *let fly* at them with shotguns —Gerald Priestland⟩ **b :** to loose an arrow **4 :** to give unrestrained expression to an emotion ⟨*let fly* with some observations that shook space enthusiasts —*Time*⟩ ⟨she was *letting fly* on the trombone —*Irish Digest*⟩ — **let go 1 a :** to cast off or drop ⟨the mooring lines are *let go* —*Lamp*⟩ ⟨more windjammers *let go* their anchors on the reef —Marjory S. Douglas⟩ **b :** to release one's hold on or break away from ⟨he *let go* the ladder and jumped —K.M.Dodson⟩ ⟨tons of riverbank *let go* . . . into the stream —S.H.Adams⟩ **c :** to cease to pay attention to **:** dismiss from one's mind ⟨had not made a career . . . of being young, but she had not *let* herself *go*, either —Hamilton Basso⟩ ⟨did the best he could, and *let it go* at that⟩ **d :** to dismiss from employment **:** FIRE ⟨couldn't do the work so they had to *let him go*⟩ **2 :** to give out **:** EMIT ⟨the great whistle *let go* a defiant blast —Frederick Way⟩ **3 a :** to abandon self-restraint **:** give uninhibited expression to impulses or emotions **:** cut loose ⟨one of those actors who are too anxious to be thought gentlemen to *let* themselves *go* —T.C.Worsley⟩ ⟨*let* himself *go* in his letters as though he were talking to his correspondent —*Atlantic*⟩ ⟨in Port Royal they *let go* with a roar after the long watches at sea —H.E.Rieseberg⟩ ⟨once home, she thought, . . . she could really *let go* —Nancy Hale⟩ **b :** to discharge matter or wind from the body **4 a :** to relax one's hold ⟨the dog had him by the throat and wouldn't *let go*⟩ **b :** to release a line or drop anchor ⟨at the command "*let go* and haul" we came smartly about on a new tack⟩ ⟨found a good anchorage in the lagoon and *let go*⟩ **5 :** to let fly ⟨*Punch let go* with a special diatribe —*Saturday Rev.*⟩ — **let into :** to let in ⟨have large windows *let into* most of the walls —Fay King⟩ ⟨flower beds *let into* the asphalt —Elizabeth Taylor⟩ ⟨stranger walked in, asked to be *let into* the game —*Amer. Guide Series: Md.*⟩ — **let loose 1 a :** to turn loose or free from restraint **:** let go **:** LIBERATE ⟨floating mines, evidently *let loose* by French patrols —P.W. Thompson⟩ ⟨an entomologist who was *let loose* on the same small area —C.W.M.Swithinbank⟩ ⟨the rancors *let loose* by war —J.D.Hicks⟩ **b :** to give rise to **:** set off ⟨the great success of the pioneer lines *let loose* a torrent of speculative buying —O.S.Nock⟩ **2 :** to let fly ⟨I do now *let loose* my opinion —Shak.⟩ ⟨*let loose* a torrent of invective —Albert Dasnoy⟩ ⟨*let loose* a tremendous outburst of laughter —Walter O'Meara⟩ ⟨a machine gun *let loose* on me —Mack Morriss⟩; *specif* **:** to pour down rain ⟨get the shocks into the stack before the skies *let loose* —Irving Dilliard⟩ **3 :** to throw off restraint **:** let go **:** give way ⟨the friction clutch would *let loose* at its appointed tension —F.J.Haskin⟩ — **let one have it 1 :** to subject to vigorous assault ⟨hauled back and *let him have it* full in the solar plexus⟩ ⟨held her tongue until the company left and then she really *let him have it*⟩; *specif* **:** SHOOT ⟨took careful aim and *let him have it* right between the eyes⟩ ⟨the musketeers advanced to within sixty paces of the enemy and then *let them have it* —Tom Wintringham⟩ — **let slide :** to cease to pay attention to **:** let go — **let slip :** to allow to escape; *esp* **:** to impart (information) inadvertently ⟨*let slip* one day that he had once been married —Nevil Shute⟩ — **let the cat out of the bag :** to reveal hitherto undisclosed information ⟨his vacation plans were a secret but he *let the cat out of the bag* by purchasing deep-sea fishing tackle⟩
[4]**let** \"\ *n* -s [[3]*let*] *Brit* **1 a :** an act of leasing or renting **b :** LEASE **2 :** a rented house or apartment
-let \lət, *usu* -əd·+V\ *n suffix* -s [ME *-let, -lette*, fr. MF *-elet*, fr. OF, fr. *-el* + *-et* (dim. suffix)] **1 :** small one ⟨book*let*⟩ ⟨stream*let*⟩ **2 :** article worn on — in names of articles of dress ⟨ank*let*⟩ ⟨wrist*let*⟩
let bug *or* **let dab** *vi* [prob. fr. [3]*let* + *bug* (origin unknown) or *dab*] *Scot* **:** to disclose information — usu. used with a negative ⟨didna mean to *let bug* about it —J.J.Bell⟩
[1]**letch** \'lech\ *n* -ES [ME *lache, leche* stream flowing through boggy land, bog (attested in place names), fr. OE *læcc, lecc*, fr. *leccan* to wet, moisten — more at LEAK] *dial Brit* **:** a muddy ditch or pool **:** BOG, SWAMP
[2]**letch** \"\ *n* -ES [perh. back-formation fr. *letcher*, alter. of *lecher*] **:** CRAVING ⟨full of politics and a ~ for fishing —W.A. White⟩; *specif* **:** sexual desire ⟨develops a ~ for an attractive Circassian lady —Anthony West⟩
let down *vt* **1 a :** to allow to descend gradually **:** LOWER ⟨*let* the wagons *down* the steep slope by means of ropes snubbed around trees —G.R.Stewart⟩ **b** (1) **:** to lengthen (a garment) by releasing a fold of material ⟨*let down* a skirt⟩ (2) **:** to reduce the amount of (a fold) so as to lengthen a garment ⟨*let* a hem *down*⟩ **c :** to release (formed milk secretion) within the udder **2 a :** to fail to support **:** desert in a moment of need **:** FORSAKE, BETRAY ⟨peasants who had *let down* the revolutionary cause —*Times Lit. Supp.*⟩ ⟨senators felt that they had been *let down* by their own administration —Harry Conn⟩ ⟨will not *let* each other *down* at the conference table any more than we did on the battlefield —R.M.Makins⟩ **b :** to fall short of the expectations of **:** go back on a promise to **:** DISAPPOINT, FAIL ⟨the plot is good but the end *lets* you *down*⟩ ⟨the White mountains wouldn't *let* me *down* —G.M. Smith⟩ ⟨had two appointments with the crown prince and *let* him *down* on both occasions —George Mikes⟩ ⟨sorry for the kid, and tried to *let* him *down* easy —Dorothy C. Fisher⟩ **3 :** to thin out **:** DILUTE: as **a :** to reduce the intensity of (a colored pigment) by the addition of colorless pigment **b :** to reduce the viscosity of (a paint or varnish) by adding thinner **4 a :** to put (a horse) out of action by having a sinew broken **b :** to hang low and straight — used of the posterior parts of an animal's body ⟨the hocks are well *let down*⟩ ⟨a sow well *let down* in the hams⟩ **c :** to reduce the weight of (an animal in show condition) **:** make less fat ⟨highly fitted cattle . . . may have to be *let down* carefully to develop into useful breeders —W.A.Cochell⟩ ~ *vi* **1 :** to slacken exertion or mental tension **:** RELAX ⟨all through the crisis she never once *let down*⟩ **2 a :** to bring an airplane down in a glide esp. as a prelude to landing it ⟨throttle back . . . until you're *letting down* about 200 feet a minute —J.N.Bell⟩ **b :** to come down gradually esp. for a landing ⟨the plane *let down* through heavy overcast —*Time*⟩
[1]**letdown** \'·,·\ *n* [*let down*] **1 a :** a source or mood of mental depression **:** DISCOURAGEMENT, DISAPPOINTMENT ⟨the enterprise . . . has been a big ~ to those of us who had high hopes for it —E.R.Bentley⟩ ⟨the balance of the collection is a sad ~ —J.F.McComas⟩ ⟨came home . . . with a vague feeling of ~ about Italian art —R.M.Coates⟩ **b :** a slackening of effort **:** RELAXATION, DEFECTION ⟨the sudden ~ from discipline —Dixon Wecter⟩ ⟨at that time of day, a general air of ~ hung over the kitchen —Joseph Wechsberg⟩; *specif* **:** a lapse from high moral standards ⟨how hard as stone people are about other folks' ~*s* —Dorothy C. Fisher⟩ **2 :** a drop in amount or volume **:** DECLINE, SLUMP ⟨an amazing buying rush was resumed after a brief ~ —*N.Y.Times*⟩ ⟨the ~ in steel production . . . brought moderate declines in sales —*Newsweek*⟩ ⟨a normal seasonal decline is expected but no general business ~ is in sight⟩ **3 :** the descent of an airplane from cruising altitude to the point at which a landing approach is begun ⟨cross-country flying and instrument ~*s* at strange airfields —*Crowsnest*⟩ **4** *usu* **let–down** \"\ **:** a physiological response of a lactating mammal to suckling or allied stimuli whereby increased intramammary pressure forces previously secreted milk from the acini and finer tubules into the main collecting ducts whence it can be drawn through the nipple
[2]**letdown** \"\ *adj* **1 :** characterized by mental lassitude **:** DEPRESSED, DISPIRITED ⟨the ~ feeling that comes with emptying ashtrays after a party⟩ **2 :** of or relating to the gradual descent of an airplane ⟨~ procedure⟩ ⟨the first ~ point after Honolulu —*Sperryscope*⟩
[1]**le·thal** \'lēthəl\ *adj* [L *lethalis, letalis*, fr. *letum* death + *-alis* -al; prob. akin to L *lenis* soft, mild — more at LET] **1** *archaic* **:** of or relating to spiritual death ⟨discoursing of sinners and their ~ end —Charles Reade⟩ **2 a :** of, relating to, or causing death ⟨the two convicted men will soon enter the ~ chamber —William Mayer⟩ ⟨in mice the mean ~ dose was more than twice as large as the mean paralyzing dose —*Science*⟩ ⟨the ~ fire that destroyed the building and all its occupants⟩ **b :** capable of causing death **:** DEADLY ⟨wished I had a gun or some ~ weapon, that I might destroy him —Bram Stoker⟩ ⟨prohibits the transportation in interstate . . . commerce of ~ munitions —*U.S.Code*⟩ ⟨the increasing quantity of ~ carbon monoxide poured into the air by the internal-combustion motor —Lewis Mumford⟩ ⟨gathering edible mushrooms . . . is a pleasant but potentially ~ pastime —*Pfizer Spectrum*⟩ **3 :** causing damage or destruction **:** DEVASTATING ⟨showed a ~ skill in his dissection of the . . . book —*Times Lit. Supp.*⟩ ⟨a ~ attack by the opposition caused him to resign⟩ ⟨used the ~ veto ten times to block action in the security council —*Time*⟩ **syn** see DEADLY
[2]**lethal** \"\ *n* -s **1 :** a lethal substance **2 a :** an abnormality of genetic origin causing the death of the organism possessing it usu. before maturity **b :** LETHAL GENE
lethal gene *or* **lethal factor** *n* [prob. trans. of F *gène létal* or *facteur létal*] **:** a gene that in some (as homozygous) conditions may prevent development or cause the death of an organism or its germ cells
le·thal·i·ty \lē'thaləd·ē\ *n* -ES **:** the quality or state of being lethal **:** DEADLINESS ⟨modern weapons have greater range, accuracy, speed, and ~ than anything ever dreamed of before —W.P.Corderman⟩
le·thal·ly \'lēthəlē, -li\ *adv* **:** in a deadly manner ⟨this remarkable document . . . is a ~ dull volume —R.A.Billington⟩
le·thar·gic \lə'thärjik, le'-, -tháj-, -jēk\ *adj* [prob. fr. MF *lethargique*, fr. L *lethargicus*, fr. Gk *lēthargikos*, fr. *lēthargos* lethargy + *-ikos* -ic] **1 a :** of, relating to, or characterized by lethargy **:** SLOW-MOVING, SLUGGISH ⟨bullfrogs . . . were quite ~ after storage —A.C.Giese⟩ ⟨the market . . . was even more ~ than they indicated —*Fortune*⟩ ⟨the ~ sullen power of the ocean —Norman Mailer⟩ **b :** LISTLESS, INDIFFERENT, APATHETIC, DULL ⟨the weak and ~ government of Spain —Bernard DeVoto⟩ ⟨a ~ entrepreneur in the egg business —Roger Eddy⟩ **2 :** causing lethargy **:** SOPORIFIC ⟨yielded to the ~ music and fell asleep⟩

syn LETHARGIC, SLUGGISH, TORPID, COMATOSE: LETHARGIC implies a state of sleepiness or drowsiness that makes for slowness in reaction, responses, or movements and that may be constitutional, temporary, or induced by disease or injury ⟨a *lethargic* effect to compare somewhat with the effect of insulin —*Jour. of Nervous and Mental Diseases*⟩ ⟨she did look — not exactly sleepy, but *lethargic*, relaxed. All her movements were peculiarly slow —Margery Sharp⟩ ⟨a people grown *lethargic* from economic abundance —V.L.Parrington⟩ SLUGGISH describes a similar state but often implies criticism ⟨*sluggish* transportation⟩ ⟨*sluggish* pond⟩ ⟨*sluggish* digestion⟩ ⟨England has become unenterprising and *sluggish* because England has been so prosperous and comfortable —H.G. Wells⟩ ⟨we are apt to scorn our neighbor because his rate of motion is faster or more *sluggish* than our own —A.L.Guérard⟩ TORPID and COMATOSE both imply an aberration, more or less lasting, from the normal; TORPID literally implies the numb or benumbed state of a hibernating animal, but in its more common extended sense it implies a lack of energy, responsiveness, or vigor commonly associated with healthy, active individuals ⟨Oxford was *torpid* also, droning along in its eighteenth-century grooves —Van Wyck Brooks⟩ ⟨it would be a *torpid* and spiritless reader . . . who would pass by everything sensational —F.L.Mott⟩ ⟨as a reviver of the half-dead, or the merely *torpid*, Mencken's only rival . . . was Bernard Shaw —DeLancey Ferguson⟩ COMATOSE literally suggests the state of profound insensibility of a coma ⟨the almost *comatose* condition which had first intervened never developed into a fatal diabetic coma —Havelock Ellis⟩; in extended use COMATOSE implies immobility, stagnation, extreme lethargy, often due to a paralyzing external force ⟨the tradition of art remained *comatose*. Here and there a genius appeared and wrestled with the coils of convention —Clive Bell⟩

le·thar·gi·cal·ly \-jək(ə)lē, -jēk-, -li\ *adv* **:** in a lethargic manner **:** SLUGGISHLY, APATHETICALLY

lethargic encephalitis *n* **:** ENCEPHALITIS LETHARGICA

leth·ar·gize \'lethə(r),jīz\ *vt* -ED/-ING/-S *archaic* **:** to make lethargic **:** BENUMB

[1]**leth·ar·gy** \'lethə(r)jē, -ji\ *n* -ES [alter. (influenced by LL *lethargia*) of ME *litargie*, fr. MF or ML; MF *litargie*, fr. ML *litargia*, *lethargia*, fr. LL *lethargia*, fr. Gk *lēthargia*, fr. *lēthargos* lethargy (fr. *lēthē* forgetfulness) + *-ia* -y] **1** *archaic* **:** a comatose torpor **:** abnormal drowsiness ⟨seized with a ~, in which he continued till Friday evening, and then expired, much lamented —*Boston Gazette*⟩ **2 :** the quality or state of being lazy or indifferent **:** LASSITUDE, APATHY ⟨the hot moist air of the tropics spreads a feeling of ~ and indolence over everything —G.H.Reed b.1887⟩ ⟨in spite of his urgent pleas . . . for supplies and men a disheartening ~ was displayed —J.C.Fitzpatrick⟩ ⟨an ancient people, sunk in ~ and refusing to be inspired —Joseph Frank⟩

[2]**lethargy** \"\ *vt* -ED/-ING/-ES *archaic* **:** LETHARGIZE ⟨his discernings are *lethargied* —Shak.⟩

le·the \'lē(,)thē\ *n* -S [L, fr. Gk *lēthē*] **:** OBLIVION, FORGETFULNESS ⟨severances of soul for which there is neither balm nor ~ —W.R.Greg⟩

le·the·an \'lēthēən, lə'th-,lē'th-\ *adj, usu cap* [L *Lethaeus* of Lethe, Lethean (fr. Gk *lēthaios*, fr. *Lēthē* Lethe, place of oblivion in the lower world, fr. *lēthē* forgetfulness) + E *-an*; akin to Gk *lanthanesthai* to forget, *lanthanein* to escape notice — more at LATENT] **:** of, relating to, or causing forgetfulness ⟨the *Lethean* sensuousness of Keats —Wylie Sypher⟩

lethied *adj* [alter. of *Lethe* + E *-ed*] *obs* **:** LETHEAN

le·thif·er·ous \(')lē¦thif(ə)rəs\ *adj* [L *lethifer*, *letifer* lethiferous (fr. *letum* death + *-fer* -ferous) + E *-ous* — more at LETHAL] *archaic* **:** LETHAL

le·thoc·er·us \lə'thäsərəs\ *n, cap* [NL, fr. *letho-* (fr. Gk *lētho-*, fr. *lēthē* forgetfulness) + *-cerus*] **:** a genus of very large predaceous aquatic bugs (family Belostomatidae) — compare GIANT WATER BUG

le·thri·nus \lə'thrīnəs\ *n, cap* [NL] **:** a genus (the type of the family Lethrinidae) of percoid fishes that are related to those of the family Sparidae from which they are distinguished by possession of a long scaleless snout, are widely distributed in warm southern seas, and include several important food fishes and others which are regarded as dangerously toxic

let in *vt* **1 :** to insert or embed in (a surface) ⟨*lets in* diagonal sheathing at each corner of the house⟩ **2 :** to involve or commit unfavorably ⟨the provisions . . . could still *let* us *in* for trouble —Elmer Davis⟩ ⟨smiled at all her schemes, little dreaming that . . . she was *letting* him *in* for some £20,000 —Elizabeth Montizambert⟩ **3 :** to share information with or allow to participate ⟨learned a lot more . . . and I'll *let* you in on it —Rex Ingamells⟩

let-in \'=,=\ *adj* [*let in*] **:** shortened and widened by the cutting and sewing in of additional pieces — used of pelts

let off *vt* **1 a :** to touch off **:** IGNITE, EXPLODE ⟨felt like a boy who wanted to *let off* crackers —I.L.Idriess⟩ ⟨explosions produced by *letting off* small charges of dynamite backstage —W. L. Gresham⟩; *specif* **:** FIRE ⟨*let off* their guns at British ships —G.F.Hudson⟩ **b :** to give vent to **:** get off ⟨before I left I *let off* a dissent —O.W.Holmes †1935⟩ **2 a :** to release from something, esp. a penalty **:** PARDON, EXCUSE ⟨the offender was *let off* with a severe reprimand —Harvey Graham⟩ ⟨you have promised to sing one song . . . and I cannot *let* you *off* —W.H.Hudson †1922⟩ **b :** to release from duty ⟨had *let* the men *off* for the last quarter of the day —Mary Austin⟩ **3 :** to neglect an opportunity to dismiss or score against (an opponent)

let-off \'=,=\ *n* -S [*let off*] **1 :** an act or instance of letting off ⟨spend the rest of his life in gaol, and a damned lucky *let-off* it is for him —Ngaio Marsh⟩; *specif* **:** neglect of a chance to dismiss or score against an opponent **2 a :** a device for releasing a strand (as yarn from a warp beam) to a loom at a regulated tension **b :** the release of the cocked hammer of a gun by the sear in firing **c :** the discontinuance of contact between an escape wheel tooth and a pallet in a watch

let on *vi* **1 a :** to make acknowledgment **:** ADMIT ⟨knew what the matter was but never *let on*⟩ **b :** to reveal one's presence ⟨the others were up in the tree house all the time and didn't *let on* —Agnes N. Keith⟩ **2 :** to repeat confidential information **:** TATTLE ⟨the jealous woman has *let on* to an old bum —Charlotte Armstrong⟩ **3 :** PRETEND ⟨ain't half as sick as she *lets on* —Edna Ferber⟩

let-on \'=,=\ *n* -S [*let on*] *Scot* **:** SHAM

[1]**let out** *vt* **1** *chiefly Brit* **:** to make known **:** REVEAL ⟨never *let out* his plans —Lord Dunsany⟩ **2 a :** to extend in dimension **:** LOOSEN; *esp* **:** to release (extra material) so as to enlarge a garment ⟨the man who *lets out* the seams in my clothing —J.A. Maxwell⟩ **b :** to cut (a pelt) in strips and reassemble into a longer narrower piece with better color and texture — compare TAPE 3 **3** *archaic* **:** to furnish for temporary use at a fee **:** LOAN ⟨*let out* their coin upon large interest —Shak.⟩ ⟨a girl who *let out* chairs for hire —J.M.Jephson & L.A.Reeve⟩ **4 a :** to release from further responsibility ⟨the old curmudgeon has found a new scapegoat and that *lets me out*⟩ **b :** to release from an obligation **:** let off ⟨Japan was to be . . . *let out* of paying reparations —*Time*⟩ **5 a :** to release from restraint **:** allow to gather speed ⟨*let* the car *out* a bit —Steve McNeil⟩ **b :** to let go **:** FIRE ⟨some workers without tenure guarantee will probably be *let out* —Henry Giniger⟩ ~ *vi* **1 :** to lash out **2 :** to conclude a session or performance **:** turn loose a group of people **:** break up ⟨waiting for school to *let out* —B.A.Williams⟩ ⟨after the theatres *let out*, a . . . throng trooped in for midnight supper —Robert Shaplen⟩

[2]**let out** \'=,=\ *n* -S *chiefly Irish* **:** a lavish entertainment

let-out \(')=¦=\ *adj* [[1]*let out*] *of furs* **:** lengthened by letting-out

let·o·vic·ite \,led·ə'vi,sīt\ *n* -S [G *letovicit*, fr. *Letovice*, Czechoslovakia, its locality + G *-it* -ite] **:** a mineral $(NH_4)_3H(SO_4)_2$ consisting of an acid ammonium sulfate

lets *pres 3d sing of* LET, *pl of* LET

let's \(')lets, *when not followed by a pause often* (,)les *in rapid speech*\ [by contr.] **:** let us

lett \'let, *usu* -ed·+V\ *n* -S *usu cap* [G *Lette*, fr. Latvian *Latvi*] **1 a :** a people closely related to the Lithuanians and mainly inhabiting Latvia **b :** a member of such people **2 :** LATVIAN 2

let·ta·ble \'led·əbəl, -etəb-\ *adj* [[3]*let* + *-able*] *chiefly Brit* **:** capable of being rented or leased

letted *past of* LET

[1]**let·ter** \'led·ə(r), -etə-\ *n* -S *often attrib* [ME *lettre*, *letter*, fr. OF *lettre*, fr. L *littera*, *litera* letter, *litterae*, pl., epistle, writing, literature; perh. akin to L *linere* to daub, smear — more at LIME] **1 a :** a conventional symbol usu. written or printed representing alone or in combination a simple or compound speech sound, constituting one of the units of an alphabet, and often including the arabic numbers — compare ACROPHONY, DACTYLOLOGY, SEMAPHORE **b letters** *pl* **:** ALPHABET ⟨teach a child his ~*s*⟩ **c** *obs* **:** ALLITERATION ⟨I will something affect the ~, for it argues facility —Shak.⟩ **2 a :** a written or printed message intended for the perusal only of the person or organization to whom it is addressed **:** MISSIVE ⟨a business ~ should preferably be typed⟩ **b :** such a message enclosed in an addressed envelope and usu. sealed ⟨a table on which were several ~*s* — evidently this was where mail was left for those in the house —Millen Brand⟩ **c :** an official communication conferring authority or status ⟨a ~ from the admiral admits him to the naval base⟩ ⟨~ of absolution⟩, conveying information or instructions ⟨circular ~ outlining requirements for admission⟩ ⟨pastoral ~ calling upon the people to resist —W.E.McManus⟩ ⟨his contribution to the book was a ~ from New York⟩, serving as an introduction ⟨asked her minister for a ~ to the new church⟩, or attesting to length, quality, or terms of employment ⟨service ~⟩ ⟨~ of recommendation⟩ ⟨~ of appointment⟩ **d** (1) *Roman & civil law* **:** RESCRIPT (2) **:** a written communication issued from a court in attestation of an appointment or status or rights or duties ⟨parliament is summoned by the king's . . . ~ issued out of chancery —T.E.May⟩ — usu. used in pl. ⟨~*s* of adoption⟩ ⟨~*s* of citizenship⟩ **3 letters** *pl but sing or pl in constr* **a :** literary expression **:** LITERATURE, BELLES LETTRES ⟨a polished novel which shows British ~*s* at its best —*Hunting's Monthly List*⟩ ⟨good ~*s* have some significance in the health of the state —Ezra Pound⟩ ⟨words exist before the art of ~*s* —John Dewey⟩ **b :** scholarly attainment **:** LEARNING ⟨man of ~*s*⟩ ⟨more a friend of ~*s* than a learned man himself —R.W.Southern⟩ **4 :** the outward sense or significance **:** literal terms ⟨rigorous insistence on the ~ of the contract —Alvin Johnson⟩ ⟨a decision dealing with human beings cannot be based on the ~ of the law alone —F.M.Hechinger⟩ — opposed to *spirit* **5 a :** a single piece of type **b :** a style of type ⟨roman ~⟩ **c :** TYPE ⟨a font of body ~⟩; *esp* **:** a supply of type ⟨can't set it without any ~⟩ **6 :** the initial of a school or college awarded to a student for achievement usu. in athletics ⟨a rugged physique that helped him win football and basketball ~*s* in college —Howard Rushmore⟩ — **to the letter** *adv* **:** to the minutest detail **:** METICULOUSLY ⟨followed his instructions *to the letter*⟩ ⟨seeing his bargains carried out *to the letter* —Norman Douglas⟩

[2]**letter** \"\ *vb* -ED/-ING/-S *vi* **1** *archaic* **:** to write or carry letters ⟨our people go backwards and forwards . . . ~*ing* and messaging —Charles Dickens⟩ **2 :** to win a school letter for athletic prowess ⟨as a freshman he ~*ed* in football —Tom Siler⟩ ~ *vt* **1 :** to set down in letters **:** PRINT ⟨few painters alive can ~ a respectable caption on a portrait —P.M.Hollister⟩ — often used with *out* ⟨streamers on which are ~*ed out* the names of historic battles —Elbridge Colby⟩ **2 a :** to mark with letters **:** INSCRIBE ⟨~ a poster⟩ ⟨~ a squad car⟩ **b :** to append letters to ⟨numbers were ~*ed* on all the books —Helen V. Samuelson⟩ ⟨twelve companies, ~*ed* from A to M, skipping J—W.H.Baumer⟩; *specif* **:** to impress alphabetical letters on (a page or book cover) near the fore edge parallel to the same letters of the thumb index

[3]**letter** \"\ *n* -S [[3]*let* + *-er*] *chiefly Brit* **:** one that rents or leases

letter board *n* **:** a board (as a sliding shelf in a rack) used for storage of standing type

letter book *n* **:** a book in which letters or copies of letters are kept esp. to provide a running account of a business or enterprise ⟨the general's *letter books* give an intimate picture of the campaign⟩

letter box *n* **:** MAILBOX; *esp* **:** a box provided by the post office for the deposit of letters and other first-class mail

lettercard \'=,=\ *n* [prob. trans. of F *carte-lettre*] **:** a postcard that folds and seals like a letter sheet with the message inside

letter box

letter carrier *n* **:** MAIL CARRIER

letter case *n* **:** a usu. folding leather case for carrying letters ⟨stuffing my watch, *letter case*, loose change and handkerchief into my pockets —W.J.Locke⟩

letter drawer *n* **:** a file drawer for letters usu. having a partition that can be moved back as correspondence accumulates

let·tered \'led·ə(r)d, -etə-\ *adj* [ME, fr. *letter* + *-ed*] **1 a :** possessed of learning **:** EDUCATED ⟨spread their translations before the ~ public —G.C.Sellery⟩ **b :** of, relating to, or characterized by learning **:** CULTURED ⟨a man of ~ tastes —Benjamin Disraeli⟩ **2 :** inscribed with or as if with letters ⟨the walls of the lower grade schoolroom were covered with . . . ~ statements —Oliver LaFarge⟩ ⟨~ tortoise⟩ **3 :** consisting of letters ⟨~ cipher⟩

let·ter·er \'led·ərə(r), -etə-\ *n* -S **:** one that letters: as **a :** a commercial artist who does lettering **b :** a craftsman who paints company names or other lettering on commercial vehicles **c :** an artisan who cuts incised or raised letters and designs on monumental stones **d :** a craftsman who copies the magnified outlines of lead type as patterns for steel type

letterer-siwe disease \'led·ərə(r)'zēvə-\ *n, usu cap L&S* [after Erich *Letterer* *b*1895 Ger. pathologist and Sture A. *Siwe* *b*1897 pediatrician and professor in Sweden, who first described it] **:** an acute disease of children characterized by fever, hemorrhages, and other evidences of a disturbance in the reticuloendothelial system and by severe bone lesions esp. of the skull

let·ter·et \¦led·ə¦ret\ *n* -S **:** a short letter

letter founder *n* **:** TYPEFOUNDER

let·ter·gae \¦letər¦gā\ *n* -S [prob. fr. [3]*let* + *-er* + *gae*; fr. the phrase *let gae (the tune)* raise the tune] *Scot* **:** PRECENTOR

letter hand *n* **:** a style of medieval handwriting used in public letters

letterhead \'=,=\ *also* **letter heading** *n* **1 :** a sheet of printed or engraved stationery usu. giving the name and address of the organization and the nature of the enterprise and often including the title of the sender **2 :** the heading at the top of a letterhead

lettering *n* -S **1 :** the act or process of inscribing or marking with letters ⟨taught herself ~ . . . and was promoted to the studio —*Mademoiselle*⟩; *specif* **:** the impressing of a title on the backbone of a book **2 :** the letters or calligraphy used in an inscription ⟨anthology shows examples of modern ~ as used in contemporary advertising —*Brit. Book News*⟩ ⟨~ can be condensed, elongated, slanted . . . to fill any need —Harry Roth⟩

lettering pen *n* **:** a pen with a nib end especially shaped for forming the thick or thin strokes of letters in calligraphy and freehand lettering

let·ter·less \'led·ə(r)ləs\ *adj* **1** *archaic* **:** devoid of learning **:** ILLITERATE **2 :** devoid of correspondence **3 :** devoid of inscription

letter lichen *n* **:** a lichen (as a member of the genus *Graphis*) in which the apothecium assumes a form like written characters

lettering pens

letter mail *n* **:** first-class mail

let·ter·man \'==,man, -,maa(ə)n, -,mən\ *n, pl* **lettermen :** an athlete who has earned a letter in a school sport

letter missive *n, pl* **letters missive** [ME *lettres missives*, *letter missive*] **:** a letter from a superior authority addressed to a particular individual or group and conveying a command, recommendation, permission, or invitation

letter of advice : ADVICE 5a

letter of attorney [ME] **:** POWER OF ATTORNEY

letter of credence *or* **letters of credence** [ME *letter of credance*, prob. part trans. of ML *litterae de credentia*, *litterae credentiae*] **:** a formal document furnished a diplomatic agent for presentation to the government to which he is sent attesting to his power to act for his government or head of state — compare RECREDENTIAL

letter of credit : a letter addressed by a banker to a correspondent certifying that a person named therein is entitled to draw on him or his credit up to a certain sum — called also *traveler's letter of credit, circular letter of credit, circular note* **2 :** a letter addressed by a banker to a person to whom credit is given authorizing him to draw on the issuing bank or on a bank in his country up to a certain sum and guaranteeing to accept the drafts if duly made — called also *commercial letter of credit, confirmed credit, confirmed letter of credit*

letter of delegation : a letter delegating authority esp. to collect a debt

letter of hypothecation : HYPOTHECATION CERTIFICATE

letter of instruction : a form of order dealing only with the broader phases of operations and issued by or to higher commanders for the guidance and control of a large military command

letter of intent : a written statement of the intention to enter into a formal agreement; *esp* **:** a written authorization enabling officers of the federal government in time of imperative need for war materials and supplies to order the making or furnishing of such materials and supplies before the issuance of a formal contract and providing reimbursement for the contractor's expenses if no contract is subsequently issued

letter package *n* **:** a package sent by international mail at the first-class rate

letter paper *n* **:** paper of a size suitable for writing letters

letter-perfect \¦==¦==\ *adj* **:** correct to the smallest detail ⟨*letter-perfect* as to the duration of notes, nuances, and phrasing —Samuel Chotzinoff⟩; *specif* **:** VERBATIM ⟨gave a *letter-perfect* rendition of the soliloquy⟩

letter post *n* **:** a class of mail in the United Kingdom comprising chiefly letters and postcards and corresponding to first-class mail in the U. S.

letterpress \'==,=\ *n* **1 a :** the process of printing direct from an inked raised surface upon which the paper is impressed — called also *printing, relief printing, typographical printing*; compare ELECTRONOGRAPHY, INTAGLIO, PLANOGRAPHY, STENCIL **b :** work done by this process **c :** a machine for letterpress printing **2 :** COPYING PRESS **3** *chiefly Brit* **:** reading matter as distinct from pictorial illustrations **:** TEXT ⟨lively pencil sketches . . . dodge in and out among the ~ —*Manchester Guardian Weekly*⟩

letter rate *n* **:** the rate of postage for first-class mail

letters *pl of* LETTER, *pres 3d sing of* LETTER

letters close \-'klōs\ *n pl* [trans. of F *lettres closes*, fr. MF, trans. of ML *litterae clausae*] **:** letters issued by a government or sovereign to a private person in a private matter — distinguished from *letters patent*

letters credential *n pl* [part trans. of ML *litterae credentiales*] **:** LETTER OF CREDENCE

letter sheet *n* **:** a sheet of stationery that is folded and sealed with the message inside and serves as its own envelope for mailing

lettershop \'==,=\ *n* **:** an independent agency that handles secretarial and office work (as mailing, mimeographing, and bookkeeping) on a job basis

letters of administration : a formal written communication from a court evidencing the right of an administrator to administer the goods or estate of a deceased person

letters of horn·ing \-'hȯrniŋ\ [*horning* act of proclaiming a person an outlaw by blowing three blasts upon a horn, fr. *horn* (instrument) + *-ing*] *Scots law* **:** a process of a court directing a debtor to pay or perform according to the terms of the letters under penalty of being proclaimed an outlaw by the blowing of three blasts upon a horn

letters of marque *also* **letter of marque** [ME *letters of marc*, prob. part trans. of ML *litterae de marqua*] **:** written authority granted to a private person by a government to seize the subjects of a foreign state or their goods by way of retaliation for injuries; *specif* **:** a license or extraordinary commission granted by a government to a private person to fit out an armed vessel to cruise as a privateer or corsair at sea and plunder the enemy — called also *letters of marque and reprisal*

letters of request [ME] **1 :** a written request from one government or sovereign to another to aid an injured person in seeking redress, with a promise to reciprocate **2** *Eng eccl law* **:** an instrument by which an inferior court waives jurisdiction over a case and requests a higher court to hear it

letters overt *n pl* [trans. of AF *lettres overtes*, trans. of ML *litterae patentes*] **:** LETTERS PATENT

letterspace \'==,=\ *vt* **:** to insert or leave a space between the letters of (a word)

letterspacing *n* **:** spacing between letterspaced characters

letters patent *n pl* [ME, part trans. of AF & ML; AF *lettres patentes*, trans. of ML *litterae patentes*] **:** written communications usu. signed and sealed from a government or sovereign of a nation conferring upon a designated person a grant (as a right, title, status, property, authority, privilege, monopoly, franchise, immunity, or exemption) that could not otherwise be enjoyed in a form readily open for inspection by all seeking confirmation of the grant conferred — distinguished from *letters close*

letters rogatory *n pl* **:** a formal written request by a court or judge to a court or judge in a foreign jurisdiction to summon and cause to be examined a specified witness within its jurisdiction and transmit his testimony for use in a pending action — compare DEDIMUS

letters testamentary *n pl* **:** a written communication from a court or officer informing an executor of his appointment and authority to execute the will of the testator

letterweight \'==,=\ *n* **:** PAPERWEIGHT

letterwinged kite \'==,=-\ *n* **:** an Australian kite (*Elanus scriptus*) with a black edging on the underwing that resembles the letter M when the bird is in flight

letterwood \'==,=\ *n* [trans. of F *bois de lettres*; fr. the fanciful resemblance of its markings to letters of the alphabet] **1 :** the mottled wood of a So. American tree (*Brosimum aubletii*) used for veneer **2 :** the tree that yields letterwood

letter writer *n* **:** one that writes letters; *specif* **:** one whose employment is letter writing ⟨a professional *letter writer* spread his papyrus on a table under the candlelight —Alice Parmelee⟩

let·tic \'led·ik\ *adj, usu cap* [*Lett* + *-ic*] **:** [1]LETTISH

letting *n* -S **1** *chiefly Brit* **:** an act of letting or leasing **2** *chiefly Brit* **:** a tenement let or to be let

letting-in \¦==¦=\ *n* -S **:** the process of shortening and widening pelts by cutting in strips and stitching

letting-out \¦==¦=\ *n* -S **:** the process of lengthening pelts by cutting them in narrow diagonal strips that are nailed to a board in a stepped-down layout and stitched together to improve the marking and appearance of the fur for garments

[1]**lett·ish** \'led·ish\ *adj, usu cap* [prob. fr. G *lettisch*, fr. *Lette* Lett + G *-isch* -ish] **:** of or relating to the Latvians or their language

[2]**lettish** \"\ *n* -ES *cap* **:** LATVIAN 2

letto- *comb form, usu cap* [*Lett* + *-o-*] **:** Lettish and ⟨*Letto-Lithuanian* parentage⟩

let·tre bâ·tarde \¦le·trəbə¦tärd\ *n, pl* **lettres bâtardes** \"\ [F, lit., bastard letter] **1 :** a Gothic letter with the angles rounded **2 :** BÂTARDE

let·tre de ca·chet \¦le·trədə,ka¦shā\ *n, pl* **let·tres de cachet** \"\ [F] **:** a letter bearing an official (as a royal) seal and usu. authorizing imprisonment without trial of a named person ⟨these leaflets . . . were simply *lettres de cachet* issued by the Ogpu for action by the Gestapo —Anthony West⟩

let·tre de cré·ance \¦le·trədəkrā¦äⁿs\ *n, pl* **lettres de créance** \"\ [F, fr. MF, trans. of ML *litterae credentiae*] **:** LETTER OF CREDENCE

lett·som·ite \'letsə,mīt\ *n* -S [William G. *Lettsom* †1887 Eng. mineralogist + E *-ite*] **:** CYANOTRICHITE

let·tuce \'led·əs, -etəs\ *n* -S [ME *letuse*, fr. OF *laitues*, pl. of *laitue*, fr. L *lactuca*, fr. *lact-*, *lac* milk; fr. its milky juice — more at GALAXY] **1 a :** a plant of the genus *Lactuca*; *specif* **:** a common garden vegetable (*L. sativa*) the succulent leaves of which are used esp. in salads — see COS LETTUCE, HEAD LETTUCE, LEAF LETTUCE **b :** any of several plants (as members of the genera *Claytonia* and *Valerianella*) having succulent foliage **2** *slang* **:** GREENBACKS

lettuce aphid *n* **:** an aphid (esp. *Macrosiphum barri*) that is a pest of lettuce

lettuce bird *n* **:** an American goldfinch (*Spinus tristis*)

lettuce cabbage *n* **:** CHINESE CABBAGE

lettuce green *n* **:** a variable color averaging a moderate yellow green that is greener, lighter, and stronger than average moss green or mosstone and yellower, lighter, and stronger than average pea green or spinach green

lettuce mildew *n* **:** a destructive disease of lettuce caused by a downy mildew (*Bremia lactucae*)

lettuce opium *n* **:** LACTUCARIUM

lettuce saxifrage *n* **:** a saxifrage (*Saxifraga micranthidifolia*) of the eastern U. S. having foliage that resembles lettuce

let up *vi* [[3]*let* + *up*] **1 a :** to diminish or slow down **:** SLACKEN, RELAX ⟨the wind's *letting up* a little⟩ ⟨not one of us should *let up* in our drive for standardizing our procedures —H.H.

Helm) ⟨free to . . . *let up* and enjoy ourselves —A.L.Rowse⟩ **b** : to become idle : CEASE, STOP ⟨pitched horseshoes the whole evening and never *let up* until it was too dark to see⟩ ⟨took shelter under a carriage shed until the rain *let up* —Oliver LaFarge⟩ **2** : to ease up or become less severe — used with *on* ⟨able to *let up* slightly on armament expenditures —D.M.Keezer⟩ ⟨remove some of these restrictions, *let up* a bit on people —T.P.Whitney⟩ ⟨*let up* on him — he didn't mean any harm⟩

letup \'⸗,⸗\ *n* -s [*let up*] **1 a** : a lessening of effort or intensity : SLACKENING, ABATEMENT ⟨they labored without ~, forming two constantly moving lines —Hamilton Basso⟩ ⟨during the six-day ~ in ground fighting —*Wall Street Jour.*⟩; *specif* : a break in inclement weather ⟨the rain continued without ~ —Hilbert Schenck⟩ **b** : a reduction in quantity or quality ⟨seems to be no ~ in the flow of nature books —Dorothy H. Jenkins⟩ ⟨a major achievement to sustain without ~ . . . 100 minutes of running jokes —*Newsweek*⟩ ⟨no ~ in the billingsgate between Berlin and Moscow —H.C.Wolfe⟩ **2** : an act or instance of relaxation : abandonment of restraint ⟨allowed myself the ~ of a drive in the park —O.W.Holmes †1935⟩

leu \'leü\ *n, pl* **lei** \'lā\ [Romanian *leu*, lit., lion, fr. L *leon-, leo* — more at LION] **1** : the basic monetary unit of Romania — see MONEY table **2** : a coin representing one leu

leuc- *or* **leuco-** *also* **leuk-** *or* **leuko-** *comb form* [NL, fr. Gk *leuk-, leuko-* white, fr. *leukos* — more at LIGHT] **1** : white : colorless : weakly colored ⟨*leuc*augite⟩ ⟨*leuco*plast⟩ ⟨*leuko*cyte⟩ — often in names of chemical compounds derived from (as by reduction) or related to a dye or other colored compound ⟨*leuc*aurin⟩ ⟨*leuco*methylene blue⟩ **2** : leukocyte ⟨*leuko*penia⟩ **3** : white matter of the brain ⟨*leuco*tomy⟩

leu·ca·den·dron \,lükə'dendrən\ *n, cap* [NL, fr. *leuca-* (irreg. fr. Gk *leukos* white) + *-dendron*] : a large genus of evergreen trees and shrubs (family Proteaceae) native to the Cape of Good Hope that have silvery white leaves and dioecious capitate flowers — see SILVER TREE

leu·cae·na \lü'sēnə\ *n, cap* [NL, fr. Gk *leukainein* to make white, become white, fr. *leukos* white] : a small genus of tropical trees (family Leguminosae) that have pods resembling those of the acacia and 10 stamens — see LEAD TREE

leuc·au·gite \(')lük+\ *n* [*leuc-* + *augite*] : a white or grayish augite that resembles diopside

leucemi·a *or* **leucaemia** *var of* LEUKEMIA

leu·cet·ta \lü'sedə\ *n, cap* [NL, irreg. fr. Gk *leukos* white] : a genus of calcareous sponges (order Asconosa) of leuconoid structure

leuch \'lyük\ *Scot past of* LAUGH

leuch·ten·berg·ite \'lȯiktən,bər,gīt\ *n* -s [G *leuchtenbergit*, fr. Maximilian, Duke of *Leuchtenberg* †1852 + G *-it* -ite] : a clinochlore that often resembles talc and contains little or no iron

leuc·ich·thys \lü'kikthəs, lü'si-\ *n, cap* [NL, fr. *leuc-* + *-ichthys*] : a genus of whitefishes comprising the lake herrings and ciscoes that differ from members of the genus *Coregonus* in having a large mouth with a long and often projecting lower jaw

leu·ci·fer \'lüsəfə(r)\ *n, cap* [NL, alter. (influenced by NL *leuc-*) of L *lucifer* morning star — more at LUCIFER] : a genus of free-swimming slender macruran crustaceans that is sometimes made the type of a distinct family

leu·cine \'lü,sēn, -üsᵊn\ *n* -s [ISV *leuc-* + *-ine*] : a white crystalline amino acid $(CH_3)_2CHCH_2CH(NH_2)COOH$ that is obtained by the hydrolysis of most dietary proteins (as casein or zein) and is also made synthetically and that in its levorotatory L-form is essential in the nutrition of animals and man; α-amino-γ-methyl-valeric acid

leu·cite \-,sīt\ *n* -s [obs. G *leucit* (now *leuzit*), fr. *leuc-* + *-it* -ite] : a white or gray mineral $KAlSi_2O_6$ consisting of a potassium aluminum silicate occurring in igneous rocks (as recent lavas) usu. in trapezohedral crystals with a glassy fracture (hardness 5.5–6.0, sp. gr. 2.45–2.50) — called also *amphigene*

leu·cit·ic \(')lü¦sid·ik\ *adj* : relating to, containing, or resembling leucite

leu·ci·tite \'lüsə,tīt\ *n* -s [obs. G *leucitit* (now *leuzitit*), fr. obs. G *leucit* leucite (now *leuzit*) + G *-it* -ite] : a basaltic rock chiefly composed of leucite with augite, some magnetite, and no feldspar

leu·ci·to·he·dron \,lüsə(,)tō'hēdrən\ *n* -s [ISV *leucite* + *-o-* + *-hedron*] : a trapezohedron or tetragonal trisoctahedron

leu·ci·toid \'lüsə,tȯid\ *n* -s [ISV *leucite* + *-oid*] : LEUCITOHEDRON

leu·cit·o·phyre \lü'sidə,fī(ə)r\ *n* -s [ISV *leucite* + *-o-* + *-phyre*; prob. orig. formed as G *leuzitophyr*] : a porphyry with leucite phenocrysts

leu·co \'lü(,)kō\ *adj* [ISV, fr. *leuc-*] : relating to or being a colorless or weakly colored compound derived from or related to a dye or other colored compound — compare LEUC- 1

leuco- — see LEUC-

leu·co·anthocyanin \¦lü(,)kō+\ *n* [*leuc-* + *anthocyanin*] : a colorless precursor of an anthocyanin

leuco base *n* [ISV *leuco* + *base*] : a colorless or weakly colored amine that is formed by reduction of a dye (as a triphenylmethane dye) or its carbinol derivative and that on oxidation and treatment with acids usu. gives back the dye

leucoblast *var of* LEUKOBLAST

leu·cob·ry·um \lü'käbrēəm\ *n, cap* [NL, fr. *leuc-* + *-bryum* (fr. Gk *bryon* moss) — more at BRY-] : a genus of mosses that is related to *Dicranum* though sometimes made type of a separate family and is characterized by a tufted habit of growth resulting in the formation of thick cushiony masses and by great reduction in chlorophyll with many void cells resulting in a dull grayish white or greenish white coloration of the plant — see WHITE MOSS

leu·co·chal·cite \,lükō'kal,sīt\ *n* -s [obs. G *leucochalcit* (now *leukochalcit*), fr. G *leuc-* + *chalc-* + *-it* -ite] : a mineral $Cu_2(AsO_4)(OH).H_2O(?)$ consisting of a basic arsenate of copper crystallizing in the form of white silky needles

leu·co·choly \'lükə,kälē\ *n* -ES [*leuc-* + *-choly* (as in *melancholy*)] : a state of feeling that accompanies preoccupation with trivial and insipid diversions ⟨~ . . . though it seldom laughs or dances, nor ever amounts to what one calls joy or pleasure, yet is a good easy sort of a state —Thomas Gray⟩

leu·co·ci·din \,lükə'sīdᵊn, '⸗,⸗⸗\ *n* -s [ISV *leuc-* + *-cide* + *-in*] : a substance (as produced by bacteria) destroying leukocytes

leu·co·crat·ic \¦lükə¦krad·ik\ *adj* [G *leukokrat* leucocratic (fr. *leuk-* leuc- + *-krat*, fr. Gk *kratein* to rule, prevail) + E *-ic*; akin to Gk *kratos* strength — more at HARD] *of a mineral or rock* : having a light color — compare MELANOCRATIC, MESOCRATIC

leu·cocri·num \lü'käkrənəm, ,lükə'krīnəm\ *n, cap* [NL, fr. *leuc-* + Gk *krinon* lily] : a genus of plants (family Liliaceae) of the western U.S. having a short rootstock, leaves like those of the crocus, and large white umbellate flowers — see SAND LILY

leucocyt- *or* **leucocyto-** — see LEUKOCYT-

leu·co·cyt·al \¦lükə¦sīd·ᵊl\ *or* **leu·co·cy·ta·ry** \-d·ərē\ *adj* : LEUKOCYTIC

leucocyte *var of* LEUKOCYTE

leu·co·cy·the·mia *also* **leu·co·cy·thae·mia** \,lükə,sī'thēmēə\ *n* -s [NL, fr. *leuc-* + *cyt-* + *-emia*] : LEUKEMIA — **leu·co·cy·the·mic** *also* **leu·co·cy·thae·mic** \¦⸗⸗¦⸗⸗¦mik\ *adj*

leucocytoblast *var of* LEUKOCYTOBLAST

leucocytopoiesis *var of* LEUKOCYTOPOIESIS

leucocytosis *var of* LEUKOCYTOSIS

¹**leu·co·cy·to·zo·an** \¦lükə,sīd·ə¦zōən\ *adj* [NL *Leucocytozoon* + E *-an*, adj. suffix] : of or relating to the genus *Leucocytozoon* or to leucocytozoa

²**leucocytozoan** \"\ *n* -s [NL *Leucocytozoon* + E *-an*, n. suffix] : LEUCOCYTOZOON

leu·co·cy·to·zo·on \⸗⸗¦⸗⸗'zō,än, -ōən\ *n* [NL, fr. *leuc-* + *cyt-* + *-zoon*] **1** *cap* : a genus of sporozoans parasitic in birds — see HAEMOPROTEIDAE **2** *pl* **leucocyto·zoa** \-ōə\ : a member of the genus *Leucocytozoon*

leu·co·derm \'lükə,dərm\ *n* -s [*leuc-* + *-derm* (fr. Gk *derma* skin) — more at DERM-] **1** : a person with a white or light skin **2** *usu cap* : a member of a hypothetical Caucasoid race

leucoderma *var of* LEUKODERMA

leucoencephalitis *var of* LEUKOENCEPHALITIS

leuco ester *n* : a water-soluble sodium salt of the sulfuric acid ester of the leuco compound of a vat dye that is applied to textiles and then oxidized in acid solution to the corresponding vat dye — compare DYE table I

leu·co·indigo \¦lü(,)kō+\ *n* [ISV *leuco* + *indigo*] : INDIGO WHITE

leu·co·jum \lü'kōjəm\ *n, cap* [NL, fr. Gk *leukoion* stock (*Matthiola incana*), fr. *leuk-* leuc- + *ion* violet — more at VIOLET] : a genus of bulbous herbs (family Amaryllidaceae) that are native to the Old World, are widely cultivated for their early spring bloom, and have a regular perianth with equal segments and stamens with long filaments — see SNOWFLAKE

leu·co·lyt·ic \¦lükə¦lid·ik\ *adj* [*leuc-* + *-lytic*] : inducing lysis of white blood cells — used of drugs and infective agents

leu·co·ma *also* **leu·ko·ma** \lü'kōmə\ *n* -s [LL *leucoma*, fr. Gk *leukōma*, fr. *leuk-* leuc- + *-ōma* -oma] : a dense white opacity in the cornea of the eye

leu·co·maine \'lükə,mān\ *n* -s [ISV *leuc-* + *-maine* (as in *ptomaine*); orig. formed as F *leucomaïne*] : a basic substance normally produced in the living animal body as a decomposition product of protein matter — compare PTOMAINE

leu·con \'lü,kän\ *n* -s [NL, fr. Gk *leukon*, neut. of *leukos* white — more at LIGHT] : a sponge or sponge larva having a complex structure in which the flagellated layer is restricted to numerous small interstitial chambers intercalated between the incurrent and excurrent canals and the paragaster is reduced or lacking — compare ASCON, SYCON — **leu·co·noid** \'lükə,nȯid\ *adj or n*

leu·co·nostoc \¦lükə+\ *n* [NL, fr. *leuc-* + *Nostoc*] **1** *cap* : a genus of saprophytic bacteria (family Lactobacillaceae) including several that are pests in sugar refineries because of the habit of forming slime in sugar solutions **2** -s : any bacterium of the genus *Leuconostoc*

leucopenia *var of* LEUKOPENIA

leu·coph·a·nite \lü'käfə,nīt\ *also* **leu·co·phane** \'lükə,fān\ *n* -s [*leucophanite* fr. *leucophane* (fr. Sw *leukophan*, fr. *leuk-* leuc- + *-phan* -phane) + *-ite*] : a mineral $(Na, Ca)_2BeSi_2(O, F, OH)_7$ consisting of a beryllium sodium calcium silicate with fluorine occurring in glassy greenish tabular crystals

leu·co·phoe·ni·cite \lükō'fēnə,sīt\ *n* -s [*leuc-* + *phoenic-* (fr. Gk *phoinik-, phoinix* purple) + *-ite* — more at PHOENICIAN] : a mineral $Mn_7Si_3O_{12}(OH)_2$ consisting of a manganese silicate

leu·co·phore \'lükə,fō(ə)r\ *n* -s [ISV *leuc-* + *-phore*] : a white chromatophore — compare GUANOPHORE

leu·co·phos·phite \,lükə'fä,sfīt\ *n* [*leuc-* + *phosph-* + *-ite*] : a mineral approximately $K_2(Fe,Al)_7(PO_4)_4(OH)_{11}.6H_2O$ consisting of a hydrous basic phosphate of potassium, iron, and aluminum

leu·co·plast \'lükə,plast\ *n* -s [ISV *leuc-* + *-plast*; orig. formed as G *leukoplast*] : a colorless plastid; *specif* : a nonpigmented plastid that occurs esp. in the cytoplasm of interior plant tissues and is capable under proper conditions of developing into a chromoplast — see AMYLOPLAST, ELAIOPLAST

leu·co·plas·tid \,lükə'plastəd, '⸗⸗,⸗⸗\ *n* [*leuc-* + *plastid*] : LEUCOPLAST

leucopoiesis *var of* LEUKOPOIESIS

leu·cop·te·rin \lü'käptərən\ *n* [ISV *leuc-* + *pterin*] : a crystalline alkali-soluble compound $H_2NC_6N_4(OH)_3$ that constitutes the white pigment of cabbage butterflies and other lepidoptera and wasps and is convertible into xanthopterin on reduction; 2-amino-4,6,7-trihydroxy-pteridine

leu·co·py·rite \,lükə'pī,rīt\ *n* [*leuc-* + *pyrite*] : LOELLINGITE

leucorrhea *or* **leucorrhoea** *var of* LEUKORRHEA

leu·co·ryx \'lükə(,)riks\ *n, pl* **leucoryxes** *also* **leucoryx** [NL, fr. *leuc-* + Gk *oryg-, oryx* leucoryx] : a large chiefly pale brownish white antelope of No. Africa (*Oryx leucoryx*) related to the gemsbok

leu·co·sin \'lükəsən\ *n* -s [ISV *leucos-* (fr. Gk *leukos* white) + *-in* — more at LIGHT] : a substance believed to be a carbohydrate occurring in the form of whitish lumps as a food reserve in many yellow-green algae of the class Chrysophyceae

leucosis *var of* LEUKOSIS

leu·co·so·le·nia \,lükəsō'lēnēə\ *n, cap* [NL, fr. *leuc-* + Gk *sōlēn* channel, pipe + NL *-ia* — more at SYRINGE] : a genus (the type of the family Leucosolenidae) of small ascon sponges that grow in colonies on rocks near the seashore

leu·co·sphe·nite \⸗⸗'sfē,nīt\ *n* -s [ISV *leuc-* + *sphen-* + *-ite*; prob. orig. formed as G *leukosphenit*] : a mineral $Na_4BaTi_2Si_{10}O_{27}$ consisting of a sodium barium silicotitanate occurring in white wedge-shaped crystals

leu·co·stic·te \⸗⸗'stik(,)tē\ *n* [NL, fr. *leuc-* + *-sticte* (fr. Gk *stiktos* tattooed, spotted, fr. *stizein* to tattoo) — more at STICK] **1** *cap* : a genus consisting of the rosy finches **2** -s : any bird of the genus *Leucosticte*

leucotaxine *var of* LEUKOTAXINE

leu·coth·o·e \lü'käthə,wē\ *n* [NL, fr. L *Leucothoe*, legendary Persian princess supposed to have been changed by Apollo into a sweet-scented shrub] **1** *cap* : a large genus of American and Asiatic shrubs of the family Ericaceae with herbage that contains a poisonous substance similar to that found in shrubs of the genus *Kalmia* and with flowers in terminal and axillary one-sided racemes **2** -s : any plant of the genus *Leucothoe*

leu·co·tome \'lükə,tōm\ *n* -s [*leuc-* + *-tome*] : a narrow rotating blade in a cannula for use in lobotomy

leu·cot·o·my \lü'käd·əmē\ *n* -ES [ISV *leuc-* + *-tomy*] : LOBOTOMY

leucotoxic *var of* LEUKOTOXIC

leu·cov·o·rin \lü'kävərən\ *n* -s [*leuco-* (fr. NL *Leuconostoc*, genus name of *Leuconostoc citrovorum*) + *-vor-* (fr. NL *citrovorum*, specific epithet of *Leuconostoc citrovorum*) + *-in* — more at LEUCONOSTOC, CITROVORUM FACTOR] : a crystalline synthetic acid $C_{20}H_{23}N_7O_7$ derived from folic acid and used in the form of its calcium salt esp. in treating some anemias and toxic symptoms arising from the use of folic acid antagonists; N^5-formyl-tetrahydro-pteroylglutamic acid — called also *folinic acid-SF*

leu·cox·ene \lü'käk,sēn\ *n* -s [G *leukoxen*, fr. *leuk-* leuc- + *-xen* -xene] : a mineral consisting mostly of rutile and partly of anatase or sphene occurring in some igneous rocks from the alteration of ilmenite

leu·cyl \'lüsəl\ *n* -s [ISV *leucine* + *-yl*] : the acid radical $(CH_3)_2CHCH_2CHNH_2CO–$ of leucine

leud \'lüd\ *n, pl* **leuds** \-dz\ *or* **leu·des** \-,dēz\ [ML *leudes* (pl.), of Gmc origin; akin to OHG *liuti* people (pl. of *liut* person, people) — more at LIBERAL] : a feudal tenant or vassal in the ancient Frankish kingdoms

leugh \'lyük\ *Scot past of* LAUGH

leuk \'yük\ *chiefly Scot var of* LOOK

leuk- *or* **leuko-** — see LEUC-

leuk·ane·mia \¦lük+\ *n* [NL, fr. *leuc-* + *anemia*] **1** : LEUKEMIA **2** : LEUKOSIS 2

leu·ke·mia *also* **leu·kae·mia** \lü'kēmēə\ *or* **leu·ce·mia** *or* **leu·cae·mia** \" *also* -ü'sē-\ *n* -s [NL, fr. *leuc-* + *-emia*] : an acute or chronic disease of unknown cause in man and other warm-blooded animals that involves the blood-forming organs, is characterized by an abnormal increase in the number of leukocytes in the tissues of the body with or without a corresponding increase of those in the circulating blood, and is classified according to the type of leukocyte most prominently involved

leu·ke·mic *also* **leu·kae·mic** \(')lü¦kēmik, -mek\ *adj* [*leukemia* + *-ic*] **1** : of, relating to, or affected by leukemia ⟨~ mice⟩ **2** : characterized by an increase in white blood cells ⟨~ blood⟩ ⟨transmissible ~ . . . diseases of fowls —*Experiment Station Record*⟩

leu·ke·mid \lü'kēməd\ *n* -s [ISV *leukem-* (fr. NL *leukemia*) + *-id*] : a skin lesion of leukemia

leu·ke·mo·gen \lü'kēməjən, -,jen\ *n* -s [*leukemia* + *-o-* + *-gen*] : a substance tending to induce the development of leukemia — compare CARCINOGEN

leu·ke·mo·genesis \lü¦kēmō+\ *n* [*leukemia* + *-o-* + *genesis*] : induction or production of leukemia

leu·ke·mo·gen·ic \⸗¦⸗¦⸗'jenik\ *adj* [*leukemia* + *-o-* + *-genic*] : causing or tending to induce leukemia ⟨~ effects of ionizing radiation —*Science*⟩

leu·ke·moid \lü'kē,mȯid\ *adj* [*leukemia* + *-oid*] : resembling leukemia but not involving the same changes in the blood-forming organs ⟨a ~ reaction in malaria⟩

leu·ker·gy \'lü(,)kərjē\ *n* -ES [ISV *leuc-* + *-ergy*; prob. orig. formed as Pol *leukergia*] : the clumping of white blood cells that accompanies some inflammations and infections

leu·ko·blast *also* **leu·co·blast** \'lükə,blast\ *n* [ISV *leuc-* + *-blast*] : a developing leukocyte : a cellular precursor of a leukocyte

leu·ko·blas·to·sis \,⸗⸗,bla'stōsəs\ *n, pl* **leukoblasto·ses** \-ō,sēz\ [NL, fr. ISV *leukoblast* + NL *-osis*] : LEUKOSIS

leukocyt- *or* **leukocyto-** *also* **leucocyt-** *or* **leucocyto-** *comb form* [NL, fr. ISV *leukocyte*] : leukocyte ⟨*leukocyto*penia⟩ ⟨*leukocyt*osis⟩

leu·ko·cyte *also* **leu·co·cyte** \'lükə,sīt, *usu* -īd·+V\ *n* -s [ISV *leuc-* + *-cyte*] **1** : a white or colorless nucleated cell of the blood that occurs to the number of 5000 to 10,000 in each cubic millimeter of normal human blood and that is classified into two main groups comprising (1) highly phagocytic cells with densely granular cytoplasm and complexly segmented nucleus and (2) cells with nearly clear cytoplasm and simple or kidney-shaped nucleus, including some that are immunologically active — called also respectively (1) *granulocyte* (2) *agranulocyte*; compare ERYTHROCYTE **2** : a cell (as a histiocyte) of the tissues comparable to or identical with a leukocyte of the blood

leu·ko·cyt·ic *also* **leu·co·cyt·ic** \¦⸗⸗¦sid·ik\ *adj* **1** : of, relating to, or involving leukocytes **2** : characterized by an excess of leukocytes

leu·ko·cy·to·blast *also* **leu·co·cy·to·blast** \'lükə,sīd·ə,blast, ⸗⸗¦⸗,⸗\ *n* [*leukocyt-* + *-blast*] : a cellular precursor of a leukocyte — compare LYMPHOBLAST, MYELOBLAST — **leu·ko·cy·to·blas·tic** \¦⸗⸗¦⸗¦blastik\ *adj*

leu·ko·cy·to·gen·e·sis \,⸗⸗,⸗⸗'jenəsəs\ *n, pl* **leukocytogeneses** \-ə,sēz\ [NL, fr. *leukocyt-* + L *genesis*] : LEUKOPOIESIS

leu·ko·cy·toid \¦⸗⸗¦sīd,ȯid\ *adj* : resembling a leukocyte

leu·ko·cy·toly·sin \,lükə,sī'täləsən, ¦lükə,sīd·ə¦līsᵊn\ *n* [ISV *leukocyt-* + *lysin*] : a specific lytic antibody that dissolves white blood cells

leu·ko·cy·tol·y·sis \,lükə,sī'täləsəs\ *n, pl* **leukocytolyses** \-ə,sēz\ [NL, fr. *leukocyt-* + *-lysis*] : destruction of leukocytes — **leu·ko·cytolytic** \¦⸗⸗+\ *adj*

leu·ko·cy·to·pe·nia \,lükə,sīd·ə'pēnēə\ *n* [NL, fr. *leukocyt-* + *-penia*] : LEUKOPENIA

leu·ko·cy·to·poi·e·sis *also* **leu·co·cy·to·poi·e·sis** \-,pȯi'ēsəs\ *n, pl* **leukocytopoie·ses** *also* **leucocytopoie·ses** \-ē(,)sēz\ [NL, fr. *leukocyt-* + *-poiesis*] : LEUKOPOIESIS

leu·ko·cy·to·sis *or* **leu·co·cy·to·sis** \,lükə,sī'tōsəs\ *n, pl* **leukocyto·ses** *or* **leucocyto·ses** \-ō,sēz\ [NL, fr. *leukocyt-* + *-osis*] : an increase in the number of leukocytes in the circulating blood that occurs normally (as after meals) or abnormally (as in some infections) — **leu·ko·cy·tot·ic** *or* **leu·co·cy·tot·ic** \⸗⸗¦⸗¦täd·ik\ *adj*

leu·ko·der·ma *also* **leu·co·der·ma** \,lükə'dərmə\ *n* -s [NL, fr. *leuc-* + *-derma*] : a skin abnormality that is characterized by a usu. congenital lack of pigment in spots or bands and produces a patchy whiteness — compare VITILIGO

leu·ko·encephalitis *also* **leu·co·encephalitis** \¦lü(,)kō+\ *n* [NL, fr. *leuc-* + *encephalitis*] : inflammation of the white matter of the brain — compare STAGGER 4

leu·koly·sin \lü'käləsən, ¦lükə¦līsᵊn\ *n* -s [*leuc-* + *lysin*] : LEUKOCYTOLYSIN

leukoma *var of* LEUCOMA

leu·kon \'lü,kän\ *n* -s [NL, fr. Gk, neut. of *leukos* white — more at LIGHT] : a body organ consisting of the white blood cells and their precursors — compare ERYTHRON

leuk·onych·ia \,lükō'nikēə\ *n* -s [NL, fr. *leuc-* + *-onychia*] : a white spotting, streaking, or discoloration of the fingernails caused by injury or ill health

leu·ko·pe·nia \,lükō'pēnēə\ *n* -s [NL, fr. *leuc-* + *-penia*] : a condition in which the number of leukocytes circulating in the blood is abnormally low and which is most commonly due to a decreased production of new cells in conjunction with various infectious diseases, as a reaction to various drugs or other chemicals, or in response to irradiation — **leu·ko·pe·nic** \¦⸗⸗¦pēnik\ *adj*

leu·ko·plakia \,lükō'plākēə, -lak-\ *n* -s [NL, fr. *leuc-* + Gk *plak-, plax* flat surface + NL *-ia* — more at PLEASE] : a condition commonly considered precancerous in which thickened white patches of epithelium occur on the mucous membranes esp. of the mouth, vulva, and kidney pelvis; *also* : one of the thickened patches — **leu·ko·plakic** \¦⸗⸗¦plakik\ *adj*

leu·ko·poi·e·sis *or* **leu·co·poi·e·sis** \,lükə,pȯi'ēsəs\ *n, pl* **leukopoie·ses** *or* **leucopoie·ses** \-ē,sēz\ [NL, fr. *leuc-* + *-poiesis*] : the formation of white blood cells

leu·ko·poi·et·ic *or* **leu·co·poi·et·ic** \¦⸗⸗¦⸗¦ed·ik\ *adj* [*leuc-* + *-poietic*] : relating to, characterized by, or inducing the formation of white blood cells

leu·kor·rhea *also* **leu·kor·rhoea** *or* **leu·cor·rhea** *or* **leu·corrhoea** \,lükə'rēə\ *n* -s [NL, fr. *leuc-* + *-rrhea*] : a white, yellowish, or greenish white viscid discharge from the vagina resulting from inflammation or congestion of the uterine or vaginal mucous membrane — **leu·kor·rhe·al** *also* **leu·kor·rhoe·al** *or* **leu·cor·rhe·al** *also* **leu·cor·rhoe·al** \¦⸗⸗¦rēəl\ *adj*

leu·ko·sarcoma \¦lükə+\ *n* [NL, fr. *leuc-* + *sarcoma*] : lymphosarcoma accompanied by leukemia — **leu·ko·sarcomatosis** \"+\ *n*

leu·ko·sis *or* **leu·co·sis** \lü'kōsəs\ *n, pl* **leuko·ses** *or* **leuco·ses** \-ō,sēz\ [NL, fr. *leuc-* + *-osis*] **1** : LEUKEMIA **2** : any of several poorly differentiated diseases of poultry commonly grouped as the avian leukosis complex that involve disturbed blood formation and are distinguished individually by special manifestations (as paralysis, tumor formation, leukemia, and eye damage) — see BIG LIVER DISEASE, FOWL PARALYSIS, LYMPHOMATOSIS, OSTEOPETROSIS, PEARL EYE

leu·ko·tax·ine *or* **leu·co·tax·ine** \,lükə'tak,sēn, -,sən\ *n* -s [*leuc-* + Gk *taxis* arrangement, order (fr. *tassein, tattein* to arrange) + E *-ine* — more at TACTICS] : a crystalline polypeptide that is obtained from the fluid at sites of inflammation in the body and that increases the permeability of capillaries and migration of leukocytes

leu·kot·ic *or* **leu·cot·ic** \(')lü¦käd·ik\ *adj* [fr. *leukosis*, after such pairs as *narcosis*: *narcotic*] : characterized by or inducing the diseased blood condition found in avian leukosis

leu·ko·tox·ic *or* **leu·co·tox·ic** \¦lükə¦täksik\ *adj* [ISV *leuc-* + *toxic*] : of or relating to a toxin destructive to leukocytes — **leu·ko·toxicity** \"+\ *n*

leu·ko·toxin \¦⸗⸗¦⸗sən\ *n* [ISV *leuc-* + *toxin*] : a substance specif. destructive to leukocytes

leu·ma \'lümə\ *n* -s [G, fr. LGk *loimē* pestilence; akin to OE *lǣssa* less — more at LESS] : SHIPPING FEVER 2c

lev \'lef\ *n, pl* **le·va** \'levə\ [Bulg, lit., lion, fr. OBulg *livŭ*, prob. fr. OHG *lewo*, fr. L *leo* — more at LION] **1** : the basic monetary unit of Bulgaria — see MONEY table **2** : a coin representing one lev

lev- *or* **levo-** *also* **laev-** *or* **laevo-** *comb form* [F *lévo-*, fr. L *laevus* left; akin to Gk *laios* left, OSlav *lěvŭ*] **1** *usu* *levo-* *also laevo-*, *usu ital* : levorotatory — in names of chemical compounds ⟨*lev*an⟩ ⟨*levo*-limonene⟩ ⟨*levo*-tartaric acid⟩; symbol (–)- ⟨(–)-tartaric acid⟩; compare L- **2** : left : on the left side : to the left ⟨*levo*version⟩

lev *abbr* levant

le·vade \lə'väd\ *n* -s [G, fr. F *lever* to raise (fr. L *levare*) + *-ade* — more at LEVER] : a show-ring movement in which a horse raises the forequarters, brings the hindquarters under him, and balances with haunches deeply bent and forelegs drawn up

le·val·loi·sian \¦levə¦lȯizēən, -ȯizhən\ *also* **le·val·lois** \lə'val(,)wä\ *adj, usu cap* [*levalloisian* fr. *Levallois*-Perret, suburb of Paris, France + E *-ian*; *levallois* fr. *Levallois*-Perret] : of or relating to a culture tradition overlapping the late Acheulean and early Mousterian and notable for a technique of stone-tool manufacture by the striking of flakes from a flat flint nodule

le·val·loi·so-mousterian \¦levə¦lȯi(,)zō+\ *adj, usu cap L&M* [*levalloiso-* (fr. *levalloisian*) + *mousterian*] : of or relating to a culture with Levalloisian and Mousterian tool traditions

lev·an \'le,van\ *n* -s [*lev-* + *-an*] : any of a group of sparingly soluble levorotatory polysaccharides $(C_6H_{10}O_5)_n$ composed of levulose units of the furanose type and formed esp. from sucrose solutions by the action of various bacteria (as *Bacillus subtilis* or *B. mesentericus*) — compare DEXTRAN

lev·ance and cou·chance \ˈlevən(t)sənˈkau̇chən(t)s\ *also* **lev·an·cy and cou·chan·cy** \-vənsē...chənsē\ *n* [*levance and couchance* alter. (influenced by *-ance*) of *levancy and couchancy*, fr. *levancy* (fr. *levant* — in *levant and couchant* — + *-cy*) + *and* + *couchancy* (fr. *couchant* — in *levant and couchant* — + *-cy*)] **:** the state of being levant and couchant

1le·vant \ləˈvant\ *adj, often cap* [*Levant,* the countries of the eastern Mediterranean, fr. ME *levaunt* East, Orient, fr. MF *levant,* fr. pres. part. of *lever* to raise (*se lever* to rise), fr. L *levare;* fr. the direction of the sunrise — more at LEVER] **:** LEVANTINE, EASTERN

2levant \ˈ"\ *n* -S [*Levant,* the countries of the eastern Mediterranean] **1 :** LEVANTER 2 **2** *usu cap* **:** LEVANT MOROCCO

3levant \ˈ"\ *vt* -ED/-ING/-S **:** to give (leather) the finish of Levant morocco

4levant *n* -S [perh. fr. Sp *levantar* to break (camp), raise, fr. OSp, to raise, irreg. fr. *levar,* fr. L *levare*] *obs* **:** a wager made with intent not to pay if lost

5le·vant \ləˈvant\ *vi* -ED/-ING/-S *chiefly Brit* **:** to default a losing bet or a debt and abscond ⟨his Buddhist friend has ~*ed* after taking my name and address —Rudyard Kipling⟩

lev·ant and cou·chant \ˌlevəntənˌkau̇chənt\ *adj* [alter. of ME *couchant and levant,* part trans. of MF *couchant et levant* lying down and rising up, fr. *couchant* (pres. part. of *coucher* to lay down, *se coucher* to lie down) + *et* and + *levant* (pres. part. of *lever* to raise, *se lever* to rise) — more at COUCH] **:** rising up and lying down — used of trespassing beasts and indicating that they have been long enough on land to lie down and rise up to feed, such time being held to include a day and night at the least and being required as grounds for legal distraint

levant cotton *n, usu cap L* **:** an annual Old World cotton (*Gossypium herbaceum*) that has heart-shaped 5-lobed to 7-lobed leaves, yellow flowers with purplish centers, and small fruits with large seeds and short grayish lint and that is sometimes considered to be one of the ancestors of modern short-staple commercial cottons

levant dollar *n, usu cap L* [so called fr. its wide circulation in the Levant] **:** MARIA THERESA DOLLAR

1le·vant·er \ləˈvantə(r)\ *n* -S [*Levant,* the countries of the eastern Mediterranean + E *-er*] **1** *cap* **:** a native or inhabitant of the Levant **2 :** a strong easterly Mediterranean wind ⟨the Mediterranean squadron battling its way into Valletta harbor through the high steep seas of a ~ —C.S.Forester⟩

2levanter \ˈ"\ *n* -S [*5levant* + *-er*] **:** one that levants to avoid paying a debt or a bet

3levanter \ˈ"\ *n* -S [*3levant* + *-er*] **:** a leather dresser who works up or imitates the grain of levant skins

1levan·tine \ˈlevənˌtīn, -tēn, ləˈvan-\ *adj, usu cap* [*Levant,* the countries of the eastern Mediterranean + E *-ine*] **:** of or relating to the Levant

2levantine \ˈ"\ *n* -S **1** *cap* **:** a native or inhabitant of the Levant; *esp* **:** a cosmopolitan descendant of Frenchmen or Italians who is often a middleman between Europeans and the indigenous peoples **2 a :** a silk fabric formerly made in the Levant **b :** a twilled cotton with a glazed finish used chiefly for linings

levan·tin·ism \-ī,nizəm, -ē,n-\ *n* -S *usu cap* **:** customs, interests, ideas, or attitudes characteristic of Levantine peoples

levant morocco *n, usu cap L* **:** leather from sheep, goat, or seal skins with drawn grain pattern used for bookbinding — called also *Levant*

levant red *n, often cap L* **:** TURKEY RED

levant sponge *or* **levantine sponge** *n, usu cap L* **:** TURKEY CUP SPONGE

levant wormseed *n, usu cap L* **1 :** the buds of a European wormwood (*Artemisia cina*) used as an anthelmintic **2 :** the plant bearing Levant wormseed

levant wormseed oil *n, usu cap L* **:** a yellow essential oil obtained from the flowers of Levant wormseed for use as an anthelmintic

le·va·ri fa·ci·as \ləˌvärēˈfākēˌas\ *n* [NL, you should cause to be levied] **:** a common-law writ of execution for the satisfaction of a judgment debt out of the goods and lands or profits of the lands of the judgment debtor — compare FIERI FACIAS

lev·arterenol \ˌlev+\ *n* [*lev-* + *arterenol*] **:** levorotatory norepinephrine

le·va·tor \ləˈvād·ə(r), -vād-\ *n, pl* **lev·a·to·res** \ˌlevəˈtōr-(ˌ)ēz\ *or* **levators** [NL, fr. ML, lever, one that levies, fr. L *levatus* (past part. of *levare* to raise) + *-or* — more at LEVER] **:** a muscle that serves to raise a body part — compare DEPRESSOR

1le·vee \ˈlevē, -vi; ləˈvē, -ˈvā\ *n* -S [F *lever,* fr. MF, action of rising from bed, fr. *lever* to rise from bed, raise, fr. L *levare* to raise] **1 a :** a reception held by a person of distinction on rising from bed ⟨the Sun King had one nobleman to hand him his stockings, another his shirt, in his morning ~ —Saul Bellow⟩ **b** *Brit* **:** an afternoon assembly at which the king or his representative receives only men **c :** a fashionable party or reception usu. in honor of a particular person ⟨the years of ~*s* and parades and other suave peacetime occasions —Gladys B. Stern⟩ ⟨young ladies who were invited to ~*s,* as the college receptions were then called —Mary A. Allen⟩ ⟨they were dressed as if for a ~ —A.J.Liebling⟩ **2** *archaic* **:** the act or action of arising from or as if from bed ⟨the sun's ~ —Thomas Gray⟩ **3** *obs* **:** the guests gathered at a levee

2levee *vt* **leveed; leveed; leveeing; levees** *obs* **:** to court (the great or powerful) by attending or seeking entry to levees

3lev·ee \ˈlevē, -vi\ *n* -S [F *levée,* fr. MF *levee* levee, action of raising, fr. OF, action of raising, fr. fem. of *levé,* past part. of *lever* to raise] **1 a :** an embankment designed to prevent flooding ⟨the Mississippi river ~*s* have often had to be sandbagged⟩ **b :** a river landing place **:** PIER, QUAY **2 :** a small continuous dike or ridge of earth for confining the irrigation checks of land to be flooded **3 :** the very low ridge sometimes built up by streams on their floodplains on either side of their channels **4 :** a red-light district esp. in Chicago **syn** see WHARF

4levee \ˈ"\ *vt* **leveed; leveed; leveeing; levees :** to provide with a levee ⟨*leveed* the stream channel⟩ ⟨*leveed* banks⟩

levee en masse *var of* LEVY EN MASSE

1lev·el \ˈlevəl\ *n* -S [ME *livel, level,* fr. MF *livel,* fr. (assumed) VL *libellum,* fr. L *libella,* dim. of *libra* pound, weight, balance] **1 a :** a device for finding a horizontal line or plane by means

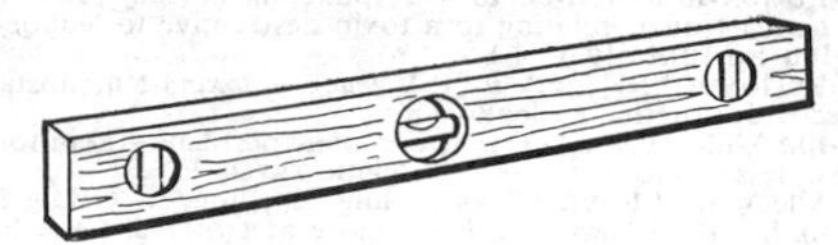

level 1a

of a bubble in a nonfreezing liquid (as alcohol or ether) that shows adjustment to the horizontal by movement of the bubble to the center of a glass tube that is slightly bowed up from the horizontal longitudinally **b :** a surveyor's telescope on which is mounted a sensitive bubble tube and which indicates a horizontal line of sight when the bubble is centered by means of leveling screws **c** [prob. fr. *2level*] **:** a measurement of the difference of altitude of two points by means of a level ⟨take a ~⟩ **2 :** horizontal state or condition **:** uniform altitude ⟨brings the tilted surface to a ~⟩; *esp* **:** equilibrium of a fluid marked by a horizontal surface of even altitude ⟨water tries to find its own ~⟩ **3 :** an approximately horizontal line or surface: as **a :** such a line or surface taken as an index of altitude ⟨wall charts arranged at eye ~ —J.K.Blake⟩ ⟨we were then 400 feet beneath the ~ of the fields overhead —Andrew Finn⟩ **b :** an area of country unbroken by noticeable elevations or depressions ⟨a side-hill village, spilling from the ~ of a plateau down a sharp incline into the valley —*Amer. Guide Series: Vt.*⟩ **4 :** a position in any scale of achievement, importance, significance, or value **:** PLANE, RANK: as **a :** a degree of artistic, intellectual, or spiritual meaning ⟨the ~ of insight is generally very high —S.E.Hyman⟩ ⟨the ~ of excellence achieved in the novel . . . provides an imposing yardstick against which the film repeatedly will be measured —Arthur Knight⟩ ⟨different ~*s* or orders of truth —J.W.Krutch⟩ **b :** a measure of personal worth or dignity ⟨I don't feel that it's necessary to quarrel with people. One puts himself on their ~ in that way —J.C.Powys⟩ **c :** a rank in an organization or hierarchy ⟨stipulated that the meeting should be on the ~ of foreign ministers —*N.Y. Times*⟩ ⟨had a genius for . . . using her associates at all ~*s* in . . . building her own career —Harrison Smith⟩ ⟨only on the provincial and state ~ had a certain regrouping taken place —*Americana Annual*⟩ ⟨handled major problems of the union on a national ~ —*Current Biog.*⟩ **d :** social standing or precedence ⟨the social ~*s* . . . were laid upon one's position in the university rather than money —Virginia D. Dawson & Betty D. Wilson⟩ **5 a :** a line or surface that cuts perpendicularly all plumb lines that it meets and hence would everywhere coincide with a surface of still water **b :** the plane of the horizon or a line in it **6 :** an open stretch of water in a canal or river (as between two canal locks) **7** [*2level*] *obs* **:** the act of aiming a gun or other missile-firing weapon **8 a :** a horizontal passage in a mine intended for regular working and transportation — compare ADIT **b :** the horizontal plane containing a main level and other workings (as crosscuts and drifts) ⟨the 700-foot ~⟩ — compare DRIFT 6 **9 :** a characteristic and fairly uniform concentration of a constituent of the blood or other body fluid ⟨a normal blood-sugar ~⟩ **10 :** the magnitude of a quantity considered in relation to an arbitrary reference value (as volts or decibels) ⟨a scale of auditory magnitudes has been derived from loudness tests and can be used whenever the loudness ~ of a sound is known —J.C.Steinberg & W.A.Munson⟩ ⟨video signal ~ is usually referred to in terms of volts, while audio ~ is measured in volume units —H.E.Ennes⟩ **11 :** ENERGY LEVEL **12 a :** a degree of ability or aptitude or measure of performance ⟨the student who has not reached an advanced ~ —A.S.Hornby⟩ ⟨they slow the game down to a tempo corresponding to their ~ of fitness —W.J.Finn⟩ **b :** a grade of mental or emotional development or maturity ⟨evidence as to ~*s* of personality development (e.g., anal, oral) —G.P.Murdock⟩ **13 :** a plane of economic activity, prices, or production ⟨production, employment, and national income were at record peacetime ~*s* —*Collier's Yr. Bk.*⟩ ⟨continued high ~ of private capital investments —Fritz Sternberg⟩ **14 :** a natural or fit position in relation to others — used in the phrase *one's level* ⟨the peso . . . was allowed to seek its own ~ —*Collier's Yr. Bk.*⟩ — **on the level :** bona fide **:** GENUINE, HONEST ⟨the deal seems to be *on the level*⟩ ⟨gained wide credit for acting always *on the level*⟩

2level \ˈ"\ *vb* **leveled** *or* **levelled; leveled** *or* **levelled; leveling** *or* **levelling** \-v(ə)liŋ\ **levels** [ME *levellen,* fr. *livel, level,* n. — more at 1LEVEL] *vt* **1 :** to make (a line or surface) horizontal **:** even off **:** make flat or level ⟨they are the natural highways of all nations . . . ~*ing* the ground and removing obstacles from the path of the traveler —H.D. Thoreau⟩ **2 a :** to bring to a horizontal aiming position ⟨a second sentry . . . ~*ed* his halberd at the parson's breast —Max Peacock⟩ ⟨hesitates to ~ his barrage directly —C.H. Stoddard⟩ **b :** AIM, DIRECT ⟨bitter taunts that his wife had ~*ed* at him —J.C.Powys⟩ ⟨two major criticisms have been ~*ed* at the program —*N.Y. Times*⟩ ⟨jokes, ridicule, and ill-natured gossip were ~*ed* against the daring females who succeeded in getting employment —Langston Day⟩ **3 :** to bring to a common level or plane (as of rank or condition) **:** EQUALIZE ⟨love ~*s* all ranks —W.S.Gilbert⟩ ⟨social differences in the plantation country of the South were ~*ed* down to some extent after the Civil War —Hans Kurath⟩ **4 a :** to lay level with the ground **:** FLATTEN, RAZE ⟨a mysterious fire ~*ed* the tower —*Amer. Guide Series: Pa.*⟩ ⟨the cyclone of 1889 ~*ed* the entire city —*Amer. Guide Series: Minn.*⟩ **b :** to knock down **:** lay prone ⟨brought his fist up quickly under my chin and ~*ed* me backwards on the bed —Shea Murphy⟩ **5 :** to make even, equal, or uniform (as in color) **6 :** to alter by linguistic or phonetic leveling (sense 2) **7 :** to find the heights of different points in (a piece of land) esp. with a surveyor's level **:** to make a contour of by means of a level — sometimes used with *over* or *up* ~ *vi* **1 :** to attain or come to a level — often used with *down, out,* or *up* ⟨the deck of the *Janet* ~*ed* a little as she slowed down —Arnold Gifford⟩ ⟨the trail turned south there and ~*ed* out —W.V.T.Clark⟩ **2 a :** to aim a gun or other weapon horizontally ⟨they ~ **:** a volley, a smoke and the clearing of smoke —Robert Browning⟩ **b** *obs* **:** to direct attention or effort at an object **3 :** to bring persons or things to a level ⟨your levelers wish to ~ down as far as themselves; but they cannot bear ~*ing* up to themselves —Samuel Johnson⟩ **4 :** to impart color evenly or with uniform shade ⟨dyes that ~ readily⟩ **5 :** to be made identical by linguistic or phonetic leveling (sense 2) **6 :** to form a smooth film free of brush marks — used of paints **7 :** to deal frankly and without artifice **:** speak candidly and openly ⟨I'll ~ with you. From you I hold back nothing —Richard Brooks⟩

3level \ˈ"\ *adj* [1*level*] **1 a :** having no part higher than another **:** conforming to the curvature of the earth's ocean surfaces ⟨these low, ~ landscapes . . . are characteristic of the continent as a whole —*Atlas of Australian Resources*⟩ ⟨this land is so ~ that before the erection of . . . fences snow-sailing was a popular and very exciting sport —*Amer. Guide Series: Minn.*⟩ **b :** coinciding or parallel with the plane of the horizon **:** HORIZONTAL ⟨the bottom of the excavation must be ~ —J.R.Dalzell⟩ **2 a :** even or unvarying in height ⟨secure the advantage of a ~ temperature —*Oil*⟩ **b :** equal in advantage, progression, or standing ⟨where every democratic dream had been fulfilled, and where all men had started ~ —W.B.Yeats⟩ ⟨another rider drew ~ with the squire —T.B. Costain⟩ ⟨sitting down as a ~ member of the dairyman's household seemed at the outset an undignified proceeding —Thomas Hardy⟩ **c :** proceeding monotonously or uneventfully ⟨their ~ life is but a smoldering fire, unquenched by want, unfanned by strong desire—Oliver Goldsmith⟩ **d** (1) **:** PENETRATING, STEADY, UNFLINCHING, UNWAVERING ⟨she gave him a ~ look —Louis Auchincloss⟩ (2) **:** CALM, QUIET, UNEXCITED ⟨finished his bottle and began to speak in ~ tones and with a quiet final authority —Honor Tracy⟩ ⟨it was not in ~ and sober mood that the heir was expected but in a stew of high excitement —Francis Hackett⟩ **e :** contested on even terms **:** exhibiting no handicap ⟨the race was clearly ~⟩ **3 :** maintaining equilibrium **:** BALANCED, JUST, STEADY ⟨a longtime producer, who, from seeing so many actors come and go, keeps a ~ head about them —*N.Y. Times*⟩ ⟨arrive at a justly proportioned and ~ judgment on this affair —Sir Winston Churchill⟩ **4 :** distributed evenly **:** of a uniform shade ⟨a badly prepared fabric cannot be expected to give ~ dyeing —R.S.Horsfall & L.G.Lawrie⟩ **5 a :** uttered with stress on two or more syllables that is heavy and equal or apprehended as equal ⟨pronounced *impossible* with ~ stress⟩ ⟨~ stress is characteristic of the French language⟩ **b :** uttered at a pitch that remains the same for an entire syllable or for more than one ⟨a kind of ~ whine —Robert Browning⟩ **6 :** being a surface perpendicular to all lines of force in a field of force so that no energy is transformed in moving a mass along it **:** EQUIPOTENTIAL **7 a :** suited to a particular plane of ability or achievement — usu. used in combination ⟨college-*level* institutes and higher-than-college-*level* academies—Joseph Alsop⟩ **b :** conducted at or proper to a particular organizational rank or status — usu. used in combination ⟨the nature and extent of top-*level* thinking with respect to planned action —J.F.H.Turton⟩ **8 :** evenly matched in appearance and qualities ⟨"a nice ~ lot," said the colonel . . . as they watched the first four companies —Rudyard Kipling⟩ ⟨by only keeping white hounds and by most careful and judicious mating he obtained a ~ pack in 20 years —B.V.Fitzgerald⟩ **9 :** bona fide **:** untainted by devious motive or intent to deceive ⟨the game is ~⟩ **10 :** of or relating to the spreading out of a cost or charge in even payments over a period of time rather than making a single lump sum payment ⟨~ premium plans are offered widely by insurance companies⟩

syn FLAT, PLAIN, PLANE, EVEN, SMOOTH, FLUSH: LEVEL in its literal meanings is almost entirely limited to the notion of conforming to or paralleling either the curvature line of the surface of the earth or the nearly identical line horizon to horizon; its stress is on the notion of a plane through either of these lines and its connotation not so precise that no minor irregularity of surface is possible. Its suggestion is usu. a favorable one ⟨a *level* and convenient lot⟩ FLAT stresses the notion of an unbroken horizontal surface; it indicates lack of a break in surface contour and may be deprecatory ⟨*flat* uninteresting prairies⟩ No longer common, the adjective PLAIN in this sense is likely to apply to terrain and have about the same implications as the noun PLAIN. PLANE, a close cognate of PLAIN, similarly has the connotations of the noun PLAIN. In mathematical use it contrasts with *solid* or *spherical.* EVEN stresses lack of noteworthy breaks or irregularities in surfaces although it does not indicate, as SMOOTH does, complete lack of any roughnesses, ruptures, or irregularities. SMOOTH stresses a completely regular surface lacking irregularities perceptible to touch or sight, roughnesses, dents, ridges, breaks, or inept jointures. SMOOTH has no suggestion of a given plane. FLUSH may stress lack of designed breaks in an even surface, like panels, ridges, molding strips, or cornices; it may suggest the setting or embedding of one thing into another leaving an uninterrupted plane ⟨bolts set *flush*⟩ — **level best :** very best ⟨did his *level best* to make money at it —F.L.Allen⟩

4level *adv, obs* **:** in a level line or manner

level–coil *n* [by folk etymology (influence of *3level* and *1coil*) fr. MF *lever le cul* to raise or remove the rump, displace from a seat] **1** *obs* **:** an old game in which the players at a given signal replace each other in seats amid a general scramble and tumult **2** *obs* **:** a noisy sport or melee

level crossing *n, Brit* **:** GRADE CROSSING

leveled *or* **levelled** *past of* LEVEL

lev·el·er *or* **lev·el·ler** \ˈlev(ə)lə(r)\ *n* -S **1 :** one that levels: as **a :** a scraper for leveling ground ⟨large automatic ~*s* like the land plane —O.W.Israelsen⟩ **b :** an adjustable attachment on row-cultivating tools for leveling off ridges left by the cultivators **2 a** *usu leveller, usu cap* **:** one of a group of radicals arising in the Parliamentary army during the English Civil War and advocating a program of constitutional reform designed to secure equality before the law for all men esp. in political and economic rights together with religious toleration as opposed to all forms of church establishment ⟨the *Levellers* . . . objected to political privilege on the part of the nobility —G.H.Sabine⟩ **b :** one advocating or held to advocate the leveling of differences of rank, privilege, or possession among men; *esp* **:** one favoring the removal of political or social inequalities ⟨determined ~*s* of society, the Swedish dislike any sort of ostentation —*Harper's Bazaar*⟩ ⟨the republicans, the ~*s,* the fanatics, — all ranged themselves on the side of the new ideas —George Bancroft⟩ **c :** something that tends to reduce or eliminate differences among men ⟨for us housewives, a ration card was the great ~ —Joan Comay⟩ ⟨war has always been the great ~ —*Harper's*⟩

level–headed \ˌ==ˌ==\ *adj* **:** exhibiting balance and deliberation **:** COOL ⟨the more *level-headed* leaders distrusted this flamboyant orator —Desmond Ryan⟩ — **level–head·ed·ness** \ˌ==ˌ===\ *n*

leveling *or* **levelling** *n* -S [fr. gerund of *2level*] **1 :** the action of one that levels **2 :** a change in the spelling or pronunciation of a word or word form or element to conform with that of a different although often related one **:** obliteration of a phonetic or linguistic distinction ⟨Middle English *sang* (singular) and *sungen* (plural) have both become *sang* by ~ in modern English⟩ ⟨~ of *riding* and *writing* is frequent in American speech⟩ **3 :** the finding of a horizontal line, the ascertaining of differences of elevation between points on the earth's surface, or the establishing of grades (as for a railway roadbed) by use of a surveyor's level **4 :** the establishment of a standard time for a job or a piecework operation by time-study computations based on the actual performance of workers in order to fix incentive pay rates or appraise workers' efficiency **5 :** the formation of a smooth film free of brush marks — used of paints

leveling rod *n* **:** a graduated rod used in measuring the vertical distance between a point on the ground and the line of sight of a surveyor's level

leveling screw *n* **:** one of three or more adjusting screws for bringing an instrument or other object into level

lev·el·ism \ˈlevəˌlizəm\ *n* -S *archaic* **:** disposition or endeavor to level distinctions of rank

lev·el·ly \-vəl(l)ē, -)i\ *adv* **:** in a level manner

lev·el·man \ˈlevəlmən, -ˌman\ *n, pl* **levelmen :** a surveyor who operates a leveling instrument

level measure *n* **:** dry measure obtained by filling a container level with the top — called also *struck measure*

levelness *n* -ES **:** the quality or state of being level

level off *vt* **:** to make smooth or even ⟨dry ingredients are heaped into the utensil, then *leveled off* with a knife —Ida B. Allen⟩ ⟨bulldozers quickly *leveled off* the site⟩ ~ *vi* **1 :** to reach a constant rate or unvarying volume, total, or amount **:** attain equilibrium **:** STABILIZE ⟨populations often *level off* as they press harder on natural resources⟩ ⟨the signs are that unemployment is *leveling off* —*Wall Street Jour.*⟩ **2 :** to change a flight path to horizontal after a climb, glide, or dive **3 :** to approach a limit ⟨the plate current in a vacuum tube *levels off* as the applied voltage is increased⟩

level premium *n* **:** one of a series of equal installments by which the premium on an insurance policy may be paid rather than in a lump sum

levels *pl of* LEVEL, *pres 3d sing of* LEVEL

level–wind \ˌ==ˌ=\ *n* **:** a device for winding a fishing line evenly on a multiplying reel

1lever \ˈlevə(r), ˈlēv-\ *n* -S [ME *lever, levour,* fr. OF *levier,* fr. *lever* to raise, fr. L *levare;* akin to L *levis* light, having little weight — more at LIGHT] **1 a :** a bar used for prying or dislodging something **:** CROWBAR **b :** any means, instrument, or agency used for achieving a purpose (as by inducing or compelling action or providing motive) **:** TOOL ⟨attempts to use food as a political ~ —*Time*⟩ ⟨could use the girl's action as a ~ to make her lawyer . . . turn over the letters —Erle Stanley Gardner⟩ ⟨others misuse the interview as a ~ to force the employee to resign —R.S.Brown⟩ ⟨shies away from reflection . . . and seeks out the ~*s* of power — and those who control them —Dwight Macdonald⟩ **2 a :** a rigid piece that transmits and modifies force or motion when forces are applied at two points and it turns about a third; *specif* **:** a bar of metal, wood, or other rigid substance used to exert a pressure or sustain a weight at one point of its length by the application of a force at a second and turning at a third on a fulcrum **b :** a projecting piece by which a mechanism is operated or adjusted ⟨gearshift ~⟩ ⟨to increase speed move the starting ~ to the right⟩ **3 :** LEVER TUMBLER **4 :** a supported or hanging position in which a gymnast's body while extended or bent at right angles at the hips is held parallel to the floor

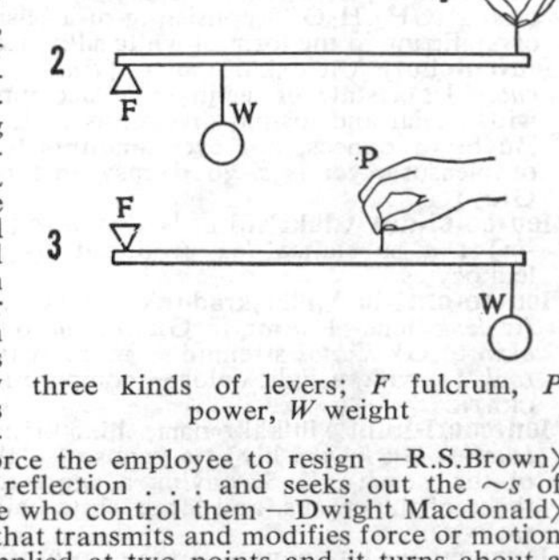

three kinds of levers; *F* fulcrum, *P* power, *W* weight

2lever \ˈ"\ *vb* **levered; levered; levering** \-v(ə)riŋ\ **levers** *vi* **1 :** to pry or work with or as if with a lever ⟨~*ing* at the rock —F.V.W.Mason⟩ **2 :** to operate a lever ~ *vt* **1 :** to pry, raise, or move with or as if with a lever ⟨~*ed* the other boot off with his bare toes —Richard Llewellyn⟩ ⟨like every alliance . . . it can be ~*ed* into action only with difficulty —A.A.Berle⟩ **2 :** to operate as a lever ⟨~*s* the throttles back until the engines are turning out 44 inches at 2400 revolutions —Richard Thruelsen⟩

lever action *n* **:** a rifle action that is manually operated by an external lever

lever·age \ˈlev(ə)rij, ˈlēv-, -rēj\ *n* -S **1 a :** the action or mechanical effect of a lever ⟨its weight is greatly aggravated by the ~ caused by its projection —*Harper's*⟩ **b :** an arrangement or system of levers **2 :** EFFECTIVENESS, POWER, INFLUENCE ⟨would have had little bargaining ~ while the blast furnaces were cold —*Christian Science Monitor*⟩ ⟨serious criticism has failed of ~ —Louis Kronenberger⟩ **3 :** the intensified speculative effect of market fluctuations on a company's common stock caused by its outstanding bonds and preferred stock on which the interest rate is fixed ⟨the majority of the large closed-end companies do have senior securities outstanding in varying amounts, and accordingly the companies have varying degrees of ~ —H.V.Prochnow⟩

lever arm *n* **:** the perpendicular distance from the fulcrum of a lever to the line of action of the effort or to the line of action of the weight

lev·er·et \ˈlev(ə)rət\ *n* -S [ME, fr. (assumed) MF *levret*, fr. MF *levre* hare (fr. L *lepor-, lepus*) + *-et* — more at LAPIN] **1 :** a hare in its first year **2** *obs* **:** MISTRESS, LIGHT-O'-LOVE

lever·man \ˈlevə(r)mən, ˈlēv-\ *n, pl* **levermen :** a man who operates levers or controls: as **a :** TOWERMAN ⟨a ~ on duty in the switch tower nearby was suspended soon after the accident —*N.Y. Times*⟩ **b :** a sawmill deckman **c :** a sawmill worker who controls the mechanism that transfers lumber from one set of conveyor rolls to another or from rolls to platform — called also *rollerman* **d :** an operator of a donkey engine for moving logs **e :** a member of a forging crew who handles billets during forging

lever scales *n pl* **:** STEELYARD

lever shears *n pl* **:** shears constructed on the principle of the lever — called also *alligator shears, crocodile shears*

lever tumbler *n* **:** an internal member of a lock usu. of flat sheet metal that is moved by a key to operate the bolt — distinguished from *pin tumbler* and *sliding tumbler*

lever watch *n* **:** a watch with lever escapement having a vibrating lever to connect the action of the escape wheel with that of the balance

leverwood \ˈ==,=\ *n* **:** HOP HORNBEAM

levet *n* -S [prob. fr. It *levata* call to arms, action of raising, fr. fem. of *levato*, past part. of *levare* to raise, fr. L — more at LEVER] *obs* **:** REVEILLE

levi·able \ˈlevēəbəl\ *adj* [ME *levyable*, fr. *levien* to levy + *-able*] **1 :** that may be levied ⟨the fine . . . is ~ not upon the string or succession of oaths, but upon each individual malediction —A.P.Herbert⟩ **2 :** that may be levied upon ⟨~ goods⟩

¹le·vi·a·than \ləˈvīəthən\ *n* -S [ME, fr. LL, fr. Heb *liwyāthān*] **1 a** *often cap* **:** a sea monster often symbolizing evil in the Old Testament and in Christian literature ⟨thou didst crush the heads of ~ —Ps 74:14 (RSV)⟩ **b** (1) **:** any of various large sea animals ⟨this ~ of animals is the great Blue Whale —Weston LaBarre⟩ (2) a large oceangoing ship ⟨the modern ~ would be a commercial failure were the traveling public not willing to pay . . . for the extra speed, comfort, and luxury —W.D.Winter⟩ **c** *archaic* **:** a wealthy or powerful man **2** *or* **leviathan state** *usu cap L* [so called fr. the use of the word *Leviathan* to designate the state in the book *Leviathan* (1651) by Thomas Hobbes †1679 Eng. philosopher] **:** the political state; *esp* **:** an all-powerful state usu. held to be characterized by a vast bureaucracy and machinery of coercion and exercising totalitarian control over its citizens ⟨the oppression of *Leviathan* at its worst —*Times Lit. Supp.*⟩ ⟨the prostration of the judiciary before the Nazi *Leviathan* —Karl Loewenstein⟩ ⟨millions . . . surrendered their right of private judgment to the *Leviathan state* —Geoffrey Bruun⟩ **3 :** the largest or most massive thing of its kind **:** the monster of a class ⟨America has come to look like . . . a ~ of mechanized power —Irwin Edman⟩ ⟨published that ~ of school books —G.H.Genzmer⟩ ⟨~ shovels . . . dig their wide trench as they crawl —Frederick Simpich †1950⟩

²leviathan \"\ *adj* **:** of enormous size **:** MONSTROUS, VAST ⟨the ~ proportions of international scandal —Paul Murray⟩ ⟨show the volume and pressure of that ~ intelligence —Christopher Morley⟩

leviathan stitch *n* **:** a double cross-stitch producing an 8= pointed figure usu. worked in wool on canvas

leviathan stitch

levied *past of* LEVY

levi·er \ˈlevēə(r)\ *n* -S **:** one that levies

levies *pl of* LEVY, *pres 3d sing of* LEVY

¹lev·i·gate \ˈlevə,gāt\ *vt* -ED/-ING/-S [L *levigatus*, past part. of *levigare*, fr. *levis* smooth + *agere* to drive — more at LIME, AGENT] **1** *archaic* **:** to polish or make smooth **2 a :** to grind to a fine smooth powder while in moist condition ⟨by first *levigating* the zinc oxide with a small amount of glycerin a smooth paste is obtained —*Art of Compounding*⟩ **b :** to separate (fine powder) from coarser material by suspending in a liquid ⟨whiting is pure finely divided calcium carbonate prepared by wet-grinding and *levigating* natural chalk —R.N.Shreve⟩

²lev·i·gate \ˈlevəgət, -və,gāt\ *adj* [L *levigatus*] *bot* **:** GLABROUS

lev·i·ga·tion \,levəˈgāshən\ *n* -S [ME *levygacyon*, fr. L *levigation-, levigatio*, fr. *levigatus* + *-ion-, -io* -ion] **:** the action or process of smoothing or levigating

lev·i·ga·tor \ˈ==,gād·ə(r)\ *n* -S **1 :** a workman who levigates (as pigments) **2 :** a levigating tool

lev·in \ˈlevən\ *n* -S [ME *levene*; prob. akin to Goth *lauhmuni* lightning, *liuhath* light — more at LIGHT] *archaic* **:** LIGHTNING

le·vin tube *also* **le·vine tube** \ləˈvēn-\ *n, usu cap L* [after Abraham Louis *Levin* †1940 Am. physician who invented it] *med* **:** a tube designed to be passed into the stomach or duodenum through the nose

levi·rate \ˈlevərət, ˈlēv-, -,rāt\ *n* -S *often attrib* [L *levir* husband's brother + E *-ate*; akin to OE *tācor* husband's brother, OHG *zeihhur*, Gk *daēr*, Skt *devr*] **:** the marriage of a widow by the brother or occas. the heir of her deceased husband sometimes (as among the ancient Hebrews) constituting a compulsory custom — compare JUNIOR LEVIRATE, SORORATE — **levi·rat·ic** \;==ˈrad·ik\ *adj*

Le·vi's \ˈlē,vīz\ *trademark* — used for heavy blue denim pants that are reinforced at strain points with copper rivets and have close-fitting legs

le·vis·ti·cum \ləˈvistəkəm\ *n, cap* [NL, fr. LL, lovage — more at LOVAGE] **:** a genus of European herbs (family Umbelliferae) with yellow flowers and dorsally flattened fruit — see LOVAGE

lev·i·tate \ˈlevə,tāt\ *vb* -ED/-ING/-S [*levity* + *-ate*] *vi* **:** to rise or float in the air esp. in seeming defiance of gravitation (as objects at a spiritualistic seance) ~ *vt* **:** to lift, suspend, or cause to move in the air esp. in seeming defiance of gravitation ⟨*levitating* being the term used by spiritualistic mediums for causing chairs and tables to rise into the air without apparent motivation —Alva Johnston⟩ ⟨we are *levitated* between acceptance and disbelief —Sean O'Faolain⟩ **syn** see RISE

lev·i·ta·tion \,==ˈtāshən\ *n* -S [*levity* + *-ation*] **:** a rising-or lifting in the air ⟨speed and the special ~ that skates give to the human form —H.E.Clurman⟩ ⟨the use of hydrogen gas for ~ —*Manchester Guardian Weekly*⟩; *esp* **:** the rising or lifting of a person or thing by means held to be supernatural ⟨reported that he had seen manifestations of ~, had heard accordions play without being touched by human hands —M.L.Bach⟩ — **lev·i·ta·tion·al** \;==ˈtāshən°l, -shnəl\ *adj*

lev·i·ta·tive \ˈ==,tād·iv\ *adj* [*levitate* + *-ive*] **:** having the ability to rise by levitation **:** marked by or relating to levitation

lev·i·ta·tor \ˈ==,tād·ə(r)\ *n* -S **:** one that levitates

le·vite \ˈlē,vīt, *usu* -īd·+V\ *n* -S [ME, fr. LL *Levita, Levites*, fr. Gk *Leuitēs*, fr. *Leui* Levi, third son of Jacob and ancestor of the Levites (fr. Heb *Lēwī*) + *-itēs* -ite] **1** *usu cap* **:** a member of the Hebrew tribe of Levi **:** a descendant of Levi; *specif* **:** a non-Aaronic descendant of Levi assigned to assist the Levitical priests of the family of Aaron in the care of the tabernacle and later of the temple **2** *sometimes cap* **:** a Christian cleric in orders below those of priest; *specif* **:** DEACON 1

le·vit·i·cal \ləˈvid·əkəl, -it|, |ēk-\ *also* **le·vit·ic** \|ik, |ēk\ *adj, usu cap* [*levitical* fr. LL *leviticus* levitical (fr. Gk *leuitikos*, fr. *Leuitēs* Levite + *-ikos* -ic) + E *-al*; *levitic* fr. LL *leviticus*] **1 a :** of, characteristic of, or relating to the Levites **b :** qualified as a Levite **2 :** of, relating to, or characteristic of the book of Leviticus **3 a :** of or relating to Hebrew dogma or ritual ⟨*Levitical* questions⟩ **b :** PRIESTLY **4 :** AARONIC 2 — **le·vit·i·cal·ly** \|ək(ə)lē, |ēk-, -li\ *adv, usu cap*

levitical degrees *n pl, usu cap L* **:** the degrees of kinship within which marriage is forbidden in Leviticus 18

lev·i·ty \ˈlevəd·ē, -ətē, -i\ *n* -ES [L *levitat-, levitas* lightness in weight, frivolity, fr. *levis* light + *-itat-, -itas* -ity — more at LIGHT] **1 a :** excessive or unseemly frivolity **:** lack of fitting seriousness **:** TRIFLING ⟨light without ~ and serious without solemnity, always within the limits of classically disciplined form —*New Yorker*⟩ ⟨there was about him something that made ~ seem out of place —O.S.J.Gogarty⟩ **b :** lack of steadiness **:** CHANGEABLENESS, FICKLENESS, INCONSTANCY ⟨that emotional seriousness will not transform intellectual ~ —W.C.Brownell⟩ ⟨pitted its gravity and longevity against the ~ and evanescence of the brisk fire —Charles Dickens⟩ **2 a :** the quality or state of being light in weight ⟨the qualities of warmth, ~, and least resistance to the air —William Paley⟩ **b :** a positive property of lightness opposed to gravity and formerly believed to be a characteristic of some physical objects ⟨it will no longer be lightness in the sense of very little weight, but positive and active lightness; we call this ~ —George Adams & Olive Whicher⟩ ⟨substitutes for universal gravity a polarity of gravity and ~, the latter a nonmechanical . . . force apparent . . . in certain volcanic phenomena and the growth of plants —*Times Lit. Supp.*⟩

le·vo *or* **lae·vo** \ˈlē(,)vō\ *adj* [*lev-*] **:** LEVOROTATORY

levo- — see LEV-

le·vo·glucosan \¦lē(,)vō+\ *n* [*lev-* + *glucosan*] **:** a levorotatory crystalline anhydride $C_6H_{10}O_5$ of glucose that is best prepared by treating the beta form of phenyl glucoside with alkali, and that regenerates glucose on heating with water; 1,6-anhydro-β-D-glucose — compare GLUCOSAN; GLUCOSE illustration

le·vo·gyrate \¦lēvō+\ *or* **le·vo·gyre** \ˈlēvō+,-\ *adj* [*levogyrate* fr. *lev-* + *gyrate*, adj.; *levogyre* ISV *lev-* + *-gyre* (fr. L *gyrus* circular motion) — more at GYRE] **:** LEVOROTATORY

le·vo·pimaric acid \¦=(,)=+ . . . -\ *n* [*levopimaric* ISV *lev-* + *pimaric* (in *pimaric acid*)] **:** a crystalline levorotatory resin acid $C_{19}H_{29}COOH$ occurring esp. in oleoresins from pine trees and isomerizing readily to abietic acid on heating or treatment with acids

le·vo·rotation \¦lēvō+\ *n* [*lev-* + *rotation*] **:** left-handed or counterclockwise rotation — used chiefly of the plane of polarization of light; opposed to *dextrorotation*; compare OPTICAL ROTATION

le·vo·rotatory *or* **le·vo·rotary** \"+\ *adj* [*lev-* + *rotatory* or *rotary*] **:** turning toward the left hand or counterclockwise; *esp* **:** rotating the plane of polarization of light toward the left hand ⟨~ crystals⟩ ⟨~ sugar solutions⟩ — opposed to *dextrorotatory*; compare OPTICALLY ACTIVE

lev·u·li·nate \ˈlevyələ,nāt\ *n* -S [*levulinic* (in *levulinic acid*) + *-ate*] **:** a salt of levulinic acid

lev·u·lin·ic acid \¦==¦linik-\ *n* [*levulinic* ISV *levulin* substance yielding levulose on hydrolysis (ISV *levul-* — fr. *levulose* — + *-in*) + *-ic*] **:** a crystalline keto acid $CH_3CO(CH_2)_2COOH$ obtained by action of dilute acids on hexoses (as levulose) and on substances (as starch or sucrose) that yield hexoses on hydrolysis

lev·u·lose \ˈ==,lōs *also* -ōz\ *n* -S [ISV *lev-* + *-ule* + *-ose*] **:** levorotatory D-fructose obtained usu. by hydrolysis either of inulin from dahlia tubers or from the Jerusalem artichoke or of sucrose

¹levy \ˈlevē, -vi\ *n* -ES [ME *levee, levy*, fr. MF *levee* levy, action of raising, fr. OF, action of raising, fr. fem. of *levé*, past part. of *lever* to raise — more at LEVER] **1 a :** the imposition or collection of an assessment, tax, tribute, or fine ⟨make a ~ on all meat, out of which to pay the running costs of the . . . organization —*Sydney (Australia) Bull.*⟩; *specif* **:** the taking of property on execution to satisfy a judgment ⟨it authorizes a ~ upon property of the witness —E.D.Dickinson⟩ **b :** an amount levied **:** IMPOST, TAX ⟨a direct food ~ was imposed —Leonard Mason⟩ **2 a :** the enlistment or conscription of men for military service **:** MUSTER ⟨the ~ of the militia, which had previously been confined to the countryside, was extended to Paris —Evelyn Cruickshanks⟩ **b :** the troops raised by a levy ⟨defeat followed by victory had transmuted green *levies* into veteran soldiers —Peter Rainier⟩ ⟨*levies*, who were eating the village out of hearth and home —Marguerite Steen⟩

²levy \"\ *vb* -ED/-ING/-ES [ME *levyen, levien*, fr. *levee, levy*, n.] *vt* **1 a :** to impose or collect (as a tax or tribute) by legal process or by authority **:** EXACT ⟨we cannot ~ unlimited drafts on the future to avoid bankruptcy in the present —W.R.Inge⟩ ⟨there will be no European army if the exclusive right to ~ taxes is left to individual governments —*European Federation Now*⟩ ⟨the time-honored graft that policemen usually ~ on prostitutes —Green Peyton⟩ ⟨*levied* a heavy fine for contempt of court⟩ **b :** to exact or require (as a service) by authority or power ⟨upon those did Solomon ~ a tribute of bond service unto this day —1 Kings 9:21 (AV)⟩ **2 :** to enlist or conscript for military service ⟨go ~ men and make prepare for war —Shak.⟩ ⟨the armies of the early 17th century were mercenary, rapidly *levied*, disbanded again, haphazard —Hilaire Belloc⟩ **3 :** to carry on (war) **:** MAKE, WAGE ⟨treason against the U.S. shall consist only in ~*ing* war against them, or in adhering to their enemies, giving them aid and comfort —*U.S.Constitution*⟩ ⟨only a skirmish in the general war *levied* upon social distinctions —V.L.Parrington⟩ **4** *law* **a :** to seize in satisfaction of a legal claim or judgment **b :** to carry into effect (as a writ of execution) **:** ENFORCE **c :** to arrange (a fine) in settlement of a suit to establish title to land ⟨she was also prohibited from ~*ing* a fine —Joshua Williams⟩ ~ *vi* **1 :** to seize real or personal property or subject it to attachment or execution **:** make a levy ⟨*levied* on the judgment debtor's property under an execution⟩ **2 :** to draw for provisions or resources — usu. used with *on* ⟨I have *levied* on many writers for my essential conception of American culture —Max Lerner⟩ ⟨had *levied* on their cellars to produce new offerings —A.J.Liebling⟩

³levy \"\ *n* -ES [by shortening & alter. fr. *eleven pence* (approximate value of the coin)] **1 :** a Spanish real — used esp. in Pennsylvania, Maryland, and Delaware **2 :** the sum of 12½ cents

levy court *n* **:** a body of magistrates exercising in some states (as Delaware) the functions performed in other states by county commissioners ⟨the *Levy Court* of each county shall meet at the courthouse . . . three times in every year —*Del. Revised Statutes*⟩

levy en masse \¦levē-, -vi- + *pronunc at* EN MASSE\ *also* **le·vée en masse** \" *or* ləˈvā-\ *or* **levy in mass** *n, pl* **levies en masse** *also* **levées en masse** *or* **levies in mass** [*levy en masse & levy in mass* trans. of F *levée en masse*, fr. *levée* levy + *en masse*; *levée en masse* fr. F] *international law* **:** the spontaneous act of the people of a territory not yet occupied by an enemy force of taking up arms for self-defense upon the approach of an enemy without having had time to organize in accordance with recognized rules of warfare

le·vyn·ite \lāˈvē,nīt\ *or* **le·vyne** \lāˈvēn\ *n* -S [*levynite* fr. *levyne* (irreg. fr. Armand *Lévy* †1841 Fr. mineralogist + E *-ine*) + *-ite*] **:** a white or light-colored mineral $NaCa_3Al_7Si_{11}O_{36}.15H_2O$ that occurs in rhombohedral crystals and is a hydrous calcium aluminum silicate

¹lew \ˈlü\ *adj* [ME *lew, lewe* lukewarm, warm, fr. OE *hlēow* warm; akin to ON *hlȳr* lukewarm — more at LEE] **1** *now dial* **:** LUKEWARM **2** *now dial Brit* **:** ²LEE 1

²lew \"\ *n* -S *now dial Brit* **:** a place of shelter **:** the side sheltered (as from the wind)

lewd \ˈlüd\ *adj* [ME *lewed, lewede* vulgar, base, laical, fr. OE *lǣwede* laical] **1** *obs* **a :** of, relating to, or characteristic of common and ignorant people **:** VULGAR **b :** BASE, EVIL, WICKED — used of persons and their conduct **c :** POOR, WORTHLESS — used of things **2 a :** sexually unchaste or licentious **:** DISSOLUTE, LASCIVIOUS **b :** suggestive of or tending to moral looseness **:** inciting to sensual desire or imagination **:** INDECENT, OBSCENE, SALACIOUS ⟨moralists looked upon it as a ~ distraction —Lewis Mumford⟩ ⟨loud, ~ dissonances from the . . . orchestra in the pit —*Time*⟩ ⟨the hawk stood . . . with his ~ purple tongue lolling from his open beak —Liam O'Flaherty⟩

lewd·ly *adv* [ME *lewedly* ignorantly, badly, fr. *lewed, lewede* + *-ly*] **:** in a lewd manner

lewd·ness *n* -ES [ME *lewednesse* ignorance, wickedness, fr. *lewed, lewede* + *-nesse* -ness] **:** the quality or state of being lewd

lewd·ster \ˈlüdztə(r), -dst-\ *n* -S *archaic* **:** a lewd person

lew·is \ˈlüəs\ *n* -ES [prob. fr. the name *Lewis*] **:** an iron dovetailed tenon that is made in sections, can be fitted into a dovetail mortise, and is used in hoisting large stones — called also *lewisson*

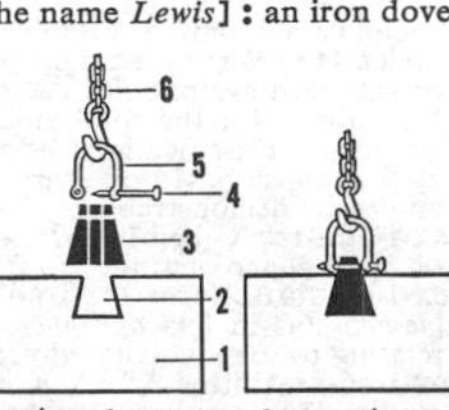

lewis: *1* stone, *2* mortise, *3* tenon, *4* bolt, *5* link, *6* chain to pulleys

lewis acid *n, usu cap L* [after Gilbert N. *Lewis* †1946 Am. chemist] **:** ²ACID 2c

lewis base *n, usu cap L* **:** ¹BASE 8c

lewis bolt *n* **:** a bolt with an enlarged head leaded into masonry as a foundation bolt or into a stone for use as a lewis

lewis gun *n, usu cap L* [after Isaac N. *Lewis* †1931 Am. army officer and inventor] **:** a gas-operated air-cooled machine gun fed by a drum magazine and first used in World War I ⟨dropped my stick with a clatter like a *Lewis gun* —Angus Mowat⟩

lew·i·sia \lüˈizh(ē)ə\ *n* [NL, fr. Meriwether *Lewis* †1809 Am. explorer + NL *-ia*] **1** *cap* **:** a large genus of herbs (family Portulacaceae) of western No. America with linear woolly leaves and large pink flowers — see BITTERROOT **2** -S **:** any plant of the genus *Lewisia*

lew·i·sian \(ˈ)lü¦izh(ē)ən\ *adj, usu cap* [*Lewis*, northern part of the island of Lewis with Harris, Outer Hebrides + E *-ian*] **:** of, relating to, or constituting a division of the Precambrian — see GEOLOGIC TIME table

¹lew·is·ite \ˈlüə,sīt\ *n* -S [William J. *Lewis* †1926 Eng. mineralogist + E *-ite*] **:** a mineral consisting of a titanian romeite related to pyrochlore

²lewisite \"\ *n* -S [Winford Lee *Lewis* †1943 Am. chemist + E *-ite*] **:** a colorless to amber to dark brown liquid vesicant that sometimes has an odor like that of geraniums, that is made by reaction of acetylene with arsenic trichloride, and that was developed for use as a war gas but has never been so used; dichloro-2-chloro-vinyl-arsine

lewis–langmuir theory \¦lüəˈslaŋ,myü(ə)r-\ *n, usu cap both Ls* [after Gilbert N. *Lewis* †1946 and Irving *Langmuir* †1957 Am. chemists] **:** a chemical theory of atomic structure: the atom consists of a positive nucleus surrounded by concentric cubic shells at the corners of which the electrons are located — compare OCTET

lew·is·son \ˈlüəsən\ *n* -S [by alter.] **:** LEWIS

lew·is's woodpecker \ˈlüəsəz-\ *n, usu cap L* [after Meriwether *Lewis* †1809] **:** a woodpecker (*Asyndesmus lewis*) of western No. America with the upper parts greenish black, the breast and collar gray, and the face and abdomen rich red

lew·is·ton·ite \ˈlüəstə,nīt\ *n* -S [*Lewiston*, Utah, its locality + E *-ite*] **:** a mineral $(Ca,K,Na)_5(PO_4)_3(OH)$ consisting of a basic phosphate of calcium, potassium, and sodium

lewth \ˈlüth\ *n* -S [ME *-lewth*, fr. OE *hlēowth, hlȳwth*, fr. *hlēow* warm — more at LEW] *now dial Brit* **:** shelter or protection from the weather **:** WARMTH

lew–warm \ˈ=¦=\ *adj* [ME, fr. *lew* + *warm*] *dial Brit* **:** LEW 1

lex \ˈleks\ *n, pl* **le·ges** \ˈlā(,)gās, ˈlē(,)jēz\ [L *leg-, lex* law — more at LEGAL] **1** *Roman law* **a :** LEX PUBLICA **b :** LEX PRIVATA **2 :** LAW

lex *abbr* lexical; lexicon

lex actus *var of* LEX LOCI ACTUS

lex com·mis·so·ria \-,kämə'sōrēə\ *n* [LL] *Roman & civil law* **:** a penalty clause for nonperformance of a contract: as **a :** a provision that a pledge shall be forfeited if a loan is not repaid **b :** a condition that money paid on a contract of sale shall be forfeited and the sale rescinded if remaining payments are defaulted

lex do·mi·ci·lii \-,dämə'kilē,ē\ *n* [NL, law of the domicile] **:** the law of the domicile by which the rights of persons are sometimes governed (as where a person dies leaving personal property)

lex·eme \ˈlek,sēm\ *n* -S [*lexicon* + *-eme*] **:** a meaningful speech form that is an item of the vocabulary of a language — **lex·em·ic** \(ˈ)lek¦sēmik\ *adj*

lex fo·ri \-ˈfōr(,)ē\ *n* [NL, law of the court] **:** the law of the court in which a proceeding is brought

lex ge·ne·ra·lis \-,genəˈrāləs\ *n* [NL, general law] *Roman & civil law* **:** a law of general application as contrasted with one applicable to a particular person

le·xia \ləˈhēə\ *n* -S [perh. fr. obs. Sp *lexia* lye (now *lejia*), fr. L *lixiva*, fem. of *lixivus* consisting of lye — more at LIQUID] **:** a soft light-colored raisin produced chiefly in Spain and Australia from white vinifera grapes that are treated with a caustic solution and sometimes with olive oil before drying

-lex·ia \ˈleksēə\ *n comb form* -S [NL, fr. Gk *lexis* word, speech] **:** reading of (such) a kind or with (such) an impairment ⟨*bradylexia*⟩ ⟨*dyslexia*⟩

lex·i·cal \ˈleksəkəl, -sēk-\ *also* **lex·ic** \-sik,-sēk\ *adj* [*lexical* fr. *lexicon* + *-al*; *lexic* back-formation fr. *lexical*] **1 a :** of or relating to words, word formatives, or the vocabulary of a language as distinguished from its grammar and construction ⟨~ elements like *book, run,* and so on —Sol Saporta⟩ ⟨~ research is not so much linguistic research as research in the culture of a community —R.I.McDavid⟩ **b :** uttered with heavy stress when devoid of context or when emphatic ⟨\ˈand\ or \ˈaa(ə)nd\ is the ~ pronunciation of *and*, which in context usu. has \ə\ for vowel or no vowel at all and often has not two consonants but one, which is \n\ or by environmental assimilation \m\ or \ŋ\⟩ ⟨a distinction may be present in ~ pronunciation which disappears in connected speech —A.F.Hubbell⟩ **2 :** of or relating to a lexicon or to lexicography ⟨~ methods aim to list all the relevant forms —A.F. Parker-Rhodes⟩ — **lex·i·cal·i·ty** \,leksəˈkaləd·ē, -lətē, -i\ *n* -ES — **lex·i·cal·ly** \-sək(ə)lē, -sēk-, -li\ *adv*

lexical meaning *n* **:** the meaning of the base (as the word *play*) in a paradigm (as *plays, played, playing*) — compare GRAMMATICAL MEANING

lex·i·cog·ra·pher \,leksəˈkägrəfə(r)\ *n* -S [LGk *lexikographos* compiler of a glossary (fr. LGk *lexikon* lexicon + Gk *-graphos* one that writes) + E *-er* — more at -GRAPHER] **:** an author or compiler of a dictionary ⟨~: . . . a harmless drudge that busies himself in tracing the original, and detailing the signification of words —Samuel Johnson⟩

lex·i·co·graph·ic \¦leksəkō¦grafik, -sēk-, -kə¦g-, -fēk\ *or* **lex·i·co·graph·i·cal** \-fəkəl, -fēk-\ *adj* [*lexicography* + *-ic* or *-ical*] **:** of or relating to lexicography ⟨~ methods⟩ ⟨~ history⟩ — **lex·i·co·graph·i·cal·ly** \-fək(ə)lē, -fēk-, -li\ *adv*

lex·i·cog·ra·phist \,leksəˈkägrəfəst\ *n* -S [*lexicography* + *-ist*] **:** LEXICOGRAPHER

lex·i·cog·ra·phy \-fē, -fi\ *n* -ES [fr. *lexicographer*, after such pairs as E *geographer: geography*] **1 :** the editing or making of a dictionary **2 :** the principles and practices of dictionary making ⟨a martyr, by my ~, is on all fours with a fool who risks and loses his life in any other showy but useless way —H.L. Mencken⟩

lex·i·co·log·i·cal \¦leksəkō¦läjəkəl, -sēk-, -kə¦l-, -jēk-\ *or* **lex·i·co·log·ic** \-jik,-jēk\ *adj* **:** of or relating to lexicology

lex·i·col·o·gist \,leksəˈkäləjəst\ *n* -S **:** a specialist in lexicology

lex·i·col·o·gy \-jē,-ji\ *n* -ES [F *lexicologie*, fr. *lexico-* (fr. LGk *lexiko-*, fr. *lexikon*) + *-logie* -logy] **:** the science of the derivation and signification of words **:** a branch of linguistics that treats of the signification and application of words

lex·i·con \ˈleksə,kän, -sək-, -sēkən,-sēkən\ *n, pl* **lexi·ca** \-kə\ *or* **lexicons** [LGk *lexikon*, fr. neut. of *lexikos* of words, fr. Gk *lexis* word, speech (fr. *legein* to speak) + *-ikos* -ic — more at LEGEND] **1 :** a book containing an alphabetical or other systematic arrangement of the words in a language or of a considerable number of them and their definitions **:** DICTIONARY, WORDBOOK ⟨for the making of the great ~ of the Greek language —*Times Lit. Supp.*⟩ **2 :** the vocabulary of a language, of an individual speaker, of a set of documents, of a body of speech, of a subject, or of an occupational or other group ⟨in her financial ~, five cents was as valuable as five dollars —Calder Willingham⟩ ⟨the realization that Marxism is not a complete ~ of progress —*New Republic*⟩ ⟨the missile . . . will become more and more important in the whole ~ of war —H.W.Baldwin⟩ **3 :** COMPENDIUM, ACCOUNT, RECORD ⟨the ~ of human struggle, through which she had searched to decipher a meaning, dissolved for her and floated away —Helen Howe⟩ ⟨in the bright ~ of LP, I know of no other pair of standard symphonies . . . so essentially satisfying —Irving Kolodin⟩ **4 :** the total stock of morphemes in a language ⟨linguistic classifications established on the basis of ~ (as against those based on grammar) are more apt to prove right and to be demonstrable —N.A.McQuown⟩

lex·i·con·ize \-kə,nīz\ *vt* -ED/-ING/-S **1 :** to make a lexicon of (a language or subject) **2 :** to incorporate in a lexicon

lex·i·co·statistic *or* **lex·i·co·statistical** \¦leksə(,)kō+\ *adj* [*lexico-* (as in *lexicographer*) + *statistic* or *statistical*] **:** of, relating to, or involving glottochronology (sense 2)

lex·i·co·statistics \"+\ *n pl but sing in constr* [*lexico-* + *statistics*] **:** GLOTTOCHRONOLOGY 2

lex·i·graph·ic \¦leksə¦grafik\ *or* **lex·i·graph·i·cal** \-fəkəl\ *adj* **:** of or relating to lexigraphy — **lex·i·graph·i·cal·ly** \-fək(ə)lē\ *adv*

lex·ig·ra·phy \lek'sigrəfē\ *n* [Gk *lexis* word + E *-graphy*] **1 :** the art or practice of defining words **2 :** a system of writing (as that of the Chinese) in which each character represents a word

lex·i·phan·ic \¦leksə¦fanik\ *adj* [*Lexiphanes* (bombastic speaker in the dialogue *Lexiphanes* by Lucian, 2d cent. A.D. Greek satirist) + E *-ic*] *archaic* **:** using ostentatiously recondite words **:** BOMBASTIC, PRETENTIOUS

lex·i·phan·i·cism \,==¦fanə,sizəm\ *n* -S *archaic* **:** pretentious phraseology or an instance or example of such phraseology

lex lo·ci ac·tus \¦lek,slōkē'aktəs, -ē'äk-\ *or* **lex actus** *n* [*lex loci actus* fr. NL, law of the place of the act; *lex actus* fr. NL, law of the act] **:** the law of the place where an act is done or a transaction takes place

lex loci ce·le·bra·ti·o·nis \-,kelə,brād·ē'ōnəs\ *n* [NL, law of the place of the ceremony] **:** the law of the place where a contract esp. of marriage is made

lex loci con·trac·tus \-.kən·'traktəs\ *n* [NL, law of the place of the contract] **:** the law of the place where a contract is made or is to be performed

lex loci de·lic·ti \-də'liktē\ *n* [NL] **:** the law of the place of the wrong or tort

lex loci rei si·tae \-¦rā'si,tī\ *or* **lex si·tus** \-'si,tüs\ *n* [*lex loci rei sitae* fr. NL, law of the place of the situated property; *lex situs* fr. NL, law of the site] **:** the law of the place where a property is situated

lex loci so·lu·ti·o·nis \-,sə,lütē'ōnəs\ *n* [NL] **:** the law of the place of performance of a contract

lex mer·ca·to·ria \-,mərkə'tōrēə\ *or* **lex mer·ca·to·rum** \-rəm\ *n* [*lex mercatoria* fr. ML, lit., mercantile law; *lex mercatorum* fr. NL, lit., law of merchants] **:** LAW MERCHANT

lex non scrip·ta \¦lek,snän'skriptə, -nōn-\ *n* [LL, unwritten law] **:** unwritten law; *esp* **:** the common law as distinguished from statutory law

lex pri·va·ta \,lekspr̄ə'väd·ə\ *n* [NL, private law] *Roman law* **:** a provision (as a restriction or obligation) of a private contract — called also *lex*

lex pu·bli·ca \(')lek'spüblәkə, -'spəb-\ *n* [ML, public law] **1** *Roman law* **:** a law passed by a popular assembly **2** *Roman law* **:** a written law

lex sa·li·ca \(')lek(s)'saləkə\ *n, usu cap S* [ML] **:** SALIC LAW

lex scrip·ta \(')lek(s)'skriptə\ *n* [LL, written law] **:** the written or statute law

lex ta·li·o·nis \¦lek,stalē'ōnəs\ *n* [NL, law of retaliation] **:** the law of retaliation equivalent to an offense; *esp* **:** the principle of retributive justice based on the Mosaic law of "eye for eye, tooth for tooth" in Exod 21:23–25 — called also *talion*

¹ley *archaic var of* LYE

²ley *var of* LEA

ley·den blue \'līdᵊn-\ *n, often cap L* [fr. *Leiden, Leyden,* city in the southwest Netherlands] **:** COBALT BLUE

leyden jar *n, usu cap L* [so called fr. its having been invented in Leiden] **:** the earliest form of electrical condenser consisting essentially of a glass jar coated part way up both inside and outside with metal foil and having the inner coating connected to a conducting rod passed through the insulating stopper

ley·dig cell \'līdig-\ *also* **ley·dig's cell** \-dig(z)-\ *n, usu cap L* [after Franz *Leydig* †1908 Ger. zoologist] **:** an interstitial cell of the testis usu. considered the chief source of testicular androgens and perhaps other hormones

ley·dig's duct \-digz-\ *n, usu cap L* **:** MESONEPHRIC DUCT

ley farming \'lē-,'lā-\ *n* [*²ley*] **:** the growing of grass or legumes in rotation with grain or tilled crops as a soil conservation measure

ley pewter \'lā-\ *n* [perh. fr. the name *Ley*] **:** pewter containing a relatively large percentage of lead

ley·ton \'lāt'n\ *adj, usu cap* [fr. *Leyton,* municipal borough, northeastern suburb of London, England] **:** of or from the municipal borough of Leyton, England **:** of the kind or style prevalent in Leyton

le·za \'lēzə\ *n* -S [origin unknown] **:** the heavy hard gray to grayish brown smooth lustrous wood of an Indian tree (*Lagerstroemia tomentosa*) used for furniture, flooring, and paneling

lez·ghi·an *also* **les·ghi·an** \'lezgēən, 'leskē-\ *n* -S *usu cap* [Russ *Lezgin,* n., Lezghian + E *-ian,* n. suffix] **1 :** a division of the peoples of the Caucasus that includes the Avars, the Lakhs, and the Kyurins **2 :** a member of the Lezghian people

lez·gin·ka \lez'giŋkə\ *n* -S [Russ, fr. *Lezgin*] **:** a courtship dance of the Caucasus mountains in which the woman moves with graceful ease while the man dances wildly about her

lf *abbr* **1** leaf **2** leaflet **3** lightface

LF *abbr* **1** ledger folio **2** left field **3** left foot **4** left forward **5** left front **6** lettering faded **7** lineal feet **8** load factor **9** lock forward **10** *often not cap* low frequency

LFA *abbr* local freight agent

LFB *abbr* left fullback

LFC *abbr, often not cap* low-frequency current

LFD *abbr* least fatal dose

l–form \'=,=\ *n, usu cap L* **:** a filterable form of certain bacteria commonly regarded as a specialized reproductive body appearing chiefly when the environment is unfavorable and much resembling typical pleuropneumonia organisms

lft *abbr* leaflet

lg *abbr* **1** large **2** long

LG *abbr* **1** landing ground **2** large grain **3** left guard **4** lifeguard

lge *abbr* large

lgr *abbr* **1** larger **2** longer

lgt *abbr* light

lgth *abbr* length

LH *abbr* **1** left hand **2** lighthouse **3** lower half **4** luteinizing hormone

LHA *abbr* **1** local hour angle **2** lord high admiral

lha·sa \'läsə *also* 'lasə\ *adj, usu cap* [fr. *Lhasa,* Tibet] **:** of or from Lhasa, the capital of Tibet **:** of the kind or style prevalent in Lhasa

lhasa ap·so \,==¦ap(,)sō\ *also* **lhasa** *or* **lhasa terrier** *n, usu cap L, often cap A* [*apso* fr. Tibetan] **1 :** a Tibetan breed of small terrier lionlike in appearance with a dense coat of long hard straight hair, a heavy fall over the eyes, heavy whiskers and beard, and a well-feathered tail curled over its back **2** *pl* **lhasa apsos :** a terrier of the Lhasa apso breed

LHB *abbr* left halfback

LHC *abbr* lord high chancellor

l–head \'=,=\ *adj, cap L* **:** having the intake and exhaust valves in compartments of the block to the same side of the cylinder head ⟨an *L-head* gasoline engine⟩

lho·ke \'lō(,)kä\ *n* -S *usu cap* **:** the Tibeto-Burman language of Bhutan

lho·ta \'lōd·ə\ *n, pl* **lhota** *also* **lhotas** *usu cap* **1 :** one of several Naga peoples of the Assam-Burma frontier region **2 :** a member of the Lhota people

LHT *abbr* lord high treasurer

¹li \'lē\ *n, pl* **li** *also* **lis** [Chin (Pek) *li³*] **:** any of various Chinese units of distance; *esp* **:** one equal to about ⅓ mile

²li \"\ *n* -S [Chin (Pek) *li³* propriety] **:** one of the cardinal virtues in Confucianism that consists of propriety or correct behavior as the outward expression of an inner harmony with the ethical principles of nature

³li \"\ *n, pl* **li** *or* **lis** *usu cap* [Chin (Pek) *li³*, lit., rude, rustic] **1 :** an ethnic group that is culturally a branch of the early Tai people of southern China and that forms the largest ethnic group next to the Chinese in Hainan Island in southeast China **2 :** a member of the Li people

LI *abbr* **1** light infantry **2** low intensity

Li *symbol* lithium

li *abbr* link

li·a·bil·i·ty \,līə'biləd·ē, -lətē, -i\ *n* -ES **1 a :** the quality or state of being liable ⟨the ~ of an insurer⟩ **b :** LIKELIHOOD ⟨the ~ to take to their beds at the drop of a hat —Osbert Lancaster⟩ **2 :** something for which one is liable: as **a** (1) **:** an amount that is owed whether payable in money, other property, or services — compare ACCRUED LIABILITY, CAPITAL LIABILITY, CONTINGENT LIABILITY, CURRENT LIABILITY, FIXED LIABILITY (2) **liabilities** *pl* **:** pecuniary obligations **:** DEBTS — compare ASSET **b :** an obligation or duty which is owed by one person to another to refrain from some course of conduct injurious to the latter or to perform some act or to do something for the benefit of the latter and for breach of which the law gives a remedy to the latter (as damages, restitution, specific performance, injunction) **:** accountability and responsibility to another enforceable by legal civil or criminal sanctions **3 :** something that works as a disadvantage **:** DRAWBACK ⟨effects on the growing self of a . . . child that will be his *liabilities* instead of assets —Bingham Dai⟩ ⟨the very traits which made him a success . . . are likely to be serious *liabilities* at a later stage —P.B.Sears⟩ **syn** see DEBT

liability insurance *n* **:** insurance against loss resulting from liability for injury or damage to the persons or property of others

liability limit *n* **:** the maximum amount which a liability insurance company agrees to pay as a result of a single accident or injury to a single person

li·a·ble \'līəbəl, *esp in sense 3* 'lībəl\ *adj* [fr. (assumed) AF, fr. OF *lier,* to bind, tie (fr. L *ligare*) + *-able* — more at LIGATURE] **1 a :** bound or obligated according to law or equity **:** RESPONSIBLE, ANSWERABLE ⟨~ for the debts incurred by his wife⟩; *also* **:** subject to appropriation or attachment ⟨all his property is ~ to pay his debts⟩ **b** (1) **:** subject to control by — used with *to* ⟨~ to the driving laws of the state⟩ (2) **:** being in a position to incur — used with *to* ⟨~ to the death penalty⟩ ⟨those who do not vote are ~ to fines —*Americana Annual*⟩ **c** *obs* **:** belonging to ⟨all that we find . . . ~ to our crown and dignity —Shak.⟩ **2** *obs* **:** SUITABLE, FIT, APT **3 :** exposed or subject to some usu. adverse contingency or action **:** LIKELY ⟨~ to fall⟩ ⟨~ to be hurt⟩ ⟨these values are ~ to fluctuate with every change in the current market —J.A.Hobson⟩

syn SUBJECT, OPEN, EXPOSED, SUSCEPTIBLE, PRONE, SENSITIVE, INCIDENT: LIABLE, now rather wide in its use, may retain its original legalistic suggestion and imply the consequences of the actions of legal authority ⟨*liable* to military service⟩ ⟨*liable* to be fined⟩ or range variously between this use and employment as a very close synonym for LIKELY; however used, it often though by no means always implies that the likely development will be unpleasant ⟨*liable* to be burned at the stake for . . . heresy —Agnes Repplier⟩ ⟨a palatal semiconsonant . . . *liable* to pass into another consonant —W.J.Entwistle & W.A.Morison⟩ SUBJECT may imply a great likelihood of the development that is indicated; more than the others it may although it does not always indicate that the development has happened or must happen ⟨another mystery . . . how, *subject* to the life he describes, he was able to become a poet —Osbert Sitwell⟩ ⟨rivers and streams . . . *subject* to great floods —Bram Stoker⟩ OPEN does not stress the probability of the ensuing development that is indicated; it stresses the ease with which that development may occur and esp. the lack of shield, guard, or defense against an unpleasant development ⟨another modern tendency in education . . . perhaps somewhat more *open* to question —Bertrand Russell⟩ ⟨standing thus alone . . . *open* to all the criticism which descends on the lone operator —Bruce Catton⟩ OPEN and EXPOSED are often interchangeable but OPEN makes no necessary implication about the presence or existence of the development, simply indicating lack of defense; in some but not all uses, EXPOSED indicates actual presence of the influencing force without indication of lack of defense ⟨*exposed* to streptococcus infection⟩ SUSCEPTIBLE changes the focus of attention and suggests not a temporary situation but an inherent or essential characteristic of the person or thing involved which makes the indicated influence or development likely ⟨fell in love with her . . . was already in a highly *susceptible* state and tumbled immediately —H.S.Canby⟩ ⟨a nature . . . perhaps even less *susceptible* than other men's characters of essential change —Walter Pater⟩ PRONE suggests a more positive predisposition of the subject toward the influence or development, a predisposition which is not merely receptive to the influence or development but which invited it ⟨you may well warn me against such an evil. Human nature is so *prone* to fall into it —Jane Austen⟩ ⟨I think that girls are less *prone* than boys to punish oddity by serious physical cruelty —Bertrand Russell⟩ SENSITIVE does not suggest a predisposition toward so much as a very readily perceptive or impressionable nature likely to be influenced by stimuli that might be without effect in another situation ⟨the founding of the university by the greatest capitalist in America made it *sensitive* to charges of capitalistic influence and inclined to lean backward to avoid them —R.M.Lovett⟩ ⟨so sweet and *sensitive* that she feels influences more acutely than other people do —Bram Stoker⟩ SENSITIVE may imply that the matter being perceived and calling forth a reaction is unpleasant ⟨raised her voice to a squeaking tone that was very painful to a *sensitive* ear —Ellen Glasgow⟩ INCIDENT may be mentioned in this series only because it indicates the fact of concomitant or ensuing result and implies nothing more than the existence of this fact ⟨economic factors *incident* to the depression —J.B.Conant⟩ **syn** see in addition RESPONSIBLE

li·a·ble·ness *n* -ES **:** the quality or state of being liable ⟨mutability and ~ to change —Ralph Wardlaw⟩

li·ag·o·ra \lī'agərə\ *n, cap* [NL, after *Liagora,* a nereid, fr. Gk *Leiagorē*] **:** a genus of marine red algae (family Helminthocladiaceae) characterized by the branched cylindrical thallus and by calcification of the gelatinous matrix so that it is often brittle and of a chalky texture

li·aise \lē'āz\ *vi* -ED/-ING/-S [back-formation fr. *liaison*] **1 :** to establish liaison ⟨told me to go to Bonn and ~ with the newly formed government —C.W.Thayer⟩ **2 :** to act as a liaison officer ⟨*liaising* with the next unit's guard posts—Earle Birney⟩

li·ai·son \'lēə,z|än, 'lē(,)ā,z|, lē'ā,z| *also* ÷'lāə,z| *or* -,s| *or* |ōn *or* |ōn *or* |ōⁿ *or* |äⁿ *or* ,=ə'= *or* ,=(,)ā'= *or* 'lēəlzən *or* lē'ālzᵊn *or* ÷'lāəlzən *or* |sən *or* |sᵊn\ *n* -S *often attrib* [F, fr. MF, fr. *lier* to bind, tie + *-aison* -ation (fr. L *-ation-, -atio*) — more at LIABLE] **1 a :** a close bond or connection ⟨the farmers and the labor people ended up supporting the same people but without much of a ~ between them —Tilford Dudley⟩ **:** RELATIONSHIP, INTERRELATIONSHIP ⟨a proper ~ between the school and the ordinary experience of the students —*Nat'l Catholic Educational Assoc. Bull.*⟩ ⟨establish any kind of ~ with the top men who were running trade and business —H.W.Carter⟩ **b :** an illicit sexual relationship between a man and a woman **2 :** the pronunciation at the end of the first of two consecutive words the second of which begins with a vowel sound and follows without pause of a consonant sound not present in the first word in other positions (as of \z\ in French \lāzāmē\ for *les amis* by contrast to \lāpwä\ for *les pois,* or in eastern New England of \r\ in \fārōf\ for *far off* by contrast to \fākrī\ for *far cry*) **3 a :** intercommunication established and maintained between parts of an armed force to ensure mutual understanding, unity of action, and esp. prompt and effective support by artillery and air units ⟨a ~ officer⟩ ⟨doing ~ work in the front lines⟩ **b :** any intercommunication for establishing and maintaining mutual understanding ⟨such ~ work as we have goes on between theological liberals in both groups —W.L.Sperry⟩

liaison aircraft *n* **:** a light airplane or helicopter used by military forces for courier and staff work behind the lines and for limited reconnaissance and artillery spotting over battle lines

li·ana \lē'änə, -'anə\ *or* **li·ane** \-n\ *n* -S [F *liane,* fr. F dial. *liône, lieune, liane,* prob. fr. *lier* to bind, tie — more at LIABLE] **:** a climbing plant that roots in the ground with woody lianas being characteristic of tropical rain forests and herbaceous lianas of temperate regions — **li·anoid** \-,nȯid\ *adj*

li·ang \lē'äŋ, -'aŋ\ *n, pl* **liang** *also* **liangs** [Chin (Pek) *liang³*] **:** an old Chinese unit of weight equal to ¹⁄₁₆ catty and equivalent to a little more than an ounce avoirdupois — called also *tael*

liangle *var of* LEEANGLE

liao·yang \lē'aù¦yäŋ\ *adj, usu cap* [fr. *Liaoyang,* Manchuria] **:** of or from the city of Liaoyang, Manchuria **:** of the kind or style prevalent in Liaoyang

li·ar \'lī(ə)r, -īə\ *n* -S [ME *lier, liar,* fr. OE *lēogere,* fr. *lēogan* to lie + *-ere* -er — more at LIE] **:** one that usu. knowingly and habitually utters falsehood **:** one that lies

liard \lē'är\ *n* -S [MF, after Guigues *Liard,* 15th cent. Frenchman who coined them] **:** a French coin of the 15th to the 18th centuries orig. of base silver but of copper from the time of Henry IV and worth ¼ of a sou

liar dice *n* **:** a poker-dice game in which a player's cast is concealed by a screen or his hands and he may bluff by announcing a better hand than he has

liar paradox *n* **:** a semantical paradox associated with the Cretan philosopher Epimenides (†7th cent. B.C.) and occurring when someone says "I am lying" or "I am now asserting a falsehood" which is a true statement if it is false and a false one if it is true — compare EPIMENIDEAN, RUSSELL'S PARADOX

¹li·as *also* **ly·as** \'līəs\ *n* -ES *often attrib* [ME *lyas,* fr. MF *liois,* prob. fr. *lie* dregs; fr. the appearance — more at LEE] **:** a kind of blue limestone found esp. in southwestern England

²lias *adj, usu cap* [fr. *Lias* oldest division of the European Jurassic system, fr. *¹lias*] **:** of or relating to a subdivision of the European Jurassic — see GEOLOGIC TIME table

li·as·sic \(')lī¦asik\ *adj, usu cap* [*²lias* + *-ic*] **:** LIAS

li·atris \lī'a·trəs, 'līə·t-\ *n* [NL] **1** *cap* **:** a genus of perennial American herbs (family Compositae) having aromatic often cormous roots, linear grassy leaves, and spikes of rose-purple or white discoid heads of perfect tubular flowers — see BLAZING STAR, BUTTON SNAKEROOT **2** -ES **:** any of several herbs of *Liatris* or the closely related genus *Trilisa* (as wild vanilla and the button snakeroot) sometimes used in medicine

lib \'lib\ *vt* **libbed; libbed; libbing; libs** [ME *libben;* akin to MD & MLG *lubben* to castrate; perh. akin to OE *lēaf* leaf — more at LEAF] *now dial Brit* **:** CASTRATE

lib *abbr* **1** [L *liber*] book **2** liberal **3** [L *libra*] pound **4** library; librarian

li·bate \'lībāt, ='=\ *vb* -ED/-ING/-S [L *libatus,* past part. of *libare* to pour as an offering] *vi* **:** to pour out a libation or make libation to **~** *vi* **1 :** to make libation **2 :** to drink alcoholic drink ⟨sat up with three *libating* guests who would not leave⟩

li·ba·tion \lī'bāshən\ *n* -S [L *libation-, libatio,* fr. *libatus* (past part. of *libare* to pour as an offering) + *-ion-, -io* -ion; akin to Gk *leibein* to pour, drip, Lith *lieti* to pour] **1 :** the act of pouring a liquid (as wine) either on the ground or on a victim in a sacrifice to a deity **2 a :** a liquid (as wine) serving as a libation or poured out in or as if in the manner of a libation ⟨pours water on the ground as a ~ to Mother Earth —J.G. Frazer⟩; *also* **:** the amount of such a liquid ⟨poured . . . a generous ~ of paraffin on the embers —Mary Webb⟩ **b :** a drink (as of wine) often taken ceremoniously ⟨the copious ~*s* of Burgundy in which he had indulged —T.L.Peacock⟩ ⟨consuming a final ~ at the bar —F.V.W.Mason⟩ ⟨a ~ in celebration of their long marriage⟩ — **li·ba·tion·al** \-shənᵊl,-shnəl\ *adj* — **li·ba·tion·ary** \-shə,nerē\ *adj*

li·ba·tion·er \-sh(ə)nə(r)\ *n* -S **:** one that pours a libation

lib·bard \'libə(r)d\ *archaic var of* LEOPARD

lib·bet \'libət\ *n* -S [origin unknown] *now dial Brit* **:** a torn and hanging strip **:** TATTER, RAG — usu. used in pl. ⟨torn all to ~*s*⟩

li·bec·cio \lə'bechē,ō, -e(,)chō\ *or* **li·bec·chio** \-ekē,ō, -e(,)kō\ *n* -S [It, fr. colloq. Ar *labāj, labash,* fr. Gk *lib-, lips,* fr. *leibein* to pour, drip — more at LIBATION] **:** a southwest wind

¹li·bel \'lībəl\ *n* -S [ME, fr. MF, fr. L *libellus,* dim. of *liber* book — more at LEAF] **1 a** *obs* **:** a written declaration, bill, certificate, request, or supplication **b :** the written statement made in civil law and admiralty law practice and in proceedings in ecclesiastical and occas. other courts by the plaintiff of his cause of action and the relief he seeks — compare DECLARATION **c** *Scots law* **:** the part of an indictment stating the grounds of the charge **d** *Scots law, archaic* **:** the punishment attached to an offense **2** *obs* **:** a brief piece of writing (as a little book or short treatise) **3 a** *archaic* **:** a handbill or circular esp. attacking or defaming someone **b** (1) **:** a written or oral defamatory statement or a representation or suggestion that conveys an unjustly unfavorable impression ⟨his criticism was a ~ of the writer⟩ ⟨the photograph is more a ~ than a reproduction⟩ (2) **:** a statement or representation published without just cause or excuse, expressed either in print or in writing or by pictures, effigies, or other signs and tending to expose another to public hatred, contempt, or ridicule **:** defamation of a person by means of written statements, pictures, or other visible signs **:** the publication of such writings or pictures as are of a blasphemous, treasonable, seditious, or obscene character — compare PRIVILEGED COMMUNICATION 2, SLANDER (3) **:** the act, tort, or crime of publishing such a libel

²li·bel \"\ *vb* **libeled** *or* **libelled; libeled** *or* **libelled; libeling** *or* **libelling** \-b(ə)liŋ\ **libels** *vi* **1 :** to spread defamation **:** make libelous statements — often used with *against* or *on* **2 :** to institute legal proceedings by a libel **~** *vt* **1 :** to hurt the reputation of by malicious or unfair issue of any false or harmful representation **:** issue a libel against **:** make a libelous statement or insinuation about or representation of **2 a :** to proceed against in law by filing a libel (as against a ship or goods) **b :** to allege in a libel **syn** see MALIGN

li·bel·ant *or* **li·bel·lant** \'lībəlant\ *n* -S **1 :** one that institutes a suit by a libel **2 :** one who makes or publishes a libel **:** LIBELER

li·bel·ee *or* **li·bel·lee** \,lībə¦lē\ *n* -S **:** one against whom a libel has been filed — compare DEFENDANT

li·bel·er *or* **li·bel·ler** \'lībələ(r)\ *n* -S **:** one that libels

li·bel·ist *or* **li·bel·list** \-ləst\ *n* -S **:** LIBELER

li·bel·lu·la \lī'belyələ, lə'-\ *n* [NL, dim. of *libella* dragonfly, fr. L, level (instrument); fr. the horizontal position of the wings — more at LEVEL] **1** *cap* **:** a genus of large often brightly colored dragonflies usu. with dark blotches on the wings that is the type of the family Libellulidae and in older classifications includes all the dragonflies **2** -S **:** any dragonfly of the genus *Libellula* **:** SKIMMER

li·bel·lu·li·dae \,lībə'lülə,dē\ *n pl, cap* [NL, fr. *Libellula,* type genus + *-idae*] **:** a large family of dragonflies having the abdomen triangular in cross section and females without a well-developed ovipositor — see LIBELLULA

li·bel·ous *or* **li·bel·lous** \'lībələs\ *adj* [*¹libel* + *-ous*] **:** constituting or including a libel **:** DEFAMATORY ⟨a ~ statement⟩ ⟨a ~ book⟩ ⟨claimed the movie was ~ —*Associated Press*⟩ ⟨a ~ portrait⟩ — **li·bel·ous·ly** *or* **li·bel·lous·ly** *adv*

libels *pl of* LIBEL, *pres 3d sing of* LIBEL

li·ber \'lībə(r), 'li,be(ə)r\ *n, pl* **li·bri** \'lī,brī, 'li(,)brē\ *or* **libers** [L, inner bark of a tree, pith of papyrus, book — more at LEAF] **1 :** BAST **2 :** a book of records (as of deeds or wills)

li·be·ra \'lēbə,rä\ *n* -S *usu cap* [L (first word of the responsory), imper. of *liberare* to set free — more at LIBERATE] **:** a Roman Catholic responsory that is sung usu. at funerals after the Mass and prior to the final prayers for the deceased

¹lib·er·al \'lib(ə)rəl\ *adj* [ME, fr. MF, ML & L; MF, fr. ML & L; ML *liberalis* of or constituting liberal arts, fr. L, of freedom, of a freeman, noble, generous, fr. *liber* free + *-alis* -al; akin to OE *lēodan* to grow, *lēod* people, OHG *liotan* to grow, *liut* person, people, ON *lothiun* shaggy, Goth *lindan* to grow, Gk *eleutheros* free, Skt *rodhati, rohati* he climbs, grows; basic meaning: growing] **1 a :** of, belonging to, being, or consisting of liberal arts or one of the liberal arts ⟨the studies are ~, not in one of the technical fields⟩ **b** *archaic* **:** of, belonging to, or befitting a man of free birth; *also* **:** of, belonging to, or befitting one that is a gentleman in social rank **c :** of, belonging to, or befitting a free man ⟨the ~ occupations of the gentry of ancient Rome⟩ **2 a :** marked by generosity, bounteousness, openhandedness **:** not stinting ⟨a ~ giver⟩ ⟨a man of ~ nature⟩ **b :** bestowed in a generous and openhanded way **:** ABUNDANT, BOUNTIFUL, AMPLE ⟨a ~ donation⟩ ⟨a ~ quantity⟩ ⟨receiving ~ rewards for the risks they took —*Amer.*

Guide Series: N.H.⟩ **c :** LARGE, FULL ⟨possessed a ~ lip⟩ ⟨a ~ bosom⟩ **3 a :** free from restraint or check **:** unchecked by a sense of the decorous, the fitting, or the polite ⟨possessed a ~ tongue that was always offending people⟩ **b** *obs* **:** lacking significant moral restraints **:** LICENTIOUS **4 a :** not strict or rigorous ⟨a ~ attitude toward one's children⟩ **b :** not confined or restricted to the exact or literal ⟨a ~ translation of the Greek text⟩ **5 a :** not narrow in mind **:** BROAD-MINDED, OPEN-MINDED **b :** not bound by authoritarianism, orthodoxy, or traditional or established forms in action, attitude, or opinion ⟨a man of ~ views who would not mind making significant changes in the social or economic structure if he felt it was for the best⟩ ⟨~ in his interpretation of his duties as a governor⟩ ⟨theologians, even the most ~, will rally to the defense of theology —A.L.Guérard⟩ **c** [F *libéral,* fr. MF *liberal*] **:** of, favoring, or based upon the principles of liberalism ⟨the ~ theory of progress —M.Q.Sibley⟩ ⟨the issue of ~ constitutionalism —G.H.Sabine⟩ ⟨the ~ emphasis upon the inalienable rights of the individual —J.H.Hallowell⟩ ⟨the Prussian monarchy was not ~, but it was progressive and enterprising —Stringfellow Barr⟩ — compare CONSERVATIVE, RADICAL 3a **d** *usu cap* **:** of, belonging to, or constituting a political party advocating or associated with the principles of political liberalism: as (1) **:** of or constituting a political party in the United Kingdom evolving from the Whigs and associated during the period of its status as one of the two major British parties of the 19th and early 20th centuries with ideals of individual esp. economic freedom, greater individual participation in government, and constitutional, political, and administrative reforms designed to secure these objectives ⟨the English *Liberal* party was rent asunder by the explosives of modern nationalism —C.J.Friedrich⟩ ⟨*Liberal* representation in Parliament has been reduced to a tiny handful —Henry Slesser⟩ — compare CATHOLIC, CONSERVATIVE, LABOR, RADICAL 3c(1), TORY, UNIONIST, WHIG (2) **:** of or constituting a major political party in another member nation of the British Commonwealth ⟨the Province of Quebec . . . is the stronghold of the *Liberal* party —C.E.Silcox⟩ ⟨launched the *Liberal* government's policy in Australia's federal election campaign —A.E.Norman⟩ ⟨*Liberal* opposition to Labor proposals in the New Zealand parliament⟩ (3) **:** of or constituting a minor political party active chiefly in New York and associated with social reform and support of policies favorable to organized labor ⟨the anticommunist stand taken by the founders of the *Liberal* party⟩

syn PROGRESSIVE, ADVANCED, RADICAL agree in application to a person or thing freed from or opposed to what is established or orthodox. LIBERAL, the most general term, suggests an emancipation from convention, tradition, or dogma that extends from a belief in altering institutions to fit altering conditions to a preference for lawlessness; on the one hand it suggests a commendable pragmatism, tolerance, and broad-mindedness and on the other a highly questionable unorthodoxy, experimentalism, or positive irresponsibility ⟨a *liberal* Episcopalian, preferred a non-Gothic auditorium in which the congregation could hear well, rather than merely view distant ritual —Robert Berkelman⟩ ⟨the prevailing *liberal* movement of the time was Benthamite in its emphasis on legal and social reform, and denounced tradition as the chief obstacle to progress —Michael Polanyi⟩ ⟨don't let us be hampered by routine and red tape and precedent, let's . . . put a *liberal* interpretation on our duties —W.S.Gilbert⟩ ⟨if *liberal,* in respect to language, means "tolerant of change", this book is *liberal.* If it means "not strict", the book is not *liberal,* or at least not intentionally so —J.B.McMillan⟩ ⟨the strict school of rabbis allowed divorce only on the ground of adultery; the *liberal* school, on almost any ground —J.C.Swaim⟩ PROGRESSIVE implies an opposition to the reactionary or backward, a willingness to forsake past methods or beliefs in the interests of improvement or amelioration ⟨one *progressive* publisher is now experimenting with plastic bindings —*Third Degree*⟩ ⟨the party direction must be moderate and yet *progressive* and dynamic —*N.Y.Times*⟩ ⟨the struggle . . . between the conservative and the *progressive* mind —G.G.Coulton⟩ ⟨to *progressive* leadership — a leadership which has sought . . . to advance the lot of the average American citizen —F.D.Roosevelt⟩ ⟨much *progressive* economic and social legislation designed to benefit the masses and to break the power of the privileged —A.C. Gordon⟩ ADVANCED usu. applies to something high in a scale of development or ahead of its time often suggesting mental daring. It can favorably suggest the extremely liberal or progressive or unfavorably suggest something new and experimental to the point of foolishness or bizarreness ⟨the economic interests of the *advanced* and backward peoples —J.A.Hobson⟩ ⟨the most *advanced* nuclear weapons —V.M.Barnett⟩ ⟨the continuing notion among many *advanced* writers that only difficult writing is good writing —F.L.Allen⟩ ⟨to her own generation she seemed *advanced* in realism and in daring —F.L. Pattee⟩ RADICAL usu. suggests extremeness to the point of a sharp break with the already established and esp. in its political application a desire to uproot and destroy; it is often interchangeable with *revolutionary* ⟨*radical* innovators, challenging the authority of the past —G.C.Sellery⟩ ⟨*radical* and experimental music —Humphrey Searle⟩ ⟨of mild nature and inclined to oppose *radical* changes in the established order —*Amer. Guide Series: Maine*⟩ ⟨*radical* and revolutionary views of the state⟩

syn GENEROUS, BOUNTIFUL, BOUNTEOUS, OPENHANDED, MUNIFICENT, HANDSOME: LIBERAL suggests openhandedness and lack of close stinting in giving ⟨*liberal* gifts to his nephews⟩ ⟨a *liberal* legacy to his servant⟩ ⟨*liberal* grants from the legislature⟩ ⟨a *liberal* serving of pie⟩ GENEROUS may suggest some pleasing personality trait like magnanimity, warmheartedness, willingness to aid, altruism, or forgetfulness of self ⟨he ladled out food with such a *generous* hand that the Indians named him 'Big Spoon' —*Amer. Guide Series: Md.*⟩ ⟨if she gave a friend a present — and this must have happened every day, for she was *generous* beyond the dreary bounds of common sense —Osbert Sitwell⟩ ⟨such a kindly, smiling, tender, gentle, *generous* heart of her own, as won the love of everybody who came near her —W.M.Thackeray⟩ BOUNTIFUL suggests lavish, abundant, and unremitting giving or providing ⟨spare not now to be *bountiful,* call your poor to regale with you . . . give your gold to the hospital, let the weary be comforted, let the needy be banqueted —Alfred Tennyson⟩ BOUNTEOUS has about the same suggestion as BOUNTIFUL but seems somewhat less likely to be applied to persons ⟨the *bounteous* yields of cotton, alfalfa, small grains, sorghums, melons, lettuce, dates, and citrus fruits for which the state is noted —*Amer. Guide Series: Ariz.*⟩ OPENHANDED suggests free and unguarded generosity; its antonym is *closefisted* ⟨*openhanded* to all appeals for charity⟩ MUNIFICENT may suggest princely or lordly lavishness and richness in giving ⟨had been most *munificent* to his soldiers. He had doubled their ordinary pay. He had shared the spoils of his conquests with them —J.A.Froude⟩ ⟨guaranteed by the United States government in terms of *munificent* land grants —Irving Stone⟩ HANDSOME may imply either that a gift is large and impressive or that the giver is magnanimous or gracious ⟨final decision to join the Allies was based on their favorable military position . . . as well as on the *handsome* prizes which she was offered —C.E.Black & E.C.Helmreich⟩ ⟨this method of dealing with her, if not lavish, was suitable, and in fact *handsome* —Edith Wharton⟩

²**liberal** \"\ *n* -s **:** one that is liberal: as **a :** one that is open-minded or not strict in his observance of orthodox, traditional, or established forms or ways **b** *usu cap* **:** a member or supporter of a Liberal party ⟨Conservatives, Labourites, and *Liberals* have two whips each in the House of Lords —F.A. Ogg & Harold Zink⟩ ⟨in Australia *Liberals* and Conservatives coalesced . . . in the face of the growth of Labour —Barbara & Robert North⟩ ⟨a preference for the Democratic presidential nominee among *Liberals* in New York⟩ ⟨in most European countries, the *Liberals* today are a right-wing party —A.M. Schlesinger b. 1917⟩ **c :** an adherent or advocate of liberalism esp. in terms of individual rights and freedom from arbitrary authority ⟨writing as a theological ~⟩ ⟨Manchester *Liberals* . . . fought factory legislation as a cardinal sin —Louis Filler⟩ ⟨the ~'*s* concern for individual or minority rights and freedoms —F.W.Coker⟩ — compare PROGRESSIVE

liberal arts *n pl* [trans. of ML *liberales artes*] **1 :** the studies comprising the trivium and quadrivium in the middle ages **2 :** the studies (as language, philosophy, history, literature, abstract science) esp. in a college or university that are presumed to provide chiefly general knowledge and to develop the general intellectual capacities (as reason or judgment) as opposed to professional, vocational, or technical studies ⟨a *liberal arts* curriculum⟩ ⟨a *liberal arts* college⟩; *also* **:** the humanities ⟨studied mainly the sciences and the *liberal arts*⟩ — see HUMANITY 3c

liberal catholic *n, cap L&C* **:** a person or group rejecting the authority of the Roman Catholic Church in specific matters of doctrine, discipline, or church government but accepting the body of its teachings or its forms of worship

liberal education *n* **:** education based on the liberal arts and intended to bring about the improvement, discipline, or free development of the mind or spirit — compare GENERAL EDUCATION

lib·er·al·ism \ˈlib(ə)rə,lizəm\ *n* -s **1 :** the quality or state of being liberal: as **a :** lack of strictness or rigor ⟨treats his children with a certain ~⟩ **b :** BROAD-MINDEDNESS, OPEN-MINDEDNESS ⟨an outlook marked by ~ and tolerance⟩ **2 :** principles, theories, or actions that are liberal: as **a** *often cap* **:** a movement in modern Protestantism emphasizing intellectual liberty and the spiritual and ethical content of Christianity ⟨nineteenth century *Liberalism* . . . introduced historical method in the interpretation of the gospels —C.H.Moehlman⟩ — compare FUNDAMENTALISM, MODERNISM **b :** a theory in economics emphasizing individual freedom from restraint esp. by government regulation in all economic activity and usu. based upon free competition, the self-regulating market, and the gold standard ⟨the decline of mercantilism produced a period characterized notably by the ideas and policy of ~⟩ — called also *economic liberalism;* compare CAPITALISM, COLLECTIVISM, FREE ENTERPRISE, INDIVIDUALISM, LAISSEZ-FAIRE, MERCANTILISM, SOCIALISM **c :** a political philosophy based on belief in progress, the essential goodness of man, and the autonomy of the individual and standing for tolerance and freedom for the individual from arbitrary authority in all spheres of life esp. by the protection of political and civil liberties and for government under law with the consent of the governed ⟨the touchstone that enables us to recognize ~ is the question of toleration —M.R.Cohen⟩ ⟨the classic ~ . . . derived from French rationalism and Benthamite utilitarianism —C.H.Driver⟩ ⟨~ had always claimed to stand for the greatest social good —G.H.Sabine⟩ — compare CATHOLICISM 4, COMMUNISM 2, CONSERVATISM 1b, FASCISM 2a, INDIVIDUALISM, SOCIALISM **d** *usu cap* **:** the principles or policies of a Liberal party ⟨the individualism of British *Liberalism* —L.D.Epstein⟩ ⟨nonconformist religion . . . was traditionally associated with political *Liberalism* —G.D.H.Cole⟩ **e :** an attitude or philosophy favoring individual freedom for self-development and self-expression ⟨a positive and noble impulse . . . of intellectual ~ was its immanent zeal for truth —F.C.Sell⟩

lib·er·al·ist \-ləst\ *n* -s **:** LIBERAL

lib·er·al·is·tic \ˈ;lib(ə)rə;listik\ *also* **lib·er·al·ist** \ˈlib(ə)rələst\ *adj* **:** of or belonging to, being marked by, or tending toward liberalism ⟨the ~ philosophy of the eighteenth century⟩

lib·er·al·i·ty \,libəˈralədˌē, -lətē, -i\ *n* -ES [ME *liberalite,* fr. MF *liberalité,* fr. L *liberalitat-, liberalitas,* fr. *liberalis* liberal + *-itat-, -itas* -ity — more at LIBERAL] **1 :** the quality or state of being liberal in giving, granting, or yielding **:** GENEROSITY ⟨gifts to charity marked by a great ~⟩; *also* **:** an instance of such liberality **:** a liberal gift **:** GRATUITY ⟨almost financially ruined by his *liberalities*⟩ **2 :** the quality or state of being liberal in attitude or principle ⟨coeducation was introduced in 1870, early evidence of the institution's ~ and vigor —*Amer. Guide Series: Mich.*⟩ ⟨my grandmother was proud of her ~ in not objecting to his marrying into what she called 'Trade' —Bertrand Russell⟩ **3** *archaic* **:** LIBERALS **4 :** FULLNESS, AMPLENESS, BROADNESS ⟨a ~ of mouth and feature⟩ ⟨crossing areas of knowledge so as to insure a genuine ~ of awareness —J.P.Elder⟩

lib·er·al·iza·tion \,lib(ə)rələˈzāshən, -,līˈz-\ *n* -s **:** the act of liberalizing or the state of being liberalized ⟨the ~ of citizenship requirements —Cecil Hobbs⟩ ⟨college entrance requirements had . . . undergone considerable ~ —Alfred Kähler⟩

lib·er·al·ize \ˈlib(ə)rə,līz\ *vb* -ED/-ING/-S [¹*liberal* + *-ize*] *vt* **1 :** to make liberal or more liberal: as **a :** to imbue with liberal ideas, principles, or attitudes ⟨somewhat *liberalized* politically after he was exposed to a variety of opposing opinions⟩ **b :** to alter in the direction of breaking away from orthodoxy, tradition, or an established pattern ⟨~ the ritual of the church⟩ ⟨~ a college curriculum⟩ **c :** to make less strict or rigorous ⟨~ the immigration laws⟩ **d :** to make larger, freer, fuller, or more comprehensive (as in coverage or scope) ⟨*liberalized* health and hospitalization coverage by insurance companies —*Trends*⟩ ⟨studies to ~ the mind⟩ ⟨an effort to ~ foreign trade —*Time*⟩ **2 :** to free from official control **:** DECONTROL ~ *vi* **:** to become liberal or more liberal in ideas, principles, attitudes, or affiliations

lib·er·al·iz·er \-zə(r)\ *n* -s **:** one that liberalizes

liberal jew *n, usu cap L&J* **:** REFORM JEW

liberal judaism *n, usu cap L&J* **:** REFORM JUDAISM

lib·er·al·ly \ˈlib(ə)rəlē, -li\ *adv* **:** in a liberal manner ⟨gave ~ to charity⟩ ⟨~ endowed with relatives⟩ ⟨~ educated⟩ ⟨a great esplanade ~ provided with seats —F.J.Haskin⟩

lib·er·al·ness *n* -ES **:** LIBERALITY

liberal republican *n, usu cap L&R* **:** a member of a political party of dissident Republicans formed in opposition to the first Grant administration ⟨the Democratic convention accepted . . . the ticket of the *Liberal Republicans* —H.R.Penniman⟩

liberal unionist *n, usu cap L&U* **:** a member of a British political group seceding from the Liberals over opposition to home rule for Ireland and maintaining existence as a separate party during the late 19th century ⟨the Conservatives and *Liberal Unionists* were . . . in power —G.M.Trevelyan⟩

¹**liberate** *adj* [L *liberatus,* past part. of *liberare*] *obs* **:** LIBERATED, FREE

²**lib·er·ate** \ˈlibə,rāt, *usu* -ād.+V\ *vt* -ED/-ING/-S [L *liberatus,* past part. of *liberare,* fr. *liber* free — more at LIBERAL] **1 a :** to give release (as from restraint or bondage) **:** set at liberty **:** let loose **:** FREE ⟨~ a slave⟩ ⟨~ him from economic worry —Will Durant⟩ ⟨*liberated* great, new, and unexpected forces —Drew Middleton⟩; *specif* **:** to free (as a country) from control or domination by a foreign power **b** *in Hinduism & Buddhism* **:** to provide with salvation or grant salvation to **2 :** to free from combination **:** SEPARATE, DISENGAGE ⟨use of the acid sintering material is necessary to ~ the zinc —R.B.Fulton⟩ **3** *slang* **:** to acquire by some legally irregular means **:** STEAL ⟨played in Army bands . . . rarely traveled with fewer than three *liberated* pianos —*Time*⟩ ⟨a . . . barricade was constructed . . . with material *liberated* from a nearby construction site —Thorne Dreyer⟩ **syn** see FREE

lib·er·a·tion \,libəˈrāshən\ *n* -s [ME *liberacion,* fr. L *liberation-, liberatio,* fr. *liberatus* + *-ion-, -io* -ion] **:** the act of liberating or the state of being liberated ⟨eliminated affectation and propaganda from her work . . . results of this ~ give to these poems of her last decade a variety, spontaneity, and depth —R.S.Hillyer⟩ ⟨the slow oxidation . . . with the ~ of appreciable quantities of iodine —W.H.Dowdeswell⟩ ⟨complete ~ of the mind from what is nonmental —Samuel Alexander⟩; *specif* **:** the act of freeing from control or domination by a foreign power or the state of being freed from such power ⟨the struggle for the ~ of France in the early 1940's —*Current Biog.*⟩

lib·er·a·tion·ism \-shə,nizəm\ *n* -s **:** principles or attitudes advocating liberation; *esp* **:** the principles of those opposed to a state or established church and esp. in England advocating disestablishment

lib·er·a·tion·ist \-sh(ə)nəst\ *n* -s **:** one that favors or advocates liberationism

lib·er·a·tive \ˈlibə,rād·iv, -b(ə)rəd·-\ *adj* **:** liberating or tending toward liberation

lib·er·a·tor \ˈlibə,rād·ə(r), -ātə-\ *n* -s [L, fr. *liberatus* + *-or*] **:** one that liberates ⟨came as a ~ against the . . . man, who for a century or two had imposed his military and economic will on these peoples —*Saturday Rev.*⟩ ⟨the aspect not simply of an earthly ~ but of a divine redeemer —Maurice Samuel⟩

lib·er·a·to·ry \ˈlib(ə)rə,tōrē\ *adj* [L *liberatus* (past part. of *liberare* to set free) + E *-ory* — more at LIBERATE] **:** tending, serving, or attempting to liberate

¹**li·be·ria** \līˈbirēə, -bēr-\ *adj, usu cap* [fr. *Liberia,* country in western Africa] **:** of or from Liberia **:** of the kind or style prevalent in Liberia **:** LIBERIAN

²**liberia** \"\ *n* -s *often cap* **:** a dark grayish brown that is very slightly redder and deeper than Rembrandt and slightly less strong and very slightly redder than average chocolate brown

¹**li·be·ri·an** \-rēən\ *adj, usu cap* [*Liberia,* Africa + E *-ian*] **:** LIBERIA

²**liberian** \"\ *n* -s *usu cap* **:** a native or inhabitant of Liberia

liberian rubber *n, usu cap L* **:** a low-grade resinous rubber collected in parts of tropical western Africa from a native fig tree (*Ficus vogelii*)

libers *pl of* LIBER

¹**lib·er·tar·i·an** \,libə(r)ˈterēən, -ta(a)r-, -tār-\ *n* -s [¹*liberty* + *-arian*] **1 :** an advocate of the doctrine of free will — contrasted with *necessitarian* **2 :** one who upholds the principles of liberty; *specif* **:** one who upholds the principles of individual liberty of thought and action ⟨private judgment and constitutional authority . . . authoritarians have left but little scope for the former, ~*s* would always cut down the latter to the smallest proportions —C.H.McIlwain⟩

²**libertarian** \ˈ;=;==\ *adj* **:** of or belonging to a libertarian: as **a :** advocating a theory of free will ⟨a ~ doctrine⟩ **b** (1) **:** advocating or advancing liberty ⟨a ~ ruler⟩ (2) **:** based on or embodying principles of liberty ⟨a ~ rule of law⟩ ⟨the ~ tradition⟩

lib·er·tar·i·an·ism \,=ˈ==ə,nizəm\ *n* -s **:** the theories or practices of a libertarian ⟨a new and extreme ~ arising which . . . goes almost to the length of anarchy in rejecting any state —Norman Thomas⟩

li·ber·ti·cid·al \lə;bərd·ə;sīdᵊl\ *adj* [F *liberticide* + E *-al*] **:** LIBERTICIDE

¹**li·ber·ti·cide** \ləˈbərd·ə,sīd\ *adj* [F, fr. *liberté* liberty + *-i-* + *-cide* killing (fr. *-cide,* n. comb. form) — more at LIBERTY] **:** destroying or tending to destroy liberty

²**liberticide** \"\ *n* -s **1 :** the destruction of liberty **2 :** a destroyer of liberty

lib·er·tin·age \ˈlibə(r),tēnij, -nēj, ,==ˈ==\ *n* -s [¹*libertine* + *-age*] **:** libertinism esp. in religious matters or in conduct ⟨his lifelong untidiness, ribald small talk, obscure ~ —Glenway Wescott⟩

¹**lib·er·tine** \ˈlibə(r),tēn, ,==ˈ=, *chiefly Brit* -tīn\ *n* -s [ME *libertyn,* fr. L *libertinus,* fr. *libertinus,* adj.] **1 a** *obs* **:** a manumitted slave **:** FREEDMAN **b** *usu cap* **:** a member of a first-century Jerusalem synagogue composed of the descendants of Jews who had been carried in captivity to Rome and later freed ⟨members of the synagogue of the *Libertines* disputed with Stephen according to Acts 6: 9 (AV)⟩ **2** *usu cap* **a :** one of a political party in Geneva that until its fall in 1555 championed the ancient liberties of the city against the rule of Calvin and the French refugees — called also *Perrinist* **b :** one of a 16th century pantheistic sect in France and the Netherlands that denied the distinction between good and evil **3 :** a freethinker esp. in religious matters — usu. used disparagingly **4 :** one that is markedly unrestrained esp. by convention or morality; *esp* **:** one leading a dissolute life

²**libertine** \"\ *adj* [L *libertinus* of a freedman, fr. *libertus* freedman (fr. *liber* free) + *-inus* -ine — more at LIBERAL] **:** of, belonging to, or being a libertine: as **a :** freethinking in religion — usu. used disparagingly **b** *archaic* **:** free from restraint **:** UNCONTROLLED **c** (1) **:** showing unusual freedom from conventions or usual or standard patterns of behavior (2) **:** morally loose in conduct **:** LICENTIOUS, PROFLIGATE, DISSOLUTE

lib·er·tin·ism \ˈlibə(r),tē,nizəm, ,==ˈ=-\ *n* -s **:** the quality or state of being libertine or a libertine or the principles or behavior of a libertine: **a :** licentiousness in conduct **:** marked disregard of conventional moral restraints **b :** freethinking in religious matters; *esp* **:** excessive or blameworthy freethinking of this kind **c** *archaic* **:** freedom from restraint **:** LIBERTY

lib·er·ty \ˈlibə(r)d·ē, -)tē, -i\ *n* -ES *often attrib* [ME *liberte,* fr. MF *liberté,* fr. L *libertat-, libertas,* fr. *liber* free + *-tat-, -tas* -ty — more at LIBERAL] **1 :** the quality or state of being free: **a** (1) **:** freedom from usu. external restraint or compulsion **:** the power to do as one pleases (2) **:** a condition of legal nonrestraint of natural powers — compare PRIVILEGE 1e **b :** exemption from subjection to the will of another claiming ownership or services — compare BONDAGE, SERFDOM, SLAVERY **c :** freedom from arbitrary or despotic control **d :** the power of choice **:** freedom from necessity **:** freedom from compulsion or constraint in the act of willing something **e** (1) **:** CIVIL LIBERTY (2) **:** POLITICAL LIBERTY (3) **:** INDIVIDUAL LIBERTY (4) **:** PERSONAL LIBERTY **2 :** a figure representing a personification of liberty (as on a coin) **3 a :** a right or immunity enjoyed by prescription or by grant (as from a sovereign power) **:** PRIVILEGE, EXEMPTION, FRANCHISE **b :** LEAVE, PERMISSION ⟨granted the boy ~ to go out⟩ **c :** a place within which certain immunities are enjoyed or jurisdiction is exercised; *specif* **:** a district of some British cities within which the exclusive privilege or franchise of executing legal process was by royal grant vested in one or more persons exempting them from the jurisdiction of the sheriff **d :** permission to go freely within the limits ⟨given the ~ of the house⟩ ⟨allowed only the ~ of his prison cell⟩ **4 :** action or an action or license that goes beyond a usu. acceptable, proper, or wise limit: as **a** (1) **:** action or an action or privilege in or as if in violation of the laws of strict etiquette or propriety **:** FAMILIARITY ⟨guilty of many *liberties* in his dealings with his superiors⟩ ⟨take undue ~ with a stranger⟩ (2) **:** an undue intimacy **:** an improper familiarity esp. with another's person **b :** an action that goes beyond the limits of prudence ⟨took *liberties* with his health⟩ **c :** action or an action that goes beyond the limits of strict accuracy or conformity (as to a rule) ⟨a certain ~ in his translation⟩ ⟨took *liberties* in the way he played the game⟩ **5 :** a short authorized absence from naval duty usu. for less than 48 hours — compare LEAVE **6 :** a strong blue that is redder and deeper than sèvres and redder and darker than cerulean blue (sense 1b) — called also *regatta* — **at liberty 1 :** FREE ⟨set the prisoners *at liberty*⟩ ⟨*at liberty* to do what one likes⟩ **2 :** at leisure **:** UNOCCUPIED, UNUSED

liberty bond *n, usu cap L* **:** a bond of a Liberty loan

liberty cap *n* **:** a limp close-fitting conical cap resembling that given to a Roman slave upon his manumission and adopted as the cap of French revolutionists and as a symbol of liberty esp. in the U.S. before 1800 — compare BONNET ROUGE

liberty cap as worn by the French revolutionists

liberty freighter *n* **:** LIBERTY SHIP

liberty green *n* **:** a moderate yellow green that is greener and paler than average moss green and yellower and paler than average pea green or apple green (sense 1a)

liberty hall *n* **:** a place where one can do as one likes ⟨his friends were all for the authoritarianism of home life; the last thing they wished was *liberty hall* —Elizabeth Bowen⟩; *esp* **:** a house where a guest is encouraged to act with unusual freedom

liberty horse *n* **:** a circus horse that performs tricks (as wheeling, circling, running in file) in a group and without a rider

liberty loan *n, usu cap 1st L* **:** one of the five U.S. government gold bond issues authorized by acts of Congress between April 24, 1917 and March 3, 1919

lib·er·ty·man \ˈ===,man\ *n, pl* **libertymen** *Brit* **:** a sailor having permission to go ashore

liberty of contract : FREEDOM OF CONTRACT

liberty of speech : FREEDOM OF SPEECH

liberty of the press : FREEDOM OF THE PRESS

liberty pole *n* **:** a tall flagstaff surmounted by a liberty cap, the flag of a republic, or other object regarded as a symbol of liberty

liberty ship *n, usu cap L* **:** a cargo ship of a type built in the U.S. during World War II

liberty tea *n* [so called fr. its having been used as a substitute for tea by the American colonists to evade the British tea tax] **:** WHORLED LOOSESTRIFE

li·be·rum ma·ri·ta·gi·um \ˌlēbə,rüm,marəˈtägē,üm\ *n* [ML] : FRANKMARRIAGE

li·be·rum veto \ˈlibərəm-\ *n* [L *liberum* (neut. of *liber* free) + E *veto* — more at LIBERAL] : a veto exercised by a single member (as of a legislative body) under rules requiring unanimous consent ⟨the anarchic potentialities of the *liberum veto* —C.J. Friedrich⟩

li·beth·en·ite \ləˈbethə,nīt\ *n* -s [G *libethenit*, fr. *Libethen*, Czechoslovakia + G *-it* -ite] : an olive green orthorhombic mineral $Cu_2(PO_4)(OH)$ consisting of a basic copper phosphate and occurring in small prismatic crystals or in globular or reniform masses (hardness 4, sp. gr. 3.6–3.8)

libi·dibi \ˌlibēˈdibē, ˌlēbēˈdēbē\ *or* **libi·divi** \-ˈdivē, -ˈdēvē\ *n* -s [AmerSp *libidivi*, alter. of Sp *dividivi* — more at DIVI-DIVI] : DIVI-DIVI

li·bid·i·nal \ləˈbidᵊnəl\ *adj* [NL *libidin-*, *libido* + E *-al*] : of or belonging to the libido ⟨acting out of ~ or hostile impulses —R.M.Dorn⟩ — **li·bid·i·nal·ly** \-nəlē, -li\ *adv*

li·bid·i·ni·za·tion \-ˌ==əˈzāshən, -ˌīˈz-\ *n* -s : the act of libidinizing or the state of being libidinized : investment with libido ⟨may lead to a ~ of sleep and may develop into a craving for sleep —Emanuel Windholz⟩

li·bid·i·nize \=ˈ==,īz\ *vt* -ED/-ING/-S [NL *libidin-*, *libido* + E *-ize*] : to feel toward or treat as if a source or avenue of sexual gratification : invest with libido ⟨a woman in labor suffers injury to the most highly *libidinized* organs of the body —*Diseases of the Nervous System*⟩

li·bid·i·nous \ləˈbidᵊnəs\ *adj* [ME *lybydynous*, fr. MF *libidineus*, fr. L *libidinosus*, fr. *libidin-*, *libido* + *-osus* -ous] **1** : having or marked by lustful desires : characterized by lewdness : LUSTFUL, LASCIVIOUS ⟨indulged in ~ orgies —Samuel Putnam⟩ **2** [influenced in meaning by NL *libido*] : of or belonging to the libido ⟨the struggles against ~ temptation —*Psychological Abstracts*⟩ ⟨identification and ~ ties between individuals, the latter being reduced to forms of sexual love —Abram Kardiner⟩ — **li·bid·i·nous·ly** *adv* — **li·bid·i·nous·ness** *n* -ES

li·bi·do \ləˈbē(,)dō *also* ÷ˈlibə,dō *or* ˈlibē,dō *or* ləˈbī(,)dō\ *n* -s [NL, fr. L, desire, lust, fr. *libēre* to please — more at LOVE] **1 a** : emotional or psychic energy that in psychoanalytic theory is derived from primitive biological urges and that is usu. goal-directed ⟨described the relation of person to person with the aid of the concept of ~, the grossest manifestation of which is sexual love —Abram Kardiner⟩ **b** : desire for sexual outlet or gratification ⟨may be prompted to take a second wife not by an excessive ~ —R.H.Loure⟩ **c** : frequency of sexual outlet ⟨during the nonbreeding season in the young ram there occurs a similar marked decline in ~ —*Nature*⟩ ⟨therapy . . . to stimulate ~ in bulls during the season of the year when sexual activity is depressed —*Veterinary Bull.*⟩ **2** : lustful desire or striving ⟨the will . . . has a strong ~ of its own —L.J.A. Mercier⟩

lib–lab \ˈlib,lab\ *n* -s *usu cap both Ls* [*Liberal-Labor*] **1** : a member of the British Liberal party in the late 19th century belonging to or supporting the trade-union movement **2** : a political liberal associated with policies favorable to organized labor

libo·ce·drus \ˌlībəˈsēdrəs, ˌlib-\ *n, cap* [NL, fr. Gk *liboi* tears (fr. *leibein* to pour) + L *cedrus* cedar; fr. the resinous nature of the tree — more at LIBATION, CEDAR] : a genus of trees (family Pinaceae) having leaves that resemble those of the sequoia — see INCENSE CEDAR

libr *abbr* librarian

li·bra *in senses 1 & 2* ˈlībrə *or* ˈlēb-, *in sense 3* ˈlēbrə *or* -ēvrə\ *n* [ME, fr. L, lit., balance, unit of weight] **1** -s *usu cap* : the 7th sign of the zodiac — see SIGN table, ZODIAC illustration **2** *pl* **li·brae** \ˈlī(,)brē, ˈlē,brī\ [L] : an ancient Roman unit of weight equal to 327.45 grams or 0.7221 pound avoirdupois **3** -s [Sp & Pg, fr. L] **a** : any of various Spanish or Portuguese units of weight varying around 460 grams or 1.01 pounds avoirdupois **b** : the Colombian unit equal to 500 grams **c** : the Venezuelan unit equal to 1 kilogram **d** : the basic monetary unit of Peru from 1898 to 1930; *also* : a gold coin worth one libra

li·brar·i·an \līˈbrerēən, -bra(a)r-, -brār-\ *n* -s [*library* + *-an*] **1 a** : a specialist in the care or management of a library **b** : one whose vocation is working with library books (as by cataloging) **2** : one whose special task is the management of any body of literature (as the musical scores for an orchestra)

li·brar·i·an·ship \-,ship\ *n* : the office or duties of a librarian

li·brary \ˈlī,brerē, -b(r)ərē, -,brē, -ri *also* ÷-,ber- *sometimes* -,bər·ē *or* -,bər·i\ *n* -ES *often attrib* [ME *librarie*, fr. ML *librarium & libraria*, fr. neut. & fem. respectively of L *librarius* of books, fr. *libr-*, *liber* book + *-arius* -ary — more at LEAF] **1 a** : a room, a section or series of sections of a building, or a building itself given over to books, manuscripts, musical scores, or other literary and sometimes artistic materials (as paintings or musical recordings) usu. kept in some convenient order for use but not for sale ⟨the house contained a ~ besides the living, dining, and kitchen areas⟩ ⟨a college ~⟩ — see PUBLIC LIBRARY **b** (1) : a collection of books, manuscripts, or other literary materials kept (as in a library) for study or reading or a collection of paintings, musical scores, musical recordings, photographs, maps, or films kept for convenient use, study, or enjoyment ⟨a ~ of early American travel books⟩ ⟨a ~ of Bach recordings⟩ ⟨a private ~ of manuscript plays⟩ (2) : an institution for the custody or administration of such a collection ⟨the *Library* of Congress⟩ (3) : a collection suggesting a library (as a reference library) ⟨the most complete ~ of illustrations available in book form —*advt*⟩ ⟨a ~ of color chips —*Amer. Fabrics*⟩ **c** : RENTAL LIBRARY **d** (1) : CANON 3c ⟨the goal of going through the entire Shakespeare ~ —Lewis Funke⟩ (2) : a series of books of some similarity issued by a publisher ⟨a Hawthorne ~⟩ (3) : a series of reference materials bearing on the same matter (as programs, routines, and subroutines in digital computing) **e** : MORGUE 2a **f** : something suggesting a library esp. in being a receptacle of wide or miscellaneous information ⟨men and women . . . who are oral *libraries* for neighborhood history and gossip —*Amer. Guide Series: Tenn.*⟩ **2** *Brit* : a business established to conduct transactions for others : AGENCY; *esp* : a theater ticket agency

library binder *n* : one that binds and rebinds books in durable cloth for frequent use

library binding *n* : an esp. strong durable cloth bookbinding suitable for use by a circulating library; *also* : the production of books so bound — compare EDITION BINDING

library buckram *n* : a fabric used for library bindings

library corner *n* : a corner of a book-cover turn-in in which the surplus cloth is folded under for greater strength instead of being cut away as in ordinary binding

library edition *n* : a set of books uniform in size and format usu. of the works of one author

library of congress classification *n, usu cap L&1st C* : a library classification using the letters of the alphabet plus numbers for its notation — compare DECIMAL CLASSIFICATION, EXPANSIVE CLASSIFICATION

library paste *n* : a thick white smooth adhesive made from starch and used esp. on paper and paperboard

library school *n* : a school specializing in the teaching of library science

library science *n* : the study or the principles and practices of library care and administration or of any division of it (as bibliography or reference work)

library steps *n pl* : a portable set of often folding steps used to gain access to the high shelves of a library

library steps

library van *n* : BOOKMOBILE

¹li·brate \ˈlī,brāt, -,brət\ *n* -s [ML *librata*, fr. ML *libra* English pound (fr. L, balance, libra) + L *-ata* (fem. of *-atus* -ate)] : land having a value of a pound a year

²li·brate \-,brāt\ *vb* -ED/-ING/-S [L *libratus*, past part. of *librare*, fr. *libra* balance] *vi* **1** : to vibrate as a balance does before resting in equilibrium **2** : to stay poised ~ *vt, archaic* : to cause to librate : BALANCE, WEIGH

li·bra·tion \līˈbrāshən\ *n* -s [L *libration-*, *libratio*, fr. *libratus* + *-ion-*, *-io* -ion] **1** : the action or state of librating **2** *obs* : the act or process of weighing **3** : an oscillation in the apparent aspect of a secondary body (as a planet or a satellite) as seen from the primary object around which it revolves caused by the inclination of its axis of rotation, variations in its orbital speed, real irregularities in its rotation, or changes in the observer's position on the primary body — see LIBRATION OF THE MOON

libration of the moon : the combination of four libration effects that causes parts of the side of the moon turned to the earth to be alternately visible and invisible so that as much as 59 percent of the moon's entire surface can be observed from the earth

li·bra·to·ry \ˈlībrə,tōrē\ *adj* : moving like a balance as it tends to an equipoise : BALANCING

li·bret·tist \ləˈbred·əst, -etəst\ *n* -s [F or It; F *librettiste*, fr. It *librettista*, fr. *libretto* + *-ista* -ist] : the writer of a libretto

li·bret·to \ləˈbred·(,)ō, -e(,)t\ *n, pl* **libret·tos** \-ōz\ *or* **libret·ti** \-ē\ [It, dim. of *libro* book, fr. L *libr-*, *liber* — more at LEAF] **1** : the text of a work (as an opera) for the musical theater **2** : the book containing a libretto

li·bre·ville \ˈlēbrə,vēl, -vil, ˌ==ˈ=\ *adj, usu cap* [fr. *Libreville*, Gabon] : of or from Libreville, the capital of Gabon : of the kind or style prevalent in Libreville

libri *pl of* LIBER

libri·form \ˈlībrə,fȯrm, ˈlib-\ *adj* [ISV *libri-* (fr. L *libr-*, *liber* inner bark of a tree, pith of papyrus, book) + *-form* — more at LEAF] : resembling phloem fibers

libs *pres 3d sing of* LIB

li·bur·ni·an \(ˈ)līˈbərnēən\ *adj, usu cap* [*Liburnia*, ancient district of Illyria (fr. L) + E *-an*] : of or belonging to Liburnia, an ancient country on the northeast coast of the Adriatic

liburnian galley *n, usu cap L* : a fast light large-sailed sharp-prowed galley invented by the Liburnian pirates

lib·ya \ˈlibēə\ *adj, usu cap* [fr. *Libya*, country in northern Africa] : of or from Libya : of the kind or style prevalent in Libya : LIBYAN

¹lib·y·an \-ēən\ *adj, usu cap* [*Libya*, ancient territory variously conceived in northern Africa (fr. L *Libye*, *Libya*, fr. Gk *Libyē*) + E *-an*] **1** : of, relating to, or characteristic of ancient Libya **2** : of, relating to, or characteristic of the ancient Libyans **3** [*Libya*, country in northern Africa + E *-an*] : of, relating to, or characteristic of modern Libya or its people

²libyan \"\ *n* -s *usu cap* **1 a** : a member of any of the peoples indigenous in historical ancient times to the region immediately west of Egypt **b** : a member of any of the peoples that in historical ancient times were indigenous to No. Africa west from Egypt to the Atlantic **2** *in some ethnological classifications* : a member of a branch of the Mediterranean subrace comprising some or all of the Libyans and those peoples (as the Berbers) believed to be descended from them without substantial mixture with other stocks and also comprising the people believed to have been the principal racial stock of prehistoric Egypt and perhaps of adjoining parts of prehistoric northeastern Africa **3** : a Berber language of ancient No. Africa **4** : a native or inhabitant of modern Libya

libyan alphabet *n, usu cap L* : an alphabet of consonantal characters of simple geometric form of uncertain origin but perhaps derived in part from the Punic or neo-Punic alphabet in which several hundred inscriptions in the Libyan language are known from the late pre-Christian period and the first several centuries of the Christian era principally from what are now Tunisia and eastern Algeria — called also *Numidian alphabet*; see TIFINAGH

libyan cat *n, usu cap L* : KAFFIR CAT

libyco–berber \ˌlibə(,)kō+\ *n, adj, usu cap L&B* [*Libyco-* (fr. L *Libycus* of Libya, fr. Gk *Libykos*, fr. *Libyē* Libya) + *Berber*] : BERBER 2

libyo- *comb form, usu cap* [*Libya*] : Libyan and ⟨*Libyo*-Phoenician⟩ ⟨*Libyo*-Teutonic⟩

lib·y·the·idae \ˌlibəˈthēə,dē\ *n pl, cap* [NL, fr. *Libythea*, type genus (perh. fr. Gk *Libys* Libyan + *thea* appearance, aspect) + *-idae*] : a small family comprising the snout butterflies and often considered a subfamily of Nymphalidae

lic *abbr* **1** license; licensed **2** licentiate

li·ca·nia \ləˈkānēə, līˈ-\ *n, cap* [NL, modif. (with some letter rearrangement) of Galibi *caligni* (tree of the genus *Licania*)] : a large genus of tropical American trees (family Rosaceae) having alternate simple leaves and small panicled flowers

li·can·ic acid \ləˈ|kanik-, (ˈ)lī|\ *n* [NL *Licania* + E *-ic*] : a crystalline unsaturated keto acid $C_4H_9(CH{=}CH)_3(CH_2)_4COCH_2CH_2COOH$ that in the form of the glyceride is the chief component of oiticica oil and that may be hydrogenated to stearic acid

li·car·e·ol \ləˈka(a)rē,ōl, līˈ-, -,ōl\ *n* -s [ISV *licare-* (fr. NL *Licaria*, genus of trees of the family Lauraceae) + *-ol*] : levorotatory linalool

lice *pl of* LOUSE

li·cens·able \ˈlīsᵊnsəbəl\ *adj* : capable of being licensed or of receiving a license ⟨licenses to import most ~ commodities from hard-currency areas —*Foreign Commerce Weekly*⟩

¹li·cense *or* **li·cence** \ˈlīsᵊn(t)s\ *n* -s *see sense 5* [ME *licence*, fr. MF, fr. L *licentia*, fr. *licent-*, *licens* (pres. part. of *licēre* to be permitted, be for sale) + *-ia* -y; akin to Latvian *līkt* to come to terms] **1** : permission to act ⟨go from hence without their ~ —Daniel Defoe⟩ **2 a** : unusual freedom of action permitted because of extenuating circumstances or special prerogatives ⟨in the decoration the Chinese silversmiths had been allowed the utmost ~ —Osbert Lancaster⟩ ⟨reason and common sense were given full ~ to take no notice of pedants —Stuart Hampshire⟩ ⟨had a stranger's ~ to go everywhere —Nadine Gordimer⟩ **b** (1) : excessive freedom : the abuse of liberties granted ⟨a wave of municipal reform . . . for the correction of what was regarded as ~ —Havelock Ellis⟩ ⟨Caesar's legions . . . were enjoying their victory in the ~ which is miscalled liberty —J.A.Froude⟩ ⟨freedom of the press also carries the grave responsibility that it not be turned into ~ —*Time*⟩ (2) : abusive disregard for rules of personal conduct : LICENTIOUSNESS ⟨like most women of that character and those circumstances her ~ was peculiarly unlimited —Tennessee Williams⟩ ⟨prenuptial chastity in one tribe and adolescent ~ in another —Ruth Benedict⟩ **3 a** (1) : a right or permission granted in accordance with law by a competent authority to engage in some business or occupation, to do some act, or to engage in some transaction which but for such license would be unlawful ⟨a ~ to sell liquor⟩ ⟨a marriage ~⟩ ⟨a ~ to practice medicine⟩ (2) : a document evidencing a license granted **b** : authority or permission of one having no possessory rights in land to do something on that land which would otherwise be unlawful or a trespass — distinguished from *lease* **c** : the grant by a patent holder to another of any of the rights embodied in the patent short of an assignment of a fractional interest therein and short of assigning all the rights protected by the patent **d** : the grant of some but not all of the rights embraced in a copyright **e** *Canad* : a free miner's certificate **4** : a deviation from strict fact, form, or rule utilized by an artist or writer on the assumption that it will be permitted for the sake of the advantage or effect gained ⟨permitting myself a certain ~ of treatment, the better to round out the picture —S.H.Adams⟩ ⟨has little truck with those who have taken literary ~ —D.L.Horner⟩ **5** *pl* **license** *chiefly Midland* **a** : formal permission from local authorities **b** : a document embodying such permission ⟨get a pair o' *license* fer to marry —J.W.Riley⟩

²license *also* **licence** \"\ *vt* -ED/-ING/-S [ME *licencen*, fr. *licence*, n.] **1 a** : to grant or issue a license to (someone) usu. after special qualifications have been met ⟨was *licensed* and later ordained to the ministry —J.C.Brauer⟩ **b** : to permit or authorize esp. by formal license ⟨patented processes were freely *licensed* in a general effort to do everything and anything to help win the war —Marquis James⟩ **2 a** : to accord permission or consent to : ALLOW ⟨at a wedding everybody seemed *licensed* to kiss everyone else —Irwin Shaw⟩ ⟨a popular novelist may be *licensed* to draw on his imagination —A.T. Quiller-Couch⟩ ⟨an able man, *licensed* by the times to do pretty much as he pleased —J.H.Hanford⟩ **b** [MF *licencier*, fr. *licence*, n.] *archaic* : to give permission for departure to : DISMISS ⟨thus *licensed*, the chief . . . left the presence chamber —Sir Walter Scott⟩ **syn** see AUTHORIZE

license bond *n* : a surety bond required by law as a condition precedent to the pursuit of a specified business or profession

li·censed *also* **li·cenced** \-ᵊn(t)st\ *adj* **1** : having a license : permitted or authorized by license ⟨a ~ bureau of judges —Harry Lewis⟩ ⟨a ~ preacher⟩; *specif* : having a liquor license ⟨a ~ hotel⟩ **2** : permitted an unusual freedom : PRIVILEGED ⟨status of a sort of ~ amateur jester —Harvey Graham⟩

licensed premises *n pl but sing or pl in constr, Brit* : an establishment in which alcoholic beverages and tobacco are permitted to be retailed and consumed

li·cens·ee \ˌlīsᵊnˈsē\ *n* -s : a licensed person: as **a** : a person who is on the property of another with the consent of its possessor whether by permission or invitation — compare INVITEE, TRESPASSER **b** : a person who is on the property of another with the consent of the possessor but solely for purposes in which the possessor has no business or pecuniary interest — compare GUEST 2b **c** : a person (as a fireman in the course of his duty) who is on the property of another by authority of law **d** : a person having a liquor license

li·cense·less \-ᵊn(t)sləs\ *adj* : having no license

license plate *or* **license tag** *n* : a plate or tag of metal, leather, or some other durable material attesting that a license has been secured and usu. bearing a registration number

li·cens·er \ˈlīsᵊnsə(r)\ *n* -s : one that licenses

li·cen·sor \ˈlīsᵊnsə(r); ˌ==ˈsȯ(ə)r, -ō(ə)\ *n* -s : one that grants a license

li·cen·sure \ˈlīsᵊnshər, -,shu̇(ə)r\ *n* -s [²*license* + *-ure*] **1** : the granting of licenses esp. to practice a profession **2** : the system of granting licenses (as for professional practice) in accordance with established standards

¹li·cen·ti·ate \līˈsenchēət, -ē,āt, *esp in sense 1b* līˈs-\ *n* -s [ML *licentiatus*, fr. past part. of *licentiare* to allow, fr. L *licentia* license — more at LICENSE] **1 a** : one who has a license to practice a profession; *esp* : one who has a license granted by a university or other degree-conferring body ⟨with a year and a half off to become a ~ in canon law —*Time*⟩ **b** : an academic degree ranking below that of a doctor given by some European institutions of higher education ⟨as a part of his work toward the ~ . . . prepared a critical edition of two late 14th century commentaries —T.A.Kirby⟩ **2** : one licensed to preach in some churches (as the Presbyterian) but not yet installed as a pastor

²licentiate *adj* [ML *licentiatus*, past part.] **1** *obs* **a** : given permission : ALLOWED **b** : licensed to preach **2** *obs* : taking unusual liberties : DISORDERLY, UNGOVERNED ⟨would count me the most ~ loose strayer under heaven —Thomas Nash⟩

³li·cen·ti·ate \-ē,āt\ *vt* -ED/-ING/-S [ML *licentiatus*, past part.] : to give liberty, permission, or scope to ⟨were *licentiated* to go a-begging —Isaac D'Israeli⟩

li·cen·ti·ate·ship \-ēət,ship\ *n* : the quality or state of a licentiate

li·cen·ti·a·tion \(,)lī,senchēˈāshən\ *n* -s : the act of licensing esp. to practice medicine

li·cen·tious \(ˈ)līˈsenchəs\ *adj* [L *licentiosus*, fr. *licentia* + *-osus* -ous] **1** : marked by the absence of legal or moral restraints : hostile or offensive to accepted standards of conduct ⟨the ~ practice . . . of making depredations upon foreign nations —Thomas Hutchinson⟩ ⟨the lying and ~ character of our newspapers —Thomas Jefferson⟩ **2** : marked by lewdness : LASCIVIOUS, UNCHASTE ⟨ribaldry . . . too well suited to the taste of a profane and ~ pit —T.B.Macaulay⟩ ⟨a more depraved ~ lot of rascals don't exist —C.B.Nordhoff & J.N. Hall⟩ **3** : marked by neglect of or disregard for strict rules of correctness ⟨verse . . . somewhat ~ in number of syllables —Henry Hallam⟩ ⟨English speech was never more syntactically ~ —Havelock Ellis⟩ — **li·cen·tious·ly** *adv*

li·cen·tious·ness *n* -ES : the quality or state of being licentious ⟨the utmost ~ of the press and of the stage —T.B.Macaulay⟩

lich \ˈlich\ *n* -s [ME *lich*, *lik* body, corpse, fr. OE *līc* — more at LIKE] *dial Brit* : a dead body : CORPSE — used chiefly in combination ⟨*lich*-house⟩

lich bird *n* : a nightjar (*Caprimulgus europaeus*)

lichee *var of* LITCHI

¹li·chen \ˈlīkən *sometimes chiefly Brit* ˈlichən\ *n* -s [L, fr. Gk *leichēn*, *lichēn*, prob. fr. *leichein* to lick — more at LICK] **1** : any of numerous complex thallophytic plants that constitute the group Lichenes, that are made up of an alga and a fungus growing in symbiotic association on various solid surfaces (as rocks or the bark of trees), that consist of a branching thallus which is not differentiated into stem and leaves but which may be crustose, fruticose, or foliaceous and which contains algal gonidia embedded in a meshwork of fungal hyphae, and that include organisms important in the weathering and breakdown of rocks and some that are sources of foods or dyes — see ASCOLICHENES, BASIDIOLICHENES; ICELAND MOSS, REINDEER MOSS; ARCHIL, LITMUS **2** : any of several skin diseases characterized by the eruption of flat papules; *esp* : LICHEN PLANUS

²lichen \"\ *vt* -ED/-ING/-S : to cover over with or as if with lichens ⟨they lay till all their bones were . . . ~*ed* into color with the crags —Alfred Tennyson⟩ ⟨look down upon the ~*ed* walls of this lovely building —R.M.Lockley⟩ ⟨~*ed* history, an immeasurably vast continuity —R.L.Mittenbuhler⟩

li·che·na·les \ˌlīkəˈnā(,)lēz\ *n pl, cap* [NL, fr. L *lichen* + NL *-ales*] *in some esp former classifications* : an order of fungi comprising the lichens

li·che·nes \līˈkē(,)nēz\ *n pl, cap* [NL, fr. pl. of L *lichen*] : a major category of thallophytes comprising the lichens now usu. treated as an independent group more or less coordinate with Algae and Fungi — compare LICHENALES

lichen green *n* : a light greenish gray that is yellower, lighter, and stronger than French gray and bluer than ash gray

li·chen·i·fi·ca·tion \lī,kenəfəˈkāshən ,līkən-\ *n* [ISV ¹*lichen* + *-i-* + *-fication*] : the process by which skin becomes hardened and leathery or lichenoid usu. as a result of chronic irritation; *also* : a patch of skin so modified

li·chen·i·fied \līˈkenə,fīd, ˈlīkən-\ *adj* [¹*lichen* + *-ify* + *-ed*] : HARDENED, LEATHERY ⟨~ eczema⟩

li·chen·in \ˈlīkənən\ *n* -s [¹*lichen* + *-in*] : a gelatinous polysaccharide $(C_6H_{10}O_5)_n$ composed of glucose units and found esp. in several species of moss and lichen and in cereal grains and bulbs

lichen is·lan·di·cus \ˌ==,īˈslandəkəs\ *n* [NL, lit., Icelandic lichen] : ICELAND MOSS

li·chen·ism \ˈlīkə,nizəm\ *n* -s : symbiosis between certain algae and fungi that produces lichens

li·chen·ist \-nəst\ *n* -s : LICHENOLOGIST

li·chen·oid \-,nȯid\ *adj* : resembling lichen ⟨~ dermatitis⟩

li·chen·o·log·ic \ˌlīkənōˈläjik\ *or* **li·chen·o·log·i·cal** \-jəkəl\ *adj* : of or relating to lichenology

li·chen·ol·o·gist \ˌlīkəˈnäləjəst\ *n* -s : a specialist in lichenology

li·chen·ol·o·gy \-jē\ *n* -ES [ISV ¹*lichen* + *-o-* + *-logy*] : the study of lichens

li·chen·oph·a·gous \ˌlīkəˈnäfəgəs\ *adj* [¹*lichen-* + *-o-* + *-phagous*] : feeding on lichens

li·chen·op·o·ra \ˌlīkəˈnäpərə\ *n, cap* [NL, fr. ¹*lichen* + *-o-* + *-pora*] : a genus of bryozoans (class Gymnolaemata) usu. forming small laminate colonies on shells

li·chen·ous \ˈlīkənəs\ *also* **li·chen·ose** \-,nōs\ *adj* [¹*lichen* + *-ous* or *-ose*] **1 a** : of, relating to, or resembling lichens **b** : abounding in or covered with lichens ⟨a stone seat stood at one end, a fountain at the other, both ~ and crumbling —Frederic Prokosch⟩ **2** : of or relating to lichen : LICHENOID

lichen pla·nus \ˌ==ˈplānəs, -lān-\ *n* [NL, lit., flat lichen] : a skin disease characterized by an eruption of wide flat papules covered by a horny glazed film, marked by intense itching, and often accompanied by lesions on the oral mucosa

lichens *pl of* LICHEN

li·cheny \ˈlīkənē\ *adj* [¹*lichen* + *-y*] : LICHENOUS 1 ⟨the bald patch . . . gleamed like a brown pebble through his ~ hair —Gerald Durrell⟩

lich fowl *n* : a nightjar (*Caprimulgus europaeus*)

lich–gate *var of* LYCH-GATE

lich–house \ˈ=,=\ *n* [ME *lich hus*, fr. *lich* corpse + *hus*, *hous* house — more at LICH, HOUSE] : MORTUARY

¹lichi *var of* LITCHI

²lichi *var of* LECHWE
lich owl *n, Brit* **:** BARN OWL
lich stone *n* **:** a stone on which to rest a coffin at the lych-gate
licht \ˈlikt\ *Scot var of* LIGHT
lich·ten·berg figure \ˈliktən,bərg-\ *n, cap L* [after Georg Christoph *Lichtenberg* †1799 Ger. physicist and writer] **:** a pattern of branching lines formed by fine powder (as of sulfur) dusted over an insulating surface across which an electric-leakage discharge has recently taken place
lich·tit \ˈliktət\ *Scot var of* LIGHTED
licht·ly \-ktli\ *Scot var of* LIGHTLY
licht·some \-ktsəm\ *Scot var of* LIGHTSOME
lic·it \ˈlisət, *usu* -əd·+V\ *adj* [MF *licite*, fr. L *licitus*, fr. past part. of *licēre* to be permitted — more at LICENSE] **:** not forbidden by law **:** ALLOWABLE, PERMITTED **syn** see LAWFUL
lic·i·ta·tion \,lisəˈtāshən\ *n* -s [L *licitation-, licitatio*, fr. *licitatus* (past part. of *licitari* to bid a price, freq. of *licēre* to be for sale) + *-ion-, -io* -ion — more at LICENSE] **1 :** the act of offering for sale or bidding at an auction **2 :** ⁷CANT 2
lic·it·ly *adv* **:** in a licit manner **:** LEGALLY
¹lick \ˈlik\ *vb* -ED/-ING/-S [ME *licken*, fr. OE *liccian*; akin to OS *likkon* to lick, OHG *leckōn*, ON *sleikja*, L *lingere*, Gk *leichein* to lick, Skt *leḍhi, reḍhi* he licks] *vt* **1 a** (1) **:** to draw or pass the tongue over ⟨kept trying to ~ his swollen lips with a dry tongue —Ray Duncan⟩ ⟨a few of the reporters ~*ed* their pencils nervously —*Time*⟩ ⟨~ a postage stamp⟩ (2) **:** to flicker or play over like a tongue **:** LAP ⟨a brick wall perpetually ~*ed* by smoke —Andrew Buchanan⟩ ⟨walked down to the sea where it ~*ed* the beach —Richard Sale⟩ **b :** to take into the mouth with or as if with the tongue **:** lap up ⟨watched the cat ~ the flecks of cream from the rim of the bowl⟩ ⟨sauntered down the street ~*ing* ice-cream cones⟩ **2 a :** to strike repeatedly esp. as a punishment **:** BEAT, THRASH ⟨taken her to her pa and said if he didn't ~ her, they would —Helen Eustis⟩ **b :** DEFEAT, OVERCOME **:** get the better of ⟨if you ~ me, you take what money I have —William Faulkner⟩ ⟨when its road-building program is completed, it will ~ one of its major problems —Mary R. Johnson⟩ ⟨a man's not ~*ed* when he's got a wife like this —Caroline Slade⟩ ⟨we've got the outfit to ~ the wilderness —S.H.Adams⟩ **3 :** to give a finished appearance to ⟨carefully leveled, ~*ed*, snipped artificial lawns —John Muir †1914⟩ ~ *vi* **1 :** to lap with the tongue or in the manner of a tongue ⟨the surf ~*ed* at the seawall —Isa Glenn⟩ **2 :** to dart like a tongue ⟨the pain ~*ed* over . . . in short little spasms —Gordon Merrick⟩ ⟨a huge puff of smoke-fringed flame filled the doorway, ~*ing* outward toward me —Ralph Ellison⟩ **3 :** to move at top speed ⟨rattled down the stony track as hard as he could ~ —T.A.Browne⟩ **syn** see CONQUER — **lick into shape :** to give proper form to **:** train or drill into orderly form ⟨a civilian can be *licked into shape* as a soldier by the manual of arms —Dixon Wecter⟩ — **lick one's chops :** to anticipate with relish ⟨a banker *licks his chops* over the increase in the earnings on each dollar —George Shea⟩ — **lick one's wounds :** to tend one's injuries **:** recover from defeat ⟨those gray silent ships which carried the war to the enemy . . . while the fleet *licked its wounds* —E.L.Beach⟩
²lick \"\ *n* -s **1 a** (1) **:** an act or instance of licking ⟨a quick ~ at the frosting bowl⟩ (2) **:** an amount held on the tongue ⟨the cat took a ~ of milk⟩ **b** (1) **:** a quick often careless application of something as if by a stroke of the tongue **:** a small amount of something seemingly so applied **:** the least bit **:** ⁴DAB 2 ⟨ready, down to the last ~ of paint —Mollie Panter-Downes⟩ ⟨a ~ of rain beat against the window —E.L. Thomas⟩ ⟨how long have you known I can't read a ~ —James Street⟩ (2) **:** a trace of some characteristic or quality ⟨has a faint ~ of the charlatan about him⟩ **c :** something that darts like a tongue ⟨the campfire played its little ~*s* of light against a tree trunk —A.B.Guthrie⟩ **2 a** (1) **:** a sharp hit **:** BLOW ⟨hit the board a hard ~ with the blunt end of an ax —Bruce Siberts⟩ (2) *dial Brit* **:** WHIPPING, BEATING — usu. used in pl. ⟨he was ready to take his ~*s* like a man⟩ **b :** an effective effort **:** CRACK 11, THRUST — usu. used in pl. ⟨treasure was often found in the last few ~*s* with the pick and shovel —W.P.Webb⟩ ⟨give the cameraman a chance to put in some heavy artistic ~*s* —John McCarten⟩ **c :** the smallest effort or act esp. of work **:** STROKE ⟨ain't had a ~ of work since November —Edna Ferber⟩ ⟨the truth is that neither . . . has ever done a ~ —Hamilton Basso⟩ **3 a** (1) **:** a place where salt is found on the surface of the earth and wild animals resort to lick it up (2) **:** a salt spring or a salt brook **b :** an artificial often medicated saline preparation given to sheep and cattle to lick **4** *West* **:** SYRUP, MOLASSES ⟨piles flapjacks before me up to my chin, with plenty of butter and ~ —F.B.Gipson⟩ **5** *in swing music* **:** a musical figure; *specif* **:** an interpolated and usu. improvised figure or flourish **6 :** a strand of hair usu. fixed neatly in place ⟨slicking his dark hair . . . in immaculate shiny ~*s* —John Phillips⟩ — **lick and a promise :** a perfunctory performance of a task ⟨gives his job little more than a *lick and a promise* —Jack Iams⟩ ⟨breakfast over, I gave the house a *lick and a promise* —Kathleen Thomas⟩
lick·er \ˈlikə(r)\ *n* -s [ME *lykkare*, fr. *lykken, licken* to lick + *-are* -er] **:** one that licks
licker-in \ˌlikəˈ(r)in\ *n* -s **:** a drum or cylinder in a carding machine that takes the lap from the feed rollers
lick·er·ish \ˈlik(ə)rish, -rēsh\ *adj* [alter. (influenced by *-ish*) of *lickerous*] **1 a :** fond of good food **:** eager to taste or enjoy ⟨he drank . . . rather by way of good fellowship than from a ~ appetite —W.E.Heitland⟩ **b :** having a craving **:** DESIROUS ⟨their own ~ affection to gold —Jonathan Swift⟩ **2** *obs* **:** tempting to the appetite **:** DAINTY ⟨and wouldst thou seek again to trap me here with ~ baits —John Milton⟩ **3 :** having or suggesting lustful desires **:** LECHEROUS ⟨they responded with . . . frank, ~ stares —Shelby Foote⟩ — **lick·er·ish·ly** *adv* — **lick·er·ish·ness** *n* -ES
lickerous *adj* [ME *likerous*, fr. (assumed) ONF, var of OF *lechereus* — more at LECHEROUS] *obs* **:** LICKERISH
lickety-split \ˌlikədˈē;ˈ\ *also* **lickety-brindle** \-ˈ;ᵊ\ *or* **lickety-cut** \-ˈ;ˈ\ *adv* [prob. irreg. fr. ¹*lick* + *split* or *brindle* or *cut*] **:** with a rush **:** RAPIDLY ⟨you climb astride a little trolley and rattle out of the place *lickety-split* —Claudia Cassidy⟩
¹licking *n* -s [ME, fr. gerund of *licken* to lick — more at LICK] **1 :** the act of one that licks (as by lapping with the tongue) **2 a :** a sound thrashing **:** a beating at the hands of another **:** DRUBBING ⟨when I was cornered and fought, even a ~ wasn't a hundredth as bad as I thought it would be —John Reed⟩ **b :** a severe setback **:** DEFEAT ⟨American industries competing with import industries took their ~ —A.H.Hansen⟩ ⟨in the long run . . . apathetic voters would take the ~ —*Time*⟩ **3 :** the act or process of taking the lap from the feed roller in a carding machine by the licker-in
²licking *adv* [fr. pres. part. of *lick* (to hit)] *dial* **:** EXCEEDINGLY ⟨a ~ big frame of light wood —Eden Phillpotts⟩ ⟨eaten with a spoon . . . I only remember that it was — and is — ~ good —Della Lutes⟩
licking disease *or* **licking sickness** *n* **:** pica of cattle
licking stone *n* **:** a lick in brick form
lick-log \ˈ;ˌ\ *n* -s **:** a felled tree in which troughs are cut and filled with salt for cattle
lickpenny \ˈ;ˌ;\ *n* [ME *lickpeny*, fr. *licken* to lick + *peny* penny] *archaic* **:** something that uses up money ⟨law is a ~ —Sir Walter Scott⟩

lick-log

lick·some \ˈliksəm\ *dial Eng var of* LIKESOME
lick-spigot *n* [¹*lick*] **1** *obs* **:** TAPSTER **2** *obs* **:** LICKSPITTLE
lickspit \ˈ;ˌ\ *n* [¹*lick* + *spit* (spittle)] **:** LICKSPITTLE **syn** see PARASITE
¹lickspittle \ˈ;ˌ;\ *n* [¹*lick* + *spittle*] **:** an abject parasite or toady ⟨they were . . . hired hands and ~*s* —R.P.Warren⟩ **syn** see PARASITE
²lickspittle \"\ *vb* -ED/-ING/-S *vt* **:** to act servilely toward **:** FLATTER, TOADY ⟨*lickspittled* everyone in the hope of advancement⟩ ~ *vi* **:** to flatter or toady to someone in a servile manner ⟨hated to see anyone ~⟩
lic·noph·o·ra \likˈnäfərə\ *n, cap* [NL, fr. Gk *liknon* winnowing fan + NL *-phora*] **:** a genus of peritrichous ciliate protozoans that have a posterior attaching disk and a very large fanlike anterior membranellar zone extending to the cytopharynx and are commensal
lic·o·rice *also* **li·quo·rice** \÷ˈlik(ə)rish, ÷ -rēsh, ÷ -rəs\ *n* -s [ME *licoris, licorice*, fr. OF *licorece, licorice*, fr. LL *liquiritia*, alter. of L *glycyrrhiza*, fr. Gk *glykyrrhiza*, fr. *glykys* sweet + *rhiza* root — more at DULCET, WORT] **1 a** *or* **licorice root :** a dried root of gummy texture and sweet rather astringent flavor that is the source of extracts used to mask unpleasant flavors (as of drugs) or to impart pleasing flavors (as to confections or tobacco) **b :** an extract of licorice commonly prepared in the form of a gummy or rubbery paste **2 a** (1) **:** a tall perennial leguminous herb (*Glycyrrhiza glabra*) of the Mediterranean region that has odd-pinnate leaves with ovate leaflets and stalked racemes of blue flowers and that is widely cultivated in southern Europe for its long thick sweet roots which are the source of licorice (2) **:** any of several other plants of the genus *Glycyrrhiza* **b :** any of various plants resembling members of the genus *Glycyrrhiza* — usu. used in combination; see INDIAN LICORICE
licorice fern *n* **:** any of several ferns of the genus *Polypodium* having rootstocks of a sweetish flavor
licorice powder *n* **:** a laxative composed of powdered senna and licorice, sulfur, fennel oil, and sugar
licorice root *n* **1 :** LICORICE 1a **2 :** WILD LICORICE 1
licorice vine *n* **:** INDIAN LICORICE
lic·tor \ˈliktər, -ˌtȯ(ə)r\ *n* -s [L; perh. akin to *ligare* to bind — more at LIGATURE] **:** a Roman officer bearing the fasces as the insignia of his office whose duties included attendance upon the chief magistrates appearing in public, clearing the way and causing due respect to be paid to them, and also the apprehension and punishment of criminals
lic·to·ri·an \(ˈ)likˈtōrēən\ *adj* **:** of, relating to, or resembling a lictor
lic·u·a·la \ˌlikyəˈwälə, -wālə\ *n, cap* [NL, fr. Makassar *lekowala* (palm of the genus *Licuala*)] **:** a genus of tropical Asiatic dwarf fan palms having prickly petioles and large branching spikes of flowers
lic·u·ry *or* **lic·u·ri** \ˈlikərē\ *n, pl* **licuries** *or* **licuris** [Pg *licuri, licuri*, fr. Tupi] **:** OURICURY
licury wax *n* **:** OURICURY WAX
¹lid \ˈlid\ *n* -s [ME, fr. OE *hlid* lid, gate, opening; akin to OFris *hlid* cover, eyelid, OHG *lit, hlit* cover, ON *hlith* opening, door, gate, Goth *hleithra* hut, tent, OE *hleonian, hlinian* to lean — more at LEAN] **1 :** something that covers the opening of a hollow container (as a vessel or box) **:** a movable cover ⟨a trunk ~⟩ ⟨a piano ~⟩ ⟨simple pine chests with lift ~*s* —*Antiques*⟩ **2 :** EYELID **3** *dial* **:** either cover of a book **4 a :** the operculum in mosses **b :** the cap of a pyxidium **5** *slang* **:** HAT ⟨in a slaphappy painter's cap that looked like an Italian officer's ~ —Saul Bellow⟩ **6 :** a force that confines or represses ⟨if he doesn't clamp the ~ down hard on his feelings —Constance Foster⟩; *specif* **:** an official curb or check ⟨clapped a ~ on further release of information⟩ ⟨votes to clamp a four-month ~ on wages and prices —*Current History*⟩ ⟨the ~ was clamped on . . . gambling in nightclubs —*Newsweek*⟩
²lid \"\ *vt* **lidded; lidded; lidding; lids :** to cover with or as if with a lid ⟨the classified fruit is then *lidded* . . . ready for shipment —*Westralian Farmers Co-op Gazette*⟩ ⟨she . . . *lidded* her eyes —Wright Morris⟩
lid cell *n* **1 :** one of the terminal cells closing the neck of an archegonium until the maturation of the egg cell **2 :** the uppermost cell of the antheridium in ferns
lid·ded \ˌlidəd\ *adj* [¹*lid* + *-ed*] **1 :** having a lid ⟨milk is left in a heavy ~ mug —Hamlin Garland⟩ **2 :** having or covered with lids — used of the eyes chiefly in combination ⟨her blue-*lidded* eyes —Calder Willingham⟩ ⟨his weather-*lidded* eyes watched the floor —Helen Rich⟩
lid·der \ˈlidə(r)\ *n* -s **:** one that fastens lids to packed containers
lid·less \ˈlidləs\ *adj* **1 :** having no lid ⟨a ~ container⟩ **2 :** without or as if without covering by the eyelids **:** SLEEPLESS, WATCHFUL ⟨to an eye like mine, a ~ watcher of the public weal —Alfred Tennyson⟩
li·do \ˈlē(ˌ)dō\ *n* -s [fr. the *Lido*, town and fashionable sea resort near Venice, Italy] **1 :** a luxuriously equipped and fashionable beach resort ⟨a *Lido* for Dubliners —George Burrows⟩ **2 :** a well-equipped swimming pool (as on an ocean liner)
lid·o·caine \ˈlidəˌkān\ *n* -s [acetanil*id* + *o-* + *-caine*] **:** a crystalline compound $(CH_3)_2C_6H_3NHCOCH_2N(C_2H_5)_2$ derived from acetanilide that is used in the form of its hydrochloride as a local anesthetic
¹lie \ˈlī\ *vb* **lay** \ˈlā\ **lain** \ˈlān\ *or archaic* **lien** \ˈlī(ə)n\ **ly·ing** \ˈlīiŋ\ **lies** [ME *liggen, ligen, lien*, fr. OE *licgan*; akin to OHG *ligen* to lie, ON *liggja* to lie, L *lectus* bed, Gk *lechos* bed, *lechesthai* to lie down, OIr *lige* bed, grave, OSlav *ležati* to lie] *vi* **1 a :** to be or to stay at rest in a horizontal position **:** be prostrate **:** REST, RECLINE ⟨~ motionless⟩ ⟨~ asleep⟩ ⟨~ dead⟩ ⟨~*s* in his grave⟩ **b :** to assume a horizontal position — often used with *down* **c** *archaic* **:** to reside temporarily **:** stay for the night **:** LODGE, SOJOURN, SLEEP **d** *archaic* **:** to have sexual intercourse — used with *with* **e :** to stay without moving (as in concealment) ⟨~ in wait for deer⟩ ⟨~ in ambush⟩ **f** *of a game bird* **:** to remain still at the approach of hunters or dogs ⟨~ to the gun⟩ ⟨~ to a point⟩ **2 a :** to be in a helpless or defenseless state ⟨the town *lay* at the mercy of the invader⟩ ⟨*lying* in prison⟩ **b :** to remain subject — used with *under* ⟨the house *lay* under a curse⟩ ⟨*lying* under a cruel despotism⟩ **3** *of an inanimate thing* **:** to be or remain in a flat or horizontal position upon a broad support ⟨books *lying* on the table⟩ ⟨snow ~*s* on the fields⟩ ⟨leaves *lay* thick on the ground⟩ **4 :** to have direction **:** STRETCH, EXTEND ⟨the route *lay* to the west⟩ ⟨thought of the empty hours that *lay* ahead⟩ ⟨the grain of the wood *lay* crosswise⟩ **5 a :** to occupy a certain relative place or position **:** become situated ⟨easterly oases . . . ~ close to or below sea level —W.B.Fisher⟩ ⟨the song ~*s* well within his range⟩ ⟨meadows *lying* along the river⟩ ⟨mountains *lay* between us and our goal⟩ ⟨that way madness ~*s* —Shak.⟩ **b :** to have a place in relation to something else ⟨motive that *lay* behind his actions⟩ ⟨question ~*s* outside the scope of our inquiry⟩ ⟨real reason ~*s* deeper⟩ **c :** to have an effect through mere presence, weight, or relative position ⟨remorse *lay* heavily on his conscience⟩ ⟨her years *lay* lightly upon her⟩ ⟨your time will not ~ heavy upon your hands —Jonathan Swift⟩ **d** *law* **:** to be sustainable or admissible **:** be capable of being maintained ⟨action for libel will ~ in such cases⟩ ⟨appeal usually ~*s* to the supreme or high court of the colony —W.E.Simnett⟩ **6 a :** to remain at anchor or becalmed ⟨fleet *lying* in the harbor⟩ **b :** to assume or maintain a position in relation to the wind ⟨able to ~ closer to the wind than the other yachts⟩ ⟨the more a ship is trimmed by the stern the farther she will ~ off the wind —*Manual of Seamanship*⟩ **c :** ¹LAY 5a **7 :** to have place **:** EXIST ⟨choice *lay* between fighting or surrendering⟩ **:** BELONG, PERTAIN, CONSIST — used with *in* ⟨felt that his future *lay* in teaching⟩ ⟨tried with all the strength that *lay* in him⟩ **8 :** REMAIN ⟨field *lying* fallow⟩ ⟨machinery *lying* idle⟩ ⟨talent *lay* hid⟩; *esp* **:** to remain unused ⟨unsold goods *lying* on the shelves⟩ ⟨money *lying* in the bank⟩ or uncared-for ⟨left his tools *lying* about⟩ ⟨dishes *lying* in the sink⟩ **9 a** *now dial* **:** to be still **:** SUBSIDE ⟨near dark, the wind ~*s* —G.S.Perry⟩ **b** *of wind* **:** to blow from a certain direction ⟨came out to see where the wind *lay*⟩ **10** *obs* **:** to engage in some occupation or live in a specified way — used with *at* or *about* ~ *vt* **1** *now chiefly dial* **:** to cause to lie **:** LAY **2** *of a ship* **:** to make headway along (as a course) — **lie low 1 :** to lie prostrate, defeated, or disgraced **2 :** to stay in hiding **:** strive to avoid notice ⟨better *lie low* until this affair blows over⟩ **3 :** to bide one's time **:** remain secretly ready for action
²lie \"\ *n* -s **1 :** the position or situation in which something lies ⟨~*s* of a golf ball⟩ ⟨~ of a ball in lawn bowling⟩ ⟨~ of a stone in curling⟩ ⟨~ of fibers in felted pulp⟩ ⟨~ of the cards in a bridge deal⟩ **2** *chiefly Brit* **:** topographical features and situation **:** SLOPE ⟨~ of the land⟩ **3 :** the haunt of an animal or a fish **:** COVERT ⟨a fine trout ~⟩ **4** *Brit* **:** an act or instance of lying or resting (as in bed) ⟨I have clearly in mind the coldest ~ I have so far met —Thomas Skelton⟩; *esp* **:** a period of lying in bed beyond the usual time of arising ⟨why didn't you take a ~ in your bed a morning like that —Michael McLaverty⟩ **5 :** the angle of the blade or clubhead with the shaft of a hockey stick or golf club
³lie \"\ *vb* **lied; lied; ly·ing** \ˈlīiŋ\ **lies** [ME *ligen, leyen, lien*, fr. OE *lēogan*; akin to OHG *liogan* to lie, ON *ljūga*, Goth *liugan*, OSlav *lŭgati* to lie, Lith *lūgoti* to request] *vi* **1 :** to make an untrue statement with intent to deceive **:** tell a lie ⟨man is the only animal . . . that habitually ~*s* —Leo Stein⟩ **2 :** to create a false or misleading impression **:** convey an untruth ⟨unless these figures ~⟩ ⟨that thermometer must be *lying*⟩ ~ *vt* **:** to bring about by lying **:** affect in a specified way by telling lies ⟨men have been *lied* out of office⟩ ⟨managed to ~ himself out of trouble⟩
syn LIE, PREVARICATE, EQUIVOCATE, PALTER, FIB can mean to tell an untruth directly or indirectly. LIE is direct and blunt, imputing dishonesty ⟨children sometimes *lie* to avoid punishment⟩ ⟨the camera can cheat and *lie* with all the success and assurance of a confidence trickster —Richard Harrison⟩ PREVARICATE is commonly used to evade the insulting bluntness of LIE, but also can imply evasion of truth as by quibbling or confusing the issue ⟨he could *prevaricate* no longer, and, confessing to the gambling, told her the truth —Thomas Hardy⟩ EQUIVOCATE implies evasion by the use of words or remarks with double meanings in the hope that an incorrect one will be understood ⟨he was wholly in sympathy with Congregationalism, and had no mind to conceal or *equivocate* concerning its democratic tendencies —V.L.Parrington⟩ or by the use of talk which avoids committing one to anything. PALTER implies a falseness or unreliability in statements or dealings ⟨if insanity is not to be a defense, let us say so frankly and even brutally, but let us not mock ourselves with a definition that *palters* with reality —B.N.Cardozo⟩ FIB is often used as an innocuous equivalent of LIE but more often implies telling a trivial, insignificant, or socially necessary untruth ⟨the government admitted the laboratory, but . . . may be *fibbing* patriotically, of course —*Time*⟩
— **lie in one's throat** *or* **lie in one's teeth :** to lie flatly, maliciously, or outrageously
⁴lie \"\ *n* -s [ME *lige, leye, lie*, fr. OE *lyge*; akin to OHG *lugī* lie, ON *lygi*; derivatives fr. the root of E ³*lie*] **1 a :** an assertion of something known or believed by the speaker to be untrue **:** a deliberate misrepresenting of fact with intent to deceive ⟨his story was a tissue of ~*s*, evasions, and exaggerations⟩ ⟨his decent reticence is branded as hypocrisy, his circumlocutions are roundly called ~*s* —W.S.Maugham⟩ ⟨believes . . . that men have petty larceny forever in their hearts and ~*s* forever in their mouths —Bergen Evans⟩ ⟨any printed ~ that any notorious villain pens —Charles Dickens⟩ **b :** an untrue or inaccurate statement that may or may not be believed true by the speaker ⟨often suspected that history was mostly ~*s* anyway⟩ **2 :** something that misleads or deceives ⟨his pose of humility was a ~⟩ **3 :** a charge of lying ⟨threw the ~ in his face⟩
lie-abed \ˈ;ˌ;\ *n* -s **:** one given to rising late
lie along *vi* **1** *archaic* **:** to lie flat or at full length **2 :** to careen under pressure of the wind
lie athwart *vi* **:** to ride at anchor or mooring with head to the wind across the tide
lie back *vi* **1 :** to lean backward against a support ⟨*lay back* in his chair and dozed off⟩ **2 :** to cease from strenuous effort or activity ⟨after a busy life he was content to *lie back* and take life easy⟩
lie-back \ˈ;ˌ\ *n* [*lie back*] **:** LAY-BACK
lie·be·ner·ite \ˈlēb(ə)nəˌrīt\ *n* -s [F *liebenerite*, fr. L. *Liebener*, 19th cent. Fr. mineralogist + F *-ite*] **:** a variety of pinite
lie·ber·kühn's gland *also* **lieberkühn's crypt** \ˈlēbə(r)ˌk(y)ünz-, -kǖnz-\ *n, usu cap L* [after Johann N. *Lieberkühn* †1756 Ger. anatomist] **:** any of the tubular glands of the intestinal mucous membrane
lie·ber·mann-bur·chard reaction \ˈlēbərmənˈbu̇(ə)rˌkärt-\ *n, usu cap L&B* [after Karl T. *Liebermann* †1914 Ger. chemist and H. *Burchard*, 19th cent. Ger. chemist] **:** a test for unsaturated steroids (as cholesterol) and triterpenes based on the formation of a series of colors (as pink to blue to green) with acetic anhydride in the presence of concentrated sulfuric acid
lieb·frau·milch \ˈlēpˌfrau̇ˌmilk, -ˌmiu̇k\ *also* **lieb·frau·en·milch** \lēpˈfrau̇ən-\ *n* -s *usu cap* [G; *liebfraumilch*, alter. of *liebfrauenmilch*, fr. *Liebfrauenstift* (lit., foundation of the Virgin Mary), religious foundation in Worms, Germany, where the wine was first produced + *milch* milk] **:** a white wine of the Rhenish variety from Worms in Rheinhessen, Germany; *also* **:** a similar wine from elsewhere in Germany often blended to approximate a standard
lie·big condenser \ˈlēbig-\ *n, usu cap L* [after Baron Justus

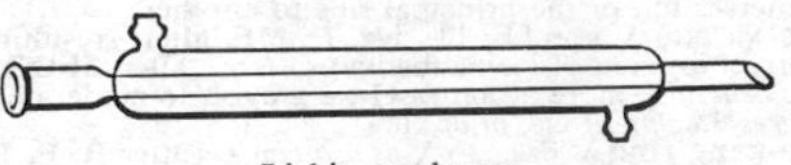
Liebig condenser

von *Liebig* †1873 Ger. chemist, who described it] **:** a condenser for use in distillation that consists of two tubes one inside the other with space between for circulation of water
lie·big·ite \ˈlēbiˌgīt\ *n* -s [Baron Justus von *Liebig* + E *-ite*] **:** an apple-green mineral $Ca_2U(CO_3)_4.10H_2O$ consisting of hydrous uranium calcium carbonate and occurring as concretions or coatings
lieb·lich \ˈlēplik, -ik\ *adj* [G, pleasant, charming, attractive, fr. MHG *lieplich* friendly, affectionate, pleasure, fr. *liep* dear, beloved (fr. OHG *liob*) + *-lich* -ly — more at LIEF] **:** sweet in tone — used in organ-stop names ⟨~ gedeckt⟩
lie by *vi* **1 :** to intermit activity, work, or progress **:** REST ⟨we *lay by* during the heat of the day⟩ ⟨the ship was forced to *lie by* for several days for repairs⟩ **2 :** to be in a state or condition of disuse ⟨his dogs and guns *lay by* that season⟩
lie-by \ˈ;ˌ\ *n* -s [*lie by*] *Brit* **:** a railroad siding for passing
liech·ten·stein \ˈliktənˌstīn\ *adj, usu cap* [fr. *Liechtenstein*, principality in central Europe] **:** of or from the principality of Liechtenstein **:** of the kind or style prevalent in Liechtenstein
¹lied *past of* LIE
²lied \ˈlēt\ *n, pl* **lie·der** \ˈlēdə(r)\ [G, song, fr. OHG *liod* — more at LAUD] **:** a German folk song; *specif* **:** a German art song of the 19th century (as by Schubert, Hugo Wolf) in which a lyric text is set to a well-considered usu. through-composed melody and accompaniment with all three elements contributing nearly equally to the total effect
Lie·der·kranz \ˈlēdəˌkran(t)s, -rän-\ *trademark* — used for a soft surface-ripened cheese with a somewhat strong pungent flavor and odor
lie detector *n* **:** a device using instruments to register changes in blood pressure, strength of pulse beat or respiratory movements, or increased perspiration as indicative of emotional excitement assumed to accompany lying under questioning; *esp* **:** KEELER POLYGRAPH
lie down *vi* **1** *archaic* **:** to go to bed for the night **2 :** to lie on a bed for a brief rest **:** take a nap **3** *obs* **:** lie in **4 :** to submit meekly or abjectly to defeat, disappointment, or insult ⟨they will not take this violation of their rights *lying down*⟩ **5 :** to fail to perform or to neglect one's part deliberately ⟨*lie down* on the job⟩
lie-down \ˈ;ˌ\ *n* -s [*lie down*] **:** a lying down or period of lying down **:** NAP, REST
¹lief \ˈlēf, -ēv\ *adj* -ER/-EST [ME *lef, leef, leif, lif*, fr. OE *lēof*; akin to OHG *liob* dear, beloved, ON *ljūfr*, Goth *liufs* dear, beloved, OE *lufu* love — more at LOVE] **1** *archaic* **:** DEAR, BELOVED **2** *obs* **:** PLEASING, AGREEABLE, ACCEPTABLE **:** PRECIOUS — used with dative of personal pronoun ⟨death me ~*er* were than such despite —Edmund Spenser⟩ **3** *archaic* **:** WILLING, GLAD
²lief \"\ *n* -s [ME *lef, leef, leif, lif*, fr. OE *lēof*, fr. *lēof*, adj.] **1** *archaic* **:** BELOVED, SWEETHEART **2** *obs* **:** DEAR — used as a title of respect in addressing a superior
³lief \ˈlē|v, ˈli|, |f\ *adv* -ER/-EST [ME *lef, leef, leif, lif*, fr. *lef, leef, lif*, adj.] **:** GLADLY, WILLINGLY, FREELY — used in the phrases *had as lief, would as lief, had liefer,* or *would liefer* ⟨I had as ~ go as not⟩ ⟨far ~*er* by his dear hand had I die —Alfred Tennyson⟩ ⟨he would as ~ have the Germans as neighbors as the British —Manfred Nathan⟩ ⟨frankly, I'd just as ~ stay⟩
lief·ly \ˈlē|vlē, ˈli|, |flē\ *adv* [¹*lief* + *-ly*] **:** WILLINGLY, GLADLY
¹liege \ˈlēj *sometimes* -ēzh\ *adj* [ME *lige, liege, lege*, fr. OF

lige (fr. — assumed — ML *liticus,* fr. LL *litus* serf — alter. of *laetus* — + L *-icus* -ic) & *liege,* fr. LL *laeticus,* fr. *laetus* serf (of Gmc origin; akin to OLF *leto* serf, OS *lat,* OFris *let*) + L *-icus* -ic; prob. akin to OE *lǣtan* to let — more at LET] **1 a :** having the right to feudal allegiance and service ⟨a vassal's responsibilities to his ~ lord⟩ **b :** obligated to render feudal allegiance and service ⟨a right to call on every ~ subject to render assistance —Sir Walter Scott⟩ **2 :** bound by obligations resembling those existing between a feudal lord and his vassal **:** FAITHFUL, LOYAL ⟨master of his own impulses, as a soloist should be, and not ~ to the conductor —Irving Kolodin⟩ ⟨all the ~ people of Pennsylvania —Thomas McKean⟩

²liege \"\ *n* -s [ME *lige, liege, lege,* fr. *lige, liege, lege,* adj.] **1 a :** a vassal bound to feudal service and allegiance **:** LIEGE MAN 1 **b :** a loyal subject (as in a monarchy) **2 :** a liege lord **:** a feudal superior to whom allegiance and service are due **:** a lord paramount

³li·ège *or* **li·ege** \lē'āzh, -'ezh\ *adj, usu cap* [fr. *Liège,* Belgium] **:** of or from the city of Liège, Belgium **:** of the kind or style prevalent in Liège

liege man *n* [ME] **1 :** a vassal serving his lord under a solemn obligation and entitled to receive protection from him ⟨you shall become true *liege men* to his crown —Shak.⟩ **2 :** a devoted adherent and follower ⟨he's the *liege man* of his division commander on discipline —J.W.Bellah⟩

liege pou·stie \'lēj¦püstē, -paüs-\ *n* [ME *lege pouste,* fr. MF *lige poesti, lige pousté,* lit., liege power] **:** the state of good health requisite under Scots law to the exercise of full legal powers esp. in the transfer of property (as by deed or will) — compare DEATHBED DEED

lieger *archaic var of* LEDGER 4

lie in *vi* **:** to be in childbed ~ *vt, obs* **:** COST

¹lien *archaic past part of* LIE

²lien \'lē(ə)n\ *n* -s [MF, band, tie, bond, fr. L *ligamen* band, tie, fr. *ligare* to bind, tie — more at LIGATURE] **1 :** a charge upon real or personal property for the satisfaction of some debt or duty ordinarily arising by operation of law **:** a right in one to control or to hold and retain or enforce a charge against the property of another until some claim of the former is paid or satisfied ⟨the owner of the cargo has a ~ on the vessel for any injury —David Davis⟩ ⟨efforts to effect a release of the federal tax ~ —J.D.Johnson⟩ **2 a :** MORTGAGE **b :** the security interest created by a mortgage ⟨the ~ of a mortgage⟩

³li·en \'līən, 'lī,en\ *n* -s [L — more at SPLEEN] **:** SPLEEN

lien·able \'lē(ə)nəbəl\ *adj* [*²lien* + *-able*] **:** capable of being subjected to or made the subject of a lien ⟨a ~ article⟩

li·enal \(')lī¦ēnᵊl, 'līən-\ *adj* [ISV *³lien* + *-al*] **:** of or relating to the spleen **:** SPLENIC

li·en·cu·lus \lī'eŋkyələs\ *n, pl* **liencu·li** \-yə,lī\ [NL, dim. of L *lien* spleen — more at SPLEEN] **:** a small accessory or supplementary spleen

lien·ee \(')lē¦nē, ¦lēə¦nē\ *n* -s [*²lien* + *-ee*] **1 :** one whose property is subject to a lien **2** *Austral* **:** LIENHOLDER

lienholder \'≈(≈),≈≈\ *n* **1 :** one having a valid lien **2 :** one having an inchoate lien capable of being perfected **:** a lien claimant

lien·or \'lē(ə)nər, (')lē¦nō(ə)r, ¦lēə¦n-\ *n* -s [*²lien* + *-or*] **1 :** LIENHOLDER **2** *Austral* **:** LIENEE 1

li·eno·renal ligament \¦līə(,)nō, lī¦ē(,)nō + . . .-\ *n* [*³lien* + *-o-* + *renal*] **:** a mesenteric fold passing from the spleen to the left kidney and affording support to the splenic artery and vein

li·en·ter·ic \¦līən-¦terik\ *adj* [F or L; F *lientérique,* fr. L *lientericus,* fr. Gk *leienterikos,* fr. *leienteria* + *-ikos* -ic] **:** containing or characterized by the passage of undigested or partially digested food — used of feces or diarrhea

li·en·tery \'līən-,terē, lī'entərē\ *n* -ES [MF or ML; MF *lienterie,* fr. ML *lienteria,* fr. Gk *leienteria,* fr. *leios* smooth + *enteron,* intestine + *-ia -y* — more at LIME, INTER-] **:** lienteric diarrhea

lie off *vi* **1 :** to keep a little away from the shore or another ship **2 :** to cease work for a time **:** rest during a period of exertion **3 :** to hold back in the early part of a race

lie over *vi* **1** *of a ship* **:** lie along **2 a :** to remain unpaid when overdue **b :** to await disposal or attention at a later time ⟨several jobs *lying over* from last week⟩

¹li·er \'lī(ə)r, -īə\ *n* -s [*¹lie* + *-er*] **:** one that lies (as in ambush)

²lier \'li(ə)r\ *archaic var of* LEHR

lier *comparative of* -LY

li·erne \lē'ərn, -'e(ə)rn\ *n* -s [F, fr. MF, fr. *lier* to bind, tie — more at LIABLE] **:** a rib in Gothic vaulting that does not spring from the impost and is not a ridge rib but passes from one boss or intersection of the principal ribs to another

lierre \lē'e(ə)r\ *n* -s [F, lit., ivy, fr. MF, alter. (resulting fr. incorrect division of *l'ierre* the ivy) of *ierre,* alter. of OF *edre,* fr. L *hedera* — more at HEDERA] **:** a grayish to moderate olive

lies *pres 3d sing of* LIE, *pl of* LIE

lie·se·gang ring \'lēzə,gäŋ-\ *n, usu cap L* [after R. E. *Liesegang* †1947 Ger. chemist] **:** one of a series of usu. concentric bands of a precipitate that are separated by clear spaces and that are often formed in gels by periodic or rhythmic precipitation — usu. used in pl.

-liest *superlative of* -LY

lie to *vi, of a ship* **:** to stay as nearly stationary as feasible with head to windward ⟨*lying to* all night waiting for daylight to check their position —Stanley Rogers⟩

lieu \'lü\ *n* -s [MF, fr. L *locus* — more at STALL] **:** PLACE, STEAD — **in lieu** *adv* **:** INSTEAD ⟨a small monetary payment . . . is given *in lieu* —Wilfred Whitely⟩ — **in lieu of** *prep* **:** in the place of **:** instead of ⟨the mumbling cant that . . . the characters employ *in lieu of* English —John McCarten⟩ ⟨rendered three days' work . . . *in lieu of* rent —G.G.Coulton⟩ ⟨striking out the words "one year" and inserting *in lieu thereof* the words "six months" —*U.S. Code*⟩

lieu lands *n pl* **:** public lands that a patentee has a right to locate and select in place of lands within the limits of a previous grant which are occupied by persons given special protection by the law

lie up *vi* **1 :** to stay in bed or at rest ⟨his doctor insists . . . the patient should *lie up* for 5 weeks —*Lancet*⟩ **:** keep to one's room, den, or covert ⟨the lions were *lying up* after feeding⟩ **2** *of a ship* **:** to go into or remain in a dock (as for repairs)

lieut *abbr, often cap* lieutenant

lieu·ten·an·cy \lü'tenənsē, -si, *Brit usu* lef't- *or* ləf't- *or esp in the navy* le't- *or* lə't-\ *n* -ES [ME *lieutenauncie,* fr. MF *lieutenancie,* fr. *lieutenant* + *-cie* -cy] **1 :** the office, rank, or commission of a lieutenant ⟨the earl . . . had recently been turned out of the ~ of the county —T.B.Macaulay⟩ ⟨jumped at a chance for a second ~ in the marines —*Time*⟩ **2** *obs* **:** a territorial unit under the jurisdiction of a lieutenant **3 :** the term of office of a lieutenant **4** *usu cap, obs* **:** the body of deputies to the lord lieutenant of an English county ⟨addresses from the *Lieutenancy,* grand juries, and corporations in our county —*London Gazette*⟩

lieu·ten·ant \-tenənt\ *n* -s [ME *lieutenaunt,* fr. MF *lieutenant,* fr. *lieu* place + *tenant* holding, fr. pres. part. of *tenir* to hold, fr. L *tenere* — more at LIEU, THIN] **1 a :** an officer representing and exercising powers on behalf of a higher official (as a king) — compare LORD LIEUTENANT **b :** a representative of or substitute for another in the performance of duty **c :** ASSISTANT 2b ⟨the president's intimate friend and most trusted ~ —*Harper's*⟩ **2 a :** a military officer — see FIRST LIEUTENANT, FLIGHT LIEUTENANT, SECOND LIEUTENANT **b :** a naval officer ranking just below a lieutenant commander and above a lieutenant junior grade **c :** a Salvation Army officer — see FIRST LIEUTENANT 2, SECOND LIEUTENANT **d :** a fire or police department officer ranking below a captain **3 :** the adult assistant leader of a Girl Guide or Ranger company and formerly of a Girl Scout troop

lieutenant colonel *n* **1 :** an army, marine, or air force officer ranking just below a colonel and above a major **2 :** a Salvation Army officer ranking above a brigadier and below a colonel

lieutenant commander *n* **:** a naval officer ranking below a commander and above a lieutenant

lieutenant commissioner *n* **:** a Salvation Army officer ranking above a colonel and below a commissioner

lieutenant general *n* [MF, lit., general lieutenant] **1 :** VICE-REGENT ⟨name the Prince of Piedmont as *lieutenant general* —*The New Republic*⟩ **2 :** an army, marine, or air force officer ranking just below a general and above a major general

lieutenant governor *n* **:** a deputy or subordinate governor: as **a :** an elected official serving as deputy to the governor of an American state and as his successor in case of death or removal from office and usu. presiding over the upper house of the state legislature **b :** the formal head of the government of a Canadian province appointed by the federal government as the representative of the crown and resembling the governor-general in power and function ⟨the power of the *lieutenant governors* to reserve provincial bills for the approval of the Dominion government —Alexander Brady⟩

lieutenant junior grade *n, pl* **lieutenants junior grade :** a naval officer ranking below a lieutenant and above an ensign

lieu·ten·ant·ry \-tenəntrē\ *n* -ES **:** LIEUTENANCY ⟨strip you out of your ~ —Shak.⟩

lieu·ten·ant·ship \-tenənt,ship\ *n* [ME *lieutenauntship,* fr. *lieutenaunt* + *-ship*] *archaic* **:** LIEUTENANCY 1

lieve \'lēv, 'liv\ *dial var of* LIEF

lieves \'lēvz, 'livz\ *New Eng var of* ³LIEF

liev·rite \'lēv,rīt\ *n* -s [G *lievrit,* fr. C.H. *Lelièvre,* 19th cent. Fr. mineralogist + G *-it* -ite] **:** ILVAITE

¹life \'līf\ *n, pl* **lives** \-īvz\ [ME *lif,* fr. OE *līf;* akin to OHG *līb* life, ON *līf* life, OE *libban, lifian* to live — more at LIVE] **1 a :** animate being **:** the quality that distinguishes a vital and functional being from a dead body or purely chemical matter ⟨~ is the immediate gift of God —William Blackstone⟩ ⟨my ability to give ~ to an animal —Mary W. Shelley⟩ — compare DEATH 1 **b :** the principle or force by which animals and plants are maintained in the performance of their functions and which distinguishes by its presence animate from inanimate matter **c** (1) **:** the state of a material complex or individual characterized by the capacity to perform certain functional activities including metabolism, growth, reproduction, and some form of responsiveness or adaptability (2) **:** a specific aspect of the process of living or performing the functions involved in living ⟨the physical and emotional ~ of a boy —Harrison Smith⟩ ⟨the cowboy's sex ~ was intermittent —D.B.Davis⟩ **2 :** the course of existence **:** the sequence of physical and mental experiences that make up the existence of an individual **:** the totality of actions and occurrences constituting an individual experience ⟨emotions provoked by particular events in his ~ —T.S.Eliot⟩ ⟨interests . . . that have occupied his ~ —F.R.Leavis⟩ ⟨children . . . are the joy of our *lives* —Agnes S. Turnbull⟩ **3 :** BIOGRAPHY 1 ⟨a shilling ~ will give you all the facts —W.H.Auden⟩ ⟨a full-length ~⟩ **4 a :** the earthly state of human existence as distinguished from the spiritual state after death ⟨all those who in this transitory ~ —*Bk. of Com. Prayer*⟩ **b :** a spiritual form of eternal existence transcending physical death ⟨he who hears my word . . . has passed from death to ~ —Jn 5:24 (RSV)⟩ ⟨his craving . . . for release into the ~ to come —Rodney Gilbert⟩ **5 a :** the duration of the earthly existence of an individual; *specif* **:** the period from birth to death ⟨his habits were such as promise a long ~ —T.B.Macaulay⟩ ⟨early in ~ he had married⟩ **b :** a specific phase of earthly existence ⟨parents . . . had more effect on your child ~ —*Glamour (Australia)*⟩; *esp* **:** the period from an event until death ⟨six senators appointed for ~⟩ **c :** a sentence of imprisonment for the remaining portion of the convict's earthly existence ⟨if found guilty . . . he could get ~ —George Quint⟩ **d :** continued existence and right to function (as in a political office) ⟨the secretary of state . . . whose ~ depends on such a fickle thing as votes —E.O.Hauser⟩ ⟨fighting for his political ~ —*N.Y. Times*⟩ **6 :** a way or manner of living; *esp* **:** one associated with an occupation, location, or time ⟨a continent where the rural ~ is predominant —P.E.James⟩ ⟨she will have a wretched ~ with this young scamp —L.C.Douglas⟩ ⟨the ~ of the colonists is visible to the eye —R.W.Hatch⟩ **7 :** someone held to be as dear to one as existence — usu. used as a term of endearment ⟨my bride, my wife, my ~ —Alfred Tennyson⟩ **8 :** something held to be essential to animate existence or to a livelihood ⟨the words that I have spoken to you are spirit and ~ —Jn 6:63 (RSV)⟩ ⟨the fishing village drew its ~ from the sea⟩ **9 :** a vital or living being; *specif* **:** PERSON ⟨many youthful *lives* miss the opportunities for education —Ernest & Pearl Beaglehole⟩ **10 :** the force or principle that animates and usu. tends to shape the development of something ⟨the ~ of the constitution . . . has been not logic but experience —F.A.Ogg & Harold Zink⟩ **11 :** energy and liveliness in action, thought, or expression **:** ANIMATION, SPIRIT ⟨gives thy gestures grace and ~ —William Wordsworth⟩ ⟨there was little ~ in her voice —Winston Churchill⟩ ⟨there is still ~ in the old conceptions of loyalty —Leslie Rees⟩ ⟨breathe ~ into books for children —Rumer Godden⟩ **12 :** the form or pattern of something as it exists in reality ⟨a drawing from the ~⟩ ⟨screen motion was a little faster and more jerky than ~ —Otis Ferguson⟩ ⟨pictures show the family to the ~ —May L. Becker⟩ **13 :** a person whose life is insured (as by a life-insurance policy); *esp* **:** one considered with regard to his prospects for a long existence ⟨an insurance doctor had pronounced him a first-class ~ —E.M.Lustgarten⟩ **14 a :** the period of duration of something held to resemble a natural organism in structure or functions ⟨throughout the ~ of the republic —C.L.Jones⟩ ⟨ended the Labour government's ~ within . . . one year —Herbert Dorn⟩ **b :** the period of time during which a material object is fit for use or the efficient performance of its functions **:** the number of times an object may be used efficiently ⟨the ~ of the road was hardly a year —*Amer. Guide Series: N.H.*⟩ ⟨the ~ of a battleship was set at twenty years —C.E.Black & E.C.Helmreich⟩ ⟨tool ~ varied greatly with the microstructure of the steels being machined —F.H.Colvin⟩ **c :** the period of existence (as of an ion) — compare HALF-LIFE **d :** the period of time during which a legal document or relationship (as a marriage) is in force and effect **e :** the period of time during which something (as a book or a play) continues to be popular ⟨making a few books tremendously popular but shortening the *lives* of all —J.D.Hart⟩ ⟨the permanent ~ of distinguished minor fiction —E.K.Brown⟩ **f :** the property (as resilience, elasticity, springiness) of an inanimate substance resembling the animate quality of a living being ⟨the ~ of a bow⟩ ⟨an elastic belt that had lost most of its ~⟩ **g :** the length of time that the usefulness or quality of a packaged product lasts before deterioration begins ⟨lengthen the ~ of packaged fresh meat cuts —V.J.Hillery⟩ ⟨shelf ~ of baked pies —Lou Bisno⟩ **15 :** living beings; *esp* **:** the living things of a particular kind, quality, or environment ⟨bird ~⟩ ⟨plant ~⟩ ⟨forest ~⟩ **16 a :** human activities: as (1) **:** the active or practical part of human existence ⟨if a student is to be prepared for ~, he must be prepared for making a living —*Bull. of Bates Coll.*⟩ (2) **:** social activities ⟨entered the ~ of the court⟩ **b :** the activity and movement characterizing the presence of living beings ⟨sidewalk cafes just now stirring to midmorning ~ —P.E.Deutschman⟩ **c :** the activities of a given sphere, area, or time ⟨economic and commercial ~ was almost wholly at a standstill —R.A.Hall b.1911⟩ ⟨~ in the Mediterranean war theater⟩ ⟨participate in local, state, and national ~ —John Lodge⟩ ⟨his private ~⟩ **17 :** one that inspires or excites spirit and vigor and is usu. held to provide a principal basis for enjoyment or success ⟨the ~ of the party⟩ ⟨he was the ~ of the enterprise⟩ **18 a :** another chance or a continued opportunity given to one likely to lose; *esp* **:** an opportunity given a batter in cricket and baseball to reach a base or to continue at bat because of a fielding error **b :** one of several turns limited in number by the rules of a game (as English pool) during which a player may continue in the game until he makes a mistake (as hitting the wrong ball or pocketing his own ball) **19** *cap, Christian Science* **:** ²GOD b(6) **20 :** something resembling animate life: as **a :** continued active existence and development ⟨British Columbia's chance for a separate political ~ —R.W.Van Alstyne⟩ ⟨upon circulation . . . the ~ and prosperity of a newspaper depends —F.L.Mott⟩ **b :** a state characterized by the functioning of the mechanical parts (as of a motor) ⟨the engine coughed into ~ —B.R.Ingram⟩ **21 :** conscious existence supposed to be a quality of the soul or as the soul's nature and being — **for dear life** *adv* **:** so as to save or as if trying to save one's life **:** with might and main ⟨a giant octopus . . . was holding on *for dear life* with a dozen legs —C.L.Carmer⟩ — **on your life** *adv* **:** by all means **:** under any or all circumstances ⟨obey them *on your life* —John Buchan⟩ **:** on any account — usu. used in negative constructions ⟨have any of them appreciated one jot or one tittle of it? not *on your life* —Louis Auchincloss⟩

²life \"\ *adj* **1 :** of or relating to animate being ⟨manifestations of ~ instincts —Abram Kardiner⟩ ⟨~ processes⟩ **2 :** for or lasting throughout the duration of existence **:** LIFELONG ⟨~ income⟩ ⟨~ tenure⟩ ⟨a ~ member⟩ ⟨~ aims⟩ **3 :** using a living model ⟨a ~ class⟩ **4 :** of, relating to, or provided by life insurance ⟨a ~ policy⟩

life-and-death *also* **life-or-death** \¦≈≈¦≈\ *adj* **:** involving or culminating in life or death **:** having vital importance as if involving life or death ⟨engaged in a *life-and-death* struggle —Fitzroy Maclean⟩ ⟨the desperate *life-and-death* battle between workers and owners —*Yale Rev.*⟩ ⟨the *life-and-death* power of the Senate Appropriations Committee —Douglass Cater⟩

life annuity *n* **:** an annuity payable during the lifetime of the annuitant — called also *single life annuity;* compare ANNUITY, JOINT LIFE ANNUITY, JOINT LIFE AND SURVIVOR ANNUITY

life arrow *n* **:** an arrow for carrying a line to a boat or ship

life assurance *n, chiefly Brit* **:** LIFE INSURANCE

life belt *n* **1 :** a life preserver in the form of a buoyant belt **2 :** SAFETY BELT

lifeblood \'≈,≈\ *n* **1 :** blood regarded as the seat of vitality ⟨a gaping wound issuing ~ —Shak.⟩ **2 :** something that gives or is held to give life and energy **:** a vital or life-giving force ⟨water is the ~ of India —Chester Bowles⟩ ⟨fuel oil has come to be the ~ of their civilization —K.R.Greenfield⟩

lifeboat \'≈,≈\ *n* **1 :** a strong buoyant boat esp. designed for use in saving shipwrecked people ⟨the cart, bearing the ~, was on its way down the beach —J.C.Lincoln⟩ **2 :** a boat carried by a ship for use in emergency; *esp* **:** a quarter boat kept in readiness for lowering in an emergency ⟨the ~s are arranged along almost the full length of the uppermost deck —F.E.Dodman⟩

lifeboat falls *n pl* **:** ropes and blocks used with davits for lowering a lifeboat

lifeboat gun *n* **:** a gun used for shooting a lifeline to a ship in distress

life·boat·man \'≈,≈mən, -,man\ *n, pl* **lifeboatmen :** a member of the crew of a lifeboat

life breath *n* **:** the breath that sustains life ⟨giving *life breath* to the skeleton —*Spectator*⟩

life buoy *n* **:** a float usu. consisting of a ring of buoyant material to support persons who have fallen into the water

life buoy

life car *n* **:** a watertight boat or chamber traveling on a rope and usu. used to haul persons through surf too heavy for an open boat

life cast *or* **life mask** *n* **:** a cast taken from the face of a living person — compare DEATH MASK

life cycle *n* **1 :** the series of stages or changes in form and functional activity through which an organism passes between successive recurrences of a specified primary stage — compare NUCLEAR CYCLE **2 :** LIFE HISTORY 1a **3 :** a series of significant periods (as infancy and adolescence) through which an individual, group, or culture passes during its lifetime ⟨the *life cycle* of the family⟩ ⟨the Apache *life cycle*⟩

life estate *or* **life interest** *n* **:** an estate or interest in property held only during or measured by the term of the life of a specified natural person — compare LIFE TENANT, REMAINDER, REVERSION

life everlasting *n* **1 :** LIFE 4b **2 a :** EVERLASTING 3 **b :** PEARLY EVERLASTING **c :** ORPINE

life expectancy *n* **:** an expected number of years of life based on statistical probability ⟨the normal *life expectancy* in the U. S. has been raised —G.R.Cowgill⟩ ⟨the *life expectancy* of the average new book —David Dempsey⟩ — called also *expectation of life*

life-force \'≈¦≈\ *n* **:** ÉLAN VITAL ⟨freedom . . . has always been the *life-force* of western civilization —Harold Butler⟩ ⟨the conflict between the *life-force* of his characters —Arthur Miller⟩

life-form \'≈,≈\ *n* **:** the body form characterizing a kind of organism (as a species) at maturity ⟨trees are commonly the dominant *life-form* in moist cool areas⟩

life·ful \'līffəl\ *adj* [ME *lifful,* fr. *lif* life + *-ful* — more at LIFE] **:** full of or giving vitality ⟨~ eyes⟩

life-giving \'≈,≈≈\ *adj* **:** giving or having power to give life and spirit **:** INVIGORATING ⟨returning the *life-giving* humus to the land —Louis Bromfield⟩ ⟨the *life-giving* streams of foreign investment by private companies —*Lamp*⟩

¹lifeguard \'≈,≈\ *n* [*¹life* + *guard*] **:** one that guards or protects a person's life; *specif* **:** an expert swimmer employed (as at a beach or pool) to safeguard bathers and to prevent drownings ⟨seen a ~ work over a half-drowned man —Zane Grey⟩

²lifeguard \"\ *vt* **:** to guard or protect the life of (a person) ~ *vi* **:** to serve as a lifeguard

life guardsman *n, usu cap L&G* **:** a member of a body of soldiers assigned to guard the British monarch

life gun *n* **:** a device used esp. in rescue work to extend a line of rope to an otherwise inaccessible place

life history *n* **1 a :** a history of the stages or changes through which an organism passes in its development from the egg, spore, or other primary stage until its natural death **b :** one series of these changes often constituting a life cycle **2 :** the history of an individual's development in his social environment ⟨the technique of collecting *life histories* in social research⟩ — compare CASE HISTORY 1

lifehold \'≈,≈\ *adj* **:** held for life or as a life estate

life income policy *n* **:** a life-insurance policy providing for a stated life income to the beneficiary beginning at the death of the insured

life instinct *n* **:** unconscious or biological tendencies toward maintenance and increase of organic existence

life insurance *n* **:** insurance providing for payment of a stipulated sum to a designated beneficiary upon death of the insured

life jacket *n* **:** a life preserver in the form of a sleeveless jacket **:** LIFE VEST

lifeleaf \'≈,≈\ *also* **liveleaf** \'≈,≈\ *n* **:** AIR PLANT 2

life·less \'līfləs\ *adj* [ME *lifles,* fr. OE *līflēas,* fr. *līf* life + *-lēas* -less — more at LIFE] **:** having no life: **a :** having ceased to live **:** deprived of life **:** DEAD ⟨a ~ carcass⟩ **b :** of a kind that is without life **:** INANIMATE ⟨as cold and ~ as marble —W.M.Thackeray⟩ ⟨animate the ~ clay —Mary W. Shelley⟩ **c :** lacking qualities expressive of life and vigor **:** COLORLESS, DULL ⟨a speech more ~ . . . than most of its mechanical type —S.H.Adams⟩ ⟨a ~ voice⟩ **d :** having the appearance of being dead ⟨that ~ but yet breathing creature —Anthony Trollope⟩ **e :** destitute of living beings ⟨the plain lay dark . . . and ~ —O.E.Rölvaag⟩

life·less·ly *adv* **:** in a lifeless manner

life·less·ness *n* -ES **:** the quality or state of being lifeless

lifelike \'≈,≈\ *adj* **:** like a living being or a real object **:** accurately representing or imitating real life ⟨a ~ portrait⟩ ⟨~ dialogue⟩

life·like·ness *n* -ES **:** the quality or state of being lifelike ⟨~ of expression⟩

lifeline \'≈,≈\ *n* **1 a :** a line to which persons may cling to save or protect their lives: as (1) **:** one stretched along the deck or from the yards of a ship — see SHIP illustration (2) **:** one attached to a ship or buoy for the use of people in the water (3) **:** one stretched through surf for the use of bathers **b :** a line attached to a diver's helmet for use chiefly in raising and lowering him in the water **c :** a rope line by which a person may be lowered to safety (as from a burning building) **2 :** something held to resemble a line used for the saving or protection of life ⟨the . . . program is the very ~ by which an alcoholic can pull himself back to a normal position in life —*Alcoholics Anonymous Grapevine*⟩ **3** *usu cap* **:** LINE OF LIFE **4 a :** a land, sea, or air route regarded as indispensable to life; *esp* **:** one held necessary to supply or communicate with a usu. distant outpost or to maintain an empire ⟨severing the Mediterranean ~ of the empire —Malcolm Wheeler-Nicholson⟩

lifelong \'≈¦≈\ *adj* **:** lasting or continuing through life ⟨the ~ relations between master and slave —V.L.Parrington⟩ ⟨my ~ friend⟩ ⟨whose ~ study of Mediterranean . . . art —S.L. Faison⟩

life·man \'līfmən\ *n, pl* **lifemen :** one who practices lifemanship

life·man·ship \'⸗⸗,ship\ *n* **:** the art or practice of achieving superiority or an appearance of superiority over other people (as in conversation or business) by perplexing and demoralizing them — compare GAMESMANSHIP, ONE-UPMANSHIP

life mast *n* **:** LIFE CAST

life master *n, usu cap L&M* **:** a player of the highest rank in U.S. contract bridge tournament play ⟨develop promising players into *Life Masters* —J.P.Dunne & A.A.Ostrow⟩ — compare MASTER POINT

life net *n* **:** a strong net or sheet (as of canvas) held by firemen or others to catch persons jumping from burning buildings

life-of-man \,⸗⸗ˈ⸗\ *n, pl* **life-of-mans :** any of several plants found in the U.S.: as **a :** SPIKENARD 2a **b :** BUSH HONEYSUCKLE **c :** ORPINE **d :** MOUNTAIN ASH

life of ri·ley \-ə(v)'rīlē, -li\ *usu cap R* **:** a carefree way of living characterized by ease, comfort, and often luxury ⟨living the *life of Riley*⟩

life-or-death *var of* LIFE-AND-DEATH

life peer *n* **:** a British peer whose title is not hereditary ⟨the bill . . . calls for the creation of *life peers* — both men and women —*Associated Press*⟩

life peerage *n* **:** the rank or dignity of a life peer ⟨ten men who are to receive *life peerages* —T.P.Ronan⟩

life plant *n* **:** AIR PLANT 2

life preserver *n* **1 :** a device (as a life belt, life ring, or life vest) designed to save a person from drowning by buoying up the body while in water **2 :** BLACKJACK 4 ⟨beaten and bruised with *life preservers* —Charles Reade⟩

lif·er \'līfə(r)\ *n* -s **1 :** one sentenced to imprisonment or similar punishment for life **2 :** LIFE 5c

life raft *n* **:** a very buoyant raft usu. made of wood or an inflatable material and designed to be used by people forced into the water (as from a sinking ship)

¹liferent \'⸗ˌ⸗\ *n* [ME (Sc) *lifrent*, fr. *lif* life + *rent* — more at LIFE, RENT] **:** a right in Scots law regarded either as a personal servitude or as a usufruct to use and enjoy while preserving the substance of usu. heritable property

²liferent \"\ *vt* **:** to grant a liferent of

liferenter \'⸗ˌ⸗⸗\ *n* **:** a person holding a liferent

liferent escheat *n* **:** the forfeiture under Scots law to the superior of the annual profits from property held by liferent during the life or duration of the outlawry (as for debt) of the liferenter

life raft

life·rent·rix \'⸗,rentriks\ *n, pl* **liferentrix·es** \-triksəz\ *or* **liferentri·ces** \-trə,sēz\ [*¹liferent* + *-trix*] **:** a female liferenter

life ring *n* **:** a ring-shaped life preserver usu. made of cork and other buoyant materials

liferoot \'⸗,⸗\ *n* **:** GOLDEN RAGWORT

lifesaver \'⸗,⸗⸗\ *n* **1 a :** one trained to save lives of drowning persons **b** *chiefly Brit* **:** LIFEGUARD **2 :** one that saves a person from a serious predicament or difficulty usu. at a critical time ⟨the fellowship income is a ~ to me —F.A.Perry⟩

¹lifesaving \'⸗,⸗⸗\ *n* [*life* + *saving*, fr. gerund of *save*] **:** the art or practice of saving or protecting lives esp. of drowning persons ⟨a course in ~⟩

²lifesaving \"\ *adj* **:** that engages in or is designed for lifesaving ⟨a ~ squad⟩

life scout *n* **:** a boy scout who has earned ten merit badges — compare EAGLE SCOUT, STAR SCOUT

life sentence *n* **:** LIFE 5c

life-size *also* **life-sized** \'⸗ˌ⸗\ *adj* **:** of natural size **:** equal in size to the form of a living being or an object in real life ⟨a *life-size* bronze figure of a woman —*Amer. Guide Series: N.C.*⟩ ⟨a *life-size* London bus —*Newsweek*⟩ ⟨two *life-sized* statues of the king —*Literary Digest*⟩

life·some \'līfsəm\ *adj* **:** full of animation and vigor **:** SPRIGHTLY ⟨the speeches . . . are very witty and ~ —Hartley Coleridge⟩

life space *n* **:** the physical and psychological environment of an individual or group

life-span \'⸗,⸗\ *n* **1 :** the duration of existence of an individual ⟨the effect on his *life-span* of the great pressure under which her husband works —George Lawton⟩ **2 :** the average length of life of a kind of organism or a material object esp. in a particular environment or under specified circumstances ⟨some insects whose *life-span* is no longer than a season —*Nat'l Geographic*⟩ ⟨the *life-span* of the daily political cartoon —E.W.Kenworthy⟩ ⟨the whole *life-span* of the commonwealth —*So. Atlantic Quarterly*⟩

life-style \'⸗,⸗\ *n* **:** STYLE 4c(2)

life table *n* **:** MORTALITY TABLE

life tenant *n* **:** a tenant having possession (as of property) for the duration of his life — compare LIFE ESTATE, REMAINDER, REVERSION

lifetime \'⸗,⸗\ *n* [ME *liftime*, fr. *lif* life + *time* — more at LIFE, TIME] **1 :** the time that a life continues **:** the duration of the existence of a living being or a thing ⟨a ~ of writing nonfiction —Stuart Chase⟩ ⟨these edifices . . . possess only a limited ~ —Osbert Sitwell⟩ ⟨during its ~ the university has absorbed several other institutions —*Amer. Guide Series: Md.*⟩ **2 a :** the duration of the existence of an ion or subatomic particle **b :** HALF-LIFE

life tree *n* **:** TREE OF LIFE

life vest *n* **:** a life preserver designed as a vestlike garment of buoyant or inflatable material — compare MAE WEST

life·ward \'līfwə(r)d\ *adv* **:** toward life ⟨the world had turned ~ from death —Bernard De Voto⟩

lifeway \'⸗,⸗\ *n* **:** LIFE 6 ⟨the ~*s* of these rural New Mexicans —Ruth Underhill⟩ ⟨practices suitable to their hunting ~ —Laura Thompson⟩

lifework \'⸗ˌ⸗\ *n* **:** the entire or principal work of one's lifetime; *also* **:** a work extending over a lifetime ⟨influenced him to choose government service as a ~ —*Current Biog.*⟩ ⟨spent his last . . . years waging an exhausting literary battle to defend his ~ —*Infantry Jour.*⟩

life vest

lif·ey \'līfi\ *adj* [ME *lify*, fr. *lif* life + *-y*] *now chiefly Scot* **:** full of life **:** SPIRITED

life zone *n* **:** a biogeographic zone

LIFO *abbr* last in, first out

¹lift \'lift\ *n* -s [ME *luft, lift*, fr. OE *lyft* air, sky — more at LOFT] *now chiefly Scot* **:** HEAVENS, SKY ⟨the sweet calm moon in the midnight ~ —John Wilson †1854⟩

²lift \"\ *vb* -ED/-ING/-S [ME *liften*, fr. ON *lypta*; akin to MLG *lüchten* to lift, MHG *lüften*; derivative fr. the root represented by OE *lyft* air — more at LOFT] *vt* **1 a :** to raise from a lower to a higher position (as from the ground into the air) **:** move away from the pull of gravitation **:** ELEVATE 1 ⟨the elevator ~*s* pedestrians ninety feet up the steep face of the cliff —*Amer. Guide Series: Oregon*⟩ ⟨did not ~ his head from his book —D.M.Davin⟩ ⟨~*ed* his pen from the paper⟩ **b :** to raise in rank, condition, or position ⟨~*ed* him to national recognition⟩ ⟨millions of families . . . have been ~*ed* from poverty —F.L.Allen⟩ **c :** to raise or project above surrounding objects ⟨a . . . church building ~*s* a tall clock tower —*Amer. Guide Series: Texas*⟩ ⟨the highest of these peaks . . . ~*s* its majestic cone far into the zone of permanent snow —P.E.James⟩ **d :** to raise in rate or amount ⟨~ prices of commodities —L.C.Jauncey⟩ **2** *now chiefly dial* **:** to attend to the collection of (as a payment due) ⟨the laird ~*ed* his rent —Charles Gibbon⟩ **3** *archaic* **:** to cut up (a swan) **4 a :** to take up and remove (as a tent or camp) **b :** to put an end to (a blockade or siege) by withdrawing or causing the withdrawal of investing forces **c** (1) **:** to revoke by an authoritative act **:** RESCIND ⟨urged the . . . government to ~ the embargo on the shipment of arms —*Current Biog.*⟩ (2) **:** to revoke or confiscate usu. temporarily or for a specified time ⟨~ a passport⟩ **d :** to take (as a bus ticket) esp. in order to issue a replacement **5 :** to take from its proper place: **a :** STEAL ⟨had his pocketbook ~*ed*⟩: as (1) **:** to carry or drive off (as cattle) by theft ⟨I'll never ~ no more cattle —R.M.Daw⟩ (2) **:** PLAGIARIZE **b :** to take out of normal setting ⟨~ a word out of context⟩ ⟨the writer ~*ed* an episode from history⟩ **6** *chiefly Scot* **:** to take up and carry (a coffin) in a funeral procession **7 :** to take up from the ground: **a :** to dig (root crops) ⟨tubers should not be ~*ed* when there are blight spots on the leaves —*New Zealand Jour. of Agric.*⟩ **b :** to loosen and remove (as seedlings) from the seedbed or from a nursery ⟨don't ~ bulbs before leaves are brown —*Sydney (Australia) Bull.*⟩ **8 :** to remove by scalping ⟨~ the hair⟩ **9 :** to pay off (an obligation) ⟨~ a mortgage⟩ **10 :** to soften and swell (as a film of paint or size) **11 :** FACE-LIFT **12 :** to call in (hounds) for withdrawal from the chase or for redirection in hunting **13 a :** to shift (artillery fire) from one area to another usu. at greater range **b :** to withhold (fire) from an area ⟨~ the fire prior to the advance of the infantry —*Organized Reserve Corps Army Training Bull.*⟩ **14 :** to move from one place to another (as by an airlift) **:** TRANSPORT ⟨~*ed* the staff and students . . . to California and back —*Collier's Yr. Bk.*⟩ **15 :** to remove (a fingerprint) from a surface usu. by the use of plastics and powders **16 a :** to remove (a form) from a printing press **b :** to remove (as matter in a form) for use in another job ~ *vi* **1 a :** RISE ⟨a hundred-passenger airliner ~*s* from a New York airport —Seth Babits⟩ ⟨a blue jay ~*ed* suddenly from the rubbish heaps —Clemence Dane⟩ **b :** to appear elevated (as above surrounding objects) ⟨white church spires ~ above green valleys —Gladys Taber⟩ ⟨green mountains which ~ above the desert —*Holiday*⟩ **2 a :** to rise and disperse — used chiefly of fog or clouds **b :** to cease temporarily — used of rain ⟨the rain slackened, ~*ed*, and finally left off —H.E.Bates⟩ **3 :** WARP — used of a floor **4 :** to shake slightly — used of a sail **5 :** PICK 5 **6 :** to rise after pitching — used of a ball ⟨on such a wicket . . . the ball is liable to ~ sharply —*Calling All Cricketers*⟩ **7 :** to remain intact when raised from a supporting surface — used of printing type in a locked-up form

syn LIFT, RAISE, REAR, ELEVATE, HOIST, HEAVE, and BOOST can mean, in common, to move from a lower to a higher place or position. LIFT, when it does not merely apply to any moving upward or causing to rise as by picking up, can suggest both a moving upward with a certain effort or a moving upward as in aspiring ⟨*lift* a book to dust under it⟩ ⟨*lift* a log onto a truck⟩ ⟨the tall buildings *lifted* their spires above the surrounding plain⟩ RAISE can be interchanged with LIFT but often suggests strongly a bringing of something to a vertical or a high position for which it is designed or fitted ⟨*raise* a chair above his head⟩ ⟨*raise* a flag⟩ ⟨*raise* a building⟩ ⟨*raise* a civilization to eminence⟩ REAR can sometimes esp. in figurative use be interchanged with RAISE, but can also suggest a certain literal or figurative suddenness in the movement from a lower to higher position, as of something jutting ⟨*raise* children to be responsible adults⟩ ⟨*rear* children to a happy adulthood⟩ ⟨the horse *reared*, its front feet flailing high in the air⟩ ⟨the building *reared* thirty-odd stories high⟩ ELEVATE can, in a certain literary style, be interchanged with LIFT or RAISE, but generally suggests exaltation, uplifting, or enhancing ⟨*elevate* a hand and an eyebrow⟩ ⟨an instructor *elevated* to a professorship⟩ ⟨*elevate* your standards of good conduct⟩ ⟨*elevate* his thoughts⟩ HOIST usu. implies the raising aloft of something of considerable weight esp. by mechanical means ⟨lay the heavy weights on the ground and subsequently have to *hoist* them up again —C.S.Forester⟩ ⟨the boat rocked as the admiral *hoisted* his bulk inboard —A.B.Mayse⟩ ⟨it takes five power winches to *hoist* this mammoth expanse of canvas on the five 62-foot center poles of Douglas fir —*Monsanto Mag.*⟩ HEAVE suggests strain and great effort ⟨he looked like a massive, slow-footed bear as he *heaved* himself out of the car —Jean Stafford⟩ ⟨nature's way of creating a mountain peak — first the *heaving* up of some blunt monstrous bulk of rumpled rock —C.E. Montague⟩ ⟨his men *heaved* and *heaved*, but they couldn't get that anchor off the bottom —C.L.Carmer⟩ BOOST suggests lifting or assisting to move upward by a push or other help from below ⟨*boosted* him through the skylight on the new roof —*Amer. Guide Series: La.*⟩ **syn** see in addition STEAL

— lift at *obs* **:** to rise in or stir up hostility to **— lift one's voice** *or* **lift up one's voice :** to cry aloud **:** call out ⟨thousands . . . *lifted their voices* to demand an end to uncertainty —Julian Dana⟩

³lift \"\ *n* -s *often attrib* [ME, fr. *liften*, v.] **1 :** the unit or weight that may be lifted at one time **:** QUANTITY ⟨a ~ of sheet steel⟩ ⟨610,000 pounds of daily cargo ~ —*N.Y. Times*⟩ **2 a :** the action or an instance of lifting ⟨the clear ~ of a girl's voice —Cliff Farrell⟩ ⟨a ~ of her eyebrows⟩ **b :** the action or an instance of rising as if lifting something ⟨the ~ and boom of the waves —Sacheverell Sitwell⟩ ⟨the ~ and sweep of the hills to the sky —John Connell⟩ **c :** the action or habit of carrying (a part of the body) in an upright position **:** elevated carriage ⟨the proud ~ of her head⟩ **d :** the lifting up of a dancer usu. by her partner ⟨in a superb ~ at the end —*Dance Observer*⟩ — compare ELEVATION 1d **3 a :** a device for lifting: **a :** a rope leading from a masthead to the extremity of a yard below and used chiefly to raise and support the yard — see SHIP illustration **b :** a device (as a handle or knob) used to raise a window **c :** a hinged handle used on chests **d :** the part used to lift the bar in some early door latches **4 a :** an act of stealing **:** THEFT 1 **b** *obs* **:** THIEF **5 a :** the action or an instance of assistance (as in the attainment of a higher position) **b :** a ride along one's way in a vehicle going in the same direction ⟨gave her ~*s* in his car between there and the village —Elizabeth Taylor⟩ ⟨the rain-drenched couple raising their thumbs for a ~ —E.D.Radin⟩ **6** *dial Eng* **:** a gate (as in a wall or fence) that is opened by lifting **7 :** one of the layers forming the heel of a shoe — see TOP LIFT **8** *dial Eng* **:** a cut of meat usu. from the thigh **9 a :** one of a series of levels or stepped workings in a mine; *also* **:** the vertical distance apart of such workings **b :** one of a series of sections or slices successively removed from a temporary pillar in a mine **10 :** a rise in position or condition **:** a favorable advance ⟨people . . . most deserving of such a ~ in fortune —F.L.Allen⟩ ⟨another ~ in transport costs —*Sydney (Australia) Bull.*⟩ **11 :** a usu. slight rise or elevation (as of the ground) ⟨came down from the little ~ in the ground where they were standing —W.C.Williams⟩ **12 :** the distance or extent to which something (as the water in a canal lock) rises ⟨the vertical ~ of the lower lock is 25 feet —*Civil Engineering*⟩ **13 :** an apparatus or machine used for hoisting: as **a :** a set of pumps used in a mine **b :** DUMBWAITER 2 ⟨a ~ for books in a library⟩ **c** *chiefly Brit* **:** ELEVATOR 1 ⟨heard him ring for the ~ —J.D.Beresford⟩ **d :** an apparatus for raising an automobile from the ground to a higher level (as for repair or parking) **e :** a conveyor for carrying people up or down a mountain slope ⟨three new ~*s* highlight New Hampshire's extension of ski facilities —Judith D. Beal⟩ — see ALPINE LIFT, CHAIR LIFT, SKI LIFT **f :** a mechanism for raising certain parts of farm implements above the ground ⟨a tractor with a power ~⟩ **14 a :** an elevating power or influence ⟨the great ~ of the thing . . . is what still compels in this great picture —F.J.Mather⟩ **b :** an elevation of the spirits produced by such an influence ⟨needs the ~ that the right clothes can give —*Springfield (Mass.) City Library Bull.*⟩ ⟨got a tremendous ~ from the experience —W.P.Webb⟩ ⟨a sudden ~ of excitement —Oliver La Farge⟩ **15 :** the portion of the escapement action in a timepiece in which the escape tooth imparts an impulse to the pallets **16 a :** the distance between the terminal limits of yarn or thread wound on a bobbin **b :** the traverse of a piece of mechanism in winding a bobbin **17 :** the component of the total aerodynamic force acting on an airplane or airfoil that is perpendicular to the relative wind and that for an airplane constitutes the upward force that opposes the pull of gravity **18 :** the cope of a foundry mold **19 :** a stack of brick in the kiln **20 :** a single haul of a lift net; *also* **:** the fish taken in such a haul **21 :** the amount of concrete placed at a single time in the building of a structure (as a wall, pier, abutment) **22 :** a pile of sheets (as of paper) constituting a number convenient for handling in a single printing operation ⟨when a ~ of printed sheets is removed from the press —R.W.Polk⟩ **23 a :** an organized movement of men and equipment or of supplies by some form of transportation ⟨move 1332 troops with their equipment in a single ~ —E.A. Suttles⟩ ⟨our ship carried a diverse and colorful fragment of . . . the second ~ —Gordon Merrick⟩ ⟨a food ~⟩ **b :** ¹AIRLIFT ⟨says the Korea ~ is the longest in the world —Frederick Graham⟩ ⟨how the Berlin ~ works —Charles Gardner⟩

— on the lift *adv (or adj), South & Midland* **:** in a weak condition (as from illness, hunger, or exposure) **:** unable to rise or stand without support

lift·able \'liftəbəl\ *adj* **:** capable of being lifted

lift bridge *n* **:** a drawbridge whose movable parts are lifted

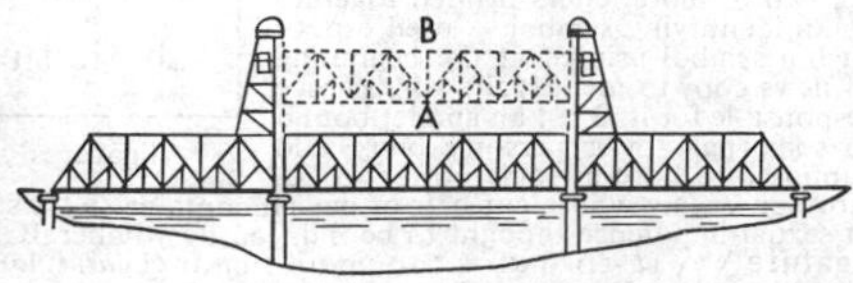

vertical lift bridge: *A* normal position, *B* raised

vertically or by rotating about a horizontal axis — compare BASCULE BRIDGE, SWING BRIDGE

lifted *past of* LIFT

lifted stem turn *n* **:** a stem turn in which the inside ski is unweighted, lifted, and set down parallel with the outside stemming ski

lift·er \'liftə(r)\ *n* -s **1 a :** one that lifts **b :** THIEF — see SHOPLIFTER **2 :** a machine or device for lifting: as **a :** a hoisting apparatus (as a bucket wheel in a paper mill or a device in a harvesting machine for elevating grain) **b :** a cam or other device used for lifting an engine valve **c :** a foundry tool for lifting loose sand from the mold; *also* **:** a contrivance that is attached to a cope to hold the sand together when the cope is lifted **d :** a removable handle for lifting lids in a kitchen range or stove **e :** a root-crop harvesting machine consisting essentially of a pair of spaced inclined bars that pass through the soil with low pointed ends foremost **f :** a piece in a lever-tumbler lock that moves the tumblers when the master key or skeleton key is inserted and turned exactly as they are moved by the ordinary key

lift gate *n* **:** an upper rear panel (as on a station wagon) that opens upward as a tailgate opens downward

lift ground *n* **:** a substance painted or drawn on the plate in etching to cause the acid-resistant ground coated over it to break down in water or acid exposing the painted parts to the biting action

lifting *pres part of* LIFT

lifting bolt *n* **:** an eyebolt to which a hook or other tackle is attached for lifting heavy machinery

lift·man \'lif(t)mən\ *n, pl* **liftmen** *chiefly Brit* **:** an elevator operator

lift net *n* **:** a bag or basket-shaped net designed to be fished vertically through the water (as in taking smelts)

lift-off \'⸗,⸗\ *n* -s [fr. *lift off*, v.] **:** a vertical takeoff by an aircraft or a rocket missile or vehicle

lift pump *also* **lifting pump** *n* **:** SUCTION PUMP

lifts *pres 3d sing of* LIFT, *pl of* LIFT

lift-slab \'⸗,⸗\ *adj* **:** of, relating to, or being a method of concrete building construction in which floor and horizontal roof slabs are cast one on top of the other usu. at ground level and then lifted to their proper heights after the concrete has developed the necessary strength

lift truck *n* **:** a small truck or a hand- or power-operated dolly equipped (as with a forklift or platform) for lifting and transporting loads (as about a shop or freight depot) — see FORK TRUCK

lift valve *n* **:** a valve whose direction of movement is perpendicular to the plane of its seat

lift van *n* **:** a large strong waterproof shipping case in which household or other goods may be sealed and shipped as a unit

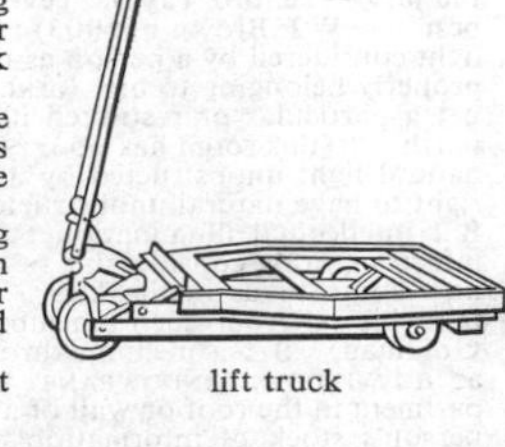

lift truck

lift wall *n* **:** the cross wall at the head of a canal lock

lig \'lig\ *dial Brit var of* LIE

lig·a·ment \'ligəmənt\ *n* -s [ME, fr. ML & L; ML *ligamentum* ligament of the body, fr. L, band, tie, fr. *ligare* to bind, tie + *-mentum* -ment — more at LIGATURE] **1 a :** a tough band of tissue that serves to connect the articular extremities of bones or to support or retain an organ in place and is usu. composed of coarse bundles of dense white fibrous tissue parallel or closely interlaced, pliant, and flexible, but inextensile **b :** any of various folds or bands of pleura, peritoneum, or mesentery connecting parts or organs **c :** a chitinous elastic band in bivalve mollusks connecting the valves along a line adjacent to the umbones and serving to open the valves — see RESILIUM **2 :** something that ties or unites one thing or part to another ⟨the law of nations, the great ~ of mankind —Edmund Burke⟩

lig·a·men·tal \,⸗⸗'mentᵊl\ *adj* **:** LIGAMENTOUS

lig·a·men·ta·ry \-tərē\ *adj* **:** LIGAMENTOUS

ligament of cooper *usu cap C* [after Sir Astley P. *Cooper* †1841 Eng. surgeon] **:** COOPER'S LIGAMENT

ligament of the ovary : a rounded cord of fibrous and muscular tissue extending from each superior angle of the uterus to the inner extremity of the ovary of the same side

ligament of treitz *usu cap T* [after Wilhelm *Treitz* †1872 Austrian physician] **:** TREITZ'S MUSCLE 1

ligament of wins·low \-'winz(,)lō, -'vin(t)(,)slō\ *usu cap W* [after Jakob B. *Winslow* †1760 Dan. naturalist] **:** a ligament of the posterior surface of the knee formed by the expansion of the tendons of the semimembranosus and other muscles

ligament of zinn \-'zin, -'tsin\ *usu cap Z* [after Johann G. *Zinn* †1759 Ger. physician] **:** the common tendon of the inferior rectus and the internal rectus muscles of the eye

lig·a·men·tous \,ligə'mentəs\ *adj* **1 :** of or relating to a ligament **2 :** forming or formed of a ligament **— lig·a·men·tous·ly** *adv*

lig·a·men·tum \,⸗⸗'mentəm\ *n, pl* **ligamen·ta** \-tə\ [ML — more at LIGAMENT] **:** LIGAMENT 1

ligamentum fla·vum \-'flāvəm\ *n, pl* **ligamenta fla·va** \-və\ [NL, lit., yellow ligament] **:** any of a series of ligaments of yellow elastic tissue connecting the laminae of adjacent vertebrae from the axis to the sacrum

ligamentum nu·chae \-'n(y)ükē\ *n, pl* **ligamenta nuchae** [NL, lit., ligament of the back of the neck] **:** a median ligament of the back of the neck that is rudimentary in man but highly developed and composed of yellow elastic tissue in many quadrupeds where it assists in supporting the head

ligan *or* **ligen** *var of* LAGAN

lig·and \'ligənd, 'līg-\ *also* **ligand group** *n* -s [L *ligandus*, gerundive of *ligare* to bind, tie — more at LIGATURE] **:** a group, ion, or molecule coordinated to the central atom in a coordination complex

li·gas \lē'gäs\ *n* -ES [Tag *ligás*] **:** a poisonous Philippine tree (*Semecarpus perrottetii*) of the family Anacardiaceae that has hard wood and yields an illuminating resin

li·gate \'lī,gāt\ *vt* -ED/-ING/-S [L *ligatus*, past part. of *ligare* to bind,tie — more at LIGATURE] **:** to tie with a ligature

li·ga·tion \lī'gāshən\ *n* -s [MF, fr. LL *ligation-, ligatio*, fr. L *ligatus* + *-ion-, -io* -ion] **1 :** the action of binding; *specif* **:** the surgical process of tying up a blood vessel **2 :** something that binds **:** CONNECTION, LIGATURE

lig·a·tive \'ligəd·iv\ *adj* [L *ligatus* + E *-ive*] *linguistics* **:** CONNECTIVE, BINDING ⟨the ~ article in Tagalog⟩

¹lig·a·ture \'ligəchə(r), -gə,chü(ə)r, -ü̇ə\ *n* -s [ME, fr. MF, fr. LL *ligatura* tie, bond, fr. L *ligatus* (past part. of *ligare* to bind, tie) + *-ura* -ure; akin to MLG *lik* band, MHG *geleich* joint, limb, Alb *lith* I tie] **1 a :** something that is used to bind; *specif* **:** a thread, wire, or other material used in surgery (as for tying the blood vessels) **b :** something that unites or connects **:** BOND ⟨having no ~ of race and family affection to bind them together —Horace Bushnell⟩ **2 :** the action of binding or tying ⟨the ~ of an artery⟩ **3 a** *in mensural notation* **:** a compound note form indicating a group of musical notes or tones to be sung to one syllable **b :** a flexible metal band with its adjusting screws that holds in place the reed of single reed woodwind instruments (as of a clarinet) **4 a :** a character consisting of two or more letters combined into one or joined by a tie **b :** a connecting line or stroke (as ‿ or ⁀) used to indicate that two successive sounds are pronounced as one syllable **c :** two or more letters printed together as an identifying symbol — used esp. of such a symbol printed at the beginning of news copy to identify the wire service responsible for it **5 a :** an amulet bound to some part of a person's body and supposed to have a magic power to destroy an enemy whose cut hair or nails it contains **b :** a state of sexual impotence thought to be induced by witchcraft

fi fl ff ffi ffl ct st ch sp sh th tt

ligatures

²ligature \"\ *vt* -ED/-ING/-S **:** to tie up **:** BIND ⟨*ligaturing* the blood vessels —*Veterinary Record*⟩

li·geance \'līj ən(t)s, 'lēj-\ *n* -s [ME *legeaunce*, fr. MF *ligeance*, fr. *lige* liege + *-ance* — more at LIEGE] **1** *archaic* **:** ALLEGIANCE **2** *now chiefly Brit* **:** the jurisdiction or territory of a liege lord or of a sovereign

li·ger \'līgə(r)\ *n* -s [*lion* + *tiger*] **:** a hybrid between a male lion and a female tiger — compare TIGON

ligg \'lig\ *now dial Brit var of* LIE

lig·gat *or* **lig·get** \'ligət\ *n* -s [ME *lidgate*, fr. OE *hlidgeat*, fr. *hlid* covering, door, gate + *geat* gate — more at LID, GATE] *Scot* **:** GATE; *esp* **:** SWING GATE

lig·ger \'ligə(r)\ *n* -s [*lig*, *ligg* + *-er*] **1** *dial Eng* **:** a float that usu. consists of a bundle of reeds with baited line attached for pike fishing **2** *dial Eng* **:** a footbridge (as of a plank) across a ditch or drain

¹light \'līt, *usu* -īd.+V\ *n* -s [ME *liht*, *light*, fr. OE *lēoht*, *līht;* akin to OHG *lioht* light, ON *ljōs*, Goth *liuhath*, L *luc-*, *lux* light, *lucēre* to shine, Gk *leukos* white, Skt *rocate* he shines] **1 a :** something that makes vision possible ⟨God said, "Let there be ~"; and there was ~ —Gen 1:3 (RSV)⟩ **b :** the sensation aroused by stimulation of the visual pathways **:** BRIGHTNESS, LUMINOSITY ⟨that ~ we see is burning in my hall —Shak.⟩ **c :** an electromagnetic radiation in the wavelength range including infrared, visible, ultraviolet, and X rays and traveling in a vacuum with a speed of about 186,281 miles per second; *specif* **:** the part of this range that is visible to the human eye and extends approximately from a wavelength of 3900 angstroms to a wavelength of 7700 angstroms **2 a :** the light of the sun **:** DAYLIGHT ⟨was up each morning at the first ~ —Frank O'Connor⟩ **b :** DAWN **3 :** a specific material source of light: as **a :** a heavenly body ⟨as night fell the ~s in the sky multiplied⟩ **b :** CANDLE ⟨put a ~ in the window⟩ **c :** ELECTRIC LAMP ⟨turned on all the ~s in the house⟩ **4** *archaic* **:** EYESIGHT ⟨when I consider how my ~ is spent ere half my days in this dark world —John Milton⟩ **5 a :** spiritual illumination that is a divine attribute or the embodiment of divine truth ⟨the ~ shines in the darkness, and the darkness has not overcome it —Jn 1:5 (RSV)⟩ ⟨Jesus is the ~ —Eliza E. Hewitt⟩ ⟨Celestial *Light*, shine inward —John Milton⟩ **b :** INNER LIGHT **c :** ultimate truth **:** ENLIGHTENMENT ⟨reaching out and groping for a pathway to the ~ —B.N.Cardozo⟩ **d :** a doctrine or set of beliefs representing true Christianity — used esp. in Scotland in the phrases *old light* and *new light* **6 a :** open view **:** public knowledge ⟨brought to ~ —languages that were hitherto practically unknown —A.V.W.Jackson⟩ **b :** a particular aspect or appearance presented to view ⟨an accused person's own testimony may put him in a very bad ~ before the jury —Telford Taylor⟩ ⟨every owner saw his dogs in the best ~ —W.F.Brown b. 1903⟩ **7 a :** a source or measure of light considered by a person as necessary for his vision and as properly belonging to him ⟨asked him not to stand in her ~⟩ **b :** a particular or restricted illumination ⟨this studio has a north ~⟩ ⟨this room has poor ~⟩ ⟨~ of the fire⟩ **c** (1) **:** the natural light unobstructed by a building or wall (2) **:** a legal right to have natural unobstructed light (3) **:** ANCIENT LIGHT **8 :** intellectual illumination **:** something that enlightens or informs ⟨throw considerable ~ on some of the problems that now confront us in the U.S. —J.B.Conant⟩ ⟨could proudly take his ~ from such unembarrassed conservatism —Eric Goldman⟩ **9 :** a medium through which light is admitted: as **a :** WINDOW, WINDOWPANE **b :** SKYLIGHT **c :** a glass compartment in the roof or wall of a greenhouse **10 lights** *pl* **:** a person's stock of information or ideas **:** philosophy of life **:** STANDARDS ⟨the attitude that one should worship according to one's ~s —Adrienne Koch⟩ ⟨tried to make him behave himself according to English ~s —G.B.Shaw⟩ **11 :** a conspicuous or dominant person in a particular country, place, or field of endeavor **:** LUMINARY ⟨one of the leading ~s of the French court —R.A.Hall b. 1911⟩ ⟨the leading and lesser ~s of U.S. diplomacy —*Time*⟩ ⟨some literary ~ from the book world —Arthur Miller⟩ **12 :** a particular look or aspect of the eye ⟨an ugly ~ came into his eye —Gretchen Finletter⟩ ⟨listened with a fiery ~ burning in her eyes —Sherwood Anderson⟩ **13 a :** a source of light used as a signal: as (1) **:** LIGHTHOUSE ⟨the keeper of the Eddystone *Light*⟩ (2) **:** a ship's blinker light ⟨called the flagship on the ~ to announce she was reporting for duty⟩ (3) **:** TRAFFIC SIGNAL ⟨turn left at the next ~⟩ **b :** a signal esp. of a traffic light ⟨stopped by a red ~⟩ ⟨given the green ~ to go ahead with his plan⟩ **14 :** something that gives life or individuality to a person **:** vital spark ⟨hide his ~ under a bushel⟩ ⟨the ~ of individual human character shining through these events —Leslie Rees⟩ **15 a :** a quality of animation, brilliance, or intensity ⟨a man of deep shadows and dazzling ~ —O.S.J.Gogarty⟩ ⟨almost any crowd shows higher ~s than this one —Katherine F. Gerould⟩ **b** (1) **:** the part of a picture that represents those objects or areas upon which the light is supposed to fall — opposed to *shade;* compare CHIAROSCURO (2) **:** the part of a work of sculpture that provides a reflecting surface for light **16 :** a flame or spark by which something (as a cigarette, cigar, or pipe) may be lighted ⟨took out a cigarette and asked him for a ~⟩ **17 :** LIGHTFACE **18 lights** *pl* **a :** FOOTLIGHTS **b :** an illuminated display of a performer's name on a theater marquee ⟨dreamed of seeing her name in ~s⟩ — **in the light of 1 :** from the point of view of ⟨advised his students to read the old authors and to criticize them *in the light of* their enhanced anatomical knowledge —Harvey Graham⟩ **2 :** in view of ⟨were fascinated — particularly *in the light of* his recent attack on modern poets —Harvey Breit⟩ ⟨*in the light of* the current news his argument seems well taken —R.A.Smith⟩

²light \"\ *adj*, *usu* -ER/-EST [ME *liht*, *light*, fr. OE *lēoht*, *līht;* akin to OFris *liacht* bright, OS & OHG *lioht* bright, OE *lēoht*, n., light — more at ¹LIGHT] **1 a** *archaic* **:** burning brightly **:** BLAZING — used of fire ⟨piled those ancient books together and set them all on a ~ fire —John Jortin⟩ **b :** having light **:** BRIGHT ⟨the rooms are airy and ~⟩ ⟨still ~ when he arrived⟩ **2 a :** having a high lightness of color ⟨though her hair was dark, she had ~ eyes⟩ **b :** having a light complexion ⟨~er than his brother⟩

³light \"\ *vb* **lighted** \-īd.əd, -ītəd\ *or* **lit** \'lit, *usu* -id.+V\ **lighted** *or* **lit; lighting; lights** [ME *lihten*, *lighten*, fr. OE *lȳhtan*, *līhtan*, *līehtan;* akin to OS *liohtian* to light, OHG *liuhten*, Goth *liuhtjan;* causative-denominative fr. the root of E ²*light*] *vi* **1** *now dial* **:** to emit light **:** be burning ⟨the two candles . . . were still ~*ing* —Eamonn O'Neill⟩ **2 :** to become filled with light **:** BRIGHTEN — usu. used with *up* ⟨people ~ up when he speaks with or to them —E.K.Lindley⟩ ⟨his face *lit* up at the small triumph —W.J.McKee⟩ **3 a :** to become ignited **:** take fire ⟨the match ~s easily⟩ **b :** to ignite something (as a cigarette, cigar, or pipe) — usu. used with *up* ⟨a small yellow flame flickered where a smoker was ~*ing* up —A.P.Gaskell⟩ ~ *vt* **1 :** to set fire to **:** cause to burn **:** IGNITE, KINDLE ⟨*lit* a cigarette⟩ ⟨struck a match and ~*ed* the lamp —Ellen Glasgow⟩ — sometimes used with *up* ⟨~ up a cigarette⟩ **2 a :** to attend or conduct with or as with a light **:** GUIDE ⟨all our yesterdays have ~*ed* fools the way to dusty death —Shak.⟩ **b :** to give light to **:** fill with light or furnish with lights **:** ILLUMINATE ⟨the chapel . . . *lit* by a three-light east window —*Country Life*⟩ — often used with *up* ⟨~ up the sky⟩ **3 :** to cause to glow **:** ANIMATE, BRIGHTEN ⟨a quick animation *lit* her face —Clarissa F. Cushman⟩ — often used with *up* ⟨one shining smile *lit* up the whole place for me —Margaret Biddle⟩ — **light a shuck** *also* **light a rag** *chiefly South & Midland* **:** to leave in haste **:** run away

⁴light \"\ *adj*, *usu* -ER/-EST [ME *liht*, *light*, fr. OE *lēoht*, *līht;* akin to OHG *līhti* light, ON *lēttr*, Goth *leihts*, L *levis* light, Gk *elachys* small, Skt *laghu*, *raghu* fast, light, slight] **1 a :** having little weight **:** not heavy ⟨~ enough for even a very small child to manage alone —Betty Pepis⟩ **b :** less heavy than others of its kind ⟨a ~ overcoat⟩ ⟨a ~ log⟩ **c :** designed to move swiftly or to carry a comparatively small load ⟨a ~ truck⟩ ⟨a ~ airplane⟩ **d :** being of small specific gravity **:** having relatively little weight in proportion to bulk ⟨~ as a feather⟩ ⟨aluminum is a ~ metal⟩ **e :** containing less than the legal, standard, or usual weight ⟨~ coin⟩ **2 a :** of slight extent or little importance **:** TRIVIAL ⟨shows the ~*est* incidence and intensity of infection —J.H.Fischthal⟩ ⟨attests in what ~ esteem we held the tank —S.L.A.Marshall⟩ **b :** not abundant **:** INCONSIDERABLE ⟨a ~ rain⟩ ⟨the early voting was ~⟩ ⟨trading on the commodity exchange was ~⟩ ⟨has relatively ~ traffic and few billboards —*Amer. Guide Series: Md.*⟩ ⟨a ~ breakfast⟩ **3 a** (1) **:** not oppressive **:** easily broken or disturbed ⟨a ~ and fitful sleep⟩ (2) **:** easily aroused **:** not weighed down by sleep ⟨a ~ sleeper⟩ **b :** barely moving or existing **:** exerting a minimum of force or pressure **:** GENTLE ⟨a ~ touch⟩ ⟨a ~ breeze⟩ ⟨that ~ irregular breathing —Aldous Huxley⟩ **c :** resulting from a very slight pressure **:** FAINT, INDISTINCT ⟨a ~ impression⟩ ⟨a ~ stroke of the pen⟩ ⟨the print was too ~ to read⟩ **4 a :** capable of being borne **:** easily endurable ⟨a ~ illness⟩ ⟨a ~ misfortune⟩ **b :** able to be performed with little effort **:** demanding comparatively little energy or strength ⟨contributed to the family income by doing ~ work —M.S. Kendrick⟩ **5 :** capable of moving or acting swiftly and dexterously **:** NIMBLE ⟨although her hands were old and often tremulous, they were ~ at whatever they performed —Elizabeth M. Roberts⟩ ⟨a healthy stout man in a hurry, ~ on his feet —Glenway Wescott⟩ **6** *now Scot* **:** delivered of a child — used always in the comparative **7 a :** showing a lack of seriousness **:** FRIVOLOUS, GIDDY ⟨had forfeited by his ~ conduct and his intemperate opinions —Ellen Glasgow⟩ ⟨~ stories, risky anecdotes were discouraged —Gamaliel Bradford⟩ **b :** lacking in stability or steadiness **:** FICKLE, CHANGEABLE ⟨a ~ man, in whom no person can place any confidence —W.E.H.Lecky⟩ **c :** sexually promiscuous **:** WANTON ⟨their thoughts strayed to ~ women —John Steinbeck⟩ **8 :** free from care **:** not burdened by suffering **:** BUOYANT, CHEERFUL ⟨more pleased and ~ of mind than she had been —W.M. Thackeray⟩ **9 :** intended to amuse and entertain **:** demanding little mental effort of the reader, listener, or spectator ⟨one generation's ~ reading often becomes another's heavy text —J.D.Hart⟩ ⟨standard ~ ballet music — inoffensive until it overdoes the waltz —Arthur Berger⟩ **10** *of a beverage* **a :** having a comparatively low alcoholic content ⟨~ wines and beers⟩ **b :** having a low concentration of flavoring congenerics **:** characterized by a relatively mild flavor **:** not heavy **11 a :** capable of being easily digested ⟨a ~ soup⟩ **b :** well leavened **:** not soggy or heavy ⟨~ bread⟩ **c :** full of air **:** FLUFFY ⟨well beaten eggs make a ~ omelet⟩ ⟨a ~ soufflé⟩ **12 :** lightly armed or equipped ⟨a fairly ~ cavalry, not fully armored —Tom Wintringham⟩ **13 :** easily pulverized **:** LOOSE, POROUS ⟨a ~ soil⟩ **14 a** *of the head* **:** having a sensation of lightness or instability **:** DIZZY, GIDDY, DISORDERED **b** *now dial Brit* **:** light in the head **:** LIGHT-HEADED, GIDDY ⟨he's a bit ~ since his accident⟩ **15 :** carrying a small cargo or none at all **:** not heavily burdened ⟨the ship returned ~⟩ **16 :** characterized by a relatively small capital investment and the use of relatively simple machinery and usu. devoted to the production of consumer goods ⟨moving into the ~*er* industries like furniture manufacture —Sam Pollock⟩ **17 :** not heavy or massive in construction or appearance ⟨despite its size, the building is ~ and graceful⟩ **18 a** *of a syllable* **:** UNACCENTED, WEAK — contrasted with *heavy* **b :** designating the second-strongest of the three degrees of stress recognized by some linguists ⟨the stress on the last syllable of "basketball" is ~⟩ **c** *of a vowel* **:** articulated without raising of the back of the tongue ⟨the front vowels and \ä\ are ~⟩ — compare DARK **d** *of an l sound* **:** CLEAR 2b **19** *of sound* **:** having a clear usu. soft and airy quality without heaviness ⟨afraid that she would ruin her small ~ voice if she persisted in singing heavy operatic music —*Current Biog.*⟩ **20** *of poultry* **:** losing weight — see GOING LIGHT **21 :** of, relating to, or containing atoms of normal mass or less than normal mass — used of isotopes ⟨deuterium has twice the mass of ordinary ~ hydrogen atoms⟩ **22** *of a domino* **:** having a comparatively small number of pips ⟨the 6-3 is ~*er* than the 6-6⟩ **23 :** being in debt to the pot in a poker game ⟨three chips ~⟩ **syn** see EASY

⁵light \"\ *adv*, *usu* -ER/-EST [ME *lihte*, *lighte*, *light*, fr. OE *lēohte*, *līhte*, fr. *lēoht*, *līht*, adj.] **:** in a light manner **:** LIGHTLY ⟨experienced campers travel ~ —*Boy Scout Handbook*⟩ — often used in combination ⟨*light*-clad⟩ ⟨*light*-loaded⟩

⁶light \"\ *vb* **lighted** *or* **lit; lighted** *or* **lit; lighting; lights** [ME *lihten*, *lighten*, fr. OE *līhtan*, *līohtan;* akin to OFris *lichta* to lighten, MD *lichten*, OHG *lihten;* causative-denominative fr. the root of E ⁴*light*] *vi* **1 :** to climb downward (as from a horse) **:** DISMOUNT — now usu. used with *down* ⟨every time he *lit* down from his saddle —W.F.Harris⟩ **2 :** to descend on a surface **:** fall to the ground **:** PERCH, SETTLE ⟨laying waste every foot of the field they ~*ed* in —O.E.Rölvaag⟩ **3 :** to come down suddenly **:** fall unexpectedly (as of a blow, good fortune, or bad fortune) — usu. used with *on* or *upon* ⟨when he got that far . . . Nemesis *lit* on him —Elmer Davis⟩ **4 :** to come or arrive by chance **:** HAPPEN — usu. used with *on* or *upon* ⟨~*ed* upon the lonely spot quite by accident —Lady Barker⟩ **5** *now dial Brit* **a :** to come to pass **:** occur by chance **b :** to experience good or bad fortune or success **:** FARE — often used with *on* ~ *vt* **1** *archaic* **:** to ease of a burden or load **:** LIGHTEN ⟨~ this weary vessel of her load —Edmund Spenser⟩ **2** *now dial Eng* **:** to deliver of a child **3 :** HAUL, MOVE ⟨~ the sail out to windward —G.S.Nares⟩ — **light into :** to attack forcefully ⟨has *lit into* the Administration's tax bill with some sparkling epithets —*Wall Street Jour.*⟩ ⟨*lit into* that food until I'd finished off the heel of the loaf —Helen Eustis⟩

light adaptation *n* **:** the adjustments including narrowing of the pupillary opening, decrease in visual purple, and dispersion of melanophores by which the retina of the eye is made efficient as a visual receptor under conditions of strong illumination — compare DARK ADAPTATION

light air *n* **:** wind having a speed of 1 to 3 miles per hour — see BEAUFORT SCALE table

light airplane *n* **:** LIGHTPLANE

light-armed \'≈'≈\ *adj* **:** armed with light weapons

light artillery *n* **:** guns and howitzers of no more than 105-millimeter caliber

light battery *n* **:** a battery of light artillery

light-beam pickup *n* **:** a phonograph pickup using a beam of light to couple the stylus to a light-sensitive converting element

lightboat \'≈,≈\ *n* **:** LIGHTSHIP

light bob *n* [⁴*light* + *bob* (nickname for *Robert*)] *Brit* **:** a light infantry soldier

light bomber *n* **:** a bomber of relatively light weight (as under 100,000 pounds) that is designed primarily to carry a moderate bombload against tactical targets (as bridges, barracks, convoys, and supply dumps) and is used also for strafing and rocketing ground targets — compare MEDIUM BOMBER, HEAVY BOMBER

light box *n* **:** a device for providing a strong uniform light on a surface (as for examining negatives or transparencies)

light bread *n*, *chiefly South & Midland* **:** wheat bread in loaves made from white flour leavened with yeast

light breeze *n* **:** wind having a speed of 4 to 7 miles per hour — see BEAUFORT SCALE table

light bridge *n* **:** ¹BRIDGE 3m(1)

light-brown apple moth *n* **:** a variable yellow and brown tortricid moth (*Tortrix postvittana*) that damages apple leaves in Australia and New Zealand

light brunswick green *n*, *often cap B* **:** a green that is yellower and paler than holly green (sense 1), lighter, stronger, and slightly yellower than deep chrome green, and yellower, lighter, and stronger than average hunter green or middle Brunswick green — called also *royal green;* compare DEEP BRUNSWICK GREEN

light bulb *n* **:** INCANDESCENT LAMP

light chrome green *n* **:** a green that is yellower and less strong than holly green (sense 1), yellower and darker than golf green, yellower, lighter, and stronger than average hunter green, and lighter and stronger than deep or medium chrome green — called also *navy green*, *Windsor green;* compare DEEP CHROME GREEN

light chrome yellow *n* **:** a strong yellow that is slightly less strong than yolk yellow and greener and stronger than gamboge — called also *Cologne yellow*, *gallstone*, *lemon chrome yellow*, *oxgall*, *Paris yellow*, *ultramarine yellow*, *zinc yellow*

light comedy *n* **:** comedy characterized by delicacy and wit

light cruiser *n* **:** a naval cruiser whose principal armament usu. consists of 6-inch guns — compare HEAVY CRUISER

light curve *n* **:** a curve expressing graphically the fluctuations in light of a variable star or other astronomical body (as a planet or asteroid)

light displacement *n* **:** the displacement of a ship completely equipped but unladen

light-draft \'≈'≈\ *adj*, *of a ship* **:** capable of operating in shallow waters

light due *or* **light duty** *n* **:** a toll levied on ships in certain waters for the upkeep of lighthouses and lightships

light-duty \'≈'≈≈\ *adj* **1 :** designed for occasional or moderate service only — used of a tool or a machine **2 :** capable of being done by a light-duty device

lighted *past of* LIGHT

¹light·en \'līt^ən\ *vb* **lightened; lightened; lightening** \-t(ᵊ)niŋ\ **lightens** [ME *lihtenen*, *lightenen*, fr. *liht*, *light*, adj., light, bright — more at LIGHT (bright)] *vt* **1 a :** to throw light on **:** make light or clear **:** ILLUMINATE ⟨a moon riding high ~*ed* their path to the beach —Ernest Beaglehole⟩ **b :** to make brighter **:** lessen the darkness of ⟨~ the picture for consumption abroad —U.T.Holmes⟩ ⟨the good news ~*ed* his gloom⟩ **2** *archaic* **:** to illuminate intellectually or spiritually **:** ENLIGHTEN ⟨have power on this dark land to ~ it —Alfred Tennyson⟩ **3 :** to make lighter (as a shade or tint) ⟨~*ed* the blue paint before applying it to the wall⟩ ~ *vi* **1 a** *archaic* **:** to shine brightly **:** glow with light ⟨my lamp ~s in the tower —Sir Walter Scott⟩ **b :** to grow lighter **:** BRIGHTEN ⟨her face would ~ directly you entered the room —Osbert Sitwell⟩ **2 :** to give out flashes of lightning ⟨this dreadful night that thunders, ~s, opens graves, and roars —Shak.⟩

²lighten \"\ *vb* -ED/-ING/-S [ME *lihtenen*, *lightenen*, fr. *liht*, *light*, adj., light (not heavy) — more at LIGHT (not heavy)] *vt* **1 a :** to relieve of a burden in whole or in part ⟨~s the ship⟩ ⟨the good news ~*ed* his mind⟩ **b :** to reduce in weight or quantity **:** LESSEN ⟨every student educated at private expense ~s the burden on the state —T.L.Hungate⟩ ⟨decide to ~ their holdings of rayon goods —S.B.Hunt⟩ **2 :** to make happier **:** CHEER, GLADDEN ⟨the time since I wrote last has been ~*ed* by two jolly dinners —H.J.Laski⟩ **3 :** to make less wearisome **:** ALLEVIATE ⟨no companionship to ~ his work —Robertson Davies⟩ ⟨afraid of intruding upon a sorrow that I could not ~ —Oscar Wilde⟩ ~ *vi* **1 :** to become light or less heavy **:** become less burdensome ⟨some correspondents believe censorship has ~*ed* somewhat —*N.Y. Times*⟩ ⟨as the war debt ~*ed*, economic and commercial development was rapid —*Amer. Guide Series: La.*⟩ **2 :** to become more cheerful ⟨his mood ~*ed* and brightened as he figured things out —O.E. Rölvaag⟩ **syn** see RELIEVE

light·en·er \-t(ᵊ)nə(r)\ *n* -s **:** one that lightens

light engine *n* **:** a locomotive operating without cars attached or with caboose only

lightening *n* -s [fr. gerund of ²*lighten*] **:** a sense of decreased weight and abdominal tension felt by a pregnant woman on descent of the fetus into the pelvic cavity prior to labor

lightening hole *n* **:** a hole cut in a plate or structural member of a ship to reduce its weight without reducing its strength

light equation *n* **:** the 498.6 seconds required by light to traverse a distance equal to the mean radius of the earth's orbit

¹light·er \'līd.ə(r), -ītə-\ *n* -s [ME, fr. (assumed) MD *lichter* (whence D), fr. MD *lichten* to lighten, unload + *-er* — more at LIGHT (to ease of a burden)] **:** a large usu. flat-bottomed boat or barge that is mainly used in unloading or loading ships not lying at wharves or in transporting freight around a harbor

²lighter \"\ *vt* -ED \-ING\ -S **:** to convey by or as if by a lighter ⟨goods have to be ~*ed* half a mile or more between ship and shore —W.R. Moore⟩ ⟨they could ~ the stuff down to Colon —D.B.Chidsey⟩

³lighter \"\ *n* -s [³*light* + *-er*] **1 :** one that lights or sets fire ⟨a ~ of lamps⟩ ⟨excelled as a ~ of fires —D.L.Busk⟩ ⟨a pressurized can of charcoal ~⟩ **2 :** a device for lighting a fire; *esp* **:** a mechanical or electrical device used for lighting cigarettes, cigars, or pipes

⁴lighter *comparative of* LIGHT

light·er·age \-əríj, -rēj\ *n* -s [ME, fr. *lighter* + *-age*] **1 :** a price paid for lightering **2 :** the loading, unloading, or transportation of goods by means of a lighter ⟨organized the ~ service of the harbor —Joseph Conrad⟩ **3 :** the boats engaged in lightering

lighterage limits *n pl* **:** the area of a harbor within which lighter service is regularly provided under certain conditions and charges

lighterman \'līd.ə(r)mən\ *n*, *pl* **lightermen :** a person employed on a lighter

light·er-out \'līd.ə'rau̇t\ *n* -s [*light out*, v. + *-er*] **:** a worker who inspects the lining of beer barrels by inserting a light through the side hole and looking through the top

lighter-than-air \'≈≈≈'≈\ *adj* **:** of less weight than the air displaced — used of aircraft

lightest *superlative of* LIGHT

lightface \'≈,≈\ *n* **:** a typeface or font of characters having comparatively light thin lines (as *this*) — compare BOLDFACE

lightfaced \'≈'≈\ *adj* **:** of or referring to lightface

lightfast \'≈,≈\ *adj* **:** resistant to light and esp. to sunlight; *specif* **:** colorfast to light

light·fast·ness *n* -ES **:** ability to resist change by light and esp. by sunlight; *specif* **:** resistance to fading or change of color by light ⟨violet shades of outstanding ~⟩ ⟨testing dyed materials for ~⟩

light field artillery *n* **:** LIGHT ARTILLERY

light filter *n* **:** COLOR FILTER

light-fingered \'≈'≈≈\ *adj* **1 :** adroit and skillful in stealing esp. by picking pockets **2 :** having a light and dexterous touch ⟨a *light-fingered* burglar who can crack the combination of a bank vault —Harry Hansen⟩ **:** NIMBLE ⟨the *light-fingered* thoughtfulness, the ironic lyricism of the most civilized playwright of the era —*Time*⟩ — **light-fin·gered·ness** *n* -ES

light flux *n* **:** LUMINOUS FLUX

light-foot \'≈,≈\ *adj* [ME *lightfot*, fr. *light* + *fot* foot — more at LIGHT (not heavy), FOOT] **:** LIGHT-FOOTED ⟨impressed by their *light-foot* walk and their easy carriage —John Buchan⟩

light-footed \'≈'≈≈\ *adj* [ME *liht fotyd*, fr. *liht*, *light* + *fotyd*, *foted*, footed fr. *fot* foot + *-ed*] **1 :** having a light and springy step ⟨a *light-footed* girl⟩ **2 :** moving gracefully and nimbly ⟨this last, incredibly *light-footed*, transparent opera —Curt Sachs⟩ — **light-foot·ed·ly** *adv* — **light-foot·ed·ness** *n*

light·ful \'lītfəl\ *adj* [ME *lihtful*, *lightful*, fr. *liht*, *light* light + *-ful* — more at LIGHT] *archaic* **:** full of light **:** BRIGHT ⟨the hall within was ~ and airy —A.Conan Doyle⟩ — **light·ful·ness** *n*

light-grasp \'≈,≈\ *n* **:** the light-gathering power of a telescope

light green SF yellowish *or* **light green SF** *n*, *usu cap L&G& Y* **:** an acid triphenylmethane dye used chiefly as a biological stain and color for foods — see DYE table (under *Acid Green 5*)

light grège *n* **:** PIPING ROCK

light gunmetal *n* **:** PELICAN 4

light-handed \'≈'≈≈\ *adj* [ME *lyghte handyd*] **1 :** having a light or delicate hand or touch ⟨the translation . . . is very good, being *light-handed*, apparently effortless, and generally unobtrusive —*New Yorker*⟩ **2** *archaic* **:** having little to carry **3 :** SHORTHANDED — **light-hand·ed·ness** *n*

light harness *n* **:** a class of show or race horses

light-headed \'≈'≈≈\ *adj* **1 :** disordered in the head **:** DELIRIOUS **:** DIZZY ⟨so *light-headed* from no sleep that my head felt big as the sky —R.P.Warren⟩ **2 :** lacking in maturity or seriousness **:** FRIVOLOUS, HEEDLESS ⟨like the teen-agers they are, tender, graceful, *light-headed* —Walter Goodman⟩ — **light-head·ed·ly** *adv* — **light-head·ed·ness** *n* -ES

light·heart·ed \ˈ;ˌ=\ *adj* [ME *ligt-herted*] **1 :** free from care or anxiety **:** GAY, HIGH-SPIRITED ⟨~ and cheerful to an irrepressible degree —Merran McCulloch⟩ — opposed to *heavyhearted* **2 :** cheerfully optimistic and hopeful **:** CASUAL ⟨this ~ trust in evolution —M.R.Cohen⟩ ⟨like other old races . . . they can be ~ in the midst of misery and joke at their own expense —H.J.Forman⟩ **syn** see GLAD

light·heart·ed·ly *adv* **:** in a lighthearted manner ⟨~ overlooks some of the less noble but basic facts of international life —S.L.Sharp⟩ ⟨sending them out to continue the war that was so ~ entered upon —C.S.Forester⟩

light·heart·ed·ness *n* **:** the quality or state of being lighthearted ⟨scientists are unduly sensitive to any suspicion of ~ in serious journals —T.H.Savory⟩ ⟨smiled innocently at their ~ —Robert Hichens⟩

light heavyweight *n* **1** *also* **light heavy :** a boxer weighing more than 160 but not over 175 pounds **2 :** a wrestler weighing more than 174 but not over 191 pounds

light–heeled \ˈ;ˌ=\ *adj* **1** *archaic* **:** lively in walking or running **:** BRISK, NIMBLE ⟨the villain is much *lighter-heel'd* than I, I followed fast, but faster he did fly —Shak.⟩ **2** *archaic* **:** UNCHASTE, WANTON

lighthouse \ˈ=,=\ *n* **:** a tower or other building equipped to guide navigators by means of a powerful light that gives a continuous or interrupted signal

lighthouse keeper \ˈ=,=,==\ *n* **:** one who maintains a lighthouse and operates the light and fog signals

light housekeeping \(ˈ)ˈ=,=,==\ *n* **1 :** domestic work restricted to the less laborious duties (as dusting or using a vacuum cleaner) **2 :** housekeeping in a room or apartment with limited facilities for cooking

lighthouse tube *n* **:** a triode that is shaped like a tiered lighthouse and that develops ultrahigh-frequency power — called also *megatron*

lighthouse

light·ing \ˈlīd·iŋ, -ītˌ, |ēŋ\ *n* -s [ME *lihting, lighting,* fr. OE *lihting,* fr. *lihten* to light + *-ing* — more at LIGHT (to illuminate)] **1 a :** ILLUMINATION ⟨the only ~ comes through a small window⟩ **b :** the action of setting on fire **:** IGNITION ⟨the ~ of the candle⟩ ⟨the ~ of the fire⟩ **2 :** an incidence or disposition of light (as in a painting) ⟨a good portrait except for the ~ of the hands⟩ **3 :** an artificial supply of light or the apparatus providing it

light·ish \ˈlīd·ish\ *adj* **:** rather light ⟨the lean, *lightish*-haired young man —Kay Boyle⟩

lightkeeper \ˈ=,==\ *n* **:** one who is in charge of a lighthouse or lightship

light·less \ˈlītləs\ *adj* [ME *lihtles, lightles,* fr. OE *lēohtlēas,* fr. *lēoht* light + *-lēas* -less — more at LIGHT] **1 :** receiving no light **:** without illumination **:** DARK ⟨came up the ~ stairs —James Jones⟩ **2 :** giving no light ⟨tells us of ~ stars, "visible" only to radio antennae —*Scientific American Reader*⟩

light·less·ness *n* -ES **:** the quality or state of being lightless **:** DARKNESS

light lock *n* **:** LIGHT TRAP

¹light·ly *adv* [ME *lihtly, lightly,* fr. OE *lēohtlīce,* fr. *lēohtlīc,* adj., light, fr. *lēoht* light + *-līc* -ly (adj. suffix) — more at LIGHT (not heavy)] **1 :** with little weight **:** with little force or pressure **:** not heavily or severely **:** BUOYANTLY, GENTLY ⟨wearing its mantle of history ~ —Richard Joseph⟩ ⟨~ kneaded to produce a fine texture —*Amer. Guide Series: N.C.*⟩ ⟨that odd superstition that the dead sleep ~ —Margery Allingham⟩ ⟨these sixty years he wears ~ —I.A.Gordon⟩ ⟨the little boat floated ~ on the sea⟩ **2 :** in a small degree or quantity **:** to no great extent or amount ⟨land ~ wooded with a varied growth —*Amer. Guide Series: La.*⟩ ⟨~ infected with the disease, recovering quite promptly —Morris Fishbein⟩ ⟨~ damaged⟩ ⟨~ fried eggs⟩ **3 :** with little effort or difficulty **:** EASILY, READILY ⟨did not get off so ~ —Jean Stafford⟩ ⟨much more deeply rooted and much less ~ resolved —Marjorie Grene⟩ **4 :** with agility **:** NIMBLY, SWIFTLY ⟨leaped ~ over the extended tongues of wagons and buggies —Sherwood Anderson⟩ **5 :** without strong cause or reason ⟨the experiment which had so nearly ended in disaster was not to be ~ repeated —J.T.McNish⟩ ⟨not a man to propose anything ~ —Bernard DeVoto⟩ **6 :** with indifference or lack of care **:** SLIGHTINGLY, UNCONCERNEDLY ⟨she says it ~ but she means it —Walter Havighurst⟩ ⟨a terrific responsibility, and one that we do not take ~ —*N. Y. Times Mag.*⟩ **7 :** without dejection **:** CHEERFULLY, GAILY ⟨an end that shall ~ and joyfully meet its translation —Walt Whitman⟩ ⟨not his words, for they were spoken ~ enough —J.E.Simmons⟩

²light·ly \ˈliktli\ *vt* -ED/-ING/-ES [ME (Sc) *lightlien,* fr. *lihtly, lightly* frivolous, fr. OE *lēohtlic* light] *chiefly Scot* **:** to make light of **:** treat slightingly **:** BELITTLE

light machine gun *n* **:** an air-cooled machine gun of not more than .30 caliber

light marching order *n* **:** an equipment of troops consisting of at most a canteen and haversack with arms and ammunition

light meat *n* **:** light-colored meat (as veal)

light metal *n* **:** a metal or alloy of low density (as aluminum, magnesium, titanium and beryllium, and alloys composed predominantly of one or more of these metals)

light meter *n* **:** a small portable illuminometer usu. of the photovoltaic type **:** EXPOSURE METER

light–minded \ˈ;ˌ=\ *adj* **:** lacking in moral earnestness **:** FRIVOLOUS, TRIFLING ⟨felt that it was a *light-minded* room, a room for sinning in evening clothes —Sinclair Lewis⟩ ⟨completely *light-minded* and unmoral and the events . . . are those of a racy morning tabloid —Rosemary Benét⟩

light–mind·ed·ly *adv* **:** in a light-minded manner

light–mind·ed·ness *n* **:** the quality or state of being light-minded

¹lightness *n* -ES [ME *lihtnesse, lightnesse,* fr. OE *līhtnes,* fr. *lēoht, līht* bright + *-nes* -ness — more at LIGHT (bright)] **1 :** the quality or state of being illuminated **:** ILLUMINATION ⟨the ~ of the room⟩ ⟨the ~ of the sky⟩ **2 :** the attribute of object colors by which the object appears to reflect or transmit more or less of the incident light and which varies for surface colors from black as a minimum to white as a maximum and for transparent volume colors from black to colorless

²lightness *n* -ES [ME *lihtnesse, lightnesse,* fr. *liht, light* light + *-nesse* -ness — more at LIGHT (not heavy)] **1 :** the quality or state of being light or having little weight ⟨the primary object of the Gothic vault was its appearance of immaterial ~ —Nikolaus Pevsner⟩ ⟨the ~ of the bread⟩ **2 :** a lack of seriousness or dignity **:** LEVITY ⟨the ~ of tone with which I uttered such serious words —E.J.Goodman⟩ **3 a :** ease of movement **:** NIMBLENESS ⟨trotted up the stair with much ~ —John Brown⟩ **b :** an ease and gaiety of style or manner ⟨a charming ~ of speech —Shane Leslie⟩ ⟨a ~ of inflection that made the statement seem disarming —H.V.Gregory⟩ **4 :** an absence of heaviness or pressure ⟨a comparable feathery ~ of touch —A.M.Daintrey⟩ **5 :** GRACEFULNESS ⟨the ~ of her figure⟩

¹light·ning \ˈlītniŋ, -nēŋ\ *n* -s [ME *lightning, lightening,* fr. gerund of *lihtenen, lightenen* to lighten — more at LIGHTEN (illuminate)] **1** *obs* **:** the action of giving light **:** ILLUMINATION, ENLIGHTENMENT ⟨a ~ before death —Shak.⟩ **2 :** the flashing of light produced by a discharge of atmospheric electricity from one cloud to another or from a cloud to the earth; *also* **:** the discharge itself **3** *slang* **:** cheap whiskey of poor quality **4 :** a sudden stroke of good fortune; *esp* **:** a nomination or selection for high political office ⟨a multiplicity of candidates, including favorite sons hoping for real ~ to strike —*Time*⟩ **5** *often cap* **:** one of a class of racing sailboats about 19 feet in length that are sloop-rigged and have a centerboard

²lightning \"\ *adj* **:** moving with or having the speed and suddenness of lightning ⟨the jargon of the auctioneer as he works with ~ rapidity —*Amer. Guide Series: N.C.*⟩ ⟨the ~ speed of modern warfare —F.D.Roosevelt⟩ ⟨superb fighters, masters of the ~ raid —Seth Agnew⟩ ⟨made ~ descents on the native villages —Tom Marvel⟩

³lightning \"\ *vi* **lightninged; lightninged; lightning; lightnings :** to discharge a flash of lightning ⟨it is *lightning* more than ever⟩ ⟨it ~*ed* terribly last night⟩

lightning arrester *n* **1 :** any of various devices for protecting an electrical apparatus and its operator from injury by a momentary abnormal rise of voltage caused by lightning or other surges **2 :** a protective device usu. used in parallel with a radio set to carry accumulations of static electricity and minor lightning discharges to the ground without going through the radio set

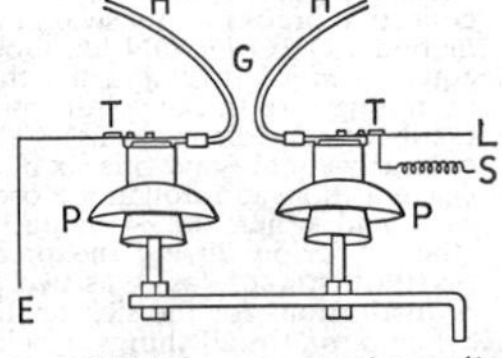

horn lightning arrester (sense 1): *G* spark gap; *H,H,* diverging horns; *P,P,* insulators; *T,T,* terminals; *E* ground; *L* line; *S* station

lightning bug *n* **:** FIREFLY

lightning calculator *n* **:** a person able to solve arithmetical problems mentally with extraordinary speed

lightning chess *n* **:** RAPID TRANSIT

lightning conductor *n* **:** a conductor leading from a lightning rod to the ground

lightning pains *n pl* **:** intense shooting or lancinating pains occurring in locomotor ataxia

lightningproof \ˈ==;=\ *adj* **:** protected from lightning

lightning rod *n* **1 :** a metallic rod set up on a building or mast and connected with the moist earth or water below to diminish the chances of destructive effect by lightning **2 :** a person or object that serves to divert attack from another ⟨serves as the *lightning rod* for complaints by our friends and allies abroad —Dorothy Fosdick⟩

lightning stone *or* **lightning tube** *n* **:** FULGURITE

lightning storm *n* **:** THUNDERSTORM ⟨the *lightning storm* in the night had touched off the fire —Hugh Fosburgh⟩

lightning switch *n* **:** a switch used in an antenna circuit (as during lightning storms) to connect the antenna to the ground instead of to the radio set

lightning war *n* **:** a war marked by surprise and speed of movement and intended to achieve victory quickly for the attacking power — compare BLITZKRIEG

light of the moon : the period between the new moon and the full moon

light oil *n* **1 :** an oil of low specific gravity or relatively low boiling point (as below about 200° C): as **a :** a flammable product obtained by the distillation of coal tar and containing aromatic hydrocarbons, phenols, and pyridine **b :** a somewhat similar product recovered from wash oil after the scrubbing of coke-oven gas and used as a source of benzene and other aromatic hydrocarbons **c :** naphtha or other flammable petroleum distillate **2 :** a crude petroleum having a high Baumé gravity (as 30° or higher)

light–o'–love *also* **light–of–love** \ˈ==;=\ *n, pl* **light–o'–loves** *also* **light–of–loves 1 :** a light woman **:** PROSTITUTE ⟨couldn't disapprove of me any more obviously if I were a *light-o'-love* you'd picked up on the street —B.A.Williams⟩ **2 :** LOVER, PARAMOUR

light opera *n* **:** opera that has a usu. gay and relatively trivial subject matter and a conventional and tuneful musical treatment — compare COMIC OPERA

light out *vi* [⁶*light*] **:** to leave in a hurry **:** start quickly ⟨after the spring roundup, ranch hands *light out* for the nearest cow town and a good time —S.E.Fletcher⟩

light pillar *n* **:** a white halo extending vertically above and below the sun or moon and caused by reflection from the upper and under surfaces of snow crystals

lightplane \ˈ=,=\ *n* **:** a small and comparatively lightweight airplane; *esp* **:** a privately owned passenger airplane — called also *light airplane*

light plot *n* **:** a plan and complete set of instructions for lighting a stage production (as a play or opera)

light pressure *n* **:** the radiation pressure of light

lightproof \ˈ=;=\ *adj* **:** impenetrable by light

light quantum *n* **:** PHOTON; *esp* **:** one of luminous radiation

light railway *n* **:** a railroad not properly equipped for ordinary heavy traffic: **a :** a railroad restricted to light traffic under British statutory laws **b :** a narrow-gage railroad

light red *n* **1 a :** a red that is lighter than moderate or grayish red **b :** a dark pink **2 :** BURNT OCHER 2 **3 :** any of various pale red or reddish orange pigments; *esp* **:** a calcined yellow ocher

light red silver ore *or* **light ruby silver ore** *n* **:** PROUSTITE

light repair *n* **:** a repair to freight cars in revenue service requiring no more than 20 man-hours of work

light repeater *n* **:** a device for conveying information on the condition of a railroad signal light

lightroom \ˈ=,=\ *n* **:** the chamber in a lighthouse that contains the lamp

lights \ˈlīts\ *n pl* [ME *lihtes, lightes,* fr. *liht, light,* adj., light (not heavy) — more at LIGHT] **1** *now dial* **:** LUNGS ⟨his liver began to grow into his ~ and the doctors couldn't save him —L.P.Hartley⟩ **2 :** the lungs of a slaughtered animal

light sails *n pl* **:** the sails carried on a sailing ship only in light winds

light·scot \ˈlīt,skät\ *n* [trans. of OE *lēohtgesceot, lēohtsceot*] *Old Eng law* **:** a tax of half a penny per hide of land for church candles

light sensitization *n* **:** PHOTOSENSITIZATION

lightship \ˈ=,=\ *n* **:** a ship that is equipped with various signaling and warning devices including a brilliant light at the masthead and that is moored off a shoal or place of dangerous navigation where a lighthouse is impracticable

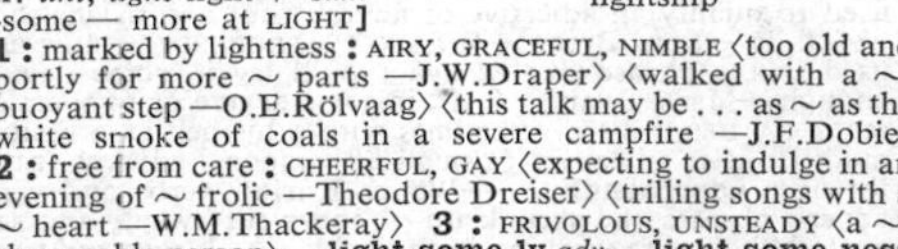

lightship

light sickness *n* **:** a disease of animals caused by photosensitization

light–skirts \ˈ=,=\ *n pl but sing in constr* **:** a loose woman

¹light·some \ˈlītsəm\ *adj* [ME *lihtsum, lightsum,* fr. *liht, light* light + *-sum* -some — more at LIGHT] **1 :** marked by lightness **:** AIRY, GRACEFUL, NIMBLE ⟨too old and portly for more ~ parts —J.W.Draper⟩ ⟨walked with a ~, buoyant step —O.E.Rölvaag⟩ ⟨this talk may be . . . as ~ as the white smoke of coals in a severe campfire —J.F.Dobie⟩ **2 :** free from care **:** CHEERFUL, GAY ⟨expecting to indulge in an evening of ~ frolic —Theodore Dreiser⟩ ⟨trilling songs with a ~ heart —W.M.Thackeray⟩ **3 :** FRIVOLOUS, UNSTEADY ⟨a ~, changeable person⟩ — **light·some·ly** *adv* — **light·some·ness** *n* -ES

²lightsome \"\ *adj* [ME *lihtsum, lightsum,* fr. *liht, light* light + *-sum* -some — more at LIGHT (not heavy)] **1 :** giving light **:** LUMINOUS ⟨~ clouds and shining seas —P.B.Shelley⟩ **2 :** not dark or gloomy **:** well lighted **:** BRIGHT ⟨a school with spacious ~ rooms⟩ **3** *archaic* **:** CLEAR, LUCID ⟨with plain and ~ brevity —John Milton⟩ **4** *archaic* **:** light in color ⟨~ green of ivy and holly —J.R.Lowell⟩

lights–out \ˈ;=\ *n, pl* **lights–out 1 :** a command or signal (as a bell or bugle call) for putting out lights **2 :** a prescribed bedtime for persons living under discipline (as in a boarding school or army camp) ⟨the only place where he could hide to study after *lights-out* —H.H.Martin⟩ ⟨while away the hours before *lights-out* —*English Digest*⟩

light splitter *n* **:** BEAM SPLITTER

light stand *n* **:** a small stand or table on which a light is put

light stone *n* **:** a grayish to dark grayish yellow that is very slightly redder than golden green — called also *Portland stone*

light–struck \ˈ;=\ *adj* **:** having reference to a light-sensitive photographic material fogged by accidental exposure to light

lighttight \ˈ=;=\ *adj* **:** LIGHTPROOF

light–time \ˈ=,=\ *n* **:** the time required for light to travel from any specified heavenly body to the earth

light trap *n* **1 a :** a passageway (as for a photographic darkroom) provided with double doors, curtains, or bends to allow passage of a person while excluding light **b :** a device (as for a photographic apparatus) that allows free passage of air or movement of a sliding part but excludes light — called also *light lock* **2 :** a device for collecting or destroying insects that consists of a bright light in association with a suitable trapping or killing medium

light valve *n* **:** an electromagnetically operated device whose light transmission varies in accordance with an electrical quantity (as current) and that is used esp. in recording sound on motion-picture film

light verse *n* **:** verse that is written mainly to amuse and entertain and that is often marked by qualities of wit, elegance, and lyric beauty

light vessel *n* **:** LIGHTSHIP

light wedgwood *n, often cap W* **:** a grayish blue — distinguished from *dark Wedgwood*

¹lightweight \ˈ=,=\ *n* [⁴*light* + *weight*] **1 :** one of less than average weight: as **a :** a boxer weighing more than 126 but not over 135 pounds **b :** a wrestler weighing more than 134 but not over 145 pounds **2 a :** a person lacking in strength of character or intellectual depth ⟨shows up its author as a ~ —C.J.Rolo⟩ ⟨if she hadn't been the ~, the weakling she was —Donn Byrne⟩ **b :** a person inadequately qualified for the position he fills or the duties he is charged with ⟨the muddled thinking of a ~ in diplomacy —*Times Lit. Supp.*⟩

²lightweight \"\ *adj* **1 :** of or relating to a lightweight ⟨a ~ bout⟩ ⟨the ~ championship⟩ **2 :** having less than average weight without fully corresponding lessening of strength, warmth, or other desirable quality ⟨~ aluminum railroad cars⟩ ⟨a ~ sweater⟩ **3 :** lacking in earnestness or profundity **:** not to be taken seriously ⟨a ~ kid who gets by on bare maintenance mentality —*Mademoiselle*⟩ ⟨~ discourses on long dead and justly forgotten court ladies —*Saturday Rev.*⟩

lightweight aggregate *n* **:** an aggregate for structural concrete, mortar, or plaster that weighs less than the usual rock aggregate

light well *n* **:** a shaft designed to admit light to the interior rooms of a building

light wine *n* **:** TABLE WINE

light within *n, pl* **lights within** *usu cap L&W* **:** INNER LIGHT

light·wood \ˈlīt,wu̇d, *Southern usu* ˈlīd·|əd *or* -ītˌ| *or chiefly dial* |ərd\ *n* **1** *chiefly South* **:** a dry wood that burns readily **:** KINDLING WOOD; *esp* **:** coniferous wood abounding in pitch **2 a :** an Australian acacia (*Acacia melanoxylon*) — called also *blackwood* **b :** any of several trees (as the candlewood) containing flammable volatile substances

light–year \ˈ;=\ *n* [¹*light*] **:** a unit of length in interstellar astronomy equal to the distance that light travels in one year in a vacuum or 5,878,000,000,000 miles

light yellowwood *n* **1 :** any of several timber trees with yellow wood: as **a** *southern Africa* **:** a podocarp (*Podocarpus thunbergii*) **b** *Austral* (1) **:** SASSAFRAS 3a(2) (2) **:** a flindersia (*Flindersia oxleyana*) (3) **:** ARBORVITAE 1 **2 :** the wood of a light yellowwood tree

lig·ia \ˈlijēə, lə'jīə\ *n, cap* [NL, prob. after *Ligia,* a siren in ancient Greek mythology, fr. Gk *Ligeia*] **:** a genus of large dark-colored active terrestrial isopod crustaceans (the type of the family Ligiidae) having long antennae and uropods and living about wharves and among rocks along seacoasts — see WHARF MONKEY

lign– *or* **ligni–** *or* **ligno–** *comb form* [L *lign-, ligni-,* fr. *lignum* — more at LIGNEOUS] **1 :** wood ⟨*ligni*form⟩ ⟨*ligni*vorous⟩ ⟨*ligno*graphy⟩ **2** [ISV, fr. *lignin*] **:** lignin ⟨*ligno*protein⟩ ⟨*ligno*sulfonic acid⟩

lign·al·oe \lī'na(,)lō, lig'-\ *or* **lign·al·oes** \-ōz\ *n* [ME *ligne aloes,* fr. MF *lignaloe, lignaloes,* fr. ML *lignum aloes,* lit., wood of the aloe] **1 :** AGALLOCH **2 :** LINALOA

lignaloe oil *n* **:** LINALOE OIL

ligne \ˈlēnʸ\ *n* -s [F, lit., line, fr. L *linea* — more at LINE] **:** any of various units of measure: as **a :** a French unit for watch movements equal to 0.0888 inch **b :** a Swiss unit for watches equal to 0.0802 inch **c :** LINE 9a(2)

lig·ne·ous \ˈlignēəs\ *adj* [L *ligneus,* fr. *lignum* wood (fr. *legere* to gather) + *-eus* -eous — more at LEGEND] **:** of or resembling wood **:** WOODY

lig·nes·cent \(ˈ)lig'nes°nt\ *adj* [*lign-* + *-escent*] **:** somewhat woody **:** tending toward woodiness

lig·ni·fi·ca·tion \,lignəfə'kāshən\ *n* -s **:** the action or process of being or becoming lignified

lig·ni·fy \ˈlignə,fī\ *vb* -ED/-ING/-ES [F *lignifier,* fr. *lign-* + *-fier* -fy] *vt* **:** to convert into wood or woody tissue ~ *vi* **:** to become wood or woody by chemical and physical changes in the cell walls that convert some or all of the constituents into lignin or lignocellulose — compare CUTICULARIZED, CUTINIZED, SUBERIZATION

lig·nin \ˈlignən\ *n* -s [*lign-* + *-in*] **1 :** an amorphous substance or mixture that together with cellulose forms the woody cell walls of plants and the cementing material between them and thus gives them added mechanical strength, that is a polymeric material characterized by a higher carbon content than cellulose and by propyl-benzene units, methoxyl groups, and hydroxyl groups, and that is not hydrolyzed by acids but is soluble in hot alkali and bisulfite and is readily oxidizable **2 :** any of various usu. brown products obtained from wood or woody plants by separation from cellulosic materials and often other organic materials: as **a :** a brown amorphous insoluble powder recovered from the black liquor resulting from the sulfate or soda process of making cellulosic pulp and used chiefly as a binder, filler, and extender (as in phenolic resins) — called also *alkali lignin* **b :** a brown amorphous powder recovered from sulfite liquor and composed usu. of ligninsulfonates — called also *sulfite lignin*

ligninsulfonate \;==;==,=\ *or* **lig·no·sulfonate** \;lignō+\ *n* [*lignin* or *lign-* + *sulphonate*] **:** a salt of a ligninsulfonic acid

ligninsulfonic acid \;==(,)=;==-\ *or* **lig·no·sulfonic acid** \;lignō+ . . . -\ *n* [ISV *lignin* or *lign-* + *sulfonic*] **:** any of various sulfonic acids derived from lignin; *esp* **:** those found as calcium or other soluble salts in sulfite liquor and used chiefly in tanning, as dispersing agents, and as raw materials for the manufacture of vanillin

lig·ni·per·dous \;lignə;pərdəs\ *adj* [*lign-* + L *perdere* to destroy + E *-ous* — more at PERDITION] **:** that destroys wood ⟨a ~ insect⟩

lig·nite \ˈlig,nīt, *usu* -īd·+V\ *n* -s [F, fr. *lign-* + *-ite*] **:** a variety of coal intermediate between peat and bituminous coal that is of comparatively recent origin, contains much volatile matter, and is usu. brownish black; *esp* **:** such coal in which the texture of the original wood is distinct — called also *brown coal, wood coal* — **lig·nit·ic** \(ˈ)lig;nid·|ik, -itˌ, |ēk\ *adj*

lig·ni·tif·er·ous \;lignə;tif(ə)rəs\ *adj* [ISV *lignite* + *-i-* + *-ferous*] **:** containing lignite

lig·ni·tize \ˈlignə,tīz\ *vt* -ED/-ING/-S [*lignite* + *-ize*] **:** to convert into lignite

lig·no·cellulose \;lignō+\ *n* [ISV *lign-* + *cellulose*] **:** any of several closely related substances constituting the essential part of woody cell walls and consisting of cellulose intimately associated with lignin — **lig·no·cellulosic** \"+\ *adj*

lig·no·cer·ic acid \;lignə;serik-\ *n* [*lignoceric* ISV *lign-* + *cer-* + *-ic*] **:** a crystalline fatty acid $CH_3(CH_2)_{22}COOH$ found esp. in wood tar (as from beechwood) and in the form of esters in many fats, fatty oils, and waxes

lig·no·sae \lig'nō(,)sē\ *n pl, cap* [NL, fr. L, fem. pl. of *lignosus* woody, fr. *lign-* + *-osus* -ous] *in some classifications* **:** a phylum comprising all those plants that are fundamentally woody and remain predominantly so — compare HERBACEAE

lig·no–tuber \;lig(,)nō+\ *n* [*lign-* + *tuber*] **:** BURL 2a

lig·num \ˈlignəm\ *n, pl* **lignums** \-mz\ *also* **lig·na** \-nə\ [NL, fr. L, wood — more at LIGNEOUS] **1 :** woody tissue **2 :** any of various trees (as lignum vitae) **3** *Austral* **:** any of various polygonaceous plants

lignum aloes *n pl but usu sing in constr* [ME, fr. ML, lit., wood of the aloe] **:** LIGNALOE

lig·num vi·tae \ˈlignəm'vīd·|ē, -ītˌ, |ī\ *n, pl* **lignum vitaes** [NL, fr. LL, a tree, lit., wood of life] **1 :** any of several trees of the genus *Guaiacum:* as **a :** a tropical American tree (*G. officinale*) found esp. in the West Indies **b :** BASTARD LIGNUM VITAE **2 :** the wood of lignum vitae **3** *Austral* **:** any of various hardwood trees (as members of the genera *Metrosideros, Acacia, Eucalyptus,* and *Vitex*) **4 :** SANDARAC TREE 1

lig·ro·in *also* **lig·ro·ine** \ˈligrəwən\ *n* -s [origin unknown] **:** any of several petroleum naphtha fractions boiling usu. in the range 20° to 135°C that commonly have a specified boiling range whether narrow (as for petroleum pentane or petroleum hexane) or wide (as 40° to 75°C) and that are used chiefly as solvents

ligul- or **liguli-** *comb form* [NL [1]*ligula*] **1 :** ligule ⟨*ligular*⟩ ⟨*liguliform*⟩ **:** ligulate ⟨*liguliflorous*⟩ **2** [NL [2]*Ligula*] **:** the genus Ligula ⟨*liguloid*⟩

[1]**lig·u·la** \ˈligyələ\ *n, pl* **ligu·lae** \-yə͵lē\ *also* **ligulas** [NL, fr. L, small tongue, small strap, spoon — more at LIGULE] **1 :** LIGULE **2 :** a band of white matter in the wall of the fourth ventricle of the brain **3 :** the distal lobed part of the labium of an insect consisting typically of a pair of median glossae and a pair of lateral paraglossae

[2]**ligula** *n* [NL, fr. L, small tongue, small strap, spoon] **1** *cap* **:** a genus of tapeworms (family Diphyllobothriidae) that lack external evidence of segmentation, are extremely short-lived intestinal parasites of fish-eating birds or rarely of man as adults, and develop almost to maturity in the body cavity of freshwater fishes **2** -s **:** a larval tapeworm developing reproductive organs and living in the body cavity of a fish

lig·u·lar \ˈligyələ(r)\ *adj* [*ligul-* + *-ar*] **:** LIGULATE

lig·u·lar·ia \͵ligyəˈla(a)rēə\ *n, cap* [NL, fr. L *ligula* small tongue, small strap, spoon + NL *-aria* — more at LIGULE] **:** a genus of Old World herbs (family Compositae) resembling the groundsel and having the margins of the involucral bracts overlapping — see LEOPARD PLANT

lig·u·late \ˈligyələt, -yə͵lāt\ *adj* [L & NL *ligula* + E *-ate*] **1 :** shaped like a strap — used of the narrow flat corollas of the ray flowers in a composite plant **2 :** furnished with ligules, ligulae, or ligulate corollas

lig·u·lat·ed \-ˌād·əd\ *adj* [L & NL *ligula* + E *-ate* + *-ed*] **:** LIGULATE

lig·ule \ˈli͵gyül\ *n* -s [NL *ligula*, fr. L, spoon; akin to L *lingere* to lick — more at LICK] **1 a :** a thin appendage of a foliage leaf; *esp* **:** one forming a membranous projection from the top of the leaf sheath of a grass **b :** a ligulate corolla of a ray floret in a composite head **c :** a membranous scale on the leaf above the sporangium in *Selaginella* and *Isoetes* **d :** a scale associated with the ovule in *Araucaria* **2 :** a lobe like a tongue on the parapodia of an annelid

lig·u·li·flo·rous \͵ligyələ¦flōrəs, -lȯr-\ *adj* [ISV *ligul-* + *-florous*] **:** having ligulate flowers

lig·u·loid \ˈligyə͵lȯid\ *adj* [*ligul-* + *-oid*] **:** of or relating to the genus *Ligula*

lig·ure \ˈli͵gyü(ə)r\ *n* -s [LL *ligurius*, fr. Gk *ligyrion*] **:** a precious stone that is prob. the jacinth ⟨the third row a ~, an agate, and an amethyst —Exod 28:19 (AV)⟩

[1]**li·gu·ri·an** \lə̇ˈgyu̇rēən\ *n* -s *cap* **1 :** a native or inhabitant of ancient Liguria **2 :** a language known from a small body of inscriptions from the area inhabited by the ancient Ligurians and generally considered as having affinities with Indo-European **3 :** a native or inhabitant of modern Liguria

[2]**ligurian** \"\ *adj, usu cap* **1** [*Liguria*, country in southwestern Europe + E *-an*] **:** of, relating to, or characteristic of ancient Liguria or its people **2** [*Liguria*, compartimento of Italy + E *-an*] **:** of, relating to, or characteristic of the modern Italian compartimento of Liguria or its people

lig·u·rite \ˈligyə͵rīt\ *n* -s [F *ligurite*, fr. *Liguria*, compartimento of Italy + F *-ite*] **:** an apple-green variety of sphene

li·gus·ti·cum \lə̇ˈgəstə̇kəm\ [NL, fr. L, lovage — more at LOVAGE] *syn of* LEVISTICUM

li·gus·tra·les \͵ligəˈstrā(͵)lēz\ [NL, fr. *Ligustrum*, type genus + *-ales*] *syn of* OLEALES

li·gus·trum \-trəm\ *n, cap* [NL, fr. L, privet, perh. fr. *Ligus* Ligurian] **:** a large genus of Old World shrubs (family Oleaceae) having smooth entire leaves and terminal panicles of white flowers — see PRIVET

lig·u·us \ˈligyüəs\ *n, cap* [NL] **:** a genus of large spiral pulmonate arboreal snails of Florida and the West Indies much prized by shell collectors for their polished shining shells that are banded with many colors

lig·y·da \ˈlijədə\ [NL, irreg. after *Ligeia*, a siren in ancient Greek mythology, fr. Gk] *syn of* LIGIA

lih·yan·ic \lēˈyanik\ *or* **lih·yan·i·an** \-ānēən\ *or* **lih·yan·ite** \-ā͵nīt\ *n* -s *usu cap* [Ar *Liḥyān* + E *-ic* or *-ian* or *-ite*] **:** a Semitic language of western Arabia known from inscriptions of the 2d and 1st centuries B.C.

li·ja \ˈlē(͵)hä\ *n* -s [Sp] **:** any of several filefishes

lik·abil·i·ty \͵līkəˈbilədē\ *n* **:** the quality or state of being likable

lik·able *or* **like·able** \ˈlīkəbəl\ *adj* **:** that can be liked or attracts liking ⟨a friendly ~ man⟩ ⟨a ~ feature of the book⟩ ⟨a gay and ~ humor —*N.Y. Times*⟩ — **lik·able·ness** *n* -ES

[1]**like** \ˈlīk\ *vb* -ED/-ING/-S [ME *liken*, fr. OE *līcian*; akin to OHG *lihhēn* to please, ON *līka*, Goth *leikan*; derivative fr. the root of the second constituent of OE *gelīc* like, alike — more at [3]LIKE] *vt* **1** *chiefly dial* **:** to be suitable, pleasing, or agreeable to (a person) ⟨at first in heart it *liked* me ill —Sir Walter Scott⟩ ⟨till then, if it ~*s* you —Andrew Lang⟩ **2 a :** to feel attraction toward or take pleasure in **:** have a liking for ⟨which friend he ~*s* best⟩ **:** FAVOR ⟨~*s* some vegetables and dislikes others⟩ **:** ENJOY ⟨~*s* doing business with them⟩ **b :** to affect favorably **:** agree with **:** SUIT ⟨I like onions but they don't ~ me⟩ **:** BECOME ⟨she likes red but it doesn't ~ her⟩ — usu. used in negative constructions **3 :** to feel toward or concerning **:** REGARD — used with *how* ⟨how would you ~ to lose your job⟩ ⟨how do you ~ her new hat⟩ ⟨learning how he *liked* the new worker⟩ **4 :** to wish to have **:** WANT ⟨do not ~ anybody to touch my things —Marjorie Osterman⟩ — often used with a conditional auxiliary ⟨would ~ a drink⟩ ⟨would ~ you to do it⟩ ⟨would ~ it returned soon⟩ ⟨isn't as widely circulated as we would ~ for it to be —E.B.Atwood⟩ ⟨would ~ for you to look this over⟩ **:** INCLINE, PREFER ⟨cases in which the doctor ~*s* to give an injection⟩ ~ *vi* **1** *obs* **:** to be in a healthy condition **:** THRIVE ⟨quinces . . . will not ~ in our cold parts —William Lawson⟩ **2** *now dial* **:** APPROVE — used with *of* or *with* ⟨I daredn't do't; my master wouldn't ~ of it —Anne Baker⟩ **3 :** to feel inclined **:** CHOOSE ⟨had salmon almost any time he *liked* —Edison Marshall⟩ **4 :** to feel liking **:** find oneself attracted ⟨would rather ~ than criticize —E.A.Weeks⟩

syn LOVE, ENJOY, RELISH, FANCY, DOTE: LIKE is a general term indicating a viewing or regarding with favor and without aversion, but without great warmth of feeling ⟨*liked* inns, and farmers, and loafers on the river —H.S.Canby⟩ LOVE (opposed to *hate*) does imply ardent attachment and great warmth ⟨I *love* Henry, but I cannot *like* him; and as for taking his arm I should as soon think of taking the arm of an elm tree —R.W. Emerson⟩ ⟨they *loved* Maurice too, but more mildly. And, very temperately, they *liked* their Aunt Rome —Rose Macaulay⟩ ⟨*loved* to roam and was passionately fond of beauty both in nature and in art —H.E.Starr⟩ ENJOY suggests taking pleasure or satisfaction in possessing, using being with, or appreciating what one likes or loves ⟨*enjoy* a finer degree of civilization than the individuals and the nations around us —Havelock Ellis⟩ ⟨seemed to *enjoy* the beautiful site of that building —Willa Cather⟩ RELISH applies to an enjoying and savoring of something that gives one peculiar satisfaction or gratification ⟨a paradox that the happiest, most vigorous, and most confident ages which the world has ever known—the Periclean and the Elizabethan—should be exactly those which created and which most *relished* the mightiest tragedies —J.W.Krutch⟩ ⟨a few hundred (not more) choice-loving connoisseurs *relish* him as the most perfect opportunist in prose —Christopher Morley⟩ FANCY may apply to a liking or a taking pleasure in something appealing to one's imagination or to one's personal tastes or whims ⟨yachts, horses, whatever he *fancied* —George Meredith⟩ ⟨would he really *fancy* a little farm somewhere inland, or would he die of the landlocked loneliness —Frank Ritchie⟩ DOTE may indicate an excessive or compulsive fondness and liking, often foolish or infatuated ⟨he *doted* on his daughter Mary; she could do no wrong —Walter Havighurst⟩ ⟨you know how servants are. They *dote* on such yarns —L.C. Douglas⟩

[2]**like** \"\ *n* -s **1 :** a feeling of attraction toward a person or thing **:** LIKING — usu. used in pl. ⟨has so many ~*s* in life—and almost as many dislikes —*Times Lit. Supp.*⟩ ⟨he now takes violent ~*s* to people —H.J.Laski⟩ **2 :** something that one likes ⟨black in summer is one of her ~*s* —*Holiday*⟩

[3]**like** \"\ *adj, sometimes* **liker**; *sometimes* **likest** [ME *lik*, *ilik*, alter. (influenced by ON *glīkr*, *līkr*) of *ilich*, fr. OE *gelīc* like, alike; akin to OHG *gilīh* like, alike, ON *glīkr*, *līkr*, Goth *galeiks*; all fr. a prehistoric Gmc compound having a first constituent represented by OE *ge-* (perfective, associative, and collective prefix) and a second constituent represented by OE *līc* body, OHG *līh*, ON *līk*, Goth *leik*; akin to Lith *lygus* like, equal — more at CO-] **1 a :** the same or nearly the same (as in nature, appearance, or quantity) ⟨members of the cat family have ~ dispositions⟩ ⟨fabrics of ~ consistency⟩ **:** equal or nearly equal ⟨gave one six blows and the other a ~ number⟩ ⟨gave a thousand dollars before and a ~ sum now⟩ ⟨his own card and others of ~ value —J.B.Pick⟩ **:** CORRESPONDING ⟨the ~ period during the preceding year⟩ **:** IDENTICAL, INDISTINGUISHABLE ⟨as ~ as two peas⟩ **:** SIMILAR ⟨hospitals and ~ institutions for the sick or disabled⟩ — formerly used with *as, unto, of* ⟨in all things it behoved him to be made ~ unto his brethren —Heb. 2:17 (AV)⟩; formerly and sometimes now used with *to, with* ⟨~ to the soft caress bestowed . . . by loving fingers —*Phoenix Flame*⟩ ⟨an old Greek was a being of ~ passions with a modern Englishman —E.A.Freeman⟩ **b :** of a form, kind, appearance, or effect resembling or suggesting — used postpositively in combination ⟨a box*like* seedpod⟩ ⟨a home*like* atmosphere⟩ ⟨a life*like* statue⟩ ⟨dog*like* existence⟩; used with a hyphen after nouns in *-ll* ⟨bell-*like*⟩ and often in nonce or infrequent compounds ⟨president-*like*⟩ ⟨opium-*like*⟩ **c :** faithful to a subject or original ⟨the finished portrait being ever so ~⟩ **2 a :** LIKELY ⟨the importance of statistics as the one discipline ~ to give accuracy of mind —H.J.Laski⟩ **b :** being about or as if about — used with the infinitive ⟨it's ~ to drive me crazy⟩ **3 :** of the kind befitting or characteristic of — used postpositively in combination ⟨lady*like* behavior⟩ ⟨lawyer*like* argumentation⟩ — **like as we lie :** having each played an equal number of golf strokes — **something like :** something nearly or altogether as it should be

syn ALIKE, SIMILAR, ANALOGOUS, COMPARABLE, AKIN, PARALLEL, UNIFORM, IDENTICAL: LIKE is a general word indicating resemblance or similarity ranging from virtual identity in all characteristics to a chance resemblance in only one ⟨convincing only to himself, or to a limited circle of *like* minds —*Times Lit. Supp.*⟩ ALIKE is similar to LIKE but is less likely to be used for the chance, farfetched resemblance and is generally limited to use in a predicate or postposed situation after a compounded substantive modified ⟨their resemblance as brother and sister . . . they looked utterly *alike* —Sinclair Lewis⟩ SIMILAR often stresses the likenesses between different things, implying that differences may be overlooked or ignored for a time ⟨Virginia creeper or the deceptively *similar* poison ivy —*Amer. Guide Series: Md.*⟩ ⟨regard the attraction which illusion has for us as *similar* to that which a flame at night has for a moth —M.R. Cohen⟩ ANALOGOUS indicates presence of some likeness which makes it feasible or permissible to draw from it an analogy, a sustained or appropriate comparison ⟨the two new states would have a position *analogous* to that of British Dominions —*Manchester Guardian Weekly*⟩ ⟨quite *analogous* to the emotionalizing of Christian art is the example afforded by the evolution of the Latin hymn —H.O.Taylor⟩ COMPARABLE indicates a likeness on one point or a limited number of points which permits a limited or casual comparison or matching together ⟨the Syrians . . . with Arabian coffee, served thick and strong in tiny cups, as a national drink *comparable* to the Englishman's tea —*Amer. Guide Series: R.I.*⟩ COMPARABLE is esp. likely to be used in connection with considerations of merit, standing, rank, or power ⟨neither in military nor industrial terms is China *comparable* to the other three great powers —Vera M. Dean⟩ AKIN, limited to use in postpositive situations, indicates an essential likeness, sometimes the sort of likeness found in kinship, in common descent from an original ancestor, prototype, or ancestral stock ⟨the Mongols of Outer Mongolia . . . are *akin* to those of the neighboring Buryat-Mongol A.S.S.R. —*Foreign Affairs*⟩ ⟨real nursery tales, *akin* to Brer Rabbit —*Times Lit. Supp.*⟩ ⟨science . . . is *akin* to democracy in its faith in human intelligence and cooperative effort —H.J.Muller⟩ PARALLEL is used to indicate the fact of similarities over a course of development throughout a history or account or the fact of resemblances or likenesses permitting a setting or bracketing together as though side by side ⟨the almost *parallel* growth of the Twin Cities —*Amer. Guide Series: Minn.*⟩ ⟨*parallel* to the classic and academic Italian school was one with a more distinctive native feeling —Paul Manship⟩ ⟨*parallel* to the powers of the king were the powers of the father in the individual household —Ralph Linton⟩ UNIFORM suggests a likeness and similarity throughout, a lack of noticeable variation wherever things in question occur or operate ⟨one of the most fundamental social interests is that law shall be *uniform* and impartial —B.N.Cardozo⟩ ⟨schools . . . no longer expect all children to learn to read at a *uniform* rate —*Education Digest*⟩ IDENTICAL indicates either the fact of being the same person or thing or, in connection with things copied, reproduced, or repeated, an exact correspondence with no significant difference being involved ⟨George Eliot and Mary Ann Evans were *identical*⟩ ⟨the interests of workers and their employers were not altogether *identical* —M.R.Cohen⟩ ⟨his home life and his life as a man of letters are never *identical* —H.S.Canby⟩

[4]**like** \"\ *n* -s [ME *lik, like, ilik, ilike*, fr. *lik, ilik*, adj. — more at [3]LIKE] **1 a :** a person or thing similar or equal to the one referred to **:** sort of person **:** KIND ⟨made it hard for you and your ~ —C.S.Lewis⟩ **:** COUNTERPART ⟨not less talented than his French or English ~ —*New Republic*⟩ **:** EQUAL ⟨scarcely expect to hear its ~ again —A.N.Whitehead⟩ — usu. used with a possessive adjective **b** *archaic* **:** a person or thing similar to another — used chiefly in proverbial expressions ⟨~ breeds like⟩ **2 :** a stroke in golf that will make equal the number of strokes played by opposing players or sides — **the like :** something similar **:** SUCHLIKE ⟨fastened with a paper clip or *the like*⟩ ⟨did you ever hear *the like*⟩ ⟨taking everything he needed . . . grease gun, wrenches, and *the like* —Danforth Ross⟩ — compare ET CETERA — **the like of** *or* **the likes of :** a person or thing like ⟨won't take such talk from *the likes of him*⟩ ⟨upon *the likes of* them that schools and colleges depend —F.L.Allen⟩ **:** anything to equal ⟨did you ever see *the likes of* that boy⟩ ⟨a mass of . . . information *the like of* which has never been collected before —*Times Lit. Supp.*⟩

[5]**like** \"\ *adv, sometimes* -ER/-EST [ME *lik, like, ilik, ilike*, fr. *lik, ilik*, adj. — more at [3]LIKE] **1** *archaic* **:** ALIKE, EQUALLY — used to qualify an adjective or adverb ⟨hut and palace show ~ filthily —Lord Byron⟩ **2 :** LIKELY, PROBABLY — now usu. used in the phrase *like enough* ⟨you'll try it, some day, ~ enough —Mark Twain⟩ **3 a :** in some degree or to some extent **:** RATHER — used sometimes with a hyphen as a limiting modifier after adjectives ⟨a small-*like* wagon⟩, adverbs ⟨saunter over nonchalantly ~ —Walter Karig⟩, verbs and verb-adverb phrases ⟨he shrunk up ~ and went away⟩, and sentences ⟨they were working in the field, ~⟩ **b** *substand* **:** sort of **:** in a way — used before and after nouns sometimes with a hyphen usu. to suggest uncertainty as to the exactness of description ⟨little sort of pictures ~ on his hat⟩ ⟨valley surrounded with ~ little mountains⟩ **c** *substand* **:** in a specified manner or degree — used after adjectives sometimes with a hyphen ⟨raise the children decent ~⟩ ⟨he spoke knowing-*like*⟩ **4 :** NEARLY ⟨the real rates . . . are more ~ 18 per thousand —B.K.Sandwell⟩ — **as like as not** *or* **like as not :** in all likelihood **:** PROBABLY ⟨like as not, her estimate won't be very good —S.L.Payne⟩

[6]**like** \"\ *prep* [ME *lik, like, ilik, ilike*, fr. *lik, ilik*, adj. & *lik, like, ilik, ilike*, adv. — more at [4]LIKE, [5]LIKE] **1 :** of the character of: **a :** typical of ⟨was ~ him to remember us at Christmas⟩ ⟨isn't that just ~ a man⟩ **b :** that compares with **:** EQUALING — usu. used in negative constructions ⟨no place ~ home⟩ ⟨no fool ~ an old fool⟩ ⟨nothing ~ a warm bath for relaxing⟩ ⟨never saw anything ~ it⟩ **c :** of a like nature with **:** comparable to — used in questions and noun clauses ⟨what is she ~⟩ ⟨learn what skiing is ~⟩ **d :** of the kind indicated by **:** of such a character as ⟨was autocratic but dictators are ~ that⟩ ⟨have great respect for a man ~ that⟩ **:** of the kind represented by ⟨keep people ~ him in line⟩ **2 :** in or after the manner of: **a :** in a manner befitting ⟨returned home ~ a dutiful son⟩ ⟨act ~ gentlemen⟩ ⟨treated him ~ a hero⟩ **b :** in the manner indicated **:** in such a manner as ⟨stop crying ~ this⟩ ⟨can't do it ~ that⟩ **c :** in what manner — used in questions and noun clauses ⟨take the wheel and see what it drives ~⟩ **3 a :** the same as or similar to (as in structure, character, appearance, or effect) ⟨foxes are ~ dogs⟩ ⟨she looks ~ her sister⟩ ⟨understood the English character, so much ~ his own —W.C.Ford⟩ ⟨our notion of fair play, ~ theirs, includes the opponent —Margaret Mead⟩ **:** of a character or in a manner suggesting ⟨vitamins that are ~ candy —*Jour. Amer. Med. Assoc.*⟩ ⟨the mist is thick ~ white cotton —Vicki Baum⟩ **:** RESEMBLING, APPROACHING ⟨has done something ~ justice to its complexity —Lewis Mumford⟩ **b :** the same as or similar to that of ⟨heard sounds ~ a motor running⟩ **4** — used correlatively with the force of *as . . . so* ⟨~ master, ~ man⟩ **5 a :** as though there would be **:** indicative of the probable occurrence of ⟨looks ~ rain⟩ ⟨looks ~ good fishing⟩ **b :** as though he, she, or it were or might be ⟨felt ~ a hypocrite⟩ ⟨looks ~ a smart boy⟩ **:** as is characteristic of or usual to ⟨sounds ~ thunder⟩ ⟨tastes ~ grape to me⟩ ⟨feeling ~ himself again⟩ **6 :** such as ⟨traditional concerns ~ law and literature —G.B.Saul⟩ **7** — used to form intensive or ironic phrases ⟨worked ~ a house afire⟩ ⟨rub out . . . a backache ~ nobody's business —Fannie Hurst⟩ ⟨sold ~ hot cakes⟩ ⟨screamed ~ hell⟩ ⟨fight ~ the devil⟩ ⟨hurt ~ anything⟩ ⟨~ fun he did⟩ — **like a book** *adv* **1 :** in formal often pedantic language ⟨talks *like a book*⟩ **2 :** with complete understanding ⟨can read his mind *like a book*⟩ — **like that 1 :** of that kind **:** in that manner ⟨small towns *like that*⟩ ⟨talked *like that*⟩ **2 :** in close accord ⟨no great family in the city he's not just *like that* with —C.B.Kelland⟩

[7]**like** \"\ *conj* [[5]*like*] **1 a** *archaic* **:** as of or in the manner of one that is ⟨the look is vivid still nor seems ~ dead —Thomas Creech⟩ **b** — used in intensive phrases ⟨waved ~ mad⟩ ⟨dancing ~ crazy⟩ **2 :** in the same way or manner as or to the same degree or extent as ⟨impromptu programs where they ask questions much ~ I do on the air —Art Linkletter⟩ — often followed by a noun or pronoun representing an incomplete clause whose verb would be the same as that of the main clause ⟨took to figures ~ a duck to water⟩ ⟨looks ~ they can raise better tobacco —Caroline Gordon⟩ ⟨looks ~ he will get the job⟩ **3 :** as if **:** as though ⟨wore his clothes ~ he was . . . afraid of getting dirt on them —*St. Petersburg (Fla.) Independent*⟩ ⟨was ~ he'd come back from a long trip⟩ ⟨acted ~ she felt sick⟩ — used esp. with intransitive verbs of the senses ⟨sounded ~ the motor had stopped⟩ **4 :** in accordance with the way in which **:** the way that ⟨the violin now sounds ~ an old masterpiece should —*Baton*⟩ **:** in the manner that ⟨did it ~ he told me to⟩ **5 a :** of the kind that ⟨wanted a doll ~ she saw in the store window⟩ **:** such as ⟨anomalies ~ just had occurred —*New Republic*⟩ **b :** similar to ⟨it was a little ~ when the war came —Gouverneur Paulding⟩ **6 :** for example ⟨when your car gives trouble — ~ when the motor won't start⟩ ⟨things that were beginning increasingly to come up — ~ next week every rifle . . . had to be turned in —James Jones⟩

[8]**like** \"\ *or* **liked** \-kt\ *verbal auxiliary* [[3]*like*] *now substand* **:** came near **:** was near — used with the perfect infinitive sometimes in the reduced form without *have* ⟨had four quarrels and ~ to have fought one —Shak.⟩ ⟨these fellows . . . had ~ to a been whipped —Anne Royall⟩ ⟨it *liked* to killed me —John Dos Passos⟩ and sometimes in that form with a substandard past participle identical with a past tense form ⟨I *liked* to have went crazy —Stetson Kennedy⟩ ⟨so loud I ~ to fell out of bed —Helen Eustis⟩

[9]**like** *vt* -ED/-ING/-S [[3]*like*] *obs* **:** LIKEN ⟨~ me to the peasant boys of France —Shak.⟩

[10]**like** *chiefly South & Midland var of* LACK

likeable *var of* LIKABLE

like as *conj* [ME, fr. *lik*, like, adv. + *as* — more at [5]LIKE] *chiefly dial* **:** in the way or manner that **:** AS ⟨*like as* a father pitieth his children, so the Lord pitieth them —Ps.103:13 (AV)⟩ ⟨an eddy there . . . *like as* you'd expect —C.S.Forester⟩ — now usu. used with *if* ⟨it was . . . *like as* if the films suddenly came for real —Richard Llewellyn⟩

liked *past of* LIKE

like·li·head \ˈlīklē͵hed\ *n* [ME *liklihede*, fr. *likli* likely + *-hed, -hede* -hood (akin to ME *-hod, -had* -hood)] *archaic* **:** LIKELIHOOD

like·li·hood \ˈlīklē͵hu̇d, -li͵-\ *n* [ME *liklihod*, fr. *likli* likely + *-hod, -had* -hood] **1** *obs* **:** LIKENESS **2 :** PROBABILITY ⟨in all ~ it will rain⟩ **3** *chiefly Brit* **:** appearance of probable success **:** PROMISE

like·li·ness \-lēnə̇s, -lin-\ *n* -ES [ME *liklinesse*, fr. *likli* likely + *-nesse* -ness] **:** LIKELIHOOD

[1]**like·ly** \ˈlīklē, -li\ *adj* -ER/-EST [ME *likli*, fr. ON *glīkligr*, *līkligr* likely, probable, fr. *glīkr*, *līkr* like, alike + *-ligr* -ly — more at [3]LIKE] **1 :** of such a nature or so circumstanced as to make something probable ⟨any approach more ~ of success⟩ **:** in a fair way — usu. used with a following infinitive ⟨any . . . government would be subject to the same dangers and ~ to meet the same fate—Elmer Davis⟩ **2 a :** seeming to justify belief or expectation ⟨if there is failure in one quarter . . . it is a ~ sign of failure in the other —R.P.Blackmur⟩ **:** CREDIBLE ⟨a ~ story⟩ **b :** having a better chance of existing or occurring than not **:** having the character of a probability ⟨tell the road authorities of their ~ future demands —John Kemp⟩ ⟨it is ~ that modern farming methods are increasing the quantities of small animals —*Amer. Guide Series: Ark.*⟩ **3 :** apparently fit or adapted for something expressed or implied **:** SUITABLE, QUALIFIED ⟨a ~ place to fish⟩ ⟨the more ~ district for discovery of prehistoric remains —Edward Clodd⟩ ⟨thrusting their spears . . . into *likely*-looking water —Wilfred Thesiger⟩ **4 :** giving promise of success or excellence **:** PROMISING ⟨sifted . . . the universities for ~ men —*Science Digest*⟩ **5** *now dial* **:** AGREEABLE, HANDSOME ⟨a ~ child . . . thoroughly nice, cheerful, obliging —Frances G. Patton⟩ **syn** see PROBABLE

[2]**likely** \"\ *adv* [ME *likli*, fr. *likli*, adj.] **:** in all probability **:** PROBABLY ⟨a popular dance hall was more ~ her choice than his —Valentine Williams⟩ ⟨they will ~ betray themselves by loud breathing —*Scribner's*⟩ ⟨more than ~ pictures it in terms of assembly lines —*Item*⟩ — **as likely as not** *or* **likely as not :** as like as not

like-minded \ˈ≈¦≈≈\ *adj* **:** having a like disposition or purpose **:** of the same mind or habit of thought — **like-mind·ed·ly** *adv* — **like-mind·ed·ness** *n*

lik·en \ˈlīkən\ *vb* **likened; likened; likening** \-k(ə)niŋ\ **likens** [ME *liknen*, fr. *lik* like + *-nen* -en — more at [3]LIKE] *vt* **:** to represent as similar **:** COMPARE ⟨~ life to a pilgrimage⟩ ~ *vi* **:** to be or become like ⟨once knew a lady that ~*ed* surprisingly to you —M.A.Bianchi⟩

like·ness *n* -ES [ME *liknesse*, fr. OE *līcnes*, prob. short for *gelīcnes*, fr. *gelīc* like, alike + *-nes* -ness — more at [3]LIKE] **1 :** the quality or state of being like **:** RESEMBLANCE, SIMILARITY ⟨should have known you anywhere from your ~ to your father —Archibald Marshall⟩ ⟨the ~*es* that hold people together . . . are greater than the unlikenesses that would make them foes —Max Gilstrap⟩ **2 :** APPEARANCE, FORM, GUISE, SEMBLANCE, SHAPE ⟨low-hanging clouds took on the ~ of a wintry sky —H.A.Chippendale⟩ ⟨modeling . . . its gods after its own ~ —Agnes Repplier⟩ **3 :** a usu. visual representation (as of a person) **:** COPY, EFFIGY, PORTRAIT ⟨her ~ has appeared on the cover of a . . . magazine —*Newsweek*⟩ ⟨a bronze bust . . . which is an excellent ~ —W.G. MacCallum⟩

[1]**liker** *comparative of* LIKE

[2]**lik·er** \ˈlīkə(r)\ *n* -s [[1]*like* + *-er*] **:** one that likes ⟨the ~ does not like . . . in accordance with mere tradition —George Saintsbury⟩

likes *pres 3d sing of* LIKE, *pl of* LIKE

like·some \ˈlīksəm\ *adj* [[1]*like* + *-some*] *now dial* **:** pleasing to the mind or senses **:** AGREEABLE ⟨a ~ girl⟩ ⟨seemed quite ~⟩

likest *superlative of* LIKE

like·ways \ˈlīk͵wāz\ *adv* [[3]*like* + *-ways*] *now dial* **:** LIKEWISE ⟨and ~ what a pleasure —Charles Dickens⟩

likewise \ˈ≈͵≈\ *adv* [ME, fr. [3]*like* + *wise*, n.] **1 :** in like manner **:** SIMILARLY ⟨when the prime minister resigns, all the lords of the admiralty do ~ —*Encyc. Americana*⟩ **2 :** in addition **:** MOREOVER, BESIDES ⟨a governor who is ~ High Commissioner for the Pacific —*Colliers Yr. Bk.*⟩ **3 :** so am I or so do I — used informally to express agreement with a sentiment expressed by another ⟨would answer "*Likewise*" when someone said "Pleased to meet you"⟩

li·kin *also* **le·kin** *or* **li·ken** \ˈlēˈkēn\ *n* -s [modif. of Chin

(Pek) *li²-chin¹*, fr. *li²* one thousandth of a tael + *chin¹* money] **:** a former Chinese provincial tax at inland stations on imports or articles in transit

lik·ing \ˈlīkiŋ, -kēŋ\ *n* -s [ME, fr. OE *līcung* pleasure, fr. *līcian* to be pleasing to + *-ung* -ing — more at ¹LIKE] **1 :** an inclination to be pleased with a person or thing **:** favorable regard ⟨had a greater ~ for law —E.M.Coulter⟩ **:** FANCY ⟨took a ~ to the newcomer⟩ **:** PREFERENCE ⟨the ~ for independent dwellings has persisted —*Amer. Guide Series: Minn.*⟩ **:** RELISH, TASTE ⟨the hot night was not to his ~ —Irving Kolodin⟩ **2** *archaic* **:** the bent of one's desire **:** PLEASURE, WILL ⟨had married him against his ~ —Shak.⟩ **3** *archaic* **:** bodily condition **:** HEALTH ⟨their young ones are in good ~ —Job 39:4 (AV)⟩ — **on liking** *adv* **:** on condition of pleasing and being pleased ⟨his policy to engage a servant *on liking*⟩

li·lac \ˈlīlək, -ī,lak, -,läk\ *n* -s [obs. F *lilac* (now *lilas*), fr. Ar *laylak*, *līlak*, fr. Per *nīlak* bluish, fr. *nīl* blue, indigo, fr. Skt *nīla* dark blue] **1 a :** a plant of the genus *Syringa; esp* **:** a European shrub (*S. vulgaris*) that is often found as an escape in No. America and has cordate ovate leaves and large panicles of fragrant pink-purple flowers **b :** any of various cultivated shrubs that are derived directly or by hybridization from members of the genus *Syringa* (as *S. vulgaris, S. persica, S. josikea, S. emodi,* and *S. amurensis*) and have white, pink, purple, or blue flowers **2 a :** any of several Australian plants of the genus *Melia* having purple flowers; *esp* **:** CHINABERRY 2 **b :** BLUEBLOSSOM **3 a :** a variable color averaging a moderate purple that is redder and paler than heliotrope, paler than average amethyst, and bluer and paler than cobalt violet **b :** a moderate pink to light grayish red that is very slightly lighter than corinthian pink

lilac daphne *n* **:** a daphne (*Daphne genkwa*) of China and Korea that blooms before the leaves emerge

li·la·ceous \(ˈ)lī¦lāshəs\ *adj* [*lilac* + *-aceous*] **:** of or resembling the color lilac

lilac gray *n* **:** a light purplish gray that is less strong and very slightly redder than orchid haze

lilac leaf miner *n* **:** the larva of a minute gracilariid moth (*Gracilaria syringella*) that mines and rolls the leaves of the lilac

lilac mildew *n* **:** a powdery mildew (*Microsphaera alni*) that attacks the leaves of the lilac

lilacthroat \ˈ⸗(,)⸗,⸗\ *n* **:** a metallic green So. American hummingbird (genus *Heliodoxa*) with a triangular lilac throat patch

lil·ae·op·sis \,lilēˈäpsəs\ *n, cap* [NL, fr. *Lilaea*, genus of plants belonging to the family Juncaginaceae + *-opsis*] *in some classifications* **:** a small genus of perennial creeping aquatic or marsh herbs (family Umbelliferae) with the leaves obsolete and the petioles altered into hollow cylindrical or subulate septate phyllodia and with small umbels of minute white flowers

li·las \lēˈlä\ *n* -ES [F, lilac] **:** LILAC 3

lil·i·a·ce·ae \,lilēˈāsē,ē\ *n pl, cap* [NL, fr. *Lilium*, type genus + *-aceae*] **:** a large family of monocotyledonous plants (order Liliales) characterized by a regular perianth of separate segments, superior ovary, loculicidal capsular fruit, and usu. bulbous stem base

lil·i·a·ceous \¦⸗⸗¦āshəs\ *adj* [LL *liliaceus*, fr. L *lilium* lily + *-aceus* -aceous — more at LILY] **1 :** of, relating to, or resembling lilies **2 a :** of or relating to the family Liliaceae **b :** having a regular corolliform perianth similar to that of plants of the genus *Lilium*

lil·i·a·les \,⸗⸗ˈā(,)lēz\ *n pl, cap* [NL, fr. *Lilium* + *-ales*] **:** an order of monocotyledonous plants with complete, perfect, and typically trimerous flowers, a compound ovary, and seeds with an oily or fleshy endosperm — see AMARYLLIDACEAE, IRIDACEAE, LILIACEAE

lil·ied \ˈlilēd, -lid\ *adj* [¹*lily* + *-ed*] **1** *archaic* **:** resembling a lily in whiteness or fairness ⟨soft ~ fingers —Samuel Warren⟩ **2 :** full of or covered with lilies ⟨~ pool and grassy acres —George Eliot⟩ **3 :** bearing or decorated with the emblematic or heraldic fleur-de-lis ⟨the ~ banner of France —S.R. Gardiner⟩

lilies *pl of* LILY

lil·i·i·flo·rae \,lilē,īˈflō(,)rē, -lō(,)-\ *n* [NL, fr. *lilii-* (fr. *Lilium*) + *-florae* (fr. L *flor-, flos* flower — more at BLOW (to bloom)] *syn of* LILIALES

lil·i·um \ˈlilēəm\ *n* [NL, fr. L, lily] **1** *cap* **:** a large genus (the type of the family Liliaceae) of herbaceous plants having scaly bulbs, whorled or scattered leaves, showy flowers with a perianth of six segments, versatile anthers, a 3-lobed stigma, and a capsular fruit — see LILY **2** -s **:** any plant of the genus *Lilium*

¹lill \ˈlil\ *vb* -ED/-ING/-S [perh. alter. of *loll*] *vt, now dial Eng* **:** to allow (the tongue) to hang ⟨~ out their tongue like a calf —James Mabbe⟩ ~ *vi, now dial Eng* **:** to hang out **:** PROTRUDE ⟨a tongue ~*ing* out of the mouth —John Florio⟩

²lill \ˈ"\ *n* -s [perh. alter. of ²*lilt*] *Scot* **:** a hole of a wind instrument

³lill \ˈ"\ *or* **lill pin** *n* -s [*lill* perh. short for ¹*lilliputian*] **:** a very small pin

lille \ˈlēl, *esp before pause or consonant* -ē(ə)l\ *adj, usu cap* [fr. *Lille*, city in northern France] **:** of or from the city of Lille, France **:** of the kind or style prevalent in Lille

lille lace *n, usu cap 1st L* **:** a bobbin lace having a hexagonal mesh ground and simple patterns outlined with a heavy flat thread

lil·li·an·ite \ˈlilēə,nīt\ *n* -s [G *lillianit*, fr. *Lillian* mine, Leadville, Colo. + G *-it* -ite] **:** a mineral $Pb_3Bi_2S_6$ consisting of a steel gray sulfide of lead and bismuth

¹lil·li·put \ˈlilə(,)pət, -lē(,)-\ *adj, sometimes cap* [fr. *Lilliput*, imaginary country in Swift's *Gulliver's Travels* (1726) inhabited by people six inches high] **:** LILLIPUTIAN 2 ⟨these ~ frogs —John Burroughs⟩

²lilliput \ˈ"\ *n* -s *sometimes cap* **:** LILLIPUTIAN 2 ⟨would the Arabs show much respect for ~*s* when they seem ready to challenge giants —Hal Lehrman⟩

¹lil·li·pu·tian \¦⸗⸗¦pyüshən\ *adj, sometimes cap* [*Lilliput*, imaginary country + E *-ian*, adj. suffix] **1 :** of, relating to, or characteristic of the imaginary country Lilliput **2 :** of, relating to, or characteristic of the Lilliputians: **a :** extremely small ⟨displaying . . . all of that ~ wardrobe —Hamlin Garland⟩ **b :** SMALL-MINDED, PETTY ⟨the ~ senators —W.A. White⟩

²lilliputian \ˈ"\ *n* -s *often cap* [*Lilliput*, imaginary country + E *-ian*, n. suffix] **1 :** an inhabitant of the imaginary country Lilliput **2 :** one that resembles a Lilliputian: **a :** a tiny person **b :** a petty or small-minded person ⟨the ~*s* that now misrule the destiny of America —B.J.Davis⟩

lil·loo·et \ˈliləwət, -,wet\ *n, pl* **lillooet** *or* **lillooets** *usu cap* **1 a :** a Salishan people of the Fraser river valley in British Columbia **b :** a member of such people **2 :** the language of the Lillooet people

lil·ly-low \ˈlili,lō\ *n* [alter. of *low* (flame)] *chiefly dial Eng* **:** a bright flame

lil·ly·pil·ly \ˈlilē,pilē\ *n* -ES [origin unknown] **:** a plant of the genus *Eugenia; esp* **:** an Australian tree (*E. smithii*) with hard fine-grained wood

¹lilt \ˈlilt\ *vb* -ED/-ING/-S [ME *lulten*] *vt* **1 :** to begin to sing, sound, or play **:** STRIKE — often used with *up* ⟨~ up your pipes —Allan Ramsey †1758⟩ **2 :** to sing in a lively cheerful manner ⟨~*ing* a tune to supply the lack of conversation —Emily Brontë⟩ ~ *vi* **1 :** to sing or speak in a rhythmical manner ⟨whose shrill voice I have heard this half hour ~*ing* in the . . . kitchen —Sir Walter Scott⟩ **2 a :** to move in a lively springy manner ⟨a young man . . . ~*ing* a little in his walk —Rudyard Kipling⟩ **b :** to sway gently from side to side (as in some dances)

²lilt \ˈ"\ *n* -s **1 :** a spirited and usu. gay song or tune ⟨a well-known rollicking Irish ~ —Samuel Lover⟩ ⟨the wordless music of a ~ —Brian George⟩ **2 :** a rhythmical swing, flow, or cadence ⟨the lines go with a ~ —R.L.Stevenson⟩ ⟨the ~ of the train as it picked up speed —John Masters⟩ **3 :** a springy movement indicative of buoyant spirits ⟨a ~ in her step⟩

lilting *adj* [fr. pres. part. of ¹*lilt*] **:** characterized by a rhythmical swing or cadence **:** BUOYANT ⟨the flute broke into a light ~ air —J.G.Frazer⟩ ⟨swinging down the street with an easy, ~ stride —*Longman's Mag.*⟩ — **lilt·ing·ly** *adv* — **lilt·ing·ness** *n* -ES

lilting skip *n* **:** a skip with sideward swaying

¹lily \ˈlilē, -li\ *n* -ES [ME *lilie*, fr. OE, fr. L *lilium*, of non-IE origin; akin to the source of Gk *leirion* lily] **1 a :** any of numerous erect perennial leafy-stemmed bulbous herbs that constitute the genus *Lilium*, are native to the northern hemisphere, and are widely cultivated for their showy and unscented flowers **b :** any of various other plants of the family Liliaceae that usu. have showy flowers suggesting those of plants of the genus *Lilium* — used chiefly in combination; compare DAY LILY, LILY OF THE VALLEY, MARIPOSA LILY, PLANTAIN LILY **c :** any of various plants of other families (as Amaryllidaceae, Iridaceae) of the order Liliales including several that are cultivated for their showy and often fragrant flowers — usu. used in combination; compare BUTTERFLY LILY 1, SPIDER LILY **2 :** any of various plants with showy flowers: as **a :** the scarlet anemone that grows wild in Palestine — used chiefly in biblical references **b :** WATER LILY **c :** CALLA 2 **3 :** one that resembles the lily in whiteness, fairness, purity, or fragility ⟨a virgin, a most unspotted ~ —Shak.⟩ **4 a :** the conventional or heraldic fleur-de-lis considered as the symbol of France — usu. used in pl. ⟨the golden *lilies* of France —Gilbert Parker⟩ **b** *obs* **:** the north-pointing end of a compass needle **5 :** ROYAL SPADE **6 :** a pontoon airstrip consisting of interlocked hexagonal metal drums

lily

²lily \ˈ"\ *adj* **:** resembling a lily in whiteness, fairness, purity, or fragility ⟨my lady's ~ hand —John Keats⟩

lily family *n* **:** LILIACEAE

lily green *n* **:** a moderate yellow green that is greener and lighter than average moss green and yellower and paler than average pea green or apple green

lily iron *n* **1 :** a harpoon with a detachable barbed head used esp. in swordfishing **2 :** the head of a lily iron

lilylike \ˈ⸗⸗,⸗\ *adj* **:** resembling a lily ⟨~ in her stateliness and sweetness —Alfred Tennyson⟩

lily-livered \¦⸗⸗¦⸗⸗\ *adj* [¹*lily* + *livered*; fr. the whiteness of the lily and fr. the former belief that the choleric temperament depends on the body's producing large quantities of yellow bile] **:** lacking courage **:** COWARDLY ⟨*lily-livered* poltroons lacking even the . . . courage of a rabbit —P.G.Wodehouse⟩

lily of the incas *usu cap I* **:** PERUVIAN LILY

lily of the nile *usu cap N* [*Nile*, river in northeast Africa] **:** AGAPANTHUS 2

lily of the valley *n, pl* **lilies of the valley 1 :** a low perennial herb (*Convallaria majalis*) of the family Liliaceae having usu. two large oblong lanceolate leaves and a raceme of fragrant nodding bell-shaped white flowers — compare FALSE LILY OF THE VALLEY **2 :** the dried rhizome and roots of the lily of the valley used as a cardiac tonic

lily-of-the-valley shrub \¦⸗⸗⸗⸗¦⸗⸗-\ *n* **:** MOUNTAIN FETTERBUSH

lily-of-the-valley tree *n* **1 :** SWEET PEPPERBUSH **2 :** MOUNTAIN FETTERBUSH **3 :** SOURWOOD

lily pad *n* **:** a floating leaf of a water lily

lily thorn *n* **:** PRICKLY APPLE

lily-trotter \ˈ⸗⸗,⸗⸗\ *n* **:** any of various birds of the family Jacanidae that have feet adapted for running on floating vegetation

lily of the valley

lilyturf \ˈ⸗⸗,⸗\ *n* **:** a plant of either of two genera (*Liriope* and *Ophiopogon*) used as an ornamental

¹lily-white \ˈ⸗⸗¦⸗\ *adj* [ME *lilie-whit*, fr. *lilie* lily + *whit* white] **1 :** white as a lily **:** pure white **2 a :** designed to maintain a color line by excluding Negroes ⟨overruled the rank and file on the basis of the *lily-white* clause in the union ritual —John Beecher⟩ **b :** characterized by or favoring the exclusion of Negroes esp. from politics ⟨began to identify themselves with a *lily-white* movement which would expel Negroes from the organization —H.R.Penniman⟩ — opposed to BLACK-AND-TAN **3 :** lacking faults or imperfections **:** IRREPROACHABLE, PURE, INNOCENT ⟨will show the jury he isn't as *lily-white* as he would have them believe —George Norris⟩

²lily-white \ˈ"\ *n* **:** a member of a lily-white organization; *esp* **:** a member of a faction of the Republican party in the southern U.S. favoring the exclusion of Negroes from political life — opposed to *black and tan*

lim *abbr* limit; limited

¹lima \ˈlēmə\ *adj, usu cap* [fr. *Lima*, Peru] **:** of or from Lima, the capital of Peru **:** of the kind or style prevalent in Lima

²li·ma \ˈlīmə\ *n, cap* [NL, fr. L *lima* file; fr. the shape of the shell — more at LIME] **:** a genus of bivalve mollusks (suborder Pectinacea) that is the type of the family Limidae comprising the file shells

³li·ma \ˈlēmə\ *usu cap* — a communications code word for the letter *l*

li·ma bean \ˈlīmə-\ *also* **lima** *n* -s [fr. *Lima*, Peru] **1 a :** any of various bush or tall-growing beans that are derived from a perennial tropical American species (*Phaseolus limensis*) and that are widely cultivated for their large flat edible usu. pale green or whitish seeds **b :** SIEVA BEAN **2 :** the seed of any lima bean

lima-bean pod borer *n* **:** the larva of a small European pyralidid moth (*Etiella zinckenella*) introduced into No. America that bores into the green pods of many legumes including lima beans

li·ma·cea \līˈmāshēə\ *n pl, cap* [NL, fr. *Limac-, Limax*, type genus + *-ea* (fr. L, neut. pl. of *-eus* -eous)] *in old classifications* **:** a natural group comprising the terrestrial slugs

lim·a·cel *or* **lim·a·celle** \,liməˈsel\ *n* -s [F *limacelle*, fr. *limace* slug (fr. L *limac-, limax*) + *-elle* -el (fr. L *-ella*)] **:** the small internal shell of slugs of *Limax* and related genera

li·mac·i·dae \līˈmasə,dē\ *n pl, cap* [NL, fr. *Limac-, Limax*, type genus + *-idae*] **:** a family of gastropod mollusks — see LIMAX

li·mac·i·form \-,fȯrm\ *adj* [prob. fr. (assumed) NL *limaciformis*, fr. L *limac-, limax* slug + *-iformis* -iform] **:** resembling a slug — used esp. of insect larvae

lim·a·cine \ˈlimə,sīn, ˈlīm-, -sən\ *adj* [NL *limacinus*, fr. L *limac-, limax* slug + *-inus* -ine] **:** of, relating to, or resembling a slug

li·ma·cod·i·dae \,līməˈkädə,dē\ [NL, fr. *Limacodes*, included genus (fr. L *limac-, limax* slug + NL *-odes*) + *-idae*] *syn of* EUCLEIDAE

lim·a·coid \ˈlimə,kȯid\ *adj* [NL *limacoides*, fr. L *limac-, limax* slug + *-oides* -oid] **:** like a slug **:** LIMACINE

li·ma·çon \,lēməˈsōⁿ, ˈlimə,sän\ *n* -s [F, lit., snail, fr. OF, dim. of *limaz* snail, slug, fr. L *limac-, limax* slug] **:** a plane curve consisting of the collection of points obtained by taking a fixed distance in both directions along a half line from a fixed point on a circle measured from its second intersection with the circle

li·man \lēˈmän\ *n* -s [Russ, fr. Turk, harbor, fr. Gk *limenion* small harbor, dim. of *limen-, limēn* harbor] **:** a bay or estuary at the mouth of a river **:** LAGOON

li·man·da \ləˈmandə\ *n, cap* [NL, fr. F *limande* dab, fr. OF, irreg. fr. *lime* dab, file, fr. L *lima* file — more at LIME] **:** a genus of flounders that have the eyes on the right side, a humped nose, small scales, and the undersurface often brightly colored and that include certain excellent food fishes of northern temperate seas (as the rusty dab)

li·ma·tion \līˈmāshən\ *n* -s [L *limation-, limatio*, fr. *limatus* (past part. of *limare* to file, fr. *lima* file) + *-ion-, -io* -ion] **:** FILING, POLISHING

li·ma wood \ˈlēmə-, ˈlīmə-\ *n, usu cap L* [fr. *Lima*, Peru] **:** a soluble red wood derived from a tree (*Caesalpinia tinctoria*) of Ecuador and Peru and used in dyeing

¹li·max \ˈlī,maks\ *n, cap* [NL *Limac-, Limax*, fr. L *limac-, limax* slug, fr. (assumed) Gk *leimak-, leimax* (whence LGk *leimak-, leimax* slug) — more at LIME] **:** a genus (the type of the family Limacidae) of gastropod mollusks containing typical slugs including several troublesome garden pests and formerly including most of the slugs

²limax \ˈ"\ *adj* **:** resembling a slug — used esp. of small amoebas that form a single broad anterior pseudopodium and flow sluggishly forward

¹limb \ˈlim\ *n* -s [ME *lim*, fr. OE; akin to ON *limr* member of the body, *lim* limb of a tree, L *limit-, limes* boundary, limit, *limus* sidelong, *limin-, limen* threshold, Gk *leimōn* meadow, *limen-, limēn* harbor, *ōlenē* elbow — more at ELL] **1** *now dial Brit* **:** an organ or member of the body **2 a :** one of the projecting paired appendages (as an arm, wing, fin, or parapodium) of an animal body made up of diverse tissues (as epithelium, muscle, and bone) derived from two or more germ layers and concerned esp. with movement and grasping but sometimes modified into sensory or sexual organs **b :** a leg or arm of a human being ⟨a froufrou of petticoats concealing their upper ~*s* —Godfrey Winn⟩ ⟨lost the use of his ~*s*⟩ ⟨artificial ~*s* — better elbows and wrists, legs capable of producing a smooth walking cadence —R.M.Yoder⟩ ⟨packed so close together in a boat already leaking that they could hardly move a ~ —B.N.Cardozo⟩ **3 :** a large primary branch of a tree ⟨the knotty ~*s* of an enormous oak —P.B.Shelley⟩ **4 :** a person that is an active member or agent ⟨choose such ~*s* of noble counsel —Shak.⟩ ⟨lame the ~*s* of the democracy —J.A.Froude⟩ ⟨~ of the law⟩ **5 :** a branch or arm of something ⟨a ~ of the sea⟩ ⟨a ~ of a cross⟩ ⟨the Stanleyville ~ is a completely detached rail segment —Tom Marvel⟩ ⟨elongation of the ~*s* of the letters —F.W.Goudy⟩ **6 :** a mischievous child **:** a young scamp ⟨his folks likely fretting themselves to prostration over him, the ungrateful ~ —Helen Eustis⟩ **7 :** either part of an archery bow from the handle to the tip ⟨upper ~⟩ ⟨lower ~⟩ **8 :** one of the two parts of an anticline or syncline on either side of the axis — **out on a limb :** in an exposed and dangerous position with little chance of retreat ⟨was not quite willing to go *out on a limb* for a little piece of paper —John Steinbeck⟩ ⟨like other venture-loving businessmen, he occasionally finds himself *out on a limb* —*Time*⟩

²limb \ˈ"\ *vt* -ED/-ING/-S **:** to cut or tear off the limbs of **:** DISMEMBER; *esp* **:** to cut off the limbs of (a felled tree) ⟨after being felled and ~*ed* —W.F.Driver⟩

³limb \ˈ"\ *n* -s [L *limbus* border — more at LIMP] **1 :** EDGE, BORDER: as **a :** the graduated margin of an arc or circle in an instrument for measuring angles **b :** the graduated staff of a leveling rod **2 :** the outer edge of the apparent disk of a celestial body or a portion of the edge ⟨the east ~ of the sun⟩ **3 a :** the expanded portion of an organ or structure: as (1) **:** the spreading upper portion of a gamosepalous calyx or a gamopetalous corolla as distinguished from the lower tubular portion (2) **:** the broad terminal portion of a petal as contrasted with the narrow basal part (3) **:** a leaf blade **b :** the margin or the terminal portion of the leaf in mosses when different in color or structure from the median or basal portion

¹lim·ba \ˈlimbə\ *n, pl* **limba** *or* **limbas** *usu cap* **1 a :** a peasant people of Sierra Leone traditionally distantly affiliated with their neighbors as far afield as Fouta Djallon in French Guinea **b :** a member of such people **2 :** a West-Atlantic language of the Limba people

²limba \ˈ"\ *n* -s [prob. native name in West Africa] **1 :** a tall whitish-trunked West African tree (*Terminalia superba*) — called also *afara, korina* **2 :** the straight-grained wood of the limba tree

lim·bal \ˈlimbəl\ *adj* [*limbus* + *-al*] **:** LIMBIC

lim·bate \ˈlim,bāt\ *adj* [LL *limbatus* bordered, fr. L *limbus* border + *-atus* -ate] **:** having a part of one color surrounded by an edging of another color ⟨a ~ leaf⟩

lim·ba·tion \limˈbāshən\ *n* -s [*limbate* + *-ion*] **:** LIMBUS

limb bud *n* **:** a proliferation of embryonic tissue shaped like a mound from which a limb develops

lim·beck *also* **lim·bec** \ˈlim,bek\ *n* -s [ME *lambyke, lembike*, modif. of MF *alambic* & ML *alembicum* — more at ALEMBIC] **:** ALEMBIC ⟨shelves filled with jars, bottles, phials and ~*s* —Josephine Pinckney⟩

limbed \ˈlimd\ *adj* [ME *-limed*, fr. *lim* limb + *-ed*] **:** having limbs; *specif* **:** having limbs of a specified character — usu. used in combination ⟨broad-*limbed*⟩ ⟨strong-*limbed*⟩

¹lim·ber \ˈlimbə(r)\ *n* -s [ME *lymour*] **1** *now dial Eng* **:** the shaft of a cart, wagon, or carriage — usu. used in pl. **2 a :** a horse-drawn 2-wheeled vehicle to which a gun or caisson may be attached by means of a lunette that is slipped over a pintle and that includes a pole to which the horses are joined and an ammunition chest that serves as a seat for cannoneers **b :** a similar vehicle designed to be drawn by a tractor

²limber \ˈ"\ *vb* -ED/-ING/-S *vt* **:** to attach a gun or caisson to the limber preparatory to moving to a new position ~ *vi* **:** to put together the limber and the gun or caisson — usu. used with *up*

³limber \ˈ"\ *adj, often* -ER/-EST [origin unknown] **1 a :** capable of being shaped **:** FLEXIBLE, PLIABLE ⟨diamond necklaces . . . as ~ as a ribbon collar —*New Yorker*⟩ ⟨loosen their already ~ credit terms —*Newsweek*⟩ **b :** lacking in firmness **:** PLIANT, UNTRUSTWORTHY ⟨put me off with ~ vows —Shak.⟩ **2 a :** having a resilient and supple quality of body or movement **:** AGILE, NIMBLE ⟨with his ~ springiness and his arms dangling from half-length sleeves —W.B.Furlong⟩ **b :** having a lively and supple quality of mind or style ⟨your sharpened eye and ~*er* imagination —Edwin Denby⟩ ⟨delightfully ~ renditions —Whitney Balliett⟩ **3** *now dial* **:** FLABBY, LIMP, WEAK **syn** see SUPPLE

⁴limber \ˈ"\ *vb* **limbered; limbered; limbering** \-b(ə)riŋ\ **limbers** *vt* **:** to cause to become limber **:** make flexible or pliant **:** LOOSEN — often used with *up* ⟨~*ed* his mental and moral muscles —Janet Whitney⟩ ⟨for the musician to ~ up his smallest joint —J.M.Barzun⟩ ~ *vi* **:** to become limber esp. by engaging in light exercise — usu. used with *up*

⁵limb·er \ˈlimə(r)\ *n* -s [²*limb* + *-er*] **:** a logger who trims limbs from felled trees — called also *brusher, brutter*

limber board *n* [*limber* (as in *limbers*) + *board*] **:** one of the movable planks used to cover the bilge-water passages on each side of a keelson — see SHIP illustration

limber chain *n* [*limber* (as in *limbers*) + *chain*] **:** a chain used to clean limber holes

limber chest *n* [¹*limber* + *chest*] **:** an ammunition box or chest on the limber

limberham \ˈ⸗⸗,⸗\ *n* [³*limber* + *ham*] *archaic* **:** a supple-jointed obsequious person

limber hole *n* [*limber* (as in *limbers*) + *hole*] **:** a drain hole near the bottom of a frame or other structural member of a ship — see SHIP illustration

lim·ber·ly *adv* [³*limber* + *-ly*] **:** in a limber manner ⟨turns about ~ and marches away —Saul Bellow⟩

limberneck \ˈ⸗⸗,⸗\ *n* [³*limber* + *neck*] **:** a botulism of poultry and other birds characterized by paralysis of the neck muscles and pharynx that interferes with swallowing and with raising or controlling the head — compare DUCK SICKNESS

lim·ber·ness *n* -ES [³*limber* + *-ness*] **:** the quality or state of being limber

limber pine *n* [³*limber* + *pine*] **:** a pine (*Pinus flexilis*) of the Pacific coast of No. America that has the needles in bundles of five and densely clustered at the branchlet ends and the cones with a very short stalk

limber rope *n* [*limber* (as in *limbers*) + *rope*] **:** a rope passing through the limbers of a ship to keep them clear of dirt

lim·bers \ˈlimbə(r)z\ *n pl* [modif. of F *lumière* (sing.), fr. OF *lumiere* light, opening, fr. L *luminare* window, fr. *lumin-, lumen* light — more at LUMINARY] **:** gutters or conduits on each side of the keelson to afford a passage for water to the pump well

lim·bic \ˈlimbik\ *adj* [F *limbique*, fr. *limbe* limbus (fr. NL *limbus*, fr. L, border) + *-ique* -ic] **:** of, relating to, or forming a limbus

limbic lobe *n* [part trans. of F *lobe limbique*] **:** the marginal medial portion of the cortex of a cerebral hemisphere

lim·bif·er·ous \(ˈ)limˈbif(ə)rəs\ *adj* [prob. fr. F *limbifère* limbiferous (fr. *limbe* limbus + *-i-* + *-fère* -ferous) + E *-ous*] **:** having a border or margin

limbing *pres part of* LIMB

limb·less \ˈlimləs\ *adj* [¹*limb* + *-less*] **:** having no limbs

limb·meal \'liməl\ *adv* [ME *limmele*, fr. OE *limmǣlum*, fr. *lim* limb + *-mǣlum* -meal] *now dial Eng* **:** limb from limb **:** in pieces

lim·bo \'lim(,)bō\ *n* -s [ME, fr. ML, abl. of *limbus* limbo, fr. L, border — more at LIMP] **1** *often cap* **:** a region believed to exist on the border of hell as the abode of souls barred from heaven through no fault of their own (as the souls of just men who died before the coming of Christ or the souls of unbaptized infants) **2 a :** a place or state of restraint or confinement ⟨trapping travelers in an airless ~ —Sam Boal⟩ ⟨trapped by its own sense of inadequacy in a ~ of boredom —William Murray⟩ **b :** a place or state of neglect or oblivion ⟨the ~ of forgotten things⟩ ⟨vanished into the ~ of profitless products —S.H.Adams⟩ ⟨disappeared into the ~ of lost ships —E.L. Beach⟩ **c :** an intermediate or transitional place or state **:** a middle ground ⟨the infinitely complex pattern of business practices which occupies the ~ between competition and monopoly —S.M.Fine⟩ ⟨half-man, half-child, and yet neither, the adolescent occupies a special human ~ —*New Republic*⟩

limbs *pl of* LIMB, *pres 3d sing of* LIMB

lim·bu \'lim(,)bü\ *n, pl* **limbu** *or* **limbus** *usu cap* **1 a :** a Mongoloid people chiefly of Nepal **b :** a member of such people **2 :** the Tibeto-Burman language of the Limbu people

lim·burg·er cheese \'lim,bərgər, -bōgə(r, -bəigə(r\ *also* **limburger cheese** *or* **limburg cheese** *n* -s *usu cap L* [*limburger* fr. Flem, one belonging to Limburg, fr. *Limburg*, province in northeast Belgium + Flem *-er* (akin to D *-er*); *limburg* fr. *Limburg*, province in northeast Belgium] **:** a semisoft surface-ripened cheese that has a rind of pungent odor and a creamy-textured body of strong flavor

lim·bus \'limbəs\ *n* -ES [ML, fr. L, border] **1 :** LIMBO **2** [NL, fr. L, border] **:** a border distinguished by color or structure: as **a :** a circumference or margin of a bivalve shell or of an insect wing external to the closed cells **b :** the marginal region of the cornea of the eye by which it is continuous with the sclera

limby \'limē\ *adj, often* -ER/-EST [1*limb* + *-y*] **:** having many or prominent limbs ⟨this figured birch tends to be ~, requiring pruning —*Jour. of Forestry*⟩

1**lime** \'līm\ *n* -s [ME *lim*, fr. OE *līm*; akin to OHG *līm* birdlime, ON *lim* lime (calcium oxide), L *lima* file, *linere* to smear, *levis* smooth, Gk *leios* smooth, LGk *leimak-*, *leimax* slug, Russ *slina* saliva, Skt *layate* he clings, sticks] **1 :** BIRDLIME **2 a :** a caustic highly infusible solid that consists essentially of calcium oxide often together with magnesia, that is obtained usu. in the form of white to grayish lumps or pebbles by calcining limestone, seashells (as oyster or conch shells), coral, or other forms of calcium carbonate, and that is used chiefly in building (as in mortar, plaster, and brick), in agriculture, in metallurgy, in the chemical and related industries, and in the treatment of water, sewage, and trade wastes — called also *burnt lime, caustic lime, quicklime* **b :** HYDRATED LIME **c :** HYDRAULIC LIME **d :** CALCIUM — not used systematically ⟨~ nitrate⟩ ⟨carbonate of ~⟩ **3 :** limestone or other form of calcium carbonate with or without magnesium carbonate **4 a :** a pit or the liquid it contains in which skins are limed **b :** the process of liming in leather manufacturing

2**lime** \"\ *vt* -ED/-ING/-S [ME *limen*, fr. OE *-līman*; akin to OHG *līmen* to cement, ON *līma*; denominative fr. the root of E 1*lime*] **1** *archaic* **:** to bind together **:** CEMENT ⟨who gave his blood to ~ the stones together —Shak.⟩ **2 :** to smear with a sticky substance (as birdlime) ⟨would have found twigs *limed* for him —Sir Walter Scott⟩ **3 :** to entangle or catch with or as if with birdlime ⟨birds are *limed* with the sticky sap of wild fig trees smeared on splinters of bamboo —C.D.Forde⟩ ⟨*limed* soul . . . struggling to be free —Shak.⟩ **4 a :** to coat with a solution of lime and water **:** WHITEWASH ⟨their gaudy-hued houses and *limed* picket fences —*Time*⟩ **b :** to apply ground limestone or other forms of lime to (land) **:** fertilize with lime ⟨can ~ it, cross-plow it, manure it —F.D.Roosevelt⟩ **c :** to treat with lime: as (1) **:** to steep in a lime solution in order to remove hair (as in tanning) or to dissolve proteins (as in gluemaking) (2) **:** to add lime to in order to precipitate impurities **d :** to coat (as the inside of water pipes) with calcareous scale ⟨hard water ~*s* pipes⟩

3**lime** \"\ *adj* [1*lime*] **:** of, relating to, or containing lime or limestone

4**lime** \"\ *vi* -ED/-ING/-S [prob. alter. of 6*line*] *archaic* **:** COPULATE ⟨how the raging lion is to ~ with the yearning unicorn —W.H.Auden⟩

5**lime** \"\ *n* -s [alter. of earlier *line*, fr. *lind* — more at LIND] **:** LINDEN 1a

6**lime** \"\ *n* -s [F, lime (the fruit), fr. Prov *limo*, fr. Ar *līm*] **1 :** a spiny tropical tree (*Citrus aurantifolia*) with elliptic oblong narrowly winged leaves **2 :** the small globose fruit of the lime that is greenish yellow when ripe and has a very acid pulp that yields a juice used as a flavoring agent and as a source of ascorbic acid — compare LEMON **3** *or* **lime yellow :** a grayish to moderate yellow — called also *justic, old fustic*

lime·ade \'lī'mād\ *n* -s **:** a beverage of lime juice sweetened and mixed with plain or carbonated water

lime anthracnose *n* **:** a blighting and fruit spotting disease of the lime in the West Indies caused by a fungus (*Colletotrichum gloeosporioides*)

lime–ash \'=,=\ *n, dial Eng* **:** ashes and lime mixed for flooring

lime·berry \'līm- — *see* BERRY\ *n* **1 :** a spiny Malayan shrub (*Triphasia trifolia*) of the family Rutaceae with small pleasantly flavored red berries **2 :** the fruit of the limeberry shrub

lime blue *n* **1 :** a blue pigment stable toward lime: as **a :** a mixture of copper hydroxide and lime that is no longer used **b :** a mixture of ultramarine or methylene blue and gypsum **2 a :** AZURITE BLUE **b :** FRENCH BLUE

lime boil *n* **:** a process (as in bleaching cotton) of boiling with water containing lime

limeburner \'=,==\ *n* [ME *limbrennere*, fr. *lim* lime + *brennere* burner] **:** one that burns limestone or shells to make lime

limed ginger \'līmd-\ *n* **:** ginger rootstocks coated with lime — called also *bleached ginger*

limed oak *n* **:** oak that has been treated with a lime paste rubbed into the grain to give it a special finish

limed rosin *n* **:** CALCIUM RESINATE

lime glass *n* **:** a glass containing a substantial proportion of lime that is used in most commercial glass products (as bottles, tumblers, and window glass)

lime green *n* **1 :** LINDEN GREEN **2 :** TILLEUL GREEN **3 :** a grayish greenish yellow to light olive **4 :** a variable color averaging a strong yellow green

lime–juic·er \'līm,jüsə(r)\ *n* [*lime juice* (noun phrase, fr. 6*lime* + *juice*) + *-er*; fr. the use of lime juice on British ships as a beverage to prevent scurvy] **1** *Austral* **:** an Englishman newly arrived in Australia **2** *slang* **a :** a British ship ⟨ship aboard a British *lime-juicer* —J.C.Lincoln⟩ **b :** an English sailor ⟨*lime-juicers* beating their way aft with a belaying pin —Joseph Hergesheimer⟩ **c :** ENGLISHMAN ⟨exhibits less of that deadly stuffiness than many another *lime-juicer* —*New Republic*⟩

limekiln \'=,=\ *n* [ME *limkilne*, fr. *lim* lime + *kilne* kiln] **:** a kiln or furnace for reducing limestone or shells to lime by burning

lime·less \'līmləs\ *adj* **:** having no lime ⟨these allegedly ~ oceans —*Yale Rev.*⟩

1**lime·light** \'līm,līt, *usu* -īd.+V\ *n* **1 a :** a stage lighting instrument producing its illumination by means of an oxyhydrogen flame directed on a cylinder of lime and usu. equipped with a lens to concentrate the light in a beam **b :** the intense white light produced by such an instrument ⟨as the branches burn they glow with the dazzling white of ~ —M.A.Wilson⟩ **c** *Brit* **:** SPOTLIGHT ⟨his genial smile was spotted on everyone in turn, like a ~, with an orange slide over it, at a theatre —Osbert Sitwell⟩ **2 :** the light of public attention **:** the center of the stage ⟨held the ~ in this period and set the pace, tone, and temper of the movie medium —Lewis Jacobs⟩ ⟨in the ~⟩

2**limelight** \"\ *vt* **:** to center attention on **:** SPOTLIGHT ⟨pleased and flattered . . . to be so studied, so ~*ed* —Hamlin Garland⟩

lime·light·er \-īd.ə(r)\ *n* [1*limelight* + *-er*] **:** one who is or wants to be in the limelight ⟨a perfect modern pantheon of ~*s* —*Saturday Rev.*⟩

limelike \'=,=\ *adj* **:** resembling the lime ⟨~ fruit⟩

lime liniment *n* [1*lime*] **:** CARRON OIL

lime·man \'līmmən\ *n, pl* **limemen 1 :** a slaughterhouse worker who removes fat and flesh from hides by washing them in clear water, soaking them in lime, and rewashing them **2 :** LIMER

lime mortar *n* **:** a mortar made of lime, sand, water, and occas. a small quantity of cement

lime myrtle *n* **:** LIMEBERRY

li·men \'līmən\ *n* -s [L *limin-, limen* threshold; intended as trans. of G *schwelle* — more at LIMB] **:** THRESHOLD 3 ⟨make urgent the appetites and needs which are smoldering below the ~ of awareness —R.M.Lindner⟩

li·me·ña \lə'mānyə\ *n* -s *cap* [Sp, fem. of *limeño*] **:** a female native or resident of Lima, Peru

lim·e·ni·tis \,limə'nīd·əs\ *n, cap* [NL, fr. Gk *limenitis* harbor goddess, fem. of *limenitēs* harbor god, fr. *limen-*, *limēn* harbor + *-itēs* -ite — more at LIMB] **:** a holarctic genus of butterflies (family Nymphalidae) comprising mainly dark butterflies with a white wing bar but including also the two important mimics, viceroy (*L. archippus*) and red-spotted purple (*L. astyanax*)

lime nitrogen *n* **:** CALCIUM CYANAMIDE — used chiefly commercially

li·me·ño \lə'mān(,)yō\ *n* -s *cap* [Sp, fr. *Lima*, Peru] **:** a male native or resident of Lima, Peru

lime oil *n* **:** either of two essential oils obtained from limes and used chiefly as flavoring materials: **a :** an oil obtained by steam distillation of the juice of the crushed fruit **b :** a yellow oil resembling lemon oil and obtained by expression of the fresh peel of the fruit

lime peel *n* **1 :** a variable color averaging a strong yellow green that is yellower and duller than viridine yellow and greener and darker than parrot green **2** *of textiles* **:** a moderate yellow green that is lighter, stronger, and slightly yellower than average moss green and yellower and stronger than average pea green

lime pit *n* [ME *lymepit*, fr. *lyme, lim* lime + *pit*] **1 :** a limestone quarry **2 :** a pit where lime is made **3 :** a pit where lime is used (as in liming hides)

lime putty *n* **:** a cement that consists of lump lime slaked with water to the consistency of cream and left to harden by evaporation until it becomes like soft putty

lime·quat \'līm,kwät\ *n* -s [6*lime* + kum*quat*] **1 :** a hybrid between the lime and the kumquat **2 :** the fruit of the limequat tree

1**lim·er** \'līmə(r)\ *n* -s [ME, fr. MF *limier*, fr. OF *liemier*, fr. *lien* leash, band, tie + *-ier* -er — more at LIEN] *archaic* **:** a leash hound; *esp* **:** BLOODHOUND

2**limer** \"\ *n* -s [2*lime* + *-er*] **1 :** one that snares birds with birdlime **2 :** one that uses or applies lime; *esp* **:** a tannery worker who soaks hides and skins in lime solution to loosen the hair — called also *limeman*

1**lim·er·ick** \'lim(ə)rik, -rēk\ *adj, usu cap* [fr. *Limerick*, city and county in southwest Ireland] **1 :** of or from the city of Limerick, Ireland **:** of the kind or style prevalent in Limerick **2 :** of or from County Limerick, Ireland **:** of the kind or style prevalent in County Limerick

2**limerick** \"\ *n* -s [fr. *Limerick*, Ireland; prob. fr. its use by a group of Irish poets writing in Limerick in the 18th cent.] **:** a light verse form of 5 anapestic lines of which lines 1, 2, and 5 are of 3 feet and rhyme and lines 3 and 4 are of 2 feet and rhyme

3**limerick** \"\ *n* -s *usu cap* [fr. *Limerick*, Ireland] **:** a fishhook of a shape first made in Ireland — see FISHHOOK illustration

limerick lace *also* **limerick** *n* -s *usu cap 1st L* **:** a lace of Irish origin made by embroidering or darning patterns on net; *esp* **:** TAMBOUR LACE

1**limes** *pl of* LIME, *pres 3d sing of* LIME

2**li·mes** \'lī,mēz\ *n, pl* **lim·i·tes** \'limə,tēz\ [L *limit-, limes* — more at LIMB] **:** a boundary or line of fortifications; *specif* **:** one of the fortified frontiers of the ancient Roman Empire

lime soap *n* **:** an insoluble soap that is formed as a troublesome curd when ordinary soap is used in hard water but that may be specially prepared for use in lubricating greases, in waterproofing agents, and in the paint industry — compare CALCIUM STEARATE

lime–soda feldspar *n* **:** PLAGIOCLASE

limestone \'=,=\ *n* **1 :** a rock that is chiefly formed by accumulation of organic remains (as shells or coral), that consists mainly of calcium carbonate though sometimes also containing magnesium carbonate, and that is extensively used in building, agriculture, and metallurgy and yields lime when burned — compare CALCITE, CHALK, DOLOMITE, OOLITE **2 :** HAIR BROWN

limestone sink *n* **:** SINK 5b

lime sulfur *n* **:** a fungicide and insecticide containing calcium polysulfides usu. obtained by boiling sulfur with lime and water

lime tree *n* **1 :** LINDEN 1a **2 :** OGEECHEE LIME 2 **3 :** LIME

li·met·ta oil \lə'med·ə-\ *or* **li·mette oil** \-et-\ *n* [*limetta* fr. NL (former specific epithet or varietal epithet of the lime *Citrus aurantifolia*), prob. fr. F *limette* lime, fr. *lime* + *-ette*; *limette* fr. F] **:** LIME OIL

li·met·tin \lə'met°n\ *n* -s [ISV *limett-* (fr. NL *limetta*) + *-in*] **:** CITROPTEN

1**lime–twig** \'=,=\ *n* [ME *lyme twig*, fr. *lyme, lim* lime + *twig*] **1 :** a twig covered with birdlime to catch birds **2 :** SNARE, TRAP ⟨called her beauty *lime-twigs* —John Donne⟩

2**lime–twig** \"\ *vt, archaic* **:** ENSNARE, CATCH ⟨allowed his mind to be *lime-twigged* and ruffled and discomposed by words —W.S.Landor⟩

lime uranite *n* [prob. trans. of G *kalkuranit*] **:** AUTUNITE

1**limewash** \'=,=\ *n* **:** a solution of lime and water used as a substitute for paint

2**limewash** \"\ *vt* **:** to cover (as walls or cupboards) with limewash **:** WHITEWASH

limewater \'=,==\ *n* **1 :** an alkaline water solution of calcium hydroxide that absorbs carbon dioxide from the air forming a film of calcium carbonate on the surface of the liquid and that is used in medicine as an antacid and ingredient of external washes — compare MILK OF LIME **2 :** natural water containing considerable amounts of calcium carbonate or calcium sulfate in solution

limewood \'=,=\ *n* **:** the wood of the linden tree

limey \'līmē, -mi\ *n* -s *often cap* [*lime-* (fr. *lime-juicer*) + *-y*] **1** *slang* **:** an English sailor **2** *slang* **:** ENGLISHMAN ⟨among us ~*s* —Maurice Ashley⟩

lime yellow *n* **:** 6LIME 3

lim·ia \'limēə\ *n, cap* [NL] **:** a genus of West Indian topminnows including several that are sometimes kept in tropical aquariums

li·mic·o·lae \lī'mikə,lē\ *n pl, cap* [NL, fr. LL, pl. of *limicola* mud-dweller, fr. LL *limi-* (fr. L *limus* mud) + L *-cola* dweller, inhabitant; akin to L *linere* to smear — more at LIME, -COLOUS] **1** *in some esp former classifications* **:** an order or suborder of migratory birds comprising the sandpipers and related forms (family Scolopacidae) or often being made coextensive with the suborder Charadrii **2** *in some esp former classifications* **:** a group of Oligochaeta comprising the more aquatic and typically smaller oligochaete worms — compare TERRICOLAE

li·mic·o·line \-ə,līn, -,lən\ *adj* [NL *Limicolae* + E *-ine*] **:** shore-inhabiting **:** of or relating to the Limicolae

li·mic·o·lous \(')lī¦mikələs\ *adj* [*limi-* (fr. LL, fr. L *limus* mud) + *-colous*] **:** living in mud

lim·i·dae \'limə,dē\ *n pl, cap* [NL, fr. *Lima*, type genus + *-idae*] **:** a family of mollusks comprising the file shells and belonging to the suborder Pectinacea

limier *comparative of* LIMY

limiest *superlative of* LIMY

li·min·al \'limən°l, 'līm-\ *adj* [ISV *limin-* (fr. L *limin-, limen* threshold) + *-al* — more at LIMEN] **1 :** of or relating to the limen ⟨~ research⟩ **2 :** situated at the limen **:** barely perceptible ⟨observation of ~ hues is beset with difficulties —Elsie Murray⟩ **3 :** having the lowest amount necessary to produce a particular effect **:** possessing the minimal quantity ⟨an electron must be given a certain ~ amount of energy before it can escape from the metal —Therald Moeller⟩

lim·i·nary \'limə,nerē\ *adj* [F *liminaire*, fr. LL *liminaris*, fr. L, of a threshold, fr. *limin-, limen* threshold + *-aris* -ar — more at LIMB] **:** placed at the beginning (as of a book) **:** INTRODUCTORY, PRELIMINARY ⟨~ quotations from the Greek or Latin —Gouverneur Paulding⟩

lim·i·ness \'līmēnəs\ *n* -ES **:** the quality or state of being limy

liming *pres part of* LIME

1**lim·it** \'limət, *usu* -əd·+V\ *n* -s [ME *limite*, fr. MF, fr. L *limit-, limes* boundary, limit — more at LIMB] **1 a :** a geographical or political boundary **:** BORDER, FRONTIER ⟨at the exact northern ~ of this valley —*Amer. Guide Series: Minn.*⟩ ⟨just outside the three-mile ~ —Beverly Smith⟩ — often used in pl. ⟨kept within the ~*s* of Detroit —*Amer. Guide Series: Mich.*⟩ **b limits** *pl* **:** the place or area enclosed within a boundary **:** BOUNDS ⟨into the ~*s* of the North they came —John Milton⟩ ⟨the first collegiate foundation in the ~*s* of the present U.S. —K.B. Murdock⟩ **2 a :** something that bounds, restrains, or confines — usu. used in pl. ⟨simple-minded because of the ~*s* to his experience —Margaret F. Richey⟩ ⟨discover the relationships of meanings within the ~*s* of his form —W.V.O'Connor⟩ ⟨cooperate within ~*s*⟩ **b :** the utmost extent **:** a point beyond which it is impossible to go ⟨pushed to the ~ to meet these demands —R.E.Barnaby⟩ ⟨a veteran operator who can be trusted to the ~ —Tris Coffin⟩ ⟨the sky's the ~⟩ **3 :** LIMITATION ⟨the sadness is without ~ —Shak.⟩ ⟨her opportunity is practically without ~ other than the limitation of her own ability —G.W.Johnson⟩ **4 :** a determining feature or differentia in logic **5 :** a prescribed maximum or minimum amount, quantity, or number ⟨the store set a ~ of five pounds of coffee to a customer during the sale⟩ ⟨suggested lowering the age ~ for voting from 21 to 18⟩: as **a :** the maximum quantity of game or fish that may be taken legally in a specified period ⟨so many ducks that ~ bags are almost routine among competent hunters —Scott Young⟩ **b** (1) **:** a maximum established for a gambling bet, raise, or payoff ⟨playing blackjack, two cents' ~ —Hamilton Basso⟩ (2) **:** an agreed time for ending a card game ⟨set a ~ of 1 a.m.⟩ **6 a :** a number such that the numerical difference between it and a mathematical function will be arbitrarily small for all values of the independent variables sufficiently close to but not equal to certain prescribed numbers or sufficiently large positively or negatively ⟨the ~ of $(x^2-1) \div (x-1)$ as x approaches 1 is 2⟩ **b :** a number such that if Sn represents the *nth* term of an infinite sequence the numerical difference between Sn and the number will be arbitrarily small for n sufficiently large ⟨the ~ of the sequence ½, ⅔, ¾, . . . , $\frac{n}{n+1}$ as n becomes large is 1⟩ **c :** either of the two numbers substituted in an antiderivative for the independent variable in evaluating a definite integral **7 :** the maximum or minimum permissible dimension (as of a machine part or manufactured object) ⟨the plungers and cylinders of the injection system are fitted to extremely close ~*s* —William Landon⟩ **8 :** something that is exasperating or intolerable **:** LAST STRAW — used with *the* ⟨I've seen bad weather, but this is the ~⟩ **9 :** the full duration of a ball game or prizefight — used with *the* ⟨a good pitcher but he couldn't go the ~⟩ ⟨although he went the ~ he lost the fight on points⟩

2**limit** \"\ *vt* -ED/-ING/-S [ME *limiten*, fr. MF *limiter*, fr. L *limitare*, fr. *limit-, limes* boundary, limit] **1 :** to assign to or within certain limits **:** fix, constitute, or appoint definitely **:** ALLOT, PRESCRIBE ⟨no end is ~*ed* to damned souls —Christopher Marlowe⟩ — now used chiefly in legal terms **2** *obs* **:** to assign (a duty) to someone ⟨'tis my ~*ed* service —Shak.⟩ **3 a :** to set bounds or limits to **:** CONFINE ⟨~*s* itself to fresh water —Richard Semon⟩ ⟨must ~ itself to functions which are consistent with the needs of collective defense —A.O.Wolfess⟩ ⟨the town is pleasantly ~*ed* —William Sansom⟩ ⟨persons whose musical experience is ~*ed* —Virgil Thomson⟩ **b :** to curtail or reduce in quantity or extent ⟨could ~ production and marketing of dairy products —*Wall Street Jour.*⟩ ⟨medical science knows how to ~ these evils —C.W.Eliot⟩ **4** *archaic* **:** to be or act as a boundary to ⟨a stone wall ~*s* the farm on the west⟩

syn RESTRICT, CIRCUMSCRIBE, CONFINE: LIMIT stresses the fact of existence of boundaries, checks to expansion, or exclusions which either are not passed over or cannot or may not be; it is a general term with less power of suggestion than others in this set ⟨the airplane has possibilities so many that fancy cannot *limit* them —B.N.Cardozo⟩ ⟨*limiting* the purposes for which public funds could be appropriated —*Americana Annual*⟩ RESTRICT may imply a narrow limitation, a more sharp and severe constriction or checking than LIMIT ⟨the decision to restrain French influence . . . and to *restrict* it to the frontiers of his own choosing —Hilaire Belloc⟩ ⟨combinations have arisen which *restrict* the very freedom that Bentham sought to attain —O.W.Holmes †1935⟩ CIRCUMSCRIBE may suggest a bounding circle, often close and narrow, preventing free outward range or activity, in other words, an encompassing restriction ⟨think that the emotional range . . . of drama is limited and *circumscribed* by verse —T.S.Eliot⟩ ⟨the Government's . . . imposition of restrictions and quotas that have *circumscribed* the conduct of publishing so radically —*Times Lit. Supp.*⟩ CONFINE is the strongest in this set in indicating bounds not to be passed; it suggests close cramping restriction, hindrance by encircling environment, or exclusion seemingly arbitrary or, at any rate, positive ⟨strong congressional leaders have always sought to *confine* the President to mere administration —Alan Barth⟩ ⟨must *confine* himself to inferior jobs allotted to his kind —Ruth Benedict⟩

lim·it·able \-məd·əbəl, -mətəb-\ *adj* **:** capable of being limited — **lim·it·able·ness** *n* -ES

lim·i·tar·i·an \,limə'ta(a)rēən, -ter-\ *n* -s [1*limit* + *-arian* (as in *trinitarian*)] **:** one that limits or restricts; *specif* **:** one who holds that Christ died only for the elect or that not all men are to be saved

lim·i·tary \'limə,terē, -ri\ *adj* **1** *archaic* **:** subject to limits **:** limited in capacity ⟨poor ~ creature calling himself a man of the world —Thomas DeQuincey⟩ **2** *archaic* **a :** of or relating to a boundary **b :** ENCLOSING, LIMITING ⟨imagined isles beyond the ~ ocean —R.C.Trench⟩

lim·i·ta·tion \,limə'tāshən\ *n* -s [ME *limitacioun*, fr. MF or L; MF *limitation*, fr. L *limitation-, limitatio*, fr. *limitatus* (past part. of *limitare* to limit) + *-ion-, -io* -ion] **1 :** the action of limiting ⟨without any other express ~ or restraint —John Locke⟩ ⟨fighting to restore the doctrine of ~ to its high place among the nations —*New Republic*⟩ **2 :** the quality or state of being limited ⟨itself conditioned by our inescapable human ~ —M.R.Cohen⟩ **3 a :** a restriction or restraint imposed from without (as by law, custom, or circumstances) ⟨all railroads have weight and height ~*s*, because of tunnels, bridges and so forth —*Westinghouse News*⟩ ⟨still further ~*s* on the work of the editors of the news —F.L.Mott⟩ **b :** a restrictive weakness or lack of capacity ⟨the ~*s* of the power of speech —B.N. Cardozo⟩ ⟨within the ~*s* of black and white —Hunter Mead⟩ ⟨the ~ of materials, their strength, their resistance to strain —Mary Austin⟩ **4 :** a time assigned for something; *specif* **:** a certain period limited by statute after which actions, suits, or prosecutions cannot be brought in the courts **5 a :** the limiting or marking out of the bounds of an estate in property **b :** the creation by deed or devise of a lesser estate or estates out of a fee **c :** an exception to the usual rules for the descent of titles of nobility or honor — **lim·i·ta·tion·al** \¦==¦tāshən°l, -shnəl\ *adj*

lim·i·ta·tive \'limə,tād·iv, -,təd·-\ *adj* [ML *limitativus*, fr. L *limitatus* + *-ivus* -ive] **:** serving to limit or restrict **:** LIMITING, RESTRICTIVE ⟨a ~ enumeration of the categories of work on which prisoners might be employed —J.S.Pictet⟩; *esp* **:** having reference in logic to a third quality of judgment besides affirmative and negative

limit bid *n* **:** a bid in bridge understood to mean that the bidder can barely expect to make the contract and has no values in reserve

limit dextrin *n* **:** a nonreducing dextrin obtained by the exhaustive action of an enzyme (as beta-amylase on amylopectin or phosphorylase on glycogen) — called also *residual dextrin*

1**limited** *adj* [fr. past part. of 2*limit*] **1 a :** confined within limits **:** restricted in extent, number, or duration ⟨the product of ~ rainfall —Samuel Van Valkenburg & Ellsworth Huntington⟩ ⟨~ markets of one thousand —V.G.F.Reynolds⟩ ⟨such enterprises should have a ~ life —Leslie Rees⟩ **b** *of a train* (1) **:** having a limited number of cars and making a limited number of stops in order to provide fast through service

(2) **:** offering superior accommodations or service and faster transportation **2 :** characterized by enforceable limitations prescribed (as by custom or a constitution) upon the scope or exercise of powers ⟨the government of the United States . . . though ~ in its powers, is supreme —John Marshall⟩ ⟨England has been great . . . under the present ~ monarchy —Edmund Burke⟩ — compare ABSOLUTE 3, CONSTITUTIONAL 4, DIVINE RIGHT 1 **3 :** narrow and unimaginative **:** lacking in originality of thought ⟨a thorough good sort; a bit ~; a bit thick in the head —Virginia Woolf⟩ — **lim·it·ed·ly** *adv* — **lim·it·ed·ness** *n* -ES

²limited *n* -S **:** a limited train

limited–access highway *n* **:** EXPRESSWAY

limited atonement *n* **:** a theological doctrine that the reconciliation effected between God and man by the sufferings of Jesus Christ was efficacious for some but not all men — compare GENERAL ATONEMENT

limited company *or* **limited–liability company** *n, Brit* **:** a company in which the liability of each shareholder is limited to the par value of his stock or to an amount fixed by a guarantee

limited divorce *n* **:** a divorce a mensa et thoro

limited edition *n* **:** an edition of a book or other publication limited to a specified number of copies and usu. printed in a special format

limited fee simple *n, pl* **limited fees simple 1 :** a fee simple estate in land that may last forever but is limited to terminate automatically whenever certain circumstances in existence when the estate is created cease to exist **:** a base, qualified, or determinable fee simple estate **2 a :** a fee simple estate that is defeasible and may come to an end for any reason (as by reentry after breach of a condition subsequent upon which the estate was limited) **b :** a reversion or remainder estate in land or a conditional fee-tail estate

limited liability *n* **1 :** the liability of shareholders in a corporation or a limited company **2 :** a liability (as of shipowners) limited by statute or treaty

limited owner *n* **:** a person having an ownership that is not absolute or perfect (as one for a limited period)

limited partner *n* **:** a partner whose liability to creditors of the partnership is usu. limited to the amount of capital he has contributed to the partnership providing he has not held himself out to the public as a general partner and has complied with other requirements of law **:** SPECIAL PARTNER

limited partnership *n* **:** a partnership having one or more general partners and one or more limited partners — called also *special partnership;* compare GENERAL PARTNERSHIP

limited payment insurance *n* **:** life insurance for which premiums are collected over a limited period (as 20 years)

limited policy *n* **:** an insurance policy specif. excluding certain classes or types of loss

limited service *n* **1 :** a military classification for equipment not considered suitable for use in combat areas **2 :** a military classification for personnel considered not acceptable for combat service

limited war *n* **1 :** a war with an objective less than the total defeat of the enemy's armed forces **2 :** a war limited to a relatively small area

lim·it·er \ˈlimәd·ә(r), -ətә-\ *n* -S [alter. (influenced by *-er*) of ME *limitour,* fr. *limiten* to limit + *-our* -or] **:** one that limits ⟨continue to rely on competition as the principal ~ of private economic power —E.S.Mason⟩: as **a :** CURRENT LIMITER **b :** an electronic device for limiting a train of electrical oscillations to a uniform prescribed amplitude

limites *pl of* LIMES

limit gage *n* **:** a gage that serves to determine whether the measured part is within prescribed limits of tolerance

¹limiting *adj* [fr. pres. part. of ²*limit*] **1 :** functioning as a limit **:** CONFINING, RESTRICTIVE ⟨abandoned the ~ dramatic plot —Douglas Cleverdon⟩ **2** *of a modifying word* **:** serving to limit the application of the modified noun without reference to quality, kind, or condition (as *this* in *this book, which* in *which book*) or to express the absence of limitation (as *any* in *any book*) — distinguished from *descriptive*

²limiting *n* -S [fr. gerund of ²*limit*] **:** the process by which an electronic signal is held within prescribed limits or by which the relationship between the outgoing and incoming signal in a device is no longer linear

limiting factor *n* **1 :** the factor that limits the reaction rate in any physiological process governed by many variables **2 :** the environmental factor that is of predominant importance in restricting the size of a population ⟨lack of winter browse is a *limiting factor* for many deer herds⟩

lim·it·less \ˈlimәtlәs\ *adj* **:** having no limits **:** UNBOUNDED, INEXHAUSTIBLE ⟨humanity with its ~ desires —Mary Webb⟩ ⟨the view plunged into the ~ horizon —William James⟩ ⟨had a ~ war chest —Hodding Carter⟩ — **lim·it·less·ly** *adv* — **lim·it·less·ness** *n* -ES

limit of accommodation 1 : AMPLITUDE OF ACCOMMODATION **2 :** RANGE OF ACCOMMODATION

limit of liability : the maximum amount for which an insurance company may be held liable under a given policy

limit order *also* **limited order** *n* **:** an order to buy securities at a specified maximum price or sell them at a specified minimum price

lim·i·trophe \ˈlimә,trōf\ *adj* [F, fr. LL *limitrophus* set apart to furnish subsistence to troops stationed on the frontiers, irreg. fr. L *limit-, limes* boundary, limit + Gk *trophos* feeder, fr. *trephein* to nourish — more at LIMB, ATROPHY] **1 :** situated on a border or frontier **:** ADJACENT, NEIGHBORING ⟨disputes between ~ powers —*Contemporary Rev.*⟩ ⟨this territory is ~ to the Union —A.J.Bruwer⟩ **2 :** MARGINAL, INCIPIENT, BORDERLINE ⟨~ plasmolysis⟩

limits *pres 3d sing of* LIMIT, *pl of* LIMIT

limit switch *n* **:** a switch that operates as an automatic control to prevent a mechanism or process from going beyond a prescribed limit

li·miv·o·rous \(ˈ)lī;miv(ә)rәs\ *adj* [prob. fr. (assumed) NL *limivorus,* fr. LL *limi-* (fr. L *limus* mud) + L *-vorus* -vorous; akin to L *linere* to smear — more at LIME] **:** swallowing mud for the organic matter contained in it

lim·ma \ˈlimә\ *n, pl* **lim·ma·ta** \-әd·ә\ [LL, fr. Gk *leimma* Pythagorean semitone, remnant, fr. *leipein* to leave — more at LOAN] **1** *in ancient Greek music* **:** a semitone in the Pythagorean scale that is less than half a whole step and is designated as the difference between a perfect fourth and two whole steps or 256/243 — called also *diesis* **2** [LGk *leimma,* fr. Gk] **:** a pause in Greek verse equivalent to one mora — symbol Λ, ʌ, ∧

¹lim·mer \ˈlimәr\ *n* -S [ME (Sc)] **1** *chiefly Scot* **:** a worthless unprincipled fellow **:** SCOUNDREL **2** *chiefly Scot* **:** a loose or immoral woman **:** PROSTITUTE

²limmer \"\ *adj, chiefly Scot* **:** SCOUNDRELLY, UNPRINCIPLED

lim·mock \ˈlimәk\ *adj* [prob. alter. of ³*limber*] *dial Eng* **:** LIMBER, LIMP

lim·mu \ˈli(,)mü\ *n* -S [Assyr] **:** EPONYM 1b

limn \ˈlim\ *vt* **limned** \-md\ **limned; limning** \-m(n)iŋ\ **limns** [ME *limnen* to illuminate (a manuscript), alter. of *luminen,* modif. of MF *enluminer* to illuminate (a manuscript), light up, fr. OF, modif. (influenced by OF *en-*) of L *illuminare* to light up, illuminate, embellish — more at ILLUMINATE] **1 a :** to draw or paint upon a canvas or other flat surface ⟨not every ancestral likeness had been ~*ed* by the brush of a maestro —R.P.Warren⟩ **b :** to outline in clear sharp detail **:** DELINEATE ⟨sees the tanker ~*ed* in her periscope sights —E.L. Beach⟩ ⟨the sweep of the main avenues sprang forth ~*ed* in light —H.T.Desa⟩ ⟨its contours framed in a luminous aureole rather than ~*ed* —Norman Douglas⟩ **2 :** to describe or portray in symbols (as words or notes) ⟨testimony ~*ed* a desperate situation —*Time*⟩ ⟨~*s* the complete domination and degradation of the state —Murray Seasongood⟩ **syn** see REPRESENT

limn- *or* **limni-** *or* **limno-** *comb form* [NL, fr. Gk, pool, marshy lake, fr. *limnē;* akin to Gk *limen-, limēn* harbor — more at LIMB] **:** freshwater lake **:** pond ⟨*limni*meter⟩ ⟨*limno*logy⟩

lim·naea \lim'nēә\ *syn of* LYMNAEA

limnaeid *var of* LYMNAEID

lim·nae·i·dae \lim'nēә,dē\ *syn of* LYMNAEIDAE

lim·nal \ˈlimnәl\ *adj* [*limn-* + *-al*] **:** of or relating to lakes

lim·nan·tha·ce·ae \,lim(,)nan'thāsē,ē\ *n pl, cap* [NL, fr. *Limnanthes,* type genus + *-aceae*] **:** a family of aquatic or marsh herbs (order Geraniales) that have pinnate leaves, long-peduncled small flowers, and polycarpellary fruit — see LIMNANTHES — **lim·nan·tha·ceous** \;≈(,)≈¦thāshәs\ *adj*

lim·nan·thes \limˈnan,thēz, -an(t)thēz\ *n, cap* [NL, fr. *limn-* + *-anthes*] **:** a genus (the type of the family Limnanthaceae) of western No. American annual herbs having trimerous flowers and entire petals that are shorter than the sepals — see MEADOW-FOAM

¹lim·neph·i·lid \(ˈ)lim¦nefәlәd\ *adj* [NL *Limnephilidae*] **:** of or relating to the Limnephilidae

²limnephilid \"\ *n* -S [NL *Limnephilidae*] **:** an insect of the family Limnephilidae

lim·ne·phil·i·dae \,limnә'filә,dē\ *n pl, cap* [NL, fr. *Limnephilus,* type genus (fr. Gk *limnē* pool + NL *-philus*) + *-idae*] **:** a family of large caddis flies whose larvae live usu. in ponds or slow streams

lim·ner \ˈlim(n)ә(r)\ *n* -S [ME *lympner,* alter. (influenced by *-er*) of *limnour,* alter. of *luminour,* fr. *luminen* to illuminate (a manuscript) + *-our* -or] **1 a :** an illuminator of medieval manuscripts ⟨illustrated by sedulous ~*s* —*Times Lit. Supp.*⟩ **b :** one that draws or paints; *esp* **:** a self-taught itinerant artist ⟨among the last of the traveling ~*s* —Esther Forbes⟩ **2 :** one who describes or portrays (as in words) ⟨in such terms does Carlyle, the fine, vivid ~ that he is, introduce the Abbot —E.V.Lucas⟩

lim·netic \(ˈ)lim¦ned·ik\ *also* **lim·nic** \ˈlimnik\ *adj* [ISV *limn-* + *-etic* or *-ic*] **:** of, relating to, or inhabiting the pelagic part of a body of fresh water ⟨~ worms⟩

lim·ne·tis \limˈnēd·әs\ *n, cap* [NL, fr. Gk *limnētis,* fem. of *limnētēs* living in marshes, fr. *limnē* marshy lake] **:** a genus of phyllopod crustaceans (order Conchostraca) including numerous small almost spherical forms that have only the first pair of feet in the male provided with a clasping organ

lim·nim·e·ter \limˈnimәd·ә(r)\ *or* **lim·nom·e·ter** \-näm-\ *n* [ISV *limn-* + *-meter*] **:** a sensitive form of tide gage for measuring variations of level in lakes

-lim·ni·on \ˈlimnē,än, -ēәn\ *n comb form, pl* **-limnia** [NL, fr. Gk *limnion* small lake, dim. of *limnē* marshy lake] **:** lake **:** water ⟨hypo*limnion*⟩

lim·nite \ˈlim,nīt\ *n* -S [G *limnit,* fr. *limn-* + *-it* -ite] **:** BOG IRON ORE

limno- — see LIMN-

lim·no·bi·um \limˈnōbēәm\ *n, cap* [NL, fr. Gk *limnobion,* neut. of *limnobios* living in a lake, fr. *limn-* + *bios* mode of life — more at QUICK] **:** a genus of American aquatic herbs (family Hydrocharitaceae) that have flowers with spathes — see FROGBIT 2

lim·noc·ni·da \limˈnäknәdә\ *n, cap* [NL, fr. *limn-* + Gk *knidē* nettle — more at CNIDA] **:** a genus of small freshwater hydrozoan jellyfishes (suborder Trachomedusae) found in central Africa

lim·nod·ri·lus \limˈnädrәlәs\ *n, cap* [NL, fr. *limn-* + LGk *drilos* leech] **:** a common genus of the family Tubificidae comprising aquatic oligochaete worms of the eastern U.S.

lim·no·graph \ˈlimnә,graf, -rȧf\ *n* [ISV *limn-* + *-graph*] **:** a record made on a limnimeter

lim·no·log·i·cal \¦limnә¦läjәkәl\ *also* **lim·no·log·ic** \-jik\ *adj* **:** of or relating to limnology — **lim·no·log·i·cal·ly** \-jәk(ә)lē\ *adv*

lim·nol·o·gist \limˈnälәjәst\ *n* -S [ISV *limnology* + *-ist*] **:** a specialist in limnology

lim·nol·o·gy \-jē\ *n* -ES [ISV *limn-* + *-logy*] **:** the scientific study of physical, chemical, meteorological, and biological conditions in fresh waters esp. of ponds and lakes

limnometer *var of* LIMNIMETER

lim·no·pi·the·cus \,limnōpә'thēkәs, -ō'pithәkәs\ *n, cap* [NL, fr. *limn-* + *-pithecus*] **:** a genus of fossil nonbrachiating gibbons from the Lower Miocene of eastern Africa

lim·no·plankton \¦limnō+\ *n* [ISV *limn-* + *plankton*] **:** the plankton of fresh waters esp. of lakes — **lim·no·planktonic** \"+(,)≈¦≈≈\ *adj*

lim·nor·chis \limˈnórkәs\ *n, cap* [NL, fr. *limn-* + *Orchis*] *in some classifications* **:** a genus of No. American orchids closely related to *Habenaria* that have greenish or whitish flowers with an entire lip

lim·no·ria \,limnә'rīә\ *n* [NL, fr. Gk *Limnōreia,* one of the Nereids] **1** *cap* **:** a genus (the type of the family Limnoriidae) of isopod crustaceans that contains the gribble **2** -S **:** any isopod of the genus *Limnoria*

lim·nos·ce·lis \limˈnäsәlәs\ *n, cap* [NL, fr. *limn-* + Gk *skelis, schelis* rib of beef; akin to Gk *skelos* leg — more at CYLINDER] **:** a genus of very primitive Lower Permian reptiles (order Cotylosauria) of the southwestern U.S. that are clumsily built creatures about five feet long somewhat like lizards and now thought to be very near the point of divergence between amphibians and reptiles

limns *pres 3d sing of* LIMN

li·mo·do·rum \,limә'dōrәm\ *n* [NL, fr. Gk *leimodōron,* a plant, perh. broomrape (genus *Orobanche*), fr. *leimo-* (fr. *leimōn* meadow) + *dōron* gift; akin to Gk *didonai* to give — more at LIMB, DATE] *syn of* CALOPOGON

¹li·moges \lēˈmōzh, lә'-\ *adj, usu cap* [fr. *Limoges,* city in west central France] **:** of or from the city of Limoges, France **:** of the kind or style prevalent in Limoges

²limoges \"\ *n, usu cap* **1 :** LIMOGES ENAMEL **:** LIMOGES WARE **2 :** a superior variety of china — compare HAVILAND

limoges enamel *n, usu cap L* **:** enamelware in which the enamel is applied over the entire surface of the metal with the various colors being juxtaposed

limoges ware *n, usu cap L* **1 :** LIMOGES ENAMEL **2 :** articles of porcelain made at Limoges

li·moid \ˈlī,mȯid\ *adj* [NL *Lima* + E *-oid*] **:** like or relating to the genus *Lima* or the family Limidae

¹li·mon \lēˈmōⁿ\ *n* -S [F, loess, silt, fr. OF, silt, fr. *lum, lun* mud, fr. L *limus;* akin to L *linere* to smear — more at LIME] **:** LOESS

²li·mon \ˈlīmәn\ *n* -S [blend of ⁶*lime* and *lemon*] **:** a hybrid citrus fruit produced by crossing a lime and a lemon

li·mon·ci·llo \,lēmōnˈsē(,)(y)ō\ *n* -S [AmerSp, dim. of Sp *limón* lemon, fr. Ar *laymūn*] **1 a :** any of several tropical American fruit or timber trees **b** *Puerto Rico* **:** BAYBERRY 1 **2** *Southwest* **:** any of several yellow-flowered composite plants (genus *Pectis*) with strongly lemon-scented foliage; *esp* **:** CHINCHWEED

li·mon·ci·to \-sē(,)tō\ *n* -S [PhilSp, dim. of Sp *limón* lemon] *Philippines* **:** LIMEBERRY

lim·o·nene \ˈlimә,nēn, ˈlīm-\ *n* -S [ISV *limon-* (as in *limonin*) + *-ene*] **:** a liquid terpene hydrocarbon $C_{10}H_{16}$ that has an odor like a lemon and exists in a dextrorotatory form occurring in many essential oils (as orange, lemon, or celery-seed oil), in a levorotatory form occurring esp. in pine-needle oils, and in the racemic form dipentene; 1,8-*para*-menthadiene

lim·o·nin \ˈlimәnәn, ˈlīm-\ *n* -S [F *limonine,* fr. *limon* lemon + *-ine* — more at LEMON] **:** a bitter lactone $C_{26}H_{30}O_8$ found esp. in lemon seeds, in the pulp and seeds of navel oranges, and in the bark of amur cork trees

li·mo·nite \ˈlīmә,nīt\ *n* -S [G *limonit,* fr. Gk *leimōn* meadow + G *-it* -ite — more at LIMB] **:** a naturally occurring hydrous ferric oxide that was formerly thought to be a distinct mineral $2Fe_2O_3.3H_2O$ but that is now known to have a variable composition and to consist of a mixture of several minerals (as goethite, lepidocrocite, hematite) with or without presumably adsorbed additional water, that may in some cases be principally goethite and in other cases essentially ferric oxide gel, or that may be bog iron ore or a brown, yellow, or red ocher in which impurities are very common — **li·mo·nit·ic** \¦≈≈¦nid·ik\ *adj*

li·mo·nit·iza·tion \,≈≈,nīd·ә'zāshәn\ *n* -S **:** the alteration of a mineral or rock to limonite usu. by weathering

li·mo·ni·um \līˈmōnēәm\ *n, cap* [NL, fr. Gk *leimōnion* sea lavender, fr. *leimōn* meadow] **:** a genus of annual or perennial sometimes shrubby herbs (family Plumbaginaceae) with leaves usu. radical and flowers in cymose panicles or spikes and subtended by scaly bracts — see SEA LAVENDER

li·mo·ni·us \līˈmōnēәs\ *n, cap* [NL, prob. fr. Gk *leimōnios* of a meadow, fr. *leimōn* meadow] **:** a genus of click beetles whose larvae include many wireworms that are economic pests

li·mo·sa \līˈmōsә\ *n, cap* [NL, fr. L, fem. of *limosus* muddy, fr. *limus* mud + *-osus* -ose; akin to L *linere* to smear — more at LIME] **:** a genus of birds (family Scolopacidae) comprising the godwits

li·mo·sel·la \,līmә'selә\ *n, cap* [NL, fr. L *limosus* muddy + *-ella*] **:** a small genus of widely distributed aquatic herbs (family Scrophulariaceae) having stems that root at the nodes, small entire leaves, and very small solitary scapose flowers — see MUDWORT

limosi *usu cap, var of* LEMOSI

li·mos·phere \ˈlimә,sfi(ә)r\ *n* [*limo-* (fr. L *limus* mud) + *sphere*] **:** an apical body near the blepharoplast of the spermatozoid of some bryophytes comparable to the acroblast in animals

li·mous \ˈlīmәs\ *adj* [ME *lymous,* fr. L *limosus,* fr. *limus* mud + *-osus* -ose] *archaic* **:** MUDDY, SLIMY

lim·ou·sine \ˈlimә,zēn, ,≈≈ˈ≈\ *n* -S [F, lit., cloak, fr. *Limousin,* region in west central France] **1 :** an automobile having an enclosed compartment seating three or more passengers and orig. a driver's seat outside and covered with a roof but later a driver's seat enclosed but separated from the passengers' compartment by a glass usu. movable partition **2 :** a small bus (as for transporting passengers to or from an airport) ⟨the wide seats in the airline's ~ were built to hold three people —J.S.Redding⟩ **3 :** a large luxurious sedan; *esp* **:** one for hire and seating five persons behind the driver

¹limp \ˈlimp\ *vi* -ED/-ING/-S [prob. fr. ME *lympen* to fall short; akin to OE *limpan* to happen, OHG *gilimpfan* to be fitting, MHG *limpfen* to limp, OE *lempheal*t lame, MHG *lampen* to dangle, L *limbus* border, Skt *lambate* it hangs down, L *labi* to glide, slide — more at SLEEP] **1 a :** to walk lamely **:** HOBBLE ⟨leaning on the old-fashioned ebony cane . . . she ~*ed* across the floor —Ellen Glasgow⟩ **b :** to go unsteadily **:** FALTER, STUMBLE ⟨the conversation ~*ed* for some time —Henry Green⟩ ⟨this comparison admittedly ~*s* as much as any —Alfred Einstein⟩ ⟨his logic ~*s* woefully —Hudson Hoagland⟩ ⟨a deliberately ~*ing* meter and desperately forced rhymes —William DuBois⟩ **2 a :** to proceed slowly or with difficulty esp. as the result of a disabling accident or storm ⟨~*ed* into the harbor with her hold full of water —*Amer. Guide Series: Mich.*⟩ ⟨the plane ~*ed* in over the edge of the strip, its engine coughing badly —Howard Hunt⟩ **b :** to barely make headway ⟨capable of ~*ing* along, hovering around the subsistence level —R.C.Doty⟩ ⟨commerce ~*ed* toward a standstill —*Time*⟩

²limp \"\ *n* -S **:** the action of limping ⟨walked with a ~⟩

³limp \"\ *adj, usu* -ER/-EST [akin to ¹*limp*] **1 a :** having no defined shape **:** SLACK, SOFT ⟨a ~ body that seemed to have been poured into his clothes as if it were sand —Edith Sitwell⟩ ⟨letting his body go completely ~ with ecstasy —Liam O'Flaherty⟩ ⟨~ as a rag⟩ **b :** DROOPING, EXHAUSTED ⟨as a result of this protracted session he now felt fairly ~ —J.R.Parker⟩ ⟨~ with fatigue⟩ **2 :** lacking in strength or firmness **:** FLABBY, SPIRITLESS ⟨made a ~ gesture as if waving away all desire to know —G.K.Chesterton⟩ ⟨small, rather ~ jokes —Wolcott Gibbs⟩ ⟨a ~ young man who finds most of his enjoyment in witnessing the pains and loves of others —*New Yorker*⟩ **3 a** *of a book cover* **:** lined with very flexible paper rather than rigid board **b** *of a binding or a book* **:** having limp covers

lim·pa \ˈlimpә\ *n* -S [Sw] **:** rye bread made with molasses or brown sugar

limp·er \-pә(r)\ *n* -S **:** one that limps

lim·pet \ˈlimpәt, *usu* -әd·+V\ *n* -S [ME *lempet,* fr. OE *lempedu,* fr. ML *lampreda* limpet, lamprey — more at LAMPREY] **1 :** a marine gastropod mollusk with a low conical shell broadly open beneath that browses over rocks or timbers chiefly between tidemarks and adheres very tightly when disturbed; *specif* **:** a member of the families Acmaeidae and Patellidae in which the uncoiled shell apex is imperforate — compare KEYHOLE LIMPET, SLIPPER LIMPET **2 :** a person who clings tenaciously to someone or something ⟨disconcert the studio loafer and the studio ~ —Osbert Sitwell⟩ **3** *or* **limpet bomb** *or* **limpet mine :** an explosive designed to cling to the hull of a ship ⟨saboteurs stuck *limpet mines* on two gunrunning yachts —*Newsweek*⟩

lim·pid \ˈlimpәd\ *adj* [F or L; F *limpide,* fr. L *limpidus,* fr. *limpa, lumpa* water — more at LYMPH] **1 a :** completely free from cloudiness or other obstacles to the passage of light ⟨the water itself is so ~ that you can get no concept of depth by peering down into it —Thomas Barbour⟩ ⟨a ~ stream, through which we see to the very bottom —Lindley Murray⟩ **b :** clear and simple in style **:** readily intelligible ⟨absolute simplicity of subject is matched by ~ and artless style —C.S.Kilby⟩ **2 :** absolutely serene and untroubled ⟨still shows the benign effects of a ~ childhood —*Time*⟩ ⟨my conscience ~ —Geoffrey Household⟩ **syn** see CLEAR

lim·pid·i·ty \limˈpidәd·ē, -әtē, -i\ *n* -ES [LL *limpiditat-, limpiditas,* fr. L *limpidus* + *-itat-, -itas* -ity] **:** the quality or state of being limpid ⟨its marvelous simplicity and ~, its ruthless abstinence from the pleasures of mere rhetoric —Irving Kristol⟩

lim·pid·ly *adv* **:** in a limpid manner ⟨state all this in ~ clear English —John Gillin⟩

lim·pid·ness *n* -ES **:** the quality or state of being limpid **:** LIMPIDITY ⟨lake waters under rock, unfathomable in ~ —George Meredith⟩

limp·ing·ly *adj* [*limping* (pres. part. of ¹*limp*) + *-ly*] **:** in a limping manner ⟨had a smattering of college German and could get along ~ —W.A.White⟩

limping standard *n* **:** a monetary system under which both gold and silver are legal tender but only one metal is given free coinage

limp·kin \ˈlimpkәn\ *n* -S [¹*limp* + *-kin*] **:** a large brown wading bird (*Aramus pictus*) that resembles a bittern but has a longer slightly curved bill, longer neck and legs, and white stripes on head and neck — see COURLAN

limp·ly *adv* **:** in a limp manner

limp·ness *n* -ES **:** the quality or state of being limp

limp·sy *also* **limp·sey** \ˈlimpsē\ *or* **lim·sy** \-msē\ *adj* [³*limp* + *-sy* (as in *tipsy*)] **1** *dial* **:** limp esp. from lack of physical strength **:** WEAK ⟨suddenly the half-frozen and lifeless body fell ~ in their hands —Walt Whitman⟩ **2** *dial* **:** lacking in energy **:** LAZY

li·mu \ˈlē(,)mü\ *n* -S [Hawaiian] *Hawaii* **:** a water plant; *esp* **:** any of more than 70 various edible seaweeds

limu–eleele \-,ālā'ā(,)lā\ *n* -S [Hawaiian *limu-'ele 'ele*] *Hawaii* **:** an edible marine green alga (*Enteromorpha intestinalis*)

limu–kohu \-ˈkō(,)hü\ *n* -S [Hawaiian] *Hawaii* **:** an edible brown alga (*Asparagopsis sandjordiana*)

li·mu·li·dae \lәˈmyülә,dē\ *n pl, cap* [NL, fr. *Limulus,* type genus + *-idae*] **:** a family (order Xiphosura) comprising the king crab and various related extinct forms

¹lim·u·loid \ˈlimyә,lȯid\ *adj* [NL *Limulus* + E *-oid*] **:** like or relating to the king crabs

²limuloid \"\ *n* -S **:** KING CRAB

lim·u·lus \-lәs\ *n* [NL, fr. L *limus* sidelong + *-ulus* — more at LIMB] **1** *cap* **:** the type genus of Limulidae comprising the king crabs or in some classifications including solely the No. American king crab **2** *pl* **limuluses** \"\ *or* **limu·li** \-yә,lī\ *also* **limuluses :** KING CRAB

limy \ˈlīmē, -mi\ *adj, usu* -ER/-EST [¹*lime* + *-y*] **1 :** smeared with or consisting of lime **:** VISCOUS **2 :** containing lime or limestone ⟨a ~ soil⟩ **3 :** resembling or having the qualities of lime

¹lin \ˈlin\ *vi* **linned; linned; linning; lins** [ME *linnen,* fr. OE *linnan;* akin to OHG *bilinnan* to cease, ON *linna* to cease, Goth *aflinnan* to go away — more at LESS] *now dial Brit* **:** to come to a stop **:** CEASE

²lin \"\ *dial var of* ¹LINE

³lin \"\ *var of* LINN

⁴lin \"\ *n* -S [Chin (Pek) *lin²*] **:** a female unicorn — used in Chinese mythology

lin *abbr* **1** lineal **2** linear **3** liniment

lin·able *also* **line·able** \ˈlīnәbәl\ *adj* [⁴*line* + *-able*] **:** lying or arranged in a straight line

li·na·ce·ae \līˈnāsē,ē\ *n pl, cap* [NL, fr. *Linum,* type genus + *-aceae*] **:** a widely distributed family of herbs, shrubs, or trees (order Geraniales) having regular pentamerous flowers with the stamens twice as many as the petals and a fruit that is a capsule or a drupe — see LINUM — **li·na·ceous** \(ˈ)lī¦nāshәs\ *adj*

lin·age *also* **line·age** \'līnij, -nēj\ *n* -s [³*line* + -*age*] **1 :** the number of lines of printed matter or of written matter estimated in terms of the number of lines it would occupy in print **2 :** payment for literary matter at so much a line (as by newspapers or periodicals) ⟨the ~ of many magazines is about 15 cents⟩ ⟨offered him a chance to do several articles on ~⟩ **3 :** the amount of space occupied (as by advertising matter in a newspaper or periodical) usu. measured in terms of agate lines

li·na·loe \lē'nälōā\ *also* **li·na·loa** \-ōä\ *n* -s [MexSp *lináloe*, fr. Sp, agalloch, fr. ML *lignum aloes*, lit., wood of the aloe] **:** the wood of any of several trees of the genus *Bursera* esp. of a Mexican tree (*B. aloexylon*) that yields a perfume and is used to some extent in furniture and cabinetwork

linaloe oil *n* **:** any of several chemically similar essential oils used in perfumery and as sources of linalool: as **a :** a colorless or pale yellow oil obtained from linaloe or the wood of other trees of the family Burseraceae — called also *Mexican linaloe oil* **b :** BOIS DE ROSE OIL

lin·al·o·ol \lə'nalō,ōl, -,ōl, ,linə'lül\ *also* **lin·a·lol** \'linə,lōl, -lōl\ *n* -s [ISV *linaloe* + -*ol*] **:** a fragrant liquid unsaturated tertiary alcohol $C_{10}H_{17}OH$ that occurs both free and in the form of esters in many essential oils and that exists in dextrorotatory form obtained esp. from bois de rose oil or coriander oil, in levorotatory form obtained esp. from Mexican linaloe oil and the oil from a Japanese cinnamon, and in racemic form obtained by isomerization of geraniol or synthetically all optically isomeric and all used in perfumes, soaps, and flavoring materials

lin·a·lyl \'linə,lil, -lēl\ *n* -s [ISV *linal-* (fr. *linalool*) + -*yl*] **:** a radical $C_{10}H_{17}$ derived from linalool by removal of the hydroxyl group

linalyl acetate *n* **:** a fragrant liquid ester $CH_3COOC_{10}H_{17}$ that is found esp. in bergamot oil, lavender oil, and petitgrain oil, that is also made from linalool, and that is used similarly to linalool

lin·a·mar·in \,linə'ma(a)rən, -mer-\ *n* -s [ISV *lin-* (fr. L *linum* flax) + *amar-* (fr. L *amarus* bitter) + -*in*; orig. formed as F *linamarine* — more at LINEN, AMAROID] **:** a bitter crystalline cyanogenetic glucoside $(CH_3)_2C(CN)OC_6H_{11}O_5$ occurring esp. in flax and the lima bean and yielding acetone cyanohydrin and glucose on hydrolysis — called also *phaseolunatin*

li·nan·thus \lī'nan(t)thəs\ *n*, *cap* [NL, fr. *lin-* (fr. L *linum*) + -*anthus*] **:** a genus of delicate herbs (family Polemoniaceae) of the western U.S. having opposite usu. palmately divided leaves

li·nar·ia \lī'na(a)rēə, -ner-\ *n* [NL, fr. *lin-* (fr. L *linum*) + -*aria*] **1** *cap* **:** a genus of herbs and undershrubs (family Scrophulariaceae) having a personate spurred corolla — see TOADFLAX **2** -s **:** any plant of the genus *Linaria*

li·na·rite \'līnə,rīt, lə'nä,-\ *n* -s [G *linarit*, fr. *Linares*, Spain, its locality, + G -*it* -ite] **:** a mineral $PbCu(SO_4)(OH)_2$ consisting of a basic lead copper sulfate occurring in deep blue monoclinic crystals

¹linch \'linch\ *or* **linch·et** \-chət\ *Brit var of* ¹LYNCH

²linch \"\ *var of* LINGE

linch·pin *also* **lynch·pin** \'linch,pin\ *n* [ME *lynspin*, fr. *lyns*, *lins* linchpin (fr. OE *lynis*) + *pin*; akin to OS *lunisa* linchpin, OHG *lun*, Skt *āṇi* — more at ELL] **1 a :** a pin inserted in an axletree outside of the wheel to prevent the latter from slipping off **b :** a linking device (as for making a plow rig fast to a tractor) that consists essentially of a metal pin that can be fitted into sockets in the objects to be linked and usu. has some locking device to prevent shifting **2 :** something that serves to hold together the elements of a situation ⟨the ~ in the prosecution's case was a subpoenaed canceled check —Joel Sayre⟩ ⟨the ~ in this entire policy is clearly collaboration —Joseph Barnes⟩

linch·pinned \-pind\ *adj* **:** supplied or secured with linchpins

¹lin·coln \'liŋkən\ *adj*, *usu cap* [fr. *Lincoln*, city in Lincolnshire, England] **:** of or from the city of Lincoln, England **:** of the kind or style prevalent in Lincoln

²lincoln \"\ *adj*, *usu cap* [fr. *Lincolnshire* or *Lincoln*, county in eastern England] **:** LINCOLNSHIRE

³lincoln \"\ *adj*, *usu cap* [fr. *Lincoln*, Nebraska] **:** of or from Lincoln, the capital of Nebraska **:** of the kind or style prevalent in Lincoln

⁴lincoln \"\ *n* [²*lincoln*] **1** *usu cap* **:** an English breed of long-wool mutton type sheep similar to the Leicester but heavier and having a larger and bolder head with a characteristic tuft of wool on the forehead — see LINCOLN LAMB **2** *or* **lincoln longwool** -s *usu cap 1st L & often cap 2d L* **:** a sheep of the Lincoln breed

lincoln day *n*, *usu cap L&D* [after Abraham *Lincoln* †1865 16th president of the U.S.] **:** LINCOLN'S BIRTHDAY

lin·coln·esque \,liŋkə'nesk\ *adj*, *usu cap* **:** resembling or resembling that of Abraham Lincoln ⟨a *Lincolnesque* pose⟩

lincoln green *n* [¹*lincoln*] **1** *usu cap L* **:** a woolen of Lincoln green formerly worn by foresters **2** *often cap L* **:** a moderate olive green that is yellower and paler than forest green (sense 2), yellower, lighter, and slightly stronger than cypress and greener and slightly duller than holly green (sense 2)

lin·coln·i·an \(')liŋ'kōnēən\ *adj*, *usu cap* [Abraham *Lincoln* + E -*an*] **:** of or relating to Abraham Lincoln or to his character or style

lin·coln·i·ana \liŋ,kōnē'anə, ,liŋkənē, -'änə, -'ānə *also* 'ānə\ *n pl*, *usu cap* **:** matter (as papers, books, letters, relics) relating to Abraham Lincoln

lin·coln·ite \'liŋkə,nīt\ *n* -s *usu cap* **:** a follower or adherent of Abraham Lincoln or of his policies **:** a person oriented toward or serving the Northern side in the Civil War

lincoln lamb *n*, *usu cap 1st L* [²*lincoln*] **1 :** a crossbred Argentine sheep developed from the Lincoln breed **2 :** the pelt of the young lamb of the Lincoln lamb commonly processed as fur

lincoln red *n* [²*lincoln*] **1** *or* **lincoln red shorthorn a** *usu cap L&R&S* **:** a British breed of red dual-purpose cattle that is sometimes considered a variety of the Shorthorn breed **b** *usu cap L & often cap R&S* **:** an animal of this breed **2** *often cap L* **:** CARTHAMUS RED

lincoln rocker *n*, *usu cap L* [after Abraham *Lincoln*] **:** a high-backed upholstered rocking chair with open arms that was popular in the middle of the 19th century

lincoln's birthday *n*, *usu cap L&B* [after Abraham *Lincoln* †1865 16th president of the U. S.] **:** February 12 observed as a legal holiday in many of the states of the U. S.

lin·coln·shire \'liŋkən,shi(ə)r, -,shiə, -,shə(r)\ *adj*, *usu cap* [fr. *Lincolnshire* or *Lincoln*, county in eastern England] **:** of or from the county of Lincoln, England **:** of the kind or style prevalent in Lincoln

lincoln's sparrow *also* **lincoln's finch** *n*, *usu cap L* [after Thomas *Lincoln* †1883 friend of Audubon (who named it)] **:** a small No. American sparrow (*Melospiza lincolni*) similar to the song sparrow but having a buff band on the breast

Lin·crus·ta Wal·ton \,lin,krəstə'wōlt³n, -ltən\ *trademark* — used for a heavy fabric coated with thickened and colored linseed oil, stamped with decorative designs, and used to cover walls and ceilings

linc·tus \'liŋktəs\ *n* -ES [NL, fr. L, past part. of *lingere* to lick — more at LICK] **:** a syrupy or sticky preparation containing medicaments exerting a local action on the mucous membrane of the throat

lind \'lind\ *n* -s [ME *linde*, fr. OE *lind*; akin to OHG *linta* linden, ON *lind* linden, and prob. to OE *līthe* mild, gentle — more at LITHE] *archaic* **:** LINDEN 1

lin·dack·er·ite \lin'dakə,rīt\ *n* -s [G *lindackerit*, fr. Joseph *Lindacker*, 19th cent. Austrian chemist who analyzed it + G -*it* -ite] **:** a light green mineral $Cu_6Ni_3(AsO_4)_4(SO_4)(OH)_4 \cdot 5H_2O$ consisting of a hydrous basic nickel copper sulfate and arsenate and occurring either as tabular crystals or massive

lin·dane \'lin,dān\ *n* -s [T. van der *Linden*, 20th cent. Du. chemist who isolated four isomers of benzene hexachloride + E -*ane*] **:** an insecticide consisting of not less than 99 percent of the gamma isomer of benzene hexachloride used esp. against agricultural pests but also in medicine (as in the treatment of scabies by application to the skin)

lin·den \'lindən\ *n* -s [prob. fr. (assumed) obs. E *linden*, adj., made of linden wood, fr. ME *linden*, fr. OE, fr. *lind* + -*en*] **1 :** a tree of the genus *Tilia*: as **a :** a large European tree (*T. europaea*) that is usu. thought to be a natural hybrid and is much used for ornamental and street planting — called also *European linden*, *lime* **b :** a tall forest tree (*T. americana* or *T. glabra*) of eastern and central No. America — called also *American linden*, *basswood*; see TREE illustration **2 :** the light soft fine-grained white wood of linden; *esp* **:** BASSWOOD 1b

linden borer *n* **:** a common spotted longicorn beetle (*Saperda vestita*) whose larva bores in the linden and whose imago eats the twigs and petioles causing the leaves to fall

linden family *n* **:** TILIACEAE

linden green *or* **linden yellow** *n* **:** a moderate greenish yellow that is greener and duller than citron yellow, redder and paler than Javel green, and paler than oil yellow

linden looper *also* **linden inchworm** *n* **:** a yellow black-lined looper that is the larva of a moth (*Erannis tiliaria*) of the family Geometridae and that frequently defoliates the linden

linde process \'lind-\ *n*, *usu cap L* [after Carl von *Linde* †1934 Ger. physicist] **:** a process of liquefying air or other gas by repeated compression and expansion producing cooling by the Joule-Thomson effect

lin·der \'lində(r)\ *n* -s [prob. of Scand origin; akin to ON *lindi* belt, girdle; akin to ON *lind* linden] *dial* **:** a woolen undershirt or vest

lin·dera \'lindərə\ *n*, *cap* [NL, fr. Johann *Linder* †1723 Swed. botanist] **:** a small genus of evergreen or deciduous shrubs (family Lauraceae) that are native to Asia and No. America and sometimes cultivated as ornamentals with small yellow flowers in nearly sessile axillary clusters — see SPICEBUSH

lin·der·man joint \'lində(r)mən-\ *n*, *usu cap L* [prob. fr. the name *Linderman*] **:** a joint used in making wooden boxes that is similar to a tongue-and-groove joint and is usu. glued

lind·gren·ite \'lin(d)grə,nīt\ *n* -s *often cap L* [Waldemar *Lindgren* †1939 Am. geologist + E -*ite*] **:** a mineral $Cu_3(MoO_4)_2(OH)_2$ consisting of a basic molybdate of copper

lind·ley·an \'lin(d)lēən\ *adj*, *usu cap* [John *Lindley* †1865 Eng. botanist + E -*an*] **:** of, relating to, or devised by the English botanist John Lindley ⟨the *Lindleyan* system of classification⟩

lin·do \'lin(,)dō\ *n* -s [Sp, pretty, fr. L *legitimus* legitimate — more at LEGITIMATE] **:** any of several bright-colored So. American tanagers

lind·strom·ite *or* **lind·ström·ite** \'linztrə,mīt, -n(t)st-\ *n* -s *usu cap* [Sw *lindströmit*, fr. Gustaf *Lindström* †1916 Swed. mineral analyst + Sw -*it* -ite] **:** a mineral $PbCuBi_3S_6$ consisting of a sulfide of bismuth, copper, and lead

lind·worm \'lin,dwərm\ *also* **lin·dorm** \-dȯrm\ *n* -s [*lindworm* part trans. of Dan & Sw *lindorm*; *lindorm* fr. Dan & Sw, fr. ON *linnormr*, fr. *linnr* serpent + *ormr* serpent; perh. akin to OE *līthe* mild, gentle — more at LITHE, WORM] **:** a fabulous monster usu. resembling a wingless wyvern

¹lin·dy \'lindē, -di\ *n* -ES [prob. fr. *Lindy*, nickname of Charles A. *Lindbergh* b1902 Am. aviator who made the first solo nonstop transatlantic flight in 1927] **:** a jitterbug dance originating in Harlem and later developing many local variants of tap steps, two-steps, balance, and grapevine

²lindy \"\ *vi* -ED/-ING/-ES **:** to dance the lindy

¹line \'līn\ *n* -s [ME, fr. OE *līn* — more at LINEN] **1 a** *archaic* **:** spun or woven flax **:** linen material **b** *obs* **:** linen clothing **2 a** *obs* **:** the fiber of flax **b :** long fibers of flax hackled and ready for spinning **3** *archaic* **:** a flax plant (*Linum usitatissimum*)

²line \"\ *vt* -ED/-ING/-s [ME *linen*, fr. ¹*line*] **1 :** to cover the inner surface of ⟨~ cloak with silk⟩ ⟨*lined* the cheese box with cheesecloth⟩ **2 :** to put something in the inside of **:** FILL, SUPPLY ⟨and then the justice, in fair round belly with good capon *lined* —Shak.⟩ **3 :** to serve as the lining of ⟨silk hangings *lined* the walls⟩ **4** *obs* **a :** to cover the outer surface of **:** PAD **b :** to place persons or things along the side of for security **:** strengthen by adding something **:** FORTIFY **5 :** to strengthen (a book) after sewing, trimming, and usu. backing by applying glue to the back and affixing lining material (as super, leather, or flannel) and paper — often used with *up* — **line one's pockets :** to take money freely esp. from questionable sources ⟨*lined his pockets* on the new school contract⟩

³line \"\ *n* -s [ME, partly fr. OF *ligne* (fr. L *linea*, fr. fem. of *lineus* made of flax or linen, fr. *linum* flax, linen + -*eus* -eous) & partly fr. OE *līne*; OE *līne* akin to OHG *līna* rope; derivative fr. the root of OE *līn* spun or woven flax — more at LINEN] **1 a :** THREAD, STRING, CORD, ROPE: as (1) **:** a comparatively strong slender cord — often used in combination ⟨hand*line*⟩ ⟨a hard hemp ~⟩ (2) **:** LEASH, LEAD (3) *archaic* **:** a cord or nerve of the body (4) **:** a thread of a spider's web (5) **:** CLOTHESLINE (6) **:** a rope used on shipboard (as for hauling, towing, mooring); *specif* **:** a piece of rope that has been cut from a coil for a particular use (7) **:** a rope of about 150 fathoms length that is attached to a whaling harpoon (8) **:** a single 50-fathom skein of the rope used to make up a skate of a fisherman's setline or groundline **b** (1) **:** a device for catching fish consisting of a cord (as of silk or linen) together with baited hooks, sinkers, floats, and other appurtenances — see HANDLINE (2) **:** scope for activity **:** ROPE **c :** a length of material (as cord, wire, or steel tape) that is used esp. in measuring and leveling ⟨used a ~ to level the foundation⟩ **d :** cordage as a material ⟨makers of fine linen ~⟩ ⟨only the strongest ~ will serve⟩ **e :** REIN 1 — usu. used in pl. ⟨dropped the ~*s* over the horse's head⟩ **f :** piping for conveying a fluid (as steam, gas, water, oil) from one location to another ⟨blew out the main ~⟩ ⟨installed a new sewage ~⟩; *broadly* **:** HOSE, PIPE **g** (1) **:** a wire or pair of wires connecting one telegraph or telephone station with another or a whole system of such wires (2) **:** the principal circuits of an electric power system **2 a** (1) **:** a row of written or printed characters or of spacing material esp. when extending across a page or column ⟨70 ~*s* of crabbed gothic script⟩ ⟨the last ~ on the page⟩ (2) **:** a row of type (as for printing a line) (3) **:** SLUG 2b(4), 2b(5), 2c **b :** a unit in the rhythmic structure of verse that is formed by the grouping together of a number of the smallest units of the rhythm (as syllables, stress-groups, metrical feet) according to some principle or norm supplied by the nature or a convention of that kind of verse and that constitutes a rhythmic unit intermediate between the foot and the larger structural units into which lines in turn may be composed or combined either by continuous stichic repetition in series or by arrangement in systematic patterns (as strophes or stanzas) **c :** a brief bit of writing **:** a short letter **:** NOTE ⟨dropped him a ~ confirming the date⟩ ⟨jotted down a few ~*s*⟩ **d lines** *pl* **:** a certificate of marriage **:** MARRIAGE LINES **e :** the words making up a part in a drama — usu. used in pl. ⟨spent four hours a day memorizing his ~*s*⟩ **f lines** *pl* **:** a task usu. assigned as a school punishment that consists of writing out or sometimes memorizing or translating a specified number of lines of writing (as classical verse) **3 a :** something (as a ridge, seam, furrow, band of color) that is distinct, elongated, narrow, and rather uniform in width ⟨~*s* of color in stratified rock⟩ ⟨growth ~*s* in a tree trunk⟩ **b :** a narrow crease on the visible part of the body **:** WRINKLE ⟨face seamed with ~*s*⟩ **c :** the course or direction of something in motion or treated as if in motion ⟨the ~ of flight of a bullet⟩ ⟨~*s* of flow⟩ **:** ROUTE **d** (1) **:** a real or imaginary straight line oriented in terms of at least temporarily stable points of reference or arrangement in such a line ⟨sight along the ~ from the fence corner to the blasted oak⟩ ⟨the reserves advanced to the ~ of the guns⟩ ⟨waiting in ~ for tickets⟩ (2) **:** an oriented state of harmonious agreement ⟨had to bring the doubters into ~⟩ ⟨it was difficult to get everyone into ~⟩ ⟨hardly in ~ with our policy⟩ **e :** a boundary or limit esp. of a plot of ground — usu. used in pl. ⟨had a surveyor run property ~*s*⟩ **f** (1) **:** the track and roadbed of a railway (2) **:** condition of track as to uniformity of direction on tangents or variation on curves **g** (1) **:** a sharp image of the slit in a spectrograph produced by light of a particular wavelength or a narrow range of wavelengths, the position of the image providing data from which the wavelength can be determined (2) **:** a similar image in a mass spectrograph whose position provides data that can be used to determine the mass of an isotope **4 a :** a course of conduct, action, or thought ⟨took a firm ~ with his nephew⟩ ⟨his decision took the ~ of duty⟩ **b :** an individual's field of intellectual, artistic, or business activity or interest ⟨modern art is his ~⟩ ⟨completely out of my ~⟩ **c :** a field of business or professional activity ⟨worked in the plumbing ~⟩ ⟨men used to want their sons to enter one of the professional ~*s*⟩ **d** *slang* **:** an individual's characteristic form of glib and often persuasive address ⟨had a ~ to make angels weep⟩ **5 a** (1) *obs* **:** a basis or standard by which one lives **:** rule of conduct (2) **:** a bounding restriction (as on personal conduct) **:** LIMIT, RESTRAINT ⟨really overstepped the ~ of good taste⟩ **b** *archaic* **:** position in life **:** LOT, RANK **c :** FORTUNE, CHANCE, LUCK — usu. used in the phrase *hard lines* ⟨it was hard ~*s* to have such a sudden setback⟩ **6 :** any of various things that are or may be considered as arranged in a row or sequence: as **a** (1) **:** a succession of ancestors or descendants of an individual **:** FAMILY, RACE, LINEAGE ⟨descended from a noble ~⟩ ⟨the sire of an evil ~⟩ (2) **:** a strain produced and maintained by selective breeding ⟨a high-fat ~ of cattle⟩ (3) **:** a chronological series **b :** a series of related positions that may be represented by a continuous line which does not intersect itself **:** CHAIN 3b ⟨a ~ of mountain peaks⟩ ⟨extended the ~ of fire towers⟩ ⟨the intricate ~ of the coast⟩ **c** (1) *obs* **:** TRENCH, RAMPART (2) **:** dispositions made to cover extended military positions and presenting a front to the enemy — usu. used in pl. (3) **:** a military formation in which the different elements are abreast of each other — contrasted with *column* (4) **lines** *pl*, *Brit* **:** a row or block of tents or small buildings for troops in cantonment **d :** naval ships arranged in a regular order **:** a regular ordering of ships; *esp* **:** an arrangement of ships abreast **e** (1) **:** the combatant forces of an army as distinguished from the staff corps and services of supply and in Great Britain from the household troops (2) **:** the force of a regular navy **f** (1) **:** officers of the U.S. Navy eligible for command at sea as distinguished from officers of the staff (2) **:** officers of the U. S. Army belonging to a combatant branch **g :** a rank of objects that are or are accounted to be of one kind ⟨a ~ of small houses⟩ ⟨a ~ of trees along the stream⟩ **h** (1) **:** a group of public conveyances (as buses, ships, or airplanes) plying regularly under one management over a route ⟨several stage ~*s* were started⟩; *broadly* **:** a system of transportation together with its equipment, routes, and appurtenances ⟨the eastern freight ~*s*⟩ (2) **:** the company or organization owning or conducting a transportation line **i :** a rhythmic succession of musical notes or tones ⟨a musical ~⟩ ⟨the melodic ~⟩ **j** (1) **:** an arrangement of manufacturing or assembling operations designed to permit sequential occurrence on various stages of production ⟨a carefully engineered production ~⟩ (2) **:** the personnel of an organization responsible for its stated objective (as by manning a production line) — compare STAFF (3) **:** the channel of communication within an organization **k** (1) **:** the 7 players, including center, 2 guards, 2 tackles, and 2 ends, who in offensive football play line up on or within one foot of the line of scrimmage (2) **:** the players who in defensive play line up within one yard of the line of scrimmage **l** *slang* **:** RED-LIGHT DISTRICT **7 :** a narrow elongated mark drawn or projected (as with pencil or graver): as **a** (1) **:** a circle of latitude or longitude on a map (2) **:** EQUATOR — usu. used with *the* ⟨passing the ~⟩ **b** (1) **:** STRAIGHT LINE — used esp. technically when confusion with *curve* is unlikely (2) **:** a locus of points whose coordinates depend on a single independent variable **:** CURVE 5a **:** the intersection of two surfaces **c :** a mark recording a boundary, division, or contour (as on a map) **d :** any of the horizontal parallel strokes on a music staff, on and between which the notes are placed **e :** a mark (as by pencil, brush, or graver's tool) that forms part of the formal design of a picture as distinguished from the shading or coloring **f :** a heavy horizontal line on a bridge score that divides the honor score from the trick score **g** (1) **:** a demarcation of a limit with reference to which the playing of some game (as football) or sport (as racing) is regulated — usu. used in combination; see END LINE, FREE THROW, GOAL LINE, SIDELINE; RUGBY illustration (2) **:** LINE OF SCRIMMAGE **8 a :** a defining outline **:** CONTOUR, LINEAMENT ⟨the rising ~ of the hills⟩ — often used in pl. ⟨the sleek ~*s* of blooded stock⟩ **b :** the general style of an artistic composition with respect to the sequence or arrangement of its outlines, contours, and other elements — usu. used in pl. **c lines** *pl* **:** the outlines of a ship from stem to stern and from keel to sheer strake whether visualized from a sectional plan or viewed directly **d :** a plan or sketch of something done or to be done **:** MODEL — usu. used in pl. ⟨brief notes on the ~*s* of a guidebook⟩ ⟨explained the ~*s* of his foreign policy⟩ **e :** the contour or lineament of a specific instrumental or voice part in music and its horizontal motion as distinguished from the overall vertical harmonic structure ⟨the soaring tenor ~⟩ ⟨the bass ~ of the harmony⟩ **f :** one of four imaginary areas on a fencer's body when confronting an opponent that is determined as being the quarter of defense and attack in a given position of the blades **g :** the style or cut of a garment ⟨a dress cut on the princess ~⟩ — often used in pl. **h :** the visible design or outline of a dancer's body **9** [trans. of F *ligne*] **a** (1) **:** a disused unit of length equal to ½ inch (2) **:** a unit of measure for buttons equal to 1/40 inch — called also *ligne* **b :** MAXWELL **c** (1) **:** AGATE LINE (2) *chiefly Brit* **:** PICA — used to indicate the size of large type ⟨288-point type is often called 24-*line* type⟩ (3) **:** the top-to-bottom or belly-to-back dimension of a text letter used as a unit to denote the relative size of a larger esp. initial letter or of a cut appearing with matter set in such text letters ⟨this 72-point ornament will be a 9-*line* initial when set with 8-point text type or a 12-*line* initial when set with 6-point text type⟩ (4) **:** one line of text type used as a unit for measuring the body size of a larger character set with it — used in combination ⟨a 3-*line* initial⟩ ⟨a 10-*line* ornament⟩ **d :** the unit of fineness of halftones expressed as the number of screen lines to the linear inch with the lower numbers (as 60-line) denoting coarse and the higher numbers (as 120-line) fine **10 a :** a stock of goods on hand and available for sale or bought for resale usu. including more than one kind of thing but of varied quality and price ⟨a new store carrying a ~ of fancy groceries⟩ ⟨a new ~ of accessories⟩ ⟨a full ~ of electrical supplies⟩ **b** (1) **:** kinds of insurance available (2) **:** the amount of insurance written (as by several companies) on a single risk **c :** amount of credit available to a single borrower **11 a :** an indication (as of a trend or intention) based on insight or investigation ⟨tried to get a ~ on his brother's plans⟩ **b :** the trail of scent left by a quarry **12 a :** a complete game of 10 frames in bowling — called also *string* **b :** a hand won in gin rummy; *also* **:** the points gained by winning a hand **13 a :** a strip on a craps layout on which are placed side bets to the effect that the caster of the dice will pass — called also *pass line* **b :** FLIGHT LINE — **down the line** *adv* (*or adj*) **1 :** to or toward the center of town **:** DOWNTOWN **2 :** all the way **:** FULLY, COMPLETELY ⟨are prepared to back the president *down the line*⟩ — **in line :** in or into a lineal arrangement: as **a :** in a straight line **:** in or into alignment **b :** in or into a state of harmonious conformity **c :** in or into order or control — **in line for** *prep* **:** due or in a position to attain or receive ⟨*in line for* a promotion⟩ — **in line with** *prep* **:** in agreement or concordance with ⟨*in line with* our previous policy⟩ — **on the line** *adv* (*or adj*) **1 a :** on a level with the eye of a spectator — used of the arrangement of a picture in an exhibition **b :** in full view and at hazard ⟨put his future *on the line* when he backed this policy⟩ **2 :** on the border between two categories of a classification **3 :** IMMEDIATELY **:** without delay ⟨paid cash *on the line*⟩ **4 :** into prostitution ⟨she lost her job and went *on the line*⟩ — **on the lines of :** similar to **:** closely resembling **:** LIKE — **out of line :** not in a lineal arrangement: as **a :** not in a straight line **:** out of alignment **b :** not in a state of harmonious conformity ⟨prices and wages were badly *out of line*⟩ **c :** not in order or concord **:** badly behaved ⟨sorry if I was *out of line* last evening⟩

⁴line \"\ *vb* -ED/-ING/-s [ME *linen*, fr. ³*line*] *vt* **1** *archaic* **a :** to tie or make fast with a line **b :** to measure, sound, or examine with a line (2) **:** to reach or extend like a line **2 :** to mark with a line or lines **:** deface with lines ⟨time that ~*s* the faces of the fair⟩ **3 :** to depict with lines **:** portray esp. in outline **:** DRAW **4 :** to place, be placed, or be in a line along **:** place or form a line or lines along ⟨pedestrians ~ the walks⟩ ⟨shabby houses *lining* mean streets⟩ **5 :** to form into a line or lines **:** bring into physical alignment, into agreement with some standard, or into concord (as with an idea) — often used with *up* ⟨*lined* up the troops to face the river⟩ ⟨*lining* up support for the candidate⟩ ⟨we will ~ up an invincible resistance⟩ **6 :** to track (wild bees) to their nest by following their line of flight **7 :** LINE OUT **8 :** to throw or hit (as a baseball) so as to cause to travel swiftly and not far above the ground ~ *vi* **1 a :** to form a line : come together into a line — often used with *up* ⟨*lined* up and marched away⟩ **b :** to share a common boundary : ADJOIN ⟨their lands *lined* on the brook⟩ **2 :** to fish with a line ⟨seining and *lining*⟩ **3 :** to hit a line drive in baseball **4 :** ALIGN

⁵line \"\ *adj* [³*line*] **:** LINEAL, LINEAR: as **a** (1) **:** made up of or delineated by means of lines ⟨a ~ sketch⟩ — see LINE ENGRAVING (2) **:** involving or consisting of line work ⟨~ copy⟩ **b** (1) **:** having authority and responsibility flowing in a direct unbroken line between superior and subordinate persons in an organization ⟨the machinery of policy formulation is controlled by ~ executives⟩ (2) **:** belonging to personnel of the line of an organization ⟨the nature of ~ authority becomes apparent from the scalar principle —Harold Koontz & Cyril O'Donnell⟩ (3) **:** STRAIGHT-LINE

⁶line \"\ *vt* -ED/-ING/-S [ME *linen,* modif. of MF *aligner* to impregnate, align — more at ALIGN] **:** COVER, IMPREGNATE — used of a canine male

lin·ea \ˈlinēə\ *n, pl* **line·ae** \-ēˌē\ [L, line — more at LINE (cord)] **:** a line or linear body structure — see LINEA ALBA

linea al·ba \-ˈalbə\ *n, pl* **lineae al·bae** \-lˌbē\ [NL, lit., white line] **:** a median vertical tendinous line on the mammalian abdomen formed of fibers from the aponeuroses of the two rectus abdominis muscles and sometimes visible externally as a furrow

lineable *var of* LINABLE

lineae al·bi·can·tes \-ˌalbəˈkanˌtēz\ *n pl* [NL, lit., whitish lines] **:** whitish marks in the skin esp. of the abdomen and breasts that usu. follow pregnancy

¹lin·eage \ˈlinēij, -ēēj\ *n* -S [ME *linage,* fr. MF *linage, lignage,* fr. OF, fr. *ligne* line of descent, line, cord + *-age* — more at LINE (cord)] **1 a :** descent in a line from a common progenitor ⟨a person of unknown ~⟩ **b :** derivation or source of origin ⟨the characters reveal the play's ~⟩ **:** line of descent or tradition **:** BACKGROUND ⟨conceptions of ancient ~⟩ **2 :** a group of persons (as a family or clan) tracing descent from a common ancestor who is regarded as its founder **:** a unilineal descent group — compare MAXIMAL LINEAGE, MINIMAL LINEAGE **3 :** the number of lines on a score sheet that a set of bowling pins can withstand **syn** see ANCESTRY

²lineage *var of* LINAGE

line ahead *n, Brit* **:** COLUMN 4a

¹lin·eal \ˈlinēəl\ *adj* [ME, fr. LL *linealis,* fr. L *linea* line + *-alis* -al] **1 :** of or relating to a line **:** measured on or ascertained by a line **:** having the direction of a line **:** LINEAR ⟨~ magnitude⟩ ⟨50 ~ feet of walk⟩ **2 :** composed of or arranged in lines ⟨~ designs⟩ ⟨a ~ rather than a literal translation⟩ **3 a :** consisting of or being in a direct male or female line of ancestry or descent ⟨a ~ descent⟩ ⟨~ heirs⟩ ⟨a ~ ancestor⟩ — distinguished from *collateral* **b :** relating to or derived from ancestors in the direct line ⟨~ rights⟩ ⟨~ dignity⟩ **:** HEREDITARY ⟨a ~ feud⟩ **c :** descended in a direct line **:** being in a line of succession through lineage **4 a :** belonging to one lineage ⟨~ relatives⟩ **b :** of, relating to, or dealing with a lineage ⟨written in ~ terminology⟩ ⟨a ~ chief⟩ **5 :** of or relating to the line or officers of the line in an army or navy — **lin·eal·i·ty** \ˌlinēˈalədē\ *n* -ES — **lin·eal·ly** \ˈlinēəlē, -li\ *adv*

²lineal \"\ *n* -S **:** a lineal descendant

lineal measure *n* **:** LINEAR MEASURE

lineal promotion *n* **:** promotion of an officer by seniority according to lineal rank

lineal rank *n* **:** the rank of an officer in his arm of the service — distinguished from *relative rank*

¹lin·ea·ment \ˈlinēəmənt\ *n* -S [ME *liniament,* fr. L *lineamentum,* fr. *linea* line + *-mentum* -ment] **1 a :** an outline, feature, or contour of a body or figure and esp. of a face — usu. used in pl. **b :** the distinguishing or characteristic feature of something immaterial — usu. used in pl. ⟨the ~s of Christian life⟩ **2** *archaic* **:** a small amount **:** RUDIMENT, TRACE **3 :** a topographic feature; *esp* **:** one that is rectilinear — **lin·ea·men·tal** \ˌ⸗⸗⸗ˈmentᵊl\ *adj*

²lineament \"\ *vt* -ED/-ING/-S **:** to give lineaments to **:** form lineaments on or in ⟨a harsh land ~*ed* by frost and wind⟩ — **lin·ea·men·ta·tion** \ˌ⸗⸗⸗mənˈtāshən\ *n* -S

lin·ear \ˈlinēə(r)\ *adj* [L *linearis,* fr. *linea* line + *-aris* -ar] **1 a :** of or relating to a line: as (1) **:** following a straight course **:** being or going in a straight direction (2) *of music* **:** HORIZONTAL (3) *of a unit of measure* **:** involving a single dimension **:** not square or cubic **b :** consisting of or arranged in a line: as (1) **:** capable of being represented by a straight line on a graph — used of a relationship between two variables such that a change in one is accompanied by a proportional change in the other ⟨the relation between urban population percentage and propensity to compete is not ~ —V.O.Key⟩ ⟨this series of samples may have been drawn from a population in which there is a ~ relation between age and height —G.W.Snedecor⟩ ⟨many sweeping systems of cosmology have been based on this ~ (directly proportionate) relationship between the distance of galaxies and their speed —*Time*⟩ (2) **:** having or showing a linear relationship ⟨instead of a ~ trend we find merely temporary fluctuations —P.A.Sorokin⟩ (3) *of painting* **:** characterized by an emphasis on line; *broadly* **:** having forms that are painted flat and evenly and with precise fully indicated outlines (4) **:** consisting of an open and usu. long straight chain of atoms ⟨a ~ molecule⟩ ⟨~ polymers⟩ **2 a** (1) **:** resembling a line esp. in extended length and narrow uniform width **:** long and slender ⟨a wire is a ~ conductor⟩ ⟨a ~ leaf⟩ — see LEAF illustration (2) **:** intermediate between linear and a specified characteristic — used in combination ⟨a *linear*-ensate leaf⟩ ⟨petals *linear*-obovate⟩ **b** *of a human body* **:** ECTOMORPHIC — opposed to *lateral* **3 a :** giving a scale reading directly proportional to the quantity measured — used of a measuring instrument **b :** being, giving, or involving a response directly proportional to the input — used esp. in connection with electronic devices ⟨the amplifier must . . . have a pronounced ~ response several octaves greater, in treble and bass, than you require in practical use —David Sarser⟩ ⟨the crystal detector is not ~, so that a given increase in rectified current does not indicate a directly proportional increase in field strength —*Radio Amateur's Handbook*⟩ **4 :** of, relating to, or constituting a segmental phoneme

linear accelerator *n* **:** an accelerator in which particles are propelled in a straight line and receive successive increments of energy through the application of alternating potentials to a series of electrodes and gaps

linear content *n* **:** LENGTH

linear differential equation *n* **:** an equation of the first degree only in respect to the dependent variable or variables and their derivatives

linear equation *n* [prob. trans. of F *équation linéaire;* fr. the fact that every such equation in two variables in Cartesian coordinates represents a straight line] **:** an equation of the first degree in any number of variables

linear function *n* **:** a mathematical function in which the variables appear only in the first degree, multiplied by constants, and combined only by addition and subtraction

lin·ear·ism \ˈlinēəˌrizəm\ *n* -S **:** LINEARITY; *esp* **:** the condition of having linear historical continuity without significant fluctuation or deviation ⟨it is doubtful whether true ~ exists in any social process or evolution⟩

lin·ear·is·tic \ˌ⸗⸗⸗ˈristik\ *adj* **:** having a linear quality **:** characterized by linearity

lin·ear·i·ty \ˌlinēˈarədē *also* -ˈer-\ *n* -ES **:** the quality or state of being linear: as **a :** the condition of extending along or in a line **b :** one to one correspondence between diverse and often opposed elements **c :** the faithfulness with which an output signal of an electronic reproducing system reproduces an input signal; *specif* **:** the faithfulness with which the shape and arrangement of the elements in a television picture reproduce the shape and arrangement of the original televised image

lin·ear·iza·tion \ˌlinēərəˈzāshən\ *n* -S **1 :** the process of linearizing or the condition of being linear **2 :** a thing made linear

lin·ear·ize \ˈ⸗⸗⸗ˌrīz\ *vt* -ED/-ING/-S **:** to give a linear form to **:** make linear **:** project in linear form ⟨a heterogeneous catalyst . . . not only can ~ polyethylene —*Chem. and Engineering News*⟩

lin·ear·ly *adv* **:** in a linear manner **:** so as to be or appear linear

linear measure *n* **1 :** a measurement of length **2 :** a system of such measures (as the inch, foot, yard system)

linear momentum *n* **:** the momentum of translation being a vector quantity in classical physics equal to the product of the mass and the velocity of the center of mass

linear perspective *n* **:** perspective projection in which an object is represented on a surface by means of lines from points of the object through the drawing surface to a common point of intersection

linear programming *n* **:** a theory of maximization of linear functions of a large number of variables subject to constraints used esp. in the administrative and economic planning of industrial and military operations

¹lineate *vt* -ED/-ING/-S [ML *lineatus,* past part. of *lineare,* fr. L, to make straight, fr. *linea* line — more at LINE (cord)] **1** *obs* **:** to mark with lines **2** *obs* **:** DELINEATE

²lin·eate \ˈlinēət, -ēˌāt\ *or* **lin·eat·ed** \-ēˌād·əd\ *adj* [*lineate* fr. ML *lineatus; lineated* fr. past part. of ¹*lineate*] **:** marked with lines or stripes

lin·ea·tion \ˌlinēˈāshən\ *n* -S [ME *lineacion* outline, fr. LL *lineation-, lineatio,* fr. L, line, fr. *lineatus* (past part of *lineare*) + *-ion-, -io* -ion] **1 a :** the action of marking with lines or outlining **:** DELINEATION **b :** a depiction in outline **2 :** an arrangement of lines **:** MARKINGS **3 :** arrangement (as of verse) by or in lines

lineback \ˈ⸗ˌ⸗\ *n* **:** an animal (as some Hereford cattle) having a stripe of distinctive color along the spine

linebacker \ˈ⸗ˌ⸗⸗\ *n* [³*line* + *backer*] **:** a football player stationed within one to four yards of the line of scrimmage and expected to make quick tackles close to the line of scrimmage on running plays and to protect against short passes

linebacking \ˈ⸗ˌ⸗⸗\ *n* [*linebacker* + *-ing*] **:** the action, ability, or manner of playing linebacker on a football team

line block *n* **:** LINECUT

line bonus *n* **:** a bonus (as of 10, 20, or 25 points) scored in gin rummy for each hand won

¹linebred \ˈ⸗ˌ⸗\ *adj* [fr. past part. of *linebreed*] **:** produced by or subjected to linebreeding

²linebred \"\ *n* -S **:** a linebred individual

line·breed \ˈlīnˌbrēd\ *vb* [back-formation fr. *linebreeding*] *vi* **:** to practice linebreeding ~ *vt* **:** to interbreed by linebreeding **:** produce by linebreeding

line·breed·ing \-diŋ\ *n* [³*line* + *breeding*] **:** the breeding of individuals within a particular line of descent: **a :** moderately close inbreeding (as between aunt and nephew, between cousins) **b :** any of various schemes of breeding designed to perpetuate the desirable characters of a superior animal by interbreeding its descendants — compare INBREEDING

line camp *n, West* **:** a camp for the use of employees working on the outlying parts of a large ranch

linecasting \ˈ⸗ˌ⸗⸗\ *n* **:** the act or process of producing type in the form of metal slugs — called also *slugcasting*

line chief *n* **:** a noncommissioned aviation officer (as in the U.S. Air Force) who supervises the upkeep of a flight line — compare LINE CREW

line crew *n* **:** a maintenance crew on an airfield flight line

linecut \ˈ⸗ˌ⸗\ *n* **:** a relief printing plate made by photographing a design (as a pen-and-ink drawing composed of lines of varying thickness and sometimes grains, dots, stipples, cross-hatching) onto a plate or film and then photographing the negative onto a sensitized usu. zinc or copper plate that is then developed with the lines that will form the relief printing surface being protected with an acid resist and the rest of the plate surface being etched down; *also* **:** a print made from a linecut — called also *line block, line engraving, line plate*

¹lined \ˈlīnd\ *adj* [ME, fr. past part. of *linen* to line (as a cloak)] **1 :** having a lining or liner **2 :** depicted with a lining of a specified color — used of heraldic representations ⟨the mantling gules, ~ ermine⟩

²lined \"\ *adj* [fr. past part. of ⁴*line*] **1 :** marked or covered with lines **2 :** depicted with a line attached to the collar — used of a heraldic representation of an animal

line drawing *n* **:** a drawing made with pen, crayon, or other pointed instrument in solid lines or solid masses as copy for linecuts

line drive *n* **:** a batted baseball hit in a nearly straight line and typically not far above the ground — called also *liner*

line drop *n* **:** a voltage drop along an electric transmission or distribution line due to the impedance of the circuit

line engraver *n* **:** one engaged in line engraving **:** a maker of line engravings

line engraving *n* **1 a :** engraving in metal in which the effects are produced by lines of different widths and closeness; *also* **:** a plate so engraved **b :** a picture produced by intaglio printing from such an engraving **2 :** the photomechanical process by which linecuts are made; *also* **:** LINECUT

line etching *n* **:** LINECUT

line fence *n* **:** a fence built along the boundary or property line of a farm or ranch

line-firing \ˈ⸗ˌ⸗⸗\ *n* **:** the application of a firing iron in parallel lines over the skin of a horse in cases of chronic inflammation of the tendons of the leg

line frequency *n* **:** the number of lines scanned per second by the sawtooth wave of current used in television for horizontal scanning with an electron beam — compare FRAME FREQUENCY

line gauge *n* **:** a printer's ruler on which measurements have been marked in picas, usu. in other point sizes, and sometimes in inches

line geometry *n* **:** the geometry that assumes the line instead of the point as the element of space

line graph *n* **:** a graph in which points representing values of a variable for suitable values of an independent variable are connected by a broken line

line-haul \ˈ⸗ˌ⸗\ *n* **:** the actual transporting of items (as freight) between terminals as distinguished from pickup, delivery, and other terminal services

line integral *n* **:** the limit of the sum of products formed by dividing a given arc into *n* parts and multiplying the length of each part by the value of the function to be integrated at any point in this part, the number of parts increasing indefinitely and the length of each part approaching zero

line·less \ˈlīnləs\ *adj* **:** free from lines **:** lacking a line

line letter *n* **:** a method of reproducing text matter for the blind by embossing on paper the outlines of the roman letters ⟨point systems mostly superseded *line letter* before the 20th century⟩ — compare BRAILLE

line loss *n* **:** a loss of electric energy due to heating of line wires by the current

line·man \ˈlīnmən\ *n, pl* **linemen 1 :** CHAINMAN 4 **2 :** one who sets up or repairs electric wire communication or power lines — called also *linesman* **3 :** any football player except the quarterback in a T-formation (as a guard, tackle, end, or center) whose position is within one yard of the line of scrimmage when the ball is snapped

lineman's loop knot *n* **:** BUTTERFLY KNOT

line measure *n* **:** LINE GAUGE

linemen's pliers *n pl* **:** stout pliers with cutting edges on the jaws used esp. for cutting wire

lineman's loop knot

¹lin·en \ˈlinən\ *adj* [ME, fr. OE *linen,* fr. *lin* flax, spun or woven flax + *-en;* akin to OHG & ON *lin* flax, Goth *lein* linen cloth; all fr. a prehistoric Gmc word borrowed fr. L *linum* flax, linen, prob. of non-IE origin; akin to the source of Gk *linon* cord, flax] **1 a :** made of flax ⟨waxed ~ thread⟩ **b :** being or made of linen ⟨~ cloth⟩ ⟨a ~ blouse⟩ **2 :** like that of linen ⟨a ~ finish⟩

²linen \"\ *n* -S [ME, fr. *linen,* adj.] **1 a :** cloth made of flax and noted for its strength, coolness, and luster though somewhat subject to creasing — see BUTCHER LINEN **b :** thread or yarn spun from flax **2 a :** clothing (as shirts, underwear) or household articles (as sheets, tablecloths) made or orig. made of linen cloth and now usu. of other fabrics (as cotton, rayon) ⟨washed out her ~ every evening⟩ ⟨had a good stock of ~*s*⟩ **b** *obs* **:** a piece bandage of linen cloth **c** *archaic* **:** a wrapping of linen for the dead **:** GRAVECLOTHES — often used in pl. **3 :** LINEN PAPER

linen closet *n* **:** a closet with deep shelves and drawers for the storage of domestic linens (as towels, tablecloths, and sheets)

linen decency *n, obs* **:** commonplace and prosperous conventionality as symbolized by fine linen

linendraper \ˈ⸗⸗ˌ⸗⸗\ *n, chiefly Brit* **:** a retail dealer in yard goods

linen finish *n* **:** a finish on paper resembling the texture of linen cloth

linenfold \ˈ⸗⸗ˌ⸗\ *n* **:** a carved or molded ornament (as for paneling) representing a fold or scroll of linen

linenfold

lin·en·ized \ˈlinəˌnīzd\ *adj* **:** made or finished to resemble linen cloth or weave

linen paper *n* **1 :** paper made from linen fibers **2 :** paper with a linen finish

linen pattern *or* **linen scroll** *n* **:** LINENFOLD

linen press *n* **1 :** a large cupboard or cabinet for the storage of domestic linens **2 :** a press consisting of a flat bed upon which damp linen is placed for flattening through pressure applied with a large wooden screw

linen tester *n* **:** a small magnifier used esp. for counting threads in fabrics

lin·eny \ˈlinənē\ *adj* [²*linen* + *-y*] **:** resembling linen cloth

lineo- *comb form* [L *linea* line — more at LINE (cord)] **:** line ⟨*lineograph*⟩ **:** linear and ⟨*lineocircular*⟩

line of action 1 : the line along which a force or the resultant of any number of forces may be considered to act **2 :** the locus of all points of contact between two interacting teeth of a pair of gears

line of affection *usu cap A* **:** a short horizontal line on the Mount of Mercury that runs from the percussion toward the center of the palm and that is held by palmists to indicate affection for a member of the opposite sex — see LINE OF MARRIAGE, PALMISTRY illustration

line of apollo *usu cap A* [after *Apollo,* Graeco-Roman god of manly beauty, of poetry and music, and of the wisdom of oracles, sometimes regarded as a sun god — more at APOLLO] **:** LINE OF THE SUN

line of apsides : the major axis of an elliptical orbit

line of battle : the position of troops or ships arranged for or as if for delivery of an attack or reception of a charge

line-of-battle ship \ˈ⸗⸗ˈ⸗⸗-\ *n* **:** SHIP OF THE LINE

line of beauty : HOGARTH'S LINE

line of brilliancy : LINE OF THE SUN

line of columns : a group of parallel columns (as of soldiers or ships) whose fronts are in a straight line

line of communication *or* **line of communications :** the net of land, water, and air routes connecting a field of action (as a military front) with its bases of operations and supplies

line of credit : an amount up to which a financial institution will extend credit to a borrower

line of defense 1 : an artificial or natural barrier that can be readily employed for defense against invasion or attack (as a line of fortifications, a river, or a narrow pass) **2 :** an organization of military land forces with which a nation seeks to maintain its integrity against armed aggression or invasion ⟨the standing army usu. forms a nation's first *line of defense*⟩

line of departure : a line which units of a military force are ordered to cross at a certain time to coordinate an attack

line of destiny *usu cap D* **:** LINE OF FATE

line of distance : the perpendicular extending from the eye to the plane of perspective and having as its foot the center of vision

line of duty : all that is authorized, required, or normally associated with some field of responsibility (as of a policeman, fireman, or soldier) — used esp. in connection with assessment of responsibility for or classification of sickness, injury, or death of persons subject to a line of duty ⟨it is now customary to consider any sickness or injury of a member of an armed service that is suffered while on active duty to have been incurred in the *line of duty* in the absence of personal fault or neglect or of existence of the condition prior to entry into service⟩

line of elevation : the prolongation of the axis of the bore when an artillery piece is laid

line off *vt* **:** to separate with or into lines **:** mark off ⟨*line* several columns *off*⟩

line of fate *usu cap F* **:** a line located on the center of the palm that often runs straight from the wrist to the Mount of Saturn and that is usu. held by palmists to indicate according to its direction and strength the nature and degree of a person's success in life esp. as a result of outside influences — called also *line of Destiny, line of Saturn;* see PALMISTRY illustration

line officer *n* **:** an officer of the line of an army or navy

line of fire : the flight path of a projectile fired from a gun

line of flow 1 : a field line of the velocity vector in a flowing fluid **2 :** the path of any particle in an ensemble of particles moving under one law

line of flux : FIELD LINE

line of force : a field line in a field of force (as a magnetic field, an electric field, a gravitational field)

line of fortune : LINE OF THE SUN

line of head *usu cap H* **:** a line that begins on the Mount of Jupiter or at the start of the line of Life or on the Mount of Mars and runs across the palm and that is usu. held by palmists to indicate intellectual strength, temperament, and the quality and direction of talents — see PALMISTRY illustration

line of health *usu cap H* **:** LINE OF MERCURY

line of heart *usu cap H* **:** a line that runs across the palm at the base of the mounts parallel to the line of head and that is usu. held by palmists to indicate the strength and nature of a person's affections and emotional nature — called also *mensal line;* see PALMISTRY illustration

line of induction : a field line in a field of magnetic induction

line of influence *sometimes cap I* **:** one of a series of lines that appear on the Mount of Venus inside and parallel or perpendicular to the Life line and that are usu. held by palmists to indicate influences on a person's life from outside factors esp. by relatives or close friends

line of intuition *usu cap I* **:** a line located at the side of the hand and formed almost as a semicircle from the Mount of Mercury to the Mount of Luna that is usu. held by palmists to indicate a sensitive and impressionable nature and often a strong faculty of intuition

line of least resistance 1 : the shortest distance between the center of an underground charge of explosive and the open air **2 :** the easiest line of conduct

line of life *usu cap 2d L* **:** a line that rises under the Mount of Jupiter and runs down the palm in an arc around the Mount of Venus and that is usu. held by palmists to indicate the duration, vitality, and events of life — see PALMISTRY illustration

line of liver *usu cap 2d L* **:** LINE OF MERCURY

line of march 1 : the route along which a column (as of troops) advances ⟨driver ants destroying everything along their *line of march*⟩ **2 :** the arrangement of troops in column for a march

line of marriage *usu cap M* **1 :** a relatively long line of Affection that when corroborated by the lines of Life or Fate is usu. held by palmists to indicate the event and the approximate time of marriage or sometimes a very important love affair **2 :** LINE OF AFFECTION

line of mars *usu cap M* [after *Mars,* Roman god of war and agriculture, fr. L *Mart-, Mars*] **:** a line on the hand that rises on the lower Mount of Mars and forms an arc around the Mount of Venus inside the line of Life and that is usu. held by palmists to strengthen the line of Life and sometimes to indicate martial qualities — called also *line of Protection;* see PALMISTRY illustration

line of mercury *usu cap M* [after *Mercury,* Roman god of commerce, fr. L *Mercurius*] : a line on the hand that usu. begins on the Mount of Mercury and often runs straight down the hand to the rascettes and that is usu. held by palmists to indicate the condition of the liver and the digestive system and the presence of maladies or physical and mental qualities associated with them — called also *Hepatica, Hepatic line, line of Health, line of Liver;* see PALMISTRY illustration

line of metal : the line of sight passing along the upper surface of the tube of a cannon

line of nodes : a straight line joining the two opposite nodes of an astronomical orbit

line of position 1 : LINE OF SITE **2** : a locus of all possible positions of a ship for the conditions given — see SUMNER LINE **3** : a line along which an aircraft is known (as by ground reference or celestial fix) to be flying and which when crossed with another line of position will establish the precise position of the aircraft

line of pressure *or* **line of resistance** : a broken line joining the points of resultant pressure between the voussoirs of an arch or buttress

line of protection *usu cap P* : LINE OF MARS

line of saturn *usu cap S* [after *Saturn*, Roman god connected with the sowing of seed, fr. L *Saturnus*] : LINE OF FATE

line of scrimmage : an imaginary line for each side in American football that is parallel to the goal lines and passes through the point of the ball nearest the side's own goal line when the ball is laid on the ground with its long axis parallel with the side lines preparatory to a scrimmage

line of sight 1 *or* **line of sighting** : a linear projection toward a target of the straight line obtained when the sights of a firearm are in perfect alignment : the axis of the line of vision of a sight (as of an artillery piece) or other angle-measuring instrument **2** : LINE OF VISION **3 a** : a line from an observer's eye to a distant point (as on the celestial sphere) toward which he is looking or directing an observing instrument **b** : a line joining the earth or the sun and a distant astronomical body **4** : the straight path between a radio transmitting antenna and receiving antenna when unobstructed by the horizon ⟨reports of receptions far beyond the *line of sight* beyond which the signals should not have gone —*Science News Letter*⟩

line of site : a straight line from the muzzle of an artillery piece to a target

line of success : LINE OF THE SUN

line of supply : the routes (as roads, railways, rivers) in the rear of an army by which the army is supplied

line of the sun *or* **line of sun** *usu cap S* : a line that may begin on any part of the hand but ascends the palm to the Mount of Apollo and that is usu. held by palmists to indicate possession of exceptional talents leading toward success in life — called also *line of Apollo, line of brilliancy, line of fortune, line of success;* see PALMISTRY illustration

line of travel 1 : WALKING LINE **2** *usu cap T* : a line that rises from the rascettes high into the Mount of the Moon and esp. when strengthened by other markings on the hand is usu. held by palmists to indicate restlessness and travel

line of vision : a straight line joining the fovea of the eye with the fixation point

lin·eo·late \ˈlinēə,lāt\ *or* **lin·eo·lat·ed** \-ād·əd\ *adj* [*lineolate* fr. NL *lineolatus*, fr. L *lineola* small line (dim. of *linea* line) + *-atus* -ate; *lineolated* fr. NL *lineolatus* + E *-ed* — more at LINE (cord)] : marked with fine lines ⟨a ~ parrakeet⟩

line organization *n* : the part of a business organization that forms an integrated whole concerned with the production of the goods or services that are the stock in trade of the organization — often distinguished from *staff*

line out *vt* **1 a** : to mark (as a casting) with lines indicating material to be removed **b** : to indicate with or as if with lines : OUTLINE ⟨followed the route he had *lined out*⟩ **c** : DEACON 1 **2 a** : to plant (young nursery stock) in rows or lines for growing on **b** : to arrange in an extended line ⟨*lined* his cattle *out* along the trail⟩ **3** *dial* : SCOLD, PUNISH, REBUKE ~ *vi* **1** : to move rapidly usu. in a particular direction ⟨*lined out* for home without a backward glance⟩ ⟨the plane climbed and *lined out* east —W.B.Mowery⟩ **2** : to make an out by hitting a baseball in a line drive that is caught ⟨cut into the first ball and *lined out* —Ring Lardner⟩

line–out \ˈ=,=\ *n* -s [fr. the phrase *line out* "to line up, form a line"] : a play in rugby which is used to restart the game after the ball has gone into touch and in which the forwards of both teams form two close lines at right angles to the touchline and the ball is thrown between them

line pattern *n* : a virus disease of peach and cherry characterized by faint leaf mottling in more or less regular lines

line plate *n* : LINECUT

¹lin·er \ˈlīnə(r)\ *n* -s [partly fr. ME (Sc), fr. ME *linen* to line, measure with a line, mark with a line + *-er;* partly fr. ³*line* + *-er*] **1** : a person that makes or draws lines: as **a** *Scot* : an official that traces the boundaries of estates **b** : a worker that draws line detail (as in wheel dressing or ornamenting pottery ware) **c** : a writer employed at a fixed rate per line : PENNY-A-LINER **2** : something with which lines are made: as **a** : a sable brush used by coach painters **b** : FITCH 2 **c** : a small grease pencil used to delineate lines in theatrical makeup **3** : one that uses a line (as a man or a boat in fishing) — often used in combination ⟨a hand ~⟩ **4** : something that has a position fixed with reference to or on a particular line; *esp* : LINE TREE **5 a (1)** : a ship belonging to a regular line of ships ⟨a transatlantic ~⟩ **(2)** : SHIP OF THE LINE **b** : an aircraft belonging to an airline **6** : LINE DRIVE **7 a** : a small plant or seedling intended for lining out for further growth in the nursery row before being set out in its final growing place **b** : a plant that is to be budded in the nursery

²liner \"\ *n* -s [²*line* + *-er*] **1** : one that lines something: as **a** : a worker that applies, inserts, or attaches a lining (as in or into a carton, garment, suitcase) **b** : a machine that lines up the backbones of books **2** : something used to line or back another part: as **a** : a replaceable tube to fit inside an engine cylinder or a bushing for a bearing **b** : a facing placed between two surfaces or between a surface and some damaging agent to diminish wear, avoid overheating, or serve as reinforcement ⟨a tire ~⟩ ⟨an asbestos ~ for the kitchen range⟩ ⟨a flexible water and vapor proof drum ~⟩ **c** : a slab on which small pieces of material (as marble or tile) are fastened for grinding **d** : paper or other material that is used to cover board (as shelving or the bottom of a drawer) and often decorated **e** : a removable insert (as of glass, metal, or paper) in a container ⟨covered silver butter dish with glass ~⟩ **f** : an insert in the cover of a container that serves to make a hermetic seal between cover and container **g** : a removable and usu. warm lining for a garment (as a coat or pair of gloves) **h** : an outside ply of a combination paperboard or of a corrugated board; *also* : the smoother or more finished ply of a two-ply paperboard (as pasteboard) **3** : a narrow strip of plate to fill in between a frame and an outer strake of a ship **4** : a casing for a drilled oil well that does not extend to the surface **5** : a supplementary or explanatory text accompanying a recording

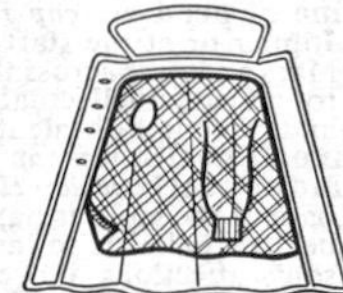
liner 2g

linerboard \ˈ=,=\ *n* : paperboard used as a facing on corrugated or solid fiberboard

line rider *n* **1** : a ranch employee who patrols boundaries, turning back stray cattle, repairing fences, and checking conditions (as of grazing or water supply) **2** : a worker who patrols along a petroleum pipeline to inspect and make minor repairs

liner–up \ˈ=,=\ *n, pl* **liners–up** [²*line up* + *-er*] : one that lines up the backbones of books

lines *pl of* LINE, *pres 3d sing of* LINE

line scale *n* : a scale in front of a typewriter platen against whose vertical lines typed characters may be aligned and against whose top edge paper and typing may be straightened

line screen *n* : SCREEN 10a

lineshaft \ˈ=,=\ *n* : a main shaft in a shop or factory usu. bearing pulleys by which machines are driven

lineside \ˈ=,=\ *adj* : adjacent to a railway line ⟨~ equipment for handling mail⟩

linesides \ˈ=,=\ *n pl but sing or pl in constr* [³*line* + *sides*, pl. of *side*] **1 a** : LARGEMOUTH BLACK BASS **b** : SPOTTED BLACK BASS **2** : BLACK SEA BASS 1

lines·man \ˈlīnzmən\ *n, pl* **linesmen** [*line's* (gen. of ³*line*) + *man*] **1** : a soldier of the line **2** : LINEMAN 2 **3** : an official who assists a referee esp. in various goal and net games: as **a** : a lawn tennis official who decides whether a ball falls inside or outside of the line or lines he is assigned to watch **b** : a football official whose duties include marking the distance gained or lost in the progress of each play, observing defensive holding of eligible forward pass receivers, marking the point where the ball goes out-of-bounds, and noting violations of the scrimmage formation **c** : a soccer official who assists the referee in deciding where and when a ball is out-of-bounds and which team is entitled to a kick-in, goal kick, or corner kick **d** : a touch judge in rugby **e** : either of two volleyball officials who are stationed at diagonally opposite corners of the court to assist the referee in determining out-of-bounds balls and illegal serves **f** : either of two officials assigned esp. to determine off side violations at the zone lines and at center in professional ice hockey **4** : LOFTSMAN; *esp* : one who specializes in laying down full-size line plans of ships

line space *n* : the space provided for a single line of typewriting

line space lever *or* **line spacer** *n* : the lever on a typewriter that operates the spacing ratchet and revolves the platen to a new line of writing and that is used to throw the carriage to a new line

line spectrum *n* : an optical spectrum more or less separated into sharply defined regions — used esp. of atomic spectra

line squall *n* : a squall or thunderstorm occurring along a squall line; *also* : a line of squalls or thunderstorms

line storm *n, chiefly New Eng* : an equinoctial storm

line–throwing gun \ˈ=,==-\ *n* : LYLE GUN

line tree *n* : a tree lying in a boundary line; *specif* : one intersected by a survey line and marked (as by blazing) for subsequent identification of a boundary point — called also *sight tree*

¹line up *vb* [⁴*line* + *up*] *vi* : to assume an orderly linear arrangement ⟨*line up* for inspection⟩ ~ *vt* : to put into alignment: as **a** : to put in correct adjustment for smooth running or perfect fitting **b** : to arrange in a line ⟨*line* the silverware *up*⟩ **c** : to assemble and make available ⟨*lined* a lot of support *up* for the reform candidate⟩ **d** : to check, mark, or correct the position of printed matter on (a press sheet)

²line up *vt* [²*line* + *up*] : to cover (a surface of a book's coverboard or backbone) by applying and affixing a liner

lineup \ˈ=,=\ *n* -s [¹*line up*] **1** : a line of persons arranged for inspection; *esp* : a muster containing suspects whose identification is sought by the police **2 a (1)** : a list of players who will take part in a game (as of football or baseball) and of their positions **(2)** : the players on such a list **b** : an arrangement of persons or sometimes of things usu. having a common purpose or sentiment ⟨the ~ at a ticket-office window⟩ ⟨the ~ of political factions⟩ **3** : the condition or manner of being lined up **4 a** : the act of lining up a printed sheet **b** : a sheet that has been lined up

lin·e·us \ˈlinēəs\ *n, cap* [NL, perh. irreg. fr. L *linea* line — more at LINE (cord)] : a genus of long slender nemertine worms (order Heteronemertea) sometimes attaining an extended length of 75 feet

line voltage *n* : the voltage of a power transmission circuit or distribution circuit up to the point of transformation or utilization

linewalker \ˈ=,==\ *n* : a worker who patrols a petroleum line on foot to inspect and make minor repairs — compare LINE RIDER

liney *var of* LINY

¹ling \ˈliŋ\ *n* -s [ME *linge, lenge;* akin to D *leng* ling, G *länge*, ON *langa;* derivative fr. the root of E ¹*long*] **1** : any of various fishes of the family Gadidae: as **a** : a large fish (*Molva molva*) of shallow seas of northern Europe and Greenland that is commonly salted and dried for food or a closely related and similarly used deep-sea fish **b** : the American burbot **c** : any of several American hakes (genus *Urophycis*) **2** : any of various fishes belonging to families other than Gadidae: as **a** : LINGCOD **b** : a fish of the family Ophidiidae **c** : COBIA

²ling \"\ *n* -s [ME *lyng*, fr. ON; akin to OE ²*-ling*] **1** : a heath plant; *esp* : the common Old World heather (*Calluna vulgaris*) **2** : a growth of heather or other heaths

³ling \ˈliŋ\ *also* **ling ko** \-ˈkō\ *n* -s [Chin (Pek) *ling²*] : WATER CHESTNUT 1

¹-ling \liŋ, lēŋ\ *n suffix* -s [ME, fr. OE; akin to OHG *-ling*, ON *-lingr*, Goth *-lings*, OE *-ing* — more at -ING (one of a specified kind)] **1** : one belonging to or associated with a (specified) group or condition or marked by a (specified) quality ⟨hire*ling*⟩ ⟨dar*ling*⟩ ⟨nest*ling*⟩ **2** : young, small, or inferior one ⟨duck*ling*⟩ ⟨gos*ling*⟩ ⟨prince*ling*⟩

²-ling \" *or* **-lings** \-ŋz\ *adv suffix* [*-ling* fr. ME, fr. OE; *-lings* fr. ME *-linges*, fr. *-ling* + *-es*, gen. sing. ending of nouns (functioning adverbially, as in *nedes* needs, *alweyes* always); akin to OHG *-lingūn* -ling, OE *-lō* strap, Lith *lenkti* to bend — more at -s] : in (such) a direction or manner : to (such) an extent ⟨east*ling*⟩ — chiefly in adverbs of state or manner ⟨dark*ling*⟩

³-ling *pres part of* -LE

ling *abbr* linguistic, linguistics

lin·ga·la \liŋˈgälə\ *n* -s *usu cap* : a Bantu language widely used in trade and public affairs in the Congo — compare TSHILUBA

lin·gam \ˈliŋgəm\ *or* **lin·ga** \-gə\ *n* -s [Skt *liṅga* (nom. *liṅgam*), lit., mark, characteristic] **1** : a stylized phallic symbol often depicted in conjunction with the yoni, connoting maleness, vitality, and creative power, and being an emblem of the Indian god Siva **2** : lingam and yoni

lin·ga·yat *also* **lin·ga·yit** \liŋˈgäyət\ *n* -s *usu cap* [Kanarese *liṅgāyata*, fr. Skt *liṅga*] : a member of an Indian religious sect characterized by worship of the god Siva, wearing of the lingam, denial of caste distinctions, and burial of the dead

ling·berry \ˈliŋ- — *see* BERRY\ *n* [²*ling* + *berry*] : MOUNTAIN CRANBERRY

lingbird \ˈ=,=\ *n* [²*ling* + *bird*] *dial Eng* : MEADOW PIPIT

lingcod \ˈ=,=\ *n* [¹*ling* + *cod*] : a large greenish-fleshed scorpaenid fish (*Ophiodon elongatus*) of the Pacific coast of No. America that is an important food fish closely related to the typical greenlings — called also *cultus*

linge \ˈlinj\ *vt, past or past part* **linged** [origin unknown] *dial chiefly Brit* : STRIKE, FLOG

¹lin·gel *also* **lin·gle** \ˈliŋ(g)əl\ *n* -s [ME *liniolf*, fr. MF *ligneul*, fr. L *lineola* small line, dim. of *linea* line — more at LINE (cord)] *now Scot* : a shoemaker's thread

²lingel *also* **lingle** \"\ *n* -s [ME *lingell* leather of a horse's harness] *Scot* : a little thong of leather

lin·ger \ˈliŋgə(r)\ *vb* **lingered; lingered; lingering** \-g(ə)riŋ\ **lingers** [ME (northern dial.) *lengeren* to dwell, freq. of *lengen* to tarry, prolong, fr. OE *lengan* to prolong; akin to OHG *lengen* to make long, ON *lengja;* causative fr. the root of E ¹*long*] *vi* **1** : to remain or wait long : be slow in parting or in quitting something : DELAY, LOITER, TARRY **2 a** : to remain alive although suffering or gradually dying ⟨would not have thee ~ in thy pain —Shak.⟩ ⟨the old man ~*ed* several months after his stroke⟩ **b** : to remain existent though waning in strength, importance, or influence ⟨winter ~*ed*⟩ ⟨old customs ~⟩ **3** : to be slow to act : PROCRASTINATE, DAWDLE, HESITATE ⟨charged that he ~*ed* in settling the estate to increase his fees⟩ **4** : to move slowly : SAUNTER ⟨~*ing* homeward⟩ **5** *now dial Eng* : LONG, HANKER — usu. used with *after* ~ *vt* **1** *obs* : to put off : POSTPONE, DEFER **2** *obs* : to make extended : PROTRACT, PROLONG **3** : to spend or pass (as a period of time) slowly and often in suffering or distress — often used with *out* ⟨~*ed* out several more years⟩ **syn** see STAY

lin·ger·er \-gərə(r)\ *n* -s : one that lingers

¹lin·ge·rie \,länjəˈrā, ,läⁿzhə-, ,laⁿzhə-, ,lanjə-, -ˈrē, ˈ=,=,= *also* ˈ==rē *or* ˈ==ri *sometimes* ,lōⁿzhə-; *by many, vowels other than* a *in the first syllable and* ē *or* i *in the last are regarded as substand*\ *n* -s [F, fr. MF, fr. *linge* linen (fr. *linge*, adj., made of linen, fr. L *lineus* made of flax or linen) + *-erie* -ery — more at LINE (cord)] **1** *archaic* : linen articles or garments **2** : intimate feminine apparel (as nightwear and underwear)

²lingerie \"\ *adj* : having a frilly dainty finish or style like that characteristic of fine underwear for women ⟨a tailored black suit with a white ~ blouse⟩ ⟨sheer fabric and ~ detail⟩

lin·ger·ing·ly *adv* : in a lingering manner : slowly or for a prolonged period

lingier *comparative of* LINGY

lingiest *superlative of* LINGY

ling ko *var of* LING

¹lin·go \ˈliŋ(,)gō\ *n, pl* **lingoes** *also* **lingos** [prob. fr. Prov *lengo, lingo* tongue, language, fr. L *lingua* — more at TONGUE] : language or speech that is thought of as strange: as **a** : a foreign language esp. when of purely local or remote usage ⟨became skilled in several tribal ~*es*⟩ **b** : the special vocabulary of a particular field of interest : the jargon, cant, or argot of a particular interest group or class of persons ⟨seaman's ~⟩ ⟨hospital ~⟩ **c** : language or style in utterance that is characteristic of an individual ⟨the shouted invective that is the basis of her ~⟩ **syn** see DIALECT

²lingo *or* **lin·goe** \"\ *n, pl* **lingoes** [prob. fr. F *lingot* ingot] *weaving* : a metal weight attached to the bottom of cords in a jacquard harness

lin·goa wood \liŋˈgōə-\ *also* **lingoa** *n* -s [*lingoa* fr. native name in the Moluccas] : AMBOYNA 1

ling·on·berry \ˈliŋən- — *see* BERRY\ *also* **lingon** \ˈliŋən, ˈlin-,gŏn\ *or* **lin·gen·berry** \ˈliŋən- — *see* BERRY\ *or* **lingen** *n* [*lingonberry & lingenberry* fr. Sw *lingon* mountain cranberry + E *berry; lingon & lingen* fr. Sw *lingon;* akin to ON *lyng* heather — more at LING] : MOUNTAIN CRANBERRY

lin·got \ˈliŋgət\ *n* -s [ME (Sc) *lingat*, fr. MF *lingot*, prob. fr. OProv, fr. *lenga* tongue, fr. L *lingua*] *archaic* : an ingot of metal

lin·go·um \liŋˈgōəm\ [NL, fr. the native name (in the Moluccas) of lingoa wood] *syn of* PTEROCARPUS

lings *pl of* LING

¹-lings *pl of* -LING

²-lings — see -LING

ling·tow \ˈliŋ,tō\ *n* [prob. fr. Sc *ling* line (fr. F *ligne*) + E *tow* — more at LINE (cord)] *Scot* : a rope used by smugglers for packing burdens

lingu- *or* **lingua-** *or* **lingui-** *or* **linguo-** *comb form* [L *lingu-*, fr. *lingua*] **1** : language ⟨*lingui*potence⟩ ⟨*lingu*ist⟩ **2** : tongue ⟨*linguo*papillitis⟩ **3 a** : produced by the tongue and — in terms referring to speech sounds ⟨*linguo*dental⟩ ⟨*lingua*nasal⟩ ⟨*linguo*nasal⟩ ⟨*linguo*palatal⟩ **b** : lingual and ⟨*linguo*maxillary⟩ **4** : lingually ⟨*linguo*distal⟩

lin·gua \ˈliŋgwə\ *n, pl* **lin·guae** \-ŋ,gwē\ [L, tongue, language] : a tongue or organ resembling a tongue in structure or function: as **a** : GLOSSA **b** : HYPOPHARYNX

lin·guae·form \ˈliŋgwē,fȯrm\ *adj* [by alter. (influence of L *linguae*, gen. of *lingua* tongue)] : LINGUIFORM

lingua fran·ca \-ˈfraŋkə\ *n, pl* **lingua francas** \-kəz\ *or* **linguae fran·cae** \-an,sē\ [It, lit., Frankish language] **1** : a common language that consists of Italian mixed with French, Spanish, Greek, and Arabic and is spoken in the ports of the Mediterranean — compare SABIR **2** : any of various hybrid or other languages that are used over a wide area as common or commercial tongues among peoples of diverse speech (as Hindustani, Swahili) — compare JARGON 2c, KOINE, PIDGIN **3** : something (as a system of common interests or social symbols) that functions like a common language in making individuals comprehensible to one another ⟨some tradition where a *lingua franca* of symbols, dogma, style, and learning survives —Stephen Spender⟩

lingua ge·ral \-zhəˈräl\ *n, pl* **lingua gerals** [Pg *lingua geral*, lit., general language] : a trade language based on Tupi and used in inland Brazil

lin·gual \ˈliŋg(yə)wəl\ *adj* [ML *lingualis*, fr. L *lingua* + *-alis* -al] **1 a** : of or relating to the tongue ⟨~ inflammation⟩ : resembling a tongue **b** : lying near or next to the tongue ⟨a ~ blood vessel⟩ ⟨the ~ surface of the teeth⟩ **c** *of a speech sound* : produced by the tongue; *sometimes* : dental or cerebral (sense 3a) **2** : LINGUISTIC

lingual artery *n* : an artery arising from the external carotid between the superior thyroid and facial arteries and supplying the tongue

lingual bone *n* : HYOID BONE

lin·gua·le \liŋˈgwa(,)lē, -wā(-, -wä(-\ *n* -s [NL, fr. ML, neut. of *lingualis*] : the midpoint of the upper border of the mandible — compare GNATHION 1

¹lin·gua·lis \liŋˈgwaləs, -wāl-, -wäl-\ *adj* [ML] : LINGUAL

²lingualis \"\ *n* -ES [NL, fr. ML *lingualis*, adj.] : the tongue musculature : the intrinsic muscles of the tongue

lin·gual·ly \ˈliŋgwəlē *sometimes* -gyəw-\ *adv* : in a lingual manner : toward the tongue

lingual nerve *n* : a branch of the mandibular division of the trigeminal nerve supplying the anterior two thirds of the tongue and responding to stimuli of pressure, touch, and temperature

lingual tonsil *n* : a variable mass or group of small nodules of lymphoid tissue lying at the base of the tongue just anterior to the epiglottis

lin·gua·ta \liŋˈgwäd·ə, -wād·ə\ *n pl, cap* [NL, fr. LL, neut. pl. of *linguatus* tongued, eloquent, fr. L *lingua* tongue + *-atus* -ate] *in some esp former classifications* : a large suborder of Salientia including all toads and frogs having a tongue and separate openings for the eustachian tubes — compare AGLOSSA 1, PHANEROGLOSSA

lin·guat·u·la \liŋˈgwachələ\ *n, cap* [NL, fr. LL *linguatus* + NL *-ula*] : a genus of tongue worms that includes a cosmopolitan parasite (*L. serrata*) of the nasal and respiratory passages of various canines, sheep and goats, the horse, and occasionally man

lin·guat·u·lid \-ləd\ *n* -s [NL *Linguatulida*] : a tongue worm of the genus *Linguatula; broadly* : TONGUE WORM

lin·gua·tu·li·da \,liŋgwəˈtülədə, -wəˈtyü-\ *n pl, cap* [NL, fr. *Linguatula* + *-ida*] : a group of wormlike pseudosegmented parasitic animals that are considered to constitute a separate phylum, a class of Arthropoda, or esp. formerly an order of Arachnida, that lack eyes, circulatory system, and respiratory organs, that live as adults in the respiratory passages or body cavity of reptiles, birds, or mammals, and that undergo larval development in the visceral tissues of similar hosts and that comprise the tongue worms

lin·guat·u·lo·sis \liŋ,gwachəˈlōsəs\ *n, pl* **linguatulo·ses** \-ō,sēz\ [NL, fr. *Linguatula* + *-osis*] : infestation with or disease caused by tongue worms

lin·gue \ˈliŋgwā\ *n* -s [AmerSp, fr. Araucanian *lige*] : a Chilean timber tree (*Persea lingue*) that is closely related to the avocado, has a bark which is a locally important source of tannin, and yields a lustrous pale brown timber esteemed for cabinetwork and joinery

lin·guet \ˈliŋ,gwet\ *n* -s [by alter.] : LANGUET

lingui- — see LINGU-

lin·gui·form \ˈliŋgwə,fȯrm\ *adj* [*lingu-* + *-form*] : having the form of a tongue : tongue-shaped

lin·guip·o·tence \liŋˈgwipəd·ən(t)s\ *n* [*lingu-* + *potence*] : mastery of languages

lin·guist \ˈliŋgwəst\ *n* -s [L *lingu-* + E *-ist*] **1** : a person accomplished in languages and esp. in living languages : one who is facile in several languages **2** : a student of or expert in linguistics

lin·guist·er \-tə(r)\ *n* -s [*linguist* + *-er*] : INTERPRETER

lin·guis·tic \liŋˈgwistik, -tēk\ *also* **lin·guist·i·cal** \-tәkəl, -tēk-\ *adj* [*linguist* + *-ic* or *-ical*] **1** : of or relating to language or to the knowledge or study of languages : relating to linguistics or to the affinities of languages ⟨~ studies⟩ ⟨the ~ point of view⟩ **2** : constituting language ⟨nonliterary ~ acts —Joshua Whatmough⟩

lin·guis·ti·cal·ly \-tək(ə)lē, -tēk-, -li\ *adv* : from the linguistic point of view : in respect to language or linguistics

linguistic atlas *n* : a publication containing or consisting of a set of maps upon which are recorded dialectal variations of pronunciation, vocabulary, inflection, and idiom — called also *dialect atlas*

linguistic form *n* : a meaningful unit of speech (as an allomorph, morpheme, word, phrase, clause, sentence) — called also *speech form*

linguistic geographer *n* : a specialist in linguistic geography

linguistic geography *n* : local or regional variations of a language or dialect as a field of study or knowledge — called also *dialect geography*

lin·guis·ti·cian \,liŋgwəˈstishən\ *n* -s [*linguistic* + *-an*] : LINGUIST 2

linguistic island *n* [trans. of G *sprachinsel*] **:** SPEECH ISLAND

lin·guis·tics \liŋ'gwistiks, -tēks\ *n pl but usu sing in constr* **:** the study of human speech in its various aspects (as the units, nature, structure, and modification of language, languages, or a language including esp. such factors as phonetics, phonology, morphology, accent, syntax, semantics, general or philosophical grammar, and the relation between writing and speech) — called also *linguistic science, science of language;* compare PHILOLOGY

lin·guist·ry \'liŋgwəstrē\ *n* -ES [*linguist* + *-ry*] **:** knowledge or study of languages

lin·gu·la \'liŋgyələ\ *n* [NL, fr. L, small tongue, object like a tongue, fr. *lingua* tongue + *-ula* — more at TONGUE] **1** *pl* **lingu·lae** \-yə,lē\ **:** a tongue-shaped process or part: as **a :** a ridge of bone in the angle between the body and the greater wing of the sphenoid **b :** an elongated prominence of the vermiform process of the cerebellum **c :** a dependent projection of the upper lobe of the left lung **2 a** *cap* **:** the type genus of Lingulidae comprising burrowing brachiopods with very long contractile pedicles that have existed from at least Ordovician time **b** *pl* **lingulae :** any brachiopod of the genus *Lingula* — **lin·gu·lar** \-lə(r)\ *adj*

lin·gu·late \'liŋgyə,lāt\ *also* **lin·gu·lat·ed** \-ād·əd\ *adj* [*lingulate* fr. L *lingulatus*, fr. *lingula* + *-atus* -ate; *lingulated* fr. L *lingulatus* + E *-ed*] **:** shaped like a tongue or a strap

lin·gu·lel·la \,liŋgyə'lelə\ *adj, usu cap* [fr. *Lingulella*, subdivision of the European Cambrian, fr. NL, genus of brachiopods, fr. *Lingula*, genus of burrowing brachiopods + *-ella*] **:** of or relating to a subdivision of the European Cambrian — see GEOLOGIC TIME table

¹lin·gu·lid \'liŋgyələd\ *adj* [NL *Lingulidae*] **:** of or relating to Lingulidae

²lingulid \"\ *n* -S [NL *Lingulidae*] **:** a brachiopod of the family Lingulidae

lin·gu·li·dae \liŋ'gyülə,dē\ *n pl, cap* [NL, fr. *Lingula*, type genus + *-idae*] **:** a family of brachiopods (order Atremata) that includes the earliest recorded Lower Cambrian animal fossils and is represented by a few recent forms — see LINGULA 2

lin·gu·lif·er·ous \,liŋgyə¦lif(ə)rəs\ *adj* [NL *Lingula* + E *-iferous*] **:** containing or made up of shells of brachiopods of *Lingula* or related genera ⟨~ rocks⟩

¹lin·gu·loid \'liŋgyə,lȯid\ *adj* [NL *Lingula* + E *-oid*] **:** like or like that of a brachiopod of the genus *Lingula*

²linguloid \"\ *n* -S **:** a brachiopod resembling or related to those of the genus *Lingula*

³linguloid \"\ *adj* [NL *lingula* + E *-oid*] **:** LINGULATE

linguo- — see LINGU-

lin·guo·version \¦liŋgwə+\ *n* [*lingu-* + *version*] **:** displacement of a tooth to the lingual side of its proper occlusal position

¹lingy \'liŋē\ *adj* -ER/-EST [²*ling* + *-y*] **:** covered with or abounding in heaths, esp. heather **:** HEATHY, HEATHERY

²lin·gy \'linjē\ *adj* [origin unknown] *dial Eng* **:** SUPPLE, ACTIVE

lin·hay \'linē\ *n* -S [origin unknown] *dial chiefly Eng* **:** a shed usu. with a lean-to roof and one or more open sides

linier *comparative of* LINY

liniest *superlative of* LINY

lin·i·ment \'linəmənt\ *n* -S [ME *lynyment* ointment, fr. LL *linimentum*, fr. L *linere, linire* to smear + *-mentum* -ment — more at LIME] **:** a liquid or semiliquid alcoholic, oily, or saponaceous preparation of a consistency thinner than an ointment for application to the skin with friction esp. as an anodyne or a counterirritant **:** EMBROCATION

¹li·nin \'līnən\ *n* -S [ISV *lin-* (fr. L *linum* flax) + *-in* — more at LINEN] **1 :** a bitter white crystallizable substance with purgative qualities obtained from the purging flax **2 :** a protein obtained from flaxseed

²linin \"\ *n* -S [ISV *lin-* (fr. L *linum* thread, flax) + *-in;* orig. formed in G] **:** the feebly-staining portion of the reticulum of the nucleus of a resting cell in which chromatin granules appear to be embedded that is variously construed as chromatin in a particular physical state or in fixed preparations as precipitated protein

¹lin·ing \'līniŋ, -nēŋ\ *n* -S [ME, fr. gerund of *linen* to line (as a cloak)] **1 :** material or an arrangement of material used to line something: as **a :** a layer (as of fabric) inserted under, usu. following the lines of, and made temporarily or permanently fast to the principal material of a garment ⟨a coat with a warm fur ~⟩ — see ²LINER 2g **b** (1) **:** the material used in reinforcing the backbone of a book (2) **:** PASTEDOWN (3) **:** a sheet of paper or other material placed immediately under a pastedown **c :** LINING LEATHER **d** *or* **lining cloth :** extra canvas sewed on a part of a sail exposed to chafing **e :** an attached or loose sheet or an applied coating on all or part of the inner surfaces of a container **2** *archaic* **:** CONTENTS **3 linings** *pl, now dial Eng* **:** UNDERCLOTHES; *esp* **:** DRAWERS **4 :** the act of providing something with a lining **:** the process of inserting a lining

²lining \"\ *n* -S [fr. gerund of ⁴*line*] **1 :** an act or instance or the process of lining: **a :** the fixing of boundaries of estates in a burgh in Scotland by the lines; *also* **:** the erection or alteration of a building by permission of a dean of guild **b :** ordering in a line or lines **:** ALIGNMENT **c :** marking or tracing lines on a surface **d :** fishing with hook and line — often used in combination ⟨made his living hand-*lining*⟩ **e :** measuring or checking with a line **2 :** a product of lining; *esp* **:** ornamentation in the form of narrow lines ⟨wheels brightened with crimson ~⟩

lining bar *n* [²*lining*] **:** a crowbar the working end of which has a square section and ends in a pinch, wedge, or diamond point

lining figure *n* [²*lining*] **:** an arabic numeral that aligns with the base of a type line or printed line — called also *modern figure*

lining leather *n* [¹*lining*] **:** lightweight leather for lining leather goods (as shoes, handbags)

lining–out stock \'ˌ=ˌ=-\ *n* [*lining-out* fr. gerund of *line out*] **:** small or seedling plants for use as liners

lining page *n* [¹*lining*] **:** the exposed side of a pastedown in a book

¹link \'liŋk\ *n* -S [ME, fr. OE *hlinc;* akin to OE *hlanc* lank — more at LANK] **1 a** *now dial Brit* **:** a ridge of land **:** stretch of rising ground **b links** *pl, chiefly Scot* **:** sandy level or undulating land built up along a coastline **2 links** *pl but sing or pl in constr* **a** *archaic* **:** a seaside golf course **:** a golf course built on coastal links **b :** GOLF COURSE

²link \"\ *n* -S [ME, of Scand origin; akin to ON *hlekkr* chain, link; akin to ON *hlykkr* bend, noose — more at LANK] **1 :** a connecting structure (as a loop by which something is made fast): as **a links** *pl, obs* **:** FETTERS **b** (1) **:** a single ring or division of a chain (2) **:** one of the standardized links of a surveyor's chain being 7.92 inches long and serving as a measure of length **c :** CUFF LINK **d :** BOND 3e **e :** an intermediate rod or piece for transmitting force or motion; *esp* **:** a short connecting rod with a hole or pin at each end **f :** the fusible member of a fuse designed to melt when an excessive current flows **g :** a metal unit that connects the cartridges of an automatic weapon and with them forms a feed belt **2 :** something analogous to a link of chain (as in form, function, or serial arrangement): as **a** (1) **:** one of the segments into which sausage in continuous casing is usu. constricted (as by tying) at regular intervals (2) **:** a small sausage resembling one of the links of a chain of sausage but not being part of a chain (3) **links** *pl* **:** a chain of sausages **b :** a unifying element **:** a means of connecting or communicating ⟨the letters that were the last ~ with her past⟩ ⟨love of nature forms a ~ with our pioneer ancestors⟩ **c :** a constructive part of a mechanism having at least two elements belonging to different pairs **d :** a unit in a communication system (as a radio transmitter and receiver operating together to form part of a more extensive communication system) **3 links** *pl, dial* **:** a winding of a river or watercourse; *also* **:** the ground along such a winding **4 :** a step in ballroom dancing involving weaving forward and back in the manner of the grapevine

³link \"\ *vb* -ED/-ING/-S [ME *linken*, fr. ²*link*] *vt* **1 :** to couple or connect by or as if by a connecting element ⟨to ~ the new settlements on the Pacific with the settled east —R.H.Brown⟩ ⟨none of the subjects that ~*ed* us together could be talked about —Nevil Shute⟩ ⟨~*ing* the human heart to the life of the earth —Laurence Binyon⟩ — often used with *up* ⟨the . . . elaborate network of schools ~*ed* up with industry —A.R. Williams⟩ **2** *dial Brit* **:** to take (a person) by the arm usu. as an escort **:** walk arm in arm with **3** *chiefly Brit* **:** LOOP 3 ~ *vi* **1 :** to become coupled or connected esp. by means of a connecting element ⟨a piston ~*s* to a drive shaft by means of a connecting rod⟩ — often used with *up* ⟨the two families ~ *up* through the marriage of a daughter and son⟩ **2 :** to form a connection or association ⟨the newer company ~*ed* with several older ones in self-protection⟩; *esp* **:** to join company — often used with *up* ⟨~*ed* up with two young waitresses . . . off for the evening —Earle Birney⟩ **syn** see JOIN

⁴link \"\ *adj* [²*link*] **1 :** relating to or made of links ⟨a ~ fence⟩ ⟨~ sausage⟩ **2 :** serving to connect; *specif* **:** functioning as a linguistic connective

⁵link \"\ *n* -S [perh. modif. of ML *linchinus, lichinus* candle, lamp, alter. of L *lychnus*, fr. Gk *lychnos;* akin to Gk *leukos* bright, white — more at LIGHT] **1 :** a torch (as of tow and pitch) formerly used to light a person on his way through the streets **2 :** LINKBOY, LINKMAN **3** *obs* **:** a black coloring agent or blacking sometimes considered to have been lampblack

⁶link \"\ *vi* [origin unknown] *Scot* **:** to trip along **:** walk or move smartly and quickly

⁷link \"\ *adj* [Yiddish, fr. MHG *linc, lenc* left, awkward, ignorant; akin to OHG *lenka* left hand and prob. to L *languēre* to be languid — more at SLACK] **:** not devout **:** lax in respect to religious observances

link·able \-kəbəl\ *adj* **:** capable of being linked

link·age \-kij, -kēj\ *n* -S **1 :** the manner or style of being fitted together or united: as **a :** the manner in which atoms or radicals are linked in a molecule **b :** BOND 3e **2 :** the quality or state of being linked; *esp* **:** a relationship between genes that causes them to be manifested together in inheritance through concurrence of characters that they separately control, and that is usu. considered to result from the location of such genes on the same chromosome **3 a :** a system of links; *specif* **:** a system of links or bars which are jointed together and more or less constrained by having a link or links fixed and by means of which straight or approximately straight lines or other point paths may be traced **b :** the product of the magnetic flux through an electrical coil by its number of turns with the magnetic flux and the coil being connected like two links of a chain and each unit of flux threading through one turn of the coil to contribute one unit to the linkage

linkage group *n* **:** a group of genes that tend to be inherited as a unit

link and pin coupler *n* **:** an early device for coupling railroad cars consisting of a heavy metal pin inserted through a metal link

linkboy \'ˌ=ˌ=\ *n* **:** an attendant formerly employed to bear a torch or other light to light the way of a person abroad in the streets at night

linked \'liŋkt\ *adj, of genes* **:** exhibiting genetic linkage **:** tending to be inherited together

link·er \'liŋkə(r)\ *n* -S **:** one that links; *esp* **:** a worker who makes or joins links by hand or machine

¹linking *n* -S [fr. gerund of ³*link*] **:** LIAISON 2

²linking *adj* [fr. pres. part. of ³*link*] **:** being a speech sound that has an analogue in the spelling and that is pronounced before a vowel-initial word that follows without pause but not before a consonant or a pause ⟨*r*-droppers often have a ~ \r\ in *four eighths*⟩ ⟨in French there is a ~ \z\ before the *autres* of *les autres*⟩

link·is·ter *or* **link·ster** \'liŋk(ə)stə(r)\ *dial var of* LINGUISTER

link·man \'liŋkmən\ *n, pl* **linkmen 1 :** LINKBOY **2 :** an attendant (as at a theater) who summons vehicles and shows passengers to and from them

link motion *n* **:** motion imparted by a linkage (as in some steam locomotive engines to operate the slide valve); *also* **:** LINKAGE 3a

link relative *n* [²*link*] **:** the ratio usu. expressed in percent of any value of a statistical variable evaluated at equal intervals of time (as annual crop yield) to the value for the immediately preceding interval

links *pl of* LINK, *pres 3d sing of* LINK

links–and–links \¦=ˌ=¦=\ *also* **links–links** \'=ˌ=\ *adj* **1 :** of, relating to, or being a circular or flat knitting machine for producing purl or fancy stitches **2 :** produced on a links-and-links machine ⟨*links-and-links* patterns⟩

links·man \'liŋksmən\ *n, pl* **linksmen** [*links* (pl. of ¹*link*) + *man*] **:** GOLFER

linkup \'=ˌ=\ *n* -S [fr. the phrase *link up*] **1 :** establishment of contact ⟨planned a ~ with the eastern allies near the river⟩ **2 :** something that serves as a linking device or factor ⟨the new highway will provide an east-west ~⟩

link verb *or* **linking verb** *n* **:** a verb (as *be, become, seem, feel, grow*) that connects a predicate with a subject **:** copulative verb

linkwork \'=ˌ=\ *n* **1 :** something (as a chain or a fabric of metal mesh) consisting of interlocking links **2 :** LINKAGE 3a

link–worming \'=ˌ=\ *n* **:** the protection of rope cables (as on a ship) with windings of chain

linky \'liŋkē\ *adj* -ER/-EST [¹*link* + *-y*] *Scot, of land or country* **:** resembling or made up of links

lin·lith·gow·shire \lin'lithgō,shi(ə)r\ *or* **lin·lith·gow** \(,)gō\ *adj, usu cap* [fr. *Linlithgowshire, Linlithgow*, county in Scotland] **:** WEST LOTHIAN

¹linn *also* **lin** \'lin\ *n* -S [ME *lyn*, alter. of *linde* — more at LIND] **:** LINDEN 1

²linn *also* **lin** \"\ *n* -S [ScGael *linne* pool; akin to W *llyn* lake and perh. to Gk *plein* to sail, float — more at FLOW] **1** *chiefly Scot* **:** a pool or collection of water; *esp* **:** one below a fall of water **2** *chiefly Scot* **:** WATERFALL, CATARACT **3** *chiefly Scot* **:** a steep ravine **:** PRECIPICE

lin·naea \lə'nēə\ *n* [NL, fr. Carolus *Linnaeus* (Latinized form of Carl von *Linné*) †1778 Swed. botanist] **1** *cap* **:** a monotypic genus of creeping evergreen subshrubs (family Caprifoliaceae) of the northern parts of both hemispheres with small exstipulate leaves and the flowers borne in pairs at the end of elongated peduncles and having the corolla campanulate — see TWINFLOWER **2** -S **:** a plant of the genus *Linnaea*

lin·nae·an *or* **lin·ne·an** \-ēən\ *adj, usu cap* [prob. fr. (assumed) NL *linnaeanus*, fr. *Linnaeus* + L *-anus* -an] **:** of, relating to, or following the method of the Swedish botanist Carl von Linné who established the system of binomial nomenclature

linnaean species *n, usu cap L* **:** a taxonomic species distinguished on morphological grounds; *specif* **:** one of the large species delimited on broad morphological grounds by Linnaeus or another of the early naturalists — compare MACROSPECIES

lin·nae·ite *or* **lin·ne·ite** \lə'nē,īt\ *n* -S [G *linneit*, fr. Carl von *Linné* + G *-it* -ite] **:** a mineral Co_3S_4 of pale steel-gray color and metallic luster that occurs in isometric crystals and also massive and that is essentially a cobalt sulfide

linned *past of* LIN

lin·ne·on \'linē,än\ *n* -S [NL, fr. Carl von *Linné* + Gk *-on* (neuter n. & adj. suffix)] **:** MACROSPECIES

lin·net \'linət, *usu* -əd·+V\ *n* -S [MF *linette*, fr. *lin* flax (fr. L *linum*) + *-ette;* fr. the fact that it likes to feed on flaxseed — more at LINEN] **1 :** a common small Old World finch (*Carduelis cannabina* or *Acanthis cannabina*) having plumage that varies greatly according to age, sex, and season and is sometimes pied or nearly white **2 :** any of various finches (as of the genera *Spinus* and *Chloris*) that are closely related to the common linnet — usu. used in combination ⟨green ~⟩ ⟨pine ~⟩ **3** *chiefly West* **:** HOUSE FINCH

linnet hole *n* [*linnet* modif. (influenced by *linnet*) of F *lunette* small opening — more at LUNETTE] **:** one of the small holes connecting a glass-melting furnace with its arch

lin·ney *or* **lin·ny** \'linē\ *var of* LINHAY

linning *pres part of* LIN

li·no \'lī(,)nō\ *n* -S **1** [by shortening] *chiefly Brit* **:** LINOLEUM **2** [by shortening fr. *Linotype*] *chiefly Brit* **:** a machine for setting type

li·no·cut \'līnə,kət\ *n* [*lino* + *cut*] **:** a printing surface made by cutting a design on a mounted piece of linoleum; *also* **:** a print made from it — compare BLOCK PRINT

li·nog·na·thus \lə'nägnəthəs\ *n, cap* [NL, fr. *lino-* (fr. Gk, fr. *linon* thread, cord, flax) + *-gnathus* — more at LINEN] **:** a cosmopolitan genus of sucking lice including parasites of several domestic mammals

li·no·le·ate \lə'nōlē,āt\ *n* -S [ISV *linoleic* (in *linoleic acid*) + *-ate*] **:** a salt or ester of linoleic acid

lin·o·le·ic acid \¦linə¦lēik-, lə'nōlēik-\ *n* [*linoleic* ISV *lin-* (fr. Gk. fr. *linon* flax) + *oleic* (in *oleic acid*)] **:** a liquid unsaturated fatty acid $C_{17}H_{31}COOH$ that occurs in the form of glycerides in linseed oil, soybean oil, cottonseed oil, and other drying and semidrying oils, that is used chiefly in making salts for use as driers in paints and varnishes, and that is considered one of the fatty acids essential in animal nutrition; *cis*-9, *cis*-12-octadecadienoic acid

li·no·le·in \lə'nōlēən\ *n* -S [ISV *linoleic* + *-in*] **:** a glycerol ester of linoleic acid; *esp* **:** glycerol tri-linoleate

lin·o·le·nate \,linə'lē,nāt, -le-,-\ *n* -S [*linolenic* (in *linolenic acid*) + *-ate*] **:** a salt or ester of linolenic acid

lin·o·le·nic acid \¦linə¦lenik-, -lenik-\ *n* [*linolenic* ISV *linoleic* + connective *-n-* + *-ic*] **:** a liquid unsaturated fatty acid $C_{17}H_{29}COOH$ that occurs in the form of glycerides along with glycerides of linoleic acid esp. in linseed oil, perilla oil, and other drying oils and that is considered one of the fatty acids essential in animal nutrition; 9,12,15-octadeca-trien-oic acid

lin·o·le·nin \,=ˌ=ˈlēnən, -lenən\ *n* -S [*linolenic* + *-in*] **:** a glycerol ester of linolenic acid; *esp* **:** glycerol tri-linolenate

li·no·le·um \lə'nōlēəm *sometimes* -lyəm\ *n* -S *often attrib* [L *linum* flax + *oleum* oil — more at OIL] **1 :** a floor covering made by laying on a burlap or canvas backing a mixture of solidified linseed oil with gums, cork dust or wood flour or both, and usu. pigments **2 :** a material similar to linoleum in use and qualities but made with substitutes for the linseed oil, the filler, or both

linoleum–block printing *n* **:** relief printing from a carved linoleum block — compare BLOCK PRINT

linoleum brown *n* **:** BEESWAX 3

linoleum knife *n* **:** a knife with a short stiff blade ending in a sharp curved point that is used esp. for cutting and trimming linoleum

linoleum knife

li·no·lic acid \lə'nōlik-\ *n* [by alter.] **:** LINOLEIC ACID

lin·on \'linən, lē'nōⁿ\ *n* -S [F, fr. *lin* flax, linen] **:** a fine lawn of linen or cotton

li·nop·ter·is \lə'näptərəs\ *n, cap* [NL, fr. *lino-* (fr. Gk, fr. *linon* net, cord, flax) + *-pteris*] **:** a genus of fossil ferns abundant in the coal measures and distinguished by their reticulate venation

li·no·type \'līnə,tīp\ *vi* [*Linotype*] **:** to operate a Linotype machine ~ *vt* **:** to set by means of a Linotype machine

Li·no·type \"\ *trademark* **1** — used for a keyboard-operated typesetting machine that uses circulating matrices and produces each line of type in the form of a solid metal slug **2 :** matter produced by a Linotype machine or printing done from such matter

li·no·typ·er \-pə(r)\ *or* **li·no·typ·ist** \-pəst\ *n* **:** one that operates the keyboard of a Linotype machine

li·nox·yn \lə'näksən\ *n* -S [ISV *lin-* (fr. L *linum* flax) + *oxy-* + *-n* (fr. *-in*) — more at LINEN] **:** an elastic solid that is formed when linseed oil is oxidized and is used chiefly in cements, adhesives, and linoleum

lins *pres 3d sing of* LIN, *pl of* LIN

¹lin·sang \'lin,saŋ\ [NL, fr. Malay, linsang] *syn of* PRIONODON

²linsang \"\ *n* -S [Malay] **1 :** any of various Asiatic viverrid mammals of *Prionodon* and related genera that resemble long-tailed cats and differ from the related civets and genets in the absence of a second upper molar **2 :** an African viverrid mammal (*Poiana poensis*) related to the Asiatic linsangs

lin·seed \'lin,sēd\ *n* [ME, fr. OE *linsǣd*, fr. *lin* flax + *sǣd* seed — more at LINEN, SEED] **1 :** FLAXSEED **2 :** the common agricultural flax plant

linseed cake *n* **:** the residue that remains when oil is expressed or extracted from flaxseed and that is used chiefly as a cattle feed

linseed meal *n* **:** ground linseed or linseed cake

linseed oil *n* **:** a yellowish drying oil that is expressed or extracted from flaxseed, contains large proportions of glycerides of linolenic, linoleic, and oleic acids, and is used chiefly in paint and varnish, in printing ink, in linoleum — compare BLOWN OIL 1, BOILED OIL

linseed tea *n* **:** a demulcent tea made by infusing flaxseed

lin·sey \'linzē, -zi\ *n* -S [ME *lynesey, lynsy*, prob. fr. *Lynsey* Lindsey, village in Suffolk, England, where it was made] **:** LINSEY-WOOLSEY

lin·sey–wool·sey \'linzē'wůlzē, -zi . . . zi\ *n* -S *often attrib* [ME *lynsy wolsye*, prob. fr. *lynesey, lynsy* linsey + *wolsye* (fr. *wolle* wool + *-sey, -sy, -sye* — as in *lynesey, lynsy*) — more at WOOL] **1 a :** a formerly used textile of wool and linen **b :** a coarse sturdy fabric with cotton warp and woolen filling **2 :** something incongruously mingled **:** disordered or nonsensical speech or action ⟨what *linsey-woolsey* hast thou to speak to us again —Shak.⟩

lin·stock \'linz,täk, -n,st-\ *n* [earlier *lyntstock*, by folk etymology (influence of ¹*lint*) fr. D *lontstok*, fr. *lont* match, rag + *stok* stick; akin to OHG *stoc* stick — more at LUNT, STOCK] **:** a pointed forked staff shod with iron at the foot formerly used to hold a lighted match for firing cannon

¹lint \'lint\ *n* -S [ME, perh. fr. L *linteum* linen cloth, fr. neut. of *linteus* made of linen, irreg. fr. *linum* flax, linen — more at LINEN] **1** *chiefly Scot* **:** FLAX 1 **2 a :** a soft fleecy material (as for poultices and dressings for wounds) made from linen usu. by scraping **b :** fuzz consisting usu. of fine ravelings and short fibers of yarn and fabric; *esp* **:** an accumulation of dust and fuzz on a floor **c :** fluff or fuzz of any material (as paper) **3** *dial* **:** the actual netting of a fishnet **4 a :** a fibrous coat of thickened convoluted hairs borne by the seeds of cotton plants and constituting the staple of cotton fiber after ginning — compare LINTER 1 **b** *or* **lint cotton :** virgin cotton

²lint \"\ *vi* -ED/-ING/-S **1 :** to leave lint adhering to a surface after contact **:** give off or deposit lint ⟨found that his napkin had ~*ed*⟩ **2 :** PICK *vi* 5

lint bells *n pl but sing or pl in constr* **:** the common agricultural flax plant

lin·tel \'lint³l\ *n* -S [ME, fr. MF, modif. of LL *limitaris* threshold (influenced in meaning by L *limin-, limen* threshold), fr. L *limitaris*, adj., constituting a boundary, fr. L *limit-, limes* boundary, limit + *-aris* -ar — more at LIMB] **:** a horizontal architectural member spanning and usu. carrying the load above an opening

lin·teled *or* **lin·telled** \-³ld\ *adj* **:** having a lintel

lintel

¹lin·ter \'lintə(r)\ *n* -S [alter. of *lean-to*] **1** *chiefly NewEng* **:** a cow stable built either in or as an extension of a barn **2** *North* **:** LEAN-TO

²lint·er \"\ *n* -S [¹*lint* + *-er*] **1 a :** a machine for removing residual fuzz from cottonseed that has been ginned **b :** a worker who operates such a machine **2 linters** *pl* **:** the fuzz of short fibers that adheres to cottonseed after ginning and is recovered and used for many purposes (as batting, padding, or a source of cellulose) that do not require long fibers

lint·er·man \-(r)mən\ *n, pl* **lintermen :** the operator of a linter

linthead \'=ˌ=\ *n* **1** *chiefly South* **:** a cotton-mill worker **2** *chiefly South* **:** a Southern lower class white person — usu. used disparagingly

lin·tie \'lintī\ *n* -S [*lint-* (in *lintwhite*) + *-ie*] *chiefly Scot* **:** LINNET

lint·less \'lintləs\ *adj* **:** free from lint ⟨immaculately ~ corners⟩ ⟨a ~ wild cotton⟩

lin·tol \'lint³l\ *Brit var of* LINTEL

lin·ton·ite \'lint³n,īt, -tən,-\ *n* -S [Laura A. *Linton* †1915 Am. scientist + E *-ite*] **:** a green mineral that is a variety of thomsonite

lintseed \'=ˌ=\ *n* **:** FLAXSEED; *esp* **:** an inferior flaxseed obtained from flax plants grown for fiber

lint·white \'lint,(h)wīt\ *n* [ME *lynkwhyt*, by folk etymology (influence of *whyt, whit* white) fr. OE *linetwige*, prob. fr. *line-* (fr. *līn* flax) + *-twige* (perh. akin to OHG *zwīgōn* to pluck, OE *twig* branch, twig); prob. fr. the fact that it likes to feed on flaxseed — more at LINEN, TWIG] **:** LINNET 1

lint-white \'ˌ=ˌ=\ *adj* [¹*lint* + *white*] **1 :** of the color of dressed flax **2 :** of the color flax
linty \'lintē\ *adj* -ER/-EST [¹*lint* + *-y*] **:** like lint **:** full of or covered with lint
li·num \'līnəm\ *n* [NL, fr. L, flax — more at LINEN] **1** *cap* **:** the type genus of Linaceae comprising herbaceous annual or perennial plants that have small sessile leaves, terminal or axillary racemes of flowers with fugacious petals, and capsular fruits — see FLAX 1 **2** -S **:** any plant of the genus *Linum; esp* **:** any plant of this genus cultivated for ornament or growing wild as distinguished from the common agricultural flax
li·nus \'līnəs\ *n* -ES [Gk *linos*] **:** a dirge or lamentation of ancient Greece
liny *also* **liney** \'līnē\ *adj* **linier; liniest** [³*line* + *-y*] **:** like a line or streak **:** marked with or full of lines
lin·y·phi·idae \ˌlinə'fīəˌdē\ *n pl, cap* [NL, fr. *Linyphia*, type genus (fr. Gk *linyphos* linen weaver — fr. *linon* linen, cord, flax + *hyphos* web — + NL *-ia*) + *-idae* — more at LINEN, WEAVE] **:** a large family of small spiders that weave horizontal sheet webs
linz \'lin(t)s, -nz\ *adj, usu cap* [fr. *Linz*, city in northwest Austria] **:** of or from the city of Linz, Austria **:** of the kind or style prevalent in Linz
linz·er torte \-(t)sə(r)-, -zə(r)-\ *n, usu cap L* [G, lit., Linz torte] **:** a baked torte made of a rich pastry dough composed of chopped almonds, butter, flour, cocoa, sugar, eggs, and spices, filled with jam or preserves, and topped with a lattice — compare SACHER TORTE
lio- — see LEIO-
li·on \'līən\ *n* -S *often attrib* [ME *leon, lion*, fr. OF, fr. L *leon-, leo*, fr. Gk *leōn*, prob. of non-IE origin] **1 a :** a large carnivorous chiefly nocturnal mammal (*Felis leo*) of the cat family that is now found mostly in open or rocky areas of Africa but also in southern Asia and that has a tawny body with a tufted tail and a shaggy blackish or dark brown mane in the male **b :** any of several other animals of the genus *Felis; esp* **:** COUGAR **2 :** a person felt to resemble a lion esp. in courage, ferocity, dignity, or dominance ⟨he that trusts to you, where he should find you ~s, finds you hares —Shak.⟩ ⟨they tame the ~s in the Army, not appease them —James Jones⟩ ⟨outsmarted the other old financial ~s —Meridel Le Sueur⟩ **3 a** *usu cap* **:** a lion that is a symbol of a country, people, or individual ⟨British *Lion*⟩ ⟨*Lion* of Judah⟩ ⟨*Lion* of St. Mark⟩ **b :** a heraldic representation of a lion rampant **4 :** any of several old coins bearing the figure of a lion (as a gold coin of Philip VI of France) — see SAINT ANDREW **5 a lions** *pl, Brit* (1) **:** the principal sights of a city or country (2) *obs* **:** the world or experience of the world **b :** a person who is a center of attention or an object of admiration, interest, or curiosity ⟨they were fountains of interesting gossip, and the ~s of the meal —Arnold Bennett⟩ ⟨one must certainly have the ~ of the moment at one's parties —Victoria Sackville-West⟩ **6 :** a light to moderate yellowish brown **7** *usu cap* [*Lions* (*club*)] **:** a member of one of the major service clubs **8 :** a cub scout of the fourth rank comprising boys at least 10 years old — **lion in the way** *also* **lion in the path :** a dangerous obstacle; *esp* **:** a danger invented or exaggerated as an excuse for inaction ⟨the indecisive man alw ıys sees a *lion in the way*⟩ — **lion's mouth :** a place or situation of great danger ⟨test pilots fly constantly into the *lion's mouth*⟩ — **lion's share :** the largest part ⟨the central government collects and spends the *lion's share* of the citizens' tax dollar —Cabell Phillips⟩ ⟨slyly sneaked the *lion's share* of buttered toast at tea —Jean Stafford⟩

lion

li·on·cel \'līənˌsel\ *n* -S [F, fr. MF, dim. of *lion*] **:** a heraldic representation of a small lion rampant usu. as one of a group of at least three
lion dollar *n* [trans. of D *leeuwendaalder;* fr. the lion rampant on the obverse] **:** DOG DOLLAR
li·on·esque \ˌlīə¦nesk\ *adj* **:** having the characteristics of a lion
li·on·ess \'līənəs\ *n* -ES [ME *liones, leonesse*, fr. OF *lionesse, leonesse*, fr. *lion, leon* lion + *-esse* -ess — more at LION] **:** a female lion ⟨hardly a literary lion or ~ whom she did not admire —*Times Lit. Supp.*⟩
li·on·et \'līənət, ˌ==¦net\ *n* -S [MF, dim. of *lion*] **:** a young or small lion
lion-fish \'=ˌ=ˌ=\ *n* **1 :** any of several scorpion fishes (genus *Pterois*) of the tropical Pacific brilliantly striped and barred with elongated fins and venomous dorsal spines **2 :** STONEFISH
lionheart \'=ˌ=ˌ=\ *n* **:** a lionhearted person
lionhearted \¦=ˌ=¦==\ *adj* **:** having a courageous heart **:** BRAVE ⟨band of ~ fighters —Stuart Cloete⟩ — **lionheartedly** *adv* — **li·on·heart·ed·ness** *n* -ES
lion-hunter \'=ˌ=ˌ==\ *n* **1 :** one that hunts lions esp. for sport **2 :** a person who seeks the company of celebrities ⟨included in her makeup some of the impulses of the *lion-hunter* and of the social climber —J.W.Krutch⟩
li·on·ism \'līəˌnizəm\ *n* -S **:** the practice of lionizing or the state of being lionized
li·on·iza·tion \ˌlīənə'zāshən, -ˌnī'-\ *n* -S **:** the act of lionizing
li·on·ize \'==ˌnīz\ *vb* -ED/-ING/-S *see -ize in Explan Notes, vt* **1 :** to treat or regard as a celebrity or object of interest ⟨the opera-mad city *lionized* the new tenor⟩ **2** *Brit* **a :** to show the sights of a place to **b :** to visit or view the sights of ~ *vi* **1** *Brit* **:** to visit or view the sights **2 :** to seek the company of celebrities ⟨this tendency of human nature to ~ —A.J.Todd⟩ — **li·on·iz·er** \-zə(r)\ *n* -S
lionlike \'=ˌ=ˌ=\ *adj* **:** resembling a lion
lion lizard *n* [so called fr. its crest that resembles a lion's mane] **:** BASILISK 3
li·on·ly *adj, archaic* **:** LIONLIKE
lion-mask \'=ˌ=ˌ=\ *n* **:** a decorative motif consisting of a conventionalized lion's face found esp. in 18th century English furniture
lion monkey *or* **lion marmoset** *n* **:** any of several So. American marmosets (genus *Leontocebus*) having tufted tails and well-marked neck ruffs of long hair **:** TAMARIN — called also *leoncito*
lion of england *usu cap E* **:** a heraldic representation of a lion passant gardant or (as on the shield of England)
lion-paw foot \'=ˌ=ˌ=-\ *n* **:** a foot in the form of a lion's paw found esp. in 18th century English furniture — see LION-MASK illustration

lion-mask with lion-paw foot

lion's beard *n* **:** a pasqueflower (*Pulsatilla ludoviciana*) of No. America
lion's-ear \'==ˌ=\ *n, pl* **lion's-ears 1 :** a mint of the genus *Leonotis; esp* **:** a common tropical mint (*L. nepetaefolia*) **2 :** any of various woolly-leaved So. American plants constituting two genera (*Culcitium* and *Espeletia*) of the family Compositae **3 :** MOTHERWORT 1
lion's face *n, pl* **lion's faces** *or* **lions' faces :** a heraldic representation of a lion's head affronté without any of the neck showing but usu. with part of the mane visible — compare LEOPARD'S FACE
lion's foot *n* **1 :** a plant having leaves so shaped or lobed as to suggest a lion's foot; *specif* **:** a plant of the genus *Prenanthes* (esp. *P. serpentaria*) — see GALL OF THE EARTH 1 **2 :** EDELWEISS 1
lion's-heart \'==ˌ=\ *n, pl* **lion's-hearts :** DRAGONHEAD
li·on·ship \'līənˌship\ *n* **:** the quality or state of being a social lion
lion's-mouth \'==ˌ=\ *n, pl* **lion's-mouths 1 :** SNAPDRAGON **2 :** FOXGLOVE 1 **3 :** TOADFLAX 1
lion's-snap \'==ˌ=\ *n, pl* **lion's-snaps :** SNAPDRAGON
lion's-tail \'==ˌ=\ *n, pl* **lion's-tails 1 :** LION'S-EAR 1 **2 :** MOTHERWORT 1
lion's-tooth \'==ˌ=\ *or* **lion's-teeth** *n, pl* **lion's-tooths** *or* **lion's-teeth 1 :** DANDELION **2 :** FALL DANDELION
lion-tailed \'=ˌ=¦=\ *adj* **:** having a tufted tail
lion-tailed macaque *or* **lion-tailed monkey** *n* **:** a black Indian macaque (*Macaca silenus*) that has a pale gray ruff of long hairs around the face and a tuft at the tip of the tail
lion-tawny \'=ˌ=¦==\ *adj* **:** of the color lion
li·o·pel·mid \ˌlīə'pelməd, -ˌmid\ *adj* [NL *Liopelmidae*] **:** of or relating to the Liopelmidae
li·o·pel·mi·dae \-ˌməˌdē\ *n pl, cap* [NL, fr. *Liopelma*, type genus (fr. *leio-* + Gk *pelma* sole of the foot) + *-idae* — more at FELL] **:** a family of primitive frogs with four toes on the forefeet, five on the hind feet, and no webs that includes a genus (*Liopelma*) with a single New Zealand species (*L. hamiltoni*) — see ASCAPHUS
liou·ville's theorem \(ˈ)lyü¦vēlz-\ *n, usu cap L* [after Joseph *Liouville* †1882 Fr. mathematician] **:** a theorem in fluid dynamics: the density of any selected part of a stream of fluid that does no work and that has no work done on it remains constant as that part moves along its stream line
¹lip \'lip\ *n* -S [ME *lippe, lip*, fr. OE *lippa;* akin to OFris *lippa* lip, OHG *leffur* & *lefs*, OSw *læpi*, Norw *lepe*, and prob. to L *labium, labrum* lip, and to L *labi* to slide, glide — more at SLEEP] **1 a :** either of the two fleshy folds which surround the orifice of the mouth in man and many other vertebrates and in man are organs of speech essential to certain articulations; *also* **:** the pink or reddish margin of a human lip composed of nonglandular mucous membrane **b :** this part of the mouth considered as an organ of speech — used chiefly in pl. ⟨taken down from the ~s of his mother or teacher —H.E.Scudder⟩ **2** *slang* **:** saucy or impudent speech ⟨I'll have none of your ~⟩ **3 :** EMBOUCHURE 2 **4 :** an edge of a wound **5 :** either of a pair of fleshy folds surrounding an orifice **6 :** a liplike anatomical part or structure: as **a :** LABIUM **b :** LABELLUM 1 **7 a :** the edge or margin of a hollow vessel or cavity (as a cup, bell, or crater) esp. if it shows a slight flare ⟨slept that night on the ~ of a dead volcano —Negley Farson⟩ — see BELL illustration **b :** an edge, rim, or margin esp. when projecting or overlapping ⟨that narrow ~ of rock on the mountain's face —N.C. McDonald⟩ ⟨on the ~ of the Plymouth beach —Sean O'Dwyer⟩ ⟨the car roared up across the ~ of the hill —Thomas Wolfe⟩ **c** as (1) **:** the edge in a flue pipe (as in a pipe organ) across which a current of air is forced causing a wave motion in the air within the pipe that produces the tone (2) *Brit* **:** the lower part of the roof near a face in a coal mine (3) **:** the sharp cutting edge on the end of an auger, drill, or similar tool (4) **:** a projection of the top of a railhead at a joint caused by flow of metal under the action of traffic (5) **:** a low parapet erected on the downstream edge of a millrace or dam apron to minimize scouring of the river bottom **8 :** a short open spout or drip (as on a pitcher) **9 :** the lapping of water at the margin
²lip \"\ *adj* **1 a** *of utterance* **:** coming from the lips only without thoughtfulness or without sincerity of intent ⟨~ comfort⟩ ⟨~ devotion⟩ ⟨~ praise⟩ — compare LIP-LABOR, LIP SERVICE, LIP-WORSHIP **b** *of a person* **:** speaking or otherwise expressing oneself without thought as to the meaning of the words used or without sincerity ⟨~ comforter⟩ — compare LIP SERVER, LIP-WORSHIPER **2 :** produced with the participation of the lips or one of the lips **:** LABIAL ⟨~ consonants⟩
³lip \"\ *vb* **lipped; lipped; lipping; lips** *vt* **1 a :** to touch with the lips **:** put the lips to; *specif* **:** KISS ⟨a hand that kings have *lipped* and trembled kissing —Shak.⟩ **b :** to take into the mouth by action of the lips (as by nipping or sucking) — sometimes used with *up* **2 a :** to utter esp. in a murmuring voice **b** *slang* **:** SING **3 :** to fill in the chinks of ⟨~ a wall⟩ **4 :** to set a piece of wood in (an archer's bow) where a flaw has been cut out **5 :** to notch the edge of ⟨~ a sword⟩ **6 :** to lap against **:** LAVE ⟨the water *lipped* the shingle —R.P. Warren⟩ **7 :** to rise above (as the horizon or the top of a hill or cliff) ⟨*lipping* the rim of a long hill street —Thomas Wolfe⟩ **8 :** to form a lip on (as machine work) **9 :** to strike a golf ball so that it hits the edge of (the cup) but fails to drop in **10 :** to put (snuff) behind the lip ~ *vi* **1 a :** to flow over the lip of a container or vessel — used with *over* or *in* **b :** to have liquid flowing over the brim or edge — used with *over* **2 :** to form or take the form of a lip **3 :** to lap with a splashing noise **:** PLASH **4 :** to use the lips; *specif* **:** to adjust one's lips to the mouthpiece of a wind instrument — sometimes used with *up* **5 :** to apply the lips (as in kissing) — used with *at*
lip- *or* **lipo-** *comb form* [NL, fr. Gk, fr. *lipos* — more at LEAVE] **1 :** fat **:** fatty tissue **:** fatty **:** ADIP- ⟨*lip*ectomy⟩ ⟨*lipo*cardiac⟩ ⟨*lipo*cele⟩ **2 :** lipide
LIP *abbr* life insurance policy
li·pa-li·pa \'lēpə¦lēpə\ *n* -S [native name in the Sulu islands] **:** a dugout with planked sides used by natives of the Sulu islands
li·pan \lē'pän, li-\ *n, pl* **lipan** *or* **lipans** *usu cap* **1 a :** an Apache people of eastern New Mexico and western Texas **b :** a member of such people **2 :** the Athapaskan language of the Lipan people
lipar- *or* **liparo-** *comb form* [Gk, fr. *liparos*, fr. *lipos* fat — more at LEAVE] **:** fatty **:** fat ⟨*lipar*ocele⟩ ⟨*lipar*oid⟩ ⟨*lipar*ous⟩
li·par·i·an \lə'perēən, -pa(a)r-, -pär-\ *adj, usu cap* [*Lipari* islands, group of islands in the Tyrrhenian sea north of the coast of Sicily + E *-an*] **:** of, relating to, or characteristic of the Lipari islands
¹lip·a·rid \'lipərəd, -ˌrid\ *adj* [NL ²*Liparidae*] **:** of or relating to the Liparididae
²liparid \"\ *n* -S [NL ²*Liparidae*] **:** a fish of the family Liparididae
¹li·par·i·dae \lə'parəˌdē\ [NL, fr. *Liparis* genus of moths (fr. Gk *liparos* fatty, shiny, bright) + *-idae* — more at LIPAR-] *syn of* LYMANTRIIDAE
²liparidae \"\ [NL, fr. *Liparis*, genus of scorpaenoid fishes (fr. Gk *liparos*) + *-idae*] *syn of* LIPARIDIDAE
lip·a·rid·i·dae \ˌlipə'ridəˌdē\ *n pl* [NL, fr. *Liparid-, Liparis*, type genus + *-idae*] **:** a family of scorpaenoid fishes containing the sea snails
lip·a·ris \'lipərəs\ *n, cap* [NL, fr. Gk *liparos* fatty, shiny, bright — more at LIPAR-] **:** a genus of terrestrial orchids having two broad shining leaves and terminal racemes of irregular flowers — see TWAYBLADE
lip·a·rite \-ˌrīt\ *n* -S [G *liparit*, fr. *Lipari* islands + G *-it* -ite] **:** RHYOLITE
li·pase \'līˌpās, 'li-, -āz\ *n* -S [ISV *lip-* + *-ase*] **:** any of a class of enzymes that accelerate the hydrolysis or synthesis of fats or the breakdown of lipoproteins and that occur in both animals (as in pancreatic juice) and plants (as in the castor bean) — compare ESTERASE
lipbrush \'=ˌ=\ *n* **:** a small brush for applying lipstick
lip-deep \'=¦=\ *adj* **1 :** plunged in to or as if to the lips **2 :** no deeper than the lips **:** INSINCERE **:** SHALLOW
li·pe·mia *also* **li·pae·mia** \lə'pēmēə\ *n* -S [NL, fr. *lip-* + *-emia, -aemia*] **:** the presence of an excess of fats or lipides in the blood; *specif* **:** HYPERCHOLESTEROLEMIA — **li·pe·mic** *also* **li·pae·mic** \-mik\ *adj*
li·peu·rus \lə'pyürəs\ *n, cap* [NL, irreg. fr. *lip-* + *-urus*] **:** an extensive genus of bird lice that are parasites of various birds
lip fern *n* [so called fr. the liplike indusium] **:** a fern of the genus *Cheilanthes*
liph·i·sti·idae \ˌlifə'stīəˌdē\ *n pl, cap* [NL, fr. *Liphistius*, type genus + *-idae*] **:** a family of primitive spiders belonging to the suborder Liphistiomorphae
¹li·phis·ti·o·morph \lə'fistēəˌmȯrf\ *adj* [NL *Liphistiomorphae*] **:** of or relating to the Liphistiomorphae
²liphistiomorph \"\ *n* **:** a spider of the suborder Liphistiomorphae
li·phis·ti·o·mor·phae \=ˌ===ˈmȯrˌfē\ *n pl, cap* [NL, fr. *Liphistius*, genus of spiders + *-o-* + *-morphae*] **:** a suborder comprising the primitive spiders that retain abdominal segmentation
lip·id \'lipəd\ *also* **lip·ide** \'liˌpīd, -ˌpəd\ *n* -S [ISV *lip-* + *-id, -ide;* orig. formed as F *lipide*] **:** any of a group of substances that in general are soluble in ether, chloroform, or other solvent for fats but are only sparingly soluble in water, that with proteins and carbohydrates constitute the principal structural components of living cells, and that are considered to include fats, waxes, phosphatides, cerebrosides, and related and derived compounds and sometimes steroids and carotenoids — called also *lipin, lipoid*
lip·i·do·plast \'lipədəˌplast\ *also* **lip·i·do·plas·tid** \ˌ===+\ *n* -S [ISV *lipide* + *-o-* + *-plast* or *plastid*] **:** ELAIOPLAST
lip·i·do·sis \ˌlipə'dōsəs\ *n, pl* **lipido·ses** \-ˌsēz\ [NL, fr. ISV *lipid* + NL *-osis*] **:** LIPOIDOSIS
lip·i·do·some \'lipədəˌsōm\ *n* -S [ISV *lipide* + *-o-* + *-some*] **:** a fatty inclusion body of cytoplasm
lipid pneumonia *or* **lipoid pneumonia** *n* **:** pneumonia caused by the aspiration or absorption into the lungs of oily substances (as nose drops or mineral oil) and usu. found to be chronic
lip·in \'lipən\ *n* -S [*lip-* + *-in*] **:** LIPID; *esp* **:** a complex lipid (as a phosphatide or a cerebroside)
lipizzan *often cap, var of* LIPPIZAN
lipizzaner *usu cap, var of* LIPPIZANER
lip-labor \'=ˌ==\ *n, archaic* **:** action with the lips (as in speaking) — used esp. to designate the saying of prayers by rote or repetitively with little or no thought about their meaning
lip·less \'lipləs\ *adj* **:** having no lips
liplike \'=ˌ=\ *adj* **:** resembling a lip esp. in forming a fleshy fold or margin
lip microphone *n* **:** a microphone worn on the speaker's lip
¹lipo- — see LIP-
²lipo- *comb form* [F, fr. LL, fr. Gk, fr. *leipein* to leave, be lacking — more at LOAN] **1 :** lacking **:** without ⟨*lipo*graphy⟩ **2 :** leaving **:** abandoning ⟨*lipo*xenous⟩
li·po·blast \'lipəˌblast, 'lipə-\ *n* [ISV *lip-* + *-blast*] **:** a connective-tissue cell destined to become a fat cell
li·po·ca·ic \ˌ==¦kāik\ *n* -S [*lip-* + Gk *kaiein* to burn + E *-ic* — more at CAUSTIC] **:** a lipotropic preparation from the pancreas
li·po·chon·dri·on \ˌ==¦kändrēən\ *n, pl* **lipochon·dria** \-drēə\ [NL, fr. *lip-* + Gk *chondrion* granule, dim. of *chondros* grain — more at GRIND] **:** GOLGI BODY
li·po·chrome \'==ˌkrōm\ *n* [ISV *lip-* + *-chrome*] **:** any of the naturally occurring pigments soluble in fats or in solvents for fats; *esp* **:** CAROTENOID
li·po·dystrophy \ˌ==+\ *n* [ISV *lip-* + *dystrophy*] **:** a disorder of fat metabolism esp. involving loss of fat from or deposition of fat in tissue — compare LIPOIDOSIS
li·po·fus·cin \ˌ=='fəsᵊn, -'fyüsᵊn\ *n* -S [ISV *lip-* + *fuscin*, a brown animal pigment, fr. L *fuscus* dark brown, blackish + ISV *-in* — more at DUSK] **:** any of several brown pigments that are similar to the melanins and are found in various tissues (as of the heart) in a state of exhaustion or of senility
¹li·po·genesis \ˌ==+\ *n* [NL, fr. *lip-* + L *genesis*] **:** formation of fat in the living body esp. when excessive or abnormal
²lipogenesis \"\ *n* [NL, fr. ²*lipo-* + L *genesis*] **:** acceleration of development by the omission of certain ancestral stages — compare BRADYGENESIS, TACHYGENESIS
li·pog·e·nous \lə'päjənəs, lī'-\ *also* **li·po·gen·ic** \¦lipə¦jenik, ¦lī-\ *adj* [*lip-* + *-genous, -genic*] **:** producing or tending to produce fat ⟨the ~ effect of estrogens⟩
lip·o·gram \'lipəˌgram, 'lī-\ *n* [MGk *lipogrammatos*, adj., lacking a letter, fr. Gk *lipo-* ²lipo- + *-grammatos* (fr. *grammat-, gramma* letter) — more at GRAM] **:** a writing composed of words not having a certain letter (as the *Odyssey* of Tryphiodorus which had no alpha in the first book, no beta in the second, and so on)
lip·o·gram·mat·ic \¦==grə'mad·ik\ *adj* [MGk *lipogrammatos* + E *-ic*] **:** being a lipogram **:** having the character of a lipogram
lip·o·gram·ma·tism \ˌ=='gramə,tizəm\ *n* -S [MGk *lipogrammatos* + E *-ism*] **:** the practice of writing lipograms
lip·o·gram·ma·tist \-məd·əst\ *n* -S [MGk *lipogrammatos* + E *-ist*] **:** a writer of lipograms
li·pog·ra·phy \lə'pägrəfē, lī-\ *n* -ES [²*lipo-* + *-graphy*] **:** inadvertent omission (as of a letter or syllable) in writing
li·po·ic acid \lə'pōik-\ *n* [*lip-* + *-ic*] **:** any of several microbial growth factors occurring esp. in yeast and liver; *specif* **:** the crystalline alpha variety $C_7H_{13}S_2COOH$ that together with cocarboxylase and other factors is essential for the oxidation of alpha-keto acids (as pyruvic acid to acetic acid) during metabolic changes in the body; 6,8-epi-dithio-octanoic acid — compare THIOCTIC ACID
¹li·poid \'līˌpȯid, 'li- *or* **li·poi·dal** \lə'pȯidᵊl, lī-\ *adj* [ISV *lip-* + *-oid* (adj. suffix) or *-oidal*] **:** FATLIKE
²lipoid \"\ *n* -S [ISV *lip-* + *-oid* (n. suffix)] **:** a fatlike substance: as **a :** a mixture extracted from biological tissue by ether **b :** LIPID **c :** LIPIN
li·poid·ic \lə'pȯidik, lī-\ *adj* [ISV ²*lipoid* + *-ic*] **:** LIPOID
li·poi·do·sis \ˌlīˌpȯi'dōsəs, ˌli-\ *n, pl* **lipoido·ses** \-ˌsēz\ [NL, fr. ISV ²*lipoid* + NL *-osis*] **:** a disorder of fat metabolism esp. involving the deposition of fat in an organ (as the liver or spleen) — compare LIPODYSTROPHY
li·pol·y·sis \lī'päləsəs, lə-\ *n, pl* **lipoly·ses** \-ˌsēz\ [NL, fr. *lip-* + *-lysis*] **:** the hydrolysis of fat
li·po·lyt·ic \¦lipə¦lid·ik, ¦lī-\ *adj* [ISV *lip-* + *-lytic*] **:** of, relating to, causing, or resulting from lipolysis ⟨lipase is a ~ enzyme⟩
li·po·ma \lī'pōmə, lə-\ *n, pl* **lipo·mas** \-məz\ *or* **lipoma·ta** \-məd·ə\ [NL, fr. *lip-* + *-oma*] **:** a tumor consisting of fatty tissue — **li·pom·a·tous** \-'pämədəs, -pōm-\ *adj*
li·po·ma·to·sis \lī,pōmə'tōsəs, lə-\ *n, pl* **lipomato·ses** \-ˌsēz\ [NL, fr. *lipomat-, lipoma* + *-osis*] **:** any of several abnormal conditions marked by local or generalized deposits of fat or replacement of other tissue by fat; *specif* **:** the presence of multiple lipomas
li·po·mi·cron \līpə'mīˌkrän, ˌli-, -'mi,k-\ *n* [NL, fr. *lip-* + *chylomicron*] **:** a chylomicron esp. in the blood of an insect
li·po·nys·sus \ˌ=='nisəs\ [NL, fr. *lip-* + *-nyssus* (fr. Gk *nyssein, nyttein* to prick, sting) — more at NUMEN] *syn of* BDELLONYSSUS
li·po·phage \'==ˌfāj\ *n* [*lip-* + *-phage*] **:** a cell (as a phagocyte) that takes up fat — **li·po·pha·gia** \ˌ=='fājēə\ *n* -S — **li·po·phag·ic** \¦==¦fajik\ *adj*
li·po·phan·er·o·sis \ˌ==ˌfanə'rōsəs\ *n* [NL, fr. *lip-* + *phaner-* + *-osis*] **:** fatty degeneration of cells involving the unmasking of cellular lipoids
li·po·phil·ic \¦==¦filik\ *also* **li·po·phile** \'==ˌfīl\ *adj* [*lip-* + *-philic, -phile*] **:** relating to or having strong affinity for fats or other lipids **:** promoting the solubilization or absorption of lipids ⟨the ionic type of emulsifier is composed of an organic ~ group and a hydrophilic group —W.C.Griffin⟩ — compare HYDROPHILIC, HYDROPHOBIC, OLEOPHILIC
li·po·phore \'==ˌfō(ə)r\ *n* -S [*lipochrome* + *chromatophore*] **:** a pigment cell or chromatophore containing a lipochrome pigment
li·po·protein \ˌlipə, ˌlipə+\ *n* [*lip-* + *protein*] **:** any of a class of widely distributed conjugated proteins that contain a considerable percentage of lipid and that have the solubility and mobility properties of alpha globulins or beta globulins — compare PROTEOLIPID
li·po·sarcoma \ˌ==+\ *n* [NL, fr. *lip-* + *sarcoma*] **:** a sarcoma arising from immature fat cells of the bone marrow
li·po·sis \lī'pōsəs, lə-\ *n, pl* **lipo·ses** \-ˌsēz\ [NL, fr. *lip-* + *-osis*] **:** OBESITY
li·po·si·tol \lī'pōsəˌtȯl, lə-, -ˌtōl\ *n* -S [*lip-* + *inositol*] **:** any of several phosphatides occurring in plants (as soybeans) and in animals esp. in the brain and spinal cord and containing the meso form of inositol in combination
li·po·soluble \ˌlipə, ˌlipə+\ *adj* [ISV *lip-* + *soluble*] **:** soluble in fats or oils **:** FAT-SOLUBLE, OIL-SOLUBLE ⟨~ bismuth preparations⟩
li·po·some \'==ˌsōm\ *n* -S [ISV *lip-* + *-some*] **:** one of the fatty droplets in the cytoplasm esp. of an egg
li·po·thym·ia \ˌlipə'thimēə, ˌli-\ *or* **li·poth·y·my** \lə'päthəmē\ *n, pl* **lipothymias** *or* **lipothymies** [F & LL; F *lipothymie*, fr. LL *lipothymia*, fr. Gk, fr. *lipothymein* to faint (fr. *lipo-* ²lipo- + *thymos* spirit, mind, courage) + *-ia* -y — more at FUME] **:** FAINTNESS, FAINTING — **li·po·thym·i·al** \¦lipə¦thimēəl\ *adj* — **li·po·thym·ic** \-mik\ *adj*
li·po·trop·ic \ˌlipə¦träpik, ¦li-, -trōp-\ *also* **li·po·troph·ic** \-äfik, -ōf-\ *adj* [ISV *lip-* + *-tropic* or *-trophic*] **:** tending to prevent abnormal deposition of fats or deposition of abnormal fats or to accelerate their removal if present
li·pot·ro·pism \lə'pä·trəˌpizəm\ *n* [*lip-* + *-tropism*] **:** the state or tendency of being lipotropic
li·po·typh·la \ˌlīpə'tiflə, li-\ *n pl, cap* [NL, fr. *lip-* + *-typhla* (fr. Gk *typhlon* cecum) — more at TYPHL-] **:** a suborder of insectivores comprising the moles, hedgehogs, and true shrews and having the pubic symphysis short and the postorbital process undeveloped — compare MENOTYPHLA
li·pox·e·nous \lə'päksənəs, lī-\ *adj* [²*lipo-* + *-xenous*]

: abandoning the host — used of various parasitic fungi (as ergot) — **li·pox·e·ny** \-nē\ *n* -ES

li·pox·i·dase \-ksə,dās, -āz\ *n* -S [*lip-* + *oxidase*] : a crystallizable protein enzyme that catalyzes the oxidation primarily of unsaturated fatty acids or unsaturated fats by oxygen and secondarily of carotenoids to colorless substances and that occurs esp. in soybeans and cereals

1lipped \'lipt\ *adj* [ME, fr. *lippe, lip* lip + *-ed* — more at LIP] **1 a** : having a lip : having a raised edge resembling a lip **b** : having a lip (of such a kind) ⟨a virgin purest ~ —John Keats⟩ **2** : LABIATE

2lipped *past of* LIP

lip·pen \'lipən\ *vb* -ED/-ING/-S [ME *lipnien, lipnen*] *chiefly Scot, vi* : to have faith or trust : TRUST, RELY, CONFIDE — usu. used with *to* ⟨too merry a lass at times to ~ to entirely —R.L. Stevenson⟩ ~ *vt* : ENTRUST ⟨had done wrong in ~*ing* a boat to such a young crew —William Black⟩

1lip·per \'lipər\ *vi* -ED/-ING/-S [prob. of imit. origin] *Scot* **1** : RIPPLE **2** *of a boat* : to become sunk to the gunwale — used with *with*

2lip·per \-pə(r)\ *n* -S **1** : a slight roughness or ruffling of the sea **2** : a light spray from small waves

3lipper \"\ *n* -S [*2lip* + *-er*] **1** : an implement for making a lip on a glass vessel **2** : one that shapes the lip of a glass or earthen vessel

4lipper \"\ *n* -S [origin unknown] : a thin piece of blubber used to wipe the decks of a whaler

5lipper \"\ *vt* -ED/-ING/-S : to wipe with a lipper — used with *up* or *off* ⟨~ up the decks⟩

lip·per·ings \-pəriŋz\ *n pl* [fr. pl. of *lippering*, gerund of *5lipper*] : oil and refuse cleaned from a whaling ship's deck with a lipper : SLUMGULLION

lip·pia \'lipēə\ *n, cap* [NL, fr. Augustin *Lippi* †1705 French physician and traveler + NL *-ia*] : a large genus of tropical American herbs, shrubs, and small trees (family Verbenaceae) having small flowers in heads or spikes

lippie *var of* LIPPY

lip·pi·ness \'lipēnəs, -pin-\ *n* -ES **1** : the state or quality of being lippy **2** : saucy or impertinent language

1lip·ping \'lipiŋ\ *n* -S [*1lip* + *-ing*] **1** : outgrowth of bone in liplike form at a joint margin (as in degenerative arthritis) **2** : a piece of wood set in an archer's bow where a flaw has been cut out **3** : EMBOUCHURE 2a

2lipping *pres part of* LIP

lip·pi·tude \'lipə,tüd, -ə·,tyüd\ *n* -S [F, fr. L *lippitudo*, fr. *lippitus* (past part. of *lippire* to be blear-eyed, fr. *lippus* blear-eyed) + *-udo* -ude — more at LEAVE] *archaic* : soreness or blearedness of the eyes

lip·pi·zan *also* **lip·iz·zan** \,lipət'sän\ *n* -S *often cap* [*Lippiza, Lipizza* + E *-an*] : LIPPIZANER 2

lip·pi·zan·er *also* **lip·iz·zan·er** \,lipət'sänər\ *or* **lip·pi·za·na** \-nə\ *or* **lip·piz·zan·er** \-nər\ *n* -S [*Lippizaner, Lipizzaner, Lippizzaner* fr. G, fr. *Lippiza, Lipizza, Lippizza*, stud in northwestern Yugoslavia (formerly the Austrian Imperial Stud) where the strain was developed; *Lippizana* fr. It, fr. *Lippiza*] **1** *usu cap* : a strain or breed of shapely spirited chiefly white horses developed by crossbreeding Spanish, Danish, Italian, and Arab stock at the Austrian Imperial Stud at Lippiza near Trieste **2** *often cap* : a horse of the Lippizaner strain or breed used esp. in specialty display and dressage

lip plug *n* : LABRET

lipp·mann process \'lipmən-\ *n, usu cap L* [after Gabriel *Lippmann* †1921 French physicist] : a method of color photography depending upon the interference of light waves and employing in the camera an extremely fine-grain photographic plate in contact with a mercury reflector

1lip·py *also* **lip·pie** \'lipē, -pi\ *n, pl* **lippies** [*lip* (Sc var. of *3leap*) + *-y, -ie*] : an old Scotch unit of capacity equal to ¼ Scotch peck

2lip·py \'lipē, -pi\ *adj, usu* -ER/-EST [*1lip* + *-y*] **1 a** *of a dog* : having hanging lips when hanging lips are not acceptable by the standard of the breed or having lips excessively hanging by the standard of the breed **b** *of a person* : having an excessively prominent lip **2** : impudent or impertinent in speech ⟨~ adolescents⟩

lip-read \'ˌ=,=\ *vt* : to understand by lipreading ⟨a surprising vocabulary of words which they could *lip-read* quite successfully —*Lancet*⟩ ~ *vi* : to read lips ⟨teaching the deaf child to *lip-read* and to talk —Grace Coolidge⟩

lip-reader \'=,==\ *n* : one that can understand the words or meaning of a speaker by lipreading

lipreading \'=,==\ *n* : the catching of the words or meaning of a speaker by watching the movements of his lips without hearing his voice (as by a deaf person) — compare ORAL METHOD

lip rouge *n* : rouge for the lips

lip-rounding \'=,==\ *n* : ROUNDING 1c

lips *pl of* LIP, *pres 3d sing of* LIP

lipsalve \'=,=\ *n* : an ointment for the lips

lip server *n* : one that practices lip service

lip service *n* : service consisting only of avowed expressions of adherence, devotion, or allegiance : service by words but not by deeds ⟨pay *lip service* to the principles of competitive business but . . . permit big business to deny access to scarce raw materials to independent businessmen —Henry Wallace⟩ ⟨were . . . established as accepted religions provided their followers did *lip service* to the cult of the emperor —Brooke P. Church⟩

1lipstick \'=,=\ *n* [*1lip* + *stick*] : a waxy solid preparation or rouge put up in stick form for use as a cosmetic on the lips; *also* : a stick of such a preparation with its case

2lipstick \"\ *vb* -ED/-ING/-S *vt* **1** : to apply lipstick to **2** : to form by applying lipstick ⟨she had loops ~*ed* above a rather thin upper lip —Earle Birney⟩ ~ *vi* : to apply lipstick

lip stop *n* **1** : FLUE STOP 1 **2** : either of the sounds \p\ and \b\

lip strike *n* : the part of a lock that makes contact with the lip of a bolt or fastener

lip sync *n* [*lip synchronization*] **1** : LIP SYNCHRONIZATION **2** : the relationship that exists between sound and action in a sound motion picture when the two are in synchrony **3** : sound in a sound motion picture that is perceived as proceeding from concurrent action in distinction from sound that is heard but perceived not to be proceeding from concurrent action : synchronous dialogue

lip-sync *adj* [*lip sync*] : of, relating to, or produced by lip synchronization or lip sync

lip synchronization *n* **1** : recording of sound simultaneously with photographing of action so as to secure perfect synchrony of both (as when a motion picture is projected) **2** : recording of sound and photographing of action at separate times but utilizing techniques designed to secure synchrony of sound and action when the two are combined

lip-teeth \'=,=\ *adj* : LABIODENTAL

li·pu·ria \lə'pyùrēə\ *n* -S [NL, fr. *lip-* + *-uria*] : the presence of fat in urine

lipwork \'=,=\ *n* **1** *obs* : KISSING **2** : unthinking or insincere use of words : vain repetition

lip-worship \'=,==\ *n* : worship in utterance but not in deed : affirmation of devotion or fidelity without corresponding action

lip-worshiper \'=,===\ *n* : one that worships in utterance only : one affirming devotion or fidelity without corresponding action

liq *abbr* **1** liquid **2** liquor

li·quate \'lī,kwāt *also* 'li-, *usu* -ād.+V\ *vb* -ED/-ING/-S [L *liquatus*, past part. of *liquare*; akin to L *liquēre* to be fluid — more at LIQUID] *vt* : to cause (a metal or other substance that is more fusible than a substance with which it is combined) to separate out by the application of heat — often used with *out* ⟨*liquating* the impure metal out⟩ ~ *vi* : to become separated from a less fusible substance by being subjected to heat — often used with *out* ⟨metallic lead that readily ~*s out*⟩

li·qua·tion \lī'kwāshən, lə-, -āzhən\ *n* -S [LL *liquation-, liquatio*, fr. L *liquatus* + *-ion-, -io* -ion] : the process of separating a fusible substance (as a metal) from one less fusible by the application of heat

liq·ue·fa·cient \,likwə'fāshənt\ *n* -S [L *liquefacient-, liquefaciens*, pres. part. of *liquefacere* to liquefy, fr. *liquēre* to be fluid + *facere* to make — more at LIQUID, DO] : something that serves to liquefy or to promote liquefaction

liq·ue·fac·tion \,==ˈfakshən\ *n* [ME, fr. LL *liquefaction-, liquefactio*, fr. L *liquefactus* (past part. of *liquefacere*) + *-ion-, -io* -ion] **1** : the process of making or becoming liquid : conversion of a solid into a liquid by heat or of a gas into a liquid by cold or pressure **2** : the state of being liquid

liq·ue·fac·tive \,==ˈfaktiv\ *adj* [*liquefaction* + *-ive*] : relating to or causing liquefaction

liq·ue·fi·a·ble \,==ˈfīəbəl\ *adj* [*liquefy* + *-able*] : capable of being liquefied

liquefied petroleum gas *n* : a compressed gas consisting of flammable light hydrocarbons (as propane and butane) obtained esp. as a by-product in the refining of petroleum or the manufacture of natural gasoline and used chiefly as a domestic and industrial fuel, as a motor fuel, and as a raw material for chemical synthesis (as of synthetic rubber) — abbr. *LPG*; called also *bottled gas, LP gas*

liq·ue·fi·er \'likwə,fī(ə)r, -īə\ *n* -S : one that liquefies: as **a** : an apparatus for liquefying gases **b** : a worker who operates compressors for liquefying gases (as chlorine gas)

liq·ue·fy *also* **liq·ui·fy** \'likwə,fī\ *vb* -ED/-ING/-S [MF *liquefier*, modif. (influenced by MF *-fier* -fy) of L *liquefacere* — more at LIQUEFACIENT] *vt* : to reduce to a liquid state — used both of solids and gases ~ *vi* : to become liquid

li·quesce \li'kwes\ *vb* -ED/-ING/-S [L *liquescere*] : LIQUEFY

li·ques·cence \-ˈsᵊn(t)s\ *n* -S : the quality or state of being liquescent

li·ques·cent \-sᵊnt\ *adj* [L *liquescent-, liquescens*, pres. part. of *liquescere* to become fluid, incho. of *liquēre* to be fluid — more at LIQUID] : being or becoming or tending to become liquid

1li·queur *R* li'kər, lē'-, + V -kər·; *-R* -kə̄, + V -kər· *or* -kō *also* -kər; -'k(y)ù(ə)r, -ùə\ *n* -S [F, liquid, liquor, liqueur, fr. OF *licour, liqueur* liquid — more at LIQUOR] **1** : an alcoholic beverage often used as an after-dinner drink and as a cocktail ingredient, flavored with various aromatic substances and usu. sweetened, and made chiefly by steeping and distilling the flavoring substances in spirit — compare CORDIAL **2** : a solution of sugar and aged wine used to induce second fermentation in the production of champagne

2liqueur \"\ *vt* -ED/-ING/-S : to treat or mix with liqueur

liqueur d'or \-'dȯr\ *n, pl* **liqueurs d'or** [F, lit., gold liqueur] : a sweet colorless French liqueur flavored primarily with lemon and containing tiny golden flecks — compare DANZIGER GOLDWASSER

liqueur green *n* : a light to moderate greenish yellow that is greener and stronger than dyer's broom or acacia

liqueur jaune \-'zhōn\ *n, pl* **liqueurs jaunes** \"\ [F, lit., yellow liqueur] : a liqueur resembling yellow Chartreuse

liqueur verte \-'vert\ *n, pl* **liqueurs vertes** \"\ [F, lit., green liqueur] : a liqueur resembling green Chartreuse

1liq·uid \'likwəd\ *adj* [ME, fr. MF *liquide*, fr. L *liquidus*, fr. *liquēre* to be fluid; akin to L *lixa* water, lye, *lixivus* consisting of lye, OIr *fliuch* damp, W *gwlith* dew, *gwlyb* wet] **1 a** (1) : that is extremely fluid without being gaseous so as to flow freely typically in the manner of water and to have a definite volume without having a definite shape except such as is temporarily given by a container and such as is readily lost (as by an upset or overflow) and that is only slightly compressible and incapable of indefinite expansion in such a way that constituent molecules while moving with extreme ease upon each other do not tend to separate from each other in the manner characteristic of the molecules of gases ⟨water and milk and blood are ~ substances⟩ (2) : WATERY ⟨sailing over the ~ depths of the seas⟩ **b** : brimming with tears ⟨sorrow which made the eyes of many grow ~⟩ **2 a** : bright and clear to the vision ⟨the ~ air of a spring morning⟩ ⟨shining with a ~ luster⟩ **b** *obs* : clearly evident : MANIFEST **c** *chiefly Scots law* (1) *of an account or obligation* : UNDISPUTED (2) *of a debt* : ascertained and constituted against a debtor by a written obligation or by a court decree **3 a** (1) : that is smooth and musical in tone : that has a flowing quality entirely free of harshness or discord or abrupt breaks ⟨the ~ song of a robin in the early evening⟩ (2) : that is smooth and unconstrained in movement ⟨the ~ grace of a ballerina⟩ **b** *of a consonant* (1) : that is frictionless and capable of being prolonged like a vowel (as \l\, some varieties of \r\, and in some classifications \n\, \m\, \ŋ\) (2) : CONTINUANT **4** : tending to become altered (as in form or content) : not fixed : not stable ⟨~ political agreements that were quite without real significance⟩ **5** : that is cash or capable of being readily converted into cash ⟨~ assets⟩

syn FLUID: LIQUID implies a flow characteristic of water and implies a substance, as water, with definite volume but no definite form except that given by its container; figuratively, it is opposed to *harsh* or, sometimes, *fixed* or *rigid* ⟨its coal and *liquid* fuel —*Current Biog.*⟩ ⟨*liquid* soap⟩ ⟨the *liquid* sweetness of the thrush —H.J.Laski⟩ FLUID implies flowing of any kind and extends to gases, to highly viscous substances, or to something usu. solid but liquefied, as by heating or dissolving; figuratively, it is, more commonly than LIQUID, opposed to *rigid* or *fixed* ⟨the memory of him would become as *fluid* as water and trickle out of her mind —Ellen Glasgow⟩ ⟨a more *fluid* oil paint on canvas —*Nat'l Gallery of Art*⟩ ⟨representatives whose task it should be not to codify and embalm the laws, but to keep them *fluid* —D.C.Peattie⟩ ⟨our moral notions are always *fluid* —J.E.E.Dalberg-Acton⟩

2liquid \"\ *n* -S [F *liquide*, fr. MF, fr. *liquide*, adj.] **1** : a liquid substance — compare GAS, SOLID **2** : a liquid consonant

liquid air *n* : air in the liquid state but usu. richer in oxygen than gaseous air that is obtained as a faintly bluish transparent mobile intensely cold liquid by compressing purified air and cooling it by its own expansion to a temperature below the boiling points of its principal components nitrogen and oxygen and is used chiefly as a refrigerant and as a source of oxygen, nitrogen, and inert gases (as argon)

liquid-air trap *n* : a tube which is immersed in liquid air and through which gases are passed to have vaporous impurities removed by condensation or sublimation

liq·uid·am·bar \'likwə,dambə(r)\ *n* [NL, fr. L *liquidus* liquid + ML *ambar* amber — more at LIQUID, AMBER] **1 a** *cap* : a genus of trees (family Hamamelidaceae) with small monoecious flowers and a globose fruit composed of many woody carpels — see SWEET GUM **b** -S : any tree of the genus *Liquidambar* **2** *also* **liq·uid·am·ber** \"\ : a storax or a resin from the sweet gum

liquid ammonia *n* : a heavy liquid that has a high vapor pressure at ordinary temperatures, that causes freezing when brought into contact with the skin, that is obtained by compressing anhydrous gaseous ammonia, and that is used in refrigeration and as a solvent (as in the study of ammono compounds) and as a source of gaseous ammonia

liq·ui·date \'likwə,dāt, *usu* -ād.+V\ *vb* -ED/-ING/-S [LL *liquidatus*, past part. of *liquidare* to melt, fr. L *liquidus* liquid — more at LIQUID] *vt* **1 a** (1) : to determine by agreement or by litigation the precise amount of (indebtedness, damages, accounts) ⟨was prepared to pay the debt as soon as it was *liquidated*⟩ (2) : to determine the liabilities and apportion assets toward discharging the indebtedness of (as a firm that is going out of business) ⟨decided to ~ the corporation by the end of the year⟩ **b** : to settle (a debt) by payment or other adjustment or settlement ⟨made every effort to stabilize the economy by *liquidating* the national debt⟩ **2** : to get rid of : dispose of ⟨any remaining doubts or objections can be easily *liquidated*⟩; *esp* : to get rid of by force or violence and esp. by killing ⟨ruthlessly ~*s* all opponents of the regime⟩ **3** *archaic* : to make clear : make plain : make unambiguous or less ambiguous ⟨time only can ~ the meaning —Alexander Hamilton⟩ **4** : to convert (assets) into cash ⟨*liquidated* his securities⟩ ~ *vi* **1** : to liquidate debts or damages or accounts **2** : to determine (as of a firm that is going out of business) liabilities and to apportion assets toward discharging indebtedness

liquidating dividend *n* : a final payment to a stockholder (as by a firm that is going out of business) that is usu. a simple return of the stockholder's capital

liq·ui·da·tion \,likwə'dāshən\ *n* -S **1** : the action or process of liquidating or of being liquidated **2** : the condition of being liquidated

liq·ui·da·tor \'==,dād·ə(r), -ātə-\ *n* -S : one that liquidates; *esp* : an individual appointed by law to liquidate assets (as of a bankrupt company) — compare RECEIVER

liquid bleach *n* : a liquid containing bleaching agents; *esp* : a solution of sodium hypochlorite used for bleaching (as in laundry and textile work), disinfecting, and deodorizing — compare BLEACH LIQUOR

liquid compass *n* : a compass in which the compass card and magnets rest on a pivot in a bowl filled with liquid

liquid crystal *n* : a mesomorphic substance (as para-azoxyanisole) having observable optical anisotropy like a crystal as evidenced by double-refraction polarization but having such low viscosity as to behave mechanically like a liquid — compare CYBOTAXIS

liquid extract *n* : FLUIDEXTRACT

liquid fire *n* : a flammable liquid composition of chemicals that can be shot in a flaming stream (as against tanks or into fortified positions)

liquid glue *n* : a fluid preparation of glue (as of animal glue with a chemical liquefier in water)

liquid gold *n* : a liquid preparation (as a suspension of finely divided gold in an oil) for decorating ceramic ware with gold or gold color

li·quid·i·ty \li'kwidəd·ē, -ətē, -i\ *n* -ES [F or L; F *liquidité*, fr. L *liquiditat-, liquiditas*, fr. *liquidus* liquid + *-itat-, -itas* -ity — more at LIQUID] **1** : the quality or state of being liquid **2** : the quality or state of possessing liquid assets ⟨a bank that has progressively increased its ~⟩

liquidity preference *n* : preference for actual cash rather than for income-yielding investments; *specif* : this preference insofar as it affects the relationship between cash balances and interest rates

liq·uid·ize \'likwə,dīz\ *vt* -ED/-ING/-S : to cause to be liquid

liq·uid·ly *adv* : in a liquid manner ⟨laughed ~⟩ : like a liquid ⟨silk that rippled ~⟩

liquid measure *n* **1** : a unit or series of units for measuring liquid capacity — see MEASURE table **2** : a measure for liquids

liq·uid·ness *n* -ES : the quality or state of being liquid

liquid oxygen *n* : a pale blue transparent mobile magnetic liquid obtained by compressing gaseous oxygen and used chiefly in liquid-oxygen explosives and as the oxidizer in rocket propellants — called also *lox*

liquid-oxygen explosive *n* : a blasting explosive that consists essentially of a cartridge containing combustible material (as carbon black or lampblack) and immersed in liquid oxygen shortly before use

liquid petrolatum *also* **liquid paraffin** *n* : a transparent oily liquid obtained usu. by distilling petroleum fractions boiling between 330°C and 390°C and used chiefly in medicine for treating constipation and esp. formerly as a demulcent and solvent for nose and throat medication — called also *mineral oil, white mineral oil*

liquid rosin *n* : TALL OIL

liquid sugar *n* : a thick saturated solution of usu. refined cane or beet sucrose that is often partially or fully inverted to prevent crystallization

liq·ui·dus \'likwədəs\ *also* **liquidus curve** *n* -ES [L *liquidus* liquid — more at LIQUID] : a curve usu. on a temperature-composition diagram for a binary system that over a range of temperatures between the melting points of the pure components relates compositions of the liquid phase to the solid phase in equilibrium with the liquid phase and that indicates temperatures above which only the liquid phase can exist — compare SOLIDUS, SOLVUS

liquify *var of* LIQUEFY

1li·quor \'likə(r)\ *n* -S [ME *licour, liquour*, fr. OF *licour, liqueur*, fr. L *liquor*, fr. *liquēre* to be fluid — more at LIQUID] : a liquid substance: as **a** : something drunk as a beverage (as water, milk, fruit juice); *esp* : a usu. strong distilled alcoholic beverage (as whiskey, rum) rather than a fermented one (as wine, beer) **b** (1) : the liquid in which meat or vegetables have been cooked : BROTH (2) : the juice of meat given off during cooking and often combined with a thickening agent and spices and served with the meat : GRAVY (3) : a dressing or sauce served with foods (4) : the juice contained in oysters or clams **c** : sugarcane sap that has not been crystallized to sugar **d** : a solution of a medicinal substance usu. in water — distinguished from *tincture* **e** : a solution or emulsion or suspension used or obtained in an industrial process : BATH 2b ⟨scouring ~ for wool⟩ ⟨dye ~⟩ ⟨waste ~*s*⟩: as (1) : a solution of a chemical used in digesting raw materials for cellulosic pulp ⟨soda ~⟩ — see SULFITE LIQUOR (2) : the liquid drained from such pulp at the end of the cook — see BLACK LIQUOR (3) : AMMONIA LIQUOR (4) : BLEACH LIQUOR (5) : IRON LIQUOR (6) : FAT LIQUOR — **in liquor** : DRUNK ⟨men *in liquor* must be handled differently at the country club —Bernard De Voto⟩

2liquor \"\ *vb* **liquored; liquored; liquoring** \-k(ə)riŋ\ **liquors** *vt* **1** : to treat with a liquid substance: as **a** *archaic* (1) : to dress (as leather) with an oily or greasy liquid substance (2) : to cover or smear with a greasy or oily lubricant **b** : to steep or soak in or with a liquid (as in various industrial processes or as in the preparation of some foods) **2** : to ply with alcoholic liquor (as whiskey, rum) — usu. used with *up* ⟨had been pretty well ~*ed* up by his friends by the time she found him⟩ ~ *vi* : to drink alcoholic liquor esp. in large quantities — usu. used with *up* ⟨sit down amid a lot of bottles and ~ up —Coulton Waugh⟩ ⟨after they had been married awhile he started up his ~*ing* again —Helen Rich⟩

li·quor am·nii \'lī,kwȯr'amnē,ī\ *n* [NL] : AMNIOTIC FLUID

liquor cabinet *n* : a cabinet or closet in which alcoholic beverages and the materials for mixing drinks are kept

liquored up *also* **liquored** *adj* : DRUNK ⟨a *liquored up* lumberjack, returning from a spree —H.J.Barnes⟩

liquor head *n* : DRUNKARD

liquorice *var of* LICORICE

li·quor·ish \'lik(ə)rish\ *adj* [*1liquor* + *-ish*] **1** : LICKERISH **2 a** : inclined to drink liquor (as whiskey, rum) : showing an appetite for liquor **b** : alcoholic in composition ⟨a somewhat ~ drink⟩ — **li·quor·ish·ly** *adv* — **li·quor·ish·ness** *n* -ES

1liquorous *obs var of* LICKERISH

2li·quor·ous \'lik(ə)rəs\ *adj* [*1liquor* + *-ous*] **1** : LIQUORISH 2 ⟨a ~ old man⟩ ⟨a ~ beverage⟩ **2** : that results from or resembles an intoxicated condition ⟨~ speech⟩ ⟨this rising state of ~ ecstasy —Richard Scowcroft⟩

li·quory \-k(ə)rē, -ri\ *adj* [*1liquor* + *-y*] : marked by or given to or prompted by the drinking of strong liquor : BOOZY, LIQUORISH ⟨the glittering ~ boom which the heavy-spending war years had brought on —*Life*⟩ ⟨~ joy⟩

1li·ra \'lirə, 'lē-\ *n* [It, fr. L *libra* balance, unit of weight] **1** *pl* **li·re** \'lē(,)rā\ *also* **li·ras** \'lirəz, 'lē-\ **a** : the basic monetary unit of Italy — see MONEY table **b** : a coin or note representing one lira **2** *pl* **li·ras** \'lirəz, 'lē-\ *also* **li·re** \'lē(,)rā\ [Turk, fr. It] **a** : a Syrian pound — see MONEY table **b** : the basic monetary unit of Malta and Turkey — see MONEY table **3** *pl* **li·roth** *or* **li·rot** \'lē,rōt(h)\ *also* **li·res** \-(,)rās\ *or* **li·re** \-(,)rā\ [NHeb, fr. It] : the former Israeli pound

2li·ra \'lērə\ *n* -S [It, fr. L, lyre — more at LYRE] **1** : LYRE 1 **2** : HURDY-GURDY 1 **3** : a bowed stringed musical instrument dating from about the 15th century and related to the viol and having additional free vibrating strings

3li·ra \'līrə\ *n, pl* **li·ras** \-rəz\ *also* **li·rae** \-(,)rē\ [NL, fr. L, furrow — more at LEARN] : a ridge (as on some shells) resembling a fine thread or a hair — **li·rate** \-,rāt, -rət\ *adj* — **li·ra·tion** \lī'rāshən\ *n* -S

lire \'lī(ə)r, 'lī(-, -ē(-, -ēə\ *n* -S [ME, fr. OE *līra* muscle, fleshy part of the body — more at LEG] *dial Brit* : BRAWN, MUSCLE

li·rel·la \lə'relə, lī-\ *n* -S [NL, dim. of L *lira* furrow — more at LEARN] : an elongated apothecium in lichens that has a furrow along the middle — **li·rel·late** \-,lāt\ *adj*

lir·i·o·den·dron \,lirēə'dendrən\ *n* [NL, fr. Gk *leirion, lirion* lily + NL *-dendron* — more at LILY] **1** *cap* : a genus of No. American and Asiatic trees (family Magnoliaceae) with 4-lobed smooth shining leaves and large greenish yellow flowers resembling tulips — see TULIP TREE **2** -S : any tree of the genus *Liriodendron*

lir·i·o·my·za \-'mīzə\ *n, cap* [NL, fr. Gk *leirion, lirion* lily + NL *-myza*] : a genus of agromyzid flies having larvae that are leaf miners and that include several economically important pests of cultivated plants — see PEA LEAF MINER

li·ri·o·pe \lə'rīə(,)pē\ *n, cap* [NL, after *Liriope*, a nymph in Roman mythology] **:** a genus of stoloniferous scapose grass-leaved herbs (family Liliaceae) with short thick rhizomes and small whitish or blue or violet flowers in racemes or spikes and with a superior ovary — see LILYTURF

lir·i·pipe \'lirə,pīp\ *also* **lir·i·poop** \-,püp\ *n* [ML *liripipium*] **1 :** a very long tippet orig. an extension of the peak of a hood and later attached to a medieval chaperon or forming part of the old clerical and academic dress **2** *obs* **:** something (as a lesson, a role) to be learned

1**lirk** \'lirk\ *n* -s [ME (northern dial.) *lerk*] *Scot* **:** WRINKLE

2**lirk** *vb* -ED/-ING/-S *Scot* **:** WRINKLE

li·roc·o·nite \lī'räkə,nīt\ *n* -s [F, fr. Gk *leiros* resembling a lily, delicate (fr. *leirion* lily) + *konia* powder (fr. *konis* dust) + F *-ite* — more at LILY, INCINERATE] **:** a basic hydrous aluminum copper arsenate $Cu_2Al(AsO_4)(OH)_4.4H_2O$ occurring in monoclinic crystals of a sky-blue or verdigris-green color (hardness 2–2.5, sp. gr. 2.88–2.99)

1**lis** \'lēs\ *n, pl* **lis** *or* **lisses** [F, lit., lily, fr. OF, fr. pl. of (assumed) *lil*, fr. L *lilium* — more at LILY] **:** FLEUR-DE-LIS

2**lis** *var of* LISS

3**lis** *pl of* LI

li·sa \'lēsə\ *n* -s [Sp, fr. OSp *liça*] **1 :** either of two gray mullets (*Mugil cephalus* or *M. curema*) of the tropical western Atlantic highly regarded as table fishes **2** *also* **lisa fran·ce·sa** \-frän'sāsə\ [*lisa francesa* fr. Sp, lit., French lisa] **:** TENPOUNDER 1

li·saw \'lē,sȯ\ *also* **li·shaw** \-,shȯ\ *n, pl* **lisaw** *or* **lisaws** *usu cap* **:** LISU

lis·bon \'lizbən\ *adj, usu cap* [fr. *Lisbon*, Portugal] **:** of or from Lisbon, the capital of Portugal **:** of the kind or style prevalent in Lisbon

lis·e·ran purple \'lizərən-\ *n* [*liseran* prob. by shortening & alter. fr. *alizarin*] **:** a strong reddish purple that is bluer, lighter, and stronger than average fuchsia purple and redder and paler than purple orchid or phlox purple

lish \'lish\ *adj* [origin unknown] *dial Brit* **:** lithe and quick **:** NIMBLE

li·si \'lēsē\ *n* -s [native name in the Solomon islands] **:** a Solomon islands canoe built of planks and with a high upturned stem and stern

lisk \'lisk\ *n* -s [ME *leske*, of Scand origin; akin to ON *ljōski* groin, OSw & ODan *liuske;* akin to OE *lēosca* groin, MLG *lēsche* groin, MD *liese* thin skin, G dial. (Switzerland) *lösch* loose, OE *losian* to get lost — more at LOSE] *dial Brit* **:** GROIN

lis·keard·ite \li'skär,dīt, -kȧ,d-\ *n* -s [*Liskeard*, town in Cornwall, England, its locality + E *-ite*] **:** a mineral (Al, Fe)$_3$-$(AsO_4)(OH)_6.5H_2O$ consisting of a basic hydrous arsenate of aluminum and iron

lisle \'līl, *esp before pause or consonant* 'līəl\ *or* **lisle thread** *n* -s [fr. *Lisle* (now *Lille*), France, where it was first manufactured] **:** a smooth tightly twisted thread usu. made in two or more plies of long-staple cotton and used chiefly in making hosiery, underwear, and gloves

1**lisp** \'lisp *sometimes in mockery* 'lithp\ *vb* -ED/-ING/-S [ME *wlispen, lispen*, fr. OE *-wlyspian;* akin to MD & OHG *lispen* to speak unclearly, stammer, stutter, lisp, Norw dial. *leispa*, Sw *läspa*] *vi* **1 a :** to pronounce the sibilants *s* and *z* imperfectly esp. by giving them the sound of *th* ⟨imperfect adjustment of the organs of speech causes children to ~⟩ ⟨some people ~ when they first wear an upper denture —H.E. Kessler⟩ **b :** to speak falteringly or with a lisp ⟨look you ~, and wear strange suits —Shak.⟩ ⟨children often ~ when they first learn to talk⟩ **2 :** to make a sound resembling a lisp ⟨bits of dirty newspaper ~*ed* along —Elizabeth Taylor⟩ ~ *vt* **:** to utter falteringly or with a lisp ⟨at his mother's knee first ~*s* his ABC's⟩ ⟨*l* is ~*ed* for the *r* which the baby can't pronounce —E.C.Smith⟩ ⟨demurely lowers her eyes and ~*s* a soft reply⟩

2**lisp** \"\ *n* -s **1 :** a speech defect or affectation characterized by the imperfect pronunciation of sibilants, esp. the substitution of interdental sounds **:** act of lisping ⟨spoke with an engaging ~ —Charles Dickens⟩ **2 :** a sound resembling a lisp ⟨the rhythmic ~ of sandal straps —L.C.Douglas⟩

lis pen·dens \'li'spen,denz\ *n* [L] **1 :** a pending lawsuit **2 :** a written notice usu. required by law to be recorded in a public registry office of a pending lawsuit identifying the principals, the court, and the specific property in controversy **3 :** the legal doctrine that one dealing with or purchasing an interest in property involved in pending litigation with actual or constructive knowledge of the existence of that litigation is subject to all the rights of others adjudicated in that litigation

lisp·er \'lispə(r)\ *see pronunc at* LISP\ *n* -s [ME *lyspare*, fr. *lispen* to lisp + *-are* -er] **:** one that lisps

1**lisp·ing** \-piŋ\ *n* -s [ME, fr. gerund of *lispen* to lisp] **1 :** defective pronunciation of sibilants ⟨interdental ~⟩ **2 :** 2LISP 2 ⟨the first ~*s* of Greek art —Florence Simmonds⟩ ⟨low ~*s* of the summer rain —H.W.Longfellow⟩

2**lisping** *adj* [fr. pres. part. of 1*lisp*] **:** characterized by a lisp or lisping — **lisp·ing·ly** *adv*

lis·pund \'lispənd\ *or* **lis·pound** \-,paůnd, -,pənd\ *n* -s [LG *lispund*, fr. MLG *lispunt, livespunt*, fr. *lis, lives* Livonian + *punt* pound; akin to OHG *phunt* pound — more at POUND] **:** any of various units of weight of the Shetland and Orkney islands varying from 12 to 30 or more pounds

liss *or* **lis** \'lis\ *n, pl* **lisses** [IrGael *lios*, fr. MIr *liss, less;* akin to W *llys* court] **:** an ancient Irish fortification or storage place enclosed by a circular mound or trench or both

liss- *or* **lisso-** *comb form* [NL, fr. Gk *lissos, lispos, lisphos;* prob. akin to OE *līm* lime — more at LIME] **:** smooth ⟨*Lis*sencephala⟩ ⟨*Lisso*flagellata⟩

lis·sa·jous figure \,lēsə'zhü-\ *also* **lissajous curve** *n, usu cap L* [after Jules A. *Lissajous* †1880 Fr. physicist] **:** any of an infinite variety of curves formed by combining two mutually perpendicular simple harmonic motions, commonly exhibited by the oscilloscope, and used in studying frequency, amplitude, and phase relations of harmonic variables

lis·sam·phib·ia \,li,sam'fibēə\ *n pl, cap* [NL, fr. *liss-* + *Amphibia*] **:** a primary division of smooth-skinned amphibians comprising the existing orders — compare STEGOCEPHALIA

lis·sau·er's tract \'li,saůə(r)z-\ *n, usu cap L* [after Heinrich *Lissauer* †1891 Ger. neurologist] **:** a slender column of white matter between the dorsal gray column and the periphery of the spinal cord

lisse \'lēs\ *n* -s [F *lice, lisse* heddle, warp, lisse, fr. L *licia*, pl. of *licium* thread, thrum] **:** a silk gauze used for dresses and trimmings

lis·sen·ceph·a·la \,li(,)sen'sefələ, ,sən-, -,sᵊn-\ *n pl, cap* [NL, fr. *liss-* + *-encephala* (fr. Gk *enkephalos* brain) — more at ENCEPHAL-] *in some classifications* **:** eutherian mammals having a brain with few or no cerebral convolutions and including the edentates, bats, insectivores, and rodents

lis·sen·cephalic \,li(,)sensə'falik, -lēk\ *or* **lis·sen·ceph·a·lous** \-(,)sen'sefələs, -,sən-, -,sᵊn-\ *adj* [*liss-* + *encephalic, -encephalous*] **1 :** having a smooth cerebrum without convolutions **2** [NL *Lissencephala* + E *-ic* or *-ous*] **:** of or relating to the Lissencephala — **lis·sen·ceph·a·ly** \,=(,)='sefəlē\ *n*

lisses *pl of* LIS

lis·so·flagellata \,lisō+\ *n pl, cap* [NL, fr. *liss-* + *Flagellata*] *in some esp former classifications* **:** an order or other major division of Mastigophora comprising all the flagellates that lack a protoplasmic collar — compare CHOANOFLAGELLATA — **lis·so·flagellate** \"+\ *n* -s

1**lis·some** *also* **lis·som** \'lisəm\ *adj* [alter. of *lithesome*] **1 :** easily flexed **:** SLENDER, LITHE, LIMBER ⟨~ girl⟩ ⟨as ~ as a hazel wand —Alfred Tennyson⟩ **2 :** quick and light in action **:** NIMBLE ⟨~ grace of the cat tribe —James Stevenson-Hamilton⟩ **syn** see SUPPLE

2**lis·some** \'lisəm\ *adv* **:** in a lissome manner **:** SUPPLELY, NIMBLY ⟨*lissome*-swaying hips —Ednah P. Hayes⟩

lis·some·ness *n* -ES **:** the quality or state of being lissome

lis·sot·ri·chi \li'sä·trə,chī\ [NL, fr. *liss-* + *-trichi*] *syn of* LEIOTRICHI

lis·sot·ri·chous \-kəs\ *adj* [*liss-* + *-trichous*] **:** LEIOTRICHOUS

lis·sot·ri·chy \-,kē\ *n* -ES [*liss-* + *-trichy*] **:** the racial characteristic of having straight hair

lissu *usu cap, var of* LISU

1**list** \'list\ *vb* **listed** *or* **list; listed** *or* **list; listing; lists** [ME *lusten, lysten, listen*, fr. OE *lystan;* akin to OS *lustian* to desire, long for, OHG *lusten*, ON *lysta;* causative-denominatives fr. the root of E 1*lust*] *vt* **:** to give pleasure to **:** GRATIFY, SUIT ⟨could have my being while it ~*ed* me —W.J.Locke⟩ ~ *vi* **:** to have a desire or inclination **:** CHOOSE, WISH ⟨allowed that mind of mine to stray thereafter as it ~*ed* —Rafael Sabatini⟩

2**list** \"\ *n* -s [ME, prob. fr. *listen*, v.] **1** *archaic* **:** INCLINATION, CRAVING, DESIRE ⟨which I have neither ~ nor leisure to recount —Thomas Fuller⟩ **2** *archaic* **:** personal inclination **:** WILL ⟨by the law of the land, and not the arbitrary ~ . . . of any man living —Edmund Hickeringill⟩

3**list** \"\ *vb* **listed** *or* **list; listed** *or* **list; listing; lists** [ME *listen*, fr. OE *hlystan* — more at LISTEN] *vi* **:** to give ear **:** LISTEN ⟨she talks and I am fain to ~ —Robert Frost⟩ ~ *vt, archaic* **:** to listen to **:** HEAR ⟨teach your ears to ~ me with more heed —Shak.⟩

4**list** \"\ *n* -s [ME *liste, list*, fr. OE *līste;* akin to MLG *līste* edge, border, OHG *līsta*, Alb *leth* edge, bank, border] **1 a** *obs* **:** a strip of cloth ⟨gartered with a red and blue ~ —Shak.⟩ **b :** a band or strip of any material; *esp* **:** a narrow strip of wood cut from the edge of a plank or board **c :** LISTEL **d** *archaic* **:** LISTER RIDGE **e** (1) **:** the first thin coat of tin applied in the manufacture of tin plate (2) **:** a rim of tin left on an edge of tin plate after it is coated **2 lists** *pl but sing or pl in constr* [influenced in meaning by MF *lice* lists, of Gmc origin; akin to OHG *līsta* edge, border] **a :** a tilting arena or the palisade enclosing it ⟨give proof of your knightly worth in the ~*s* tomorrow —Rafael Sabatini⟩ **b :** an arena for any kind of combat ⟨entered the ~*s* against the bull —Frank Yerby⟩ **c :** a controversy or field of competition ⟨enter the ~*s* . . . for or against practical programs of population resettlement —Ethel Albert⟩ ⟨a thick skin and a ready wit make him a good candidate for the political ~*s*⟩ ⟨one of Ireland's major industries . . . has now entered the dollar-earning ~*s* —E.M.Woolf⟩ **3** *obs* **a :** a line marking a limit or extent **:** BOUNDARY ⟨the very ~, the very utmost bound of all our purposes —Shak.⟩ **b :** a railing or railed enclosure esp. used as an exercising ground ⟨a ~ to ride horses in, much frequented by the gallants in summer —John Evelyn⟩ **4 a** *chiefly Brit* **:** a strip forming the edge of a woven fabric **:** SELVAGE ⟨pieces having tightly woven ~*s* which curl badly should be sewn together . . . and dyed in tubular form —C.M.Whittaker & C.C.Wilcock⟩ **b** *archaic* **:** a material resembling selvage ⟨have had ~ nailed round my doors, and stopping every crack —Mary Delany⟩ **5 :** a streak of color **:** STRIPE ⟨a hackle with a blue or dun ~ —J.E.Leisenring⟩; *specif* **:** a dark stripe along the midline of a horse's back

5**list** \"\ *vt* **listed** *or* **list; listed** *or* **list; listing; lists** [ME *listen, liste, list*, n.] **1** *obs* **:** to put a border around **:** EDGE **2 :** to cut away a narrow strip (as sapwood) from the edge of ⟨staves, air-dried and ~*ed* —F.P.Hankerson⟩ **3 a :** to prepare (land) for a crop or check (soil) from blowing by making ridges and furrows with a lister — compare LISTING 2 **b :** to plant (a field) with a lister

6**list** \"\ *n* -s [F *liste*, fr. MF, group of people, roster, fr. OIt *lista* band, stripe, row, group, roster, of Gmc origin; akin to OHG *līsta* edge, border — more at 4LIST] **1 a :** a simple series of words or numerals (as the names of persons or objects) ⟨guest ~⟩ ⟨grocery ~⟩ ⟨there were 109 publications . . . but the casualty ~ was long, too —*Amer. Guide Series: Wash.*⟩; *specif* **:** an official roster **:** ROLL ⟨drawing up a ~ for . . . party nomination —Richard Scammon⟩ — compare ACTIVE LIST, BLACKLIST, RETIRED LIST **b :** INDEX, CATALOG, CHECKLIST ⟨the card catalog in a library . . . is used mainly as a finding ~ —Saul Herner⟩ ⟨the . . . disc jumped to the top of the hit ~ in ten days —R.G.Hubler⟩ ⟨the publisher added the book to his ~⟩ ⟨put eggs on the shopping ~⟩ ⟨check the ~ of qualifications for a job⟩ **c :** the total number to be considered or included ⟨among the essentials of true democracy, responsible citizenship comes high on the ~⟩ ⟨added spelling reform to the ~ of his interests —W.B.Shaw & E.S.Bates⟩ **2 :** a record of individual holdings of real and personal property subject to taxation ⟨tax the grand ~ a definite percentage . . . for school revenue —*Amer. Guide Series: Vt.*⟩ **3 :** the total register of securities admitted to trading on a stock exchange ⟨there were many . . . strong individual stocks in the ~ —*Springfield (Mass.) Union*⟩ **4 :** LIST PRICE ⟨set your own ~, take a big markup and still undersell the field —*Office Appliances*⟩

7**list** \"\ *vb* -ED/-ING/-S *vt* **1 a :** to make a list of **:** ENUMERATE ⟨~ five reasons why you enjoyed the book⟩ ⟨it is now possible . . . to ~ all the amino acids necessary —*Americana Annual*⟩ ⟨~ the specialized agencies of the United Nations⟩ **b :** to include on a list **:** REGISTER, RECORD: as (1) **:** to enter (taxable property) on an official list (2) **:** to enter (a stock or other security) in the list of those officially admitted to dealings on the exchange (3) **:** to place (property) in the hands of a real-estate agent for sale or rent (4) **:** to enter in a price list **c :** to declare to be **:** GIVE ⟨increased confidence . . . was ~*ed* as a reason for the increase in spending —*Dun's Rev.*⟩ ⟨twenty-four books . . . two of them ~*ed* as essential library acquisitions —Anthony Boucher⟩ **d :** to put in writing **:** SHOW ⟨the only membership he ~*s* is in a professional society⟩ **2 a** *obs* **:** to put into a category **:** CLASSIFY ⟨virtues are ~*ed* in the rank of invisible things —Thomas Traherne⟩ **b :** to put (oneself) down — used with *as* ⟨~*s* himself as a political liberal⟩ **3** *archaic* **:** to recruit or appoint into or as if into military service ⟨will ~ you for my soldier —Sir Walter Scott⟩ ~ *vi* **1** *archaic* **:** to enlist in or as if in the armed forces ⟨he is going to ~ with us, and be our clergyman —George Borrow⟩ **2 :** to become entered in a catalog with a selling price ⟨the wrench alone ~*s* at $3 —*Industrial Equipment News*⟩

8**list** \"\ *vb* -ED/-ING/-S [origin unknown] *vi* **:** to lean to one side **:** CANT, TILT ⟨she ~*s* steeply to port —H.W.Baldwin⟩ ⟨the trees . . . all ~*ed* to leeward —Frances G. Patton⟩ ~ *vt* **:** to cause to list ⟨shift tanks and bulldozers in transport's holds, ~*ing* the ships —K.M.Dodson⟩

9**list** \"\ *n* -s **1 :** a deviation from the vertical **:** CANT, TILT ⟨water flooding into the hold gave the ship a heavy ~ to starboard⟩ ⟨there was a faint forward ~ to his body as he walked —Lawrence Williams⟩ **2 :** a tendency to incline **:** LEANING ⟨a . . . political ~ to the left —Paul Woodring⟩

list·able \'listəbəl\ *adj* [7*list* + *-able*] **:** capable of being listed; *specif* **:** TAXABLE

1**list·ed** \'listəd\ *adj* [ME, fr. *liste, list* edge + *-ed* — more at LIST (edge)] **1 :** striped or banded with color ⟨~ pig⟩ **2 :** planted or prepared for planting with a lister ⟨~ corn⟩ ⟨~ ground⟩ **3 :** reduced in width by having a strip removed from the edge ⟨used of a board ⟨~ barrel staves⟩

2**listed** *adj* [fr. past part. of 7*list*] **:** incorporated in a list; *specif* **:** admitted to trading on a stock exchange ⟨~ securities⟩ ⟨~ stock⟩

list·ee \li'stē\ *n* -s [7*list* + *-ee*] **:** one that is included in a list

lis·tel \'listᵊl\ *n* -s [F, fr. It *listello*, dim. of *lista* band, stripe — more at LIST (roll)] *archit* **:** a narrow band or list **:** FILLET

1**lis·ten** \'lisᵊn\ *vb* **listened; listened; listening** \-s(ᵊ)niŋ\ **listens** [ME *listnen*, alter. (influenced by *listen* to listen, fr. OE *hlystan*, fr. *hlyst* hearing) of OE *hlysnan;* akin to OHG *lūstrēn* to listen, ON *hlust* hearing, ear, OIr *cluas* ear, Skt *śroṣati* he hears, OE *hlūd* loud — more at LOUD] *vt, archaic* **:** to give ear to **:** HEAR ⟨lady, vouchsafe to ~ what I say —Shak.⟩ ~ *vi* **1 :** to pay attention to sound **:** prepare oneself to hear ⟨stood erect and quiet as if ~*ing* —O.E.Rölvaag⟩ ⟨partial heart block may be determined by ~*ing* with the stethoscope —H. G.Armstrong⟩ ⟨he'd ~ nervously to the gunfire —Ira Wolfert⟩ ⟨liked to follow him about and talk with him or ~ to him ask . . . devastating questions of their elders —Irwin Edman⟩ — often used in imperative ⟨~ to this from a great philosopher —Brand Blanshard⟩; used dial. with *at* ⟨~ at that mother bird —J.H.Stuart⟩ ⟨got a radio . . . we could ~ at —Vereen Bell⟩ **2 :** to hear with thoughtful attention **:** consider seriously **:** HEED ⟨have heard but not ~*ed* —R.L.Shayon⟩ ⟨frame an issue to which voters would ~ —F.L.Paxson⟩ ⟨had not the slightest intention of ~*ing* to the grievances of the colonies —H.E.Scudder⟩ **3 :** to be alert to catch an expected sound — usu. used with *for* ⟨~*ed* for his step in the hall⟩ **4** *slang* **:** to make an impression on a listener **:** SOUND ⟨it doesn't ~ right —Mark Reed⟩ ⟨it ~*s* to me as though the wise guys had been giving him a tip to lay off —*New Republic*⟩ ⟨why do some bands ~ better than others —*Musical Enterprise*⟩

2**listen** \"\ *n* -s **:** an act of listening ⟨listened, and with each ~ the game grew clearer —Rudyard Kipling⟩

lis·ten·able \-s(ᵊ)nəbəl\ *adj* **:** agreeable to the ear ⟨produces highly ~ music —Norman Cousins⟩

lis·ten·er \-s(ᵊ)nə(r)\ *n* -s **1 :** one that listens ⟨to enjoy conversation means to be a good ~ as well as a good talker⟩ ⟨this book . . . is not intended to appeal to the musicologist nor yet to the untrained ~ —Ralph Hill⟩ ⟨dogs make good ~*s* on a frontline patrol⟩ **2 :** one that sets himself to hear ⟨~*s* wrote in to congratulate the radio actor on his performance⟩; *specif* **:** AUDITOR 5

listener-in \'=(=)=;'=\ *n, pl* **listeners-in** [*listen in* + *-er*] **:** one that listens in **:** AUDITOR, EAVESDROPPER

lis·ten·er·ship \'=(=)=,ship\ *n* **:** the extent of a radio audience or the appeal of a radio program in number of listeners ⟨broadcasting in so many languages . . . it is hard even to guess at our ~ —Osmond Dowling⟩ ⟨nor were they or the company disappointed by the ~ of the program —*Advertising Age*⟩

listen in *vi* **1 :** to tune in to or monitor a transmission ⟨*listened in* last night to Continental stations —B.L.K. Henderson⟩ ⟨*listen in* on the submarine-bell receivers for the noises made by the propellers of passing vessels —*Scientific American*⟩ ⟨*listen in* on the enemy's communications line⟩ **2 :** to give ear to a conversation without participating in it ⟨I remember *listening in* while a foreman and his girl workers were discussing who was going to work —Sam Pollock⟩; *esp* **:** EAVESDROP ⟨*listen in* on a party line⟩ ⟨when they speak from a telephone booth in a hotel, everybody sitting in the lobby *listens in* —A.T.Weaver⟩

1**lis·ten·ing** \'lis(ᵊ)niŋ\ *n* -s [ME *listning*, fr. gerund of *listnen* to listen] **:** the act of one that listens; *esp* **:** the monitoring of a foreign broadcast ⟨methods used internally to combat foreign ~ —Tangye Lean⟩

2**listening** *adj* [fr. pres. part. of 1*listen*] **1 :** alert to or receptive of sound ⟨two underwater ~ stations —J.W.Cross⟩; *specif* **:** receiving radio broadcasts ⟨~ homes . . . were presumably exposed to the product's other forms of advertising —T.J. Allard⟩ **2 :** facilitating the reception of sound ⟨~ galleries⟩ ⟨wore his ~ button in his ear —William Faulkner⟩

listening post *n* **1 :** a center for gathering intelligence concerning an adversary ⟨a master hand at reading political riddles, with a thousand *listening posts* throughout the country —Charles Michelson⟩ ⟨establishment of normal diplomatic relations . . . will give us *listening posts* behind the bamboo curtain —N.D.Palmer⟩; *specif* **:** a concealed forward military position occupied during periods of reduced visibility for the purpose of detecting enemy activity by listening **2 :** a shortwave radio station capable of monitoring foreign broadcasts ⟨a *listening post*, whither high-powered radio sets daily brought news and views direct from all the continents —*Christian Science Monitor*⟩

1**list·er** \'listə(r)\ *n* -s [7*list* + *-er*] **:** one that lists or catalogs: as **a :** ASSESSOR 2 ⟨once every four years the ~*s* . . . reappraise all the real and personal property in the township —J.A. Kouwenhoven⟩ **b :** an employee of a woodworking establishment who estimates the cost of materials and labor for work done **c :** a laundry worker who itemizes the articles in bundles of soiled laundry

2**lister** \"\ *n* -s [5*list* + *-er*] **1 :** a double-moldboard plow that throws a ridge of earth both ways, is frequently equipped to prepare a seedbed at the bottom of the furrow by means of a small subsoiling attachment, and is used mainly in growing sorghum, corn, and cotton in the central and southern great plains where rainfall is limited — called also *middlebreaker, middle-burster, middlebuster, middlesplitter* **2** *or* **lister-planter** \'=,=;=\ **:** a lister plow with an attachment for dropping seeds into the furrow

lis·tera \'listərə\ *n, cap* [NL, after Martin *Lister* †1712 Eng. physician] **:** a genus of opposite-leaved orchids native to the north temperate and arctic zones and having racemose greenish flowers without spurs — see TWAYBLADE

lis·ter bag *also* **lys·ter bag** \'listə(r)-\ *n, usu cap L* [after Col. William J. *Lyster* †1947 Am. army medical officer] **:** a canvas water bag used esp. for supplying troops with chemically treated drinking water

lister cultivator *n* [2*lister*] **:** a cultivator usu. having blades designed to throw soil toward the roots of a crop, two heavy furrow balance wheels, and two wheels to hold the machine on the ridges

1**lis·ter·el·la** \,listə'relə\ [NL, fr. Joseph *Lister* †1912 Eng. surgeon and bacteriologist + NL *-ella*] *syn of* LISTERIA

2**listerella** \"\ *n* -s **:** LISTERIA 2

lis·te·ria \li'stirēə\ *n* [NL, fr. Joseph *Lister* + NL *-ia*] **1** *cap* **:** a genus of small gram-positive flagellated bacterial rods (family Corynebacteriaceae) of which the chief and type species (*L. monocytogenes*) causes infectious mononucleosis in man and a wide variety of infections in mammals **2** -s **:** any bacterium of the genus *Listeria* — called also *listerella*

lis·te·ri·an \(')li;stirēən\ *adj, often cap* [Joseph *Lister* + E *-ian*] **:** of or relating to listerism or to Joseph Lister

lis·te·ri·o·sis \(,)li,stirē'ōsəs\ *also* **lis·ter·el·lo·sis** \,listərə'lōsəs\ *n, pl* **listerio·ses** *also* **listerello·ses** \-ō,sēz\ [NL, fr. *Listeria* or *Listerella* + *-osis*] **:** a serious commonly fatal disease of a great variety of wild and domestic mammals and birds and occas. man caused by a bacterium (*Listeria monocytogenes*) and taking the form of a severe encephalitis accompanied by disordered movements usu. ending in paralysis, fever, monocytosis, and sometimes abortion — compare CIRCLING DISEASE

lis·ter·ism \'listə,rizəm\ *n* -s *often cap* [Joseph *Lister* + E *-ism*] **1 :** the use of an antiseptic on the field of a surgical operation **2 :** aseptic and antiseptic surgery

lis·ter·ize \-,rīz\ *vt* -ED/-ING/-S *often cap* [Joseph *Lister* + E *-ize*] **:** to treat by means of listerian methods

lister ridge *n* **:** a raised strip of ground thrown up by a lister to form a seedbed

l'i·stes·so tem·po \lē'ste(,)sō'tem(,)pō\ *adv* [It] **:** in the same tempo as before — used as a direction in music

listful *adj* [3*list* + *-ful*] *obs* **:** ATTENTIVE ⟨the shepherd swains . . . with greedy ~ ears —Edmund Spenser⟩

1**list·ing** \'listiŋ\ *n* -s [ME, fr. *liste, list* strip, selvage + *-ing* — more at LIST (strip)] **1 :** 4LIST 4a **2 a :** the furrowing of soil esp. for seedbeds in which row crops are sown in the furrows **b :** the method of planting crops in a furrow with a lister **3 :** a narrow strip cut from the edge of a board

2**listing** *n* -s [fr. gerund of 7*list*] **1** *archaic* **:** ENLISTMENT **2 a :** an act or instance of making or including in a list or catalog; *specif* **:** the admission of securities to trading on a securities exchange **b :** 6LIST 1 ⟨made a ~ of the ten most intelligent animals —Charles Mulvey⟩ ⟨an important annotated ~ —*Middle East Jour.*⟩ **3 a :** an authorization to a real-estate broker to sell or rent property **b :** a broker's record of available properties **c :** a piece of property listed with a real-estate broker

list·less \'listləs\ *adj* [ME *listles*, fr. *list* desire + *-les* -less — more at LIST (desire)] **:** characterized by lack of inclination or impetus to exertion **:** LANGUID, SPIRITLESS ⟨~ stance⟩ ⟨~ voice⟩ ⟨a cold and ~ day of autumn —Edith Sitwell⟩ ⟨hearings . . . have been ~, seldom drawing more than two committee members —*New Republic*⟩ **syn** see LANGUID

list·less·ly *adv* **:** in a listless manner ⟨shook hands rather ~ —A.S.Crockett⟩

list·less·ness *n* -ES **:** the quality or state of being listless

list price *n* **:** the basic price of an item as published in a catalog, price list, or advertisement but subject to trade, quantity, and other discounts

lists *pres 3d sing of* LIST, *pl of* LIST

list system *n* **:** a system of proportional representation under which a voter chooses between party lists each containing as many names as there are representatives to be chosen and the number of candidates declared elected from each list is determined by the percentage cast for each list out of the total vote ⟨all of the *list systems* . . . give the voter little or no discretion in choosing particular candidates —H.F.Gosnell⟩ — compare HARE SYSTEM, PREFERENTIAL VOTING, SINGLE TRANSFERABLE VOTE

li·su *or* **lis·su** \'lē;sü\ *n, pl* **lisu** *or* **lisus** *or* **lissu** *or* **lissus**

usu cap **1 a :** a Tibeto-Burman people inhabiting the hilly Salween drainage in the Yunnan-Burma borderlands **b :** a member of such people **2 :** the north Lolo dialect of the Lisu people

liszt·i·an \'listēən\ *adj, usu cap* [Franz von *Liszt* †1886 Hungarian piano virtuoso and composer + E *-ian*] **:** of, relating to, or characteristic of Franz Liszt or his music

¹lit \'lit\ *vt* **lited** *or* **litted**; **lited** *or* **litted**; **liting** *or* **litting**; **lits** [ME *liten, litten,* fr. ON *lita* to dye, fr. *litr* color — more at LITMUS] *Scot* **:** DYE

²lit \"\ *n* -s [ME, fr. ON *litr* color] *Scot* **:** DYE, DYESTUFF

³lit *adj* [fr. past part. of ³*light*] **:** LIGHTED: as **a :** ILLUMINATED ⟨a brightly ~ room⟩ **b :** IGNITED ⟨~ candle⟩ ⟨~ firecracker⟩ **c** *slang* **:** intoxicated by liquor or narcotics ⟨not exactly ~ but considerably exalted —Hans Zinsser⟩

lit *abbr* **1** liter **2** literal; literally **3** literary **4** literature

lit·a·ny \'lit(ᵊ)nē, -ni\ *n* -ES [alter. (influenced by LL *litania* litany) of ME *letanie,* fr. OF, fr. LL *litania,* fr. LGk *litaneia,* fr. Gk, entreaty, supplication, fr. *litaneuein* to entreat, supplicate, fr. *litanos* entreating, fr. *litē* supplication; akin to OE *līm* lime — more at LIME] **1 a :** a liturgical prayer consisting of a series of invocations and supplications either read or sung usu. with alternate responses by clergy and congregation **b :** a liturgical procession during which clergy and congregation sing or chant prayers **2 :** a ritualistic repetition of prayers usu. of praise and supplication ⟨in his morning ~ he could pray to be kept from lasciviousness —Carl Van Doren⟩ **3 :** a recital or chant having the resonant or repetitive qualities associated with a litany ⟨the author recites his ~ of the great mysteries — birth, death, flood, water, sky —Sidney Alexander⟩ ⟨the shrill *litanies* of shopboys —James Joyce⟩ ⟨rehearsed her ~ of symptoms —John Dollard & N.E.Miller⟩

li·tas \'lē,täs\ *n, pl* **li·tai** \-,tā\ [Lith] **1 :** the basic unit of monetary value of Lithuania from 1923 to 1940 **2 :** a silver coin representing one litas

li·tchi \'lī(,)chē, 'lē(-\ *n* [Chin (Pek) *li⁴ chih¹*] **1** *or* **litchi nut** *or* **li·chee** *also* **lee·chee** *or* **li·chi** *or* **ly·chee** \"\ -s **:** the fruit of a Chinese tree (*Litchi chinensis*) that is about one inch in diameter and has a hard scaly outer covering and a small hard seed surrounded by white translucent watery flesh which on drying becomes firm, sweetish, and black and constitutes the edible part of the fruit **2 a** *cap* **:** a genus of Chinese trees (family Sapindaceae) with pinnate leaves and regular greenish white flowers in terminal panicles **b** -s **:** any tree of the genus *Litchi*; *esp* **:** a tree (*L. chinensis*) often cultivated in the Philippines, India, and elsewhere for its edible fruits

lit clos \'lē'klō\ *n* [F, lit., enclosed bed] **:** a free-standing or built-in French bed enclosed in wooden panels

LitD *abbr or n* -s **:** a doctor of literature

lit de re·pos \-dərə'pō\ *n* [F, lit., bed of repose] **:** CHAISE LONGUE

¹lite \'līt\ *n* -s [ME *lut, lit,* fr. OE *lȳt,* n. & adj. — more at LITTLE] *dial Eng* **:** LITTLE

²lite \"\ *adj* [ME *lut, lit,* fr. OE *lȳt*] *dial Eng* **:** FEW, LITTLE

³lite \"\ *vi* -ED/-ING/-S [ME *liten,* of Scand origin; akin to ON *hlīta* to rely on, trust; akin to OE *hleonian* to lean — more at LEAN] *dial Eng* **1 :** WAIT, EXPECT **2 :** RELY, TRUST

-lite *also* **-lyte** \,līt, *usu* -īd·+V\ *n comb form* [F *-lite,* alter. of *-lithe,* fr. Gk *lithos* stone] **1 a :** mineral **:** rock **:** fossil in stone ⟨cryo*lite*⟩ ⟨rhyo*lite*⟩ ⟨dendro*lite*⟩ **b :** -LITH 1b ⟨albo*lite*⟩ **2 :** -LITH 2 ⟨phlebo*lite*⟩

li·ter *or* **li·tre** \'lēd·ə(r), -ētə-\ *n* -s [F *litre,* alter. of *litron,* an old measure, modif. of ML *litra,* fr. Gk, a weight, a coin] **:** a metric unit of capacity equal to the volume occupied by one kilogram of water at 4° C and at the standard atmospheric pressure of 760 millimeters equivalent to 1 cubic decimeter — see METRIC SYSTEM table

lit·er·a·cy \'lid·ərəsē, 'litər-, 'li·trə-, -si\ *n* -ES ['*literate* + *-cy*] **1 :** the quality or state of being literate **2 :** an ability to read a short simple passage and answer questions about it

¹lit·er·al \'lid·ərəl, 'litər-, 'li·trəl\ *adj* [ME, fr. MF, fr. ML *litteralis, literalis,* fr. L, of a letter, of writing, fr. *littera, litera* letter & *litterae, literae* epistle, writing + *-alis* -al — more at LETTER] **1 a :** according with the letter of the scriptures ⟨amillennialists recognize the need for ~ interpretation —*Bibliotheca Sacra*⟩ **b :** adhering to fact or to the ordinary construction or primary meaning of a term or expression **:** ACTUAL, OBVIOUS ⟨the need for a ~ breathing spell forces the fish to let go —L.P.Schultz⟩ ⟨a ~ solitude like a desert —G.K.Chesterton⟩ ⟨liberty in the ~ sense is impossible —B.N.Cardozo⟩ ⟨reactionary in the ~ sense of the word, but did not agree . . . how far back they wanted to go —William Petersen⟩ **c :** being without exaggeration or embellishment **:** PLAIN, UNADORNED ⟨~ prose⟩ ⟨a love of ~ truth —Robert Graves⟩ **d :** characterized by a concern mainly with facts **:** PROSAIC, UNIMAGINATIVE ⟨the opposite of a liberal education . . . is a ~ education —Sidney Hook⟩ ⟨if a painter tells a story . . . even the most ~ person will have no difficulty in understanding what the artist is trying to say —Huntington Hartford⟩ ⟨statue . . . dressed as he had been when alive, in accordance with the ~ standards of late-century monumental sculpture —J.T.Soby⟩ ⟨a ~ and academic reading of a classic score —Virgil Thomson⟩ **2 a :** of, relating to, or expressed in letters ⟨the distress signal SOS has no ~ meaning⟩ ⟨~ coefficient⟩ ⟨cryptographic codes may be either ~ or numerical⟩ **b :** resulting from the mistaken use or omission of a letter ⟨~ error⟩ **3 :** reproduced word for word **:** EXACT, VERBATIM ⟨~ translation⟩

²literal \"\ *n* -s **:** a small error usu. of a single letter in writing or printing ⟨in setting type, allow enough space so that a line will accommodate any ~ the proofreader may find⟩

literal contract *n, civil law* **:** an obligation fully evidenced by writing and binding upon the party signing and promising therein

lit·er·al·ism \'lid·ərə,lizəm, 'litərə,-, 'li·trə,-\ *n* -s **1 :** adherence to the explicit substance of an idea or expression ⟨Biblical ~ . . . has never realized that no historic document is self-explanatory —W.L.Sperry⟩ ⟨the book employed Marxian dialectics with ruthless ~ —Leo Gurko⟩ ⟨the spirit of legalistic ~ —J.C.Swaim⟩ **2 :** fidelity to observable fact **:** REALISM ⟨picturesque scenery painted with laborious ~ —*Amer. Guide Series: Pa.*⟩

lit·er·al·ist \-ləst\ *n* -s **:** one that advocates or practices literalism ⟨the ~ wants to hear cowbells in his music —H.A. Overstreet⟩; *specif* **:** ¹FUNDAMENTALIST 1 ⟨others of the early church fathers . . . were not ~s in regard to the Mosaic account of creation —V.A.Rice & F.N.Andrews⟩

lit·er·al·is·tic \¦==,=¦listik\ *adj* **:** of or relating to literalism — **lit·er·al·is·ti·cal·ly** \-tək(ə)lē\ *adv*

lit·er·al·i·ty \,lid·ə'raləd·ē, ,litə-, -ətē, -i\ *n* -ES **:** LITERALNESS

lit·er·al·ize \'lid·ərə,līz, 'litərə,-, 'li·trə,-\ *vt* -ED/-ING/-S **:** to make literal ⟨disposition to ~ metaphors —R.A.Vaughan⟩

lit·er·al·ly \'lid·ərəlē, 'litər(ə)l-, 'li·trə-, -li\ *adv* **1 a :** in the literal sense **:** without metaphor or exaggeration **:** EXPLICITLY ⟨he can always be taken seriously; he cannot always be taken ~ —E.R.Bentley⟩ ⟨interpret the Bible figuratively as well as ~ —R.W.Murray⟩ **b :** in the literal meaning of the term **:** ACTUALLY, REALLY ⟨broke the . . . ice ~ by jointly blasting the formidable frozen barrier —Alexander Kendrick⟩ ⟨migrations of passenger pigeons . . . crossed here by the millions, ~ darkening the sky —*Amer. Guide Series: Mich.*⟩ **2 :** with exact equivalence **:** VERBATIM ⟨simultaneous interpreters translate the speaker's words ~⟩ **3 :** in effect **:** VIRTUALLY ⟨a collection of . . . devices that will ~ make your hair stand on end —Horace Sutton⟩ ⟨this boy ~ rode roughshod over the patient —L.E.Hinsie⟩

lit·er·al·ness \-rəlnəs\ *n* -ES **:** the quality or state of being literal

lit·er·ar·i·ly \¦lid·ə¦rerəlē, ¦litə¦r-,-li\ *adv* **:** in a literary manner

lit·er·ar·i·ness \'==,rēnəs, -rin-\ *n* -ES **:** the quality or state of being literary

lit·er·ary \'lid·ə,rerē, 'litə,r-, -ri\ *adj* [in sense 1, fr. L *littera, litera* letter + E *-ary;* in other senses, fr. F *littéraire,* fr. L *litterarius,* *literarius* of writing, fr. *litterae, literae* writing + *-arius* -ary — more at LETTER] **1** *archaic* **:** ¹LITERAL 2a **2 a :** of, relating to, or having the characteristics of humane learning ⟨the educational system should provide a ~ as well as a rational education —G.K.Chalmers⟩ ⟨~ institution⟩ **b :** of, relating to, or having the characteristics of literature ⟨renouncing the dogma that Latin was the ~ language of Italy, began to write in Tuscan —G.C.Sellery⟩ ⟨described his types in the grand ~ manner, with great subtlety and penetration —William Stephenson⟩ ⟨a ~ magazine may deal with . . . anything at all, so long as each article is a piece of literature —R.G.Howarth⟩ **c :** BOOKISH 2 ⟨this work is too wordy, and the dialogue has a muffled ~ flavor —T.G.Bergin⟩ **d :** of or relating to books ⟨~ agent⟩ ⟨~ manuscripts⟩ **3 a :** having a firsthand knowledge of literature **:** WELL-READ ⟨he is ~, given to quoting to himself rather long stretches of remembered lines —F.J.Hoffman⟩ **b :** of, relating to, or concerned with men of letters or with writing as a profession ⟨a new star in the ~ firmament —*Yankee*⟩ ⟨for her admirable series of ~ biographies she has chosen . . . nineteenth-century poets —Harrison Smith⟩ ⟨was rather ~ in college —Scott Fitzgerald⟩ **4** *of a painting or sculpture* **:** characterized by a primary interest in depicting an event, story, or allegory **:** ANECDOTAL

literary apabhramsa *n* **:** APABHRAMSA C

lit·er·ary·ism \-rē,izəm\ *n* -s **:** an instance of or tendency to use excessive refinement of expression in written compositions ⟨every ~ . . . fritters away a scrap of the reader's patience —Ezra Pound⟩

literary property *n* **1 a :** the property an author or those claiming under him has in the written product of his intellectual skill and labor either before or after general publication and either at common law or under statutory copyright **b :** the written product of an author or any copy thereof **2 :** the property an author or those claiming under him has in his work under common law prior to copyright consisting chiefly of his right to control the use, enjoyment, and disposition of such work for profit or any purpose, this right being superseded by statutory copyright and lost by dedication of such work to the public — compare COPYRIGHT

¹lit·er·ate \'lid·ərət, 'litərət, 'li·trət, *usu* -əd·+V\ *adj* [ME *literat,* fr. L *litteratus, literatus,* adj. & n., fr. *litterae, literae* epistle, writing, literature + *-atus* -ate — more at LETTER] **1 a :** characterized by or possessed of learning **:** EDUCATED, CULTURED ⟨one of the more ~ analysts working in this area —Webster Schott⟩ ⟨citizens . . . highly ~ in economic matters —Alan Valentine⟩ ⟨the familiar magic in words and miracles in perception that are Shakespeare's . . . provide the mind with a ~ and often gusty evening —*New Republic*⟩ ⟨it is a ~ community, with several good museums and its own symphony orchestra⟩ **b :** able to read and write — opposed to *illiterate* ⟨a large percentage of the world's adult population is ~ in some language⟩ **2 a :** versed or immersed in literature or creative writing **:** LITERARY ⟨a novel . . . of the former master of satire, who nevertheless is always ~ and engrossing —Harvey Breit⟩ **b :** dealing with literature or belles lettres ⟨innovators in this form of ~ publishing —Seymour Krim⟩ **c :** well executed or technically proficient **:** POLISHED, LUCID ⟨though it is . . . always cinematically ~, the picture is longer on talk than on action —*Time*⟩ ⟨assembling doctoral findings into a ~ thesis —J.P.Elder⟩

²literate \"\ *n* -s [L *litteratus, literatus*] **1 a :** an educated person **b :** one who can read and write **2 :** one admitted to holy orders in the Church of England without having a university degree

lit·er·ate·ly *adv* **:** in a literate manner

lit·e·ra·ti \,lid·ə'räd·(,)ē, ,litə-, -'rä¦, ¦(,)t¦, ¦i *also* -'rā,tī\ *n pl* [obs. It & L; obs. It *litterati,* fr. L, pl. of *litteratus*] **1 :** the educated class **:** INTELLIGENTSIA ⟨these ~ educated to admire the spirit of classical antiquity —C.J.Friedrich⟩ ⟨the Indian ~ —Selig Harrison⟩ **2 :** MEN OF LETTERS ⟨hegira of many of the ~ to Europe, where they hoped to live the creative life and produce . . . poems and novels —C.I.Glicksberg⟩; *specif* **:** AVANT-GARDE 2 ⟨professed intense scorn for its crackpot ~ and painters —S.J.Perelman⟩

lit·e·ra·tim \-'räd·əm, -ātəm\ *adv (or adj)* [ML, fr. L *littera, litera* letter — more at LETTER] **:** letter for letter

lit·er·a·tion \,lid·ə'rāshən, ,litə'-\ *n* -s [L *littera, litera* letter + E *-ation* — more at LETTER] **:** the representation of sounds or words by letters

lit·e·ra·to \,==¦rä¦d·(,)ō, -'nä¦, ¦(,)tō\ [It, fr. L *litteratus, literatus* literate — more at LITERATE] *sing of* LITERATI

lit·er·a·tor \'lid·ə,rād·ə(r), 'litə-, -,rātə-\ *n* -s [L *litterator, literator* grammarian, critic, fr. *litteratus, literatus* + *-or*] **1** *archaic* **:** one who engages in textual criticism or descriptive bibliography **2** [modif. of F *littérateur* — more at LITTERATEUR] **:** LITTERATEUR

lit·er·a·ture \'lid·ərə,chu̇(ə)r, 'litərə-, 'li·trə-, 'lid·ə(r),ch-, -,chu̇ə, -,chə(r), -rə,tyu̇-, -rə,tu̇-\ *n* -s *often attrib* [ME *litterature,* fr. L *litteratura, literatura* writing, grammar, learning, fr. *litteratus, literatus* literate + *-ura* -ure] **1** *archaic* **:** knowledge of books **:** literary culture ⟨in many things he was grotesquely ignorant; he was a man of very small ~ —W.D. Howells⟩ **2 :** the production of literary work esp. as an occupation ⟨continually dissociated himself from ~ . . . as a profession —Philip Rahv⟩ **3 a :** writings in prose or verse; *esp* **:** writings having excellence of form or expression and expressing ideas of permanent or universal interest ⟨~ stands related to man as science stands to nature —J.H.Newman⟩ ⟨our conceptions of types of character and the manifold variations of these types is due mainly to ~ —John Dewey⟩ **b :** the body of written works produced in a particular language, country, or age ⟨they speak a . . . sonorous and flexible language, and their ~ is not unworthy of their language —H. T.Buckle⟩ ⟨that superb mess of thought and observation, lust, rhetoric, and pedantry, that we call Renaissance ~ —Clive Bell⟩ **c :** the body of writings on a particular subject ⟨the ~ on field sports is a mass of technicalities held together with a sticky kind of nature loving —J.M.Barzun⟩ ⟨any scientist . . . will answer that at the beginning of an attack on any problem his first task is to look up the existing ~ —T.H.Savory⟩ **d :** leaflets, handbills, circulars, or other printed matter of any kind ⟨asked for volunteers to distribute campaign ~⟩ ⟨induced to migrate by glowing real-estate development ~ —*Amer. Guide Series: Tenn.*⟩ **4 :** the aggregate of musical compositions ⟨programs . . . representing within any one year the greatest possible breadth of musical ~ —William Schuman⟩; *specif* **:** compositions of regional or historical significance or for any particular instrument or group of instruments ⟨a cross section of the Brahms piano ~ —*Saturday Rev.*⟩

literature search *n* **:** the methodical investigation of all published sources for information bearing on a usu. scientific or technological subject ⟨it is in chemistry that the *literature search* has attained full stature —*New Technical Books*⟩

lit·e·ra·tus \,lid·ə'räd·əs, ,litə-, -rä-, -təs\ *n* -ES [L *litteratus, literatus* literate — more at LITERATE] **:** a member of the literati

liters *pl of* LITER

lites *pl of* LITE, *pres 3d sing of* LITE

lith \'lith\ *n* -s [ME, fr. OE; akin to MD *lit, let* limb, part of the body, OHG *lid,* ON *lithr,* Goth *lithus* limb, L *lituus* crooked staff carried by augurers, Toch A & B *lit-* to go away, fall down, OE *eln* ell — more at ELL] **1** *Scot* **:** JOINT, LIMB, MEMBER — often used in the phrase *lith and limb* **2** *Scot* **:** DIVISION, SEGMENT

lith- *or* **litho-** *comb form* [L, fr. Gk, fr. *lithos*] **1 :** stone ⟨*lith*anthrax⟩ ⟨*litho*phyte⟩ ⟨*litho*graph⟩ **2 :** calculus ⟨*lith*osis⟩ ⟨*litho*logy⟩ **3** [NL *lithium*] **:** lithium ⟨*lith*ic⟩ ⟨*lith*emia⟩

-lith \,lith\ *n comb form* -s [NL *-lithus* & F *-lithe,* fr. Gk *lithos* stone] **1 a :** stone **:** structure or implement of stone ⟨cyclo*lith*⟩ ⟨mono*lith*⟩ ⟨eo*lith*⟩ **b :** artificial stone **:** cement ⟨grano*lith*⟩ **2** *med* **:** calculus ⟨angio*lith*⟩ ⟨nephro*lith*⟩ **3 :** -LITE 1a ⟨cocco*lith*⟩ ⟨zoo*lith*⟩

lith *abbr* lithograph; lithography

li·tham \lē'thäm\ *n* -s [Ar *lithām*] **:** a strip of cloth wound round the head covering all but the eyes and worn by Tuaregs of the Sahara desert

lith·arge \'li,thärj, -äj, =='=\ *n* -s [ME *litarge, litharge,* fr. MF, fr. L *lithargyrus,* fr. Gk *lithargyros,* fr. *lith-* stone + *argyros* silver — more at ARGENT] **1 :** lead monoxide obtained in flake or powdered form by processes carried out at temperatures above the melting point of the oxide; *broadly* **:** LEAD MONOXIDE — compare MASSICOT 1 **2** *also* **lith·ar·gite** \-,jīt\ **:** lead monoxide occurring native in the form of red crystals — compare MASSICOT 2

¹lithe \'līth, 'lith\ *adj* -ER/-EST [ME *lithe, lith,* fr. OE *līthe* mild, gentle; akin to OS *līthi* mild, gentle, OHG *lindi,* L *lentus* flexible, slow, W *llathr* bright, smooth, Skt *latā* vine, liana; basic meaning: flexible] **1** *chiefly Scot* **:** mild and soothing **:** GENTLE, SERENE ⟨sang the mass with ~ devotion —Bruce Marshall⟩ **2 a :** agile and lissome **:** easily flexed **:** SUPPLE, RESILIENT ⟨~ dancing girls⟩ ⟨saw the ~ mechanic's body . . . flex like a drawn bow —Waldo Frank⟩ ⟨the long palette knife, with its thin blade of ~ steel —Oscar Wilde⟩ **b :** characterized by effortless grace ⟨charming and ~ in writing —*Times Lit. Supp.*⟩ **syn** see SUPPLE

²lithe \'līth\ *vt* -ED/-ING/-S *dial* **:** to make thick (as broth)

³lithe \"\ *vb* -ED/-ING/-S [ME *lithen,* fr. ON *hlýtha;* akin to OE *hlȳdan* to make a noise, shout, OFris *hlēda* to make a noise, shout, OHG *hlūten* to make a noise, OE *hlūd* loud — more at LOUD] *archaic* **:** LISTEN, HEAR

⁴lithe \"\ *n* -s [perh. alter. of *lewth*] *Scot* **:** a sheltered place **:** SHELTER

lithe·ly *adv* [¹*lithe* + *-ly*] **:** in a supple manner **:** FLEXIBLY, RESILIENTLY

li·the·mia *also* **li·thae·mia** \lə'thēmēə\ *n* -s [NL, fr. *lith-* + *-emia, -aemia*] **:** a condition in which excess uric acid is present in the blood — **li·the·mic** *also* **li·thae·mic** \-mik\ *adj*

lithe·ness *n* -ES [ME *lithnes,* fr. *lith, lithe* lithe + *-nes* -ness — more at LITHE] **:** the quality or state of being lithe **:** SUPPLENESS, FLEXIBILITY

lith·er \'lithə(r)\ *adj* [ME, bad, wicked, wretched, lazy, fr. OE *lȳthre* bad, wicked, wretched; akin to OE *loddere* beggar, MLG *lüder* dissolute person, *lodder* shiftless person, OHG *lottar* insignificant, empty, MHG *liederlich* slight, insignificant, OIr *lott* whore] **1** *now dial Eng* **:** disinclined to exertion **:** SLOTHFUL, LAZY **2** *now dial Eng* **a :** easily displaced **:** YIELDING ⟨winged through the ~ sky —Shak.⟩ **b :** supple and active **:** AGILE ⟨boys . . . are made that ~ —Maxwell Gray⟩

lith·er·ness *n* -ES [ME *lithernesse* wickedness, laziness, fr. *lither* + *-nesse* -ness] *now dial Eng* **:** the quality or state of being lither **:** LAZINESS

lithe·some \'līthsəm, 'lith-\ *adj* [¹*lithe* + *-some*] **:** characterized by agile grace ⟨an altogether more ~ and none the less useful wolfhound —*Nat'l Geographic*⟩ **syn** see SUPPLE

lithe·some·ness *n* -ES **:** the quality or state of being lithesome

lithi- *or* **lithio-** *comb form* [NL *lithium*] **:** lithium ⟨*lithio*philite⟩ ⟨*lithi*ate⟩

lith·ia \'lithēə\ *n* -s [NL, fr. *lith-* + *-ia* (as in *magnesia*)] **1 :** lithium oxide Li_2O obtained as a white crystalline substance (as by burning lithium in oxygen) **2** [NL, fr. *lithium* + *-a*] **:** LITHIASIS 1

lithia emerald *n* **:** HIDDENITE

lithia mica *n* **:** LEPIDOLITE

li·thi·a·sis \lə'thīəsəs\ *n, pl* **lithia·ses** \-,sēz\ [NL, fr. Gk, fr. *lith-* + *-iasis*] **1 :** the formation or presence of stony concretions in the body (as in the urinary tract and gall bladder) — usu. used in combination ⟨chole*lithiasis*⟩ ⟨nephro*lithiasis*⟩ **2 :** an abnormal development of sclerotic or grit cells in a plant (as the pear)

lith·i·ate \'lithē,āt, *usu* -ād·+V\ *vt* -ED/-ING/-S [*lithi-* + *-ate*] **:** to combine or impregnate with lithium or a lithium compound ⟨*lithiated* water⟩

lithia water *n* **:** a mineral water characterized by the presence of lithium salts (as lithium carbonate or lithium chloride)

lith·ic \'lithik, -ēk\ *adj* [Gk *lithikos,* fr. *lith-* + *-ikos* -ic] **1 :** of or relating to stone ⟨eruptions in which only old ~ debris is expelled —*Jour. of Geol.*⟩; *esp* **:** made of stone ⟨~ artifacts⟩ **2** [*lith-* + *-ic*] **:** of or relating to lithium — **lith·i·cal·ly** \-thək(ə)lē, -ēk-, -li\ *adv*

-lith·ic \¦lithik, -ēk\ *adj comb form* [*lithic*] **1 :** relating to or characteristic of a (specified) stage in man's use of stone as a cultural tool ⟨Neo*lithic*⟩ ⟨pre*lithic*⟩ ⟨techno*lithic*⟩ **2** *bot* **:** stone ⟨epi*lithic*⟩

li·thid·i·o·nite \lə'thidēə,nīt\ *n* -s [It *litidionite,* fr. Gk *lithidion* pebble (dim. of *lithos* stone) + It *-ite*] **:** a mineral $(Cu,Na_2,K_2)Si_3O_7$ consisting of a rare silicate of alkalies and copper

lithier *comparative of* LITHY

lithiest *superlative of* LITHY

lith·i·fi·ca·tion \,lithəfə'kāshən\ *n* -s [fr. *lithify,* after such pairs as E *edify: edification*] **:** the conversion of unconsolidated sediments into solid rock

lith·i·fy \'==,fī\ *vb* -ED/-ING/-ES [*lith-* + *-ify*] *vt* **:** to change to stone **:** PETRIFY ⟨coal is carbonized and *lithified* vegetation —H.A.Meyerhoff⟩ ~ *vi* **:** to become changed into stone ⟨sands ~ into sandstones —C.M.Nevin⟩

lithing *pres part of* LITHE

lith·i·oph·i·lite \,lithē'äfə,līt\ *n* -s [*lithi-* + *phil-* + *-ite*] **:** a mineral $LiMnPO_4$ consisting of a phosphate of lithium and manganese usu. containing iron and being isomorphous with triphylite

lith·i·oph·o·rite \-fə,rīt\ *n* -s [G *lithiophorit,* fr. *lithi-* + *phor-* + *-it* -ite] **:** a mineral $LiMn_3Al_2O_9.3H_2O(?)$ consisting of hydrous oxide of manganese, aluminum, and lithium

li·this·tid \lə'thistəd, -,tid\ *adj* [NL *Lithistida*] **:** of, relating to, or resembling the Lithistida or related sponges

li·this·ti·da \-,stədə\ *n pl, cap* [NL, fr. (assumed) Gk *lithistos* (verbal of Gk *lithizein* to resemble a stone, fr. *lith-* + *-izein* -ize) + NL *-ida*] *in former classifications* **:** an order of sponges (class Demospongiae) comprising well-preserved fossil sponges with a massive reticulate skeleton of fused siliceous spicules

lith·ite \'li,thīt\ *n* -s [*lith-* + *-ite*] **:** a calcareous concretion esp. in a tentaculocyst or lithocyst

lith·i·um \'lithēəm\ *n* -s [NL, fr. *lith-* + *-ium*] **:** a soft silver-white univalent element of the alkali metal group that is the lightest metal known, that occurs combined in several minerals (as amblygonite, spodumene, lepidolite, zinnwaldite), in many mineral waters, and in plant ashes, that is obtained as the metal by electrolysis of fused lithium chloride, and that is used chiefly in nuclear reactions, in metallurgy for removing gases from molten metals and making light alloys, and in the manufacture of lithium compounds — symbol *Li;* see ELEMENT table

lithium aluminum hydride *n* **:** a white flammable solid $LiAlH_4$ soluble in ether that is made by the reaction of lithium hydride and anhydrous aluminum chloride and that is used as a reducing agent esp. for organic compounds [as a carboxylic acid (RCOOH) to an alcohol (RCH_2OH)]

lithium carbonate *n* **:** a crystalline salt Li_2CO_3 used in the glass and ceramic industries and in medicine in the treatment of manic-depressive psychosis

lithium chloride *n* **:** a hygroscopic crystalline salt LiCl used chiefly in the manufacture of metallic lithium, in welding fluxes, and in the form of an aqueous solution for controlling humidity in air conditioning

lithium hydride *n* **:** a flammable crystalline solid LiH that is usu. bluish owing to traces of metallic lithium, that is made by direct union of lithium and hydrogen at high temperatures, and that is used chiefly as a source of hydrogen and in the synthesis of lithium aluminum hydride and other lithium compounds

lithium perchlorate *n* **:** a crystalline salt $LiClO_4$ useful as an oxidizer in solid rocket propellant systems

¹litho \'li,thō\ *n* -s [by shortening] **1 :** LITHOGRAPH **2 :** LITHOGRAPHY

²litho \"\ *adj* [by shortening] **:** LITHOGRAPHIC

³litho \"\ *vt* -ED/-ING/-S [by shortening] **:** LITHOGRAPH

litho- — see LITH-

lith·o·bi·o·mor·pha \,lithō,bīə'mȯrfə\ *n pl, cap* [NL, fr. *lith-* + *bi-* + *-morpha*] **:** a large order of centipedes having lateral spiracles and 15 pairs of legs in the adult and 7 pairs in the newly hatched young

li·tho·bi·us \lə'thōbēəs\ *n, cap* [NL, fr. *lith-* + Gk *bios* life — more at QUICK] **:** a large nearly cosmopolitan genus (the type of the family Lithobiidae) of centipedes having the body composed of nine long and six short segments and living usu. under stones or logs

lith·o·car·pus \,lithə'kärpəs, -kȧp-\ *n, cap* [NL, fr. *lith-* + *-carpus*] **:** a large genus of chiefly Asiatic evergreen trees (family Fagaceae) differing from *Quercus* mainly in the erect staminate catkins — see OAK, TANBARK OAK

lith·o·cholic acid \¦lithə+-\ *n* [ISV *lith-* + *cholic*] **:** a crystalline bile acid $C_{23}H_{38}(OH)COOH$ found esp. in man and the ox; 3-hydroxy-cholanic acid

lith·o·chro·my \'lithə,krōmē\ *n* -ES [*lith-* + *-chromy*] **:** the art of painting on stone

lith·o·clase \ˈ⸗⸗ˌklās, -āz\ *n* -s [F, fr. *lith-* + *-clase*] **:** a natural fracture in rock
lith·o·culture \ˈlithə+ˌ-\ *n* [*lith-* + *culture*] **:** culture of the Stone Age
lith·o·cyst \ˈ"+ˌ-\ *n* [ISV *lith-* + *cyst*] **1 :** a sac containing lithites that is found in many medusae and other invertebrates and is held to be an auditory organ **2 :** a cell that includes a cystolith
li·tho·des \ləˈthō,dēz\ *n, cap* [NL, fr. Gk *lithōdēs* resembling stone, fr. *lith-* + *-ōdēs* -ode] **:** a genus (the type of the family Lithodidae) of anomuran crabs that live in cold water toward the poles or in the deep sea
lith·o·des·ma \ˌlithəˈdezmə\ *n, pl* **lithodesma·ta** \-məd·ə\ [NL, fr. *lith-* + Gk *desma* bond — more at DESMA] **:** a small shelly plate connected with the resilium in many bivalve shells
¹**lith·o·did** \ˈlithədəd, -ōd\ *adj* [NL *Lithodes* & *Lithodidae*] **:** of or relating to the genus *Lithodes* or the family Lithodidae
²**lithodid** \"\ *n* -s **:** a crab of the genus *Lithodes* or the family Lithodidae
li·thod·o·mous \ləˈthädəməs\ *adj* [Gk *lithodomos* mason + E *-ous*] **:** burrowing in rock
li·thod·o·mus \-məs\ [NL, fr. Gk *lithodomos* mason, fr. *lith-* + *-domos* (fr. *demein* to build) — more at TIMBER] *syn of* LITHOPHAGA
lith·o·facies \ˌlithə+\ *n* [NL, fr. *lith-* + *facies*] **:** a facies characterized by a particular lithologic aspect
lith·o·gen·e·sis \"+\ *n* [NL, fr. *lith-* + *genesis*] **1 :** the science of the formation of rocks **2 :** the formation of calculi
li·thog·e·nous \ləˈthäjənəs\ *adj* [*lith-* + *-genous*] **:** that produces stone ⟨~ polyp⟩
lith·o·glyph \ˈlithəˌglif\ *n* [Gk *lithoglyphia*, fr. *lith-* + *glyphein* to engrave, carve + *-ia* -y — more at CLEAVE (split)] **1 :** an engraving on stone **2 :** an engraved stone
lith·o·glyp·tics \ˌ⸗⸗+\ *n pl but usu sing in constr* [*lith-* + *glyptics*, pl. of ¹*glyptic*] **:** the art or process of engraving gems
¹**lith·o·graph** \ˈlithəˌgraf, -raa(ə)f,-raif,-räf\ *vt* -ED/-ING/-S [back-formation fr. *lithography*] **1 :** to produce, copy, or portray by lithography **2 :** to inscribe or record by inscribing on stone or ware
²**lithograph** \"\ *n* [back-formation fr. *lithography*] **:** a print made by lithography ⟨a show of drawings and ~*s* —Arnold Bennett⟩
li·thog·ra·pher \ləˈthägrəfə(r), ˈlithəˌgrafə(r)\ *n* -s **:** one that lithographs **:** one engaged in lithography
lith·o·graph·ic \ˌlithəˈgrafik, -fēk\ *adj* [*lithography* + *-ic*] **:** of, done by, or used in lithography ⟨the ~ printing⟩ ⟨the ~ principle⟩ ⟨~ paper⟩ — **lith·o·graph·i·cal·ly** \-fək(ə)lē, -fēk-,-li\ *adv*
lithographic crayon *n* **:** a crayon or stylus of compressed grease and coloring matter used by lithographers for drawing a design on stone or metal
lithographic limestone *n* **:** a fine-grained dense limestone with conchoidal fracture formerly used in lithography
lithographic varnish *n* **:** a heat-thickened linseed oil of various viscosities used in lithography
li·thog·ra·phy \ləˈthägrəfē, -fi\ *n* -ES [G *lithographie*, fr. *lith-* + *-graphie* -graphy] **1 a :** the process of printing from a plane surface (as a smooth stone or metal plate) on which the image to be printed is ink-receptive and the blank area ink-repellent — compare OFFSET **b :** the art of making designs on lithographic surfaces **2 :** a planographic process **:** PLANOGRAPHY
lith·o·gra·vure \ˌlithəgrəˈvyu̇(ə)r, -grāˌv-, -ü̇ə\ *n* [*lith-* + *gravure*] **:** a process of photoengraving on stone
lith·oid \ˈliˌthȯid\ *also* **li·thoi·dal** \ləˈthȯidᵊl\ *adj* [*lithoid* fr. Gk *lithoeidēs*, fr. *lith-* stone + *-oeidēs* -oid; *lithoidal* fr. Gk *lithoeidēs* + E *-al*] **:** resembling a stone
lithoing *pres part of* LITHO
Lith·ol \ˈliˌthōl, -ōl\ *trademark* — used for any of a group of organic pigments most of which consist essentially of salts of difficultly soluble azo compounds; see DYE table I (under *Pigment Red 49, 52,* and *57*)
lith·ol·a·paxy \liˈthäləˌpaksē, ˈlithələ-\ *n* -ES [*lith-* + Gk *lapaxis* evacuation (fr. assumed Gk *lapaktos* — verbal of *lapassein* to empty — + *-sis*) + E *-y* — more at LAPACTIC] **:** the operation of crushing a urinary calculus in the bladder and removing the fragments
lith·o·log·ic \ˌlithəˈläjik\ *also* **lith·o·log·i·cal** \-jəkəl\ *adj* **:** of or relating to lithology — **lith·o·log·i·cal·ly** \-k(ə)lē\ *adv*
li·thol·o·gy \ləˈthäləjē, -ji\ *n* -ES [*lith-* + *-logy*] **1 :** the study of rocks **2 :** the character of a rock formation or of the rock found in a geological area or stratum expressed in terms of its structure, mineral composition, color, and texture ⟨a relation between the fossil content of a stratum and its ~ —F.J. Pettijohn⟩
lith·o·man·cy \ˈlithəˌmansē\ *n* -ES [F *lithomantie*, fr. *lith-* + *-mantie* -mancy] **:** divination by stones or by charms or talismans of stone
lith·o·marge \-ˌmärj, -äj\ *n* -s [*lith-* + L *marga* marl] **:** a smooth compact common kaolin
lith·o·meteor \ˌ⸗⸗+\ *n* [*lith-* + *meteor*] **:** a conglomeration of small solid particles (as of dust or sand) that is suspended in the atmosphere and often produces a dry haze
lith·o·mor·phic \ˌ⸗⸗ˈmȯrfik\ *adj* [*lith-* + *-morphic*] *of soils* **:** deriving color from parent material
¹**lith·on·trip·tic** \ˌli,thänˈtriptik\ *also* **lith·o·trip·tic** \ˌlithəˈ-\ *adj* [*lithontriptic* modif. (influenced by Gk *tribein* to rub) of Gk *lithōn thryptikos* stone-crushing; *lithotriptic* alter. (influenced by *lith-*) of *lithontriptic*] **:** having the quality of or used for dissolving or destroying stone in the bladder or kidneys
²**lithontriptic** \"\ *also* **lithotriptic** \"\ *n* -s **:** a lithontriptic agent
lith·o·pe·di·on \ˌlithəˈpēdēˌän\ *n* -s [NL, fr. *lith-* + Gk *paidion* small child, dim. of *paid-, pais* child — more at FEW] **:** a fetus calcified in the body of the mother
li·thoph·a·ga \ləˈthäfəgə\ *n, cap* [NL, fr. *lith-* + *-phaga*] **:** a genus of elongated bivalve mollusks (family Mytilidae) comprising the date mussels that live and bore in limestone and coral — compare PHOLAS
li·thoph·a·gous \-gəs\ *adj* [*lith-* + *-phagous*] **:** consuming stone ⟨~ mollusks⟩
lith·o·phane \ˈlithəˌfān\ *n* -s [ISV *lith-* + *-phane* (as in *diaphane*)] **:** porcelain impressed with figures that are made distinct by transmitted light (as from a lampshade) — **lith·o·phan·ic** \ˌ⸗⸗ˈfanik\ *adj*
lith·o·phile \ˈlithəˌfīl\ *adj* [*lith-* + *-phile*] **:** tending to be concentrated in the silicate outer shell of the earth ⟨uranium is a typical ~ element —*Jour. of Geol.*⟩
li·thoph·i·lous \ləˈthäfələs\ *adj* [ISV *lith-* + *-philous*] **:** growing or living in stony places ⟨~ plants⟩ ⟨~ insects⟩
lith·o·photogravure \ˌlithō+\ *n* [*lith-* + *photogravure*] **:** a photomechanical process in which a photolithographic transfer is made on a stone ruled with very fine lines to produce halftone effects
lith·o·phy·sa \ˌ⸗⸗ˈfīsə\ *n, pl* **lithophy·sae** \-ˌsē\ [NL, fr. *lith-* + Gk *physa* bubble — more at PUSTULE] **:** a spherulitic cavity often with concentric chambers that is observed in some rhyolitic lavas — **lith·o·phy·sal** \ˌ⸗⸗ˈ⸗sᵊl\ *adj*
lith·o·phyte \ˈlithəˌfīt\ *n* -s [F, fr. *lith-* + *-phyte*] **1** *archaic* **:** a plant or a plantlike organism having a hard stony structure or skeleton **2 :** a plant or a plantlike organism that grows on the surface of rocks — **lith·o·phyt·ic** \ˌ⸗⸗ˈfid·ik\ *adj*
lith·o·pone \ˈlithəˌpōn\ *n* -s [ISV *lith-* + Gk *ponos* work, artifact] **:** a white pigment consisting essentially of a mixture of zinc sulfide and barium sulfate precipitated by mixing solutions of barium sulfide and zinc sulfate and used chiefly in paint, printing ink, and linoleum and as a filler in paper, rubber, and plastics — compare CADMIUM LITHOPONE
lith·o·print \ˈ⸗⸗+ˌ-\ *vt* [*lith-* + *print*] **:** to print (as typewritten matter) by offset or photo-offset
lith·o·printing \ˈ⸗⸗+ˌ-\ *also* **lith·o·print** \ˈ⸗⸗+ˌ-\ *n* [*lith-* + *printing, print*] **:** photo-offset printing
lith·ops \ˈliˌthäps\ *n* [NL, fr. *lith-* + *-ops*] **1** *cap* **:** a genus of stemless succulent southern African plants (family Aizoaceae) that are sometimes grown for ornament and that have the leaves in pairs forming a stonelike body with a fissure on top from which the sessile usu. solitary flower emerges **2** *pl* **lithops :** any plant of the genus *Lithops* — called also *living stone, stoneface, stone life face*

litho purple *n* [¹*litho*] **:** a grayish to dark purple
lithos *pl of* LITHO, *pres 3d sing of* LITHO
lith·o·sere \ˈlithə+ˌ-\ *n* [*lith-* + *sere*] **:** an ecological sere originating on rock
li·tho·si·an \ləˈthōsēən\ *adj* [NL *Lithosiidae* + E *-an*] **:** of or relating to the Lithosiidae
li·tho·si·id \-sēəd\ *n* -s [NL *Lithosiidae*] **:** a moth of the family Lithosiidae
lith·o·si·idae \ˌlithəˈsīəˌdē\ *n pl, cap* [NL, fr. *Lithosia*, type genus (fr. Gk *lithōsis* petrifaction, fr. *lithoun* to become petrified — fr. *lithos* stone — + *-sis*) + *-idae*] **:** a large family of moths closely related to the Arctiidae but lacking normal ocelli and sometimes included as a subfamily in Arctiidae
lith·o·sol \ˈlithəˌsȯl, -ōl\ *n* -s *sometimes cap* [*lith-* + L *sol*um ground, soil — more at SOLE] **:** an azonal group of shallow soils consisting of imperfectly weathered rock fragments usu. on steep mountain slopes or high plateaus
lith·o·sper·mum \ˌ⸗⸗ˈspərməm\ *n, cap* [NL, fr. Gk *lithospermon* gromwell, fr. *lith-* + *-spermon* (fr. *sperma* seed) — more at SPERM] **:** a genus of herbs (family Boraginaceae) having a regular tubular corolla and polished white stony nutlets — see CORN GROMWELL, PUCCOON
lith·o·sphere \ˈ⸗⸗+ˌ-\ *n* [ISV *lith-* + *sphere*] **:** the solid part of the earth; *specif* **:** the outer part of the solid earth composed of rock essentially like that exposed at the surface and believed to be about 50 miles in thickness — compare ATMOSPHERE, HYDROSPHERE
¹**lith·o·tham·ni·oid** \ˌ⸗⸗ˈthamnēˌȯid\ *adj* [NL *Lithothamnion* + E *-oid*] **:** of or relating to the genus *Lithothamnion*
²**lithothamnioid** \"\ *n* -s **:** an alga of the genus *Lithothamnion*
lith·o·tham·ni·on \ˌ⸗⸗ˈ⸗nēən\ *n* [NL, fr. *lith-* + Gk *thamnos* bush + *-ion* (dim. suffix)] **1** *cap* **:** a genus of crustose reef-forming red algae (family Corallinaceae) that are abundant in post-Jurassic geologic strata and are represented by numerous recent forms growing chiefly on rocks and other algae **2** -s **:** any plant of the genus *Lithothamnion*
lith·o·tome \ˈ⸗⸗ˌtōm\ *n* -s [F, fr. MGk *lithotomon*, fr. Gk *lith-* + *-tomon* -tome] **1 :** a knife used for lithotomy **2** [*lith-* + *-tome*] **:** a stone so formed as to appear as if cut by art
li·thot·o·mist \ləˈthäd·əməst, -ätə-\ *n* -s [F *lithotomiste*, fr. *lithotomie* + *-iste* -ist] **:** a specialist in lithotomy
li·thot·o·mize \-ˌmīz\ *vt* -ED/-ING/-S [*lithotomy* + *-ize*] **:** to subject to lithotomy
li·thot·o·my \-mē, -mi\ *n* -ES [LL *lithotomia*, fr. Gk, fr. *lithotomein* to quarry, perform a lithotomy, fr. *lith-* + *-tomein* (fr. *temnein* to cut) — more at TOME] **:** the operation of cutting into the urinary bladder for removal of a stone
lith·o·tope \ˈlithəˌtōp\ *n* -s [*lith-* + *-tope*] **:** an area of relatively uniform conditions of rock deposition
lithotriptic *var of* LITHONTRIPTIC
lith·o·trite \ˈlithəˌtrīt\ *n* -s [back-formation fr. *lithotrity*] **:** an instrument for performing lithotrity
li·thot·ri·tist \ləˈthä·trətəst\ *n* -s [*lithotrity* + *-ist*] **:** a specialist in lithotrity
lith·o·tri·tor \ˈlithəˌtrīd·ə(r)\ *n* -s [alter. (influenced by L *tritor* one that rubs) of earlier *lithotriptor*, fr. *lithotriptic* + *-or*] **:** LITHOTRITE
li·thot·ri·ty \ləˈthä·trəd·ē\ *n* -ES [*lithotritor* + *-y*] **:** the breaking of a stone in the bladder into small pieces capable of being voided or washed out
lith·o·type \ˈlithəˌtīp\ *n* [*lith-* + *type*] **1 :** a letterpress printing plate made of shellac, fine sand, tar, and linseed oil; *also* **:** an imprint made from it **2 :** an etched stone surface for printing a design in relief; *also* **:** an imprint made from it
li·thox·yl *or* **li·thox·yle** \ləˈthäkˌsil\ *also* **li·thox·y·lite** \-ˌsəˌlīt\ *n* -s [*lithoxyl, lithoxyle* fr. Sw *lithoxylon*, fr. *lith-* + Gk *xylon* wood; *lithoxylite* fr. *lithoxyl* + *-ite*] **:** petrified wood
liths *pl of* LITH
-liths *pl of* -LITH
liths·man \ˈlithsmən\ *n, pl* **lithsmen** [OE *lithsmann*, fr. ON *lithsmann-, lithsmathr* warrior, sailor, fr. *liths* (gen. of *lith* people, host) + *mann-, mathr* man; akin to ON *litha* to go — more at LEAD] **:** a sailor in the navy during the period of the Danish kings of England
lith·u·a·nia \ˌlith(y)əˈwānēə, -nyə\ *adj, usu cap* [fr. *Lithuania*, country in eastern Europe] **:** of or from Lithuania **:** of the kind or style prevalent in Lithuania **:** LITHUANIAN
¹**lith·u·a·ni·an** \-nēən, -nyən\ *adj, usu cap* [*Lithuania* + E *-an*] **1 a :** of, relating to, or characteristic of Lithuania, a country of eastern Europe **b :** of, relating to, or characteristic of the Lithuanians **2 :** of, relating to, or characteristic of the Lithuanian language
²**lithuanian** \"\ *n* -s *cap* **1 :** a native or inhabitant of Lithuania **2 :** a Baltic language of the Lithuanian people and the official language of Lithuania — see INDO-EUROPEAN LANGUAGES table
¹**lith·u·an·ic** \-ˈwanik\ *adj, usu cap* [*Lithuania* + E *-ic*] **:** LITHUANIAN
²**lithuanic** \"\ *n* -s *cap* **:** LITHUANIAN 2
lit hum *abbr, often cap L&H* [ML *literae humaniores*] the humanities
li·thu·ria \ləˈthyu̇rēə\ *n* -s [NL, fr. *lith-* + *-uria*] **:** excess of uric acid or of its salts in the urine
lithy \ˈlīthē, ˈlithē, -i\ *adj* -ER/-EST [ME *lethy, lithy;* akin to MHG *ledic, ledec* free, unhindered, ON *lithugr*, and perh. to OE *lith* limb — more at LITH] *now dial Eng* **:** easily bent **:** PLIABLE, SUPPLE
lit·i·ga·ble \ˈlid·əgəbəl, ˈlitə-\ *adj* [*litigate* + *-able*] **:** capable of being litigated
¹**lit·i·gant** \-gənt\ *adj* [L *litigant-, litigans*, pres. part. of *litigare*] **:** contending in law **:** engaged in a lawsuit ⟨the parties ~⟩
²**litigant** \"\ *n* -s **:** one engaged in a lawsuit ⟨right of ~*s* . . . to be unhampered in the quest for justice —*Jour. of the Amer. Judicature Society*⟩
lit·i·gate \ˈlid·əˌgāt, ˈlitə-, *usu* -ād·+V\ *vb* -ED/-ING/-S [L *litigatus*, past part. of *litigare*, fr. *lit-, lis* lawsuit (fr. OL *stlit-, stlis*) + *-igare* (fr. *agere* to drive, lead, act, do); perh. akin to Gk *stellein* to set up — more at STALL, AGENT] *vi* **:** to carry on a legal contest by judicial process ⟨only states can ~ before this court —R.H.Heindel⟩ ⟨the great *litigating* public —Geoffrey Lincoln⟩ ~ *vt* **1** *archaic* **:** to enter into controversy over ⟨the point indeed has been much *litigated* —Horace Walpole⟩ **2 :** to make the subject of a lawsuit **:** contest in law **:** prosecute or defend by pleadings, evidence, and debate in a court ⟨the restraining order is being *litigated* —H.J.Ruttenberg⟩ ⟨~ the validity of a state statute —*Harvard Law Rev.*⟩
litigated motion *n* **:** a motion at law that can be decided only after notice to an opposing party entitled to be heard — compare EX PARTE
lit·i·ga·tion \ˌ⸗⸗ˈgāshən\ *n* -s [LL *litigation-, litigatio*, fr. L *litigatus* (past part. of *litigare*) + *-ion-, -io* -ion] **1** *archaic* **:** DISPUTE ⟨was, after some ~, obliged to consent —Henry Fielding⟩ ⟨a matter of ~ among psychologists —William James⟩ **2 a :** the act or process of litigating ⟨losses arising from ~ in a civil antitrust suit —*Wall Street Jour.*⟩ ⟨~ over an estate⟩ **b :** the practice of taking legal action ⟨my lawyer is bound by all his affections to encourage me in ~ —G.B.Shaw⟩ ⟨he enjoyed ~ —Louis Auchincloss⟩ **3 :** a controversy involving adverse parties before an executive governmental agency having quasi-judicial powers and employing quasi-judicial procedures
lit·i·ga·tor \ˈ⸗⸗ˌgād·ə(r), -ātə-\ *n* -s [L, fr. *litigatus* + *-or*] **:** one that litigates **:** LITIGANT
li·ti·gi·os·i·ty \ləˌtijēˈäsəd·ē\ *n* -ES [fr. *litigious*, after such pairs as E *ponderous: ponderosity*] **:** the quality or state of being litigious
li·ti·gious \ləˈtijəs\ *adj* [ME, fr. MF *litigieux*, fr. L *litigiosus*, fr. *litigium* quarrel, dispute (fr. *litigare*) + *-osus* -ous] **1 a :** marked by an inclination to quarrel **:** DISPUTATIOUS, CONTENTIOUS ⟨the ~ and acrimonious spirit . . . fostered by a training in medieval logic —R.W.Southern⟩ **b :** fond of litigation **:** prone to engage in lawsuits ⟨pertinacious and ~ in collecting their alleged dues —F.D.Smith & Barbara Wilcox⟩ **2 a** *obs* **:** inviting controversy **:** DISPUTABLE ⟨an age . . . that hath almost lost piety in the chase of some ~ truths —Joseph Hall⟩ **b :** liable or subject to litigation ⟨not known to be ~ when purchased —James Muirhead⟩ **3 :** of, relating to, or marked by litigation ⟨able to trace the story of the . . . heirs through the ~ tangle of a dozen generations —J.T.Winterich⟩ — **li·ti·gious·ly** *adv* — **li·ti·gious·ness** *n* -ES
liting *pres part of* LIT *or of* LITE
li·ti·o·pa \ləˈtīəpə\ *n, cap* [NL, fr. Gk *litos* plain, simple + *opē* opening, hole] **:** a genus of minute marine gastropod mollusks (suborder Taenioglossa) commonly living among seaweeds
li·tis·con·test \ˌlīd·əskənˈtest\ *vt* [back-formation fr. *litiscontestation*] *Scots law* **:** to bring to litiscontestation
li·tis·con·tes·ta·tion \ˌ⸗⸗+\ *n* [ME *litiscontestacioun*, fr. MF *litiscontestation*, fr. ML *litis contestation-, litis contestatio*, lit., attestation of a lawsuit] **1 :** a legal process by which controverted issues are established and a joinder of issues arrived at **2 :** the issues involved in a law case **3 :** the stage of pleading by which a party contests a suit — **li·tis·con·tes·ta·tion·al** \ˌ⸗⸗ˌ⸗ˌ⸗ˈtāshənᵊl, -shnəl\ *adj*
lit·mus \ˈlitməs\ *n* -ES [of Scand origin; akin to ON *litmosi* herbs used in dyeing, fr. *litr* color + *mosi* moss; akin to OE *wlite* face, OHG *antlizzi* face, ON *lita* to look, Goth *wlits* face, figure, *wlaiton* to spy, look, L *voltus, vultus* facial expression, appearance, face, MW *gwelet* to see — more at MOSS] **:** a coloring matter that turns red in acid solutions and blue in alkaline solutions, is obtained from several lichens (as *Roccella tinctoria, R. fuciformis*, or *Lecanora tartarea*), is usu. formed with powdered chalk or gypsum into small blue cakes, and is used as an acid-base indicator — compare ARCHIL, AZOLITMIN
litmus milk *n* **:** milk colored with litmus and used as a culture medium for determining acid or alkali production
litmus paper *n* **:** unsized paper colored red, blue, or violet by treating with an aqueous infusion of litmus for use as an acid-base indicator
li·to·mo·soi·des \ˌlīd·ōməˈsȯiˌdēz, ˌlid··\ *n, cap* [NL] **:** a genus of filariid worms including a form (*L. carinii*) that is parasitic in the cotton rat and is much used in research on chemotherapy and other problems concerning human filariases
li·top·tern \lĭˈtäpˌtərn\ *n* -s [NL *Litopterna*] **:** one of the Litopterna
li·top·ter·na \ˌ⸗(ˌ)⸗ˈtərnə\ *n pl, cap* [NL, fr. Gk *litos* plain, smooth + *pterna* heel] **:** an order of extinct So. American Cenozoic ungulates with one or three functional toes
litorina [NL, fr. L *litor-, litus* seashore + NL *-ina*] *syn of* LITTORINA
litorinidae [NL *Litorina* + *-idae*] *syn of* LITTORINIDAE
li·to·tes \ˈlīd·əˌtēz, ˈlid·-; līˈtōd·ēz\ *n, pl* **litotes** [Gk *litotēs*, fr. *litos* simple, plain; akin to Gk *leios* smooth — more at LIME] **1 :** understatement in which an affirmative is expressed by the negative of the contrary (as in "He's not a bad ballplayer") — opposed to *hyperbole* **2 :** an example of litotes ⟨the ~ in this passage⟩
lit-par-lit \ˈlēˌpärˈlē\ *adj* [F, lit., bed-by-bed] **:** of, relating to, or having the form of foliated or fissile rock that has been intruded by many thin sheets or stringers of magma
li·tra \ˈlī·trə\ *n, pl* **li·trae** \-ˌtrē\ [Gk] **1 :** a unit of value of ancient Sicily based on the value of a pound of bronze **2 :** a silver coin worth one litra
¹**litre** *var of* LITER
²**li·tre** \ˈlē·trā\ *n* -s [Sp] **:** a poisonous Chilean shrub (*Lithraea caustica*) of the family Anacardiaceae that has hardwood used in cabinetwork
lits *pres 3d sing of* LIT, *pl of* LIT
lit·sea \ˈlitsēə\ *n, cap* [NL, fr. F *litsé* shrub of the genus *Litsea*, fr. Chin (Cant) *lei tsai* cherry, lit., small plum] **:** a genus of aromatic shrubs or trees (family Lauraceae) having small evergreen leaves, short racemes of flowers, and berrylike fruits — see MANGEAO
lit·ster \ˈlitstər\ *n* -s [ME *litestere*, fr. *liten, litten* to dye + *-stere* -ster — more at LIT] *Scot* **:** DYER
Litt D *abbr or n* -s [ML *litterarum doctor*] **:** a doctor of letters
litted *past of* LIT
¹**lit·ten** \ˈlitᵊn\ *n* -s [ME *lytton, letton*, fr. OE *līctūn*, fr. *līc* body, corpse + *tūn* enclosure, field, village — more at LIKE, TOWN] *dial Eng* **:** CHURCHYARD; *esp* **:** a churchyard used as a cemetery
²**litten** \"\ *adj* [*lit* (past part. of ³*light*) + *-en*] *archaic* **:** LIGHTED ⟨like a cloud of ~ gold —*Blackwood's*⟩ — often used in combination ⟨dim-*litten* chamber —William Morris⟩
¹**lit·ter** \ˈlid·ə(r), ˈlitə-\ *n* -s [ME *litere, liter* bed, litter, fr. OF *litiere*, fr. *lit* bed, fr. L *lectus* — more at LIE] **1 a :** a vehicle consisting of a usu. covered and curtained couch in which a single passenger is carried ⟨as Rome became powerful and captured many slaves, the usual conveyance in the city was a ~ carried on the shoulders of four men —Edwin Tunis⟩ **b :** a bed, stretcher, basket, or other device for carrying a sick or injured person ⟨the wounded general . . . was moved to the rear first by wagon, then by ~ —John Mason Brown⟩ **2 a :** material (as straw or hay) used esp. as bedding for animals ⟨fibrous peat is also used as . . . ~ material for bedding stock and for stable and poultry yards —J.A.DeCarlo & Maxine M. Otero⟩ **b :** the uppermost slightly decayed layer of organic matter on the forest floor ⟨rain . . . is absorbed by the spongelike mass of ~ and then seeps into the soil —*London Calling*⟩ — compare DUFF, HUMUS **3 a :** the offspring at one birth of a multiparous animal ⟨a ~ of puppies⟩ **b** *archaic* **:** an act of animal parturition ⟨the female produces from three to six young ones at a ~ —Samuel Williams⟩ **4 a :** refuse or rubbish lying scattered about ⟨the ~ of rusty cans and foul rags —Van Wyck Brooks⟩ **b :** an untidy accumulation of objects lying about ⟨an old pamphlet among the ~ of the abbot's study —J.H.Blunt⟩

Roman litter

²**litter** \"\ *vb* -ED/-ING/-S *vt* **1 a :** to supply (an animal) with material for bedding ⟨keep him warm by ~*ing* him up to the belly with fresh straw —Edward Topsell⟩ **b :** to cover (as a floor) with material for bedding ⟨a loose stable, well ~*ed* down with fresh straw —*Sporting Mag.*⟩ **2 :** to produce a litter of ⟨wolves ~*ed* their young in the deserted farmhouses —Samuel Smiles⟩ **3 a :** to strew with scattered articles ⟨the great majority ~*s* the scene with papers, boxes, cans . . . —*Phoenix Flame*⟩ **b :** to scatter about in disorder ⟨~*ed* his clothing all over the floor⟩ **c :** to lie about in disorder ⟨pieces of stuccoed tracery . . . ~*ed* the garden —Charles Lever⟩ ~ *vi* **1 :** to produce a litter ⟨a horrible desert . . . where the she wolf still ~*ed* —T.B.Macaulay⟩ **2 :** to strew litter ⟨don't ~⟩
lit·te·rae clau·sae \ˈlid·əˌrēˈklȯˌzē\ *n pl* [NL] **:** LETTERS CLOSE
litterae hu·ma·ni·o·res \-hyüˌmanēˈōˌrēz\ *n pl* [ML, lit., more humane letters] **:** HUMANITIES
lit·ter·a·teur \ˌlid·ərəˈtər, ˌlitər-, +V -ˈtər-; -tə(r *also* -tu̇(ə)r *or* -tüə\ *n* -s [F *littérateur*, fr. L *litterator, literator* grammarian, critic — more at LITERATOR] **:** one that devotes himself to literary pursuits; *esp* **:** a professional writer ⟨a distinguished Danish ~⟩ ⟨a satire on life among the ~*s* —Carlos Baker⟩
litterbug \ˈ⸗⸗ˌ⸗\ *n* [²*litter* + *bug*] **:** one that litters a street, park, or other public area with waste paper, trash, or garbage ⟨hand out summonses impartially to ~*s*, whether they are motorists, pedestrians, or throwers of refuse from apartment windows —Charles Grutzner⟩ ⟨don't be a ~⟩
litter carrier *n* **1 :** one that carries a litter **:** STRETCHER-BEARER **2 :** a box or bed with a dumping mechanism suspended from wheels on an overhead track that is used to move manure (as from a stable to a spreader)
lit·ter·er \ˈlid·ərə(r), -itə-\ *n* [²*litter* + *-er*] **:** LITTERBUG
littermate \ˈ⸗⸗ˌ⸗\ *n* **:** a product of a multiple birth considered in relation to other members of the same litter
lit·tery \ˈlid·ərē, ˈlitə-, -ri\ *adj* [¹*litter* + *-y*] **1 :** of, relating to, or having the character of litter ⟨let nothing ~ nor dusty go inside the room —Emily Holt⟩ **2 :** covered with litter **:** UNTIDY ⟨he took me into his library, a rough, ~, but considerable collection —Thomas Carlyle⟩

litting *pres part of* LIT

¹lit·tle \'lid·ᵊl, -itᵊl *sometimes when not heavily stressed* (,)lil *esp when a vowel follows*\ *adj, in sense 1 usu* **lit·tler** \-id·ᵊlə(r), -it(ᵊ)l-\ *usu* **lit·tlest** \-id·ᵊləst, -it(ᵊ)l-\ *in senses 2 & 3 usu* **less** \'les\ *or* **less·er** \'lesə(r)\ *usu* **least** \'lēst\ [ME *lutel, litel, littel*, fr. OE *lȳtel*; akin to OE *lȳt* little, few, OS *luttil* small, miserable, OHG *luzzil* little, ON *lūta* to bow down, Goth *liuts* hypocritical, W *lludded* fatigue, Lith *liūsti* to be sad] **1 :** not big **:** not great: as **a** (1) **:** small in size **:** DIMINUTIVE, TINY ⟨has ~ feet⟩ (2) **:** short in stature ⟨a pompous ~ man⟩ (3) **:** that has not attained the full growth of maturity ⟨a ~ child⟩ (4) **:** that is viewed as tiny or as short; *esp* **:** that seems brief ⟨had only a ~ month to wait⟩ (5) **:** small in comparison with related forms — used in vernacular names (as of animals) **b :** small in number **:** comprising only a few individuals (as members or inhabitants) ⟨a ~ group of people⟩ ⟨a ~ herd of buffalo⟩ ⟨a ~ village⟩ **c :** small in rank or condition **:** lacking distinction ⟨~ magistrates much occupied with picayune matters⟩ ⟨big businessmen trampling on the ~ fellow⟩ **d :** contemptibly limited (as in scope or outlook) **:** PALTRY, MEAN, NARROW ⟨disgusted with the pettiness of ~ minds⟩ **e** (1) **:** small in a way that arouses in the speaker or writer a feeling of tenderness, pity, or sympathy (as through real or supposed defenselessness) ⟨my dear ~ mother⟩ ⟨bless your ~ heart⟩ ⟨stood there trying to warm her poor ~ hands⟩ ⟨hurt his ~ knee⟩ (2) **:** small or trivial in a way that amuses the speaker or writer (as by arousing a mood of playfulness or bantering) ⟨what ~ game are you up to now⟩ ⟨used to enjoy her ~ tricks⟩ ⟨a funny ~ way of smiling⟩ (3) **:** small in a way that arouses in the speaker or writer a feeling of exasperation or disapprobation (as through paltriness, meanness, deviousness) ⟨couldn't stand her mean ~ accusations⟩ ⟨know all about your ~ scheme⟩ **2 :** not much: as **a :** that exists only in a small amount or to a slight or limited extent or degree ⟨has ~ money⟩ ⟨have ~ space to work in⟩ ⟨~ change for the better⟩ **:** barely any **:** SCANTY ⟨have ~ hope left⟩ ⟨has ~ love for her⟩ ⟨can do it with but ~ effort⟩ **b :** short in duration **:** BRIEF ⟨had ~ sleep⟩ ⟨there is ~ time left⟩ **c :** that exists in or to an appreciable though not extensive amount, extent, or degree **:** some but not much — used with *a* ⟨fortunately I still have a ~ money left⟩ ⟨don't worry, you still have a ~ time⟩ **3 :** small in importance or interest **:** TRIFLING, TRIVIAL ⟨mentioned a lot of ~ points that I found not worth attention⟩ **syn** see SMALL

²little \"\ *adv* **less** \"\ **least** \"\ [ME *lutel, litel, littel*, fr. OE *lȳtel*, fr. *lȳtel*, adj.] **1 a :** to only a slight or limited extent or degree **:** not to any great extent or degree **:** only slightly **:** not much **:** not very much ⟨said ~ more than what you already know⟩ ⟨loved her ~⟩ ⟨a once popular writer who is now ~ heard from⟩ ⟨facts that were ~ known at the time⟩ **b :** not at all **:** not in the least — used prepositively as an emphatic negative esp. with a verb of knowing, thinking, believing, caring ⟨he ~ knows or cares what may happen⟩ **2 :** INFREQUENTLY, RARELY ⟨has been seeing her very ~⟩

³little \"\ *n* -s [ME *lutel, litel, littel*, fr. OE *lȳtel*, fr. *lȳtel*, adj.] **1 :** something not very extensive (as in amount, quantity, duration): **a** (1) **:** a small amount or quantity ⟨worked hard to earn what ~ he could⟩ **:** not much ⟨pointed out that ~ had been accomplished⟩ (2) **:** only a small amount or quantity **:** something far short of everything **:** something constituting only a tiny fraction of all **:** practically nothing ⟨lost most of her money and has to be satisfied with ~ of what life offers⟩ ⟨remembered ~ of the past⟩ ⟨knows ~ of what has happened⟩ ⟨has learned to be happy with ~⟩ **b :** an appreciable though not extensive amount or quantity **:** a considerable amount or quantity — used with preceding *a* ⟨spent a lot of money but still has a ~ in the bank⟩ **2 a :** a short time ⟨after a ~ she glanced at him⟩ ⟨stepped out into the garden for a ~⟩ ⟨will be back in a ~⟩ **b :** a short distance ⟨had traveled quite far and a ~ still remained to be covered⟩ — **a little** *adv* **1 a :** for a short time ⟨remain with me *a little*⟩ **b :** for or at a short distance ⟨can walk *a little* and then catch a cab⟩ ⟨the two buildings are set *a little* apart from each other⟩ **2 :** to an appreciable though not extensive amount or degree **:** to a considerable though not great extent or degree **:** SOMEWHAT, RATHER ⟨found the play *a little* dull⟩ ⟨liked her *a little*⟩ **3 :** from time to time though not frequently **:** SOMETIMES, OCCASIONALLY ⟨still gets around to seeing her *a little*⟩ — **by little and little :** little by little — **in little** *adv* **:** on a small scale; *esp* **:** in miniature ⟨a painting done *in little*⟩

little anteater *n* **:** SILKY ANTEATER

little auk *n* **:** DOVEKIE 2

little barley *n* **:** an annual barley (*Hordeum pusillum*) that is native to western No. America and widespread in the southern states and in tropical America and that has flattened glumes and the lemmas of the lateral spikelets raised on pedicels

little bittern *n* **:** any of several small bitterns (genus *Ixobrychus*); *esp* **:** a European bittern (*I. minutus*) with dark upper parts and buffy white underparts and wing coverts

little bitty *adj, dial* **:** SMALL, TINY

little black ant *n* **:** a tiny slender glossy black ant (*Monomorium minimum*) that usu. nests out of doors and invades houses in search of food (as sweets)

little blue heron *n* **:** a small American heron (*Florida caerulea*)

little bluestem *n* **:** a forage grass (*Andropogon scoparius*) of central No. America — called also *bluejoint turkeyfoot*

little-boys' breeches \'=,=-\ *n pl but sing or pl in constr* **:** DUTCHMAN'S-BREECHES

little brain *n* **:** CEREBELLUM

little brown bat *n* **:** a small widely distributed No. American bat (*Myotis leucifugus*) having rich bronzy brown fur, flight membranes partially furred, and moderately long bluntly pointed ears

little brown crane *n* **:** a crane (*Grus canadensis canadensis*) of western No. America that is a variety of the sandhill crane distinguished by its smaller size and shorter bill

little buckeye *n* **:** RED BUCKEYE

little bull bat *n* **:** a small Central American mastiff bat (*Noctilis albinenter*)

little bustard *n* **:** a bustard (*Otis tetrax*) of Mediterranean countries

little by little *adv* **:** by small degrees or amounts **:** a little at a time **:** GRADUALLY ⟨*little by little* they got to know each other⟩ ⟨added the water *little by little*⟩

little casino *n* **:** the two of spades in the game of casino which scores one point for the player who takes the card in a trick

little cat *n* **:** a hand recognized in some poker games that consists of an eight, seven, six, five, and three, contains no pairs, is composed of two or more suits, and ranks next below a big cat

little cherry *or* **little cherry disease** *n* **:** a virus disease of sweet cherries characterized by angular pointed fruits of about half normal size which retain the brilliant red color of immaturity beyond the normal picking time

little chief hare *n* [trans. of Chipewyan *bucka-thrae-gga-yaze*] **:** a pika (*Ochotona princeps*) of No. America

little corporal *n* **:** billiards played with three balls and a small wooden pin in which caroms count as in ordinary billiards but the knocking down of the pin by the cue ball after contact with an object ball scores five points

little-ease \'=,=\ *n* **:** a place of confinement (as an extremely small prison cell) or a confining device (as a pillory) making it impossible for a prisoner to have even ordinary comfort or freedom of movement

little englander *n, usu cap L & E* **:** an Englishman opposed to territorial expansion of the British Empire and usu. anticipating the gradual voluntary secession of existing possessions therefrom

little eng·land·ism \-'iŋ(g)lən,dizəm *sometimes* -'eŋ(g)-\ *n, usu cap L&E* **:** the policies and convictions of Little Englanders

little entrance *n, usu cap L&E* **:** an entrance in the liturgy of the Eastern Church during which the book of the Gospel is brought in

little finger *n* **:** the fourth finger of the hand

little folk *n* **:** LITTLE PEOPLE

little grebe *n* **:** a small European grebe (*Podiceps ruficollis*)

little greenshank *n* **:** a small sandpiper (*Totanus stagnatilis*) of eastern Asia that resembles the lesser yellowlegs

little gull *n* **:** a European black-headed gull (*Larus minutus*) that is the smallest of the true gulls

littlehead porgy \'==,=-\ *n* **:** a silvery porgy (*Calamus proridens*) of Florida and the West Indies that is brilliantly marked with violet-blue and orange

little hours *n pl* **:** the offices of prime, terce, sext, and none

little house *n* **:** PRIVY 2

little housefly *n* **:** LESSER HOUSEFLY

little ice age *n, often cap L&I&A* **:** an episode of glacial expansion whose maximum extension occurred in the 17th and 18th centuries

little italy *n, pl* **little italies** *usu cap L&I* **:** a quarter or section (as in a city) populated chiefly by Italian immigrants or by persons of Italian descent

little joe *n, usu cap L&J* **:** a throw of four in the game of craps

little joker *n* **1 :** JOKER 2a **2 :** a playing-card joker rated lower in scoring value than a big joker

little king *n* **:** a very small wren (*Nannus troglodytes*) that is of a dark brown color barred and mottled with black and that has a short erect tail and is common throughout Europe

littleleaf \'==,=\ *adj* **:** having little leaves — used as a qualifying epithet esp. in the vernacular names of some plants ⟨~ lilac⟩

little leaf \"\ *n* **:** a plant disorder characterized by small and often chlorotic and distorted foliage: as **a :** a zinc-deficiency disease of deciduous woody plants (as grape, peach, or pecan) **b** *usu* **little-leaf disease :** a destructive disease of southern pines (as *Pinus echinata*) of unknown cause

little league *n, often cap both Ls* **:** a commercially sponsored baseball league made up of teams whose players are boys from 8 to 12 years old — compare PONY LEAGUE

little leaguer *n, often cap both Ls* **:** one that belongs to or plays in a little league

little locust bird *n* **:** a pratincole (*Glareola nordmanni*) that resembles a long-legged swallow

little magazine *n* **:** a literary usu. noncommercial magazine typically small in format that esp. features experimental writing or other literary expression appealing to a relatively limited number of readers

little magpie *n* **:** MAGPIE LARK

little mary *n, often cap M, slang* **:** STOMACH, BELLY

littlemouth porgy \'==,=-\ *n* **:** SHEEPSHEAD PORGY

littleneck \'==,=\ *or* **littleneck clam** *n* [fr. *Littleneck* Bay, inlet of Long Island Sound, N.Y.] **:** the young of the quahog when large enough to be eaten raw

lit·tle·ness *n* -ES [ME *litelnesse*, fr. OE *lȳtelnes*, fr. *lȳtel* little + *-nes* -ness] **1 :** the quality or state of being little ⟨the ~ of the world in the vast emptiness of space⟩ **2 :** an act marked by littleness; *esp* **:** a mean or petty act ⟨a life of envy, filled with ~*es*⟩

little office *n, often cap L&O* **:** a usu. invariable office resembling but shorter than the daily canonical office and designed to honor a special saint or mystery of religion; *esp* **:** such an office honoring the Virgin Mary

little one *n* **:** young offspring; *esp* **:** CHILD

little owl *n* **:** a small squat owl (*Athene noctua*) common in Europe and having a flattened head and face, dark brown upper parts spotted and barred with white, and whitish underparts streaked with dark brown

little peach *n* **:** a virus disease of the peach tree characterized typically by a dwarfing of the fruit and delay in ripening and by yellowing of the leaves and finally by death of the tree

little people *n* **:** tiny imaginary beings (as fairies, elves, leprechauns) of folklore

little pickerel *n* **:** GRASS PICKEREL

little piked whale *n* **:** PIKED WHALE

little potato *n* **:** RHIZOCTONIA DISEASE 2

littler *comparative of* LITTLE

little red fox *n* **:** a small Australian fruit bat (*Pteropus scapulatus*) with short chocolate-brown fur and transparent wing membranes

little review *n* **:** LITTLE MAGAZINE; *esp* **:** a little magazine featuring nonfiction and critical writing

little rock \'==,=\ *adj, usu cap L&R* [fr. *Little Rock*, Ark.] **:** of or from Little Rock, the capital of Arkansas **:** of the kind or style prevalent in Little Rock

little russian *n, usu cap L&R* **1 :** UKRAINIAN **2 :** RUTHENIAN

lit·tle's disease \'lid·ᵊlz-, -itᵊlz-\ *n, usu cap L* [after William J. *Little* †1894 Eng. physician that described it] **:** SPASTIC PARALYSIS

little sister of the poor *usu cap L&S&P* [trans. of F *Petite Sœur des Pauvres*] *Roman Catholicism* **:** a member of a religious community founded in Brittany, France, about 1840 and devoted esp. to the care of old people

little skate *n* **:** a ray (*Raja erinacea*) small in size and brown above mottled with black spots that is common in American coastal waters of the Atlantic

little slam *n* **:** the winning of all tricks except one in a card game (as bridge) — called also *small slam*

little snowball *n* **:** BUTTONBUSH

little snowy *n* **:** SNOWY EGRET

little spotted skunk *n* **:** any of a number of small skunks (genus *Spilogale*) that have a coat of marbled black and white and that are common and widely distributed in the southwestern U.S. and in Mexico

littlest *superlative of* LITTLE

little staggerweed *n* **:** DUTCHMAN'S-BREECHES

little stint *n* **:** a small sandpiper (*Pisobia minuta*)

little striker *n* **:** LEAST TERN

little stroke *n* **:** a usu. transient blockage of one or more arteries in the cerebrum causing temporary numbness or impaired function of a part, slowed mentation, speech defects, dizziness, and nausea — called also *strokelet;* compare APOPLEXY

little sugar pine *n* **1 :** WESTERN WHITE PINE 1 **2 :** SUGAR PINE

little tern *n* **:** a very small cosmopolitan tern (*Sterna albifrons*)

little theater *n* **1 :** a small theater for legitimate productions that is designed for a relatively small group or community; *esp* **:** such a theater in which usu. noncommercial and low-cost productions are presented that are often experimental or otherwise designed for a relatively limited audience and that have usu. small often amateur casts **2 :** drama of a kind that is best suited to production in a little theater; *esp* **:** drama that is usu. noncommercial and low in production costs and that is often experimental or otherwise designed for a relatively limited audience

little toe *n* **:** the outermost and smallest digit of the foot

little tuna *also* **little tunny** *n* **:** a small active pelagic tuna (*Euthynnus alletteratus*) circumtropical in distribution and widely known as a sport fish — called also *false albacore*

little vehicle *n, usu cap L&V* [trans. of Skt *hīnayāna*] **:** HINAYANA — usu. used with *the* ⟨reverted to the pure form of Buddhism known as the *Little Vehicle*⟩

Lit·tle·way Lockstitch \,litᵊl,wā-\ *trademark* — used for a shoe constructed by a method in which the upper and lining are attached to the insole by means of staples that do not penetrate to the upper surface of the insole and the outsole is attached to the insole by means of a lockstitch

little whaup *n* **:** WHIMBREL

little white heron *n* **:** SNOWY EGRET

little woman *n* **:** WIFE — not often in formal use

lit·tling \'lid·ᵊliŋ, 'lit(ᵊ)l-\ *n* -s ['*little* + *-ing*] *Scot* **:** a young child or young animal

lit·tlish \-lish\ *adj* **:** somewhat little **:** comparatively little

¹lit·to·ral \'lid·ərəl, 'litə-; ¦==¦ral, -räl, -ral\ *adj* [L *littoralis, litoralis*, fr. *littor-, littus, litor-, litus* seashore + *-alis* -al] **:** of or relating to or on or near a shore esp. of the sea: **a :** of, relating to, or being the biogeographic zone that includes (1) the intertidal and eulittoral regions on a seacoast or (2) the marginal part of a body of fresh water extending downward to the limit of rooted vegetation **b :** inhabiting or growing on or near a seacoast **c :** composed of material deposited near a shore and within the zone affected by waves and coastal currents

²littoral \"\ *n* -s [It *littorale*, fr. *littorale*, adj., of the seashore, fr. L *littoralis, litoralis*] **:** a coastal region including both the land along the coast and the water near the coast **:** the shore zone between high and low watermarks

littoral cell *n* **:** one of the reticuloendothelial cells lining the sinuses of various reticular organs of the body

littoral current *n* **:** a current moving along and roughly parallel to a shore

littoral right *n* **:** the right of one owning littoral land to have access to and use of the shore and water — compare RIPARIAN RIGHT

lit·to·ri·na \,lid·ə'rīnə, -rēnə\ *n, cap* [NL, fr. L *littor-, littus* seashore + NL *-ina*] **:** the type genus of Littorinidae comprising the typical littoral marine periwinkles — **lit·to·ri·noid** \'==;=,nȯid\ *adj*

lit·to·rin·i·dae \,=='rinə,dē\ *n pl, cap* [NL, fr. *Littorina*, type genus + *-idae*] **:** a large nearly cosmopolitan family of snails (suborder Taenioglossa) that have broad conical shells with round aperture and horny operculum, that are chiefly littoral in salt water or brackish or fresh water and are remarkably resistant to desiccation, and that feed on algae — **lit·to·ri·nid·i·an** \-,rə'nidēən\ *n* -s

lit·tre's gland \'lē·trəz-\ *n, usu cap L* [after Alexis *Littre* †1726 Fr. physician] **:** one of the mucous glands in the submucous tissue of the urethra

lit·trow spectrograph \'li·,trō-\ *n, usu cap L* [after Joseph Johann von *Littrow* †1840 Austrian astronomer and mathematician] **:** a spectrograph in which dispersion is produced by a prism backed by a reflecting metallic film so that the light traverses the prism twice

lit·u·ate \'lichəwət, *usu* -əd·+V\ *adj* [L *lituus* crooked staff carried by augurs + E *-ate* — more at LITH] *bot* **:** forked with the points turned slightly outward ⟨~ fungi⟩

lit·u·ite \-,wīt\ *n* -s [NL *Lituites*] **:** a fossil of the genus *Lituites*

Lit·u·i·tes \,=='wīd·,ēz\ *n, cap* [NL, fr. L *lituus* + NL *-ites*] **:** a genus of Ordovician nautiloid mollusks with the shell fully coiled when young but with the later increments forming a straight tube — **lit·u·i·toid** \'==wə,tȯid\ *adj*

lit·u·ol·i·dae \,=='wälə,dē\ *n pl, cap* [NL, fr. *Lituola*, type genus (dim. of L *lituus* curved staff) + *-idae*] **:** a family of imperforate foraminiferans that are related to those of the family Fusulinidae and have shells divided into cells and composed chiefly of sand grains cemented together

lit up *adj, slang* **:** DRUNK

lit·u·rate \'lichə,rāt, -,rət, *usu* -d·+V\ *adj* [LL *lituratus*, past part. of *liturare* to erase, fr. L *litura* smear, erasure, fr. *litus* (past part. of *linere, linire* to smear) + *-ura* -ure — more at LIME] *biol* **:** SPOTTED

li·tur·gi·cal \lə'tərjəkəl, -təj-, -təij-, -jēk-\ *also* **li·tur·gic** \-jik, -ēk\ *adj* **1 a :** of, relating to, or having the characteristics of liturgy ⟨~ vestments⟩ ⟨a ~ service⟩ **b :** being in accordance with officially prescribed form **:** RUBRICAL ⟨ceremonies conducted in strict ~ form⟩ **2 :** using or favoring the use of liturgy ⟨a ~ Christian sect⟩ — **li·tur·gi·cal·ly** \-jək(ə)lē, -jēk-, -li\ *adv*

lit·ur·gi·cian \,lid·ə(r)'jishən\ *n* -s **:** a student of liturgics

li·tur·gics \lə'tərjiks, -təj-, -təij-\ *n pl but usu sing in constr* **1 :** the study of liturgies; *esp* **:** LITURGIOLOGY 1 **2 :** a branch of practical theology concerned with the forms of worship and their practice

li·tur·gi·o·log·i·cal \lə¦tərjēə¦läjəkəl\ *adj* **:** of or relating to liturgiology or a liturgiology

li·tur·gi·ol·o·gist \-,=='äləjəst\ *n* -s **:** a specialist in liturgiology

li·tur·gi·ol·o·gy \-jē\ *n* -ES [*liturgy* + *-o-* + *-logy*] **1 :** the history, doctrine, and interpretation of liturgies **2 :** a treatise on liturgies

lit·ur·gism \'lid·ə(r),jizəm, 'litə(-\ *n* -s **:** strict or excessive adherence to liturgy

lit·ur·gist \-,jəst\ *n* -s **1 :** one who favors or adheres to a liturgy **2 :** a student or compiler of liturgies **3 :** one who leads in liturgical worship — **lit·ur·gis·tic** \'==;jistik, -tēk\ *adj*

lit·ur·gy \'lid·ə(r)jē, 'litə(-, -ji\ *n* -ES [LL *liturgia*, fr. Gk *leitourgia* public service, divine service, liturgy, fr. *leit-* (fr. *leōs* people) + *-ourgia* -urgy] **1 a :** a rite or series of rites, observances, or procedures prescribed for public worship in the Christian church in accordance with authorized or standard form **b :** a Eucharistic rite or service **c :** ceremonial or ritualistic worship **2 :** a system or series of ceremonial or ritualistic actions done according to a prescribed arrangement ⟨the scoop and stretch of her fingers . . . might have been part of a witch's ~ —Richard Llewellyn⟩ **3** [Gk *leitourgia*] **:** a public service or office imposed upon the wealthy citizens of ancient Athens **syn** see FORM

lit·vak \'lit,väk, -vək\ *n* -s *cap* [Yiddish, fr. Pol *Litwak* fr. *Litwa* Lithuania] **:** a Lithuanian Jew

litz wire \'lits-\ *n* [part trans. of G *litzendraht*, fr. *litze* braid, cord, lace + *draht* wire] **:** a wire composed of individually enameled copper strands braided together to reduce skin effect and consequent high-frequency resistance

liv·a·bil·i·ty *also* **live·a·bil·i·ty** \,livə'biləd·ē, -ətē, -i\ *n* **1 :** survival expectancy **:** VIABILITY — used esp. of poultry and domestic livestock ⟨breeders are coming to select for ~ as well as for high egg production —W.F.Hollander⟩ **2 :** suitability for human living — used of housing and environment ⟨your city . . . can have the power to enforce a reasonable level of ~ in all of its homes —J.W.Lund⟩ ⟨something a town may gain in size will compensate for loss of ~ —*Atlantic*⟩

liv·able *also* **live·able** \'livəbəl\ *adj* ['*live* + *-able*] **1 :** VIABLE **2 :** suitable for living ⟨a very ~ house⟩ **3 :** BEARABLE, ENDURABLE ⟨found life scarcely ~⟩ — **liv·able·ness** *n* -ES

¹live \'liv\ *vb* -ED/-ING/-s [ME *liven*, fr. OE *libban, lifian*; akin to OHG *lebēn* to live, ON *lifa*, Goth *liban*, L *caelebs* unmarried] *vi* **1 :** to be alive **:** have the life of an animal or plant ⟨the child *lived* and grew⟩ **2 :** to continue alive ⟨the longer I ~, I find the folly and the fraud of mankind grow more and more intolerable —Tobias Smollett⟩ ⟨*lived* to a ripe and vigorous old age⟩ ⟨had nine children of whom only five *lived*⟩ **3 :** to maintain oneself **:** FEED, SUBSIST ⟨*lived* on peanut-butter sandwiches and milk, but was very contented —*Current Biog.*⟩ ⟨a man must always ~ by his work —Adam Smith⟩ ⟨many of our customers *lived* on high inventories —*Monsanto Chemical Co. Annual Report*⟩ ⟨*lived* on his relatives⟩ ⟨*lived* by his wits⟩ **4 :** to conduct, direct, or pass one's life ⟨had religiously *lived* up to that standard —C.L.Jones⟩ ⟨I *lived* and cared only for science —Harrison Brown⟩ **5 :** to occupy a home **:** DWELL, RESIDE ⟨~*s* in the suburbs⟩ ⟨the houses in which they *lived*, the ceremonies of their courts, he cannot accurately figure to himself —Matthew Arnold⟩ **6 :** to attain eternal life or beatitude ⟨I am the resurrection and the life; he who believes in me, though he die, yet shall he ~ —Jn 11:25 (RSV)⟩ **7 :** to survive oblivion **:** remain in human memory or record ⟨though you die in combat gory, ye shall ~ in song and story —W.S.Gilbert⟩ ⟨and yet the past ~*s* in us all —W.R.Inge⟩ ⟨the desire of man to ~ on through his deeds, characteristic of the erection of pyramids —John Dewey⟩ **8 :** to flourish in human life or consciousness **:** retain effect, existence, or vigor ⟨his name cannot die while courage and honor ~ among men⟩ **9 :** to outlast storm or danger **:** remain afloat or operative — used of a ship or airplane ⟨the 20 to 25 Jap torpedo planes managed to ~ long enough to launch four torpedoes —Ira Wolfert⟩ **10 :** to realize the possibilities of life amply **:** attain fulfillment or satisfaction ⟨the boy who is mentally awake ~*s* more in a day than a dull boy does in a month —*Boy Scout Handbook*⟩ ⟨I smile when I find people cheerfully talking of "happiness" as something to be desired in life. I have *lived* —Havelock Ellis⟩ **11 :** COHABIT ⟨for 18 months she had *lived* with that Canadian colonel —Fred Majdalany⟩ ~ *vt* **1 :** to pass through or spend the duration of ⟨we do not ~ out our lives unattended by divinity —*Amer. Scholar*⟩ ⟨*lived* an unforgettable hour that seemed a lifetime⟩ **2 :** ENACT, PRACTICE ⟨what other men were preaching, he *lived* —P.E.More⟩ ⟨images and ideas which can be *lived* and defended —Stephen Spender⟩ **3 :** to exhibit vigor, gusto, or enthusiasm in ⟨seized life with both hands and *lived* every minute of it —H.W.Glover⟩ **syn** see RESIDE — **live it up :** to live with gusto and usu. fast and loose ⟨*lived it up* with wine and song —*Newsweek*⟩ — **live up to :** to be equal to **:** compare in quality or worth with

²live \'līv\ *adj* -ER/-EST [short for *alive*] **1 :** having life **:** LIVING ⟨she purged a ~ eel —Robert Burton⟩ ⟨ships ~ cattle⟩ **2 :** abounding with life **:** VITAL, VIVID ⟨the portrait is . . . always ~ and spirited —*Times Lit. Supp.*⟩ ⟨a ~ appreciation of the role of cultural forces in history —L.A.White⟩ ⟨he saw an oldening, flaccid face with ~ eyes —Maurice Walsh⟩ **3 :** exerting force or containing energy: as **a :** AFIRE, GLOWING ⟨tossed a ~ cigarette from the car⟩ **b :** connected to electric power ⟨a thousand-volt wire, ~ and burning with its power —Adria Langley⟩ **c :** charged with explosives and containing shot or a bullet ⟨a ~ shell⟩ ⟨a ~ cartridge⟩ ⟨~ ammunition⟩; *also* **:** UNDISCHARGED, UNEXPLODED ⟨a ~ bomb⟩ **d :** imparting or driven by power **:** having motion ⟨the ~ center of a lathe⟩ ⟨~ conveyor rolls⟩ **e :** charged with fissionable material ⟨the pile was built up . . . with alternating layers of ~ and dead blocks —L.R.Hafstad⟩ **4 :** living in thought or controversy **:** of continuing interest **:** open to debate **:** not settled or decided **:** UNCLOSED ⟨long-standing denominational disputes still were ~ issues —Oscar Handlin⟩ **5 :** being in a pure native state: as **a** *of a mineral* **:** NATIVE, VIRGIN **b** *of rock* **:** UNWROUGHT, UNQUARRIED **6 a :** of bright vivid color **b :** of normal brightness or luster — used of timber and lumber **7 :** highly reverberant — used of a room or enclosed space in which sound is produced — compare ANECHOIC, DEAD 10 **8 a** *of a playing card* **:** available for play because still in the hands or stock **b :** being in play ⟨a ~ ball⟩ **9** *of rubber* **:** SPRINGY, RESILIENT **10 a :** not yet printed from or plated **:** to be held for possible further or future printing — used of a printing surface **b :** not yet typeset; *also* **:** typeset but not yet proofread **c :** used for storing or holding live matter **11 a :** of or relating to a performance done without mechanical reproduction by phonograph or cinema **:** presented directly by musicians or actors in concert hall or theater or on radio or television **:** not recorded or filmed **b :** present and responsive — used of a radio or television studio audience

liveability *var of* LIVABILITY

liveable *var of* LIVABLE

live axle *n* **:** the driving axle of any self-propelled vehicle ⟨the usual front axle of a passenger car is a dead axle and the rear axle is a *live axle* —*Principles of Automotive Vehicles*⟩

live-bearer \ˈlīv+,-\ *n* **:** a fish that brings forth living young rather than eggs

live-bearing \ˈ≈¦≈≈\ *adj* **:** bringing forth living young **:** VIVIPAROUS

live birth *n* **:** birth in such a state that acts of life are manifested after the extrusion of the whole body — compare STILLBIRTH

live-born \ˈ≈¦≈\ *adj* **:** born in such a state that acts of life are manifested after the extrusion of the whole body — compare STILLBORN

live-box \ˈ≈,≈\ *n* **:** a box or pen suspended in water to keep aquatic animals alive

1lived *past of* LIVE

2lived \¦līvd, ¦livd\ *adj* [ME, fr. *lif* life + *-ed* — more at LIFE] **:** having a life of a specified kind or length — usu. used in combination ⟨short-*lived*⟩ ⟨tough-*lived*⟩

li·ve·do \lə'vē,dō, lī-\ *n* -s [L, fr. *livēre* to be blue — more at LIVID] **:** a bluish usu. patchy discoloration of the skin

live down *vt* **:** to live so as to refute, overcome, or cause to be forgotten (as a mistake, misconduct, slander) ⟨managed to *live* his youthful follies *down*⟩

live-forever \ˈ≈≈¦≈≈\ *n* -s **1 :** SEDUM 2 **2 :** PEARLY EVERLASTING

live hole *n* **:** one of the flues in a clamp of bricks

live in *vi* **:** to lodge in one's place of employment — used of a servant

live·ing·ite \ˈliviŋ,īt, ˈlīv-\ *n* -s [George D. *Liveing* †1924, Eng. chemist + E *-ite*] **:** a mineral $Pb_5As_8S_{17}$ consisting of a sulfide of arsenic and lead

liveleaf *var of* LIFELEAF

livelihead *n* [ME *livelihed, livelihede,* fr. *lively* + *-hed, -hede* (var. of *-hod, -had* -hood)] **1** *obs* **:** living presence **:** LIFE **2** *obs* **:** LIVELIHOOD

live·li·hood \ˈlīvlē,hu̇d, -vli-,-\ *n* [alter. (influenced by *1lively* & *-hood*) of ME *livlod, livelode* course of life, livelihood, fr. OE *līflād* course of life, fr. *līf* life + *lād* course, journey — more at LIFE, LODE] **1 :** means of support or subsistence ⟨even then I had a low opinion of politics as a ~ —W.A.White⟩ ⟨for almost 30 years the inhabitants . . . have obtained their ~ from granite —*Amer. Guide Series: Minn.*⟩ ⟨by canny foraging on farm gardens, the rabbit still maintains a comfortable ~ —*Amer. Guide Series: Va.*⟩ **2** *obs* **:** income-producing property **:** ESTATE, PATRIMONY **3** [*1lively* + *-hood*] *obs* **:** LIVELINESS

syn see LIVING

live·li·ly \-lәlē, -li\ *adv* [*1lively* + *-ly*] **:** in a lively manner

live-line \ˈ≈,≈\ *vi* [fr. the phrase *live line*] **:** to fish by allowing the bait or lure to drift with the current on a slack line

live·li·ness \ˈlīvlēnәs, -lin-\ *n* -ES [ME *livelinesse,* fr. *lively* + *-nesse* -ness] **:** the quality or state of being lively

live load *n* **1 :** the load (as furniture and persons) to which a structure is subjected in addition to its own weight not including wind load, earthquake shocks, and such effects as the centrifugal force acting on railroad bridges located on curves, tractive effort, and impact due to sudden application of the load — compare DEAD LOAD **2 :** the weight of passengers or cargo carried by a vehicle

1live·long \ˈliv,≈, ˈlīv-\ *adj* [ME *lef long,* fr. *lef* dear + *long* — more at LIEF, LONG] **:** WHOLE, ENTIRE, COMPLETE — usu. used of a period of time ⟨sat in the *livelong* day he sat in his loom, his ear filled with its monotony —George Eliot⟩

2live·long \ˈliv,≈\ *n* -s [*1live* + *long* (adv)] **1 :** ORPINE **2 :** PEARLY EVERLASTING

1live·ly \ˈlīvlē, -li\ *adj, usu* -ER/-EST [ME, fr. OE *līflīc,* fr. *līf* life + *-līc* -ly — more at LIFE] **1** *obs* **:** LIVING **2 :** ANIMATED, VIVID, BRISK, KEEN, VIGOROUS ⟨is a ~ and fluent conversationalist —Arthur Knight⟩ ⟨the school's great tradition of ~ teaching —N.M.Pusey⟩ ⟨two Californians . . . were ~ entries —S.H.Adams⟩ ⟨a Glasgow journalist with a ~ mind and ready wit —Gilbert Harding⟩ **3 :** ACTIVE, INTENSE ⟨a ~ sense of the ludicrous —T.L.Peacock⟩ ⟨roused his *liveliest* disgust —John Buchan⟩ ⟨a ~ trade in farm products —H.E.Starr⟩ **4 :** BRILLIANT, FRESH, GAY ⟨the ~ charm of Florentine and Venetian artists —*Amer. Guide Series: N.Y. City*⟩ ⟨a ~, flashing wit⟩ ⟨it was moist and overgrown with mosses, ferns, creepers, and low shrubs, all of the *liveliest* green —W.H.Hudson †1922⟩ **5 :** ENLIVENING, TANGY **:** not flat **:** SPARKLING ⟨many a peer of England brews *livelier* liquor than the Muse —A.E.Housman⟩ **6 a :** quick to rebound **:** RESILIENT **b** *of a baseball* **:** capable of traveling an excessively great distance when hit ⟨the pitchers know they are throwing that ~ ball —Ted Williams⟩ **c :** riding lightly on the sea **:** responding readily to the helm ⟨a ~ boat⟩ **7 a :** full of life, movement, or incident ⟨the Detroit river . . . surface was ~ with craft of all descriptions —*Amer. Guide Series: Mich.*⟩ **b :** requiring alertness or activity because of danger or opposition ⟨enemy artillery made things ~ for a while⟩ ⟨speakers from across the aisle gave them a ~ time⟩

syn ANIMATED, VIVACIOUS, SPRIGHTLY, GAY: LIVELY may suggest briskness, alertness, keenness, or energy ⟨the *liveliest,* the most provocative, and the most curiously informed study of the current political situation . . . written with energy and with racy humor —H.S.Commager⟩ ⟨boomtowns, stomping dances, big talk, hope unlimited, a veritable explosion of moving, building, and working, kept things *lively* —Russell Lord⟩ ANIMATED is close to LIVELY and may apply to the spirited, sparkling, or quite active ⟨even the hardest of his friends . . . became *animated* when he took her hand, tried to meet the gay challenge in her eyes and to reply cleverly to the droll word of greeting on her lips —Willa Cather⟩ ⟨an *animated* chatter, like the bubbles of champagne made articulate —Joseph Hergesheimer⟩ VIVACIOUS suggests a very active liveliness, often sportive, compelling, or alluring ⟨they began to laugh and play, and turn heels over head, showing themselves jolly and *vivacious* brats —Nathaniel Hawthorne⟩ ⟨remember her as very pretty and *vivacious.* I never met a girl with as much zip as she had in those days —Ring Lardner⟩ SPRIGHTLY, close to VIVACIOUS, may suggest a liveliness that is alert and spirited ⟨the thrill of his enthusiasm made him walk with an elastic step. He was *sprightly,* vigorous, fiery in his belief in success —Stephen Crane⟩ ⟨Mrs. Thomas, *sprightly* again, laughed with Dylan as they recounted old stories the day's visits had recalled, and waved greetings to friends —J.M.Brinnin⟩ GAY suggests demonstrative carefreeness, sometimes marked by merriment or exuberance ⟨three *gay* girls, overflowing with life, health, and youth; and full of spirits and mischief —Herman Melville⟩ ⟨a *gay* world with its country squires and their horses and racing, its Madeira drinking, its promenades and dancing and assemblies —V.L. Parrington⟩

2lively \"\ *adv, usu* -ER/-EST [ME, fr. *lively,* adj.] **:** in a lively manner ⟨now then, step ~ there⟩

liv·en \ˈlīvәn\ *vb* **livened; livened; livening** \-v(ә)niŋ\ **livens** [*2live* + *-en*] *vt* **:** ENLIVEN — often used with *up* ~ *vi* **:** to become lively or more lively — often used with *up* — **liv·en·er** \-v(ә)nә(r)\ *n* -s

live·ness *n* -ES [*2live* + *-ness*] **:** the quality or state of being live; *esp* **:** the reverberant quality of a room

live oak *n* **:** any of several American evergreen oaks: as **a :** a medium-sized oak (*Quercus virginiana*) that is native to eastern No. America from Virginia southward to the eastern coast of Mexico, is often cultivated as a shelter and shade tree because of its rapid growth and wide-spreading shapely form, and is noted for its extremely hard tough durable wood once much used in shipbuilding **b :** any of various western No. American oaks (as canyon live oak, coast live oak, interior live oak) with evergreen foliage and hard durable wood

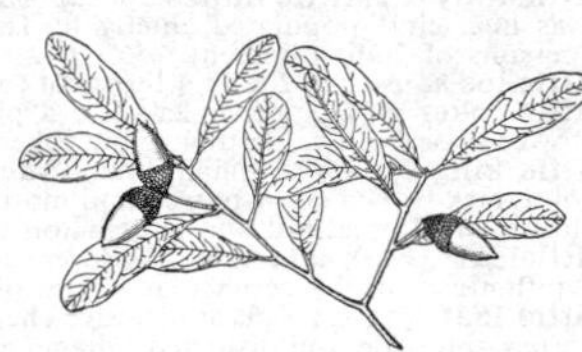

leaves and acorns of live oak

live-oak·er \ˈ≈¦ōkә(r)\ *n* -s *South* **:** one engaged in live-oak lumbering

live out *vi* **:** to lodge elsewhere than where employed — used of a servant

live parking *n* **:** the parking of a vehicle with a driver or operator in attendance

1liv·er \ˈlivә(r)\ *n* -s [ME, fr. OE *lifer;* akin to OFris *livere* liver, OHG *lebra,* ON *lifr,* and perh. to Gk *lipos* fat — more at LEAVE] **1 a :** a large very vascular glandular organ of vertebrates that secretes bile and causes important changes in many of the substances contained in the blood which passes through it (as by converting sugars into glycogen which it stores up until required and in forming urea), in man being the largest gland, from 40 to 60 ounces in weight, of a dark red color, occupying the upper right portion of the abdominal cavity immediately below the diaphragm to whose curvature its upper surface conforms, being divided by fissures into five lobes, and receiving blood both from the hepatic artery and the portal vein and returning it to the systemic circulation by the hepatic veins — see DIGESTION illustration **b :** any of various large compound glands associated with the digestive tract of invertebrate animals and prob. concerned with the secretion of digestive enzymes **2** *archaic* **:** the liver regarded as determining the quality or temper of a man ⟨hot ~s and cold purses —Shak.⟩ — compare WHITE-LIVERED **3 :** the liver of an animal (as a calf or pig) eaten as food by man **4 :** disease or disorder of the liver; *esp* **:** BILIOUSNESS ⟨had a touch of ~ —Christopher Isherwood⟩ **5** *or* **liver brown** *or* **liver maroon :** a grayish reddish brown that is redder and deeper than average taupe brown — called also *autumn oak* **6 :** a liver-colored substance (as any of several sulfur compounds) — called also *hepar*

2liver \"\ *adj* **:** of a dark chestnut color — used esp. of horses and dogs

3liver \"\ *vi* **livered; livered; livering** \-v(ә)riŋ\ **livers :** to become thick and rubbery like liver **:** GEL — used esp. of paints, varnishes, and printing inks

4liver \"\ *vt* -ED/-ING/-S [ME *liveren,* partly fr. OF *livrer,* fr. L *liberare* to free; partly short for ME *deliveren* — more at LIBERATE, DELIVER] *now dial Eng* **:** DELIVER

5liver \"\ *n* -s [ME, fr. *liven* to live + *-er*] **1 :** one that lives esp. in a specified way ⟨my father was a good ~ —W.A. White⟩ ⟨the typical American cheap ~ abroad —Herbert Gold⟩ ⟨the grossest of evil ~s —W.J.Locke⟩ **2 :** RESIDENT

6liver *comparative of* LIVE

liverberry \ˈ≈≈- — *see* BERRY\ *n* **1 :** TWISTED-STALK **2 :** the fruit of twisted-stalk

liver cell *n* **:** one of the secretory cells characteristic of the liver

liv·ered \¦livә(r)d\ *adj* [*1liver* + *-ed*] **:** having a liver of a specified character — usu. used in combination ⟨lily-*livered*⟩

liver extract *n* **:** an extract of the water-soluble constituents of fresh mammalian liver used in treatment of anemia

liver fluke *n* **:** any of various trematodes (as *Fasciola hepatica*) that invade the mammalian liver — compare AMERICAN FLUKE, CHINESE LIVER FLUKE

liver fungus *n* **:** BEEFSTEAK FUNGUS

liv·er·ied \ˈliv(ә)rēd, -rid\ *adj* [*livery* + *-ed*] **:** wearing a livery

livering *n* -s [ME *levering,* fr. *lever, liver* liver + *-ing* — more at LIVER] *obs* **:** a pudding or sausage of liver

liv·er·ish \ˈliv(ә)rish\ *adj* **1 :** like liver esp. in color ⟨arabesques of a ~ bronzy hue —Mary Austin⟩ **2 a :** suffering from liver disorder **:** BILIOUS ⟨looked pretty ~ but was all right next morning⟩ ⟨was feeling ~⟩ **b :** causing biliousness ⟨and Turkish coffee which though ~ stuff he always drank —John Galsworthy⟩ **c :** seeming or acting bilious **:** CRABBED, MELANCHOLY ⟨a gloomy, ~ sort of man —P.B.Kyne⟩ — **liv·er·ish·ness** *n* -ES

liverleaf \ˈ≈≈,≈\ *n* **:** HEPATICA 1b

liv·er·less \-lәs\ *adj* **1 :** lacking a liver **2 :** deficient in liver function or in courage or temper

liver lily *n* **:** an iris (*Iris versicolor*) of the eastern U. S.

liver line *n, usu cap 1st L* **:** LINE OF MERCURY

liver maroon *n* **:** LIVER 5

liver of antimony *archaic* **:** a brown powder obtained by heating an antimony sulfide with an alkaline sulfide

liver of sulfur : SULFURATED POTASH

liver oil *n* **:** a fatty oil obtained from liver; *usu* **:** FISH-LIVER OIL

liv·er·pool \ˈlivә(r),pül\ *adj, usu cap* [fr. *Liverpool,* England] **1 :** of or from the city of Liverpool, England **:** of the kind or style prevalent in Liverpool **2 :** of or relating to a usu. white or cream-colored ceramic ware made in Liverpool potteries beginning in the early 18th century

liver·pool bit *n, usu cap L* **:** a curb bit with a straight shank

liverpool rummy *n, usu cap L* **:** a card game of the contract rummy group

1liv·er·pud·li·an \¦livә(r)¦pәdlēәn\ *adj, usu cap* [*Liverpudl-* (alter. — influenced by *puddle* — of *Liverpool,* England) + E *-ian*] **1 :** of, relating to, or characteristic of Liverpool, England **2 :** of, relating to, or characteristic of the people of Liverpool

2liverpudlian \"\ *n* -s *cap* **:** a native or inhabitant of Liverpool

liver rot *n* **:** a disease that is caused by liver flukes esp. in sheep and cattle and is marked by sluggishness, anemia, and wasting and by great local damage to the liver due to the presence of the worms and their by-products — compare BLACK DISEASE

livers *pl of* LIVER, *pres 3d sing of* LIVER

liver sausage *or* **liver pudding** *n* **:** a sausage consisting of cooked ground liver and lean pork trimmings seasoned with condiments and herbs and stuffed into casings and boiled or smoked

liver spots *n pl* **:** CHLOASMA

liverwort \ˈ≈≈,≈\ *n* **1 :** a bryophyte of the class Hepaticae **2 :** HEPATICA 1b

liverwort lettuce *n* **:** FALSE WINTERGREEN

liv·er·wurst *R* ˈlivә(r),wәrst, -,wu̇rst, -*R* -,wәst, -,wu̇ost, *R* & -*R* -,wu̇st *also* -,wә(r)st *sometimes* -,wu̇sht\ *n* -s [part trans. of G *leberwurst,* fr. *leber* liver + *wurst* sausage — more at BRATWURST] **:** LIVER SAUSAGE

1liv·ery \ˈliv(ә)rē, -ri\ *n* -ES [ME *livere,* fr. OF *livree,* lit., distribution, delivery, fr. fem. of *livré,* past part. of *livrer* to deliver — more at LIVER] **1** *archaic* **:** the apportioning of provisions esp. to servants or the rations so given **2 a :** the distinctive clothing or badge formerly given by a person of rank or wealth to be worn by his retainers esp. in wartime service **b :** LIVERY COLOR 1 **c liveries** *pl, in Scottish heraldry* **:** LIVERY COLOR 2a **d :** a servant's uniform ⟨a chauffeur in ~⟩ **e :** distinctive dress (as of an organization, profession, occupation) ⟨the ~ of the guild members⟩ ⟨the sisters wear a white habit and scapular with a black veil, the ~ of St. Dominic —T.P. McCarthy⟩ **:** CLOTHES, GARB, GARMENTS ⟨if he can dress his endeavors in the ~ of patriotism, . . . he can cover the scandals of his own character —J.A.Froude⟩ **f :** LIVERY COMPANY **3** *archaic* **a :** one's retainers or retinue **b :** the members of a British livery company **4 a** *obs* **:** the ration of provender given a horse **b :** the feeding, stabling, and care of horses for pay **:** BOARDING **c :** a stable keeping horses and usu. carriages for hire **d :** a concern offering vehicles of any of various kinds for rent ⟨a canoe ~⟩ ⟨an automobile ~⟩ ⟨a bicycle ~⟩ **5 a :** the act of delivering legal possession of property (as lands or tenements) — compare GRANT 3a, LIVERY OF SEIZIN **b** *Eng law* (1) **:** the delivery of the possession of lands released from a court dealing with wardships (2) **:** the writ by which such possession is obtained

2livery \"\ *adj* **1 :** issued as livery **2 :** constituting livery ⟨a chauffeur's visored ~ cap⟩ **3 :** kept for hire ⟨~ limousines⟩

3livery \"\ *adj* [*1liver* + *-y*] **1 a :** resembling liver **b :** suggesting liver disorder **:** LIVERISH ⟨he returned a captain, unwounded, but thin and yellow, with the ~ look that confirmed the stories —Edna Ferber⟩ **2 :** HEAVY, CLINGING, GUMMY — used of soil ⟨heavy soil plows up in ~ slices in winter —F.D. Smith & Barbara Wilcox⟩

livery color *n* **1 :** the color or one of the colors of the clothing issued by a feudal superior to his retainers or by a person of wealth or rank to his servants **2 livery colors** *pl* **a :** the principal metal and the principal color of an escutcheon of arms often used also as the principal colors of a flag or ensign or of a personal standard as well as of the liveries of the armiger's servants **b :** the principal colors of the flag of a political unit (as a nation) sometimes not identical with its armorial colors **:** the national or civic colors

livery company *n* **:** any of various London craft or trade associations that are descended from medieval guilds

livery cupboard *n* **:** a free-standing cupboard used for the storage of food and drink esp. in the middle ages

livery·man \ˈ≈(≈)≈mәn\ *n, pl* **livery·men** \-mәn, -,men\ **1** *archaic* **:** a liveried retainer **2 :** a freeman of the city of London entitled to wear the livery of the company to which he belongs and to enjoy other privileges (as to vote for some of the chief London municipal officials) **3 :** the keeper of a vehicle-rental service

livery of seizin *Eng law* **:** a now disused ceremony for conveyance of land by the symbolic transfer of a key, twig, or turf or by symbolic entry of the grantee

livery stable *n* **:** a stable where horses and vehicles are kept for hire and where stabling is provided

1lives *pl of* LIFE, *pres 3d sing of* LIVE

2lives \ˈlivz\ *North var of* LIEF

live-sawed \ˈ≈¦≈\ *adj* **:** sawed through without being turned — used of a log

livest *superlative of* LIVE

live steam *n* **:** steam direct from a boiler and under full pressure

livestock \ˈ≈,≈\ *n* **:** animals of any kind kept or raised for use or pleasure; *esp* **:** meat and dairy cattle and draft animals — opposed to *dead stock*

live storage *n* **:** storage of property permitting use at will by the owner

liv·e·tin \ˈlivәdәn\ *n* -s [anagram of *vitellin*] **:** a protein obtained from egg yolk

live trap *n* **:** a trap for catching an animal alive and uninjured

livetrap \ˈ≈,≈\ *vt* [*live trap*] **:** to capture (an animal) with a live trap (as for removal to another area for restocking)

liveweight \ˈ≈¦≈\ *n* **:** the weight of an animal while living

live well *n* **1 :** a well for keeping fish alive in a fishing boat by allowing seawater to circulate through it **2 :** LIVE-BOX

live wire *n* **1 :** an energized electrical conductor **2 :** an alert, active, aggressive person ⟨a *live wire,* full of American know-how —C.W.Mills⟩

liveyere *var of* LIVYER

liv·id \ˈlivәd\ *adj* [F *livide,* fr. L *lividus,* fr. *livēre* to be blue; akin to OIr *lī* color, W *lliw* color, OE *slāh* sloe, OHG *slēha* sloe, Russ *sliva* plum] **1 :** discolored by or as if by bruising **:** BLACK-AND-BLUE ⟨~ flesh⟩ **2 :** of the color lead — compare LIVID BROWN, LIVID PINK, LIVID PURPLE, LIVID VIOLET **3 :** ASHEN, PALLID, GHASTLY, GRAY ⟨as I imprinted the first kiss on her lips, they became ~ with the hue of death —Mary W. Shelley⟩ **4 :** LURID ⟨world of sideshow freaks among whom he has a large and rather ~ acquaintance —J.S.Sandoe⟩ — **li·vid·i·ty** \lә'vidәd·ē, -әtē, -i\ *n* -ES — **liv·id·ness** *n* -ES

livid brown *n* **:** a grayish red that is bluer and less strong than bois de rose, yellower and paler than blush rose, and bluer and duller than Pompeian red

liv·id·ly *adv* **:** in a livid manner

livid pink *n* **:** a grayish pink

livid purple *n* **:** a grayish reddish purple that is redder and duller than heather (sense 2a) and deeper than Campanula violet

livid violet *n* **:** a light grayish red that is bluer and very slightly lighter than ashes of rose

liv·ier \ˈlivyә(r), -vēә-\ *n* -s [prob. fr. *lives* (pl. of *life*) + *-ier*] *dial Eng* **:** the holder of a lease granted for one or more lifetimes

1liv·ing \ˈliviŋ\ *adj* [ME, fr. pres. part. of *liven* to live — more at LIVE] **1 a :** having life **:** not dead ⟨all ~ things by definition have irritability and response —Weston LaBarre⟩ ⟨swore by the ~ God that he spoke truth⟩ ⟨the skin is a ~ tissue —Morris Fishbein⟩ ⟨and he stood between the dead and the ~; and the plague was stopped —Num 16: 48 (RSV)⟩ **b :** now or still having life **:** CONTEMPORARY, SURVIVING ⟨not in the memory of ~ men had such another opportunity offered⟩ ⟨the ~ orders of insects⟩ **c :** ACTIVE, EFFECTIVE, FUNCTIONING, PRODUCTIVE, VITAL ⟨the past of mankind . . . abides as a ~ reality in our present —P.E.More⟩ ⟨educators who think of the liberal-arts tradition in a ~ and creative fashion —H.D. Gideonse⟩ ⟨a suffix that continues to form new compounds remains ~ in the language⟩ **2 a :** exhibiting the life or motion of nature or its life-giving powers ⟨it was a land of high, rolling prairies, wide valleys, and sweet ~ water —F.B.Gipson⟩ ⟨drinking this champagne water is pure pleasure, so is breathing the ~ air —John Muir †1914⟩ ⟨the happy ~ sunlight —Edith Sitwell⟩ **b :** BURNING ⟨then on the ~ coals red wine they pour —John Dryden⟩ **3 :** remaining uncut or unquarried **:** NATIVE ⟨in places the track was hewn out of the ~ rock —*Geog. Jour.*⟩ **4 a :** full of life or vigor **:** LIVELY ⟨visualized anatomy as a ~ subject —H.R.Viets⟩ **b :** true to life or reality **:** VIVID ⟨no mere historical curiosity but a ~ and moving work of art —Edward Sackville-West⟩ ⟨seek through the flesh: you will not find the ~ likeness of the mind —D.C. Babcock⟩ **c :** animated by thought or purpose bearing directly on life **:** vitally inspired or relevant **:** moved or formed by significant aims ⟨a working library, a ~ library —Virginia Woolf⟩ **5 :** appropriate, designed, or adequate for living ⟨rug and wood paneling define the ~ area —Edgar Kaufmann⟩ **6 :** having or using live performers (as actors or musicians) rather than mechanical recordings ⟨baffled in the effort to detect the ~ performance from the . . . record —R.D.Darrell⟩ ⟨there would be a renaissance of the ~ theater —*Theatre Arts*⟩ **7 :** VERY — used as an intensive ⟨history . . . scares the ~ daylights out of school kids —*Nicholas County (W. Va.) News Leader*⟩ ⟨beat the ~ tar out of him⟩

2living \"\ *n* -s [ME, fr. gerund of *liven*] **1 :** the condition of being alive or the action of a being that has life ⟨~ in the same house became unbearable⟩ ⟨the ascetic with a passion for ~ —H.S.Canby⟩ **2 :** the passing of one's life in a particular way **:** conduct or manner of life ⟨the art of ~ is thus recognized as a subject which concerns everyone —Herbert Spencer⟩ ⟨the collegiate way of ~ —J.B.Conant⟩ ⟨utter impatience with totalitarian ~ —G.P.Musselman⟩ ⟨was conspicuous for loose ~⟩ **3 a :** means of subsistence **:** LIVELIHOOD ⟨we both earn our ~s —Virginia Woolf⟩ ⟨bees, too, are here . . . getting a ~ among the blue flowers of the sea holly —Robert Lynd⟩ **b** *archaic* **:** an estate or income-producing property **c** *Brit* **:** 1BENEFICE 1 ⟨the diaries of clergymen in quiet country ~s —*Sydney (Australia) Bull.*⟩

syn LIVELIHOOD, SUBSISTENCE, SUSTENANCE, MAINTENANCE, SUPPORT, KEEP, BREAD, OR BREAD AND BUTTER: LIVING is general in meaning but is now limited to use in a few idioms ⟨to make a *living* selling books⟩ ⟨to take a *living* from the soil⟩ LIVELIHOOD often applies to the wages, salary, or income from which one lives or to the profession or craft whereby one earns his wages or salary ⟨provided with a modest *livelihood*⟩ ⟨while the profession is of necessity a means of *livelihood* or of financial reward, the devoted service which it inspires is motivated by other considerations —R.M.MacIver⟩ ⟨stock raising is his *livelihood*⟩ ⟨education is a preparation for life, not merely for a *livelihood*, for living not for *a* living —George Sampson⟩ SUBSISTENCE suggests living with only the barest necessities ⟨*subsistence* wages are the lowest needed to sustain life⟩ ⟨if he could raise enough corn and pork for *subsistence*, he cared for nothing more —*Amer. Guide Series: N.C.*⟩ SUSTENANCE applies to whatever sustains life; it ranges from indicating food and other necessities for bare subsistence to more liberal provision ⟨the purely *sustenance* type of farming in which the farmer merely supplies his own needs —Samuel Van Valkenburg and Ellsworth Huntington⟩ ⟨Irish parents who had come to this country in search of more *sustenance* than they could glean from the barren soil of Connemara —Russel Crouse⟩ MAINTENANCE applies to a complex of necessities like food, lodging, clothing, and cleaning or to money sufficient to provide them ⟨*maintenance* for his separated wife⟩ ⟨the hospital had advertised for a general resident doctor at $300 a month and *maintenance* —Greer Williams⟩ ⟨monthly allowances to parents for the *maintenance*, care, training, education, and advancement of the child —*Current Biog.*⟩ SUPPORT may apply to means of maintenance or to the person who provides the means ⟨his scanty wages are his parent's sole *support*⟩ KEEP is a somewhat colloquial synonym for MAINTENANCE and is applicable to animals as well as persons ⟨hired men could no longer be had for ten or fifteen dollars a month and *keep* —W.A.White⟩ BREAD and BREAD AND BUTTER are synecdoches for LIVING or SUSTENANCE ⟨give us this day our daily *bread* Mt 6: 11 (RSV)⟩ ⟨earning one's *bread and butter* at the mill⟩

living death *n* **:** life emptied of joys and satisfactions **:** extreme wretchedness ⟨what happened . . . at the Nazi camp adds little to the all too familiar *living-death* literature —*Time*⟩

living fossil *n* **:** an animal or plant (as the king crab or the gingko tree) that has remained essentially unchanged from earlier geologic times and whose near relatives are usu. extinct — compare RELICT

living language *n* **:** a language in use as a vernacular ⟨any world language must be a *living language* —Charlton Laird⟩

liv·ing·ly *adv* [ME, fr. *living* + *-ly*] **:** VITALLY, REALISTICALLY

liv·ing·ness *n* -ES [¹*living* + *-ness*] **:** VITALITY, VIGOR, VIVIDNESS ⟨what he likes in nature is perhaps more than anything else the mere sense of ~ —J.W.Beach⟩ ⟨his memory stored up an amazing gallery of faces and figures, and he got these down with supreme ~ —Sheldon Cheney⟩

living newspaper *n* **:** a theatrical presentation often using a medley of techniques (as staged and filmed episodes) to dramatize social and economic problems — compare EPIC DRAMA

living picture *n* **:** TABLEAU, PANTOMIME

living pledge *n* **:** the transfer of possession of an estate to a lender to be held by him until the debt is paid out of the rents and profits — compare MORTGAGE

living rock *n* **1 :** MESCAL 1 **2 :** a cactus (*Ariocarpus fissuratus*) of the southwestern U.S. and adjacent Mexico that resembles the related mescal

living room *n* **1 :** a room in a residence used for the common social activities of the occupants — compare DRAWING ROOM, PARLOR, SITTING ROOM **2 :** space in which to live **:** LEBENSRAUM ⟨surplus populations would demand *living room* —W.P. Webb⟩

living space *n* **1 :** territory needed or sought for occupation by a nation whose population is expanding **:** LEBENSRAUM ⟨countries which had the doubtful honor of being regarded as belonging to Germany's *living space* —Paul Einzig⟩ **2 :** habitable space in a dwelling ⟨only actual rooms can be called *living space* —J.R.Dalzell⟩

living standard *n* **:** STANDARD OF LIVING ⟨to provide a minimum *living standard* for our 150 million people —M.S.Eccles⟩

living stone *n* **:** LITHOPS 2

liv·ing·ston·ite \ˈliviŋstə,nīt\ *n* -S [David *Livingstone* †1873 Scot. missionary and explorer + E *-ite*] **:** a mineral $HgSb_4S_7$ consisting of a lead-gray mercury antimony sulfide resembling stibnite

living trust *n* **:** a trust created by the transfer of property by its owner to a living or existing person to hold as trustee **:** a trust inter vivos — compare TESTAMENTARY TRUST

living unit *n* **:** an apartment or house for use by one family

living wage *n* **1 :** a subsistence wage **2 :** a wage sufficient to provide the necessities and comforts held to comprise an acceptable standard of living

li·vi·sto·na \,livəˈstōnə\ *n, cap* [NL, fr. *Liviston*, estate near Edinburgh, Scotland] **:** a genus of Asiatic, Malaysian, and Australian fan palms — see CHINESE FAN PALM

¹li·vo·ni·an \ləˈvōnēən, -nyən\ *adj, usu cap* [*Livonia*, district in Latvia + E *-an*] **1 a :** of, relating to, or characteristic of Livonia **b :** of, relating to, or characteristic of the people of Livonia **2 :** of, belonging to, or in the Livonian language

²livonian \"\ *n* -S *cap* **1 :** a native or inhabitant of Livonia **2 :** a Finno-Ugric language of the Livonian people — see URALIC LANGUAGES table

li·vor \ˈlī,vȯ(ə)r, -,vər\ *n* -S [L, fr. *livēre* to be blue + *-or* — more at LIVID] **1** *obs* **:** MALIGNITY, SPITE **2** *archaic* **:** livid condition

li·vrai·son \,lēvrāˈzōⁿ\ *n* -S [F, lit., delivery, fr. OF, fr. L *liberation-, liberatio* action of freeing — more at LIBERATION] **:** FASCICLE 2

li·vre \ˈlēvə(r), -vr(ᵊ), -v(rə)\ *n* -S [F, fr. L *libra* balance, unit of weight] **1 :** a former French unit of value worth a pound of silver in the reign of Charlemagne **2** *or* **livre tour·nois** \-tu̇rnˈwä\ **:** the livre of Tours that from 1667 until replaced by the franc in 1795 was the only legal French livre and consisted of 20 sous of 12 deniers each

liv·yer \ˈlivyər\ *or* **liv·yere** *or* **live·yere** \(ˈ)livˈye(ə)r\ *n* -S [alter. of *livier*] **:** a permanent settler of northeastern Canada who lives by trapping, trading, or fishing

li·wa \ˈlēwə\ *n* -S [Ar *liwā'*] **:** a large administrative district in any of several Muslim countries

lix·iv·i·al \(ˈ)likˈsivēəl\ *adj* [*lixivium* + *-al*] *archaic* **:** relating to or like lixivium **:** obtained by lixiviation **:** ALKALINE

lix·iv·i·ate \-vē,āt, *usu* -ād.+V\ *vt* -ED/-ING/-S [*lixivium* + *-ate*] **:** to extract a soluble compound from (a solid mixture) by washing or percolation **:** LEACH

lix·iv·i·a·tion \(,)=,==ˈāshən\ *n* -S **:** the process of lixiviating **:** PERCOLATION

lix·iv·i·ous \(ˈ)=ˈsivēəs\ *adj* [L *lixivius* made of lye, fr. *lixa* lye, water + *-ivus* -ive — more at LIQUID] *archaic* **:** LIXIVIAL

lix·iv·i·um \=ˈ=ēəm\ *n, pl* **lixiv·ia** \-ēə\ *or* **lixiviums** [LL, lye, fr. neut. of L *lixivius*] *archaic* **:** a solution (as lye) obtained by lixiviation

liz·ard \ˈlizə(r)d\ *n* -S [ME *lesard, liserd*, fr. MF *laisarde*, fr. L *lacerta* — more at LEG] **1 a :** any member of the suborder Lacertilia of the reptilian order Squamata characterized in distinction from the snakes by a fused inseparable lower jaw, a single temporal opening, two pairs of well differentiated functional limbs which may be lacking in burrowing forms, external ears, and eyes with movable lids and having a scaly or tuberculate skin, replaceable teeth that lack true sockets and are fused to the ridge of the jaw in agamid lizards and the chameleons and to the side of the jaw in most other lizards — compare ACRODONT, GILA MONSTER, PLEURODONT **b :** any relatively long-bodied reptile with legs and tapering tail (as a crocodile or dinosaur) **c :** a similarly shaped amphibian (as a newt or salamander) **2 :** a domestic greenish bronze canary with a yellow crown and scaly-appearing plumage **3 :** ALLIGATOR 6b **4** *or* **lizard green :** a moderate green that is yellower and paler than sea green (sense 1a) and lighter and slightly bluer than laurel green (sense 1) **5 :** a rope with a thimble or block spliced into one or both of the ends used as a fairlead in handling a ship's rigging **6** *usu cap* **:** ALABAMIAN — used as a nickname **7 :** leather made from lizard skin **8 :** LOUNGE LIZARD ⟨the lonely wives and the ~*s* with the thin mustaches —Willard Robertson⟩

typical lizard

lizard bronze *n* **:** OLD MOSS

lizard fish *n* **:** any of various slender marine fishes having a scaly head like that of a lizard and a large mouth and constituting the family Synodontidae

lizard flower *or* **lizard orchis** *n* **:** any of several European plants of the genus *Orchis*

lizard's–tail \ˈ==,=\ *n, pl* **lizard's–tails :** a No. American herbaceous perennial plant (*Saururus cernuus*) with small white apetalous flowers — called also *breastweed*

lizard's-tail

lizard's–tail family *n* **:** SAURURACEAE

lizardtail \ˈ==,=\ *n* **1 :** LIZARD'S-TAIL **2 :** a Californian white-woolly herb (*Eriophyllum stoechadifolium*) of the family Compositae with yellow flowers

lizari *or* **lizary** *var of* ALIZARI

liz·zie \ˈlizē, -zi\ *n* -S [(*tin*) *lizzie*] *slang* **:** a small and relatively inexpensive automobile

LJ *abbr* lord justice

LJJ *abbr* lords justices

lju·blja·na \lēˈüblēˈänə, lēˈüblēə,näˈ\ *adj, usu cap* [fr. *Ljubljana*, Yugoslavia] **:** of or from the city of Ljubljana, Yugoslavia **:** of the kind or style prevalent in Ljubljana

lkg *abbr* leakage

lkr *abbr* locker

¹'ll \(ə)l, ᵊl\ *vb* [by contr.] **:** SHALL, WILL ⟨*I'll* leave it to you —Noel Coward⟩ ⟨you'*ll* remember —Anne Brooks⟩ ⟨when'*ll* he go⟩

²'ll \ᵊl\ *conj* [by contr.] **:** TILL ⟨wait'*ll* he leaves⟩

LL *abbr* **1** large letter **2** leased line **3** lending library **4** limited liability **5** live load **6** *often not cap* [L *loco laudato*] in the place cited **7** loose leaf **8** lord lieutenant **9** lower left

ll *abbr* **1** leaves **2** [L *leges*] laws **3** lines

lla·ma \ˈlämə, ˈyä-\ *n, pl* **llamas** *also* **llama** [Sp, fr. Quechua] **1 :** any of several wild and domesticated So. American ruminants related to the camels but smaller and without a hump; *specif* **:** the domesticated variety of the guanaco that is about three feet high at the shoulder with a coat of long coarse woolly hair varying in color from black to white and that has been used for centuries in the Andes as a beast of burden and a source of wool — compare ALPACA, VICUÑA **2 :** cloth made from the llama's hair

llan·dei·lo \lanˈdī(,)lō\ *adj, usu cap* [fr. *Llandeilo*, subdivision of the European Ordovician, fr. *Llandeilo*, So. Wales] **:** of or relating to a subdivision of the European Ordovician — see GEOLOGIC TIME table

llan·do·ve·ri·an \ˈlandəˈvirēən\ *adj, usu cap* [fr. *Llandoverian*, subdivision of the European Silurian, fr. *Llandovery*, Wales + E *-ian*] **:** of or relating to a subdivision of the European Silurian — see GEOLOGIC TIME table

lla·ne·ro \läˈne(,)rō, yä-\ *n* -S [Sp, fr. *llano* + *-ero* -er] **:** a cowboy or herdsman in Spanish America

lla·no \ˈlä(,)nō, ˈla(-, ˈyä(-\ *n, pl* **llanos** [Sp, plain, fr. L *planum*, fr. neut. of *planus* level, flat — more at FLOOR] **:** an extensive plain in Spanish America or southwestern U.S. generally with few trees — compare CAMPO

llan·virn \(ˈ)lanˈvi(ə)rn, -ˈvərn\ *adj, usu cap* [fr. *Llanvirn*, subdivision of the European Ordovician] **:** of or relating to a subdivision of the European Ordovician — see GEOLOGIC TIME table

lla·re·ta \yəˈrād.ə\ *n* [Sp, fr. Quechua *yareta*] **:** YARETA

llau·tu \ˈlau̇(,)tü\ *n* -S [Sp *llautu, llauto*, fr. Quechua *lláutu*] **:** a fringed cord of vicuña wool worn wound about the head by ancient Peruvians as an emblem of nobility

LLB *abbr or n* -S [NL *legum baccalaureus*] **:** a bachelor of laws

LLD *abbr or n* -S [NL *legum doctor*] **:** a doctor of laws

l level *n, usu cap 1st L* **:** the energy level of an electron in the L-shell

llew·el·lin setter \lüˈe|lən-, ləˈwel|\ *n, usu cap L* [after R.L. Purcell-*Llewellin*, 19th cent. Eng. dog breeder] **:** a strain of English setter noted for its field-trial performance

LLI *abbr* latitude and longitude indicator

LLJJ *abbr* lords justices

LLM *abbr or n* -S [NL *legum magister*] **:** a master of laws

lloyd–geor·gian \ˈlȯidˈjȯrj(ē)ən\ *also* **lloyd–george·ite** \-ȯr,jīt\ *adj, usu cap L&G* [David *Lloyd George* †1945 British statesman + E *-ian* or *-ite*] **:** of or associated with the statesman David Lloyd George or his policies

lloyd's bushtit \ˈlȯidz-\ *n, usu cap L* [fr. the name *Lloyd*] **:** a gray black-marked bushtit (*Psaltritus minimus lloydi*) of the southwestern U.S. and adjacent Mexico

LLR *abbr* line of least resistance

llyn \ˈlin\ *n* -S [W — more at LINN] **:** a lake or pool in Wales

LM *abbr* **1** land mine **2** long meter **3** lord mayor

lm *abbr* lumen

LMD *abbr* long meter double

LMG *abbr* light machine gun

lmn *abbr* lineman

lmt *abbr* limit

LMT *abbr* **1** length, mass, time **2** local mean time

LMTD *abbr* logarithmic mean temperature difference

ln *symbol* natural logarithm

Ln *symbol* lanthanide

ln *abbr* **1** lane **2** lien **3** loan

LNC *abbr* local naval commander

LND *abbr* limiting nose dive

lng *abbr* lining

¹lo \ˈlō\ *interj* [ME, fr. OE *lā*] — used to call attention ⟨~, all ye miserable sinners . . . hearken unto my words —Harold Fleming⟩ or to express wonder or surprise ⟨pulled aside the napkin and ~, there were roses —Gladys B. Stern⟩

²lo \"\ *n* -S *usu cap* [¹*lo*, taken as a proper name in the phrase *Lo, the poor Indian* in *Essay on Man* I, 99, by Alexander Pope †1744, Eng. poet] **:** a No. American Indian ⟨appeared again at the head of our train in the company of thirty or forty other *Los* —G.W.Perrie⟩

LO *abbr* **1** liaison officer **2** lubricating oil

lo *abbr* lord

¹loa \ˈlōə\ *n* [NL, of African origin; akin to Kongo *lowa, loba* eye worm] **1** *cap* **:** a genus of African filarial worms (family Dipetalonematidae) infecting the subcutaneous tissues and blood of man, transmitted by the bite of flies of the genus *Chrysops*, and associated with urticarial and other allergic manifestations — compare CALABAR SWELLING; see EYE WORM **2** -S **:** any worm of the genus *Loa*

²loa \lōˈwä\ *n, pl* **loa** *or* **loas** [Haitian Creole *lwa*] **:** a Haitian voodoo cult deity of African origin

LOA *abbr* length over all

loach \ˈlōch\ *n* -ES [ME *loche, loch*, fr. MF *loche*] **:** any of a family (Cobitidae) of small Old World freshwater fishes closely related to the Cyprinidae but resembling catfishes in appearance and habits

¹load \ˈlōd\ *n* -S [ME *lod, lood* act of loading, load (influenced in meaning by *laden* to load), fr. OE *lād* course, way, journey, carrying, support — more at LADE, LODE] **1 :** an item or collection of things, material, animals, or passengers carried **: a :** whatever is put on a man or pack animal to be carried **:** PACK ⟨the supply men hiked their ~*s* up on their shoulders —Burgess Scott⟩ **b :** whatever is put in a ship or vehicle or airplane for conveyance **:** a collection of freight or passengers **:** CARGO ⟨one more stop before he finished delivering his ~⟩; *specif* **:** a quantity of material assembled or packed as a shipping unit sometimes with a specified character or arrangement ⟨each ~ of 50 disks is packaged in a . . . glass vial —*Modern Packaging*⟩ ⟨a car with a transverse ~⟩ **c (1) :** the quantity that can be or customarily is carried at one time by an often specified means of conveyance ⟨a dump truck with a full ~ of sand⟩; *specif* **:** a measured quantity of a commodity fixed for each type of carrier ⟨a ~ of plain tiles is 1000 —*Gregory's Handbook for Australian Builders*⟩ — often used in combination ⟨a boat*load* of tourists⟩ ⟨an arm*load* of bundles⟩ ⟨arrived by the jeep*load*⟩ (2) *Midland* **:** an armful esp. of firewood **d :** the mineral matter transported by a stream as visible sediment or in solution **2 a :** a mass or weight supported by something ⟨a roof sagging under its ~ of snow⟩ ⟨branches bent low by their ~ of fruit⟩ **b :** the forces to which a structure is subjected because of weights carried on the supports or the overturning moments to which a structure is subjected by wind pressure on the vertical surfaces ⟨the external forces, or ~*s*, to which a roof truss is subjected consist of the weights of materials of construction, snow, ice, and wind pressure together with the reactions developed at the supports as a result of these ~*s* —F.E.Kidder & Harry Parker⟩ ⟨the most accurate way of determining the full ~ on each tire is to weigh each axle of a fully loaded truck — *Armstrong Tires Data Bk.*⟩ — see DEAD LOAD, LIVE LOAD **c :** the amount of stress put on something ⟨the ~ on a glued joint⟩ ⟨this normal instinctive fear which adds its ~ to the burden of the nervous system —H.G.Armstrong⟩ **3 :** something borne or conveyed in a manner suggesting a material load: as **a :** something that weighs down the mind or spirits ⟨a ~ of care⟩ ⟨took a great ~ off his mind⟩ **b :** a burdensome or laborious responsibility ⟨carry his share of the ~ in a democratic society —*Bull. of Bates Coll.*⟩ ⟨his heavy ~ of day-to-day work —*N.Y.Times*⟩ **c :** the content of thought or feeling carried (as by a piece of writing) ⟨a work which has acquired an enormous ~ of sentimental values —Hunter Mead⟩ **4** *slang* **:** an intoxicating amount of liquor drunk **:** a state of intoxication ⟨he'd come in with a small ~ on, but he was never really high —Roderick Lull⟩ **5 :** a large quantity **:** LOT — usu. used in pl. ⟨a singing comedienne with . . . ~*s* of energy —*New Yorker*⟩ **6 a :** a charge or cartridge for a firearm: (1) **:** a charge of powder (2) **:** a charge of shot in a shotshell (3) **:** a fully loaded cartridge **b :** the quantity of material loaded into a device or machine at one time ⟨a washer that takes a 10 pound ~⟩ ⟨put three ~*s* through the dryer⟩ **7 :** external resistance overcome by a machine or prime mover ⟨at all ~*s* less than full capacity, the turbine operates at better efficiency with individual nozzle control — B.G.A.Skrotzki & W.A.Vopat⟩ **8 a :** power output (as of an engine, motor, power plant, or source of electric current) or power consumed (as by a device or circuit) **b :** a device or group of devices to which power is delivered **9 :** something (as a railway freight car) that contains a load ⟨a train of thirty empties and ten ~*s* —Elton Brown⟩ **:** one that is loaded **10 a** (1) **:** the amount of work that a person carries or is expected to carry ⟨workers . . . willing to adapt to work ~*s* set by time study methods —J.A.Morris b. 1918⟩ ⟨counseling duties in addition to normal teaching ~*s* —Bates Boyle⟩ ⟨patient ~ of physicians in private practice⟩ ⟨the case ~ of social workers⟩ ⟨a regular student with an academic ~ of 12 semester hours⟩ (2) **:** the amount of authorized work to be performed by a machine, a group, a department, or a factory **b :** the demand upon the operating resources of a system (as a telephone exchange, postal system, or railroad) ⟨the ~ in a refrigeration system is the name applied to the quantity of heat that must be removed per unit of time —B.H.Jennings⟩ **:** the number or quantity (as of persons, vehicles) accommodated (as by an institution, transportation system) at one time ⟨the population ~ on the land —Russell Lord⟩ ⟨care for the potential ~ of senile mental cases —*Psychological Abstracts*⟩ ⟨traffic reaching its peak ~ during rush hours⟩ **11** *slang* **:** a full view **:** EYEFUL; *also* **:** EARFUL — used in the phrase *get a load of* ⟨get a ~ of this new convertible —Bennett Cerf⟩ **12 :** BURDEN 10 ⟨the worm ~ in rats⟩ **13 :** an amount added to the selling price of an article, service, or security to represent selling or delivery expense and profit of the distributor — called also *loading*

²load \"\ *vb* -ED/-ING/-S [ME *loden*, fr. *lod, lood*, n.] *vt* **1 a :** to put a load in or on (a means of conveyance) **:** to fill with material, animals, or passengers to be transported ⟨had ~*ed* the moving van by noon⟩ ⟨~ the plane with cargo⟩ ⟨steamboats ~*ed* down with goods and passengers —*Amer. Guide Series: Minn.*⟩ **b :** to place in or on a means of conveyance **:** pack or stow as a load ⟨~ the freight into the car⟩ ⟨~*s* his family into the car for a ride⟩ **2 a :** to encumber or oppress with something heavy, laborious or disheartening **:** weigh down **:** BURDEN — often used with *with* ⟨a railway president . . . would not ~ himself with departmental minutiae —W.J. Cunningham⟩ ⟨a business that was ~*ed* down with debts⟩ ⟨~ human life with frustration and grief —David Cort⟩ **b :** to place as a burden or obligation **:** SADDLE — often used with *on* ⟨~ more work on him⟩ **c :** ⁴GUM *vt* 4 **d :** to play a card (as in the game of hearts) that will increase the count against (an opponent who takes the trick) **3 a :** to place or be a material weight or physical stress on ⟨grapes ~ down the vines⟩ ⟨~ the springs to the limit⟩ **b :** to increase the weight of by adding something heavy ⟨the stockwhip was . . . ~*ed* with shot at the butt —H.L.Davis⟩ **c :** to add a conditioning substance esp. a mineral salt to (something) for body or some other property: as (1) **:** to add filler to (paper) **:** FILL (2) *of textiles* **:** WEIGHT 1c ⟨silk which has been ~*ed* with . . . metallic salts —*Irish Digest*⟩ **d :** to weight (dice) to fall unfairly **e :** to pack with one-sided or prejudicial influences or assumptions or numbers **:** give a determining slant or proportion to **:** BIAS ⟨the system was heavily ~*ed* in favor of royalty, aristocracy, and priesthood —A.L.Kroeber⟩ ⟨the situation is a little ~*ed* against the male of the species —John Gould⟩ ⟨so ~*ed* his questions that a witness had to answer as desired or appear unpatriotic⟩ ⟨the jury comes in ~*ed* to soak an anarchist — Maxwell Anderson⟩ **f :** to weight (as a test or experimental situation) with factors influencing validity or outcome **g :** to charge with emotional associations or significance ⟨the sentiment that ~*s* such words as *mother*⟩ **4 a :** to supply in abundance or excess ⟨a prewar custom of ~*ing* visitors with gadgets —DeWitt Morrill⟩ ⟨an uncle . . . who, like all pawnbrokers, was ~*ed* with trumpets —E.J.Kahn⟩ ⟨their questions were ~*ed* with insinuation —Jean Stafford⟩ **:** HEAP ⟨an enameled plate that was ~*ed* high with potatoes —Liam O'Flaherty⟩ **:** PACK ⟨clearly written and ~*ed* with pictures and diagrams —*Dun's Rev.*⟩ ⟨~ up on them while the price is low⟩ **b** (1) **:** to apply (as a pigment) heavily ⟨the ~*ed* streaks of orange and cinnabar —F.J.Mather⟩ (2) **:** to color (a painting) thickly (3) **:** to make (as a color) opaque by mixing in white **c :** to put runners on (first, second, and third bases) in baseball ⟨the pitcher ~*ed* the bases by walking three batters⟩ **d :** to fill (a person) with fanciful information ⟨the pilot warmed to his opportunity, and proceeded to ~ me up in the good old-fashioned way —Mark Twain⟩ **5 a :** to put a load in (a device or piece of equipment) **:** supply with the material to be used or processed ⟨~ his corncob pipe⟩ ⟨~, unload, and reload the washer by hand⟩: as (1) **:** to place a charge or cartridge in (the chamber of a firearm) **:** assemble the components of (a cartridge) (2) **:** to transfer (germinated grain) from the working floor to dry in a kiln (3) **:** to insert photographic film in (as a holder or magazine) **:** place a holder or magazine in (as a camera or machine) **b :** to place or insert as a load in a device, machine, or container ⟨~ the cloth into a dye vat⟩ **6 a :** to increase the resistance in the working of ⟨~ a windmill for a 15-mile wind —F.E.Kidder & Harry Parker⟩ **b** (1) **:** to change (as by introducing a loading coil) the resonance frequency or wavelength of (a radio transmitter) (2) **:** to introduce (loading coils) or distribute (induction) along an electrical conductor (3) **:** to add to a power-absorbing device (as a resistance or antenna) to (a telephone line) in order to reduce attenuation and distortion (4) **:** to add (as a circuit element or antenna) to a circuit to absorb power **7 :** to change (as an alcoholic drink) by adding an adulterant or drug **8 a :** to add loading to (an insurance premium) **b :** to add a sum to (as the selling price of a book or security) after profits and expenses are accounted for ⟨~*ed* prices⟩ ⟨waiters can ~ checks more deftly than any of their colleagues on the European Continent —T.H.Fielding⟩ — *vi* **1 :** to receive a load **:** take on cargo or passengers ⟨trucks were ~*ing* with mail at the platform in back⟩ ⟨stopped behind a school bus that was ~*ing*⟩ **2 :** ⁴GUM *vi* 2 **3 :** to put a load on or in a carrier, device, machine, or container; *specif* **:** to insert the charge or cartridge in the chamber of a firearm **4 :** to go or go in as a load **:** make one's way as a passenger ⟨the nurses were called . . . to ~ into the boat —Lonnie Coleman⟩ **:** be suitable for loading a carrier, device, or machine ⟨razor blades that ~ without handling⟩ **syn** see BURDEN — **load the dice :** to prejudice the outcome **:** place one at an advantage or disadvantage **:** present an argument one-sidedly ⟨the victim has already *loaded the dice* against himself by . . . previous actions —*Economist*⟩ ⟨a survey of labor-management relations which doesn't *load the dice* in favor of management —*Infantry Jour.*⟩

³load *var of* LODE

load–bearing tile \ˈ=,==-\ *n* **:** tile capable of carrying superimposed loads for use in masonry construction

load binder *n* **:** ²BOOMER

load chart *n* **:** a schematic and graphic device to indicate the amount of authorized work yet to be performed by a machine, a group, or any other producing unit in a factory

load dispatcher *n* **:** a worker whose duty is seeing that the demand on a utility system (as for gas, electricity, or water) is continuously supplied

load displacement *n* **:** the displacement of a ship when loaded to the extent for which it was designed

loaded *adj* [fr. past part. of ²*load*] **1** *slang* **:** DRUNK ⟨celebrated by getting ~ on champagne⟩ **2 :** containing an explosive charge ⟨a ~ cigar⟩ **3** *of a quadruped's shoulder* **:** having the upper muscles excessively developed or lumpy **4 :** full to bursting with strong feeling (as anger) **5 :** having a large amount of money — **loaded for bear :** supplied with all one needs for success **:** amply prepared ⟨learning that every outfit . . . was at full strength, sober, and *loaded for bear* —E.G.Love⟩

loaded line *n* **:** a telephone or telegraph line that has exceptionally high inductance distributed uniformly or introduced at regular intervals

¹**load·en** \ˈlōdᵊn\ *dial var of* LOADED

²**loaden** \"\ *vt* [¹*load* + *-en*] *now dial* **:** ²LOAD

load·er \ˈlōdə(r)\ *n* -s [ME *loder*, fr. *loden* to load + *-er* — more at LOAD] **1 :** a person whose work is loading: as **a :** one who loads articles or materials to be transported into or onto the means of conveyance **b :** one who charges processing equipment with material **c :** one who fills containers or instruments with a specified quantity of material **2 :** a device or machine used for loading ⟨an automatic bobbin ~⟩; *specif* **:** a machine (as a belt or bucket conveyor or a power scoop shovel) that picks up loose material (as snow or gravel) and loads it upon a vehicle or into a container within the same unit **3 :** an attendant who loads guns for a hunter ⟨many Highland folk still look to the grouse season for some welcome ready money, by working as . . . ~*s* —Colin Gibson⟩

load·er·man \-mən\ *n, pl* **loadermen :** a logger who operates the machinery for hoisting and loading logs

load factor *n* **1 :** the ratio of average to maximum load; *specif* **:** the ratio of the average load carried by a power station or system for a given period to the maximum load during that period **2 :** the ratio stated as a percentage between the freight or passenger capacity of a vehicle or line and its actual utilization ⟨averaged a passenger *load factor* of about 92 percent —*Boeing Mag.*⟩

loading *n* -s [fr. gerund of ²*load*] **1 a :** a cargo, weight, or stress placed on something; *specif* **:** WING LOADING **b :** the amount of freight loaded during a specified period **:** SHIPMENT — usu. used in pl. ⟨quarterly ~*s* of inland barges averaging ten million tons⟩; *esp* **:** CARLOADING **2** *or* **loading charge :** LOAD 13; *specif* **:** an amount added to the net or pure premium of an insurance policy to provide for business expenses, future contingencies, and profits or bonuses **3 :** material used to load paper, cloth, leather, or rubber **:** FILLER, STUFFING **4 :** a cartridge or charge for a firearm consisting of particular components or characteristics **5 a :** the amount or degree to which something is or can be loaded ⟨the maximum axle ~⟩ ⟨an average ~ of 0.2 percent boric acid —*Rev. of Applied Entomology*⟩ **b :** the relative contribution of each component factor in a psychological test or in an experimental, clinical, or social situation

loading chute *n* **:** an inclined plane fenced in on each side up which cattle or other livestock can be driven for loading into trucks or other means of conveyance

loading coil *n* **:** a coil inserted in a tuned electrical circuit to increase its inductance

loading density *n* **:** the quantity of powder per unit volume of a cartridge case

loading tool *n* **:** a device for loading ammunition by hand

load·less \ˈlōdləs\ *adj* **:** having no load

load limit *n* **:** the maximum recommended or permitted weight of a vehicle determined by combining the tare weight with the load weight

load line *n* **1** *or* **load waterline a :** the line on the outside of a ship to which it sinks in the water when loaded or safely loaded **b** *also* **load line mark :** a mark representing the safe load line **2 :** one of a set of marks graduated in accordance with international standards and required by law in most maritime countries to be cut and painted amidships on the sides of a seagoing cargo ship to indicate the greatest draft to which it can be safely loaded under various conditions (as tropical fresh water or North Atlantic winter) — see PLIMSOLL MARK

Load·om·e·ter \(ˈ)lōˈdäməd·ə(r)\ *trademark* — used for an instrument that records the weight borne by a wheel of a vehicle passing over it

loads *pl of* LOAD, *pres 3d sing of* LOAD

loadstar *var of* LODESTAR

loadstone *var of* LODESTONE

load water plane *n* **:** the horizontal plane of a ship at the load waterline — abbr. *LWP*

¹**loaf** \ˈlōf\ *n, pl* **loaves** \-ōvz\ *also* **loafs** \-ōfs\ [ME *lof*, *laf*, fr. OE *hlāf* bread, loaf; akin to OHG *hleib*, *leib* bread, loaf, ON *hleifr*, Goth *hlaifs*] **1 a :** a shaped or molded mass of bread ⟨a ~ of white bread⟩ ⟨~ bread and rolls⟩ **b :** a hollowed crust of a loaf of bread with a specified filling ⟨oyster ~⟩ **2 :** a regularly molded often rectangular mass ⟨a ~ of cheese⟩ ⟨dried banana *loaves*⟩: as **a :** a conical mass of sugar ⟨sugar ~⟩ **b :** a baked dish consisting usu. of a specified main ingredient (as ground meat or fish) held together with soft crumbs or eggs and a liquid (as milk or tomato sauce) ⟨beef ~⟩ ⟨salmon ~⟩ **3 a :** a thick lump or mass ⟨her dark hair piled into an overhanging ~ —William Sansom⟩ **b** *Brit* **:** a head of a vegetable (as cabbage) **4** *or* **loaf of bread** *slang Brit* **:** HEAD, MIND ⟨going to be a useful boy, so long as you use your ~ —Robert Westerby⟩

²**loaf** \"\ *vb* -ED/-ING/-S [prob. back-formation fr. ¹*loafer*] *vi* **:** to spend time in idleness **:** to lounge or loiter about or along **:** do no work ⟨fired when he ~*ed* on the job⟩ ⟨cast the fly and ~ and dream —Henry van Dyke⟩ ⟨a place where the cows ~, usually near water, shade, or shelter —*Plan & Profit with Herefords*⟩ ⟨got up slowly from the settee in the corner and ~*ed* across the . . . lobby —Raymond Chandler⟩ ⟨the herring gull . . . ~*s* along on slow wingbeats —Brooks Atkinson⟩ ~ *vt* **:** to spend in idleness ⟨crowds of men who had come to ~ the evening away —Sherwood Anderson⟩—**loaf one's way :** to proceed on a course in an idle manner ⟨the bright ones *loaf their way* through and acquire habits of indolence instead of an education —*College English*⟩

³**loaf** \"\ *n* -s **:** a time spent at loafing ⟨went camping for a good ~⟩

loaf cake *n* **:** a cake (as a pound cake) baked in a loaf pan

loaf cheese *n* **:** process cheese molded in the form of a usu. rectangular loaf

loaf·er \ˈlōfə(r)\ *n* -s [perh. short for *landloafer*, modif. of G *landläufer* vagabond, tramp, fr. *land* + *läufer* runner, walker] **:** one that loafs **:** IDLER ⟨neighborhood ~*s* tipped their chairs within reach of the cracker barrel —S.T.Williamson⟩

²**loafer** \"\ *or* **loafer wolf** *n* -s [by folk etymology fr. Sp *lobo* wolf, fr. L *lupus* — more at WOLF] **:** TIMBER WOLF

Loafer \"\ *trademark* — used for a low leather step-in shoe with an upper resembling the moccasin but with a broad flat heel

loaf·er·ish \ˈlōf(ə)rish\ *adj* **:** befitting or having the appearance of a loafer ⟨stood around in ~ indifference⟩ ⟨~ looking men standing on the street corner⟩

loafing barn *or* **loafing shed** *n* **:** a barn or shed for cattle in which they range at will on a heavy bedding of straw rather than occupy fixed stanchions

loaf·ing·ly *adv* **:** in a loafing manner

loaf pan *n* **:** a deep rectangular pan of metal or glass used for baking food in the form of loaves

loaf sugar *n* **:** refined sugar molded into loaves or small cubes or squares

lo·a·i·a·sis \ˌlōəˈīəsəs\ *or* **lo·i·a·sis** \lōˈīə-\ *n, pl* **loaia·ses** *or* **loia·ses** \-ˌsēz\ [NL, fr. *Loa* + *-iasis*] **:** infestation with or disease caused by an eye worm (*Loa loa*) that migrates through the subcutaneous tissue and across the cornea of the eye — compare CALABAR SWELLING

loa loa \ˈlōəˈlōə\ *n* [NL, fr. *Loa loa*, species of worm that causes the disease] **:** LOAIASIS

¹**loam** \ˈlōm, ˈlüm\ *n* -s [ME *lom*, *lam*, fr. OE *lām*; akin to OS *lēmo* clay, mud, OHG *leimo* clay, mud, OE *līm* lime — more at LIME] **1 a** *obs* **:** clayey earth **:** CLAY **b :** a mixture composed chiefly of moistened clay (as for plastering, making bricks) **c :** a coarse strongly bonded molding sand used in founding **2 :** SOIL, TOPSOIL; *specif* **:** a usu. fertile and humus-rich soil consisting of a friable mixture containing from 7 to 27 percent clay, 28 to 50 percent silt, and less than 52 percent sand **3 :** BROCCOLI BROWN

²**loam** \"\ *vt* -ED/-ING/-S **:** to cover, smear, or fill with loam

loam board *n* **:** a board of definite profile used to strickle a mold in loam or to strike up its core on a core barrel

loam·i·ness \ˈlōmēnəs, ˈlüm-, -min-\ *n* -ES **:** the quality or state of being loamy

loam·less \ˈlōmləs, ˈlüm-\ *adj* **:** having no loam ⟨a ~ yard⟩

loam mold *n* **:** a foundry mold made of siliceous sand, clay, and organic matter in proper proportions and used in making iron castings

loamy \ˈlōmē, ˈlüm-, -mi\ *adj, usu* -ER/-EST **:** consisting of, like, or of the character of loam

¹**loan** \ˈlōn\ *n* -s [ME *loon*, *lon*, *lan*, fr. ON *lān*; akin to OE *lǣn* loan, *lēon* to lend, OHG *lēhan* borrowed property, *līhan* to borrow, lend, ON *ljā* to lend, grant, Goth *leihwan* to lend, L *linquere* to leave, Gk *leipein* to leave, Skt *riṇakti* he leaves; basic meaning: to leave] **1 a :** money lent at interest ⟨was authorized to make ~*s* upon farm commodities —F.D.Roosevelt⟩ ⟨a bond issue is a typical form of major business ~⟩ **b :** something lent for the borrower's temporary use on condition that it or its equivalent be returned ⟨life's not our own, — 'tis but a ~ to be repaid —Charles Swain⟩ **2 a :** the grant of temporary use made by a lender ⟨able to get the ~ of a car to take them back —George Farwell⟩ **b :** the temporary duty of a person transferred by a superior to the service of another for a limited time ⟨he had been on ~ to the navy during the war, away from the campus —C.O.Gorham⟩ **3 :** LOANWORD

²**loan** \"\ *vb* -ED/-ING/-S *vt* **1 :** to lend (money) at interest **2 :** LEND 1a ⟨~*ed* her the clothes to wear and primped her to look nice —Carson McCullers⟩ **3 :** LEND 1c ⟨our pink-cheeked conducting officer . . . who had been ~*ed* by the Red Signal Corps for the trip —E.P.Snow⟩ **4** *dial* **:** BORROW 1 ⟨can I ~ a ladder from you for a day or so⟩ ~ *vi* **:** to lend money at interest ⟨in times of distress, ~ to good customers —N.S.B. Gras⟩

³**loan** \"\ *n* -s [ScGael *lōn*; akin to OIr *loun* provision] *Scot* **:** PROVISIONS

⁴**loan** \"\ *n* [ME (Sc) *lone*, alter. of *lane* — more at LANE] *dial Brit* **:** LOANING

loan·able \ˈlōnəbəl\ *adj* **:** that may be loaned; *esp* **:** available for loan at a certain time at interest ⟨~ funds⟩

loanblend \ˈ=,=\ *n* **:** a word some of whose constituents are native and others of foreign origin — called also *hybrid*

loan crowd *n* **:** a group of stock exchange members meeting to borrow or lend stocks

lo and behold *interj* — used to express wonder or surprise ⟨there, *lo and behold*, in the window . . . was a 'To Let' board —A.P.Herbert⟩

loan·er \ˈlōnə(r)\ *n* -s **1 :** one that loans **2 :** something lent (as in place of an article left for repair)

loan farm *n* [trans. of Afrik *leningsplaas*] *southern Africa* **:** a piece of land held from the government on payment of an annual quitrent

loan form *n* **:** a form borrowed by one language from another ⟨English *their* and *get* are *loan forms* from Old Norse⟩ — compare LOANWORD

loan·ing \ˈlōniŋ\ *n* -s [ME *loning*, fr. *lone* lane, loaning + *-ing* — more at LOAN] **1** *dial Brit* **:** a way between fields **:** LANE **2** *dial Brit* **:** an open space near a farm or village where cows are often milked **:** PADDOCK

loan office *n* **:** an office at which loans are negotiated or at which the accounts of loans are kept and the interest paid to the lender

loan–out \ˈ=,=\ *n* -s [fr. *loan out*, v.] **:** the loan to another motion-picture studio of a player under contract in exchange for money or the services of another player

loan paper *n* **:** a paper similar in characteristics and use to bond paper but often somewhat heavier and stronger

loan shark *n* **:** one who lends money to individuals at extortionate interest rates

loan–shark \ˈ=,=\ *vi* [*loan shark*] **:** to lend money as a loan shark

loanshift \ˈ=,=\ *n* **:** a change in the meaning of a word under the influence of another language (as when a word meaning "pedal extremity" acquires also the meaning "12-inch unit of length" under the influence of English "foot"); *also* **:** a word that has undergone such a change in meaning **:** CALQUE 1

loan translation *n* [trans. of G *lehnübersetzung*] **:** a compound, derivative, or phrase introduced into a language through translation of the constituent parts of a term in another language (as *neogrammarian* from German *junggrammatiker*, *reason of state* from French *raison d'état*) — called also *calque*

loan value *n* **:** the amount which the owner may borrow against a life insurance policy, equal to the cash value less interest to the end of the current policy year

loanword \ˈ=,=\ *n* [trans. of G *lehnwort*] **:** a word taken from another language and at least partly naturalized **:** a borrowed or adopted word — called also *loan*

loas *pl of* LOA

lo·a·sa \ˈlōəsə\ *n* [NL] **1** *cap* **:** a genus (the type of the family Loasaceae) of tropical American prickly herbs having 10 staminodia and a 3- to 5-valved capsule **2** -s **:** any plant or flower of the genus *Loasa*

lo·a·sa·ce·ae \ˌlōəˈsāsēˌē\ *n pl, cap* [NL, fr. *Loasa*, type genus + *-aceae*] **:** a family of mainly herbaceous bristly hairy sometimes climbing plants (order Parietales) having regular pentamerous flowers with numerous stamens — **lo·a·sa·ceous** \ˌ==ˈsāshəs\ *adj*

loasa family *n* **:** LOASACEAE

loath *or* **loth** *also* **loathe** \ˈlōth, -t͟h\ *adj* [ME *loth*, *lath* hostile, loathsome, averse, fr. OE *lāth* hostile, loathsome; akin to OFris & OS *lēth* hated, loathsome, OHG *leid*, ON *leithr* hated, loathsome, OIr *liuss* aversion, disgust, and perh. to Gk *aleitēs* sinner] **:** characterized by unwillingness to do something contrary to one's tastes, likes, sympathies, or ways of thinking ⟨when he suggested a meal, I was nothing ~ —H.G. Wells⟩ — usu. used predicatively or postpositively with an infinitive ⟨seemed ~ to enter, yet drawn by some desire stronger than his reluctance —Willa Cather⟩ ⟨a spirit of camaraderie . . . that made us ~ to part —Jack Hulbert⟩ **syn** see DISINCLINED

loathe \ˈlōt͟h\ *vt* -ED/-ING/-S [ME *lothen*, fr. OE *lāthian*, fr. *lāth*, adj.] **:** to feel strong aversion for **:** have extreme disgust at **:** DETEST, ABHOR ⟨~ writing harp parts, because they mean writing out so many notes —Deems Taylor⟩ ⟨sickened of it and *loathed* it —Arnold Bennett⟩ **syn** see HATE

loath·er \-t͟hə(r)\ *n* -s **:** one that loathes something

loath·ful \-thfəl\ *adj* [ME *lothful* hateful, loathsome, reluctant, fr. *loth* evil, harm, hatred (fr. OE *lāth*, fr. *lāth*, adj.) + *-ful*] *now Scot* **:** SHRINKING, RELUCTANT, BASHFUL

loath·ing \ˈlōt͟hiŋ, -t͟hēŋ\ *n* -s [ME *lothing*, fr. gerund of *lothen* to loathe] **:** a feeling of aversion, abhorrence, or detestation **:** extreme digust **:** ANTIPATHY ⟨the crew was divided between admiration and ~ —Elinor Wylie⟩

loath·ing·ly *adv* **:** in the manner of one who feels loathing

¹**loath·ly** \ˈlōthlē, -th-, -li\ *adj* [ME *lothly*, fr. OE *lāthlic*, fr. *lāth* hostile, loathsome + *-lic* -ly] **:** LOATHSOME, REPULSIVE ⟨the ~ lady . . . changes back again into her original lovely and youthful self —Boris Ford⟩

²**loathly** \"\ *adv* [ME *lothly*, fr. OE *lāthlīce*, fr. *lāthlīc*, adj.] **:** UNWILLINGLY

loath·ness \ˈlōthnəs, -t͟h-\ *n* -ES [ME *lothnesse*, *lathnesse* harmfulness, unpleasantness, reluctance, fr. *loth*, *lath* hostile, loathsome, averse + *-nesse* -ness] **:** the quality or state of being loath **:** RELUCTANCE

loath·some \ˈlōthsəm, -t͟h-\ *adj* [ME *lothsum*, fr. *loth* evil, harm, hatred + *-sum* -some — more at LOATHFUL] **:** exciting loathing **:** DISGUSTING: **a :** offensive to the senses **:** NAUSEATING, FOUL ⟨rot with some ~ disease —W.S.Maugham⟩ **b :** repulsive to sensibility or conscience **:** ODIOUS, ABHORRENT ⟨what is holy and what is ~ are in like manner set aside —W.G. Sumner⟩ **syn** see OFFENSIVE

loath·some·ly *adv* [ME *lothsumly*, fr. *lothsum* + *-ly*] **:** in a loathsome manner ⟨~ ugly⟩

loath·some·ness *n* -ES [ME *lothsumnesse*, fr. *lothsum* + *-nesse* -ness] **1 :** the quality or state of being loathsome **2 :** something loathsome **3** *archaic* **:** LOATHING

loathy \ˈlōt͟h|ē, -th|, |i\ *adj* [obs. *loath* evil, harm, hatred (fr. ME *loth*) + *-y* — more at LOATHFUL] **:** LOATHSOME ⟨~ examples of age, sickness, and death —E.W.Hopkins⟩

loaves *pl of* LOAF

loaves and fishes *n pl* [so called fr. the 5 barley loaves and 2 fishes with which Jesus miraculously fed a multitude of 5000 (John 6) that he later reproached for their greater interest in the food than in him (John 6: 26)] **:** material gain ⟨concentrating on how to get *loaves and fishes*, the schools . . . make out of our youngsters precisely what their parents wish them to become —B.I.Bell⟩

¹**lob** \ˈläb\ *n* -s [prob. of LG or Flem origin; akin to Flem *lobbe* simpleton, LG *lubbe* coarse, awkward person, MLG *lobbe* thick underlip; akin to OE *lobbe*, *loppe* spider, Fris *lob*, *lobbe* hanging mass of fat or flesh, G dial. *loppen* to be loose, Sw dial. *lubbe* plump figure, ON *lūfa* thick hair — more at SLOBBER] **1** *now dial Brit* **:** a dull heavy person **:** LOUT ⟨a great fat ~ that had no life in him at all —Samuel Lover⟩ **2** *archaic* **:** a loosely hanging object **3** *dial Brit* **:** a large amount

²**lob** \"\ *vb* **lobbed**; **lobbed**; **lobbing**; **lobs** *vt* **1** *archaic* **:** to let hang heavily **:** DROOP ⟨their poor jades ~ down their heads —Shak.⟩ ⟨goggling at her grandmother with her mouth *lobbed* wetly open —Norman Lindsay⟩ **2 :** to throw, hit, or propel slowly in or as if in a high arc ⟨*lobbing* hand grenades over the rock —Burtt Evans⟩: as **a :** to return (a tennis ball) in a high arc usu. over an opposing player's head **b :** to bowl or throw (a cricket ball) underhand usu. slowly **c** (1) **:** to throw (a baseball) in a soft easy manner ⟨~ the ball in⟩ (2) **:** to hit (a baseball) in a slow high arc ⟨~ a few practice flies to the outfield⟩ **3 :** COB 3 ~ *vi* **1 :** to move slowly and heavily ⟨rockets . . . *lobbed* shoreward —K.M.Dodson⟩ **2 :** to hit a tennis ball easily in a high arc **3** *Austral* **:** to arrive at a place ⟨just *lobbed* in town —R.M.Daw⟩

³**lob** \"\ *n* -s [²*lob*] **1 :** a cricket ball bowled or thrown underhand usu. slowly **2 :** a tennis ball hit slowly in a high arc

⁴**lob** \"\ *also* **lobb** *n* -s [origin unknown] **1 :** a step or stair in a mine **2 :** a mineral vein descending like steps

⁵**lob** \"\ *n* -s [origin unknown] *slang Brit* **:** a container for valuables; *esp* **:** TILL

lob- *or* **lobi-** *or* **lobo-** *comb form* [*lobe*] **:** lobe ⟨*lob*ectomy⟩ ⟨*lobi*form⟩ ⟨*lobi*gerous⟩ ⟨*lobo*tomy⟩

lo·ba \ˈlōbə\ *n* -s [prob. native name in the Philippines] **:** a Manila copal hardened somewhat by delaying collection of the resin usu. for one to three months after tapping the tree

lo·bal \ˈlōbəl\ *adj* [*lob-* + *-al*] **:** LOBED

lo·bar \ˈlōbə(r), -ˌbär,-ˌbȧ(r\ *adj* [*lob-* + *-ar*] **:** of or relating to a lobe **:** LOBATE

lo·bar·ia \lōˈba(a)rēə\ *n, cap* [NL, fr. *lob-* + *-aria*] **:** a genus of foliaceous lichens (family Stictaceae) — see LUNGWORT

lobar pneumonia *n* **:** acute pneumonia involving one or more lobes of the lung characterized by sudden onset, chill, fever, difficulty in breathing, cough, and blood-stained sputum, marked by consolidation, and normally followed by resolution and return to normal of the lung tissue

lo·ba·ta \lōˈbäd·ə, -ˈbād·ə\ *n pl, cap* [NL, fr. *lob-* + *-ata*] **:** an order of ctenophores (class Tentaculata) with the body compressed in the vertical plane and produced into two large oral lobes and four pointed processes

lo·ba·tae \-d·ˌē\ [NL, fr. *lob-* + L *-atae* (fem. pl. of *-atus* -ate)] *syn of* LOBATA

lo·bate \ˈlōˌbāt, *usu* -ād.+V\ *also* **lo·bat·ed** \-ād·əd\ *adj* [*lobate* fr. NL *lobatus*, fr. *lob-* + L *-atus* -ate; *lobated* fr. NL *lobatus* + E *-ed*] **1 a :** having lobes ⟨a ~ leaf⟩ **b :** resembling a lobe ⟨a ~ tongue⟩ **2 a** *of a fish* **:** having the integument of the fin continued on the bases of the fin rays **b** *of a bird* **:** having lateral membranous flaps — **lo·bate·ly** *adv*

lo·ba·tion \lōˈbāshən\ *n* -s **1 a :** the quality or state of being lobed **b :** the formation of lobes or lobules **2 a :** LOBE **b :** LOBULE

¹**lob·ber** \ˈläbə(r)\ *n* -s [²*lob* + *-er*] **:** one that lobs

²**lobber** \"\ *var of* ¹LOPPER

¹**lob·by** \ˈläbē, -bi\ *n* -ES [ML *lobium*, *lobia*, *laubia* covered walk, gallery, portico, of Gmc origin; akin to OHG *louba*, *louppea* protective roof, porch — more at LODGE] **1 a :** a corridor or hall connected with a larger room or series of rooms and used as a passageway or waiting room ⟨ignorant where the narrow *lobbies* led —Emily Brontë⟩ ⟨this ~ of many doors at the head of the windowed staircase —Elizabeth Bowen⟩ ⟨the small ~ of the post office —Willard Robertson⟩: as (1) one of the two corridors or anterooms of the British House of Commons to which members go to vote when the House divides on a motion ⟨time and again, on issues of foreign policy, Labor and Conservative MPs have gone into the same ~ —*New Republic*⟩ (2) **:** a large hall serving as a foyer or anteroom ⟨a hotel ~⟩ ⟨a theater ~⟩ (3) **:** an anteroom of a capitol **b** *archaic* **:** a small room or enclosure: as (1) **:** a small apartment on board ship (2) **:** a small enclosed pen for cattle (3) **:** a watchman's enclosure in or outside a factory **2 a :** the persons who frequent the lobbies of a legislative house to do business with the members; *specif* **:** persons not members of a legislative body and not holding government office who attempt to influence legislators or other public officials through personal contact **b :** a particular group of such persons representing a special interest

²**lobby** \"\ *vb* -ED/-ING/-ES *vi* **1 :** to conduct activities (as engaging in personal contacts or the dissemination of information) with the objective of influencing public officials and esp. members of a legislative body with regard to legislation and other policy decisions ⟨~ for their proposals when they reached the floor of the legislature —Gladys M. Kammerer⟩ **2 :** to attempt to secure a desired objective by the use of methods resembling or held to resemble those of a political lobbyist ⟨members successfully *lobbied* among the convention delegates —*New Republic*⟩ ~ *vt* **1 :** to influence or attempt to influence with regard to policy decisions and esp. proposals for legislation ⟨wine, dine, and ~ the legislature —*Newsweek*⟩ **2 a :** to promote and esp. to secure the passage of (as legislation) by influencing public officials ⟨the man who *lobbied* the prohibition law through Congress —Herbert Asbury⟩ **b :** to advance or otherwise secure favorable treatment for (as a desired project) by influencing public officials before the beginning or following the completion of the legislative process

lob·by·er \-bē(r)\ *n* -s **:** one that lobbies **:** LOBBYIST

lob·by·gow \ˈläbēˌgau̇\ *n* -s [origin unknown] *slang* **:** an errand boy **:** MESSENGER

lob·by·ism \ˈläbēˌizəm\ *n* -s **:** the activities of a lobbyist or the practice of lobbying

lob·by·ist \-ēəst\ *n* -s **:** one who lobbies; *specif* **:** a person employed and compensated for lobbying

lob·by·man \-mən\ *n, pl* **lobbymen :** one who serves as an attendant or porter in a lobby; *specif* **:** one employed in the lobby of a theater to take tickets and give information

lobcock \ˈ=,=\ *n* [¹*lob* + *cock*] *now dial Eng* **:** a stupid blundering person **:** LOUT

lobe \ˈlōb\ *n* -s [MF, fr. LL *lobus*, fr. Gk *lobos* — more at SLEEP] **1 :** a curved or rounded projection or division: as **a :** a more or less rounded projection of a body organ or part ⟨~ of the ear⟩ — see EAR illustration **b :** a division of a body organ marked off by a fissure on the surface (as of the brain, lungs, liver) **c :** a division or projection of a plant organ ⟨~ of a leaf⟩ **d :** a rounded projection or dome of a building **2 a :** a membranous flap on the sides of the toes of some birds (as the coot) **b :** a portion of a suture in a cephalopod shell that forms an angle or curve whose convexity is directed away from the orifice — opposed to *saddle* **c :** one of the longitudinal divisions of the body or of the lateral divisions of the glabella in a trilobite **3 :** a projecting part of a cam wheel or of a noncircular gear wheel in a machine **4 :** a great rounded marginal projection from a continental ice sheet **5 a :** one of the inflated bags at the stern of a kite balloon that acts either as a fin or as a stabilizer **b :** one of the sections into which the envelope of a balloon is sometimes divided by the tension of the internal rigging **6 :** a portion of the radiation pattern of a directional antenna representing an area of stronger transmission of radio signals

lo·bec·to·my \lōˈbektəmē, -mi\ *n* -ES [ISV *lobe* + *-ectomy*] **:** surgical removal of a lobe of an organ or gland; *specif* **:** excision of a lobe of a lung

lobed \ˈlōbd\ *adj* **:** having lobes **:** LOBATE — used chiefly of leaves

lobe–finned fish \'=,=-\ *also* **lobe–fin** \'=,=\ *n* **:** CROSSOPTERYGIAN

lobefoot \'=,=\ *n, pl* **lobefoots :** a bird having lobate toes; *esp* **:** NORTHERN PHALAROPE

lobe·less \'lōbləs\ *adj* **:** lacking lobes

lobe·let \-lət\ *n* -s **:** a small lobe

lo·be·lia \lō'bēlyə, -lēə\ *n* [NL, fr. Matthias de *Lobel* †1616 Flemish botanist + NL *-ia*] **1 a** *cap* **:** a large genus (the type of the family Lobeliaceae) of herbaceous plants of wide distribution that have the corolla tube split **b** -s **:** any plant or flower of this genus **2** -s **:** the leaves and tops of a lobelia (*L. inflata*) — see INDIAN TOBACCO **3** *or* **lobelia blue** -s **:** a strong violet that is bluer than clematis, bluer and paler than pansy, and bluer and stronger than royal purple (sense 2)

lobelia

lo·be·li·a·ce·ae \lō,bēlē'āsē,ē\ *n pl, cap* [NL, fr. *Lobelia*, type genus + *-aceae*] **:** a family of widely distributed herbs, shrubs, or trees (order Campanulales) that are characterized by the irregular corolla and often syngenesious anthers and are esp. abundant in the Pacific islands — **lo·be·li·a·ceous** \=;==-'āshəs\ *adj*

lobelia family *n* **:** LOBELIACEAE

lobelia violet *n* **:** a grayish purple that is redder, lighter, and stronger than telegraph blue, bluer, lighter, and stronger than mauve gray, and bluer and lighter than average rose mauve

lo·be·line \'lōbə,lēn, -lən, lō'bē-\ *n* -s [NL *Lobelia* + E *-ine*] **:** a poisonous crystalline alkaloid $C_{22}H_{27}NO_2$ obtained from lobelia and used chiefly as a respiratory stimulant — called also *alpha-lobeline*

lo·bel·lat·ed \lōbə;lād·əd\ *adj* [*lobe* + L *-ellus* (dim. suffix) + E *-ate* + *-ed*] **:** LOBULATE

lo·bel's catchfly \'lōbəlz-\ *n, usu cap L* [after Matthias de *Lobel* — more at LOBELIA] **:** a European annual herb (*Silene armeria*) with hollow stems and deep rose flowers that is adventive in eastern No. America — called also *flybane, garden catchfly, sweet william catchfly*

lobes *pl of* LOBE

lobi *pl of* LOBUS

lobi– — see LOB-

lob·ing \'lōbiŋ\ *n* -s **:** LOBATION

[1]**lo·bi·ped** \'lōbə,ped\ *adj* [ISV *lob-* + *-ped*] **:** having lobate toes

[2]**lobiped** \"\ *n* -s **:** LOBEFOOT

lob·lol·ly \'läb,lälē, -lē\ *n* [prob. fr. E dial. *lob* to bubble while boiling + obs. E dial. *lolly* broth, soup] **1** *dial* **a :** a thick gruel **b :** an unsightly miry mess **:** MUDHOLE ⟨when the fall rains came there wouldn't be anything here but a ~ —R.P.Warren⟩ ⟨made *loblollies* by treading and treading in one spot —William Faulkner⟩ **2** *now dial* **:** a clownish person **:** LOUT **3 :** LOBLOLLY PINE

loblolly bay *n* **1 :** an ornamental evergreen shrub or small tree (*Gordonia lasianthus*) of the southern U.S. **2 :** an endemic Jamaican tree (*Haemocharis haematoxylon*) of the family Theaceae

loblolly boy *n, archaic* **:** a surgeon's attendant on shipboard

loblolly pine *n* **1 :** a tall spreading pine (*Pinus taeda*) of the central and southeastern U.S. with reddish brown fissured bark, leaves in groups of three, sessile cones having the umbones of the scales prolonged into spines, and a full bushy upper head — called also *frankincense pine* **2 :** any of several shrubby to tall arboreal pines of the U.S.

loblolly tree *n* **:** a West Indian or tropical American tree having more or less leathery leaves (as *Pisonia subcordata, Cordia alba, Cupania glabra*)

lo·bo \'lō,bō\ *or* **lobo wolf** *n* -s [Sp *lobo* wolf — more at LOAFER] **:** TIMBER WOLF ⟨prepared to fight the fiercest panther or a pack of ~*s* —J.F.Dobie⟩

lobo– — see LOB-

lo·bo·la *or* **lo·bo·lo** \'lōbələ\ *n* -s [native name in southern Africa] **:** bride-price esp. among the Bantu-speaking peoples of southern Africa

lo·bo·podium \,lōbə+\ *or* **lo·bo·pod** \'==,päd\ *n, pl* **lobopodia** *or* **lobopodiums** *or* **lobopods** [NL *lobopodium*, fr. *lob-* + *podium*] **:** a broad thick pseudopodium with a core of endoplasm

lo·bo·sa \lō'bōsə\ *n pl, cap* [NL, fr. *lob-* + L *-osa* (fem. of *-osus* -ous)] *in many classifications* **:** an order of protozoans having thick irregular pseudopodia — **lo·bose** \'lō,bōs\ *adj*

lo·bo·ste·mon \,lōbə'stē,män\ *n, cap* [NL, fr. *lob-* + Gk *stēmōn* warp, thread — more at STAMEN] **:** a genus of southern African perennial herbs or shrubs (family Boraginaceae) that have alternate, sessile, and usu. hairy leaves and white, pink, or blue infundibuliform flowers in scorpioid cymes or dense heads and are sometimes cultivated as greenhouse ornamentals

lo·bot·o·mize \lō'bäd·ə,mīz\ *vt* -ED/-ING/-S **:** to incise a lobe of the brain of

lo·bot·o·my \-_mē, -mi\ *n* -ES [ISV *lob-* + *-tomy*] **:** incision into the brain (as into the frontal lobes) to sever nerve fibers for the relief of certain mental disorders and tension — called also *leucotomy*

lobs *pl of* LOB, *pres 3rd sing of* LOB

lob·scouse \'läb,skau̇s\ *n* -s [origin unknown] **:** a sailor's dish prepared by stewing or baking bits of meat with vegetables, hardtack, and other ingredients

lobsided *var of* LOPSIDED

lob's pound *n* [[1]*lob*] **1** *dial Eng* **:** PRISON **2** *dial Eng* **:** DIFFICULTY, DISGRACE **3 :** BITTERSWEET 3b — compare LOBSTER RED

[1]**lob·ster** \'läbstə(r), -bst-\ *n* -s *see sense 1* [ME *lopster, lobster*, fr. OE *loppestre*, fr. *loppe, lobbe* spider — more at LOB] **1** *pl also* **lobster a :** a large marine decapod crustacean of the family Homaridae commonly used for food; *esp* **:** a member of the genus *Homarus* including the American lobster (*H. americanus*) and the European lobster (*H. vulgaris*) of the Atlantic coasts and the very small cape lobster (*H. capensis*) of southern Africa **b :** SPINY LOBSTER **c** *Austral* **:** the common freshwater crayfish **2** *archaic* **a :** a British soldier — called also *boiled lobster* **b :** a uniformed police officer — called also *unboiled lobster* **3 :** a person regarded with contempt: as **a** *archaic* **:** a man unduly responsive to female wiles **:** one willing to pay for female company **b :** a stupid or awkward person **:** LUMMOX, CLOWN **4 :** BITTERSWEET 3b

American lobster

[2]**lobster** \"\ *vi* -ED/-ING/-S **:** to fish for or catch lobsters

lobsterback \'==,=\ *n* [so called fr. the red uniforms] *archaic* **:** a British soldier

lobster car *n* **:** a slatted container in which live lobsters are kept under water awaiting sale or transportation

lobster caterpillar *or* **lobster** *n* -s **:** a caterpillar that has extremely long thoracic legs and two long caudal processes, rests in a grotesque position, and feeds on many trees and shrubs — see LOBSTER MOTH

lobster claw *n* **:** an incompletely dominant genetic anomaly in man marked by variable reduction of the skeleton of the extremities and cleaving of the hands and feet into two segments resembling lobster claws

lobster crab *n* **:** PORCELAIN CRAB

lob·ster·ling \'läbstə(r)liŋ, -bst-\ *n* -s **:** a young lobster

lob·ster·man \-mən\ *n, pl* **lobstermen :** one whose business is catching lobsters

lobster moth *n* **:** a European moth (*Stauropus fagi*) of the family Notodontidae that is the adult of the lobster caterpillar

lobster new·burg *or* **lobster new·burgh** \-'n(y)ü,bərg, -bə̄g, -əig\ *n, usu cap N* [*Newburg, Newburgh* of unknown origin] **:** cooked lobster meat heated usu. in a chafing dish in a sauce of cream, egg yolk, and sherry

lobster pot *n* **:** an oblong cage with slat sides and a funnel-shaped net used as a trap for catching lobsters

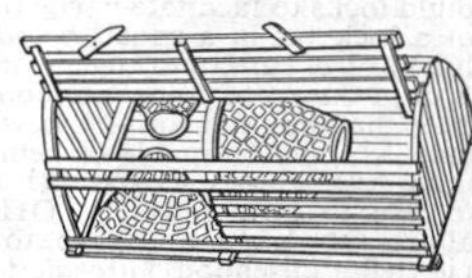
lobster pot (Maine)

lobster red *n* **:** a strong red that is yellower and paler than Goya, bluer, lighter, and slightly stronger than average cherry red, and yellower and deeper than geranium (sense 3a)

lobster roll *n* **:** lobster salad in a long roll

lobster shift *or* **lobster trick** *n* **1 :** a tour of duty esp. in newspaper work that covers the late evening or early morning hours **:** GRAVEYARD SHIFT **2 :** the skeleton staff left on duty in a newspaper office from the time one edition has gone to press until work begins on the next edition

lobster–tail \'==,=\ *n* **:** jointed armor for the lower part of the body

lobster thermidor *n, pl* **lobsters thermidor :** a mixture of cooked lobster meat, mushrooms, cream, egg yolks, and sherry stuffed into a lobster shell with or without a covering of Parmesan cheese and oven-browned

lobster trap *n* **:** LOBSTER POT

lob·stick \'läbz,tik, -b,st-\ *var of* LOPSTICK

lobtail \'=,=\ *vi* [[1]*lob* + *tail*] *of a whale* **:** to beat the surface of the water with the flukes

lob·u·lar \'läbyələ(r)\ *adj* **:** of, relating to, or resembling a lobule — **lob·u·lar·ly** *adv*

lob·u·lar·ia \,==='la(a)rēə\ *n, cap* [NL, fr. *lobulus* + *-aria*] **:** a genus of Mediterranean herbs (family Cruciferae) with forked pubescence and small white flowers in racemes — see SWEET ALYSSUM

lobular pneumonia *n* **:** BRONCHOPNEUMONIA

lob·u·late \'läbyələt, -,lāt, *usu* -d·+V\ *also* **lob·u·lat·ed** \-,lād·əd\ *adj* **:** made up of, divided into, or provided with lobules

lob·u·la·tion \,=='lāshən\ *n* -s **1 a :** the quality or state of being lobulate **b :** the formation of or division into lobules **2 :** LOBULE

lob·ule \'läb(,)yül\ *n* -s [*lobe* + *-ule*] **1 :** a small lobe ⟨the ~ of the ear⟩ **2 :** a subdivision of a lobe; *specif* **:** one of the small masses of tissue of which various organs (as the liver) are built up

lob·u·lose \'läbyə,lōs\ *or* **lob·u·lous** \-ləs\ *adj* **:** having lobules

lob·u·lus \-ləs\ *n, pl* **lobu·li** \-,lī\ [NL, fr. F or E *lobule*] **1 a :** LOBE **b :** LOBULE **2 :** ALULA 2b

lo·bus \'lōbəs\ *n, pl* **lo·bi** \-,bī\ [NL, fr. Gk *lobos*] **:** LOBE

–lo·bus \ləbəs\ *n comb form* **:** one having a (specified) kind of lobe — in generic names ⟨Chaeno*lobus*⟩ ⟨Gono*lobus*⟩

lobworm \'=,=\ *n* [[1]*lob* + *worm*] **:** LUGWORM

loc *abbr* **1** local **2** location **3** [L *loco*] in the place

loca *pl of* LOCUS

[1]**lo·cal** \'lōkəl\ *adj* [ME *locale*, fr. MF *local*, fr. LL *localis*, fr. L *locus* place (fr. OL *stlocus*) + *-alis* -al — more at STALL] **1 :** characterized by or relating to position in space **:** having a definite spatial form or location ⟨a ~ body⟩ ⟨a ~ heaven and hell⟩ ⟨give to airy nothing a ~ habitation and a name —Shak.⟩ **2 :** characterized by, relating to, or occupying a particular place **:** characteristic of or confined to a particular place **:** not general or widespread ⟨~ politics⟩ ⟨a ~ custom⟩ **3 :** relating to what is local **:** not broad or general ⟨a person of ~ ideas⟩ ⟨a ~ point of view⟩ **4 :** current only in a particular section of a country — used of words or expressions whether dialect or standard (as *you-all, down East, the food is all*) **5 a :** primarily serving the needs of a particular limited district, often a community or minor political subdivision ⟨all-weather ~ roads⟩ ⟨a ~ bus line⟩ **b :** applicable in or relating to such a district only ⟨~ transportation costs⟩ ⟨~ taxes⟩ **c** *of a public conveyance* **:** making all the stops on its run ⟨a ~ train⟩ — compare EXPRESS **d** *of an act, law, statute* **:** limited in operation to only part of the territory subject to the legislative power (as a town, district, county) **6 :** involving or affecting only a restricted area or portion of the organism **:** not general ⟨a ~ ailment⟩ ⟨~ anesthesia⟩

[2]**local** \"\ *n* -s **:** a local person or thing ⟨found the ~*s* somewhat dour and unfriendly⟩: as **a :** a local train, elevator, or other public conveyance **b :** a local or particular branch, lodge, or chapter of an organization (as a labor union or a college fraternity) **c :** a local company or team (as of ballplayers) — usu. used in pl. ⟨the ~*s* play tomorrow⟩ **d** (1) **:** a newspaper story or item of interest mainly to readers who live in the town or city where the paper is published (2) **:** a radio or television program sent out from one station only **e** (1) **:** a stamp for paying postage within a restricted area (2) **:** a carrier's stamp issued by a private carrier (3) **:** a precanceled stamp precanceled in the city where it is used — compare BUREAU **f** *Brit* **:** a nearby or neighborhood pub **g** (1) **:** LOCAL ANESTHESIA (2) **:** LOCAL ANESTHETIC

[3]**local** \"\ *vt* **localed** *or* **localled; localed** *or* **localled; localing** *or* **localling; locals** *Scots law* **:** to impose as a local charge; *specif* **:** to assign to the landholders of a parish their individual shares in the payment of (the parish minister's stipend)

local action *n* **1 :** voltaic action at an electrode of an electrolytic cell consisting of currents set up in the electrolyte between chemically different areas due to impurities on its surface **2 :** a legal action that by its nature must have arisen in a particular place (as an action of trespass or replevin or one against a municipal corporation) — compare TRANSITORY ACTION

local agent *n* **:** a person or firm authorized to act as agent for one or more property insurance companies in a particular community and usu. paid by commission

local allegiance *n* **:** allegiance due to the government of a state in which an alien temporarily resides

local anesthesia *n* **:** loss of sensation in a limited and usu. superficial area esp. from the effect of a local anesthetic

local anesthetic *n* **:** an anesthetic for topical and usu. superficial application **:** an anesthetic intended to produce local anesthesia

local color *n* **1 :** the color belonging to an object under normal daylight and not caused by accidental influences (as of reflection or shadow) **2 :** color in writing derived from the presentation of the features and peculiarities of a particular locality and its inhabitants

local colorist *n* **:** a writer who makes much use of local color esp. as derived from the quaint or picturesque

lo·cale \lō'kal *sometimes* lə'- *or* -kȧl\ *n* -s [modif. of F *local*, fr. *local*, adj. — more at LOCAL] **1 :** a place or locality esp. when viewed in relation to a particular event or characteristic ⟨the actual ~ of the crime⟩ ⟨a healthful ~ esp. helpful to asthmatics⟩ **2 :** LOCATION, SITE, SITUATION ⟨the ~ and period of the story⟩ ⟨a universe that has no real ~ or date —Edmund Wilson⟩

local freight *n* **:** a freight train performing local services including picking up and setting out cars, switching, and loading and unloading less-than-carload freight at way stations

local government *n* **1 a :** the government of a specific local area (as a city, county, or town) constituting a subdivision of a nation, state, or other major political unit ⟨no tradition of autonomy in *local government* —J.A.Corry⟩ ⟨every state is divided into *local government* areas —F.A.Ogg & P.O.Ray⟩ **b** *or* **local self–government :** self-government in local affairs by a political subdivision as distinguished from administration of the area by the central government ⟨a law passed by the appropriate legislature may abolish *local government* —J.A.Corry⟩ ⟨customary to think of Britain as the home of *local self-government* —C.J.Friedrich⟩ — compare HOME RULE **2 :** the body of persons exercising the functions of government in a local territorial unit and constituting the unit as an active agency ⟨in the performance of such powers the *local government* is acting as the state's agent —J.E.Pate⟩ **3 :** a branch of political science dealing with the government of local areas ⟨college-level courses in *local government*⟩

lo·cal·ism \'lōkə,lizəm\ *n* -s **1 :** affection for a particular place **:** concern with local affairs **:** SECTIONALISM; *specif* **:** the tendency to place local interests above national **2 :** something characteristic of a locality; *esp* **:** a local idiom or peculiarity of speaking or acting

lo·cal·ist \-,ləst\ *n* -s **1 :** one that is strongly or unduly concerned with purely local matters **2 :** one that attributes the origin of disease to local causes

lo·cal·is·tic \'lōkə;listik, -tēk\ *adj* **:** locally oriented or limited **:** concerned or associated with a particular locality ⟨a ~ theory of disease⟩ ⟨the colonist's ~ defense of home —W.L.Miller⟩

lo·cal·ite \'==,līt\ *n* -s **:** a native or resident of a locality under consideration **:** LOCAL

lo·cal·itis \,=='līd·əs\ *n* -ES [[1]*local* + *-itis*] **:** undue concern (as on the part of a military commander) with a particular area or the problems of a particular situation resulting in failure to visualize adequately the whole of which it is a part

lo·cal·i·ty \lō'kaləd·ē, -ətē, -i\ *n* -ES [F *localité*, fr. LL *localitat-, localitas*, fr. *localis* local + *-itat-, -itas* -ity — more at LOCAL] **1 a :** the fact or condition of having a location in space or time ⟨every real object has ~ as one of its attributes⟩ **b** *archaic* **:** restriction to a particular place **:** LOCALIZATION **2 :** a particular spot, situation, or location: as **a :** the place from which something (as a sample of a mineral or a specimen of a plant) was obtained or is available ⟨type *localities* should be exactly specified⟩ ⟨a ~ rich in mineral springs⟩ **b :** a place having or considered in respect to a particular feature ⟨*localities* of heavy rainfall⟩ **c :** a political subdivision of a state **:** LOCAL GOVERNMENT **3 a :** space or place reference **:** orientation in respect to space ⟨a strong sense of ~⟩ **b :** a phrenological indication for the faculty of observing and recognizing places and their relative positions **4** *Scots law* **a :** the provision by a marriage contract of a liferent in lands to a wife **b :** the assignment to the landholders of a parish of their individual shares in the payment of the parish minister's stipend

lo·cal·iz·able \'lōkə,līzəbəl, ,=='===\ *adj* **:** capable of being localized

lo·cal·iza·tion \,lōkələ'zāshən, -lī'-\ *n* -s **:** an act of localizing or the state of being localized: as **a :** the reference of a sense impression to some particular locality in the body or of a perceived object to a definite locality in space **b :** the reference of an event to a particular position in a temporal series **c** (1) **:** restriction (as of a lesion) to a limited area of the body (2) **:** restriction of functional centers (as of sight, smell, or speech) to a particular section of the brain

lo·cal·ize \'lōkə,līz\ *vb* -ED/-ING/-S *see -ize in Explan Notes* [[1]*local* + *-ize*] *vt* **1 :** to make local or orient locally: as **a :** to fix in or assign or confine to a definite place or locality ⟨hot applications helped to ~ the infection⟩ ⟨it was not hard to ~ the origins of this legend **b** to give local significance to; *esp* **:** to write up (a news story of more than local significance) or rewrite (a press release or wire service story) so that local significance is played up ~ *vi* **1 :** to collect or accumulate in or be restricted to a specific or limited area ⟨iodine tends to ~ in the thyroid⟩ ⟨anger *localized* sharply on the new tax⟩ ⟨the infection *localized* with the formation of a definite abscess⟩

localized vector *n* **:** a vector (as a force) requiring for its description not only its magnitude and direction but also its axis, the line along which its representative segment lies

lo·cal·iz·er \-zə(r)\ *n* -s **:** one that localizes; *esp* **:** a radio transmitter used in blind landing to keep an airplane aligned with the runway

local law *also* **local act** *n* **:** a law passed by a legislative body and intended to apply only to one part of the area under its jurisdiction — distinguished from *general law;* compare BYLAW

localled *past of* LOCAL

localling *pres part of* LOCAL

lo·cal·ly \'lōkəlē, -li\ *adv* [ME *localliche*, fr. *localle* local + *-iche* -y] **1 :** in relation to position in space **2 :** in relation or respect to a particular place or situation **3 :** in or about an area under consideration **:** NEARBY ⟨much corn is grown ~⟩ **4 :** in the region of origin **:** in the place where native or grown ⟨a fruit used ~ to flavor brandy⟩

lo·cal·ness *n* -ES **:** the quality or state of being local; *esp* **:** concern with local matters

local officer *n* **:** a layman in a Salvation Army corps who voluntarily undertakes part-time duties and serves without pay

local option *n* **:** the privilege or power granted by a legislature to a political subdivision (as a town) to determine by popular vote of the citizens of the subdivision whether a law on a controversial issue (as the sale of liquor or the fluoridation of the water supply) shall apply in the subdivision

local preacher *n* **:** a layman licensed by his church to preach in a specified district

local rate *n* **:** a transportation rate for a shipment that does not leave the lines of the originating carrier

local road *or* **local street** *n* **:** a way used primarily for access to adjacent property

locals *pl of* LOCAL, *pres 3d sing of* LOCAL

local self–government *n* **:** LOCAL GOVERNMENT 1b

local service airline *n* **:** an airline that connects cities or larger terminals with smaller communities or makes all or most stops between larger terminals — called also *feeder line*

local time *n* **:** time expressed with respect to the celestial meridian of a particular place being the same for all points along the same meridian of longitude — usu. distinguished from *standard time* and *Greenwich time*

local union *n* **1 :** a local branch of a trade union (as a national or international union) made up of many branches **2 :** a trade union that exists only in a particular locality and is not affiliated with a larger union

lo·cant \'lōkənt\ *n* -s [*location* + *-ant*] **:** the portion of a chemical name that designates the position of an atom or group in a molecule (as *β-* in *β-naphthylamine, m-* in *m-xylene, 2-* in *2-butanol*, or *l-* in *glucose-1-C*[14])

lo·car·no \lō'kär(,)nō\ *n* -s *usu cap* [fr. the *Locarno* Pact, a series of treaties and conventions between Germany on the one hand and Belgium, France, Great Britain, Italy, Poland, and Czechoslovakia on the other, signed in Locarno, Switzerland on Dec. 1, 1925] **:** a nonaggression pact or other arrangement for international peace and security usu. based upon a mutual guarantee of borders by and provision for arbitration of disputes among the signatory nations ⟨proposed an Asian *Locarno* —*Christian Science Monitor*⟩ ⟨pleasant daydreams about *Locarnos* and mutual self-restraint pacts —Delmer Hubbell⟩

lo·cat·able \(')lō¦kād·əbəl\ *adj* **:** possible to locate

lo·cate \'lō,kāt *also* ='=; *usu* -ād·+V\ *vb* -ED/-ING/-S [L *locatus*, past part. of *locare*, fr. *locus* place — more at STALL] *vi* **1 :** to take up one's residence **:** establish oneself or one's business **:** SETTLE ⟨the company *located* north of town⟩ ⟨their parents *located* in Ohio⟩ **2** *of a Methodist minister* **:** to retire from clerical life or duties ~ *vt* **1 :** to determine or indicate the place of **:** define the site or limits of (as by a survey) ⟨*locating* the lines of the property⟩ **2 a :** to set or establish in a particular spot or position **:** STATION ⟨*located* himself behind the screen⟩ ⟨carefully *located* the clock in the exact center of the mantel⟩ **b :** to establish in a charge or office **3 a :** to seek out and discover the position of ⟨*located* the children in the attic⟩ ⟨try to ~ the source of the sound⟩ **b :** to find the place of or assign a place to in a sequence ⟨*locating* the reigns of the pastoral kings⟩ **c :** to determine the position of (a mathematical object) ⟨~ a decimal point⟩ ⟨~ a point in a plane⟩ **4** *civil law* **:** to let out by a contract of location

lo·cat·er \-ād·ə(r)\ *n* -s **:** one that locates

lo·ca·tio \lō'kād·ē,ō\ *n* -s [L (also, location)] *Roman, civil, & Scots law* **:** LETTING, LEASING

locatio con·duc·tio \-kən'dəktē,ō\ *or* **locatio et conductio** \-,etkən-\ *n* [L, letting (and) hiring] *Roman & civil law* **:** a contract of letting and hiring

lo·ca·tion \lō'kāshən\ *n* -s [L *location-, locatio*, fr. *locatus* (past part. of *locare* to place, lease) + *-ion-, -io* -ion — more at LOCATE] **1 a :** an act or the process of locating ⟨devoted all her time to the ~ of the missing money⟩ **b :** the act or process of marking out an area of land **:** the surveying of a tract of land (as for settlement) **2 a :** a position or site occupied or available for occupancy (as by a building) or marked by some distinguishing feature ⟨a sheltered ~⟩ ⟨much of the charm of the house was in its ~⟩ ⟨discovered the ~ of the hiding place⟩ **b :** an area or tract of land: as (1) **:** a tract of land whose bounds have been officially designated (as for settlement or for a mining claim) (2) *Austral* **:** FARM, STATION (3) *Africa* **:** a segregated area of a town or city in which natives are required to live **c :** the center line and grade line of a railway established preparatory to its construction **d :** a place outside of a motion-picture studio where a picture or part of it is filmed — used chiefly in the phrase *on location* **3 :** a letting for hire **:** a contract for the use of something (as a house, a vehicle, the service of a person) for hire — **lo·ca·tion·al** \-shənᵊl, -shnəl\ *adj* — **locationally** \-ᵊlē, -əlē, \|i\ *adv*

locatio rei \-ˈrāˌ\ *n* [L, letting of a thing] *law* **:** a bailment of a chattel for use and for hire

¹loc·a·tive \ˈläkəd·iv, -ətiv\ *n* -s [L *locus* place + E *-ative* (as in *vocative*)] **:** the locative case or a word in that case

²locative \"\ *adj* [F *locatif,* fr. MF, fr. L *locatus* + MF *-if* -ive] **1 :** serving or tending to locate ⟨a ~ impulse⟩ **2** [¹*locative*] **:** belonging to or being a grammatical case that denotes place or the place where or wherein

lo·ca·tor \ˈlōˌkād·ə(r), -ātə- *also* ≈ˈ≈\ *n* -s [L, fr. *locatus* (past part. of *locare* to locate, lease) + *-or* — more at LOCATE] **:** one that locates: as **a** *civil & Scots law* **:** one that lets for hire — compare CONDUCTOR 4 **b :** one that locates land or a mining claim **c :** a device used to designate location (as a card or file used to show location of records) **d :** JIG 4b **e :** RADIOLOCATOR

loc cit \ˈlōkˈsit, ˈläk-\ *abbr* [L *loco citato*] in the place cited

lo·cel·late \lōˈse(ˌ)lāt, -lət\ *adj* [NL *locellus* + E *-ate*] **:** divided into locelli — often used in combination ⟨a bi*locellate* ovary⟩

lo·cel·lus \-eləs\ *n, pl* **locel·li** \-eˌlī\ [NL, fr. LL, compartment, dim. of L *locus* place — more at STALL] **1 :** a secondary compartment of a unilocular ovary of various legumes formed by a false partition **2 :** either of the two cavities of a pollen sac

¹loch \ˈläk, ˈläk\ *n* -s [ME (Sc) *louch, locht,* fr. ScGael *loch;* akin to OIr *loch* lake, pond — more at LAKE] **1** *Scot* **:** LAKE **2** *Scot* **:** a bay or arm of the sea esp. when nearly landlocked

²loch \ˈläk\ *n* -s [origin unknown] *Brit* **:** a fissure or void cavity in a mineral vein esp. of a lead mine

loch·aber ax \läkˈ\|äbə(r)-, läˈk\|, \|abə(r)-\ *n, usu cap L* [fr. *Lochaber,* district in Scotland] **:** a weapon formerly used by Scottish Highlanders consisting of a pole with a long ax head often provided with a hook at its end

Loch-aber ax

loch·age \ˈläkij\ *or* **loch·a·gus** \läˈkāgəs\ *n, pl* **lochages** \-jəz\ *or* **locha·gi** \-äˌjī\ [Gk *lochagos,* fr. *lochos* + *-agos* (fr. *agein* to lead, drive) — more at AGENT] **:** the commander of a lochus

loch·an \ˈläkən\ *n* -s [ScGael, dim. of *loch*] *Scot* **:** a small lake **:** POND

loche \ˈlōch\ *n* -s [F] **1** *archaic* **:** LOACH **2** [CanF, fr. F, loach] **:** the New World burbot

lo·chet·ic \lōˈked·ik\ *adj* [LGk *lochētikos,* fr. *lochan* to lie in wait (fr. *lochos* ambush, lochus) + *-ikos* -ic — more at LOCHUS] **:** lying in wait for prey — used esp. of insects

lo·chia \ˈlōkēə, ˈläkēə\ *n, pl* **lochia** [NL, fr. Gk, fr. neut. pl. of *lochios* of childbirth, fr. *lochos* childbirth, ambush, lochus — more at LOCHUS] **:** a discharge from the uterus and vagina following delivery — **lo·chi·al** \-ēəl\ *adj*

loch le·ven trout \-ˈlēvən-\ *n, usu cap both Ls* [fr. *Loch Leven,* Scotland] **:** a trout native to Loch Leven and other lakes of southern Scotland and northern England that is a variety (*Salmo trutta levenensis*) of the European brown trout; *broadly* **:** any brown trout introduced into and established in No. American waters

loch·us \ˈläkəs\ *n, pl* **lochi** \-äˌkī\ [NL, fr. Gk *lochos* ambush, childbirth, lochus; akin to Gk *lechos* bed — more at LIE] **:** a small division of an ancient Greek army comprising about 100 to 200 men — see LOCHAGE

lochy \ˈläkī\ *adj* [¹*loch* + *-y*] *Scot* **:** having many lakes

loci *pl of* LOCUS

lo·ci·a·tion \ˌlōsēˈāshən\ *n* -s [*local* + *faciation*] **:** a subunit of an ecological faciation, one such subunit in each faciation being distinguishable from others in relative abundance of the dominant species

¹lock \ˈläk\ *n* -s [ME *lok, lokk,* fr. OE *locc;* akin to OFris & OS *lok* lock of hair, OHG *loc,* ON *lokkr* lock, L *luctari, luctare* to struggle, wrestle, *luxus* dislocated, Gk *lygos* withe, *lygizein* to bend, twist, Lith *lugnas* flexible; basic meaning: to bend] **1 a :** a tuft, tress, or ringlet of hair as it grows **b locks** *pl* **:** the hair of the head **c** *obs* **:** a tress of false or artificial hair **2 :** a cohering bunch of wool, cotton, flax, or other natural fiber **:** TUFT, FLOCK: as **a locks** *pl* **:** short inferior wool obtained in small bunches (as from the legs) and not part of the coherent fleece **b :** the cotton lint contained in a single cell of a cotton boll; *also* **:** a cell of a cotton boll **3 :** a usu. small quantity esp. of hay or straw **:** BUNDLE, HEAP

²lock \"\ *n* -s [ME *lok,* fr. OE *loc;* akin to OE *lūcan* to lock, close, OHG *loh* enclosure, prison, cave, opening, OHG *lūhhan* to close, ON *loka* lock of a door, *lūka* to close, Goth *galūkan* to enclose, *usluk* opening, OE *locc* lock of hair — more at ¹LOCK] **1 a :** a fastening (as for a door, box, trunk lid, drawer) in which a bolt is secured by any of various mechanisms and can be released by inserting and turning a key or by operating a special device (as a combination, time clock, automatic release button, magnetic solenoid) **b** *obs* **:** HOBBLE, SHACKLE **c :** the mechanism by which the charge or cartridge of a firearm is exploded — often used in combination; see GUNLOCK, MATCHLOCK **2 a** *obs* **:** a movable barrier across a stream **b** *archaic* **:** the space of water between the piers of a bridge **c** (1) **:** an enclosure (as in a canal, river, or dock) with gates at each end used in raising or lowering boats as they pass from level to level (2) **:** AIR LOCK 1 **3 a :** a locking or fastening together **:** a closing of one thing upon another **b :** a group of objects (as vehicles) intricately massed together so as to impede the freedom or mobility of individual objects **:** a block or jam esp. of traffic **c** (1) **:** a hold in wrestling secured on one part of the body ⟨an arm*lock*⟩ ⟨a leg *lock*⟩ (2) *obs* **:** STRATAGEM, TRICK (3) *obs* **:** DIFFICULTY, DILEMMA **d :** plaster forced through laths to form a key **e** *archaic* **:** a receiver or place for receipt of stolen goods **f** *or* **lock seam :** a joint made by folding over two or more lapped edges of sheet metal **g :** the contact of a tooth of the escape wheel of a timepiece with the locking surface of the pallet; *specif* **:** the amount by which the escape tooth overlaps the pallet at the instant it leaves the impulse face **h** (1) **:** the joint at which two panels of a rail fence are locked together (2) **:** the triangular area in a field formed by the corner panels of a rail fence **4** [by shortening] **:** OARLOCK, ROWLOCK **5 :** LOCK FORWARD

³lock \"\ *vb* -ED/-ING/-S [ME *lokken,* fr. *lok,* n.] *vt* **1 :** to fasten the lock of ⟨~ the door⟩ **:** make fast with or as if with a lock ⟨closed and ~*ed* the box⟩ — often used with *up* ⟨don't forget to ~ up all the doors and windows⟩ ⟨~ up the house⟩ **2 a :** to fasten in or out or to make secure or inaccessible by means of or as if by means of locks **:** confine or shut in or out ⟨~ oneself in⟩ ⟨~ up the prisoners⟩ ⟨~*ed* their secrets in her heart⟩ ⟨~*ing* the child in his arms⟩ ⟨a ship ~*ed* fast in ice⟩ **b :** to hold fast or inactive **:** OVERCOME, FIX ⟨a mind ~*ed* in contemplation⟩ ⟨sleep ~*ing* the tired eyelids⟩ **3 :** to make fast by or as if by the interlacing or interlocking of parts ⟨~*ing* arms across the table⟩: as **a :** to make fast or rigid by the engaging of parts or the action of a restraint esp. friction ⟨~ the wheels of a carriage⟩ **b :** to hold in a close embrace ⟨~*ed* in each other's arms⟩; *also* **:** to grapple in combat ⟨~*ed* in a death struggle⟩ **c :** to fasten (imposed letterpress matter) securely in a chase or on the bed of a press by tightening the quoins; *also* **:** to attach (a curved printing plate) to the plate cylinder of a rotary press — usu. used with *up* **4 :** to invest (capital) where conversion into money is not easy — usu. used with *up* ⟨had his resources ~*ed up* in the canal scheme⟩ **5 a :** to move or permit to pass (as a ship) by raising or lowering in a lock — often used with *in, out, down, up,* or *through* **b :** to provide (as a canal) with locks **c :** to divide off (a portion of a river) by a lock — used with *off* ~ *vi* **1 :** to become locked **:** become fixed or fast by or as if by means of a lock ⟨the door ~*s* easily⟩ **2 :** INTERLACE, INTERLOCK ⟨the sections ~ into one another⟩ **3 a** *of a vehicle* **:** to permit the fore wheels to swivel round with more or less freedom in turning **b** *of wheels* **:** to have such freedom of motion **4 a :** to build locks to facilitate navigation **b :** to go or pass by means of a lock (as in a canal) ⟨~*ed* into the new canal⟩ — **lock horns 1** *of cattle* **:** to engage or interlock the horns in fighting **2** *of persons* **:** to come into conflict ⟨will probably *lock horns* over the appointment of a new supervisor⟩

⁴lock \"\ *adj* **:** capable of being made fast **:** LOCKABLE

⁵lock \"\ *vt* -ED/-ING/-S [D *locken,* fr. MD; akin to OE *lōccian* to attract, entice, OHG *lockōn, lucchen* to entice, allure, ON *lokka,* and prob. to OHG *liogan* to lie — more at LIE (tell a falsehood)] *archaic* **:** ALLURE, ENTICE, SEDUCE

lock·able \ˈläkəbəl\ *adj* **:** capable of being locked ⟨a desk with one ~ drawer⟩

lock·age \-kij, -kēj\ *n* -s [²*lock* + *-age*] **1 a :** an act or the process of passing something (as a boat) through a lock **b :** something passed or passing through a lock; *esp* **:** the quantity (as of logs) that can be locked at one time **2 :** the construction of a system of locks (as in a canal); *also* **:** a system of locks **3 :** toll paid for passing through a lock or locks (as of a canal) **4 :** the vertical distance through which a boat is raised or lowered in passing through a lock or series of locks; *also* **:** the volume of water involved in the process

lockaid gun \ˈ≈ˌ≈-\ *n* [²*lock* + *aid*] **:** a tool consisting of a barrel with a thin vibrator blade used to force open a lock

lock-and-block system \ˌ≈≈ˈ≈-\ *n, Brit* **:** a railway block system in which the signals permitting a train to enter a block are locked while a train is in the block and automatically unlocked as it leaves the block

lock bolt *n* **1 :** BOLT 2b **2 a :** a bolt or pin employing a special locking collar instead of a nut **b :** a bolt for securing an adjustable part of a machine in a desired position

lockbox \ˈ≈ˌ≈\ *n* **:** a box (as a strongbox or safe-deposit box) that locks; *esp* **:** a post-office box that is accessible to the renter by means of a key

lock corner *n* **:** a corner (as of a wood or metal box) secured by dovetail or other interlocking construction

lock-down \ˈ≈ˌ≈\ *n* [fr. *lock down,* v.] **:** a strip of wood with holes in the ends through which pins are driven to hold together a raft of logs

lock·e·an *also* **locke·i·an** *or* **lock·i·an** \ˈläkēən\ *adj, usu cap* [John *Locke* †1704 Eng. philosopher + E *-an, -ian*] **:** of or relating to John Locke or to his theories or philosophical system

lock·e·an·ism *also* **lock·i·anism** \-ēəˌnizəm\ *n* -s *usu cap* **:** the philosophical system of John Locke that denies the existence of innate ideas and asserts that the mind orig. resembles a tabula rasa so that all knowledge comes from experience specif. from sense perception and from reflection upon the relations of apprehended ideas and the operations of the mind itself, maintains that the primary qualities of objects (as extension, figure, number, motion, rest) inhere in the objects independently of being perceived and that the secondary qualities (as color, sound, odor) are caused by external objects but do not resemble them, and holds that political sovereignty is based on the consent of the governed

locked *adj* [fr. past part. of ³*lock*] **1 :** fastened or united by locking ⟨a ~ closet⟩ **2 a :** *of a joint* **:** held rigidly in the position assumed during complete extension ⟨struck a blow with a ~ wrist⟩ **b** *of the knee joint* **:** having a restricted mobility and incapable of complete extension

locked groove *n* **:** a final closed groove on a recording disc

locked-in \ˈ≈ˈ≈\ *adj* [fr. past part. of *lock in*] **:** unalterably fixed ⟨a *locked-in* finish⟩

locked jaw *var of* LOCKJAW

locked jury *n* **:** a jury considering a case under orders not to separate and to communicate with no one except the court or its officers

locked-wire rope *or* **locked-coil wire rope** *n* **:** a rope esp. adapted for haulage and rope transmission having a smooth cylindrical surface and made by drawing the outer wires to such shape that each one interlocks with the other so that the wires lie in concentric layers about a wire core

lock·er \ˈläkə(r)\ *n* -s [ME *lokker,* fr. *lokken* lock + *-er* — more at LOCK] **1 :** a container used for safekeeping or storage and usu. capable of being locked: as **a :** a drawer, cupboard, or compartment that may be closed with a lock; *esp* **:** one for individual storage use ⟨gym ~*s*⟩ **b :** a chest or compartment on shipboard for compact stowage of articles of a particular class ⟨a boatswain's ~⟩ ⟨forward paint ~*s*⟩; *esp* **:** an enclosed storage space (as for valuable cargo) **c** *South* **:** LINEN CLOSET **d :** one of the compartments available for rent in a locker plant designed for storing quick-frozen foods for extended periods usu. at or below 0° F and at 80% relative humidity **2** *archaic* **:** a locking device **3 :** one that locks: as **a :** British customs employee in charge of a warehouse **b :** a locking device for use on a vehicle wheel

locker paper *n* **:** a flexible protective paper for wrapping food for quick-freezing and storage

locker plant *n* **:** a refrigeration and storage establishment consisting of quick-freezing equipment and storage lockers rentable for food storage

locker room *n* **:** a room devoted to storage lockers; *esp* **:** one in which participants in a sport have individual lockers for their clothes and special equipment and change into and out of sports costume

locke's solution \ˈläk(s)-\ *or* **locke solution** *n, usu cap L* [after Frank S. *Locke,* 19th-20th cent. Brit. physiologist] **:** a solution isotonic with blood plasma that contains the chlorides of sodium, potassium, and calcium and sodium bicarbonate and dextrose and is used similarly to physiological saline

lock·et \ˈläkət, *usu* -əd·+V\ *n* -s [MF *loquet* latch, fr. MD *loke* latch, bolt + MF *-et* (dim. suffix); akin to OE *loc* bolt, lock — more at LOCK] **1** *obs* **:** a crossbar of a window **2 :** a part of a scabbard where a belt hook fastens **3 :** a group of set jewels **4 :** a catch or spring for fastening something (as a necklace) **5 a :** a small and often ornate case usu. of precious metal having space for a memento (as a miniature or a lock of hair) and worn typically suspended from a chain or necklace **b :** a patch of distinctive color (as white) on the throat or chest of a cat

locket 5a

lockfast \ˈ≈ˌ≈\ *adj* [ME (Sc) *lokfast,* fr. *lok* lock + *fast*] *Scot* **:** made fast by a lock

lock forward *n* **:** the middle player in the third row of the scrum in rugby

lock-grained \ˈ≈ˈ≈\ *adj, of lumber* **:** having interlaced grain

lock handle *also* **locking handle** *n* **:** a handle that can be locked in a fixed position

lockhole \ˈ≈ˌ≈\ *n* **:** KEYHOLE

lock hospital *n, Brit* **:** a hospital for the treatment of venereal diseases

lockhouse \ˈ≈ˌ≈\ *n* **:** a house for the person in charge of a canal or river lock

lockian *usu cap, var of* LOCKEAN

lockier *comparative of* LOCKY

lockiest *superlative of* LOCKY

locking *pres part of* LOCK

locking plate *n* **:** the count wheel used in one type of clock striking train — distinguished from *rack*

locking ring *n* **:** a screw collar connecting the tube and jacket of some types of guns of minor caliber

lockjaw \ˈ≈ˌ≈\ *also* **locked jaw** *n* **:** an early symptom of tetanus characterized by spasm of the jaw muscles and inability to open the jaws **:** TRISMUS; *broadly* **:** TETANUS

lock-joint \ˈ≈ˌ≈\ *n* **:** a joint in which the elements joined are interlocked (as in a dovetail joint) with or without other fastening (as glue, solder, or pinning)

lockkeeper \ˈ≈ˌ≈≈\ *n* **:** a person in charge of a lock (as on a canal) ⟨the ~ . . . came to the rescue with his boathook —Thomas Hughes⟩

lockless \ˈläkləs\ *adj* **:** having no lock ⟨a ~ cabin⟩ ⟨a long ~ stretch of water⟩

lockmaker \ˈ≈ˌ≈≈\ *n* **:** one that makes locks

lockmaking \ˈ≈ˌ≈≈\ *n* **:** the process of making locks

lock·man \ˈläkmən\ *n, pl* **lockmen 1** *Scot* **:** a public executioner **2 :** a coroner's summoner in the Isle of Man **3 :** LOCKKEEPER, LOCKMASTER

lockmaster \ˈ≈ˌ≈≈\ *n* **:** a person who immediately directs the operation of a lock (as of a canal) ⟨the ~ . . . relays word to the control tower that we are ready to start our lift —J.H. Winchester⟩

Lock·nit \ˈläkˌnit\ *trademark* — used for a fabric knitted with an interlocking stitch that resists runs

locknut \ˈ≈ˌ≈\ *n* **1 :** a nut screwed down hard on another to prevent it from slacking back **2 :** a nut so constructed that it locks itself when screwed up tight **3 :** a nut screwed against the end of a pipe fitting to hold it securely and prevent leakage **4 :** a nut used with an electrical conduit for locking it into a junction box or fitting

lock on *vt* **:** to sight and follow (a target) automatically by means of a radar beam ⟨will automatically follow, through any gyrations, the object on its screen to which it has been *locked on* —*New Republic*⟩

lock out *vt* **1 :** to withhold employment from (a body of employees) in order to gain concessions **2 :** to shut out from by or as if by a locked door ⟨meters are usually *locked out* of the system when premises are to be left vacant⟩

¹lockout \ˈ≈ˌ≈\ *n* -s [*lock out*] **:** an act of locking out or the condition of being locked out: as **a :** the withholding of employment by an employer and the whole or partial closing of his business establishment in order to gain concessions from employees — compare STRIKE **b :** involuntary closure of secure premises (as a bank vault) due to failure of an intricate time-lock device either by chance or as a result of tampering

²lockout \"\ *adj* **:** serving to prevent operation of a device or part of it ⟨the ~ circuit breaker operates when there is an excessive current flowing —Ernest Venk & William Landon⟩

lockpick \ˈ≈ˌ≈\ *n* **:** PICKLOCK

lockpin \ˈ≈ˌ≈\ *n* **:** a peg or pin that is inserted through a hole or holes and locks two parts together

lock plate *n* **:** a plate to which the several parts of the lock of some firearms are attached and by which the whole is fastened to the stock by screws

lock rail *n* **:** a horizontal stiffening member of a paneled door in or to which the lock is fixed

lock·ram \ˈläkrəm\ *n* -s [ME *lokerham,* alter. (influenced by *bukeram, bokeram* buckram) of *Locronan,* town in Brittany where it was made] **1 :** a coarse plain-woven linen of French origin formerly used in England (as for clothing) **2** *or* **lock·rum** \"\ *dial* **:** NONSENSE

locks *pl of* LOCK, *pres 3d sing of* LOCK

lock seam *n* **:** LOCK 3f

lockset \ˈ≈ˌ≈\ *n* **1 :** a complete lock system including the lock mechanism together with knobs, keys, plates, strikes, and other accessories **2 :** a jig or template used to prepare a door for receiving a lock

locks·man \ˈläksmən\ *n, pl* **locksmen 1** *Scot* **:** TURNKEY **2 :** LOCKKEEPER

locksmith \ˈ≈ˌ≈\ *n* [ME *loksmith,* fr. *lok* lock + *smith* — more at LOCK, SMITH] **:** a worker who makes or repairs locks

locksmithing \ˈ≈ˌ≈≈\ *n* **:** the work or business of a locksmith

lockspit \ˈ≈ˌ≈\ *n* [³*lock* + *spit* (spadeful)] *Brit* **:** a small trench cut to indicate the line to be followed in further work (as in making a railroad or a line of fortifications)

lockstep \ˈ≈ˌ≈\ *n* **:** a mode of marching in step by a body of men (as prisoners) going one after another as closely as possible

lock stile *n* **:** the stile on the free edge of a door that receives the lock — compare LOCK RAIL

¹lockstitch \ˈ≈ˌ≈\ *n* [²*lock* + *stitch*] **:** a sewing machine stitch formed by the looping together of two threads one on each side of the material being sewn

²lockstitch \"\ *vt* **:** to sew on or together with a lockstitch ⟨~*ing* the border of the cuff⟩ ~ *vi* **:** to sew with a lockstitch ⟨most modern sewing machines ~⟩

lock, stock, and barrel *adv* [so called fr. the three principal parts of a flintlock] **:** WHOLLY, COMPLETELY ⟨sold his property *lock, stock, and barrel*⟩ ⟨took over the duties of his predecessor *lock, stock, and barrel*⟩

lock strike *n* **:** a metal fastening on a doorframe into which the bolt of a lock is projected to secure the door

lock tender *n* **1 :** LOCKKEEPER **2 :** a worker in charge of an air lock (as of a caisson)

lock time *n* **:** the interval between the releasing of the hammer on a firearm and the striking of the primer by the firing pin

lock turtle *or* **lock tortoise** *n* **:** BOX TORTOISE

lockup \ˈ≈ˌ≈\ *n* -s [fr. *lock up,* v.] **1 :** an act of locking or the state of being locked ⟨~ occurs regularly at six o'clock⟩ **2 :** something that is or is intended to be locked: as **a :** JAIL; *esp* **:** a local jail where persons are detained prior to court hearing **b** *Brit* **:** a shop or store without living quarters **c** *chiefly Brit* **:** rented storage space (as a locker or garage) that may be locked by the user **d** (1) **:** a credit obligation (as a renewed note) or other investment in which capital is locked up (2) **:** a stamp or other philatelic item bought speculatively for anticipated appreciation in value **3 a :** the operation of locking up imposed letterpress matter **b :** the quality of such locking up ⟨a secure ~ for foundry⟩

lock washer *n* **:** a washer (as a spring washer or a tooth lock washer) placed underneath a nut or screwhead to prevent loosening

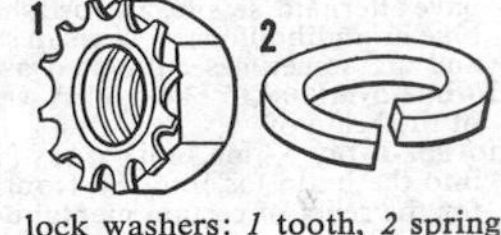

lock washers: *1* tooth, *2* spring

lockwire \ˈ≈ˌ≈\ *n* **:** wire thrust through matching holes (as in a nut and bolt) to lock parts together, the ends often being secured by a metal seal

lockwork \ˈ≈ˌ≈\ *n* **:** the mechanism on or in locks **:** the parts of a lock

locky \ˈläkē\ *adj* -ER/-EST **:** having or characterized by locks ⟨a loose ~ fleece⟩

locn *abbr* location

¹lo·co \ˈlō(ˌ)kō\ *n* -s *often cap* [by shortening] **:** LOCOFOCO 2

²loco \"\ *n, pl* **locoes** *or* **locos** [MexSp, fr. Sp, adj., crazy] **1 :** LOCOWEED **2** *or* **loco disease :** LOCOISM **3 a :** an animal affected by locoism **b :** a mentally disordered person

³loco \"\ *vt* -ED/-ING/-S **1 :** to poison with locoweed **2 :** to make or cause to be frenzied or crazy

⁴loco \"\ *adj* [Sp] *slang* **:** out of one's mind **:** FRENZIED ⟨went ~ with rage⟩ **:** CRAZY ⟨a ~ idea⟩

⁵loco \"\ *adv (or adj)* [It (*al*) *loco,* lit., at the passage] **:** in the register as written — used as a direction in music; compare OTTAVA

⁶loco \"\ *n* -s [by shortening] **:** LOCOMOTIVE

loco- *comb form* [F, fr. MF, fr. L *loco,* abl. of *locus* place — more at STALL] **1 :** from place to place ⟨*locomotion*⟩ **2 :** place ⟨*locodescriptive*⟩

lo·co ci·ta·to \ˈlō(ˌ)kōsīˈtā(ˌ)tō, ˈlä(ˌ)kōsəˈtä(ˌ)tō\ *adv* [L] **:** in the place cited **:** in the passage quoted — abbr. *loc. cit.*

lo·co·descriptive \ˌlōkō+\ *adj* [*loco-* + *descriptive*] **:** describing a locality or a particular place

locoed *adj* [fr. past part. of ³*loco*] **1** *West, of an animal* **:** affected by locoism **2** *West, of a person* **:** ECCENTRIC, CRAZY, INSANE

lo·co·fo·co \ˌlōkōˈfō(ˌ)kō\ *n* -s [prob. fr. ¹*locomotive* (self-propelled) + It *foco, fuoco* fire, fr. L *focus* fireplace, hearth — more at FOCUS] **1 :** a match or cigar developed during the 19th century and capable of being ignited by friction on any hard dry rough surface ⟨~*s* . . . were a decided improvement over the lucifers —*Springfield (Mass.) Union*⟩ — compare LUCIFER, SAFETY MATCH **2** *usu cap* [so called fr. a meeting of New York City Democrats on Oct. 22, 1835, to which the radical members came provided with matches to forestall a reported plot by their adversaries to disrupt the meeting by putting out the lights] **a :** a member of a radical group of New York Democrats organized in 1835 in opposition to the regular party organization ⟨editorials that, in the fashion of the northern *Locofocos,* called for . . . freedom of banking —Joseph Dorfman⟩ **b :** DEMOCRAT 2 ⟨the two great belligerents — the *Locofocos* and Whigs —*Diplomatic Correspondence of Texas*⟩

lo·co·fo·co·ism \-ˈfōkōˌizəm\ *n* -s *often cap* **:** the principles of the Locofocos ⟨the most arrant democracy and ~ that I ever happened to hear —Nathaniel Hawthorne⟩

lo·co·ism \ˈlōkōˌizəm\ *n* -s [²*loco* + *-ism*] **1 :** a disease of horses, cattle, and sheep caused by chronic poisoning with locoweeds and characterized by motor and sensory nerve damage resulting in peculiarities of gait, impairment of vision, lassitude or extreme excitement, emaciation, and ultimately paralysis and death if not controlled **2 :** any of several intoxications of domestic animals (as alkali disease) that are sometimes confused with locoweed poisoning

¹lo·co·mo·bile \ˌlōkəˈmōˌbēl\ *adj* [F, fr. *loco-* + *mobile*] **:** having the power to move about **:** SELF-PROPELLING ⟨a ~ crane⟩ — **lo·co·mo·bil·i·ty** \ˌ===ˈbiləd·ē\ *n*

²locomobile \"\ *n* [F, fr. *locomobile*, adj.] **:** a self-propelling vehicle or engine

lo·co·mote \ˈlōkəˌmōt, ˌ==ˈ=\ *vi* -ED/-ING/-S [back-formation fr. *locomotion*] **:** to move about ⟨*locomoting* down the road with a peculiar halting stride⟩

lo·co·mo·tion \ˌlōkəˈmōshən\ *n* [*loco-* + *motion*] **1 :** an act or the power of moving from place to place **:** progressive movement (as of an animal body) **2 :** TRAVEL

¹lo·co·mo·tive \ˌlōkəˈmōd·iv, -mōt|, |ēv *also* |əv; *by railroad men sometimes* ˌlək-\ *adj* [F, fr. MF, fr. *loco-* + LL *motivus* moving, capable of moving — more at MOTIVE] **1 a :** of or relating to locomotion ⟨the ~ faculty typical of animal life⟩ **b :** having the ability to move independently from place to place ⟨a ~ mollusk⟩ **c :** functioning in locomotion **:** LOCOMOTOR ⟨~ organs include flagella, cilia, pseudopodia, and limbs⟩ **2 a :** of or relating to travel ⟨a positive ~ mania⟩ **b :** traveling much or frequently ⟨having lately led a very ~ existence⟩ **3 :** of, relating to, or being a machine (as an engine) that moves about by operation of its own mechanism ⟨a ~ crane⟩ — **lo·co·mo·tive·ly** \|əvlē, -li\ *adv* — **lo·co·mo·tive·ness** \|ivnəs, |ēv- *also* |əv-\ *n* -ES

²locomotive \"\ *n* **1 a** *archaic Brit* **:** LOCOMOBILE **b :** a self-propelled vehicle or combination of self-propelled vehicles operating under a single control, running on rails, utilizing any of several forms of energy for producing motion, and used for moving railroad cars — compare DIESEL-ELECTRIC LOCOMOTIVE, ELECTRIC LOCOMOTIVE, STEAM LOCOMOTIVE, TURBINE-ELECTRIC LOCOMOTIVE, TURBINE LOCOMOTIVE **2 :** a cheer characterized by a slow beginning and a progressive increase in speed and used esp. at school and college sports events

locomotive engineer *n* **:** ENGINEER 4b

lo·co·mo·tive·man \ˌ===ˈ==ˌman\ *n, pl* **locomotivemen** *Brit* **:** ENGINEER 4b

locomotive works *n pl but sing or pl in constr* **:** a plant for building locomotives

lo·co·mo·tiv·i·ty \ˌlōkəmōˈtivəd·ē\ *n* **:** locomotive power **:** capacity for independent movement

¹lo·co·mo·tor \ˌlōkəˈmōd·ə(r), -mōtə-\ *n* [*loco-* + L *motor* one that moves — more at MOTOR] **:** one that has power of locomotion

²locomotor \"\ *also* **lo·co·mo·to·ry** \ˌ==ˈmōd·ərē\ *adj* **1 :** of or relating to locomotion **:** functioning in or concerned with locomotion **:** LOCOMOTIVE 1 **2 :** affecting or involving the organs concerned with locomotion ⟨~ incoordination⟩

locomotor ataxia *n* **:** TABES DORSALIS

locos *pl of* LOCO, *pres 3d sing of* LOCO

locoweed \ˈ==ˌ=\ *n* [²*loco* + *weed*] **1 :** any of several leguminous plants (genera *Astragalus* and *Oxytropis*) of western No. America that cause locoism in livestock **2 :** any of several noxious or poisonous plants other than those causing locoism: as **a** *West* (1) **:** a plant (as white snakeroot or rayless goldenrod) associated with alkali disease (2) **:** WATER HEMLOCK 1 (3) **:** any of several wild larkspurs of western No. America that are poisonous to livestock **b** *slang* **:** HEMP 1; *also* **:** MARIJUANA

¹lo·cri·an \ˈlōkrēən, ˈläk-\ *adj, usu cap* [*Locris*, region in the central part of ancient Greece (fr. L, fr. Gk *Lokris*) + E *-an*] **:** of or relating to Locris in ancient Greece

²locrian \"\ *adj, usu cap* [*Locri*, ancient city in southwestern Italy (fr. L) + E *-an*] **:** of or relating to the ancient city of Locri

locrian mode *n, usu cap L* [¹*Locrian*] **:** an authentic ecclesiastical mode represented on the white keys of the piano by an ascending scale from B to B but not actually used because its pentachord and tetrachord comprise respectively the forbidden diminished fifth and augmented fourth — see MODE illustration

loc·tal *or* **lok·tal** \ˈläktᵊl\ *adj* [fr. *Loktal*, a trademark] **:** having, being, or fitting an 8-pin vacuum-tube base having a central guide pin with a groove that fits into a spring catch in the socket to hold the tube firmly in place

loc·u·la·ment \ˈläkyələmənt\ *n* -S [L *loculamentum* receptacle, fr. *loculus* compartment, receptacle, coffin + *-mentum* -ment — more at LOCULUS] **:** LOCULUS b

loc·u·lar \ˈläkyələ(r)\ *adj* [ISV *locul-* (fr. NL *loculus*) + *-ar*] **:** having or composed of loculi — usu. used in combination ⟨*multilocular*⟩

loc·u·late \-yəlȯt, -yəˌlāt\ *or* **loc·u·lat·ed** \-ˌlād·əd\ *adj* [NL *loculus* + E *-ate* or *-ated* (fr. *-ate* + *-ed*)] **:** having, forming, or divided into loculi ⟨a ~ pocket of pleural fluid⟩ ⟨a ~ ovary⟩

loc·u·la·tion \ˌläkyəˈlāshən\ *n* -S **1 :** the condition of being or the process of becoming loculate ⟨a gradual ~ of bony tissue⟩ **2 :** a group of loculi usu. isolated from surrounding structures (as by a fibrous tissue septum) ⟨the development of ~s in empyema⟩

loc·ule \ˈläˌkyül\ *n* -S [F, fr. L *loculus* compartment, receptacle, coffin — more at LOCULUS] **:** LOCULUS — used chiefly in botany

loc·uled \-ld\ *adj* **:** LOCULATE

loc·u·li·ci·dal \ˌläkyələˈsīdᵊl\ *adj* [NL *loculus* + E *-i-* + *-cidal*] *of a capsular fruit* **:** dehiscent longitudinally so as to bisect each loculus — compare CIRCUMSCISSILE, SEPTICIDAL; see FRUIT illustration — **loc·u·li·ci·dal·ly** \-ᵊlē\ *adv*

loc·u·lus \ˈläkyələs\ *n, pl* **locu·li** \-yəˌlī\ [NL, fr. L, compartment, receptacle, coffin, dim. of *locus* place — more at STALL] **:** a small chamber or cavity: as **a :** a recess in an ancient tomb or catacomb for the reception of a body or a funeral urn **b** (1) **:** one of the cells of the compound ovary of a plant (2) **:** the cavity of a pollen sac (3) **:** a spore-bearing chamber in the stroma of a fungus **c** (1) **:** one of the spaces between the septa of the theca of an anthozoan (2) **:** one of the chambers in the shell of a foraminifer (3) **:** an egg case (as of a mollusk) (4) **:** a sucker on a haptor **d :** a small sinus in a bone (as in the mastoid bone)

lo·cum \ˈlōkəm\ *n* -S **1** [by shortening] **:** LOCUM TENENS **2** [by shortening] **:** LOCUM TENENCY

lo·cum·ship \-mˌship\ *n* -S [*locum* + *-ship*] **:** LOCUM-TENENCY

locum-te·nen·cy \-ˈtēnənsē, -ˈtenə-\ *n* -ES [ML *locum tenentia*, fr. *locum tenent-, locum tenens* + L *-ia* -y] **:** the position or duties of a locum tenens

locum te·nens \-ˈtēˌnenz, -ˈte|, |nənz\ *n, pl* **locum tenen·tes** \-təˈnenˌtēz\ [ML, lit., one holding an office] **:** one filling an office for a time or temporarily taking the place of another **:** SUBSTITUTE, DEPUTY — used esp. of a physician or clergyman

lo·cus \ˈlōkəs\ *n, pl* **lo·ci** \ˈlōˌsī, -ˌsē, -ˌkē\ *also* **lo·ca** \ˈlōkə\ [L — more at STALL] **1 :** PLACE, LOCALITY; *esp* **:** the place connected with a particular event having legal import — used esp. in legal phrases **2** [by shortening] **:** LOCUS CLASSICUS **3** [NL, fr. L] **a :** the regular linear position occupied in a chromosome by any one gene or its allele **b :** the point in a chromosome associated with a particular hereditary character **4** [NL, fr. L] *math* **:** the collection of all points whose location is determined by some stated law

locus clas·si·cus \-ˈklasəkəs\ *n, pl* **lo·ci classi·ci** \-ˌsīˈklasəˌsī\ [L] **:** a classical passage **:** a standard passage important for the elucidation of a word or subject

lo·cus poe·ni·ten·ti·ae \-ˌpenəˈtenchēˌē\ *n, pl* **loci poenitentiae** [LL, lit., place of repentance] **:** an opportunity to withdraw or resile from an inchoate obligation before it is completed **:** an opportunity to change one's mind or to decide not to commit an intended crime

locus si·gil·li \-səˈjiˌlī\ *n, pl* **loci sigilli** [L] **:** the place of or for the seal — abbr. *L. S.*

locus stan·di \-ˈstandē, -nˌdī\ *n, pl* **loci standi** [L, lit., place to stand] **:** a right to appear in a court or before any body on a given question **:** a right to be heard

lo·cust \ˈlōkəst\ *n* -S [ME, fr. L *locusta* locust, lobster; perh. akin to L *lacertus* muscle — more at LEG] **1 :** a grasshopper of the family Acrididae; *esp* **:** any of numerous migratory grasshoppers that often travel in vast swarms and strip the areas through which they pass of all vegetation **2 :** CICADA 2 **3 a** *or* **locust tree :** any of various hard-wooded trees of the family Leguminosae: as (1) **:** CAROB 1a (2) **:** a tall tree (*Robinia pseudoacacia*) of eastern No. America that has pinnately compound leaves, drooping racemes of fragrant white flowers, and strong stiff wood that is remarkably resistant to decay — called also *black locust, honey locust* (3) **:** COURBARIL 1 (4) **:** HONEY LOCUST 1a(1) (5) *NewZeal* **:** KOWHAI **b :** any of various trees of other families resembling a locust — used with a qualifying term ⟨bastard ~⟩ **c :** the wood of a locust tree

lo·cus·ta \lōˈkəstə\ *n, cap* [NL, fr. L, locust] **1 :** a genus of short-horned grasshoppers including the common migratory locust of the Old World **2** *in some esp former classifications* **:** a variously limited genus of long-horned grasshoppers

lo·cus·tal \-tᵊl\ *adj* [NL *Locusta* + E *-al*] **:** of or relating to locusts or to the genus *Locusta*

lo·cus·tar·i·an \ˌlōkəˈsta(a)rēən\ *n* -S [NL *Locustariae*, old name designating a group of saltatorial insects (fr. *Locusta* + L *-ariae*, fem. pl. of *-arius* -ary) + E *-an*] **:** LOCUST 1, CICADA 2

locust bean *n* **1 :** CAROB 1b **2 :** AFRICAN LOCUST

locust bean gum *n* **:** CAROB GUM

locust bean gum powder *or* **locust bean flour** *n* **:** CAROB FLOUR

lo·cust·berry \ˈlōkəst- — *see* BERRY\ *n* **1 :** any of several nances (genus *Byrsonima*) of extreme southern Florida and the West Indies **2 :** the acid drupe of a locustberry sometimes used as food

locust bird *n* **1** *India* **:** ROSE-COLORED STARLING **2** *Africa* **a :** GRACKLE **b :** WHITE STORK **c :** a pratincole (*Glareola nordmanni*)

locust borer *also* **locust beetle** *n* **:** a brownish black yellow-barred long-horned beetle (*Megacyllene robiniae*) whose larvae bore in the wood of the black locust tree

locust eater *n* **1 :** DIAL BIRD **2 :** ROSE-COLORED STARLING

lo·cus·telle \ˌlōkəˈstel\ *n* -S [F, dim. of *locuste* locust, fr. L *locusta* — more at LOCUST] **:** GRASSHOPPER WARBLER

¹lo·cus·ti·dae \lōˈkəstəˌdē\ [NL, fr. *Locusta* + *-idae*] *syn of* ACRIDIDAE

²locustidae \"\ [NL, fr. *Locusta* + *-idae*] *syn of* TETTIGONIIDAE

locust leaf miner *n* **:** a small orange and black beetle (*Xenochalepus dorsalis*) that skeletonizes the leaves of the black and honey locust or its larva that mines within the leaves

locustlike \ˈ==ˌ=\ *adj* **:** like a locust; *esp* **:** like a migratory locust in voracity, swarming habit, or numbers

locust lobster *n* [*locust* fr. It. *locusta* locust, lobster, fr. L — more at LOCUST] **:** a decapod crustacean of the family Scyllaridae; *esp* **:** a large edible crustacean (*Scyllarus arctus*) of the Mediterranean sea that somewhat resembles a lobster

locust plant *n* **:** a wild senna (*Cassia marilandica*)

locust pod *n* **:** CAROB 1b

locust shrimp *n* **:** SQUILLA 2

locust tree *n* **:** LOCUST 3a

lo·cu·tion \lōˈkyüshən\ *n* -S [ME *locucioun*, fr. L *locution-, locutio*, fr. *locutus* (past part. of *loqui* to speak) + *-ion-, -io* -ion] **1 :** a particular form of expression **:** a peculiarity of phrasing; *esp* **:** a word, phrase, or expression characteristic of a region, group, or cultural level ⟨~s which nearly all . . . hill people use daily —*Amer. Guide Series: Ark.*⟩ **2** *obs* **:** the act of uttering **:** SPEECH ⟨and give ~ from a thousand tongues —W.L.Lewis⟩ **3 :** style of discourse **:** PHRASEOLOGY ⟨the vein of Homeric feeling and the general style of ~ . . . would be maintained —George Grote⟩

lo·cu·tor·ship \lōˈkyüd·ə(r)ˌship\ *n* [L *locutor* speaker (fr. *locutus* — *-or*) + E *-ship*] **:** the office of spokesman

LOD *abbr* **1 :** line of dance **2 :** line of direction **3 :** line of duty

lod·di·ge·sia \ˌlädəˈjēzēə\ *n, cap* [NL, fr. Conrad *Loddiges* †1826 Eng. nurseryman + NL *-ia*] **:** a genus of hummingbirds containing one species (*L. mirabilis*) of Peru in which the two outer tail feathers are very long and devoid of webs except at the ends

lode *also* **load** \ˈlōd\ *n* -S [ME *lod, lode*, fr. OE *lād* way, course, journey, carrying, support; akin to ON *leith* way, course, OE *līthan* to go — more at LEAD] **1** *dial Eng* **a :** COURSE, PATH, ROAD **b :** WATERWAY, CANAL; *also* **:** an open drain ⟨down that long dark ~ . . . he and his brothers skated home —Charles Kingsley⟩ **2 :** a deposit of ore: as **a :** a mineral deposit that fills a fissure in the country rock **b :** an ore deposit occurring in place within definite boundaries separating it from the adjoining rocks — called also *lead, vein;* compare PLACER **3 :** something that resembles a lode ⟨found a new ~ of moral strength —A.C.Fields⟩ ⟨had struck a ~ of human kindliness —Marcia Davenport⟩ ⟨his letters are an astonishingly rich ~ of information —J.M.England⟩

lode·man·age \ˈlōdmənij\ *n* S [ME *lodmanage*, fr. *lodman* pilot (fr. OE *lādman*, fr. *lād* + *man*) + *-age*] **:** PILOTAGE

lo·den \ˈlōdᵊn\ *or* **loden cloth** *n* -S *sometimes cap L* [G *loden*, fr. OHG *lodo, ludo* coarse cloth] **:** a thick woolen cloth of Tyrolean origin that is heavily fulled to make it wind and water resistant and is used for outer clothing

lode·star *or* **load·star** \ˈlōdˌstär, -tä\ *n* [ME *lodsterre, lodesterre*, fr. *lod, lode* lode + *sterre* star — more at STAR] **1 :** a star that leads or guides; *esp* **:** POLESTAR 1 **2 :** someone or something that serves as a guiding star or as a focus of hope or attention ⟨a strangely compelling . . . human ~ whose influence half the time was unsuspected —Struthers Burt⟩ ⟨inconstancy and opportunism were the ~s of the day —*Saturday Rev.*⟩

lodestone *or* **loadstone** \ˈ=ˌ=\ *n* [*lode, load* + *stone*] **1 :** magnetite possessing polarity **2 :** something that strongly attracts **:** MAGNET ⟨was a scholastic ~ himself, and students . . . flocked to his classes —T.S.Lovering⟩ ⟨devotion to the law — the ~ of his life —*Newsweek*⟩

¹lodge \ˈläj\ *vb* -ED/-ING/-S [ME *loggen*, fr. OF *logier*, fr. *loge*, n.] *vt* **1 a :** to provide temporary quarters for **:** give a place to sleep to **:** show hospitality to ⟨there were some in which two or three hundred people . . . could without difficulty be *lodged* and fed —T.B.Macaulay⟩ **b :** to establish or settle in a place ⟨the troops *lodged* themselves in the enemy's outworks⟩ **c :** to serve as a habitation or shelter for ⟨every house was proud to ~ a knight —John Dryden⟩ **d :** to rent lodgings to **:** ACCOMMODATE 4b ⟨hoped they would ~ him for the winter⟩ **2 :** to serve as a receptacle for **:** CONTAIN ⟨a sinus *lodging* the nerve and artery of the part⟩ **3 :** to drive or track (a deer) to covert **4 :** to beat flat on the ground ⟨though bladed corn be *lodged* and trees blown down —*Shak.*⟩ **5 a :** to cause to reach an intended or a fixed position or place usu. by throwing, discharging, or thrusting ⟨two bullets were found *lodged* in the table —*Newsweek*⟩ ⟨the limit of my ambition is to ~ a few pebbles where they will be hard to get rid of —Robert Frost⟩ **b :** to deposit in passing ⟨a fish bone that was *lodged* in his throat⟩ **6 a :** to place in custody **:** INCARCERATE ⟨his scurrilities may ~ him in the pillory —H.M.Reichard⟩ ⟨just 45 days after the perpetration of the crime, every participant was securely *lodged* behind bars —D.D.Martin⟩ **b :** to deposit for safeguard or preservation ⟨agents collect the rent for the land, and ~ it in the bank —G.B.Shaw⟩ ⟨wrote a full account of our transaction and *lodged* it with a trusty man —J.H.Wheelwright⟩ **7 :** to place or vest esp. in a source, means, or agent ⟨we shall reach the best results if we ~ power in a group —B.N. Cardozo⟩ ⟨small family unit of the patriarchal type with formal authority *lodged* in the father —John Dollard⟩ **8 :** to lay or deposit before a proper authority or person **:** FILE, DELIVER ⟨the defendant then *lodged* an appeal —Priscilla Hughes⟩ ⟨fled to his solicitors to ~ his defense —Clive Arden⟩ ⟨strong protests *lodged* by a number of religious groups —B.L.Fox⟩ **9 :** to fell (a tree) so as to cause to become caught against another when falling **:** HANG UP **~** *vi* **1 a :** to occupy a place temporarily **:** stay overnight **:** SLEEP ⟨he would ~ on the cot in the spare room upstairs —Elmer Davis⟩ **b** (1) **:** to have a residence **:** DWELL, STAY ⟨~ over a bookbinder's shop —T.B.Costain⟩ (2) **:** to be a lodger ⟨the entire year of the major's *lodging* with them —Glenway Wescott⟩ **2 :** to seek covert ⟨found the place where the deer had *lodged*⟩ **3 :** to come to a rest **:** stop or settle and remain ⟨bullets pinged . . . *lodged* in the walls of houses, zipped through windows —Green Peyton⟩ ⟨could hardly have marveled more if real stars had fallen and *lodged* on his coat —Van Wyck Brooks⟩ ⟨it had *lodged* in his memory —Victor Canning⟩ **4 :** to fall or lie down — used esp. of grass or grain ⟨buckwheat . . . tends to ~ by late fall —R.E.Trippensee⟩ **syn** see RESIDE

²lodge \"\ *n* -S [ME *loge, logge*, fr. OF *loge*, of Gmc origin; akin to OHG *louba, louppea* sheltered roof, porch, prob. fr. *loub* leaf, foliage — more at LEAF] **1 a** *now chiefly dial* **:** a small or temporary dwelling; *esp* **:** a rude shelter or abode (as a hut, cabin, tent) **b** *obs* **:** a place of confinement or detention ⟨books of controversy . . . have always been confined in a separate ~ from the rest —Jonathan Swift⟩ **c** *dial Eng* **:** OUTBUILDING **2 a** *obs* **:** the workshop of a body of freemasons **b :** the meeting place of a branch of a fraternal organization ⟨a Masonic ~⟩ **c :** the body of members composing a branch of a fraternal organization **3 a :** a house set apart for residence in the hunting or other special season ⟨had a hunting and fishing ~ on the peak —Nard Jones⟩ **b :** an inn or resort hotel ⟨gave half-hour magic shows at mountain ~s and dude ranches —*Current Biog.*⟩ **c :** a recreation center of a camp or vacation spot often containing dining facilities ⟨in the evening we gathered in the main ~ —Wright Morris⟩ **4 a :** a house on an estate orig. for the use of a gamekeeper, caretaker, porter, or similar person but now often used to house guests of the owner **b :** a shelter for an employee (as a gatekeeper or porter of an institution or a factory) ⟨the beautiful fountain . . . which conceals the ~ of the attendant of the square —O.S.J.Gogarty⟩ **c :** the residence of the head of a college (as at Cambridge University) **5 :** a den or lair esp. of gregarious animals that often involves constructive work ⟨a beaver's ~⟩ ⟨a buck's ~⟩ **6** *archaic* **:** a place to put or hold something **:** a place of temporary sojourn ⟨earth is our ~, and heaven our home —Isaac Watts⟩ **7 :** a theater loge ⟨the theater lent its ~ —Robert Browning⟩ **8 a :** a dwelling, cabin, hut, or tent of the No. American Indians **:** WIGWAM — compare HOGAN, TEPEE, WICKIUP **b :** the regular occupants of a lodge **:** a family of No. American Indians ⟨a tribe of 200 ~s comprising about 1000 individuals⟩ **9 :** a local union; *also* **:** a branch of a national union

lodge·able \-jəbəl\ *adj* **:** suitable to be used for lodging ⟨~ quarters⟩

lodged \-jd\ *adj* **:** lying down — used of a heraldic beast of the chase

lodgepole \ˈ=ˌ=\ *n* **:** a pole used (as by the Plains Indians of No. America) in the construction of a lodge

lodgepole needle miner *n* **:** the larva of a very small gelechiid moth (*Coleotechnites milleri*) that mines in the leaves of lodgepole pine in western No. America and sometimes causes extensive defoliation

lodgepole pine *also* **lodgepole** *n* **:** either of two pines of western No. America that have needles in pairs and short ovoid usu. asymmetric cones: **a :** a scrubby coastal pine (*Pinus contorta*) with thick deeply furrowed bark and hard strong coarse-grained medium-light wood — called also *beach pine* **b :** a taller straight pine of the interior that has thin and little-furrowed bark and soft weak fine-grained lightweight wood and that is usu. considered to be a variety (*Pinus contorta* var. *latifolia*) of the coastal lodgepole though sometimes treated as a separate species (*P. murrayana*)

lodg·er \ˈläjə(r)\ *n* -S **1** *archaic* **a :** one that lives or dwells in a place **:** INHABITANT, OCCUPANT **b :** one that passes the night in a place (as at an inn) **2 :** one that occupies a rented room in another's house **:** a person who lives in lodgings ⟨took in permanent ~s⟩ ⟨the eternal ~, nowhere really at home —Oscar Handlin⟩; *specif* **:** one who by agreement with the owner of housing accommodations acquires no property, interest, or possession therein but only the right in accordance with the agreement to live in and occupy a room or other designated portion therein that still remains in the owner's legal possession — compare GUEST **3 :** something that becomes fixed or lodged in a place

lodges *pres 3d sing of* LODGE, *pl of* LODGE

lodg·ing \ˈläjiŋ, -jēŋ\ *n* -S [ME *logging*, fr. gerund of *loggen* to lodge — more at LODGE] **1 a :** a place to live **:** DWELLING, HABITATION ⟨high wages that go at once for ~ —Marjory S. Douglas⟩ **b :** a place in which to settle or come to rest **:** LODGMENT ⟨must not allow the recklessness of despair to find any ~ in our hearts —A.E.Stevenson b.1900⟩ **2 a** (1) **:** sleeping accommodations ⟨itinerant schoolteacher who found board and ~ in the house of his pupils' parents —*Amer. Guide Series: La.*⟩ ⟨accepting a night's ~ in the barn —*Amer. Guide Series: Mich.*⟩ (2) **:** a temporary place to stay ⟨find a ~ for the night⟩ **b :** a room or rooms in the house of another used as a place of residence — usu. used in pl. ⟨bent his footsteps toward his ~s —Gilbert Parker⟩ **3 lodgings** *pl* **a** *obs* **:** quarters for soldiers **:** CAMP **b** *Brit* **:** the living quarters of a college or university student who is neither staying with his family nor living on campus **4 :** the act of lodging ⟨had a regard for me from the time of my first ~ in their house —Benjamin Franklin⟩

lodging house *n* **:** a house where lodgings are provided and let that is often somewhat arbitrarily defined for the purpose of regulation under a particular statute or ordinance

lodging knee *n* **:** a horizontal wooden knee for securing a deck beam to a ship's side

lodging-room \ˈ==ˌ=\ *n* **:** a place for sleeping that often accommodates more than one person **:** BEDROOM ⟨we have one *lodging-room* with two single beds —Dorothy Wordsworth⟩

lodg·ment *or* **lodge·ment** \ˈläjmənt\ *n* -S [MF *logement*, fr. OF, fr. *logier* to lodge + *-ment* — more at LODGE] **1 a** *obs* **:** quarters for soldiers **b** *obs* **:** an entrenchment or other defensive work thrown up on a captured advance position as protection against attack **c** (1) **:** the occupation and holding of a position in hostile or disputed territory ⟨had a very stiff fight all day to make any ~ at all —Sir Winston Churchill⟩ (2) **:** an act resembling that of a lodgment by armed troops ⟨they were able to find ~ in corners where no monastery could have supported itself —R.W.Southern⟩ **2 a :** a place usu. a building for lodging or protecting something **:** SHELTER ⟨a hut built years ago for temporary ~ of cattlemen herding —Horace Kephart⟩ **b** (1) **:** ACCOMMODATIONS, LODGINGS ⟨found temporary ~s in Paris —W.H.Auden⟩ (2) *archaic* **:** accommodations provided in an inn ⟨the miserable ~ and miserable fare of a provincial inn —Washington Irving⟩ **3 a :** the act, fact, or manner of lodging **b :** a placing, depositing, or coming to rest ⟨the ~ of the balloon in the tree⟩ **4 a :** an accumulation or collection of something deposited in a place or remaining at rest ⟨the plains on both sides are covered at this season by heavy ~s of water —Henry Beveridge⟩ **b :** a place of rest or deposit **:** a securely established position ⟨O.K. has gained ~ in practically all civilized languages —Thomas Pyles⟩ **c :** a firm emplacement of glacial till

lodgment area *n* **:** an initial base of operations resulting from the consolidation of two or more beachheads or airheads

lo·dha \ˈlō(ˌ)dä\ *n, pl* **lodha** *or* **lodhas** *usu cap* [Hindi *lodhā* agriculturist] **1 :** a low caste numerous in Madhya Pradesh and Uttar Pradesh **2 :** a member of the Lodha caste

lodh bark \ˈlōd-\ *n* [Hindi *lodh*, fr. Skt *lodhra, rodhra;* akin to Skt *rudhira* red — more at RED] **:** the bark of an East Indian tree (*Symplocos racemosa*) that is a source of a yellow dye and is used locally as a mordant

lod·i·cule \ˈlädəˌkyül\ *n* -S [L *lodicula* coverlet, dim. of *lodic-, lodix* cover] *in the grass flower* **:** one of the two (rarely three) delicate membranous hyaline scales at the base of the ovary which by their swelling assist in anthesis

lod·o·my \ˈlädəmi\ *Scot var of* LAUDANUM

lodz \ˈlädz, ˈlüj, ˈwüj\ *adj, usu cap* [fr. *Łódź*, Poland] **:** of or from the city of Lodz, Poland **:** of the kind or style prevalent in Lodz

loe \ˈlü\ *Scot var of* LOVE

loef·fler's syndrome \ˈleflə(r)z-\ *also* **loeffler's pneumonia** *n, usu cap L* [after Wilhelm *Löffler* b1887 Swiss physician] **:** a mild pneumonitis marked by transitory pulmonary infiltration and eosinophilia and usu. characterized by an allergic reaction

loel·ling·ite *also* **löl·ling·ite** \ˈleliŋˌīt\ *n* -S [G *löllingit*, fr. *Lölling*, town in Austria, its locality + G *-it* -ite] **:** a mineral $FeAs_2$ consisting of a tin-white iron arsenide that is isomorphous with arsenopyrite and usu. occurs massive — called also *leucopyrite*

lo·e·some \'lüsəm\ *Scot var of* LOVESOME

loess \'les, 'ləs, 'lō,es\ *also* **löss** \'les, 'ləs\ *n* -ES [G *löss*, alter. of *lösch*, fr. G dial. (Switzerland) *lösch*, adj., loose; akin to OHG *lōs* loose — more at -LESS] : an unstratified deposit of loam that ranges to clay at the one extreme and to fine sand at the other, is usu. of a buff or yellowish brown color, covers extensive areas in No. America, Europe, and Asia, is now generally believed to be chiefly deposited by the wind, is usu. calcareous, often contains shells, bones, and teeth of mammals as well as concretions of calcium carbonate and occas. of iron oxide, and makes an excellent soil where adequately watered

loess·i·al \'lesēəl, 'ləs-, lō'es-\ *also* **loess·al** \-səl\ *adj* : relating to or consisting of loess

loess·land \'les,land, 'ləs,-, 'lō,es,-\ *n* : land whose surface is of loess

loe·we·ite \'lāvə,īt\ *or* **loe·wig·ite** \-vi,gīt\ *n* -S [*loeweite* fr. G *löweit*, fr. Karl J. *Löwe* †1890 Ger. chemist + G *-it* -ite; *loewigite* fr. G *löwigit*, alter. of *löweit*] : a mineral $Na_4Mg_2(SO_4)_4.5H_2O$ consisting of hydrous magnesium sodium sulfate occurring in pale yellow cleavable masses

L of C *abbr* line of communications

¹loft \'lȯft *also* 'läft\ *n* -S [ME, fr. OE, fr. ON *lopt* air, upper story; akin to OE *lyft* air, OS & OHG *luft*, Goth *luftus*] **1 a** *archaic* : the upper regions : SKY ⟨they are only birds — swifts in the ~ of the morning —Walter de la Mare⟩ **b** *obs* : the ceiling of a room **2** : a room or floor above another : an upper room or story : an attic room : ATTIC ⟨moved into a student ~ —Saul Bellow⟩ ⟨a slated cottage . . . containing a kitchen, two bedrooms and a ~ —J.M.Mogey⟩ **3 a** : a gallery in a church or hall ⟨below the organ ~ —H.S.Morrison⟩ **b** (1) : one of the upper floors of a warehouse or business building esp. when not partitioned ⟨stock clerk in a garment ~ —William DuBois⟩ (2) : a work space in an industrial or manufacturing building **c** : an upper part of a barn used esp. for storing hay : HAYLOFT ⟨climbing painfully up into the ~ to pitch down some hay —F.B.Gipson⟩ **4** : a coop or house for pigeons; *also* : a stock of pigeons **5 a** (1) : the backward slant of the face of a golf-club head (2) : HEIGHT 2b(1) ⟨won't give the ball enough ~ —Johnny Revolta⟩ **b** : the act of lofting : a lofting stroke **6** : the resilience of textile fibers esp. wool

²loft \"\ *vb* -ED/-ING/-S *vt* **1 a** : to place or store in a loft ⟨the remainder of the crop which was measured and *~ed* —George Washington⟩ **b** : to house in a loft ⟨*~ed* his pigeons on the roof⟩ **2** *obs* : to build or furnish with a loft **3 a** (1) : to strike (a ball) so as to cause to rise sharply : toss usu. in an arc ⟨*~ed* a pop fly to short center field —W.B.Furlong⟩ ⟨*~ing* stones at street lights —Maxwell Griffith⟩ (2) : to cause to rise or advance : PROMOTE ⟨was *~ed* to a new job —*Time*⟩ **b** : to shoot (a taw) in an arched course through the air **c** : to release (a bowling ball) in such a way as to cause to drop onto the alley beyond the foul line **4** : to cause (as a golf ball) to rise high into the air **5** : to lay out a full-sized working drawing of the lines and contours of (as a ship's hull or an airplane's wing) ~ *vi* **1 a** : to hit or throw a ball high into the air **b** : to rise high into the air when struck **2** : to loft a bowling ball

loft building *n* : a large building usu. of more than one story whose open floor space without partitions allows maximum adaptability of use (as for the display of merchandise or light manufacturing)

loft–dried \'=,=\ *adj* : dried by hanging in a drying loft ⟨*loft-dried* writing paper⟩

loft·er \-tə(r)\ *n* -S : an iron golf club whose face is laid back sufficiently for lofting the ball — called also *lofting iron*

loft·i·ly \-t°lē, -t°li, -təl-\ *adv* : in a lofty manner ⟨bore herself still more ~ and resolved to snub him explicitly if he addressed her again —G.B.Shaw⟩

loft·i·ness \-tēnəs, -tin-\ *n* -ES : the quality or state of being lofty ⟨with the ~ of a patriot of old Rome —George Meredith⟩ ⟨soap imparts to silk material a bulk and ~ difficult to obtain with synthetic softening agents —H.C.Speel & H.H.Mosher⟩

lofting *n* -S [fr. gerund of ²*loft*] : the process of lofting an airplane or ship or a part of one

lofting iron *n* : LOFTER

loft·less \-tləs\ *adj* : having no loft

loftly *adv* [by alter.] *obs* : LOFTILY

loft·man \-tmən\ *n, pl* **loftmen 1** : a worker in a drying loft **2** : FLYMAN 2

lofts·man \-tsmən\ *n, pl* **loftsmen** : one who lays out to scale the lines (as of an airplane and its parts) preparatory to the making of blueprints and tools — called also *linesman*

lofty \-tē, -ti\ *adj* -ER/-EST [ME, fr. ¹*loft* + *-y*] **1** : having a haughty overbearing manner : characterized by arrogance and pride : SUPERCILIOUS ⟨looked down upon him with the *loftiest* contempt —Charles Dickens⟩ ⟨expected to treat this exhibition with an attitude of ~ scorn —Ralph Linton⟩ **2 a** : elevated in character and spirit : dignified of mien and bearing : elegant of speech : NOBLE, STATELY ⟨of unquestionable integrity and ~ standards of judgment —Paul Moor⟩ ⟨he was handsome, with fine, even features, a ~ brow —Aline B. Saarinen⟩ ⟨trees, or the sight of them, excites their minds to ~ thinking —W.F. Hambly⟩ **b** : elevated in station or position : SUPERIOR ⟨the bright bar or kitchen . . . where the less ~ customers of the house were in the habit of assembling —George Eliot⟩ ⟨the insignia of a particularly ~ secret society —Jean Stafford⟩ **3** : extending or rising high in the air : having great or imposing height : TOWERING ⟨a ~ perpendicular cliff —E.V.Lucas⟩ ⟨a ~ and magnificent spire —Edwin Benson⟩ **4** : having full-bodied, firm, and resilient textile fibers **5** : having little practical application or value : ESOTERIC ⟨basic precepts are not ~ abstractions far removed from matters of daily living —D.D. Eisenhower⟩ **syn** see HIGH

¹log \'lȯg *also* 'läg\ *n* -S *often attrib* [ME *logge*, prob. of Scand origin; akin to Norw *låg* fallen tree, ON *lāg*; akin to ON *liggja* to lie — more at LIE] **1 a** : a usu. bulky piece or length of unshaped timber; *esp* : a tree trunk or a length of a trunk or branch trimmed and ready for sawing and usu. over six feet long — compare BILLET, BOLT **b** : a stick of wood cut for fuel (as in a fireplace) usu. two to three feet in length with all or part of the bark on it ⟨a birch ~⟩ **c** : a heavy piece of wood or sometimes other material attached to the leg (as of a prisoner or an animal) so as to restrain movement **d logs** *pl, slang Austral* : a jail esp. when of rude construction **2** : one of several devices (as the common one consisting of a log chip and log line) designed to gauge the speed of a ship **3** [short for *logbook*] **a** : a daily record of a ship's speed or progress or the full record of a ship's voyage including notes on the ship's position at various times and including notes on the weather and on important incidents occurring during the voyage **b** : any of various other journals or records in which are noted sequential data on the speed or progress or performance of something: (1) : a record of a flight by an airplane or of the operating history of an airplane or of a piece of its equipment or of the flying time of a pilot or other aircrew member (2) : a record of the performance of an engine or boiler or similar piece of equipment (3) : a record of the progress made in drilling an oil well including notes on formations penetrated and on the casing used and including other pertinent data (4) : a record of camera shots taken esp. in motion pictures (5) : a minute-by-minute record of what is broadcast by a radio station

²log \"\ *vb* **logged; logged; logging; logs** *vt* **1 a** (1) : to cut down for use as logs ⟨*logged* most of the trees in the area⟩ (2) : to cut up into logs : saw into logs ⟨*logging* the timber into 7-foot lengths⟩ **b** : to cut down the trees of (a region) and remove the felled trees from for use as logs ⟨had *logged* off most of that part of the country⟩ **2** : to make a note or record of (the speed, progress, performance, or other sequential details of something) esp. in a journal or other record of data : enter details of or about in a log ⟨*logged* the ship's speed at 10 knots⟩ **3 a** : to move (an indicated distance) or attain (an indicated speed) as noted in a log ⟨the ship *logged* 100 miles that day⟩ ⟨the plane *~s* 600 miles an hour⟩ **b** (1) : to sail a ship or fly an airplane for an indicated distance or an indicated period of time) ⟨asked how many hours he had *logged*⟩ (2) : to have or arrive at a record of (an indicated distance or an indicated period of time) in sailing a ship or flying an airplane : have (an indicated record) to one's credit ~ *vi* : to fell trees and cut them up into logs and transport the logs to sawmills or a place of sale

³log \'läg\ *vb* **logged; logged; logging; logs** [origin unknown] *dial Eng* : OSCILLATE, ROCK

⁴log \'lȯg *also* 'läg\ *abbr or n* -S logarithm

log *abbr* **1** logic **2** logistic

log- or logo- *comb form* [Gk, fr. *logos* word, reason, speech, account — more at LEGEND] : word : thought : speech : discourse ⟨*logo*gram⟩ ⟨*logo*latry⟩ ⟨*logo*mania⟩

-log — see -LOGUE

¹lo·gan \'lōgən\ *n* -S [by shortening] *NewEng* : POKELOGAN

²logan \"\ *n* -S [by shortening] : LOGANBERRY

³logan *var of* LAGAN

lo·gan·berry \'lōgən- — *see* BERRY\ *n* [James H. *Logan* †1928 Am. lawyer and horticulturist + E *berry*] **1 a** : a red-fruited upright-growing dewberry regarded as a variety (*Rubus ursinus loganobaccus*) of the western dewberry or as a hybrid of the western dewberry and the red raspberry **b** : the berry borne by a loganberry **2** : PRUNE PURPLE

lo·ga·nia \lō'gānēə\ *n* [NL, fr. James *Logan* †1751 Irish botanist + NL *-ia*] **1** *cap* : the type genus of the family Loganiaceae comprising Australian and New Zealand herbs and subshrubs that are sometimes cultivated for their clusters of pentamerous white to flesh-colored flowers **2** -S : any plant of the genus *Logania*

lo·ga·ni·a·ce·ae \lō,gānē'āsē,ē\ *n pl, cap* [NL, fr. *Logania*, type genus + *-aceae*] : a family of herbs, shrubs, and trees (order Gentianales) distinguished by the opposite stipulate leaves and the bilocular superior ovary — **lo·ga·ni·a·ceous** \=,=,=ˈāshəs\ *adj*

lo·ga·nin \'lōgənən\ *n* -S [ISV *logan-* (fr. NL *Loganiaceae*, family to which nux vomica belongs) + *-in*] : a crystalline glucoside $C_{17}H_{26}O_{10}$ obtained esp. from nux vomica and the buckbean

log·an stone *or* **log·gan stone** \'lägən-\ *n* [prob. alter. of *logging*, pres. part. of ³*log*] : ROCKING STONE

lo·gan tent \'lōgən-\ *n, usu cap L* [after Sir William Edmond *Logan* †1875 Canadian geologist] : a pyramidal tent that is about seven feet wide and seven feet high and that is made roomy by a vertical back wall about two feet high

Logan tent

¹log·a·oe·dic \,lägə'ēdik\ *adj* [LL *logaoedicus*, fr. LGk *logaoidikos*, fr. *log-* + *aoidē* music, poetry (fr. *aeidein* to sing) + *-ikos* -ic — more at ODE] : having a metrical rhythm marked by the mixture of several meters; *specif* : having a rhythm that uses both dactyls and trochees or anapests and iambs

²logaoedic \"\ *n* -S : a logaoedic piece of verse

log·a·rithm \'lȯgə,rithəm *also* 'läg-\ *n* -S [NL *logarithmus*, fr. *log-* + Gk *arithmos* number — more at ARITHMO-] : the exponent that indicates the power to which a number must be raised to produce a given number ⟨if $B^2=N$, then 2 is the ~ of *N* (to the base *B*)⟩ ⟨4 is the ~ of 16 to the base 2⟩ — abbr. *log*; see ANTILOGARITHM, COMMON LOGARITHM, NATURAL LOGARITHM; compare BASE 6d

log·a·rith·mic \,=='rithmik, -mēk\ *also* **log·a·rith·mi·cal** \-məkəl, -mēk-\ *adj* **1** : of, involving, or expressed in terms of a logarithm **2** : using, based on, or relating to a logarithmic scale — **log·a·rith·mi·cal·ly** \-mək(ə)lē, -mēk-, -li\ *adv*

logarithmic curve *n* : a graph in which the ordinate is the logarithm of the abscissa

logarithmic decrement *n* : the natural logarithm of the decrement for a series of exponentially damped oscillations

logarithmic function *n* : a function that is a logarithm

logarithmic paper *n* : graph paper in which actual distances on one or both axes are proportional to the logarithm of the quantities to which they correspond

logarithmic scale *n* : a scale on which actual distances from the origin are proportional to the logarithms of the corresponding scale numbers rather than to the numbers themselves

logarithmic spiral *n* : EQUIANGULAR SPIRAL

logbook \'=,=\ *n* [¹*log* (device for gauging a ship's speed) + *book*] : LOG 3

log chip *also* **log ship** *n* : a thin flat usu. triangular piece of wood that is typically like a quadrant of a circle and that usu. has a radius of 5 or 6 inches and is loaded with lead on the arc so as to float point up and that is attached to a log line by cords from each corner and is tossed into the water so that the log line may run out from the log reel when the motion of a ship through the water or the velocity of a current is being gauged

logcock \'=,=\ *n* **1** : PILEATED WOODPECKER **2** : IVORY-BILLED WOODPECKER

log drive *n* : DRIVE 1f

log driver *n* : one that guides logs in a drive downstream working with a pike pole from a river bank or a boat or on the floating logs

log driving *n* : the occupation of a log driver

loge \'lōzh, 'lōj\ *n* -S [F — more at LODGE] **1 a** : a small compartment : BOOTH, STALL, ENCLOSURE ⟨the doorkeeper peered out from his ~ just inside the entrance to the building⟩ **b** : a box in a theater **2 a** : a small area (as in a room) that is partitioned off from a larger area (as by a railing) **b** : the forward section of a mezzanine or balcony in a theater when this section is in some way (as by an aisle or railing) partitioned off from the part farther back

log fixer *n* : ROSSER a

log frame *n* : a sawing machine; *specif* : one having a gang of saws for cutting a log into boards

loggan stone *var of* LOGAN STONE

logged *adj* [fr. past part. of ²*log*] **1** : made heavy or sluggish so that movement is impossible or difficult ⟨his feet . . . feeling ~ as a landed sailor's —William Sansom⟩ **2** : made sodden : soaked or permeated with something; *specif* : WATERLOGGED ⟨a graveyard of rotting ~ ships⟩ ⟨the boat still rolled and pitched, but sickishly now because it was so ~ down with water —Roy Sparkia⟩

log·ger \'lȯgə(r) *also* 'läg-\ *n* -S [¹*log* + *-er*] **1 a** : one who is engaged in the action or business of logging — called also *lumberjack*; compare LUMBERMAN **b** : a worker who insulates petroleum pipelines and tanks and still towers against heat radiation and absorption **2** [²*log* + *-er*] : a device that automatically records data esp. about temperature or humidity or barometric pressure or other physical conditions

log·ger·head \'lȯgə(r),hed *also* 'läg-\ *n* [prob. fr. E dial. *logger* block of wood (fr. ¹*log* + *-er*) + *head*] **1** *now chiefly dial* **a** : BLOCKHEAD, DUMBBELL **b** : HEAD; *esp* : a large cumbrous head **2** *or* **loggerhead turtle a** : any of various very large marine turtles (family Cheloniidae); *esp* : a carnivorous turtle (*Caretta caretta*) that is common in the warmer parts of the Atlantic ocean from Brazil to Cape Cod **b** : ALLIGATOR SNAPPER **c** : a snapping turtle (*Chelydra serpentina*) **3** : an iron tool consisting of a long handle terminating in a ball or bulb that is heated and used to melt tar or to heat liquids **4** : an upright piece of round timber which is fixed in a whaleboat and around which a turn of the line is taken when it is running out too fast **5** : a disease of cotton characterized by a shortening of the internodes of stems and branches **6 loggerheads** *pl but sing or pl in constr, dial Eng* : any of several herbs of the genus *Centaurea* — **at loggerheads** *adv (or adj)* : in or into a state of strong antagonistic usu. quarrelsome disagreement ⟨*at loggerheads* with the people of his village —Harold Hobson⟩ ⟨the story of an energetic subordinate *at loggerheads* with his superiors —*Times Lit. Supp.*⟩ ⟨confusions which put old friends *at loggerheads* —L.C.Douglas⟩ — **to loggerheads** *adv (or adj), archaic* : at loggerheads

log·ger·head·ed \'=,=,hedəd\ *adj, now chiefly dial* : BLOCKHEADED, STUPID

loggerhead shrike *n* : a shrike (*Lanius ludovicianus*) of the southeastern U.S.

loggerhead sponge *n* : a massive sponge (*Spheciospongia vespera*) of the West Indies and Florida that attains a weight of 700 pounds but is of little commercial importance

log·gets *or* **log·gats** \'lägəts\ *n pl but usu sing in constr* [prob. fr. ¹*log* + *-et* + *-s*] : a game formerly played in England in which players threw pieces of wood at a stake driven into the ground

log·gia \'läj(ē)ə, 'lȯj-\ *n, pl* **loggias** \-əz\ *also* **log·gie** \-jā\ [It, fr. F *loge* — more at LODGE] : a roofed open gallery or arcade in the side of a building esp. when facing upon an open court; *specif* : such a gallery or arcade set at a height of one or more stories and not projecting from the surface of the building but forming an integral part of the building **syn** see BALCONY

loggia

logginess *var of* LOGINESS

logging *n* -S [fr. gerund of ²*log*] : the occupation of felling trees and cutting them up into logs and transporting the logs to sawmills or to a place of sale

logging wheel *n* : one of a pair of large wheels from 7 to 12 feet in diameter that are used for hauling logs

log·gish \'lȯgish *also* 'läg-\ *adj* : resembling or suggestive of a log ⟨everything was still, with that ~ inanimate thing lying there —Sheila Kaye-Smith⟩

log glass *n* : a small hourglass used to time the running out of a log line

loggy *var of* LOGY

logia *pl of* LOGION

-lo·gia \'lōj(ē)ə\ *n comb form* -S [L, fr. Gk — more at *-logy*] : -LOGY

log·ic \'läjik, -jēk\ *n* -S [ME *logik*, fr. MF *logique*, fr. L *logica*, fr. Gk *logikē*, fr. fem. of *logikos* of speech, argumentative, logical, fr. *logos* word, reason, speech, account + *-ikos* -ic — more at LEGEND] **1 a** (1) : a science that deals with the canons and criteria of validity in thought and demonstration and that traditionally comprises the principles of definition and classification and correct use of terms and the principles of correct predication and the principles of reasoning and demonstration : the science of the normative formal principles of reasoning : the science of correct reasoning — see FORMAL LOGIC, MATERIAL LOGIC (2) : a system of formal principles of deduction or inference (3) : semiotic or a branch of semiotic; *esp* : SYNTACTICS (4) : the formal principles of a branch of knowledge ⟨the ~ of art⟩ **b** (1) : a particular mode of argumentation or reasoning viewed as valid or faulty according to its apparent agreement with or departure from accepted principles of logic ⟨she spent quite a long time explaining the situation, but he failed to see her ~⟩ (2) : relevance or propriety (as of a quality, a procedure) judged as present or absent according to apparent conformity or lack of conformity with the dictates of logic ⟨could not understand the ~ of such a deed⟩ **c** : interrelation or connection or sequence (as of facts or events) esp. when seen by rational analysis as inevitable, necessary, or predictable ⟨by the ~ of events, anarchy leads to dictatorship⟩ **2** : something that convinces or proves or that obviates argument or makes argument useless and that is by its nature quite apart from or beyond or opposed to the use of reason as a means of arriving at decisions or settling disputes or attaining truth **3** : an exposition of or treatise on logic

log·i·cal \-jəkəl, -jēk-\ *adj* [ML *logicalis*, fr. L *logica* + *-alis* -al] **1 a** : of or relating to logic : having the nature of logic ⟨~ argumentation⟩ **b** : that agrees with accepted principles of logic : that is in harmony with sound reasoning ⟨a ~ conclusion⟩ **c** : that is in accordance with inferences reasonably drawn from preceding or surrounding or predictable facts or events or circumstances ⟨a ~ result⟩ ⟨a ~ candidate⟩ **d** : analytical and not factual or empirical : FORMAL ⟨a ~ statement⟩ ⟨a ~ expression⟩ **2** : that is capable of reasoning or that uses reason in a way that agrees with accepted principles of logic ⟨a ~ thinker⟩ — **log·i·cal·ly** \-jək(ə)lē, -jēk-, -li\ *adv* — **log·i·cal·ness** *n* -ES

logical implication *or* **logical entailment** *n* : IMPLICATION 2b(2)

log·i·cal·i·ty \,läjə'kaləd·ē\ *n* -ES : the quality or state of being logical : logical character : LOGICALNESS

log·i·cal·iza·tion \,läjəkələ'zāshən\ *n* -S : the act of logicalizing or state of being logicalized

log·i·cal·ize \'läjəkə,līz\ *vt* -ED/-ING/-S : LOGICIZE

logical positivism *or* **logical empiricism** *n* : a philosophical movement holding that meaningful statements are either a priori and analytic or a posteriori and synthetic and that metaphysical theories are strictly meaningless or have only emotive force — compare CONFIRMABILITY THEORY, VERIFIABILITY PRINCIPLE

logical presumption *n* : PRESUMPTION OF FACT

logical realism *n* : REALISM 2a

logical reason *n* : DISCURSIVE REASON

logical subject *n* : the subject of a sentence that expresses the actual agent of an expressed or implied action (as *father* in "it is your father speaking") or that is the thing about which something is otherwise predicated (as *to do right* in "it is sometimes hard to do right") — called also *real subject*; distinguished from *grammatical subject*

logical syntax *n* : SYNTAX 3b

logical truth *n* : FORMAL TRUTH

lo·gi·cian \lō'jishən, lə'-\ *n* -S [ME *logicien*, fr. MF, fr. *logique* logic + *-ien* -ian — more at LOGIC] : one that is skilled in logic

log·i·cism \'läjə,sizəm\ *n* -S [ISV *logic* + *-ism*] **1** : a philosophical system marked by special emphasis on logic **2 a** : a philosophical thesis according to which logic is an autonomous discipline that is not reducible to psychology — opposed to *psychologism* **b** : a philosophical thesis according to which mathematics is reducible to logic — compare INTUITIONISM — **log·i·cist** \-səst\ *n* -S

log·i·cize \'läjə,sīz\ *vb* -ED/-ING/-S [*logic* + *-ize*] *vi* : to use logic : REASON ⟨incapable of *logicizing*⟩ ~ *vt* : to make logical : convert to logical form ⟨*logicized* the argument⟩

log·ic·less \'läjikləs\ *adj* : devoid of logic

log·i·co- *comb form* [*logical*] : logical : logical and ⟨*logico*-mathematical⟩

log·ics \-ks\ *n pl but usu sing in constr* : LOGIC

¹lo·gie \'lōgi\ *n* -S [by shortening] *chiefly Scot* : KILLOGIE

²lo·gie \'lōgē\ *n* -S [after David *Logie*, 19th cent. Brit. inventor] : a piece of imitation jewelry designed for use in theater productions

logier *comparative of* LOGY

-logies *pl of* -LOGY

logiest *superlative of* LOGY

lo·gi·ly \'lōgəlē, -li *sometimes* 'lȯg- *or* 'läg-\ *adv* : in a logy manner

lo·gi·ness *also* **log·gi·ness** \-gēnəs\ *n* -ES : the quality or state of being logy

lo·gi·on \'lōjē,än, -ōgē- 'läg-\ *n, pl* **logia** \-ēə\ *or* **logions** [Gk, saying, oracle, dim. of *logos* word, speech — more at LEGEND] : a usu. short pointed pregnant saying or observation esp. of a religious teacher; *esp* : one of the agrapha

¹lo·gis·tic \lō'jistik, lə'-, -tēk\ *or* **lo·gis·ti·cal** \-təkəl, -tēk-\ *adj* [*logistic* prob. fr. F *logistique*, fr. ML & LL; ML *logisticus* rational, fr. LL, of computation, fr. Gk *logistikos* calculatory, rational, fr. *logistēs* calculator, reasoner (fr. *logizein* to calculate, fr. *logos* word, reason, account + *-izein* -ize) + *-ikos* -ic; *logistical* fr. ML *logisticus* + *-al* — more at LEGEND] **1** : of or relating to logic or logicism **2** : of or relating to logistic or logistics **3** : of, represented by, or relating to a logistic curve — **lo·gis·ti·cal·ly** \-tək(ə)lē\ *adv*

²logistic \"\ *n* -S [F *logistique*, fr. Gk *logistikē*, fr. fem. of *logistikos*] **1** : the science or art of calculating esp. arithmetically **2 a** : ALGEBRA 2 **b** : SYMBOLIC LOGIC **3** : LOGISTIC CURVE

logistic curve *n* : a curve representing a function involving an exponential and shaped like the letter S ⟨a mass of data on growth of subhuman and human populations, of the number of governmental functions, growth of production, inventions, state laws and so on, to show that their growth and diffusion follows the *logistic curve* —P.A.Sorokin⟩

lo·gis·ti·cian \,lōjə'stishən\ *n* -S : a specialist in logistic or logistics

lo·gis·tics \lō'jistiks, lə'-, -tēks\ *n pl but often sing in constr* [F *logistique* + E *-s* — more at LOGISTIC] **1 :** LOGISTIC 1, 2 **2 :** military science in its planning and handling and implementation of personnel (as in classification, movement, evacuation) and matériel (as in production, distribution, maintenance) and facilities (as in construction, operation, distribution) and other related factors

log jack *n* **1 :** HAUL-UP **2 :** a tool like a cant hook that is used to raise or hold up a log that is being sawed so as to avoid pinching the saw

logjam \'=,=\ *n* **1 :** a jamming up of logs into a deadlocked jumble in a watercourse (as in a river during a drive) **2 :** the condition of being jammed into immobility **:** DEADLOCK, IMPASSE ⟨trying to break the ~ in negotiations⟩ **:** STOPPAGE, BLOCKAGE ⟨a ~ of news dispatches⟩ ⟨extended the Congressional session to clear a legislative ~⟩

log line *n* **:** a line that is usu. made of cord (as hemp, braided cotton twine) and that is used in gauging the speed of a ship or the velocity of a water current; *esp* **:** such a line that is divided into knots (sense 8a) and that has a log chip attached to one end and that runs out from a log reel

¹log-log \'='=\ *n, pl* **log-logs** [⁴*log*] **:** the logarithm of a logarithm

²log-log \"\ *adj* **1 :** involving or expressed in terms of log-logs **2 :** using, based on, or relating to a log-log scale

log-log paper *n* **:** logarithmic paper having logarithmic scales both horizontally and vertically — compare SEMILOGARITHMIC

log-log scale *n* **:** a scale on which actual distances from the origin are proportional to the log-logs of the corresponding scale numbers rather than to the numbers themselves

log·man \'lȯgmən *also* 'läg-\ *n, pl* **logmen :** LOGGER

logo \'lō(,)gō *also* 'lä(,)-\ *n* -s [by shortening] **:** LOGOTYPE

logo- — see LOG-

log·o·dae·da·ly \,lägō'dedᵊlē, -'ded-\ *n* -ES [LL *logodaedalia*, fr. LGk *logodaidalia*, fr. Gk *logodaidalos* skilled in verbal legerdemain (fr. *log-* speech, word + *daidalos* skillful, ingeniously formed) + *-ia* -y — more at CONDOLE] **:** arbitrary or capricious coinage of words

log·o·gram \'lȯgə,gram *also* 'läg-, -raa(ə)m\ *n* [*log-* + *-gram*] **:** a letter or character or symbol or sign used to represent an entire word (as *$* represents *dollar*): **a :** a graphic sign that represents a complete word or morpheme but without providing separate phonetic representation of the individual phonemes or syllables composing the word or morpheme (as *&* represents *and*) **b :** an often conventionalized picture or a symbol that represents an object not easily indicated by a simple picture ⟨in some countries, a ~ in the form of the torch of learning stands for a school —O.R.Bontrager⟩

log·o·gram·mat·ic \¦lȯgəgrə¦mad·ik *also* ¦läg-\ *adj* [*logogram* + *-matic* (as in *grammatic*)] **:** of, relating to, or marked by the use of logograms **:** consisting of logograms — **log·o·gram·mat·i·cal·ly** \-d·ək(ə)lē\ *adv*

log·o·graph \'lȯgə,graf, -rȧf *also* 'läg-\ *n* [*log-* + *-graph*] **:** LOGOGRAM

lo·gog·ra·pher \lō'gägrəfə(r)\ *n* -s [Gk *logographos* prose writer (fr. *log-* + *-graphos* writer, fr. *graphein* to write) + E *-er* — more at CARVE] **:** a prose writer in ancient Greece

log·o·graph·ic \¦lȯgə¦grafik *also* ¦läg-\ *adj* [*logograph* + *-ic*] **:** of, relating to, or marked by the use of logographs **:** consisting of logographs **:** LOGOGRAMMATIC ⟨Japanese, which uses a combination of ~ and syllabic writing —Robert Lado⟩ — **log·o·graph·i·cal·ly** \-fək(ə)lē\ *adv*

log·o·griph \'lȯgə,grif *also* 'läg-\ *n* -s [*log-* + Gk *griphos* reed fish basket, riddle — more at CRIB] **:** a word puzzle (as an anagram)

lo·go·li \lō'gōlē\ *n, pl* **logoli** *or* **logolis** *usu cap* **1 :** one of the peoples of the Bantu Kavirondo group **2 :** a member of the Logoli people

log·o·mach·ic \¦lȯgə¦makik\ *also* **log·o·mach·i·cal** \-akəkəl\ *adj* **:** of, relating to, or marked by a logomachy

lo·gom·a·chist \lō'gäməkəst\ *or* **log·o·mach** \'lägə,mak\ *n* -s **:** one given to logomachy

lo·gom·a·chy \lō'gäməkē\ *n* -ES [Gk *logomachia*, fr. *log-* + *-machia* -machy] **1 a :** a dispute over or about words **b :** contention in words that are used wholly or almost wholly without real awareness of their meaning or that have little or no actual relation to reality **:** contention made up wholly or almost wholly of pure verbiage **2 :** a game of making words (as in anagrams)

log·o·mania \¦lȯgə *also* ¦lägə+\ *n* [NL, fr. *log-* + *mania*] **:** abnormal talkativeness **:** LOGORRHEA

log·o·pe·dia \,lȯgə'pēdēə *also* ,läg- *or* ,lȯg-\ *n* -s [NL, fr. *log-* + ortho*pedia*] **:** LOGOPEDICS

log·o·pe·dic \¦==¦pēdik\ *adj* [*log-* + ortho*pedic*] **:** of or relating to logopedics

log·o·pe·dics \,==¦pēdiks\ *n pl but sing or pl in constr* [*log-* + ortho*pedics*] **:** the scientific study and treatment of speech defects

log·or·rhea \,lȯgə'rēə *also* ,läg-\ *n* -s [NL, fr. *log-* + *-rrhea*] **:** pathologically excessive and often incoherent talkativeness — **log·o·rrhe·ic** \¦==¦rēik\ *adj*

lo·gos \'lō,gäs, 'lä,gäs, 'lō,gōs, 'lȯ,gōs\ *n, pl* **lo·goi** \-gȯi\ [Gk, word, reason, speech, account — more at LEGEND] **1** *often cap* **:** reason or the manifestation of reason conceived in ancient Greek philosophy as constituting the controlling principle in the universe: **a :** a moving and regulating principle in the universe together with an element in man by which according to Heraclitus this principle is perceived **b :** a cosmic governing or generating principle according to the Stoics that is immanent and active in all reality and that pervades all reality **c :** a principle that according to Philo is intermediate between ultimate or divine reality and the sensible world **2** *usu cap* **:** the actively expressed creative revelatory thought and will of God identified in the prologue of the Gospel of St. John and in various Christian doctrinal works with the second person of the Trinity

log·o·thete \'lȯgə,thēt *also* 'läg-\ *n* -s [ML *logotheta*, fr. LGk *logothetēs*, fr. *log-* + *-thetēs* (fr. *tithenai* to set, place) — more at DO] **:** one of various functionaries (as an administrator) under the Byzantine emperors

logo·type \'lȯgə,tīp *also* 'läg-\ *n* [*log-* + *type*] **1 :** a genotype designated subsequent to the publication of a generic name **2 a :** a single piece of type faced with two or more separate letters or figures (as *in, on, re, the, and, 1963*) — compare LIGATURE **b :** a single piece of type or a single plate faced with a term (as the name of a newspaper, an advertiser's trademark, a company name and address)

log perch *n* **:** a darter (*Percina caprodes*) about six inches long found in lakes and streams about Lake Superior esp. southward and eastward

log reel *n* **:** a usu. small wooden reel around which a log line is wound

log·roll \'lȯ,grōl *also* 'lä,-\ *vb* [back-formation fr. *logrolling*] *vi* **:** to take part in logrolling ~ *vt* **:** to promote or get acceptance or passage of (legislation) by logrolling ⟨~*ed* his tax bill through⟩ — **log·roll·er** \-lə(r)\ *n* -s

log·roll·ing \-liŋ\ *n* -s [¹*log* + *rolling*] **1 a** (1) **:** the act or process of rolling logs; *esp* **:** the act or process of rolling logs into one place to be burned when land is being cleared (2) **:** a gathering of neighbors and friends to assist each other in rolling logs into one place to be burned **b** (1) **:** the act or process of causing a floating log to rotate by treading (as in the course of a drive) (2) **:** a sport in which a person tries to retain his balance while standing on and rotating a floating log with his feet and while trying at the same time to dislodge usu. a single competitor on the same log **2 :** the exchanging of assistance or favors (as political assistance or favors); *specif* **:** the trading of votes by legislators to secure favorable action on projects of interest to each one ⟨passed by a majority obtained by ~ among a combination of interests —Joseph Dorfman⟩ ⟨~ . . . secures a certain protection for local interests —C.J.Friedrich⟩ — compare BACK SCRATCHING, PORK BARREL

log rule *n* **1 a :** a table showing the estimated number of board feet of lumber that can be sawed from logs of various lengths and diameters **b :** a formula by which the estimated number of board feet may be ascertained **2 :** SCALE RULE

log run *n* **1 :** the total merchantable product cut from softwood logs including all grades **2 :** the total merchantable product cut from hardwood logs except the lowest grade

log runner *n* **:** one of two small Australian oscine birds of the genus *Orthonyx* of terrestrial habits

logs *pl of* LOG, *pres 3d sing of* LOG

log scale *n* **1 :** the board-foot content of logs as determined by a log rule **2 :** SCALE RULE

log ship *var of* LOG CHIP

log slate *n* **:** a folding slate sometimes used for preliminary noting of data to be later copied into a logbook

log slip *n* **:** a gangway used in logging

log tooth *n* **:** a chain link with one or more projecting teeth used in a chain for transporting logs

log turner *n* **:** NIGGER 5

lo·gu·do·rese \¦lōgədə¦rēz, -ēs\ *n* -s *usu cap* [It, fr. *logudorese* of Logudoro, fr. *Logudoro*, district in central Sardinia + It *-ese*] **:** the dialect of Sardinian spoken in the Logudoro district

-logue *or* **-log** \,lȯg *also* ,läg\ *n comb form* -s [ME *-loge*, *-logue*, fr. OF *-logue*, fr. L *-logus*, fr. Gk *-logos*, fr. *legein* to speak — more at LEGEND] **1 a :** discourse, talk ⟨duo*logue*⟩ **b :** performance, recital ⟨piano*logue*⟩ **2 :** student, specialist ⟨Sino*logue*⟩

log washer *n* **:** a mechanical trough washer for separating a material (as ore) from clay and earth

logway \'=,=\ *n* **:** a gangway used in logging

logwood \'=,=\ *n* **1 a** (1) **:** a tree (*Haematoxylon campechianum*) of Central America and the West Indies (2) **:** the very hard brown or brownish red heartwood of this tree that is used in preparing a dye (3) **:** a dye prepared from this heartwood as a water extract or as a solid extract obtained by evaporation or as crystals and used in dyeing various materials (as mordanted silk or wool or cotton or as leather or fur or hair) black — see DYE table I (under *Natural Black 1*); HEMATEIN, HEMATOXYLIN **b :** a tree (*Condalia obovata*) of Texas and adjacent Mexico that has spatulate entire mucronate leaves forming dense chaparral thickets and yielding a yellow dye — called also *brasil* **2 :** a blackish purple to purplish black — called also *admiral, bluewood, campeachy wood*

logwood black *n* **:** a rich black formed esp. on silk by mordanting with a salt of iron and dyeing with logwood

logwood printing black *n, often cap L&P&B* **:** a natural dye — see DYE table I (under *Natural Black 4*)

lo·gy *also* **log·gy** \'lōgē, -gi *sometimes* 'lȯg- *or* 'läg-\ *adj, usu* -ER/-EST [perh. fr. D *log* heavy, unwieldy, cumbersome + E *-y*; akin to MLG *luggich* lazy, sleepy] **1 :** marked by sluggishness and lack of vitality **:** slowed down esp. physically or mentally to a condition of dullness or numbed languidness or lethargy **:** heavily listless **:** DOPEY, GROGGY, TORPID ⟨was ~ from eating too much⟩ ⟨took a sleeping tablet and felt ~ the next morning⟩ **2 :** lacking resilience **:** not recovering quickly when stress is released **:** having low snap ⟨a ~ piece of rubber⟩

-lo·gy \lajē, -ji\ *n comb form* -ES [ME *-logie*, fr. OF, fr. L *-logia*, fr. Gk, fr. *logos* word, reason, speech, account + *-ia* -y — more at LEGEND] **1 :** oral or written expression ⟨phraseo*logy*⟩ **2 :** doctrine, theory, science ⟨socio*logy*⟩ **3 :** discourse, treatise ⟨insecto*logy*⟩

lo·han \'lō'hän\ *n, pl* **lohan** *or* **lohans** *often cap* [Chin (Pek) *lo²-han⁴*, short for *a¹-lo²-han⁴*, fr. Skt *arhan*, nom. masc. of *arhat* — more at ARHAT] **:** ARHAT

lo·har \'lō'här\ *n, pl* **lohar** *or* **lohars** *often cap* [Hindi *lohār*, fr. Skt *lohakāra* blacksmith, fr. *loha* copper, iron + *kāra* maker, worker, fr. *karoti* he does, makes; akin to Skt *rudhira* red — more at RED, KARMA] **:** one of a numerous Hindu caste whose usual occupation is ironworking or carpentering

lo·hoch *or* **lo·hock** \'lō,häk\ *or* **lo·och** \'lō,äk\ *n* -s [MF *looch*, fr. Ar *la'ūq* anything licked] **:** LINCTUS

loiasis *var of* LOAIASIS

loin \'lȯin\ *n* -s [ME *loyne*, fr. MF *loigne*, fr. (assumed) VL *lumbea*, fr. L *lumbus* loin; akin to OE *lendenu* loins, OHG *lentī, lentin* kidneys, loins, ON *lend* loin, OSlav *lędvĭje* loins] **1 a :** the part of the body of a human being or quadruped lying on each side of the spinal column between the hipbone and the false ribs — usu. used in pl.; see HORSE illustration **b :** a cut of meat (as mutton or pork) comprising this part of one or both sides of an animal carcass with the adjoining half of the vertebrae included but without the adjoining flank — see LAMB illustration **2 loins** *pl* **a :** the upper and lower abdominal regions and the region about the hips **b** (1) **:** the pubic region (2) **:** the generative organs

loincloth \'=,=\ *n* **:** a cloth worn about the loins often as the sole article of clothing in warm climates esp. among primitive peoples

loin disease *n* **:** aphosphorosis of cattle often complicated by botulism

loir \'lȯi(ə)r, 'lwär\ *n* -s [F, fr. L *glir-, glis*] **:** a large European dormouse (*Glis glis*)

loi·ter \'lȯid·ə(r), -ȯitə-\ *vi* -ED/-ING/-s [ME *loteren, loiteren*, prob. fr. MD *loteren* to shake, wiggle, be loose (whence D *leuteren* to dawdle); prob. akin to OE *lūtian* to lurk, *lūtan* to bend, stoop, OHG *luzēn* to lurk, ON *lūta* to bow down — more at LITTLE] **1 :** to interrupt or delay an activity or an errand or a journey with or as if with aimless idle stops and pauses and purposeless distractions ⟨asked him not to ~ on the way home⟩ **:** fritter away time in the course of doing something or proceeding somewhere ⟨don't ~ on the job⟩ **:** take more time than is usual or necessary **:** be markedly or unduly slow in doing something or going somewhere **:** DAWDLE, LINGER **2 a :** to remain in or near a place in an idle or apparently idle manner **:** hang around aimlessly or as if aimlessly ⟨vagrants found ~*ing* outside the building⟩ ⟨~*ing* in the clubhouse —Furman Bisher⟩ ⟨~*ed* in the shade of the awnings —Sherwood Anderson⟩ **b :** to be unnecessarily slow in leaving **:** fitfully put off leaving **:** hang back **:** stay around without real necessity **:** lag behind ⟨a crowd of people, who ~*ed* to hear the bloodcurdling threats the prisoner shouted —Willa Cather⟩ **syn** see DELAY

loiter away *also* **loiter out** *vt* **:** to spend (time) in an idle aimless way **:** fritter away ⟨*loitered away* the whole afternoon⟩

loi·ter·ing·ly *adv* **:** in a manner that is marked by loitering **:** with loitering ⟨moved ~ down the street⟩

loja bark *var of* LOXA BARK

lo·kao \lō'kä(,)ō\ *n* -s [Chin (Pek) *lu⁴ kao¹*, lit., green ointment] **:** a green dye obtained from the bark of Eurasian buckthorns (esp. *Rhamnus utilis* and *R. globosa*) — called also *Chinese green*

loke \'lōk\ *n* -s [perh. fr. (assumed) ME, fr. OE *loca* enclosure, stronghold; akin to OE *loc* lock on a door — more at LOCK] *dial Eng* **:** a short narrow lane often coming to a dead end **:** a private road **:** BLIND ALLEY, LANE

lo·ke·la·ni \,lōkə'länē\ *n* -s [Hawaiian, fr. *loke* rose (fr. E *rose*) + *lani* heavenly] **:** a small fragrant pink or red rose common in Hawaii

lo·ko·no \lō'kō(,)nō\ *n* -s **:** an Arawakan language of British Guiana

lok·shen \'lȯkshən\ *n pl but sing or pl in constr* [Yiddish (pl. of *loksh* noodle), fr. Russ dial *loksha*, of Turkic origin; akin to Uigur & Kazan Tatar *lakča* noodles, Chavash *läškä*] **:** NOODLES

loktal *var of* LOCTAL

lol·i·gin·i·dae \,lälə'jinə,dē\ *n pl, cap* [NL, fr. *Loligin-*, *Loligo*, type genus + *-idae*] **:** a family of elongated cylindrical squids having the body tapering to a point and the arms partially retractile — see LOLIGO

lo·li·go \lō'lī(,)gō\ *n, cap* [NL, fr. L *lolligo, loligo* cuttlefish] **:** a genus (the type of the family Loliginidae) including numerous somewhat flattened cylindrical squids

lol·i·um \'lōlēəm, 'läl-\ *n, cap* [NL, fr. L, darnel] **:** a genus of grasses characterized by two-ranked many-flowered spikelets — see DARNEL, RYEGRASS

¹loll \'läl *also* 'lȯl *sometimes* 'lōl\ *vb* -ED/-ING/-s [ME *lollen*, prob. of imit. origin like ME *lullen* to lull — more at LULL] *vi* **1 :** to hang loosely or laxly **:** DROOP, DANGLE ⟨his head ~*ing* on his shoulders —Norman Mailer⟩ ⟨the ~*ing* stalk of every sun-weary flower —Osbert Sitwell⟩ **2 :** to recline, lean, or move in a lax, lazy, or indolent manner **:** IDLE, LOUNGE, SPRAWL ⟨jaded people ~*ing* supine in carriages —G.B.Shaw⟩ ⟨knocks off for several days and ~*s* about in pajamas at home —E.P.Snow⟩ ⟨~*ing* about the beach —Oliver Herford⟩ **3 :** *of the tongue* **:** to hang out **:** PROTRUDE ⟨their dogs . . . lay tired, with ~*ing* tongues —Adrian Bell⟩ ~ *vt* **:** to let roll out or down or back and forth **:** to let droop or dangle ⟨~*s* his tired tongue —Carl Sandburg⟩ — often used with *out* ⟨~*ed* his tongue out in derision⟩

²loll \"\ *n* -s *archaic* **:** act or posture of lolling

lollapalooza *var of* LALAPALOOZA

lol·lard \'lälə(r)d *also* 'lȯl-\ *n* -s *usu cap* [ME, fr. MD *lollaert*, fr. *lollen* to mutter, mumble, doze + *-aert* -ard — more at LULL] **1 :** one of various heretics in the Netherlands in the 14th century akin to the Fraticelli and the Beghards **2 :** one of the followers of Wycliffe in England and Scotland in the 14th and 15th centuries traveling as itinerant lay preachers throughout the land, denouncing ecclesiastical and temporal abuses, and preaching a spiritual message based on a primary appeal to the Bible

lol·lard·ism \-(r),dizəm\ *n* -s *usu cap* **:** LOLLARDY

lol·lardy \-,dē\ *also* **lol·lard·ry** \-drē\ *n* -ES *usu cap* [ME *Lollardie, Lollardrie*, fr. *Lollard* + *-ie* -y or *-rie* -ry] **:** the principles, beliefs, and practices of the Lollards

löllingite *var of* LOELLINGITE

lol·ling·ly *adv* **:** in a lolling manner **:** in a relaxed way

lol·li·pop *or* **lol·ly·pop** \'lälē,päp, -li,-\ *n* [prob. fr. ¹*loll* (to protrude the tongue) + *-i-* + *pop*] **:** a piece of hard candy to be dissolved in the mouth: **a :** a candy held in the mouth **b :** a lump of candy on the end of a stick that may be inserted in and removed from the mouth — see ALL-DAY SUCKER

lol·lop \'läləp\ *vi* -ED/-ING/-s [¹*loll* + *-op* (as in *wallop, gallop*)] **1** *dial Eng* **:** to loll, lounge, or move loungingly **:** SLOUCH ⟨these men, women, and children loll and ~ about —Osbert Sitwell⟩ **2 :** to proceed with a bounding or bobbing motion ⟨watching a rabbit ~ across —Adrian Bell⟩ ⟨the jeep ~*ed* and slewed in low low —Dan Wickenden⟩ ⟨the ~*ing* gait of the wolves —George Moore⟩

lol·ly \'lälē, -li\ *n* -ES [short for *lollipop*] **1** *Brit* **:** a piece of candy; *esp* **:** HARD CANDY **2** *also* **lolly ice :** soft ice or ice and snow that is ground down from floes or formed in turbulent seawater

lollygag *var of* LALLYGAG

lo·lo \'lō(,)lō\ *n, pl* **lolo** *or* **lolos** *usu cap* [Chin (Pek) *lo² lo²*] **1 :** NOSU **2 :** the Tibeto-Burman language of the Nosu people

¹lo·ma \'lōmə\ *n* -s [Sp, fr. *lomo* loin, back of an animal, fr. L *lumbus* loin — more at LOIN] *chiefly Southwest* **:** a broad-topped hill

²loma \"\ *n, pl* **loma** *or* **lomas** *usu cap* **1 a :** a people of the border regions of Liberia, Sierra Leone, and the Republic of Guinea **b :** a member of such people **2 :** a Mande language of the Loma people

lo·mas \'lō,mäs\ *or* **lomas de za·mo·ra** \-thäsä'mȯrə\ *adj, usu cap L&Z* [fr. *Lomas* or *Lomas de Zamora*, Argentina] **:** of or from the city of Lomas, Argentina **:** of the kind or style prevalent in Lomas

lo·ma·tia \lō'māsh(ē)ə\ *n, cap* [NL, fr. Gk *lōmat-, lōma* hem, fringe + NL *-ia*] **:** a small genus of low-growing Chilean and Australian trees (family Proteaceae) some of which yield dyes from their sap and wood used locally for furniture — see LOMATIOL

lo·ma·tine \'lōmətən, -əd·ən\ *or* **lo·mat·i·nous** \lō'matᵊnəs\ *adj* [ISV *lomat-* (fr. Gk *lōmat-, lōma* hem, fringe) + *-ine*; akin to L *lorum* strap — more at LORE] **:** LOBED ⟨the ~ toes of some birds⟩

lo·mati·ol \lō'māshē,ōl, -,ȯl\ *n* -s [NL *Lomatia* + E *-ol*] **:** a yellow crystalline pigment $C_{15}H_{14}O_4$ that surrounds the seeds of Australian trees of the genus *Lomatia* and that is a hydroxy derivative of lapachol

lo·ma·ti·um \lō'māshēəm\ *n, cap* [NL, fr. Gk *lōmation* small border, dim. of *lōmat-, lōma* hem, fringe] **:** a genus of perennial herbs (family Umbelliferae) resembling parsley and having leaves that are for the most part finely and ternately compound and winged fruit that is oblong to orbicular

¹lom·bard \'läm,bärd, -bȧd, -,bə(r)d\ *n* -s *often attrib* [ME *Lumbarde*, fr. MF *lombard*, fr. OIt *lombardo*, fr. L *Langobardus, Longobardus*] **1** *cap* **a :** a member of a Teutonic people invading Italy in A.D. 568, settling in the Po Valley, and establishing a kingdom **b :** a person descended from the Teutonic Lombards; *broadly* **:** a native of the part of Italy settled by the Lombards **2 a** *usu cap* **:** a Lombard engaged in banking or moneylending; *broadly* **:** BANKER, MONEYLENDER **b** *sometimes cap* **:** the place of business of a Lombard **:** BANK, PAWNSHOP

²lombard \"\ *n* -s [Sp *lombarda*, fr. fem. of *lombardo* Lombard, fr. It] **:** a cannon used in the 15th and 16th centuries

lombard architecture *n, usu cap L* **1 :** a round-arched architecture of northern Italy that is believed to date from the 8th century **2 :** the architecture of northern Italy including the Lombard, the later Romanesque, the Gothic, and other styles

lom·bard·esque \¦läm,bär¦desk, -bȧ¦d-, -,bə(r)¦d-\ *adj, usu cap* [It *lombardesco*, fr. *lombardo* + *-esco* -esque] **1 :** of or relating to a Lombard type or school **2 :** of or relating to any of several Italian Renaissance painters named Lombardi or Lombardo

¹lom·bar·dic \(')läm¦bärdik, -bȧd-, -dēk\ *adj, usu cap* [¹*Lombard* + *-ic*] **1 :** of or relating to the Lombards or to the region of northern Italy formerly constituting the kingdom of the Lombards **2 :** belonging to or characteristic of a medieval Italian writing developed from the Roman cursive

²lombardic \"\ *n* -s *usu cap* **:** a Lombardic script

LOMBARDIC

lombard loan *n, usu cap 1st L*, *Brit* **:** a loan on stock-exchange securities usu. made by a central bank to commercial banks

lombard school *n, usu cap L* **:** any of several Renaissance schools of painting in cities (as Mantua, Milan, Padua) of northern Italy

lom·bar·dy poplar \'läm,bärdē-, -bȧdē-, -di-\ *n, usu cap L* [fr. *Lombardy*, district in northern Italy] **:** a staminate variety (*Populus nigra italica*) of the black poplar distinguished by its columnar fastigiate shape and strongly ascending branches

lom·bro·sian \(')läm¦brōzhən\ *adj, usu cap* [Cesare *Lombroso* †1909 Ital. physician and criminologist + E *-ian*] **:** of or relating to the doctrines of Lombroso esp. that a criminal represents a distinct anthropological type with definite physical and mental stigmata and that he is the product of heredity, atavism, and degeneracy ⟨*Lombrosian* school⟩ ⟨a *Lombrosian* approach to criminology⟩

lo·ment \'lō,ment\ *also* **lo·men·tum** \lō'mentəm\ *n* -s [NL *lomentum*, fr. L, cosmetic wash made fr. bean meal, fr. *lotus* (past part. of *lavare* to wash) + *-mentum* -ment — more at LYE] **:** a dry indehiscent one-celled fruit (as of the tick trefoil) that is produced from a single superior ovary and breaks transversely into numerous segments at maturity — see FRUIT illustration

lo·mi·lo·mi \'lōmē'lōmē\ *n* -s [Hawaiian] **:** a vigorous massage usually used by the Hawaiians to relieve pain and fatigue

lomilomi salmon *n* **:** a Hawaiian dish consisting of salmon worked with the fingers, mixed with onions, and seasoned

lo·mi·ta \lō'mēd·ə\ *n* -s [Sp, dim. of *loma* hill — more at LOMA] **:** a low broad hill

lomonite *var of* LAUMONTITE

lon *abbr* longitude

lonch- *or* **loncho-** *comb form* [NL, fr. Gk, fr. *lonchē* spear-head, lance] **:** lance ⟨*Lonch*ocarpus⟩ ⟨*Lonch*ma⟩

lon·cho·car·pus \,läŋkə'kärpəs\ *n, cap* [NL, fr. *lonch-* + *-carpus*] **:** a large genus of chiefly tropical American trees and shrubs (family Leguminosae) that have pinnate leaves and red and white flowers with the wings and keel united

lon·chop·ter·i·dae \,läŋ,käp'terə,dē\ *n pl, cap* [NL, fr. *Lonchoptera*, type genus (fr. *lonch-* + *-ptera*) + *-idae*] **:** a family of small two-winged flies with porrect antennae and lanceolate wings

lon·chura \läŋ'kyürə\ *n* [NL, fr. *lonch-* + *-ura*] **1** *cap* **:** a large genus of weaverbirds including the well-known cowry bird **2** -s **:** any bird of *Lonchura* or a closely related genus

lon·don \'ləndən\ *adj, usu cap* [fr. *London*, England] **:** of or from London, the capital of England ⟨a *London* newspaper⟩ ⟨*London* church bells⟩ **:** of the kind or style prevalent in London ⟨morning came, cold, with a high, gray, *London* sky —John Galsworthy⟩

london bridge *n, usu cap L&B* [fr. *London Bridge,* a bridge built in 1209 across the Thames river in London, England] **:** an old singing game in which one of a line of children passing under an arch formed by uplifted arms is captured by a downward swoop of the arms at the end of the refrain

london broil *n, usu cap L* **:** broiled flank steak sliced diagonally across the grain

london brown *n, often cap L* **:** CARBUNCLE 3

lon·don·der·ry \ˌləndənˌderē, -ri\ *adj, usu cap* [fr. *Londonderry,* county borough in Ireland] **1 :** of or from the county borough of Londonderry, Northern Ireland **:** of the kind or style prevalent in Londonderry **2 :** of or from County Londonderry, Northern Ireland **:** of the kind or style prevalent in County Londonderry

lon·don·er \ˈləndənə(r)\ *n* -s *cap* [ME *londynere,* fr. *London* England + ME *-ere* -er] **:** a native or resident of London, England

lon·don·ese \ˌləndəˌnēz, -ēs\ *n, usu cap* [*London,* England + E *-ese*] **:** the dialect of London; *esp* **:** COCKNEY 2b

lon·don·esque \-ˌnesk\ *adj, usu cap* [*London,* England + E *-esque*] **:** characteristic of London

london forces *n pl, usu cap L* [after Fritz Wolfgang *London* †1954 Am. physicist born in Germany] **:** nonchemical interactions between atoms or molecules

lon·don·ish \ˈləndənish\ *adj, usu cap* [*London,* England + E *-ish*] **:** relating to or characteristic of London

london ivy *n, usu cap L* **:** the smoke or the thick fog of London

lon·don·iza·tion \ˌləndənəˈzāshən\ *n* -s *usu cap* **:** the act or process of londonizing

lon·don·ize \ˈləndəˌnīz\ *vt* -ED/-ING/-S *often cap* [*London,* England + E *-ize*] **1 :** to cause to acquire a quality distinctive of London or a trait distinctive of Londoners **2 :** to cause to conform to or imitate London fashions

london particular *n, usu cap L* **:** an extremely thick London fog

london plane *or* **london plane tree** *n, usu cap L* **:** a rapid-growing smoke resistant tree (*Platanus × acerifolia*) that is a hybrid between the Oriental plane and a common American sycamore (*P. occidentalis*) and is used for street and shade-tree planting

london pride *n, usu cap L* **1 :** a hardy perennial saxifrage (*Saxifraga umbrosa*) native to western Europe **2 :** SWEET WILLIAM **3 :** MALTESE CROSS 2 **4 :** SOAPWORT

London Purple *trademark* — used for an arsenical insecticide obtained as a by-product of the dye industry

london rocket *n, usu cap L* **:** a European herb (*Sisymbrium irio*) that sprang up in London after the great fire of 1666 and is occas. adventive in No. America

london smoke *n, often cap L* **:** a nearly neutral slightly olive black that is very slightly lighter and less neutral than Chaetura black

lon·dony \ˈləndənē\ *adj, usu cap* [*London,* England + E *-y*] **:** marked by or tending to suggest characteristics of London

lone \ˈlōn\ *adj* [ME, by shortening (resulting fr. incorrect division of *alon, alone* alone as *a lon, a lone*) of *alon, alone* — more at ALONE] **1 a :** having no company **:** LONESOME, SOLITARY ⟨here and there a ~ traveler could be seen walking up the winding roads —H.A.Chippendale⟩ ⟨a ~ horseman carried the mail —*Amer. Guide Series: N.H.*⟩ **b :** preferring solitude **:** disposed to isolation ⟨the hermit, the ~ soul, does not build but seeks a cave —John Dewey⟩ ⟨a ~ wolf⟩ **c :** having no husband **:** being unmarried or widowed ⟨a big city is full of ~ women⟩ **2 :** ONLY, SOLE ⟨constitutes the ~ industry of the community —*Amer. Guide Series: Vt.*⟩ ⟨the annual picnic in many companies furnishes the ~ contact with employees' families —*Dun's Rev.*⟩ ⟨the *Lone Star State*⟩ **3 :** situated by itself **:** ISOLATED, REMOTE ⟨the ~ oak tree against the sky —Howard Troyer⟩ ⟨this ~ outpost on the keys —*Amer. Guide Series: Fla.*⟩ **syn** see ALONE, SINGLE — **one's lone :** one's self ⟨walks by *its* wild *lone* —E.B.White⟩ ⟨if he doesn't come I couldn't live here *my lone* —Michael McLaverty⟩

lone hand *n* **1 a :** a hand in certain partnership card games strong enough to be played out alone by the person holding it after his partner has laid aside his own hand **b :** a person playing such a hand **2 :** a course of action, policy, or enterprise carried out by a country, group, or individual without allies or associates

lone·li·hood \ˈlōnlēˌhu̇d\ *n* **:** LONELINESS

lone·li·ly \-lәlē\ *adv* **:** in a lonely manner

lone·li·ness \ˈlōnlēnəs, -lin-\ *n* -ES **1 a :** the fact or condition of being alone **:** ISOLATION ⟨had become frightened by the ~ of her position in life —Sherwood Anderson⟩ ⟨the impersonality and ~ of modern mass civilization —C.B.Forcey⟩ **b :** a seclusion from others **:** a deliberately selected state of solitude **:** SEPARATENESS ⟨holding herself aloof in chosen ~ —P.E. More⟩ **2 :** a remoteness from human habitation **:** BLEAKNESS, DESOLATENESS ⟨the ~ of the spot was set off by the unbroken snow around it⟩ **3 :** a state of dejection or grief caused by the condition of being alone ⟨felt so forlorn, so helpless, filled as she was with gnawing ~ —O.E.Rölvaag⟩ ⟨often the artist has an aching sense of great ~ —J.R.Oppenheimer⟩

lone·ly \-lē, -li\ *adj, usu* -ER/-EST [*lone* + *-ly*] **1 a :** being without company **:** lacking companions or associates **:** LONE ⟨a ~ fisherman stood below on a tuft of gravel —Frederic Prokosch⟩ ⟨young men who brought their girls there to dance as well as ~ ones who danced with the hostesses —Edmund Wilson⟩ **b :** cut off from company or neighbors **:** SOLITARY ⟨a ~ little town far off upon the verge of Lapland night —G.D. Brown⟩ ⟨the train stopped frequently at ~ little stations —Robert Hichens⟩ **2 :** not frequented by human beings **:** DESOLATE ⟨dangerous and ~ portions of . . . coast —A.F. Harlow⟩ ⟨a ~ road⟩ **3 :** affected by loneliness **:** dejected and unhappy as a result of being alone ⟨so far from home . . . so ~ and terribly unhappy —Eric Linklater⟩ ⟨a poor sick ~ old woman —W.M.Thackeray⟩ ⟨~ for his family⟩ **4 :** producing a condition or feeling of loneliness ⟨it's a ~ thing to be a champion —G.B.Shaw⟩ **syn** see ALONE

lone·ness *n* -ES **:** the quality or state of being lone **:** ISOLATION ⟨space that was absolute meaninglessness and absolute cold, and absolute dark ~ —Waldo Frank⟩ ⟨to face the ~ of their days —Marsden Hartley⟩

lon·er \ˈlōnə(r)\ *n* -s [*lone* + *-er*] **:** one that avoids others: as **a :** a person who keeps to himself ⟨a ~ with no close friends⟩ ⟨a political ~ who joins no factions⟩ **b :** a solitary animal ⟨the black bear is elusive, speedy . . . a ~, a nomad, and harmless —E.J.Kahn⟩

lone scout *n* **:** a boy or girl scout who lives in a rural community that does not have a regular scout organization

1lone·some \ˈlōnsəm\ *adj* [*lone* + *-some*] **1 a :** being in a state of loneliness **:** affected by sadness or dejection as a result of lack of companionship or separation from others ⟨was ~ for the female society of my kind —W.A.White⟩ ⟨enjoyed being abroad but was ~ for his family⟩ **b :** causing a feeling of loneliness ⟨how ~ and silent the house had seemed —Gretchen Finletter⟩ **2 a :** REMOTE, UNFREQUENTED ⟨like one that on a ~ road doth walk in fear and dread —S.T.Coleridge⟩ **b :** lacking companionship **:** separated from others of its kind **:** LONE ⟨had no industries, few towns of any size, no fences, no roads, and only a ~ railroad line or two —*Newsweek*⟩ ⟨two cruisers ahead and to port of the carrier, and one ~ destroyer on her starboard —C.A.Lockwood⟩ **syn** see ALONE

2lonesome \"\ *n* -s **:** SELF ⟨be nice if we had the patch all to our ~s —Wallace Stegner⟩ ⟨working by his ~ in the fields —Mary Webb⟩

lone·some·ly *adv* **:** in a lonesome manner

lone·some·ness *n* -ES **:** the quality or state of being lonesome

lone star *adj, usu cap L&S* [fr. the *Lone Star* state, nickname for Texas; fr. the single star of its flag] **:** TEXAS

lone star tick *n* **:** a widely distributed No. American ixodid tick (*Amblyomma americanum*) that attacks various mammals and is regarded as a potential spotted fever vector

lone troop *n* **:** a girl scout troop that is not under the jurisdiction of a girl scout council

lone wolf *n* **1 :** a wolf that hunts or prowls alone **2 :** a person who prefers to work, act, or live alone ⟨American painters are *lone wolves* who fear to lose their individuality by working together and trading ideas —Manny Farber⟩ ⟨in all things a *lone wolf,* apparently wanting no friends and seeking to influence no man —C.W.M.Hart⟩

lone-wolf \ˈ=ˈ=\ *vi* [*lone wolf*] **:** to proceed on one's own in the manner of a lone wolf **:** work, act, or live alone ⟨bade the men stay by Location No. 1 while he *lone-wolfed* it to Location No. 2 —*Infantry Jour.*⟩

1long \ˈlȯŋ *also* ˈläŋ\ *adj* **lon·ger** \-ŋgə(r)\ **lon·gest** \-ŋgəst\ [ME *long, lang,* fr. OE; akin to OHG *lang* long, ON *langr,* Goth *langs,* L *longus,* MPer *drang,* Skt *dīrgha* — more at INDULGE] **1 a :** extending for a considerable distance **:** having great length ⟨oaks in ~ and imposing avenues —*Amer. Guide Series: La.*⟩ ⟨a ~ coastline⟩ ⟨the ~ trip from New York to London was made in remarkably short time⟩ **b :** having greater length than usual ⟨a large oval man, with a ~ oiled mustache —Lawrence Durrell⟩ ⟨a ~ car⟩ ⟨~ fingers⟩ **c :** having greater height than usual **:** TALL ⟨walked over to the ~ French windows and looked out —May Sarton⟩ ⟨a ~, lean individual —F.V.W.Mason⟩ ⟨a race of ~ gaunt men —Sherwood Anderson⟩ **d :** having a greater length than breadth **:** ELONGATED ⟨a ~ skull⟩ ⟨a ~ face⟩ **e :** longer than desirable or necessary **:** too long ⟨the dress is ~ on her⟩ ⟨the column is two lines ~⟩ ⟨his first serve was ~⟩ **2 a :** having a specified length ⟨the table was six feet ~⟩ **b :** forming the chief linear dimension ⟨the ~ side of the building⟩ ⟨placed the sofa the ~ way of the room⟩ **3 a :** extending over a considerable time ⟨even after ~ experience editing has never become easy —E.S. McCartney⟩ ⟨a ~ tradition of national consciousness —Vera M. Dean⟩ ⟨a ~ friendship⟩ **b :** having a specified duration ⟨the play was two hours ~⟩ **c :** prolonged beyond the usual time **:** not interrupted ⟨drank in ~, greedy swallows —Scott Fitzgerald⟩ ⟨the occasional shutting of a door would peal in ~ reverberations —T.L.Peacock⟩ ⟨a ~ look⟩ ⟨a ~ breath⟩ ⟨the four enemies who were lifting the ~ yell as they came racing for him —W.N.Burns⟩ **4 a :** containing many items in a series ⟨a ~ and strong list of candidates was put forward —S.H.Adams⟩ ⟨the ~ series of combat operations —Mack Morriss⟩ ⟨played a ~ list of comedy and farcical roles —W.P. Eaton⟩ **b :** having a specified number of units ⟨a book 300 pages ~⟩ **c :** consisting of a greater number or amount than usual **:** LARGE ⟨this son was a man of 40 or thereabouts, was married, and had a ~ family —A.T.Quiller-Couch⟩ ⟨now reverenced as a master . . . because his pictures fetch ~ prices —Clive Bell⟩ **5 a** *of a speech sound* **:** having a relatively long duration ⟨the vowel of *dark* is ~*er* than the vowel of *dock* when the *r* is not pronounced⟩ **b :** indicating the member of a pair of similarly spelled vowel or partly vowel sounds that is descended from a vowel long in duration but that now is not long in duration or does not have duration as its chief distinguishing feature ⟨~ *a* in *fate*⟩ ⟨~ *e* in *equal*⟩ ⟨~ *i* in *sign*⟩ ⟨~ *o* in *ode*⟩ ⟨~ *u* in *fuse*⟩ **c** (1) *of a syllable in Greek or Latin verse* **:** of relatively extended duration (2) *of a syllable in English verse* **:** STRESSED **6 a :** lasting too long **:** TEDIOUS ⟨a ~ lecture⟩ ⟨a ~ explanation⟩ **b :** seeming to pass slowly and heavily ⟨those ~ grim years between the fall of France and the battle of El Alamein —R.K.Dickson⟩ ⟨hung parasitically round the court in the ~ days of its poverty —A.M.Young⟩ **7 :** having the capacity to reach or extend or travel a considerable distance ⟨the ~ voice of the hounds —Thomas Wolfe⟩ ⟨a ~ northeast wind —Marjory S. Douglas⟩ ⟨a fighter with a ~ left jab⟩ ⟨hits a ~ ball⟩ ⟨~ sight⟩ **8** *of a number or unit of measure* **:** larger or longer than the standard ⟨a ~ mile⟩ **9 a :** extending far into the future ⟨a ~ view of the problem⟩ ⟨the thoughts of youth are ~, ~ thoughts —H.W.Longfellow⟩ **b :** extending beyond what is known or easily verified ⟨a ~ guess⟩ **c :** far off in time **:** REMOTE ⟨a ~ date⟩ **d :** payable after a considerable period ⟨a ~ note⟩ **10 :** consisting of or containing long straw ⟨~ fodder⟩ **11 :** esp. strong in or esp. well furnished with — used with *on* ⟨deficient in logic but ~ on human understanding —Stuart Chase⟩ ⟨~ on ancestry and short on cash —Clement Eaton⟩ **12** *of betting odds* **a :** marked by an unusual degree of difference between the amounts wagered on each side ⟨odds of 30 to 1 or even ~*er*⟩ **b :** of or relating to the larger amount wagered ⟨take the ~ end of the bet⟩ **13 :** subject to great odds **:** having little likelihood of success ⟨strike out for himself, be independent, take a ~ chance for a large reward —W.P.Webb⟩ **14 :** holding securities or goods in anticipation of an advance in prices ⟨~ of cotton⟩ ⟨be on the ~ side of the market⟩ **15** *of a beverage* **:** served in a tall glass **:** constituting a large measure ⟨a ~ drink⟩ **16 :** adequate in amount **:** capable of meeting consumer needs ⟨corn is in ~ supply⟩ **17** *of fractional paper sizes* **:** having a longer dimension equal to the shorter dimension of the full-size sheet ⟨~ quarto⟩ **18 a :** flowing readily **:** FLUID ⟨a ~ printing ink⟩ **b :** yielding a readily flowing mixture ⟨a ~ carbon black⟩ **19 :** TELEPHOTO — **at long last** *adv* **:** after a long wait **:** FINALLY ⟨*at long last* they sighted land⟩ — **at the longest** *adv* **:** at the outside limit of time ⟨will take two hours *at the longest*⟩ — **long in the tooth :** past one's best days **:** OLD ⟨as fighters go, he is a sere and yellowed leaf and *long in the tooth* —Gilbert Millstein⟩

2long \"\ *adv* -ER/-EST [ME *longe, lange,* fr. OE, fr. *long, lang,* adj.] **1 :** for or during a long time ⟨children know what a story or play is ~ before they know what an essay is —George Sampson⟩ ⟨a quiet picturesque resort, ~ the gathering place of artists —*Amer. Guide Series: Mich.*⟩ **2 :** at or to a long distance **:** FAR — used chiefly in combination ⟨*long*-removed⟩ ⟨*long*-traveled⟩ **3 :** for the duration of a specified period ⟨all summer ~⟩ ⟨all his life ~⟩ ⟨all day ~⟩ **4 :** at a point of time far before or after a specified moment or event ⟨~ before the discovery of America⟩ ⟨his diary was deciphered ~ after his death⟩ **5 :** after or beyond a specified time — used in the comparative ⟨didn't stay ~*er* than five o'clock⟩ ⟨the city held out ~*er* than a year under siege⟩

3long \"\ *n* -s [ME *long, lang,* fr. *long, lang,* adj.] **1 :** a long period of time ⟨expected the train before ~⟩ **2** [ME, fr. ML *longa* — more at LONGA] *in mensural notation* **:** a note that in imperfect time is one half the length of a large note and twice the length of a breve, and in perfect time is one third the length of a large note and three times the length of a breve **3 :** a long syllable **4 :** one who purchases or operates on the long side of the market — compare BULL 2a **5 :** a long signal (as in Morse code) ⟨tapped out a ~ and a short⟩ ⟨blew two ~s on his whistle⟩ **6 a longs** *pl* **:** long trousers ⟨was proudly wearing his first pair of ~s⟩ **b :** a size in men's clothing (as suits, coats, slacks) for the person who is above average in height **7 longs** *pl* **:** LONG-TERM BONDS — **the long and short** *or* **the long and the short :** the sum and substance **:** GIST **:** WHOLE

4long \"\ *vi* -ED/-ING/-S [ME *longen, langen,* fr. OE *longian, langian;* akin to OS *langōn* to long, OHG *langēn,* ON *langa;* derivative fr. the root of E *1long*] **:** to feel a strong desire or craving **:** wish for something intensely **:** YEARN ⟨~ for summer to come⟩ ⟨when I look at her dancing, I ~ to dance with her —Anne D. Sedgwick⟩ ⟨~s for the big sales that a sensational book or a novelty may seem to promise —August Frugé⟩

syn LONG, YEARN, HANKER, PINE, HUNGER, and THIRST mean in common to have a strong desire (for something). LONG implies wishing for something with one's whole heart ⟨however much you may *long* for a cigarette —Agnes M. Miall⟩ ⟨*long* for peace and security after war and disorder⟩ ⟨for the first time in her life she had ceased *longing,* ceased striving —Ellen Glasgow⟩ YEARN adds to LONG the idea of eagerness, tenderness, or passionateness ⟨*yearn* for something to believe in⟩ ⟨they often became homesick and *yearned* for their old associations —V.G.Heiser⟩ ⟨gazed into his faded blue eyes as if *yearning* to be understood —Joseph Conrad⟩ ⟨*yearned* for the return of a lover⟩ HANKER suggests somewhat disparagingly that one is made uneasy or restless by a desire ⟨he *hankered* after other, strange delights —Robertson Davies⟩ ⟨no *hankering* to be the founder of a new system of philosophy —M.R.Cohen⟩ ⟨all who enjoy or *hanker* after a life in the open air —*Brit. Book News*⟩ ⟨*hanker* after illicit pleasures⟩ PINE suggests a languishing or other more or less adverse physical effect from usu. fruitless longing ⟨one realizes all the pleasure of the present good; the other converts it into pain by *pining* after something better —T.L.Peacock⟩ ⟨some people *pine* for adventure, stalk it, woo it with lures —Sylvia Berkman⟩ ⟨the job he had always *pined* for —*Time*⟩ HUNGER and THIRST suggest a compelling craving ⟨could even a mother have *hungered* more acutely for the sight of a daughter? —Ellen Glasgow⟩ ⟨people *thirsting* for conquest —Julien Benda⟩ ⟨she was *thirsting* to hear the whole of the story —Winston Churchill⟩

5long \"\ *vi* -ED/-ING/-S [ME *longen,* fr. *along* (*on*) because (of) — more at ALONG OF] *archaic* **:** to be suitable or fitting ⟨give thee everything that ~s unto the daughter of a king —William Morris⟩

long *abbr* **1** longeron **2** longitude; longitudinal

lon·ga \ˈläŋgə\ *n* -s [ML, fr. fem. of L *longus* long — more at LONG] **:** LONG 2

long account *n* **1 :** the account of a purchaser of securities on margin **2 :** the aggregate of margin purchases in a given security or commodity or in a delivery month or of the market as a whole

longaeval *var of* LONGEVAL

1long ago *adv* [*2long* + *ago*] **:** in the distant or comparatively distant past **:** not recently ⟨*long ago* changed their nomadic way of life for a settled one⟩ ⟨left for work *long ago*⟩

2long ago *n* **:** the distant past ⟨the excitement and uncertainties of the campaign, even the triumph of the election, seem incidents of the *long ago* —*New Yorker*⟩

long-ago \ˌ==ˈ=\ *adj* [*1long ago*] **:** belonging to a time long gone ⟨those *long-ago* dresses that had made such lovely sounds —Bruce Marshall⟩

lon·gan \ˈläŋgən\ *or* **lun·gan** \ˈləŋ-\ *n* -s [Chin (Pek) *lung² yen³,* lit., dragon's eye] **1 :** a pulpy fruit related to the litchi and produced by an East Indian tree (*Euphoria longana*) **2 :** a tree that bears the longan

long-and-short-haul clause \ˈ==ˈ=ˈ=-\ *n* **:** a clause in U.S. laws regulating railroad rates providing that the total rate for a distance less than and included in a longer distance shall not be higher than that for the longer distance except when specially authorized by public regulatory authorities

long-and-short work \ˈ==ˈ=-\ *n* **:** ashlar quoins arranged alternately horizontally and vertically (as to finish off rubblework)

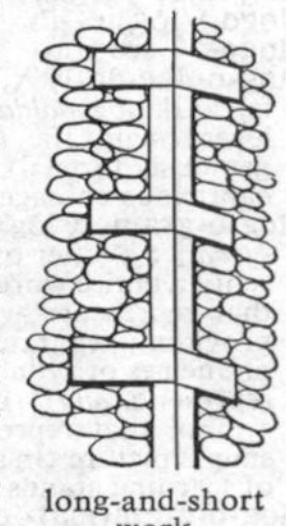

long-and-short work

lon·ga·nim·i·ty \ˌläŋgəˈniməd·ē\ *n* -ES [LL *longanimitas,* fr. *longanimis* long-suffering (fr. *longus* long + *animus* soul, mind, spirit) + *-itas* -ity — more at ANIMATE] **:** a disposition to bear injuries patiently **:** FORBEARANCE ⟨bears his trials with ~⟩ **syn** see PATIENCE

lon·gan·i·mous \läŋˈganəməs\ *adj* [LL *longanimus, longanimis*] **:** able to bear injuries patiently **:** FORBEARING

long appoggiatura *n* **:** a grace note that is played on the beat with half the time value taken from the principal note following it — see APPOGGIATURA illustration

long ballot *n* **:** BLANKET BALLOT

long barrow *n* **:** a neolithic burial mound of oval, wedge, or very much elongated shape — compare ROUND BARROW

1long beach *adj, usu cap L&B* [fr. *Long Beach,* Calif.] **:** of or from the city of Long Beach, Calif. ⟨the *Long Beach* harbor⟩ **:** of the kind or style prevalent in Long Beach

2long beach *n, often cap L&B* **:** a light yellowish brown that is lighter and slightly redder and stronger than khaki and paler and slightly yellower than walnut brown

longbeak \ˈ=ˌ=\ *n* **:** DOWITCHER

longbeard \ˈ=ˌ=\ *n* **1 :** a man with a long beard **2 :** BELLARMINE

long beech fern *n* **:** a beech fern (*Phegopteris dryopteris*)

longbill \ˈ=ˌ=\ *n* **:** a bird with a long bill (as a snipe)

long bill *n* **:** a bill of exchange that runs for more than 30 and often more than 60 days — compare SHORT BILL

long-billed curlew \ˈ=ˌ=-\ *n* **:** HEN CURLEW

long-billed dowitcher *n* **:** a rather large dowitcher (*Limnodromus griseus scolopaceus*) of western No. America that has a long bill and that breeds along the arctic coast of Alaska and winters south into Mexico

long-billed marsh wren *n* **:** a marsh wren (*Telmatodytes palustris palustris*) that is predominantly dark brown to blackish brown above with buffy sides and white underparts and is widely distributed in No. America east of the Rocky mountains

longboat \ˈ=ˌ=\ *n* **:** the largest boat carried by a merchant sailing ship

long bone *n* **:** one of the elongated bones that form the characteristic support of the vertebrate limb and consist of an essentially cylindrical shaft containing marrow and terminating at each end in an enlarged head for articulation with other bones

longbow \ˈ=ˌ=\ *n* **1 :** a wooden bow drawn by hand and usu. 5½ to 6 feet long **2 :** the great bow of medieval England that sometimes reached a length of 6 feet, 7 inches, had a drawing weight of 100 pounds, and shot a cloth-yard shaft of 37 inches

long bowls *n pl but sing in constr* **:** a game whose object is bowling a skittle ball along the ground for a given distance in the fewest bowls — **at long bowls :** at a distance — used of ships cannonading at a distance from their target

long buchu *n* **1 :** a southern African shrub (*Barosma ensata*) whose leaves furnish an adulterant of buchu **2 :** BUCHU

long cards *n pl* **:** cards held in bridge or whist by a player in a suit of which the other players have none

long-case clock *n* **:** GRANDFATHER CLOCK

long-chain \ˈ=ˈ=\ *adj* **:** having a relatively long chain of atoms (as carbon atoms) in the molecule

long clam *n* **1 :** SOFT-SHELL CLAM **2 :** RAZOR CLAM

long-clawed prawn \ˈ=ˌ=-\ *n* **:** RIVER PRAWN

longcloth \ˈ=ˌ=\ *n* **:** a fine bleached cotton cloth with a close plain weave and a soft finish that is used chiefly for children's wear and underwear

long column *n* **:** a column so slender that it will fail under longitudinal load by bending rather than by crushing and typically having a length of 20 to 30 times the diameter

long count *n, often cap L&C* **:** a system of dating in the Maya calendar according to the time in numbers of baktuns, katuns, tuns, uinals, and days elapsed since an arbitrary point prior to 3000 B.C. — compare SHORT COUNT

long-crested jay \ˈ=ˌ==-\ *n* **:** a jay (*Cyanocitta stelleri diademata*) that is a variety of the Steller's jay, is distinguished chiefly by an intensely iridescent blue abdomen and rump and bluish white streaks on the head, and is found from Wyoming to New Mexico

long cross *n* **:** LATIN CROSS 1

long-cycled *also* **long-cycle** \ˈ=ˈ=\ *adj* **:** having an aecial or uredinial stage or both intervening between the pycnial and telial stages (as certain rusts) — opposed to *short-cycled*

long dance *n* **:** a longways dance; *specif* **:** RINKAFADDA

long-day \ˈ=ˈ=\ *adj* **:** responding to a long photoperiod — used of plants

1long-distance \ˈ=ˈ==\ *adj* [fr. the phrase *long distance*] **1 a :** situated a long distance away ⟨a *long-distance* friend⟩ **b :** covering a long distance ⟨a *long-distance* race⟩ ⟨*long-distance* vision⟩ **2 :** of or relating to telephone communication with a distant point ⟨a *long-distance* call⟩ ⟨*long-distance* night rates⟩

2long-distance \ˈ=ˈ==\ *adv* **:** by long-distance telephone ⟨called her up *long-distance*⟩

3long-distance \"\ *vt* **1 :** to make a long-distance telephone call to ⟨didn't think it was worth while *long-distancing* you in Washington —Mary Manning⟩ **2 :** to express or communicate by means of a long-distance telephone call ⟨wrote, wired or *long-distanced* their desire to move in immediately —*Life*⟩

long distance *n* [*1long-distance*] **1 :** communication by long-distance telephone ⟨decided it by *long distance*⟩ **2 :** a telephone operator or exchange that gives long-distance connections ⟨had to ask *long distance* for his number⟩

long division *n* **:** arithmetical division in which the several steps corresponding to the division of parts of the dividend by the divisor are indicated in detail

long dog *n, dial Eng* **:** GREYHOUND; *esp* **:** a greyhound mongrel

long dozen *n* **:** one more than a dozen **:** THIRTEEN

long draft *n* **:** a system of spinning yarn or drafting roving that eliminates one or more reducing or roving processes

long-drawn-out \ˈ=ˈ=ˈ=\ *also* **long-drawn** \ˈ=ˈ=\ *adj* **:** extended to a great length esp. of time **:** PROTRACTED ⟨the most critical times of that *long-drawn-out* contest —Clement Attlee⟩ ⟨the *long-drawn* trials of vigilance and exertion —Mark Sullivan⟩

1longe *or* **lunge** \ˈlənj, ˈlōⁿzh, ˈläⁿzh, ˈlänj\ *n* -s [F *longe,* fr. OF, fr. fem. of *lonc* long, fr. L *longus* — more at LONG] **:** a long rein or strap used to lead or guide a horse in training — called also *longeing rein*

2longe *or* **lunge** \"\ *vt* **longed** *or* **lunged; longed** *or* **lunged; longeing** *or* **lunging; longes** *or* **lunges :** to guide or exercise (a horse) by means of a longe

3longe \'lənj, 'länj\ *n* -s [by shortening & alter.] **1 :** LAKE TROUT b **2 :** MUSKELLUNGE

longear \'=,=\ *n, West* **:** an unbranded calf

long–eared \'=¦=\ *adj* **1 :** having long ears **2 :** ASININE **:** STUPID ⟨an evil, heavy-laden, *long-eared* age —Thomas Carlyle⟩

long–eared bat *n* **:** any of numerous bats having very long ears (as members of the nearly cosmopolitan genus *Plecotus* in which the ears may equal the forearm in length)

long–eared fox *n* **1 :** a small carnivorous mammal (*Otocyon megalotis*) of southern Africa that is related to the typical foxes but is distinguished by very large erect ears and the presence of four molars in each jaw **2 :** DESERT FOX 2

long–eared jerboa *n* **:** a central Asian jerboa (*Euchorentes naso*) that is ocherous or russet and has a snout like that of a pig

long–eared owl *n* **:** an owl of the northern hemisphere (*Asio otus*) that has conspicuous ear tufts and mottled coloration; *esp* **:** a slender long-winged and long-tailed American owl (*Asio otus wilsonianus*)

longear sunfish *or* **long–eared sunfish** *n* **:** a sunfish (*Lepomis megalotis*) of the central and southern U. S. that is brilliant in color with a long opercular flap

longed *past of* LONG

longeing rein *or* **lunging rein** *n* **:** LONGE

1longer *comparative of* LONG

2lon·ger \'läŋgə(r)\ *n* -s [origin unknown] **:** a row of barrels stowed fore and aft

lon·ge·ron \'länjərən\ *n* -s [F, longitudinal girder, longeron, fr. *allonger* to make long — more at ALLONGE] **:** a fore-and-aft member of the framing of an airplane fuselage that is usu. continuous across a number of points of support

long ess *var of* LONG S

longest *superlative of* LONG

lon·ge·val *also* **lon·gae·val** \län'jēvəl\ *adj* [L *longaevus* + E *-al*] *archaic* **:** long lasting

lon·gev·i·ty \län'jevəd·ē, lȯn-, -ətē, -i\ *n* -ES [LL *longaevitas*, fr. L *longaevus* long-lived (fr. *longus* long + *aevum* age, lifetime) + *-itas* -ity — more at LONG, AYE] **1 a :** a long duration of individual life ⟨his ~ was remarkable, considering the fact that he had been sickly as a child⟩ ⟨~ of metal parts is increased by this new process —*Report: General Motors Corp.*⟩ **b :** length of life ⟨studies in ~⟩ **2 :** long continuance **:** SENIORITY ⟨~ in office is also an asset —Spencer Parratt⟩ ⟨held a remarkable record for parliamentary ~ —*Time*⟩

longevity pay *n* **:** additional wages or other compensation given on the basis of length of service

lon·ge·vous \(')län¦jēvəs\ *adj* [L *longaevus*] **:** LONG-LIVED ⟨his ~ royal grandfather —*Time*⟩

long face *n* **:** a facial expression of sadness or melancholy usu. affected or exaggerated ⟨go around with a *long face* feeling sorry for yourself —Gregor Felsen⟩

long–fed \'=¦=\ *adj, of cattle* **:** kept on a fattening ration for a period of four or more months — compare SHORT-FED

long field *n* **:** the part of a cricket field near the boundary behind the bowler; *also* **:** a fielder stationed there — called also *deep field*

longfin \'=,=\ *n* **:** any of several long-finned fishes: as **a** *Austral* **:** a member of the family Serranidae **b :** ARCTIC GRAYLING **c :** ALBACORE

long–finned tuna *or* **long–finned tunny** \'=,=-\ *n* **:** ALBACORE

longfin pompano *n* **:** a common pompano (*Trachinotus palometa*) of the warm western Atlantic that is marked by elongated fins and tail

long fold *adj* **:** LONG GRAIN

long·ford \'lȯŋfə(r)d, 'läŋ-\ *adj, usu cap* [fr. *Longford* county, Ireland] **:** of or from County Longford, Ireland **:** of the kind or style prevalent in County Longford

long four *n* **:** a candle weighing a quarter of a pound

long·ful \'lȯŋfəl *also* 'läŋ-\ *adj* ['*long* + *-ful*] *dial* **:** LENGTHY

long game *n* **:** the phase of golf in which distance driving is a factor of first importance — compare SHORT GAME

long glass *n* **:** a nautical telescope

long grain *adj, of paper and paperboard* **:** having the machine direction running the long way of the sheet — called also *long fold;* compare BROAD FOLD

long green *n, slang* **:** paper money **:** CASH ⟨the boy will have plenty of the *long green* in a couple of years —Raymond Chandler⟩

long hair *also* **long–haired cat** *n* **:** a domestic cat having long silky outer fur and conforming in basic characteristics to the Persian type — compare SHORTHAIR

longhair \'=,=\ *n* [back-formation fr. *long-haired*] **1 a :** a man who wears his hair long **b :** an American Indian (as a Navaho) who has not attended school ⟨the ~*s* of the Southwest, if sometimes rejected for illiteracy, are sought to man jackhammers and bulldozers —Elizabeth S. Sergeant⟩ **2 a :** an artistically gifted person or one seriously interested in any of the arts; *esp* **:** a composer, performer, or lover of classical music ⟨the great and the unknown who make music in Manhattan go there — from ~*s* to hot pianists, drummers, and vibraharpists —*Newsweek*⟩ **b :** an impractical or unworldly intellectual **:** a scholar remote from everyday life ⟨described the younger writers as lugubrious and timid ~*s* huddling in chill academies —Irving Howe⟩ ⟨problems the hard-boiled businessmen seem willing to leave to the ~*s* —H.A.Wolff⟩ ⟨books are for women and ~*s* —Ellery Queen⟩

long–haired \'=¦=\ *adj* **1 :** having long hair **2 :** characterized by a devotion to abstract theory and impractical ideas ⟨making the crusader seem a *long-haired* dreamer who has never met a payroll —John Lardner⟩ ⟨were called reformers, cranks, enthusiastics, *long-haired* idealists —S.V.Benet⟩ **3 :** comprising, produced by, or appealing to aesthetes, idealists, or intellectuals ⟨the advanced guard of writers, the holy few who can only appeal endlessly to a limited and *long-haired* audience —Harrison Smith⟩ ⟨playing together in informal *long-haired* jam sessions —*Newsweek*⟩ ⟨*long-haired* fiction —*Time*⟩ **4 :** of, devoted to, or having the characteristics of classical music ⟨*long-haired* pianist⟩ ⟨*long-haired* audience⟩ ⟨*long-haired* concerto⟩

long–haired chimpanzee *n* **:** a chimpanzee (*Pan satyrus schweinfurthii*) that has exceptionally long hair and is found in forested country north and east of the Congo river

longhand \'=,=\ *n* **:** the characters used in ordinary writing **:** HANDWRITING — compare SHORTHAND

long handle *n* **:** the full force of the bat in cricket ⟨the batsman used the *long handle*⟩ ⟨give the bowling the *long handle*⟩

long haul *n* **1 :** a long distance; *specif* **:** transportation of goods between two distant points ⟨the furniture was crated for the *long haul* between New York and Chicago⟩ **2 :** a considerable period of time — used with *the* ⟨many old wives' rules are still valid for the *long haul* from cradle to the grave —Ernestine Evans⟩ ⟨over the *long haul* there is every reason to believe that the number of college students will increase steadily —R.C. Story⟩

longhead \'=,=\ *n* **1 :** a head with a low cephalic index **2 :** a dolichocephalic person

longheaded \'=¦==\ *adj* **1 :** having unusual foresight or wisdom **2 :** DOLICHOCEPHALIC — **long·head·ed·ly** *adv* — **long·head·ed·ness** *n* -ES

long hop *n* **:** a bowled ball in cricket that pitches short and takes a relatively long flight after rebounding

longhorn \'=,=\ *n* **1 :** a long-horned animal **2 a** (1) *cap* **:** an English breed of heavy beef cattle with low wide horns that is now little raised (2) *usu cap* **:** an animal of this breed **b :** any of certain practically extinct long-horned cattle of Spanish derivation formerly common in southwestern U. S. esp. in Texas **3** *or* **longhorn cheese :** mild cheddar cheese of a specified form and weight

long–horned beetle *also* **longhorn beetle** \'=,=-\ *n* **:** any of various beetles that constitute the family Cerambycidae and are usu. distinguished by their very long antennae

long–horned grasshopper *n* **:** any of various grasshoppers that constitute the family Tettigoniidae and are distinguished by their very long antennae — see KATYDID

long horse *n* **1 :** a vaulting apparatus that is similar to a side horse but has one end elongated and is placed for vaulting in the direction of its length **2 :** a gymnastic event on the long horse

long horse

longhouse \'=,=\ *n* **1 a :** a communal dwelling often over 100 feet long used by some No. American Indians (as the Iroquois) **b :** a similar dwelling used by some peoples of the Pacific **2 :** a major council of some No. American Indians (as Iroquois)

long hundred *n* **:** a unit of quantity for countable objects (as fish) equal to 120 objects or to some other number larger than 100

long hundredweight *n* **:** HUNDREDWEIGHT b — see MEASURE table

long hunter *n* **:** a resident of an eastern frontier settlement of late 18th century America accustomed to spending long continuous periods hunting in the mountains of Tennessee and Kentucky

longi- *comb form* [ME, fr. L, fr. *longus* — more at LONG] **1 :** long ⟨*longi*caudal⟩ ⟨*longi*pennate⟩ ⟨*longi*rostrine⟩ **2 :** longitudinal ⟨*longi*section⟩

lon·gi·col·lous \¦länjə¦käləs\ *adj* [*longi-* + L *collum* neck + E *-ous*] **:** having a long beak or neck ⟨a ~ perithecium⟩

lon·gi·cone \'länjə,kōn\ *n* [ISV *longi-* + *cone*] **:** a long conical shell characteristic of certain cephalopods; *also* **:** an animal having such a shell — **lon·gi·con·ic** \¦=¦känik\ *adj*

1lon·gi·corn \'länjə,kȯrn\ *adj* [NL *Longicornia*] **1 :** of or relating to the Cerambycidae **2** [*longi-* + *-corn*] **:** having long antennae

2longicorn \"\ *n* **:** LONG-HORNED BEETLE

lon·gi·cor·nia \,länjə'kȯ(r)nēə\ *n pl, cap* [NL, fr. *longi-* + L *-cornia*, neut. pl. of *-cornis* -corn] *in former classifications* **:** a group of beetles coextensive with Cerambycidae

long·ie \'lȯŋi\ *var of* LUNGIE

long·ies \'lȯŋēz *also* 'läŋ-\ *n pl* ['*long* + *-ie* + *-s*] **1 :** long underwear **2 :** long pants for boys

lon·gi·fo·lene \,länjə'fō,lēn\ *n* -s [ISV *longifol-* (fr. NL *longifolia* — specific epithet of *Pinus longifolia* — fr. *longi-* + *-folia*, fr. L *folium* leaf) + *-ene* — more at BLADE] **:** a liquid tricyclic sesquiterpene $C_{15}H_{24}$ occurring in various turpentines (as from *Pinus longifolia*, *P. ponderosa*, or *P. torreyana*)

lon·gil·o·quence \län'jiləkwən(t)s\ *n* [*longi-* + *-loquence* (as in *grandiloquence*)] **:** LONG-WINDEDNESS

long·ing \'lȯŋiŋ, -ŋēŋ *also* 'läŋ-\ *n* -s [ME *longing, langing*, fr. OE *langung*, fr. *longian, langian* to long + *-ung* -ing — more at LONG] **:** an eager desire esp. for something remote or unattainable **:** CRAVING ⟨this first sight of him must answer for the amassed ~*s* of 20 years —Anne S. Mehdevi⟩ ⟨pined away with ~ for ancient Greece —W.A.Kaufmann⟩

long·ing·ly *adv* **:** in a longing manner

long·ing·ness *n* -ES **:** LONGING, DESIRE

lon·gin·ian \län'jinēən\ *adj, usu cap* [Dionysius Cassius *Longinus*, 3d cent. A.D. Greek philosopher and rhetorician + E *-ian*] **:** of or characteristic of Longinus ⟨the perennial dialectic between Horatian technique and *Longinian* inspiration —Harry Levin⟩

lon·gin·qui·ty \län'jiŋkwəd·ē\ *n* -ES [L *longinquitas*, fr. *longinquus* distant (fr. *longus* long) + *-itas* -ity — more at LONG] *archaic* **:** remoteness in space or time

long iron *n* **1 :** a golf iron (as a No. 1, No. 2, or No. 3 iron) that has a long shaft and relatively slight loft and is used for hitting a long relatively low ball **2 :** a shot or stroke made with a long iron — compare SHORT IRON

1lon·gi·ros·trine \¦länjə¦rästrən, -rä,strīn\ *adj* [*longi-* + *rostr-* + *-ine*] **:** having a long jaw

2longirostrine \"\ *n* -s **:** a long-jawed creature; *specif* **:** one of the long-jawed primitive proboscideans of the family Gomphotheriidae

lon·gi·section \¦länjə+\ *n* [*longi-* + *section*] **:** a longitudinal section

long·ish \'lȯŋish, -ēsh *also* 'läŋ-\ *adj* ['*long* + *-ish*] **:** somewhat long **:** moderately long ⟨followed by a ~ courtship — a couple of years or more —Robert Reid⟩ ⟨the ~ hair, the mustache and Vandyke, the bohemian air —Claudia Cassidy⟩

lon·gis·si·mus dor·si \län'jisəməs'dȯrsē\ *n* [NL, lit., the longest of the back] **:** the middle and largest division of the sacrospinalis muscle

lon·gi·tude \'länjə,tüd, -ə,tyüd\ *n* -s [ME, fr. L *longitudo*, fr. *longi-* + *-tudo* -tude] **1 a :** measure or distance along the longest line **:** LENGTH **b** *archaic* **:** long duration **2 a :** angular distance measured on a great circle of reference from the intersection of the adopted zero meridian with this reference circle to the similar intersection of the meridian passing through the object — used esp. in astronomy and geodesy; see CELESTIAL LONGITUDE, GALACTIC LONGITUDE **b :** the arc or portion of the earth's equator intersected between the meridian of a given place and the prime meridian (as from Greenwich, England) or sometimes from the capital of a country (as from Washington or Paris) and expressed either in degrees or in time, the length of a degree varying as the cosine of the latitude so that it is 69.65 statute miles at the equator and 53.43 miles at 40 degrees latitude ⟨the ~ of New York is 74 degrees or 4 hours 56 minutes west of Greenwich⟩

longitude by account *or* **longitude by dead reckoning :** the approximate longitude of a ship as calculated by dead reckoning

longitude of node : the angular distance of the node of a planet's or comet's orbit eastward along the ecliptic from the vernal equinox

longitude of perihelion : the heliocentric longitude of the perihelion point of a planet's or comet's orbit as usu. measured along the ecliptic to the orbit's node and thence along the orbit to the perihelion point

longitude signal *n* **:** a telegraphic or radio time signal sent out from a station whose longitude is known and received at other stations whose longitude is to be determined from the differences in local time

1lon·gi·tu·di·nal \¦länjə¦tüdᵊnəl, -ə¦tyü-\ *adj* [F, fr. MF, fr. L *longitudin-, longitudo* longitude + MF *-al*] **1 :** of or relating to the lengthwise dimension **:** AXIAL ⟨the ~ extent of the building⟩ ⟨~ stability⟩ ⟨the ~ strength of a beam⟩ **2 a :** extending in length **:** placed or running lengthwise — opposed to *transverse* ⟨contour plowing has largely replaced ~ plowing on sloping land⟩ **b :** extending along or relating to the anteroposterior axis of a body or part ⟨a fish with yellow ~ stripes⟩ **c :** ECTOMORPHIC **3 :** extending over a period of time; *specif* **:** dealing with the growth and change of an individual or group over a period of years ⟨a ~ study of juvenile delinquents over a five-year period⟩ — **lon·gi·tu·di·nal·ly** \-ᵊnəlē, -li\ *adv*

2longitudinal \"\ *n* -s **1 :** a longitudinally located body part (as a sinus or nerve) **2 :** LONGERON **3 :** one of the fore-and-aft continuous or intercostal girders used in large merchant ships and in nearly all warships to give the required strength and stiffness

longitudinal bulkhead *n* **:** a bulkhead that extends fore and aft

longitudinal crevasse *n* **:** a crevasse roughly parallel to the direction of ice movement that forms where a glacier spreads laterally

longitudinal fault *n* **:** a geological fault with its strike parallel to that of the regional structure

longitudinal framing *n* **:** ISHERWOOD SYSTEM

longitudinal metacenter *n* **:** the point in a vertical line through the center of gravity of a ship where this line is intersected by a second vertical line through the center of buoyancy when the ship is inclined at a very small angle in a fore-and-aft direction

longitudinal metacentric height *n* **:** the distance between the center of gravity of a ship and the longitudinal metacenter

longitudinal system *n* **:** a method of constructing steel ships in which the required strength and stiffness in a fore-and-aft direction is obtained by working in longitudinals — compare ISHERWOOD SYSTEM

longitudinal valley *n* **:** a valley parallel to adjacent folds or mountain ridges **:** STRIKE VALLEY

longitudinal wave *n* **:** a wave (as a sound wave) in which the particles of the medium vibrate in the direction of the line of advance of the wave

long jack *n, usu cap J* [fr. the name *Jack*] **1 :** an Australian tree (*Flindersia oxleyana*) with smooth bark and yellow wood **2 :** the wood of the long Jack tree

longjaw \'=,=\ *or* **longjaws** *n* **1 a :** a cisco (*Leucichthys alpenae*) of Lake Huron and Lake Erie **b :** any of various other ciscoes of the Great Lakes **2 :** NEEDLEFISH

long–jawed \'=¦=\ *adj* **1 :** having a long jaw **2** *of rope* **:** having lost most of its twist

long jenny *n* **:** a losing hazard in English billiards in which the ball is played in a corner pocket from the far end of the table — compare SHORT JENNY

long john *n, usu cap J* [fr. the name *John*] **:** a timber tree (*Triplaris surinamensis*) of the family Polygonaceae found along the lower Amazon and in the Guianas

long johns *n pl* [fr. the name *John* + *-s*] **:** long underwear

long jump *n, Brit* **:** BROAD JUMP

long knife *n, usu cap L&K* **:** BIG KNIFE

longl *abbr* longitudinal

1longleaf \'=,=\ *n* **:** LONGLEAF PINE

2longleaf \"\ *adj* **:** made from longer leaves rather than the small tip leaves ⟨~ tea⟩

longleaf pine *also* **long–leaved pine** \'=,=-\ *n* **1 :** a large pine (*Pinus palustris*) of the southern U.S. that has very long dark green leaves, long cones, thin orange-brown bark, and gnarled twisted limbs and that is an important timber tree and the chief New World source of naval stores — called also *Georgia pine* **2 :** the rather heavy tough coarse-grained reddish orange wood of the longleaf pine — called also *southern pine*

longleaf willow *n* **:** any of several willows (as a sandbar willow) with slender elongated leaves

long leg *n* **:** a fielding position in cricket on the leg side relatively far from the batsman; *also* **:** a player fielding in this position — compare SHORT LEG; see CRICKET illustration

long–legged bat \'=,=(=)-\ *n* **:** a small brown bat (*Myotis volans*) of western North America

long–legged duck *n, South* **:** TREE DUCK

longlegs \'=,=\ *n pl but sing or pl in constr* **1 :** STILT **2 :** DADDY LONGLEGS

longline \'=,=\ *n* **:** a long heavy fishline with numerous baited hooks that sometimes extends for several miles and that may be used as a setline or arranged to drift with current or tide

long–line \'=¦=\ *adj* **:** of or relating to long-distance communication or transportation ⟨*long-line* telephone workers⟩ ⟨*long-line* trains⟩ ⟨*long-line* trucking⟩

long–liner \'=,==\ *n* [*longline* + *-er*] **:** one that fishes with a longline

long–lining \'=,==\ *n* **:** fishing with a longline

long–lived \'lȯŋ¦līvd, -livd *also* 'läŋ-\ *adj* [ME *longe lived*, fr. *longe* long + *lived*] **1 a :** having a long life ⟨a *long-lived* man⟩ **:** typically having long life ⟨a *long-lived* family⟩ **b :** capable of having a long life by reason of constitutional peculiarities ⟨a *long-lived* tree⟩ **2 :** lasting a long time **:** ENDURING ⟨a successful textbook is *long-lived* and stays in print for several years —*Education Digest*⟩ — **long–lived·ness** *n* -ES

long logger *n* **:** a logger in the western American coastal fir and redwood regions

long·ly *adv* [ME *longly, langly*, fr. *long, lang* long + *-ly* — more at LONG] **:** at or to a considerable length **:** for a considerable distance ⟨the lawn sloping ~ up to the brick house —Ross Lockridge⟩

long mark *n* **:** MACRON

long measure *n* **:** LINEAR MEASURE

long meter *also* **long measure** *n* **:** a quatrain in iambic tetrameter lines with the second and fourth lines rhyming and often the first and third lines rhyming — compare BALLAD METER

long moss *n* **:** SPANISH MOSS

longneck \'=,=\ *n* **1** *North* **:** PINTAIL 1 **2** *Eng* **:** LITTLE BITTERN

long–neck clam \'=,=-\ *n* **:** SOFT-SHELL CLAM

long–necked turtle \'=,=-\ *n* **:** a common Australian turtle (*Chelodina longicollis*) that is distinguished by a greatly elongated neck and a peculiar garlicky odor

long·ness *n* -ES [ME *longnesse, langnesse*, fr. OE *langnes*, fr. *long, lang* long + *-nes* -ness] **:** the quality or state of being long

long nine *n* **:** a long thin cheap cigar formerly made in the U.S. and packed in barrel lots for shipment

longnose dace *also* **long–nosed dace** \'=,=-\ *n* **:** a common dace (*Rhinichthys cataractae*) that is olive green to dusky brown above with dark blotches on the sides and pale underparts and is common in clean swift streams of the central U.S.

long–nosed cattle louse *n* **:** a widely distributed sucking louse (*Linognathus vituli*) that feeds on cattle

long–nosed squirrel *n* **:** any of several Oriental squirrels that have the snout prolonged: as **a :** a member of a genus (*Dremomys*) of brightly mottled arboreal forms **b :** a short-tailed ground squirrel (genus *Rhinosciurus*) of Malaysia

longnose gar *also* **long–nosed gar** *n* **:** a gar (*Lepisosteus osseus*) that has a snout more than twice as long as the rest of its head and is widely distributed in rivers and lakes of the eastern and north central sections of the U.S.

longnose sucker *or* **long–nosed sucker** *n* **:** NORTHERN SUCKER

long nutmeg *n* **:** MACASSAR NUTMEG

lon·go·bard \'läŋgə,bärd\ *n, pl* **longobards** \-dz\ *or* **longobar·di** \,==bär,dī, -dē\ *cap* [L *Longobardi, Langobardi*] **:** LOMBARD — **lon·go·bar·dic** \,==¦bärdik\ *adj, usu cap*

long of *prep* [by shortening] *dial* **:** along of

long off *n* **:** a fielding position in cricket on the off side of the field well behind the bowler; *also* **:** a player fielding in this position — see CRICKET illustration

long–oil \'=¦=\ *adj* **:** containing a relatively high proportion of drying oil to resin ⟨spar varnishes are *long-oil* varnishes⟩ — compare OIL LENGTH

long on *n* **:** a fielding position in cricket on the on side of the field well behind the bowler; *also* **:** a player fielding in this position — see CRICKET illustration

long particular meter *n* **:** an iambic hymn meter of six four-foot lines to the stanza

long pennant *n* **:** a long narrow piece of bunting generally carried at the masthead of a government vessel in commission

long pepper *n* **1 a :** the fruit of an eastern Asiatic pepper (*Piper longum*) consisting of elongated spikes that are ground to produce a condiment somewhat sweeter and more aromatic but less pungent than common pepper **b :** any of several plants of the genus *Piper* (as the kava) **2 a :** a hot pepper (*Capsicum frutescens longum*) with extremely pungent slender elongated drooping red or yellow fruits that are the chief source of cayenne pepper **b :** the fruit of a long pepper

long–period variable *n* **:** an intrinsic variable star whose light fluctuations are fairly regular and require many months or several years to complete one cycle

long pig *n* **:** a human victim of a cannibal feast

long play *n* **:** a long-playing record

long–playing \'=¦==\ *adj* **:** of or relating to a microgroove record having a diameter of 10 or 12 inches and turning at 33⅓ revolutions per minute

long primer *n* **:** an old size of type (approximately 10 point) between bourgeois and small pica — compare POINT SYSTEM

long pull *n* **:** LONG RUN

long purples *n pl* **:** MALE ORCHIS ⟨with fantastic garlands did she come of crow-flowers, nettles, daisies, and *long purples* — Shak.⟩

long–range \'=¦=\ *adj* **1 :** involving or taking into account a long period of time ⟨the *long-range* inadequacy of the world's resources of coal, gas, oil, and uranium —Farrington Daniels & R.A.Morgen⟩ ⟨a *long-range* study for development of a national postwar monetary and fiscal program —*Current Biog.*⟩ **2 a :** relating to long distances ⟨*long-range* travel⟩ **b :** designed for or fit for long distances ⟨*long-range* rockets⟩

long rate *n* **:** TERM RATE

long ream *n* **:** twenty quires of paper of 25 sheets each

long rifle *n* **:** KENTUCKY RIFLE

long robe *n* **:** the legal profession ⟨gentlemen of the *long robe*⟩

long roll *n* **:** a prolonged roll of the drums formerly the signal for troops to fall in immediately

longroot \'=,=\ *n* **:** PINE-BARREN SANDWORT

long run *n* **:** a period of time sufficiently long to permit all factors in a situation to exercise their full influence — used

chiefly in the phrase *in the long run* ⟨it is obvious that in the *long run* automation will be of great benefit to us all —John Diebold⟩
longs *pl of* LONG, *pres 3d sing of* LONG
long s *also* **long ess** *n* **:** a form of the letter *s* once generally used in writing and printing but now used only for archaic effect

ſ, ʃ
long s

longs and shorts *n pl* **:** LONG-AND-SHORT WORK
long scale *n* **:** GLOVER SCALE
long·schat pine \ˈlȯŋ,shät- *also* ˈläŋ,shät-\ *n* [*longschat* fr. ¹*long* + *shat*, n.] **:** a common pitch pine (*Pinus rigida*) of eastern No. America
longshanks \ˈ⸗,⸗\ *n pl but sing or pl in constr* **:** STILT
longship \ˈ⸗,⸗\ *n* **:** a long ship similar to a galley used by the old Northmen
longshore \ˈ⸗¦⸗\ *adj* [short for ¹*alongshore*] **:** of or belonging to the seacoast or a seaport ⟨the ~ herring season started with a swing —G.G.Carter⟩ ⟨~ work⟩
longshore current *n* **:** LITTORAL CURRENT
long·shore·man \ˈ⸗¦⸗mən\ *n, pl* **longshoremen** [*longshore* + *man*] **:** one who is employed at a seaport to work at the loading and unloading of ships
long·shor·ing *pronunc at* LONGSHORE + iŋ\ *n* -s [*longshoreman* + *-ing*] **:** the act or occupation of working as a longshoreman
long-short story \ˈ⸗ˈ⸗ˈ⸗-\ *n* **:** a short story of more than average length **:** a prose narrative intermediate between a short story and a short novel
long shot *n* **1 :** an entry (as in a horse race) that seems to have little chance of winning ⟨looking over the *long shots* with his last two dollars —Tom O'Reilly⟩ ⟨a *long shot* won the race⟩ **2 :** a bet in which the chance of winning is very slight but in which one can win much more than he wagers ⟨the lure of the *long shot* is practically irresistible to the average human being —C.B.Davis⟩ **3 :** a venture or act involving great risk but promising a great reward if successful ⟨was attracted by such *long shots* as expeditions to search for buried treasure⟩ **4 :** a motion-picture shot made with the camera at a considerable distance from the scene — **by a long shot** *adv* **:** by a great deal ⟨his labors haven't ended there — not *by a long shot* —J.D.Adams⟩
long·shucks \ˈlȯŋ,shəks *also* ˈläŋ-\ *n pl but sing or pl in constr*, *also* **longshucks pine :** LOBLOLLY PINE 1
long sight *n* **:** HYPEROPIA
longsighted \ˈ⸗¦⸗⸗\ *adj* **:** FARSIGHTED — **long·sight·ed·ness** *n* -ES
long since *adv* [²*long*] **1 :** LONG AGO ⟨he *long since* gave up the attempt to climb the mountain⟩ **2 :** for a long time ⟨has *long since* been recognized as a great writer⟩
long six *n* **:** a candle weighing a sixth of a pound
long-sleev·er \ˈläŋˈslēvə(r)\ *n* -s *Austral slang* **:** a large drink esp. of beer
long smut *n* **:** a disease of the ovaries of sorghum and millet caused by fungi of the genus *Tolyposporium*
long·some \ˈlȯŋsəm *also* ˈläŋ-\ *adj* [ME *longsum, langsum*, fr. OE, fr. *long, lang* long + *-sum* -some — more at LONG] **:** tediously long ⟨~ hours of overwork —William Barnes⟩ — **long·some·ly** *adv* — **long·some·ness** *n* -ES
long splice *n* **:** a splice without an appreciable increase of circumference that is used when the rope must run over a sheave or through a hole
longspur \ˈ⸗,⸗\ *n* [fr. the length of its hind claws] **:** any of several long-clawed fringillid birds chiefly of the genus *Calcarius* that inhabit the arctic regions and the Great Plains of No. America, are usu. strikingly marked with black, white, and ocher in the male, and travel in immense flocks during migration — see ALASKA LONGSPUR, CHESTNUT-COLLARED LONGSPUR, LAPLAND LONGSPUR, MC COWN'S LONGSPUR, SMITH'S LONGSPUR
long-spurred violet \ˈ⸗,⸗-\ *n* **:** a violet (*Viola rostrata*) of northeastern No. America that has lilac-purple flowers with a long slender spur
long stack *n, NewEng* **:** an oblong haystack with a ridged top
long-standing \ˈ⸗¦⸗⸗\ *adj* **1 :** having existed for a long time ⟨aroused hope that the *long-standing* conflict between the two organizations would be ended —*Collier's Yr. Bk.*⟩ **2 :** capable of existing for a long time ⟨might . . . become a *long-standing* demonstration of how to occupy a military base —*Harper's*⟩
long-staple \ˈ⸗¦⸗⸗\ *adj* **:** having relatively long fibers
long-stemmed \ˈ⸗¦⸗\ *adj* **1 :** having a long stem or trunk ⟨strolled on beneath the *long-stemmed* trees —George Meredith⟩ **2 :** tall and slender ⟨a *long-stemmed* redhead of breathtaking loveliness —C.J.Rolo⟩
longstone \ˈ⸗,⸗\ *n* **:** MENHIR
long stop *n* **:** a fielding position in cricket directly behind the wicketkeeper; *also* **:** a fielder occupying this position
long-straw pine *n* **1 :** LONGLEAF PINE **2 :** LOBLOLLY PINE
long-sufferance \ˈ⸗ˈ⸗(⸗)⸗\ *n, archaic* **:** LONG-SUFFERING **syn** see PATIENCE
¹**long-suffering** \ˈ⸗ˈ⸗(⸗)⸗\ *n* **:** long and patient endurance of offense ⟨it shows much *long-suffering* in you to put up with him —Thomas Hardy⟩ **syn** see PATIENCE
²**long-suffering** \ˈ⸗ˈ⸗(⸗)⸗\ *adj* **:** showing patience under long provocation ⟨a *long-suffering* wife abused by an evil husband —J.D.Hart⟩ — **long-suf·fer·ing·ly** *adv*
long suit *n* **1 a :** a holding of more than the average number of cards in a suit (as four or more cards in bridge) **b :** the suit of which one has the most cards in a hand **2 :** the activity or quality in which a person excels ⟨cooking is her *long suit*⟩
long sweetening *n, South & Midland* **:** sweetening in liquid form (as molasses) — compare SHORT SWEETENING
long tackle *n* **:** TOP BURTON
long-tackle block *n* **:** a block that has a long assemblage of ropes and pulleys
longtail \ˈ⸗,⸗\ *n* **1 a :** an animal (as a dog) that has an uncut tail **b :** GREYHOUND **2 a :** OLD-SQUAW **b :** TROPIC BIRD
long-tailed blue \ˈ⸗,⸗-\ *n, archaic* **:** a blue tailcoat
long-tailed chat *n* **:** a long-tailed yellow-breasted chat (*Icteria virens longicauda*) that is found in the Pacific coast region of the U.S.
long-tailed cuckoo *n* **:** KOEL
long-tailed duck *n* **:** OLD-SQUAW
long-tailed jaeger *n* **:** a relatively small and very graceful jaeger (*Stercorarius longicaudus*) that has extremely long middle tail feathers
long-tailed mealybug *n* **:** a mealybug (*Pseudococcus adonidum*) that is a minor pest of citrus and avocado in California and certain other regions
long-tailed paca *n* **:** FALSE PACA
long-tailed pangolin *n* **:** an African pangolin (*Manis macrura*) that has a tail nearly twice the length of its body
long-tailed porcupine *n* **:** a porcupine (*Trichys lipura*) of Borneo and Sumatra that has short spines and a long tail
long-tailed shrew *n* **:** an American shrew of the genus *Sorex*
long-tailed skipper *n* **:** any butterfly of the genus *Urbanus* or *Chioides* (family Hesperiidae) marked by a prolongation of the posterior margin of each hindwing which suggests a tail
long-tailed tiger cat *n* **:** MARGAY
long-tailed tit *or* **long-tailed titmouse** *n* **:** a small titmouse (*Aegithalos caudatus*) of Europe and northern Asia with a long tail and plumage largely pink and white — called also *bottle tit*
long-tailed weasel *n* **:** the common American weasel (*Mustela frenata*) that occurs in various races from Central America to well within the arctic circle and is distinguished from related forms by its large size and long black-tipped tail — compare ERMINE
long-term \ˈ⸗ˈ¦⸗\ *adj* **1 :** extending over or involving a relatively long period of time ⟨the *long-term* reconstruction of countries damaged by war —W.S.Sayre⟩ ⟨*long-term* earnest championing of American art — Aline B. Saarinen⟩ — opposed to *short-term* **2 a :** of, relating to, or constituting a financial gain, loss, operation, or obligation based on a term usu. of more than 10 years **b :** of or relating to capital assets held for more than six months
long-term bond *n* **:** a financial obligation that runs for at least five years and usu. for a much longer period
long-termer \ˈ⸗ˈ¦⸗⸗\ *n* **:** one serving a long term esp. of imprisonment
longtime \ˈ⸗,⸗\ *adj* **:** LONG-STANDING ⟨a ~ friend⟩
long·tim·er \ˈ⸗¦tīmə(r)\ *n* [*long time* + *-er*] **1 :** one that has been in a place, position, or activity for a long time **:** OLD-TIMER, OLD HAND **2 :** a prisoner serving a long term **:** LONG-TERMER
long-toed stint \ˈ⸗,⸗-\ *n* **:** a small sandpiper (*Erolia subminuta*) that breeds in eastern Siberia and winters in southeastern Asia
long tom *n* [fr. *Tom*, nickname for *Thomas*] **1** *usu cap L&T* **a :** a long pivot gun formerly carried on the deck of a warship ⟨the *Long Tom* roared from his pivot and the grapeshot fell like hail —J.J.Roche⟩ **b :** a large gun having a long range used on land; *esp* **:** a U.S. 155 millimeter rifled gun used during World War II **2 a** *Eng* **:** LONG-TAILED TIT **b :** any of several Australian needlefishes **3 :** a trough for washing gold-bearing earth
long ton *n* **:** TON 1a — see MEASURE table
long tongue *n* **1 :** WRYNECK **2** *dial* **:** GOSSIP
long·ton hall \ˈlȯŋtən-, ˈläŋtən-\ *n, usu cap L&H* [fr. *Longton Hall*, Staffordshire, England] **:** a faintly greenish glassy English 18th century soft-paste porcelain often glazed in rich blue with decoration in opaque white enamel
longue \ˈlȯŋ\ *n* -s [alter. of ⁴*lunge*] **:** LAKE TROUT b
lon·gueur \lōⁿ'gœr(·)\ *n* -s [F, lit., length, fr. OF *longour*, fr. *lonc, long* long, fr. L *longus* — more at LONG] **:** a dull and tedious passage or section (as of a book, play, or musical composition) — usu. used in pl. ⟨written in a style with ~s as thick as treacle —H.J.Laski⟩ ⟨his ~s, his exactions upon the deep understanding of his performers and of his listeners —J.N.Burk⟩
lon·gu·lite \ˈläŋgyə,līt\ *n* -s [G *longulit*, fr. L *longulus* rather long (fr. *longus* long) + G *-it* -ite] **:** a crystallite of elongated form
long vacation *n, chiefly Brit* **:** the summer vacation of universities and law courts
long view *n* **:** an examination of or approach to a problem or situation that emphasizes the long-range factors involved ⟨the indispensable task of supplying *long views* about the problems of society —Zechariah Chafee⟩
longwall system \ˈ⸗,⸗-\ *n* [*longwall* fr. ¹*long* + *wall*] **:** a method of coal mining in which the working face extends entirely across the seam, the work proceeds either away from or toward the main shaft, and the roof is allowed to cave in behind the workers
¹**longways** \ˈ⸗,⸗\ *adv* [¹*long* + *-ways*] **1 :** LENGTHWISE ⟨the books lie upright, ~, or diagonally on the shelves —Stephen Spender⟩ **2** *dancing* **:** in two straight lines ⟨this number is danced ~⟩
²**longways** \"\ *or* **longways dance** *also* **longway** \ˈ⸗,⸗\ *or* **longway dance** *n* **:** a folk dance in which the basic formation is two lines of couples facing each other usu. with men on one side and women on the other — compare CONTREDANCE
long whist *n* **:** whist played under the rule that 10 points constitute a game
long-winded \ˈ⸗¦⸗⸗\ *adj* **1 :** having the capacity to take a long sustaining breath **:** not easily subject to loss of breath ⟨men of endurance, deep-chested, *long-winded*, tough —R.W.Emerson⟩ **2 a :** tediously long in speaking or writing ⟨the most *long-winded* master of modern letters —*Time*⟩ **b :** LONG-DRAWN-OUT, TEDIOUS ⟨it begins with "in short" and proceeds to be *long-winded* —A.T.Quiller-Couch⟩ — **long-wind·ed·ly** *adv* — **long-wind·ed·ness** *n* -ES
longwise \ˈ⸗,⸗\ *adv* **:** LENGTHWISE
longwood \ˈ⸗,⸗\ *n* **:** a veneer flitch of substantial length
long-wool *or* **long-wooled** \ˈ⸗¦⸗\ *adj* [*long* + *wool* or *wooled*, fr. *wool* + *-ed*] **:** of or relating to a class of domestic sheep that have long but coarse wool ⟨Leicester, Cotswold, and Lincoln are breeds of *long-wool* sheep⟩
longwool \ˈ⸗,⸗\ *n* **:** a long-wool sheep
long·xuyen \ˈlau̇ŋ¦swēn\ *adj, usu cap* [fr. *Longxuyen*, So. Vietnam] **:** of or from the city of Longxuyen, So. Vietnam **:** of the kind or style prevalent in Longxuyen
long yearling *n* **:** an animal between one and two years old esp. when nearer two than one
long·yi \ˈläŋ,yē\ *var of* LUNGI
lo·nic·era \lōˈnisərə, ˌlänəˈsirə\ *n, cap* [NL, after Adam *Lonicerus* (Lonitzer) †1586 Ger. botanist] **:** a genus (family Caprifoliaceae) of erect or climbing shrubs comprising the honeysuckles that have a tubular or infundibuliform corolla and fruit in the form of a berry — compare HONEYSUCKLE
lonk \ˈläŋk\ *n* [by shortening & alter. fr. *Lancashire*, England] **1** *usu cap* **:** an English breed of large hardy black-faced mutton type sheep **2** -s *often cap* **:** an animal of the Lonk breed
lon·tar \ˈläntə(r)\ *also* **lontar palm** *n* -s [Malay *lontar*, fr. Jav *ron-tal*, fr. *ron* leaf + *tal* Palmyra palm] **:** PALMYRA 1
¹**loo** \ˈlü\ *interj* [by shortening] **:** HALLOO
²**loo** \"\ *vb* -ED/-ING/-s *now dial* **:** HALLOO
³**loo** \"\ *n* -s [short for obs. E *lanterloo*, fr. F *lanturelu, lanturlu* piffle, twaddle, fr. *lanturelu, lanturlu*, meaningless syllables occurring in the refrain of a song of the early 17th century] **1 :** an ancient card game in which after contributions are made to a pool three or five cards are dealt to each player and the winner of each trick or the majority of tricks takes an agreed portion of the pool with the losing players being obligated to contribute an agreed amount to the next pool **2 :** money staked at loo **3 :** an instance of being looed
⁴**loo** \"\ *vt* -ED/-ING/-s **:** to obligate to contribute an agreed sum to a new pool at loo as a result of failing to win a trick
⁵**loo** \"\ *var of* LEW
⁶**loo** \"\ *n* -s [perh. modif. of F *lieux d'aisance*] **:** TOILET 5
loo·by \ˈlübē\ *n* -ES [ME *loby*; prob. akin to Flem *lobbe* simpleton — more at LOB] **:** an awkward clumsy fellow often characterized by laziness and stupidity **:** LUBBER
looby-loo \ˌlübēˈlü\ *n* [fr. *looby-loo*, meaningless syllables in the text of the song] **:** a singing game in which children move arms, legs, and head in accordance with the words of the song
looch *var of* LOHOCH
lood \ˈlüd\ *Scot var of* LOUD
loo·ey *or* **loo·ie** \ˈlüē\ *n* -s [by shortening & alter.] *slang* **:** LIEUTENANT
loof \ˈlüf\ *n* -s [ME *lofe*, fr. ON *lōfi* — more at GLOVE] *chiefly Scot* **:** the palm of the hand
loofah *var of* LUFFA
¹**look** \ˈlu̇k\ *vb* -ED/-ING/-s [ME *looken, loken*, fr. OE *lōcian*; akin to MD *loeken* to look, OS *lōcōn*] *vt* **1 :** to make sure or take care (that something is done) ⟨censor to ~ that no man lived idly —Edward Gee⟩ **2 :** to ascertain by the use of one's eyes ⟨I will ~ what time the train starts⟩ **3 a :** to exercise the power of vision upon **:** EXAMINE, OBSERVE, PERCEIVE **b** *archaic* **:** to look up ⟨if I ~*ed* a word today —John Adams⟩ **c** *dial* **:** to count (as sheep) esp. to determine whether any have strayed **4** *archaic* **:** to search for **:** SEEK ⟨at her leisure hours she ~*s* goose eggs —Samuel Johnson⟩ **5 :** EXPECT ⟨I never ~ to have a mistress that I shall love half as well —Henry Brooke⟩ **6** *dial* **:** to pick over ⟨she ~*ed* the spinach⟩ **7** *archaic* **:** to influence or bring into a place or condition by the exercise of the power of vision ⟨thou has *look'd* thyself into my grace —Shak.⟩ **8 :** to express by use of the eyes or by an expression of the countenance ⟨not an eye to ~ comfort to you —Douglas Jerrold⟩ ⟨the friar ~*ed* his surprise —Robert Brennan⟩ **9 :** to have an appearance that befits or accords with ⟨the actors . . . ~*ed* the parts they were called upon to play —*Linguaphone Mag.*⟩ ⟨he ~*ed* a typical sturdy John Bull —C.H.Driver⟩ ⟨she ~*ed* her age⟩ **~** *vi* **1 a :** to exercise the power of vision ⟨he ~*s*⟩ ⟨~ before you leap⟩ — used in the imperative as an interjection esp. to call attention ⟨~, here he comes⟩ **b :** to exercise this power in a particular direction **:** direct the eyes or one's attention upon someone or something ⟨from my elevated station I ~*ed* down —Thomas De Quincey⟩ ⟨~*ed* from one to the other —Carson McCullers⟩ ⟨~*ed* abroad for their inspiration —O. Elfrida Saunders⟩ ⟨~ at the map⟩ ⟨if we ~ at the successful serious novels of the last decade —Lionel Trilling⟩ **c :** to direct the eyes in a manner indicative of a specified feeling ⟨~*ed* sadly upon him⟩ **2 :** to have the appearance of being **:** appear to the eye **:** SEEM ⟨her . . . lips ~*ed* parched and unnatural —Ellen Glasgow⟩ ⟨his face ~*ed* almost gray —T.B.Costain⟩ ⟨it ~*s* as if . . . varnishes will meet very severe competition during the coming year —C.L. Boltz⟩ ⟨it begins to ~ as though the social scientist . . . is actually a dialectician —R.M.Weaver⟩ **3 a :** to have a specified direction **:** afford a specified outlook **:** open on or into something ⟨a village that ~*ed* across the river —Ernest Hemingway⟩ ⟨the little terrace which ~*ed* seaward —John Buchan⟩ **b :** to face or turn in a specific direction ⟨their nostrils . . . ~ downwards —T.H.Huxley⟩ **4 :** to gaze in wonder or surprise **:** STARE ⟨you should have seen them ~⟩ **5 :** to show a tendency **:** to tend or point in a specific direction ⟨the evidence ~*s* to acquittal⟩ **syn** see EXPECT, SEE — **look after 1 :** to follow with the eyes **:** look in the direction of ⟨and with dimm'd eyes *look after* him —Shak.⟩ **2** *archaic* **:** to search for **:** SEEK ⟨the knave . . . hath all those requisites in him that folly and green minds *look after* —Shak.⟩ **3 :** to attend to **:** take care of **:** see to the safety or well-being of **:** TEND ⟨sent to . . . *look after* his interests —G.C.Sellery⟩ ⟨somebody . . . who *looked after* the children —Eden Phillpotts⟩ ⟨I daresay you can *look after* yourself —Andrew Young⟩ **4 :** to busy or concern oneself with **:** pay heed to **:** CONSIDER — **look a gift horse in the mouth :** to criticize and find fault with a gift — **look alive :** to be alert or quick — usu. used in the imperative — **look at :** to hold a mental attitude toward **:** CONSIDER, REGARD, VIEW ⟨his teachings are *looked at* too narrowly by many people⟩ ⟨easy to *look at* scientists in other countries as competitors —R.L.Meier & Eugene Rabinowitch⟩ — **look black :** to express anger or hostility by the use of one's eyes **:** FROWN, SCOWL — **look down one's nose :** to view with arrogance, disdain, or disapproval — usu. used with *at* ⟨the older residents have traditionally *looked down their noses* at the newcomers —A.G.Mezerik⟩ ⟨critics who *look down their noses* at these stories —Upton Sinclair⟩ — **look for 1 :** to await with hope or anticipation ⟨tell them they may *look for* me any day —Jane W. Carlyle⟩ ⟨finality is not to be *looked for* in . . . translation —J.C.Swaim⟩ **2 :** to search for **:** SEEK ⟨we had been *looking for* a house —Dana Burnet⟩ ⟨that's where you *look for* grouse in October —Corey Ford⟩ — **look forth** [ME *loken forth*, fr. *looken, loken* to look + *forth*] **:** to look out (as from a window) ⟨the warden . . . from old Baliol's tower *looks forth* —Sir Walter Scott⟩ — **look forward 1 :** to look into the future ⟨*looked forward* with the same ease that most people slip backward —John Mason Brown⟩ **2 a :** to look into the future with expectation (as of an event or development) ⟨*looked forward* to a hard year —J.S.Dickey⟩ ⟨*looked forward* to the time when under true Communism there would be no state —F.A. Ogg & Harold Zink⟩ **b :** to anticipate with pleasure or satisfaction ⟨they certainly *look forward* to meeting him⟩ ⟨did not *look forward* to living in the splendor of Government House —*Current Biog.*⟩ — **look here** *or* **look-a-here** — used in the imperative as an interjection to call attention and often to preface a protest, reprimand, or order — **look in the eye** *or* **look in the face :** to meet with a steady gaze as an indication of courage, confidence, or defiance — **look into 1 :** to inspect closely **:** examine carefully **:** INVESTIGATE ⟨*look into* the trade and investment opportunities —*advt*⟩ ⟨*look into* the population problem —A.L.Guérard⟩ ⟨decided to *look into* his background —Frank O'Leary⟩ **2 :** to consult (as a book) in a rapid or cursory manner ⟨*looked into* the chronicles of the middle ages —T.B.Macaulay⟩ ⟨have just *looked into* the . . . essay —O.W. Holmes †1935⟩ — **look like** *chiefly Brit* **:** to give promise of **:** show a likelihood of — used with a gerund ⟨the new age *looks like* being tougher than the old —Patrick Balfour⟩ ⟨at two months he *looked like* developing into a healthy . . . bird —*Sydney (Australia) Bull.*⟩ — **look of** *obs* **:** to direct one's gaze upon — **look on 1** *obs* **:** to regard favorably **:** ESTEEM ⟨I am not *look'd on* in the world —Shak.⟩ **2 :** to look upon ⟨people who now *look on* him as a reactionary —F.D. Roosevelt⟩ ⟨the average American . . . too often *looks on* books as furniture —John Barkham⟩ — **look the other way :** to direct one's attention away from something of which one disapproves or which one chooses to ignore — **look through 1 a :** to direct one's gaze through (as an opening or a transparent substance) ⟨we *looked through* the window⟩ ⟨the child *looked through* the screen door⟩ **b :** to see through ⟨he *looks* quite *through* the deeds of men —Shak.⟩ **c :** to gaze at as if through empty space **:** ignore haughtily or insolently ⟨the two Chinese spokesmen *looked* . . . *through* the correspondents they once knew —Peggy Durdin⟩ **2 :** to gaze over the whole of ⟨if one *looks* . . . *through* Russian history —Bernard Pares⟩; *esp* **:** to examine cursorily usu. from beginning to end ⟨the press service . . . *looked through* its files —Bruce Bliven b.1889⟩ ⟨they read or *looked through* a . . . number of weekly journals —M.K.Adler⟩ **3** *obs* **:** to be visible through ⟨that our drift *look through* our bad performance —Shak.⟩ — **look to 1 :** to direct one's attention to ⟨psychologists have tended to *look to* childhood for the sources of their troubles —D.M.Davin⟩ **2 :** to take care of **:** attend to ⟨ordered his own surgeon to *look to* the hurts of the captive —T.B.Macaulay⟩ **3 a :** to direct one's gaze at ⟨we *looked to* the sky at intervals —John Tyndall⟩ **b :** to keep watch upon ⟨constable, *look to* your prisoner —Maria Edgeworth⟩ **4 a :** to direct one's expectations to ⟨the American people *look to* the president for a unifying lead —D.W.Brogan⟩ **b :** to rely upon; *esp* **:** to count upon for something ⟨those who . . . *looked to* the printed word for inspiration —*Amer. Guide Series: N.J.*⟩ ⟨newspapers . . . no longer *look to* their subscribers as the major source of revenue —D.M.Potter⟩ **5 :** to look forward to ⟨can *look to* quiet in my old age —J.A.Froude⟩ — **look toward** *or* **look towards 1 :** to gaze or face in the direction of ⟨*looked towards* the speaker⟩ ⟨the city *looks toward* the river⟩ **2 :** to prepare for **:** ANTICIPATE ⟨*looked toward* the union of . . . some of the former provinces —C.L.Jones⟩ ⟨a definite policy *looking toward* the reduction of the number of public houses —D.W. McConnell⟩ — **look upon 1 :** to hold an opinion of **:** CONSIDER, REGARD ⟨each family *looked upon* this zone as personal property —L.S.B.Leakey⟩ ⟨generally *looks upon* a victim of airsickness as an object of ridicule —H.G.Armstrong⟩ **2 :** to direct one's gaze at **:** OBSERVE ⟨the graceful madrona . . . is beautiful to *look upon* —*Amer. Guide Series: Oregon*⟩ — **look up to :** to have a feeling of veneration or admiration for **:** regard with deference **:** RESPECT ⟨the non-Russian Slavs . . . were to *look up* to the Russians —A.M.Dragnich⟩ ⟨still *looked up to* him as their leader —T.B.Macaulay⟩
²**look** \"\ *n* -s [ME, fr. *looken* to look] **1 a :** the act of looking **:** the direction of the eyes toward something in order to see it **b :** a deliberate act of looking **:** GLANCE ⟨darted a quick ~ at me —Kenneth Roberts⟩ ⟨he was hers for a ~ or the speaking of a word —Ethel Wilson⟩ **c :** an examination of something with or as if with the eyes **:** the direction of one's attention toward something ⟨this final ~ at the present regime —J.K.Fairbank⟩ ⟨a brief ~ at the origins and development of . . . a great liberating movement —M.D.Geismar⟩ **2 a :** the appearance or expression of the countenance ⟨a round face carrying a ~ of Alpine simplicity —Osbert Sitwell⟩ ⟨wearing an ugly ~ on his face —F.B.Gipson⟩ **b :** the appearance of a person; *esp* **:** an attractive or healthy appearance — usu. used in pl. ⟨she's lost what ~*s* she ever had —Ellen Glasgow⟩ **3 :** the state or form in which something appears and which is often indicative of its nature or quality ⟨have a manufactured ~ — A.M.Young⟩ ⟨the rough-hewn rural ~ of the conventional academy —J.P.Marquand⟩ **4 :** a distance usu. encompassed by a single act of looking ⟨a long ~ of river —S.H.Holbrook⟩ **syn** see APPEARANCE
look around *vi* **1 :** to look in several directions **:** gaze about ⟨*looked around* in awe⟩ **2 :** to make a comprehensive examination of something (as a place or situation) **:** INVESTIGATE ⟨*looked around* before deciding which car to purchase⟩
look back *vi* **1 :** to turn and look at something in the direction from which one is coming or from which one's face is turned ⟨*looked back* and saw their pursuers gaining upon them⟩ **2 :** to turn one's mind or thoughts to the past **:** reflect on past events ⟨inclined to *look back* to their African origins —Oscar Handlin⟩ ⟨an era which the future will *look back* upon as another golden age —*New Englander*⟩ ⟨when I *look back* on my tolerance at the time —O.S.J.Gogarty⟩ **3 :** to show signs of retrogression or interrupted progress — usu. used in the negative ⟨from that time the industry has never *looked back* —L.D.Stamp⟩
look down *vb* [ME *looken doun*, fr. *looken* to look + *doun* down] *vi* **1 a :** to direct one's gaze in a downward direction esp. from an elevated position ⟨the gods *looked down* from on high⟩ ⟨*looked down* upon the servants . . . as if they had been

pygmies —Jonathan Swift⟩ **b :** to become located in a position that affords a downward view ⟨the window *looks down* upon the courtyard⟩ ⟨the high plains *looked down* upon the lower areas —R.A.Billington⟩ **2 :** to assume an attitude of contempt or scorn — usu. used with *on* ⟨tended to *look down* on the other Italians —William Barrett⟩ ⟨the liberal arts colleges *looked down* on teacher training —F.M.Hechinger⟩ ~ *vt* **:** to overcome (someone) by use of the eyes ⟨never could *look* the boy *down* —Charles Dickens⟩

look-down \ˈ=,=\ *n* -s [*look down*] **:** the superficial appearance of paper as seen under reflected light — compare LOOK-THROUGH

lookdown fish \ˈ=,=-\ *also* **lookdown** *n* -s [*look down*] **:** any of several deep-bodied compressed silvery carangid fishes comprising a genus (*Argyreiosus*) widely distributed in warm seas and having high truncated foreheads

looked *adj* [²*look* + *-ed*] *obs* **:** LOOKING ⟨lean-*look'd* prophets whisper fearful change —Shak.⟩

look·ee *or* **looky** \ˈlu̇kē, -ki\ *interj* [alter. of the imperative expression *look ye*, fr. ¹*look* + *ye*] — used to call attention

look·er \ˈlu̇kə(r)\ *n* -s [ME *loker*, fr. *looken, loken* to look + *-er*] **1 a** *obs* **:** one (as a keeper, steward, or bailiff) that looks after or has charge of something **b** *dial* **:** HERDSMAN **2 a :** one that looks ⟨a ~ down into the wells of human loneliness —J.F.Dobie⟩ ⟨millions of free ~*s* on TV —*Time*⟩ **b** *Brit* **:** INSPECTOR — usu. used in combination ⟨cloth ~*s*⟩ ⟨glass ~⟩ **c :** one that seeks out and appraises timber **3 a :** one having features or an appearance of a specified kind ⟨she's a good ~ —S.H.Adams⟩ ⟨that skin does its best to make him a handsome ~ —*Bookman*⟩ **b :** a woman of great physical beauty or attractiveness ⟨what a ~ she is —*New Yorker*⟩

looker-on \ˌ=ˈ=\ *n, pl* **lookers-on** [*look on* + *-er*] **:** ONLOOKER ⟨*lookers-on* often see what familiarity obscures for the participants —Walter Moberly⟩

look in *vi* [ME *loken in*, fr. *looken, loken* to look + *in*] **1 :** to direct one's gaze to the interior of something ⟨children . . . *look in* at the open door —H.W.Longfellow⟩ **2 :** to enter (as a room or building) for the purpose of seeing someone **:** make a short call **:** VISIT ⟨persuaded him to *look in* for a cup of tea whenever he visited the hamlet —Flora Thompson⟩ ⟨the doctor *looked in* frequently⟩ **3 :** to watch television

look-in \ˈ=,=\ *n* -s [*look in*] **1 :** the action or an instance of looking in **:** a usu. brief view ⟨had a good *look-in*. Saw everything with minute care —Abanindranath Tagore⟩ ⟨gave me a curious *look-in* on peace-time labor problems —*Collier's*⟩ **2 :** a chance of success ⟨handicapped by lack of condition, he never had a *look-in* —*New Yorker*⟩ **3 :** a share in something ⟨some bargain between the rival contenders for a *look-in* at Shanghai's customs receipts —*Literary Digest*⟩

looking \ˈ==\ *adj* [fr. pres. part. of ¹*look*] **:** having a specified look or appearance ⟨the detergent . . . left their clothes dirty ~ —Vance Packard⟩ ⟨the most disagreeable ~ character has the tenderest heart —*Modern Language Notes*⟩ — often used in combination ⟨angry-*looking*⟩ ⟨good-*looking*⟩

looking glass *n* [*looking* (gerund of ¹*look*) + *glass*] **1 a :** a mirror usu. made of glass with a backing of some reflecting substance (as mercury) ⟨had first seen her face in the *looking glass* —Jean Stafford⟩ **b :** the glass used in such a mirror ⟨little pieces of *looking glass* —Leslie Thomas⟩ **2 :** something held to resemble or to perform the functions of a looking glass **:** MIRROR 1b(1)

looking-glass plant *n* **:** an Asiatic tree (*Heritiera littoralis*) whose leaves are silvery beneath

look on *vi* **:** to be a spectator **:** OBSERVE, WATCH ⟨the world *looks on* and laughs —Mark Pattison⟩

look out *vb* [ME *loken out*, fr. *looken, loken* to look + *out*] *vi* **1 :** to gaze from within something (as a building) to the outside **:** put one's head out of a window or similar aperture ⟨*looked out* at the window⟩ **2** *archaic* **:** to venture out **:** make a brief excursion **3 a :** to be on the lookout or the watch (as against some danger) **:** exercise vigilance **:** be on guard ⟨there's danger ahead. *Look out*⟩ — often used with following *for* ⟨the good sailor will *look out* for shoals⟩ **b :** to watch diligently (as for a person) **:** gaze about in search **:** be on the alert (as for the presence of something) — used with following *for* ⟨*look out* for some old andirons when you visit the antique shop⟩ ⟨the mole-rats . . . which I had been urged to *look out* for and to collect —Douglas Carruthers⟩ **c :** to take care or be concerned with the welfare (as of a person) — used with following *for* ⟨*look out* for the baby while I go shopping⟩ ⟨the female *looks out* for the young⟩ **4** *obs* **:** to show itself **:** APPEAR ⟨the business of this man *looks out* of him —Shak.⟩ **5 :** to have or provide an outlook ⟨the little room which *looks out* on the . . . yew hedge —Patricia Wingfield⟩ ⟨homes and churches *looking out* on the placid village green —Budd Schulberg⟩ ~ *vt, chiefly Brit* **:** to search for or find by using the eyes **:** look up ⟨I have some letters of his . . . I'll *look* them *out* —Clemence Dane⟩ ⟨discover how few words I need to *look out* —O.W.Holmes †1935⟩

lookout \ˈ=,=\ *n* -s *often attrib* [*look out*] **1 :** one engaged in keeping watch **:** SCOUT, WATCHMAN ⟨the ~ sang out from his perch high in the shrouds —W.P.Schramm⟩ ⟨~*s* in their towers are watching the forests —*Pomona (Calif.) Progress-Bull.*⟩ ⟨sent ~*s* . . . along the road to catch the first glimpse of the approaching delegates —Dorothy C. Fisher⟩ ⟨gambling-house ~*s* . . . pass him in without question —Joseph Mitchell⟩ **2 :** an elevated place or structure affording a wide view and often used for keeping watch: as **a :** CROW'S NEST 1 **b :** one used for the detection of forest fires — called also *primary lookout* **c :** BELVEDERE **3 :** the action of keeping watch **:** a careful looking or watching (as for an object or event) ⟨a sharp ~ must be kept for traffic —Cornelius Vanderbilt b. 1898⟩ ⟨keeping a keen ~ for opportunities of expanding —A.P.Ryan⟩ **4 :** a usu. distant view **:** PROSPECT ⟨the traveller feels . . . disgusted with the ugliness of the ~ —*English Illustrated Mag.*⟩ **5** *chiefly Brit* **:** a prospective condition **:** a probability for the future **:** OUTLOOK ⟨it would be a sad ~ for the Australian dramatist if there were no little theaters —Leslie Rees⟩ ⟨growing thin and wizen in a solitary prison is a poor ~ —W.S.Gilbert⟩ **6 :** a matter of care or concern to one individual as opposed to others ⟨his ~ that the message gets through, not theirs —Stuart Chase⟩ **7 :** a short wooden bracket or cantilever used to support an overhanging portion of a roof or a bay window or a balcony — **on the lookout :** in the process or state of watching ⟨*on the lookout* for thieves —L.C. Douglas⟩ ⟨those in charge will have to be continuously *on the lookout* —*Auckland (New Zealand) Weekly News*⟩ ⟨be *on the lookout* for every little flaw —Robertson Davies⟩

look over *vt* [ME *loken over*, fr. *looken, loken* to look + *over*] **1 :** to inspect or examine usu. in a cursory way ⟨took a stroll about the town to *look it over* —H.A.Chippendale⟩ ⟨his scripts are *looked over* for accuracy —*Saturday Rev.*⟩ **2 :** to eliminate from consideration **:** DISREGARD, OVERLOOK, PARDON ⟨I'm only a private — perhaps you'll *look over that* —*Strand*⟩

look-over \ˈ=,==\ *n* -s [*look over*] **:** a cursory examination or survey ⟨the table . . . was given a final *look-over* —James Reynolds⟩

looks *pl of* LOOK, *pres 3d sing of* LOOK

look-see \ˈ=,=\ *n* [²*look* + *see*, v.] **:** a general survey **:** a tour of inspection **:** INVESTIGATION ⟨my quick *look-see* at a large and complicated situation —*Survey Graphic*⟩ ⟨animals . . . will stir in their hibernation and venture out for a stretch and a *look-see* —*Science News Letter*⟩

look-through \ˈ=,=\ *n* -s [fr. the phrase *look through*] **:** the texture and formation of a sheet of paper when examined by transmitted light — compare LOOK-DOWN

look up *vb* [ME *looken up*, fr. *looken* to look + *up*] *vi* **1 :** to raise the eyes **:** turn the face upward ⟨*looked up* from his book⟩ **2 :** to cheer up **:** take courage ⟨cheer up yourself, *look up* —Shak.⟩ **3 :** to improve in prospects or condition ⟨lived on the wife's income until business *looked up* again —George Santayana⟩ ⟨chances to control the Senate are *looking up* —T.R.Ybarra⟩ ~ *vt* **1 :** to search for ⟨required to *look up* the said Indian and bring him before some one of the magistrates —*Plymouth Colonial Records*⟩ ⟨*look up* the book and send it to me⟩ **2 a :** to consult (as a reference work) in order to find out information about something ⟨if you wish to do some further reading on this . . . subject, *look up* my book —W.J.Reilly⟩ **b :** to search for in a reference work ⟨*look up* an unfamiliar word in the dictionary⟩ ⟨*look* this number *up* in the phone book⟩ **c :** to find out information about (as by consulting a reference work) ⟨seized a timetable and *looked up* the trains —Gilbert Parker⟩ **3 :** to seek out; *esp* **:** to discover the whereabouts of and make a call on **:** visit briefly ⟨if I'd known you were in the regiment . . . I'd have *looked* you *up* —James Jones⟩ ⟨I *looked up* a man in the Bureau of Internal Revenue —W.H.Upson⟩

looky *var of* LOOKEE

¹**loom** \ˈlüm\ *n* -s *often attrib* [ME *lome*, fr. OE *gelōma* tool, utensil; akin to MD *allame* tool] **1** *now chiefly Scot* **:** TOOL **2** *now chiefly Scot* **:** an open vessel **:** RECEPTACLE **3 :** a frame or machine for interlacing at right angles two or more sets of threads or yarns to form a cloth — compare WARP, WEFT **4 :** the art or occupation of weaving ⟨sends her for consolation to the ~ and distaff —Samuel Johnson⟩ **5** [prob. fr. Scand origin; akin to ON *hlummr* handle of an oar] **a :** the part of an oar which is inboard from the oarlock usu. including the handle **b :** the part of an oar between the blade and handle **6 :** flexible tubing usu. nonmetallic for protecting and insulating electric wires

²**loom** \ˈ"\ *vt* -ED/-ING/-S **:** WEAVE — **loom the web :** to mount the warp on a loom

³**loom** \ˈ"\ *adj* [origin unknown] **:** moderate in force **:** GENTLE — used of a gale

⁴**loom** \ˈ"\ *vi* -ED/-ING/-S [origin unknown] **1 a :** to come into sight esp. above the surface (as of the sea or land) in enlarged or distorted and indistinct form often as a result of atmospheric conditions ⟨the foothills were beginning to ~ ahead through the dust-haze —E.E.Shipton⟩ ⟨could avert a collision should a southbound ship ~ out of the murk ahead —R.S.Porteous⟩ ⟨the hull of the ship . . . ~*ed* up suddenly —T.B.Costain⟩ **b :** to come into view **:** make an appearance ⟨the figure of a shepherd suddenly ~*ed* before me —Robert Gibbings⟩ ⟨another merchandising consideration . . . has ~*ed* up during the last few years —*Amer. Fabrics*⟩ **c :** to take shape as an impending occurrence ⟨fit . . . for the struggle which ~*ed* ahead —Roy Lewis & Angus Maude⟩ **d :** to appear in an impressively great or exaggerated form ⟨the . . . political drives of the Italian people ~*ed* large in prose fiction —T.G.Bergin⟩ ⟨the oceans ~ large in the visions of those who specialize in geopolitics —R.E.Coker⟩ **2** *obs* **:** to move slowly up and down — used of the sea or a vessel

⁵**loom** \ˈ"\ *n* -s **1 :** the indistinct and exaggerated appearance of something (as land or a ship) seen on the horizon or through fog or darkness ⟨watching for distant sails or the first ~ of the land —Sarah O. Jewett⟩ ⟨could make out the ~ of land in the darkness —G.A.Stansfield⟩ **2 a :** a looming shadow or reflection ⟨the pale gray ~ of the stadium —J.J.Godwin⟩ ⟨turned and saw the dim ~ of the cliffs above me —William Beebe⟩ **b :** the glow in the sky created by a light whose beam is below the horizon

⁶**loom** \ˈ"\ *n* -s [of Scand origin; akin to Norw *lom* loon] **1 :** LOON **2 a :** AUK **b :** GUILLEMOT **c :** PUFFIN

loom·ery \ˈlüm(ə)rē\ *n* -ES [⁶*loom* + *-ery*] **:** a breeding place of looms

loomfixer \ˈ=,==\ *n* **:** a textile worker who adjusts and repairs looms

looming *n* -s **:** a mirage in which images of objects below the horizon appear in distorted form

¹**loon** \ˈlün\ *n* -s [ME *loun*] **1 :** a worthless person **:** IDLER, LOUT, RASCAL **2** *chiefly Scot* **a :** a man of low station **:** MENIAL **b :** MISTRESS, HARLOT **c :** BOY, LAD ⟨the family . . . consisted of three ~*s* and a lassie —S.R.Crockett⟩ **3 a :** a crazy person **b :** SIMPLETON

²**loon** \ˈ"\ *n* -s [of Scand origin; akin to Norw *lom* loon, ON *lōmr* — more at LAMENT] **1 :** any of several fish-eating diving birds that belong to the genus *Gavia* and the order Gaviiformes and that are found in the northern part of the northern hemisphere **2 :** GREBE 1

¹**loo·ny** *or* **loo·ney** *or* **lu·ny** \ˈlünē, -ni\ *adj* **loonier** *or* **lunier; looniest** *or* **luniest** [*lun-* (fr. *lunatic*) + *-y*] **:** CRAZY, FOOLISH

²**loony** *or* **looney** *or* **luny** \ˈ"\ *n, pl* **loonies** *or* **looneys** *or* **lunies :** a loony person **:** LUNATIC

loony bin *n* **:** an insane asylum **:** MADHOUSE

¹**loop** \ˈlüp\ *n* -s [ME *loupe*; perh. akin to MD *lupen* to lie in wait, watch, peer] *archaic* **:** a small narrow opening (as in a wall) **:** LOOPHOLE ⟨massy walls . . . exhibited ~*s* for archers —Ann Radcliffe⟩

²**loop** \ˈ"\ *n* -s *often attrib* [ME *loupe*, of unknown origin] **1 a :** a fold or doubling of a line (as a thread, cord, or rope) leaving an aperture between the parts through which another line can be passed or into which a hook may be hooked **b :** such a fold of cord or ribbon serving as an ornament (as on a uniform) — see SHOULDER LOOP **c :** LOOP KNOT **2 a :** something (as a figure, course, formation, or structure) having the shape of a loop ⟨the ~ of the "a" was formed with some irregularity —F.W.Crofts⟩ ⟨saw the ~ of a river —John Buchan⟩ ⟨the driveway turns in a ~ before a fine . . . gate —*Amer. Guide Series: Va.*⟩ **b :** a turning area for cars, locomotives, or trains at the end of a railway or a street railway **c :** the portion of a lasso forming a noose ⟨the ~ settled over his prey —P.B.Kyne⟩ **d** (1) **:** a school figure in which a skater executes a semicircle followed immediately by a complete revolution around his vertical axis finishing with a second semicircle and thus tracing an oval within a larger circle while remaining on the same edge throughout (2) **:** a figure resembling a small figure eight made by following the first loop with a second one executed on the same edge of the opposite foot **e :** a surgical electrode in the form of a loop **f :** a maneuver in which an airplane starting from straight and level flight passes successively through a climb, inverted flight, a dive, and then returns to normal flight — called also *inside loop*; compare OUTSIDE LOOP **g :** a curved sand bar enclosing or nearly enclosing a body of water **h :** a road constituting a detour or an arm of a cloverleaf off a main thoroughfare ⟨graveled side ~*s* so that you can park off the highway —Mary Richards⟩ **3 :** a ring or curved piece made of some material (as wood, metal, or cloth) and used to form a fastening or a handle **:** EYE, STAPLE ⟨jeans with five belt ~*s* —*advt*⟩ **4 a :** the portion of a vibrating string, air column, or other vibrating body between two nodes **b :** the middle point of such a portion **5 :** a fingerprint in which some of the papillary ridges make a single backward turn without any twist — compare ARCH 3e, WHORL; see FINGERPRINT illustration **6** [prob. fr. the *Loop*, important business district in Chicago, Illinois] **:** the main business section or the most congested part of a city ⟨a large ~ spread over many blocks —Norman Katkov⟩ **7 :** a closed electric circuit: as **a :** one cell of a mesh or lattice **b :** a power feeder that returns to the point of origin and can thus feed in either direction **8 :** a wire usu. of platinum bent at one end into a small loop (usu. 4 millimeters in inside diameter) and used in transferring microorganisms — compare NEEDLE **9 :** an athletic conference or league **10 :** a lateral movement made by a defensive player when the ball is snapped in football **11 :** an 18-hole round of golf **12 :** LOOP ANTENNA **13 :** a portion of film or magnetic tape — **for a loop** *adv* **1 :** into a state of amazement, excitement, or confusion ⟨members of the cast were thrown *for a loop* when they caught sight of him —Cornelia O. Skinner⟩ ⟨that strange poetic touch which knocks the Japanese *for a loop* —*Time*⟩ **2 :** into a usu. sudden and unexpected reversal of fortune or a state of distress ⟨any such attempt would knock our whole economy *for a loop* —L.H.Keyserling⟩ — **on the loop** *adv (or adj)* **:** with the controller so adjusted that the motors are parallel

³**loop** \ˈ"\ *vb* -ED/-ING/-S *vi* **1 :** to form a loop ⟨the river ~*s* around the city⟩ **2 :** to move (as through the air) in loops ⟨the ring-billed gulls ~ above . . . the lake —*Amer. Guide Series: Minn.*⟩ ⟨a grenade came ~*ing* through the air —Lionel Shapiro⟩ **3 :** to execute a loop in an airplane ~ *vt* **1 a :** to place (something) within a loop **:** make a loop on or about ⟨~*ed* his finger with string⟩ ⟨lakes that ~ the town . . . like a chain of beads —*Amer. Guide Series: Minn.*⟩ **b :** to fasten with a loop ⟨the car is ~*ed* to the bag by steel cables —H.W.Baldwin⟩ — often used with *up* ⟨~ up a curtain⟩ **c :** to make a loop in or of ⟨~ a string⟩ **2 :** to furnish with loopholes **3 :** to join (two courses of loops) in knitting **4 :** to connect (electric conductors) so as to complete a loop **5 :** to cause (an airplane) to go into a loop **6 :** to cause to move esp. through the air in a course resembling or characterized by a loop ⟨~*ed* the grenade into the enemy trench⟩ ⟨~*ed* a long forward pass downfield⟩ — **loop the loop 1 :** to make a complete loop on a loop-the-loop **2 :** to perform a loop in an airplane

loop antenna *also* **loop aerial** *n* **:** a coil antenna usu. consisting of a single turn

loop-back \ˈ=,=\ *n* **:** HOOP BACK

looped \-pt\ *adj* [²*loop* + *-ed*] **1 :** having, formed in, or characterized by loops ⟨blend of carpet rayon and wool in a random ~ pile —*advt*⟩ **2 :** heavily intoxicated **:** DRUNK

loop·er \ˈlüpə(r)\ *n* -s [³*loop* + *-er*] **1 :** any of numerous usu. rather small smooth hairless caterpillars that are mostly larvae of moths of the family Geometridae, that lack prolegs on the middle segments of the body, and that move with a looping movement in which the anterior and posterior prolegs are alternately made fast and released — called also *inchworm, measuring worm, spanworm* **2 :** one that loops: as **a :** a machine that forms loops or loops things together: (1) **:** one that joins knitted edges esp. of hosiery (2) **:** one that transfers knitted loops from one knitting machine to another **b :** a worker who sews loops on garments **c :** a hosiery worker who closes toes and heels or joins ribbed tops **d :** one that hangs or ties tobacco on sticks so that it may be hung in the curing barns **e :** a ball that is pitched, hit, or thrown in a wide curve

loop·ful \-p,fu̇l\ *n* -s **:** the amount held in a loop; *specif* **:** the amount taken up in a standard four millimeter loop used by bacteriologists ⟨place a ~ of . . . culture on a clean slide —*Methods for Medical Laboratory Technicians*⟩

loop hinge *n* **:** a hinge constructed by looping two pieces of metal together (as on chests)

¹**loop·hole** \ˈlü,pōl, -üp,hōl\ *n* [¹*loop* + *hole*] **1 a :** a small opening (as in a wall or parapet) through which small arms may be discharged ⟨its attic was a fort, with ~*s* instead of windows —*Amer. Guide Series: Texas*⟩ **b :** a similar opening to admit light and air or to permit observation **2 a :** an outlet or means of escape; *esp* **:** one constituted by an ambiguity or an omission in the text through which the intent of a statute, contract, or obligation may be evaded ⟨this amendment would close a ~ in the law —*U.S. Code*⟩ ⟨tax ~*s* which would cost the government . . . millions of dollars —Robert Wallace⟩

²**loophole** \ˈ"\ *vt* **:** to make loopholes in ⟨on the day of the fight this fort was extensively *loopholed* —*Scribner's*⟩

loop in *vt* **:** to connect (as an electric cable) in circuit

looping snail *n* **:** a land snail of the genus *Truncatella*

loop jump *n* **:** a figure skating jump in which the skater takes off from the back outside edge of one skate, makes a full turn in the air, and lands on the back outside edge of the same skate

loop knot *n* **:** any of several knots (as the bowline) used to form a fixed loop in a cord or rope

loop of hen·le \-ˈhenlē, -lə\ *usu cap H* [after F. G. J. *Henle* †1885 Ger. pathologist] **:** the part of a vertebrate nephron that lies between the proximal and distal convoluted tubules, leaves the cortex of the kidney descending into the medullary tissue, then bending back and reentering the cortex, and presumably plays a role in water resorption

loop of retrogression : the loop in the apparent path of a planet, asteroid, or comet caused by its retrograde motion near opposition to the sun

loops *pl of* LOOP, *pres 3d sing of* LOOP

loop stitch *n* **:** a needlework stitch (as chainstitch or lazy daisy stitch) having one or more loops as part of the design and method of working

loop-the-loop \ˌ==ˈ=\ *n* [fr. the phrase *loop the loop*] **:** an amusement-park device consisting of a railway running on a largely elevated course that includes at least one portion forming an upright circle over which the passengers ride head downward

loop winding *n* **:** LAP WINDING

loopy \ˈlüpē\ *adj* -ER/-EST [²*loop* + *-y*] **1 :** having or characterized by loops ⟨the fine puff of smoke . . . floating off in a ~ ring —*Cosmopolitan*⟩ **2 a :** slightly crazy **b :** confused in one's thoughts and actions esp. as a result of mild intoxication ⟨what with the beer . . . we were all kind of ~ —Gwen Bentley⟩

loos *pl of* LOO, *pres 3d sing of* LOO

¹**loose** \ˈlüs\ *adj* -ER/-EST [ME *loos, lous*, fr. ON *lauss* loose, free — more at -LESS] **1 a :** not rigidly fastened or securely attached **:** lacking a firm or tight connection **:** ready to move or come apart from an attachment ⟨~ planks in a bridge⟩ ⟨sloping sides covered with . . . ~ rock —F.J.R.Rodd⟩ **b** (1) **:** lightly secured or made fast; *esp* **:** having worked partly free from attachments ⟨a ~ tooth⟩ ⟨the knife had a ~ blade⟩ ⟨~ masonry⟩ (2) **:** having relative freedom of movement or arrangement as a result of being only locally restrained or fixed ⟨~ ribbons fluttering from her hat⟩ ⟨the slamming of a ~ shutter⟩ **c :** produced freely and accompanied by raising of mucus **:** not dry or harsh **:** PRODUCTIVE ⟨a ~ cough⟩ **d :** easily altered or removed **:** not fast ⟨a ~ dye⟩ ⟨a ~ color⟩ **e :** permitting some freedom of movement — usu. used of a stable or a box stall **f :** not clinging close to the figure **:** not tight-fitting ⟨~ clothing⟩ **2 :** free from a state of confinement or restraint: **a :** free from bonds, fetters, or confining limits ⟨a ~ convict⟩ ⟨a horse ~ of his tether⟩ ⟨a lion ~ in the streets⟩ **b :** free from constraint or obligation **:** at liberty **:** not bound (as by duty or habit) ⟨if . . . your thoughts are ~ of state affairs —Joseph Addison⟩ **c :** not assigned to special use or service **:** subject to free disposal **:** having no assigned place or employment ⟨~ hours⟩ ⟨~ funds⟩ **d :** not bound together **:** not brought together in a bundle, container, or binding **:** not secured in a setting or joined in a fixed combination ⟨~ papers⟩ ⟨~ hair⟩ ⟨~ milk⟩ **e** *archaic* **:** DISCONNECTED, DETACHED, RANDOM ⟨a good deal of ~ information —Thomas Carlyle⟩ ⟨~ pages⟩ **f :** not joined to anything else ⟨a ~ line⟩ **3 :** not dense, close, or compact in structure or arrangement: as **a :** composed of particles capable of free movement ⟨~ earth⟩ ⟨the action of the tides carried away the ~ soil —*Amer. Guide Series: Maine*⟩ **b :** not in close order **:** UNSERRIED ⟨with horse and chariots ranked in ~ array —John Milton⟩ ⟨~ flocks drifting slowly from the neighboring jungle —William Beebe⟩ **c :** having wide spaces or interstices ⟨a cloth of ~ texture⟩ **d :** ³LAX 3c **e :** lacking compactness or smooth integration of build ⟨a strong, ~, round-shouldered, shuffling, shaggy fellow —Charles Dickens⟩ **4 a :** lacking in restraint or power of restraint ⟨a ~ tongue⟩ ⟨~ bowels⟩ **b :** lacking in moral restraint; *esp* **:** characterized by immorality **:** LEWD, UNCHASTE, WANTON ⟨~ writings⟩ ⟨a ~ life⟩ ⟨a ~ woman⟩ **5 a :** not tightly drawn or stretched **:** SLACK ⟨drive a pony cart with ~ reins⟩ ⟨a ~ belt⟩ ⟨~ skin⟩ **b :** having a flexible or relaxed character (as from weakness or agility) ⟨my knees ~ under me —R.L.Stevenson⟩ ⟨walked with a ~ swinging stride —E.T. Thurston⟩ **6 a :** lacking in precision, exactness, or care **:** inaccurate or indeterminate in construction **:** lacking in system or logic ⟨a ~ style⟩ ⟨~ reasoning⟩ ⟨a ~ analogy⟩ ⟨a ~ thinker⟩ **b :** lacking in rigidity (as of construction) and permitting freedom of interpretation ⟨a ~ working agreement⟩ ⟨a ~ construction of the Federal Constitution⟩ **7 :** characterized by limited cohesion between constituent elements and permitting a wide area of freedom of action ⟨a ~ federation of sovereign principalities —F.A.Ogg & Harold Zink⟩ **8 a :** not in strict accordance with the rules **:** being without special care ⟨~ practice⟩ **b :** characterized by poor quality **:** inefficient or unskilled in performance ⟨~ play⟩ **c :** having players relatively wide apart ⟨a ~ formation in football⟩ — compare TIGHT **d :** disputed as to possession **:** gone from control (as of a player or team) ⟨a ~ ball⟩ ⟨a ~ puck⟩ **9 :** LAX 4 **10 a :** expressed in or characterized by loose sentences ⟨~ style⟩ **b :** OPEN 18

²**loose** \ˈ"\ *vb* -ED/-ING/-S [ME *loosen, losen, lousen*, fr. *loos, lous*, adj. — more at ¹LOOSE] *vt* **1 a :** to let loose **:** set free **:** release from or as if from restraint ⟨the railroad had him arrested . . . but the judge *loosed* him with a warning —S.H. Adams⟩ ⟨war has again been *loosed* —Arthur Geddes⟩ ⟨the corn dance . . . should ~ downpours upon the dry country —Oliver La Farge⟩ **b :** to free (as the lips or tongue) from restraint **c :** to give absolution to ⟨whatever you ~ on earth shall be *loosed* in heaven —Mt 16:19 (RSV)⟩ **2 a :** to make loose **:** UNBIND, UNDO, UNTIE ⟨~ a knot⟩ ⟨*loosed* the laces of her shoe —B.A.Williams⟩ **b** *archaic* **:** DISSOLVE ⟨by assuming vows no pope will ~ —P.B.Shelley⟩ **3 :** to cast loose **:** DETACH ⟨*loosed* the boat from its moorings —George Eliot⟩ ⟨~ a rope⟩ **4 :** to let fly (as an arrow) **:** DISCHARGE (as a gun) **:** send forth (something) as a missile ⟨a hail of bullets and arrows was *loosed* into the flanks of the . . . advance guard —*Amer. Guide Series: Pa.*⟩ ⟨the destroyer had *loosed* a salvo of 4.7-inch shells

at her target —*Crowsnest*⟩ — often used with *off* ⟨the little boys had *loosed* off a pistol —Victoria Sackville-West⟩ **5 :** to make less rigid, tight, or strict **:** RELAX, SLACKEN ⟨the old bonds of authority have been *loosed* by the war —Bertrand Russell⟩ ⟨limbs had been *loosed* by grievous labor of combat —Alexander Pope⟩ **6** *chiefly Scot* **:** to free or obtain by payment of a fee **7** *Scots law* **:** to stop (an arrestment) from taking effect **:** WITHDRAW **~** *vi* **1 :** to let fly a missile (as an arrow) **:** discharge a gun **:** FIRE — often used with *off* ⟨almost *loosed* off at it before I saw it was a cow —Ernest Hemingway⟩ **2 :** to weigh anchor **:** set sail **3** *dial chiefly Eng* **:** to become dismissed ⟨every day when the school **~***s* —James Hogg⟩

3**loose** \"\ *n* -s [partly fr. 1*loose* & partly fr. 2*loose*] **1 :** the release of an arrow from a bow ⟨with a strong bow the ~ is easier to do well than with a weak one —A.E.Hodgkin⟩ **2** *obs* **:** the conclusion or outcome of a matter **:** ISSUE **3** *obs* **:** the state or condition of looseness; *esp* **:** freedom from or abandonment of moral restraint **4 :** loose rock or rock that may easily be loosened **5 :** open forward play in rugby — often used with *the;* contrasted with *tight* ⟨the North forwards . . . were so lively in the ~ that they neutralized the advantage gained by the visitors in the tight —*Rugger*⟩ — **give a loose to** *or* **give loose to :** to give freedom, full vent, or free rein to ⟨*gave* his usual *loose to* gaiety and mirth —Henry Fielding⟩ — **on the loose** *adv* (*or adj*) **1 :** in a state of freedom **:** without limits or restrictions as to movement ⟨the more warlike tribes were still *on the loose* —Oliver La Farge⟩ ⟨a dangerous animal . . . left *on the loose* —F.B.Gipson⟩ **2 :** without moral restraint (as on behavior); *esp* **:** in a state characterized by unrestrained and usu. dissolute behavior ⟨the rowdy element, . . . drunken poachers and sailors *on the loose* —*Saturday Rev.*⟩ ⟨she began shop-lifting and going *on the loose* again —Samuel Butler †1902⟩

4**loose** \"\ *adv* [1*loose*] **:** LOOSELY ⟨our manners sit more ~ upon us —Joseph Addison⟩

loose accent *n* **:** PIECE ACCENT

loose–bodied \ˈlüs¦bädēd\ *adj, of a dress* **:** hanging loosely; *specif* **:** made without stays

loose–box \ˈ=,=\ *n, Brit* **:** BOX STALL

loose change *n* **:** coins or bills of low denominations and likely to be carried loose (as in one's pocket)

loose constructionist *n* **:** an advocate of loose construction (as of a statute or constitution); *specif* **:** one favoring a liberal construction of the Constitution of the U.S. to give broader powers to the federal government — compare ELASTIC 4a; STRICT CONSTRUCTIONIST

loose coupling *n* **:** a coupling of two circuits such that any change of current in one produces relatively small change in the other

loose cover *n, chiefly Brit* **:** SLIPCOVER 1

loose end *n* **1 :** something left hanging loose **:** a fragment or piece of something remaining unused ⟨cut the *loose ends* of string after you have tied the package⟩ **2 :** a fragment of unfinished business ⟨committees will be tying up the technical *loose ends* of the . . . conference's final act —Frank Gorrell⟩ — **at loose ends** *or* **at a loose end 1 :** lacking a settled occupation or regular employment **:** uncertain of one's future course of action ⟨feeling himself *at loose ends* — no job, no immediate prospects —Dixon Wecter⟩ ⟨*at a loose end* for a time, he had been finally pitchforked into the car business —Robert Westerby⟩ **2 :** not knowing what to do with oneself **:** UNSETTLED ⟨all day long he had been *at loose ends* —Hamilton Basso⟩ ⟨being *at a loose end* that afternoon, he went to a movie⟩

loose fit *or* **loose fit–up** *n* **:** a fit with sufficient clearance to permit free play or in the extreme to rattle ⟨a *loose fit-up* of bearings in a groove⟩

loose–footed \ˈ=¦==\ *adj* **:** having the foot loose **:** not having or not secured to a boom — used of a sail

loose head *n* **:** the end player in the front line of a rugby scrum whose team is to put the ball in play

loose–housing system *n* **:** a system of dairy cattle management in which animals are kept at liberty in a loafing barn usu. with access to an open yard and are taken to separate areas or buildings for milking and feeding — compare MILKING PARLOR

loose–joint butt *n* **:** a single knuckle hinge with the pin secured in one of the halves and easily separated by sliding the pieces apart along the axis of the pin

loose-joint butt

loose–jointed \ˈ=¦==\ *adj* **1 :** having joints apparently not closely articulated **2 :** capable of or characterized by unusually free movements ⟨the easy, *loose-jointed* grace of the trained athlete —S.E.White⟩ **3 :** poorly constructed **:** CLUMSY ⟨a *loose-jointed* paragraph⟩

loose–leaf \ˈ=¦=\ *adj* **1 a :** having leaves secured in book form in a mechanical cover whose backbone may be opened for the removal, rearrangement, or replacement of leaves ⟨a *loose-leaf* notebook⟩ ⟨a *loose-leaf* ledger⟩ ⟨a *loose-leaf* encyclopedia⟩ — compare POST BINDER, RING BINDER, SPRING BINDER **b :** of, belonging to, or using articles having such leaves ⟨*loose-leaf* paper⟩ ⟨*loose-leaf* systems in bookkeeping⟩ **2 :** concerned with or used in the sale of tobacco as loose hands rather than in packed hogsheads ⟨a *loose-leaf* auction⟩ ⟨the hogshead and *loose-leaf* systems of marketing —*Experiment Station Record*⟩ ⟨make purchases . . . in the many *loose-leaf* warehouses —*Burley Tobacco Grower*⟩

loose–lipped \ˈ=¦=\ *adj* **:** LOOSE-TONGUED ⟨are not so *loose-lipped* and fond of gossip —Virginia Woolf⟩

loose·ly *adv* [ME *losly, lously, lousely,* fr. *loos, lous* loose + *-ly*] **:** in a loose manner ⟨lizard skulls with ~ built jaws —W.E. Swinton⟩ ⟨a union of ~ federated states⟩ ⟨these novels could be ~ grouped as mysteries —J.D.Hart⟩ ⟨played ~ with the truth —John Sparkman⟩

loose milk *n* **:** milk that is sold in bulk out of a large container

loos·en \ˈlüsᵊn\ *vb* -ED/-ING/-S [ME *losnen, loosnen,* fr. *loos, lous* loose + *-nen* -en] *vt* **1 :** to set free **:** release from restraint **:** let loose ⟨~ the tongues of the . . . prisoners —*Saturday Rev.*⟩ **2 :** to make looser **:** free from or lessen the tightness, firmness, or fixedness of ⟨~ a screw⟩ ⟨refused to ~ his control of charity funds —*Fortnight*⟩ ⟨~ social ties⟩ ⟨a liming process . . . ~*s* the hair —*Amer. Guide Series: Pa.*⟩ **3 :** to relax or free costiveness from or relax (the bowels) **4 a :** to weaken the attachment or adhesion between **:** DETACH ⟨the ivy creeping up the wall . . . does not ~ its ancient stones —Newman Smyth⟩ **b :** to separate the particles of or make less firmly packed ⟨a cultivator . . . will ~ hard-packed earth —*Monsanto Mag.*⟩ **5 :** to cause or permit to become less strict **:** relax the severity of ⟨~ the regulations governing investment in foreign countries⟩ ⟨~ discipline⟩ **~** *vi* **:** to become loose or looser ⟨even after his catastrophe his grip of his soul did not ~ —Hugh Walpole⟩ ⟨the dynastic and religious entanglements . . . have ~*ed* or disappeared —Edward Sapir⟩

loos·en·er \-s(ᵊ)nə(r)\ *n* -s **:** one that loosens

loose·ness \-snəs\ *n* -ES [ME *losenes,* fr. *loos, lous, lose* loose + *-nes* -ness] **:** the quality or state of being loose ⟨the ~ of the upper body clothing —J.H.Shaw⟩ ⟨~ of the bowels⟩ ⟨their speech may create the illusion of ~ but their behavior is straitlaced —John Mason Brown⟩ ⟨detect some vagueness and ~ in his thought —H.J.Muller⟩

loosen up *vi* **1 :** to become more liberal or generous with money ⟨*loosen up,* and be a big, kindly, generous human being —*Motor Print*⟩ **2 :** to become less tense or reserved **:** RELAX ⟨wanted them to *loosen up* and have a good time —Jean Boley⟩ ⟨the way you *loosen up* and forget you're a highbrow —Sinclair Lewis⟩ **~** *vt* **:** to introduce more freedom or flexibility into ⟨the private business policies which are helping to *loosen up* the economy —S.H.Slichter⟩

loose–pin butt *n* **:** a butt hinge with a removable pin — see BUTT HINGE illustration

1**looser** *comparative of* LOOSE

2**loos·er** \ˈlüsə(r)\ *n* -s **:** one that looses ⟨the sail ~*s* sent aloft —S.B.Luce⟩

loose rate *n* **:** a piece or incentive rate yielding high earnings for expenditure of effort

looses *pres 3d sing of* LOOSE, *pl of* LOOSE

loose scrum *n* **:** a scrum formed around a ball that is in play

loose sentence *n* **:** a usu. complex sentence in which the principal clause comes first and the latter part of which contains subordinate modifiers or trailing elements (as in "I saw him yesterday while I was walking down the street") — compare PERIODIC SENTENCE

loose side *n* **:** the convex face of a sheet of veneer characterized by distortion of tissue caused in cutting — compare TIGHT SIDE

loose smut *n* **:** a smut disease of grains in which the entire head is transformed into a dusty mass of spores with only the rachis remaining after the spores mature — compare COVERED SMUT

loosest *superlative of* LOOSE

loosestrife \ˈ=,=\ *n* [2*loose* + *strife;* intended as trans. of Gk *lysimacheios* loosestrife, understood as a compound formed from Gk *lysis* action of loosing, deliverance & Gk *machē* battle, strife — more at LYSIMACHIA] **1 :** a plant of the genus *Lysimachia* (esp. *L. vulgaris*) **2 :** a plant of the genus *Lythrum; esp* **:** PURPLE LOOSESTRIFE **3 :** a plant of the genus *Steironema; esp* **:** FRINGED LOOSESTRIFE

loosestrife family *n* **:** LYTHRACEAE

loose–tongued \ˈ=¦=\ *adj* **:** free of speech **:** given to unrestrained talk

loose wall *n* **:** SEEDY TOE

loosing *n* -s [ME *losing, lousing,* fr. gerund of *loosen, losen, lousen* to loose] **:** the act of releasing; *specif* **:** the absolution or remission of sins ⟨a notable example of binding and ~ by the minister —G.W.Sprott⟩

1**loot** \ˈlüt\ *Scot past of* LET

2**loot** \"\ *Scot var of* LOUT

3**loot** \", *usu* -üd·+V\ *n* -s [Hindi *lūṭ,* fr. Skt *luṇṭati* he robs, plunders] **1 :** goods esp. articles of considerable value taken in war (as from the enemy or a captured city) **:** BOOTY, PLUNDER, SPOILS ⟨those who have fought solely for booty and ~ —R.E.Sherwood⟩ **2 :** something held to resemble goods of value seized in war: as **a :** anything taken by force or violence (as in a robbery) ⟨the accumulated ~ of all the sea rovers —H.E.Rieseberg⟩ **b :** illicit gains by public officials **c :** articles having or held to have great value ⟨the rich ~ of . . . wedding gifts —R.L.Shayon⟩ ⟨a rich ~ of factual material —F.L.Mott⟩ **d :** MONEY ⟨would not . . . spend all that ~ on her —Langston Hughes⟩ **3 :** the action of looting ⟨general ~ of church land —Hilaire Belloc⟩

4**loot** *vb* -ED/-ING/-S *vt* **1 a :** to plunder or sack (as a conquered city) in war **b :** to rob esp. on a large scale and usu. by violence or corruption ⟨~*ed* a bank⟩ ⟨corrupt politicians ~*ed* the nation's forest and mineral reserves⟩ **2 :** to seize and carry away by force esp. in war ⟨the enemy soldiers ~*ed* the treasures of the art museums⟩ **~** *vi* **:** to perform the action of robbing or plundering esp. in war **syn** see ROB

5**loot** \"\ *n* -s [by shortening & alter.] *slang* **:** LIEUTENANT

loo·ten \ˈlütᵊn\ *Scot past of* LET

loot·er \ˈlüd·ə(r), -ütə-\ *n* -s **:** one that loots

loo·tie \ˈlüd·ē\ *also* **loo·tie·wal·lah** \¦==¦wälə\ *n* -s [*lootie* fr. Hindi *lūṭī,* fr. *lūṭ; lootiewallah* fr. Hindi *lūṭīwālā,* fr. *lūṭī* + *-wālā* man — more at WALLAH] *India* **:** one that engages in looting or marauding — usu. used in pl.

loots·man \ˈlütsmən\ *n, pl* **lootsmans** [modif. of D *loodsmannetje,* dim. of *loodsman* pilot, fr. MD, fr. ME *lodesman,* fr. *lodes* (gen. of *lode* course) + *man* — more at LODE] **:** REMORA

1**lop** \ˈläp\ *n* -s [ME *loppe,* of unknown origin] **:** the smaller branches and twigs (as of a tree) that have been cut off **:** trimmings; *esp* **:** such parts of a tree that are not measured for timber ⟨the timber merchant who bought the trees did not wish to take away the ~ and top —H.C.W.Bouring⟩

2**lop** \"\ *vb* **lopped; lopped; lopping; lops** *vt* **1 a :** to cut off branches or twigs from (as a tree or vine) **:** remove dead parts or superfluous growth from **:** TRIM **b** *archaic* **:** to cut off the head or limbs of (a person) **2 a :** to cut (as branches or twigs) from a tree or bush — often used with *off* ⟨cut down the small tree and *lopped* the branches off —W.H.Hudson †1922⟩ **b :** to cut (the limbs or head) from a person ⟨~*s* the head of his enemy into a wine cask —Burke Wilkinson⟩ — often used with *off* ⟨the hasty decision to ~ off part of a limb —C.L.Boltz⟩ **c :** to cut (as a portion or part) from something ⟨decided to ~ the dog's tail⟩ — often used with *off* ⟨*lopped* off the border provinces of the empire⟩ **3 :** to remove esp. superfluous parts from **:** eliminate as unnecessary, superfluous, or undesirable — usu. used with *off* ⟨about 100,000 jobs . . . have been *lopped* off the federal payroll —Daniel Bell⟩ ⟨*lopped* off a billion dollars in excise revenues —*U. S. News & World Report*⟩ **~** *vi* **:** to perform the action of cutting off

3**lop** \"\ *n* -s [ME *loppe,* of Scand origin; akin to OSw *loppa* flea; perh. akin to ON *hlaupa* to jump, leap — more at LEAP] *dial Eng* **:** FLEA

4**lop** \"\ *vi* **lopped; lopped; lopping; lops** [perh. imit.] **1 :** to hang downward esp. in a loose or limp manner **:** flop or sway about loosely **:** DROOP **2 :** to move or act in a lazy and usu. slouching manner **3 :** to move with short leaps **:** BOUND ⟨a rabbit . . . *lopped* among the darkening cabbages —H.E. Bates⟩ ⟨used to ~ around in the gymnasium after badminton or handball —Dorothy Baker⟩

5**lop** \"\ *adj* [4*lop*] **:** hanging down **:** PENDENT ⟨~ ears⟩

6**lop** \"\ *n* [5*lop*] **1** *usu cap* **:** a variety or breed of domestic rabbits having very large ears that are usu. too heavy to be carried erect and fall to the side of the head **2** -s *often cap* **:** a rabbit of the Lop breed

7**lop** \"\ *n* -s [prob. imit.] **:** a condition of the sea in which the waves are short and choppy

8**lop** \"\ *vi* **lopped; lopped; lopping; lops :** to break in short choppy waves — used of the sea ⟨the tide high and *lopping* rhythmically against the side —Darrell Berrigan⟩

LOP *abbr* line of position

lo·pa·rite \ˈlōpə,rīt\ *n* -s [Russ *loparit,* fr. *Lopar'* Lapp (prob. fr. Sw *Lappar* Lapps, pl. of *Lapp*) + *-it* -ite] **:** a perovskite containing alkalies and cerium

lop down *vi* **:** to sit or lie down **:** FLOP 2a ⟨thought she'd just *lop down* a few minutes on the old sofa —Harriet B. Stowe⟩

1**lope** \ˈlōp\ *n* -s [ME, alter. of *loup,* fr. ON *hlaup;* in senses 2 and 3, prob. influenced by D *loop* course, run, stride, fr. MD; ON *hlaup* akin to MD *loop,* OHG *hlouf* course; derivative fr. the root of ON *hlaupa* to jump, leap] **1** *obs* **:** LEAP **2 :** an easy natural gait of a horse resembling a canter **3 :** an easy bounding gait capable of being sustained for a considerable period ⟨the ~ of a wolf⟩

2**lope** \"\ *vb* -ED/-ING/-S [ME *lopen,* alter. of *loupen,* fr. ON *hlaupa;* in sense 2, prob. influenced by D *loopen* to run, fr. MD *lopen* — more at LEAP (v.)] *vi* **1** *obs* **:** LEAP **2 a :** to go or move at a lope ⟨the hares and rabbits *loped* away —Charles Kingsley⟩ ⟨*loped* up the trail —Donald Keith⟩ **b :** to ride at a lope **~** *vt* **:** to cause (as a horse or pony) to lope ⟨*loped* our jaded horses along at a brisk pace —Theodore Roosevelt⟩

lop–eared \ˈ=¦=\ *adj* **:** having ears that droop ⟨*lop-eared* rabbits⟩ ⟨a shaggy, mean-eyed, *lop-eared* . . . pony —C.T. Jackson⟩

lop·er \ˈlōpə(r)\ *n* -s **1 :** one that lopes; *esp* **:** a saddle horse having the loping gait **2 :** the vertical sliding pieces that when pulled out support the fall front of a desk or secretary

lo·pe·zia \lōˈpēzēə\ *n, cap* [NL, prob. fr. J. *López,* 16th cent. Span. colonial official + NL *-ia*] **:** a genus of Mexican and Central American herbs and subshrubs (family Onagraceae) having alternate leaves and small irregular mostly red racemose flowers

lo·pez·ite \ˈlōpə,zīt\ *n* -s [Emiliano *López,* 20th cent. Chilean mineral collector + E *-ite*] **:** a mineral $K_2Cr_2O_7$ consisting of a dichromate of potassium and found in the nitrate deposits of Chile

loph- *or* **lopho-** *comb form* [NL, fr. Gk, fr. *lophos*] **:** crest **:** tuft **:** comb ⟨*lopho*phytosis⟩ ⟨*Loph*ura⟩

-loph \ˌläf\ *n comb form* -s [Gk *lophos*] **:** crest ⟨ecto*loph*⟩

lophi- *or* **lophio-** *comb form* [NL, fr. Gk *lophion* small crest, dim. of *lophos*] **:** small crest or tuft ⟨*Lophio*don⟩ ⟨*Lophio*mys⟩

lo·phi·id \ˈlōfēəd, -ē,id\ *n* -s [NL *Lophiidae*] **:** a fish of the family Lophiidae

lo·phi·idae \ləˈfīə,dē\ *n pl, cap* [NL, fr. *Lophius,* type genus + *-idae*] **:** a family of large-headed marine fishes comprising the anglers and often made coextensive with a suborder Lophioidea of the order Pediculati

lo·phine \ˈlō,fēn, -,fən, ˈlä-\ *n* -s [prob. fr. F, fr. *loph-* + *-ine*] **:** a crystalline nitrogenous base $(C_6H_5)_3C_3HN_2$ that emits light when a solution of it in warm alcoholic potassium hydroxide absorbs oxygen; 2, 4, 5-triphenyl-imidazole

lo·phi·o·don \ləˈfīə,dän\ *n, cap* [NL *Lophiodont-, Lophiodon,* fr. *lophi-* + *-odont-, -odon* -odon] **:** a genus of large European Eocene perissodactyls related to the tapir

1**lo·phi·o·dont** \ˈlōfēə,dänt\ *also* **lo·phi·o·don·toid** \¦===ˈdän·,tȯid\ *adj* [*lophiodont* fr. NL *Lophiodont-, Lophiodon; lophiodontoid* fr. NL *Lophiodont-, Lophiodon* + E *-oid*] **:** of or relating to the genus *Lophiodon*

2**lophiodont** \"\ *n* -s [NL *Lophiodont-, Lophiodon*] **:** an animal of the genus *Lophiodon*

lo·phi·oi·dea \,lōfēˈȯidēə\ *n pl, cap* [NL, fr. *Lophius* + *-oidea*] *in some classifications* **:** a suborder of Pediculati coextensive with the Lophiidae

lo·phi·o·mys \ləˈfīə,mis\ *n, cap* [NL, fr. *lophi-* + *-mys*] **:** a genus of atypical rodents of northeastern and eastern Africa having the temporal fossae of the skull bridged by plates of bone — compare CRESTED HAMSTER

lo·phi·os·to·ma·ta·ce·ae \,lōfē,ästəməˈtāsē,ē\ *n pl, cap* [NL, fr. *Lophiostomat-, Lophiostoma,* type genus (fr. *lophi-* + *-stomat-, -stoma* -stoma) + *-aceae*] **:** a family of ascomycetous fungi (order Sphaeriales) distinguished by the elongated laterally compressed opening of the perithecium

lo·phi·us \ˈlōfēəs\ *n, cap* [NL, fr. Gk *lophos* crest] **:** the type genus of Lophiidae

1**loph·o·branch** \ˈläfə,braŋk, ˈlōf-\ *n* -s [NL *Lophobranchii*] **:** LOPHOBRANCHIATE

2**lophobranch** \"\ *adj* [NL *Lophobranchii*] **:** LOPHOBRANCHIATE

1**loph·o·branchiate** \¦==+\ *adj* [NL *Lophobranchii* + E *-ate*] **:** of or relating to the Lophobranchii

2**lophobranchiate** \"\ *n* -s **:** a lophobranchiate fish

loph·o·bran·chii \,==ˈbraŋkē,ī\ *n pl, cap* [NL, fr. *loph-* + *-branchii* (fr. Gk *branchion* gill) — more at BRANCHIA] *in some classifications* **:** an order of small teleost fishes that comprise the sea horses and pipefishes and are coextensive with the family Syngnathidae and that are sometimes considered a suborder of Thoracostei

loph·o·dermium \,==ˈdərmēəm\ *n, cap* [NL, fr. *loph-* + *-dermium* (fr. Gk *derma* skin) — more at DERM-] **:** a genus of ascomycetous fungi (order Phacidiales) having filiform one-celled ascospores in perithecia which are finally erumpent

1**loph·o·dont** \ˈ==,dänt\ *adj* [ISV *loph-* + *-odont*] **:** having or constituting molar teeth with transverse ridges on the grinding surface ⟨~ rodents⟩ — opposed to *bunodont*

2**lophodont** \"\ *n* -s **:** an animal (as an ungulate) having lophodont teeth

lo·phoph·o·ral \ləˈfäf(ə)rəl\ *adj* **:** of or relating to a lophophore

loph·o·phore \ˈläfə,fō(ə)r, ˈlōf-\ *n* -s [*loph-* + *-phore*] **:** an organ usu. of a circular or horseshoe shape that surrounds the mouth and bears the tentacles and that serves to engulf food particles and provide a respiratory current in bryozoans, brachiopods, and a few marine worms

lo·phoph·o·rus \ləˈfäf(ə)rəs\ *n, cap* [NL, fr. *loph-* + *-phorus*] **:** a genus consisting of the monals

loph·o·phyl·lid \¦läfə¦filəd, ¦lōf-\ *or* **loph·o·phyl·li·did** \-lədəd, -,did\ *adj* [*lophophyllid* fr. NL *Lophophyllidium; lophophyllidid* irreg. fr. NL *Lophophyllidiidae* (family of tetracorals including the genus *Lophophyllidium*), fr. *Lophophyllidium,* type genus + *-idae*] **:** of or relating to *Lophophyllidium*

loph·o·phyl·lid·i·um \,==fəˈlidēəm\ *n, cap* [NL, fr. *loph-* + *phyll-* + *-idium*] **:** a genus (sometimes made the type of a family Lophophyllidiidae) of tetracorals common and widely distributed in central No. American Upper Carboniferous formations

lo·phoph·y·ton \ləˈfäfə,tän\ [NL, fr. *loph-* + Gk *phyton* plant; fr. its occurrence as a parasite on the comb of fowls — more at PHYT-] *syn of* ACHORION

loph·o·phytosis \,läfō, ,lōfō+\ *n* [NL, fr. *loph-* + *phytosis*] **:** favus of fowls

lo·phor·nis \ləˈfȯrnəs\ *n, cap* [NL, fr. *loph-* + *-ornis*] **:** a genus of hummingbirds consisting of the coquettes

lo·phor·tyx \-,tiks\ *n, cap* [NL, fr. *loph-* + Gk *ortyx* quail — more at OREORTYX] **:** a genus consisting of the helmet quails

lo·phos·te·on \ləˈfästē,än\ *n, pl* **lophos·tea** \-ēə\ *or* **lophos·teons** [NL, fr. *loph-* + *-osteon*] **:** the keel-bearing part of a bird's sternum

lo·phot·i·dae \ləˈfäd·ə,dē\ *n pl, cap* [NL, fr. *Lophotes,* type genus (irreg. fr. Gk *lophos* crest) + *-idae*] **:** a monotypic family of elongated ribbonlike deep-sea fishes (order Allotriognathi) — compare OARFISH

lo·phot·ri·chous \ləˈfä·trəkəs\ *or* **lo·phot·ri·chate** \-kət\ *also* **loph·o·trich·ic** \¦läfə¦trikik, ¦lōf-\ *adj* [*lophotrichous* fr. *loph-* + *-trichous; lophotrichate* fr. *loph-* + *trich-* + *-ate; lophotrichic* fr. *loph-* + *trich-* + *-ic*] **:** having a tuft of flagella at one end

-lophs *pl of* -LOPH

lo·phu·ra \ləˈfyùrə\ *n, cap* [NL, fr. *loph-* + *-ura*] **:** a genus of pheasants consisting of the firebacks

lop·o·lith \ˈläpə,lith\ *n* -s [Gk *lopos* shell, husk + E *-lith;* akin to Gk *lepein* to peel — more at LEPER] **:** a laccolith in which the base is basin-shaped instead of being horizontal

lopped *past of* LOP

1**lop·per** \ˈläpə(r)\ *vb* -ED/-ING/-S [ME *lopren,* of Scand origin; akin to Icel *hleypir* rennet, Norw dial. *løyper,* Sw dial. *löper,* Dan *løbe,* all fr. ON *hleypa* to cause the coagulation of, causative of *hlaupa* to undergo coagulation, jump, leap — more at LEAP] *North* **:** COAGULATE, CLOT, CURDLE — used esp. of milk

2**lopper** \"\ *n* -s [2*lop* + *-er*] **1 :** one that lops ⟨a great oak . . . spoiled of boughs by the ~'s ax —Thomas Jackson⟩ **2 :** pruning shears having handles about two feet long

loppered milk *n* [ME *lopred milk,* fr. *lopred* (past part. of *lopren*) + *milk*] *North* **:** CLABBER

lopping *n* -s [fr. gerund of 2*lop*] **:** something cut off; *esp* **:** a branch cut from a tree or bush — usu. used in pl.

lopping shears *n pl* **:** pruning shears made with handles 24 to 30 inches in length and used for cutting branches of trees and shrubs

lopping shears

1**lop·py** \ˈläpē, -pi\ *adj* [ME, fr. *loppe* flea + *-y* — more at LOP (flea)] *dial Brit* **:** infested with fleas

2**loppy** \"\ *adj* [4*lop* + *-y*] **:** hanging loosely **:** LIMP

3**loppy** \"\ *adj* [7*lop* + *-y*] **:** CHOPPY — used of the sea

lops *pl of* LOP, *pres 3d sing of* LOP

lopseed \ˈ=,=\ *n* [5*lop* + *seed*] **:** a perennial Asiatic herb (*Phryma leptostachya*) adventive in No. America

lopseed family *n* **:** PHRYMACEAE

lopsided \ˈ=¦==\ *also* **lobsided** \ˈ=¦==\ *adj* [5*lop* + *sided*] **1 :** leaning to one side (as from a defect of structure) ⟨looked rather ~ with three boats swung on the port side and no boat at all on the starboard side —H.A.Chippendale⟩ ⟨small, wormy, ~ apples —Joseph Mitchell⟩ **2 :** lacking in balance or symmetry **:** poorly proportioned **:** disproportionately heavy on one side ⟨~ economic development⟩ ⟨a ~ vote of 373 to 9⟩ ⟨a ~ personality⟩ — **lop·sid·ed·ly** *adv* — **lop·sid·ed·ness** *n* -ES

lopstick \ˈ=,=\ *n* [1*lop* + *stick*] *Canad* **:** a tree with branches trimmed so that it may serve as a landmark or memorial

loq *abbr* loquitur

lo·qua·cious \lōˈkwāshəs\ *adj* [L *loquac-, loquax* loquacious (fr. *loqui* to speak) + E *-ious*] **1 a :** given to excessive talking **:** GARRULOUS ⟨the brandy made him a bit ~ —Sherwood Anderson⟩ **b :** full of excessive talk **:** WORDY ⟨the prolonged and ~ death scene —C.W.Cunnington⟩ ⟨the ~ cluttered plot —*Newsweek*⟩ **2 :** BABBLING, NOISY ⟨sometimes a ~ brook would run right through it —Christopher Rand⟩ **syn** see TALKATIVE

lo·qua·cious·ly *adv* **:** in a loquacious manner

lo·qua·cious·ness *n* -ES **:** the quality or state of being loqua-

cious : TALKATIVENESS ⟨a ~ at times rising to eloquence —Walter Cerf⟩
lo·quac·i·ty \lō'kwasəd-ē, -ətē, -i\ *n* -ES [L *loquacitat-, loquacitas*, fr. *loquac-, loquax* + *-itat-, -itas* -ity] **1 :** LOQUACIOUSNESS, GARRULITY ⟨had lost his usual ~ and quaint humor —Charles Kingsley⟩ **2 :** an instance of loquacity ⟨knew what they were doing in all their ramblings and *loquacities* —C.E.Montague⟩
lo·quat \'lō,kwät, ⸗'⸗\ *n* -S [Chin (Cant) *lō-kwat*] **1 :** an Asiatic evergreen tree (*Eriobotrya japonica*) now cultivated in most tropical or subtropical regions for its fruit — called also *Japanese medlar, Japanese plum, nispero* **2 :** the fruit of the loquat used for preserves, jams, and jellies
lo·quence \'lōkwən(t)s\ *or* **lo·quen·cy** \-nsē\ *n, pl* **loquences** *or* **loquencies** [L *loquentia*, fr. *loquent-, loquens* + *-ia* -y] *archaic* : SPEECH, DISCOURSE
lo·quent \-kwənt\ *adj* [L *loquent-, loquens*, pres. part. of *loqui* to speak] *archaic* **:** using speech **:** SPEAKING — **lo·quent·ly** *adv*
lo·qui·tur \'läkwəd·ə(r), -ətə-\ [L, he speaks, she speaks, 3d pers. sing. pres. indic. of *loqui* to speak] **:** begins to speak — used as a stage direction usu. after the name of the player
lor \'lȯ(ə)r, -ȯ(ə)\ *substand var of* LORD
lora *pl of* LORUM
lo·ral \'lōrəl, -ȯr-\ *adj* [²*lore* + *-al*] **:** of or relating to a lore
lo·ran \'lōr,an, 'lȯ,r-, ⸗'⸗\ *n* -S [*long-range navigation*] **:** a system of long-range navigation in which pulsed signals sent out by two pairs of radio stations of known position are used by navigators to determine the geographical position of a ship or an airplane
lor·an·dite \'lärən,dīt\ *n* -S [Hung *lorandit*, fr. Eotvös *Lorand*, 19th cent. Hung. physicist + Hung *-it* -ite] **:** a cochineal red monoclinic mineral $TlAsS_2$ consisting of a thallium sulfarsenide
lo·ran·skite \lə'ran,skīt\ *n* -S [G *loranskit*, fr. A. M. *Loranski*, 19th cent. Russ. mine inspector + G *-it* -ite] **:** a mineral (Y,Ce,Ca,Zr?)(Ta,Zr?)O_4(?) consisting of a black oxide of yttrium, cerium, calcium, tantalum, and zirconium
lo·ran·tha·ce·ae \,lō,ran'thāsē,ē, ,lō-\ *n pl, cap* [NL, fr. *Loranthus*, type genus + *-aceae*] **:** a family of parasitic or hemiparasitic shrubs or trees (order Santalales) comprising the mistletoes that are natives chiefly of tropical regions, have thick leathery mostly opposite and sometimes scaly leaves, and are attached to their hosts by haustoria
lo·ran·thus \lə'ran(t)thəs\ *n, cap* [NL, fr. L *lorum* strap + NL *-anthus* — more at LORE] **:** a very large mostly tropical genus (the type of the family Loranthaceae) of hemiparasitic plants distinguished by the baccate or drupaceous fruit
lor·cha \'lȯrshə\ *n* -S [Pg] **:** a three-masted sailing ship used in Chinese, Thai, and Philippine waters that has a hull built on a European model and rigging like that of a Chinese junk with batten lugsails

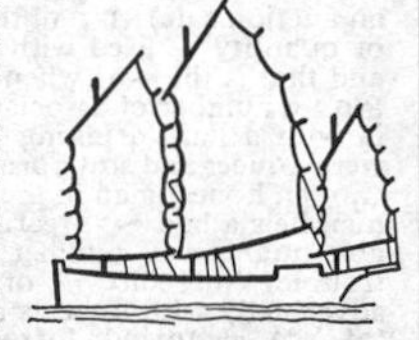
lorcha

¹**lord** \'lȯ(ə)rd, -ȯ(ə)d, *sometimes chiefly Brit* 'lȧd *esp in exclamations & in the form of address "My Lord" used by lawyers in court* \ *n* -S [ME *lord, loverd*, fr. OE *hlāford*, fr. *hlāf* bread, loaf + *weard* keeper, guard — more at LOAF, WARD] **1 :** one having power and authority over others: **a :** a ruler by hereditary right or preeminence to whom service and obedience are due : GOVERNOR, PRINCE, SOVEREIGN ⟨~ among earls —Alfred Tennyson⟩ ⟨our late sovereign ~ —John Keats⟩ **b :** one of whom a fee or estate is held in feudal tenure **:** the proprietor of feudal land — compare MANOR, MESNE LORD **c :** a proprietor or owner of land or houses ⟨~ of few acres and those barren too —John Dryden⟩ — compare LANDLORD **d** *obs* **:** the male head of a household **:** a master of servants ⟨that evil servant shall say in his heart, my ~ delayeth his coming —Mt 24:48 (AV)⟩ **e :** HUSBAND ⟨my sour husband, my hardhearted ~ —Shak.⟩ **f :** one that has achieved mastery by virtue of superior strength or conquest ⟨last in the field and almost ~*s* of it —Shak.⟩ ⟨pain is a terrible ~⟩ **g :** a man who exercises leadership or great power in a particular business or occupation ⟨press ~*s*⟩ ⟨money ~*s*⟩ ⟨the ~*s* of the art today —Bernard Smith⟩ ⟨a warning from the vice ~*s* . . . not to meddle in their affairs —Bosley Crowther⟩ **2** *cap* **a :** ²GOD ⟨the *Lord* will not hold him guiltless who takes his name in vain —Exod 20:7 (RSV)⟩ — often used as an interjection to express surprise or pity ⟨*Lord*, what fools these mortals be —Shak.⟩ **b :** CHRIST ⟨they have taken the *Lord* out of the tomb, and we do not know where they have laid him —Jn 20:2 (RSV)⟩ **3 :** a man of rank or high position: as **a :** a tenant in capite of the king or other feudal superior — compare BARON 1 **b :** any of various titled noblemen in Great Britain — used as a courtesy title for the younger son of a duke or marquess ⟨*Lord* Eustace Percy, younger son of a duke of Northumberland⟩ and as a mode of reference for (1) a baron ⟨*Lord* Graves, Baron of Gravesend⟩ or (2) on all but formal occasions a peer of the rank of marquess, earl, or viscount or one so styled as a courtesy title ⟨addressing the marquess of Hartington as *Lord* Hartington⟩ **c lords** *pl, usu cap* **:** the lords temporal and spiritual that constitute the upper house of the British Parliament ⟨only two or three bills thrown out by the *Lords* have ever been forced through by the Commons —George Orwell⟩ **4 :** a planet having controlling power or influence astrologically over a particular sign, house, or hour **5 :** a person chosen to preside over a festival — compare LORD OF MISRULE **6** *Brit* **:** a humpbacked person **7 :** a male harlequin duck — compare LORD-AND-LADY
²**lord** \"\ *vb* -ED/-ING/-S [ME *lorden*, fr. *lord*, n.] *vi* **:** to behave like a lord **:** act in a lordly manner **:** put on airs ⟨supreme the spectral creature ~*ed* —Robert Browning⟩ — usu. used with formulary *it* ⟨~*ing* it in a stucco palace —Clifton Fadiman⟩ ⟨~*ing* it around the bar —Edna Ferber⟩ ⟨the film director has ~*ed* it over the interpreter of Shakespeare —Walter Goodman⟩ ~ *vt* **1** *archaic* **:** to rule as lord of ⟨all the revels he had ~*ed* there —John Keats⟩ **2** *archaic* **a :** to grant the title of lord to **:** ENNOBLE ⟨those that hath for any services been ~*ed* — George Wither⟩ **b :** to address by the title of lord ⟨every spoken tongue should ~ you —Alfred Tennyson⟩
lord admiral *n* **:** LORD HIGH ADMIRAL
lord advocate *n* **:** the chief law officer of the crown in Scotland who in practice delegates his powers as principal prosecutor in criminal matters to the solicitor general and the four advocates-depute
lord almoner *n* **:** LORD HIGH ALMONER OF ENGLAND
lord-and-lady \'⸗⸗'⸗⸗\ *n, pl* **lords-and-ladies :** HARLEQUIN DUCK
lord baltimore cake *n, usu cap L&B* [prob. after *Lord Baltimore* (George Calvert) †1632 Eng. proprietor in America] **:** a usu. gold butter cake with a filling of macaroons, nuts, and cherries and a boiled frosting — compare LADY BALTIMORE CAKE
lord bird *n* **:** HARLEQUIN DUCK
lord chamberlain *or* **lord chamberlain of the household** *n* **:** a royal officer and government official in England whose duties include the appointment of professional men and tradesmen for the court, the regulation of the royal theaters and chapels royal, and the licensing of all plays produced publicly in England
lord chancellor *n, pl* **lords chancellor :** a British officer of state who presides over the House of Lords in both its legislative and judicial capacities, serves as the head of the British judiciary, and is usu. a leading member of the cabinet ⟨judicial appointments are made on the advice of the *lord chancellor* —W.H.Wickwar⟩ — called also *lord high chancellor;* compare MASTER OF THE ROLLS
lord chief justice of england *cap E* **:** the presiding judge of the King's Bench Division of the High Court of Justice in England
lord clerk register *n* **:** an officer of state in Scotland who has custody of the archives
lord commissioner *n, pl* **lords commissioners :** a member of a board exercising the powers of a high British office of state that has been put in commission
lord commissioner of admiralty : one of the lords commissioners including the first lord, the sea lords, and the civil lord who perform the executive duties of the former office of lord high admiral in England
lord commissioner of the treasury : one of the lords commissioners who perform the duties of the former office of lord high treasurer of England — see FIRST LORD OF THE TREASURY
lord fauntleroy *adj, usu cap L&F* [after *Lord Fauntleroy*, boy hero of Frances Hodgson Burnett's novel *Little Lord Fauntleroy* (1886)] **:** resembling or suggestive of Lord Fauntleroy (as in style of clothing or haircut)
lord great chamberlain of england *cap E* **:** a hereditary great officer of state in England whose duties were orig. financial but are now mainly ceremonial
lord harry *n, usu cap L&H* [fr. *Harry*, nickname for the name *Henry*] **:** DEVIL 1
lord high admiral *n* **:** a great officer of state formerly at the head of the naval administration of Great Britain
lord high almoner of england *cap E* **:** an ecclesiastical officer of the royal household in Great Britain who distributes the royal bounty
lord high chancellor *n* **:** LORD CHANCELLOR
lord high commissioner *n* **:** a commissioner who represents the British crown at the General Assembly of the Church of Scotland
lord high constable *n* **:** a great officer of state in England now appointed only for rare occasions (as coronations)
lord high steward *n* **:** an English officer of state now appointed only for rare occasions (as a coronation or the trial of a peer)
lord high treasurer of england *cap E* **:** the former third great officer of the crown whose duties are now executed by the Treasury Board
lord·ing \'lȯ(ə)rdiŋ, -ȯ(ə)d-\ *n* -S [ME, alter. of *loverding*, fr. OE *hlāfording*, fr. *hlāford* lord + *-ing* — more at LORD] **1** *archaic* **:** LORD ⟨have a care for yourselves, ~*s* —Charles Kingsley⟩ **2** *obs* **:** LORDLING
lord-in-waiting \'⸗⸗'⸗⸗\ *n, pl* **lords-in-waiting :** a man chosen from a noble family to serve as a personal attendant in the household of the British sovereign or of the prince of Wales
lord justice *or* **lord justice of appeal** *n, pl* **lords justices** *or* **lords justices of appeal :** a judge of the Court of Appeal in England
lord justice clerk *n, pl* **lord justice clerks :** JUSTICE CLERK
lord justice general *n, pl* **lord justices general :** JUSTICE GENERAL
lord keeper of the great seal : LORD CHANCELLOR
lord keeper of the privy seal : LORD PRIVY SEAL
lord·less \'lȯ(ə)rdləs, -ȯ(ə)d-\ *adj* [ME *lordles*, alter. of *loverdles*, fr. OE *hlāfordlēas*, fr. *hlāford* lord + *-lēas* -less] **:** having no lord **:** lacking a master
lord·let \-lət\ *n* -S **:** LORDLING
lord lieutenancy *n* **:** the office of a lord lieutenant
lord lieutenant *n, pl* **lords lieutenant** *or* **lord lieutenants 1 :** an official of the crown in English counties formerly having extensive military powers and now serving as the principal justice of the peace and keeper of the county records **2 :** LORD LIEUTENANT OF IRELAND
lord lieutenant of ireland *cap I* **:** the English viceroy in Ireland before 1922
¹**lordlike** \'⸗,⸗\ *adj* [ME *lordlik*, fr. ¹*lord* + *lik* like] *archaic* **:** LORDLY
²**lordlike** *adv, obs* **:** in a manner befitting a lord
lord·li·ly \'lȯ(ə)rdləlē, -ȯ(ə)d-\ *adv* **:** in a lordly manner
lord·li·ness \-lēnəs, -lin-\ *n* -ES [ME *lordlynes*, fr. ¹*lordly* + *-nes* -ness] **1 :** the quality or state of being a lord **2 a :** the manner and behavior suitable to a lord **:** DIGNITY **b :** an attitude of superiority toward inferiors **:** HAUGHTINESS
lord·ling \-liŋ\ *n* -S [ME, alter. of *loverdling*, fr. *loverd* lord + *-ling* — more at LORD] **:** a petty or insignificant lord ⟨a poor ~ of uncertain prospects —J.M.Barzun⟩
¹**lord·ly** *adj, usu* -ER/-EST [ME, alter. of *loverdlich*, fr. OE *hlāfordlic*, fr. *hlāford* lord + *-līc* -ly] **1 a :** of, relating to, or administered by a lord ⟨~ or absolute monarchy is the best and most natural government —John Hall⟩ **b :** having the characteristics of a lord **:** DIGNIFIED, HONORABLE ⟨more ~ than all emperors and kings condensed into one —C.H. Spurgeon⟩ ⟨its ~ and patrician detachment —Irwin Edman⟩ **c** (1) **:** befitting a lord **:** NOBLE ⟨the generous public spirit . . . responsible for this ~ gift of land —Lewis Mumford⟩ (2) **:** suitable for a lord **:** GRAND, STATELY ⟨one of the *lordliest* sites on earth —R.L.Duffus⟩ ⟨heir to a ~ fortune —Dumas Malone⟩ **2 :** having or affecting a feeling of superiority **:** ARROGANT, HAUGHTY, IMPERIOUS ⟨a ~ indifference to making money by his writings —Leslie Stephen⟩ ⟨a ~ nation that will not trust thee but for profit's sake —Shak.⟩ **syn** see PROUD
²**lordly** \"\ *adv* [ME, fr. *lordly*, adj.] **:** in a lordly manner
lord lyon king of arms *or* **lord lyon :** LYON KING OF ARMS
lord marcher *n, pl* **lords marchers** [ME *lord marchier*, fr. ¹*lord* + *marchier* marcher] **:** MARCHER 2
lord mayor *n* **:** the mayor of a large city esp. in the British Commonwealth
lord of appeal in ordinary : a life peer with eminent legal qualifications appointed to act as one of the principal members of the House of Lords in its proceedings as a court of last resort ⟨authorized the appointment of . . . nine *lords of appeal in ordinary* —F.A.Ogg & Harold Zink⟩
lord of council and session : a judge of the Court of Session in Scotland
lord of erection *Scots law* **:** the lord or superior of a temporal lordship created by secularization of an ecclesiastical benefice at the time of the Reformation — called also *titular*
lord of misrule [ME *lorde of mysrewle*] **1 :** one chosen to preside over the Christmas revels at court, in noble households, and elsewhere in England esp. in the 15th and 16th centuries — called also *Abbot of Misrule;* compare ABBOT OF UNREASON **2 :** the presiding officer of a popular festival
lord of regality [ME (Sc) *lord of regalite*] **:** one formerly granted rights of regalities by a Scottish king
lord of session : LORD OF COUNCIL AND SESSION
lord of the admiralty : LORD COMMISSIONER OF ADMIRALTY
lord of the articles [ME (Sc)] **:** one of a standing committee of the Scottish Parliament charged with the drafting and preparation of the acts or bills for laws
lord of the ascendant : a planet whose house is rising in the east
lord of the bedchamber 1 : a lord in waiting in the British royal household **2 :** either of two lords in attendance in the household of the prince of Wales
lord of the treasury : LORD COMMISSIONER OF THE TREASURY
lord·ol·a·try \lȯ(ə)r'däl·ə·trē, lȯ(ə)'-, -ri\ *n* -ES [¹*lord* + *-o-* + *-latry*] **:** adulation of a lord because of his rank or title ⟨the extent and prevalence of ~ in this country —W.M.Thackeray⟩
lord ordinary *n, pl* **lords ordinary :** one of the five judges constituting the Outer House of the Court of Session in Scotland
lor·do·sis \lȯ(ə)r'dōsəs, lȯ(ə)'-\ *n, pl* **lordo·ses** \-,sēz\ [NL, fr. Gk *lordōsis*, fr. *lordos* bent backward + *-ōsis* -osis; akin to OE *belyrtan* to deceive, MHG *lürzen* to deceive, *lerz, lurz* left, located on the left side, ScGael *lorcach* lame] **1 :** abnormally exaggerated forward curvature of the spine — opposed to *kyphosis* **2 :** the state of one affected with lordosis
lor·dot·ic \-'däd·ik, -ätik\ *adj* [fr. *lordosis*, after such pairs as E *hypnosis: hypnotic*] **:** of or relating to lordosis
lord president *n, pl* **lord presidents 1 :** LORD PRESIDENT OF THE COUNCIL **2 :** the presiding officer of the Court of Session in Scotland — compare JUSTICE GENERAL
lord president of the council : a British officer of state who has only nominal official duties as presiding member of the Privy Council in the United Kingdom but who is often made a member of the cabinet and entrusted with special functions
lord privy seal *n* **:** a British officer of state who has only nominal official duties as custodian of the privy seal but who is often made a member of the cabinet and given special functions
lord proprietor *or* **lord proprietary** *n, pl* **lords proprietors** *or* **lords proprietary :** a person granted a royal charter for the establishment and government of an American colony in the 17th century
lord provost *n* **:** the chief magistrate of a large city in Scotland
lord rector *n* **:** the titular head of a Scottish university — compare CHANCELLOR 2a
lord register *n* **:** LORD CLERK REGISTER
lords *pl of* LORD, *pres 3d sing of* LORD
lords-and-ladies \'⸗⸗'⸗⸗\ *n pl but sing or pl in constr* **1 :** CUCKOOPINT **2 :** JACK-IN-THE-PULPIT 1
lord's day *n, usu cap L & often cap D* [ME *Lordes day*, trans. of LL *dominica dies*, trans. of Gk *kyriakē hēmera;* fr. the Christian belief that Christ arose from the dead on Sunday] **:** SUNDAY ⟨nobody has ever . . . knitted a stitch in this house on the *Lord's day* —Ellen Glasgow⟩
lord·ship \'lȯ(ə)rd,ship, -ȯ(ə)d-\ *n* [ME, fr. OE *hlāfordscipe*, fr. *hlāford* lord + *-scipe* -ship — more at LORD] **1 a :** the rank or dignity of a lord — used as a title with *your* or periphrastically with *his* or *their* ⟨his *Lordship* is not at home⟩ ⟨if it please your *Lordship*⟩ **b :** the authority or power of a lord **:** DOMINION, SOVEREIGNTY ⟨the ~ of God over time —F.V.Filson⟩ ⟨this claim to racial ~ —*Times Lit. Supp.*⟩ **2 :** the domain or territory belonging to or under the jurisdiction of a lord **:** SEIGNIORY ⟨wandered from ~ to ~ and country to country —A.R.Wagner⟩ **3 a :** a royalty on minerals **b :** a royalty on the sales of books
lords ordainers *n pl* **:** ORDAINERS
lord spiritual *n, pl* **lords spiritual** [ME *lord spirituel*] **:** an English bishop or archbishop who is a member of the House of Lords — compare LORD TEMPORAL
lord's room *n* **:** a box for spectators of rank at the back of and overlooking the stage of an Elizabethan theater
lord's supper *n, usu cap L&S* [ME *Lordis sopere*, trans. of LL *dominica cena*, trans. of Gk *kyriakon deipnon*] **:** EUCHARIST 1a
lord's table *n, usu cap L & often cap T* [trans. of Gk *trapeza Kyriou*] **:** ALTAR 2a
lord steward of the household : the highest officer of the royal household of England who is a peer and privy councilor, presides at the Green Cloth, and has charge of the hall, kitchen, pantry, ewery, cellars, and almonry
lord temporal *n, pl* **lords temporal** [ME *lord temporel*] **:** a member of the House of Lords who is not an ecclesiastic ⟨in the fifteenth century the lords spiritual outnumbered the *lords temporal* —F.A.Ogg & Harold Zink⟩ — compare LORD SPIRITUAL
lord treasurer *n* **:** LORD HIGH TREASURER OF ENGLAND
lord trier *n, pl* **lords triers :** a member of the House of Lords sitting in judgment on a peer
lordy \'lȯ(ə)rdē, -ȯ(ə)dē, -di\ *interj* [¹*lord* + *-y*] — used to express surprise, astonishment, or strength of feeling
¹**lore** \'lō(ə)r, -ȯ(ə)r, -ōə, -ȯ(ə)\ *n* -S [ME, fr. OE *lār;* akin to OHG *lēra* doctrine, OE *leornian* to learn — more at LEARN] **1** *archaic* **:** something that is taught **:** LESSON, DOCTRINE, INSTRUCTION ⟨men admire virtue who follow not her ~ —John Milton⟩ ⟨we have learnt a different ~ —S.T.Coleridge⟩ **2 :** something that is learned: **a :** knowledge gained through study ⟨have plied their book diligently and know all about some one branch or another of accepted ~ —R.L.Stevenson⟩ **b :** knowledge or wisdom gained through experience ⟨learned for themselves the ~ of swift hunting in the dusk —Alan Devoe⟩ ⟨skilled in the ~ of frocks —Arnold Bennett⟩ **c :** traditional and unscientific knowledge or belief transmitted usu. by word of mouth ⟨provides ~ about words which is as pleasant as it is unreliable —Charlton Laird⟩ **3 a :** a body of knowledge relating to a particular field of learning ⟨using anatomical and physiological ~ —John Dewey⟩ ⟨basic in all modern attitudes toward earth ~ —K.F.Mather⟩ **b :** a body of traditions relating to a person, institution, or place ⟨lectured on Scottish ~ —Ashley Halsey⟩ ⟨the ~ of baseball heroes⟩ **syn** see KNOWLEDGE
²**lore** \"\ *n* -S [NL *lorum*, fr. L, strap; akin to Gk *eulēra* reins, Arm *lar* rope, and prob. to Gk *eilein* to wind, roll — more at VOLUBLE] **1 a :** the space between the eye and bill in a bird **b :** the corresponding region in a reptile or fish **2 :** the anterior part of the gena of an insect
¹**lo·re·al** \'lōrēəl, -ȯr-\ *adj* [irreg. fr. ²*lore* + *-al*] **:** LORAL
²**loreal** \"\ *n* -S **:** a scale lying between the nasal and the eye of a snake
lorel *n* -S [ME, fr. *loren* (past part. of *lesen* to lose), fr. OE, past part. of *lēosan* to lose — more at LOSE] *obs* **:** a worthless person
lore·lei \'lȯrə,lī, 'lär-, 'lōr-\ *n* -S *usu cap* [after the *Lorelei*, siren of German legend said to inhabit the Lorelei rock on the right bank of the Rhine south of Koblenz and to entice boatmen to their destruction by her beauty and her singing] **:** SIREN 2 ⟨art is a temptation, a seduction, a *Lorelei* —H.L. Mencken⟩
lore·less \'lō(ə)rləs, -ȯ(ə)r-, -ōə-, -ȯ(ə)\ *adj, archaic* **:** lacking learning or knowledge
lo·rentz-fitzgerald contraction \'lōr,en(t)s-\ *n, usu cap L&F&G* [after Hendrik A. *Lorentz* †1928 Du. physicist and George F. *FitzGerald* †1901 Irish physicist] **:** FITZGERALD CONTRACTION
lorentz transformation *n, usu cap L* **:** the transformation of a physical formula applicable to a phenomenon as observed by one observer so as to apply to the same phenomenon as observed by another observer in uniform motion relative to the first in accordance with the theory of relativity
lo·renz curve \'lōr,en(t)s-\ *n, usu cap L* [prob. after Charlotte *Lorenz* b1895 Ger. statistician] **:** a curve formed by plotting the cumulative distribution of the amount of a variable against the cumulative frequency distribution of the individuals having the amount (as for indicating the degree of concentration of salary income among a number of individuals)
lo·rette \lə'ret, lō-\ *n* -S [F, fr. Notre Dame de *Lorette*, section of Paris] **:** a French courtesan esp. of the Second Empire period ⟨a sumptuous scene where ~*s*, actresses, respectable women . . . could satisfy their curiosity as to each other — Arnold Bennett⟩
lorette pruning system *n, usu cap L* [after Louis *Lorette* †1925 Fr. horticulturist who originated it] **:** a system of summer pruning of fruit trees to encourage the development of fruiting spurs
lo·ret·to·ite \lə'red·ə,wīt\ *n* -S [*Loretto*, Tennessee + E *-ite*] **:** a mineral $Pb_7O_6Cl_2$(?) consisting of a lead oxychloride occurring in honey-yellow bladed aggregates (hardness 3, sp. gr. 7.6)
lo·ret·to nun \lə'red·(,)ō-\ *n, usu cap L* [fr. *Loreto*, city in Italy famous for its Holy House, said to have been the home of the Virgin Mary in Nazareth] **:** a member of a congregation of religious women founded by Mary Teresa Ball near Dublin, Ireland, in 1822 — called also *Lady of Loretto*
l organism *n, usu cap L* **:** L-FORM
lor·gnette \lȯ(r)n'yet\ *n* -S [F, fr. *lorgner* to take a sidelong look at (fr. MF, fr. *lorgne* cross-eyed) + *-ette*] **:** a pair of eyeglasses or opera glasses with a handle

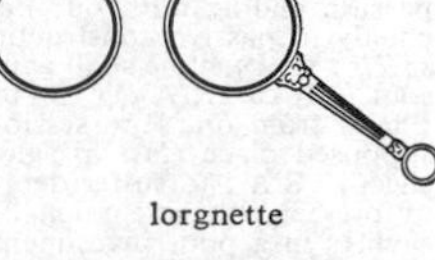
lorgnette

lor·gnon \lȯrn'yōⁿ\ *n* -S [F, fr. *lorgner*] **:** LORGNETTE ⟨aped the city lady's use of a ~ by looking through a doughnut stuck on a fork — Sinclair Lewis⟩
lo·ri \lō'rē\ *n* -S [modif. of F *loris*] **:** LORIS
lo·ri·ca \lə'rīkə\ *n, pl* **lori·cae** \-ī,sē\ [L, fr. *lorum* strap — more at LORE] **1 :** a Roman cuirass of leather or metal **2** [NL, fr. L] **:** a hard protective case or shell (as of a rotifer) **3** [NL, fr. L] **:** the cell wall or two valves of a diatom
lor·i·car·ia \,lȯrə'ka(a)rēə\ *n, cap* [NL, fr. LL *loricaria*, fem. of *loricarius* of a cuirass, fr. L *lorica* cuirass + *-arius* -ary] **:** a genus (the type of the family Loricariidae) of catfishes
lor·i·car·i·an \,⸗⸗'ka(a)rēən\ *adj or n* [NL *Loricaria* + E *-an*] **:** LORICARIID
¹**lor·i·car·i·id** \-rēəd\ *adj* [NL *Loricariidae*] **:** of or relating to the family Loricariidae
²**loricariid** \"\ *n* -S [NL *Loricariidae*] **:** a catfish of the family Loricariidae
lor·i·ca·ri·idae \,⸗⸗kə'rīə,dē\ *n pl, cap* [NL, fr. *Loricaria*, type genus + *-idae*] **:** a family of small So. American armored catfishes having the sides and back covered with angular bony plates, the air bladder with a bony capsule, and the mouth small and with thick fringed lips — **lor·i·car·i·oid** \,⸗⸗'ka(a)rē,ȯid\ *adj or n*

1lor·i·ca·ta \ˌlȯrəˈkād·ə, -ād·ə\ *n pl, cap* [NL, fr. L, neut. pl. of *loricatus*] **:** any of several groups of animals with a lorica (as the armadillos or the loricate rotifers)

2loricata \"\ *n pl, cap* [NL, fr. L, neut. pl. of *loricatus*] **:** an order of large long-tailed reptiles (as alligators, crocodiles, gavials) having four limbs adapted to swimming or walking, a tough skin stiffened with bony plates and horny epidermal scales, teeth implanted in sockets and confined to the margins of the jaws, the quadrate bone immovably fixed to the skull, and the heart completely four-chambered

3loricata \"\ [NL, fr. L, neut. pl. of *loricatus*] *syn of* AMPHINEURA

4loricata \"\ [NL, fr. L, neut. pl. of *loricatus*] *syn of* PALINURA

1lor·i·cate \ˈlȯrəˌkāt, *usu* -ād·+V\ *vt* -ED/-ING/-S [L *loricatus*, past part. of *loricare* to arm with a cuirass, fr. *lorica* cuirass, lorica] **:** to enclose in or cover with a protecting substance

2lor·i·cate \-kət, -ˌkāt, *usu* -d·+V\ *or* **lor·i·cat·ed** \ˌ==ˈkād·əd, -ātəd\ *adj* [L *loricatus*] **1 :** having a lorica **2** [NL *Loricata*] **:** of or relating to the Loricata

3loricate \"\ *n* -s [NL *Loricata*] **:** a loricate animal

lor·i·ca·ti \ˌ==ˈkād·ˌī\ [NL, fr. L, masc. pl. of *loricatus*] *syn of* 2LORICATA

lor·i·ca·tion \ˌ==ˈkāshən\ *n* -s [L *lorication-*, *loricatio*, fr. *loricatus* + *-ion-*, *-io* -ion] **1 :** the quality or state of having a lorica **2 :** a loricate covering

lor·i·keet \ˈlȯrəˌkēt\ *n* -s [*lory* + *-keet* (as in *parrakeet*)] **:** any of numerous small arboreal usu. brush-tongued parrots that are found mostly in Australasia and that feed largely upon the nectar of flowers

lor·i·let \ˈlȯrəˌlet\ *n* -s [*lory* + *-let*] **:** a small short-tailed parrot of New Guinea and northern Australia that is dark green with yellow flanks and red and blue markings on the head — called also *fig parrot*

lor·i·mer \ˈlȯrəmə(r)\ *or* **lor·i·ner** \-rənə(r)\ *n* -s [ME *lorimer*, *loriner*, fr. OF *lormier*, *lorenier*, fr. *lorain* strap holding a horse's saddle (fr. LL *loramentum* harness, straps, fr. L *lorum* strap + *-mentum* -ment) + *-ier* -er] **:** a maker of bits, spurs, and metal mountings for bridles and saddles

lor·i·ot \ˈlȯrēət, -ēˌō\ *n* -s [F, fr. MF, alter. of *loriol*, fr. *l'oriol* the loriot, the oriole, fr. OF, fr. *l'* the (contr. of *le*, def. art., the, fr. L *ille* that one, that) + *oriol* loriot, oriole — more at LARIAT, ORIOLE] **:** the golden oriole of Europe

lo·ris \ˈlōrəs, *in sense 1* " *or* lōˈrē\ *n* [F, perh. fr. obs. D *loeris* booby, simpleton] **1** -ES **:** either of two small nocturnal slow-moving lemurs: **a :** a slim-bodied lemur (*Loris gracilis*) of southern India and Ceylon — called also *slender loris* **b :** a stockier heavier-limbed lemur (*Bradicebus tardigradus*) of India and the East Indies that has a dusky dorsal stripe — called also *slow loris* **2** *cap* [NL, fr. F] **:** a genus (the type of the family Lorisidae) that comprises the slender loris — **lo·ri·sid** \ˈlōrəsəd\ *adj or n*

lo·ris·i·dae \ləˈrisəˌdē\ *n pl, cap* [NL, fr. *Loris*, type genus + *-idae*] **:** a family of lemurs comprising the lorises and related forms (as the galagos and pottos)

lo·ris·i·form \-fȯrm\ *adj* [NL *Lorisiformes*] **:** resembling a loris

lo·ris·i·for·mes \ˌ===ˈfȯrˌmēz\ *n pl, cap* [NL, fr. *Loris* + *-iformes*] *in some classifications* **:** a division of Lemuroidea comprising the lorises and related forms

lor·mery \ˈlȯrmərē\ *n* -ES [ME *lormerie*, fr. MF, fr. OF, fr. *lormier* lorimer + *-ie* -y] *archaic* **:** metalware made by lorimers

lorn \ˈlȯ(ə)rn, -ō(ə)n\ *adj* [ME, fr. *loren*, past part. of *lesen* to lose] **1** *archaic* **:** LOST, RUINED **2 a :** left alone **:** ABANDONED, FORSAKEN ⟨thus to be cast out, thus ~ to die —John Keats⟩ ⟨one large brass saucepan lay ~ near the doorstep —Arnold Bennett⟩ **b :** DESOLATE, LONELY ⟨never vaunted her ~ condition —Dorothy Parker⟩ **syn** see ALONE

lorn·ness \ˈ=nəs\ *n* -ES **:** the quality or state of being lorn

lo·ro \ˈlōr(ˌ)ō\ *n* -s [AmerSp, fr. Sp, parrot, prob. fr. Carib *loro*, *roro*] **:** PARROT FISH

lorraine cross *n, usu cap L* **:** CROSS OF LORRAINE

lor·rain·er \ləˈrānə(r), lōˈ-,-lȯˈ-\ *n* -s *usu cap* [*Lorraine*, region in western Europe + E *-er*] **:** a native or inhabitant of Lorraine

lor·rain·ese \ləˌrāˈnēz, ¦lō,r-, -ēs\ *adj, usu cap* [*Lorraine* + E *-ese*] **1 :** of, relating to, or characteristic of Lorraine **2 :** of, relating to, or characteristic of the people of Lorraine

lor·ry \ˈlȯrē, ˈlär-, -ri\ *n* -ES [prob. fr. ²*lurry*] **1 a :** a large low horse-drawn wagon without sides and with a platform that slightly overhangs the four small heavy wheels **b** *Brit* **:** MOTORTRUCK; *esp* **:** one with low or open sides and sometimes a canvas cover **2 :** any of various trucks running on rails: as **a** *Brit* **:** a light easily movable flatcar for the use of workmen on railroads **b :** LARRY

lorry-hop \ˈ==ˌ=\ *vi, Brit* **:** to hitchhike esp. on lorries

lo·rum \ˈlōrəm, ˈlȯr-\ *n, pl* **lo·ra** \-rə\ [NL, fr. L, strap — more at LORE] **1 :** ²LORE **2 a :** a transverse piece in the proboscis of a bee in which the base of the submentum rests **b :** a similar structure in other insects **c :** an elongated sclerite in the dorsal wall of the pedicel of a spider

lo·ry \ˈlōrē\ *n* -ES [Malay *luri*, *nuri*] **:** any of numerous parrots of Australia, New Guinea, and the adjacent islands that belong mostly to the genera *Domicella*, *Trichoglossus*, *Chalcopsitta*, and *Eos*, often have the tongue papillose at the tip and the mandibles less toothed than in other parrots, and feed mostly on soft fruits and the nectar of flowers

los·able *also* **lose·able** \ˈlüzəbəl\ *adj* **:** capable of being lost — **los·able·ness** *n* -ES

los angeleno \(ˌ)lōˌs+ˌ-\ *also* **los an·ge·le·an** \(ˌ)lōˌsanjəˈlēən *also* -aŋgəˈl-\ *n, cap L&A* [*los angeleno* fr. AmerSp *los angeleño*, fr. *Los Angeles*, California + Sp *-eño* (suffix added to place names to form names of inhabitants); *los angelean* fr. *Los Angeles*, California + E *-an*] **:** ANGELENO

los an·ge·les \lōˈsanjələs, -saan- *also* lȯˈ- *or* ləˈ- *or* -saŋg(ə)l- *or* -saiŋ- *sometimes* -jəˌlēz *or* -gəˌlēz\ *adj, usu cap L&A* **:** of or from the city of Los Angeles, Calif. ⟨a *Los Angeles* freeway⟩ **:** of the kind or style prevalent in Los Angeles

lösch·ia \ˈlərshēə, ˈlesh-\ [NL, fr. F. *Lösch*, 19th cent. Ger. zoologist + NL *-ia*] *syn of* ENTAMOEBA

lo·schmidt number \ˈlōˌshmit-\ *n, usu cap L* [after Joseph *Loschmidt* †1895 Austrian physicist] **:** the number of molecules per unit volume of an ideal gas at 0°C and a pressure of 1 atmosphere, its value for 1 cubic centimeter being about 2.7×10^{19}; *sometimes* **:** AVOGADRO NUMBER

lose \ˈlüz\ *vb* **lost**; **lost** \ˈlȯst *also* ˈläst\ **losing**; **loses** [alter. (prob. influenced in pronunciation by ¹*loose*) of ME *losen* to lose, get lost, perish, destroy, fr. OE *losian* to get lost, perish, destroy, fr. *los* destruction; akin to OE *lēosan* to lose, OHG *forliust* destruction, ON *losa* to loosen, Goth *fralusnan* to perish, L *luere* to atone for, Gk *lyein* to unbind, release, dissolve, Skt *lunāti* he cuts off] *vt* **1 :** to bring to destruction **:** RUIN, DESTROY ⟨what to ourselves in passion we propose, the passion ending doth our purpose ~ —Shak.⟩ — now used chiefly in passive constructions ⟨ship was *lost* on the reef⟩; *specif* **:** DAMN ⟨if he shall gain the whole world and ~ his own soul —Mt 16:26 (AV)⟩ **2 :** to fail to keep at hand or accessible **:** miss from one's possession **:** miss from its customary or supposed place ⟨*lost* his gloves⟩ ⟨little Bopeep has *lost* her sheep⟩ **3 a :** to suffer deprivation of **:** part with esp. in an unforeseen or accidental manner ⟨~ a leg in an auto crash⟩ ⟨~ savings in a poor investment⟩ ⟨*lost* his job⟩ **b :** to become deprived of or lacking in (a quality) ⟨has *lost* her beauty⟩ ⟨if salt has *lost* its taste, how can its saltness be restored —Mt 5:13 (RSV)⟩ ⟨the ceremony has *lost* its original meaning⟩ **4 a :** to suffer deprivation through the death or removal of or final separation from (a person) ⟨*lost* a son in the war⟩ ⟨village *losing* its young men through emigration⟩ **b :** to fail to keep (a patient) from dying ⟨have *lost* few pneumonia cases since penicillin came into use⟩ **c :** to become deprived of the services or useful presence of (as soldiers) through death, injury, desertion, capture ⟨the victors *lost* more men than the defeated⟩ **d :** to fail to keep control of or allegiance of ⟨~ votes⟩ ⟨the sect is *losing* its younger members⟩ **5 a :** to fail to use **:** be unable to make proper use of **:** let slip by **:** WASTE ⟨~ time in hunting for mislaid tools⟩ **:** MISS ⟨hated to ~ a day's fishing⟩ ⟨*lost* no opportunity to point out faults⟩ ⟨~ the tide⟩ ⟨sarcasm was *lost* on him⟩ **b :** to fail to win, gain, or obtain ⟨~ a prize⟩ ⟨~ a hooked fish⟩ ⟨~ a contest⟩ ⟨~ a lawsuit⟩ **:** undergo defeat in ⟨*lost* every battle but the last⟩ **c :** to fail to catch with the senses or the mind ⟨*lost* part of what he said⟩ **6 :** to cause the loss of ⟨one careless statement *lost* him the election⟩ ⟨leading from the king will ~ two tricks⟩ **7 :** to fail to keep, sustain, or maintain ⟨*lost* his balance⟩ ⟨the writer seems to have *lost* his touch⟩ ⟨*lost* his temper⟩ ⟨~ interest in a game⟩ ⟨~ poise⟩ ⟨*lost* his footing on the path and fell⟩ ⟨~ caste⟩ ⟨*lost* count of the minutes⟩ **8 a :** to cause to miss one's way or bearings ⟨you could not ~ him anywhere in London⟩ ⟨soon *lost* himself in the maze of streets⟩ **b :** to make (oneself) withdrawn from immediate reality ⟨*lost* himself in daydreaming⟩ **9 a :** to wander or go astray from **:** miss so as not to be able to find ⟨*lost* his way⟩ ⟨the ships *lost* each other in the fog⟩ **b :** to draw away from **:** shake off **:** OUTSTRIP ⟨*lost* his pursuers⟩ **10 :** to fail to keep in sight or in mind ⟨*lost* the thief in the crowded street⟩ ⟨the fielder *lost* the ball in the sun⟩ ⟨an intention that was soon *lost*⟩ **11 :** to free oneself from **:** get rid of ⟨dieting to ~ weight⟩ ⟨~ a cold⟩ **12 :** to make (itself) hidden or obscured ⟨the river ~*s* itself in the marshes⟩ ~ *vi* **1 :** to undergo deprivation of something of value ⟨investors *lost* heavily⟩ or deterioration of a valuable quality ⟨the story ~*s* considerably in translation⟩ **2 :** to undergo defeat **:** fail to win a goal or a contest ⟨able to ~ with good grace⟩ ⟨better to have loved and *lost* than never to have loved at all —Alfred Tennyson⟩ **3** *of a timepiece* **:** to run slow — **lose ground :** to become at a disadvantage **:** fall behind **:** fail to advance or improve — **lose one's cud :** to cease ruminating **:** refuse feed — **lose one's heart :** to fall in love ⟨*lost her heart* to a charming ne'er-do-well⟩

lo·sel \ˈlōzəl\ *n* -s [ME, fr. *losen* (past part. of *lesen* to lose), alter. of *loren* (past part. of *lesen* to lose), fr. OE, past part. of *lēosan* to lose — more at LOSE] **:** a worthless person

lo·sel·ry \-rē\ *n* -ES *archaic* **:** the character or action of a losel

lose out *vi* **:** to fail to win in competition **:** fail to receive an expected reward or gain ⟨afraid of *losing out* to more unscrupulous competitors⟩ ⟨*lost out* in the hurdles⟩

los·er \ˈlüzə(r)\ *n* -s **:** one that loses: as **a :** one that consistently loses or is likely to lose or is behind (as in a game or competition) ⟨a cheerful ~⟩ **b** *Brit* **:** LOSING HAZARD **c :** a card that may be expected to lose a trick or that does lose a trick in bridge ⟨discarded his club ~*s* on the established spades in dummy⟩ **d :** one that is convicted of a penal offense

loses *pres 3d sing of* LOSE

lo·sey·ite \ˈlōzēˌīt\ *n* -s [Samuel R. *Losey* †1906? Am. mineral collector + E *-ite*] **:** a mineral $(Mn,Zn)_7(CO_3)_2(OH)_{10}$ composed of a basic carbonate of manganese and zinc

1losh \ˈläsh\ *n* -ES *often attrib* [Russ *los'* elk; akin to OHG *elaho* elk — more at ELK] **1 :** elk hide **2 :** a hide dressed only with oil ⟨~ leather⟩

2losh \"\ *interj* [euphemism for *lord*] — used as a mild oath in Scots dialect

losing *adj* [fr. pres. part. of *lose*] **:** likely to result in failure or defeat ⟨~ strategy⟩ ⟨fighting a ~ battle⟩ **:** likely to lose **:** causing defeat ⟨~ cards⟩ ⟨three ~ tricks in his hand⟩

losing hazard *n* **:** the pocketing of the cue ball after it strikes an object ball in English billiards

1loss \ˈlȯs *also* ˈläs\ *n* -ES [ME *los*, prob. back-formation fr. *lost*, past part. of *losen* to lose, get lost, perish, destroy — more at LOST] **1 a :** the act or fact of losing **:** failure to keep possession **:** DEPRIVATION ⟨precautions against ~ or theft of property⟩ ⟨~ of a leg⟩ ⟨~ of sight⟩ ⟨~ of reputation⟩ ⟨~ of caste⟩ ⟨virtual ~ of three divisions of infantry⟩ **b :** the harm or privation resulting from losing or being separated from something or someone ⟨bore up bravely under the ~ of both parents⟩ ⟨the explosion caused a temporary ~ of hearing⟩ ⟨embittered by the ~ of his wife's affection⟩ **c :** an instance of losing ⟨his retirement was a serious ~ to the company⟩ ⟨her death was a ~ to all who knew her⟩ **d** *obs* **:** LACK, DEFAULT **2 :** a person or thing or an amount that is lost: as **a losses** *pl* **:** killed, wounded, or captured soldiers **b :** power or energy wasted in a machine, apparatus, or system ⟨friction ~⟩ ⟨heat ~ due to faulty insulation⟩ **c** (1) **:** the power diminution of a circuit element corresponding to conversion of electric power into heat by resistance (2) **:** ATTENUATION **3 a :** the act or fact of failing to gain, win, obtain, or utilize ⟨~ of a battle⟩ ⟨~ of opportunity⟩ ⟨~ of a game⟩ ⟨~ of a night's sleep⟩; *specif* **:** an amount by which the cost of an article or service exceeds the selling price — opposed to *profit* ⟨forced to sell all the stock at a ~⟩ ⟨railroad claimed to be operating at a ~⟩ **b :** a yardage disadvantage in football that results when an offensive play ends behind the line of scrimmage **4 :** decrease in amount, magnitude, or degree ⟨temperature ~⟩ ⟨~ in altitude⟩ — opposed to *gain* **5 a :** the state or fact of being destroyed or placed beyond recovery **:** DESTRUCTION, RUIN, PERDITION ⟨quitted all to save a world from utter ~ —John Milton⟩ ⟨~ of a ship with all hands⟩ ⟨~ of life in war⟩ **b** *obs* **:** a cause of ruin or destruction **6 :** the amount of an insured's financial detriment due to the occurrence of a stipulated contingent event (as death, injury, destruction, or damage) in such a manner as to charge the insurer with a liability under the terms of the policy — **at a loss :** unable to determine **:** PUZZLED, UNCERTAIN ⟨*at a loss* for a remedy⟩ ⟨*at a loss* for words to describe the situation⟩ — **for a loss** *adv* **:** into a state of depression, distress, or exhaustion ⟨at times gets me down and throws me *for a loss* —Christian Gauss⟩

2löss *var of* LOESS

loss-and-gain account \ˈ==ˌ=-\ *n* **:** INCOME ACCOUNT 2

loss constant *n* **:** an amount added to an insurance premium (as in a workmen's compensation policy) in consideration of the high loss ratio usu. sustained on small risks

los·sen rearrangement \ˈläsᵊn-\ *n, usu cap L* [prob. after Wilhelm *Lossen* †1906 Ger. chemist] **:** the conversion of a hydroxamic acid RCONHOH to an amine RNH_2, a urea $(RNH)_2CO$, a urethane $RNHCOOC_2H_5$, or a similar derivative by way of an intermediate isocyanate RNCO

loss·er \ˈlȯsə(r) *also* ˈläs-\ *n* -s [¹*loss* + *-er*] **:** an element inserted into an electric circuit (as of an amplifier) for providing impedance so as to prevent resonant electric oscillation

loss factor *n* **1 :** the ratio of the average to the maximum power loss in a circuit variably loaded over a given period **2 :** the product of the dielectric constant of a capacitor dielectric by the alternating-current power factor

loss leader *n* **:** an article sold at a loss in order to draw customers

loss·less \ˈlȯsləs *also* ˈläs-\ *adj* **:** being without loss **:** suffering no loss

loss ratio *n* **:** the ratio between insurance losses incurred and premiums earned during a given period

loss reserve *n* **:** an insurance company's reserve representing the discounted value of future payments to be made on losses which have already occurred

lossy \ˈlȯsē *also* ˈläsē\ *adj* [¹*loss* + *-y*] **1 :** of, relating to, or constituting a material capable of damping out an unwanted mode of oscillation and having little effect on a desired mode **2 :** highly dissipative of electrical energy ⟨a ~ medium⟩

lost *adj* [fr. past part. of *lose*] **1 a :** not made use of **:** WASTED ⟨~ hours⟩ **:** MISSED ⟨~ opportunity⟩ **b :** not gained or won ⟨~ battle⟩ ⟨~ race⟩ **c :** not claimed **:** FORFEITED ⟨~ annuity⟩ ⟨~ option⟩ **2 a :** having wandered from the path **:** unable to find the way ⟨~ child⟩ **b :** no longer visible ⟨the plane was soon ~ in the distance⟩ ⟨~ in the crowd⟩ **c :** lacking assurance or self-confidence **:** uncertain as to direction or location **:** BEWILDERED ⟨felt ~ on the first day on the job⟩ ⟨**:** HELPLESS ⟨~ without his glasses⟩ ⟨only the intellectually ~ who ever argue —Oscar Wilde⟩ **3 :** ruined or destroyed physically or morally **:** DAMNED ⟨~ ship⟩ ⟨~ soul⟩ **:** DESPERATE ⟨wild ~ manner of occasionally clasping his head in his hands —Charles Dickens⟩ ⟨crying out such ~ and terrible words —Virginia Woolf⟩ **4 a :** parted with ⟨~ limb⟩ **:** gone out of one's possession or control **:** MISLAID ⟨~ book⟩ **b :** no longer possessed ⟨~ honor⟩ ⟨~ reputation⟩ ⟨~ memory⟩ **c :** no longer known ⟨~ tunnel⟩ ⟨~ city⟩ or practiced ⟨~ art⟩ **5 a :** taken away or beyond reach or attainment **:** DENIED — used with *to* ⟨Asia Minor and the Balkans went the way of other regions ~ to the faith —Kemp Malone⟩ ⟨his career is ~ to history after that date⟩ **b :** HARDENED, INSENSIBLE — used with *to* ⟨~ to all sense of honor⟩ ⟨~ to shame⟩ **6 :** affected by or occupied with something so as to be unaware of one's surroundings **:** RAPT ⟨~ in revery⟩ ⟨~ in admiration⟩ **7** *of a golf ball* **:** that cannot be found within five minutes

lost ball *n* **:** a bowled ball in cricket that has been hit by a batsman and cannot be found or recovered by the fielding side counting six or more runs to the batsman's credit

lost cause *n* **:** a cause that has lost all prospect of success ⟨*lost cause* of the Southern Confederacy⟩ ⟨a frequent champion of *lost causes*⟩

lost-color process \ˈ=ˌ¦==-\ *n* **:** a technique of pottery decoration found in Central and So. America and involving the covering of areas with wax before dipping in dye so that on subsequent firing the waxed areas lose the applied color and revert to the original color

lost motion *n* **1 :** the lag between the motion of a driver and that of a follower in a mechanism due to yielding or looseness **2 :** inefficient or poorly directed expenditure of energy or time

lost·ness *n* -ES **:** the quality or state of being lost ⟨that ~ which is the extreme product of individualism —T.L.Cook⟩

lost river *n* **:** a surface stream that flows into an underground passageway

lost-wax process \ˈ=¦=-\ *n* [*lost-wax* trans. of F *cire perdue*] **:** CIRE PERDUE

1lot \ˈlät, *usu* -ȧd·+V\ *n* -s [ME, fr. OE *hlot*; akin to OHG *luz* share of land, ON *hlutr* lot, share, *hlautr*, Goth *hlauts* lot, Lith *kliudyti* to cause to hook on, and perh. to L *claudere* to close — more at CLOSE] **1 :** an object (as a piece of wood, pebble, die, straw) used as one of the counters in determining a question by the chance fall or choice of one or more of them — see SORTILEGE **2 a :** the use of lots or an equivalent process (as counting off) as a means of deciding something ⟨one was chosen by ~ to represent the group⟩ **b :** the choice resulting from such process ⟨the ~ fell on the youngest member⟩ **3 a :** something that comes to or happens to one upon whom a choice by lot has fallen **:** SHARE, PART, ALLOTMENT ⟨the will provided for equal ~*s* for all the children⟩ ⟨you have neither part nor ~ in this matter —Acts 8:21 (RSV)⟩ **b :** one's way of life or one's share of worldly reward or privation determined by chance, fate, or divine providence **:** FORTUNE, DESTINY ⟨the ~ of man, to suffer and to die —Alexander Pope⟩ ⟨a policeman's ~ is not a happy one —W.S.Gilbert⟩ ⟨one of those women who have always been resigned to the limitations of their ~ —Nadine Gordimer⟩ **4** *obs* **a :** a customs fee **:** TAX, DUTY **5** *obs* **a :** a lottery prize **b :** a prizewinning lottery ticket **6 a :** an allotment or portion of land set aside for a special purpose ⟨each settler was awarded a ~⟩ ⟨pasture ~⟩ ⟨burial ~⟩ ⟨circus ~⟩ ⟨used-car ~⟩ **b :** a measured parcel of land having fixed boundaries and designated on a plot or survey ⟨farm cut up into house ~*s*⟩ ⟨building ~⟩ **c :** a parcel of land in fact used for, intended for, or appropriated to a common purpose ⟨manufacturing ~⟩ ⟨refuse ~⟩ **d** *chiefly North* **:** a small pasture **e** *chiefly South & Midland* **:** COW PEN, BARNYARD **f :** PARKING LOT **g :** a motion-picture studio and its adjoining property **7 a :** a number of units of an article ⟨stationery ~⟩ or a parcel of articles offered as one item (as in an auction sale) **b :** all the members of a present group, kind, or quantity — used with *the* ⟨one more suitcase to carry out and that is the ~⟩ ⟨when you've seen one you've seen the ~⟩ **8 a :** a number of associated persons **:** CREW, SET, CROWD ⟨got in with a hard-drinking poker-playing ~⟩ ⟨his wife's family were a queer and stubborn ~⟩ ⟨nothing but a ~ of busybodies⟩ ⟨not an honest man in the ~⟩ **b :** KIND, SORT ⟨stay away from him, he's a bad ~⟩ ⟨recruits were a sorry ~⟩ **9 :** a considerable quantity or number **:** GREAT DEAL ⟨~ of money⟩ ⟨~ of trouble⟩ ⟨there are ~*s* of books on the subject⟩ — often used adverbially with *a* ⟨feels a ~ better now⟩ **syn** see FATE

2lot \"\ *vb* **lotted**; **lotted**; **lotting**; **lots** [ME *lotten*, fr. *lot*, n.] *vi* **:** to cast or draw lots ~ *vt* **1 :** to form or divide into lots ⟨~ land⟩ ⟨~ fruit for market⟩ — often used with *out* ⟨~ out goods in parcels⟩ **2 :** ALLOT, APPORTION **3** *obs* **:** to draw lots for — **lot on** *or* **lot upon** *now chiefly dial* **:** to count on **:** look forward to **:** EXPECT, PLAN

lot *abbr* lotion

1lo·ta *or* **lo·tah** \ˈlōd·ə, -ōtə\ *n* -s [Hindi *lotā*] **:** a small usu. spherical water vessel of brass or copper used in India

2lota \"\ *n, cap* [NL, fr. F *lotte* burbot] **:** a genus of fishes (family Gadidae) consisting of the burbots

lote \ˈlōt\ *or* **lotebush** \ˈ=ˌ=\ *also* **lo·ti·bush** \ˈlōd·ēˌ=\ *or* **lotewood** \ˈlōt·ˌwu̇d\ *n, pl* **lotes** *or* **lotebushes** [origin unknown] **1 :** a low spiny shrub (*Condalia obtusifolia*) of Mexico and southern Texas having edible fruit and roots from which a soap substitute is made — called also *Texas buckthorn* **2 :** JUJUBE 2

loth *var of* LOATH

lo·tha·rin·gian \ˌlōthəˈrinj(ē)ən\ *adj, usu cap* [ML *Lotharingia* Lorraine, region in western Europe + E *-an*] **:** of or relating to Lorraine

lo·thar·io \lōˈtha(a)rēˌō, -ther-,-thär-,-thär-,-thȧr-\ *n* -s *often cap* [after *Lothario*, seducer in the play *The Fair Penitent* (1703) by Nicholas Rowe †1718 Eng. dramatist] **:** a gay deceiver or seducer **:** LIBERTINE, RAKE

lo·tic \ˈlōd·ik, -ōtik\ *adj* [L *lotus* action of washing or bathing (fr. *lautus*, *lotus*, past part. of *lavere* to wash) + E *-ic*] **:** of, relating to, or living in actively moving water (as in stream currents or waves) — compare LENTIC

lo·ti·form \ˈlōd·əˌfȯrm\ *adj* [ISV *lotus* + *-iform*] **:** having the form of a lotus petal

lo·tion \ˈlōshən\ *n* -s [L *lotion-*, *lotio*, fr. *lautus*, *lotus* (past part. of *lavere* to wash) + *-ion-*, *-io* -ion — more at LYE] **1 :** the act of washing **:** ABLUTION **2 :** a liquid usu. aqueous medicinal preparation containing one or more insoluble substances and applied externally for skin disorders **3 :** a liquid cosmetic preparation usu. containing alcohol and a cleansing, softening, or astringent agent and applied to the skin esp. of the face and hands ⟨hand ~⟩ ⟨after-shave ~⟩

lo·tio ni·gra \ˈlōshēˌōˈnīgrə\ *n* [NL] **:** BLACK WASH 1

lo·ti·um \ˈlōshēəm\ *n* -s [L, urine, fr. *lautus*, *lotus*, past part. of *lavere* to wash] **:** urine formerly used as a cosmetic for the hair

lot·ment \ˈlätmənt\ *n* -s [²*lot* + *-ment*] *now dial* **:** an allotment of land

lo·tong \ˈlōˌtȯŋ\ *or* **lu·tong** \ˈlüˌ-\ *n* -s [Malay *lotong*] **:** a common black langur (*Presbytis obscurus* or *P. maurus*) of southeastern Asia and the East Indies

lo·toph·a·gi \lōˈtäfəˌjī,lōˈ-\ *n pl, sometimes cap* [L, legendary people who ate the lotus and encouraged travelers who visited them to do the same, fr. Gk *Lōtophagoi*, fr. *lōtos* lotus + *-phagoi* (pl. of *-phagos* -phagous)] **:** LOTUS-EATERS

lo·toph·a·gous \-gəs\ *adj* [*lotophagi* + *-ous*] **:** relating to or characteristic of lotus-eaters — **lo·toph·a·gous·ly** *adv*

lo-trap \ˈlō+ˌ-\ *n* [alter. of *low* + *trap*] **:** LOW-HOUSE

lots \ˈläts\ *adv* [fr. pl. of ¹*lot*] **:** to or by a considerable number or amount **:** MUCH ⟨~ more fun⟩ ⟨feeling ~ better⟩

lotted *past of* LOT

lot·ter \ˈläd·ə(r), -ätə-\ *n* -s **:** one that separates into lots; *specif* **:** one that appraises merchandise to be auctioned and assembles it into salable lots

lot·tery \ˈläd·ərē, -ätərē, -ä·trē, -ri\ *n* -ES *often attrib* [MF *loterie*, fr. MD, fr. *lot* lot + *-erie* -ery (fr. OF); akin to OE *hlot* lot — more at *lot*] **1 :** a scheme for the distribution of prizes by lot or chance; *esp* **:** a scheme by which prizes are distributed to the winners among those persons who have paid for a chance to win them usu. as determined by the numbers on tickets as drawn at random (as from a lottery wheel) — see DUTCH LOTTERY, INTEREST LOTTERY **2 :** the occasion of selection of prizes by lot **3 :** an event or affair whose outcome is or seems to be determined by chance ⟨regarded marriage as a ~⟩

lottery bond *n* **:** a bond issued by an interest lottery

lottery wheel *n* **:** a revolving drum or hollow cylinder in which lottery tickets are mixed and from which the winning numbers are drawn — called also *policy wheel*

lotting *pres part of* LOT

lot·to *also* **loto** \ˈläd·(ˌ)ō, -ä(ˌ)tō\ *n* -s [F or It; F *loto*, fr. It *lotto* lotto, lottery, fr. F *lot* lot, share, fr. OF, of Gmc origin; akin to OE *hlot* lot — more at LOT] **:** a game played usu. for a pool with cards bearing rows of numbers in which a caller draws numbered counters from a stock and each player covers the corresponding numbers if they appear on his card, the winner being the one who first covers one complete row

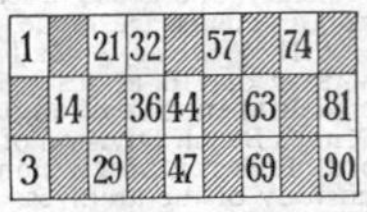

a card used in lotto

lo·tu·ko \lōˈtü(ˌ)kō\ *also* **la·tu·ka** \ləˈtükə\ *n, pl* **lotuko** *or*

lotukos *usu cap* **1 a :** a group of Negro peoples east of the Nile in Southern Sudan **b :** a member of any of such peoples **2 :** the Nilotic language of the Lotuko peoples

lo·tus *also* **lo·tos** \ˈlōd·əs, -ōtəs\ *n* [L & Gk; L *lotus*, fr. Gk *lōtos*, fr. Heb *lōṭ* myrrh] **1** -ES **:** the fruit in legendary Greek history eaten by the Lotophagi and supposed to cause a state of dreamy content and complete forgetfulness of home and friends; *also* **:** the shrub bearing this fruit — see LOTUS TREE **2** -ES **a :** LOTUS TREE **b :** SWEET CLOVER **3** -ES **:** any of various water lilies including several represented in ancient Egyptian and Hindu art and religious symbolism: as **a :** INDIAN LOTUS; *broadly* **:** NELUMBO 2 **b :** EGYPTIAN LOTUS 1 **4** -ES **:** an ornament used in ancient decoration (as in Egyptian capitals) and generally asserted to have been suggested by the Egyptian lotus (sense 1) **5** [NL, fr. L] **a** *cap* **:** a genus of widely distributed upright herbs or subshrubs (family Leguminosae) with pinnate leaves and solitary, twin, or umbellate flowers **b** -ES **:** any plant of the genus *Lotus*

American lotus

lotus bird *n* **:** a jacana (*Irediparra gallinacea*) of Australia

lotus-eater *or* **lotos-eater** \ˈ=ˌ=\ *n* [trans. of Gk *Lōtophagoi*] **:** one who gives himself up to indolence and daydreams ⟨a paradise for gourmets, *lotus-eaters*, and just plain tourists —T.H.Fielding⟩

lotus eye *n* **:** the eye (as of a Buddha) shaped or drawn in eastern art in the form of a lotus petal

lo·tus·in \ˈlōd·əsən\ *n* -S [NL *Lotus* + E *-in*] **:** a yellow crystalline cyanogenetic glucoside $C_{28}H_{31}NO_{16}$ obtained from a No. African leguminous plant (*Lotus arabicus*)

lotus land *n* **1 :** a place inducing dreaming and idleness **2 :** a state or an ideal marked by indolent self-indulgence and irresponsibility ⟨beguile the United States into living in a *lotus land* of isolation —M.W.Childs⟩

lotus lily *n* **:** WATER CHINQUAPIN

lotus tree *n* **:** any of several trees reputed to have furnished the lotus mentioned by the ancients: as **a :** a shrubby deciduous jujube tree (*Ziziphus lotus*) of the Mediterranean region that produces small yellow fruits **b :** a tall nettle tree (*Celtis australis*) of the same region that somewhat resembles a beech but produces a small sweet globose fruit **c :** an Asiatic persimmon (*Diospyros lotus*) that is sometimes cultivated for its small rounded yellow or purplish fruits; *also* **:** the common American persimmon (*D. virginiana*)

louch \ˈlau̇ch, ˈlüch\ *vi* -ED/-ING/-S [origin unknown] *dial Brit* **:** SLOUCH

louche \ˈlüsh\ *adj* [F, lit., cross-eyed, squint-eyed, fr. L *luscus* one-eyed] **:** SQUINTING, OBLIQUE **:** DEVIOUS, PERVERSE, SINISTER ⟨you've got to keep yourself free of any suggestion of ~ behavior —Anthony West⟩

lou·cheux \lüˈshō\ *n, pl* **loucheux** *usu cap* [F, fr. *louche*] **:** KUTCHIN 2

1**loud** \ˈlau̇d\ *adj* -ER/-EST [ME, fr. OE *hlūd*; akin to OS *hlūd* loud, OHG *hlūt* loud, ON *hljōth* silence, attention, hearing, Goth *hliuma* ear, L *cluēre* to be named, be called, Gk *klytos* famous, Skt *śṛnoti* he hears] **1 a :** marked by intensity or volume of sound — opposed to *soft* ⟨where ears are willing, talk tends to be ~ and long —Aldous Huxley⟩ ⟨~ and protracted singing —John Burroughs⟩ **b :** producing a loud sound ⟨the marten was ~ beside them —David Walker⟩ **2 a :** CLAMOROUS, INSISTENT **:** NOISY, VEHEMENT, EMPHATIC ⟨giving ~ lip service . . . as a means of drowning the voice of conscience —B.G.Gallagher⟩ ⟨small but determinedly ~ groups are mistaken for vast multitudes and are causing irreparable harm —M.R.Cohen⟩ **b** *obs* **:** EVIDENT, MANIFEST, OBVIOUS — used chiefly of a lie **3 :** obtrusive or offensive in appearance or smell **:** violating taste or propriety **:** FLASHY, NOISOME, OBNOXIOUS ⟨came along in the ~*est* pinstripe suit in history —John O'Reilly⟩ ⟨a ~ fish smell which one night's hard rain hadn't even dented —Raymond Chandler⟩ ⟨he was stout, ~, red, bluff, and free from any drawback of delicacy —Charles Dickens⟩ **4 :** uttered with the normal speaking voice; *specif* **:** produced by vibration of the vocal cords ⟨~ vowels⟩ ⟨~ voiced consonants⟩ — compare ALOUD, OUT LOUD

syn LOUD, STENTORIAN, EARSPLITTING, HOARSE, RAUCOUS, STRIDENT, and STERTOROUS, all applying to sounds, agree in meaning great in volume or unpleasant in effect. LOUD suggests a volume above normal, sometimes suggesting vehemence or obtrusiveness ⟨a *loud* cry⟩ ⟨a *loud* blast on a trumpet⟩ ⟨*loud* demands for reform⟩ ⟨a *loud* and unpleasant person⟩ STENTORIAN, chiefly applying to voices, implies exceedingly great power and range ⟨a *stentorian* voice, husky from much bawling of orders —F. Tennyson Jesse⟩ ⟨a few words, rendered either completely inaudible or painfully *stentorian* according to the whim of the microphone —*Times Lit. Supp.*⟩ ⟨blowing his nose in *stentorian* tones —O.E. Rölvaag⟩ EARSPLITTING adds the idea of a physically oppressive loudness, esp. shrillness, as of screams or shrieks ⟨suddenly he trumpeted, an *earsplitting* sound in the close stall —W.V.T.Clark⟩ ⟨an *earsplitting* cry of terror⟩ HOARSE implies harshness, huskiness, or roughness of tone, sometimes suggesting an accompanying or causal loudness ⟨the *hoarse* growling of the mob —Kenneth Roberts⟩ ⟨voice came to my ears . . . tense and *hoarse* with an overmastering rage —Jack London⟩ ⟨the *hoarse* bellow of the bull whistle —*Amer. Guide Series: N.C.*⟩ RAUCOUS implies a loud, harsh, grating tone, esp. of voice, often implying rowdiness ⟨the voices often become *raucous* or shrill and any proper dignity of the spirit suffers —W.R.Benét⟩ ⟨music of the city, *raucous*, jazzy, witty, dramatic —Howard Hanson⟩ ⟨women . . . gathering along the platform with thin, bright, *raucous* laughter —William Faulkner⟩ ⟨the *raucous* vitality of a mining boomtown —Seth Agnew⟩ STRIDENT adds to RAUCOUS the idea of a rasping, discordant but insistent quality, esp. of voice ⟨scurrying traffic whose *strident* voice mingles whistle blasts with the hollow clang of bell buoys and the screams of softly wheeling gulls —*Amer. Guide Series: N.Y. City*⟩ ⟨a sort of a *strident*, metallic quality about her revealed in the high pitch of her voice —Claire Sterling & Max Ascoli⟩ ⟨her vocal attack often sounds *strident* and explosive —*Newsweek*⟩ STERTOROUS, usu. not applied to sounds made by the voice, suggests the loud snoring, or sounds like snoring made in breathing, esp. when it is difficult, by persons or animals in sleep, in a coma, or with marked asthmatic difficulties ⟨the *stertorous* breathing of the owl —Osbert Sitwell⟩ ⟨the horse is trembling . . . its breathing *stertorous* like groaning —William Faulkner⟩

2**loud** \"\ *adv* -ER/-EST [ME *loude*, fr. OE *hlūde*; akin to OS *hlūdo* loudly, OHG *hlūto*; derivative fr. the root of E 1*loud*] **:** with loud sound or offensive appearance, manner, or smell ⟨who screams ~*est* . . . when the dinner consists of canned tuna fish —A.C.Spectorsky⟩ ⟨Eskimo-tanned furs smell out ~, especially in a warm room —*Newsweek*⟩

loud·en \ˈlau̇dᵊn\ *vb* -ED/-ING/-S *vi* **:** to become loud **:** grow audible **:** intensify in sound ~ *vt* **:** to make loud **:** intensify the sound of

lou·der·back \ˈlau̇də(r)ˌbak\ *n* [after George D. *Louderback* †1957 Am. geologist] **:** a tilted fault block capped by a lava flow

loud-hailer \ˈ=ˈ==\ *n* **:** BULLHORN

loud·ish \ˈlau̇dish\ *adj* **:** rather loud

loud·ly *adv, sometimes* -ER/-EST [ME, fr. 1*loud* + *-ly*] **:** in a loud, noisy, or emphatic manner ⟨the large birds laughed so ~ that the goldfinch became annoyed —James Thurber⟩ ⟨the white man's examples . . . spoke to the Indians more ~ than words —*Amer. Guide Series: Minn.*⟩

loudmouth \ˈ=ˌ=\ *n* **:** a foolish noisy person **:** BRAGGART ⟨why do you expect your children not to fall for the phony or the ~ —L. Ruth Middlebrook⟩

loudmouthed \ˈ=ˈ=\ *adj* **:** given to loud and idle talk **:** noisily offensive ⟨his ~ tabloids spiel sex, crime, and the workingman's cause —*Time*⟩

loud·ness *n* -ES [ME *lowdenesse* quality of being loud, fr. OE *hlūdnys*, fr. *hlūd* loud + *-nys*, *-nes* -ness] **:** the attribute of a sound that determines the magnitude of the auditory sensation produced by the sound and that in a musical sound depends upon both the energy-flux density and the pitch

loud pedal *n* **:** DAMPER PEDAL

loudspeaker \ˈ=ˈ==\ *n* **:** an electroacoustic device similar to a telephone receiver in operation but amplifying sound (as in public-address systems, radio and television receivers, and phonographs) — see CONE SPEAKER, ELECTRODYNAMIC SPEAKER

lou·ey *or* **lou·ie** *var of* LOOEY

lough \ˈläk, ˈläḵ\ *n* -S [ME, of Celt origin; akin to OIr *loch* lake, pond — more at LAKE] **1** *now chiefly Irish* **:** LAKE **2** *now chiefly Irish* **:** a bay or inlet of the sea

lough·lin·ite \ˈlöflə̇ˌnīt *also* ˈläf-\ *n* -S [Gerald F. *Loughlin* †1946 Am. geologist + E *-ite*] **:** a mineral $MgSi_2O_5.nH_2O$ consisting of a hydrous silicate of magnesium resembling asbestos

lou·is \ˈlüē\ *n, pl* **louis** [F, fr. *Louis* XIII †1643 king of France] **:** LOUIS D'OR

louis d'or \-ˈdȯr\ *n, pl* **louis d'or** [F, fr. *louis* + *d'or* of gold, golden] **1 :** a French gold coin first struck in 1640 and issued up to the Revolution **2 :** the French 20-franc gold piece issued after the Revolution

louis heel *n, usu cap L* [prob. after *Louis* XV †1774 king of France] **:** a French heel usu. two inches or less in height

lou·i·si·ana \lüˌ|ēzēˈanə, ˌ|lü|, |ˌēz-, -lüˌēz-, lüˌēz-, ləˌwēz-, *sometimes* ˌlüzēˌa-\ *adj, usu cap* [fr. *Louisiana*, state in the southern U.S., fr. F *Louisiane*, former French territory extending from the Mississippi river to the Rocky mountains, fr. *Louis* XIV †1715 king of France] **:** of or from the state of Louisiana ⟨a *Louisiana* bayou⟩ **:** of the kind or style prevalent in Louisiana **:** LOUISIANIAN

Louis heel

louisiana cypress *n, usu cap L* **:** a bald cypress (*Taxodium distichum*)

louisiana grass *n, usu cap L* **:** CARPET GRASS 1

louisiana heron *n, usu cap L* **:** an American heron (*Hydranassa tricolor ruficollis*) that is slaty above and white beneath

louisiana muskrat *n, usu cap L* **:** an American muskrat that is restricted to the coastal marshes of Louisiana, is usu. considered to constitute a distinct subspecies, and is distinguished from the typical form by somewhat smaller size, skin with heavier leather, and hair duller and without reddish cast

louisiana tanager *n, usu cap L* **:** WESTERN TANAGER

louisiana water thrush *n, usu cap L* **:** a No. American water thrush (*Seiurus motacilla*)

1**lou·i·si·an·i·an** \-zēˈanēən\ *also* **lou·i·si·an·an** \-anən\ *n* -S *cap* [*Louisiana* + E *-an*, n. suffix] **:** a native or resident of Louisiana

2**louisianian** \"\ *also* **louisianan** \"\ *adj, usu cap* [*Louisiana* + E *-an*, adj. suffix] **1 :** of, relating to, or characteristic of the state of Louisiana **2 :** of, relating to, or characteristic of the people of Louisiana **3 :** AUSTRORIPARIAN

lou·is qua·torze \ˈlüēkəˈtȯrz\ *adj, usu cap L&Q* [F *Louis Quatorze* (Louis XIV) †1715 king of France] **:** of, relating to, or having the characteristics of the reign of Louis XIV of France: as **a :** marked by imposing dignity and return to the ancient orders and details in architecture with emphasis on regularity and rich interior decoration **b :** exhibiting elaborate carving, gilding, and often inlay in furniture with Roman motifs in ornamentation and a combination of straight and curved lines in design — compare BOULLE **c :** florid and tending to rococo and rocaille in decorative art

louis quinze \-ˈkaⁿz\ *adj, usu cap L&Q* [F *Louis Quinze* (Louis XV) †1774 king of France] **:** of, relating to, or having the characteristics of the reign of Louis XV of France: as **a :** exhibiting irregularly curved lines and surfaces in interior ornamentation **b :** marked by curved lines and rich upholstery in furniture

louis seize \-ˈsez\ *adj, usu cap L&S* [F *Louis Seize* (Louis XVI) †1793 king of France] **:** of, relating to, or having the characteristics of the reign of Louis XVI of France: as **a :** approaching the antique more and more in architecture while taking on a greater lightness **b :** reverting to the straight line in decoration **c :** showing the influence of frescoes of Pompeii and Herculaneum in interior ornamentation **d :** marked by straight lines, light and simple construction, and pastoral motifs in ornamentation of furniture

louis treize \-ˈtrez\ *adj, usu cap L&T* [F *Louis Treize* (Louis XIII) †1643 king of France] **:** of, relating to, or having the characteristics of the reign of Louis XIII of France: as **a :** of developed Renaissance style in architecture but retaining much Gothic picturesqueness **b :** of square and angular design in furniture

lou·is·ville \ˈlüēˌvil, *esp in the South* -ēvəl\ *adj, usu cap* [fr. *Louisville*, city in north central Kentucky] **:** of or from the city of Louisville, Ky. ⟨*Louisville* officials⟩ **:** of the kind or style prevalent in Louisville

lou·is·vill·ian \ˌ=ˈvilyən\ *n* -S *cap* [*Louisville*, Kentucky + E *-an*] **:** a native or resident of Louisville, Kentucky

1**louk** \ˈlük\ *vb* -ED/-ING/-S [ME *lowken*, *luken* to weed, pull out, fr. OE *lūcan* to pull up (a weed); akin to MLG *lūken* to pull, OHG *liochan* to pluck, pull out, ON *lok* weeds, L *lugēre* to mourn — more at LUGUBRIOUS] *dial Eng* **:** WEED

2**louk** \ˈlau̇k\ *vt* -ED/-ING/-S [origin unknown] *dial Eng* **:** BEAT, WHIP, STRIKE

3**louk** \"\ *n* -S *dial Eng* **:** 3BLOW 1a

1**loun** \ˈlün\ *Scot var of* 1LOON

2**loun** \ˈlau̇n\ *or* **lound** \-nd\ *chiefly Scot var of* LOWN

1**loun·der** \ˈlündər\ *n* -S [origin unknown] *chiefly Scot* **:** a severe blow

2**lounder** \"\ *vb* -ED/-ING/-S *chiefly Scot* **:** to beat or thrash heavily

1**lounge** \ˈlau̇nj\ *vb* -ED/-ING/-S [origin unknown] *vi* **:** to act or move idly or lazily **:** to stand, sit, or recline indolently **:** LOAF, LOLL, SAUNTER ⟨for whole days at a time he would ~ in his Windsor chair in the kitchen —George Orwell⟩ ⟨*lounged* out from the office and looked him over —S.E.White⟩ ~ *vt* **:** to pass (time) idly — usu. used with *away* ⟨returned to Rome to ~ away the remainder of his days —J.A.Froude⟩

2**lounge** \"\ *n* -S **1 :** a place for lounging: as **a :** a room in a private home or public building for informal gathering and conversation or other leisure occupations **:** LIVING ROOM, PARLOR ⟨these paints are particularly suitable for ~, dining room, and bedrooms —*Australian Home Beautiful*⟩ **:** LOBBY, WAITING ROOM ⟨had the "plush" furnishings and atmosphere and most of the amenities of the ~ of a world airport —Sam Pollock⟩ ⟨in the U. N.'s corridors and ~*s*, where the doubtful are influenced —*Time*⟩ **b :** COCKTAIL LOUNGE **c :** a room in a public building often combining lounging, smoking, and toilet facilities **d :** a room or place on a train, ship, or airplane offering club or lounging facilities ⟨had gathered her lonely charges in the ~ at the rear of the plane —Henry La Cossitt⟩ **2** *archaic* **:** a lounging gait or posture **:** SAUNTER, SLOUCH **3 :** a long couch on which one person may recline or several may sit ⟨threw herself on the ~ and buried her face in her hands —Winston Churchill⟩ — compare DAVENPORT, DAYBED, DIVAN, SOFA

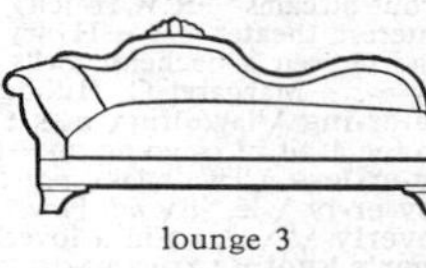

lounge 3

3**lounge** \"\ *archaic var of* LUNGE

lounge car *n* **:** a railroad passenger car with lounging often movable seats and facilities for serving refreshments — called also *club car, club-lounge car;* compare PARLOR CAR

lounge chair *n* **:** EASY CHAIR

lounge lizard *n* **1 :** LADIES' MAN, FOP **2 :** a social parasite

loung·er \ˈlau̇njə(r)\ *n* -S **1 :** one that lounges **:** IDLER ⟨the ~*s* at the bar were beginning to show signs of leaving —Haldane Macfall⟩ **2 :** an article of clothing (as a jacket or shoes) or of furniture (as a couch) meant for comfort and leisure use

lounge suit *n, chiefly Brit* **:** BUSINESS SUIT

1**lounging** *adj* [fr. pres. part. of 1*lounge*] **1 :** INDOLENT, SLACK ⟨how different is that quick springy figure from our young men's ~ style —George Meredith⟩ **2** [fr. gerund of 1*lounge*] **:** fit for leisure use or wear ⟨~ pajamas⟩ — **loung·ing·ly** *adv*

2**lounging** *n* -S [fr. gerund of 1*lounge*] **:** IDLING, SAUNTERING

loungy \ˈlau̇njē\ *adj* [1*lounge* + *-y*] **:** suitable for lounging **:** IDLE

1**loup** \ˈlau̇p, ˈlōp, ˈlüp\ *vb* -ED/-ING/-S [ME *loupen* to leap — more at LOPE (v.)] *chiefly Scot* **:** LEAP, FLEE

2**loup** \"\ *n* -S [ME — more at LOPE (n.)] *chiefly Scot* **:** LEAP

loup-cer·vier \ˈlüsə(ˌ)fē, ˌlüserˈvyā\ *n, pl* **loup-cerviers** *or* **loup-cervier** [CanF, fr. F, lynx, fr. L *lupus cervarius*, lit., deer wolf, fr. *lupus* wolf + *cervarius* of deer, fr. *cervus* deer, stag + *-arius* -ary — more at HART] **:** CANADA LYNX

loupe \ˈlüp\ *n* -S [F, loupe, gem of imperfect brilliancy, fr. MF, gem of imperfect brilliancy, prob. of Gmc origin; akin to Fris *lob*, *lobbe* hanging mass of fat or flesh — more at LOB] **:** a small magnifying glass used by jewelers and watchmakers

loup-ga·rou \ˌlügəˈrü\ *n, pl* **loups-garous** [MF, fr. OF *leu garoul*, fr. *leu* wolf (fr. L *lupus*) + *garoul*, *garulf* werewolf, of Gmc origin; akin to OE *werwulf* werewolf, OHG *werwolf* — more at WOLF, WEREWOLF] **:** WEREWOLF

louping ill *n* [*louping* fr. gerund of 1*loup*] **:** a tick-borne virus disease of sheep and other domestic animals and rarely man that is related to or identical with the Russian spring-summer encephalitis of man and occurs characteristically as a meningoencephalitis accompanied by muscular tremors and spasms followed by varying degrees of paralysis

loup-the-dyke \ˌ=ˈ=ˌ=\ *adj* [fr. the phrase *loup the dyke*, fr. 1*loup* + *the* + *dyke*] *Scot* **:** GIDDY, UNSETTLED

lour *var of* LOWER

1**lourd** *n* -S [obs. *lourd*, adj., dull, stupid, fr. ME *lourde*, fr. MF *lourd*, fr. L *luridus* pale yellow, sallow — more at LURID] *obs* **:** LOUT, SOT

2**lourd** \ˈlu̇rd\ *adv* [alter. (influenced by 1*-ed*) of Sc *loor*, *lour*, alter. of E dial. *liever*] *Scot* **:** RATHER — used in the phrases *had lourd* and *wad lourd*

lour·dan \ˈlərdᵊn\ *var of* LURDAN

loure \ˈlu̇(ə)r\ *n* -S [F, dance in slow triple or sextuple time, bagpipe, fr. MF, bagpipe, perh. fr. ON *lūthr* trumpet] **:** a dance in slow triple or sextuple time; *also* **:** the music for such a dance

lou·rie \ˈlu̇rē\ *n* -S [Afrik *loerie*, fr. Malay *luri*, *nuri* lory] **:** any of several touracos of southern Africa

lou·ro \ˈlō(ˌ)rü\ *n* -S [Pg, lit., laurel, fr. L *laurus* — more at DAPHNE] **:** a tree of the genus *Ocotea*

loury *var of* LOWERY

1**louse** \ˈlau̇s\ *n, pl* **lice** \ˈlīs\ *see sense 3* [ME *lous* (pl. *lys*), fr. OE *lūs* (pl. *lȳs*); akin to OHG & ON *lūs* louse, W *llau* lice] **1 :** any of various small wingless usu. flattened insects that are parasitic on warm-blooded animals and constitute the orders Anoplura and Mallophaga — compare BIRD LOUSE, SUCKING LOUSE; BODY LOUSE, CRAB LOUSE, HEAD LOUSE **2 a :** any of various small usu. sluggish arthropods that live on various animals or plants and suck their blood or juices — usu. used in combination; compare BEE LOUSE, CARP LOUSE, FISH LOUSE, PLANT LOUSE, WHALE LOUSE **b :** any of several somewhat similar arthropods that are not parasitic — usu. used in combination; compare BOOK LOUSE, WOOD LOUSE **3** *pl* **louses :** a person regarded as extremely contemptible for parasitic or other odious low conduct **:** BASTARD, HEEL, RAT, STINKER ⟨what a beast, what a cad, what a ~ he had been —Walter Karig⟩ ⟨while all the time she was withering her inner self with ". . . you ~! You perfect ~" —Catherine Hubbell⟩

2**louse** \ˈlau̇s, ˈlau̇z\ *vt* -ED/-ING/-S [ME *lowsyn*, fr. *lous*, *lows*, n.] **:** to pick lice from ⟨one old crone was alternately pinching a pretty child's cheeks and *lousing* her hair —I.L.Idriess⟩

louse·berry \ˈlau̇s- — *see* BERRY\ *n* **:** a European spindle tree (*Euonymus europaeus*) yielding berries formerly believed to repel insects

louse fly *n* **:** an insect of the family Hippoboscidae

louse up *vb* [2*louse*] *vt* **:** to foul up **:** mess up **:** SNARL, UNDO ⟨won't play it with a partner who *louses it up* —John Brooks⟩ ⟨the triteness which *louses up* most novels today —Paul Engle⟩ ~ *vi* **:** to fall into confusion **:** make a mess ⟨just where any famous singer will *louse up* in any famous opera —M.M.Hunt⟩

lousewort \ˈ=ˌ=\ *n* **1 :** a plant of the genus *Pedicularis* formerly reputed to cause sheep feeding upon it to be subject to vermin **:** WOOD BETONY **2 :** RATTLE 3a

lou·si·ci·dal \ˌlau̇səˈsīdᵊl\ *adj* **:** louse-killing — used of an insecticide ⟨the larvicidal and ~ action of DDT —*Yr. Bk. of General Therapeutics*⟩

lou·si·cide \ˈlau̇səˌsīd\ *n* -S [1*louse* + *-i-* + *-cide*] **:** a louse-killing insecticide **:** PEDICULICIDE ⟨DDT powder is highly effective and longer lasting than any other ~ in use —*Jour. Amer. Med. Assoc.*⟩

lous·i·ly \ˈlau̇zəlē, -li\ *adv* **:** in a lousy manner **:** MEANLY, CONTEMPTIBLY

lous·i·ness \-zēnə̇s, -zin-\ *n* -ES **1 :** PEDICULOSIS **2 :** VILENESS **3 :** a defect of silk fabric marked by fuzziness and specks caused by splitting of the fiber

lous·ter \ˈlau̇stə(r)\ *vi* -ED/-ING/-S [origin unknown] *dial Eng* **:** to bustle or scramble about **:** work actively

lousy \ˈlau̇zē, -zi\ *adj* -ER/-EST [ME, fr. *lous* louse + *-y*] **1 :** infested with or marked by the presence of lice ⟨the ragged, ~ tribesmen —T.E.Lawrence⟩ ⟨~ disease⟩ **2 a :** totally repulsive or abominable **:** CONTEMPTIBLE, FILTHY, VILE ⟨a ~ way of getting even⟩ **b :** miserably poor or inferior ⟨he believes that, contrary to the popular conception, women are ~ spies —*Infantry Jour.*⟩ ⟨forgive me for writing on this ~ paper —O.W.Holmes †1935⟩ ⟨observed that it was a ~ war, but better than no war at all —J.P.Roche⟩ — often used as an intensive ⟨get that third rocker after a ~ six months in grade —Walt Sheldon⟩ **3 :** amply supplied **:** REPLETE ⟨the concert halls . . . with violinists —Virgil Thomson⟩ ⟨the avenue was ~ with pawnshops —Charles Jackson⟩ ⟨they all thought the Americans were ~ with money —Maxwell Griffith⟩ **4** *of silk* **:** fuzzy and specked because of splitting of the fiber

1**lout** \ˈlau̇t, *usu* -au̇d·+V\ *vi* -ED/-ING/-S [ME *louten*, fr. OE *lūtan*; akin to ON *lūta* to bow down — more at LITTLE] **1 :** to bow in courtesy or respect ⟨I uncovered and ~*ed* as I passed —A.Conan Doyle⟩ **2 :** to bend in submission **:** YIELD ⟨have rubbed shoulders with kings and noblemen and ~*ed* to none of them —*Times Lit. Supp.*⟩

2**lout** \"\ *n* -S [perh. fr. ON *lūtr* bent down, stooped, fr. *lūta* to bow down] **:** an awkward clownish fellow **:** OAF, YOKEL ⟨married to some ~ of a shopkeeper —Frank O'Connor⟩ ⟨see that a few ~*s* don't spoil the fun for everybody —*Vancouver (Canada) Province*⟩ **syn** see BOOR

3**lout** \"\ *vt* -ED/-ING/-S **:** to treat as a lout **:** subject to contumely **:** DERIDE, SCORN ⟨I am ~*ed* by a traitor villain —Shak.⟩

louth \ˈlau̇th\ *adj, usu cap* [fr. *Louth*, county in northeast Ireland] **:** of or from County Louth, Ireland **:** of the kind or style prevalent in County Louth

lout·ish \ˈlau̇d·ish, -au̇t|, |ēsh\ *adj* **:** resembling or suggesting a lout **:** CLOWNISH, COARSE ⟨his ~ flights of fancy —Francis Hackett⟩ — **lout·ish·ly** *adv* — **lout·ish·ness** *n* -ES

lou·tre \ˈlüd·ə(r)\ *n* -S [F, otter, fr. L *lutra*] **:** OTTER 4

lou·troph·o·ros \lüˈträfəˌräs\ *n, pl* **loutropho·roi** \-ˌrȯi\ [Gk, lit., carrying water for a bath, fr. *loutron* bath, water for a bath (fr. *louein* to wash) + *-phoros* -phore — more at LYE] **:** a tall long-necked water vase with two handles used in ancient Athens for bringing water for the ceremonial bath on the eve of marriage and often buried in the grave of one dying while betrothed

louty \ˈlau̇d·ē\ *adj* -ER/-EST [2*lout* + *-y*] **:** LOUTISH

lou·var \ˈlüˌvär\ *n* -S [It dial. (Calabrian & Sicilian) *lùvaru*, prob. fr. L *ruber* red — more at RED] **:** a large plump voracious scombroid fish (*Luvarus imperialis*) cosmopolitan in warm seas

lou·ver *or* **lou·vre** \ˈlüvə(r)\ *n* -S [ME *lover*, fr. MF *lovier*] **1 a :** a roof lantern or turret often with slatted apertures for escape of smoke or admission of light in a medieval building **b** *obs* **:** a dovecote resembling a louver **2 a :** an opening in wall or ceiling for ventilation or cooling provided with one or more slanted fins to exclude rain and sun and often made so that the fins may be closed at will — compare BRISE-SOLEIL **b :** a fin or shutter of a

louver 2a

louver **3 :** a fixed or adjustable louver for cooling of an enclosed engine or motor (as of an airplane, automobile, or machine) **4 :** a finned or vaned device to deflect or control a flow of air or the radiation of light ⟨ceiling fixtures with ~s seem to diffuse and soften light⟩ ⟨electric fans are often fitted with circular ~s to direct the airstream⟩ **5 :** a closure using adjustable slanted louvers ⟨pulled the ~s in our room as tight as they'd go, but in a couple of hours the water had washed in over our shoes —Land Kaderli⟩

lou·vered *or* **lou·vred** \-və(r)d\ *adj* **1 :** set sloping in the manner of the boards or slats of a louver ⟨~ wooden shutters are very much a part of almost every dwelling —Harold Sinclair⟩ **2 :** furnished with louvers ⟨has . . . controlled ventilation and diffused lighting from a ~ ceiling —*Architectural Rev.*⟩

lov·able *also* **love·able** \ˈləvəbəl\ *adj* [ME *lufabyll, luffable*, fr. *loven, luffen* to love + *-able* — more at LOVE] **:** gifted with traits and qualities that attract affection ⟨she was both likable and ~ —Oliver LaFarge⟩ — **lov·able·ness** *n* -ES — **lov·ably** \-blē, -li\ *adv*

lov·age \ˈləvij\ *n* -S [ME *lovache*, fr. AF, modif. of LL *levisticum*, alter. of L *ligusticum*, fr. neut. of *ligusticus* Ligurian, fr. *Ligus* Ligurian] **:** any of several aromatic perennial herbs of the family Umbelliferae: as **a :** a stout branched glabrous herb (*Levisticum officinale*) that is native to southern Europe and is sometimes cultivated for its rhizomes which are used as a carminative, its stalks and foliage which are used as a potherb, a substitute for celery, or a tea, its seeds which are used for flavoring and in confectionery, and its flowering tops which yield an oil used in flavoring and perfumery — called also *sea parsley* **b :** any of several white-flowered herbs of regions constituting a genus (*Ligustrum*) and having large aromatic roots; *esp* **:** a coarse herb (*L. scoticum*) of rocky or marshy coasts of northwestern Europe and eastern No. America from Greenland to New York with fleshy leaves sometimes used as a potherb — called also *Scotch lovage, sea parsley*

lovage oil *n* **:** a yellow-brown aromatic essential oil obtained from the root or other parts of lovage and used in flavoring and in perfumery

lov·at \ˈləvət\ *n* -S [prob. fr. *Lovat*, locality in Inverness-shire, Scotland] **:** a predominantly dusty green color mixture in fabrics (as tweeds) orig. intended to blend with the Scottish landscape

¹love \ˈləv\ *n* -S [ME, fr. OE *lufu*; akin to OHG *lupa* love, OE *lēof* dear, L *lubēre, libēre* to please, Skt *lubhyati* he desires] **1 a :** the attraction, desire, or affection felt for a person who arouses delight or admiration or elicits tenderness, sympathetic interest, or benevolence **:** devoted affection ⟨a mother's ~ for her child⟩ **b :** an assurance of love ⟨give my ~ to your father when you get home⟩ **2 a :** warm attachment, enthusiasm, or devotion (as to a pursuit or a concrete or ideal object) ⟨inherited his father's ~ of the sea —G.H.Burnham⟩ ⟨just so much instruction in Latin as would suffice to show which boys and girls had a ~ of the subject —Bertrand Russell⟩ **b :** the object of such attachment or devotion ⟨a born crusader and his ~ was language —Charlton Laird⟩ ⟨events and people are his ~, festivals, law terms, battles, licences, royalty — but especially people —G.W.Stonier⟩ **3 a :** the benevolence attributed to God as resembling a father's affection for his children **b :** men's adoration of God in gratitude or devotion **4 a :** the attraction based on sexual desire **:** the affection and tenderness felt by lovers ⟨the entrance of ~ into sex life . . . was an advance along the road of human civilization as important as the emancipation of slaves —Theodor Reik⟩ ⟨his ~ had been woven of sentiment rather than passion —Ellen Glasgow⟩ **b :** a god or personification of love (as Cupid, Amor, or Eros) or a figured representation of one (as in art or imaginative conception) ⟨on the other side a *Love* with a flaring torch and head reversed —S.T.Coleridge⟩ **c :** an amorous episode **:** AMOUR, LOVE AFFAIR ⟨tremendous curiosity about her jealously guarded life and ~s —Bosley Crowther⟩ **d :** the sexual embrace **:** COPULATION ⟨many cocottes pay their coachmen either partly or wholly in ~ —Arnold Bennett⟩ **5 :** a beloved person **:** DARLING, DEAR, SWEETHEART — often used as an endearment ⟨come on, ~, let's go in and see what's doing —Lilian Balch⟩ **6** *obs* **:** a thin silk fabric formerly worn in token of mourning or a border made of this stuff **7 :** a score of zero in tennis and some other games **:** NOTHING ⟨if the server wins the first point, the score is fifteen-~ —Clement Wood & Gloria Goddard⟩ ⟨opened the match with a ~ victory on his own service —*N.Y. Times*⟩ **8** *cap, Christian Science* **:** GOD **9 :** a delightful or superb example, instance, or occurrence ⟨we had a perfect ~ of a sounding-boat —Mark Twain⟩ ⟨it's a ~, isn't it —Marguerite Steen⟩ **syn** see ATTACHMENT — **for love** *adv* **:** for pleasure **:** without stakes **:** without reward of money or material gain ⟨play cards *for love*⟩ ⟨headed the hospital's building campaign *for love*⟩ — **for love or money :** at any price **:** on any consideration — used with a negative ⟨couldn't get him to go along *for love or money*⟩ — **in love :** inspired by tender or ardent affection **:** ENAMORED, DEVOTED ⟨haven't you ever been *in love* . . . so that nothing else in the world matters at all —Louis Bromfield⟩ ⟨the ardor that makes a woman fall *in love* with a religion or an idea —Ellen Glasgow⟩ ⟨*in love* with his work, entranced by everything connected with it, grateful for his fame and fortune —*Saturday Rev.*⟩ — **of all love** *or* **of all loves** *obs* — used in entreaty

²love \"\ *vb* -ED/-ING/-S [ME *loven*, fr. OE *lufian*; akin to OHG *lubōn* to love; denominative fr. the root of E ¹*love*] *vt* **1 :** to feel affection for **:** hold dear **:** CHERISH ⟨the lonely and ailing old bachelors and widowers . . . all ~ her —G.S. Perry⟩ **2 a :** to feel a lover's passion, devotion, or tenderness for ⟨*loved* his wife devotedly —Ruth P. Randall⟩ **b :** to engage in sex play — sometimes used with *up* **c :** to copulate with **3 a :** to cherish or foster with divine love and mercy ⟨I have *loved* you with an everlasting love —Jer 31:3 (RSV)⟩ **b :** to feel reverent adoration for (God) ⟨but showing steadfast love to thousands of those who ~ me and keep my commandments —Exod 20:6 (RSV)⟩ **4 a :** to like or desire actively **:** be strongly attracted or attached to **:** delight in ⟨the sculptor must ~ the feel of stone —Leslie Rees⟩ ⟨he ~s the limelight —Eudora Welty⟩ ⟨some leading social scientists ~ their IBM machines too much —C.K.Kluckhohn⟩ **b :** to take pleasure or satisfaction in **:** LIKE — used with an infinitive as object ⟨*loved* to indulge his grief in true romantic fashion —J.W. Beach⟩ ⟨the poor folk would still ~ to emigrate to the U. S. —Frank Gorrell⟩ **5 :** FONDLE, CARESS ⟨mother nuzzled my cheek and throat and I *loved* her back⟩ **6 :** to thrive in **:** PREFER — used of plants and animals ⟨the rose ~s sunlight⟩ ⟨central Asian wild pheasants ~ impenetrable jungles —Douglas Carruthers⟩ **7 :** CHOOSE, PREFER, LIKE ⟨would ~ to have some lemonade⟩ ~ *vi* **:** to feel affection or experience desire ⟨the poet must learn to ~ before he can begin to hate —C.D.Lewis⟩ **syn** see LIKE

³love \"\ *usu cap* — a communications code word for the letter *l*

loveable *var of* LOVABLE

love affair *n* **1 :** a romantic attachment or episode between lovers ⟨a niece caught up in her first *love affair* —Hugh Walpole⟩ **2 :** a lively enthusiasm ⟨my *love affair* with aviation —Arthur Godfrey⟩

love apple *n* [prob. trans. of MF *pomme d' amour*] **:** TOMATO

love arrow *n* **:** ¹DART 3a

lovebird \ˈ=,=\ *n* **1 :** any of various small parrots that show great affection for their mates, that include esp. members of the genera *Agapornis* of Africa, *Loriculus* of Asia, and *Psittacula* of So. America, that are usu. chiefly green or delicate gray, and that are often kept as cage birds — compare BUDGERIGAR **2 :** a strong yellow green that is yellower than viridine yellow and lighter, stronger, and slightly greener than parrot green

love child *n* **:** an illegitimate child **:** BASTARD ⟨the uneasy tenderness of a devout churchwoman dandling her daughter's *love child* —Jan Struther⟩

¹loved \ˈləvd\ *adj* [ME, fr. past part. of *loven* to love] **:** held dear **:** CHERISHED ⟨death . . . deprived him of a ~ companion —W.C.Ford⟩

²loved \"\ *n, pl* **loved :** one that is loved

love dart *n* **:** ¹DART 3a

love-entangle *or* **love-entangled** \ˈ==ˈ==\ *n* -S **1 :** LOVE-IN-A-MIST 1 **2 :** a stonecrop (*Sedum acre*) **3 :** a virgin's bower (*Clematis vitalba*) of Europe

love feast *n* **:** a meal eaten in common in token of brotherly love: as **a :** ²AGAPE 1 **b :** a modern religious service in imitation of the ancient agape **c :** a banquet, gathering, or celebration held to reconcile differences and promote good feeling or show someone affectionate honor ⟨hotel lobbies were crowded with milling politicians as the annual *love feast* of the Kansas Republicans drew near —*Emporia* (Kans.) *Gazette*⟩ ⟨the affair was a *love feast*, garnished with the floral offerings, the numberless recalls, the encores, and all the rest —*Musical America*⟩

loveful *adj, obs* **:** LOVABLE, LOVING

love game *n* **:** a game (as in tennis) won without loss of a point

love god *n* **:** CUPID

love grass *n* **:** a grass of the genus *Eragrostis* that is esp. useful for forage and for the prevention of erosion — called also *bay grass*

love-in-a-mist \ˈ====ˈ=\ *n* **1 :** a European garden plant (*Nigella damascena*) having the flowers enveloped in numerous finely dissected bracts **2 :** a tropical American passionflower (*Passiflora foetida*) with finely dissected bracts **3 :** SNOW-IN-SUMMER a

love-in-idleness \ˈ==ˈ===\ *n* **:** WILD PANSY

love-in-winter \ˈ==ˈ==\ *n* **:** PIPSISSEWA

love knot *n* [ME *love knotte*, fr. ¹*love* + *knotte* knot] **:** a decorative or stylized knot sometimes used as an emblem of love — called also *lover's knot, true lover's knot*

love·less \ˈləvləs\ *adj* [ME *loveles*, fr. ¹*love* + *-les* -less] **1 :** UNLOVING **2 :** UNLOVED **3 :** UNLOVELY — **love·less·ly** *adv*

love·less·ness *n* -ES **1 :** want of love for others **2 :** failure to receive the love of others **3 :** UNATTRACTIVENESS, UNLOVELINESS

love letter *n* **:** a letter expressing a lover's affection

love-lies-bleeding \ˈ=,=ˈ==\ *n* **1 :** a cultivated plant of the genus *Amaranthus* (esp. *A. caudatus*) **2 :** BLEEDING HEART 1 **3 :** PHEASANT'S-EYE 1

love life *n* **:** the activities, habits, and relationships centering in the affections and esp. in sexual life

love-light \ˈ=,=\ *n* **:** the radiance of affection ⟨and yet her eyes had that brooding *love-light* —John Galsworthy⟩

love·li·head \ˈləvlē,hed\ *n* [¹*lovely* + *-head* (as in *godhead*)] **:** LOVELINESS

love·li·ly \-lə̇lē\ *adv* [ME *lovelyly*, fr. ¹*lovely* + *-ly*] **:** in a lovely manner

love·li·ness \ˈləvlēnə̇s, -lin-\ *n* -ES [ME *luflynes*, fr. *lufly*, *lovely* lovely + *-nes* -ness] **:** the quality or state of being lovely **:** BEAUTY ⟨that dead first wife . . . who was all undemanding ~ —Mark Schorer⟩

love·ling \-liŋ\ *n* -S **:** DARLING

lovelock \ˈ=,=\ *n* **:** a long lock or curl of hair usu. hanging alone over the shoulder and worn esp. in the 17th and 18th centuries — compare EARLOCK

love·lorn \ˈləv,lȯrn, -ȯ(ə)n\ *adj* **:** bereft of love or of a lover — **love·lorn·ness** \-nnə̇s\ *n* -ES

¹love·ly \ˈləvlē, -li\ *adj, usu* -ER/-EST [ME, fr. OE *luflic*, fr. *lufu* love + *-līc* -ly — more at LOVE] **1** *obs* **:** disposed to affectionate or amorous love **2 :** meriting love by moral or ideal worth **3 :** delightful for beauty, harmony, or grace **:** attractive because of natural charm ⟨a strange shy ~ girl —John Masefield⟩ ⟨and the stars are ~ and gleaming on the lightless heavenly floor —William Morris⟩ ⟨conservation and wise use of resources can make a wealthy people in a ~ land —H.W.Odum⟩ ⟨then we remember that harsh unflurried, that harsh unembittered laughter, and we look up the ~ lines in the book —Edmund Wilson⟩ **4 :** most pleasing **:** GRAND, SWELL ⟨a good man and a ~ preacher —Ruth Suckow⟩ ⟨if you go, the chances are you'll have a ~ time —Wolcott Gibbs⟩ **syn** see BEAUTIFUL

²lovely *adv* [ME, beautifully, affectionately, willingly, fr. OE *luflīce* affectionately, willingly, fr. *luflīc*, adj.] *obs* **:** BEAUTIFULLY

³love·ly *n* -ES [ME, beautiful one, fr. *lovely*, adj.] **1 :** a beautiful girl or woman; *esp* **:** a professional beauty (as a show girl) ⟨swept off his feet by this tempestuous young ~ —*Irish Digest*⟩ ⟨the world of impresarios, stage *lovelies*, and night club music —*Times Lit. Supp.*⟩ **2 :** a lovely object ⟨hemstitched *lovelies* that are soft, smooth, and lint-free —*Sears, Roebuck Cat.*⟩ **3 :** an outstanding or egregious example **:** BEAUTY

lovely fir *or* **lovely red fir** *n* **:** AMABILIS FIR

lovemaking \ˈ=,==\ *n* [ME *love makinge*, fr. ¹*love* + *makinge* making] **1 :** wooing or courtship between lovers ⟨in his comedies . . . there is the finest ~ in the world —*Modern Language Notes*⟩ **2 :** amorous dalliance **:** SEXUAL INTERCOURSE **3 :** the courtship practices of animals ⟨idly watched the splashing and ~ of the distant ducks⟩

love·man \ˈləv,man\ *n, pl* **lovemans** [²*love* + *man*] **:** CLEAVERS

love match *n* **:** a marriage prompted chiefly by affection

lovemate \ˈ=,=\ *n* **:** LOVER

love nest *n* **:** a dwelling of lovers; *esp* **:** a place where illicit lovers live or meet ⟨a sordid *love nest* on a back street —Martha Gellhorn⟩

love object *n* **:** a person on whom affection is centered or on whom one is dependent for affection or needed help

love parrakeet *or* **love parrot** *n* **:** LOVEBIRD

love-philter \ˈ=,==\ *n* **:** PHILTER

love-potion \ˈ=,==\ *n* **:** PHILTER

love-powder \ˈ=,==\ *n* **:** a powder used as a philter

lov·er \ˈləvə(r)\ *n* -S [ME, fr. *loven* to love + *-er*] **1 a :** a person in love ⟨a man came down to where his ~ was —J.C. Hall⟩; *esp* **:** a man in love with a girl or woman ⟨her heart went out to him as to a ~ —Sheila Kaye-Smith⟩ **b lovers** *pl* **:** two persons in love with each other ⟨he'd sit with his arm round her waist and she with her head on his shoulder just like ~s —W.S.Maugham⟩ **2 :** an affectionate or benevolent friend ⟨not an ardent denominational ecclesiastic, but a broad-souled and eager ~ of men —O.M.Buck⟩ **3 :** an enthusiastic amateur **:** DEVOTEE ⟨as a ~ of truth, the national propaganda of all the belligerent nations sickened me —Bertrand Russell⟩ ⟨a lifelong ~ of the woodcock runs and trout streams —R.W.Hatch⟩ ⟨a variety of subjects that will interest theater ~s —Henry Hewes⟩ **4 :** PARAMOUR ⟨she had chosen a bachelor girl's life, although she had children by ~s —Margaret C. Hubbard⟩

lov·er·ing \ˈləv(ə)riŋ\ *n* -S **:** LOVEMAKING ⟨she dearly loved to see a bit of ~ going on —Mary Webb⟩

lov·er·less \ˈləvə(r)ləs\ *adj* **:** having no lover

¹lov·er·ly \-lē, -li\ *adj* [*lover* + *-ly*] **:** befitting a lover

²loverly \"\ *adv* **:** in a lover's manner

lover's knot *n* **:** LOVE KNOT

lovers' lane *n* **:** a lane or place favored by lovers for seclusion and dalliance

lover's leap *n* **1 :** a cliff or high point from which disappointed and despairing lovers plunge to death **2 :** the move of a man in backgammon from ace point to twelve point in one throw of the dice

lover's-pride \ˈ==ˈ=\ *n, pl* **lover's-prides :** PERSICARIA

loverwise \ˈ==,=\ *adv* **:** in the manner of a lover

loves *pl of* LOVE, *pres 3d sing of* LOVE

love scene *n* **:** a scene between lovers (as in a play)

love seat *n* **:** a double chair, sofa, or settee for two persons

love set *n* **:** a set in tennis won without loss of a game

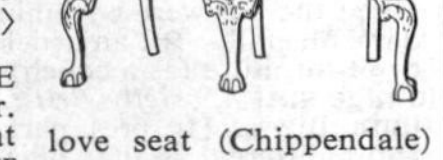

love seat (Chippendale)

love-sick \ˈ=,=\ *adj* **1 :** languishing with love **:** YEARNING ⟨strong men behaved like *love-sick* boys before her beauty⟩ **2 :** expressing a lover's longing ⟨while the nightingales their *love-sick* ditty sing —John Dryden⟩ — **love·sick·ness** *n*

love·some \ˈləvsəm\ *adj* [ME *lovesom, lufsom*, fr. OE *lufsum*, fr. *lufu* love + *-sum* -some — more at LOVE] **1 :** CHARMING, WINSOME **:** BEAUTIFUL, LOVELY ⟨a woman young and ~, and shaped exceeding fair —William Morris⟩ **2 a :** FRIENDLY, AFFECTIONATE **b :** AMOROUS

love song *n* **:** a lyrical, musical, or poetic expression of love esp. of man for woman

love spoon *n* [trans. of W *llwy serch*] **:** a wooden spoon often with double bowl formerly carved by a Welsh suitor as an engagement gift for his promised bride

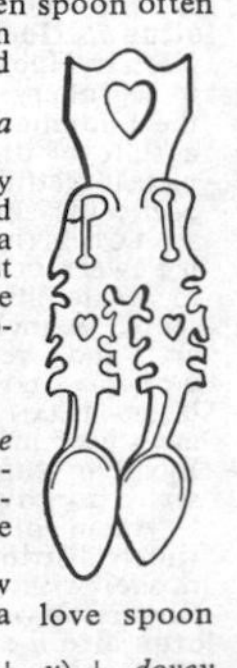

love spoon

love's test *n* **:** a common everlasting (*Antennaria plantaginifolia*) of eastern No. America

love·ston·ite \ˈləv,stō,nīt\ *n* -S *usu cap* [Jay *Lovestone*, 20th cent. Am. union leader expelled from the Communist party in 1929 + E *-ite*] **:** a member of a faction of the American Communist party deviating from party policy esp. on the question of accepting and working with established trade unions

love story *n* **:** a tale of lovers

love vine *n* **:** DODDER

love wave *n, usu cap L* [after A. E. H. *Love* †1940 Eng. mathematician] **:** a seismic disturbance consisting of horizontal transverse vibrations of the earth's crust propagated near the surface

loveworthy \ˈ=,==\ *adj* **:** meriting love ⟨saw how utterly ~ she was and had always been —Sheila Kaye-Smith⟩

¹lovey-dovey \ˈləvēˈdəvē\ *n* -S [*lovey*- (fr. ¹*love* + *-y*) + *-dovey* (fr. ¹*dove* + *-y*)] **:** SWEETHEART

²lovey-dovey \"\ *adj* **:** SENTIMENTAL, SOFT **:** SACCHARINE, MUSHY

¹lov·ing \ˈləviŋ, -vēŋ\ *adj* [ME *lovyng*, alter. of *lovende*, fr. OE *lufiende*, pres. part. of *lufian* to love — more at LOVE] **1 :** feeling or expressing love **:** AFFECTIONATE ⟨eyes at once critical and ~ —John Galsworthy⟩ — often used in combination ⟨a peace-*loving* people⟩ ⟨a fun-*loving* couple⟩ **2 :** marked by careful attention to detail **:** PAINSTAKING ⟨devoting ~ attention to details —*Time*⟩ ⟨the ~ protection of the liberty of the individual —Brand Blanshard⟩ — **lov·ing·ness** *n* -ES

²loving \"\ *n* -S [ME, fr. gerund of *loven* to love — more at LOVE] **:** a lover's action or attitude

loving cup *n* [¹*loving* + *cup*] **1 :** a large ornamental vessel with two or more handles that is used for ceremonial drinking (as in welcome) by assembled companions **2 :** a loving cup given someone as a token of friendship or honor or presented as a trophy to the winner in sporting or other competition

loving-kindness \ˌ==ˈ==\ *n* **:** tender and benevolent affection **:** favoring mercy ⟨the cause of wisdom and *loving-kindness* in education —*Times Lit. Supp.*⟩

lov·ing·ly *adv* **1 :** in a loving manner **:** FONDLY, AFFECTIONATELY ⟨looked ~ into the handsome face —Israel Zangwill⟩ **2 :** with close attention to detail **:** PAINSTAKINGLY ⟨the mountain shoes so ~ made by hand —Claudia Cassidy⟩

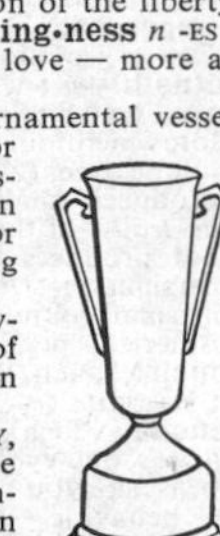

loving cup

lo·voz·e·rite \lōˈväzə,rīt\ *n* -S [Russ *lovozerit*, fr. *Lovozero*, village in the Kola peninsula, northwest Russia + Russ *-it* -ite] **:** a mineral $(Na,K)_2(Mn,Ca)ZrSi_6O_{16}.3H_2O$ consisting of a hydrous silicate of alkalies, manganese, calcium, and zirconium

¹low \ˈlō\ *n* -S [ME, fr. OE *hlāw, hlǣw* — more at LAW] *archaic* **:** HILL, MOUND; *specif* **:** a burial mound

²low \" *sometimes* ˈlü\ *vb* -ED/-ING/-S [ME *loowen*, fr. OE *hlōwan*; akin to OLF *luon, luogin* to moo, OHG *hluoen* to moo, L *calare* to call, summon, Gk *kalein* to call, Lith *kalbà* language] *vi* **1** *of cattle* **:** to make the usu. deep sustained sound characteristic of cows and other bovine animals **:** MOO **2 :** to make a sound suggestive of the lowing of cattle ⟨that's what I would say, and they would ~ with pleasure —E.L. Burdick⟩ ~ *vt* **:** to utter with a lowing sound

³low \"\ *n* -S **:** the usu. deep sustained sound characteristic of cows and other bovine animals ⟨the ~ of herds —William Wordsworth⟩

⁴low \ˈlō\ *adj* -ER/-EST [ME *low, lowe*, fr. *lah*, fr. ON *lāgr*; akin to OFris *lēch* low, MD *lage*, MHG *læge* low, flat, Russ *lezt'* to climb, and perh. to ON *liggja* to lie — more at LIE] **1 a** (1) **:** having a relatively small upward extension **:** extending upward or outward relatively little ⟨a man of ~ stature⟩ ⟨a ~ building⟩ ⟨a ~ wall⟩ ⟨~ relief⟩ (2) **:** situated, placed, or passing relatively little above the line, point, or plane with relation to which reckoning is made ⟨a ~ bridge⟩ ⟨a bird of ~ flight⟩ (3) *now chiefly dial* **:** not tall **:** SHORT ⟨a ~, fat man —Vance Randolph & G.P.Wilson⟩ ⟨about forty, ~, corpulent —Anne Royall⟩ (4) **:** having a low neck **:** DÉCOLLETÉ ⟨a ~ dress⟩; *also* **:** LOW-CUT ⟨a ~ shoe⟩ (5) **:** articulated with a wide opening between the comparatively flat tongue and the palate **:** OPEN ⟨the sounds \ä\ \a\ are ~⟩ **b** (1) **:** situated relatively below the normal level, surface, or base of measurement, or the mean elevation ⟨~ ground⟩ ⟨the ~ levels in a mine⟩ (2) **:** of or relating to the lowlands esp. near the seashore — now used chiefly in fixed phrases ⟨the *Low* Countries⟩ (3) **:** having less than or being below or farthest below the usual or normal height ⟨the water is ~ in the reservoir⟩ — compare LOW TIDE, LOW WATER (4) **:** being near the horizon ⟨the afternoon sun is ~ at four o'clock in winter⟩ **c** (1) **:** DEAD, LIFELESS — now usu. used in the phrase *lay low* ⟨keen swords and sharp arrows laid the enemy ~⟩ (2) **:** PROSTRATE — usu. used in the phrase *lay low* ⟨laid ~ for weeks by a severe illness⟩ ⟨laid him ~ with one mighty stroke of his staff⟩ (3) **:** ABASED, HUMBLED — usu. used in the phrase *bring low* ⟨added that he kept a list of all his opponents and . . . would bring them ~ —Evelyn G. Cruickshanks⟩ (4) **:** not prosperous **:** POOR, EMBARRASSED, BACKWARD ⟨sought to account for the ~ state of the higher studies in this country⟩ ⟨was ~ financially —Arthur Godfrey⟩ **d :** passing far downward ⟨a ~ swoop⟩ ⟨a ~ obeisance⟩ **2 a** (1) **:** of or relating to the lower classes **:** socially or economically humble or inferior ⟨a person of ~ birth⟩ ⟨women of ~ degree —H.M. Parshley⟩ ⟨loved by all his parishioners, high and ~⟩; *also* **:** associated with lower class status **:** IGNOBLE, PLEBEIAN ⟨these tasks become . . . too ~ to be performed by the native —B.K. Sandwell⟩ (2) **:** ranking as poor or inferior by some standard **:** INFERIOR ⟨a man of ~ intelligence⟩ ⟨results in the domination of news by ~ intellectual and moral standards —F.L.Mott⟩ ⟨groups of the population with ~ personal hygiene —E.C. Faust⟩ (3) **:** lacking dignity or elevation **:** ORDINARY, COMMONPLACE, PROSAIC ⟨distinguished between the high and the ~ style . . . the latter assigned to the realism of every day life —William Barrett⟩ ⟨have used abbreviations freely in this letter. Do you think them ~ —O.W.Holmes †1935⟩ (4) **:** characterized by burlesque, horseplay, and broad or farcical humor **:** bordering on farce ⟨~ comedy⟩ (5) **:** culturally inferior by some standard **:** little advanced in civilization ⟨savages of a ~ Negrito type —*Encyc. Americana*⟩ (6) **:** having a relatively simple organization **:** not highly developed in the scale of biological evolution ⟨~ organisms⟩ ⟨no remains of . . . ~ forms of man have been found here —S. E.Morison & H.S.Commager⟩ (7) *usu cap* **:** Low Church ⟨who was very *Low*, would forget for a moment her annoyance at the ecclesiastical lace —Osbert Lancaster⟩ **b** (1) **:** morally reprehensible **:** BASE, MEAN ⟨that was a ~ trick⟩ ⟨marked by a certain ~ cunning⟩; *also* **:** striking below the belt **:** FOUL ⟨a ~ blow⟩ (2) **:** DEGRADED, ABANDONED, DISSOLUTE, DISREPUTABLE ⟨a ~ public house —*Newsweek*⟩ ⟨intrigues with ~ women —Benjamin Franklin⟩ (3) **:** lacking in or reflecting lack of refinement or breeding **:** COARSE, VULGAR ⟨~ in her tastes and aspirations, ~ in her likes and dislikes —Joseph Furphy⟩ ⟨sporting events of a ~ type —G.M.Trevelyan⟩ ⟨scenes of would-be comedy from illiterate ~ characters —Leslie Rees⟩ ⟨that's a ~ word⟩ (4) **:** not conforming to some standard of correctness or propriety ⟨the ~ language is the everyday language —Miguel Covarrubias⟩ **c** (1) **:** lacking strength, health, or vitality **:** FEEBLE, WEAK ⟨he was very ~ —Granville Toogood⟩ ⟨a ~ pulse⟩ (2) **:** not rich or highly seasoned **:** not nourishing **:** PLAIN, SIMPLE ⟨a ~ diet⟩ (3) **:** lacking spirit or vivacity **:** DEPRESSED, DEJECTED ⟨felt too ~ even to remonstrate —Louis Auchincloss⟩ **:** marked by dejection or depression ⟨in a ~ state of mind —J.C.Lincoln⟩ ⟨better than he thought in ~ moments —*Times Lit. Supp.*⟩ **d :** UNFAVOR-

ABLE, DISPARAGING ⟨had a ~ opinion of his talents⟩ **3 :** deficient, inferior, or unusually small in quantity, intensity, value, or degree: as **a :** less than normal **:** not intense **:** MODERATE ⟨~ barometric pressure⟩ ⟨~ speed⟩ ⟨~ visibility⟩ ⟨a ~ fever⟩ ⟨a ~ conductor of heat⟩ ⟨valleys . . . ~ in lime —Walter Bally⟩ **b** (1) **:** not loud **:** SOFT ⟨spoke in a very ~ voice —Katharine N. Burt⟩ (2) **:** depressed in musical pitch **:** FLAT (3) **:** relating to those musical notes or tones in the contra-octave esp. in singing ⟨~ G⟩ **c** (1) **:** numerically small **:** not high in amount ⟨the illiteracy rate is very ~⟩ ⟨a ~ number⟩ ⟨deal me a ~ card⟩ (2) **:** being beneath a rate, amount, or value considered normal, standard, or adequate by some criteria ⟨persons of ~ income group⟩ ⟨~ wages⟩ ⟨~ prices⟩; *specif* **:** CHEAP ⟨that's a very ~ price for that suit⟩ (3) **:** relatively small or too small **:** MODERATE ⟨gave me a very ~ estimate⟩ (4) **:** nearly exhausted **:** DEPLETED, SHORT ⟨left me when the coal was ~ —*New Republic*⟩ ⟨the stores being so ~ —R.L.Stevenson⟩ ⟨very ~ in pocket⟩ **d :** being near or not very distant from the equator ⟨the ~ northern latitudes⟩ **e :** being relatively near the beginning of a series of chemical compounds arranged in order of increasing molecular weight or of increasing valence of the chief constituent ⟨~*er* fatty acids⟩ — compare HIGH 1b 7 **f :** designed for slow or usu. the slowest speed; *specif* **:** giving the lowest ratio of propeller-shaft to engine-shaft speed and the highest amplification of torque ⟨~ gear⟩ **g :** not lively **:** SLOW ⟨published . . . at very ~ tempo because of lack of funds —Mortimer Graves⟩ ⟨a steady, dignified ~ dance —Anatole Chujoy⟩ **4 :** very low **:** marking a nadir **:** LOWEST ⟨surely the ~ point of the entire period —Philles Nash⟩ ⟨organized religion has reached a ~ point in its history —*Humanist*⟩ **syn** see BASE

5**low** \"\ *n* -s [ME, fr. *lah*, fr. *lah*, adj. — more at 4LOW] **1 :** something that is low: as **a :** a piece of low-lying level ground — usu. used in pl. ⟨many ~*s* growing dense reedbeds —Douglas Carruthers⟩ **b :** LOW SPEED **c** (1) **:** the lowest card of the trump suit or the lowest trump card in play counting one point in all forms and related games (2) **:** the lowest number, card, or score in a game; *also* **:** the player having low **d :** a domain of low barometric pressure — compare CYCLONE 1a **e :** lowest prices of a movement ⟨buy stocks at the ~⟩ **f :** a nadir of decline or degradation ⟨whose report card marks a new ~ —Ralph Linton⟩ ⟨prestige, power, and reputation plummet to new ~*s* —Neal Stanford⟩ ⟨membership is at an all-time ~ —*Sydney (Australia) Bull.*⟩

6**low** \"\ *adv* -ER/-EST [ME *lowe*, fr. *lahe*, *lage*, fr. *lah*, adj. — more at 4LOW] **1 :** in or to a low position **:** not on high **:** near the ground ⟨the village is nestled ~ in the foothills of the great range⟩ **2 :** to or toward a low position **:** in a low direction or course ⟨aim your blows ~⟩ **3 a :** in subjection, poverty, or disgrace ⟨brought ~ by misfortune⟩ **b** (1) **:** in a low or poor condition **:** HUMBLY, MEAGERLY ⟨on that income you must live very ~⟩ (2) **:** at a low rate ⟨don't value yourself too ~⟩ **4 :** at a relatively low price **:** CHEAPLY ⟨sell wheat ~⟩ **5 a :** with a low voice or sound **:** not loudly **:** SOFTLY ⟨speak ~⟩ **b :** with a low musical pitch or tone **6** *archaic* **:** LATE

7**low** *or* **lowe** \"\ *n* -s [ME, fr. ON *log*, *logi* flame; akin to OFris *loga* flame, MHG *lohe* flame, Goth *liuhath* light — more at LIGHT] *chiefly Scot* **:** FLAME, BLAZE, GLOW

8**low** *or* **lowe** \"\ *vb* [ME *lowen*, fr. ON *loga*, fr. *logi*, n.] *Scot* **:** FLAME, BLAZE, GLOW

9**low** \'laů\ *vb* -ED/-ING/-S [by shortening] *dial* **:** ALLOW

lo·wa \'lō(w)ə\ *n* -s [Hindi *lavā*] **:** an Indian quail of the genus *Perdicula*

low·an \'lōən\ *n* -s [native name in Australia] *Austral* **:** LEIPOA

low·ance \'laůən(t)s\ *n* -s [short for *allowance*] *dial Brit* **:** food or drink or the equivalent in money given to a worker in addition to his wages

low-angle fault *n* **:** a geological fault with its dip less than 45 degrees

low-back \'ˌ\ *adj*, *of a vowel* **:** uttered with the back of the tongue low in the mouth ⟨a *low-back* \ä\⟩

lowball \'ˌ\ *n* **:** a form of draw poker in which the lowest-ranking poker hand wins the pot, the ace being always the lowest-ranking card, straights and flushes not counting, and the best possible hand being A, 2, 3, 4, 5 regardless of suits

low beam *n* **:** the short-range focus of a vehicle headlight that directs the light below the eye level of oncoming drivers — contrasted with *high beam*; distinguished from *parking lights*

low-bed \'ˌ\ *or* **lowboy** \'ˌ\ *adj*, *of a vehicle* **:** having a bed only a few inches above the roadway ⟨a *low-bed* truck⟩ ⟨a *low-bed* trailer⟩

1**lowbell** \'ˌ\ *n* [perh. fr. 4*low* + *bell*] **1 :** a small bell (as for the neck of a sheep or cow) **2** *archaic* **:** a bell used with a sudden casting of light to frighten, stupefy, and capture birds

2**lowbell** *vt*, *obs* **:** to frighten or capture by or as if by the use of a lowbell

low bindweed *n* **:** a feebly twining herb (*Convolvulus spithamaeus*) of eastern No. America with oval leaves and white flowers

low birch *n* **:** DWARF BIRCH

low blood pressure *n* **:** HYPOTENSION

low blow *n* **:** a blow below the belt line in boxing

low blueberry *n* **:** LOWBUSH BLUEBERRY

lowborn \'ˌ\ *adj* **:** born in a low condition or rank ⟨~ rich or . . . blue-blooded poor —Clement Greenberg⟩

lowboy \'ˌ\ *n* **:** a dressing table about three feet high with drawers and similar to but smaller than the lower part of a highboy

lowboy

low-braced \'ˌ\ *adj*, *archery* **:** UNDERSTRUNG

low brass *n* **1 :** brass low in zinc content **2 :** brass containing about 20 percent zinc — compare HIGH BRASS

lowbred \'ˌ\ *adj* **:** bred or resembling one bred in a low condition of life **:** characteristic or indicative of such breeding **:** RUDE, VULGAR ⟨a ~ man⟩

1**lowbrow** \'ˌ\ *n* [4*low* + *brow*] **:** a person who does not possess or have pretensions to strong or advanced intellectual interests **:** one who lacks intellectual sophistication ⟨detective novels appeal to . . . highbrows as well as ~*s* —W.O.Aydelotte⟩

2**lowbrow** \"\ *adj* **:** of, relating to, or suitable for a lowbrow ⟨a ~ book⟩ ⟨a ~ program⟩ ⟨America had two types, ~ and highbrow —W.V.O'Connor⟩

low-browed \'ˌ\ *adj* [4*low* + *browed*] **1 :** being a person with a low brow or a low forehead ⟨*low-browed* Neanderthaloids⟩ **2 :** LOWBROW

low·brow·ism \'lō,braů,izəm\ *n* -s **:** the quality or state of being a lowbrow **:** the attitudes or traits characteristic of a lowbrow ⟨persistent ~ apparent in our slang —Sidney Baker⟩

low-budget \'ˌ\ *adj* **:** suited to or made on a low budget ⟨a *low-budget* picture⟩ ⟨folk who were enjoying the *low-budget* campsites —W.L.Gresham⟩ ⟨a *low-budget* menu⟩

lowbush \'ˌ\ *adj* **1 :** forming a very low or procumbent bush ⟨~ members of the genus *Rubus*⟩ **2 :** borne on a lowbush plant ⟨tangy ~ beach plums⟩

lowbush blackberry *also* **low blackberry** *n* **:** DEWBERRY

lowbush blueberry *also* **low blueberry** *n* **1 :** any of several low-growing No. American blueberries that are usu. considered to constitute a single highly variable species (*Vaccinium angustifolium*), have narrow serrulate leaves and sweet bluish black fruit with a heavy light blue bloom, and commonly form very large colonies by means of stolons **2 :** the fruit of a lowbush blueberry

low-central \'ˌ\ *adj* **:** LOW-MIXED

low church *adj*, *usu cap L&C* **:** tending toward or stressing the heritage of Protestant Christianity including its emphasis on the recovery of the orig. Christian gospel and personal service to its cause together with the minimization or outright rejection of sacerdotalism, sacramentarianism, and other forms of ceremonial ritualism — compare HIGH CHURCH

low churchman *n*, *usu cap L&C* **:** a person holding or advocating Low Church views

low-class \'ˌ\ *adj* **:** LOWER-CLASS

low comedian *n* **:** a comedian that specializes in a broad type of humor

low cornel *n* **:** DWARF CORNEL a

low-cost \'ˌ\ *adj* **:** obtainable at a low cost ⟨abundant and *low-cost* money —*U.S. News & World Report*⟩ ⟨*low-cost* housing⟩

low country *n* **:** a low-lying country or region; *specif* **:** the part of a southern state extending from the seacoast inland to the fall line

low-country \'ˌ\ *adj* [*low country*] **:** of, relating to, or proceeding from a low country or region ⟨retain at least a trace of her *low-country* accent —Hamilton Basso⟩

low cudweed *n* **:** MARSH CUDWEED

low-cut \'ˌ\ *adj* **1 :** having an outline or border that is cut or shaped low as contrasted with other styles of the same article ⟨a *low-cut* neckline⟩ **2** *of a shoe* **:** having uppers that do not extend up as far as the ankle ⟨a *low-cut* oxford⟩

lowdah *var of* LAODAH

low-down \'ˌ\ *adj* [4*low* + *down*, adv.] **1 :** quite or very low ⟨there would come a shy, *low-down* little knock on the door —Flora Thompson⟩ **2 :** CONTEMPTIBLE, MEAN, BASE ⟨couldn't have looked like that if he had been bad and *low-down* —Anne G. Winslow⟩ ⟨a *low-down* sneak⟩ ⟨it's right *low-down*, now, right wrong —Elizabeth M. Roberts⟩

lowdown \'ˌ\ *n* -s **:** the actual facts **:** inside information **:** DOPE ⟨give the ~ on American life —M.D.Geismar⟩ ⟨in a position to give you folks the real ~ —Erle Stanley Gardner⟩

low dutch *n*, *cap L&D* **1 :** LOW GERMAN 1 **2 :** a dialect of Dutch spoken in America by immigrants from the Netherlands

lowe *var of* LOW

lowed *past of* LOW

low·ell \'lōəl *also* 'lōil\ *n* -s *usu cap* [fr. *Lowell*, city in northeast Massachusetts] **:** a cheap cotton cloth made in Lowell, Mass., in the 19th century

low-end \'ˌ\ *adj* **1 :** of low grade ⟨*low-end* woolens⟩ ⟨*low-end* pelts⟩ ⟨*low-end* glass ware⟩ **2 :** manufacturing low grade goods esp. of cloth ⟨a *low-end* mill⟩

low enema *n* **:** an enema in which the injected material goes no higher than the rectum — compare HIGH ENEMA

1**low·er** *or* **lour** \'laů(ə)r, -aůə, *esp in the South* -aůwə(r; *sometimes* 'lō(ə)r *or* 'lōə\ *vi* -ED/-ING/-S [ME *louren*; akin to MD *loeren* to lie in wait, watch, MHG *lūren*] **1 :** to look sullen **:** FROWN ⟨~*ing* at the pavement —G.B.Shaw⟩ **2 a :** to be dark, gloomy, and threatening ⟨the clouds ~⟩ **b :** to become covered with dark and threatening clouds ⟨a rising wind and ~*ing* sky⟩ **c :** to show threatening signs of approach ⟨dark ~*s* the tempest overhead —H.W.Longfellow⟩ ⟨great thunderheads ~*ing* as they came —Mary Austin⟩ **3** *archaic* **:** to lie in wait

2**lower** *or* **lour** \"\ *n* -s [ME *lour*, fr. *louren*, v.] **:** a lowering look; *also* **:** a lowering or gloomy sky or aspect of weather

3**low·er** \'lō(ə)r, -ōə\ *adj* [fr. *lower*, compar. of 4*low*] **1 :** relatively low in position, amount, or degree ⟨a ~ berth⟩ ⟨a ~ estimate⟩ ⟨a ~ boiling point⟩ **2 a :** being or relating to something or someone of popular or inferior origin or rank ⟨the ~ chamber of a legislative body⟩ ⟨~ officeholders⟩ **b :** less differentiated in structure **:** less highly advanced in the scale of development through evolution ⟨the ~ animals⟩ ⟨~ organisms⟩ **c** *also* **low :** of or relating to a phase of an educational system that must be completed before the next one is entered ⟨~ school⟩ ⟨~ division⟩ ⟨~ freshmen⟩ **3 a** (1) **:** situated or regarded as being situated below the level of another part or place ⟨the ~ middle class⟩ ⟨the ~ settlements⟩ (2) **:** situated or believed to be situated beneath the surface of the earth ⟨the ~ world⟩ (3) **:** being the southern part of an area ⟨the center of the financial district in ~ Manhattan —*Current Biog.*⟩ ⟨the ~ South⟩ **b** *usu cap* **:** being an earlier epoch or series of the period or system named ⟨*Lower* Carboniferous⟩ ⟨*Lower* Cretaceous⟩ ⟨*Lower* Permian⟩ ⟨*Lower* Silurian⟩ — contrasted with *Upper* **c :** farther from the source ⟨the ~ Nile⟩ ⟨the ~ Mississippi⟩ **d** *usu cap* **:** living on lower ground, not so far inland, farther downstream, or farther south than others of the same group ⟨the *Lower* Creek⟩ **4 :** more recent ⟨assigns a ~ date for this event⟩

4**lower** \"\ *vb* -ED/-ING/-S *vi* **1 :** to move to a lower level **:** descend to a lower stage **:** let oneself down ⟨came and ~*ed* by her —A.B.Guthrie⟩ ⟨the river ~*ed* as rapidly as it rose⟩ **2 :** to diminish or decrease in value, amount, intensity, or degree ⟨predicted that prices would gradually ~⟩ ⟨voice ~*ed* into the sound of rain —James Still⟩ **3 :** to lower a boat or sail ⟨~*ed* for a bull sperm whale —H.A.Chippendale⟩ — often used with *away* ⟨as you ~ away, you can gather the jib as it comes down —Peter Heaton⟩ ~ *vt* **1 a :** to let descend by its own weight **:** let down ⟨~ a bucket⟩ ⟨~ a sail⟩ ⟨into this the general ~*ed* his portly form —D.G.Gerahty⟩ **b :** to depress as to direction ⟨~ the aim of a gun⟩ **c** (1) **:** to depress the surface of (as by carving, scraping) (2) **:** to remove (a part) in so doing **d :** to reduce the height of ⟨~ a wall⟩ **2 a :** to reduce in value or amount ⟨~ the price of goods⟩ ⟨~ the rate of interest⟩ **b** (1) **:** to bring down in quality, character, or reputation **:** DEGRADE ⟨~*ed* himself by his actions⟩ ⟨novels and tales likely to ~ taste —*Times Lit. Supp.*⟩ (2) **:** ABASE, HUMBLE **:** bring down in rank ⟨~*ed* the proud grandees and exalted the commoners⟩ **c :** to make less elevated as to objective ⟨~*ed* his aspirations⟩ — often used in the phrase *lower one's sights* ⟨nothing would be more fatal . . . than to ~ our sights —J.B.Conant⟩ **3 a :** to move (the tongue) down away from the palate **b :** to replace (a sound) with an allophone or phoneme of lower tongue position ⟨\ē\ was ~*ed* to \i\ before \r\⟩ — **lower the boom :** crack down ⟨*lowered the boom* last week on congressional junketing —*Time*⟩ ⟨right pleasant about it, but he really *lowered the boom* —Maxwell Griffith⟩

5**lower** \"\ *n* -s **:** the lower member of a pair: as **a :** a lower berth **b :** a lower denture

low·er·able \'lō(ə)rəbəl\ *adj* **:** capable of being lowered

lower angle *n* **:** SECOND ANGLE

Low·er·a·tor \'lōə,rād·ə(r)\ *trademark* — used for a machine for conveying loads vertically to a lower level

lower austral *adj*, *usu cap L&A* **:** of, relating to, or constituting a division of the Austral Zone including the Austroriparian and Lower Sonoran subdivisions

lower boom *n* **:** a spar run out from each side of a ship at anchor to secure boats clear of the side — see SHIP illustration

lower bridge *n* **:** the lower platform of a ship's bridge having two levels

lower case *n* **:** the lower one of a pair of type cases containing small letters and usu. also figures, punctuation marks, spaces, quads — compare UPPER CASE

1**lowercase** \'ˌ\ *adj* [*lower case*] **1** *of a letter* **:** having as its typical form a f g or *b n i* or **q z r** rather than A F G or *B N I* or **Q Z R** — abbr. *lc*; compare CAPITAL **2 :** set, printed, written, or otherwise rendered in lowercase letters — abbr. *lc*

2**lowercase** \"\ *n* **:** lowercase letters — abbr. *lc*; compare UPPERCASE

3**lowercase** \"\ *vt* **:** to print or set in lowercase; *also* **:** to change (as a capital letter) to a lowercase letter — abbr. *lc*

lower chamber *n* **:** LOWER HOUSE ⟨the House of Assembly resembles . . . the *lower chambers* in the other Dominions —Alexander Brady⟩

lower chinook *n*, *usu cap L&C* **:** a Chinookan language of the Clatsop and Chinook peoples

lower class *n* **1 :** a social class occupying a position below the middle class and having the lowest status in a society: as **a :** a feudal and post-feudal grouping of people composed principally of laborers and peasants **b :** a class composed chiefly (as in England) of manual workers **:** WORKING CLASS **c :** a socioeconomic grouping (as in the U.S.) characterized chiefly by low income, lack of education, and performance of unskilled manual labor **2 lower classes** *pl* **:** an aggregate of social groupings comprising subdivisions of the lower class

lower-class \'ˌ\ *adj* [*lower class*] **1 :** of or relating to the lower class **2 :** belonging to or associated with the lower class and its possession of or inclination toward such characteristics as a low material standard of living, social instability, little emphasis on convention and the proprieties, and a low level of personal ambition and of aspiration esp. toward education — compare MIDDLE-CLASS, UPPER-CLASS **3 :** being an inferior or low-ranking specimen of its kind **:** ranking low in some scale or by some standard ⟨after a couple of summers of seasoning in *lower-class* minor circuits —L.E.Davis⟩ ⟨an invitation to a *lower-class* embassy —Lillian Hellman⟩

low·er·class·man \'ˌ\mən\ *n*, *pl* **lowerclassmen** [fr. the phrase *lower class* "freshman or sophomore class" + *man*] **:** UNDERCLASSMAN

lower court *n* **:** a court whose decisions are subject to review or to appeal to a higher court **:** the court that first hears or tries cases **:** an inferior court

lower covert *n* **:** a covert on the undersurface of the wing or tail of a bird — usu. used in pl.

lower criticism *n* [so called fr. its primary or foundational character as contrasted with the higher criticism which utilizes its results] **:** study of the Bible that aims at reconstructing the original biblical texts **:** TEXTUAL CRITICISM — compare HIGHER CRITICISM

lower culmination *n*, *astron* **:** the crossing of a circumpolar object over that part of the celestial meridian between the visible pole and the horizon

lower deck *n* **1 a :** the lowest deck in ships with two or three decks **:** a deck below the main deck **b :** next to the lowest deck in ships with four or more decks — see DECK illustration **2** *chiefly Brit* **a :** the quarters of the enlisted personnel of a ship **b :** the enlisted personnel **3 :** a deck of a newspaper headline below the top deck

lowered *past of* LOWER

low·er·er \'lō(ə)rə(r)\ *n* -s [4*lower* + *-er*] **:** one that lowers

lower functional calculus *n* **:** functional calculus in which quantification is applied only to variables of individuals or arguments — called also *functional calculus of the first order*

lower fungus *n* **:** any of numerous fungi with hyphae absent or rudimentary and nonseptate and never forming a compact tissue (as in the Phycomycetes) — compare HIGHER FUNGUS

lower house *n* **:** the popular and often the larger and more representative branch of a legislative body having two chambers ⟨the *lower house* of the Dominion Parliament is known as the House of Commons —F.A.Magruder⟩

1**low·er·ing** *also* **lour·ing** \'laů(ə)riŋ, -rēŋ *esp in the South* -aůwər-\ *adj* [ME *louring*, fr. pres. part. of *louren* to lower, frown — more at LOWER] **:** dark and threatening **:** GLOOMY, SULLEN, FROWNING ⟨a ~ expression in her black eyes —Liam O'Flaherty⟩ ⟨it was a ~ May day —Sylvia T. Warner⟩

2**lowering** *n* -s [fr. gerund of 4*lower*] **:** the act or an instance of making low or lower ⟨a ~ of trade restrictions —*Current Biog.*⟩

low·er·ing·ly *also* **lour·ing·ly** *adv* [1*lowering* + *-ly*] **:** in a lowering manner **:** DARKLY, GLOOMILY ⟨looked at him ~⟩

lower larynx *n* **:** the syrinx of a bird

lower limb *n* **:** the edge of a celestial body that is nearest the horizon

lower mars *n*, *usu cap L&M* [3*lower* + *Mars*, Roman god of war and agriculture, fr. L *Mart-*, *Mars*] **:** a Mount located inside the line of Life beneath the Mount of Jupiter and above the Mount of Venus that when well developed is usu. held by palmists to indicate active courage and a martial spirit and sometimes an aggressive or quarrelsome nature — compare UPPER MARS; see PALMISTRY illustration

lower mast *n* **:** the lowest part of a compound mast composed of two or more poles — compare TOPMAST

low·er·most \'lō(ə)r,mōst *also chiefly Brit* -ˌməst\ *adj* **:** LOWEST ⟨at the ~ point of her flight —Sacheverell Sitwell⟩

lower orders *n pl* **:** LOWER CLASSES ⟨you had the marks of the *lower orders* on you —Anthony West⟩

lower plants *n pl* **:** plants (as the algae and fungi) having simple structure and reproductive processes

lowers *pres 3d sing of* LOWER, *pl of* LOWER

lower sonoran *adj*, *usu cap L&S* **:** of, relating to, or being the warmer part of the Sonoran life zone that adjoins the Tropical zone — compare UPPER SONORAN

lower transit *n* **:** the apparent crossing of a celestial body over the half of the meridian that lies between the celestial poles and contains the observer's zenith

lower umpqua *n*, *usu cap L&U* **:** KUITSH

low·ery *also* **loury** \'laů(ə)rē, -ri *esp in the South* -aůwər-\ *adj* [2*lower* + *-y*] **:** CLOUDY, GLOOMY, LOWERING ⟨a ~ sky⟩

lowest *superlative of* LOW

lowest common denominator *n* **1 :** the lowest common multiple of two or more denominators **2 :** something (as a quality or level of taste) that typifies or is common, acceptable, or comprehensible to all or the greatest possible number of individuals ⟨the committee system . . . reduces all ideas to the *lowest common denominator* —M.W.Straight⟩ ⟨broadcasting . . . falls into the error of producing programs at the *lowest common denominator* —Franklin Dunham⟩ ⟨living together in boredom, men exhibit their *lowest common denominator* —Clement Greenberg⟩ ⟨the quest by . . . the movies and the radio for *lowest common denominators* —John Collier b. 1884⟩

lowest common multiple *n* **:** the smallest common multiple of two or more numbers or the common multiple of lowest degree of two or more polynomials

lowes·toft ware \'lōz,tȯft-, -ˌtäft-, -ˌtəft-\ *or* **lowestoft** *n* -s *usu cap L* [fr. *Lowestoft*, city in eastern England] **1 :** a soft china made at Lowestoft, England from 1757 to 1802 **2 :** Chinese porcelain specially decorated (as with armorial bearings) for the English trade — called also *Chinese export porcelain*

low explosive *n* **:** a deflagrating or nondetonating explosive **:** PROPELLANT

low-flung \'ˌ\ *adj*, *archaic* **:** very degraded **:** LOW-DOWN

low franconian *n*, *cap L&F* **:** the West Germanic language that was used by the Franks inhabiting the region around the lowest part of the Rhine and that survives into modern times as a group of Low German dialects of northwestern Germany and as one of the principal linguistic strains from which Dutch (sense 1b) has evolved — compare FRANCONIAN

low frequency *n* **:** a radio frequency in the next to lowest range of the radio spectrum — see RADIO FREQUENCY table

low-frequency \'ˌ\ *adj* [*low frequency*] **:** of or relating to low frequency or a radio wave having such a frequency

low-front \'ˌ\ *adj*, *of a vowel* **:** low and front ⟨\a\⟩

low gallonage sprayer *n* **:** CONCENTRATE SPRAYER

low german *n*, *cap L&G* [trans. of G *niederdeutsch*] **1 :** the German dialects of northern Germany esp. as used since the end of the medieval period **:** PLATTDEUTSCH — compare HIGH GERMAN, MIDDLE LOW GERMAN, OLD SAXON **2 :** the West Germanic languages other than High German — compare DUTCH

low-grade \'ˌ\ *adj* [fr. the phrase *low grade*] **1 :** being of a grade or quality rated as inferior ⟨*low-grade* materials⟩ ⟨*low-grade* minds —*English Jour.*⟩ ⟨*low-grade* ore⟩ **2 :** being near the lower extreme of the range in which it may occur ⟨a *low-grade* fever is a slight fever⟩ ⟨a *low-grade* imbecile exhibits extreme deviation from normal⟩ — compare HIGH-GRADE

low ground *n*, *chiefly South* **:** 1BOTTOM 6 — often used in pl.

low-headed \'ˌ\ *adj* **:** CHAMAECEPHALIC

low-heat cement *n* **:** a portland cement specially prepared to develop a relatively low amount of heat of hydration during the setting and hardening period

low hop clover *n* **:** a nearly prostrate European clover (*Trifolium procumbens*) with yellow flowers

low-house \'ˌ\ *n* **:** the trap house on the right side of a skeet shooting range that projects the target from a point 3½ feet above the ground — called also *lo-trap*; compare HIGH-HOUSE

low hurdles *n pl but sing or pl in constr* **:** a track event of 220 yards or 200 meters distance with ten 2 ft. 6 in. hurdles to be surmounted — compare HIGH HURDLES, HURDLE RACE

lowing *pres part of* LOW

low·ish \'lōish\ *adj* **:** rather low ⟨an ignorant woman of ~ mentality —Rosamond Lehmann⟩ ⟨a ~ neckline —Marion Miller⟩

low-key \'ˌ\ *adj* [fr. the phrase *low key*] **1 :** of low intensity **:** RESTRAINED, LOW-KEYED **2** *photog* **:** having or producing dark tones only with little contrast ⟨a *low-key* picture⟩ — compare KEY 10d

low-keyed \'ˌ\ *adj* **:** subdued or restrained in mood, treatment, or quality ⟨a *low-keyed* little movie —*Newsweek*⟩ ⟨writes a cool, *low-keyed* prose —John Woodburn⟩ ⟨a little masterpiece of *low-keyed* eloquence —*Theatre Arts*⟩

1**low·land** \'lōlənd, 'lō,land, -aa(ə)nd\ *n* [4*low* + *land*] **:** land that is low with respect to the neighboring country **:** a low or level country; *specif*, *dial* **:** BOTTOM 6 — often used in pl.

2**lowland** \"\ *adj* **1 :** of, relating to, or characteristic of a lowland : inhabiting or growing in lowlands ⟨a ~ area⟩ ⟨~ speech⟩ 2 *usu cap* [fr. the *Lowlands*, southern and eastern part of Scotland] : of, relating to, or typical of the Lowlands of Scotland or the speech of that area

low·land·er \-də(r)\ *n* **1** : a native or inhabitant of a lowland region **2** *usu cap* : an inhabitant of the Lowlands of Scotland — compare HIGHLANDER

lowland fir *also* **lowland white fir** *n* : a lofty tree (*Abies grandis*) of the coast region of No. America with long curving branches, deep green leaves, and soft wood

lowland plover *n* : GOLDEN PLOVER

lowland rice *n* : rice grown on land that is flooded or irrigated — compare UPLAND RICE

lowland scots *n, cap L&S* : Scots spoken in the Lowlands

low latin *n, cap both Ls* : postclassical Latin in its later stages

low-level \ˈ=ˌ==\ *adj* [fr. the phrase *low level*] **1** : being on a low level (as of importance or rank) ⟨sees only *low-level* Chinese officials —*Newsweek*⟩ ⟨restricting itself to such *low-level* generalization —P.B.Rice⟩ **2** : occurring, done, or placed at a relatively low level ⟨*low-level* bombing and strafing raids⟩

low-life \ˈ=ˌ=\ *adj* [fr. the phrase *low life*] : of or relating to the world of low social life ⟨his realism turned naturally to *low-life* adventure —V.L.Parrington⟩ ⟨recalling *low-life* pictures of the old Dutch painters —Van Wyck Brooks⟩

lowlife \ˈ=ˌ=\ *n, pl* **lowlifes** *also* **lowlives** [fr. the phrase *low life*] **1** : a person of low social, cultural, or economic status ⟨wanted to transcribe completely the conversation of the ~*s* —Sinclair Lewis⟩ **2** : a person of criminal or low moral character : a shady or disreputable person ⟨among the ~*s* of the underworld —J.V. Ten Eyk⟩ ⟨finds his wife has deserted him and with a dirty ~ too —Ethel Wilson⟩

low·li·head \ˈlōlē,hed\ *n* [ME *lowliheed*, fr. *lowli*, lowly + *-heed*, *-hed*, *-hede* -hood (akin to ME *-hod*, *-had* -hood)] *archaic* : lowly state ⟨this charnel life, this ~ —Sidney Lanier⟩

low·li·ly \-lәlē\ *adv* [ME *lawlyly*, fr. *lawly*, lowly + *-ly*] : in a lowly manner

low·li·ness \ˈlōlēnә̇s\ *n* -ES [ME *lowlinesse*, fr. *lowli*, lowly + *-nesse* -ness] : the quality or state of being lowly

low-lived \ˈlō¦līvd\ *adj* : living a low life : suggestive of a low life : MEAN, CONTEMPTIBLE ⟨a *low-lived* creature⟩ ⟨a *low-lived* trick⟩

low-loss \ˈ=¦=\ *adj* : having low resistance and electric power loss ⟨a *low-loss* radio condenser⟩

¹low-low \ˈ=ˈ=\ *adj* [⁴*low* + ⁴*low*] **1** : slower than ordinary low gear and thereby adapted to heavy loads or steep grades ⟨a *low-low* gear⟩ **2** *of tide* : lower than the normal low

²low-low \ˈ"\ *n* : low-low gear ⟨tried to shift into *low-low* —Hugh Fosburgh⟩

¹low·ly \ˈlōlē, -li\ *adv* [ME, fr. ⁴*low* + *-ly*, adv. suffix] **1** : in a lowly manner : HUMBLY, MEEKLY, MODESTLY ⟨bowed ~ before her⟩ **2** : in a low position, manner, or degree ⟨affected rams are usually ~ fertile —*Fertility of Sheep*⟩ ⟨rare records . . . ~ priced —*advt*⟩ **3** : in a low voice : not loudly

²lowly \ˈ"\ *adj* -ER/-EST [ME, fr. ⁴*low* + *-ly*, adj. suffix] **1 a** : humble in manner or spirit : MODEST, MODERATE, MEEK ⟨taught him to be ~ and reverent⟩ **b** : of or relating to a low social or economic rank ⟨a man of ~ birth⟩ ⟨they were too ~ to associate with me —G.B.Shaw⟩ **c** : low in the scale of biological or cultural evolution ⟨a ~ society of the present day —*Notes & Queries on Anthropology*⟩ ⟨accepted the possibility that ~ . . . animals might be generated spontaneously —S.F. Mason⟩ **d** : ranking low in some hierarchy ⟨a ~ instructor in government —Fred Rodell⟩ ⟨a ~ parish priest⟩ **e** : low in order of importance, value, or esteem ⟨need not trouble himself with the ~ business of reading and writing if he had a good scribe —G.B.Jeffery⟩ ⟨made from a ~ railroad spike —*R-Mor-Plate*⟩ **f** : not lofty or sublime : PROSAIC, COMMONPLACE ⟨using great words on the *lowlier* subject, contrives to make them appropriate —A.T.Quiller-Couch⟩ **2** : low in position or growth : being relatively close to the ground ⟨the starvation need of air and light allotted to the ~ growths —William Beebe⟩ **syn** see HUMBLE

low-lying \ˈ=¦==\ *adj* **1** : having little upward extension or elevation : lying or rising relatively little above the ground or other base ⟨*low-lying* sand islands —*Amer. Guide Series: Fla.*⟩ ⟨*low-lying* hills⟩ **2** : lying below the normal level, surface, or the base of measurement or mean elevation ⟨*low-lying* haze and clouds —Alexander Forbes⟩ ⟨supplies to the *low-lying* cities of the state —*Amer. Guide Series: La.*⟩

low mallow *n* : DWARF MALLOW

low mass *n, often cap L&M* : a mass that is not sung but said in the simplest ceremonial form often without music or choir and with but one priest and one acolyte

low-melting \ˈ=¦==\ *adj* : melting at a relatively low temperature

lowmen *n pl, obs* : dice loaded to turn up low numbers

low-minded \ˈ=¦==\ *adj* : inclined in mind to low or unworthy things : showing a vulgar mind ⟨to my, perhaps *low-minded*, taste, they are by far the most successful pieces in the book —J.R.Hulbert⟩

low-mixed \ˈ=¦=\ *adj, of a vowel* : uttered (as \ә\) with the middle of the tongue low and intermediate between front and back

low moor *n* : a wet lowland rich in calcium and potassium and characterized by abundant moisture-loving grasses, reeds, rushes, and sedges

¹lown \ˈlau̇n\ *vb* -ED/-ING/-S [ME (Sc) *lownen*, of Scand origin; akin to Sw *lugna* to calm, quiet, OIcel *lygna*; derivative fr. the root of OSw *lughn*, n., calm, OIcel *logn*; akin to Goth *liuhath* light — more at LIGHT] *dial* : CALM, QUIET

²lown \ˈ"\ *adj* [ME (Sc) *lowne*, of Scand origin; akin to OSw *lughn*, adj., calm, Norw *logn*, OIcel *lygn*; derivative fr. the root of OSw *lughn*, n., calm, OIcel *logn*] *dial* : CALM, QUIET, STILL ⟨a ~ spring night —Maristan Chapman⟩

³lown \ˈ"\ *n* -S *dial* : CALM, QUIET, STILLNESS

⁴lown \ˈlün\ *chiefly Scot var of* ¹LOON

lownd \ˈlau̇nd\ *dial var of* ²LOWN

low-neck \ˈ=ˌ=\ *n* : a low-necked dress

low-necked *also* **low-neck** \ˈ=¦=\ *adj* : having a low-cut neckline

low·ness *n* -ES [ME *lownesse*, fr. ⁴*low* + *-nesse* -ness] : the quality or state of being low

lowp \ˈlau̇p, ˈlōp, ˈlüp\ *var of* ¹LOUP

low-pass filter *n* : an electric-circuit filter that transmits only frequencies below a prescribed frequency limit

low pitch *n* : DIAPASON NORMAL

low-pitched \ˈ=¦=\ *adj* **1** : pitched in a low key : being of low tone or dynamics ⟨a *low-pitched* voice⟩ **2** : having a low ratio of height to span ⟨a *low-pitched* roof⟩; *also* : LOW-STUDDED

low-pressure \ˈ=¦==\ *adj* **1 a** : having, employing, exerting, or operating under a relatively small pressure ⟨a *low-pressure* burner⟩ **b** : having or resulting from a low atmospheric pressure ⟨a *low-pressure* system⟩ ⟨a *low-pressure* storm⟩ — compare CYCLONE **2** : not strenuous, intense, or aggressive in manner or approach : EASYGOING ⟨find a wonderfully *low-pressure* feeling about the whole area —Richard Joseph⟩ ⟨*low-pressure* circulation methods —*U.S. News & World Report*⟩ ⟨a *low-pressure* and thoroughly diverting report —C.W.Morton⟩ — compare HIGH-PRESSURE

low-quarter shoe *n, chiefly South* : LOW SHOE

low-rate \ˈ=ˌ=\ *vt, chiefly South & Midland* : BELITTLE, CENSURE, DEPRECIATE, DISPARAGE ⟨you *low-rate* me too much —Lonnie Coleman⟩ ⟨*low-rating* the achievements of his . . . friends —Lee Rogow⟩

low relief *n* [trans. of F *bas-relief*] : BAS-RELIEF

¹low·rie \ˈlau̇rē\ *n* -S [fr. *Lowrie*, nickname fr. the name *Lawrence*] *Scot* : FOX ⟨has greedy ~ been among thy sheep —David Sillar⟩

²low·rie \ˈlōri\ *Austral var of* LORY

low·ry process \ˈlau̇rē-\ *n, usu cap L* [after C. B. *Lowry*, who devised it] : an empty-cell wood-treating process involving an injection of creosote without a preliminary vacuum in excess of the amount required and removal of the excess by a quick high vacuum

lows *pl of* LOW, *pres 3d sing of* LOW

low-salt diet *n* : LOW-SODIUM DIET

low saxon *n, cap L&S* : the Germanic dialects of northwest Germany between the Rhine and the Elbe

lowse *adj* ˈlōs, *v.* ˈlōz\ *dial Brit var of* LOOSE

low-set \ˈ=¦=\ *adj, of an animal* : STOCKY, BLOCKY, COBBY; *specif* : having the legs short with heavily developed musculature

low shoe *n* : a low-cut shoe; *esp* : OXFORD

low sick *adj, South & Midland* : seriously ill

low side window *n* : a window in medieval churches that is narrow, near the ground, and out of the line of the other windows — called also *lychnoscope*

low·sin \ˈlōzә̇n\ *n* -S [E dial. (northern) *lowsin*, *lowsing*, gerund of *lowse* to loose, stop work, fr. ME *loosen*, *losen*, *lousen* to loose — more at LOOSE] *dial Brit* : an act of stopping work ⟨seen my last ~ —Charles Murray⟩

low-slung \ˈ=¦=\ *adj* : having relatively small upward extent : being relatively close to the ground, floor, or other base ⟨the furniture was all *low-slung* and functional —Edmund Wilson⟩ ⟨this *low-slung* modernistic building —*Women's Wear Daily*⟩ ⟨*low-slung* beef cattle —J.F.Sembower⟩; *specif* : having a low floor to facilitate loading and to maintain stability on curves at high speed ⟨made up of *low-slung* tubular cars holding 600 passengers —*Time*⟩

low-sodium diet *n* : a diet restricted to foods naturally low in sodium content and prepared without added salt that is used esp. in the management of certain circulatory or kidney disorders

low speed *n* : slow speed; *esp* : the slowest speed — used esp. of an automobile with three forward speeds

low-spirited \ˈ=¦===\ *adj* **1** *archaic* : lacking in ardor or in courage **2** : DEJECTED, DEPRESSED ⟨found his friend ailing and *low-spirited*⟩

low-spir·it·ed·ness *n* : the quality or state of being low-spirited

low-strung \ˈ=¦=\ *adj* : having less than a fistmele between bow and bowstring ⟨a *low-strung* bow⟩

low-studded \ˈ=¦==\ *adj* : furnished or built with short studs ⟨a *low-studded* house⟩

low sunday *n, usu cap L&S* [ME *low-sonday*, fr. ⁴*low* + *sonday* Sunday] : the Sunday following Easter

low-temperature \ˈ=¦=...\ *adj* : relating to or carried out at very low or relatively low temperatures ⟨*low-temperature* refrigeration⟩ ⟨*low-temperature* carbonization of coal below about 1300°F⟩

low-tension \ˈ=¦==\ *adj* **1** : having a low potential or voltage **2** : constructed to be used at low voltage ⟨a *low-tension* coil⟩ ⟨a *low-tension* transmission line⟩

low-test \ˈ=¦=\ *adj* : having a low volatility — used esp. of gasoline

low tide *n* : the farthest ebb of the tide : the tide at its lowest

lowveld \ˈ=ˌ=\ *n* : GRASSVELD

low voltage *n* **1** : voltage low enough to be considered safe for indoor domestic use and typically 120 volts or less **2** : voltage below that required for normal operation

low-warp \ˈ=¦=\ *adj* : having the warp threads strung horizontally ⟨*low-warp* tapestry⟩

low water *n* **1** : a low stage of the water (as in a river or lake); *specif* : LOW TIDE **2** : a depressed, degraded, or embarrassed state ⟨the country was patently at a moral and religious *low water* —W.L.Sperry⟩ ⟨found itself in *low water* after a checkered . . . career —W.J.Thorne⟩

low-water line *or* **low-water mark** *n* **1** : a line or mark indicating low water **2** *usu* **low-water mark** : something that marks a nadir of decline or degradation ⟨the *low-water mark* of political infamy was the killing of statewide civil service —*New Orleans States*⟩

low week *n, usu cap L&W* : the week beginning with Low Sunday

low wine *n* : a weak liquor produced by the first distillation of wash : first run of the still — often used in pl.; compare FEINTS

lowy \ˈlōē\ *n* -ES [MF *louee*, *liuee* space of a league, fr. OF, fr. *liue* league, fr. LL *leuga* — more at LEAGUE] : BANLIEUE

¹lox \ˈläks\ *n* -ES [*liquid oxygen*] : LIQUID OXYGEN

²lox \ˈ"\ *n, pl* **lox** *or* **loxes** [Yiddish *laks*, fr. MHG *lahs* salmon, fr. OHG — more at LAX] : smoked salmon

lox- *or* **loxo-** *comb form* [NL, fr. Gk, fr. *loxos*; akin to MIr *losc* lame, OE *eln* ell — more at ELL] : oblique ⟨*lox*odograph⟩ ⟨*Loxo*soma⟩

loxa bark \ˈläksә-, ˈlōhә-\ *or* **lo·ja bark** \ˈlōhә-\ *n* [fr. *Loxa*, *Loja*, province in southwest Ecuador] : PALE BARK

lox·ia \ˈläksēә\ *n, cap* [NL, fr. *lox-* + *-ia*] : a genus constituted by the crossbill

lox·o·clase \ˈläksә,klās, -āz\ *n* -S [G *loxoklas*, fr. *lox-* + *-klas* -clase] : an orthoclase containing considerable sodium

lox·o·cosm \ˈläksә,käzәm\ *n* [ISV *lox-* + *-cosm*] : a device to show how the inclination of the earth's axis causes the day's length to vary from season to season

lox·od·o·graph \läkˈsädә,graf, -räf\ *n* [*lox-* + Gk *hodos* way, course + E *-graph* — more at CEDE] : an apparatus for recording a ship's course by magnetism and photography or other registering device

¹lox·o·dont \ˈläksә,dänt\ *also* **lox·o·don·tous** \¦==ˈdäntәs\ *adj* [*loxodont* fr. NL *Loxodonta*; *loxodontous* fr. NL *Loxodonta* + E *-ous*] : having shallow hollows between the ridges of the molar teeth

²loxodont \ˈ"\ *n* -S [NL *Loxodonta*] : an elephant with loxodont teeth

lox·o·don·ta \ˌ==ˈdäntә\ *n, cap* [NL, fr. *lox-* + *-odonta*] : a genus of Elephantidae comprising the African elephants and extinct related forms

lox·o·drome \ˈläksә,drōm\ *n* -S [ISV, back-formation fr. *loxodromic*] : RHUMB LINE ⟨a sailor who has chosen a direction on the compass and keeps it steadily is following a ~ —Hugo Steinhaus⟩

lox·o·drom·ic \¦==ˈdrämik\ *also* **lox·o·drom·i·cal** \-mәkәl\ *adj* [*loxodromic* prob. fr. (assumed) NL *loxodromicus*, fr. Gk *lox-* + *drom-* + L *-icus* -ic; *loxodromical* fr. *loxodromic* + *-al*] : relating to a rhumb line or to sailing on rhumb lines — **lox·o·drom·i·cal·ly** \-mәk(ә)lē\ *adv*

loxodromic curve *n* : RHUMB LINE

¹lox·o·loph·o·dont \¦läksә¦läfә,dänt\ *adj* [NL *Loxolophodont-*, *Loxolophodon* genus of extinct ungulates in some classifications, fr. *lox-* + *loph-* + *-odont-*, *-odon* -odon] : having molar teeth with oblique crests connecting the anterior inner tubercle with the two outer tubercles and with the posterior inner tubercle rudimentary or absent — used esp. of several extinct ungulates

²loxolophodont \ˈ"\ *n* -S [NL *Loxolophodont-*, *Loxolophodon*] : a loxolophodont animal

lox·om·ma \läkˈsämә\ *n, cap* [NL, fr. *lox-* + *-omma*] : a genus of primitive Permian labyrinthodont amphibians (order Rhachitomi) that are commonly considered remotely ancestral to the modern salientians and are found in the coal measures of England and Bohemia

lox·om·moid \-sä,mȯid\ *n* -S [prob. fr. NL *Loxommoidea* (group including the genus *Loxomma*), fr. *Loxomma* + *-oidea*] : a member of the genus *Loxomma*

lox·os·ce·les \läkˈsäsә,lēz\ *n, cap* [NL, fr. *lox-* + Gk *-skelēs* (fr. *skelos* leg) — more at CYLINDER] : a genus of So. American spiders including a species (*L. laeta*) which is common about buildings and whose bite causes a local necrosis of tissue and sometimes systemic symptoms of poisoning

lox·o·so·ma \,läksәˈsōmә\ *n, cap* [NL, fr. *lox-* + *-soma*] : a genus (the type of the family Loxosomatidae) comprising solitary members of the Ectoprocta

lox·y·gen \ˈläksә̇jәn\ *n* -S [*liquid oxygen*] : LIQUID OXYGEN

loy \ˈlȯi\ *n* -S [IrGael *lāighe*; akin to Gk *lachainein* to dig] **1** : a long narrow spade used in Ireland **2** : a tool with a broad chisel point for digging post holes

¹loyal \ˈlȯi(ә)l ˈlȯ(i)yәl\ *adj, sometimes* -ER/-EST [MF, fr. OF *loial*, *leial*, fr. L *legalis* legal, of or relating to law — more at LEGAL] **1 a** : faithful to the lawful government or to the sovereign to whom one is subject : unswerving in allegiance ⟨the army remains ~⟩ ⟨no one can be hired until the administrator certifies that the individual is ~ to the United States —Arthur Schlesinger b. 1917⟩ ⟨there is no ~*er* subject of Her Grace than myself —J.H.Wheelwright⟩ **b** : faithful and devoted to a private person; *esp* : faithful to a person to whom fidelity is held to be due ⟨gentle, solicitous, and ~ slaves —Margaret Leech⟩ ⟨a ~ husband⟩ **2** : displaying or reflecting loyalty ⟨explained with a ~ little sob —Elinor Wylie⟩ ⟨~ utterances⟩ **3** : faithful or tenacious in adherence to a cause, ideal, practice, or custom ⟨a very ~ churchgoer⟩ ⟨~ in habits and attitudes to a vanished age —J.W.Krutch⟩ ⟨the Syrians . . . are still ~ to milk, butter, cheese, and lamb —*Amer. Guide Series: R.I.*⟩ **4** *obs* : LAWFUL, LEGITIMATE **syn** see FAITHFUL

²loyal \ˈ"\ *n* -S : a loyal subject or follower — usu. used in pl. ⟨those he considers to be his true-blue ~*s* —*Time*⟩

loy·al·ism \-ә,lizәm\ *n* -S : the principles or conduct of a loyalist : display of loyalty ⟨represents outspoken ~ —*Times Lit. Supp.*⟩

loy·al·ist \-әlә̇st\ *n* -S : a person who is or remains loyal to a political cause, party, government, or sovereign: as **a** : an American opposed to separation from Great Britain during the Revolution : TORY ⟨a descendant of ~*s* who left the American colonies for Canada —*Current Biog.*⟩ **b** : an adherent to the Union cause during the Civil War esp. in a southern state **c** *usu cap* : an adherent to the constitutional republican government during the Spanish Civil War (1936–1939) ⟨rushed to help the *Loyalists* —E.O.Hauser⟩

loy·al·ly \-әlē, -әli\ *adv* : in a loyal manner

loy·al·ness \-(ә)lnә̇s\ *n* -ES : the quality or state of being loyal

loyal opposition *n* : a minority party esp. in a legislative body whose opposition to the party in power is constructive, responsible, and bounded by loyalty to fundamental interests and principles ⟨a well-fortified minority will tend to improve . . . legislative debate and can become a genuine *loyal opposition* —*Amer. State Legislatures*⟩; *specif* : the minority party in the British parliament — often used in the phrase *His Majesty's loyal opposition*

loy·al·ty \ˈlȯi(ә)ltē, ˈlȯ(i)yәl- -ti\ *n* -ES *often attrib* [ME *loyaltee*, fr. MF *loialté*, fr. OF *loialté*, *leialté*, *lealté*, fr. *loial*, *leial* loyal + *-té* -ty] : the quality, state, or an instance of being loyal : fidelity or tenacious adherence (as to a government, principle, practice, or custom) ⟨~ is . . . essentially personal and moral, based on individual choice . . . and may find expression in a dozen forms —Francis Biddle⟩ ⟨why these products had failed to build brand ~ —Vance Packard⟩ ⟨~ is the absence of subversive tendencies or liaisons —L.A.Huston⟩ ⟨~ is . . . agreement with the party platform and program —E.S.Griffith⟩ ⟨~ to friends⟩ ⟨a ~ check⟩ **syn** see FIDELITY

loyalty board *n* : a board (as of a government agency) established and authorized to inquire into the loyalty to the government of the U.S. of persons employed or considered for employment by the U.S. government or by international organizations of which the U.S. is a member and to make usu. advisory determinations in such cases

loyalty oath *n* : a usu. mandatory oath affirming the loyalty of its taker (as to a sovereign, government, or party principles) ⟨ruled the Genevese . . . with the help of *loyalty oaths* and the gibbet —*Times Lit. Supp.*⟩ ⟨the *loyalty oath* will be abandoned at the next Democratic convention —*Newsweek*⟩; *esp* : an oath often required of public employees or applicants for public employment in the U.S. typically affirming that the signer upholds the U.S. or state constitutions and is not knowingly a member of any of a number of organizations held to be subversive

loy·o·lite \lȯiˈō,līt, lȯ(i)ˈyō,-, ˈlȯiә,-, ˈlō(i)yә,-\ *n* -S *usu cap* [Saint Ignatius of *Loyola* †1556 Span. ecclesiastic who founded the Jesuit order + E *-ite*] : JESUIT

lo·zen \ˈlōzᵊn, ˈläz-\ *n* -S [modif. of MF *losange*, fr. OF, diamond-shaped heraldic figure] *Scot* : a lozenge-shaped window pane

¹loz·enge \ˈläz|zᵊnj, |әnj *sometimes* ˈlō| *or* |s|\ *n* -S [ME *losenge*, fr. MF *losange*, fr. OF, diamond-shaped heraldic figure] **1** : a figure with four equal sides and two acute and two obtuse angles : DIAMOND, RHOMBUS **2** : something having the form of a lozenge: as **a** (1) : a small flat lozenge-shaped candy; *esp* : one made from sugar and gum, variously flavored, and sometimes medicated ⟨took a throat ~ for his cough⟩ (2) : PASTILLE **b** : a diamond-shaped decorative element or motif **c** (1) : a diamond-shaped heraldic figure usu. with the upper and lower angles slightly acute (2) : a diamond-shaped escutcheon now commonly used only by women **d** (1) : one of the diamond-shaped facets on a cut gem (2) : a cut with lozenge-shaped outline

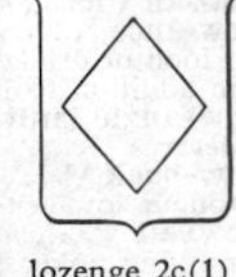

lozenge 2c(1)

²lozenge \ˈ"\ *adj* : marked with or composed of a lozenge : LOZENGED

lozenged \-jd\ *or* **lozenge-shaped** \¦==ˌ=\ *adj* : shaped like a lozenge

lozenge file *n* : a die-sinker's small file with a lozenge-shaped cross section and teeth on all four faces

lozenge molding *n* : a molding used in Norman architecture characterized by lozenge-shaped ornaments

loz·eng·er \-jә(r)\ *n* -S [by alter.] *dial* : LOZENGE 2a

lozengewise \ˈ==ˌ=\ *adv* : in the shape of a lozenge : so as to form a lozenge or a lozenge pattern

loz·engy \-jē\ *adj* [MF *losengié*, fr. OF, fr. *losenge*, *losange* diamond-shaped heraldic figure] *heraldry* : divided into lozenge-shaped compartments

lo·zi \ˈlōzē\ *n, pl* **lozi** *or* **lozis** *usu cap* **1 a** : a Bantu-speaking people in Northern Rhodesia known for their woodcarving — called also *Barotse* **b** : a member of such people **2** : a Bantu language of the Lozi people that is closely related to Sotho and is used as a lingua franca in Barotseland

lp *abbr* **1** ladyship **2** lordship

LP \ˈelˈpē\ *trademark* — used for a microgroove phonograph record ordinarily having a diameter of 10 or 12 inches, turning at 33⅓ revolutions per minute, and requiring a playing time of about 10 to 30 minutes

LP *abbr* **1** landplane **2** large paper; large post **3** liquefied petroleum **4** long picot **5** long primer **6** lord provost **7** loss of pay **8** low-pass **9** low point **10** low pressure

LPF *abbr* leukocytosis-promoting factor

LPG *abbr* liquefied petroleum gas

lp gas *n, usu cap L&P & sometimes cap G* [*l*iquefied *p*etroleum *gas*] : LIQUEFIED PETROLEUM GAS

LPM *abbr* long particular meter

LPP *abbr* large paper proofs

LPS *abbr* lord privy seal

LPW *abbr* lumens per watt

lr *abbr* lira

LR *abbr* **1** large ring **2** left rear **3** living room **4** lock rail **5** log run **6** long range **7** lower right

lrg *abbr* large

LRRP *abbr, often not cap* lowest required radiated power

LS *abbr* **1** landing ship **2** land service **3** leading seaman **4** left side **5** legal scroll **6** letter signed **7** library science **8** listed securities **9** local sunset **10** [L *locus sigilli*] the place of the seal **11** longitudinal section **12** long shot **13** loudspeaker **14** low speed **15** lump sum

l's *or* **ls** *pl of* L

LSC *abbr, often not cap* [L *loco supra citato*] in the place cited above

lsd *abbr* leased

LSD *or* **LSD 25** *n* -S : LYSERGIC ACID DIETHYLAMIDE

LSD *abbr* **1** landing ship dock **2** *often not cap* [L *librae, solidi, denarii*] pounds, shillings, pence

l-shaped \ˈ=¦=\ *adj, cap L* : having the shape of a capital L

l-shell \ˈ=ˌ=\ *n, usu cap L* : the second innermost shell of electrons surrounding an atomic nucleus — compare K-SHELL, M-SHELL

LSM *abbr* landing ship medium

LSO *abbr* landing signal officer

l square *n, cap L* : a carpenter's square

LSR *abbr* local sunrise

LSS *abbr* **1** lifesaving service **2** lifesaving station

LST *abbr* **1** landing ship tank **2** local sidereal time **3** local standard time

lt *abbr* **1** *often cap* lieutenant **2** light

LT *abbr* **1** landed terms **2** left tackle **3** legal tender **4** letter telegram **5** line telegraphy **6** local time **7** long ton **8** low tension

LTA *abbr* lighter than air

ltd *abbr, often cap* limited

ltg *abbr* lightning

ltge *abbr* lighterage

lthr *abbr* leather

LTI *abbr* light transmission index

LTL *abbr* less-than-truckload
ltng *abbr* lightning
ltr *abbr* **1** letter **2** lighter
lu \'lü\ *n, pl* **lu** *usu cap* **:** a Tai ethnic group inhabiting chiefly the extreme southwest part of Yunnan province in southern China and adhering to a Buddhist religion
lu *abbr* lumen
Lu *symbol* lutetium
lu·ah *or* **lu·ach** \lü,ä k\ *n, pl* **lu·hoth** *or* **lu·hot** *or* **lu·choth** *or* **lu·chot** \lü kōt(h)\ [Heb *lūaḥ*, lit., board, tablet (pl. *lūḥōt*)] **:** JEWISH CALENDAR
lu·au \'lü'aü, '=,=\ *n* -s [Hawaiian *lu'au*] **1 :** a feast with Hawaiian food and usu. Hawaiian entertainment **2 :** cooked young taro leaves usu. with coconut cream and chicken or octopus
lub *abbr* lubricant; lubricating
lu·ba \'lübə\ *n, pl* **luba** *or* **lubas** *usu cap* **1 a :** an African Negro people of southern Belgian Congo **b :** a member of such people **2 :** any of numerous Bantu languages spoken in Belgian Congo; *esp* **:** TSHILUBA
[1]**lub·ber** \ləbə(r)\ *n* -s [ME *lobre*, *lobur*, prob. of Scand origin; akin to Sw dial. *lubber* fat lazy fellow, *lubbe* plump figure — more at LOB] **1** *also* **lub·bard** \'ləbə(r)d\ **:** a big clumsy fellow; *esp* **:** a worthless idler **2 :** a clumsy or unskilled seaman — compare LANDLUBBER
[2]**lubber** \"\ *vi* **lubbered; lubbered; lubbering** \-b(ə)riŋ\ **lubbers :** to act in a lubberly manner esp. when managing a boat
[3]**lubber** \"\ *adj* **1** *also* **lub·bard** \ləbə(r)d\ **:** LUBBERLY **2 :** [3]BLUBBER ⟨his thick ~ lips were drawn heavily downward —Hall Caine⟩
lubber fiend *n* **:** a helpful goblin that does household chores at night
lubber grasshopper *n* **:** either of two very large stout clumsy short-winged No. American grasshoppers: **a :** a grasshopper (*Romalea microptera*) of the southeastern U.S. **b :** a grasshopper (*Brachystola magna*) of the southwestern U.S. and adjacent Mexico
lubberland \'=,=\ *n* **:** COCKAIGNE
lubber line *also* **lubber's line** *or* **lubber mark** *or* **lubber's point** *n* **:** a fixed line on the compass or other directional indicator of a ship or airplane that is aligned with the longitudinal axis of the ship or plane
lub·ber·li·ness \'ləbə(r)lēnəs, -lin-\ *n* -ES **:** the quality or state of being lubberly
[1]**lub·ber·ly** *adj* [[1]*lubber* + *-ly*] **1 a :** resembling or having the characteristics of a lubber **:** CLUMSY, LAZY, LOUTISH, STUPID ⟨emerged a ~ mediocrity —C.J.Rolo⟩ **b :** not seamanlike ⟨of all landlubbers, the most ~ —Herman Melville⟩ **2 :** appropriate to or fit for a lubber ⟨unfit for anything but some ~ shoreside pursuit —LaSelle Gilman⟩ **3** *of a ship* **a :** handled ineptly **b :** not shipshape
[2]**lubberly** \"\ *adv* **:** in a lubberly manner
lubber's hole *n* **:** a hole in a ship's top near the mast through which one may go farther aloft without going over the rim by the futtock shrouds
lube \'lüb\ *n* -s [short for *lubricating oil*] **:** a lube oil or other lubricant
lü·beck *or* **lu·beck** *or* **lue·beck** \'lü,bek\ *adj, usu cap* [fr. *Lübeck*, city in northern Germany] **:** of or from the city of Lübeck, Germany **:** of the kind or style prevalent in Lübeck
lube oil *n* [short for *lubricating oil*] **:** a lubricating oil obtained from petroleum
lu·blin \'lüblən\ *adj, usu cap* [fr. *Lublin*, city in eastern Poland] **:** of or from the city of Lublin, Poland **:** of the kind or style prevalent in Lublin
lu·bra \'lübrə\ *n* -s [native name in Tasmania] **:** an aboriginal girl or woman of Australia
lu·bric \'lübrik\ *or* **lu·bri·cal** \-brəkəl\ *adj* [*lubric* fr. MF *lubrique*, fr. L *lubricus*; *lubrical* fr. *lubric* + *-al*] *archaic* **:** LUBRICIOUS
[1]**lu·bri·cant** \'lübrəkənt\ *adj* [L *lubricant-*, *lubricans*, pres. part. of *lubricare* to lubricate, fr. *lubricus* slippery — more at SLEEVE] **:** serving to lubricate
[2]**lubricant** \"\ *n* -s **1 :** a substance capable of reducing friction, heat, and wear when introduced as a film between solid surfaces (as oil or grease for metal bearings, graphite for sprocket chains, soap or paraffin for wood surfaces, cutting compound for lathe tools); *esp* **:** such a substance interposed between moving parts of machinery — compare CUTTING FLUID **2 :** an emulsion, oil, or dressing applied to fibers and yarns to make processing easier and less damaging **3 :** something that lessens or prevents friction or difficulty ⟨a man who believed in the smile as a social ~ —Margery Allingham⟩ ⟨a kind of literary ~, that will ease the reading alone —Dudley Fitts⟩
lu·bri·cate \-,kāt, *usu* -ād.+V\ *vb* -ED/-ING/-S [L *lubricatus*, past part. of *lubricare*] *vt* **1 :** to make smooth, slippery, or oily in motion, action, or appearance ⟨this small amount of chemical ~*s* the wax crystals —Desmond Reilly⟩ ⟨in drilling an oil well, mud is used to ~ the cutting bit —*Westinghouse News*⟩ **2 :** to apply a lubricant to **:** treat with a lubricant ⟨~ the bearings⟩ ⟨~ the economic system with a sufficiency of purchasing power —Hugh Dalton⟩ ⟨~ the skin with cold cream⟩ **3** *slang* **:** to ply with drink ⟨*lubricated* them with continuous champagne —Horace Sutton⟩ **4** *slang* **:** BRIBE ⟨*lubricated* a dishonest official⟩ ~ *vi* **1 :** to act as a lubricant ⟨oil ~*s* efficiently most of the time⟩ **2** *slang* **:** to drink or get drunk ⟨the *lubricating* kept right on, not so badly, but more than anyone could carry —Ethel Merman⟩
lubricating oil *n* **:** an oil (as a petroleum distillate or a fatty oil) used as a lubricant
lu·bri·ca·tion \,==ˈkāshən\ *n* -s **:** the act or process of lubricating or the state of being lubricated
lu·bri·ca·tive \'==,kād.iv\ *adj* **:** acting or capable of acting as a lubricant
lu·bri·ca·tor \-,kād.ə(r), -ātə-\ *n* -s **:** one that lubricates: as **a :** GREASER, OILER **b :** LUBRICANT **c :** an oil container or other device for applying a lubricant
lu·bri·ca·to·ry \-kə,tōrē, *chiefly Brit* ¦==¦kātəri *or* -ā.tri\ *adj* [*lubricate* + *-ory*] **:** serving to lubricate
lu·bri·cious \lü'brishəs\ *or* **lu·bri·cous** \'lübrəkəs\ *adj* [*lubricious* alter. (influenced by *-ious*) of *lubricous*, fr. ML *lubricus*, fr. L, slippery] **1 a :** marked by wantonness **:** LECHEROUS ⟨eluding the *lubricous* embraces of her wealthy employer —*Amer. Mercury*⟩ ⟨some *lubricous* fellows . . . who made companions of these serving maids —E.L.Masters⟩ **b :** sexually stimulating **:** SALACIOUS ⟨a little ~ book . . . on a bed table by a pink-shaded lamp —Graham Greene⟩ ⟨exploited in full ~ detail by the metropolitan tabloids —John Woodburn⟩ **2** [influenced in meaning by L *lubricus*] **a :** having a smooth or slippery quality ⟨the skin of the cephalopods is thin and *lubricous* —R.B.Todd⟩ **b :** marked by uncertainty or instability **:** ELUSIVE, SHIFTY ⟨how ~ a friend and changeable a partisan —Robert Ferguson⟩ — **lu·bri·cious·ly** *adv*
lu·bric·i·ty \lü'brisəd.ē, -ətē, -i\ *n* -ES [MF *lubricité* lasciviousness, slipperiness, fr. ML & LL; ML *lubricitat-*, *lubricitas* lasciviousness, fr. LL, slipperiness, instability, fr. L *lubricus* slippery + *-itat-*, *-itas* -ity] **1 a :** LASCIVIOUSNESS, SENSUALITY ⟨a life of futile ~ —*Dial*⟩ **b :** something that stimulates to lewdness; *specif* **:** PORNOGRAPHY ⟨laws have been singularly ineffectual in eradicating ~ —*Christian Science Monitor*⟩ **2 a :** freedom from friction **:** SLIPPERINESS, SMOOTHNESS ⟨the scented ~ of soap —Sydney Smith⟩ **b :** a property that lessens friction ⟨the ~ of oil⟩ **3 :** INSTABILITY ⟨the ~ of fortune⟩
lu·bri·fy \'lübrə,fī\ *vt* -ED/-ING/-S [F *lubrifier*, fr. MF, fr. L *lubricus* + MF *-fier* -fy] *archaic* **:** LUBRICATE
lu·bri·to·ri·um \,=='tōrēəm, -tȯr-\ *n* -s [*lubri-* (as in *lubricate*) + *-torium* (as in *sanatorium*)] **:** a station or room for lubricating motor vehicles
lu·can *or* **lu·kan** \'lükən\ *adj, usu cap* [*lucan* fr. LL *lucanus*, fr. *Lucas* Luke, the Evangelist regarded as the author of the third Gospel in the New Testament (fr. Gk *Loukas*) + L *-anus* -an; *lukan* fr. *Luke* + E *-an*] **:** of, relating to, or having the characteristics of the Evangelist Luke or the Gospel ascribed to him
[1]**lu·ca·nid** \lü'kānəd\ *adj* [NL *Lucanidae*] **:** of or relating to the Lucanidae
[2]**lucanid** \"\ *n* -s [NL *Lucanidae*] **:** a beetle of the family Lucanidae

lu·can·i·dae \=ˈkanə,dē\ *n pl, cap* [NL, fr. *Lucanus*, type genus + *-idae*] **:** a family of insects comprising the stag beetles
lu·ca·nus \=ˈkānəs\ *n, cap* [NL, perh. fr. LL, daylight, fr. L *luc-*, *lux* light + *-anus* -an — more at LIGHT] **:** a genus (the type of the family Lucanidae) of beetles
lu·carne \lü'kärn, -kȧn\ *n* -s [alter. (influenced by F *lucarne* dormer window, fr. MF, alter. — influenced by MF *luiserne*, *luserne* lantern, fr. L *lucerna* lamp — of *lucanne*) of earlier *lucane*, fr. MF *lucanne*, fr. OF, fr. (assumed) OFrk *lūkinna*, fr. *lūk* something that closes (akin to MD *luke* something that closes, fence) + *-inna*, dim. suffix; akin to OE *lūcan* to close — more at LOCK] **:** DORMER WINDOW
lu·cayo \lü'kī(,)ō, -kā(-\ *also* **lu·cayan** \-kāən, -kīən\ *n, pl* **lucayo** *or* **lucayos** *also* **lucayan** *or* **lucayans** *usu cap* [*Lucayo* fr. AmerSp, fr. Arawak; *Lucayan* fr. AmerSp *Lucayo* + E *-an*] **1 a :** an extinct aboriginal Arawakan tribe of the Bahamas **b :** a member of such tribe **2 :** the language of the Lucayo people
luce \'lüs\ *n* -s [ME, fr. MF *lus*, fr. LL *lucius*] **1 :** a pike esp. when full grown **2 :** a heraldic representation of a pike
lu·cen·cy \'lüsᵊnsē, -nsi\ *n* -ES [*lucent* + *-cy*] **:** the quality or state of being lucent **:** LUMINOSITY ⟨a color . . . with the ~ of porcelain —John Hersey⟩
lu·cent \-sᵊnt\ *adj* [L *lucent-*, *lucens*, pres. part. of *lucēre* to shine — more at LIGHT] **1 :** glowing with light **:** LUMINOUS, RADIANT ⟨the sun's ~ orb —John Milton⟩ **2 :** marked by clarity or translucence **:** CLEAR ⟨watches the underwater world . . . through the ~ membrane —*Time*⟩ ⟨reveal his ~ style —*Amer. Guide Series: Ind.*⟩ **syn** see BRIGHT
lu·cent·ly *adv* **:** in a lucent manner
lucern *n* -s [prob. modif. of G *lüchsern* of a lynx, fr. *luchs* lynx, fr. OHG *luhs* — more at LYNX] *obs* **:** LYNX
lu·cer·nal \(')lü¦sərnᵊl, -¦sən-,-¦əin-\ *adj* [L *lucerna* lamp + E *-al*] **:** of or relating to a lamp ⟨~ microscope⟩
lu·cer·nar·ia \,lüsər'na(a)rēə\ *n, cap* [NL, fr. L *lucerna* lamp + NL *-aria*] **:** a widely distributed genus (the type of the family Lucernariidae) of north Atlantic littoral sessile or creeping scyphozoan jellyfishes that have a bell-shaped body prolonged at the margin into eight lobes each with a group of short tentacles — **lu·cer·nar·i·an** \¦==¦na(a)rēən\ *adj or n*
lu·cer·na·ri·da \,lü(,)sərnə'rīdə\ *also* **lu·cer·nar·i·id·ea** \,lüsər,na(a)rē'īdēə\ [NL, fr. *Lucernaria* + *-ida* or *-idea*] *syn of* STAUROMEDUSAE
lu·cerne *also* **lu·cern** \lü'sərn, -sən, -əin\ *n* -s [F *luzerne*, fr. Prov *luserno*, prob. fr. OProv *luzerna* lamp, fr. L *lucerna*; prob. fr. the shiny seeds; akin to L *lucēre* to shine — more at LIGHT] *chiefly Brit* **:** ALFALFA
lucerne flea *n* **:** a springtail (*Sminthurus viridis*) that damages alfalfa esp. in Australia
luces *pl of* LUX
luchot *or* **luchoth** *pl of* LUAH
lu·chu·an \lü'chüən\ *n* -s *cap* [fr. *Luchu* islands (Ryukyu islands), southwest of Kyushu, Japan + E *-an*] **:** a native of the Ryukyu islands related to the Japanese but with a Malayan or Ainu admixture
luci- *comb form* [L, fr. *luc-*, *lux* — more at LIGHT] **:** light ⟨*lucimeter*⟩
lu·ci·an·ic \,lüshē¦anik\ *adj, usu cap L* [*Lucian*, 2d cent. A.D. Greek satirist and wit + E *-ic*] **:** of, relating to, or resembling Lucian or his writings ⟨interrogative, ironical, *Lucianic* scepticism —Douglas Bush⟩
lu·ci·ble \'lüsəbəl\ *adj* [LL *lucibilis*, fr. L *lucēre* to shine + *-ibilis* -able] *archaic* **:** LUCENT
lu·cid \'lüsəd\ *adj* [L *lucidus*; akin to L *lucēre* to shine — more at LIGHT] **1 a :** suffused with light **:** BRIGHT, LUMINOUS, RADIANT ⟨satellites burning in a ~ ring —William Wordsworth⟩ ⟨wrap the hills from feet to flank in ~ haze —J.A. Symonds⟩ ⟨the lamps . . . seemed dim in that ~ twilight —C.P. Snow⟩ **b :** penetrated with light **:** TRANSLUCENT ⟨descended into the valleys to bathe in ~ streams —Elinor Wylie⟩ ⟨rain hit on the windshield, the fine ~ drops moving back slowly —H.D. Skidmore⟩ **2 :** having, manifesting, or marked by full use of one's faculties **:** ORIENTED, RATIONAL, SANE ⟨seemed to recover himself, for a ~ gleam came into his eyes —Jack London⟩ ⟨his ~ hours —W.M.Thackeray⟩ **3 :** clear to the understanding **:** readily intelligible **:** lacking ambiguity ⟨his style is ~ and he always makes his meaning clear —A.S.Hornby⟩ ⟨far more persuasive and ~ as a speaker than as a writer —A.J.Toynbee⟩ ⟨the ~ exactness of the epithets —J.L.Lowes⟩ **syn** see CLEAR
lu·ci·da \'lüsədə\ *n, pl* **luci·dae** \-,dē\ [NL, fr. L, fem. of *lucidus* lucid] **:** the brightest star of a constellation or other group
lucid interval *n* [trans. of ML *lucidum intervallum*] **1 :** a temporary period of rationality between periods of insanity or delirium **2 :** a period of calm or normal activity between periods of confusion
lu·cid·i·ty \lü'sidəd.ē, -ətē, -i\ *n* -ES [LL *luciditat-*, *luciditas* brightness, L *lucidus* + *-itat-*, *-itas* -ity] **1 :** the quality or state of being lucid esp. in thought or style ⟨combined idealistic turbulence with ~ of expression —Maurice Edelman⟩ ⟨clearness in the narrow sense — the thin ~ of what passes at times for scientific statement —C.E.Montague⟩ **2 :** the presumed state of being able to perceive the truth directly and instantaneously **:** CLAIRVOYANCE ⟨just before one dies there comes a strange ~ —Robert Graves⟩ ⟨when the spirit is drawn to ~ by the immediacy of death —Graham Greene⟩
lu·cid·ly *adv* **:** in a lucid manner **:** CLEARLY ⟨the outstanding scientist who is also able to write ~ for the layman —James Stokley⟩
lu·cid·ness *n* -ES **:** LUCIDITY
lucies *pl of* LUCY
lucifee *var of* LUCIVEE
lu·ci·fer \'lüsəfə(r)\ *n* -s [ME *lucifer* morning star & *Lucifer* fallen rebel archangel, devil, fr. OE, fr. L *lucifer* morning star, fr. *lucifer*, adj., light-bearing (prob. trans. of Gk *phōsphoros* light-bearing, morning star), fr. *luci-* + *-fer* (adj. comb. form) — more at -FER] **1** *usu cap* **:** DEVIL **2** *usu cap* **:** a person resembling Lucifer esp. in evil or pride ⟨the background of the local *Lucifer* was eminently respectable —M.D.Geismar⟩ ⟨a true man, and proud as a *Lucifer* —Thomas Hardy⟩ **3** *also* **lucifer match :** a friction match having as active substances antimony sulphide and potassium chlorate ⟨holding up a lighted ~ to a gas fixture on the wall —R.P.Warren⟩
[2]**lucifer** \"\ [NL, fr. L, morning star] *syn of* LEUCIFER
lu·cif·er·ase \lü'sifə,rās, -āz\ *n* -s [ISV *luciferin* + *-ase*] **:** an enzyme that is associated with luciferin and that catalyzes its oxidation
lucifer hummingbird *n, usu cap L* [*lucifer* fr. NL (specific epithet of *Calothorax lucifer*), fr. L] **:** a bronze green fork-tailed hummingbird (*Calothorax lucifer*) of southwestern No. America that has a purple gorget in the male
[1]**lu·ci·fe·ri·an** \¦lüsə¦firēən\ *n* -s *usu cap* [*Lucifer* †A.D.371? bishop of Cagliari, Sardinia + E *-an*, n. suffix] **:** an adherent of a schismatic sect of the early Christian church advocating a rigorous attitude toward repentant Arians
[2]**luciferian** \"\ *adj, usu cap* [*Lucifer* †A.D.371? + E *-an*, adj. suffix] **:** of or relating to the Luciferians of the early Christian church
[3]**luciferian** \"\ *adj, usu cap* [ML *luciferianus*, fr. *Lucifer* the devil, Satan (fr. L *lucifer* morning star) + L *-ianus* -an] **:** of, relating to, or having the quality of evil or pride attributed to Lucifer **:** DEVILISH, SATANIC ⟨gave him at times a certain *Luciferian*, a dreadful, but an heroic aspect —Hervey Allen⟩
[4]**luciferian** \"\ *n* -s *usu cap* [[1]*lucifer* + *-an*] **:** a member of a 19th century party of Satan worshipers believed to hold black masses
lu·cif·er·in \lü'sifərən\ *n* -s [ISV *lucifer-* (fr. L *lucifer* light-bearing) + *-in*] **:** a pigment believed to be related to the flavin pigments that is found in luminescent organisms (as fireflies) and that furnishes practically heatless light in undergoing oxidation promoted by luciferase
lu·cif·er·ous \-f(ə)rəs\ *adj* [L *lucifer* light-bearing + E *-ous*] **1** *archaic* **:** bringing or giving light **2** *archaic* **:** affording insight **:** ILLUMINATING
lu·cif·ic \-fik\ *adj* [LL *lucificus*, fr. L *luci-* + *-ficus* -fic] *archaic* **:** producing light
lu·ci·form \'lüsə,fȯrm\ *adj* [ML *luciformis*, fr. L *luci-* + *-formis* -form] **:** of, relating to, or having the characteristics of light **:** LUMINOUS
lu·cif·u·gous \lü'sifyəgəs\ *also* **lu·cif·u·gal** \-gəl\ *adj*

[*lucifugous* fr. L *lucifugus*, fr. *luci-* + *-fugus* (fr. *fugere* to flee); *lucifugal* fr. L *lucifugus* + E *-al* — more at FUGITIVE] **:** avoiding light ⟨a ~ creature of the darkness —Anatole Broyard⟩
lu·ci·gen \'lüsəjən\ *n* -s [*luci-* + *-gen*] **:** a lamp or torch giving a bright light by burning a spray of oil mixed with hot air
lu·cil·ia \lü'silēə\ *n, cap* [NL] **:** a genus of blowflies comprising the greenbottle flies
[1]**lu·ci·na** \lü'sīnə\ *n* -s *usu cap* [*Lucina*, Roman goddess of childbirth] *archaic* **:** MIDWIFE
[2]**lucina** \"\ *n* [NL, prob. fr. L *Lucina*, Roman goddess of childbirth] **1** *cap* **:** a genus (the type of the family Lucinidae) of chiefly tropical edible bivalve mollusks having a white orbicular shell and a very long cylindrical foot that is sometimes placed with related forms in a superfamily (Lucinacea) of the order Eulamellibranchia **2** -s **:** any mollusk of the genus *Lucina* — **lu·cine** \'lü,sīn, -,sən\ *n* -s — **lu·ci·noid** \'lüsə,nȯid\ *adj*
lu·cio·per·ca \,lüs(h)ēō'pərkə\ *n, cap* [NL *lucio-* (fr. LL *lucius* pike) + L *perca* perch — more at PERCH] **:** a genus of usu. large freshwater fishes (family Percidae) including several Old World pike perches that are excellent food fishes — see FOGAS, ZANDER
Lu·cite \'lü,sīt\ *trademark* — used for an acrylic resin or plastic consisting essentially of polymerized methyl methacrylate
lu·ci·vee \'lüsə,vē\ *n* -s [modif. of CanF *loup-cervier* — more at LOUP-CERVIER] *NewEng* **:** CANADA LYNX
[1]**luck** \'lək\ *n* -s [ME *lucke*, fr. MD *luc*; akin to MLG *lucke* luck, MHG *gelücke*] **1 a :** a purposeless, unpredictable, and uncontrollable force that shapes events favorably or unfavorably for an individual, group, or cause **:** FATE, FORTUNE ⟨~ is still a factor in the growth of nations as well as men —Samuel Van Valkenburg & Ellsworth Huntington⟩ **b :** a chance combination of circumstances or conditions operating for or against the individual **:** ACCIDENT ⟨seems less an act of divine providence than plain bad ~ —*Time*⟩ ⟨the ~ of the cards was against him —W.P.Webb⟩ ⟨the ~ of the hunt was with some of these teams —C.W.Nimitz⟩ **c :** customary or characteristic fortune as evidenced by a series of successes or mishaps ⟨his hard ~ followed him throughout his life⟩ ⟨it was his ~ to go through the war without a scratch⟩ ⟨just our ~ to get a fellow like that —James Hilton⟩ **2 a :** good fortune **:** favoring chance ⟨through a combination of ~ and hard work he rose to the top⟩ **b :** favorable outcome **:** SUCCESS ⟨having no ~ at all with the . . . operator on the other end of the line —R.M.Blough⟩ ⟨admired a lilac in his backyard and said I had no ~ with them —Nell G. Ahern⟩ ⟨his purchase of the Nicaragua right of way had better ~ —F.L.Paxson⟩ **3 :** something believed to bring good luck **:** CHARM ⟨jutting from her topmast was a bunch of heather, which was the ship's ~ —G.G.Carter⟩ **syn** see CHANCE — **down on one's luck :** badly off as a result of a series of unlucky chances ⟨a model who is desperately *down on her luck*, professionally and otherwise —*Theatre Arts*⟩ — **in luck :** FORTUNATE, LUCKY — **out of luck :** UNLUCKY
[2]**luck** \"\ *vb* -ED/-ING/-S [ME *lukken* to chance, happen, fr. *lucke*, n.] *vi* **1 :** to prosper or succeed esp. through chance or good fortune ⟨~*ed* out on the exam⟩ **:** happen or come upon something desirable through good fortune ⟨~*ed* into a really valuable find⟩ — usu. used with *out*, *on*, or *into* **2 :** to take action relying on one's luck — usu. used with *out* or *through* ⟨just ~ through without any plan or policy⟩ ~ *vt* **:** to carry out (an action) relying on one's luck **:** VENTURE, RISK — often used with *it* ⟨~ it through⟩ ⟨~ it out⟩
luck·en \'ləkən\ *adj* [ME (Sc) *lukkin*, fr. past part. of *luken*, *louken* to lock, fasten, fr. OE *lūcan* to lock — more at LOCK] *Scot* **:** CLOSED, LOCKED
lucken gowan *n, chiefly Scot* **:** GLOBEFLOWER
luck·i·ly \'ləkəlē, -li\ *adv* **:** in a lucky manner **:** by good luck **:** FORTUNATELY ⟨~ the man . . . was available —D.L.Busk⟩
luck·i·ness \-kēnəs, -kin-\ *n* -ES **:** the quality or state of being lucky
luck·less \'ləkləs\ *adj* **:** being without luck **:** generally unfortunate or unlucky **:** suffering extreme ill-fortune ⟨the resting place of some ~ wanderer —*Amer. Guide Series: Calif.*⟩ ⟨the ~ enlisted man who has to go in and slug hand to hand —P.J. Searles⟩ ⟨the ~ candidate was a picture of depression —S.H. Adams⟩ **syn** see UNLUCKY
luck·less·ly *adv* **:** in a luckless manner **:** UNFORTUNATELY
luck·less·ness *n* -ES **:** the quality or state of being luckless
luck·now \'lək,naù\ *adj, usu cap* [fr. *Lucknow*, city in northern India] **:** of or from the city of Lucknow, India **:** of the kind or style prevalent in Lucknow
luckpenny \'=,==\ *also* **luck money** *n, Brit* **:** a small sum or piece of money passed back from the seller to the purchaser after a bargain has been made ⟨bargaining and clutching after their ~ —Augusta Gregory⟩
[1]**lucky** \'ləkē, -ki\ *adj, often* -ER/-EST [[1]*luck* + *-y*] **1 :** having luck **:** meeting with success **:** generally enjoying good fortune ⟨~ enough to get quarters in the town's most imposing edifice —Marquis James⟩ ⟨~ in having a lingo that hadn't yet settled into a literary language —Harold Rosenberg⟩ ⟨those who are poorer, weaker, less ~ than oneself —J.C.Powys⟩ **2 :** producing or resulting in good by chance **:** conducive to success **:** FAVORABLE ⟨a ~ sudden combination of chance mutations —Theodosius Dobzhansky⟩ ⟨regard a book-club choice as a ~ accident —John Baker⟩ ⟨a ~ hour⟩ **3 :** having a quality believed to produce good luck ⟨considered a ~ dish to eat —*Amer. Guide Series: La.*⟩ ⟨~ coin⟩ ⟨~ star⟩ **4** *chiefly Scot* **:** FULL, OVERFULL, AMPLE
syn LUCKY, FORTUNATE, HAPPY, and PROVIDENTIAL can all signify meeting with a success that is unforeseen or is not the direct result of merit and can also apply to an action producing or something resulting from such success. LUCKY stresses almost exclusively the agency of chance ⟨the *lucky* winner of a grand prize in a lottery⟩ ⟨a *lucky* turn of the cards⟩ ⟨the *lucky* day on which one wins a prize⟩ ⟨a *lucky* ten dollars found in the rubbish heap⟩ FORTUNATE, often interchangeable with but occurring less in speech than LUCKY, often implies less a positive luck than an encouraging absence of common, pervasive mischance or the unexpected presence of extremely favorable circumstances, sometimes even suggesting the active intervention of a higher power ⟨a *fortunate* turn of the cards⟩ ⟨a business *fortunate* in its location⟩ ⟨the *fortunate* day on which he made a good marriage⟩ ⟨the *fortunate* winner of a scholarship⟩ HAPPY, in this connection, can signify being or bringing good fortune and a consequent joy ⟨the *happy* faculty of learning from experience⟩ ⟨the *happy* results of hard work⟩ ⟨a *happy* choice of employees⟩ PROVIDENTIAL, often interchangeable with LUCKY or FORTUNATE, more often implies a good fortune resulting from the help or interference of providence ⟨it was certainly most *providential* that I looked up at that instant, as the monster would probably, in less than a minute, have seized and dragged me into the river —William Bartram⟩ ⟨a *providential* investment bringing good returns when most needed⟩
[2]**lucky** \"\ *adv, Scot* **:** GENEROUSLY **:** TOO ⟨it's ~ long⟩
[3]**lucky** \"\ *n* -ES **1 a :** something that is lucky **b :** something kept to bring luck **2** *slang Brit* **:** ESCAPE, GETAWAY
[4]**lucky** *or* **luck·ie** \"\ *n, pl* **luckies** [prob. fr. [1]*lucky*] *Scot* **:** an old woman; *specif* **:** GRANNY
lucky bag *n* **1 :** GRAB BAG **2 :** a locker or compartment on a warship where stray articles are stowed until claimed or disposed of
lucky bone *n* **1** *dial* **:** WISHBONE **2** *dial* **:** BONE; *esp* **:** one from the head of a sheep or hog worn or carried to bring good luck
lucky dad *n, Scot* **:** GRANDFATHER
lucky dip *n, Brit* **:** GRAB BAG ⟨there were *lucky dips* . . . into which small hands were plunged —W.J.MacQueen-Pope⟩
lucky minnie *n, Scot* **:** GRANDMOTHER
lucky stone *n* **:** a stone held to bring good luck (as a perforated pebble or an otolith of a fish)
lu·come window \'lükəm-\ *n* [obs. E *lucome* dormer window (alter. of earlier *lucane*) + E *window* — more at LUCARNE] **:** a wide gable-end window in early American houses
lu·cra·tive \'lükrəd.iv, -ətiv\ *adj* [ME *lucratif*, fr. MF, fr. L *lucrativus*, fr. *lucratus* (past part. of *lucrari* to gain, fr. *lucrum* gain, profit) + *-ivus* -ive] **1 a :** producing wealth **:** MONEY-MAKING, PROFITABLE ⟨a ~ literature meant novels and nothing else —G.B.Shaw⟩ ⟨a ~ business⟩ ⟨a ~ property⟩ **b :** worthwhile as a military target ⟨many ~ artillery targets —*Infantry*

Army Reserve Training Bull.⟩ ⟨a ~ target for an atom bomb —R.W.Stokley⟩ **2** *archaic* **:** having or marked by a love of gain **:** AVARICIOUS, GREEDY **3** *Roman & civil law* **:** acquired, received, or had without burdensome conditions ⟨a ~ title⟩ ⟨~ ownership⟩ — **lu·cra·tive·ly** \-əvlē, -li\ *adv* — **lu·cra·tive·ness** \-ivnəs\ *n* -ES

lucrative interest *n* **:** interest representing the creditor's possible profits from his having the use of his own money

lucrative succession *n, Scots law* **:** the succession of an heir who has during the lifetime of the ancestor accepted without adequate consideration any part of the estate which he would otherwise have inherited

lu·cre \'lükə(r)\ *n* -S [ME, fr. L *lucrum;* akin to OE *lēan* reward, OHG *lōn,* ON *laun* (pl.) rewards, Goth *laun* reward, OIr *lōg* reward, price, Gk *leia* booty, prey, Skt *lotra* booty] **1 a :** monetary gain **:** PROFIT, REWARD **b :** MONEY ⟨set aside some ~ for shopping and souvenirs —Winston Brebner⟩ **2** *archaic* **:** the process of gaining **:** ACQUISITION — used esp. in the phrase *lucre of gain*

lu·cre·tian \lü'krēshən\ *adj, usu cap* [T. *Lucretius* Carus †55B.C. Roman philosophical poet + E *-an*] **:** of, relating to, or having the characteristics of Lucretius or the Epicurean philosophic system expounded by him ⟨dry, steely, *Lucretian* aloofness —*Modern Philology*⟩

lu·crum ces·sans \'lükrəm'se,sanz\ *n* [*lucrum cessans* fr. ML, ceasing profit; *lucrum interceptum* fr. NL, intercepted profit] **1** *or* **lucrum in·ter·cep·tum** \-,intə(r)'septəm\ *Roman & canon law* **:** the interest or damages awarded for loss of reasonably expected profits or for loss of use of property **2** *Scots law* **:** damages for loss of expected gain or profits as distinguished from an actual loss

luctation *n* -S [L *luctation-, luctatio,* fr. *luctatus* (past part. of *luctari* to struggle) + *-ion-, -io* -ion — more at LOCK] *obs* **:** ENDEAVOR, STRUGGLE

luc·tif·er·ous \(')lək¦tif(ə)rəs\ *adj* [L *luctifer* mournful (fr. *luctus* sorrow + *-fer* -ferous) + E *-ous*] *archaic* **:** bearing sorrow **:** MOURNFUL

luctual *adj* [L *luctus* sorrow (fr. *luctus,* past part. of *lugēre* to mourn) + E *-al* — more at LUGUBRIOUS] *obs* **:** SAD, SORROWFUL

lu·cu·brate \'lük(y)ə,brāt\ *vi* -ED/-ING/-S [L *lucubratus,* past part. of *lucubrare* to work by lamplight, compose by night; akin to L *lucēre* to shine — more at LIGHT] **:** to discourse learnedly in writing **:** EXPATIATE ⟨~ in various scholarly journals⟩ — compare ELUCUBRATE — **lu·cu·bra·tor** \-,brād·ə(r), -ātə-\ *n* -S

lu·cu·bra·tion \,==ˈbrāshən\ *n* -S [L *lucubration-, lucubratio* study or composition at night, fr. *lucubratus* + *-ion-, -io* -ion] **1 :** the act of lucubrating **:** laborious study **:** MEDITATION ⟨after long ~ I have hit upon such an expedient —Oliver Goldsmith⟩ **2 :** the product of study or meditation as expressed in speech or writing **:** weighty or pretentious statement of ideas ⟨bring his moldy and moth-eaten ~s before the public —Nathaniel Hawthorne⟩ ⟨his oratorical ~s on the subject of age —*New Republic*⟩

lucubratory *adj* [L *lucubratorius* connected with study at night, fr. *lucubratus* + *-orius* -ory] *obs* **:** laboriously thought out or expressed

lu·cu·lent \'lükyələnt\ *adj* [ME, fr. L *luculentus,* fr. *luc-, lux* light — more at LIGHT] **1** *archaic* **:** emitting light **:** BRILLIANT, SHINING ⟨a ~ flame —John Evelyn⟩ **2 :** transparently clear in thought or expression **:** CONVINCING, EVIDENT ⟨a ~ oration —Robert Burton⟩ ⟨so ~ a commentary —J.G.Lockhart⟩ **3** *obs* **:** ILLUSTRIOUS, RESPLENDENT ⟨most debonair and ~ lady —Ben Jonson⟩ — **lu·cu·lent·ly** *adv*

lu·cul·lan \lü'kələn\ *or* **lu·cul·li·an** \-lēən\ *adj, usu cap* [L *lucullanus, lucullianus,* fr. Lucius Licinius *Lucullus,* 1st cent. B.C. Roman general, patron of learning, and epicure + L *-anus, -ianus* -an] **1 :** of or relating to Lucullus **2 :** LAVISH, LUXURIOUS — used esp. of food ⟨cornflakes or shredded wheat with bananas or fresh sliced peaches, thought by us to be a *Lucullan* treat —Mary McCarthy⟩

lucullan marble *n, usu cap L* [trans. of L *marmor luculleum;* prob. fr. its being especially liked by Lucullus] **:** LUCULLITE

lu·cul·lite \-,līt\ *n* -S [G *lucullan* lucullite (fr. L *Lucullanus* Lucullan) + E *-ite*] **:** an Egyptian marble colored black by carbon

¹lu·cu·ma \'lük(y)əmə\ [NL, fr. Sp *lúcuma* eggfruit] *syn of* POUTERIA

²lucuma \"\ *n* -S [Sp *lúcuma* eggfruit, fr. Quechua *lúcuma, lucma*] **:** a plant or fruit of the genus *Pouteria* **:** EGGFRUIT

lu·cu·mi \,lükə¦mē\ *n, pl* **lucumi** *or* **lucumies** *usu cap* **1 a :** a group of people in Cuba who are members of a secret society of African origin **b :** a member of such a group **2 :** the secret language used by the Lucumi derived from Yoruba

lu·cus a non lu·cen·do \'lükə,sā¦nänlü'sen,dō\ [NL, a grove from not being light; fr. the practice ascribed to ancient Roman etymologists of deriving words from their semantic opposites, as *lucus* ("grove") from *lucēre* ("to shine, be light") because a grove is not light] **:** an illogical explanation or absurd derivation **:** NON SEQUITUR ⟨the whole discussion may seem a *lucus a non lucendo* for all the light it throws upon the effect of the classics on mediaeval literature —H.O.Taylor⟩

lu·cy \'lüsē, -si\ *n* -ES [LL *lucius*] **:** LUCE 2

lucy light *n, usu cap 1st L* [after St. *Lucy* †A.D.303 virgin and martyr of Syracuse in Sicily whose feast day is December 13] **:** December 13 Old Style, the shortest day — called also *St. Lucy's day;* contrasted with *Barnaby bright*

lucy sto·ner \-ˈstōnə(r)\ *n, pl* **lucy stoners** *usu cap L&S* [*Lucy Stone* †1893 Am. woman suffragist + E *-er*] **:** a female advocate of women's rights; *esp* **:** a married woman who uses her maiden name as a surname ⟨the *Lucy Stoners* and women's rights fighters of her own class at college —Mary McCarthy⟩

ludd·ism \'lə,dizəm\ *also* **ludd·it·ism** \-,dīd·,izəm\ *n* -S *usu cap* [*luddism* fr. Ned *Ludd fl*1779 half-witted Leicestershire workman who destroyed stocking frames + E *-ism; ludditism* fr. *luddite* + *-ism*] **:** the beliefs or practices of the Luddites

ludd·ite \'lə,dīt\ *n* -S *usu cap* [Ned *Ludd* + E *-ite*] **:** a member of a group of early 19th century English workmen engaged in attempting to prevent the use of laborsaving machinery by destroying it

ludefisk *or* **ludfisk** *var of* LUTEFISK

lu·der·ick \'lüd(ə)rik\ *n* -S [native name in Gippsland, Australia] **:** a silvery gray Australian percoid food fish (*Girella tricuspidata*) of shallow coastal seas and estuaries and tidal rivers — called also *black bream, blackfish*

lü·ders' line *also* **lue·ders' line** \'lü¦də(r)z-, 'lē¦\ *n, usu cap 1st L* [after W. *Lüders fl*1859 Ger. scientist, its discoverer] **:** a line or any of a definite system of line markings appearing on the smooth surface of tough material (as metal) strained beyond its elastic limit and caused by flow of the material

lu·dhi·a·na \,lüdē¦änə\ *adj, usu cap* [fr. *Ludhiana,* city in northwest India] **:** of or from the city of Ludhiana, India **:** of the kind or style prevalent in Ludhiana

lu·dib·ri·ous \lü'dibrēəs\ *adj* [L *ludibriosus* derisive, fr. *ludibrium* derision (fr. *ludus* play) + *-osus* -ose] **1** *obs* **:** RIDICULOUS **2** *archaic* **:** MOCKING, SCORNFUL

ludicro- *comb form* [L *ludicrus* + E *-o-*] **:** ludicrous and ⟨*ludicro*pathetic⟩ ⟨*ludicro*serious⟩ ⟨*ludicro*splenetic⟩

lu·di·crous \'lüdəkrəs\ *adj* [L *ludicrus,* fr. *ludus* game, play, sport; akin to L *ludere* to play, Gk *loidoros* abusive] **1** *archaic* **:** relating to, characterized by, or designed for play or amusement **:** not serious **:** FRIVOLOUS, JOKING ⟨the most attractive of all ~ compositions —Samuel Johnson⟩ **2 a :** amusing or laughable through obvious absurdity, incongruity, exaggeration, or eccentricity ⟨an unchangeable grin that gave still more ~ effect to the comic alarm and sorrow of their features —Nathaniel Hawthorne⟩ **b :** meriting derisive laughter or scorn as absurdly inept, false, or foolish ⟨common sense making transparently clear what was ~ in every fallacy —Edgar Johnson⟩ ⟨how ~ it was to leave the substance of power in a single ruler —*Times Lit. Supp.*⟩ ⟨this act of ~ cruelty —Edmund Burke⟩ **syn** see LAUGHABLE

lu·di·crous·ly *adv* **:** in a ludicrous manner **:** ABSURDLY

lu·di·crous·ness *n* -ES **:** the quality or state of being ludicrous

lu·di·fi·ca·tion \,lüdəfə'kāshən\ *n* -S [L *ludification-, ludificatio,* fr. *ludificatus* (past part. of *ludificare* to deceive, make sport of, fr. *ludus* game, play, sport + *-ficare* -fy) + *-ion-, -io* -ion] *archaic* **:** an act of deception or mockery

lud·lam·ite \'lədlə,mīt\ *n* -S [Henry *Ludlam* †1880 Eng. mineralogist + E *-ite*] **:** a mineral (Fe, Mg, Mn)$_3$ (PO$_4$)$_2$.4H$_2$O that is a hydrous iron phosphate with magnesium and manganese replacing some of the iron and that occurs in small green transparent monoclinic crystals

lud·lo·vi·an \'ləd¦lōvēən\ *adj, usu cap* [fr. *Ludlovian,* subdivision of the European Silurian, fr. ML *Ludlovia* (Ludlow), Shropshire, England + E *-an*] **:** of or relating to a subdivision of the European Silurian — see GEOLOGIC TIME table

Lud·low \'ləd,lō\ *trademark* — used for a machine that casts type and material slugs from matrices set by hand in a special stick

lu·do \'lü,dō\ *n* -S [L, I play, 1st pers. sing. pres. indic. of *ludere* to play] **:** a form of pachisi played chiefly in the British Isles

lud·wig·ia \ləd'wigēə\ *also* **lud·vig·ia** \-'vig-\ *n, cap* [NL, fr. Christian G. *Ludwig* †1773 Ger. botanist + NL *-ia*] **:** a genus of perennial herbs (family Onagraceae) chiefly of tropical or warm regions that have 4-parted flowers and a short capsular fruit

lud·wig·ite \'ləd,wi,gīt\ *n* -S [G *ludwigit,* fr. Ernst *Ludwig* †1915 Austrian chemist + G *-it* -ite] **:** a mineral (Mg, Fe)$_2$-FeBO$_5$ consisting of an iron magnesium borate occurring in fibrous masses of a blackish green color

lud·wig's angina \ lüd(,)vigz-\ *n, usu cap L* [after Wilhelm F. von *Ludwig* †1865 Ger. physician] **:** an acute streptococcal or sometimes staphylococcal infection of the deep tissues of the floor of the mouth and adjoining parts of the neck and lower jaw marked by severe rapid swelling that may close the respiratory passage and accompanied by chills and fever

lud·wigs·ha·fen \'lüd(,)vigz,häfən, ,=(,)=ˈ==\ *adj, usu cap* [fr. *Ludwigshafen* am Rhein, city in southwest Germany] **:** of or from the city of Ludwigshafen am Rhein, Germany **:** of the kind or style prevalent in Ludwigshafen am Rhein

luebeck *usu cap, var of* LÜBECK

lue·ne·burg·ite \'lünə,bər,gīt\ *n* -S [G *lüneburgit,* fr. *Lüneburg,* Germany, its locality + G *-it* -ite] **:** a mineral Mg$_3$B$_2$-(OH)$_6$(PO$_4$)$_2$.6H$_2$O consisting of a hydrous basic phosphate of magnesium and boron

lu·er syringe \'lüə(r)-\ *n, usu cap L* [after *Luer* †1883 Fr. instrument maker] **:** a glass syringe with a glass piston that has the apposing surfaces ground and that is used esp. for hypodermic injection

lu·es \'lü,ēz\ *n, pl* **lues** [NL, fr. L, plague; akin to Gk *lyein* to unbind, release, dissolve — more at LOSE] **:** SYPHILIS

lu·et·ic \lü'ed·ik\ *adj* [fr. *lues,* after such pairs as E *herpes: herpetic*] **:** SYPHILITIC — **lu·et·i·cal·ly** \-ək(ə)lē\ *adv*

luf·bery *also* **luf·ber·ry** \'ləf,berē, -,bərē, -ri\ *vi* -ED/-ING/-S [after Raoul G. V. *Lufbery* †1918 Am. aviator] **:** to go into or fly in a Lufbery circle

lufbery circle *also* **lufberry circle** *n, usu cap L* **:** a military flying formation or maneuver in which two or more airplanes follow each other closely in circular line or ascending spiral

¹luff \'ləf\ *n* -S [ME *luff, loff,* fr. MF *lof,* prob. fr. (assumed) MD *loef* (whence D *loef*); akin to MLG *lōf* side of a ship toward the wind, ON *lōfi* palm of the hand — more at GLOVE] **1 a** *obs* **:** the side of a ship toward the wind **b :** the act of sailing a ship closer to the wind **c :** the forward edge of a fore-and-aft sail **d** *archaic* **:** the fullest and roundest part of a ship's bow **e :** LUFF TACKLE **2 :** a radial or in-and-out movement of the load being carried by a crane produced by raising or lowering the jib

²luff \"\ *vb* -ED/-ING/-S [ME *loven,* fr. *luff, loff,* n.] *vi* **1 :** to turn the head of a ship toward the wind **:** sail nearer the wind — often used with *up* **2 :** to move the jib of a crane in and out ~ *vt* **1 :** to point higher into the wind than (another yacht) when racing in order to avoid being overtaken on the windward side **2 :** to move (the jib of a crane) in and out

³luff \"\ *n* -S [by shortening & alter.] *slang* **:** LIEUTENANT

luf·fa \'ləfə\ *n* [NL, fr. Ar *lūf*] **1** *cap* **:** a genus of tropical climbing herbs (family Cucurbitaceae) with white flowers and large fruits **2** *or* **loo·fah** \'lüfə\ -S **a :** a plant of the genus *Luffa* **b :** the fruit of such a plant **:** DISHCLOTH GOURD **3** *or* **loofah** -S **:** the fibrous skeleton of the luffa fruit used as a sponge — called also *vegetable sponge*

luff tackle *n* [¹*luff*] **:** a tackle that has a single and a double block with the standing part of the fall fixed to the single block thus multiplying the power three or four times according as the single or the double block is movable — see TACKLE illustration

luff upon luff : a luff tackle on the fall of another

luft·mensch \'lüft,mench\ *n, pl* **luftmensch·en** \-chən\ [Yiddish *luftmentsh,* fr. *luft* air (fr. MHG, fr. OHG) + *mentsh* person, human being, fr. MHG *mensch, mensche,* fr. OHG *mennisco;* akin to OFris *mānniska* person, human being, MD *mensche,* OS *mennisco;* all fr. a prehistoric WGmc noun derived from the adjective represented by OE *mennisc* human, ON *mennskr,* Goth *mannisks;* all fr. a prehistoric Gmc compound whose first constituent is represented by OE *man, mann* man and whose second constituent is represented by OE *-isc* -ish — more at LOFT, MAN] **:** an impractical contemplative person having no definite trade, business, or income **:** DREAMER ⟨the ~ who personifies the quixotic, speculative principle in Jewish life —Irving Howe⟩

¹lug \'ləg\ *n* -S [ME *lugge*] **1** *dial Eng* **:** ROD, POLE **2** *now dial Eng* **a :** a varying measure of length usu. 16½ feet **b :** a square lug

²lug \"\ *vb* **lugged; lugged; lugging; lugs** [ME *luggen,* prob. of Scand origin; akin to Norw *lugge* to pull by the hair, Sw *lugga* to pull by the hair, Norw & Sw *lugg* tuft of hair] *vt* **1 a** *now chiefly dial* (1) **:** to give a pull to (as the ear or hair) (2) **:** to pull esp. by the ear or hair **b :** to pull with force **:** DRAG ⟨*lugged* the little wretch . . . out of the room —Samuel Butler †1902⟩ ⟨*lugged* the feed trough out into the open —Marjorie K. Rawlings⟩ **2 :** to carry with great effort ⟨*lugged* those boxes all over the city till they seemed full of marble —Dan Browne⟩ ⟨preferred to ~ his own suitcase —Horace Sutton⟩ **3 :** to bring in or introduce in a ponderous or forced manner ⟨~ a story into the conversation⟩ ~ *vi* **1 a :** to pull with effort **:** TUG **b** *of a horse* **:** to bear down on the bit **2 :** to move heavily or by jerks ⟨printers' rollers ~ when sticky⟩ **3** *of a racehorse* **:** to swerve from the course toward or away from the inside rail ⟨kept *lugging* in toward the rails —G.F.T.Ryall⟩ **4** *archaic* **a :** to draw one's sword **b :** to take out one's money or purse

³lug \'ləg\ *n* -S **1** *archaic* **a :** an act of lugging **b :** something that is lugged **2 :** a box or basket holding 25 to 40 pounds of fruit or vegetables; *specif* **:** a box having an inside width of 13½ inches, an outside length of 17½ inches, and a depth of from 4¼ to 7¾ inches **3 lugs** *pl* **:** superior airs **:** affectations of importance ⟨no ~s about him . . . nothing hoity-toity —Louis Auchincloss⟩ ⟨the way these doctors and profs and preachers put on ~s about being "professional men" —Sinclair Lewis⟩ **4 :** LUGSAIL **5** *slang* **:** an exaction of money **:** a political assessment — used in the phrase *put the lug on* ⟨put the ~ on state employees —*Newsweek*⟩

⁴lug \'ləg, *dial* 'lüg\ *n* -S [ME (Sc) *lugge,* perh. fr. ME *luggen,* v.] **1** *Scot* **:** the earflap of a cap or bonnet **2** *now chiefly dial* **:** EAR ⟨I got ears . . . first-class ~ —C.B.Kelland⟩ ⟨a great clout in the ~ —J.M.Synge⟩ **3 :** something that projects like an ear: as **a :** a projection or handle by which something may be grasped or carried **b :** a projection on a casting to which a bolt or other part may be fitted **c :** a leather loop on a harness saddle through which the shaft passes **d :** a projection or ridge on the rim of a wheel (as of a tractor) or on a rubber tire to increase traction **4 :** a small projecting part of a larger member; *esp* **:** the part of a windowsill or doorsill that tails into the masonry on each side of the opening **5 :** a fitting of copper or brass to which electrical wires are soldered or connected **6 :** a rounded nut that covers the end of a bolt (as for holding an automobile wheel in place) **7 lugs** *pl* **:** a poor grade of tobacco leaves from the lower part of the stem of the plant — compare LEAF 1c(4) **8** *slang* **a :** a heavy clumsy fellow **:** BLOCKHEAD, GOOD-FOR-NOTHING ⟨cuff the daylights out of a moronic ~ —James Wallace⟩ **b :** an ordinary commonplace person ⟨walk among the people, just another ~ —Stephen Longstreet⟩ ⟨just another poor ~ who'd cracked up and was talking to himself —*Scribner's*⟩

⁵lug \'ləg\ *n* -S [origin unknown] **:** LUGWORM

lu·gan·da \lü'gandə, -gän-\ *n, usu cap* **:** GANDA 2

lug·ba·ra \lüg'bärə\ *n, pl* **lugbara** *or* **lugbaras** *usu cap* **1 a :** a people living along the border of Uganda and the Belgian Congo **b :** a member of such people **2 :** a Central Sudanic language of the Lugbara people

lug bolt *n* [⁴*lug*] **1 :** a bolt terminating in a long flat extension or hook instead of a head — called also *strap bolt* **2 :** a bolt for fastening a lug

lug brick *n* [⁴*lug*] **:** paving brick having lugs on one side and one end to control the space between adjacent bricks when laid in a pavement

lug chair *n* [⁴*lug*] *Brit* **:** WING CHAIR

¹luge \'lüzh\ *n* -S [F, fr. F dial. (Savoy & Switzerland)] **:** a small sled used for coasting esp. in Switzerland

²luge \"\ *vi* -ED/-ING/-S **:** to coast on a luge — **lug·er** \-zhə(r)\ *n* -S

lug foresail *n* [perh. fr. ⁴*lug*] **:** a foresail without a boom

lug·gage \'ləgij, -gēj\ *n* -S *often attrib* [²*lug* + *-age*] **1 :** something that is lugged; *esp* **:** the belongings that a traveler carries with him ⟨his only ~ what he could carry in a red plaid cotton handkerchief —*Amer. Guide Series: Minn.*⟩ ⟨brought as part of their ~ toasting irons, waffle irons, and gridirons —M.R. Werner⟩ **2 a :** suitcases, traveling bags, and other articles containing a traveler's belongings **:** BAGGAGE ⟨both running-boards were piled with traps and ~ —D.L.Sharp⟩ ⟨stowing space under the beds for hand ~ —Horace Sutton⟩ **b :** empty suitcases and other containers for a traveler's belongings esp. as offered for sale ⟨a shop that sells fine ~⟩

lug·gage·less \-ləs\ *adj* **:** having no luggage

luggage tan *n* **:** a variable color averaging a strong brown that is yellower, lighter, and slightly less strong than average russet, yellower and paler than rust, and yellower, stronger, and slightly lighter than gold brown

luggage van *n, Brit* **:** BAGGAGE CAR

lug·gar *also* **lug·ger** \'ləgə(r)\ *n* -S [Hindi *lagar, lagaṛ*] **:** any of several large Asiatic falcons of dull brown color; *esp* **:** a gyrfalcon (*Falco jugger*) of India that somewhat resembles the American prairie falcon

lugged \'ləgd\ *adj* [ME (Sc) *lwgyt* having earflaps, fr. *lugge* earflap + *-yt,* alter. of ME *-ed,* adj. suffix — more at LUG] **:** having lugs

¹lug·ger \'ləgə(r)\ *n* -S [²*lug* + *-er*] **:** one that lugs: as **a :** a worker in a slaughterhouse or meat-packing establishment who carries meat to and from various processing operations **b :** an agricultural worker who carries containers filled with farm products from the field to a central point **c** *slang* **:** a person employed by a gambling house to bring players to it

²lugger \"\ *n* -S [*lug-* (fr. *lugsail*) + *-er*] **:** a small fishing or coasting boat that carries one or more lugsails and that has two or three masts with or without jibs or topsails

lug·gie \'ləgi\ *n* -S [⁴*lug* + *-ie*] *chiefly Scot* **:** a small wooden pail or dish with a handle

lugging *pres part of* LUG

lug hook *n* [prob. fr. ²*lug*] **:** a device consisting of a pair of pointed dogs pivoted at the middle of a short bar for carrying small logs or railroad ties

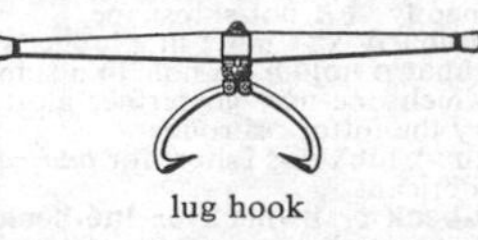

lug hook

lu·gol's solution \'lü,gōlz-\ *n, usu cap L* [after J. G. A. *Lugol* †1851 Fr. physician] **:** a deep brown aqueous solution that has an odor of iodine, that contains approximately 5 grams of iodine and 10 grams of potassium iodide in 100 milliliters, and that is used chiefly in medicine for the internal administration of iodine and esp. in veterinary practice as a disinfectant; *also* **:** any of several similar solutions (as an aqueous or alcoholic solution containing iodine and potassium iodide for use as a microscopic stain)

lug pole *n* [¹*lug*] **:** a pole on which a kettle is hung in a fireplace

lugs *pres 3d sing of* LUG, *pl of* LUG

lug·sail \'ləgsəl (*usual nautical pronunc*), -,sāl\ *n* [perh. fr. ⁴*lug* + *sail*] **:** a four-sided sail bent to a yard that hangs more or less obliquely on a mast slung at about a third or quarter of its length from the forward end and hoisted and lowered with the sail — called also *lug;* compare BALANCE LUGSAIL, DIPPING LUG, SPLIT LUG, STANDING LUG

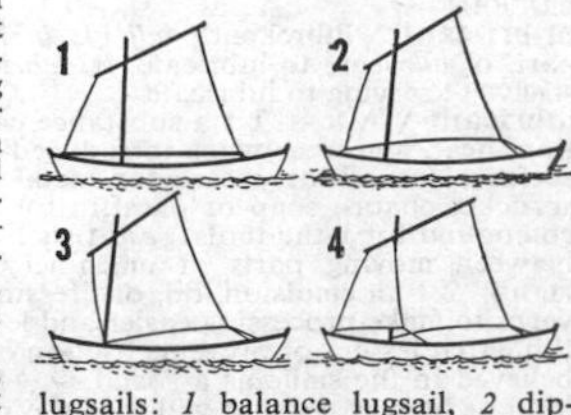

lugsails: *1* balance lugsail, *2* dipping lug, *3* standing lug, *4* split lug

lug sole *n* [⁴*lug*] **:** a thick rubber sole that has deep indentations in a pattern designed to provide good footing and is used on sport and work shoes

lu·gu·bri·os·i·ty \lə,gübrē'äsəd·ē, lü-,-ətē,-i\ *n* -ES [fr. *lugubrious,* after such pairs as E *curious. curiosity*] **:** the quality or state of being lugubrious

lu·gu·bri·ous \==ˈbrēəs\ *adj* [L *lugubris* lugubrious, connected with mourning (fr. *lugēre* to mourn) + E *-ous;* akin to Gk *lygros* mournful, Skt *rujati* he breaks, hurts] **1 :** expressive of, marked by, or giving rise to grief or sorrow **:** MOURNFUL ⟨~ notices on the passing of old friends —*Time*⟩; *esp* **:** exaggeratedly or affectedly mournful ⟨~ literary posturings —G.A.Wagner⟩ **2 :** disposed to gloom **:** DISMAL ⟨a certain ~ element in English taste —Bernard Leach⟩ — **lu·gu·bri·ous·ly** *adv* — **lu·gu·bri·ous·ness** *n* -ES

lugworm \'=,=\ *n* [⁵*lug* + *worm*] **:** any of several large marine polychaetous annelids (genus *Arenicola*) that have a row of tufted gills along each side of the back, burrow in sandy beaches between tide marks in America and Europe, and are used for bait

LUHF *abbr, often not cap* lowest useful high frequency

luhot *or* **luhoth** *pl of* LUAH

luian *usu cap, var of* LUWIAN

lu·id·ia \lə'widēə\ *n, cap* [NL] **:** a large genus of chiefly tropical active starfishes (order Phanerozonia) with long slender rather flabby rays — see MUD-STAR

lui-haai \'lā¦hī\ *n* -S [Afrik, fr. *lui* lazy (fr. D, fr. MD *loy, loey*) + *haai* shark, fr. D, fr. MD *haey* — more at HAYE] **:** a small blunt-snouted striped shark (*Poroderma africanum*) of the East African coast — called also *striped dogfish*

lu·i·se·ño *or* **luiseño** \,lüē'sān(,)yō\ *n, pl* **luiseño** *or* **luiseños** *usu cap* [AmerSp, fr. San *Luis* Rey de Francia, mission in California + Sp *-eño* (suffix added to place names to form names of inhabitants)] **1 a :** a Shoshonean people of southwestern California **b :** a member of such people **2 :** the language of the Luiseño people

lu·jau·vrite \'lü,yaův,rīt\ *or* **lu·jaur·ite** \-aů,rīt\ *n* -S [G *luijaurit,* fr. *Luijaur Urt, Lujavr Urt,* Lapland, its locality + G *-it* -ite] **:** a melanocratic nepheline-syenite rock

lukan *usu cap, var of* LUCAN

luk·ban \lůk'bän\ *n* -S [Tag *lukbán*] **:** SHADDOCK

luke \'lük\ *adj* [ME *luke, lewk;* akin to OE *hlēow* warm — more at LEW] *archaic* **:** LUKEWARM

lukewarm \'=¦=\ *adj* [ME, fr. *luke* + *warm*] **1 :** moderately warm **:** neither cold nor hot **:** TEPID ⟨~ water⟩ ⟨~ food⟩ **2 :** lacking in real conviction **:** not wholly committed to a cause or belief **:** HALFHEARTED, INDIFFERENT ⟨seemed ~ or capable of a divided allegiance —Hilaire Belloc⟩ ⟨although he never openly repudiated a protectionist policy he soon grew ~ in its support —V.L.Parrington⟩ — **luke·warm·ly** *adv* — **luke·warm·ness** *n* -ES

luke·warm·ish \'=¦==\ *adj* **:** somewhat lukewarm

lukewarmth \'=,=\ *n* **:** LUKEWARMNESS

lu·ki·ko \lü'kē(,)kō\ *n* -S *usu cap* [native name in Uganda] **:** a native legislative and judicial council in various African provinces

lu·lab *or* **lu·lav** *also* **lu·lov** \'lü,läv, -,ləv\ *n, pl* **lu·la·bim** *or* **lu·la·vim** \,lülə'vēm\ *or* **lu·labs** *or* **lu·lavs** \'lü,lävz, -ləvz\ *also* **lu·lo·vim** \lü'lōvəm, -vēm\ *or* **lu·lovs** [Heb *lūlābh* branch]**:** the traditional festive palm branch that is carried and waved during the festival of Sukkoth — compare ETHROG

lu·le \'lü(,)lā\ *n, pl* **lule** *or* **lules** *usu cap* **1 :** a group of peoples of northern Argentina **2 :** a member of any of the Lule peoples

1lull \ˈləl\ vb -ED/-ING/-S [ME *lullen;* prob. of imit. origin like MLG *lollen* to lull, MD *lollen* to mumble, doze, Latvian *leluot* to rock a child, Skt *lolati* he moves to and fro] vt **1 a :** to make quiet : cause to sleep or rest peacefully : SOOTHE ⟨sat ~ing the child —George Eliot⟩ ⟨~ed him to sleep with an interminable canticle —Rudyard Kipling⟩ **b :** to bring to a state of comparative calm ⟨~ed the raging seas⟩ **2 :** to induce a false sense of security and well-being in : cause to relax one's vigilance : lessen tension in ⟨~ them into an apathetic sense of security —Raymond Holden⟩ ⟨~ the group into contentment —Oscar Handlin⟩ ⟨~ed our minds with things we wanted to see again —H.D.Skidmore⟩ ~ *vi* **:** to diminish in force or intensity : SUBSIDE, ABATE ⟨the afternoon breeze ~ed and finally dropped off altogether —O.E.Rölvaag⟩ ⟨this conversation would ~ for awhile —Richard Church⟩ **syn** see CALM

2lull \"\ n -s **1** *archaic* **:** something that lulls or soothes; *specif* : LULLABY **2 a :** a temporary cessation or lessening of the wind or of a storm ⟨a ~ in the rain⟩ **b :** a period of intensified quiet ⟨the ~ before the storm⟩ ⟨a dark still summer ~ —Kay Boyle⟩ **3 :** a temporary drop in activity ⟨the business ~ will end by midyear —*Look*⟩ ⟨when a ~ comes in the creative activity —Ralph Linton⟩ **4 :** a relaxed or dazed state of mind

3lull \"\ n -s [LG *lull;* akin to D *lul* mouth of a pump, baby bottle, D *lullen* to suck, prattle (fr. MD *lollen* to mumble, doze)] **:** a tube through which blubber is passed to tubs in the hold of a whaling ship

1lull·a·by \ˈlələ,bī\ n -ES [obs. E *lulla, lullay, lully,* interj. used to lull a child (fr. ME, prob. fr. *lullen* to lull) + E *bye,* interj.] **1 :** a soothing refrain; *specif* : a song to quiet children or lull them to sleep **2** *obs* **:** GOOD-NIGHT

2lullaby \"\ vt -ED/-ING/-ES **:** to soothe or quiet with or as if with a lullaby ⟨the rhythm of motion *lullabied* his brain —Tom Hopkinson⟩

lull·er \ˈlələ(r)\ n -s **:** one that lulls

lul·li·an \ˈləlēən\ adj, *usu cap* [Raymond *Lully* †1315 Catalan ecclesiastic and scholastic philosopher + E *-an*] **:** of or relating to Lully or the teachings in which he combated the separation of faith and reason and endeavored to demonstrate the exclusive truth of Christianity

lull·i·loo \ˈlələ,lü\ vi -ED/-ING/-S [imit.] **:** to shout joyously in the manner of various African peoples ⟨~ed with cries of joy —Sir Richard Burton⟩

lull·ing·ly adv **:** in a lulling manner

1lu·lu \ˈlü,lü\ n -s [prob. fr. *Lulu,* nickname fr. the name *Louise*] *slang* **:** a person or thing remarkable or wonderful : STANDOUT ⟨his first idea was a ~ —Frederic Wakeman⟩ ⟨a really low class here that is a ~ —August Hollingshead⟩ ⟨a ~ of a mistake⟩ ⟨told you this ~ of a story and made a total donkey out of you —Calder Willingham⟩

2lulu \"\ n -s [Samoan *lūlū*] **:** a Samoan barn owl

lu·lu·ai \ˌlüləˈwī\ n -s [native name in eastern New Guinea] **:** a village headman or chief in New Guinea

lu·lu·bae·an \ˌlü,lüˈbēən\ n -s *cap* **1 :** one of several early peoples who intruded into Assyria and introduced their dialects into the area **2 :** a member of the Lulubaean people

lum \ˈləm\ n -s [origin unknown] *chiefly Scot* **:** CHIMNEY

lumb- *or* **lumbo-** *comb form* [L *lumb-,* fr. *lumbus* — more at LOIN] **1 :** loin ⟨*lumbodynia*⟩ **2 :** lumbar and ⟨*lumbosacral*⟩

lum·ba·go \ˌləmˈbā,gō\ n -s [L, fr. *lumbus* loin] **:** muscular rheumatism involving the lumbar muscles and usu. accompanied by pain

lum·bang \lümˈbäŋ\ n -s [Tag *lumbáng*] **1 :** CANDLENUT **2 :** a tree (*Aleurites trisperma*) of the Philippine islands whose nuts yield a valuable oil

lumbang oil n **:** CANDLENUT OIL

lum·bar \ˈləmbə(r), -,bär, -,bȧ(r\ adj [NL *lumbaris,* fr. L *lumbus* loin + *-aris* -ar] **1 :** of, relating to, or near the loins or the group of vertebrae lying between the thoracic vertebrae and the sacrum **2 :** of, relating to, or indicating the region of the abdomen lying on either side of the umbilical region and above the corresponding inguinal — see ABDOMINAL REGION illustration

lumbar artery n **:** any artery of the four or five pairs arising from the back of the aorta opposite the lumbar vertebrae and supplying the muscles of the loins, the skin of the sides of the abdomen, and the spinal cord

lumbar ganglion n **:** one of the small ganglia of the lumbar part of the sympathetic nerves

lum·bar·i·za·tion \ˌləmbərəˈzāshən, -,rīˈ-\ n -s **:** a condition marked by fusion of the first sacral and last lumbar vertebrae

lumbar nerve n **:** one of the five pairs of the spinal nerves of the lumbar region in man one of which passes out below each lumbar vertebra and the upper four of which unite by connecting branches into a lumbar plexus

lumbar puncture n **:** a spinal puncture in the lumbar region

lumbar vein n **:** any vein of the four pairs collecting blood from the muscles and integument of the loins, the walls of the abdomen, and adjacent parts and emptying into the vena cava

lumbar vertebra n **:** one of the vertebrae situated between the thoracic vertebrae above and the sacrum below that in man are five in number

lum·ba·yao *also* **lum·ba·yau** \ˌlümbäˈyaů\ n -s [Bisayan *lumbayaw*] **:** a Philippine timber tree (*Tarrietia javanica*) whose wood is one of those sold as Philippine mahogany

1lum·ber \ˈləmbə(r)\ vi **lumbered; lumbered; lumbering** \-b(ə)riŋ\ **lumbers** [ME *lomeren;* prob. akin to Sw dial. *loma* to walk with slow and heavy steps, ME *lame* — more at LAME] **1 :** to move heavily or clumsily : move as if burdened ⟨the airplane . . . now proceeded to ~ slowly along —Noel Coward⟩ ⟨~ed a little in his walk —Kenneth Roberts⟩ ⟨the story ~s to a permanent standstill shortly after it begins —*New Yorker*⟩ **2** [prob. imit.] **:** to make a rumbling sound

2lumber \"\ n -s [perh. alter. of *1lombard;* fr. the use of pawnshops as storehouses of disused property] **1 a :** surplus or disused articles (as furniture) that are stored away : things cumbrous, bulky, or useless **b :** something superfluous, without value, or needlessly cumbersome ⟨get rid of the useless ~ that blocks our highways of thought —John Dewey⟩ ⟨this ~ of facts, conjectures, alternate possibilities —J.G.Cozzens⟩ ⟨useless words . . . dropped as worthless linguistic ~ —T.D. Weldon⟩ **2 a :** timber or logs esp. after being prepared for the market — compare ROUGH LUMBER, SHIPLAP, SURFACED LUMBER, WORKED LUMBER **b :** one of several structural materials prepared in a form similar to lumber ⟨insulating ~⟩ ⟨metal ~⟩ **3 :** superfluous flesh — used esp. of a dog

3lumber \"\ vb **lumbered; lumbered; lumbering** \-b(ə)riŋ\ **lumbers** vt **1 :** to cover or fill with or as if with lumber : clutter up : burden unnecessarily : ENCUMBER ⟨the constitution . . . was ~ed with obsolete provisions —*Americana Annual*⟩ ⟨did not wish to ~ his mind with the rubbish that most men seemed to rejoice in —Van Wyck Brooks⟩ **2 :** to heap together in disorder ⟨all those things ~ed in the closet⟩ **3 :** to log and saw the timber of ⟨this . . . valley was ~ed, hard, in 1915 —R.M.Neal⟩ ~ *vi* **1 :** to cut logs in the forest : saw logs into lumber for the market ⟨colonists were squatting on their land, ~ing in their woods —*Amer. Guide Series: Md.*⟩ **2 :** to become stored away and useless ⟨another large box to ~ with the odd and the antiquated —Peter Maggs⟩

4lumber \"\ adj **1 :** of, made of, or containing lumber ⟨~ pile⟩ **2 :** dealing in lumber ⟨~ business⟩ ⟨~ camp⟩

lumber-core \ˈ==,=\ adj **:** involving the use of or having a central layer of substantial lumber ⟨plywood of *lumber-core* construction⟩

lum·ber·dar \ˌləmbə(r)ˈdär, -dȧ(r\ n -s [Hindi *lambardār,* fr. *lambar* rank (fr. E *number*) + *-dār* holder — more at BHUMIDAR] **:** a village headman in India

lum·ber·er \ˈləmbərə(r)\ n -s [*3lumber* + *-er*] **:** one employed in lumbering

1lumbering adj [fr. pres. part. of *1lumber*] **1 :** ponderous and graceless in appearance ⟨the enormous ~ palaces of commerce —Edith Sitwell⟩ ⟨the ~ deal table — Charles Dickens⟩ **2 a :** slow-moving : having a heavy gait : CLUMSY, CUMBERSOME ⟨the big ~ two-wheel carts piled high with supplies —Green Peyton⟩ ⟨the ~, swag-bellied trot of an old milker —F.D.Davison⟩ **b :** DULL, SLOW-WITTED ⟨could always outwit his ~ brain —Liam O'Flaherty⟩ **3 :** lacking in grace, subtlety, or fluency of expression ⟨~ and irregular hexameters —Gilbert Highet⟩ ⟨cutting through involved ~ sentences —S.T.Williamson⟩ **syn** see AWKWARD

2lumbering n -s [fr. gerund of *3lumber*] **:** the business of cutting or getting timber or logs from the forest for lumber, of processing it for sale, and of marketing it

lum·ber·ing·ly adv [*1lumbering* + *-ly*] **:** in a lumbering manner ⟨pursued her ~, but she was agile as a monkey —Booth Tarkington⟩

lum·ber·ing·ness n -ES **:** the quality or state of being lumbering

lumberjack \ˈ==,=\ n [*2lumber* + *jack* (man)] **1 a :** LOGGER **b :** a worker who piles lumber in a yard or shed **2 :** a tripod or other stand usu. surmounted by a spike and used as a fulcrum in raising boards to the tops of lumber piles

lumber jacket n **:** one of the various jackets adapted from those worn by lumbermen and usu. made hip-length and single-breasted with a waistband and patch pockets

lumber kiln n **:** a room in which timber or lumber is dried by artificial heat

lum·ber·less \ˈləmbə(r)ləs\ adj **:** having no lumber

lum·ber·ly adj [*1lumber* + *-ly*] **:** LUMBERING

lum·ber·man \ˈ==mən\ n, pl **lumbermen :** one who is engaged in lumbering esp. in a supervisory or managerial capacity — compare LOGGER

lumbermen's overs n pl **:** thick felt boots combined with heavy rubber arctics worn esp. by lumbermen

lumber room n **1 :** a room in which unused furniture and other discarded articles are kept : STOREROOM **2 :** something resembling a lumber room ⟨go through life . . . filling the *lumber room* of their minds with odds and ends of a grudge here, a jealousy there —J.L. Liebman⟩

lum·ber·some \ˈləmbə(r)səm\ adj [*1lumber* + *-some*] **:** CUMBERSOME ⟨a massive ~ grizzly —*Scribner's*⟩

lumber wagon n, *chiefly North* **:** a long springless box wagon for miscellaneous hauling esp. in farm work

lumberyard \ˈ==,=\ n **:** a yard where a stock of lumber is kept for sale

lumbermen's overs

lumbo- — see LUMB-

lum·bo·dorsal fascia \ˌləm(,)bō+-\ n [*lumbodorsal* fr. *lumb-* + *dorsal*] **:** a large fascial band on each side of the back extending from the iliac crest and the sacrum to the ribs and the intermuscular septa of the muscles of the neck, adhering medially to the vertebral spines, and continuing laterally with the aponeuroses of certain of the abdominal muscles

lum·bo·sacral \"+\ adj [*lumb-* + *sacral*] **:** relating to the lumbar and sacral regions or parts; *specif* : indicating a ligament connecting the last lumbar vertebra and the sacrum

lum·bri·cal \ˈləmbrəkəl\ adj [NL *lumbricalis,* fr. L *lumbricus* earthworm + *-alis* -al] **:** being one of or constituting the lumbricales

lum·bri·ca·lis \ˌləmbrəˈkāləs\ n, pl **lumbrica·les** \-,lēz\ [NL, fr. *lumbricalis* lumbrical] **:** one of the four small muscles in the palm of the hand that arises from and is accessory to one of the deep flexor tendons and is inserted at the base of the digit to which the tendon passes; *also* : one of four similar muscles in the sole of the foot

1lum·bri·cid \ˈləmbrəsəd, -,sid\ adj [NL *Lumbricidae*] **:** of or relating to the Lumbricidae or earthworms

2lumbricid \"\ n -s [NL *Lumbricidae*] **:** one of the Lumbricidae : EARTHWORM

lum·bric·i·dae \ˌ=ˈbrisə,dē\ n pl, *cap* [NL, fr. *Lumbricus,* type genus + *-idae*] **:** a family of segmented worms (order Oligochaeta) containing most of the earthworms of Eurasia and No. America and including important genera (as *Lumbricus, Allolobophora,* and *Eisenia*) — see EARTHWORM

lum·bric·i·form \-,fȯrm\ adj [NL *Lumbricus* + E *-iform*] **:** resembling an earthworm : VERMIFORM

lum·bri·ci·na \ˌləmbrəˈsīnə, -sēnə\ n pl, *cap* [NL, fr. *Lumbricus* + *-ina*] *in former classifications* **:** a division of oligochaete worms approximately equal to Neoligochaeta

lum·bri·cine \ˈləmbrə,sēn, -,sən\ adj [NL *Lumbricina*] **:** having an arrangement of setae resembling that in *Lumbricus* — used of an oligochaete worm that has eight bristles per segment usu. arranged in pairs — compare PERICHAETINE

1lum·bri·coid \-,kȯid\ adj [NL *lumbricoides* (specific epithet of the roundworm *Ascaris lumbricoides*), fr. L *lumbricus* earthworm + *-oides* -oid] **:** resembling an earthworm

2lumbricoid \"\ n -s **:** a creature (as an ascarid) that resembles an earthworm

lum·bri·co·mor·pha \ˌləmbrəkəˈmȯrfə\ n pl, *cap* [NL, fr. *lumbrico-* (fr. *Lumbricus*) + *-morpha*] *in former classifications* **:** a division of oligochaete worms approximately equal to Neoligochaeta

lum·bri·cu·li·dae \ˌ==ˈkyülə,dē\ n pl, *cap* [NL, fr. *Lumbriculus,* type genus (fr. L *lumbricus* earthworm + NL *-ulus*) + *-idae*] **:** a family of small usu. reddish aquatic oligochaete worms somewhat resembling the Lumbricidae

lum·bri·cus \ˈləmbrəkəs\ n, *cap* [NL, fr. L, earthworm, intestinal worm] **1 :** a genus of earthworms that is the type of the family Lumbricidae **2** -ES **:** EARTHWORM

lum·brous \ˈləmbrəs\ adj [*1lumber* + *-ous*] **:** LUMBERING

lume \ˈlüm, ˈlüm\ *Scot var of* 1LOOM

lu·men \ˈlümən\ n, pl **lu·mi·na** \-mənə\ *also* **lumens** [NL *lumin-, lumen,* fr. L, light, air well, opening] **1 :** the cavity or passageway of a tubular organ ⟨the ~ of a blood vessel or the intestine⟩ **2 :** the space enclosed by the walls of a cell and in a living cell occupied by the protoplast **3 :** the bore of a tube (as of a hollow needle or catheter) **4 :** a unit of luminous flux equal to the light emitted in a unit solid angle by a uniform point source of one candle

lumen-hour \ˈ==,=\ n **:** a unit of luminous energy equal to a lumen of luminous flux acting for one hour

lum hat n, *Scot* **:** STOVEPIPE HAT

lumi- *prefix* [irreg. fr. L *lumin-, lumen* light] **:** formed by irradiation ⟨*lumichrome*⟩ ⟨*lumisterol*⟩

lu·mi·chrome \ˈlümə,krōm\ n [*lumi-* + *-chrome*] **:** a blue fluorescent crystalline compound $C_{12}H_{10}N_4O_2$ that is a derivative of alloxazine, that is formed from riboflavin by ultraviolet irradiation in neutral or acid solution or by the action of microorganisms (as *Pseudomonas riboflavina*), and that is found in the urine and milk of ruminants

lu·miere blue \lümˈye(ə)r-, (ˈ)lüm|ye\ n [*lumiere* fr. F *lumière* light, fr. LL *luminaria* lamps, pl. of *luminare* lamp] **:** a light bluish green that is darker than average aqua green (sense 1), bluer and paler than average turquoise green, and bluer, lighter, and stronger than robin's-egg blue (sense 2)

lumiere green n [*lumiere* fr. F *lumière* light] **:** SKY GREEN

lu·mi·flavin \ˌlümə+\ n [*lumi-* + *flavin*] **:** a yellow-green fluorescent crystalline compound $C_{13}H_{12}N_4O_2$ that is a derivative of isoalloxazine and that is formed from riboflavin by ultraviolet irradiation in alkaline solution

lumin- *or* **lumini-** *or* **lumino-** *comb form* [ME *lumin-,* fr. L *lumin-, lumen* light] **1 :** light ⟨*luminiferous*⟩ ⟨*luminometer*⟩ **2 :** lumen ⟨*luminal*⟩ **3 :** luminescence ⟨*luminol*⟩

lu·mi·naire \ˌlüməˈna(a)(ə)r, -ne|, |a\ n -s [F, lighting, lights, fr. LL *luminaria* lamps, pl. of *luminare* lamp] **:** a complete lighting unit including lamp, shade, reflector, fixture, and other accessories

lu·mi·nal *also* **lu·me·nal** \ˈlümənᵊl\ adj [*lumin-* + *-al*] **:** of or relating to a lumen

Luminal \ˈlümə,nal, -,nȯl, -mənᵊl\ *trademark* — used for phenobarbital

lu·mi·nance \-nən(t)s\ n -s [*lumin-* + *-ance*] **1 :** the quality or state of being luminous **2 :** the luminous intensity of a surface in a given direction per unit of projected area (as the word *reflectance* refers to the effective physical reflectance of a surface for a given quality of light, so the word ~ refers to the effectiveness of a given light on the eye, regardless of its origin —R.M.Evans) ⟨the photographic quantities that are of interest to the photographer are ~ of the object photographed and illuminance of the sensitive plate or film —A.R.Greenleaf⟩

lu·mi·nar·ism \-nə,rizəm\ n -s [*luminarist* + *-ism*] **1 :** the concern with or skill in the portrayal of effects of light and shade in painting — compare PLEINAIRISM **2** *often cap* **:** LUMINISM 2

lu·mi·nar·ist \-,rəst\ n -s [F *luminariste,* fr. *luminaire* lighting, lights + *-iste* -ist] **1 :** an artist who is esp. concerned with the effects of light and the portrayal of them in painting : an artist skilled in the rendition of effects of light and shade **2** *often cap* **:** LUMINIST 2

1lu·mi·nary \ˈlümə,nerē, -ri\ n -ES [ME *luminarye,* fr. MF & LL; MF *luminaire* lighting, lights, fr. LL *luminaria* lamps, pl. of *luminare* lamp, fr. L, window, fr. *lumin-, lumen* light; akin to L *lucēre* to shine — more at LIGHT] **1 :** one that is an inspiration to others : one who has achieved success in his chosen field : LEADING LIGHT ⟨played host to a huge gathering of international *luminaries* —Edmund Stevens⟩ ⟨staff will . . . consist of the *luminaries* in the field and be doing the most significant research —Alfred Friendly⟩ **2 :** an artificial light : ILLUMINATION ⟨lighting of the big new structure with mercury-vapor *luminaries* on lofty standards —*Motor Transportation in the West*⟩ **3 :** a body that gives light; *esp* : one of the heavenly bodies ⟨as *luminaries* . . . the total amount of light they afford during the night is far inferior to that afforded by our single moon —H.P.Wilkins⟩

2luminary \"\ adj [*lumin-* + *-ary*] **:** of, relating to, or characterized by light ⟨at an unearthly height one ~ clock against the sky —Robert Frost⟩

lu·mi·nate \-,nāt\ vt -ED/-ING/-S [L *luminatus,* past part. of *luminare* to illuminate, light up, fr. *lumin-, lumen* light] **:** ILLUMINATE — **lu·mi·na·tion** \ˌ==ˈnāshən\ n -s

lu·mine \ˈlümən\ vt -ED/-ING/-S [ME *luminen* to illuminate (a manuscript) — more at LIMN] **:** ILLUMINE ⟨a smile of joy *lumined* his wrinkled features —J.F.Cooper⟩

lu·mi·nesce \ˌlüməˈnes\ vi -ED/-ING/-S [back-formation fr. *luminescent*] **:** to exhibit luminescence

lu·mi·nes·cence \-sᵊn(t)s\ n -s [ISV *lumin-* + *-escence;* orig. formed as G *lumineszenz*] **1 :** an emission of light that is not ascribable directly to incandescence and therefore occurs at low temperatures, that is produced by physiological processes (as in the firefly), by chemical action, by friction, by electrical action (as the glow of gases in vacuum tubes when subjected to electric oscillations of high frequency or as the glow of certain bodies when subjected to cathode rays), by certain bodies while crystallizing, by suddenly and moderately heating certain bodies previously exposed to light or to cathode rays, or by exposure to light, or that occurs in radioactivity — compare FLUORESCENCE, PHOSPHORESCENCE **2 :** the light produced by luminescence

lu·mi·nes·cent \ˌ==ˈnesᵊnt\ adj [ISV *lumin-* + *-escent*] **:** relating to, exhibiting, or adapted for the production of luminescence

luminescent paint n **:** LUMINOUS PAINT

lumini- — see LUMIN-

lu·mi·nif·er·ous \ˌ==ˈnif(ə)rəs\ adj [*lumin-* + *-ferous*] **:** transmitting, producing, or yielding light

lu·mi·nism \ˈlümə,nizəm\ n -s [*luminist* + *-ism*] **1 :** LUMINARISM 1 **2** *often cap* **:** any of several schools of artists active in France in the second half of the 19th century esp. concerned with effects of light and technical problems involved in rendering them — compare DIVISIONISM, IMPRESSIONISM, NEO-IMPRESSIONISM, POINTILLISM

lu·mi·nist \-nəst\ n -s [F *luministe,* fr. L *lumin-, lumen* light + F *-iste* -ist] **1 :** LUMINARIST 1 **2** *often cap* **:** an adherent or follower of a theory, method, or practice of luminism (sense 2)

lumino- — see LUMIN-

lu·mi·nol \-,nōl,-,nōl\ n -s [*lumin-* + *-ol*] **:** an almost white to yellow crystalline compound $C_8H_7N_3O_2$ that gives a brilliant bluish luminescence when it is treated in alkaline solution with an oxidizing agent (as hydrogen peroxide) and that is used in chemical analysis (as in testing for blood spots); 5-amino-2,3-dihydro-1,4-phthalazine-dione

lu·mi·nom·e·ter \ˌ==ˈnäməd·ə(r)\ n [*lumin-* + *-meter*] **:** ILLUMINOMETER

lu·mi·no·phor \ˈlümənə,fō(ə)r\ n -s [ISV *lumin-* + *-phore*] **:** a luminescent substance : PHOSPHOR

lu·mi·no·scope \-,skōp\ n [ISV *lumin-* + *-scope*] **:** an instrument used for detecting rare metals in the soil by means of ultraviolet light and developed in the U.S.S.R.

lu·mi·nos·i·ty \ˌ==ˈnäsəd·ē, -ətē, -i\ n -ES [fr. *luminous,* after such pairs as E *curious: curiosity*] **1 a :** the quality or state of being luminous ⟨the rare few . . . who give to accurate reporting the ~ of poetry —D.C.Peattie⟩ **b :** something luminous ⟨mind is a constant ~ —John Dewey⟩ **2 a :** the relative quantity of light **b :** BRIGHTNESS 2a **3 :** the quantity of radiation emitted by a star or other celestial source usu. expressed in terms of the sun's intensity or in centimeter-gram-second units **4 :** the luminous efficiency of radiant energy : the ratio of light to heat in radiant energy — used in psychophysics

luminosity curve n **:** a curve expressing the product of relative spectral energy distribution by visibility

lu·mi·nous \ˈlümənəs\ adj [ME, fr. L *luminosus* full of light, fr. *lumin-, lumen* light + *-osus* -ose — more at LUMINARY] **1 a :** emitting or seeming to emit a steady suffused light that is reflected or produced from within ⟨the sole elements of the cosmos would seem to be ~ objects — the nebula, the stars, the planets —Lincoln La Paz⟩ ⟨he had recourse to the ~ dial of his watch —Elizabeth Bowen⟩ ⟨his eyes were ~ . . . they blazed like mortal stars —Elinor Wylie⟩ ⟨there was his face, serene, ~, often smiling —A.N.Whitehead⟩ **b :** bright and shining : CLEAR, TRANSLUCENT ⟨feeling for ~ effect that her early landscapes show —F.E.Hyslop⟩ ⟨every note in her huge range is perfect, ~, and golden —Robert Evett⟩ ⟨few foresaw the ~ future of the young man —C.G.Bowers⟩ **c :** yellow, flaring, and illuminating ⟨such a flame is also ~ —R.H. Wright⟩ **2 :** bathed in or exposed to steady light : ILLUMINATED ⟨shed a faintly ~ glow upon the upturned still face —Djuna Barnes⟩ ⟨stretched out on their backs lazily inviting the ~ American weather —Thomas Wolfe⟩ ⟨gazing up into the foliage . . . ~ with the bright sunlight —W.H.Hudson †1922⟩ **3 a :** enlightened and intelligent : edifying and inspiring ⟨full of ~ ideas of statesmanship —Samuel Alexander⟩ ⟨her own fine and ~ genius —J.P.Bishop⟩ ⟨the ~ moment when men's imaginations see alike —Lillian Smith⟩ ⟨the splendor of a profound and ~ intellect —Gertrude Atherton⟩ **b :** very easily understood : clearly intelligible ⟨convert the new situation from the obscure into the clear and ~ —John Dewey⟩ ⟨his prose is simple and ~ . . . and his text is based on wide reading —Howard M. Jones⟩ **syn** see BRIGHT

luminous efficiency n **:** the ratio of the total luminous flux radiated by any source to the total radiant flux from that source commonly expressed in lumens per watt

luminous energy n **:** energy transferred by or in the form of visible radiation — compare RADIANT ENERGY

luminous flux n **:** radiant flux in the visible-wavelength range usu. expressed in lumens instead of watts — called also *light flux*

luminous-flux density n **:** the luminous energy in a beam of light passing a unit normal section per unit time — called also *intensity of light*

luminous intensity n **:** a quantity used to specify the light-giving power of a source (as a lamp) and usu. expressed in candles ⟨a point source whose *luminous intensity* is one candle emits one lumen of luminous flux per steradian of solid angle⟩

lu·mi·nous·ly adv **:** in a luminous manner ⟨this unshakable determination, so ~ apparent in him —Robert Cutler⟩ ⟨told the facts ~ for all of us⟩

luminous moss n **:** an acrocarpous moss (*Schistostega osmundacea*) occurring in caves and dark holes in the woods and glowing by reflected light

lu·mi·nous·ness n -ES **:** LUMINOSITY

luminous paint n **:** a paint containing a phosphor (as zinc sulfide activated with copper) and so able to glow in the dark either for a time after exposure to ultraviolet radiation or indefinitely by excitation with a radioactive material (as radium) if one has been incorporated with the phosphor

lu·mis·ter·ol \lüˈmistə,rōl, -ōl\ n [*lumi-* + *sterol*] **:** a crystalline compound stereoisomeric with ergosterol from which it is formed by ultraviolet irradiation as an intermediate product in the production of tachysterol and vitamin D_2

lum·me *or* **lum·my** \ˈləmē\ *interj* [contr. of *love me* (in the exclamation *Lord love me!*)] *Brit* — used to express surprise, interest, or approval

lum·mi \ˈləmē, -mi\ n, pl **lummi** *or* **lummis** *usu cap* **1 a :** a Salishan people of northwestern Washington **b :** a member of such people **2 :** the language of the Lummi people

lum·mox \ˈləməks\ n -ES [origin unknown] : a heavy, ungainly, and often stupid or lazy person

lum·my \ˈləmē, -mi\ adj -ER/-EST [prob. fr. lumme] slang Brit : FIRST-RATE

1lump \ˈləmp\ n -S [ME; prob. akin to obs. D lompe piece, lump, D lomp rag, MHG lumpe rag, and perh. to MHG lampen to dangle — more at LIMP] 1 a (1) : a compact mass usu. of indefinite size and shape ⟨a queer ~ of a house —Thomas Hardy⟩ ⟨a ~ of coal⟩ ⟨a ~ of sugar⟩ ⟨it is a ridge, a high and uneven ~ of land —Norman Cousins⟩ (2) : the amount of clay or dough needed for one vessel or one baking ⟨all men's honors lie like one ~ before him to be fashioned —Shak.⟩ b : something resembling a lump ⟨everything is technique which is not the ~ of experience itself —Mark Schorer⟩ ⟨everybody has a ~ of loneliness —R.H.Newman⟩ 2 a obs : an aggregation of things : CLUMP b : a great amount or quantity ⟨a really nice ~ of salvage money —R.S.Porteous⟩ c : a vast mass or majority ⟨few candidates ever started with such a ~ who did not get the nomination —R.L.Strout⟩ ⟨the great ~ of radio listeners . . . let it run all day —Atlantic⟩ 3 : PROTUBERANCE, SWELLING, BUMP 2a ⟨came to with nothing more than a ~ on his head⟩ 4 : a thickset heavy person; specif : one who is stupid or dull ⟨a hearty ~ of a lad —Robertson Davies⟩ 5 Brit : a wave raised when a body of water is cut up by the wind 6 Brit : a length of gray goods 7 **lumps** pl a : BEATINGS ⟨he'd taken enough ~s —John & Ward Hawkins⟩ ⟨on the back waterways the single small craft takes its ~s —A.W.Baum⟩ b : COMEUPPANCE ⟨self-appointed specialists on women are given their ~s —Brendan Gill⟩ ⟨the good guys . . . were as usual giving the bad guys their ~s —Time⟩ — **by the lump** or **in the lump** adv : as a whole ⟨taken in the lump, the . . . team ran well and up to form —Manchester Guardian Weekly⟩ — **in a lump** or **in one lump** adv : all at one time ⟨not a set which is apt to be bought in one lump —J.S.Wilson b. 1913⟩ — **lump in one's throat** : a constriction of the throat usu. caused by emotion ⟨seemed to be a lump in my throat almost all the time —Kenneth Roberts⟩

2lump \"\ vb -ED/-ING/-S vt 1 : to throw into a mass : group or unite in a body or sum without discrimination : consider as a whole without distinction of the parts ⟨the town harbor is all the northeast coast's little fishing caves . . . ~ed together —Charles Rawlings⟩ ⟨promise that you won't ~ me with all the rest in there —Louis Auchincloss⟩ ⟨~ men together according to degrees of orthodoxy —Barbara Ward⟩ 2 a : to make into lumps : HILL ⟨plowed fields, one of which was ~ed up for melon planting —C.A.Murray⟩ b : to make lumps on or in ⟨his pockets and the front of the shirt were ~ed . . . with various articles —Vincent McHugh⟩ 3 : to move noisily and clumsily : sit heavily ⟨~ed his huge bulk down opposite —G. G.Carter⟩ 4 : LOAD ⟨did not hesitate to ~ coal at Newcastle —I.L.Idriess⟩ ~ vi 1 : to become formed into lumps ⟨the cushion ~ed up into uncomfortable hard wads⟩ 2 : to move oneself usu. noisily and clumsily : sit down heavily ⟨would loll and ~ on the sofa —Harold Nicolson⟩

3lump \"\ adj : consisting of one whole : not divided into parts ⟨pay by agreement a yearly ~ sum —G.G.Coulton⟩ ⟨300 dollars coming to you in a ~ check —Edmund Schiddel⟩

4lump \ˈləmp, ˈlu̇mp\ vt -ED/-ING/-S [perh. fr. obs. D lompen to beat, prob. fr. lompe lump] dial Eng : to beat severely : THRASH

5lump \ˈləmp\ vt -ED/-ING/-S [origin unknown] : to put up with or get used to ⟨if you don't like it you can ~ it —W.S. Maugham⟩

lump coal n : bituminous coal in the large lumps remaining after a single screening that is often designated by the size of the mesh over which it passes and by which the minimum size lump is determined ⟨¾-inch lump coal⟩ ⟨2-inch lump coal⟩

lum·pen \ˈlu̇mpən, ˈləm-\ adj [G lumpen- (in lumpenproletariat degraded and contemptible section of the proletariat), fr. lump contemptible person & lumpen rag, fr. MHG lumpe rag] : of, relating to, or being an amorphous group of dispossessed and uprooted individuals set off by their inferior status from the economic and social class with which they are identified ⟨exclusion of the rootless ~ proletariat from a leading role in the revolutions —Amer. Polit. Sci. Rev.⟩ ⟨the new unemployed intelligentsia . . . will not become ~ intellectuals —Daniel Bell⟩

1lump·er \ˈləmpə(r)\ vi -ED/-ING/-S [prob. alter. (influenced by 1lump) of 1lumber] dial Eng : to walk awkwardly : STUMBLE ⟨they ~ed straight into the night —Thomas Hardy⟩

2lumper \"\ n -S [2lump + -er] 1 a : a laborer employed to handle freight (as in loading a ship) b : one who unloads fish from a commercial fishing boat 2 chiefly Irish : a large kind of potato 3 : a taxonomist who regards organisms as recognizably divided into relatively large complex readily separated units which may include much variability within their bounds — compare SPLITTER 4 : a textile worker; specif : one who tends a cotton opener 5 : a worker in a quarry or a stonecutting establishment who assists with the hoisting of blocks of stone

lumpfish \ˈ=,=\ n [obs. E lump lumpfish (prob. fr. D lomp blenny, loach, fr. MD lompe cod) + E fish; prob. akin to obs. D lompe piece, lump] : a soft thick clumsy marine fish (Cyclopterus lumpus) of both coasts of the northern No. Atlantic whose color is usu. translucent sea green but sometimes purplish above or in the males brilliant red and yellow — compare CYCLOPTERIDAE

lump·i·ly \ˈləmpəlē, -li\ adv : in a lumpy manner : with lumps ⟨the cereal had been cooked a bit ~⟩

lump·i·ness \-pēnə̇s, -pin-\ n -ES : the quality or state of being lumpy

lump·ing·ly adv [lumping (pres. part. of 2lump) + -ly] : with heavy movements : CLUMSILY

lump·ish \ˈləmpish\ adj [ME lumpisch, fr. 1lump + -isch, -ish -ish] 1 : being stupid or sluggish in speech or action ⟨the long frontier struggles added courage . . . a doggedness which was never ~ —John Buchan⟩ ⟨the hitherto ~ girl pleaded with real inspiration —Victoria Sackville-West⟩ 2 obs : being low in spirits : DEJECTED ⟨she is ~, heavy, melancholy —Shak.⟩ 3 : having a heavy appearance : awkward and clumsy of movement ⟨the great bulk of them . . . were joyless matrons and their ~ daughters —Alistair Cooke⟩ ⟨the prime beef cow, with the ~ awkward Brahma and the Shorthorn —Green Peyton⟩ 4 : LUMPY 1 ⟨her heavy riding jacket was ~ across her square solid shoulders —H.E.Bates⟩ 5 a : having or producing a dull heavy often unpleasant sound or tone ⟨lifeless and ~ as the bagpipes drowsy drone —Robert Lloyd⟩ b : having a tedious pedantic style of writing : BORING ⟨written in "translator's English" of a peculiarly ~ kind —Howard M. Jones⟩ ⟨the novels therefore . . . are ~ and dull —Virginia Woolf⟩ — **lump·ish·ly** adv — **lump·ish·ness** n -ES

lump·kin \ˈləm(p)kə̇n\ n -S [after Tony Lumpkin, ignorant young man in the comedy She Stoops to Conquer (1773) by Oliver Goldsmith †1774 Brit. author] : a clumsy often stupid person : a blundering fool

lump lime n : quicklime in lumps as it comes from vertical kilns in calcining limestone

1lumps \ˈləmps\ n pl but sing in constr [fr. pl. of 1lump] : a disease of canaries that is marked by development of multiple cystic tumors from the feather follicles and is probably of genetic origin

2lumps pres 3d sing of LUMP

lumpsucker \ˈ=,==\ n [obs. E lump lumpfish + E sucker] : a fish of the family Cyclopteridae

lump-sum \ˈ=ˈ=\ adj [fr. the phrase lump sum] : consisting of a single sum of money ⟨has made generous lump-sum settlements —O.J.Hale⟩ ⟨purchased or acquired . . . for a lump-sum price —Jour. of Accountancy⟩

lumpy \ˈləmpē, -pi\ adj -ER/-EST [1lump + -y] 1 a : filled with lumps ⟨unfortunately the gravy was ~⟩ b (1) : covered with lumps : characterized by a rough surface ⟨severe acne which had left his skin ~ —Norman Mailer⟩ ⟨over the somewhat ~ plain abundantly dotted with pine and juniper —Gladys A. Reichard⟩ (2) : characterized by choppy waves ⟨fishing and sailing on the ~ waters —F.J.Mather⟩ 2 : having a thickset clumsy appearance ⟨the ~ man with bowed head —J.T.Soby⟩ 3 : characterized by a thick cut — used esp. of a gem 4 a : LUMPISH 5a ⟨his solos tended to come out in an unaccustomed series of ~ almost blatant phrases —Whitney Balliett⟩ b : uneven and often crude in style ⟨peppered with short ~ tracts on rural education —New Yorker⟩ ⟨a ~ drawing of two hands —A.J.Liebling⟩

lumpy crab n : a small stoutly built red crab (Xanthias taylori) with rough tuberculated carapace and chelae that is common between the tide lines along the California coast

lumpy jaw also **lump jaw** n : ACTINOMYCOSIS; esp : actinomycosis of the head in cattle

lumpy skin disease n : a highly infectious disease of African cattle that is marked by mild fever, loss of condition, and the development of inflammatory nodules in the skin and mucous membranes tending to become necrotic and ulcerous, is prob. due to a filterable virus, and may be transmitted by insects

lumpy wool n : an exudative dermatitis of sheep marked by crusting and matting of the wool that is due to an actinomycete (Actinomyces dermatonomus or Nocardia dermatonomus)

lu·mut \ˈlü,müt\ n pl [native name in Guam] : seaweeds used as food in Guam

1luna n -S [ME, fr. ML, fr. L, moon — more at LUNAR] obs : silver as used in alchemy

2lu·na \ˈlünə\ n -S [Hawaiian, lit., high, above] Hawaii : FOREMAN; esp : a foreman of a plantation

lu·na·cy \ˈlünəsē, -si\ n -ES [lunatic + -cy] 1 a : insanity interrupted by lucid intervals that was formerly supposed to be influenced by the changes of the moon ⟨grating so harshly all his days of quiet with turbulent and dangerous ~ —Shak.⟩ b : any form of insanity; also : the state of being a lunatic ⟨if they examined him for ~, they'd have him in a straitjacket in two minutes —Irwin Shaw⟩ c : insanity amounting to lack of capacity or of responsibility in the eyes of the law but in some states not including idiocy 2 a : wild foolishness : extravagant folly ⟨the Florida boom was also the first ~ to feel the full power of the press agent —Alva Johnston⟩ b : ABSURDITY, STUPIDITY ⟨the ~ of the . . . partisan political debate over Far Eastern policy —H.R.Isaacs⟩ ⟨the economic ~ of a divided national structure —Emrys Hughes⟩ c : gay madness : GIDDINESS ⟨for handsome ~ . . . a cap with white ostrich spilling over the face —Lois Long⟩ **syn** see INSANITY

luna moth \ˈlünə-\ also **luna** n -S often cap L [NL luna (specific epithet of Actias luna), fr. L, moon] : a large American moth (Actias luna) that has long extensions like tails on the hind wings which are mainly light green with a transparent spot surrounded by rings of light yellow, blue, and black and has a larva which feeds esp. on walnut, hickory, maple, and sweet gum and spins a thin papery cocoon before pupating

luna park n, usu cap L&P [fr. Luna Park, Coney Island, Brooklyn, N.Y., noted for its illumination] : a place felt to resemble the amusement center Luna Park ⟨the entire yard is illuminated by floodlights like a Luna Park —Nat'l Geographic⟩

lu·nar \ˈlünə(r), -,när, -,nä(r\ adj [L lunaris, fr. luna moon + -aris -ar; akin to OSlav luna moon, MIr lūan moon, L lucēre to shine — more at LIGHT] 1 a : of, taking place on, or relating to the moon ⟨~ craters⟩ ⟨a direct ~ hit —Edwin Diamond⟩ : resembling the surface of the moon ⟨the odd ~ landscape of the great glacier —John Hunt⟩ ⟨his imagery is cold and ~, shadows on sand —Kathleen Raine⟩ b : ORBED, CRESCENT, LUNATE ⟨who grasps the struggling heifer's ~ horns —Alexander Pope⟩ c : measured by the moon's revolutions ⟨~ month⟩ 2 [1luna + -ar] : relating to or containing silver

lunar appulse n : PENUMBRAL LUNAR ECLIPSE

lunar bone n [trans. of NL os lunare] : LUNATUM

lunar caustic n : silver nitrate esp. when fused, toughened (as by addition of hydrochloric acid or potassium nitrate), and molded into sticks or small cones for use in medicine as a caustic

lunar cycle n : METONIC CYCLE

lunar day n 1 : the rotation period of the moon on its axis equal to the sidereal month of about 27⅓ days 2 : the interval of about 24 hours and 50 minutes of sidereal time between successive transits of the moon across the meridian of any fixed observer

lunar dial n : a dial for showing the hour of night by the shadow of a gnomon in moonlight

lunar distance n : the angular distance from the moon to a planet or star used to determine longitudes at sea

lu·nare \lüˈna(a)rē, -närē\ n, pl **lunar·ia** \-na(a)rēə, -ärēə\ [NL, fr. L, neut. of lunaris lunar] : LUNATUM

lunar eclipse n : an eclipse in which the moon near the full phase passes partially or wholly through the umbra of the earth's shadow — see ECLIPSE illustration

lunar ecliptic limit n : a distance along the ecliptic averaging about 11 degrees on each side of either of the moon's nodes within which the sun must be at full moon in order for a lunar eclipse to occur

lunar equation n : the correction of the epacts by +1 every 300 years 7 times in succession and then by +1 after the next 400 years made because of the error in the lunar cycle in relation to the Gregorian calendar — compare SOLAR EQUATION

lu·nar·ia \lüˈna(a)rēə\ n [NL, fr. LL, henbane, fr. L luna moon + -aria (fem. sing. of -arius -ary)] 1 cap : a genus of herbs (family Cruciferae) having cordate leaves and broad siliques 2 -S : any plant of the genus Lunaria — called also honesty, satinpod

1lu·nar·i·an \lüˈna(a)rēən\ n -S usu cap [lunar + -an, n. suffix] 1 : a supposed inhabitant of the moon 2 : an authority on lunar astronomy 3 usu cap : one that has a well-developed Mount of the Moon bulging outward toward the center of the palm and that is usu. held by palmists to be characterized by imagination, desire for travel, and idealism ⟨the Lunarian is not often seen in pure development —W.G. Benham †1944⟩

2lunarian \"\ adj [lunar + -an, adj. suffix] : of, relating to, or existing on the moon

lunar inequality n 1 : one of many variations in the moon's motion from a true ellipse caused by the perturbation of the sun or the planets 2 : one of the nearly inappreciable fluctuations of the magnetic needle from its mean position due apparently to the moon

lu·nar·i·um \lüˈna(a)rēəm, -ˈner-, -ˈnär-\ n -S [NL, fr. L luna + NL -arium] : a device for illustrating the motion and phases of the moon

lunar letter n : MOON LETTER

lunar mansion n : any of the 28 ancient astronomical and astrological divisions of the ecliptic each of which contains the moon on successive days

lunar month n 1 : SIDEREAL MONTH 2 : SYNODIC MONTH

lunar sigma n : the Greek letter sigma in the form C

lunar star n : a star whose geocentric distances from the moon are given in nautical almanacs and are used in computing longitudes

lunar tables n pl 1 : mathematical tables for computing the moon's position at any past or future time 2 : tables used in navigation for correcting an observed lunar distance on account of refraction and parallax

lunar theory n : the theory of the moon's motion as deduced from the law of gravitation with its many perturbations

lunar tide n : the part of a terrestrial tide due to the mutual attraction between earth and moon

1lu·na·ry \ˈlünərē, -ri\ n -ES [ME lunarie, a plant, fr. LL lunaria henbane] 1 : HONESTY 3 2 : a moonwort (Botrychium lunaria)

2lunary \"\ adj [modif. (influenced by E -ary) of Sp lunar or L lunaris; Sp lunar fr. L lunaris — more at LUNAR] : LUNAR 1a ⟨drawn up the spectre of a planet from the limbo of ~ souls —E.A.Poe⟩

lunar year n : a period of 12 lunar months

lunas pl of LUNA

1lu·nate \ˈlü,nāt, -nə̇t, usu -d+V\ also **lu·nat·ed** \-,nād·ə̇d\ adj [lunate fr. L lunatus, past part of lunare to bend in a crescent, fr. luna moon; lunated fr. L lunatus + E -ed] : shaped like a crescent

2lunate \"\ n -S : an ancient crescent-shaped stone implement

lunate bone n [prob. trans. of (assumed) NL os lunatum] : LUNATUM

lu·nate·ly adv : in the shape of a crescent

1lu·na·tic \ˈlünə,tik\ also **lu·nat·i·cal** \(ˈ)lüˈnad·ə̇kəl\ adj [lunatic fr. ME lunatik, fr. OF or LL; OF lunatique, fr. LL lunaticus, fr. L luna moon; lunatical fr. lunatic + -al — more at LUNAR] 1 a obs : affected with lunacy b : having or controlled by an unsound mind : MAD c : designed for the treatment or care of insane persons ⟨~ asylum⟩ 2 a : wildly foolish : given to or marked by extravagant folly ⟨pure fantasy unrelated to reality is dangerous, ~, and irresponsible —Rex Warner⟩ ⟨consuming with ~ speed the assets of the earth —Herbert Agar⟩ b : gaily mad : GIDDY ⟨performed . . . with wonderful precision and ~ brightness —New Yorker⟩ ⟨the light ~ touch which she uses to satirize fur fashion shows and torch singers —Virginia Forbes⟩ 3 of a horse : MOON-BLIND

2lunatic \"\ n -S [ME lunatik, fr. lunatik, adj.] 1 a : a person affected with lunacy or of unsound mind b : one who is wildly eccentric : one capable of crazy actions or extravagances : CRACKPOT ⟨all sorts of political ~s whom no one would dream of taking seriously —G.B.Shaw⟩ ⟨he is a ~ when it comes to fishing⟩ 2 : a person whose abnormal mental condition renders him incapable or irresponsible before the law (as an insane person or one non compos mentis)

lu·nat·i·cal·ly \lüˈnad·ə̇k(ə)lē, -natə̇-, -li\ adv : in a lunatic manner

lunatic fringe n : the members of a group (as a political or social movement) espousing extreme, eccentric, or fanatical views : an extreme or wild group on the periphery of a larger group or of a movement ⟨he's . . . a true liberal but he has not been associated with the lunatic fringe of radical experimentation —John Dos Passos⟩ ⟨the lunatic fringe in American thought —H.J.Laski⟩

lu·na·tion \lüˈnāshən\ n -S [ME lunacioun, fr. ML lunation-, lunatio, fr. L luna moon + -ation-, -atio -ation] : the period of time averaging 29 days, 12 hours, 44 minutes, and 2.8 seconds elapsing between two successive new moons : SYNODIC MONTH

lu·na·tum \lüˈnād·əm\ n, pl **luna·ta** \-ād·ə\ [NL, fr. L, neut. of lunatus lunate] 1 : the second bone on the radial side of the proximal series of the carpus 2 in certain amphibia : a carpal bone probably representing the radiale

1lunch \ˈlənch\ n -ES often attrib [prob. short for 1luncheon] 1 archaic : a piece of food 2 a : a light meal usu. in the middle of the day : LUNCHEON b : a light meal taken at any time of the day or night at a selected place ⟨midnight ~⟩ ⟨picnic ~⟩ c : the regular midday meal when the principal meal is eaten in the evening 3 : food prepared for lunch 4 : a place where food is cooked and sold : LUNCHROOM ⟨dairy ~⟩

2lunch \"\ vb -ED/-ING/-ES vi : to eat lunch ⟨~ed at a restaurant⟩ ~ vt : to provide lunch for ⟨insisted on ~ing them before they left⟩

1lunch·eon \ˈlənchən\ n -S often attrib [perh. alter. of nuncheon] 1 archaic : a piece of food : CHUNK ⟨cramming a huge ~ of piecrust into his mouth —Sir Walter Scott⟩ 2 a : a light meal at midday : LUNCH ⟨school over, we hurried home to a cold ~ —Lyman Abbott⟩ b : a light meal of more formal character usu. for a group of people in a public dining room (as at a club meeting or a business meeting) ⟨a handful of university press people . . . habitually attended the annual ~s —Saturday Rev.⟩

2luncheon \"\ vi -ED/-ING/-S : to eat luncheon

luncheon bar n, Brit : SNACK BAR ⟨standing at the little luncheon bar like a pelican in a wilderness —John Galsworthy⟩

lunch·eon·ette \,lənchəˈnet, usu -ed·+V\ n -S : a place where light lunches are sold

lun·cheon·less \ˈlənchənlə̇s\ adj : having no luncheon

luncheon meat n : ready-to-eat meat molded (as in a loaf) and packaged by a packing house

lunch·er \ˈlənchə(r)\ n -S : one that lunches ⟨looking around at the bustling ~s —Dawn Powell⟩

lunch·less \ˈlənchlə̇s\ adj : having no lunch ⟨so anxious to be on time, they had been waiting ~ —Cleveland (Ohio) Plain Dealer⟩

lunchroom \ˈ=,=\ n : a small restaurant specializing in food ready to serve or quickly prepared

lunchtime \ˈ=,=\ n : a time for eating lunch ⟨worked for a living and had a regular ~ —Frederick Skerry⟩

lunch wagon also **lunch cart** n : DINER 2b

lun·da \ˈlündə, ˈlün-\ n, pl **lunda** or **lundas** usu cap 1 a (1) : a Bantu-speaking people along the Congo-Angola border (2) : any of the affiliates of the historical Lunda Empire (as the peoples of Balovale District in Northern Rhodesia) b : a member of one of the Lunda peoples 2 : one of the Bantu languages of the Lunda peoples

lun·den·si·an \(ˈ)lənˈdensēən\ adj, usu cap [prob. fr. (assumed) NL lundensis of or relating to Lund (fr. Lund, city in southwest Sweden) + E -an] : of or relating to a 20th century school of theological thought associated with the faculty at the University of Lund in Sweden and characterized by emphasis on Agape as the heart of the Christian message

lun·dy·foot \ˈləndē,fu̇t\ n, usu cap [after Lundy Foot fl1776 Irish tobacconist] : a variety of snuff

1lune \ˈlün\ n -S [ME loyne, lune, fr. MF loigne, longe, fr. OF longe, fr. lonc long, fr. L longus — more at LONG] : a hawk's leash

2lune \"\ n -S [L luna moon — more at LUNAR] 1 : the part of a plane surface bounded by two intersecting circular arcs or of a spherical surface bounded by two great circles 2 : something in the shape of a half-moon

lunes \ˈlünz\ n pl [F, pl. of lune crazy whim, fr. MF, crazy whim, moon, fr. L luna moon] : fits of lunacy or frenzy : crazy or unreasonable whims ⟨these dangerous, unsafe lunes of the king —Shak.⟩

lu·nette \lüˈnet\ n -S [in sense 1, prob. fr. (assumed) MF lunette (whence F lunette horseshoe having the front semicircular part only), lit., small object resembling a full moon or a crescent moon, fr. OF lunete small object resembling a full moon or a crescent moon, reflecting part of a circular mirror, fr. lune moon (fr. L luna) + -ete -ette; in other senses, fr. F lunette small opening, lunettes (pl.) blinders for a horse, spectacles, fr. OF lunete] 1 : a horseshoe having the front semicircular part only 2 a : an opening in a vault esp. for a window b : the surface at the upper part of a wall that is partly surrounded by a vault which the wall intersects and that is often filled by a window, by several windows, or by mural painting 3 : a blinder esp. for a vicious horse 4 a **lunettes** pl : SPECTACLES b : a convexo-concave lens for spectacles 5 : a fieldwork consisting of two faces forming a salient angle and two parallel flanks — compare REDAN 6 a : the figure or shape of a crescent moon ⟨peered through the ~s made by the screen wipers —Margery Allingham⟩ b : an ornament of crescent shape ⟨a gold ~ set with diamonds⟩ 7 : a watch crystal having a curved top glass streamlined to allow clearance to the watch hands 8 : a gold or gilt clip or a crystal case of crescent shape used to hold the Host upright in the monstrance 9 : a ring in the trail plate of a towed vehicle (as a gun carriage) that is used to attach the towed vehicle to the limber 10 : a small open frame with a glass bottom carried by divers 11 : a broad low somewhat crescentic mound of loamy or sandy material formed by the wind

1lung \ˈləŋ\ n -S [ME lunge, fr. OE lungen; akin to OHG lungun lung, ON lungu (pl.) lungs, Goth leihts light — more at LIGHT] 1 a : one of the usu. two compound saccular organs that constitute the basic respiratory organ of air-breathing vertebrates, that arise from the ventral wall of the embryonic alimentary canal, each developing into a somewhat conical sac surrounded by a serous membrane continuous with the pleura, depending from the bronchus by which it is continuous with the pharynx and from the pulmonary artery and vein, being suspended in and normally occupying the entire lateral parts of the thorax, and consisting essentially of an inverted tree of intricately branched bronchioles that communicate with thin-walled terminal alveoli swathed in a network of delicate capillaries between which and the air inspired into the alveoli the actual gaseous exchange of respiration takes place, and that in man are somewhat flattened with a broad base resting against the diaphragm that closes the thoracic cavity posteriorly and have the right lung divided into three lobes and the left into two lobes b : any of various respiratory organs of invertebrates — compare BOOK LUNG 2 : something that supplies air for breathing: as a Brit : an open space in or near a city ⟨area of hill and moor which serves like a giant ~ the great urban populations —Gerald Nethercot⟩ b : a device for enabling individuals abandoning a submarine to rise to the surface c : a mechanical device for regularly introducing fresh air into and withdrawing stale air from the lung : RESPIRATOR — see IRON LUNG

²lung \'lu̇ŋ\ *n* -s [Chin (Pek) *lung²*] : DRAGON 3c

lungan *var of* LONGAN

lung book *n* : BOOK LUNG; *esp* : the functional laminated part of a book lung

¹lunge \'lənj\ *vb* -ED/-ING/-S [by shortening & alter. fr. obs. *allonge* to make a thrust with a sword, fr. F *allonger* to extend (an arm), make long, fr. OF *alongier* to make long — more at ALLONGE] *vt* **1** *archaic* : to deliver (as a kick or thrust) suddenly — often used with *out* ⟨*lunged* out a kick —W.M. Thackeray⟩ **2** : to cause to make or move with a lunge : thrust or push with a lunge ⟨strode mightily through, waving his free arm, *lunging* his portfolio —Katherine A. Porter⟩ ~ *vi* **1 a** : to make a thrust or pass with a foil **b** : to tackle an opponent in field hockey **2** : to make a forceful forward movement : PLUNGE, SURGE ⟨*lunged* forward and opened the door for her —J.P.Marquand⟩ ⟨*lunged* in with a heavy black iron tray —Katherine Mansfield⟩

²lunge \"\ *n* -s **1 a** : a sudden thrust or pass (as with a sword or foil) **b** : a one-handed tackling stroke in field hockey **2** : the act of plunging forward : a forceful often abrupt movement ahead : SURGE ⟨she made a ~ at a door —Elizabeth Bowen⟩ ⟨clattering ~ from the electric shovel —George Farwell⟩ ⟨feeling the long easy ~ of the ship —Vincent McHugh⟩ ⟨no one can read a page . . . without feeling its ~, its force —John Mason Brown⟩ **3** : a movement for position in gymnastics or dancing in which one foot is advanced as far as possible with the knee bent and directly over the instep while the other foot remains stationary

³lunge *var of* LONGE

⁴lunge \'lənj\ *n* -s [short for *muskellunge*] **1** : LAKE TROUT b **2** : MUSKELLUNGE

lunged \ˈləŋd\ *adj* [¹*lung* + *-ed*] **1** : having lungs : PULMONATE **2** : having lungs of a specified kind or number ⟨deep-*lunged*⟩ ⟨one-*lunged*⟩

lun·geous \'lənjəs, 'lu̇n-\ *adj* [prob. fr. ¹*lunge* + *-ous*] *dial Eng* : rough and violent; *also* : ILL-TEMPERED

¹lung·er \'lənjə(r)\ *n* -s [¹*lunge* + *-er*] **1** : one that lunges **2** : a safety belt that is equipped with side swivels and rope handles which may be held by two assistants or suspended from the ceiling to give support to a gymnast when learning aerial stunts and that is sometimes equipped with ball bearings so that lateral rotation within the belt is possible

²lung·er \'ləŋə(r)\ *n* -s [¹*lung* + *-er*] : one suffering from a chronic disease of the lungs; *esp* : one that is tubercular

lunger disease *n* : a chronic progressive pneumonia of sheep consistently fatal and of unknown etiology

lung fever *n* : PNEUMONIA

lungfish \'=,=\ *n* : a fish of the order Dipneusti or Cladistia that breathes by a modified lunglike air bladder as well as gills — see CERATODUS; compare LEPIDOSIREN, PROTOPTERUS

lung fluke *n* : a fluke invading the lungs; *esp* : an Old World form (*Paragonimus westermanii* or *P. kellicotti*) attacking man and producing lesions that are comparable to those of tuberculosis and that are acquired by eating inadequately cooked freshwater crustaceans which act as intermediate hosts

lung·ful \'ləŋ,fu̇l\ *n, pl* **lungfuls** *or* **lungs·ful** \-ŋ,fu̇lz, -ŋz,fu̇l\ : the amount of air in the lungs at one time ⟨climb up . . . for even deeper *lungsful* of fresh air —Joyce M. Batten⟩

lun·gi *or* **lun·gyi** \'lu̇ŋgē, ˈlŋjē\ *also* **long·gyi** \'lȯl\, 'lōl\ *n* -s [Hindi *luṅgī*, fr. Per] **1** : a usu. cotton cloth used esp. in India, Pakistan, and Burma for articles of clothing (as sarongs, skirts, and turbans) **2** : a piece of cotton cloth usu. 2½ yards long that is folded about the body and tied at the waist and that is worn esp. in India

lung·ie \'ləŋi\ *n* -s [Norw *langve, langvi, lomvi*, fr. ON *langvē*, fr. *langr* long + *-vē*, a bird; akin to OHG *wio* kite and perh. to ON *veithr* hunt, hunting, fishing — more at LONG, GAIN] *Scot* : MURRE

lunging rein *n* [*lunging* fr. gerund of ²*longe*] : LONGE

lungis *n* -ES [MF *longis* slow-moving person, tall awkward person (influenced in meaning by MF *long*, fr. L *longus*), fr. LL *Longinus*, Roman soldier who according to an apocryphal gospel (Gospel of Nicodemus 7:8) pierced Christ's side with a spear during the crucifixion — more at LONG] *obs* : a dull lazy fellow : LOUT

lung·less \'ləŋləs\ *adj* : having no lungs

lung lichen *or* **lung moss** *n* : LUNGWORT 3

lunglike \'=,=\ *adj* : resembling a lung esp. in function

lungoor *var of* LANGUR

lung plague *n* : contagious pleuropneumonia of cattle

lungs *pl of* LUNG

lung sickness *n* : LUNG PLAGUE

lungworm \'=,=\ *n* : any of various nematodes that infest the lungs and air passages of mammals: as **a** : a member of the genus *Dictyocaulus* **b** : the swine lungworm (*Metastrongylus elongatus*) that causes bronchitis and serves as an intermediate host of the swine-influenza virus

lungworm disease *n* : HOOSE 2

lungwort \'=,=\ *n* [ME *lungwurt*, fr. OE *lungenwyrt*, fr. *lungen* lung + *wyrt* wort — more at LUNG, WORT] **1** : any of several plants once thought helpful in pulmonary diseases: as **a** : BLACK HELLEBORE **b** : MULLEIN **c** : WALL HAWKWEED **2 a** : a European herb (*Pulmonaria officinalis*) with hispid leaves and small blue flowers **b** : VIRGINIA COWSLIP **3** : a widely distributed lichen (*Lobaria pulmonaria*) formerly used in the treatment of bronchitis and now to some extent in perfumes and in tanning extracts

lungy \'ləŋē, -ŋi\ *adj* [¹*lung* + *-y*] *slang* : CONSUMPTIVE

lu·ni·solar \ˈlünə+\ *adj* [L *luna* moon + E *-i-* + *solar* — more at LUNAR] : relating or attributed to the moon and the sun jointly or to the mutual relations of sun and moon

lunisolar period *n* : a period of 532 years at the end of which in the Julian calendar the new and full moons and the eclipses recur on the same days of the week, month, and year as in the previous period

lunisolar precession *n* : the principal component of the precession of the equinoxes due to the joint action of moon and sun

lu·ni·tidal interval \"+-\ *n* : the interval between the transit of the moon and the time of the lunar high tide next following

lun·ker \'ləŋkə(r)\ *n* -s [origin unknown] : something large of its kind — used esp. of a fish ⟨a ~ bass⟩

lunk·head \'ləŋk,=\ *also* **lunk** *n* -s [*lunkhead* prob. fr. *lunk-* (alter. of ¹*lump*) + *head*; *lunk* short for *lunkhead*] : a dull-witted person : DOLT ⟨these . . . ~s couldn't come up to Shakespeare —Mark Twain⟩ — **lunk·headed** \'=;=\ *adj*

lu·noid \'lü,nȯid\ *adj* [L *luna* moon + E *-oid*] : LUNATE

¹lunt \'lənt\ *n* -s [D *lont* match, rag; akin to MLG *lunte* match, wick] **1** *chiefly Scot* : SLOW MATCH; *also* : LINK, TORCH **2** *chiefly Scot* : SMOKE; *also* : hot vapor

²lunt \"\ *vb* -ED/-ING/-S *vt* **1** *chiefly Scot* : to smoke tobacco in (a pipe) **2** *chiefly Scot* : to set fire to : light up : KINDLE ~ *vi* **1** *chiefly Scot* : to emit smoke **2** *chiefly Scot* : to catch fire

lu·nu·la \'lünyələ\ *n, pl* **lunu·lae** \-,lē\ [NL, fr. L, crescent-shaped ornament worn by a woman, fr. *luna* moon + *-ula*] **1** : LUNULE **2** [L] : one of various crescent-shaped ornaments usu. of bronze, copper, or silver found in archaeological sites of the early Bronze Age

lu·nu·lar \-lə(r)\ *adj* [ISV *lunula* + *-ar*] : of or relating to a lunule : LUNULATE

lu·nu·lar·ia \,=='la(a)rēə\ *n, cap* [NL, fr. L *lunula* + NL *-aria*] : a genus of liverworts (family Marchantiaceae) with crescent-shaped gemma cups

lu·nu·late \'lünyə,lāt, -lət, *usu* -d·+V\ *also* **lu·nu·lat·ed** \-,lād·əd\ *adj* [*lunulate* fr. NL *lunulatus*, fr. L *lunula* + *-atus* -ate; *lunulated* fr. NL *lunulatus* + E *-ed*] : resembling a small crescent ⟨a ~ process⟩ : having crescent-shaped markings ⟨a ~ markings on a bug⟩

lu·nule \'lün(,)yül\ *n* -s [NL *lunula*] : a body part that suggests a crescent: as **a** [F, fr. L *lunula*] : the whitish mark at the base of a fingernail **b** : an impressed or modified area in front of the beak on the outside of many bivalve shells **c** : a small area above the antennae on the front of some of the true flies **d** : the crescentic unattached border of a semilunar valve **e** : one of the openings in the test of the keyhole urchins

lu·nu·let \'lünyələt\ *n* -s [NL *lunula* + E *-et*] : LUNULA

lu·nu·mi·del·la \,lünyəmə'delə\ *n* -s [Sinhalese *luṇu-midella*, fr. *luṇu* salt + *midella* (any of various species of *Barringtonia*)] **1** : a tree (*Melia dubia*) of Asia, Africa, and Australasia having reddish white wood similar to toon **2** : the wood of the lunumidella tree

luny *var of* LOONY

lun·yie \'lün(y)i\ *Scot var of* LOIN

lu·nyo·ro \lün'yōrō\ *n, pl* **lunyoro** *or* **lunyoros** *usu cap* : NYORO

luo *or* **lu·oh** *also* **lwo** \lə'wō\ *n, pl* **luo** *or* **luos** *or* **luoh** *or* **luohs** *usu cap* **1 a** : a scattered pastoral people along various tributaries of the Nile and on the eastern shore of Lake Victoria **b** : a member of such people **2** : a Nilotic language of the Luo people

lu·or·a·wet·lan \lə,wȯrə'wetlən\ *n* -s *usu cap* : a language family of the extreme northeast of Asia comprising Chukchi, Koryak, and Kamchadal — see PALEOSIBERIAN

lu·pa·nar \lü'pānə(r)\ *n* -s [L, fr. *lupa* prostitute, she-wolf, fem. of *lupus* wolf — more at WOLF] : BROTHEL

lu·pa·nine \'lüpə,nēn, -nən\ *n* -s [*lupan-* (irreg. fr. *lupine*) + *-ine*] : a bitter crystalline poisonous alkaloid $C_{15}H_{24}N_2O$ found in various lupines

lu·pe \'lü(,)pā\ *n* -s [Samoan] : a Polynesian fruit pigeon (*Globicera pacifica*)

lu·pe·ol \'lüpē,ȯl, -ōl\ *n* -s [ISV *lupe-* (irreg. fr. *lupine*) + *-ol*; prob. orig. formed in G] : a crystalline triterpenoid alcohol $C_{30}H_{49}OH$ found esp. in yellow lupine, gutta-percha and balata, and shea butter

lu·per·ca·lia \,lüpə(r)'kālēə, -ālyə\ *n* -s *usu cap* [L, fr. neut. pl. of *lupercalis* of or relating to the Luperci, fr. *luperci* + *-alis* -al] : an ancient Roman festival celebrated February 15 to ensure fertility for the people, fields, and flocks — **lu·per·ca·lian** \;==;kālēən, -lyən\ *adj*

lu·per·ci \lü'pər,sī\ *n pl, usu cap* [L, prob. fr. *lupus* wolf] : priests of the cult of the ancient Roman rural god Faunus whose festival was the Lupercalia

lu·pet·i·dine \lü'ped·ə,dēn, -dən\ *n* -s [ISV *lu-* (fr. *lutidine*) + *-pe-* + *-tidine* (fr. *lutidine*)] : any of the dimethyl derivatives $(CH_3)_2C_5H_8NH$ of piperidine all of which are colorless alkaline liquids

lu·pi·form \'lüpə,fȯrm\ *adj* [*lupus* + *-iform*] : resembling lupus

¹lu·pine *also* **lu·pin** \'lüpən\ *n* -s [ME *lupine*, fr. L *lupinus*, *lupinum*, fr. *lupinus*, adj.] **1 a** : a plant of the genus *Lupinus* **b** : the seed of a lupine plant (as of the lupine *L. albus*) used as food from earliest times **2** : a light purplish blue that is bluer and paler than average periwinkle and bluer than zenith

²lu·pine \-,pīn, -pən\ *adj* [L *lupinus*, fr. *lupus* wolf + *-inus* -ine] : of, relating to, or resembling a wolf : WOLFISH ⟨his death touched off a ~ scuffle for succession —*Time*⟩

lupine maggot *n* : the maggot of a two-winged fly (*Hylemya lupini*) that develops in and damages the stem of lupines esp. in the southeastern U.S.

lu·pin·ine \'lüpə,nēn, -nən\ *n* -s [ISV ¹*lupine* + *-ine*] : a crystalline weakly poisonous alkaloid $C_{10}H_{19}NO$ found esp. in lupines

lu·pi·no·sis \,==ˈnōsəs\ *n* -ES [NL, fr. L *lupinus, lupinum* lupine + NL *-osis*] : acute liver atrophy of cattle and other mammals due to poisoning by ingestion of various lupines

lu·pi·nus \lü'pīnəs\ *n, cap* [NL, fr. L, lupine] : a genus of herbs (family Leguminosae) with digitate or unifoliolate leaves and white, yellow, blue, or purple flowers in long racemes

lu·pis \lü'pēs\ *n* -ES [Cebuan] *Philippines* : the finest quality of abaca used for delicate fabrics

lu·poid \'lü,pȯid\ *adj* [ISV *lupus* + *-oid*] : LUPIFORM

lu·pous \'lüpəs\ *adj* [*lupus* + *-ous*] : of, relating to, or affected with lupus

lu·pu·lic acid \lə'pyülik-\ *or* **lu·pu·lin·ic acid** \ˈlüpyə;linik-\ *n* [*lupulic* fr. *lupul-* (fr. *lupulin*) + *-ic*; *lupulinic* fr. *lupulin* + *-ic*] : either of two acidic compounds obtained from lupulin: **a** : HUMULONE **b** : LUPULON

lu·pu·lin \'lüpyələn\ *n* -s [*lupul-* (fr. NL *lupulus* — specific epithet of the hop plant *Humulus lupulus* — fr. L *lupus* hop plant, wolf + *-ulus*) + *-in*] : a fine yellow resinous powder on the strobiles of hops that contains humulone and lupulon

lu·pu·line \-,līn, -lən\ *or* **lu·pu·li·nous** \ˈ==;līnəs\ *adj* [prob. fr. (assumed) NL *lupulinus*, fr. NL *lupulus* + L *-inus* -ine] : resembling a cluster of hops

lu·pu·lon \'lüpyə,län\ *also* **lu·pu·lone** \-,lōn\ *n* -s [ISV *lupul-* (fr. NL *lupulus*) + *-one*] : a bitter crystalline antibiotic $C_{26}H_{38}O_4$ that is obtained from lupulin and is effective against fungi and various bacteria

lu·pus \'lüpəs\ *n* -ES [ML, fr. L, wolf — more at WOLF] : any of several diseases (as lupus erythematosus or lupus vulgaris) characterized by skin lesions

lupus er·y·thema·to·sus \-,erə,thēmə'tōsəs, -them-\ *n* [NL, lit., erythematous lupus] : a systemic disease of unknown cause and unpredictable course that is characterized esp. by fever, skin rash, and arthritis, often by acute hemolytic anemia, by small hemorrhages in the skin and mucous membranes, by inflammation of the pericardium, and in serious cases by involvement of the kidneys and central nervous system

lupus vul·ga·ris \-,vəl'ga(a)rəs\ *n* [NL, lit., common lupus] : tuberculous disease of the skin marked by formation of soft brownish nodules with ulceration and scarring

¹lur \'lü(ə)r\ *n, pl* **lur** *or* **lurs** *usu cap* **1** : a chiefly nomadic Muslim people of undetermined ethnological origin inhabiting a wild part of the Zagros mountains of Iran — see PERSIAN 1b **2** : a member of the Lur people

²lur \"\ *n, pl* **lur** *or* **lurs** *usu cap* : ALUR

³lur \'lu̇(ə)r\ *also* **lu·re** \-ürə\ *n, pl* **lurs** \-ü(ə)rz\ *also* **lu·ren** \-ürən\ [Dan & Sw & Norw *lur*, fr. ON *lūthr* trumpet] : a large bronze roughly S-shaped trumpet of the Bronze Age in Scandinavian countries ⟨the oldest metal musical instruments of Europe are the signal horns called ~s —*Science News Letter*⟩

lur

¹lurch \'lərch, -əch, -əich\ *vb* -ED/-ING/-ES [ME *lorchen*, prob. alter. of *lurken* to lurk — more at LURK] *vi* **1** *dial chiefly Eng* : to loiter about a place furtively : PROWL, SNEAK ⟨~ about the place looking sinister —Anthony Carson⟩ **2** *obs* : CHEAT, STEAL ~ *vt* **1** *obs* : to obtain by fraud or stealth : FILCH, STEAL ⟨put lately into many men's heads . . . his own ambitious ends to ~ a crown —John Milton⟩ **2** *archaic* : to do out of something : CHEAT, ROB ⟨in the brunt of seventeen battles . . . he ~*ed* all swords of the garland —Shak.⟩

²lurch \"\ *n* -ES *archaic* : an act of lurching or a state of watchful readiness ⟨the enemy of human happiness, always lying at ~ to make prey of the young —J.P.Kennedy †1870⟩

³lurch \"\ *n* -ES [MF *lourche*, n., a game & *lourche*, adj., deceived, prob. of Gmc origin; akin to MHG *lerz, lurz* left, located on the left side, *lürzen* to deceive — more at LORDOSIS] **1** *obs* : an act or instance of cheating : FRAUD **2** *obs* **a** : an act or instance of discomfiture : SETBACK, ROUT **b** *obs* : one's sphere of control : POWER ⟨David, when he had Saul in his ~, might . . . have cut off his head —Thomas Goodwin⟩ **3 a** : a decisive defeat in which a player wins a game by more than twice his opponent's score; *specif* : a defeat in which a player wins a cribbage game before his opponent has progressed halfway toward the goal — compare GAMMON, RUBICON **b** *obs* : an old table game that may have resembled backgammon — **in the lurch** *adv (or adj)* **1** *obs* : in a defenseless position : at a disadvantage ⟨he took me *in the lurch* —Thomas D'Urfey⟩ **2** : in a vulnerable, difficult, or embarrassing position without support — used with *leave* ⟨at the peak of the noonday rush the cashier stalked out and left him *in the lurch*⟩ ⟨the U.S. cannot . . . leave the British *in the lurch* in their struggle against this exhibition of nationalism —Neal Stanford⟩

⁴lurch \"\ *vt* -ED/-ING/-ES **1** : to defeat by a lurch (as in cribbage) — compare SKUNK **2** *archaic* : to leave in the lurch : DISAPPOINT, DESERT ⟨fortune . . . hath ~*ed* generals in her time —*Sporting Mag.*⟩

⁵lurch \"\ *n* -ES [origin unknown] **1 a** : a sudden roll of a ship to one side (as in heavy weather) **b** : an act or instance of swaying or tipping ⟨a sudden ~ of the vehicle threw the two men together —John Morrison⟩ ⟨felt a great ~ of joy —Marcia Davenport⟩ **c** : a gait characterized by a sway or stagger ⟨walk with the same slow, complacent ~ —Rebecca West⟩ **2** : BENT, DRIFT, INCLINATION, TENDENCY, URGE ⟨showed a decided ~ toward a solitary life⟩

⁶lurch \"\ *vi* -ED/-ING/-ES **1 a** : to roll or tip abruptly : CANT, PITCH ⟨the schooner ~*ed* in the uneasy chop —Kenneth Roberts⟩ ⟨ramshackle outbuildings, ~*ing* rose arches —Elizabeth Taylor⟩ ⟨the glen seemed to ~ forward and become a defile —John Buchan⟩ **b** : to move with a series of lurches : CAREEN, SWAY ⟨landing craft ~*ed* toward shore —*Time*⟩ ⟨international group . . . ~*ed* for days over lunar roads to watch the sacred right of franchise exercised —*Punch*⟩ ⟨she slouched off . . . the cub ~*ing* along contentedly beside her —C.G.D.Roberts⟩ **2 a** : to move unsteadily or in a series of stops and starts : STAGGER ⟨a visiting . . . celebrity, somewhat bemused by whiskey, ~*ed* across the room —Ian Bevan⟩ ⟨horses ~*ing* in deep mud —Adrian Bell⟩ **b** : to give a sudden or involuntary movement : JERK, LUNGE ⟨rubbed the sleep out of his eyes and ~*ed* upright —Julian Dana⟩ ⟨~*ed* forward with a bullet in his head —E.V.Burkholder⟩ ⟨the pain ~*ed* in him —Ernest Hemingway⟩ **3** : to move in an awkward or uncertain fashion : BLUNDER, STUMBLE ⟨we're not all . . . ~*ing* along on mere instinct —Anne D. Sedgwick⟩ ⟨Congress ~*ed* toward adjournment —*Time*⟩

lurch·er \-chə(r)\ *n* -s [¹*lurch* + *-er*] **1** *archaic* : a petty thief : PILFERER **2** *obs* : GLUTTON **3 a** *archaic* : LURKER, SPY **b** *Austral* : a street loiterer : HOODLUM **4** *Brit* : a mongrel dog; *esp* : a cross between a greyhound and a collie often used by poachers

lurch·ing·ly *adv* [*lurching* (pres. part. of ⁶*lurch*) + *-ly*] : in a lurching manner : JERKILY, SWAYINGLY

lur·dane \'lərdᵊn\ *n* -s [ME *lurdan*, fr. MF *lourdin* dullard, fr. *lourd* dull, stupid — more at LOURD] *archaic* : an idle or lubberly fellow

¹lure \'lu̇(ə)r, -u̇ə\ *n* -s [ME, enticement, falconer's lure, fr. MF *loire, loirre* falconer's lure, fr. OF, of Gmc origin; akin to MLG *lōder* bait, MHG *luoder*; akin to OE *lathian* to invite, OHG *ladōn*, ON *latha*, Goth *lathon* to call, invite, and perh. to Gk *laimos* wanton, impudent, greedy] **1** : a bunch of feathers roughly resembling a bird, attached to a long cord, often baited with raw meat, and used by a falconer to recall a hawk **2 a** : an alluring prospect : inducement to pleasure or gain : ENTICEMENT, INCENTIVE ⟨~ of adventure⟩ ⟨~ of a pleasant climate⟩ ⟨threw out all the ~s of her beauty . . . to make a prize of his heart —T.L.Peacock⟩ ⟨prohibited all inheritance taxes . . . as a ~ to wealthy settlers —C.P.Curtis⟩ ⟨textbooks . . . designed as ~s to learning —Sloan Wilson⟩ **b** (1) : drawing power : APPEAL, ATTRACTION ⟨a situation that has, in itself, an intense and universal ~ —Louis Kronenberger⟩ ⟨salmon . . . have for him a quite irresistible ~ —J.E.Sayers⟩ ⟨the high-pitched song of fine thin glass, the ~ of its translucent depths —Martin James⟩ ⟨the sets and costumes lack ~ —*Time*⟩ (2) *archaic* : a blandishment used in an attempt to gain control ⟨time stoops to no man's ~ —A.C.Swinburne⟩ **3** : a heraldic figure of two wings joined with the tips downward with a leash attached ⟨a pair of wings inverted conjoined in ~ or —E.E.Reynolds⟩ **4 a** : a device or decoy for attracting animals to capture ⟨uses about three kinds of ~s, one being oil catnip which actually makes a bobcat . . . easy to get in a trap —*Fur-Fish-Game*⟩; *specif* : live or artificial bait used for catching fish ⟨fishermen casting every kind of ~ you've ever seen —Stewart Beach⟩ — compare ⁵FLY 4 **b** : TRAP, SNARE ⟨this flamboyant role . . . is a ~ and pitfall for an ambitious singing actress —Douglas Watt⟩ ⟨party leaders sought to . . . set a special ~ for the state's support —*U.S. News & World Report*⟩ **c** : a structure resembling a tassel on the head of pediculate fishes that is often luminous and is used to attract prey

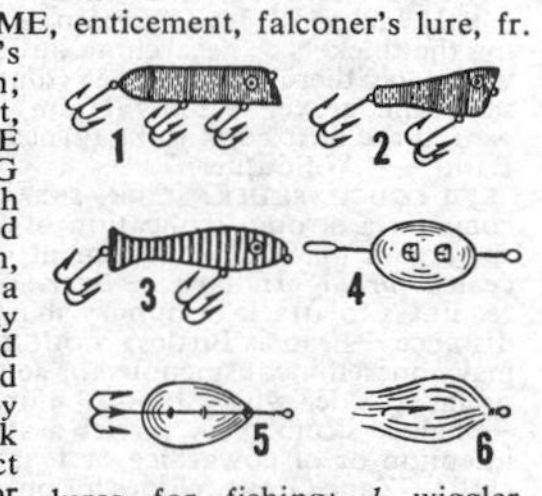

lures for fishing: *1* wiggler, *2* plunker, *3* minnow, *4* spinner, *5* spoon, *6* bucktail

²lure \"\ *vb* -ED/-ING/-S [ME *luren*, fr. MF *loirier*, fr. OF, fr. *loire, loirre*, n.] *vt* **1** *archaic* **a** : to recall (a hawk) by means of a lure **b** : to call (as a hawk) to the lure ⟨O for a falconer's voice to ~ this tercel-gentle back again —Shak.⟩ **2** : to tempt with a promise of pleasure or gain : ALLURE, ATTRACT, ENTICE, INVITE ⟨don't let money ~ you into a job you don't like —W.J.Reilly⟩ ⟨the magic of a full moon had *lured* me from my laboratory —William Beebe⟩ ⟨*lured* able . . . men to his staffs —W.T.Ridder⟩ ⟨raised almost half a million dollars to ~ new industries to their town —T.E.Murphy⟩ — often used with *on* or *onward* ⟨knowledge . . . keeps *luring* him on —H.A. Overstreet⟩ ⟨towering cliffs . . . challenge him, ~ him onward —G.I.Bell⟩ ~ *vi* **1** *archaic* : to call a hawk to the lure **2** *obs* : to call loudly : HALLOO

syn ENTICE, INVEIGLE, DECOY, TEMPT, SEDUCE: LURE may mean to draw into danger, evil, or difficulty by ruse or wiles ⟨it was not money that *lured* the adolescent husbandman to the cities, but the gay life —H.L.Mencken⟩ ⟨*lured* into the imperfect world of coarse uncompleted passion —Oscar Wilde⟩ or merely to offer an inducement ⟨salt mines, which *lured* the Celts to settle on prehistoric encampments —Claudia Cassidy⟩ ENTICE may suggest artful coaxing ⟨she appeared to be playing with the bird, possibly amusing herself by trying to *entice* it on to her hand —W.H.Hudson †1922⟩ ⟨the fellow — for all his gentle voice — was a deceiver; *enticing* people to follow him about and listen to his prattle —L.C.Douglas⟩ INVEIGLE may mean persuading one against his will or better judgment ⟨I hope to be able to call and see you there, instead of *inveigling* you into these surreptitious meetings, even although they have the charm of secrecy —William Black⟩ DECOY means to lead into danger or entrap by artifice ⟨the islanders had been living in relative opulence from the wreckage of ships which they had skillfully *decoyed* to destruction on the reefs —Thomas Barbour⟩ TEMPT means to arouse a desire sometimes contrary to one's conscience or better judgment ⟨"I was forgetting," she said. "I am forbidden tea. I mustn't drink it." She looked at the cup, tremendously *tempted*. She longed for tea. An occasional transgression could not harm her —Arnold Bennett⟩ ⟨seated bolt upright in a chair that would have *tempted* a good-humored person to recline —G.B.Shaw⟩ SEDUCE means to lead astray, usu. from propriety, duty, or morality ⟨the hideous beast whose craft had *seduced* me into murder —E.A.Poe⟩ ⟨watching the seditious crew of "Congress men" *seducing* the colonials into unnatural rebellion against the best of kings and fathers —V.L.Parrington⟩ or to delude ⟨words when used with the gift of magic can *seduce* a reader into belief that has no roots in reality —Rose Feld⟩

³lure \"\ *n* -s [short for *velure*] : a heated pad for lustering felt hats

⁴lure \"\ *vt* -ED/-ING/-S : to rub (felt) with a lure

lure·ment \-mənt\ *n* -s [²*lure* + *-ment*] : ALLUREMENT

luren *pl of* LUR

¹lur·er \'lu̇(ə)rə(r)\ *n* -s [³*lure* + *-er*] : a worker who rubs felt hats with a lure

²lurer \"\ *n* -s [²*lure* + *-er*] : one that lures

lu·ri \'lu̇rē\ *n, pl* **luri** *or* **luris** *usu cap* : ALUR

lu·rid \'lu̇rəd\ *adj* [L *luridus* pale yellow, sallow; prob. akin to L *lutum* dyer's rocket, yellow] **1 a** : wan and ghastly pale in appearance : LIVID ⟨frightened to death by the ~ waxworks —Sara H. Hay⟩ ⟨the leaves . . . shone ~, livid — they looked as if dipped in sea water —Virginia Woolf⟩ ⟨lights around the two effigies threw them up into ~ distinctness —Thomas Hardy⟩ **b** *archaic* : dingy brown or yellowish brown — used of a plant **c** : of any of several light or medium grayish colors ranging in hue from yellow to orange **2** : shining with the red glow of fire seen through smoke or cloud : suffused with red ⟨~ flames of burning chateaux —C.A. & Mary Beard⟩ ⟨the sun, shining through the smoke . . . seemed blood-red, and threw an unfamiliar ~ light upon everything —H.G.Wells⟩ **3 a** : causing horror or revulsion : HIDEOUS, GRUESOME ⟨~ examples of debauchery and vice —Liam O'Flaherty⟩ ⟨the tabloids gave all the ~ details of floating wreckage and dismembered bodies⟩ **b** : highly colored : EXTRAVAGANT, GAUDY, SENSATIONAL ⟨~ emotionalism and tear-jerking nostalgia —Leslie Rees⟩ ⟨his readings of standard symphonic works seemed ~ and supercharged —Douglas Watt⟩ ⟨~ as any melodrama —S.H.Holbrook⟩ ⟨paperbacks in the usual ~ covers —T.R.Fyvel⟩

lu·rid·ly *adv* **:** in a lurid manner ⟨somewhat ~ described as the sun-blistered, almost uninhabitable refuge of men and women of mystery —Raymond Holden⟩

lu·rid·ness *n* -ES **:** the quality or state of being lurid

lur·ing·ly *adv* [*luring* (pres. part. of 2*lure*) + *-ly*] **:** in an enticing manner

1lurk \ˈlərk, -ə̄k,-əik\ *vi* -ED/-ING/-S [ME *lurken;* akin to Norw *lurke* to move slowly, sneak away, MHG *lūren* to lie in wait, watch — more at LOWER] **1 a :** to lie in ambush **:** PROWL, SKULK ⟨guerrillas ~ in the mountains⟩ ⟨unlicensed traders ~*ing* along the shore —R.A.Billington⟩ ⟨below the surface ~ little beasts of prey —Alice Duncan-Kemp⟩ **b :** to move furtively or inconspicuously **:** SNEAK, STEAL ⟨shall I ~ about this country like a thief —Henry Fielding⟩ ⟨cook ~*s* down before daylight to scour her pots and pans —W.M.Thackeray⟩ **c :** to be constantly present or persist in staying **:** REMAIN, LINGER ⟨melancholy that ~*s* in the eyes of cripples —Ellen Glasgow⟩ ⟨bass which ~ among the cypress knees —*Amer. Guide Series: Tenn.*⟩ ⟨the excitement of the first act still ~*ing* in the air —Richard Fletcher⟩ **2 a :** to be hidden but capable of being discovered **:** be potentially present ⟨wants what he sees, not what may be ~*ing* in the future —Gertrude Atherton⟩ ⟨in the play ~*ed* a wholesome plea for freedom —Leslie Rees⟩ ⟨the obviously genuine humor which ~*ed* behind his utterances —Alvin Redman⟩; *specif* **:** to constitute a latent threat ⟨malaria ~*ed* in the marshy lands —*Amer. Guide Series: Va.*⟩ ⟨these prisoners represent sinister influences that will ~ in the world long after their bodies have returned to dust —R.H.Jackson⟩ **b :** to remain out of sight **:** lie hidden ⟨beating the thickets . . . searching out some spring calves he knew were ~*ing* there —P.B.Kyne⟩ ⟨diamonds were said to ~ in the sand and gravel —Emily Hahn⟩ ⟨treasures . . . might have ~*ed* in the next book to be turned from Greek or Arabic into Latin —R.W.Southern⟩

syn COUCH, SKULK, SLINK, SNEAK: these five words have in common a strong implication of furtive action. LURK often suggests a place of concealment ⟨mountain defiles that concealed *lurking* Indians —*Amer. Guide Series: Oregon*⟩ or a readiness to attack ⟨a hungry shark that was *lurking* at a little distance —Francis Birtles⟩ COUCH (archaic in this sense) is to make oneself inconspicuous for some reason ⟨no vast obscurity or misty vale, where bloody murder . . . can *couch* for fear —Shak.⟩ SKULK usu. carries a strong implication of sinister intention or of cowardice or fear ⟨coyotes *skulking* near the cattle —Zane Grey⟩ ⟨eludes his pursuers and *skulks* off through the swamp —*Amer. Guide Series: Ark.*⟩ ⟨to be eternally conscious of enemies on every side; to *skulk* behind hedges; to hide in holes and corners —Kenneth Roberts⟩ SLINK implies cautious movement to evade observation ⟨a cat *slunk*, a padding shadow, across the white space —Ruth Park⟩ ⟨his way of *slinking* round a corner like a fox —Edith Sitwell⟩ ⟨Hagen *slunk* down the dark stairs, past a sound of snoring —Berton Roueché⟩ SNEAK may add a suggestion of deliberate intent to enter or leave a place or position by sly, indirect, usu. underhanded methods ⟨I *sneak* out of the house and go to a Dairy Company's tea shop —Arnold Bennett⟩ ⟨had to *sneak* into his old laboratory at night with a key he still keeps —D.C. Peattie⟩ ⟨typhoid fever . . . *sneaks* in when sanitation fails —Justina Hill⟩

2lurk \ˈ"\ *n* -S *slang Brit* **:** a method of fraud **:** a trick esp. of a beggar or swindler

lurk·er \-kə(r)\ *n* -S [ME, fr. *lurken* to lurk + *-er*] **1 :** one that lurks **2 :** a rowboat used by English pilchard fishermen

lurk·ing *adj* **1 :** CONCEALED, LATENT ⟨~ danger⟩ ⟨examples of what the nature reporter with the ~ camera may capture —Walt Disney⟩ ⟨~ smile⟩ ⟨search for ~ ambiguities, latent meanings —C.I.Glicksberg⟩ **2 :** PERSISTENT, LINGERING ⟨a ~ skepticism in the breast of the public teacher —Isaac Taylor⟩ ⟨was now far too important . . . to have any ~ regrets —Elinor Wylie⟩ — **lurk·ing·ly** *adv*

1lur·ry \ˈlərē\ *n* -ES [by shortening & alter. fr. *liripipe*] *now dial Eng* **1 :** something repeated by rote (as a formula or canting speech) ⟨turn prayer into a kind of ~ —John Milton⟩ **2 :** a jumble of sounds **:** TUMULT

2lurry \ˈ"\ *vb* -ED/-ING/-ES [origin unknown] *dial Eng* **:** DRAG

3lurry \ˈ"\ *dial Brit var of* LORRY

lurs *pl of* LUR

1lu·sa·tian \lüˈsāshən\ *n* -S *usu cap* [*Lusatia*, former region in eastern Germany between the Elbe and the Oder + E *-an*, n. suffix] **1 :** a native or inhabitant of Lusatia **2 :** WENDISH

2lusatian \ˈ"\ *adj* [*Lusatia* + E *-an*, adj. suffix] **:** of or relating to the language or people of Lusatia

lu·scin·ia \lüˈsinēə\ *n, cap* [NL, fr. L, nightingale] **:** a genus consisting of the nightingales

lus·cious \ˈləshəs\ *adj* [ME *lucius, licius*, perh. by shortening & alter. fr. *delicious*] **1 a :** having a delicious taste or smell **:** juicy and sweet **:** TOOTHSOME, AROMATIC ⟨pears, peaches, and grapes as large, as photogenic, and as ~ —*Better Homes & Gardens*⟩ ⟨~ steaks smothered in onions —Howard Taubman⟩ ⟨pastries and cakes, each more ~ than the other —Anna A. Coombs⟩ ⟨go on producing ~ green fodder even when all other forms of pasture have long since burned up —Henry Wynmalen⟩ **b** *archaic* **:** excessively sweet **:** CLOYING ⟨the last cup . . . is by no means improved by the ~ lump of half-dissolved sugar usu. found at the bottom of it —Sir Walter Scott⟩ **2 :** having sensual appeal **:** arousing sexual desire **:** VOLUPTUOUS, SEDUCTIVE ⟨goddesses, whose round ~ legs and bare feet dangle fetchingly from the clouds —Mary McCarthy⟩ ⟨a picture of a ~ girl getting her dress ripped off by a gunman —F.L.Allen⟩ **3 :** richly luxurious or highly appealing to the senses ⟨a ~ quilted silk eiderdown on the bed —Christopher Isherwood⟩ ⟨~ beauty of tone —Winthrop Sargeant⟩ ⟨the ~ poetry of the garden scene —Arthur Knight⟩; *specif* **:** excessively ornate **:** FLORID ⟨rich and ~ phrases, thick with imagery —Ruth Park⟩ ⟨arrangement . . . too ~ to be thoroughly in key with the master's style —Harold Rogers⟩ **syn** see DELIGHTFUL

lus·cious·ly *adv* **:** in a luscious manner

lus·cious·ness *n* -ES **:** the quality or state of being luscious

1lush \ˈləsh\ *adj* -ER/-EST [ME *lusch* lax, soft, tender, prob. alter. of *lasche* soft, watery, fr. MF, lax, slack, indolent — more at LACHES] **1 a :** vigorously growing **:** producing an abundance of juicy green foliage **:** SUCCULENT, LUXURIANT ⟨~ grass⟩ ⟨~ crops flourished in the rich virgin soil —L.H.Beck⟩ ⟨a ~ and flowery growth of sky-blue delphinium —Louis Bromfield⟩ **b :** characterized by or capable of supporting flourishing vegetation **:** GREEN, FERTILE ⟨a country of ~ pastures and frequent rain —Henry Williamson⟩ ⟨gray cliffs ~ with tropical verdure —David Fairchild⟩ ⟨~ land where farm ground sells at top prices —G.P.Musselman⟩ **2 a :** displaying sturdy vigor or intensity **:** LUSTY, THRIVING ⟨the ~ growth of bureaucracy in . . . collective farms —John Fischer⟩ ⟨the ~ idealism of the prewar period —F.B.Millett⟩ ⟨pictures of ~ organic communities —R.E.Coker⟩ **b :** characterized by abundance **:** GENEROUS, PLENTIFUL ⟨~ appropriations⟩ ⟨~ campaign contributions —Fulton Lewis⟩ ⟨an increasingly ~ supply of aids and suggestions —V.M.Rogers⟩ **c :** characterized by or offering great financial gain **:** PROSPEROUS, PROFITABLE ⟨the ~ profit level of the war years —Gardner Jackson⟩ ⟨able-bodied men . . . hired away by the ~ war industries —R.E.Outman⟩ ⟨firms might lose out on ~ contracts —*Wall Street Jour.*⟩ **3 :** LUSCIOUS: as **a :** AROMATIC, SAVORY, DELICIOUS ⟨a perfume that smells fruity and ~ —*New Yorker*⟩ ⟨made a ~ lattice-topped pie —Myrl C. Boyle⟩ **b :** appealing to the senses **:** SENSUOUS ⟨this pleasant morning . . . ~ with summer languor —Ben Hecht⟩ ⟨using full, ~ orchestras for his accompaniments —*Metronome Yearbook*⟩ ⟨the cop's nasty voice . . . turned ~ with respect —David Driscoll⟩; *specif* **:** VOLUPTUOUS ⟨a ~ blonde with honey-colored hair —S.J.Perelman⟩ **c :** richly ornate **:** LUXURIOUS, OPULENT, SUMPTUOUS ⟨stayed at the Waldorf and had a ~ time —Frances Crane⟩ ⟨cars of ~ design —Alan Moorehead⟩ ⟨business and industrial worlds provide equally ~ salaries —Jeanne K. Beaty⟩ ⟨~, imaginative descriptions of the pageantry in the daily life of the Vatican —Richard McLaughlin⟩; *esp* **:** excessively ornate ⟨a restrained realism which makes other passages seem ~ —Richard Plant⟩ ⟨~ overelaboration and rampant colorism —Wilder Hobson⟩ ⟨sincere and moving despite their ~ sentimentality —*Musical Digest*⟩ **syn** see PROFUSE

2lush \ˈ"\ *n* -ES [origin unknown] **1** *slang* **:** intoxicating liquor **:** DRINK ⟨a good fellow that loveth his ~ —Charles Lever⟩ **2 :** an habitual heavy drinker **:** DRUNKARD, ALCOHOLIC ⟨a lazy ~ with an inordinate appetite for alcohol —Henry Von Rhau⟩ ⟨it becomes the policeman's lot to drive the ~*es* home —A.C. Spectorsky⟩

3lush \ˈ"\ *vb* -ED/-ING/-ES *vi, slang* **:** to indulge in liquor **:** DRINK — often used with *up* ⟨~*ing* up on some autumnal nut-brown ale —Douglass Wallop⟩ ~ *vt* **1** *slang* **:** to drink up (liquor) ⟨shouldn't ~ champagne on an empty stomach —D.G.Gerahty⟩ — often used with *up* **2** *slang* **:** to ply with liquor — often used with *up* ⟨~ themselves up with dry martinis and large whiskeys —*Blackwood's*⟩

lush·burg \ˈləsh,bərg\ *n* -S [ME *lussheburgh*, fr. *Luxemburg*, medieval county and duchy in western Europe] **:** a lightweight imitation of the English silver penny imported from Luxemburg in the reign of Edward III

lu·shei *also* **lu·shai** \(ˈ)lüˈshā\ *n, pl* **lushei** *or* **lusheis** *usu cap* **1 a :** a nomadic Chin or Kuki people of southern Assam **b :** a member of such people **2 :** the Tibeto-Burman language of the Lushei people

lush·er \ˈləshə(r)\ *n* -S *slang* **:** DRUNKARD, SOT

lush·ings \ˈləshə̇nz, ˈlu̇sh-, -shiŋz\ *n pl* [prob. alter. of *lashings*] *dial Brit* **:** PLENTY, ABUNDANCE ⟨you can have both grub and liquor here in ~ —Hume Nisbet⟩

lush·ly *adv* **:** in a lush manner **:** EXTRAVAGANTLY, LUXURIANTLY

lush·ness *n* -ES **:** the quality or state of being lush **:** EXTRAVAGANCE, LUXURIANCE

lush worker *n, slang* **:** one that robs drunks

lushy \ˈləshē, -shi\ *adj* -ER/-EST **:** LUSH

lu·si·an \ˈlüsēən\ *n* -S *cap* [by shortening] **:** LUSITANIAN

1lu·si·ta·nian \ˌlüsəˈtānēən, -nyən\ *n* -S *cap* [*Lusitania*, ancient region corresponding approximately to the greater part of modern Portugal and the Spanish provinces of Salamanca and Cáceres + E *-an*, n. suffix] **1 :** a native or inhabitant of Lusitania **2 :** PORTUGUESE

2lusitanian \ˈ"\ *adj, usu cap* [*Lusitania* + E *-an*, adj. suffix] **1 :** of, relating to, or characteristic of a region of the Iberian peninsula formerly known as Lusitania and almost coinciding with modern Portugal **2 :** PORTUGUESE

lu·si·ta·no-american \ˌlüsəˈtā(ˌ)nō+\ *n, cap L&A* [*Lusitano-* Portuguese, Portuguese and (fr. NL, fr. L *lusitanus* Lusitanian, fr. *Lusitania*) + *American*] **:** a Brazilian wholly or partly of Portuguese descent

lusk·ish \ˈləskish\ *adj* [obs. E *lusk* sluggard (fr. ME, fr. *lusken* to lie hid, be lazy) + E *-ish*] *archaic* **:** somewhat lazy **:** SLUGGISH — **luskishness** *n* -ES *archaic*

luso- *comb form, usu cap* [Pg, fr. *lusitano* Portuguese, fr. L *lusitanus* Lusitanian] **:** Portuguese and ⟨*Luso*-Brazilian⟩

lu·so·ry \ˈlüs(ə)rē, -üz-, -ri\ *adj* [L *lusorius*, fr. *lusus* (past part of *ludere* to play) + *-orius* -ory — more at LUDICROUS] *archaic* **1 :** used in play **2 :** composed in a playful style

1lust \ˈləst\ *n* -S [ME, fr. OE; akin to OHG *lust* pleasure, desire, ON *losti* sexual desire, Goth *lustus* desire, L *lascivus* wanton, playful, Gk *lilaiesthai* to yearn, Skt *laṣati* he yearns, *lasati* he plays] **1** *obs* **a :** PLEASURE, GRATIFICATION, DELIGHT ⟨gazing upon the Greeks with little ~ —Shak.⟩ **b :** personal inclination **:** WISH, WHIM ⟨when I am hence, I'll answer to my ~ —Shak.⟩ **c :** VIGOR, FERTILITY ⟨the increasing ~ of the earth or of the plant —Francis Bacon⟩ **2 :** sexual desire esp. of a violent self-indulgent character **:** LECHERY, LASCIVIOUSNESS ⟨love comforteth, like sunshine after rain, but ~'s effect is tempest after sun —Shak.⟩ ⟨two lonely people . . . drawn together by the nature of their ~*s* (not love) —James Stern⟩ **3 a :** an intense longing **:** CRAVING ⟨an unquenchable ~ to dominate —B.I.Bell⟩ ⟨an insatiable ~ for land —P.W.Gates⟩ ⟨extremest commercialism and the ~*s* of a great city —Robert Russell⟩ ⟨the sea . . . instilling in the restless spirit a ~ for adventure —George Theotokas⟩ **b :** EAGERNESS, ENTHUSIASM ⟨restore your vigor and ~ for living —*Nat'l Geographic*⟩ ⟨was candor incarnate, with a ~ for iconoclasm —W.A.White⟩ **syn** see DESIRE

2lust \ˈ"\ *vb* -ED/-ING/-S [ME *lusten*, fr. *lust*, n.] *vi* **:** to have an intense desire or need **:** have a desire as a ruling passion **:** CRAVE, LONG, YEARN ⟨his bulky body ~*ed* for sleep with every muscle and nerve —S.V.Benét⟩ — often used with *after* ⟨scented . . . a chance of return to the old detective work that his soul ~*ed* after —Rudyard Kipling⟩; *specif* **:** to have a sexual urge ~ *vt, obs* **:** to make a choice of **:** PLEASE ⟨I kings create . . . and, whom I ~, do heap with glory —Edmund Spenser⟩

1lus·ter *or* **lus·tre** \ˈləstə(r)\ *n* -S [ME *lustre*, fr. L *lustrum* — more at LUSTRUM] **:** LUSTRUM 2

2luster *or* **lustre** \ˈ"\ *n* -S [MF *lustre*, fr. OIt *lustro*, fr. *lustrare* to brighten, fr. L; akin to L *lucēre* to shine — more at LIGHT] **1 a :** a glow of reflected light **:** GLOSS, SHEEN ⟨pearl with a beautiful ~⟩ ⟨~ of an enameled surface⟩ ⟨the highest . . . ~ always points to the straight, smooth hairs which are especially apparent in goat hair, such as mohair —Werner Von Bergen⟩; *specif* **:** the appearance of the surface of a mineral as affected by or dependent upon peculiarities of its reflecting qualities ⟨the ~ of minerals can be divided into two types, metallic and nonmetallic —C.S.Hurlbut⟩ ⟨the ~ of micas is splendent, on cleavage faces sometimes pearly —L.V.Pirsson⟩ **b :** a coating or substance that gives luster to a surface ⟨old glass sometimes acquires an iridescent ~ due to weathering⟩ ⟨~*s* are overglaze colors of metallic oxides in an oily medium —D.W.Olson⟩ **2 a :** a glow of light from within **:** LUMINOSITY, SHINE ⟨~ of the stars⟩ ⟨Blue Grotto of the magical ~ —Claudia Cassidy⟩ **b :** an inner beauty **:** RADIANCE ⟨one of those figures of spirit and light that leave an unforgettable ~ in the mind —Gordon Webber⟩ **3 a :** BRILLIANCE, DISTINCTION, RENOWN ⟨many Metropolitan stars were on hand to add ~ to the season —Ann M. Lingg⟩ ⟨his ~, after all, derives not merely from the victories . . . but also from the nobility with which he invested the Arab world —H.M.Sachar⟩ **b** *obs* **:** a distinction that imparts luster ⟨knighthood, which is . . . a ~ to a family —Thomas Habington⟩ **4 a :** a glass pendant used esp. to ornament a candlestick or chandelier **b :** a decorative object (as a chandelier) hung with glass pendants **5 a** *chiefly Brit* **:** a fabric with cotton warp and a filling of luster wool, mohair, or alpaca **b :** LUSTER WOOL **6 :** LUSTERWARE

luster 4b

3luster *or* **lustre** \ˈ"\ *vb* **lustered** *or* **lustred**; **lustered** *or* **lustred**; **lustering** *or* **lustring** \-t(ə)riŋ\ **lusters** *or* **lustres** *vi* **:** to have luster **:** become lustrous **:** GLINT, GLEAM ⟨their feathers ~*ed* in the moonlight as they passed —*Westminster Gazette*⟩ ~ *vt* **1 :** to give luster or distinction to ⟨names that have ~*ed* American literature —W.R.Benét⟩ **2 :** to coat or treat with a substance that imparts luster ⟨~*ed* Majolica was first made by the Arabs and Saracens —Ernst Rosenthal⟩ ⟨~*ed* cotton is . . . weaker than cotton mercerized without tension —G.S.Fraps⟩

4lust·er \ˈləstə(r)\ *n* -S [2*lust* + *-er*] **:** one that lusts

5luster *n* -S [L *lustrum* cave, bog — more at POLLUTE] *obs* **:** CAVE

luster blue *n* **:** a moderate blue that is redder and duller than average copen and redder and deeper than azurite blue or Dresden blue

lus·ter·er \ˈləstərə(r)\ *n* -S **:** one that lusters textiles

lus·ter·less \ˈləstə(r)ləs\ *adj* **:** lacking luster **:** DULL ⟨hair that is dry and ~ —Morris Fishbein⟩ ⟨a lifeless, ~, and spiritless conformity —*New Republic*⟩

lusterware \ˈ==,=\ *n* **:** pottery decorated by applying to the glaze metallic compounds which become iridescent metallic films in the process of firing — called also *luster pottery*

luster wool *n* **:** coarse glossy wool from long-wool sheep (as Lincoln and Leicester) — called also *braid wool*

lust·ful \ˈləstfəl\ *adj* **1 :** full of lust **:** excited or characterized by lust **:** having or expressing powerful unsatisfied desire or craving ⟨~ of power⟩ ⟨looked with ~ eyes upon butter, bread, and pancakes, but eschewed them —W.A.White⟩; *esp* **:** LECHEROUS, LIBIDINOUS ⟨a sensuous grace that roused his ~ nature⟩ **2** *archaic* **:** full of vigor or enthusiasm **:** LUSTY

lust·ful·ly \-fəlē, -li\ *adv* **:** in a lustful manner

lust·ful·ness *n* -ES **:** the quality or state of being lustful

lustick *adj* (*or adv*) [D *lustig*, fr. MD *lustich* — more at LUSTY] *obs* **:** LUSTY, MERRY

lustier *comparative of* LUSTY

lustiest *superlative of* LUSTY

lust·i·head \ˈləstē,hed\ *n* -S [ME *lustyheed*, fr. *lusty* + *-heed*, *-hed*, *-hede* -hood (akin to ME *-hod*, *-had* -hood)] *archaic* **:** LUSTIHOOD

lust·i·hood \-,hu̇d\ *n* -S [*lusty* + *-hood*] **1 :** vigor of body or spirit **:** ROBUSTNESS ⟨to view the panorama of freedom-in-controversy, to hear the pleasing sounds of its ~ —*New Yorker*⟩ **2 :** sexual inclination or capacity ⟨marveled that one hour should bring together such loveliness as hers and his ~ —J.P.Bishop⟩

lust·i·ly \ˈləstə̇lē, -li\ *adv* [ME, fr. *lusty* + *-ly*] **:** in a lusty manner **:** VIGOROUSLY, ENTHUSIASTICALLY

lust·i·ness \-tēnə̇s, -tin-\ *n* -ES [ME *lustinesse*, fr. *lusty* + *-nesse* -ness] **:** the quality or state of being lusty **:** VIGOR, ENTHUSIASM

lusting *pres part of* LUST

lust·less \ˈləstlə̇s\ *adj* [ME *lustles*, fr. 1*lust* + *-les* -less] *obs* **:** lacking vigor **:** LISTLESS, FLACCID ⟨in his ~ limbs . . . a shaking fever reigned continually —Edmund Spenser⟩

lust·ly *adj* **:** LUSTFUL

lus·tral \ˈləstrəl\ *adj* [L *lustralis*, fr. *lustrum* + *-alis* -al] **1 :** of, relating to, or used for purification ⟨~ water⟩ ⟨congregating at this spot and hour for their ~ summer rites —Norman Douglas⟩ **2** *archaic* **:** of or relating to a lustrum **:** QUINQUENNIAL

lus·trate \ˈlə,strāt, *usu* -ād.+V\ *vt* -ED/-ING/-S [L *lustratus*, past part. of *lustrare* to lustrate, brighten, fr. *lustrum*] **:** to cleanse or purify by lustration

lus·tra·tion \(ˌ)ləˈstrāshən\ *n* -S [L *lustration-, lustratio*, fr. *lustratus* + *-ion-, -io* -ion] **1 a :** a purificatory ceremony performed as a preliminary to entering a holy place, as a means of removing bloodguiltiness, on the occasion of a birth, marriage, or death, or as a means of ceremonially cleansing a house, a city, army, or a whole people on some special occasion ⟨~ with water is a prominent feature in Babylonian cult —W.L. Wardle⟩ **b :** an act or instance of cleansing esp. by moral or spiritual purification ⟨the ~ of penitents —Lawrence Durrell⟩ ⟨the Deluge as a type of the world's ~ —F.W.Farrar⟩ **c :** an act of washing **:** ABLUTION ⟨had not lost the . . . habit of personal ~ —D.W.Bone⟩ **2** *archaic* **:** a tour of inspection **:** SURVEY ⟨have made a last ~ of all my walks and haunts, and taken a long farewell —Francis Jeffrey⟩

lus·tra·to·ry \ˈləstrə,tōrē\ *adj* **:** LUSTRAL 1

lustre *var of* LUSTER

lustrical *adj* [L *lustricus* lustral (fr. *lustrum* + *-icus* -ic) + E *-al*] *obs* **:** LUSTRAL

1lus·tring \ˈləstriŋ\ *n* -S [modif. (influenced by *-ing*) of It *lustrino* — more at LUTESTRING] **:** LUTESTRING

2lustring *n* -S [fr. gerund of 3*luster*] **:** a finishing process (as calendering) for giving yarns and cloth a glossy surface or appearance

lus·trous \ˈləstrəs\ *adj* [2*luster* + *-ous*] **1 :** having a gloss or shine **:** GLEAMING, LUMINOUS ⟨Siamese silk in ~ colors —*New Yorker*⟩ ⟨the ~ flame within the opal —Owen Wister⟩ ⟨her eyes were ~ in her pale face —A.J.Cronin⟩ **2 :** shining or radiant through qualities of character or in reputation **:** BRILLIANT, GLAMOROUS, ILLUSTRIOUS ⟨set a ~ example for others to follow —Russell Grenfell⟩ ⟨verse . . . both ~ and deep —Mark Van Doren⟩ ⟨~ actors of the period —H.W. Wind⟩ ⟨it would be hard . . . to make the waterfront saloon setting of "Anna Christie" ~ —John Mason Brown⟩ **syn** see BRIGHT

lus·trous·ly *adv* **:** in a lustrous manner

lus·trous·ness *n* -ES **:** the quality or state of being lustrous

lus·trum \ˈləstrəm\ *n, pl* **lus·trums** \-trəmz\ *or* **lus·tra** \-trə\ [L; akin to L *lucēre* to shine — more at LIGHT] **1 a :** a purification of the whole Roman people made in ancient times after the census which was taken every five years **b :** the Roman census **2 :** a period of five years **:** QUINQUENNIUM ⟨from 1797–1802 they shared a ~ of sympathy and love —George Mallaby⟩

lusts *pl of* LUST, *pres 3d sing of* LUST

lusty \ˈləstē, -ti\ *adj* -ER/-EST [ME; akin to MD *lustich* pleasant, merry, MHG *lustic* pleasant, merry, ON *lostigr* willing, ready; all fr. a prehistoric NGmc-WGmc adjective derived from the noun represented by OE *lust* pleasure with the suffix represented by OE *-ig* -y — more at LUST, -Y] **1** *archaic* **:** MERRY, JOYOUS **2 :** LUSTFUL ⟨had his moments of ~ passion —Winthrop Sargeant⟩ ⟨~ greed in their veins —*Amer. Guide Series: Mich.*⟩ ⟨with the ~ appetite of a buccaneer —Nancy Hale⟩ **3 :** full of vitality **:** ROBUST, FLOURISHING ⟨his six brothers were tall and healthy and ~ —Walter Macken⟩ ⟨when the missing chemicals were replaced, the cane planters began to get ~ crops —Marjory S. Douglas⟩ ⟨a ~ young city sprawling on the lake front —P.W.Gates⟩ ⟨progressive spirit of the ~ young Whig party —V.L.Parrington⟩ **4 a :** full of strength **:** POWERFUL ⟨it was such a ~ shock that it unsettled another rock up the mountain —Burtt Evans⟩ ⟨a tart, ~ wine of the country —John Kobler⟩ ⟨a ~ factor in the wage-price spiral —H.A.Wolff⟩ **b :** unusually large in size **:** CORPULENT, MASSIVE ⟨a huge florid figure of a ~ man —Erle Stanley Gardner⟩ ⟨this ~ veteran of some 700 years is 19 feet in circumference —J.A.M.Muir⟩ **5 :** full of energy or activity **:** FORCEFUL, VIGOROUS ⟨hammers the piano in a ~, untrained way —Donita Ferguson⟩ ⟨people poured forth to give him ~ cheers —Allan Nevins & H.S.Commager⟩ ⟨the ~ days of Elizabethan England swarm to life —*N.Y. Times*⟩ ⟨in the tradition of the great satirists, the ~ haters —H.R.Hays⟩ **syn** see VIGOROUS

lu·sus \ˈlüsəs\ *n* -ES [NL, fr. L, game, fr. *lusus*, past part. of *ludere* to play — more at LUDICROUS] **:** a deviation from the normal **:** FREAK; *esp* **:** SPORT 6

lu·ta·ceous \(ˈ)lüˈtāshəs\ *adj* [L *lutum* mud + E *-aceous*] **:** formed from or having the fine texture of mud **:** CLAYEY — used of conglomerate rock

lu·ta·nist *or* **lu·te·nist** \ˈlüt(ᵊ)nə̇st\ *n* -S [ML *lutanista*, fr. *lutana* lute (prob. fr. MF *lut, leut*) + *-ista* -ist] **:** one who plays a lute

1lute \ˈlüt, *usu* -üd.+V\ *n* -S *often attrib* [ME, fr. MF *lut, leut*, fr. OProv *laut* fr. Ar *al-ʽūd* the oud, fr. *al* the + *ʽūd* oud] **1 :** a stringed musical instrument of Oriental origin that has a large pear-shaped body and a neck with a fretted fingerboard having from 6 to 13 pairs of strings tuned by pegs set in the head and is played by plucking the strings with the fingers **2 :** a harpsichord stop

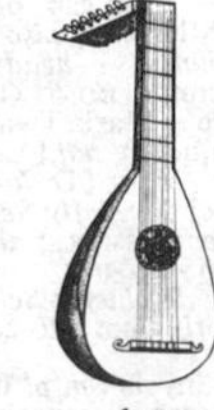

lute

2lute \ˈ"\ *vb* -ED/-ING/-S *vi* **1 :** to play a lute **2 :** to sound like a lute ~ *vt* **:** to play on a lute **:** express by means of a lute

3lute \ˈ"\ *n* -S [ME, fr. L *lutum* mud, clay — more at POLLUTE] **1 :** a substance (as cement or clay) for packing a joint or coating a porous surface to produce imperviousness to gas or liquid **2 :** a packing ring (as of rubber for a fruit jar) **3 :** SEAL 2c(2)

4lute \ˈ"\ *vt* -ED/-ING/-S [ME *luten*, fr. L *lutare*, fr. *lutum* mud, clay] **1 :** to seal or cover with lute ⟨~ a pipe joint⟩ ⟨*luted* his boat with grafting wax —R.L.Cook⟩; *specif* **:** to fill a crevice in half-dry ceramic ware) with wet clay **2 :** to fasten with lute ⟨in the neck of the steel cylinder . . . there was *luted* a vertical glass tube —P.G.Tait⟩

5lute \ˈ"\ *n* -S [D *loet*] **1 :** a straight-edged piece of wood for striking off superfluous clay from a brick mold **2 :** a usu. wooden implement resembling a rake without teeth used in leveling off freshly poured concrete

6lute \ˈ"\ *vt* -ED/-ING/-S **:** to level off (freshly poured concrete) with a lute

lute- *or* **luteo-** *comb form* [NL *luteum* (in *corpus luteum*), fr. L, neut. of *luteus* yellowish, luteous] **:** corpus luteum ⟨*luteal*⟩ ⟨*luteotrophic*⟩

lu·te·al \'lüdēəl, 'lütē-\ *adj* [*lute-* + *-al*] **:** of, relating to, or involving the corpus luteum

lutecium *var of* LUTETIUM

lu·te·fisk \'lüdə,fisk, 'lütə-\ *also* **lu·de·fisk** \'lüdə-\ *or* **lut·fisk** \'lüt,f-\ *or* **lud·fisk** \'lüd,f-\ *n* -s [*lutefisk* fr. Norw, fr. *lute* to wash in lye solution + *fisk* fish; *lutfisk* fr. Sw, fr. *luta* to wash in lye solution + *fisk* fish; *ludefisk* & *ludfisk* fr. Dan *ludefisk*, fr. *lude* to wash in lye solution + *fisk* fish; Norw *lute*, Sw *luta*, Dan *lude* akin to ON *laug* bath, hot spring; Norw & Sw & Dan *fisk* fr. ON *fiskr* fish — more at LYE, FISH] **:** stockfish that has been soaked in lye water, skinned, boned, and boiled

lu·te·in \'lüdēən, 'lütē-\ *n* -s [NL *luteum* (in *corpus luteum*) + E *-in*] **1 :** a red-orange crystalline carotenoid alcohol $C_{40}H_{54}(OH)_2$ occurring esp. in plants usu. with carotenes and chlorophylls but also in animal fat, egg yolk, and corpus luteum; a dihydroxy-α-carotene — called also *xanthophyll* **2 :** a preparation (as a hormone) from corpus luteum

lu·te·in·ization \,=ənə'zāshən, -,nī'z-\ *n* -s [ISV *lutein* + *-ization*] **:** the process of luteinizing

lu·te·in·ize \'==ə,nīz\ *vb* -ED/-ING/-S [ISV *lutein* + *-ize*] *vt* **:** to cause the production of corpora lutea in ~ *vi* **:** to undergo transformation into corpus luteum

luteinizing hormone *n* **:** a hormone of protein-carbohydrate composition that is obtained from the anterior lobe of the pituitary gland and that in the female stimulates the development of corpora lutea and together with follicle-stimulating hormone the secretion of progesterone and in the male the development of interstitial tissue in the testis and the secretion of testosterone — abbr. *LH;* called also *interstitial-cell-stimulating hormone*

lutenist *var of* LUTANIST

lu·teo \'lüdē,ō, 'lütē-\ *adj* [*luteo-*] **:** of, relating to, or being a series of coordination complexes (as of cobalt or chromium) ⟨~ chromic salts⟩ — compare LUTEO- 2

luteo- *comb form* [ISV, fr. L *luteus* yellowish, luteous] **1 :** yellowish **:** yellowish and ⟨*luteo*fuscous⟩ ⟨*luteo*virescent⟩ **2 :** being one of a series of coordination complexes (as of cobalt or chromium) that contain six molecules of ammonia or their equivalent and that in most cases are yellow ⟨*luteo*cobaltic chloride $[Co(NH_3)_6]Cl_3$⟩

lu·teo·fulvous \¦lüd·ēō+\ *adj* [*luteo-* + *fulvous*] **:** tawny yellow

lu·teo·fuscous \"+\ *adj* [*luteo-* + *fuscous*] **:** dusky or blackish yellow

lu·te·o·lin \'lüd·ēələn, 'lütē-, -,lin\ *n* -s [ISV *luteol-* (fr. NL *luteola* — specific epithet of the dyer's rocket *Reseda luteola* — fr. L, fem. of *luteolus* yellowish) + *-in*] **:** a yellow crystalline pigment $C_{15}H_{10}O_6$ occurring usu. as a glycoside in many plants (as dyer's rocket); a tetrahydroxy-flavone

lu·te·o·lous \lü'tēələs\ *adj* [L *luteolus*, fr. *luteus* yellowish, luteous] *biol* **:** slightly yellow **:** YELLOWISH

lu·te·o·ma \,lüd·ē'ōmə\ *n, pl* **luteo·mas** \-məz\ *or* **luteoma·ta** \-məd·ə\ [NL, fr. *lute-* + *-oma*] **:** an ovarian tumor derived from corpus luteum

lu·teo·rufescent \¦lüd·ēō+\ *adj* [*luteo-* + *rufescent*] **:** reddish yellow

lu·teo·trophic \,lüd·ēə¦träfik, -rōf-\ *or* **lu·teo·trop·ic** \-¦träpik\ *adj* [*lute-* + *-trophic* or *-tropic*] **:** acting on the corpora lutea

lu·teo·trophin \,==='trōfən, -räf-\ *or* **lu·teotro·pin** \-rōpən\ *or* **luteotrophic hormone** *n* -s [*luteotrophin*, *luteotropin* fr. *luteotrophic*, *luteotropic* + *-in*] **:** LACTOGENIC HORMONE

lu·te·ous \'lüd·ēəs, 'lütē-\ *adj* [L *luteus*, fr. *lutum* dyer's rocket, yellow + *-eus* -eous — more at LURID] **:** of any of several colors averaging light to moderate greenish yellow

lu·teo·virescent \¦lüd·ēō+\ *adj* [*luteo-* + *virescent*] **:** greenish yellow

lut·er \'lüd·ə(r), 'lütə-\ *n* -s [[4]*lute* + *-er*] **:** one that applies lute; *specif* **:** a worker who seals coke-oven doors with lute — called also *dauber*, *paster*

lutes *pl of* LUTE, *pres 3d sing of* LUTE

lu·tes·cent \(')lü¦tes°nt\ *adj* [L *luteus* yellowish, luteous + E *-escent*] **:** YELLOWISH

lutescent warbler *n* **:** ORANGE-CROWNED WARBLER

lute stern *n* [perh. fr. [1]*lute*] **:** a transom stern particularly adapted for landing on beaches used on small fishing boats in the south of England

lute·string \'lüt,striŋ\ *n* [by folk etymology fr. It *lustrino* sequin, glossy fabric, fr. *lustro* luster — more at LUSTER] **:** a plain glossy silk formerly much used for women's dresses and ribbons

lu·te·tium *also* **lu·te·cium** \lü'tēsh(ē)əm\ *n* -s [*lutetium* fr. NL, fr. L *Lutetia*, town in Gaul (now Paris) + NL *-ium; lutecium* fr. NL, fr. F *Lutèce* (fr. L *Lutetia*) + NL *-ium*] **:** a trivalent metallic element of the rare-earth group usu. associated with ytterbium in the purification steps leading to its isolation — symbol *Lu;* see ELEMENT table

lutfisk *var of* LUTEFISK

luth \'lüth\ *n* -s [F, lit., lute, fr. MF *lut*, *leut* — more at LUTE] **:** LEATHERBACK

[1]**lu·ther·an** \'lüth(ə)rən, -thərn\ *n* -s *usu cap* [Martin *Luther* †1546 Ger. religious reformer + E *-an*, n. suffix] **:** a follower or adherent of Luther or of the doctrines and practices of the Lutheran Church

[2]**lutheran** \"\ *adj, usu cap* [Martin *Luther* + E *-an*, adj. suffix] **:** of or relating to Luther or his doctrines or to the Lutheran Church

lu·ther·an·ism \-th(ə)rə,nizəm\ *n* -s *cap* **:** the doctrines or religious principles taught by Luther or held by the Lutheran Church

lutheran window *n, usu cap L* [*Lutheran* by folk etymology (influence of [2]*lutheran*) fr. earlier *lucane* — more at LUCARNE] **:** DORMER WINDOW

lu·ther·ism \'lüthə,rizəm\ *n* -s *usu cap* [Martin *Luther* + E *-ism*] **1 :** LUTHERANISM **2 :** something characteristic of Luther or his followers

lu·thern \'lüthə(r)n\ *n* -s [prob. by folk etymology (influence of [2]*lutheran*) fr. earlier *lucane* — more at LUCARNE] **:** DORMER WINDOW

lu·thi·er \'lüd·ēə(r)\ *n* -s [F, fr. *luth* lute (fr. MF *lut*, *leut*) + *-ier* -er — more at LUTE] **1 :** a lute maker **2 :** a maker of stringed instruments (as violins)

lu·ti·an·i·dae \¦lüshē'anə,dē, ,lütē'-\ *syn of* LUTJANIDAE

lu·ti·dine \'lüd·ə,dēn, -,dən\ *n* -s [approximate anagram of *toluidine*] **:** any of the dimethyl derivatives $C_5H_3(CH_3)_2N$ of pyridine that are usu. associated with pyridine and the picolines in the bases of coal tar and that are found also in gas liquor

lu·ti·din·ic acid \¦==¦dinik-\ *n* [*lutidinic* ISV *lutidine* + *-ic*] **:** a crystalline acid $C_5H_3N(COOH)_2$ that is isomeric with quinolinic acid and cinchomeronic acid and is made by oxidizing one of the lutidines; 2,4-pyridine-dicarboxylic acid

luting *n* -s [fr. gerund of [4]*lute*] **:** [3]LUTE

lut·ist \'lüd·əst, -ütəst\ *n* -s **1 :** a lute player **2 :** a maker of lutes

[1]**lu·tjanid** \lü'chānəd, -an-\ *adj* [NL *Lutjanidae*] **:** of or relating to the Lutjanidae

[2]**lutjanid** \"\ *n* -s [NL *Lutjanidae*] **:** a member of the Lutjanidae

lu·tjan·i·dae \-'chanə,dē\ *n pl, cap* [NL, fr. *Lutjanus*, type genus + *-idae*] **:** a large family of active carnivorous marine percoid fishes chiefly of rocks and reefs along tropic shores that includes a number of important food fishes — compare SNAPPER

lu·tja·nus \-'chānəs\ *n, cap* [NL, prob. fr. Malay dial. *lutjang*, a fish] **:** a genus of marine percoid fishes that is the type of the family Lutjanidae and includes both important food fishes and a few highly toxic forms

lu·ton \'lüt°n\ *adj, usu cap* [fr. *Luton*, city in southeast central England] **:** of or from the city of Luton, Bedfordshire, England **:** of the kind or style prevalent in Luton

lutong *var of* LOTONG

lu·tra \'lü·trə\ *n, cap* [NL, fr. L *lutra*, *lytra* otter] **:** a genus (family Mustelidae) comprising the common otters of Europe and America

lu·trar·ia \lü'tra(a)rēə\ *n, cap* [NL, fr. L *lutra* otter + NL *-aria*] **:** a genus of edible clams (family Mactridae) related to the surf clams — see OTTER SHELL

lu·tre·o·la \lü'trēələ\ *n, cap* [NL, dim. of L *lutra* otter] *in some classifications* **:** a genus of Mustelidae that comprises the minks and is usu. included as a subgenus in *Mustela*

lu·trine \'lü,trīn, 'lü·trən\ *adj* [ML *lutrinus*, fr. L *lutra* otter + *-inus* -ine] **:** of or relating to the otters

lu·tu·am·i·an \,lüd·ə'wamēən\ *n, pl* **lutuamian** *or* **lutuamians** *usu cap* **1 a :** an Indian people of Oregon and northern California **b :** a member of such people **2 :** a language family of Oregon comprising Klamath and Modoc

lutulent *adj* [L *lutulentus*, fr. *lutum* mud + *-ulentus* -ulent — more at POLLUTE] *obs* **:** TURBID

lutz \'lůts\ *n* -ES *usu cap* [prob. irreg. fr. Gustave *Lussi* b1898 Swiss figure skater, its inventor] **:** a figure-skating jump in which the skater makes his takeoff from the back outside edge of one skate, rotates counterclockwise, and lands on the back outside edge of the other skate

lu·var·i·dae \lü'varə,dē\ *n pl, cap* [NL, fr. *Luvarus*, type genus (fr. It dial. *lùvaru* louvar) + *-idae* — more at LOUVAR] **:** a family of scombroid fishes comprising the louvar

lu·wi \'lü(,)wē\ *n, pl* **luwi** *or* **luwis** *usu cap* **1 :** an ancient people of the southern coast of Asia Minor **2 :** a member of the Luwi people

[1]**lu·wi·an** \'lüwēən\ *also* **lu·ian** \'lüyən\ *or* **lu·vi·an** \-üvēən\ *adj, usu cap* [*Luwi* + E *-an*, adj. suffix] **1 :** of, relating to, or characteristic of the Luwi or their country (Luya) **2 :** of, relating to, or characteristic of the Luwian language

[2]**luwian** \"\ *n* -s *usu cap* **:** the Anatolian language of the Luwi people known chiefly from quotations in Hittite documents — see INDO-EUROPEAN LANGUAGES table

[1]**lux** *vt* -ED/-ING/-ES [F *luxer*, fr. L *luxare*] *obs* **:** LUXATE

[2]**lux** \'ləks\ *n, pl* **lux** *or* **luxes** [L, light — more at LIGHT] **:** a unit of illumination equal to the direct illumination on a surface that is everywhere one meter from a uniform point source of one candle **:** a unit of illumination that is equal to one lumen per square meter

lux·ate \'lək,sāt, *usu* -ād·+V\ *vt* -ED/-ING/-S [L *luxatus*, past part. of *luxare*, fr. *luxus* dislocated — more at LOCK (of hair)] **:** to throw out of place or joint **:** DISPLACE, DISLOCATE ⟨the . . . fractured and *luxated* teeth were removed —*Dental Abstracts*⟩ ⟨a *luxated* patella⟩

lux·a·tion \,lək'sāshən\ *n* -s [LL *luxation-*, *luxatio*, fr. L *luxatus* + *-ion-*, *-io* -ion] **:** the act of luxating or state of being luxated **:** DISPLACEMENT, DISLOCATION

luxe \'ləks\ *n* -s [L *luxus* — more at LUXURY] **:** the quality or state of being sumptuous **:** LUXURY, ELEGANCE ⟨furs and Edwardian ~ —Cyril Connolly⟩ — compare DELUXE

lux·em·bourg *or* **lux·em·burg** \'ləksəm,bůrg, -bůəg *also* 'lük- *or* -,bərg *or* -,bəg *or* -,bəig; 'ləksəm,bərg, -bəg,-bəig *also* -bůrg *or* -bůəg\ *adj, usu cap* [*Luxembourg*, *Luxemburg*, city and grand duchy in western Europe] **:** of or from the grand duchy of Luxembourg or the city of Luxembourg, its capital **:** of the kind or style prevalent in Luxembourg **:** LUXEMBOURGIAN

lux·em·bourg·er *or* **lux·em·burg·er** \-gə(r)\ *n* -s *cap* **:** a native or inhabitant of the duchy of Luxembourg

[1]**lux·em·bourg·i·an** *or* **lux·em·burg·i·an** \¦==¦gēən\ *adj, usu cap* **1 :** of, relating to, or characteristic of Luxembourg **2 :** of, relating to, or characteristic of the people of Luxembourg

[2]**luxembourgian** \"\ *n* -s *cap* **:** the Germanic speech of Luxembourg

luxmeter \'=,==\ *also* **lux·om·e·ter** \lək'sämǝd·ǝ(r)\ *n* [*luxmeter* ISV *lux* + *-meter; luxometer* fr. *lux* + *-o-* + *-meter*] **:** an illuminometer giving its indications in luxes

lux·u·ri·ance \(,)ləg'zhůrēən(t)s, (,)lək'shůr-\ *n* -s [fr. *luxuriant*, after such pairs as E *assistant: assistance*] **:** the quality or state of being luxuriant **:** RICHNESS, PROLIFERATION

lux·u·ri·an·cy \-nsē, -si\ *n* -ES [*luxuriant* + *-cy*] *archaic* **:** LUXURIANCE

lux·u·ri·ant \-nt\ *adj* [L *luxuriant-*, *luxurians*, pres. part. of *luxuriare* to luxuriate] **1 a :** yielding or capable of yielding abundance **:** FRUITFUL, PRODUCTIVE ⟨placid undulating ~ country —J.C.Powys⟩ **b :** characterized by abundant growth **:** LUSH, FLOURISHING ⟨this damp and mild climate makes possible the most ~ forest growth —C.D.Forde⟩ ⟨*Canna indica* was planted and it flourished, growing a most ~ crop —Edward Samuel⟩ ⟨regular features, ~ side-whiskers and mustache —F. L.Hise⟩ **2 a :** exuberantly rich and varied **:** PROLIFIC, INVENTIVE ⟨all the ~ human life that pours out upon a traveler who knocks on many doors —J.T.Flexner⟩ ⟨a ~ mythology has . . . populated the universe with explanatory spirits —S.C.Pepper⟩ ⟨~ and vital imagery —Eunice Glenn⟩ **b :** excessively elaborate **:** FLORID ⟨a master of ~ prose . . . too often entangled in his own metaphors —Nicolas Slonimsky⟩ **3 :** characterized by luxury **:** LUXURIOUS, ELEGANT ⟨gay companies in ~ restaurants —Theodore Dreiser⟩ **syn** see PROFUSE

lux·u·ri·ant·ly *adv* **:** in a luxuriant manner

lux·u·ri·ate \-ē,āt, *usu* -ād·+V\ *vi* -ED/-ING/-S [L *luxuriatus*, past part. of *luxuriare*, fr. *luxuria* luxury] **1 a :** to grow profusely **:** FLOURISH, THRIVE ⟨in the nearby conservatory ~ tropical plants —Aubrey Drury⟩ **b :** to develop extensively **:** PROLIFERATE, EXPAND ⟨this globe . . . that ~*s* into a million forms of riotously breeding life —Will Durant⟩ ⟨around these ~*s* a free and unsymmetrical, yet ordered decoration of spiral curves —O. Elfrida Saunders⟩ ⟨the art department . . . had *luxuriated* as an easy refuge for the football player and the dilettante —F.H.Taylor⟩ **2 a :** to abandon oneself to pleasure **:** live luxuriously **:** indulge oneself ⟨we have taken a very charming little cottage . . . for the whole summer and I am going to ~ there in wanton splendor —H.J.Laski⟩ ⟨gives few interviews . . . ~*s* in no autographing parties —J.K. Hutchens⟩ **b :** to find enjoyment **:** take delight **:** REVEL ⟨was *luxuriating* in a good cigar —B.L.K.Henderson⟩ ⟨*luxuriated* in the admiration and intellectual comradeship of newfound friends —W.R.Parker⟩ ⟨tried to ~ in his own self-pity —Hanama Tasaki⟩

lux·u·ri·ous \-,ēəs\ *adj* [ME, fr. MF *luxurieux*, fr. L *luxuriosus*, fr. *luxuria* luxury, excess + *-osus* -ose] **1 :** of, relating to, or expressive of esp. unrestrained gratification of the senses ⟨gave a cautious sniff, and then a ~ one —Jan Struther⟩ ⟨the bottomland corn . . . rustled thickly, a ~, arousing sound —Max Steele⟩ ⟨that sense of tears in mortal things, that sort of ~ melancholy —Norman Birkett⟩; *often* **:** LECHEROUS, SENSUAL, VOLUPTUOUS ⟨a peep show presenting the choicest erotic fantasies evolved in the course of the most ~ civilizations —*Saturday Rev.*⟩ **2 a :** pleasure loving **:** fond of luxury or self-indulgence **:** SYBARITIC ⟨a ~ nobility having regard neither for toil nor for temperance —J.D.Hart⟩ ⟨a sophisticate who defends his ~ tastes and his simple conviction that the best is quite good enough for him —R.A.Cordell⟩ **b :** characterized by opulence, sumptuousness, or rich abundance ⟨imagined . . . her husband installed in a ~ suite of rooms —W.S. Maugham⟩ ⟨~ privileges which seem to be reserved for . . . officials —H.S.Canby⟩ ⟨never before . . . has the work been led so suavely, so powerfully, or with so ~ a sound —Virgil Thomson⟩ ⟨a ~ cargo of wine, olive oil, and candied tropic fruits —Elinor Wylie⟩; *specif* **:** excessively ornate ⟨a ~ piece of late romantic writing, heavily orchestrated —Edward Sackville-West & Desmond Shawe-Taylor⟩ **3 :** LUXURIANT ⟨~ vegetation⟩ ⟨tossed his ~ black mane —Eleanor Clark⟩

syn LUXURIOUS, SUMPTUOUS, and OPULENT can apply to something obviously or ostentatiously rich or magnificent. LUXURIOUS implies choice and costly and is often used to refer to that which provides unusual physical ease and gratification ⟨a *luxurious* home with every comfort⟩ ⟨a mass of gorgeous upholstery and a labyrinth of *luxurious* architecture —G.K. Chesterton⟩ ⟨the place is *luxurious*, with gay cabañas on the shore of a lake, with fencing and riding teachers, beautiful flower gardens, and various recreational facilities —*Amer. Guide Series: Maine*⟩ ⟨lighting a cigarette and stretching out his legs in *luxurious* contentment —J.C.Powys⟩ ⟨evenings of *luxurious* quiet after toil —Adrian Bell⟩ SUMPTUOUS implies extravagantly rich, splendid, or luxurious ⟨a velvet gown, *sumptuous* and wine-purple, with a white ruff that stood up . . . high and stiff —Edmund Wilson⟩ ⟨*sumptuous* as the processional colors of the forest —Elinor Wylie⟩ ⟨a *sumptuous* breakfast of hot cakes, fresh eggs and coffee and prime cold venison —Walter O'Meara⟩ OPULENT stresses an extreme richness or sometimes a flaunting luxuriousness ⟨the *opulent* court of an Indian rajah⟩ ⟨*opulent* color, used mainly in pictures of nudes and still life —Eric Newton⟩ ⟨wild *opulent* growth —Duncan Phillips⟩ ⟨the table spread with *opulent* hospitality . . . the baked ham at one end and the saddle of roast mutton at the other, with fried chicken, oysters, crabs, sweet potatoes, jellies, custards —V.L.Parrington⟩ **syn** see in addition SENSUOUS

lux·u·ri·ous·ly *adv* **:** in a luxurious manner

lux·u·ri·ous·ness *n* -ES **:** the quality or state of being luxurious

[1]**lux·u·ry** \'ləksh(ə)rē, 'ləgzh-, -ri\ *n* -ES [ME *luxurie*, fr. MF, fr. L *luxuria* luxury, excess; akin to L *luxus* luxury, excess, and prob. to L *luxus* dislocated — more at LOCK (of hair)] **1** *archaic* **:** LECHERY, LUST ⟨stained with adulterous ~ —John Marston⟩ **2 a :** an habitually sumptuous environment or way of life ⟨princes of the Renascence lavished upon private ~ . . . enormous amounts of money —Lewis Mumford⟩ **b :** an elegant appointment or material aid to the achievement of luxury ⟨the sharp gaze of a woman . . . condemned the details of this chamber that imitated every ~ —Arnold Bennett⟩ **c :** a nonessential item or service that contributes to luxurious living **:** an indulgence in ornament or convenience beyond the indispensable minimum **:** EXTRAVAGANCE ⟨expensive shotguns and other *luxuries* —Thomas Munro⟩ ⟨sent her off . . . in a taxi, which was evidently a ~ for her: she protested about the expense —Edmund Wilson⟩ ⟨allowing no money to be wasted on whims and *luxuries* until necessities have been thoroughly served —G.B.Shaw⟩ **3 :** a means or source of pleasurable experience or personal satisfaction **:** COMFORT, SELF-INDULGENCE ⟨dropping into a plush-covered armchair, a ~ she seldom allowed herself —L.P.Hartley⟩ ⟨for the rich and titled, snobbery is not a superfluous ~, but a necessity —Aldous Huxley⟩ ⟨the Senate is small and can afford the ~ of very loose rules —D.W.Brogan⟩ ⟨Western European states . . . could no longer afford the ~ of full independence and freedom of action in foreign affairs —F.L.Schuman⟩ **4 :** LUXURIOUSNESS ⟨a period of ~, when racecourses, wine cellars, and balls reached their apogee —*Amer. Guide Series: Va.*⟩ ⟨nobody wants to banish ~ of language from the theater —Kenneth Tynan⟩ ⟨the fabrics . . . lacked richness and ~ of handling —E.I.Cohen⟩

[2]**luxury** \"\ *adj* **:** of or relating to luxury or luxuries or catering to luxurious tastes **:** SUMPTUOUS, NONESSENTIAL ⟨~ liner⟩ ⟨~ resort⟩ ⟨~ goods⟩ ⟨laughter, a ~ reflex, is without survival value —Isaac Rosenfeld⟩

luxury consumption *n* **:** the absorption of nitrogen or potash from the soil by a crop in excess of crop needs

lux·us \'ləksəs\ *n* -ES [L, luxury, excess] **:** SUPERFLUITY

luzern *obs var of* LUCERNE

lu·zu·la \'lüzyələ\ *n, cap* [NL, fr. It *luzziola*, *lucciola* (in *erba luzziola*, *erba lucciola* adder's-tongue)] **:** a genus of perennial herbs (family Juncaceae) resembling grass or rushes and having leaves and young stems frequently hairy and flowers crowded, umbeled, or in spikes — see WOOD RUSH

lv *abbr* **1** lava **2** leave

LV *abbr* **1** legal volt **2** licensed victualer **3** light vessel **4** low voltage

lve *abbr* leave

lvov \lə'vōf\ *adj, usu cap* [fr. *Lvov*, city in western Ukraine, U.S.S.R.] **:** of or from the city of Lvov, U.S.S.R. **:** of the kind or style prevalent in Lvov

lvs *abbr* leaves

LW *abbr* **1** left wing **2** long wave **3** low water

LWB *abbr* long wheelbase

lwe·na \lə'wānə\ *n, pl* **lwena** *or* **lwenas** *usu cap* **1 a :** a people of Angola and the Kabompo district of Northern Rhodesia **b :** a member of such people **2 :** a Bantu language of the Lwena people

LWL *abbr* **1** length at waterline **2** load waterline

LWM *abbr* low-water mark

[1]**lwo** *or* **lwoo** \lə'wō\ *n* -s *usu cap* **:** a division of the Nilotic languages including Shilluk, Acholi, Alur, Lango, and Luo

[2]**lwo** *usu cap, var of* LUO

LWP *abbr* load water plane

lx *abbr* lux

LXX [fr. the Roman numeral for 70] *symbol* Septuagint

ly *abbr* langley

[1]**-ly** \lē,li\ *adj suffix, usu* -ER/-EST [ME *-lich*, *-ly*, *-li*, fr. OE *-lic*, *-līc;* akin to OFris & OS *-līk* -ly, MD *-lijc*, OHG *-līh*, *-lih*, ON *-ligr;* all fr. a Gmc noun represented by OE *līc* body, corpse — more at LIKE] **1 :** like in appearance, manner, or nature **:** having the characteristics of ⟨queen*ly*⟩ ⟨father*ly*⟩ ⟨woman*ly*⟩ **2 :** expressing regular recurrence in stated units of time **:** every ⟨hour*ly*⟩ ⟨dai*ly*⟩ ⟨week*ly*⟩

[2]**-ly** \"; *in -l(e)ly words pronunciation of only one l is usual if the nucleus of the next-to-the-last syllable is an unstressed vowel or a syllabic l, less frequent if the nucleus is a stressed vowel*\ *adv suffix, usu* -ER/-EST [ME *-liche*, *-ly*, *-li*, fr. OE *-līce*, *-lice*, fr. *-līc*, *-lic* (adj. suffix)] **1 :** in a (specified) manner ⟨slow*ly*⟩ **:** in the manner of a ⟨soldier*ly*⟩ **:** from a (specified) standpoint

ly·all·pur \'līl,pů(ə)r, ,=='=\ *adj, usu cap* [fr. *Lyallpur*, Pakistan] **:** of or from the city of Lyallpur, Pakistan **:** of the kind or style prevalent in Lyallpur

ly·am \'līəm\ *n* -s [ME *lyame*, *lyeme*, fr. MF *liem* leash, bond, fr. L *ligamen* band, tie — more at LIEN] *archaic* **:** LEASH

lyam-hound \'==,=\ *n, archaic* **:** BLOODHOUND

ly·art \'līərt\ *also* **ly·ard** \-rd\ *adj* [ME, fr. MF *liart*, fr. OF] **1** *chiefly Scot* **:** streaked with gray **2** *chiefly Scot* **:** VARIEGATED

lyas *var of* LIAS

lyc- *or* **lyco-** *comb form* [NL, fr. Gk *lyk-*, *lyko-*, fr. *lykos* — more at WOLF] **:** wolf ⟨*Lyco*podium⟩

ly·cae·na \lī'sēnə\ *n, cap* [NL, fr. Gk *lykaina*, fem. of *lykos* wolf] **:** a genus (the type of the family Lycaenidae) comprising small slender butterflies with the upper surface of the wings usu. metallic blue, green, or copper and the undersurface dull or cryptic

[1]**ly·cae·nid** \-nəd\ *adj* [NL *Lycaenidae*] **:** of or relating to the family Lycaenidae

[2]**lycaenid** \"\ *n* -s **:** a butterfly of the family Lycaenidae

ly·cae·ni·dae \-nə,dē\ *n pl, cap* [NL, fr. *Lycaena*, type genus + *-idae*] **:** a family of small often brilliantly colored butterflies having the forelegs short in the male and including the blues, coppers, and hairstreaks

ly·can·thrope \'līkən,thrōp; lī'kan(t)hrəp, -n,thrōp\ *n* -s [NL *lycanthropus*, fr. Gk *lykanthrōpos* werewolf, fr. *lyk-* + *anthrōpos* man, human being — more at ANTHROP-] **1 :** a person displaying lycanthropy **2 :** WEREWOLF

ly·can·throp·ic \¦līkən¦thräpik\ *adj* **:** of or relating to lycanthropy

ly·can·thro·pist \lī'kan(t)thrəpəst\ *n* -s **:** LYCANTHROPE

ly·can·thro·pous \(')=¦==pəs\ *adj* **:** LYCANTHROPIC

ly·can·thro·py \-pē\ *n* -ES [NL *lycanthropia*, fr. Gk *lykanthrōpia*, fr. *lykanthrōpos* werewolf + *-ia* -y] **1 :** a delusion that one has become or has assumed the characteristics of a wolf or other predatory animal **2 :** the assumption of the form and characteristics of a wolf held to be possible through the practice of witchcraft or magic

ly·ca·on \lī'kāən, -ā,än\ *n, cap* [NL, fr. L, mythological king of Arcadia who was transformed into a wolf, fr. Gk *Lykaōn*] **:** a genus of animals containing the African hunting dog

ly·cée \(')lē¦sā\ *n* -s [F, fr. MF, lyceum, fr. L *Lyceum*] **:** a state-maintained secondary school esp. in France that prepares students for the university

ly·ce·um \(')lī¦sēəm, 'lī,sēəm\ *n* -s *often attrib* [L *Lyceum*, gymnasium near ancient Athens where Aristotle taught, fr. Gk *Lykeion*, fr. neut. of *Lykeios*, epithet of Apollo whose temple was nearby] **1 :** a place for holding lectures or public discussions **2 a :** an institution or movement providing public lectures, concerts, and entertainments and generally furthering education **b :** a local branch of such a lyceum **3 :** a secondary school in continental Europe; *specif* **:** LYCÉE **4** *Brit* **:** a bombastic and outmoded theatrical style

lychee *var of* LITCHI

lych-gate *or* **lich-gate** \'lich,=\ *n* [ME *lycheyate*, fr. *lyche*, *lich* lich + *yate* gate] **:** a roofed gate in a churchyard under which a bier rests during the initial part of the burial service

lych-gate

lych·nis \'liknəs\ *n* [NL, fr. L, a red flower, fr. Gk; akin to

Gk *lychnos* lamp, *leukos* bright, white — more at LIGHT] **1** *cap* **:** a large genus of herbs (family Caryophyllaceae) having sepals united into a tube or cup, usu. 5 styles, and fruit in the form of a capsule with 5 or 10 teeth — compare SILENE **2** -ES **:** any plant of the genus *Lychnis*

lych·no·scope \ˈliknə,skōp\ *n* [Gk *lychnos* lamp + E *-scope*] **:** LOW SIDE WINDOW — **lych·no·scop·ic** \ˌ≈≈ˈskäpik\ *adj*

¹ly·cian \ˈlish(ē)ən *sometimes* ˈlisēən\ *adj, usu cap* [L *lycius*, adj & n., Lycian (fr. Gk *lykios*, fr. *Lykia* Lycia, ancient district in Asia Minor) + E *-an*] **1 :** of, relating to, or characteristic of ancient Lycia, a region of southern Asia Minor **2 :** of, relating to, or characteristic of the people of Lycia

²lycian \"\ *n* -s *usu cap* [L *Lycius*, n., Lycian + E *-an*] **1 :** a native or inhabitant of ancient Lycia **2 :** an Anatolian language known from a small body of inscriptions from southwestern Asia Minor dating from the 5th and 4th centuries B.C. — see INDO-EUROPEAN LANGUAGES table

¹lycid \ˈlīsəd, ˈlis-\ *adj* [NL *Lycidae*] **:** of or relating to the family Lycidae

²lycid \"\ *n* -s **:** a beetle of the family Lycidae

lyc·i·dae \ˈlisə,dē\ *n pl, cap* [NL, fr. *Lycus*, type genus (fr. Gk *lykos* wolf) + *-idae* — more at WOLF] **:** a family of soft-bodied mainly tropical beetles that are usu. marked with a bold pattern of orange or brown and black, have disagreeable qualities to many predators, and are mimicked by numerous edible insects

lyci·um \ˈlis(h)ēəm\ *n, cap* [NL, fr. Gk *lykion*, a thorn from Lycia, fr. neut. of *Lykios* Lycian] **:** a genus of shrubs or trees (family Solanaceae) having simple leaves and tubular campanulate flowers — see MATRIMONY VINE

lyco- — see LYC-

ly·cod·i·dae \līˈkädə,dē\ [NL, fr. *Lycodes*, type genus (fr. Gk *lykōdēs* wolflike, fr. *lyk-* lyc- + *-ōdēs* -ode) + *-idae*] *syn of* ZOARCIDAE

ly·co·pene \ˈlīkə,pēn\ *n* -s [ISV *lycop-* (fr. NL *Lycopersicon*) + *-ene*; orig. formed as G *lycopen*] **:** a red crystalline open-chain unsaturated hydrocarbon $C_{40}H_{56}$ that is the coloring matter of the tomato and many berries and other fruits and is isomeric with carotene

ly·co·per·da·ce·ae \,līkō(,)pərˈdāsē,ē\ *n pl, cap* [NL, fr. *Lycoperdon*, type genus + *-aceae*] **:** a family of fungi (order Lycoperdales) comprising the puffballs and having a spherical fruiting body with a flexible peridium of two or three layers enclosing a chambered gleba that appears solid and white when young and at maturity is filled with masses of powdery dark spores

ly·co·per·da·les \-ä(,)lēz\ *n pl, cap* [NL, fr. *Lycoperdon*, genus of fungi + *-ales*] **:** a small order of basidiomycetes comprising the puffballs, earthstars, and sometimes a few other closely related fungi and having a fleshy often globose fruiting body filled at maturity with a mass of dustlike spores

ly·co·per·doid \ˌ≈≈ˈpər,dȯid\ *adj* [NL *Lycoperdon* + E *-oid*] **:** of, relating to, or resembling the genus *Lycoperdon*

ly·co·per·don \ˌ≈≈ˈ≈,dän\ *n, cap* [NL, fr. *lyc-* + Gk *perdesthai* to break wind — more at FART] **:** a genus of fungi (family Lycoperdaceae) whose fruiting body tapers toward a base consisting of spongy mycelium

lycoperdon nut *n* **:** a subterranean fungus (*Elaphomyces cervinus*) resembling a puffball — compare HART'S TRUFFLE

ly·co·per·si·con \-ˈpərsə,kän\ *n, cap* [NL, irreg. fr. Gk *lykopersion*, an Egyptian plant] **:** a genus of So. American herbs (family Solanaceae) having anthers projected into sharp or narrow sterile tips — see TOMATO

ly·co·per·si·cum \-səkəm\ [NL, fr. *Lycopersicon*] *syn of* LYCOPERSICON

ly·co·phore \ˈlīkə,fō(ə)r\ *n* -s [prob. fr. *lyc-* + *-phore*] **:** DECACANTH

ly·co·pod \-,päd\ *n* -s [NL *Lycopodium*] **:** a plant of the genus *Lycopodium* or of the order Lycopodiales

ly·co·po·di·a·ce·ae \ˌ≈≈,pōdēˈāsē,ē\ *n pl, cap* [NL, fr. *Lycopodium*, type genus + *-aceae*] **:** a family of plants (order Lycopodiales) characterized by leaves without ligules, variably rounded strobili, and homosporous reproduction — compare CLUB MOSS

ly·co·po·di·a·les \-ā(,)lēz\ *n pl, cap* [NL, fr. *Lycopodium*, genus of plants + *-ales*] **:** an order of plants (subdivision Lycopsida) coextensive with the family Lycopodiaceae or extended to include also Selaginellaceae and Isoetaceae

ly·co·po·din·e·ae \,līkəpōˈdinē,ē\ *n pl, cap* [NL, fr. *Lycopodium*, genus of plants + *-ineae*] **:** a class of plants coextensive with the subdivision Lycopsida

ly·co·po·di·tes \,līkəpōˈdīd·(,)ēz\ *n, cap* [NL, fr. *Lycopodium* + *-ites*] **:** a genus of fossil plants that resemble present-day lycopods

ly·co·po·di·um \,līkəˈpōdēəm\ *n* [NL, fr. *lyc-* + *-podium*] **1** *cap* **:** a large genus (the type of the family Lycopodiaceae) of erect or creeping plants that have evergreen one-nerved leaves in four to many ranks and are often used in Christmas decorations — see CLUB MOSS, GROUND FIR, GROUND PINE **2** *or* **lycopodium powder :** a fine yellowish flammable powder composed of the spores of a club moss (as *Lycopodium clavatum*) and used as a dusting powder for the skin and for the surface of hand-rolled pills and as a component of fireworks and flashlight powders

¹ly·cop·sid \(ˈ)līˈkäpsəd\ *adj* [NL *Lycopsida*] **:** of or relating to the Lycopsida

²lycopsid \"\ *n* -s [NL *Lycopsida*] **:** a plant of the subdivision Lycopsida

ly·cop·si·da \līˈkäpsədə\ *n pl, cap* [NL, fr. L *lycopsis*, a plant + NL *-ida*] **:** a subdivision of Tracheophyta coextensive with the class Lycopodineae comprising vascular plants (as the club mosses and related forms) with small leaves, sessile and adaxial sporangia, and no leaf gaps in the primary vascular cylinder — compare PSILOPSIDA, PTEROPSIDA, SPHENOPSIDA

ly·cop·sis \-səs\ *n, cap* [NL, fr. L, a plant, bugloss, fr. Gk *lykopsis*, prob. fr. *lyk-* lyc- + *-opsis*] **:** a genus of bristly herbs (family Boraginaceae) with small blue flowers in terminal scorpioid racemes — see BUGLOSS

ly·co·pus \ˈlīkəpəs\ *n, cap* [NL, fr. *lyc-* + *-pus*] **:** a small genus of nonaromatic mints having two stamens in each flower — see BUGLEWEED, WATER HOREHOUND

ly·co·rine \līˈkōrən, ˈlīkə,rīn\ *n* -s [NL *Lycoris*, genus of plants (fr. L, a woman's name) + E *-ine*] **:** a poisonous crystalline alkaloid $C_{16}H_{17}NO_4$ found in the bulbs of the common daffodil and several other amaryllids

ly·co·sa \līˈkōsə\ *n, cap* [NL, fr. L *lycos*, a spider, fr. Gk *lykos*, lit., wolf — more at WOLF] **:** a genus (the type of the family Lycosidae) of spiders including the wolf spiders

¹ly·co·sid \-səd\ *adj* [NL *Lycosidae*] **:** of or relating to the family Lycosidae

²lycosid \"\ *n* -s [NL *Lycosidae*] **:** a spider of the family Lycosidae

ly·cosi·dae \līˈkōsə,dē, -käs-\ *n pl, cap* [NL, fr. *Lycosa*, type genus + *-idae*] **:** a cosmopolitan family of relatively large active ground spiders that catch their prey by pursuit rather than in a web

¹lyc·tid \ˈliktəd\ *adj* [NL *Lyctidae*] **:** of or relating to the family Lyctidae

²lyctid \"\ *n* -s [NL *Lyctidae*] **:** a beetle of the family Lyctidae

lyc·ti·dae \-tə,dē\ *n pl, cap* [NL, fr. *Lyctus*, type genus + *-idae*] **:** a family of small elongate wood-boring beetles — see POWDER-POST BEETLE

lyc·tus \-təs\ *n* [NL, fr. L, ancient city in Crete, fr. Gk *Lyktos*] **1** *cap* **:** the type genus of the family Lyctidae **2** -ES **:** any beetle of the genus *Lyctus*

lydd·ite \ˈli,dīt\ *n* -s [*Lydd*, England, near which it was first tested + E *-ite*] **:** a high explosive composed chiefly of picric acid

ly·del·la \līˈdelə\ *n, cap* [NL, fr. *Lyda*, genus of flies (fr. L *Lydus* Lydian, fr. Gk *Lydos*) + *-ella*] **:** a genus of small tachinid flies including one (*L. stabulans grisescens*) of importance in the biological control of the European corn borer

lyd·ga·tian line \(ˈ)lidˈgāshən-\ *n, usu cap 1st L* [John *Lydgate* †*ab*1451 Eng. poet + E *-ian*] **:** BROKEN-BACKED LINE

¹lyd·i·an \ˈlidēən\ *adj, usu cap* [L *lydius* Lydian (fr. Gk *lydios*, fr. *Lydia*, ancient country in Asia Minor) + E *-an*] **1 a :** of, relating to, or characteristic of Lydia, an ancient country of western Asia Minor **b :** of, relating to, or characteristic of the people of Lydia **2 :** of, relating to, or characteristic of the music of Lydia ⟨soft *Lydian* airs —John Milton⟩

²lydian \"\ *n* -s *cap* [L *lydius*, adj., Lydian + E *-an*] **1 :** a native or inhabitant of ancient Lydia **2 :** an Anatolian language known from a small body of inscriptions from Asia Minor dating from the 4th century B.C. or earlier — see INDO-EUROPEAN LANGUAGES table

lydian mode *n, usu cap L* [trans. of Gk *harmonia lydia*] **1 :** a Greek mode consisting of two disjunct tetrachords represented on the white keys of the piano by a descending diatonic scale from C to C — see GREEK MODE illustration **2** [trans. of ML *modus Lydius*] **:** an authentic ecclesiastical mode represented on the white keys of the piano by an ascending diatonic scale from F to F — see MODE illustration

lydian stone *n, usu cap L* [trans. of L *lapis lydius*, trans. of Gk *lydia lithos*] **:** TOUCHSTONE

lydian tetrachord *n, usu cap L* **:** a descending tetrachord in ancient Greek music consisting of a half step followed by two whole steps

lyd·ite \ˈli,dīt\ *n* -s [G *lydit*, fr. *Lydien* Lydia + G *-it* -ite] **:** TOUCHSTONE

¹lye \ˈlī\ *n* -s [ME *lye, leye, lie*, fr. OE *lēag, lēah*; akin to MD *lōghe* lye, OHG *louga* lye, ON *laug* bath, hot spring, L *lavare, lavere* to wash, bathe, OIr *lūaith* ashes, Gk *louein* to wash, Arm *loganam* I bathe] **1 a :** a strong alkaline liquor that contains chiefly potassium carbonate obtained by leaching wood ashes with water and that has been used esp. in soapmaking and washing **b :** a strong alkaline solution (as of sodium hydroxide or potassium hydroxide) ⟨caustic ~⟩ — compare ²CAUSTIC 1 **2 :** a solution obtained by lixiviation **:** a solid caustic — called also *concentrated lye*

²lye \"\ *vt* **lyed; lyed; lying; lyes :** to treat with lye

lye hominy *n* **:** hominy prepared from kernels of grain that have been soaked in lye to remove the hulls

lyeng \lēˈeŋ\ *n, pl* **lyeng** *or* **lyengs** *usu cap* **1 :** a Naga people chiefly in an area northwest of Manipur valley **2 :** a member of the Lyeng people

lye-peeled \ˈ≈ˌ≈\ *adj* **:** subjected to lye peeling

lye peeling *n* **:** the process of removing the peels of fruits and vegetables by immersion in a lye solution

ly·ery \ˈlīəri\ *adj* [*lyer*, alter. of *lire* + *-y*] *dial Eng* **:** having little fat in the flesh — used of cattle

¹ly·gae·id \(ˈ)līˈjēəd\ *adj* [NL *Lygaeidae*] **:** of or relating to the family Lygaeidae

²lygaeid \"\ *n* -s [NL *Lygaeidae*] **:** a true bug of the family Lygaeidae

ly·gae·idae \līˈjēə,dē\ *n pl, cap* [NL, fr. *Lygaeus*, type genus (fr. Gk *lygaios* shadowy) + *-idae*] **:** an extensive family of plant-sucking often brilliantly colored true bugs — see CHINCH BUG

ly·ge·um \līˈjēəm\ *n, cap* [NL, fr. Gk *lygos* flexible twig, withe — more at LOCK (tuft of hair)] **:** a genus of grasses having two or three one-flowered spikelets that unite to form a hard false fruit — see ESPARTO

ly·gi·nop·te·ris \,līgəˈnäptərəs\ *n, cap* [NL, fr. Gk *lyginos* of withe (fr. *lygos* withe + *-inos* -ine) + NL *-pteris*] **:** a genus of Carboniferous seed ferns having a stem with mesarch siphonostele, large accumulation of pith, and marked development of secondary wood

ly·go·des·mia \,līgōˈdezmēə\ *n, cap* [NL, fr. Gk *lygo-* (fr. *lygos* withe) + *desmos* band, bond, *desmē* bundle + NL *-ia* — more at DESM-] **:** a genus of wiry-stemmed No. American weedy herbs (family Compositae) — see SKELETON WEED 2

ly·go·di·um \līˈgōdēəm\ *n, cap* [NL, fr. Gk *lygōdēs* like a willow (fr. *lygos* willow, withe) + NL *-ium*] **:** a genus of mostly tropical ferns (family Schizaeaceae) characterized by twining fronds that have mostly opposite pairs of pinnae below and sporophylls above — see CLIMBING FERN

ly·go·so·ma \,līgəˈsōmə\ *n, cap* [NL, fr. Gk *lygo-* (fr. *lygos* withe) + NL *-soma*] **:** a genus of scincoid lizards having a slender form with limbs reduced or lacking

ly·gus \ˈlīgəs\ *n* [NL] **1** *cap* **:** a large genus of small plant-sucking mirid bugs some of which are vectors of virus diseases of plants **2** *pl* **lygus :** LYGUS BUG

lygus bug *n* **:** a bug of the genus *Lygus* (as the tarnished plant bug)

¹lying *pres part of* LIE *or of* LYE

²lying *adj* [ME *leghynge*, fr. pres. part. of *leghen, leyen* to lie — more at LIE] **1 :** given to falsehood ⟨a ~ witness⟩ **2 :** calculated to mislead **:** FALSE, UNTRUE ⟨a whole world of false conceptions and ~ sentimentality —Harrison Smith⟩ ⟨silly newspapers and magazines for the circulation of ~ advertisements —G.B.Shaw⟩ **syn** see DISHONEST

lying-in \ˌ≈≈ˈ≈\ *n, pl* **lyings-in** *or* **lying-ins** [ME *lyynge yn*, fr. *lyynge, liynge*, gerund of *lien, ligen* to lie + *yn, in* in (adv.) — more at LIE, IN] **:** the state attending and consequent to childbirth **:** CONFINEMENT

ly·ing·ly *adv* [ME *leeiyyngli*, fr. *leeiyyng, leghynge* lying + *-li* -ly] **:** in a lying manner **:** FALSELY

lying press *n* **:** a press in which sheets or books are held by lateral pressure for various bookbinding operations — called also *laying press*

lyke-wake \ˈlī,kwāk\ *n* [ME *lych wake*, fr. *lych, lich* lich + *wake*] *now chiefly Scot* **:** the night watch kept over a corpse — compare ²WAKE 3a

lyle gun \ˈlī(ə)l-\ *n, usu cap L* [after David A. *Lyle* †1937 Am. officer, U. S. Army, its inventor] **1 :** a mounted gun that resembles a small brass cannon and is used to fire a projectile attached to a line of rope to an extreme range of about 700 yards in rescue operations at sea **2 :** a firing device that resembles a short shotgun and is used to propel a weight attached to a line of rope in rescue operations at sea or on land (as in fire fighting) — called also *line-throwing gun*

lym *n* -s [ME *lyam*, fr. *lyame, lyeme* leash — more at LYAM] *obs* **:** BLOODHOUND

ly·man·tria \līˈman·trēə\ *n, cap* [NL, fr. Gk *lymantēr* destroyer + NL *-ia*] **:** the type genus of Lymantriidae

¹ly·man·tri·id \-ēəd\ *adj* [NL *Lymantriidae*] **:** of or relating to the family Lymantriidae

²lymantriid \"\ *n* -s [NL *Lymantriidae*] **:** a moth of the family Lymantriidae

ly·man·tri·idae \,līmənˈtrīə,dē\ *n pl, cap* [NL, fr. *Lymantria*, type genus + *-idae*] **:** a family of moths comprising certain typical tussock moths and having larvae that are distinguished by a dense coat of often urticating hairs and that include many destructive pests which attack trees and other economic plants

lyme \ˈlīm\ *var of* LYAM

lyme grass \ˈ≈-\ *n* [prob. fr. obs. E *lyme* birdlime (fr. ME *lyme, lim* birdlime) + E *grass* — more at LIME] **:** a grass of the genus *Elymus*

lyme-hound \ˈ≈ˌ≈\ *var of* LYAM-HOUND

lym·naea \limˈnēə, ˈ≈≈≈\ *n, cap* [NL, irreg. fr. Gk *limnaios* of the marsh, fr. *limnē* marsh, pool — more at LIMN-] **:** a genus of snails formerly almost coextensive with the family Lymnaeidae but now comprising comparatively few species of dextrally coiled freshwater snails that include some of importance as intermediate hosts of flukes of medical or veterinary interest — compare FOSSARIA, GALBA

¹lym·nae·id \-ēəd\ *adj* [NL *Lymnaeidae*] **:** of or relating to the family Lymnaeidae

²lymnaeid \"\ *n* -s [NL *Lymnaeidae*] **:** a snail of the family Lymnaeidae

lym·nae·idae \limˈnēə,dē\ *n pl, cap* [NL, fr. *Lymnaea*, type genus + *-idae*] **:** a family of thin-shelled air-breathing freshwater snails (suborder Basommatophora) that have an elongate ovoidal shell with a large opening and a simple lip and that include numerous species important as intermediate hosts of trematode worms

lymph \ˈlim(p)f\ *n, pl* **lymphs** \-m(p)fs, -mps\ [L *lympha*, alter. of earlier *limpa, lumpa*, modif. of Gk *nymphē* nymph — more at NUPTIAL] **1** *archaic* **:** a spring or stream of water **:** pure clear water ⟨dips her shining ankles in the ~ —E.R.B.Lytton⟩ ⟨receive the baptismal ~ —George Borrow⟩ **2** *archaic* **:** the sap of plants ⟨that moved the pure and subtle ~ through the . . . veins of leaf and flower —William Cowper⟩ **3** [NL *lympha*, fr. L, water] **:** a pale coagulable fluid that bathes the tissues, passes into lymphatic channels and ducts, and is discharged into the blood by way of the thoracic duct, and that consists of a liquid portion resembling blood plasma, numerous white blood cells, and normally no red blood cells — compare CEREBROSPINAL FLUID, CHYLE

lymph- *or* **lympho-** *comb form* [NL *lympha*] **1 :** lymph ⟨*lympho*genic⟩ **2 :** lymphatic tissue ⟨*lymph*enteritis⟩ **3 :** lymphocytes ⟨*lympho*protease⟩ ⟨*lympho*taxis⟩

lym·phad \ˈlim,fad\ *n* -s [ScGael *long-fhada*, fr. *long* ship + *fada* long] **1 :** a small one-masted galley **2 :** a heraldic representation of a lymphad

lymphad 2

lym·pha·den \ˈlim(p)fə,den\ *n* -s [NL, fr. *lymph-* + Gk *adēn* gland — more at ADEN-] **:** LYMPH GLAND

lymph·ad·e·ni·tis \,lim,fadᵊnˈīd·əs, ,lim(p)fə,deˈnī-\ *n* -ES [NL, fr. *lymphaden* + *-itis*] **:** inflammation of lymph glands

lym·phad·e·noid \(ˈ)limˈfadᵊn,ȯid, ˈlim(p)fəˈde,nȯid\ *adj* [NL *lymphaden* + E *-oid*] **:** resembling or having the properties of a lymph gland

lymph·ad·e·no·ma \,lim,fadᵊnˈōmə, ,lim(p)fə,deˈnō-\ *n, pl* **lymphadenomas** \-məz\ *or* **lymphadenoma·ta** \-məd·ə\ [NL, fr. *lymphaden* + *-oma*] **1 :** LYMPHOMA **2 :** HODGKIN'S DISEASE

lymph·ad·e·nop·a·thy \-ᵊnˈäpəthē, -eˈnä-\ *n* [NL *lymphaden* + E *-o-* + *-pathy*] **:** abnormal enlargement of lymph glands

lymph·ad·e·no·sis \-ᵊnˈōsəs, -eˈnō-\ *n, pl* **lymphadeno·ses** \-ō,sēz\ [NL, fr. *lymphaden* + *-osis*] **:** any of certain abnormalities or diseases affecting the lymphatic system: as **a :** leukosis involving lymphatic tissues **b :** LYMPHATIC LEUKEMIA **c :** INFECTIOUS MONONUCLEOSIS

lymphangi- *or* **lymphangio-** *comb form* [NL, fr. *lymphangion* lymphatic vessel, fr. *lymph-* + Gk *angeion* vessel, blood vessel — more at ANGI-] **:** lymphatic vessels ⟨*lymphangi*ectasis⟩ ⟨*lymphangio*logy⟩

lym·phan·gi·al \(ˈ)limˈfanjēəl\ *adj* [*lymphangi-* + *-al*] **:** of or relating to the lymphatic vessels

lymph·an·gi·o·ma \,lim,fanjēˈōmə\ *n, pl* **lymphangiomas** \-məz\ *or* **lymphangioma·ta** \-məd·ə\ [NL, fr. *lymphangi-* + *-oma*] **:** a tumor formed of dilated lymphatic vessels — compare ANGIOMA — **lym·phan·gi·om·a·tous** \(ˌ)≈ˌ≈≈ˈämədəs, -ˈōm-\ *adj*

lym·phan·gi·tis \,lim,fanˈjīd·əs\ *n, pl* **lymphangit·i·des** \-ˈjidə,dēz\ [NL, fr. *lymphangi-* + *-itis*] **:** inflammation of the lymphatic vessels

lymphangitis ep·i·zo·ot·i·ca \-,epəzəˈwäd·əkə\ *n* [NL] **:** EPIZOOTIC LYMPHANGITIS

lymphangitis ul·ce·ro·sa \-,əl(t)səˈrōsə\ *n* [NL] **:** PSEUDOGLANDERS

¹lym·phat·ic \(ˈ)limˈfad·ik, -at|, |ēk\ *adj* [L *lymphaticus* frantic, frenzied, fr. *lympha*, *lumpa* water, water goddess, modif. of Gk *nymphē* nymph, water goddess; influenced by Gk *nympholēptos* frenzied, caught by nymphs — more at NUPTIAL, NYMPHOLEPT] **1 a :** of, relating to, or produced by lymph, lymphoid tissue, or lymphocytes ⟨~ nodules⟩ ⟨~ infiltration⟩ **b :** conveying lymph ⟨a ~ channel⟩ **2** *or* **lym·phat·i·cal** \|əkəl, |ēk-\ *archaic* **:** FRENZIED **3 a** *of a person* **:** having a dull pallid complexion and slack often puffy tissues suggestive of or accompanied by a lymphatic temperament **b** *of a temperament* **:** characterized by lack of energy and indisposition to physical or mental exertion ⟨a beautiful and stupid woman of ~ type —E.C.Bentley⟩ ⟨the bacon hog is less ~ and more active and animated —A.L.Anderson⟩ — **lym·phat·i·cal·ly** \|ək(ə)lē, |ēk-, -li\ *adv*

²lymphatic \"\ *n* -s **1** *or* **lymphatical** *archaic* **:** LUNATIC **2 :** a vessel that contains or conveys lymph, that originates as an interfibrillar or intercellular cleft or space in a tissue or organ, and that if small has no distinct walls or walls composed only of endothelial cells and if large resembles a vein in structure — see THORACIC DUCT

lymphatic leukemia *n* **:** leukemia marked by proliferation of lymphoid tissue, abnormal increase of leukocytes in the circulating blood, and enlargement of lymph nodes

lym·pha·tism \ˈlim(p)fə,tizəm\ *n* -s [ISV *lymphat-* (fr. ¹*lymphatic*) + *-ism*] **1 :** lymphatic temperament **2 :** STATUS LYMPHATICUS

lymphato- *comb form* [ISV *lymphat-* (fr. ¹*lymphatic*) + *-o-*] **:** lymphatic tissue ⟨*lymphato*lysin⟩ ⟨*lymphato*lysis⟩

lymph cell *also* **lymph corpuscle** *n* **:** a cell in lymph; *specif* **:** LYMPHOCYTE

lymph·ede·ma *also* **lymph·oe·de·ma** \ˈlim(p)f+\ *n* [NL, fr. *lymph-* + *edema* or *oedema*] **:** edema due to faulty lymphatic drainage

lymph follicle *n* **:** LYMPH GLAND; *esp* **:** LYMPH NODULE

lymph gland *or* **lymph node** *n* **:** one of the rounded masses of lymphoid tissue surrounded by a capsule of connective tissue that occur in various parts of the body in the course of the lymphatic vessels and that consist of a reticulum of connective tissue fibers in the meshes of which are contained numerous small round cells each having a large round deeply staining nucleus and when carried off by the lymph flowing through the gland becoming a lymphocyte

lymph heart *n* **:** a contractile muscular expansion of a lymphatic vessel that serves to drive the lymph toward the veins (as in some amphibians)

lymph nodule *n* **:** a small simple lymph gland

lympho- — see LYMPH-

lym·pho·blast \ˈlim(p)fə,blast\ *n* [ISV *lymph-* + *-blast*] **1 :** a cell giving rise to lymphocytes **2 :** a primitive undifferentiated hemocyte — used only by those who consider that all blood cells have a common origin; compare MYELOBLAST — **lym·pho·blas·tic** \ˌ≈≈ˈblastik\ *adj*

lym·pho·blas·to·ma \ˌ≈≈,blaˈstōmə\ *n, pl* **lymphoblastomas** \-məz\ *or* **lymphoblastoma·ta** \-məd·ə\ [NL, fr. ISV *lymphoblast* + NL *-oma*] **:** any of several diseases of lymph glands marked by the formation of tumorous masses composed of mature or immature lymphocytes

lym·pho·blas·to·sis \-ōsəs\ *n, pl* **lymphoblasto·ses** \-ō,sēz\ [NL, fr. ISV *lymphoblast* + NL *-osis*] **:** the presence of lymphoblasts in the peripheral blood (as in acute lymphatic leukemia or infectious mononucleosis)

lym·pho·cys·tis disease \,lim(p)fəˈsistəs-\ *n* [NL *lymphocystis*, fr. *lymph-* + Gk *kystis* bladder, pouch — more at CYST] **:** a skin disease of the walleye that is characterized by ulceration and the formation of irregular pinkish lumps in skin and fins and is usu. held to be of virus origin

lym·pho·cyte \ˈlim(p)fə,sīt\ *n* -s [ISV *lymph-* + *-cyte*] **:** a colorless weakly motile cell produced in lymphoid tissue that is the typical cellular element of lymph and constitutes 20 to 30 percent of the leukocytes of normal human blood where it occurs either as the small lymphocyte of about 0.01 millimeter in diameter with large round deeply staining nucleus and narrow rim of clear cytoplasm or as the less common large lymphocyte that is regarded by some as an immature stage of the small one — **lym·pho·cyt·ic** \ˌ≈≈ˈsid·ik\ *adj*

lymphocytic choriomeningitis *n* **:** an acute virus disease characterized by fever, nausea and vomiting, headache, stiff neck, and slow pulse, marked by the presence of numerous lymphocytes in the cerebrospinal fluid, and transmitted esp. by rodents and bloodsucking insects

lym·pho·cy·to·genesis \,lim(p)fə,sīd·ə+\ *n* [NL, fr. ISV *lymphocyte* + NL *-o-* + L *genesis*] **:** LYMPHOPOIESIS

lym·pho·cy·to·ma \ˌ≈≈,sīˈtōmə\ *n, pl* **lymphocytomas** \-məz\ *or* **lymphocytoma·ta** \-məd·ə\ [NL, fr. ISV *lymphocyte* + NL *-oma*] **1 :** a tumor in which lymphocytes are the dominant cellular elements **2 :** LYMPHOCYTOMATOSIS

lym·pho·cy·to·ma·to·sis \-,tōməˈtōsəs\ *n, pl* **lymphocytomato·ses** \-ō,sēz\ [NL, fr. *lymphocytomat-*, *lymphocytoma* + *-osis*] **:** an abnormal condition characterized by the formation of lymphocytomas; *specif* **:** a neoplastic disease of the common fowl marked by lymphocytoma formation and extensive lymphocytic infiltration of the tissues that is commonly regarded as a manifestation of the avian leukosis complex but may be an independent infective process

lym·pho·cy·to·pe·nia \-,sīd·əˈpēnēə\ *n* -s [NL, fr. ISV *lymphocyte* + NL *-o-* + *-penia*] **:** a decrease in the normal number of lymphocytes in the circulating blood

lym·pho·cy·to·poiesis \,lim(p)fə,sīd·ə+\ *n, pl* **lymphocytopoieses** [NL, fr. ISV *lymphocyte* + NL *-o-* + *-poiesis*] **:** formation of lymphocytes usu. in the lymph glands

lym·pho·cy·to·sis \-,sīˈtōsəs\ *n, pl* **lymphocyto·ses** \-ō,sēz\ [NL, fr. ISV *lymphocyte* + NL *-osis*] **:** increase in the number of lymphocytes in the blood usu. associated with chronic inflammations and some infectious diseases (as tuberculosis and syphilis) — compare GRANULOCYTOSIS, MONOCYTOSIS

lym·pho·cy·tot·ic \¦==sī¦täd·ik\ *adj* [fr. NL *lymphocytosis*, after such pairs as NL *hypnosis*: E *hypnotic*] **:** of or relating to lymphocytosis

lymphoedema *var of* LYMPHEDEMA

lym·phog·e·nous \(ˈ)limˈfäjənəs\ *also* **lym·pho·gen·ic** \ˌlim(p)fə¦jenik\ *adj* [*lymph-* + *-genous* or *-genic*] **1 :** producing lymph or lymphocytes **2 :** arising or resulting from lymphocytes or lymphatics ⟨a ~ spread of infection⟩

lym·pho·granuloma \ˌlim(p)fə+\ *n, pl* **lymphogranulomas** *or* **lymphogranulomata** [NL, fr. *lymph-* + *granuloma*] **1 :** a granuloma or a nodular swelling of a lymph node **2** *or* **lymphogranuloma ve·ne·re·um** \-vəˈnirēəm\ *also* **lymphogranuloma in·gui·nale** \-ˌiŋgwəˈna(ˌ)lē, -ā(-, -äl-\ [*lymphogranuloma venereum* fr. NL, venereal lymphogranuloma; *lymphogranuloma inguinale* fr. NL, inguinal lymphogranuloma] **:** a contagious venereal disease that is caused by various strains of a rickettsia (*Chlamydia trachomatis*) and is marked by swelling and ulceration of lymphatic tissues in the iliac and inguinal regions

lym·pho·gran·u·lo·ma·to·sis \ˌlim(p)fəˌgranyəˌlōməˈtōsəs\ *n, pl* **lymphogranulomato·ses** \-ōˌsēz\ [NL, fr. *lymphogranulomat-*, *lymphogranuloma* + *-osis*] **1 :** the development of benign (as in sarcoidosis) or malignant (as in Hodgkin's disease) lymphogranulomas in various parts of the body **2 :** a condition characterized by lymphogranulomas

lymph·oid \ˈlimˌfȯid\ *adj* [ISV *lymph-* + *-oid*] **1 :** of, relating to, or resembling lymph **2 :** of, relating to, or resembling the tissue characteristic of the lymph glands

lymphoid cell *n* **:** the characteristic lymphocyte-producing cell of the lymph glands

lym·phoid·o·cyte \limˈfȯidəˌsīt\ *n* -s [ISV *lymphoid* + *-o-* + *-cyte*] **:** HEMOCYTOBLAST

lym·phol·y·sis \limˈfäləsəs\ *n, pl* **lympholy·ses** \-əˌsēs\ [NL, fr. *lymph-* + *lysis*] **:** the destruction of lymph cells

lym·pho·lyt·ic \ˌlim(p)fəˈlid·ik\ *adj* **:** causing or characterized by lympholysis

lym·pho·ma \limˈfōmə\ *n, pl* **lymphomas** \-məz\ *or* **lympho·ma·ta** \-məd·ə\ [NL, fr. *lymph-* + *-oma*] **:** a tumor of lymphoid tissue — **lym·phoma·tous** \(ˈ)lim¦fäməd·əs, -fōm-\ *adj*

lym·pho·ma·toid \limˈfōməˌtȯid\ *adj* [NL *lymphomat-*, *lymphoma* + E *-oid*] **:** characterized by or resembling lymphomas ⟨a ~ tumor⟩

lym·pho·ma·to·sis \(ˌ)limˌfōməˈtōsəs\ *n, pl* **lymphomato·ses** \-ōˌsēz\ [NL, fr. *lymphomat-*, *lymphoma* + *-osis*] **:** the presence of multiple lymphomas in the body; *specif* **:** a phase of the avian leukosis complex in which the viscera are infiltrated with lymphocytes and lymphomas are widely distributed in the various organs — see NEUROLYMPHOMATOSIS

lym·pho·ma·tot·ic \(ˌ)=¦=¦==¦täd·ik\ *adj* [fr. NL *lymphomatosis*, after such pairs as NL *hypnosis*: E *hypnotic*] **:** of or relating to lymphomatosis

lym·pho·path·ia ve·ne·re·um \ˌlim(p)fəˈpathēəvəˈnirēəm\ *n* [NL, lit., venereal lymph disease] **:** LYMPHOGRANULOMA 2

lym·pho·pe·nia \-ˈpēnēə\ *n* -s [NL, fr. *lymph-* + *-penia*] **:** reduction in the number of lymphocytes circulating in the blood of man or animals

lym·pho·poi·e·sis \-ˌpȯiˈēsəs\ *n, pl* **lymphopoie·ses** \-ēˌsēz\ [NL, fr. *lymph-* + *-poiesis*] **:** the formation of lymphocytes or lymphatic tissue

lym·pho·poi·et·ic \¦==pȯi¦ed·ik\ *adj* [ISV *lymph-* + *-poietic*] **:** of or relating to lymphopoiesis

lym·pho·sarcoma \ˌlim(p)fō+\ *n* [NL, fr. *lymph-* + *sarcoma*] **:** a malignant lymphoma tending to metastasize freely esp. along the regional lymphatic drainage

lym·pho·spo·rid·i·o·sis \"+spəˌridēˈōsəs\ *n, pl* **lympho·sporidio·ses** \-ōˌsēz\ [NL, fr. *lymph-* + *sporidium* + *-osis*] **:** EPIZOOTIC LYMPHANGITIS

lymph·ous \ˈlim(p)fəs\ *adj* [*lymph* + *-ous*] **:** resembling lymph

lymphs *pl of* LYMPH

lymph sac *n* **:** an extensive dorsal subcutaneous space that opens into a lymph heart of a frog or toad

lymph-vascular \ˈ=¦===\ *adj* [*lymphatic* + *vascular*] **:** of, relating to, or containing lymphatic vessels

lyn *or* **lynn** *var of* ²LINN

lyn·ce·an \(ˈ)lin¦sēən, ˈlin(t)sē-\ *adj* [L *Lynceus* of Lynceus, sharp-sighted (fr. Gk *Lynkeios*, fr. *Lynkeus*, mythological member of the Argonauts who was famous for his sharpness of sight) + E *-an*] *archaic* **:** SHARP-SIGHTED

¹**lynch** \ˈlinch\ *or* **lyn·chet** \ˈlinchət\ *n, pl* **lynches** *or* **lynchets** [*lynch* alter. of *linch*, alter. of ¹*link*; *lynchet* alter. of *linch* + *-et*] **1** *Brit* **:** a terrace or ridge on the face of a down **2** *Brit* **:** a ridge or strip of unplowed land forming a boundary between fields

²**lynch** \ˈlinch\ *vt* -ED/-ING/-ES [*lynch* law] **1 a** *archaic* **:** to beat or otherwise do physical violence to by mob action ⟨had been ~*ed*, tarred and feathered, and sent down the Missouri on a frail raft —*Lawrence (Kansas) Republican*⟩ **b :** to hang or otherwise kill by mob action in punishment of a presumed crime or offense ⟨had recently been ~*ed* by burning —S.C.Webster⟩ **2 :** to subject to scorn, defamation, or ridicule by violent attack in speech or writing ⟨liberalism . . . had not been condemned in the court of human reason, but ~*ed* outside of it —M.R. Cohen⟩ —**lynch·er** \-chə(r)\ *n* -s

lynching *n* -s **1 a :** the act of a mob or group that lynches **b :** an instance of this act **2 :** LYNCH LAW

lynch law *n* [prob. after William *Lynch* †1820 Am. vigilante] **:** the act or practice by a self-constituted court of condemning a person and usu. inflicting death upon him for a presumed crime or offense without due process of law

lynchpin *var of* LINCHPIN

lyn·cine \ˈlinˌsīn\ *adj* [L *lync-*, *lynx* + E *-ine*] **:** of or relating to a lynx

lynn·ha·ven \linˈhāvən\ *n* [fr. *Lynnhaven*, Va.] **:** a large oyster typically from Virginia or Maryland waters — compare BLUEPOINT

lynx \ˈliŋ(k)s\ *n* [L, fr. Gk; fr. its light color or its sharp sight; akin to OE *lox* lynx, OHG *luhs*, MD *los*, Lith *lūšis* lynx, Skt *ruśat* light, Gk *leukos* white, bright — more at LIGHT] **1 a** *pl* **lynx** *or* **lynxes :** any of various wildcats that have relatively long legs, a short stubby tail, and often tufted ears and that yield a valuable fur varying in color from pale grayish buff to black-spotted tawny: as (1) **:** the common lynx (*Lynx lynx*) of northern Europe and Asia (2) **:** BAY LYNX (3) **:** CANADA LYNX (4) **:** SPOTTED LYNX **b** *cap* [NL, fr. L] **:** the genus of Felidae or subgenus of *Felis* comprising these animals **2** *pl* **lynx** *or* **lynxes :** the fur or pelt of a lynx

lynx 1a(1)

lynx cat *n* **1 :** a pale grayish very slightly spotted lynx (*Lynx uinta*) of the intermountain region of the western U.S. and southern British Columbia **2** *Southwest* **:** BAY LYNX

lynx-eyed \ˈ=¦=\ *adj* **:** SHARP-SIGHTED ⟨*lynx-eyed* for scandal or for romance —Donn Byrne⟩

lynxlike \ˈ=ˌ=\ *adj* **:** resembling a lynx esp. in alertness

lyo- *comb form* [prob. fr. NL, fr. Gk *lyein* to loose, dissolve, release + NL *-o-* — more at LOSE] **1 :** lacking **:** rudimentary in ⟨*Lyomeri*⟩ **2 :** looseness **:** dispersion ⟨*lyophilic*⟩

ly·om·eri \līˈäməˌrī\ *n pl, cap* [NL, fr. *lyo-* + *-meri* (fr. Gk *meros* part) — more at MERIT] **:** a small order of fragile soft-bodied deep-sea fishes with large mouth and minute eyes — see GULPER, PELICAN FISH

ly·om·er·ous \(ˈ)lī¦ämərəs\ *adj* [NL *Lyomeri* + E *-ous*] **:** of or relating to the Lyomeri

ly·on bean \ˈlīən-\ *n, usu cap L* [after William S. *Lyon* †1916 Am. botanist] **:** a tropical Asian plant (*Stizolobium niveum*) grown in the southern U.S. and elsewhere for forage

lyon court \"-\ *n, usu cap L&C* [*lyon*, obs. var. of *lion*] **:** a lawcourt and administrative office in Scotland that is headed by the Lord Lyon King of Arms, has jurisdiction over the bearing and display of armorial ensigns, and maintains the public registers of Scottish armorial bearings and genealogies — called also *Court of the Lord Lyon*

ly·o·ne·tia \ˌlīəˈnēsh(ē)ə\ *n, cap* [NL, fr. Pierre *Lyonet* (also, *Lyonnet*) †1789 Dutch entomologist + NL *-ia*] **:** a genus of moths that is the type of the family Lyonetiidae

¹**ly·o·netid** \¦==¦ned·əd\ *adj* [NL *Lyonetiidae*] **:** of or relating to the family Lyonetiidae

²**lyonetid** \"\ *n* -s **:** a moth of the family Lyonetiidae

ly·o·ne·ti·idae \ˌlīənəˈtīəˌdē\ *n pl, cap* [NL, fr. *Lyonetia*, type genus + NL *-idae*] **:** a family of very small tineoid lepidoptera whose larvae are leaf miners

ly·on herald \ˈlīən-\ *n, usu cap L&H* [ME (Sc. dial.) *leon heraud*, fr. *leon* lion + *heraud* herald; fr. the representation of a lion on the royal shield — more at LION, HERALD] **1 :** the chief of the royal heralds in medieval and 16th century Scotland **2 :** LYON KING OF ARMS

ly·o·nia \līˈōnēə\ *n, cap* [NL, fr. John *Lyon* †*ab*1818 Scot. gardener and collector of American plants + NL *-ia*] **:** a genus of upright shrubs (family Ericaceae) that have white or pinkish flowers in axillary or terminal clusters with urceolate or cylindric corolla, anthers opening by terminal pores, and a capsular many-seeded fruit

ly·on king of arms \ˈlīən-\ *also* **lyon** *n, pl* **lyon kings of arms** *also* **lyons** *usu cap L&K&A* [*lyon*, obs. var. of *lion*] **:** the chief officer of arms in Scotland who sits as judge in Lyon Court, grants patents of arms, supervises the Scottish heralds and pursuivants in the preparation and conduct of state, public, and royal ceremonial, and is also controller of the royal messengers-at-arms

ly·on·naise \ˈlīəˌnāz, ˌ==ˈ=\ *adj* [F (*à la*) *lyonnaise* in the manner of Lyons, fr. fem. of *lyonnais* of Lyons, fr. *Lyon* Lyons, France] **:** prepared or seasoned with onions and sometimes parsley ⟨~ potatoes⟩ ⟨potatoes ~⟩

lyon office *n, usu cap L&O* [*lyon*, obs. var. of *lion*] **:** the administrative and clerical section of the Lyon Court in Scotland

ly·ons \(ˈ)lē¦ōⁿ, ˈlīənz\ *or* **lyon** \(ˈ)lē¦ōⁿ, *F* lyōⁿ\ *adj, usu cap* [fr. *Lyons* (F *Lyon*), France] **:** of or from the city of Lyons, France ⟨*Lyons* silk⟩ **:** of the kind or style prevalent in Lyons

lyons blue *n, often cap L* **:** a strong blue that is redder and deeper than Sèvres, redder and darker than cerulean blue (sense 1b), and slightly greener and lighter than liberty

¹**ly·o·phile** \ˈlīəˌfīl\ *adj* [ISV *lyo-* + *-phile*] **1 :** LYOPHILIC **2** *also* **ly·o·phil** \-ˌfil\ **:** of, relating to, or obtained by lyophilization ⟨~ process⟩

²**lyophile** \"\ *vt* -ED/-ING/-S **:** LYOPHILIZE

ly·o·phil·ic \¦==¦filik\ *adj* [*lyo-* + *-philic*] **:** of, relating to, or having a strong affinity between a dispersed phase and the liquid in which it is dispersed ⟨~ colloidal systems such as rubber and benzene are not easily coagulated⟩ — opposed to *lyophobic*; compare HYDROPHILIC

ly·oph·i·li·za·tion \(ˌ)līˌäfələˈzāshən, -fəˌlīˈz-\ *n* -s [ISV *lyophilize* + *-ation*] **:** the process of lyophilizing or the state of being lyophilized

ly·oph·i·lize \līˈäfəˌlīz\ *vt* -ED/-ING/-S [ISV *lyophil-* (fr. ¹*lyophile*) + *-ize*] **:** to dry (as tissue or serum) in a frozen state under high vacuum esp. for preservation **:** FREEZE-DRY

ly·o·phobic \¦==¦fōbik *also* -¦fäb-\ *also* **ly·o·phobe** \ˈ==ˌfōb\ *adj* [*lyophobic* fr. *lyo-* + *-phobic*; *lyophobe*, ISV *lyo-* + *-phobe*] **:** of, relating to, or having a lack of strong affinity between a dispersed phase and the liquid in which it is dispersed ⟨~ systems such as colloidal metals in water are easily coagulated⟩ — opposed to *lyophilic*; compare HYDROPHOBIC

ly·o·po·ma \ˌlīəˈpōmə\ *n* [NL, fr. *lyo-* + Gk *pōma* lid, operculum] *syn of* INARTICULATA

ly·o·po·ma·ta \ˌlīəˈpōməd·ə\ *n pl* [NL, fr. *lyo-* + *-pomata* (fr. Gk *pōmat-*, *pōma* lid, operculum) — more at POMACENTRIDAE] *syn of* INARTICULATA

ly·o·trop·ic \ˌlīə¦träpik\ *adj* [*lyo-* + *-tropic*] **:** relating to or dependent on the forces existing between components in a solution and not on their properties as individuals

lyotropic series *n* **:** HOFMEISTER SERIES

ly·ra \ˈlīrə\ *n* -s [L, lyre, fr. Gk] **1 a :** ²LIRA **b :** a glockenspiel with a lyre-shaped frame **2** *also* **lyre** \ˈlī(ə)r, ˈlīə\ [NL *lyra*, fr. L] **:** a triangular area of the ventral surface of the corpus callosum between the posterior pillars of the fornix

lyrachord *var of* LYRICHORD

ly·rate \ˈlīˌrā¦t, -ˌrə¦, *usu* ¦d.+V\ *also* **ly·rat·ed** \ˈlīˌrād.əd, -ātəd\ *adj* **:** having or suggesting the shape of a lyre ⟨a ~ leaf⟩ ⟨the bird's ~ tail⟩ — see LEAF illustration — **ly·rate·ly** *adv*

lyraway \ˈ==ˌ=\ *adv* [*lyra* + *-way*] **:** according to the lute tablature instead of musical notation ⟨play ~ on the viola da gamba⟩

lyre \ˈlī(ə)r, ˈlīə\ *n* -s [ME *lire*, fr. OF, fr. L *lyra*, fr. Gk] **1 a :** a stringed musical instrument of the harp class used by the ancient Greeks esp. to accompany song and recitation and made with a hollow body and two curved arms that are joined at the top by a yoke and four to ten strings that are struck with a plectrum — compare CITHARA, LIRA **b :** a musical instrument or device resembling the lyre **2 :** MUSIC LYRE

lyre-back \ˈ=ˌ=\ *n* **:** a decorative motif in the form of a lyre used esp. in the splat of American chairs of the late 18th and early 19th centuries

lyre bat *n* **:** a small long-eared bat (*Lyroderma lyra*) of eastern Asia

lyrebird \ˈ=ˌ=\ *n* **:** either of two Australian passerine birds of the genus *Menura*; *esp* **:** a bird (*M. novaehollandiae*) of New South Wales that is about the size of a grouse, is generally brown in color with rufous color on the throat, wings, tail coverts, and tail, and is distinguished in the male by 16 very long tail feathers spread out during courtship in the shape of a lyre

lyrebird

lyre crab *n* **:** TOAD CRAB

lyreflower \ˈ=ˌ=\ *n* **:** BLEEDING HEART 1

lyre-guitar \¦=¦=ˌ=\ *n* **:** a guitar with six strings

lyre·man \ˈ=mən\ *n* -s [*lyre* + *man*] **:** DOG-DAY CICADA

lyre pheasant *n* **:** LYREBIRD

lyre snake *n* **:** a weakly venomous colubrid snake (*Trimorphodon lambda*) that has posterior grooved poison fangs in the upper jaw and a lyre-shaped blotch on the nape of the neck and is found in desert areas of southwestern No. America

lyretail \ˈ=ˌ=\ *n* **:** LYREBIRD

lyre-tailed \ˈ=ˌ=\ *adj* **:** having a lyrate tail

lyre-tailed nightjar *n* **:** a So. American goatsucker (*Hydropsalis brasiliana*) having a lyrate tail that it opens and shuts while in flight

lyre turtle *n* **:** LEATHERBACK 1

¹**lyr·ic** \ˈlirik, -rēk\ *adj* [MF or L; MF *lyrique*, fr. L *lyricus*, fr. Gk *lyrikos*, fr. *lyra* lyre + *-ikos* -ic] **1 :** of or relating to a lyre or harp **2** *of verse* **a :** suitable to sing to the lyre **b :** suitable for being set to music and sung **:** MELODIC **3 a :** characterized by or expressive of direct usu. intense personal emotion ⟨the ~ writer virtue depends upon the intensity with which the personal vision is rendered —R.P.Warren⟩ ⟨a ~ and tender dance —*Dance Observer*⟩ ⟨a ~ and personal response to life —A.M.Mizener⟩ **b :** rhapsodic and unrestrained in manner or style ⟨publish ~ prose saying how gay an occasion it was —Katherine A. Porter⟩ ⟨the ~ typewriters of literary ghosts —Merriman Smith⟩ ⟨exploded with ~ wrath —*Time*⟩ **4 :** *of a singing voice* **:** having a relatively light, pure, melodic quality ⟨~ soprano⟩ ⟨~ tenor⟩ — compare COLORATURA, DRAMATIC

²**lyric** \"\ *n* -s [MF or L; MF *lyrique*, fr. L *lyricum*, fr. neut. of *lyricus* adj.] **1 a :** a lyric composition ⟨a tender and gay little ~ which she had sung to crowded drawing rooms —S.H. Adams⟩; *specif* **:** a lyric poem ⟨a third ~ of twenty lines —Malcolm Cowley⟩ **b lyrics** *pl* **:** the words of a popular song or musical-comedy number ⟨rereading the ~s slowly and savoring the ingenious metrical tricks that make these songs unique —William Zinsser⟩ **2** [MF *lyrique*, fr. L *lyricus*, fr. Gk *lyrikos*, fr. *lyrikos*, adj.] *archaic* **:** a lyric poet

lyr·i·cal \-rəkəl, -rēk-\ *adj* **:** LYRIC — **lyr·i·cal·ly** \-rək(ə)lē, -rēk-, -li\ *adv* — **lyr·i·cal·ness** \-kəlnəs\ *n* -ES

lyric caesura *n* **:** a feminine caesura that follows an unstressed syllable required by the meter (as in Housman's "they cease not fighting ‖ east and west") — contrasted with *epic caesura*

lyric drama *n* **:** OPERA

lyri·chord *also* **lyra·chord** \ˈlirəˌkȯrd, ˈlīr-\ *n* [*lyrichord* fr. *lyre* + harp*sichord*; *lyrachord*, alter. (influenced by E *lyra*) of *lyrichord*] **:** a harpsichord having its strings sounded by revolving wheels instead of being plucked

lyr·i·cism \ˈlirəˌsizəm\ *n* -s **1 a :** the quality or state of being lyric **:** SONGFULNESS ⟨the magical union of sound and hush that is ~ at its most subtle best —David Morton⟩ ⟨~ teaches ideas to dance instead of plodding along like a Ph.D. thesis —Peter Viereck⟩ **b :** a personal direct intense style or quality in poetry or the other arts ⟨reminds us with quiet ~ of life itself —Irwin Edman⟩ ⟨paintings in which shape and color are manipulated with restraint to produce a quiet and grave ~⟩ **2 :** unrestrained enthusiasm **:** exaggeration of style or feeling ⟨the sort of author who inspires ~ or invective, not judicious interpretation —*Time*⟩ ⟨the extravagance of their claims and the ~ of their expression —*Times Lit. Supp.*⟩ ⟨pages of a rather hysterical ~ about the dead child —Aldous Huxley⟩

lyr·i·cist \-səst\ *n* -s **:** a writer of lyrics

lyr·i·cize \-ˌsīz\ *vb* -ED/-ING/-S *vi* **1 :** to write or sing lyrics **2 :** to write in a lyric style ~ *vt* **:** to treat in a lyric manner ⟨making a revel of life and *lyricizing* death, hardship, and villainy —W.J.Fisher⟩

lyric theater *n* **1 :** OPERA HOUSE **2 :** a theatrical production involving music; *esp* **:** OPERA

ly·ri·form \ˈlīrəˌfȯrm\ *adj* [ISV *lyri-* (fr. L *lyriforme*, fr. *lyre* (fr. MF *lire*) + *-iforme* -iform] **:** shaped like a lyre

lyriform organ *n* **:** a cuticular groove that is connected with a nerve ending in many spiders, often occurs in groups on the legs and sternum, and is thought to be an organ of hearing

lyr·ism \ˈliˌrizəm\ *n* -s [¹*lyric* + *-ism*] **:** LYRICISM

lyr·ist *in sense 1* ˈlīrəst, *in sense 2* ˈlir-\ *n* -s [L *lyristes*, fr. Gk *lyristēs*, fr. *lyra* lyre + *-istēs* -ist] **1 :** a player on the lyre **2** [¹*lyric* + *-ist*] **:** LYRICIST

ly·ru·rus \līˈrürəs\ *n, cap* [NL, fr. Gk *lyra* lyre + NL *-urus*] **:** a genus of birds including the black grouse

lys- *or* **lysi-** *or* **lyso-** *comb form* [NL, fr. Gk *lys-*, *lysi-* loosening, dissolution, fr. *lysis*, fr. *lyein* to loosen, dissolve + *-sis* — more at LOSE] **1 :** loosening or dissolution or decomposition ⟨*lysigenous*⟩ ⟨*lysin*⟩ **2** *usu* **lyso-** [ISV *lysin* + *-o-*] **:** lysin ⟨*lysogen*⟩

ly·sate \ˈlīˌsāt\ *n* -s [ISV *lys-* (fr. NL *lysis*) + *-ate*] **:** the product resulting from lysis

lyse \ˈlīs, -īz\ *vb* -ED/-ING/-S [irreg. fr. *lysis*] *vt* **:** to cause to undergo lysis **:** produce lysis in ⟨blood cells may be *lysed* —K.F.Maxcy⟩ ~ *vi* **:** to undergo lysis

-lyse — see -LYZE

ly·sen·ko·ism \ləˈseŋ(ˌ)kōˌizəm\ *n* -s *usu cap* [Trofim Denisovich *Lysenko* b1898 Russ. geneticist + E *-ism*] **:** a biological doctrine asserting the fundamental influence of somatic and environmental factors on heredity in contradiction of orthodox genetics

ly·ser·gic acid \ləˈ¦sərjik-, (ˈ)lī¦\ *n* [*lys-* + *ergot* + *-ic*] **:** a crystalline tetracyclic acid $C_{15}H_{15}N_2COOH$ obtained from ergotic alkaloids by hydrolysis; *also* **:** LYSERGIC ACID DIETHYLAMIDE

lysergic acid di·eth·yl·amide \-ˌdīˈethələˌmīd\ *n* [*lysergic acid* + *diethyl* + *amide*] **:** a crystalline compound $C_{15}H_{15}N_2CON(C_2H_5)_2$ that causes psychotic symptoms similar to those of schizophrenia — called also *LSD*, *LSD 25*

ly·si·gen·ic \ˌlīsə¦jenik\ *also* **ly·si·ge·net·ic** \-jə¦ned·ik\ *adj* [*lys-* + *-genic* or *-genetic*] **:** LYSIGENOUS

ly·sig·e·nous \(ˈ)lī¦sijənəs\ *adj* [*lys-* + *-genous*] **:** formed by the breaking down of adjoining cells — used esp. of some intercellular spaces; compare SCHIZOGENOUS — **ly·sig·e·nous·ly** *adv*

ly·si·lo·ma \ˌlīsəˈlōmə\ *n, cap* [NL, fr. *lys-* + Gk *lōma* border, fringe; fr. the fact that in ripening the sides of the pod are loosened; akin to L *lorum* strap — more at LORE] **:** a small genus of tropical American trees (family Leguminosae) with pinnate leaves, few stamens, and a flat straight pod — see SABICU

ly·si·mach·ia \ˌlīsəˈmakēə\ *n, cap* [NL, fr. L, a plant, fr. Gk *lysimacheios* loosestrife, fr. *Lysimachos* Lysimachus *fl* 5th or 4th cent.B.C. Greek doctor] **:** a widely distributed genus of herbs (family Primulaceae) with leafy stems, leaves opposite or whorled, and yellow flowers — see LOOSESTRIFE 1, MONEYWORT

ly·sim·e·ter \līˈsimәd·ə(r)\ *n* [ISV *lys-* + *meter*] **:** a device for measuring the percolation of water through soils and determining the soluble constituents removed in the drainage

ly·sin \ˈlīsᵊn\ *n* -s [ISV *lys-* + *-in*] **:** any of various substances (as an antibody) capable of causing lysis

ly·sine \ˈlīˌsēn\ *n* -s [ISV *lys-* + *-ine*; prob. orig. formed as G *lysin*] **:** a crystalline basic amino acid $H_2N(CH_2)_4CH(NH_2)COOH$ that is obtained in its dextrorotatory L form by hydrolysis of many proteins (as from blood), by fermentation, or by synthesis and resolution of the racemic form and that is essential in the nutrition of animals and man; α, ε-diamino-caproic acid

ly·sis \ˈlīsəs\ *n, pl* **ly·ses** \-īˌsēz\ [NL, fr. Gk, act of loosing, loosening, dissolution, remission of fever — more at LYS-] **1 :** the gradual decline of a disease process **:** DEFERVESCENCE; *specif* **:** the gradual lowering of fever — compare CRISIS **2 :** a process of disintegration or dissolution (as of bacteria or blood cells)

-ly·sis \ləsəs\ *n comb form, pl* **-lyses** \ləˌsēz\ [NL, fr. L & Gk; L, loosening, fr. Gk, fr. *lysis*] **1 :** decomposition ⟨electro*lysis*⟩ ⟨hydro*lysis*⟩ ⟨pyro*lysis*⟩ **2 :** destruction **:** disintegration **:** dissolution — esp. of material associated with living organisms ⟨bio*lysis*⟩ ⟨auto*lysis*⟩ ⟨proteo*lysis*⟩ **3 a :** relief or reduction ⟨neuro*lysis*⟩ **b :** detachment (as in the surgical operation of freeing from adhesions) ⟨cardio*lysis*⟩ ⟨gastro*lysis*⟩ **c :** paralysis ⟨glosso*lysis*⟩

lyso- — see LYS-

ly·so·gen \ˈlīsəjən, -ˌjen\ *n* -s [*lys-* + *-gen*] **:** an antigen that stimulates the production of lysins

ly·so·genesis \ˌlīsə+\ *n* [NL, fr. *lys-* + L *genesis*] **:** the production of lysins or of the phenomenon of lysis

ly·so·genetic \¦==+\ *adj* [fr. NL *lysogenesis*, after L *genesis*: E *genetic*] **:** of or relating to lysogenesis

ly·so·gen·ic \ˌlīsə¦jenik\ *adj* [*lys-* + *-genic*] **:** harboring a prophage as hereditary material ⟨~ bacteria⟩ — **ly·so·ge·nic·i·ty** \ˌ==jəˈnisəd·ē, -ətē, -i\ *n* -ES

Ly·sol \ˈlīˌsōl, -sōl\ *trademark* — used for a disinfectant consisting of a brown emulsified solution containing cresols

ly·so·lecithin \¦līsō+\ *n* [*lys-* + *lecithin*] **:** a hemolytic substance formed from a lecithin by the removal of one fatty acid unit per molecule by enzymatic hydrolysis esp. with lecithinase A or bacterial toxins

ly·so·zyme \ˈlīsəˌzīm\ *n* -s [*lys-* + *-zyme*] **:** a basic protein that is present in egg white and in biological secretions (as tears, saliva, and the latex of some plants) and that functions as a mucolytic enzyme and is capable of attacking the capsules of various bacteria

lys·sa \ˈlisə\ *n* -s [NL, fr. Gk, rage, madness, rabies in dogs; akin to Gk *leukos* white — more at LIGHT] **:** RABIES, HYDROPHOBIA

lys·sa·ci·na \ˌlisəˈsīnə\ *n pl, cap* [NL, fr. Gk *lyssa* madness + *akis* barb, spicule, needle + NL *-ina* — more at ACIDANTHERA] *in some classifications* **:** an order of Hyalospongiae comprising those members of the Hexasterophora with spicules separate or incompletely fused — compare DICTYONINA — **lys·sa·cine** \ˈ==ˌsīn\ *adj or n*

lys·sic \ˈlisik\ *adj* [NL *lyssa* + E *-ic*] **:** of or relating to rabies **:** HYDROPHOBIC

lyster bag *usu cap L, var of* LISTER BAG

ly·syl \ˈlīsəl\ *n* -s [*lysine* + *-yl*] **:** the acid radical $H_2N(CH_2)_4CH(NH_2)CO_2$– of lysine

¹**-lyte** \ˌlīt, *usu* -īd.+V\ *n comb form* -s [Gk *lytos* that may be untied, soluble, verbal of *lyein* to loosen, dissolve — more at LOSE] **:** a substance capable of undergoing lysis (sense 2) ⟨electro*lyte*⟩ ⟨hydro*lyte*⟩

²**-lyte** — see -LITE

lythe \ˈlīth\ *n, pl* **lythe** *or* **lythes** [origin unknown] *Brit* **:** any of several food fishes; *esp* **:** POLLACK

ly·thra·ce·ae \līˈthrāsēˌē\ *n pl, cap* [NL, fr. *Lythrum*, type genus + *-aceae*] **:** a family of herbs, shrubs, and trees (order Myrtales) having flowers with crumpled corolla, a hypanthium, and often unequal stamens — **ly·thra·ceous** \(ˈ)lī¦thrāshəs\ *adj*

ly·thra·les \lī'thrā(,)lēz\ [NL, fr. *Lythrum* + *-ales*] *syn of* MYRTALES

ly·thrum \'līthrəm\ *n, cap* [NL, fr. Gk *lythron* gore; fr. the color of the flowers; akin to L *lutum* mud — more at POLLUTE] **:** a genus (the type of the family Lythraceae) of herbs and subshrubs having purple or rose-pink flowers with 4 to 8 petals and a 2-celled capsule — see LOOSESTRIFE 2

lyt·ic \'lid·ik, 'lit|, |ēk\ *adj* [Gk *lytikos* able to loose, fr. *lytos* soluble, that may be untied + *-ikos* -ic] **:** of or relating to lysis or a lysin **:** productive of or effecting lysis esp. of cells ⟨~ antibodies⟩ ⟨~ mechanism in the cell⟩ — **lyt·i·cal·ly** \-k(ə)lē, -li\ *adv*

-lyt·ic \'‚=‚=\ *adj suffix* [Gk *lytikos* able to loose] **:** of, relating to, or effecting lysis (sense 2) ⟨electro*lytic*⟩ ⟨hydro*lytic*⟩

lyt·ta \'lid·ə\ *n* [L, fr. Gk, *lytta, lyssa* madness, rabies — more at LYSSA] **1** *pl* **lyttae :** a fibrous and cartilaginous rod lying within the longitudinal axis of the tongue in many carnivorous mammals (as the dog) **2** *cap* [NL, fr. L] **:** a widespread genus of blister beetles (family Meloidae) containing the Spanish fly — compare CANTHARIS

lyx- *or* **lyxo-** *comb form* [*lyxose*] **1 :** related to lyxose ⟨*lyxo*flavin⟩ **2** *usu* **lyxo-**, *usu ital* **:** having the stereochemical arrangement of atoms or groups found in lyxose ⟨D-*lyxo*-3-hexulose⟩

lyx·o·flavin \'liksə+\ *n* [*lyx-* + *flavin*] **:** a yellow crystalline compound $C_{17}H_{20}N_4O_6$ isolated from heart muscle and stereoisomeric with riboflavin but derived from lyxose

lyx·ose \'lik,sōs, -ōz\ *n* -s [anagram of *xylose*] **:** a crystalline aldose sugar $HOCH_2(CHOH)_3CHO$ that is the epimer of xylose and that is prepared by degradation of galactose methods

-lyze *also* **-lyse** \,līz\ *vb comb form* -ED/-ING/-S [ISV, prob. irreg. fr. NL *-lysis* + ISV *-ize* or *-ise*] **:** to produce or undergo lytic disintegration or dissolution ⟨electro*lyze*⟩ ⟨pyro*lyze*⟩ ⟨solvo*lyze*⟩

LZ *abbr* landing zone

¹m \'em\ *n, pl* **m's** *or* **ms** \'emz\ *often cap, often attrib* **1 a :** the 13th letter of the English alphabet **b :** an instance of this letter printed, written, or otherwise represented **c :** a speech counterpart of orthographic *m* (as *m* in *mimic, small, comfort*, or French *muet*) **2 :** 1000 — see NUMBER table **3 :** a printer's type, a stamp, or some other instrument for reproducing the letter *m* **4 :** someone or something arbitrarily or conveniently designated *m* esp. as the 12th or when j is used for the 10th the 13th in order or class **5 :** something having the shape of the capital letter M **6 a :** EM 2 **b :** PICA **7 :** an antigen of human blood that shares a common genetic locus with the N antigen — **have an M under one's girdle** *obs* **:** to show courtesy by using the title Mr., Mrs., or Miss

²m *abbr, often cap* **1** Mach **2** [L *magister*] master **3** magistrate **4** magnetic **5** maiden **6** maiden over **7** mail **8** [F *main*] hand **9** majesty **10** make **11** male **12** [L *manipulus*] handful **13** [It *mano*] hand **14** manual **15** March **16** mare **17** maritime **18** mark **19** marker **20** marquis **21** married **22** martyr **23** masculine **24** mass **25** master **26** mate **27** maxwell **28** May **29** mean **30** measure **31** mechanical **32** medical **33** [L *medicinae*] of medicine **34** medium **35** mega- **36** melts at **37** member **38** memorandum **39** meridian **40** [L *meridies*] noon **41** metal **42** meter **43** metropolitan **44** [It *mezzo*] half **45** micro- **46** middle **47** mil **48** mile **49** military **50** mill **51** [L *mille*] thousand **52** milli- **53** million **54** mine **55** minim **56** minor **57** minute **58** [L *misce*] mix **59** miscellaneous **60** mist **61** [L *mistura*] mixture **62** model **63** modulus **64** molar; mole **65** molecular weight **66** moment **67** Monday **68** monoplane **69** monsieur **70** monsoon **71** month **72** moon **73** morning **74** morphine **75** mortar **76** mortgage **77** [L *mortis*] of death **78** mother **79** motor **80** mountain **81** mucoid **82** mud **83** muscle **84** mustard gas **85** muster **86** myopia

³m *symbol, cap* **1 a** place for the insertion of a given name of a bridegroom (as in a ceremonial statement) or of a male person — compare ³N 1 **b** place for the insertion of two or more usu. given names of a person — compare NN **2** *ital* mutual inductance **3** metal — used esp. of a univalent cation; see BASE 8a, GENERAL FORMULA

m- \'med·ə, -etə\ *abbr* meta-

¹'m \m\ *vb* [by contr.] **:** AM ⟨I'*m* going⟩

²'m \ .im, .əm\ *pron* [by contr.] **:** HIM ⟨show'*m* the way to the fairgrounds⟩

³'m *after "yes"* əm, *after "no"* m\ *n* -s [by contr.] **:** MADAM ⟨yes'*m*⟩

ma \'mä, 'mȯ, 'mà, 'ma, 'maa\ *n* -s [short for *mama*] **:** MOTHER

mA *abbr* milliangstrom

ma *abbr* **1** major **2** milliampere

MA \(')e¦mā\ *abbr or n* -s Master of Arts

MA *abbr, often not cap* **1** mental age **2** meter angle **3** middle ages **4** military academy **5** military attaché **6** military aviator **7** mill annealed **8** mountain artillery **9** my account

maa \'ma, 'maa, 'mä, 'mà\ *n or vi* [imit.] **:** BAA

MAA *abbr* master-at-arms

ma'a·ba·ra \'mäbə¦rä\ *n, pl* **ma'aba·rot** *or* **ma'aba·roth** \-rōt(h), -ōs\ [NHeb *ma'bārāh*, fr. Heb, crossing, ferry] **:** a transitional settlement or village for immigrants in Israel

maal *sometimes cap, var of* MĀL

ma'am *also* **mam** *or* **ma'm** \'mam, -aa(ə)-, -ä-, -à- *sometimes* ¦məm; *in some areas where both -ä- and -a- or -aa(ə)- occur -ä- is substand or dial; after "yes" often* ,əm; *often* ,məm *by British servants*\ *n* -s [by contr.] **:** MADAM 1

ma'amselle *n* -s [modif. of F *mademoiselle* — more at MADEMOISELLE] **:** MADEMOISELLE

maanhaar-jackal \'män,här+\ *n* [part trans. of Afrik *maanhaarjakkals*, fr. *maanhaar* mane (fr. *maan* mane + *haar* hair) + *jakkals* jackal] **:** AARDWOLF

maar \'mär\ *n* -s [G] **:** a volcanic crater that is produced by explosion in an area of low relief, is generally more or less circular, and often contains a lake, pond, or marsh

maa·rad \'mä,rad\ *n* -s [origin unknown] **:** a brownish long-staple cotton developed in Egypt from American pima cotton

maa·rib *or* **maa·riv** \'märiv, 'mäər-, 'mīr-\ *n, pl* **maa·ri·bim** *or* **maa·ri·vim** \,mäə(,)rē¦vēm\ [Heb *ma'ărībh* bringing evening] **:** the daily evening liturgy of the Jews — compare MINHAH, SHAHARITH

maas·bank·er \'mäs,baŋkə(r)\ *n* [Afrik, fr. *maas* net, mesh + *bank* bank, shoal, shelf + *-er*] **:** a horse mackerel (*Trachurus trachurus*) that is an important commercial food fish in southern Africa

MAB *abbr* medical advisory board

¹ma·ba \'mäbə\ *n, cap* [NL, fr. Tongan & Fijian, a tree of the genus Maba] **:** a widely distributed genus of tropical trees and shrubs (family Ebenaceae) having dioecious trimerous flowers and very hard wood resembling ebony

²maba \"\ *n* -s *usu cap* **:** one of a mixed negroid people of Muslim culture who in the 17th century established the powerful sultanate of Wadai east of Lake Chad — compare KANURI

MABA *abbr* meta-aminobenzoic acid

mabe \'māb\ *n* -s [origin unknown] **:** a cultured pearl that is essentially hemispherical in form

ma·bi \(')mä¦bē\ *n* -s [AmerSp *mabí*] **1 :** a nakedwood (*Colubrina reclinata*) with orange-brown bark and dark brown heartwood tinged with yellow **2 :** a beverage prepared from the bark of the mabi

ma·bo·lo \mə'bō(,)lō\ *n* -s [PhilSp, fr. Tag *mabulo*] **:** CAMAGON

ma·bu·ya \mə'büyə\ *n* [NL, fr. AmerSp, lizard of the genus Mabuya] **1** *cap* **:** a genus of insectivorous lizards (family Scincidae) common about houses in Central and So. America **2** -s **:** a lizard of the genus *Mabuya*

mab·yer \'mabyə(r)\ *n* -s [Corn *mabyar*, fr. *map, mab* son, boy + *yar* hen] *Cornwall* **:** a young hen **:** PULLET

¹mac *var of* MACK

²mac \'mak\ *n* -s *usu cap* [fr. *Mac-, Mc-*, common patronymic prefix in many Scotch and Irish surnames] **:** FELLOW — used informally to address a man whose name is unknown ⟨look, *Mac*, I don't hear a word you're saying —Maritta Wolff⟩

³mac *or* **mack** \"\ *n* -s [by shortening] **1** *Brit* **:** MACKINTOSH **2 :** MACKINAW

mac *abbr* **1** macadam **2** macerate

MAC *abbr, sometimes not cap* **1** maximum allowable concentration **2** model airplane club

ma·cá \mə'kä\ *n, pl* **macá** *or* **macás** *usu cap* [Sp, of AmerInd origin] **1 a :** a people or group of peoples of the Gran Chaco in Paraguay and Argentina **b :** a member of such people or group of peoples **2 :** the language of the Macá people

ma·caa·sim *or* **ma·kaa·sim** \mə'kä,sēm\ *n* -s [Tag *makaasim*, perh. fr. *asim* sourness] **1 :** any of several chiefly Philippine hardwood trees of the genus *Eugenia* **2 :** the hard heavy fine-grained durable wood of a macaasim tree

ma·ca·bi \,makə¦bē\ *n* -s [Sp *macabí*] **1 :** a bonefish (*Albula vulpes*) **2 :** TENPOUNDER 1

ma·ca·bre *also* **ma·ca·ber** \mə'käb(rə), -kàb(-, *chiefly before a pause* -brᵊ, *chiefly before a vowel following without pause* -br (*br beginning the syllable to which the following vowel belongs*); *sometimes*- bə(r)\ *adj* [F, fr. (*danse*) *macabre* dance of death, fr. MF (*danse*) *macabré*, (*danse de*) *Macabré*, fr. *Macchabées* Maccabees, 2d–1st cent. B.C. Jewish patriots; prob. fr. their being associated with death because of a passage in 2 Macc (12:43–46) that is important in the development of the concepts of purgatory and prayers for the dead] **1 :** concerned with death or having death as a subject **:** comprising or including a personalized representation of death ⟨German baroque poems containing ~ blazons, describing . . . the parts of the dead body —Leo Spitzer⟩ — compare DANSE MACABRE **2 :** concerned with or dwelling unduly on the grim, grisly, or gruesome **:** designed to produce an effect of horror ⟨a ~ presentation of a tragic story⟩ — often used absolutely ⟨a writer specializing in the ~⟩ **3 :** tending to produce horror in a beholder **:** HORRIBLE, DISTRESSING, UNPLEASANT ⟨this ~ procession of starving peasants⟩ ⟨government couldn't resist the ~ impulse to set down a huge, modern atomic establishment . . . in such an old-time, idyllic spot —Conrad Richter⟩ — **ma·ca·bre·ly** \-b(rə)lē *sometimes* -bə(r)lē\ *adv*

ma·ca·ca \mə'käkə\ *n, cap* [NL, fr. Pg, female monkey, fem. of *macaco* monkey] **:** a genus of Old World monkeys consisting of the macaques

ma·ca·ca·hu·ba *or* **ma·ca·cu·uba** \mə,käkə'(h)übə\ *n* -s [Pg *Macacaúba*, fr. Tupi] **:** QUIRA

ma·ca·co \mə'kä(,)kō\ *n* -s [Pg, fr. a native word in Africa] **1 :** any of various Old World monkeys or lemurs or New World monkeys **2** *obs* **:** MACAQUE

ma·ca·cus \mə'kākəs, -käk-\ [NL, fr. Pg *macaco* monkey] *syn of* MACACA

mac·ad·am \mə'kadəm\ *n* -s [after John L. McAdam †1836 Brit. engineer] **1 :** macadamized roadway or pavement **2 :** the broken stone used in macadamizing

mac·a·damia \,makə'dāmēə, -dam-\ *n* [NL, fr. John Macadam †1865 Australian chemist born in Scotland + NL *-ia*] **1** *cap* **:** a small genus of Australian evergreen trees (family Proteaceae) including one (*M. ternifolia*) that is widely cultivated in warm regions for its edible nut **2** -s **a** *or* **macadamia tree :** any tree of the genus *Macadamia* **b :** MACADAMIA NUT

macadamia nut *n* **:** the hard-shelled nut of the macadamia tree somewhat resembling a filbert and eaten raw or roasted — called also *Queensland nut*

mac·ad·am·iza·tion \mə,kadəmə'zāshən, -də,mī'z-\ *n* -s **:** the act or process of macadamizing

mac·ad·am·ize \mə'kadə,mīz\ *vt* -ED/-ING/-S [*macadam* + *-ize*] **:** to construct or finish (a road) by compacting into a solid mass a layer of small broken stone on a convex well-drained roadbed using fine stone dust and water as a cement or now usu. cement grout or bituminous material as a binder

macadam road *n* **:** MACADAM 1; *esp* **:** a road surfaced with a bituminous binder

ma·ca·na \mə'känə\ *n* -s [Sp, fr. Taino] **:** a wooden weapon or agricultural tool widely employed by the Indians of So. America and the Antilles, usu. made like a flattened club or sword, and sometimes edged or headed with stone

mac·a·nese \¦makə¦nēz, -ēs\ *n, pl* **macanese** *usu cap* [*Macao*, Portuguese colony on the southeastern end of Macao island at the mouth of the Pearl river in southeastern China + E *-nese* (as in *Japanese*)] **:** one of a population of Portuguese-Chinese stock who live in Macao on the coast of southern China

¹ma·cao \mə'kau̇\ *adj, usu cap* [fr. *Macao* city & colony, China] **:** of or from the city or colony of Macao, China **:** of the kind or style prevalent in Macao

²macao \"\ *n* -s [fr. *Macao* colony] **:** a card game like baccarat except that only one card is dealt to each player

ma·caque \mə'kak, -käk\ *n* -s [F, fr. Pg *macaco* — more at MACACO] **:** any of numerous short-tailed Old World monkeys of *Macaca* and related genera having distinct ischial callosities and usu. tufted eyebrows and being found chiefly in southern Asia and the East Indies but including some that range northward into northern China and Japan and others (as the Barbary ape) that extend into northwest Africa and the tip of Europe; *esp* **:** RHESUS

macaranduba *var of* MASSARANDUBA

mac·a·rize \'makə,rīz\ *vt* -ED/-ING/-S [Gk *makarizein*, fr. *makar, makarios* blessed, happy + *-izein* -ize] **:** to pronounce happy or blessed **:** FELICITATE, LAUD

mac·a·ro·ni \,makə'rōnē, -ni\ *n, pl* **macaronis** *or* **macaronies** [It dial. (Naples) *maccarone* dumpling, small cake, macaroni] **1 :** an alimentary paste composed chiefly of semolina dried in the form of slender tubes or small fancy shapes ⟨~ shells⟩ ⟨elbow ~⟩; *esp* **:** tubular alimentary paste having a diameter of .11 to .27 inches — distinguished from *spaghetti*; compare VERMICELLI **2 a :** a member of a class of traveled young Englishmen of the late 18th and early 19th centuries that affected foreign ways **b :** a precious affected young man **:** EXQUISITE, FOP, DANDY ⟨spruce ~*s*, and pretty to see, tidy and dapper and gallant —J.W.Palmer⟩ **c** *or* **macaroni penguin :** ROCK HOPPER **3** *chiefly Austral* **:** something droll or extravagant **:** foolish chatter **:** NONSENSE **4** *slang* **:** ITALIAN

¹mac·a·ron·ic \¦makə¦ränik\ *adj* [NL *macaronicus*, fr. It. dial. *maccarone* dumpling, macaroni (regarded as coarse peasant fare) + L *-icus* -ic] **1** *archaic* **:** having the characteristics of a jumble or medley **:** MIXED ⟨will look on the architecture . . . as belonging to the ~ order —James Dallaway⟩ **2 a :** characterized by a mixture of vernacular words with Latin words or with non-Latin words having Latin endings ⟨many carols are ~ and in them Latin and English . . . are often combined with a syntactical accuracy —E.K.Chambers⟩ **b :** characterized by a mixture of two languages — **mac·a·ron·i·cal·ly** \-nək(ə)lē\ *adv*

²macaronic \"\ *n* -s **:** macaronic composition or language **:** a confused mixed-up piece of writing

mac·a·ro·nism \,makə'rō,nizəm\ *n* -s [*macaroni* + *-ism*] **:** FOPPISHNESS

macaroni wheat *n* **:** DURUM WHEAT

mac·a·roon \¦makə¦rün\ *n* -s [F *macaron*, fr. It dial. (Naples) *maccarone* dumpling, small cake, macaroni] **1 :** a small cake composed chiefly of the white of eggs, sugar, and ground almonds or almond paste or coconut **2** *obs* **:** MACARONI 1

ma·cart·ney \mə'kärtnē\ *n* -s *usu cap* [after George, 1st Earl Macartney †1806 Brit. diplomat] **1 :** FIREBACK 1 **2 :** MACARTNEY ROSE

macartney rose *n, usu cap M* [after George, 1st Earl *Macartney*] **:** a tall-growing rambling Chinese evergreen rose (*Rosa bracteata*) that has hairy branches, strong hooked prickles, and large solitary fragrant white flowers above prominent bracts and that has been introduced into and naturalized in warmer parts of Europe and America

macassar *usu cap, var of* MAKASSAR

macassar agar–agar *n, usu cap M* [fr. *Macassar* (Makassar) city on southwestern Celebes Island, and strait between Celebes and Borneo, Indonesia] **:** an East Indian agar-agar derived from seaweeds of the genus *Eucheuma* (esp. *E. muricatum*)

macassar ebony *also* **macassar** *n* -s **:** EBONY 1; *esp* **:** the ornately streaked and mottled wood of an East Indian ebony tree (*Diospyros macassar*)

macassarese *usu cap, var of* MAKASSARESE

macassar mace *n, usu cap 1st M* **:** mace derived from Macassar nutmeg

macassar nutmeg *n, usu cap M* **:** the seed of an East Indian tree (*Myristica argentea*) that is sometimes used as an adulterant of or substitute for nutmegs — called also *long nutmeg*

macassar oil *n, often cap M* **:** a soft fat obtained from seeds of the kusam and used in cooking, in illumination, and as a hair dressing; *also* **:** any of several similar oils or oily preparations used as hair dressings

ma·cau·lay·an \mə'kȯlēən\ *adj, usu cap* [Thomas Babington *Macaulay*, 1st Baron *Macaulay* †1859 English writer and statesman + E *-an*] **:** of, relating to, or resembling the English writer Macaulay ⟨a *Macaulayan* style⟩

ma·cau·lay·ism \-ē,izəm\ *n* -s *usu cap* [Thomas B. *Macaulay* + E *-ism*] **:** a Macaulayan style or turn of phrase

ma·caw \mə'kȯ\ *n* -s [Pg *macau*, prob fr. *macaúba* macaw palm, on the fruit of which they feed] **:** any of numerous parrots of *Ara* and related genera that are now confined to So. and Central America but were formerly also represented in the West Indies, include some of the largest of parrots, and have a very long tail, a naked space around the eyes, a strong hooked bill with which they crack hard nuts, a harsh voice, and brilliantly and contrastingly colored plumage

ma·ca·wood \mə'kä,wu̇d, -kȯ,w-\ *n* [*macacahuba* + *wood*] **:** QUIRA

macaw palm *or* **macaw tree** *n* [Pg *macaúba*, fr. Tupi *macahiba, macahuba*] **:** any of several So. American palms of the genus *Acrocomia* with nuts that yield a violet-scented oil used in perfumery and in some cases nutritious edible oils

mc·bur·ney's point \mək'bərnēz-, mak\ *n, usu cap M&B* [after Charles *McBurney* †1913 Am. surgeon] **:** a point on the abdominal wall between the right anterior superior iliac spine and the umbilicus where most pain is elicited by pressure in acute appendicitis

mac·ca·be·an *also* **mac·ca·bae·an** \¦makə¦bēən\ *adj, usu cap* **1** [Judas *Maccabaeus*, 2d cent. B.C. Jewish patriot + E *-an*] **:** of or relating to Judas Maccabaeus **2** [*Maccabees* or *Maccabaei* 2d–1st cent. B.C. family of Jewish patriots + E *-an*] **:** of or relating to the Maccabees

mac·ca·bee \'makə,bē\ *n, pl* **maccabees** *usu cap* [after *Maccabees*, 2d–1st cent. B.C. family of Jewish patriots] **:** a member of any of various fraternal orders — see KNIGHT OF THE MACCABEES

mac·ca·boy \'makə,bȯi\ *also* **mac·ca·baw** \-bȯ\ *or* **ma·cou·ba** \mə'kübə\ *n* -s [modif. of F *macouba*, fr. *Macouba*, district in Martinique where it is made] **:** a snuff from Martinique

macca crab \'makə-\ *n* [*macca* of unknown origin] *Jamaica* **:** DECORATOR CRAB

mc·car·thy·ism \mə'kärthē,izəm *sometimes* -rd·ē-\ *n* -s *usu cap M&2dC* [Joseph R. *McCarthy* †1957 Am. politician + E *-ism*] **:** a political attitude of the mid-twentieth century closely allied to know-nothingism and characterized chiefly by opposition to elements held to be subversive and by the use of tactics involving personal attacks on individuals by means of widely publicized indiscriminate allegations esp. on the basis of unsubstantiated charges

mc·car·thy·ite \-ē,īt\ *also* **mc·car·thy·ist** \-ēəst\ *n* -s *usu cap M&2dC* [Joseph R. *McCarthy* + E *-ite* or *-ist*] **:** a person approving of or practicing McCarthyism

mc·cart·ney rose \mə'kärtnē-\ *or* **mccartney's rose** *n, usu cap M & 2d C* [after George, 1st Earl *Macartney* †1806 Brit. diplomat] **:** MACARTNEY ROSE

mc·car·ty \mə'kärd·ē\ *n* -ES *usu cap M & 2d C* [by folk etymology (influence of the name McCarty) of MexSp *mecate* — more at MECATE] *West* **:** MECATE

mac·chi \'mäkē\ *n* -s [It *macchia*] **:** MAQUIS 1

mac·chia \'mäkēə\ *n, pl* **mac·chie** \-ē,ā\ [It — more at MAQUIS] **:** MAQUIS 1

mc·clel·lan saddle \mə'klelən-\ *also* **mcclellan** *n, usu cap M & 2d C* [after George B. *McClellan* †1885 Am. army officer] **:** a saddle with moderately high leather-covered pommel and cantle developed during the Civil War and long used by the cavalry of the U. S. Army

mac·cles·field \'makəlz,fēld, -l,sf-\ *n, usu cap* [fr. *Macclesfield*, England, where it was originally made] **:** a silk with small allover patterns used esp. for neckties

mc·clin·tock's tables \mə'klintəks-\ *n pl, usu cap M & 2d T* [after Emory *McClintock* †1916 Am. mathematician and actuary] **:** tables of mortality among annuitants based on the experience of 15 American insurance companies and published in 1896

mac·co \'ma(,)kō\ *archaic var of* ²MACAO

mc·cown's longspur \mə'kau̇nz-\ *also* **mc·cown's bunting** \mə'kau̇nz-\ *n, usu cap M & 2d C* [after John P. *McCown*, 19th cent. Am. army officer] **:** a brownish gray longspur (*Rhynchophanes mccowni*) of central No. America with black markings on head, back, and throat and predominantly white underparts

mc·coy \mə'kȯi\ *n* -s, *usu cap M & 2d C* [alter. (influenced by the name *McCoy*) of Sc *Mackay* (in *the real Mackay* the true chief of the Mackay clan — a position often a matter of dispute between the two branches of the clan)] **:** the real or genuine thing **:** something that is neither an imitation nor an inferior substitute — used with the definite article

mac·cus \'makəs, 'mak-\ *n, pl* **mac·ci** \-ä(,)kē, -ak,sī\ [L, prob. fr. Oscan] **:** a stock character of Roman comedy representing a stupid greedy country fellow

mc·dou·gall furnace \mək'dügəl-\ *n, usu cap M&D* [after *McDougall*, 19th cent. Brit. engineer] **:** a roasting furnace consisting of a vertical cylindrical shaft containing several superposed hearths over which ore entering at the top is made to pass consecutively by mechanical rabbles rotating around a central shaft

¹**mace** \'mās\ *n* -s [ME, fr. MF, fr. (assumed) VL *mattia*; akin to L *mateola* mallet, OHG *medela* plow, Skt *matya* harrow] **1 a :** a heavy staff or club made wholly or partly of metal, often spiked, and used esp. in the middle ages for breaking armor **b :** a club used as an offensive weapon ⟨a policeman's ~⟩ **2 :** a staff borne by, carried before, or placed near a magistrate or other dignitary as an ensign of his authority **3 :** MACE-BEARER **4 :** a knobbed mallet used by curriers in dressing leather to make it supple **5 a :** a rod with a flat wooden head formerly used in billiards instead of a cue **b :** a similar rod used in bagatelle

mace 2

²**mace** \"\ *vt* -ED/-ING/-s **:** to strike with or as if with a mace ⟨the boxer *maced* his opponent with a left hook⟩

³**mace** *n* -s [ME *mace, macis*, fr. MF *maci, macis*, fr. L *macir* reddish rind of an Indian root, fr. Gk *makir, makeir*] **1 :** a fragrant and highly aromatic spice consisting of the dried arillode of the nutmeg **2 :** the dried arillode of various other nutmeg trees used as spice — usu. used with a qualifying term ⟨Bombay ~⟩

⁴**mace** \"\ *n, pl* **mace** [Malay *mas, ĕmas* mace, gold, fr. Skt *māṣa* bean, weight] **1** *archaic* **:** a small gold coin of Malaysia **2 :** a Chinese unit of weight and a corresponding unit of value equal to one tenth of a tael

⁵**mace** \"\ *n* -s [origin unknown] **1** *or* **mace·man** \-smən\ *pl* **macemen** *slang* **:** SWINDLER **2** *slang* **:** SWINDLING

⁶**mace** \"\ *vt*, -ED/-ING/-s *slang* **:** CHEAT, SWINDLE; *esp* **:** to force political contributions from (public employees)

mace–bearer \'=,=\ *n* **:** an officer who carries a mace (as before a dignitary); *esp* **:** the sergeant at arms of the British House of Commons

mace butter *n* [³*mace*] **:** NUTMEG BUTTER

ma·cé·doine \¦masə¦dwän, -sā¦-\ *n* -s [F, fr. *Macédoine* Macedonia (perh. in allusion to the mixture of races there)] **1 a :** a mixture of fruits or vegetables cut in pieces and dressed and served as a salad or cocktail in a jellied dessert or in a sauce or garnish **b :** a dish having a garnish of macédoine ⟨a chicken ~⟩ **2 :** a confused mixture **:** MEDLEY

¹**mac·e·do·nian** \¦masə¦dōnēən\ *adj, usu cap* [*Macedonia*, region in the central Balkan peninsula + E *-an*] **:** belonging or relating to Macedonia

²**macedonian** \"\ *n* -s *cap* **1 :** a native or inhabitant of ancient Macedonia **2 a :** a native or inhabitant of modern Macedonia **b :** one that is of Macedonian descent **3 :** the Slavic language of the modern Macedonian people **4 :** the language of ancient Macedonia of uncertain affinity but generally assumed to be Indo-European

³**macedonian** \"\ *n, usu cap* [*Macedonius*, 4th cent. bishop of Constantinople and patriarch of the Eastern Church + E *-an*] **:** a follower of the bishop Macedonius, who held the Holy Ghost to be a creature like the angels and a servant and minister of the Father and the Son

macedonian cry *or* **macedonian call** *n, usu cap M* [¹*Macedonian*; fr. the vision of St. Paul at Troas (Acts 16:9) wherein a man appealed to him to go to Macedonia to help the people there] **:** an outcry for help

macedonian–persian \¦=¦=¦==¦=\ *adj, usu cap M&P* **:** relating to or involving both Macedonia and Persia

macedonian pine *n, usu cap M* **:** BALKAN PINE

mac·e·don·ic \¦masə¦dänik\ *adj, usu cap* [L *Macedonicus*, fr. Gk *Makedonikos*, fr. *Makedonia* Macedonia + *-ikos* -ic] **:** MACEDONIAN

mace–head \'=,=\ *n* **:** MATTOIR

ma·ceió \¦masā¦ō\ *adj, usu cap* [fr. *Maceió*, Brazil] **:** of or from the city of Maceió, Brazil **:** of the kind or style prevalent in Maceió

ma·cel·lum \mə'seləm\ *n, pl* **macel·la** \-lə\ [L, fr. Gk *makellon* enclosure, meat market, market, fr. Heb *mikhalāh* enclosure, pen] **:** an ancient Roman market or market building; *esp* **:** a meat market

mace oil *n* **1 :** an essential oil obtained by distillation from mace and similar in properties to nutmeg oil **2 a :** NUTMEG OIL a **b :** NUTMEG BUTTER

mac·er \'māsə(r)\ *n* -s [ME, fr. *mace* + *-er*] **:** MACE-BEARER; *specif* **:** a court officer in Scotland charged with keeping order, executing warrants, and similar duties

mac·er·al \¦masə¦ral\ *n* -s [prob. fr. L *macer* soft, weak + E *-al*] **:** a fragment of plant debris in coal

¹**mac·er·ate** \'masə,rāt, *usu* -ād·+V\ *vb* -ED/-ING/-s [L *maceratus*, past part. of *macerare* to soften, fr. *macer* soft, weak — more at MEAGER] *vt* **1 :** to cause (the body or its flesh) to waste away by or as if by excessive fasting **2 a :** to cause (solid matter) to become soft or separated into constituent elements by steeping in fluid ⟨flax *macerated* in water⟩ ⟨fibrous food *macerating* in the cow's rumen⟩ **b :** to cause (a solid object) to soften and fray as if long soaked in water ⟨a mallet with ends *macerated* by pounding⟩ ~ *vi* **:** to soften and wear away esp. as a result of being wetted or steeped

²**mac·er·ate** \'masərət\ *n* -s **:** a product of macerating **:** something prepared by maceration ⟨examining the chromosomes in a liver ~⟩ — compare HOMOGENATE

mac·er·a·tion \,masə'rāshən\ *n* -s [L *maceration-, maceratio*, fr. *maceratus* + *-ion-, -io* -ion] **1 :** an act or the process of macerating something: **a :** a process of extracting fragrant oils that is similar to enfleurage but differs in the use of hot fat in which the flower petals are immersed **b :** the extraction of a drug by allowing it to stand in contact with a solvent **2 :** the condition of being macerated ⟨the fetus was recovered in an advanced state of ~⟩

mac·er·a·tive \'masə,rād·iv\ *adj* **:** characterized or accompanied by maceration ⟨~ degeneration of tissue⟩

mac·er·a·tor \-ād·ə(r)\ *n* -s **:** one that macerates; *esp* **:** an apparatus for converting paper or fibrous matter into pulp

maces *pl of* MACE, *pres 3d sing of* MACE

mac·far·lane \mək'färlən\ *n* -s *often cap M & sometimes cap F* [prob fr. the name *MacFarlane*] **:** a heavy caped overcoat with slit sides

macfarlane

mac·gil·li·vray's warbler \mə'giləvrāz-\ *n, usu cap M* [after William *MacGillivray* †1852 Scot. naturalist] **:** a warbler (*Oporornis tolmiei*) of western No. America that is similar and closely related to the eastern mourning warbler

mc·gov·ern·ite \mə'gəvə(r),nīt\ *n* -s *often cap M&G* [J.J. *McGovern* †1915 Am. mine foreman + E *-ite*] **:** a mineral $Mn_9(AsO_3)_2SiO_3(OH)_2$ consisting of a basic silicate and arsenite of manganese that is found at Sterling Hill, N.J.

mach *n* -s *usu cap* [by shortening] **:** MACH NUMBER

mach *abbr* machine; machinery; machinist

mach·ae·rid·ia \,makə'ridēə\ *n pl, cap* [NL, fr. L *machaera* sword, dagger (fr. Gk *machaira*) + NL *-idia*] **:** a small group of Ordovician and Devonian animal fossils that are wormlike and bilaterally symmetrical but enclosed by plates suggesting those of echinoderms, are considered structurally comparable to the dipleurula and ancestral to modern echinoderms, being then made a class of Echinodermata, or are regarded as aberrant barnacles and included among the Cirripedia

ma·chae·ro·dus \mə'kirədəs, -ker-\ *syn of* MACHAIRODUS

mach·air *or* **mach·ar** \'makər\ *n* -s [ScGael *machair* & IrGael *machaire*] *Scot & Irish* **:** a flat or low-lying plain or field

¹**ma·chai·ro·dont** \mə'kīrə,dänt\ *also* **ma·chae·ro·dont** \-kir-, -ker-\ *adj* [*machairodont*, fr. Gk *machaira* sword, dagger + E *-odont*; *machaerodont*, fr. L *machaera* sword, dagger (fr. Gk *machaira*) + E *-odont*] **:** of or relating to the genus *Machairodus* **:** like a saber-toothed tiger

²**machairodont** \"\ *also* **machaerodont** \"\ *n* -s **:** a member of the genus *Machairodus* **:** SABER-TOOTHED TIGER

ma·chai·ro·dus \-.dəs\ *n, cap* [NL, fr. Gk *machaira* sword, dagger + NL *-odus*] **:** a genus of extinct felid mammals distinguished by extreme development of the canine teeth, comprising the saber-tooth tigers, and usu. considered to constitute a subfamily of Felidae or in some classifications a distinct family

ma·chan *or* **ma·chaan** \mə'chän\ *n* -s [Hindi *macān* platform, scaffold, fr. Skt *mañca*] *India* **:** a platform (as in a tree) used for observation in tiger hunting

ma·chan·cha \mə'chänchə\ *n* -s [AmerSp] **:** a venomous Peruvian snake (*Bothrops barnetti*) related to the fer-de-lance

mach angle \'mäk-, 'mȧk-\ *n, usu cap M* [after Ernst *Mach* †1916 Austrian physicist and philosopher] **:** half of the vertex angle of a Mach cone whose sine is the ratio of the speed of sound to the speed of a moving body

mach cone *n, usu cap M* [after Ernst *Mach*] **:** the conical pressure wave front produced by a body moving at a speed greater than that of sound

mache *n* -s [by shortening and alter.] **:** PAPIER-MÂCHÉ

ma·cheer \mə'chi(ə)r\ *n* -s [modif. of Sp *mochila* — more at *mochila*] *West* **:** MOCHILA

ma·che·te \mə'shed·ē, -'che| *sometimes* -shā| *or* -chā| *or* -shet

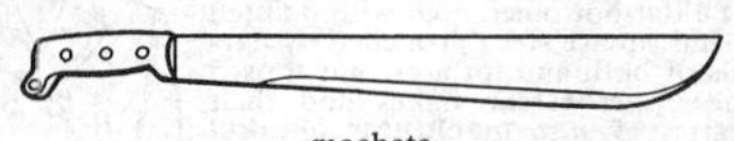

machete

or +V -shed·\ *n* -s [Sp *machete*] **1** *also* **ma·chette** \-shet, +V -ed·\ *or* **match·et** \'machət, +V -əd·\ **:** a large heavy knife usu. made with a blade resembling a broadsword often two or three feet in length and used esp. in So. America and the West Indies for cutting cane and clearing paths **2 :** a small four-stringed Portuguese guitar that is the forerunner of the ukulele

¹**ma·chi** \'mächē\ *n* -s [Jap, town, city] **:** a Japanese town or commercial center; *esp* **:** the lowest administrative division which is coordinate with the purely rural mura

²**machi** \"\ *n* -s [AmerSp, fr. Araucan *machi, mache*] **:** an Araucanian shaman, usu. female

mach·i·a·vel \¦makēə¦vel *sometimes* ¦mäk- *or* ¦mȧk-\ *n* -s *usu cap* [after Niccolò *Machiavelli* †1527 Italian statesman and political philosopher] **:** MACHIAVELLIAN

¹**mach·i·a·vel·li·an** \¦=¦=¦veléən, -lyən\ *adj, usu cap* [Niccolò *Machiavelli* + E *-an*] **1 :** of or relating to Machiavelli or his political theory (as the doctrine that any means however lawless or unscrupulous may be justifiably employed by a ruler in order to establish and maintain a strong central government) **2 :** resembling or suggesting the principles of conduct laid down by Machiavelli **:** characterized by political cunning, duplicity, or bad faith

²**machiavellian** *n* -s *usu cap* **:** an adherent to the political doctrine of Machiavelli **:** a person characterized by Machiavellian behavior esp. in political matters

mach·i·a·vel·li·an·ism \,=¦=¦velēə,nizəm, -lyə,n-\ *n* -s *usu cap* **:** the political doctrine of Machiavelli

mach·i·a·vel·li·an·ist \-,nəst\ *n* -s *usu cap* **:** MACHIAVELLIAN

mach·i·a·vel·li·an·ly \¦=¦=¦veléənlē, -lyə-, -li\ *adv, usu cap* **:** in a Machiavellian manner

mach·i·a·vel·lic \¦=¦=¦velik, -lēk\ *adj, usu cap* [Niccolò *Machiavelli* + E *-ic*] **:** MACHIAVELLIAN

mach·i·a·vel·lism \-¦ve,lizəm\ *n* -s *usu cap* [Niccolò *Machiavelli* + E *-ism*] **:** MACHIAVELLIANISM

ma·chic·o·late \mə'chikə,lāt, ma'-\ *vt* -ED/-ING/-s [ML *machicolatus*, past part. of *machicolare*, fr. OF *machicoller*, fr. *machicoleis* machicolation, fr. *macher* to crush (of imit. origin) + *col* neck, fr. L *collum* — more at COLLAR] **:** to furnish (as a turret) with machicolations

ma·chic·o·la·tion \mə,chikə'lāshən, (,)ma,ch-\ *n* -s **1 a :** an opening between the corbels that support a projecting parapet or in the floor of a gallery or the roof of a portal for shooting or dropping missiles upon assailants attacking below **b :** a parapet containing such openings — see BATTLEMENT illustration **2 :** a construction imitating medieval machicolation

ma·chi·co·tage \¦mashəkō¦täzh\ *n* -s [F, fr. *machicoter* to embellish plain song (fr. *machicot*, a former choir official in the chapter of Notre Dame in Paris, France) + F *-age*] **:** the embellishment of the solo part of plain song by the insertion of ornaments between the authentic tones

ma·chi·cou·lis \¦mäshə(,)kü¦lē, ¦mash-, ,==¦külē\ *n, pl* **machicou·lis** \-lē(z)\ *or* **machicou·lises** \-lēz\ [F *mâchicoulis*, *mâchecoulis*, fr. MF *machicoulis, machecoulis*, alter. of OF *machicoleis* — more at MACHICOLATE] **:** MACHICOLATION

-machies *pl of* -MACHY

ma·chi·guen·ga \,mächə'geŋgə\ *n, pl* **machiguenga** *or* **machiguengas** *usu cap* [Sp, of AmerInd origin] **1 a :** an Arawakan people of southern Peru **b :** a member of such people **2 :** the language of the Machiguenga people

ma·chi·la *also* **ma·chil·la** \mə'shēlə\ *n* -s [Pg, perh. fr. Tamil *macil, mañcil* stage in a journey, fr. Hindi *manzil*, fr. Ar] **:** a hammock slung on a pole used for carrying passengers in many parts of Africa

ma·chil·i·dae \mə'kilə,dē\ *n pl, cap* [NL, fr. *Machilis*, type genus + *-idae*] **:** a cosmopolitan family of primitive insects (order Thysanura) with dorsally convex body, contiguous compound eyes, and three ocelli

ma·chi·lis \mə'kīləs, 'makəl-\ *n, cap* [NL] **:** an Old World genus of very primitive insects that is the type of the family Machilidae

machilla *var of* MOCHILA

ma·chin \mə'chēn\ *n* -s [Tag *matsing*] **:** a grayish brown long-tailed macaque (*Macaca philippinensis*) of the Philippines

ma·chin·abil·i·ty \mə,shēnə'biləd·ē, -lətē, -i\ *n* **:** the quality or state of being machinable

ma·chin·able *also* **ma·chine·able** \mə'shēnəbəl\ *adj* **:** capable of or suitable for being machined

machi·nal \mə'shēnᵊl, 'makən-\ *adj* [L *machinalis*, fr. *machina* machine + *-alis* -al] *archaic* **:** of or relating to machines **:** MECHANICAL

mach·i·nate \'makə,nāt, ÷'mashə-, ÷'maish-, *usu* -ād·+V\ *vb* -ED/-ING/-s [L *machinatus*, past part. of *machinari*, fr. *machina* machine, plan, trick, artifice — more at MACHINE] *vi* **:** PLOT, SCHEME, CONTRIVE ~ *vt* **:** to scheme or contrive to bring (something undesirable) about **:** plan to do (something harmful) **:** PLOT

mach·i·na·tion \,=='nāshən\ *n* -s [L *machination-, machinatio*, fr. *machinatus* + *-ion-, -io* -ion] **1 :** an act or instance of machinating **2 :** a scheming or crafty action, subtle maneuver, or artful design intended to accomplish some end; *esp* **:** one regarded as evil or reprehensible — usu. used in pl. ⟨thwart the vast insidious ~s of some baffled fiend —George Santayana⟩ **3** *obs* **:** use or construction of machinery; *also* **:** a mechanical appliance **syn** see PLOT

mach·i·na·tor \'==,nād·ə(r), -ātə-\ *n* -s [L, fr. *machinatus* + *-or*] **:** one that machinates **:** a plotter or artful schemer

¹**ma·chine** \mə'shēn\ *n* -s [MF, fr. L *machina*, fr. Gk (Dor dial.) *machana* (Attic *mēchanē*), fr. (Dor dial.) *machos* means, expedient (Attic *mēchos*) — more at MAY] **1 a** *archaic* **:** a structure or constructed thing whether material or immaterial **:** ERECTION, HANDIWORK **b** (1) *archaic* **:** SHIP, BOAT (2) **:** CONVEYANCE, VEHICLE ⟨brought his ~ to a halt with a flourish⟩ **c** *obs* **:** APPLIANCE, DEVICE **d** *archaic* **:** a military engine (as a siege tower or catapult) **e :** any of various apparatuses formerly used in the production of theatrical stage effects **f** (1) **:** an assemblage of parts that are usu. solid bodies but include in some cases fluid bodies or electricity in conductors and that transmit forces, motion, and energy one to another in some predetermined manner and to some desired end (as for sewing a seam, printing a newspaper, hoisting a load, or maintaining an electric current) (2) **:** an instrument (as a lever) designed to transmit or modify the application of power, force, or motion (3) **:** a mechanical device of the particular kind relevant or under consideration ⟨run up the seams on the ~⟩ (4) *Brit* **:** a power-driven printing press ⟨in the printing office the hand press is spoken of as the "press" and the machine press as the "~" —John Southward⟩ **2 a :** a living organism or one of its functional systems ⟨the intricate hearing ~ of the bat⟩ **:** bodily mechanism — used esp. when the whole is thought of as a system of more or less mechanically interacting parts ⟨disease alters the balance of the human ~⟩ **b :** a person or organization that acts like a machine esp. in responding automatically and without intelligence or feeling or as though responding mechanically to activating stimuli ⟨thought of the lower animals as mere ~s without sense or sensibility⟩ ⟨making ~s of men⟩ **c** (1) **:** a combination of persons acting together (as for a common end) together with the agencies they use ⟨the entire social ~⟩ ⟨building a powerful war ~⟩ (2) **:** a highly organized group that, under the leadership of a boss or a small clique, controls the policies and activities of a political party esp. for private rather than for public ends **3 :** a literary device or contrivance (as a supernatural agency) introduced for dramatic effect; *also* **:** an agency so introduced

syn MACHINE, ENGINE, APPARATUS, APPLIANCE signify, in common, a device, often complex, for doing work beyond human physical or mental limitations or faster than human hand or mind. MACHINE applies to a construction or organization whose parts are so connected and interrelated that it can be set in motion and perform work as a unit ⟨those most practical *machines* of our modern life, the dynamo and the telephone —Havelock Ellis⟩ ⟨calculators, billers, duplicators, and other business *machines*⟩ ⟨the finest *machine* in the world is useless without a motor to drive it —C.C.Furnas⟩ ⟨as by no means a cold and calculating thinking *machine* —W.L.Sperry⟩ Although in an earlier and still common use ENGINE can signify any device or contrivance to multiply force or speed ⟨metal-wheeled chariots . . . soon appeared as the newest and most powerful *engines* of war —R.W.Murray⟩ ⟨television, our newest and potentially greatest *engine* of enlightenment —Gilbert Seldes⟩ more generally ENGINE applies to a particular kind of machine, usu. one which turns one form of physical power into another more useful, sometimes, however, applying to both a power-generating unit and the total working unit moved by the power unit ⟨gasoline *engines*⟩ ⟨airplane *engines*⟩ ⟨these *engines* were built to pump out mines —C.F.Kettering & Allen Orth⟩ ⟨a fire *engine*⟩ ⟨a steam *engine* pulling a hundred cars⟩ APPARATUS is more general than the other words, applying to any more or less complicated mechanism or unit of organization for effecting a given work, whose parts may be many or few, delicate or crude ⟨*apparatus* (heavy generators, transformers, etc)—*Time*⟩ ⟨substances such as glass, crystal, and flint are linked with *apparatuses* of one kind or another (compasses, barometers, spectrums, and hourglasses) —Louise Bogan⟩ ⟨a table . . . covered with his writing *apparatus* —Osbert Sitwell⟩ ⟨a professional historical journal . . . equipped with an *apparatus* of footnotes —*Times Lit. Supp.*⟩ ⟨the pipes, fixtures, and other *apparatus* inside buildings for bringing in the water supply and removing the liquid and water-borne wastes —*Water & Sewage Control Engineering*⟩ APPLIANCE is often interchangeable with APPARATUS but usu. designates a simple useful machine the power for which can be supplied readily, commonly, therefore, suggesting the electrical appliance ⟨sometimes a bow is drawn with the assistance of the feet, or of a ring-handled dagger, or other *appliance* —*Notes & Queries on Anthropology*⟩ ⟨among those *appliances* reflecting the greatest sales increases were driers and freezers —*Dun's Rev.*⟩ ⟨vacuum cleaners and home *appliances*⟩

²machine \"\ *vb* -ED/-ING/-S *vt* **1 :** to subject to or produce or finish by the action of machinery: as **a :** to turn, shape, plane, mill, or otherwise reduce or finish (as a metal blank or casting) by machine-operated cutting tools **b** *Brit* **:** to print with a power-driven press **2 :** to fashion as if by machinery **:** cause to conform to a fixed pattern **:** STANDARDIZE **~** *vi* **:** to be machinable ⟨brass **~***s* easily⟩

ma·chine·able \-nəbəl\ *var of* MACHINABLE

machine bolt *n* **:** a metal rod with a usu. square or hexagonal wrench head at one end and threads at the other that is commonly available in a size range of from ¼ inch to 3 inches in diameter — see BOLT illustration

machine buff *n* **:** a cut of leather from which a thin layer of the grain surface has been removed leaving a portion of the grain and which is used esp. for upholstery

machine calender *n* **:** a calender stack with all metal rolls placed in the line of flow of the paper between the driers and the winder — compare SUPERCALENDER

machine cannon *n* **:** MACHINE GUN; *esp* **:** one using projectiles larger than used in small arms

machine carbine *n* **:** an automatic carbine **:** SUBMACHINE GUN

machine chest *n* **:** the chest that in papermaking holds the stock coming from the jordan and ready to go to the paper machine

machine-coated \ˌ=ˌ=ˌ=\ *adj, of paper* **:** coated on a paper machine as an integral part of the papermaking operation and not on a separate machine

machined *adj* **:** made or finished by or as if by machine

machine direction *n* **:** the direction in which the stock flows onto the paper machine wire **:** the circumferential direction of a roll of paper; *also* **:** the corresponding dimension of a sheet cut from it — called also *grain, grain direction;* compare CROSS DIRECTION

machine-dried \ˌ=ˌ=ˌ=\ *adj, of paper* **:** completely dried by contact with steam-heated drums

machine file *n* **:** a file with the tang replaced by a round shank designed to be clamped in the chuck of a power-driven machine

machine finish *n* **:** a moderately smooth finish applied to book and cover papers by passing them through the calender rolls of a paper machine — abbr *M.F.*

machine-glazed \ˌ=ˌ=ˌ=\ *adj, of paper* **:** given a high finish on one side only by drying the web in continuous contact with a highly polished heated cylinder (as of a Yankee machine) — abbr. *M.G.*

machine gun *n* **:** an automatic gun firing small-arms ammunition that has a cooling device which permits delivery of sustained fire for relatively long periods and a highly stable mount which permits fire over masks and friendly troops — compare AUTOMATIC RIFLE

machine-gun \ˌ=ˈ=ˌ=\ *vb* [*machine gun*] *vt* **:** to shoot at or kill with a machine gun **~** *vi* **:** to fire a machine gun

machine gunner *n* **:** a member of a crew that serves a machine gun **:** an operator of a machine gun

machine-hour \ˌ=ˈ=ˌ=\ *n* **:** the operation of one machine for one hour used as a basis for cost finding and for determining operating effectiveness

ma·chine·less \məˈshēnləs\ *adj* **:** lacking or done without machines; *esp, of a permanent wave* **:** prepared without use of curlers attached to a heating unit **:** COLD-WAVED

machinelike \ˌ=ˈ=ˌ=\ *adj* **:** resembling a machine esp. in precise regularity of action or stereotyped uniformity of product

ma·chine·ly \məˈshēnlē\ *adv* **:** as if by a machine

machine-made \ˌ=ˈ=ˌ=\ *adj* **1 :** made by machinery — distinguished from *handmade* **2 :** STEREOTYPED, MECHANICAL

ma·chine·man \məˈshēnmən, -nˌman\ *n, pl* **machinemen :** one who operates or tends a machine: as **a** *Brit* **:** PRESSMAN **b :** an operator of a rock drill

machine manager *or* **machine minder** *n, Brit* **:** PRESSMAN

machine operator *n* **:** a worker assigned to or skilled in the operation of a particular kind or class of industrial machine — sometimes distinguished from *machinist*

machine pistol *n* **:** a light inexpensive submachine gun

machine rest *n* **:** a fixed support for holding a firearm while it is fired (as for determining the accuracy of the weapon or checking ammunition loadings)

machine rifle *n* **:** AUTOMATIC RIFLE

machine room *n, Brit* **:** a printing pressroom

ma·chin·ery \məˈshēn(ə)rē, -ri\ *n* -ES [¹*machine* + *-ery*] **1 :** machines as a functioning unit: as **a** *obs* **:** a setup of machines for producing theatrical stage effects **b** (1) **:** the constituent parts of a machine or instrument **:** WORKS ⟨a fine watch with precise and delicate **~**⟩ (2) **:** equipment, stock, or range of machines ⟨the **~** at the mill⟩ ⟨modern textile **~**⟩ **c** *archaic* **:** the machines introduced into a literary work (as a poem) **2 a :** the means and appliances by which something is kept in action or a desired result is obtained ⟨the **~** of the human body⟩ ⟨the **~** of communications⟩ **b :** the system of instrumentalities and organized activities by means of which an organization functions or a social or other process is carried on ⟨the complex **~** of modern society⟩ ⟨the **~** of negotiation⟩; *esp* **:** the apparatus of government ⟨the United Nations set up **~** for mediation⟩ **syn** see EQUIPMENT

machine screw *n* **:** a screw with slotted head or socket head used for holding metal parts together

machine shop *n* **:** a workshop in which work is machined to size and assembled

machine steel *also* **machinery steel** *n* **:** steel of a grade suitable for the working parts of machines — distinguished from *tool steel*

machine tap *n* **:** a tap operated by machinery

machine telegraphy *n* **:** a system of telegraphy employing an automatic transmitter **:** automatic telegraphy

machine tender *n* **:** the working supervisor of a papermaking machine

machine tool *n* **:** a usu. power-driven machine designed for shaping solid work by tooling either by removing material (as in a lathe or milling machine) or by subjecting to deformation (as in a punch press) ⟨the *machine tool* industry⟩ ⟨heavy-duty *machine tools*⟩

machine-tooled \ˌ=ˈ=ˌ=\ *adj* **:** made or finished with or as if with a machine tool **:** finely and precisely finished or shaped ⟨a *machine-tooled* accuracy of statement⟩

machining *n* -s **1 :** an act or instance of running a machine (as a sewing machine or printing press) **2 :** machine work

ma·chin·ism \məˈshēˌnizəm\ *n* -s [¹*machine* + *-ism*] **:** preoccupation with or dependence on machines (as in economics or politics)

ma·chin·ist \-ˌnəst\ *n* -s [prob. fr. F *machiniste,* fr. *machine* + *-iste* -ist] **1 a** (1) *archaic* **:** an inventor or builder of machines (2) **:** a worker who fabricates, assembles, or repairs machinery **b :** a craftsman skilled in the use of machine tools — sometimes distinguished from *machine operator* **c :** MACHINE OPERATOR **2** *archaic* **:** a person in charge of the mechanical aspects of a theatrical production (as lighting, technical machines, and handling of scenery) **3 :** a member of a political machine **4 a :** MACHINIST'S MATE **b :** a warrant officer (as in the U. S. Navy) whose specialty is supervision of the operation, maintenance, and repair of machinery and engines

machinist's hammer *n* **:** a cross-peen, ball-peen, or straight-peen hammer

machinist's mate *n* **:** a petty officer in the engineer's department of the U. S. Navy

ma·chin·ize \məˈshēˌnīz\ *vt* -ED/-ING/-S [¹*machine* + *-ize*] **:** to make like a machine **:** convert or organize into a machine ⟨the *machinizing* of party politics⟩

ma·chi·no·fac·ture \məˈshēnōˌfakchə(r), -ksh-\ *n* -s [¹*machine* + *-o-* + *-facture* (as in *manufacture*)] **1 :** making or building by means of machines **2 :** a product of machine activity

mach·ism \ˈmäˌkizəm, -k-\ *n* -s *usu cap* [Ernst *Mach* †1916 Austrian physicist and philosopher + E *-ism*] **:** the theories of the physicist and philosopher Mach; *specif* **:** his empiriocriticism

mach·me·ter *pronunc at* MACH NUMBER + ˌmēd·ə(r)\ *n, usu cap* [*mach* + *-meter*] **:** an airspeed indicator calibrated to read Mach number directly

mach number \ˈmäk-, ˈmak- *sometimes chiefly Brit* ˈmak-\ *n, usu cap M* [after Ernst *Mach*] **:** a number representing the ratio of the speed of a body to the speed of sound in the surrounding atmosphere ⟨for subsonic speeds the *Mach number* is less than 1 (as 0.80) and for supersonic speeds it is greater than 1 (as 1.31 or 5)⟩

macho·polyp *or* **macho·zooid** \ˌmakō+\ *n* [Gk *machē* battle, fight + *-o-* E *polyp* or *zooid* — more at -MACHY] **:** a defensive zooid of a hydroid colony, having an abundance of stinging organs but no mouth

ma·chree \məˈkrē, -k-\ *n* -s [IrGael *mo chroidhe* my heart, my dear] *Irish* **:** my dear

macht·po·li·tik \ˈmäktˌpōlēˌtēk, -äkt-\ *n* -s [G, fr. *macht* power (fr. OHG *maht*) + *politik* politics, fr. F *politique* — more at MIGHT, POLITICS] **:** POWER POLITICS; *specif* **:** a doctrine in political theory advocating the use of power and esp. of physical force by a political state in the attainment of its objectives ⟨an internationalism based on realpolitik and **~** —*New Republic*⟩ — compare REALPOLITIK

mach wave *n, usu cap M* [after Ernst *Mach* †1916 Austrian physicist and philosopher] **:** the envelope of wave fronts propagated from an infinitesimal disturbance in a supersonic flow field

-ma·chy \məkē, -ki\ *n comb form* -ES [Gk *-machia,* fr. *machē* battle, fight (fr. *machesthai* to battle, fight) + *-ia* -y] **:** warfare **:** contest between or by means of ⟨logo*machy*⟩

machy *abbr* machinery

machzor *var of* MAHZOR

m acid *n, usu cap M* **:** a crystalline sulfonic acid $NH_2C_{10}H_5(OH)SO_3H$ made by alkaline fusion of a disulfonic acid of alpha-naphthylamine and used as a dye intermediate; 5-amino-1-naphthol-3-sulfonic acid

ma·ci·gno \məˈchēn(ˌ)yō\ *n* -s [It, millstone, flysch, fr. (assumed) VL *machineus,* fr. L *machina* machine — more at MACHINE] **:** FLYSCH

mac·i·len·cy \ˈmasələnsē\ *also* **mac·i·lence** \-n(t)s\ *n, pl* **macilencies** *also* **macilenc·es :** macilent condition; *esp* **:** leanness of body

mac·i·lent \-nt\ *adj* [L *macilentus,* fr. *macies* leanness — more at EMACIATE] **:** THIN, EMACIATED, LEAN

macing *pres part of* MACE

mc·in·tire \ˈmakənˌtī(ə)r\ *n* -s *usu cap M&I* [after Samuel *McIntyre* †1811 Am. architect and woodcarver] **:** a style of late 18th and early 19th century American furniture and interior architecture distinguished by the discreet use of carving esp. on vertical elements and the employment of rich veneering

macintosh *var of* MACKINTOSH

¹mack *interj* [perh. euphemism for (*Saint*) *Mary*] *obs* — used as a mild oath

²mack \ˈmak\ *n* -s [prob. modif. of F *maquereau,* fr. OF *makerel* — more at MACKEREL] *slang* **:** PIMP ⟨accomplished courtesans were attended by their . . . **~***s* —Herbert Asbury⟩

³mack *var of* MAC

mackallow *n* -s [ScGael *macaladh* fostering after being weaned] *obs Scot* **:** goods held in trust by a foster parent for a child

mc·kay \məˈkā\ *adj, usu cap M&K* [after Gordon *McKay* †1903 Am. inventor and industrialist] **:** of, relating to, or used in the McKay process

mack·ay·ite \ˈmakēˌīt\ *n* -s [John W. *MacKay* †1902 Am. miner and financier + E *-ite*] **:** a mineral $Fe_2(TeO_3)_3.nH_2O$(?) consisting of a hydrous tellurite of iron

mc·kay process \məˈkā-\ *n, usu cap M&K* [after Gordon *McKay*] **:** a process of shoe manufacture in which the outsole is sewn to the insole, the needle going through outsole, shoe upper, lining, and insole and forming a chain stitch

¹mack·er·el \ˈmak(ə)rəl\ *n, pl* **mackerel** *or* **mackerels** [ME *makerel,* fr. OF, prob. fr. *makerel* pimp, modif. of MD *makelaer* go-between, broker, pimp, fr. *makelen* to act as go-between, broker or pimp (fr. *maken* to make, do) + *-aer* -er; fr. the belief that mackerel act as pimps for the herring in the schools they accompany — more at MAKE] **1 a :** a fish (*Scomber scombrus*) of the No. Atlantic that is green above with dark blue bars and silvery below, reaches a length of about 18 inches, and in both Europe and America is one of the most important food fishes, being caught chiefly when it leaves the high seas and approaches the coasts in great schools to spawn — see BLINKER, SPIKE, TINKER **b :** a fish of the suborder Scombroidea; *esp* **:** a comparatively small member of this group as distinguished from a bonito or tuna **2 :** any of various fishes more or less resembling members of the Scombroidea — usu. used with a qualifying term ⟨snake **~**⟩ ⟨horse **~**⟩ ⟨Atka **~**⟩

²mackerel \"\ *adj* **:** TICKED — used esp. of a coat pattern of tabby cats in which the dark bars are not solid

³mackerel *n* -s [ME *makerel,* fr. MF — more at ¹MACKEREL] *obs* **:** PIMP

mackerel-back \ˈ=(=)=ˌ=\ *or* **mackerel-backed sky** \ˈ=(=)=ˌ=-\ *n* **:** MACKEREL SKY

mackerel bait *n* **:** jellyfish and other small oceanic creatures on which mackerel feed

mackerel bird *n* **1** *Brit* **:** WRYNECK **2** *Brit* **:** a young kittiwake

mackerel breeze *or* **mackerel gale** *n* **:** a wind that ruffles the water and is held to favor the catching of mackerel with hook and line

mackerel cock *n, Irish* **:** MANX SHEARWATER

mack·er·el·er \ˈmak(ə)rələ(r)\ *n* -s **:** a fisherman or boat engaged in mackerel fishing

mackerel goose *n* **:** PHALAROPE

mackerel gull *n* **:** TERN

mack·er·el·ing \ˈmak(ə)rəliŋ\ *n* -s **:** mackerel fishing

mackerel midge *n* **:** the young of various rocklings

mackerel scad *also* **mackerel shad** *n* **:** any of several small carangid fishes of a cosmopolitan genus (*Decapterus*); *esp* **:** a common western Atlantic fish (*D. macarellus*) that is of a silvery color and plumbeous below

mackerel scale *n* **:** any of the somewhat angular cloudlets forming one variety of mackerel sky

mackerel shark *n* **:** a shark of the family Lamnidae esp. of the genus *Isurus; specif* **:** PORBEAGLE — see BONITO SHARK

mackerel sky *n* **:** a sky covered with rows of altocumulus or cirrocumulus clouds resembling the patterns on a mackerel's back

mackerel tuna *n* **:** LITTLE TUNA

mack·ie line \ˈmakē-\ *n, usu cap M* [after Alexander *Mackie,* 19th cent. scientist] **:** a light outline at the edge of dense or dark parts of a photographic image caused by a retardation of development in the edge area — compare ADJACENCY EFFECT

mack·i·naw \ˈmakəˌnȯ\ *n* -s *sometimes cap* [fr. *Mackinaw* City, Michigan, formerly the site of an important trading post] **1** *or* **mackinaw boat :** a flat-bottomed boat with pointed prow and square stern propelled by oars or sails or both and formerly much used on the upper Great Lakes and their tributaries **2** *also* **mackinaw blanket :** a heavy woolen blanket in solid colors or stripes formerly distributed by the U.S. government to the Indians **3 a** *also* **mackinaw cloth :** a heavy single or double cloth of wool or wool and other fibers often with face and back of different colors or with a plaid design and usu. heavily napped and felted for warmth **b** *also* **mackinaw coat :** a short usu. double-breasted and belted coat or jacket of mackinaw or similar heavy fabric — called also *blanket-coat* **4** *usu* **mackinaw trout :** LAKE TROUT b

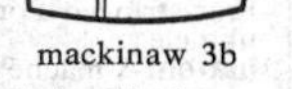

mackinaw 3b

mack·i·nawed \-ȯd\ *adj* **:** dressed in a mackinaw

mc·kin·ley·ism \məˈkinlēˌizəm\ *n* -s *usu cap 1st M&K* [William *McKinley* †1901, 25th president of the U.S.] **:** the political policies advocated by or associated with William McKinley

mack·in·tosh *also* **mac·in·tosh** \ˈmakənˌtäsh\ *n* -ES [after Charles *Macintosh* †1843 Scot. chemist and inventor] **1** *chiefly Brit* **:** RAINCOAT **2 :** a lightweight waterproof fabric orig. of rubberized cotton

mack·in·toshed \-sht\ *adj* **:** dressed in a mackintosh

mack·in·tosh·ite \-ä,shīt\ *n* -s [James B. *Mackintosh* †1891 Am. chemist + E *-ite*] **:** an altered metamict uranothorite

¹mack·le \ˈmakəl\ *n* -s [F *macule,* spot, stain, mackle, fr. L *macula* spot, stain] **:** a blur or double impression on a printed sheet

²mackle \"\ *vb* -ED/-ING/-S **:** BLUR

mack's cement \ˈmak(s)-\ *n, usu cap M* [after L. *Mack,* 19th cent. scientist] **:** a cementing material made by the complete dehydration of gypsum and the addition of a small percentage of calcined sodium sulfate and potassium sulfate

ma·cle \ˈmakəl\ *n* -s [F, wide-meshed net, mascle, macle, fr. OF, mesh, lozenge voided — more at MASCLE] **1 :** CHIASTOLITE **2 a :** a twinned crystal **b :** a flat often triangular diamond that is usu. a twinned crystal **3 :** a dark or discolored spot (as in a mineral specimen)

mac·leaya \məˈklāə\ *n, cap* [NL, after Alexander *MacLeay* †1848 Brit. entomologist and colonial statesman] **:** a genus of Asiatic herbs (family Papaveraceae) with pinnately lobed glaucous leaves and tall showy panicles of cream-colored apetalous flowers — see PLUME POPPY

ma·cled \ˈmakəld\ *adj* **1** *of a mineral* **:** marked like chiastolite **2** *of a crystal* **:** having a twin structure **3 :** SPOTTED — used chiefly of minerals

mc·leod \məˈklau̇d\ *or* **mcleod tool** *n* -s [fr. the name *McLeod*] **:** a combination hoe and rake used esp. by the U.S. Forest Service in fire fighting

mcleod gauge *n, usu cap M&L* [after Herbert *McLeod* †1923 Eng. chemist] **:** a sensitive instrument for measuring the pressure of a highly rarefied gas by compressing a portion of the gas in a closed capillary tube and applying Boyle's law

ma·clu·ra \məˈklu̇rə\ *n* -s [NL, after William *Maclure* †1840 Am. geologist] **:** OSAGE ORANGE

ma·clu·rin \-rən\ *n* -s [ISV *maclur-* (fr. NL *Maclura*) + *-in;* orig. formed in G] **:** a light yellow crystalline pigment $C_6H_3(OH)_2COC_6H_2(OH)_3$ found esp. in old fustic **:** a pentahydroxy-benzophenone

ma·clu·rite \-ü,rīt\ *n, cap* [NL, after William *Maclure*] **:** a genus of Ordovician gastropod mollusks known from their usu. large flat spiral shells

mac·nab cypress \mәkˈnab-\ *also* **macnab's cypress** *n, usu cap M & often cap N* [after James *MacNab* †1878 Scot. botanist] **:** a bushy evergreen tree (*Cupressus macnabiana*) of the Pacific coast of No. America

ma·co \ˈmä(ˌ)kō\ *n* -s [after *Maho* or *Mako* Bey, 19th cent. Egyptian official] **:** EGYPTIAN COTTON — used esp. of the natural undyed state ⟨black hose with **~** feet⟩

ma·cock *or* **may·cock** \ˈmāˌkäk\ *n* -s [fr. *mawcawk, mahawk* (in some Algonquian language of Virginia)] **:** an inferior melon or other cucurbit formerly cultivated by the Indians of eastern No. America

ma·con \ˈmäˈkōⁿ\ *n* -s *usu cap* [F *mâcon,* fr. *Mâcon,* France] **:** a still Burgundy wine that is made in the department of Saône-et-Loire, France, in both a red variety and a white variety

ma·con·ite \ˈmākəˌnīt\ *n* -s [*Macon* county, Georgia + E *-ite*] **:** a vermiculite from No. Carolina

macouba *n* -s **:** MACCABOY

ma·coun wild-rye *also* **macoun rye grass** \məˈkün-\ *n, usu cap M* [fr. the name *Macoun*] **:** a native perennial forage grass (*Elymus macounii*) of western No. America

macoute *obs var of* MACUTA

mac·quar·ie perch \məˈkwärē-\ *n* [after Lachlan *MacQuarie* †1824 British army officer and governor of New South Wales, Australia] **:** a locally important food fish (*Macquaria australasica*) of the family Serranidae that is reddish brown above and yellow below and is restricted to the upper reaches of the Murray river system of Australia

macquarie pine *n, usu cap M* [after Lachlan *MacQuarie*] **:** HUON PINE

mac·que·reau \ˌmakˈrō\ *n, pl* **macque·reaux** \-ō(z)\ [F *maquereau,* fr. OF *makerel* — more at MACKEREL] **:** PIMP, PROCURER

macr- *or* **macro-** *comb form* [F & L, fr. Gk *makr-, makro-* long, fr. *makros* — more at MEAGER] **1 :** long ⟨*macro*biotic⟩ ⟨*macro*diagonal⟩ **2 :** large ⟨*macr*ergate⟩ ⟨*macro*molecule⟩ ⟨*macro*gamete⟩ ⟨*macro*mastia⟩ ⟨*macro*gnathism⟩ ⟨*macro*podia⟩ — often used to contrast with *micr-* **3 :** macrodiagonal ⟨*macro*dome⟩ **4 :** including and more comprehensive than ⟨*Macro*-Khoisan⟩ — used of a language group

mac·ra·can·tho·rhyn·chi·a·sis \ˌmakrəˌkan(t)thə(ˌ)riŋˈkīəsəs\ *n* -ES [NL, fr. *Macracanthorhynchus* + *-iasis*] **:** infestation with or disease caused by an acanthocephalid worm of the genus *Macracanthorhynchus*

mac·ra·can·tho·rhyn·chus \-ˈriŋkəs\ *n, cap* [NL, fr. *macr-* + *acanth-* + *-rhynchus*] **:** a genus of Acanthocephala that includes the common acanthocephalan of swine

mac·rad·e·nous \(ˈ)maˈkradᵊnəs\ *adj* [*macr-* + *aden-* + *-ous*] **:** having large glands

mac·ra·me \ˈmakrəˌmā, məˈkrämē\ *n* -s [F or It; F *macramé,* fr. It *macramè,* fr. Turk *makrama, mahrama* napkin, kerchief, face towel, fr. Ar *migramah* embroidered veil] **1 :** a coarse lace or decorative fringe made by knotting threads or cords in a geometrical pattern — see MACRAME KNOT **2** *also* **macrame cord :** cord for or suitable for making macrame

macrame knot *n* **:** an ornate knot often used in making macrame

macrame knot

mac·ran·drous \(ˈ)maˈkrandrəs\ *adj* [*macr-* + *-androus*] **:** having oogonia and antheridia borne on the same plant or on plants of similar size and form — used of green algae of the family Oedogoniaceae; compare NANNANDROUS

mac·rau·che·nia \ˌmaˌkrȯˈkēnēə\ *n, cap* [NL, fr. Gk *makrauchen* long-necked (fr. *makr-* macr- + *auchēn* neck) + NL *-ia*] **:** a genus (the type of the family Macraucheniidae) of long-necked three-toed Pleistocene mammals (order Litopterna) of So. America that had a complete dentition of 44 teeth without a diastema and with pitted incisors like those of the horse, the external nostrils far back, cervical vertebrae resembling those of camels, and other characters suggesting rhinoceroses

mac·ren·ce·phal·ic \ˌmaˌkr+ -\ *also* **mac·ren·ceph·a·lous** \ˌmaˌkr+\ *adj* [*macr-* + *encephalic* or *encephalous*] **:** having a large or long brain case

mac·ro \ˈma(ˌ)krō\ *adj* [*macr-*] **1 :** large, thick, or excessively developed ⟨**~** layer of the cerebral cortex⟩ ⟨the book as the **~** unit of thought —Eugene Garfield⟩ **2 :** of or involving large quantities **:** intended for use with large quantities ⟨a **~** procedure in analysis⟩ ⟨carrying out a test on a **~** scale⟩ **:** GROSS ⟨the **~** appearance of a specimen⟩

mac·ro·analysis \ˌma(ˌ)krō+\ *n* [ISV *macr-* + *analysis*] **:** chemical analysis not on a small or minute scale **:** qualitative or quantitative analysis dealing with quantities usu. of the order of grams — opposed to *microanalysis*

macro-axis \"+\ *n* [*macr-* + *axis*] **:** the longer lateral axis of an orthorhombic or triclinic crystal

mac·rob·del·la \ˌmaˌkräbˈdelə\ *n, cap* [NL, fr. *macr-* + *-bdella*] **:** a genus of large active aquatic blood-sucking leeches resembling and closely related to the Old World medicinal leech

mac·ro·bi·an \(ˈ)maˈkrōbēən\ *adj* [Gk *makrobios* (fr. *makr-* macr- + *bios* life) + E *-an* — more at QUICK] **:** LONG-LIVED

mac·ro·bi·o·sis \ˌmakrōˌbīˈōsəs\ *n* -ES [NL, fr. LGk *makrobiōsis,* fr. *makr-* macr- + *-biōsis* -biosis] **:** LONGEVITY

mac·ro·bi·ot·ic \ˌmakrōˌbīˈäd·ik *also* -ˌbē-\ *adj* [Gk *makrobiotos* long-lived (fr. *makr-* macr- + *-biotos,* fr. *bios* life) + E *-ic*] **:** LONG-LIVED; *esp, of a seed* **:** surviving in the dormant state for many years — compare MESOBIOTIC

mac·ro·bi·ot·ics \ˌ⸗⸗(ˌ)⸗ˈäd·iks\ *n pl but sing or pl in constr* **:** the art of prolonging life

mac·ro·bi·o·tus \ˌmakrəˈbīəd·əs\ *n, cap* [NL, fr. Gk *makrobiotos*] **:** a genus of bear animalcules having the body naked, transparent, and containing numerous fat globules that resemble enormous blood corpuscles

mac·ro·blast \ˈmakrə,blast\ *n* [ISV *macr-* + *-blast*] **1 :** MEGALOBLAST **2 :** an erythroblast destined to produce macrocytes

mac·ro·brachium \ˌmakrō+\ *n, cap* [NL, fr. *macr-* + *brachium*] **:** a genus of large stout chiefly tropical shrimps including one (*M. jamaicensæ*) that occurs in freshwaters of Florida and the Gulf coast to Brazil and sometimes attains a length of 17 inches and a weight of over 3 pounds

mac·ro·car·pa \ˌmakrəˈkärpə\ *n* -s [NL *macrocarpa* (specific epithet of *Cupressus macrocarpa*), fr. *macr-* + *-carpa* (fr. Gk *karpos* fruit) — more at HARVEST] **:** a New Zealand evergreen shrub or tree (*Cupressus macrocarpa*) that is used for hedges and that sometimes causes abortion in cattle that browse on it

mac·ro·cen·trus \ˌmakrōˈsen·trəs\ *n, cap* [NL, fr. Gk *makrokentros* with a long sting, fr. *makr-* macr- + *kentron* sting — more at CENTER] **:** a genus of polyembryonic braconid wasps which are larval parasites of other insects and some of which are important in the biological control of noxious pests (as the oriental peach moth)

mac·ro·ceph·a·lous \ˌmakrōˈsefələs\ *or* **mac·ro·ce·phal·ic** \-səˈfalik\ *adj* [F *macrocéphale* (fr. Gk *makrokephalos* having a long head, fr. *makro-* macr- + *-kephalos* -cephalous) + E *-ous* or *-ic*] **1 a :** having an exceptionally large head ⟨a ~ idiot⟩ **b** *of a cranium* **:** exceptionally or abnormally large **2** *of a dicotyledonous embryo* **:** having the cotyledons consolidated

¹**mac·ro·ceph·a·lus** \ˌ⸗⸗ˈsefələs\ [NL, fr. Gk *makrokephalos* having a long head] *syn of* PHACOCHOERUS

²**macrocephalus** \"\ *n, pl* **macrocepha·li** \-ˌlī\ [NL, fr. Gk *makrokephalos* having a long head] **:** a macrocephalous person or skull

mac·ro·ceph·a·ly \-lē\ *n* -ES [F *macrocéphalie*, fr. *macrocéphale* + *-ie* -y] **:** the quality or state of being macrocephalous

mac·ro·chaeta \ˌmakrō+\ *n, pl* **macrochaetae** [NL, fr. *macr-* + *-chaeta*] **:** any of various large bristles occurring on the bodies of insects that are used as a basis for classification — distinguished from *microchaeta*

mac·ro·chei·ra \ˌmakrōˈkīrə\ *n, cap* [NL, fr. Gk *makrocheir* long-armed, fr. *makr-* macr- + *cheir* hand — more at CHIR-] **:** a genus of deep sea spider crabs (family Majidae) consisting of the giant crab of Japan

mac·roch·e·lys \məˈkräkələs\ *n, cap* [NL, fr. *macr-* + Gk *chelys* tortoise — more at CHELYS] **:** a genus of turtles consisting of the alligator snapper

mac·ro·chemical \ˌmakrō+\ *adj* [*macr-* + *chemical*] **:** of, relating to, or using the methods of macrochemistry — **mac·ro·chemically** \"+\ *adv*

mac·ro·chemistry \"+\ *n* [*macr-* + *chemistry*] **:** chemistry studied or applied without the use of the microscope or of microanalysis — contrasted with *microchemistry*

mac·ro·chi·res \ˌmakrōˈkī(ˌ)rēz\ *n pl, cap* [NL, fr. Gk *makrocheir* long-armed] *in some classifications* **:** a group of birds including the swifts and hummingbirds and sometimes also the goatsuckers

mac·ro·chiroptera \ˌmakrō+\ [NL, fr. *macr-* + *Chiroptera*] *syn of* MEGACHIROPTERA

mac·ro·cinematography \"+\ *n* [*macr-* + *cinematography*] **:** photomacrography in which the product is a motion picture

mac·ro·climate \"+\ *n* [*macr-* + *climate*] **:** the overall climate of a region usu. a large geographic area — distinguished from *microclimate* — **mac·ro·climatic** \"+\ *adj*

mac·ro·conidium \"+\ *n, pl* **macroconidia** [NL, fr. *macr-* + *conidium*] **:** a large usu. multinucleate conidium of a fungus — compare MICROCONIDIUM

mac·ro·conjugant \"+\ *n* [*macr-* + *conjugant*] **:** the larger member of a pair of conjugating protozoans of unequal size

mac·ro·cosm \ˈmakrə,käzəm\ *n* -s [F *macrocosme*, fr. ML *macrocosmos, macrocosmus*, fr. *macr-* + Gk *kosmos* order, universe] **1 :** the great world **:** the universe in its entirety — contrasted with *microcosm* **2 :** a complex regarded as a whole world in itself ⟨to consider the state as the ~ of the family⟩ ⟨the great ~ of pain —Henry Miller⟩

mac·ro·cos·mic \ˌ⸗⸗ˈkäzmik\ *adj* **:** of, relating to, or constituting a macrocosm — **mac·ro·cos·mi·cal·ly** \-mək(ə)lē\ *adv*

mac·ro·cosmos \ˌmakrə+\ *n* [ML — more at MACROCOSM] **:** MACROCOSM

mac·ro·cranial \ˌmakrō+\ *adj* [*macr-* + *cranial*] **:** having a large or long skull

mac·ro·crystalline \"+\ *adj* [*macr-* + *crystalline*] **:** consisting of or having crystals large enough to be determined by the eye or a simple lens

mac·ro·cyclic \"+\ *adj* [*macr-* + *cyclic*] **1** *of an organic chemical* **:** containing a ring structure of large size consisting usu. of 15 or more atoms **2** *of a rust fungus* **:** having one or more binuclear spores in addition to teliospores and sporidia **:** having a long or complex life cycle

mac·ro·cyst \ˈmakrō,sist\ *n* [ISV *macr-* + *cyst*] **:** a large spore case or cyst; *esp* **:** a young encysted resting plasmodium of a slime mold — compare MICROCYST

mac·ro·cys·tis \ˌmakrōˈsistəs\ *n* [NL, fr. *macr-* + *-cystis*] **1** *cap* **:** a genus of brown algae (family Laminariaceae) that are often very large and consist of a slender stipe with pinnate fronds and floats — see GIANT KELP **2** *pl* **macrocystis :** any plant of the genus *Macrocystis*

mac·ro·cyte \ˈmakrə,sīt\ *n* -s [ISV *macr-* + *-cyte*] **:** an exceptionally large red blood cell occurring chiefly in anemias (as pernicious anemia)

mac·ro·cyt·ic \ˌmakrōˈsid·ik\ *adj* **:** of or relating to macrocytes; *specif, of an anemia* **:** characterized by macrocytes in the blood ⟨pernicious anemia is a ~ anemia⟩

mac·ro·cy·to·sis \ˌmakrō,sīˈtōsəs\ *n, pl* **macrocyto·ses** \-ō,sēz\ [NL, fr. ISV *macrocyte* + NL *-osis*] **:** the occurrence of macrocytes in the blood

mac·ro·diagonal \ˌmakrō+\ *n* [*macr-* + *diagonal*] **:** MACRO⸗AXIS

mac·ro·dome \ˈmakrə,dōm\ *n* [*macr-* + *dome*] **:** the dome of a crystal having planes parallel to the longer lateral axis — compare BRACHYDOME, CLINODOME

mac·ro·dont \-,dänt\ *adj* [ISV *macr-* + *-odont*] **:** having large teeth usu. with a dental index of over 44 — **mac·ro·don·tia** \ˌmakrəˈdänch(ē)ə\ *or* **mac·ro·don·tism** \ˈmakrə,dän,tizəm\ *n* -s

mac·ro·economic \ˌmakrō+\ *adj* [*macr-* + *economic*] **:** of, relating to, or based on macroeconomics ⟨~ decisions⟩

mac·ro·economics \"+\ *n pl but usu sing in constr* [*macr-* + *economics*] **:** study of the economic system as a whole esp. with reference to its general level of output and income and the interrelations among sectors of the economy—opposed to *microeconomics*

mac·ro·element \"+\ *n* [*macr-* + *element*] **:** MACRONUTRIENT

mac·ro·ergate \"+\ *also* **mac·rer·gate** \(ˈ)maˈkrər,gāt\ *n* [ISV *macr-* + *ergate*] **:** a member of a caste of atypically large worker ants

mac·ro·etch \ˈmakrō,ech\ *vt* [*macr-* + *etch*] **:** to etch (metal) for examination with the naked eye

mac·ro·evolution \ˌma(ˌ)krō+\ *n* [*macr-* + *evolution*] **:** evolutionary change involving relatively large and complex steps (as transformation of one species to another) — distinguished from *microevolution;* compare SALTATORY EVOLUTION — **macroevolutionary** *adj*

mac·ro·fauna \ˌmakrō+\ *n* [NL, fr. *macr-* + *fauna*] **1 :** a large or widely distributed fauna **:** the fauna of a macrohabitat **2 :** animals large enough to be seen by the naked eye ⟨the ~ of a sewage filtration bed⟩ — compare MESOFAUNA, MICROFAUNA — **mac·ro·faunal** \"+\ *adj*

mac·ro·flora \"+\ *n* [NL, fr. *macr-* + *flora*] **1 :** a large or widely distributed flora **:** the flora of a macrohabitat **2 :** plants large enough to be seen by the naked eye ⟨the ~ of a coral reef⟩

mac·ro·fossil \ˌmakrō+\ *n* [*macr-* + *fossil*] **:** a fossil large enough to be observed by direct inspection — compare MICROFOSSIL

mac·ro·gamete \ˌma(ˌ)krō+\ *n* [ISV *macr-* + *gamete*] **:** the larger and usu. female gamete of a heterogamous organism — compare MICROGAMETE

mac·ro·gametocyte \"+\ *n* **:** a gametocyte producing macrogametes

mac·rog·a·my \məˈkrägəmē\ *n* -ES [*macr-* + *-gamy*] **1 :** HOLOGAMY **2 :** syngamy between fully developed vegetative cells (as in certain protozoa or algae) — compare MICROGAMY

mac·roglia \(ˈ)maˈkräglēə, ˌmakrəˈglīə\ *n* -s [NL, fr. *macr-* + *neuroglia*] **:** neuroglia made up of astrocytes — **mac·rogli·al** \-ēəl,-īəl\ *adj*

mac·ro·glos·sia \ˌmakrōˈgläsēə, -lȯs-\ *n* -s [NL, fr. *macr-* + *-glossia*] **:** pathological and commonly congenital enlargement of the tongue

mac·ro·graph \ˈmakrə,graf, -ráf\ *n* [*macr-* + *-graph*] **:** a usu. photographic graphic reproduction of an object that may be slightly reduced, of natural size, or magnified up to a limit of about 10 diameters

mac·ro·graph·ic \ˌmakrəˈgrafik\ *adj* **:** of, relating to, being, or involved in macrography

mac·rog·ra·phy \məˈkrägrəfē\ *n* -ES [*macr-* + *-graphy*] **1 a :** a tendency to write unusually large **b :** unusually large writing **2 :** examination or study with the naked eye — opposed to *micrography* **3 :** the art or process of making macrographs

mac·ro·habitat \ˌmakrō+\ *n* [*macr-* + *habitat*] **:** a habitat of sufficient extent to present considerable variation of environment, contain varied ecological niches, and support a large and usu. complex flora and fauna

mac·ro·lecithal \ˌmakrō+\ *adj* [*macr-* + *lecithal*] **:** MEGALECITHAL

mac·ro·lepidoptera \"+\ *n pl, cap* [NL, fr. *macr-* + *Lepidoptera*] *in some esp former classifications* **:** a major division of Lepidoptera comprising the butterflies and the noctuid, bombycid, sphingid, and geometrid moths together with certain related moths and including most of the large lepidopters and none of the minute forms — now usu. used descriptively without taxonomic implications and then often not capitalized; compare MICROLEPIDOPTERA — **mac·ro·lepidopterous** \"+\ *adj*

mac·ro·linguistics \"+\ *n* [*macr-* + *linguistics*] **:** the study of phenomena connected in any way with language

mac·rol·o·gy \məˈkräləjē\ *n* -ES [L *macrologia*, fr. Gk *makrologia*, fr. *makrologein* to use many words, fr. *makr-* macr- + *-logein* (fr. *logos* word, speech) + *-ia* -y — more at LEGEND] **:** PLEONASM 1

mac·ro·mania \ˌmakrō+\ *n* [NL, fr. *macr-* + *mania*] **:** a delusion that things (as parts of the patient's body) are larger than they really are — **mac·ro·maniacal** \"+\ *adj*

mac·ro·mas·tia \ˌmakrōˈmastēə\ *n* -s [NL, fr. *macr-* + *-mastia*] **:** excessive development of the mammary glands

mac·ro·mere \ˈmakrō,mi(ə)r\ *n* -s [*macr-* + *-mere*] **:** any of the large blastomeres of the vegetative hemisphere of an embryo that result from the unequal segmentation of a telolecithal egg — opposed to *micromere;* see BLASTULA illustration

mac·ro·mesentery \ˌmakrō+\ *n* [*macr-* + *mesentery*] **:** PROTOCNEME

mac·ro·method \"+\ *n* [*macr-* + *method*] **:** a method (as of analysis) not involving the use of very small quantities of material — opposed to *micromethod*

mac·ro·molecular \"+\ *adj* [ISV *macr-* + *molecular*] **:** of or relating to a macromolecule **:** consisting of or characterized by macromolecules ⟨~ compounds⟩

mac·ro·molecule \"+\ *n* [ISV *macr-* + *molecule*] **:** a very large molecule (as of a protein, cellulose, rubber, or other natural or synthetic high polymer) ⟨possess more reliable information on the structure of atoms and small molecules than on the structure of colloidal particles and ~s —*Physics Today*⟩ ⟨~s with a diameter of about 100 A (=10^{-5} mm) . . . can be seen in electron micrographs —Felix Haurowitz⟩

macro-moth \ˈmakrō+,-\ *n* [*macr-* + *moth*] **:** a moth belonging to the Macrolepidoptera

mac·ro·mutant \ˌmakrō+\ *n* [*macr-* + *mutant*] **:** an organism that has undergone macromutation

mac·ro·mutation \"+\ *n* [*macr-* + *mutation*] **:** complex mutation involving concurrent alteration of numerous characters — compare MACROEVOLUTION — **mac·ro·mutational** \"+\ *adj*

macron \ˈmāˌkrän, ˌkrən *also* ˈma|\ *n* -s [Gk *makron*, neut. of *makros* long — more at MEAGER] **:** a mark ¯ placed over a vowel to indicate that the vowel is long or placed over a syllable or used alone to indicate a stressed or long syllable in a foot of verse

mac·ro·nuclear \ˌma(ˌ)krō+\ *adj* [*macronucleus* + *-ar*] **:** of or relating to a macronucleus

mac·ro·nucleate *also* **mac·ro·nucleated** \"+\ *adj* [NL *macronucleus* + E *-ate* or *-ated* (fr. *-ate* + *-ed*)] **:** having a macronucleus

mac·ro·nucleus \"+\ *n* [NL, fr. *macr-* + *nucleus*] **:** a relatively large densely staining nucleus that is believed to exert a controlling influence over the trophic activities of most ciliated protozoans — distinguished from *micronucleus*

mac·ro·nutrient \"+\ *n* [*macr-* + *nutrient*] **:** a chemical element (as potassium, calcium, magnesium, nitrogen, phosphorus, sulfur) of which relatively large quantities are essential to the growth and welfare of a plant — called also *macroelement, major element;* compare MICRONUTRIENT

mac·ro·phage \ˈmakrə,fāj\ *n* -s [F, fr. *macr-* + *-phage*] **:** a large phagocyte; *specif* **:** HISTIOCYTE — **mac·ro·phag·ic** \ˌmakrəˈfajik\ *adj*

macrophagic system *n* **:** RETICULOENDOTHELIAL SYSTEM

mac·roph·a·gous \(ˈ)maˈkräfəgəs\ *adj* [*macr-* + *-phagous*] **:** feeding on relatively large particulate matter — compare MICROPHAGOUS

mac·ro·phoma \ˌmakrə+\ *n, cap* [NL, fr. *macr-* + *Phoma*] *in some classifications* **:** a genus of imperfect fungi with large pycniospores that is now usu. included in *Sphaeropsis*

mac·ro·photograph \ˌmakrō+\ *n* [*macr-* + *photograph*] **:** PHOTOMACROGRAPH

mac·ro·photography \"+\ *n* [ISV *macr-* + *photography*] **:** PHOTOMACROGRAPHY

mac·ro·phyl·lous \ˌmakrōˈfiləs\ *adj* [*macr-* + *-phyllous*] **:** having large or elongated leaves with usu. many veins or a much-branched main vein — compare MICROPHYLLOUS

mac·ro·phylogeny \ˌma(ˌ)krō+\ *n* [*macr-* + *phylogeny*] **:** an assumed rapid differentiation of major systematic categories through complex reorganization and mutation of the genes

mac·ro·physics \ˌmakrō+\ *n pl but sing or pl in constr* [ISV *macr-* + *physics*] **:** the part of physics that deals with bodies large enough to be directly and individually observed and measured

mac·ro·phyte \ˈmakrə,fīt\ *n* -s [*macr-* + *-phyte*] **:** a member of the macroscopic plant life esp. of a body of water — **mac·ro·phyt·ic** \ˌmakrəˈfid·ik\ *adj*

mac·ro·pinacoid \ˌmakrō+\ *n* [ISV *macr-* + *pinacoid*] **:** a pinacoid having faces parallel to the longer lateral and the vertical axis — **mac·ro·pinacoidal** \"+\ *adj*

mac·ro·plankton \"+\ *n* [ISV *macr-* + *plankton*] **:** macroscopic plankton comprising the larger planktonic organisms (as jellyfish, crustaceans, sargassums) — **mac·ro·planktonic** \"+\ *adj*

¹**ma·crop·o·did** \məˈkräpədəd\ *adj* [NL *Macropodidae*] **:** of or relating to the Macropodidae

²**macropodid** \"\ *n* -s **:** a macropodid animal **:** KANGAROO, WALLABY

mac·ro·pod·i·dae \ˌmakrəˈpädə,dē\ *n pl, cap* [NL, fr. *Macropod-, Macropus*, type genus + *-idae*] **:** a family of diprotodont marsupial mammals comprising the kangaroos, wallabies, and rat kangaroos that are all saltatory animals with long hind limbs and weakly developed forelimbs and are typically inoffensive terrestrial herbivores

mac·rop·o·dous \(ˈ)maˈkräpədəs\ *also* **mac·rop·o·dal** \-dᵊl\ *adj* [*macr-* + *-podous* or *podal*] **1** *of a plant embryo* **:** having an enlarged or elongated hypocotyl **2** *of a plant or plant part* **:** having a long stem or stalk ⟨a ~ leaf⟩

mac·ro·pol·y·cyte \ˌmakrōˈpälə,sīt\ *n* -s [*macr-* + *poly-* + *-cyte*] **:** an exceptionally large neutrophil with a much⸗lobulated nucleus that appears in the blood in pernicious anemia

mac·ro·pore \ˈmakrə,pō(ə)r\ *n* [*macr-* + *pore*] **:** a pore (as in coal) of comparatively large size; *esp* **:** a pore in soil of such size that water drains from it by gravity and is not held by capillary action — **mac·ro·porosity** \ˌma(ˌ)krō+\ *n* — **mac·ro·po·rous** \ˌmakrəˈpōrəs, (ˈ)maˈkräpərəs\ *adj*

mac·ro·prism \ˈmakrō+,-\ *n* [*macr-* + *prism*] **:** a crystal prism that makes a relatively great intercept on the macro-axis

mac·ro·procedure \ˌmakrō+\ *n* [*macr-* + *procedure*] **:** a procedure (as for analysis) not involving the use of very small quantities of material — opposed to *microprocedure*

mac·rop·sia \məˈkräpsēə\ *also* **mac·rop·sy** \ˈma,kräpsē\ *n, pl* **macropsias** *also* **macropsies** [NL *macropsia*, fr. *macr-* + *-opsia*] **:** a condition of the eye in which objects appear to be unnaturally large — opposed to *micropsia*

ma·crop·sis \məˈkräpsəs\ *n, cap* [NL, fr. *macr-* + *-opsis*] **:** a genus (the type of the family Macropsidae) of leafhoppers that includes the plum leafhopper

mac·rop·ter·ous \(ˈ)maˈkräptərəs\ *adj* [Gk *makropteros* having long wings, fr. *makr-* macr- + *-pteros* -pterous] **1 :** having long or large wings—used of birds or insects **2 :** having large or long fins — used of fishes — **mac·rop·tery** \-tərē\ *n*

mac·rop·tic \(ˈ)maˈkräptik\ *adj* [*macr-* + *optic*] **:** affected with macropsia

mac·ro·pus \ˈmakrəpəs\ *n, cap* [NL, fr. *macr-* + *-pus*] **:** the type genus of Macropodidae comprising the typical kangaroos and wallabies

mac·ro·pyg·ia \ˌmakrōˈpijēə\ *n, cap* [NL, fr. *macr-* + *-pygia*] **:** a large genus of long-tailed pigeons that resemble cuckoos — see CUCKOO DOVE

mac·ro·pyramid \ˌmakrō+\ *n* [*macr-* + *pyramid*] **:** a crystal pyramid that corresponds to the analogous macroprism

mac·ro·rham·pho·si·dae \ˌmakrō,ramˈfōsə,dē, -ōzə-\ *n pl, cap* [NL, fr. *Macrorhamphosus*, type genus + *-idae*] **:** a family of long-snouted fishes (order Solenichthyes) consisting of the bellows fishes

mac·ro·rham·pho·sus \-ōsəs,-ōzəs\ *n, cap* [NL, fr. *macr-* + *rhamph-* + L *-osus* -ous] **:** the type genus of Macrorhamphosidae

mac·ro·rhi·nus \ˌmakrōˈrīnəs\ [NL, fr. *macr-* + *-rhinus*] *syn of* MIROUNGA

mac·ro·sce·lid·i·dae \ˌmakrōsəˈlidə,dē\ *n pl, cap* [NL, fr. *Macroscelides*, type genus (fr. *macr-* + *scel-* + L *-ides*, patronymic suffix) + *-idae* — more at -IDE] **:** a family of African insectivores comprising the elephant shrews and constituting sometimes with the addition of the Tupaiidae a suborder (Menotyphla) of Insectivora

mac·ro·scian \(ˈ)maˈkräsh(ē)ən\ *adj* [Gk *makroskios* (fr. *makr-* macr- + *-skios*, fr. *skia* shadow) + E *-an* — more at SHINE] **:** having or casting a long shadow ⟨that ~ day which I had dreaded for so long —Osbert Sitwell⟩

mac·ro·sclereid \ˌmakrō+\ *n* [*macr-* + *sclereid*] **:** one of the columnar sclereids that often form an outer layer in various fruits and seeds and occur also in the stems of some xerophytes — called also *rod cell;* compare OSTEOSCLEREID

mac·ro·scop·ic \ˌmakrəˈskäpik, -pēk\ *also* **mac·ro·scop·i·cal** \-pəkəl, -pēk-\ *adj* [ISV *macr-* + *-scopic, -scopical*] **1 :** large enough to be observed by the naked eye — opposed to *microscopic* **2 :** being in the large or taken in the large **:** considered in terms of large units or elements ⟨a ~ equation⟩ **3 :** MEGASCOPIC 2a — **macroscopically** *adv*

mac·ro·segment \ˌmakrō+\ *n* [*macr-* + *segment*] **:** a continuum of speech between two perceptible pauses

mac·ro·seism \ˈmakrō,sīzəm *sometimes* -sez- *or* -säz- *or* -sēz-\ *n* [ISV *macr-* + *-seism*] **:** a severe or major earthquake — compare MICROSEISM — **mac·ro·seis·mic** \ˌmakrōˈsīzmik *also* |sm- *sometimes* -ˈse| *or* -ˈsā| *or* -ˈsē|s\ *adj*

mac·ro·seismograph \ˌmakrō+\ *n* [*macroseism* + *-o-* + *-graph*] **:** a seismograph specially adapted for recording large earthquakes

mac·ro·si·phum \ˌmakrōˈsīfəm\ *n, cap* [NL, fr. *macr-* + Gk *siphōn* tube — more at SIPHON] **:** a genus of large often pink or green aphids including a number of economically important plant pests some of which are vectors of virus diseases (as mosaic) — see ENGLISH GRAIN APHID, PEA APHID, ROSE APHID

mac·ros·mat·ic \ˌma,kr+-\ *also* **macro-osmatic** \ˌma(ˌ)krō+\ *adj* [*macr-* + *osmatic*] **:** having the sense or organs of smell highly developed ⟨dogs are ~ animals⟩

mac·ro·so·mat·ic \ˌmakrəsōˈmad·ik\ *or* **mac·ro·so·ma·tous** \-rəˈsōməd·əs\ *adj* [*macr-* + *somatic* or *-somatous*] **:** having a usu. abnormally large body

mac·ro·so·mia \ˌmakrəˈsōmēə\ *n* -s [NL, fr. *macr-* + *-somia*] **:** GIGANTISM

mac·ro·species \ˌmakrō+\ *n* [*macr-* + *species*] **:** a large and usu. polymorphic biological species markedly discontinuous from its congeners **:** a polytypic species — compare LINNAEAN SPECIES, MICROSPECIES

mac·ro·splanchnic \"+\ *adj* [ISV *macr-* + *splanchnic;* orig. formed as It *macrosplàncnico*] **:** ENDOMORPHIC 2 — opposed to *microsplanchnic;* compare NORMOSPLANCHNIC

mac·ro·spo·range \ˌmakrōspəˈranj, -krəˈspōr,anj\ *n* [NL *macrosporangium*] **:** MEGASPORANGIUM

mac·ro·sporangium \ˌmakrō+\ *n* [NL, fr. *macr-* + *sporangium*] **:** MEGASPORANGIUM

mac·ro·spore \ˈmakrə,spō(ə)r\ *n* [*macr-* + *spore*] **1 :** MEGASPORE **2 :** the larger of two forms of spores produced by certain protozoans (as radiolarians) — **mac·ro·spo·ric** \ˌmakrəˈspōrik\ *adj*

mac·ro·spo·ri·um \ˌmakrəˈspōrēəm\ *n, cap* [NL, fr. *macr-* + *-sporium*] *in some classifications* **:** a genus of imperfect fungi that are sometimes included in the genus *Alternaria* but that differ from members of that genus in having the dark greenish brown muriform spores borne singly rather than in chains

mac·ro·sporophyll *also* **mac·ro·sporophyl** \ˌmakrə+\ *n* -s [*macr-* + *sporophyll, sporophyl*] **:** MEGASPOROPHYLL

mac·ro·stachya \ˌmakrōstakēə, -ták-\ *n, cap* [NL, fr. *macr-* + *Stachys*] **:** a form genus of Paleozoic fossil plants based on strobiles that are now regarded as fructifications of plants of the genus *Calamites*

mac·ros·te·les \məˈkrästə,lēz\ *n, cap* [NL, fr. *macr-* + *-steles* (perh. fr. Gk *stēlē* stela)] **:** a genus of leafhoppers some of which transmit virus diseases to plants — see SIX-SPOTTED LEAFHOPPER

mac·ro·sto·mia \ˌmakrəˈstōmēə\ *n* -s [NL, fr. *macr-* + *-stomia*] **1 :** the condition of having an abnormally large mouth **2** *also* **mac·ros·to·mus** \məˈkrästəməs\ *pl* **mac·rosto·mi** \-tə,mī, -,mē\ **:** an abnormally large mouth

mac·ro·structural \ˌmakrō+\ *adj* **:** of or relating to macrostructure

mac·ro·structure \"+\ *n* [ISV *macr-* + *structure*] **:** the structure (as of metal, a body part, or the soil) revealed by visual examination with little or no magnification

mac·ro·sty·lous \ˌmakrōˈstīləs\ *adj* [*macr-* + *-stylous*] *of a flower* **:** having long styles; *specif* **:** having long styles and short stamens — compare MESOSTYLOUS, MICROSTYLOUS

mac·ro·sudanic \ˌmakrō+\ *n, cap* [*macr-* + *Sudanic*] **:** CHARI-NILE

mac·ro·taxonomy \ˌma(ˌ)krō+\ *n* [*macr-* + *taxonomy*] **:** taxonomy of larger biologic units (as family, order, class)

mac·ro·there \ˈmakrō,thi(ə)r\ *n* -s [NL *Macrotherium*] **:** a member of the genus *Macrotherium*

mac·ro·the·ri·um \ˌmakrōˈthirēəm\ *n, cap* [NL, fr. *macr-* + *-therium*] **:** a widely distributed genus of Miocene and Pliocene chalicotheres (order Perissodactyla) formerly supposed to be generalized edentates — compare CHALICOTHERIIDAE

mac·ro·therm \ˈmakrə,thərm\ *n* -s [*macr-* + *-therm*] **:** MEGATHERM

mac·ro·tia \maˈkrōsh(ē)ə, -ōd·ēə\ *n* -s [NL, fr. Gk *makr-* + Gk *ōt-, ous* ear + NL *-ia* — more at EAR] **:** excessive largeness of the ears

mac·ro·tome \ˈmakrə,tōm\ *n* [*macr-* + *-tome*] **:** an apparatus for making large sections of anatomical specimens

mac·ro·tous \(ˈ)maˈkrōd·əs\ *adj* [*macr-* + Gk *ōt, ous* ear + E *-ous*] **:** having large ears

mac·ro·trich·i·um \ˌmakrōˈtrikēəm\ *n, pl* **macrotrich·ia** \-ēə\ [NL, fr. *macr-* + Gk *trich-, thrix* hair + NL *-ium* — more at TRICHINA] **:** one of the larger hairs found esp. along the veins of the wings of various insects — compare MICROTRICHIUM

macroura *syn of* MACRURA

mac·ro·za·mia \ˌmakrōˈzāmēə\ *n* [NL, fr. *macr-* + Gk (Dor dial.) *zamia* loss (Attic *zēmia*)] **1** *cap* **:** a genus of Australian cycads with erect trunks, pinnate leaves, large cones, and in some forms edible nuts **2** -s : any tree of the genus *Macrozamia*

mac·ro·zoospore \ˈmakrə+\ *n* [*macr-* + *zoospore*] : one of the larger zoospores produced by algae (as members of the genus *Ulothrix*) that bear zoospores of markedly different size — compare MICROZOOSPORE

ma·cru·ra \məˈkrurə\ *n pl, cap* [NL, fr. *macr-* + *-ura*] *in some classifications* : a suborder of Decapoda comprising crustaceans (as shrimps, lobsters, prawns) with well-developed abdomens — compare BRACHYURA — **ma·cru·ral** \-ürəl\ *adj* — **ma·cru·ran** \-ürən\ *adj or n* — **ma·cru·roid** \-ü,rȯid\ *adj*

ma·cru·ri·dae \-ürə,dē\ *n pl, cap* [NL, fr. *Macrurus*, type genus + *-idae*] : a family of fishes (order Anacanthini) comprising the grenadiers

macru·rous \(ˈ)maˈkrürəs, məˈk-\ *adj* [*macr-* + *-urous*] **1** : having a long tail **2** [NL *Macrura* + E *-ous*] : of or relating to the Macrura

ma·cru·rus \məˈkrürəs\ *n, cap* [NL, fr. *macr-* + *-urus*] : the type genus of Macruridae

mac·ta·tion \makˈtāshən\ *n* -s [LL *mactation-, mactatio*, fr. L *mactatus* (past part. of *mactare* to honor, sacrifice, slay, slaughter, fr. *mactus* worshiped, honored) + *-ion-, -io* -ion] : an act of killing; *esp* : the ritual slaughter of a sacrificial victim

mac·tra \ˈmaktrə\ *n, cap* [NL, fr. Gk *maktra* kneading trough, fr. *massein* to knead — more at MINGLE] : the type genus of Mactridae formerly including most members of the family but now restricted to a few somewhat triangular, usu. thin-shelled surf clams — **mac·troid** \-,trȯid\ *adj*

mac·tri·dae \-trə,dē\ *n pl, cap* [NL, fr. *Mactra*, type genus + *-idae*] : a widely distributed family of marine clams (suborder Tellinacea) that have closely fitting or slightly gapping shells with two cardinal teeth in each valve and fused ensheathed siphons of equal length and that comprise the surf clams — compare LUTRARIA, MACTRA, SPISULA

macu *also* **maku** \mäˈkü, məˈ-\ *n, pl* **macú** *or* **macús** *usu cap* [Pg, of AmerInd origin] **1 a** : a Puinavean people of northwestern Amazonas, Brazil **b** : a member of such people **2** : the language of the Macú people

ma·cu·ca \məˈkükə\ *n* -s [Pg, fr. Tupi] : any of several So. American tinamous (esp. *Tinamus major*)

macul- *or* **maculo-** *also* **maculi-** *comb form* [ME *macul-*, fr. L, fr. *macula*] **1** : spot : blotch ⟨*macul*ation⟩ ⟨*maculi*form⟩ **2** : spotted and : macular and ⟨*maculo*petechial lesions⟩ ⟨*maculo*anesthetic⟩

mac·u·la \ˈmakyələ\ *n, pl* **macu·lae** \-,lē\ *also* **maculas** [L] **1** : BLOTCH, SPOT, STAIN; *esp* : MACULE 2 **2** : any of various anatomical structures having the form of a spot differentiated from surrounding tissues: as **a** : MACULA ACUSTICA **b** : MACULA LUTEA — see EYE illustration

macula acu·sti·ca \-əˈküstəkə\ *n, pl* **maculae acusti·cae** \-tə,sē\ [NL, lit., acoustic spot] : either of two small areas of sensory hair cells in the ear located (1) in the saccule and (2) in the utricle that are covered with gelatinous material on which are located crystals or concretions of calcium carbonate and that are associated with the perception of equilibrium — called also respectively (1) *macula sacculi*, (2) *macula utriculi*

mac·u·la·cy \ˈmakyələsē\ *n* -ES [*maculate* + *-cy*] : a smirched, unclean, bespotted state

macula lu·tea \-ˈlüd·ēə\ *n, pl* **maculae lute·ae** \-ē,ē\ [NL, lit., yellow spot] : a small yellowish area lying slightly lateral to the center of the retina that constitutes the region of maximum visual acuity and is made up almost wholly of retinal cones

mac·u·lar \ˈmakyələ(r)\ *adj* **1 a** : of or relating to a spot or spots **b** [NL *macula* (*lutea*) + E *-ar*] : mediated by the macula lutea ⟨~ vision⟩ **2** : marked with a spot or spots : SPOTTY

¹mac·u·late \-,lāt\ *vt* -ED/-ING/-S [ME *maculaten*, fr. L *maculatus*, past part. of *maculare*, fr. *macula* spot] **1** *archaic* : SPOT, SPECKLE **2** *archaic* : BESMIRCH, DEFILE

²mac·u·late \-lət\ *or* **mac·u·lat·ed** \-,lād·əd\ *adj* [*maculate* fr. L *maculatus*, past part.; *maculated* fr. L *maculatus* + E *-ed*] **1** : marked with spots : BLOTCHED **2** : BESMIRCHED, DEFILED, IMPURE

mac·u·la·tion \,makyəˈlāshən\ *n* -s [ME *maculacion*, fr. L *maculation-, maculatio*, fr. *maculatus* + *-ion-, -io* -ion] **1** *archaic* : the act of spotting or staining or the condition of being spotted or stained **2 a** : SPOT, STAIN, BLEMISH ⟨indurated ~*s* on the cheeks⟩ **b** : the system or arrangement of spots and markings on an animal or plant

mac·u·la·ture \ˈmakyələ,chü(ə)r\ *n* -s [F, fr. L *maculatus* + F *-ure*] : an impression made from an intaglio engraved plate to remove ink from the recessed areas

mac·ule \ˈma(,)kyül\ *n* -s [F, fr. L *macula*] **1** : MACULA 2 **2** : a patch of skin exhibiting altered coloration but usu. not elevated above the general surface that forms a characteristic feature of various diseases (as smallpox)

mac·u·lic·o·lous \,makyəˈlikələs\ *also* **macu·li·cole** \ˈmakyələ,kōl, məˈkyülə,-\ *adj* [*macul-* + *-colous* or *-cole*] *of a fungus* : having pycnidia produced in localized masses so as to form definite spots on a host plant

maculo- — *see* MACUL-

mac·u·lo·papular \ˌmakyə(,)lō+\ *adj* [*macul-* + *papular*] *of a skin lesion* : combining the characteristics of macules and papules — **mac·u·lo·papule** \"+\ *n*

mac·u·lose \ˈmakyə,lōs\ *adj* [L *maculosus*, fr. *macula* spot + *-osus* -ose] : SPOTTED

ma·cum·ba \məˈkümbə\ *n* -s [Pg] **1** : a Brazilian fetishistic ritual or cult that is largely of African origin and combines sorcery with dancing, drumming, and chanting **2** : the Brazilian popular music or dance based upon macumba

ma·cu·pa \məˈküpə\ *n* -s [Sp, fr. Tag & Bisayan] **1** *Philippines* : OTAHEITE APPLE **2** *Philippines* : the heavy red wood of the otaheite apple tree

ma·cu·shi \məˈküshē\ *or* **ma·cu·si** \-üsē\ *also* **ma·ku·shi** *or* **ma·ku·si** *n, pl* **macushi** *or* **macushis** *or* **macusi** *or* **macusis** *usu cap* **1 a** : a Cariban people of Brazil and British Guiana **b** : a member of such people **2** : the language of the Macushi people

ma·cush·la \məˈküshlə, -kush-, -(,)lä\ *n* -s [IrGael *mo chuisle*, lit., my vein, my blood] *Irish* : DARLING — used usu. as a noun of address

ma·cu·ta *also* **ma·cu·te** \məˈküd·ə\ *n* -s [Pg *macuta*, fr. Kimbundu *mukuta*, fr. Kongo *nkuta* cloth] **1** : an old west African unit of value **2** : an old copper coin equal to 50 reis issued by Portugal for its African colonies; *also* : a corresponding unit of value **3** : a 5-centavo coin of Angola issued in 1927; *also* : a corresponding unit of value ⟨4-*macuta* coins⟩

¹mad \ˈmad, -aa(ə)-, -ai-\ *adj* **madder**; **maddest** [ME *medd, madd*, fr. OE *gemǣd, gemǣded*, past part. of (assumed) *gemǣdan* to make silly or mad, fr. *gemād* silly, mad; akin to OS *gimēd* foolish, crazy, OHG *gimeit* foolish, crazy, ON *meitha* to hurt, mutilate, Goth *gamaidans*, acc. pl., crippled, wounded, OIr *māel* bald, dull, W *moel* bald, Skt *methati* he hurts; basic meaning: chop, chop off] **1 a** : disordered in mind : CRAZY, INSANE ⟨the man was ~ and had berserk fits of superhuman strength and rage —Charles Kingsley⟩ **b** : arising from, indicative of, or marked by mental disorder ⟨no lunatic in a ~ fit, but a sane man fighting for his soul —Bram Stoker⟩ **2 a** : completely unrestrained by reason and judgment : utterly foolish : SENSELESS ⟨she's ~ . . . to throw away money and position for some hole-and-corner existence with a good-looking lawyer's clerk —Clara Morris⟩ **b** : arising from or indicative of a lack of reason and judgment : RASH ⟨was so astounded by this ~ project on the part of her husband . . . that she had not a word to say —William Black⟩ **c** : incapable of being explained, interpreted, or accounted for : ILLOGICAL ⟨facts which fairly shriek for explanation; for without an explanation they're ~, irrational, utterly incredible —W.H.Wright⟩ **3 a** : carried away by intense anger : ENRAGED, FURIOUS ⟨was so ~ . . . that I thought I could shoot the man —Liam O'Flaherty⟩ **b** : keenly displeased : ANGRY, IRKED ⟨looked ~ for a second but then . . . began to laugh —Robert Lowry⟩ ⟨~ as a wet hen⟩ **4 a** : carried away by enthusiasm, infatuation, or desire ⟨men were ~ for her and any girl liked men's attentions —Barnaby Conrad⟩ ⟨was not fundamentally ~ about a home and kids —Rex Ingamells⟩ ⟨the students were all perfectly ~ on highbrow music —Arnold Bennett⟩ **b** : arising from or marked by intense enthusiasm, infatuation, or desire ⟨a nation . . . engaged in the ~ pursuit of wealth —*Saturday Rev.*⟩ ⟨has been having a ~ vogue in Europe and is constantly written about —*New Yorker*⟩ **5** : affected with rabies : RABID ⟨a ~ dog⟩ **6** : marked by wild or irresponsible gaiety and merriment : HILARIOUS ⟨of their childhood, of the ~ pranks they played —Winston Churchill⟩ **7 a** : intensely excited, distraught, or frantic ⟨driving him ~ with jealousy —Edmund Wilson⟩ **b** : arising from or indicative of intense excitement or distress ⟨tried to reach it in a ~ resolve to claw into the wood with my nails —Jack London⟩ **8** : marked by intense and often chaotic activity : WILD, FURIOUS ⟨a ~ scramble for the sides of the ship —A.C.Whitehead⟩ **syn** see ANGRY

²mad \"\ *vb* **madded**; **madded**; **madding**; **mads** [ME *madden*, fr. *medd, madd*, adj.] *vi, archaic* : to act in an insane or furious manner : RAGE ~ *vt* : to make mad: **a** *archaic* : to make insane **b** : to make angry : EXASPERATE

³mad \"\ *n* -s [¹*mad*] **1** : ANGER, FURY ⟨the fight had taken all the ~ out of me —H.E.Giles⟩ **2** : a fit or mood of angry temper ⟨had worked up a ~ before he bayoneted the corporal —R.O.Bowen⟩ ⟨still had a bit of a ~ on —William Forrest⟩

MAD *abbr* magnetic airborne detector

¹mad·a·gas·can \ˌmadəˈgaskən, -gaas-\ *adj, usu cap* [*Madagascar*, island in the Indian ocean southeast of Africa + E *-an*] **1** : of, relating to, or characteristic of Madagascar **2** : of, relating to, or characteristic of the people of Madagascar

²madagascan \"\ *n* -s *cap* : a native or inhabitant of Madagascar

mad·a·gas·car \-kə(r)\ *adj, usu cap* [fr. *Madagascar*, island in the Indian ocean] **1** : of or from Madagascar : of the kind or style prevalent in Madagascar **2** : MALAGASY

madagascar bean *n, usu cap M* **1** : HYACINTH BEAN **2** : LIMA BEAN

madagascar cat *n, usu cap M* : a small lemur (*Lemur catta*) having the tail barred with black

mad·a·gas·car·i·an \ˌ==ˌ=ˈska(a)rēən\ *adj, usu cap* [*Madagascar* island + E *-ian*] : MALAGASY

madagascar jasmine *n, usu cap M* : a twining vine (*Stephanotis floribunda*) native to Madagascar that is used as an ornamental in warm regions and in greenhouses and has thick dark green waxy leaves and waxy white flowers in clusters along the stem

madagascar periwinkle *n, usu cap M* : PERIWINKLE 1c

madagascar rubber vine *or* **madagascar rubber** *n, usu cap M* : a woody vine (*Cryptostegia madagascariensis*) with large whitish or pink flowers that is native to Madagascar and is grown in the tropics as an ornamental and for its milky juice that yields rubber

¹mad·am \ˈmadəm\ *n, pl* **madams** \-əmz\ *or* **mes·dames** \(ˈ)māˈdäm, -dam, -daa(ə)m, -dȧm\ *see numbered senses* [ME *madame, madame*, fr. OF *ma dame*, lit., my lady] **1** : LADY — used as a form of respectful or polite address formerly to a woman of rank or position but now to any woman ⟨~, I swear I use no art at all —Shak.⟩ ⟨right this way, ~⟩ **2** : MISTRESS 2 — used as a conventional title of courtesy formerly with the given name but now usu. with the surname ⟨how did thy master part with *Madam* Julia —Shak.⟩ ⟨with one accord lament for *Madam* Blaize —Oliver Goldsmith⟩ **3** *pl* **madams**, *archaic* : a woman affecting ostentatious refinement ⟨was far too pampered a ~ —Thomas Hood †1845⟩ **4** *pl* **madams a** *obs* : PROSTITUTE ⟨a gentleman who mistook a kept ~ for a lady —*Gentleman's Mag.*⟩ **b** : the female head of a house of prostitution : BAWD ⟨the hard-bitten ~ of the house where the prostitute works —Brendan Gill⟩ **5** *pl* **madams** : the female head of a household : WIFE ⟨every once in a while the ~ and I will order a book that we've read about —H.S.Truman⟩

²madam \"\ *vt* -ED/-ING/-S *archaic* : to address as madam ⟨they ~ each other with genteel petulance —*Examiner*⟩

ma·dame \(ˈ)maˈdam, -daa(ə)m *also* məˈd- *sometimes* məˈdäm *or* məˈdam; *before a surname* " *or* ˌmadəm\ *n, pl* **mes·dames** \(ˈ)māˈdäm, -dam, -daa(ə)m, -dȧm\ *or* **madames** *see numbered senses* [fr. OF *ma dame*, lit., my lady] **1** *pl* **madames**, *archaic* : a French married woman ⟨would tell you which ~ loved a monsieur —Ben Jonson⟩ **2** : a female member of the French royal family; *specif* : the eldest daughter of the French king or of the dauphin **3** *pl* **mesdames** : MISTRESS — used as a title that is prefixed to the surname of a woman who is not of English-speaking nationality or that is assumed by a professional woman (as a musician) esp. to imply European antecedents **4** *pl* **madames** : MADAM 4b ⟨the wrong side of the tracks, among coal miners and ~*s* of sporting houses —Heath Bowman⟩

ma'·dan \ˈmäˌdän\ *n, pl* **ma'dan** *or* **ma'dans** *usu cap* **1** : an Arab people inhabiting the marshland below Baghdad along the Tigris and Euphrates rivers **2** : a member of the Ma'dan people

mad·a·pol·lam *or* **mad·a·pol·am** \ˌmadəˈpäləm\ *n* -s [fr. *Madapollam*, suburb of Narsapur, India, where it was originally made] : a soft plain cotton now woven in various weights in England

mad apple *n* **1** : EGGPLANT **2** : THORN APPLE 2 **3** : DEAD SEA APPLE

madar *var of* MUDAR

mad·a·ro·sis \ˌmadəˈrōsəs\ *n, pl* **madaro·ses** \-ō,sēz\ [NL, fr. *madarōsis* baldness, madarosis, fr. *madaroun* to make bald (fr. *madaros* wet, bald) + *-sis*; akin to Gk *madan* to be wet, be bald — more at MEAT] : loss of the eyelashes or of the hair of the eyebrows

mad·a·rot·ic \ˌmadəˈräd·ik\ *adj* [fr. NL *madarosis*, after such pairs as NL *hypnosis*: E *hypnotic*] : of, related to, or affected with madarosis

¹madbrain \ˈ=ˌ=\ *n* [¹*mad* + *brain*] *archaic* : one who is mad-brained

²madbrain *adj, obs* : MAD-BRAINED

mad-brained \ˈ=ˈbrānd\ *adj* : marked by hotheadedness : RASH

¹madcap \ˈ=ˌ=\ *n* [¹*mad* + *cap*] : one who is madcap

²madcap \"\ *adj* : marked by impulsiveness, recklessness, or rashness ⟨the ~ girl ran up to her mother —W.M.Thackeray⟩ ⟨the venture was a sound proposition . . . no ~ haphazard scheme —*Irish Digest*⟩

madded *past of* MAD

mad·den \ˈmadᵊn, ˈmaad-,ˈmaid-\ *vb* **maddened**; **maddened**; **maddening** \-d(ᵊ)niŋ\ **maddens** [¹*mad* + *-en*] *vi* : to become or act as if mad ⟨whole populations ~*ing* to avenge the cause —H.H.Milman⟩ ~ *vt* **1** : to drive mad : CRAZE ⟨guards do not have time to wrestle with bathers ~*ed* by fear —Charles Price⟩ **2** : to make intensely angry : ENRAGE ⟨~*ed* statesmen and diplomats by his tactlessness and his colossal cheek —Roger Pippett⟩

maddening *adj* [fr. pres. part. of *madden*] **1** : tending to craze ⟨~ pain . . . can rarely be alleviated but by opium —J.M. Good⟩ **2 a** : tending to infuriate ⟨was facing a horrible death . . . a ~ waste of life —Upton Sinclair⟩ **b** : tending to vex : IRRITATING ⟨the ceaseless tinny tumult of the jukebox was ~ —John McNulty⟩ — **mad·den·ing·ly** *adv* — **mad·den·ing·ness** *n* -ES

¹mad·der \ˈmadə(r)\ *n* -s [ME *madder, mader*, fr. OE *mædere*; akin to MD *mēde* madder, OHG *matara*, ON *mathra* madder, and perh. to Pol *modry* dark blue, Czech *modrý* blue] **1** : any of several herbs of the genus *Rubia*; *esp* : a Eurasian herb (*Rubia tinctorum*) with verticillate leaves and small yellowish panicled flowers succeeded by berries **2 a** : the root of the madder plant used formerly in dyeing chiefly because of its content of alizarin in the form of the glycoside ruberythric acid **b** : a dye prepared from this root but later replaced by synthetic alizarin — compare GARANCINE, TURKEY RED 1a

branch of madder

²mad·der \", ˈmaad-,ˈmaid-\ *comparative of* MAD

³mad·der \ˈmadə(r)\ *or* **meth·er** \ˈmethə-\ *n* -s [IrGael *meadar* churn, madder] : a square wooden drinking cup used in Ireland

madder bleach *n* : a method of bleaching cotton goods in order to secure a pure white ground for printing by boiling several times with alkalis and then using bleach powder

madder blue *n* : a grayish violet to grayish purple

madder brown *n* : CASTILIAN BROWN

madder carmine *n* : a moderate red to purplish red that is very slightly bluer and less strong than pomegranate purple

madder crimson *n* : a vivid red that is bluer and deeper than apple red, yellower and stronger than carmine, bluer and darker than Castilian red or pimento, and bluer and deeper than scarlet — called also *crimson madder*

madder family *n* : RUBIACEAE

madder indian red *n, often cap I* : TUSCAN RED

madder lake *n* **1** : MADDER ROSE **2 a** : a purplish red pigment prepared formerly from madder and usu. alum **b** : a cherry red pigment prepared from alizarin and usu. a compound of aluminum — see DYE table (under *Pigment Red 83*)

madder orange *n* : a strong orange that is lighter and stronger than pumpkin, redder than cadmium orange, and lighter and stronger than mandarin orange — called also *orange madder*

madder pink *n* : MADDER ROSE

madder purple *n* : a moderate to dark red

madder red *n* : ENGLISH RED

madder rose *n* : a strong purplish red that is redder than average bright rose — called also *casino pink, madder lake, madder pink, pink madder, rose madder*

madder scarlet *n* : a strong yellowish pink that is darker and much redder than salmon pink, redder and deeper than melon, and redder than peach red — called also *scarlet madder*

madder violet *n* : a dark purple that is bluer, lighter, and stronger than average prune, bluer and less strong than mulberry (sense 2a), and bluer and lighter than plum (sense 6b) — called also *eveque, old helio*

madderwort \ˈ==ˌ=\ *n* : a plant of the family Rubiaceae

madder yellow *n* : DUTCH PINK 3

maddest *superlative of* MAD

mad·ding \ˈmadiŋ, ˈmaad-,ˈmaid-, -dēŋ\ *adj* [fr. pres. part. of ²*mad*] **1** : acting as if mad : FRENZIED, RAVING ⟨far from the ~ crowd's ignoble strife —Thomas Gray⟩ **2** : inciting to madness : MADDENING ⟨her courage and loyalty balanced ~ defects —Anne Green⟩

mad·dish \-dish,-dēsh\ *adj* [¹*mad* + *-ish*] **1** *obs* : acting like a madman **2** : somewhat mad

mad·dle \-dᵊl\ *vb* -ED/-ING/-S [irreg. fr. ¹*mad*] *vi, dial Eng* : to go mad ~ *vt, dial Eng* : CRAZE, CONFUSE

mad-dog skullcap *or* **mad-dog weed** *n* : an American mint (*Scutellaria lateriflora*) that yields a resinoid used esp. formerly as a tonic and antispasmodic — called also *blue pimpernel, blue skullcap*; see SCUTELLARIN

mad·dox rod \ˈmadəks-\ *n, usu cap M* [after Ernest E. Maddox †1933 Brit. ophthalmologist] : a transparent cylindrical glass rod or one of a series of such rods placed one above another for use in testing the eyes for heterophoria

made *adj* [ME *mad*, fr. past part. of *maken* to make — more at MAKE] **1 a** : artificially produced by a manufacturing process ⟨bought a few ~ goods — rope and nails —G.W.Brace⟩ **b** : artificially produced by excavation, grading, or filling ⟨the successive beds of ~ ground —T.H.Huxley⟩ **c** : INVENTED, FICTITIOUS ⟨reads like a ~ story —J.H.Newman⟩ **2** : assured of success ⟨now am I a ~ man forever —Christopher Marlowe⟩ **3** : fully trained — used esp. of a horse or dog ⟨a regular supply of ~ Argentine ponies at a moderate price —John Board⟩ **4** : specially fitted, designed, or adapted ⟨a situation ~ for misunderstanding —Broadus Mitchell⟩

made-beaver \ˈ=ˈ==\ *n* **1** : a unit of value equivalent to the value of one beaver skin used in the early days of the Canadian fur trade **2** : a token representing the value of a made-beaver — called also *beaver*

made dish *n* : a dish of food prepared from several ingredients (as meat, vegetables, and herbs) ⟨this beef casserole is a tasty *made dish*⟩

mad·e·fac·tion \ˌmadəˈfakshən\ *n* [LL *madefaction-, madefactio*, fr. L *madefactus* (past part. of *madefacere*) + *-ion-, -io* -ion] *obs* : WETTING ⟨to all ~ there is required an imbibition —Francis Bacon⟩

madefy *vt* -ED/-ING/-ES [ME *madifien*, fr. MF *madefier*, fr. L *madefacere*, fr. *madēre* to be wet + *facere* to make, do — more at MEAT, DO] *obs* : WET, MOISTEN

¹ma·dei·ra \məˈdirə *sometimes* -derə\ *n* -s *usu cap* [Pg, fr. *Madeira* islands] **1** : an amber-colored dessert wine of Madeira — compare BUAL, MALMSEY, SERCIAL **2** : a wine similar to Madeira

²madeira \"\ *adj, usu cap* [fr. *Madeira*, island group in the eastern Atlantic ocean off the coast of Morocco] : of, relating to, or characteristic of the Madeira islands or their inhabitants

³madeira \"\ *n* -s *usu cap* [modif. (influenced by ¹*madeira*) of Sp *madera* wood, fr. L *materia* wood, material, matter — more at MATTER] **1** : MAHOGANY 1a(1)&3a **2** *also* **madeira nut** : ENGLISH WALNUT 1

madeira chair *n, usu cap M* : a wickerwork chair orig. made in Madeira

madeira embroidery *n, usu cap M* : an eyelet and cutwork embroidery usu. having floral designs in white on white linen

madeira mahogany *n, usu cap 1st M* : canary wood from Madeira

¹ma·dei·ran \məˈdirən *sometimes* -der-\ *adj, usu cap* [*Madeira* islands + E *-an*] : MADEIRA

²madeiran \"\ *n* -s *usu cap* : a native or inhabitant of the Madeira islands

madeira roach *or* **madeira cockroach** *n, usu cap M* : a large cockroach (*Leucophaea maderae*) that is widely distributed in warm regions

madeira vine *n, usu cap M* : a vine (*Boussingaultia baselloides*) with shining entire leaves and small white flowers

madeira-vine family *n, usu cap M* : BASELLACEAE

madeira wood *n, usu cap M* [³*madeira*] **1** : MAHOGANY 1a(1), 3a **2** : WHITE IRONWOOD 1b

mad·e·leine \ˈmadᵊlən, ˈmadᵊlˌān\ *n* -s [F, prob. after *Madeleine* Paulmier, 19th cent. Fr. pastry cook] : a small rich cake baked in a tin shaped like a shell

made mast *n* : a mast composed of several longitudinal pieces held together by iron bands at intervals of about 3 feet

ma·de·moi·selle \ˌmadəmə'zel *also* ˌmadmwəˈz- *or* ˌma(a)d-mwəˈz- *or* ˌma(a)d(,)mwäˈz- *or* ˌma(a)d(,)mwəˈz- *or* ˌma(a)d-maˈz- *or* ˌma(a)mˈz- *or* ˌma(a)mwəˈz- *or* ˌmadəmˈz-\ *n, pl* **mademoiselles** \-lz\ *or* **mes·de·moi·selles** \ˌmädəmə'zel, -dəmwəˈ-, -dmwəˈ-, -d(,)mwäˈ-, -d(,)mwəˈ-, -dməˈ-\ [F, fr. OF *ma damoisele*, lit., my (young) lady] **1 a** : an unmarried French woman ⟨attractive ~*s* in national costume . . . serve twenty-nine varieties of wine —*Scots Mag.*⟩ **b** : a French governess or nurse ⟨was spending the summer in a chalet . . . with her four children, her sister, a ~, and a cook —Maddy Vegtel⟩ **2** : a female member of the French royal family: **a** : the eldest daughter of the king's eldest brother **b** : the eldest daughter of the king **c** : the highest-ranking unmarried princess of the blood royal **3** : MISS — often used as a title prefixed to the name of an unmarried woman who is not of English-speaking nationality **4** : any of several silvery marine fishes with a strong second anal spine that form a genus (*Bairdiella*) of the family Sciaenidae; *esp* : a fish (*B. chrysura*) of the southern U.S.

made-over \ˈ=ˈ==\ *adj* [fr. past part. of *make over*] : fashioned again : REMADE, REMODELED ⟨hostels range from *made-over* barns to comparatively luxurious houses —*Life*⟩

made-to-measure \ˈ=ˈ=ˈ==\ *adj* : fashioned to measurements specifically required ⟨one may have one's personal idiosyncrasies built into the *made-to-measure* garment —S.D. Barney⟩

made-to-order \ˈ=ˈ=ˈ==\ *adj* **1** : produced to supply a special or an individual demand : made in addition to the regular stock or line; *specif* : MADE-TO-MEASURE ⟨*made-to-order* footgear —Edna Ferber⟩ — opposed to *ready-made* **2** : fashioned or created in or as if in accordance with or as if with a preconceived plan ⟨in a few years Bonn will be a spick-and-span *made-to-order* capital —Joseph Wechsberg⟩

made-up \ˈ=ˈ=\ *adj* [fr. past part. of *make up*] **1** *obs* : CONSUMMATE, COMPLETE ⟨remain assured that he's a *made-up* villain —Shak.⟩ **2** : marked by the use of makeup ⟨applied a small handkerchief carefully to her *made-up* eyelashes —Dorothy Sayers⟩ **3** : fancifully conceived or falsely devised ⟨the style . . . seemed to be too formal, too *made-up*, insufficiently spontaneous —Aldous Huxley⟩ **4 a :** fully manufactured ⟨a *made-up* garment consists of more than one class of fabric —S.D.Barney⟩ **b** *of a necktie* **:** made with a permanently tied bow ⟨swallowed his pride and used a *made-up* tie —J.M.Barrie⟩ **5 :** firmly resolved **:** DECIDED ⟨an audience with stubbornly *made-up* minds —*Progressive Labor World*⟩

made-work \'=,=\ *n* **:** work designed to provide employment as distinguished from work that is inherently necessary or permanently valuable ⟨heavy government spending, *made-work*, and an unbalanced budget —John Fischer⟩

madge \'maj\ *n* -s [prob. fr. *Madge*, nickname for *Margaret*] **1 :** BARN OWL **2** *dial Brit* **:** MAGPIE

ma·dhab \mə'dab\ *n* -s [Ar *madhhab* opinion] **:** a school of Muslim jurisprudence

mad–headed \'=;==\ *adj* **:** MAD-BRAINED

madhouse \'=,=\ *n* **1 :** a house where insane persons are detained and treated **:** an insane asylum **2 :** a place or scene of bewildering uproar or confusion ⟨before we bought a television . . . the place used to be a ~ —Bennett Cerf⟩

ma·dhu·ca \mə'dükə\ *n* [NL, fr. Skt *madhūka* mahua — more at MAHUA] **1** *cap* **:** a genus of East Indian trees (family Sapotaceae) several of which yield valuable oils and timber — see ILLUPI, MAHUA **2** -s **:** any tree of the genus *Madhuca*

mad·hya·mi·ka \mäd'(h)yəmə̇kə\ *n* -s *usu cap* [Skt *mādhyamika*, fr. *madhyama* middle, superlative of *madhya* middle — more at MID] **1** *or* **madhyamaka :** one of the two major philosophical systems of Mahayana Buddhism holding against both realism and nihilism that ultimate reality has no definable characteristic and is beyond both knowing and being — compare YOGACARA **2 :** an adherent of Madhyamika

ma·di \'mädē\ *n, pl* **madi** *or* **madis** *usu cap* **1 a :** a Negro people of the upper Nile region north of Lake Albert **b :** a member of such people **2 :** a central Sudanic language of the Madi people

ma·dia \'mädēə\ *n, cap* [NL, fr. Sp *madia, madi*, a Chilean species of *Madia*, fr. Araucan *Madi*] **:** a genus of sticky herbs (family Compositae) having heads with deeply grooved bracts investing the achenes — see MELOSA, TARWEED

madia oil *n* **:** an oil made from the seeds of the melosa and used as a substitute for olive oil

mad·id \'madə̇d\ *adj* [L *madidus*, fr. *madēre* to be wet — more at MEAT] **:** WET, MOIST ⟨his large deep blue eye, ~ and yet piercing —Benjamin Disraeli⟩

mad·i·son \'madəsən\ *adj, usu cap* [fr. *Madison*, Wis.] **:** of or from Madison, the capital of Wisconsin ⟨*Madison* shoppers⟩ **:** of the kind or style prevalent in Madison

madison avenue *adj, usu cap M&A* [fr. *Madison avenue*, New York city, the center of the Amer. advertising business] **:** of, relating to, or having the characteristics of the American advertising industry ⟨taking full advantage of modern *Madison Avenue* advertising techniques —*Newsweek*⟩ ⟨dress more conservative than *Madison Avenue* junior executives —Robert Sylvester⟩

¹mad·i·so·ni·an \ˌmadə'sōnēən\ *adj, usu cap* [James *Madison* †1812, 4th U.S. president + E *-ian*] **:** of or relating to James Madison or to his political principles

²madisonian \"\ *n* -s *usu cap* **:** a follower of James Madison **:** an adherent of the political principles of Madison ⟨persons who at that time were staunch Federalists and since that time have been staunch . . . *Madisonians* —*Annals of 14th Congress*⟩

³madisonian \"\ *n* -s *cap* [*Madison*, Wis. + E *-ian*] **:** a native or resident of Madison, Wisconsin

mad itch *n* **:** PSEUDORABIES

mad·ling \'madliŋ\ *n* -s [¹*mad* + *-ling*] **:** a mad person **:** DOTARD, FOOL, SIMPLETON

mad·ly *adv* [ME, fr. *medd, madd, mad* mad + *-ly* — more at MAD] **:** in a mad manner: as **a :** in an insane manner ⟨drew his sword and rushed ~ on the justiciary —J.R.Green⟩ **b :** in a foolish or rash manner ⟨the help of that single power he had ~ rejected —T.B.Macaulay⟩ **c :** in a vigorous or energetic manner ⟨worked ~ throwing the boxes in at the door of the express car —Sherwood Anderson⟩ **d :** to an excessive or extreme degree ⟨finds herself ~ in love with a young American —B.R.Redman⟩ ⟨boasts a pedigree that is almost ~ aristocratic —Francis Steegmuller⟩

mad·man \'mad,man, 'maad-,'maid-, -ˌmən, -ˌmaa(ə)n\ *n, pl* **madmen** [ME *madd man*] **1 :** a man who is insane **:** LUNATIC ⟨there are *madmen* . . . in whom it is difficult to find any trace of hallucination —Henry Maudsley⟩ **2 :** a man who is rash or foolish ⟨the casual skill with which these *madmen* diced with danger —J.E.Macdonnell⟩

mad money *n* **:** carfare carried by a girl on a date to provide a means of escaping her escort in the event of unwanted familiarities; *broadly* **:** a small sum carried by a woman for emergency use

mad·nep \'=,nep\ *n* -s [¹*mad* + E dial. *nep, neep* turnip, parsnip, fr. ME *nepe* — more at NEEP] **1** *obs* **:** COW PARSNIP **2 :** WILD PARSNIP

mad·ness *n* -ES [ME *maddnesse*, fr. *madd* mad + *-nesse* -ness — more at MAD] **1 :** the quality or state of being mad: as **a :** INSANITY ⟨undergoes a period of ~ in a mental hospital —W.E.Allen⟩ **b :** extreme folly **:** RASHNESS ⟨to grant such a demand would be strategic ~ —H.W.Baldwin⟩ **c :** intense anger **:** RAGE ⟨his editorials . . . often goaded the opposition to ~ —W.E.Smith⟩ **d :** complete involvement in or concern with the pursuit of an object or activity ⟨trivial by-products of her age's industrial ~ —Sherwood Anderson⟩ **e :** ECSTASY, ENTHUSIASM ⟨poetry has nothing to do with reasoning but is a sort of divine ~ —Irving Babbitt⟩ **2 :** any of several ailments of animals (as dogs) marked by frenzied or irrational behavior; *specif* **:** RABIES

¹ma·don·na \mə'dänə\ *n* -s [It, fr. OIt *ma donna*, lit., my lady] **1** *archaic* **:** LADY — used as a form of respectful or polite address ⟨good ~, why mournest thou —Shak.⟩ **2** *obs* **:** an Italian woman **3 :** a picture, statue, or other representation of the Virgin Mary ⟨artisans readying the giant religious floats with their jeweled life-sized ~s —Barnaby Conrad⟩

²madonna \"\ *adj* **:** of, relating to, or being a woman's hair style in which the hair is pulled back smoothly from a middle part

madonna lily *n, usu cap M* **:** a white lily (*Lilium candidum*) with bell-shaped to broad funnel-shaped flowers formerly extensively forced for spring blooming — called also *Annunciation lily, Lent lily*; compare BERMUDA LILY

ma·do·qua \mə'dōkwə\ *n* [Amharic *mēdaqqwa*] **1** -s **:** ROYAL ANTELOPE **2** *cap* **:** a genus comprising some small antelopes of eastern and northeastern Africa

mador *n* -s [L, moisture, fr. *madēre* to be wet + *-or* — more at MEAT] *obs* **:** SWEAT

ma·drague \mə'drag\ *n* -s [F, fr. Prov *madrago*, fr. Ar *mazrabah*] **:** a large fishpound or a seine used to capture tuna in the Mediterranean

¹ma·dras \mə'dras, -räs, -raa(ə)s, -rȧs; 'madrəs, 'maad-\ *adj, usu cap* [fr. *Madras*, India] **:** of or from the city of Madras, India **:** of the kind or style prevalent in Madras

²madras \"\ *n* -ES *sometimes cap, often attrib* **1 a** (1) **:** a fine plain-woven shirting and dress fabric usu. of cotton with small usu. woven designs (as stripes, checks) in bright colors or in white (2) **:** a light open usu. cotton fabric that has a heavy usu. woven design and that is used for curtains and draperies **b :** MADRAS HANDKERCHIEF **2 :** SUNN

ma·dra·sah *or* **ma·dra·sa** \mə'drasə\ *n* -s [Ar *madrasah*, lit., place of study] **:** a Muslim school or college or university

madras gram *n, usu cap M* **:** HORSE GRAM

madras handkerchief *n, sometimes cap M* **:** a large usu. cotton kerchief in bright usu. solid colors that is often worn as a turban

madras hemp *n, usu cap M* **:** SUNN

ma·drasi *also* **ma·dras·si** *pronunc at* ¹MADRAS +ē\ *n, pl* **madrasi** *or* **madrasis** [Hindi *madrasī*] **1** *usu cap* **:** a native or inhabitant of Madras in the subcontinent of India **2** *sometimes cap* **:** a native hired usu. as an unskilled laborer in the subcontinent of India

mad·re·po·ra \ˌmadrə'pōrə, mə'drepərə\ [NL, fr. It, madrepore — more at MADREPORE] *syn of* ACROPORA

mad·re·po·rar·ia \ˌmadrəpə'ra(a)rēə, mə,drep-\ *n pl, cap* [NL, fr. *Madrepora* + *-aria*] **:** an extensive order of Anthozoa including most species that produce stony corals and that resemble the actiniarians in the general structure of the soft parts but that usu. form colonies and always have an ectodermal calcareous skeleton — **mad·re·po·rar·i·an** \ˌmadrəpə'ra(a)rēən, mə,drep-\ *adj or n*

mad·re·pore \'madrə,pō(ə)r\ *n* [F *madrépore*, fr. It *madrepora*, fr. *madre* mother (fr. L *mater*) + *-pora* (fr. *poro* pore, fr. L *porus*) — more at MOTHER, PORE] **:** any of various stony reef-building corals (order Madreporaria) of tropical seas that assume a variety of branching, encrusting, or massive forms and that include the staghorn corals, the brain corals, and the mushroom corals

¹mad·re·po·ri·an \ˌmadrə'pōrēən\ *adj* [*madrepore* + *-ian*] **:** MADREPORIC

²madreporian \"\ *n* -s **:** MADREPORE

mad·re·por·ic \ˌmadrə'pȯrik\ *also* **mad·re·po·rit·ic** \-ˌpə'rid·ik, mə,drep-\ *adj* **:** of, relating to, or like a madrepore or a madreporite

madreporic body *or* **madreporic plate** *or* **madreporic tubercle** *n* **:** MADREPORITE

mad·re·por·i·form \ˌmadrə'pȯrə,fȯrm\ *adj* [ISV *madrepore* + *-iform*] **:** resembling a madrepore

mad·re·por·ite \'madrə,pȯr,īt, mə'drepə,rīt\ *n* -s [ISV *madrepore* + *-ite*] **:** a perforated or porous body that is situated at the distal end of the stone canal in echinoderms and that may be internal or inconspicuously buried in the body wall (as in holothurians) or may be a conspicuous convex plate on the dorsal side of the body (as in many starfishes)

ma·drid \mə'drid\ *adj, usu cap* [fr. *Madrid*, Spain] **:** of or from Madrid, the capital of Spain **:** of the kind or style prevalent in Madrid

madrid sweet clover *n, usu cap M* **:** a biennial sweet clover native to Spain and introduced for use as a forage and hay crop in the southern U. S.

mad·ri·gal \'madrəgəl, 'maad-,-rēg-\ *n* -s [It *madrigale*, fr. ML *matricale*, fr. neut. of (assumed) ML *matricalis* simple, fr. LL, of the womb — more at MATRIC] **1 :** a medieval short lyrical poem esp. of love **2 a :** a polyphonic part-song originating in the 14th century that has parts for three or more voices and is marked by the use of a secular text and a freely imitative style and counterpoint and that in its later development esp. in the 16th and 17th centuries is often marked by a distinct melody in the upper voice and by being designed for accompaniment by strings that either double or replace one or more of the voice parts — compare MOTET **b :** a part-song of any kind; *esp* **:** GLEE

mad·ri·gal·er *also* **mad·ri·gal·ler** \-lə(r)\ *n* -s **:** MADRIGALIST

mad·ri·gal·esque \ˌ==gə'lesk\ *adj* [F, fr. It *madrigalesco*, fr. *madrigale* + *-esco* -esque] **:** relating to or having the characteristics of a madrigal

mad·ri·galian \ˌ==galēən, -gāl-, -lyən\ *adj* [*madrigal* + *-ian*] **:** of or relating to madrigals

mad·ri·gal·ist \'==,gələst\ *n* -s **:** a composer of madrigals

ma·drih *or* **ma·drich** \mä'driḵ\ *n, pl* **madri·him** *or* **madri·chim** \ˌmädri'ḵēm\ [NHeb *madhrīkh*, fr. Heb, guide, leader] **:** a leader or teacher in Israeli youth groups

madri·le·ña \ˌmadrə'lānyə, ˌmäthr-\ *n* -s *often cap* [Sp, fem. of *madrileño*] **:** a female native or resident of Madrid, Spain

¹mad·ri·lene \'madrə,lēn, ˌ=='=\ *n* -s *cap* [Sp *madrileño*] **:** MADRILENIAN

²ma·dri·lene \'madrə,len, -lān\ *n* -s [F *(consommé) madrilène*, lit., Madrid consommé] **:** a consommé flavored with tomato and served hot or cold

¹mad·ri·le·nian \ˌmadrə'lēnēən, -nyən\ *adj, usu cap* [Sp *madrileño* of Madrid (fr. *Madrid*) + E *-ian*] **:** of or from Madrid, Spain **:** of the kind or style prevalent in Madrid

²madrilenian \"\ *n* -s *cap* **:** a native or resident of Madrid, Spain

madri·le·ño \ˌmadrə'lān(ˌ)yō, ˌmäthr-\ *n* -s *often cap* [Sp, fr. *Madrid*, Spain] **:** a native or resident of Madrid, Spain **:** MADRILENIAN

ma·dro·na *or* **ma·dro·ne** *or* **ma·dro·no** \mə'drōnə\ *n* -s [Sp & MexSp *madroño*] **1 :** a plant of the genus *Arbutus*: as **a :** an evergreen tree or shrub (*A. menziesii*) of the Pacific coast of No. America that has a smooth bark and thick shining leaves and edible red berries **b :** a tree or shrub (*A. xalapensis*) of the Mexican border **2 :** DAGAME **3 :** STRAWBERRY TREE 1

madrona apple *n* **:** one of the red berries borne by the madrona

mads *pres 3d sing of* MAD, *pl of* MAD

mad staggers *n pl* **:** STAGGERS

madstone \'=,=\ *n* **:** a stony concretion (as a hair ball taken from the stomach of a deer) supposed to counteract the poisonous effects of the bite of an animal (as one affected with rabies)

madtom \'=,=\ *n* -s [¹*mad* + *tom* (cat)] **:** any of several small freshwater catfishes (family Ameiuridae) that are widely distributed in the central and eastern U.S. and have poisonous pectoral spines capable of inflicting painful wounds

mad·u·ra \'majərə\ *adj, usu cap* [fr. *Madura*, India] **:** of or from the city of Madura, India **:** of the kind or style prevalent in Madura

madura foot *n, usu cap M* **:** maduromycosis of the foot

madu·rese \ˌmadə'rēz, ˌmajə;-, mə,dü;-, -ēs\ *n, pl* **madurese** *usu cap* [*Madura* + E *-ese*] **1 a :** an Indonesian people inhabiting Madura and adjacent regions on Java **b :** a member of the Madurese people **2 :** the Austronesian language of the Madurese people

ma·du·ro \mə'dü(ˌ)rō\ *n* -s [Sp, fr. *maduro* ripe, mature, fr. L *maturus* — more at MATURE] **:** a dark-colored relatively strong cigar

mad·u·ro·mycosis \ˌmajə(ˌ)rō+\ *n* [NL, fr. *Madura*, India + NL *-o-* + *mycosis*] **:** a destructive chronic disease usu. restricted to the feet, marked by swelling and deformity resulting from the formation of granulomatous nodules drained by sinuses connecting with the exterior, and caused esp. by an aerobic form of actinomycetes and sometimes by true fungi — compare NOCARDIOSIS

madweed \'=,=\ *n* **:** MAD-DOG SKULLCAP

madwoman \'=,==\ *n, pl* **madwomen :** an insane woman

madwort \'=,=\ *n* **1 :** a cress of the genus *Lobularia* **2 :** GERMAN MADWORT **3 :** GOLD OF PLEASURE **4 :** a plant of the genus *Alyssum*

madzoon *var of* MATZOON

¹mae \'mā\ *adj, adv, or n* [ME (northern dial.) *ma*, fr. OE *mā* — more at MORE] *Scot* **:** MORE

²mae \'ma, 'maa, 'mā\ *Scot var of* BAA

maeander *var of* MEANDER

mae·an·dra \mē'andrə\ *n, cap* [NL, fr. L *maeander, maeandrus* twist, winding — more at MEANDER] **:** a large genus of massive reef-building corals including many brain corals — **mae·an·droid** \-'=,drȯid\ *adj*

mae·an·drine \-,drīn, -'drən\ *adj* [NL *Maeandra* + E *-ine*] **:** of or relating to the genus *Maeandra* — **mae·an·drin·i·form** \ˌ=;(ˌ)=drinə,fȯrm\ *adj* — **mae·an·dri·noid** \=;'=drə,nȯid\ *adj*

mae·ce·nas \mə'sēnəs, mē'- *also* mī'-\ *n* -ES *usu cap* [L, after Gaius *Maecenas* †8 B.C. Roman statesman and patron of literature] **:** a generous benefactor; *esp* **:** a munificent patron of literature or art ⟨opera has never really paid its way anywhere, but in Europe government subventions have replaced the . . . vanished *Maecenases* —James Hinton⟩

mae·ce·nas·ship \-nəs,ship\ *n, usu cap* **:** the status of being a Maecenas

mae·ce·na·tism \-nə,tizəm\ *n* -s *usu cap* [Gaius *Maecenat-, Maecenas* + E *-ism*] **:** PATRONAGE

mæg·bote *or* **maeg·bot** *also* **mag·bote** \'mag,bōt\ *n* -s [OE *mǣgbōt*, fr. *mǣg* kinsman, relative + *bōt* compensation; akin to OS & OHG *māg* kinsman, ON *māgr* relative by marriage, Goth *megs* son-in-law, Gk *periēmektein* to be unwilling, Lith *mėgti* to like; basic meaning: friendly — more at BOOT] *Anglo-Saxon law* **:** compensation paid to the kinsmen of a man slain

mael·strom \'mālztrəm, -lst- *also* -lz,trām *or* -l,strām\ *n* -s [obs. D (now *maalstroom*), fr. *malen* to grind, turn (fr. MD) + *strom* stream, fr. MD *strōm*; akin to OHG *malan* to grind, and to OHG *stroum, strōm* stream — more at MEAL, STREAM] **1 :** a powerful often destructive water current that usu. moves in a circular direction with extreme rapidity sucking in objects within a given radius **:** WHIRLPOOL ⟨tried to shoot the canoe across a stretch of treacherous ~ —*Harper's*⟩ **2 :** something resembling a maelstrom ⟨the ancient taboos were gone, lost in the ~ of war —Coulton Waugh⟩ ⟨childhood playmates in the country . . . later separated in the ~ of city life —J.D.Hart⟩ ⟨couldn't fuse his thoughts out of the ~ of thinking —Herbert Elliston⟩

mael·zel's metronome \'meltsəlz-\ *n, usu cap 1st M* [after Johann N. Maelzel (Mälzel) †1838 Ger. musician, its inventor] **:** METRONOME

maen \'mān\ *Scot var of* MOAN

mae·nad *also* **me·nad** \'mē,nad\ *n* -s [L *maenad-, maenas*, fr. Gk *mainad-, mainas*, lit., madwoman, fr. *mainesthai* to be mad; akin to Gk *menos* spirit — more at MIND] **1 a :** a woman participating in the orgiastic Dionysian rites **:** BACCHANTE **b :** a frenzied female dancer **2 :** an unnaturally excited or distraught woman ⟨a figure scarcely human, a tragic *Maenad* —R.L.Stevenson⟩ — **mae·nad·ic** \mē'nadik\ *adj*

mae·nad·ism \'=,na,dizəm\ *n* -s **:** the practices of the maenads

mae·ni·dae \'mēnə,dē\ *n pl, cap* [NL, *Maena*, type genus (fr. L, a kind of small sea fish, fr. Gk *mainē*) + *-idae*] **:** a small family of slender percoid marine fishes including the picarels

mae·o·ni·an \(')mē'ōnēən\ *adj, usu cap* [*Maeonia*, ancient country in Asia Minor (fr. L, fr. Gk *Maionia*) + E *-an*] **:** of or relating to ancient Maeonia afterward called Lydia and reputed to be the birthplace of Homer

maerl \'mer(ə)l, mä'er-\ *n* -s [F *maërl, maërle*, fr. Bret *merl, maërl* marl, maerl, fr. MF *marle* marl — more at MARL] **:** lime-producing red seaweeds principally of the genus *Lithothamnion* used esp. in France to reduce acidity of the soil

¹mae·sto·so \mī'stō(ˌ)sō, ˌmīə's-, -)zō\ *adj (or adv)* [It, majestic, fr. *maestà* majesty (fr. L *majestat-, majestas*) + *-oso* -ous — more at MAJESTY] **:** majestic and stately and usu. moderate in tempo — used as a direction in music

²maestoso \"\ *n* -s **:** a composition or movement in the maestoso style or tempo

maestral *obs var of* MISTRAL

mae·stro \'mī(ˌ)strō *sometimes* mä'e(-\ *n, pl* **maestros** \-rōz\ *or* **mae·stri** \-rē\ [It, lit., master, fr. L *magister* — more at MASTER] **:** one who is accomplished in a specialized field; *esp* **:** a master or teacher of an art (as music) ⟨when the ~ was active as one of the world's more famous operatic conductors —Claudia Cassidy⟩ ⟨contributors include some ~s in the delightful art of the spoof or parody —*Atlantic*⟩ ⟨that did not always mean that the ~ himself had actually painted the picture —H.W.Van Loon⟩

maestro di cap·pel·la \-dēkə'pelə\ *n* [It] **:** CHOIRMASTER

maestro-sastre \ˌmīstrō;sästrē\ *n* [Sp, fr. *maestro* master + *sastre* tailor] **:** MASTER-TAILOR

mae·ter·linck·ian \ˌmā|də(r)ˌliŋkēən, ˌme|, |tə- *sometimes* ˌmä| *or* ˌma| *or* ˌmȧ|\ *adj, usu cap* [Maurice *Maeterlinck* †1949 Belgian poet, dramatist, and essayist + E *-ian*] **:** of, characteristic of, or resembling Maeterlinck or his writings ⟨writing a symbolic *Maeterlinckian* drama —Agnes Repplier⟩

mae west \'mā'west\ *n, usu cap M&W* [after *Mae West b*1892 Am. actress noted for her full figure] **:** a yellow life jacket inflatable by means of two cartridges of carbon dioxide that is worn by fliers in flights over water

maf·fick \'mafik, -fēk, *esp in pres part* -fək\ *vi* -ED/-ING/-S [back-formation fr. *Mafeking*, town in Union of So. Africa (used attrib. in such phrases as *Mafeking night*), site of a siege by the Boers during the Boer war that was relieved by British troops on May 17, 1900; fr. the rejoicing that the lifting of the siege caused in England] **:** to celebrate with boisterous rejoicings and hilarious behavior ⟨the reaction to better news caused a ~*ing* such as has rarely been seen—Nancy Mitford⟩

maf·fle \'mafəl\ *vb* -ED/-ING/-S [ME *mafflen*, prob. of imit. origin] *vi, now dial Eng* **:** to speak indistinctly **:** MUMBLE, STAMMER ~ *vt, now dial Eng* **:** to cause to become confused or bewildered

ma·fia *or* **maf·fia** \'mäfēə, 'maf-\ *n* -s *usu cap* [fr. *Mafia, Maffia*, a secret criminal society of Sicily, fr. It, fr. It dial. (Sicily) *mafia* boldness, bluster, swagger, prob. fr. Ar *maḥyah* boasting] **1 :** a secret society of political terrorists ⟨browbeaten into joining this industrial *Mafia* —Benjamin Stolberg⟩ ⟨charges of a Soviet *Mafia* operating in Europe⟩ **2 :** a secret organization composed chiefly of criminal elements and usu. held to control racketeering, peddling of narcotics, gambling, and other illicit activities throughout the world ⟨the *Mafia* . . . concentrated on gambling, prostitution, and blackmail rackets among Italian immigrants, but prohibition brought an eruption of activity on a national scale —Stanley Frank⟩

maf·ic \'mafik\ *adj* [magnesium + L *ferrum* + E *-ic* — more at FARRIER] **:** of or relating to a group of minerals characterized by magnesium and iron and usu. by their dark color

maf·ite \-,fīt\ *n* -s [*mafic* + *-ite*] **:** a mafic mineral

ma·foo *also* **ma·fu** \'mä'fü\ *n* -s [Chin (Pek) *ma³ fu¹* groom, fr. *ma³* horse + *fu¹* laborer] **:** a Chinese stable boy or groom

maf·tir \'mäf,ti(ə)r, =='=\ *n* -s [Heb *maphṭīr* one that dismisses] **:** the reader of the Haftarah

ma·fura *or* **ma·fur·ra** \mə'fərə\ *n* -s [of Bantu origin; akin to Sotho & Ronga *mafura*, lit., fat, oil] **:** an East African tree (*Trichilia emetica*) having capsular fruit whose seeds yield a fatty substance resembling cocoa butter that is used for soap and candles

¹mag \'mag, -aa(ə)g, -aig\ *n* -s [short for *magpie*] **1** *dial Eng* **:** the European magpie **2 :** *now dial Brit* **:** TALK, CHATTER

²mag \"\ *vi* **magged; magged; magging; mags** *dial Brit* **:** to talk incessantly **:** CHATTER ⟨always *magging* about progress —John Morrison⟩

³mag \"\ *n* -s [origin unknown] *dial Brit* **:** HALFPENNY

⁴mag \'mag, -aa(ə)g, -aig\ *n* -s [by shortening] *slang* **:** MAGAZINE ⟨liked the plots and intrigues of the mystery ~s —*Newsweek*⟩

⁵mag \"\ *n* -s [by shortening] *slang* **:** MAGNETO ⟨all that's needed is to take the ~ out and give it a wipe —Agatha Christie⟩

mag *abbr* **1** magazine **2** magnet; magnetic; magnetism **3** magneto **4** magnitude

ma·ga \'mägə\ *n* -s [Skt] **:** a member of the priestly caste among the Sauras of India

ma·ga·dhi \'mägədē\ *n* -s *cap* **:** the Prakrit language of Magadha

mag·a·dis \'magədə̇s\ *n* -ES [Gk, of non-IE origin] **:** an ancient Greek musical instrument having twenty strings and the capability of being played in octaves

mag·a·dize \-,dīz\ *vi* -ED/-ING/-S [Gk *magadizein*, fr. *magadis* + *-izein* -ize] **1 :** to sing or play in octaves ⟨the Greek practice of *magadizing*, in which . . . lay the fundamental principle of polyphony —H.E.Wooldridge⟩ **2 :** to play on the magadis

ma·ga·hat \ˌmägə'hät\ *n, pl* **magahat** *or* **magahats** *usu cap* [native name in southern Negros] **1 :** a Bisayan people inhabiting the hills of southern Negros, Philippine islands **2 :** a member of the Magahat people

mag·a·hi \'magəhē\ *n* -s *cap* **:** an Indic dialect of west Bihar

ma·ga·li \mə'gälē\ *n, pl* **magali** *or* **magalis** *usu cap* **:** one of the numerous more isolated peoples of Arabia

ma·ga·ni \mə'gänē\ *n* -s *often cap* [native name in the Philippines] **:** a class of warriors of Mindanao — called also *bagani*

¹mag·a·zine \'magə;zēn, ˌmaig-\ *n* -s [MF, fr. OProv, fr. Ar *makhāzin*, pl. of *makhzan* storehouse, fr. *khazana* to store up] **1 a :** a place where goods or supplies are stored **:** WAREHOUSE ⟨each hamlet . . . possesses a ~ inside which families deposit all their provisions —H.T.Norris⟩ ⟨in the compting rooms and fur ~s of the concern —Walter O'Meara⟩ **b** *archaic* **:** a country or district esp. rich in natural resources or produce ⟨set down in a perfect ~ of fruit and vegetables, grain and wine—Leitch Ritchie⟩ **c** *archaic* **:** a city viewed as a marketing center ⟨islands . . . are now converted into complete ~s for all kinds of European goods —*Gentleman's Mag.*⟩ **2 a :** a place to store ammunition: as (1) **:** a building in which ammunition and explosives are kept on a military installation (2) **:** a compartment of a ship used to store ammunition and explosives **b** *archaic* **:** something resembling a place to store ammunition ⟨stored his ~ of malice with weapons equally sharp —Samuel Johnson⟩ **3 a :** the contents stored in a magazine: as (1) **:** an accumulation of munitions of war ⟨a large ~ of darts and arrows —Edward Gibbon⟩ (2) **:** a stock or store of provisions or goods ⟨~ of flesh, milk, butter, and cheese —Daniel Defoe⟩ **b :** something resembling the contents of a magazine ⟨truth becomes . . . a new weapon in the ~ of power —R.W.Emerson⟩ **4 a** (1) **:** a periodical that usu. contains a miscellaneous collection of articles, stories, poems, and pictures and is directed at the general reading public (2) **:** a periodical containing special material directed at a group having a particular hobby, interest, or profession (as education, photography, or medicine) or at a particular age group (as children, teen-agers) ⟨alumni ~⟩ — compare LITTLE MAGAZINE **b :** a special section of a newspaper usu. appearing on Sunday ⟨seek a much wider audience for the paper . . . through an enlarged ~ —Bruce Bliven b. 1889⟩ **5 :** a supply chamber: as **a :** a holder that is incorporated in or attachable to a gun and that contains cartridges to be fed into the gun chamber by the operation of the piece — see CLIP e **b :** a lighttight chamber containing plates, sheet film, or rollable film for use in or on a camera or containing both feed and take-up spools for film for use in or on a motion-picture camera or projector **c :** the chambers to hold circulating matrices in a typesetting machine

²magazine \"\ *vt* -ED/-ING/-S *archaic* **:** to store in or as if in a magazine **:** store up for use

mag·a·zine·let \ˌ==ˈlət\ *n* -S **:** a small periodical

mag·a·zin·er \ˌ==ˈzēnə(r)\ *n* -S **:** MAGAZINIST

magazine safety *n* **:** a safety mechanism on an automatic pistol that makes firing impossible unless the magazine is in the weapon

mag·a·zin·ish \ˌ==ˈzēnish\ *adj* **:** characteristic of magazine writing **:** somewhat superficial or shallow ⟨the book seems too slick, too ~⟩

mag·a·zin·ist \-nəst\ *n* -S **:** one who writes for or edits a magazine ⟨usually the newspaper journalist rather than the ~ . . . has published his drama-filled memoirs —R.E.Wolseley⟩

mag·a·ziny \-nē\ *adj* **:** MAGAZINISH

mag·da·len \ˈmagdələn\ *or* **mag·da·lene** \-ˌlēn\ *n* -S *often cap* [after Mary *Magdalen* or *Magdalene*, woman whom Jesus healed of evil spirits (Lk 8:2), considered identical with a reformed prostitute (Lk 7:36 ff.)] **1 :** a reformed prostitute **2 :** a house of refuge or reformatory for prostitutes

¹mag·da·le·nian \ˌmagdəˈlēnēən, -nyən\ *adj, usu cap* [F *Magdalénien*, fr. *Magdalén-* (fr. *La Madeleine*, rock shelter on the Vézère river in southwestern France, the type station of Magdalenian culture) + F *-ien* -ian] **:** of or belonging to a late Paleolithic period characterized by implements of flint (as scrapers, gravers, saws, and knives) and of bone and ivory (as borers, needles, harpoons, and hooks), carving, and polychrome painting in caves of southern France and northern Spain

²magdalenian \"\ *n* -S *usu cap* **:** one of a late Paleolithic people producing a distinct culture

mag·de·burg \ˈmägdəˌbu̇rg, ˈmagdəˌbərg\ *adj, usu cap* [fr. *Magdeburg*, Germany] **:** of or from the city of Magdeburg, Germany **:** of the kind or style prevalent in Magdeburg

magdeburg hemisphere *n, usu cap M* **:** either of a pair of hemispherical cups forming when placed together a cavity from which the air can be withdrawn by an air pump and used to illustrate the pressure of air

Magdeburg hemispheres

mage \ˈmāj\ *n* -S [ME, fr. L *magus* — more at MAGIC] **1 :** MAGICIAN **2 :** MAGUS

¹ma·gel·lan \məˈjelən\ *adj, usu cap* [fr. the Straits of *Magellan*, strait between the southern tip of the mainland of So. America and the Tierra del Fuego archipelago that connects the Atlantic and Pacific oceans] **:** MAGELLANIC

²magellan \"\ *n* -S *usu cap* [after Ferdinand *Magellan* (Pg Fernando de Magalhães) †1521 Port. navigator who led the first expedition to circumnavigate the globe] **:** a world traveler ⟨a modern *Magellan* can leave . . . in a giant clipper of the air —*Saturday Rev.*⟩

magellan barberry *n, usu cap M* **:** a So. American evergreen shrub (*Berberis buxifolia*) with grooved slender branchlets, entire leaves, orange-yellow flowers, and dark purple fruit that is grown for ornament

mag·el·lan·ic \ˌmajəˈlanik\ *adj, usu cap* [Straits of *Magellan* + E *-ic*] **:** of, relating to, or characteristic of the Straits of Magellan or that general area of the southern hemisphere

magellanic cloud *n, usu cap M&C* **:** either of the two nearest galaxies to the Milky Way system located within 25 degrees of the south celestial pole and appearing as conspicuous patches of light resembling detached portions of the Milky Way but actually more than 200,000 light-years distant

ma·gen da·vid \mäˈgän(ˌ)däˈvēd, ˈmȯgənˈdȯvəd *sometimes* ˈmāgənˈdāvəd\ *also* **mo·gen da·vid** \ˈmȯgənˈdȯvəd\ *n, pl* **magen davids** *also* **mogen davids** *usu cap M&D* [Heb *māghēn Dāwīdh*, lit., shield of David, fr. *Dāwīdh* David †*ab*973B.C. king of Judah and Israel] **:** a figure in the shape of a six-pointed star formed by two intersecting equilateral triangles and widely used as a symbol of Judaism — called also *Shield of David, Star of David*

ma·gen·ta \məˈjentə\ *n* -S [fr. *Magenta*, town in northern Italy, site of a battle between the Austrian and the Franco-Sardinian armies on June 4, 1859; fr. its having been discovered shortly after the battle and fr. the red color of fuchsine, reminiscent of the blood spilled at Magenta] **1 :** FUCHSINE **2 a :** a deep purplish red that is bluer and stronger than American beauty, bluer, lighter, and stronger than hollyhock, and bluer and deeper than Harvard crimson (sense 2); *specif* **:** one of the subtractive primaries **b :** FUCHSIA RED **c** *of textiles* **:** a dark to deep purplish red that is redder and slightly darker than Indian lake

magenta rose *n* **:** a moderate purplish red that is bluer and deeper than average rose or solferino, redder and deeper than violine pink, and bluer and duller than average fuchsia rose

mag·er·ful \ˈmagərfəl\ *adj* [prob. by alter.] *Scot* **:** MASTERFUL

¹magged *past of* MAG

²magged \ˈmagd, -aa(ə)gd, -aigd\ *adj* [prob. fr. E dial., tired, exhausted, of unknown origin] **:** WORN, FRAYED ⟨a ~ rope⟩

mag·gid \ˈmägid\ *n, pl* **mag·gid·im** \mäˈgēdəm, -ēm\ [Heb *maggīdh* narrator] **:** an itinerant Jewish preacher whose discourse on a biblical text is usu. embellished by parables drawn from the rabbinical commentaries and from Jewish folklore and is often delivered in a chant

mag·gie's drawers \ˈmagēz-, ˈmaigēz-\ *n pl, usu cap M* [fr. *Maggie*, nickname for *Margaret*] **1** *slang* **:** the red flag waved across the target by a marker on the target range when a shot has completely missed the target **2** *slang* **:** a miss when scoring targets

magging *pres part of* MAG

mag·gio·re \mäˈjō(ˌ)rā\ *adj* [It, lit., greater, fr. L *major*— more at MAJOR] **:** MAJOR 7

¹mag·got \ˈmagət, ˈmaig-, *usu* -əd.+V\ *n* -S [ME *mathek, maddock, magotte* worm, grub, maggot, of Scand origin; akin to ON *mathkr* maggot, worm; akin to OE & Goth *matha* maggot, worm, OHG *mado* maggot, MLG *maddik* earthworm, and perh. to Arm *mat'il* louse] **1 a :** a soft-bodied legless grub that is the larva of various dipterous insects (as the housefly), that lacks a head capsule, has posterior complex respiratory apertures, and develops usu. in decaying organic matter or as a parasite in plants or animals — see MYIASIS **b :** something resembling a maggot ⟨a dead city spored with the ~s of helmeted figures —Bernard Frizell⟩ **2 a :** a sudden usu. eccentric idea **:** WHIM ⟨got some ~ in her head about being loved for her own sake —D.C.Murray⟩ **b :** a fixed idea **:** OBSESSION ⟨a decent and civilized lieutenant whose personal ~ was to spend the war in magnificent action —John McCarten⟩ **3 :** an old English country dance tune usu. coupled with someone's name ⟨My Lady Winwood's *Maggot*⟩

²maggot \"\ *n* -S [short for *maggotpie*] *dial Eng* **:** MAGPIE

maggot–pated *adj, obs* **:** having little sense **:** SILLY

maggotpie *n* [prob. fr. *Magote* (nickname for *Margaret*) + *pie* (magpie)] *obs* **:** MAGPIE

mag·got·ry \ˈmagətrē\ *n* -ES **:** stupid absurdity ⟨seemed somehow to come from all the . . . uncountable small ~ of the earth —Thomas Wolfe⟩

maggot snipe *n* **:** TURNSTONE

mag·goty \ˈmagəti\ *adj* **1 :** infested with maggots ⟨five small sacks of ~ apricots —Josephine Johnson⟩ **2** *chiefly Brit* **:** filled with absurd whims **:** FREAKISH

magh \ˈmäg\ *n* -S *usu cap* [Skt *māgha*] **:** a month of the Hindu year — see MONTH table

mag·hem·ite \magˈheˌmīt, ˈmagəˌm-\ *n* -S [*magnetite* + *hematite* + *-ite*] **:** a magnetic mineral consisting of ferric oxide and constituting a member of the magnetite series

ma·ghre·bi *or* **ma·ghri·bi** \ˈməgrəbē\ *n, pl* **maghrebi** *or* **maghrebis** *or* **maghribi** *cap* [Ar *maghribīy*, lit., western] **1 :** a native or inhabitant of the Maghreb, a region including northwestern Africa, esp. Morocco, Algeria, and Tunis, and formerly also Moorish Spain **2 :** the Arabic dialect spoken in western No. Africa

ma·ghreb·i·an \məˈgrebēən\ *or* **ma·ghrib·i·an** \-grib-\ *adj, usu cap* [*Maghreb, Maghrib* northwestern Africa and Spain + E *-ian*] **1 :** of, relating to, or characteristic of the Maghreb **2 :** of, relating to, or characteristic of the people of the Maghreb

maghzen *var of* MAKHZAN

magi *pl of* MAGUS

¹ma·gi·an \ˈmājēən\ *n* -S *usu cap* [L *magus* + E *-ian* — more at MAGUS] **:** MAGUS

²magian \"\ *adj* **1** *usu cap* **:** of or relating to the Magi **2 :** MAGICAL

ma·gi·an·ism \-əˌnizəm\ *n* -S *usu cap* **:** the beliefs and practices of the Magi

¹mag·ic \ˈmajik, -jēk\ *n* -S [ME *magik*, fr. MF *magique*, fr. L *magice*, fr. Gk *magikē*, fr. fem. of *magikos*, adj.] **1 a :** the use of means (as ceremonies, charms, spells) that are believed to have supernatural power to cause a supernatural being to produce or prevent a particular result (as rain, death, healing) considered not obtainable by natural means and that also include the arts of divination, incantation, sympathetic magic, and thaumaturgy **:** control of natural forces by the typically direct action of rites, objects, materials, or words considered supernaturally potent **b magics** *pl* **:** magic beliefs or practices **:** CHARM 1b ⟨in their crafts, their dances, their rituals of harvest, their local ~s for comfort and ease —Waldo Frank⟩ ⟨masters of poems and small ~s who could make . . . spells and runes —Leah B. Drake⟩ **2 a :** an extraordinary power or influence seemingly from a supernatural source ⟨a thinker who proposed to test men and measures by the ~ of sincerity —V.L.Parrington⟩ ⟨he was our leader and our ~ —Ralph Ellison⟩ ⟨our dynamic economy that uses so completely the ~ of mass production —P.M.Mazur⟩ **b :** something that seems to cast a spell or to give an effect of otherworldliness **:** ENCHANTMENT ⟨all the mystery, ~ and romance which belong to royalty alone —J.E.P.Grigg⟩ ⟨the lake with its gray melancholy, its brooding ~ of an untouched world —Anita Leslie⟩ ⟨the right word gives us a sense of mystery and ~ —C.S.Kilby⟩ **3 :** the art of producing unusual illusions by legerdemain ⟨entertained with acts of jugglery and ~⟩

syn WITCHCRAFT, WITCHERY, WIZARDRY, SORCERY, THAUMATURGY, ALCHEMY: MAGIC applies to any supernatural power or art or to any natural power or art seeming to have miraculous results; it is often used in connection with effecting a result or influencing a tendency ⟨*magic*, the attempt of man to govern the forces of nature directly, by means of a special lore —C.S.Coon⟩ ⟨*magic* may be loosely defined as an endeavor through utterance of set words, or the performance of set acts, to control or bend the powers of the world to man's will —J.B.Noss⟩ ⟨words when used with the gift of *magic* can seduce a reader into belief that has no roots in reality —Rose Feld⟩ WITCHCRAFT and WITCHERY, often applicable to deeds of women rather than men, apply to doings of witches, the former suggesting use, usu. malevolent, of spells, enchantments, and guile, the latter suggesting enchanting allure ⟨thus with *witchcraft* I am crowned and wrapped in marvels round and round —Elinor Wylie⟩ ⟨the *witchery* of the soft blue sky —William Wordsworth⟩ ⟨the *witchery* of legend and romance —Ben Riker⟩ WIZARDRY, usu. used of men's acts or accomplishments, suggests power to enchant with or as if with supernatural skill, power, or craft ⟨the *wizardry* of my past wonder, the enchantment of romance —John Galsworthy⟩ ⟨the museum staff's *wizardry* at exhibit making —W.C.Fitzgibbon⟩ SORCERY suggests use of incantation, charm, or spell to produce an effect, often harmful ⟨there was a highly institutionalized means of covert aggression at the disposal of the Indians. This was *sorcery* —A.I. Hallowell⟩ ⟨the storyteller's *sorcery* of catapulting historical datum into dramatic detail —Frederic Morton⟩ THAUMATURGY is applicable to any performance of miracles, esp. by incantation ⟨who see *thaumaturgy* in all that Jesus did —Matthew Arnold⟩ ALCHEMY may apply to transmutation of substances according to the secret laws of early chemical inquiry or to similar processes ⟨called *alchemy*, an attempt to transmute other metals into gold, to discover the elixir of life —Rumer Godden⟩ ⟨the *alchemy* of moonlight turned all the jungle to perfect growth, growth at rest —William Beebe⟩

²magic \"\ *adj* [ME *magik*, fr. MF *magique*, fr. L *magicus*, fr. Gk *magikos*, fr. *magos* magus, wizard, sorcerer (of Iranian origin; akin to OPer *magush* sorcerer) + *-ikos* -ic] **1 :** of or relating to the occult **:** supposedly having supernatural properties or powers ⟨the witch doctor is there to give them some ~ medicine to drink —J.G.Frazer⟩ ⟨engravings on harpoons and awls . . . may have been ~ signs, protective against adverse influence —Hugo Obermaler⟩ **2 a :** having unusually distinctive qualities resembling the supernatural **:** producing startling and amazing effects ⟨with this ~ piece of paper, was free to go as I could —W.G.Shepherd⟩ ⟨the popular impression that a ~ method has been invented for mastering a strange language in six weeks —F.N.Robinson⟩ ⟨a man who really had the ~ touch —Leonard Bernstein⟩ **b :** giving a feeling of enchantment ⟨it was the most ~ moment of the day . . . full of meaning and loveliness —Olive Johnson⟩

³magic \", *esp in pres part* -jək\ *vt* **magicked; magicked; magicking; magics :** to affect or influence by or as if by magic **:** BEWITCH ⟨the light of those autumn days was *magicked* —Hervey Allen⟩ ⟨had *magicked* them free of their prison —Pamela Frankau⟩

mag·i·cal \-jəkəl, -jēk-\ *adj* [¹*magic* + *-al*] **1 :** MAGIC 1 ⟨~ techniques take over . . . in order to ensure the success of the enterprise —O.G.Simmons⟩ **2 :** resembling magic **:** having an effect like magic **:** produced by or as if by magic ⟨that ~ hush that comes before the start of every performance of a play —Marc Connelly⟩ ⟨the ~ transformation of egg into omelet —Walter O'Meara⟩ ⟨the disappearance in the fall of the common chimney swift is so sudden as to seem almost ~ —Roy Bedichek⟩ ⟨writes with a ~ simplicity which leaves one amazed —Marvin Lowenthal⟩

mag·i·cal·ly \-k(ə)lē, -li\ *adv* **:** in the manner of magic **:** by or as if by magic ⟨England was ~ small, the channel to be taken in a stride —Thomas Wolfe⟩

magic carpet *n* **:** a legendary rug or carpet capable of transporting one who stood on it to any place desired

magic circle *n* **1 :** a circle drawn by a magician about any person or place protecting it from demons raised by incantations **2** *also* **magic cube :** an arrangement of numbers in rings and radial ranks in a circle or in a number of cubes forming a larger perfect cube devised on the principle of the magic square to add up to the same number along different ranks or diagonals

Magic Eye *trademark* — used for a small cathode-ray tube with a controlled beam used as an indicator of maximum response in tuning a radio receiver

ma·gi·cian \məˈjishən\ *n* -S [ME *magicien*, fr. MF, fr. *magique* magic + *-ien* -ian — more at MAGIC] **1 :** one skilled in magic; *esp* **:** one who uses charms, incantations, and spells ⟨the village ~ is called in to secure the safety and fertility of a garden —C.D.Forde⟩ — compare SORCERER **2 :** one who entertains an audience by tricks of illusion and sleight of hand **3 :** one whose skill or art seems to be magical ⟨both loved music, and this boy . . . was a ~ with his instrument —Willa Cather⟩ ⟨authors . . . are word ~s; they do strange things with human emotions —Allan McMahan⟩

magic lantern *n* **:** an early form of optical projector of still pictures using a transparent slide

magic music *n* **:** a game in which a player is guided in finding a hidden object by music whose volume is increased or decreased according as he moves nearer or farther away

mag·i·co-religious \ˌmajəˌkō+\ *adj* [²*magic* + *-o-* + *religious*] **:** of, belonging to, or having the character of a body of magical practices intended to cause a supernatural being to produce or prevent a specific result (as an increase of the crops)

magic realism *n* [trans. of G *magischer realismus*] **:** the meticulous and realistic painting of fantastic images

magic square *n* **:** a square containing a number of integers so arranged that the sum of the numbers in each row, column, and diagonal is always the same

4	9	2
3	5	7
8	1	6

6	3	10	15
9	16	5	4
7	2	11	14
12	13	8	1

magic squares

magic tree *n* **:** a showy-flowered Peruvian shrub (*Cantua buxifolia*) of the family Polemoniaceae used in Europe for ornament

magilp *var of* MEGILP

ma·gin·da·nao \məˌgindəˈnau̇\ *also* **ma·gin·da·naw** \-ˈnȯ\ *n, pl* **magindanao** *or* **magindanaos** *also* **magindanaw** *or* **magindanaws** *usu cap* **1 a :** a Moro people inhabiting central Mindanao, Philippines **b :** a member of such people **2 :** the Austronesian language of the Magindanao people being closely related to or a dialect of Maranao

ma·gi·not line \ˈmazhəˌnō, -ajə-\ *n, usu cap M&L* [fr. the *Maginot Line* (trans. of F *ligne Maginot*), a series of fortifications on the northeastern frontier of France begun in 1927, after André *Maginot* †1932 Fr. politician who was minister of war when the fortifications were begun] **:** a defensive barrier or entrenched position that gives a false sense of security ⟨hiding behind a *Maginot Line* of atomic bombs —L.A. DuBridge⟩ ⟨maintain prestige by withdrawing behind a *Maginot Line* of social caste⟩

ma·gis·ter \məˈjistə(r)\ *n* -S [L — more at MASTER] **:** a master or teacher in ancient Rome or at a medieval university

¹mag·is·te·ri·al \ˌmajəˈstirēəl\ *adj* [LL *magisterialis* of authority, fr. L *magisterium* + *-alis* -al] **1 a** (1) **:** of, relating to, or having the characteristics of a master or teacher **:** AUTHORITATIVE ⟨a ~ survey of the evolution of man as a social animal —*Times Lit. Supp.*⟩ ⟨bespeak a sort of ~ attitude toward language which has been lost in the intervening centuries —R.M.Weaver⟩ (2) **:** marked by a dignified or sedate manner or aspect ⟨modeled on the British reviews . . . it imitated their ~ air —Van Wyck Brooks⟩ ⟨the dark ~ tone of academic eating places —Emily Coleman⟩ (3) **:** marked by a pompous or overbearing manner or aspect ⟨was ~ in petty rebuke —V.L.Parrington⟩ ⟨the ~ condescension found in so much biography these days —*Times Lit. Supp.*⟩ **b :** of, relating to, or required for a master's degree ⟨the student submitting a novel or a book of poems as his ~ thesis —Malcolm Cowley⟩ **2** *obs* **:** of, relating to, or having the characteristics of a master designer or workman **3** *obs* **:** of or relating to a magistery **4 :** of or relating to a magistrate, his office, or his duties **:** administered or conducted by a magistrate **:** holding the office of a magistrate

²magisterial *n* -S *obs* **:** MAGISTERY

magisterial district *n* **:** an administrative county division in Kentucky, Virginia, and West Virginia

mag·is·te·ri·al·ly \ˌmajəˈstirēəlē, -li\ *adv* **1 a :** with an authoritative manner because of knowledge and experience **:** MASTERFULLY ⟨could assert that light is corpuscular . . . so ~ that astronomical expeditions could be organized —Alvin Johnson⟩ **b :** with a lordly air **:** DICTATORIALLY ⟨it will not do to say ~, "Take the child away!" —J.L.Lowes⟩ **2 :** in the position or with the authority of a magistrate

magisterialness *n* -ES *obs* **:** the quality or state of being magisterial

mag·is·te·ri·um \ˌmajəˈstirēəm\ *n* -S [ML] **1** *obs* **:** MAGISTERY **2** *Roman Catholicism* **:** the church's teaching power or function

mag·is·tery \ˈ==ˌsterē\ *n* -ES [ML *magisterium*, fr. L, office of a supervisor, office of tutor or guardian, instruction, fr. *magister* master — more at MASTER] **1 :** a principle of nature having transmuting or curative powers **:** PHILOSOPHERS' STONE ⟨the that hath water turned to ashes, hath the *Magistery*, and the true Philosophers' stone —James Howell⟩ **2** *obs* **:** MASTERSHIP, AUTHORITY **3** *obs* **a :** PRECIPITATE 1 **b :** any of various white precipitates from metallic solutions ⟨a white precipitate of bismuth subnitrate was formerly known as ~ of bismuth⟩

mag·is·tra·cy \ˈ==strəsē, -si\ *n* -ES [*magistrate* + *-cy*] **1 :** the quality or state of being a magistrate **2 :** the office of a magistrate **:** magisterial power and dignity ⟨outlaws who . . . set at defiance the justice and ~ of the country —Sir Walter Scott⟩ **3 :** the collective body of magistrates ⟨escorted with great pomp . . . by the ~ of the city —T.B.Macaulay⟩

¹mag·is·tral \-strəl\ *adj* [LL *magistralis*, fr. L *magistr-*, *magister* + *-alis* -al] **1 :** of, relating to, or characteristic of a master **:** AUTHORITATIVE, MAGISTERIAL 1a ⟨the ~ order, accuracy, and clarity of the physical sciences themselves —Lewis Mumford⟩ ⟨she has the dignity, the ~ presence, of an heroic figure of tragedy —*New Republic*⟩ **2 a :** concocted or prescribed by a physician to meet the needs of a particular case — opposed to *officinal* **b** *obs* **:** EFFECTUAL, SOVEREIGN

²magistral \"\ *n* -S *obs* **:** a sovereign medicine

mag·is·tral·i·ty \ˌ==ˈstraləd·ē\ *n* -ES [NL *magistralitas*, fr. LL *magistralis* + L *-itas* -ity] **:** magistral quality, position, or character

mag·is·tral·ly \ˈ==strəlē\ *adv* **:** in a magistral manner ⟨his summing up . . . is ~ succinct —Mary W. Hess⟩

mag·is·trand \ˈ==ˌstrand\ *n* -S [ML *magistrandus*, gerundive of *magistrare* to grant a master's degree, fr. ML (*artium*) *magister* master of arts — more at MASTER] *Scot* **:** a fourth and final year student in a university who will receive a master of arts degree — used officially at Aberdeen

mag·is·trate \-ˌstrāt, -strət, *usu* -d.+V\ *n* -S [ME *magistrat*, fr. L *magistratus*, fr. *magistr-*, *magister* master + *-atus* -ate — more at MASTER] **:** a public official entrusted with administration of the laws: as **a :** a principal official exercising governmental esp. executive powers over a major political unit (as a nation) ⟨the president of the federal council . . . and the vice-president are the first ~s of the confederation —*Statesman's Yr. Bk.*⟩ **b :** a local official exercising administrative and often judicial functions ⟨the ~ in South Africa is . . . the senior representative of the government in his district —Leo Marquard⟩ **c :** a local judiciary official having limited original jurisdiction esp. in criminal cases: (1) **:** JUSTICE OF THE PEACE (2) **:** the judge of a police court

mag·is·trate·ship \-ˌship\ *n* **:** the office of a magistrate; *also* **:** the tenure in office of a magistrate

magistratic *obs var of* MAGISTRATICAL

mag·is·trat·i·cal \ˌmajəˈstrad·əkəl\ *adj* **:** MAGISTERIAL 4 — **mag·is·trat·i·cal·ly** \-ək(ə)lē\ *adv*

mag·is·tra·ture \ˈ==ˌstrāchər, -strəˌchu̇(ə)r\ *n* -S [F, fr. MF, fr. *magistrat* office of a magistrate (fr. L *magistratus*) + *-ure*] **:** MAGISTRACY

mag·le·mo·se \ˈmagləˌmōsə, ˈmau̇l-, ˈmägl-\ *adj, usu cap* [fr. *Maglemose*, locality on the western coast of Sjælland, Denmark, type station of Maglemosian culture] **:** MAGLEMOSIAN

mag·le·mo·sian *or* **mag·le·mo·sean** \ˌ==ˈmōsēən, -ōshən, -ōzhən\ *adj, usu cap* [*Maglemose*, Denmark + E *-ian, -an*] **:** of or belonging to a Mesolithic culture of northern Europe characterized by bone and stone implements

mag·ma \ˈmagmə, ˈmaig-\ *n* -S [in sense 1, fr. L, fr. Gk; in other senses, NL, fr. L; akin to Gk *massein* to knead — more at MINGLE] **1** *archaic* **:** DREGS, SEDIMENT **2 a :** a crude mixture of mineral or organic matter in the state of a thin paste **b :** something resembling magma ⟨melt back into the primitive ~ of confusion . . . the best and sharpest instruments which the mind has forged —D.C.Williams⟩ **3 a :** molten rock material that is liquid or pasty originating within the earth **:** the molten material or mass from which an igneous rock results by cooling and crystallization — compare LAVA **b :** the glassy base of an eruptive rock **4 :** a suspension of a large amount of precipitated material in a small volume of a watery vehicle ⟨bismuth ~ is commonly known as milk of bismuth⟩ **5 :** a mass of raw sugar and syrup obtained in sugar refining by mixing — compare MASSECUITE

magma chamber *n* **:** the underground space usu. deep below the earth's surface occupied by magma that may ascend from it to or toward the surface

mag·mat·ic \(ˈ)magˈmad·ik, (ˈ)maig-\ *adj* [ISV *magmat-* (fr. NL *magmat-*, *magma*) + *-ic*] **:** of, relating to, or derived from magma ⟨water may fall originally as rain, or it may be ~ water from the bowels of the earth which ascends to the surface as the steam of volcanoes or in hot springs —*Nat'l Geographic*⟩ — compare METEORIC

magn *abbr* **1** magnetic; magnetism **2** magneto

mag·na \ˈmagnə, ˈmaig-, ˈmäg-, ˈmäg-\ *n* -S [*magna* (*cum* *laude*)] **:** a college or university degree magna cum laude; *also* **:** a person receiving such a degree

mag·na char·ta *or* **mag·na car·ta** \ˌmagnə ˈkär|d·ə, ˌmaig-, -kä|, |tə\ *n, pl* **magna chartas** *or* **magna cartas** *usu cap M&C* [fr. *Magna Charta* or *Magna Carta*, a charter of rights granted by King John of England on June 15, 1215, fr. ML, lit., great charter] **:** a statement of principles that is embodied in a document (as an agreement or legislative act) and usu. establishes procedures or guarantees rights ⟨the original Wagner Act was the *Magna Charta* of labor —A.F.Whitney⟩ ⟨these Articles of Capitulation were regarded by . . . the colonists as their *Magna Charta* —*Times Lit. Supp.*⟩

mag·na cum laude \ˌmagnə, ˌmaig-, ˌmäg-, ˌmág- +\ *adv (or adj)* [L, with great praise] **:** with great distinction — used as a mark of meritorious achievement in the academic requirements for graduation from school or college; compare CUM LAUDE, SUMMA CUM LAUDE

mag·na·flux \ˈmagnəˌfləks, ˈmaig-\ *vt* **:** to test by the Magnaflux method ⟨~ all spindle blades —*Electrical World*⟩

Mag·na·flux \"\ *trademark* — used for a method of testing a ferrous metal for defects by magnetizing the material and observing the patterns assumed by iron powder applied either dry or in liquid suspension

mag·na·nim·i·ty \ˌmagnəˈnimәd·ē, ˌmaig-, -mətē, -i\ *n* -ES [ME *magnanimite*, fr. MF *magnanimité*, fr. L *magnanimitat-, magnanimitas*, fr. *magnanimus* + *-itat-, -itas* -ity] **1 a :** a loftiness of spirit enabling one to sustain danger and trouble with tranquillity, firmness, and courage ⟨can bear whatever happens with manlike ~ —James Harris⟩ ⟨was not wanting in a sense of the ~ of warriors —Walter Pater⟩ **b** *archaic* **:** a loftiness of ambition and outlook ⟨that ~ of soul which delights in bold enterprises —William Robertson †1793⟩ **2 a :** a nobility of feeling that is superior to meanness, pettiness, or jealousy and that disdains revenge or retaliation **:** generosity of mind ⟨nothing pays richer dividends than ~ —W.E.Binkley⟩ ⟨an opportunity for ~ . . . to unite a country that seems at times to be hopelessly divided —M.W.Childs⟩ ⟨~, which was her chosen attitude, was often a strain to her —Mary Austin⟩ **b :** an instance of magnanimity — usu. used in pl. ⟨all her thoughts may like the linnet be . . . dispensing round their *magnanimities* of sound —W.B.Yeats⟩

mag·nan·i·mous \(ˈ)magˈnanəməs, (ˈ)maig-\ *adj* [L *magnanimus*, fr. *magnus* great + *animus* spirit — more at MUCH, ANIMATE] **1 :** showing or suggesting a lofty and courageous spirit ⟨the irreproachable lives and ~ sufferings of their followers —Joseph Addison⟩ **2 :** showing or suggesting nobility of feeling and generosity of mind **:** incapable of meanness or pettiness **:** FORGIVING ⟨even his enemies admitted that he was ~ to the point of knight-errantry —G.K.Chesterton⟩ ⟨too sincere for dissimulation, too ~ for resentment —Ellen Glasgow⟩ — **magnan·i·mous·ly** *adv* — **mag·nan·i·mous·ness** *n* -ES

mag·nate \ˈmagˌnā|t, ˈmaig-, -ˌnə|, *usu* |d·+V\ *n* -S [ME *magnates*, pl., fr. LL, fr. L *magnus* great — more at MUCH] **1 a :** a person of rank **:** NOBLEMAN, PEER ⟨the king surrounded by his ~s was enthroned —L.G.W.Legg⟩ **b :** a person of influence or distinction ⟨the county ~s and the peasants who farmed their land —Sam Pollock⟩ ⟨a smart little luncheon party at which my grandfather was entertaining an important local ~ —Osbert Lancaster⟩ **2 :** a person prominent in the management of a large industry or enterprise ⟨a tobacco ~ who had crashed in competition —*Times Lit. Supp.*⟩ ⟨a ~ of the first order in the world of industry and commerce —Ernest Barker⟩

mag·nate·ship \-ˌship\ *n* **:** the status or position of a magnate

magnes *n* -ES [ME, fr. L, fr. Gk *Magnēs (lithos)*, lit., stone from Magnesia] **1** *obs* **:** MAGNET **2** *obs* **:** magnetic power

mag·ne·sia \magˈnēshə, -ēzh| *sometimes* |ēsh|\ *n* -S [ME, fr. ML, fr. Gk *magnēsia*, any of several ores and amalgams, fr. fem. of *Magnēs* of Magnesia, ancient city in Asia Minor] **1** *obs* **:** an ingredient of the philosophers' stone sometimes described as a plasmic saltish fluid or gum composed of the four elements **2** *archaic* **:** MANGANESE **3 a :** a white highly infusible solid consisting of magnesium oxide MgO that occurs naturally as periclase, is obtained in various forms (as a light bulky slightly alkaline reactive powder or a heavier refractory solid) usu. by calcining magnesite or a basic magnesium carbonate or magnesium hydroxide, and that is used chiefly in making firebrick and other refractories, in magnesium oxychloride cements, insulation, fertilizers, and rubber, and in medicine and pharmacy esp. as an antacid and mild laxative **b :** MAGNESIUM — not used systematically ⟨carbonate of ~⟩ ⟨citrate of ~⟩ **4 :** MAGNESIUM CARBONATE — not used systematically

magnesia al·ba \-ˈalbə\ *n* [NL, lit., white magnesia] **:** MAGNESIUM CARBONATE b

magnesia cement *n* **:** MAGNESIUM OXYCHLORIDE CEMENT

mag·ne·sial \ˌ=ˈnēsh(ē)əl, -zh(ē)əl\ *adj* **:** MAGNESIAN

magnesia magma *n* **:** MILK OF MAGNESIA

mag·ne·sian \|ən| *sometimes* |ēən\ *adj* [*magnesia & magnesium* + *-an*] **:** of, relating to, or characterized by magnesia or magnesium ⟨the British ~ limes are slow-slaking —A.D.Cowper⟩

magnesian limestone *n* **:** DOLOMITE

mag·ne·sic \=ˈnēsik\ *adj* [ISV *magnes-* (fr. NL *magnesium*) + *-ic*] **:** of, relating to, or containing magnesium ⟨natural ~ waters⟩

magnesio- *comb form* [ISV, fr. NL *magnesium*] **:** magnesium ⟨*magnesio*chromite⟩

mag·ne·sio·chromite \magˈnēsh|(ˌ)ō, maig-, -ēzh| *sometimes* |ē(ˌ)ō+\ *n* [*magnesio-* + *chromite*] **:** a mineral $MgCr_2O_4$ consisting of an oxide of magnesium and chromium isomorphous with chromite — called also *magnochromite*

mag·ne·sio·copiapite \"+\ *n* [*magnesio-* + *copiapite*] **:** a mineral $MgFe_4(SO_4)_6(OH)_2.20H_2O$ consisting of a hydrous basic sulfate of magnesium and iron and isomorphous with copiapite and cuprocopiapite

mag·ne·sio·ferrite \"+\ *n* [*magnesio-* + *ferrite*] **:** a magnetic usu. black mineral $MgFe_2O_4$ consisting of an oxide of magnesium and iron and constituting a member of the magnetite series — called also *magnoferrite*

mag·ne·site \ˈmagnəˌsīt\ *n* -S [F *magnésite*, fr. NL *magnesium* + F *-ite*] **:** a mineral $MgCO_3$ that consists of magnesium carbonate, that is isomorphous with siderite and calcite, and that is used chiefly in making refractories and magnesia

mag·ne·sium \magˈnēzēəm, maig- *also* -zhəm\ *n* -S [NL, fr. ML *magnesia* + NL *-ium*] **:** a silver-white light malleable ductile bivalent metallic element that occurs abundantly in nature but always in combination in minerals (as magnesite, dolomite, carnallite, olivine, spinel), in sea and mineral waters, and in animals and plants (as in bones and seeds and in the form of chlorophyll in the green parts of plants), that is obtained chiefly by electrolysis of fused salts containing magnesium chloride or by thermal reduction of magnesia, that is used in unalloyed form in metallurgical and chemical processes and also (as in the form of powder, flakes, or ribbons) in photography, signaling, and pyrotechny because of the intense white light it produces on burning to form magnesia, and that is used structurally esp. in the form of light alloys (as in airplanes) — symbol *Mg;* compare ALKALINE-EARTH METAL

magnesium bomb *n* **:** an incendiary bomb made with a light magnesium case and a cone of Thermit powder that burns fiercely when detonated, ignites the magnesium case, and maintains a temperature of over 3000°F for 10 minutes

magnesium carbonate *n* **:** a carbonate of magnesium: as **a :** the very white crystalline normal salt $MgCO_3$ that occurs naturally as magnesite and also in the form of dolomite, is prepared artificially by precipitation usu. as the trihydrate $MgCO_3.3H_2O$, and is used chiefly in paint and printing ink, as a filler (as in paper and rubber), as an addition to table salt to prevent caking, and in medicine and pharmacy **b :** a crystalline hydrated basic salt obtained by precipitation (as by heating a solution or suspension of the trihydrate) and used in thermal insulation and for many of the same purposes as normal salt

magnesium chloride *n* **:** a bitter deliquescent crystalline salt $MgCl_2$ that usu. crystallizes with six molecules of water, that occurs in seawaters, natural brines, and salt deposits, that is obtained by recovery from seawater, brines, or carnallite or by chlorination of magnesia, and that is used chiefly in producing magnesium metal and magnesium oxychloride cements and as a fireproofing agent

magnesium–chlorophoenicite *n* **:** a mineral $(Mg,Mn)_5(AsO_4)_2(OH)_7$ consisting of a basic arsenate of magnesium usu. with manganese

magnesium citrate *n* **:** a crystalline salt used in the form of a lemon-flavored acidulous effervescent solution as a saline cathartic

magnesium fluoride *n* **:** a crystalline salt MgF_2 occurring naturally as sellaite but also made synthetically and used chiefly as a flux and as a coating for optical glass to cut down reflection

magnesium hydroxide *n* **:** a slightly alkaline crystalline compound $Mg(OH)_2$ that occurs naturally as brucite, is obtained by hydration of magnesia or by precipitation (as from seawater by lime in the production of magnesium chloride) as a white difficultly soluble powder, and is used chiefly in medicine

magnesium nitrate *n* **:** a very soluble deliquescent crystalline oxidizing salt $Mg(NO_3)_2.6H_2O$ used chiefly in catalysts and fireworks

magnesium oxide *n* **:** MAGNESIA 3a

magnesium oxychloride cement *n* **:** a cement that is used only for interior work (as floors in hospitals and public buildings), is made by adding in proper proportions a strong solution of magnesium chloride to magnesia, and when used with small stones, wood flour, or cork sets to a hard mass in a short time and takes a high polish

magnesium perchlorate *n* **:** a deliquescent crystalline explosive salt $Mg(ClO_4)_2$ used as a drying agent

magnesium silicate *n* **:** any of various silicates of magnesium: as **a :** a tetrasilicate $Mg_3Si_4O_{10}(OH)_2$ found in nature as talc from which it is obtained usu. in fibrous or micaceous forms for use chiefly as a filler or extender (as in paints) **b :** a trisilicate approximately $Mg_2Si_3O_8.n\,H_2O$ obtained by precipitation as a white powder and used chiefly in medicine as a gastric antacid adsorbent and coating (as in the treatment of ulcers)

magnesium sulfate *n* **:** any of several sulfates of magnesium; *esp* **:** the normal salt $MgSO_4$ occurring in nature as the hydrates kieserite and epsomite and also as double salts (as langbeinite) — see EPSOM SALTS

mag·net \ˈmagnət, ˈmaig-, *usu* -əd·+V\ *n* -S [ME *magnete*, fr. MF, fr. L *magnet-, magnes*, fr. Gk *Magnēs (lithos), Magnētis (lithos)*, lit., stone of Magnesia, ancient city in Asia Minor] **1 a :** a variety or a piece of magnetite or magnetic iron ore having naturally the property of attracting iron **:** LODESTONE — called also *natural magnet* **b :** a body having the property of attracting iron and producing a magnetic field external to itself; *specif* **:** a mass of iron, steel, or alloy that has this property artificially imparted, that usu. has two poles of opposite nature situated near its ends so that when brought close to a similar body the unlike poles attract each other while the like poles repel each other, and that in the form of a bar or needle (as a compass needle) suspended so that it may rotate freely around a vertical axis assumes a direction nearly north and south — compare BAR MAGNET, ELECTROMAGNET, FIELD MAGNET, NORTH POLE, SOUTH POLE **2 :** something that attracts ⟨this new steel plant has also acted as a ~ in attracting . . . new industrial development to the region —J.L.Street b. 1902⟩ ⟨the pot-bellied stove is a ~ for the tellers of tall stories —*Amer. Guide Series: N.H.*⟩

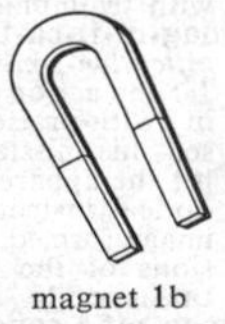

magnet 1b

magnet- *or* **magneto-** *comb form* [ˈ*magnetic*] **1 :** magnetic force ⟨*magneto*meter⟩ **2 :** magnetism **:** magnetic ⟨*magneto*-electric⟩ ⟨*magnet*on⟩ **3 :** magnetoelectric ⟨*magneto*telegraph⟩

ˡmag·net·ic \(ˈ)magˈned·|ik, (ˈ)maig-, -et|, |ēk *sometimes* məgˈn-\ *adj* [F & LL; F *magnétique*, fr. LL *magneticus*, fr. L *magnet-, magnes* magnet + *-icus* -ic] **1 a :** of or relating to a magnet or to magnetism **b :** possessing the ability or power to attract **:** endowed with extraordinary charm **:** ARRESTING, CAPTIVATING ⟨so ~ a man —W.A.White⟩ ⟨an idea so ~ that he cannot divest himself of it —W.P.Webb⟩ **2 a :** of, relating to, or characterized by the earth's magnetism **b :** referred to magnetic north as a reference line ⟨a course of 71° ~ corrected for wind —*Pilots' Radio Handbook*⟩ **3 :** magnetized or capable of being magnetized **:** capable of being attracted by a magnet ⟨~ chips of steel produced by a tool⟩ ⟨a ~ alloy⟩ **4 :** actuated by magnetic attraction **5 :** having, susceptible to, or induced by animal magnetism ⟨as if he had been in a ~ slumber —Charles Dickens⟩

²magnetic *n* -S *obs* **:** MAGNET

mag·net·i·cal \(ˈ)magˈned·|əkəl, (ˈ)maig-, -et|, |ēk- *sometimes* məgˈn-\ *adj* [LL *magneticus* + E *-al*] *archaic* **:** MAGNETIC

mag·net·i·cal·ly \-ək(ə)lē, -ēk-, -li\ *adv* **:** in a magnetic manner **:** by the use of magnetism ⟨her dark eyes shone ~ in the light of the chandeliers —Hudson Strode⟩ ⟨~ attracted to the city —Robert Moses⟩

magnetic amplifier *n* **:** a device in which an alternating current in the secondary is modulated by variations of core reluctance due to varying a direct current in the primary so that the secondary modulations may be of much greater amplitude than the primary and thus make the device an amplifier

magnetic amplitude *n* **:** AMPLITUDE 3b

magnetic axis *n* **:** the straight line joining the two poles of a magnet (as the magnetic poles of the earth)

magnetic bearing *n* **:** a bearing relative to magnetic north

magnetic blowout *n* **:** extinction of an electric arc when deflected by a magnetic field

magnetic brake *n* **:** a friction brake controlled by means of an electromagnet

magnetic chart *n* **:** a chart showing the magnetic declination, inclination, or intensity over a given geographical area

magnetic chuck *n* **:** a chuck in which the workpiece is held by magnetic forces

magnetic circuit *n* **:** a closed path followed by magnetic flux (as through the field magnet and armature of a dynamo)

magnetic clutch *n* **1 :** a clutch in which the coupling is between solid parts drawn together by electromagnetic force **2 :** MAGNETIC FLUID CLUTCH

magnetic compass *n* **:** COMPASS 4a; *broadly* **:** a compass whose operation depends upon an element that senses the earth's magnetic field

magnetic cooling *n* **:** application of the magnetocaloric effect to the attainment of low temperatures

magnetic course *n* **:** the course on which an airplane is intended to be flown that is measured from magnetic north and that is the true course as laid out on the chart

magnetic cutter *n* **:** a cutting head in recording phonograph records that uses attraction and repulsion of pieces of magnetized metal to swing the cutting stylus

magnetic damping *n* **:** mechanical damping produced by the reaction of a magnetic field with eddy currents due to relative motion of conductor and field

magnetic declination *or* **magnetic deviation** *n* **:** DECLINATION 6

magnetic dip *n* **:** DIP 3b

magnetic elements *n pl* **:** the magnetic declination, the magnetic dip, and the magnetic intensity or one of its components at any point on the earth's surface

magnetic equator *n* **:** ACLINIC LINE — compare GEOMAGNETIC EQUATOR

magnetic field *n* **:** a region subject to the influence of magnetism that is manifested by the mechanical forces that it exerts upon electricity moving across it and upon the poles of magnets placed in it

magnetic fluid *n* **1 :** a hypothetical fluid formerly assumed to account for magnetic phenomena **2 :** a mixture of finely divided iron with oil or other suitable liquid that is characterized by its marked increase in viscosity when subjected to a strong magnetic field — compare MAGNETIC FLUID CLUTCH

magnetic fluid clutch *n* **:** a fluid clutch in which the coupling fluid consists of finely divided ferromagnetic material suspended in oil or other liquid and is rendered practically solid when subjected to a strong magnetic field between the driving and the driven surfaces

magnetic flux *n* **:** the product of the average component of magnetic induction perpendicular to any given surface in a magnetic field by the area of that surface usu. expressed in maxwells or webers

magnetic flux density *n* **:** MAGNETIC INDUCTION 2

magnetic focusing *n* **:** the converging of a stream of electrons by means of a suitable magnetic field — compare MAGNETIC LENS

magnetic force *n* **1 :** the mechanical force exerted by a magnetic field upon a magnetic pole placed in it **2 :** MAGNETIZING FORCE **3 :** MAGNETIC INTENSITY

magnetic head *n* **:** an electromagnet used in magnetic recording for converting electrical signals into a magnetic record on tape or wire, converting a magnetic recording into electrical signals, or erasing a magnetic recording

magnetic heading *n* **:** the heading measured clockwise from magnetic north

magnetic hysteresis *n* **:** HYSTERESIS 1c

mag·ne·ti·cian \ˌmagnəˈtishən, ˌmaig-\ *n* -S **:** MAGNETIST; *esp* **:** one skilled in making magnetic measurements (as of rocks)

magnetic inclination *n* **:** DIP 3b

magnetic induction *n* **1 :** induction of magnetism in a body when it is in a magnetic field or in the magnetic flux set up by a magnetomotive force — symbol *B* **2 :** the product of the magnetic permeability of a medium by the intensity of magnetic field in it — called also *magnetic flux density*

magnetic intensity *n* **:** a vector quantity pertaining to the condition at any point under magnetic influence (as of a magnet, an electric current, or an electromagnetic wave) measured by the force exerted in a vacuum upon a free unit north pole placed at the point in question — called also *magnetic force*

magnetic iron *or* **magnetic iron ore** *n* **:** MAGNETITE

magnetic lag *n* **:** the failure of the magnetization in a magnetic substance to keep up with the magnetizing force as it varies

magnetic latitude *n* **1 :** the angle whose tangent is one half the tangent of the magnetic dip at any given point **2 :** GEOMAGNETIC LATITUDE

magnetic lens *n* **:** an electron lens that focuses electron beams by means of a magnetic field

magnetic memory *n* **1 :** the deviation of a body from normal behavior under magnetization due to its previous magnetic history **2 :** magnetic retentivity

magnetic meridian *n* **:** a line on the earth's surface approximating a great circle passing through the north and south magnetic poles

magnetic mine *n* **:** a naval mine designed to explode by the magnetic effect caused by the hull of a passing metal ship

magnetic moment *n* **:** the vector whose vector product by the intensity of the ambient magnetic field gives the resulting mechanical moment or torque — used of a magnet, a current-bearing electric circuit, or a magnetic dipole

magnetic needle *n* **:** a bar magnet or a set of bar magnets so suspended as to indicate the direction of the magnetic field in which it is placed; *esp* **:** such a magnet that is slender and pointed at the ends and used as a compass

magnetic north *n* **:** the northerly direction of the magnetic meridian at any given point distinguished from the true or geographic north

magnetic oxide *or* **magnetic oxide of iron** *n* **:** FERROSOFERRIC OXIDE

magnetic parallel *n* **:** ISOCLINIC LINE

magnetic permeability *n* **:** PERMEABILITY 4

magnetic pickup *n* **:** a phonograph pickup using the stylus vibration to move a piece of metal in a magnetic field and generating an electrical voltage in a coil of wire

magnetic pole *n* **1 :** one of the poles of a magnet **2 :** either of two nonstationary regions on the earth which sometimes move many miles in a day, toward which the isogonic lines converge, and at which the dip is plus or minus 90 degrees

magnetic potential *n* **:** the scalar quantity characteristic of a point in a magnetic field whose negative gradient equals the intensity or strength of the magnetic field and which represents the work required to bring a unit north pole from a point infinitely remote up to the point in question

magnetic potentiometer *n* **:** an instrument for measuring differences of magnetic potential between points in a magnetic field

magnetic printing *n* **:** the transfer in magnetic recording of a recorded signal from a position on the recording medium to a nearby position on the same or another medium due to proximity

magnetic profile *n* **:** a profile usu. at right angles to the geologic structure showing magnetic anomalies revealed by a geophysical survey

magnetic pyrites *n* **:** PYRRHOTITE

magnetic quantum number *n* **:** an integer that expresses the quantized angular momentum of an atom or molecule spinning in a magnetic field as a multiple of $h/2\pi$, when *h* is the Planck constant

magnetic recorder *n* **:** a device for carrying out magnetic recording or a device that is usu. incorporated with it for reproducing magnetically recorded sound by moving the magnetized material so that it induces a current which when amplified actuates a loudspeaker

magnetic recording *n* **:** the process of recording sound, data (as for a computer), or a television program by producing varying local magnetization of a moving tape, wire, or disc

magnetic reproducer *n* **:** a device for reproducing material recorded on a magnetic tape, wire, or disc

magnetic resonance *n* **1 :** the response of electrons, atoms, molecules, or nuclei to certain discrete radiation frequencies as a result of space quantization in a magnetic field **2 :** the operating principle of the cyclotron and similar accelerators in which ions and particles are accelerated at every half revolution by an electric field in resonance with the revolving frequency of the ions or particles

magnetic rigidity *n* **:** a measure of the momentum of an electric particle moving normally across a magnetic field (as in a cyclotron) equal to the product of the radius of curvature by the intensity of the field

mag·net·ics \magˈned·|iks, maig-, -et|, |ēks\ *n pl but sing in constr* **:** the science of magnetism

magnetic shell *n* **:** a theoretical layer or shell so magnetized that one surface is entirely of north and the other of south polarity with the lines of induction extending through the thickness of the layer

magnetic shielding *n* **:** protection from the influence of an external magnetic field

magnetic sound *n* **:** sound recorded magnetically instead of photographically on a motion-picture film

magnetic storm *n* **:** a marked temporary disturbance of the earth's magnetic field held to be related to sunspots

magnetic survey *n* **:** a determination made by means of magnetic surveying

magnetic surveying *n* **:** the process of determining the magnetic elements at various points on the earth's surface including local variations (as for making isomagnetic charts or as a means of prospecting for ore)

magnetic susceptibility *n* **:** SUSCEPTIBILITY 3a

magnetic tape *n* **:** a ribbon of thin paper or plastic coated with fine magnetic iron oxide powder mixed with a binder, made usu. ¼ inch in width and about two thousandths of an inch in thickness, and used in magnetic recording

magnetic tape recorder *n* **:** TAPE RECORDER

magnetic valve *n* **:** a valve operated electromagnetically usu. by a solenoid whose axis is perpendicular to the valve seat

magnetic variation *n* **:** DECLINATION 6

magnetic viscosity *n* **:** a property of magnetizable substances because of which a certain time is required for the magnetization to reach an equilibrium value under a given magnetizing force

magnetic wire *n* **:** a thin wire (as of stainless steel) used in magnetic recording

magnetic wire recorder *n* **:** WIRE RECORDER

mag·net·ism \ˈmagnəˌtizəm, ˈmaig-\ *n* -S [NL *magnetismus*, fr. L *magnet-, magnes* magnet + *-ismus* -ism — more at MAGNET] **1 a :** a class of physical phenomena that includes the attraction for iron observed in lodestone and a magnet, that is believed to be inseparably associated with moving electricity, that is exhibited by both magnets and electric currents, and that is characterized by fields of force in which both magnets and electric currents experience mechanical forces — compare DIAMAGNETISM, PARAMAGNETISM, TERRESTRIAL MAGNETISM **b :** a science that deals with magnetic phenomena **2 :** an ability to attract **:** a power to charm ⟨the ~ and the glamorous oratorical gifts that make him a hero to so many —Woodrow Wyatt⟩ ⟨a personal ~ that made him irresistible —A.E.Wier⟩ ⟨the ~ of America was in her free institutions —R.J.Purcell⟩ ⟨the ~ of courage and devotion —Ambrose Bierce⟩ **3** [F or G; F *magnétisme*, fr. G *magnetismus*] : ANIMAL MAGNETISM

mag·net·ist \-,tәst\ *n* -s [*magnet* + *-ist*] : one who studies magnetism

mag·net·ite \-,tīt\ *n* -s [G *magnetit*, fr. *magnet* + *-it* -ite] : a black isometric mineral of the spinel group consisting of ferrosoferric oxide and constituting an important iron ore that is strongly attracted by a magnet and sometimes possesses polarity — called also *magnetic iron;* see LODESTONE

magnetite series *n* : a series of isomorphous minerals in the spinel group consisting of magnetite, magnesioferrite, franklinite, jacobsite, trevorite, and maghemite

mag·net·it·ic \¦==¦tid·ik\ *adj* : containing magnetite

mag·ne·tiz·abil·i·ty \,==,tīzә'bilәd·ē, -әtē, -i\ *n* : the quality or state of being magnetizable

mag·ne·tiz·able \¦==¦tīzәbәl\ *adj* : capable of being magnetized

mag·ne·ti·za·tion \,=nәd·ә'zāshәn, -nәtә'z-, -nә,tī'z-\ *n* -s **1** : a magnetizing or state of being magnetized; *also* : degree to which a body is magnetized ⟨the ~ of earth⟩ **2** : intensity of magnetic force measured by magnetic moment per unit of volume

magnetization curve *n* : a graph representing changes in the condition of a magnetizable substance with magnetizing force *H* as abscissa and either magnetization *I* or induction *B* as ordinate

mag·ne·tize \'magnә,tīz, 'maig-\ *vb* -ED/-ING/-S *see -ize in Explan Notes* [F or G; F *magnétiser*, fr. G *magnetisieren*, fr. *magnet* + *-isieren* -ize] *vt* **1** : to bring under the influence of animal magnetism ⟨*magnetized* by her husband into the state termed clairvoyance —Horace Greeley⟩ **2** : to attract like a magnet : exert a powerful influence upon : CAPTIVATE, CHARM ⟨cities which don't expect to ~ visitors don't build coliseums —Robert Moses⟩ ⟨with his patrician air and his flashing wit . . . he *magnetized* the crowd —Van Wyck Brooks⟩ ⟨that dauntless company of moderns whose spirits have been *magnetized* by . . . polar exploration —John Mason Brown⟩ **3** : to communicate magnetic properties to : convert into a magnet ⟨~ a needle⟩ ~ *vi* : to become magnetized ⟨are advantageous because they will not ~ —W.F.Cloud⟩

mag·ne·tiz·er \-,tīzә(r)\ *n* -s : one that magnetizes

magnetizing current *n* : a current that magnetizes or energizes a magnetic core : EXCITING CURRENT

magnetizing force *n* : magnetic intensity applied to points within a magnetizable substance — called also *magnetic force*

mag·ne·to \mag'nēd·(,)ō, maig-, -ē(,)tō\ *n* -s [short for *magnetoelectric machine*] : a magnetoelectric machine; *esp* : an alternator with permanent magnets used to generate the current for the ignition in an internal-combustion engine or for ringing a telephone bell

mag·ne·to- *in pronunciations below*, =¦== mag¦nēd·(,)ō *or* maig- *or* -¦nē(,)tō *or* -¦ned·(,)ō *or* -¦ne(,)tō *or* -,tә\ — see MAGNET-

mag·ne·to·caloric effect \¦== +-\ *n* [*magnet-* + *caloric*] : a reversible change in the temperature of a thermally insulated magnetizable substance in a magnetic field of varying intensity with the temperature rising or falling according as the field intensity is increased or decreased

magneto: *1* permanent magnet, *2* pole pieces, *3* armature core, *4* armature shaft, *5* armature winding, *6* slip ring, *7* collector brush

mag·ne·to·chemical \"+\ *adj* [*magnet-* + *chemical*] : of or relating to magnetochemistry

mag·ne·to·chemistry \=¦==+\ *n* [ISV *magnet-* + *chemistry*] : a branch of science that deals with the relation of magnetism to chemical phenomena

mag·ne·toelastic \=¦==+\ *adj* [*magnet-* + *elastic*] : relating to magnetoelasticity

mag·ne·to·elasticity \=,==+\ *n* [*magnet-* + *elasticity*] : the effect of elastic strain upon the magnetization of a ferromagnetic elastic material (as when the magnetization of a steel spring varies as it vibrates) — compare MAGNETOSTRICTION

mag·ne·to·electric \=¦==+\ *adj* [*magnet-* + *electric*] : relating to or characterized by electromotive forces developed by magnetic means ⟨~ induction⟩

mag·ne·to·generator \=,==+\ *n* [*magnet-* + *generator*] : MAGNETO

mag·ne·to·gram \=¦==,gram\ *n* [*magnet-* + *-gram*] : an automatic record of magnetic phenomena made by a magnetograph

mag·ne·to·graph \-,graf\ *n* [*magnet-* + *-graph*] **1** : an automatic instrument for recording (as by photography) states and variations of a terrestrial magnetic element **2** : MAGNETOGRAM — **mag·ne·to·graph·ic** \=¦==¦grafik\ *adj*

mag·ne·to·hydrodynamic \=¦==+\ *adj* [*magnet-* + *hydrodynamic*] : of or relating to phenomena arising from the motion of electrically conducting fluids in the presence of electric and magnetic fields ⟨~ methods of power generation⟩ ⟨~ wave motion⟩

mag·ne·to·hydrodynamics \"+\ *n pl but sing in constr* : a branch of physics that deals with magnetohydrodynamic phenomena

mag·ne·to·ionic \=¦==+\ *adj* [*magnet-* + *ionic*] : of or relating to the joint effect of atmospheric ionization and the earth's magnetic field upon the propagation of electromagnetic waves

mag·ne·to·mechanical ratio \"+-\ *n* [*magnet-* + *mechanical*] : GYROMAGNETIC RATIO

mag·ne·tom·e·ter \,magnә'tämәd·ә(r), ,maig-, -mәtә-\ *n* [*magnet-* + *-meter*] : an instrument for measuring magnetic intensity, esp. of the earth's magnetic field

mag·ne·to·metric \=¦== *at* MAGNETO- +\ *adj* [*magnet-* + *-metric*] : of or relating to the magnetometer or magnetometry

mag·ne·tom·e·try \,magnә'tämәtrē, ,maig-, -ri\ *n* -ES [ISV *magnet-* + *-metry*] : a science of measuring the intensity of magnetic fields and of determining the direction of lines of force; *also* : use of the magnetometer

mag·ne·to·motive force \=¦== *at* MAGNETO- +-\ *n* [*magnet-* + *motive*] : a force that is the cause of a flux of magnetic induction and is the total of the magnetic potential differences along the entire length of a magnetic line of force or is the line integral between two points or around a circuit of the intensity of the magnetic field

mag·ne·ton \'magnә,tän, 'maig-\ *n* -s [ISV *magnet-* + *-on;* orig. formed as F *magnéton*] : a unit of the quantized magnetic moment of a particle (as an atom) — see BOHR MAGNETON, NUCLEAR MAGNETON

magneto-optic \=¦==¦==+\ *also* **magneto-optical** \=¦==¦===\ *adj* [*magnet-* + *optic, optical*] : relating to the influence of a magnetic field upon light (as in the Faraday effect and the Kerr effect)

magneto-optics \=,=='==\ *n pl but sing in constr* : a branch of physics dealing with the influence of a magnetic field upon light

Mag·ne·to·phon \='== at MAGNETO- + ,fän\ *trademark* — used for a tape recorder

mag·ne·to·photophoresis \=,==+\ *n* [NL, fr. *magnet-* + *photophoresis*] : photophoresis under the influence of a magnetic field

mag·ne·to·plumbite \"+\ *n* [*magnet-* + L *plumbum* lead + E *-ite* — more at PLUMB] : a mineral $(Pb, Mn)(Fe, Mn, Ti)_6O_{10}$(?) consisting of an oxide of ferric iron with lead, manganese, and titanium occurring in acute black metallic hexagonal pyramids

mag·ne·to·resistance \"+\ *n* [*magnet-* + *resistance*] : the change in electrical resistance due to the presence of a magnetic field — **mag·ne·to·resistive** \=¦==+\ *adj*

mag·ne·to·static \=¦==+\ *adj* [ISV *magnet-* + *static*] : of, being, or relating to a stationary magnetic field

mag·ne·to·statics \=,==+\ *n pl but sing in constr* : a branch of physics that deals with magnetostatic properties — compare ELECTROSTATICS

mag·ne·to·striction \"+\ *n* [ISV *magnet-* + *-striction* (as in *constriction*)] : the change in the dimensions of a ferromagnetic body caused by a change in its state of magnetization

magnetostriction oscillator *also* **magnetostrictive oscillator** *n* : an electric oscillator in which the frequency is controlled by the mechanical vibrations induced in a body by magnetostriction

mag·ne·to·strictive \=¦==¦striktiv\ *adj* [ISV *magnetostriction* + *-ive*] : relating to, operated by, or using magnetostriction ⟨a ~ vibrator⟩

mag·ne·tron \'magnә,trän, 'maig-\ *n* -s [blend of *magnet* and *-tron*] : a diode vacuum tube in which the flow of electrons is controlled by an externally applied magnetic field to generate power at microwave frequencies

magnets *pl of* MAGNET

mag·ni·fi·able \¦magnә¦fīәbәl, ¦maig-\ *adj* : capable of being magnified

mag·nif·ic \mag'nifik, maig-, -fēk *sometimes* mәg-\ *also* **mag·nif·i·cal** \-fәkәl, -fēk-\ *adj* [MF *magnifique*, fr. L *magnificus* — more at MAGNIFICENCE] **1** *obs* : having renown : ILLUSTRIOUS **2** : MAGNIFICENT 2a **3** *obs* : intending to impress or extol : HIGH-SOUNDING ⟨those ~ odes and hymns —John Milton⟩ **4 a** : imposing in size or splendor : EXALTED **b** : showing pomposity ⟨commenced the conversation in the most ~ style —S.T.Coleridge⟩ **5** *obs* : royally generous : MUNIFICENT — **mag·nif·i·cal·ly** \-fәk(ә)lē, -fēk-, -li\ *adv*

mag·nif·i·cat \mag'nifә,kat, maig-, -fē,k-, *sometimes* mәg- *or* -kä| *or* -kā|; män'yifә,kä|, män . . . kä|, -yēf-, -fē,k; *usu* |d·+V\ *n* -s [fr. the *Magnificat*, a canticle sung at vespers in the Roman Catholic Church, fr. ME, fr. L, magnifies (3d sing pres. indic. of *magnificare* to magnify, extol), in *magnificat anima mea Dominum* my soul magnifies the Lord, the first words of the canticle, derived fr. Luke 1:46 ff.] : a song or hymn of praise ⟨a thrush was pouring forth a ~ to the spring —Rafael Sabatini⟩

magnificate *vt* -ED/-ING/-S [L *magnificatus*, past part. of *magnificare* — more at MAGNIFY] *obs* : MAGNIFY ⟨~ the church with triumphal pomp and ceremony —Andrew Marvell⟩

mag·ni·fi·ca·tion \,magnәfә'kāshәn, ,maig-\ *n* -s [LL *magnification-, magnificatio*, fr. L *magnificatus* + *-ion-, -io* -ion] **1** : the act or process of magnifying: as **a** : the act of enlarging with praise : LAUDATION ⟨next to the glorification of himself, his mission was the ~ of his country —*Quarterly Rev.*⟩ **b** : the apparent enlargement or reduction of an object by an optical instrument, being the ratio of the dimensions of an image formed by the instrument to the corresponding dimensions of the object — compare ANGULAR MAGNIFICATION, DIAMETER 1c **2** : the quality or state of being magnified

mag·nif·i·cence \mag'nifәsәn(t)s, maig-, mәg-\ *n* -s [ME, fr. MF, fr. L *magnificentia*, fr. *magnificus* noble, splendid, magnificent (fr. *magnus* great + *-i-* + *-ficus* -fic) + *-entia* -ence — more at MUCH] **1** — used as a title of respect applied to kings and other distinguished persons ⟨your *Magnificence* has blood on your hands —Samuel Shellabarger⟩ **2** *archaic* : the virtue recognized in medieval ethics of unostentatious liberality in expenditures of money **3 a** : lavish display in one's surroundings or appointments : SPLENDOR, SUMPTUOUSNESS ⟨easily impressed by ~ —Arnold Bennett⟩ ⟨the wooden ~ of Georgian columns —Thomas Wolfe⟩ ⟨no greater ~ than a Greek robe of virgin white —Elinor Wylie⟩ **b** *obs* : a brilliant ceremony **4** *obs* : greatness of reputation ⟨and for the heavens' wide circuit, let it speak the Maker's high ~ —John Milton⟩ **5** : spectacular beauty : GRANDEUR, SPLENDOR ⟨a sublimely awful scene of power and ~, a world of mountains piled upon mountains —Mark Van Doren⟩ ⟨spring had descended in full force . . . with a gentle ~ —Horace Sutton⟩ **6** : nobleness of expression

mag·nif·i·cen·cy \-nsē\ *n* -ES [L *magnificentia*] **1** *obs* : MAGNIFICENCE **2** *archaic* : something magnificent — usu. used in pl. ⟨it deserves to be mentioned among the rare *magnificencies* of ancient Rome —Richard Lassels⟩

¹mag·nif·i·cent \-nt\ *adj* [L *magnificent-* (in *magnificentior* more magnificent — irreg. compar. of *magnificus* — , back-formation fr. *magnificentia* magnificence)] **1 a** : great in deed or exalted in place : characterized by wonderful or splendid achievements — now used only as an epithet applied to former famous rulers ⟨Lorenzo the *Magnificent*⟩ **b** : having dignity and stateliness : displaying ceremonial pomp ⟨after them came the nobility in their coronation robes which was a most ~ sight —*Saturday Rev.*⟩ **2 a** : characterized by lavish display : exhibiting sumptuousness : BRILLIANT ⟨the ~ pavilion with its painted ceilings, flamboyant gilt decorations, and extravagant chandeliers —S.P.B.Mais⟩ ⟨~ red damask hangings round the chancel and choir —George Santayana⟩ **b** : characterized by ostentatious expenditure : EXTRAVAGANT ⟨the ~ luncheon bill was reverently borne in, on silver —Sinclair Lewis⟩ ⟨offered his brother . . . a ~ bribe, nothing less than the half of his kingdom —C.S.Forester⟩ **3** : strikingly beautiful : superb of form or shape : SPLENDID ⟨heavily built man with a ~ pair of shoulders —Robert Graves⟩ ⟨a ~ dapple-gray horse, with glossy hair —Virginia Woolf⟩ ⟨from the road there was a ~ view of the country lying to the south —Sherwood Anderson⟩ **4** : impressive to the imagination : INSPIRING, NOBLE ⟨a ~ illustration of the public's instinct for the quality of a leader —F.D.Roosevelt⟩ ⟨admonished all to know the truth for the ~ purpose of becoming free —Philip Wylie⟩ **5** : exceptionally fine ⟨valley crops were ~ that year —Julian Dana⟩ ⟨a really ~ soup —Gordon Sager⟩ ⟨our frontiers have turned out some ~ people —Russell Lord⟩ **syn** see GRAND

²magnificent \"\ *n* -s : one who is eminent ⟨seen escorting two ~s of literary New York —Thomas Beer⟩

magnificent bird of paradise : a showy bird of paradise (*Ptiloris magnificus*) of northern Australia and New Guinea with the male having a golden yellow nape, a blood red patch on the back, and shining blackish green on the breast

magnificent frigate bird *n* : a frigate bird (*Fregata magnificens*) that is widespread in tropical American waters and throughout the Caribbean

mag·nif·i·cent·ly *adv* : in a magnificent manner : GRANDLY, IMPRESSIVELY ⟨behaved so simply and ~ —C.L.Carmer⟩ ⟨an age . . . ~ confident in the future —S.C.Burchell⟩

mag·nif·i·cent·ness *n* -ES : the quality or state of being magnificent

mag·nif·i·co \mag'nifә,kō\ *n, pl* **magnificoes** *or* **magnificos** [It, fr. *magnifico*, adj., magnificent, fr. L *magnificus* — more at MAGNIFICENCE] **1** : a nobleman of Venice **2 a** : a person of importance, high position, or distinguished appearance and manner ⟨pithy character sketches of the whole gallery of Victorian ~es —*Newsweek*⟩ **b** : something superlative of its kind ⟨a pudding . . . is considered by Russians to be the supreme ~ of all national desserts —Alexandra Kropotkin⟩

mag·ni·fi·er \'magnә,fī(ә)r, 'maig-, -fīә\ *n* -s : one that magnifies; *specif* : a lens or combination of lenses

mag·ni·fy \-,fī\ *vb* -ED/-ING/-S [ME *magnifien*, fr. MF *magnifier*, fr. L *magnificare*, fr. *magnificus* noble, splendid, magnificent — more at MAGNIFICENCE] *vt* **1 a** : to praise highly : EXTOL, LAUD ⟨while they *magnified* the art, they often belittled the artist —Havelock Ellis⟩ ⟨history, in every country, is so taught as to ~ that country —Bertrand Russell⟩ **b** : to increase the importance of : cause to be held in greater esteem or respect ⟨on that day the Lord *magnified* Joshua in the sight of all Israel —Jos 4:14 (NCE)⟩ **2 a** : to make greater : add to : INTENSIFY, HEIGHTEN ⟨real drama . . . will use ugliness to ~ beauty —Alan Mickle⟩ ⟨felt her every weakness *magnified* and revealed in the fine mirror —Ethel Wilson⟩ **b** : to give a distorted view of : EXAGGERATE ⟨a simple mistake in judgment was often *magnified* to the proportions of a major crime —B.F.Fairless⟩ ⟨*magnified* the peril —Arnold Bennett⟩ ⟨material comfort and ease was *magnified* in contrast with the pains and risk of experimental creation —John Dewey⟩ **3** : to enlarge in fact or in appearance ⟨the microscope *magnified* the object 100 diameters⟩ ~ *vi* **1** : to have the power of causing objects to appear larger than they are : to increase the apparent dimensions of objects ⟨a glass that *magnifies* greatly⟩ **2** *now dial Brit* : to have importance : MATTER, SIGNIFY **syn** see EXALT — **magnify oneself against** : to oppose with pride ⟨if indeed you *magnify yourselves against* me and make my humiliation an argument against me —Job 19:5 (RSV)⟩

magnifying glass *n* : a lens that magnifies the apparent dimensions of objects seen through it

magnifying power *n* : magnification esp. as applied to visual instruments

mag·nil·o·quence \mag'nilәkwәn(t)s, maig-\ *n* -s [L *magniloquentia*, fr. *magniloquus* magniloquent (fr. *magnus* great + *-i-* + *-loquus*, fr. *loqui* to speak) + *-entia* -ence — more at MUCH] : the quality or state of being magniloquent ⟨an air of ~ hardly suited to the simple rusticity of its theme —John McCarten⟩

mag·nil·o·quent \-nt\ *adj* [back-formation fr. *magniloquence*] : characterized by a high-flown often bombastic style, manner, or quality esp. in language : GRANDILOQUENT : OSTENTATIOUS ⟨continues his comic oration . . . bent on the choice of ~ phrase —E.K.Brown⟩ — **mag·nil·o·quent·ly** *adv*

mag·ni·to·gorsk \mag'nēd·ә,gȯrsk\ *adj, usu cap* [fr. *Magnitogorsk*, U.S.S.R.] : of or from the city of Magnitogorsk, U.S.S.R. : of the kind or style prevalent in Magnitogorsk

mag·ni·tude \'magnә,tüd, 'maig-, -nә-,tyüd\ *n* -s [ME, fr. L *magnitudo*, fr. *magnus* great + *-i-* + *-tudo* -tude — more at MUCH] **1** *obs* : greatness of character or position : NOBILITY **2 a** (1) : greatness of size or extent : VASTNESS ⟨cannot wage a war of such ~ . . . without inaugurating a new epoch —A.N. Whitehead⟩ ⟨the ~ of his literary output —H.W.H.Knott⟩ ⟨the ~ of the shift away from centralized planning of all economic activity —Harry Schwartz⟩ (2) : SIZE 3a(1) ⟨negative accelerations of any considerable ~ in aircraft are seldom encountered —H.G.Armstrong⟩ ⟨able to operate only over distances of very small ~ —G.W.Gray b. 1886⟩ (3) : QUANTITY, NUMBER ⟨the savings in amounts of metal . . . will be of dramatically significant ~s —*Amer. Fabrics*⟩ **b** : VOLUME, LOUDNESS ⟨the ~ of the total sound made . . . was astounding —William Beebe⟩ **3** : the importance, quality, or caliber of something ⟨a seaside curiosity of the first ~ —Charles Gordon⟩ ⟨disappointing work by a writer of first ~ —Richard Plant⟩ ⟨this is no bad test of the stature, or rather the ~, of a poet —David Daiches⟩ ⟨this court can be insensible neither to the ~ nor delicacy of this question —John Marshall⟩ **4** : a number representing the intrinsic or apparent brightness of a celestial body on a logarithmic scale in which a difference of one unit corresponds to the multiplication or division of the brightness of light by 2.512+ and a difference of five units corresponds to the multiplication or division by 100 ⟨a star of ~ 3.0 is approximately 2.512 times brighter than a star of ~ 4.0⟩ ⟨a star of ~ 1.0 is 100 times brighter than one of ~ 6.0⟩ — compare ABSOLUTE MAGNITUDE, APPARENT MAGNITUDE, VISUAL MAGNITUDE **5** : a number assigned to a quantity by means of which the quantity may be compared with other quantities of the same class **6** : the amount of energy released at the source of an earthquake or indicated by the intensity of an earthquake at one place and usu. represented by a number on an arbitrary scale **syn** see SIZE

mag·ni·tu·di·nous \¦==¦tüdәnәs, -¦tyü-\ *adj* [L *magnitudin-, magnitudo* magnitude + E *-ous*] : having magnitude

mag·no- *in pronunciations below*, ¦==¦mag(,)nō *or* ¦maig(,)nō *or* -nә\ *comb form* [ISV, fr. *magnesia* & NL *magnesium*] **1** : magnesia ⟨*magno*chromite⟩ **2** : magnesium ⟨*magno*ferrite⟩ ⟨*magno*phorite⟩

mag·no·chromite \,== *at* MAGNO- +\ *n* [G *magnochromit*, fr. *magno-* + *chromit* chromite] : MAGNESIOCHROMITE

mag·no·ferrite \"+\ *n* [G *magnoferrit*, fr. *magno-* + *ferrit* ferrite] : MAGNESIOFERRITE

¹mag·no·lia \mag'nōlyә, maig-\ *n* [NL, fr. Pierre *Magnol* †1715 French botanist + NL *-ia*] **1** *cap* : a genus (the type of the family Magnoliaceae) of No. American and Asian shrubs and trees that have entire evergreen or deciduous leaves and usu. showy white, yellow, rose, or purple flowers appearing in early spring often before the leaves, having many ovoid pistils borne on a sessile receptacle, and being followed by a follicular fruit **2** -s : any tree or shrub of the genus *Magnolia* **3** -s : TULIP TREE 1 **4** -s : the dried bark of any plant of the genus *Magnolia* (esp. *M. virginiana*) used in folk medicine

²magnolia \"\ *adj, sometimes cap* [so called fr. the traditional popularity of magnolia trees on old southern plantations] : of, relating to, or resembling the South of pre-Civil War days ⟨smile at the sentimentalities of the ~ tradition —W.S. White⟩

mag·no·li·a·ce·ae \=,nōlē'āsē,ē\ *n pl, cap* [NL, fr. *Magnolia*, type genus + *-aceae*] : a family of shrubs and trees (order Ranales), having bisexual flowers, stamens arranged spirally, and numerous simple pistils spirally arranged on an elongated axis — **mag·no·li·a·ceous** \(,)=¦==¦āshәs\ *adj*

magnolia warbler *n* : a No. American warbler (*Dendroica magnolia*)

mag·noph·o·rite \mag'näfә,rīt\ *n* -s [*magno-* + *phor-* + *-ite*] : a mineral $NaKCaMg_5Si_8O_{23}OH$ of the amphibole group consisting of silicate of sodium, potassium, calcium, and magnesium

¹mag·num \'magnәm, 'maig-\ *n* -s [L, neut. of *magnus* great — more at MUCH] **1** : a large wine bottle holding about ⅖ of a gallon **2** [fr. *Magnum*, a trademark] : a magnum cartridge or firearm

²magnum \"\ *adj* : high-powered due to a larger case and larger powder charge than other cartridges of approximately the same caliber — used of cartridges and of weapons designed to use the cartridges

magnum opus *n* [L] : a great work; *esp* : a literary or artistic work of importance : the greatest achievement of an artist ⟨a golden opportunity to finish his *magnum opus* under the conditions of leisure —Saxe Commins⟩

mag·nus effect \'magnәs-, 'maignәs-\ *n, usu cap M* [after Heinrich G. *Magnus* †1870 Ger. chemist and physicist] : the sideways thrust on a rotating cylinder placed with its axis perpendicular to a current of air which has been utilized to propel ships and in aviation as a lift — compare ROTOR SHIP

magnus hitch *n* [*magnus* of unknown origin] : a rolling hitch that is similar in form to a clove hitch and is used to hitch a rope or line to a larger rope or to a spar

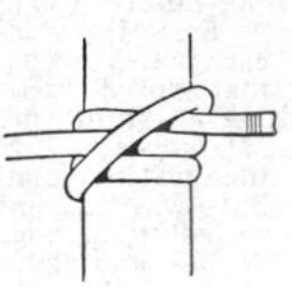
magnus hitch

ma·got \mә'gō, ma'-, mä'-\ *n* -s [F, fr. MF, fr. *magog*, *magot* deformed creature, fr. *Magog*, a nation represented in the NT as one that will be deceived by Satan (Rev 20:8), fr. *Magog*, described in the OT as a land from which the people under their king Gog wished to set forth to destroy Jerusalem (Ezek 38 & 39)] **1** : BARBARY APE **2** : a small grotesque figure of Chinese or Japanese style or workmanship

¹mag·pie \'mag,pī, 'maig-\ *n* [*Mag* (nickname for *Margaret*) + *pie* (magpie)] **1** : any of numerous birds of *Pica* and several other genera of the family Corvidae that are closely related to the jays but have a long graduated tail and usu. black-and-white plumage: as **a** : the common European magpie (*Pica pica*) **b** : a closely similar American magpie (*P. pica hudsonia*) of the Rocky Mountain region **c** : YELLOW-BILLED MAGPIE **2** : any of several birds of the family Cracticidae having black-and-white plumage suggesting the true magpies: as **a** : PIPING CROW **b** : a related bird (*Gymnorhina hypoleuca*) that occurs in Tasmania and southeastern Australia and has been introduced into New Zealand **3** : one who chatters endlessly or foolishly **4** : the black-and-white ceremonial dress of an Anglican bishop

²magpie \"\ *adj* **1** : pied like a magpie **2 a** : having characteristics or traits resembling those attributed to the magpie; *esp* : addicted to indiscriminate collecting ⟨have on occasions been thankful for her ~ ways —L.A.G.Strong⟩ **b** : MISCELLANEOUS ⟨~ collection of bric-a-brac —Louis Bromfield⟩ ⟨his eye roved uneasily over the ~ litter of his room —C.D.Lewis⟩

³magpie \"\ *vt* **magpied; magpied; magpieing; magpies** : to garner up like a magpie : pilfer and hoard ⟨those memories . . . have been *magpied* together from glittering little trivia —Basil Marriott⟩ ⟨admits *magpieing* ideas from others and using them later as his own⟩

magpie diver *n* : SMEW

magpie finch *n* : a small mannikin of variegated color; *esp* : the African mannikin (*Lonchura cucullata*)

magpie goose *n* **:** a black-and-white Australian swan goose (*Anseranas semipalmata*)
magpie lark *n* **:** a black-and-white passerine bird (*Grallina cyanoleuca*) of Australia of uncertain affinities
magpie moth *n* **:** either of two black-and-white moths: **a :** a European geometrid moth (*Abraxas grossulariata*) whose larva feeds on currant and gooseberry bushes **b :** any of several Australian and New Zealand moths of the genus *Nyctemera* having hairy larvae that feed on many plants
magpie robin *n* **:** any of several varicolored Asiatic singing birds of the genus *Copsychus; esp* **:** a bird (*C. saularis*) ranging from India to the Philippines
magpie shrike *n* **1 :** a So. American black-and-white tanager (*Cissopis leveriana*) **2 :** any of several Australian crow shrikes
mags *pl of* MAG, *pres 3d sing of* MAG
mags·man \ˈmagzmən\ *n, pl* **magsmen** [¹*mag* + *man*] *slang chiefly Brit* **:** SWINDLER
ma·gua·ri \məˈgwärē\ *n* -s [Pg *maguari, maguari,* fr. Tupi] **:** a So. American varicolored stork (*Euxenura galatea*)
ma·guey \məˈgā, ˈmag,wā\ *n* -s [Sp, fr. Taino] **1 a :** any of various fleshy-leaved agaves: as (1) **:** a Mexican agave (as *Agave atrovirens*) that is used as a source of pulque (2) *Philippines* **:** the agave (*A. cantala*) that yields cantala (3) **:** the common century plant (*A. americana*) **b :** a plant of the closely related genus *Furcraea* **2 a :** any of several hard fibers derived from magueys; *esp* **:** CANTALA **b** *or* **maguey rope** *chiefly West* **:** a rope of maguey fiber or horsehair
maguey worm *n* **:** AGAVEWORM
ma·gus \ˈmāgəs\ *n, pl* **ma·gi** \ˈmā,jī *sometimes* ˈma,-\ [ME, fr. L, fr. Gk *magos* — more at MAGIC] **1 :** a member of a hereditary priestly class among the ancient Medes and Persians whose doctrines included belief in astrology **:** a Zoroastrian priest; *specif, usu cap* **:** one of the traditionally three wise men from the East who according to the Gospel of Matthew paid homage to the infant Jesus **2 :** an adept in occult arts **:** MAGICIAN, SORCERER
¹**magyar** \ˈmag,yär, ˈmaiˌ, ˈmäˌ, ˈmaˌ, |á(r *also* |gy|ə(r) *or* (*with no* ˈmai| *variant*) |(,)j| *or* |d(,)y|\ *n* -s *cap* [Hung] **1 :** a member of the dominant ethnic group of Hungary — compare HUN, HUNGARIAN **2 :** the language of the Magyars that is Finno-Ugric in affiliation — see URALIC LANGUAGES table
²**magyar** \"\ *adj, usu cap* **:** of or relating to the Magyars or Magyar **:** HUNGARIAN
magyar·ization \,≈(,)≈rəˈzāshən, -,rīˈz-\ *n* -s *usu cap* **1 :** the act or process of being magyarized ⟨the hard fight against *Magyarization* —J.S.Roucek⟩ **2 :** the quality or state of being magyarized ⟨bring about the *Magyarization* of the non-Magyar elements —W.J.Ehrenpreis⟩
magyar·ize \ˈ≈(,)≈,rīz\ *vt* -ED/-ING/-S *often cap* **1 a :** to make Magyar in quality, traits, or culture **b :** to bring under the control of Magyars **2 :** to modify or alter (a word) to conform to language characteristics distinctive of Magyar
mah *abbr* mahogany
¹**maha** *usu cap, var of* OMAHA
²**ma·ha** \ˈmä(,)hä, ˈmähə\ *n* -s [Sinhalese *maha* large, great, fr. Skt *mahat*] **1 :** a Ceylonese langur (*Presbytis ursina*) **2 :** SAMBAR
mahagua *var of* MAJAGUA
ma·ha·jan *or* **ma·ha·jun** \məˈhäjən\ *n* -s [Hindi *mahājan,* fr. Skt *mahājana,* lit., great person, fr. *mahat* great + *jana* people, person — more at MUCH, KIN] *India* **:** MONEYLENDER
¹**ma·hal** \məˈhäl\ *n* -s [Ar *maḥall* place] **1** *India* **a :** SUMMER HOUSE **b :** a private apartment or lodging **2 a :** a territorial division in India **b :** a division of a farm or hunting preserve in India
²**mahal** \"\ *n* -s [prob. after *Mahal,* name of a fine grade of Persian carpet] **:** NEW COCOA
ma·ha·la \məˈhälə\ *n* -s [Yokuts *mokel* women] *West* **:** SQUAW
mahala mat *n* [so called fr. its use by squaws for making mats] **:** a prostrate much-matted shrub (*Ceanothus prostratus*) of the Pacific coast of the U. S.
ma·ha·leb \ˈmä(h)ə,leb\ *also* **mahaleb cherry** *n* -s [Ar *maḥlab*] **:** a small slender European cherry (*Prunus mahaleb*) that has pure white fragrant flowers in racemes and small inferior fruits from which a dye and a cordial are sometimes made and that is grown for use as an understock in grafting cultivated cherries — called also *St. Lucie cherry*
ma·hant \məˈhənt\ *n* -s [Hindi *mahant,* fr. Prakrit *mahanta-,* fr. Skt *mahat* great] *India* **:** a religious superior **:** ELDER
ma·ha·ra·ja *or* **ma·ha·ra·jah** \,mä(h)əˈräjə, -räzhə\ *n* -s [Skt *mahārāja,* fr. *mahat* great + *rājan* king — more at RAJA] **:** a Hindu prince ranking above a raja; *esp* **:** a ruler of one of the principal native states of India
ma·ha·ra·ni *or* **ma·ha·ra·nee** \,mä(h)əˈränē\ *n* -s [Hindi *mahārānī,* fr. *mahā* great (fr. Skt *mahat*) + *rānī* queen — more at RANI] **1 :** the wife of a maharaja **2 :** a Hindu princess ranking above a rani; *esp* **:** a sovereign princess of one of the principal native states of India
ma·ha·rash·tri \məˈhäˈräsh(,)trē\ *n* -s *cap* [Skt *Mahārāṣṭrī* — more at MARATHI] **:** the Prakrit language of the region of Maharashtra in western India
ma·ha·san·ghi·ka \məˈhäˈsəŋgəkə\ *n* -s *usu cap* [Skt *mahāsāṃghika,* masc. pl., name of a Buddhist school] **:** an adherent of an early Buddhist sect from which Mahayana Buddhism developed
mahaseer *also* **mahasir** *var of* MAHSEER
ma·hat·ma \məˈhätmə, -hat-\ *n* -s [Skt *mahātman,* lit., great-souled, wise, fr. *mahat* great + *ātman* soul — more at MUCH, ATMAN] **1 :** a person held worthy of reverence for high-mindedness, wisdom, and selflessness **2 :** one of a class of Indian and Tibetan sages held by Theosophists to possess superior knowledge and powers **3 :** a person of great prestige in some field of endeavor ⟨a kind of ~ of music —Ward Morehouse⟩
ma·ha·ya·na \,mä(h)əˈyänə\ *n* -s *cap* [Skt *mahāyāna* the great vehicle, fr. *mahat* great + *yāna* vehicle — more at HINAYANA] **:** a branch of Buddhism made up of various syncretistic sects that are found chiefly in Tibet, Nepal, China, and Japan, have vernacular scriptures based on a Sanskrit canon, believe in a god or gods, and usu. teach the bodhisattva ideal of compassion and universal salvation — called also *Great Vehicle;* compare HINAYANA, LAMAISM
mah·di \ˈmädē\ *n* -s *usu cap* [Ar *mahdīy* rightly or divinely guided] **1 :** a messianic guide who according to Muslim tradition will appear prior to the last day and lead the community of the faithful to salvation **2 :** a Muslim leader who assumes a messianic role
mah·dism \ˈmä,dizəm\ *n* -s *usu cap* **:** belief in or devotion to a Mahdi
mah·dist \-dəst\ *n* -s *usu cap* **:** an adherent of Mahdism
ma·hi·can *or* **mo·hi·can** \məˈhēkən, mō'-\ *n, pl* **mahican** *or* **mahicans** *or* **mohican** *or* **mohicans** *usu cap* [Mahican, lit., wolf] **1 a :** an Indian people of the upper Hudson river valley and eastward into the valley of the Housatonic **b :** a member of such people **2 :** an Algonquian language of the Mahican people
ma·hi·ma·hi \ˈmäheˈmähē\ *n, pl* **mahimahi** [Hawaiian, Tahitian, & Marquesan] **:** DOLPHIN 2
¹**mah-jongg** *or* **mah jong** \(ˈ)mäˈjlôŋ, -ˈzhl, läŋ\ *n* -s [fr. *Mah-Jongg,* a trademark] **1 :** a game of Chinese origin usu. played by 4 persons with 144 tiles that are drawn and discarded until one player secures a winning hand of 4 sets of 3 tiles and a pair **2 :** a winning hand in mah-jongg
²**mah-jongg** \"\ *vi* -ED/-ING/-S **:** to win a mah-jongg game
mahlstick *var of* MAULSTICK
ma·hoe \məˈhō\ *n* -s [F *mahot, maho,* fr. Taino *maho*] **1** *also* **ma·ho** \"\ **:** any of various chiefly tropical trees with strong bast fibers: as **a** (1) **:** MAJAGUA (2) **:** PORTIA TREE **b :** any of several trees of the family Thymelaeaceae; *esp* **:** a West Indian tree (*Daphnopsis caribaea*) **c :** any of several trees of the genus *Sterculia; esp* **:** a So. American tree (*S. pruriens*) that yields a pale brown lustrous straight-grained wood **2** *also* **maho :** the wood or fiber of a mahoe **3** [Maori] **:** a small shrubby New Zealand tree (*Melicytus ramiflorus*) of the family Violaceae with dark green alternate leaves and few-seeded purple berries — called also *whitey wood*
ma·hog·a·nize \məˈhägə,nīz\ *vt* -ED/-ING/-S *see -ize in Explan Notes* **:** to cause to resemble mahogany usu. by staining ⟨a mahoganized cabinet⟩
ma·hog·a·ny \-nē, -ni\ *n* -ES *often attrib* [origin unknown] **1 :** the wood of any of various chiefly tropical trees of the family Meliaceae: **a** (1) **:** the durable yellowish brown to reddish brown usu. moderately hard and heavy wood of a West Indian tree (*Swietenia mahagoni*) that is readily worked, takes a high polish when dressed, can be cut to show numerous striking figures because of its well differentiated structural elements and overlapping grain, and is widely used for cabinetwork and fine finish work — called also *Cuban mahogany, Dominican mahogany* (2) **:** the similar wood of any other tree of the genus *Swietenia* — called also *Honduras mahogany* **b :** any of several African woods more or less similar to New World mahogany: (1) **:** the rather hard heavy usu. odorless wood of trees of the genus *Khaya* — called also *African mahogany* (2) **:** the rather lightweight cedar-scented wood of trees of the genus *Entandrophragma* that varies in color from pinkish to deep reddish brown — called also *African scented mahogany, cedar mahogany, sapele mahogany* **2 :** any of various woods resembling or substituted for mahogany obtained from trees of the family Meliaceae — not used technically without a qualifying term; see PHILIPPINE MAHOGANY **3** *also* **mahogany tree a :** a tree of the genus *Swietenia; esp* **:** a West Indian tree (*S. mahagoni*) **b :** an African tree of the family Meliaceae that yields mahogany **c :** a tree not belonging to the family Meliaceae that yields mahogany **4 a :** TABLE ⟨ranged around the ~ are union and company representatives —Lawrence Galton⟩; *esp* **:** DINING TABLE ⟨other families did not welcome us to their ~ —W.M.Thackeray⟩ **b :** COUNTER 4b, BAR 5a ⟨every interval sees twenty orchestral players with their elbows on the ~ —Charles Reid⟩ **5** *also* **mahogany brown** *or* **mahogany red :** a moderate reddish brown that is yellower and slightly darker and less strong than roan, less strong than oxblood, redder and deeper than russet tan, and redder and slightly deeper than rustic brown **6 a** *dial Eng* **:** a Cornish drink made of gin and treacle **b :** a strong drink made of brandy and water
mahogany acid *n* **:** any of several dark-colored oil-soluble mixtures of sulfonic acid derivatives of petroleum that are obtained as by-products in refining white oils with sulfuric acid or made as primary products by sulfonation of petroleum distillates and are used as such or in the form of salts chiefly as emulsifying agents, as rust-proofing agents, and as additives to lubricants
mahogany bean *n* **:** POD MAHOGANY
mahogany birch *n* **:** SWEET BIRCH
mahogany family *n* **:** MELIACEAE
mahogany gum *n* **:** any of various eucalypts; *specif* **:** JARRAH
mahogany rot *n* **1 :** the tuber-rotting phase of late blight; *broadly* **:** LATE BLIGHT **2** *also* **mahogany browning :** a physiological disease of potato tuber due to long exposure to low temperature
mahogany snapper *n* **:** a small brown West Indian snapper (*Lutanus mahogoni*)
mahogany soap *n* **:** a salt of a mahogany acid; *esp* **:** a sodium salt of such an acid
ma·ho·li \məˈhōlē\ *n* -s [Tswana *mogwêlê*] **:** MOHOLI LEMUR
ma·ho·nia \məˈhōnēə\ *n* [NL, fr. Bernard McMahon †1816 Am. botanist + NL *-ia*] **1** *cap* **:** a genus of No. American and Asiatic shrubs of the family Berberidaceae that have unarmed branches and pinnate leaves and are sometimes included in the genus *Berberis* — see AGARITA, OREGON GRAPE **2** -s **:** any shrub of the genus *Mahonia*
ma·hon stock \məˈhōn-\ *n, usu cap M* [fr. *Mahón,* Minorca, Spain] **:** VIRGINIAN STOCK
mahos *pl of* MAHO
ma·hout \məˈhaut\ *n* -s [Hindi *mahāwat, mahāut,* fr. Skt *mahāmātra* of great eminence, fr. *mahat* great + *mātra* measure, fr. *māti* he measures — more at MUCH, MEASURE] **:** a keeper and driver of an elephant
mahratta *or* **mahratti** *usu cap, var of* MARATHA
mah·ri \ˈmärē\ *also* **mah·ra** \-rə\ *n, pl* **mahri** *or* **mahris** *also* **mahra** *or* **mahras** *cap* [Ar *mahrīy* or *mahrah*] **1 :** a native or inhabitant of the Mahra region of the Arabian peninsula **2 :** the Semitic language of the Mahri people
mah·seer *also* **mah·sir** \ˈmä,si(ə)r\ *or* **mah·sur** \-sə(r)\ *or* **ma·ha·seer** *or* **ma·ha·sir** \məˈhä,si(ə)r\ *n, pl* **mahseer** [Hindi *mahāsir,* prob. fr. Skt *mahat* big, great + *śiras* head — more at CEREBRAL] **:** a large Indian freshwater cyprinid food and sport fish (*Barbus mosal*)
mah·sud \mäˈsüd\ *n* -s *usu cap* **:** a member of a people of northwestern Pakistan related to the Wazir
ma·hua \ˈmä(h)wə\ *or* **moh·wa** \ˈmō(w)ə\ *n* -s [Hindi *mahūā,* fr. Skt *madhūka,* fr. *madhu* sweet, honey, mead — more at MEAD] **:** any of several East Indian trees of the genus *Madhuca* (esp. *M. latifolia* or *M. indica*) with nectar-filled flowers that are used for food and in preparing an intoxicating drink — compare ILLUPI
mahua butter *var of* MOWRAH BUTTER
ma·huang \ˈmäˈhwäŋ\ *n* -s [Chin (Pek) *ma² huang²*] **:** any of several Chinese plants of the genus *Ephedra* (esp. *E. sinica*) yielding ephedrine
mah·zor *or* **mach·zor** \mäkˈzō(ə)r, ˈmäkzə(r)\ *n, pl* **mahzorim** *or* **machzo·rim** \,mäkzōˈrēm\ *or* **mahzors** *or* **machzors** [Heb *maḥăzōr,* lit., cycle] **:** a Hebrew prayer book containing the Jewish liturgy for festivals — compare SIDDUR
mai \ˈmī\ *n* -s [Jap] **:** a slow Japanese folk or theater dance featuring hand gestures — distinguished from *odori*
ma·ia \ˈmā(y)ə, ˈmīə\ [NL, fr. L, a large crab, fr. Gk] *syn of* MAJA
ma·ian·the·mum \māˈ(y)an(t)thəməm, mīˈa-\ *n, cap* [NL, fr. L *maius* May + NL *-anthemum* — more at MAY (month)] **:** a genus of perennial herbs (family Liliaceae) having slender rhizomes and an erect stem bearing a few leaves and a terminal raceme of small white flowers — see FALSE LILY OF THE VALLEY
¹**maid** \ˈmād\ *n* -s [ME *maide,* short for *maiden*] **1 a :** an unmarried girl or woman esp. when young **:** VIRGIN **b** *obs* **:** a male virgin **2 a :** a girl or woman employed to do domestic work in a home, hotel, motel, or institution **b :** CHARWOMAN **3** *Brit* **:** a young ray or skate
²**maid** \"\ *vb* -ED/-ING/-S **1 :** to attend as bridesmaid **2 :** to serve as maid
mai·dan *also* **mei·dan** \mīˈdän\ *n* -s [Hindi *maidān,* fr. Ar] **:** an Asiatic or African parade ground or esplanade
¹**maid·en** \ˈmādᵊn\ *n* -s [ME, fr. OE *mǣden, mægden,* fr. *mægth, mægeth;* akin to OS *magath* maiden, OE *mago, magu* son, man, servant, MD *maget, maecht* maiden, OHG *magad* maiden, ON *mǫgr* son, youth, *mær* maiden, Goth *magus* boy, child, *magaths* virgin, OIr *mug* serf, *macc* son, Latvian *mač* small] **1 :** MAID, VIRGIN ⟨supposedly a place for the ~s of that era to catch a beau —Frances H. Eliot⟩ **2** *obs* **:** MAIDSERVANT **3** *archaic* **:** a former Scottish beheading device resembling the guillotine **4** *Scot* **:** HARVEST DOLL **5 :** MAIDEN OVER **6 :** a mare, stallion, or gelding that has never won a race **7 :** *chiefly Brit* **:** WHIP 3a
²**maiden** \"\ *adj* [ME, fr. *maiden,* n.] **1** *of a girl or woman* **a :** UNMARRIED ⟨~ aunt⟩ **b :** VIRGIN **2 :** of, relating to, or befitting a maiden ⟨~ innocence⟩ ⟨~ loveliness⟩ **3 :** FIRST, EARLIEST ⟨convulses his audience with his ~ speech —*Brit. Book News*⟩ ⟨her ~ voyage —H.A.Chippendale⟩ **4 a :** INTACT, FRESH, UNTAKEN, UNTRIED, UNUSED ⟨records were of any and all manufacture . . . some were ~; none had been played more than six times —C.G.Burke⟩ ⟨the ~ city (as it was named from its successful resistance to the siege) —Sam Pollock⟩ **b :** of or relating to a horse that has never won a race ⟨yesterday she shed her ~ certificate when she won the sixth race —*Johannesburg Sunday Express*⟩ **c** *Eng law* **:** of or relating to an assize or session without cases to be tried or formerly one resulting in no sentence of death **5** *of a female animal* **a :** never yet mated **b :** never having borne young **syn** see YOUTHFUL
maiden cane *n* **:** a grass (*Panicum hemitomon*) of moist or low coastal areas of the southern U.S. that is propagated by extensively creeping rootstocks
maiden duck *n, Brit* **:** SHOVELER
maidenhair \ˈ≈≈,≈\ *or* **maidenhair fern** *n* [*maidenhair* fr. ME *maidenheer,* fr. *maiden* + *heer* hair; intended as trans. of LL *capillus Veneris,* lit., Venus's hair] **:** a fern of the genus *Adiantum:* as **a :** VENUSHAIR **b :** a palmately branched No. American fern (*A. pedatum*) with fronds having divergent recurved branches borne on a lustrous reddish or blackish stipe
maidenhair spleenwort *n* **:** a rock-inhabiting small fern (*Asplenium trichomanes*) of the north temperate zone and Hawaii with slender pinnate black-stiped fronds
maidenhair tree *n* **:** GINKGO
maidenhair-tree family *n* **:** GINKGOACEAE
maidenhair-vine \ˈ≈≈,≈\ *n* **:** WIRE PLANT
maidenhead \ˈ≈≈,≈\ *n* [ME *maidenhed, maidenhede,* fr. ¹*maiden* + *-hed, -hede* -hood (akin to ME *-hod, -had* -hood] **1 a :** the quality or state of being a maiden **:** intact virginity **b :** unused or uncontaminated condition **:** FRESHNESS, PURITY ⟨pious pledges to safeguard the ~ of scholarship —William Manchester⟩ **2** *obs* **:** the first stage or first use of something **3 :** HYMEN
maidenhead spoon *n* [obs. E *maidenhead* ornamental representation of the head of the Virgin Mary (fr. ME *maidenhed,* fr. ¹*maiden* + *hed* head) + E *spoon*] **:** a 16th century silver or silver-gilt spoon with handle terminating in a bust of the Virgin Mary
maid·en·hood \ˈmādᵊn,hu̇d\ *n* [ME *maidenhod,* fr. OE *mægdenhād,* fr. *mægden* maiden + *-hād* -hood] **1 :** the quality or state of being a maid or virgin **:** GIRLHOOD ⟨thoughts and emotions of maturing youth and ~ —H.A.Overstreet⟩ **2** *obs* **:** intact virginity
maid·en·ish \-ᵊnish\ *adj* **1 :** of or resembling a girl **:** GIRLISH **2 :** OLD-MAIDISH ⟨a short, fair, rather ~ woman —Saul Bellow⟩
maid·en·ism \-ᵊn,izəm\ *n* -s **:** a girlish trait or mannerism
maiden lady *n* **:** an unmarried and usu. middle-aged woman
maid·en·li·ness \-ᵊnlēnəs, -lin-\ *n* -ES [¹*maidenly* + *-ness*] **:** conduct or traits befitting a maiden ⟨though she heard the remembered voice, her ~ had not permitted that she should show herself —Arnold Bennett⟩
¹**maid·en·ly** \-ᵊnlē, -li\ *adj* [ME] **:** of, resembling, or suitable to a maiden **:** GENTLE, MODEST, TIMID, VIRGINAL
²**maidenly** \"\ *adv, archaic* **:** in a maidenly manner
maiden name *n* **:** the surname of a woman before she is married
maiden oak *n* **:** DURMAST
maiden over *n* **:** a cricket over in which no runs are scored from hits
maiden pink *n* **:** a low-growing stoloniferous Eurasian pink (*Dianthus deltoides*) having single crimson-eyed flowers
maiden plum *n* **:** a West Indian guao (*Comocladia integrifolia*) with edible purplish drupes
maidens *pl of* MAIDEN
maiden's-blush \ˈ≈≈ˈ≈\ *n, pl* **maiden's-blushes 1** *Austral* **:** a pink-flowered timber tree (*Echinocarpus australis*) of the family Tiliaceae **2** *Austral* **:** a timber tree (*Euroschinus falcatus*) of the family Anacardiaceae
maidenship *n, obs* **:** the rank or standing of a maiden
maid·hood \ˈmād,hu̇d\ *n* [ME *maidhod,* fr. OE *mægthād,* fr. *mægth* maiden + *-hād* -hood — more at MAIDEN] **1 :** MAIDENHOOD **2 :** the status or occupation of a maidservant
maiding *pres part of* MAID
maid-in-waiting \ˈ≈≈ˈ≈≈\ *n, pl* **maids-in-waiting :** a young woman of a queen's or princess's household appointed to wait upon or attend her
maid·ish \ˈmādish\ *adj* **:** MAIDENISH ⟨you would think a small ~ mind had pored over the task —Audrey Barker⟩ — **maid·ish·ness** *n* -ES
maid of all work 1 : a domestic who does general housework **2 :** a person or thing put to a wide variety of uses ⟨the prime minister is the general *maid of all work* in the cabinet —H.J. Laski⟩ ⟨a patrol boat is a sort of *maid of all work,* ready to do anything —A.P.Herbert⟩
maid of honor 1 : an unmarried lady usu. of noble birth whose duty it is to attend a queen or a princess **2 :** a bride's principal unmarried wedding attendant — distinguished from *matron of honor;* compare BRIDESMAID **3 :** a pastry of puff paste filled with a rich custard flavored with almond paste and lemon
mai·dou \mīˈdü\ *n* -s [native name in Burma and Indochina] **:** a tree (*Pterocarpus pedatus*) of Burma and Indochina whose wood resembles amboyna but is of coarser figure and darker brown
maids *pl of* MAID, *pres 3d sing of* MAID
maidservant \ˈ≈,≈≈\ *n* **:** a female servant
maid's-hair \ˈ≈,≈\ *n, pl* **maid's-hairs :** YELLOW BEDSTRAW
mai·du \ˈmī(,)dü\ *n, pl* **maidu** *or* **maidus** *usu cap* [Maidu, lit., person, man] **1 a :** an Indian people of the Feather and American river valleys of California **b :** a member of such people **2 :** a Pujunan language of the Maidu people **3 :** PUJUNAN
maidy \ˈmādē\ *n* -ES **:** a little maid
ma·ieu·tic \māˈyüd‚ik, mī-, -üt|, |ēk\ *adj* [Gk *maieutikos,* lit., of midwifery, fr. (assumed) *maieutos* (verbal of *maieuesthai* to act as midwife, fr. *maia* midwife) + *-ikos* -ic; akin to Gk *mētēr* mother — more at MOTHER] **:** of or relating to the dialectic method practiced by Socrates in order to elicit and clarify the ideas of others
¹**mai·gre** \ˈmāgrə, *F* mägrᵊ\ *or* meeg- *or* -g(r)ə\ *adj* [F, maigre, meager, fr. MF — more at MEAGER] **1 :** being a day on which the eating of flesh is forbidden by the Roman Catholic Church **2 :** constituting a food that contains no flesh nor juices of flesh and so may be eaten on maigre days
²**mai·gre** \"\ *or* **mai·ger** \-gə(r)\ *also* **mea·gre** \ˈmēgə(r)\ *n, pl* **maigres** \-gərz, *F* -grᵊ\ *or* -g(rə)\ *or* **maigers** \-gə(r)z\ [F *maigre,* fr. MF, perh. fr. *maigre,* adj.] **1 :** a large European marine food fish (*Sciaena aquila*) **2 :** a member of the percoid family Sciaenidae **:** CROAKER 2, DRUM 5 — called also *bar*
maijd *var of* MAJID
mai·idae \ˈmā(y)ə,dē, ˈmīə-\ [NL, fr. *Maia,* type genus + *-idae*] *syn of* MAJIDAE
maik \ˈmāk\ *Scot var of* MAKE
¹**mail** \ˈmāl\ *n* -s [ME *maill, male,* fr. OE *māl* terms, agreement, pay, fr. ON *māl* speech, language, agreement; akin to OE *mǣl* speech, conversation, *mæthel* assembly, OS & OHG *mahal* assembly, judgment, Goth *mathl* meeting place, market, OE *mōt* meeting — more at MEET] *now chiefly Scot* **:** PAYMENT, RENT, TRIBUTE, TAX
²**mail** \ˈmāl, *esp before pause or consonant* -āəl\ *n* -s *often attrib* [ME *male,* fr. OF, of Gmc origin; akin to MD *māle* bag, traveling bag, OHG *malaha, malha* wallet, bag] **1** *chiefly Scot* **:** BAG, WALLET, TRAVELING BAG **2 a :** the bags of letters and the other postal matter conveyed under public authority from one post office to another **b :** the postal matter consigned at one time to or from one person or one post office or conveyed by a particular train, airplane, or ship ⟨the ~ for the city⟩ ⟨the doctor's ~ was late that day⟩ ⟨the letter just made the 7 o'clock ~⟩ **c :** a conveyance that transports mail ⟨the train was a fast ~⟩ **3** *or* **mails** *pl* **a :** a nation's postal system — compare POST 3 **b :** postal matter collectively ⟨in colonial days newspapers were not considered part of the ~s⟩
³**mail** \"\ *vb* -ED/-ING/-S [²*mail*] *vt* **:** to send by mail ⟨~ a letter home⟩ ~ *vi* **:** to send postal matter by mail ⟨many advertisers ~ to carefully chosen lists of prospects⟩
⁴**mail** \"\ *n* -s [ME *maile, maille,* fr. MF, fr. OF, fr. L *macula* spot, mesh of a net] **1 a** *obs* **:** a ring or plate constituting the basic unit of the medieval warrior's defensive armor **b :** armor made of metal links or plates — compare CHAIN MAIL, PLATE ARMOR **2 a :** the hard enclosing covering of various animals (as of a tortoise or a lobster) **b** *archaic* **:** the full-grown breast feathers esp. of a hawk **3 :** a metal or glass eye in a heddle through which the thread of the warp passes
⁵**mail** \"\ *vt* -ED/-ING/-S **:** to arm with mail
⁶**mail** \"\ *vt* -ED/-ING/-S [perh. fr. ²*mail* or ⁴*mail*] **1** *obs* **:** ENVELOP **2 :** to wrap up (a hawk) **:** BIND
⁷**mail** *n* -s [F, mail, maul, fr. MF, hammer, maul — more at MAUL] *obs* **:** MALL
⁸**mail** \ˈmāl\ *Scot var of* MOLE
mail·abil·i·ty \,māləˈbiləd‚ē\ *n* **:** the quality or state of being mailable
mail·able \ˈmāləbəl\ *adj* [³*mail* + *-able*] **:** adapted for mailing **:** legally admissible as mail
mailbag \ˈ≈,≈\ *n* **1 :** a letter carrier's shoulder bag **2 :** a pouch used in the shipment of mail
mailbox \ˈ≈,≈\ *n* **1 :** a public box for deposit of outgoing mail **2 :** a box at or near a dwelling for the occupants' mail — see BOX illustration

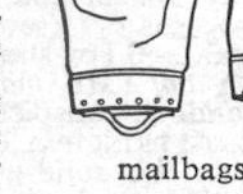
mailbags 2

mail carrier *n* **1 :** one that carries mail between post offices **2 :** one that delivers mail along an established route

mail–cheeked \'=,chēkt\ *adj* [4*mail* + *-cheeked* (fr. 1*cheek* + *-ed*)] **:** having the sides of the head armored — used esp. of a fish of the order Scleroparei

mailclad \'=,=\ *adj* **:** protected by or as if by a coat of mail

mail clerk *n* **1 :** one who does clerical work (as selling stamps or sorting or canceling mail) in a post office **2 :** a mail sorter on a railway mail car **3 :** an employee who handles mail in a private or government establishment that is not part of the post-office department

mail crane *n* **:** a crane or arm at trackside in a railroad station for pouches of mail consigned to or left by moving trains

mail drop *n* **1 a :** a receptacle for mail esp. at the place of delivery **b :** a slot (as in a chute) for deposit of mail **2 :** an address used by an agent who transmits secret communications (as for an espionage apparatus)

ma·i·le \'mīē,lā\ *n* -s [Hawaiian] **:** a Pacific island vine (*Alyxia olivaeformis*) of the family Apocynaceae with fragrant leaves and bark that are used for decoration and in Hawaii for leis

mailed \'mā(ə)ld\ *adj* [ME, fr. *maile* mail (armor) + *-ed*] **1 :** protected or armed with mail **2 :** protected by an outer covering (as of scales or plates) ⟨a ~ fish⟩

mailed catfish *n* **:** ARMORED CATFISH

mailed fist *n* [trans. of G *gepanzerte faust*] **:** armed or overbearing force **:** POWER, VIOLENCE ⟨this was my first experience with a *mailed fist* clothed in the kid glove —G.B.Oxnam⟩

mail edition *n* **:** an early-morning edition of a metropolitan newspaper for out-of-city distribution — compare CITY EDITION

1mail·er \'mālər\ *n* -s [ME *mailler*, fr. *maill* mail (rent) + *-er*] *Scot* **:** a cotter who pays rent

2mail·er \'mālə(r)\ *n* -s [2*mail* & 3*mail* + *-er*] **1 a :** a user of the mails ⟨a wide variety of mechanical equipment is in use by large ~*s*⟩ **b :** one who addresses and otherwise prepares material that is to be mailed **2** *archaic* **:** a boat that carries mail **3 :** MAILING MACHINE **4 a :** a container (as a paperboard tube) for mailing something in **b :** an advertising leaflet for enclosure with letter mail

mail flag *n* **:** a flag displayed by a ship carrying mail

1mail·ing \'māliŋ\ *n* -s [ME *mailling*, fr. *maill* mail (rent) + *-ing*] **1** *Scot* **:** a rented farm **2** *Scot* **:** the rent paid for a farm

2mailing *n* -s [fr. gerund of 3*mail*] **1 :** the act of sending by mail ⟨on the day of ~ he had not appeared⟩ **2 :** the mail dispatched at one time by a sender ⟨large ~*s* which once took weeks now can be made ready for the post office overnight —*Dun's Rev.*⟩ **3 :** something sent by mail ⟨over a million domestic postcards, circulars, parcels, and other ~*s* reached the Dead Letter Office —*Canada Yr. Bk.*⟩

mailing machine *n* **:** any of various machines that help prepare mail (as by stamping, addressing, or weighing)

mailing piece *n* **:** a piece of advertising matter (as a form letter, leaflet, or catalog) for distribution by mail

maill \'māl\ *var of* 1MAIL

mail·less \'mālləs\ *adj* **:** not armored with mail

mail·lot \ma'yō\ *n* -s [F, lit., swaddling cloth, fr. MF, prob. alter. of *maillol*, fr. *maille* laced band, mesh, mail — more at MAIL (armor)] **1 :** tights for dancers, acrobats, or gymnasts **2 :** JERSEY 2 **3 :** a woman's one-piece usu. strapless bathing suit

maillot 3

mail·man \'mā(ə)l,man, -aa(ə)n\ *n, pl* **mail·men :** MAIL CARRIER

mail messenger *n* **:** one who works for the post-office department under contract transporting mail between a post office and a postal transportation terminal (as at an airfield or railroad station)

mail order *n* **:** an order for goods that is received and filled by mail

mail-order house *n* **:** a retail establishment whose business is conducted by mail

mail-rider \'=,==\ *n* **:** a horseback rider who carries mail

mails *pl of* MAIL, *pres 3d sing of* MAIL

mail shell *n* [4*mail*] **:** CHITON

1maim \'mām\ *vt* -ED/-ING/-S [ME *maynen*, *maymen*, *maynhen*, *mayhaymen*, fr. OF *mahaignier*, *maynier*, prob. of Gmc origin; akin to MHG *meidem*, *meiden* gelding, Goth *gamaidans*, acc. pl., crippled — more at MAD] **1 :** to commit the felony of mayhem upon **2 :** to wound seriously **:** MUTILATE, DISABLE, DISFIGURE ⟨he was a puritan, ~*ed* by the narrow orthodoxy of his childhood —Douglas Stewart⟩

syn MAIM, CRIPPLE, MUTILATE, BATTER, MANGLE apply, in common, to an injuring (of a body or an object) so severe as to leave permanent or lasting effects. MAIM implies the loss or destruction of the usefulness of a limb or member ⟨an arm hanging useless, *maimed* in a car accident⟩ CRIPPLE usu. implies the loss of an arm or leg or the serious impairment of its use but can apply to any injury seriously impairing normal mobility or functioning ⟨a boy *crippled* by the loss of a leg⟩ ⟨hands *crippled* by arthritis⟩ ⟨a battleship, *crippled* by cruisers the night before, lay smoking and floundering within sight —Ira Wolfert⟩ MUTILATE implies the cutting, esp. cutting off, or the removal of a part essential to completeness and lessening the perfection, beauty, or pleasing wholeness of the thing ⟨looking exactly like a company of dolls a cruel child had *mutilated*, snapping a foot off here, tearing out a leg here, and battering the face of a third —Richard Jefferies⟩ ⟨never *mutilate* a book by tearing out pages or removing illustrations —L.R.McColvin⟩ BATTER and MANGLE do not suggest loss, as of a limb, but rather an injuring which disfigures, usu. excessively, BATTER implying a pounding or harsh beating, MANGLE implying a tearing, twisting, or hacking ⟨a procession of *battered* automobiles —Oscar Handlin⟩ ⟨to bring up cannon and *batter* the forts into surrender —P.G.Mackesy⟩ ⟨people who have disregarded the warnings and been *mangled* by sharks —V.G.Heiser⟩ ⟨a smashed truck and *mangled* driver —G.R.Stewart⟩ ⟨his face and head were frightfully *mangled* with long cuts, evidently made by an axe —A.F.Harlow⟩

2maim *n* -s [ME *maheym*, *mayme*, *mayne*, fr. MF *mahaing*, *mahaim*, fr. OF, fr. *mahaignier*, v.] **1** *obs* **:** the loss of a limb or member of the body or of the use of it **:** serious physical injury ⟨the beggars . . . look upon their ~*s* as . . . purses, which will always give them money —J.R.Lowell⟩ **2** *obs* **:** a serious defect or mutilation **:** a major lack

3maim \'mām\ *adj, archaic* **:** MAIMED

maimed \-md\ *adj* [ME *maymed*, *mayned*, fr. past part. of *maymen*, *maynen* to maim] **:** CRIPPLED, MUTILATED ⟨the ~ right hand twisted and clutched —P.B.Kyne⟩ — **maimed·ness** *n* -ES

maim·er \-mə(r)\ *n* -s **:** one that maims ⟨a worse killer and ~ than . . . botulism, typhoid, and trichinosis —Jeff McDermid⟩

mai·mon \'mī'mōn\ *n* -s [It *maimone*, fr. Ar *maymūn*, fr. Gk *mimō* ape] **:** MANDRILL

1mai·mon·i·de·an \mī,mīnə'dēən\ *adj, often cap* [*Maimonides* (Moses ben Maimon) †1204 Jewish philosopher + E *-an*] **:** of or relating to Moses Maimonides

2maimonidean \"\ *n* -s *usu cap* **:** a follower of Moses Maimonides

mai·mul \(')mī,mül\ *n, pl* **maimul** *usu cap* **:** a member of a Muslim caste of net workers and fishermen in the Bengal area

1main \'mān\ *n* -s [ME, fr. OE *mægen*; akin to OS & OHG *magan*, *megin* strength, main part, ON *magn*, *megin*, strength, *mega* to be able — more at MAY] **1 :** physical strength **:** POWER — used in the phrase *with might and main* **2 a** [by shortening] **:** MAINLAND **b** [short for obs. E *main sea*, fr. 2*main* + *sea*] **:** HIGH SEA **3** [2*main*] **:** the chief or principal part **:** the essential point ⟨the ~ of the lady's history —Robert Browning⟩ ⟨he is one of those writers who, in the ~, leave me cold —J.D.Adams⟩ **4** *obs* **:** END, PURPOSE, OBJECT **5 :** a pipe, duct, or circuit to or from which lead tributary branches of a utility system and which carries their combined flow ⟨water ~⟩ ⟨gas ~⟩ ⟨sewer ~⟩ ⟨electric ~⟩ — compare BUS BAR, LATERAL **6** [by shortening] **a :** MAINMAST **b :** MAINSAIL

2main \"\ *adj* [ME *mayn*, fr. OE *mægen-*, fr. *mægen*, n.] **1 :** outstanding, conspicuous, or first in any respect **:** GREAT, PREEMINENT **:** PRINCIPAL ⟨the ~ office is located in New York⟩ ⟨just inside the solid-glass ~ doors —Sylvia Gray⟩ ⟨the ~ reason that any businessman can understand —*Wall Street Jour.*⟩ **2** *now chiefly dial* **:** large in amount, effect, or extent **:** GREAT **3 a** *obs* **:** having or manifesting great strength or power **:** MIGHTY ⟨soaring on ~ wing —John Milton⟩ **b :** fully exerted **:** SHEER ⟨keep her in bed by ~ force —Edna Ferber⟩ **4** *obs* **:** of or relating to wide reaches or expanse (as of sea or land) **5 :** connected with or located near the mainmast or mainsail **6 :** expressing the chief predication in a complex sentence ⟨~ clause⟩ ⟨~ predicate⟩ ⟨~ verb⟩ **syn** see CHIEF

3main \"\ *n* -s [prob. fr. 2*main*] **1 a :** a number exceeding four and not exceeding nine called by the caster in the game of hazard before throwing **b :** LINE 13a **2 a :** an archery match **b** *archaic* **:** a boxing match **c** *archaic* **:** a lawn bowling match **3 :** a cockfight series consisting of an odd number of matches ⟨got himself a fighting cock . . . and was making himself a little money in the chicken ~*s* —Erskine Caldwell⟩

4main \"\ *adv* [prob. fr. 2*main*] *now dial* **:** VERY, EXTREMELY ⟨it was ~ hot —R.L.Stevenson⟩

main battery *n* **:** the guns of heaviest caliber on a warship

main brace *n* [ME *mayne brase*, fr. *mayne*, *mayn* main + *brase*, *brace* brace — more at BRACE] **1 :** the brace attached to a sailing ship's main yard **2 :** the brace that transmits the load most directly from one of its terminal joints to the other

main chance *n* **:** the chance that seems to promise most advantage ⟨one eye on heaven and one on the *main chance* —W.M.Thackeray⟩

main couple *n* **:** the principal truss in a roof

main course *n* **:** the mainsail of a square-rigged ship

main crop *n* **:** a fruit or vegetable crop gathered in the prevailing season as distinguished from an early or late harvest

main deck *n* **:** the principal deck of a ship: **a :** the highest complete deck on a naval vessel extending the full length and width of the ship **b :** the deck next below the upper or the shelter deck on a merchant ship usu. located at the end of the transverse framing; *often* **:** the uppermost continuous deck so constructed that it is possible to close securely all openings — see DECK illustration, SHIP illustration

main drain *n* **:** the principal lengthwise pipe of a ship's bilge drainage system

main droite \maⁿ'drwät\ *adv (or adj)* [F, lit., right hand, fr. *main* hand (fr. L *manus*) + *droite*, fem. of *droit* right, direct, straight, fr. L *directus* direct, straight — more at MANUAL, DIRECT (adj.)] **:** with the right hand — used as a direction in keyboard music; abbr. *M.D.*

maine \'mān\ *adj, usu cap* [fr. *Maine*, state in the northeastern U.S., prob. fr. F, historical region of France] **:** of or from the state of Maine **:** of the kind or style prevalent in Maine

maine cat *n, usu cap M, chiefly NewEng* **:** ANGORA CAT

main·er \-nə(r)\ *n* -s *cap* [*Maine* state + E *-er*] **:** a native or resident of the state of Maine

main gauche \maⁿgōsh\ *adv (or adj)* [F, lit., left hand, fr. *main* hand + *gauche* left — more at GAUCHE] **:** with the left hand — used as a direction in keyboard music; abbr. *M.G.*

main guard *n* **1 :** the keep of a castle **2 a :** the principal guard of a garrison **b** *Brit* **:** the building or barrack in which a main guard is lodged **3 :** the chief guard of an army from which all other guards are detached — not now used technically **4 :** a support of an outpost

main guy *n* **1** [2*main* + *guy* (rope)] **:** the principal guy rope of a circus tent **2** [2*main* + *guy* (person)] **:** CHIEF, LEADER

main hatch *n* **:** a ship's principal hatch usu. just forward of the mainmast

main·ite \'mā,nīt\ *n* -s *cap* [*Maine* state + E *-ite*] **:** MAINER

main·land \'mān,land, -aa(ə)nd, -,lənd\ *n* [ME *mayn land*, fr. *mayn* main + *land*] **:** a continuous body of land constituting the chief part of a country or continent

main·land·er \-də(r)\ *n* -s **:** a dweller on the mainland ⟨any ~ — Hawaii's term for a resident of continental United States — will find its stores . . . stocked with the latest mainland fashions —Jack Teehan⟩

main line *n* **1 :** a principal highway or railroad line or the chief artery of a branching system **2** *slang* **a :** a principal vein ⟨a shot of heroin in the *main line*⟩ **b :** the injection of a narcotic into a principal vein ⟨still cool and stepping dainty off my last *main line* —Herbert Gold⟩

main·line \'mān,līn\ *vi* [*main line*] *slang* **:** to inject a narcotic drug (as heroin) into a principal vein — **mainliner** \-līnə(r)\ *n* -s *slang*

mainly *adv* [ME *mainliche*, *maynly*, fr. *main*, *mayn*, adj., main + *-liche*, *-ly* -ly] **1** *obs* **:** in a strong or forceful manner **2 :** in the principal respect **:** for the most part **:** CHIEFLY **3** *now dial Eng* **:** very much **:** VERY, EXCEEDINGLY

main·mast \'mānmast *(usual nautical pronunc)*, -n,mast, -,maa(ə)st, -,mast\ *n* **:** a sailing ship's principal mast usu. second from the bow — see SHIP illustration

main·our \'mānə(r)\ *or* **man·ner** \'manə(r)\ *n* -s [ME *manor*, fr. AF *mainoure*, *meinoure*, fr. OF *manuevre*, *manœuvre* manual labor — more at MANEUVER] *Old Eng law* **:** something stolen found on the thief's person or in his immediate possession — **with the mainour** *or* **in the mainour** *adv (or adj)* **:** in the act **:** FLAGRANTE DELICTO, RED-HANDED

main·per·na·ble \'mānpə(r)nəbəl\ *adj* [ME, fr. AF *meinpernable*, fr. *mainprendre* + *-able*] **:** capable of being mainprised

main·per·nor \-pə(r)nə(r)\ *n* -s [ME *meinpernour*, fr. AF, fr. *mainprendre* (v.) + *-our* -or] **:** one who gives an undertaking of mainprise

1main·prise \'mān,prīz\ *n* -s [ME *meinprise*, fr. AF, fr. *mainprendre* to accept surety, fr. OF *main* hand (fr. L *manus*) + *prendre* (past part. *pris*) to take — more at MANUAL, PRIZE (act of capturing)] **:** an undertaking given to a magistrate or court that even without having an accused in custody one will be liable for the appearance of the accused on a fixed day to defend any and all charges to be brought against him — compare BAIL

2mainprise \"\ *vt* -ED/-ING/-S [ME *mainprisen*, *meinprisen*, fr. AF *meinprise*, n.] **:** to release or procure the release of on mainprise

main·pri·sor \-zə(r)\ *n* -s [ME *mainprisour*, fr. *mainprisen* (v.) + *-our* -or] **:** MAINPERNOR

1mains \'mānz\ *n pl but sing in constr* [short for *domains*, pl. of *domain*] *dial Brit* **:** the home farm of a manor

2mains \"\ *adj* [fr. *mains*, pl. of 1*main*] **:** of or relating to electric power mains ⟨~ voltage⟩ ⟨~ frequency⟩

main·sail \'mānsəl *(usual nautical pronunc)*, -n,sāl\ *n* [ME *mayne saile*, fr. *mayne*, *mayn* main + *saile*, *sail* sail] **:** the principal sail on the mainmast — compare MAIN COURSE; see SAIL illustration

main sequence *n* **:** the broad band of the spectrum-luminosity diagram which contains the great majority of stars and the sun and for which the absolute visual magnitudes range from about —3 for stars of spectral type B to 12 for stars of spectral type M

main shaft *n* **:** a principal drive shaft (as in a machine shop or in a motor vehicle) — distinguished from *countershaft*

mainsheet \'=,=\ *n* [ME *mayne shete*, fr. *mayne*, *mayn*, adj., main + *shete* sheet] **:** a rope by which the mainsail is trimmed and secured — see SHIP illustration

mainspring \'=,=\ *n* **1 :** the chief spring in a mechanism; *esp* **:** the coiled driving spring of a watch or clock **2 :** the chief or most powerful motive, agent, or cause ⟨the ~ was useful common sense —Van Wyck Brooks⟩

mainstay \'=,=\ *n* [ME *mayne stay*, fr. *mayne*, *mayn* main + *stay*] **1 :** a ship's stay extending from the maintop forward usu. to the foot of the foremast — see SHIP illustration **2 :** chief support **:** principal reliance ⟨she has been a ~ of several small luncheon clubs —Robert Rice⟩ ⟨cotton is the ~ of the surrounding country —*Amer. Guide Series: La.*⟩

main stem *n* **:** a main trunk or channel: as **a :** the main course of a river or stream ⟨apt to miss this offshoot to the left because the *main stem* to the creek went straight ahead through the trees —N.C.McDonald⟩ **b :** the main line of a railroad **c :** the main street of a city or town **d :** BIG TIME 2 ⟨much of his career has been off the musical *main stem* —*Time*⟩

mainstream \'=,=\ *n* **:** the prevailing current or direction of activity or influence ⟨the ~ of medieval learning in the universities passed by the alchemists —S.F.Mason⟩ ⟨within the ~ of the western democratic tradition —Max Beloff⟩

main street *adj, usu cap M&S* [2*main* + *street* (n.); influenced in meaning by *Main Street* (1920), novel by Sinclair Lewis †1951 Am. novelist and playwright that portrays materialistic provincialism as a characteristic of American life in a small town] **:** of or relating to the mediocre, materialistic, or drab aspects of average U.S. town and city life ⟨the popularity of the *Main Street* theme —*Nation*⟩

main street·er \-,strēd·ə(r)\ *n, usu cap M&S* **:** a representative of Main Street attitudes ⟨with millions of other native *Main Streeters* in the army, I used to wonder how it would be to get back on Main Street in my own little town —Dale Kramer⟩

maint \'mānt\ *adj* [F, fr. OProv *mant*, *maint*] *archaic* **:** MANY

maint *abbr* maintenance

main·tain \(')mān·'tān, mən-\ *vt* -ED/-ING/-S [ME *maintenen*, *maintenen*, fr. OF *maintenir*, fr. ML *manutenēre*, fr. L *manu tenēre* to know for certain, lit., to hold in the hand, fr. *manu* (abl. of *manus* hand) + *tenēre* to hold — more at MANUAL, THIN] **1 :** to keep in a state of repair, efficiency, or validity **:** preserve from failure or decline ⟨exercise . . . sufficient to ~ bodily and mental vigor —H.G.Armstrong⟩ **2 a :** to sustain against opposition or danger **:** back up **:** DEFEND, UPHOLD ⟨only fast ironclad cruisers could ~ the position of the Union against other naval powers —H.K.Beale⟩ **b :** to uphold in argument **:** contend for ⟨~*s* his logical position⟩ **3 :** to persevere in **:** carry on **:** keep up **:** CONTINUE ⟨members of the . . . tribe ~ native customs with ceremonial dances —*N.Y. Times*⟩ ⟨the husband could be certain of ~*ing* a certain standard of living —*Saturday Rev.*⟩ ⟨in addition to ~*ing* his news schedule he served as a fire warden —*Current Biog.*⟩ **4 :** to provide for **:** bear the expense of **:** SUPPORT ⟨the lady of beauty is ~*ed* as the pampered wife of a wealthy man —Lucy Crockett⟩ ⟨two homes, with 145 beds, are ~*ed* for the aged and indigent —*Americana Annual*⟩ **5 :** to affirm in or as if in argument **:** ASSERT, DECLARE ⟨~*ed* that this government was untrustworthy —*Collier's Yr. Bk.*⟩ ⟨was ~*ing* . . . that "modern society could hardly look worse" —*Saturday Rev.*⟩ **6 :** to assist (a party to legal action) so as to commit maintenance

syn ASSERT, DEFEND, VINDICATE, JUSTIFY: MAINTAIN indicates firm, convinced, persistent upholding of something as true, just, valid, or acceptable ⟨*maintain* that the whole educational scheme of our schools and colleges should be recast, and that a much larger portion of it should be devoted to modern languages and to history —R.B.Merriman⟩ ⟨stubbornly *maintained* his views in any argument even to insisting upon certain observations which subsequently were shown to be practically impossible —Witmer Stone⟩ ASSERT may indicate a setting forth of something as true, valid, or existent with or without aggressive determination to convince and to silence opposition ⟨that rigid sect which *asserts* that all real science is precise measurement —Havelock Ellis⟩ ⟨in Elizabethan drama, the critic is rash who will *assert* boldly that any play is by a single hand —T.S.Eliot⟩ ⟨what I content myself with *asserting* here you can scarcely deny —A.T.Quiller-Couch⟩ DEFEND may apply to a stating as true in the face of attack, objection, or disbelief, often as a calm apologist without the aggressiveness suggested by ASSERT ⟨*defended* his action by saying it was the best and quickest way —S.H.Holbrook⟩ ⟨called upon to *defend* his action against Russian charges that undesirable persons remained in office —*Current Biog.*⟩ VINDICATE suggests an adducing with force, cogency, logic, truth, or evidence that overwhelms doubt, hesitancy, denial, or opposition ⟨the aesthetic apologies by which artists and art critics *vindicate* artistic activity —Bernard Smith⟩ ⟨have all *vindicated* ourselves and received responsible positions —John Dos Passos⟩ JUSTIFY indicates an appeal to a standard of law or right or to an accepted rule or measure to show the truth, validity, or propriety of something ⟨*justified* the right of revolution not upon the ground of hostile acts of the people but upon usurpations of authority upon the part of those to whom such authority has been delegated —W.S.Myers⟩ ⟨*justified* his seizure of power on the grounds of an alleged conspiracy by the government to control the elections —*Americana Annual*⟩

main·tain·able \-tānəbəl\ *adj* [ME *mayntenable*, fr. *mayntenen*, *maintenen*, v. + *-able*] **:** capable of being maintained

maintained school *n* **:** a publicly supported elementary or secondary school in Great Britain

main·tain·er \-nə(r)\ *n* -s [alter. (influenced by E *-er*) of ME *mayntenour*, fr. AF, fr. *maintenir*, v. + *-our* -or] **1 :** one that maintains **2 :** MAINTAINOR

maintaining power *n* **:** a device supplying a driving force for maintaining a watch or clock in operation during winding

main·tain·or \mān-'tānə(r)\ *n* -s [ME *meyntenour*, fr. AF *meyntenour*, *maintenour* maintainer] **:** one guilty of maintenance

1main·te·nance \'mānt(ə)nən(t)s, -t'nən-\ *n* -s [ME *meyntenaunce*, *maintenaunce*, fr. MF *maintenance* act of maintaining, fr. OF, fr. *maintenir*, v. + *-ance*] **1** *obs* **:** BEARING, DEPORTMENT ⟨lustier ~ than I did look for —Shak.⟩ **2 a :** the act of providing means of support for someone ⟨the small man looked to his neighboring lord for a protection and ~ which the state could not give —W.C.Dickinson⟩ **b :** the provisions, supplies, or funds needed to live on **:** means of sustenance ⟨at least half of them are living parasitically on the other half instead of producing ~ for themselves —G.B.Shaw⟩ **3 a** [ME *meyntenaunce*, *mayntenaunce*, fr. AF *mayntenaunce*, fr. OF *maintenance* act of maintaining, protection] **:** an officious or unlawful intermeddling in a cause depending between others by assisting either party with money or means with which to carry it on — see CHAMPERTY **b :** the right of a seaman to food and quarters **4 :** the labor of keeping something (as buildings or equipment) in a state of repair or efficiency **:** CARE, UPKEEP ⟨the mere ~ of the fences . . . gives much to do —Richard Jefferies⟩ **5 a :** the upholding or defense of an attitude, opinion, or cause ⟨the ~ of this belief was not rational —Abram Kardiner⟩ **b :** the action of preserving or supporting (as a condition or institution) ⟨will facilitate the ~ of peace —C.L.Jones⟩ **syn** see LIVING

2maintenance \"\ *adj* **:** designed or adequate to maintain a living body in a stable condition without providing reserves for growth, functional change, or healing effect ⟨established the experimental animals on a ~ ration for calcium⟩ ⟨the patient may often be kept going indefinitely on a ~ ration of digitalis⟩

maintenance bond *n* **:** a contract of insurance against loss from lack of durability of construction work

maintenance man *n* **:** a worker who keeps buildings, shops, or equipment in good repair

maintenance of membership : a stipulation of some labor union contracts requiring persons who are members when the contract is adopted or who join during its life to pay dues until its expiration on penalty of discharge but not requiring nonmembers to join

maintenance of way : the upkeep and repair of a railroad's fixed property (as track and bridges)

main·top \'=,=\ *n* [ME *mayne toppe*, fr. *mayne*, *mayn*, adj., main + *toppe* top (platform)] **:** a platform about the head of the mainmast of a square-rigged ship — see SHIP illustration

main·top·man \'=,=mən\ *n, pl* **maintopmen :** a mariner assigned to duty on a ship's mainmast or maintop

main-topmast \mān·'täpməst *(usual nautical pronunc)*, -p,mast, -,maa(ə)st\ *n* [ME *mane toppe maste*, fr. *mane*, *mayn* main + *toppe maste* topmast] **:** a ship's mainmast spar between the mainmast itself and the main-topgallant mast — see SHIP illustration

main topsail schooner *n* **:** a schooner carrying a square foretopsail and topgallant sail

main track *n* **:** a track on which railroad trains travel from city to city — compare SIDING 3

main-truck \'=,=\ *n* [2*main* + *truck*] **:** the truck of a ship's mainmast

main wales *n* **:** two or more strakes of the thickest planking lying at the widest part of a wooden ship's hull and extending its entire length and supporting the main deck

main yard *n* [ME *mayne yerde*, fr. *mayne*, *mayn*, adj., main + *yerde* yard] **:** the yard on which a ship's mainsail is extended

mainz \'mīn(t)s\ *adj, usu cap* [fr. *Mainz*, Germany] **:** of or from the city of Mainz, Germany **:** of the kind or style prevalent in Mainz

mai·oi·dea \mā'ōidēə, mī'-\ [NL, fr. *Maia*, genus of crabs + *-oidea*] *syn of* OXYRHYNCHA

maiolica *var of* MAJOLICA

mai·pu·re \mī'pü(,)rā\ *n, pl* **maipure** *or* **maipures** *usu cap* [AmerSp *maipure*, *maipuru*, of AmerInd origin] **1 a :** an

Arawakan people of the upper Orinoco in Venezuela **b :** a member of such people **2 :** the language of the Maipure people
mair \ˈmār\ *chiefly Scot var of* MORE
ma·i·re \ˈmīē,rā\ *n* -s [Maori] **:** any of several New Zealand trees with dense heavy wood: as **a :** a New Zealand tree of the genus *Olea* — usu. used with a descriptive qualifier; compare BLACK MAIRE, WHITE MAIRE **b :** a small light-barked tree (*Eugenia maire*) with white flowers followed by red berries **c :** a small and often shrubby tree (*Mida myrtifolia*) that is related to the Asiatic sandalwood and has glossy glabrous usu. alternate leaves and small brownish green flowers in axillary clusters followed by small red drupes
mais *pl of* MAI
mai·son-dieu \ˌmā,zōⁿˈdyə̄\ *n, pl* **maisons-dieu** \ˈ"\ [ME *mesondieu, masondewe,* fr. MF *meson-Dieu, maison-Dieu,* fr. OF, fr. *maison* house + *Dieu* God (fr. L *deus* god) — more at DEITY] **:** HOSTEL, HOSPITAL
mai·so·nette *also* **mai·son·nette** \ˌmāzōˈnet\ *n* -s [F *maisonnette,* fr. OF, dim. of *maison* house, fr. L *mansion-, mansio* dwelling, habitation — more at MANSION] **1 :** a small house **2 :** an apartment often of two stories
maist \ˈmāst\ *dial Brit var of* MOST
mais·ter \ˈmāstə(r)\ *now dial var of* MASTER
maist·ly *dial var of* MOSTLY
maistry *obs var of* MASTERY
mai·thi·li \ˈmīd·əlē\ *n* -s *usu cap* **1 :** an Indic dialect of north Bihar **2 :** a cursive script derived from Devanagari
maî·tre d' \ˌmā·d·ə(r)ˈdē *also* -ā·trəˈdē\ *n, pl* **maître d's** [by shortening] **:** MAÎTRE D'HÔTEL
maî·tre d'armes \ˌmā·trəˈdärm, māt'd-\ *n, pl* **maîtres d'armes** [F, lit., master of arms] **:** a teacher of fencing
maî·tre d'hô·tel \ˌmā·trə(,)dōˈtel, ˌmāt(,)d-\ *n, pl* **maîtres d'hôtel** [F, lit., master of house, fr. MF *maistre d'ostel*] **1 a :** a head steward (as of a great house or a hotel) **:** MAJORDOMO **b :** HEADWAITER **2** *or* **maître d'hôtel butter :** a sauce of melted butter, chopped parsley, salt, pepper, and lemon juice
maize \ˈmāz\ *n* -s [Sp *maíz,* fr. Taino *mahiz, mays*] **1 :** INDIAN CORN **2** *or* **maize yellow :** a variable color averaging a light yellow that is redder and duller than jasmine or chrome lemon and redder and very slightly darker than popcorn **3 :** MILO
maize billbug *n* **:** a weevil (*Sphenophorus maidis*) sometimes destructive to corn
maizebird \ˈ-,-\ *n* **:** REDWING BLACKBIRD
maize dance *n* **:** an American Indian ritual dance in supplication or in thanksgiving for a successful maize harvest
maize mildew *n* **:** a downy mildew (*Sclerospora maydis*) attacking Indian corn
maize oil *n* **:** CORN OIL
maiz·er \ˈmāzə(r)\ *or* **maize thief** *n, pl* **maizers** *or* **maize thieves :** REDWING BLACKBIRD
maize smut *n* **:** BOIL SMUT
maj *abbr* **1** major **2** majority
¹ma·ja \ˈmä(,)hä\ *n* -s [Sp, fem. of *majo*] **:** a Spanish belle of the lower class — compare MAJO
²ma·ja \ˈmājə\ *n, cap* [NL, fr. L *maia,* a large crab, fr. Gk] **:** a nearly cosmopolitan genus of crabs that is the type of the family Majidae
ma·ja·gua *or* **ma·ha·gua** \məˈhägwə\ *n* -s [AmerSp (also, *demajagua, damajagua*), fr. Taino] **:** either of two malvaceous trees that are often considered variant forms of a single species: **a :** an irregularly spreading or shrubby tree (*Hibiscus tiliaceus*) that is widely distributed along tropical shores, yields a light tough wood used esp. for canoe outriggers and a fibrous bast used for cordage and caulking, and is often cultivated for ornament or for its useful products — called also *balibago, purau* **b :** an erect forest tree (*H. elatus*) of the West Indian uplands yielding a moderately dense timber with the heartwood variegated in purple, metallic blue, and olive that is in demand esp. for cabinetwork and gunstocks — called also *blue mahoe*
ma·jes·tic \məˈjestik, -tēk\ *also* **ma·jes·ti·cal** \-təkəl, -tēk-\ *adj* [*majesty* + *-ic* or *-ical*] **:** having, exhibiting, or marked by majesty or dominion **:** IMPERIAL, REGAL **syn** see GRAND
ma·jes·ti·cal·ly \-tək(ə)lē, -tēk-, -li\ *adv* **:** in a majestic manner
maj·es·ty \ˈmajəstē, -ti\ *n* -ES [ME *maieste, magestee,* fr. OF *majesté,* fr. LL *majestat-, majestas,* fr. L, sovereign power, dignity, authority, fr. a base akin to L *major* greater (compar. of *magnus* great) + *-tat-, -tas* -ty — more at MUCH] **1 a** *cap* **:** the sovereign greatness, authority, or dominion of God ⟨seated at the right hand of the throne of the *Majesty* in heaven —Heb 8:1 (RSV)⟩ **b :** sovereign power, authority, or dignity **:** kingly greatness ⟨the kingdom of truth is a threat to every historical ~ —Reinhold Niebuhr⟩ ⟨a tyrannous sun, whose ~ was almost insupportable, lorded it over the world —James Stephens⟩ **c :** the person of a sovereign ⟨and watching, one knew that ~ had passed⟩ **2** [ME *mageste,* fr. MF or ML; MF *majesté,* fr. ML *majestat-, majestas,* fr. L] — used with *your* in addressing reigning sovereigns and their consorts and with *his, her,* or *their* as a periphrastic designation of these ⟨he had pleaded with her ~ to let him study the art of war in the tented field —A.B.Feldman⟩ ⟨Your *Majesty*⟩ ⟨Their *Majesties* of England —Frank Yerby⟩ **3** [MF *maiesté,* fr. ML *majestat-, majestas*] **:** a representation in graphic or plastic art of God the Father, of Christ, of the Virgin, or of the three persons of the Trinity enthroned in glory **4 a :** royal dignity, bearing, or aspect **:** STATELINESS ⟨there is a ~ that surrounds a president in Soviet eyes —M.W.Straight⟩ **b :** august or commanding power, effect, or appearance **:** GRANDEUR ⟨the luminous band of the Milky Way that stretches in quiet ~ all around the sky —B.J.Bok⟩ ⟨stood up straight, in all the ~ of his giant stature —Liam O'Flaherty⟩ ⟨this link between mortals and forces shaping their lives was the mighty concern which gave a kind of ~ to . . . his plays —John Mason Brown⟩ **5 :** greatness or splendor of quality or character (at his best in sudden ~ of phrase —Virginia Woolf) ⟨nightingales disturbed the ~ of great nights —F.M.Ford⟩
¹majid \ˈmājəd, ˈmaj-\ *also* **mai·id** \ˈmā(y)əd, ˈmīəd\ *adj* [NL *Majidae* or *Maiidae*] **:** of or relating to the Majidae
²majid \"\ *also* **maiid** \"\ *n* -s **:** a crab of the family Majidae **:** a typical spider crab
maji·dae \ˈmājə,dē, ˈmaj-\ *n pl, cap* [NL, fr. *Maja,* type genus + *-idae*] **:** a large family of oxyrhynchan crabs that includes most of the spider crabs
maj·lis *also* **mej·lis** *or* **mej·les** *or* **mej·liss** \majˈlis, mej-, -les\ *n* -ES [Per *majlis* assembly, council, fr. Ar] **:** a council, assembly, or tribunal in No. Africa or southwestern Asia; *specif* **:** a house of parliament (as in Iran or Iraq) **:** PARLIAMENT
ma·jo \ˈmä(,)hō\ *n* -s [Sp] **:** a Spanish dandy of the lower class — compare MAJA
ma·jol·i·ca *also* **ma·iol·i·ca** \məˈjäləkə *sometimes* -ˈyäl-\ *n* -s [It *maiolica,* fr. ML *Majolica* Majorca, largest of the Balearic islands, Spain, where this ware was made, alter. of LL *Majorica*] **:** earthenware covered with an opaque tin glaze and decorated on the glaze before firing with color oxides; *esp* **:** early Italian ware of this type
majolica blue *n, often cap M* **1 :** a dark blue that is redder and duller than Flemish blue or Peking blue and less strong and very slightly greener than Japan blue **2** *of textiles* **:** a moderate blue that is greener and duller than average copen or Dresden blue and redder and duller than pompadour
majolica earth *n, often cap M* **:** INDIAN RED 2b
ma·joon \məˈjün\ *n* -s [Hindi *maʿjūn,* lit., kneaded, fr. Ar] **:** an East Indian narcotic confection that is made of hemp leaves, henbane, datura seeds, poppy seeds, honey, and ghee and that produces effects like those of hashish and opium — called also *bhang*
¹ma·jor \ˈmājə(r)\ *adj* [ME *majour,* fr. L *major* larger, greater, compar. of *magnus* large, great — more at MUCH] **1 :** greater in dignity, rank, importance, or interest **:** SUPERIOR ⟨regarded him as one of the ~ poets of his generation —Douglas Cleverdon⟩ ⟨the minor and ~ arts are flourishing —*Saturday Rev.*⟩ **2 :** greater in number, quantity, or extent **:** LARGER ⟨output of salt showed marked increases by all of the ~ . . . producing countries —*Americana Annual*⟩ ⟨the ~ part of this work was undertaken by him —H.W.H.Knott⟩ **3 :** of full legal age ⟨~ children⟩ **4 :** notable or conspicuous in effect or scope **:** CONSIDERABLE, PRINCIPAL — compare NEGLIGIBLE ⟨on a ~ military offensive —*Collier's Yr. Bk.*⟩ ⟨so that no single country produced any of the ~s weapons exclusively in its own territory —Denis Healey⟩ **5 :** involving grave risk **:** SERIOUS ⟨a ~ illness⟩ ⟨a ~ operative procedure⟩ **6 a :** of or relating to a subject of academic study chosen as a field of specialization **b :** of or relating to a secondary-school course requiring a maximum of classroom hours **7 a** *of a scale* **:** having half steps between the third and fourth and the seventh and eighth degrees **b** *of a key* **:** based (as in its harmonic relations) on such a scale — opposed to *minor;* used after the name of a keynote ⟨sonata in C *major*⟩ ⟨the F-*major* symphony⟩ **c** *of an interval* (1) **:** greater by a half step than minor **:** of a size equal to the distance between the keynote and a (specified) degree of the major scale — used of the second, third, sixth, and seventh — compare PERFECT (2) **:** greater by a comma — used of one whole step in an untempered scale compared with another ⟨C–D is a ~ step, greater than the minor step D–E⟩ — compare TEMPERAMENT **d** *of a mode in mensurable music* **:** having the large divided into longs
²major \"\ *n* -s [ML, fr. L, adj.] **1** *archaic* **:** MAJOR PREMISE **2 :** a person of full legal age **3 a :** one that is superior in rank, importance, station, or performance ⟨minor poets are legion; the ~s are few and far between⟩ **b :** one of the larger or more important members or units of a kind or group ⟨night baseball in the ~s is here to stay —John Drebinger⟩ ⟨much effort is made to "standardize" movies . . . the ~s possess a near monopoly —R.A.Brady⟩ **c :** MAJOR SUIT ⟨there is a laydown grand slam in either ~ —Florence Osborn⟩ **4** [prob. fr. F, fr. ML, magnate, chief] **:** an army, marine, or air-force officer ranking just below a lieutenant colonel and above a captain **5 :** a Salvation Army officer ranking above a senior captain and below a senior major **6 a :** a subject of academic study chosen as a field of specialization ⟨took English literature as his ~⟩ **b :** a student specializing in such a field ⟨he is a history ~⟩
³major \"\ *vi* -ED/-ING/-s **:** to pursue an academic major ⟨~*ing* in history at the university —John Dos Passos⟩
major air command *n* **:** any of the principal subdivisions of the U.S. Air Force that are directly responsible to air force headquarters — compare AIR COMMAND
ma·jo·ra·na \ˌmājəˈrānə\ *n, cap* [NL] **:** a genus of herbs (family Labiatae) that is sometimes included in the genus *Origanum* but is distinguished by having the flowers in verticels arranged in dense continuous spikes or heads
ma·jor·a·tion \ˌmājəˈrāshən\ *n* -s [ML *majoration-, majoratio,* fr. *majoratus* (past part. of *majorare* to increase, fr. L *major,* adj.) + L *-ion-, -io* -ion] **:** ENLARGEMENT, INCREASE
major axis *n* **:** the axis passing through the foci of an ellipse
major bass *n* **1 :** a 32-foot bourdon organ pipe **2 :** a 16-foot pedal open diapason organ pipe
¹ma·jor·can \məˈjȯrkən\ *adj, usu cap* [*Majorca* island, Spain + E *-an*] **1 :** of, relating to, or characteristic of the Balearic island of Majorca, Spain **2 :** of, relating to, or characteristic of the people of Majorca
²majorcan \"\ *n* -s *cap* **:** a native or inhabitant of Majorca
major canon *n* **:** a resident canon of a cathedral or collegiate church receiving a stipend — compare HONORARY CANON, MINOR CANON
major diameter *n* **:** the largest diameter of a screw thread measured at the crest of a male thread and at the root of a female thread
ma·jor-do·mo \ˌmājə(r)ˈdō(,)mō\ *n* -s [Sp *mayordomo* or obs. It *maiordomo,* fr. ML *major domus,* lit., chief of the house, fr. *major,* n. + L *domus,* gen. of *domus* house — more at TIMBER] **1 :** a man having charge of a great household (as a royal or princely establishment) **:** a head steward or palace official **2 :** BUTLER, STEWARD **3** *Southwest* **:** MAYORDOMO
major element *n* **:** MACRONUTRIENT
ma·jor·ette \ˌmājəˈret\ *n* -s [by shortening] **:** DRUM MAJORETTE
major excommunication *n, Roman Catholicism* **:** absolute exclusion of a person from the church and in extreme cases even from social intercourse with church members — distinguished from *minor excommunication*
major feria *n* **:** GREATER FERIA 1
major flute *n* **:** an open flute stop of large scale usu. of 8-foot pitch in a pipe organ
major form class *n* **:** any one of the parts of speech of traditional grammar (as noun, verb, or preposition)
major general *n* [prob. fr. F *major général,* fr. *major* (officer) + *général,* adj., general] **:** an army, marine, or air-force officer ranking just below a lieutenant general and above a brigadier general
¹ma·jor·i·tarian \məˌjȯrəˈta(a)rēən, -jär-, -ter-, -tär-\ *adj* [*majority* + *-arian* (as in *humanitarian*)] **:** of, characterized by, or believing in majoritarianism ⟨~ politics⟩ ⟨~ principle⟩ ⟨~ party system⟩
²majoritarian \"\ *n* -s **:** one that believes in or advocates majoritarianism ⟨a ~ . . . holds the many more likely to be in possession of reason and truth than the few —*Va. Quarterly Rev.*⟩
ma·jor·i·tar·i·an·ism \-ēə,nizəm\ *n* -s **:** the philosophy or practice according to which the decisions of an organized group should be made by a numerical majority of its members ⟨combine ~ with philosophies that are essentially aristocratic —J.R.Pennock⟩ ⟨an unchecked ~ can sweep a dictator to power during a transient mob hysteria —Peter Viereck⟩
ma·jor·i·ty \məˈjȯrəd·ē, -jär-, -ətē, -i\ *n* -ES [MF *majorité,* fr. ML *majoritat-, majoritas,* fr. L *major,* adj. + *-itat-, -itas* -ity] **1** *obs* **:** the quality or state of being greater **:** SUPERIORITY ⟨whose . . . great name in arms holds from all soldiers chief ~ and military title capital —Shak.⟩ **2 :** the status of being of full legal age ⟨graduated . . . before he had attained his ~ —W.L.Burrage⟩ **3 a :** a number greater than half of a total ⟨the ~ of the human race is still today on the sidelines, watching and wondering —A.J.Toynbee⟩ — distinguished from *plurality* **b :** the excess of such a greater number over the remainder of the total **:** EDGE, MARGIN ⟨resulted in giving him a ~ of 98 out of a total of 504 votes cast —Joseph Schafer⟩ **c :** the preponderant quantity or share ⟨the ~ of the wool used in the U. S. is imported —F.J.Soday⟩ **4 :** all dead persons ⟨the end comes: he joins the ~ —W.H.Auden⟩ **5 :** the group or party whose votes preponderate **6** [prob. fr. F *majorité,* fr. *major* (officer) + *-ité* -ity] **:** the military office, rank, or commission of a major ⟨*majorities* and colonelcies were thick as June blackberries —Dixon Wecter⟩
²majority \"\ *adj* **:** of, relating to, or constituting a majority ⟨each committee is therefore composed of ~ and minority members —F.A.Ogg & P.O.Ray⟩
majority leader *n* **:** the leader of the majority party in a legislative body ⟨appointment as *majority leader* of the Senate⟩ — compare MINORITY LEADER
majority rule *n* **:** a political principle providing that a majority usu. constituted by fifty percent plus one of the members of a politically organized group shall have the power to make decisions binding upon the whole group ⟨democratic doctrines of political equality and *majority rule* —C.V.Shields⟩
ma·jor·ize \ˈmājə,rīz\ *vi* -ED/-ING/-s *rugby* **:** to convert a try
major key *n* **:** a musical key or tonality in the major mode
major league *n* **1 a :** a league of highest classification in U.S. professional baseball **b :** a league of major importance in any of various other sports (as basketball or ice hockey) **2 :** BIG LEAGUE 2 ⟨a petty blackmailer going up to the *major leagues* —Gordon & Mildred Gordon⟩
major mitch·ell \ˌ-ˈmichəl\ *n, usu cap both Ms* [after *Major* Sir Thomas *Mitchell* †1855 Brit. explorer in Australia] *Austral* **:** PINK COCKATOO
major order *n* **1 :** any of three orders in the Roman Catholic Church: **a :** PRIESTHOOD **b :** DIACONATE **c :** SUBDIACONATE — compare MINOR ORDER **2 :** any of three orders in the Eastern Church or the Anglican Church: **a :** EPISCOPATE **b :** PRIESTHOOD **c :** DIACONATE
major party *n* **:** a political party whose electoral strength is sufficiently great to permit it to win control of a government usu. with comparative regularity and when defeated to constitute the principal opposition to the party in power ⟨caused splinter parties to form from both of the *major parties* —D.D. McKean⟩ — compare MINOR PARTY, THIRD PARTY
major penalty *n* **:** a five-minute suspension of a player in ice hockey with no substitute allowed — compare MINOR PENALTY
major piece *n* **:** a queen or rook in chess — compare MINOR PIECE
major planet *n* **:** any of the four largest planets of the solar system ⟨Jupiter, Saturn, Uranus, and Neptune are the *major planets*⟩ — compare ASTEROID, TERRESTRIAL PLANET
major premise *n* **:** the premise of a syllogism containing the major term
major prophet *n* **:** the author of one of the three chief prophetic books of the Old Testament ⟨Ezekiel, Isaiah, and Jeremiah are usually ranked as the *major prophets* of the Hebrews⟩
major seminary *n* **:** SEMINARY 2b(2)
major seventh chord *n* **:** a chord consisting of a major triad and a major seventh — see SEVENTH CHORD illustration
ma·jor·ship \ˈmājə(r),ship\ *n* -s [²*major* + *-ship*] *archaic* **:** ¹MAJORITY 6
major suit *n* **:** either of two bridge suits of superior scoring value: **a :** SPADES **b :** HEARTS — compare MINOR SUIT
major surgery *n* **:** surgery involving a risk to the life of the patient; *specif* **:** an operation upon an organ within the cranium, chest, abdomen, or pelvic cavity — compare MINOR SURGERY
major tenace *n* **:** ace and queen of a suit held in one hand in some card games (as bridge) — compare MINOR TENACE
major term *n* **:** the term of a syllogism constituting the predicate of the conclusion
major triad *n* **1 :** a musical triad whose frequencies are in the proportions 4:5:6 **2 :** a musical triad consisting of a fundamental tone with its major third and perfect fifth — see TRIAD illustration
ma·jus·cu·lar \məˈjəskyələ(r)\ *adj* **:** of, relating to, or resembling a majuscule
¹majus·cule \ˈmajə,skyül, məˈjə-\ *adj* [F, fr. L *majusculus* rather large, fr. *majus-,* stem of *major* larger, greater — more at MAJOR (adj.)] **:** written in or in the size or style of majuscules ⟨~ script⟩
²majuscule \"\ *n* -s [F, n. & adj.] **:** a large letter (as a capital or uncial) — compare MINUSCULE
ma·jus la·ti·um \ˌmä(,)yüsˈlād·ē,üm\ *n, usu cap L* [L, lit., greater Latium, fr. *majus* greater (neut. of *major*) + *Latium,* ancient country of Italy] **:** the right of Roman citizenship granted to the holder of a magistracy in a territorial unit outside Rome and to his wife, children, and parents — compare JUS LATII, MINUS LATIUM
mak \ˈmak\ *Scot var of* MAKE
makaasim *var of* MACAASIM
mak·able \ˈmākəbəl\ *adj* **:** capable of being made ⟨~ contract in bridge⟩
ma·kah \ˈmä(,)kä\ *n, pl* **makah** *or* **makahs** *usu cap* **1 a :** an Indian people forming a subdivision of the Nootka **b :** a member of such people **2 :** the dialect of the Makah people
ma·ka·hi·ki \ˌmäkəˈhēkē\ *n* -s [Hawaiian] **:** a period of several months which was celebrated each fall in ancient Hawaii with athletic contests, religious rites, and payment of tribute to chiefs and during which all warfare was tabooed
ma·kai \məˈkī\ *adv (or adj)* [Hawaiian, fr. *ma* toward + *kai* sea] *Hawaii* **:** toward the sea **:** SEAWARD
ma·kai·ra \məˈkīrə\ *n, cap* [NL, perh. fr. Gk, fem. of *makar* blessed] **:** a genus of large active marine fishes (family Istiophoridae) comprising the marlins
mak·ar \ˈmakər\ *n* -s [ME *maker,* maker, poet — more at MAKER] *chiefly Scot* **:** POET
ma·ka·ra \ˈməkərə\ *n* -s [Skt] **:** a water monster of Hindu religious myth that is represented in religious art as having the body of a crocodile and head of an antelope and as being the steed of Varuna and the emblem of Kamadeva
ma·kas·sar *or* **ma·cas·sar** \məˈkasə(r), -aas-\ *n, pl* **makassar** *or* **makassars** *or* **macassar** *or* **macassars** *usu cap* [fr. *Makassar* (*Macassar*), city on southwestern Celebes island, and strait between Celebes and Borneo, Indonesia] **1 :** MAKASSARESE **2 :** the Austronesian language of the Makassarese people
ma·kas·sar·ese *also* **ma·cas·sar·ese** \məˌkasəˈrēz, -aas-, -ēs\ *n, pl* **makassarese** *also* **macassarese** *usu cap* [*Makassar* (*Macassar*), city and strait, + E *-ese*] **1 :** an Indonesian people living in and around the port of Makassar in the southwestern part of Celebes **2 :** a member of the Makassarese people
ma·ka·tea \ˌmäkəˈtāə\ *n* -s [Tuamotu] **:** a broad uplifted coral reef surrounding an island in the south Pacific
¹make \ˈmāk\ *vb* **made** \ˈmād\ **made; making; makes** [ME *maken,* fr. OE *macian;* akin to OFris *makia* to build, make, MD *maken* to make, do, OHG *mahhōn* to join, prepare, do, make, MIr *maistrid* he butters, W *maeddu* to conquer, Gk *magēnai* to be kneaded, OSlav *mazati* to anoint; basic meaning: to knead, press] *vt* **1 a** *obs* **:** BEHAVE, ACT — used with *it* and an adverb or adjective complement **b :** to seem to begin (an action) **:** BEGIN ⟨*made* to go⟩ **2 a** *archaic* **:** to bring about — used with *that* **b :** to cause to happen to or be experienced by someone ⟨~ us some sport⟩ ⟨~ trouble for him⟩ **c :** to cause to exist, occur, or appear **:** bring to pass **:** CREATE, CAUSE ⟨God *made* heaven and earth⟩ ⟨~ a disturbance⟩ ⟨his entrance *made* a sensation⟩ ⟨*making* a fuss over nothing⟩ ⟨~ mischief⟩ **d :** to give rise to **:** favor the growth or occurrence of ⟨good fences ~ good neighbors —Robert Frost⟩ ⟨lending money is a good way to ~ enemies⟩ ⟨haste ~s waste⟩ **e :** to fit, intend, or destine by or as if by creating ⟨laws were *made* for men, not men for laws⟩ ⟨ham and eggs were *made* for each other⟩ ⟨was never *made* to be an actor⟩ **f** *chiefly South & Midland* **:** to plant and raise (a crop) ⟨*made* a crop of oats⟩ **3** *obs* **:** to give birth to **4 a :** to bring (a material thing) into being by forming, shaping, or altering material **:** FASHION, MANUFACTURE ⟨~ a gun⟩ ⟨~ a suit of clothes⟩ ⟨~ a toy⟩ ⟨~ bricks without straw⟩ ⟨~ a railing out of water pipes⟩ **b :** COMPOSE, WRITE ⟨~ verses⟩ ⟨~ a sonnet⟩ ⟨~ an epigram⟩ **c :** to lay out and construct ⟨~ a road⟩ ⟨~ a park⟩ **5 :** to frame or formulate in the mind **:** form as a result of calculation or design ⟨~ plans for vacation⟩ ⟨~ a diagram⟩ **6 :** to put together from components or ingredients **:** CONSTITUTE ⟨~ bread with whole wheat flour⟩ ⟨house *made* of stone⟩ ⟨a chance to show the stuff he is *made* of⟩ **7 a :** to compute or estimate to be **:** find by calculation to be ⟨I ~ it 23 miles to the border from here⟩ **b :** to form and hold in the mind ⟨~ no doubt that he is guilty⟩ ⟨*made* no scruple of joining the enterprise⟩ **8 a :** to lay and set alight (a fire) **b :** to set in order ⟨~ beds⟩ **:** FIX, PREPARE ⟨~ coffee⟩ ⟨~ dinner⟩ ⟨~ camp⟩ **c :** to shuffle (a deck of cards) in preparation for the next deal **9 a** *dial* **:** to cure (as fish) by smoking or drying **b :** to cause (hay) to be cut and cured **10 a :** to cause to be or become **:** put in a certain state or condition ⟨trying to ~ the matter clear to everyone⟩ ⟨was *made* leader of the expedition⟩ ⟨*made* him sorry he had spoken so quickly⟩ ⟨*made* the scene real for us⟩ ⟨*made* himself useful around the place⟩ **b :** APPOINT, ORDAIN ⟨*made* him bishop⟩ ⟨*made* him a member of his cabinet⟩ **11 a :** ENACT, ESTABLISH ⟨~ laws⟩ ⟨~ a rule⟩ **b :** to execute in an appropriate manner **:** draw up ⟨~ a will⟩ ⟨~ a deed of transfer⟩ **c :** SET, NAME ⟨~ a price for the lot⟩ ⟨~ spades trumps⟩ **d :** to cause (an occurrence in time or the hour of the day) to be announced, indicated, or observed ⟨~ eight o'clock by striking eight bells⟩ ⟨~ sunset by hauling down the colors with ceremonies⟩ **12** *chiefly Brit* **:** to train to a requisite standard of efficiency ⟨~ a horse⟩ ⟨~ a falcon⟩ **13 a** *now dial* **:** to make fast **:** SHUT, BAR ⟨at this time the doors are *made* against you —Shak.⟩ **b :** to take possession of (a point) in backgammon by occupying with two or more men **c** (1) **:** to cause (an electric circuit) to be completed or closed (2) **:** to bring about (a contact) **d** (1) **:** to convert (a split) into a spare in bowling ⟨*made* the 3-10 split⟩ (2) **:** to score (a spare) by means of a split in bowling ⟨~ a spare by getting the 3-10 split⟩ **14** *obs* **a :** BRING ⟨have they *made* you to this —Ben Jonson⟩ **b :** PUT ⟨dangerous to ~ them hence —Ben Jonson⟩ **15 a :** to conclude as to the nature or meaning of something ⟨hardly knew what to ~ of his actions⟩ **b :** to regard as being **:** think to be ⟨not the fool some ~ him⟩ **16 a :** to carry out (an action indicated or implied by the object) **:** PERFORM ⟨~ war⟩ ⟨time to ~ a move⟩ ⟨~ an incision⟩ ⟨~ a promise⟩ ⟨~ amends⟩ ⟨~ a speech⟩ ⟨~ music⟩ ⟨~ apologies⟩ ⟨*made* a crackling noise⟩ ⟨*made* plans to go away⟩ ⟨~ preparations for the trip⟩ ⟨~ a bid⟩ **b :** to perform with a bodily movement ⟨~ a bow⟩ ⟨~ a jump⟩ ⟨~ a sweeping gesture⟩ **c :** to achieve by traversing **:** TRAVERSE ⟨~ a long detour⟩ ⟨mailman *making* his rounds⟩ **17 a :** to produce as a result of action, effort, or behavior with respect to something ⟨~ a mess of the job⟩ ⟨managed to ~ a joke of his losses⟩

⟨must be *made* an example of⟩ ⟨*made* a practice of getting up early⟩ — often used with *of it* ⟨tried to ~ a thorough job of it⟩ ⟨decided to ~ a night of it⟩ **b :** EAT ⟨*made* a good breakfast⟩ ⟨*made* a hasty lunch of soup and a sandwich⟩ **c** (1) *archaic* **:** to turn into another language by translation ⟨*making* these two authors English —John Dryden⟩ (2) *obs* **:** INTERPRET **18 :** to cause to act in a certain way **:** COMPEL — used with infinitive without *to* ⟨*made* him return the money⟩ but with *to* in passive constr. ⟨*made* to see the error of his ways⟩ **19 :** to cause or assure the success or prosperity of ⟨the night that either ~*s* me or fordoes me quite —Shak.⟩ ⟨anyone he takes a liking to is *made*⟩ **20 a :** to amount to in significance ⟨~*s* a great difference⟩ ⟨~*s* no matter⟩ ⟨doesn't ~ good sense⟩ **b :** to form the essential being of **:** be sufficient to constitute ⟨clothes ~ the man⟩ ⟨stone walls do not a prison ~ —Richard Lovelace⟩ **c :** to form by an assembling of individuals ⟨~ a quorum⟩ ⟨two more ~*s* an even dozen⟩ **:** EQUAL ⟨twice two ~*s* four⟩ ⟨two nickels ~ a dime⟩ **d :** to count as ⟨~ a fourth at bridge⟩ ⟨that ~*s* the third time he has failed⟩ **21 a :** to be or be capable of being changed or fashioned into ⟨rags ~ the best paper⟩ ⟨oak ~*s* good flooring⟩ **b :** to develop into **:** be or become useful as **:** serve as ⟨she will ~ a fine wife⟩ ⟨worried men ~ poor soldiers⟩ ⟨a collie ~*s* a good watchdog⟩ ⟨rabbit ~*s* a good stew⟩ ⟨*made* a very good witness⟩ **c :** FORM 6b **22 a :** REACH, ATTAIN, ACHIEVE ⟨tried to ~ the airfield with one motor failing⟩ ⟨*made* an average of 200 miles a day⟩ ⟨can ~ 80 miles per hour⟩ ⟨a story that *made* the front page⟩ ⟨~ a home run⟩ — often used with *it* ⟨you will never ~ it to the other shore in this weather⟩ **b :** to gain the rank of ⟨*made* corporal after a few months⟩ **c :** to gain a place on ⟨*made* the varsity soccer team⟩ **23 :** to gain (as money) by working, trading, or dealing ⟨~ a living⟩ ⟨~ a profit⟩ ⟨*made* his fortune in railroads⟩ **24 a :** to act so as to win or acquire ⟨~ acquaintances in his new job⟩ ⟨~*s* friends easily⟩ **b** *dial* **:** STEAL **c :** to score (points) in a game or sport **25 a :** to fulfill (a contract) in a card game **:** win (a specified number of points, tricks) at cards ⟨~ two spades⟩ **b :** to win a trick with (a card) **26 a :** to get sight of **:** make out ⟨*made* an enemy cruiser coming on astern⟩ **b :** to visit in the course of a journey **:** include in a route or itinerary ⟨intended to ~ Paris on the way to Vienna⟩ **c :** CATCH ⟨in time to ~ the morning train⟩ **d** *slang* **:** RECOGNIZE, IDENTIFY ⟨afraid the cops would ~ him from his fingerprints⟩ **27 a :** to persuade to consent to sexual intercourse **:** SEDUCE 3 ⟨nine to one he would ~ her on the first try —Mary McCarthy⟩ **b :** to copulate with **:** LAY 1c **~** *vi* **1** *archaic* **:** to compose poetry **2 a :** BEHAVE, ACT ⟨*made* as though he were angry⟩ ⟨don't ~ as if you didn't hear me⟩ **b :** to begin or seem to begin a certain action ⟨*made* as though to hand it to me⟩ ⟨he *made* as though he would have gone further —Lk 24:28 (AV)⟩ **c :** to act so as to be or to seem to be — used with adj. complement ⟨~ merry⟩ ⟨*made* fast to the dock⟩ ⟨*made* ready to depart⟩ **d** *slang* **:** to play a part **:** do an imitation ⟨~ like a bird⟩ ⟨~ like a detective⟩ **3 :** to set out **:** PROCEED, HEAD ⟨last seen *making* for the river⟩ ⟨*made* after the fox⟩ **4 :** to increase in height or size ⟨the tide is *making* now⟩ ⟨water was *making* fast in forward bilges⟩ ⟨light was *making* in the east⟩ **5** *now dial* **:** to concern or busy oneself **:** INTERFERE — used in the phrase *to meddle or make* ⟨I'll neither meddle nor *make* with them further —Charlotte Brontë⟩ **6 :** to reach or extend in a certain direction ⟨the forest ~*s* up nearly to the snow line⟩ **7 :** to have weight or effect **:** TELL ⟨courtesy ~*s* for safer driving⟩ ⟨ignored evidence that *made* against his theory⟩ **8 :** to undergo manufacture or processing ⟨bolts are *making* in this shop⟩ ⟨hay ~*s* better in small heaps⟩ **9** *of ore in a mine* **:** APPEAR, OCCUR ⟨the ore ~*s* at the intersection of a vein by a cross fissure⟩

syn MAKE, FORM, SHAPE, FASHION, FABRICATE, MANUFACTURE, and FORGE can mean in common to cause something to come into being. MAKE can comprise any such action whether by an intelligent or blind agency and resulting in either material or immaterial existence ⟨*make* a boat⟩ ⟨*make* a treaty⟩ ⟨*make* a choice⟩ ⟨*make* friends⟩ ⟨*make* an impression⟩ FORM suggests a definite outline, structure, or plan ⟨*form* a figure out of clay⟩ ⟨*form* a plan⟩ ⟨*form* a league of states⟩ ⟨*form* character by training⟩ SHAPE suggests an outside agency impressing a particular form upon something ⟨a blacksmith *shapes* horseshoes out of metal⟩ ⟨*shape* a boat out of a block of wood⟩ ⟨*shape* a shoe on a last⟩ ⟨*shape* a good career out of a few talents⟩ FASHION suggests both an intelligent agency and a certain inventive power or ingenuity ⟨*fashion* a cabinet out of orange crates⟩ ⟨*fashion* a work of art out of odds and ends of scrap wood, paint, and pieces of metal⟩ FABRICATE stresses a uniting of parts or materials in a whole, often according to a standardized pattern, often with skill in construction, and in figurative extension often suggesting the imaginative constructing of a falsehood ⟨*fabricate* doors and windows for a series of identical houses⟩ ⟨*fabricate* a temporary scaffolding out of tree branches to buttress a wall⟩ ⟨*fabricate* a cock-and-bull story for the press⟩ MANUFACTURE stresses the making of something by labor, usu. by machinery, now applying to any making using raw materials and a fixed process, often extending to connote laborious, mechanical construction as opposed to skillful creation ⟨*manufacture* a pair of shoes⟩ ⟨*manufacture* airplane parts⟩ ⟨*manufacture* standard plots for a series of cheap novels⟩ FORGE still can suggest the smithy or the making of something by sudden strong uniting of elements under intense heat ⟨*forge* a chain⟩ ⟨*forged* a novel out of his own intense suffering⟩ More often, however, it implies a devising with a certain effort to give the appearance of truth or reality, extending in this use to comprise counterfeiting of documents in handwriting ⟨*forge* a lie to avoid punishment⟩ ⟨*forge* a signature on a check⟩

— **make a bag** *of a pregnant animal* **:** to undergo enlargement of the udder prior to parturition — **make a clean breast :** to make a full disclosure or confession ⟨decided to *make a clean breast* of his part in the affair⟩ — **make a dent in :** to produce an inconsiderable effect upon ⟨his gambling losses hardly *made a dent in* his huge fortune⟩ ⟨unable even to *make a dent in* his complacency⟩ — **make a face :** to express or betray a feeling (as of disgust, chagrin) or an attitude (as of defiance, derision) by distorting one's features **:** GRIMACE — **make a leg :** to bow and scrape — **make a long arm :** to extend the arm **:** reach out **:** exert oneself — **make a long nose :** to thumb one's nose — **make a market :** to stand ready to buy or sell (a security) within a set price range so that dealing may proceed without undue price fluctuations — **make a mouth :** to accustom a colt to the bit — **make a play for :** to attempt to capture ⟨*make a play for* the tourist trade with performances of native dances —*Time*⟩ — **make away with 1 :** to carry off **2 :** SPEND, DISSIPATE **3 :** DESTROY, KILL **4 :** CONSUME, EAT ⟨*made away with* the whole pie⟩ — **make believe :** PRETEND, FEIGN — **make bold :** VENTURE, DARE ⟨*made bold* to predict a successful trip to outer space⟩ — **make bones :** to show hesitation, uncertainty, or scruple ⟨*makes no bones* about his dislike of his in-laws⟩ ⟨how silly to *make bones* of trifles —Virginia Woolf⟩ — **make book 1 :** to accept bets at calculated odds on all the entrants in a race or contest **:** lay odds **2 :** to make a business of accepting bets — **make default :** to fail in a legal obligation (as appearing and answering in a legal proceeding or at a trial) — **make do :** to get along or manage with the means at hand however inadequate or unsatisfactory ⟨must still *make do* with temporary expedients —Walter Moberly⟩ — **make ends meet :** to live within one's income — **make even :** to typeset (a piece of copy) so that the last word ends a full line **:** to reach a point in correcting set type where the reset matter either ends a paragraph or ends a line with a word that ended a line in the old setting — **make foul water :** to sail in such shallow water that the ship's keel stirs the mud at the bottom — **make free 1 :** to adopt an unduly intimate or familiar manner ⟨if he *makes free* stop him⟩ **2 :** to help oneself without restraint ⟨my roommate *makes free* with my neckties⟩ — **make fun of :** to make an object of amusement or laughter **:** RIDICULE, MOCK — **make game** *of a hunting dog* **:** to sniff about eagerly at the scent of game — **make good :** to make valid or complete ⟨*made good* his escape⟩: as **a :** to make up or compensate for (a deficiency) ⟨*make good* previous neglect of his child⟩ **b :** INDEMNIFY ⟨the insurance company *made good* the loss⟩ **c :** to carry out (a promise or prediction) **:** FULFILL **d :** PROVE, VERIFY ⟨*make good* a charge⟩ **e :** to prove to be capable and efficient ⟨*made good* in his first job⟩ **:** justify by success a course of action or an expectation **:** SUCCEED ⟨the play *made good* at the box office⟩ — **make haste :** HASTEN, HURRY ⟨members of the committee *make haste* to tell her how glad they are —Agnes M. Miall⟩ — **make hay :** to make use of offered opportunity esp. in gaining an early advantage — **make hay of :** to throw into disorder **:** DEMOLISH, OVERTHROW ⟨new evidence *makes hay of* the accepted theory⟩ — **make head 1 :** to make progress esp. against resistance **2 :** to rise in armed revolt **3 :** to build up pressure (as in a steam boiler) — **make heavy weather :** to experience difficulty in making progress **:** FLOUNDER, LABOR ⟨*made heavy weather* with his algebra⟩ — **make hole :** to drill an oil well — **make light of :** to treat as of little account — **make love 1 :** WOO, COURT **2 a :** NECK, PET **b :** to engage in sexual intercourse — **make much of 1 :** to treat as of importance **:** EXPLOIT **2 :** to treat with obvious affection or special consideration **:** fuss over **:** FLATTER, PET — **make of** *or* **make over** *dial* **:** to praise lavishly **:** show much affection for ⟨I like to be *made of*⟩ ⟨paused to *make over* the baby⟩ ⟨felt loved and *made over*⟩ — **make one's law** *Old Eng law* **:** to adduce the sworn statements of compurgators to clear oneself of a charge — **make one's mark :** to achieve success or fame ⟨*made his mark* as a literary critic —Eric Partridge⟩ — **make one's number :** to signal the number by which the ship is designated on a register — **make one's peace :** to reconcile oneself **:** come to terms ⟨*making his peace* with his mother and promising to fight no more —William Du Bois⟩ ⟨the worker . . . fulfills himself by *making his peace* with the system —W.N. Whyte⟩ — **make one's way :** ADVANCE; *specif* **:** to gain standing in a trade, profession, or other means of livelihood ⟨world in which these youngsters have to live and *make their way* —Robert Reid⟩ — **make places** *of two bells* **:** to make a particular shift of position in successive changes in change ringing so as to allow a third bell to be struck successively before, between, and after them — **make play with 1 :** use vigorously or effectively ⟨*making play with* political issues in comedy⟩ **2 :** to act brilliantly or showily in using **:** make an effect with ⟨*makes* great *play with* fashionable critical terms⟩ — **make public :** DISCLOSE — **make ready :** to prepare and adjust the form and press for printing — **make sail 1 a :** to raise or spread sail **b :** to set additional sail **2 :** to set out on a voyage — **make shift :** to try to get along or succeed under difficulties or with inferior means — **make something of :** to start a fight or a quarrel over **:** show resentment concerning **:** CHALLENGE ⟨I said you cheated — do you want to *make something of* it⟩ — **make strange** *now dial* **:** to act in an unfriendly or surprised manner ⟨*make strange* of a request⟩ — **make sure 1** *obs* **:** BETROTH **2 :** to reach or attain certainty ⟨telephoned to *make sure* of the time⟩ **3 :** to expect strongly **:** be certain or convinced ⟨we *made sure* you were not coming today⟩ — **make the best of 1 :** to use or dispose of to the best advantage ⟨could never *make the best of* his opportunities⟩ **2 :** to regard or treat (something unsatisfactory or unfavorable) as favorably as possible ⟨*make the best of* a bad bargain⟩ — **make the blood boil :** to arouse anger or indignation — **make the fur fly 1 :** to take part in a cat-and-dog fight **2 :** to cause a lively disturbance **3 :** to hustle about in doing a temporary job (as cleaning a room) — **make the grade 1** *of a person* **:** to make good **:** SUCCEED **2** *of a thing* **:** to come up to some standard **:** win acceptance — **make the most of :** to show or use to the best advantage ⟨wanted to *make the most of* his first vacation in three years⟩ — **make time 1 :** to travel at a certain rate of speed ⟨*make* fast *time*⟩ **2 :** to go quickly ⟨have to *make time* to get to the bank before it closes⟩ — **make tracks 1 :** to proceed at a walk or run **2 :** to go in a hurry **:** run away **:** FLEE — **make use of :** to put to use **:** USE, EMPLOY — **make water 1** *of a boat* **:** LEAK **2 :** URINATE — **make way 1 :** to open or give room for passing or entering **:** yield passage **:** fall back or move aside **2 :** to make progress — **make weight** *of a boxer* **:** to lose sufficient weight to remain eligible for a specified weight division — **make with** *slang* **:** PRODUCE, PERFORM — usu. used with *the* and in place of the idiomatic or normal verb ⟨start *making with* the answers⟩ ⟨let's not *make with* the jokes⟩ ⟨*making with* the tears⟩ ⟨*make with* the boyish charm⟩

²**make** \"\ *n* -s [ME *mak, maken,* fr. *maken,* v.] **1 a :** the manner or style in which a thing is composed or constructed ⟨needed a tool of a heavier ~⟩; *esp* **:** the quality or perfection of cutting of a gem **b :** the origin of a manufactured article ⟨an automobile of a well-known ~⟩ **2 :** the physical, mental, or moral constitution of a person ⟨had the look and ~ of a prizefighter⟩ ⟨men of his ~ are rare⟩ **3 a :** the act of producing or manufacturing ⟨the ~ cycle in the production of a fuel gas⟩ **b :** the actual yield or amount produced (as by an oil well or a mine) over a specified period **:** OUTPUT **4 :** the declaration of trumps in the game of bridge-whist **5 :** the closing or completing of an electric circuit **6 :** act of shuffling; *also* **:** turn to shuffle ⟨it's your ~ while your partner deals⟩ **7** *slang* **:** a military promotion or appointment ⟨list of ~*s*⟩ — **on the make** *adv (or adj)* **1 :** in the process of forming, growing, or improving **2 :** in quest of a higher social or financial status **:** in an aggressively and alertly opportunistic frame of mind **3 :** in search of sexual adventure

³**make** \"\ *n* -s [ME *make, mak,* fr. OE *gemaca* — more at MATCH] **1** *now dial Brit* **:** EQUAL, MATCH **2** *now dial Brit* **:** one who is a companion or mate; *esp* **:** SPOUSE

⁴**make** \"\ *n* -s [origin unknown] *dial Brit* **:** HALFPENNY

make and mend *n, Brit* **:** a period (as an afternoon) given the hands on a ship for work on their clothing or as a period of leisure without set duties **:** HALF-HOLIDAY ⟨*make and mends* were granted in celebration of the royal birthday⟩

make·bate \ˈmāk,bāt\ *n* -s [¹*make* + obs. *bate* strife, discord, fr. ME, fr. *baten* to contend, argue, beat the wings — more at BATE] *archaic* **:** one that excites contentions and quarrels

¹**make-believe** *also* **make-belief** \ˈ=(,)=\ *n* -s **1 :** a pretending to believe (as in the play of children) **:** a mere pretense **:** FICTION ⟨*make-believe* of the theater⟩ **2 :** one who makes believe **:** PRETENDER

²**make-believe** \"\ *adj* [fr. the phrase *make believe*] **:** FEIGNED ⟨lived in a private *make-believe* world⟩ **:** INSINCERE ⟨*make-believe* friendship⟩

¹**make-do** \ˈ=,=\ *adj* [fr. the phrase *make do*] **:** MAKESHIFT, IMPROVISED, TEMPORARY ⟨*make-do* airfield⟩

²**make-do** \"\ *n* -s **:** something that is made use of or made to serve instead of something better or more suitable ⟨housing had the flimsy quality of wartime *make-do* —Robert Zimmerman⟩

make down *vi, dial* **:** RAIN, SNOW **~** *vt* **:** to prepare (a folding berth) for night occupancy

make-down \ˈ=,=\ *n* -s [*make down*] **:** the arrangement of sleeping space (as in a pullman car) to accommodate a given number of passengers

ma·ke·ev·ka \məˈkā(y)əfkə\ *adj, usu cap* [fr. *Makeevka,* U.S.S.R.] **:** of or from the city of Makeevka, U.S.S.R. **:** of the kind or style prevalent in Makeevka

makefast \ˈ=,=\ *n* -s [fr. the phrase *make fast*] **:** something to which a boat is fastened (as a buoy or a post)

make-game \ˈ=,=\ *n* [fr. the phrase *make game (of)*] *archaic* **:** an object of ridicule **:** LAUGHINGSTOCK

make·ham's law \ˈmākəmz-\ *n, usu cap M* [after William *Makeham,* 19th cent. Brit. mathematician] **:** an actuarial rule: the mortality risk of a person at any age over 20 is equal to a constant plus a simple exponential function of the age

make-hawk \ˈ=,=\ *n* **:** a trained hawk used to teach inexperienced ones their work

make·less \ˈmākləs\ *adj* [ME, fr. *make, mak* match + *-less* — more at MAKE (match)] *now dial* **:** having no mate or match

make off *vi* **1 :** DEPART ⟨said good-bye and *made off* to his next appointment⟩ **2 :** to run away **:** ESCAPE ⟨the animals *make off* when danger appears⟩ — **make off with :** to take away **:** carry off ⟨*made off with* first prize⟩ **:** GRAB, STEAL ⟨*made off with* the whole herd of cattle⟩

make-or-break \ˈ=ˈ=ˈ=\ *adj* **:** allowing of no mean between full success and complete disaster ⟨*make-or-break* attempt⟩

make out *vt* **1 :** to draw up or prepare in writing ⟨*make out* a list⟩ **:** fill in (as a printed form) by writing ⟨*make* the check *out* to me⟩ **2** *now chiefly dial* **:** ACCOMPLISH, ACHIEVE **3** *obs* **:** to count as or complete (a total) **4** *now chiefly dial* **:** to make shift **:** MANAGE **:** try successfully ⟨*made out* to accomplish the voyage —Washington Irving⟩ **5 :** to find or grasp the meaning of ⟨trying to *make* the blurred writing *out*⟩ **:** UNDERSTAND, INTERPRET ⟨tried to *make out* what had actually happened⟩ **6 a :** DEMONSTRATE, ESTABLISH ⟨a good case can be *made out* in his defense⟩ ⟨malicious intent was clearly *made out* in this case⟩ **b :** to form an idea or opinion about **:** CONCLUDE ⟨how on earth do you *make* that *out*⟩ **7 :** to represent as being ⟨not the villain he is often *made out*⟩ **:** pretend to be true ⟨*made out* that he had been working all morning⟩ **8 :** to represent or delineate in detail ⟨every feature of the landscape faithfully *made out*⟩ **9 :** to see and identify with effort or difficulty **:** DISCERN ⟨you can just *make it out* from this hill⟩ **10** *dial* **:** INTEND, PLAN ⟨*make out* to go to town tomorrow⟩ **~** *vi* **1** *now dial Brit* **:** to go or get out **:** ESCAPE **2 a :** SUCCEED, THRIVE ⟨*made out* very well as a salesman⟩ **b :** to get along ⟨how are you *making out* in your new apartment⟩ **c :** to make shift ⟨*make out* with patched gear . . . and still get the job done —F.B.Gipson⟩

make over *vt* **1 :** to transfer the title of (property) **:** CONVEY, ASSIGN ⟨*made* his estate *over* to his brother⟩ **2 a :** REMAKE, REMODEL, RENOVATE ⟨*made over* her mother's dress for herself⟩ ⟨*made* the entire house *over*⟩ **b :** to alter the character of **:** REFORM ⟨what good ever came of trying to *make* anyone *over* —Ellen Glasgow⟩ **c :** to change the text or arrangement of (a printed page)

make-over \ˈ=,==\ *n* -s [*make over*] **:** something that is made over or made afresh: as **a :** an altered or restyled garment **b :** revised or fresh news copy for a new edition of a newspaper

make-peace \ˈ=,=\ *n* [fr. the phrase *make peace*] **:** PEACEMAKER

mak·er \ˈmākə(r)\ *n* -s [ME, fr. *maken* to make + *-er* — more at MAKE] **:** one that makes: as **a** *usu cap* **:** ²GOD ⟨calling loudly on his *Maker*⟩ **b** *archaic* **:** one that writes verses **:** POET **c :** a person who makes a promissory note **d :** a declarer in bridge **e :** a tool used in calking ships' plates to close up the joint after splitting the edge of the overlapping plate **f :** MANUFACTURER ⟨~ of auto parts⟩

makeready \ˈ=,==\ *n* -ES [fr. the phrase *make ready*] **:** final preparation and adjustment (as of a form and press for printing, a die for stamping, bindery machinery for folding); *also* **:** material (as underlays and overlays) used in making ready

maker's mark *n* **:** the hallmark on a piece of English gold, silver, or plate denoting the person or firm responsible for its production

maker-up \ˈ==ˈ=\ *n, pl* **makers-up** [*make up* + *-er*] **:** one that makes up: as **a :** one who arranges set type in form for printing **b** *chiefly Brit* **:** an assembler or packer of manufactured goods **c** *chiefly Brit* **:** a garment maker or manufacturer

makes *pres 3d sing of* MAKE, *pl of* MAKE

¹**make·shift** \ˈmāk,shift\ *n* [fr. the phrase *make shift*] **1** *obs* **:** a shifty person **2 :** a temporary expedient **:** SUBSTITUTE **3 :** the act or practice of making shift ⟨reduced to ~ and petty economizing⟩ **syn** see RESOURCE

²**makeshift** \"\ *also* **make·shifty** \-tē\ *adj* **1** *obs* **:** SHIFTY **2 :** serving as makeshift **:** characterized by makeshift ⟨~ living arrangement⟩ ⟨~ government policy⟩ — **make·shift·ness** \-f(t)nəs\ *n* -ES

make up *vt* **1 a :** to draw up in complete form **:** COMPILE **b :** INVENT ⟨*make up* a plot⟩ ⟨story was partly true and partly *made up*⟩ **:** IMPROVISE ⟨*made* new verses *up* as he went along⟩ **c :** to set (an account) in order **:** BALANCE **2 a** *obs* **:** BUILD, CONSTRUCT **b :** to produce or complete by fitting together or assembling ⟨*make up* a suit⟩ ⟨*make up* a train of cars⟩ **c :** to arrange type matter into (columns or pages) for a book or newspaper **d :** to put together from ingredients **:** COMPOUND, MIX ⟨*make up* a fresh batch of dough⟩ ⟨*make up* a bottle of cough medicine⟩ **e :** to lay and light (a fire) **3 :** to form into **:** wrap or fasten up ⟨*make* the books *up* into a parcel⟩ ⟨separate mailbags are *made up* for each city on the route⟩ **4 a :** to set in order **:** PREPARE ⟨*make* a bed *up* in the guest room⟩ **:** ARRANGE ⟨*make up* a room⟩ **b :** to shuffle (a deck) for dealing **5 a :** to compensate for (a deficiency) ⟨add some more water to *make up* the difference⟩ **b :** to act so as to correct (an omission) or remove (a deficiency in the record) ⟨*make up* a history examination⟩ **:** compensate for ⟨time taken off must be *made up* by overtime⟩ **c :** REPRINT, REPLACE ⟨*make* imperfect copies or sheets *up*⟩ **6 a** *of parts or quantities* **:** to combine to produce (a sum or a whole) **b :** CONSTITUTE, COMPOSE ⟨a party largely *made up* of peasants and artisans⟩ ⟨all the things that go to *make up* a national culture⟩ **7 :** SETTLE, DECIDE ⟨*made up* his mind to sell the house⟩ ⟨*make up* a quarrel⟩ ⟨glad that he has *made it up* with his family⟩ **8 a :** to prepare (as an actor) in physical appearance for a role ⟨came in *made up* as an Egyptian queen⟩ **b :** to apply cosmetics to ⟨no time to *make up* her face⟩ **9 :** to get (an animal) into condition for marketing **~** *vi* **1 :** to become reconciled **:** become friends again ⟨kiss and *make up*⟩ **2 a :** ADVANCE, APPROACH ⟨rapidly *making up* to the pier⟩ **b :** GATHER, RISE ⟨black clouds were *making up* in the east⟩ ⟨a storm seems to be *making up*⟩ **3 a :** to act ingratiatingly or flatteringly **:** curry favor ⟨*made up* to his aunt for a new bicycle⟩ **b :** to make love **:** make advances **:** COURT ⟨suspected of *making up* to his housekeeper⟩ **4 :** COMPENSATE ⟨hurried to *make up* for lost time⟩ **:** PAY, ATONE ⟨tried to *make up* for his neglect⟩ **5 :** to apply cosmetics ⟨began to *make up* at the age of thirteen⟩

makeup \ˈ=,=\ *n* -s [*make up*] **1 a :** the way in which the parts or ingredients of something are put together **:** COMPOSITION ⟨chemical ~ of a cleaning fluid⟩ ⟨the present ~ of the cabinet favors big business⟩ **b :** innate character or personality **:** physical, mental, and moral constitution ⟨defeat was attributed to certain defects in the national ~⟩ **2 :** an invented story **:** FICTION, LIE ⟨came down here to . . . try and show that the blessed miracle was a ~ —G.B.Shaw⟩ **3 a :** the act or the operation of making up ⟨a compositor working on ~⟩ **b :** the arrangement of printed matter ⟨a book in attractive ~ and binding⟩ **c :** reprinted or replacement matter **4 a :** cosmetics (as lipstick, face powder, mascara, eye shadow) used to color and beautify the face or the features ⟨evening ~⟩; *also* **:** a cosmetic applied to other parts of the body ⟨leg ~ for a tanned appearance⟩ **b :** the total of cosmetics, wigs, facial and body padding, and other items often strongly applied or emphasized for projection beyond bright lighting that give an actor or actress the appearance of the character being portrayed; *also* **:** a similar application of cosmetics for persons appearing on television or making other public appearances **c :** the act or process of applying cosmetics ⟨classes in ~ for models⟩ **d :** the appearance resulting from applying cosmetics ⟨her ~ had a natural look⟩ **5 a :** COMPENSATION, REPLACEMENT; *specif* **:** material added in a manufacturing process to replace material that has been used up ⟨a daily ~ of fresh acid⟩ **b :** the screw thread at the end of a pipe for the attachment of fittings **6 :** a special examination in which a student may make up for absence or failure at a regular examination

makeup clerk \ˈ=,=-\ *n* **:** one who prepares insurance claims for investigation and adjustment

makeup man *n* **1 :** a compositor or editorial worker that makes up **2 :** one who applies makeup to actors **3 :** a worker who fills orders or requisitions **4 :** a worker who prepares ingredients for such products as plastic coating solutions, artificial leather, or ice cream

makeup pay *n* **:** an amount paid to a piece-rated or incentive worker to bring his earnings up to a guaranteed minimum

makeup rule *n* [*make up*] **:** a steel rule with projecting top used (as in making up) to push apart lines of type

makeup water *n* [*make up*] **:** water supplied (as to a steam boiler) to compensate for loss by evaporation and leakage

makeweight \ˈ=,=\ *n* **1 a :** something thrown into a scale to bring the weight to a desired value **b :** a thing or a person of little worth or independent value thrown into a gap or empty place to fill out a whole ⟨some of the stories in the collection are mere ~*s*⟩ **2 :** COUNTERWEIGHT, COUNTERPOISE ⟨America's power as a ~ in the international scales —J.R. Chamberlain⟩

make-work \ˈ=,=\ *n* [fr. the phrase *make work*] **:** work devised chiefly to provide for the employment of labor ⟨older men have jobs which are *make-work* because no one can bring himself to discharge them —David Riesman⟩

ma·khor·ka \məˈkȯrkə\ *n* -s [Russ] **:** a coarse tobacco (*Nicotiana rustica*) grown esp. in the Ukraine

makh·zan *or* **makh·zen** *also* **magh·zen** \'makzən\ *n* -s [Ar *makhzan*] **:** the native Moroccan government; *collectively* **:** privileged peoples from whom Moroccan state officials are recruited
maki \'make͞, 'mäke͞\ *n* -s [F, prob. fr. Malagasy *máky*] **:** LEMUR
ma·ki·mo·no \ˌmäkə'mō(ˌ)nō, ˌmak-, -mōnə\ *n* -s [Jap, fr. *maki* scroll, roll + *mono* thing] **:** a picture, pictured story, or writing mounted on paper and usu. rolled in a scroll — compare KAKEMONO
[1]**mak·ing** \'mākiŋ, -kēŋ\ *n* -s [ME, fr. OE *macung*, fr. *macian* to make + *-ung* -ing — more at MAKE] **1 a :** the act or process of forming, causing, manufacturing, or coming into being ⟨a mind given to image-*making*⟩ ⟨laws already made or in the ~⟩ ⟨landed in a situation not of his own ~⟩ **b :** ORIGINATION, GROWTH ⟨when the modern age of science and technology was in the ~⟩ **2 :** a process or means of advancement or success ⟨misfortune was the ~ of him⟩ **3 :** something that is made: as **a :** a quantity produced at one time **:** BATCH ⟨~ of bread⟩ **b makings** *pl* **:** the slack and dirt produced in coal mining **4 a :** POTENTIALITY ⟨he had the ~ of a hero⟩ — often used in pl. ⟨has the ~*s* of a fine ballplayer⟩ **b makings** *pl* **:** the material from which something is to be made ⟨the ~*s* for a new suit⟩; *specif* **:** paper and tobacco for cigarettes
[2]**making** \"\ *adj* [fr. pres. part. of [1]*make*] **1 :** that makes — often used in combination ⟨contact-*making* parts of a switch⟩ **2 :** required to be made to specification ⟨a ~ order for goods not carried in stock⟩
making iron *n* **:** a chisel-shaped tool used by caulkers of ships to finish the seams after the oakum has been driven in
making–up day \'==ˌ=-\ *n* [fr. pres. part. of *make up*] **:** the first day of settlement on which contango agreements are made on the London stock exchange
making–up price *n* **:** the price at which stock is carried over on an account from one settlement to another on the London stock exchange
ma·ki·ri·ta·re \məˌkērē'tärē\ *n, pl* **makiritare** *or* **makiritares** *usu cap* **1 a :** a Cariban people of Venezuela **b :** a member of such people **2 :** the language of the Makiritare people
mak·luk \'makˌlək\ *n* -s [Esk *makliok, muklok*] **:** a large seal; *specif* **:** BEARDED SEAL
ma·ko \'mä(ˌ)kō\ *or* **mako shark** *n* -s [Maori *mako*] **:** any of several sharks of the genus *Isurus:* as **a :** BONITO SHARK **b :** a large vigorous shark (*I. oxyrhynchus*) of the Atlantic that is held to be dangerous to man but is highly esteemed as a sport fish
ma·ko·ma·ko \'mäkōˌmä(ˌ)kō, 'məkəˌmək\ *or* **ma·ko** \'mä-(ˌ)kō\ *n* -s [Maori] **1 :** a New Zealand tree (*Aristotelia racemosa*) of the family Elaeocarpaceae having a small red berry that turns black at maturity and is used for making wine — called also *wineberry* **2 :** the New Zealand bellbird
ma·kon·de \mə'kōn(ˌ)dā\ *n, pl* **makonde** *or* **makondes** *usu cap* **1 a :** a Bantu-speaking people of southeastern Tanganyika Territory and northern Mozambique known esp. for their sculptured masks **b :** a member of such people **2 :** KONDE 3
ma·ko·pa \mə'kōpə\ *n* -s [Tag & Bikol] **:** the Otaheite apple or its wood
ma·ko·re \ˌmäkə'rā\ *n* -s [native name in southern Africa] **:** a large tree of southern Africa (*Mimusops leckellii*) that yields a wood resembling cherry but having a pronounced black mottle — called also *cherry mahogany*
mak·ro·skel·ic \ˌmakrə'skelik\ *adj* [Gk *makro-* macr- + *skelos* leg + E *-ic* — more at CYLINDER] **:** having long legs in proportion to the trunk with a skelic index of 95 to 100
maku *usu cap, var of* MACÚ
ma·kua *also* **ma·kwa** \mə'kwä\ *n, pl* **makua** *or* **makuas** *usu cap* **1 a :** a Bantu-speaking people of Portuguese East Africa **b :** a member of such people **2 :** a Bantu language of the Makua people
makushi *or* **makusi** *usu cap, var of* MACUSHI
ma·ku·tu \'mäkü,tü\ *n* -s [Maori] *NewZeal* **:** a magic spell **:** CURSE, SORCERY
[1]**mal** \'mäl, -a-, -ä-\ *n* -s [F & It; F *mal*, fr. OF, fr. *mal*, adv., badly; It *mal, male*, fr. *male*, adv., badly; OF *mal* badly & It *male* badly fr. L *male*, fr. *malus* bad] **:** DISEASE, SICKNESS — used chiefly in combination ⟨~ de mer⟩ ⟨petit ~⟩
[2]**mål** *or* **maal** *n* -s *sometimes cap* [Norw *mål*, lit., speech, fr. ON *māl*] **:** LANDSMÅL
[1]**mal-** *comb form* [ME, fr. MF *mal*, adj., bad & *mal*, adv., badly; MF *mal* bad, fr. OF, fr. L *malus;* MF *mal* badly, fr. OF, fr. L *male*, fr. *malus* bad — more at SMALL] **1 a :** bad **:** evil ⟨*mal*practice⟩ **b :** badly **:** evilly ⟨*mal*odorous⟩ **2 a :** irregular **:** abnormal ⟨*mal*formation⟩ **b :** irregularly **:** abnormally ⟨*mal*formed⟩ **3 a :** poor **:** inadequate ⟨*mal*adjustment⟩ **b :** poorly **:** inadequately ⟨*mal*nourished⟩
[2]**mal-** *or* **malo-** *comb form* [ISV, fr. *malic* (in *malic acid*)] **:** malic acid ⟨*mal*amide⟩ ⟨*malo*nitrile⟩
[1]**mala** *pl of* MALUM
[2]**ma·la** \'mālə\ *n, pl* **ma·lae** \-(ˌ)lē\ [NL, fr. L, jaw, cheek — more at MAXILLA] **1 :** a single lobe of the maxilla of an insect **2 a :** the grinding surface of a mandible of an insect **b :** the third segment of a mandible of some myriapods
ma·la·ano·nang \məˌläə'nōˌnäŋ\ *n* -s [Tag] **:** a Philippine timber tree (*Shorea malaanonan*) with light yellow wood
[1]**mal·a·bar** \ˌmalə¦bär, -bä(r\ *adj, usu cap* [fr. *Malabar*, coast of southwestern India] **:** of or from the Malabar coast **:** of the kind or style prevalent in Malabar
[2]**malabar** *n* -s **1** *cap* **:** a native or inhabitant of the Malabar coast of southwestern India **2** *often cap* **:** [2]BAY 2
malabar almond *n, usu cap M* **1 :** a tropical Asian evergreen tree (*Terminalia catappa*) that is widely grown in warm regions for ornament and for the edible kernel of the seed of its drupaceous fruit — called also *country almond, Indian almond* **2 :** the edible almond-shaped kernel of the seed of the Malabar almond
malabar nightshade *or* **malabar spinach** *n, usu cap M* **:** a plant of the genus *Basella; esp* **:** an Asiatic climbing plant (*B. alba*) with fleshy shining leaves and small white racemose flowers that is grown in the tropics as a potherb and in temperate regions as an ornamental vine
malabar nut *n, usu cap M* **1 :** an East Indian shrub (*Adhatoda vasica*) of the family Acanthaceae having leaves, root, and seed that are used as a source of an antipyretic and antispasmodic **2 :** the seed of the Malabar nut
malabar rat *n, usu cap M* **:** BANDICOOT 1
malabar squirrel *n, usu cap M* **:** a giant squirrel (*Ratufa indica malabarica*) of southern India
mal·a·bath·rum \ˌmalə'bathrəm\ *n* -s [L *malabathrum, malobathrum*, fr. Gk *malabathron*, modif. of Skt *tamālapattra* garcinia leaf, fr. *tamāla* garcinia (perh. fr. *tamas* darkness) + *pattra* leaf, wing, feather; akin to Skt *patati* he flies — more at TEMERITY, FEATHER] **1 :** the leaf of a plant (*Cinnamomum malabathrum*) used esp. in making a perfumed ointment **2 :** an ointment prepared from malabathrum
mal·absorption \¦mal+\ *n* [[1]*mal-* + *absorption*] **:** faulty absorption of nutrient materials from the alimentary canal
malac *abbr* malacology
malac- *or* **malaco-** *comb form* [L *malac-*, fr. Gk *malak-, malako-*, fr. *malakos;* akin to MIr *malcad* decay, Russ *molchat'* to be silent, L *molere* to grind — more at MEAL] **:** soft ⟨*malac*oid⟩ ⟨*malaco*phyllous⟩
[1]**mal·a·can·thid** \¦malə¦kan(t)thəd\ *adj* [NL *Malacanthidae*] **:** of or relating to the Malacanthidae
[2]**malacanthid** \"\ *n* -s [NL *Malacanthidae*] **:** a fish of the family Malacanthidae
mal·a·can·thi·dae \ˌ==ˌ'kan(t)thəˌdē\ *n pl, cap* [NL, fr. *Malacanthus*, type genus + *-idae*] **:** a family of long compressed to fusiform short-headed marine percoid fishes that are often brightly colored and that include excellent food fishes
mal·a·can·thus \-thəs\ *n, cap* [NL, irreg. fr. *malac-* + *-acanthus*] **:** the type genus of the family Malacanthidae
ma·lac·ca cane \mə'lakə-\ *also* **malacca** *n* -s *often cap* [fr. *Malacca*, city and settlement in Malaya] **:** an often mottled cane obtained from an Asiatic rattan palm (*Calamus rotang*) and used esp. for making walking sticks and umbrella handles
ma·lac·can \-kən\ *adj, usu cap* [*Malacca*, Malay Peninsula + E *-an*] **:** of or relating to Malacca on the Malay peninsula
malacca weasel *n, usu cap M* **:** RASSE
ma·la·ce·ae \mə'lāsēˌē\ *n pl, cap* [NL, fr. *Malus*, type genus + *-aceae*] *in some classifications* **:** a family of shrubs and trees comprising members of the family Rosaceae (as the apple, quince, pear) that have the carpels united and adnate to the calyx tube
mal·a·chite \'maləˌkīt\ *n* -s [alter. of earlier *melochite*, fr. ME *melochites*, fr. L *molochites*, prob. fr. Gk *molochitēs*, fr. *molochē, malachē* mallow + *-itēs* -ite — more at MALLOW] **:** a mineral $Cu_2CO_3(OH)_2$ consisting of a green basic carbonate of copper that is an ore of copper and is used to make ornamental objects (as vases) — compare AZURITE
malachite green *n* **1 a :** a pigment made of ground malachite **b :** a similar pigment made synthetically **2** *sometimes cap M&G* **:** a triphenylmethane basic dye prepared from benzaldehyde and dimethylaniline and used chiefly in coloring paper bluish green, in making organic pigments, in industrial and biological stains, and also in medicine as an antiseptic — called also *Victoria green; see* DYE table I (under *Basic Green 4, Pigment Green 4, Solvent Green 1*) **3** *also* **malachite :** a moderate yellowish green that is greener, stronger, and slightly lighter than tarragon, lighter and stronger than average almond green, and deeper and slightly yellower than verdigris — called also *Bremen green, copper green, green verditer, Hungarian green, iris green, mineral green, mountain green, Olympian green, shale green, Tyrolese green, verditer green*
ma·la·cia \mə'lāsh(ē)ə\ *n* -s [NL, fr. Gk *malakia* softness, fr. *malakos* soft + *-ia*] **:** abnormal softening of a tissue — often used in combination ⟨osteo*malacia*⟩
mal·a·cich·thy·es \ˌmalə'sikthēˌēz\ *n pl, cap* [NL, fr. *malac-* + Gk *ichthyes* (pl. of *ichthys* fish) — more at ICHTHUS] **:** a small order of fishes including solely the family Icosteidae and being of uncertain systematic relations though possibly a specialized or degenerate offshoot of Percoidea
mal·a·clem·ys \-'kleməs\ *n, cap* [NL, irreg. fr. *malac-* + *-clemys* (fr. Gk *klemmys* tortoise)] **:** a genus of moderate-sized No. American edible terrapins (family Testudinidae) comprising the diamondback terrapins
malaco- — see MALAC-
mal·a·cob·del·la \ˌmaləˌkäb'delə\ *n, cap* [NL, fr. *malac-* + *-bdella*] **:** a genus of broad nemertean worms (order Bdellonemertea) that resemble leeches and are commensal in the gill cavity of clams and other mollusks
[1]**mal·a·cob·del·lid** \¦==¦=ˌdeləd\ *adj* [NL *Malacobdella* + E *-id*, adj. suffix] **:** of or relating to the genus *Malacobdella*
[2]**malacobdellid** \"\ *n* -s [NL *Malacobdella* + E *-id*, n. suffix] **:** a worm of the genus *Malacobdella*
mal·a·co·cotylea \ˌmalə(ˌ)kō+\ [NL, fr. *malac-* + *-cotylea* (fr. Gk *kotylē* cup, anything hollow) — more at KETTLE] *syn of* DIGENEA
mal·a·coid \'maləˌkȯid\ *adj* [*malac-* + *-oid*] **1** *of a living body* **:** having a soft or mucilaginous structure or texture ⟨the ~ plasmodia of slime molds⟩ **2 :** of, relating to, or resembling malacia ⟨~ alteration of bone⟩
mal·a·co·lite \'maləkəˌlīt\ *n* -s [F *malacolithe*, fr. *malac-* + *-lithe* -lite] **:** DIOPSIDE; *esp* **:** a pale translucent diopside
mal·a·co·log·i·cal \¦==¦lïjəkəl\ *adj* **:** of or relating to malacology
mal·a·col·o·gist \ˌ=='käləjəst\ *n* -s **:** a specialist in malacology
mal·a·col·o·gy \-jē\ *n* -ES [F *malacologie*, contr. of *malacozoologie*, fr. *malacozoo-* (fr. NL *Malacozoa* zoological group in some classifications including soft-bodied animals such as the mollusks, fr. *malac-* + *-zoa*) + *-logie* -logy] **:** a branch of zoology dealing with mollusks — compare CONCHOLOGY
mal·a·con \'maləˌkän\ *also* **mal·a·cone** \-ˌkōn\ *or* **mal·a·kon** \-ˌkän\ *n* -s [G *malakon*, fr. Gk, neut. of *malakos* soft] **:** a brown altered form of zircon
mal·a·coph·i·lous \¦==¦käfələs\ *adj* [*malaco-* mollusk (fr. *malacology*) + *-philous*] **:** adapted to pollination by snails — used esp. of the flowers of some arums; compare ANEMOPHILOUS, ENTOMOPHILOUS
mal·a·co·phyl·lous \¦==(ˌ)kō¦filəs\ *adj* [prob. fr. (assumed) NL *malacophyllus*, fr. NL *malac-* + *-phyllus* -phyllous] **:** having soft or fleshy leaves ⟨~ xerophytes⟩
mal·a·cop·o·da \ˌ=='käpədə\ [NL, fr. *malac-* + *-poda*] *syn of* ONYCHOPHORA
[1]**mal·a·cop·te·ryg·i·an** \¦malə¦käptə¦rij(ē)ən\ *adj* [NL *Malacopterygii* + E *-an*, adj. suffix] **:** of or relating to the Malacopterygii
[2]**malacopterygian** \"\ *n* -s [NL *Malacopterygii* + E *-an*, n. suffix] **:** a teleost fish of the division Malacopterygii
mal·a·cop·te·ryg·ii \ˌ-ˌ'rijēˌī\ *n pl, cap* [NL, fr. *malac-* + *-pterygii*] *in some classifications* **:** an extensive division of teleost fishes having soft fin rays — **mal·a·cop·te·ryg·ious** \-'rij(ē)əs\ *adj*
mal·a·co·so·ma \ˌmalə(ˌ)kō'sōmə\ *n, cap* [NL, fr. *malac-* + *-soma*] **:** a genus of moths (family Lasiocampidae) including the common tent caterpillars
mal·a·cos·tra·ca \ˌmalə'kästrəkə\ *n pl, cap* [NL, fr. Gk *malakostraka*, neut. pl. of *malakostrakos* soft-shelled, fr. *malak-* malac- + *-ostrakos* (fr. *ostrakon* shell) — more at OYSTER] **:** a major subclass of Crustacea including most of the well-known marine, freshwater, and terrestrial members of the group (as lobsters, crabs, shrimps, sow bugs, beach fleas) — **mal·a·cos·tra·can** \¦==¦kästrəkən\ *adj or n* — **mal·a·cos·tra·cous** \-kəs\ *adj*
mal·a·cotic \¦==¦kädˌik\ *adj* [*malacia* + *-otic*] *of a tooth* **:** exhibiting malacia **:** SOFT
mal·adaptation \¦mal+\ *n* [[1]*mal-* + *adaptation*] **:** poor or inadequate adaptation ⟨a secular, urban civilization . . . exposing the individuals to many more shocks and rebuffs, and to frequent feelings of ~ —*Social Thought From Lore To Science*⟩
mal·adapted \"+\ *adj* [[1]*mal-* + *adapted*] **:** unsuited or poorly suited by nature, character, or design to a particular use, purpose, or situation ⟨their buildings were empty classic shells, woefully ~ to the functions they serve —Lewis Mumford⟩
mal·adaptive \"+\ *adj* [[1]*mal-* + *adaptive*] **1 :** marked by poor or inadequate adaptation ⟨cultures have . . . disappeared from the stage of history in consequence of ~ practices —G.P. Murdock⟩ **2 :** not conducive to adaptation ⟨so long as destructive, unconscious motivations persist, ~ behavior will plague the person —L.R.Wolberg⟩
mal·a·dive \'maladiv\ *adj* [MF *maladif*, fr. OF, fr. *malade* sick + *-if* -ive] **1 :** of, relating to, or affected by illness or disease **:** SICKLY, FEEBLE ⟨a ~ condition⟩ ⟨her ~step⟩ **2 :** marked by or expressive of moral weakness or unwholesomeness ⟨a ~ apology⟩ ⟨~ poetry⟩
mal·adjusted \¦mal+\ *adj* [[1]*mal-* + *adjusted*] **:** poorly or inadequately adjusted; *specif* **:** lacking harmony with one's environment from failure to reach a satisfactory adjustment between one's desires and the conditions of one's life ⟨~ persons⟩ ⟨the ~ child⟩
mal·adjustive \"+\ *adj* [[1]*mal-* + *adjustive*] **:** not conducive to adjustment ⟨~ behavior⟩
mal·adjustment \"+\ *n* [[1]*mal-* + *adjustment*] **:** poor, faulty, or inadequate adjustment: as **a :** failure (of a mechanical part) to assume the proper, exact, or conforming position for adequate functioning ⟨the clutch is subject to . . . ~*s* upon use —Joseph Heitner⟩ **b :** a state of disharmony, imbalance, or disequilibrium ⟨~ between the customs of the East and the innovations of the West —*Orient Bk. World*⟩ ⟨~ between urban standards and rural poverty —Peter Scott⟩ ⟨~ in production and consumption with attendant unemployment, poverty, and waste —J.A.Hobson⟩ **c :** lack of harmony between the individual and his environment from failure to reach a satisfactory adjustment between one's desires and the conditions of one's life ⟨emotional ~*s*⟩ ⟨sexual ~⟩ ⟨symptoms of ~ . . . in early childhood —*Psychological Abstracts*⟩ **d :** an irregularity or anomaly resulting from economic instability ⟨~*s* . . . of the world wheat industry —A.F.Vass⟩ ⟨~*s* and inequities in wage rates —H.S.Truman⟩
mal·administer \"+\ *vt* [[1]*mal-* + *administer*] **:** to administer improperly, poorly, or inefficiently ⟨~ the public relief program⟩
mal·administration \"+\ *n* [[1]*mal-* + *administration*] **:** incompetent or corrupt administration; *specif* **:** inefficiency or corruption in public office ⟨awake to the dangers and disgrace of the existing ~ —J.A.Froude⟩ ⟨charging the mayor with ~⟩
mal·a·droit \¦malə¦drȯit\ *adj* [F, fr. MF, fr. *mal* badly + *adroit* — more at MAL-, ADROIT] **1 :** marked by a lack of dexterity or skill **:** CLUMSY ⟨a ~ movement of my hand . . . caused the car to swerve —C.H.Whiteley⟩ ⟨a ~ translation⟩ **2 :** revealing a lack of perception, judgment, or finesse **:** TACTLESS, INEPT, BUNGLING ⟨embittered by ~ introductions —Sara H. Hay⟩ ⟨~ propaganda⟩ **syn** see AWKWARD
mal·a·droit·ly *adv* **:** in a maladroit manner ⟨groping ~ for solutions —*New Republic*⟩
mal·a·droit·ness *n* **:** the quality or state of being maladroit ⟨the ~ of some . . . gifts —Graham Greene⟩
mal·a·dy \'malədē, -di\ *n* -ES [ME *maladie*, fr. OF, fr. *malade* sick (fr. L *male habitus* undernourished, feeble, fr. *male* badly + *habitus*, past part. of *habēre* to have, hold) + *-ie* -y — more at MAL-, GIVE] **1 :** a disease, distemper, disorder, or indisposition of the animal body proceeding from impaired or defective functions ⟨told by his physicians that he had a fatal ~ —Willa Cather⟩ **2 :** an unwholesome or disordered state or condition ⟨some deep ~ of the soul —Van Wyck Brooks⟩ ⟨analyze the nature and the causes of the ~ from which the nation suffers —Reinhold Niebuhr⟩ ⟨the critical ~ of our age —Louis Kronenberger⟩
malae *pl of* MALA
[1]**mala fide** \¦malə¦fīdē, ¦mälə¦fē(ˌ)dā\ *adv* [LL, in bad faith] **:** with or in bad faith **:** falsely and maliciously ⟨the debates . . . are reported *mala fide* —T.E.May⟩
[2]**mala fide** \"\ *adj* **1 a :** acting with intent to deceive or defraud ⟨a *mala fide* agent⟩ **b :** holding by a title known to lack legal sanction ⟨a *mala fide* possessor⟩ ⟨*mala fide* settlers . . . swore they had established residence —R.G.Lillard⟩ **2 :** SPECIOUS, INSINCERE ⟨a *mala fide* proposal⟩
mala fi·des \ˌmalə'fīˌdēz, ˌmälə'fēˌdās\ *n* [LL, bad faith] **:** bad faith **:** purpose to deceive or defraud ⟨the *mala fides* of the company is generally apparent for the jury —Ira Carlisle⟩
[1]**mal·a·ga** *or* **má·la·ga** \'maləgə\ *adj, usu cap* [fr. *Málaga*, city in southern Spain] **:** of or from the city of Málaga, Spain **:** of the kind or style prevalent in Málaga
[2]**malaga** \"\ *n* -s **1** *usu cap* **a :** any of several aromatic usu. sweet white or red dessert wines made in the province of Málaga, Spain **b :** a similar wine made elsewhere (as in California) that is a deep amber-colored blend of juices from several kinds of grapes **2** *often cap* **:** a dark red to deep reddish brown
malaga red *n, often cap M* **:** OXBLOOD — distinguished from *Malaga 2*
[1]**mal·a·gasy** \¦malə¦gasē\ *n, pl* **malagasy** *also* **malagasies** *cap* **1 a :** a people of Madagascar thought to be descended from Bantu-speaking, Malayan, and Arab peoples **b :** a member of such people **c :** a native or inhabitant of Madagascar or of the Malagasy Republic **:** MADAGASCAN **2 :** the Austronesian language of the Malagasy people
[2]**malagasy** \"\ *adj, usu cap* **1 a :** of, relating to, or characteristic of the Malagasy **b :** of, relating to, or characteristic of the Malagasy Republic **2 :** of, relating to, or being a biogeographic region or subregion that includes Madagascar and adjacent islands and is esp. characterized by the presence of various lemurs and by numerous mammals and birds different from those of the African mainland
mala·gue·na \ˌmalə'gānyə, ˌmäl-, ÷ -gwā-; *there is no* w *in the Spanish pronunc*\ *n* -s [Sp *malagueña*, fr. fem. of *malagueño* of or relating to Málaga, fr. *Málaga*, city in southern Spain] **1 :** a folk tune native to Málaga which is similar to a fandango and to which stanzas of four octosyllabic verses are sung **2 :** a Spanish couple dance similar to a fandango
malagueta pepper *or* **malaguetta pepper** *also* **malagetta pepper** *var of* MELEGUETA PEPPER
mal·a·hack \'maləˌhak\ *vt* [prob. fr. [1]*mal-* + connective *-a-* + *hack*] *dial* **:** to cut or carve awkwardly
mala in se *pl of* MALUM IN SE
mal·aise \(')ma¦lāz\ *or* **mal·ease** \(')ma¦lēz\ *n* -s [*malaise* fr. F, fr. OF, fr. *mal* bad + *aise* comfort; *malease* alter. (influenced by *ease*) of *malaise* — more at MAL-, EASE] **1 :** a sense of physical ill-being **:** an indefinite feeling of generalized debility or lack of health often indicative of or accompanying the onset of an illness ⟨marked ~ and prostration are not features of the common cold in adults —Yale Kneeland⟩ ⟨menstruation . . . gives rise to a characteristic ~ in some women —*Jour. Amer. Med. Assoc.*⟩ **2 :** a vague sense of mental or moral ill-being or uneasiness ⟨without being able to analyze the source of his ~, he felt that something ominous was impending —S.N.Behrman⟩ ⟨the symptoms of his generation's ~ —Janet Flanner⟩
malakon *var of* MALACON
malakostraca *or* **malakostraka** *syn of* MALACOSTRACA
ma·lam·bo \mə'lam(ˌ)bō\ *n* -s [AmerSp & Pg, malambo tree] **:** the yellowish aromatic bark of a So. American shrub (*Croton malambo*) used in medicine and perfumery
mal·a·mute *or* **mal·e·mute** \'maləˌmyüt\ *n* -s *sometimes cap* [after *Malemute, Malemiut*, Alaskan Eskimo people that developed the breed] **:** a sled dog of northern No. America; *esp* **:** ALASKAN MALAMUTE
mal·an·ders *or* **mal·len·ders** \'malənda(r)z\ *n pl but usu sing in constr* [ME *malawnder* (sing.) sore on a horse's knee, fr. MF *malandre*, fr. L *malandria* sore on a horse's neck] **:** a chronic eczema occurring usu. on the posterior or flexion surface of the knee of a horse's foreleg — compare SALLENDERS
ma·lan·ga \mə'läŋgə\ *n* -s [AmerSp, prob. fr. Kongo, pl. of *elanga* water lily] **1 :** TARO **2 :** YAUTIA
ma·la·nia \mə'lānēə\ *n, cap* [NL, fr. Daniel F. *Malan* †1959 So. African political leader + NL *-ia*] **:** a genus of living coelacanth fishes represented by a single specimen taken in shallow water north of Madagascar — compare LATIMERIA
ma·la·pa·ho \ˌmälə'pä(ˌ)hō\ *n* -s [Tag *malapahò*] **1 :** any of several Philippine trees of the genus *Dipterocarpus* **2 :** a wood, resin, or fiber of a malapaho tree
[1]**mal·a·pert** \¦malə¦pərt\ *adj* [ME, fr. MF, unskillful, ill-taught, fr. *mal* badly + *apert* able, skillful, modif. (influenced by *L ad-*) of L *expertus* expert — more at MAL-, EXPERT] **:** impudently bold **:** SAUCY ⟨untutored lad, thou art too ~ —Shak.⟩ ⟨returning the woman's stare with a look of ~ challenge —Llewelyn Powys⟩ — **mal·a·pert·ness** *n*
[2]**malapert** \"\ *n* -s **:** a malapert person ⟨the ~ knew well enough I laughed at her —Richard Steele⟩
ma·la prax·is \¦mālə'praksəs\ *n* [NL, bad practice] **:** MALPRACTICE
mala prohibita *pl of* MALUM PROHIBITUM
[1]**mal·a·prop** \'maləˌpräp\ *n* -s [after Mrs. *Malaprop*, character noted for her misuse of words in the comedy *The Rivals* (1775) by Richard B. Sheridan †1816 Irish dramatist, fr. E *malapropos*] **:** MALAPROPISM
[2]**malaprop** \"\ *or* **mal·a·prop·i·an** \¦==¦präpēən, -pröp-\ *adj* **:** marked by the use of malapropisms ⟨a ~ use of words —Alexander Bain⟩ ⟨the ~ adolescent . . . pries at him with personal questions ("Was your wife a lymphomaniac?") —*Time*⟩
mal·a·prop·ism \'==ˌpräˌpizəm\ *n* -s [[1]*malaprop* + *-ism*] **1 :** a usu. humorous misapplication of a word or phrase; *specif* **:** a blundering use of a word that sounds somewhat like the one intended but is ludicrously wrong in the context **2 :** an example of malapropism (as in "an allegory on the banks of the Nile" or "if I reprehend anything in this world, it is the use of my oracular tongue and a nice derangement of epitaphs") ⟨renowned for her ~*s* —John Galsworthy⟩
[1]**mal·ap·ro·pos** \ˌmaˌlaprə'pō, ='==ˌ=\ *adv* [F *mal à propos*, lit., not to the purpose, inappropriate] **:** in an inappropriate or irrelevant manner **:** UNSEASONABLY, INOPPORTUNELY ⟨listening distractedly, answering ~ —P.L.Fermor⟩
[2]**malapropos** \"\ *adj* **:** INAPPROPRIATE, INOPPORTUNE
mal·ap·te·ru·rus \məˌlaptə'rürəs\ *n, cap* [NL, irreg. fr. *malac-* + *pter-* + *-urus*] **:** a genus consisting of the electric catfish
[1]**ma·lar** \'mālə(r)\ *adj* [NL *malaris*, fr. L *mala* jaw, cheek + *-aris* -ar — more at MAXILLA] **1 :** of or relating to the cheek or the side of the head **2 :** indicating the zygomatic bone
[2]**malar** \"\ *n* -s **:** ZYGOMATIC BONE
malari- *or* **malario-** *comb form* [*malaria*] **:** malaria ⟨*malari*oid⟩ ⟨*malario*logy⟩ ⟨*malario*metry⟩
ma·lar·ia \mə'lerēə, -la(ə)r-, -lār-\ *n* -s [It, fr. *mala aria* bad air, fr. *mala* (fem. of *malo* bad, fr. L *malus*) + *aria* air — more at SMALL, ARIA] **1** *archaic* **a :** air infected with a noxious substance capable of causing disease; *esp* **:** an unhealthy exhalation from marshy soils **:** MIASMA **b :** a febrile disease believed to be caused by air infected with such noxious exhalations —

often used with *the* ⟨a horrid thing called the ~ —Horace Walpole⟩ **2 a :** an acute or chronic disease caused by the presence of sporozoan parasites (genus *Plasmodium*) in the red blood cells, transmitted from infected man to uninfected man by the bite of anopheline mosquitoes, and characterized by periodic attacks of chills and fever that coincide with mass destruction of blood cells and the release of toxic substances by the parasite at the end of each reproductive cycle ⟨~ remains the greatest single cause of debilitation and death throughout the world —*Jour. Amer. Med. Assoc.*⟩ — see FALCIPARUM MALARIA, VIVAX MALARIA **b :** any of various more or less similar diseases of birds and mammals caused by blood protozoans — see BIRD MALARIA

ma·lar·i·ae \mə'lerē,ē\ *n* -s [NL (specific epithet of *Plasmodium malariae*), gen. of *malaria*, fr. It] **:** the quartan malaria parasite (*Plasmodium malariae*) ⟨~ infection⟩

malariae malaria *n* **:** malaria caused by a malaria parasite (*Plasmodium malariae*) and marked by recurrence of paroxysms at 72-hour intervals — called also *quartan malaria*

malaria germ *n* **:** MALARIA PARASITE

1ma·lar·i·al \mə'lerēəl, -la(a)r-, -lār-\ *also* **ma·lar·i·an** \-rēən\ *adj* [*malaria* + *-al* or *-an*] **:** of, relating to, infected by, or resembling malaria ⟨~ fever⟩ ⟨~ conditions in areas newly occupied by troops —*Atlantic*⟩

2malarial \"\ *n* -s **:** one infected with malaria

malarial cachexia *n* **:** a generalized state of debility that is marked by anemia, jaundice, splenomegaly, and emaciation and results from long-continued chronic malarial infection

malarial catarrhal fever *n* **1 :** heartwater of sheep **2 :** ICTEROHEMATURIA

malarial fever *n* **1 :** malaria of man **2 a :** INFECTIOUS ANEMIA **b :** TEXAS FEVER

ma·lar·i·al·ize \mə'lerēə,līz, -la(a)r-, -lār-\ *vt* -ED/-ING/-S **:** to infect with malaria for the purpose of inducing fever in the treatment of some diseases

malarial mosquito *or* **malaria mosquito** *n* **:** a mosquito that transmits the malaria parasite — compare ANOPHELES

malaria parasite *n* **:** a protozoan of the sporozoan genus *Plasmodium* being transmitted to man or to certain other mammals or birds by the bite of a mosquito in which its sexual reproduction takes place, multiplying asexually in the vertebrate host by schizogony in the red blood cells or in certain tissue cells, causing destruction of red blood cells and the febrile disease malaria, or producing gametocytes by sporogony that if taken up by a suitable mosquito initiate a new sexual cycle — compare MEROZOITE, OOKINETE, PHANEROZOITE, SCHIZONT, SPOROZOITE

ma·lar·i·oid \mə'lerē,ȯid, -la(a)r-, -lār-\ *adj* [*malari-* + *-oid*] **:** resembling malaria

ma·lar·i·ol·o·gist \=,==ˈäləjəst\ *n* -s **:** a specialist in the study, treatment, or prevention of malaria

ma·lar·i·ol·o·gy \-jē\ *n* -ES [ISV *malari-* + *-logy*] **:** the scientific study of malaria

ma·lar·io·met·ric \mə,lerēə,me·trik, -la(a)r-, -lār-\ *adj* **:** of or relating to malariometry

ma·lar·i·om·e·try \=,=='ämə·trē\ *n* -ES [*malari-* + *-metry*] **:** the determination of the endemic level of malarial infection in an area or a population

ma·lar·io·therapy \=,'=rēō+\ *n* [ISV *malari-* + *therapy*] **:** the treatment of disease by raising the body temperature through infecting the patient with malaria

ma·lar·i·ous \mə'lerēəs, -la(a)r-, -lār-\ *adj* [*malaria* + *-ous*] **:** full of or infected with malaria ⟨~ regions⟩ ⟨a ~ patient⟩ ⟨the highly ~ jungles of Burma or New Guinea —*Atlantic*⟩

ma·lar·key *also* **ma·lar·ky** \mə'lärkē, -lākē, -ki\ *n, pl* **malarkeys** *also* **malarkies** [origin unknown] **:** insincere or pretentious talk or writing designed to impress one and usu. to distract attention from ulterior motives or actual conditions **:** NONSENSE ⟨column after column of . . . unmitigated ~ —Polly Adler⟩ ⟨masters of ~ for the masses —*Time*⟩

malar point *n* **:** the most prominent point on the zygomatic bone — see CRANIOMETRY illustration

malars *pl of* MALAR

mal·assimilation \ˌmal+\ *n* [*1mal-* + *assimilation*] **:** MALABSORPTION

malate \'ma,lāt, 'mā,-\ *n* -s [F, fr. *mal-* 2mal- + *-ate*] **:** a salt or ester of malic acid

mal·a·thi·on \ˌmalə'thī,än *sometimes* mə'lāthēən\ *n* [fr. *Malathion*, a trademark] **:** a thiophosphate insecticide $C_{10}H_{19}O_6PS_2$ that has a lower mammalian toxicity than parathion and is also a valuable acaricide

mal·a·vogue \ˌmalə'vōg\ *vt* [origin unknown] *dial chiefly Irish* **:** to treat or punish severely

ma·la·wi \mə'läwē\ *adj, usu cap* [fr. *Malawi*, country in southeastern Africa] **:** of or from the country of Malawi **:** of the kind or style prevalent in Malawi —**ma·la·wi·an** \-ēən\ *n* -s *cap* [*Malawi*, Africa + E *-an*] **:** a native or inhabitant of Malawi — **malawian** *adj, usu cap*

ma·lax \'mā,laks, mə'l-\ *vt* -ED/-ING/-ES [ME *malaxen*, fr. L *malaxare* to soften, fr. Gk *malaxai*, aor. infin. of *malassein*, fr. *malakos* soft — more at MALAC-] **:** MALAXATE

malax·age \'mā,laksij, mə'l-\ *n* -s [F, fr. *malaxer* to malaxate, knead (fr. L *malaxare*) + *-age*] **:** the act or process of softening a material (as clay) by moistening and working it

malax·ate \'maləksāt, mə'lak-\ *vt* -ED/-ING/-S [L *malaxatus*, past part. of *malaxare*] **:** to soften and incorporate (as plaster, clay, or drug ingredients of pills) by rubbing, kneading, or rolling, and simultaneously mixing with a thinner substance

malax·a·tion \ˌmalak'sāshən, mə,lak's-\ *n* -s [LL *malaxation-*, *malaxatio* act of softening, fr. L *malaxatus* + *-ion-*, *-io* -ion] **1 :** the act or process of reducing to a soft mass by malaxating **2 :** the process by which parasitic and predatory hymenoptera chew their victims previous to feeding by the adult or larvae

mal·ax·a·tor \'maləksād·ə(r)\ *n* -s [*malaxate* + *-or*] **:** one that malaxates; *esp* **:** a machine or mill for grinding, kneading, or stirring into a pasty mass

ma·lax·er·man \mə'laksə(r)mən\ *n, pl* **malaxermen** [*malaxer-* (fr. *malax* + *-er*) + *man*] **:** one that mixes fireclay

ma·lax·is \mə'laksəs\ *n, cap* [NL, fr. Gk, act of softening, fr. *malassein* to soften] **:** a genus of terrestrial orchids with solid tubers that produce simple stems bearing one or few leaves and a raceme of tiny mostly greenish flowers — see GREEN ADDER'S-MOUTH

1ma·lay \mə'lā, 'mā,lā\ *n* [obs. D *Malayo* (now *Maleier*) fr. Malay *Mĕlayu*] **1** -s *cap* **:** a member of a people of the Malay peninsula, eastern Sumatra, parts of Borneo, and some small adjacent islands **2** -s *cap* **:** the Austronesian language of the Malays widely used as a trade language **3 a** *usu cap* **:** an Asiatic breed of tall upright exhibition game fowls with walnut comb and small wattles, very long legs, naked face and throat, and distinctive mahogany red and black plumage **b** -s *often cap* **:** any bird of the Malay breed

2malay \"\ *adj, usu cap* **1 a :** of, relating to, or characteristic of Malaya **b :** of, relating to, or characteristic of Malaysia **2 :** of, relating to, or characteristic of the Malays **3 :** of, relating to, or characteristic of the Malay language

ma·laya \mə'lāə *also* (')mā¦l- *sometimes* -āyə\ *adj, usu cap* [fr. *Malaya*, federation of states in the southern part of the Malay peninsula] **:** of or from Malaya **:** of the kind or style prevalent in Malaya **:** MALAYAN

mal·a·ya·lam \ˌmalə'yäləm\ *n* -s *usu cap* **1 :** the Dravidian language of Kerala, southern India, closely related to Tamil **2 :** the script normally used in writing Malayalam

mal·a·ya·li \-lē\ *n, pl* **malayalis** \-lēz\ *or* **malaya·lim** \-ləm\ *usu cap* **1 :** a Malayalam-speaking inhabitant of the Malabar coast of India **2 :** MALAYALAM

1ma·lay·an \mə'lāən, (')mā¦l- *sometimes* -āyən\ *n* -s *cap* [*1Malay* + E *-an*, n. suffix] **1 :** a native or inhabitant of Malaya **2 :** DEUTERO-MALAY

2malayan \"\ *adj, usu cap* [*1Malay* + E *-an*, adj. suffix] **1 :** of, relating to, or characteristic of the Malays **2 :** of, relating to, or constituting the subdivision of the biogeographic Oriental region that includes the Malay peninsula, the Philippines, and the Indo-Malayan archipelago to Wallace's line

malayan bear *or* **malay bear** *n, usu cap M* **:** SUN BEAR

malayan forge *n, usu cap M* **:** a hand-operated forge with a vertical double piston bellows used esp. in Malaysia

malay apple *n, usu cap M* **1 :** the edible fruit of a tree (*Eugenia malaccensis*) of Asia and Polynesia **2 :** the tree that bears Malay apples

malay camphor *n, usu cap M* **:** BORNEO CAMPHOR

ma·lay·ic \-ā(y)ik\ *adj, usu cap* [*1malay* + *-ic*] **:** MALAYAN

malayo- *comb form, usu cap* [*2malay* + *-o-*] **:** Malayan and ⟨*Malayo*-Indonesian⟩

1ma·layo–indonesian \mə¦lā(,)ō, (¦)mā¦l-+\ *adj, usu cap M&I* **1 :** of, relating to, or characteristic of both the Malays and the Indonesians **2 :** AUSTRONESIAN

2malayo–indonesian \"\ *n, cap M&I* **:** a member of the Malay people of Indonesia

1ma·layo–polynesian \mə¦lā(,)ō, (¦)mā¦l-+\ *adj, usu cap M&P* **1 :** of, relating to, or characteristic of both the Malays and the Polynesians **2 :** AUSTRONESIAN

2malayo–polynesian \"\ *n, cap M&P* **1 :** a member of the Malay people of Polynesia **2 :** AUSTRONESIAN

ma·lay·sia \mə'lāzh(ē)ə, -āsh-\ *adj, usu cap* [fr. *Malaysia*, country in southeastern Asia] **:** of or from the country of Malaysia **:** of the kind or style prevalent in Malaysia

1ma·lay·sian \-(ē)ən\ *adj, usu cap* [*Malaysia*, Asia + E *-an*] **1 :** of, relating to, or characteristic of Malaysia **2 :** of, relating to, or characteristic of the natives or inhabitants of Malaysia **3 :** of, relating to, or characteristic of the deutero-Malays

2malaysian \"\ *n* -s *cap* **1 :** a native or inhabitant of Malaysia **2 :** DEUTERO-MALAY

malay squirrel *n, usu cap M* **:** a squirrel (*Callosciurus prevostii*) found in the Malay peninsula that has a dark back and a lighter belly separated by broad white lateral stripes

malay wild dog *n, usu cap M* **:** a wild dog (*Cuon javanicus*) found in Malaysia and adjacent islands and closely related to the red dog

mal·behavior \¦mal+\ *n* [*1mal-* + *behavior*] **:** behavior that is regarded as socially unacceptable ⟨few forms of ~ . . . are not in history and essence a variation or deflection of normal mechanisms —A.L.Gesell & Frances Ilg⟩

mal·brouck \'mal,brůk\ *n* -s [F *malbrouk*, *malbrouch*, prob. fr. *Malbrouk*, figure in an 18th century French song who was popularly identified with John Churchill, 1st Duke of Marlborough †1722 Eng. military commander] **:** a West African arboreal monkey (*Cercopithecus cynosurus*)

mal·chus \'malkəs\ *n* -ES [F, fr. LL *Malchus*, high priest's servant whose ear St. Peter cut off with a sword (Jn 18: 10), fr. Gk *Malchos*] **:** a short sword resembling an anlace

mal·conduct \(¦)mal+\ *n* [*1mal-* + *conduct*] **:** bad conduct; *esp* **:** dishonesty in managing public affairs ⟨must be convicted of ~ before he can be removed —Gouverneur Morris⟩

mal·conformation \¦=+\ *n* [*1mal-* + *conformation*] **:** imperfect or abnormal formation ⟨the inherent ~ of the Carlovingian Empire —F.T.Palgrave⟩; *esp* **:** disproportion between bodily structures ⟨~ of head and shoulders⟩

mal·construction \"+\ *n* [*1mal-* + *construction*] **:** poor or faulty construction

1mal·content \"+\ *n* [MF, fr. *malcontent*, adj.] **1 :** a discontented person: **a :** one who bears a grudge from a sense of grievance or thwarted ambition ⟨lord of folded arms . . . liege of all loiterers and ~s —Shak.⟩ ⟨every peevish, moody ~ —Nicholas Rowe⟩ ⟨in the drama of the early 17th century . . . the ~ is the man who has been unable to achieve an "advancement" commensurate with his abilities —H.B.Parkes⟩ ⟨~s . . . bitter and almost choking with self-pity —E.W.Griffiths⟩ **b :** one who is disaffected with an established order or government or in active opposition to it **:** REBEL ⟨harebrained scheme of a small group of ~s —William Plutte⟩ **2 :** *archaic* **:** DISCONTENT ⟨the ~ of Job —Sir Thomas Browne⟩

2malcontent \"\ *adj* [MF, fr. OF, fr. *mal* badly + *content* — more at MAL-, CONTENT] **:** marked by a restless, moody, or bitter dissatisfaction with the existing state of affairs **:** DISCONTENTED ⟨you stand pensive, as half ~ —Shak.⟩ ⟨~ satire —*New Republic*⟩; *specif* **:** disaffected with an established order or government ⟨a ~ group of political exiles⟩

mal·contented \"+\ *adj* [prob. fr. MF *malcontent*, adj. + E *-ed*] **:** MALCONTENT ⟨young men who are ~, unsettled, and influenced by the more extreme racial sentiments —Michael Banton⟩ — **mal·contentedly** \"+\ *adv* — **mal·contentedness** \"+\ *n*

1mal·dan·id \(')mal¦danəd\ *adj* [NL *Maldanidae*] **:** of or relating to the Maldanidae

2maldanid \"\ *n* -s [NL *Maldanidae*] **:** a worm of the family Maldanidae

mal·dan·i·dae \mal'danə,dē\ *n pl, cap* [NL, fr. *Maldane*, type genus + *-idae*] **:** a family of slender cylindrical polychaete worms having rudimentary parapodia, lacking differentiated gills, and living in sand tubes

mal de ca·de·ras \ˌmaldəkə'derəs\ *n* [AmerSp, lit., disease of the hips] **:** an infectious disease of horses in So. America caused by a protozoan parasite (*Trypanosoma equinum*) in the blood and characterized by rapid emaciation, anemia, blood-colored urine, paresis, and edema

mal del pin·to \ˌmal,del'pin·(,)tō\ *n* [AmerSp, lit., disease of the spotted one] **:** PINTA

mal de mer \ˌmaldə'me(ə)r\ *n* [F] **:** SEASICKNESS

mal·development \¦mal+\ *n* [*1mal-* + *development*] **:** abnormal growth or development **:** DYSPLASIA

mal di gom·ma \ˌmaldē'gōmə, -gämə\ *n* [It, lit., gum disease] **:** a foot rot or collar rot of citrus plants caused by a fungus (*Phytophthora parasitica*)

mal·distribution \"+\ *n* [*1mal-* + *distribution*] **:** bad or faulty distribution: as **a :** undesirable inequality or unevenness of placement or apportionment (as of population, wealth, or resources) over an area or among the members of a group ⟨these islands suffer from a ~ of population—Amry Vandenbosch⟩ ⟨the ~ of wealth inherent in the profit system —*N.Y. Times*⟩ **b :** inequitable or inefficient delivery or conveyance (as of goods) to the members of a group ⟨~ of steel and its diversion to the giant affiliates of the ruling steel mills —Gunther Stein⟩

mal·dive islands \ˌmal,dīv-, -ōl-, -,div-\ *adj, usu cap M&I* [fr. *Maldive Islands*, country in Northern Indian Ocean] **:** of or relating to the Maldive Islands **:** of the kind or style prevalent in the Maldive Islands

1mal·div·i·an \(')mal¦divēən, (')mōl-\ *also* **mal·di·van** \'=,dīvən, -,dəv-\ *adj, usu cap* [*Maldive* Islands, in Indian Ocean southwest of Ceylon + E *-an*, adj. suffix] **1 :** of, relating to, or characteristic of the Maldive Islands **2 :** of, relating to, or characteristic of Maldivians

2maldivian \"\ *also* **maldivan** \"\ *n* -s *cap* [*Maldive* Islands + E *-an*, n. suffix] **:** a native or inhabitant of the Maldive Islands

mal·don·ite \'mōldə,nīt\ *n* -s [*Maldon*, Victoria, Australia, its locality + E *-ite*] **:** a mineral of variable composition but approximately Au_2Bi consisting of an alloy of gold and bismuth

mal·duck \'maldək\ *n* [prob. alter. (influenced by *duck*) of *mallemuck*] *Brit* **:** FULMAR

1male \'māl, *esp before pause or consonant* -āəl\ *adj* [ME, fr. MF *male*, *masle*, adj. & n., fr. L *masculus*, adj. & n., dim. of *mas*, adj. & n., male] **1 a** (1) **:** of, relating to, or being the sex that begets young by performing the fertilizing function in generation **:** of, relating to, or being the sex that produces relatively small usu. motile gametes (as sperms, spermatozoids, spermatozoa) by which the eggs of a female are made fertile **:** exhibiting maleness ⟨a ~ animal⟩ ⟨~ sex organs⟩ — symbol ♂ (2) **:** STAMINATE; *esp* **:** having only staminate flowers and not producing fruit or seeds ⟨a ~ holly⟩ ⟨a ~ bittersweet⟩ **b** (1) **:** of, relating to, or characteristic of one that is male, esp. a man **:** VIRILE ⟨a deep ~ voice⟩ **:** having a quality (as strength, vigor, courage) associated with one that is male ⟨full of ~ energy⟩ ⟨spoke to her with ~ directness⟩ (2) **:** made up of male individuals, esp. men **:** consisting of males ⟨a ~ choir⟩ ⟨the ~ population of the city⟩ **2** *of a gem* **:** having a rich and dark coloring ⟨a ~ sapphire⟩ **3 :** MASCULINE 2b(2) **4 :** designed for fitting into a corresponding female part which is hollow ⟨a ~ hose coupling⟩ **5 :** relating to a dialect or having speech forms used only by men ⟨~ language⟩ **6 :** of, associated with, or being the formal, active, or generative principle of the cosmos — compare YANG

syn MALE, MASCULINE, MANLY, MANLIKE, MANNISH, MANFUL, and VIRILE all mean belonging to or like a male of the species, esp. human. MALE, opposing *female*, applies to humans, animals, or plants, and always indicates sex ⟨a *male* collie⟩ ⟨a *male* willow⟩ ⟨a *male* child⟩ ⟨a *male* chorus⟩ MASCULINE, opposing *feminine*, is sometimes interchangeable with MALE ⟨the *masculine* half of the audience⟩ and is used to distinguish grammatical gender ⟨a *masculine* noun⟩ ⟨a *masculine* inflection on an adjective⟩ but most commonly applies to qualities that seem esp. to distinguish the male from the female ⟨a very *masculine* voice⟩ ⟨the *masculine* firmness, the quiet force of his style —Henry James⟩ ⟨his *masculine* longing to command —Edith Sitwell⟩ ⟨his wife was a great *masculine* virago —Tobias Smollett⟩ MANLY, usu. opposing *boyish*, *childish*, or *effeminate*, suggests the finer qualities of a man, esp. courage, independence, and mature physical characteristics or mental firmness or forthrightness ⟨a *manly* refusal to avoid difficulties⟩ ⟨a boy's love is likely to be divided between a gun and a watch; but the more active and *manly* choose the gun —H.D.Thoreau⟩ ⟨the country, with its rugged virtues and its *manly* independence —W.G.O'Donnell⟩ ⟨a sculptor had a model so perfect in *manly* symmetry and strength —G.G.Coulton⟩ MANLIKE is often close to *human* in a general sense ⟨one of the more *manlike* apes⟩ but is generally used to suggest characteristically masculine qualities or, sometimes, foibles ⟨sturdy, sunburnt creatures, in petticoats, but otherwise *manlike* —Nathaniel Hawthorne⟩ ⟨a boy *manlike* in stature, strength, and a strong tendency to try to dominate⟩ MANNISH applies chiefly to women, or things belonging to them, that have certain manlike qualities ⟨a great many women, brave in *mannish* clothes —Louis Bromfield⟩ ⟨at one time bobbed her hair, which had made her head a little too *mannish* —Edmund Wilson⟩ MANFUL adds to MANLY a greater stress on sturdiness or resoluteness ⟨we should be shabby fellows if we spent any serious proportion of our 13,000 days in shirking or whining or sponging on the more *manful* part of mankind —C.E.Montague⟩ ⟨worked like a *manful* soldier —Charles Dickens⟩ ⟨a *manful* handling of a trying situation⟩ VIRILE, stronger than MASCULINE and opposing *impotent*, suggests qualities belonging to esp. well-developed manhood, as marked aggressiveness, masterfulness, forcefulness, or, specifically, male sexuality or procreativeness ⟨the religion is *virile*, aggressive, and growing —L.C.May⟩ ⟨the robust, *virile* Elizabethan era —Rosette Hargrove⟩ ⟨he would have preferred brutality, which was *virile*, . . . rather than this sad, sedulous defeat —Audrey Barker⟩ ⟨the *virile* story of a little man, his big wife, and his bigger bull —*Atlantic*⟩

2male \"\ *n* -s [ME, fr. MF *male*, *masle*, adj. & n.] **:** an individual (as a man, boy, male animal, staminate plant) that begets young **:** an individual that produces relatively small usu. motile gametes by which the eggs of a female are fertilized **:** an individual possessing the qualities of maleness **:** male individual

3ma·le \'mälā\ *n, pl* **ma·ler** \-lər\ *or* **male** *or* **males** *usu cap* **:** a member of a Dravidian animistic people of Bengal

male alto *n* **:** a male singer singing falsetto — called also *countertenor*

malease *var of* MALAISE

ma·le·ate \mə'lēˌāt, *usu* -ād·+V\ *n* -s [ISV *maleic* (in *maleic acid*) + *-ate*] **:** a salt or ester of maleic acid

male bamboo *n* **:** an East Indian bamboo grass (*Dendrocalamus strictus*) forming great clumps often 50 feet high

maleberry \'=- — *see* BERRY\ *n* **1 :** PEABERRY **2 :** PRIVET ANDROMEDA

mal·e·branch·ism \¦malə¦bran,chizəm\ *n* -s *usu cap* [F *malebranchisme*, fr. Nicolas de *Malebranche* †1715 Fr. metaphysician + F *-isme* -ism] **:** a philosophical system based on the premise that the mind cannot have knowledge of anything external to itself except through its relation to God

mal·e·branch·ist \-,chəst\ *n* -s *usu cap* [F *malebranchiste*, fr. Nicolas de *Malebranche* †1715 + F *-iste* -ist] **:** an advocate of or believer in Malebranchism

mal·e·cite *or* **mal·i·seet** \'malə,sēt, ,=='=\ *n, pl* **malecite** *or* **malecites** *or* **maliseet** *or* **maliseets** *usu cap* [prob. fr. Micmac *Malisit*] **1 a :** an Indian people of New Brunswick, Canada, and of the northernmost part of northeastern Maine **b :** a member of such people **2 :** an Algonquian language of the Malecite and Passamaquoddy peoples

malecontent *archaic var of* MALCONTENT

mal·e·di·cent \¦malə¦dīs°nt\ *adj* [L *maledicent-*, *maledicens*, pres. part. of *maledicere* to speak evil] **1** *archaic* **:** addicted to speaking evil **2** *archaic* **:** SLANDEROUS

1mal·e·dict \'malə,dikt\ *adj* [LL *maledictus* (past part. of *maledicere* to curse), fr. L, past part. of *maledicere* to speak evil] *archaic* **:** ACCURSED

2maledict \"\ *vt* -ED/-ING/-S [LL *maledictus* (past part. of *maledicere* to curse), fr. L, past part. of L *maledicere* to speak evil, fr. *male* badly + *dicere* to speak, say — more at MAL-, DICTION] *archaic* **:** EXECRATE, CURSE

mal·e·dic·tion \ˌ=='dikshən\ *n* -s [ME *malediccioun*, fr. LL *malediction-*, *maledictio*, fr. *maledictus* (past part. of *maledicere* to curse) + L *-ion-*, *-io* -ion] **:** CURSE, EXECRATION ⟨the ~s of great poets, whose hate confers an unwelcome immortality —John Buchan⟩

mal·e·dic·tive \¦==¦diktiv\ *adj* [*2maledict* + *-ive*] **1 :** marked by cursing **:** invoking evil **2 :** ACCURSED

mal·e·dic·to·ry \-t(ə)rē\ *adj* [*2maledict* + *-ory*] **:** MALEDICTIVE 1

mal·e·fac·tion \¦malə¦fakshən *sometimes* (')mal¦fak-\ *n* [*malefactor* + *-ion*] **:** CRIME, OFFENSE ⟨is most commonly attributed to the ~ of a maternal relative —Abram Kardiner⟩

mal·e·fac·tor \'malə¦faktə(r) *sometimes* (')mal¦f- *or* -,tō(ə)r *or* -,tō(ə)\ *n* [ME *malefactour*, fr. L *malefactor*, fr. *malefactus* (past part. of *malefacere* to do evil, fr. *male* badly + *facere* to do) + *-or* — more at DO] **1 :** one who commits an offense against the law; *esp* **:** FELON **2 :** one who does ill toward another **:** EVILDOER ⟨a sinister ~ abusing his power —*Iron Age*⟩ **syn** see CRIMINAL

mal·e·fac·tress \-,trəs\ *n* -ES [*malefactor* + *-ess*] **:** a female malefactor

male fern *n* **:** a fern (*Dryopteris filix-mas*) of Europe and No. America producing an oleoresin that is used in expelling tapeworms — compare ASPIDIUM

ma·lef·ic \mə'lefik\ *adj* [L *maleficus*, fr. *male* badly + *-ficus* -fic] **1 :** of, having, or exerting an unfavorable or malignant influence ⟨a ~ force⟩ **:** BALEFUL **2 :** MALICIOUS

mal·e·fice \'maləfəs\ *n* -s [ME, fr. L *maleficium*, fr. *maleficus*] **1 :** a piece of evil sorcery **:** an evil spell or enchantment ⟨a magic power working against mysterious ~s —Joseph Conrad⟩ **2** *archaic* **:** a piece of mischief **:** an evil deed

ma·lef·i·cence \mə'lefəsən(t)s\ *n* -s [It *maleficenza*, fr. L *maleficentia*, fr. *maleficus* + *-entia* -ence] **1 a :** the commission of harm or evil **:** EVILDOING ⟨the punishment of ~⟩ **b :** a harmful or evil act ⟨guilty of more than one ~⟩ **2 :** the quality or state of being maleficent ⟨recognized the ~ of the plan⟩

ma·lef·i·cent \-nt\ *adj* [fr. *maleficence*, after such pairs as E *benevolence: benevolent*] **1 a :** working harm or evil **:** EVIL, BALEFUL ⟨believes that he is surrounded at every step by ~ spirits —J.G.Frazer⟩ **b :** productive of harm or evil **:** HURTFUL, INJURIOUS ⟨the man does leave his mark behind him, ineffaceable, beneficial to all, ~ to none —*Harper's*⟩ **2 a :** that commits or is disposed to commit offenses or crimes ⟨were surrounded by ~ nations⟩ **b :** having the nature of an offense or crime **:** CRIMINAL ⟨guilty of a ~ act⟩

1maleficiate *adj* [ML *maleficiatus*, past part. of *maleficiare* to bewitch, injure, fr. L *maleficium* evil spell] *obs* **:** placed under an evil spell; *esp* **:** made impotent by sorcery

2maleficiate *vt* -ED/-ING/-S [ML *maleficiatus*, past part. of *maleficiare*] *obs* **:** to put under an evil spell; *esp* **:** to make impotent by sorcery

male griffin *n* **:** a griffin (sense 1 b) sometimes borne in coats of arms that is without wings and that has clusters of rays or spikes issuing from various parts of its body

ma·le·ic acid \mə'lēik, -lāik-\ *n* [*maleic* fr. F *maléique* (in *acide maléique* maleic acid), alter. of *malique* malic (in *acide malique* malic acid) — more at MALIC ACID] **:** a crystalline unsaturated dicarboxylic acid HOOCCH=CHCOOH obtained usu. by catalytic oxidation of benzene or naphthalene or by dehydration of malic acid and used chiefly in making polyester resins; *cis*-butene-dioic acid — compare CIS-TRANS ISOMERISM a, FUMARIC ACID

maleic anhydride *n* **:** a crystalline cyclic acid anhydride $C_4H_2O_3$ that gives rise to maleic acid on reaction with water, that reacts readily with dienes in the Diels-Alder reaction, and that is used chiefly in the manufacture of alkyd and other resins and in the manufacture of modified drying oils

maleic hydrazide *n* : a crystalline cyclic hydrazide $C_4H_4N_2O_2$ made by reaction of hydrazine with maleic acid or anhydride and used to retard plant growth and the sprouting of potatoes, onions, and root crops (as carrots or beets) in storage
male incense *n, obs* : a frankincense of esp. high quality
malekite *usu cap, var of* MALIKITE
male menopause *n* : climacteric in the male
malemute *sometimes cap, var of* MALAMUTE
male·ness *n* -ES : the qualities (as of form, physiology, behavior) that distinguish an individual that produces small usu. motile gametes from one that produces eggs : MASCULINITY — opposed to *femaleness*; see SEX
malengine *n* [ME *malengin*, fr. MF, deceit, fr. OF, fr. *mal* bad + *engin* skill — more at MAL-, ENGINE] **1** *obs* : evil machination **2** *obs* : GUILE, DECEIT
mal·en·ten·du \mälänˈtändü\ *n* -S [F, fr. *mal entendu* misunderstood, fr. *mal* badly + *entendu*, past part. of *entendre* to understand, interpret, be attentive — more at MAL-, INTEND] : MISUNDERSTANDING ⟨through some ~ arrived an hour late⟩
male nutmeg *n* : MACASSAR NUTMEG
mal·eo \ˈmalē,ō\ *n, pl* **maleo** *or* **maleos** [Galelarese (language of northern Halmahera) *mĕleo*] : a megapode (*Macrocephalon maleo*) of Celebes that lays its eggs in holes in sandy beaches
male orchis *n* : a Eurasian orchid (*Orchis mascula*) with showy pink or purple flowers in a loose spike
male pronucleus *n* : the nucleus that remains in a male gamete after reduction and that contains only one half of the number of chromosomes characteristic of its species — compare FEMALE PRONUCLEUS
maler *pl of* MALE
males *pl of* MALE
males·her·bia \,maləˈzərbēə, ,maləsˈhər-, malˈzər-\ *n, cap* [NL, fr. Chrétien G. de Lamoignon de *Malesherbes* †1794 Fr. statesman + NL *-ia*] : a genus of So. American herbs or undershrubs (family Malesherbiaceae) that have capsular fruit and large yellow racemose flowers with a tubular calyx exceeding the corolla
males·her·bi·a·ce·ae \,═(═),══ˈāsē,ē\ *n pl, cap* [NL, fr. *Malesherbia*, type genus + *-aceae*] : a family of plants (order Parietales) coextensive with the genus *Malesherbia*
male shield fern *n* : MALE FERN
male–sterile \ˈ═;══\ *adj* : having male gametes lacking or nonfunctional ⟨a *male-sterile* plant⟩
ma·le·ta \məˈlād·ə\ *n* -S [Sp, bag, purse, fr. MF *malette*, fr. OF *malete*, fr. *male* bag + *-ete* -ette — more at MAIL, -ETTE] *Southwest* : a usu. rawhide bag
maletolt *var of* MALTOLTE
ma·lev·o·lence \məˈlevələn(t)s\ *n* -S [MF *malivolence*, fr. L *malivolentia*, *malevolentia*, fr. *malivolent-*, *malivolens*, *malevolent-*, *malevolens* malevolent + *-ia* -y] **1** : the quality or state of being malevolent ⟨slander that arose from pure ~⟩ **2** : behavior marked by or indicative of intense often vicious ill will ⟨an era full of selfishness and ~⟩ **syn** see MALICE
ma·lev·o·lent \-lənt\ *adj* [L *malivolent-*, *malivolens*, *malevolent-*, *malevolens*, fr. *male* badly + *volent-*, *volens*, pres. part. of *velle* to will — more at MAL-, WILL] **1** : having, showing, or indicative of intense often vicious ill will : filled with or marked by deep-seated spite or rancor or hatred ⟨a gossipy ~ old woman⟩ ⟨a ~ lie⟩ **2** : productive of harm or evil : HURTFUL, INJURIOUS ⟨have lived ~ and criminal lives and have been despised by men and punished by society —E.G.Conklin⟩ — **ma·lev·o·lent·ly** *adv*
malevolous *adj* [L *malevolus*, fr. *male* badly + *-volus* (fr. *velle*)] *obs* : MALEVOLENT
mal·fea·sance \malˈfēzᵊn(t)s\ *also* **mal·fai·sance** \ˈmalfəˈzäⁿs\ *n* -S [E ¹*mal-* + obs. E *feasance* doing, execution, fr. MF *faisance*, fr. OF, fr. *fais-* (stem of *faire* to make, do, fr. L *facere*) + *-ance* — more at DO] **1** : WRONGDOING, MISCONDUCT, MISBEHAVIOR; *specif* : the doing by a public officer under color of authority of his office of something that is unwarranted, that he has contracted not to do, and that is legally unjustified and positively wrongful or contrary to law — called also *malpractice*; distinguished from *misfeasance*, *nonfeasance* **2** : an act or instance of wrongdoing esp. by a public officer under color of authority of his office
mal·fea·sant \malˈfēzᵊnt\ *n* -S [fr. *malfeasance*, after such pairs as E *assistance: assistant*] : one that is guilty of malfeasance
mal·form \ˈ═+\ *vt* [¹*mal-* + *form*, v.] : to cause to be badly or imperfectly formed : cause to be formed in such a way as to deviate from the normal or usual : give an abnormal, anomalous, or otherwise irregular and defective formation or structure to ⟨a virus that ~s tobacco leaves⟩ ⟨in his chair sat a personality ~*ed* beyond decency by greed and pride —Clemence Dane⟩
mal·formation \ˈ═+\ *n* [¹*mal-* + *formation*] **1** : the condition of being malformed ⟨suffered from a ~ of character⟩ ⟨congenital ~⟩ **2** : something that is malformed : an instance of being malformed ⟨all kinds of queer ~*s* in our physical and psychological makeup —H.A.Overstreet⟩
mal·formed \ˈ═;═\ *adj* [¹*mal-* + *formed* (past part. of *form*, v.)] : formed in such a way as to deviate with undesirable or pernicious results from the normal or usual : having a formation or structure that is abnormal, anomalous, or otherwise irregular and defective : badly or imperfectly formed : MISSHAPEN ⟨walked with a limp that was caused by a ~ foot —F.V.W.Mason⟩
¹**mal·function** \"+\ *vi* [¹*mal-* + *function*, v.] : to function badly or imperfectly : fail to operate in the normal or usual manner ⟨designed a rifle that would not ~⟩ ⟨the parachute ~*ed*, opening too late⟩ ⟨attributable to some ~*ing* of the nervous system —Edward Sapir⟩
²**malfunction** \"\ *n* **1** : the action or fact of malfunctioning ⟨altitudes where ~ of the plane becomes evident⟩ **2** : an instance of malfunctioning ⟨three ~*s* had been reported and rectified before the rocket was finally launched⟩
mal·gache *or* **mal·gach** *also* **mal·gash** \(ˈ)malˈgash\ *n, pl* **malgache** *or* **malgach** *or* **malgaches** *also* **malgashes** *usu cap* [F *malgache*] : MALAGASY
mal·gré \(ˈ)malˈgrā\ *prep* [F, fr. OF *maugré* — more at MAUGRE] : DESPITE ⟨one bar where a decent drink is to be obtained, ~ the monstrous regiment of women —R.S.Hillyer⟩
malgré lui \,═,═ləˈwē\ *adv* [F, in spite of himself] : despite himself ⟨extraordinary talents, which somehow always crop out to show him at his best *malgré lui* —*Saturday Rev.*⟩
mal·gu·zar \,mälgəˈzär\ *n* -S [Hindi *mālguzār*, fr. Ar *māl* property, rent + Per *guzār* payer] : MALIK
mal·heur \maˈlər\ *n* -S [F, fr. OF *maleur*, fr. *mal* bad + *eür* fortune, fr. L *augurium* augury — more at MAL-, AUGURY] *archaic* : MISFORTUNE
¹**ma·li** *also* **mal·lee** *or* **mal·ly** *or* **mol·ly** \ˈmälē\ *n, pl* **malis** *also* **mallees** *or* **mallies** *or* **mollies** [Hindi *mālī*, fr. Skt *mālika* gardener] : one belonging to a caste in the subcontinent of India whose usual occupation is gardening
²**mali** \"\ *adj, usu cap* [*Mali*, republic in west Africa] : of or from the Republic of Mali : of the kind or style prevalent in Mali
ma·li·an \ˈmälēən\ *n* -S *cap* [*Mali*, country in western Africa + E *-an*] : a native or inhabitant of Mali — **malian** *adj, usu cap*
mal·ic acid \ˈmalik, ˈmālik-\ *n* [*malic* fr. F *malique*, fr. L *malum* apple + F *-ique* -ic — more at MALUS] : a crystalline hydroxy dicarboxylic acid HOOCCH(OH)CH$_2$COOH known in three optically isomeric forms; hydroxy-succinic acid: (1) the levorotatory L-form found in various plant juices (as in apples, grapes, rhubarb) and formed as an intermediate in the Krebs cycle; (2) the dextrorotatory D-form usu. obtained by resolution of the racemic form; (3) the racemic form made by hydration of maleic acid or fumaric acid
¹**mal·ice** \ˈmaləs\ *n* -S [ME, fr. OF, fr. L *malitia*, fr. *malus* bad — more at SMALL] **1 a** (1) : intention or desire to harm another usu. seriously through doing something unlawful or otherwise unjustified : willfulness in the commission of a wrong : evil intention ⟨ruined her reputation and did it with ~⟩ ⟨rejoiced out of pure ~ in seeing others suffer⟩ — compare IMPLIED MALICE, MALICE AFORETHOUGHT, MALICE IN FACT (2) : conscious and deliberate transgression esp. of a moral code viewed as established by God accompanied by an evil intention ⟨theologians hold that the gravity of an offense against divine law depends on the degree of ~ involved⟩ (3) : revengeful or unfriendly feelings : ILL WILL, ENMITY ⟨in spite of all he has had to put up with from them, he bears them no ~⟩ **b** : sportive intention or desire to discomfit others (as by teasing or joking) : playful mischievousness ⟨with smiling ~ asked her where she had been⟩ **2** *obs* **a** : BADNESS; *esp* : WICKEDNESS **b** : HARMFULNESS
syn MALEVOLENCE, ILL WILL, SPITE, DESPITE, MALIGNANCY, MALIGNITY, SPLEEN, GRUDGE: MALICE may apply either to a deep-seated, often unjustified, innate desire to bring pain and suffering to others or to enjoy contemplating it or to a passing impish mischievousness not arising from a hardened vindictive nature ⟨from such persons no repentance was to be looked for. They were impelled by a *malice* or a fanaticism which clemency could not touch or reason influence —J.A. Froude⟩ ⟨she was clever, witty, brilliant, and sparkling beyond most of her kind; but possessed of many devils of *malice* and mischievousness —Rudyard Kipling⟩ MALEVOLENCE may suggest a cold deep hatred or enmity underlying wishes for evil for others ⟨their society is organized by a permanent, universal animosity and *malevolence*; sullen suspicion and resentment are their chief motives, ill will and treachery their chief virtues —H.J.Muller⟩ ILL WILL may suggest a feeling of enmity, antipathy, or resentment directed against a person or thing, often with cause; it differs from MALEVOLENCE in not implying a lasting character trait ⟨Catherine could not believe it possible that any injury or any misfortune could provoke such *ill will* against a person not connected, or, at least, not supposed to be connected with it —Jane Austen⟩ SPITE suggests petty ill will and mean envy and resentment ⟨a man full of the secret *spite* of dullness, who interrupted from time to time, and always to check or disorder thought —W.B.Yeats⟩ DESPITE, now not common, may imply more pride and disdain but less pettiness than SPITE ⟨not in *despite* but softly, as men smile about the dead —G.K.Chesterton⟩ MALIGNANCY and MALIGNITY imply deep passion and relentless driving force ⟨employed by the envy, jealousy and *malignity* of his enemies, to ruin him with the queen —Hilaire Belloc⟩ ⟨he is cruel with the cruelty of petrified feeling, to his poor heroine; he pursues her without pity or pause, as with *malignity* —Matthew Arnold⟩ ⟨blinded by *malignancy* against the class of manual worker —Cecil Sprigge⟩ SPLEEN indicates choleric ill will with wrathful release of latent spite ⟨his just fame was long obscured by partisan *spleen* —V.L.Parrington⟩ ⟨venting their *spleen* against the United States in so venomous a manner —T.R.Fyvel⟩ GRUDGE suggests cherished ill will with deep resentment at a real or imagined slight, affront, humiliation, or other cause of chagrin ⟨she had never been close to Uncle Claude and had held a *grudge* against him for ending her companionship with Ralph —Jean Stafford⟩ ⟨the secret *grudges* that the relations of men whom he had killed or dishonored bore against him —Robert Graves⟩
²**malice** *vi* -ED/-ING/-S *obs* : to regard with malice ~ *vi, obs* : to harbor or cherish malice
malice aforethought *or* **malice prepense** *n* [*malice aforethought* trans. of AF *malice purpensee*; *malice prepense* alter. of earlier *malice prepensed* (trans. of AF *malice purpensee*), fr. E *malice* + obs. E *prepensed* premeditated — more at PREPENSE] : deliberate malice : premeditated malice; *specif* : malice in fact or implied malice in the intention of one who has had sufficient time to act with premeditation in the doing of something unlawful (as in doing serious bodily harm to another person or as in murdering another person)
mal·ice·ful \ˈ══fəl\ *adj, archaic* : MALICIOUS
malice in fact *law* : malice actually existing or proved by direct evidence to have existed in the intention of a person in the commission of unjustified injury or harm to another — distinguished from *implied malice*
ma·li·cious \məˈlishəs\ *adj* [ME, fr. OF *malicius*, fr. L *malitiosus*, fr. *malitia* malice + *-osus* -ose] : given to, marked by, or arising from malice ⟨took a ~ pleasure in emphasizing this point and in watching me wince —Rudyard Kipling⟩ — **ma·li·cious·ly** *adv* — **ma·li·cious·ness** *n* -ES
malicious abandonment *n, law* : desertion of one spouse by the other without just cause
malicious mischief *n, law* : willful, wanton, or reckless damage or destruction of another's property
malicious prosecution *n, law* : the bringing of a civil or criminal proceeding against another in a court of law without reasonable cause and with malicious intent
ma·lif·er·ous \məˈlif(ə)rəs\ *adj* [L *malum* evil (fr. *malus* bad) + E *-iferous* — more at SMALL] *archaic* : having an unhealthful effect : UNWHOLESOME
¹**ma·lign** \məˈlīn\ *adj* [ME *maligne*, fr. MF, fr. L *malignus*, fr. *male* badly + *-ignus* (as in *benignus* benign) — more at MAL-] **1 a** : evil in nature, influence, or effect : INJURIOUS, BALEFUL ⟨prompted by ~ motives⟩ ⟨living in a ~ environment⟩ **b** : MALIGNANT, VIRULENT ⟨a ~ lesion⟩ **2 a** : having or showing or indicative of intense often vicious ill will : intensely hostile : MALEVOLENT ⟨gave him a ~ look⟩ **b** : desiring or taking pleasure in the sufferings of others ⟨believed in the existence of witches and ~ spirits⟩
²**malign** \"\ *vb* -ED/-ING/-S [ME *malignen*, fr. MF *maligner*, fr. LL *malignare*, *malignari*, to act maliciously, fr. L *malignus*] *vi, obs* : to speak, think, or act malevolently ~ *vt* **1** *obs* **a** : to regard with intense ill will or with bitter dislike or hatred **b** : RESENT, BEGRUDGE **2** : to utter injuriously misleading or deliberately and injuriously false reports about : induce misunderstanding of and lower regard for by falsehood or misrepresentation ⟨gossips had ~*ed* the lady —George Meredith⟩
syn CALUMNIATE, ASPERSE, VILIFY, TRADUCE, DEFAME, SLANDER, LIBEL: MALIGN may suggest malevolent calculation as a motivating force and specific and subtle misrepresentations and falsehoods as instruments ⟨little doubt that Lytton Strachey and other British historians have *maligned* Ward in order to build up the fame of "Chinese" Gordon —Richard Watts⟩ The past participle may be less severe in suggestion and apply to the role of innocent reiteration in conditioning a reputation ⟨in view of Hans Heysen's studies of this *maligned* and slandered tree, its beauty is clear enough —Thomas Wood †1950⟩ CALUMNIATE involves malice against the victim, is used more often in connection with public affairs and figures, and suggests blackening of the general reputation ⟨*calumniating* him as a traitor in satisfying his ancient personal grudge⟩ ASPERSE may suggest continued attack on a reputation, sometimes by direct false accusation but often by covert depreciating insinuation ⟨one may not admire it, but one can no longer *asperse* the integrity of those who do —*Times Lit. Supp.*⟩ VILIFY may suggest a direct ranting or railing abuse without subtlety, an attempt to make vile and shameful ⟨should not be *vilified* in newspapers, for that is want of tact and waste of space —Rudyard Kipling⟩ ⟨his circumlocutions are roundly called lies, and his silence is *vilified* as treachery —W.S.Maugham⟩ TRADUCE is the least rich in connotation in this series. More than the preceding words, it may suggest success in derogation ⟨fear of this witch of the East [Cleopatra], shamelessly *traduced* by Octavian's agents, hagrode the popular mind —John Buchan⟩ DEFAME stresses actual loss of reputation brought about by malicious charges ⟨*defaming* and defacing, till she left not even Lancelot brave nor Galahad clean —Alfred Tennyson⟩ SLANDER connotes nasty maliciousness in motivation, oral utterance, frequently covert, and definite suffering or loss for the victim ⟨you would darkly *slander* him you cannot openly defame —E.G.Bulwer-Lytton⟩ ⟨he was rector until the new governor listened to some cock-and-bull story against him, and made him resign. He was the best preacher they ever had — he'd have been a bishop one day, if someone hadn't *slandered* him to the governor —R.A. W.Hughes⟩ LIBEL, more legalistic than the others in this series, is much the same as SLANDER in its connotations, except that it may imply issuance of the defamatory matter in wider and more permanent media than SLANDER. In legal or legalistic use denotations and connotations of words in this series vary in different jurisdictions
ma·lig·nance \məˈlignən(t)s\ *n* -S [fr. *malignant*, after such pairs as E *assistant: assistance*] : MALIGNANCY
ma·lig·nan·cy \-nənsē, -si\ *n* -ES [¹*malignant* + *-cy*] **1 a** : the quality or state of being malignant **b** : an instance of malignant behavior or malignant nature **2 a** *of a tumor* : exhibition of malignant qualities : VIRULENCE **b** : a malignant tumor **syn** see MALICE
¹**ma·lig·nant** \-nənt\ *adj* [LL *malignant-*, *malignans*, pres. part. of *malignare*, *malignari* to act maliciously] **1 a** *obs* : REBELLIOUS, DISAFFECTED, MALCONTENT **b** : evil in nature or influence or effect : INJURIOUS, BALEFUL, MALIGN ⟨astrological belief in the ~ power of the stars⟩ **c** : having or showing or indicative of intense often vicious ill will : desiring or causing or rejoicing in the sufferings of others : extremely malevolent or malicious ⟨the ~ tongues of gossipers⟩ **2** *med* : tending to produce death or deterioration ⟨~ malaria⟩: **a** *of a tumor* : unencapsulated and tending to infiltrate, metastasize, and in the absence of treatment terminate fatally — opposed to *benign* **b** : severe and rapidly progressive ⟨~ hypertension⟩ **c** : of unfavorable prognosis : not responding favorably to treatment ⟨psychotic reactions with a ~ trend⟩ — **ma·lig·nant·ly** *adv*
²**malignant** \"\ *n* -S **1** *archaic* : one that is rebellious, dis affected, or malcontent **2** *archaic, usu cap* : CAVALIER 4a
malignant catarrh *also* **malignant catarrhal fever** *n* **1** : a catarrhal fever of cattle apparently caused by a filterable virus and marked by acute edematous inflammation of the respiratory and digestive systems and sometimes of the sinuses of the head and eyes and genitourinary organs **2** : hepatic coccidiosis of the rabbit
malignant edema *n* : inflammatory edema in infections; *specif* : an acute wound infection of wild and domestic animals and rarely man that is clinically indistinguishable from blackleg and that is caused by an anaerobic toxin-producing bacterium (*Clostridium septicum*) — compare BIGHEAD, BRAXY
malignant hypertension *n* : essential hypertension characterized by acute onset, severe symptoms, rapidly progressive course, and poor prognosis
malignant jaundice *n* : canine piroplasmosis
malignant lymphoma *n* : HODGKIN'S DISEASE
malignant malaria *n* : FALCIPARUM MALARIA
malignant neutropenia *n* : AGRANULOCYTOSIS
malignant pustule *n* : localized anthrax of the skin taking the form of a pimple surrounded by a zone of edema and hyperemia and tending to become necrotic and ulcerated
malignant tumor *n* : a metastatic tumor : CANCER
maligned *past of* MALIGN
ma·lign·er \məˈlīnə(r)\ *n* -S : one that maligns
maligning *pres part of* MALIGN
ma·lig·ni·ty \məˈlignəd·ē, -ətē, -i\ *n* -ES [ME *malignitee*, fr. MF *malignité*, fr. L *malignitat-*, *malignitas*, fr. *malignus* malign + *-itat-*, *-itas* -ity — more at MALIGN] **1** : great malignancy or malice **2** : an instance of malignant or malicious behavior or nature **syn** see MALICE
ma·lign·ly *adv* : in a malign manner
maligns *pres 3d sing of* MALIGN
ma·li·hi·ni \,mälēˈhēnē\ *n* -S [Hawaiian] : a newcomer or stranger among the people of Hawaii
ma·lik \ˈmälik\ *n* -S [Hindi *mālik*, fr. Ar] **1** : a chief or leader (as in a village) in parts of the subcontinent of India : HEADMAN **2** : ZAMINDAR
ma·li·ka·na \,mäləˈkänə\ *n* -S [Hindi *mālikāna*, lit., proprietary, fr. Per, fr. Ar *mālik*] **1** : a fee paid to a malik by way of rent or duty on land **2** : a pension or allowance granted by the government to a malik
mal·i·ki \ˈmaləkē\ *n* -S *usu cap* [Ar *malikīy* of or relating to Malik, fr. *Malik* ibn-Anas †A.D.795 Moslem jurist] **1** : an orthodox school of Muslim jurisprudence predominating in No. Africa and Upper Egypt — compare HANAFI, HANBALI, SHAFI'I **2** *or* **mal·i·kite** *or* **mal·e·kite** \ˈmalə,kīt\ [*Malik* ibn-Anas †A.D.795 + E *-ite*] : a follower of the Maliki school
ma·lin·che \məˈlinchē\ *n* -S [AmerSp, fr. Nahuatl *Malintzin* (Marina) †1550? Aztec slave mistress of Hernando Cortes] : a man or boy dressed as a woman in a Mexican dance drama
ma·line \məˈlēn\ *n* -S *sometimes cap* [F, Mechlin lace, back-formation fr. *malines*, taken as a plural] : MALINES 2
ma·lines \məˈlēn\ *n, pl* **malines** *sometimes cap* [F, fr. *Malines* (Mechelen), city in northern Belgium] **1** *or* **malines lace** : MECHLIN LACE **2** : a fine stiff net that has a hexagonal mesh and that is made of silk or rayon (as for millinery) or hair (as for veils)
ma·lin·ger \məˈliŋgə(r)\ *vi* **malingered**; **malingered**; **malingering** \-g(ə)riŋ\ **malingers** [F *malingre* sickly, ailing, fr. (assumed) OF *malingre*, fr. OF *mal* badly + *haingre* thin, lean, perh. of Gmc origin; akin to MHG *hager* thin, lean; akin to Av *kasu-* little — more at MAL-] **1** : to pretend to be ill or otherwise physically or mentally incapacitated so as to avoid duty or work ⟨a ~*ing* soldier⟩ **2** : to deliberately induce, protract, or exaggerate actual illness or other incapacity so as to avoid duty or work **syn** see DODGE
ma·lin·ger·er \-gərə(r)\ *n* -S : one that malingers
ma·lin·ke \məˈliŋ(,)kā\ *n, pl* **malinke** *or* **malinkes** *usu cap* **1 a** : a people of Mandingo affiliation widespread in the western part of Africa from Portuguese Guinea into the French Sudan **b** : a member of such people **2** : a Mande language of the Malinke people
ma·li·nois \ˌmalənˈwä\ *n, pl* **malinois** *usu cap* [F, fr. *malinois*, adj., of or from Malines, fr. *Malines* (Mechelen), city in northern Belgium] : the largely fawn-colored short-haired variety of Belgian sheepdog
mal·i·now·skite \,maləˈnäf,skīt\ *n* -S [ISV *malinowsk-* (fr. E *Malinowski*, 19th cent. Russ. civil engineer) + *-ite*] : a tetrahedrite containing 13 to 16 percent of lead
mal·integration \ˌmal+\ *n* [¹*mal-* + *integration*] : defective integration ⟨~ of one group with another⟩ ⟨personality ~⟩
mal·investment \"+\ *n* [¹*mal-* + *investment*] : bad investment ⟨a ~ that nearly led to bankruptcy⟩
maliseet *usu cap, var of* MALECITE
ma·lism \ˈmā,lizəm\ *n* -S [L *malus* bad + E *-ism* — more at SMALL] : the doctrine that the world is evil
mal·i·son \ˈmaləsən, -əzən\ *n* -S [ME *malisoun*, fr. OF *maleïcon*, *maleïcon*, fr. LL *malediction-*, *maledictio* — more at MALEDICTION] : MALEDICTION, CURSE
mal·kin \ˈmó(l)kən, ˈmalk-, ˈmák-\ *n* -S [ME *malkyn*, fr. *Malkyn*, feminine name, prob. fr. *Mall* (nickname fr. the name *Maria*, *Mary*) + *-kyn*, *-kin* -kin] **1** *now dial Eng* **a** : a pole with a bundle of rags at one end used for cleaning out a baker's oven **b** : a ragged effigy : SCARECROW **2** *now dial Brit* **a** : an untidy woman : SLATTERN **b** (1) : CAT (2) : HARE
mal·kite \ˈmal,kīt\ *n* -S *usu cap* [Syr *malkā* king + E *-ite*] : MELCHITE
¹**mall** \ˈmól\ *var of* MAUL
²**mall** \ˈmól *also* ˈmäl *or* ˈmal\ *n* -S [by shortening & alter. (influenced in pronunciation by ¹*mall*) fr. *pall-mall*] **1 a** : the mallet used in the game of pall-mall **b** : the game of pall-mall **c** : an alley used for this game **2** [fr. *The Mall*, fashionable promenade in St. James's Park, London, that was originally a pall-mall alley] **a** : a usu. public area (typically a lane or similar strip) often set with trees or bushes or flowers and designed as a promenade for leisurely strolling or as a pedestrian walk **b** : a usu. paved or grassy strip between two roadways : MEDIAN STRIP ⟨a highway divided by a ~⟩
mal·la·drite \məˈlä,drīt, ˈmalə,d-\ *n* -S [It, fr. Alessandro *Malladra* †1944 Ital. geologist + It *-ite*] : a sodium fluosilicate Na_2SiF_6 occurring in minute hexagonal crystals in fumaroles in the crater of Vesuvius near Naples in Italy
mal·lan·gong \ˈmalən,gäŋ\ *n* -S [native name in Australia] : PLATYPUS
mal·lard \ˈmalə(r)d\ *n, pl* **mallard** *or* **mallards** [ME, fr. MF *malart*, *mallart*, fr. OF, prob. fr. *male*, *masle* male + *-art* -ard — more at MALE] **1** : a common and widely distributed wild duck (*Anas platyrhynchos*) of the northern hemisphere that is a dabbler, is the source of the domestic ducks, and is distinguished in the male by a greenish black head and neck, white collar, chestnut breast, grayish brown back, purple speculum, and grayish white underparts **2** *archaic* : a male mallard
mal·lard·ite \ˈmalə(r),dīt\ *n* -S [F, fr. Ernest *Mallard* †1894 Fr. mineralogist + F *-ite*] : hydrous sulfate of manganese $MnSO_4.7H_2O$
mal·le·a·bil·i·ty \,malēəˈbiləd·ē, -lyəb-, ÷-ləb-, -lətē, -i\ *n* [F *malléabilité*, fr. *malléable* malleable + *-ité* -ity] : the quality or state of being malleable
mal·lea·bil·i·za·tion \,═(═)═bələˈzāshən, -(,)bil-, -,līz-\ *n* -S [*malleabiliz-* (fr. *malleabilize*) + *-ation*] : the process of malleabilizing
mal·lea·ble \ˈmalēəbəl, -lyəb-, ÷-ləb-\ *adj* [ME *malliable*, fr. MF or ML; MF *malleable*, fr. ML *malleabilis*, fr. *malleare* to

hammer (fr. L *malleus* hammer) + L *-abilis* -able — more at MAUL] **1 :** capable of being extended or shaped by beating with a hammer or by the pressure of rollers ⟨most metals are ~⟩ — compare DUCTILE **2 :** capable of being formed or transformed **:** susceptible of being fashioned into a new or different form or shape **:** not rigidly fixed in condition or direction **:** plastically open to outside forces or influences **:** adaptable to other conditions or needs or uses **:** IMPRESSIONABLE ⟨finds a sort of ~ mind in front of him that he can play with as he will —John Masefield⟩ ⟨the ~ character of youth⟩ ⟨tactics that are ~ and vary with circumstances⟩ **syn** see PLASTIC

malleable iron *also* **malleable cast iron** *n* **:** cast iron containing usu. from 2 to 3 percent carbon and 1.5 to 0.8 percent silicon and produced by annealing white cast iron of this composition in order to convert hard brittle cementite to graphite in nodular form so that the material will have greater ductility than white iron or ordinary gray iron containing graphite in flake form

mal·lea·ble·ize *also* **mal·lea·blize** \-bə,līz\ *vt* -ED/-ING/-S **:** to make malleable ⟨*malleableizing* cast iron⟩

mal·lea·ble·ness *n* -ES **:** MALLEABILITY

mal·le·al \ˈmalēəl\ *also* **mal·le·ar** \-ēə(r)\ *adj* [prob. fr. (assumed) NL *mallealis, mallearis,* fr. NL *malleus* + L *-alis* -al or *-aris* -ar — more at MALLEUS] **:** of or relating to the malleus

¹mal·le·ate \-ē,āt\ *vt* -ED/-ING/-S [ML *malleatus,* past part. of *malleare* to hammer] **:** to beat with a hammer **:** POUND ⟨the surfaces of some fragments suggested that the clay had been poorly *malleated* —*Amer. Antiquity*⟩; *specif* **:** to beat or mark or dent (a metal) with a hammer in working or decorating

²mal·le·ate \-,āt, -ēət\ *adj* [NL *malleatus,* fr. *malleus* + L *-atus* -ate] **:** having a malleus

mal·le·a·tion \,==ˈāshən\ *n* -S [ML *malleation-, malleatio,* fr. *malleatus* (past part. of *malleare* to hammer) + L *-ion-, -io* -ion] **1 :** the action of malleating or state of being malleated **2 :** a mark or dent like one made by malleating

¹mal·lee \ˈmalē\ *n* -S [*mallee* native name in Victoria, Australia] **1** *also* **mallee box :** any of several low-growing Australian eucalypts; *esp* **:** one producing several stems from the base (as *Eucalyptus dumosa* or *E. oleosa*) **2 a :** a dense brushwood or thicket formed by mallees **b :** an area covered by mallee brushwood or a mallee thicket

²mallee *var of* MALI

mallee bird *or* **mallee fowl** *or* **mallee hen** *n* [¹*mallee*] **:** LEIPOA

mal·le·in \ˈmalēən\ *n* -S [ISV *malle-* (fr. NL *mallei* — specific epithet of the glanders-producing bacterium *Actinobacillus mallei* —, gen. of *malleus* glanders) + *-in*] **:** a product containing toxic principles of the bacillus of glanders and used to test for the presence of infection with that organism

mal·le·in·i·za·tion \,==ənə̇ˈzāshən, -,nīˈz-\ *n* -S **:** the action of malleinizing or condition of being malleinized

mal·le·in·ize \ˈ==ə,nīz\ *vt* -ED/-ING/-S [ISV *mallein* + *-ize*] **:** to test with mallein

mal·le·mock \ˈmalə,mək\ *also* **mol·le·mock** \ˈmälə,mäk\ *or* **mol·ly·mawk** \ˈmälē,mȯk\ *n* -S [D *mallemuk, mallemok,* fr. *mal* silly (fr. MD) + *mok* gull; akin to MLG *mal* silly and to ON *mār* gull — more at MEW] **:** one of several large oceanic birds (as the fulmar or petrel)

mallenders *var of* MALANDERS

mal·leo·incudal \ˌmalēō+\ *adj* [*malleo-* (fr. NL *malleus*) + *incudal*] **:** of or relating to the malleus and incus

mal·le·o·lar \məˈlēələ(r)\ *adj* [prob. fr. (assumed) NL *malleolaris,* fr. NL *malleolus* + L *-aris* -ar] **:** of or relating to a malleolus esp. of the ankle

mal·le·o·lare \mə,lēəˈla(a)rē, ,malē-, -ˈlärē\ *n* -S [NL, prob. fr. neut. of (assumed) NL *malleolaris*] **:** MALLEOLAR POINT

malleolar point *n* **:** the tip of the malleolus of the tibia

mal·le·o·lus \məˈlēələs\ *n, pl* **malleo·li** \-,lī\ [NL, fr. L, little hammer, dim. of *malleus* hammer — more at MAUL] **:** the rounded lateral projection on each bone of the leg at the ankle

mal·leo·my·ces \,malēōˈmī,sēz\ [NL, fr. *malleo-* (fr. *malleus* glanders) + *-myces*] *syn of* ACTINOBACILLUS

¹mal·let \ˈmalət, *usu* -əd·+V\ *n* -S [ME *maillet,* fr. MF, fr. OF, fr. *mail* maul, mallet + *-et* — more at MAUL] **:** a hammer that has a cylindrical typically barrel-shaped head of wood or of other soft material: as **a :** a tool with a large head for driving another tool (as a chisel) or for striking a surface without marring it **b** (1) **:** an implement with a long handle and large head used in the game of croquet for striking the ball (2) **:** an implement with a very long narrow handle and a rather narrow tapering light head used in the game of polo for striking the ball **c :** a light hammer with a small head used in playing a vibraphone or similar percussion instrument

mallet a

²mallet \"\ *vt* -ED/-ING/-S **:** to strike with or as if with a mallet ⟨end of flat portion of cleat shall be folded back over nailheads and ~*ed* flat —*Sweet's Catalog Service*⟩

³mallet \"\ *also* **mallet bark** *or* **mallet wood** *n* -S [*mallet* native name in Western Australia] **1 :** any of several Australian gum trees of the genus *Eucalyptus* esp. when rich in tannin **2 :** CALIFORNIA LAUREL

mallet cutting *n* [¹*mallet*] **1 :** LEAF-BUD CUTTING **2 :** a hardwood cutting of current season's growth with a heel of the previous season's growth

mal·le·us \ˈmalēəs\ *n* [NL, fr. L, hammer] **1** *pl* **mal·lei** \-ē,ī\ **a :** the outermost of the three auditory ossicles of mammals consisting of a head, neck, short process, long process, and handle, the short process and handle being fastened to the tympanic membrane, and the head articulating with the head of the incus — see EAR illustration **b :** one of the hard lateral pieces of the mastax of rotifers **c :** one of the middle pair of Weberian ossicles in certain fishes **2** *cap* **:** a genus of bivalve mollusks (family Pteriidae) containing the typical hammer shells **3** -ES [NL, fr. LL, a disease of animals, prob. fr. L, hammer] **:** GLANDERS

mallie *var of* MALI

mal·ling rootstock \ˈmȯliŋ-\ *n, usu cap M* [fr. East Malling Research Station, Kent, England] **:** any of several rootstocks for fruit trees developed by the East Malling Research Station, Kent, England that are propagated vegetatively and used esp. for dwarfing apple trees — see PARADISE 6

mal·lo·mys \ˈmalə,mis\ *n, cap* [NL, fr. Gk *mallos* lock of wool + NL *-mys*] **:** a genus of New Guinea giant rats often reaching a length of 2½ feet

mal·loph·a·ga \məˈläfəgə\ *n pl, cap* [NL, fr. Gk *mallos* lock of wool + NL *-phaga*] **:** an order of secondarily wingless insects comprising the bird lice — **mal·loph·a·gan** \-gən\ *adj or n* — **mal·loph·a·gous** \-gəs\ *adj*

mal·lor·quin \,ma(l)ˌyȯ(r)ˈkēn\ *adj or n, usu cap* [Sp *mallorquín,* fr. *Mallorca* Majorca, largest of the Balearic islands off the east coast of Spain + *-in* -ine (fr. L *-inus*)] **:** MAJORCAN

mal·lo·seismic \ˌmalō+\ *adj* [Gk *mallon* rather, more (compar. of *mala* very) + E *seismic* — more at MELIORATE] **:** of, relating to, or being a region subject to frequent destructive earthquakes

mal·lo·tus \məˈlōd·əs\ *n, cap* [NL, fr. Gk *mallōtos* fleecy, fr. *mallos* lock of wool] **:** a genus of tropical Asiatic and Australian trees (family Euphorbiaceae) with diclinous flowers of which the staminate ones have numerous stamens — see KAMALA

mal·low \ˈma(,)lō, -,lə; -,lōw, -lō+V\ *n* -S [ME *malwe,* fr. OE *mealwe,* fr. L *malva,* of non-IE origin; akin to the source of Gk *molochē, malachē* mallow] **1 :** a plant of the family Malvaceae: as **a :** an erect or decumbent European perennial herb (*Malva sylvestris*) with axillary clusters of rosy purple flowers **b :** DWARF MALLOW **2 :** a moderate purplish red that is bluer and less strong than average rose, paler than violine pink, and bluer and paler than magenta rose or average fuchsia rose

mallow family *n* **:** MALVACEAE

mallow pink *n* **:** a moderate purplish pink to light reddish purple

mallow purple *n* **1** *or* **mallow red :** MALLOW 2 **2 :** MAUVE 2

mallow rose *n* **:** ROSE MALLOW 1

mally *var of* MALI

¹malm \ˈmä|m, ˈmȧ| *also* |lm\ *n* -S [ME *malme,* fr. OE *mealm-;* akin to ON *malmr* metal, ore, Goth *malma* sand, OE *melu* meal — more at MEAL] **1** *dial chiefly Eng* **a :** a soft friable chalky limestone **b :** a light clayey soil containing chalk **:** MARL **2 a :** an artificial mixture of clay and chalk used in the manufacture of bricks **b :** MALM BRICK

²malm \"\ *vt* -ED/-ING/-S **1 :** to convert (clay and chalk) into artificial malm **2 :** to cover or treat (brick earth) with artificial malm

³malm \"\ *adj, usu cap* **:** of, relating to, or constituting a subdivision of the European Jurassic — see GEOLOGIC TIME table

mal·ma \ˈmalmə\ *or* **malma trout** *n* -S [*malma* native name in Kamchatka, northeast U.S.S.R.] **:** DOLLY VARDEN 2

mal·mai·son \ˌmalməˈzōⁿ\ *n* -S *usu cap* [fr. *Malmaison,* château near Paris, France] **:** any of various tender greenhouse carnations with stiff massive growth and large fully double usu. pink flowers

malmaison rose *n* **:** a vivid purplish red that is redder and paler than Indiana and redder and lighter than rubellite — called also *rose malmaison*

malm brick *n* **:** a brick made from marl or malm

mal·mi·gnatte \ˌmalmənˈyat\ *n* -S [It *malmignatta,* fr. *mal, malo* bad (fr. L *malus*) + *mignatta* leech — more at SMALL] **:** a small black venomous spider (*Latrodectus tredecimguttatus*) of southern Europe having 13 small red spots on the abdomen

malmö *or* **malmo** \ˈmal(,)mō, -l,mə(r)(·), -l,mō\ *adj, usu cap* [fr. *Malmö,* city in southwest Sweden] **:** of or from the city of Malmö, Sweden **:** of the kind or style prevalent in Malmö

malm rubber *n* **:** a soft malm brick that is capable of being worked into special shapes by cutting or rubbing

malm·sey \ˈmämzē\ *n* -S *often cap* [ME *malmesey,* fr. ML *Malmasia* Monemvasia, town off the coast of the southeastern Peloponnesus, Greece] **1 :** a sweet aromatic wine made from the malvasia grape and produced orig. around the town of Monemvasia and later elsewhere throughout the Mediterranean and in the Canary and Madeira islands **2 :** the sweetest variety of Madeira wine

malmstone \ˈ=,=\ *or* **malm rock** *n* [¹*malm*] **1** *dial chiefly Eng* **:** MALM **2** *dial Eng* **:** a cherty rock similar to flint used in building and paving

malmy \ˈmä|mi, ˈmȧ| *also* |lmi; *in sense 2 also* ˈmȯ-\ *adj* -ER/-EST [¹*malm* + *-y*] **1** *dial Eng* **:** containing malm **:** resembling malm **2** *dial Eng* **:** SOFT, MELLOW

mal·nourished \(ˈ)mal+\ *adj* [¹*mal-* + *nourished*] **1 :** exhibiting the physical and physiological results of an inadequate diet **2 :** UNDERNOURISHED

mal·nourishment \"+\ *n* [¹*mal-* + *nourishment*] **:** MALNUTRITION

mal·nutrition \ˌ=+\ *n* [¹*mal-* + *nutrition*] **:** faulty nutrition due to inadequate or unbalanced intake of nutrients or their impaired assimilation or utilization

ma·lo \ˈmälō\ *n* -S [Hawaiian] **:** a loincloth that is now worn by Hawaiian men only on ceremonial occasions — compare MARO

malo- — see ²MAL-

ma·lo animo \ˈmä,lōˈanə,mō\ *adv* [L, with bad intent] **:** with evil or wrongful intent **:** MALICIOUSLY — used in English law esp. with respect to forgery

mal·observation \ˌmal+\ *n* [¹*mal-* + *observation*] **:** erroneous observation or interpretation **:** MISREADING

ma·lo·ca \məˈlōkə\ *n* -S [Pg, fr. AmerSp, raid, attack fr. Araucanian *malocan* to fight] **:** a large communal dwelling of some So. American Indian peoples (as in Brazil); *also* **:** the group inhabiting such a dwelling

mal·occluded \ˌmal+\ *adj* [¹*mal-* + *occluded*] **:** characterized by malocclusion

mal·occlusion \"+\ *n* [¹*mal-* + *occlusion*] **:** improper occlusion; *esp* **:** an abnormality in the occlusal relations of teeth or dentures

mal·odor \(ˈ)mal+\ *n* [¹*mal-* + *odor*] **:** an offensive odor

¹mal·odor·ant \maˈlōdərənt\ *n* -S [*malodor* + *-ant*] **:** an ill-smelling substance

²malodorant \(ˈ)ˌ=ˈ===\ *adj* **:** MALODOROUS

mal·odorous \(ˈ)mal+\ *adj* [¹*mal-* + *odorous*] **1 :** having a bad odor **:** RANK, FETID, STINKING ⟨stone castles and ~ hovels —T.B.Costain⟩ ⟨the flavor . . . like that of many ~ cheeses, is delicate —Marjorie K. Rawlings⟩ **2 :** highly improper **:** SCANDALOUS ⟨methods, questionable when not ~ —John Mason Brown⟩

ma·lo·ji·llo \ˌmäləˈhē(,)(y)ō\ *or* **ma·lo·ji·lla** \-_(y)ə\ *n* -S [*malojillo* fr. AmerSp, dim. of *malojo* forage plant, fr. Sp *malhojo* waste grass, fr. *mal, malo* bad (fr. L *malus*) + *-hojo* leaf (fr. L *folium*); *malojilla* fr. AmerSp, dim. of *maloja* forage plant, fem. of *malojo* — more at SMALL, BLADE] **:** PARA GRASS

mal·o·nate \ˈmalə,nāt, -,nət\ *n* -S [ISV *malonic* (in *malonic acid*) + *-ate*] **:** a salt or ester of malonic acid

ma·lo·nic acid \məˈlōnik-, -ˈlänik-\ *n* [*malonic* fr. F. *malonique* (in *acide malonique* malonic acid), alter. of *malique* malic (in *acide malique* malic acid) — more at MALIC ACID] **:** a crystalline dicarboxylic acid $CH_2(COOH)_2$ obtained by oxidation of malic acid but usu. made by hydrolysis of cyanoacetic acid and used esp. in the form of its diethyl ester in organic synthesis (as of barbiturates and vitamins of the B complex)

mal·o·nyl \ˈmalə,nil, -nēl\ *n* -S [ISV *malonic* (in *malonic acid*) + *-yl*] **:** the bivalent radical $CH_2(CO)_2$ of malonic acid

malonylurea \ˈ==,==ˈ==\ *n* [*malonyl* + *urea*] **:** BARBITURIC ACID

ma·loo climber \ˈmä,lü-\ *also* **maloo** *n* -S [*maloo* fr. Hindi *māl* garland, rope, fr. Skt *mālā* garland] **:** an East Indian climbing shrub (*Bauhinia vahlii*) with a tough fibrous bark that is used in rope manufacture

mal·o·pe \ˈmalə(,)pē\ *n, cap* [NL, fr. L, mallow] **:** a small genus of chiefly European annual herbs (family Malvaceae) having flowers subtended by three large cordate bracts

mal·pa·is \ˌmälpäˈēs\ *n* -ES [Sp *mal pais* bad country] **1** *Southwest* **:** rough country underlain by dark esp. basaltic lava **:** BADLANDS **2** *Southwest* **:** basaltic lava

mal·pigh·ia \malˈpigēə\ *n, cap* [NL, fr. Marcello *Malpighi* †1694 Ital. anatomist + NL *-ia*] **:** a genus of tropical American shrubs and trees (family Malpighiaceae) having a glandular calyx and drupaceous fruit — see JIQUI

mal·pigh·i·a·ce·ae \ˌ=,==ˈāsē,ē\ *n pl, cap* [NL, fr. *Malpighia,* type genus + *-aceae*] **:** a family of tropical herbs, shrubs, or trees (order Geraniales) having stinging hairs, usu. opposite leaves, and yellow or red flowers with prominently clawed petals and often winged or lobed tricarpellary fruit — **mal·pigh·i·a·ceous** \ˌ=,==ˈāshəs\ *adj*

mal·pigh·i·an \(ˈ)malˈpigēən\ *adj, usu cap* [Marcello *Malpighi* †1694 + E *-an*] **:** of, relating to, or discovered by Marcello Malpighi

malpighian cell *n, usu cap M* **:** PALISADE CELL

malpighian corpuscle *also* **malpighian body** *n, often cap M* **1 :** the part of a nephron that consists of Bowman's capsule and its included glomerulus **2** *also* **malpighian follicle :** any of the small masses of adenoid tissue formed around the branches of the splenic artery in the spleen

malpighian layer *n, usu cap M* **:** the deeper part of the epidermis consisting of cells whose protoplasm has not yet changed into horny material

malpighian pyramid *n, usu cap M* **:** any of the conical masses forming the medullary substance of the kidney, projecting as papillae into the renal pelvis, and being made up of bundles of straight uriniferous tubes that open at the apex of the pyramid

malpighian tubule *also* **malpighian tube** *or* **malpighian vessel** *n, usu cap M* **:** one of the group of long blind vessels opening into the posterior part of the alimentary canal in most insects and some other arthropods and functioning primarily as excretory organs

malpighian tuft *n, usu cap M* **:** GLOMERULUS

mal·posed \(ˈ)malˈpōzd\ *adj* [fr. *malposition,* after such pairs as E *composition: composed*] **:** characterized by malposition ⟨~ teeth⟩

mal·position \ˌmal+\ *n* [¹*mal-* + *position*] **:** wrong or faulty position **:** MISPLACEMENT

¹mal·practice \(ˈ)=+\ *n* [¹*mal-* + *practice*] **1 a :** a dereliction from professional duty whether intentional, criminal, or merely negligent by one rendering professional services that results in injury, loss, or damage to the recipient of those services or to those entitled to rely upon them or that affects the public interest adversely **b :** the failure of one rendering professional services to exercise that degree of skill and learning commonly applied under all the circumstances in the community by the average prudent reputable member of the profession with the result of injury, loss, or damage to the recipient of those services or to those entitled to rely upon them **2 :** an injurious, negligent, or improper practice **:** MALFEASANCE, WRONGDOING ⟨cheating and fixing and other ~*s* —F.A. Wrensch⟩ ⟨bewailing some current academic ~ with the English language —D.J.Lloyd⟩

²malpractice \"\ *vi* **:** to engage in or commit malpractice ⟨the death of the boy . . . is laid at his door as a *malpracticing* doctor —Rose Feld⟩

mal·practitioner \ˌ=+\ *n* [¹*mal-* + *practitioner*] **:** one who engages in or commits malpractice

mal·praxis \(ˈ)=+\ *n* [¹*mal-* + *praxis*] **:** MALPRACTICE

mal·presentation \"+\ *n* [¹*mal-* + *presentation*] **:** abnormal presentation of the fetus at birth

mals *pl of* MAL

malster *var of* MALTSTER

¹malt \ˈmȯlt\ *n* -S *often attrib* [ME, fr. OE *mealt;* akin to OHG *malz* malt, OS & ON *malt;* derivative fr. the root of E ¹*melt*] **1 :** a material that consists of grain (as barley or oats) softened by steeping in water, allowed to germinate in order to develop the enzyme diastase which is capable of saccharifying the starch of the material itself and of raw grain mixed with it, usu. dried in a kiln, and often ground and that is used esp. in brewing and distilling and as a nutrient and digestive — compare GREEN MALT, WORT **2 a :** MALT LIQUOR **b :** MALT WHISKEY **3 :** MALTED MILK

²malt \"\ *vb* -ED/-ING/-S [ME *malten,* fr. *malt,* n.] *vt* **1 :** to convert into malt ⟨~ barley⟩ **2 :** to make or treat with malt or malt extract ⟨~ beer⟩ ~ *vi* **1 :** to become malt **2 :** to make grain into malt

mal·ta \ˈmȯltə\ *adj, usu cap* [fr. *Malta,* island in the Mediterranean sea south of Sicily] **:** of or from the country of Malta **:** of the kind or style prevalent in Malta

malta fever *n, usu cap M* **:** brucellosis caused by a bacterium (*Brucella melitensis*)

maltalent *n* [ME, fr. MF, fr. OF, fr. *mal* bad + *talent* disposition — more at TALENT] *archaic* **:** ILL WILL, MALICE

malta orange *or* **maltese orange** *n, usu cap M* **:** BLOOD ORANGE

malt·ase \ˈmȯl,tās, -āz\ *n* -S [ISV ¹*malt* + *-ase*] **:** an enzyme that accelerates the hydrolysis of maltose and other alpha-glucosides to glucose and that is found in plants, animals, yeast, and bacteria **:** an alpha-glucosidase

malted *n* -S [fr. past part. of ²*malt*] **:** MALTED MILK

malted milk *n* [*malted* fr. past part. of ²*malt*] **1 :** milk that has been malted; *specif* **:** a soluble easily digested powder prepared from dried milk and malted cereals **2 :** a beverage made by dissolving malted milk in milk or other liquid often with ice cream and flavoring added

malt·er \ˈmȯltə(r)\ *n* -S [²*malt* + *-er*] *now dial Brit* **:** MALTSTER

¹mal·tese \(ˈ)mȯlˈtēz, -ēs\ *n, pl* **maltese** [*Malta* + E *-ese,* n. suffix] **1** *cap* **:** a native or inhabitant of Malta **2** *cap* **:** the Semitic language of the Maltese people **3** *usu cap* **:** any of various animals or breeds of animals originating in or believed to have originated in Malta: as **a :** a breed of asses **b :** a breed of large-uddered usu. hornless milch goats **c :** a breed of white long-coated toy dogs with black nose and very dark eyes **d :** a breed of erect hen-type pigeons with a turned-up fanlike tail **e :** MALTESE CAT

²maltese \"\ *adj, usu cap* [*Malta* + E *-ese,* adj. suffix] **1 a :** of, relating to, or characteristic of Malta **b :** of, relating to, or characteristic of the people of Malta **2 :** of, relating to, or characteristic of the Maltese language

maltese cat *n, usu cap M* **:** a bluish gray domestic short-haired cat

maltese cross *n, usu cap M* **1 a :** a cross formée **b :** a cross resembling the cross formée but having the outer face of each arm indented in a V — called also *cross of eight points* **2 :** a Eurasian garden perennial (*Lychnis chalcedonica*) having scarlet or rarely white flowers in dense terminal heads — called also *scarlet lychnis* **3 a :** a star wheel with teeth shaped like a Maltese cross used with a finger stop wheel to limit the uncoiling of a watch mainspring — called also *Geneva stop* **b :** a similar device in a motion-picture projector used to advance a film one or more frames at a time

Maltese cross 1b

maltese lace *n, usu cap M* **:** a lace of Maltese origin: **a :** a fine bobbin lace of silk **b :** a guipure with geometric designs

malt extract *n* **1 :** a sugary mucilaginous substance obtained from wort **2 a :** a sweet light-brown syrupy liquid prepared by infusing malt with water and evaporating and used chiefly in medicine and foods; *also* **:** a powder made by drying this liquid **b :** a weak alcoholic preparation made like beer but darker in color and thicker in consistency

mal·tha \ˈmalthə\ *also* **mal·thite** \-,thīt\ *n* -S [*maltha* fr. L, soft mixture of wax and pitch, fr. Gk *maltha, malthē;* akin to Gk *malthakos* soft; *malthite* fr. *maltha* + *-ite* — more at MILD] **:** a black viscid substance intermediate between petroleum and asphalt — called also *earth pitch, mineral tar*

mal·the \ˈmal(,)thē\ [NL, fr. Gk *malthē,* a large fish] *syn of* OGCOCEPHALUS

mal·thi·dae \ˈ=thə,dē\ [NL, fr. *Malthe* + *-idae*] *syn of* OGCOCEPHALIDAE

malthouse \ˈ=,=\ *n* [ME *malthous,* fr. OE *mealthūs,* fr. *mealt* malt + *hūs* house — more at MALT, HOUSE] **:** a building in which malt is made

¹mal·thu·sian \malˈth(y)üzhən, ÷mȯl-, -zēən\ *n* -S *usu cap* [Thomas R. *Malthus* †1834 Eng. economist + E *-an,* n. suffix] **:** a supporter of Malthus or Malthusianism

²malthusian \(ˈ)=ˈ=(=)=\ *adj, usu cap* [Thomas R. *Malthus* †1834 + E *-an,* adj. suffix] **:** of or relating to Malthus or Malthusianism

mal·thu·sian·ism \-,nizəm\ *n* -S *usu cap* **:** the doctrines of Malthus holding esp. that population tends to increase at a faster rate than its means of subsistence and that widespread poverty and degradation of the lower classes inevitably result unless the population is preventively checked by moral restraint or positively checked esp. by disease, famine, or war

malt·i·ness \ˈmȯltēnə̇s, -tin-\ *n* -ES **:** the quality or state of being malty

malt·ing \ˈmȯltiŋ\ *n* -S [ME, fr. gerund of *malten* to malt — more at MALT] **1 :** the act or process of making or of becoming malt; *specif* **:** the conversion of the starches of a distillery mash from starch to fermentable sugar by the enzymes of the malt **2 :** MALTHOUSE

malt liquor *n* **:** a fermented liquor (as beer) made with malt

malt·man \ˈ=mən\ *n, pl* **maltmen** [ME, fr. ¹*malt* + *man*] **:** MALTSTER

mal·to \ˈmal(,)tō\ *n, pl* **malto** *or* **maltos** *usu cap* **1 a :** a Dravidian people of Bengal **b :** a member of such people **2 :** the language of the Malto people

malt·ol \ˈmȯl,tȯl, -tōl\ *n* -S [ISV ¹*malt* + *-ol*] **:** a crystalline compound $C_6H_6O_3$ derived from gamma-pyrone, found esp. in pine needles, larch bark, and chicory, and formed when streptomycin is hydrolyzed and when barley and other grains are roasted

mal·tolte *or* **male·tolt** \ˈmal,tōlt\ *n* -S [MF *maletoulte, maltoute* additional duty or tax, fr. OF *mauthoste,* fr. *mau, mal* bad + *toste, tolte, toute* pillage, tax, fr. (assumed) VL *tollita,* fem. of (assumed) VL *tollitus,* past part. of L *tollere* to lift up, take away — more at MAL-, TOLERATE] **:** an arbitrary customs duty levied by the British crown during the late medieval period in addition to the regular port charges

malt·ose \ˈmȯl,tōs\ *n* -S [F, fr. E ¹*malt* + F *-ose*] **:** a crystalline dextrorotatory fermentable reducing disaccharide sugar $C_{12}H_{22}O_{11}$ formed esp. from starch by the action of beta-amylase (as in saliva and malt), as an intermediate product in metabolism, and in brewing and distilling and used chiefly in foods and in biological culture media; 4-α-glucosyl-glucose — called also *malt sugar;* compare GLUCOSE illustration

mal·treat \(ˈ)mal+\ *vt* [F *maltraiter,* fr. MF, fr. *mal* badly + *traiter* to treat, handle, manage, fr. L *tractare* — more at MAL-, TREAT] **:** to treat ill **:** treat roughly **:** ABUSE, MISTREAT, MISUSE ⟨whenever women felt ~*ed* and humiliated —Theodor Reik⟩ ⟨a machine that had already been ~*ed* —Bryan Morgan⟩ — **mal·treater** *n* — **mal·treatment** *n*

malts *pl of* MALT, *pres 3d sing of* MALT

malt shop *n* **:** an ice-cream shop specializing in malted milks

malt·ster \'mȯltstə(r)\ *also* **mal·ster** \-lstə(r)\ *n* -s [ME *maltestere, malstere,* fr. ¹*malt* + *-stere* -ster] **:** a maker of malt

malt sugar *n* **:** MALTOSE

malt vinegar *n* **:** the product made by fermentation without distillation of an infusion of barley malt or cereals whose starch has been converted by malt

malt whiskey *n* **:** whiskey made from malted barley in a pot still

maltworm \'⸗,⸗\ *n, archaic* **:** TIPPLER, TOPER

malty \'mȯltē, -ti\ *adj* -ER/-EST [¹*malt* + *-y*] **1 :** containing or resembling malt **2 :** addicted to malt liquor

ma·lum \'mäləm\ *n, pl* **ma·la** \-lə\ [L, fr. neut. of *malus* bad — more at SMALL] **:** an offense against right or law **:** EVIL, WRONG

malum in se \-in'sā\ *n, pl* **mala in se** [NL, offense in itself] **:** an offense that is evil or wrong from its own nature or by the natural law irrespective of statute — compare MALUM PROHIBITUM

malum pro·hi·bi·tum \-prō'hibəd·əm\ *n, pl* **mala prohibi·ta** \-əd·ə\ [NL, prohibited offense] **:** an offense prohibited by statute but not inherently evil or wrong — compare MALUM IN SE

malungeon *usu cap, var of* MELUNGEON

mal·union \(')mal+\ *n* [¹*mal-* + *union*] **:** incomplete or faulty union (as of the fragments of a fractured bone)

mal·united \¦⸗+\ *adj* [¹*mal-* + *united*] **:** united in a position of abnormality or deformity — used of the fragments of a broken bone

ma·lus \'māləs\ *n, cap* [NL, fr. L, apple tree, fr. *malum* apple, fr. Gk (Dor) *malon;* akin to Gk (Attic) *mēlon* apple] **:** a genus of trees or shrubs (family Rosaceae) of the north temperate zone sometimes included in the genus *Pyrus* but distinguished by having the soft pubescent leaves revolute or plicate in the bud, flower clusters lacking a stout central column, styles more or less joined at the base, and fruit without grit cells

mal·va \'malvə\ *n* [NL, fr. L, mallow — more at MALLOW] **1** *cap* **:** a genus of Old World herbs (family Malvaceae) having palmate leaves and tribracteate flowers with naked reniform indehiscent carpels **2** -s **:** a plant of the genus *Malva* — see COMMON MALLOW

mal·va·ce·ae \mal'vāsē,ē\ *n pl, cap* [NL, fr. *Malva,* type genus + *-aceae*] **:** a family of herbs, shrubs, and trees (order Malvales) characterized by monadelphous stamens and one-celled anthers — compare COTTON, OKRA — **mal·va·ceous** \(')⸗¦vā-shəs\ *adj*

mal·va·les \mal'vā(,)lēz\ *n pl, cap* [NL, fr. *Malva* + *-ales*] **:** an order of dicotyledonous plants characterized by volvate calyx, usu. numerous stamens, and a polycarpellary ovary

mal·va·sia \,malvə'zēə, -'sēə\ *n* -s [It, fr. *Monemvasia,* town off the coast of the southeastern Peloponnesus, Greece] **1 :** a grape that yields the wine known as malmsey **2 :** MALMSEY — **mal·va·si·an** \¦⸗¦⸗ən\ *adj*

mal·vas·trum \mal'vastrəm\ *n, cap* [NL, irreg. fr. L *malva* mallow] **:** a large genus of herbs and shrubs (family Malvaceae) characterized by red or yellow flowers and capitate stigmas — see FALSE MALLOW

mal·ver·sa·tion \,malvə(r)'sāshən\ *n* -s [MF, fr. *malverser* + *-ation*] *civil & Scots law* **:** misbehavior, corruption, extortion, disloyalty, embezzlement, misappropriation, or breach of trust in an office of public trust, an agency, or a commission; *broadly* **:** corrupt administration

malverse *vi* [F *malverser,* fr. MF, fr. *mal* badly + *verser* to turn, occupy oneself, fr. L *versare* to turn, transform, fr. *versus,* past part. of *vertere* to turn — more at WORTH] *civil & Scots law, obs* **:** to be guilty of malversation

mal·vi \'malvē\ *n* -s *cap* **:** the Indic dialect of Malwa

mal·vi·din \'malvədən\ *n* -s [ISV *malv-* (fr. L *malva* mallow) + *-idin*] **:** an anthocyanidin widely distributed in plants esp. in the form of its glucosides malvin and oenin and also in the free form in grapes and usu. obtained as the violet-brown crystalline chloride $C_{17}H_{15}ClO_7$

mal·vin \'malvən\ *n* -s [ISV *malv-* (fr. L *malva*) + *-in*] **:** an anthocyanin pigment found esp. in the European wild mallow and in species of primrose and obtained usu. as the reddish brown chloride $C_{29}H_{35}ClO_{17}$

mal·voi·sie \'malvə(,)zē, ¦malv,wä¦zē\ *n* -s [F, fr. MF *malvesie,* fr. *Malvesie* Monemvasia] **:** MALMSEY

¹mam \'mam\ *n* -s [of baby-talk origin — more at MAMMA] *chiefly Brit* **:** MOM

²mam *or* **ma'm** *var of* MA'AM

³mam \'mäm\ *n, pl* **mam** *or* **mams** *usu cap* [Sp *mame,* of AmerInd origin] **1 a :** an Indian people of southwestern Guatemala **b :** a member of such people **2 :** a Mayan language of the Mam people

MAM *abbr* milliampere minute

mama *var of* MAMMA

ma·mak \'mä,mäk\ *n, pl* **mamak** *or* **mamaks** *usu cap* **:** one of several forest peoples of Sumatra related to the Toala of Celebes

ma·ma·loi \,mämäl'wä\ *n* -s [Haitian creole *mamalwa,* fr. *mama* mother + *lwa* loa] **:** a voodoo priestess esp. of Haiti — compare PAPALOI

ma·ma·mu \mə'mä(,)mü\ *n* -s [Hawaiian *mamamo*] **:** a large-eyed Indo-Pacific porgy (*Monotaxis grandoculis*) highly esteemed as food in the Pacific islands

ma·ma·ni \'mämənē\ *n* -s [Hawaiian *māmane*] **:** a tree (*Sophora chrysophylla*) of the Hawaiian mountain regions having very hard durable wood much valued for posts and building

ma·ma·nua \mə'mänwə\ *n, pl* **mamanua** *or* **mamanuas** *usu cap* **1 :** a negritoid or Veddoid people inhabiting northern Mindanao, Philippines **2 :** a member of the Mamanua people

mama's boy *or* **mamma's boy** *n* **:** a boy or man whose behavior is unnaturally good or overcautious; *esp* **:** one who is delicate, unaggressive, or overdependent on others

mam·ba \'mämbə, 'mam-\ *n* -s [Zulu *im-amba*] **:** any of several tropical and southern African venomous snakes of the genus *Dendraspis* related to the cobras but lacking a dilatable hood; *esp* **:** a southern African snake (*D. angusticeps*) that has a light or olive-green phase and a black phase, that attains in the latter phase a length of 12 feet, and that is dreaded because of its quickness and readiness to inflict its often fatal bite

¹mam·bo \'mäm(,)bō\ *also* **mam·bu** \-bü\ *n* -s [Haitian creole] **:** a Haitian voodoo priestess

²mambo \"\ *sometimes* 'mam-\ *n* -s [AmerSp] **:** a complex staccato usu. fast dance related to the rumba and of Cuban origin; *also* **:** the style of music for this dance

³mambo \"\ *vi* -ED/-ING/-S **:** to dance the mambo

mam·e·lière \,mamәl'ye(ə)r\ *n* -s [F, fr. MF *mameliere,* fr. *mamele* breast, nipple (fr. L *mamilla*) + *-iere* -ier — more at MAMMILLA] **:** one of two round steel plates or a single plate used to cover the breasts in medieval armor

mam·e·lon \'mamələn\ *n* -s [F, lit., nipple, fr. MF, dim. of *mamele*] **:** a dome-shaped protuberance or elevation: as **a :** a small rounded hill esp. of lava formed over a fumarole **b :** a fortified mound or hillock **c :** one of the three rounded protuberances on the cutting ridge of recently erupted incisor teeth

mam·e·lu·co \,mamə'lü(,)kō\ *n* -s [Pg *mameluco, mamaluco,* modif. (influenced by *mameluco* Mamluk, fr. Ar *Mamlūk*) of Tupi *Mamaruca*] **:** a Brazilian mestizo; *specif* **:** the offspring of a white man and an Indian woman — compare CABOCLO

mamey *or* **mamie** *var of* MAMMEE

ma·mie tay·lor \'māmē'tālə(r)\ *n, usu cap M&T* [prob. fr. the name *Mamie Taylor*] **:** a drink consisting of Scotch whisky, lime juice, and ginger ale served in a tall glass with ice

mamilla *var of* MAMMILLA

mamillaria *syn of* MAMMILLARIA

mamillate *or* **mamillated** *var of* MAMMILLATE

mam·luk \'mam,lük\ *or* **mam·e·luke** *also* **mam·e·luk** \-mə,-\ *n* -s [*mamluk,* fr. Turk & Ar; *mameluke,* fr. Turk *memlûk,* fr. Ar *mamlūk,* lit., slave; *mameluke* & *mameluk,* fr. F *mameluk,* fr. Ar *mamlūk*] **1** *usu cap* **:** a member of a former Egyptian military class orig. made up of a body of Caucasian slaves converted to Islam who gained great political power in Egypt, occupied the sultanate from 1250 to 1517, were defeated by Napoleon in 1798, and were exterminated or dispersed in 1811 by Mehemet Ali **2** *usu mameluke, often cap* **a :** a white or yellow slave in Muslim countries **b :** a member of a body of slave soldiers

¹mam·ma *or* **ma·ma** \'mämə, 'māmə *sometimes* 'məmə, *chiefly Brit* mə'mä\ *also* **mom·ma** \'məmə\ *n* -s [of baby-talk origin like E *mam* mother, G dial. *mamme* mother, L *mamma* mother, female breast, Gk *mamma, mammē* mother, IrGael & W *mam,* Alb *mēmë,* Russ *mama*] **1 :** MOTHER **2** *slang* **:** WOMAN, WIFE

²mam·ma \'mamə\ *n, pl* **mam·mae** \-a,mē\ [L, mother, breast — more at ¹MAMMA] **:** a glandular organ for secreting milk characteristic of all mammals but normally rudimentary in the male **:** a mammary gland and its accessory parts

mam·mal \'maməl\ *n* -s [NL *Mammalia*] **:** one of the Mammalia

mam·ma·lia \mə'mālēə, -lyə\ *n pl, cap* [NL, fr. LL, neut. pl. of *mammalis* of the breast, fr. L *mamma* breast + *-alis* -al] **:** the highest class of Vertebrata comprising man and all other animals that nourish their young with milk, that have the skin usu. more or less covered with hair, that have mammary glands, a mandible articulating directly with the squamosal, a chain of small ear bones, a brain with four optic lobes, a muscular diaphragm separating the heart and lungs from the abdominal cavity, only a left aortic arch, warm blood containing red cells without nuclei except in the fetus, and embryos developing both amnion and allantois, and that except in the monotremes reproduce viviparously — compare ALLOTHERIA, EUTHERIA, METATHERIA, PROTOTHERIA, THERIA

¹mam·ma·li·an \-ēən, -yən\ *n* -s [NL *Mammalia* + E *-an*] **:** one of the Mammalia

²mammalian \"\ *adj* **:** of, relating to, or characteristic of mammals **:** belonging to the Mammalia

mam·ma·lif·er·ous \¦mamə¦lif(ə)rəs\ *adj* [NL *Mammalia* + E *-ferous*] **:** containing mammalian remains ⟨a ~ deposit⟩ ⟨a ~ stratum⟩

mam·mal·i·ty \mə'maləd·ē, ma'-\ *n* -ES [*mammal* + *-ity*] **:** the quality or state of being mammalian

mam·ma·log·i·cal \¦mamə¦läjəkəl\ *adj* **:** of or relating to mammalogy

mam·mal·o·gist \mə'maləjəst, ma'-\ *n* -s **:** a specialist in mammalogy

mam·mal·o·gy \-jē, -ji\ *n* -ES [ISV, blend of NL *Mammalia* and ISV *-logy*] **:** a branch of zoology dealing with mammals

mam·ma·plas·ty \'mamə,plastē\ *n* -ES [²*mamma* + *-plasty*] **:** plastic surgery of the breast

mam·ma·ry \'mam(ə)rē, -ri\ *adj* [L *mamma* female breast + E *-ary* — more at MAMMA] **:** of, relating to, lying near, or affecting the mammae

mammary gland *n* **:** one of the large compound glands that are characteristic of mammals, are regarded as highly specialized sebaceous glands, are modified in the female to secrete milk for the nourishment of the young, are situated on the ventral aspect of the body, vary in number from 2 to 22, and usu. terminate in a nipple

mammary pouch *n* **:** the marsupium of a monotreme as distinguished from that of a marsupial

mammary ridge *n* **:** either of a pair of longitudinal ectodermal thickenings in the mammalian embryo that extend from the base of the anterior to the posterior limb buds and are the source of the mammary glands — called also *milk line*

mamma's boy *var of* MAMA'S BOY

mam·mate \'ma,māt\ *adj* [L *mammatus,* fr. *mamma* breast + *-atus* ate] **:** MAMMIFEROUS

mam·ma·to·cumulus \mə¦mād·ō, ma¦mād·ō+\ *n* [NL, fr. L *mammatus* of the breast + NL *-o-* + *cumulus*] **:** a cumulus or cumulostratus storm cloud having breast-shaped protuberances below — called also *festoon cloud*

mam·ma·tus \mə'mād·əs, ma'-\ *adj* [NL, fr. L, of the breast] **:** of, relating to, or being a cloud whose lower surface is in the form of pouches

mam·me \'mamā\ *n, pl* **mamme** *or* **mammes** [It dial., pl. of *mamma,* lit., breast, fr. L; fr. the shape of the fruit — more at MAMMA] **:** the overwintering crop of the caprifig maturing in the spring — compare MAMMONI, PROFICHI

mam·mea \mə'mēə, ma'-\ *n, cap* [NL, fr. Sp *mamey* mammee — more at MAMMEE] **:** a genus of American and Asiatic trees (family Guttiferae) that have a valvate 2-parted calyx and 2⸗celled or 4-celled ovary becoming a large drupaceous fruit

mam·mec·to·my \mə'mektəmē, ma'-\ *n* -ES [ISV *mamm-* (fr. L *mamma* breast) + *-ectomy*] **:** MASTECTOMY

mam·mee *or* **ma·mey** *or* **mam·ie** *or* **mam·mey** \(')ma¦mē *sometimes* -¦mā, *esp attributively* 'mamē\ *n, pl* **mammees** \-ēz\ *or* **mameys** \-āz\ *or* **mamey·es** \mə'mā,ās\ *or* **mamies** *or* **mammeys** [Sp *mamey,* fr. Taino] **1** *also* **mammee apple a :** a tropical American tree (*Mammea americana*) having a globular or ovoid fruit with thick russet or reddish leathery rind and yellow or reddish juicy flesh **b :** the fruit of this tree — called also *tropical apricot* **2 a :** MARMALADE TREE **b** *also* **mammee sapota** *or* **mammee colorado :** the fruit of this tree **3 :** SAPODILLA

mam·mer \'mamə(r)\ *vi* -ED/-ING/-S [ME *mameren, memeren,* of imit. origin] **1** *now dial Eng* **:** STAMMER, MUTTER **2** *now dial Eng* **:** WAVER, HESITATE

mam·met \'mamət\ *var of* MAUMET

mammey *var of* MAMMEE

mammies *pl of* MAMMY

mam·mi·fer \'mamәfә(r)\ *n* -s [F *mammifère* adj. & n., fr. L *mamma* breast + F *-ifère* -iferous — more at MAMMA] *archaic* **:** MAMMAL

mam·mif·er·ous \mə'mif(ə)rəs, ma'-\ *adj* [F *mammifère* + E *-ous*] **:** having breasts **:** MAMMALIAN

mam·mi·form \'mamə,fȯrm\ *adj* [L *mamma* breast + E *-iform*] **:** having the form of a breast or nipple **:** MAMMILLARY

mam·mil·la *also* **ma·mil·la** \mə'milə, ma'-\ *n, pl* **mammillae** *also* **mamil·lae** \-i,lē\ [L, breast, nipple, dim. of *mamma, mama* breast — more at MAMMA] **:** NIPPLE

mam·mil·lar \'mamələ(r)\ *adj* [LL *mamillaris,* fr. L *mamilla* breast, nipple + *-aris* -ar] **:** MAMMILLARY

¹mam·mil·lar·ia \,mamə'la(a)rēə\ *n* [NL, fr. L *mammilla* breast, nipple + NL *-aria*] *syn of* CACTUS

²mammillaria \"\ *n* [NL, fr. L *mammilla* + NL *-aria*] **1** *cap* **:** a genus of succulents (family Cactaceae) characterized chiefly by the nipple-shaped protuberances on their surface and formerly including many species now separated into several other genera (as *Coryphantha, Cochemia, Dolichothele*) **2** -s **:** any cactus of *Mammillaria* or a related genus

mam·mil·lary \'mamə,lerē, -ri\ *adj* [L *mammilla* breast, nipple + E *-ary* — more at MAMMILLA] **1 :** of or relating to the breasts **2 a :** having the form of a rounded eminence **b :** composed of concretions shaped somewhat like breasts **:** studded with mammiform protuberances ⟨limonite frequently occurs in ~ masses⟩

mammillary body *n* **:** either of two small rounded eminences on the undersurface of the brain behind the tuber cinereum forming terminals of the anterior pillars of the fornix — called also *corpus albicans*

mam·mil·late \'mamə,lāt\ *or* **mam·mil·lat·ed** \-ād·əd\ *also* **mam·il·late** \-āt\ *or* **mam·il·lat·ed** \-ād·əd\ *adj* [LL *mammillatus, mamillatus,* fr. L *mammilla, mamilla* breast, nipple + *-atus* -ate, -ated — more at MAMMILLA] **1 :** having nipples or small protuberances like nipples **2 a :** having the form of a bluntly rounded protuberance **b** *usu mammillated* **:** having a hummocky rock surface with many smoothly rounded knobs or mounds formed esp. as a result of glacial erosion ⟨the *mammillated* variety of glaciated surface —C.A. Cotton⟩

mam·mil·la·tion \,⸗⸗'lāshən\ *n* -s [LL *mamillatus* + E *-ion*] **1 :** a mammillate or mammilliform protuberance **2 :** the condition of having nipples or protuberances resembling nipples

mam·mil·li·form \mə'milə,fȯrm, ma'-\ *adj* [L *mammilla* + E *-iform*] **:** nipple-shaped

mam·mi·tis \ma'mīd·əs, ma'-\ *n, pl* **mam·mit·i·des** \-mid·ə,dēz\ [NL, fr. ²*mamma* + *-itis*] **:** MASTITIS

¹mam·mock \'mamək\ *n* -s [origin unknown] **1** *now dial* **:** a broken piece **:** SHRED, SCRAP, FRAGMENT **2** *now dial* **:** MESS, LITTER

²mammock \"\ *vt* -ED/-ING/-S **1** *now dial* **:** to tear into fragments **:** MANGLE; *esp* **:** to break or cut (as bread or meat) into ragged pieces **2** *now dial* **:** to rumple or make untidy **:** DISARRANGE, MESS

mam·mo·gen \'maməjən, -,jen\ *n* -s [²*mamma* + *-o-* + *-gen*] **:** any of certain hypothetical hormonal factors that stimulate mammary development and are usu. held to be produced in the pituitary gland — compare LACTOGENIC HORMONE

mam·mo·gen·ic \¦mamə¦jenik\ *adj* [²*mamma* + *-o-* + *-genic*] **:** stimulating or inducing mammary development — **mam·mo·gen·i·cal·ly** \-nək(ə)lē\ *adv*

mam·mon \'mamən\ *n* -s *often cap* [LL *mammona,* fr. Gk *mamōna,* fr. Aram *māmōnā* riches] **:** material wealth or possessions esp. having an evil power or debasing influence **:** WEALTH, MONEY ⟨you cannot serve God and ~ —Mt 6:24 (RSV)⟩ ⟨materialism was in the saddle; *Mammon* ruled the hearts and minds of men —C.I.Glicksberg⟩

mam·mo·ni \'mämə,nē\ *n, pl* **mammoni** *or* **mammonis** [It dial., pl. of *mammone,* lit., large breast, aug. of *mamma* breast — more at MAMME] **:** the autumn crop of the caprifig — compare MAMME, PROFICHI

mam·mon·ish \'mamənish\ *adj* **:** actuated or prompted by a devotion to money getting or the service of mammon

mam·mon·ism \-ə,nizəm\ *n* -s **:** devotion to the pursuit of wealth **:** the service of mammon

mam·mon·ist \-,nəst\ *n* -s **:** one devoted to the ideal or the pursuit of wealth — **mam·mon·is·tic** \¦mamə¦nistik\ *adj*

mam·mon·ite \'⸗⸗,nīt\ *n* -s **:** MAMMONIST — **mam·mon·it·ish** \-īd·ish\ *adj*

mam·mon·te·us \mə'mäntēəs, ma'-\ [NL, fr. Russ *mamont, mamot* mammoth + L *-eus* -eous] *syn of* MAMMUTHUS

mam·mose \'ma,mōs\ *n* -s [origin unknown] *Del. & N.J.* **:** a young sturgeon

¹mam·moth \'maməth\ *n* -s [Russ *mamot, mamont, mamant,* perh. fr. a Yakut word derived fr. Yakut *mamma* earth; fr. the belief that the mammoths burrowed in the earth like moles] **1 :** any of numerous extinct elephants widely distributed in the Pleistocene and distinguished from recent elephants by having molars with cementum filling the interstices of the numerous high narrow ridges of enamel and usu. by the large size, very long upcurved tusks, and well-developed body hair — compare WOOLLY MAMMOTH **2 :** something that is immense of its kind **:** GIANT ⟨a company that is a ~ of the industry⟩ ⟨a diesel-powered ~ of the highways⟩

mammoth (restored)

²mammoth \"\ *adj* **1 :** resembling a mammoth in size and weight ⟨a ~ bull elephant⟩ **2 :** characterized by extreme size, ponderous or preponderant weight, bulk, dimension, strength, or force **:** GIGANTIC ⟨the ~ hydrogen bomb explosion —*N.Y. Times*⟩ ⟨a ~ parade⟩ ⟨~ watermelons, cabbages, and tomatoes —Alan Moorehead⟩ ⟨the ~ optimism of the man —*Saturday Rev.*⟩ ⟨a ~ undertaking⟩ **syn** *see* HUGE

mammoth red clover *or* **mammoth clover** *n* **:** a clover (*Trifolium pratense perenne*) that is a variety of red clover, is distinguished from the typical red clover by stouter, coarser, more prolific growth and darker later-flowering heads, and is cultivated chiefly for forage

mammoth redwood *n* **:** REDWOOD 3a

mammothrept *n* -s [Gk *mammothreptos* child brought up by his grandmother, fr. *mammē* mother, grandmother + *-o-* + *threptos,* verbal of *trephein* to bring up, nourish — more at MAMMA, ATROPHY] *obs* **:** a spoiled child **:** INFANT

mammoth tree *n* **:** BIG TREE

mam·mo·trop·ic \¦mamə¦träpik\ *adj* [ISV ²*mamma* + *-o-* + *-tropic*] **:** MAMMOGENIC

mam·mu·lar \'mamyələ(r)\ *adj* [L *mammula* small breast (dim. of *mamma* breast) + E *-ar* — more at MAMMA] **:** consisting of small papillae ⟨~ excrescences⟩

mam·mut \'mamət\ *n, cap* [NL, fr. G, mammoth, fr. F *mammouth,* fr. Russ *mamot, mamont* — more at MAMMOTH] **:** the proboscidean genus comprising the mastodons and being the type and in some classifications sole genus of a family (Mammutidae) closely related to the Elephantidae

mam·mu·thus \'maməthəs\ *n, cap* [NL, fr. G *mammut* or F *mammouth* mammoth] **:** the genus of Elephantidae comprising the mammoths

mam·my \'mamē, -mi\ *n* -ES [alter. of ¹*mamma*] **1 :** MAMMA **2 a :** a Negro woman serving as a nurse to white children esp. formerly in the Southern states ⟨in the Richmond of the 1880's a ~ still ruled over every household in which there were children —J.B.Cabell⟩ **b :** a Negro woman — often taken to be offensive

mammy chair *n* **:** a basket or chair (as of canvas) attached to a cargo boom and used to convey persons to and from boats alongside ship in an open roadstead (as on the west coast of Africa)

mammy coot *n* **:** PURPLE GALLINULE

mammy wagon *or* **mammy lorry** *n* **:** a small open-sided bus or light truck used to transport passengers or goods in West Africa

ma·mo \'mä(,)mō\ *n* -s [Hawaiian] **:** any of several black Hawaiian honeycreepers that constitute a genus (*Drepanis*) of the family Drepanididae, are distinguished by yellow feathers above and below the tail which were used in choice featherwork, and are now wholly extinct

ma·mo·na \mə'mōnə\ *n* -s [Pg] **:** CASTOR-OIL PLANT

ma·mon·ci·llo \,mämən'sē(,)(y)ō\ *n* -s [AmerSp, dim. of Sp *mamón* mamoncillo, prob. fr. a native name in Venezuela] **:** GENIP 2

ma·mo·ty \'mämәd·ē\ *n* -ES [Tamil *mammaṭṭi,* alter. of *man⸗veṭṭi,* fr. *maṇ* earth + *veṭṭi* spade] **:** a hand tool used for digging and cultivating in southeastern Asia

mam·pa·lon \'mampə,län\ *n* -s [native name in Indonesia] **:** a short-tailed web-footed reddish brown viverrid mammal (*Cynogale bennettii*) of Malaysia and adjacent islands that resembles an otter in appearance and habits — called also *otter civet*

mam·pus \'mampəs\ *n* -ES [origin unknown] *dial Brit* **:** a very large number **:** MULTITUDE ⟨a ~ of folk were there⟩

mams *pl of* MAM

mam·sell *or* **mam'·selle** \mam'zel\ *n* -s [F *mam'selle,* contr. of *mademoiselle* — more at MADEMOISELLE] **:** MADEMOISELLE

ma·mu·shi \mə'müshē\ *n* -s [Jap] **:** a small venomous pit viper (*Agkistrodon blomhoffi*) that is marked with dark brown blotches on a pale gray ground, is widely distributed in the Japanese islands, and is represented by identical or closely related forms on the adjacent Asiatic mainland

mam·zer *also* **mom·ser** *or* **mom·zer** \'mämzə(r)\ *n* -s [LL *mamzer,* fr. Heb *mamzēr*] **1 :** a child of a union not sanctioned by biblical law as interpreted by the rabbis **2** [Yiddish *mamzer,* fr. Heb *mamzēr*] **:** BASTARD

¹man \'man, -aa(ə)-, *as suffix* -,ə-, *in exclamations* -,ai-\ *n, pl* **men** \'men, *in compounds* -mən *or* ,men\ [ME, fr. OE *man, mon;* akin to OS & OHG *man* human being, man, ON *mathr,* Goth *manna,* Skt *manu* human being, man, OSlav *mǫžĭ* man, and perh. to OE *gemynd* mind — more at MIND] **1 a :** a member of the human race **:** a human being **:** PERSON — usu. used of males except in general or indefinite applications with collective adjectives or in the pl. ⟨every ~ must now do his duty⟩ ⟨all *men,* both male and female —David Hume †1776⟩; often used interjectionally to express intensity of feeling ⟨~, what a relief⟩ ⟨~, oh ~⟩ ⟨~, can that fellow shoot baskets⟩ **b** (1) **:** the human race **:** MANKIND **:** human beings personified as an individual — used without an article ⟨~ is a greedy beast⟩ (2) **:** a bipedal primate mammal (*Homo sapiens*) that is anatomically related to the great apes but is distinguished by notable development of the brain with a resultant capacity for articulate speech and abstract reasoning, marked erectness of body carriage with corresponding alteration of muscular balance and loss of prehensile powers of the foot, and shortening of the arm with accompanying increase in thumb size and opposability, that is usu. considered to occur in a variable number of freely interbreeding races, and that is the sole recent representative of the natural family Hominidae;

Figs 1 and 2 MUSCULAR SYSTEM OF MAN

Fig 1, FRONT VIEW. Fig 2, BACK VIEW. The sides marked A show the muscles of the first layer located immediately below the skin. Those marked B show the important muscles of the deeper layers. Where a muscle is shown in only one of the figures, that fact is indicated following the name: as, temporal (fig 1)

Head and Neck

1 frontalis
2 occipitalis
3 temporal (fig 1)
4 orbicularis of eye
5 greater zygomaticus
6 lesser zygomaticus
7 angular head of the quadratus of upper lip (fig 1)
8 nasalis (fig 1)
9 orbicularis of mouth (fig 1)
10 triangularis of chin (fig 1)
11 quadratus of lower lip (fig 1)
12 mentalis (fig 1)
13 masseter (fig 1)
14 buccinator (fig 1)
15 anterior auricularis
16 superior auricularis
17 posterior auricularis
a parotid gland
18 mylohyoid (fig 1)
19 digastric
20 platysma
21 sternocleidomastoid
22 omohyoid (fig 1)
23 sternohyoid (fig 1)
24 trapezius
25 splenius of head (fig 2)
26 splenius of neck (fig 2)
27 levator of scapula (fig 2)
28 supraspinatus (fig 2)

Trunk

29 greater pectoralis (fig 1)
30 deltoid
31 latissimus dorsi
32 anterior serratus
33 external oblique
34 rectus abdominis (fig 1)
35 umbilicus (fig 1)
36 abdominal aponeurosis (fig 1)
37 linea alba (fig 1)
38 subclavius (fig 1)
39 lesser pectoralis (fig 1)
40 posterior superior serratus (fig 1)
41 internal oblique
42 infraspinatus (fig 2)
43 lesser teres (fig 2)
44 greater teres (fig 2)
45 greater rhomboideus (fig 2)
46 lesser rhomboideus (fig 2)
b scapula (fig 2)
c 9th rib (fig 2)
d 10th rib (fig 2)
e 11th rib (fig 2)
f 12th rib (fig 2)
47 posterior inferior serratus (fig 2)
48 lumbodorsal fascia (fig 2)
49 sacrospinalis (fig 2)

Upper Extremity

50 biceps of arm
51 triceps of arm
52 brachialis
53 lacertus fibrosus
54 long radial extensor of wrist
55 brachioradialis
56 radial flexor of wrist
57 long palmaris (fig 1)
58 flexor of digits (fig 1)
59 ulnar flexor of wrist
60 short palmaris
61 short radial extensor of wrist
62 long flexor of thumb (fig 1)
63 pronator quadratus (fig 1)
64 short flexor of thumb (fig 1)
65 long palmaris (cut across in fig 1)
66 first dorsal interosseus
67 first lumbricalis (fig 1)
68 fibrous sheaths of the tendons
69 adductor of the little finger
70 annular ligament of the carpus
g head of humerus (showing bicipital groove)
71 common extensor of digits (fig 1)
72 ulnar extensor of wrist (fig 1)
73 long extensor of thumb
h medial epicondyle of humerus (fig 2)
i lower end of radius (fig 2)
j lower end of ulna (fig 2)
74 tendons of extensors of thumb (fig 2)
75 adductor of thumb (fig 2)
76 tendons of extensors of digits and wrist (fig 2)
77 pronator teres (fig 2)
78 palmar aponeurosis (fig 2)

Lower Extremity

k anterior superior spine of ilium (fig 1)
79 iliacus (fig 1)
80 gluteus medius
81 tensor of fascia lata
82 rectus femoris (fig 1)
83 psoas major (fig 1)
84 pectineus (fig 1)
85 sartorius
86 long adductor of thigh (fig 1)
87 great adductor of thigh
88 gracilis
89 vastus lateralis
90 vastus medialis
91 gluteus minimus (fig 1)
92 superior extremity of rectus femoris (fig 1)
93 inferior extremity of rectus femoris (fig 1)
m head of femur (fig 1)
94 inferior extremities of psoas and iliacus (fig 1)
95 tendon of rectus femoris
n patella (fig 1)
o head of fibula (fig 1)
p medial condyle of femur (fig 1)
r tuberosity of tibia (fig 1)
96 anterior tibialis
97 medial head of gastrocnemius (fig 1)
98 soleus
99 long extensor of digits (fig 1)
100 long peroneus
101 short peroneus (fig 1)
102 long flexor of digits (fig 1)
103 long extensor of hallux (fig 1)
104 annular ligament of ankle (fig 1)
105 short extensor of digits (fig 1)
106 abductor of hallux (fig 1)
s ilium
t greater trochanter
107 gluteus maximus (fig 2)
108 biceps of thigh (fig 2)
109 semitendinosus (fig 2)
110 semimembranosus (fig 2)
111 plantaris (fig 2)
112 lateral head of gastrocnemius (fig 2)
113 long flexor of digits (fig 2)
114 third peroneus (fig 2)
115 tendon of posterior tibialis (fig 2)
116 Achilles' tendon (fig 2)
u tuberosity of calcaneus
117 piriformis (fig 2)
118 superior gemellus and inferior gemellus (fig 2)
119 internal obturator (fig 2)
120 quadratus of thigh (fig 2)

Fig 3 SKELETON OF ADULT MAN

(a few small or internal bones are omitted)

Head

bones of the cranium

A top of skull showing sutures
1 frontal
2 parietal
3 squamous portion of occipital
4 greater wing of sphenoid
5 squamous portion of temporal
6 ethmoid

bones of the external face

7 nasal
8 lacrimal
9 vomer
10 maxilla
11 mandible
12 zygomatic

principal features of the bones of the head

13 coronoid process of mandible
14 condyloid process of mandible
15 styloid process of temporal
16 mastoid process
17 zygomatic arch
a coronal suture
b sphenofrontal suture
c sphenosquamosal suture
d squamous suture
e sphenoparietal suture
f lambdoid suture
g occipitomastoid suture
h sagittal suture
i superior temporal ridge
k inferior temporal ridge
l hyoid bone

Chest

bones of the breast

18 manubrium
19 gladiolus
20 xiphoid process

true ribs

21 *to* 27 first to seventh ribs inclusive

false ribs

28 *to* 30 eighth to tenth ribs inclusive
31 *and* 32 floating ribs
m costal cartilage

Trunk

spinal column

33 first thoracic vertebra
34 twelfth thoracic vertebra
35 fifth lumbar vertebra
36 fifth sacral vertebra
37 coccyx

Upper Extremity

shoulder

38 clavicle
39 scapula

arm

40 humerus
41 ulna
42 radius
(*p*) bones of forearm in prone position
(*r*) same in supine position

bones of the hand

(43) bones of right hand (dorsal surface)
(44) bones of left hand (volar surface)
B bones of the left hand (dorsal surface)
(*s*) carpus
(*t*) metacarpus
(*u*) phalanges of thumb and fingers

bones of the carpus

45 lunatum
46 pisiform
47 triquetrum
48 hamatum
49 capitatum
50 navicular
51 lesser multangulum
52 greater multangulum

bones of the metacarpus

53 *to* 57 first to fifth metacarpal bones
I thumb
II index finger
III middle finger
IV ring finger
V little finger

phalanges

58 first phalanx of thumb
59 second phalanx of thumb
60 ungual tuberosity
61 first phalanx of index
62 second phalanx of index
63 third phalanx of index

Lower Extremity

bones and principal parts of pelvic girdle

64 ilium
65 ischium
66 pubis
67 sacrum
68 brim of pelvis
69 pelvic cavity

bones of the leg

70 femur
71 patella
72 tibia
73 fibula

bones of the feet

(74) bones of left foot (dorsal surface)
C bones of right foot (plantar surface)
(*x*) tarsus
(*y*) metatarsus
(*z*) phalanges of toes

bones of the tarsus

75 talus
76 calcaneus
w tuberosity of calcaneus
77 cuboid
78 *to* 80 cuneiform bones
81 navicular bone

bones of the metatarsus

82 *to* 86 first to fifth metatarsal bones
87 sesamoid bones
VI big toe
VII *to* IX second to fourth toes
X little toe

phalanges

88 first phalanx of big toe
89 second phalanx of big toe
90 first phalanx of little toe
91 second phalanx of little toe
92 third phalanx of little toe

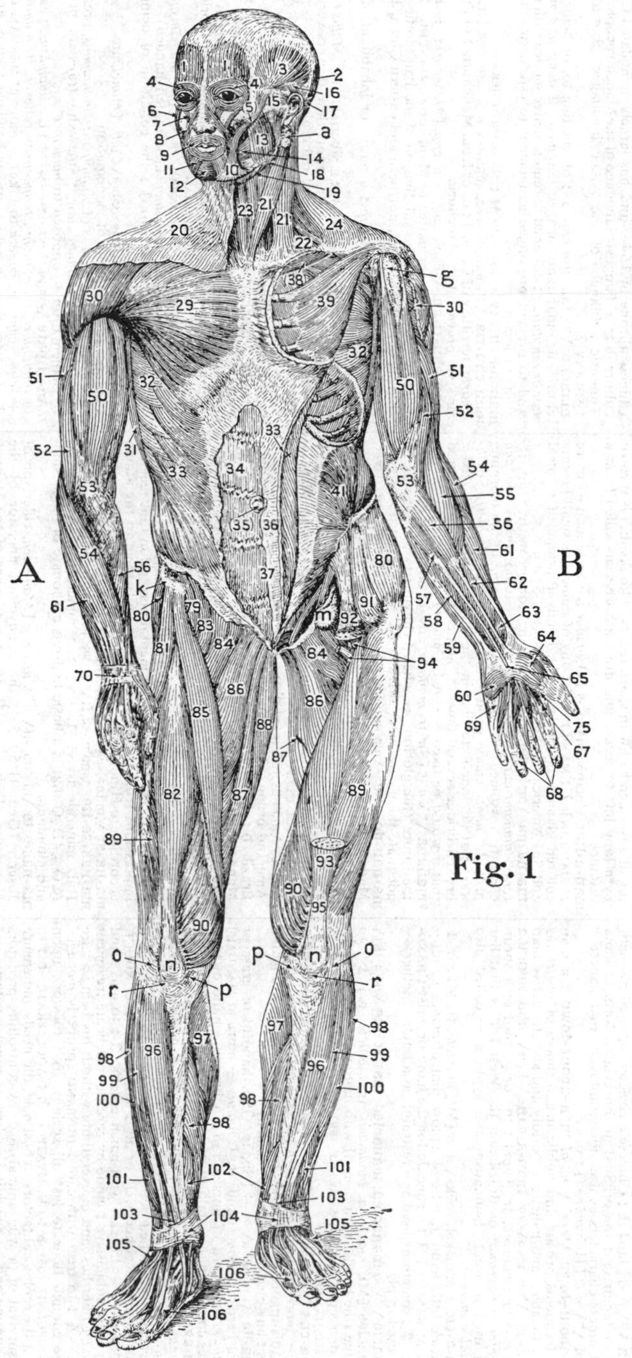

Fig. 1

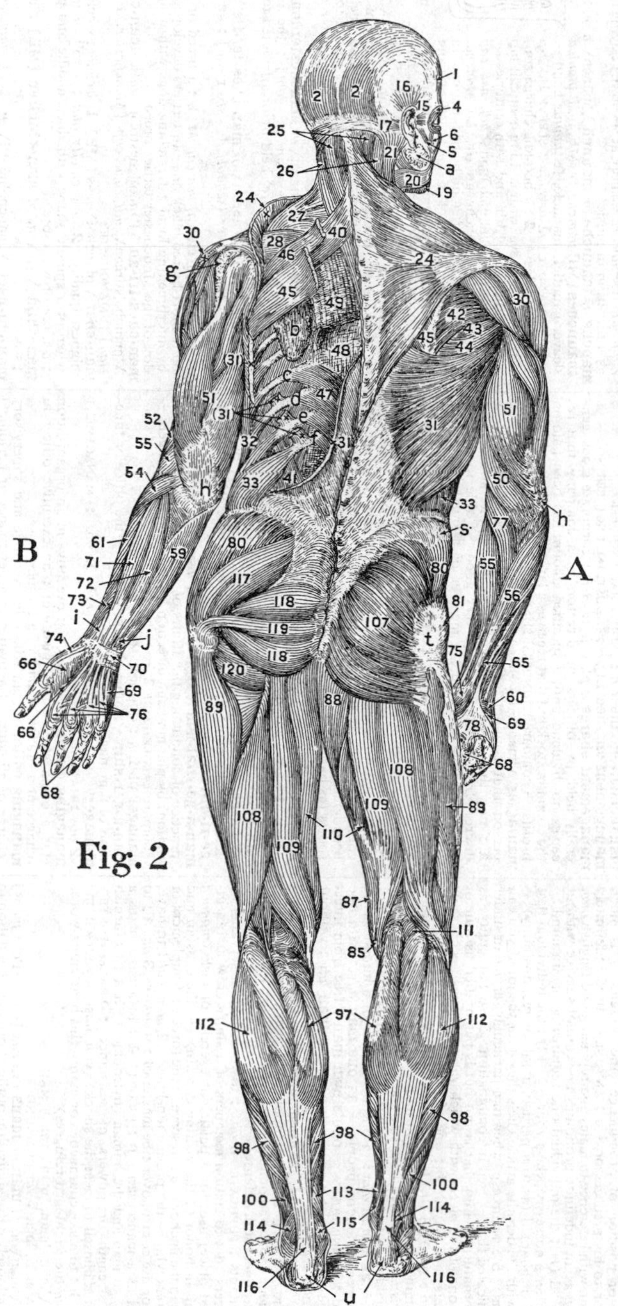

Fig. 2

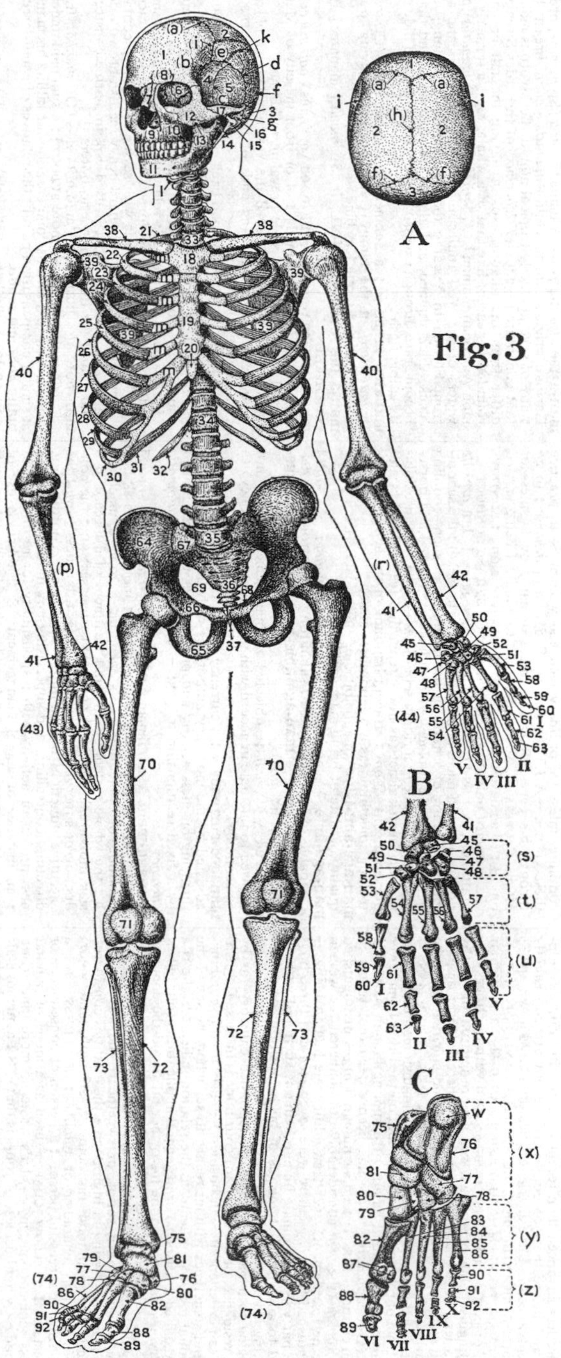

Fig. 3

broadly **:** any living or extinct member of the family Hominidae comprising recent man and various extinct Old World forms that are less advanced than recent man esp. in brain development and in erectness of body carriage but are consistently more advanced in these characteristics than any known ape — compare AFRICANTHROPUS, HOMO, PITHECANTHROPUS; FLORISBAD MAN, PEKING MAN, RHODESIAN MAN **c** (1) **:** a particular aspect or part of the human being — used with qualifiers esp. to distinguish a higher from a lower, a more spiritual or worthy from a less, or a grosser from a more ethereal aspect or part ⟨qualities that differentiate the inward and spiritual from the outward and worldly ~⟩ — see INNER MAN, OUTER MAN (2) **:** one endued with the qualities that distinguish man on the one hand from purely spiritual entities and on the other from lower animals **:** an individual having or assuming human nature or form ⟨God appearing as ~ has been a recurrent theme in human culture⟩ **2 a** (1) **:** a male human being — distinguished from *woman* ⟨the *men* considerably outnumbered the women in the new settlement⟩ (2) **:** an adult male human being — distinguished from *boy* ⟨there were seven *men* and three boys in the party⟩ (3) **:** a male human being as such and without regard to any special status (as of birth, position, or office) ⟨the king is but a ~, as I am —*Shak.*⟩ **b :** a male human being belonging to a particular and usu. specified category (as by birth, residence, or membership) ⟨our hope is in these English*men*⟩ ⟨an experienced ~ of business⟩ — usu. used in combination and sometimes without regard to sex when the sex of the individual is not significant to the relation indicated ⟨she is a highly skilled drafts*man*⟩ or in general applications ⟨our fellow country*men* have each done his or her bit to aid the common cause⟩ **c** (1) **:** HUSBAND ⟨I'll have to ask my ~⟩ — now chiefly dial. except in the phrase *man and wife* (2) *chiefly dial* **:** a man that is lover, suitor, or sweetheart ⟨he was her ~⟩ **d** (1) **:** one possessing in high degree the qualities considered distinctive of manhood (as courage, strength, and vigor) (2) *obs* **:** manly character or quality **:** MANLINESS **e :** a prosperous or successful person **:** a person of consequence or high estate **f :** FELLOW, CHAP — used as a mode of familiar address ⟨come, come, my ~, let's waste no more time⟩ ⟨but, my good ~, what business of yours is that⟩ **3 :** a human male that serves or is subordinate to another or others: as **a :** liege man **:** VASSAL **b** *men pl* **:** members of a military or other fighting force ⟨the guerrillas had upward of 7000 *men*⟩; *esp* **:** members of the ranks of an organized force as distinguished from officers ⟨the enemy lost heavily in officers, *men*, and matériel⟩ **c :** a man that is in personal attendance on another person (as a manservant, valet, or groom) **d** *men pl* **:** the working force (as of a factory) as distinguished from the employer and usu. the management ⟨the *men* have been on strike for several weeks⟩ **e** *Brit* **:** UNDERGRADUATE **4 :** INDIVIDUAL, ONE: as **a :** the male individual in question — used in place of a pronoun ⟨the good ~ fell ill⟩ **b :** the holder of an office or position of prominence ⟨the present ~ is much inferior to his predecessor⟩ **c :** ANYONE — used indefinitely but usu. with reference to males and replacing Old English *man* or *mon* as an indefinite pronoun ⟨a ~ cannot survive without hope⟩ **d** (1) **:** the individual one requires or has in mind — used after a possessive ⟨he's your ~⟩ (2) **:** the individual best suited or adapted (as to a particular job or responsibility) — used with the definite article ⟨he's the ~ for the job if you can get him⟩ **5 :** a ship esp. when in a particular service or under an indicated flag — used in combination **6** *obs* **:** an entity (as a supernatural being) that is not but is personified as human **7 a :** one of the pieces with which various games (as chess or checkers) are played **b :** one of the players on a team ⟨nine *men* on a side⟩ **8** *Brit* **a :** a conical heap of stones set up on a mountain top **b :** the mountain top itself ⟨Scafell *Man*⟩ **9** *Christian Science* **:** the compound idea of infinite Spirit **:** the spiritual image and likeness of God **:** the full representation of Mind — **as a man** *adv* **:** in one's character of a human being **:** as a person among people — **as one man** *adv* **:** with one accord **:** UNANIMOUSLY — **one's own man :** free from interference or control **:** INDEPENDENT — **to a man** *adv* **:** without exception

²**man** \"\ *vt* **manned; manned; manning; mans** [ME *mannen*, fr. *man*, n.] **1 a :** to supply with men **:** furnish with a sufficient force or complement of men (as for management, service, operation, defense) ⟨~ a fleet⟩ **b** *obs* **:** to furnish with inhabitants **:** POPULATE **c** *obs* **:** to furnish with servants or followers **d :** to station members of a ship's crew at (an indicated place) usu. for a particular exercise or task ⟨*manned* the rail in honor of the visiting captain⟩ ⟨~ the capstan and heave in the anchor⟩ **e :** to serve in the force or complement of ⟨workers who ~ the production lines⟩ **2** *now dial* **:** to have, gain, or use control over **:** be master of **:** MANAGE **3** *obs* **a :** to attend as a manservant **b :** ESCORT **4 :** to accustom (as a hawk) to man and the human environment **5 a :** to furnish with strength or powers of resistance **:** BRACE, FORTIFY ⟨*manned* himself to meet the shock⟩ ⟨you must ~ yourself, my boy⟩ **b :** to make courageous or manly ⟨his heartening words *manned* the frightened refugees⟩

³**man** \ˈmän, ˈman, ˌmən\ *var of* MAUN

⁴**man** \ˈmän, ˈman\ *var of* MAUND

⁵**man** \ˈman\ *n, pl* **man** *or* **mans** *usu cap* [Chin (Pek) *man*²] **1 a :** a loosely defined division of the aboriginal population in China usu. comprising the tribes living in the south and southwest **b :** one of these tribes or peoples (as the Yao or Miao) **2 :** any of the primitive mountain tribes of Vietnam; *esp* **:** YAO

man *abbr* **1** manila **2** [L *manipulus*] handful **3** manual **4** manufacture

¹**ma·na** \ˈmänə\ *n* -s [of Melanesian & Polynesian origin; akin to Hawaiian & Maori *mana*] **:** impersonal supernatural force or power that may be concentrated in objects or persons and that may be inherited, acquired, or conferred

²**mana** \"\ *n* -s [Jap] **1 :** Chinese characters as used phonetically in Japanese **:** the original unabbreviated form of kana **2 :** Chinese characters as used ideographically in Japanese

³**mana** \"\ *n* -s [Heb *māneh*] **:** MINA

man–about–town \ˌ＝＝ˈ＝\ *n, pl* **men–about–town :** a man who frequents private and public urban places of resort (as clubs, theaters, and balls) **:** a worldly and socially active man

man·a·ca \ˈmanəkə\ *or* **man·a·can** \-kən\ *also* **manaca root** *n* -s [Pg *manacá*, fr. Tupi] **:** the dried root of a shrub (*Brunfelsia hopeana*) of Brazil and the West Indies that has been used to treat rheumatism and syphilis — called also *vegetable mercury*

¹**man·a·cle** \ˈmanəkəl, -nēk-\ *n* -s [ME *manicle*, fr. MF, fr. L *manicula* little hand, handle of a plow, dim. of *manus* hand — more at MANUAL] **1 :** a shackle for the hand or wrist **:** HANDCUFF **2 :** something used as a restraint (as a fetter or tether) — usu. used in pl.

²**manacle** \"\ *vt* **manacled; manacled; manacling** \-k(ə)liŋ\ **manacles** [ME *maniclen*, *manaclen*, fr. *manicle*, n.] **1 :** to confine (the hands) with or as if with handcuffs **2 :** to make fast or secure **:** BIND, SHACKLE, FETTER; *broadly* **:** RESTRAIN **syn** see HAMPER

man·a·cus \ˈmanəkəs\ *n* [NL, modif. of D *manneken* little man — more at MANIKIN] **1** *cap* **:** a genus consisting of manakins distinguished by having the throat feathers elongated **2** -ES **:** any bird of the genus *Manacus*

ma·na·da \məˈnädə\ *n* -s [Sp, fr. OSp, handful of grass or grain, herd, fr. *mano* hand, fr. L *manus* — more at MANUAL] *Southwest* **:** a herd of horses; *esp* **:** a breeding band of wild horses consisting of a stallion, several mares, and young stock

¹**man·age** \ˈmanij, -nēj, *esp in pres part* -nəj\ *vb* -ED/-ING/-S [It *maneggiare*, fr. (earlier) *maneare*, fr. *mano* hand, fr. L *manus* — more at MANUAL] *vt* **1 :** to train or handle (a horse) in graceful or studied action or stance **2 :** to control and direct **:** handle either well or ill **:** cope with **:** CONDUCT, ADMINISTER ⟨~s his skis with much grace⟩ **3 :** to make and keep (one) submissive **:** guide by careful or delicate treatment ⟨*managed* her husband in everything without his being aware of it⟩ **4 :** to treat with care **:** HUSBAND ⟨properly *managed* we've enough flour to last tili spring⟩ **5 :** to work upon **:** MANIPULATE: as **a :** CULTIVATE 1 **b :** ADULTERATE **c :** to adjust the ecological factors to best meet the needs and ensure the survival of (a wild animal) usu. by controlling predators and hunting and by providing shelter or supplementary food supplies **6 :** to bring about by contriving **:** succeed in doing or accomplishing ⟨don't know how I'll ~ it but I'll be there⟩ — often followed by an infinitive ⟨human life on earth cannot continue unless we ordinary men and women ~ to practice these virtues —A.J.Toynbee⟩ ~ *vi* **1** *obs, of a horse* **:** to go through his paces **2 a :** to direct or carry on business or affairs **:** SUPERVISE, ADMINISTER **b :** to admit of being carried on **3 :** to achieve one's purpose **:** get on or along **:** CONTRIVE ⟨he *managed* only by careful planning⟩ **syn** see CONDUCT

²**manage** \"\ *n* -s [It *maneggio*, fr. *maneggiare*] **1 a** *archaic* **:** the action and paces of a trained riding horse **b :** the schooling or handling of a horse or the technique of such schooling or handling **c :** a place where horses are trained and horsemanship practiced **:** a riding school **:** MANEGE 1 **d :** an exhibition or theatrical act (as in a circus) that features horses and horsemanship **2** *obs* **:** efficient handling or the action of controlling something (as a weapon or a state)

man·age·abil·i·ty \ˌmanijəˈbiləd·ē, -nēj-, -lətē, -i\ *n* **:** the quality or state of being manageable

man·age·able \ˈmanijəbəl, -nēj-\ *adj* [¹*manage* + *-able*] **:** capable of being managed **:** submitting to control **:** GOVERNABLE, TRACTABLE — **man·age·able·ness** *n* -ES — **man·age·ably** \-blē, -li\ *adv*

man·aged \-jd\ *adj* **:** subjected to management; *esp* **:** not allowed to fluctuate in accord with natural laws ⟨~ money⟩ ⟨a ~ economy⟩

managed currency *n* **:** a currency whose purchasing power is adjusted by the monetary authorities with the purpose of influencing business activity and prices rather than determined by a fixed relationship to gold — contrasted with *automatic currency*

man·age·ment \ˈmanijmənt, -nēj-\ *n* -s [¹*manage* + *-ment*] **1 :** the act or art of managing: as **a :** more or less skilled handling of something (as a weapon, a tool, a machine) **b :** the whole system of care and treatment of a disease or a sick individual ⟨the ~ of contagious diseases⟩ **c :** the conducting or supervising of something (as a business); *esp* **:** the executive function of planning, organizing, coordinating, directing, controlling, and supervising any industrial or business project or activity with responsibility for results **2** *obs* **:** an instance or act of management **3 :** judicious use of means to accomplish an end **:** conduct directed by art or craft **:** skillful and often devious treatment **:** INTRIGUE **4 a :** the collective body of those who manage or direct any enterprise or interest **:** the board of managers **b :** employer representation in an employer-employee relationship — opposed to *labor* **5** *archaic* **:** moderation (as in conduct) from respect for the feelings of another **:** CONSIDERATION, INDULGENCE

man·age·men·tal \ˌ＝＝ˈmentᵊl\ *adj* **:** of, relating to, or constituting management

management consultant *n* **:** one that advises business or industrial firms in the conduct of their affairs and in devising and installing more satisfactory procedures for their use

management engineer *n* **:** INDUSTRIAL ENGINEER

management engineering *n* **:** INDUSTRIAL ENGINEERING

management shares *n pl, chiefly Brit* **:** corporate stock generally held by officers or directors of a company that receives no dividend until a specified amount has been paid on the common stock but that receives a large share of the residual profits — compare FOUNDERS' SHARES

man·ag·er \ˈmanijə(r), -nēj-\ *n* -s **:** one that manages **:** a person that conducts, directs, or supervises something: as **a :** one that conducts business or household affairs with discreet frugality and care ⟨a very good ~, able to make a little go a long way⟩ **b :** a member of a small group of a legislative body (as a house of the British Parliament) appointed to perform some special duty **c :** a person whose work or profession is the management of a specified thing (as a business, an institution, or a particular phase or activity within a business or institution) **d :** a receiver appointed under English law by a court of equity to carry on under the court's control a business for the benefit of creditors or other beneficiaries **e** (1) **:** a person that in various professional sports (as baseball or boxing) is in overall charge of a team or athlete (2) **:** a student or other person that in collegiate sports supervises equipment and records under the direction of a coach **f :** a person appointed by elected officials to supervise the activities of a civic corporate body — see CITY MANAGER

man·ag·er·ess \-j(ə)rəs\ *n* -ES **:** a female manager

man·a·ge·ri·al \ˌmanəˈjirēəl\ *adj* **:** of, relating to, or characteristic of a manager ⟨~ qualities⟩ ⟨~ problems⟩ — **man·a·ge·ri·al·ly** \-ēəlē, -li\ *adv*

man·a·ge·ri·al·ism \ˌ＝＝ˈjirēəˌlizəm\ *n* -s **:** the philosophy or practice of conducting the affairs of an organized group (as a nation) by planning and direction by professional managers — compare LAISSEZ-FAIRE 2

manager plan *n* **:** COUNCIL-MANAGER PLAN

man·a·ger·ship \ˈmanijə(r)ˌship, -nēj-\ *n* **:** the office or function of a manager

managery *n* -ES [¹*manage* + *-ry*] **1** *obs* **:** MANAGEMENT **2** *obs* **:** MANEGE 1,2

managing director *n* **:** the chief executive in an organization (as a bank, steel works, institute) **:** an executive officer in charge of a branch or part of a business

managing editor *n* **:** an editor in executive and supervisory charge of all editorial activities of a newspaper or periodical

ma·na·gua \məˈnägwə\ *adj, usu cap* [fr. *Managua*, Nicaragua] **:** of or from Managua, the capital of Nicaragua **:** of the kind or style prevalent in Managua

man·a·hoac \ˈmanəˌhōk\ *n, pl* **manahoac** *or* **manahoacs** *usu cap* **1 :** a Siouan people of northern Virginia **2 :** a member of the Manahoac people

ma·na·ism \ˈmänəˌizəm\ *n* -s [¹*mana* + *-ism*] **:** belief in mana

ma·na·is·tic \ˌ＝＝ˈistik\ *adj* **:** of, relating to, characteristic of, or exhibiting manaism

ma·nak \ˈmaˌnak\ *n* -s [Esk] **:** an Eskimo implement consisting of a wooden ball with sharp recurved hooks that is thrown by a long line to secure and draw ashore seals killed from a distance

man·a·kin \ˈmanəkən\ *n* -s [D *manneken* little man — more at MANIKIN] **1 :** MANIKIN **2 :** any of numerous small brightcolored clamatorial birds of the family Pipridae of Central and So. America — compare MANNIKIN

¹**ma·ña·na** \məˈnyänə\ *adv* [Sp, lit., tomorrow, fr. OSp, fr. (*cras*) *mañana* early tomorrow, fr. *cras* tomorrow + *mañana* early, fr. (assumed) VL *maneana*, fr. L *mane* in the morning, prob. fr. *manis*, *manus* good — more at MATURE] *chiefly Southwest* **:** at an indefinite time in the future ⟨a hunter passed a broken bridge several times . . . and every time he was assured that it would be fixed ~ —A.L.Campa⟩

²**mañana** \"\ *n* -s [Sp, fr. *mañana*, adv.] **:** an indefinite time in the future ⟨the glorious ~ when behaviorists will give us an adequate theory of the creative artist —Eliseo Vivas⟩

ma·nan·do·nite \məˈnandəˌnīt\ *n* -s [*Manandona* river, Madagascar + E *-ite*] **:** a mineral $Li_4Al_{14}B_4Si_6O_{29}(OH)_{24}$ (?) that is a basic borosilicate of lithium and aluminum

man·a·no·say \ˌmanəˈnō(ˌ)sā\ *or* **man·a·nose** \ˈmanəˌnōz\ *n* -s [prob. of Algonquian origin; akin to *man-* to gather (in some Algonquian language of Virginia)] *chiefly Midland* **:** SOFT-SHELL CLAM

ma·nao \məˈnä(ˌ)ō\ *n, pl* **manao** *or* **manaos** *usu cap* [Pg, of AmerInd origin] **1 a :** an Arawakan people of northwestern Brazil **b :** a member of such people **2 :** the language of the Manao people

man ape *n* **1 :** GREAT APE **2 :** any of various fossil primates that are intermediate in characters between recent man and the great apes

¹**manas** *pl of* MANA

²**man·as** \ˈmanəs, ˈmənəs\ *n* -ES [Skt, fr. *manyate* he thinks — more at MIND] **:** the faculty of mental perception that receives impressions from the senses and transmits them to the atman according to Hinduism — **ma·nas·ic** \məˈnasik\ *adj*

ma·na·si \ˌmänəˈsē\ *n* -s *usu cap* **:** a dialect of Chiquitoan

ma·nas·se·ite \məˈnasēˌīt\ *n* -s [Ernesto *Manasse* †1922 Ital. mineralogist + E *-ite*] **:** a mineral $Mg_6Al_2(OH)_{16}(CO_3).4H_2O$ that is a basic hydrous carbonate of magnesium and aluminum

ma·nas·site \məˈnaˌsīt\ *n* -s *usu cap* [*Manasseh*, elder son of Joseph (Gen 41:50–52), the eponymous ancestor of the Manassites (Josh 17) + E *-ite*] **:** a member of the Hebrew tribe of Manasseh — compare EPHRAIMITE

man–at–arms \ˈ＝＝ˈ＝\ *n, pl* **men–at–arms :** SOLDIER; *esp* **:** a heavily armed and usu. mounted soldier

man·a·tee *also* **man·a·ti** \ˈmanəˌtē\ *n* -s [Sp *manatí*, prob. of Cariban origin; akin to Galibi *manati*, *manaté* breast, teats] **:** any of several chiefly tropical aquatic herbivorous mammals that constitute a genus (*Trichechus*) of the order Sirenia and differ from the dugong esp. in having the tail broad and rounded instead of like that of a whale; *esp* **:** a formerly common American mammal (*T. latirostris* syn. *T. manatus*) of the waters of the West Indies and neighboring mainland coasts from Florida to Yucatan that is about 10 feet long, nearly black, thick-skinned, and almost free from hair and that has become rare through excessive killing for its fat and hide or for its edible flesh

manatee grass *n* **:** a submerged aquatic herb (*Cymodocea manatorum*) of the family Cymodoceaceae having pointed rootstocks and terete leaf blades

man·a·tus \ˈmanətəs\ [NL, fr. Sp *manatí* manatee] *syn of* TRICHECHUS

ma·naus *or* **ma·ná·os** *or* **ma·naos** \məˈnaùs\ *adj, usu cap* [fr. *Manaus* or *Manáos*, Brazil] **:** of or from the city of Manaus, Brazil **:** of the kind or style prevalent in Manaus

ma·nav·el·ins *also* **ma·nav·il·ins** \məˈnavələnz\ *n pl* [origin unknown] *slang* **:** odds and ends of food **:** LEFTOVERS; *also* **:** fancy or made dishes

manback \ˈ＝ˌ＝\ *n* **:** the human back esp. as a bearer of burdens

man·bark·lak *also* **man·bark·lac** \ˈmanˌbärˌklak\ *n* -s [D *manbarklak*, fr. native name in Surinam] **1 :** any of numerous usu. large tropical American trees constituting a genus (*Eschweilera*) that is closely related to *Lecythis* and has smooth leathery leaves, brightly colored flowers in panicles or racemes, and large operculate fruits with sessile seeds often containing bitter kernels **2 :** the very hard heavy reddish brown wood of various manbarklaks that is used esp. in marine construction and valued for its resistance to borers

man·bote *also* **man·bot** \ˈmanˌbōt\ *n* -s [OE *manbōt*, fr. *man* + *-bōt* compensation — more at BOOT] **:** a sum paid under Old English law to a lord as compensation for killing his man; *also* **:** similar compensation paid to the relatives of a murdered man

manc *abbr* mancando

man·ca·la \mänˈkälə, ˈmäŋkələ\ *n* -s [Ar *manqalah*, fr. *naqala* to move] **:** any of various games that are widely played in Africa and southern Asia and in areas (as parts of Oceania or of the New World) influenced by African or Asiatic cultures and that involve competition between two players in the distribution of pieces (as beans or pebbles) into rows of holes or pockets (as in a board) under various rules that permit accumulation of pieces by capture — called also *wari;* see CHUBA

man·can·do \(ˈ)mänˈkän(ˌ)dō\ *also* **man·can·te** \-(ˌ)tā\ *adj (or adv)* [*mancando* fr. It, verbal of *mancare* to lack, fr. *manco* lacking, left-handed, fr. ML *mancus* lacking in weight, fr. L, having a crippled hand, maimed, infirm, prob. fr. *manus* hand; *mancante* fr. *mancare* — more at MANUAL] **:** dying away — used as a direction in music

manche *or* **maunche** *or* **maunch** \ˈmänch\ *n, pl* **manches** *or* **maunches** [ME *manche*, fr. MF, fr. L *manica* sleeve, gauntlet, manacle, fr. *manus* hand — more at MANUAL] **1** *archaic* **:** SLEEVE 1a; *esp* **:** a hanging sleeve **2 :** a heraldic charge consisting of a sleeve with a long pendent lap worn in the 12th, 13th, and 14th centuries

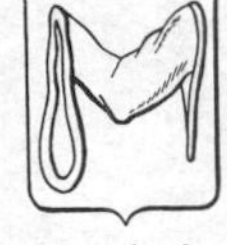

manche 2

man·che·gan \(ˈ)mänˈchāgən\ *adj, usu cap* [Sp *manchego* Manchegan (fr. *La Mancha*, region consisting of a high arid plateau in New Castile, Spain) + E *-an*] **:** of or from La Mancha **:** of the kind or style prevalent in La Mancha ⟨the *Manchegan* plain⟩ ⟨a *Manchegan* knife⟩

¹**man·ches·ter** \ˈmanˌchestə(r), ˈmaan-, -nchəs-\ *adj, usu cap* [fr. *Manchester*, England] **:** of or from the city of Manchester, England **:** of the kind or style prevalent in Manchester

²**manchester** \"\ *n* -s *usu cap* **1** *Brit* **:** cotton textiles ⟨*Manchester* goods⟩ ⟨a sales clerk in the *Manchester* department⟩ **2 :** MANCHESTER TERRIER

man·ches·ter·ism \-təˌrizəm\ *or* **manchesterdom** *n* -s *usu cap* [*Manchester* (*school*) + *-ism* or *-dom*] **:** the principles or doctrines (as laissez-faire) held by or attributed to a school of English economists

man·ches·ter·ist \-tərəst\ *or* **man·ches·ter·ite** \-təˌrīt\ *n* -s *usu cap* [*Manchester* (*school*) + *-ist* or *-ite*] **:** an adherent of Manchesterism

manchester terrier *n, usu cap M* **1 :** a breed of small lightly built short-haired black and tan terriers developed in England by interbreeding local rat-catching dogs with whippets **2 :** a dog of the Manchester terrier breed

man·ches·tri·an \(ˈ)manˈchestrēən\ *also* **man·ches·te·rian** \ˌmanchəˈstirēən\ *adj, usu cap* [*Manchester*, England + E *-ian*] **:** ¹MANCHESTER

man·chet \ˈmanchət\ *n* -s [ME] **1** *archaic* **:** wheaten bread of highest quality **2** *now chiefly dial* **:** a roll of manchet esp. when of a spindle shape with thick middle and pointed ends **:** a piece of white bread

man–child \ˈ＝ˌ＝\ *n, pl* **men–children** [ME] **:** a male child **:** SON

man·chi·neel \ˌmanchəˈnē(ə)l\ *n* -s [F *mancenille*, fr. Sp *manzanilla*, lit., small apple — more at MANZANILLA] **:** a poisonous tropical American tree (*Hippomane mancinella*) of the family Euphorbiaceae having smooth pale-brown bark, close-grained figured yellowish brown wood that is sometimes used for cabinetwork, small greenish flowers in a stiff spike, a blistering milky juice, and apple-shaped fruit

¹**man·chu** \(ˈ)manˈchü, maan-\ *n, pl* **manchu** *or* **manchus** **1** *usu cap* **a :** a member of the native Mongolian race of Manchuria that is related to the Tungus, was orig. nomad but conquered China and established a Manchu dynasty on the Chinese throne in 1644, and has largely assimilated Chinese culture **b :** the Tungusic language of the Manchu people **c :** the Tungusic subfamily of the Altaic languages **2** *often cap* **:** SHERRY 2

²**manchu** \"\ *adj, usu cap* **1 :** of, relating to, or being Manchuria, its inhabitants, or their language **2** *slang, of a military law or regulation* **:** designed to require active service with troops and to prevent prolonged assignment to esp. desirable positions or locations

manchu cherry *n, usu cap M* **:** NANKING CHERRY

man·chu·ria \(ˈ)manˈchùrēə, maan-\ *adj, usu cap* [fr. *Manchuria*, territory of China] **:** of or from Manchuria **:** of the kind or style prevalent in Manchuria

¹**man·chu·ri·an** \-ēən\ *adj, usu cap* [*Manchuria* + E *-an*] **1 :** of, relating to, or native to Manchuria **:** MANCHU **2 :** of, relating to, or being the subdivision of the Palaearctic region that includes Manchuria, northern and eastern China, Korea, and Japan

²**manchurian** \"\ *n* -s *cap* **:** a native or inhabitant of Manchuria **:** MANCHU

manchurian crab *n, usu cap M* **:** a Siberian crab (*Malus baccata mandshurica*) that produces fragrant white flowers very early in the season followed by small red crab apples

manchurian dog *also* **manchurian dogskin** *n, usu cap M* **:** the skin of Chinese dogs dressed and processed for use as fur

manchurian tiger *n, usu cap M* **:** a long-haired tiger of northeastern Asia that is often considered to constitute a distinct subspecies (*Felis tigris longipilis*) of the Asiatic tiger

manchurian wolf *n, usu cap M* **1 :** a wolf of northern China that is regarded as a variety of the common Old World wolf (*Canis lupus*) **2 :** MANCHURIAN DOG

man·ci·nism \ˈman(t)səˌnizəm\ *n* -s [It *mancinismo*, fr. *mancino* left-handed (fr. *manco* lacking, left-handed) + *-ismo* -ism — more at MANCANDO] **:** the condition of being lefthanded

man·ci·pa·ble \ˈman(t)səpəbəl\ *adj* [*mancipate* + *-able*] **:** subject to or capable of mancipation

man·ci·pant \-pənt\ *n* -s [L *mancipant-*, *mancipans*, pres. part. of *mancipare*] *Roman law* **:** one who transfers property by mancipation — opposed to *mancipee*

man·ci·pate \-səˌpāt\ *vt* -ED/-ING/-S [L *mancipatus*, past part. of *mancipare*, fr. *mancip-*, *manceps* purchaser, fr. *manus* hand + *-cip-*, *-ceps* (fr. *capere* to take) — more at MANUAL, HEAVE] **1** *obs* **:** to place in subjection or bondage **:** BIND, RESTRICT **2** *Roman law* **:** to transfer by mancipation

man·ci·pa·tion \ˌ⸗⸗ˈpāshən\ *n* -s [L *mancipation-, mancipatio,* fr. *mancipatus* + *-ion-, -io* -ion] **1** *obs* **a :** the act of enslaving **b :** involuntary servitude : SLAVERY **2** *Roman law* **a :** an early form of ceremonial conveyance under the jus civile involving the balance scales, bronze money, a balance holder, and five citizens as witnesses in which persons and property (as Italic lands, slaves, beasts of burden, rural praedial servitudes, children under potestas, and various women) subject to the ceremony were transferred by one Roman citizen into the power and control of another — compare MANCIPIUM **b :** MANCIPATORY WILL

man·ci·pa·to·ry \ˈman(t)səpəˌtōrē\ *adj* **:** of, relating to, or involving mancipation

mancipatory will *n, Roman law* **:** an early form of will wherein a conveyance was made by the ceremony of mancipation by the owner of the family property to the buyer thereof who was charged with transferring the inheritance to an unknown heir or legatee named in a sealed document written by the testator

man·ci·pee \ˌman(t)səˈpē\ *n* -s [*mancipate* + *-ee*] *Roman law* **:** one who receives property by mancipation — opposed to *mancipant*

man·cip·i·um \manˈsipēəm\ *n, pl* **mancip·ia** \-ēə\ [L, fr. *mancip-, manceps* purchaser — more at MANCIPATE] **1** *Roman law* **a** (1) **:** the status of a freeman subject to the power and control of the head of a Roman family similar to that of a slave except that he could not be abused or killed without legal cause (2) **:** the power or control so exercised by such head of family over such freeman **b :** a form of quiritarian as opposed to bonitarian ownership of property common in early Roman law **c :** MANCIPATION **2 :** SLAVE

man·ci·ple \ˈman(t)səpəl\ *n* -s [ME, fr. OF *mancipe, manciple,* fr. L *mancipium*] **:** a steward or purveyor esp. for a college or monastery

man·co \ˈmaŋ(ˌ)kō\ *n* -s [by shortening] *Scot* **:** CALAMANCO

man·co·no \ˌmäŋkəˈnō\ *n* -s [Sp *mancono,* fr. Bisayan] **1 :** a Philippine timber tree (*Xanthostemon verdugonianus*) of the family Myrtaceae **2 :** the heavy hard wood of the mancono

¹man·cu·ni·an \(ˈ)manˈkyünēən, -nyən\ *adj, usu cap* [LL *Mancunium* Manchester + E *-an*] **1 :** of, relating to, or characteristic of Manchester, England **2 :** of, relating to, or characteristic of the people of Manchester

²mancunian \"\ *n* -s *cap* **:** a native or resident of Manchester, England

man·cus \ˈmaŋkəs\ *n* -ES [OE, fr. ML *mancusus,* fr. Ar *manqūsh* engraved] **:** an Anglo-Saxon unit of value equal to 30 silver pence; *also* **:** a piece of gold or silver worth 30 pence

-man·cy \ˌman(t)sē, ˌmaan-, -si\ *n comb form* -ES [ME *-mancie, -mauncie,* fr. OF *-mancie,* fr. L *-mantia,* fr. Gk *manteia,* fr. *manteuesthai* to divine, prophesy + *-ia* -y; akin to Gk *mainesthai* to rage, rave — more at MIND] **:** divination in a (specified) manner or by means of (something specified) ⟨chiro*mancy*⟩

¹mand *var of* MAUND

²mand \ˈmand\ *n* -s [Hindi *mārnwā, marnwā,* fr. Skt *maḍaka*] **:** RAGI

M and A *abbr* management and administration

¹man·dae·an \manˈdēən\ *n* -s *usu cap* [Mandaean *mandayyā* having knowledge + E *-an*] **1 :** a member of a Gnostic sect that regards John the Baptist as the Messiah and that is found in regions of the lower Tigris and Euphrates **2 :** a form of Aramaic found in documents written by Mandaeans

²man·dae·an \(ˈ)⸗¦⸗⸗\ *adj, usu cap* **1 :** of, relating to, or characteristic of the Mandaeans or Mandaeanism **2 :** of, relating to, or characteristic of the Mandaean language

man·dae·an·ism \manˈdēəˌnizəm\ *n* -s *usu cap* **:** the beliefs of the Mandaeans

man·da·ic \manˈdāik\ *n* -s *usu cap* [Mandaean *mandayyā* having knowledge + E *-ic*] **:** MANDAEAN 2

man·da·la \ˈməndələ\ *n* -s [Skt *maṇḍala* circle] **:** a graphic mystic symbol of the universe that is typically in the form of a circle enclosing a square and often bearing symmetrically arranged representations of deities and is used chiefly in Hinduism and Buddhism as an aid to meditation

¹man·da·lay \ˌmandəˈlā, -aan-\ *adj, usu cap* [fr. *Mandalay,* Burma] **:** of or from the city of Mandalay, Burma **:** of the kind or style prevalent in Mandalay

²mandalay \"\ *n* -s *often cap* **:** PILGRIM BROWN

man·da·ment \ˈmandəmənt\ *n* -s [L *mandare* to command + E *-ment* — more at MANDATE] **:** COMMAND, INJUNCTION

¹man·da·mus \manˈdāməs, maan'- *sometimes* -dām- *or* -dam- *or* -däm-\ *n* -ES [L, we enjoin, 1st pl. pres. indic. of *mandare* to enjoin — more at MANDATE] **1 a :** the mandate of the sovereign under early English law commanding a subject to perform some act or duty **b :** the prerogative writ issued under English law in the absence of any other legal remedy by the King's Bench Division of the High Court of Justice in the king's name to a public officer to enforce the performance by him of some public duty **2 :** the extraordinary writ issued under constitutions and regulated by statute when there is no other adequate remedy at law, in equity, or under statute by a court of superior jurisdiction to an inferior tribunal, to a corporation, or to any person commanding the performance of some clear public duty imposed by law **:** a statutory extension of such a remedy

²mandamus \"\ *vt* -ED/-ING/-ES **:** to serve or coerce with a mandamus

man·dan \ˈman,dan, -ˌdən\ *n, pl* **mandan** *or* **mandans** *usu cap* **1 a :** a Siouan people ranging between the Heart and Little Missouri rivers in No. Dakota **b :** a member of such people **2 :** the language of the Mandan people

man·dant \ˈmandənt\ *n* -s [L *mandant-, mandans,* pres. part. of *mandare* to command — more at MANDATE] **:** MANDATOR

man·da·pa \ˈməndəpə\ *or* **man·da·pam** \-pəm\ *n* -s [Skt *maṇḍapa*] **:** a general gathering area in an Indian temple that is comparable to the narthex of a western church

man·dar \mänˈdär\ *vt* -ED/-ING/-s [Sp, lit., to command, fr. L *mandare*] **:** to control (a bull) by aggressive action in bullfighting

¹man·da·rin \ˈmandərən, -aan-\ *n* -s [Pg *mandarim,* modif. (influenced by *mandar* to command, fr. L *mandare*) of Malay *mĕntĕri,* fr. Skt *mantrin* counselor, fr. *mantra* counsel; akin to Skt *manyate* he thinks — more at MANDATE, MIND] **1 a :** a public official under the Chinese Empire of any of nine superior grades that were filled by individuals from the ranks of lesser officeholders that passed examinations in Chinese literary classics **b** (1) **:** a pedantic official (2) **:** BUREAUCRAT **c :** a person of position and influence esp. in intellectual or literary circles; *often* **:** an elder and often traditionalist or reactionary member of such a circle **2** *cap* **a :** the primarily northern dialect of Chinese used by the court and the official classes under the Empire **b :** the chief dialect of China that is spoken in about four fifths of the country and has a southern variety centering about Nanking, a western variety centering about Chengtu, and a northern now standard variety centering about Peking **3 :** a small grotesque seated image in Chinese costume with the head so fixed as to continue nodding when set in motion **4** *also* **man·da·rine** \"\ **a** *or* **mandarin tree** *or* **mandarin orange** [F *mandarine,* fr. Sp *mandarina,* prob. fr. *mandarin* mandarin, fr. Pg *mandarim;* prob. fr. the color of a mandarin's robes] (1) **:** a small spiny Chinese citrus tree (*Citrus reticulata*) having slender twigs and lanceolate leaves, small white flowers, and yellow to reddish orange loose-skinned fruits (2) **:** any of several cultivated citrus trees that are selections or hybrids of the Chinese mandarin — see SATSUMA, TANGERINE **b** *or* **mandarin orange** (1) **:** the fruit of a mandarin tree — called also *kid-glove orange, tangerine* (2) **:** a yellow or pale orange mandarin — distinguished from *tangerine* **c** *usu* **mandarine :** a sweet liqueur flavored with the dried peel of mandarins **5 :** MANDARIN PORCELAIN **6 a :** MANDARIN RED **b :** MANDARIN ORANGE 2

²mandarin \"\ *adj* **1 :** of, relating to, or typical of a mandarin ⟨~ graces⟩ **2 :** resembling or styled after that of a mandarin ⟨~ styles⟩ **3** *of literary style or work* **:** marked by polished ornate complexity in the use of language

man·da·rin·ate \-əˌnāt\ *n* -s [prob. fr. F *mandarinat,* fr. *mandarin* (fr. Pg *mandarim*) + *-at* -ate] **1 :** the body of mandarins **:** mandarins as a group or class **2 :** the office or dignity of a mandarin **3 :** rule by mandarins

mandarin collar *n* **:** a narrow stand-up collar usu. open in front

mandarin duck *n* **:** a brightly marked crested Asiatic duck (*Aix galericulata*) that is closely related to the New World wood duck and is often domesticated

man·da·rin·ism \-ˌnizəm\ *n* -s [prob. fr. F *mandarinisme,* fr. *mandarin* + *-isme* -ism] **1 :** government by mandarins **2 :** the character or spirit of the mandarins

mandarin oil *n* **:** a fragrant yellow essential oil expressed from the peel of mandarin oranges and used chiefly in flavoring and perfumery

mandarin orange *n* **1 :** MANDARIN 4a, 4b **2 :** a strong orange that is darker than pumpkin, redder and duller than cadmium orange, and redder and deeper than cadmium yellow

mandarin porcelain *n* **:** an oriental porcelain ware usu. with showy decorations often including figures in the costume of the mandarin

mandarin red *n* **:** a strong reddish orange that is yellower and paler than poppy or paprika and slightly redder, lighter, and stronger than fire red

man·da·tary \ˈmandəˌterē\ *n* -ES [LL *mandatarius,* fr. L *mandatus* + *-arius* -ary] **1 :** a person to whom a legal mandate is given — distinguished from *mandator* **2 :** a member nation of the League of Nations to which a mandate over territory is given

¹man·date \ˈmanˌdāt, -aan- *sometimes* -ndət, *usu* -d.+V\ *n* -s [MF & L; MF *mandat,* fr. L *mandatum,* fr. neut. of *mandatus,* past part. of *mandare* to commit to one's charge, order, enjoin, command, prob. irreg. fr. *manus* hand + *-dere* to put — more at MANUAL, DO] **1** [ML *mandatum,* fr. L, command, mandate] **:** MAUNDY **2 a** (1) **:** a formal order from a superior court or official to an inferior one; *esp* **:** the order or command that embodies the decision of a U. S. appellate court when final judgment is not entered and is sent to the court below (2) **:** MANDAMUS **b** *archaic* **:** a papal ordinance in an individual case (as preferment to a benefice) **c** (1) **:** a contract under Roman law by which one agrees to perform gratuitously some act for another who agrees to indemnify him (2) **:** a contract of agency under civil law in which one undertakes to perform some act for another whether gratuitously or for a reward; *esp* **:** a gratuitous bailment in which the bailee undertakes to do something in respect to the thing bailed — distinguished from *deposit* **3 a :** an authoritative command, order, or injunction **:** a clear instruction, authorization, or direction ⟨acting under the ~ of the statute in question⟩ **b :** the authorization to act or approval given by a constituency to its elected representative ⟨accepted the ~ of the people⟩ **4 a :** an order or commission granted by the League of Nations as mandator to a member nation as its mandatary for the establishment of a responsible government over former German colonies or other conquered territory **b :** a mandated colony or territory

²mandate \"\, *in sense 1* ⸗ˈ⸗\ *vt* -ED/-ING/-s **1** *Scot* **:** to commit (as a sermon) to memory **2 :** to administer or assign (as a colony) under a mandate

man·da·tee \ˌmanˌdāˈtē, -ndə¦-\ *n* -s **:** one to whom a mandate is assigned

man·da·tor \manˈdād·ə(r)\ *n* -s [LL, fr. L *mandatus* + *-or*] **:** one that gives a mandate (as under Roman or civil law) **:** MANDANT — compare MANDATORY

man·da·to·ri·ly \ˈmandəˌtōrəlē, -aan-, -tȯr-, -li\ *adv* **:** so as to be mandatory **:** OBLIGATORILY

¹man·da·to·ry \-rē, -ri\ *adj* [LL *mandatorius,* fr. L *mandatus* + *-orius* -ory] **:** containing, constituting, or relating to a mandate; *esp* **:** OBLIGATORY — opposed to *directory*

²mandatory \"\ *n* -ES **:** MANDATARY; *esp* **:** one holding a mandate from the League of Nations

mandatory injunction *n* **:** an injunction entered at the conclusion of an equity case compelling the defendant to do some positive act or to cease to do something he has done, thereby compelling him in effect to undo it — compare PROHIBITORY INJUNCTION

man·da·tum \manˈdād·əm\ *n, pl* **manda·ta** \-d·ə\ [L — more at MANDATE] **:** MANDATE

man-day \ˈ⸗¦⸗\ *n, pl* **man-days 1 :** the labor of one man in one normal working day **2 :** a unit consisting of a hypothetical average man-day

man·da·ya \mänˈdīyə\ *n, pl* **mandaya** *or* **mandayas** *usu cap* **1 a :** a people inhabiting southern Mindanao, Philippines **b :** a member of such people **2 :** the Austronesian language of the Mandaya people

M and B *abbr* matched and beaded

M and D *abbr* medicine and duty

man·de \ˈmän(ˌ)dā\ *n, pl* **mande** *also* **mandes** *usu cap* **1 :** MANDINGO 1, 2 **2 :** a branch of the Niger-Congo language family including Malinke, Bambara, Dyula, Kono, Vai, Mende, Kpelle, Loma, Mano, and Susu spoken in French West Africa, Sierra Leone, and Liberia, with their center in the upper Niger valley — called also *Mandingo*

man·de·ism \manˈdēˌizəm\ *n* -s *usu cap* [F *Mandéisme,* fr. *Mandéen* Mandaean (fr. Mandaean *mandayyā* having knowledge) + *-isme* -ism] **:** MANDAEANISM

mandel- *or* **mandelo-** *comb form* [ISV, fr. *mandelic* (*acid*)] **:** mandelic acid ⟨*mandel*amide⟩ ⟨*mandelo*nitrile⟩

man·del·ate \ˈmandəˌlāt\ *n* -s [*mandel-* + *-ate*] **:** a salt or ester of mandelic acid

man·del·ic acid \manˈdelik-, -dēlik-\ *n* [part trans. of G *mandelsäure,* fr. *mandel* almond (fr. ML *mandala,* alter. of LL *amandula*) + *säure* acid — more at ALMOND] **:** a crystalline hydroxy acid $C_6H_5CH(OH)COOH$ that is known in three optically different isomeric forms, that is obtainable in the levorotatory D-form from amygdalin by hydrolysis but is usu. made in the racemic form by reaction of benzaldehyde with hydrocyanic acid and then hydrochloric acid, and that is used chiefly in the form of its salts as a bacteriostatic agent for genitourinary tract infections; phenyl-glycolic acid

man·di·ble \ˈmandəbəl, -aan-\ *n* -s [MF, fr. LL *mandibula,* fr. L *mandere* to chew — more at MOUTH] **1 a :** JAW 1a; *esp* **:** a lower jaw consisting of a single bone or completely fused bones **b :** the lower jaw with its investing soft parts — see FISH illustration **c :** either the upper or lower segment of the bill of a bird **2 :** any of various invertebrate mouthparts serving to hold or bite into food materials: as **a :** either member of the anterior part of mouth appendages of an arthropod often forming strong biting jaws **b :** one of the paired corneous or calcified cutting plates on the proboscis of certain polychaete worms

mandibul- *or* **mandibuli-** *or* **mandibulo-** *comb form* [LL *mandibula*] **:** mandible **:** mandibular and ⟨*mandibulo*pharyngeal⟩ ⟨*mandibuli*form⟩

man·dib·u·la \manˈdibyələ, maan-\ *n, pl* **mandibu·lae** \-yəˌlē\ [LL] **:** MANDIBLE

man·dib·u·lar \-yələ(r)\ *adj* [LL *mandibula* + E *-ar*] **:** of, relating to, or located near a mandible

mandibular angle *n* **:** an angle formed by the junction at the gonion of the posterior border of the ramus and the inferior border of the body of the mandible

mandibular arch *n* **:** the first visceral arch of the vertebrate embryo

mandibular artery *n* **:** INFERIOR ALVEOLAR ARTERY

mandibular canal *n* **:** a bony canal within the mandible that gives passage to blood vessels and nerves serving the area

mandibular nerve *n* **:** a division of the trigeminal nerve that supplies sensory fibers to the mandible and its teeth and motor fibers to the muscles of mastication

man·dib·u·lary \-yəˌlerē\ *adj* [LL *mandibula* + E *-ary*] **1 :** MANDIBULAR **2 :** being or functioning like a mandible

man·dib·u·la·ta \manˌdibyəˈlād·ə, -lād·ə\ *n pl, cap* [NL *Mandibulata,* fr. *mandibul-* + *-ata*] *in some classifications* **:** a subphylum or superclass of Arthropoda comprising arthropods with mandibles on the second postoral somite and usu. preoral true antennae and including the crustaceans, myriopods, insects, and a few related forms — compare CHELICERATA, TRILOBITA

¹man·dib·u·late \manˈdibyələt, -yəˌlāt, *usu* -d.+V\ *adj* [*mandibul-* + *-ate*] **1 a :** having mandibles ⟨~ insects⟩ **b** *of a vertebrate* **:** having a lower jaw **2** [NL *Mandibulata*] **:** of or relating to the Mandibulata

²man·dib·u·late \-yəˌlāt\ *n* -s **:** a mandibulate animal; *esp* **:** one of the Mandibulata

man·dib·u·lat·ed \-ˌlād·əd\ *adj* [*mandibul-* + *-ate* + *-ed*] *of an arthropod* **:** MANDIBULATE

man·dib·u·la·tion \manˌdibyəˈlāshən\ *n* -s [*mandibul-* + *-ation*] **:** handling of nesting material by a bird with its bill

man·dib·u·li·form \manˈdibyələˌfȯrm\ *adj* [ISV *mandibul-* + *-form*] **:** having the form or function of a mandible — used esp. of the maxillae of an insect when hard and adapted for biting

man·dil·ion \manˈdilyən\ *n* -s [MF *mandillon,* dim. of *mandil* cloak, fr. OSp, towel, rag, horseblanket, apron, prob. fr. LGk *mandēlion, mandilion, mantēlion, mantilion* towel, napkin, fr. L *mantelium,* alter. of *mantelum,* prob. fr. *manus* hand + *-telum* (fr. *tergēre* to rub off, wipe off) — more at MANUAL, TERSE] **:** a loose outer garment of the 16th and 17th centuries: as **a :** a soldier's cloak usu. with hanging sleeves **b :** a servant's sleeveless garment similar to a tabard

man·din·go \manˈdiŋ(ˌ)gō\ *n, pl* **mandingo** *or* **mandingoes** *or* **mandingos** *usu cap* **1 a :** a people widely spread over West Africa centering in the upper Niger valley and including the Bambara, Dyula, and Malinke **b :** a member of such people **2 :** the language of the Mandingo people **3 :** MANDE 2

man·din·ka \manˈdiŋkə\ *n, pl* **mandinka** *or* **mandinkas** *usu cap* **:** MALINKE

mandioc *or* **mandioca** *var of* MANIOC

man·dir \ˈmənˌdir\ *n* -s [Hindi, fr. Skt *mandira*] **:** a Hindu temple

mand·len \ˈmän(d)lən\ *n pl* [Yiddish, pl. of *mandel,* lit., almond, fr. MHG — more at MANDELIC ACID] **:** small pieces of baked or fried dough used in soups

man·doer *also* **man·dor** *or* **man·dur** \(ˈ)mänˈdü(ə)r, -dȯ(ə)r\ *n* -s [D & Indonesian; D *mandoer,* fr. Indonesian *mandur,* fr. Pg *mandador,* lit., one that commands, fr. L *mandator* — more at MANDATOR] **:** a native foreman or overseer (as of a sugar plantation or a gang of miners) esp. in Malaysia, Java, and the Dutch East Indies

man·do·la \manˈdōlə\ *also* **man·do·ra** \-ōrə\ *or* **man·dore** \manˈdō(ə)r, -dȯ(-, ˈ⸗,⸗\ *n* -s [*mandola, mandora* fr. It, fr. F *mandore,* modif. of LL *pandura,* a three-stringed lute; *mandore* fr. F — more at BANDORE] **:** a 16th and 17th century lute with a pear-shaped body that is the ancestor of the smaller mandolin of the present day

¹man·do·lin *also* **man·do·line** \ˌmandəˈlin, -aan-, ˈ⸗dᵊlən\ *n* -s [It *mandolino,* dim. of *mandola*] **:** a musical instrument of the lute family that has a pear-shaped body and fretted neck and from four to six pairs of strings and is played with a plectrum — see MANDOLA

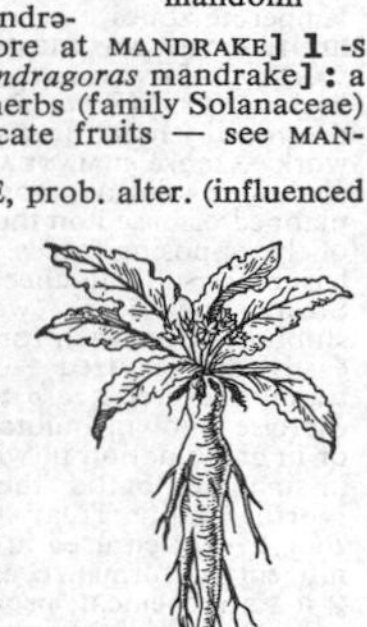
mandolin

²mandolin \"\ *adj* **:** resembling a mandolin in shape — used of rabbits with narrow forequarters and broad and deep hindquarters

man·do·lin·ist \-nəst\ *n* -s **:** a mandolin player

man·dom \ˈmandəm\ *n* -s [¹*man* + *-dom*] **:** MANKIND

man·dor·la \ˈmänˌdȯrˌlä\ *n* -s [It, lit., almond, fr. LL *amandula* — more at ALMOND] **:** a panel or contour in the shape of an almond; *usu* **:** an almond-shaped aureole **:** VESICA PISCIS ⟨Christ seated in a ~⟩

man·drag·on \ˈmanˌdragən\ *n* [alter. (influenced by *dragon*) of obs. *mandrag,* fr. ME *mandragge* — more at MANDRAKE] *archaic* **:** MANDRAKE

man·drag·o·ra \manˈdragərə, ˌmandrə-ˈgōrə, -aan-, -ˈgȯrə\ *n* [ME — more at MANDRAKE] **1 :** MANDRAKE 1 **2** *cap* [NL, fr. L *mandragoras* mandrake] **:** a small genus of acaulescent Eurasian herbs (family Solanaceae) with campanulate flowers and baccate fruits — see MANDRAKE 1a

man·drake \ˈmanˌdrāk, -aan-\ *n* [ME, prob. alter. (influenced by ¹*drake*) of *mandragge, mandragora,* fr. OE *mandragora,* fr. L *mandragoras,* fr. Gk] **1 a :** an herb (*Mandragora officinarum*) of southern Europe and northern Africa that has ovate leaves, whitish or purple flowers followed by globose yellow fruits which were formerly supposed to have aphrodisiac properties, and a large forked root which has been credited with human attributes and made the subject of many superstitions **b** (1) **:** the root of this plant formerly used esp. to promote conception, as a cathartic, or as a narcotic and soporific (2) **:** a solution or draft of mandrake root (as in wine) formerly used as a narcotic (3) **:** a fake or substitute for this root (as one carved from the root of a bryony) **2 :** any of several other plants; *esp* **:** MAYAPPLE 1 **b :** PODOPHYLLUM 2

Old World mandrake

¹man·drel *also* **man·dril** \ˈmandrəl\ *n* -s [prob. modif. of F *mandrin*] **1** *Brit* **:** a miner's pick **2 a :** a usu. tapered or cylindrical axle, spindle, or arbor that is inserted into a hole in a piece of work so as to support the work during machining **b :** a metal bar that serves as a core around which metal or other material may be cast, molded, forged, bent, or otherwise shaped **3 :** any of a train of jointed units intended to be pulled through an underground duct as each joint is made to ensure perfect alignment or through a steel pipe in process of welding to ensure a smooth interior **4 :** the shaft and bearings on which a tool (as a dental grinding disk or circular saw) is mounted **5 :** a temporary interior support for a thin-walled tube (as a tubular steel pile to be filled later with concrete) being driven into something

²mandrel \"\ *vt* -ED/-ING/-s **:** to turn with a mandrel

mandrel press *n* **:** a press that drives mandrels into holes prepared to receive them

man·drill \ˈmandrəl\ *n* -s [prob. fr. ¹*man* + *drill* (baboon)] **:** a large fierce gregarious baboon (*Mandrillus mormon*) of western Africa with large red ischial callosities and in the male blue ridges on each side of the red-bridged nose

man·drin \ˈmandrən\ *n* -s [F] **:** a stylet for a catheter

man·dru·ka *also* **man·drou·ka** \manˈdrükə\ *n* -s [fr. *Mandruka* (*Mandrouka*), locality near Bengasi, Libya] **:** a deep-water honeycomb sponge of close fiber and small root

mands *pl of* MAND

M and S *abbr* maintenance and supply

mandt's guillemot \ˈmänts-\ *n, usu cap M* [after Martin Wilhelm von *Mandt* †1858 Ger. physician and naturalist] **:** a guillemot that constitutes the northern subspecies (*Cepphus grylle mandtii*) of the black guillemot of the north Atlantic

man·dua \ˈmanjəwə\ *n* -s [Hindi *mārnwā, marnwā* — more at MAND] **:** RAGI

man·du·ca·ble \ˈmanjəkəbəl\ *adj* [LL *manducabilis,* fr. *manducare* + *-abilis* -able] *archaic* **:** capable of being chewed **:** EATABLE

man·du·cate \ˈmanjəˌkāt\ *vt* -ED/-ING/-s [L *manducatus,* past part. of *manducare* — more at MANGER] *archaic* **:** MASTICATE, CHEW, EAT

man·du·ca·tion \ˌ⸗⸗ˈkāshən\ *n* -s [LL *manducation-, manducatio,* fr. L *manducatus* + *-ion-, -io* -ion] **1 a** *obs* **:** the taking of food **:** EATING **b :** COMMUNION 2c **2 :** the act of chewing — now used chiefly of invertebrate animals

man·du·ca·to·ry \ˈmanjəkəˌtōrē, -tȯr-\ *adj* **:** relating to, employed in, or adapted for chewing ⟨the ~ apparatus of crustaceans⟩

mandur *var of* MANDOER

man·dy·as \mänˈthēəs, -ˈdē-\ *n* -ES [LL *mandya,* fr. Gk *mandya, mandyas, mandyē, mandyēs,* of non-IE origin] **:** an outer garment resembling a cloak or cope worn in the services of Eastern Orthodox churches

¹mane \ˈmān\ *n* -s [ME, fr. OE *manu;* akin to OE *mene* necklace, OHG *mana* mane, *menni* necklace, ON *mön* mane, *men* necklace, L *monile* necklace, OIr *muin-* neck, Skt *manyā,* and perh. to L *mont-, mons* mountain — more at MOUNT] **1 :** the long and heavy hair growing around the neck of some mammals ⟨the lion's ~⟩ — see HORSE illustration **2 :** long heavy hair on a person's head ⟨his large features and rich ~ of hair —Osbert Lancaster⟩ **3 :** the full feathering on the back of the head and neck of some fancy pigeons

2**mane** \"\ *chiefly Scot var of* MOAN

3**ma·ne** \'mä(,)nā\ *adv* [L, fr. *manis, manus* good — more at MATURE] : in the morning — used esp. in pharmacy

man–eater \'ˌ=ˌ==\ *n* : one that has or is thought to have an appetite for human flesh: as **a** : CANNIBAL 1 **b** *or* **man–eater shark** : a large voracious shark; *esp* : a shark (*Carcharodon carcharias*) that reaches a length of over 30 feet, is found in all warm seas, and has been known to attack and devour human beings **c** : NEWT, SALAMANDER; *esp* : HELLBENDER **d** : a large feline (as a lion or tiger) that has acquired the habit of feeding on human flesh **e** : a man-eating crocodile: as (1) : SALT-WATER CROCODILE (2) : NILE CROCODILE

man–eating \'=ˌ==\ *adj* : eating or having an appetite for human flesh

man–eating shark *n* : MAN-EATER b

ma·ne·bach twin \'mänəˌbäk-\ *n, usu cap M* [fr. *Manebach*, Thuringia, Germany] : a monoclinic twin crystal having the basal pinacoid as the twinning plane and composition face

maned \'mānd\ *adj* [1*mane* + *-ed*] **1** : having a mane **2** : CRINED

maned rat *n* : CRESTED HAMSTER

maned sheep *n* : AOUDAD

maned wolf *or* **maned dog** *n* : a yellowish red So. American wild dog (*Chrysocyon brachyurus*, syn. *jubatus*) with black nape, lower jaw, and feet

man·een \'maˌnēn\ *n* -S [1*man* + *-een* (fr. IrGael *-īn*, dim. suffix)] *Irish* : a little man

ma·nege *also* **ma·nège** \ma'nezh, mə'n-\ *n* -S [F *manège*, fr. It *maneggio* — more at MANAGE] **1** : a school for teaching horsemanship and for training horses : a riding academy **2** : the art of horsemanship or of training horses **3** : the movements or paces of a trained horse

maneh *n* -S [Heb *māneh*] : 1MINA

mane·less \'mānləs\ *adj* : having no mane

ma·nent \'mäˌnent\ [L, they remain, 3d pl. pres. indic. of *manēre* to remain — more at MANSION] : remain on stage — used as a stage direction to specify that named characters do not leave the stage; compare EXEUNT

ma·ne·ri·al \mə'nirēəl\ *adj* [ML *manerium* manor (fr. OF *manoir*) + E *-al* — more at MANOR] *archaic* : MANORIAL

ma·nes \'mäˌnās, 'māˌnēz\ *n pl* [L; perh. akin to L *manus* good — more at MATURE] **1** *often cap* : the spirits of the dead and gods of the lower world in ancient Roman belief — compare LEMURES **2 a** : ancestral spirits worshiped as gods **b** *sing in constr* : the spirit of a dead person regarded as an object to be venerated or appeased

manesheet \'ˌ=ˌ=\ *n* [1*mane* + *sheet*] : a covering for the upper part of a horse's head

man·ess \'manəs\ *n* -ES [1*man* + *-ess*] *archaic* : WOMAN

ma·net \'mäˌnet\ [L, he remains, 3d sing. pres. indic. of *manēre* to remain — more at MANSION] : remains on stage — used as a stage direction to specify that a named character does not leave the stage; compare 1EXIT

ma·net·ti \mə'ned·ē\ *n* -S *usu cap* [after Saverio *Manetti* †1784 Ital. botanist] : a vigorous China rose (*Rosa chinensis manetti*) used chiefly as a grafting stock

ma·net·tia \-ēə\ *n, cap* [NL, after Saverio *Manetti*] : a genus of tropical American vines (family Rubiaceae) with showy tubular flowers that are white, yellow, or red

manettia vine *n* : a Brazilian vine (*Manettia bicolor*) with red and yellow flowers that is used as an ornamental in warmer temperate zones

1**ma·neu·ver** *also* **ma·noeu·vre** *or* **ma·noeu·ver** \mə'n(y)üvə(r)\ *n* -S [F *manœuvre*, fr. OF *manuevre*, *maneuvre* work done by hand, fr. ML *manuopera, manopera*, fr. L *manu operare* to do work by hand, fr. *manu* (abl. of *manus* hand) + *operare* to work — more at MANUAL, OPERATE] **1 a** : a military, naval, or air force evolution, movement, or change of position; *esp* : one planned or based on the position of an enemy, the relationship of the opposing forces, and factors of terrain or weather ⟨the leisurely ~*s* and checkmate of royal mercenary armies —Stringfellow Barr⟩ ⟨well emplaced, they sometimes proved stubborn, but when forced into an open war of ~, they were easily disorganized —Irwin Shaw⟩ **b** : an armed forces training exercise; *esp* : an extended and large-scale training exercise involving military, naval, and air force units separately or in combination in which theoretically hostile forces engage in simulated battle ⟨the eighty U.S. ships participating in the North Atlantic Treaty Organization's first naval ~ —*Current Biog.*⟩ — often used in pl. ⟨the Third Army turned in a magnificent performance at the Louisiana ~*s* —Green Peyton⟩ **2 a** : a movement, procedure, or method of working usu. involving skillful operation and expert physical management ⟨the simplest ~ to actuate the normal eustachian tube is to swallow —H.G.Armstrong⟩ **b** : a manipulation to accomplish a change of position; *specif* : rotational or other movement applied to a fetus within the uterus to alter its position and facilitate delivery **3 a** : an evasive movement : a change of position or shift of tactics ⟨because his area of ~ seems so small . . . his fight lacks the heroic cast —W.W.Whyte⟩ ⟨permits no room for concession or ~ —Harry Schwartz⟩ **b** : an intended and controlled variation from a straight and level flight path in the operation of an aircraft ⟨certain acrobatic ~*s* such as outside spins, inverted spins, outside loops, pushovers, and inverted flight —H.G.Armstrong⟩ **4 a** : a management of affairs : an action taken as one of a series of actions intended to gain a tactical end ⟨this ~ almost cost him the nomination —H.L.Mencken⟩ ⟨his stubborn and tactless ~*s* —A.L.Funk⟩ **b** : an adroit and clever management of affairs often using trickery and deception ⟨unable to meet the ~*s* of the speculative railroad wrecker —W.C.Ford⟩ **syn** see TRICK

2**maneuver** *also* **manoeuvre** *or* **manoeuver** \"\ *vb* **maneuvered; maneuvered; maneuvering** \-v(ə)riŋ\ **maneuvers** [F *manœuvrer*, fr. OF *manovrer, manuvrer* to do work by hand, fr. L *manu operare*] *vi* **1 a** : to perform a movement in military, naval, or air force tactics : make changes in position in order to secure an advantage in attack or defense ⟨the regiment ~*ed* for several days before it was ready to attack⟩ **b** : to make a series of changes in direction and position for a specific purpose (as in changing course, in switching tracks, or in docking) ⟨a small freight train, having left some cars on the main line, is ~*ing* upon the siding —G.R.Stewart⟩ ⟨the ferry had to ~ in order to dock⟩ **2 a** : to use stratagems : SCHEME ⟨~*ed* successfully to get him to ask her to the dance⟩ **b** : to change ground or shift tactics : jockey for position ⟨had more freedom to ~ than has his emancipated successor —R.M. Weaver⟩ ⟨political parties checkmated one another and ~*ed* for advantage —F.A.Ogg & Harold Zink⟩ ~ *vt* **1 a** : to change the tactical disposition of : cause to execute tactical movements ⟨large bodies of troops were ~*ed* —*Survey Graphic*⟩ **b** : to perform tactical or acrobatic evolutions with (an airplane) **2** : to manage or manipulate into or out of a position or condition ⟨~*ed* him into a car —*Time*⟩ ⟨~*ed* myself into being asked to play —Lloyd Alexander⟩ ⟨~*ed* the cork out with his thumb —Kay Boyle⟩ **3 a** : to guide or direct with adroitness and design ⟨~*ed* her guests until the talk at the table became general —Jean Stafford⟩ **b** : to bring about or secure as a result of skillful management ⟨~*ed* out of the Highway Commission the funds to build the state medical school —*Today*⟩ — **ma·neu·ver·er** \-v(ə)rə(r)\ *n* -S

ma·neu·ver·abil·i·ty \məˌn(y)üv(ə)rə'biləd·ē, -ətē, -i\ *n* **1 a** : the quality or state of being maneuverable ⟨destroy our ~ and our bargaining power —A.E.Stevenson †1965⟩ ⟨~ is an essential quality in a racing car⟩ **b** : the quality of an airplane that determines the rate at which attitude and direction of flight can be changed without loss of control **2** : the quality or state of being able to be used for maneuvering ⟨the harbor had considerable more ~ now —Russell Thacker⟩

ma·neu·ver·able \mə'n(y)üv(ə)rəbəl\ *adj* **1** : capable of maneuvering ⟨a ~ foreign policy⟩ **2** : capable of being maneuvered ⟨a highly ~ ship⟩

maneuvering board *n* : a printed compass rose with polar coordinates that is used together with parallel rulers and dividers to solve problems of relative movement of ships or airplanes such as arise in changing station in formation or mooring — called also *mooring board*

manf *abbr* manufacturer

manfish \'ˌ=ˌ\ *n, pl* **menfish** : MERMAN

man–for–man defense *n* : MAN-TO-MAN DEFENSE

man·fre·da \man'frēdə\ *n* [NL, prob. fr. the name *Manfred*] **1** *cap* : a genus of perennial American herbs that are closely related to and often included among those of the genus *Agave* from which they are distinguished chiefly by the bulbous stem base and annually decaying leaves — see AMOLE **2** -S : any plant of the genus *Manfreda*

man friday *n, pl* **men friday** *or* **men fridays** *often cap M & usu cap F* [after *Friday*, native servant of Robinson Crusoe, hero of the novel *Robinson Crusoe* (1719), by Daniel Defoe †1731 Eng. journalist and novelist] : a valued aide or employee who gives efficient and devoted service and is usu. entrusted with a wide range of tasks : RIGHT-HAND MAN ⟨the *man Friday* of the party leader is seldom a capable successor —K.R.Popper⟩

man·ful \'manfəl\ *adj* [ME, fr. 1*man* + *-ful*] **1** : of, relating to, or befitting a man : MANLY ⟨let your recreations be ~, not sinful —George Washington⟩ **2** : having or showing courage and resolution : BRAVE, NOBLE ⟨his life has been one ~ struggle against poverty —Anthony Trollope⟩ **syn** see MALE

man·ful·ly \-fəlē, -li\ *adv* [ME, fr. *manful* + *-ly*] : in a manful manner : RESOLUTELY ⟨shoulder ~ the burden of teaching every freshman the elements of self-expression —H.N. Francis⟩

man·ful·ness *n* -ES [ME, fr. *manful* + *-ness*] : the quality or state of being manful

man fungus *n* : EARTHSTAR

mang \'maŋ\ *var of* AMANG

1**man·ga** \'mäŋgə, 'maŋ-\ *n* -S [MexSp, fr. Sp, sleeve, fr. L *manica* — more at MANCHE] *Southwest* : PONCHO

2**man·ga** \'maŋgə\ *n* -S [Pg — more at MANGO] : MANGO

man·ga·bei·ra \ˌmaŋgə'bārə\ *n* -S [Pg, fr. *mangaba* fruit of the mangabeira, fr. Tupi *mangaba, mangahiba*] : a Brazilian vine (*Hancornia speciosa*) of the family Apocynaceae having a milky juice that yields a rubber

mangabeira rubber *n* : rubber obtained from the mangabeira

man·ga·bey \'maŋgəˌbā\ *also* **man·ga·by** \-bē\ *n* -S [fr. *Mangaby*, Madagascar] : a long-tailed arboreal African monkey of the genus *Cercocebus*

1**man·ga·ian** \mäŋ'(g)īyən, -'(g)īən\ *adj, usu cap* [*Mangaia* Island, Cook islands + E *-an*] **1** : of, relating to, or characteristic of the island of Mangaia **2** : of, relating to, or characteristic of the people of Mangaia

2**mangaian** \"\ *n* -S *cap* : a native or inhabitant of Mangaia Island

mangan– *or* **mangano–** *also* **mangani–** *comb form* [G *mangan*, fr. F *manganèse* — more at MANGANESE] : manganese : manganese and ⟨*mangan*ate⟩ ⟨*mangano*columbite⟩ ⟨*mangani*ferous⟩

man·ga·na \män'gänə\ *n* -S [Sp, back-formation fr. *manganilla* trick, ruse, fr. (assumed) VL *manganella*, fr. pl. of (assumed) VL *manganellum*, dim. of LL *manganum* contrivance, device, philter, fr. Gk *manganon* mangonel, philter — more at MANGONEL] *chiefly Southwest* : a throw with a lariat designed to catch a horse by the forefeet : FOREFOOTING

man·gan–alluaudite \ˌmaŋgən+\ *n* [*manganese* + *alluaudite*] : a mineral $(Na,Mn)PO_4$ that consists of phosphate of manganese and sodium and is isomorphous with alluaudite

man·gan·apatite \"+\ *n* [G *manganapatit*, fr. *mangan* manganese + *apatit* apatite] : a dark bluish green apatite containing manganese

man·ga·nate \'maŋgəˌnāt\ *n* -S [ISV *mangan-* + *-ate*] : any of several classes of salts containing manganese in the anion: as **a** : a salt of manganic acid obtained as a green mass usu. by fusion of manganese dioxide with an alkali — called also *manganate(VI)* **b** : MANGANITE

man·gan·berzeliite \ˌmaŋgən+\ *n* [G *manganberzeliit*, fr. *mangan* manganese + *berzeliit* berzeliite] : a mineral $Mn_2(Ca,Na)_3(AsO_4)_3$ that consists of arsenate of calcium, sodium, and manganese, and is isomorphous with berzeliite

man·gan·blende \'maŋgənˌblend\ *n* [G, fr. *mangan* manganese + *blende*] : ALABANDITE

man·gan·brucite \ˌmaŋgən+\ *n* [Sw *manganbrucit*, fr. *mangan* manganese + *brucit* brucite] : a manganiferous brucite

man·gan·ei·sen \'maŋgəˌnīzᵊn\ *n* -S [G, fr. *mangan* manganese + *eisen* iron, fr. OHG *īsan* — more at IRON] : an alloy of manganese and iron

man·ga·nese \'maŋgəˌnēz, -aiŋ-, -ēs\ *n* -S *often attrib* [F *manganèse*, fr. It *manganese*, fr. *manganese* magnesia, modif. of ML *magnesia* — more at MAGNESIA] **1 a** : a black oxide of the metallic element manganese; *esp* : PYROLUSITE **b** : any of various ores of the metallic element manganese ⟨gray ~⟩ ⟨red ~⟩ **2** : a grayish white polyvalent metallic element that is ordinarily hard and brittle, resembles iron but is not magnetic, occurs in nature alloyed in meteoric iron and combined in many minerals (as pyrolusite, psilomelane, manganite, hausmannite, rhodochrosite) and as a trace element in plants and animals, is obtained in a state of high purity by electrolysis or by electric-furnace reduction of ore with aluminum or silicon or in the form of alloys (as ferromanganese or spiegeleisen) by smelting, and is used chiefly in making steel — symbol *Mn*; see ELEMENT table

manganese black *n* : manganese dioxide esp. when used as a pigment

manganese brown *n* **1** : a natural or synthetic brown oxide or hydroxide of manganese used as a pigment or produced on the fiber in dyeing **2** *or* **manganese bister** : SHERRY 2

manganese chloride *n* : a chloride of manganese; *esp* : MANGANOUS CHLORIDE

manganese dioxide *n* : a dark brown or gray-black insoluble compound MnO_2 found in nature as pyrolusite, made synthetically (as by decomposition of manganous nitrate or by chemical or electrolytic precipitation), and used chiefly as an oxidizing agent and a depolarizer in dry cells, in glassmaking and ceramics, as a pigment, and as a starting material for other manganese compounds (as permanganates and driers for varnishes and paints)

manganese epidote *n* : PIEDMONTITE

manganese green *n* : barium manganate $BaMnO_4$ used as a pigment — called also *Cassel green*

manganese heptoxide *n* : a compound Mn_2O_7 obtained as a dark green explosive oil by action of concentrated sulfuric acid on permanganates — called also *manganese(VII) oxide*

manganese oxide *n* : an oxide of manganese; *esp* : MANGANESE DIOXIDE

manganese sesquioxide *n* : a compound Mn_2O_3 obtained as a black powder by heating manganese dioxide or manganous salts in air — called also *manganese(III) oxide, manganic oxide*

manganese spar *n* **1** : RHODONITE **2** : RHODOCHROSITE

manganese steel *n* **1** : steel containing manganese **2** : HADFIELD MANGANESE STEEL

manganese sulfate *n* : a sulfate of manganese; *esp* : MANGANOUS SULFATE

manganese tetroxide *n* : a compound Mn_3O_4 or $MnMn_2O_4$ found in nature as hausmannite and obtained as a reddish brown powder by strongly heating manganese oxides or hydroxides in air — called also *manganomanganic oxide, red manganese oxide*

manganese velvet brown *n* : BURNT UMBER 2

manganese violet *n* : a moderate purple that is redder and duller than heliotrope (sense 4a), bluer, lighter, and stronger than average amethyst, bluer and stronger than cobalt violet, and bluer and deeper than average lilac (sense 3a) — called also *Burgundy violet, mineral violet, Nuremberg violet, permanent violet*

man·ga·ne·sian \ˌmaŋgə'nēzhən, -zēən\ *adj* : of, relating to, or containing manganese

man·gan·hedenbergite \ˌmaŋgən+\ *n* [Sw *manganhedenbergit*, fr. *mangan* manganese + *hedenbergit* hedenbergite — more at MANGAN-] : a hedenbergite containing manganese

mangani– — see MANGAN-

man·gan·ic \maŋ'ganik\ *adj* [ISV *mangan-* + *-ic*] : of, relating to, or derived from manganese — used esp. of compounds in which this element is trivalent and of the acid in which it is hexavalent; compare MANGANOUS

manganic acid *n* : an acid H_2MnO_4 known only in solution and esp. in the form of its salts (as potassium manganate)

manganic hydroxide *n* : a compound MnO(OH) occurring in nature as manganite and obtained synthetically as a brown powder by precipitation and drying; manganese oxide and hydroxide

manganic oxide *n* : MANGANESE SESQUIOXIDE

man·ga·nif·er·ous \ˌmaŋgə'nif(ə)rəs\ *adj* [*mangan-* + *-iferous*] : containing manganese ⟨~ rocks⟩

man·ga·nite \'maŋgəˌnīt\ *n* -S [*mangan-* + *-ite*] **1** : an ore of manganese MnO(OH) consisting of manganic hydroxide in brilliant steel-gray or iron-black orthorhombic crystals or massive — called also *gray manganese ore* **2** : any of a series of unstable salts made by reaction of manganese dioxide with a base ⟨calcium ~⟩ — called also *manganate(IV)*

man·gan·ja \män'gänjə\ *n, pl* **manganja** *or* **manganjas** *usu cap* : NYANJA

mangano– — see MANGAN-

man·ga·no·calcite \ˌmaŋgə(ˌ)nō+\ *n* [G *manganokalzit*, fr. *mangan-* + *kalzit* calcite] **1** : a rhodochrosite containing calcium **2** : a calcite containing manganese

man·ga·no·columbite \"+\ *n* [*mangan-* + *columbite*] : a manganiferous columbite

man·ga·no·langbeinite \"+\ *n* [It, fr. *mangan-* + *langbeinite*] : a mineral $K_2Mn_2(SO_4)_3$ consisting of a very rare sulfate of potassium and manganese found in lava at Vesuvius

man·ga·no·manganic oxide \"+ . . . -\ *n* [ISV *mangan-* + *manganic*] : MANGANESE TETROXIDE

man·ga·no·phyl·lite \ˌmaŋgənō'fiˌlīt\ *n* [G *manganophyll* manganophyllite (fr. *mangan-* + *-phyll*) + E *-ite*] : a manganiferous biotite

man·ga·no·siderite \ˌmaŋgə(ˌ)nō+\ *n* [G *manganosiderit*, fr. *mangan-* + *siderit* siderite] : an intermediate member of the isomorphous series siderite–rhodochrosite

man·ga·no·site \ˌmaŋgə'nōˌsīt, man'ganə,-\ *n* -S [G *manganosit*, fr. *mangan-* + connective *-s-* + *-it* -ite] : a mineral MnO consisting of manganous oxide occurring in small emerald green octahedrons that turn black on exposure (hardness 5–6, sp. gr. 5.18)

manganoso– *comb form* [ISV *mangan-* + *-oso-* (fr. L *-osus* -ous)] : MANGANOUS

man·ga·no·tantalite \ˌmaŋgə(ˌ)nō+\ *n* [G or Sw *manganotantalit*, fr. *mangan-* + *tantalit* tantalite] : a manganiferous tantalite

man·ga·nous \'maŋgənəs, man'ganəs\ *adj* [*mangan-* + *-ous*] : of, relating to, or derived from manganese — used esp. of compounds in which this element is bivalent; compare MANGANIC

manganous chloride *n* : a pink deliquescent crystalline salt $MnCl_2$ used chiefly as a flux and a catalyst

manganous hydroxide *n* : a crystalline amphoteric compound $Mn(OH)_2$ that is found in nature as pyrochroite, that is obtained synthetically as a white precipitate by adding alkali to a solution of a manganous salt, and that rapidly turns brown in air by oxidation

manganous oxide *n* : an insoluble monoxide MnO of manganese found in nature as manganosite and obtained as a green easily oxidizable powder by heating other oxides of manganese in a current of hydrogen — called also *manganese(II) oxide*

manganous sulfate *n* : an almost white salt $MnSO_4$ that is usu. obtained as the rose-colored efflorescent crystalline tetrahydrate by treating manganese dioxide with sulfuric acid and powdered coal and that is used chiefly as a fertilizer and spray for plants

manganous sulfide *n* : a compound MnS found in nature as alabandite and obtained synthetically usu. as an easily oxidizable flesh-colored precipitate

man·gan·pectolite \ˌmaŋgən+\ *n* [G *manganpectolith*, fr. *mangan* manganese + *pectolith* pectolite] : a manganiferous pectolite

man·gar \'məŋgə(r)\ *n, pl* **mangar** *or* **mangars** *usu cap* **1** : a people of Nepal **2** : a member of the Mangar people

1**mang·a·re·van** \ˌmäŋ(g)ə'rāvən\ *adj, usu cap* [*Mangareva* island, Gambier islands, French Polynesia + E *-an*] **1 a** : of, relating to, or characteristic of the island of Mangareva or the Gambier islands **b** : of, relating to, or characteristic of the people of Mangareva or the Gambier islands **2** : of, relating to, or characteristic of the Mangarevan language

2**mangarevan** \"\ *n* -S *cap* **1** : a native or inhabitant of Mangareva or the Gambier islands **2** : the Mangarevan language — compare AUSTRONESIAN, POLYNESIAN

mangas *pl of* MANGA

mang·be·tu \mäŋ'be(ˌ)tü\ *also* **mang·bat·tu** \-ba(-\ *or* **mangbet·tu** \-be(-\ *or* **mom·but·too** \mäm'bə(-\ *n, pl* **mangbetu** *or* **mangbetus** *usu cap* **1 a** : a people dwelling about the headwaters of the Uele river in northern Zaire and sometimes regarded as a distinctive racial type **b** : a member of such people **2** : a Central Sudanic language of the Mangbetu people

mange \'mānj\ *n* -S [ME *manjewe*, fr. MF *mangeue* appetite, itching, fr. *mangier* to eat — more at MANGER] **1** : any of various more or less severe, persistent, and contagious skin diseases that are marked esp. by eczematous inflammation and loss of hair and that affect domestic animals or sometimes man; *esp* : a skin disease caused by a minute parasitic mite of *Sarcoptes, Psoroptes, Chorioptes*, or related genera that burrows in or lives on the skin or of *Demodex* that lives in the hair follicles or sebaceous glands — see CHORIOPTIC MANGE, DEMODECTIC MANGE, PSOROPTIC MANGE, SARCOPTIC MANGE; ITCH 1b, SCABIES; compare SCAB **2** *archaic* : a constant irritating desire : ITCH

man·ge·ao \ˌmän(g)ā'aü\ *n* -S [Maori] : a New Zealand timber tree (*Litsea calicaris*) that has tough hard wood with dark grayish brown bark and flowers in 4- to 5-flowered umbels arranged in axillary racemes

man·gel \'maŋgəl\ *n* -S [short for *mangel-wurzel*] : BEET; *specif* : MANGEL-WURZEL

mangel–wurzel \'ˌ==ˌwərzəl\ *also* **mangold–wurzel** \'maŋgəl(d)w-, -ˌgōl-\ *n* -S [G *mangelwurzel* (alter. of *mangoldwurzel*) & *mangoldwurzel*, fr. *mangold* beet (fr. OHG *mānegolt*) + *wurzel* root, fr. OHG *wurzala*] **1** : a large coarse yellow to reddish orange beet extensively grown as food for cattle **2** : the fleshy so-called root of the mangel-wurzel that consists of enlarged hypocotyl and root and is less rich in sugar than either the common beet or the sugar beet

mange mite *n* : any of the small parasitic mites that infest the skin of animals and cause mange

man·ger \'mānjə(r)\ *n* -S [ME *manger, mangeour*, fr. MF *maingeure*, fr. *mangier* to eat, fr. L *manducare* to chew, eat, devour, fr. *manducus* glutton, fr. *mandere* to chew, eat — more at MOUTH] **1** : a trough or open box in which feed or fodder is placed for horses or cattle to eat **2** : a perforated raised floor on which an anchor chain rests in the chain locker of a ship

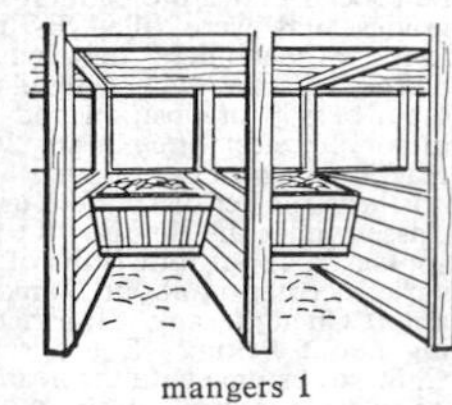

mangers 1

manger board *n* : a low athwartship partition aft of the hawseholes that prevents seawater from running aft on the deck of a ship

mangey *var of* MANGY

man·gif·era \man'jif(ə)rə\ *n, cap* [NL, fr. ISV *mango* + L *-fera*, fem. of *-fer* -ferous] : a large genus of tropical Asiatic trees (family Anacardiaceae) that have coriaceous entire leaves, small paniculate flowers, and a fleshy drupaceous fruit with a fibrous mesocarp — see MANGO

man·gi·ly \'mānjəlē, -li\ *adv* : in a mangy manner

man·gi·ness \-jēnəs, -jin-\ *n* -ES : the quality or state of being mangy

1**man·gle** \'maŋgəl, -aiŋ-\ *vt* **mangled; mangled; mangling** \-g(ə)liŋ\ **mangles** [ME *manglen*, fr. AF *mangler*, freq. of OF *mahaignier, maynier* to maim — more at MAIM] **1 a** : to cut, bruise, or hack with repeated blows or strokes : make a ragged or torn wound or series of wounds on ⟨the trees had been whittled and chewed and *mangled* with a dull ax —Wallace Stegner⟩ ⟨rocks *mangled* the feet of the animals —*Amer. Guide Series: Nev.*⟩ **b** : to destroy the shape of by a violent blow or crash ⟨the *mangled* coaches —*Associated Press*⟩ **2** : to spoil, mutilate, or make incoherent through bungling, ignorance, or deliberate falsification ⟨*mangling* a phrase out of its true context —F.L.Mott⟩ ⟨they altered the sequence, they *mangled* the text —Barbara Ward⟩ ⟨the pianist *mangled* the concerto⟩ **syn** see MAIM

²**mangle** \"\ *n* -s [Sp, fr. Taino] **1 :** MANGROVE **2 :** any of several trees or shrubs (as *Avicennia nitida* and *Laguncularia racemosa*) that resemble the mango

³**mangle** \"\ *n* -s [D *mangel*, fr. G, fr. MHG, dim. of *mange* mangonel, mangle, fr. LL *manganum* — more at MANGONEL] **1 :** a machine for ironing laundry work by passing it between heated rollers **2 :** a machine for applying starch or other sizing material to textiles and then smoothing and drying them **3 :** a machine resembling a hand wringer for rolling rubber latex into sheets **4 :** a cylinder machine that makes stereotype molds from dry flong by impressing it on a form **5 :** PADDER 1b

⁴**mangle** \"\ *vt* -ED/-ING/-S [D *mangelen*, fr. G *mangeln*, fr. *mangel*, n.] **:** to press or smooth (as damp linen) with a mangle

mangle gearing *n* **:** a mechanism for producing reciprocating motion consisting of a rack with teeth on both sides and around the ends or a row of pegs engaging a pinion that rotates continuously in one direction

¹**man·gler** \-g(ə)lə(r)\ *n* -s [¹*mangle* + *-er*] **:** one that mangles or mutilates; *specif* **:** a machine for chopping or mincing (as meat or sugarcane)

²**mangler** \"\ *n* -s [⁴*mangle* + *-er*] **:** one that smooths or presses with a mangle; *esp* **:** an operator of a mangle for starching and pressing cloth, mercerizing it, or giving it a finish

man·go \ˈmaŋ(ˌ)gō, -aiŋ-\ *n, pl* **mangoes** *or* **mangos** [Pg *manga*, fr. Tamil *mān-kāy*] **1 a :** a yellowish red oblong to pear-shaped tropical fruit that has a firm skin and hard central stone and is widely cultivated for its very juicy, aromatic, and pleasantly subacid pulp but in seedling and wild strains is often exceedingly fibrous and has a distinct flavor of turpentine **b :** a large evergreen tree (*Mangifera indica*) that is native to India, has alternate coriaceous leaves and small yellow or reddish flowers in branching terminal panicles, and produces mangoes and inferior grayish timber **2 :** any of several chiefly tropical shrubs or trees that produce edible fruits resembling mangoes — usu. used in combination; compare WILD MANGO **3 a** (1) **:** a vegetable (as a sweet pepper) stuffed (as with shredded cabbage) and then pickled (2) **:** a pickled mango melon **b** *chiefly Midland* **:** a large round sweet pepper **4 :** any of a genus (*Anthracothorax*) of hummingbirds

mango bird *n* **:** an oriole (*Oriolus kundoo*) that is native to India

man-god \ˈ=ˌ=\ *n, sometimes cap M&G* **1 :** one who is both human and divine **2 a :** a man who is made a god **b :** a god in human form

mango fly *n* **:** any of various tabanid flies (genus *Chrysops*) that are vectors of filarial worms (as the eye worm)

man·gold \ˈmaŋgəld, -ˌgōld\ *n* [short for *mangold-wurzel*] **:** MANGEL-WURZEL

mangold-wurzel *var of* MANGEL-WURZEL

mango melon *n* **:** a muskmelon (*Cucumis melo chito*) that bears fruit resembling oranges and is used for pickles and preserves — called also *lemon cucumber*

man·go·nel \ˈmaŋgəˌnel\ *n* -s [ME *mangnel*, *mangonel*, fr. MF *mangunel*, *mangonel*, prob. fr. ML *manganellus*, dim. of LL *manganum* ballista, mangonel, fr. Gk *manganon* philter, ballista; akin to Gk *manganeuein* to deceive, MIr *meng* deception, ruse, Toch A *mañk* guilt, error, Skt *mañju* beautiful; basic meaning: to beautify] **:** a military engine formerly used for throwing missiles (as stones or javelins)

mangonism *n* -s [F *mangonisme*, fr. L *mangon-*, *mango* dealer that gives a false appearance to his wares (of Gk origin; akin to *manganeuein* to deceive) + F *-isme* -ism — more at MANGONEL] *obs* **:** a method of training or treating plants contrary to natural conditions of growth

mango-squash \ˈ=(ˌ)=ˌ=\ *n* **:** CHAYOTE

man·go·steen \ˈmaŋgəˌstēn\ *n* -s [Malay *mangustan*] **1 a :** the dark reddish brown fruit of an East Indian tree (*Garcinia mangostana*) with thick rind enclosing numerous carpels and juicy flesh having a flavor suggestive of both peach and pineapple **b :** a tree that bears mangosteens **2 :** the pericarp of the mangosteen fruit used as an astringent

mango weevil *n* **:** a weevil (*Sternochetus mangiferae*) whose larvae feed in and destroy the seeds of mangoes

man·grove \ˈmaŋˌgrōv, -an-,\ *n, often attrib* [prob. fr. Pg *mangue* (fr. Sp *mangle*, fr. Taino) + E *grove*] **1 :** a tropical maritime tree or shrub of the genus *Rhizophora* (esp. *R. mangle*) bearing fruit that germinates while still on the tree with the hypocotyl growing to a considerable length before detachment and having numerous prop roots that ultimately form an impenetrable mass and play an important role in land building **2 :** any of various other plants that resemble the mangrove; *specif* **:** a tree of the genus *Avicennia* — see BLACK MANGROVE

mangrove cutch *or* **mangrove cutch :** ¹CUTCH 2

mangrove crab *n* **:** any of numerous usu. small active tropical American crabs (family Grapsidae) that live in mangrove swamps climbing about the trees and sometimes feeding on their leaves

mangrove cuckoo *n* **:** a cuckoo (*Coccyzus minor*) of the West Indies and the Florida keys

mangrove family *n* **:** RHIZOPHORACEAE

mangrove fish *or* **mangrove skipper** *n* **:** MUDSKIPPER

mangrove mullet *n* **:** SEA MULLET 1a

mangrove oyster *n* **:** a small oyster (*Ostrea frons*) that grows in clumps on mangrove roots along Floridian and West Indian shores

mangrove snapper *n* **:** GRAY SNAPPER

mangrove swamp *also* **mangrove** *n* **:** a brackish-water coastal swamp of tropical and subtropical areas that is usu. dominated by shrubby halophytes and is partly inundated by tidal flow

mangt *abbr* management

¹**mangue** \ˈmaŋ\ *n* -s [F] **:** KUSIMANSE

²**man·gue** \ˈmäŋ(ˌ)gā\ *n, pl* **mangue** *or* **mangues** *usu cap* [Sp, of AmerInd origin] **1 a :** a Chorotegan people of southwestern Nicaragua **b :** a member of such people **2 :** the language of the Mangue people

man·gum terrace \ˈmaŋgəm-\ *n* [after P. H. *Mangum*, 19th cent. Am. farmer] **:** a broad low ridged terrace that is used as part of a farm's water-disposal system

man·gun \(ˌ)manˈgün\ *n, pl* **mangun** *or* **manguns** *usu cap* **1 :** a Tungusic people of the Amur river region in Siberia **2 :** a member of the Mangun people

man·gwe \ˈman(ˌ)gwā\ *n* -s [native name in Africa] **:** SOUTH AFRICAN YELLOWWOOD

man·gy *also* **man·gey** \ˈmānjē, -ji\ *adj, usu* **mangier**; *usu* **mangiest** [*mange* + *-y*] **1 a :** infected with or as if with the mange ⟨a ~ dog⟩ **b :** relating to, characteristic of, or resulting from the mange ⟨a ~ appearance⟩ ⟨a ~ itch⟩ **2 a :** having many worn-out or bare spots **:** SEEDY, SHABBY ⟨aging but resolute, with ~ hair —W.A.White⟩ ⟨knelt on the ~ rug —Elizabeth Taylor⟩ ⟨as ~ a lawn as ever anyone paid taxes on —R.M.Yoder⟩ **b :** having a mean and wretched appearance or quality **:** SQUALID ⟨the meanest hotel and the *mangiest* restaurant —P.E.Deutschman⟩ **3** *obs* **:** CONTEMPTIBLE, MISERABLE — used as a generalized term of disapproval

man·gyan \mänˈgyän\ *n, pl* **mangyan** *or* **mangyans** *usu cap* [Tag *Mangyán*] **1 a :** any of several peoples of Mindoro, Philippines — compare HANUNÓO **b :** a member of any such peoples **2 :** any of the Austronesian languages of the Mangyan peoples

manhandle \ˈ=ˌ==\ *vt* [¹*man* + *handle*] **1 :** to move or manage by human force ⟨~ their car out of a ditch —*Scots Mag.*⟩ **2 :** to handle roughly ⟨~ citizens who . . . failed to hang out the flag —Dixon Wecter⟩

man-harness knot *n* **:** a loop knot tied in the bight of a rope to aid in hauling

man-hater \ˈ=ˌ==\ *n* **1 :** a person who hates mankind **:** MISANTHROPE **2 :** a person who avoids the society of men

¹**man·hat·tan** \manˈhatᵊn, maan-, mən-\ *n, pl* **manhattan** *or* **manhattans 1** *usu cap* **a :** an Algonquian Indian people formerly inhabiting the present site of New York city **b :** a member of such people **2** *also* **manhattan cocktail** *often cap M* [fr. *Manhattan*, borough of New York city] **:** a cocktail consisting of Italian vermouth, rye or bourbon whiskey, and a dash or two of bitters stirred with cracked ice, strained, and served with a maraschino cherry

²**manhattan** \(ˈ)manˈhatᵊn, -aan-, mənˈh-\ *adj, usu cap* **:** of or from the borough of Manhattan, New York, N.Y. ⟨a *Manhattan* skyscraper⟩ **:** of the kind or style prevalent in Manhattan

manhattan clam chowder *n, usu cap M* **:** chowder made of minced clams, salt pork, vegetables, esp. tomatoes, with water, and seasoned with herbs — compare NEW ENGLAND CLAM CHOWDER

man·hat·tan·ese \manˌhatᵊnˈēz, maan-, mən-, -ēs\ *n, pl* **manhattanese** *cap, often attrib* [*Manhattan* borough + E *-ese*] **1 :** a New Yorker who lives on Manhattan Island — usu. used in pl. **2 :** English as spoken by the Manhattanese

man·hat·tan·ite \=ˈhatᵊnˌīt\ *n* -s *cap* [*Manhattan* borough + E *-ite*] **:** a native or resident of Manhattan borough, New York, N.Y.

manhead \ˈ=ˌ=\ *n* **:** MANHOLE 1

manhole \ˈ=ˌ=\ *n* **1 :** a hole through which a man may go; *esp* **:** one to gain access (as for cleaning or repair) to an underground or enclosed structure (as a sewer, electric conduit, steam boiler) — see SEPTIC TANK illustration **2 :** ²SCUTTLE 1a

man·hood \ˈmanˌhu̇d, -aan-\ *n* [ME *manhode*, fr. *man* + *-hode* -hood] **1 :** the condition of being a human being **:** human quality or nature ⟨make moral postulates that rest less on his scientific knowledge than on his simple ~ —Weston La Barre⟩ **2 :** manly qualities **:** COURAGE, BRAVERY, RESOLUTION ⟨send ~ out of him in fear —G.D.Brown⟩ ⟨society everywhere is in conspiracy against the ~ of every one of its members —R.W.Emerson⟩ **3 a :** the condition of being an adult male ⟨the thing for which he had striven since ~ —Mary K. Hammond⟩ ⟨grew to ~ in a frontier town⟩ **b :** the condition of being a male as distinguished from a female ⟨has become the symbol of ~, which is socially valued —H.M.Parshley⟩ **c :** VIRILITY **d :** male genitalia **4 :** MEN; *esp* **:** the adult males ⟨Ireland's ~ . . . were distributed among the prisons of England —O.S.J.Gogarty⟩ ⟨Britain's strength lies in her own ~, standing on her own shores —M.W. Straight⟩ **5 :** mature status **:** MATURITY ⟨grew up to ~ under the protection of Great Britain —F.H.Underhill⟩ ⟨combat aviation has grown to ~ —H.H.Arnold & I.C. Eaker⟩

manhood suffrage *n* **:** suffrage of all male citizens not under a civil disability (as for crime or lunacy)

man-hour \ˈ=ˈ=\ *n* **:** a unit of one hour's work by one man used esp. as a basis for cost finding and wages ⟨should save countless thousands of dollars and *man-hours* —*Advt*⟩

manhunt \ˈ=ˌ=\ *n* **:** an organized and usu. intensive hunt or search for a man esp. if charged with a crime ⟨at the time of the crime, a gigantic ~ was staged —*Springfield (Mass.) Daily News*⟩

man hunter *n* **:** one that hunts men

ma·ni \ˈmänē\ *n, pl* **mani** *or* **manis** [Sp *maní*, fr. Taino] **:** PEANUT

ma·nia \ˈmānēə *sometimes* -nyə\ *n* -s [ME, fr. LL, fr. Gk *mainesthai* to be mad; akin to Gk *menos* spirit — more at MIND] **1 :** excitement of psychotic proportions manifested by mental and physical hyperactivity, disorganization of behavior, and elevation of mood; *specif* **:** the manic phase of manic-depressive psychosis **2 a :** excessive or unreasonable enthusiasm **:** a violent desire, passion, or partiality **:** CRAZE ⟨has a ~ for building and transforming —Arnold Bennett⟩ ⟨seized by a ~ for acquisition —Erico Verissimo⟩ ⟨enamel vases, for which our middle classes so long had a ~ —Albert Dasnoy⟩ ⟨letters from citizens who had the ~ of print —Winston Churchill⟩ **b :** something that is the object of a mania ⟨prizefighting, horse racing, and dog racing are national ~s —T.H.Fielding⟩ ⟨demobilization became the ~ of the day —Demaree Bess⟩

syn MANIA, DELIRIUM, FRENZY, and HYSTERIA denote in common a state of mind in which there is a loss of control over emotional, nervous, or mental processes. MANIA implies insanity, esp. when manifested as the manic phase of manic-depressive psychosis. DELIRIUM implies cerebral excitement precipitated by toxic factors in disease or drugs or occurring in the course of a prolonged mental disorder and manifest in delusions, illusions, hallucinations, incoherence, and restlessness. FRENZY usu. applies to the physical symptoms of mania or any symptoms resembling them. HYSTERIA is a functional psychic disorder simulating organic disease and is manifest in such physical symptoms as disturbances of sensation, motion, and visceral functions expressed typically as functional paralysis of a limb, nausea, emotional instability. **syn** see in addition INSANITY

man·i·a·ble \ˈmanēəbəl\ *adj* [MF, fr. OF, fr. *manier* to caress, handle (fr. *main* hand, fr. L *manus*) + *-able* — more at MANUAL] **1** *obs* **:** capable of being handled or worked **:** PLIABLE **2 :** MANAGEABLE, TRACTABLE ⟨some more definite and more ~ problem —Clive Bell⟩

¹**ma·ni·ac** \ˈmānēˌak\ *or* **ma·ni·a·cal** \məˈnīəkəl\ *adj* [*maniac* fr. LL *maniacus*, fr. Gk or LGk *maniakos*, fr. *mania*; *maniacal* fr. LL *maniacus* + E *-al*] **1 a :** affected with madness **:** MAD, INSANE ⟨a ~ killer⟩ **b :** indicating or suggestive of madness **:** characteristic of or like that of a maniac ⟨stared back from ~ little eyes —Farley Mowat⟩ ⟨~ desires to impose the national will upon other populations —Lewis Mumford⟩ ⟨that ~ glint in a housewife's scheming eye —Howard Spring⟩ **2 :** characterized by ungovernable excitement or frenzy **:** FRANTIC, VIOLENT ⟨under the feet of a ~ mob stampeding out into the bush —Arthur Grimble⟩ — **ma·ni·a·cal·ly** \-k(ə)lē, -li\ *adv*

²**maniac** \"\ *n* -s **1 :** LUNATIC, MADMAN ⟨believe the crime was the work of a sex ~ —*Associated Press*⟩ **2 :** a person characterized by an inordinate or ungovernable enthusiasm, passion, or partiality for something ⟨our own circle of fishing ~s —*Ford Times*⟩ ⟨amateur map ~s should revel in this book —*Scientific American*⟩

³**maniac** \"\ *n* -s [*m*athematical *a*nalyzer, *n*umerical *i*ntegrator *a*nd *c*omputer] **:** a high-speed electronic digital computer

¹**man·ic** \ˈmanik, -nēk *sometimes* ˈmān-\ *adj* [Gk *manikos*, fr. *mania* mania + *-ikos* -ic] **1 :** affected with mania ⟨a ~ individual⟩ **2 :** relating to, suggestive of, or like mania ⟨displayed a ~ excitement⟩ ⟨transitions from ~ self-assertions to painful self-doubt —Irving Howe⟩

²**manic** \"\ *n* -s **:** a manic individual

¹**manic-depressive** \ˈ=‚=ˈ=‚=\ *adj* [ISV *manic* + *depressive*; orig. formed as G *manisch-depressiv*] **:** relating to, characterized by, or exhibiting features similar to manic-depressive psychosis

²**manic-depressive** \"\ *n* **:** a manic-depressive individual

manic-depressive psychosis *or* **manic-depressive reaction** *n* **:** a major mental disorder manifested either by mania or by psychotic depression or by alternating mania and depression

¹**man·i·chae·an** *or* **man·i·che·an** \ˌmanəˈkēən\ *adj, usu cap* [LL *Manichaeus* member of the Manichean sect (fr. LGk *Manichaios*, fr. *Manichaios* Manes †ab276A.D. Persian sage who founded the sect) + E *-an*] **1 :** of or relating to Manichaeism or the Manichaeans ⟨the *Manichaean* debt to Zoroastrianism⟩ **2 :** characterized by or reflecting belief in Manichaeism ⟨*Manichaean* influences in Augustinian doctrines⟩ ⟨anti-Semitism of the current type . . . is a complete and irrational philosophy of life based on a *Manichaean* conception of the world —*Times Lit. Supp.*⟩

²**manichaean** *or* **manichean** \"\ *or* **man·i·chee** \ˈmanəˌkē\ *n* -s *usu cap* **1 :** a member of the religious sect adhering to Manichaeism **2 :** a believer in religious or philosophical dualism

man·i·chae·ism *or* **man·i·che·ism** \ˈmanəˌkēˌizəm\ *also* **man·i·chae·an·ism** *or* **man·i·che·an·ism** \ˌmanəˈkēəˌnizəm\ *or* **man·i·chee·ism** \ˈmanəˌkēˌizəm\ *n* -s *usu cap* [*Manichaeus* (Manes) *or Manichaean* + E *-ism*] **1 :** a syncretistic religious dualism originating in Persia, widely held in the Roman empire during the third and fourth centuries A.D. and in central and eastern Asia for a longer period, and teaching as a saving wisdom given through the Hebrew prophets, Jesus, and Mani that a cosmic conflict exists between a good realm of light and an evil realm of darkness, that matter and flesh are in the realm of darkness, and that man's duty is to aid the forces of good by practicing asceticism esp. by avoiding procreation and animal food **2 :** a dualistic interpretation of the world dividing it between good and evil powers or regarding matter as inherently evil

man·i·chae·is·tic \ˌmanəkēˈistik\ *adj, usu cap* [*Manichaeus* + E *-istic*] **:** of, relating to, or resembling Manichaeism

ma·ni·co·ba rubber \ˌmänəˈsōbə-\ *n* [Pg *maniçoba* any of several trees yielding Ceará rubber, fr. Tupi *manisoba* leaf from such trees] **1 :** CEARÁ RUBBER **2** *also* **manicoba** -s **:** any of several trees of the genus *Manihot* that yield Ceará rubber

man·i·cole \ˈmanəˌkōl\ *n* -s [of Arawakan origin; akin to Jucuna *manakóla* manicole, Tariána *mánaka*] **:** ASSAI

¹**man·i·cure** \ˈmanəˌkyu̇(ə)r, -u̇ə\ *n* -s *often attrib* [F, fr. L *manus* hand + F *-icure* (as in *pédicure* pedicure) — more at MANUAL, PEDICURE] **1 :** MANICURIST **2 :** a treatment for the care of the hands and nails usu. including massage of the hand and cleaning, shaping, and polishing of the nails

²**manicure** \"\ *vt* -ED/-ING/-S **1 :** to care for (hands and nails) with a manicure **2 :** to trim closely and evenly ⟨wants that lawn *manicured* —Steve McNeil⟩

man·i·cur·ist \-u̇rəst\ *n* -s **:** a person who gives manicure treatments

man·i·dae \ˈmanəˌdē\ *n pl, cap* [NL, fr. *Manis*, type genus + *-idae*] **:** a family of mammals that is coextensive with the order Pholidota and that includes the pangolins

ma·ni·enie grass \ˌmänēəˈnē(ˌ)ā-\ *n* [Hawaiian *mānienie*] **:** BERMUDA GRASS

ma·nière cri·blée \məˈnyerkrēˈblā\ *n* [F, lit., criblé manner] **:** an engraving technique orig. used in the 15th century in which round holes punched in a block or plate produce a white spotted background in the print — called also *dotted manner*

manière noire \-ˈnwär\ *n* [F, lit., black manner] **:** the act or process of producing an overall texture in aquatint by scratching the plate directly with a wire brush or other device or by ruling closely set parallel lines in several directions on the ground before etching

¹**man·i·fest** \ˈmanəˌfest *sometimes* |ˈfəst *or chiefly in southern U. S. & Brit* -nil *or* -nē\ *adj* [ME, fr. MF or L; MF *manifeste*, fr. L *manifestus*, *manufestus*, fr. *manus* hand + *-festus* (as in *infestus* hostile) — more at MANUAL, DARE] **1 a :** capable of being readily and instantly perceived by the senses and esp. by the sight **:** not hidden or concealed **:** open to view ⟨the earth's convexity had now become strikingly ~ —E.A.Poe⟩ **b :** capable of being easily understood or recognized at once by the mind **:** not obscure **:** OBVIOUS ⟨the wisdom of the new rule was so ~ that it was accepted as a conclusive precedent —Frederick Pollock⟩ **c :** being the part or aspect of a phenomenon that is directly observable **:** concretely expressed in behavior **:** OVERT ⟨witchcraft has ~ and latent functions for the individual and for social groups —*Psychological Abstracts*⟩ **2** *obs* **:** bearing evident marks or signs — used with *of* **syn** see EVIDENT

²**manifest** \"\ *vb* -ED/-ING/-S [ME *manifesten*, fr. MF or L; MF *manifester*, fr. L *manifestare*, fr. *manifestus*] *vt* **:** to show plainly **:** make palpably evident or certain by showing or displaying ⟨~*ed* precisely the same bone structure as the mask of the great author —Osbert Sitwell⟩ ⟨choice ~s itself in society in small increments —Lewis Mumford⟩ ~ *vi* **:** to produce a physical disturbance indicating the presence of a ghost or spirit **:** APPEAR ⟨observe a number of striking phenomena which . . . were then actively ~*ing* —Hereward Carrington⟩ ⟨when the atmosphere is heavy, it is hard for the spirits to ~ —M.L.Bach⟩ **syn** see SHOW

³**manifest** \"\ *n* -s [MF or It; MF *manifeste*, fr. It *manifesto* — more at MANIFESTO] **1 :** MANIFESTATION, INDICATION ⟨the Eightieth Congress had just been a ~ of Republican intentions —V.L.Albjerg⟩ **2 :** MANIFESTO ⟨this ~ . . . is neither conservative nor too radical —Ernest Harms⟩ **3 a :** a list or invoice of cargo for any of several forms of transportation (as a ship or plane) usu. containing marks or indications of contents or commodity, consignee, and other pertinent information for use at terminals or a customhouse **b :** a list (as of passengers, destinations, baggage weights) in air transportation for each flight **c :** a list of cars by location, number, owners' initials, and contents in a train, accompanying the train and teletyped to yards and terminals **4 :** a fast freight train usu. carrying merchandise, perishables, or livestock

man·i·fest·able \-təbəl\ *adj* **:** capable of being manifested

man·i·fes·tant \ˌmanəˈfestənt\ *n* -s [F, fr. pres. part. of *manifester* to manifest — more at MANIFEST] **:** one who makes or participates in a manifestation ⟨the ~s paraded past the docks —J.H.Rosny⟩

man·i·fes·ta·tion \ˌmanəfəˈstāshən, -ˌfeˈ-\ *n* -s [ME *manifestacion*, fr. LL *manifestation-*, *manifestatio*, fr. L *manifestatus* (past part. of *manifestare* to manifest) + *-ion-*, *-io* -ion — more at MANIFEST] **1 a :** the act, process, or an instance of manifesting **:** DISPLAY, SHOW, EXPRESSION ⟨demanded some ~ of repentance on the part of abjured heretics⟩ ⟨love on a high level of ~ —John Dewey⟩ **b :** something that manifests or constitutes an expression of something else **:** a perceptible, outward, or visible expression ⟨heat and light . . . had been regarded as ~s of the escape of phlogiston —S.F.Mason⟩ ⟨the extent of the . . . disease cannot always be determined by its clinical ~s —*Encyc. Americana*⟩ ⟨violent brushwork and strident color are the ~ of a desperate intensity of vision —David Sylvester⟩ **c :** one of the forms, guises, or appearances in which an individual (as a spirit, divine being, or personality) is manifested ⟨in his West African ~ is the god of good fortune —M.J.Herskovits⟩ ⟨various ~s of the same god were known by different names —*History of Ukraine*⟩ ⟨dominated by four separate ~s of her own sick personality —William Peden⟩ ⟨another prophet, a new ~ of God —M.L. Bach⟩ **d :** an occult phenomenon ⟨the ~s here were of materialization —G.H.Estabrooks⟩; *specif* **:** MATERIALIZATION ⟨a good ghost story, with all the appropriate ~s —*Time Lit. Supp.*⟩ **2 :** a public demonstration or display of power and purpose (as by a political party or adherents to some cause) ⟨meetings, parades, and other such ~s —H.M.Parshley⟩

man·i·fes·ta·tive \ˌmanəˈfestədˌiv\ *adj* [F or ML; F *manifestatif*, fr. ML *manifestativus*, fr. L *manifestatus* + *-ivus* -ive] **:** serving to manifest **:** DEMONSTRATIVE — **man·i·fes·ta·tive·ly** \-d‧əvlē\ *adv*

manifest content *n, psychoanalysis* **:** the content of a dream as it is recalled by the dreamer

manifest destiny *n, often cap M&D* **:** an ordering of human history regarded as inevitable and obviously apparent that leads a people or race to expand to geographic limits held to be natural or to extend sovereignty over a usu. indefinite area ⟨a step in our *manifest destiny*, one of several acts of our territorial expansion —Lancaster Pollard⟩ ⟨a believer in *manifest destiny* in Asia —*New Republic*⟩ ⟨the *manifest destiny* school of historians —C.J.Friedrich⟩; *also* **:** the doctrine of or belief in such inevitable expansion ⟨that peculiar type of historical mysticism that we in America call *manifest destiny* —Donald Heiney⟩

man·i·fest·er \ˈmanəˌfestə(r)\ *n* -s **:** one that manifests

man·i·fest·ly *adv* **:** in a manifest manner **:** PLAINLY, OBVIOUSLY ⟨from the sound of his replies, was ~ shaving —John Galsworthy⟩

man·i·fest·ness *n* -ES **:** the quality or state of being manifest

¹**man·i·fes·to** \ˌmanəˈfe(ˌ)stō\ *n, pl* **manifestos** *or* **manifestoes** [It, fr. *manifestare* to manifest, declare, proclaim, fr. L, to manifest — more at MANIFEST] **1** *obs* **:** DEMONSTRATION, EVIDENCE **2 :** a public declaration of intentions, motives, or views **:** a public statement of policy or opinion ⟨if other writers are impressed with his recipe they form a school, and perhaps issue a ~ —Susanne K. Langer⟩ ⟨gave me an opportunity to write a ~ —H.J.Laski⟩ ⟨professors signed a ~ repudiating various charges —F.L.Paxson⟩ ⟨impelled the . . . government of Russia to issue *manifestos* —F.A.Ogg & Harold Zink⟩

²**manifesto** \"\ *vi* -ED/-ING/-ES **:** to issue a manifesto

¹**man·i·fold** \ˈmanəˌfōld\ *adj* [ME *manifold*, *manifald*, fr. OE *manigfeald*, fr. *manig* many + *-feald* -fold — more at MANY] **1 a :** marked by diversity or variety **:** numerous and varied ⟨performs the ~ duties required of him —J.H.Ferguson⟩ ⟨reveal its ~ attractions for the visitor —*London Calling*⟩ ⟨~ industries put the city in line with other important industrial centers —Samuel Van Valkenburg & Ellsworth Huntington⟩ **b :** NUMEROUS, MANY ⟨brought forth fruit ~ —J.G.Edwards⟩ **2 :** comprehending or uniting various features, kinds, characteristics **:** MULTIFARIOUS ⟨the romantic symphony, with its ~ melodic content —P.H.Lang⟩ **3 :** being so in many ways **:** rightfully so-called for many reasons ⟨a ~ liar⟩ **4 :** consisting of many of one kind combined **:** operating many of one kind of object ⟨a ~ bell pull⟩

²**manifold** \"\ *adv* [ME *manifold*, *manifald*, fr. *manifold*, *manifald*, adj.] **:** many times **:** a great deal **:** MANYFOLD ⟨will increase your blessings ~⟩

³manifold \"\ *n* [ME *manifold, manifald,* fr. *manifold, manifald,* adj.] **1 :** something that is manifold: as **a :** a whole uniting or consisting of many diverse elements ⟨the ~ of aspirations, passions, frustrations —Harry Slochower⟩ ⟨the unspeakably rich ~ of goings-on —Erwin Schrödinger⟩ ⟨bring into one picture the ~ of his character —John Buchan⟩ **b** [trans. of G *mannigfaltigkeit*] *Kantianism* **:** the totality of unorganized experience as it is presented in sense **c :** a metal chest with many valves by which watertight compartments, pumps, and the drains may be so connected that any or all of the pumps may be used to pump out any compartment **d :** a pipe fitting with several lateral outlets for connecting one pipe with others; *specif* **:** EXHAUST MANIFOLD **e :** AGGREGATE 5 **2** *dial chiefly Eng* **:** the third stomach of a ruminant — usu. used in pl.

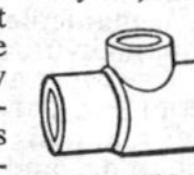
manifold 1d

⁴manifold \"\ *vb* -ED/-ING/-S [¹*manifold*] *vt* **1 :** to make many or several copies of esp. by the process of manifold writing ⟨~ a letter⟩ **2 :** to make manifold **:** MULTIPLY ⟨~*ed* many times the work which could be done⟩ **3 :** to collect or distribute (a fluid) or to assemble (as sources of supply) by means of a manifold ~ *vi* **:** to make several or many copies (as of a manuscript) **:** do manifold writing

man·i·fold·er \-də(r)\ *n* **:** one that manifolds; *esp* **:** a contrivance for manifold writing

man·i·fold·ly *adv* [ME *manyfaldly,* fr. *manifold, manifald* manifold + *-ly*] **:** in a manifold manner

man·i·fold·ness *n* -ES **:** the quality or state of being manifold ⟨the intricacy and ~ of things —J.A.Thomson & Patrick Geddes⟩

manifold paper *n* **:** a lightweight paper used with carbon paper to produce multiple copies

man·i·hot \'manə,hät\ *n, cap* [NL, fr. F, cassava, of Tupian origin — more at MANIOC] **:** a genus of economically important herbs or shrubs (family Euphorbiaceae) orig. tropical American but now widespread in the tropics, having alternate entire or palmate leaves, apetalous monoecious flowers and 3-seeded capsular fruit — see BITTER CASSAVA, CEARÁ RUBBER, SWEET CASSAVA

¹man·i·kin \'manəkən, -nēk-\ *n* -S [D *manneken, mannekijn,* little man, fr. MD *mannekijn,* dim. of *man;* akin to OE *man, mon* man — more at MAN] **1 :** MANNEQUIN **2 a :** a little man **:** DWARF, PYGMY ⟨a bright-eyed little ~, naked like all his people —C.S.Forester⟩ **3 :** a model of the human body commonly in detachable pieces for exhibiting the parts and organs, their position, and relations

²manikin \"\ *adj* **:** DIMINUTIVE, DWARF, PUNY

¹ma·nila *also* **ma·nil·la** \mə'nilə\ *adj* [fr. *Manila,* Philippines] **1** *usu cap* **:** of or from the city of Manila, Philippines **:** of the kind or style prevalent in Manila **2** [*Manila (paper)*] **a :** made of manila paper or board ⟨a ~ envelope⟩ ⟨a ~ folder⟩ ⟨~ cards⟩ **b** *usu cap* [*Manila (hemp)*] **:** made from Manila hemp ⟨*Manila* rope⟩ ⟨*Manila* yarn⟩

²manila \"\ *also* **manilla** *n* -S **1** [*Manila (hemp)*] **a** *sometimes cap* **:** ABACA **:** **b** *or* **manilla** \"\ [*Manila (rope)*] **:** a rope of manila **c** *or* **manilla** [*Manila (paper)*] **:** manila paper or board **2** *also* **manila cigar** *usu cap M* **:** a cigar or cheroot made of tobacco grown in the Philippines ⟨always carried on him about six or seven large *Manilas* —Osbert Sitwell⟩ **3** *usu cap* **:** MANILA COPAL **4 :** a light yellowish brown that is lighter, stronger and slightly redder than khaki, yellower and slightly darker than walnut brown, yellower and paler than cinnamon, and stronger than fallow

manila copal *or* **manila resin** *n, usu cap M* **:** a copal from any of several trees of the genus *Agathis* (esp. *A. alba*) usu. from the Philippines or Indonesia that varies from soft to hard depending on whether it is gathered after intentional tapping or accidental wounding of the trees and that is used chiefly in varnish — see BOEA, LOBA, MELENGKET, PONTIANAK; compare DAMMAR, KAURI

manila elemi *n, usu cap M* **:** an elemi obtained in the Philippines and parts of southeastern Asia from a tree (*Canarium luzonicum*)

manila grass *n, usu cap M* **:** a tropical Asiatic grass (*Zoisia matrella*) common in the Philippines and used more recently in America as a lawn grass

manila hemp *or* **manila fiber** *n, usu cap M* **:** ABACA

manila maguey *n* **:** CANTALA

ma·nila·man \-'-‚mən\ *n, pl* **manilamen** *cap* [*Manila,* Philippines + E *man*] **:** a native of the Philippines; *esp* **:** a sailor hailing from Manila, Philippines ⟨a nondescript crew such as lascars or *Manilamen* —Herman Melville⟩

manila paper *or* **manilla paper** *n, often cap M* **:** a strong and durable paper of a yellowish or buff color and smooth finish made from Manila hemp; *also* **:** a paper of similar color and finish regardless of fiber content

manila tamarind *n, usu cap M* **:** the edible pods of camachile

man·il·kara \,manəl'ka(a)rə\ *n, cap* [NL, fr. Malayan *manilkāra*] **:** a genus (family Sapotaceae) that was formerly included in *Mimusops* and comprises chiefly New World tropical timber trees some of which yield valuable gums — see BULLY TREE, MASSARANDUBA

ma·nil·la \mə'nē(y)ə, -ēlyə\ *n* -S [Pg *manilha* or Sp *manilla,* prob. fr. Catal *manilla,* dim. of *mà* hand, fr. L *manus* — more at MANUAL] **:** a piece of metal shaped like a horseshoe orig. mainly of copper alloys but later of iron used by some peoples of western Africa for ornamental purposes and as a medium of exchange esp. in conjunction with ceremonial exchanges

ma·nille \mə'nil\ *n* -S [modif. of Sp *malilla,* dim. of obs. Sp *mala* manille, fr. fem. of Sp *malo* bad, fr. L *malus* — more at SMALL] **:** the second highest trump in various card games esp. when it is a card that would have lower or the lowest rank if its suit were not trumps (as the seven of trumps in ombre or the nine of trumps in klaberjass)

ma·ni·ni \mə'nēnē\ *n* -S [Hawaiian] **:** CONVICT FISH; *esp* **:** a black-and-white form (*Hepatus triostegus*)

man·i·nose \'manə,nōz\ *var of* MANANOSAY

man–in–the–ground \'-‚-‚-\ *n* **:** BIGROOT

man in the moon [ME *mon in the mone*] **:** a fancied figure of a man or man's face suggested by the dark and bright areas of the moon

man in the street : an average or ordinary man **:** an average person ⟨carried Labor Party views to the *man in the street* —*Current Biog.*⟩; *specif* **:** an ordinary man without specialized knowledge of the field in question or of mediocre intellectual tastes or accomplishments ⟨simplify a message sufficiently to be understood by the *man in the street* —*Newsman*⟩ ⟨said that the *man in the street* tended to look upon book reading as a highbrow activity —*N.Y. Times*⟩

man·i·oc \'manē,äk *also* 'män-\ *or* **man·i·o·ca** \,manē'ōkə\ *also* **man·di·oc** \'mandē,äk\ *or* **man·di·o·ca** \,mandē'ōkə\ *n* -S [F *manioc* & Sp & Pg *mandioca,* of Tupian origin; akin to Tupi *maniaca, manioca, mandioca* cassava, Guarani *mandióg*] **:** CASSAVA

man·i·ple \'manəpəl\ *n* -S [ME *manaple,* fr. ML *manipulus,* fr. L, handful, sheaf, fr. *manus* hand; fr. its having been originally held in the hand — more at MANUAL] **1 :** an ecclesiastical vestment consisting of a narrow cloth band or scarf hanging from the left arm and symbolizing the napkin that deacons of the early church used in their table ministrations **2** [L *manipulus,* fr. *manipulus* handful, sheaf; fr. the ancient Roman custom of using a pole with a handful of hay attached as a standard for a company of soldiers] **a :** a subdivision of the Roman legion consisting of either 120 or 60 men **b** *obs* **:** a small body of soldiers **:** COMPANY **3** [L *manipulus*] *archaic* **:** HANDFUL

maniple 1

maniplies *var of* MANYPLIES

ma·nip·u·la·bil·i·ty \mə,nipyələ'biləd·ē\ *n* **:** the quality or state of being manipulable

ma·nip·u·la·ble \mə'nipyələbəl\ *adj* [*manipul*ate + *-able*] **:** MANIPULATABLE

ma·nip·u·lan·dum \mə,nipyə'landəm\ *n, pl* **manipulan·da** \-də\ [NL, fr. E *manipulate* + L *-andum* (neut. of *-andus,* 1st conj. gerundive ending)] *psychol* **:** something that is or is to be manipulated ⟨the instigator and ~ of behavior, the matrix within which all action must be described —R.R.Sears⟩

ma·nip·u·lar \mə'nipyələ(r)\ *adj* [L *manipularis,* fr. *manipulus* maniple + *-aris* -ar] **1 :** of or relating to the ancient Roman maniple **2** [influenced in meaning by *manipulation*] **:** MANIPULATORY ⟨~ operations⟩

ma·nip·u·lat·able \-yə,lād·əbəl\ *adj* **:** capable of being manipulated ⟨~ variables —S.C.Dodd⟩

ma·nip·u·late \mə'nipyə,lāt *sometimes* ÷ -pə,-\ *vt* -ED/-ING/-S [back-formation fr. *manipulation*] **1 :** to treat, work, or operate with the hands or by mechanical means **:** handle or manage esp. with skill or dexterity ⟨was a spastic child and found it difficult to ~ a pencil —*Current Biog.*⟩ ⟨a cat was trained to ~ an electric device —J.H.Masserman⟩ ⟨~ an injured limb⟩ **2 a :** to treat or manage with the mind or intellect ⟨nature may be so *manipulated* that mathematical laws may be applied to it —M.R.Cohen⟩ ⟨if we can only quantify our material and ~ it statistically —S.L.Payne⟩ ⟨expert both in *manipulating* the dialectic processes and in applying them to theology —H.O.Taylor⟩ **b** (1) **:** to control the action or course of by management **:** utilize by controlling and managing ⟨providence has strangely *manipulated* events toward this end —Agnes S. Turnbull⟩ ⟨wealth is *manipulated* much as it is in our society —Abram Kardiner⟩ ⟨*manipulating* a situation to achieve certain advantages —F.G.Hawley⟩ (2) **:** to control, manage, or play upon by artful, unfair, or insidious means esp. to one's own advantage ⟨*manipulated* the Indians for national purposes, involving them in successive wars —H.M.Hyman⟩ ⟨knew how to ~ his weaknesses —Mary Deasy⟩ ⟨being used and *manipulated* by the knowing men around him —*New Republic*⟩ (3) **:** to force (prices) up or down by matched orders, wash sales, fictitious reports, or similar methods ⟨groups who ~ the prices —Vicki Baum⟩ **3 :** to change by artful or unfair means so as to serve one's purpose **:** tamper with **:** DOCTOR ⟨considerably *manipulated* by the suppression . . . of a number of passages —Henry Fielding⟩ ⟨suspected that the police reports were *manipulated* —Evelyn G. Cruickshanks⟩ ⟨voting lists were *manipulated* —W.O.Douglas⟩ **syn** see HANDLE

ma·nip·u·la·tion \-‚-‚-'lāshən\ *n* -S [F, fr. *manipule* apothecary's handful (fr. L *manipulus* handful) + *-ation* — more at MANIPLE] **1 :** the act, process, or an instance of manipulating: as **a :** the act or an instance of handling with the hands or mechanical means ⟨accidents sometimes occurred through carelessness in ~ by the drivers —O.S.Nock⟩ ⟨~ by crushing, grinding, firing —Lewis Mumford⟩ **b :** manual examination and treatment of body parts; *esp* **:** adjustment of faulty structural relationships by manual means (as in the reduction of fractures or dislocations or the breaking down of adhesions) **c :** management or handling directed toward some object ⟨it needs careful ~ to prevent its being washed away —*Amer. Guide Series: Minn.*⟩ ⟨a passion for the ~ of language as music —F.A.Swinnerton⟩ ⟨used as a tool for the description and ~ of cultural data —Ralph Linton⟩ **d :** management with use of unfair, scheming, or underhanded methods esp. for one's own advantage ⟨swing the balance of political power . . . by ~ —Paul Blanshard⟩ ⟨~ is one of the dirtiest words in the new lexicon —W.H.Whyte⟩ **e :** activity by an individual or group intended to influence the behavior of market prices **2 :** the condition of being manipulated ⟨vulnerability to psychological ~ —M.W.Straight⟩

ma·nip·u·la·tive \-'-‚-,lād·|iv, -‚lə|, |t|, |ēv *also* |əv\ *adj* **:** of, relating to, or performed by manipulation ⟨~ practices⟩ — **ma·nip·u·la·tive·ly** \|əvlē, -li\ *adv*

ma·nip·u·la·tor \-,lād·ə(r), -ātə-\ *n* -S **:** one that manipulates: as **a :** a mechanical device for handling objects as desired without touching them with the hands **b :** a person engaged in activities designed to influence by artificial means the prices of stocks or commodities **c manipulators** *pl* **:** the thumb and index finger whose combined action largely controls the blade in fencing

ma·nip·u·la·to·ry \mə'nipyələ,tōrē, -tȯr-, -ri\ *adj* **:** MANIPULATIVE

man·i·pur \,manə'pu̇(ə)r, ,mən-\ *n* [fr. *Manipur,* state in India] **1** *usu cap* **:** an Indian breed of small speedy ponies of mixed Mongolian and Arab ancestry **2** -S *often cap* **:** an animal of the Manipur breed

man·i·pu·ri \,-‚-'pu̇rē\ *n, pl* **manipuri** *or* **manipuris** *usu cap* [fr. *Manipur* state] **1 a :** a people inhabiting the Manipur region of Assam near the Burma border **b :** a member of such people **c :** MEITHEI 2 **2 :** a dance form associated esp. with Manipur in northern India and characterized by a gentle lyrical style — compare BHARATA NATYA, KATHAK, KATHAKALI **3 :** MANIPUR

¹manis *pl of* MANI

²ma·nis \'mānəs\ *n, cap* [NL, prob. fr. L *manes* spirits of the dead; fr. their nocturnal habits — more at MANES] **:** the type genus of Manidae comprising the pangolins or restricted to the five-toed Asiatic pangolin

ma·nism \'mä,nizəm, 'mā,-\ *n* -S [*manes* + *-ism*] **:** the worship of the spirits of deceased humans **:** ANCESTOR CULT

ma·nis·tic \mä'nistik, mā'-\ *adj* [*manes* + *-istic*] **:** of or relating to manism

man·it \'manət\ *n* -S [by shortening & alter.] **:** MAN-MINUTE

man·i·to·ba \,manə'tōbə\ *adj, usu cap* [fr. *Manitoba,* province of Canada] **:** of or from the province of Manitoba **:** of the kind or style prevalent in Manitoba **:** MANITOBAN

manitoba maple *n, usu cap 1st M* **:** BOX ELDER

¹man·i·to·ban \-bən\ *adj, usu cap* [*Manitoba,* Canada + E *-an*] **1 :** of, relating to, or characteristic of Manitoba, Canada **2 :** of, relating to, or characteristic of the people of Manitoba

²manitoban \"\ *n* -S *cap* **:** a native or inhabitant of the province of Manitoba, Canada

man·i·tou *or* **man·i·tu** \'manə,tü\ *also* **man·i·to** \-,tō\ *n* -S [of Algonquian origin; akin to Ojibwa *manito* spirit, god, Natick *manitto,* Shawnee *maneto*] **1 a :** one of the Algonquian deities or spirits dominating the forces of nature **b :** an image or spirit of such a deity **2 :** a supernatural force or spiritual energy which gives power to spirits, deities, and natural forces

ma·niu \mä'nē'ü\ *n* -S [AmerSp *mañiú*] **:** a Patagonian timber tree (*Saxegothaea conspicua*) of the family Taxaceae that yields wood valued for interior work

ma·ni wall \'mänē-\ *n* [*mani* fr. Tibetan, a prayer carved on the stones in such walls, fr. Skt *maṇi* jewel (as in *om maṇi padme hūṃ* Oh, the jewel on the lotus, Amen — the words of the prayer)] **:** a wall made of stones inscribed with a Lamaist prayer

man jack *n* **:** individual man **:** single one **:** MAN ⟨under suspicion . . . every *man jack* of us —Ngaio Marsh⟩ ⟨as good as any *man jack* —Norman Mailer⟩

man·jak \'man,jak\ *n* -S [Calinago] **:** asphalt found esp. on Barbados and used for making varnish and insulating electric cables and for fuel

man·ka·to \man'kād·ō\ *n* -S *usu cap* [fr. *Mankato,* Minn.] **:** a substage of the Wisconsin glacial stage

man–keen \'-‚-\ *adj* [¹*man* + *keen*] **1** *dial Eng, of an animal* **:** disposed to attack human beings **:** SAVAGE **2** *dial Eng, of a woman* **:** love-smitten **:** fond of men

man·kie \'maŋki\ *n* -S [by shortening & alter.] *Scot* **:** CALAMANCO

man–killer \'-‚-‚-\ *n* [ME, fr. ¹*man* + *killer*] **:** one that kills humans

¹mankind \(')‚-'-, *in sense 2* '-‚-\ *n sing but sing or pl in constr* [ME, fr. ¹*man* + *kind*] **1 :** the human race **:** the totality of human beings ⟨~ speaks many languages —Leonard Bloomfield⟩ ⟨~ have agreed in admiring great talents —James Boswell⟩ **2 :** men as distinguished from women

²mankind *adj, obs* **:** having masculine traits **:** like a virago

³mankind *adj* [origin unknown] *obs* **:** FIERCE, SAVAGE, FURIOUS

man·less \'manləs\ *adj* **1 :** destitute of men ⟨an unaccountably ~ cocktail party —*Time*⟩ **2** *obs* **:** UNMANLY — **man·less·ly** *adv* — **man·less·ness** *n* -ES

man·li·hood \'manlē,hu̇d\ *n* [*manly* + *-hood*] **:** MANLINESS

¹manlike \'-‚-\ *adj* [ME, fr. *man* + *like*] **1 :** resembling man **:** having the form or nature of a man ⟨hairy ~ creatures —*Blue Bk.*⟩ **2 :** befitting or belonging to a man **:** MANLY, MANNISH, MASCULINE ⟨simple, vigorous . . . ~ passion —*Forum*⟩ **syn** see MALE

²manlike \"\ *adv* **:** as a man **:** MANFULLY ⟨meet the danger ~⟩

man·like·ly *adv* [¹*manlike* + *-ly*] **:** in the manner of a man

man·like·ness *n* **:** the quality or state of being like a man

man·li·ly \'manlәlē\ *adv* **:** in a manly manner

man·li·ness \-nlēnəs\ *n* -ES [ME *manlines,* fr. *manly* + *-nes* -ness] **:** the quality or state of being manly

man·ling \-nliŋ\ *n* -S [¹*man* + *-ling*] **:** a little man

man lock *n* **:** AIR LOCK 1a

¹man·ly \'manlē, -aan-, -li\ *adj* -ER/-EST [ME, fr. *man* + *-ly* (adj. suffix)] **1 a :** having qualities appropriate to a man **:** not effeminate or timorous **:** bold, resolute, and open in conduct or bearing ⟨neither altogether coward nor brave, neither ~ nor sissified —John Reed⟩ **b** (1) **:** belonging to or appropriate in character to a man ⟨~ sports⟩ ⟨beer is a ~ drink —Giles Playfair⟩ ⟨a big booming ~ voice⟩ (2) **:** of undaunted courage **:** GALLANT, BRAVE ⟨seemed a big ~ thing to say —R.P. Warren⟩ ⟨not a very ~ thing . . . to come here and browbeat a woman —A. Conan Doyle⟩ ⟨a ~ disregard of his enemies —H.E.Scudder⟩ **2** *obs* **:** ADULT, MATURE **syn** see MALE

²manly *adv* [ME, fr. *man* + *-ly* (adv. suffix)] **:** in a manly manner: as **a** *obs* **:** COURAGEOUSLY **b** *obs* **:** EXCELLENTLY

man–made \'-'-\ *adj* **:** manufactured, created, or constructed by man ⟨*man-made* verbal systems —A.H.S.Korzybski⟩ ⟨*man-made* laws⟩; *specif* **:** SYNTHETIC ⟨*man-made* fibers⟩

man midwife *n, archaic* **:** ACCOUCHEUR

man–milliner \'-'-‚-‚-\ *n, pl* **man–milliners** *or* **men–milliners :** a man who makes or sells millinery

man–minute \'-‚-‚-\ *n* **:** a unit of measurement (as in time-motion study) consisting of the amount of work done by one worker in one minute

mann– *or* **manno–** *comb form* [ISV, fr. *manna*] **1 :** manna ⟨*mann*ite⟩ ⟨*mann*ose⟩ **2 :** related to mannose ⟨*mann*an⟩ **3 :** *manno-, usu ital* **:** having the stereochemical arrangement of atoms or groups found in mannose ⟨D-*manno*-3-hexulose⟩ ⟨*manno*-saccharic acid⟩

man·na \'manə\ *n* -S [ME, fr. OE, fr. LL, fr. Gk, fr. Heb *mān*] **1 a :** food miraculously supplied to the Israelites in their journey through the wilderness **b :** divinely supplied spiritual nourishment **c :** something of value that falls one's way **:** WINDFALL ⟨the seasonal ~ of flying ants and palm grubs are . . . joyfully accepted for the cooking pot —Norman Lewis⟩ ⟨onto the pavement fell a strange ~ of caramels and razors —Constantine FitzGibbon⟩ **2 a :** the sweetish dried exudation of the European flowering ash and related plants that contains mannitol as its chief constituent and has been used medicinally as a laxative and demulcent **b :** a similar product from various other plants (as a tamarisk) **3 a :** MANNA LICHEN **b :** MANNA GRASS **c :** MANNA ASH

manna ash *n* **:** any of several European ashes yielding manna; *esp* **:** an ash (*Fraxinus ornus*) that has flowers with sepals and greenish white petals — called also *flowering ash*

manna grass *n* **:** a grass of the genus *Glyceria*

manna gum *n* **1 :** an Australian eucalypt (*Eucalyptus viminalis*) that yields a false manna **2 :** LERP

manna insect *or* **manna scale** *n* **:** a scale insect (*Trabutina mannipara*) causing production of manna on the tamarisk

manna lichen *n* **1 :** any of several Old World lichens of the genus *Lecanora* (esp. *L. esculenta, L. affinis,* and *L. fruticulosa*) that have semicrustaceous scaly-foliose or fruticose thalli that roll up and are blown about often in large quantities over the African and Arabian deserts and are much used there for food by man and animals **2 :** a lichen (*Gyrophora esculenta*) used in Japan for food

man·nan \'ma,nan, -‚nən\ *n* -S [ISV *mann-* + *-an*] **:** any of several polysaccharides that yield mannose on hydrolysis and occur in the cell walls of many plants (as in ivory nuts and other seeds and in the wood esp. of coniferous trees) and in micro-organisms (as yeast)

manna sugar *n* **:** MANNITOL

manned *adj* [fr. past part. of ²*man*] **:** carrying or performed by a man ⟨a ~ earth satellite is a necessary research step —H.M. Schmeck⟩ ⟨~ stellar explorations⟩ ⟨~ space flight —*Science*⟩

man·ne·quin \'manəkən\ *n* -S [F, fr. D *manneken, mannekijn,* little man — more at MANIKIN] **1 a :** an artist's, tailor's, or dressmaker's lay figure **b :** DUMMY 3a(1) **2 :** a woman who models clothing **:** MODEL

¹man·ner \'manə(r)\ *n* -S [ME *manere,* fr. OF *maniere,* fr. (assumed) VL *manuaria,* fr. fem. of LL *manuarius* of the hand, fr. L *manus* hand + *-arius* -ary — more at MANUAL] **1 a :** KIND, SORT ⟨what ~ of man is he⟩ ⟨what ~ of train had borne him homeward —Ben Riker⟩ **b :** KINDS, SORTS — now used in the phrase *all manner of* ⟨observed all ~ of important people —Oscar Handlin⟩ ⟨picked up all ~ of more or less useful information —J.B.Benefield⟩ **c** *obs* **:** NATURE, CHARACTER, CONDITION — used in the phrase *the manner of* ⟨the ~ of their work and weary pain —Edmund Spenser⟩ **2 a** (1) **:** a characteristic or customary mode of acting **:** natural or normal behavior **:** HABIT, USAGE, CUSTOM ⟨stopped to speak, after the ~ of the country —Ellen Glasgow⟩ ⟨spoke to all the children, as was his ~⟩ (2) **:** the mode or method in which something is done or happens **:** a mode of procedure or way of acting **:** WAY, MODE, FASHION ⟨the ~ of entering the water . . . is important —John Tassos⟩ ⟨responded in a lively ~⟩ ⟨the ~ in which traits are transmitted⟩ ⟨in a haphazard and very far from complete ~ —R.W.Steel⟩ (3) **:** method of artistic execution or mode of presentation esp. as distinguished from the matter presented **:** STYLE, FORM ⟨examples of several earlier ~*s* —*Times Lit. Supp.*⟩ ⟨offers plenty of room for many jazz ~*s* —Wilder Hobson⟩ (4) **:** a method or style characterizing a period or phase of an artist's work ⟨a group of pictures done in his early ~⟩ (5) **:** a character that marks an artist's work as uniquely his own **:** a distinctive or personal character, quality, or tone ⟨style belongs to the age, his ~ to the poet —J.P.Bishop⟩ ⟨~ has been replaced by style —R.B.West⟩ ⟨a ~ of her own —Henry Reed b.1914⟩ **b** (1) **manners** *pl, archaic* **:** the habitual conduct or moral character of a person (2) **manners** *pl* **:** social conduct or rules of conduct as shown in the prevalent customs **:** social conditions **:** mode of life ⟨the brutal ~*s* of an age given to bear-baiting and similar amusements⟩ ⟨the novel is a study in the ~*s* of a class⟩; *specif* **:** the morality of a time as reflected in its prevalent customs or social practices ⟨the licentious ~*s* of a corrupt society⟩ (3) **manners** *pl, archaic* **:** good customs or mode of life **c** (1) **:** characteristic or distinctive bearing, air, or deportment ⟨had . . . ~ as distinct from *manners* — a certain poise, genial but always extremely self-possessed —Joyce Cary⟩ (2) **manners** *pl* **:** habitual conduct or deportment in social intercourse evaluated according to some conventional standard of politeness or civility **:** BEHAVIOR ⟨never guilty of bad ~*s*⟩ ⟨watch your ~*s*⟩ (3) **manners** *pl* **:** good manners ⟨it wouldn't have been ~*s* —Ruth Park⟩ (4) *of an animal* **:** ACTION, DEPORTMENT — usu. used in pl. ⟨the dog pointed with excellent ~*s*⟩ (5) **manners** *pl, archaic* **:** forms of courtesy or respect — usu. used in the phrase *to make one's manners* ⟨made their ~*s* to the squire —S.H.Adams⟩ (6) **:** a distinguished or stylish air ⟨taught to acquire a ~ suitable to her station⟩ **syn** see METHOD — **by any manner of means** *or* **by no manner of means :** in any or no way whatever **:** not at all ⟨are you angry with me? *By no manner of means*⟩ — **in a manner** *or* **in a manner of speaking :** so to speak **:** as it were ⟨he's *in a manner* stone dead —Horace Kephart⟩ ⟨the problem is only asleep, *in a manner of speaking*⟩ — **to the manner born 1** *obs* **:** born to follow or obey a certain practice or custom **2 :** fitted by birth, rearing, or long training or experience to occupy some post or position ⟨was *to the manner born* in the court circles of Versailles —C.G.Bowers⟩

²manner *var of* MAINOUR

man·ner·able \'manərəbəl\ *adj, dial* **:** POLITE, MANNERLY

man·nered \'manə(r)d\ *adj* [ME *manered,* fr. *manere* manner + *-ed*] **1 :** having manners of a specified kind — usu. used in combination ⟨well-*mannered* folk of comfortable means —Robert Shaplen⟩ **2 a** *archaic* **:** dealing with or portraying social manners or customs ⟨no hand at describing costumes, a great requisite in . . . ~ pictures —Charles Lamb⟩ **b** (1) **:** having or displaying a particular or individual manner or style ⟨delightfully ~ . . . lithographs of earlier American life —*Times Lit. Supp.*⟩ ⟨beautifully ~ without ever verging on the precious —Vernon Jarratt⟩ (2) **:** having an artificial or stilted character **:** not natural or spontaneous ⟨~, but imaginative —Dorothy Sayers⟩ ⟨find it either cold and ~ —C.J. Rolo⟩ ⟨brief, ~ and unlikeliest idiom —*Times Lit. Supp.*⟩

man·ner·ing \-nəriŋ\ *n* -s [¹*manner* + *-ing*] **:** a preliminary training (as of a colt) in manners

man·ner·ism \ˈmanəˌrizəm\ *n* -s [¹*manner* + *-ism*] **1 a :** exaggerated or affected emulation of or adherence to a particular style or manner **:** stilted or artificial quality **:** ARTIFICIALITY, PRECIOSITY ⟨refined almost to the point of ~ —Winthrop Sargeant⟩ ⟨avoids all tiresome ~ —Gouverneur Paulding⟩ ⟨an almost unrelieved ~ and melancholy have taken hold of mid-century poetry —Louise Bogan⟩ **b** *often cap* **:** an art style in late 16th century Europe characterized by spatial incongruity and excessive elongation of the human figures **2 :** a characteristic mode or peculiarity of action, bearing, or treatment ⟨each of us has his own ~*s* in sleeping —Geoffrey Jefferson⟩ ⟨free of ~*s* copied from the great —David Sylvester⟩ ⟨some of the birds' curious customs and ~*s* —E.A.Armstrong⟩

man·ner·ist \-ˌrəst\ *n* -s [¹*manner* + *-ist*] **1 :** an artist whose works show a strong tendency to imitation, to obedience to the rules of a school, or to a mannerism of his own **2** *often cap* **:** any of the artists of late 16th century Europe practicing mannerism

man·ner·is·tic \ˌmanəˈristik\ *also* **man·ner·is·ti·cal** \-təkəl\ *adj* **:** exhibiting or characterized by mannerisms; *esp, psychiatry* **:** characterized by stylized, individualized, often bizarre patterns or traits of behavior — **man·ner·is·ti·cal·ly** \-tək(ə)lē\ *adv*

man·ner·ize \ˈmanəˌrīz\ *vt* -ED/-ING/-s **:** to make manneristic

man·ner·less \ˈmanə(r)ləs\ *adj* [ME *maner-les*, fr. *manere* manner + *-les* -less — more at MANNER] **:** destitute of manners **:** UNMANNERLY — **man·ner·less·ness** *n* -ES

man·ner·li·ness \-lēnəs, -lin-\ *n* -ES **:** the quality or state of being mannerly

¹**man·ner·ly** \-lē, -li\ *adj* [ME *manerly*, fr. *manere* manner + *-ly*] **1** *obs* **:** DECOROUS, SEEMLY, MORAL **2 :** showing good manners **:** CIVIL, RESPECTFUL, POLITE ⟨pleasant to record that they were agreeable and ~ —A.W.Long⟩

²**mannerly** \"\ *adv* [ME *manerly*, fr. *manerly*, adj.] **1** *obs* **:** DECENTLY, DECOROUSLY **2 :** with good manners **:** POLITELY, RESPECTFULLY, CIVILLY ⟨will always pull ~ over to the curb —Christopher Morley⟩

manners *pl of* MANNER

man·ner·some \ˈmanə(r)səm\ *adj* [¹*manner* + *-some*] *chiefly dial* **:** MANNERLY ⟨required that they be ~ and quiet —Edward Kimbrough⟩

man·nes·mann process \ˈmänəsˌmän-, ˈmanəsmən-\ *n, usu cap M* [after Reinhard M. *Mannesmann* †1922 Ger. industrialist and inventor] **:** a process of making seamless tubes from metal billets by piercing

man·ness \ˈmannəs\ *n* -ES **:** the distinctive or differential characteristics of man

mann·heim \ˈmanˌhīm, ˈmän-\ *adj, usu cap* [fr. *Mannheim*, Germany] **:** of or from the city of Mannheim, Germany **:** of the kind or style prevalent in Mannheim

man·nich reaction \ˈmänik-\ *n, usu cap M* [after Carl *Mannich* †1947 Ger. chemist] **:** the condensation typically of ammonia or a primary or secondary amine with formaldehyde and a ketone to form a beta-amino ketone

man·nie \ˈmani\ *n* [¹*man* + *-ie*] **1** *chiefly Scot* **:** a small or undersized man **2** *chiefly Scot* **:** a small boy **:** LAD

man·ni·kin \ˈmanəkən\ *n* -s [D *manneken, mannekijn* — more at MANIKIN] **1 :** MANIKIN **2 :** any of numerous small weaverbirds (genus *Lonchura*) of Africa, Asia, and Australasia

manning *n* -s [fr. gerund of ²*man*] **1 :** the act or action of supplying with men ⟨money destined for the equipping and ~ of the fleet —T.B.Macaulay⟩ **2 :** CREW ⟨found a post for him in our ~ —*Scots Mag.*⟩

manning table *n* **:** a survey chart or inventory for scheduling manpower requirements in an industrial plant typically showing each operation with number of workers and time required, each worker classified as to job, experience, handicaps, and the minimum time for training a replacement

man·nish \ˈmanish, -aan-, -nēsh\ *adj* [ME, fr. *man* + *-ish*] **1 a :** resembling a man as distinguished from a woman **:** UNWOMANLY, MASCULINE ⟨those ~ women —H.M.Parshley⟩ **b :** resembling or suggesting that of a man ⟨a ~ jacket⟩ ⟨low-heeled ~ oxfords —W.H.Wright⟩ ⟨~ pajamas⟩ ⟨a ~ hair-do⟩ **c :** peculiar to or characteristic of a man as distinguished from a woman ⟨with true ~ arrogance⟩ **2 :** relating to or characteristic of an adult male as distinguished from a child **syn** see MALE

man·nish·ness *n* -ES **:** the quality or state of being mannish

man·ni·tan \ˈmanəˌtan\ *n* -s [ISV *mannite* + *-an*] **:** an anhydride (as styracitol) $C_6H_{12}O_5$ of mannitol that with fatty acids forms esters useful as emulsifying agents

man·nite \ˈmaˌnīt\ *n* -s [F, fr. *mann-* + *-ite*] **:** MANNITOL — not used systematically

man·ni·tol \ˈmanəˌtōl, -tōl\ *n* -s [ISV *mannite* + *-ol*] **:** a slightly sweet crystalline hexahydroxy alcohol $C_6H_8(OH)_6$ known in three optically isomeric forms obtainable by reduction of mannose; *esp* **:** the levorotatory D-form that is the principal constituent of the manna of manna ash and is found also in many other higher plants, algae, and fungi but is usu. manufactured along with sorbitol and that is used chiefly in the form of the hexanitrate and in aqueous solution for intravenous administration as a diagnostic test of kidney function

mannitol hexanitrate *n* **:** an explosive crystalline ester $C_6H_8(NO_3)_6$ made by nitration of mannitol and used in blasting caps and in medicine in admixture with a carbohydrate (as lactose) in the treatment of angina pectoris and vascular hypertension

manno- — see MANN-

man·nonic acid \məˈnänik, -ˈnōn-\ *n* [ISV *mann-* + *-one* + *-ic*] **:** a syrupy acid $C_5H_6(OH)_5COOH$ formed by oxidizing mannose

man·nose \ˈmaˌnōs\ *n* -s [ISV *mann-* + *-ose*] **:** an aldose sugar $HOCH_2(CHOH)_4CHO$ known in dextrorotatory, levorotatory, and racemic forms that are epimers of the corresponding forms of glucose; *esp* **:** the D-form obtained usu. by the hydrolysis of the mannan in ivory nut turnings or in impure form by treatment of D-glucose with alkali

man·nu·ron·ic acid \ˌmanyəˈränik-\ *n* [ISV *mann-* + *uronic*] **:** an aldehyde-acid $HOOC(CHOH)_4CHO$ related to mannose and obtained by hydrolysis of alginic acid

¹**ma·no** \ˈmä(ˌ)nō\ *n* -s [Sp, lit., hand, fr. L *manus* — more at MANUAL] **:** a handstone used as the upper millstone for grinding maize and other grains — compare METATE

²**mano** \"\ *n, pl* **mano** *or* **manos** *usu cap* **1 a :** a Negro people inhabiting the northern tip of the central province of the Republic of Liberia, West Africa, and the adjacent territory of French West Africa to the north **b :** a member of such people **2 :** a Mande language of the Mano people

³**ma·no** \məˈnō\ *n* -s [Hawaiian *manō* shark] *Hawaii* **:** any of several large sharks (as the man-eater)

mano- *comb form* [F, fr. Gk, loose, sparse, infrequent, fr. *manos* — more at MONK] **:** gas **:** vapor ⟨*manograph*⟩

ma·no·bo \məˈnō(ˌ)bō\ *n, pl* **manobo** *or* **manobos** *usu cap* **1 a :** any of several closely related peoples inhabiting central Mindanao, Philippines **b :** a member of any of such peoples **2 :** any of the closely related Austronesian languages of the Manobo peoples

ma·no des·tra \ˈmänōˈdestrə\ *n* [It] **:** the right hand — abbr. *M D, D M;* used as a direction in music for keyboard playing

manoeuvre *or* **manoeuver** *var of* MANEUVER

man-of-all-work \ˈ==ˈ=ˌ=\ *n, pl* **men-of-all-work :** a domestic employee who performs all kinds of work and services about the home

man of god *cap G* [ME] **1 :** a godly man; *specif* **:** SAINT **2 :** a minister or other ecclesiastic ⟨a *man of God* and unquestionably a trustworthy man —Earl Hamner⟩

man of law [ME] **:** LAWYER

man of letters 1 : a learned man **:** SCHOLAR **2 :** a literary man **:** AUTHOR, LITTÉRATEUR

man of parts : a talented or gifted man **:** a man of notable endowments or capacity ⟨no *man of parts* . . . would accept so feeble a role —H.S.Truman⟩ ⟨not in the nature of a *man of parts* to stick to the same plodding trade —Harriette Wilson⟩

man of straw 1 : an imaginary argument of no substance advanced in order to be easily confuted or an imaginary adversary advancing such an argument ⟨seems to be looking for a *man of straw* to belabor —*Jour. of Forestry*⟩ **2 :** a person usu. without means or position who is vested with some nominal or fictitious post or responsibility as a cover in proceedings of doubtful legality or to shield the real author of an action **:** FRONT, DUMMY ⟨a *man of straw* who appears to any summons that may be brought against the paper —F.M.Ford⟩

man of the cloth : a minister or other ecclesiastic

man-of-the-earth \ˈ===ˈ=\ *n, pl* **men-of-the-earth** *or* **men-of-the-earths 1 :** an American morning glory (*Ipomoea pandurata*) having an enormous starchy root — called also *manroot, wild potato* **2 :** a long rooted morning glory (*Ipomoea leptophylla*) of the western U. S.

man of the house : the chief male in a household

man of the woods 1 [trans. of Malay *orang hutan*] **:** ORANGUTAN **2** *Austral* **:** OLD MAN 3

man of the world 1 : a man familiar with the ways of the world and typically free from sentimentality, excessive delicacy of feelings, or illusions **:** a practical or worldly man of much experience ⟨his greatest vanity was that he was a *man of the world* —F.A.Swinnerton⟩ **2 :** a man of the world of fashion or high life ⟨began his career as a *man of the world* at the . . . court —R.A.Hall b.1911⟩

man-of-war \ˈ==ˈ=\ *n, pl* **men-of-war 1 :** a combatant warship of a recognized navy **2 :** MAN-O'-WAR BIRD

man-of-war fish *n* **:** a small fish (*Nomeus gronovii*) of the family Nomeidae that is common in the Gulf of Mexico and that lives among the tentacles of the Portuguese man-of-war

man·o·graph \ˈmanəˌgraf, -ráf\ *n* [ISV *mano-* + *-graph*] **:** an optical device for making an indicator card for high speed of an engine

ma·noir \maˈnwär\ *n* -s [F, fr. OF, habitation, manor — more at MANOR] **:** a manor house or country residence in a French-speaking country

ma·no·le·ti·na \məˌnōləˈtēnə\ *n* -s [Sp, fr. *Manolete* (Manuel R. Sánchez) †1947 Spanish matador + *-ina* (fr. fem. of *-ino* -ine, fr. L *-inus*)] **:** a right-handed pase in bullfighting in which a piece of the muleta is held by the left hand behind the back

ma·nom·e·ter \məˈnämədə(r), -mətə-\ *n* [F *manomètre*, fr. *mano-* + *-mètre* -meter] **1 :** an instrument for measuring the pressure of gases and vapors commonly by balancing the pressure against a column of liquid (as mercury) in a U-tube or against the elastic force of a spring or an elastic diaphragm (as in an aneroid barometer) **:** PRESSURE GAUGE **2 :** an instrument for measuring blood pressure **:** SPHYGMOMANOMETER — **man·o·met·ric** \ˌmanəˈmetrik, -rēk\ *also* **man·o·met·ri·cal** \-rəkəl, -rēk-\ *adj* — **man·o·met·ri·cal·ly** \-rək(ə)lē, -rēk-, -li\ *adv* — **ma·nom·e·try** \məˈnämətrē\ *n* -ES

manometer 1

manometric flame *n* **:** a flame produced by a device in which pressure variations due to sound waves are communicated to the gas feeding the flame and cause it to fluctuate in height so that when viewed in a revolving mirror the image of the flame appears as a luminous band with deep serrations corresponding roughly to the sound vibrations

ma·no·min \ˈmänəˌmin\ *n* -s [Ojibway *mânomin*, fr. *mâno* good + *min* grain, seed] **:** WILD RICE 1

man on horseback [after the *Man on Horseback*, nickname of Georges E. J. M. Boulanger †1891 Fr. chauvinistic general and demagogue; fr. his frequent appearance before the Paris crowds mounted on a black horse] **1 :** a man typically a military figure whose ambitions, personal popularity, and pretensions to be destined to save the nation or lead it to greatness mark him as a potential dictator ⟨endangered by *men on horseback* or rabble-rousers —Telford Taylor⟩ ⟨used to advantage by the first rascally *man on horseback* who comes along —*New Yorker*⟩ **2 :** DICTATOR, CAUDILLO; *esp* **:** a military dictator ⟨the *man on horseback* . . . comes to power by way of a coup, usually with army support —Bruce Bliven b. 1889⟩

man on the street : MAN IN THE STREET

man·op·to·scope \maˈnäptəˌskōp\ *n* [L *manus* hand + E *opt-* + *-scope* — more at MANUAL] **:** a device for determining ocular dominance

man·or \ˈmanə(r)\ *n* -s [ME *maner*, fr. OF *manoir* habitation, manor, fr. *manoir* to sojourn, dwell, fr. L *manēre* to remain, sojourn — more at MANSION] **1 a :** the house or hall of an estate **:** MANSION ⟨quarreled good-naturedly over the location of the ~ —Frank Yerby⟩ **b :** the house of a lord with the land belonging to it **:** a landed estate **2 a** (1) **:** a unit of English rural territorial organization; *esp* **:** a unit of English social, economic, and administrative organization in the middle ages consisting of an estate under a lord enjoying a variety of rights over land and tenants including the right to hold court and usu. having tenants of varying degrees of freedom and servitude and marked by a large degree of economic self-sufficiency (2) **:** a basically similar unit of social, economic, and administrative organization varying in specific features from region to region (as in medieval Europe) **b :** a tract of land in No. America occupied by tenants who pay a fee-farm rent to the proprietor; *specif* **:** a tract of land in New York granted by the king of Great Britain in colonial days either by patent or in confirmation of grants from the States-General of Holland to proprietors holding by perpetual rent in money or in kind

man orchid *n* **:** MALE ORCHIS

manor house *n* **:** the house of the lord of a manor

ma·no·ri·al \məˈnōrēəl, -nōr-\ *adj* **1 :** of or relating to a manor ⟨~ accounts⟩ ⟨~ documents⟩ ⟨~ custom⟩ **2 :** based on the manor ⟨a ~ economy⟩

manorial court *n* **:** a local court held by the lord of a manor in medieval England and colonial America

ma·no·ri·al·ism \-ēəˌlizəm\ *n* -s **:** a system of economic, social, and political organization based on the medieval manor — compare FEUDALISM

ma·no·ri·al·ize \-ˌlīz\ *vt* -ED/-ING/-s **:** to cause to conform or subject to the tenure of the manorial system ⟨*manorialized* estates created by the Norman lords —F.M.Stenton⟩

manorial system *n* **:** MANORIALISM

manos *pl of* MANO

ma·no si·ni·stra \ˌmä(ˌ)nōsəˈnē(ˌ)strä\ *n* [It] **:** the left hand — used as a direction in music; abbr. *MS, SM*

man·o·stat \ˈmanəˌstat\ *n* -s [*mano-* + *-stat*] **:** a device for automatically maintaining a constant pressure within an enclosure — **man·o·stat·ic** \ˌ==ˈstad·ik\ *adj*

man-o'-war bird \ˈ==ˈ=-\ *or* **man-o'-war hawk** *n* **1 :** FRIGATE BIRD **2 :** SKUA **3 :** ALBATROSS

man power *n* **1 a :** power available from or supplied by the physical effort of man **b :** a unit of power assumed to be the rate at which a man can perform mechanical work; *sometimes* **:** one tenth of a horsepower **2** *usu* **manpower** \ˈ=ˌ==\ **:** the strength (as of a nation, community, or industry) expressed in terms of available persons **:** personnel available or competent to serve **:** human resources ⟨requires a tremendous amount of engineering *manpower* —*Controller*⟩ ⟨the largest single supplier of educated *manpower* —T.D.Durrance⟩ ⟨*manpower* problems⟩; *specif* **:** the strength of a nation in terms of persons available for military service

¹**man·qué** \(ˈ)mänˈkā, -äŋ-\ *adj* [F, fr. past part. of *manquer* to lack, fr. It *mancare* — more at MANCANDO] **:** failing to achieve a desired status through the force of circumstances or some inner flaw **:** short of or frustrated in the fulfillment of one's aspirations **:** UNSUCCESSFUL — used postpositively ⟨an artist ~, now condemned to the operation of a candy store —Wolcott Gibbs⟩ ⟨already he was spoken of as the great man ~ —J.C.Smith⟩ ⟨the best writing in his book hints to me of a poet ~ —*Saturday Rev.*⟩

²**manque** \ˈmäⁿk, -äŋk\ *n* -s [F, lit., lack, defect, fr. *manquer*] **:** the low numbers (1 to 18) in roulette when a bet is placed on them

man·quel·ler \ˈmanˌkwelə(r)\ *n* -s [ME, fr. ¹*man* + *queller* killer, fr. *quellen* to kill, quell + *-er* — more at QUELL] *archaic* **:** a killer of men **:** MURDERER, HOMICIDE

man·rent \ˈmanˌrent\ *n* [ME (Sc), alter. of *manred, manreden*, fr. OE *manrǣden*, fr. *man* + *rǣden* condition — more at MAN, KINDRED] *archaic* **:** HOMAGE — usu. used in the phrases *bond of manrent* or *band of manrent*

manroot \ˈ=ˌ=\ *n* **1 :** MAN-OF-THE-EARTH **2 :** BIGROOT

manrope \ˈ=ˌ=\ *n* **:** a side rope (as to a ship's gangway or ladder) used as a handrail

manrope knot *n* **:** a double wall knot with a double crown

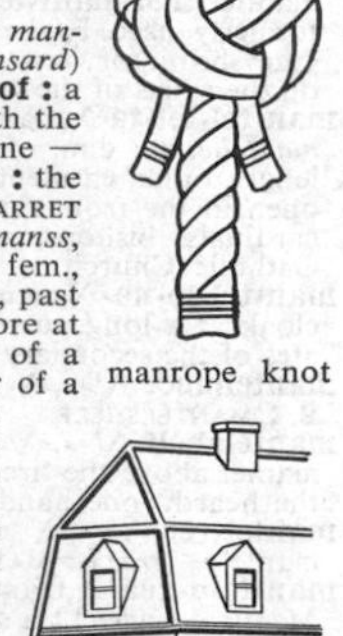

manrope knot

mans *pres 3d sing of* MAN, *pl of* MAN

man·sa·ka \mänˈsäkə\ *n* -s *usu cap* **:** MANDAYA

man·sard \ˈmanˌsärd, -sȧd\ *n* -s [F *mansarde*, after François *Mansart* (*Mansard*) †1666 Fr. architect] **1** *or* **mansard roof :** a roof having two slopes on all sides with the lower slope steeper than the upper one — compare CURB ROOF, GAMBREL ROOF **2 :** the story formed by a mansard roof **:** GARRET

manse \ˈman(t)s, -aa(ə)n-\ *n* -s [ME *manss*, fr. ML *mansa, mansus, mansum*, fr. fem., masc. & neut. respectively of L *mansus*, past part. of *manēre* to remain, dwell — more at MANSION] **1** *archaic* **:** the dwelling of a householder **:** the house of the holder of a homestead **2 :** the residence of a clergyman; *esp* **:** the house assigned to or occupied by a Presbyterian clergyman **3 :** a hide of land

manservant \ˈ=ˌ==\ *n, pl* **menservants :** a male servant: as **a :** an indentured male servant **b :** VALET

mans·field·ite \ˈmanzˌfēlˌdīt, -n(t)s,f-\ *n* -s [George R. *Mansfield* †1947 Amer. geologist + E *-ite*] **:** a mineral $Al(AsO_4).2H_2O$ that consists of hydrous arsenate of aluminum and is isomorphous with scorodite

mansard 1

manshift \ˈ=ˌ=\ *n* **1 :** SHIFT 2b(2) **2 :** a unit of work output equal to that of one man working through one shift ⟨output per ~ is an inadequate criterion of the human effort employed in raising coal —*Economist*⟩

man·si \ˈmänsē\ *n, pl* **mansi** *or* **mansis** *cap* [Russ, fr. Vogul *manśi*] **:** VOGUL 1

man·sion \ˈmanchən, ˈmaan-\ *n* -s [ME *mansioun*, fr. MF *mansion*, fr. L *mansion-, mansio* act of staying or sojourning, habitation, dwelling, fr. *mansus* (past part. of *manēre* to remain, sojourn, dwell) + *-ion-, -io* -ion; akin to OIr *ainmne* patience, Gk *menein* to remain, Toch A&B *mäsk-* to be] **1 a** *obs* **:** the act of remaining or dwelling **:** STAY ⟨the solidness of the earth is for the station and ~ of living creatures —Francis Bacon⟩ **b** *archaic* **:** a place where one remains or dwells **:** ABODE ⟨on whose high branches . . . the birds of broadest wing their ~ form —Alexander Pope⟩ **2 a** *or* **mansion house :** a structure serving as a dwelling or lodging place: as (1) **:** the house of the lord of a manor (2) **:** a large imposing residence ⟨we'll build a house to last; not a ~ but a big house just the same —E.A.McCourt⟩ ⟨the governor's ~⟩ **b :** a separate apartment, compartment, lodging, or room in a large structure ⟨in my Father's house are many ~*s* —Jn 14:2 (RSV)⟩ **3** *obs* **:** a stopping or halting place **:** STAGE **4 a :** HOUSE 3b **b :** one of the 28 parts into which the moon's monthly course through the heavens is divided **5** [influenced in meaning by F maison, lit., house] **:** one of a series of permanent structures used to represent various settings (as a castle or cave) in the staging of medieval or Renaissance plays esp. in France

man·sion·ary \-chəˌnerē\ *n* -ES [LL *mansionarius*, fr. L *mansion-, mansio* + *-arius* -ary] **:** SEXTON

man·sion·ry \-chənrē\ *n* -ES **:** MANSIONS

man-size \ˈ=ˌ=\ *or* **man-sized** \ˈ=ˈ=\ *adj* **1 :** suitable for or requiring a man ⟨a *man-size* job⟩ **2 :** LARGE-SCALE ⟨a *man-size* model⟩

manslaughter \ˈ=ˌ==\ *n* [ME, fr. ¹*man* + *slaughter*] **:** the slaying of a human being; *specif* **:** the unlawful killing of a human being without express or implied malice

manslayer \ˈ=ˌ==\ *n* [ME *manslaer, mansleer*, fr. ¹*man* + *slaer, sleer* slayer — more at SLAYER] **:** one who commits homicide

man's motherwort *n* **:** CASTOR-OIL PLANT

man·so \ˈmän(ˌ)sō, ˈman-\ *n* -s *usu cap* [Sp, fr. *manso* tame, gentle, fr. (assumed) VL *mansus*, alter. of L *mansuetus* — more at MANSUETE] **1 :** a Tanoan people of the southwestern U.S. and Mexico **2 :** a member of the Manso people

man·son·el·la \ˌman(t)səˈnelə\ *n, cap* [NL, fr. Sir Patrick *Manson* †1922 Brit. physician and parasitologist + NL *-ella*] **:** a genus of filarial worms (family Dipetalonematidae) including one (*M. ozzardi*) that is common and apparently nonpathogenic in human visceral fat and mesenteries in So. and Central America

man·so·nia \manˈsōnēə\ *n* [NL, fr. Sir Patrick *Manson* + NL *-ia*] **1** *cap* **:** a widespread genus of mosquitoes which carry filarial worms and whose larvae and pupae obtain oxygen directly from plants under water **2** -s **:** a mosquito of the genus *Mansonia*

man·son's disease \ˈman(t)sənz-\ *n, usu cap M* [after Sir Patrick *Manson*] **:** SCHISTOSOMIASIS MANSONI

manstealing \ˈ=ˌ==\ *n* -s **:** KIDNAPPING

manstopper \ˈ=ˌ==\ *n* **:** a bullet capable of causing a shock sufficient to stop a soldier advancing in a charge

man·suete \(ˈ)manˈswēt\ *adj* [ME, fr. L *mansuetus*, past part. of *mansuescere* to tame, fr. *manus* hand + *suescere* to accustom; akin to Gk *ēthos* custom — more at MANUAL, ETHICAL] *archaic* **:** GENTLE, TAME

man·sue·tude \ˈman(t)swəˌtüd, -ə-,tyüd\ *n* -s [ME, fr. L *mansuetudo*, fr. *mansuetus* tame + *-udo* -ude] **:** the quality or state of being gentle **:** MEEKNESS, TAMENESS ⟨his matchless knowledge of the human heart and his infinite ~ —W.J. Locke⟩

mansura *adj, usu cap* [fr. El *Mansura*, Egypt] **:** EL MANSURA

man·sworn \ˈmanˌswō(ə)rn, -swȯ(ə)n\ *adj* [ME, fr. past part. of *mansweren* to swear falsely, fr. OE *mānswerian*, fr. *mān* crime, guilt, sin, false oath + *swerian* to swear; akin to OFris & OS *mēn* crime, guilt, false oath, OHG & ON *mein* crime, guilt, false oath, OE *mān*, adj., criminal, bad, false — more at MEAN] *now dial* **:** FORSWORN, PERJURED

¹**mant** \ˈmant\ *vb* -ED/-ING/-s [ScGael *mannd*, n., stammer] *chiefly Scot* **:** STAMMER

²**mant** \"\ *n* -s [ScGael *mannd*] *chiefly Scot* **:** a speech impediment **:** STAMMER

³**mant** *n* -s [F *mante*, fr. MF, fr. OProv *manta*, fr. (assumed) VL, blanket, cloak, alter. of LL *mantus* cloak, back-formation fr. L *mantellum*] *obs* **:** MANTILLA; *also* **:** MANTEAU

man·ta \ˈmantə, ˈmän-\ *n* [Sp, lit., blanket, cloak, fr. (assumed) VL, blanket, cloak] **1** -s *chiefly Southwest* **:** a plain cotton fabric **2** -s **a :** a square piece of cloth or blanket used in southwestern U.S. and Latin America usu. as a cloak, head covering, or shawl **b :** a piece of canvas or other heavy cloth used to cover a loaded packsaddle or to wrap loads for carrying **3 a** *also* **manta ray** -s [AmerSp, fr. Sp, blanket; fr. the method of catching the fish in traps resembling large blankets] **:** DEVILFISH 1 **b** *cap* [NL, fr. AmerSp] **:** a genus of rays containing the typical devilfishes **4 a** *pl* **manta** *or* **mantas** *usu cap* **:** an Indian people of coastal Ecuador **b :** a member of such people

man-tailored \ˈ=ˈ==\ *adj, of a woman's suit or coat* **:** made with the trim severe simplicity associated with men's coats and suits

man·teau \(ˈ)manˈtō\ *n* -s [F, fr. OF *mantel* — more at MANTLE] **1** *obs* **:** MANTUA **2 :** a loose cloak, coat, or robe

man·teel \(ˈ)manˈtē(ə)l\ *n* -s [F *mantille*, fr. Sp *mantilla* — more at MANTILLA] *archaic* **:** a cloak or a cape worn by women

man·te·idae \manˈtēəˌdē\ *n pl, cap* [NL, fr. *Mante-, Mantis*, type genus + *-idae*] **:** a family of carnivorous insects sometimes esp. formerly made coextensive with Manteodea but now usu. restricted to mantises with black-barred wings, a rather long pronotum, and a frontal shield that is narrow in proportion to its height

man·tel \ˈmantᵊl, -aan-\ *n* -s [MF *mantel, manteau* cloak, mantle, mantel — more at MANTLE] **1 a :** the beam, stone, or arch serving as a lintel to support the masonry above a fire-

place ⟨a high ~ has some advantage in producing a more effectual ventilation —Thomas Tredgold⟩ **b :** the finish around a fireplace covering the front and sometimes the two sides of the chimney ⟨the skill of our craftsmen is reflected in . . . the wood ~s —*Sweet's Catalogue Service*⟩ **2 :** the usu. ornamental shelf above a fireplace ⟨stepped to the ~ and rested his elbows on it —Eudora Welty⟩
man·te·let \-t(ᵊ)lət, *usu* -əd·+V\ *n* -s [ME, fr. MF, dim. of *mantel, manteau* cloak] **1 :** a very short cape, cloak, or mantle **2** *or* **mant·let** \-tlət, *usu* -əd·+V\ **:** a movable shelter formerly used by besiegers as a protection when attacking ⟨they bring forward ~s and pavises and the archers muster on the skirts of the woods —Sir Walter Scott⟩
man·tel·let·ta \ˌmantᵊlˈed·ə\ *n* -s [It, prob. modif. of ML *mantelletum*, dim. of L *mantellum* cloak, mantle] **:** a knee-length outer garment that is sleeveless but has armholes, is open in the front but fastened at the neck, and is worn by cardinals, bishops, and other high prelates of the Roman Catholic Church
man·tel·lo·ne \ˌmantᵊlˈōnē\ *n* -s [It, augm. of *mantello* cloak] **:** a long purple cloak worn over the cassock by prelates of the secondary rank attached to the papal court
mantelpiece \ˈ==,=\ *n* **1 :** a mantel with its side elements **2 :** MANTELSHELF
mantelshelf \ˈ=,=\ *n, pl* **mantelshelves :** the part of a mantel above the fireplace that serves as a shelf ⟨standing by the hearth, one hand on the ~ —Gertrude Atherton⟩
manteltree \ˈ==,=\ *n* [ME *mantelltree*, fr. *mantell, mantel* mantel + *tree*] **:** MANTEL 1a
man·te·o·dea \ˌmantēˈōdēə\ *n pl, cap* [NL, fr. *Mante-, Mantis* + *-odea*] **:** a suborder of Orthoptera often considered a separate order, comprising predaceous insects with the forelegs specialized for seizing prey and including the mantises — see MANTEIDAE
mant·er \ˈmantər\ *n* -s [¹*mant* + *-er*] *chiefly Scot* **:** STAMMERER
¹**man·tic** \ˈmantik\ *n* -s [Gk *mantikē*, fr. fem. of *mantikos* prophetic] **:** the art or science of divination
²**mantic** \ˈ"\ *adj* [Gk *mantikos*, fr. *mantis* prophet, seer + *-ikos* -ic — more at MANTIS] **:** of or relating to the faculty of divination **:** PROPHETIC
man·ti·core \ˈmantəˌkō(ə)r\ *also* **man·ti·cho·ra** *or* **man·ti·co·ra** \ˌ==ˈkōrə\ *or* **man·ti·ger** \ˈ=tijə(r)\ *n* -s [ME *manticore, mantichora*, fr. L *mantichora*, fr. Gk *martichōras, martichoras*, of Iranian origin; akin to OPer *martiya* man, and to OPer *khvar-* to eat, Av *khwar-*] **:** a legendary animal having the head of a man often with horns, the body of a lion, and the tail of a dragon or scorpion
¹**man·tid** \ˈmantəd\ *adj* [NL *Mantidae*] **:** of or relating to mantids
²**mantid** \ˈ"\ *n* -s **:** MANTIS 1
¹**man·ti·dae** \-təˌdē\ [NL, fr. *Mantis*, type genus + *-idae*] *syn of* MANTEIDAE
²**mantidae** \ˈ"\ [NL, fr. *Manta*, type genus + *-idae*] *syn of* MOBULIDAE
man·tilla \manˈtē(y)ə, -tilə\ *n* -s [Sp, dim. of *manta* blanket, cloak — more at MANTA] **1 :** a light scarf often of black lace worn over the head and shoulders esp. by Spanish and Latin American women **2 :** a short light cape or cloak

mantilla 1

manting *pres part of* MANT
man·tis \ˈmantəs, -aan-\ *n* [NL, fr. Gk, lit., prophet; fr. the posture of such insects, with the forelimbs extended as though in prayer; akin to Gk *mainesthai* to be mad — more at MANIA] **1** *pl* **mantis·es** \-ˌtəsəz\ *or* **man·tes** \-ˌtēz\ **:** an insect of *Mantis* or a related genus (suborder Manteodea) that has a long prothorax, feeds upon other insects, clasps its prey in upheld forelimbs as if in prayer, and is harmless to man **2** *cap* **:** a genus of insects containing the typical mantises
man·tis·ia \manˈtisēə\ *n, cap* [NL, fr. *Mantis*, genus of insects + *-ia*; fr. the resemblance of the flowers to the insect] **:** a genus of East Indian herbs (family Zingiberaceae) having very irregular flowers with lateral filamentous staminodia and a 1-celled ovary — see DANCING-GIRLS
man·tis·pa \manˈtispə\ *n* [NL, fr. *Mantis* + *pagana* (specific epithet of *Mantis pagana*), fr. L, fem. of *paganus* of the country — more at PAGAN] **1** *cap* **:** the type genus of Mantispidae **2** -s **:** any insect of the genus *Mantispa*
¹**man·tis·pid** \-pəd\ *adj* [NL *Mantispidae*] **:** of or relating to the Mantispidae
²**mantispid** \ˈ"\ *n* -s **:** an insect of the family Mantispidae
man·tis·pi·dae \-pəˌdē\ *n pl, cap* [NL, fr. *Mantispa*, type genus + *-idae*] **:** a family of insects (order Neuroptera) having the prothorax elongated and the first pair of legs developed after the manner of a mantis
mantis prawn *or* **mantis shrimp** *n* **:** SQUILLA
man·tis·sa \manˈtisə\ *n* -s [L *mantissa, mantisa*, fr. Etruscan, prob. of Celt origin; akin to OIr *mēit* size, W *maint*; akin to OIr *mār* large — more at MORE] **1** *obs* **:** an addition of little value or importance **2 :** the decimal part of a logarithm
¹**man·tle** \ˈmantᵊl, -aan-\ *n* -s [ME *mantel, mentel*; partly fr. OE *mentel*; partly fr. OF *mantel*; both fr. L *mantellum*] **1 a :** a loose sleeveless garment worn over other clothes **:** an enveloping robe or cloak ⟨brought a heavy ~ and covered her from head to foot —William Black⟩ **b :** a mantle regarded as a symbol of preeminence or authority ⟨take off the ~ of authority and drop it on younger shoulders —H.H.Arnold & I.C.Eaker⟩ **2 a :** something that covers, enfolds, or envelops ⟨the green ~ of the standing pool —Shak.⟩ ⟨the ~ of night made it easier for them to forget their youth —T.B.Costain⟩ **b** (1) **:** the fold or lobe or pair of lobes of the body wall in a mollusk or brachiopod lining the shell in shell-bearing forms, bearing the shell-secreting glands, and usu. forming a cavity between itself and the body proper that holds the respiratory organs (2) **:** the soft external body wall that lines the test or the shell of a tunicate or barnacle **c :** the outer wall and casing of a blast furnace above the hearth **d :** CEREBRAL CORTEX **3 :** MANTLING **4 :** the back, scapulars, and wings of a bird when distinguished from other parts of the plumage by a distinct and uniform color (as in some gulls) **5 :** a penstock for a waterwheel **6 a :** the external layers of meristematic cells in a stem apex often equivalent to the combined tunica and corpus **b :** the fungal network around an ectotrophic mycorhiza that replaces the root hairs as an absorbing system **7 a :** a lacelike hood or sheath of some refractory material that gives light by incandescence when placed over a flame **b :** a thin zone at the border of a flame **c :** HEATING MANTLE **8 a :** MANTLEROCK **b :** the part of the earth's interior beneath the lithosphere and above the central core from which it is separated by a discontinuity at a depth of about 1800 miles **9 :** MANTEL
²**mantle** \ˈ"\ *vb* **mantled; mantled; mantling** \-t(ᵊ)liŋ\ **mantles** [ME *mantellen*, fr. *mantel*, n.] *vt* **1 :** to conceal by covering **:** make obscure ⟨its venerable trunk is richly *mantled* with ivy —J.G.Strutt⟩ **2 :** to cover with or as if with a mantle ⟨the land is *mantled* with glacial deposits —W.W.Atwood b.1906⟩ **3 :** to cause to blush **:** give a glowing color to ~ *vi* **1 a** *of a hawk* **:** to spread one wing and then the other over the corresponding outstretched leg **b** *obs* **:** to spread out — used of wings **2 :** to become covered with a coating (as of scum or froth) ⟨the poison *mantled* in the cup —Alexander Pope⟩ **3 :** to spread over a surface ⟨seldom o'er a breast so fair *mantled* a plaid with modest care —Sir Walter Scott⟩ **4 :** BLUSH, COLOR ⟨her rich face *mantling* with emotion —Benjamin Disraeli⟩
mantle cavity *n* **:** the cavity between the mantle and the body proper of a mollusk or brachiopod in which the respiratory organs lie
man·tled \ˈmantᵊld, -aan-\ *adj* [¹*mantle* + *-ed*] **1 :** furnished or covered with or as if with a mantle ⟨places *mantled* with coarse, bouldery gravel —P.E.James⟩ ⟨cool, forest-*mantled* hills⟩ **2 :** ornamented with a mantling
mantled ground squirrel *n* **:** a common ground squirrel (*Citellus lateralis*) of western No. America that is reddish brown above with black and buff lateral stripes and resembles a large chipmunk in habits and appearance
mantle fiber *n* **:** one of the apparent fibers that pass between the centromeres of the chromosomes and the poles of the mitotic spindle and that appear to draw the chromosomes apart
mantlerock \ˈ==,=\ *n* **:** unconsolidated residual or transported material that overlies or covers the solid rock in place — called also *regolith*; compare LATERITE, SAPROLITE
mantlet *var of* MANTELET
mantling *n* -s [fr. gerund of ²*mantle*] **1 :** a heraldic representation of a mantle behind and around a coat of arms — called also *lambrequin* **2 :** MANTLE 4
man·to \ˈmanˌtō\ *n* -s [Sp, fr. LL *mantus* — more at MANT] **1 :** a usu. black shawl worn esp. by Spanish or Latin American women as a covering for head and shoulders **2 a :** a nearly horizontal or gently inclined sheetlike body of ore — called also BLANKET DEPOSIT **b :** a pipe-shaped ore body
man·to·dea \manˈtōdēə\ *or* **man·toi·dea** \-ˈtȯidēə\ [NL, fr. *Mantis* + *-odea* or *-oidea*] *syn of* MANTEODEA
¹**man·toid** \ˈmanˌtȯid\ *adj* [NL *Mantoidea*] **:** of, relating to, or resembling the Manteodea
²**mantoid** \ˈ"\ *n* -s **:** MANTIS 1
man·tol·o·gy \manˈtäləjē\ *n* -ES [Gk *mantis* prophet + E *-o-* + *-logy* — more at MANTIS] *archaic* **:** DIVINATION
man-to-man \ˈ==ˈ=\ *adj* **:** characterized by frankness and honesty ⟨their discussions had been straightforward *man-to-man* talks —J.Hendrick⟩
man-to-man defense *n* **:** a system of defense in various sports (as football and basketball) in which each defensive player guards a specified opponent — compare ZONE DEFENSE
man·toux test \(ˈ)manˈtü-\ *n, usu cap M* [after Charles *Mantoux* †1947 French physician] **:** an intracutaneous test for hypersensitivity to tuberculin and thus for past or present infection with tubercle bacilli — compare TUBERCULIN TEST
man·tra \ˈmantrə, ˈmən-\ *also* **man·tram** \-trəm\ *n* -s [Skt *mantra*, lit., speech, hymn, incantation, fr. *manyate* he thinks — more at MIND] **1 :** a Vedic hymn or prayer **2 :** a verbal spell, ritualistic incantation, or mystic formula used devotionally in popular Hinduism and Mahayana Buddhism
man-trap \ˈ=,=\ *n, pl* **man-traps 1 :** a trap for catching men; *specif* **:** a trap designed to catch trespassers **2 :** something (as a carelessly built scaffold) likely to bring about injury or death to the unwary **3 :** a source of potential danger or difficulty ⟨his innocence of all the tricks and *man-traps* in the rigorous profession of politics —Herbert Agar⟩
mants *pres 3d sing of* MANT, *pl of* MANT
man·tua \ˈmanchəwə\ *n* -s [modif. (influenced by *Mantua*, Italy) of F *manteau* — more at MANTLE] **1 :** a usu. loose-fitting gown or robe worn open at the front to show the underdress or petticoat and popular esp. with women in the 17th and 18th centuries **2** [fr. *Mantua*, Italy] **:** a silk dress fabric orig. made in Italy
mantua-maker \ˈ===,==\ *n* **:** one that makes mantuas; *broadly* **:** DRESSMAKER
¹**man·tu·an** \ˈmanchəwən\ *n* -s *cap* [L *Mantuanus*, adj. & n., fr. *Mantua*, Italy + L *-anus* -an] **:** a native or inhabitant of Mantua, Italy
²**mantuan** \ˈ"\ *adj, usu cap* [L *Mantuanus*] **:** of or relating to the Italian city of Mantua
man·ty \ˈmantē\ *chiefly Scot var of* MANTUA
man·tzu \ˈmänt(ˌ)sü\ *or* **man·tse** \-ˌtsə\ *n, pl* **mantzu** *or* **mantzus** *or* **mantse** *or* **mantses** *usu cap* **:** ⁵MAN
manu \ˈmaˌnü\ *n* -s *usu cap* [Skt — more at MAN] **:** one of a series of progenitors of human beings and authors of human wisdom in Hindu mythology
¹**man·u·al** \ˈmanyə(wə)l\ *adj* [ME *manuel*, fr. MF, fr. L *manualis*, fr. *manus* hand + *-alis* -al; akin to OE & ON *mund* hand, OHG *munt*, Gk *marē* hand, Alb *marr* I take] **1 a :** of, relating to, or involving the hands ⟨~ dexterity⟩ **b :** designed for use or operation with the hands **:** worked by hand ⟨an engine with a ~ choke⟩ **2 a :** requiring or involving physical skill and energy ⟨~ labor⟩ **b :** engaged in an activity or occupation requiring or involving physical skill and energy ⟨~ workers⟩ **3** *obs* **:** AUTOGRAPH **4 :** existing in fact or deed **:** ACTUAL — used of legal possession or occupation **5 :** using signs and the manual alphabet in teaching the deaf — compare ORAL
²**manual** \ˈ"\ *n* -s [ME *manuel*, fr. LL *manuale*, fr. L, neut. of *manualis*, adj.] **1 a :** a small book capable of being carried in the hand or conveniently handled: as (1) **:** a book containing the forms of religious ceremonies used in the medieval Christian church (2) **:** a book used by underwriters and agents that gives classifications, rates, forms, and rules for writing insurance (3) **:** a book containing in concise form the principles, rules, and directions needed for the mastery of an art, science, or skill **b :** a concise treatise based on a larger work **:** HANDBOOK **2 :** the prescribed movements in the handling of a weapon or other military item during a drill or ceremony ⟨the ~ of arms⟩ ⟨the ~ of the guidon⟩ **3 :** a keyboard for the hands ⟨upper ~ of a harpsichord⟩; *specif* **:** one of the several keyboards of a pipe-organ console controlling a separate division of the instrument ⟨solo ~⟩ ⟨swell ~⟩ **4 :** PRIMARY 3a
manual alphabet *n* **:** an alphabet used in dactylology
ma·nu·a·lii \ˌmänəwəˈlēˌē\ *n* -s [Samoan, fr. *manu* bird + *alii* master] **:** a gallinule (*Porphyrio porphyrio samoensis*) of Samoa
man·u·al·ism \ˈmanyə(wə)ˌlizəm\ *n* -s **:** the teaching of deaf persons by the manual method
man·u·al·ist \-ləst\ *n* -s **1 :** one who works with the hands **2 :** one who uses or advocates the use of the manual method in teaching the deaf
man·u·a·li·ter \ˌmanyəˈwaləd·ə(r)\ *adv* [NL, fr. ML, by hand, fr. L *manualis* manual] **:** on the manuals only — used as a direction in organ music; compare PEDALITER
man·u·al·ly \ˈmanyə(wə)lē, -li\ *adv* [ME, fr. *manuel, manual* + *-ly*] **:** with or by means of the hands **:** by manual methods
manual method *n* **:** a method of teaching the deaf that mainly employs signs and the manual alphabet
manual rate *n* **:** an insurance rate based on the experience of a probable class of risks and published in a manual
manual training *n* **:** a course of training given in an elementary or secondary school to develop skill in using the hands and to teach practical arts (as woodworking, metalworking)
¹**ma·nu·an** \məˈnüən\ *adj, usu cap* [*Manua* islands, American Samoa + E *-an*] **1 :** of, relating to, or characteristic of the Manuan islands of American Samoa **2 :** of, relating to, or characteristic of the people of the Manuan islands of American Samoa
²**manuan** \ˈ"\ *n* -s *cap* **:** a native or inhabitant of the Manuan islands of American Samoa
man·u·ary \ˈmanyəˌwerē\ *adj* [LL *manuarius*, fr. L *manus* hand + *-arius* -ary — more at MANUAL] *archaic* **:** MANUAL
ma·nu·bri·al \məˈnübrēəl\ *adj* [NL *manubrium* + E *-al*] **:** of, relating to, or shaped like a manubrium
ma·nu·bri·um \-brēəm\ *n, pl* **manu·bria** \-ēə\ *also* **manubriums** [NL, fr. L, handle, fr. *manus* hand] **1 :** a process or part shaped like a handle: **a** *also* **manubrium ster·ni** \-ˈstərˌnī\ **:** the cephalic segment of the sternum of man and many other mammals which is a somewhat triangular flattened bone with whose anterolateral borders the clavicles articulate **b :** a median anterior process of the sternum of a bird **c :** the process of the malleus of the ear **d :** the process bearing the mouth of a hydrozoan **:** HYPOSTOME **e :** the base of the spring of an arthropod of the order Collembola **2 :** a cylindrical cell that projects from the middle of the inner wall of each of the eight shields composing the wall of the antheridium of a stonewort and that ultimately bears the antheridial threads
man·u·cap·tion \ˌmanyəˈkapshən\ *n* [ML *manucaption-, manucaptio*, fr. *manucaptus* (past part. of *manucapere* to go bail for, fr. L *manus* hand + *capere* to take) + L *-ion-, -io* -ion — more at MANUAL, HEAVE] **1 :** MAINPRISE **2 :** a writ for the production in court of an alleged felon **3 :** seizure in hand
man·u·cap·tor \-ptə(r)\ *n* [ML, fr. *manucaptus* + L *-or*] **:** MAINPERNOR
man·u·cap·ture \-pchə(r)\ *n* [ML *manucaptus* + E *-ure*] **:** a taking into physical possession **:** SEIZURE
man·u·code \ˈmanyəˌkōd\ *n* [F, fr. NL *manucodiata*, fr. Malay *manuq dewata*, lit., bird of the gods] **:** any of various birds of paradise; *esp* **:** a chiefly iridescent black or greenish bird (genus *Manucodia*) of Australia and New Guinea
¹**manucodiata** *n* -s [NL] *obs* **:** BIRD OF PARADISE
²**man·u·co·di·a·ta** \ˌmanyəˌkōdēˈäd·ə, -ˈād·ə\ [NL, fr. ¹*manucodiata*] *syn of* PARADISAEA
man·u·duc·tion \ˌmanyəˈdəkshən\ *n* -s [ML *manuduction-, manuductio*, fr. L *manus* hand + *duction-, ductio* action of leading, fr. *ductus* (past part. of *ducere* to lead) + *-ion-, -io* -ion — more at TOW] **1 :** the act of guiding or leading (as by the hand) ⟨the ground over which he had accepted my hurried ~ —W.E.Gladstone⟩ **2 :** something that guides or leads **:** INTRODUCTION ⟨a pleasant and scholarly ~ into alchemical byways —F.O.Taylor⟩
man·u·duc·tive \ˌ==ˈdəktiv\ *adj* [*manuduction* + *-ive*] **:** leading by or as if by the hand
man·u·duc·tor \ˈ==ˌdəktə(r)\ *n* -s [LL, fr. L *manus* hand + *ductor* leader, fr. *ductus* + *-or*] **:** DIRECTOR; *esp* **:** the director of a band or choir
man·u·duc·to·ry \ˌ==ˈdəkt(ə)rē\ *adj* [*manuduction* + *-ory*] **:** MANUDUCTIVE
man·u·fac·tor \ˌmanyəˈfaktə(r)\ *n* [LL *manufactus* made by hand + E *-or* — more at MANUFACTURE] *archaic* **:** MANUFACTURER
¹**man·u·fac·to·ry** \ˌman(y)əˈfakt(ə)rē, -ri\ *n* [LL *manufactus* + E *-ory*] **1** *archaic* **:** a product of manufacture ⟨a fleet . . . being the natural ~ of this country —Thomas Paine⟩ **2** *archaic* **:** MANUFACTURING ⟨clothed in woolens apparently of their own ~ —J.J.Henry⟩ **3 :** FACTORY 2a ⟨his father had started a match ~ in a barn —E.J.Benton⟩
²**manufactory** *adj, obs* **:** of or relating to manufacture
man·u·fac·tur·able \ˌ==ˈfakchərəbəl, -ksh-\ *adj* **:** capable of being manufactured ⟨aircraft, electronics, and a thousand other ~ wonders —C.M.Wilson⟩
manufacturage *n* -s *obs* **:** MANUFACTURE
man·u·fac·tur·al \ˌman(y)əˈfakchərəl, -ksh(ə)r-\ *adj* **:** of or relating to manufacture
¹**man·u·fac·ture** \ˌman(y)əˈfakchə(r), -ksh-\ *n* -s [MF, fr. LL *manufactus* made by hand (fr. L *manu* — abl. of *manus* hand — + *factus*, past part. of *facere* to make, do) + MF *-ure* — more at MANUAL, DO] **1 :** something made from raw materials by hand or by machinery ⟨hemp and tow cloth were familiar household ~s —V.S.Clark⟩ ⟨imports most ~s used by consumers or needed for internal development —D.L.Cohn⟩ **2 a :** the process or operation of making wares or other material products by hand or by machinery esp. when carried on systematically with division of labor ⟨families engaged in domestic ~ often lived and worked in one room —J.W.Krutch⟩ ⟨the ~ of furniture⟩ ⟨steel ~⟩ **b :** a productive industry using mechanical power and machinery **3** *obs* **:** a manual occupation or trade **4** *archaic* **:** FACTORY ⟨all my prospects were built on a ~ I had erected —Daniel Defoe⟩ **5 :** the act or process of making, inventing, devising, or fashioning **:** PRODUCTION, CREATION ⟨the ~ of blood goes on constantly in the human body —Morris Fishbein⟩ ⟨a true appreciation of the ~ of a movie and of a star —Horace Sutton⟩ ⟨his ideas about the ~ of this world and his hopes for his future —Rudyard Kipling⟩
²**manufacture** \ˈ"\ *vb* **manufactured; manufactured; manufacturing** \-kchəriŋ, -ksh(ə)r-\ **manufactures** [F *manufacturer*, fr. *manufacture*, n.] *vt* **1 :** to make (as raw material) into a product suitable for use ⟨the wood . . . is *manufactured* into fine cabinetwork —*Amer. Guide Series: Oregon*⟩ ⟨~ iron into steel⟩ **2 a :** to make from raw materials by hand or by machinery ⟨were *manufacturing* beautiful jewelry of gold, silver, shell, and precious stones —R.W. Murray⟩ ⟨a substitute for milk . . . *manufactured* from the soya bean —V.G.Heiser⟩ **b :** to produce according to an organized plan and with division of labor ⟨*manufacturing* 7000 cars in one day —*Amer. Guide Series: Mich.*⟩ **3 :** to make up sometimes with the intent to deceive **:** INVENT, FABRICATE ⟨the speech is evidently *manufactured* by the historian —Edward Gibbon⟩ **4 a :** to produce as if by manufacturing **:** CREATE ⟨is busy *manufacturing* a new culture —D. W.Brogan⟩ ⟨the strain of *manufacturing* conversation for at least ten minutes —Wilfred Fienburgh⟩ **b :** to produce from different and usu. less specialized materials in the living body ⟨green plants ~ carbohydrates⟩ ~ *vi* **:** to engage in manufacture **syn** see MAKE
manufactured gas *n* **:** a combustible gaseous mixture (as carbureted water gas or producer gas) made from coal, coke, or petroleum products for use as a fuel, illuminant, or raw material for synthesis — compare NATURAL GAS
man·u·fac·tur·er \ˌ==ˈfakchərə(r), -ksh(ə)rə-\ *n* -s **:** one that manufactures: as **a** *archaic* **:** a worker in a factory ⟨wages of mechanics, artificers, and ~s are . . . higher than those of common laborers —Adam Smith⟩ **b :** an employer of workers in manufacturing **:** the owner or operator of a factory ⟨a leading automobile ~⟩ **c :** one who changes the form of a commodity or who creates a new commodity
manufacturer's agent *n* **:** an agent middleman operating on a contractual basis within an exclusive territory who sells for a manufacturing client noncompeting but related goods and who has limited authority over price and terms of sale
manufacturer's joint *n* **:** the seam where the two sides of a fiberboard container are joined by the manufacturer usu. by gluing, stitching, or taping
manufacturing *adj* **1 :** engaged in manufacture ⟨an important ~ city⟩ ⟨a ~ establishment⟩ **2 :** of or relating to manufacture ⟨a series of ~ projects⟩
ma·nu for·ti \ˌmäˌnüˈfȯ(r)d·ˌē, -ȯ(r)ˌtī\ *adv* [L, with strong hand] **:** with such force as constitutes the crime of breaking the peace — compare VI ET ARMIS
ma·nu·ka \ˈmänəkə\ *n* -s [Maori] **:** either of two New Zealand woody plants that often tend to overgrow grazing land and form dense scrub: **a :** NEW ZEALAND TEA TREE **b :** KANUKA
ma·nul \ˈmänəl\ *n* -s [Mongolian] **:** a small wildcat (*Felis manul*) of the mountains of Mongolia, Siberia, and Tibet that has soft grayish white fur marked with a few blackish transverse bands on the loins and is often held to be the source of the long-haired varieties of the domestic cat — called also *Pallas's cat*
ma·nu·ma \ˌmänəˈmä\ *n* -s [Samoan *manumā*, fr. *manu* bird + *mā* shame] **:** a bright-colored fruit pigeon (*Ptilinopus perousii*) of Samoa and the Fiji islands
ma·nu·mea \ˌmänəˈmāə\ *n* -s [Samoan] **:** TOOTH-BILLED PIGEON
man·u·mise \ˈmanyəˌmīz\ *vt* -ED/-ING/-S [irreg. fr. L *manumissus*, past part.] *archaic* **:** MANUMIT
man·u·mis·sion \ˌ==ˈmishən\ *n* [ME, fr. MF, fr. L *manumission-, manumissio*, fr. *manumissus* (past part. of *manumittere*) + *-ion-, -io* -ion] **:** the act or process of manumitting; *esp* **:** formal emancipation from slavery ⟨was true to his profession of humanitarian and liberal principles and advocated the ~ of the slaves —A.L.Harris⟩
man·u·mit \ˌ==ˈmit, *usu* -id·+V\ *vt* **manumitted; manumitted; manumitting; manumits** [ME *manumitten*, fr. MF *manumitter*, fr. L *manumittere*, fr. *manu* from the hand (abl. of *manus* hand) + *mittere* to send, let go — more at MANUAL, SMITE] **:** to set free **:** LIBERATE; *esp* **:** to release from slavery ⟨four million slaves had been *manumitted* by a stroke of the presidential pen —H.M.Gloster⟩ **syn** see FREE
man·u·mit·ter \ˈ==ˌmid·ə(r)\ *n* -s **:** one that manumits
man·u·motive \ˈmanyə+\ *adj* [L *manus* hand + E *motive*] *of a vehicle* **:** moved by a hand-operated mechanism
ma·nur·able \məˈn(y)u̇rəbəl\ *adj* **:** capable of being manured
ma·nur·age \məˈnyu̇rij, -ēj\ *n* -s **:** the cultivation or occupation of land
ma·nur·ance \-rən(t)s\ *n* -s [ME *manouraunce*, fr. *manouren* + *-aunce* -ance] **1 a** *obs* **:** the tenure, occupation, or control of land **b** *archaic* **:** the cultivation of land **2** *obs* **:** the cultivation or training of the mind
¹**ma·nure** \məˈn(y)u̇(ə)r, -u̇ə\ *vt* -ED/-ING/-S [ME *manouren*, fr. MF *manouvrer*, lit., to do work by hand, fr. L *manu operare* — more at MANEUVER] **1** *obs* **:** to have the possession or management of (as land) **2** *archaic* **a :** to subject (land) to cultivation **:** TILL **b :** to develop (as the mind) by instruction and discipline **:** TRAIN **3 :** to apply manure to **:** enrich by the application of a fertilizing substance ⟨the fields were *manured*, the fodder was all in —Hugh MacLennan⟩
²**manure** \ˈ"\ *n* -s *often attrib* **:** material that fertilizes land; *esp* **:** refuse of stables and barnyards consisting of mammal and bird excreta with or without litter — compare FERTILIZER
ma·nur·er \-rə(r)\ *n* -s **:** one that manures
manure salts *n pl but sing or pl in constr* **:** a variable mixture of salts that contains a high percentage of chloride and from 20 to 30 percent of potash K_2O and is used as a fertilizer

ma·nu·ri·al \mə'n(y)u̇rēəl\ *adj* **:** of, relating to, or having the characteristics of manure — **ma·nu·ri·al·ly** \-ēəlē\ *adv*

¹ma·nus \'mānəs\ *n, pl* **manus** [NL, fr. L, hand — more at MANUAL] **1 a :** the distal segment of the forelimb of a vertebrate including the carpus and forefoot or hand **b :** the enlarged proximal part of the propodus of the chela of an arthropod **2** [L, lit., hand] *Roman law* **a :** ownership of property **b :** power over a person; *specif* **:** the power and rights of a husband and citizen over his wife in a case of marriage by coemptio, confarreation, or usus

²manus *pl of* MANU

³ma·nus \'mä,nüs\ *n, pl* **manus** *usu cap* [fr. *Manus* Island in the Admiralty islands] **1 a :** a people inhabiting Manus Island **b :** a member of such people **2 :** an Austronesian language of the Manus people

manus chris·ti \-'kri,stī\ *n, pl* **manus christi** *usu cap C* [ML, lit., hand of Christ] **:** a cordial made by boiling sugar usu. with rose water or violet water and formerly given to feeble persons

¹man·u·script \'manyə,skript *sometimes* 'manə-\ *adj* [L *manu scriptus* written by hand, fr. *manu* (abl. of *manus* hand) + *scriptus*, past part. of *scribere* to write — more at MANUAL, SCRIBE] **:** written by hand or typed **:** not printed ⟨~ poems⟩ ⟨a ~ map⟩

²manuscript \"\ *n* -s [ML *manuscriptum*, fr. neut. of L *manu scriptus*] **1 :** a composition written by hand: as **a :** a composition written before the invention or adoption of printing **b :** a handwritten copy of an ancient author or work **c :** a handwritten composition that has not been printed **2 :** a written or typewritten document as distinguished from a printed copy; *esp* **:** the copy of a writer's work from which printed copies are made **3 :** HAND 6a **4 :** writing as opposed to print **:** written documents or written characters — abbr. *MS*

man·u·script·al \ˌ⸗⸗'skriptəl\ *adj, archaic* **:** of, relating to, or existing in manuscript

manuscript catalog *n* **1 :** a handwritten catalog of books or other items usu. in some systematic order **2 :** a catalog of manuscripts

man·u·scrip·tion \,manyə'skripshən\ *n* -s [LL *manuscription-, manuscriptio*, fr. L *manus* hand + *scription-, scriptio* writing, fr. *scriptus* + *-ion-, -io* -ion] **:** writing done by hand

manuscript ticket *n* **:** a transportation ticket (as for theatrical troupes) sold at through rates but with stopover privileges and permitting installment payments at designated places en route

manuscript writing *n* **1 :** calligraphy based on the handwriting found in medieval manuscripts **2 :** writing that consists of unjoined letters made with lines and circles and that is often taught in elementary school

ma·nu·si·na \,mänə'sēnə\ *n* -s [Samoan, fr. *manu* bird + *sina* white] **:** a pure white tern (*Gygis alba*) of Polynesia

ma·nu·ta·gi \'täge, -täŋē\ *n* -s [Samoan *manutagi*, fr. *manu* bird + *tagi* cry] **:** a fruit pigeon (*Ptilinopus porphyraceus fasciatus*) of Samoa

manutenency *n* [ML *manutenentia*, fr. L *manus* hand + *tenentia* tenancy — more at MANUAL, TENANCY] *obs* **:** SUPPORT

man·u·terge \'manyə,tərj\ *or* **man·u·ter·gi·um** \ˌ⸗⸗'tərjēəm\ *n, pl* **manu·terg·es** \'⸗⸗,tərjəz\ *or* **manuter·gia** \ˌ⸗⸗'tərjēə\ [LL *manutergium*, fr. L *manus* hand + *-tergium* (fr. *tergēre* to wipe off, rub off) — more at TERSE] **:** a small towel used in Christian liturgies at the lavabo

man·van·ta·ra \man'vantərə\ *n* -s [Skt, fr. *maver* man + *antara* interval, period of time] **:** one of the 14 intervals in Hinduism that constitute a kalpa

¹man·ward \'⸗wə(r)d\ *adv* [ME, fr. ¹*man* + *-ward*] **:** toward man ⟨a good man, in the old . . . phrase, Godward and ~ —Sir Walter Scott⟩

²manward \"\ *adj* **:** directed toward man ⟨~ activities and relations —A.M.Fairbairn⟩

manway \'⸗,⸗\ *n* **:** a small passageway admitting a man ⟨a ~ in a coal mine⟩

manwise \'⸗,⸗\ *adv* [¹*man* + *-wise*] **:** in the manner of men

man-woman \'⸗,⸗⸗\ *n, pl* **men-women 1** *obs* **:** HERMAPHRODITE **2 :** a mannish woman

¹manx \'maŋ(k)s, -aiŋ(-\ *adj, usu cap* [alter. of earlier *Manisk*, fr. a Scand adj. whose first constituent is *Mana* Isle of Man in the Irish sea off the northwestern coast of England (fr. OIr), and whose second constituent is represented by ON *-iskr* -ish] **1 a :** of, relating to, or characteristic of the Isle of Man **b :** of, relating to, or characteristic of the people of the Isle of Man **2 :** of, relating to, or characteristic of the Manx language

²manx \"\ *n, pl* **manx** *cap* **1 :** a native or inhabitant of the Isle of Man **2 :** the Celtic language of the Manx people now almost completely displaced by English — see INDO-EUROPEAN LANGUAGES table

manx cat *n, usu cap M* **:** a short-haired domestic cat having the tail externally lacking though represented internally by a few rudimentary vertebrae and constituting a distinct breed

manx·man \'⸗mən, -man,-,maa(ə)n\ *n, pl* **manxmen** \-,mən, -,men\ *cap* **:** a native or inhabitant of the Isle of Man

manx shearwater *n, usu cap M* **:** a small black-and-white shearwater (*Puffinus puffinus*) common in the eastern north Atlantic

manxwoman \'⸗,⸗⸗\ *n, pl* **manxwomen** *cap* **:** a woman who is a native or inhabitant of the Isle of Man

¹many \,menē, -ni *sometimes* ,mən-\ *adj* **more** \(ˈ)mō(ə)r, -ȯ(ə)r, -ōə,-ȯ(ə)\ **most** \(ˈ)mōst\ [ME *many, mony* many a, many, fr. OE *manig, mænig, monig*; akin to OS & OHG *manag* many a, many, ON *mangr*, Goth *manags* many a, many, OIr *menicc* frequent, Skt *magha* gift, OSlav *mŭnogŭ* much] **1 :** consisting of or amounting to a large but indefinite number **:** not few ⟨~ people expressed fear⟩ ⟨worked hard for ~ years⟩ ⟨a country with ~ natural resources⟩ ⟨the ~ advantages of an education⟩ **2 :** one of a large but indefinite number regarded distributively — used before *a, an,* or *another* or in an inverted construction to modify a singular noun ⟨~ a man hoped for better days⟩ ⟨remained a mystery for ~ a year⟩ ⟨~ another student made the same mistake⟩ ⟨~ is the time she scolded the boy⟩ — **as many :** the same in number ⟨saw three plays in *as many* days⟩

²many \"\ *pron, pl in constr* [ME *many, mony* many a one, many, fr. OE *manig, mænig, monig*, fr. *manig, mænig, monig*, adj.] **:** a large number of persons or things ⟨~ are called but few are chosen —Mt 22:14 (RSV)⟩ ⟨~ of the statements are true⟩

³many \"\ *n, pl in constr* [¹*many*] **1 :** a large but indefinite number of units or individuals ⟨a good ~ of the books were novels⟩ ⟨a great ~ of the tourists were from the East⟩ **2 :** the great majority of people **:** MASSES, MULTITUDE — often used with preceding *the* ⟨nothing but contempt for the ~⟩ **3** *obs* **:** COMPANY, HOST, RETINUE ⟨the chiefs divide and wheeling east and west before their ~ ride —John Dryden⟩ **4** *usu cap* **:** something that is manifold **:** PLURALITY ⟨philosophers have largely proclaimed the One to be reality and the *Many* to be appearance —H.M.Kallen⟩

man·yat·ta \mən'yad·ə\ *n* -s [native name in Kenya] *southern Africa* **:** a kraal esp. in Kenya

man-year \'⸗'⸗\ *n, pl* **man-years :** the work of one man in a year composed of a standard number of working days of standard length

¹manyfold \'⸗⸗,⸗\ *adj* [by alter.] **:** MANIFOLD ⟨took the form of ~ reparation, of penal and exemplary damages —Frederick Pollock & F.W.Maitland⟩

²manyfold \"\ *adv* [¹*many* + *-fold*] **:** by many times **:** to a considerable degree or extent ⟨provision for education and health care has increased ~ —Abram Bergson⟩

many-headed \'⸗⸗'⸗⸗\ *adj* **1 :** having many heads **2 :** of or relating to the people ⟨expelled a king in order to set up a *many-headed* tyranny —John Russell †1878⟩ — usu. used as a generalized expression of disapproval

many·ness \'menēnəs, -nin-\ *n* -ES **:** the quality or state of being many **:** MULTIPLICITY

many-one \'⸗⸗'⸗\ *adj, of a relation in logic* **:** constituted so that if the first term is given only one thing can be the second term whereas if the second term is given any of many things can be the first term ⟨the relation "sired-by" is *many-one* since many offspring may be sired by one animal but each offspring has only one sire⟩ — compare ONE-MANY, ONE-ONE

manyplies \'⸗⸗,⸗\ *also* **mani·plies** \"\ *n pl but usu sing in constr* [¹*many* + *plies*, pl. of *ply* (fold)] **:** OMASUM

many-sided \'⸗⸗'⸗⸗\ *adj* **1 :** having many sides **:** MULTILATERAL ⟨*many-sided* figures⟩ **2 a :** having many aspects or bearings ⟨a *many-sided* topic⟩ **b :** having many interests or aptitudes ⟨*many-sided* men⟩ **syn** see VERSATILE

many·sid·ed·ness *n* -ES **:** the quality or state of being many-sided ⟨the loftiness and ~ of English theological thought —Leo Zander⟩

many-valued \'⸗⸗'⸗⸗\ *adj* [trans. of G *mehrwertig*] **:** having, demanding, or satisfied by three or more values ⟨*many-valued* logics⟩ — see TRUTH-VALUE

man·za·na \man'zänə\ *n* -s [AmerSp, fr. Sp, apple, block of houses, fr. OSp *mazana, maçana* apple, fr. L (*mala*) *Matiana*, fr. *mala* apples + *Matiana*, neut. pl. of *Matianus* of Matius, fr. C. *Matius*, 1st cent. B.C. Roman writer on gastronomy + L *-anus* -an] **:** any of several units of land area used esp. in Central America that average around 1.7 acres

man·za·ni·lla \,manzə'nē(y)ə, -ēlyə\ *n* -s [Sp, lit., chamomile, dim. of *manzana* apple] **1 :** a pale aromatic dry sherry from the Sanlucar vineyards at the mouth of the Guadalquivir, Spain **2 a :** any of several weedy plants of the family Compositae esp. of the genera *Bidens, Stemmodontia*, and *Trixis* **b :** any of several Mexican trees or shrubs esp. of the genera *Quercus* and *Ximenia*

man·za·ni·llo \-ē(,)(y)ō, -ēl(,)yō\ *n* -s [Sp, dim. of *manzano* apple tree, fr. *manzana* apple] **1 :** MANCHINEEL **2 :** any of several Mexican shrubs or trees esp. of the genera *Euphorbia, Rhus*, and *Xylosma*

man·za·ni·ta \-ēd·ə\ *n* -s [AmerSp, dim. of *manzana* apple] **1 :** any of various California shrubs of the genus *Arctostaphylos* (esp. *A. pungens* or *A. tomentosa*) **2 :** MADRONA

¹mao·mao \'mau̇,mau̇\ *n* -s [Samoan *ma'oma'o*] **:** a Samoan honey eater (*Gymnomyza samoensis*)

²maomao \"\ *n* -s [Maori] **:** a New Zealand surf fish (*Ditrema violacea*) that somewhat resembles a flounder, is typically blue in color, and is a superior food fish

mao·ri \'mau̇(ə)rē, -ri\ *n* **1** *pl* **maori** *or* **maoris** *usu cap* **a** (1) **:** a Polynesian people native to New Zealand (2) **:** a member of such people **b :** the Austronesian language of the Maori **2** -s **:** a brilliantly colored Australian marine percoid food fish (*Ophthalmolepis lineolatus*)

mao·ri·an \-rēən\ *adj, usu cap* [*Maori* + *-an*] **:** NEW ZEALAND

maori cabbage *n, usu cap M* **:** the wild cabbage of New Zealand

maori hen *n, usu cap M* **:** WEKA

mao·ri·land·er \-,landə(r)\ *n* -s *cap* [*Maoriland* New Zealand (fr. *Maori* + *land*) + *-er*] **:** a native or inhabitant of New Zealand

mao·ri·tanga \,mau̇rē'täŋə\ *n* -s *usu cap* [Maori] **1 :** the traditions and ideals and culture of the Maori people **2 :** Maori nationalism

¹map \'map\ *n* -s [ML *mappa*, fr. L, napkin, of Sem origin; akin to Heb *mĕnaphā* fan] **1 a** (1) **:** a drawing or other representation that is usu. made on a flat surface and that shows the whole or a part of an area (as of the surface of the earth or some other planet or of the moon) and indicates the nature and relative position and size according to a chosen scale or projection of selected features or details (as countries, cities, bodies of water, mountains, deserts) — compare CHART (2) **:** a similar drawing or other representation of the celestial sphere that indicates the nature and relative position and size of stars or planets or other celestial features or phenomena **b :** something (as a significant outward appearance, a pointed or concise verbal description) that indicates or delineates or reveals by representing or showing with a clarity suggestive of that of a map ⟨thus is his cheek the ~ of days outworn —Shak.⟩ **2** *slang* **:** FACE — **put on the map :** to give great prominence of fame to (as a city, a region) **:** make widely known ⟨discovery of rich uranium deposits really *put* that section of the country *on the map*⟩ — **wipe off the map :** to utterly destroy (as a city, a region) **:** ANNIHILATE ⟨threatened a nuclear attack that would *wipe* the country *off the map*⟩

²map \"\ *vt* **mapped; mapped; mapping; maps 1 a :** to make a map of **:** show or establish the features or details of with clarity like that of a map ⟨~ the surface of the moon⟩ ⟨sorrow was *mapped* on her face⟩ **b :** to make a survey of or travel over for or as if for the purpose of making a map ⟨a remote section they haven't even begun to ~⟩ **c :** to assign to every element of (a mathematical set) an element of the same or another set ⟨a set is called denumerable if it can be *mapped* . . . onto the set of all the natural numbers —A.H.Wallace⟩ **2 :** to arrange, delineate, or plan the details of **:** show or plan in detail ⟨*mapped* a program⟩ — often used with *out* ⟨*mapping* out what he hoped to accomplish⟩

MAP *abbr* **1** maximum average price **2** medical aid post

ma·pau *also* **ma·pou** \'mä,pau̇\ *n* -s [Maori *mapau*] **:** a New Zealand tree (*Rapanea urvillei*) of the family Myrsinaceae that has reddish brown leaves and small white flowers and a light wood that is much used for fuel

map crack *n* **:** a minute crack (as on the surface of mortar, concrete, plaster)

ma·ple \'māpəl\ *n* -s *often attrib* [ME, fr. OE *mapul-*; akin to ON *mǫpurr* maple and perh. to OHG *mazzaltra* maple] **1 a** (1) **:** a tree or shrub of the genus *Acer* — see BOX ELDER, NORWAY MAPLE, SILVER MAPLE, SUGAR MAPLE, SWAMP MAPLE, SYCAMORE (2) **:** the wood of a maple tree; *esp* **:** the hard light-colored close-grained wood of the sugar maple that is used extensively for flooring, furniture, and small items (as turnings and handles) — compare BIRD'S-EYE MAPLE, CURLY 2 (3) **:** the flavor of maple sap or its products (as syrup or sugar) **b** *Austral* (1) **:** SILKY BEECH (2) **:** QUEENSLAND MAPLE (3) **:** a tree closely related to the Queensland maple **2 a :** a light brown **b :** a grayish yellow

maple bladder-gall mite *n* **:** an eriophyid mite (*Vasates quadripes*) producing swellings on maple leaves

maple borer *n* **:** an insect or insect larva that bores into maple trees

maple cream *or* **maple butter** *n* **:** maple syrup boiled to the concentration of soft sugar, cooled, and stirred to a creamy consistency

maple-face *n, obs* **:** a blotchy face

maple family *n* **:** ACERACEAE

maple honey *n* **:** maple syrup of light color boiled to a density of strained honey

maple leaf cutter *n* **:** the larva of a tiny incurvariid moth (*Paraclemensia acerifoliella*) that infests the leaves of maples and constructs a case of bits of leaves

mapleleaf viburnum \'⸗⸗,⸗-\ *or* **maple-leaved viburnum** *n* **:** DOCKMACKIE

maple-leaved \ˌ⸗⸗'⸗\ *adj* **:** having leaves like those of most maples

maplelike \'⸗⸗,⸗\ *adj* **:** resembling maple

maple silkwood *n* **:** QUEENSLAND MAPLE

maple sugar *n* **1 :** sugar made by boiling maple syrup to the hard sugar stage and then stirring immediately to promote crystallization **2 :** a moderate yellowish brown that is lighter and very slightly redder than Bismarck brown, lighter and slightly yellower and stronger than cinnamon brown, and redder, lighter, and slightly stronger than bronze

maple syrup *n* **:** syrup made by concentrating the sap of the sugar maple or various other maples

maple worm *n* **:** a grub that is the larva of a saturniid moth (*Anisota rubicunda*) and that defoliates maples

ma·po \'mä,pō\ *n* -s [AmerSp] **:** a small goby (*Bathygobius soporator*) of the south Atlantic coast and the West Indies

map·pable \'mapəbəl\ *adj* **:** capable of being represented on or by a map

mapped *past of* MAP

mappe·monde \(ˈ)map'mōnd\ *n* -s [ME *mappemounde* map of the world, fr. MF *mappemonde*, fr. ML *mappa mundi*, fr. *mappa* map + L *mundi*, gen. of *mundus* world — more at MAP] **:** a medieval map of the world

map·pen \'mapən\ *adv* [contr. of *mayhappen*] *dial Eng* **:** PERHAPS, POSSIBLY, MAYBE

map·per \'mapə(r)\ *n* -s **1 :** CARTOGRAPHER **2 :** a fire insurance company clerk who keeps maps showing the location of buildings on which the company has written insurance and data about the coverage

mapping *pres part of* MAP

map projection *n* **:** PROJECTION 1

maps *pl of* MAP, *pres 3d sing of* MAP

map turtle *also* **map terrapin** *n* **:** a small aquatic turtle (*Graptemys geographica*) of the central and eastern U.S. that is olive-colored and marked by delicate yellow tracings

ma·pu·che \mə'püchē\ *n, pl* **mapuche** *or* **mapuches** *usu cap* **1 a :** an Araucanian people of southern Chile **b :** a member of such people **2 :** the language of the Mapuche people

MAQ *abbr* money allowance for quarters

ma·quette \ma'ket, mə'-\ *n* -s [F, fr. It *macchietta*, dim. of *macchia* sketch, fr. *macchiare* to sketch, blot, speckle, fr. L *maculare* to spot, stain, fr. *macula* spot] **:** a usu. small preliminary model of something designed esp. to gauge the general appearance or composition of the thing that is planned: as **a :** a wax or clay model of a contemplated piece of sculpture **b :** a model of a room and its furnishings and decorative patterns **c :** a model of a building

ma·qui \'mä(,)kē\ *n* -s [Sp, fr. Mapuche] **:** a Chilean shrub (*Aristotelia maqui*) of the family Elaeocarpaceae that has evergreen foliage and berries from which a wine is made

ma·quil·lage \ˌmakē'(y)äzh, ˌmäk-\ *n* -s [F, fr. *maquiller* to make up, paint one's face + *-age*] **:** MAKEUP 4

ma·quis \(ˈ)ma'kē, (ˈ)mä'-\ *n, pl* **maquis** \-ē(z)\ [F, fr. It *macchie*, pl. of *macchia* thicket, spot, fr. L *macula* spot] **1** *also* **ma·qui** \"\ **a :** thick scrubby underbrush profuse along the shores of the Mediterranean and esp. profuse in the island of Corsica **b :** an area or zone marked by such underbrush **2** *often cap* **a :** a member of an underground movement or organization; *esp* **:** a French guerrilla fighter in World War II resisting the Nazis **b :** a band or unit of maquis

ma·qui·sard \ˌmakē'zär(d),\ *n* -s *often cap* [F, fr. *maquis* + *-ard*] **:** MAQUIS 2

¹mar \'mär, 'mȧ(r\ *vt* **marred; marred; marring; mars** [ME *marren*, fr. OE *mierran* to obstruct, waste; akin to OHG *merren* to obstruct, Goth *marzjan* to offend, and prob. to Skt *mṛṣyate* he forgets] **1 a :** to detract from the good condition or perfection or wholeness or beauty of **:** cause to be injured or damaged or defaced or blemished **:** SPOIL, IMPAIR ⟨will in no way ~ the enjoyment of your stay —Richard Joseph⟩ ⟨is too good a book to be *marred* by small defects —R.A.Smith⟩ ⟨all these gifts and qualities . . . were *marred* by prodigious faults —Virginia Woolf⟩ ⟨left a smudge that *marred* the lustrousness of the piano's polished surface⟩ ⟨the scenic beauty of this region is now *marred* by commercial signs —*Amer. Guide Series: Tenn.*⟩ **b** *archaic* **:** to inflict serious bodily harm on **:** severely disfigure **:** MUTILATE, MANGLE **c** *obs* **:** to bring to utter destruction **:** cause to be completely ruined **2** *archaic* **:** to get in the way of **:** HAMPER, IMPEDE, BLOCK **3** *obs* **:** BEWILDER, PERPLEX **syn** see INJURE

²mar \"\ *n* -s **:** something that mars **:** INJURY, DEFACEMENT, BLEMISH ⟨the importance of avoiding dust and ~s on photographic plates —*Science*⟩

mar *abbr* **1** marine **2** maritime **3** married

MAR *abbr* microanalytical reagent

¹ma·ra \mə'rä\ *n* -s [AmerSp *mará*, perh. fr. Araucanian] **:** a long-legged long-eared rodent (*Dolichotis magellanica*) closely related to the cavies and widely distributed in southern So. America

²mara \'marə\ *n* -s *usu cap* [by shortening] **:** MARACAIBO 1a

mar·a·bou *or* **mar·a·bout** \'marə,bü\ *n* -s [F *marabout*, lit., marabout] **1 a** *or* **marabou stork :** a large stork of the genus *Leptoptilos*: as (1) **:** an African stork (*L. crumeniferus*) (2) **:** ADJUTANT BIRD **b :** a soft feathery fluffy material prepared from the long coverts of marabous or usu. from turkey feathers and used esp. for trimmings ⟨all these ladies wearing ~ —*New Yorker*⟩ **2 a :** a thrown silk usu. dyed in the gum **b :** a fabric made of this silk

mar·a·bout \'marə,bü(t)\ *n* -s [F, fr. Pg *marabuto*, fr. Ar *murābiṭ*] **1** *often cap* **:** a Muslim monk or hermit esp. in Africa **:** Muslim ascetic **:** Muslim holy man or saint **2 :** a tomb or shrine erected to a marabout

mar·a·bout·ism \-ü(d·),izəm, -ü,ti-\ *n* -s *sometimes cap* **1 :** the way of life of a Muslim holy man **2 :** veneration of Muslim holy men

ma·raca \mə'räkə, -rakə\ *n* -s [Pg *maracá*, prob. fr. Tupi] **:** a dried gourd or a rattle like a gourd containing dried seeds or pebbles that has a handle and is used as a percussion instrument often in pairs

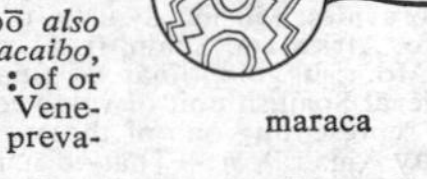

maraca

¹mar·a·cai·bo \ˌmarə'kī(,)bō *also* ˌmer-\ *adj, usu cap* [*Maracaibo*, city in northwest Venezuela] **:** of or from the city of Maracaibo, Venezuela **:** of the kind or style prevalent in Maracaibo

²maracaibo \"\ *n* -s *usu cap* **1 a** *also* **maracaibo coffee :** a coffee grown in Venezuela **b :** cacao from Venezuela **2** *also* **maracaibo lignum vitae :** VERA

maracaibo bark *n, usu cap M* **:** an inferior variety of cinchona bark

maracaibo boxwood *n, usu cap M* **:** ZAPATERO 2

mar·a·can \'marə,kan, -kən\ *n* -s [Pg *maracanã*, prob. fr. Tupi] **:** a Brazilian macaw

mar·a·cock \-,käk\ *n* [fr. *maracock, maracaw* (in some Algonquian language of Virginia), fr. Carib *merecuyá* granadilla, fr. Tupi *maracuyá*] **:** MAYPOP

ma·rae \mə'rī\ *n, pl* **marae** *or* **maraes** [Tahitian & Maori] **1 :** a Polynesian temple enclosure used for worship or sacrifice or other religious ceremonies **2 :** a square or similar open area before a Maori tribal or family meetinghouse used for formal reception of guests or other formal functions

marajuana *var of* MARIJUANA

ma·ral \mə'räl\ *n* -s [Per *marāl*] **:** an Asiatic red deer

ma·ran \mə'ran\ *n* [*Marans*, town in western France] **1** *usu cap* **:** a French breed of domestic fowls that lay many large dark brown eggs **2** -s *often cap* **:** a fowl of the Maran breed

ma·ra·nao *also* **mar·a·naw** \ˌmarə'nau̇\ *n, pl* **maranao** *or* **maranaos** *also* **maranaw** *or* **maranaws** *usu cap* [Sp, fr. Maranao *Maranáw*, fr. *ranaw* lake] **1 a :** a Moro people inhabiting the area around Lake Laneo and certain parts of central Cotabato province, Mindanao, Philippines, and northern Borneo **b :** a member of such people **2 :** the Austronesian language of the Maranao people

ma·rang \'mä,räŋ, 'ma,raŋ\ *n* -s [Tag] **1 :** a Philippine tree (*Artocarpus odoratissima*) resembling the breadfruit **2 :** the fruit of the marang tree consisting of a mass of small seeds embedded in a white sweetish edible pulp

ma·ra·nham jaborandi \ˌmarən'yam-, -yau̇n-\ *n, usu cap M* [*Maranhão*, state in northeast Brazil + E *jaborandi*] **:** JABORANDI 1b

marano *usu cap, var of* MARRANO

ma·ran·ta \mə'rantə\ *n* [NL, fr. Bartolomeo *Maranta* †1571 Ital. physician and botanist] **1 a** *cap* **:** a genus (the type of the family Marantaceae) of tropical American herbs with tuberous starchy roots and large sheathing leaves and regular flowers with a single petaloid filament bearing a one-celled anther **b** -s **:** any plant of the genus *Maranta* **2** -s **:** starch prepared from the rootstocks of an American arrowroot (*Maranta arundinacea*)

mar·an·ta·ce·ae \,marən'tāsē,ē\ *n pl, cap* [NL, fr. *Maranta*, type genus + *-aceae*] **:** a family of tropical monocotyledonous perennial herbs (order Musales) having a pronounced swelling at the junction of the petiole and leaf blade — **mar·an·ta·ceous** \ˌ⸗⸗'tāshəs\ *adj*

ma·ran·tic \mə'rantik\ *adj* [Gk *marantikos*, fr. (assumed) Gk *marantos* (verbal of Gk *marainein* to waste away) + Gk *-ikos* -ic] **:** of, relating to, or marked by marasmus **:** MARASMIC

ma·ra·ra \mə'rärə\ *n* -s [native name in Australia] **:** an Australian tree (*Weinmannia lachnocarpa*) of the family Escalloniaceae that is prominently buttressed at the base and has opposite compound leaves of 3-toothed leaflets and yields a light hard wood

maras *pl of* MARA

ma·ras·ca \mə'raskə\ *or* **marasca cherry** *n* -s [It *marasca*] **:** a Dalmatian bitter wild cherry (*Prunus cerasus marasca*) from the fermented juice of which maraschino liqueur is made — compare SOUR CHERRY

mar·a·schi·no \,marə'skē,nō, -'shē-\ *n* -s [It, fr. *marasca*] **1** *often cap* **:** a sweet liqueur made orig. in Dalmatia that is distilled from the fermented juice of the marasca and often flavored (as with bitter almonds, jasmine, or vanilla) and that is used as a cocktail ingredient, in cooking, and in preserving cherries **2** *or* **maraschino cherry** *often cap M* **a :** a usu. large cherry preserved in true or imitation maraschino **b :** MARASCA

ma·ras·ma \mə'razmə\ *n* -S [It, fr. LL *marasmus*] **:** MARASMUS

ma·ras·mic \-mik\ *adj* [*marasmus* + *-ic*] **:** of, relating to, or marked by marasmus **:** MARANTIC

ma·ras·mi·us \-mēəs\ *n, cap* [NL, fr. LL *marasmus*] **:** a genus of mostly small-sized white-spored mushrooms (family Agaricaceae) having a tough leathery stem and cap and lacking both ring and volva — see FAIRY RING, THREAD BLIGHT

ma·ras·moid \-,mȯid\ *adj* [*marasmus* + *-oid*] **:** resembling marasmus

ma·ras·mus \-,məs\ *n* -ES [LL, fr. Gk *marasmos*, fr. *marainein* to waste away — more at SMART] **:** progressive emaciation esp. in the young because of malnutrition due chiefly to faulty assimilation and utilization of food

ma·ra·tha *also* **mah·rat·ta** \mə'rädə, -radə\ *or* **mah·rat·ti** \-d·ē\ *n, pl* **maratha** *or* **marathas** *usu cap* [Hindi *Marhaṭā*, *Marhaṭṭā* & *Marathi Marāṭhā*, fr. Skt *Mahārāṣṭra*, fr. *mahat* great + *rāṣṭra* kingdom; akin to Skt *rājan* king — more at MUCH, RAJA] **1 :** a Scytho-Dravidian people of the south central part of the subcontinent of India **2 :** a member of the Maratha people

ma·ra·thi \-d·ē\ *n* -S *usu cap* [Marathi *Marāṭhī*, fr. Skt *Mahārāṣṭrī*, fr. *Mahārāṣṭra*] **:** the chief Indic language of southern and eastern Bombay state

¹mar·a·thon \'marə,thän *also* 'mer- *sometimes* -,thən\ *n* -S *sometimes cap* [*Marathon*, ancient town in east central Greece where in 490 B.C. the Greeks won a victory over the Persians of which the news was carried to Athens by a long-distance runner] **1 a :** a long-distance race: (1) **:** a footrace run on an open course of now usu. 26 miles 385 yards (2) **:** a race other than a footrace (as for swimmers, skaters) marked by esp. great length **b :** a competition in which participants vie with each other to see who can last the longest in doing something **:** a contest that tests the stamina and endurance of the contestants **:** an endurance contest ⟨a dance ~⟩ ⟨a speechmaking ~⟩ **2 :** an activity that tests or demonstrates the stamina or endurance power of the performer ⟨after a ~ of autographing some 4000 copies of the first volume of his memoirs —*Time*⟩

²marathon \"\ *also* **mar·a·tho·ni·an** \,==ˈthōnēən\ *or* **mar·a·thon·ic** \-ˈthänik\ *adj, sometimes cap* **:** belonging to or suggestive of or suited for a marathon race or competition or other activity: **a :** marked by unusual length of time ⟨a ~ session of Congress⟩ or distance ⟨a ~ hike⟩ or extent ⟨a speech with a ~ opening sentence⟩ **b :** such as tests or demonstrates the stamina or endurance power of the performer ⟨*marathonic* lungpower —*Newsweek*⟩ ⟨besides being amused by her performance, we were stunned by the *marathonian* ebullience —Stanley Kauffmann⟩

³marathon \"\ *vi* -ED/-ING/-S **:** to run a marathon or take part in marathon competition or activity ⟨an exhibition of ~*ing*⟩ — **mar·a·thon·er** \-nə(r)\ *n* -S

⁴marathon \"\ *n* -S **:** a strong orange that is darker than pumpkin and redder and duller than cadmium orange

ma·rat·tia \mə'rad·ēə\ *n, cap* [NL, fr. Giovanni Francesco *Maratti* †1777 Ital. botanist + NL *-ia*] **:** the type genus of Marattiaceae comprising ferns with the sporangia in two rows forming a synangium

ma·rat·ti·a·ce·ae \=,==ˈāsē,ē\ *n pl, cap* [NL, fr. *Marattia*, type genus + *-aceae*] **:** a family (coextensive with the order Marattiales) of chiefly tropical eusporangiate ferns with mostly pinnate often gigantic fronds and thick stipules and abaxial sori — **ma·rat·ti·a·ceous** \=,==ˈāshəs\ *adj*

ma·rat·ti·a·les \=,==ˈā(,)lēz\ *n pl, cap* [NL, fr. *Marattia* + *-ales*] **:** an order of lower ferns (class Filicineae) comprising the Marattiaceae

¹ma·raud \mə'rȯd\ *vb* -ED/-ING/-S [F *marauder*, fr. *maraud* vagabond] *vi* **:** to roam about and make irregular sudden small-scale attacks, raids, or incursions for or as if for the sake of obtaining loot **:** rove about and pillage ⟨were told to watch out for ~*ing* bands of Indians⟩ ~ *vt* **:** to subject to marauding **:** RAID, PILLAGE — now usu. used in passive ⟨a poverty-stricken ~*ed* countryside⟩

²maraud \"\ *n* -S *archaic* **:** the act of marauding

ma·raud·er \-də(r)\ *n* -S **:** one that marauds **:** PLUNDERER

mar·a·ve·di \,marəˈvādē\ *n* -S [Sp *maravedí*, fr. Ar *Murābiṭīn* Almoravides, Muslim dynasty of the 11th and 12th centuries in No. Africa and Spain, fr. pl. of *murābiṭ* marabout] **1 :** an old Moorish gold dinar of Spain and Morocco **2 a :** a medieval Spanish unit of value equal to $^1/_{34}$ real **b :** a copper coin representing one of these units

ma·ray \mə'rā\ *n* -S [native name in Australia] **:** a Pacific round herring (*Etrumeus jacksoniensis*) occurring in great numbers off the coast of Australia

marbelize *var of* MARBLEIZE

¹mar·ble \'märbəl, 'mäb-\ *n* -S [ME *marbel*, fr. OF *marbre*, fr. L *marmor*, fr. Gk *marmaros* marble, rock, prob. fr. *marainein* to waste away — more at SMART] **1 a :** limestone that is crystallized in varying degrees by metamorphism, that ranges from granular to compact in texture, that is white or tinted or veined or mottled with various colors (as bluish gray, red, yellow, green) or is sometimes black, that is capable of taking a usu. high polish, and that is extensively used esp. in architecture and sculpture **b :** something composed of or made from this limestone: as (1) **:** a piece (as a block, slab, shaft) of this limestone ⟨a table top of ~⟩; *esp* **:** a commemorative monument (as an inscribed tablet, pillar, shaft, or tomb) made from this limestone ⟨read the inscription on the ~⟩ (2) **:** a piece of sculpture carved from this limestone ⟨a museum with a splendid collection of ancient Greek ~*s*⟩ **c :** something resembling (as in hardness, rigidity, coldness, smoothness) or suggestive of marble this limestone ⟨had a heart of ~ and paid no attention to her tears⟩ **2 a :** a little ball made of a hard substance (as agate, glass, porcelain, baked clay, steel) typically ranging from about ½ inch to about 1 inch in diameter; *esp* **:** such a little ball used in various games **b marbles** *pl but sing in constr* **:** a children's game that is played with these little balls and that consists typically in trying to knock out of a certain area one or more of the balls arranged inside a circle or in a row by hitting the balls with another ball usu. propelled by the thumb **3 :** MARBLING **4 marbles** *pl, slang* **a :** elements of common sense ⟨the old man losing his ~*s* one by one —J.F.Powers⟩ ⟨persons who are born without all their ~*s* —Arthur Miller⟩ **b :** food thrown up by the stomach

²marble \"\ *vt* **marbled; marbled; marbling** \-b(ə)liŋ\ **marbles :** to make like marble esp. in coloration **:** MARBLEIZE **:** STREAK, BLOTCH, MOTTLE; *specif* **:** to give a veined or mottled appearance to (as paper, book edges, book end papers, tiles, glass) by staining or varying the composition of or by some other process

³marble \"\ *adj* **1 :** composed of or made from marble ⟨a ~ floor⟩ ⟨~ top⟩ **2 a :** resembling (as in hardness, rigidity, coldness, smoothness) or suggestive of marble ⟨had a ~ heart incapable of human warmth⟩ ⟨the still evening and the ~ calm of the lake⟩ **b :** MARBLED ⟨~ paper⟩ ⟨~ glass⟩

marble bone *or* **marble bone disease** *n* **:** OSTEOPETROSIS

marble bones *n pl but sing in constr* **:** OSTEOPETROSIS

marble cake *n* **:** a cake made with light and dark batter so as to have a streaked or mottled appearance suggestive of marble

marbled *adj* [partly fr. ¹*marble* + *-ed*, partly fr. past part. of ²*marble*] **1 a :** done in or covered with marble ⟨the ~ likeness of the emperor⟩ ⟨the ~ exterior of the building⟩ **b :** marked by an extensive use of marble as an architectural or decorative feature ⟨an ancient ~ city⟩ **2 :** having markings or a coloration that resembles or is suggestive of marble ⟨a dog with a handsome ~ coat⟩; *specif* **:** having a veined, streaked, or mottled appearance through being subjected to a process of marbling ⟨~ endpapers⟩ ⟨~ glass⟩ ⟨~ slate⟩ ⟨~ calfskin⟩ **3 :** marked by an intermixture of fat and lean ⟨a well ~ cut of meat⟩

marbled cat *or* **marbled tiger cat** *n* **:** a long-tailed brightly patterned cat (*Felis marmorata*) of southeastern Asia and the East Indies

marbled godwit *n* **:** a large American godwit (*Limosa fedoa*) that is reddish or yellowish brown in color and has a long straight or slightly upcurved bill

marbled murrelet *n* **:** a murrelet (*Brachyramphus marmoratus*) that is dusky and has white underparts mottled with brown and that is found from Alaska to Vancouver

marbled polecat *n* **:** TIGER WEASEL

marbled sculpin *n* **:** CABEZONE 1

marblehearted \ˈ=,==\ *adj* **:** devoid of and coldly resistant to kindness, sympathy, pity, friendliness, or affection ⟨a ~ tyrant⟩

mar·ble·ization \,märbələ'zāshən, ,mäb-, -,lī'z-\ *n* -S **:** the process of becoming marbleized or the condition of being marbleized

mar·ble·ize *also* **mar·bel·ize** \'märbə,līz, 'mäb-\ *vt* **marbleized** *also* **marbelized; marbleized** *also* **marbelized; marbleizing** *also* **marbelizing; marbleizes** *also* **marbelizes :** MARBLE — **mar·ble·iz·er** \-,līzə(r)\ *n* -S

mar·bler \-b(ə)lə(r)\ *n* -S **:** one that marbles (as paper, the edges of a book)

marbles *pl of* MARBLE, *pres 3d sing of* MARBLE

marble thrush *n* **:** MISTLE THRUSH

marblewood \ˈ==,=\ *n* **1 a :** a large Asiatic tree (*Diospyros kurzii*) that has a hard mottled wood — called also *Andaman marble* **b** (1) **:** NATIVE OLIVE 1a (2) **:** an Australian timber tree of the genus *Albizzia* **2 :** the wood of a marblewood

marbling *n* -S [fr. gerund of ²*marble*] **1 :** the action or process of making like marble esp. in coloration **2 :** coloration or markings resembling or suggestive of marble **3 :** an intermixture of fat and lean in a cut of meat esp. when evenly distributed ⟨the quality of a cut of meat can often be judged from its degree of ~⟩

mar·bly \'märb(ə)lē, 'mäb-, -li\ *adj, sometimes* -ER/-EST [¹*marble* + *-y*] **1 :** MARBLE 2a ⟨the ~ calm of the lake⟩ **2 :** MARBLED 1b ⟨a ~ building⟩

¹marc *obs var of* ³MARK

²marc \'märk, 'mäk\ *n* -S [F, fr. MF, fr. *marchier* to trample under foot — more at MARCH] **1 a :** the residue remaining after a fruit (as grapes or olives) has been subjected to pressing — compare POMACE 1 **b :** an insoluble residue remaining after extraction of a substance (as a drug) with a solvent **2 :** a brandy that is made by distilling the skins of grapes or the pulp of apples after the wine or cider is made — called also *eau-de-vie de marc*; compare GRAPPA

marc *abbr* marcato

mar·can *or* **mar·kan** \'märkən, 'mäk-\ *adj, usu cap* [*marcan* fr. LL *Marcus* Mark, evangelist traditionally regarded as author of the second gospel + E *-an*; *markan* fr. *Mark* + E *-an*] **:** of or characteristic of the Evangelist Mark or the Gospel ascribed to him ⟨carefully studied the *Marcan* text⟩

mar·can·do \mär'kän(,)dō\ *adv* (*or adj*) [It, verbal of *marcare* to mark, accent] **:** MARCATO

mar·ca·site \'märkə,sīt, ¦==ˈzēt\ *n* -S [ME *marchasite*, fr. ML *marcasita*, fr. Ar *marqashīthā*, fr. Syr *marqēshīthā*, perh. fr. Assyr *markhashītu* of or belonging to Markhashi, fr. *Markhashi*, region perhaps located in northeast Persia] **1 a :** any of several minerals with a metallic luster; *esp* **:** crystallized iron pyrites — not used technically **b :** a mineral consisting of iron disulfide FeS_2 having the same composition as iron pyrites and resembling it in appearance but differing from it by its orthorhombic crystallization and its lower specific gravity (4.85–4.90) — called also *white iron pyrites* **2 a :** a piece of marcasite (as crystallized iron pyrites) used in making ornaments esp. costume jewelry **b :** an ornament (as a piece of costume jewelry) made of marcasite — **mar·ca·sit·i·cal** \¦==ˈsid·əkəl\ *adj*

mar·ca·tis·si·mo \,märkəˈtisə,mō\ *adv* (*or adj*) [It, superl. of *marcato*] **:** with very strong accentuation — used as a direction in music

mar·ca·to \mär'käd·(,)ō\ *adv* (*or adj*) [It, past part. of *marcare* to mark, accent, of Gmc origin; akin to OHG *marcōn* to determine the boundaries of — more at MARK] **:** with strong accentuation — used as a direction in music

¹mar·cel \(ˈ)mär¦sel, (ˈ)mä¦s-\ *or* **marcel wave** *n* -S [after *Marcel* Grateau †1936 Fr. hairdresser] **:** a deep soft wave or series of such waves made in the hair by the use of a heated curling iron

²marcel \"\ *vb* **marcelled; marcelled; marcelling; marcels** *vt* **:** to make a marcel in ⟨regularly *marcelled* her hair⟩ ~ *vi* **:** to make a marcel ⟨skilled at *marcelling*⟩

mar·cel·la \mär'selə, mä's-\ *n* -S [prob. alter. of ²*marseilles*] **:** an English cotton fabric made with a quilted or honeycomb face and used esp. for clothing, trimming, or bedspreads

mar·cel·ler \-lə(r)\ *n* -S **:** a hairdresser who makes marcels

mar·ces·cence \mär'ses'n(t)s\ *n* -S [fr. *marcescent*, after such pairs as E *competent: competence*] **:** the quality or state of being marcescent

¹mar·ces·cent \-nt\ *adj* [L *marcescent-, marcescens*, pres. part. of *marcescere* to wither, incho. fr. *marcēre* to wither; akin to MHG *mern* to dip bread in wine or water, MIr *mraich*, *braich* malt, and prob. to Gk *marainein* to waste away — more at SMART] *of a plant part* **:** withering without falling off ⟨~ leaves⟩

²marcescent \"\ *n* -S **:** a plant that has marcescent parts

marc·gra·via \märk'grāvēə, mäk'-\ *n, cap* [NL, fr. Georg *Markgraf* †1644 Ger. naturalist and traveler in So. America + NL *-ia*] **:** a genus (the type of the family Marcgraviaceae) of tropical American epiphytic woody vines that have vegetative shoots with 2-ranked closely appressed sessile leaves and flowering shoots with spreading petiolate leaves

marc·gra·vi·a·ce·ae \=,==ˈāsē,ē\ *n pl, cap* [NL, fr. *Marcgravia*, type genus + *-aceae*] **:** a small family of often epiphytic tropical American shrubs, trees, or vines (order Parietales) that have usu. pendulous flowers and petals united into a hood and sometimes functioning as nectaries — **marc·gra·vi·a·ceous** \(ˈ)=¦==ˈāshəs\ *adj*

¹march \'märch, 'mäch\ *n* -ES *usu cap* [ME, fr. OF *march*, *marz*, fr. L *martius*, fr. *martius* of Mars, fr. *Mart-, Mars*, Roman god of war and agriculture] **:** the third month of the Gregorian calendar — abbr. *Mar.*; see MONTH table

²march \"\ *n* -ES [ME *marche*, fr. OF, of Gmc origin; akin to OHG *marha* boundary — more at MARK] **1 a** (1) **:** a border region **:** BORDERLAND, FRONTIER (2) **:** BOUNDARY **b :** TERRITORY; *esp* **:** the territory (as a province) of an official's jurisdiction **2** *usu cap* **:** MARCH KING OF ARMS

³march \"\ *vi* -ED/-ING/-ES [ME *marchen*, fr. MF *marchir*, fr. OF, fr. *marche*, n.] **:** to have a contiguous location **:** have common borders or frontiers **:** lie continuously parallel or adjacent ⟨a region that ~*es* with Canada on the north and the Pacific on the west⟩ **:** lie extended ⟨mountain ranges that ~ along the horizon on every side —*Amer. Guide Series: Vt.*⟩

⁴march \"\, *as a command in drilling often* 'härch *or* 'häch\ *vb* -ED/-ING/-ES [MF *marcher*, *marchier* to march, trample under foot, fr. OF *marchier* to trample under foot, prob. of Gmc origin; akin to OE *mearcian* to mark, determine the boundaries of, OHG *marcōn* to determine the boundaries of — more at MARK] *vi* **1 a** (1) **:** to move along steadily with a regular measured stride; *esp* **:** to move along steadily with a rhythmic stride and in step with one or more others so moving ⟨enviously watched the column of soldiers ~*ing* smartly up the street⟩ (2) **:** to begin to move along steadily in this manner **:** begin such movement **:** set out or start marching ⟨said his troops would ~ at the crack of dawn⟩ **b :** to be in accord **:** move along in harmonious agreement **:** JIBE ⟨wherever his sympathies ~*ed* with the facts —Walter Lippmann⟩ **2 a** (1) **:** to move from one point to another usu. by walking esp. in a direct purposeful manner and without delaying ⟨heard a noise upstairs and ~*ed* up to see what was going on⟩ (2) **:** to go along **:** PROCEED, TRAVEL ⟨can ~ off to distant times and places —*Newsweek*⟩ ⟨hundreds of ships which had ~*ed* into the gulf —K.M. Dodson⟩ **b :** to make steady progress **:** move right along **:** go forward **:** move ahead **:** ADVANCE ⟨engines that ~ down the assembly line each day —A.H.Raskin⟩ ⟨forces that ~ inexorably toward greater social justice⟩ **3** *obs* **:** to have status **:** have rating **:** RANK ⟨~ in the first rank of magnificence —Robert Johnson⟩ ~ *vt* **1 a :** to cause to march ⟨~*ed* a division of foot troops forty honest miles in a day —H.H. Arnold & I.C.Eaker⟩ ⟨discipline that could ~ men past the point of exhaustion —Bruce Catton⟩ **b :** to bring or conduct somewhere esp. in a peremptory or unceremonious way or by force ⟨can remember him ~*ing* us all off from the schoolhouse —A.E.Coppard⟩ ⟨~*ed* them promptly to the jailhouse⟩ **2 :** to cover (an indicated distance or area) by marching **:** TRAVERSE ⟨~*ed* the ten remaining miles in record time⟩

⁵march \"\ *n* -ES [MF *marche*, fr. *marcher*, *marchier*, v.] **1 a** (1) **:** the action of marching ⟨were too tired to begin another ~⟩ (2) **:** the distance covered within a specific period of time by marching ⟨the city was at least a day's ~ away⟩ (3) **:** a regular measured stride or rhythmic step used in marching ⟨heard the ~ of the soldiers as they filed past⟩ **b** (1) **:** forward movement **:** steady advance **:** PROGRESS ⟨the ~ of time and events⟩ ⟨the ~ of science⟩; *esp* **:** forward movement of a marching unit esp. a military unit ⟨could not check the ~ of troops into their country⟩ (2) **:** direction of movement **:** COURSE ⟨did not like the current ~ of public opinion⟩ **c :** a long usu. tiring journey usu. on foot ⟨were not happy at the thought of a ~ to the top of the mountain⟩ **2 :** an instrumental or vocal composition that is in duple rhythm (as ⁴⁄₄ time) or triply compound rhythm (as ⁶⁄₈ time) with a strongly accentuated beat and that is designed or suitable for the accompaniment and guidance of marching **3 :** the taking of all five tricks by one side in the game of euchre — **on the march :** moving along steadily **:** ADVANCING ⟨saw that industrial improvement was *on the march*⟩ **:** MARCHING ⟨troops that were constantly *on the march*⟩ — **steal a march on** *also* **get a march on :** to get ahead of or win an advantage over esp. unexpectedly and with sly adroitness ⟨*stole a march on* his competitors by being the first to put the product on the market⟩

march *abbr, often cap* marchioness

mar·chant \'märchənt\ *archaic var of* MERCHANT

mar·chan·tia \mär'shantēə\ *n* [NL, fr. Nicolas *Marchant* †1678 Fr. botanist + NL *-ia*] **1** *cap* **:** the type genus of Marchantiaceae comprising liverworts that reproduce asexually by gemmae and have stalked antheridiophores **2** -S **:** any liverwort of the genus *Marchantia*

mar·chan·ti·a·ce·ae \=,==ˈāsē,ē\ *n pl, cap* [NL, fr. *Marchantia*, type genus + *-aceae*] **:** a family of liverworts (order Marchantiales) with prostrate usu. dichotomously branched thalli and archegonia on specialized upright branches — see MARCHANTIA — **mar·chan·ti·a·ceous** \=¦==ˈāshəs\ *adj*

mar·chan·ti·a·les \=,==ˈā(,)lēz\ *n pl, cap* [NL, fr. *Marchantia* + *-ales*] **:** an order of Hepaticae comprising liverworts in which the gametophyte is differentiated internally into ventral storage tissue sometimes enclosing primitive conducting tissue and into a dorsal region of air chambers and in which the sporophyte has a jacket layer that is only one cell thick — see MARCHANTIACEAE

march brown *n, usu cap M & often cap B* **1 :** a mayfly (*Ecdyurus venosus*) mostly brown and striped with yellow **2 :** an angler's fly made to imitate the March brown mayfly

mär·chen \'me(ə)rkən, *G* 'meer\ *n, pl* **märchen** [G, fr. MHG *merechyn* short verse narrative, fr. *mære* report, narrative (fr. OHG *mārī*, *māri*, fr. *māri* famous) + *-chyn*, dim. suffix, fr. OHG *-chīn*; akin to OE *mǣre* famous, ON *mærr* famous, OE *māra* larger, more — more at MORE, -KIN] **:** TALE; *esp* **:** FOLKTALE

march·er \'märchə(r), 'mäch-\ *n* -S [ME *marchier*, *marchere*, fr. *marche* border region + *-er*, *-ier*, *-ere*, *-iere* -er] **1 :** one that inhabits a border region **2 :** a lord enjoying royal liberties and having jurisdiction over territory in the English marches — called also *lord marcher*

marches *pl of* MARCH, *pres 3d sing of* MARCH

mar·che·sa \mär'käzə\ *n, pl* **marche·se** \-(,)zā\ [It, fem. of *marchese*] **:** an Italian woman holding the rank of a marchese **:** MARCHIONESS

mar·che·se \-(,)zā\ *n, pl* **marche·si** \-(,)zē\ [It, fr. ML *marcensis*, fr. *marca* border region, of Gmc origin; akin to OHG *marha* boundary — more at MARK] **:** an Italian nobleman next in rank above a count **:** MARQUIS

mar·chesh·van \mär'keshvən\ *n* -S *usu cap* [Heb *marḥeshwān*] **:** HESHVAN

mar·chet \'märchət\ *or* **mar·che·ta** \mär'käd·ə\ *also* **merchet** \'mərchət\ *n* -S [ME *merchet*, fr. AF, fr. L *mercatus* trade, market place — more at MARKET] **:** a fee paid to a British feudal lord by his tenant for marrying off a daughter or son esp. to one outside the lord's jurisdiction or for the lord's waiving the droit du seigneur

march fly *n, usu cap M* **1 :** a fly of the family Bibionidae that usu. appears in early spring **2** *Austral* **:** HORSEFLY

marching fire *n* **:** ASSAULT FIRE

marching flank *n* **:** the flank of a military command farthest from the pivot when executing a change of direction

marching orders *n pl* **1 :** orders to set out on a march **:** orders to proceed ⟨the division got its *marching orders* one day before the attack⟩ **2 :** a notice of dismissal (as from a job) ⟨did very poor work and soon got his *marching orders*⟩

mar·chio·ness \'märsh(ə)nəs, 'mäsh-\ *n* -ES [ML *marchionissa*, *marcionissa*, fr. *marchion-*, *marchio* marquis (fr. *marca* border region) + LL *-issa* -ess] **1 :** the wife of a marquess **2 :** a woman who holds in her own right the rank of marquess

march king of arms *usu cap M&K&A* [²*march*] **:** an English king of arms of the late medieval period who had jurisdiction in the west of England and in Wales and Cornwall and whose province was later divided between Clarenceux King of Arms and Norroy King of Arms

marchland \ˈ=,=\ *n* **:** land in or along border regions **:** BORDERLAND

march·man \ˈ=mən\ *n, pl* **marchmen** [ME *marcheman*, fr. *marche* border region + *man* — more at MARCH] **:** MARCHER 1

march–order \ˈ=,==\ *vt* **:** to ready (arms or other military equipment) for marching ⟨*march-ordered* the artillery⟩

march·pane \'märch,pān, 'mäch-\ *n* -S [It *marzapane* — more at MARZIPAN] **:** MARZIPAN

march–past \ˈ=,=\ *n, pl* **march–pasts :** a filing by **:** PROCESSION ⟨reviews with relish the *march-past* of his years —*New Yorker*⟩; *specif* **:** a ceremonious procession or parade of marching units esp. of troops that file in review before inspectors or spectators

mar·cion·ism \'märshə,nizəm\ *n* -S *usu cap* [*Marcion*, 2d cent. A.D. Christian Gnostic + E *-ism*] **:** the doctrine of the Marcionites

mar·cion·ite \-,nīt\ *also* **mar·cion·ist** \-,nəst\ *n* -S *usu cap* [LL *marcionita*, *marcionista*, fr. *Marcion* + L *-ita* -ite or L *-ista* -ist] **:** a member of an anti-Judaic Gnostic sect that flourished from the 2d century to about the 7th century A.D.

mar·co·man·ni \,märkə'ma,nī\ *n pl, usu cap* [L *Marcomani*, *Marcomanni*] **:** an ancient Germanic people related to the Suevians

¹mar·co·ni \mär'kōnē, mä'k-\ *adj, usu cap* [Guglielmo *Marconi* †1937 Ital. electrical engineer and inventor] **:** of or relating to the system of wireless telegraphy invented by Marconi ⟨a *Marconi* aerial⟩

²marconi \"\ *vt* **marconied; marconied; marconiing; marconies :** to send (a message) by radiogram

³marconi \"\ *adj, usu cap* [prob. so called fr. the resemblance of the complex system of struts and stays formerly characteristic of the Bermuda rig to the poles and stays used in wireless telegraphy] **:** of, relating to, or marked by a Bermuda rig ⟨a *Marconi* mainsail⟩

mar·co·ni·gram \-,gram\ *n* [¹*marconi* + *-gram*] **:** RADIOGRAM

mar·co·ni·graph \-,graf, -räf\ *n* [¹*marconi* + *-graph*] **:** apparatus used in Marconi wireless telegraphy

marconi rig *n, usu cap M* **:** BERMUDA RIG

mar·co po·lo sheep \'mär,kō'pō,lō-, 'mä,k-\ *or* **marco polo's sheep** *n, usu cap M&P* [after *Marco Polo* †1324? Ital. traveler] **:** an Asiatic wild sheep with exceptionally large horns that is considered to be a variety (*Ovis ammon poli*) of the argali or to constitute a distinct species (*O. poli*)

¹mar·cot \'mär,kät, =ˈ=\ *vt* **marcotted; marcotted; marcotting; marcots** [F *marcotter*, fr. *marcotte*, n.] **:** to propagate (a plant) by marcottage

²marcot \"\ *also* **mar·cotte** \"\ *n* -S [F *marcotte*, fr. MF, prob. irreg. fr. L *mergus* layer of a plant, fr. *mergere* to dip, plunge — more at MERGE] **1 :** a branch of a plant prepared for marcottage **2 :** a new plant produced by marcottage

mar·cot·tage \'mär,käd·ij, =ˈ==; ¦märkə¦täzh\ *n* -S [F, fr. *marcotter* + *-age*] **:** air layering in which the rooting medium is bound to the plant rather than enclosed in a pot or other container; *broadly* **:** AIR LAYERING

marcs *pl of* MARC

mar del pla·ta \¦mär,del¦pläd·ə\ *adj, usu cap M&P* [fr. *Mar del Plata*, city in eastern Argentina] **:** of or from the city of Mar del Plata, Argentina **:** of the kind or style prevalent in Mar del Plata

mar·di gras \'märdē¦grä, ¦mädē¦grä, -di-\ *n, usu cap M&G* [F, lit., fat Tuesday] **1 a :** the last day before Lent often marked by merrymaking and feasting and in some places (as

New Orleans) by parades esp. of grotesquely costumed individuals and by masquerade balls **b :** a carnival period (as in New Orleans) preceding Lent and often lasting for many days and climaxed on the final day before Lent **2 :** a festive celebration held on or like that often held on the last day or days before Lent and marked by merrymaking and feasting

¹mare *n* -s [ME, fr. OE; akin to OHG & ON *mara* incubus, Croatian *mora*, and prob. to Gk *marainein* to waste away — more at SMART] *obs* **:** an evil preternatural being conceived of as causing nightmare

²mare \ˈma(a)(ə)r, ˈme(ə)r, |ə\ *n* -s [ME *mare, mere*, fr. OE *mere;* akin to OHG *merha* mare, ON *merr* mare, OE *mearh* horse, OHG *marah*, ON *marr*, W *march*] **1 :** a female horse or other equine animal esp. when fully mature or of breeding age — compare FILLY **2** *chiefly Scot* **:** ¹TRESTLE 1a

³ma·re \ˈmä(ˌ)rā, |(ˌ)rē, |ri\ *n, pl* **ma·ria** \ˈrēə\ [NL, fr. L, sea — more at MARINE] **:** one of several dark areas of considerable extent on the surface of either the moon or Mars

ma·re·ca \məˈrēkə\ *n, cap* [NL, fr. Pg *marreca* wild duck] **:** a genus comprising the widgeons

mare clau·sum \-ˈklȯsəm, -ˈklau̇ˌsu̇m\ *n* [NL, closed sea] **:** a sea or other navigable body of water that is under the jurisdiction of one nation and that is closed to other nations

ma·re·han \ˈmärəˌhän\ *n, pl* **marehan** *or* **marehans** *usu cap* **1 :** a negroid people of Somaliland in the eastern part of Africa **2 :** a member of the Marehan people

mare li·be·rum \-ˈlibərəm, -ˈlēbəˌru̇m\ *n* [NL, free sea] **1 :** a sea or other navigable body of water that is open to all nations **2 :** FREEDOM OF THE SEAS

ma·rem·ma \məˈremə\ *n* -s [It, fr. ML *maritima* places near the sea, fr. L, neut. pl. of *maritimus* maritime — more at MARITIME] **:** swampy coastland

mar·eng cell \ˈmäˌreŋ-\ *n, usu cap M* [*mareng* fr. Glenn L. Martin †1955 Am. airplane manufacturer + E *engineering*] **:** a fuel container made of airplane cloth impregnated inside and outside with a synthetic rubber that tends to seal up punctures

ma·ren·go \məˈreŋ(ˌ)gō\ *adj, often cap* [F, fr. *Marengo*, village in northwest Italy; prob. fr. the serving of a chicken marengo to Napoleon after his victory over the Austrians at Marengo in 1800] **:** of, consisting of, or served with a sauce made of mushrooms, tomatoes, olives, oil, and wine ⟨sautéed chicken ~⟩

mare nos·trum \-ˈnästrəm, -ˈnäˌstru̇m\ *n* [L, our sea; fr. the fact that the Roman Empire at its greatest extent included all lands bordering on the Mediterranean] **:** a sea or other navigable body of water that belongs to a single nation or that two or more nations share by mutual agreement

mareograph *var of* MARIGRAPH

mare's nest *n, pl* **mare's nests** *or* **mares' nests 1 :** a hoax or fraud or some other nonexistent or illusory thing that seems at first to be very wonderful and full of promise but that ultimately brings ridicule on those deceived by it ⟨creating a neat little *mare's nest* in English dramatic history —R.S.Loomis⟩ ⟨spent his whole life looking for what was actually a *mare's nest*⟩ **2 :** a place, condition, or situation of great untidiness, disorder, or confusion ⟨the hold of the ship was a *mare's nest*⟩ ⟨had made a *mare's nest* of the administration⟩

mare's tail *n, pl* **mare's tails** *or* **mares' tails 1 :** a cirrus cloud that has a long slender flowing appearance **2** *pl* *mare's tails* **a :** a common aquatic plant (*Hippuris vulgaris*) with elongated shoots clothed with dense whorls of subulate leaves **b :** HORSETAIL 2 **c :** HORSEWEED 1

ma·rey's law \məˈrāz-\ *n, usu cap M* [after Étienne Jules *Marey* †1904 Fr. physiologist] **:** a statement in physiology: heart rate is related inversely to arterial blood pressure

mar·fire \ˈmärˌfī(ə)r\ *n* [perh. fr. E dial. *mar* (alter. of E ¹*mere*) + E *fire*] *dial Eng* **:** phosphorescence occurring on the sea

marg *abbr* margin; marginal

mar·ga \ˈmärgə\ *n* -s [Skt *mārga* path, fr. *mṛga* deer, gazelle] **1** *Hinduism* **:** one of several ways of approaching salvation — compare BHAKTI-MARGA **2 :** EIGHTFOLD PATH

mar·ga·rate \ˈmärgəˌrāt\ *n* -s [ISV *margaric* (in *margaric* acid) + *-ate*] **:** a salt or ester of margaric acid

mar·ga·ret grunt \ˈmärg(ə)rət-\ *n* [*margaret* by folk etymology (influence of the name *Margaret*) fr. *margate*] **:** MARGATE a

mar·gar·ic acid \märˈ|garik-, mä|, |ˈgärik-, ˈmär|gərik-, ˈmä|, -rēk-\ *n* [*margaric* fr. F *margarique*, fr. *margar-* (fr. *margarine* margarin) + *-ique* -ic] **1 :** a crystalline synthetic fatty acid $CH_3(CH_2)_{15}COOH$ intermediate between palmitic acid and stearic acid — called also *heptadecanoic acid* **2 :** a mixture of palmitic acid and stearic acid obtained from various natural fats, oils, and waxes and formerly mistaken for a single acid

mar·ga·rin \ˈmärgərən\ *n* -s [F *margarine*, fr. Gk *margaron* pearl + F *-ine* -in] **:** a glycerol ester of margaric acid; *esp* **:** glycerol tri-margarate

mar·ga·rine *also* **mar·ga·rin** \ˈmärj(ə)rən, ˈmäj| *also* |əˌrēn *sometimes* -ärg| *or* -äg| *or* ˌ=əˈrēn\ *n* -s [F, lit., margarin] **:** a food product that is used as a substitute for butter and made from a blend of refined oils esp. vegetable oils (as cottonseed oil, soybean oil) to which other ingredients (as salt, emulsifiers, vitamin A, vitamin D) are added and that is churned with ripened skim milk so as to have a consistency that permits ready spreading

mar·ga·ri·ta·ceous \ˌmärgərə|tāshəs\ *adj* [L *margarita* pearl + E *-aceous*] **:** having a satiny iridescence like that of pearl or mother-of-pearl **:** PEARLY

mar·ga·rite \ˈmärgəˌrīt\ *n* -s [ME, fr. MF, fr. L *margarita*, fr. Gk *margaritēs*, fr. *margaron* pearl (prob. fr. Skt *mañjara* pearl, cluster of blossoms) + *-itēs* -ite] **1** *archaic* **:** PEARL **2** [G *margarit*, fr. Gk *margaritēs* pearl] **:** a mineral $CaAl_4Si_2O_{10}(OH)_2$ consisting of a basic aluminum calcium silicate related to mica but low in silica and yielding brittle folia marked by a pearly luster **3** [F *margarite*, fr. Gk *margaritēs* pearl] **:** a primary form of rock crystallization in which globulites are arranged lineally like beads **4** [NL *Margarites*] **:** a top shell of the genus *Margarites*

mar·ga·ri·tes \ˌmärgəˈrīˌdēz\ *n, cap* [NL, fr. Gk *margaritēs* pearl] **:** a genus of minute top shells that are widely distributed in cold northern seas and that are an important item of diet for cod and other fishes

mar·ga·ro·des \ˌmärgəˈrōˌdēz\ *n, cap* [NL, fr. Gk *margaron* pearl + NL *-odes*] **:** a genus of scales — see GROUND PEARL

mar·ga·ro·dite \ˈmärgərōˌdīt\ *n* -s [G *margarodit*, fr. MGk *margarōdēs* like a pearl (fr. Gk *margaron* pearl + *-ōdēs* -ode) + G *-it* -ite] **:** a pearly common mica resembling talc

mar·gar·o·pus \märˈgarəpəs\ *n, cap* [NL, fr. Gk *margaros* pearl oyster (fr. *margaron* pearl) + NL *-pus*] **:** a genus of ixodid ticks that in some classifications includes the cattle tick

mar·ga·ro·san·ite \ˌmärgəˈrōsᵊnˌīt\ *n* -s [Gk *margaron* pearl + *sanis* board + E *-ite;* fr. its pearly luster and lamellar structure; prob. akin to Gk *sathē* penis, *sainein* to wag the tail, OE *thūma* thumb — more at THUMB] **:** a mineral $PbCa_2(SiO_3)_3$ consisting of a lead calcium silicate occurring in colorless lamellar masses

mar·gate \ˈmärgət\ *or* **margate fish** *n* -s [perh. fr. *Margate*, city in southeast England] **:** any of several grunts: as **a :** a variable usu. pearl gray fish (*Haemulon album*) of the tropical western Atlantic — called also *margaret grunt, margot fish* **b :** POMPON

mar·gay \ˈmär(ˌ)gā\ *n* -s [F, fr. Tupi *maracaja, maracayá*] **:** a small American spotted cat (*Felis tigrina*) resembling the ocelot and ranging from southernmost Texas to Brazil

¹marge \ˈmärj\ *n* -s [MF, fr. L *margin-, margo* border] *archaic* **:** EDGE, BORDER, MARGIN ⟨dogs ran howling along the water's ~ —Herman Melville⟩

²marge \ˈmäj\ *n* -s [by shortening & alter.] *Brit* **:** MARGARINE

¹mar·gent \ˈmärjənt\ *n* -s [ME *margente*, alter. of ¹*margin*] *archaic* **:** EDGE, BORDER, MARGIN ⟨upon the ~ of a woodland pool —W.H.Davies⟩

²margent \ˈ"\ *adj, archaic* **:** BORDERING

¹mar·gin \ˈmärjən, ˈmäj-\ *n* -s [ME, fr. L *margin-, margo* border — more at MARK] **1 a (1) :** a vertical blank column to the left or right of an area occupied or to be occupied by the main body of a printed or written text or by a group of illustrations on a page or sheet **(2) :** a straight horizontal blank area at the top or bottom of such a page or sheet **(3) :** the entire blank area running about the borders of such a page or sheet and consisting of the left and right vertical blank columns and the straight horizontal blank areas at the top and bottom **b (1) :** the blank border outside the printed design of a stamp; *also* **:** the portion of this border at the left or right side of the stamp or at the top or bottom **(2) :** the border of a sheet of stamps beyond the outside line of perforations; *also* **:** the portion of this border at the left or right side of the sheet or at the top or bottom **2 a :** the extreme edge of something and the area lying parallel to and immediately adjoining this edge esp. when in some way distinguished from the remaining area lying farther in **:** the outside limit and adjoining surface of something **:** boundary area **:** VERGE: as **(1) :** the boundary area extending along the edge of a body of water ⟨stood at the ~ of the lake⟩ or of a wooded section ⟨a village built at the ~ of a forest⟩ or of some other similar body or surface ⟨the melting ~s of a glacier⟩ **(2) :** the boundary area extending along the edge of a leaf of a plant **(3) :** the boundary area extending along the edge of an insect's wing **b :** the part of the momentary field of consciousness which is felt only vaguely and dimly **3 a :** the flat unmolded part of the stiles and rails of a paneled framing **b :** the cylindrical land of a drill the diameter of which determines the size of the hole **4 a :** something that is over and above what is strictly necessary and that is designed to provide for emergencies **:** a spare amount or measure or degree allowed or given for contingencies or special situations **:** a factor or group of factors making for ready opportunity or ample scope or personal choice in proceeding freely ⟨an enormous ~ of luxury in this country against which we can draw for our vital needs —Walter Lippmann⟩ ⟨the busy lawyer . . . had no ~ of time for meditation —Van Wyck Brooks⟩ **b (1) :** a bare minimum below which or an extreme limit beyond which something is no longer desirable or becomes impossible ⟨a joke that was on the ~ of good taste⟩ ⟨living on the ~ of respectability⟩ **(2) :** the limit below which economic activity cannot be continued under normal conditions **:** the particular condition (as with regard to the increment of return for labor or for interest on an investment) that limits the existence or continuance of an economic process other things being unchanged ⟨a ~ of production⟩ ⟨the ~ of consumption⟩ **5 a :** the difference that exists between net sales and the cost of merchandise sold and that is taken as that from which expenses must be met or profit derived or from which other obligations must be met or other advantages derived — called also *gross margin* **b :** the excess market value of collateral over the face of a loan **c (1) :** cash or collateral which is deposited with a broker to secure him from loss on a contract made on behalf of his principal and which may also constitute a partial payment of the purchase price **(2) :** a customer's equity if his account is terminated at prevailing market prices **(3) :** a speculative transaction in which the broker does part of the financing **(4) :** an allowance above or below a certain figure within which a purchase or sale is to be made **6 :** measure or degree of difference; *esp* **:** one by which a decision is made ⟨the vote was 54 to 34, a ~ of twenty⟩ ⟨the wide ~ between producers' and consumers' prices —*Economist*⟩ **syn** see BORDER, ROOM

²margin \ˈ"\ *vb* -ED/-ING/-S *vt* **1 a :** to make notes in the margin of (a page or sheet) ⟨~*ing* every other page with comments and criticism⟩ **b :** to indicate or specify (as sources) by means of marginal notes ⟨historical documents from which material was drawn were carefully ~*ed* throughout the text⟩ **2 a :** to provide with an edging or border ⟨a beautifully printed page that had been ornately ~*ed*⟩ **b :** to be situated along or lie extended along so as to form a border ⟨trees ~*ing* the shore⟩ ⟨a bright band of color ~*ing* the butterfly's wings⟩ **3 :** to deposit a margin upon (as stock); *specif* **:** to hold or keep secured by depositing or adding to a margin — often used with *up* ~ *vi* **:** to deposit additional margin — usu. used with *up*

¹mar·gin·al \ˈmärjənᵊl, ˈmäj-\ *adj* [ML *marginalis*, fr. L *margin-, margo* border + *-alis* -al — more at MARK] **1 a :** written or printed in the margin of a page or sheet ⟨~ notes⟩ **b :** having notes written or printed in the margin ⟨a ~ manuscript⟩ **2 a :** of, relating to, or constituting a margin ⟨the ~ parts of an insect's wing⟩ **b (1) :** situated at, on, or near a margin ⟨outlying ~ territorial possessions⟩; *specif* **:** occupying the borderland of a relatively stable territorial or cultural area ⟨~ groups of aborigines⟩ **(2) :** characterized by the incorporation of habits and values from two divergent cultures and by incomplete assimilation in either ⟨the ~ cultural habits of new immigrant groups⟩ **c (1) :** running round a leaf parallel and near to the margin ⟨~ leaf venation⟩ **(2) :** *of a monocarpellary ovary* **:** PARIETAL **3 :** located at the fringe of consciousness ⟨~ sensations⟩ **4 a :** close to the lower limit of qualification or acceptability ⟨possesses only ~ ability⟩ **b (1) :** having a character or capacity fitted to yield a supply of goods which when marketed at existing price levels will barely cover the cost of production ⟨~ land⟩ ⟨~ production⟩ ⟨~ producers⟩ **(2) :** of, relating to, or concerned with a limit or margin of return or reward as measured by existing price levels that is barely sufficient to yield a profit or cover the costs of production ⟨~ profits⟩ ⟨~ sales⟩

²marginal \ˈ"\ *n* -s **:** something that is marginal: as **a (1) :** a note written or printed in a margin **(2) :** a decorative border of a page or sheet **b :** a body part (as one of the plates around the edge of the carapace of a turtle, an outer tooth in the radula of a mollusk) that is marginal in relation to another part

marginal blight *or* **marginal spot** *n* **:** a disease of lettuce that is caused by a bacterium (*Pseudomonas marginalis*) and is marked by a brownish discoloration along the margins of the leaves

marginal body *or* **marginal organ** *also* **marginal dot** *n* **:** LITHOCYST

marginal convolution *also* **marginal gyrus** *or* **marginal lobe** *n* **:** the convolution on the upper border of the mesial surface of the frontal lobe of each cerebral hemisphere

marginal crevasse *n* **:** a crevasse pointing obliquely up-valley that develops on either side of some valley glaciers

marginal head *n* **:** SIDEHEAD

mar·gi·na·lia \ˌmärjəˈnālēə, ˌmäj-, -lyə\ *n pl* [NL, fr. ML, neut. pl. of *marginalis* marginal] **1 :** marginal notes **2 :** extrinsic matters **:** nonessential items ⟨interested in both the essentials and the ~ of that science⟩

mar·gin·al·ism \ˈmärjənᵊlˌizəm\ *n* -s **:** economic analysis that stresses use of marginal qualities in the determination of equilibrium

mar·gin·al·ist \-ᵊləst\ *n* -s **:** one that believes in the use of marginal analysis in economics

mar·gin·al·i·ty \ˌmärjəˈnalədē\ *n* -ES **:** the quality or state of being marginal

marginal lappet *n* **:** one of a pair of delicate flaps of tissue between which lie the sense organs of jellyfishes of the order Discomedusae

mar·gin·al·ly \ˈmärjənᵊlē, ˈmäj-, -ᵊli\ *adv* **1 :** in a marginal manner ⟨~ qualified⟩ ⟨~ normal⟩ **2 :** in, about, or toward a margin ⟨wandering ~ through distinguished gatherings —H.G.Wells⟩

marginal sea *n* **:** waters adjacent to a state and under its jurisdiction and extending outward from the coast about 3½ statute miles

marginal shield fern *n* **:** EVERGREEN WOOD FERN 1

marginal utility *n* **:** the amount of additional utility provided by an additional unit of an economic good or service

¹mar·gin·ate \ˈmärjəˌnāt\ *vb* -ED/-ING/-S [L *marginatus*, past part. of *marginare* to provide with a border, fr. *margin-, margo* border — more at MARK] **:** MARGIN — **mar·gin·ation** \ˌ==ˈnāshən\ *n* -s

²marginate \ˈ"\ *or* **mar·gin·at·ed** \-ˌādəd\ *adj* [L *marginatus*] **:** having a margin distinct in appearance or structure

margined *past of* MARGIN

mar·gi·nel·la \ˌmärjəˈnelə\ *n* [NL, fr. L *margin-, margo* border + NL *-ella*] **1** *cap* **:** the type genus of Marginellidae comprising chiefly tropical small glossy white-shelled marine snails **2** -s **:** a mollusk of the genus *Marginella* or family Marginellidae

mar·gi·nel·li·dae \-lə,dē\ *n pl, cap* [NL, fr. *Marginella*, type genus + *-idae*] **:** a large nearly cosmopolitan family of small marine snails (suborder Stenoglossa) with strong porcelaneous often somewhat pear-shaped shell having a long narrow aperture and a thickened outer lip — see MARGINELLA

margining *pres part of* MARGIN

margin of safety : an arithmetical index equal to the ultimate strength of a material minus the contemplated stress — compare FACTOR OF SAFETY

margin release key *n* **:** a key (as on a typewriter) that releases the margin stops (as for extending a line of writing)

margins *pl of* MARGIN, *pres 3d sing of* MARGIN

margin shell *n* **:** MARGINELLA 2

margin stop *or* **marginal stop** *n* **:** either of the stops (as on a typewriter) that limit the range of the printing and determine the width of the margins

margin trowel *n* **:** a small trowel having a square end for finishing angles and narrow spaces

margin trowel

mar·go·sa \märˈgōsə\ *n* -s [modif. of Pg *amargosa*, fem. of *amargoso* bitter, fr. (assumed) VL *amaricosus*, fr. L *amarus* bitter — more at AMAROID] **:** a large East Indian tree (*Melia azadirachta*) whose trunk exudes a tenacious gum and has a bitter bark used as a tonic and whose fruit and seeds yield a medicinal aromatic oil — compare CHINABERRY 2

mar·got fish \ˈmärgət-\ *n* [*margot* alter. of *margate*] **:** MARGATE

mar·gra·vate \ˈmärgrəˌvāt\ *or* **mar·gra·vi·ate** \märˈgrāvēˌāt\ *n* -s [*margravate* fr. *margrave* + *-ate; margraviate* fr. ML *margravius* margrave (fr. MD *marcgrave*) + E *-ate*] **:** the territory of a margrave

mar·grave \ˈmärˌgrāv, ˈmȧ,-\ *n* -s [D *markgraaf* governor of a border region, fr. MD *marcgrave;* akin to MLG *markgrēve* governor of a border region, OHG *marcgrāvo;* all fr. a prehistoric D-G compound whose constituents are akin to OHG *marha* boundary and *grāvo* count — more at MARK, BURGRAVE] **1 :** the military governor esp. of a German border province **2 :** a member of the German nobility corresponding in rank to a British marquess — **mar·gra·vi·al** \(ˈ)mär|grāvēəl\ *adj*

mar·gra·vine \ˈmärgrəˌvēn\ *n* -s [G *markgräfin* & D *markgravin;* G *markgräfin* fr. MHG *marcgrävinne, marcgrævinne*, fr. *marcgrāve* margrave (akin to MD *marcgrave*); D *markgravin* fr. MD *marcgravinne*, fr. *marcgrave* margrave] **:** the wife of a margrave

mar·gue·rite \ˌmärg(y)ə|rēt, ˌmȧg-\ *n* -s [F *marguerite*, fr. OF *margarite* daisy, pearl — more at MARGARITE] **1** *also* **marguerite daisy a :** DAISY 1a **b :** any of various single-flowered chrysanthemums; *esp* **:** a chrysanthemum (*Chrysanthemum frutescens*) of the Canary islands **c :** any of several cultivated plants of the genus *Anthemis* **2 :** a frosted cookie made by spreading a saltine, pastry square, or other base with a mixture of whipped white of egg and boiled sugar syrup and browning in an oven

marguerite yellow *n, often cap M* **:** a pale yellow green that is yellower, lighter, and stronger than smoke gray or oyster gray and yellower and paler than average Nile

mar·hesh·van \märˈkeshvən\ *n* -s *usu cap* [Heb *marḥeshwān*] **:** HESHVAN

¹ma·ri *or* **mar·ri** \ˈmä(ˌ)rē\ *also* **mur·ree** \ˈmə(-\ *n, pl* **mari** *or* **maris** *or* **marri** *or* **marris** *usu cap* **1 :** a Baluchi people of Baluchistan **2 :** a member of the Mari people

²ma·ri \ˈmärē\ *n, pl* **mari** *or* **maris** *usu cap* **:** CHEREMIS 1

mari- *comb form* [L, fr. *mare* — more at MARINE] **:** sea ⟨*mari*colous⟩ ⟨*mari*graph⟩

¹ma·ria \məˈrēə\ *n* -s [AmerSp *maria*, perh. fr. Sp *Maria* Mary, mother of Jesus] **:** any of several shrubs and trees of tropical America; *esp* **:** a valuable timber tree (*Calophyllum longifolium*) of Panama

²maria *pl of* ³MARE

ma·ri·a·chi \ˌmärēˈächē\ *n* -s [MexSp *mariache, mariachi*, perh. modif. of F *mariage* marriage — more at MARRIAGE] **1 a :** a group of itinerant Mexican folk musicians usu. consisting of singers, guitarists, and a violinist **b :** a musician belonging to such a group **2 :** the music performed or sung by a mariachi

ma·ri·a·lite \məˈrēəˌlīt, ˈmar-\ *n* -s [G *marialith*, fr. *Maria* (latinized form of *Marie*, fr. *Marie* vom Rath, wife of Gerhard vom Rath †1888 Ger. mineralogist) + G *-lith* -lite] **:** a mineral $Na_4Al_3Si_9O_{24}Cl$ that consists of a chlorine-bearing aluminosilicate of sodium and is isomorphous with meionite — see SCAPOLITE

¹mar·i·an \ˈma(a)rēən, ˈmer-, ˈmār-\ *adj, usu cap* [*Mary* I (*Mary* Tudor) †1558 Queen of England + E *-an*, adj. suffix] **1 :** of or relating to Mary Tudor or her reign (1553–58) ⟨the *Marian* persecution⟩ ⟨*Marian* exiles⟩ ⟨the *Marian* bishops⟩ **2** [*Mary* (the Virgin *Mary*), mother of Jesus + E *-an*, adj. suffix] **:** of, relating to, or characterized by veneration of the Virgin Mary ⟨*Marian* songs⟩ ⟨*Marian* theology as it affects the question of Christian reunion —*British Book News*⟩

²marian \ˈ"\ *n* -s *usu cap* [*Mary* (the Virgin *Mary*) + E *-an*, n. suffix] **:** one who venerates or is devoted to the Virgin Mary

ma·ri·a·nao \ˌmärēəˈnau̇\ *adj, usu cap* [fr. *Marianao*, city in western Cuba] **:** of or from the city of Marianao, Cuba **:** of the kind or style prevalent in Marianao

mar·i·anne \ˌmarēˈan, ˌmer-, ˌmār-; ˌmaarēˈaa(ə)n\ *also* **mar·i·an·na** \-ˈanə\ *n* -s *usu cap* [F, fr. *Marianne*, French republican society of the 1850s with the aim of overthrowing Napoleon III, fr. the feminine name *Marianne*] **:** the French Republic personified **:** the French people

ma·ria the·re·sa dollar \məˈrīətəˈrēˌsə-, -ˈrētəˈrē, |zə-\ *n, usu cap M&T* [after *Maria Theresa* †1780 Archduchess of Austria and Queen of Hungary] **:** an Austrian silver dollar bearing the bust of Maria Theresa and the date 1780 used as a trade coin in the Middle East

ma·ri·ca \məˈrīkə\ *n* [NL, fr. L *Marica*, goddess associated with a sacred grove at Minturnae in central Italy] **1** *cap* **:** a genus of tender perennials (family Iridaceae) resembling the iris and having flowers on the side of leaflike stems **2** -s **:** a plant of the genus *Marica*

ma·ric·o·lous \məˈrikələs\ *adj* [*mari-* + *-colous*] **:** living in the sea ⟨strictly ~ mollusks⟩

mar·i·co·pa \ˌmarəˈkōpə\ *n, pl* **maricopa** *or* **maricopas** *usu cap* **1 a :** an Indian people of the Gila river valley, Arizona **b :** a member of such people **2 :** a Yuman language of the Maricopa and Halchidhoma peoples

¹ma·rie \ˈmäri, ˈmeri\ *n* -s *often cap* [fr. the name *Marie, Mary*] *Scot* **:** MAID OF HONOR 1 ⟨yestreen the Queen had four *Maries* —Sir Walter Scott⟩

²ma·rie \məˈrē\ *n* -s [by folk etymology] **:** MARLI

ma·ri·en·gro·schen \məˈrēənˌgrōshən\ *n, pl* **mariengroschen** [G, fr. *Marie* Mary, mother of Jesus + G *groschen* — more at GROSCHEN] **:** an old German silver coin bearing a representation of the Madonna and Child first issued about 1505

maries *pl of* MARY

mar·i·gold \ˈmarəˌgōld, ˈmer- *sometimes* ˈma(a)rē,- *or* ˈmerē,- *or* ˈmārē,- *or* -ri,-\ *n* -s [ME *marigold, marygold*, fr. *Mary*, mother of Jesus + ME *gold*] **1 a :** POT MARIGOLD **b :** a plant of the genus *Tagetes:* as **(1) :** AFRICAN MARIGOLD **(2) :** FRENCH MARIGOLD **c :** any of numerous other yellow-flowered plants: as **(1) :** BUR MARIGOLD **(2) :** CORN MARIGOLD **(3) :** MARSH MARIGOLD **2 :** a flower of a marigold **3 a** *or* **marigold yellow :** CADMIUM ORANGE **b :** a variable color averaging a strong orange yellow that is yellower and deeper than nasturtium yellow (sense 2) and yellower and stronger than Spanish yellow

marigold finch *n* **:** a European goldcrest

marigold window *n* **:** a circular window with radial tracery **:** ROSE WINDOW, WHEEL WINDOW

mar·i·gram \ˈmarəˌgram\ *n* [*mari-* + *-gram*] **:** an autographic record from a marigraph

mar·i·graph \-ˌraf, -ˌräf\ *or* **mar·e·o·graph** \-rēə-\ *n* [*marigraph* fr. *mari-* + *-graph; mareograph* fr. F *maréographe*, fr. *maréo-* (fr. L *mare* sea) + *-graphe* -graph — more at MARINE] **:** a self-registering tide gage — **mar·i·graph·ic** \ˌmarə|grafik\ *adj*

mar·i·jua·na *or* **mar·i·hua·na** *also* **mar·a·jua·na** \ˌmarəˈ(h)wänə *also* ˌmer-\ *n* -s [MexSp *mariguana, marihuana*] **1 :** HEMP 1 **2 :** the dried leaves and flowering tops of the pistillate hemp plants that are the source of the drug cannabin and that are sometimes smoked in cigarettes with consequent action of the drug on the higher nerve centers to produce peculiar psychic disturbances — compare BHANG, GANJA, HASHISH

ma·rim·ba \mə'rimbə\ *n* -s [of African origin; akin to Kimbundu *marimba* xylophone, Tshiluba *madimba* xylophone, Kongo *madiumba* harmonicon] **1 :** a primitive xylophone of southern Africa and Central America with resonators beneath each bar **2 :** the modern improved form of the primitive marimba

marimba gong *n* **:** a marimba with metal instead of wooden bars

mar·i·mon·da \ˌmarə'mändə\ *n* -s [AmerSp] **:** a So. American spider monkey (*Ateles belzebuth*)

ma·ri·na \mə'rēnə\ *n* -s [It & Sp, fr. fem. of *marino* of the sea, marine, fr. L *marinus*] **1 :** a seaside promenade or esplanade ⟨the houses that front the ~ —*Atlantic*⟩ **2 :** a dock or basin providing secure moorings for motorboats and yachts ⟨municipal ~s⟩

¹mar·i·nade \ˌ'marə'nād *also* ˌ'mer-\ *vt* -ED/-ING/-S [alter. (influenced by *-ade*) of *marinate*] **:** MARINATE

²marinade \"\ *n* -s **:** a brine or pickle usu. containing vinegar or wine, oil, spices, and herbs in which a food (as meat or fish) is soaked to enrich its flavor

marinal *adj* [ML *marinalis*, fr. L *marinus* marine + *-alis* -al] **1** *obs* **:** of or relating to the sea **:** MARINE **2** *obs* **:** NAUTICAL

mar·i·nate \'marəˌnāt *also* 'mer-, *usu* -ād·+V\ *vt* -ED/-ING/-S [prob. fr. It *marinato*, past part. of *marinare* to marinate, fr. *marino* marine, fr. L *marinus*] **:** to season (as meat or fish) by steeping in a marinade ⟨~ beef⟩ ⟨*marinated* herring⟩

ma·rind \mə'rind\ *also* **marind–anim** \-əˌnim\ *n, pl* **marind** *or* **marinds** *usu cap* **1 a :** a Papuan people inhabiting the southern part of Netherlands New Guinea **b :** a member of such people **2 :** a language of the Marind people

ma·rind·ese \ˌmarən'dēz, -ēs\ *n, pl* **marindese** *usu cap* **:** MARIND

¹ma·rine \mə'rēn\ *n* -s [ME *maryn*, fr. MF *marine*, fr. OF, fr. fem. of *marin*, adj., marine, fr. L *marinus*] **1** *obs* **a :** SEASHORE **b :** a seaside promenade **2** [F, fr. OF, seashore] **a :** the mercantile and naval shipping of a country ⟨keep our ~ in a condition commensurate to its great ends —Edmund Burke⟩ ⟨to whose direction the ~ of England was entrusted when the Spanish invaders were approaching —T.B.Macaulay⟩ **b :** seagoing ships esp. in relation to nationality or class ⟨America had the largest mercantile ~ —Richard Cobden⟩ **3** [²*marine*] **:** one of a class of soldiers serving on shipboard or in close association with a naval force (as in a landing operation); *specif* **:** a member of the Marine Corps of the U.S. or of the Royal Marine forces of Great Britain ⟨tell that to the ~s — the sailors won't believe it —Sir Walter Scott⟩ ⟨the United States *Marines* . . . are trained, equipped, and used as soldiers —L.G.Winans⟩ **4** [F, fr. OF, seashore] **:** an executive department (as in France) having charge of naval affairs ⟨the French Minister of *Marine*⟩ **5** [F, fr. OF, seashore] **:** a marine picture ⟨a famous exhibition of . . . ~s —*Atlantic*⟩

²marine \"\ *adj* [ME *maryne*, fr. L *marinus*, fr. *mare* sea + *-inus* -ine; akin to OE *mere* sea, pool, OHG *meri* sea, ON *marr*, Goth *marei*, OIr *muir*, OSlav *morje*] **1 a** (1) **:** of or relating to the sea ⟨~ life⟩ ⟨~ vegetation⟩ ⟨~ wonders⟩ ⟨~ and land crabs⟩ ⟨~ and continental rocks⟩ ⟨sediments . . . both terrigenous and ~ —*Jour. of Geol.*⟩ ⟨although many of the Mollusca are still ~, there are even more which live in fresh water or upon the land —W.E.Swinton⟩ (2) *of climate* **:** having characteristics (as small temperature ranges and high relative humidity) controlled primarily by oceanic winds and air masses **b :** of or relating to the navigation of the sea **:** NAUTICAL ⟨~ navigation⟩ ⟨~ chart⟩ ⟨~ engineering⟩ **c :** of or relating to the commerce of the sea **:** MARITIME 1 ⟨~ law⟩ ⟨~ risks⟩ **2** *obs* **a :** bordering on the sea **:** MARITIME 2a **b :** belonging to the seashore **3 :** of or relating to marines ⟨~ barracks⟩

marine architect *n* **:** one whose profession is the designing of ships

marine barometer *n* **:** a barometer adapted for shipboard use that has a fixed cistern and a fine capillary section in the tube to damp out oscillations of the mercury caused by the motion of the ship

marine belt *n* **:** MARGINAL SEA

marine blue *also* **marine** *n* -s **:** a moderate purplish blue that is bluer and duller than average cornflower or gentian blue and bluer and less strong than old glory blue — called also *purple navy*

marine chronometer *n* **:** CHRONOMETER a

marine contract *n* **:** MARITIME CONTRACT

marine corps *n* [after the U.S. *Marine Corps*] **:** a dark blue that is redder and duller than Peking blue or Flemish blue and paler than Japan blue

marine engine *n* **:** an engine for propelling a ship

marine engineer *n* **1 :** an officer charged with maintenance and operation of a ship's engines and boilers **2 :** a specialist in marine engineering

marine engineering *n* **:** a branch of engineering that deals with the construction and operation of the power plant and other mechanical equipment of seagoing craft, docks, and harbor installations

marine glue *n* **:** a water-insoluble adhesive composed usu. of a mixture of rubber and shellac and often pitch or resins

marine green *n* **:** a dark to dark grayish green

marine hospital *n* **:** one of numerous hospitals operated under the Public Health Service of the U.S. Government for the care of sick and disabled seamen

marine iguana *n* **:** a shore-dwelling seaweed-eating iguana (*Amblyrhynchus cristatus*) of the Galápagos islands

marine insurance *n* **:** insurance against loss by damage or destruction of cargo, freight, merchandise, or the means or instruments of transportation and communication whether on land, sea, or air — compare INLAND MARINE INSURANCE, OCEAN MARINE INSURANCE

marine interest *n* **:** interest at a legally unrestricted rate on a maritime loan — compare BOTTOMRY

marine ivy *n* **:** either of two vines of the southern U.S.: **a :** a simple-leaved woody vine (*Ampelopsis cordata*) with small bluish fruit **b :** a vine (*Cissus incisa*) with divided unusually heavy leaves and fleshy stems

marine league *n* **:** a league used as a marine unit equal to three nautical miles — called also *sea league;* compare LAND LEAGUE

marine leg *n* **:** an elevating conveyor that can be lowered into the hold of a ship for unloading grain

marine oil *n* **1 :** FISH OIL **2** *or* **marine engine oil :** a lubricating oil for marine engines

marine perils *n pl* **:** perils relating to or arising from or upon the high seas or navigable waters — see PERILS OF THE SEA

mar·i·ner \'marənə(r) *also* 'mer-\ *n* -s [ME, fr. OF *marinier*, fr. ML *marinarius*, fr. L *marinus* marine + *-arius* -ary — more at MARINE] **1 a :** one who navigates or assists in navigating a ship **:** SEAMAN, SAILOR **b :** one who is employed as a member of a ship's company, participates in the operation of or activities aboard the ship, and contributes by his labor to a safe, comfortable, and successful voyage **2 :** a senior girl scout specializing in seamanship and watercraft

ma·ri·ne·ra \ˌmärə'nerə\ *n* -s [AmerSp, fr. Sp, fem. of *marinero* of the sea, marine, fr. *marino* of the sea, marine, fr. L *marinus;* fr. a wish to do honor to the Peruvian navy during a war with Chile in 1879–83] **:** a Peruvian couple dance with courtship mime and kerchief play

marine railway *n* **:** inclined tracks extending into the water so that a ship can be hauled up on a cradle or platform for cleaning or repairs

marine risks *n pl* **:** MARINE PERILS

mariner's chronometer *n* **:** CHRONOMETER a

mariner's compass *n* **:** a compass used in navigation consisting of two or more parallel magnetic needles or bundles of needles permanently attached to a compass card that is delicately pivoted and enclosed in a glass-covered box or bowl set in gimbals in the binnacle and that is read with reference to the lubber line on the front of the bowl

marines *pl of* MARINE

marine soap *n* **:** soap made usu. from coconut oil and used with seawater

marine store *n* **1 a :** ship supplies (as cordage, anchors, provisions) **b :** old ship material offered for sale as junk **2 :** a shop where marine stores are sold

marine superintendent *n* **:** an official of a steamship company charged with supervision of staff officers and crew and of matters relating to the operation of the company's ships

marine terrace *n* **:** a terrace formed along a seashore by the merging of wave-cut and wave-built terraces

marine toad *n* **:** AGUA

marine trumpet *n* **:** TRUMPET MARINE

marine varnish *n* **:** a spar varnish designed esp. for marine exposure and usu. made of tung oil and phenolic resin

mar·in·gouin \ˌmaranⁿ'gwaⁿ\ *n* -s [F, fr. Tupi *marigui* mosquito] **:** BLACKFLY a

ma·ri·nhei·ro \ˌmärə'nyā(ˌ)rō\ *n* -s [Pg, fr. *marinheiro*, adj., of ships, of the sea, marine, fr. *marinho* of the sea, marine, fr. L *marinus;* fr. the use of the wood in shipbuilding] **:** any of several tropical American timber trees of the genus *Guarea*

ma·ri·nism \mə'rēˌnizəm\ *n* -s *usu cap* [It *marinismo*, fr. Giambattista *Marini* †1625 Ital. poet + It *-ismo* -ism] **:** a florid bombastic literary style fashionable in 17th century Italy marked by extravagant metaphors, farfetched conceits, and forced antitheses — compare EUPHUISM, GONGORISM

¹ma·ri·nist \-ēnəst\ *n* -s *usu cap* [It *marinista*, fr. Giambattista *Marini* + It *-ista* -ist] **:** one given to Marinism ⟨disdaining the folly of the *Marinists* —Edmund Gosse⟩

²ma·rin·ist \mə'rēnəst\ *n* -s [²*marine* + *-ist*] **:** one who holds certain features of the earth's surface to be due to marine action rather than the action of other natural forces (as wind, rain, or frost) ⟨every line of escarpments was held by the ~s to be the work of sea waves —*Popular Science Monthly*⟩

ma·ri·no·ra·ma \məˌrēnə'ramə, -'rämə\ *n* -s [²*marine* + *-orama* (as in *panorama*)] **:** a panoramic representation of a sea view

mar·i·o·la \ˌmarē'ōlə\ *n* -s [MexSp] **:** a shrub (*Parthenium incanum*) that resembles guayule and yields a rubber

mar·i·ol·a·ter \ˌma(a)rē'äləd·ə(r), ˌmer-\ *n* -s *usu cap* [fr. *mariolatry*, after E *idolatry: idolater*] **:** one that practices Mariolatry

mar·i·ol·a·trous \ˌ==ˈälə·trəs\ *adj, usu cap* [*mariolatry* + *-ous*] **:** marked by Mariolatry

mar·i·ol·a·try \ˌ==ˈälə·trē\ *n* -ES *usu cap* [*Mary* (the Virgin *Mary*), mother of Jesus + E *-o-* + *-latry*] **1 :** the worship of the Virgin Mary; *specif* **:** rendition to the Virgin Mary of the kind of worship held due to God alone ⟨opposed to *Mariolatry* and superstition —B.J.Kidd⟩ ⟨the tasteless excesses of *Mariolatry* —*The Rev. of Religion*⟩ **2 :** extravagant idealization of woman arising from the worship of Mary ⟨pretty conceits of *Mariolatry* —J.R.Green⟩ ⟨preaches a sort of mellowed *Mariolatry*, a humorless exaltation of woman —H.L.Mencken⟩

mar·i·ol·o·gist \-ləjəst\ *n* -s *usu cap* **:** one versed in Mariology

mar·i·ol·o·gy \-jē\ *n* -ES *usu cap* [*Mary* (the Virgin *Mary*) + E *-o-* + *-logy*] **:** doctrine or opinion about the Virgin Mary as mother of the Son of God

mar·i·o·nette \ˌma(a)rēə'net, ˌmer-, *usu* -ed·+V\ *n* -s [F *marionnette*, fr. MF *maryonete*, fr. *Marion* (dim. of the name *Marie* Mary) + MF *-ete* -ette; prob. fr. the conception that a puppet resembles an image of the Virgin Mary] **1 :** a puppet moved by strings or by hand (as in a puppet show) ⟨the puppeteer makes a distinction . . . that a puppet is manipulated directly by hand, as in a Punch-and-Judy show, or sometimes with a rod or a stick from below; a ~ is manipulated by strings or wires, or occasionally by a rod, from above —A.H. Eaton⟩ **2 :** BUFFLEHEAD 2 **3 :** a mechanism that actuates the shuttle racks in a ribbon loom

mar·i·otte bottle \ˌmarē'ät-\ *n, usu cap M* [after Edme *Mariotte* †1684 Fr. physicist] **:** an apparatus that furnishes a flow of water under a constant head equal to the height of the bottom of the adjustable vertical tube above the level of the outlet

Mariotte bottle

mariotte's law *n, usu cap M* **:** BOYLE'S LAW

mar·i·po·sa \ˌmarə'pōsə, -ōzə\ *or* **mariposa moonfish** *n* -s [AmerSp *mariposa*, fr. Sp, butterfly, prob. fr. *María* Mary (the Virgin Mary) + Sp. *posar* to alight, fr. LL *pausare* to stop, rest — more at POSE] **:** OPAH

mariposa lily *or* **mariposa tulip** *also* **mariposa** *n* -s [prob. fr. AmerSp *mariposa*, fr. Sp, butterfly] **:** a plant of the genus *Calochortus* — compare SEGO LILY

Mar·i·po·san \ˌmarə'pōsᵊn, -ōzᵊn\ *n* -s *usu cap* [*Mariposa* county, central California + E *-an*] **:** a language family of the Penutian stock in California comprising a small number of languages all known as Yokuts

mar·i·po·site \ˌmarə'pōˌsīt\ *n* -s [*Mariposa* county, central California + E *-ite*] **:** a mineral consisting of a bright green chromium-bearing phengite

mar·i·schal \'märshəl\ *n* -s *often cap* [Sc, fr. ME *marshal, mareschal* marshal — more at MARSHAL] **:** a marshal of Scotland — compare EARL MARISCHAL

¹mar·ish \'marish\ *n* -ES [ME *mareis, marys*, fr. MF *marais, mareis*, of Gmc origin; akin to OE *mersc* marsh — more at MARSH] *archaic* **:** MARSH

²marish \"\ *adj, archaic* **:** MARSHY

¹mar·ist \'ma(a)rəst, 'mer-\ *n* -s *usu cap* [F *Mariste*, fr. *Marie* Mary (the Virgin Mary) + F *-iste* -ist] **:** a member of a Roman Catholic order founded at Lyons, France, in 1816 to do work in honor of the Virgin Mary

²marist \"\ *adj, usu cap* **1 :** of, relating to, or devoted to the service of the Virgin Mary **2 :** of or relating to the Marists

ma·ri·ta \mə'rīd·ə\ *n, pl* **mari·tae** \-d·ˌē\ [NL, fr. L *marita* married woman, wife, fem. of *maritus* married man, husband] **:** a sexually mature digenetic trematode — compare METACERCARIA, PARTHENITA

mar·i·tage \'marəd·ij\ *also* **mar·i·ta·gi·um** \ˌ=='tājēəm\ *n, pl* **maritages** \-jəz\ *also* **marita·gia** \-ēə\ [ML *maritagium*, fr. OF *mariage* maritage, marriage — more at MARRIAGE] **1 :** the property brought to a husband by a wife according to feudal custom upon her marriage **2 a :** the right of a feudal lord to dispose in marriage of the heiress, minor heir, or widow of a vassal **b** (1) **:** a payment made by a vassal in return for the lord's waiver of such right (2) **:** a fine imposed on a vassal for his violation of such right

¹mar·i·tal \'marəd·ᵊl, -ətᵊl *also* 'mer-; *chiefly Brit* mə'rītᵊl\ *adj* [L *maritalis*, fr. *maritus* husband + *-alis* -al — more at MARRY] **1 :** of or relating to marriage or the marriage state **:** CONJUGAL ⟨~ relationship⟩ ⟨~ status⟩ ⟨~ happiness⟩ ⟨~ difficulties⟩ **2 :** of or relating to a husband — **mar·i·tal·ly** \-ᵊlē, -li\ *adv*

²ma·ri·tal \-d·ᵊl\ *adj* [*marita* + *-al*] **:** of, relating to, or being a marita

marital deduction *n* **1 :** a deduction according to the provisions of the U.S. Internal Revenue Code from the taxable gross estate that amounts to the value of any property interest included therein and given by will, inheritance, survivorship or otherwise by a decedent to his or her surviving spouse provided that interest is not terminable during the life of the survivor but that is limited to one half the value of the adjusted gross estate — compare COMMUNITY PROPERTY, ESTATE TAX **2 :** the right under the U.S. gift tax law to deduct one half the value of any gift by one spouse to the other and to have gifts made by the spouses to a third person treated as though made one half by each — compare COMMUNITY PROPERTY, GIFT TAX

ma·rit·i·cid·al \mə¦rid·ə¦sīdᵊl\ *adj* [*mariti-* (fr. L *maritus* husband & L *marita* wife) + *-cide* + *-al*] **1 :** of or relating to mariticide; *esp* **:** of or relating to the killing of a husband by his wife **2 :** of or relating to the killing by a female insect of her mate

ma·rit·i·cide \=ˈ==ˌsīd\ *n* -s [*mariti-* (fr. L *maritus* husband & L *marita* wife) + *-cide*] **1 :** one that murders or kills his or her spouse **2 :** the act of a mariticide

maritimal *or* **maritimate** *adj* [L *maritimus* of the sea, maritime + E *-al* or *-ate*] *obs* **:** MARITIME

¹mar·i·time \'marəˌtīm *also* 'mer-\ *adj* [L *maritimus* of the sea, maritime, fr. *mare* sea — more at MARINE] **1 :** of or relating to navigation or commerce on the sea ⟨~ service⟩ ⟨~ power⟩ ⟨~ ancestry⟩ ⟨the national neglect of ~, as distinguished from naval, history —*Times Lit. Supp.*⟩ **2 a :** bordering on the sea ⟨a ~ province⟩ **b :** living near the seacoast ⟨~ farmers⟩ **c :** characteristic of those who live near the sea ⟨~ cultures⟩ **3 :** MARINE ⟨the kittiwakes . . . the most ~ of all gulls —Tom Weir⟩ ⟨a ~ climate⟩ **4** *archaic, of a soldier* **:** serving with a naval force **5 :** having the characteristics of a mariner ⟨he was far from having a ~ appearance —Charles Dickens⟩

²maritime *n* -s *obs* **:** a region or province that borders on the sea

maritime contract *n* **:** a contract directly relating to the navigation, business, or commerce of the sea and falling within the jurisdiction of the admiralty courts

maritime hypothec *also* **maritime hypothecation** *n* **:** MARITIME LIEN

maritime insurance *n* **:** MARINE INSURANCE

maritime interest *n* **:** MARINE INTEREST

maritime law *n* **:** law that relates to commerce and navigation on the high seas or other navigable waters and is administered by admiralty courts — compare ADMIRALTY 3

maritime lien *n* **:** the right of one having a recognized claim under maritime law against a ship or its cargo (as for services or supplies or for damages caused by collision) to require an admiralty court to seize the ship or other described property and enforce satisfaction of the claim — called also *tacit hypothec;* compare LIEN

maritime loan *n* **:** a loan or advance enforceable in a court of admiralty jurisdiction: as **a :** one giving rise to a maritime lien **b :** one secured by a bottomry or respondentia bond

maritime perils *n pl* **:** MARINE PERILS

maritime pine *n* **:** CLUSTER PINE

mar·jo·ram \'märjərəm, 'máj- *sometimes* -jəˌram\ *n* -s [alter. of ME *majorane*, fr. MF, fr. ML *majorana*] **:** any of various usu. fragrant and aromatic mints that constitute two genera (*Origanum* and *Majorana*) of the family Labiatae and that include several forms used as seasoning in cookery — compare SWEET MARJORAM, WILD MARJORAM

marjoram oil *n* **:** a yellowish essential oil obtained esp. from sweet marjoram and used chiefly in perfumes (as for soap)

¹mark \'märk, 'mák\ *n* -s [ME, fr. OE *mearc;* akin to OHG *marha* boundary, boundary land, ON *mörk* boundary land, forest, wilderness, Goth *marka* boundary, boundary land, L *margo* edge, border, boundary, OIr *mruig* boundary land, district, W *bro* region, Per *marz* boundary land, district] **1 a** (1) **:** ²MARCH 1 (2) [G, fr. OHG *marha* boundary, boundary land] **:** a tract of land held in common by a Germanic village community in primitive or medieval times ⟨a share in the common ~ . . . made up of the uncultivated land —Alfons Dopsch⟩; *also* **:** the community holding such a tract **b :** something placed or set up to serve as a guide or to indicate position: as (1) **:** a conspicuous object of known position serving as a guide for travelers ⟨a ~ for pilots⟩ (2) **:** something (as a line, notch, or fixed object) designed to record position (3) **:** one of the bits of leather or colored bunting placed on a sounding line at irregular but frequent intervals — compare DEEP (4) **:** PLIMSOLL MARK **c** (1) **:** something toward which a missile is directed **:** a thing aimed at **:** TARGET ⟨hit the ~ squarely in the center⟩ ⟨the officers, being on horseback, were . . . picked out as ~s —Benjamin Franklin⟩ (2) **:** the jack in the game of bowls; *also* **:** a proper bowling distance or position allowed for the jack (3) **:** the pit of the stomach in boxing (4) **:** a spot (as that marked by the heel of a player in making a fair catch) at which a free kick or a penalty kick is allowed in rugby football; *also* **:** a fair catch in rugby (5) **:** the starting line in a track event ⟨got off the ~ very quickly⟩ (6) **:** a position on the starting line assigned to a contestant in a track event; *also* **:** the relaxed position taken by a runner or swimmer at or slightly behind the starting line immediately prior to the position or attitude of readiness which precedes the firing of the starting gun — usu. used in pl. (7) — used as a skeet shooter's command for the release of the low-house target **d** (1) **:** an end in view **:** GOAL, OBJECT ⟨120 mph is not a hard ~ to achieve —*Ford Times*⟩ ⟨developed enough musicianship to fix his own ~s at which to aim —Marcia Davenport⟩ (2) **:** an object of attack, ridicule, or abuse **:** BUTT ⟨would have to explain and deny and make a general ~ of himself —Theodore Dreiser⟩ ⟨would have to go about, a ~ for the talkers —George Meredith⟩; *specif* **:** a prospective or actual victim of a confidence game or other swindle ⟨lead the ~ to her apartment —W.H.Murray⟩ ⟨the ~s don't know no different —W.L.Gresham⟩ (3) **:** the point desired to be made **:** the question under discussion — often used in the phrase *beside the mark* ⟨both seem curiously beside the ~ —*Times Lit. Supp.*⟩ ⟨it is beside the ~ to argue that a culture consists of something more than plastic compounds —Waldemar Kaempffert⟩ (4) **:** the actual facts or true state of affairs **:** condition of being correct or accurate ⟨was perhaps near the ~ —*Times Lit. Supp.*⟩ ⟨even the initial diagnosis was widely off the ~ —Martin Gardner⟩ (5) **:** a standard or acceptable level of performance, quality, or condition **:** NORM — usu. used in the phrase *up to the mark* ⟨weren't feeling up to the ~ lately —Michael McLaverty⟩ ⟨that's the great thing about persecution: it keeps you up to the ~ —Bruce Marshall⟩ ⟨both of these performances were very far from being up to the ~ —Claud Cockburn⟩; *also* **:** the limit of what is reasonable or acceptable ⟨wanted fifteen hundred pounds for it and I don't think that was beyond the ~ —H.J.Laski⟩ **2 a** (1) **:** something that gives evidence of something else **:** SIGN, INDICATION, TOKEN ⟨as a ~ of their change of sentiment —T.B.Costain⟩ ⟨his writings . . . bear ~s of haste —*Encyc. Americana*⟩ ⟨a sure ~ of the families' social position —Bernard Smith⟩ (2) **:** a narrow deep hollow on the surface of the crown of a horse's incisor tooth that gradually becomes obliterated by the wearing away of the crown and therefore is indicative of the animal's age and usu. disappears from the lower central incisors about the sixth year while traces may remain in the upper until the eleventh (3) **:** an impression or trace (as a scar or stain) made on something (4) **:** CHARACTERISTIC ⟨the ~ of every Christian —*Commonweal*⟩ (5) **:** a distinguishing characteristic or essential attribute in logic **:** DIFFERENTIA **b** (1) **:** a character usu. in the form of a cross made as a substitute for a signature by a person who cannot or is unwilling to write and often witnessed by another; *also* **:** a personal cipher used in place of a signature ⟨the symbols above the lion represent the ~ of . . . the chief sachem —Allan Forbes & R.M.Eastman⟩ (2) **:** a visible sign (as a badge or sign of honor, rank, office, or stigma) assumed by or put upon a person ⟨the vermilion ~ of marriage remained on her forehead —Nilima Devi⟩ ⟨other distinguishing ~s may be worn by navy men . . . who have won certain distinctions —*All Hands*⟩; *specif* **:** a small plate of gold or silver worn by a mark master Mason (3) **:** a character, device, label, brand, seal, or other sign put on an article esp. to show the maker or owner, to certify quality, or for identification **:** TRADEMARK ⟨the owner of a ~ can secure relief only where the infringer uses it on goods . . . closely resembling the owner's —*Harvard Law Rev.*⟩ (4) **:** a small heraldic bearing used or added as a distinctive sign — compare CADENCY MARK (5) **:** a written or printed symbol ⟨punctuation ~s⟩ (6) **:** an identifying mark (as an ear notch) cut on livestock with a knife — distinguished from *brand* ⟨every mountaineer knows his hogs by his ~ —*Amer. Guide Series: Tenn.*⟩ (7) **:** a brand on a log indicating ownership (8) **:** POSTMARK (9) *usu cap* [G *marke* mark, label, brand, fr. OHG *marha* boundary] — used with a numeral to designate a particular model of a weapon, machine, or article of equipment ⟨this nuclear power plant, known as *Mark I* —*Birmingham (Ala.) News*⟩ — abbr. *Mk* **c :** a number or other character used in registering or evaluating: as (1) **:** a symbol used by a teacher to represent his estimate of a student's work or conduct ⟨had several late ~s against him⟩; *esp* **:** GRADE ⟨gets excellent ~s at school⟩ ⟨the highest ~ in the class⟩ (2) **:** a figure registering a point or level reached or achieved ⟨within six months the population . . . topped the 500 ~ —J.D. Hillaby⟩ ⟨more than 125 have passed the half-century ~ —*Amer. Guide Series: Minn.*⟩ ⟨the 1954 figure is expected to be around that ~ —Wayne Hughes⟩; *specif* **:** RECORD ⟨the ~, almost twenty miles faster than the previous record, wasn't allowed —*Collier's Yr. Bk.*⟩ **3 a :** ATTENTION, NOTICE ⟨nothing worthy of ~ occurred in your absence⟩ **b :** IMPORTANCE, DISTINCTION ⟨might easily become a figure of ~ —H.J.Laski⟩ ⟨stands out as a man of ~ —John Bright †1889⟩ — often used in the phrase *make one's mark* ⟨has made his

~ in many ways —Milton MacKaye⟩ **c :** a lasting or strong impression **:** an enduring effect — usu. used in the phrase *make one's mark* ⟨had made their ~ in evolutionary history —W.E.Swinton⟩ ⟨made a ~ in western history —R.W. Southern⟩; *esp* **:** a strong favorable impression ⟨anxious to make a ~ with my first major book —Charles Breasted⟩ ⟨works that have made their ~ with the general public —William Murray⟩ ⟨as office boy I made such a ~ that they gave me the post of a junior clerk —W.S.Gilbert⟩ **d :** an assessment of merits **:** RATING ⟨would have their bad ~ against him —F.M.Ford⟩ ⟨could get higher ~*s* . . . for telling warm-hearted, democratic lies about the people —*New Republic*⟩ **syn** see CHARACTER, SIGN

²mark \"\ *vb* -ED/-ING/-S [ME *marken*, fr. OE *mearcian;* akin to OHG *marcōn* to determine the boundaries of, OS *markon,* ON *marka;* denominative fr. the root of E ¹*mark*] *vt* **1 a** (1) **:** to fix or trace the bounds or limits of **:** locate the boundaries of — usu. used with *out* ⟨~ out a mining claim⟩ (2) **:** to plot the course of **:** CHART, DELINEATE — usu. used with *out* ⟨some directions of social development have at least been ~*ed* out —John Dewey⟩ ⟨the course which Italy has ~*ed* out for herself —C.E.G.C.Emmott⟩ **b :** to set apart by or as if by a mark or boundary — usu. used with *off* ⟨~*ed* off their claims with tomahawks —*Amer. Guide Series: Pa.*⟩ ⟨trying to ~ off the legitimate province of an art —Edward Sapir⟩ ⟨a sign of heredity that ~*ed* them off as a race —Oscar Handlin⟩ **2 a** (1) **:** to designate as if by a mark **:** DESTINE, ASSIGN ⟨~*ed* for death by his doctors —*advt*⟩ ⟨~*ed* for greatness by his extraordinary talents and virtues⟩ ⟨~*ed* out by destiny for his place in history —Preston Slosson⟩ (2) **:** to make or leave a mark on ⟨his hobnails ~*ed* the floor⟩; *specif* **:** to affix a significant identifying mark (as a trademark or hallmark) to ⟨~ a bale of merchandise⟩ (3) **:** to furnish with natural marks of a specified kind ⟨wings ~*ed* with white lines⟩ (4) **:** to label (an article) with a sign or symbol (as for indicating price or quality) ⟨each garment is clearly ~*ed* for size and price⟩ ⟨all furs are plainly ~*ed* as to country of origin⟩ (5) **:** to dock and castrate (a lamb); *also* **:** to enumerate (the lambs of a flock) esp. by counting the tails removed during docking (6) **:** to enter or make notations or symbolic marks on or in (as for purposes of comment or emphasis) — usu. used with *up* ⟨~ up . . . a copy with his objections —J.G.Cozzens⟩ **b** (1) **:** to indicate or make note of in writing **:** JOT ⟨doesn't remember his exact words and nobody thought to ~ them down —Ira Wolfert⟩ ⟨~*ed* in his diary the date of his son's birth⟩ (2) **:** to indicate, express, or show by a mark or symbol ⟨~ an accent⟩; *also* **:** REGISTER, RECORD ⟨the barometer ~*ed* a continuing fall in atmospheric pressure⟩ ⟨Paris clocks ~*ed* 4:15 in the morning —C.A. Lindbergh b. 1902⟩ (3) **:** to make evident **:** SHOW, MANIFEST ⟨~*ed* his displeasure by a frown⟩ (4) **:** to indicate or fix (as a pivot point) in military drill or review (5) **:** to keep track of (the points) in a game; *also* **:** to keep score in (a game) ⟨~*ed* the match —*N.Y. Times*⟩ (6) **:** to determine the value or correctness of **:** score by means of marks or symbols **:** GRADE ⟨have you ~*ed* my paper yet⟩ (7) **:** to make notations on or attach symbolic marks to (as for purposes of comment or emphasis) ⟨asked him to ~ the offensive passages⟩ ⟨~*ing* up only those features of special interest to me —Joanna Jonsson⟩ **c** (1) **:** to be a distinguishing mark on or upon **:** CHARACTERIZE, DISTINGUISH ⟨high ideals ~ the work —*Encyc. Americana*⟩ ⟨stunted trees ~ the higher peaks⟩ (2) **:** SIGNALIZE ⟨often ~ the decisive turn in scientific thinking —J.B.Conant⟩ ⟨may ~ a change of emphasis —*New Statesman & Nation*⟩ (3) **:** to identify in a particular way **:** BRAND, STAMP ⟨~ him as an unscrupulous politician in many eyes —Carol L. Thompson⟩ **d :** to serve as an indication of the position or course of ⟨a sign ~*ing* the city limits —*Amer. Guide Series: Mich.*⟩ **3 a :** to give attention to **:** take notice of **:** OBSERVE, NOTICE ⟨~ the change that has taken place⟩ ⟨~ my words —Walter de la Mare⟩ ⟨but ~ how certain matters are beyond us —Winston Churchill⟩ **b :** to observe and remember the spot of disappearance or taking to cover of (game) **c** *Brit* **:** to keep a close watch on (a member of an opposing team) so as to hamper **~ *vi* 1 :** to notice or observe critically **:** NOTE, LOOK **2 :** to observe and remember the spot where game disappeared or took cover **3** *Brit* **:** to play close to one's opponent and in such a position as to hamper him, prevent him from receiving the ball, or tackle him if he receives it **4 :** to keep score in a game — **mark time 1 :** to keep the time of a marching step (as in military drill) by moving the feet alternately without advancing **2 :** to function or operate in a lackadaisical, listless, or unproductive manner **:** merely go through the motions of activity **:** fail to advance or progress **:** stand still ⟨the commission was just *marking time* —*Collier's Yr. Bk.*⟩ ⟨our free dynamic economy cannot *mark time* —Walter Reuther⟩ — **mark to the market :** to adjust cash deposited with a lender of securities to the prevailing market price

³mark \"\ *n* -S [ME, fr. OE *marc*, prob. of Scand origin; akin to ON *mark-, mörk* mark (weight); akin to OE *mearc* mark, sign; prob. fr. the marks on the bars — more at ¹MARK] **1 :** any of various old European units of weight used esp. for gold and silver; *esp* **:** a unit equal to about 8 ounces **2 a :** unit of value or a coin: **a :** an old English unit equal to 13*s* 4*d* **b :** an old Scottish unit of value equal to 13*s* 4*d* Scottish; *also* **:** a coin representing this unit issued by James VI and Charles II **c :** any one of various old Scandinavian or German units of value; *specif* **:** a unit and corresponding silver coin of the 16th century worth ½ taler **d** [G, fr. OHG *marha* boundary — more at ¹MARK] **:** the basic monetary unit of Germany from 1871; *also* **:** a coin representing this unit — see REICHSMARK **e** (1) **:** DEUTSCHE MARK (2) **:** the basic monetary unit of East Germany — see MONEY table **f** [Estonian, fr. G] **:** a unit of value used for a time in Estonia after World War I; *also* **:** a coin representing this unit issued 1922–26 **g** [Finn *markka*] **:** MARKKA **3 :** a division of land in Scotland orig. of the annual value of a mark

markan *usu cap, var of* MARCAN

mark degree *n* [¹*mark*] **:** the degree of a mark master Mason

mark down *vt* **:** to put a lower price on ⟨all overcoats have been *marked down* 20 percent⟩

markdown \ˈ=,=\ *n* -S [*mark down*] **1 :** a lowering of price **2 :** the amount by which an original selling price is reduced

marked \ˈmärkt, ˈmäkt\ *adj* **1 a :** having a mark ⟨a ~ card⟩ ⟨a ~ coin⟩ ⟨dotted with ~ boulders and other memorials of historic interest —*Amer. Guide Series: Texas*⟩ **b :** having a mark of a specified kind — usu. used in combination ⟨a scar-*marked* lad⟩ **2 :** having a distinctive or strongly pronounced character **:** NOTICEABLE ⟨spoke . . . with a ~ American accent —Nevil Shute⟩ ⟨a ~ feature of these occasions —*Encyc. Americana*⟩ ⟨have a ~ capacity for industrial work —*Current Biog.*⟩ ⟨found him of a very ~ physiognomy —Bram Stoker⟩ — often used in combination ⟨there is no well-*marked* nervous system —*Encyc. Americana*⟩ **3 a :** being a person on whom attention or interest is focused **:** enjoying fame or notoriety ⟨this small staff made the editor a ~ man —F.L.Mott⟩ **b :** being an object of attack, suspicion, or vengeance ⟨a ~ man to the British —*Amer. Guide Series: Mass.*⟩ **4 :** overtly signaled by a linguistic feature ⟨with most English nouns the plural is the ~ number⟩

mark·ed·ly \ˈmärkədlē, ˈmäk-, -li\ *adv* **:** in a marked manner or to a marked degree **:** NOTICEABLY, PLAINLY

mark·ed·ness \-kədnəs\ *n* -ES **:** the quality or state of being marked; *esp* **:** DISTINCTIVENESS

marked transfer *n* **:** an instrument for transferring a portion of the shares of a stockholder's certificate after being certified as good by a proper official on the London stock exchange

markee *var of* MARQUEE

mark·er \ˈmärkər, ˈmäkə(r\ *n* -S **1 :** a person who marks: as **a :** a person who marks game **b :** a person who keeps account of a game played (as of billiards or rackets) **:** SCORER; *also* **:** one who records the shots at target practice **c** (1) **:** a person who records attendance at a school or college **:** MONITOR (2) **:** a person who marks papers (as tests, compositions) for a teacher **d :** a worker who puts identifying information on articles: as (1) **:** a worker in a laundry or cleaning and dyeing establishment who marks articles with customer identification (2) **:** a worker who marks serial numbers on gun parts with a marking die (3) **:** a person who marks prices on merchandise **e :** a logger who marks trees for felling, felled trees for cutting into logs, or logs for identification in a drive **f :** a worker who marks outlines on leather parts of shoes as guides for such subsequent operations as cementing, punching of buttonholes, or fancy stitching **g :** a worker who pencils or chalks out a pattern on material (as cloth, wood, or metal) before it is cut; *also* **:** a pattern layout so made **h :** a worker who makes out merchandise tickets **2 :** something that marks or is used for marking: as **a :** an implement or attachment for marking the ground to facilitate planting in rows **b :** a contrivance for marking out a tennis court **c :** any of various sewing devices for marking or indicating guidelines ⟨a pin ~ for hemlines⟩ **d** (1) **:** a token used in gambling as a reminder (as of a bet or the next dealer) (2) **:** a promissory note or IOU given as evidence of a loan received or debt incurred **e :** a signal placed on each side of the rear of certain trains; *also* **:** a distinctive light fastened to a signal post to indicate whether the signal is permissive or absolute **f :** something (as a person, flag, stake, ship) posted at a point to indicate a position (as of a military unit, an obstacle) **g :** BOOKMARK **h :** a black or otherwise readily identifiable sheep **i :** a morphologic hereditary character used as an indicator of the presence or absence of a linked physiologic character — compare LINKAGE **j :** a geologic formation easily identified; *esp* **:** one used as a guide in well drilling **3 a :** an instrument connected with a switchboard that electrically selects an available trunk line and makes the necessary connections for long-distance calls **b** *or* **marker beacon** *or* **marker radio beacon :** a small transmitter of limited range used by an airplane to identify its position over a fixed spot on the earth **4 :** a word, morpheme, or combination of morphemes indicating the form class or grammatical function of the linguistic form that accompanies or includes it ⟨the ~*s the* and *-ed in the boy and played*⟩

marker bed *n* **:** MARKER 2j

¹mar·ket \ˈmärkət, ˈmäk-, *usu* -əd·+V\ *n* -S *often attrib* [ME, fr. ONF, fr. L *mercatus* trade, marketplace, fr. *mercatus*, past part. of *mercari* to trade, fr. *merc-, merx* ware, merchandise; akin to Oscan *amiricadut* without remuneration, and perh. to Gk *marptein* to seize, Skt *mṛśati* he touches; basic meaning: to seize] **1 a** (1) **:** a meeting together of people at a stated time and place for the purpose of traffic (as in cattle, provisions, or wares) by private purchase and sale and usu. not by auction (2) **:** the people assembled at such a meeting (3) **:** the privilege in English law of having a public market **b** (1) **:** a public place (as an open space in a town or a large building) where a market is held **:** MARKETPLACE; *specif* **:** a place where provisions are sold at wholesale ⟨the city ~⟩ ⟨fish ~⟩ (2) **:** a retail establishment usu. of a specified kind ⟨a meat ~⟩ **2** *archaic* **a :** the act or an instance of buying and selling ⟨every man will speak of the fair as his own ~ has gone in it —Laurence Sterne⟩ **b :** an object of bargaining or dealing **c :** opportunity for buying or selling — usu. used in the phrases *lose one's market* or *overstand one's market* **3 a :** the rate or price offered for commodities **:** MARKET PRICE **b :** the current bid and asked price for a security or other property ⟨ask the broker for the ~ on this stock⟩ **4 :** a sphere within which price-making forces operate and in which exchanges in title tend to be followed by actual movement of goods: as **a :** a geographical area of demand for commodities ⟨sell in the southern ~⟩ ⟨the world ~⟩ **b :** the course of commercial activity by which the exchange of commodities is effected **:** condition with respect to demand **:** extent of demand ⟨the ~ is dull⟩ ⟨the following prices . . . are eloquent of the declining ~ —*New Biology*⟩ **c :** a formal organized coming together of buyers and sellers of goods ⟨the stock ~⟩ ⟨the livestock ~⟩ **5 :** a unit of volume in the lumber trade represented by a log 19 inches in diameter at the small end inside the bark and 13 feet long and containing approximately 200 board feet — **at the market** *adv* **1 :** at the prevailing price on a stock exchange **2 :** at the best price obtainable when a broker executes a customer's order — **away from the market :** with a price limit outside the prevailing range of the market on a stock exchange ⟨these orders are *away from the market* —B.E.Shultz⟩ — **in the market** *adv (or adj)* **1** *or* **on the market :** up for sale **:** available for purchase ⟨put his house *on the market*⟩ **2 :** interested in buying **:** prepared to buy ⟨was *in the market* for a new car⟩

²market \"\ *vb* -ED/-ING/-S *vi* **1 :** to deal in a market **:** to go to market to buy or sell **~ *vt* 1 :** to expose for sale in a market **:** traffic in **:** sell in a market **2 :** SELL

mar·ket·abil·i·ty \,märkəd·əˈbiləd·ē, ,mäk-, -kətəˈbilət|, |i\ *n* **:** the quality or state of being marketable; *specif* **:** the degree to which assets can be disposed of for cash without causing a major decline in price

mar·ket·able \ˈmärkəd·əbəl, ˈmäk-, -kətəbəl\ *adj* **1 :** fit to be offered for sale in a market **:** being such as may be justly and lawfully sold or bought ⟨~ provisions⟩ **2 :** of or relating to buying or selling ⟨~ value⟩ **3 a :** wanted by purchasers **:** SALABLE ⟨furs are not ~ in that country⟩ **b :** enjoying a high degree of liquidity ⟨~ securities⟩ — **mar·ket·able·ness** *n* -ES — **mar·ket·ably** \-blē\ *adv*

marketable title *n* **:** a title that conveys property and the interest therein bargained for reasonably free from all liens and encumbrances save those excepted by the bargain, that does not expose the purchaser to litigation, and that he can readily sell or offer as security to a prudent man knowing all material facts and their legal significance **:** merchantable title

market analysis *n* **:** a phase of marketing research conducted to determine the characteristics and extent of a market

market basket *n* **1 a :** a splint, veneer, or fiberboard basket of various forms and sizes usu. having wooden or wire handles and used for fruits and vegetables **b :** any of various baskets used by shoppers for carrying purchases from a market **2 :** a distribution of goods purchased by consumers in a base period and used to measure changes in the cost of living

market bleach *n* **:** a method of bleaching simpler than madder bleaching for cotton cloth sold as white goods

market cross *n* **:** a cross or cross-shaped building set up where a market is held and often the scene of public business such as giving of notices or reading of warrants

market day *n* [ME] **:** a day fixed for holding a market ⟨public sales are held on *market days* —G.W.Johnson⟩

market economy *n* **:** an economy in which most goods and services are produced and distributed through the media of free markets and the price system

mar·ke·teer *R* ¦märkə¦ti(ə)r; -*R* ¦mäkə¦tiə, +V -iə(r) *or* -ir\ *n* -S [¹*market* + *-eer*] **:** a seller in a market **:** market dealer

mar·ket·er \ˈmärkəd·ə(r)\ *n* -S **:** one who buys or sells in a market

marketfish \ˈ=,=,=\ *n* [by folk etymology fr. *margate fish*] **:** MARGATE

market garden *n* **:** a garden usu. comprising a relatively extensive area in which vegetables are grown for market

market gardener *n* **:** a person who operates a market garden

market gardening *n* **:** gardening for market esp. with the use of a relatively extensive area

market hunter *n* **:** a person who hunts game for a livelihood

mar·ket·ing \ˈmärkəd·|iŋ, ˈmäk-, -ət|, |ēŋ\ *n* -S **1 a :** the act of selling or purchasing in a market ⟨doing all of her ~ once a week⟩ **b :** the bringing or sending of goods to market ⟨cattle ~*s* increased sharply this week⟩ **2 a :** produce for the market **b :** things purchased at a market **3 :** an aggregate of functions involved in transferring title and in moving goods from producer to consumer including among others buying, selling, storing, transporting, standardizing, financing, risk bearing, and supplying market information

marketing research *n* **:** research conducted to establish the extent and location of a market or to analyze the cost of products and processes as compared with that of alternative or competitive products or processes — compare MARKET RESEARCH

market letter *n* **:** a publication usu. issued by a specialist containing market information and advice

mar·ket·man \ˈmärkətmən\ *n, pl* **marketmen :** a dealer in a market **:** MARKETER

market order *n* **:** an order to buy or sell at the best price obtainable in the market when the order is executed

market overt *n* -S **:** an open public market authorized and regulated by law at which purchasers of goods with certain exceptions acquire good title regardless of any defects in the seller's title

marketplace \ˈ=,=,=\ *n* [ME, fr. *market* + *place*] **1 a :** an open square or place in a town where markets or public sales are held **b :** MARKET ⟨aggressive competition . . . in a freely functioning ~ —Harold Fleming⟩ **c :** the world of trade or economic activity **:** the everyday world ⟨the depression sent him out into the ~ —J.K.Hutchens⟩ ⟨here is an educational institution that has come down . . . to the ~ —Dwayne Orton⟩ **2 :** a sphere in which intangible values (as ideas) compete for acceptance ⟨the turbulent ~ of ideas —J.M. Mathes⟩ ⟨the ~ of thought —Robert Bendiner⟩

market pot *n* **:** a pot from which desilverized lead is run into pig molds in lead refining

market price *n* [ME *markett prise*] **:** a price actually given in current market dealings **:** a price at which the supply and demand are equal

market research *n* **:** the gathering of factual information as to consumer preferences for goods and services — compare MARKETING RESEARCH

market-ripe \¦=,=¦=\ *adj* **:** harvested slightly immature so as to reach the market in excellent condition **:** not fully ripe

markets *pl of* MARKET, *pres 3d sing of* MARKET

mar·ket·stead \ˈmärkət,sted\ *n* [ME *marketstede*, fr. *market* + *stede* stead — more at STEAD] *archaic* **:** MARKETPLACE

market town *n* [ME *markettown*] **:** a usu. small town that has the privilege of holding at stated times a public market

market value *n* **:** a price at which both buyers and sellers are willing to do business **:** the market or current price

market value clause *n* **:** an insurance clause providing for payment of a loss to goods at market value rather than manufacturing cost

mark·graf \ˈmärk,gräf\ *n, pl* **markgraf·en** \-fən\ [G, fr. OHG *marcgrāvo* — more at MARGRAVE] **:** MARGRAVE 2

mar·khor \ˈmär,kȯ(ə)r\ *also* **mar·khoor** \-ku̇(ə)r\ *n, pl* **markhor** *or* **markhors** [Per *mārkhōr*, lit., snake eater, fr. *mār* snake + *-khōr* eating, consuming (fr. *khurdan* to eat, consume)] **:** a wild goat (*Capra falconieri*) of mountainous regions from Afghanistan to India

mark·ing \ˈmärkiŋ, ˈmäk-, -kēŋ\ *n* -S [ME, fr. gerund of *marken* to mark — more at MARK] **1 :** the act, process, or an instance of making, placing, or assigning a mark ⟨his ~ of pronunciation was crude —J.H.Sledd & G.J.Kolb⟩ ⟨the ~ of whales helps us to follow these movements —Robert Clarke⟩ ⟨accused his teacher of unfair ~⟩ **2 a :** a mark made ⟨~*s* include name and address of the consignee —*Export Packing*⟩ ⟨the ~*s* on this bone were made by a beaver —R.W.Murray⟩; *specif* **:** POSTMARK **b :** arrangement, pattern, or disposition of marks ⟨the ~ of a bird's plumage⟩

marking felt *n* **:** a felt used in papermaking to make a design (as ribs or stripes) discernible on the face of the finished paper

marking gauge *n* **:** GAUGE 2c

marking hammer *n* **:** a tool used for marking trees or logs

marking knife *n* **:** a tool for marking out wood for sawing or chiseling

marking nut *n* **1 :** an East Indian tree (*Semecarpus anacardium*) **2 :** the nut of the marking nut that yields a blackish resinous juice used for marking cotton cloth

marking period *n* **:** a part of the school year between two dates on which students' marks are sent home

mark·ka \ˈmär,kä\ *n, pl* **markkaa** \"\ *or* **markkas** [Finn, fr. Sw *mark*, any of various old Scand. units of value; akin to ON *mark-, mörk* mark (weight) — more at MARK] **1 :** the basic monetary unit of Finland — see MONEY table **2 :** a coin representing one markka

markland \ˈ=,=\ *n* [³*mark* + *land*] **:** ³MARK 3

mark lodge *n* [¹*mark*] **:** an English lodge of mark master Masons

markman *n, pl* **markmen** [¹*mark* + *man*] *obs* **:** MARKSMAN

mark masonry *n, usu cap 2d M* [¹*mark*] **:** the institutions or work of mark lodges

mark master mason *n, usu cap 3d M* [¹*mark*] **1 a :** a Freemason of the fourth degree in the order in the U. S. **b :** a Freemason of the first degree of Royal Arch Masonry in the U. S. **2 a :** a Freemason of a distinct lodge associated with the Grand Lodge of mark Masons in England **b :** a degree conferred under the authority of the Grand Chapter in Scotland

mark of admiration : EXCLAMATION POINT

mark of cadency : CADENCY MARK

mark of exclamation : EXCLAMATION POINT

mark off *vt* **:** to mark or scribe to correct dimensions; *esp* **:** to scribe (castings) for machining and fitting **~ *vi, of dyed cloth* :** to bleed from darker into lighter areas

markoff \ˈ=,=\ *n* -S [*mark off*] **:** a mark on copy to indicate the beginning or ending of a galley or on a galley proof to indicate the beginning or ending of a page

mark of interrogation : QUESTION MARK

mark of reference : REFERENCE MARK

mark of the beast [ME *marke of the beast*, trans. of LL *character bestiae*, trans. of Gk *charagma tou thēriou*] **1 :** a mark of evil **2 :** a labeling as unorthodox or heretical

mark-on \ˈ=,=\ *n* -S [fr. *mark on*, v.] **1 :** MARKUP **2 :** profit margin

mark out *vt* **1 :** to obliterate or cancel with a mark ⟨vainly tried to *mark* the defacing stain *out*⟩ **2 :** MARK OFF

mar·kov chain *or* **mar·koff chain** \ˈmär,kȯf-\ *n, usu cap M* [after Andrei Andreevich *Markov* †1922 Russ. mathematician] **:** a usu. discrete stochastic process (as a random walk) in which the probabilities of occurrence of various future states depend only on the present state of the system or on the immediately preceding state and not on the path by which the present state was achieved

mar·kov·ni·kov rule \mär'kȯvnə,kȯf-\ *n, usu cap M* [after Vladimir V. *Markovnikov* †1904 Russ. chemist] **:** a statement in chemistry: in the addition of compounds to olefins the negative portion of the compound added (as the bromine in hydrogen bromide) becomes attached to the least hydrogenated end of the carbon-carbon double bond (as in the addition of hydrogen bromide to propylene: $CH_3CH{=}CH_2 + HBr \rightarrow CH_3CHBrCH_3$)

mark·ry \ˈmärkrē\ *n* -ES [by alter.] **:** MERCURY 2

marks *pl of* MARK, *pres 3d sing of* MARK

mark sensing *n* **:** actuation of the automatic punching of a card by pencil marks on the card

marks·man \ˈmärksmən, ˈmäk-\ *n, pl* **marksmen** [*marks* (gen. of ¹*mark*) + *man*] **1 :** one that shoots at a mark: as **a :** a person skillful or practiced at hitting a mark or target ⟨a first-class ~ with a pistol⟩ ⟨was the best ~ in the league at kicking field goals⟩ **b :** a member of the armed forces who is proficient enough in shooting to be ranked in a certain grade **2 :** a person who makes his mark instead of writing his name in signing documents

marks·man·ship \-n,ship\ *n* **:** the art or skill of a marksman esp. with firearms

marks·woman \ˈmärk,swu̇mən\ *n, pl* **markswomen** [*marks* (gen. of ¹*mark*) + *woman*] **:** a woman who shoots or is skilled in shooting at a mark

mark tooth *n* [¹*mark*] **:** an incisor tooth of a horse

mark up *vt* **1 :** to set a higher price on **:** add a markup to ⟨*marked* their umbrellas *up* during the long rainy spell⟩ **2** *chiefly Brit* **:** to add (an item) to a store or tavern account ⟨*mark up* . . . their modest reckonings —Guy McCrone⟩

markup \ˈ=,=\ *n* -S [*mark up*] **1 :** a raise in the price of an article ⟨extensive ~*s*⟩ **2 :** an amount added to the cost to determine the selling price; *specif* **:** the gross profit to cover overhead expenses and provide net profit usu. expressed as a percentage of the selling price

markweed \ˈ=,=\ *n* **:** POISON IVY

markworthy \ˈ=,==\ *adj* [¹*mark* + *worthy*; trans. of G *merkwürdig*] **:** NOTEWORTHY ⟨more ~ for its ferment of critical ideas —R.A.Hall b. 1911⟩

¹marl *R* ˈmärl, *chiefly before pause or consonant* -rəl, -*R* ˈmäl\ *n* -S [ME, fr. MF *marle*, fr. ML *margila*, dim. of L *marga*, fr. Gaulish] **1 :** a loose or crumbling earthy deposit that contains chiefly calcium carbonate or dolomite: as **a :** calcareous sand, silt, or clay; *also* **:** a deposit of unconsolidated shells **b :** a calcareous deposit in a glacial lake **2 :** CLAY, EARTH ⟨a clod of wayward ~ —Shak.⟩ **3 :** a brick made of marl

²marl \"\ *vt* -ED/-ING/-S [ME *marlen*, fr. *marl*, n.] **:** to overspread, manure, or dress with marl **:** fertilize with or as if with marl

³marl \"\ *vi* -ED/-ING/-S [by contr.] *now dial* **:** MARVEL

⁴marl \"\ *n* -S [by contr.] *now dial* **:** MARVEL

⁵marl \"\ *vt* -ED/-ING/-S [D *marlen*, back-formation fr. *marling* marline — more at MARLINE] **:** to cover or fasten with marline making a hitch at each turn to prevent unwinding

⁶marl \"\ *n* -S [by contr.] *now dial Brit* **:** ¹MARBLE

⁷marl \"\ *n* -S [origin unknown] **:** a delicate fiber obtained from peacock feathers and used in making artificial flies

⁸marl \"\ *n* -S [native name in Australia] **:** a slender grayish brown bandicoot (*Perameles myosura*) of western Australia with a long nose and long thin ears

mar·la·ceous \(')mär¦lāshəs\ *adj* [¹*marl* + *-aceous*] **:** containing or resembling marl

marl·berry \'märl- — *see* BERRY\ *n* [prob. fr. ⁶*marl* + *berry*] **:** a tropical American shrub or small tree (*Ardisia paniculata*) with brown wood and dark berries

marl·bor·ough \'märl,bər·|ə, 'mål-, -,bə·r|, |ō, -,bərə, *chiefly Brit* 'mòl-, -,brə\ *adj, usu cap* [fr. *Marlborough*, provincial district of New Zealand] **:** of or from the provincial district of Marlborough, New Zealand **:** of the kind or style prevalent in Marlborough

marlborough foot *n, usu cap M* [after George Spencer, 4th duke of *Marlborough* †1817 Eng. politician] **:** a rather heavy square foot sometimes used to terminate a Marlborough leg

marlborough leg *n, usu cap M* [after George Spencer, 4th duke of *Marlborough*] **:** a heavy straight sometimes vertically grooved chair leg common in furniture of late Chippendale style

Marlborough foot

marled \'märld\ *adj* [by contr.] **:** MARBLED

mar·li \'märlē\ *n* -S [F] **:** an often ornamented raised border of a plate or flat dish that forms a plane nearly parallel to the bottom

¹mar·lin \'märlən, 'mål-\ *n* -S [short for *marlinspike*; fr. the appearance of the beak] **1 a :** any of several large oceanic game fishes (genus *Makaira*) of the family Istiophoridae — see BLACK MARLIN, BLUE MARLIN, SILVER MARLIN, STRIPED MARLIN, WHITE MARLIN **b :** SPEARFISH **2 :** a synchronized swimming stunt in which the body executes a quarter turn with a full twist from a back layout position to a position at right angles to it

²marlin \"\ *n* -S [origin unknown] *chiefly Midland* **:** GODWIT

mar·line *also* **mar·lin** \'märlən, 'mål-\ *or* **mar·ling** \-liŋ\ *n* -S [*marline, marlin* fr. D *marlijn*, by folk etymology (influence of *lijn* line) fr. *marling; marling* fr. D, fr. *marren, meren* to tie, moor (fr. MD *maren, meren*) + *-ling* — more at MOOR] **:** a small usu. tarred line of two strands twisted loosely left-handed that is used for seizing and as a covering for wire rope

marlinespike *also* **marlinspike** *or* **marlingspike** \'==,=\ *n* **1 :** an iron tool that tapers to a point and is used to separate strands of rope or wire (as in splicing) — compare FID 1b **2 a :** TROPIC BIRD **b :** JAEGER

marlinespike hitch *n* **:** a hitch into which a marlinespike is inserted in order to draw seizing taut

marling *pres part of* MARL

marling hitch *n* **:** a knot that is used in series to lash long bundles (as rolled or folded awnings, hammocks, or sails)

marlinspike fish *n* **:** STRIPED MARLIN

marlin swordfish *n* **:** BLUE MARLIN

marlinespike hitch

marl·ite \'mär,līt\ *n* -S [¹*marl* + *-ite*] **:** a marl resistant to the action of air — **mar·lit·ic** \(')mär¦lid·ik\ *adj*

¹mar·lock \'målək\ *n* -S [origin unknown] *dial Eng* **:** FROLIC, PRANK

²marlock \"\ *vi* -ED/-ING/-S *dial Eng* **:** FROLIC, SPORT

mar·lo·vi·an \(')mär¦lōvēən\ *adj, usu cap* [Christopher *Marlowe* †1593 English dramatist + E *-ian*] **1 :** of, relating to, or characteristic of Christopher Marlowe ⟨a *Marlovian* fondness for exotic names —Louis MacNeice⟩ **2 :** of, relating to, or characteristic of the plays or poems of Marlowe ⟨the plays of the *Marlovian* genre —Alan Downer⟩

marlpit \'=,=\ *n* [ME, fr. *marl* + *pit*] **:** a pit where marl is dug

marls *pl of* MARL, *pres 3d sing of* MARL

marlstone \'=,=\ *n* **:** an indurated mixture of clay materials and calcium carbonate usu. containing from 25 to 75 percent clay

¹marly \'märlē\ *adj, usu* -ER/-EST [ME, fr. ¹*marl* + *-y*] **:** of, relating to, or resembling marl **:** abounding with marl

²marly \"\ *adj, usu* -ER/-EST [contr. of *marbly*] *dial Brit* **:** MARBLED, SPOTTED

marm \'märm, 'mām\ *n* -S [alter. of *ma'am*] *chiefly dial* **:** MADAM 1

mar·ma·lade \'märmə,lād, 'mām- *sometimes* ,==\ *n* -S [Pg *marmelada* quince conserve, fr. *marmelo* quince, fr. L *melimelum*, a kind of sweet apple, fr. Gk *melimēlon*, fr. *meli* honey + *mēlon* apple — more at MELLIFLUOUS] **1 :** a soft clear translucent jelly holding in suspension pieces or slices of fruit and fruit rind ⟨orange ~⟩ **2 :** MARMALADE TREE

marmalade box *n* **:** GENIPAP

marmalade cat *n* **:** a red tabby cat

marmalade tree *also* **marmalade plum** *n* **1 :** a tropical American tree (*Calocarpum zapota*) that has wood like mahogany, large obovate leaves, and an egg-shaped single-seeded fruit **2 :** MAMMEE

mar·ma·ri·za·tion *or* **mar·mo·ri·za·tion** \,märmərə'zāshən\ *n* -S **:** the process of being marmarized

mar·ma·rize *or* **mar·mo·rize** \'märmə,rīz\ *vt* -ED/-ING/-S [Gk *marmaros* & L *marmor* marble + E *-ize* — more at MARBLE] **:** to convert into marble **:** subject to marmarosis

mar·ma·ro·sis *or* **mar·mo·ro·sis** \,märmə'rōsəs\ *n, pl* **marmaro·ses** *or* **marmoro·ses** \-ō,sēz\ [NL, fr. Gk *marmaros* & L *marmor* marble + NL *-osis*] **:** the conversion of limestone into marble by metamorphism

mar·ma·tite \'märmə,tīt\ *n* -S [G *marmatit*, fr. *Marmato*, locality in Colombia + G *-it* -ite] **:** a mineral consisting of ferruginous sphalerite that is dark brown to black in color

mar·men·nill \'mär,mennətᵊl\ *n* -S [Icel, fr. ON, fr. *marr* sea + *-mennill* (dim. of *mann-*, *mathr* man) — more at MARINE, MAN] **:** MERMAN

mar·mite \'mär,mīt, (')mär¦mēt\ *also* **mar·mit** \'märmət\ *n* -S [F *marmite*] **1 a :** a large metal or earthenware soup kettle with a cover **b :** a small individual earthenware casserole with a cover used esp. for soups — called also *petite marmite* **2 :** the soup served in a marmite **:** PETITE MARMITE 1 **3 a :** a yeast product used in extracts for flavoring meats and soups and as a dietary supplement

marmite can *n* **:** a large insulated container used to bring hot food to frontline troops

mar·mo·lite \'märmə,līt\ *n* -S [Gk *marmairein* to flash, sparkle + E *-o-* + *-lite* — more at MORN] **:** a thin laminated usu. pale green serpentine

mar·mo·ra·ceous \¦märmə¦rāshəs\ *adj* [L *marmor* marble + E *-aceous* — more at MARBLE] **:** of, relating to, or resembling marble

mar·mo·rate \'märmə,rāt\ *or* **mar·mo·rat·ed** \-ād·əd\ *adj* [*marmorate* fr. L *marmoratus*, past part. of *marmorare* to adorn with marble, fr. *marmor* marble; *marmorated* fr. L *marmoratus* + E *-ed*] **:** veined like marble **:** MARBLED

mar·mo·ra·tion \,==¦rāshən\ *n* -S [L *marmoration-, marmoratio*, fr. *marmoratus* + *-ion-, -io* -ion] **:** incrustation with marble or variegation resembling that of marble **:** MARBLING

mar·mo·re·al \(')mär¦mōrēəl, (')må¦-, -mòr-\ *or* **mar·mo·re·an** \-ən\ *adj* [L *marmoreus* marmoreal (fr. *marmor* marble) + E *-al* or *-an*] **1 :** of, relating to, or resembling marble or a marble statue esp. in coldness, smoothness, or majesty **:** STATUESQUE ⟨art is not a ~ calm —Irwin Edman⟩ ⟨his conception of *marmorean* stillness —D.A.Stauffer⟩ **2 :** made of marble ⟨those ~ domes —Robert Browning⟩ — **mar·mo·re·al·ly** \-əlē, -li\ *adv*

mar·mo·sa \mär'mōsə\ *n, cap* [NL, fr. E *marmoset*] **:** a genus comprising the New World murine opossums

mar·mo·set \'märmə,set, 'mám-, -,zet, ,==¦=, *usu* -ed.+V\ *n* -S [ME *marmusette, marmozette*, fr. MF *marmouset*, *marmoset* grotesque figure (prob. also "marmoset" — whence F dial. *marmouset* marmoset), fr. *marmouser* to mumble, mutter, of imit. origin] **:** any of numerous soft-furred So. and Central American monkeys of the family Callithricidae that have claws instead of nails on all the digits except the great toe

mar·mot \'märmət, 'mám-, *usu* -əd.+V\ *n* -S [F *marmotte*] **1 :** a stout-bodied short-legged rodent of the genus *Marmota* that has coarse fur, a short bushy tail, and very small ears, lives in burrows, and hibernates in winter — see WOODCHUCK **2 :** a prairie dog or one of the larger ground squirrels

European marmot

mar·mo·ta \'märməd·ə\ *n, cap* [NL, fr. F *marmotte* marmot] **:** a genus of large rodents (family Sciuridae) that somewhat resemble badgers and comprise the marmots

marmot squirrel *n* **:** an American ground squirrel

mar·ne·an *or* **mar·ni·an** \'märnēən\ *adj, usu cap* [*Marne*, department in France + E *-an* or *-ian*] **:** LA TÈNE

ma·ro \'mä(,)rō\ *n* -S [Tahitian & Maori] **:** a loincloth made of sedge or flax fiber and worn by Polynesians in New Zealand and Tahiti — compare MALO

mar·o·cain \¦marə¦kān\ *n* -S [F (*crêpe*) *marocain*, lit., Moroccan crepe, fr. *crêpe* crepe + *marocain* Moroccan, fr. *Maroc* Morocco] **1 :** a dress crepe that is made with a warp of silk or rayon and a filling of other yarns and is similar to but heavier than canton crepe — called also *crepe marocain* **2 :** MOROCCO RED

mar·o·nite \'marə,nīt\ *n* -S *usu cap* [ML *Maronita*, fr. *Maron-*, *Maro*, 5th cent. Syrian monk + L *-ita* -ite] **:** an Arabic-speaking member of a Uniate church chiefly in Lebanon that was established as a separate Monothelete organization in the 7th century and has retained its old Syriac liturgy and a married clergy following its union with Rome in the 12th century

ma·roo·di *also* **ma·rou·di** \mə'rüdē\ *n* -S [Arawak *marodi*] *British Guiana* **:** GUAN

maroola *var of* MARULA

¹ma·roon \mə'rün\ *n* -S [modif. of AmerSp *cimarrón*, fr. *cimarrón*, adj., wild, savage, lit., living on mountaintops, fr. Sp *cima* top, summit, fr. L *cyma* young sprout of cabbage — more at CYME] **1** *usu cap* **a :** a fugitive Negro slave of the West Indies and Guiana in the 17th and 18th centuries **b :** a descendant of such a slave living in the West Indies and esp. in the mountains of Jamaica or in Guiana and esp. in Surinam **2** *South* **:** MAROONING PARTY **3 :** a person who is marooned ⟨books suited to the life of a ~ on a desert island —T.H.Savory⟩

²maroon \"\ *vb* -ED/-ING/-S *vt* **1 :** to put ashore on a desolate island or coast and leave to one's fate ⟨~*ed* by mutineers with only a week's supply of food⟩ **2 :** to place or leave in isolation or without hope of escape ⟨~*ed* in Europe by the chances of war —S.H.Adams⟩ ⟨~*ed* more than 200 motorists and truckers in the little community for several days —*Amer. Guide Series: Mich.*⟩ ~ *vi* **1 :** to escape from slavery ⟨they ~*ed* and fled into the hills⟩ **2** *South* **a :** PICNIC **b :** to camp out for some days **3 :** to live in idleness ⟨~*ing* about the town⟩

³maroon *or* **mar·roon** \"\ *n* -S [F *marron*, lit., Spanish chestnut] **1 :** a firework that consists of a pasteboard box wound with strong twine and filled with gunpowder ⟨the banging of ~*s* would warn us of the coming of a raid —H.G. Wells⟩ **2 a :** a variable color averaging a dark red that is yellower and duller than cranberry, average garnet, or average wine and duller and slightly yellower than pomegranate — called also *marron* **b** *of textiles* **:** a dark red to purplish red that is duller than plum violet

ma·roon·er \-nə(r)\ *n* -S [²*maroon* + *-er*] **:** BUCCANEER, PIRATE

marooning party *n, South* **:** an excursion or extended picnic **:** a camping trip — called also *maroon*

ma·ro·pa \mə'rōpə\ *n, pl* **maropa** *or* **maropas** *usu cap* [Sp, of AmerInd origin] **1 a :** a Tacanan people of northern Bolivia **b :** a member of such people **2 :** the language of the Maropa people

ma·ro·quin \'marəkən\ *n* -S [F, fr. *Maroc* Morocco] **:** MOROCCO

ma·ror *also* **mo·ror** \mä'rō(ə)r, -rò(ə)r, '==,=\ *n, pl* **maror** *also* **moror** [Heb *mārōr*] **:** the bitter herbs (as horseradish) eaten by Jews at the Passover seder to symbolize the bitterness of the Egyptian oppression of the Israelites

ma·rotte \mə'rät\ *n* -S [F, fr. MF, holy image, doll, dim. of the name *Marie* (Mary)] **1** *archaic* **:** BAUBLE 2 **2 :** a pet idea or notion ⟨it is a ~ of mine with which I will not trouble you —Victoria Sackville-West⟩

ma·rou·flage \¦märə¦fläzh\ *n* -S [F, fr. *maroufler* to glue canvas to a wall (fr. *maroufle*, a strong glue) + *-age*] **:** a process of fastening canvas to a wall with an adhesive (as white lead ground in oil)

ma·ro·vo \mə'rō(,)vō\ *n, pl* **marovo** *or* **marovos** *usu cap* **1 a :** a people inhabiting the east side of New Georgia, Solomon Islands **b :** a member of such people **2 :** an Austronesian language of the Marovo people

mar·plot \'mär,plät\ *n* [¹*mar* + *plot*] **1 :** one who frustrates or ruins a plan or undertaking by his meddling ⟨served by varmints, nitwits, and ~*s* —S.L.A.Marshall⟩ **2 :** one who endangers the success of an enterprise ⟨this small ~ had discovered a great deal too much —Rudyard Kipling⟩ — **mar·plot·ry** \-lä·trē\ *n* -ES

marq *abbr, often cap* marquess; marquis

¹marque \'märk, 'mák\ *n* -S [ME *mark*, fr. MF, fr. OProv *marca*, fr. *marcar* to mark, seize as a pledge, confiscate, fr. OIt *marcare* to mark — more at MARCATO] **1** *obs* **:** REPRISAL, RETALIATION **2 :** LETTERS OF MARQUE

²marque \"\ *n* -S [F, mark, sign, band, fr. MF, fr. *marquer* to mark, fr. OIt *marcare*] **:** a brand or make of a product — used esp. of sport cars ⟨the radiator, while still retaining the distinctive appearance of the ~ —Grenville Manton⟩

mar·quee \mär'kē, mä'-\ *n* -S [modif. (*marquise* being taken as pl.) of F *marquise*, lit., marchioness — more at MARQUISE] **1** *or* **mar·kee** \"\ **a :** a large field tent formerly used by an officer of high rank ⟨during the bitter winter of 1777–78, Washington lived and worked in this flimsy ~ —*Nat'l Geographic*⟩ **b :** a large tent set up for an outdoor party, reception, or exhibition ⟨a collation and a dance in ~*s* on the lawn —W.S.Maugham⟩ **2 a :** a permanent canopy usu. of metal and glass projecting over the entrance to a building (as a hotel) **b :** a similar canopy at a theater entrance usu. brightly lighted and displaying the title of the attraction and the names of the principal performers ⟨the electric sign on the ~ of the theater entrance —Burr Leyson⟩

mar·qués \mär'kās\ *n, pl* **marque·ses** \-āsəs, -āsəz\ [Sp *marqués* & Pg *marquês*, fr. OSp & OPg, fr. OProv *marques*, fr. *marca* boundary, boundary land, of Gmc origin; akin to OHG *marha* boundary, boundary land — more at MARK] **:** a marquess in Spanish and Portuguese-speaking countries

¹mar·que·san \(')mär¦kāzᵊn, (')må¦-, -āsᵊn\ *adj, usu cap* [*Marquesas* islands, French Oceania + E *-an*] **1 a :** of, relating to, or characteristic of the Marquesas islands **b :** of, relating to, or characteristic of the Marquesans **2 :** of, relating to, or characteristic of the Marquesan language

²marquesan \"\ *n* -S *cap* **1 :** a Polynesian of the Marquesas islands **2 :** the Austronesian language of the Marquesans

mar·quess \'märkwəs, 'mák-\ *or* **mar·quis** \", mär'kē, mä'-\ *n, pl* **mar·quess·es** \-kwəsəz\ *or* **mar·quis·es** \-kwəsəz\ *or* **mar·quis** \-kē(z)\ [ME *markis, marquis*, fr. MF *marquis*, alter. (influenced by OProv *marques* & OIt *marchese* marquis) of *marchis*, fr. *marche* boundary, boundary land, of Gmc origin; akin to OHG *marha* boundary, boundary land — more at MARQUE, MARCHESE, MARK] **1 :** a nobleman of hereditary rank in Europe and Japan; *specif* **:** a member of the second grade of the peerage in Great Britain ranking below a duke and above an earl **2** *obs* **:** MARCHIONESS

mar·quess·ate *or* **mar·quis·ate** \'märkwə,zāt, -,sāt, -,zət, -,sət\ *n* -S [F *marquisat*, fr. MF, modif. (influenced by *marquis*) of OIt *marchesato*, fr. *marchese* + *-ato* -ate] **1 :** the domain or territory of a marquess or marchioness **2 :** the rank or dignity of a marquess or marchioness

mar·que·try *also* **mar·que·te·rie** \'märkə·trē\ *n, pl* **marquetries** *also* **marqueteries** [MF *marqueterie*, fr. *marqueter* to checker, inlay (fr. *marque* sign, mark) + *-erie* -ery — more at MARQUE] **1 :** a decorative process in which elaborate usu. floral patterns are formed by the insertion of pieces of wood, shell, or ivory into a wood veneer that is then applied to the surface of a piece of furniture (as a table or cabinet) ⟨the craftsman should attempt to do his own veneering and ~ —Ernest Brace⟩ **2 :** an object decorated in marquetry ⟨a somewhat flamboyant piece of inlaid ~ —Agatha Christie⟩

mar·quise \mär'kēz\ *n* -S [F, fem. of *marquis* — more at MARQUESS] **1 :** MARCHIONESS **2 :** MARQUEE **3 a :** a gem or a ring setting or bezel usu. elliptical in shape but with pointed ends — see BRILLIANT illustration **b :** a gem cut for use in such a setting **4 :** a small upholstered sofa

mar·qui·sette \¦märk(w)ə¦zet\ *n* -S [*marquise* + *-ette*] **:** a sheer meshed fabric of leno weave that is made with variations in fiber, weight, and finishes, woven plain or with small allover designs, and is used for clothing, curtains, and mosquito nets

marquis of queens·ber·ry rules \-'kwēnz¦,ber|ē- -,b(ə)r|, |i-\ *n pl, usu cap M&Q* [fr. the *Marquis of Queensbury rules*, a code of rules governing boxing matches, after Sir John Sholto Douglas, 8th *Marquis of Queensbury* †1900 Eng. boxing patron who supervised the code's formulation in 1867 by John G. Chambers †1883 Eng. athlete] **:** a code of fair play presumed to apply in any fight ⟨recognize no *Marquis of Queensberry rules* by which moral decorum should regulate and govern their differences —Lucius Garvin⟩

mar·qui·to \mär'kē(,)tō\ *n* -S [AmerSp] *Southwest* **:** a frame of ornamental tinwork of Spanish American origin

mar·ra·kech *or* **mar·ra·kesh** \mə'rä,kesh, ¦marə¦kesh\ *adj, usu cap* [fr. *Marrakech* or *Marrakesh*, Morocco] **:** of or from the city of Marrakech, Morocco **:** of the kind or style prevalent in Marrakech

mar·ram grass \'marəm-\ *also* **marram** *n* -S [of Scand origin; akin to ON *maralmr*, a beach grass, fr. *marr* sea + *halmr* straw — more at MARINE, HAULM] **:** a beach grass (*Ammophila arenaria*)

mar·ra·nism \mə'rä,nizəm\ *or* **mar·ra·no·ism** \-ä(,)nō,i-\ *n* -S **:** the condition or behavior of a marrano

mar·ra·no *also* **ma·ra·no** \mə'rä(,)nō\ *n* -S *usu cap* [Sp *marrano*, lit., pig, prob. fr. Ar *maḥram* something prohibited; fr. the fact that the eating of pork is outlawed by the Jewish and Muslim religions] **:** a Christianized Jew or Moor of medieval Spain; *esp* **:** one who accepted conversion only to escape persecution

marred *past of* MAR

mar·ree \'ma(,)rē\ *n* -S [Maori *mere*] **:** ⁵MERE

mar·rer \'märə(r)\ *n* -S [ME, fr. *marren* to mar + *-er* — more at MAR] **:** one that mars esp. by rendering or doing carelessly or imperfectly ⟨there are more ~*s* than makers of good music⟩

mar·ri \'märē\ *n* -S [native name in Australia] **:** a very large Australian red gum (*Eucalyptus calophylla*) having white flowers and yielding tough strong yellowish brown wood whose value as lumber is somewhat impaired by the numerous gum veins

mar·ri·a·ble \'marēəbəl\ *adj* [ME *maryable*, fr. MF *mariable*, fr. *marier* to marry + *-able* — more at MARRY] *archaic* **:** MARRIAGEABLE

mar·riage \'marij, -rēj *also* 'mer-\ *n* -S [ME *mariage*, fr. MF, fr. *marier* to marry + *-age* — more at MARRY] **1 a :** the state of being united to a person of the opposite sex as husband or wife **b :** the mutual relation of husband and wife **:** WEDLOCK **c :** the institution whereby men and women are joined in a special kind of social and legal dependence for the purpose of founding and maintaining a family — see MONOGAMY, POLYGAMY **2 :** an act of marrying or the rite by which the married status is effected **:** WEDDING; *esp* **:** the wedding ceremony and attendant festivities or formalities — compare BEENA MARRIAGE, COEMPTIO, CONFARREATION, LEVIRATE **3 :** an intimate or close union **4 :** MARITAGE **5 :** the combination of a king and queen of the same suit (as in pinochle) — see ROYAL MARRIAGE

mar·riage·abil·i·ty \,marijə'bilәd·ē, -rēj-, -ətē, -i *also* ,mer-\ *n* **:** the quality or state of being marriageable

mar·riage·able \'marijəbəl, -rēj- *also* 'mer-\ *adj* **:** fit for or capable of marriage: as **a :** of an age at which marriage is allowable **b :** free from any legal disability that would prohibit or nullify entry into a marriage

marriage bed *n* **:** the bed shared by a newly wed couple

marriage broker *n* **:** one whose business is marriage brokerage — compare GO-BETWEEN

marriage brokerage *also* **marriage brokage** *n* **1 a :** the act of negotiating or arranging a marriage contract between a man and woman in return for a consideration **b :** the business of arranging such contracts **2 :** the fee paid for the services of a marriage broker any contract for which is void at common law

marriage chest *n* **:** HOPE CHEST

marriage class *n* **:** one of the divisions within a primitive social group (as a tribe) designed to foster exogamy

marriage contract *n* **1 :** an antenuptial contract **:** MARRIAGE SETTLEMENT **2 :** the contractual status of marriage between husband and wife

marriage flight *n* **:** NUPTIAL FLIGHT

marriage license *n* **:** a written authorization granted by a qualified governmental official or ecclesiastic to a named man and woman to marry

marriage line *n* **1** *usu cap M* **:** LINE OF MARRIAGE **2 marriage lines** *pl but usu sing in constr, chiefly Brit* **:** a certificate of marriage

marriage mill *n* **:** a place where it is possible to marry with a minimum of formality or delay

marriage of convenience [trans. of F *mariage de convenance*] **:** a marriage contracted rather for the advantages (as keeping an estate in a family, acquiring social position) arising out of it than because of mutual affection

marriage portion *n* **:** DOWER

marriage settlement *n* **1 :** a settlement of property by a party to a marriage or by a third person in view and in consideration of marriage **2 :** a settlement of property that benefits a husband, wife, or their issue **3 :** an agreement between husband and wife fixing or waiving their respective rights in each other's property sometimes in connection with a prospective divorce or separation and providing for their children — compare JOINTURE

¹married *adj* [ME *maried*, fr. past part. of *marien* to marry — more at MARRY] **1 a :** being in the state of matrimony **:** WEDDED ⟨a ~ couple⟩ **b :** of or relating to marriage and esp. to the marriage state **:** CONNUBIAL ⟨~ love⟩ **2 a :** UNITED, SHARED ⟨~ responsibilities⟩ ⟨our ~ voices wildly trolled —W.B. Yeats⟩ **b** *of a piece of antique furniture* **:** rebuilt of parts not originally from one piece **c** *Brit, of goods for sale* **:** available only as a unit **d** *Brit, of a motion picture print* **:** containing both the picture and sound record

²married *n* -S **:** a married person — usu. used in pl. and in combination ⟨the present-day young-*marrieds*⟩

mar·ried·ly *adv* **:** in the manner of a married couple **:** as if married

mar·ri·er *also* **mar·ry·er** \'marēə(r) *also* 'mer-\ *n* -S **:** one that marries: as **a :** a person that enters into the married state **b :** an official or clergyman who performs marriages

marries *pres 3d sing of* MARRY

marring *pres part of* MAR

marris *pl of* MARRI

mar·rite \'mä,rīt\ *n* -S [John E. *Marr* †1933 Eng. geologist + E *-ite*] **:** a mineral that occurs as a well-characterized substance of unknown composition in minute equant monoclinic crystals in the dolomite at Lengenbach, Valais, Switzerland

¹mar·ron \ma'rōⁿ, mə'-\ *n, pl* **marrons** \"\ [F] **1 a :** SPANISH CHESTNUT 2 **b marrons** *also* **marrons gla·cé** *pl* \(,)=,gla'sā, ==¦=\ **:** chestnuts preserved in syrup flavored with vanilla **2 a :** ³MAROON 2a **b :** ³MAROON 1

²marron \"\ *n* -S *usu cap* [F, modif. of AmerSp *cimarrón* — more at MAROON] **:** ¹MAROON 1

marron glacé *see* MARRON 1b\ *n* [F, lit., glazed Spanish chestnut] **:** a moderate brown that is lighter, stronger, and slightly yellower than bay, lighter and stronger than auburn, and redder, lighter, and stronger than chestnut brown — called also *witchwood*

marroon *var of* MAROON

mar·rot \'marət\ *also* **mar·rock** \-ək\ *n* -S [origin unknown] *dial Brit* **:** AUK, GUILLEMOT, PUFFIN

¹mar·row \ˈma(ˌ)rō, -rə *also* ˈmer-, *often* -rəw+V\ *n* -s [ME *mergh, margh, mary, merowe, marowe,* fr. OE *mearg, mearh;* akin to OS *marg* marrow, OHG *marg, marag,* ON *mergr,* Toch A *mäššunt,* Skt *majjan, majjā* marrow, OSlav *mozgŭ* brain] **1 a :** a soft highly vascular modified connective tissue that occupies the cavities and cancellous part of most bones and occurs in two forms: (1) **:** a whitish or yellowish marrow consisting chiefly of fat cells and predominating in the cavities of the long bones — called also *yellow marrow* (2) **:** a reddish marrow containing little fat, being the chief seat of red blood cell and blood granulocyte production, and occurring in the normal adult only in cancellous tissue esp. in certain flat bones — called also *red marrow* **b :** the substance of the spinal cord — called also *spinal marrow* **c** *archaic* (1) **:** PITH 1 (2) **:** the pulp of a fruit **2 :** the choicest part: as **a :** the choicest of food **:** table delicacies **b :** the seat or source of animal vigor or health **c :** the inmost, best, or essential part **:** ESSENCE **3** *chiefly Brit* **:** VEGETABLE MARROW

²mar·row \ˈmarə\ *n* -s [ME *marwe, maroo, marrow*] **1** *chiefly Scot* **:** COMPANION, PARTNER **2** *chiefly Scot* **:** SPOUSE, LOVER **3** *chiefly Scot* **:** one of a pair **:** MATCH, EQUAL ⟨a pair of boots that was not ~*s* —J.M.Barrie⟩

³marrow \"\ *vb* -ED/-ING/-S [ME *marrowen,* fr. *marrow,* n.] **1** *dial Brit* **:** MATCH, EQUAL ⟨this ~*s* your color⟩ **2** *dial Brit* **:** MARRY

marrow bean *n* **:** any of several garden beans that are grown primarily as field beans for their large white seeds

marrowbone \ˈ=(ˌ)=ˌ=\ *n* [ME *marybon,* fr. *mary* marrow + *bon* bone — more at MARROW, BONE] **1 :** a bone containing marrow esp. in sufficient quantity to be used in cookery **2 marrowbones** *pl* **:** KNEES

marrow cabbage *n* **:** CHOUMOELLIER

mar·rowed \ˈmarōd, -rəd *also* ˈmer-\ *adj* **:** having or filled with marrow

marrowfat \ˈ=(ˌ)=ˌ=\ *n* **1** *also* **marrowfat pea :** any of several wrinkled-seeded garden peas **2 :** a tallowy product obtained by rendering bone marrow

mar·row·ish \ˈmarōish, -rəwish *also* ˈmer-\ *adj* **:** resembling marrow

marrow kale *n* **:** MARROW-STEM KALE

mar·row·less \ˈmarōləs, -rəl- *also* ˈmer-\ *adj* **:** empty of marrow

marrow scoop *n* **:** an 18th-century table implement often of silver with a long thin bowl suitable for removing marrow from a bone

mar·row·sky \məˈrau̇skē\ *n* -s [origin unknown] **:** SPOONERISM

marrow squash *n* **:** VEGETABLE MARROW

marrow-stem kale *also* **marrow-stemmed kale** \ˈ=(ˌ)=ˌ=-\ *n* **:** any of several kales with heavy foliage and thickened meaty stems that are much used for forage in areas of moderately mild winters

mar·rowy \ˈmarəw|ē, -rō|, |i *also* ˈmer-\ *adj* **:** full of or like marrow **:** rich or pleasing in substance **:** PITHY

mar·rube \məˈrüb\ *also* **mar·rub** \ˈmarəb\ *n* -s [L *marrubium*] **:** HOREHOUND

mar·ru·bi·in \məˈrübēən\ *n* -s [ISV *marrubi-* (fr. NL *Marrubium*) + *-in*] **:** a bitter crystalline lactone $C_{20}H_{28}O_4$ obtained from horehound

mar·ru·bi·um \-ēəm\ *n, cap* [NL, fr. L, horehound] **:** a genus of Old World mints having wrinkled leaves and small white or purple flowers in dense axillary clusters — see HOREHOUND 1a

mar·ru·cin·i·an \ˌmarəˈsinēən\ *n* -s *usu cap* [L *Marrucini,* a people of ancient Italy + E *-an*] **:** a Sabellian dialect

¹mar·ry \ˈmarē, -ri *also* ˈmer-\ *vb* -ED/-ING/-ES [ME *marien,* fr. OF *marier,* fr. L *maritare,* fr. *maritus,* adj., married & *maritus,* n., husband, perh. fr. an (assumed) prehistoric word meaning "young woman" and akin to Gk *meirax* girl, boy, W *merch* daughter, girl, Skt *marya* man, young man, suitor] *vt* **1 a :** to become united in wedlock **:** constitute husband and wife according to law or custom ⟨they *married* each other soon after they met⟩ — usu. used in the passive ⟨they were *married* as mere children⟩ **b :** to dispose of (as a daughter) in wedlock **:** give in marriage — used esp. of a parent or guardian ⟨he *married* his daughter to his partner's son⟩ **c :** to take as husband or wife **:** WED ⟨he *married* the girl next door⟩ **d :** to join (persons) in wedlock **:** perform the ceremony of marriage for (a person or couple) — used of a religious or civil functionary ⟨he *married* ten couples in one week⟩ **e :** to obtain by marriage ⟨had every intention of ~*ing* wealth and security⟩ **2 :** to unite in close and usu. permanent relation: as **a** (1) **:** to join (two ropes) end to end so as to run through a block without jamming at the joint (2) **:** to place (two ropes) alongside of each other so as to be grasped and hauled on at the same time (3) **:** to join (pieces of wood) with a rope ⟨will have to use *married* wedges in launching the ship⟩ **b :** to unite two or more wines of different age, vintage, or quality either by blending or by blending and aging ~ *vi* **1 a :** to enter into the connubial state **:** take a husband or a wife **:** WED ⟨he first *married* at twenty⟩ **b :** to be a contracting party to a marriage ceremony, regardless of its validity **2 :** to enter into a close or intimate union ⟨these wines ~ well⟩ — **marry into :** to become a member of by marriage ⟨*married into* a prominent family⟩

²marry \"\ *interj* [ME *Marie,* after *Marie,* the Virgin Mary] *archaic* — used to express agreement or surprise esp. in answer to a question and sometimes with *come up* to express disbelief or disdain

marryer *var of* MARRIER

marrying *adj* **:** disposed to marry ⟨a ~ man⟩

marrymuffe *n* -s [origin unknown] *obs* **:** a coarse clothing material or a garment made of it

marry off *vt* **:** to dispose of in marriage **:** find a marriage partner for ⟨finally *married off* all his daughters⟩ ⟨*married* the youngest one *off* just recently⟩

mars \ˈmärz, ˈmȧz\ *n, usu cap* [ME, fr. *Mars,* 4th planet in order of distance from the sun, fr. L, after *Mars,* god of war and agriculture] *obs* **:** IRON — used in alchemical literature

mar·sa·la \märˈsälə\ *n* -s *usu cap* [fr. *Marsala,* town in Sicily] **1 :** a dark-colored wine resembling Spanish sherry that is usu. semisweet or sweet, is often classed as a dessert or appetizer wine, and is produced in western Sicily around the town of Marsala **2 :** a wine similar to Sicilian Marsala but made elsewhere (as in California)

mars brown *n, often cap M* [prob. fr. the planet *Mars*] **:** ARGUS BROWN

mars·de·nia \märzˈdēnēə\ *n, cap* [NL, fr. William *Marsden* †1836 Eng. orientalist + NL *-ia*] **:** a genus of tropical woody vines (family Asclepiadaceae) having small greenish purple flowers with the crown of the corolla consisting of five flat scales united at the base to the androecium — see RANK INDIGO

marse *or* **marsa** *var of* MASSA

mar·seil·lais \ˌmärsāˈyā\ *n, pl* **marseillais** *cap* [F, fr. *Marseille,* France] **:** a native or resident of Marseilles

¹mar·seilles *or* **mar·seille** \(ˈ)mär¦sā, (ˈ)mȧ¦-\ *adj, usu cap* [fr. *Marseilles,* France] **:** of or from the city of Marseilles, France **:** of the kind or style prevalent in Marseilles

²mar·seilles \märˈsā(ə)lz\ *n, pl* **marseilles** *usu cap* [fr. *Marseilles (quilting)*] **1 :** a firm reversible cotton fabric that usu. has small fancy designs and is used esp. for vests or trimmings **2 :** a heavy reversible compound fabric of cotton for bedspreads that is made with raised sometimes padded designs

marseilles soap *n, usu cap M* **:** soap from Marseilles orig. made from olive oil; *esp* **:** a mottled or marbled variety — compare CASTILE

marsh \ˈmärsh, ˈmȧsh\ *n* -ES *often attrib* [ME *mersh,* fr. OE *mersc, merisc;* akin to OFris & OS *mersk* meadowland near water, marsh, MD *mersch, maersc;* derivative fr. the root of OE *mere* sea, pool — more at MARINE] **1 :** a tract of soft wet land **:** FEN, SWAMP, MORASS; *specif* **:** such a tract of land often periodically inundated and treeless and usu. characterized by grasses, cattails, or other monocotyledons — compare BOG, LAKE, SWAMP **2** *chiefly dial* **:** a stretch of grassland **:** MEADOW

¹mar·shal *also* **mar·shall** \ˈmärshəl, ˈmȧsh-\ *n* -s [ME *marshal, mareschal,* fr. OF *mareschal,* of Gmc origin; akin to OHG *marahscalc* keeper of the horses, marshall, fr. *marah* horse + *scalc* servant; akin to OE *scealc* servant, OS *skalk,* Goth *skalks;* perh. akin to MHG *schel* jumping, angry, OHG *scelo* stallion, ON *skelkr* fear, Skt *śalabha* grasshopper, Lith *šuolys* gallop; basic meaning: to jump — more at MARE] **1 a** (1) **:** a high official in the household of a medieval king, prince, or noble orig. having charge of the cavalry and ranking subordinate to the constable but later usu. the chief officer in command of the military forces (2) **:** a great officer of state in various countries whose office was historically a continuation or development of the preceding but whose status came to be primarily honorary with only nominal or occasional duties — see EARL MARSHAL **b** (1) **:** any of various royal household officers of high rank charged with the arrangement of ceremonies or with other duties (2) **:** a person who arranges and directs the ceremonial aspects of any gathering **2 :** a military commander or general: as **a :** FIELD MARSHAL **b :** a general officer of the highest rank in some armies (as of France) **c :** an officer of the British Royal Air Force equivalent in rank to a field marshal in the army **3 a :** an officer having charge of prisoners: as (1) *archaic* **:** an officer of a British law court having charge of prisoners and sometimes being keeper of a prison (2) **:** KNIGHT MARSHAL (3) **:** PROVOST MARSHAL **b** (1) **:** a ministerial officer appointed for each judicial district of the U.S. to execute the process of the courts and perform various duties similar to those of a sheriff (2) **:** a law officer in some cities (as New York) of the U.S. entrusted with particular duties (as serving the process of justices' courts) **c** (1) **:** the administrative head of the police or fire department in some cities of the U.S. (2) **:** FIRE MARSHAL **4** *obs* **:** one in charge of horses esp. in respect to care of their diseases, shoeing, and grooming **:** GROOM, FARRIER

²marshal *also* **marshall** \"\ *vb* **marshaled** *or* **marshalled; marshaled** *or* **marshalled; marshaling** *or* **marshalling** \-sh(ə)liŋ\ **marshals** [ME *marshallen,* fr. *marshal,* n.] *vt* **1 :** to dispose (as people) in order **:** place in proper rank or position ⟨~*ing* the troops for a review⟩ ⟨~*ed* the peers to the head of the line⟩ **2 :** to arrange in order according to some planned or natural scheme ⟨carefully ~*ing* his arguments⟩: as **a :** to dispose (the parts of an heraldic composition) in due order **b** (1) **:** to fix the order of (assets) with respect to liability or availability for payment of obligations (2) **:** to fix the order of (claimants) with respect to priority of claims against a debtor's assets **c :** to assemble and dispatch (the constituent elements of a railway train) usu. in a marshaling or classification yard **3 :** to lead with ceremony **:** USHER, DIRECT ~ *vi* **:** to take form or order ⟨ideas ~*ing* neatly⟩; *esp* **:** to take one's place in a formal or ceremonious order ⟨footmen ~*ed* at the butler's heels⟩ **syn** see ORDER

mar·shal·cy \-lsē\ *n* -ES [ME *marshalcie,* fr. MF *mareschalcie, mareschaucie,* fr. *mareschal* + *-cie* -cy] **1 a :** the rank or position of a marshal **b** *obs* **:** the force a marshal commands **2** *obs* **:** FARRIERY

mar·shal·er *or* **mar·shall·er** \-sh(ə)lə(r)\ *n* -s **:** one that marshals

mar·shal·ess \-ləs\ *n* -ES **:** a marshal's wife

marshaling *adj* **1 :** used for marshaling something (as freight cars) **2** *usu* **marshalling** *of a camp or area* **:** used for assembling troops preparatory to embarkation (as in ships or aircraft) for an operation

mar·shall \ˈmärshəl\ *or* **marshall language** *n* -s *usu cap M* [fr. the *Marshall* islands in the western Pacific] **:** the Austronesian language of the Marshall islands

mar·shall·ese \ˌmärshəˈlēz, -ēs\ *n, pl* **marshallese** [*Marshall* islands + E *-ese*] **1** *cap* **:** a Micronesian native or inhabitant of the Marshall islands **2** *usu cap* **:** MARSHALL

mar·shall·ian \(ˈ)mär¦shalēən\ *adj, usu cap* [Alfred *Marshall* †1924 Brit. economist + E *-ian*] **:** of or relating to the economist Marshall or to his theories or followers

mar·shal·man \ˈmärshəlmən\ *n, pl* **marshalmen** [¹*marshal* + *man*] **:** a man who marshals something; *esp* **:** one of the subordinates of a marshal that marches ahead to clear the way for a ceremonial procession

marshal's court *n, usu cap M & often cap C* **:** EARL MARSHAL'S COURT

mar·shal·sea \ˈmärshəl(ˌ)sē\ *n* -s *usu cap* [ME *marshalcie* marshalcy, marshalsea — more at MARSHALCY] **:** a former English court held before the lord steward and the knight marshal of the royal household orig. to administer justice among the sovereign's domestic servants — compare VERGE

mar·shal·ship \ˈmärshəlˌship\ *n* [¹*marshal* + *-ship*] **:** MARSHALCY 1a

marsh arrow grass *n* **:** ARROW GRASS 1

marshbanker *var of* MOSSBUNKER

marsh bass *n* **:** LARGEMOUTH BLACK BASS

marsh bellflower *n* **:** a bellflower (*Campanula aparinoides*) that is common in marshes in the U. S. and has lanceolate linear leaves and small whitish flowers

marsh bent *or* **marsh bent grass** *n* **:** a redtop (*Agrostis alba*)

marsh·berry \ˈmärsh- — *see* BERRY\ *n* **:** EUROPEAN CRANBERRY

marsh blackbird *n* **:** REDWING BLACKBIRD

marsh bluebill *n* **1 :** LESSER SCAUP **2 :** RING-NECKED DUCK

marshbuck \ˈ=ˌ=\ *n* **:** SITATUNGA

marsh buggy *n* **:** a motor vehicle for use in swamp lands having wheels with wide treads or large rubber tires with cleats — called also *swamp buggy*

marsh cinquefoil *n* **:** a shrubby cinquefoil (*Potentilla palustris*) of wet or marshy land having pinnate serrate-margined leaves and purple flowers

marsh clematis *n* **:** BLUE JASMINE

marsh clover *n* **:** BUCKBEAN

marsh crab *n* **:** any of various crabs of the family Grapsidae that burrow in marshy areas along the Atlantic coast from southern Florida to Brazil; *esp* **:** a crab of a common genus *Sesarma*

marsh cress *n* **:** an annual or biennial cress (*Rorippa islandica*) that grows in damp places, is a troublesome weed in some localities, and has leaves which are sometimes used in salads or as a potherb — called also *yellow water cress*

marsh crocodile *n* **:** MUGGER

marsh crowfoot *n* **:** CURSED CROWFOOT

marsh cudweed *n* **:** an annual cudweed (*Gnaphalium uliginosum*) that is a common weed of low-lying or cultivated soil — called also *mouse-ear*

marsh cypress *n* **:** a bald cypress (*Taxodium distichum*)

marsh daisy *n* **:** a thrift (*Armeria maritima*)

marsh deer *n* **:** a large deer (*Blastocerus dichotomus* or *Dorcelaphus dichotomus*) of Brazil and Argentina

marsh elder *n* **1 :** GUELDER ROSE **2 :** any of various coarse shrubby plants of the genus *Iva* that are common in moist areas (as coastal salt marshes) in eastern and central No. America — see BURWEED MARSH ELDER

marshes *pl of* MARSH

marsh felwort *n* **:** an annual herb (*Lomatogonium rotatum*) of the family Gentianaceae that occurs in marshes and wet places in Eurasia and No. America and that has narrow opposite leaves and conspicuous blue or white flowers in terminal racemes

marsh fern *n* **1 :** a shield fern (*Dryopteris thelypteris*) of the north temperate zone that has pinnatifid fronds with pinnae of uniform size **2 :** SAW FERN

marsh fever *n* **:** MALARIA

marshfire \ˈ=ˌ=\ *n* **:** IGNIS FATUUS 1

marshfish \ˈ=ˌ=\ *n* **:** BOWFIN

marsh five-finger *n* **:** MARSH CINQUEFOIL

marsh fleabane *n* **1 :** a plant of the genus *Pluchea* **2** *also* **marsh fleawort** *or* **marsh groundsel :** a groundsel (*Senecio congestus*) of northern and arctic regions that has thick hollow stems, long narrow leaves sometimes used as a potherb, and dense heads of yellow flowers

marsh foxtail *n* **:** a widely distributed low pale perennial grass (*Alopecurus geniculatus*) that is widely distributed in low meadows and other wet places and that has simple or sparingly branched culms which are decumbent at the base and bear slender flower spikes

marsh frog *n* **:** PICKEREL FROG

marsh gas *n* **1 :** a combustible gas resulting from vegetable decay in marshy ground and consisting chiefly of methane — compare IGNIS FATUUS 1 **2 :** METHANE

marsh gentian *n* **1 :** a perennial Eurasian gentian (*Gentiana pneumonanthe*) having linear leaves and sky-blue flowers with an obconic corolla tube and occurring chiefly in damp open heaths **2 :** any of several No. American gentians that occur chiefly or exclusively in wet areas

marsh goose *n* **1 :** GREYLAG **2 :** HUTCHINS'S GOOSE

marsh grass *n* **:** a coarse grass common in marshes (as members of the genus *Spartina*); *esp* **:** a grass (*S. patens*) of the salt meadows in the eastern U. S.

marsh hare *n* **1 :** a small hare (*Sylvilagus palustris*) that is larger than the cottontail with slender less hairy feet and is found in marshy places along the U. S. coast from No. Carolina to Florida **2 a :** MUSKRAT **b :** the flesh of the muskrat — used esp. when offered for sale for use as human food

marsh harrier *n* **:** a harrier (*Circus aeruginosus*) widely distributed in the Old World but now nearly exterminated in England

marsh hawk *n* **1 :** a widely distributed American hawk (*Circus cyaneus hudsonius*) that forms a race of the European hen harrier, frequents open or marshy regions, feeds on frogs, snakes, and other lower vertebrates, and is seldom destructive of poultry **2 :** MARSH HARRIER

marsh hen *n* **1 :** any of various American birds of the family Rallidae (as the king rail, the clapper rail, and the American coot) **2 :** MOORHEN **3 :** BITTERN

marsh holy-rose *or* **marsh holywort** \-ˈ=ˌ=\ *n* **:** a small glabrous erect shrub (*Andromeda polifolia*) that spreads by creeping rhizomes, has dark green foliage and nodding pink flowers, and is widely distributed in wet areas of northern and arctic regions

marsh horsetail *n* **:** a highly variable and widely distributed scouring rush (*Equisetum palustre*) of wet or boggy areas of the northern hemisphere

marshier *comparative of* MARSHY

marshiest *superlative of* MARSHY

marsh·i·ness \ˈmärshēnəs\ *n* -ES **:** the quality or state of being marshy

marsh·ite \ˈmärˌshīt\ *n* -s [C. W. *Marsh,* 19th cent. Australian geologist + E *-ite*] **:** a mineral that is a cuprous iodide CuI and that occurs in oil-brown isometric crystals (hardness 2.5, sp. gr. 5.6)

marsh·land \ˈmärshˌland\ *n* [ME *mershland,* fr. OE *merscland,* fr. *mersc* marsh + *land* — more at MARSH, LAND] **:** a marshy district **:** MARSH — **marsh·land·er** \-də(r)\ *n*

marshlight \ˈ=ˌ=\ *n* **:** IGNIS FATUUS

marshlike \ˈ=ˌ=\ *adj* **1 :** resembling ignis fatuus **2** *of land* **:** low-lying and moist

marsh·locks \ˈmärshˌläks\ *n pl but sing or pl in constr* **:** MARSH CINQUEFOIL

marsh·mal·low \ˈmärshˌmelō, ˈmȧsh-, -mal-, -lə *often* -ləw+V\ *n* -s [ME *mershmalwe,* fr. OE *merscmealwe,* fr. *mersc* marsh + *mealwe* mallow — more at MARSH, MALLOW] **1 a :** a European perennial herb (*Althaea officinalis*) that is naturalized in the eastern U. S., has a dense velvety pubescence, ovate leaves and pink racemose flowers, and produces a mucilaginous root sometimes esp. formerly used in confectionery and in medicine **b :** ROSE MALLOW 1 **2 a :** a confection in the form of a sweetened paste made from the root of the marshmallow **b :** a confection made from corn syrup, sugar, albumen, and gelatin, beaten to a light creamy consistency, and usu. rolled in powdered sugar when partly dry

marshmallow

marsh·mal·lowy \-lōē, -ləwē\ *adj* **:** like marshmallow esp. in being soft and cloying

marsh·man \ˈmärshmən\ *n, pl* **marshmen :** one who dwells in marshland; *esp* **:** a member of a group living and obtaining a livelihood in an area of extensive marshland

marsh marigold *n* **:** a plant of the genus *Caltha; esp* **:** a swamp herb (*C. palustris*) of Europe and No. America that has simple nearly orbicular leaves and bright yellow flowers resembling buttercups and that is often gathered in early spring for use as a potherb — called also *cowslip*

marsh milkweed *n* **:** a joe-pye weed (*Eupatorium purpureum*) with green to purplish stems and heads of white, pink, or lavender flowers

marsh owl *n* **:** SHORT-EARED OWL

marsh parsley *n* **1 :** MILK PARSLEY **2 :** TAPE GRASS

marsh pea *n* **:** a glabrous scrambling perennial wild pea (*Lathyrus palustris*) of damp or marshy areas in Eurasia and No. America with winged stems, lanceolate and often mucronate leaflets, and rather large pale bluish or purplish flowers

marsh peep *n* **:** LEAST SANDPIPER

marsh pennywort *n* **:** an herb of *Hydrocotyle* or the closely related genus *Centella*

marsh pine *n* **:** POND PINE

marsh pink *n* **:** any of several No. American herbs of the genus *Sabbatia* (esp. *S. stellaris*)

marsh plover *n* **1 :** WOODCOCK **2 :** PECTORAL SANDPIPER

marsh pullet *n* **:** FLORIDA GALLINULE

marsh purslane *n* **:** a widely distributed herb (*Ludwigia palustris*) with reddish flowers and opposite leaves that is esp. common in moist ditches

marsh quail *n* **:** MEADOWLARK

marsh rabbit *n* **:** MARSH HARE

marsh robin *n* **:** CHEWINK

marsh rosemary *n* **:** SEA LAVENDER 1

marsh st.-john's-wort *n, usu cap S&J* **:** a perennial glabrous marsh herb (*Hypericum virginianum*) having sessile cordate or clasping leaves and pink to mauve flowers

marsh samphire *n* **:** GLASSWORT

marsh shield fern *n* **:** MARSH FERN 1

marsh snake *n* **:** a common dark-bellied snake (*Denisonia signata*) of New South Wales that is related to the Australian copperhead

marsh speedwell *n* **:** a common blue-flowered herb (*Veronica scutellata*) of the north temperate zone

marsh spike-grass *n* **:** SALT GRASS a

marsh spot *n* **:** a manganese deficiency disease of peas characterized by black cavities or lesions in the seeds esp. on the inner surface of the cotyledons

marsh stitchwort *n* **:** BOG STITCHWORT

marsh tea *n* **:** a Eurasian bog shrub (*Ledum palustre*) that is distinguished from the closely related Labrador tea by its narrow leaves which are sometimes infused for use in killing vermin and parasites and that yields an oil from which ledol is obtained

marsh tern *n* **1 :** GULL-BILLED TERN **2 :** BLACK TERN

marsh test *n, usu cap M* [after James *Marsh* †1846 Brit. chemist] **:** a sensitive test for arsenic in which a solution to be tested is treated with hydrogen so that if arsenic is present gaseous arsine is formed and then decomposed to a black deposit of arsenic (as when the gas is passed through a heated glass tube)

marsh tit *also* **marsh titmouse** *n* **:** a grayish Old World titmouse (*Parus palustris*) with black cap and chin and pale underparts

marsh treader *n* **:** any of various extremely elongated marsh or pond-surface bugs of the family Hydrometridae

marsh trefoil *n* **:** BUCKBEAN

marsh vetchling *n* **:** MARSH PEA

marsh violet *n* **:** a widely distributed creeping violet (*Viola palustris*) chiefly of damp alpine and subalpine habitats that has glabrous cordate to reniform or sometimes ovate leaves, stiff stolons, and lilac purple to white and lilac flowers

marsh warbler *n* **:** a small brown-and-white Eurasian warbler (*Acrocephalus palustris*) with a pale eye stripe

marshwort \ˈ=ˌ=\ *n* **:** FOOL'S WATERCRESS

marsh woundwort *n* **:** a hairy perennial woundwort (*Stachys palustris*) that has a creeping rootstock, usu. rosy purple flowers, and a distinctly rank odor and is widely distributed in the northern hemisphere esp. in wet or waste places

marsh wren *n* **:** any of several American wrens (genera *Cistothorus* and *Telmatodytes*) that frequent marshes

marshy \ˈmärshē\ *adj* -ER/-EST **1** *of land* **:** wet and spongy **:** like or constituting marsh ⟨a ~ field⟩ **2 :** relating to or occurring in marsh ⟨~ weeds⟩

mar·si \ˈmärˌsī\ *n pl, usu cap* [L] **1 :** a people of ancient

Italy east of Rome **2 :** a Germanic people defeated by the Roman emperor Germanicus

mar·si·an \ˈmärsēən\ *n* -s *usu cap* **:** the Sabellian dialect of the Italian Marsi

mar·sil·ea \mär'silēə\ *n, cap* [NL, after Count Luigi Ferdinando Marsigli (*Marsilius*) †1730 Ital. naturalist] **:** a widely distributed genus (the type of the family Marsileaceae) that comprises the clover ferns which are sometimes used as aquarium plants

mar·sil·e·a·ce·ae \mär,silē'āsē,ē\ *n pl, cap* [NL, fr. *Marsilea*, type genus + *-aceae*] **:** a family of water ferns that are heterosporous and have both microspores and megaspores in the same sporocarp — see MARSILEA — **mar·sil·e·a·ceous** \ˈ;==ˈāshəs\ *adj*

mar·sil·ia \mär'silēə\ *syn of* MARSILEA

mar·si·po·branch \ˈmärsəpō,braŋk\ *adj or n* [NL *Marsipobranchia*] **:** CYCLOSTOME

mar·si·po·bran·chia \,===ˈbraŋkēə\ *or* **mar·si·po·bran·chi·a·ta** \,===,braŋkē'äd·ə, -ˈād·ə\ *or* **mar·si·po·bran·chii** \,===ˈbraŋkē,ī\ [NL, fr. Gk *marsipos, marsypos* pouch + NL *-branchia* or *Branchiata* or *-branchii* (fr. L *branchia* gill) — more at MARSUPIUM, BRANCHIA] *syn of* CYCLOSTOMI *or of* AGNATHA

mars line *n, usu cap M* [fr. the planet *Mars* — more at MARS] **:** LINE OF MARS

mars orange *n* [fr. *mars* (iron)] **1** *usu cap M* **:** an orange artist's pigment made by calcining Mars yellow **2** *often cap M* **:** a moderate reddish orange that is yellower and darker than flamingo, yellower and duller than crab apple, and very slightly redder and darker than tile red (sense 2)

mars red *n* [fr. *mars* (iron)] **1** *usu cap M* **:** any of various red to orange, brown, or violet artist's pigments made by calcining Mars yellow **2** *often cap M* **a :** COLCOTHAR 2 **b :** TOTEM 3

mars·so·nia \mär'sōnēə\ [NL, fr. T. F. *Marsson* + NL *-ia*] *syn of* MARSSONINA

mars·so·ni·na \,märsə'nīnə, -ˈnēnə\ *n, cap* [NL, fr. Theodor F. *Marsson* †1892 Ger. botanist + NL *-ina*] **:** a form genus of imperfect fungi (order Melanconiales) with hyaline one-septate spores — see RING SPOT

mar·ster \ˈmärstər\ *dial var of* MASTER

¹mar·su·pi·al \(ˈ)mär'süpēəl, (ˈ)mä¦-\ *adj* [NL *marsupium* + E *-al*] **1 :** having a pouch for carrying the young **2 :** of, relating to, or constituting a marsupium **3** [NL *Marsupialia*] **:** of or relating to the Marsupialia

²marsupial \"\ *n* -s **:** a marsupial mammal **:** one of the Marsupialia

marsupial anteater *n* **:** BANDED ANTEATER

marsupial bone *n* **:** either of a pair of small bones supporting the pouch walls in many marsupials and in monotremes

marsupial frog *n* **:** any of several So. American tree frogs of *Nototrema* or related genera (family Hylidae) the females of which carry the eggs and the young in a pouch on their back

mar·su·pi·a·lia \mär,süpē'ālēə\ *n pl, cap* [NL, fr. *marsupium* + *-alia*] **:** an order comprising the lowest existing mammals except the Monotremata and containing the kangaroos, wombats, bandicoots, opossums, and related animals that with few exceptions develop no placenta, have a pouch on the abdomen of the female containing the teats and serving to carry the young, and usu. have numerous teeth (often over 44) few or none of which are preceded by functional milk teeth, a double uterus and vagina, the scrotum located in front of the penis, and a small brain — compare DIPROTODONTIA, METATHERIA, POLYPROTODONTIA

mar·su·pi·a·li·an \ˈ;=;=ˈālēən\ *adj* [NL *Marsupialia* + E *-an*] **:** MARSUPIAL 3

mar·su·pi·al·iza·tion \mär,süpēələ'zāshən\ *n* -s **:** the operation of marsupializing; *also* **:** an instance of this operation

mar·su·pi·al·ize \mär'süpēə,līz\ *vt* -ED/-ING/-S [²*marsupial* + *-ize*] **:** to open (as the bladder or a cyst) and sew by the edges to the abdominal wound to permit further treatment (as of an enclosed tumor) or to discharge pathological matter (as from a hydatid cyst)

marsupial mole *n* **:** an Australian marsupial (*Notoryctes typhlops*) closely resembling the eutherian mole in appearance and behavior

marsupial mouse *also* **marsupial rat** *n* **:** any of numerous small sharp-nosed chiefly insectivorous marsupials (family Dasyuridae) that superficially resemble mice or rats — called also *pouched mouse*

marsupial wolf *n* **:** TASMANIAN WOLF

mar·su·pi·on·ta \mär,süpē'äntə\ *n pl, cap* [NL, fr. *Marsupialia* + Gk *-onta* (nom. neut. pl. participial ending)] *in some classifications* **:** a subclass of mammals coextensive with the Prototheria and Metatheria and comprising all the nonplacental mammals

mar·su·pi·um \mär'süpēəm\ *n, pl* **marsu·pia** \-ēə\ [NL, fr. L, purse, pouch, fr. Gk *marsipion, marsypion*, dim. of *marsipos, marsypos* pouch, perh. fr. Av *marshū* belly] **1 a** (1) **:** an abdominal pouch formed by a fold of the skin and enclosing the mammary glands of most marsupials (2) **:** INCUBATORIUM 1 **b :** an analogous structure in lower animals (as fishes or crustaceans) for enclosing or carrying eggs or young **c :** PECTEN 1a **2 :** PERIGYNIUM 1

mars yellow *n* [fr. *mars* (iron)] **1** *usu cap M* **:** an iron yellow artist's pigment made usu. by precipitating an iron salt with alkali and heating the product **2** *often cap M* **:** a moderate to strong orange that is yellower and darker than carrot red and darker than zinc orange or sunburst — called also *iron yellow, siderin yellow*

¹mart \ˈmärt\ *n* -s [ME, fr. ScGael] **1** *chiefly Scot* **:** a beef animal fattened for slaughter **2** *chiefly Scot* **:** meat salted and stored for winter

²mart *n* -s [ME, after L *Mart-, Mars* Mars, ancient Roman god of war and agriculture] *obs* **:** BATTLE, CONTEST

³mart \ˈmärt, ˈmàt, *usu* -d·+V\ *n* -s [ME, fr. MD *market, marct, mart*, prob. fr. ONF *market* — more at MARKET] **1** *archaic* **:** a coming together of people to buy and sell **:** FAIR 1a **2** *obs* **:** chaffering and bargaining **:** buying and selling; *also* **:** BARGAIN **3 :** MARKET

⁴mart \"\ *vb* -ED/-ING/-S *vi, archaic* **:** MARKET, TRADE ~ *vt, archaic* **:** to deal in **:** SELL

⁵mart \"\ *n* -s [by folk etymology (influence of ³*mart*)] *obs* **:** LETTERS OF MARQUE

⁶mart \ˈmärt\ *n* -s [short for *marten*] *dial Eng* **:** MARTEN

mart *abbr* martyr; martyrology

mar·ta·ban \¦märd·ə¦bän, -ban\ *n* -s [fr. *Martaban*, town in Burma] **:** a large green glazed pottery jar orig. made in lower Burma and used esp. for domestic storage (as of water or food)

mar·ta·gon \ˈmärd·əgən\ *n* -s [ME, fr. Turk *martagân*, lit., turban] **:** TURK'S-CAP LILY a

mar·tel \ˈmär,tel\ *n* -s [MF *martel, marteau*, fr. LL *martellus*, alter. of L *martulus, marculus*; akin to L *malleus* hammer — more at MAUL] **:** HAMMER; *esp* **:** MARTEL-DE-FER

martel-de-fer \-də'fer\ *n* -s [F, lit., iron hammer] **:** a weapon like a hammer usu. with one side of the head pointed that was used esp. by horsemen in the middle ages to break armor

mar·te·lé \,märd·ᵊl'ā\ *adj (or adv)* [F, fr. It *martellato*] **:** MARTELLATO

mar·te·line \ˈmärd·ᵊlən\ *n* -s [F, dim. of *marteau* hammer — more at MARTEL] **:** a small hammer with a pointed peen used by marble workers and sculptors

¹mar·tel·la·to \¦märd·ᵊl¦äd·(,)ō\ *adj (or adv)* [It, fr. past part. of *martellare* to hammer, strike, fr. *martello* hammer, fr. LL *martellus* — more at MARTEL] **:** detached and strongly accented — used as a direction to players of bowed instruments; compare DÉTACHÉ

²martellato \"\ *n* -s **:** martellato technique, notes, or effect

mar·tel·lo tower \mär'telō-\ *or* **martello** *n* -s *sometimes cap* [alter. of Cape *Mortella* in Corsica, where such a tower was captured with difficulty by a British fleet in 1794] **:** a circular masonry fort or blockhouse

mar·tempering \ˈmär+,-\ *n* -s [*martensite* + *tempering*] **:** the process of quenching steel from above the transformation temperature in a bath at about 350°F and then cooling to room temperature after the temperature has become nearly uniform with the bath

mar·ten \ˈmär|tᵊn, ˈmà|, |d·ən, |tən\ *n, pl* **marten** *or* **martens** [ME *martryn*, fr. MF *martrine* marten fur, fr. OF, fr. fem. of *martrin* of a marten, fr. *martre* marten, of Gmc origin; akin to OE *mearth* marten, OFris *merth*, OHG *mardar*, ON *mörthr* marten; perh. akin to Lith *marti* bride, W *merch* daughter, girl — more at MARRY] **1 a** *or* **marten cat :** any of several slender-bodied carnivorous mammals (genus *Martes*) that are larger than weasels and of somewhat arboreal habits and that have a rather long tail and a coat of fine soft fur which is light-colored below and rich brown or gray above — compare AMERICAN SABLE, FISHER, PINE MARTEN, STONE MARTEN **b :** YELLOW-THROATED MARTEN **2 :** the fur or pelt of a marten

mar·te·ni·ko *or* **mar·ti·ni·co** \,märtᵊn'ē(,)kō\ *n* -s [native name in the Philippines] *Philippines* **:** a climbing perch (*Anabas scandens*)

mar·te·not \,märtᵊn'ō\ *n* -s [F, after Maurice *Martenot* *b*1898 Fr. scientist and musician] **:** ONDES MUSICALES

mar·tens·ite \ˈmär,ten,zīt\ *n* -s [Adolf *Martens* †1914 Ger. metallurgist + E *-ite*] **:** the hard constituent of which quenched steel is chiefly composed — **mar·ten·sit·ic** \¦mär,ten¦zid·ik\ *adj*

mar·tes \ˈmär,tēz\ *n, cap* [NL, fr. L, marten, of Gmc origin; akin to OHG *mard* marten — more at MARTEN] **:** a genus of carnivorous mammals (family Mustelidae) consisting of the typical martens, the sables, and the fisher

mar·te·sia \mär'tēzēə\ *n* [NL] **1** *cap* **:** a widely distributed genus of marine borers (family Pholadidae) burrowing in wood by means of a long elastic foot **2** -s **:** any borer of the genus *Martesia*

martext \ˈ=,=\ *n* [¹*mar* + *text*] **:** a blundering preacher

mar·tha wash·ing·ton chair \ˈmärthə'wäshiŋtən-, -wȯ|\ *n, usu cap M&W* [after *Martha Washington* †1802 wife of George Washington] **:** a chair that has a high flat back, upholstery on seat and back, and open arms or none, is usu. framed in mahogany, and was orig. used in the later part of the 18th century

martha washington geranium *n, usu cap M&W* [after *Martha Washington*] **:** any of numerous erect hairy pelargoniums that are widely cultivated for their showy white to crimson flowers with dark blotches on the two upper petals, are commonly treated as a species (*Pelargonium domesticum*), and are prob. complex hybrids between several southern African pelargoniums — called also *Lady Washington geranium*

martha washington table *n, usu cap M&W* [after *Martha Washington*] **:** a usu. octagonal worktable with four slender often reeded legs, drawers under elongated sides, and a deep receptacle for sewing materials under each end

Martha Washington table

mar tho·ma \ˈmär'tōmə\ *adj, usu cap M&T* [after *Mar Thoma* (Saint Thomas), one of Christ's twelve apostles] **:** of or relating to the Mar Thoma Syrian Church of India formed in the early 19th century as an offshoot of the Syrian Orthodox Church of Malabar

mar·tial \ˈmärshəl, ˈmàsh-\ *adj* [ME, fr. L *Martialis* of the god Mars, fr. *Mart-, Mars*, Roman god of war and agriculture + L *-alis* -al] **1 a :** of, relating to, or suited for war ⟨~ music⟩ **b :** belonging or relating to an army or to military life — distinguished from *civil* **c :** experienced in or inclined to war **:** WARLIKE ⟨~ men⟩ **d :** belonging or appropriate to one engaged or experienced in war or military life ⟨a ~ stride⟩ **2** *usu cap* **:** relating to or resembling Mars, the Roman god of war **3** *usu cap* **:** being or falling under the baleful astrological influence of Mars **4** *alchemy* **:** of, relating to, or like iron **:** CHALYBEATE

martial eagle *n* **:** a large African eagle (*Polemaetus bellicosus*) that is dusky brown above with snowy white breast speckled with brown and is often destructive to small livestock and poultry

mar·tial·ism \-shə,lizəm\ *n* -s **:** martial qualities

mar·tial·ist \-ləst\ *n* -s **:** a military man **:** one interested or skilled in warlike arts and techniques

mar·tial·ize \-shə,līz\ *vt* -ED/-ING/-S **:** to make martial

martial law *n* **1** *international law* **:** the law based on necessity or policy that is applied to all persons and property in occupied territory during invasion or occupation and is executed by the military authority of a belligerent acting directly or through civil courts; *esp* **:** such law when it is in accord with the laws and usages of war — compare MILITARY GOVERNMENT, MILITARY LAW **2 :** military rule exercised by a nation or state over its citizens or subjects in a situation where they are not legally enemies and when an emergency justifies such action

mar·tial·ly \-shəlē, -li\ *adv* **:** in a martial manner

mar·tial·ness \-shəlnəs\ *n* -ES **:** the quality or state of being martial

¹mar·tian \ˈmärshən, ˈmàsh-\ *adj, often cap* [L *Mart-, Mars*, the 4th planet from the sun (fr. *stella Martis*, lit., star of Mars, after *Mars* Roman god of war and agriculture; trans. of Gk *Areōs astēr*, lit., star of Ares, Greek god of war) + E *-ian*] **:** of or relating to the planet Mars or its hypothetical inhabitants

²martian \"\ *n* -s *usu cap M* **1 :** a hypothetical inhabitant of the planet Mars **2 :** one that is usu. held by palmists to be characterized by qualities of aggression or resistance and sometimes an inflammable temper as a result of prominent development of Upper Mars, Lower Mars, or the Plain of Mars

¹martin *n* -s [ME, fr. the name *Martin*] *obs* **:** APE, MONKEY

²mar·tin \ˈmär|tᵊn, ˈmà|, |d·ən, |tən\ *n* -s [MF, after Saint *Martin* †*ab*399 bishop of Tours; prob. fr. the migration of such birds around Martinmas] **1 :** a small European swallow (*Delichon urbica* syn. *Chelidon urbica*) having a moderately forked tail, bluish black head and back, and white rump and underparts **2 :** any of various swallows and flycatchers — usu. used in combination; compare PURPLE MARTIN

³martin \"\ *n* -s [by shortening] **:** FREEMARTIN

¹mar·ti·net \¦mär|tᵊn¦et, ¦mà|, |d·ən¦-, |tən¦-, *usu* -ed·+V\ *n* -s [ME *mertinet*, fr. MF *martinet*, dim. of *martin* — more at MARTIN] **1** *archaic* **:** ¹MARTIN **2 :** MARTINETA

²martinet \"\ *n* -s [MF, prob. dim. of the name *Martin*] **1 :** a military engine formerly used for throwing large stones **2 :** a line attached to the leech of a square sail to haul it close to the yard for furling

³martinet \"\ *n* -s [after Jean *Martinet*, 17th cent. Fr. army officer who devised a new system of military drill] **1 :** a system of military drill devised for the French army in the reign of Louis XIV **2 a :** a strict military disciplinarian **b :** one who lays stress on a rigid adherence to the details of forms and methods

mar·ti·ne·ta \,märtᵊn'ād·ə, -ˈed·ə\ *n* -s [AmerSp, prob. fr. Sp *martinete* night heron, prob. after Saint Martin (*San Martín*) around whose feast day the night herons migrate; fr. the similarity of the crests of the night heron and the martineta] **:** an Argentine tinamou (*Eudromias elegans*) with a long slender crest

mar·ti·ne·te \,märtᵊn'ād·ā\ *n* -s [AmerSp, fr. Sp, night heron] **:** a Cuban heron that forms a variety (*Butorides virescens maculatus*) of the green heron and feeds largely on insects

mar·ti·net·ish \¦märtᵊn¦ed·ish\ *adj* [³*martinet* + *-ish*] **:** like or characteristic of a person who is a martinet ⟨a ~ attitude⟩ ⟨~ discipline⟩

marting *pres part of* MART

mar·tin·gale \ˈmär|tᵊn,gāl, ˈmà|, |d·ən-, |tən- *sometimes* |d·iŋ,g- *or* |ti- *or* |tē-\ *n* -s [MF, perh. modif. of Ar *mirta'ah* rein] **1 :** a device for steadying a horse's head or checking its upward movement that is essentially a strap fastened to the girth, passing between the forelegs, and fastened to the bit or the back of the noseband or more commonly ending in two rings through which the reins pass **2** *or* **martingale guy** *or* **martingale stay a :** a lower stay of rope or chain for the jibboom or flying jibboom used to sustain the strain of the forestays and fastened to or rove through the dolphin striker — see SHIP illustration **b :** DOLPHIN STRIKER **3 :** any of several systems of betting in which a player increases his stake usu. by doubling each time he loses a bet

martingale backrope *n* **:** one of the stays leading from the lower end of a martingale to either bow of a sailing ship

mar·ti·ni \mär'tēnē, mà'-, -nĭ\ *also* **martini cocktail** *n* -s *sometimes cap M* [prob. fr. the name *Martini*] **:** a cocktail consisting of two or more parts gin to one of dry vermouth usu. stirred with ice and garnished with an olive, pearl onion, or slice of lemon peel

¹mar·ti·ni·can \,märtᵊn'ēkən\ *adj, usu cap* [*Martinique*, island in the West Indies + E *-an*] **1 :** of, relating to, or characteristic of Martinique **2 :** of, relating to, or characteristic of the Martinicans

²martinican \"\ *n* -s *usu cap* **:** a native or inhabitant of Martinique

martinico *var of* MARTENIKO

mar·ti·ni·quais \,mär|tᵊnə'kā\ *n, pl* **martiniquais** *cap* [F, fr. *Martinique* (island)] **:** MARTINICAN

¹mar·ti·nique \¦mär|tᵊn¦ēk, ¦mà|, |dən¦-, |tən¦-\ *adj, usu cap* [fr. *Martinique*, island in the West Indies] **:** of or relating to the island of Martinique, West Indies **:** of the kind or style prevalent in Martinique **:** MARTINICAN

²martinique \"\ *n* -s *often cap* **:** a brownish orange to light brown that is darker than caramel and very slightly yellower than sorrel

mar·tin·ist \ˈmärtᵊnəst\ *n* -s *usu cap* [*Martin* Luther †1546 Ger. religious reformer] **:** a follower of Martin Luther

mar·tin·mas \ˈmär|tᵊnməs, ˈmà|, |d·ənm-, |tənm-\ *n* -ES *usu cap* [ME *martinmasse*, fr. St. *Martin* †*ab*399 bishop of Tours + ME *masse* mass — more at MASS] **:** the feast of St. Martin occurring annually on the 11th of November

martinmas summer *or* **martin's summer** *n, usu cap M* **:** SAINT MARTIN'S SUMMER

martinmas term *n, usu cap M* **:** the first and fall term of the academic year at a Scottish university

mar·ti·noe \ˈmärtᵊn,ō\ *n* -s [modif. of NL *Martynia*] **:** UNICORN PLANT

martin process *n, usu cap M* [after Pierre E. *Martin* †1915 Fr. engineer who invented it] **:** an open-hearth process in which steel is made from pig iron usu. charged molten by adding to it wrought iron and steel scrap

martins *pl of* MARTIN

mar·tin's cement \ˈmärtᵊnz-\ *n, usu cap M* [fr. the name *Martin*] **:** a hard-finish gypsum plaster to which potassium carbonate has been added

martin snipe *n* [¹*martin*] *dial Eng* **:** GREEN SANDPIPER

martin storm *n* [¹*martin*; fr. its taking place about the time of the arrival of the martins in the spring] *chiefly Midland* **:** a windy storm in spring

mar·tite \ˈmär,tīt\ *n* -s [G *martit*, fr. ML *mart-, mars* iron + G *-it* -ite — more at MARS] **:** hematite occurring in iron-black isometric pseudomorphs after magnetite (hardness 6–7)

mar·ti·us yellow \ˈmärsh(ē)əs-\ *n* [after Karl A. *Martius* †1920 Ger. chemist] **1** *usu cap M, often cap Y* **:** a yellow dye that is a salt of a dinitro-alpha-naphthol and is used chiefly as a biological stain **2** *often cap M* **:** a light greenish yellow that is redder and paler than sulphur yellow (sense 2)

mart·let \ˈmärtlət\ *n* -s [MF, prob. alter. of *martinet* — more at MARTINET] **1 :** ²MARTIN 1 **2 :** a heraldic device consisting of a representation of a bird without visible feet and used esp. as a cadency mark to indicate a fourth son

mart·net \ˈmärt,net\ *n* -s [by contr.] **:** ³MARTINET 2

marts *pl of* MART, *pres 3d sing of* MART

mar·tyn·ia \mär'tinēə\ *n* [NL, fr. John *Martyn* †1768 Eng. botanist + NL *-ia*] **1** *cap* **:** the type genus of Martyniaceae comprising annual or perennial downy and clammy herbs with a bell-shaped bladdery calyx, spreading corolla tube, and a 2-beaked capsule **2** -s **:** any plant or flower of the genus *Martynia*

mar·tyn·i·a·ce·ae \mär,tinē'āsē,ē\ *n pl, cap* [NL, fr. *Martynia*, type genus + *-aceae*] **:** a small family of chiefly tropical American herbs (order Polemoniales) having a racemose terminal inflorescence of zygomorphic flowers with gamopetalous corollas — **mar·tyn·i·a·ceous** \=¦==ˈāshəs\ *adj*

¹mar·tyr \ˈmär|d·ər, ˈmà|d·ə(r, |tə-\ *n* -s [ME *martir, marter*, fr. OE *martir, martyr*, fr. LL *martyr*, fr. Gk *martyr-, martys* witness, martyr; akin to L *memor* mindful — more at MEMORY] **1 :** one who voluntarily suffers death as the penalty of witnessing to and refusing to renounce his religion or a tenet, principle, or practice belonging to it ⟨modern-day missionary ~*s*⟩ **2 :** one who sacrifices his life, station, or what is of great value for the sake of principle or to sustain a cause **3 a :** a great or constant sufferer (as from disease) ⟨a ~ to rheumatism⟩ **b :** one who adopts a specious air of suffering or deprivation esp. as a means of attracting sympathy or attention

²martyr \"\ *vt* -ED/-ING/-S [ME *martiren, martren*, fr. OE *martyrian, martrian*, fr. *martyr, martir*, n.] **1 :** to put to death for adhering to a belief, faith, or profession (as Christianity) **:** make a martyr of **2 :** to inflict agonizing pain upon **:** TORTURE **3** *archaic* **:** to torture to death **:** kill by a cruel means **4** *obs* **:** to mutilate or disfigure with or as if with wounds

mar·tyr·dom \ˈ==dəm\ *n* -s [ME *martirdom*, fr. OE *martyrdōm*, fr. *martyr* + *-dōm* -dom] **1 :** the state of being a martyr **:** the suffering of death on account of adherence to one's religious faith or to any cause ⟨early Christian ~⟩ **2 :** AFFLICTION, DISTRESS, TORMENT, TORTURE

martyress *n* -ES [¹*martyr* + *-ess*] *obs* **:** a female martyr

mar·tyr·ish \ˈmärd·ərish\ *adj* **:** like a martyr **:** suitable to a martyr ⟨her ~ resignation —S.N.Behrman⟩

mar·tyr·i·um \mär'tirēəm\ *n, pl* **martyr·ia** \-ēə\ [LL, testimony, martyr's shrine, fr. LGk *martyrion* martyr's shrine, fr. Gk, testimony, fr. *martyr-, martys* witness — more at MARTYR] **1 :** a building or chamber used by the early Christians as a burial place **2 :** a place where the relics of martyrs are preserved

mar·tyr·iza·tion \,märd·ərə'zāshən\ *n* -s **:** the making of or condition of becoming a martyr

mar·tyr·ize \ˈmärd·ə,rīz\ *vb* -ED/-ING/-S *see -ize in Explan Notes* [ME *martirizen*, fr. ML *martyrizare*, fr. LL *martyr* + L *-izare* -ize — more at MARTYR] *vt* **:** to make a martyr of: as **a :** to put to death for adhering to a faith or belief **b :** to cause great suffering to **:** TORMENT **c :** to give the appearance of being a martyr to ⟨an air of *martyrized* virtue⟩ ~ *vi* **:** to become or behave like a martyr

mar·tyr·ly \-d·ə(r)lē\ *adv (or adj)* **:** in the manner of a martyr **:** like a martyr

mar·tyr·ol·a·try \,märd·ə'rälə·trē\ *n* -ES [¹*martyr* + *-o-* + *-latry*] **:** undue exaltation or adulation of martyrs

mar·tyr·o·log·i·cal \¦märd·ərə¦läjəkəl\ *also* **mar·tyr·o·log·ic** \-jik\ *adj* **:** relating to martyrology or martyrs **:** registering or registered in a catalogue of martyrs

mar·tyr·ol·o·gist \,märd·ə'räləjəst\ *n* -s **:** a writer of or a specialist in martyrology **:** a historian of martyrs

mar·tyr·ol·o·gy \-jē\ *n* -ES [ML *martyrologium*, fr. LL *martyr* martyr + *-logium* (fr. Gk *-logion*, fr. *logos* word) — more at MARTYR, LEGEND] **1 :** a history or account of martyrs **:** a register of martyrs; *esp* **:** an official catalog of martyrs and saints of the Roman Catholic Church including some details of their lives and arranged by the dates of their anniversaries **2** [influenced in meaning by *-logy*] **:** a branch of ecclesiastical history that treats of the lives and sufferings of martyrs

mar·tyry \ˈmärd·ərē\ *n* -ES [LL *martyrium* testimony, martyrdom, martyr's shrine — more at MARTYRIUM] **1** *obs* **:** MARTYRDOM **2 :** a chapel or shrine erected in honor of a martyr

¹ma·ru \ˈmä(,)rü\ *n* -s [Jap] **:** a Japanese ship; *esp* **:** a Japanese merchant ship

²maru \"\ *n, pl* **maru** *or* **marus** *usu cap* **1 :** a Tibeto-Burman people of the Nmai river region in northeastern Burma **2 :** a member of the Maru people

ma·rua \mə'rüə\ *also* **marua rice** *n* -s [*marua*, native name in India] **:** RAGI

ma·ru·la *also* **ma·roo·la** \mə'rülə\ *n* -s [native name in southern Africa] **1 :** a tree (*Sclerocarya caffra*) of the family Anacardiaceae that is native to the veld and low country of Africa and that has grayish mottled bark, pinnate leaves, inconspicuous flowers in sprays, and succulent fruits resembling plums which contain an edible seed and are used locally to prepare an intoxicating beverage **2** *also* **marula plum :** the fruit of the marula

mar·um \ˈma(a)rəm\ *n* -s [L *marum, maron*, fr. Gk *maron*] **:** CAT THYME

ma·ru·mi kumquat \mə'rümē-\ *or* **marumi** *n* -s [Jap *marumi*, fr. *maru* circle + *mi* fruit] **:** any of several round-fruited kumquats usu. considered to be derived from the natural species (*Fortunella japonica*) — compare NAGAMI KUMQUAT

ma·ru·pa \mä'rü'pä\ *n* -s [Pg *marupá*, fr. Tupi] **:** a tree (*Simarouba amara*) of northern So. America and the Amazon valley that yields a light brittle lumber locally regarded as strongly resistant to insect attack

1mar·vel \'märvəl, 'māv-\ *n* -s [ME *merveille, mervaille, mervel,* fr. OF *merveille,* fr. LL *mirabilia* miracles, marvels, fr. neut. pl. of L *mirabilis* wonderful, marvelous, fr. *mirari* to wonder at + *-abilis* -able — more at SMILE] **1** *obs* : MIRACLE **2** : something that causes wonder or astonishment : a cause for surprise : PRODIGY ⟨with that ~ of architecture before our eyes —Martha Kean⟩ ⟨British scientists feel . . . that they could achieve ~s if they could enjoy the equipment which is available to American scientists —Bertrand Russell⟩ **3** : intense surprise or interest : ASTONISHMENT ⟨this childhood mood of ~ —*Publ's Mod. Lang. Assoc. of Amer.*⟩ **4** : HOREHOUND **syn** see WONDER — **for a marvel** *adv* : for a wonder : UNEXPECTEDLY

2marvel \"\ *vb* **marveled** *or* **marvelled; marveled** *or* **marvelled; marveling** *or* **marvelling** \-v(ə)liŋ\ **marvels** [ME *merveillen, mervaillen, mervelen,* fr. MF *merveillier,* fr. *merveille,* n.] *vi* : to become filled with surprise, astonishment, wonder, or amazed curiosity or perplexity ⟨~ not, my brethren, if the world hate you —1 Jn 3: 13 (AV)⟩ ⟨~*ed* to see what had been done so quickly⟩ — often used with *at* ⟨~*ed* at his dexterity⟩ ⟨~*ing* at the beauty of the scene⟩ ~ *vt* **1** : to feel astonishment or perplexity at or about ⟨~*ed* that they had escaped unhurt⟩ ⟨~*ed* what it all meant⟩ **2** *obs* : to cause to marvel : ASTONISH

3marvel \"\ *dial var of* MARBLE

mar·vel·ment \'märvəlmənt\ *n* -s [*2marvel* + *-ment*] : a source or cause for wonder

marvel-of-peru \'⸗⸗⸗'⸗\ *n* -s *usu cap P* [fr. *Peru,* country in So. America] : FOUR-O'CLOCK

mar·vel·ous *or* **mar·vel·lous** \'märv(ə)ləs, 'māv-\ *adj* [ME *merveillous,* fr. MF *merveilleus,* fr. *merveille* marvel + *-eus* -ous — more at MARVEL] **1** : causing or being such as to cause wonder : fundamentally exceptional in character or quality ⟨the ~ directional sense of migrating birds⟩ ⟨hands with a ~ capacity for healing⟩ **2 a** : being or having the characteristics of a miracle ⟨the ~ flow of water from the stone that was struck by the prophet's rod⟩ **b** : employing or concerned with the miraculous or supernatural ⟨the Gothic revival with its stress on the ~ and bizarre⟩ **3** : of the highest kind or quality : notably superior : EXCELLENT ⟨showed a ~ coolness in the face of danger⟩ ⟨has a ~ way with children⟩ — **mar·vel·ous·ly** *or* **mar·vel·lous·ly** *adv* — **mar·vel·ous·ness** *or* **mar·vel·lous·ness** *n* -ES

1mar·ver \'märvər\ *n* -s [F *marbre* marble — more at MARBLE] : a flat slab (as of metal, stone, wood) on which a gather of glass is rolled, shaped, and cooled

2marver \"\ *vt* -ED/-ING/-s : to roll (glass) on a marver

mar·wa·ri \mär'wärē\ *n* -s *usu cap* [native name in India] **1** : a member of a caste of moneylenders and merchants in India who have become the chief rivals of the Parsis as merchants and industrialists **2** : the Rajasthani dialect of Marwar

marx·ian \'märksēən, 'māk- *sometimes* -kshən\ *adj, usu cap* [Karl *Marx* †1883 Ger. political philosopher + E *-ian*] : of, developed by, or influenced by the doctrines of Marx ⟨in *Marxian* socialism . . . there is the frank acceptance of the class struggle —Jay Rumney⟩

marx·ism \-k,sizəm\ *n* -s *usu cap* [Karl *Marx* + E *-ism*] : the political, economic, and social principles and policies advocated by Marx, Friedrich Engels, or their followers *esp* : a theory and practice of socialism developed by or associated with Marx and including the labor theory of value, dialectical materialism, economic determination of human actions and institutions, the class struggle as the fundamental force in history, and a belief that increasing concentration of industrial control in the capitalist class and the consequent intensification of class antagonisms and of misery among the workers will lead to a revolutionary seizure of power by and the dictatorship of the proletariat and to the establishment of a classless society — compare BOLSHEVISM, COMMUNISM, LENINISM, REVISIONISM, STALINISM, SYNDICALISM, TITOISM

marxism-leninism \'⸗,⸗'⸗⸗,⸗⸗\ *n, usu cap M&L* : a theory and practice of communism developed by or held to be developed by Lenin from the doctrines of Marx ⟨*Marxism-Leninism* is a rather flexible doctrine, imposing . . . complex problems of interpretation —F.C.Barghoorn⟩

1marx·ist \'märksəst, 'māk-\ *n* -s *usu cap* [Karl *Marx* + E *-ist*] : a follower of Marx : an adherent of Marxism ⟨some of the keenest philosophic minds among the early Russian *Marxists* —G.L.Kline⟩

2marxist \"\ *adj, usu cap* : of, relating to, or having the characteristics of Marxism or Marxists ⟨the *Marxist* doctrine . . . based on the definition of all value as being created by labor —Paul Alpert⟩ ⟨forces inspired by *Marxist* thought threaten to engulf more and more of the free world —A.G.Meyer⟩

mary \'merē, 'mār-, 'ma(a)r-, -ri\ *n, pl* **marys** *also* **maries** *often cap* [fr. the name *Mary*] **1** *Austral & Pacific islands* : an aboriginal or native woman **2** *slang* : STOMACH, BELLY

marybud \'⸗⸗,⸗\ *n* [prob. fr. *Mary,* mother of Jesus + *bud*] *dial chiefly Eng* : any of various marigolds; *esp* : the common marsh marigold (*Caltha palustris*)

mary·gold *n* -s [ME — more at MARIGOLD] : MARIGOLD

marygold yellow *n* : CADMIUM ORANGE

Mary Jane *trademark* — used for a low-heeled broad-toed patent-leather sandal with a single-buckle ankle strap for wear esp. by young girls

mary·knoll·er \'merē,nōlə(r), 'mär-, 'ma(a)r-\ *n* -s *usu cap* [*Maryknoll,* N. Y. + E *-er*] : a priest of a Roman Catholic congregation devoted to foreign missions work that was organized in 1911 with headquarters at Maryknoll, N. Y.

1mary·land \'merələnd\ *adj, usu cap* [fr. *Maryland,* middle Atlantic state of the U. S., fr. Henrietta Maria (*Mary*) †1669 queen consort of Charles I of England + E *land*] : of or from the state of Maryland ⟨*Maryland* oysters⟩ : of the kind or style prevalent in Maryland

2maryland \"\ *or* **maryland tobacco** *n, usu cap M* : a bright tobacco that is grown in southern Maryland, air-cured, and used in cigarette and cigar manufacture

maryland dittany *n, usu cap M* : DITTANY 3

mary·land·er \-də(r), -rə,land-\ *n* -s *cap* [*Maryland* state + E *-er*] : a native or resident of the state of Maryland

mary·land·i·an \-rə,landēən\ *adj, usu cap* [*Maryland* state + E *-ian*] : MARYLAND

maryland pink *also* **maryland pinkroot** *n, usu cap M* : PINKROOT a

maryland yellowthroat *n, usu cap M* : an American warbler (*Geothlypis trichas*) with the upper parts olive, the throat and breast yellow, and the sides of the head of the adult male black

mary lily *n, usu cap M* [after *Mary,* mother of Jesus] : MADONNA LILY

mary major *n, usu cap both Ms* [fr. the coined name *Mary Major*] : JANE DOE — used in federal pleadings

mar·zi·pan \'märtsə,pän, -pan, 'märzə,pan *sometimes* ,⸗⸗'⸗\ *n* -s [G, fr. It *marzapane,* a coin of the middle ages, a measure, a fancy box for confections, marzipan, fr. Ar *mawthabān,* a coin of the middle ages, lit., seated person; fr. the seated Christ on the coin] **1** : a plastic confection of crushed almonds or almond paste, sugar, and whites of eggs that is often shaped into various forms (as animals or fruits) **2** : articles of marzipan

mas *abbr* masculine

MAS *abbr* milliampere second

ma·sa \'mäsə\ *n* -s [Sp, mash, dough, mass, fr. L *massa* lump, mass — more at MASS] : a moist mash resulting from the grinding of corn soaked in a lime and water solution and used in preparing tortillas, tamales, and similar food

ma·sai \mə'sī\ *n, pl* **masai** *or* **masais** *usu cap* **1 a** : a pastoral and hunting people in Kenya and Tanganyika, east of Lake Victoria, subdivided into a number of local communities **b** : a member of such people **2** : a Nilotic language of the Masai people

mas·a·rid·i·dae \,masə'ridə,dē\ *n pl, cap* [NL, fr. *Masarid-, Masaris,* type genus + *-idae*] *in some classifications* : a family of mainly tropical solitary wasps with clavate antennae now usu. treated as a subfamily of Vespidae

masc *abbr* masculine

mas·cagn·ite \ma'skan,yēt\ *also* **mas·cagn·ine** \-n,yēn, -nyən\ *n* -s [*mascagnite* alter. (influenced by *-ite*) of *mascagnine,* fr. G *maskagnin,* fr. Paolo *Mascagni* †1815 Ital. anatomist + G *-in* -ine] : native ammonium sulphate $(NH_4)_2SO_4$ found in volcanic districts

mas·ca·la·ge \,mäskə'lä(,)hā\ *n* -s [origin unknown] : harvesting of the bark of the cork oak

mas·cal·ly \'maskəlē\ *adj* [by alter.] : MASCULY

1mas·cara \ma'skarə *also* mə'- *or* -kerə\ *n* -s [It *mascara, maschera* mask — more at MASK] **1** : a cosmetic for coloring the eyelashes and eyebrows **2** : TUSCAN RED

2mascara \"\ *vt* -ED/-ING/-s : to apply mascara to : color with mascara ⟨saw the ~*ed* face —J.A.Michener⟩ ⟨the flick of a ~*ed* eyelash —Hal White⟩

mas·ca·rene grass \'maskə'rēn-\ *n* [*Mascarene* islands, in the Indian ocean east of Madagascar] : an Asiatic creeping perennial grass (*Zoysia tenuifolia*) introduced into the southern U. S. as a drought-resistant turf grass that has threadlike capillary leaves and flowers in a narrow compressed spike — called also *Korean velvet grass*

mas·ca·ron \'maskə,rän\ *n* -s [F, fr. It *mascherone,* aug. of *maschera* mask] : MASK 1c

mas·cle \'maskəl\ *n* -s [ME *mascle, mascule* mesh, lozenge voided, fr. OF *macle, mascle,* of Gmc origin; akin to OHG *masca* mesh — more at MESH] **1** *heraldry* : a lozenge voided **2** : a steel plate esp. of lozenge shape used in series on 13th century armor

mas·cled \-kəld\ *adj* : composed of or covered with lozenge-shaped scales : having lozenge-shaped divisions

mas·coi \'ma,skói\ *n, pl* **mascoi** *or* **mascois** *usu cap* **1 a** : a people or group of peoples of the Pilcomayo river basin in Bolivia and Paraguay **b** : a member of any of such peoples **2** : the language of any of the Mascoi peoples

mas·cot \'ma,skät, 'maa,-, -,skət\ *n* -s [F *mascotte,* fr. Prov *mascoto* charm, sorcery, fr. *masco* witch, fr. ML *masca, mascha* witch, specter] **1** : a person or thing held to bring good luck; *specif* : AMULET ⟨~s made of coral, jade . . ., and silver were worn —Diana Hawthorne⟩ — compare HOODOO **2 a** : something regarded as a cherished emblem or symbol (as of a group or institution) ⟨had a mountain lion as a ~⟩ ⟨their ~ was a gamecock —F.V.W.Mason⟩ **b** *chiefly Brit* : a radiator ornament on an automobile ⟨made him adopt a fireman and his hose as a ~ for his . . . car —David Masters⟩ **3 a** : a girl or other person usu. enjoying general favor or affection adopted by a team, regiment, or other group as a cherished symbolic figure ⟨chosen ~ of the . . . football team for two years —*Amarillo (Texas) Sunday News-Globe*⟩ **b** : a small boy chosen to accompany a team to its contests, typically wearing its uniform, and usu. obliged to perform such chores as tending bats or fetching water; *specif* : the bat boy of a baseball team

mas·cou·ten \mə'sküt³n,ma'-\ *n, pl* **mascouten** *or* **mascoutens** *usu cap* **1** : POTAWATOMI **2** : PEORIA

1mas·cu·line \'maskyələn, 'maas-, *chiefly Brit* 'mās-\ *adj* [ME *masculin,* fr. MF, fr. L *masculinus,* fr. *masculus,* adj. & n., male (dim. of *mas,* adj. & n., male) + *-inus* -ine] **1** : MALE ⟨accompanied by a ~ member of her family —Joseph Hergesheimer⟩ ⟨the woman's ~ partner —C.S.Ford & F.A.Beach⟩ **2 a** : belonging to, conforming to or constituting the class of words or grammatical forms characteristically referring to males ⟨~ nouns⟩ ⟨a ~ suffix⟩ ⟨~ gender⟩ — compare FEMININE **b** (1) *of a syllable* : STRESSED, STRONG (2) *of rhyme* : occurring in stressed final syllables **3 a** : suggestive of or being in some way like a man ⟨the brazier . . . is essentially a ~ thing —Edmund Vale⟩ ⟨the worn leather armchair . . . was as ~ and durable as the benches in a railway waiting room —Walter de la Mare⟩ ⟨the mountain stands . . . ruggedly ~ in outline —*Amer. Guide Series: N. H.*⟩ **b** *of a sign of the zodiac* : having a masculine influence **c** (1) : belonging or peculiar to or used by males ⟨the poem is almost exclusively a ~ method of expression —C.W.Cunnington⟩ ⟨a sea of languishing ~ glances —Elinor Wylie⟩ ⟨had this skill as well as the ~ ones of riding and shooting —Jean Stafford⟩ (2) : consisting of, dominated by, or made by males ⟨the invasion was a purely ~ one —Seamus MacCall⟩ ⟨have created a ~ country —H.S.Commager⟩ ⟨the industry is wholly ~ —R.H.Lowie⟩ (3) : having the qualities distinctive of or appropriate to a male : VIRILE, ROBUST, MANLY ⟨a big, active, ~ creature —Margaret Deland⟩ ⟨she cannot manage ~ men —Edward Sackville-West⟩ ⟨a contagious ~ book —*Encyc. Americana*⟩ (4) : having a mannish appearance, bearing, or quality : UNWOMANLY ⟨gaunt and ~ with . . . mousey hair plastered back above her ears —Leslie Charteris⟩ (5) *obs* : POWERFUL, STRONG **syn** see MALE

2masculine \"\ *n* -s : something that is masculine: as **a** : a male person **b** (1) : a noun, pronoun, adjective, or inflectional form or class of the masculine gender (2) : the masculine gender

masculine cadence *n* : a cadence with the final chord occurring on a strong beat

masculine caesura *n* : a caesura that follows a stressed or long syllable

masculine ending *n* **1** : a grammatical ending or a suffix marking masculine forms **2** : MASCULINE CADENCE

mas·cu·line·ly *adv* : in a masculine manner

mas·cu·line·ness \-lən(n)əs\ *n* -ES : the quality or state of being masculine

masculine protest *n* : a tendency to compensate for feelings of inferiority or inadequacy by exaggerating one's overt aggressiveness

mas·cu·lin·i·ty \,maskyə'linəd·ē, ,maas-, ,mās-, -nətē, -i\ *n* -ES [F *masculinité,* fr. *masculin* masculine + *-ité* -ity] : the quality, state, or degree of being masculine ⟨measurement of ~ or femininity —*Psychological Abstracts*⟩ ⟨alternates between a polished grace and blunt ~ —Stuart Keate⟩

mas·cu·lin·i·za·tion \,⸗⸗lənə'zāshən, -,nī'z-\ *n* -s : the state of being masculinized

mas·cu·lin·ize \'⸗⸗lə,nīz\ *vt* -ED/-ING/-s [F *masculiniser,* fr. *masculin* masculine + *-iser* -ize] : to cause (a female) to take on male characters (as by the administration of an androgen)

mas·cu·ly *or* **mas·cu·lee** \'maskyəlē\ *adj* [*mascle* + *-y*] *heraldry* : covered with mascles

mas·de·val·lia \,masdə'valēə\ *n, cap* [NL, fr. José *Masdevall* †1801 Span. physician + NL *-ia*] : a large genus of tropical American epiphytic orchids having flowers with sepals joined at the base into a tube and terminating in long narrow appendages

ma·ser \'māzə(r)\ *n* -s [*m*icrowave *a*mplification by *s*timulated *e*mission of *r*adiation] : a device that utilizes the natural oscillations of atoms or molecules for amplifying or generating electromagnetic waves in the microwave region of the spectrum

1mash \'mash, -aa(ə)sh, -aish\ *n* -ES [ME, fr. OE *māsc-, māx-;* akin to MHG *meisch* mash and prob. to OE *mixen* dung, dunghill — more at MIXEN] **1 a** : crushed malt or a meal (as of rye) steeped and stirred in hot water to produce wort **b** : any fermentable mixture from which spirits or alcohol may be distilled **2** : a mixture of ground feeds used either dry or moistened for feeding poultry or other livestock — see BRAN MASH **3 a** : a mass of mixed ingredients made soft and pulpy by beating or crushing : a soft pulpy mass of something **b** : MESS, MUDDLE, MISHMASH ⟨a ~ of stale jokes, bad acting, and dull drama —John McCarten⟩

2mash \"\ *vb* -ED/-ING/-ES [ME *mashen,* fr. *mash,* n.] *vt* **1 a** : to convert into a mash : reduce to a soft pulpy state by beating or pressure ⟨~ apples⟩ **b** : CRUSH, SMASH ⟨~es his hand in an automobile accident —Anthony West⟩ ⟨~*ed* out my cigarette —J.M.Cain⟩ **c** *South & Midland* : to press or drive down esp. forcefully ⟨~ down a rivet⟩ **2** : to subject (as crushed malt) to the action of water with heating and stirring for the purpose of preparing wort **3** *dial Eng* : to make an infusion of (tea) : STEEP ~ *vi* **1** : to perform the operation of mashing malt or other grains **2** *South & Midland* : to apply pressure : press down — usu. used with *on* ⟨~*ing* suddenly on the brake pedal —William Faulkner⟩

3mash \"\ *dial var of* 1MARSH

4mash \"\ *n* -ES [prob. fr. *2mash*] : a hammer used in breaking stone or mineral

5mash \"\ *vb* -ED/-ING/-ES [prob. fr. *2mash*] *vt* : to make amorous or flirtatious advances to : flirt with; *also* : to speak or signal to (a stranger) amorously : ACCOST ~ *vi* : to mash a person of the opposite sex

6mash \"\ *n* -ES **1** : a person who courts the affection of another or who is courted : SUITOR, SWEETHEART ⟨she's a hot-headed little virago, your ~ —Rudyard Kipling⟩ **2** : the act of mashing **3** : 2CRUSH 6 ⟨he's got an awful ~ on her⟩

MASH *abbr* mobile army surgical hospital

mas·ham \'masəm\ *n* -s *usu cap* [*Masham,* Yorkshire, northern England] : a British crossbred mutton sheep

mashed *adj* [fr. past part. of *5mash*] : ENAMORED, STUCK ⟨couldn't get ~ on him —Mary Deasy⟩

1mash·er \'mashə(r), -aash-, -aish-\ *n* -s [*2mash* + *-er*] : one that mashes: **a** : a brewery worker who mixes and cooks mash **b** : a kitchen utensil for mashing food ⟨a potato ~⟩

2masher \"\ *n* -s [*5mash* + *-er*] : a man who makes amorous advances esp. to a strange woman : WOLF, FLIRT ⟨was a born ~ —Dixon Wecter⟩ ⟨a young ~ who is forced into marriage —John McCarten⟩

masher b

mash·gi·ah *or* **mash·gi·ach** \mäsh'gē,äk, -ēək\ *n, pl* **mashgi·him** *or* **mashgi·chim** \,mäsh(,)gē'kēm\ [Heb *mashgīaḥ*] : a supervisor authorized to inspect meat stores, bakeries, public kitchens, and commissaries to ensure adherence to orthodox Jewish ritual cleanliness

mash·ie \'mashē, -aash-, -aish-,-shi\ *n* -s [perh. fr. F *massue* club, fr. (assumed) VL *mattiuca,* fr. (assumed) VL *mattia* mace — more at MACE] : an iron golf club with a rather wide blade well laid back used for medium distances and for lofting a ball (as from a close lie or from the rough) — called also *number five iron;* see IRON illustration

mashie iron *n* : an iron golf club with less loft than a mashie and a longer shaft — called also *driving mashie, number four iron;* see IRON illustration

mashie niblick *n* : an iron golf club with a loft between those of a mashie and a niblick — called also *number six iron;* see IRON illustration

1mashing *n* -s [ME, fr. gerund of *mashen* to mash, convert into a mash] **1** : the action or an act of one that mashes; *specif* : the act or process of mixing malt to produce wort or wash **2** : a quantity mashed

2mashing *n* -s [fr. gerund of *5mash*] : the act of accosting or making amorous advances ⟨flirting and ~ are the targets of a crusade —*Associated Press*⟩

mash·lum \'mashləm\ *n* -s [alter. (influenced by 1*mash*) of earlier *mesline* maslin — more at MASLIN] : a crop consisting of a mixture of a cereal and a legume

mash note *n* : a usu. sentimental or effusive note or letter expressing affection for the recipient ⟨blink at *mash notes* the girls send to each other —Bill Barker⟩ ⟨wrote him *mash notes* with fake names signed to them —Ring Lardner⟩

ma·sho·na \mə'shōnə, -shōnə\ *n, pl* **mashona** *or* **mashonas** *usu cap* : SHONA

mash·pee *or* **mash·pi** \'mash(,)pē\ *n, pl* **mashpee** *or* **mashpees** *or* **mashpi** *or* **mashpis** *usu cap* **1** : a remnant of Algonquian people from Massachusetts and Long Island living on Cape Cod **2** : a member of the Mashpee people

mash tun *or* **mash tub** *n* : a large vessel in which mashing is carried out

mash weld *n* : a spot-weld in which a number of overlapping parts (as rods) are welded in a single operation

ma·si \'mäsē\ *n* -s [Samoan] : fermented taro or breadfruit stored in an underground pit

mas·jid \'masjəd\ *n* -s [Ar] : MOSQUE

1mask \'mask, 'mȧsk\ *dial Brit var of* 1MASH, 2MASH

2mask \'mask, -aa(ə)-, -ai-, -ȧ-\ *n* -s [MF *masque,* fr. OIt *maschera,* prob. fr. (assumed) OIt *masca* witch (whence It dial. *masca*), fr. ML *masca, mascha* witch, specter] **1 a** (1) : a cover or partial cover for the face usu. made of cloth with openings for the eyes and used esp. for disguise at a ball or masquerade (2) : a person wearing a mask : MASKER **b** (1) : a figure of a head worn on the stage esp. by ancient Greek and Roman actors to identify the character and project the voice (2) : a grotesque false face worn at carnivals or similar merrymakings (3) : a representation of a face worn in dances and rituals among primitive peoples esp. for identification with supernatural powers or beings ⟨the fox ~s, the wolf ~s; symbols of the greatest possible power —Marjory S. Douglas⟩ **c** : an often grotesque head or face, used as an adornment (as on a keystone, on a fountain, or on furniture) **d** : a sculptured face or face and neck or a copy of a face made by means of a mold (as in plaster or wax) ⟨a death ~⟩ **2 a** (1) : a quality, trait, appearance, or posture that serves to conceal or disguise (as one's true or inner feelings or intentions) : PRETENSE, CLOAK ⟨friendship . . . is a ~ —Joseph Chiari⟩ ⟨an outward ~ of unfeelingness —Anthony Quinton⟩ ⟨a hideous ~ which conceals man's immorality —*Encyc. Americana*⟩ ⟨assumed a ~ of sullen stupidity —C.S.Forester⟩ (2) : a face suggestive of or resembling a mask in its immobility, expressionless character, or concealment of the inner personality or feelings ⟨they watched our progress with passive ~s —J.A.Michener⟩ ⟨gray-blue eyes that belied the habitual fixity of his fine olive ~ —F.J.Mather⟩ ⟨his face was a ~ that told nothing —W.S. Maugham⟩ ⟨his swarthy features stiffened into a ~ of foreboding —Walter O'Meara⟩ (3) : the side of a man's personality that is presented to the world as distinguished from his inner self : a person's public manner or outward bearing : POSE ⟨what goes on behind that ~ and behind the veil of conventional manners —P.E.More⟩ ⟨had recovered his ~, and was now polite, collected, watchful —W.H.Hudson †1922⟩ ⟨finds him a man of many ~s —E.A.Bloom⟩ ⟨according to the doctrine of the ~, a man's personality is the small portion of his inner self that he presents to the world's view —W.G. O'Donnell⟩ **b** : something that conceals from view; *specif* : a natural or artificial terrain feature which conceals a military force from view or protects it from fire **c** : a pharmaceutical masking agent **d** (1) : a translucent or opaque screen or a border design to vignette or partly to cover the sensitive surface in taking a photograph or the negative in printing, or an opaque sheet with an aperture to insert in the optical path in a motion-picture mechanism so as to modify the size, shape, or appearance of the picture (2) : an auxiliary image used to modify a photographic image (as for the purpose of improving color reproduction) **e** : a translucent or opaque border surrounding a television tube receiver screen **3** : a protective covering esp. for the face: as **a** : a gauze or wire screen worn over the face in outdoor games and in fencing : a similar protective covering used in glassworks, foundries and other industrial enterprises presenting special hazards to workers **b** : GAS MASK **c** : a device usu. covering the mouth and nose to facilitate or prevent the inhalation of a substance (as a gas, vapor, or spray) ⟨an oxygen ~⟩ **d** : a covering often of gauze-like material for the mouth and nose to prevent droplets from being dispersed into the air **e** : a cosmetic preparation esp. for the skin of the face that is applied moist, and produces a cleansing and tightening effect as it dries **f** : FRISKET 1 **4 a** : the head or face of an animal (as a fox, dog, cat) **b** : the lower lip of the nymph of a dragonfly and damselfly modified so as to form a prehensile organ

masks 1: *1* domino, *2* Greek tragedy, *3* Eskimo

3mask \"\ *vb* -ED/-ING/-s *vi* **1** : to take part in a masquerade : go about in a mask ⟨went ~*ing* with a group of young friends —E.P.O'Donnell⟩ **2** *obs* **a** : to assume a mask **b** : to disguise one's true character or intentions ~ *vt* **1 a** : to conceal from view (as with a screen or obstacle) ⟨trees and shrubs ~ the sandstone house —*Amer. Guide Series: Mich.*⟩ **b** : to make indistinct or imperceptible ⟨successive sounds blur and ~ each other —*Architectural Record*⟩ ⟨~s undesirable flavors —*Collier's Yr. Bk.*⟩ **c** : to cover up (as a thing, fact, state, quality, or emotion) so as to mislead concerning its true nature ⟨the lightness ~*ed* a terrible will —Edith Sitwell⟩ **2 a** : to cover for concealment or protection ⟨~*ed* before shipment with tough paper —*Plexiglass Design & Fabrication Data*⟩

b : to furnish with a protective mask (as a gas mask) **c** (1) **:** to conceal (as the position of a battery) from the enemy's sight (2) **:** to keep in check or on the defensive (as troops or a fortress) with part of one's force while conducting hostile operations elsewhere (3) **:** to prevent the delivery of fire on (a particular objective) by the interposition of a mask **d** *cookery* **:** to cover completely (as with thick sauce or mayonnaise) **e** (1) **:** to modify the size or shape of (as a photograph or an image to be photographed, printed, or projected) by means of an opaque border (2) **:** to modify densities of (a photographic image) selectively by means of an auxiliary image of the same subject for improving the accuracy of color reproduction **f** (1) **:** to prevent (an atom or group of atoms) from showing its ordinary reactions **:** BLOCK 1g ⟨to ~ hydroxyl in a sugar by converting it into methoxyl⟩ (2) **:** to modify or reduce the effect or activity of (as a process, a reaction) **g :** FLAVOR ⟨~ a pharmaceutical preparation⟩ **h :** to raise the audibility threshold of (a sound) by the simultaneous presentation of another sound **syn** see DISGUISE

mask crab *n* **:** any of various small shield-shaped crabs constituting the family Dorippidae

masked *adj* **1 a :** having its true character or quality concealed or disguised ⟨the ~ villainy of the man⟩ **b :** screened or concealed from view (as for protective or aesthetic reasons) ⟨a ~ battery⟩ **c :** failing to present or produce the usual symptoms **:** not obvious **:** DISGUISED, LATENT ⟨a ~ fever⟩; *specif* **:** affected by masking ⟨a ~ virus⟩ **2 a :** wearing or using a mask ⟨~ bandits⟩ ⟨~ dancers⟩ **b :** marked by or requiring the use of masks ⟨a ~ ball⟩

masked bobwhite *n* **:** a bobwhite of Sonora, Mexico, and nearby states having a blackish face and bright chestnut breast

masked civet *n* **:** a palm civet of a genus (*Paguma*) characterized by loss of the dorsal striped pattern

masked crab *n* **1 :** a European crab (*Corystes cassivelaunus*) with markings on the carapace resembling a human face **2 :** MASK CRAB

masked duck *n* **:** a small spiny-tailed black-faced duck (*Nomonyx dominicus*) of So. America and the West Indies

masked hunter *n* **:** a conenose (*Reduvius personatus*)

masked quail *n* **:** MASSENA QUAIL

maskeeg *var of* MUSKEG

mas·ke·gon \mə'skēgən, ma'-\ *n, pl* **maskegon** *or* **maskegons** *usu cap* [Cree *Mūskīgōk*, lit., of the swamp] **:** SWAMPY CREE

mas·ke·lyn·ite \'maskələ,nīt\ *n* -s [G *maskelynit*, fr. Nevil Story-*Maskelyne* †1911 Eng. mineralogist + G *-it* -ite] **:** a feldspar found in meteorites

¹mask·er \'maskə(r), -ás-\ *vt* -ED/-ING/-S [ME *maskeren, malskren;* akin to OE *malscrung* sorcery, OS *malsk* proud, Goth *untilamalsks* reckless] *now dial Eng* **:** to make confused or bewildered

²masker \"\ *n* -s [³*mask* + *-er*] **1 :** a person who wears a mask; *specif* **:** one who appears in disguise at a masquerade **2 :** a worker who places a covering over articles to protect them in handling or shipping or over parts of objects to protect them during the painting or treatment of surrounding areas

maskery *n* -ES [²*mask* + *-ery*] *obs* **:** the dress or disguise of a masker **:** MASQUERADE

mask–flower \'=,=\ *n* **:** a plant of the genus *Alonsoa*

mas·kil \'mä,skēl\ *n, pl* **maski·lim** \,mä(,)skē'lēm\ *often cap* [NHeb *maśkīl*, lit., enlightened, intellectual] **:** a person versed in Hebrew or Yiddish literature; *esp* **:** a follower or adherent of the Haskalah movement — **mas·kil·ic** \mə'skilik, mä'-\ *adj, often cap*

¹masking *n* -s [fr. gerund of ³*mask*] **1 :** the act or an instance of taking part in a masquerade ⟨general ~ on Feb. 18, Shrove Tuesday —*N.Y. Times*⟩ **2 a :** the act or an instance of concealing or screening from view, perception, or knowledge ⟨despite ~ of part of the data by . . . some other countries —P.A.Sorokin⟩ **b** *or* **masking piece :** a piece of scenery used to screen from a theater audience any part of the stage that should not be seen **3 :** a suppression of symptoms in plants (as in some virus diseases) under some environmental conditions

²masking *adj* [fr. pres. part. of ³*mask*] **1 :** used in, appropriate to, marked by, or given to the wearing of masks ⟨~ clubs staged a festival⟩ **2 :** tending to mask: as **a :** tending to conceal from view ⟨speeding down the other lane beyond the ~ truck —T.H.White b.1915⟩ **b :** being or relating to a flavoring or scenting substance used to cover or disguise an unpleasant taste or smell ⟨a ~ agent⟩

masking paper *n* **:** a paper used to cover parts of a surface that are to be kept bare when the remaining parts are painted (as with a spray gun)

masking pat *n* [E dial. *masking* (fr. gerund of ¹*mask*) + Sc *pat* pot, alter. of E *pot*] *Scot* **:** TEAPOT

masking tape *n* **:** a tape with an adhesive on one side used to cover a surface not to be painted

maskinonge *or* **maskalonge** *var of* MUSKELLUNGE

mas·kins \'maskənz, 'más-\ *n pl, usu cap* [¹*mass* + *-kin*] *now dial Eng* **:** ¹MASS — used in the phrase *by the Maskins*

masklike \'=,=\ *adj* **:** having the appearance of a mask ⟨a ~ expression⟩

mask stop *n* **:** the termination of a hoodmold when carved to bear more or less resemblance to a human face

¹mas·lin \'mazlən\ *n* -s [ME, fr. OE *mæslen, mæstling;* akin to MD & MHG *messinc* brass] **1** *obs* **:** BRASS **2** *or* **maslin kettle** *dial Eng* **:** a brass pot or vessel

²maslin \"\ *n* -s [alter. of earlier *mesline*, fr. ME *mastlioun, mestlioun*, fr. MF *mesteillon*, fr. OF, fr. (assumed) OF *mesteil* mixed grain (whence MF *mesteil*), fr. (assumed) VL *mixtilium* mixture, fr. (assumed) VL *mixtilis* mixed, constituting a mixture, fr. L *mixtus* mixed (past part. of *miscēre* to mix) + *-ilis* -ile — more at MIX] **1** *dial Brit* **a :** a mixture of different sorts of grain esp. wheat and rye or their flour or meal **b :** bread made with such flour **2** *dial Brit* **:** MIXTURE **3 :** MASHLUM

mas·och·ism \'mazə,kizəm, 'mas-\ *n* -s [ISV *masoch-* (fr. Leopold von Sacher-*Masoch* †1895 Ger. novelist) + *-ism*] **1 a :** a tendency to direct aggressive or destructive impulses against one's own ego in order to reduce the anxiety attendant on anticipated inevitable punishment or to gain positive gratification through identification with a loved one who was formerly a source of pain **b :** a tendency to assume a role of submissiveness and apparently to enjoy humiliation as the outcome of feelings of worthlessness **c :** a tendency to gain or to increase sexual gratification through the acceptance of physical abuse or humiliation — compare ALGOLAGNIA **d :** a tendency to take pleasure in physical or mental suffering inflicted on one by oneself or by another or in the practice of extreme self-denial or self-punishment **:** a taste for suffering ⟨there's a broad streak of puritan ~ in our character —K.S.Davis⟩ **2 :** the practice of masochistic tendencies ⟨it was a form of ~ . . . to condemn oneself needlessly to the tantrums of a capricious climate —Jean Stafford⟩

mas·och·ist \-kəst\ *n* -s [ISV *masoch-* + *-ist*] **:** one that is given to masochism

mas·och·is·tic \¦==¦kistik\ *adj* **:** relating to, marked by, or given to masochism — **mas·och·is·ti·cal·ly** \-tək(ə)lē\ *adv*

¹ma·son \'mās³n\ *n* -s [ME *mason, masoun*, fr. OF *maçon*, prob. of Gmc origin; akin to OE *macian* to make — more at MAKE] **1 :** a skilled workman who builds with stone or similar material (as brick, concrete, artificial stone) **2** *usu cap* **:** FREEMASON **3 a :** MASON BEE **b :** MASON WASP

²mason \"\ *vt* **masoned; masoned; masoning** \-s(³)niŋ\ **masons** [ME *masownen*, fr. MF *maçonner*, fr. OF, fr. *maçon*, n.] **1 :** to construct of or repair with masonry **2 :** to build stonework or brickwork about, under, in, or over ⟨~ up a well⟩ ⟨~ in a boiler⟩

mason bee *n* **:** any of numerous solitary bees that construct nests of hardened mud and sand

masoned *adj* **1 :** made or reinforced with masonry **2** *heraldry* **:** marked with lines of a distinct tincture representing masonry joints

ma·son·er \'mās(³)nə(r)\ *n* -s *now dial Eng* **:** MASON, BRICKLAYER

ma·son·ic \mə'sänik *sometimes* (')mā¦s- *or* -nēk\ *adj* **1 a** *usu cap* **:** of, belonging to, or connected with Freemasons or Freemasonry ⟨*Masonic* lodges⟩ **b :** suggestive of or resembling Freemasons or Freemasonry (as in display of fraternal spirit or secrecy) **:** like that of the Freemasons ⟨might hope for some ~ feminine support —Victoria Sackville-West⟩ ⟨comes to have a kind of ~ feeling for other diplomatists —C.J.Friedrich⟩ **2 :** of or relating to masons or their work — **ma·son·i·cal·ly** \-nək(ə)lē, -nēk-, -li\ *adv*

ma·son·ite \'mās³n,īt\ *n* -s [Owen *Mason*, 19th cent. Am. resident of Providence, Rhode Island + E *-ite*] **:** a chloritoid occurring in broad dark green plates

Ma·son·ite \"\ *trademark* — used for a fiberboard made from steam-exploded wood fiber and used typically for insulation and for paneling

mason jar *n, sometimes cap M* [after John L. *Mason*, 19th cent. Am. inventor] **1 :** a widemouthed glass jar with a porcelain-lined zinc screw cap sealed at cap edge and glass shoulder by a flat rubber ring **2 :** any of various wide-mouth jars with a screw cap used for home canning

ma·son·ry \'mās³nrē, -ri\ *n* -ES [ME *masonerie*, fr. MF *maçonnerie*, fr. *maçon* mason + *-erie* -ery] **1 a :** something that is built by a mason **:** something constructed of the materials (as stone, brick, concrete block, tiles) used by masons; *also* **:** monolithic concrete when used in place of stone, brick, block, or tile masonry **b :** the art, trade, or occupation of a mason **c :** the work of a mason ⟨the ~ showed great skill and care⟩ ⟨only where economy has banished the architect do we see ~ of any merit —Clive Bell⟩ **2** *usu cap* **:** FREEMASONRY

masonry cement *n* **:** a cement specially prepared for use in the mortar of brick and block masonry

masonry nail *n* **:** a hardened nail with spiral flutes for fastening objects to masonry by driving into the mortar joints

masonry saw *n* **:** a saw used to cut masonry units (as brick and tile)

mason's hammer *n* **:** a hammer with a moderately heavy head sharpened at one end to a chisel edge for cutting and dressing stone

mason's level *n* **:** a level longer than a carpenter's level used in laying brick and stone masonry

mason's mark *n* **:** BANKER-MARK

mason's measure *n* **:** a measure used by masons in determining quantities or volumes of masonry, no deductions being made for small openings, and corners being counted twice

mason's hammer

mason wasp *n* **:** any of various solitary wasps (as members of the genera *Eumenes* and *Sceliphron*) that construct nests of hardened mud for their young — compare POTTER WASP

masonwork \'==,=\ *n* **:** MASONRY

ma·soo·la \mə'sülə\ *or* **masoola boat** *n* -s [origin unknown] **:** a boat made of planks sewed together with strands of coir which cross over a wadding and used for landing along the coast of Madras, India

mas·o·rete *or* **mas·so·rete** \'masə,rēt\ *also* **mas·o·rite** \-,rīt\ *n* -s *usu cap* [alter. (influenced by *-ete* — as in *athlete* — and by *-ite*) of earlier *massoreth*, fr. MF, fr. Heb *māsoreth* bond (dubious reading in Ezek 20: 37) (whence NHeb *massōrāh, mĕsōrāh* Masorah)] **:** a scholar learned in the body of textual criticism of the Hebrew Bible called the Masorah; *esp* **:** one of the scribes who wrote down the Masorah

mas·o·ret·ic *or* **mas·so·ret·ic** \¦==¦red·ik\ *also* **mas·o·ret·i·cal** \-d·əkəl\ *adj, usu cap* [*masorete* + *-ic* or *-ical*] **:** of or relating to the Masorah, a vast body of notes on the occurrence of words, features of writing, directions for pronunciation, variant sources, and other textual criticism of the Hebrew Bible, written in the margins and at the end of texts by Jewish scribes between about A.D. 600 and the middle of the 10th century

masque *also* **mask** \'mask, -aa(ə)-, -ai-, -á-\ *n* -s [MF *masque* mask, masquerade, fr. OIt *maschera* mask — more at MASK] **1 a :** MASQUERADE **b** *obs* **:** a group or company of maskers **c :** MASKER **2 :** a short allegorical dramatic performance popular as court entertainment in 16th and 17th century Europe, performed by masked actors often themselves members of the court, and consisting of dumb show combined with music, dancing, and sometimes poetry culminating in a ceremonial dance participated in by the spectators

masqu·er \'maskə(r), 'másk-\ *n* -s [by alter. (influenced by *masque*)] **:** MASKER

¹mas·quer·ade \¦maskə¦rād, -aask-,-aisk-\ *n* -s [MF *mascarade, masquerade* social gathering of persons wearing masks, fr. OIt dial. *mascarada*, fr. OIt *mascara, maschera* mask + OIt dial. *-ada* -ade] **1 :** an action, appearance, bearing, or mode of life that is mere outward show concealing true character or situation **:** a pretense of being something that one is not **:** CAMOUFLAGE, DISGUISE ⟨her maturity was a childish, clever ~ —Philip O'Connor⟩ ⟨traveling about in the ~ of a bon vivant —Virginia Cowles⟩ ⟨discovers under a new ~ the ancient evil —V.L.Parrington⟩ ⟨became aware of an element of ~ in the appearance of this person —Elinor Wylie⟩ **2 a :** a social gathering of persons wearing masks, often dressed in rich fantastic costumes esp. to impersonate characters from history or legend, and amusing themselves with dancing, conversation, or other diversions **b :** a costume for wear at such a gathering

²masquerade \"\ *vi* -ED/-ING/-S **1 a :** to disguise oneself or go about disguised so as to appear to be something that one is not ⟨wasn't the first time he'd *masqueraded* as a girl —Valentine Williams⟩ ⟨looked like a young man *masquerading* in a white wig —R.H.Davis⟩ **b :** to take part in a masquerade **2 :** to pass oneself off or assume the appearance of something that one is not **:** POSE ⟨nonentities have too often *masqueraded* as philosophers —Richard Mayne⟩ ⟨wrong for editorial arguments to ~ as news reports —F.L.Mott⟩ ⟨exploitation *masquerading* as free enterprise —Herbert Agar⟩

mas·quer·ad·er \-də(r)\ *n* -s **:** one that masquerades; *esp* **:** a person taking part in a masquerade

¹mass \'mas, -aa(ə)s, -ais *sometimes* -ás\ *n* -ES *often cap* [ME *masse* mass, feast day, fr. OE *mæsse*, modif. of (assumed) VL *messa* mass, dismissal at the end of a religious service, fr. LL *missa*, fr. L, fem. of *missus*, past part. of *mittere* to send, dismiss — more at SMITE] **1 a :** a sequence of prayers and ceremonies constituting a commemorative sacrifice of the body and blood of Christ under the appearances of bread and wine **:** the Christian eucharistic rite **b :** a celebrating of the Eucharist esp. with a particular intention ⟨make a bequest for ~*es*⟩ **c :** a religious ceremony similar to or likened to the Christian mass ⟨Taoist ~*es* for the dead⟩ **2 :** a setting of certain parts of the mass considered as a musical composition — compare REQUIEM

²mass \"\ *n* -ES [ME *masse*, fr. MF, fr. L *massa* lump, mass, fr. Gk *maza* lump, mass, barley cake; akin to Gk *massein, mattein* to knead — more at MINGLE] **1 a** (1) **:** a quantity of matter cohering together so as to make one body usu. of indefinite shape ⟨a ~ of dough⟩ ⟨a ~ of ore⟩ (2) **:** an aggregate of particles or things making one body or quantity usu. of considerable size ⟨a ~ of sand⟩ (3) **:** a homogeneous pasty mixture compounded for making pills, troches, and plasters ⟨blue ~⟩ (4) *obs* **:** UNIVERSE, EARTH **b** (1) **:** the extent of body of a solid object **:** the extent of space that an object occupies **:** EXPANSE, BULK ⟨the highest mountain ~ on the globe —*Encyc. Americana*⟩ ⟨lifts its bulky ~ over the tangled summits —Wynford Vaughan-Thomas⟩ (2) **:** massive quality or effect **:** MAGNITUDE, MASSIVENESS ⟨in the face of their ~ and virtuosity, what was the use of rebelling against his frequent abuse of the language —*Time*⟩ ⟨impressed me with such ~ and such vividness —F.M.Ford⟩ ⟨presented with such ~ and vehemence —Edmund Wilson⟩ (3) **:** the principal part **:** main body ⟨the great ~ of the continent is buried under an ice cap —Walter Sullivan⟩ ⟨the ~ of our imports consists of raw materials⟩ ⟨saw the dark ~ of the van —Nevil Shute⟩; *also* **:** an unbroken expanse of something lacking bulk, density, or solid character ⟨~*es* of color on a canvas⟩ ⟨a ~ of water⟩ ⟨dense ~*es* of smoke —George Meredith⟩ (4) **:** AGGREGATE, WHOLE ⟨what chiefly appeals to me is the forest seen in the ~ —Arnold Bennett⟩ ⟨men in the ~ are pretty much alike⟩; *specif* **:** an aggregate of related objects or items ⟨a ~ of data⟩ ⟨the ~ of such published material is too great for integral translation —Mortimer Graves⟩ (5) **:** concentration of combat power ⟨the principle of ~⟩ **c** (1) **:** the quality or appearance of considerable largeness and material density (as in a painting or architectural structure) ⟨impressive use of ~ and repetition of detail —*Amer. Guide Series: Ark.*⟩ (2) **:** the shape of a building considered in three-dimensional volume as opposed to silhouette or stylistic decoration **d :** the property of a body that is a measure of its inertia, that is commonly taken as a measure of the amount of material it contains, that causes a body to have weight in a gravitational field, that along with length and time constitutes one of the fundamental quantities on which all physical measurements are based, and that according to the theory of relativity increases with increasing velocity ⟨two free bodies have equal ~ if the same force gives them the same acceleration⟩ **2 a** *obs* **:** a sum or fund of money **b :** a large quantity, amount, or number ⟨turned out a great ~ of miscellaneous material —R.A.Hall b.1911⟩ **3 a** (1) **:** MAJORITY, GENERALITY ⟨the great ~ of teachers . . . use their textbooks and dictionaries —H.R.Warfel⟩ ⟨declared the ~ of mankind did not know their own best interests⟩ ⟨more human . . . than the ~ of their countrymen —E.K.Brown⟩ (2) **:** a large body of persons in a compact body or array **:** a body of persons regarded as an aggregate ⟨a ~ of spectators jammed into the hall⟩ (3) **:** the great body of the people as contrasted with the upper classes **:** ordinary people **:** PROLETARIAT ⟨the coupling of the elite with the ~ is the key —Percy Winner⟩ — usu. used in pl. ⟨of this . . . he felt the ~*es* to be capable —H.S.Canby⟩ **b :** a military formation in which subdivisions are separated by less than normal intervals and distances — **in mass** *adv* **:** en masse ⟨will fall *in mass* on some point on the . . . thin encircling line —Fletcher Pratt⟩

³mass \"\ *vb* -ED/-ING/-ES *vt* **1 :** to form or collect into a mass **:** dispose in a mass **:** ASSEMBLE ⟨with her hair ~*ed* low on her brow —Donn Byrne⟩ ⟨eighteenth-century canvases ~*ing* a dozen gods, a hundred generals, and . . . bleeding soldiers —Sinclair Lewis⟩ **2 :** to concentrate (as troops or fire) on or in a particular area ~ *vi* **:** to gather and form into a mass **:** collect in a body ⟨could see the crowd . . . ~*ing* around the gates —A.P.Gaskell⟩

⁴mass \"\ *adj* **1 a :** of, relating to, designed for, serving, or characteristic of the mass of the people ⟨~ psychology⟩ ⟨the modern economic phenomenon of the . . . ~ market, ~ distribution —Percy Winner⟩ ⟨~ magazines⟩ ⟨~ education⟩ ⟨~ chest X-ray surveys of healthy persons —*Jour. Amer. Med. Assoc.*⟩ ⟨~ hysteria⟩ **b :** participated in, attended by, or affecting a large number of individuals ⟨weapons of ~ destruction⟩ ⟨called for ~ demonstrations against the government⟩ ⟨airplanes made a ~ raid on the target⟩ **c :** having a large-scale character **:** done in large or wholesale quantities ⟨~ plantings of varicolored tulips —*Amer. Guide Series: Mich.*⟩ ⟨~ production⟩ **2 :** arranged or disposed in a mass ⟨a good spot for ~ displays —*Packaging Manual for Self-Service Meats*⟩ **3 :** viewed as a whole **:** TOTAL, AGGREGATE ⟨the ~ effect of the design is most striking⟩

⁵mass \"\ *n* -ES [by shortening & alter.] *now dial Eng* **:** MASTER

mas·sa \'másə, 'masə\ *or* **marse** \'más\ *or* **mar·sa** \'másə\ *n* -s [by alter.] **:** MASTER — used esp. to represent southern Negro speech ⟨this Louisiana sugar planter was called ~ by a hundred Negroes —Katharine L. Bates⟩

mass absorption coefficient *n* **:** the absorption coefficient divided by the density or for a solute in solution by the density concentration

mas·sa·chu·set \,m¦asə'chüsət, m¦as'ch- *also* -üzət *sometimes* ¦ás- *or chiefly in substand speech* -'tü-; *usu* -əd·+V\ *or* **mas·sa·chu·setts** \-əts\ *n, pl* **massachuset** *or* **massachusets** *or* **massachusetts** *usu cap* [Massachuset *Massa-adchu-es-et*, a locality, lit., about the big hill, fr. *massa* big + *wadchu* hill + *-es*, dim. suffix + *-et*, locative suffix] **1 a :** an Indian people of the region of Massachusetts Bay **b :** a member of such people **2 :** an Algonquian language of the Massachuset people

mas·sa·chu·setts \¦==¦==, (')=¦==\ *adj, usu cap* [fr. *Massachusetts*, state of the northeastern U. S., fr. *Massachusetts* Bay, inlet of the Atlantic ocean on the east coast of Massachusetts, fr. *Massachusets*, pl. of *Massachuset*] **:** of or from the state of Massachusetts ⟨a *Massachusetts* industry⟩ **:** of the kind or style prevalent in Massachusetts

massachusetts ballot *n, usu cap M* **:** an Australian ballot on which the names of candidates with their party affiliations are grouped alphabetically under the title of the office they are seeking — compare INDIANA BALLOT, OFFICE-BLOCK BALLOT

massachusetts fern *n, usu cap M* **:** a delicate feathery shield fern (*Thelypteris simulata*) of the eastern U. S.

massachusetts trust *n, usu cap M* **:** an unincorporated business organization managed like and sometimes treated as a corporation (as for tax purposes) and first popular in Massachusetts in which the business capital is held in trust under a written declaration of trust publicly recorded outlining the powers and duties of the trustees and the rights of the beneficiaries and third persons, which capital or trust property is managed by the trustees for the beneficiaries who are the owners from time to time of transferable certificates resembling corporate stock evidencing an equitable interest in the trust property and the income earned by it — called also *business trust, common-law trust*

¹mas·sa·cre \'masəkə(r), 'maas-, -sēk-, *substand* -sə,krē\ *vt* **massacred; massacred; massacring** \-k(ə)riŋ, *substand* -sə,krēiŋ\ **massacres** [MF *massacrer*, fr. OF *macecrer*, fr. *maçacre*, n.] **1 :** to kill by massacre **:** SLAUGHTER ⟨the Spaniards were neatly *massacred* —Green Peyton⟩ **b :** to murder or kill (a person) esp. with violence or cruelty **2 :** MANGLE, MUTILATE ⟨some people who ordinarily ~ grammar —S.L. Payne⟩ ⟨got the knife, and *massacred* the bag —Carolyn Hannay⟩

²massacre \"\ *n* -s [MF, fr. OF *maçacre*] **1 a :** the act or an instance of killing a considerable number of human beings under circumstances of atrocity or cruelty **:** a wholesale slaughter ⟨the ~ of most of the surviving crew by natives —F.R. Dulles⟩ ⟨the Indians suffered as many ~*s* as they inflicted —R.S.Cotterill⟩ **b :** a peculiarly cruel or wanton act of murder or killing ⟨went . . . to avenge the ~ of a brother and a cousin —Elizabeth H. West⟩ **c :** a wholesale or wanton slaughter of animals ⟨a whale hunt and ~ —Brendan Maguire⟩ ⟨great ~*s* of foxes —T.B.Macaulay⟩ **2 :** an act of thorough destruction **:** MANGLING ⟨the author's ~ of traditional federalist presuppositions —R.G.McCloskey⟩ ⟨a ~ of sense and grammar⟩

mas·sa·crer \-k(ə)rə(r)\ *n* -s **:** a person who massacres

mass action *n* **1 :** action involving masses of people ⟨a period of *mass action* in which the individual has often felt lost —F.E. Hill⟩ ⟨by one single *mass action*, to improve the case of workers on a scale never attempted —F.D.Roosevelt⟩ ⟨concerted, public, *mass action* —Eugene Dennis⟩ **2 :** uncoordinated gross motor behavior **:** random or nonspecific responses characteristic esp. of infants

¹mas·sage \mə'sä|zh, -sä|, |j, *Brit usu* 'ma,s-\ *n* -s [F, fr. *masser* to massage (fr. Ar *massa* to stroke, strike) + *-age*] **:** manipulation of tissues for remedial or hygienic purposes (as by rubbing, stroking, kneading, or tapping) with the hand or other instrument (as a vibrator)

²massage \"\ *vt* -ED/-ING/-S **:** to treat by means of massage **:** RUB, KNEAD

mas·sag·er \-zhə(r), -jə-\ *n* -s **:** one that massages: as **a :** MASSEUR, MASSEUSE **b :** a massaging machine

mas·sa·ge·tae \mə'sajə,tē\ *n pl, usu cap* **:** an ancient Indo-European people of Russian Turkestan

mas·sa·ran·du·ba *also* **ma·ca·ran·du·ba** \,masərən'dübə\ *n* -s [Pg *maçaranduba*, fr. Tupi *maçarandiva*] **1 :** any of various trees of the genus *Manilkara; esp* **:** a Brazilian forest tree (*M. excelsa*) that yields a very hard durable light red to reddish brown wood and a milky juice which is a minor source of rubber **2 :** the wood of a massaranduba

mas·sa·sau·ga \,masə¦sógə\ *or* **massasauga rattler** *n* -s [irreg. fr. *Missisauga* river, Ontario, Canada] either of two pygmy rattlers: **a :** a small rattlesnake (*Sistrurus catenatus*) widely distributed from New York across Texas into Mexico that lives chiefly in moist areas and feeds on mice and amphibians **b :** a rattlesnake (*Sistrurus miliaris*) similar to but smaller than the massasauga — called also *ground rattler*

mass book *n, often cap M* **:** MISSAL

mass card *n, sometimes cap M* **:** a card sent to inform the recipient that mass will be offered for the person or intention specified

mass color *n* **:** MASSTONE

mass communication *n* **:** communication directed to or reaching the mass of the people ⟨given full publicity in the press and other means of *mass communication* —Eugene Gressman⟩ ⟨the perils inherent in the *mass communication* media —J.L.Teller⟩

mass defect *n* **:** the difference between the mass of an isotope and its mass number expressed in atomic mass units and being either positive or negative ⟨the *mass defect* of the carbon isotope $_{6}C^{12}$, mass 12.00388, is +0.00388, while that of phosphorus $_{15}P^{31}$, isotopic mass 30.984, is −0.016⟩ — compare BINDING ENERGY, PACKING FRACTION

mas·sé \(ˈ)ma¦sā\ *or* **massé shot** *n* -s [F *massé*, fr. *massé*, past part. of *masser* to make a massé shot, fr. *masse* maul, sledgehammer, fr. OF *mace* mace — more at MACE] **:** a shot in billiards made by elevating the cue and applying a large amount of English to the ball in order to effect an extreme draw or follow or to drive the cue ball around one object ball in order to strike another

masse·cuite \(ˈ)ma¦skwēt\ *n* -s [F *masse cuite*, fr. *masse* mass + *cuite*, fem. of *cuit*, past part. of *cuire* to cook, fr. L *coquere* — more at MASS, COOK] **:** a dense mass of sugar crystals mixed with mother liquor obtained by evaporation — compare MAGMA 5

massed \ˈmast, -aa(ə)st,-aist *sometimes* -ȧst\ *adj* [fr. past part. of [3]*mass*] **1 :** gathered or formed into a mass ⟨carried flame-colored . . . lilies and ~ greens —*N. Y. Herald Tribune*⟩ ⟨a staggering investment in time, in skilled labor, in ~ goods —Charlton Laird⟩ **2 :** constituting a result of massing ⟨a ~ chorus of all the clubs —*Amer. Guide Series: Texas*⟩ — **massed·ly** \-sə̇dlē, -stlē, -li\ *adv*

mas·se·na quail \məˈsēnə-\ *or* **massena partridge** *n, usu cap M* [after André *Masséna* †1817 Fr. marshal] **:** any of several varieties of a crested quail (*Cyrtonyx montezumæ*) ranging from southern Arizona to Guatemala

mass–energy equation \ˈ=¦===-\ *n* **:** an equation for the interconversion of mass and energy: $E = MC^2$ where E is energy in ergs, M is mass in grams, and C is the velocity of light in centimeters per second — called also *Einstein equation;* compare CONSERVATION OF ENERGY, CONSERVATION OF MASS

masses *pl of* MASS, *pres 3d sing of* MASS

mas·se·ter \məˈsēd·ə(r)\ *n* -s [NL, fr. Gk *masētēr*, fr. *masasthai* to chew — more at MOUTH] **:** a large muscle that raises the lower jaw and assists in mastication and that arises from the zygomatic arch and the zygomatic process of the temporal bone and is inserted into the angle and ramus of the lower jaw — **mas·se·ter·ic** \¦masə¦terik\ *adj*

mas·seur *R* maˈsər, məˈ-, +V -ˈsər·; *−R* -ˈsə̄, + *suffixal vowel* -ˈsər· *also* -ˈsə̄r, + *vowel in a word following without pause* -ˈsər· *or* -ˈsə̄ *also* -ˈsər\ *n* -s [F, fr. *masser* to massage — more at MASSAGE] **:** a man who practices massage and physiotherapy

mas·seuse \maˈsə(r)z, məˈ-, -sə̄z,-səiz,-süs,-süz\ *n* -s [F, fem. of *masseur*] **:** a woman who practices massage and physiotherapy

mass house *n, often cap M* **:** a Roman Catholic church — used formerly by Protestants

mas·si·cot \ˈmasə,kät\ *n* -s [ME *masticote*, fr. MF *massicot, masticot*, fr. OIt *marzacotto, massicotto* pottery glaze] **1 :** lead monoxide obtained as a yellow powder at temperatures below the melting point of the oxide — compare LITHARGE 1 **2 :** lead monoxide occurring native in the form of yellow crystals — compare LITHARGE 2

massier *comparative of* MASSY

massiest *superlative of* MASSY

mas·sif \(ˈ)ma¦sēf\ *n* -s [F, fr. *massif*, adj.] **1 :** a principal mountain mass **2 :** a block of the earth's crust bounded by faults or flexures and displaced as a unit without internal change **:** a large fault block of mountainous topography

mäs·sig \ˈmāsik\ *adj* [G, moderate, fr. OHG *māzīg*, fr. *māza* moderation + *-īg* -y; akin to OHG *mezzan* to measure — more at METE] **:** MODERATO — used as a direction in music

[1]**mas·sil·i·ote** \məˈsilē,ōt, -ēət\ *or* **mas·sil·i·ot** \-ēət, -ē,ät\ *n* -s *cap* [modif. (influenced by L *Massilia*, ancient Greek colony at Marseilles, France, fr. Gk *Massalia*) of Gk *Massaliōtēs*, fr. *Massalia* + *-ōtēs* -ote] **:** a native or inhabitant of the ancient Greek colony of Massilia at Marseilles, France

[2]**massiliote** \"\ *or* **massiliot** \"\ *adj, usu cap* **:** of or relating to the ancient Greek colony of Massilia or to Massiliotes

mass·i·ness \ˈmasēnə̇s, ˈmaas-, -ais- *sometimes* -ȧs- *or* -sin-\ *n* -ES [[1]*massy* + *-ness*] *archaic* **:** MASSIVENESS

massing *n* -s [fr. gerund of [3]*mass*] **1 a :** the act or an instance of gathering or forming into a mass ⟨this ~ of troops provoked sharp protests in foreign chancelleries⟩ **b :** a massive concentration or piling up (as of words, images, or other artistic devices) for the achievement of an effect ⟨the sense of horror is . . . conjured up by sheer pressure of words and ~*s* of lights and scenery —N.L.Rothman⟩ **c :** the architectural relationship between the various masses or volumes of a building ⟨emphasize ~, including proportion, profile, volume relationship and contour —Sheldon Cheney⟩ **2 :** MASS ⟨above these . . . towers the magnificent ~ of the clouds —G.R.Stewart⟩ ⟨the ~ on either side of the pass —*Amer. Guide Series: N. H.*⟩

mas·sive \ˈmasiv, -aas-, -ais-, -sēv *also* -əv\ *adj* [ME *massiffe*, fr. MF *massif*, fr. *masse* mass + *-if* -ive — more at MASS] **1 a** (1) **:** forming or consisting of a large mass **:** having a solid bulky form **:** COMPACT, WEIGHTY, HEAVY ⟨~ rocks⟩ ⟨~ walls⟩ ⟨~, sturdy furniture —C.B.Kelsey⟩ ⟨a ~ volume of 600 pages —*Times Lit. Supp.*⟩ (2) **:** not hollow or plated **:** SOLID ⟨the sheath of his long knife, and other things about him were of ~ silver —W.H.Hudson †1922⟩ **b** (1) **:** characterized by solid agglomeration of materials (as bricks or stones piled in a wall, solid pisé or concrete) ⟨a building of ~ construction⟩ (2) **:** composed of or characterized by heavy monumental forms ⟨the ~ and pointed style of the German Gothic —Frederika Blankner⟩ **c :** having no regular form but not being necessarily without a crystalline structure ⟨~ sandstone⟩ **2 a :** having a large, solid, or heavy build ⟨faced the ~ policewoman —Lois Shea⟩ **:** relatively or imposingly large ⟨eyebrows were very ~, almost meeting over the nose —Bram Stoker⟩ ⟨a ~ policeman's face —Ngaio Marsh⟩ ⟨the ~ jaw, and the unyielding mouth —Eric Linklater⟩ **b :** large in quantity, intensity, scope, or degree ⟨the most ~ odor I have ever known —Havelock Ellis⟩ ⟨had a sudden and ~ effect on book reading —*Publishers' Weekly*⟩ ⟨a surfeit of war and ~ injustice —John Barkham⟩ ⟨~ and instant retaliation —Elmer Davis⟩ **c** (1) **:** large in comparison to what is typical — used esp. of medical dosage or of an infective agent ⟨a ~ dose of penicillin⟩ (2) **:** extensive and severe — used of a pathologic condition ⟨a ~ hemorrhage⟩ ⟨a ~ collapse of a lung⟩ (3) **:** impressive or imposing in extent or depth, or through moral or intellectual excellence or grandeur **:** NOTABLE, MONUMENTAL ⟨~ simplicity — there's the pith of greatness in everything the man did —H.J.Laski⟩ ⟨a ~ simple man, above wile and above suspicion —Francis Hackett⟩ ⟨watched Grandmother move with a ~ dignity —Ellen Glasgow⟩ ⟨the most ~ American dramatist of his time —*Newsweek*⟩ ⟨it was this ~ figure . . . who became the master and innovator of his period —M.D.Geismar⟩

syn MASSIVE, MASSY, BULKY, MONUMENTAL, and SUBSTANTIAL can all mean impressively large or heavy. MASSIVE stresses bulk and solidity of construction ⟨bulky gas tanks — brown, *massive*, ugly —*Amer. Guide Series: N.Y.City*⟩ ⟨the state capitol at Austin — a *massive* pile of pink granite, bigger than the capitol at Washington —Green Peyton⟩ ⟨one of the most *massive* programs ever submitted by any president to Congress —Frank Kent⟩ MASSY, not common in spoken English, implies more ponderousness than does MASSIVE but equal solidity and strength ⟨this oak table top seems to be all of a piece, a *massy* whole —T.H.Littlefield⟩ ⟨a *massy* building of stone and orange-pink stucco —Al Hine⟩ ⟨avalanches . . . in their low *massy* thunder tones —John Muir †1914⟩ BULKY stresses size, usu. implying the occupying of a space out of proportion to the weight of an object and suggesting a consequent difficulty in the maneuvering of the object ⟨the rounded *bulky* form of a fat old lady —Lytton Strachey⟩ ⟨compartments were fitted to hold the *bulky* articles —*Amer. Guide Series: Ariz.*⟩ ⟨sitting on the floor, doubled up, *bulky* in his blue dungarees —Liam O'Flaherty⟩ MONUMENTAL suggests a great size or massiveness that is imposing ⟨this striking brick and limestone structure has *monumental* entrances flanked by chrome and frosted-glass lamps and surmounted by gilt eagles —*Amer. Guide Series: N. C.*⟩ ⟨the *monumental* six-volume work on international arbitration —L.M.Sears⟩ ⟨his commanding past, his *monumental* self-confidence —*Time*⟩ SUBSTANTIAL, though it can apply to size, stresses solidity and strength of construction, usu. implying worth, quality, or stability rather than great size or imposingness of appearance ⟨*substantial* homes for the technical employees of the two corporations —*Amer. Guide Series: Nev.*⟩ ⟨so *substantial* was the construction that a number of these buildings are standing today in a good state of preservation —*Amer. Guide Series: Ind.*⟩ ⟨this *substantial* volume, with over 700 pages of text —R.C.K.Ensor⟩

mas·sive·ly \-sə̇vlē, -li\ *adv* **:** in a massive manner

mas·sive·ness \-sivnə̇s, -sēv- *also* -səv-\ *n* -ES **:** the quality or state of being massive

mas·siv·i·ty \maˈsivəd·ē\ *n* -ES **:** MASSIVENESS

mass john \-¦jän\ *n, usu cap M&J* [[5]*mass* + *John* (the name)] *chiefly Scot* **:** a Scotch Presbyterian minister

mass–luminosity law \ˈ=¦==¦===-\ *n* **:** a statement in astronomy: there is a close correlation between the luminosities or absolute magnitudes of stars and their masses so that the more massive stars are in general the more luminous

mass man *n* **:** an average, typical, or ordinary man **:** a prototype of the mass society esp. when regarded as lacking individuality or social responsibility, as drawing his stereotyped ideas from the mass media, and as easily manipulated by economic, social, or cultural elites

mass medium *n, pl* **mass media :** a medium of communication (as the newspapers, radio, motion pictures, television) that is designed to reach the mass of the people and that tends to set the standards, ideals, and aims of the masses — usu. used in pl.

mass meeting *n* **:** a large meeting or rally of people for discussion of a public question

mass meristem *n* **:** a meristem in which cell division in three or more planes results in increase in mass — compare PLATE MERISTEM, RIB MERISTEM

mass noun *n* **:** a noun characteristically denoting in many languages a homogeneous substance or a concept without subdivisions (as *sand, butter, beer, accuracy* distinguished from *a grain of sand, a pat of butter, a glass of beer, a degree of accuracy*), having in this usage in English only the singular form, and preceded in indefinite constructions by *some* rather than *a* or *an* — compare COUNT NOUN

mass number *n* **:** an integer that expresses the mass of an isotope with the mass of the most abundant oxygen isotope taken as 16 and that designates the number of nucleons in the nucleus ⟨the symbol for carbon of *mass number* 14 is ^{14}C or C^{14}⟩ — symbol *A;* compare ATOMIC MASS

mass observation *n, usu cap M&O* **:** an orig. and chiefly British method of ascertaining public opinion and public sentiment by study of diaries and subjective writings, private comments, and interviews on general subjects, in combination with quantitative surveys and polls

mass of mercury : BLUE MASS

mass of the catechumens *often cap M&C* **:** the part of the mass up to the offertory when the catechumens were orig. dismissed

mass of the faithful *often cap M&F* **:** the part of the mass from the offertory to the end to which only the faithful were orig. admitted

mass of the presanctified *often cap M&P* **:** a special eucharistic service celebrated in the Latin rite on Good Friday only in which elements consecrated at a previous service are used

massorete *var of* MASORETE

mas·so·therapist \¦ma(,)sō+\ *n* [*massotherapy* + *-ist*] **:** one who practices massotherapy — compare MASSEUR, MASSEUSE

mas·so·therapy \"+\ *n* [ISV *masso-* (fr. *massage*) + *therapy*] **:** the practice of massage for remedial or hygienic purposes

mas·soy *or* **mas·soi** \məˈsȯi, ˈma,sȯi\ *also* **massoi bark** *or* **massoy bark** *n* -s [*massoy, massoi*, native name in Papua] **:** the aromatic bark of an East Indian tree (*Massoia aromatica*) of the family Lauraceae yielding a volatile oil

mass penny *n, often cap M* **:** a money offering as distinguished from an offering in kind made during the mass in the medieval church

mass priest *n, often cap M* [ME *masseprest*, fr. OE *mæssepreōst*, fr. *mæsse* mass + *preōst* priest] **1** *obs* **a :** a secular priest as distinguished from a monk **b :** a chantry priest **2 :** a Roman Catholic priest — usu. used disparagingly

mass–produce \ˈ==¦=\ *vt* [fr. *mass production*, after E *production: produce*] **:** to produce or manufacture in quantity; *esp* **:** to produce considerable quantities of (standardized commodities) with the use of machine techniques — opposed to *tailor-make*

mass–produced \¦==¦=\ *adj* [fr. past part. of *mass-produce*] **:** produced in considerable quantities esp. by machinery ⟨such *mass-produced* goods as shoes, clothing, and household equipment —*Atlantic*⟩

mass–producer \ˈ==¦==\ *n* [*mass-produce* + *-er*] **:** one that mass-produces

mass production *n* [[2]*mass*] **:** production of goods in considerable quantities esp. by machinery

mass ratio *n* **:** the ratio between the mass of a rocket with fuel and the mass after the fuel has been used up

mass selection *n* **:** selection as breeding stock of those members of a population exhibiting desirable qualities or elimination of those showing undesirable qualities **:** phenotypic selection — compare PROGENY TEST

mass society *n* **:** modern industrialized urbanized society **:** the society of the mass man esp. when held to be marked by anonymity, high mobility, lack of individuality, and a general dominance of impersonal relationships

mass spectrograph *n* **:** an apparatus for separating a stream of charged particles into a mass spectrum (as by magnetic or electric fields) usu. with photographic recording of the data and for thereby determining esp. the masses of isotopes

mass spectrometer *n* **:** an apparatus similar to a mass spectrograph but usu. with electrical measurement of the data for use esp. in determining abundance ratios of isotopes and in analyzing mixtures of compounds

mass spectrum *n* **:** the spectrum of a stream of charged particles (as electrons or nuclear particles) dispersed according to their mass

masstone \ˈ=,=\ *n* [[2]*mass*] **:** the full color of a pigment or a coating — called also *mass color*

mas·su·la \ˈmasyələ\ *n, pl* **massu·lae** \-,lē\ [NL, fr. L, small mass, fr. *massa* lump, mass + *-ula* — more at MASS] **1 :** a coherent mass of pollen grains (as in certain orchids) developed from a single pollen mother cell **2 :** a hardened layer of cytoplasm formed around the maturing microspore in some heterosporous ferns (as of the genus *Azolla*)

mass unit *n* **:** ATOMIC MASS UNIT

mass–wasting \ˈ=¦==\ *n* [[2]*mass* + *wasting*, n.] **:** the process involving movement of mantlerock that is controlled directly by gravity and that includes such gradual movements as creep and solifluction and such rapid movements as produce rockfalls, landslides, and mudflows

[1]**massy** \ˈmasē, -aas-, -ais- *sometimes* -ȧs- *or* -si\ *adj* -ER/-EST [ME, fr. *masse* mass + *-y* — more at MASS] **1 a** (1) **:** not hollow or plated **:** SOLID ⟨the ~ gold frame —R.P.Warren⟩ (2) **:** having mass, weight, or thickness ⟨in the Newtonian physics a ~ particle had its location altered by other particles —Victor Lowe⟩ **b** (1) **:** bulky and heavy **:** PONDEROUS, WEIGHTY ⟨a ~ shield⟩ ⟨no reader would read such ~ volumes —G.M.Trevelyan⟩ ⟨~ beams bound together with rawhide thongs —Aubrey Drury⟩ (2) **:** composed of great blocks or masses of material ⟨a ~ wall⟩ ⟨~ battlements⟩ **c :** forming a dense mass **:** spreading densely or over a large expanse ⟨the fig tree's ~ foliage —Norman Douglas⟩ ⟨~ clouds⟩ **2 :** imposingly large in build or size ⟨saw his ~ figure striding down the street⟩ **3 :** having a massive quality **:** giving an impression of massiveness ⟨rhythms connected with a ~, frequently metallic diction —Paul Rosenfeld⟩ **syn** see MASSIVE

[2]**mas·sy** \ˈmasē\ *dial var of* MERCY

[1]**mast** \ˈmast, -aa(ə)st,-aist,-ȧst\ *n* -s [ME, fr. OE *mæst;* akin to MD & OHG *mast*, L *malus* mast, MIr *maide* stick] **1 a :** a long pole or spar of timber or metal rising usu. vertically from the keel or deck of a ship and supporting the yards, booms, derricks, or gaffs **b :** a vertical or nearly vertical pole (as an upright post in various cranes or a structure to support an aerial) ⟨a television ~⟩ **c :** GIN POLE 2 **2 :** CAPTAIN'S MAST ⟨~ was always nasty business —K.M.Dodson⟩ — **at the mast** *or* **at mast** *adv* **:** on the main deck or quarter-deck by the mainmast where most assemblies of the crew are held for formal purposes — **before the mast** *or* **afore the mast** *adv* **1 :** forward of the foremast **2 :** as a common sailor ⟨shipped *before the mast* on a trading ship bound for the Orient⟩

[2]**mast** \"\ *vt* -ED/-ING/-S **:** to furnish with a mast ⟨pines . . . reserved for ~*ing* the king's navy —*Amer. Guide Series: Vt.*⟩

[3]**mast** \"\ *n* -s [ME, fr. OE *mæst;* akin to MD & OHG *mast* food, mast, OE *mete* food — more at MEAT] **1 :** nuts (as beechnuts and acorns) esp. as accumulated on the forest floor; *also* **:** an accumulation of such nuts used as food for hogs or other animals ⟨feed on the bountiful ~ of acorns on the wooded ridges —John Hightower⟩ **2 :** MAST BROWN

[4]**mast** \"\ *n* -s [modif. (influenced by [1]*mast*) of F *masse* billiard cue, maul, sledgehammer, fr. OF *mace* mace — more at MACE] *archaic* **:** a heavy billiard cue

mast- *or* **masto-** *comb form* [NL, fr. Gk, fr. *mastos* breast — more at MEAT] **1 :** breast **:** nipple **:** mammary gland ⟨*mast*itis⟩ ⟨*mast*odon⟩ **2 :** mastoid and ⟨*masto*tympanic⟩

mas·ta·ba \ˈmastəbə\ *n* -s [Ar *maṣṭabah, miṣṭabah* stone bench] **:** an Egyptian tomb of the time of the Memphite dynasties that is oblong in shape with sloping sides and is connected with a mummy chamber in the rock beneath

mast·age \ˈmastij\ *n* -s *archaic* **:** MAST, NUTS; *also* **:** a right to feed animals on the mast of a tract

mas·tax \ˈma,staks\ *n* -ES [NL, fr. Gk, mouth, jaws; akin to Gk *masasthai* to chew — more at MOUTH] **1 :** the pharynx of a rotifer usu. containing several horny pieces most commonly consisting of an incus and mallei **2 :** the lore of a bird

mast brown *n* [[3]*mast*] **:** a brownish orange that is less strong and slightly lighter than leather and yellower, lighter, and stronger than spice

mast cell *n* [part trans. of G *mastzelle*, fr. *mast* food, mast (fr. OHG) + *zelle* cell — more at MAST (nuts)] **1 :** a basophilic leukocyte **2 :** a cell similar to but larger than a basophilic leukocyte that is common in connective and other tissues and believed to produce heparin

mas·tec·to·my \maˈstektəmē, -mi\ *n* -ES [*mast-* + *-ectomy*] **:** excision or amputation of the breast

mast·ed \¦mastə̇d, -aas-,-ais-,-ȧs-\ *adj* **:** having or furnished with a mast ⟨probably was so ~ when she set forth —S.E. Morison⟩ — usu. used in combination ⟨a 4-*masted* ship⟩

[1]**mas·ter** \ˈmastə(r), -aas-, -ais-, -ȧs-\ *n* -s [ME *maister* master, teacher, ruler, fr. OE *mægester, magister* & OF *maistre*, both fr. L *magister;* akin to L *magnus* great, large — more at MUCH] **1 a** (1) **:** a male teacher **:** TUTOR; *esp* **:** SCHOOLMASTER ⟨watched my ~'*s* face pass from amiability to sternness —James Joyce⟩ (2) **:** a person qualified to teach at a medieval university (3) **:** a person who has received an academic degree higher than a bachelor's but lower than a doctor's ⟨a reception was held for the newly made ~*s* and doctors⟩ **b** (1) *often cap* **:** a religious leader whose doctrines one accepts **:** one who inspires devotion or reverence on the part of his disciples ⟨eighty disciples drawn from diverse faiths sat with their *Master* —M.L.Bach⟩ (2) **:** a great figure of the past (as in science, literature, or art) whose work serves as a model, ideal, or landmark for later generations **:** a figure of immense authority or generally recognized greatness ⟨one of the few valid studies of our literature on the scale of the ~*s* —M.D.Geismar⟩ ⟨thoughts which had already occurred to the great ~*s* of the past —Arturo Castiglioni⟩ ⟨music of the ~*s*⟩ **c :** a workman so proficient in his handicraft or trade as to be able to follow it independently and employ or supervise journeymen or apprentices; *sometimes* **:** one who has passed a licensing examination and consequently is permitted to contract for services **d** (1) **:** a person who possesses mastery (as of an art or technique) **:** an artist or performer of consummate skill ⟨one of the ~*s* of the new poetic idiom —R.W.Southern⟩ ⟨beautiful playing by a throng of ~*s* —Wilder Hobson⟩ ⟨a follower of the school of English ~*s* —*Current Biog.*⟩ (2) *archaic* **:** a painting or statue by a master — see OLD MASTER (3) **:** an anonymous artist of distinction whose work is distinguishable from other work of his time and place by its characteristic style or quality ⟨the ~ of the St. Cecilia altarpiece⟩ **e :** a person who is highly skilled, ingenious, or dexterous in some area of activity ⟨a ~ at laying out and illustrating advertisements —W.J.Reilly⟩ ⟨a ~ at dissembling⟩ ⟨a ~ of paradox⟩ ⟨a ~ of historical technique⟩ **f :** a bridge player (as in U. S. contract bridge tournaments) eligible to play in restricted contests **2 :** an individual having control, authority, or predominance over another: as **a** (1) **:** a man having control over the actions of others **:** RULER, GOVERNOR ⟨this decisive battle left him ~ of Europe⟩ ⟨the ~*s* of the little state met and drafted a defiant reply⟩ (2) **:** a sovereign ruler in relation to his ministers or diplomatic agents ⟨bear this message to the king your ~⟩ **b :** one that conquers or masters or is capable of conquering or mastering another **:** VICTOR, SUPERIOR ⟨in this young, obscure challenger the champion found his ~⟩ **c** (1) **:** a person who is licensed to take complete charge of a merchant ship **:** CAPTAIN, MASTER MARINER (2) **:** a former commissioned officer (as in the U. S. and British navies) ranking next below a lieutenant and performing the duties of the present navigating officer **d** (1) **:** a person having mastery of or control over something abstract or immaterial ⟨proved himself ~ of the situation⟩ ⟨~ of his own time⟩ (2) **:** something abstract or immaterial that exercises control or mastery ⟨the doctrine that fate is the ~ of our destinies⟩ (3) **:** a possessor or owner of something inanimate ⟨~ of a stately house and broad acres⟩ (4) **:** the owner of a slave ⟨his slaves found him a kind ~⟩ or of an animal ⟨these tribesmen are ~*s* of vast herds of sheep⟩; *also* **:** the male person whom an animal has been trained to obey ⟨pulling his two-year-old ~ from a rain-swollen river —*Springfield* (*Mass.*) *Union*⟩ **e** (1) **:** EMPLOYER ⟨the ~ eats his meal in a separate room from the laborer —J.M.Mogey⟩; *esp* **:** the employer of a domestic or personal servant ⟨informed the caller his ~ was not at home⟩ (2) **:** the person to whom an apprentice is articled **f :** a leader (as a bellwether) of a herd of animals **g** (1) *dial* **:** HUSBAND ⟨my ~ isn't home⟩ (2) **:** the male head of a household ⟨the ~ of the house⟩ (3) **:** a woman's lover or paramour ⟨the mistress produces to the court letters from her late ~ —*Time*⟩ **h :** a man who owns or controls a pack of hounds; *esp* **:** one who leads, commands, and disciplines the field in a hunt when hounds are in full cry ⟨always refer to all persons on the hunt, other than ~*s* and whips, as the field —Coles Phinizy⟩ — often used in the phrase *master of hounds* or in a phrase designating a pack of hounds of a specified kind (as *master of foxhounds, master of beagles*) **i :** a supernatural being in the mythology of a primitive people, regarded as the intermediary between men and a particular species of animals, replenishing the species, and responsible for sending animals to be killed by deserving hunters ⟨success depended . . . upon a man's satisfactory relations with the superhuman ~*s* —*Amer. Anthropologist*⟩ **3 a** (1) *archaic* **:** MR. 1a (2) *now chiefly dial* **:** [2]MISTER 2, 4 (3) **:** YOUTH, BOY — now used chiefly as a conventional title of courtesy before the name of a boy **b :** any of various members of the Scottish peerage: as (1) **:** the eldest son of a peer (as a viscount or baron) ⟨The *Master* of Ballantrae⟩ (2) **:** the heir presumptive to a peerage; *specif* **:** the eldest son of an heir apparent to an earldom **4 a** (1) **:** a presiding or administrative officer; *esp* **:** the head in an institution or society (as a college, guild, or corporation) (2) **:** an official who has custody or superintendence of a specified thing ⟨the *Master* of the Robes⟩ **b** (1) **:** any of several officers of court appointed to assist a judge (as by hearing and reporting upon matters referred to him or by recording proceedings) (2) **:** any of several clerks or recording officers of the supreme courts of England **c :** a person holding an office of authority among the Freemasons; *esp* **:** the presiding officer — called also *worshipful master* **5 a :** MASTER MATRIX **b** *or* **master copy :** a surface (as a stencil or a gelatin matrix) from which copies are printed by direct contact on a duplicating machine **c :** a master mechanism or device; *specif* **:** CASTER 1b

[2]**master** \"\ *vt* **mastered; mastered; mastering** \-t(ə)riŋ\ **masters** [ME *maistren*, fr. *maister*, n. — more at [1]MASTER] **1 a :** to become master of **:** bring under control **:** CONQUER, OVERCOME ⟨tried to ~ his stammer —Osbert Sitwell⟩ ⟨~*ed* his love for the wife of a neighbor —Stringfellow Barr⟩ **b :** to cause to obey **:** bend to one's will **:** SUBDUE, TAME ⟨~*s* his gal by knocking her down and dragging her away —M.W.Fishwick⟩ ⟨a farmer must ~ every beast on his farm —F.D.Smith &

Barbara Wilcox⟩ ⟨man has ~*ed* nature —P.L.Ralph⟩ **c** *obs* **:** to have or get possession of **:** OWN, POSSESS **d :** to act as master over **:** RULE, REGULATE, DIRECT **2 a :** to become skilled or proficient in the use of **:** achieve mastery or command of ⟨the telephone was an instrument he could not ~ —Osbert Sitwell⟩ ⟨~ a foreign language⟩ ⟨could not ~ the technique necessary for a concert pianist —*Current Biog.*⟩ **b :** to gain a thorough or perfect understanding, grasp, or knowledge of ⟨failed to ~ the windings of that river —Thomas Wood †1950⟩ ⟨could ~ any intricate detail of pertinent information —Robert White⟩ **c :** to work out **:** SOLVE ⟨~ a knotty problem⟩

[3]**master** \"\ *adj* [ME *maister*, fr. *maister*, n. — more at [1]MASTER] **1 :** being or relating to a master: as **a :** having chief authority or power **:** ruling over others **:** DOMINANT ⟨the theory of a ~ race⟩ **b :** being a master as distinguished from a journeyman or apprentice ⟨a ~ electrician⟩ ⟨a ~ plumber⟩ **c :** being a person notably or supremely proficient in something **:** consummately accomplished or skilled ⟨flute music played by a ~ minstrel —Lavinia R. Davis⟩ ⟨a ~ mathematician and craftsman —Eric Hoffer⟩ **d :** being the chief, guiding, or principal one **:** having all others subordinate to oneself **:** PRINCIPAL, CONTROLLING, RULING ⟨the fear of communism is the ~ fear —W.M.Ball⟩ ⟨anatomy and perspective are almost the ~ subjects —Reyner Banham⟩ ⟨it was the ~ design and . . . thousands of westerns would be modeled on it —Fanny K. Wister⟩ **e :** being something in a superlative degree — often used in combination ⟨a saturnine *master*-bore —D.B.W.Lewis⟩ ⟨a *master*-liar⟩ **f :** being a device or mechanism that controls the operation of another mechanism ⟨the pressure exerted by the brake fluid from the ~ cylinder acting on the rear face of the slave cylinder piston —Irving Frazee⟩ **g :** being a mechanical part or a device that establishes a dimension, weight, or other standard ⟨the use of suitable ~ gears or sample gears is necessary for reference purposes —G.F. Hessler⟩ — compare MASTER GAGE **h :** being or relating to a record (as on magnetic tape) from which duplicates or prints are intended to be made **2** *dial* **:** REMARKABLE, GREAT, NOTABLE, OUTSTANDING ⟨I've seen some ~ crops there —Adrian Bell⟩

[4]**master** \"\ *adv, chiefly dial* **:** EXCEEDINGLY, VERY ⟨a ~ long, rough road —Sarah O. Jewett⟩

[5]**master** \"\ *n* -s [[1]*mast* + *-er*] **:** a ship having a specified number of masts — usu. used in combination ⟨a two-*master*⟩

master agreement *n* **:** a collective-bargaining agreement the terms of which apply to a number of plants or companies and which may be supplemented by local agreements not conflicting with its provisions

master-at-arms \ˈ===ˈ=\ *n, pl* **masters-at-arms :** a petty officer on a man-of-war charged with the maintenance of order, discipline, the custody of prisoners, and similar duties

[1]**masterbatch** \ˈ==,=\ *n* [[3]*master* + *batch*] **:** a mixture that consists of rubber or plastic with one or more compounding ingredients in definite proportions but higher concentrations than in a normal mix and that is used for convenience in compounding

[2]**masterbatch** \"\ *vt* **:** to mix into a masterbatch

master bedroom *n* **:** the principal bedroom in a house usu. occupied by the head of the household

master builder *n* **:** a person notably proficient in the art of building ⟨the ancient Egyptians were *master builders*⟩; *specif* **:** one who has attained proficiency in one of the building crafts and is qualified or licensed to supervise building construction

master chief petty officer *n* **:** a chief petty officer of the second highest rank

master chief petty officer of the coast guard : a petty officer of the highest enlisted rank in the coast guard — see RANK table

master chief petty officer of the navy : a petty officer of the highest enlisted rank in the navy — see RANK table

master clock *n* **:** a clock that regulates or gives movement esp. by electricity to distant clocks

master container *n* **:** a primary shipping container into which is packed a number of cases each carrying units of the packaged goods

mas·ter·dom \ˈmastə(r)dəm, -aas-, -ȧes-, -ȧs-\ *n* -s [ME *maisterdom*, fr. OE *mægsterdōm* function of a teacher, fr. *mægester, magister* master, teacher, ruler + *-dōm* -dom — more at MASTER] **:** the state or position of being master **:** MASTERY, SUPREMACY

mastered *past of* MASTER

mas·ter·ful \-fəl\ *adj* [ME *maisterful*, fr. *maister* master + *-ful* — more at MASTER] **1 a :** inclined to play the master ⟨her mother was a ~ woman —R.W.Southern⟩ ⟨no one thought of asking the ~ gentleman where his authority was —J.H.Wheelwright⟩ **b :** reflecting or suggesting an imperious or domineering character ⟨a young maid who has ~ ways —E.K.Brown⟩ ⟨his eyes were . . . enticing and ~ —Jack London⟩ **2 :** marked by the display or qualities of vigor and power **:** VIGOROUS, ENERGETIC ⟨a ~ king who put down the lawless barons of the realm⟩ ⟨an epoch of ~ national impulse —Francis Hackett⟩ **3 :** having or reflecting the technical, artistic, or intellectual skill or power of a master **:** MASTERLY ⟨the beadwork of the tribes . . . is ~ —Juan Belaieff⟩ ⟨written in ~ English —George Lenczowski⟩ ⟨a ~ speaker who can move his audiences —R.D.Robinson⟩

syn DOMINEERING, IMPERIOUS, PEREMPTORY, IMPERATIVE: MASTERFUL suggests a capacity for commanding, compelling, and unruffled action or an ability to lead or command through strength, force, or skill ⟨the strong, *masterful* personality of Holmes dominated the tragic scene, and all were equally puppets in his hands —A. Conan Doyle⟩ ⟨she was ever a *masterful* woman, better fitted to command than to obey —H.O.Taylor⟩ ⟨the major was a *masterful* man; and I knew that he would not give orders for nothing —Rudyard Kipling⟩ DOMINEERING suggests attempts, successful or not, or desires, fulfilled or not, to subdue others by insolent or tyrannical behavior ⟨the European nations, arrogant, *domineering*, and rapacious, have done little to recommend the name of Christianity in Asia and Africa —W.R.Inge⟩ ⟨Gourlay had to pay for his years of insolence and tyranny; all who had irked beneath his *domineering* ways got their carrying done by Wilson —G.D.Brown⟩ IMPERIOUS suggests assumption with lordly arrogance and autocratic impatience at opposition of command and domination over others ⟨he had to go. There was something final about her *imperious* courtesy — high-and-mighty, he called it —Willa Cather⟩ ⟨a second Coriolanus, a proud, *imperious* aristocrat, contemptuous, above all men living, of popular rights —J.A.Froude⟩ PEREMPTORY suggests dictatorial curtness in insisting on instant compliance with commands or wishes and impatience at delay or demur ⟨the *peremptory* tone in which money was demanded for the cost of this fruitless march, while the petitions of the Parliament were set aside till it was granted, roused the temper of the Commons —J.R.Green⟩ ⟨"I decline to listen to another word. I've heard enough." The bishop accompanied the mandate by a *peremptory* gesture with the palm of the hand —Robert Grant †1940⟩ IMPERATIVE may be a close synonym for PEREMPTORY; it may be used in reference to urgent situations calling for firm briskness ⟨"An envelope and telegram form, quick!" Overwhelmed by my *imperative* manner, he handed me the required articles —Allen Upward⟩ ⟨he heard her *imperative* voice at the telephone; he heard her summon the doctor —Ellen Glasgow⟩

mas·ter·ful·ly \-fəlē, -li\ *adv* [ME *maisterfully*, fr. *maisterful* masterful + *-ly*] **:** in a masterful manner

mas·ter·ful·ness *n* -ES **:** the quality or state of being masterful

master gage *n* **:** a very accurate gage used only as a standard of reference for working gages

master gland *n* [so called fr. the fact that it produces hormones that modify and integrate the activity of other endocrine organs] **:** PITUITARY GLAND

master gunner *n* **:** a warrant officer in the British artillery

master gunnery sergeant *n* **:** a sergeant major in the marine corps

master-hand \ˈ=ˈ=\ *n* **1 :** the hand, ability, or agency of a master ⟨the touch of the *master-hand* . . . was conspicuously absent from the picture —Herschel Brickell⟩ **2 :** MASTER ⟨a *master-hand* at . . . fictionalized biography —*Saturday Rev.*⟩

mas·ter·hood \ˈ==,hu̇d\ *n* [ME *maystyrhod*, fr. *maystyr*, *maister* master + *-hod* -hood] **:** the quality or state of being a master

master in chancery 1 : an officer of a court of equity appointed to assist the court (as by finding the facts in a contested case or by executing a conveyance or transfer of property owned by a defendant who has refused to convey or transfer under the decree of the court) **2 :** a public officer in Massachusetts appointed by the governor with the consent of the council to take recognizances and bail

mastering *pres part of* MASTER

master key *n* **1 :** a key made so that it will open several locks differing somewhat from each other **2 :** something of decisive or key importance in the solution of a difficulty, problem, or dispute ⟨one of the *master keys* to the outcome of the . . . struggle —*Current History*⟩ ⟨the *master key* that explained the many mysteries of recent history —Oscar Handlin⟩

master-key \ˈ==,=\ *vt* [*master key*] **:** to design or fit (a series of locks) for a master key

master leaf *n* **:** BACK 2i

mas·ter·less \ˈ==ləs\ *adj* [ME *maisterles*, fr. *maister* master + *-les* -less] **1 a :** lacking a master ⟨a ~ horse⟩ **b** *archaic* **:** being without a master or other reputable means of livelihood **:** VAGABOND, VAGRANT ⟨provided harsh punishments for sturdy vagabonds and ~ men⟩ **2** *obs* **:** UNGOVERNED, UNGOVERNABLE — **mas·ter·less·ness** *n* -ES

masterlike *adj* [ME *maisterlike*, fr. *maister* master + *like*] *obs* **:** MASTERFUL, MASTERLY

mas·ter·li·ness \ˈmastə(r)lēnəs, -aas-, -ais-, -ȧs-, -lin-\ *n* -ES **:** the quality or state of being masterly

[1]**mas·ter·ly** \-lē, -li\ *adv* [ME *maisterly*, fr. *maister* master + *-ly*] **:** with the skill of a master **:** in a masterly fashion

[2]**masterly** \"\ *adj* [[1]*master* + *-ly*] **1** *obs* **:** of or relating to a master or lord; *specif* **:** DOMINEERING **2 :** suitable to or like that of a master **:** indicating thorough knowledge or superior skill and power ⟨a ~ retreat⟩ ⟨a ~ argument⟩ ⟨~ handling of a complex topic⟩ **syn** see PROFICIENT

mas·ter·man \ˈ==mən\ *n, pl* **mastermen** *dial Eng* **:** the head of a household **:** HUSBAND

master map *n* **:** an original usu. large-scale map which is made directly from surveys and from which other maps are derived

master mariner *n* [ME *maister mariner*, fr. *maister* master + *mariner, marinere* mariner] **1 :** a captain of a merchant ship **2 :** an experienced and skilled seaman certified to be competent to command a merchant ship

master mason *n* **1 :** a mason thoroughly competent in his trade and usu. in business on his own account **2** *usu cap both Ms* **a :** the third degree of Freemasonry — compare BLUE LODGE **b :** a Freemason who has been raised to the third degree

master matrix *n* **:** a matrix obtained by electroplating an original lacquer or wax recording of sound

master mechanic *n* **1 :** a foreman mechanic **2 :** a mechanic who is a thorough master of his trade

[1]**mastermind** \ˈ==ˌ=\ *n* [[3]*master* + *mind*] **1 :** a mind or person of masterly powers **:** a towering intellect ⟨the ~ of the thirteenth century —Agnes Repplier⟩ **2 :** a person who supplies the directing or creative intelligence for a project or for a group of persons undertaking a project ⟨~ of the world's first commercial jet airliner —*Newsweek*⟩

[2]**mastermind** \ˈ==,=\ *vt* **:** to be the mastermind in or of **:** DIRECT, SUPERVISE, ENGINEER ⟨~*ed* . . . crimes such as warehouse burglaries —Alan Hynd⟩ ⟨~*ing* an insidious campaign to gain dominance over the world —L.M.Clucas⟩

master of arts *usu cap M&A* **1 :** the recipient of a master's degree that usu. signifies that the recipient has passed a certain number of courses in the Judicial Committee — in the humanities — abbr. *M.A., A.M.* **2 :** the degree making one a Master of Arts — abbr. *M.A., A.M.*

master of ceremonies : a person who determines the forms to be observed on a public occasion or superintends their observance: as **a :** a court official of high rank in charge of the reception of ambassadors and other matters of protocol **b :** an official at solemn services of the Roman Catholic Church charged with the duty of seeing that all the rites are correctly executed **c :** a person who acts as host at a formal event (as a banquet or graduation exercise) making the welcoming speech, introducing speakers, and being generally responsible for the conduct of the program **d :** a person who acts as a host for a variety program or other stage entertainment introducing other performers to the audience and usu. interspersing his introductions with jokes, songs, or other specialty acts

master of request *or* **master of requests :** a principal officer in the court of requests

master of science *usu cap M&S* **1 :** the recipient of a master's degree that usu. signifies that the recipient has passed a certain number of courses in one of the sciences or in closely related sciences — abbr. *M.S., M.Sc.* **2 :** the degree making one a Master of Science — abbr. *M.S., M.Sc.*

master of the revels 1 : an officer of the English royal household from the 15th to the 18th centuries in charge of court entertainment — see REVELS OFFICE **2 :** an officer in charge of court entertainment at a monarchical household

master of the rolls [ME *Maister of the Rolles*] **:** a high official of the British judiciary having custody of the records of the Court of Chancery and important patents and grants and serving usu. as presiding judge of the Court of Appeal and also as a member of the Judicial Committee of the Privy Council — compare LORD CHANCELLOR, LORD CHIEF JUSTICE OF ENGLAND

master oscillator *n* **:** a low-power generator of alternating current that is usu. an electron-tube apparatus the output of which is fed into an amplifier

masterpiece \ˈ==,=\ *n* [prob. trans. of D *meesterstuk* or G *meisterstück*] **1 :** a piece of work attesting to a craftsman's professional skill and presented to his guild to qualify for admission to the rank of master ⟨a ~ was nothing more than a graduation piece —Virgil Thomson⟩ **2 a :** something done or made with extraordinary skill or brilliance **:** a supreme achievement ⟨a ~ of organization —O.S.Nock⟩ ⟨delicious onion sandwiches are perhaps her ~ —Jane Nickerson⟩ ⟨a ~ of ecclesiastical statesmanship —T.S.Eliot⟩ **b :** a work of art of notable excellence or brilliance **:** a supreme intellectual or artistic achievement ⟨the world's symphonic ~*s*⟩ ⟨the ~*s* of Elizabethan drama⟩ ⟨the artist may have many ~*s* —*Encyc. Americana*⟩; *specif* **:** an artist's most accomplished or climactic work marking the high point of his creativity ⟨this delay in printing what was to prove his ~ —H.S.Canby⟩ ⟨his ~ . . . scarcely fulfills one of the conditions set forth in handbooks of rhetoric —*English Jour.*⟩ **3 :** something that is a consummate example of or embodies in superlative degree some quality or trait ⟨~*s* of inept versification —*Amer. Guide Series: Mich.*⟩ ⟨his ~ of bad writing —Edmund Wilson⟩ ⟨a ~ of fence-sitting —*Amer. Guide Series: N.C.*⟩

master plan *n* **:** an overall plan into which the details of other specific plans are fitted **:** a plan giving overall guidance; *specif* **:** a graphic or verbal scheme for the development of a city, town, or other building project of an evolutionary nature

masterplate \ˈ==,=\ *n* **:** a plate (as of metal) containing stencil letters or a design to be copied by tracing

master point *n* **:** a point that is permanently credited to a bridge player for winning or placing high in a tournament, the accumulation of such points forming a basis for national ranking — compare LIFE MASTER

master policy *n* **:** a blanket insurance policy issued to an employer providing group coverage for employees — see GROUP 1

masterprize *n, obs* **:** MASTERPIECE

master-ring \ˈ==,=\ *n* **:** a cylindrical ring surrounding the plug in a master-keyed lock

masters *pl of* MASTER, *pres 3d sing of* MASTER

master's deed *n* **:** a deed of conveyance executed by a master in chancery in pursuance of an order of the court commanding one of the parties to make the conveyance or the master to do it in his name

master sergeant *n* **:** a noncommissioned officer rating in the army just below a command sergeant major and above a platoon sergeant, in the air force just below a senior master sergeant and above a technical sergeant, and in the marine corps just below a sergeant major and above a gunnery sergeant

mas·ter·ship \ˈ==,ship\ *n* [ME *maistershipe*, fr. *maister* master + *-shipe* -ship] **1 :** the authority or control of a master **:** DOMINION, SUPERIORITY ⟨sent forth the warning of his ~ —William Beebe⟩ **2 a** *obs* **:** the personality of a master — used as a title of courtesy **b :** the status, office, function, or dignity of a master ⟨the competitive examination which grants the rights to a ~ —*Current Biog.*⟩ **3 :** the skill, dexterity, or knowledge of a master **:** MASTERY ⟨with authority, eloquence, and ~ —Irving Kolodin⟩

mastersinger \ˈ==,==\ *n* [trans. of G *meistersinger*] **:** MEISTERSINGER

master-slave manipulator \ˈ==ˈ=-\ *n* **:** a manipulator for very accurate remote control of duplicated operations used esp. in handling materials in nuclear laboratories

master station *n* **:** the transmitting station in a group of synchronized transmitters in an electronic communication system (as in radio navigation) that controls the emission of all the stations — compare SLAVE STATION

masterstroke \ˈ==ˌ=\ *n* **:** a masterly action or achievement **:** brilliant performance or move ⟨by a ~, precisely timed, he helped to create the Republican party —W.O.Lynch⟩ ⟨a ~ of craftsmanship —F.J.Hynes⟩

master switch *n* **:** a switch that controls the action of relays or that makes and breaks the main supply line to a building or other installation

master-tailor \ˈ==ˌ==\ *n* **:** a salt marsh fiddler crab (*Uca princeps*) common along the coast of western Central and So. America

master tap *n* **:** a tap designed to cut dies from which other screws can be threaded

masterwork \ˈ==,=\ *n* **:** MASTERPIECE

masterwort \ˈ==,=\ *n* **:** any of several herbaceous plants (family Umbelliferae) used esp. formerly in medicine: **a :** a coarse European plant (*Imperatoria ostruthium*) with large ternate leaves **b :** a European herb (*Astrantia major*) that has dark-colored aromatic roots and leaves mostly in a basal tuft and is sometimes cultivated for its showy compound umbels of white to rosy flowers **c :** COW PARSNIP **d :** ANGELICA 2

mas·tery \ˈmast(ə)rē, -aas-, -ais-, -ȧs-, -ri\ *n* -ES [ME *maistrie*, fr. OF, fr. *maistre* master + *-ie* -y — more at MASTER] **1 a :** the status, position, or authority of a master **:** CONTROL, DOMINION, SWAY ⟨a sense of ~ and power —B.N.Cardozo⟩ ⟨obtained absolute ~ of the government —J.H.Plumb⟩ ⟨little could be done to undermine that ~ —P.G.Mackesy⟩ **b :** the upper hand in a contest or competition **:** SUPERIORITY, ASCENDANCY ⟨a violent spirit in him was struggling for the ~ —Gilbert Parker⟩ **c** *archaic* **:** superior force or power **2 a** *obs* **:** a notable achievement or feat **b :** the possession or a display of skill or technique **:** freedom from flaws or imperfections ⟨cannot attain to the ~ of the great artists —Matthew Arnold⟩ ⟨greater intellectual and stylistic ~ than ever before —A.L.Locke⟩ ⟨uses . . . with absolute ~, the rhythms of actual speech —Randall Jarrell⟩ **c :** the skill or knowledge in a subject that makes one a master in it **:** COMMAND ⟨~ . . . over the difficult art —Benjamin Farrington⟩ ⟨~ of managerial techniques —W.H.Whyte⟩ ⟨a high degree of ~ in the field —*Bull. of Meharry Med. Coll.*⟩

mast-fed \(ˈ)=ˌ=\ *adj* [[3]*mast*] **:** fed with mast

[1]**masthead** \ˈ=,=\ *n* [[1]*mast*] **1 a :** the top or head of a mast **:** the part of a mast above the hounds **b :** a sailor stationed at the masthead **2 a :** a block of matter usu. printed in the top lefthand corner of the editorial page of a newspaper or beside or near the table of contents of a periodical and consisting of the title of the publication and its address, the date of the issue, and sometimes the names of owners and editors and the subscription and advertising rates **b :** the nameplate of a newspaper or periodical

[2]**masthead** \"\ *vt* **1 :** to cause to go to or stand at the masthead as a punishment **2 :** to hoist (as a yard or flag) to the masthead

masthead bombing *n* **:** extremely low-level bombing of ships usu. with delayed-fuse bombs that explode below the waterline

mast hoop *n* **:** one of a number of hoops attached to the fore edge of a gaff sail which slip on the mast; *also* **:** one of the iron hoops used in making a made mast

mast hounds *n pl* [[1]*mast*] **:** HOUNDS

mast house *n* **:** a small deckhouse built around a mast to serve as a support for derricks or sometimes as a winch platform and used for housing electric control equipment where electric winches are fitted

-mas·tia \ˌmastēə, ˌmaas-\ *n comb form* -s [NL, fr. Gk *mastos* breast + NL *-ia* — more at MEAT] **:** condition of having (such or so many) breasts or mammary glands ⟨gyneco*mastia*⟩ ⟨tetra*mastia*⟩

mas·tic \ˈmastik, -aas-, -tēk\ *n* -s [ME *mastik*, fr. L *mastiche*, fr. Gk *mastichē*; fr. its use as chewing gum; akin to Gk *mastichan* to gnash the teeth] **1** *also* **mas·tich** \"\ *or* **mas·ti·che** \-tə,kē\ **:** an aromatic resinous exudation obtained usu. in the form of yellowish to greenish lustrous transparent brittle tears from incisions in mastic trees and used chiefly in varnishes (as for protecting oil paintings and water colors) **2 :** MASTIC TREE **3 :** any of various pasty materials used as protective coatings (as for thermal insulation or waterproofing) or as cements (as for setting tile or glass): as **a :** ASPHALT MASTIC **b :** a composition of mineral matter bound by a resinous medium in a volatile solvent **4 :** an alcoholic liquor flavored with resin mastic and aniseed **5 :** a light olive brown that is lighter, stronger, and slightly redder than drab or sponge and redder and paler than average mustard tan

mas·ti·cate \ˈmastə,kāt, -aas-, -ais-, *usu* -ād·+V\ *vb* -ED/-ING/-S [LL *masticatus*, past part. of *masticare*, fr. Gk *mastichan* to gnash the teeth; akin to Gk *masasthai* to chew — more at MOUTH] *vt* **1 :** to grind or crush (as food) with or as if with the teeth and prepare for swallowing and digestion **:** CHEW **2 a :** to reduce to pulp by crushing or kneading **b :** to work (rubber) on a machine so as to make it softer and more plastic before mixing with compounding ingredients **:** break down ~ *vi* **:** to make the motions involved in masticating food **:** CHEW

mas·ti·ca·tion \ˌ==ˈkāshən\ *n* -s [LL *mastication-, masticatio*, fr. *masticatus* + L *-ion-, -io* -ion] **:** the act or process of masticating or the state of being masticated

mas·ti·ca·tor \ˈ==,kād·ə(r)\ *n* -s [*masticate* + *-or*] **:** one that masticates: as **a :** a machine for chopping materials (as meat or rubber) into fine bits **b :** an operator of such a machine

[1]**mas·ti·ca·to·ry** \ˈ==kə,tōrē, -tȯr-, -ri, *chiefly Brit* ˌ==ˈkātəri *or* -ā·tri\ *adj* [*masticate* + *-ory*] **1 :** used for chewing **:** adapted to mastication ⟨~ limbs of an arthropod⟩ **2 :** of, relating to, or involving the organs of mastication ⟨~ paralysis⟩

[2]**masticatory** \"\ *n* -ES **:** a substance to be chewed to increase the saliva

mastic bully *n* **:** a tree (*Sideroxylon mastichodendron*) of Florida and the West Indies having hard wood used for shipbuilding

mastic gum *n* **:** MASTIC 1

mas·tic·ic \(ˈ)maˈstisik\ *adj* **:** of or relating to mastic

mas·tic·o·phis \maˈstikəfəs, ˌmastəˈkōf-\ *n, cap* [NL, fr. *mastic-* (irreg. fr. Gk *mastig-, mastix* whip) + *-ophis*] **:** a common genus of harmless New World snakes (family Colubridae) comprising the whip snakes and related forms

mastic tree *or* **mastic shrub** *n* **1 :** a small tree (*Pistacia lentiscus*) of southern Europe that yields mastic and has leaves that are used as an adulterant of sumac **2 :** GUMBO-LIMBO 1

mas·ti·cu·ra \ˌmastəˈkyu̇rə\ *n pl, cap* [NL, fr. *mastic-* (irreg. fr. Gk *mastig-, mastix* whip) + *-ura*] *in some classifications* **:** a division (usu. a suborder) of rays including the stingrays and having the tail long and like a whip — compare SARCURA — **mas·ti·cu·rous** \ˌ==ˈkyu̇rəs\ *adj*

mas·tiff \ˈmastəf, -aas-, -ais-, *sometimes* -ȧs-\ *n* -s [ME *mastif*, modif. (influenced by ME *-if* -ive) of MF *mastin*, fr. (assumed) VL *mansuetinus*, fr. L *mansuetus* tame — more at MANSUETE] **:** a very large powerful deep-chested smooth-coated dog of a very old breed used chiefly as a watchdog and guard dog

mastiff

mastiff bat *n* **1 :** a member of a nearly cosmopolitan family of bats (Molossidae) having fur like plush, narrow wings, and short ridged ears with angular tips **2 :** HARELIPPED BAT

mastig- *or* **mastigo-** *comb form* [Gk, whip, scourge, fr. *mastig-, mastix;* perh. akin to Gk *mēnyein* to make known, inform, Russ *manit'* to beckon, entice] **:** whip **:** flagellum ⟨*Mastigophora*⟩ ⟨*Mastigamoeba*⟩

mas·tig·amoeba \ˌmastəg+\ *n, cap* [NL, fr. *mastig-* + *amoeba*] **:** the type genus of the family Mastigamoebidae

mas·tig·amoe·bi·dae *n pl, cap* \ˌmastə̇gəˈmēbəˌdē\ [NL, fr. *Mastigamoeba,* type genus + *-idae*] **:** a family of amoeboid zooflagellates that have both pseudopods and a flagellum — see HISTOMONAS

mas·tig·i·um \maˈstijēəm\ *n, pl* **mastig·ia** \-jēə\ [NL, fr. Gk *mastigion* small whip, dim. of *mastig-, mastix*] **:** a defensive organ resembling a lash on the posterior parts of certain lepidopterous larvae

mas·ti·go·bran·chia \ˌmastə̇gōˈbraŋkēə\ *n, pl* **mastigo·branchi·ae** \-kēˌē\ [NL, fr. *mastig-* + *-branchia* (gill)] **:** a process of the thoracic limbs of decapod crustaceans resembling a brush and used for cleaning the gills — **mas·ti·go·bran·chi·al** \¦==¦braŋkēəl\ *adj*

mas·ti·go·neme \ˈ===ˌnēm\ *n* -S [F *mastigonème,* fr. *mastig-* + *-nème* (fr. Gk *nēma* thread) — more at NEEDLE] **:** FLIMMER

mas·ti·goph·o·ra \ˌ==ˈgäf(ə)rə\ *n pl, cap* [NL, fr. *mastig-* + *-phora*] **:** a class of Protozoa comprising organisms characterized by possession of flagella and including the subclasses Phytomastigina and Zoomastigina — **mas·ti·goph·o·rous** \¦==¦gäf(ə)rəs\ *adj*

[1]**mas·ti·goph·o·ran** \¦==¦gäf(ə)rən\ *adj* [NL *Mastigophora* + E *-an,* adj. suffix] **:** of or relating to the Mastigophora

[2]**mastigophoran** \"\ *n* -S [NL *Mastigophora* + E *-an,* n. suffix] **:** a flagellate of the class Mastigophora

mas·ti·go·phor·ic \¦==gō¦fórik\ *adj* [NL *Mastigophora* + E *-ic*] **:** bearing a flagellum

mas·ti·go·proc·tus \ˌ===ˈpräktəs\ *n, cap* [NL, fr. *mastig-* + *-proctus*] **:** a genus containing the giant whip scorpion

mas·tig·o·pus \maˈstigəpəs\ *n* -ES [NL, fr. *mastig-* + *-pus*] **:** a final larva of some shrimps and prawns that is very like the adult in form

mas·tigo·some \maˈstigəˌsōm, ˈmastəgō-\ *n* -S [*mastig-* + *-some*] **:** BASAL GRANULE

mas·ti·gote \ˈmastə̇ˌgōt\ *adj* [irreg. fr. *mastig-*] **:** having a flagellum

mas·ti·gure \ˈ==ˌgyü(ə)r\ *n* -S [NL *Mastigura* (syn. of *Uromastix*), fr. *mastig-* + *-ura*] **:** any of the large spiny-tailed herbivorous agamid lizards (genus *Uromastix*) of southern Asia and northern Africa

mas·ti·ka \ˈmastə̇kə\ *n* -S [prob. fr. Turk, lit., mastic (sense 1), fr. Gk *mastichē* — more at MASTIC] **:** MASTIC 4

masting *n* -S **:** the masts of a ship

mas·tit·ic \(ˈ)maˈstid·ik\ *adj* [*mastitis* + *-ic*] **:** of, relating to, or associated with mastitis ⟨~ milk⟩

mas·ti·tis \maˈstīdə̇s\ *n, pl* **mastit·i·des** \-ˈstid·əˌdēz\ [NL, fr. *mast-* + *-itis*] **:** inflammation of the breast or udder usu. caused by infection — see BLUE BAG, GARGET, SUMMER MASTITIS; compare BOVINE MASTITIS, CAKED BREAST

-mas·tix \ˈmastiks\ *n comb form* [Gk *mastig-, mastix* whip, scourge] **1** -ES **:** attacker of a (specified) person or thing ⟨Latino*mastix*⟩ **2** [NL, fr. Gk *mastig-, mastix*] **a :** one having (such) a whip — in generic names in zoology ⟨Uro*mastix*⟩ **b :** one having (such) a flagellum or (such or so many) flagella — in generic names in zoology ⟨Chilo*mastix*⟩

mast·less \ˈmastlə̇s, -aas-, -ais-, -ás-\ *adj* [[1]*mast*] **:** having no mast ⟨a ~ ship⟩

masto- — see MAST-

mas·to·cyte \ˈmastəˌsīt\ *n* -S [*masto-* (fr. G *mast* food, mast, fr. OHG) + *-cyte;* intended as trans. of G *mastzelle* mast cell — more at MAST (nuts)] **:** MAST CELL

[1]**mas·to·don** \ˈmastəˌdän, ˈmaas-, -ˌdən\ *n* -S [NL *Mastodont-, Mastodon* (syn. of *Mammut*), fr. *mast-* + *-odont-, -odon* -odon; fr. the nipple-shaped projections on the molar teeth] **1 :** any of numerous extinct mammals esp. of the genus *Mammut* that greatly resemble elephants, differ from the mammoths and existing elephants chiefly in the form of the molar teeth, have sometimes small tusks in the lower jaw besides those in the upper jaw, and are widely distributed in Oligocene to late Pleistocene formations **2 :** someone or something of gigantic size or unusually large size **:** GIANT ⟨military vehicles from little jeeps to six-wheel armored ~*s* —Gelett Burgess⟩ ⟨the ~*s* in the ring sweated their way into the next match —J.K. Hutchins⟩ — **mas·to·don·ic** \¦==¦dänik\ *adj*

[2]**mastodon** \"\ [NL *Mastodont-, Mastodon*] *syn of* MAMMUT

[3]**mastodon** \"\ *adj* [[1]*mastodon*] **:** MAMMOTH ⟨this is the time of the ~ movie —*Newsweek*⟩

mas·to·don·sau·rus \ˌ==ˌdänˈsórəs\ *n, cap* [NL, fr. *Mastodon* + *-saurus*] **:** a genus of Old World Triassic amphibians containing the largest known labyrinthodonts with the skull over four feet long and having at the front of the lower jaw a pair of short tusks that close into openings piercing the premaxillae

[1]**mas·to·dont** \ˈ==ˌdänt\ *adj* [NL *Mastodont-, Mastodon*] **1 :** having or being teeth like a mastodon's **2 :** of or relating to the mastodons

[2]**mastodont** \"\ *n* -S [NL *Mastodont-, Mastodon*] **:** MASTODON — **mas·to·don·tic** \¦==¦däntik\ *adj*

mas·to·don·ti·dae \ˌ==ˈdäntəˌdē\ [NL, fr. *Mastodont-, Mastodon* + *-idae*] *syn of* MAMMUTIDAE — see MAMMUT

mas·to·don·toid \¦==¦dänˌtóid\ *adj* [NL *Mastodont-, Mastodon* + E *-oid*] **:** like a mastodon

mas·to·dyn·ia \ˌ==ˈdinēə\ *n* -S [NL, fr. *mast-* + *-odynia*] **:** pain in the breast

[1]**mas·toid** \ˈmaˌstóid, ˈmaa-,\ *adj* [NL *mastoides,* fr. Gk *mastoeidēs,* fr. *mastos* breast + *-oeidēs* -oid — more at MEAT] **1 a :** resembling a nipple or breast; *specif* **:** being a process of the temporal bone behind the ear, well developed and of somewhat conical form in adult man but inconspicuous in children **b :** being any of several bony elements (as the pterotic bone) occupying a similar position in the skull of various lower vertebrates **2 :** of, relating to, in the region of, or affecting the mastoid process

[2]**mastoid** \"\ *n* -S **1 :** a mastoid bone or process **2 a :** MASTOIDITIS ⟨recovering from a severe ~⟩ — not used technically **b :** an operation for the relief of mastoiditis

mas·toi·dal \(ˈ)=¦stóidᵊl\ *also* **mas·toi·de·al** \-dēəl\ *or* **mas·toi·de·an** \-dēən\ *adj* [*mastoidal* fr. [2]*mastoid* + *-al; mastoideal, mastoidean* fr. NL *mastoideus,* adj., mastoid (fr. *mastoides* + L *-eus* -eous) + E *-al* or *-an*] **:** MASTOID

mas·toi·da·le \ˌmaˌstóiˈda(ˌ)lē, -dā-, -dä-\ *n* -S [NL, fr. *mastoides* + *-ale* (fr. L, neut. of *-alis* -al)] **:** the lowest point of the mastoid process — see CRANIOMETRY illustration

mastoid antrum *n* **:** TYMPANIC ANTRUM

mastoid cell *n* **:** one of the small cavities in the mastoid process that develop after birth and are filled with air

mas·toid·ec·to·my \ˌ=ˌstóiˈdektəmē, -mi\ *n* -ES [ISV [1]*mastoid* + *-ectomy*] **:** surgical removal of the mastoid cells or of the mastoid process

mas·toi·deo·squamous \maˈstóidēō+\ *adj* [*mastoideo-* (fr. NL *mastoideus*) + *squamous*] **:** relating to the mastoid and squamous portions of the temporal bone

mas·toid·i·tis \ˌmaˌstóiˈdīdə̇s, ˌmaa-,-\ *n, pl* **mas·toid·it·i·des** \-ˈdid·əˌdēz\ [NL, fr. *mastoides* + *-itis*] **:** inflammation of the mastoid or esp. of the mastoid cells

mas·to·do·hu·mer·a·lis \maˈstóidō,hyüməˈralə̇s, -räl-, -ral-\ *n* -ES [NL, fr. *mastoido-* (fr. *mastoides*) + *humeralis* humeral, fr. *humerus* + L *-alis* -al] **:** a long superficial muscle connecting the mastoid process and humerus in many quadruped mammals

mas·toid·ot·o·my \ˌmaˌstóiˈdädəmē, ˌmaa-,-\ *n* -ES [ISV [1]*mastoid* + *-o-* + *-tomy*] **:** incision of any part of the mastoid

mas·to·mys \ˈmastəˌmis\ *n* [NL, fr. *mast-* + *-mys*] **1** *cap, in some classifications* **:** a genus of rodents comprising the multimammate mice **2** *pl* **mastomys :** MULTIMAMMATE MOUSE

mas·to·tympanic \¦ma(ˌ)stō+\ *adj* [*mast-* + *tympanic*] **:** of, relating to, or being a bony element bounding the tympanic cavity in the skull of certain reptiles

mast partner *n* **:** wood planking or steel plating around a mast hole in a deck to give support to a mast

mast step *n* **:** a wood or steel foundation on which a mast rests

mast table *n* **:** a small compartment or locker built on the main deck around the base of one of the masts

mast tree *n* [[3]*mast*] **1 :** a tree that produces mast; *specif* **:** CORK OAK **2 :** an East Indian shade tree (*Polyalthia longifolia*) of the family Annonaceae

mas·tur·bate \ˈmastə(r)ˌbāt, usu -ād·+V\ *vb* -ED/-ING/-S [L *masturbatus,* past part. of *masturbari,* perh. fr. *manus* hand + *stuprare* to defile, deflower, fr. *stuprum* defilement, dishonor — more at MANUAL, TYPE] *vi* **:** to practice masturbation ~ *vt* **:** to practice masturbation on — **masturbat·or** \-ə(r)\ *n* -S

mas·tur·bat·ic \¦==¦bad·ik\ *adj* **:** involving masturbation

mas·tur·ba·tion \ˌ==ˈbāshən\ *n* -S [prob. fr. (assumed) NL *masturbation-, masturbatio,* fr. L *masturbatus* + *-ion-, -io -ion*] **:** erotic stimulation involving the genital organs commonly resulting in orgasm and achieved by manual or other bodily contact exclusive of sexual intercourse, by instrumental manipulation, occas. by sexual fantasies, or by various combinations of these agencies — **mas·tur·ba·tion·al** \¦==¦bāshənᵊl, -shnəl\ *adj*

mas·tur·ba·to·ry \ˈ==bəˌtōrē, -tór-, -ri\ *adj* **:** of, relating to, or involving masturbation

mastwood \ˈ=ˌ=\ *n* [[1]*mast*] **:** a poon tree (*Calophyllum inophyllum*) — called also *kamani*

[1]**masty** *adj* [ME, fattened on mast, fr. [3]*mast* + *-y*] *obs* **:** abounding in or fattened on mast

[2]**mas·ty** \ˈmastī\ *n* -ES [ME, modif. of MF *mastin* — more at MASTIFF] *now dial Eng* **:** MASTIFF

ma·sur birch \ˈmäzə(r)-, ˈmä¦ˈ\ *n* [part trans. of Sw *masurbjörk,* fr. *masur* veined wood + *björk* birch; akin to OHG *masar* gnarled excrescence on a tree — more at MAZER] **:** birch with a mottled figure cut from knotty trunks and used esp. for veneers

ma·su·ri·an \məˈzu̇rēən, -ˈsu̇-\ *n* -S *usu cap* [*Masuria,* region in Olsztyn department, northern Poland + E *-an*] **:** MAZURIAN

ma·su·ri·um \məˈzu̇rēəm, -ˈsu̇-\ *n* -S [NL, fr. *Masuria,* region in Olsztyn department, northern Poland + NL *-ium*] **:** chemical element 43 — a name now superseded by *technetium*

masut *var of* MAZUT

[1]**mat** \ˈmat, *usu* -ad·+V\ *n* -S [ME, fr. OE *matt, matte, meatte,* fr. LL *matta,* of Sem origin; akin to Heb *miṭṭāh* bed, couch] **1 :** a flat relatively thin article of usu. pliant typically coarse material and rectangular, oval, or other shape that is set or laid esp. on a horizontal surface as a protection or a support or cushion, or as a decorative feature, or marker: as **a** (1) **:** a piece of coarse fabric that is typically made by weaving or plaiting straw, hemp, rope, rushes, or other similar material, and is used as a floor covering or as an article on which to sit or lie or stand (2) **:** a piece of material that is typically made of meshed metal strips or twisted wire or of corrugated or perforated rubber so as to present a roughly ridged or furrowed surface and is placed at the entrance to a building for cleaning the bottoms of one's shoes **b :** a relatively small piece of woven, knitted, or felted cloth or of leather or finely woven or plaited straw or similar material made to have an ornamental appearance and used as a decorative and protective support (as for dishes and utensils on a table set for a meal) **c :** a piece of rubber or other material on which a lawn bowler places one foot when bowling a ball **d :** a large usu. rectangular pad or cushion several inches thick that is made of sponge rubber, kapok, felt, or other similar material typically covered with canvas or plastic and is laid out over an area of a floor (as in a gymnasium) so as to protect wrestlers, tumblers, or others engaged in gymnastic activities from injuring themselves through concussions (as from falls) **2** *obs* **:** material used in making mats **:** MATTING **3 a :** a webbing of rope yarn used to protect rigging from chafing **b :** MATTRESS 2b **c :** a mesh of heavy chain, cables, or rope used to confine debris in blasting **d :** a large slab made usu. of reinforced concrete and laid on soft ground to support a heavy building **4 a :** a sack used for packing coffee or sugar **b :** the solid part of a lace design **5 :** something made up of many strands thickly intertwined or knotted so as to form a tangled often impenetrable mass ⟨a ~ of unkempt hair⟩ ⟨a ~ of rank jungle undergrowth⟩; *specif* **:** a thick interlacing growth of vegetation either free on the surface of or overlying the margin of a body of water — **go to the mat :** to engage in a hotly fought usu. verbal and ideological struggle ⟨*go to the mat* with those whose arguments do not seem to me to be sound or fair —*Christian Century*⟩ — **on the mat** *adv* (*or adj*) **:** on the carpet ⟨summoned to Washington and put *on the mat* —*Economist*⟩

[2]**mat** \"\ *vb* **matted; matted; matting; mats** *vt* **1 :** to provide or cover with or as if with a mat or matting: as **a :** to provide with a floor mat or similar mat ⟨the room had been well *matted*⟩ ⟨*matted* the cottage floors⟩ **b** (1) **:** to cover over with the typically coarse material used in making mats ⟨*matting* chair bottoms⟩ (2) **:** to protect (as plants) by covering up with a warm coarse material — usu. used with *up* ⟨*matted* up the bushes before the cold snap began⟩ **c :** to cover over with a tangled often impenetrable mass made up of many thickly intertwined or knotted strands ⟨the old trail had become *matted* with undergrowth⟩ ⟨ivy *matted* the walls of the ancient temple⟩ **2 a** (1) **:** to cause to be thickly intertwined or knotted so as to form a tangled often impenetrable mass ⟨the boughs of the trees were *matted* together⟩ ⟨dirt and filth *matted* their hair⟩ (2) **:** to pack down or together so as to form a dense often impenetrable mass — usu. used with *down* ⟨constant tramping over the area had *matted* down the grass⟩ **b :** to cause (soft particles) to come together and adhere so as to form a soft semisolid mass ⟨*matting* curd particles in the making of cheese⟩ **3 :** to make into a floor mat or similar mat by weaving, plaiting or other interlacing ⟨native women *matting* straw⟩ ~ *vi* **1 a :** to become thickly intertwined or knotted so as to form a tangled often impenetrable mass ⟨untended weeds will eventually ~ together⟩ **b :** to become packed down or together so as to form a dense often impenetrable mass — usu. used with *down* ⟨corduroy pile has a tendency to ~ down in areas subjected to pressure or abrasion —Dorothy S. Lyle⟩ **2 :** to come together and adhere so as to form a soft semisolid mass ⟨piling curd at the side of a cheese-making vat and allowing it to ~⟩

[3]**mat** *or* **matte** \"\ *vt* **matted; matted; matting; mats** *or* **matts** *or* **mattes** [F *mater,* fr. OF, to defeat, overcome, fr. (assumed) VL *mattare,* fr. L *mattus* stupid, drunk] **1 :** to cause (as metals, glass, colors) to have a surface or finish or a general appearance that is without luster or gloss **:** give a dulled effect to **2** [[5]*mat*] **:** to provide (a picture) with a mat

[4]**mat** *or* **matt** *or* **matte** \"\ *adj* [F *mat,* fr. OF, defeated, overcome, fr. L *mattus* stupid, drunk; akin to L *madēre* to be wet — more at MEAT] **1 :** being without or deprived of luster or gloss **:** having a usu. smooth even surface free from shine or highlights ⟨~ metals⟩ ⟨~ colors⟩ ⟨~ glass⟩ ⟨the ~ white face of a circus clown⟩ **2 :** having a coarse rough rugose or granular surface ⟨a bacterium that forms ~ colonies on agar⟩

[5]**mat** *or* **matt** *or* **matte** \"\ *n* -S [F *mat* dull color, unpolished surface, fr. *mat,* adj.] **1 :** a border (as of white or gilt cardboard) that is put around a picture so as to be between the picture and its frame or so as to serve as the sole frame of the picture **2 a** (1) **:** a surface or finish (as on metals, glass, colors) that is without luster or gloss or is otherwise dulled (2) **:** a material or instrument used in producing such a surface or finish **b** *usu* **matte :** an opaque sheet or plate sometimes containing an aperture (as a keyhole) used in a motion-picture camera or printing gate to obscure a selected area of a scene during exposure **3** [by shortening] **:** MATRIX 4a

mat *abbr* **1** material **2** matinee **3** matins **4** maturity

MAT *abbr* **1** mechanical aptitude test **2** military aircraft types

mata *var of* MATTO

mat·a·be·le \ˌmad·əˈbē(ˌ)lē\ *n, pl* **matabele** *or* **matabeles** *usu cap* **:** NDEBELE

ma·ta·can \məˈtäkən\ *also* **ma·ta·co·an** \-kəwən\ *adj, usu cap* [AmerSp *Mataco* + E *-an*] **:** of or relating to the Mataco people or their language

ma·ta·chin *also* **ma·ta·chine** \ˌmäd·əˈchēn, ˌma-, -ˈshēn\ *n* -S *see sense 1b, often attrib* [It *mattaccino,* fr. *matto* madman, fool, fr. *matto* mad, crazy, fr. L *mattus* stupid, drunk] **1 a :** a sword dancer in a fantastic costume — called also *bouffon* **b** *pl* **matachi·ni** \-ē(ˌ)nē\ [MexSp *matachin,* fr. Sp, matachin (sense 1a), fr. It *mattaccino*] **:** a member of a society of Mexican-Indian dancers who perform ritual dances **2 :** a dance performed by a matachin

ma·ta·chi·na \-ˈchēnə, -ˈshē-\ *n, pl* **matachina** *or* **matachinas** [MexSp, fr. Sp *matachin* matachin (sense 1a), fr. It *mattaccino*] **:** MATACHIN 1b

[1]**ma·ta·co** \məˈtä(ˌ)kō\ *n* -S [AmerSp] **:** APAR

[2]**mataco** \"\ *n, pl* **mataco** *or* **matacos** *usu cap* [AmerSp *Mataco*] **1 a :** a people of Bolivia, Paraguay, and Argentina **b :** a member of such people **2 :** the language of the Mataco people

mat·a·dor *also* **mat·a·dore** \ˈmad·əˌdō(ə)r, -ó(ə)r, -ōə, -ó(ə)\ *n* -S [Sp, fr. *matar* to kill, prob. fr. (assumed) VL *mattare* to defeat, overcome — more at MAT] **1 :** a bullfighter who has the principal role in a bullfight and who finally kills the bull with a sword thrust after goading on and tiring the bull with a series of formalized passes with a cape **2 a** (1) **:** a principal trump in some card games (as ombre) (2) **:** a jack of clubs and each other trump held in sequence with it in the game of skat **b** (1) **:** a variation of the game of dominoes in which ends of dominoes matched in play must total seven except for four dominoes that may be played at any time (2) **:** one of the four dominoes that may be played at any time in the game of matador

mat·a·gal·pa \¦mad·ə¦galpə\ *n, pl* **matagalpa** *or* **matagalpas** *usu cap* [AmerSp] **1 a :** a people of Nicaragua, Honduras, and San Salvador **b :** a member of such people **2 :** a language of the Matagalpa people

mat·a·gal·pan \-pən\ *adj, usu cap* [AmerSp *Matagalpa* + E *-an,* adj. suffix] **:** of or relating to the Matagalpa people or their language

mat·a·go·ry \ˌmad·əˈgōrē, -gór-\ *or* **mat·a·gou·ri** \-ˈgu̇rē\ *n, pl* **matagories** *or* **matagouris** [modif. of Maori *tumatakuru*] **:** TUMATAKURU

[1]**ma·tai** \ˈmädˌī\ *n* -S [Maori] **:** a black pine (*Podocarpus spicata*) of New Zealand and Australia

[2]**matai** \"\ *n, pl* **matais** *or* **matai** [Samoan] **:** a Samoan chief bearing a hereditary title who is head of an extended family or of a village

ma·ta·jue·lo \ˌmad·əˈ(h)wā(ˌ)lō\ *n* -S [AmerSp *matejuelo*] **:** a large squirrelfish (*Holocentrus ascensionis*) of Florida and the West Indies

ma·ta·ma·ta \ˌmad·əməˈtä\ *n* -S [Pg *matamatá,* fr. Tupi] **1 :** a pleurodiran turtle (*Chelus fimbriata*) of Guiana and the northern part of Brazil that reaches a length of three feet, has a rough shell and a long neck with fleshy fimbriae on the neck and on the head, and produces eggs that yield an edible oil **2 :** any of several So. American trees of the genus *Eschweilera* of the family Lecythidaceae; *esp* **:** a tree yielding a heavy hard compact wood used for pilings and foundation construction

mat·a·sa·no \ˌmad·əˈsä(ˌ)nō\ *n* -S [AmerSp, fr. Sp *matar* to kill + *sano* healthy person, fr. *sano* healthy, fr. L *sanus* — more at MATADOR, SANE] **:** WHITE SAPOTA

mat·ax \ˈmadˌaks\ *n* -ES [*mattock* + *ax*] **:** a combination ax and mattock

mat bean *n* [*mat* prob. by folk etymology (influence of [1]*mat*) fr. Marathi *math* moth bean — more at MOTH BEAN] **:** MOTH BEAN

mat board *n* [[5]*mat*] **:** paperboard used for mounting (as pictures, specimens)

[1]**match** \ˈmach\ *n* -ES [in sense 1, fr. ME *macche* match, mate, spouse, fr. OE *mæcca, gemæcca* mate, spouse; in other senses, fr. [2]*match;* OE *mæcca, gemæcca* akin to OE *gemaca* companion, mate, spouse, OHG *gimahha* wife, ON *maki* match, mate, OE *macian* to make — more at MAKE] **1 a** (1) **:** one that can as an equal compete with, combat, or otherwise oppose another **:** an individual or group of individuals possessing the same qualities (as strength, courage, intelligence) in the same degree as an opposing individual or group ⟨a wrestler who finally met his ~⟩ ⟨a baseball team that appears to be a ~ for the world champions⟩ **:** one able to cope with another ⟨will be more than a ~ for her⟩ (2) **:** one that equals another in the extent of a shared quality (as of character) ⟨a figure that for heroism has no ~ in history⟩ **b** (1) **:** one that is exactly like another **:** one that forms an exact pair with another **:** an exact counterpart ⟨a lake that was almost the ~ of one he remembered from Switzerland⟩ (2) **:** one that closely resembles or harmonizes (as in appearance) with another ⟨wore a blouse that was a nice ~ for her skirt⟩ **c :** a pair made up of two individuals that are exact counterparts of each other or that closely resemble or harmonize (as in appearance) with each other ⟨a jacket and scarf that are a good ~⟩ **2 a :** a contest or game in which two or more individuals or groups of individuals oppose each other ⟨a golf ~⟩ ⟨a cricket ~⟩ **b :** a race between two horses belonging to different owners run in accordance with terms agreed upon by the owners **3** *obs* **:** AGREEMENT, COMPACT, BARGAIN **4 a** (1) **:** an agreement to enter into marriage (2) **:** a marriage union **b :** a person eligible to enter into marriage and viewed with regard to his or her advantages or disadvantages (as of social position, wealth) as a marriage partner for a prospective mate ⟨would make a good ~ for any man⟩ **5 a :** a device for fitting together two halves of a ceramics mold that consists of a knob on one half and a corresponding depression on the other **b :** a form shaped to support a pattern and made of plaster of paris or similar materials and sand or of a mixture of sand and litharge and boiled linseed oil **6 :** a condition in which two colors appear to have the same hue, saturation, and lightness

[2]**match** \"\ *vb* -ED/-ING/-ES [ME *macchen,* fr. *macche,* n. — more at [1]MATCH] *vt* **1 a :** to encounter esp. successfully as an antagonist or competitor **:** to meet and prove to be the equal of ⟨troops whom none could ~ in battle⟩ **b** (1) **:** to set in competition or combat with or in other opposition to **:** PIT, ARRAY ⟨~*ing* his strength against his enemy's⟩ (2) **:** to provide with a competitor or adversary of equal strength, courage, or ability ⟨was ~*ed* with someone that would really put his championship to the test⟩ **c :** to set in comparison with **:** compare the quality of ⟨almost any drama ~*ed* with his seems trivial⟩ **2 a :** to join or give in marriage ⟨thought of ~*ing* her son with an heiress⟩ **b** *obs* **:** to join in close association **:** put in close proximity **3 a** (1) **:** to pair up or put in a set as possessing equal or harmonizing attributes **:** combine as being suitable or congenial ⟨~*ed* the tie and the shirt⟩ (2) **:** to cause to be proportioned to **:** make correspond **:** ADAPT, SUIT ⟨~*ed* his generosity to her love⟩ **b** (1) **:** to be the exact counterpart of **:** equal in qualities ⟨trying to find a vase to ~ the remaining one of a pair⟩ (2) **:** to resemble sufficiently to be suitably coupled with **:** be enough like to go agreeably with **:** correspond to **:** harmonize with ⟨a coat that will ~ almost anything you choose to wear⟩ **c** (1) **:** to produce or provide with an exact counterpart of or for ⟨a climate that can't be ~*ed* anywhere else in the world⟩ (2) **:** to produce or provide with a suitable or harmonious counterpart of or for ⟨wanted to ~ the period decor with some antique furniture⟩ **4 a :** to fit together or make suitable for fitting together; *specif* **:** to furnish (boards) at the edges with a tongue and groove **b :** to couple (two electric circuits) by a device (as a transformer) that by providing equality of impedance ensures maximum transfer of power from one circuit to the other **5 a :** to flip, toss, or otherwise manipulate (coins) and compare the faces so exposed either to decide something contested or as a form of gambling ⟨~*ed* a couple of quarters to see who would pay the check⟩ **b :** to go through this process with (another person) ⟨said he would ~ him for it⟩ ~ *vi* **1 a** *archaic* **:** to enter into a marriage union **:** become married **b** *obs* **:** COUPLE, MATE **2 a :** to be an exact or close counterpart **:** be a counterpart that agreeably blends or harmonizes ⟨wore a new spring coat and a hat to ~⟩ **b :** to go together agreeably by reason of being exact or close counterparts that blend or harmonize ⟨gloves that will ~ very nicely with your coat⟩

syn MATCH, RIVAL, EQUAL, APPROACH, TOUCH signify in common, often in negative constructions, to be or come to be equivalent to (someone or something else) or come up to or nearly up to (the standard of another or the person or thing embodying it). MATCH stresses equivalence, usually a rival or competitive equivalence ⟨we are prone to imitate the vices of those whose virtues we cannot *match* —E.S.McCartney⟩ ⟨even in truth to nature, truth to life, he cannot *match* them —Laurence Binyon⟩ ⟨the beauty of his person was *matched* by the grace and dignity of his spirit —John Buchan⟩ ⟨his belief that . . . the United States can not *match* Russia in sheer number of workers —*Current Biog.*⟩ RIVAL is often interchangeable with MATCH but usually suggests rather a coming close to or a slight falling short of equivalence, often stressing more the idea of competitive effort or comparison ⟨the bright but penniless youth whose climb to fame *rivaled* the most incredible of the Alger stories —*Amer. Guide Series: Minn.*⟩ ⟨in winter it is a ski center *rivaling* its near neighbor —E.W.Smith⟩ ⟨he *rivaled* his friend Donne in fathering children —Douglas Bush⟩ ⟨political discussions that *rival* the temperature in intensity —*Amer. Guide Series: Tenn.*⟩ EQUAL is very close to MATCH in implying a sharing of the same level or plane, especially of excellence or achievement, stressing possibly a little less the idea of competition or rivalry ⟨when he went aloft to set sail or to shorten sail he performed feats which *equaled* those of circus performers —C.S.Forester⟩ ⟨few campaigns have *equaled* that of 1828 for its license and bitter personalities —W.C.Ford⟩ ⟨the contestants rode with a maniacal fury they had never seen *equaled* before —T.B.Costain⟩ APPROACH and TOUCH are almost interchangeable, implying a coming within sight of equivalence or a near equaling and both seldom carrying the idea of competition or rivalry, APPROACH possibly suggesting a somewhat greater falling short of equivalence than TOUCH ⟨though some of Shakespeare's songs *approach* purity, there is, in fact, an alloy —Clive Bell⟩ ⟨Lincoln *approached* perfection in the field of government —W.J.Reilly⟩ ⟨a new type, destined to be frequently imitated, but seldom *approached* and never exactly reproduced —Richard Garnett †1906⟩ ⟨you have pretty girls in Scotland . . . but none to *touch* Miss Westwater —John Buchan⟩ ⟨few of the academicians . . . can *touch* Catton's ability to get the feel of a period —Laurent Le Sage⟩

3**match** \"\ *n* -ES [ME *macche, mecche*, fr. MF *meiche*, perh. modif. of L *myxa* lamp wick, fr. Gk, lamp wick, nasal mucus — more at MUCUS] **1 a** *obs* **:** the wick of a candle or lamp **b** (1) **:** a wick or cord chemically prepared to burn at a uniform rate and formerly much used in firing cannon and muskets and other firearms and in igniting a train of powder (2) **:** the material used in making such a wick or cord **2 a :** a piece of cord, cloth, or paper or a splint of wood dipped in melted sulfur so as to be able to catch fire from a spark and formerly much used to light candles or lamps or to ignite fuel or to fumigate something **b :** a piece of flammable material (as wood) having a tip treated with potassium chlorate and sugar so as to ignite when touched with sulfuric acid **3 :** a short slender piece of wood or other fairly rigid flammable material tipped with a combustible mixture that bursts into flame through friction (as by being scratched against a usu. rough or specially prepared surface) and that so ignites the piece

match·able \'machəbəl\ *adj* **:** capable of being matched

matchboard \'=,=\ *or* **matched board** *n* **1 :** a board (as one of those used in laying floors) that has a groove cut along one edge and a tongue along the other so as to fit snugly with the edges of similarly cut boards of identical size **2 :** one of two molding boards to which the halves of a split foundry pattern are attached with one of the molding boards forming the cope mold and the other the drag mold

matchboarding \'=,==\ *also* **matched boarding** *n* **1 :** a quantity of matchboards **2 :** something made of matchboards

matchbook \'=,=\ *also* **matchfolder** \'=,==\ *n* **:** a small usu. paper packet or folder containing rows of paper matches

matchbox \'=,=\ *n* **:** a box for holding matches

matchcoat \'=,=\ *n* [prob. by folk etymology (influence of *coat*) fr. Powhatan *matshcore*] **:** a mantle or similar loose covering of fur, feathers, or usu. woolen cloth formerly extensively worn by American Indians

matched joint *or* **match joint** *n* **:** a line along which two matchboards are joined together

matchbooks

matched order *n* **:** one of two orders designed to create artificial activity in the stock market: **a :** an order placed by an individual through one broker to buy usu. at an above-market price a number of shares of stock that the individual intends to sell at once at the same price through another broker **b :** the order placed by the individual to sell stock that has been so bought

matched siding *n* **:** DROP SIDING

match·er \'machə(r)\ *n* -S [2*match* + -*er*] **1** *or* **matching machine :** a machine that planes boards and that forms the tongues and grooves in matchboards **2 :** one (as an assorter) whose work is matching articles (as for size, color, fit, quality)

matches *pl of* MATCH, *pres 3d sing of* MATCH

matchet *var of* MACHETE

match game *n* [1*match*] **1 :** a game played as a test of superiority (as a play-off game or a championship game) **2** [3*match*] **:** a game played with matches typically by nine players

matching *pres part of* MATCH

matching test *n* **:** an objective test consisting of two sets of items to be matched with each other for a specified attribute

match·less \'machləs\ *adj* **:** having no equal **:** UNPARALLELED, PEERLESS ⟨her ~ beauty⟩ — **match·less·ly** *adv*

matchlock \'=,=\ *n* **1 :** a device used in early muskets consisting of a slow-burning cord or wick held in an arm curving over a hole in the breech and capable of being lowered so as to ignite the charge with the glowing tip of the cord or wick **2 :** a musket equipped with a matchlock

matchmake \'=,=\ *vi* [back-formation fr. *matchmaker*] **:** to bring about a marriage esp. by scheming

matchmaker \'=,==\ *n* [1*match* + *maker*] **:** one that arranges a match: **a :** one that brings about a marriage or is given to bringing about marriages esp. by scheming **b :** one that arranges or promotes a match (as a prizefight)

matchmaking \'=,==\ *n* [1*match* + *making*, gerund of 1*make*] **1 :** the action of bringing about a marriage esp. by scheming **2 :** the action of arranging or promoting sports matches

1**matchmark** \'=,=\ *n* [1*match* + *mark*] **:** a mark placed on the adjacent separable parts of a device to aid in the reassembling of the parts

2**matchmark** \"\ *vt* **:** to make a matchmark on

match penalty *n* **:** a penalty in ice hockey consisting of a fine and a decision by league officials concerning suspension of an offending player who remains eligible for play until the decision is handed down

match plane *n* **:** a plane having cutters for making the tongues and grooves on the edges of matchboards

match plate *n* **1 :** a metal plate on the opposite sides of which the halves of a split pattern are attached **2 :** one of two metal plates to which the halves of a split pattern are attached

match play *n* **1 :** golf competition in which the winner is the person or team winning the greater number of holes — compare MEDAL PLAY **2 :** MATCH GAME

match point *n* **1 :** the last point needed to win a game of tennis or handball or similar sports match **2 :** a unit used in scoring duplicate bridge or tournament bridge and consisting of 1 point awarded to a pair of partners for each other pair making a lower score in a deal and ½ point awarded to a pair of partners for each other pair making the same score in a deal

match race *n* **:** a race between two contestants

match safe *n* **:** an ornamental or watertight matchbox

match-splint \'=,=\ *or* **match-stalk** \'=,=\ *n, chiefly Brit* **:** MATCHSTICK

1**matchstick** \'=,=\ *n* **:** the slender length of wood or other fairly rigid material used in making matches

2**matchstick** *adj* **1 :** made of or as if of matchsticks **2 :** of, relating to, or constituting stick figures ⟨how to draw buildings, animals, ~ men —*British Book News*⟩

matchweed \'=,=\ *n* [prob. fr. 3*match*] **:** any of various plants of the genus *Gutierrezia*

matchwood \'=,=\ *n* **1 :** wood used for making matches **2 :** thin brittle jagged pieces of wood **:** SPLINTERS ⟨the hurricane smashed the village to ~⟩

1**mate** *vt* -ED/-ING/-S [ME *maten*, fr. OF *mater* — more at MAT] **1** *obs* **:** OVERCOME, DEFEAT **2** *obs* **a :** to frustrate by bewildering **:** CONFOUND **b :** to effectively block or reduce to nothing **3** *obs* **:** DISPIRIT, DISCOMFIT, DAUNT

2**mate** \'māt, *usu* -ād·+V\ *vb* -ED/-ING/-S [ME *maten*, fr. MF *mater*, fr. OF *mat*, n., checkmate, fr. Ar *māt* (in *shāh māt* — expression used in chess to tell an opponent that his king has been checkmated) — more at CHECKMATE] *vt* **:** CHECKMATE 2 ~ *vi* **:** to bring about a checkmate

3**mate** \"\ *n* -S [ME *mat*, fr. MF, fr. OF] **:** CHECKMATE 1

4**mate** \"\ *interj* **:** CHECKMATE

5**mate** \"\ *n* -S [ME, prob. fr. MLG *māt, māte;* akin to OE *gemetta* guest at one's table, OHG *gimazzo* one eating at the same table, OE *mete* food — more at MEAT] **1 a** (1) **:** one that customarily associates with another **:** one engaged in the same activity or pursuit as another **:** ASSOCIATE, COMPANION, CONFRERE ⟨denounce our teachers, criticize certain of our ~*s*, and plan some new deviation from the rules —Sidney Lovett⟩ (2) **:** a fellow workman **:** PARTNER ⟨needed help from his ~*s* to get the job done⟩ (3) **:** an assistant to a more skilled workman **:** HELPER ⟨a plumber's ~⟩ **b** *archaic* **:** one that is equal in eminence or dignity to another **:** PEER **c :** FRIEND, BUDDY, PAL, CHUM ⟨boasted to his ~*s* about his girl —Ruth Park⟩ — often used in familiar address esp. by seamen ⟨give me a light, ~⟩ **2 a :** a deck officer on a merchant ship ranking below the captain **b :** an assistant to a warrant officer (as in the U.S. Navy) ranking as a petty officer **3 :** one of a pair: as **a** (1) **:** a marriage partner **:** SPOUSE; *esp* **:** a suitable or worthy partner in marriage ⟨finally found her ~⟩ (2) **:** one of a pair of animals brought together for breeding **b :** one of a pair that are matched in one or more qualities (as size, shape, color) ⟨couldn't find the ~ for the shoe⟩ **4 :** a guiding and retaining device placed opposite the point rail in some railroad switches — **go mates :** to be or become an associate or partner ⟨saw that it would be advantageous to *go mates* with him⟩

6**mate** \"\ *vb* -ED/-ING/-S *vt* **1** *archaic* **:** to equal in some quality esp. strength, courage, intelligence **:** MATCH **2 a :** to put in close association **:** join closely together **:** COUPLE ⟨*mating* words with deeds⟩ **b :** to fit (mechanical parts) together ⟨the turbine shaft is *mated* to the hollow compressor shaft —*Jet Aircraft Power Systems*⟩ ⟨watched engineers ~ . . . rocket stages —A.C.Fisher⟩ **3 :** to join together as mates: as **a :** to pair for breeding — often used with *up* ⟨~*s* fox terriers⟩ ⟨*mated* up the pigeons⟩ **b :** to join in marriage **:** take or give in marriage ⟨was finally *mated* with the man she loved⟩ ~ *vi* **1 a** (1) **:** to become joined together in marriage ⟨wondering with whom she would ~⟩ (2) **:** to become associated for breeding ⟨birds *mating* in the spring⟩ **b :** COPULATE ⟨some vigorous mature rams ~ successfully with nearly 100 ewes in a season⟩ **c :** to pair animals for breeding — often used with *up* **2** *archaic* **:** to claim equality with another **3** *archaic* **:** to go about in close association with another **:** CONSORT **4 :** to become fitted or geared together properly

7**ma·té** *or* **ma·te** \'mä(,)tā\ *n* -S [F & AmerSp; F *maté*, fr. AmerSp *mate*, fr. Quechua] **1 :** a small bottle gourd used for holding the beverage maté **2 :** an aromatic beverage used chiefly in So. America and esp. in Paraguay that has stimulant properties like those of coffee and tea and that is made by steeping the dried and ground leaves and shoots of the maté plant **3 a :** a So. American holly (*Ilex paraguayensis*) whose leaves and shoots are used in making the beverage maté — called also *Paraguay tea* **b :** leaves and young shoots of this holly dried and ground for use in making the beverage maté

8**mate** *or* **matee** *var of* MATY

ma·te·las·sé \¦mäd·ᵊl(,)ä¦sā, ¦mät(,)lä-\ *n* -S [F, fr. past part. of *matelasser* to cushion as with a mattress, fr. *matelas* mattress, fr. MF, alter. of *materas*, fr. OF — more at MATTRESS] **:** a double cloth of cotton or rayon or other fibers woven on a jacquard loom and used esp. for clothing, upholstery, and bedspreads and marked by raised floral or geometric designs with a puckered or quilted appearance achieved by the interlacing of threads in the weaving or the contracting of threads in the finishing

mate·less \'mātləs\ *adj* [5*mate* + -*less*] **:** having no mate

mate·ley \'mātlē\ *adj* [origin unknown] **:** URDÉE

mate·lot \'mat,lō\ *n* -S [F, fr. MF, fr. MD *mattenoot*, fr. *matte* mat, bed (fr. LL *matta* mat) + *noot* companion; akin to OE *nēotan* to make use of, enjoy — more at MAT, NEAT] **1** *Brit* **:** SAILOR **2 :** a deep blue that is greener and duller than Yale blue and greener and slightly lighter than royal (sense 8b) — called also *Olympian blue*

ma·te·lote \'mad·ᵊl,ōt, -at,lōt, *F* mȧtlȯt\ *n* -S [F, fr. *matelot*] **1 :** a sauce made of wine, onions, seasonings, and fish stock **2 :** fish stewed in matelote

1**ma·ter** \'mātə(r\ *n* -S [L — more at MOTHER] *chiefly Brit* **:** MOTHER

2**mat·er** \'mād·ə(r), -ātə-\ *n* -S [6*mate* + -*er*] **:** a worker who arranges shoes or hosiery in pairs for packing

ma·ter·fa·mil·i·as \¦mād·ə(r)fə'milēəs\ *n* -ES [L, fr. *mater* mother + OL *familias*, gen. of *familia* household — more at FAMILY] **:** a woman that is head of a household

1**ma·te·ri·al** \mə'tirēəl, -tēr-\ *adj* [ME *materiel, material*, fr. MF & LL; MF *materiel*, fr. LL *materialis*, fr. L *materia* matter + -*alis* -al — more at MATTER] **1 a** (1) **:** of, relating to, or consisting of matter **:** PHYSICAL ⟨the ~ universe⟩ ⟨the ~ nature of fire⟩ (2) **:** CORPOREAL, BODILY ⟨~ needs⟩ (3) **:** of, relating to, or derived from matter as the constituent of the physical universe ⟨~ forces⟩ **b** (1) **:** of or relating to the matter of a thing and not to its form ⟨the ~ aspect of being⟩ (2) **:** of or relating to the matter of reasoning and not to its form ⟨the ~ truth embodied in a premise⟩ **c :** existing only in outward manifestation and not prompted by or joined with actual intention ⟨~ heresy⟩ ⟨~ sin⟩ **2 a** (1) **:** being of real importance or great consequence **:** SUBSTANTIAL ⟨found a ~ difference between the two things⟩ ⟨a ~ point of order⟩ ⟨made a ~ correction⟩ ⟨a ~ objection⟩ (2) **:** ESSENTIAL ⟨information that is ~ to continued research⟩ (3) **:** RELEVANT, PERTINENT ⟨neglected no data that was ~⟩ **b :** requiring serious consideration by reason of having a certain or probable bearing on the proper determination of a law case or on the effect of an instrument or on some similar unsettled matter ⟨a ~ fact⟩ ⟨a ~ piece of evidence⟩ **3 a :** being of a coarse unspiritual nature **:** not lofty ⟨a grossly ~ form of love⟩ **b :** relating to or concerned esp. excessively with what is purely physical rather than intellectual or spiritual ⟨interested only in ~ progress⟩ ⟨is ~ in all his interests⟩ **4** *obs* **a :** pregnant with substance and meaning **:** SOLID, MEATY **b :** BULKY, MASSIVE **5 :** of or relating to production and distribution of goods and the social relationship of owners and laborers rather than to financial and political institutions — compare ECONOMIC INTERPRETATION OF HISTORY

syn PHYSICAL, CORPOREAL, PHENOMENAL, SENSIBLE, OBJECTIVE: MATERIAL describes whatever is formed of tangible matter and may be used in opposition to *spiritual, ideal, intangible;* it may have suggestions of the mundane, crass, or grasping ⟨one's *material* possessions⟩ ⟨busy with *material* affairs⟩ ⟨no veneration for property, no sense of *material* values —Willa Cather⟩ ⟨realistic and *material* rather than romantic and Utopian —V.L.Parrington⟩ PHYSICAL applies especially to things perceived by the senses, things susceptible of treatment in one way or another by the science of physics; it is opposed to *imaginary, psychical, mental*, or *spiritual* ⟨everything *physical* is measurable by weight, motion, and resistance —Thomas De Quincey⟩ ⟨athletic grounds and equipment represent a very substantial portion of Harvard's *physical* plant —*Official Register of Harvard Univ.*⟩ CORPOREAL applies to whatever is not only tangible and material but also has some sort of body ⟨we cannot compare our ideas with these *corporeal* substances —Frank Thilly⟩ ⟨"the mind" may be regarded as a living, growing "structure," even though it lacks *corporeal* tangibility —*Science*⟩ PHENOMENAL refers to what is or may be known or perceived through the senses rather than through thought, hypothesis, intuition, or reason alone ⟨her introspective bent has yielded more and more, in her recent writing, to a determination to capture the *phenomenal* world —B.R. Redman⟩ SENSIBLE may more strongly stress the idea of application to what is knowable through the senses and is opposed to *intelligible, conceptual*, or *notional* ⟨subject to this right of every riparian owner to use the water without stint, every owner is entitled to have the water come on to him without *sensible* diminution as regards quantity and *sensible* alteration as regards quality —F.D.Smith & Barbara Wilcox⟩ OBJECTIVE may stress apartness and individual essence, as reported by the senses, of something corporeal or sensible ⟨a chronic malady which, in forty years, produced no *objective* sign of disease —Douglas Hubble⟩ **syn** see in addition RELEVANT

2**material** \"\ *n* -S **1 a** (1) **:** the basic matter (as metal, wood, plastic, fiber) from which the whole or the greater part of something physical (as a machine, tool, building, fabric) is made ⟨had a good supply of all necessary ~*s*⟩ ⟨flax is the ~ used in making linen⟩ (2) **:** the finished stuff of which something physical (as an article of clothing) is made; *esp* **:** CLOTH **b** (1) **:** the whole or a notable part of the elements or constituents or substance of something physical ⟨the solid ~*s* of the mixture will settle to the bottom of the container⟩ or not physical ⟨the ~ of his character was basically good⟩ (2) **:** something (as data, observations, perceptions, ideas) that may through intellectual operation be synthesized or further elaborated or otherwise reworked into a more finished form or a new form or that may serve as the basis for arriving at fresh interpretations or judgments or conclusions ⟨found rich ~ for a definitive biography⟩ ⟨an experience that provided stimulating ~ for new evaluation of the theory⟩ (3) **:** something (as a group of specimens) used for or made the object of study and investigation ⟨museum ~⟩ **c :** matter viewed as the relatively formless basis of reality **2 a :** apparatus (as tools or other articles) necessary for doing or making something — usu. used in pl. ⟨needed writing ~*s*⟩ ⟨library ~*s*⟩ **b :** MATÉRIEL **3 :** the pieces other than the king that a chess player has available for attacking the pieces of his opponent at one or the other point of a game

material cause *n, Aristotelianism* **:** something out of which something is made or comes into being

material culture *n* **:** the totality of physical objects made by a people for the satisfaction of their needs; *esp* **:** those articles requisite for the sustenance and perpetuation of life

material fallacy *n* **:** a reasoning that is unsound because of an error concerning the subject matter of an argument — compare FORMAL FALLACY

material implication *n* **:** IMPLICATION 2b(1)

ma·te·ri·al·ism \mə'tirēə,lizəm, -tēr-\ *n* -S [NL *materialismus*, fr. LL *materialis* material + L -*ismus* -ism] **1 a :** a doctrine, theory, or principle according to which physical matter is the only reality and the reality through which all being and processes and phenomena can be explained — compare MENTALISM **b :** a doctrine, theory, or principle according to which the only or the highest values or objectives of living lie in material well-being and pleasure and in the furtherance of material progress **2 :** a preoccupation with or tendency to seek after or stress material things rather than intellectual or spiritual things

1**ma·te·ri·al·ist** \-ləst\ *n* -S [NL *materialista*, fr. LL *materialis* material + L -*ista* -ist] **:** one that adheres to, advocates, or is marked by materialism

2**materialist** \"\ *adj* **:** MATERIALISTIC

ma·te·ri·al·is·tic \=¦===¦listik, -tēk\ *adj* [1*materialist* + -*ic*] **:** of, relating to, or marked by materialism — **ma·te·ri·al·is·ti·cal·ly** \-tək(ə)lē, -tēk-, -li\ *adv*

ma·te·ri·al·i·ty \mə,tirē'aləd·ē, -tēr-, -ətē, -i\ *n* -ES [ML *materialitat-, materialitas* quality or state of being material, fr. LL *materialis* material + L -*itat-*, -*itas* -ity] **1 a** *obs* **:** MATTER, SUBSTANCE **b :** something that is material or the sum of things that are material esp. physically and in an outwardly apprehensible manner ⟨has the world of ~ under control —N.R.Nash⟩ **2 :** the quality or state of being material: as **a :** the quality or state of consisting of matter **:** the quality or state of being physical ⟨the ~ of the universe⟩ **b :** the quality or state of being something requiring serious consideration by reason of being either certainly or probably vital to the proper settlement of an issue ⟨questioned the ~ of the evidence⟩

ma·te·ri·al·i·za·tion \=,==ələ'zāshən, -,lī'z-\ *n* -S **1 a :** the action of materializing or of becoming materialized ⟨the ~ of thought by words⟩ ⟨resulted in the ~ of their philosophy⟩ **b :** an appearance (as of a spirit) in bodily form **:** APPARITION **2 :** something that has been materialized ⟨this old feud, of which the four stout walls in front of us were still the solid ~ bearing witness to it today —Osbert Sitwell⟩

ma·te·ri·al·ize \='===,līz\ *vb* -ED/-ING/-S *see -ize in Explan Notes*, *vt* **1 a :** to cause to have or represent as having material form or characteristics **:** give an outward externally apprehensible existence to **:** make perceptible to the senses **:** make material **:** OBJECTIFY ⟨*materializing* a vague idea by putting it into words⟩ ⟨heroic statues *materializing* glorious deeds⟩ **b :** to cause (as a spirit) to appear in bodily form **:** cause to be visible ⟨said she could ~ the spirits of the dead⟩ **2 :** to cause to be materialistic ⟨had been *materialized* by the cynicism that surrounded him⟩ ~ *vi* **1** *archaic* **:** to tend toward or favor materialism **2 a :** to assume bodily form **:** appear visibly ⟨asserted that she had seen the spirit of her dead grandmother ~ before her eyes⟩ **b :** to appear as if from nowhere **:** appear with mysterious suddenness ⟨squads of police *materialized* on street corners —*Time*⟩ **3 a** (1) **:** to come into actual existence **:** develop into something tangible ⟨promised him a great deal of money which never *materialized*⟩ (2) **:** to put in an appearance **:** show up **:** be on hand ⟨said they would come right away but they didn't ~⟩ **b :** to become actual fact **:** develop into something real **:** take shape ⟨what had once been a mere possibility now *materialized*⟩ **:** become fulfilled ⟨hopes that never *materialized*⟩ — **ma·te·ri·al·iz·er** \-,līzə(r)\ *n* -S

material logic *n* **:** logic that is valid within a certain universe of discourse or field of application because of certain peculiar properties of that universe or field — contrasted with *formal logic*

ma·te·ri·al·ly \mə'tirēəlē, -tēr-, -li\ *adv* [1*material* + -*ly*] **1 a** (1) **:** with regard to matter and not to form ⟨something that is ~ false⟩ ⟨a ~ good act⟩ (2) **:** with regard to the material cause ⟨two things that differ formally but are alike ~⟩ **b :** with regard to material substance ⟨all men are ~ equal⟩ **2** *obs* **:** soundly and to the point ⟨always spoke ~ with argument and knowledge —Earl of Chesterfield⟩ **3 :** to a significant extent or degree ⟨aided ~ in the conviction of the criminal⟩ ⟨became ~ better⟩ **4 :** so far as what is material is concerned ⟨they live well ~⟩

material·man \='===mən\ *n, pl* **materialmen :** one who supplies materials (as in the building trades)

materialman's lien *n* **:** a lien on property for materials supplied — compare MECHANIC'S LIEN

material matter *n* **:** MATTER OF A PROPOSITION a

material mode *n* **:** language that ostensively makes statements about objects, properties, and relations — contrasted with *formal mode*

ma·te·ri·al·ness *n* -ES **:** the quality or state of being material **:** MATERIALITY

materials *pl of* MATERIAL

ma·te·ria med·i·ca \mə'tirēə'medəkə, -tēr-\ *n* [NL, medical matter, trans. of Gk *hylē iatrikē*] **1 :** substances used in the composition of medical remedies **:** DRUGS, MEDICINE **2 a :** a branch of medical science that treats of the sources, nature, properties, and preparation of the drugs used in medicine **b :** a treatise on this subject

materia pri·ma \-'prīmə\ *n* [NL, first matter, trans. of Gk *prōtē hylē*] **:** indeterminate matter viewed as the material cause of the universe

1**materiate** *adj* [ML *materiatus*, past part. of *materiare* to make material] *obs* **:** composed of or involved with matter **:** MATERIAL

2**materiate** *vt* -ED/-ING/-S [ML *materiatus*, past part. of *materiare* to make material, fr. L *materia* matter — more at MATTER] *obs* **:** to provide or constitute the material or matter of **:** make material

ma·té·ri·el *or* **ma·te·ri·el** \mə¦tirē'el, ma¦-, -tēr-\ *n* -S [F *matériel*, fr. *matériel*, adj., material, fr. MF *materiel* — more at MATERIAL] **:** the equipment, apparatus, and supplies used by an organization or institution or required in some work or enterprise; *esp* **:** military equipment, apparatus, and supplies (as guns, ammunition, clothing) — distinguished from *personnel* **syn** see EQUIPMENT

ma·ter lec·ti·o·nis \'mäd·ə(r),lektē'ōnəs\ *n, pl* **ma·tres lec·tionis** \'mä·,trā,sl-\ [NL, lit., mother of reading; fr. its function of enabling a person reading aloud to give an accurate rendition of a written word] **:** the alphabetic signs א (\'\), ה (\h\), ו (\w\), and י (\y\) in Hebrew which assist in indicating the vocalization in an originally consonantal writing system

1**ma·ter·nal** \mə'tərnᵊl, -tən-,-təin-\ *adj* [ME, fr. MF & ML; MF *maternel*, fr. ML *maternalis*, fr. L *maternus* of a mother, maternal (fr. *mater* mother) + -*alis* -al — more at MOTHER]

1 *of a language* : acquired before any other language : being one's mother language ⟨English is their ~ language⟩ **2 a** (1) : of, relating to, or being like that of a mother : MOTHERLY ⟨a warm ~ affection for her guest —Dorothy Sayers⟩ ⟨~ instincts⟩ ⟨~ solicitude⟩ (2) *archaic* : being a mother : considered as a mother ⟨his ~ country⟩ (3) : suggestive of or acting like a mother ⟨my ~ waitress advised me in the selection of my lunch —Arnold Bennett⟩ **b** : belonging to a mother ⟨glanced over the ~ shoulder⟩ **3 a** : related through a mother or on a mother's side ⟨his ~ uncle⟩ **b** : inherited or derived from a mother ⟨exhibited both ~ traits of character and physical characteristics⟩ **c** : MATRILINEAL

²maternal \"\ *n* -s : MOTHER, MATRON ⟨our frustrated young ~*s* —Christopher Morley⟩

maternal inheritance *n* : matroclinous inheritance; *specif* : inheritance of characters transmitted through the cytoplasm of the egg

ma·ter·nal·ism \-nᵊl,izəm\ *n* -s : the quality or state of having or showing maternal instincts ⟨remarkable for her benevolent ~⟩

ma·ter·nal·is·tic \=¦==¦istik, -tēk\ *adj* : having or showing maternal instincts or attitudes : marked by maternalism ⟨~ care⟩

ma·ter·nal·ize \=ˈ==,īz\ *vt* -ED/-ING/-S *see -ize in Explan Notes* : to cause to be maternal

ma·ter·nal·ly \-ᵊlē, -ᵊli\ *adv* : in a maternal manner ⟨fussed ~ over the boy⟩

maternal rubella *n* : rubella that may occur in a pregnant woman and that is thought to cause developmental anomalies in the fetus when occurring during the first trimester

ma·ter·ni·ty \məˈtərnəd·ē, -tən-, -təin-, -nətē, -i\ *n* -ES *often attrib* [F *maternité*, fr. MF, fr. ML *maternitat-, maternitas* quality or state of being a mother, fr. L *maternus* of a mother, maternal + *-itat-, -itas* -ity] **1 a** (1) : the quality or state of being a mother : MOTHERHOOD (2) : the quality or state of being pregnant ⟨successive *maternities*⟩ **b** : the qualities belonging to or associated with motherhood : MOTHERLINESS, MATERNALISM **2** : a hospital or a section of a hospital designed for the care of women immediately before and during childbirth and for the care of newborn babies **3** : a usu. loose or adjustable garment worn during pregnancy

maters *pl of* MATER

mates *pres 3d sing of* MATE, *pl of* MATE

mate·ship \ˈmāt,ship\ *n* -s [⁵*mate* + *-ship*] **1** : the quality or state of being a mate; *esp* : FELLOWSHIP ⟨manliness and ~ in the face of terrible danger —Leslie Rees⟩ **2** : an Australian code of conduct that emphasizes egalitarianism and fellowship

¹matey \ˈmād·ē, -ātē, -i\ *n* -s [⁵*mate* + *-y*, n. suffix] **1** *chiefly Brit* : ⁵MATE 1c **2** *Brit* : a dockyard workman

²matey \"\ *adj* [⁵*mate* + *-y*, adj. suffix] *chiefly Brit* : cozily familiar and informal in personal relationship : friendly and companionable in an easygoing way : CHUMMY ⟨he is not a ~ fellow . . . not always at ease in a party — William Clark⟩

matey·ness *n* -ES *chiefly Brit* : easygoing friendliness : CHUMMINESS

matgrass \ˈ=,=\ *n* **1 a** : MATWEED 1 **b** : a low tufted European grass (*Nardus stricta*) with one-flowered spikelets **c** : SPINY ROLLING GRASS **2** : KNOTGRASS 1 **3** : a prostrate perennial herb (*Lippia nodiflora*) of riverbanks in the southwestern U. S. that is used as a soil binder — compare FOGFRUIT

¹math \ˈmath, -aa(ə)th, -ath\ *n* -s [fr. (assumed) ME *math*, fr. OE *mæth*; akin to OFris *meth* crop of hay, mowing of grass, OHG *mad*; derivative fr. the root of OE *māwan* to mow — more at MOW] *now dial Eng* : a mowing of a grass or hay crop; *also* : the crop gathered

²math *also* **muth** \ˈməth\ *n* -s [Hindi *maṭh*, fr. Skt *maṭha*, lit., hut] : a Hindu monastery

³math \ˈmath, -aa(ə)th\ *n* -s [by shortening] : MATHEMATICS

math *abbr* mathematical; mathematician; mathematics

math·e·mat·i·cal \,mathə¦mad·ə̇kəl, -at|, |ek- *sometimes* (ˈ)math¦m-\ *also* **math·e·mat·ic** \|ik, |ēk\ *adj* [*mathematica* fr. L *mathematicus* mathematical (fr. Gk *mathēmatikos* mathematical, scientific, fr. *mathēmat-, mathēma* learning, mathematics — fr. *mathein, manthanein* to learn — + *-ikos* -ic) + E *-al*; *mathematic* fr. L *mathematicus* mathematical; akin to OHG *muntar* prompt, awake, ON *munda* to aim, Goth *mundon* to pay attention to, Skt *medhā* intelligence, wisdom; all fr. a prehistoric IE combination whose first constituent means "mind" and is akin to Skt *manas* mind and whose second constituent is akin to the verb represented by Skt *dadhāti* he puts, places — more at MIND, DO] **1 a** : of, relating to, or having the nature of mathematics ⟨a ~ textbook⟩ ⟨~ problems⟩ **b** : derived by or in accordance with mathematics ⟨a ~ solution to a problem⟩ **c** : designed for use in connection with mathematics ⟨slide rules and other ~ instruments⟩ **2 a** : rigorously exact : perfectly accurate : ABSOLUTE ⟨hit the ~ center of the target⟩ ⟨had been leveled off with ~ precision —T.B.Costain⟩ **b** : having an exactness or a regularity of proportions that suggests calculation by mathematics ⟨a series of ~ flower beds⟩ **c** : being beyond doubt or questioning : altogether positive : DEFINITE ⟨~ proof⟩ ⟨~ certainty⟩ **3** : statistically possible but highly improbable : BARE, OUTSIDE ⟨has only a ~ chance of making the playoffs⟩ — **math·e·mat·i·cal·ly** \-ək(ə)lē, -ēk-, -li\ *adv*

mathematical geography *n* : a branch of geography that deals with the figure and motions of the earth, its seasons and tides, its measurement, and its representation on maps and charts by various methods of projection

mathematical induction *n* : INDUCTION 2b(2)

mathematical logic *n* : SYMBOLIC LOGIC

math·e·ma·ti·cian \,math(ə)məˈtishən\ *n* -s [MF *mathematicien*, fr. *mathematique* mathematical (fr. L *mathematicus*) + *-ien* -an, -ian] : a specialist or an expert in mathematics

math·e·mat·i·ci·za·tion \,=(=),mad·əsə̇ˈzāshən, -matə-, -,sī-ˈz-\ *n* -s : the action of mathematicizing or state of being mathematicized

math·e·mat·i·cize \,=(=)ˈmad·ə,sīz, -ˈmatə-,-\ *vb* -ED/-ING/-S *see -ize in Explan Notes*, *vt* : to reduce to mathematical form or subject to mathematical treatment ⟨enables us to ~ the whole of a scientific theory —J.H.Woodger⟩ ~ *vi* : to make use of mathematics or mathematical treatment : work or reason mathematically

mathematico- *comb form* [NL, fr. L *mathematicus* mathematical] : mathematical and ⟨*mathematico*logical⟩ ⟨*mathematico*physical⟩

math·e·mat·ics \,mathəˈmad·|iks, -at|, |ēks *sometimes* math-ˈma-\ *n pl but usu sing in constr, also* **math·e·mat·ic** [*mathematics* prob. fr. MF *mathematiques*, fr. pl. of *mathematique* mathematical; *mathematic* fr. ME *mathematique*, fr. L *mathematica*, fr. Gk *mathēmatikē*, fr. fem. of *mathēmatikos* mathematical, scientific — more at MATHEMATICAL] **1** : a science that deals with the relationship and symbolism of numbers and magnitudes and that includes quantitative operations and the solution of quantitative problems — see FORMALISM 1d, INTUITIONISM 3, LOGICISM 2b **2 a** : operations or processes involved in the solution of mathematical problems ⟨a problem requiring some very complicated ~⟩ **b** : application or use of mathematics ⟨your ~ are not so good⟩

math·e·ma·ti·za·tion \,=(=)məd·ə̇ˈzāshən, -mətə̇ˈz-; -məd-,ˈīˈz-, -,tīˈz-\ *n* -s [*mathematize* + *-ation*] : MATHEMATICIZATION

math·e·ma·tize \ˈ=(=)mə,tīz\ *vb* -ED/-ING/-S *see -ize in Explan Notes* [*mathemat-* (as in *mathematical, mathematics*) + *-ize*] : MATHEMATICIZE

math·e·meg \ˈmathə,meg\ *n* -s [Cree *mâthamek*] : a northern catfish that is a variety of the channel cat

mathe·sis \məˈthēsə̇s, ˈmathəs-\ *n, pl* **matheses** [ME, fr. LL, fr. Gk *mathēsis* acquisition of knowledge, fr. *mathein, manthanein* to learn — more at MATHEMATICAL] *archaic* : SCIENCE, LEARNING : mental discipline; *esp* : MATHEMATICS

mathesis uni·ver·sa·lis \-,yünəvə(r)ˈsāləs\ *n* [NL, universal mathesis] : a universal mathematics or calculus; *specif* : a system envisaged by Leibniz as a foundation for reasoning in all of the sciences

ma·thet·ic \məˈthed·ik\ *adj, archaic* [fr. *mathesis*, after such pairs as E *antithesis: antithetic*] : of or relating to science or learning

mathiola *syn of* MATTHIOLA

¹maths *pl of* MATH

²maths \ˈmaths\ *n, pl* **maths** [by shortening] *Brit* : MATHEMATICS

math·u·rin *or* **math·u·rine** \ˈmathyərə̇n\ *n* -s *usu cap* [F, fr. St. *Mathurin*, 3d cent. A.D. priest to whom the Paris convent of the Trinitarian order was dedicated] : TRINITARIAN 1

ma·ti·co \məˈtē(,)kō\ *n* -s [Sp, perh. fr. *Matico*, dim. of *Mateo* Matthew (the name); perh. fr. the discovery of its styptic qualities by a soldier named Mateo] **1** : a shrubby tropical American wild pepper (*Piper angustifolium*) with slender elongated aromatic leaves that are rich in volatile oil, gums, and tannins **2** : the leaves of the matico used esp. formerly in medicine chiefly as a stimulant and hemostatic

mat·ie \ˈmad·ē\ *n* -s [modif. of D *maatjesharing*, alter. of MD *magedekenharinc*, fr. *magedekijn* maiden, virgin, girl (fr. *maget* maiden, virgin + *-kijn* -kin) + *harinc* herring — more at MAIDEN, HERRING] : a young fat herring with roe or milt incompletely developed

ma·til·da \məˈtildə\ *n* -s [prob. fr. the name *Matilda*] *slang, Austral* : a tramp's bundle : SWAG

ma·til·dite \-,dīt\ *n* -s [It *matildite*, fr. *Matilda*, mine near Morococha, Peru + It *-ite*] : a silver bismuth sulfide $AgBiS_2$ occurring in slender gray crystals (sp. gr. 6.9)

ma·til·i·ja poppy \məˈtilē,hä-\ *n* [*Matilija* Canyon, Ventura county, California] : a tall branching subshrub (*Romneya coulteri*) of California and Mexico that is sometimes cultivated in mild climates for its silvery-blue foliage and large fragrant white flowers with yellow centers

¹mat·in \ˈmatᵊn\ *n* -s [*matins*] *archaic* : AUBADE

²matin \"\ *adj* [*matins*] **1** *often cap* : of or relating to matins ⟨a ~ hymn⟩ **2** : MATINAL ⟨the ~ clarity of the new day —T. O.Heggen⟩

mat·in·al \ˈmatᵊnᵊl\ *adj* [F, fr. OF *matinal, matinel*, fr. *matin* morning + *-al, -el* -al] : of or relating to morning esp. early morning ⟨the ~ chirping of birds⟩

mat·i·nee *or* **mat·i·née** \¦matᵊn¦ā\ *n* -s *often attrib* [F *matinée* morning, time of day before dinner, matinee, fr. OF *matinee* morning, fr. *matin* morning, fr. L *matutinum*, fr. neut. of *matutinus*, adj., of the morning, fr. *Matuta*, goddess of morning + L *-inus* -ine; akin to L *maturus* ripe — more at MATURE] **1** : a performance of a production (as a play, opera, film) or the presentation of a concert or sometimes the holding of some other event in the afternoon or occas. in the morning or at midnight **2** : a dressing gown esp. for a woman **3** *or* **matinee race** : a race (as a harness race) requiring no entrance fee and offering trophies and not money to the contestants

matinee idol *n* : an actor or other male performer widely popular among feminine audiences for his looks and charm

mat·i·ness \ˈmād·ēnə̇s, -ātē-, -inə̇s\ *n* -ES [by alter.] : MATEYNESS

mating *n* -s [fr. gerund of ⁶*mate*] **1** : the act of pairing or matching esp. sexually **2** : the period during which a seasonal-breeding animal is capable of mating

mating group *or* **mating isolate** *n* : a sexually reproducing group in which mating within the group is favored at the expense of mating outside the group

mating type *n* : a strain or clone or other isolate made up of organisms (as certain fungi or protozoans) incapable of sexual reproduction with one another but capable of such reproduction with members of other strains of the same organism and often capable of behaving as male in respect to one strain and as female in respect to another — compare MINUS, ³PLUS 5

mat·ins \ˈmatᵊnz\ *n pl but sometimes sing in constr, often cap* [ME *matines*, fr. OF, fr. LL *matutinae*, fr. L, fem. pl. of *matutinus*, adj., of the morning] **1** : a liturgical night office forming with lauds the first and chief of the canonical hours and including psalms, other scriptural and patristic readings, hymns, and prayers — see NOCTURN **2** : MORNING PRAYER

matin song *n* : AUBADE

ma·ti·po \ˈmäd·ə,pō\ *also* **ma·ti·pou** \-paü\ *n* -s [Maori *matipo*] : MAPAU

mat·ka *or* **mat·kah** \ˈmatkə\ *n* -s [Russ *matka* female animal, dim. of *mat'* mother; akin to L *mater* mother — more at MOTHER] : a female fur seal

matl *abbr* material

mat·lat·zin·ca \,matlətˈsiŋkə\ *n, pl* **matlatzinca** *or* **matlatzincas** *usu cap* **1 a** : an Otomian people of the southern part of Mexico **b** : a member of such people **2** : the language of the Matlatzinca people — **mat·lat·zin·can** \ˈ=,=¦siŋkən\ *adj, usu cap*

mat·less \ˈmatlə̇s\ *adj* [¹*mat*] : devoid of mats ⟨a ~ floor⟩

mat·lock·ite \ˈmatlə,kīt\ *n* -s [*Matlock*, Derbyshire, England, its locality, + E *-ite*] : a mineral PbFCl consisting of lead chloride and fluoride

mat·low \ˈmat,lō\ *n* -s [F *matelot* — more at MATELOT] *slang Brit* : SAILOR

mat·man \ˈmatmən\ *n, pl* **matmen** [¹*mat*] **1** : WRESTLER **2** : PITMAN 1f

matr- *or* **matri-** *or* **matro-** *comb form* [L *matr-, matri-*, fr. *matr-, mater* — more at MOTHER] : mother ⟨*matri*lineal⟩ ⟨*matro*clinous⟩ ⟨*matro*nymic⟩

ma·tra \ˈmä·trə\ *n* -s [Skt *mātrā*, lit., measure, fr. *māti* he measures — more at MEASURE] : a unit of metrical quantity equal to a short vowel in Sanskrit and other Indian languages

mat·rass *also* **mat·ras** *or* **mat·trass** \ˈma·trəs\ *n* -ES [F *matras* tall bottle, fr. MF, fr. OF *matras* arrow, fr. L *matara* javelin, fr. Gaulish; prob. akin to L *metiri* to measure — more at MEASURE] : a rounded glass flask with a long neck formerly used for dissolving substances by the application of heat or for distilling — called also *bolt head*

matres lectionis *pl of* MATER LECTIONIS

ma·tri·arch \ˈmā·trē,ärk, -,äk\ *n* -s [*matr-* + *-arch*] : a woman (as the mother of a family) having a status like that of a patriarch: as **a** (1) : a woman that rules often autocratically and usu. to the exclusion of male precedence over her immediate family or a larger group made up of her more remote descendants (2) : a woman that originates, rules over, or dominates a social group or an activity or a political entity **b** : a woman of great age and dignity

ma·tri·ar·chal \¦==¦ärkəl, -äk-\ *adj* **1** : of, relating to, or having the characteristics of a matriarch or matriarchy ⟨~ authority⟩ ⟨one of those speeches, both candid and ~ which enables one to understand why the nation adored her —Milton Waldman⟩ **2** : showing the influence of, depending on, or dominated by a matriarch or matriarchy ⟨a ~ people⟩ ⟨the ancient ~ system of government and ownership —E.A.Holt⟩ ⟨a ~ form of society⟩

ma·tri·arch·ate \ˈ==,är,kā|t, -,á,k-, -,kə|, *usu* |d·+V\ *n* -s **1 a** : rule or domination by a matriarch **b** : something (as a social group or an activity) ruled or dominated by a matriarch : the realm of a matriarch **2** : a theoretical stage or state or system in primitive society in which chief authority is held by matriarchs **3** : MATRIARCHY 2

ma·tri·archy \ˈ==,ärkē, -äk-, -ki\ *n* -ES **1** : MATRIARCHATE 1, 2 **2** : a system of social organization in which descent is traced solely or primarily through the female line and in which inheritance of property and social prerogatives is sometimes also established in the same way

¹matric \ˈmā·trik, ˈma-\ *also* **matri·cal** \-rə̇kəl\ *adj* [*matric* fr. *matrical*, after such pairs as E *anatomical: anatomic*; *matrical* fr. LL *matricalis*, fr. L *matric-, matrix* womb, uterus + *-alis* -al — more at MATRIX] : of or relating to a matrix — **matrically** *adv*

²ma·tric \məˈtrik\ *n* -s [by shortening] *Brit* : MATRICULATION

matric *abbr* matriculated; matriculation

mat·ri·car·ia \,ma·trəˈka(a)rēə\ *n* [NL *Matricaria*, fr. *matricaria* feverfew, fr. L *matric-, matrix* womb, uterus + NL *-aria*; fr. the use of the feverfew in folk medicine against menstrual disorders] **1** *cap* : a genus of chiefly Old World weedy herbs (family Compositae) that have a strong odor, a conical receptacle, and broadly involucrate heads with white rays and yellow disk flowers — see CHAMOMILE, CORN MAYWEED **2** *pl* **matricaria** *or* **matricarias** : a plant of the genus *Matricaria*

matricaria camphor *n* [NL *matricaria* feverfew + E *camphor*] : levorotatory camphor

mat·ri·cary \ˈ==,kerē\ *n* -ES [NL *Matricaria*] : MATRICARIA 2

matrices *n* -s [ME *matris*, fr. L *matric-, matrix*] : MATRIX

matri·cen·tric \¦ma·trə¦sen·trik, ¦mā-\ *adj* [*matr-* + *-centric*] : gravitating toward or centered upon the mother ⟨a ~ family pattern⟩ — compare PATRICENTRIC

matrices *pl of* MATRIX

matri·ci·dal \¦ma·trə¦sīdᵊl, ¦mā-\ *adj* : of or relating to a matricide

matri·cide \ˈ==,sīd\ *n* -s [in sense 1, fr. L *matricidium*, fr. *matri-* (fr. *matr-, mater* mother) + *-cidium* -cide (killing); in sense 2, fr. L *matricida*, fr. *matri-* + *-cida* -cide (killer) — more at MOTHER] **1** : murder of a mother by her son or daughter **2** : one that murders his mother

matri·clan \ˈmā·trə, ˈma·+,-\ *n* -s [*matr-* + *clan*] : a matrilineal clan — contrasted with *patriclan*

matri·clin·ic \¦==¦klinik\ *adj* [*matr-* + *-clinic*] : MATROCLINOUS

matri·cli·nous \-¦klīnəs\ *adj* [*matr-* + *-clinous*] : MATROCLINOUS

matri·cli·ny \ˈ==,klīnē\ *n* -ES [*matr-* + *-cliny*] : MATROCLINY

ma·tric·u·la \məˈtrikyələ\ *n* -s [LL, fr. L *matric-, matrix* list (fr. L, womb, uterus) + L *-ula* — more at MATRIX] **1** : a list or other register of the names of individuals that make up or belong to some group or category **2** : a certificate of enrollment in a matricula — **ma·tric·u·lar** \-lə(r)\ *adj*

ma·tric·u·lant \-lənt\ *n* -s [ML *matriculant-, matriculans*, pres. part. of *matriculare*] : one that is matriculating or has recently matriculated

¹ma·tric·u·late \-,lāt, *usu* -ād·+V\ *vb* -ED/-ING/-S [ML *matriculatus*, past part. of *matriculare*, fr. LL *matricula*] *vt* **1** : to admit to membership in a body, society, or institution esp. a college or university by entering the name in a register : ENROLL ⟨had been *matriculated* in the university⟩ **2** *obs* : ADOPT, NATURALIZE ~ *vi* : to become admitted to membership in a body, society, or institution (as a college or university) and have one's name officially registered after having previously met entrance requirements and typically after having successfully passed an entrance examination

²matriculate \-lə̇t, -,lāt, *usu* -d·+V\ *n* -s [ML *matriculatus*, past part. of *matriculare*] : one that has been accepted into a college or university or other institution as a student or candidate for a degree

ma·tric·u·la·tion \=,==ˈlāshən\ *n* -s [¹*matriculate* + *-ion*] **1** : the action of matriculating or the state of being matriculated **2** : an examination on which matriculation or rejection of an individual depends : entrance examination

ma·tric·u·la·tor \=ˈ==,lād·ə(r)\ *n* -s [¹*matriculate* + *-or*] : MATRICULANT

ma·tri·kin \ˈmā·trə,kin\ *n* [*matr-* + *kin*] : maternal relatives

matri·lateral \¦ma·trə, ¦mā·+\ *adj* [*matr-* + *lateral*] : related on the mother's side : MATERNAL ⟨a ~ cousin⟩ — contrasted with *patrilateral* — **ma·tri·laterally** \"+\ *adv*

matri·line \ˈ==+,-\ *n* [*matr-* + *line*] : an aggregate of matrilineages

matri·lineage \,==+\ *n* [*matr-* + *lineage*] : lineage based on or tracing descent through the maternal line — contrasted with *patrilineage*

ma·tri·lineal \¦==+\ *adj* [*matr-* + *lineal*] : relating to, based on, or tracing descent through the maternal line ⟨a ~ society⟩ — contrasted with *patrilineal* — **ma·tri·lineally** \"+\ *adv*

ma·tri·linear \"+\ *adj* [*matr-* + *linear*] : MATRILINEAL — **ma·tri·linearly** \"+\ *adv*

ma·tri·lin·e·ate \,=ˈlinēə̇t\ *n* -s [*matrilineal* + *-ate*] : MATRILINEAGE

mat·ri·liny \ˈma·trə,linē, -līnē\ *n* -ES [*matrilineal* + *-y*] : the practice of tracing descent through the mother's line — contrasted with *patriliny*

matri·local \¦ma·trə, ¦mā·+\ *adj* [*matr-* + *local*] : located at or centered around the residence of the wife's family or people ⟨a ~ village⟩ — contrasted with *patrilocal*

matri·locality \"+\ *n* [*matrilocal* + *-ity*] : residence esp. of a newly married couple with the wife's family or people — contrasted with *patrilocality*

mat·ri·mo·nial \¦ma·trə¦mōnēəl, -nyəl\ *adj* [MF or L; MF, fr. L *matrimonialis*, fr. *matrimonium* marriage] : of or relating to matrimony : MARITAL, CONJUGAL ⟨the ~ bond⟩ — **mat·ri·mo·nial·ly** \-ēəlē, -li\ *adv*

mat·ri·mo·ni·ous \-nēəs\ *adj* [*matrimony* + *-ous*] *archaic* : MATRIMONIAL

mat·ri·mo·ny \ˈma·trə,mōnē, -ni, *chiefly Brit* -rəmən-\ *n* -ES [ME *matrimony, matrimoigne*, fr. MF *matrimoine, matremoigne*, fr. L *matrimonium*, fr. *matr-, mater* mother — more at MOTHER] **1 a** : the union of man and woman as husband and wife : married state : married life : MARRIAGE **b** : this union entered into by baptized persons and so viewed by several large Christian churches as constituting one of the sacraments **2 a** : a card game played with a layout in which certain combinations of cards occur on which bets are placed **b** : a combination of a king and queen in this game

matrimony vine *n* : a shrub or vine of the genus *Lycium*; *esp* : an Asiatic shrub (*L. halimifolium*) with violet-purple flowers and orange-red berries

matri·potestal \¦ma·trē, ¦mā·+\ *adj* [*matr-* + *potestal*] : of, relating to, or being the power exercised by a matriarch or her blood relatives ⟨~ authority⟩ — contrasted with *patripotestal*

matri·sib \ˈ==+,-\ *n* [*matr-* + *sib*] : a matrilineal sib

matrix \ˈmā·triks, -rēks *sometimes* ˈma-\ *n, pl* **matri·ces** \ˈmā·trə,sēz *or* ˈma- *sometimes* ˈma·trəsəz\ *or* **matrix·es** [L, fr. *matr-, mater* mother] **1 a** *archaic* : UTERUS **b** : the intercellular substance of a tissue (as cartilage) **c** : the thickened epithelium at the base of a fingernail or toenail from which new nail substance develops **2 a** : something (as a surrounding or pervading substance or element) within which something else originates or takes form or develops ⟨an atmosphere of understanding and friendliness that is the ~ of peace⟩ **b** : a place or point of origin or growth : CRADLE ⟨viewing the East as the ~ of civilization⟩ **3** : a mass by which something is enclosed or in which something is embedded: as **a** (1) : the natural material in which a fossil, metal, gem, crystal, or pebble is embedded (2) : GANGUE (3) : GROUNDMASS **b** : an external lightly staining layer presumably composed of deoxyribonucleic acid and basic proteins that is held to surround the chromonemata of a fully differentiated chromosome **4 a** : a recessed mold from which a relief surface is cast: as (1) : STRIKE 14 (2) : a brass character used in a typesetting machine; *also* : a comparable character used in a photocomposing machine (3) : a stereotype mold (4) : an electrotype mold **b** : a hollow in a slab designed to receive a monumental brass **c** : a hob used to form a punch from which a die for striking coins and medals is made **d** : DIE 6a(1) **e** : an engraved or inscribed die or stamp used in making the impression of a seal (as on wax or clay) **f** : an electroformed impression of a phonograph record that is used for mass-producing duplicates of the original recording — see MASTER MATRIX **5 a** : a foundation for inlaid or overlaid damascened work or for similar work **b** : the principal constituent of an alloy **c** (1) : a strip or band placed so as to serve as a retaining outer wall of a tooth in filling a cavity (2) : a metal or porcelain pattern in which an inlay is cast or fused **6** : a material used to bind together the materials in an agglomerated mass (as a cement used in briquetting coal dust or in making concrete) **7** : a gem stone cut from some stone (as opal or turquoise) and the surrounding natural material **8** : the substrate on or within which a fungus grows **9** : one of a class of rectangular arrays of mathematical elements (as the coefficients of simultaneous linear equations) that are subject to special algebraic laws ⟨a ~ combines with numbers or other *matrices*⟩ **10** *in color photography* : a positive photographic image that accepts dye differentially according to density and transfers the dye to make a final color print **11 a** : a propositional function in logic **b** : TRUTH TABLE

matrix case *n* : a rectangular metal box that holds the matrices in a Monotype caster — called also *diecase*

matrix mechanics *n pl but sing or pl in constr* : a quantum mechanics based upon the application of postulates connecting frequencies and intensities of spectrum lines by the use of a matrix-involving algebra

matrix paper *n* : a bulky absorbent paper suitable for use in stereotype molds — called also *flong paper*

matro·clinal \¦ma·trō¦klīnᵊl, ¦mā-\ *adj* [*matr-* + *-clinal*] : MATROCLINOUS

matro·clin·ic \-¦klinik\ *adj* [*matr-* + *-clinic*] : MATROCLINOUS

matro·cli·nous \-¦klīnəs\ *adj* [ISV *matr-* + *-clinous*] : derived or inherited from the mother or maternal line — compare MATERNAL INHERITANCE, PATROCLINOUS

matro·cli·ny \'==,klīnē\ *n* -ES [*matr-* + *-cliny*] **:** the quality or state of being matroclinous

ma·tron \'mā·trən\ *n* -S [ME *matrone*, fr. MF, fr. L *matrona*, fr. *matr-*, *mater* mother — more at MOTHER] **1 a :** a married woman usu. a mother and usu. marked by a dignified maturity of age or manner or by considerable social distinction or by some other special prestige **b** (1) **:** a woman superintendent or manager that takes care esp. of the domestic economy of a usu. public institution (as a hospital, prison) or that supervises the maintenance of order and discipline among women and children (as in a school, police station) or that holds some similar position of responsibility and trust (2) **:** a woman guard or attendant (as in a prison for women) **c** (1) **:** an attendant in a women's or children's rest room who assists patrons and keeps the room clean (2) **:** PARLORMAID 2 **d :** the presiding or chief officer in some women's organizations — compare PATRON **2 :** BROOD MATRON

ma·tron·age \-nij\ *n* -S **1 :** the matrons of a region or country **2 :** supervision, guardianship, or attendance by a matron **3 :** MATRONHOOD

ma·tron·al \-nᵊl\ *adj* [L *matronalis*, fr. *matrona* + *-alis* -al] **:** MATRONLY

ma·tron·hood \'mā·trən,hu̇d\ *n* **:** the quality or state of being a matron

ma·tron·ize \'mā·trə,nīz\ *vb* -ED/-ING/-S *vt* **1 :** to give the qualities of a matron to **:** cause to be a matron ⟨was *matronized* by her children and her responsibilities⟩ **2 a :** to act as a matron to or toward **:** superintend or attend in the capacity of a matron; *esp* **:** CHAPERONE ⟨offered to ~ the young people⟩ **b :** to preside as a matron over ⟨*matronizing* the reception⟩ ~ *vi* **1 :** to become a matron **2 :** to fulfill the role of a matron

matronlike \'==,=\ *adj* **:** MATRONLY

ma·tron·li·ness \'mā·trənlēnəs, -lin-\ *n* -ES **:** the quality or state of being matronly

ma·tron·ly *adj* **:** relating to, having the characteristics of, or suitable to a matron ⟨her ~ expression became more severe —Ellen Glasgow⟩

matron of honor : a bride's principal married wedding attendant — distinguished from *maid of honor;* compare BRIDESMAID

ma·tron·ship \'==,ship\ *n* **1 a** *archaic* **:** the rank, dignity, or personality of a matron **b :** the position or function of a matron ⟨a candidate for the ~ of the institution⟩ **2 :** MATRONHOOD

mat·ro·nym·ic \,ma·trə'nimik, -mēk\ *n* -S [*matr-* + *-onymic* (as in *patronymic*)] **:** a name derived from that of the mother or a maternal ancestor — contrasted with *patronymic*

ma·tross \mə'träs\ *n* -ES [D *matroos* sailor, fr. MF *matelots* sailors, pl. of *matelot* sailor — more at MATELOT] **:** a onetime gunner's mate (as during the American Revolution) that assisted in loading and firing and sponging guns

mat rush *n* [¹*mat*] **:** GREAT BULRUSH a

mats *pl of* MAT, *pres 3d sing of* MAT

mat·sail \'matsəl (*usual nautical pronunc*), -,sāl\ *n* **:** a sail made of an extremely coarse fabric (as of strands of old rope) often stiffened with laths (as of bamboo) and used typically on junks

mat-shed \'=,=\ *n* **:** a usu. temporary structure with walls and sometimes a roof made of overlapping pieces of coarse matting stretched over poles

mat·ster \'matstə(r)\ *n* -S [¹*mat* + *-ster*] **:** WRESTLER

mat·su \'mat(,)sü\ *n* -S [Jap] **:** a timber pine (*Pinus massoniana*) of eastern Asia that yields a valuable ornamental resinous wood

mat·su·coc·cus \,==·'käkəs\ *n, cap* [NL, fr. Jap *matsu* + NL *-coccus*] **:** a genus of scales that includes destructive pests of forests (as pine forests)

mat·su·ya·ma \,mätsü¦yämə\ *adj, usu cap* [fr. *Matsuyama*, city in western Shikoku, Japan] **:** of or from the city of Matsuyama, Japan **:** of the kind or style prevalent in Matsuyama

matt *var of* MAT

matta *var of* MATTO

mat·ta·more \,mad·ə¦mō(ə)r\ *also* **mat·a·mo·ro** \,==·'mō,rō\ *n* -S [obs. F *matamore*, fr. Ar *maṭmūrah* something buried or hidden] **:** a subterranean storehouse

¹**matte** *var of* MAT

²**mat·te** \'mä(,)tā\ *n* -S [F & AmerSp; F *maté*, fr. AmerSp *mate* — more at MATÉ] **:** MATÉ

³**matte** \'mat, *usu* -ad·+V\ *n* -S [F] **:** a crude mixture of sulfides formed in smelting sulfide ores of metals (as copper, lead, nickel)

⁴**matte** \"\ *vt* -ED/-ING/-S **:** to convert (ore) into matte

matte box *n* [¹*matte*] **:** a holder for positioning mattes, filters, and diffusing screens on the front of a camera

¹**matted** *adj* [in part of sense 1 & all of sense 2, fr. past part. of ²*mat;* in part of sense 1, fr. ⁵*mat* + *-ed*] **1 :** covered or provided with a mat or mats ⟨a ~ floor⟩ ⟨a ~ picture⟩ **2 a :** tangled closely together **:** having the parts adhering closely together ⟨~ hair⟩ **b :** intertangled with something specified **:** tangled full of — usu. used in combination ⟨a leaf-*matted* lawn⟩

²**matted** *adj* [fr. past part. of ³*mat*] **1 :** having a dull surface **:** UNBURNISHED, LUSTERLESS **2 :** having an evenly roughened surface — used esp. of carving on furniture

mat·ted·ly *adv* [¹*matted* + *-ly*] **:** in a matted manner **:** so as to be matted ⟨~ disheveled⟩

mat·ted·ness *n* -ES [¹*matted* + *-ness*] **:** the quality or state of being matted

matted row system *n* [¹*matted*] **:** a system of growing strawberries in which all runners or all runners formed before a certain date on each plant set are allowed to develop and plants are set 1½ to 2 feet apart in rows that are 3½ to 4½ feet apart

¹**mat·ter** \'mad·ə(r), -atə-\ *n* -S [ME *matere*, fr. OF *matere*, *matiere*, fr. L *materia* matter, subject, physical substance, wood for building, fr. *mater* mother — more at MOTHER] **1 a :** a subject (as a fact, an event or course of events, or a circumstance, situation, or question) of interest or relevance **:** an object of thought or consideration: as (1) **:** a topic under active and usu. serious or practical consideration ⟨several other ~*s* will come before the committee⟩ ⟨weighed and argued the ~ for several days before reaching a decision⟩ (2) *archaic* **:** an affair (as of business) belonging to a particular person (3) **:** something that is a subject of disagreement, strife, or litigation **:** a source or topic of contention ⟨let the ~ between us be decided on its merits⟩ ⟨the ~ in dispute is basically trivial⟩ (4) **matters** *pl, archaic* **:** personal business **:** AFFAIRS (5) **matters** *pl* **:** the events or circumstances of a particular but usu. unspecified situation, occurrence, or relation ⟨planned to discuss ~*s* with her husband soon⟩ **b** (1) *obs* **:** the substance of a branch of knowledge **:** something that forms the subject of any field (2) **:** something (as facts, information, data) that constitutes material for thought, discussion, or action ⟨for years he had been assembling the ~ for a wholly new treatment of theoretical mechanics⟩ (3) **:** the subject or substance of a writing or discourse **:** MEAT, FUNDAMENTALS ⟨a graceful style was not enough to hide a paucity of ~⟩ (4) **:** something (as information or a topic of discussion) of a particular nature or involving a particular and often specified thing or relation ⟨I have ~ of the utmost importance to impart and to your ear alone⟩ ⟨the ~ under discussion⟩; *broadly* **:** something of an indicated kind or having to do with an indicated field or situation ⟨questions involving ~*s* of faith⟩ ⟨a serious ~⟩ (5) **:** something that is to be tried or proved (as in a court of law) — see MATTER IN DEED, MATTER IN PAIS, MATTER OF RECORD (6) *obs* **:** sensible or serious material as distinguished from nonsense or drollery **c** (1) *obs* **:** a reason or the grounds for something (as for action or being) (2) **:** a cause or source esp. of a feeling or an emotional reaction ⟨do you call this no ~ for wonder⟩ (3) **:** a circumstance or condition affecting a particular person or thing usu. unfavorably; *esp* **:** a circumstance or condition that requires or may be subject to mitigation, assuagement, or correction — used with the definite article ⟨what's the ~⟩ ⟨something the ~ with his generator⟩ **2 a :** the substance of which a physical object is composed **:** physical substance **:** MATERIAL, CONSTITUENT; *esp* **:** substance that is considered to constitute the observable universe, that together with energy is held to form the basis of objective phenomena, that includes among its properties extension, inertia, and gravitation, and that is indicated by experimental evidence to consist ultimately of elementary particles of comparatively few kinds **b :** material substance of a particular kind or for a particular purpose ⟨a viscid tarry ~⟩ ⟨dissolved out the mineral ~ with acid⟩ **c** (1) **:** material (as feces or urine) discharged or for discharge from the living body ⟨an obstruction interfering with passage of ~ from the intestine⟩ (2) **:** material discharged by suppuration **:** purulent matter **:** PUS **d :** physical substance as distinguished on the one hand from immaterial qualities and on the other from formed bodies **3 a** *obs* **:** the first product of creation **:** CHAOS **b :** the indeterminate subject of reality **:** the wholly or virtually passive element in the universe: (1) *among the Ionian nature philosophers* **:** a particular variety of primordial stuff; *specif* **:** one or more of the four elements (2) *in Anaximander* **:** APEIRON (3) *in atomism* **:** the totality of atoms (4) *in Plato* **:** something that is unlimited, formless, insensible, relatively nonexistent, but capable of being formed (5) *in Aristotle* **:** the absolutely formless substratum of all things having existence only in abstraction; *also* **:** the potential substance upon which form acts to produce realities **:** the receptive feminine principle that is a subject of change and development and has the power of resistance or implasticity by reason of which it yields only partially to the form-giving element ⟨in the Aristotelian metaphysics, the lower stages of existence are conceived as the ~ of the next higher stages, which are forms in relation to them; and so on to the end of the series —Frank Thilly⟩ — often distinguished from *form* (6) *in Plotinus* **:** the final weakest relatively qualityless indeterminate base and worthless emanation of the divine One (7) *in Descartes* **:** one of the two relative substances distinguished from spirit in being extended, entirely passive, and having the capacity for motion (8) *in Kant* **:** the sensible stuff, sensuous content, or manifold of experience **4 a :** MATTER OF A PROPOSITION **b :** MATTER OF A SYLLOGISM **5 :** a more or less definite amount, quantity, portion, or space — used chiefly in the phrase *a matter of* ⟨would you quarrel for a ~ of a dollar⟩ ⟨been a ~ of 10 years⟩ ⟨away he goes . . . a ~ of seven miles —Roger L'Estrange⟩ **6 a :** something written or printed or to be printed ⟨~ suitable for photocomposition⟩ **b :** type and other letterpress material set up for printing **c :** the text proper as distinguished from heads, illustrations, and notes or (as in a newspaper) from advertisements **7 :** material dispatched or to be dispatched by mail **:** MAIL ⟨third-class ~⟩ **8** *Christian Science* **:** the illusion that the objects perceived by the physical senses have the reality of substance ⟨Spirit is the real and eternal; ~ is the unreal and temporal —Mary B. Eddy⟩ — **for that matter** *also* **for the matter of that :** so far as that is concerned **:** as for that — **in the matter of :** in respect to **:** with regard to — **no matter :** not being of importance, consequence, or concern ⟨for all modern men *no matter* what their work —C.B.Forcey⟩ ⟨*no matter* how unpleasant some . . . might be —Carl Van Doren⟩

²**matter** \"\ *vb* -ED/-ING/-S *vi* **1 :** to be of importance **:** IMPORT, SIGNIFY ⟨it is not death that ~*s* but the fear of death —G.B.Shaw⟩ **2 :** to form or discharge pus **:** SUPPURATE ⟨a ~*ing* wound⟩ ~ *vt* **:** to regard as important or worthwhile **:** concern oneself about **:** care for **:** VALUE

³**matter** \"\ *n* -S [partly fr. ME *mattere* maker of mats, fr. ¹*mat* + *-ere* -er; partly fr. ³*mat* + *-er*] **:** one that mats: as **a :** a maker of mats **b :** MATTOIR

mat·ter·ate \-ə,rāt, *usu* -ād·+V\ *vi* -ED/-ING/-S [alter (prob. influenced by ¹*matter*) of *maturate*] *dial* **:** SUPPURATE, ²MATTER 2

mat·ter·ful \'==fəl\ *adj* **:** full of substance **:** containing matter of significance or interest ⟨a small but very ~ volume⟩

mat·ter·horn \'mad·ə(r),hȯ(ə)rn, -atə-, -ȯ(ə)n\ *n* [fr. *Matterhorn*, peak in the Pennine Alps on the Swiss-Italian border] **:** a high steep-sided sharp-pointed peak or mountain

matter in controversy 1 : FACT IN CONTROVERSY **2 a :** the case in controversy **:** the subject matter of litigation **:** the case with the issues of law or of fact stated **b :** the monetary value involved in a case and the pecuniary consequences to the parties involved

matter in deed 1 : matter to be proved by a deed or specialty **2 :** matter to be proved by any evidence — distinguished from *matter of law*

matter in issue 1 : FACT IN ISSUE **2 :** the ultimate fact or state of facts set forth in legal pleadings on which a verdict or finding is predicated as distinguished from the evidentiary facts offered to prove the ultimate fact or facts pleaded

matter in pais 1 : matter to be proved solely by the testimony of witnesses unsupported by any judicial record, deed, or other written or tangible evidence **2 :** matter giving rise to an equitable estoppel or estoppel in pais

mat·ter·ism \'mad·ə,rizəm, -atə-\ *n* -S **:** MATERIALISM

mat·ter·less \'mad·|ə(r)ləs, -at, -*R* *also* |ᵊl-\ *adj* **:** lacking substance or material quality

matter of a proposition *logic* **:** the particular content as opposed to the form (as that in which the proposition "All men are mortal" differs from "All A is B"): **a :** the subject and predicate — called also *material matter* **b :** the fact designated — called also *formal matter*

matter of a syllogism *logic* **1 :** the propositions of a syllogism esp. when contrasted with the form — called also *proximate matter* **2 :** the terms of a syllogism — called also *remote matter*

matter of breviary [trans. of MF *matiere de breviaire*] **:** something not open to question **:** something axiomatic

matter of course : a natural logical result or accompaniment **:** something that is to be expected with confidence

matter-of-course \¦===¦=\ *adj* [*matter of course*] **1 :** being such as is or may be expected or depended upon as a matter of course **2 :** regarding or assuming something to be a matter of course

matter of fact 1 : an actual occurrence **:** a matter that is or is demonstrable as fact **2 :** a legal matter involving primarily proof or evidence — distinguished from *matter of law*

matter-of-fact \¦===¦=\ *adj* [*matter of fact*] **1 :** adhering to or concerned with fact **:** not fanciful or imaginative ⟨a *matter-of-fact* account of the trip⟩ **2 :** free from show or affectation **:** PRACTICAL, COMMONPLACE ⟨a very *matter-of-fact* manner⟩ — **mat·ter-of-fact·ly** *adv* — **mat·ter-of-fact·ness** *n* -ES

matter of law : a legal matter involving primarily a question of law that according to the rules of law must be answered by the court in accordance with principles of law — distinguished from *matter in deed, matter of fact*

matter of record : matter appearing on the judicial record of a court or in a record required by law to be kept in a particular place

matters *pl of* MATTER, *pres 3d sing of* MATTER

matter wave *n* **:** DE BROGLIE WAVE

mat·tery \'mad·ərē, -atərē, -ri\ *adj* [ME *mattry*, fr. *matere* matter + *-y*] **:** producing or containing pus or material resembling pus ⟨eyes all ~⟩

mattes *pl of* MATTE, *pres 3d sing of* MATTE

mat·teu·cia \,mad·ē'üch(ē)ə, mə'tü-\ [NL, fr. Carlo *Matteucci* †1868 Ital. physicist + NL *-ia*] *syn of* PTERETIS

mat·the·an *or* **mat·thae·an** \mə'thēən, ma'-\ *adj, usu cap* [LL *Matthaeus*, *Mattheus* Matthew, one of the 12 apostles traditionally regarded as author of the first gospel + E *-an*] **:** of, relating to, or characteristic of the evangelist Matthew or the gospel ascribed to him

mat·thew walk·er knot \¦math(,)(y)ü'wȯk·ə(r)-\ *or* **matthew walker** *n, usu cap M&W* [prob. fr. the name *Matthew Walker*] **:** a stopper knot made by sticking the end of each strand of a rope up through the bights of the next two strands

Matthew Walker knot

mat·thi·o·la \mə'thīələ\ *n, cap* [NL, fr. Pierandrea *Mattioli* (*Matthiolus*) †1577 Ital. physician] **:** a genus of Old World herbs and subshrubs (family Cruciferae) having long terete siliques each with numerous winged seeds — see STOCK 24a

¹**matting** *n* -S [fr. gerund of ²*mat*] **1 a :** an act of interweaving or tangling together so as to make a mat **b :** the process of becoming matted **2 a :** material for mats; *esp* **:** a fabric of or resembling matted work **b :** mats or stock of mats **3** [⁵*mat* + *-ing*] **:** an ornamental border

²**matting** *n* [fr. gerund of ³*mat*] **:** a dull lusterless surface (as on gilding, metalwork, or satin)

³**matting** *pres part of* MATT *or of* MATTE

matting wicket *n* **:** a cricket wicket consisting of a usu. coir or canvas mat laid over leveled ground or other smooth base

mattins *often cap, chiefly Brit var of* MATINS

matt·ness *n* -ES **:** relative flatness of finish

mat·to \'mäd·(,)ō, 'ma-\ *also* **mat·ta** *or* **ma·ta** \'mäd·ə, 'ma-\ *n* -S [Pg *mato*, *mata*, fr. L *matta* mat — more at MAT] **:** dense tropical American forest; *also* **:** reclaimed land naturally covered with such forest

¹**mat·tock** \'mad·ək, -atək\ *n* -S [ME *mattok*, fr. OE *mattuc*, prob. fr. (assumed) VL *matteuca;* akin to L *mateola* mallet — more at MACE] **:** an implement that combines the features of an adz, ax, and pick and is used for digging, grubbing, and chopping

heads of mattocks

²**mattock** \"\ *vt* -ED/-ING/-S **:** to dig or grub with a mattock — often used with *up* or *out* ⟨~*ing* out stumps⟩

mat·toid \'mad·,ȯid\ *n* -S [It *mattoide*, fr. *matto* mad, crazy (fr. L *mattus* stupid, drunk) + *-oide* -oid — more at MAT] **:** a borderline psychopath

mat·toir \(')ma·¦twär\ *n* -S [F *matoir*, fr. *mater* to cause to have a surface without luster, mat — more at MAT] **:** a coarse punch used by engravers for making a rough surface on etching ground or on the naked copper to produce an effect after printing that is very similar to stippled lines

mat·tole \mə'tōl\ *n, pl* **mattole** *or* **mattoles** *usu cap* **1 a :** an Athapaskan people of northwestern California **b :** a member of such people **2 :** a language of the Mattole people

mat·to·wac·ca \,mad·ə'wakə\ *n* -S [prob. fr. an Algonquian language of the southeastern U. S.] **:** FALL HERRING

mattrass *var of* MATRASS

¹**mat·tress** \'ma·trəs\ *n* -ES [ME *materas*, fr. OF, fr. Ar *maṭraḥ* place where something is thrown] **1 a :** a resilient pad for use as a resting place either alone or supported (as by springs) on a bedstead, consisting in its simplest form of a large fabric sack stuffed with resilient filling (as wool or feathers) but now being usu. a product of manufacture with carefully stabilized filling of felted cotton, hair, or sponge rubber or sometimes of an arrangement of coiled springs that is permanently covered with fabric and often consolidated by tufting **b :** an inflatable airtight sack adapted to serve as a mattress when inflated and to collapse into a small space (as for packing) when not in use **2 a** *obs* **:** a protective covering esp. for plants **:** MAT **b :** a mass of interwoven brush and poles to protect a bank from erosion **c :** a supplementary or reinforcing foundation (as of brush, stumps, logs) to distribute a heavy load over soft ground

²**mattress** \"\ *vt* -ED/-ING/-ES **:** to provide, support, or protect with a mattress or mattresses ⟨~*ed* the curve of the bank to prevent undercutting⟩

mattress suture *also* **mattress stitch** *n* **:** a surgical stitch in which the suture is passed back and forth through both edges of a wound, the needle each time being reinserted on the side of egress and passing through to the side of ingress, thereby simulating the manner in which the edge of a mattress is sewed

matts *pl of* MATT, *pres 3d sing of* MATT

ma·tu·ra diamond \'mäd·ərə-\ *n, usu cap M* [fr. *Matura* (Matara), town in southern Ceylon] **:** zircon that is naturally or artificially made colorless

mat·u·rate \'machə,rāt, *usu* -ād·+V\ *vb* -ED/-ING/-S [L *maturatus*, past part. of *maturare* to make ripe, promote suppuration of, fr. *maturus* ripe] *vt* **1** *archaic* **:** to promote suppuration of (as an abscess) **2 :** to bring to ripeness or maturity **:** cause to ripen ~ *vi* **1 :** RIPEN, MATURE **2** *archaic* **:** SUPPURATE

mat·u·ra·tion \,==¦rāshən\ *n* -S [MF & ML; MF, fr. ML *maturation-*, *maturatio* process of becoming mature or ripe, fr. L *maturatus* + *-ion-*, *-io* -ion] **1** *archaic* **:** the formation of pus esp. in the ripening of a boil **2 a :** the process of bringing or coming to full development **:** the process of becoming mature **b** *obs* **:** the alchemical conversion of base metal to gold **c** *obs* **:** supposed development of one form of matter or being from another **d** (1) **:** the emergence of personal characteristics and behavioral phenomena through endogenous growth processes — compare LEARNING (2) **:** the achievement of intellectual maturity or emotional maturity **e :** the final stages of differentiation of cells, tissues, or organs: as (1) **:** the lignification of xylem in a higher plant (2) **:** the final phases of ripening of a seed **3 a :** the entire process by which diploid gonocytes are transformed into haploid gametes involving usu. two meiotic divisions in which reduction occurs accompanied in the female or followed in the male by physiological and structural changes fitting the resulting gamete or gametes for their future role **b :** SPERMIOGENESIS 1

mat·u·ra·tion·al \¦==¦rāshənᵊl, -shnəl\ *adj* **:** of, relating to, or involved in maturation ⟨~ defects⟩

maturation division *n* **:** a meiotic division

maturation factor *n* **:** VITAMIN B_{12}

¹**mat·u·ra·tive** \'machə,rād·iv\ *n* -S [ME *maturatif*, prob. fr. (assumed) ML *maturativus*, fr. *maturativus*, adj.] **:** medication formerly used to promote suppuration — compare LAUDABLE PUS

²**matu·ra·tive** \" *in sense 1; in senses 2 & 3* mə'tu̇rəd·iv *or* mə·'tyu̇-\ *adj* [ME *maturatif*, prob. fr. (assumed) ML *maturativus*, fr. L *maturatus* + *-ivus* -ive] **1** *archaic* **:** conducing to suppuration **2 :** conducing to ripeness or maturity **3 :** of or relating to germ-cell maturation

¹**ma·ture** \mə'tu̇(ə)r, mə·'tyu̇-, -u̇ə *sometimes* mə'chu̇-\ *adj* -ER/-EST [ME, fr. L *maturus* ripe, seasonable; akin to L *mane* in the morning, *manus* good, and perh. to OIr *maith* good] **1 :** involving, based on, or arrived at after slow and careful consideration ⟨a ~ argument⟩ ⟨~ reflections⟩ ⟨a ~ plan of action⟩ **2 a :** having attained the normal peak of natural growth and development **:** fully grown and developed **:** RIPE ⟨~ fruit⟩ ⟨the ~ reproducing human being⟩ ⟨a ~ ovary⟩ **:** having undergone maturation ⟨~ germ cells⟩ **b :** having attained a final or desired state usu. after a period of ripening or processing ⟨~ paper stock⟩ ⟨full-bodied ~ wines⟩ **c :** having or expressing the mental and emotional qualities that are considered normal to an adult socially adjusted human being ⟨a ~ outlook⟩ ⟨parents were willing to be ~, to take responsibility —H.S.Canby⟩ **3 :** of or relating to a condition of full development ⟨a man of ~ years⟩ **:** characteristic of or suitable to a mature individual ⟨~ responsibilities⟩ ⟨a ~ grace⟩ **4 a** *obs* **:** taking place at the proper time **b :** having reached a set limit of time **:** DUE ⟨a note that would become ~ in 18 months⟩ **5 a** *of the topography of a surface* **:** well dissected by the erosion of running water so that slopes predominate greatly over flats **b :** belonging to the middle portion of a cycle of erosion or other change in which geologic agents are at a maximum of efficiency or the entire work to be done is about half accomplished ⟨a ~ stream⟩ ⟨~ coasts⟩

²**mature** \"\ *vb* -ED/-ING/-S [MF & L; MF *maturer*, *madurer* to make ripe, promote suppuration of, fr. L *maturare*, fr. *maturus* ripe] *vt* **1** *obs* **:** SUPPURATE **2 a :** to bring or hasten to maturity ⟨summer suns *maturing* the fruit⟩ **b :** to promote full development of **:** bring to a desired state or to completion ⟨slowly *matured* his plans⟩ **c :** to fire (pottery) to the point that develops the optimum strength; *also* **:** to fuse (a glaze) completely on pottery ~ *vi* **1 :** to advance toward maturity **:** become fully developed or ripe ⟨wine and judgment ~ with age⟩ **2** *of an obligation* **:** to become due ⟨the note ~*s* next month⟩ **3** *of pottery* **:** to undergo maturing

syn DEVELOP, RIPEN, AGE: MATURE indicates attaining to a fullness of growth, an emergence from an undeveloped or incomplete stage ⟨a generation of serious students, *matured* by military service and anxious to absorb the best of what the institutions have to offer —Roy Lewis & Angus Maude⟩ ⟨he *matured* the plan and attended to the details of fitting out the expedition that destroyed the privateer —C.S.Alden⟩ DEVELOP indicates the freeing, unfolding, and growing of what has been latent, potential, or suspended ⟨the kitten's hunting instinct was not yet *developed* —Bertrand Russell⟩ ⟨there *developed* a growing hostility against special privileges granted by the government —H.S.Drinker⟩ ⟨his interest in the theater, begun while he was a chemistry student, *developed* into a lifetime vocation —*Americana Annual*⟩ RIPEN indicates attainment to a full stage of development, to the nearest possible perfection of the thing involved ⟨friendship *ripening* into love⟩ ⟨at twenty-three she was still young enough to *ripen* to a maturer beauty —Ellen Glasgow⟩ ⟨he basked and *ripened* in the sun of books till he grew as mellow as a meerschaum —Van Wyck Brooks⟩ ⟨the civil law, which was in force in most of the countries of continental Europe and their colonies, was the accepted product of the *ripened* experience of many centuries of Roman jurisprudence —*Encyc. Americana*⟩ AGE may indicate approach to a period of decline or decay in reference to people; in reference to things it may suggest withholding use until the perfective effects of time may be felt ⟨he has *aged*, suddenly, as though the burden he has been carrying for years has only now begun to tell on him —Gordon Bell⟩ ⟨*age* the wine in old wooden barrels⟩ ⟨*aging* the cheese before shipping it out⟩

ma·ture·ly *adv* **:** in a mature manner **:** with maturity ⟨expect children to act ~⟩

ma·ture·ment \-mənt\ *n* -s **:** the bringing of something to a state of maturity

ma·ture·ness *n* -ES **:** MATURITY 2, 4

ma·tur·er \mə'tu̇r(r), mə·'tyu̇- *sometimes* mə'chu̇-\ *n* -s **:** one that brings something to maturity

mat·u·res·cence \‚machə'resᵊn(t)s\ *n* -s [fr. *maturescent*, after such pairs as E *different: difference*] **:** MATURATION

mat·u·res·cent \¦==¦resᵊnt\ *adj* [L *maturescent-, maturescens*, pres. part. of *maturescere* to become ripe, fr. *maturus* ripe] **:** approaching maturity

mature soil *n* **:** a soil that has passed through the major developmental phases and become relatively stabilized esp. to the point that incorporation of organic material is approximately equal to the withdrawal of soluble material by plants

maturing *adj* **:** approaching a mature stage or state ⟨~ fruits⟩ ⟨~ promissory notes⟩ ⟨~ wines⟩

ma·tur·ism \mə'tu̇‚rizəm, mə·'tyu̇- *sometimes* mə'chu̇-\ *n* -s **:** a state characterized by full development and consequently by lack of opportunity for further growth or development ⟨the fear of economic ~⟩

ma·tu·ri·ty \-rəd·ē, -ətē, -i\ *n* -ES [ME *maturite*, fr. L *maturitat-, maturitas* ripeness, fr. *maturus* ripe + *-itat-, -itas* -ity] **1** *obs* **:** due care or consideration **:** DELIBERATENESS **2 :** the quality or state of being mature **:** full development **:** RIPENESS ⟨~ of grain⟩ ⟨~ of judgment⟩ ⟨~ of wine⟩ **3** *obs* **:** prompt action or consideration **4 :** a becoming due **:** termination of the period that a note or other obligation has to run **5 :** a stage intermediate between youth and old age that is the second of the three principal stages in a cycle of erosion or of other geologic change

maturity of chances : a system of betting in gambling games based on an assumption that observable past events influence the expected result of the next event

maturity race *n* **:** a race exclusively for 4-year-old horses

ma·tu·ti·nal \mə'tütᵊnəl, mə·'tyü-; ¦machə¦tīnᵊl\ *adj* [LL *matutinalis*, fr. L *matutinus* of the morning + *-alis* -al — more at MATINEE] **:** of, relating to, or occurring in the morning **:** EARLY — **ma·tu·ti·nal·ly** \-əlē, -ᵊlē\ *adv*

mat·u·tine \'machə‚tīn\ *adj* [ME *matutyne* of the morning, fr. L *matutinus*] **1** *archaic* **:** MATUTINAL **2** *of a star* **:** rising in or just before the dawn — **mat·u·tine·ly** *adv, archaic*

matweed \'=‚=\ *n* [¹*mat*] **1 :** any of several maritime grasses (as *Ammophila arenaria, Spartina stricta* and *Lygeum spartum*) **2 :** MATGRASS b

maty \'mād·ē\ *also* **mate** \'māt\ *or* **matee** \'mād·ē\ *n* -ES [origin unknown] **:** a native servant in India; *esp* **:** an assistant servant

mat·zah *also* **mat·za** \'mätsə\ *n, pl* **mat·zoth** \-(‚)tsōt(h), -ōs\ *or* **mat·zahs** \-‚tsəz, -əs\ *or* **mat·zot** \-(‚)tsōt, -ōs\ *also* **matzas** [Heb *maṣṣāh*] **:** MATZO

mat·zo *or* **mat·zoh** \'mätsə, -(‚)tsō *also* -(‚)tsȯ\ *n, pl* **mat·zoth** \-(‚)tsōt(h), -ōs\ *or* **mat·zos** \-‚tsəz, -əs; -(‚)tsōz, -ōs\ *or* **mat·zot** \-(‚)tsōt, -ōs\ [Yiddish *matse*, fr. Heb *maṣṣāh*] **1 :** unleavened bread eaten at the Passover — often used in the pl. with either sing. or pl. construction **2 :** a wafer of matzo

mat·zoon *also* **mad·zoon** \(')mät¦sün, -äd¦zün\ *n* -s [Arm *madzun*; akin to L *madēre* to be wet — more at MEAT] **:** a fermented milk food resembling yogurt

mau·bey \'mȯbē\ *n* -s [origin unknown] **:** a bitter drink prepared from the bark of a West Indian tree

mau·cher·ite \'mau̇chə‚rīt\ *n* -s [G *maucherit*, fr. Wilhelm *Maucher* †1930 Ger. mineral dealer + G *-it* -ite] **:** a mineral $Ni_{11}As_8$ consisting of a nickel arsenide

maud \'mȯd\ *n* -s [prob. fr. the name *Maud*] **1 :** a gray and black plaid worn in southern Scotland **2 :** a double fabric or a blanket or shawl with design like that of a maud plaid

maud·lin \'mȯdlən\ *adj* [fr. *Maudlin* Mary Magdalene, woman whom Jesus healed of evil spirits (Lk 8:2), fr. ME *Maudeleyn*, fr. OF *Madelaine*, fr. LL *Magdalena*, fr. Gk *Magdalēnē*; fr. the practice of representing Mary Magdalene in paintings as a penitent sinner with eyes swollen and red with weeping] **1** *archaic* **:** TEARFUL, WEEPING, LACHRYMOSE **2 :** tearfully or weakly emotional **:** effusively sentimental ⟨~ eloquence⟩ ⟨a ~ poet⟩ ⟨~ expressions of regret⟩ **3 :** drunk enough to be emotionally silly **:** FUDDLED ⟨a mob of ~ rummies . . . sing hymns —Joseph Mitchell⟩ **syn** see SENTIMENTAL

maud·lin·ism \-lə‚nizəm\ *n* -s **:** maudlin display or behavior or a tendency toward it ⟨a eulogy marked by ~⟩

maud·lin·ly *adv* **:** in a maudlin manner

mau·ger \'mȯgə(r)\ *adj* [perh. fr. G *mager* thin, lean, fr. OHG *magar* — more at MEAGER] *dial* **:** THIN, EMACIATED, PUNY

maught *or* **maucht** \'mȯkt, 'mäkt\ *n* -s [ME, of Scand origin; akin to ON *máttr* might, strength — more at MIGHT] *Scot* **:** MIGHT, STRENGTH, ABILITY

mau·gra·bee \'mȯgrə‚bē\ *or* **mau·gra·bin** \-bin\ *n* -s *usu cap* [Ar *maghribīy* western, North African] *archaic* **:** an African Moor

¹**mau·gre** *also* **mau·ger** \'mȯgə(r)\ *prep* [ME *maugre*, fr. OF *maugré*, fr. *maugré*, n.] *archaic* **:** in spite of **:** NOTWITHSTANDING

²**maugre** *also* **mauger** *n* -s [ME *maugre*, fr. OF *maugré* displeasure, fr. *mau, mal* bad + *gré* will, pleasure, fr. L *gratum*, neut. of *gratus* beloved, dear, agreeable — more at MAL-, GRACE] *obs* **:** ILL WILL **:** SPITE — often used as a mild imprecation

mauk \'mȯk\ *var of* MAWK

ma·u·ka \mä'ükə\ *adv (or adj)* [Hawaiian, fr. *ma* towards + *uka* uplands, upward] *Hawaii* **:** toward the mountains **:** INLAND, UPLAND

mau·kin \'mȯ‚kin\ *or* **maul·kin** \'mȯl,-\ *var of* MALKIN

¹**maul** *also* **mall** *or* **mawl** \'mȯl\ *n* -s [ME *malle, mell*, fr. OF *mail* hammer, maul, fr. L *malleus* hammer; akin to L *molere* to grind — more at MEAL] **1 a :** a weapon in the form of a heavy club often with a metal-studded head **:** MACE **b :** a heavy hammer often with a wooden head; *esp* **:** one (as a beetle, mallet, or sledge) used for driving wedges or piles **2** *obs* **:** a determined or irresistible foe **3** [²*maul*] **a** (1) *or* **maul in goal :** a play formerly used in rugby and American football in which an attacking player who had carried the ball across the goal line was prevented from touching it down for a score by a defending player (2) **:** LOOSE SCRUM **b :** a rough or rowdy brawl ⟨the toughs charged the gentry and . . . the battle became a heavy ~ —Bruce Marshall⟩

maul 1b

²**maul** *also* **mall** \"\ *vb* -ED/-ING/-S [ME *mallen*, fr. OF *maillier*, fr. *mail*, n.] *vt* **1** *obs* **:** to strike or knock down with or as if with a maul **2 a :** to beat and bruise ⟨~*ed* the boy with repeated blows⟩ **b :** to injure by or as if by beating **:** beat about **:** MANGLE ⟨the heavy seas ~*ed* the boats about⟩ **c :** to handle roughly or with lack of care and consideration ⟨this blessed language of ours is so ~*ed* —*Jour. of Accountancy*⟩; *often* **:** to fondle roughly ⟨stop ~*ing* the kitten⟩ **3 :** to split (wood) with maul and wedges ⟨planned to ~ out rails for a new fence⟩ ~ *vi* **:** to engage in mauling ⟨picking and ~*ing* at the hat in his hands⟩

³**maul** \"\ *dial var of* MALLOW

mau·la \'mau̇lə\ *n, pl* **ma·wa·li** \mə'wälē\ [Ar *mawla* (pl. *mawālī*)] **:** a recent convert to Islam; *esp* **:** a non-Arab convert extended the status of a protected client by one of the Arab peoples

mau·la·na \mau̇'länə\ *n* -s [Ar *mawlānā*] **:** a learned Muslim scholar esp. in India — often used as a form of address

maul·er \'mȯlə(r)\ *n* -s **:** one that mauls: as **a :** a splitter of rails **b** *slang* **:** FIST

maul·ey *or* **maul·ie** \'mȯlē\ *n* -s [perh. fr. ¹*maul* + *-y*] **:** HAND, FIST

mauling *n* -s [fr. gerund of ²*maul*] **:** rough treatment **:** hard usage **:** ABUSE ⟨the coast took a ~ from the storm⟩

maul oak *n* **:** CANYON LIVE OAK

maul·stick \'mȯl‚stik\ *or* **mahl·stick** \'mȯl-\ *n* [part trans. of D *maalstok*, fr. obs. D *malen* to paint (fr. MD) + D *stok* stick; akin to OHG *mālōn, mālēn* to paint; derivative (influenced in meaning by the word represented by OHG *meil* spot) fr. the root of OHG *māl* time — more at MEAL, MOLE] **:** a stick used by painters as a rest for the hand while working

maul·vi *also* **moul·vi** \'mau̇lvē\ *or* **mool·vi** \'mül-\ *n, pl* **maulvies** *or* **maulvis** [Hindi *maulvī*, fr. Ar *mawlawī*] **:** a learned teacher or doctor of Islamic law — used esp. in India as a form of address for a learned Muslim who ministers to the religious needs of others

mau·ma \'mȯmə\ *or* **mau·mer** \-mə(r)\ *dial var of* MAMMA

mau mau \'mau̇‚mau̇\ *n, pl* **mau mau** *or* **mau maus** *usu cap both Ms* [origin unknown] **:** a member or adherent of an African terroristic and revolutionary society or movement originating among the Kikuyu people of Kenya and demanding elimination of European settlers esp. in the uplands of Kenya and restoration of control to native Africans

mau·mé·né test \‚mōmə'nā-\ *n, usu cap M* [after Edme J. *Mauméné*, 19th cent. Fr. chemist] **:** a test made by determining the rise in temperature produced by adding concentrated sulfuric acid to a fatty oil under specified conditions and used for indicating the degree of unsaturation of the oil

mau·met \'mȯmət\ *n* -s [ME, fr. OF *mahommet*, fr. *Mahommet* Muhammad †A.D. 632 Arabian prophet and founder of Islam; fr. a medieval belief that Muslims worshiped images of Muhammad] **1** *obs* **:** a false god or idol **2** *now dial Brit* **a :** an odd figure **:** PUPPET, EFFIGY, IMAGE, DOLL — used also as a generalized term of abuse or contempt **b :** SCARECROW **3** *archaic* **:** a fancy pigeon with dark eyes and white or creamy feathers

mau·met·ry \'mȯmətrē\ *n* -ES [ME *maumetrie*, fr. *maumet* + *-rie* -ry] **1** *obs* **:** IDOLATRY **2** *pl* **maumetries** *obs* **:** the appurtenances of idolatry **3** *usu cap, archaic* **:** MUHAMMADANISM

maun *also* **man** \'mán, 'mȯn, mən\ *verbal auxiliary* [ME *man*, fr. ON, will, shall, 1st & 3d pers. sing. pres. indic. of *munu* — more at MUN] *chiefly Scot* **:** MUST — used with an infinitive without *to* ⟨I ~ explain to him —William Black⟩

mau·na·loa \'maünə'lōə\ *n* -s [Hawaiian] **:** a leguminous vine (*Canavalia microcarpa*) that is native to the Mascarene islands, has white, lavender, pink, or reddish flowers, and is much used for leis in Hawaii

maunch *or* **maunche** *var of* MANCHE

¹**maund** *or* **maun** \'mȯn(d), 'mänd, 'mand\ *n* -s [ME *maund* hand basket, fr. MF *mande*, fr. MD; akin to OE *mand* hand basket, MLG *mande*] **1** *now dial Brit* **:** a hand basket **:** HAMPER **2** *now dial Brit* **:** a measure, varying in quantity

²**maund** \'mȯnd\ *vb* [perh. fr. MF *mendier*, fr. L *mendicare* — more at MENDICANT] *archaic* **:** BEG

³**maund** \"\ *also* **man** *n* -s [Hindi *man*, fr. Skt *manā*] **:** any of various Indian units of weight; *esp* **:** a unit equal to 82.28 pounds

maund·age \-dij\ *n* -s [³*maund* + *-age*] **:** amount in maunds

¹**maund·er** \'mȯndə(r), 'män-\ *or* **maund·er·er** \-dərə(r)\ *n* -s [*maunder* fr. ²*maund* + *-er*; *maunderer* prob. fr. obs. E *maunder* to beg (fr. ¹*maunder*) + E *-er*] *archaic* **:** BEGGAR

²**maunder** \"\ *vi* **maundered; maundered; maundering** \-d(ə)riŋ\ **maunders** [prob. imit.] **1** *now dial Brit* **:** GRUMBLE **2 :** to move or progress slowly and uncertainly without definite aim or course **:** ramble idly **3 :** to speak indistinctly or disconnectedly **:** talk without order or evident purpose

maund·er·er \-d(ə)rə(r)\ *n* -s **:** one that maunders

maund·er·ing·ly *adv* **:** in a maundering manner **:** UNCERTAINLY, DISCONNECTEDLY

maun·dy \'mȯndē, 'män-, -di\ *n* -ES *often attrib* [ME *maunde*, fr. OF *mandé*, fr. L *mandatum* command, order; fr. the words spoken by Jesus to his disciples after washing their feet at the Last Supper, "a new commandment I give unto you, that ye love one another" (Jn 13:34 AV) — more at MANDATE] **1 :** a ceremony of washing the feet of the poor on Maundy Thursday **2 a :** alms distributed in connection with the maundy ceremony or on Maundy Thursday **b :** MAUNDY MONEY **3** *obs* **:** FEAST

maundy coins *n pl* **:** MAUNDY MONEY

maundy money *n* **:** one-penny, twopenny, threepenny, and fourpenny silver coins esp. minted for distribution to the poor by the British sovereign on Maundy Thursday

maundy thursday *n, usu cap M&T* **:** the Thursday in Holy Week being the day before Good Friday and the third day before Easter

maun·na \'mán(n)ə, 'mȯn-\ [*maun* + *na*] *Scot* **:** must not

maupe \'mȯp\ *var of* MAWP

mau·pok method \'mau̇‚päk-\ *n* [Esk *maupok*, lit., he waits] **:** an Eskimo method of hunting seals by waiting for them at breathing holes in the ice in order to spear them

maur \'mä(ə)r\ *dial var of* MORE

mau·ran·dia \mȯ'randēə\ *n* [NL, fr. Catharina Pancratia *Maurandy*, 18th cent. Span. botanist + NL *-ia*] **1** *cap* **:** a genus of slender twining herbs (family Scrophulariaceae) of Mexico and southwestern U.S. having flowers with a bell-shaped corolla that is gibbous at the base **2** -s **:** a plant of the genus *Maurandia*

mau·ran·dya \"\ *syn of* MAURANDIA

mau·rer's dot \'mau̇rə(r)z-\ *n, usu cap M* [after Georg *Maurer* b.1909 Ger. physician in Sumatra] **:** one of the coarse granulations present in red blood cells invaded by the falciparum malaria parasite

mauresque *often cap, var of* MORESQUE

¹**mau·re·ta·ni·an** \¦mȯrə¦tānēən, ¦mär-, -nyən\ *adj, usu cap* [*Mauretania*, ancient country in northern Africa + E *-an*, adj. suffix] **1 :** of, relating to, or characteristic of ancient Mauretania **2 :** of, relating to, or characteristic of the people of ancient Mauretania

²**mauretanian** \"\ *n* -s *cap* **1 :** a native or inhabitant of ancient Mauretania **2 :** MOOR

mau·ri·cio \mau̇'rēsē‚ō\ *n* -s [AmerSp] **:** a large Puerto Rican magnolia (*Magnolia splendens*) that yields high-grade lumber and an essential oil but is now becoming rare

mau·rist \'mȯrəst\ *n* -s *usu cap* [Saint *Maurus* †A.D. 584 Fr. monk and disciple of Saint Benedict + E *-ist*] *Roman Catholicism* **:** a member of the Congregation of St. Maur, an amalgamation of French Benedictine houses that was founded in 1618, became noted for its literary productivity, and lasted until the French Revolution

¹**mau·ri·ta·ni·an** \¦mȯrə¦tānēən, ¦mär-, -nyən\ *adj, usu cap* [*Mauritania*, country in western Africa + E *-an*] **1 :** of, relating to, or characteristic of Mauritania **2 :** of, relating to, or characteristic of the people of Mauritania

²**mauritanian** \"\ *n* -s *cap* **:** a native or inhabitant of Mauritania

mau·ri·tia \mȯ'rishēə\ *n, cap* [NL, fr. Count Joan *Mauritz* van Nassau-Siegen †1679 Du. general and administrator + NL *-ia*] **:** a genus of lofty So. American palms with pinnately lobed leaves, almost spineless trunks, perfectly 3-celled ovaries, and smooth seeds — see MIRITI PALM

¹**mau·ri·tian** \mȯ'rishən\ *adj, usu cap* [*Mauritius*, island in the Indian Ocean + E *-an*, adj. suffix] **:** of or relating to the island of Mauritius

²**mauritian** \"\ *n* -s *cap* **:** a native or inhabitant of Mauritius

mau·ri·tius \mȯ'rish(ē)əs\ *adj, usu cap* [fr. *Mauritius*, island in the Indian ocean] **:** of or from Mauritius **:** of the kind or style prevalent in Mauritius

mauritius hemp *also* **mauritius** *n* -ES *usu cap M* **:** a hard fiber obtained from the leaves of the giant cabuya and used chiefly for cordage and sacking; *esp* **:** this fiber as grown on the island of Mauritius

mauritius thorn *n, usu cap M* **:** a very thorny Indian shrub (*Caesalpinia sepiaria*) with red-striped yellow flowers that is used in tropical areas to form a stock-tight hedge — compare MULTIFLORA ROSE

mau·rya \'mau̇rē(y)ə\ *n* -s *usu cap* [Skt] **:** one of an ancient Indian people that established an empire extending in most of northern India and lasting from 321 to 184 B.C. — **mau·ry·an** \-ən\ *adj, usu cap*

mausole *n* -s [perh. fr. MF, fr. L *mausoleum*] *obs* **:** MAUSOLEUM

mau·so·le·an \¦mȯsə¦lēən, -ȯzə-\ *adj* [*mausoleum* + *-an*] **:** like, relating to, or being a mausoleum

mau·so·le·um \‚==¦lēəm\ *n, pl* **mausoleums** \-ēəmz\ *or* **mauso·lea** \-ēə\ [L, fr. Gk *mausōleion*, fr. *Mausōlos* Mausolus †*ab*353 B.C. ruler of Caria commemorated by a magnificent tomb at Halicarnassus] **1 a :** a magnificent tomb **b :** a tomb for more than one person **2 :** a large gloomy and usu. ornate building, room, or structure ⟨the bed, a huge and not unhandsome marvel of mahogany ~ —Edna Ferber⟩

maut \'mȯt\ *chiefly Scot var of* MALT

mau·ther \'mȯthə(r)\ *n* -s [ME *moder* maidservant] *dial Eng* **:** a young girl; *esp* **:** an awkward clumsy wench

mauve \'mōv *also* 'mȯv\ *n* -s [F, mallow, fr. L *malva*; fr. the color of mallow petals — more at MALLOW] **1 :** a basic violet dye derived from phenazine, obtained as the first synthetic aniline dye by oxidizing crude aniline containing toluidine, and formerly used chiefly for dyeing silk **2 :** a strong purple that is bluer and paler than monsignor — called also *mallow purple, mauveine, perkin's purple, perkin's violet*

mauve blush *n* **:** ATMOSPHERE 7

mauve gray *n* **:** a grayish purple that is redder and lighter than telegraph blue, redder and less strong than average orchid gray, and bluer and paler than average rose taupe

mauve·ine \'mō|vēn, |‚vēn *also* 'mȯ|\ *n* -s [*mauve* + *-ine*] **:** MAUVE

mauve pink *n* **:** a pale purplish pink that is redder and deeper than orchid tint

mauve taupe *n* **:** a variable color averaging a dark reddish gray that is darker and very slightly bluer than blue fox and bluer, darker, and slightly less strong than average rose taupe

mau·vette \mō'vet\ *n* -s [F, round-leaved geranium, fr. *mauve* mallow + *-ette*] **:** a pale purple that is redder and paler than average lavender, bluer and paler than phlox pink or wistaria (sense 2a), and bluer, lighter, and stronger than flossflower blue

mauve wine *n* **:** a variable color averaging a dark grayish red that is bluer and stronger than average rose brown and bluer, lighter, and stronger than average cordovan (sense 3b)

mau·vine \'mō|vən, |‚vēn *also* 'mȯ|\ *adj* [*mauve* + *-ine*] **:** of the color mauve

mauvy \'mōvē *also* 'mȯvē\ *also* **mauv·ish** \-vish\ *adj* [*mauve* + *-y* or *-ish*] **:** having a shading of mauve

maux \'mȯks\ *n, pl* **maux** [prob. irreg. fr. *malkin*] **1** *now dial Eng* **:** a slatternly woman **2** *obs* **:** SLUT 2a

¹**mav·er·ick** \'mav(ə)rik, -rēk\ *n* -s [after Samuel A. *Maverick* †1870 Am. pioneer in Texas who did not brand his calves] **1** *West* **:** an unbranded range animal; *esp* **:** a calf on the range that is unbranded and not following its mother **2 a :** a refractory or recalcitrant member of a political party who bolts at will and sets an independent course **b :** an intellectual or a member of a social upper class or of any other group who refuses to conform and takes an unorthodox stand

²**maverick** \"\ *vt* -ED/-ING/-S **1** *West* **:** to brand and take possession of (an animal) as a maverick **2** *West* **:** to obtain by dishonest or questionable means

³**maverick** \"\ *adj* **:** being, behaving like, or typical of a maverick **:** RECALCITRANT, UNMARKED, STRAY ⟨a ~ calf⟩ ⟨~ floating mine⟩ ⟨a ~ stand on a tax bill⟩

mav·er·ick·er \-kə(r)\ *n* -s **:** a person that in the days of the open range made a practice of seeking out and putting his brand on maverick cattle

ma·vis \'māvəs\ *also* **ma·vie** \-vē\ *n, pl* **mavises** *also* **mavies** [ME *mavys*, fr. MF *mauvis*] **1 a :** SONG THRUSH **b :** MISTLE THRUSH **2 :** BROWN THRASHER

ma·vish \'māvish\ *dial Brit var of* MAVIS

ma·vour·neen *also* **ma·vour·nin** \mə'vu̇r‚nēn\ *n* -s [IrGael *mo mhuirnín*, fr. *mo* my (fr. OIr) + *muirnín* darling; akin to OIr *mē* I, Gk *me* me — more at ME, AVOURNEEN] *Irish* **:** my darling

mav·ro·daph·ne \‚mavrə'dafnē\ *n* -s [NGk *maurodaphnē*, fr. LGk *mauros* dark, black + Gk *daphnē* laurel — more at DAPHNE] **:** a sweet red Greek dessert wine

¹**maw** \'mȯ\ *n* -s [ME *mawe*, fr. OE *maga*; akin to OHG *mago* stomach, ON *magi* stomach, W *megin* bellows, Lith *makas* purse] **1 :** the receptacle into which food is taken by swallowing: **a :** STOMACH **b :** CROP **2 a :** the hypothetical seat or symbol of voracious appetite **b** *obs* **:** APPETITE, INCLINATION **3 a :** the throat, gullet, or jaws esp. of a voracious carnivore **b :** an opening that gapes like ravenous jaws

²**maw** \"\ *n* -s [ME (Sc), fr. ON *mār* — more at MEW] *chiefly Scot* **:** SEA GULL

³**maw** \"\ *chiefly dial Brit var of* MOW

⁴**maw** \"\ *n* -s [origin unknown] **:** an early form of spoil five

⁵**maw** *chiefly South & Midland var of* MA

⁶**maw** \'mȯ\ *or* **maw seed** *n* -s [*maw* short for *maw seed*, part modif., part trans. of obs. G *magsame* poppy seed, fr. MHG *magesāme*, fr. *mage* poppy (fr. OHG *mago*) + *sāme* seed; akin to OS *mago-*, *māho* poppy, OSw *valmughi*, Gk *mēkōn*, Russ *mak*] **:** POPPY SEED; *esp* **:** that of the opium poppy which is commonly used as food for cage birds

mawali *pl of* MAULA

maw-bound \'=‚=\ *adj* [¹*maw*] *of cattle* **:** COSTIVE

mawk \'mȯk\ *n* -s [ME *mawke*, modif. of ON *mathkr* — more at MAGGOT] *dial Brit* **:** MAGGOT

maw·ken \'mȯkən\ *n, pl* **mawken** *or* **mawkens** *usu cap* **:** one of a primitive seafaring people located in the Mergui archipelago off the southern coast of Burma

maw·kin \'mȯ‚kin\ *var of* MALKIN

mawk·ish \'mȯkish, -kēsh\ *adj* [*mawk* + *-ish*] **1** *archaic* **:** somewhat sick or disordered **:** SQUEAMISH **2 :** having an unpleasant flavor; *usu* **:** having a faint sickly insipid taste often unpleasantly sweetish **:** CLOYING **3 :** marked by sickly sentimentality **:** falsely or puerilely sentimental **syn** see SENTIMENTAL

mawk·ish·ly *adv* **:** in a mawkish manner **:** so as to give a mawkish effect

mawk·ish·ness *n* -ES **:** the quality or state of being mawkish ⟨sincere and touching without ~ —A.L.Guérard⟩

mawl *var of* MAUL

mawmouth \'=‚=\ *n* [perh. fr. ¹*maw* + *mouth*] **:** any of several voracious American freshwater fishes

mawn *dial var of* MAWN

mawp \'mȯp\ *n* -s [perh. alter. of *nope*] *dial Eng* **:** BULLFINCH 1

maw·ther \'mȯthə(r)\ *var of* MAUTHER

mawworm \'=‚=\ *n* **1 :** a parasitic worm of the stomach or intestine; *esp* **:** a parasitic nematode **2 :** a mealymouthed sanctimonious hypocrite

¹**max** \'maks\ *n* -ES [origin unknown] *slang* **:** GIN

²**max** \"\ *n* -ES [short for *maximum*] *slang* **:** a perfect score (as in a scholastic recitation) or complete success

³**max** \"\ *vi* -ED/-ING/-ES *slang* **:** to make a perfect score or attain complete success

⁴**max** \"\ *n* -ES [native name in Yucatán] **:** a weevil (*Scyphophorus acupunctatus*) that feeds on the buds of henequen both as larva and adult

max *abbr* maximum

maxill- *or* **maxilli-** *or* **maxillo-** *comb form* [L *maxill-*, fr. *maxilla*] **1 :** maxilla ⟨*maxilli*ped⟩ **2 :** maxillary and ⟨*maxillo*facial⟩ ⟨*maxillo*zygomatic⟩

max·il·la \mak'silə\ *n, pl* **max·il·lae** \-i‚lē, -i‚lī\ *also* **maxillas** [L, dim. of *mala* jaw, cheek; perh. akin to Alb *mjekrë* chin, beard, Skt *śmaśru* beard, mustache] **1 a :** JAW 1a **b** [NL, fr. L] (1) **:** an upper jaw esp. of man or other mammals in which the bony elements are closely fused (2) **:** either of two membrane bone elements of the upper jaw lying lateral to the premaxillae and in higher vertebrates and man bearing most of the teeth — see FISH illustration **2** [NL, fr. L] **:** one of the first or second pair of mouthparts posterior to the mandibles in insects, myriopods, crustaceans, and closely related arthropods — see LABIUM 3a

max·il·lar·ia \‚maksə'la(a)rēə\ *n* [NL, fr. L *maxilla* jaw + NL *-aria*; fr. the resemblance of part of the flower to a chin] **1** *cap* **:** a large genus of tropical American epiphytic orchids with persistent often leathery leaves and single-flowered scapes that includes several cultivated for their large brilliantly colored flowers **2** -s **:** an orchid of the genus *Maxillaria*

1max·il·lary \'maksə,lerē, -ri, *chiefly Brit* mak'silər-\ *also* **max·il·lar** \-ˌlə(r)\ *adj* [*maxillary* fr. L *maxilla* + E *-ary; maxillar* fr. L *maxillaris*, fr. *maxilla* + *-aris* -ar] **:** of, relating to, being, or associated with a maxilla ⟨~ blood vessels⟩ ⟨a ~ element⟩

2maxillary \"\ *n* -ES **1** *or* **maxillary bone :** MAXILLA 1b(2) **2 :** a maxillary part (as a nerve or blood vessel)

maxillary artery *n* **:** either of two arteries of the face that are the terminal branches of the external carotid artery: **a :** an artery supplying the deep structures of the face (as the nasal cavities, palate, tonsils, and pharynx) and sending a branch to the meninges of the brain — called also *internal maxillary artery* **b :** an artery running up along the side of the face and nose — called also *external maxillary artery, facial artery*

maxillary gland *n* **:** one of the paired excretory organs opening at the base of the maxillae of various arthropods

maxillary nerve *n* **:** a sensory division of the trigeminal nerve supplying the upper jaw and its teeth, the mucous membrane of the palate, nasal cavities, pharynx, and skin areas of the middle part of the face

maxillary palpus *n* **:** a small several-segmented process on the outer aspect of each maxilla of an insect that is believed to have a sensory function — see INSECT illustration

maxillary sinus *or* **maxillary antrum** *n* **:** an air cavity in the body of the maxilla that communicates with the middle meatus of the nose — called also *antrum of Highmore*

max·il·li·ped \mak'silə,ped\ *or* **max·il·li·pede** \-pēd\ *n* -S [ISV *maxill-* + *-ped, -pede*] **:** one of the three pairs of appendages of crustaceans situated next behind the maxillae — **max·il·li·peda·ry** \-¦-¦pedərē, -pēd-\ *adj*

maxillo-alveolar index \mak¦si(,)lō+. . .-\ *n, anthrop* **:** the ratio multiplied by 100 of the breadth of the alveolar arch to its length

max·il·lo·palatal *or* **max·il·lo·palatine** \mak,si(,)lō+\ *n* [*maxill-* + *palatal* or *palatine*] **:** an inwardly projecting process of the maxillary bone in the skull of birds

max·il·lu·la \mak'silyələ\ *n, pl* **maxillu·lae** \-,lē\ [NL, fr. *maxilla* + *-ula*] **1 :** either member of the first pair of maxillae of a crustacean **2 :** any of several lobes or appendages of an insect's mouthparts that may be homologous to the crustacean maxillula

max·im \'maksəm\ *n* -S [ME *maxime*, fr. MF, fr. ML *maxima*, fr. L, fem. of *maximus* greatest, largest, superl. of *magnus* great, large — more at MUCH] **1 :** a mathematical or philosophical axiom **2 a :** a general truth, fundamental principle, or rule of conduct esp. when expressed in sententious form **b :** a saying of proverbial nature **3** [prob. fr. (assumed) NL *maxima*, fr. L, fem. of *maximus* greatest, largest] *or* **max·i·ma** \-səmə\ 4 **:** 3LARGE 4 **4** [L *maximus* greatest, largest] **:** a large worker or soldier of an ant that has polymorphic workers — compare MINIM

max·i·mal \'maksəməl\ *adj* [1*maxim*um + *-al*] **:** most complete or effective **:** HIGHEST, GREATEST — **max·i·mal·ly** \-məlē, -li\ *adv*

max·i·mal·ism \-mə,lizəm\ *n* -S [*maximal*ist + *-ism*] **:** the theories or practices of maximalists

max·i·mal·ist \-ˌləst\ *n* -S [F *maximaliste*, fr. *maximal-* (prob. fr. E *maximal*) + *-iste* -ist; intended as trans. of Russ *bol'shevik* Bolshevik] **:** one that believes in or advocates immediate and direct action to secure the whole of a program or set of goals; *specif* **:** a socialist advocating the immediate seizure of power by revolutionary means as opposed to gradual achievement of limited aims (as by the processes of parliamentary democracy) — compare GRADUALIST, MINIMALIST, REVISIONIST

max·i·mal·ize \-,līz\ *vt* -ED/-ING/-S **:** to increase (as a quality) to the utmost

maximal lineage *n* **:** a large kinship group comprising all the descendants of a remotest known ancestor with lineage being usu. traced only through ancestors of the same sex as the initial progenitor — contrasted with *minimal lineage*

max·i·mate \'maksə,māt\ *vt* -ED/-ING/-S [1*maximum* + *-ate*] **:** MAXIMIZE

max·i·ma·tion \,maksə'māshən\ *n* -S [*maximate* + *-ion*] **:** the act of maximizing or the quality or state of being maximized

max·imed \'maksəmd\ *adj* **:** expressed in a maxim

max·im·ist \'maksəməst\ *n* -S **:** a maker or user of or an enthusiast over maxims

max·im·ite \-,mīt\ *n* -S [Hudson *Maxim* †1927 Am. inventor and explosives expert + E *-ite*] **:** a high explosive of the picric acid class formerly used in armor-piercing shells

max·i·mi·za·tion \,maksəmə'zāshən, -sə,mī'z-\ *n* -S **:** an act of maximizing or the state of being maximized

max·i·mize \'maksə,mīz\ *vb* -ED/-ING/-S *see -ize in Explan Notes* [*maximum* + *-ize*] *vt* **1 :** to increase to the highest degree **:** bring to a maximum ⟨the importance of *maximizing* the use of locally available products⟩ ⟨must ~ educational opportunities for all⟩ **2 a :** to make the most of **:** assign a position of maximum significance or worth to ⟨*maximized* the experience of highly trained specialists⟩ ⟨~ the advantages of urban life —Lewis Mumford⟩ ⟨unwise to ~ the importance of present profits at the risk of future security⟩ **b :** to find a maximum value of (a mathematical function) **~** *vi* **:** to interpret something (as a doctrine or duty) in the broadest sense

max·i·miz·er \-zə(r)\ *n* -S **:** one that maximizes

1max·i·mum \'maksəməm\ *n, pl* **maximums** \-səməmz\ *or* **maxi·ma** \-səmə\ [L, neut. of *maximus* greatest, largest — more at MAXIM] **1 :** the greatest quantity or value attainable in a given case **:** the greatest value attained by a quantity that first increases and then begins to decrease **:** the highest point or degree **:** the time or period of highest, greatest, or utmost development — opposed to *minimum* **2 :** an upper limit allowed by law or other authority **3 a :** a number not less than any other number of a finite set of numbers **b :** a value of a mathematical function of one or more independent variables such that either increasing or decreasing any one of the independent variables by a sufficiently small amount results in a decrease in the function

2maximum \"\ *adj* **1 :** greatest in quantity or highest in degree attainable or attained ⟨~ pressure⟩ **2 :** relating to, marking, or determining a maximum ⟨maintaining a steady ~ line on the graph⟩

maximum card *n* **:** a card bearing an adhesive stamp (as a commemorative) and an enlarged picture of the same stamp issued by a government or philatelic agency for sale to collectors with cancellation of the stamp

maximum dose *n* **:** the largest dose of a medicine or drug consistent with safety

maximum fee *n* **:** a fee determined on the basis of payment at an hourly or per diem rate up to but not exceeding an agreed maximum sum for the entire task

max·i·mum·ly *adv* **:** to the greatest degree **:** to the utmost

max·i·mus \'maksəməs\ *adj* [L, greatest, largest] **:** of or being a system of ringing changes on a set of twelve bells

maxing *pres part of* MAX

ma·xixe \mə'shēsh(ə)\ *n, pl* **maxi·xes** \-ēshəz\ [Pg] **:** a ballroom dance of Brazilian origin roughly like the two-step (as in action and rhythm) — called also *Brazilian maxixe*

max·well \'mak,swel, -,swəl\ *n* -S [after James Clerk *Maxwell* †1879 Scot. physicist] **:** the cgs electromagnetic unit of magnetic flux equal to the flux per square centimeter of normal cross section in a region where the magnetic induction is one gauss — see WEBER

maxwell-boltz·mann law \¦=(,)=ˈbōltsmən-\ *n, usu cap M&B* [after J. C. *Maxwell* and Ludwig *Boltzmann* †1906 Austrian physicist] **:** the principle involved in equipartition of energy

maxwell disk *n, usu cap M* **:** one of two or more radially slit and concentric disks of different colors that may be overlapped by adjustable amounts to yield the average color when rotated rapidly

max·well·ian \(')mak¦swelēən\ *adj, usu cap* [J. C. *Maxwell* + E *-an*] **:** of, relating to, exhibiting, or constituting a Maxwellian distribution ⟨*Maxwellian* gases⟩ ⟨*Maxwellian* equilibrium⟩

maxwellian distribution *also* **maxwell distribution** *also* **maxwell-boltzmann distribution** *n, usu cap M&B* [after J. C. *Maxwell* and Ludwig *Boltzmann*] **:** an expression based on the theory of probability for the fractional number of molecules in a gas that are in equilibrium at a given temperature and have a specified range of velocities

maxwell's demon *n, usu cap M* [after J. C. Maxwell, its hypothecator] **:** a hypothetical being of intelligence but molecular order of size imagined to illustrate limitations of the second law of thermodynamics

maxwell's rule *n, usu cap M* **:** a principle of electromagnetism: every portion of an electric circuit carrying a current experiences such mechanical forces due to its own or to any superposed magnetic field as would cause the circuit to link with a maximum of magnetic flux

maxwell triangle *n, usu cap M* **:** CHROMATICITY DIAGRAM

1may \(¦)mā, ˌmā\ *vb, past* **might** \(¦)mīt, *usu* -īd.+V\ *or chiefly dial* **mought** *or* **mout** *or* **mowt** \(¦)maůt, (¦)mōl, *usu* ¦d.+V\ *or archaic 2d sing* **might·est** (with *thou*) \¦mīd·əst, ¦-tə-\ *pres sing & pl* **may** *or archaic 2d sing* **may·est** *or* **mayst** (with *thou*) \¦māəst, (¦)māst\ [ME, have power, am able (1st & 3d sing. pres. indic. of *mowen, mayen*, past *mighte, moghte*), fr. OE *mæg* (infin. *magan*, past *meahte, mihte*); akin to OHG *mag* have power, am able (infin. *magan, mugan*), ON *mā* (infin. *mega*), Goth *mag* have power, am able, Gk *mēchos* means, expedient, Skt *magha* gift, wealth, power] *vi, obs* **:** to have power **:** be able **~** *verbal auxiliary* **1** *archaic* **:** have the ability or competence to **:** CAN **2 a :** have permission to ⟨you ~ go now⟩ ⟨no one ~ enter without a ticket⟩ ⟨if I ~ interrupt to point out⟩ **:** have liberty to ⟨you ~ say what you please, I won't do it⟩ ⟨~ I ask why it is forbidden⟩ — used nearly interchangeably with *can* **b :** be in some degree likely to ⟨you ~ be right⟩ ⟨they ~ get here in time after all⟩ ⟨~ easily be the best play of the season⟩ — used sometimes to avoid bluntness in a question ⟨how old ~ you be⟩ or request ⟨~ I help you, or are you already being waited on⟩; compare MIGHT **3** — used in auxiliary function to express a wish or desire esp. in prayer, imprecation, or benediction ⟨~ he reign in health⟩ ⟨~ they all be damned⟩ ⟨~ the best man win⟩ **4** — used in auxiliary function expressing purpose or expectation ⟨I laugh that I ~ not weep⟩ ⟨flatters so that he ~ win favor⟩ or contingency ⟨he'll do his duty come what ~⟩ or concession ⟨he ~ be slow but he is thorough⟩; compare MIGHT **5 :** SHALL, MUST — used esp. in deeds, contracts, and statutes

2may \'mā\ *n* -S [ME, fr. OE *mǣg*; akin to OE *mǣg* kinsman — more at MAEGBOTE] *archaic* **:** MAIDEN

3may \"\ *n* -S [ME, fr. OF & L; OF *mai*, fr. L *maius*, fr. *Maia*, Roman goddess associated with Vulcan] **1** *usu cap* **:** the fifth month of the Gregorian calendar — see MONTH table **2** *often cap* **:** the early vigorous blooming part of human life **:** PRIME, HEYDAY **3** *usu cap* **:** the merrymaking of May Day **4 a :** green or flowering branches used for May Day decorations; *esp* **:** flowering branches of the hawthorn **b :** a plant that yields may: as (1) **:** HAWTHORN (2) *dial Eng* **:** SYCAMORE (3) **:** an evergreen rutaceous shrub (*Coleonema album*) of southern Africa with fragrant white flowers in spring — called also *Cape may* (4) **:** any of several spring-flowering spireas

4may \"\ *vi* -ED/-ING/-S *often cap* [ME *mayen*, fr. *may*, n.] **:** to take part in the festivities of May or May Day; *esp* **:** to gather flowers in May

5may \"\ *dial Eng var of* 1MAKE

1ma·ya \'mä(,)yä, 'mäyə, 'mī(,)ä, -īə\ *n* -S [Skt *māyā*] **1 :** an extraphysical wonder-working power in the Vedas **2 a :** the illusion-creating power of a god or demon **b :** the powerful force that creates the cosmic illusion that the phenomenal world is real; *broadly* **:** MAGIC, ILLUSION

2maya \'mī(y)ə *sometimes* 'mäyə *or* 'mä(y)ə\ *n, pl* **maya** *or* **mayas** *usu cap* [Sp] **1 a :** a group of people of Yucatán, British Honduras, northern Guatemala, and the state of Tabasco, Mexico whose language is Mayan **b :** a member of such people **2 a** (1) **:** a Mayan language of the ancient Maya peoples recorded in inscriptions (2) **:** YUCATEC; *esp* **:** the older form of that language known from documents of the Spanish period **b :** a system of writing used by the preconquest Maya peoples **3 :** the language of the Maya people **4 :** a brownish orange to light brown that is redder and lighter than sorrel, redder than caramel, and very slightly darker and stronger than paloma

3maya \"\ *n* -S [Tag] **:** any of several Philippine weaverbirds of the genus *Lonchura*

4maya \"\ *n* -S [AmerSp] **:** PINGUIN

maya arch *n, usu cap M* [2*Maya*] **:** a spanning structure made by corbeling opposed surfaces **:** CORBEL ARCH

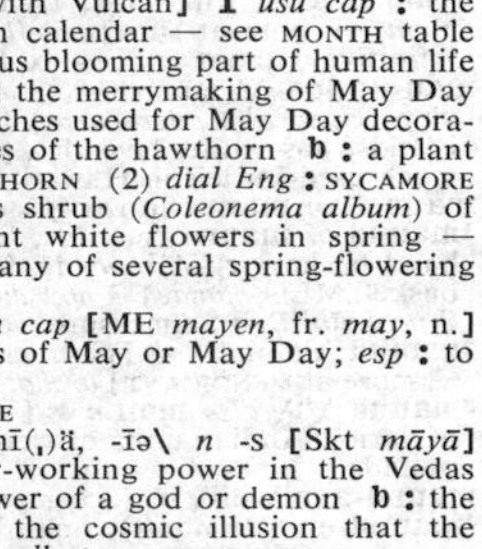

Maya arches

ma·yaca \mə'yakə\ *n, cap* [NL] **:** a small American genus (coextensive with the family Mayacaceae) of delicate mossy monocotyledonous bog plants that are related to the commelinas and have white or violet flowers

1mayan \'mī(y)ən *sometimes* 'mäyən *or* 'mä(y)ən\ *n* -S *usu cap* [2*Maya* + *-an*, n. suffix] **1 :** a language stock of Central America and Mexico consisting of Huastec, Chicomuceltec; Yucatec, Mopan; Chontal, Chol, Chorti; Tzeltal, Tzotzil, Tojolabal; Chuj; Jacaltec, Kanhobal, Motozintlec, Mam, Aguacatec, Ixil; Uspantec, Quiche, Cakchiquel, Tzutuhil; Kekchi, Pokonchi, and Pokomam **2 a :** the peoples speaking Mayan languages **b :** a member of such peoples

2mayan \"\ *adj, usu cap* [2*Maya* + *-an*, adj. suffix] **1 :** of, relating to, or constituting the Mayan language stock or peoples **:** of the kind or style characteristic of or used by the Mayan peoples **2 :** of or relating to Maya or the Maya **:** of the kind or style characteristic of or used by the Maya

ma·yan·ce \mä'yän(t)(,)sā\ *adj, usu cap* [AmerSp, fr. Sp *Maya* + *-ance* (as in *romance*, fr. L *romanice* in the Roman manner) — more at ROMANCE] **:** MAYAN

ma·ya·pis \mə'yäpəs\ *n* -ES [Tag] **:** any of several Philippine timber trees of the genera *Dipterocarpus* and *Shorea* some of which also yield resins

mayapple \'=,==\ *n, sometimes cap* **1 :** a No. American herb (*Podophyllum peltatum*) that has a poisonous rootstock and first bears a single large-lobed peltate leaf and later two similar leaves with a single large white flower at their base **2 :** the yellow egg-shaped edible but often insipid fruit of the mayapple

may basket *n, usu cap M* **:** a small basket holding a gift (as of flowers or candy) hung at the door of a favored person on May Day

1may·be \'mābē, -bi *sometimes* -¦bē; *more often in dial than in stand speech* 'mebē *or* -ebi\ *adv* [ME *may be*, fr. 1*may* + *be*, *been* to be — more at BE] **:** possibly but not surely **:** not certainly **:** PERHAPS

2maybe \"\ *n* -S **:** UNCERTAINTY, INDECISION ⟨put all the imponderables, the ifs and ~s from his mind —B.I.Kahn⟩

may beetle *or* **may bug** *n, often cap M* **:** JUNE BEETLE

may·ber·ry \'mā- — *see* BERRY\ *n, often cap* **:** an erect branching ornamental bramble (*Rubus palmatus*) with white flowers and yellow edible early-ripening fruits

maybeso \'=¦=\ *adv* [1*maybe* + *so*] *dial* **:** MAYBE

maybird \'=,=\ *n, usu cap* **:** any of various birds that tend to appear or be heard in May: as **a** *South & Midland* **:** BOBOLINK **b** *East* **:** 3KNOT **c** *dial Eng* **:** WHIMBREL **d** *Jamaica* **:** WOOD THRUSH

may blob *n, usu cap M* **:** a marsh marigold (*Caltha palustris*) — often used in pl.

maybloom \'=,=\ *n, usu cap* **:** HAWTHORN

may blossom *n, usu cap M, dial Eng* **:** LILY OF THE VALLEY

maybush \'=,=\ *n* **:** HAWTHORN

may butter *n, usu cap M* **:** butter formerly prepared in May without salt and stored for medicinal use

may cherry *n, usu cap M* **1 :** MAYDUKE **2 :** JUNEBERRY 1

1may·cock \'mā,käk\ *n* [alter. of *maracock*] **:** MAYPOP

2maycock \"\ *n, usu cap* [3*may* + *cock*] **:** BLACK-BELLIED PLOVER

may curlew *n, usu cap M, dial Eng* **:** WHIMBREL

may day *n, usu cap M&D* [ME *mayday* first day of May, fr. 3*may* + *day*] **:** the first day of May often celebrated as a springtime festival and in some countries (as the U.S.S.R.) as Labor Day

may·day \(')mā¦dā\ *usu cap* [F *m'aider* help me] — an international radiotelephone signal word used as a distress call, to introduce a distress message, or by distress traffic

mayden *archaic var of* MAIDEN

mayduke \'=¦=\ *also* **mayduke cherry** *n, usu cap M* **:** an early-ripening dark red duke cherry

mayed *past of* MAY

ma·yeng \mə'yeŋ\ *n* -S [origin unknown] **:** an Indian timber tree (*Pterospermum acerifolium*) with a reddish moderately hard and heavy wood used largely for planking

may·er \'māə(r)\ *n* -S *sometimes cap* **:** one that goes maying

mayest *archaic pres 2d sing of* MAY

mayfish \'=,=\ *n, pl* **mayfish** *or* **mayfishes :** a common marine killifish (*Fundulus majalis*) of eastern No. America

may·flower \'=,==\ *n, often cap* **1** any of various spring-blooming plants: as **a** *Brit* (1) **:** HAWTHORN (2) **:** MARSH MARIGOLD (3) **:** CUCKOOFLOWER (4) **:** GREATER STITCHWORT (5) **:** CALLA LILY **b** (1) *chiefly New England* **:** ARBUTUS 3 (2) **:** HEPATICA (3) **:** SPRING BEAUTY (4) **:** any of several No. American anemones (5) **:** MAY APPLE **2 :** a moderate red that is yellower and paler than cerise, claret (sense 3a), or average strawberry (sense 2a) and bluer and paler than Turkey red

may-flowering tulip *n, usu cap M* **:** COTTAGE TULIP

mayfly \'=,=\ *n, sometimes cap* **1 :** a slender fragile-winged short-lived imago insect of the order Plecoptera that often emerges in multitudes in spring **2 :** an artificial angling fly that simulates an ephemerid imago

mayfowl \'=,=\ *n, usu cap, dial Eng* **:** WHIMBREL

mayhap \'=¦=, ='=\ *adv* [*mayhap* fr. the phrase *may hap*, fr. 1*may* + *hap; mayhappen* fr. the phrase *may happen*, fr. 1*may* + *happen; mayhaps* alter. of *mayhap*] **:** PERHAPS, MAYBE

mayhappen \'=,==, ='==\ *also* **may·haps** \-haps\ *chiefly dial var of* MAYHAP

mayhaw \'=,=\ *n, sometimes cap* **:** a hawthorn (*Crataegus aestivalis*) of the southern U. S. that bears a juicy scarlet acid fruit often used in jellies or preserves

1may·hem \'mā,hem *also* -āəm\ *n* -S [ME *maym*, fr. AF *mahaim, mayhem* — more at MAIM] **1 a :** the malicious and permanent deprivation of another of the use of a member of his body resulting in impairment of his fighting ability and constituting a grave felony under English common law **b :** the malicious and permanent crippling, mutilation, or disfiguring of another constituting a grave felony under modern statutes but in some jurisdictions requiring a specific intent as distinguished from general malice ⟨physicians, accused . . . of sterilizing her through trickery, were ordered held for trial on charges of conspiracy to commit ~ —*Associated Press*⟩ **2 :** needless or willful damage (as in literary criticism or editorial activity)

2mayhem \"\ *vt* **mayhemed** *or* **mayhemmed; mayhemed** *or* **mayhemmed; mayheming** *or* **mayhemming; mayhems :** to commit mayhem on

may·ing \'mā(i)ŋ, -ēŋ\ *n* -S *sometimes cap* [ME, fr. gerund of *mayen* to may, take part in the festivities of May Day] **:** the celebrating of May Day

may lady *n, usu cap M, obs* **:** MAY QUEEN

may lily *n, sometimes cap M* **:** LILY OF THE VALLEY

may lord *or* **may king** *n, usu cap M, obs* **:** a youth presiding over May Day festivities

may·nard's cuckoo \'mānə(r)dz-\ *n, usu cap M* [after Charles J. *Maynard* †1929 Am. ornithologist] **:** a West Indian cuckoo (*Coccyzus minor maynardi*) that is the only form of the mangrove cuckoo reaching the southernmost U. S.

mayn't \(¦)mā(ə)nt\ [by contr.] **:** may not

1mayo \'mä(,)(y)ō, 'mä(,)yō\ *n, pl* **mayo** *or* **mayos** *usu cap* **1 :** a Taracahitian people of Sonora, Mexico **2 :** a member of the Mayo people

2mayo \'mā(,)ō\ *adj, usu cap* [fr. *Mayo*, county in northwest Ireland] **:** of or from County Mayo, Ireland **:** of the kind or style prevalent in County Mayo

mayoid \'mī,ȯid, 'mä,y-\ *n* -S *usu cap* [2*Maya* + *-oid*] **:** a linguistic subdivision of the Mayan of Guatemala, Honduras, and the states of Chiapas, Tabasco, San Luis Potosi, Tamaulipas, and Veracruz, Mexico

may·on·naise \'māə,nāz, ,==ˈ=\ *n* -S [F, perh. irreg. fr. *Mahón*, seaport of Minorca] **1 a :** a semisolid dressing made by emulsifying a mixture of raw eggs or egg yolks, vegetable oil, and vinegar or lemon juice usu. together with salt and condiments **b :** a dish (as of fish) prepared with this dressing ⟨lobster ~⟩ **2 :** GOULASH 2a

may·or \'mā(ə)r, 'me(ə)r, 'māə, 'meə\ *n* -S [ME *maire*, fr. OF, fr. L *major* larger, greater — more at MAJOR] **:** the chief magistrate of a city or borough **:** the chief executive officer of a municipal corporation in the U. S. being elected by direct popular vote and serving from one to six years, having powers that vary from the merely advisory or legislative to the strongly executive with important appointments, the veto power, and sometimes preparation of the budget, and generally serving with a council but in many American cities replaced by or subordinate to a commission or city manager — used as a title or in a mode of address and to translate various foreign titles of similar municipal officials (as the French *maire* or the German *burgomaster*); see MAYOR'S COURT

1ma·yo·ral \'mäyə¦räl, 'mīə¦-\ *n* -S [Sp, fr. *mayor* larger, greater, fr. L *major*] **:** an overseer (as of a flock, an estate, or a group of tourists) in Spain

2may·or·al \'māərəl, 'me(ə)r-\ *adj* [*mayor* + *-al*] **:** of or relating to a mayor or his office

may·or·al·ty \'māərəltē, 'me(ə)r-, -ti, *substand* ,māə'ralədē *or* ,meə'- *or* -lətē *or* -i\ *n* -ES [ME *mairaltee*, fr. MF *mairalté*, fr. OF, fr. *maire* mayor + *-al* + *-té* -ty] **1 :** the office of mayor ⟨was elected to the ~ by a large majority⟩ **2 :** the term of office as a mayor ⟨accomplished little during his ~⟩

mayor-council \¦=(=)¦==\ *adj* **:** of, relating to, or constituting a method of municipal government in which policy-making and administrative powers are vested in a usu. elective mayor and council — compare COUNCIL-MANAGER PLAN, STRONG MAYOR, WEAK MAYOR

may·or·do·mo \,māə(r)'dō(,)mō, ,meə-\ *n* -S [AmerSp, fr. Sp, majordomo — more at MAJORDOMO] *Southwest* **:** a person in charge of a group or project: as **a :** a manager of a hacienda, ranch, or estate **b :** an overseer of an irrigation system

may·or·ess \'māərəs, 'me(ə)r-\ *n* -ES [ME *meyresse*, fr. *meyre*, *maire* mayor + *-esse* -ess] **1 :** the wife or official hostess of a mayor **2 :** a woman holding the office of mayor

mayor of the palace [trans. of ML *mayor palatii*] **:** an official under the Frankish kings who orig. was the chief officer of the royal household, later prime minister, and under the later Merovingians practically sovereign

mayor's court *n* **:** a court in some cities usu. presided over by the mayor and having jurisdiction over violations of city ordinances and other petty criminal or civil matters

may·or·ship \'māə(r),ship, 'me(ə)r,-, 'meə,-\ *n* [ME *maireshipp*, fr. *maire* mayor + *-shipp*, *-shipe* -ship] **:** the office or status of a mayor

mayo·ru·na \,mīə'rünə\ *n, pl* **mayoruna** *or* **mayorunas** *usu cap* **1 a :** a people of Brazil and northeastern Peru **b :** a member of such people **2 :** the language of the Mayoruna people sometimes classed as Panoan

may pear *n, usu cap M* **:** JUNEBERRY

may pink *n, usu cap M* **1 :** COTTAGE PINK **2 :** RHODORA 2

maypole \'=,=\ *n, often cap* **:** a tall pole in an open place and wreathed with flowers forming a center for May Day sports

maypole dance *n, usu cap M* **:** a folk dance in which long ribbons are woven about a Maypole by the dancers, typically as part of a May Day festivity

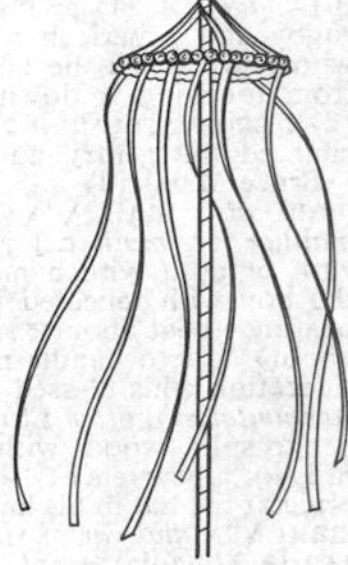

maypole

may·pop \'mā,päp\ *n* -S [alter. of 1*maycock*] **1 :** a somewhat hairy climbing perennial passionflower (*Passiflora incarnata*) of

the southern U. S. with large white to pale lavender flowers followed by a yellow edible but somewhat insipid berry about the size of a hen's egg **2 :** the fruit of the maypop
may queen *n, usu cap M* **:** a girl or young woman selected to preside over a May Day festival or other May party
may rose *n, usu cap M* **1 :** GUELDER ROSE **2 :** DAMASK ROSE
mays *pl of* MAY, *pres 3d sing of* MAY
mayst *archaic pres 2d sing of* MAY
may star *n, usu cap M* **:** STARFLOWER b
may·ten \(ˈ)mī¦ten\ *n* -s [Sp *maitén,* fr. Araucanian *mañtún*] **:** a Chilean evergreen tree (*Maytenus boaria*) having pendulous branches, slender lanceolate leaves, and minute flowers and being cultivated as an ornamental in warm countries
may·te·nus \mīˈtēnəs\ *n, cap* [NL, fr. Sp *maitén*] **:** a large genus of tropical American shrubs and trees (family Celastraceae) having evergreen leaves, small axillary flowers, and leathery capsules
maythe \ˈmāth\ *n, pl* **maythes** *but sing or pl in constr* [ME, fr. OE *mægtha, magethe*] *obs* **:** any of various weedy composite plants
maythorn \ˈ=,=\ *n, usu cap* **:** HAWTHORN
maytide *or* **maytime** \ˈ=,=\ *n, usu cap* **:** the period or month of May
may tree *n, usu cap M* **:** HAWTHORN
may·weed \ˈmā,=\ *n* [*may-* (fr. *maythe*) + *weed*] **1 :** strong-scented European chamomile (*Anthemis cotula*) that is naturalized along roadsides in the U. S. and has flower heads with a yellow disk and white rays — called also *dog fennel* **2 :** FEVERFEW
may whaup *n, usu cap M, dial Eng* **:** WHIMBREL
may whitewing *n, usu cap M* **:** WHITE-WINGED SCOTER
may wine *n, usu cap M* [trans. of G *maiwein*] **:** a punch consisting of champagne, Moselle or Rhine wine, and claret flavored with the herb woodruff
maywings \ˈ=,=\ *n pl but sing or pl in constr* **:** GAYWINGS
may–woon \(ˈ)mī¦wün\ *n* -s [Burmese *myowun,* fr. *myo* town + *wun* official, burden] **:** a Burmese provincial governor
¹maz- *or* **mazo-** *comb form* [NL, fr. Gk *mazos, mastos* — more at MEAT] **:** breast ⟨*mazalgia*⟩ ⟨*mazoplasia*⟩
²maz- *or* **mazo-** *comb form* [NL, fr. Gk *maza* placenta, fr. Gk, lump, mass, barley cake — more at MASS] **:** placenta ⟨*mazic*⟩ ⟨*mazopathia*⟩
ma·zae·di·um \məˈzēdēəm, maˈz-\ *n, pl* **mazae·dia** \-dēə\ [NL, fr. Gk *maza* lump, mass, barley cake + L *aedes* temple, house, building + NL *-ium* — more at EDIFY] **:** a fruiting body (as of some lichens) consisting of a powdery mass of free ascospores interspersed with sterile elements and enclosed in a peridium
ma·za·gran \¦mazə¦grän\ *n* -s [F, fr. *Mazagran,* village in northwest Algeria] **:** sweetened and usu. cold and diluted black coffee served in a glass
ma·za·hua \məˈzäwə\ *n, pl* **mazahua** *or* **mazahuas** *usu cap* **1 a :** an Otomian people of the states of Mexico and Michoacán, Mexico **b :** a member of such people **2 :** the language of the Mazahua people
mazal tov *var of* MAZEL TOV
ma·za·ma \məˈzämə\ *n, cap* [NL, fr. Nahuatl *maçam-, maçatl, mazatl* deer] **:** a genus of So. American deers (family Cervidae) comprising the brockets
ma·zan·de·ra·ni \¦mäzəndəˈränē\ *n, pl* **mazanderani** *or* **mazanderanis** *cap* **1 a :** a people of Mazanderan in northern Iran **b :** a member of such people **2 :** the Iranian language of the Mazanderani people
ma·za·pan \¦mäzə¦pän\ *adj, usu cap* [*Mazapan,* locality in central Mexico where remains of the culture were discovered] **:** of or belonging to a sedentary culture of Mexico centered to the northwest and west of the Valley of Mexico about A.D.1100 and characterized by plumbate and fine orange pottery
ma·zar \məˈzär\ *n* -s [Ar *mazār*] **:** a Muslim shrine or enshrined tomb
maz·ard \ˈmazə(r)d\ *n* -s [fr. obs. E *mazard* mazer, alter. (influenced by E *-ard*) of E *mazer*] *now chiefly dial* **:** HEAD, FACE ⟨a blow on the ~⟩
maz·a·rine \¦mazə¦rēn, ˈmazərən\ *n* -s [perh. after Jules *Mazarin* †1661 Fr. cardinal] **1** *now usu* **ma·za·rin** \"\ **:** a deep dish often of metal; *esp* **:** one formerly used as a liner for a serving dish and usu. pierced **2 :** MAZARINE BLUE **3** *or* **mazarine hood** [perh. after Hortense Mancini, duchess of *Mazarin* †1699] **:** a hood worn by women in the 17th century
mazarine blue *n, often cap M* **:** a deep purplish blue that is slightly redder than hyacinth blue, redder and paler than average sapphire (sense 2a), and redder, lighter, and stronger than cyanine blue (sense 1b) — called also *bellflower, Roslyn blue*
maz·a·tec \¦mazə¦tek\ *or* **maz·a·teco** \,mazəˈtā(,)kō, -te(-\ *also* **maz·a·te·ca** \-ākə,-ekə\ *n, pl* **mazatec** *or* **mazatecs** *or* **mazateco** *or* **mazatecos** *usu cap* **1 a :** a people of Oaxaca, Guerrero, and Veracruz, Mexico **b :** a member of such people **2 :** the language of the Mazatec people
maz·da·ism \ˈmazdə,izəm\ *n* -s *usu cap* [Av *Mazdāh-* Ahura Mazda, Zoroastrian deity believed to be the source of all good + E *-ism;* akin to Skt *medhā* intelligence, wisdom — more at MATHEMATICAL] **:** ZOROASTRIANISM
maz·dak·ite \ˈmazdə,kīt\ *also* **maz·dak·ean** \¦mazdə¦kēən\ *n* -s [*Mazdak,* 5th cent. A.D. Persian religious reformer + E *-ite* or *-an*] **:** a member of a communistic sect that was founded late in the 5th century by Mazdak and that advocated community of property and women, simplicity in life, and abstinence from meat
maz·da·yas·ni·an \,mazdəˈyäsnēən\ *n or adj, usu cap* **:** ZOROASTRIAN
maz·de·an \ˈmazdēən, (ˈ)maz¦d-\ *n or adj, usu cap* [Av *Mazdāh-* Ahura Mazda + E *-an*] **:** ZOROASTRIAN
maz·door *or* **maz·dur** \məzˈdu(ə)r\ *n* -s [Hindi *mazdūr,* fr. Per *muzdūr*] **:** an Indian laborer **:** COOLIE
¹maze \ˈmāz\ *vb* -ED/-ING/-S [ME *mazen, masen,* prob. fr. (assumed) OE *masian* to confuse; perh. akin to Sw *masa* to be sluggish] *vt* **1** *now chiefly dial* **:** to bring to a state of confused disorder **:** STUPEFY, DAZE **2 :** to greatly perplex **:** BEWILDER, CONFUSE ~ *vi* **:** to wander in or as if in a maze
²maze \"\ *n* -s [ME *maze, mase,* fr. *mazen, masen,* v.] **1 a** (1) **:** an intricate pattern of passages (as hedge-bordered paths) that ramifies and interconnects in a confusing way; *also* **:** a complicated winding path that is much longer than a corresponding direct route (2) **:** a path complicated by at least one blind alley and used in learning experiments and in intelligence tests **b :** something intricately and confusingly elaborate or complicated ⟨the ~ of inland waterways⟩ ⟨caught up in the ~ and whirl of political life⟩ ⟨the trials had become a legalistic ~ —*Collier's Yr. Bk.*⟩ **2** *now chiefly dial* **:** a state of bewilderment or amazement ⟨his mind was in a ~ —Liam O'Flaherty⟩

maze 1a (1)

³maze \"\ *n* -s [ME *meise,* fr. MF *maise* receptacle for herrings, fr. MLG *meise, mēse* barrel; akin to OHG *meisa* frame for carrying loads on the back, ON *meiss* basket, Skt *mesa* ram, fleece] *dial Brit* **:** any of various units of quantity of fish (as herring) from 500 to 650
mazed·ly \ˈmāz(ə)dlē\ *adv* **:** in a stupefied or bewildered manner **:** as if utterly confused
mazed·ness \-zədnəs, -z(d)n-\ *n* -ES [ME *mazednesse,* fr. *mazed* (past part. of *mazen, masen* to stupefy) + *-nesse* -ness] **:** the condition of one that is mazed or behaves mazedly
maze·ful \ˈmāzfəl\ *adj* [²*maze* + *-ful*] *archaic* **:** CONFUSING
ma·zel tov *or* **ma·zal tov** \ˈmäzəl,tōv, -tōf *also* -tōv\ *interj* [LHeb *mazāl ṭob,* lit., good luck] — used among Jews to express congratulations
maze·ment \ˈmāzmənt\ *n* -s [¹*maze* + *-ment*] **1** *obs* **:** AMAZEMENT **2 :** TRANCE, STUPOR
ma·zer \ˈmāzə(r)\ *n* -s [ME *mazer, maser* mazer, veined wood, fr. OF *mazre, mazere,* of Gmc origin; akin to OHG *masar* gnarled excrescence on a tree, ON *mösurr* maple] **:** a large drinking bowl orig. of a hard wood (as maple) and often footed and silver-mounted
mazer tree \"-\ *n* [ME *maser-tre,* fr. *mazer, maser* + *tre,* tree tree] **1 :** HEDGE MAPLE **2 :** BIRD CHERRY 1
maz·ha·bi \ˈməzəbē\ *n* -s *usu cap* [Hindi *mazhabī,* fr. Ar *madhhabīy* of or belonging to a sect, fr. *madhhab* sect] **:** an adherent of the Sikh religion of low-caste background fully assimilated into the Sikh community
mazic \ˈmazik, ˈmāz-\ *adj* [²*maz-* + *-ic*] **:** PLACENTAL
maz·i·ly \ˈmāzəlē, -lī\ *adv* [*mazy* + *-ly*] **:** in a confused or obscure fashion
mazo- — see MAZ-
mazo·car·pon \,māzōˈkär,pän, ,maz-, -,pən\ *n, cap* [NL *mazo-* (fr. Gk, fr. *maza* lump, mass, barley cake) + *-carpon* (fr. Gk *-karpon,* neut. of *-karpos* -carpous) — more at MASS] **:** a form genus of paleozoic fossil plants orig. described from sporangia alone and now included in *Sigillariostrobus*
ma·zoe lemon \məˈzōē-\ *n* [fr. *Mazoe,* town in Southern Rhodesia] *So. Africa* **:** ROUGH LEMON
mazo·pla·sia \,māzəˈplāzh(ē)ə, ,maz-\ *n* -s [NL, fr. ¹*maz-* + *-plasia*] **:** a degenerative condition of breast tissue
ma·zo·vi·an \məˈzōvēən\ *n* -s *usu cap* [*Mazovia,* ancient principality in Poland + E *-an*] **1 :** one of a Christian Polish community placed under the protection of the Teutonic knights early in the 13th century **2 :** the northeastern dialects of Polish
ma·zu·ma \məˈzümə\ *n* -s [Yiddish *mezumen,* fr. Heb *mĕzūmān, mĕzummān* fixed, appointed] *slang* **:** MONEY
ma·zur \ˈmä,zu̇(ə)r\ *or* **ma·zur·i·an** \məˈzu̇rēən\ *n* -s *usu cap* [*Mazur* fr. Pol; *Mazurian* fr. Pol *Mazur* + E *-an*] **1 :** a Pole of a Protestant community of southeastern Prussia **2 :** the Polish dialect of the Mazurs
ma·zur·ka *also* **ma·zour·ka** \məˈzərkə, -zu̇(ə)r-, -zō|, -zəl|, -zu̇ə|\ *n* -s [Russ *mazurka,* fr. Pol *mazurek* Mazur dance, fr. *Mazur*] **1 :** a Polish dance in moderate triple measure often of varied steps and figures but having characteristically a slide and hop to the side **2 :** music for the mazurka or in its rhythm usu. in moderate ¾ or ⅜ time and frequently with a strong accent on the second or third beat
mazurka jump *n* **:** a figure-skating jump in which the skater makes a vertical takeoff from the toes and bends one knee so as to cross the bent leg in front of the other in the air
ma·zus \ˈmāzəs\ *n* [NL, fr. Gk *mazos, mastos* breast; fr. the ridges on the lower lip of the flower — more at MEAT] **1** *cap* **:** a genus of low prostrate or creeping perennial herbs (family Scrophulariaceae) that have blue or white flowers in terminal one-sided racemes and are native to Asia and Australasia but often cultivated as ground covers or rock garden subjects **2** *pl* **mazus :** any plant of the genus *Mazus*
ma·zut *or* **ma·zout** *also* **ma·sut** \məˈzüt\ *n* -s [Russ *mazut*] **:** a viscous liquid residue from the distillation of Russian petroleum that is used chiefly as a fuel oil
mazy \ˈmāzē, -zi\ *adj* -ER/-EST [²*maze* + *-y*] **1 :** like or constituting a maze **:** confused or confusing because of intricate intertwining or overlapping ⟨a thousand rills their ~ progress take —Thomas Gray⟩ ⟨a gallant wig flowing in ~ ringlets —Norman Douglas⟩ **2** *dial Eng* **:** characterized by dizziness **:** GIDDY
¹maz·zard \ˈmazə(r)d\ *also* **mazzard cherry** *n* -s [origin unknown] **:** SWEET CHERRY 1; *esp* **:** wild or seedling sweet cherry used as a rootstock for grafting
²mazzard \"\ *var of* MAZARD
¹maz·zi·ni·an \(ˈ)mät¦sēnēən, -ädˈzē-\ *adj, usu cap* [Giuseppe *Mazzini* †1872 Ital. patriot + E *-an*] **:** of or relating to the Italian patriot Mazzini or his policies
²mazzinian \"\ *n* -s *usu cap* **:** a follower or adherent of Mazzini
maz·zi·nist \-sēnəst, -zē-\ *n* -s *usu cap* [Giuseppe *Mazzini* + E *-ist*] **:** MAZZINIAN
mb *abbr* millibar
MB *abbr* **1** medical board **2** medium bomber **3** motor boat **4** municipal borough **5** munitions board
MBA *abbr or n* -s **:** a master in business administration
mba·lo·lo \,embəˈlō(,)lō\ *n* -s [Fiji *mbololo*] **:** PALOLO
mba·ya \,embə¦yä\ *n, pl* **mbaya** *or* **mbayas** *usu cap* **1 a :** a Guaicuruan people of Paraguay **b :** a member of such people **2 :** the language of the Mbaya people
MBF *abbr* [L *mille* thousand] thousand board feet
MBH *abbr* [L *mille* thousand] thousands of BTU per hour
mbl *abbr* mobile
MBM *abbr* [L *mille* thousand] thousand feet board measure
mbo·ri \emˈbōrē\ *n* -s [origin unknown] **:** a mild form of surra affecting camels
MBT *abbr* mercaptobenzothiazole
mbun·du \emˈbün(,)dü\ *n, pl* **mbundu** *or* **mbundus** *usu cap* **1 :** a widespread Bantu-speaking people of Angola active in trading and known in world art circles for their wood carving esp. of miniature animal figures — called also *Ovimbundu* **2 a :** KIMBUNDU **b :** UMBUNDU
mbu·ti \emˈbüdē\ *n, pl* **mbuti** *or* **mbutis** *usu cap* **1 a :** a nomadic negroid Pygmy people of the western border of Uganda and adjacent areas to the south and west with reddish yellow skin — compare TWA **b :** a member of this people; *broadly* **:** NEGRILLO **2 :** the language of the Mbuti people
¹MC *abbr or n* -s **:** MASTER OF CEREMONIES, EMCEE
²MC *vb* **MC'd; MC'd; MC'ing; MC's :** EMCEE
mc *abbr* **1** megacycle **2** millicurie **3** millicycle
MC *abbr* **1** machinery certificate **2** magnetic course **3** marginal credit **4** marine corps **5** marked capacity **6** medical corps **7** medico-chirurgical **8** member of congress **9** member of council **10** metaling clause **11** meter-candle **12** metric carat **13** motor contact **14** motorcycle **15** movement control **16** multiple contact **17** my account
MCF *abbr* [L *mille* thousand] thousand cubic feet
mcg *abbr* microgram
MCH *abbr* mean corpuscular hemoglobin
mcht *abbr* merchant
MCI *abbr* malleable cast iron
MCO *abbr* mill culls out
MCU *abbr* medium close-up
MCV *abbr* mean corpuscular volume
MCW *abbr, often not cap* modulated continuous wave
MD *abbr or n* -s [L *medicinae doctor*] **:** a doctor of medicine
MD *abbr* **1** [F *main droite*] right hand **2** managing director **3** *often not cap* [It *mano destra*] right hand **4** medical department **5** memorandum of deposit **6** mental defective; mentally deficient **7** message dropping **8** *often not cap* months after date; month's date **9** muscular dystrophy
Md *symbol* mendelevium
m–day \ˈ=,=\ *n, usu cap M* [*m* (initial letter of *mobilization*) + *day*] **1 :** a day on which a military mobilization begins or is postulated (as in a problem in logistics) to begin **2 :** the day on which actual hostility breaks out at the commencement of a war
MDD *abbr* milligrams per square decimeter per day
mde·wa·kan·ton \,emdēˈwōkən,tän, ,medəˈw-\ *n* -s **:** a portion of the eastern forest group of the Dakota people
mdlle *abbr, often cap* mademoiselle
mdm *abbr, often cap* madam
mdme *abbr, often cap* madame
mdnt *abbr* midnight
m–dog \ˈ=,=\ *n, usu cap* [*m* (initial letter of *mine*) + *dog*] **:** a dog trained to locate buried mines
MDR *abbr* minimum daily requirement
MDS *abbr* main dressing station
mdse *abbr* merchandise
mdt *abbr* moderate
¹me \(ˈ)mē, ,mi\ *pron, objective case of* I [ME, fr. OE *mē;* akin to OHG *mih* me, ON & Goth *mik,* L *me,* Gk *me,* Skt *mā*] **1 :** I **:** a (1) — used as indirect object of a verb ⟨gave ~ a book⟩ (2) — used as indirect object in some archaic or obsolete expressions (as *meseems*) and usu. written solid with the verb element of such expressions; compare METHINKS (3) — used chiefly archaically as a vague indirect object simply to suggest the concern or involvement of the one speaking or writing ⟨tie ~ up this tress instantly —Laurence Sterne⟩ and sometimes used merely to fill out a sentence and having little or no meaning ⟨he enters ~ his name in the book —Charles Lamb⟩ **b** — used as object of a preposition ⟨stand behind ~⟩ **c** — used as direct object of a verb ⟨they know ~ very well⟩ **d** — used in comparisons after *than* and *as* when the first term in the comparison is the direct or indirect object of a verb or the object of a preposition ⟨likes him better than ~⟩ ⟨would more gladly give him the money than ~⟩ ⟨would be as helpful to you as ~⟩ **e** (1) — used in absolute or elliptical constructions ⟨who, ~⟩ esp. together with a prepositional phrase, adjective, or participle ⟨I was hungry and tired, and ~ without a cent to my name⟩ ⟨~ looking like a perfect fool, she scarcely glanced in my direction⟩ (2) — used in interjectional phrases typically to express unhappiness ⟨ah ~⟩ or surprise ⟨dear ~⟩ of the one speaking or writing or to express some other state or emotion indicated by an adjective that usu. precedes ⟨poor ~⟩ ⟨unlucky ~⟩ and that occas. follows archaically ⟨~ miserable which way shall I fly infinite wrath and infinite despair —John Milton⟩ **f** — used by speakers on all educational levels and by many reputable writers though disapproved by some grammarians in the predicate after forms of *be,* in comparisons after *than* and *as* when the first term in the comparison is the subject of a verb, and in other positions where it is itself neither the subject of a verb nor the object of a verb or preposition ⟨be thou ~, impetuous one —P.B.Shelley⟩ ⟨it's ~⟩ ⟨you're as big as ~⟩ ⟨~ and my big mouth⟩ **g** — used in substandard speech and formerly also by reputable writers as the subject of a verb which it does not immediately precede or as part of the compound subject of a verb ⟨there was left surviving only ~ —Oliver Goldsmith⟩ ⟨~ and my wife never go any more⟩ **2 :** MYSELF — used reflexively as indirect object of a verb ⟨I'm going to get ~ a wife⟩, object of a preposition ⟨I don't know whether to leave it here or take it with ~⟩, or direct object of a verb ⟨if I don't respect ~, nobody else will⟩ **3** — used like the adjective *my* with a gerund by speakers and writers on all educational levels though disapproved by some grammarians ⟨disapprove of ~ being so cheerful —S.E.White⟩
²me \"\ *n* -s **1 :** ³I **2** *dial* **:** what belongs to me
³me \ˈmē, mi\ *dial var of* MY
ME *abbr or n* -s mechanical engineer
ME *abbr* **1** *often not cap* managing editor **2** marbled edges **3** maximum effort **4** medical examiner **5** metabolizable energy **6** *often not cap* milligram equivalent; milliequivalent **7** most excellent **8** Muhammadan Era **9** muzzle energy
Me *symbol* methyl
MEA *abbr* monoethanolamine
meach \ˈmēch\ *var of* MEECH
mea·cock \ˈmē,käk\ *n* -s [origin unknown] *archaic* **:** a cowardly or effeminate man ⟨I shall be compted a ~, a milksop —John Lyly⟩
mea cul·pa \¦mäəˈku̇l(,)pä, -ä(,)ü̇'k- *sometimes* -kül- *or* ,mēəˈkəlpə\ *n, pl* **mea culpas** [L, through my fault] **:** a formal acknowledgment of personal fault or error
¹mead \ˈmēd\ *n* -s [ME *mede,* fr. OE *medu;* akin to OHG *metu* mead, ON *mjöthr,* Gk *methy* wine, Skt *madhu* sweet, honey, mead] **:** a fermented drink made of water and honey with malt, yeast, and sometimes other ingredients **:** METHEGLIN
²mead \"\ *n* -s [ME *mede,* fr. OE *mǣd*] *archaic* **:** MEADOW
mead·er \ˈmēdə(r)\ *n* -s [²*mead* + *-er*] *dial Eng* **:** MOWER
¹mead·ow \ˈme(,)dō, -,də, *often* -,dəw+V\ *n* -s *often attrib* [ME *medwe,* fr. OE *mǣdwe,* oblique case form of *mǣd;* akin to OE *māwan* to mow — more at MOW] **1 :** land in or predominantly in grass **:** GRASSLAND: as **a :** a piece of land on which grass is grown for hay or pasture **b :** a tract of moist low-lying usu. level grassland often along a watercourse — compare ¹BOTTOM 6 **c :** an upland area covered with grass and herbs and commonly surrounded by woodland ⟨cool mountain ~s⟩ **d** *dial* **:** an open swampy or marshy area often of considerable extent ⟨the New Jersey ~s⟩ **2 :** a feeding ground for fish ⟨a cod ~⟩ **3 :** MEADOW GREEN
²meadow \"\ *vt* -ED/-ING/-S **1 :** to convert into grassland **:** use for the production of hay or pasture ⟨cleared and ~ed the old orchard⟩ **2 :** to pasture (livestock) on grazing land
meadow ant *n* **:** any of several small ants that frequent open grassy land: as **a :** an ant of the genus *Lasius* **b :** PAVEMENT ANT
meadow barley *n* **:** a wild barley (*Hordeum nodosum*) that is probably native to Europe but widely distributed in No. America, grows chiefly in open meadow land, and is used chiefly for forage
meadow beauty *n* **:** DEER GRASS 2
meadow–beauty family *n* **:** MELASTOMACEAE
meadow bell *n, Brit* **:** HAREBELL
meadow bird *n* **:** BOBOLINK
meadow bright *n, dial Eng* **:** a marsh marigold (*Caltha palustris*)
meadowbrook \ˈ=,=,=\ *n* **:** a dark to dark grayish green that is bluer and slightly lighter than marine green
meadow brown *n* **:** any of several satyr butterflies; *esp* **:** a British butterfly (*Maniola jurtina*) having restricted orange markings on the upper surface of the wings of the male
meadow buttercup *n* **1 :** TALL BUTTERCUP **2 :** a marsh marigold (*Caltha palustris*)
meadow cabbage *n* **:** SKUNK CABBAGE
meadow campion *n* **:** RAGGED ROBIN
meadow cat's–tail grass *also* **meadow cat's tail** *n* **:** TIMOTHY
meadow chicken *n* **:** SORA RAIL
meadow chickweed *n* **:** FIELD CHICKWEED
meadow clary *n* **:** a tall perennial Old World salvia (*Salvia pratensis*) that has violet-blue flowers and occurs in open grasslands and waste places
meadow crake *or* **meadow drake** *n* **:** CORN CRAKE
meadow cranesbill *n* **:** a tall perennial cranesbill (*Geranium pratense*) with paired violet-blue axillary flowers that is native to northern parts of the Old World and naturalized in No. America
meadow crowfoot *n* **:** BULBOUS BUTTERCUP
meadow death camas *n* **:** a death camas (*Zygadenus venenosus*) that grows chiefly in wet grassland
mead·owed \ˈme(,)dōd, -,dəd\ *adj* [¹*meadow* + *-ed*] **:** having meadows **:** consisting of meadowland
meadow eelworm *n, chiefly Brit* **:** MEADOW NEMATODE
meadow fern *n* **1 :** SWEET GALE **2 :** SWEET FERN
meadow fescue *n* **:** a tall vigorous perennial European fescue grass (*Festuca elatior*) with broad flat leaves widely cultivated in Europe and America for permanent pasture and hay
meadow–foam \ˈ=(,)=,=\ *n* **:** a spreading herb (*Limnanthes douglasii*) of wet low-lying areas in the southwestern U. S. that is sometimes cultivated as an ornamental for its yellowish green lobed or parted succulent leaves and abundant showy white flowers
meadow foxtail *n* **:** a stout erect perennial grass (*Alopecurus pratensis*) of northern parts of the Old World that much resembles timothy, is widely cultivated for pasture and hay, and has become locally naturalized in No. America
meadow garlic *n* **:** a common wild onion (*Allium canadense*) of moist open land of eastern No. America
meadow gowan *n* **:** a marsh marigold (*Caltha palustris*)
meadow grass *n* [ME *medewe gras,* fr. *medewe, medwe* meadow + *gras* grass] **:** any of various grasses that thrive in the presence of abundant moisture: as **a :** a grass of the genus *Poa; esp* **:** KENTUCKY BLUEGRASS **b :** MEADOW FOXTAIL **c :** MANNA GRASS **d :** SKUNK GRASS
meadow grasshopper *n* **:** a grasshopper of the family Tettigoniidae
meadow green *n* **:** a dark yellowish green that is yellower and paler than holly green (sense 1), greener, lighter, and stronger than deep chrome green, and greener and lighter than average hunter green — called also *meadow*
meadow hay *n* **:** hay made from permanent and usu. natural grasslands
meadow hen *n* **1 :** AMERICAN BITTERN **2 :** AMERICAN COOT **3 a :** CLAPPER RAIL **b :** KING RAIL
mead·ow·ing \ˈmedōiŋ, -dəwiŋ\ *n* -s [¹*meadow* + *-ing*] **:** MEADOWLAND
meadowland \ˈ=,=,=\ *also* **meadow ground** *n* **:** land that is or is used as meadow
meadowlark \ˈ=,=,=\ *n* **1 :** any of several No. American birds of the genus *Sturnella* that are largely brown and buff above with a yellow breast marked with a black crescent and that are noted for their melodious sustained songs **2 :** ACORN 3
mead·ow·less \ˈmedōləs, -dəl-\ *adj* **:** lacking meadows or meadowland
meadow lily *n* **:** a common lily (*Lilium canadense*) of the eastern U. S. with nodding yellow or reddish flowers spotted with brown — see BULB illustration
meadow mouse *n* **:** any of various cricetid mice of *Microtus* and related genera; *esp* **:** a common American field mouse (*M. pennsylvanicus*)

meadow mushroom *n* **:** a common edible agaric (*Agaricus campestris*) occurring naturally in moist open organically rich soil and being the cultivated edible mushroom of commerce
meadow mussel *n* **:** an American mussel (*Volsella plicatula*) that has a ribbed shell and that is very abundant in salt marshes
meadow nematode *n* **:** any of numerous plant-parasitic nematode worms of *Pratylenchus* and related genera that were formerly considered to constitute a single variable species (*P. pratensis*) and that invade, migrate through, and multiply in the roots of various plants causing necrotic changes, rotting, and sloughing of tissues — compare ROOTKNOT NEMATODE
meadow oat grass *also* **meadow oat** *n* **:** TALL OAT GRASS
meadow ore *n* **:** BOG IRON ORE
meadow parsnip *n* **1 :** COW PARSNIP **2 :** a plant of the genus *Thaspium* **3 :** a golden alexander (*Zizia aurea*)
meadow pea *n* **:** a scrambling perennial Eurasian wild pea (*Lathyrus pratensis*) that has yellowish flowers and compressed seed pods and is cultivated as a forage plant
meadow peat *n* **:** peat formed in meadowland and predominantly from grasses and sedges
meadow phlox *n* **:** WILD SWEET WILLIAM 1
meadow pine *n* **1 :** any of several pines of the southern U. S.: as **a :** CARIBBEAN PINE **b :** LOBLOLLY PINE **2 :** a common No. American horsetail (*Equisetum arvense*) widely distributed in moist open ground
meadow pink *n* **1 :** RAGGED ROBIN **2 :** PURPLE-FRINGED ORCHID b
meadow pipit *n* **:** a common pipit (*Anthus pratensis*) that is olive brown above and largely whitish below and is widely distributed in open areas in northern and central Europe and much of Asia
meadowpride \'⸗⸗,⸗\ *n* **:** AMERICAN COLUMBO 1
meadow queen *n* **:** MEADOWSWEET 1
meadow rue *n* **:** a plant of the genus *Thalictrum*
meadow runagates *n pl but sing or pl in constr* **:** MONEYWORT
meadow rush *n* **:** a perennial bulrush (*Scirpus atrovirens*) with dark brownish green spikelets and creeping rootstocks that is a troublesome weed of wet low-lying pastures of eastern No. America
meadows *pl of* MEADOW, *pres 3d sing of* MEADOW
meadow saffron *n* **:** a plant of the genus *Colchicum*; *esp* **:** a bulbous autumn-flowering herb (*C. autumnale*) with white, lavender and white, or purple flowers — called also *autumn crocus*
meadow sage *n* **:** MEADOW CLARY
meadow salsify *n* **:** YELLOW GOATSBEARD
meadow saxifrage *n* **:** a European saxifrage (*Saxifraga granulata*) having alternate leaves and white flowers with erect sepals
meadow scabish *n* **:** COCASH 1
meadow snakegrass *n* **:** STINK GRASS 1
meadow snipe *n* **1 :** WILSON'S SNIPE **2 :** PECTORAL SANDPIPER
meadow soft grass *n* **:** VELVET GRASS
meadow sorrel *n* **:** [1]DOCK 1
meadow spittlebug *n* **:** a No. American cercopid insect (*Philaenus spumarius*) that severely damages grasses and other plants
meadowsweet \'⸗⸗,⸗\ *n* **1 :** a shrub of the genus *Spiraea; esp* **:** a No. American native or naturalized plant of this genus (as *S. alba* or *S. tomentosa*) **2 :** a plant of a genus (*Filipendula*) that is closely related to *Spiraea; esp* **:** a tall perennial Eurasian herb (*F. ulmaria*) that is sometimes cultivated for its single or double cymose white flowers
meadow vetchling *n* **:** MEADOW PEA
meadow violet *n* **:** a common violet (*Viola cucullata*) of wet or boggy land of eastern No. America with long-stemmed bluish violet or occasionally white or blue and white flowers
meadow vole *n* **:** MEADOW MOUSE
mead·ow·wink \'medō,wiŋk, -də,-\ *n* [perh. imit.] **:** BOBOLINK
mead·owy \'medōē, -dəwē, -i\ *adj* **1 :** like or like that of a meadow ⟨~ sweetness⟩ **2 :** consisting of or characterized by meadow ⟨~ shores⟩
mea·ger *or* **mea·gre** \'mēgə(r)\ *adj* [ME *megre*, fr. MF *maigre*, fr. L *macr-, macer*; akin to OE *mæger* lean, OHG *magar*, ON *magr* lean, Gk *makros* long, tall, Av *mas-* long] **1 :** destitute of or having little flesh **:** THIN, LEAN ⟨~ were his looks, sharp misery had worn him to the bones —Shak.⟩ **2 a :** lacking richness, fertility, strength, or comparable qualities **:** deficient in quantity or poor in quality **:** INFERIOR, INADEQUATE ⟨a ~ harvest⟩ ⟨stretching a ~ salary⟩ **b** *of verbal expression* **:** scanty in ideas **:** lacking strength of diction or sufficiency of imagery **3 :** dry and harsh to the touch ⟨chalk feels ~⟩ **4 :** MAIGRE
syn SCANTY, SCANT, SKIMPY, SCRIMPY, EXIGUOUS, SPARE, SPARSE: MEAGER suggests thin, pinched, slight smallness, inadequacy, barrenness, or utter lack of richness, strength, force, or fullness ⟨*meager* crops of rye, buckwheat, and potatoes scarcely provide a living for the inhabitants —Samuel Van Valkenburg & Ellsworth Huntington⟩ ⟨scientists with poor laboratories and *meager* salaries —W.A.Noyes b. 1898⟩ ⟨the child-mind is as yet too *meagre* in life-experience to confront the human enterprise —H.A.Overstreet⟩ SCANTY describes that which is barely adequate in quantity, size, extent, or degree or which only approaches adequacy ⟨the hunted wild beasts can live on *scanty* rations, going for days at a time without a mouthful —*Amer. Guide Series: Ariz.*⟩ ⟨such a *scanty* portion of light was admitted through these means that it was difficult, on first coming in, to see anything —Charles Dickens⟩ SCANT may indicate a falling or cutting short, sometimes by design, of what is desired or desirable ⟨where precipitation was too *scant* to support a solid earth covering —R.A.Billington⟩ ⟨savage people, huge in form, fierce in manner, and wearing *scant* clothing of skins —A.C.Whitehead⟩ ⟨most of the colonies gave them *scant* welcome, and many persecuted them —W.L. Sperry⟩ SKIMPY and SCRIMPY may imply niggardliness as a cause of smallness or inadequacy, the former perhaps arising from stinginess, the latter from necessitous parsimony ⟨the meal set before us upon our return to the Bear's Paw, tired and hungry, was a decidedly *skimpy* table d'hôte lunch —A.W. O'Neil⟩ ⟨the drab routine and *skimpy* meanness of the New England farm —V.L.Parrington⟩ ⟨the guests ate in silence, murmured with their food, were exceedingly well bred — more proud of their breeding than they were of the *scrimpy*, almost stingy respectability of the ménage —W.A.White⟩ EXIGUOUS describes a scanty smallness making whatever is under consideration compare most unfavorably with others of its kind ⟨in conditions the whole region, except for the river valleys that cross it, can support only a sparse and *exiguous* population who have little encouragement to cultural progress and have in fact remained backward —V.G.Childe⟩ SPARE may indicate a falling short of adequacy without, however, specific connotations, esp. depreciatory ones ⟨argument was *spare* and simple: surely the U. S. would not let a stout ally down in its hour of need —*Time*⟩ SPARSE implies thinness or lack of normal or hoped for thickness or density, with or without being therefore inadequate or insufficient ⟨the cays were little more than heaps of rock and sand, covered with coarse grass and a *sparse* growth of bush and stunted trees —C.B.Nordhoff & J.N.Hall⟩
meager lime *n* **:** lime containing a large amount of impurities (as 15 percent or more)
mea·ger·ly *adv* **:** in a meager manner **:** POORLY, INADEQUATELY ⟨very ~ represented at the conference⟩ ⟨served us grudgingly and ~⟩
mea·ger·ness *n* -ES **1 :** the quality or state of being meager ⟨~ of expression⟩ **2 :** something meager ⟨remembering these ~*es* and penny-pinchings⟩
[1]**meagre** \'mēgə(r)\ *vt* -ED/-ING/-S [*meager*] *archaic* **:** to make (as a person) thin
[2]**meagre** *var of* MAIGRE
meak \'mäk\ *n* -S [ME *meeke*] *dial Eng* **:** a long-handled bush hook **:** SCYTHE
[1]**meal** \'mēl, *esp before pause or consonant* 'mēəl\ *n* -S [ME *meel* mealtime, meal, fr. OE *mǣl* appointed time, mealtime, meal; akin to OHG *māl* time, ON *māl* measure, mealtime, Goth *mel* time, L *metiri* to measure — more at MEASURE] **1 a :** the portion of food taken at a particular time to satisfy hunger or appetite **:** REPAST **b :** an act or the time of eating a meal **2** *dial Eng* **a :** the act or time of milking **b :** the yield at a milking
[2]**meal** \"\ *vb* -ED/-ING/-S **:** EAT, FEED
[3]**meal** \"\ *n* -S [ME *mele*, fr. OE *melu*; akin to OHG *melo* meal, ON *mjöl* meal, OHG & Goth *malan* to grind, ON *mala*, L *molere* to grind, Gk *mylē* mill] **1 :** the ground seeds of a cereal grass or pulse esp. when coarsely ground and unbolted and usu. excluding flour of wheat: as **a :** OATMEAL **b** *obs* **:** the finer inner part of such ground seeds **c :** CORNMEAL **2 :** a product resembling seed meal in particle size, texture, or other quality: as **a :** a product obtained by grinding the residue remaining after removal of part of the oil from various nuts and other oily seeds — see OIL MEAL **b :** a product obtained by grinding any of various dried food products (as meat or fish) **c :** a product obtained by rapid crystallization ⟨alum ~⟩
[4]**meal** \"\ *vb* -ED/-ING/-S *vt* **1 :** to cover with meal or a mealy substance **2 :** to reduce (as the constituents of gunpowder) to powder **:** PULVERIZE ~ *vi* **:** to yield or become meal ⟨a flint corn that ~*s* well⟩
[5]**meal** *n* -S [ME *mele*, fr. OE *mēle* tub, bucket; akin to ON *mælir*, a measure] *obs* **:** a tub or bucket that is sometimes used as a measure
[6]**meal** \'mē(ə)l\ *n* -S [ON *mælir*, a measure; akin to ON *māl* measure, mealtime — more at [1]MEAL] **:** a variable weight used esp. formerly in the Orkney islands
[7]**meal** *vt* [perh. fr. (assumed) ME *melen*, fr. OE *-mǣlan*; akin to OHG *meilen* to stain; denominative fr. the root of OE *mǣl* spot, blemish — more at MOLE] *obs* **:** STAIN
[8]**meal** \'mē(ə)l\ *n* -S [ON *melr*; perh. akin to OE *melu* meal — more at [3]MEAL] *dial Eng* **:** SANDBANK, DUNE
-meal \,mēl, "mē(ə)l\ *adv comb form* [ME *-mele*, fr. OE *-mǣlum*, fr. *mǣlum*, dat. pl. of *mǣl* appointed time — more at MEAL (repast)] **:** by a (specified) portion or measure at a time ⟨inch*meal*⟩ ⟨piece*meal*⟩
meal·able \'mēləbəl\ *adj* [[4]*meal*] **:** reducible to meal
meal beetle *n* **:** the adult of the mealworm
meal·berry \'mēl- — *see* BERRY\ *n* [[3]*meal*] **:** BEARBERRY 1
meal·er \'mēlə(r)\ *n* -S [[4]*meal*] **1 :** a wooden implement for mealing powder **2** [[2]*meal*] **:** a person rooming at one place and boarding at another
meal·ie \'mēlē, -li\ *n* -S [Afrik *mielie*, fr. Pg *milho* millet, Indian corn, fr. L *milium* millet — more at MILLET] **1** *Africa* **:** INDIAN CORN — usu. used in pl. ⟨the best time to plant ~*s*⟩ **2** *or* **mealie cob** *Africa* **:** an ear of Indian corn — see GREEN MEALIES
meal·i·ness \'mēlēnəs, -lin-\ *n* -ES **:** the quality or state of being mealy; *esp* **:** possession of a mealy texture
meal·less \'mēlləs\ *adj* [[1]*meal* and [3]*meal*] **:** lacking meal or a meal ⟨the gaping ~ bin⟩ ⟨sent ~ to bed⟩
meal·man \'mēlmən\ *n, pl* **mealmen :** a dealer in meal
mealmonger \'⸗,⸗⸗\ *n* **:** MEALMAN
meal moth *or* **meal snout moth** *n* **:** any of several small widely distributed moths (as the Indian meal moth or the Mediterranean flour moth) having larvae that feed in milled and stored grain products; *esp* **:** a small golden brown moth (*Pyralis farinalis*) with dark and whitish markings
meal–mouthed \'⸗;⸗\ *adj* **:** MEALYMOUTHED 1
meal·ock \'mēlək\ *n* -S [origin unknown] *Scot* **:** a small piece or crumb of bread
meal offering *n* **:** a vegetable sacrifice among the ancient Israelites consisting of flour and salt usu. mingled with oil and frankincense
meal pennant *n* **:** a red pennant used (as in the U. S. Navy or on a yacht) to indicate that the crew is at a meal
meal plum *n* [[3]*meal*] **:** BEARBERRY 1
meal ticket *n* **1 :** a ticket authorizing the provision of a meal; *esp* **:** a card with a specified cash value that is sold by a restaurant at a discount, is redeemable at the face value in food, and constitutes a method of prepayment for meals **2 a :** a person that provides the living expenses of another ⟨only married her for a *meal ticket*⟩ **b :** someone or something that is the ultimate source of one's income ⟨had to nurse the old truck along because it was our *meal ticket*⟩ ⟨this toothpaste account was the real *meal ticket* of the agency⟩
mealtide *n* [ME *meltid*, fr. OE *mǣltīd*, fr. *mǣl* meal + *tīd* time — more at MEAL, TIDE] *obs* **:** MEALTIME
mealtime \'⸗,⸗\ *n* [ME *meeltime*, fr. *meel* meal + *time* — more at MEAL, TIME] **:** the time at which one takes a meal; *esp* **:** the usual time at which a meal is served ⟨knew that if he was not home by ~ he would get nothing to eat⟩
mealworm \'⸗,⸗\ *n* **:** the larva of various beetles of the family Tenebrionidae that infests, feeds on, and pollutes grain products (as flour and meals) but is often cultured for food for insectivorous animals, laboratory use, or as bait for fishing; *esp* **:** a pale brown to yellowish larva of a cosmopolitan beetle (*Tenebrio molitor*) — called also *yellow mealworm*
mealy \'mēlē, -li\ *adj* -ER/-EST [[3]*meal* + *-y*] **1 :** having the qualities of or resembling meal **:** soft, dry, and friable ⟨a ~ potato⟩ **2 :** containing or consisting of meal **:** FARINACEOUS **3 a :** covered with meal or with fine granules **:** FARINOSE, POLLINOSE ⟨a butterfly with ~ wings⟩ **b :** flecked with another color (as white or gray) ⟨a *mealy*-nosed mule⟩ **c :** SPOTTY, UNEVEN ⟨a ~ photographic negative⟩ **d** *of the complexion* **:** pale as if dusted with flour **:** PALLID, BLANCHED **4 :** tending to be obscure or affected in speech **:** MEALYMOUTHED
mealy amazon *n, usu cap A* **:** a large So. American parrot (*Amazona farinosa*) with the greenish upper parts of a mealy appearance
mealy–back \'⸗⸗,⸗\ *n, Austral* **:** CICADA
mealy bellwort *n* **:** MOHAWK WEED
mealy bird *or* **mealy duck** *n, dial Brit* **:** an immature old⸗squaw duck
mealybug \'⸗⸗,⸗\ *n* **:** any of numerous scales of the family Pseudococcidae that are covered with a white powdery substance and are serious pests of fruit trees and of many other cultivated plants esp. in greenhouses
mealybug wilt *n* **:** a wilt of the pineapple esp. destructive in Hawaii that is associated with the feeding of the pineapple mealybug
mealymouth \'⸗⸗,⸗\ *n* **1 :** a mealymouthed person **2** *dial Brit* **:** WILLOW WARBLER
mealymouthed \¦⸗⸗¦⸗\ *adj* **1 a :** unwilling to tell the truth in plain language **:** tending to cloak thoughts, ideas, or intents by the use of obscure or devious language ⟨a ~ hypocrite⟩; *often* **:** affectedly unwilling to use strong or coarse language **b** *of an utterance* **:** suitable to a mealymouthed person ⟨~ phrases⟩ **2** *of an animal* **:** having a zone of white behind a black muzzle — used esp. of cattle and horses — **mealy·mouthed·ly** \-¦mau̇thədlē, -thədlē, -thtlē, -thdlē\ *adv* — **mealy·mouthed·ness** \-thədnəs, -thəd n-, -th(t)n-, -th(d)n-\ *n* -ES
mealy plum aphid *n* **:** a pale green aphid (*Hyalopterus pruni*) with a powdery body surface that is native to Europe but widely naturalized on various fruit trees where it causes stunting and distortion of new growth and splitting and soiling of fruit
mealy redpoll *n* **:** a rather large pale European redpoll (*Carduelis flamea* or *Acanthis flammea*)
mealy scale *n* **:** MEALYBUG
mealy starwort *also* **mealy stargrass** *n* **:** a colicroot (*Aletris farinosa*)
mealy tree *n* **1 :** WAYFARING TREE 1 **2 :** ARROWWOOD 1a
mealywing \'⸗⸗,⸗\ *n* **:** WHITEFLY
[1]**mean** \'mēn\ *adj* -ER/-EST [ME *mene*, fr. *imene*, fr. OE *gemǣne*; akin to OHG *gimeini* common, Goth *gamains*, L *communis*; all prob. fr. a prehistoric western IE compound whose first constituent is represented by L *com-* and whose second constituent is akin to L *munus* service, gift, Skt *mayate* he exchanges — more at CO-] **1** *now dial Brit* **:** held or done in common **2 :** destitute of distinction or eminence **:** COMMON, LOW, HUMBLE **3 :** destitute of power or acumen **:** ORDINARY, INFERIOR ⟨a man of ~ intelligence⟩ **4 :** of little value or account **:** of poor or inferior quality or status **:** worthy of little or no regard **:** SHABBY, CONTEMPTIBLE ⟨the ~*er* quarters of the town⟩ ⟨living in ~ circumstances⟩ **5 :** lacking dignity of mind **:** LOW-MINDED **:** IGNOBLE, BASE **:** destitute of honor ⟨a ~ motive⟩ **6 :** PENURIOUS, STINGY, CLOSEFISTED ⟨~ hospitality⟩ **7 a :** characterized by petty selfishness or malice **:** contemptibly disobliging or unkind ⟨a ~ surly man⟩ **b :** tending to harass or distress by reason of vexatious characteristics or conditions ⟨a ~ soil to work⟩ ⟨a ~ place to drive a car in⟩ **c** *slang* **:** of a kind to impress (as an adversary or an observer) **:** EXCELLENT, EFFECTIVE ⟨pitches a ~ curve⟩ ⟨dances a ~ tango⟩ **8 a :** lowered in self-esteem **:** ASHAMED ⟨his ready cooperation made me feel ~ for what I had said⟩ **b :** SICK, UNWELL, INDISPOSED ⟨felt thoroughly ~ with a cold⟩
[2]**mean** \"\ *adv* -ER/-EST **:** in a low, petty, or contemptible way ⟨acted ~ to us⟩ ⟨a narrow *mean*-thinking busybody⟩
[3]**mean** \"\ *vb* **meant** \'ment\ *or archaic* **meaned; meant** *or archaic* **meaned; meaning; means** [ME *menen*, fr. OE *mǣnan*; akin to OHG *meinen* to have in mind, OSlav *měniti* to mention, consider] *vt* **1 :** to have in the mind esp. as a purpose or intention **:** PURPOSE, DESIGN, INTEND ⟨houses are *meant* for use⟩ ⟨~*s* to make it difficult for you⟩ ⟨*meant* to come home early⟩ **2 :** to serve or intend to convey, show, or indicate **:** SIGNIFY, DENOTE, EXPRESS ⟨what do you ~ by such conduct⟩ ⟨these words ~ nothing to me⟩ **3 :** to have significance or importance to the extent or degree of **:** count for ⟨health ~*s* everything⟩ ⟨a happy home ~*s* much to a child⟩ ⟨music ~*s* little to me⟩ ⟨success without recognition ~*s* nothing to him⟩ ⟨her happiness *meant* the world to him⟩ **4 :** to intend for or direct to a particular individual ⟨his criticism is *meant* for all of us⟩ ⟨do you ~ this for me⟩ ~ *vi* **1 :** to have an intended purpose — used chiefly with *well* or *ill* ⟨*meant* well but seldom carried anything to a conclusion⟩ **2** *obs* **:** TALK, SPEAK, TELL **3** *obs* **:** to hold an opinion **:** THINK
syn MEAN, DENOTE, SIGNIFY, and IMPORT can have, in common, the sense of to convey (an idea, an interpretation, and so on) to the mind or understanding. MEAN is the most common and general in carrying the basic sense, although it can often connote evaluation or appraisal; in applying to a term it involves the term's full content ⟨to understand what foreign words *mean*⟩ ⟨what a person's actions *mean*⟩ ⟨disunion, incoherence and inconsistency *mean* failure in design —C.W.H. Johnson⟩ ⟨to understand what an obligation *means*⟩ ⟨the term "beauty" can *mean* many things⟩ DENOTE can contrast with SIGNIFY in having as its subject something that serves as an outward sign or visible indication; in application to a term it implies the limited and defined designation of a term disentangled from connotation or unessential association ⟨slumped into a chair near the doorway, his posture *denoting* complete exhaustion —L.C.Douglas⟩ ⟨that curious love of green, which . . . in nations is said to *denote* a laxity, if not a decadence of morals —Oscar Wilde⟩ ⟨the best way to show what a term *denotes* is to point at the object it stands for⟩ SIGNIFY can contrast with DENOTE in having as its subject something of a symbolic or representative character; it can also carry a stronger implication of the importance of the conveyed meaning; in application to a term it stresses the symbolic relationship between term and idea ⟨he had hopes that her demure and reticent deportment *signified* that the effervescence of youth had evaporated —Robert Grant †1940⟩ ⟨the third figure, with a background of plow handles and mining tools, *signifies* agriculture and mining —*Amer. Guide Series: Mich.*⟩ ⟨the loss of his wife *signified* more than he could ever put into words⟩ ⟨the term "bread and butter" *signifies* the material necessities of life⟩ IMPORT can carry the idea of offering for comprehension or intellectual grasp, often, however, being virtually interchangeable with SIGNIFY; in application to a term it can stress the implications involved in the term's interpretation as distinct from its denotation ⟨the radical ideas *imported* little to conservative readers except the idea of outrageous thinking⟩ ⟨though a term's denotation may be matter of fact, in its connotations the term may *import* revolution⟩ **syn** see in addition INTEND
— mean business : to be in earnest **:** have a sober, serious, and determined intent in respect to something
[4]**mean** \"\ *vb* -ED/-ING/-S [ME *menen*, fr. OE *mǣnan* to lament, mourn for, fr. (assumed) OE *mān* lamentation, moan — more at MOAN] *vt* **1** *now chiefly Scot* **:** to complain or lament over **:** RESENT **2** *now chiefly Scot* **:** PITY **3** *now chiefly Scot* **:** to present as a complaint ~ *vi, chiefly Scot* **:** LAMENT, COMPLAIN, BEMOAN
[5]**mean** \"\ *n* -S [ME *mene*, fr. *menen* to complain or lament over] *now chiefly Scot* **:** LAMENT, COMPLAINT
[6]**mean** \"\ *n* -S [ME *mene*, fr. MF *meien, moien*, fr. OF, fr. *meien, moien*, adj. — more at [7]MEAN] **1 a :** something (as a step, stage, connection) intervening, intermediate, or intermediary ⟨so do I wish the crown, being so far off and so I chide the ~*s* that keep me from it —Shak.⟩ **b** *or* **meane** (1) **:** the middle voice in 14th century fauxbourdon; *broadly* **:** the middle (as alto or tenor) part of a harmonized musical composition (2) **:** the alto of a consort of viols (3) **:** one of the middle strings of a viol ⟨great ~⟩ **c :** a middle point or something that is in or near a middle point **:** something that falls between extremes (as of place, time, number, rate): as (1) **:** something (as prudence, temperateness) that is intermediate between excess and deficiency and represents moderation ⟨the moral ~ is no mathematical mean between extremes, but is, in any given case, relative to persons and places —Lucius Garvin⟩ (2) *Confucianism* **:** the course of moderate action between extremes in the development of the virtues of temperance and prudence (3) *Buddhism* **:** the middle way **:** the course of moderation between asceticism and self-indulgence **d** (1) **:** a quantity of the same kind as the members of a set that in some sense is representative of them all and that is located within their range in accordance with a set rule (2) **:** the mean value of a variable between given limits (3) **:** either of the middle two terms of a proportion **2 a :** something by the use or help of which a desired end is attained or made more likely **:** an agent, tool, device, measure, plan, or policy for accomplishing or furthering a purpose — usu. used in pl. but sing. or pl. in constr. ⟨secure peace by honorable ~*s*⟩ ⟨the justification of barbarous ~*s* by holy ends —H.J.Muller⟩ ⟨~*s* . . . for keeping the prices of building materials high —T. W.Arnold⟩ ⟨a continuous belt is a ~*s* of power transmission from one shaft to another⟩ **b** *obs* **:** MEDIATOR, INTERCESSOR, GO-BETWEEN — sometimes used in pl. but sing. in constr. **c** *obs* **:** favorable condition **:** OPPORTUNITY **3 means** *pl* **:** resources (as of force or wealth) available for disposal **:** material resources in such supply as to form the basis for an economically secure and sheltered life ⟨a man of ~*s*⟩; *broadly* **:** WEALTH, MONEY **4** *obs* **:** MEANTIME
syn INSTRUMENT, AGENT, INSTRUMENTALITY, ORGAN, MEDIUM, VEHICLE, CHANNEL: MEAN or MEANS, the latter now the common form in all uses, is a very general term applicable to anything employed in performing or executing some end ⟨the habit of regarding the laboring class as a mere *means* to the maintenance of the rest —G.L.Dickinson⟩ ⟨the principal *means* of transportation was . . . Afghan camels —Herbert Hoover⟩ ⟨language as a *means* of social control —J.B.Carroll⟩ ⟨faith in science as a *means* . . . to knowledge and grace —F.B.Millett⟩ INSTRUMENT may suggest a certain ready applicability to the matter under consideration rather than only the bare fact of use, and with reference to people susceptibility to use or willingness to be used ⟨tariffs and immigration restriction are chief *instruments* of this economic nationalism —J.A.Hobson⟩ ⟨the American public school as an *instrument* for strengthening the spirit of national unity —J.B.Conant⟩ ⟨extremes of corruption were reached — and here again the eunuchs were sinister and convenient *instruments* —Owen and Eleanor Lattimore⟩ AGENT in reference to natural phenomena may designate an inner capability and suggest only incidentally, if that, its being used; in reference to matters personal and social it stresses being directed by another in his interest but lacks other suggestion or value notion ⟨the bee makes honey, the spider secretes a filament; you can hardly say that any of these *agents* believes —T.S.Eliot⟩ ⟨her great lords, spiritual and temporal . . . the *agents* of her will —Henry Adams⟩ ⟨an unconscious *agent* in the hands of Providence when you recalled me —Willa Cather⟩ INSTRUMENTALITY may suggest the fact of serving as an instrument but in today's English it is likely to suggest a means or agency which is a minor part of a larger entity or under the control of a subsuming organization ⟨in the American colonies, the newspapers were a major *instrumentality* throughout the entire struggle for independence —F. L.Mott⟩ ⟨governments or subdivisions or *instrumentalities* thereof —*U. S. Code*⟩ ORGAN suggests a functioning part of a larger esp. organic whole, or more specif., a means of communication, esp. a controlled or proprietory one ⟨the Council of State was a small body that met with the king three times a

week, and it was the pivotal *organ* of government —Stringfellow Barr⟩ ⟨the Journal is the *organ* of the American Medical Association⟩ MEDIUM indicates an intermediate means, esp. a means of conveyance or communication, in connection with the latter a favored or accustomed means ⟨he had now in the periodical a *medium* for his delicate poetic talent —S.T. Williams⟩ ⟨each *medium* says something that cannot be uttered as well or as completely in any other tongue —John Dewey⟩ VEHICLE likewise indicates a means of conveying or communicating; it may be more specific and tangible than MEDIUM ⟨Roosevelt's speeches were . . . the *vehicle* by which he set in motion tremendous social and moral forces —H.L. Hopkins⟩ CHANNEL suggests a course or path of transmission or communication more forcefully than a means ⟨a petition was drafted, signed by sixty-seven scientists, and sent through proper *channels* to the President of the United States —Harrison Brown⟩ **syn** see in addition AVERAGE
— **by all means** *adv* **:** most assuredly **:** without fail **:** CERTAINLY — **by any means** *adv* **:** in any way **:** at all — **by means of** *prep* **:** through the instrumentality of **:** by the use of as a means — **by no means** *or* **by no manner of means** *adv* **:** in no way **:** not at all **:** certainly not

[7]**mean** \"\ *adj* [ME *mene*, fr. MF *meien*, *moien*, fr. OF, fr. L *medianus* — more at MEDIAN] **1 :** occupying a middle position **:** occurring between the limits or extremes: as **a** *obs* **:** intermediate in space **b :** intermediate in order, rank, or status ⟨the ~ term of a syllogism⟩ **c :** intermediate in time **d :** intermediate in kind or degree ⟨pursue a ~ course in politics⟩ **2 :** occupying a position about midway between extremes: as **a :** near the average or norm ⟨of a ~ stature⟩ **b :** of a moderate degree of excellence **:** MIDDLING, MEDIOCRE **3 :** serving as a means **:** INTERMEDIARY **4 :** having an intermediate value between two extremes **:** AVERAGE ⟨the ~ high tide is 8 feet⟩

[8]**mean** *adv* [ME *meane*, fr. *meane*, *mene* occupying a middle position, intermediate — more at [7]MEAN] **1** *obs* **:** MODERATELY **2** *obs* **:** comparatively less **3** *obs* **:** so as to fall between

[9]**mean** *vt* -ED/-ING/-S [ME *menen*, fr. *mene*, n. — more at [6]MEAN] *obs* **:** MEDIATE

mean calorie *n* [[7]*mean*] **:** CALORIE c

[1]**me·an·der** *also* **mae·an·der** \mē'andə(r), -'aan-\ *n* -S [L *maeander*, fr. Gk *maiandros*, fr. *Maiandros* (now *Menderes*), river in western Asia Minor proverbial for its winding course] **1 a :** a turn or winding of a stream **b :** a winding path or course **:** LABYRINTH **2 :** a tortuous or intricate movement or journeying **3 :** the Greek fret or key pattern originating in the period of geometric art about 1000–700 B.C. to become a permanent motif in Greek ornament

[2]**meander** \"\ *vb* **meandered; meandered; meandering** \-d(ə)riŋ\ **meanders** *vi* **1 :** to wind or turn in a course or passage **:** follow an intricate course ⟨across the ceiling ~*ed* a long crack —John Galsworthy⟩ **2 :** to wander aimlessly or casually and without urgent destination **:** RAMBLE, DRIFT ⟨~*ed* lazily through old diaries in vague search of an idea⟩ ⟨~*ing* fruitlessly from one job to another⟩ ~ *vt* **1 :** to form a meander in or of **:** cause to meander ⟨streams ~*ing* the flat plain⟩ ⟨strolling along the ~*ed* bank⟩ **2 :** to follow along the windings of (as a stream) ⟨~*ed* the lower reaches of the river⟩ **3 :** to survey a meander line on or along ⟨if such streams were not ~*ed* in connection with the public survey —*U. S. Code*⟩

meander belt *n* **:** the part of a valley bottom across which a stream shifts its channel from time to time esp. in flood

me·an·der·er \-d(ə)rə(r)\ *n* -S **:** one that meanders

me·an·der·ing·ly *adv* **:** so as to form a meander **:** without clearcut or urgent course or aim

meander line *n* **:** a usu. irregular surveyed line that is not a boundary line; *esp* **:** one following the outline of a stream, lake, or swamp

mean deviation *n* **:** the average of the absolute values of the deviations from some measure of central tendency in a statistical distribution

mean difference *n* **:** the average of the absolute values of the $n(n-1)/2$ differences that exist between pairs in a statistical distribution of n elements

mean distance *n* **:** the arithmetical mean of the maximum and minimum distances of a planet, satellite, or secondary star from its primary

me·an·dra \mē'andrə\ *or* **me·an·dri·na** \,mēən'drīnə\ *syn of* MAEANDRA

me·an·drine \mē'an,drīn, -rēn, -,drən\ *or* **me·an·droid** \-n,drȯid\ *adj* [*meandrine* ISV *meandr-* (fr. NL *Maeandra*) + *-ine; meandroid* fr. NL *Maeandra* + E *-oid*] *of a coral* **:** having a convoluted surface

me·an·drous \mē'andrəs\ *adj* **:** WINDING, FLEXUOUS, RAMBLING

meaned *past of* MEAN

[1]**meaner** *comparative of* MEAN

[2]**meaner** \'mēnə(r)\ *n* -S [[3]*mean* + *-er*] **:** one that means

mean error *n* **:** the mean deviation of a distribution of accidental errors

meanest *superlative of* MEAN

mean free path *n* **:** the average distance traversed between collisions by particles (as molecules of a gas or free electrons in metal) in a system of agitated particles — called also *free path*

mean·ie *or* **meany** \'mēnē, -ni\ *n, pl* **meanies** [[1]*mean* + *-ie*] **:** an ungracious unattractive person: as **a :** a niggardly ungenerous person **b :** a harsh carping unfair critic **c :** a theatrical or literary villain

[1]**mean·ing** \'mēniŋ, -nēŋ\ *n* -S [ME *mening*, fr. gerund of *menen* to intend — more at [3]MEAN] **1 a :** the thing one intends to convey by an act or esp. by language **:** PURPORT ⟨do not mistake my ~⟩ **b :** the thing that is conveyed or signified esp. by language **:** the sense in which something (as a statement) is understood **:** IMPORT ⟨what is its ~ to you⟩ **2 :** the thing that is meant or intended **:** INTENT, PURPOSE, AIM, OBJECT ⟨a mischievous ~ was apparent⟩ **3 :** SIGNIFICANCE ⟨a look full of ~⟩ **4 a** *or* **meaning in intension :** the logical connotation of a word or phrase **:** the intension of a term **:** what a correct definition exhibits **b** *or* **meaning in extension :** the logical denotation or extension of a term **:** the thing or class named by a word or substantive phrase **5 :** the pattern of engrams aroused by a given stimulus

[2]**meaning** \"\ *adj* [fr. pres. part. of [3]*mean*] **1 :** exhibiting a usu. specified intent or purpose ⟨a well-*meaning* man⟩ **2 :** conveying or intended to convey meaning **:** SIGNIFICANT ⟨a ~ smile⟩ — **mean·ing·ly** *adv* — **mean·ing·ness** *n* -ES

mean·ing·ful \-ŋfəl\ *adj* **1 :** having a meaning or purpose **:** capable of being understood or interpreted **:** requiring or done with understanding and intent ⟨~ work⟩ ⟨~ training⟩ ⟨a ~ experience⟩ **2 :** constructed according to the rules of a language or system of signs **:** having an assigned function in a system ⟨in a two-valued system of logic all ~ propositions are either true or false⟩ **syn** see EXPRESSIVE

mean·ing·ful·ly \-fəlē\ *adv* **:** in a meaningful manner **:** so as to be meaningful

mean·ing·ful·ness *n* -ES **:** the quality or state of being meaningful

mean·ing·less \'mēniŋlə̇s, -nēŋ-\ *adj* **1 :** lacking a meaning **:** having no significance ⟨~ jargon⟩ **2 :** having no assigned function in a given language or system of signs **:** not formed according to the rules of construction of a system **:** not being a genuine element in a sign system ⟨a word group resembling a statement is either true, false, or ~⟩ ⟨the phrase "curvature of space" is ~ in Euclidean geometry⟩ — **mean·ing·less·ly** *adv* — **mean·ing·less·ness** *n* -ES

mean life *n* **:** AVERAGE LIFE

mean line *n* [[7]*mean*] **:** BISECTRIX

[1]**mean·ly** *adv* [ME *menely*, fr. *mene* occupying a middle position + *-ly* — more at MEAN] **1** *archaic* **:** to a moderate degree **:** fairly well **:** PASSABLY, TOLERABLY **2** *obs* **:** only moderately

[2]**mean·ly** *adv* [[1]*mean* + *-ly*] **:** in a mean manner: as **a :** in a lowly manner **:** POORLY, HUMBLY, PLAINLY ⟨living ~ and without ostentation⟩ **b :** in an inferior or indifferent manner **:** BADLY ⟨troops ~ equipped⟩ **c :** in a base or ungenerous manner or with the ascription of meanness ⟨~ threatens the deepest values of all truly traditional men —W.S.White⟩

mean midnight *n* **:** midnight by mean solar time

mean moon *n* [[7]*mean*] **:** a fictitious moon imagined for purposes of calculation to revolve around the earth uniformly in the same period as that of the real moon

[1]**mean·ness** \'mēnnə̇s\ *n* -ES [[1]*mean* + *-ness*] **1 :** the quality or state of being mean (as in exhibiting baseness or stinginess) **2 :** a mean act ⟨descend to the ~*es* of frightening children and old women —Daniel Defoe⟩

[2]**meanness** \"\ *n* -ES [[7]*mean* + *-ness*] **:** the quality or state of being or constituting a mean between two extremes

mean noon *n* **:** noon by mean solar time

mean obliquity *n* **:** the average angle over a long period of time between the plane of the equator of the earth or other planet and the plane of the ecliptic

mean place *n* **:** the position of a star at a given epoch (as the beginning of a year) as affected by precession of the equinoxes and proper motion — compare STAR PLACE

mean proportional *n* [[6]*mean* + *proportional*, adj.] **1 :** GEOMETRIC MEAN **2 :** MEAN 1d(3)

mean reserve *n* **:** the arithmetical average of the initial reserve and the terminal reserve of a policy of insurance

means *pl of* MEAN, *pres 3d sing of* MEAN

mean sea level *n* [[7]*mean*] **:** SEA LEVEL 2

means grass \'mēnz-\ *n, usu cap M* [prob. fr. the name *Means*] **:** JOHNSON GRASS

mean solar day *n* **:** the interval between successive transits of the lower meridian by the mean sun containing 86,400 seconds of mean solar time

mean solar second *n* **:** a cgs unit equal to $\frac{1}{86,400}$ of a mean solar day

mean solar time *n* **:** time that is based on the motion of the mean sun and that has the mean solar second as its unit

mean spheroid *n* **:** an imaginary spheroid which is commonly assumed to be an ellipsoid of revolution but may have three unequal axes, which coincides most nearly with the actual figure of the earth at the plane of sea level, and to which trigonometrical surveys are referred

meanspirited \'=¦===\ *adj* **:** exhibiting or characterized by meanness of spirit ⟨what is essentially vulgar and ~ in politics —J.R.Lowell⟩

mean square *n* **:** the average of the squares of a set of numbers

mean square deviation *n* **:** STANDARD DEVIATION

means test *n* [fr. *means*, pl. of [6]*mean*] **1 :** a searching examination of the financial state of an unemployed person and his resident family formerly made in Great Britain when such a person had exhausted his unemployment insurance payments in order to determine his eligibility for payments from other public funds **2 :** any examination of the financial state of a person as a condition precedent to receiving social insurance, public assistance benefits, or other payments from public funds

mean sun *n* [[7]*mean*] **:** a fictitious sun supposed to move uniformly along the celestial equator completing crossings of the vernal equinox at intervals of a tropical year

meant *past of* MEAN

me·an·tes \mē'an·,tēz\ *n pl, cap* [NL, fr. L, pl. of *meant-*, *means*, pres. part. of *meare* to go — more at PERMEATE] **:** a suborder of Caudata comprising neotenous salamanders that have horny jaw sheaths and persistent gills and lack eyelids, maxillae, and hind limbs

[1]**mean·time** \'mēn·,tīm\ *n* [ME *mene-time*, fr. *mene* occupying a middle position + *time* — more at MEAN] **:** the intervening time **:** INTERVAL ⟨in the ~ had satisfied his omnivorous appetite for reading in the village library —A.C.Cole⟩

[2]**meantime** \"\ *adv* **:** MEANWHILE ⟨~ he had been attentive to his other interests —H.R.Warfel⟩

mean time *n* [[7]*mean*] **:** MEAN SOLAR TIME

meantime screw *n* [*meantime* (fr. [7]*mean* + *time*) + *screw*] **:** one of either two or four screws of precious metal set in the rim of a watch balance to regulate the speed of oscillation to very close tolerances — compare BALANCE SCREW

meantone system \'=,=-\ *n* **:** a system of tuning keyboard instruments used before the adoption of equal temperament and based on a standard interval of a mean between a major and a minor whole tone of just intonation or one half of an acoustically pure major third

mean value *n* **:** the integral of a continuous function of one or more variables over a given range divided by the measure of the range

[1]**mean·while** \'mēn,(h)wīl\ *n* [ME *mene while*, fr. *mene* occupying a middle position + *while*] **:** MEANTIME ⟨were being developed in the ~ by engineers —S.I.Hayakawa⟩

[2]**meanwhile** \"\ *adv* [ME *menewhile*, fr. *mene while*, n.] **1 :** during the intervening time **:** for the time being ⟨children who are crippled . . . ~ are cut off from ordinary opportunities —Martha M. Eliot⟩ **2 :** at the same time ⟨~ he was becoming more and more engaged in . . . the main activity of his life —W.S.Grant⟩

mean white *n* **:** POOR WHITE — usu. used disparagingly

meany *var of* MEANIE

meaow *var of* MEOW

[1]**mear** *obs var of* MERE

[2]**mear** \'mēr\ *Scot var of* MARE

mearns quail \'mərnz-\ *also* **mearns's quail** \-zə̇z-\ *n, usu cap M* [after Edgar A. *Mearns* †1916 Am. naturalist] **:** a rather pale short-tailed quail (*Cyrtonyx montezumae*) of arid uplands of the southwestern U. S. and adjacent Mexico

meas *abbr* measure

[1]**mease** \'mēz\ *vt* -ED/-ING/-S [ME *mesen*, short for *amesen*, fr. MF *amaisier*, fr. (assumed) VL *admansiare*, fr. L *ad-* + (assumed) VL *mansum* house, farm, fr. L, neut. of *mansus*, past part. of *manēre* to remain — more at MANSION] *chiefly Scot* **:** to make calm **:** PACIFY, MITIGATE

[2]**mease** \'mēz\ *dial Brit var of* [3]MAZE

mea·sle \'mēzəl\ *n* -S [sing. of *measles*] **:** a tapeworm cysticercus larva; *specif* **:** one found in the muscles of a domesticated mammal — compare TAENIA

mea·sled \'mēzəld\ *adj* [ME *meseled*, fr. *mesel* + *-ed*] **:** infected or spotted with measles — **mea·sled·ness** *n* -ES

mea·sles \'mēzəlz\ *n pl but sing or pl in constr* [ME *meseles*, pl. of *mesel* measles, spot characteristic of measles, alter. (influenced by *mesel* leper) of *masel;* akin to MD *masel* spot characteristic of measles and prob. to OHG *masar* gnarled excrescence on a tree — more at MAZER, MESEL] **1 a :** an acute contagious viral disease commencing with catarrhal symptoms, conjunctivitis, cough, and Koplik's spots on the oral mucous membrane and marked by the appearance on the third or fourth day of an eruption of distinct red circular spots which coalesce in a crescentic form, are slightly raised, and after the fourth day of the eruption gradually decline **b :** any of various other eruptive diseases (as rubella) **2** [fr. obs. E *meazel*, adj., infested with larval tapeworms in the muscles and tissues, fr. ME *mesel*, lit., leprous, fr. OF *mesel*, adj., leprous & *mesel*, n., leper — more at MESEL] **:** infestation with or disease caused by larval tapeworms in the muscles and tissues; *specif* **:** infestation of cattle and swine with cysticerci of tapeworms that as adults parasitize man — see MEASLE **3 :** a disease of apple and pear trees that is of unknown cause and is characterized by roughened bark with swellings or pustules resembling pimples

mea·sly \'mēz(ə)lē, -li\ *adj* -ER/-EST [*measles* + *-y*] **1 :** infected with measles **2** *of meat or an animal* **a :** infested with larval tapeworms **b :** TRICHINIZED **3 a :** BLIGHTED, POOR, INFERIOR ⟨sick and ~⟩ **b :** contemptibly small ⟨left only a ~ dime for a tip⟩ **syn** see PETTY

mea·sur·abil·i·ty \,mezh(ə)rə'biləd·ē, ,māzh-, -zhə(r)'-\ *n* **:** the quality or state of being measurable

mea·sur·able \'mezh(ə)rəbəl, 'māzh-, -zhə(r)b-\ *adj* [ME *mesurable* moderate, fr. MF, fr. LL *mensurabilis* measurable, fr. *mensurare* to measure + L *-abilis* -able — more at MEASURE (v.)] **1 a :** capable of being measured ⟨such ~ factors as the amount of nitrogen in air⟩; *specif* **:** large or small enough to be measured ⟨only rarely found in ~ amounts⟩ ⟨a ~ distance⟩ **b :** great enough to be worth consideration **:** SIGNIFICANT ⟨became a ~ figure on the Parisian scene —*Times Lit. Supp.*⟩ **c :** of limited duration **:** not indefinite **:** FORESEEABLE ⟨reach its goal within the ~ future —Alan Valentine⟩ **2** *of a number* **:** having an exact divisor — **mea·sur·able·ness** *n* -ES

mea·sur·ably \-blē, -li\ *adv* [ME *mesurably* moderately, fr. *mesurable* + *-ly*] **1 :** in a measure **:** to some extent ⟨the fear of immediate war has ~ abated —Quincy Howe⟩ **2 :** to a quantitatively measurable extent ⟨radiation decreased ~⟩

mea·sur·age \'mezhərij, 'māzh-\ *n* -S [ME *mesurage*, fr. MF, fr. OF, fr. *mesurer* to measure + *-age* — more at MEASURE (v.)] **:** a toll or duty levied on a ship's cargo

[1]**mea·sure** \'mezhə(r), 'māzh-\ *n* -S [ME *mesure*, fr. OF, fr. L *mensura*, fr. *mensus* (past part. of *metiri* to measure) + *-ura*

MEASURES AND WEIGHTS

UNIT	ABBR OR SYMBOL	EQUIVALENTS IN OTHER UNITS OF SAME SYSTEM	METRIC EQUIVALENT
		length	
mile	mi	5280 feet, 320 rods, 1760 yards	1.609 kilometers
rod	rd	5.50 yards, 16.5 feet	5.029 meters
yard	yd	3 feet, 36 inches	0.914 meters
foot	ft *or* ′	12 inches, 0.333 yards	30.480 centimeters
inch	in *or* ″	0.083 feet, 0.027 yards	2.540 centimeters
		area	
square mile	sq mi *or* m^2	640 acres, 102,400 square rods	2.590 square kilometers
acre	a *or* ac (seldom used)	4840 square yards, 43,560 square feet	0.405 hectares, 4047 square meters
square rod	sq rd *or* rd^2	30.25 square yards, 0.006 acres	25.293 square meters
square yard	sq yd *or* yd^2	1296 square inches, 9 square feet	0.836 square meters
square foot	sq ft *or* ft^2	144 square inches, 0.111 square yards	0.093 square meters
square inch	sq in *or* in^2	0.007 square feet, 0.00077 square yards	6.451 square centimeters
		volume	
cubic yard	cu yd *or* yd^3	27 cubic feet, 46,656 cubic inches	0.765 cubic meters
cubic foot	cu ft *or* ft^3	1728 cubic inches, 0.0370 cubic yards	0.028 cubic meters
cubic inch	cu in *or* in^3	0.00058 cubic feet, 0.000021 cubic yards	16.387 cubic centimeters
		weight	
		avoirdupois	
ton	tn (seldom used)		
short ton		20 short hundredweight, 2000 pounds	0.907 metric tons
long ton		20 long hundredweight, 2240 pounds	1.016 metric tons
hundredweight	cwt		
short hundredweight		100 pounds, 0.05 short tons	45.359 kilograms
long hundredweight		112 pounds, 0.05 long tons	50.802 kilograms
pound	lb *or* lb av *also* #	16 ounces, 7000 grains	0.453 kilograms
ounce	oz *or* oz av	16 drams, 437.5 grains	28.349 grams
dram	dr *or* dr av	27.343 grains, 0.0625 ounces	1.771 grams
grain	gr	0.036 drams, 0.002285 ounces	0.0648 grams
		troy	
pound	lb t	12 ounces, 240 pennyweight, 5760 grains	0.373 kilograms
ounce	oz t	20 pennyweight, 480 grains	31.103 grams
pennyweight	dwt *also* pwt	24 grains, 0.05 ounces	1.555 grams
grain	gr	0.042 pennyweight, 0.002083 ounces	0.0648 grams
		apothecaries'	
pound	lb ap	12 ounces, 5760 grains	0.373 kilograms
ounce	oz ap *or* ℥	8 drams, 480 grains	31.103 grams
dram	dr ap *or* ʒ	3 scruples, 60 grains	3.887 grams
scruple	s ap *or* ℈	20 grains, 0.333 drams	1.295 grams
grain	gr	0.05 scruples, 0.002083 ounces, 0.0166 drams	0.0648 grams
		capacity	
		U.S. liquid measure	
gallon	gal	4 quarts (231 cubic inches)	3.785 liters
quart	qt	2 pints (57.75 cubic inches)	0.946 liters
pint	pt	4 gills (28.875 cubic inches)	0.473 liters
gill	gi	4 fluidounces (7.218 cubic inches)	118.291 milliliters
fluidounce	fl oz *or* f ℥	8 fluidrams (1.804 cubic inches)	29.573 milliliters
fluidram	fl dr *or* f ʒ	60 minims (0.225 cubic inches)	3.696 milliliters
minim	min *or* ♏	$\frac{1}{60}$ fluidram (0.003759 cubic inches)	0.061610 milliliters
		U.S. dry measure	
bushel	bu	4 pecks (2150.42 cubic inches)	35.238 liters
peck	pk	8 quarts (537.605 cubic inches)	8.809 liters
quart	qt	2 pints (67.200 cubic inches)	1.101 liters
pint	pt	½ quart (33.600 cubic inches)	0.550 liters
		British imperial liquid and dry measure	
bushel	bu	4 pecks (2219.36 cubic inches)	0.036 cubic meters
peck	pk	2 gallons (554.84 cubic inches)	0.009 cubic meters
gallon	gal	4 quarts (277.420 cubic inches)	4.545 liters
quart	qt	2 pints (69.355 cubic inches)	1.136 liters
pint	pt	4 gills (34.678 cubic inches)	568.26 cubic centimeters
gill	gi	5 fluidounces (8.669 cubic inches)	142.066 cubic centimeters
fluidounce	fl oz *or* f ℥	8 fluidrams (1.7339 cubic inches)	28.416 cubic centimeters
fluidram	fl dr *or* f ʒ	60 minims (0.216734 cubic inches)	3.5516 cubic centimeters
minim	min *or* ♏	$\frac{1}{60}$ fluidram (0.003612 cubic inches)	0.059194 cubic centimeters

-ure; akin to OE *mǣth* measure, Gk *metron* meter, measure, Skt *māti* he measures] **1 a :** an adequate, given, or fitting amount or degree: (1) **:** commensurate or due portion **:** QUOTA ⟨all too few of the British actresses . . . have received their ~ of remembrance —*Saturday Rev.*⟩ ⟨fill the ~ of our duty to our defective fellow citizens —B.N.Cardozo⟩ (2) **:** extent or degree that is not excessive **:** not undue portion; *also* **:** a sense of proportion or restraint **:** MODERATION, TEMPERANCE ⟨with that tactlessness, that lack of ~ that were characteristic of her, went on piling question upon rhetorical question —Aldous Huxley⟩ (3) **:** fixed or suitable proportion or limit **:** BOUNDS ⟨angry beyond ~⟩ ⟨Greek love of moderation, proportion, harmony, and due ~ —Lucius Garvin⟩ ⟨the love of God is broader than the ~ of man's mind —S.D.Harkness⟩ **b** (1) **:** the dimensions, capacity, or amount of something ascertained by measuring **:** MEASUREMENTS, SIZE ⟨a slipcover made to ~⟩ ⟨took his ~ for a coat⟩ ⟨several grades of freemen according to the ~ of their wealth —John MacNeill⟩; *specif* **:** the width of a full line of print or type usu. expressed in picas (2) **:** the limit of the distance at which a fencer can reach his opponent by lunging (3) **:** the character, ability, or magnitude of a person or thing considered as a matter of observation or judgment **:** an estimate of what is to be expected (as of a person or situation) ⟨a show tailored to the ~ of its star⟩ ⟨whoever tries to . . . size him up gives an immediate ~ of himself —Max Ascoli⟩ ⟨the ~ of their tragedy is now beyond our imagination —G.F. Kennan⟩ ⟨take the ~ of the crisis⟩ **c** (1) **:** a quantity measured out esp. in relation to a standard **:** a measured quantity of a substance or article ⟨using level ~*s* is the easiest . . . way of measuring —Bee Nilson⟩ ⟨tolerance was not dealt in the same ~ to men and women —Edith Wharton⟩ **:** a quantity measuring up to a standard ⟨whether this carton of milk contains full ~ —D.M.Turnbull⟩ ⟨a play that gives the audience short ~⟩ (2) **:** AMOUNT, EXTENT, DEGREE ⟨rooks consume an enormous quantity of grubs . . . taking a fair ~ of grain by way of reward —*Brit. Birds in Colour*⟩ ⟨giving children a greater ~ of freedom⟩ ⟨in the ~ we buy abroad, profitable markets there will attract capital —T.J.Kreps⟩ **d :** the amount or kind of treatment meted out (as in retribution) ⟨the ~ which he had dealt to others should now be meted out to him —Edith Sitwell⟩ **2 a :** an instrument (as a yardstick) or a utensil (as a graduated cup) for measuring **b** (1) **:** the customary local unit (as of volume) for a particular commodity ⟨the ~ containing two Winchester bushels —Robert Forsyth⟩ (2) **:** a quantity (as of wheat, oil, beans) measured by such a unit ⟨six ~*s* of gravel⟩ (3) **:** one of a number of equal but indeterminate measured quantities ⟨at the rate . . . of 16 ~*s* of rice for 25 of salt —H.W.Hilman⟩ **c :** something used as a standard in measuring ⟨the customary load of a donkey as a ~ of weight⟩ ⟨~*s* of time are commonly derived from some kind of human endurance —*Notes & Queries on Anthropology*⟩; *esp* **:** a standard unit of length, area, or volume (as the foot, acre, cubic inch, quart) ⟨exact weights and ~*s* maintained by a governmental bureau of standards⟩ **d :** a system of standard units of measure — usu. used with a qualifier indicating the class of the system ⟨metric ~⟩, the dimension or the kind of object or substance measured ⟨long ~⟩ ⟨board ~⟩, or the locality where the system is used ⟨British ~⟩ **3 :** the act or process of measuring ⟨settled by a ~ made by a surveyor⟩ **4 a :** something having rhythmic sound or movement ⟨extolled the jury system in stately Victorian ~*s* —*Saturday Rev.*⟩: as (1) **:** MELODY, TUNE ⟨a strong, clean wind which rushed in a droning ~ through the broom sedge —Ellen Glasgow⟩ (2) **:** a round or turn of dancing **:** DANCE (3) **:** a slow and stately dance **b :** rhythmic structure **:** measured pattern of movement **:** BEAT, CADENCE ⟨a finer language, style, and ~ than the Greek which it translates —*Times Lit. Supp.*⟩: as (1) **:** poetic rhythm measured by temporal quantity or accent; *specif* **:** METER (2) **:** musical time **c :** a division or unit (as of time or stress) in a rhythmic sequence: as (1) **:** a grouping of musical beats made by the regular recurrence of primary accents and located on the staff immediately following a vertical bar — called also *bar* (2) **:** a division of a rhythmic structure (as a poem) in terms of a quantitative relation (as temporal balance) **d :** quantitative relation (as of identity, equivalence, correspondence, or balance) among elements or parts in a rhythmic structure; *esp* **:** temporal relation or balance **5** [trans. of Gk *metron*] **a :** an exact division of a quantity ⟨6 being the greatest common ~ of 42 and 12⟩ **b :** a basis of comparison **:** DENOMINATOR ⟨no common ~ between the masses of Soviet industrial hands . . . and our own working people —E.D.Laborde⟩ **6 a** (1) **:** a standard by which something intangible is determined or regulated **:** CRITERION ⟨the ~ should not be what others are doing but what is right for the individual child —Dorothy Barclay⟩ (2) **:** a directly observable quantity from which the value of another related quantity may be obtained ⟨the ~ of an angle is the subtended arc⟩ ⟨the ~ of a quantity of electricity is the mass of silver deposited by it in electrolysis⟩ **b :** a means of measuring or indicating something that cannot be directly measured, observed, or represented **:** TEST ⟨scored low in a ~ of emotional adjustment⟩ **:** INDICATION, INDEX, YARDSTICK ⟨the tastiness . . . of such foods became a ~ of the efficiency and thrift of the family —Carol Aronovici⟩ **7 measures** *pl* **:** strata of a mineral (as coal) **8 :** an action planned or taken toward the accomplishment of a purpose **:** means to an end ⟨wore steel helmets as a safety ~⟩ ⟨apply ~*s* to prevent the spread of infection⟩ **:** STEP ⟨took strong ~*s* against the rebels⟩; *specif* **:** a proposed legislative act **:** BILL ⟨sponsored an anti-inflation ~ in the senate⟩ — **beyond measure** *adv* **:** to an extreme degree **:** ABUNDANTLY, EXCESSIVELY ⟨had happiness *beyond measure*⟩ ⟨angry *beyond measure*⟩ — **for good measure** *adv* **:** in addition to the minimum required **:** as an extra ⟨added another illustration *for good measure*⟩ — **in a measure** *adv* **:** to some degree ⟨a statement that was *in a measure* both true and false⟩

²measure \"\ *vb* **measured; measured; measuring** \-zh(ə)-riŋ\ **measures** [ME *mesuren*, fr. OF *mesurer*, fr. LL *mensurare*, fr. L *mensura* measure — more at ¹MEASURE] *vt* **1 a :** to choose or control (as one's words or acts) with cautious restraint **:** REGULATE, WEIGH ⟨~ his acts and words with an iron will —H.E.Scudder⟩ **b :** to regulate or adjust by a rule or standard **:** GOVERN ⟨the demand for the commodity *measuring* the amount produced⟩ ⟨~ our efforts not by what we feel like doing but by what the situation demands⟩ **2 a :** to allot or distribute as if by measure **:** deal out **:** METE — often used with *out* ⟨laws that . . . ~ out their rewards and punishments with calm indifference —P.E.More⟩ **b :** to apportion in measured amounts; *also* **:** to separate (as from a stock) or add (as to a mixture) by measure — often used with *off* or *out* ⟨~ out the ingredients carefully⟩ ⟨~ off three cups of flour⟩ and sometimes with *in* ⟨~ in the vinegar last⟩ **3 a :** to lay off, mark, or fix (a specified distance or extent) by making measurements ⟨~ three-foot intervals between the plantings⟩ ⟨~ off a half-acre plot for a house lot⟩ **b :** to lay off, mark, or fix the exact dimensions or plan of by making measurements ⟨~ out the lines for the foundations⟩ ⟨~ the course for the 200-meter race⟩ ⟨~ off the trunk into logs of 6, 12, or 18 feet⟩ **4 a :** to ascertain the quantity, mass, extent, or degree of in terms of a standard unit or fixed amount usu. by means of an instrument or container marked off in the units **:** measure the dimensions of **:** take the measurements of ⟨~ the depth, height, and width of the cabinet⟩ ⟨~ the snowfall⟩ ⟨~ the speed of the car⟩ ⟨~ the luminosity of a star⟩ ⟨~ the temperature of the oven⟩ **b :** to compute the size of (an area, object) from dimensional measurements ⟨~ the surface area⟩ **5 :** to judge or estimate the extent, strength, worth, or character of (as a quality, action, or person) ⟨~ intelligence⟩ ⟨~ the gravity of the crisis⟩ ⟨~ the value of the counseling program⟩ ⟨*measured* his opponent before announcing his candidacy⟩ ⟨~ success by salary⟩; *specif* **:** to appraise in comparison with something taken as a criterion — often used with *against* ⟨~ himself not against adults but against age-mates —Margaret Mead⟩ **6** *archaic* **:** to travel over **:** TRAVERSE ⟨the public mind had now *measured* back again the space over which it had passed between 1640 and 1660 —T.B.Macaulay⟩ **7 :** to be a means (as an instrument or standard) of measuring **:** serve as the measure of **:** INDICATE ⟨the piles of sun-bleached linen that *measured* the housewife's pride —Ruth Davidson⟩ ⟨the atomic number . . . ~*s* both the number of protons and of electrons —James Jeans⟩ **8 :** to bring into competition or contest ⟨~ his skill with his rival's in a duel⟩ **9 :** to look (a person) up and down **:** view appraisingly ⟨his eyes *measured* me for the first time —Christopher Isherwood⟩ ~ *vi* **1 :** to take or make a measurement **:** measure something ⟨the shepherd ~*s* from the time the ewes lambed —Lewis Mumford⟩ **2 :** to have a specified measurement or measurements ⟨the cloth ~*s* two yards⟩ ⟨the bedroom ~*s* 10 feet by 12⟩ **3 :** to be comparable ⟨a success that ~*s* with their aims⟩ **4 :** to admit of being measured ⟨~*s* more easily if spread on a table⟩ — **measure one's length :** to fall or lie flat ⟨tripped on a guy wire and *measured his length* on the roof —Frederick Way⟩ — **measure swords 1 :** to compare the length of swords before fighting **2 :** to fight with swords **3 :** CONTEND, CONTEST — usu. used with *with*

mea·sured \'mezhə(r)d, 'māzh-\ *adj* [ME *mesured*, partly fr. *mesure* measure + *-ed*, partly fr. past part. of *mesuren* to measure] **1 :** marked by due proportion ⟨the ~ beauty of classical Greek art⟩ **2 a :** RHYTHMICAL ⟨the ~ flash of the beacon⟩; *specif* **:** METRICAL ⟨the free and the ~ forms of verse⟩ **b :** slow and steady **:** DELIBERATE ⟨went about their work with ~ steps⟩ **3 :** LIMITED ⟨its fundamental poverty and ~ capacity for development —H.L.Hoskins⟩ **4 :** CALCULATED ⟨spoke with ~ insolence —*Time*⟩

measured drawing *n* **:** an architectural scale drawing of an existing structure

mea·sured·ly *adv* **:** in a measured manner or to a measured degree ⟨nodded as ~ as the jouncing taxi would permit —Hamilton Basso⟩

measured mile *n* **:** a distance of one mile the limits of which have been accurately measured and marked ⟨tested his mileage meter by the *measured mile*⟩

measured music *n* **1 :** MENSURAL MUSIC **2 :** music characterized by a pattern of regularly recurring accents — compare PLAINSONG

mea·sured·ness *n* -ES **:** the quality or state of being measured

mea·sure·less \'mezhə(r)ləs, 'māzh-\ *adj* [ME *mesureles*, fr. *mesure* measure + *-les* less] **1 :** having no observable limit **:** IMMEASURABLE, BOUNDLESS ⟨looked out at the ~ expanse of sea⟩ **2 :** very great ⟨treated them with ~ contempt⟩ — **mea·sure·less·ly** *adv* — **mea·sure·less·ness** *n* -ES

measure line *n* **:** a line of known or ascertainable length put into or allowed to remain in a picture (as a linear perspective or a photograph) and often used in the determination or measurement of other lines

mea·sure·man \'mezhə(r)mən, 'māzh-\ *n, pl* **measuremen :** a worker whose job is measuring: as **a :** a paper mill worker who measures and inspects pulpwood to determine its value and its best uses **b :** one who measures rooms to estimate the amount of floor covering needed

mea·sure·ment \'mezhə(r)mənt, 'māzh-\ *n* -S **1 :** the act or process of measuring something ⟨a meter for the ~ and pricing of yard goods⟩ ⟨~ of progress in learning to read⟩ ⟨attitude ~⟩; *esp* **:** MENSURATION **2 a :** a figure expressing extent that is obtained by measuring **:** DIMENSION ⟨the room's ~*s* are 30 x 15⟩ **b :** an area, quantity, degree, or capacity obtained by measuring ⟨the ~ of the field is five acres⟩ ⟨the ~ of the jug is two quarts⟩ ⟨the temperature ~ is 72°⟩ **3 :** a system of measures **:** ¹MEASURE 2d ⟨giving serious consideration to the adoption of metric ~⟩

measurement cargo *also* **measurement goods** *or* **measurement freight** *n* **1 :** cargo or goods charged for carriage by bulk rather than weight **2 :** a cargo measuring less than 40 cubic feet per long ton or weighing less than 56 pounds per cubic foot

measure of curvature : CURVATURE 2

measure of damage : the method under applicable principles of law for estimating or ascertaining with reasonable certainty the damages sustained by any party in any litigation

mea·sur·er \'mezh(ə)rə(r), 'māzh-\ *n* -S **:** one that measures: as **a :** a worker who measures cloth before or after dyeing and finishing **b :** an operator of a hide measuring machine **c :** one who checks the size of hats **d :** a worker who measures iron or steel before and after rolling to check the measurements specified for rails, rods, or sheets **e :** a worker who takes and records measurements of garments that may change shape during cleaning or dyeing **f :** one that measures the land used for crops in order to compute the payments due contract farmers or the wages of farm laborers

measures *pl of* MEASURE, *pres 3d sing of* MEASURE

measure signature *n* **:** TIME SIGNATURE

measure up *vi* **1 :** to have necessary or fitting qualifications ⟨how the diets of American families *measure up* by nutrition standards —*U.S. Govt. Manual*⟩ **:** be equal — often used with *to* ⟨*measure up* to their expectations⟩ ⟨*measure up* to the demands of public office⟩ **2 :** to be the equal (as in ability or achievement) — used with *to* ⟨in science and learning the Incas did not *measure up* to the Mayas —R.W.Murray⟩

measuring *pres part of* MEASURE

measuring cup *n* **:** a cup having a capacity usu. of a half pint and marked so that portions may be accurately determined

measuring cup

measuring glass *n* **:** a graduated medicine or dispensing glass

measuring machine *n* **:** a machine for measuring; *esp* **:** a machine for the accurate mechanical or optical measurement of distances on standards of length, gauges, and other parts and commonly made to measure to an accuracy of 0.0001 inch or higher

measuring pitcher *n* **:** a pitcher containing up to a quart and marked so that portions may be accurately determined

measuring wheel *n* **:** ODOMETER

measuring worm *n* **:** LOOPER 1

¹meat \'mēt, *usu* -ēd.+V\ *n* -S *often attrib* [ME *mete*, fr. OE; akin to OHG *maz* food, ON *matr*, Goth *mats* food, L *madēre* to be wet, Gk *madaros* wet, *mastos* breast, Skt *madati* it bubbles, he rejoices; basic meaning: drip, be fat] **1 a :** something eaten by man or beast for nourishment **:** FOOD ⟨and to every beast of the earth . . . I have given every green herb for ~ —Gen 1:30 (AV)⟩ ⟨it was ~ and drink to him to be the guardian of a secret —John Buchan⟩ **b :** the edible part of a nut, fruit, or egg ⟨~ of half apple showing tooth marks still fresh, not turned brown —Leslie Ford⟩ **2** *obs* **:** a particular dish prepared or served as food **3 a :** animal tissue used as food: (1) **:** FLESH 2b ⟨preferring ~ to fish⟩ (2) **:** FLESH 1b; *specif* **:** flesh of domesticated cattle, swine, sheep, and goats — distinguished esp. in legal and commercial usage from *meat by-product* and from flesh of other kinds of mammals (3) **:** the edible soft parts of any animal — usu. used with a qualifying term ⟨crab ~⟩ ⟨the dark ~ of poultry⟩ **b :** meat prepared for the table ⟨spiced ~⟩ ⟨~ loaf⟩ ⟨have another slice of ~⟩ **4** *archaic* **:** any of the usual daily meals; *esp* **:** DINNER **5 a** *archaic* **:** game animals **:** QUARRY **b :** favorite or appropriate object of pursuit **:** principal delight ⟨if you like your stories restrained and nontheatrical, this is your ~ —I.T.Marsh⟩ ⟨if a baby hippopotamus was born at the zoo, that was my ~ —St. Clair McKelway⟩ **6 :** food for thought **:** solid substance **:** MATTER ⟨this is a volume of first-rate caliber, full of ~ —H.L. Hoskins⟩ ⟨the real ~ is found in the last two chapters —*Times Lit. Supp.*⟩ ⟨to him ideas are not fleshless, misty abstractions but the meaning, the ~, and the mainspring action of men —Kathleen Sproul⟩ **7** *chiefly South & Midland* **:** PORK; *esp* **:** BACON

²meat \"\ *vt* -ED/-ING/-S *now dial* **:** to supply with food

meat- *or* **meato-** *comb form* [LL *meatus*] **:** meatus ⟨*meat*ic⟩ ⟨*meato*tomy⟩

me·a·tal \mē'ād·ᵊl\ *adj* [*meat*us + *-al*] **:** of, relating to, or forming a meatus

meat ant *n* **:** a large Australian ant (*Iridomyrmex detectus*) that is a household pest

¹meat-ax \'‚‚\ *n* **1 :** CLEAVER 1a **2 :** a harsh or violent attack on a problem; *esp* **:** a rough slashing reduction of an appropriation or budget ⟨your advertising policy and budget get the *meat-ax* —Derek Brooks⟩

²meat-ax \"\ *vt* **:** to assail murderously **:** chop down **:** DESTROY, DEVASTATE ⟨the House has *meat-axed* the mutual security bill —*N.Y. Times*⟩

meatball \'‚‚\ *n* **1 :** a small ball of chopped or ground meat often mixed with bread crumbs and vegetables and browned in a skillet **2 :** a clumsy, dull, or unattractive person ⟨it was too bad the army had sent such a ~ to be administrator —John Hersey⟩ **3 :** a pennant (as in the U.S. Navy) for battle efficiency or for an athletic championship

meatbird \'‚‚\ *n* **1 :** CANADA JAY **2 :** CLARK NUTCRACKER

meat by-product *n* **:** a usable product other than flesh (sense 1a) obtained from slaughter animals including edible organ meats and various inedible products (as hair, bone, or fertilizer) — distinguished esp. in legal and commercial usage from *meat* 3a(2)

meat chopper *n* **:** MEAT GRINDER

meatcutter \'‚‚‚\ *n* **:** one that cuts meat

meat·ed \'mēd·əd\ *adj* [¹*meat* + *-ed*] **:** having flesh or meat of a specified kind — used chiefly in combination ⟨*well-meated*⟩ ⟨*lightly-meated*⟩

meat fly *n* **:** FLESH FLY

meat grinder *n* **1 :** a device for cutting meat fine **2 :** something that reduces, pulverizes, or destroys: as **a :** a devastating military action or stratagem ⟨the American public has watched the *meat grinder* in action on the Russian front, killing millions of troops —*New Republic*⟩ **b :** a process (as an official investigation or examination) or a system that may have ruinous effect ⟨if you went into public life you often put your career and your reputation in a political *meat grinder* —*Saturday Rev.*⟩

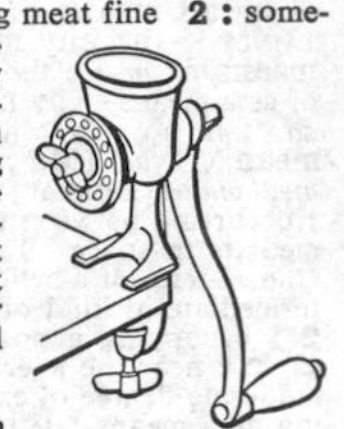

meat grinder 1

¹meath *obs var of* ¹MEAD

²meath \'mēth, 'mēth\ *adj, usu cap* [fr. *Meath*, county of eastern Ireland] **:** of or from County Meath, Ireland **:** of the kind or style prevalent in County Meath

meat hawk *n* **:** CANADA JAY

meathead \'‚‚\ *n* **:** a stupid blundering person ⟨getting letters from that ~ she's married to —W.R.Burnett⟩

meat house *n* **1 :** a small building for meat storage esp. on a farm **2 :** SMOKEHOUSE

me·at·ic \mē'ad·ik\ *adj* [*meat-* + *-ic*] *bot* **:** having intercellular spaces ⟨~ phloem⟩

meatier *comparative of* MEATY

meatiest *superlative of* MEATY

meat·i·ly \'mēd·ᵊlē\ *adv* **:** in a meaty manner

meat·i·ness \-d·ēnəs\ *n* -ES **:** the quality or state of being meaty

meat·less \'mētləs\ *adj* **:** having no meat or substance

meatman \'‚‚\ *n, pl* **meatmen :** a vendor of meat **:** BUTCHER

meat meal *n* **:** a poultry feed made of cooked, dried, and ground animal tissue

meato- — see MEAT-

meat offering *n* **:** a sacrifice of food; *specif* **:** MEAL OFFERING ⟨and when any will offer a *meat offering* unto the Lord, his offering shall be of fine flour —Lev 2:1 (AV)⟩

meat-packer \'‚‚‚\ *n* **:** a concern engaged in meat-packing

meat-packing \'‚‚‚\ *n* **:** the wholesale meat industry including slaughtering, processing, and distribution to retailers

meat safe *n, Brit* **:** SAFE 1a

meat scrap *n* **:** a by-product of meat-packing made of bits and trimmings of meat freed from fat, dehydrated, and reduced to a meal and used as a rich source of protein in animal rations

meat spot *n* **:** an old discolored blood spot in a hen's egg

meat tea *n, Brit* **:** HIGH TEA

meat type *n* **:** a type of hog esp. suitable for the production of pork without excessive early fattening — compare LARD TYPE

me·a·tus \mē'ād·əs, -ātəs\ *n, pl* **meatuses** *or* **meatus** [LL, fr. L, passage, going, fr. *meatus*, past part. of *meare* to go — more at PERMEATE] **:** a natural body passage **:** CANAL, DUCT

meat wagon *n* **1** *slang* **:** AMBULANCE **2** *slang* **:** DEAD WAGON

meatworks \'‚‚\ *n pl but sing or pl in constr* **1 :** SLAUGHTERHOUSE **2 :** PACKINGHOUSE

meaty \'mēd·ē, 'mēt|, |i\ *adj* -ER/-EST **1 :** full of meat **:** FLESHY ⟨a sloping ~ jaw —Thomas Wolfe⟩ **2 :** rich in matter **:** furnishing solid food for thought or appreciation **:** SUBSTANTIAL ⟨the announcement was ~ enough as it stood —Alzada Comstock⟩ ⟨uncommonly fine voices go to work on these ~ scores —Douglas Watt⟩

me·bos \'mē‚bäs\ *n* -ES [Afrik *mebos*, prob. fr. Jap *umeboshi* preserved plum] *Africa* **:** a confection of salted and sugared dried apricots

mec *or* **mech** \'mek\ *n* -S [by shortening] **:** MECHANIC

mec- *or* **meco-** *comb form* [ISV, fr. Gk *mēko-*, fr. *mēkos* length; akin to Gk *makros* long — more at MEAGER] **:** length **:** long ⟨*Meco*donta⟩ ⟨*meco*meter⟩

me·ca·te \mə'käd·ē\ *n* -S [MexSp, fr. Nahuatl *mecatl* cord, rope] **1** *West* **:** a rope usu. of horsehair that is used for leading or tying or as hackamore reins **2 :** an old unit of land area formerly used in the Yucatan region equal to about 400 square meters or ⅒ acre

¹mec·ca *also* **mek·ka** \'mekə\ *adj, usu cap* [fr. *Mecca*, Saudi Arabia] **:** of or from Mecca, a capital of Saudi Arabia **:** of the kind or style prevalent in Mecca

²mecca \"\ *n* -S *often cap* [fr. *Mecca*, Saudi Arabia, birthplace of Muhammad and holy city of Islam] **1 :** a place regarded as the center of an activity or interest or as the goal of its practitioners or connoisseurs ⟨a white frame building that is the ~ of trout fishermen from all over the nation —Corey Ford⟩ ⟨he was good, good enough to play the Armistice day taps at Arlington, the *Mecca* of all army buglers —James Jones⟩ ⟨London . . . bookstores spell *Mecca* for the collector and manna for the reader —David & Marian Greenberg⟩ **2 :** TUSCAN BROWN

mecca balsam *n, usu cap M* **:** BALM OF GILEAD 2a

¹mec·can \'mekən\ *adj, usu cap* [*Mecca*, Saudi Arabia + *-an*] **1 :** of, relating to, or characteristic of the city of Mecca **2 :** of, relating to, or characteristic of the people of Mecca

²meccan \"\ *n* -S *cap* **:** a native or inhabitant of Mecca

Mec·cano \mə'ka(‚)nō, me'-, -kä(-\ *trademark* — used for a steel construction set for children

mech *abbr* mechanic; mechanical; mechanics; mechanism; mechanized

mechan- *or* **mechano-** *comb form* [ME *mechan-*, fr. MF or L, fr. Gk *mēchan-*, fr. *mēchanē* machine — more at MACHINE] **:** machine ⟨*mechano*logy⟩ ⟨*mechano*morphic⟩ **:** mechanical ⟨*mechan*ize⟩ ⟨*mechano*therapy⟩ **:** mechanical and ⟨*mechano*-chemical⟩

¹me·chan·ic \mə'kanik, -nēk\ *adj* [prob. fr. MF *mechanique*, *mecanique*, adj. & n., fr. L *mechanicus*, fr. Gk *mēchanikos*, fr. *mēchanē* machine + *-ikos* -ic — more at MACHINE] **1 :** of or relating to hand work or manual skill ⟨fighting is, indeed, a ~ trade —Douglas Jerrold⟩ **2** *archaic* **a :** of or relating to laborers or artisans **b :** BASE, COARSE, VULGAR **3 a :** having or resembling the action of a machine **b :** resembling a machine in routine, dull, or involuntary performance **:** AUTOMATIC, UNINSPIRED ⟨from blank to blank a threadless way I pushed ~ feet —Emily Dickinson⟩ **4 :** agile, inventive, or resourceful like a good workman ⟨a roving artisan who lives by his ~ wits —Carl Van Doren⟩ **5 :** of, relating to, or constituting mechanistic thought or theory ⟨the dull ~ view of utility —*Fortune*⟩

²mechanic \"\ *n* -S [prob. fr. MF *mechanique*, *mecanique*] **1** *obs* **a :** manual labor or employment **b :** HANDICRAFT **2 a :** a manual worker **:** ARTISAN ⟨these Englishmen had not been ~*s* or fishermen or sailors in England —H.E.Scudder⟩ ⟨carpenters, masons, and other ~*s* —J.R.Dalzell⟩ **b :** a man skilled in the construction or operation of machines or vehicles run by machines **:** MACHINIST ⟨the machines are placed in the hands of four well-trained ~*s* who do the assembling and make the final adjustments —*Geyer's Topics*⟩ ⟨automobile ~⟩ **c** *archaic* **:** a base or vulgar fellow **:** PLEBEIAN ⟨slaves and "base ~*s*" —John Dewey⟩ **3 :** a safety belt used in practicing for a trapeze performance **4 :** a dishonest manipulator of cards, dice, or other gaming implements

¹me·chan·i·cal \-nəkəl, -nēk-\ *adj* [ME *mechanicall*, fr. MF or L; MF *mechanique*, *mecanique* (fr. L *mechanicus*) + ME *-all* -al] **1 a :** of, relating to, or concerned with machinery or tools ⟨~ design⟩ ⟨nothing is more exasperating to the farmer than to be frustrated in his plans by lack of essential supplies —*Country Life*⟩ ⟨became one of the skilled ~ superintendents of his day —Edna Yost⟩ ⟨the public had recognized the need for education in agriculture and the ~ and industrial arts —J.B.Conant⟩ : produced or operated by a machine or tool ⟨agitate a substance by ~ shaking⟩ ⟨a ~ saw⟩ **b** : of or relating to manual operations **2** : of or relating to artisans, craftsmen, or machinists **3 a** : done as if by a machine : seeming to be uninfluenced by will or emotion : AUTOMATIC, INVOLUNTARY ⟨busy in a leisurely ~ way —Douglas Stewart⟩ ⟨writers . . . learned but narrow in their range of feeling, dry, ~, timid, subservient —Van Wyck Brooks⟩ **b** : absorbed in, concerned with, or devoted to technicalities or minutiae ⟨nor was capacity shown for anything above a ~ handling of the matter —H.O.Taylor⟩ **4 a** : relating to, governed by, or in accordance with mechanics ⟨the belief that the whole universe is a ~ contrivance in which nothing can happen except in absolute accordance with the eternal and unalterable laws of mechanics —M.R.Cohen⟩ ⟨one of the first applications of ~ energy in Texas manufacturing was the use of water power in pioneer sawmills and gristmills —*Amer. Guide Series: Texas*⟩ **b** : relating to the quantitative relations of force and matter as distinguished from mental, vital, and chemical ⟨the ~ pressure of a wind of about 800 miles per hour could be tolerated by the well supported body —H.G. Armstrong⟩ **5** : relying on mechanics for theory or hypothesis ⟨~ physiologists⟩ ⟨~ determinism⟩ **6** : AUTOMATIC ⟨a ~ stoker⟩ **7** : caused by, resulting from, or relating to a process that involves a purely physical as opposed to a chemical change ⟨~ weathering⟩ ⟨~ erosion⟩ **8** *of pulp* : made from groundwood — contrasted with *chemical* **syn** see SPONTANEOUS

²mechanical \"\ *n* -s **1** *obs* : MECHANIC 2a **2** *also* **mechanical scheme** : a piece of finished copy consisting typically of type proofs, hand lettering, and art positioned and mounted for photomechanical reproduction in a letterpress, offset, or other printing plate — called also *paste-up*

mechanical advantage *n* : the advantage gained by the use of a mechanism in transmitting force; *specif* : the ratio of the force that performs the useful work of a machine (as a lever or a hydraulic press) to the force that is applied to the machine

mechanical analysis *n* : an analysis of soil by screening to determine its percentage composition by grain sizes

mechanical aptitude *n* : aptitude for understanding and using machines or tools

mechanical art *n* : TRADE 3a(1)

mechanical binding *n* : a binding (as for a notebook, catalog, price list) holding pages together by spiral wire, plastic combs, or metal rods

mechanical construction *n* : mathematical construction requiring means besides ruler and compass or involving figures other than straight lines and circles — opposed to *geometrical construction*

mechanical drawing *n* **1** : drawing done with the aid of instruments (as square and compass) — compare FREEHAND 1 **2** : a drawing made with instruments

mechanical engineer *n* : an engineer whose training or occupation is in mechanical engineering — abbr. *M.E.*

mechanical engineering *n* : a branch of engineering concerned primarily with the generation, transmission, and utilization of heat and mechanical power and with the production of tools, machinery, and their products

mechanical equivalent of heat : the value of a unit quantity of heat in terms of mechanical work units with its most probable value in cgs measure being 4.1855×10^7 ergs per calorie — symbol *J*; called also *Joule's equivalent*

mechanical heart *n* : a mechanism designed to maintain the flow of blood to the tissues of the body during a surgical operation on the heart

me·chan·i·cal·i·ty \mə̇,kanə'kaləd·ē\ *n* -ES : MECHANICALNESS

me·chan·i·cal·ize \mə̇'kanəkə,līz\ *vt* -ED/-ING/-S [¹*mechanical* + *-ize*] : to make mechanical

me·chan·i·cal·ly \-nək(ə)lē, -nēk-, -li\ *adv* : in a mechanical manner

mechanical mixture *n* : a mixture whose components are separable by mechanical means as distinguished from a chemical compound

me·chan·i·cal·ness *n* -ES : the quality or state of being mechanical ⟨was calmed by the ~ of the tasks at home —Sinclair Lewis⟩

mechanical pencil *n* : a pencil whose lead is projected by a screw or other device

mechanical property *n* : a property that involves a relationship between stress and strain or a reaction to an applied force

mechanical refrigeration *n* : the abstraction of heat by means of a working substance subjected to refrigerating thermodynamic cycles in which the energy is supplied by a mechanical compressor : cooling produced by a machine instead of by melting ice

mechanical stage *n* : a stage on a compound microscope equipped with a mechanical device for moving a slide lengthwise and crosswise or for registering the slide's position by vernier for future exact repositioning

mechanical test *n* : a test for determining a mechanical property

mechanical tissue *n* : tissue serving as a supporting framework in plants — compare PARENCHYMA, PROSENCHYMA

mechanic art *n* : MECHANICS 2b

mech·a·ni·cian \,mekə'nishən\ *n* -S [¹*mechanic* + *-ian*] : ARTISAN, MECHANIC, MACHINIST

mechanico- *comb form* [ISV, fr. L *mechanicus* mechanic, mechanical — more at MECHANIC] **1** : mechanical ⟨*mechanico*therapy⟩ **2** : mechanical and ⟨*mechanico*chemical⟩

me·chan·ics \mə̇'kaniks, -nēks\ *n pl but sing or pl in constr* **1** : a branch of physical science that deals with energy and forces and their relation to the equilibrium, deformation, or motion of solid, liquid, and gaseous bodies — see CELESTIAL MECHANICS, MATRIX MECHANICS, QUANTUM MECHANICS, WAVE MECHANICS; compare DYNAMICS, ENERGETICS, KINEMATICS, KINETICS, STATICS **2 a** : the practical application of mechanics to the design, construction, or operation of machines or tools or their products **b** : fabrication by any manual trade or craft — called also *mechanic art* **3** : working structure or mechanism : functioning system ⟨knows the ~ of the lathe intimately⟩ ⟨the ~ of the general circulation of the atmosphere —*Climate & Man*⟩ ⟨provides an adequate ~ of meaning and value —R.P.Blackmur⟩ ⟨my enjoyment of our own parties is still dimmed by the ~ of hospitality —Doris F. Bernays⟩ ⟨liberals without much grasp of the ~ of politics —H.J.Hanham⟩ **4** : routine procedure : technical details or method ⟨leaves the ~ of his agency almost solely in the hands of subordinates —*New Republic*⟩

mechanics' institute *n* : a school for adult working men formerly common in Great Britain and the U.S.

mechanic's lien *n* : a lien against a building and its site to assure payment for construction work and material — compare MATERIALMAN'S LIEN

mech·a·nism \'mekə,nizəm\ *n* -S [LL *mechanisma* contrivance, fr. Gk *mēchanē* machine + *-isma* -ism — more at MACHINE] **1 a** : a piece of machinery : a structure of working parts functioning together to produce an effect ⟨the valve ~ to operate the valve when it is in the engine block —Joseph Heitner⟩ ⟨~ of a watch⟩ **b** : a process or technique for achieving a result sometimes by cooperative effort: as (1) : a political practice or stratagem ⟨the ~s of peace —F.D.Roosevelt⟩ ⟨little thought is given to the real ~ of Communism —Norman Cousins⟩ ⟨the political ~s normal to a nation at war —R.A.Dahl⟩ (2) : a body process or function ⟨may be important in the ~ of onset of labor —J.P.Greenhill⟩ (3) : a creative method (as in the arts) ⟨have shown singularly little curiosity about the actual ~ of poetic inspiration —Herbert Read⟩ (4) : the combination of mental processes by which a result is obtained ⟨the ~ of invention⟩; *esp* : MECHANISM OF DEFENSE (5) : a systematic social or economic procedure ⟨banks provide the ~ which assures the smooth circulation of short-term credits —R.B.Westerfield⟩ **2** : mechanical operation or action ⟨he acknowledges nothing besides matter and motion; so that all must be performed either by ~ or accident —Richard Bentley †1742⟩ **3 a** : nature or a natural process conceived as like a machine or as functioning purely in accordance with mechanical laws **b** : a philosophical doctrine that holds that natural processes and esp. the processes of life are mechanically determined and capable of complete explanation by the laws of physics and chemistry — compare TELEOLOGY, VITALISM **4 a** : the fundamental physical or chemical processes involved in or responsible for an action, reaction, or other natural phenomenon ⟨meteorologists believe that this pressure jump is the ~ responsible for storms and tornadoes —*Think*⟩ ⟨the complicated ~ that governs planets and satellites decreed that the moon should slow down —Waldemar Kaempffert⟩ **b** : a sequence of steps in a chemical reaction ⟨the most satisfactory evidence for the proposed ~ of chlorination —G.W.Wheland⟩ ⟨there are . . . many different ~s by which catalysts operate —Farrington Daniels & R.A.Alberty⟩ **5** : an approach to language study based on an objective methodology in recording and classifying linguistic phenomena on the basis of observable forms — compare MENTALISM

mech·a·nis·mic \¦==¦nizmik\ *adj* : of, relating to, or involving a mechanism

mechanism of defense : an unconscious mental process (as identification, projection, or repression) that enables the ego to reach compromise solutions to problems it is unable to resolve

mech·a·nist \'mekənə̇st\ *n* -S [*mechan-* + *-ist*] **1** *archaic* : MECHANIC **2** : an adherent or practitioner of a mechanistic system; *esp* : an adherent of the philosophical doctrine of mechanism

mech·a·nis·tic \¦==¦nistik, -tēk\ *adj* **1** : mechanically determined ⟨a ~ universe⟩ **2 a** : of, relating to, or consistent with the theory of philosophic mechanism **b** : of, relating to, or marked by a psychological mechanism : tending to interpret conduct in terms of theoretical mechanisms **c** : finding biological and physical causes sufficient to explain social behavior **d** : of or relating to mechanism as an approach to linguistic study **3** : MECHANICAL — **mech·a·nis·ti·cal·ly** \-tə̇k(ə)lē, -tēk-, -li\ *adv*

mech·a·ni·za·tion \,mekənə̇'zāshən, -,nī'z-\ *n* -S : the act or process of mechanizing or the state of being mechanized

mech·a·nize \'mekə,nīz\ *vt* -ED/-ING/-S *see -ize in Explan Notes* [*mechan-* + *-ize*] **1** : to give the quality or structure of a machine to: as **a** *archaic* : to reduce to orderly systematic method or procedure **b** : to render automatic or routine : impart a deadening monotony to : deprive of spontaneity ⟨Americans have *mechanized* their emotions and standardized their ideas —W.G.Carleton⟩ **2 a** : to equip with machinery; *esp* : to substitute mechanical processes for human or animal labor in ⟨shuts down marginal coal mines and ~s many of the rest, with resultant unemployment for miners —E.A.Lahey⟩ **b** : to equip (a military force) with armed and armored motor vehicles (as tanks and self-propelled cannon) — distinguished from *motorize* **c** : to provide with mechanical power ⟨*mechanized* weapons⟩ **3 a** : to produce or reproduce by machine (an effect normally or basically produced directly by man) ⟨an enormous advantage . . . over the more *mechanized* stimuli of the motion picture —Marc Connelly⟩ ⟨now music is *mechanized* in its full tonal range —Siegfried Giedion⟩ **b** : to devise or create with undue reliance on technique or mechanics ⟨fail because of an application of formula, call it *mechanized* plotting —W.T. Scott⟩

mech·a·niz·er \-,nīzə(r)\ *n* -S : one that mechanizes

mechano- — see MECHAN-

mech·a·no·caloric effect \¦mekə,nō+-\ *n* [*mechan-* + *caloric*] : a change of temperature by produced mechanical means; *specif* : a fluctuation in liquid helium II at the point where the capillary film emerges from the parent liquid — compare SUPERFLUID

mech·a·no·mor·phic \¦===¦mȯrfik\ *adj* [*mechan-* + *-morphic*] : having the form or qualities of a machine : described in mechanical terms ⟨a ~ God⟩ ⟨this ~ world, the City of Destruction from which we must all flee —*Saturday Rev.*⟩

mech·a·no·mor·phism \"+¦mȯr,fizəm\ *n* -S [*mechan-* + *-morphism* (as in *anthropomorphism*)] : a conception of something (as the universe or a living creature) as operating mechanically or to be fully accounted for according to the laws of physical science

mech·a·no·therapist \"+\ *n* : one who practices mechanotherapy

mech·a·no·therapy \"+\ *n* [ISV *mechan-* + *therapy*] : the treatment of disease by manual, physical, or mechanical means

mechitarist *usu cap, var of* MEKHITARIST

mech·lin \'meklən\ *or* **mechlin lace** *n* -S *usu cap M* [fr. *Mechlin*, Belgium] : a delicate bobbin lace that is used for dresses and millinery and has floral designs outlined by a glossy cordonnet against a net ground of hexagonal mesh

me·cho·a·can \¦mechəwə¦kän\ *n* -S [Sp *mechoacán*, fr. *Michoacán* state, Mexico] : a weak jalap

Mech·o·lyl \'mekə,lil, -,lēl\ *trademark* — used for methacholine

mechs *pl of* MECH

me·cis·to·cirrus \mə,sistō'sirəs\ *n, cap* [NL, fr. *mecisto-* (fr. Gk *mēkistos*, superl. of *makros* long) + *cirrus* — more at MEAGER] : a genus of nematode worms (family Trichostrongylidae) including a common parasite (*M. digitatus*) of the abomasum of domesticated ruminants and the stomach of swine in both of which it may cause serious loss of blood and digestive disturbances esp. in young animals

meck·e·lian bar \me'kēlēən-\ *or* **meckelian cartilage** *or* **meckelian rod** *n, usu cap M* [Johann F. Meckel †1833 + E *-ian*] : MECKEL'S CARTILAGE

meckelian ganglion *n, usu cap M* [J.F.Meckel †1774 + E *-ian*] : SPHENOPALATINE GANGLION

meck·el's cartilage \'mekəlz-\ *n, usu cap M* [after Johann F. *Meckel* †1833 Ger. anatomist] : the cartilaginous axis of the mandibular arch forming no part of the jawbone but sometimes giving rise to the malleus and the bones of the middle ear

meckel's cave *n, usu cap M* [after Johann F. *Meckel* †1774 Ger. anatomist] : a space beneath the dura mater lodging the gasserian ganglion

meckel's diverticulum *n, usu cap M* [after Johann F. *Meckel* †1774 Ger. anatomist] : the proximal part of the yolk stalk when persistent as a blind fibrous tube connected with the lower ileum

meckel's ganglion *n, usu cap M* [after Johann F. *Meckel* †1774 Ger. anatomist] : SPHENOPALATINE GANGLION

meck·len·burg·ian \¦meklən¦bərgēən\ *adj, usu cap* [*Mecklenburg*, region in northern Germany + E *-ian*] : WÜRMIAN

meco- — see MEC-

¹me·co·dont \'mēkə,dänt\ *adj* [NL Mecodonta] : of or relating to the Mecodonta

²mecodont \"\ *n* -S : a member of the Mecodonta

me·co·don·ta \,==¦däntə\ *n pl, cap* [NL, fr. *mec-* + *-odonta*] *in some classifications* : a primary division of Caudata comprising salamanders having the palatal teeth inserted on the inner margin of the palatine processes in posteriorly diverging longitudinal rows

me·com·e·ter \mə̇'kämə̇d·ə(r)\ *n* [ISV *mec-* + *-meter*] : an instrument for measuring a newborn child

mecon- *or* **mecono-** *comb form* **1** : poppy ⟨*meconi*dium⟩ ⟨*mecono*psis⟩ **2** [NL *meconium*] : opium ⟨*mecon*in⟩ ⟨*meco*nology⟩ ⟨*mecono*phagy⟩

me·con·ic acid \mə̇'kānik-, -kōn-\ *n* [Gk *mēkōnikos* of a poppy, fr. *mēkōn* + *-ikos* -ic] : a crystalline acid $C_7H_4O_7$ obtained from opium; 3-hydroxy-4-pyrone-2,6-dicarboxylic acid

mec·o·nid·i·um \,mekə'nidēəm\ *n, pl* **meconid·ia** \-dēə\ [NL, fr. Gk *mēkōn* poppy + NL *-idium*; fr. the resemblance to the seed capsule of the poppy] : a gonophore produced by some hydroids that resembles a medusa and remains attached by a pedicel

mec·o·nin \'mekənən, 'mēk-\ *n* -S [F *méconine*, fr. *mécon-* + *-ine*] : a crystalline lactone $C_{10}H_{10}O_4$ found in opium

me·co·ni·um \mə̇'kōnēəm\ *n* -S [NL, fr. L, poppy juice, fr. Gk *mēkōnion*, fr. *mēkōn* poppy — more at MAW] **1** : OPIUM **2** [L, lit., poppy juice] **a** : a dark greenish mass of desquamated cells, mucus, and bile that accumulates in the bowel during fetal life and is discharged shortly after birth **b** [NL, fr. L] : a mass of fecal material discharged by some insect larvae at pupation

mec·o·nop·sis \,mekə'näpsə̇s, ,mēk-\ *n* [NL, fr. *mecon-* + *-opsis*] **1** *cap* : a genus of annual or perennial chiefly Asiatic herbs (family Papaveraceae) having flowers with stigmas forming a globular mass atop the ovary **2** *pl* **meconop·ses** \-(,)sēz\ : any plant of the genus *Meconopsis*

me·cop·tera \mə'käptərə\ *n pl, cap* [NL, fr. *mec-* + *-ptera*] : an order of primitive carnivorous insects usu. having membranous heavily veined wings, a long beak with biting mouthparts at the tip, and larvae that live in soil and including the scorpion flies and hanging flies — **me·cop·ter·an** \-tərən\ *n* -S — **me·cop·ter·ous** \-t(ə)rəs\ *adj*

mecs *pl of* MEC

med *abbr* **1** medalist **2** median **3** medical; medicine **4** medieval **5** medium

me·dad·dy-bush \mə'dadē,=\ *n* [*medaddy* of unknown origin] : FLY HONEYSUCKLE 2

me·dail·lon \mädäyōⁿ\ *n* -S [F *médaillon*, lit., medallion — more at MEDALLION] : a small round or oval serving of food (as a fillet or a savory)

me·da·ka \mə'däkə\ *n* -S [Jap] : a small Japanese freshwater poeciliid fish (*Oryzias latipes*) commonly occurring in flooded rice fields and usu. silvery brown in the wild but from pale yellow to deep red in aquarium strains

¹med·al \'medᵊl\ *n* -S [MF *medaille*, fr. OIt *medaglia*, coin worth half a denarius, medal, fr. (assumed) VL *medalia*, neut. pl. of *medalis* half, fr. LL *medialis* middle, fr. L *medius* middle, half + *-alis* -al — more at MID] **1 a** : a metal disk bearing a religious emblem or picture that represents a particular devotion or object of veneration **b** *archaic* : IMAGE, REPRESENTATION **2** : a piece of metal usu. in the form of a coin with an inscription, head, or other device issued to commemorate a person, action, or event or awarded (as to a soldier) for heroic deeds or meritorious service or (as to a student) for proficiency, skill, or excellence

medal 2 : Congressional Medal of Honor, Army

²medal \"\ *vt* **medaled** *or* **medalled**; **medaled** *or* **medalled**; **medaling** *or* **medalling** \-d(ᵊ)liŋ\ **medals** : to honor or reward with a medal : to confer a medal on ⟨~*ed* by the king —W.M.Thackeray⟩

medal bronze *n* : a moderate yellowish brown to light olive brown that is duller than Isabella and very slightly yellower than clay drab — called also *calabash*

medal chief *n* : an Indian chief honored with a medal

med·al·et \¦medᵊl¦et, 'medᵊlə̇t, *usu* |d.+V\ *n* -S [¹*medal* + *-et*] : a small medal

med·al·ist *or* **med·al·list** \'medᵊlə̇st\ *n* -S [F *medailliste*, fr. It *medaglista*, fr. *medaglia* medal + *-ista* -ist — more at MEDAL] **1** : a connoisseur or collector of medals **2** : a designer, engraver, or maker of medals **3 a** : one awarded a medal as a prize or distinction ⟨~ of the Geological Society⟩ **b** : the low scorer in qualifying medal play in a golf tournament **c** : a recipient of a medal as a prize in competitive sports

me·dal·lic \mə̇'dalik\ *adj* : of, relating to, or shown on a medal

¹me·dal·lion \mə̇'dalyən, me'-\ *n* -S [F *médaillon*, fr. It *medaglione*, aug. of *medaglia* medal — more at MEDAL] **1 a** : a large medal (as for a memorial purpose) ⟨a burnished bronze ~ three inches in diameter has been issued by the . . . diamond jubilee committee —*Numismatist*⟩ **b** : any of various large ancient Greek coins ⟨a ~ of Syracuse⟩ **2** : something resembling a large medal: as **a** : a tablet or panel in a wall or window bearing a figure shown in relief, a portrait, or an ornament **b** (1) : a design on a carpet or in lace (2) : a lace ornament in a garment **c** : a framed usu. oval or round design on a stamp or a piece of paper currency showing a portrait or denomination **3** : a perforated design punched in the tip of a shoe

²medallion \"\ *vt* -ED/-ING/-S **1** : to adorn with medallions **2** : to make a medallion of : represent in a medallion

me·dal·lion·ist \-nə̇st\ *n* -S : a maker, engraver, or worker of medallions

medal play *n* : golf competition scored by total number of strokes — compare MATCH PLAY

med·dle \'medᵊl\ *vb* **meddled**; **meddled**; **meddling** \-d(ᵊ)liŋ\ **meddles** [ME *medelen*, *medlen*, fr. OF *mesler*, *mesdler*, *medler*, fr. (assumed) VL *misculare*, fr. L *miscēre* to mix — more at MIX] *vt* **1** *obs* : to mix together : COMBINE, MINGLE **2** *dial* : to interfere with : DISTURB — *vi* **1** *obs* : to engage in combat **2 a** *archaic* : to occupy oneself : DEAL — usu. used with *with* **b** : to busy oneself intrusively or officiously : interfere without right or propriety ⟨the driving spirit of malice which forced him to ~ in other people's lives —Carl Van Doren⟩ ⟨history and psychology can ~ too much with the meanings of art —*Times Lit. Supp.*⟩

syn INTERFERE, INTERMEDDLE, TAMPER: MEDDLE suggests officiously entering into something in no way one's concern, affair, or responsibility without right, permission, or request of those concerned ⟨as Minister of Finance, Chari had no business to *meddle* in political affairs —Christine Weston⟩ ⟨it is inexpedient to *meddle* with questions of State in a land where men are highly paid to work them out for you —Rudyard Kipling⟩ INTERFERE suggests taking part obtrusively and officiously in the affairs of others so as to hinder, frustrate, check, or defeat ⟨he would not allow management or labor to *interfere* with increasing production —*Collier's Yr. Bk.*⟩ ⟨when a child persistently *interferes* with other children or spoils their pleasures, the obvious penalty is banishment —Bertrand Russell⟩ INTERMEDDLE combines connotations and denotations of MEDDLE and INTERFERE ⟨a petition to parliament sets forth how all kinds of unlearned men *intermeddle* with the practice of physic —G.G.Coulton⟩ TAMPER suggests unwarranted alteration or change, ill-advised readjustment, meddlesome experimentation, or improper influence ⟨he would suddenly leave his guests and rush back to town to see that the door had not been *tampered* with —Oscar Wilde⟩ ⟨these blank notes were slipped into the note case when examiners came along and the books were *tampered* to indicate that the notes were bearing interest —W.A.White⟩ ⟨money and sex are forces too unruly for our reason; they can only be controlled by taboos with which we *tamper* at our peril —L.P.Smith⟩

med·dler \-d(ᵊ)lə(r)\ *n* -S [ME *medeler*, fr. *medelen*, *medlen* to meddle + *-er*] : one that meddles : BUSYBODY

med·dle·some \'medᵊlsəm\ *adj* : given to meddling in the affairs of others : officiously intrusive **syn** see IMPERTINENT

med·dle·some·ly *adv* : in a meddlesome manner

meddlesome mat·tie \-'mad·ē\ *n* -S *usu cap both Ms* [after *Meddlesome Matty*, subject of a poem of the same name by Ann Taylor †1866 Am. writer] : BUSYBODY, MEDDLER ⟨when men insist that morality is more than that, they are quickly denounced, in general correctly, as *Meddlesome Matties* —Walter Lippmann⟩

med·dle·some·ness *n* -ES : the disposition or habit of a meddler

med·dling \'med(ᵊ)liŋ\ *n* -S [ME *medeling*, *medling*, gerund of *medelen*, *medlen* to meddle] : officious interference ⟨advised against surgical ~ which would do the patient no good —Harvey Graham⟩ : TAMPERING

med·dling·ly *adv* : in a meddling manner

¹mede *obs var of* MEAD

²mede \'mēd\ *n* -S *usu cap* [ME, fr. L *Medus*, fr. Gk *Mēdos*] : a native or inhabitant of ancient Media in Persia

¹me·del·lín *or* **me·dellin** \¦medᵊl¦ēn, ¦mātha¦yēn\ *adj, usu cap* [fr. *Medellín*, Colombia] : of or from the city of Medellín, Colombia : of the kind or style prevalent in Medellín

²medellin \"\ *n* -S *usu cap* : a high-grade Colombian coffee

med·fly \'med+,-\ *n, sometimes cap* [*Mediterranean* + *fly*] : MEDITERRANEAN FRUIT FLY

medi- *or* **medio-** *comb form* [L, fr. *medius* middle — more at MID] **1** : medially ⟨*medio*depressed⟩ ⟨*medio*perforate⟩ **2** : intermediate ⟨*medi*eval⟩ ⟨*medio*silicic⟩ **3** : middle or median plane ⟨*medi*ad⟩ ⟨*medio*dorsal⟩ ⟨*medio*palatal⟩ ⟨*medio*ventral⟩

¹media *pl of* MEDIUM

²me·dia \'mēdēə\ *n, pl* **medi·ae** \-dē,ē\ [NL, fr. L, fem. of *medius*, middle — more at MID] **1 a** [so called fr. the fact that the voice of these stops was regarded by ancient Greek grammarians as making them rougher than the voiceless unaspirated stops but smoother than the voiceless aspirated stops] : one of the voiced stops β, δ, γ in Greek — called also *medial, soft mute* **b** : a voiced unaspirated stop **c** : an unaspirated or lenis stop **2** : the middle coat of the wall of a blood or lymph vessel, consisting chiefly of circularly arranged muscle fibers **3** : the median vein of an insect's wing, typically having a convex anterior branch and a concave posterior branch

me·di·a·cy \ˈmēdēəsē, -si\ *n* -ES [¹*mediate* + *-cy*] : the quality or state of being mediate : MEDIATENESS, INTERMEDIACY — opposed to *immediacy*

me·di·ad \ˈmēdē,ad\ *adv* [*medi-* + *-ad*] : toward the median line or plane of a body or part

mediaeval *var of* MEDIEVAL

¹**me·di·al** \ˈmēdēəl\ *adj* [LL *medialis*, fr. L *medi-* + *-alis* -al] **1 a** : being, situated, or occurring in the middle : intermediate in position : MEDIAN **b** : extending toward the middle **2 a** : situated between the extremes of initial and final in a word or morpheme ⟨the ~ second *d* in *deeded*⟩ **b** *of a stop consonant in ancient Greek* : VOICED **c** : of or relating to the middle voice or a form in the middle voice **3** : MEAN, AVERAGE

²**medial** \"\ *n* -S **1 a** (1) : a medial sound or letter (2) : a form of a letter used medially **b** : MEDIA 1 **2** : the median vein of an insect's wing

medial cadence *n* **1** *in ecclesiastical modes* : a cadence ending on the mediant **2** : a cadence with an inverted penultimate chord

medial lemniscus *n* : a band of nerve fibers that transmits proprioceptive impulses from the spinal cord to the thalamus

me·di·al·ly \ˈmēdēəlē, -li\ *adv* : in a medial manner or position

medial moraine *n* : a moraine in the middle of a glacier parallel to its sides that is often formed by the union of lateral moraines when two glaciers coalesce

me·di·a·lu·na \,mēdēə'lünə\ *n, cap* [NL, fr. L *media luna* half-moon] : a genus of percoid fishes that includes the half-moon

media man *n* [¹*media*] : a worker in an advertising agency who studies, negotiates with, or selects publications or other media to carry an advertisement

¹**me·di·an** \ˈmēdēən\ *n* -S [MF *mediane*, fr. ML *mediana* (*vena*), fr. L *mediana* (fem. of *medianus* median) + *vena* vein] **1** : a median part (as a vein, nerve, or scale) **2** : a value in an ordered set of quantities below and above which fall an equal number of quantities or which is the arithmetic mean of the two middle values if there is no one middle number ⟨the ~ of the set 19, 20, 36, is 20, that of the set 19, 20, 21, 22 is 20.5⟩ **3 a** : a line from a vertex of a triangle to the midpoint of the opposite side **b** : a line joining the midpoints of the nonparallel sides of a trapezoid **4** : MEDIAN STRIP **syn** see AVERAGE

²**median** \"\ *adj* [MF or L; MF, fr. L *medianus*, fr. *medius* middle + *-anus* -an — more at MID] **1** : being in the middle : occupying an intermediate position : MEDIAL ⟨was presumably of the ~ sexual type —H.S.Canby⟩ **2** : equivalent in lightness to median gray **3** : of, relating to, or constituting a statistical median **4** : situated in the middle; *specif* : lying in a plane dividing a bilateral animal into right and left halves — used esp. of unpaired organs and parts ⟨~ fins⟩ **5** *phonetics* : produced without occlusion along the lengthwise middle line of the tongue — compare LATERAL — **me·di·an·ly** *adv*

³**median** \"\ *adj, usu cap* [*Media*, ancient country in southern Asia (fr. L, fr. Gk *Mēdia*) + E *-an*] **1 a** : of, relating to, or characteristic of ancient Media in Persia **b** : of, relating to, or characteristic of the people of Media **2** : of, relating to, or characteristic of the Median language

⁴**median** \"\ *n* -S *cap* **1** : a native or inhabitant of Media **2** : the Iranian language of ancient Media

median basilic vein *or* **median cubital vein** *n* : a continuation of the cephalic vein of the forearm that passes obliquely toward the inner side of the arm in the bend of the elbow to join with the ulnar veins in forming the basilic vein and is often selected for venipuncture

median gray *n* : a gray having equal lightness or darkness differences from black and white as terminal members of a series of grays and for eyes adapted to a white background reflecting about 25 percent of the incident light or for eyes adapted to it reflecting about 18 percent — called also *medium gray*

median nerve *n* : a nerve that arises by two roots from the brachial plexus and passes down the middle of the front of the arm

median plane *n* : MESIAL PLANE

median point *n* : a point so placed with reference to a number of points or objects distributed over a plane surface that the sum of its distances from all the individuals is a minimum

median segment *n* : the propodeum of a hymenopterous insect

median strip *n* : a paved or planted strip of ground dividing a highway into lanes according to direction of travel

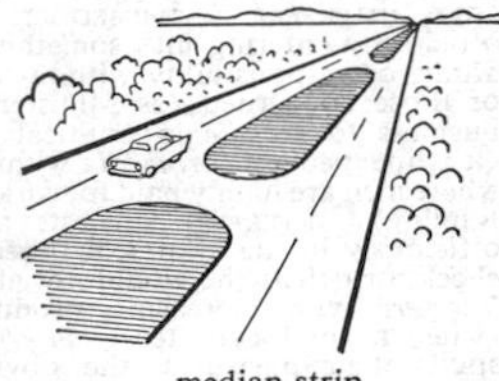

median strip

me·di·ant \ˈmēdēənt\ *n* -S [It *mediante*, fr. LL *mediant-, medians*, pres. part. of *mediare* to be in the middle — more at MEDIATE] **1** *in ecclesiastical modes* : a modulation of the authentic and the plagal modes **2** : the third musical degree of the major or minor scale (as E in the scale of C) midway between the tonic and the dominant

median vein *n* **1** : the cephalic vein in the forearm **2** : the fourth primary vein of an insect's wing falling in the middle part of the wing

me·di·as·ti·nal \,mēdēə'stīnᵊl\ *adj* [NL *mediastinum* + E *-al*] : of or relating to a mediastinum

me·di·as·ti·ni·tis \,mēdē,astə'nīd·əs\ *n, pl* **mediasti·nit·i·des** \-'nid·ə,dēz\ [NL, fr. *mediastinum* + *-itis*] : inflammation of the tissues of the mediastinum

me·di·as·ti·num \,mēdēə'stīnəm\ *n, pl* **mediasti·na** \-nə\ [NL, fr. neut. of L *mediastinus* medial, fr. *medius* middle — more at MID] **1** : the space in the chest between the pleural sacs of the lungs that contains all the viscera of the chest except the lungs and pleurae; *also* : this space with its contents **2** : a mass of connective tissue at the back of the testis being continuous externally with the tunica albuginea and internally with the interlobular septa and enclosing the rete testis

¹**me·di·ate** \ˈmēdēət, *chiefly Brit* ˈmējət *or* ˈmēdyət; *usu* -əd.+V\ *adj* [ME *mediat*, fr. LL *mediatus*, past part. of *mediare* to be in the middle, fr. L *medius* middle — more at MID] **1** : occupying a middle position : interposed between the extremes in order of time, place, or rank **2 a** *obs* : fulfilling the function of an intermediary **b** *archaic* : serving as a means : INSTRUMENTAL **3** : acting through an intervening agency : exhibiting indirect causation, connection, or relation ⟨the disease spreads by ~ as well as direct contact —*Veterinary Record*⟩ — **me·di·ate·ly** *adv* — **me·di·ate·ness** *n* -ES

²**me·di·ate** \ˈmēdē,āt, *usu* -ād.+V\ *vb* -ED/-ING/-S [in sense 1, fr. LL *mediatus*, past part. of *mediare*; in other senses, fr. ML *mediatus*, past part. of *mediare*, fr. LL, to be in the middle] *vi* **1** *archaic* : to form a connecting link : be in the middle : INTERVENE **2 a** : to interpose between parties in order to reconcile them or to interpret them to each other ⟨I want to ~ between the two of you now, because if this breach continues it will be the ruin of us all —Robert Graves⟩ **b** : to negotiate a compromise of hostile or incompatible viewpoints, demands, or attitudes : reconcile differences ⟨critics . . . who *mediated* between extreme points of view —C.I.Glicksberg⟩ ~ *vt* **1 a** : to bring about by intervention between conflicting parties : effect by action as an intermediary ⟨*mediated* a settlement satisfactory to both sides⟩ **b** : to bring accord out of by action as an intermediary ⟨endeavored to ~ East-West differences on several important issues —*Collier's Yr. Bk.*⟩ ⟨had just finished *mediating* an industrial dispute —*Current Biog.*⟩ **2 a** : to act as intermediary agent in bringing, effecting, or communicating (as a gift, result, influence) : CONVEY ⟨individuals . . . ~ the culture to the child —Margaret Mead⟩ **b** : to transmit or carry (as a physical process or effect) as intermediate mechanism or agency ⟨apparently the vast majority of papillae can ~ more than one sense quality —F.A.Geldard⟩

mediate inference *n* : a logical inference drawn from more than one proposition or premise — compare SYLLOGISM

mediating *adj* [fr. pres. part. of ²*mediate*] : performing a mediator's function : CONCILIATING, CONVEYING

me·di·a·tion \,mēdē'āshən\ *n* -S [ME *mediacioun*, fr. ML *mediation-, mediatio*, fr. *mediatus* (past part. of *mediare* to mediate) + L *-ion-, -io* -ion — more at MEDIATE] **1** : intervention between conflicting parties or viewpoints to promote reconciliation, settlement, compromise, or understanding ⟨a code . . . would not dispense with ~ between legislature and judges —B.N.Cardozo⟩ **2** : the function or activity of an intermediate means or instrumentality of transmission ⟨attains its effects . . . through the ~ of the ideological elements in society —Max Lerner & Edwin Mims⟩ **3** *international law* : intercession of one power between other powers at their invitation or with their consent to conciliate differences between them **4** : the cadence between the two reciting notes in a Gregorian psalm tone or an Anglican chant

me·di·a·tive \ˈ==,ā|d·iv, -ə|, |t|, |ēv *also* |əv\ *adj* [²*mediate* + *-ive*] : of, relating to, or used in mediation ⟨~ efforts⟩

me·di·a·tize \ˈmēdēə,tīz\ *vb* -ED/-ING/-S [G *mediatisieren*, fr. *mediat* mediate (fr. LL *mediatus*, past part. of *mediare* to be in the middle) + *-isieren* -ize — more at MEDIATE] *vt* **1** : to bring (a prince or state) down to the rank of mediate vassal from that of immediate vassal of the Holy Roman Empire : annex (a state) to another ⟨a *mediatized* prince —Cyril Connolly⟩ **2** : to put into a middle or intermediate position : make instrumental or subordinate ~ *vi* **1** : to act as mediator **2** : to become a mediate vassal of the Holy Roman Empire

me·di·a·tor \ˈ==,ād·ə(r), -ātə-\ *n* -S [ME *mediatour*, fr. MF, fr. LL *mediator*, fr. *mediatus* + *-or*] **1** : one that mediates; *esp* : one that mediates between parties at variance to reconcile them : INTERCESSOR ⟨for there is one God, and there is one ~ between God and men, the man Christ Jesus —1 Tim 2: 5 (RSV)⟩ **2** : one that transmits or conveys : a person or agency that serves as a channel or means ⟨the Arabs as depositories and ~s of ancient thought —Leonardo Olschki⟩ **3** : a mediating agent (as an enzyme or hormone) in a chemical reaction or biological process

me·di·a·to·ri·al \,mēdēə'tōrēəl, -tȯr-\ *adj* [LL *mediatorius* (fr. *mediatus* + *-orius* -ory) + E *-al*] : of, relating to, or appropriate to a mediator ⟨what she wanted was some ~ wisdom —A.D.Culler⟩

me·di·a·tor·ship \ˈ==,ād·ə(r),ship, -ātə-\ *n* : the office or function of a mediator

me·di·a·to·ry \ˈ==ə,tōrē, -tȯr-, -ri\ *adj* [LL *mediatorius*] : of, relating to, or directed toward mediation ⟨~ efforts⟩

me·di·a·tress \ˈ==,ā.trəs\ *n* -ES [*mediator* + *-ess*] : a female mediator

me·di·a·trice \,==ˈā.trəs\ *n* -S [ME, fr. MF, fr. LL *mediatric-, mediatrix*, fem. of *mediator* — more at MEDIATOR] : MEDIATRESS

me·di·a·trix \ˈ==ˈā.triks, -ēks\ *n* -ES [ME, fr. LL] : MEDIATRESS

¹**med·ic** *or* **med·ick** \ˈmedik\ *n* -S [ME *medike*, fr. L *medica*, fr. Gk *mēdikē*, fr. fem. of *mēdikos* Median, fr. *Mēdia* Media + *-ikos* -ic] : a plant of the genus *Medicago*

²**med·ic** \ˈmedik, -dēk\ *n* -S [L *medicus* physician, surgeon — more at MEDICAL] : one (as a physician, a medical student, or a military corpsman) engaged in medical work

³**medic** \"\ *adj* [L *medicus*, fr. *med-* (stem of *medērī* to heal) + *-icus* -ic — more at MEDICAL] *archaic* : MEDICAL

me·di·ca·ble \ˈmedəkəbəl, -dēk-\ *adj* [L *medicabilis*, fr. *medicare, medicari* to heal + *-abilis* -able — more at MEDICATE] **1** : CURABLE, REMEDIABLE **2** : having medicinal power : CURATIVE ⟨some ~ herb to make our grief less bitter —W.B. Yeats⟩ — **med·i·ca·bly** \-blē, -li\ *adv*

med·i·ca·go \,medə'kā,gō\ *n, cap* [NL, fr. L *medica* medic + L *-ago* (as in *plantago* plantain) — more at MEDIC, PLANTAIN] : a genus of Old World herbs (family Leguminosae) that resemble typical clovers and have pinnately trifoliolate leaves and spirally twisted seed pods — see ALFALFA

¹**med·i·cal** \ˈmedəkəl, -dēk-\ *adj* [F or LL; F *médical*, fr. LL *medicalis*, fr. L *medicus* physician, surgeon (fr. stem of *medērī* to heal + *-icus* -ic) + *-alis* -al; akin to Gk *Mēdos, Mēdē, Agamēdē*, gods of healing, Av *vī-mad-* healer, physician, L *meditari* to meditate — more at METE] **1** : of, relating to, or concerned with physicians or with the practice of medicine often as distinguished from surgery **2** : requiring or devoted to medical treatment ⟨pneumonia is a ~ disease⟩ ⟨the ~ wards of a hospital⟩ — distinguished from *surgical* **3** *archaic* : MEDICINAL — **med·i·cal·ly** \-k(ə)lē, -li\ *adv*

²**medical** \"\ *n* -S **1** : PHYSICIAN 1 **2** : a medical examination

medical examiner *n* **1** : a usu. appointed public officer who must be a person trained in medicine and whose functions are to make postmortem examinations of the bodies of persons dead by violence or suicide or under circumstances suggesting crime, to investigate the cause of their deaths, to conduct autopsies, and sometimes to initiate inquests — compare CORONER **2** : a physician employed to make medical examinations (as of applicants for military service or for life insurance or of claimants of workmen's compensation) **3** : a physician appointed to examine and license candidates for the practice of medicine in a political jurisdiction (as a state)

medical geography *n* : the study of the relation between geographic factors and disease

medical jurisprudence *n* : FORENSIC MEDICINE

medical psychology *n* : theories of personality and behavior not necessarily derived from academic psychology that provide a basis for psychotherapeutics in psychiatry and in general medicine

medical record *n* : a record of a person's illnesses and their treatment

¹**me·dic·a·ment** \məˈdikəmənt, meˈ-; ˈmedəkə-\ *n* -S [MF, fr. L *medicamentum*, fr. *medicare, medicari* to heal + *-mentum* -ment — more at MEDICATE] : a substance (as a chemical, a medicine, or an ointment) used in therapy **syn** see REMEDY

²**me·dic·a·ment** \-,ment\ *vt* -ED/-ING/-S : to treat with medicaments

med·i·ca·men·tous \,medəkə'mentəs\ *adj* [F *médicamenteux*, fr. L *medicamentosus*, fr. *medicamentum* + *-osus* -ous] : functioning as or caused by a medicament ⟨~ dermatitis⟩

med·i·cant \ˈmedəkənt, -dēk-\ *n* -S [L *medicant-, medicans*, pres. part. of *medicare, medicari* to heal] : a medicinal substance

med·i·cas·ter \ˈmedə,kastə(r)\ *n* -S [It *medicastro*, fr. *medico* physician (fr. L *medicus*) + *-astro* -aster (fr. L *-aster*) — more at MEDICAL] : a medical charlatan : QUACK

med·i·cate \ˈmedə,kāt, *usu* -ād.+V\ *vt* -ED/-ING/-S [L *medicatus*, past part. of *medicare, medicari* to heal, fr. *medicus* physician — more at MEDICAL] **1** : to treat with medicine : provide with medical care ⟨feeds, ~s, and educates the refugee community —A.J.Liebling⟩ **2 a** : to impregnate with a medicinal substance ⟨*medicated* waters⟩ ⟨authentic Chinese wines and cordials *medicated* with snake skin and tiger bone —*Amer. Guide Series: N.Y. City*⟩ **b** *archaic* : to adulterate with something noxious : DOCTOR

medicated candle *n* : DISINFECTING CANDLE

med·i·ca·tion \,medə'kāshən\ *n* -S [F or L; F *médication*, fr. L *medication-, medicatio*, fr. *medicatus* + *-ion, -io* -ion] **1** : the act or process of medicating : treatment with a medicament **2** : a medicinal substance : MEDICAMENT **syn** see REMEDY

med·i·ca·tive \ˈ==,kā|d·iv, -kə|, |t|, |ēv *also* |əv\ *adj* [ML *medicativus*, fr. L *medicatus* (past part. of *medicare, medicari* to heal) + *-ivus* -ive — more at MEDICATE] : MEDICINAL

med·i·ce·an \,medə'chēən, -də'sē-\ *adj, usu cap* [It *mediceo* Medicean (fr. the *Medici*, Ital. family powerful in Florence and Tuscany esp. fr. the 14th to 16th centuries) + E *-an*] : of or relating to the Medici family; *esp* : of or relating to a great Florentine library founded by Lorenzo de' Medici

med·i·ci blue \ˈmedə(,)chē-, -chi-\ *n, often cap M* [after the *Medici* family] : a bluish gray that is darker than clair de lune, greener and duller than average dusk (sense 3a), and deeper than puritan gray

me·dic·i·na·ble \məˈdis(ᵊ)nəbəl, meˈ-, *archaic* ˈmed(ə)sən-\ *adj* [ME *medecinable, medicinable*, fr. MF, fr. *medeciner, mediciner* to give medicine to, heal + *-able* — more at MEDICINE] : MEDICINAL

¹**me·dic·i·nal** \məˈdis(ᵊ)nəl, meˈ-, *archaic* ˈmedsənᵊl *or* ¦medə¦sīnᵊl\ *adj* [ME, fr. MF, fr. L *medicinalis*, fr. *medicina* medicine + *-alis* -al — more at MEDICINE] **1 a** : of or relating to medicine : tending to cure disease or relieve pain : used as a remedy : SANATIVE ⟨where a hot spring gushes forth, possessed, it is claimed, of ~ qualities —*Amer. Guide Series: Texas*⟩ **b** : having wholesome effect : SALUTARY ⟨a ~ phrase that he would repeat . . . in all moments of adversity —W.B. Yeats⟩ **2** *archaic* : MEDICAL

²**medicinal** \"\ *n* -S : a medicinal substance : MEDICINE

medicinal leech *n* : a large European freshwater gnathobdellid leech (*Hirudo medicinalis*) formerly much used by physicians for bleeding patients

me·dic·i·nal·ly \-nəlē, -li\ *adv* : with medicinal effect or aim : in a medicinal manner

medicinal soft soap *n* : GREEN SOAP

medicinal wafer *n* : CACHET 3

¹**med·i·cine** \ˈmedəsən, *chiefly Brit* -dsən\ *n* -S [ME *medecine, medicine*, fr. OF, fr. L *medicina*, fr. fem. of *medicinus* of a physician, medical, fr. *medicus* physician + *-inus* -ine — more at MEDICAL] **1 a** : a substance or preparation used in treating disease **b** : a person, agency, or influence that affects well-being ⟨a figure symbolic of strength and perseverance will be good ~ for the whole Western coalition —R.H.Rovere⟩ ⟨he's bad ~ —Zane Grey⟩ **2** : the science and art dealing with the maintenance of health and the prevention, alleviation, or cure of disease; *sometimes* : the branch of this field concerned with the nonsurgical treatment of disease — distinguished from *obstetrics* and *surgery* **3** : a drug or similar substance (as a potion, poison, or elixir) applied to nonmedical use **4 a** : any of various objects supposed by the No. American Indians to give control over natural or magical forces or to act as a protective or healing charm; *also* : magical power or a magical rite **b** : a similar object or agency among other primitive peoples **c** : a potent influence ⟨it's big ~ socially . . . to have one of these places —Calder Willingham⟩ **syn** see REMEDY

²**medicine** \"\ *vt* -ED/-ING/-S [ME *medecinen, medicinen*, fr. MF *medeciner, mediciner*, fr. *medecine*, medicine, n.] : to give medicine to : work a medicinal effect on ⟨the mixture was smooth and palatable . . . its gracious flavor *medicined* his mind to an immediate calm —Elinor Wylie⟩

medicine bag *n* : a bag often made of the skin of an animal patron of an Amerindian people to contain an individual's medicine and worn about the person

medicine ball *n* **1** : a large leather-covered ball stuffed with several pounds of soft material and used for conditioning exercises **2** : the exercise in which a medicine ball is thrown from one person to another

medicine bundle *n* : a bundle of sacred objects used in the ceremonies of the Plains Indians

medicine dance *n* : a ceremonial dance of the Plains Indians performed to obtain supernatural assistance

medicine dropper *n* : DROPPER 4a

medicine glass *n* : a small glass vessel graduated (as in ounces, drams, or milliliters) for measuring medicine

medicine lodge *n* **1** : a No. American Indian secret society devoted to the propitiation of supernatural beings **2** : SWEATHOUSE 1

medicine man *n* **1** : a priestly healer or sorcerer (as among Amerindian peoples) : SHAMAN **2** : the principal of a medicine show

me·dic·i·ner \məˈdis(ᵊ)nə(r), ˈmed(ə)sən-\ *n* -S [ME, fr. *medicine* + *-er*] : PHYSICIAN ⟨for the spirit there are better ~s —Witter Bynner⟩

medicine show *n* : a traveling show using entertainers to attract a crowd among which remedies or nostrums are sold ⟨his flowing mustache, fancy vest, and heavy gold chain made him appear more like the proprietor of a traveling *medicine show* than a physician with a permanent address —Willard Robertson⟩ ⟨itinerant *medicine shows* that peddle quinine and patented cures to the farm laborers —*Amer. Guide Series: Ark.*⟩

medicine song *n* : a song sung by No. American Indians in a ceremony invoking natural or magical powers

medicine woman *n* : a female healer among No. American Indians

medick *var of* MEDIC

med·i·co \ˈmedə,kō, -dē,-\ *n* -S [It *medico* or Sp *médico*, both fr. L *medicus* — more at MEDICAL] **1 a** : a medical practitioner : PHYSICIAN, SURGEON **b** : a medical student **2** : SURGEONFISH

medico- *comb form* [NL, fr. L *medicus* medical — more at MEDIC] **1** : medical ⟨*medico*psychology⟩ **2** : medical and ⟨*medico*botanical⟩ ⟨*medico*dental⟩ ⟨*medico*legal⟩

med·i·co·legal \,medə(,)kō, -dē(-+\ *adj* [NL *medico-legalis*, fr. *medico-* + L *legalis* legal — more at LEGAL] : of or relating to both medicine and law

medics *pl of* MEDIC

me·di·e·ty \məˈdīəd·ē\ *n* -ES [ME *medietee*, fr. L *medietas* — more at MOIETY] **1** : a half or moiety esp. of an ecclesiastical benefice having more than one incumbent **2** *obs* **a** : the middle or intermediate part, positon, or quality **b** : a mathematical mean

¹**medie·val** *or* **mediae·val** \,mēd¦ēvəl, ¦med-, ¦mid-; (ˈ)mē¦dēvəl, (ˈ)mi¦d-, (ˈ)me¦d-, mə'd-\ *adj* [*medi-* + L *aevum* age + E *-al*; after NL *Medium Aevum* middle ages (the period of European history extending roughly from about A.D. 500 to about 1500) — more at AYE] **1** : of, relating to, or typical or suggestive of the middle ages or their art, literature, or institutions ⟨watches her daughter fulfill the ~ rites of the coronations —Marjorie Earl⟩ ⟨the town has drowsily gone its ~ way —Richard Joseph⟩ — compare ANCIENT, MODERN **2** : ANTIQUATED, OUTMODED ⟨displayed a ~ carburetor —Nigel Dennis⟩ — **medie·val·ly** \-vəlē, -li\ *adv*

²**medieval** *or* **mediaeval** \"\ *n* -S : a person belonging to medieval times — usu. used in pl. ⟨the short shrift given the ~s is perhaps due to the desire to save space —H.R.Finch⟩

medie·val·ism \-və,lizəm\ *n* -S : medieval belief or practice : the method or spirit of the middle ages : devotion to the institutions, arts, and practices of the middle ages; *also* : a survival from the middle ages

medie·val·ist \-ləst\ *n* -S : a specialist in medieval history and culture : a devotee of medievalism : one in sympathy with the medieval spirit or with medieval attitudes or institutions : a connoisseur of medieval arts — **medie·val·is·tic** \-və¦listik, -tēk\ *adj*

medie·val·ize \,=(=)ˈēvə,līz\ *vb* -ED/-ING/-S *see -ize in Explan Notes* [*medieval* + *-ize*] *vt* : to make medieval : to give medieval quality to ~ *vi* : to study the middle ages or adopt their spirit or method

medieval latin *n, cap M&L* : the Latin used esp. for liturgical and literary purposes from the 7th to the 15th centuries inclusive — compare NEW LATIN

medieval mode *n* : ECCLESIASTICAL MODE

me·di·fixed \,mēdē+\ *adj* [*medi-* + *fixed*] *bot* : attached by the middle

me·di·glacial \"+\ *adj* [*medi-* + *glacial*] : situated between or in the midst of glaciers

medii *pl of* MEDIUS

me·dim·nus \məˈdimnəs\ *also* **me·dimn** \-ˈdim\ *n, pl* **me·dim·ni** \-m,nī\ [L *medimnus*, fr. Gk *medimnos* — more at METE] : an ancient Greek unit of capacity equal to about 1½ bushels

me·din *or* **me·dine** \məˈdēn\ *n* -S [MF *medin*, fr. Ar *mayyidī*] : MEDINO

me·di·na \məˈdēnə\ *n* -S [native name in northern Africa] : the native quarter of a North African city — compare MELLAH

me·di·nan \məˈdīnən\ *adj, usu cap* [*Medina*, N.Y. + E *-an*] : of or relating to the lowest division of the No. American Silurian — see GEOLOGIC TIME table

me·di·na worm \məˈdēnə-\ *n, usu cap M* [fr. *Médine*, French Sudan] : GUINEA WORM

¹**med·i·nese** \¦medᵊn¦ēz, -ēs\ *adj, usu cap* [fr. *Medina*, Saudi Arabia + E *-ese*] **1** : of, relating to, or characteristic of Medina, Saudi Arabia **2** : of, relating to, or characteristic of the people of Medina

²**medinese** \"\ *n, pl* **medinese** *cap* : a native or inhabitant of Medina

med·i·nil·la \,medᵊnˈilə\ *n, cap* [NL, after José de *Medinilla* y Pineda *fl*1820 Spanish governor of the Mariana islands] : a large genus of tropical Old World shrubs (family Melastomaceae) often grown for ornament and having fleshy leaves and large panicles of white or pink flowers with showy bracts

me·di·no \mə'dē(,)nō\ *n* -s [Ar *mayyidī*] **:** an old Egyptian bronze coin worth 1/40 of a piaster; *also* **:** a corresponding unit of value

me·dio \'mā(,)dyō\ *n* -s [Sp, fr. *medio*, adj., middle, half, fr. L *medius* — more at MID] **:** a coin representing one half of various Latin-American units of currency; *esp* **:** a half real

medio- — see MEDI-

me·dio·brome \'mēdēə,brōm\ *n* -s [*medi-* + *brome*, short for *bromoil*] **:** a process for altering tone values, removing distracting parts, and shifting emphasis in monochrome photographic prints by the use of oil paints

medi·oc·ra·cy \,mēdē'äkrəsē *sometimes* ,med- *or* -si\ *n* -ES [F *médiocratie*, blend of *médiocre* and *-cratie* -cracy] **:** rule by the mediocre ⟨the aristocracies must go, the *mediocracies* which take their place have to fade out —*Irish Statesman*⟩

medi·o·cre \¦mēdē¦ōkə(r) *sometimes* ¦med-\ *adj* [MF, fr. L *mediocris*, lit., halfway up a mountain, fr. *medi-* + *ocris* stony mountain; akin to Umbr *ocar*, *ukar* mountain, Gk *okris* mountaintop, edge, MIr *ochir*, *ochair* edge, L *acer* sharp — more at EDGE] **:** of a middle quality **:** of but a moderate or low degree of quality **:** INDIFFERENT, ORDINARY ⟨a best seller is the gilded tomb of a ~ talent —L.P.Smith⟩ ⟨a ~ performance⟩ ⟨received a ~ rating⟩ ⟨~ material⟩

medi·o·crist \'==,ōkrəst\ *n* -s [*mediocre* + *-ist*] **:** MEDIOCRITY 3

medi·oc·ri·ty \,==ˈäkrəd·ē, -ətē, -i\ *n* -ES [ME *mediocrete*, fr. MF *mediocrité*, fr. L *mediocritat-*, *mediocritas*, fr. *mediocris* mediocre + *-tat-*, *-tas*, -ty] **1** *archaic* **:** the quality or state of being intermediate between extremes or a quality, condition, position, or degree that is intermediate: as **a :** moderation of conduct **:** avoidance of excess or extremes **:** TEMPERANCE **b :** ability or endowment in modest degree **c :** modest fortune **:** limited or less than ample means **2 :** average capacity or worth regarded as dull, uninspired, or poor **:** conspicuous lack of distinction or excellence **:** INFERIORITY ⟨not ordinary ~ this, but planned, engineered ~ — and the social engineer's jargon is the measure of it —W.H.Whyte⟩ **3 :** a person of no outstanding distinction ⟨a most intelligent middle-aged ~ —Oscar Wilde⟩ ⟨shone among the *mediocrities* who surrounded him⟩

me·dio·palatal \¦mēdēō+\ *adj* [*medi-* + *palatal*] **:** articulated against the middle third of the hard palate or the middle third of the palate as a whole

¹medio·passive \"+\ *adj* [ISV *medi-* + *passive*] **:** of, relating to, or being a form or voice of a transitive verb which by origin is of the middle voice or is reflexive and shows by its meaning that it is developing toward passive use, or is used in both middle and passive meanings, or is used only in passive meanings

²mediopassive \"\ *n* **:** a mediopassive voice or form

med·i·tate \'medə,tāt, *usu* -ād·+V\ *vb* -ED/-ING/-S [L *meditatus*, past part. of *meditari* — more at METE] *vt* **1 :** to ponder or reflect on **:** muse over **:** CONSIDER, CONTEMPLATE ⟨*meditating* . . . the scholarly and political achievements of the last eight years —A.W.Levi⟩ **2 :** to plan or project in the mind **:** design in thought **:** INTEND, PURPOSE ⟨only looked at me in a curious sullen way, *meditating* revenge —Francis Yeats-Brown⟩ ⟨*meditated* a quick return —Jane Austen⟩ ~ *vi* **:** to keep the mind in a state of contemplation **:** dwell in thought **:** engage in studious reflection ⟨one would find her *meditating* on the values of poetry —H.V.Gregory⟩; *esp* **:** to practice religious contemplation **syn** see PONDER

med·i·tat·ing·ly *adv* **:** in a meditating manner

med·i·ta·tion \,medə'tāshən\ *n* -s [ME *meditacioun*, fr. OF *meditation*, fr. L *meditation-*, *meditatio*, fr. *meditatus* + *-ion-*, *-io* -ion] **1 :** a spoken or written discourse treated in a contemplative manner and intended to express its author's reflections or esp. when religious to guide others in contemplation **2 :** a private devotion or spiritual exercise consisting in deep continued reflection on a religious theme ⟨~ is very hard work —W.S.Maugham⟩ **3 :** the act of meditating **:** steady or close consecutive reflection **:** continued application of the mind ⟨enforced seclusion has given him opportunity for the ~ out of which this novel has come —Granville Hicks⟩

med·i·ta·tive \'==,tād·iv, -,tət|, |t|, |ēv *also* |əv\ *adj* **1 :** disposed or given to meditation ⟨there is much in them for the ~ reader —Eric Linklater⟩ **2 :** marked by, replete with, or conducive to meditation ⟨jar on the ~ silence of the morning —R.L.Stevenson⟩ — **med·i·ta·tive·ly** \-əvlē, -li\ *adv* — **med·i·ta·tive·ness** \-ivnəs, -ēv- *also* -əv-\ *n* -ES

med·i·tat·or \-,tād·ə(r), -ātə-\ *n* -s **:** one that meditates

mediterrane *also* **mediterraneal** *adj* [*mediterrane* fr. ME *mediterrayne*, fr. MF *mediterrain*, fr. L *mediterraneus*; *mediterraneal* fr. L *mediterraneus* + E *-al*] *obs* **:** INLAND, LANDLOCKED, MEDITERRANEAN

¹med·i·ter·ra·nean \,medətə¦rānēən, -nyən\ *adj* [in sense 1, fr. L *mediterraneus*, fr. *medi-* + *-terraneus* (fr. *terra* land); in other senses, fr. the *Mediterranean*, large inland sea enclosed by southern Europe, western Asia, and northern Africa — more at TERRACE] **1 :** enclosed or nearly enclosed with land ⟨it is a sea nearly as ~ as that which lies between Africa and Europe —Waldo Frank⟩ **2** *usu cap* **a :** of, relating to, characteristic of, or situated near the Mediterranean sea **b :** of or relating to the peoples or lands about the Mediterranean sea **3** *archaic* **:** situated inland **4** *usu cap* **:** of, relating to, or being the subdivision of the Palaearctic region that includes southern Europe, Persia, Asia Minor, northern Arabia, and Africa north of the Sahara **5** *usu cap* **:** of, relating to, or being a region with a climate that is marked by mild moist winters and warm to hot dry summers **6** *usu cap* **:** of or relating to the Mediterranean subrace or physical type of the Caucasian race characterized by medium or short stature, slender build, dolichocephaly, and dark complexion — compare ALPINE, ARMENOID, DINARIC, NORDIC

²mediterranean \"\ *n* -s [in sense 1, fr. *Mediterranean* sea; in sense 2, fr. ¹*mediterranean*] **1 :** a landlocked sea **2** *usu cap* **:** a person having Mediterranean physical characteristics

mediterranean anemia *n, usu cap M* **:** THALASSEMIA

mediterranean class *n, usu cap M* **:** a group of breeds of domestic fowls mostly of Spanish or Italian origin (as the Leghorns, Minorcas, and Andalusians) typically including rather lightweight nervous fowls that produce abundant white eggs — compare ASIATIC CLASS

mediterranean cypress *n, usu cap M* **:** ITALIAN CYPRESS

mediterranean fever *n, usu cap M* **:** any of several febrile conditions often endemic in parts of the Mediterranean region; *specif* **:** human brucellosis

mediterranean flour moth *n, usu cap M* **:** a small largely gray and black nearly cosmopolitan moth (*Anagasta kuehniella*) having a larva that destroys processed grain products

mediterranean fruit fly *n, usu cap M* **:** a two-winged fly (*Ceratitis capitata*) of the family Trypetidae that has black and white markings, is probably native to Africa but is now widely distributed, and has a larva which lives and feeds in ripening fruit

med·i·ter·ra·ne·an·ize \,===ˈrānēə,nīz\ *vt* -ED/-ING/-S *sometimes cap* [¹*mediterranean* + *-ize*] **:** to give a Mediterranean quality to ⟨one must ~ music, regain nature, gaiety, youth, efficacy —Maurice Boucher⟩

mediterranean release *n, usu cap M* **:** an archery release in which arrow and bowstring are drawn with three fingers and the arrow is held between the fore and middle fingers

mediterraneous *adj* [L *mediterraneus* — more at MEDITERRANEAN] **1** *obs* **:** INLAND **2** *obs* **:** SUBTERRANEAN

¹me·di·um \'mēdēəm\ *n, pl* **mediums** \-dēəmz\ *or* **me·dia** \-dēə\ [L, fr. neut. of *medius* middle — more at MID] **1 :** something lying in a middle or intermediate position: as **a :** a middle way **:** COMPROMISE ⟨try for the happy ~⟩ **b** *archaic* **:** a mathematical mean **c :** the average, usual, or common condition or amount ⟨will be leveled off to a peacetime ~ somewhere between its present employment of 7000 and its pre-Korean War level of 2500 —*Springfield (Mass.) Daily News*⟩ **2** *archaic* **:** the middle term of a syllogism **3 :** something through or by which something is accomplished, conveyed, or carried on: as **a :** a substance (as air or ether) regarded as the means of transmission of a force or effect ⟨air is the ~ that conveys sound⟩ **b :** a condition, atmosphere, or environment in which something may function or flourish ⟨a more finely perfected ~ in which . . . feelings are at liberty —T.S.Eliot⟩ **c :** an intermediate or direct instrumentality or means ⟨affirmed that the historic church was the ~ of a continuous revelation —Stringfellow Barr⟩ ⟨cattlemen seeking a ~ to combat horse thieves —R.A.Billington⟩; *esp* **:** a channel, method, or system of communication, information, or entertainment ⟨a book needs the widest possible discussion in the reviewing *media* of the country — whether magazine, newspaper, radio, television, or public platform —*Saturday Rev.*⟩ **d** *media pl but sometimes sing in constr* **:** a vehicle (as a radio or television program or a newspaper) used to carry advertising **4 a :** a proper setting or natural environment ⟨factors involved that make this slightly contaminated water better for young goldfish than a clean ~ —W.C.Allee⟩ **b :** an appropriate occupation or means of expression **:** an activity or field in which one is at home **:** MÉTIER ⟨the work of extraction and arrangement was the true ~ of the monastic scholars —R.W.Southern⟩ **5 :** a person through whom a purpose is accomplished **:** GO-BETWEEN, AGENT, INTERMEDIARY ⟨the ~ of introduction was no doubt . . . the publisher —Richard Garnett †1906⟩ **6 :** MEDIUM OF EXCHANGE **7** *pl* **mediums :** an individual through whom other persons seek to communicate with the spirits of the dead and who is held by such persons to be a channel of communication between the earthly world of the living and a nontemporal spiritual realm of the departed — compare AUTOMATIST 2b, SPIRITUALISM **8** *pl* **media a :** any nutrient system for the artificial cultivation of bacteria or other organisms or cells that is sometimes a simple substance but more commonly a complex of inorganic and organic materials in a fluid base or one rendered more or less solid by coagulation or by the addition of gelatin or agar — called also *nutrient medium* **b :** any of many fluids or solids in which organic structures are placed (as for preservation or mounting) **9 a :** the material or technical means for artistic expression (as paint and canvas, lithographic or sculptural stone, or literary or musical form) ⟨one can't have imagination until one has a ~ by which it can be expressed —J.D.Cook⟩ ⟨as his literary ~ he has chosen a biographical form which I have ventured to describe elsewhere as that of the walkie-talkie —Ernest Newman⟩ **b :** a liquid (as oil or water) with which pigment is mixed by a painter **10 :** a size of paper usu. 23x18 in. or 22x 17½ in. **11 :** a varnish spread upon the surface or back of a photographic negative before retouching or upon the surface of a print before oil coloring **12 :** a color filter used in theatrical stage lighting **13 :** a material (as paper, cloth, or activated carbon) on which solids are deposited in chemical filtration **syn** see MEAN

²medium \"\ *adj* **:** intermediate in amount, quality, position, or degree **:** AVERAGE, MEAN ⟨taxation reform helpful to the low and ~ income groups followed —*Collier's Yr. Bk.*⟩ ⟨a man of ~ height⟩ ⟨bake in a ~ oven⟩ ⟨the only car in the ~ field —*advt*⟩

medium artillery *n* **1 :** guns of greater than 105 mm. caliber but less than 155 mm. and howitzers of greater than 105 mm. caliber up to and including 155 mm. **2 :** troops that serve medium artillery

medium bomber *n* **:** a bomber of intermediate weight and range designed primarily to carry big bomb loads to strategic targets — compare HEAVY BOMBER, LIGHT BOMBER

medium chrome green *n* **:** a green that is yellower and duller than holly green (sense 1) or golf green, yellower and less strong than average hunter green, and stronger and slightly lighter than deep chrome green

medium chrome yellow *n* **:** DEEP CHROME YELLOW

medium frequency *n* **:** a radio frequency in the range between low and high frequencies of the radio spectrum — abbr *mf*; see RADIO FREQUENCY table

medium gray *n* **:** MEDIAN GRAY

me·di·um·is·tic \,mēdēə¦mistik\ *adj* **:** of, relating to, or having the qualities of a spiritualistic medium ⟨this moving of objects at a distance and without contact is one of the commonest happenings at a ~ séance —G.H.Estabrooks⟩

medium-laid \¦===¦=\ *adj* **:** having the strands twisted with a tightness between that of hard-laid and that of soft-laid rope

medium lay *n* **:** a rope lay that combines some of the wear-resistant quality of hard lay with some of the tensile strength of soft lay — called also *regular lay*

medium of exchange : something commonly accepted in exchange for goods and services and recognized as representing a standard of value — see CIRCULATING MEDIUM, MONEY

me·di·um·ship \'mēdēəm,ship\ *n* **:** the capacity, function, or profession of a spiritualistic medium ⟨his friends had been sitting weekly about a table in the hope of spiritual manifestation and one had developed ~ —W.B.Yeats⟩

medium shot *n* **:** a motion-picture shot made from or as if from a distance intermediate between that of a long shot and that of a close shot and showing a moderate amount of background

medium-term \¦===¦=\ *adj* **:** of or relating to a financial gain, loss, operation, or obligation based on a term of more than a year and usu. not more than 10 years

me·di·us \'mēdēəs\ *n, pl* **me·dii** \-dē,ī\ [NL, fr. L, adj., middle — more at MID] **:** the middle finger

med·ize \'mē,dīz\ *vb* -ED/-ING/-S *often cap* [²*Mede* + *-ize*] *vt, archaic* **:** to give a Median quality to **:** make Median ~ *vi, archaic* **:** to become Median in character **:** favor the Medes

¹med·lar \'medlə(r)\ *n* -s [ME *medeler*, fr. MF *meslier*, *medlier* medlar tree, fr. *mesle*, *medle* medlar (fruit), fr. L *mespilum*, *mespilus*, *mespila*, fr. Gk *mespilon*] **1 a :** a small Eurasian tree (*Mespilus germanica*) that is widely cultivated esp. in Europe **b :** the fruit of this tree resembling a crab apple and a much-used base for preserves **2 :** LOQUAT **3 a :** a small deciduous tree (*Vangueria infausta*) of southern Africa with few branches, with twigs and opposite leaves covered with velvety hairs, and with small greenish yellow flowers **b :** the globose fruit of this tree which has a leathery skin that is brown when ripe and a pithy flesh of a sweet-acid flavor

²medlar \"\ *n* -s [by shortening and alter.] **:** MEADOWLARK

¹med·ley \'medlē, -li\ *n* -s [ME *medle*, fr. MF *meslee*, *mesdlee*, *medlee*, fr. fem. of *meslé*, *mesdlé*, *medlé*, past part. of *mesler*, *mesdler*, *medler* to mix, quarrel, fight — more at MEDDLE] **1** *archaic* **:** COMBAT, MELEE **2 a** *archaic* **:** COMBINATION, MINGLING **b :** a heterogeneous mixture **:** HODGEPODGE, JUMBLE, MÉLANGE ⟨has a wood-smoke flavor along with the ~ of other tastes —Molly L. Bar-David⟩ ⟨his mind was confused with a ~ of thoughts —Wilson Collison⟩ ⟨a ~ of oil cans, empty cracker boxes, and whiskey bottles, loose spokes of cartwheels —Ellen Glasgow⟩ **3** *archaic* **:** a varicolored cloth of wool dyed in the raw **4 a** *archaic* **:** a musical composition put together of passages ill-matched in style or form **b :** a performance blending together a series of songs or other musical pieces ⟨a ~ of service songs —Virgil Thomson⟩ ⟨a piano ~⟩ **5** *archaic* **:** a literary miscellany

²medley \"\ *adj* [ME *medle*, fr. *medle*, n.] **1 a** *obs* **:** of a mixed color **:** MOTLEY **b** *archaic* **:** of, relating to, or consisting of medley cloth **2** *archaic* **:** of, relating to, or making up a confused or miscellaneous assemblage **:** MIXED

³medley \"\ *vt* **medleyed** *or* **medlied**; **medleyed** *or* **medlied**; **medleying**; **medleys** [¹*medley*] *archaic* **:** to make a medley of **:** MIX, MINGLE

medley relay *n* **1 :** a swimming relay race in which each member of a team of three or four uses a different stroke **2 :** a foot race in which each member of a relay team runs a different distance

medo- *comb form, usu cap* [Gk *mēdo-*, fr. *Mēdos* Mede, Median] **:** Median and ⟨*Medo*-Persian⟩ ⟨*Medo*-Scythian⟩

mé·doc \(')mā¦däk\ *n* -s *usu cap* [F, fr. *Médoc*, district in southwestern France] **:** a Bordeaux wine made in the Médoc district of France — compare BORDEAUX

med·rick \'medrik\ *n* -s [origin unknown] **:** a small gull or tern

med·ri·na·que \,medrən'yäkē, -rə'nä-\ *n* -s [Sp *medriñaque*] **1 :** a fiber from the sago palm in the Philippines **2 :** a cloth made from medrinaque fiber

me·dul·la \mə'dələ,me'-\ *n, pl* **medullas** \-ləz\ *or* **medul·lae** \-,lē\ [L; perh. akin to OE *smeoru*, *smeru* fat, grease — more at SMEAR] **1** *pl* **medullas**, *obs* **a :** the essence or pith of a matter **b :** COMPENDIUM, SUMMARY **2** *pl* **medullae a :** marrow of bone or spinal cord **b** [NL, fr. L] **:** MEDULLA OBLONGATA **3** [NL, fr. L] **a :** the inner or deep part of an organ or structure (as of a hair or kidney) **b :** the sheath of some nerve fibers **4** *pl* **medullae :** PITH **5** [NL, fr. L] **a :** the medullary layer of lichens **b :** the inner spongy layer of some fungi **c :** the central core of elongate colorless cells of the thalli of some brown algae **6** [NL, fr. L] **a :** the internal portion of some protozoans

medulla ob·lon·ga·ta \-,ä,blȯŋ'gäd·ə\ *n, pl* **medulla oblongatas** *or* **medullae oblonga·tae** \-äd·,ē\ [NL, lit., oblong medulla] **:** the somewhat pyramidal last part of the vertebrate brain developed from the posterior portion of the rhombencephalon and continuous posteriorly with the spinal cord, enclosing the fourth ventricle, and containing nuclei associated with most of the cranial nerves, major fiber tracts and decussations that link spinal with higher centers, and various centers mediating the control of involuntary vital functions (as respiration) — see BRAIN illustration

med·ul·lary \'medᵊl,erē, 'mejə,le-, mə'dələrē, -ri\ *also* **me·dul·lar** \mə'dələ(')\ *adj* [L *medullaris*, fr. *medulla* marrow + *-aris* -ar] **1 a :** of or relating to the medulla of any body part or organ **b :** containing, consisting of, or resembling marrow **c :** of or relating to the medulla oblongata or the spinal cord **d :** of, relating to, or formed of the dorsally located embryonic ectoderm destined to sink below the surface and become neural tissue **2 :** of, relating to, or composed of the pith of a plant **3 :** like marrow in consistency — used of cancers

medullary bundle *n* **:** a vascular bundle (as in plants of the family Umbelliferae) situated in the peripheral part of the pith of a stem and sometimes held to be an extension of a leaf trace

medullary canal *or* **medullary cavity** *n* **1 :** MEDULLARY GROOVE **2 :** the marrow cavity of a bone

medullary fold *n* **:** NEURAL FOLD

medullary groove *or* **medullary furrow** *n* **:** the median dorsal longitudinal groove formed in the vertebrate embryo by the medullary plate after appearance of the neural folds — called also *neural groove*

medullary layer *n* **:** the layer of loosely interwoven threads just below the algal layer in some lichens

medullary nailing *n* **:** the fixing of a fractured long bone by inserting a steel nail into the marrow cavity of the bone

medullary plate *n* **:** the longitudinal dorsal zone of epiblast in the early vertebrate embryo that constitutes the primordium of the neural tissue

medullary ray *n* **1 :** a ray of primary origin in the stele of various cryptogamous and dicotyledonous vascular plants that extends outward from the medulla often separating the vascular bundles — compare VASCULAR RAY **2 :** VASCULAR RAY

medullary sheath *n* **1 :** the layer of myelin surrounding a medullated nerve fiber **2 :** the outer layers of smaller usu. thick-walled cells that merge into the central pithy part of the core of many plant stems

medullary spot *n* **:** a small spot of irregularly arranged cells appearing as a scar in wood injured by insect boring

medullary tube *n* **:** NEURAL TUBE

medullary velum *n* **:** a thin white plate of nervous tissue forming part of the roof of the fourth ventricle

med·ul·lat·ed \'medᵊl,ād·əd, 'mejə,lā-, mə'də,lā-\ *adj* [LL *medullatus* having a marrow (fr. L *medulla* marrow + *-atus* -ate) + E *-ed* — more at MEDULLA] **1** *of a nerve fiber* **:** having a medullary sheath **2** *of other fibers* **:** having a medulla ⟨kempy wool contains many coarse ~ fibers⟩

med·ul·la·tion \,medᵊl'āshən, ,mejə'lā-\ *n* -s [*medulla* + *-ation*] **1 :** the formation of a medullary sheath or medulla **2 :** the condition of being medullated — used esp. of fibers but sometimes of animals (as sheep)

me·dul·li·spinal \mə¦dələ+\ *adj* [*medulla* + *-i-* + *spinal*] **:** relating to the spinal cord

me·dul·lo·blas·to·ma \mə,dəlō,bla'stōmə\ *n, pl* **medullo-blastomas** \-məz\ *or* **medulloblastoma·ta** \-məd·ə\ [NL, fr. *medullo-* (fr. L *medulla*) + *blast-* + NL *-oma*] **:** a malignant tumor of the central nervous system arising in the cerebellum esp. in children

medus- *or* **medusi-** *comb form* [ISV, fr. NL *medusa*] **:** medusa ⟨*medusi*ferous⟩ ⟨*medus*oid⟩

me·du·sa \mə'd(y)üsə, -üzə\ *n, pl* **medu·sae** \-(,)sē, -(,)zē\ [NL *Medusa*, a Linnaean genus of jellyfish, after *Medusa*, one of the three Gorgons, fr. L, fr. Gk *Medousa*] **:** JELLYFISH; *esp* **:** a small hydrozoan jellyfish

medusa bud *n* **:** one of the buds of a hydroid destined to develop into a gonophore or medusa

me·du·sal \-səl, -zəl\ *adj* [*medus-* + *-al*] **:** MEDUSAN

¹me·du·san \-sᵊn, -zᵊn\ *adj* [*medus-* + *-an*] **:** of, relating to, or like a medusa

²medusan \"\ *n* -s **:** MEDUSA

medusa's head *n* [after *Medusa*, one of the three Gorgons, whose hair was said to have been turned into snakes] **1 :** an edible hedgehog mushroom (*Hydnum caput-medusae*) with interwoven hymenial spines **2 :** an African euphorbia (*Euphorbia caput-medusae*) with numerous drooping slender branches **3 :** a weedy rye grass (*Elymus caput-medusae*) having long bristling awns

¹me·du·soid \mə'd(y)ü,sȯid,-,zȯid\ *adj* [*medus-* + *-oid*] **:** like a medusa

²medusoid \"\ *n* -s **:** a hydroid gonophore resembling a medusa

mee \'mē,bäs\ *var of* MEBOS

meech \'mēch\ *vi* -ED/-ING/-ES [ME *muchen*, *michen*, *mechen* to steal, skulk, prob. fr. ONF *muchier* to hide, lurk] **1** *now dial* **a :** to move in a furtive or cringing manner **:** SKULK, SNEAK **b :** to play truant **2** *now dial* **:** to complain in an ailing or peevish manner **:** WHINE

meech·er \-chə(r)\ *n* -s [ME *mucher*, *micher*, *mecher*, thief, pander, fr. *muchen*, *michen*, *mechen* + *-er*] **1** *now dial* **:** one that sneaks about or behaves dishonestly or dishonorably **:** PANDER, THIEF **2** *now dial* **:** TRUANT

meeching *adj* [fr. pres. part. of ¹*meeken*] *now dial* **:** CRINGING, SNEAKY, WHINING ⟨not going to have you do anything that will make you feel ~ afterward —W.D.Howells⟩

meed \'mēd\ *n* -s [ME *med*, *meed*, fr. OE *mēd*; akin to OE *meord* recompense, reward, wage, OS *mēda*, OHG *miata*, *mieta*, Goth *mizdo*, Gk *misthos*, OSlav *mizda*, *mŭzda* reward, Skt *mīḍha* prize, reward, contest] **1 a** *archaic* **:** the reward or wage earned by labor, service, or merit ⟨service . . . needs a receiver as well as a giver and thrives on some small ~ of welcome or honor —Freya Stark⟩ ⟨as long as slugs abound in the garden, good carbolic acid should not lack its ~ of honor —C.E.Montague⟩ **b :** the proper prize of excellence or fine performance **:** fitting return ⟨pay my ~ of tribute to him —Edna R. Johnson⟩ ⟨the old man loves us and we give him the ~ of our admiration —*Western Folklore*⟩ ⟨might pay, to the dead impresario, the ~ of parting tears —J.B.Cabell & A.J. Hanna⟩ **c :** just desert **:** fit recompense ⟨had suffered the ~ of his inhospitable conduct —G.B.Shaw⟩ **d :** AMOUNT, PORTION ⟨the plants of the jungle won success . . . by adapting their needs to the starvation ~ of air and light —William Beebe⟩ ⟨breed their own small ~ of juvenile delinquency —Sean O'Faolain⟩ **2** *archaic* **:** bribery offered or received **:** illicit gain **3** *obs* **:** MERIT, WORTH

¹meek \'mēk\ *adj* -ER/-EST [ME *meoc*, *mek*, *meek*, of Scand origin; akin to ON *mjūkr* soft, gentle — more at MUCUS] **1 :** manifesting patience and long-suffering **:** enduring injury without resentment **:** MILD ⟨~ as a mouse —Langston Hughes⟩ ⟨no longer the ~, soft native girl, but a determined woman —W.S.Maugham⟩ **2 :** deficient in spirit and courage **:** SUBMISSIVE, TAME ⟨a fine, fiery blast against ~ conformity —Orville Prescott⟩ **3 :** not violent or strong **:** GENTLE, MODERATE, WEAK ⟨~ rivulet —Green Peyton⟩ **syn** see HUMBLE

²meek \"\ *vt* -ED/-ING/-S [ME *meoken*, *meken*, fr. *meoc*, *mek*, *meek*, adj.] **:** HUMBLE, TAME ⟨man himself, ~*ed* by his Creator, may when tamed and taught, share the divine life —Anne Fremantle⟩

³meek *adv* [ME *meke*, fr. *meoc*, *mek*, *meek*, adj.] *obs* **:** MEEKLY

meek·en \'mēkən\ *vb* -ED/-ING/-S [ME *mekenen*, fr. *mek*, adj. + *-nen* -en] *vt* **:** ²MEEK ~ *vi* **:** to become meek

meek·ly *adv* [ME *meocliche*, *mekly*, fr. *meoc*, *mek* + *-liche*, *-ly* -ly] **:** in a meek manner

meek·ness *n* -ES [ME *meocnesse*, *meknesse*, fr. *meoc*, *mek* + *-nesse* -ness] **:** the quality or state of being meek **:** HUMILITY

mee·mies \'mēmēz, -miz\ *n pl but sing in constr* [by shortening] **:** SCREAMING MEEMIES ⟨you get the ~ when you're shut up in a tight spot —F.L.Harvey⟩

meen \'mēn\ *Scot var of* MOON

meer·kat *or* **mier·kat** \ˈmi(ə)rˌkat\ *n* -s [Afrik *meerkat*, fr. D, a kind of monkey, fr. MD *meercatte* monkey, fr. *meer* sea + *catte* cat; fr. the fact that monkeys came to Europe from overseas] **1 :** any of several mongooses; *esp* **:** a mongoose (*Cynictis penicillata*) of southern Africa **2 :** SURICATE

meer·schaum \ˈmi(ə)rshəm, -iəsh-, -ˌshȯm\ *n* -s [G, a species of Alcyonacea, meerschaum, fr. *meer* sea + *schaum* froth, foam] **1 :** a mineral $Mg_3Si_4O_{10}(OH)_2.4H_2O$ consisting of a hydrous magnesium silicate that is an extremely light fine soft white clayey material used for tobacco pipes and dug chiefly in Asia Minor (hardness 2–2.5, sp. gr. 2) — called also *sepiolite* **2 :** a tobacco pipe made of meerschaum **3 :** GRAVEL 3

mee·rut \ˈmārət, ˈmir-\ *adj, usu cap* [fr. *Meerut*, India] **:** of or from the city of Meerut, India **:** of the kind or style prevalent in Meerut

meer·wein–ponn·dorf reaction \ˌme(ə)rˌvīnˈpänˌdȯrf-\ *n, usu cap M&P* [after Hans *Meerwein* and Wolfgang *Ponndorf*, 20th cent. Ger. chemists] **:** the reduction of an aldehyde or ketone to the corresponding alcohol by reaction with boiling isopropyl alcohol in the presence of aluminum isopropoxide — compare OPPENAUER OXIDATION

[1]**meet** \ˈmēt, *usu* -ēd·+V\ *vb* **met** \ˈmet, *usu* -ed·+V\ **met; meeting; meets** [ME *meten*, fr. OE *mētan;* akin to OE & OS *mōt* meeting, assembly, OS *mōtian* to meet, OHG *muoz* meeting, ON *mœta* to meet, Goth *gamotjan* to meet, Arm *matčim* I approach] *vt* **1 a :** to come by accident into the presence of **:** fall in with **:** come upon **:** FIND ⟨*met* him as a stranger on a railroad journey⟩ **b :** to come near or in touch with by approach from another direction ⟨the whole delegation went to ~ them at the terminal⟩ **c :** to come into contact or conjunction with **:** JOIN ⟨there the brook ~*s* the river⟩ **d :** to present a sense impression to **:** impinge on **:** CATCH ⟨a brazen roar ~*s* the ear⟩ ⟨a pungent odor . . . *met* his nostrils —S.E. White⟩ **2 :** to collide with **:** encounter as antagonist or foe **:** fight, cope, or grapple with **:** OPPOSE ⟨*met* the heavyweight contender in a successful bout⟩ **3 :** to join (a person) in conversation, discussion, or social or business intercourse **:** enter into conference, argument, or personal dealings with **4 :** to conform to the wishes or opinions of ⟨expressed willingness to ~ him on that point⟩ **5 :** to discharge or pay fully **:** SATISFY, SETTLE ⟨could not ~ his loans —Waldo Frank⟩ ⟨did we ~ the costs —E.R.Leibert⟩ **6 :** to contend successfully with **:** cope with **:** MATCH ⟨true imaginative teaching arises to ~ the situation of the moment —A.E.Wier⟩ ⟨refiners of branded gasoline *met* the offer —S.M.Loescher⟩ ⟨this problem was *met* and solved —W.D.Leggett⟩ **7 :** to provide for **:** FILL, FULFILL ⟨natural resources . . . to ~ human needs —John Boyd Orr⟩ ⟨public and private agencies labored to ~ a critical housing shortage⟩ ⟨studied diligently to ~ the entrance requirements of his college⟩ **8 :** to be introduced to or made acquainted with ⟨an attractive sister I want you to ~⟩ ~ *vi* **1 a :** to come together usu. from different directions **:** come face to face ⟨it was in that unpropitious place they *met*⟩ **b :** to hold a session **:** convene for worship, business, or other purpose **:** ASSEMBLE, CONGREGATE ⟨the city council will ~ soon to deal with the issue⟩ **2 :** to join as contestants, opponents, or enemies ⟨the candidates *met* on many platforms to debate⟩ **3 :** to form a junction or confluence **:** follow or enter an identical course ⟨at last the two rails *met* and the golden spikes were driven —Meridel Le Sueur⟩ **4 :** to occur or appear together **:** UNITE ⟨many graces and many virtues ~ in her⟩

syn FACE, ENCOUNTER, CONFRONT: MEET, in the basic sense pertinent here, usu. implies no more than to come into the presence or company of whether by chance or design ⟨*meet* a stranger in the woods⟩ ⟨the event of my last visit to the mountain was *meeting* one of these brilliant creatures near the summit, in full song —John Burroughs⟩ ⟨as gruesome a sight as a man could *meet* in a lifetime —Marcia Davenport⟩ ⟨arrange to *meet* a friend at 2 o'clock⟩ ENCOUNTER usu. confines the meeting to one by accident or chance ⟨walked the whole of the six or seven miles . . . without *encountering* a soul —Compton Mackenzie⟩ ⟨personal reminiscences of actual incidents and people *encountered* during his 20 years of active sea life —R.W.Stallman⟩ ⟨troops moving westward by a parallel trail *encountered* the river and were delayed —*Amer. Guide Series: Fla.*⟩ ⟨this emigration *encountered* a number of obstacles —*Collier's Yr. Bk.*⟩ CONFRONT and FACE both imply a direct, usu. square, meeting in opposition. CONFRONT stresses the unavoidable, face-to-face nature of the meeting ⟨the basic question *confronting* the court —Douglass Cater⟩ ⟨the major problem *confronting* humanity —G.E.Hutchinson⟩ ⟨stared appalled at what *confronted* me —H.D.Quillin⟩ often, when the subject is personal, suggesting such a meeting resolutely entered into out of a determination to face a difficulty or settle a matter ⟨one of the most arduous tasks a conductor can *confront* —Irving Kolodin⟩ ⟨a man who can *confront* misfortune —W.S.White⟩ ⟨*confront* toil and danger —Sir Winston Churchill⟩ FACE emphasizes more the resoluteness, often courageousness, of the meeting as with something one might reasonably hesitate or dislike to meet ⟨not to avoid but to *face* the enemy⟩ ⟨the difficulties *faced* by the new government —H.C.Atyeo⟩ ⟨the government *faces* a strong storm of protest over its decision —*Current History*⟩ ⟨the ordeal he must now prepare to *face* —B.A.Williams⟩ ⟨a great many young men . . . are unwilling to *face* four years of college —*Nichols Junior College Catalogue*⟩ **syn** see in addition SATISFY

— meet her : to use the rudder to check the swing of a ship's head in a turn **— meet one halfway :** to make concessions to **:** compromise with ⟨the valley *meets him* more than *halfway* in his efforts to take the chance out of vegetable growing —*Monsanto Mag.*⟩ **— meet up with :** to encounter by chance **— meet with 1 :** to come upon **:** FIND **2 :** to join in company with **3 :** to be subjected to (fortune or vicissitude) **:** UNDERGO, EXPERIENCE **4** *obs* **:** to encounter as an enemy **:** grapple or cope with **:** OPPOSE

[2]**meet** \"\ *n* -s **1 a :** an assembling of men and hounds for a hunt **b :** a sports meeting consisting of competitive events esp. in track and field, swimming, or gymnastics contested by individuals and often by relay or other teams **c :** a sports contest of any of various other kinds ⟨basketball ~⟩ ⟨trapshooters' ~⟩ ⟨sports car ~⟩ **d :** a festival or competition of any of various other kinds ⟨singing ~⟩ **2 a :** the passage or point of passage of two trains traveling in opposite directions **b :** the point on a single track at which one train must take a siding to permit another to pass in the opposite direction **3** *Austral* **:** ASSIGNATION

[3]**meet** \"\ *adj* [ME *mete*, fr. OE *gemǣte;* akin to OHG *māza* moderation, suitability, manner, *māzi* suitable, ON *mætr* valuable, worthy, *māt* moderation, Goth *usmet* way of life, *mitan* to measure — more at METE] **1** *archaic* **:** close, exact, or scant in measure or size **2 :** SUITABLE, FIT, PROPER, APPROPRIATE ⟨he had been gradually growing more and more vile and ~ to be exterminated —Arnold Bennett⟩ **syn** see FIT

[4]**meet** *adv* [ME *mete*, fr. *mete*, adj.] *obs* **:** in a suitable manner **:** FITLY, SUFFICIENTLY

meet·er \ˈmēd·ə(r), -ētə-\ *n* -s **:** one that meets or attends a meeting

meethelp *also* **meethelper** *n* [[3]*meet* + *help*] *obs* **:** HELPMATE

[1]**meeting** *n* -s [ME, fr. gerund of *meten* to meet — more at MEET] **:** an act or process of coming together: as **a** *archaic* **:** DUEL **b :** a chance or planned encounter ⟨his first ~ with the man in many years⟩ **c** (1) **:** an assembly for religious worship ⟨attended ~ on Sunday⟩ ⟨stood in the dark across the road from a Negro church where they were holding ~ —Edwin Granberry⟩ (2) *dial Eng* **:** a congregation of religious dissenters or their house of worship (3) **:** the permanent governing organization of a congregation of the Society of Friends or that of a regional group of congregations **d :** a gathering for business, social, or other purposes ⟨a ~ of the board of directors⟩ ⟨a ~ of Congress⟩ **e :** a horse or dog-racing session extending for a stated term of days at one track ⟨begins the metropolitan racing season with a 21-day ~ in April —*Amer. Guide Series: N. Y. City*⟩ **f :** CONFLUENCE, INTERSECTION, JUNCTION ⟨the ~ of two great rivers⟩ **g :** a place of meeting **h :** a joint in carpentry or masonry

[2]**meeting** *adj* [fr. pres. part. of [1]*meet*] **1 :** that meets **:** marked by or used for meeting **2** *obs* **:** RESPONSIVE ⟨immortal verse such as the ~ soul may pierce —John Milton⟩

meeting engagement *n* **:** a collision between two advancing military forces neither of which is fully deployed for battle

meet·ing·er \ˈmētᵊnə(r), -tiŋə-\ *n* -s [[1]*meeting* + *-er*] *dial Eng* **:** a member of a nonconformist church or chapel ⟨to be a ~, you must go to chapel in all winds and weathers —Thomas Hardy⟩

meetinghouse \ˈ≈,≈\ *n* **1 :** a building used for public assembly; *esp* **:** the house of worship of any of various Protestant denominations **2 meetinghouses** *pl* **:** COLUMBINE 1a

meeting of minds : full agreement **:** CONCORD, HARMONY ⟨men . . . must make many adjustments before any *meeting of minds* is possible —Mark Starr⟩

meeting of the minds : assent by contracting parties to an agreement established as understood by both in the same sense as to terms, conditions, and subject matter

meeting rail *n* **:** the horizontal rail of a vertical sliding sash which meets the corresponding rail of the adjacent sash

meeting seed *n* [[1]*meeting*] **:** any of various aromatic seeds or small fruits formerly chewed in an effort to stay awake during religious services

meet·ly *adv* **:** FITLY, PROPERLY, SUITABLY

meet·ness *n* -ES [ME *metenes*, fr. *mete* meet + *-nes* -ness — more at MEET] *archaic* **:** the quality or state of being meet

meets *pres 3d sing of* MEET, *pl of* MEET

[1]**meg** \ˈmeg\ *n* -s *usu cap* [fr. *Meg*, nickname for *Margaret*] *chiefly Scot* **:** WOMAN: as **a :** a country girl **b :** a coarse boisterous woman

[2]**meg** \"\ *n* -s [origin unknown] **1** *obs* **:** GUINEA **2 a** *dial Brit* **:** HALFPENNY **b** *slang* **:** a one-cent piece **:** PENNY

[3]**meg** \"\ *n* -s [by shortening] **:** MEGAPHONE

[4]**meg** \"\ *vb* **megged; megged; megging; megs :** MEGAPHONE

meg *abbr* megohm

mega- *or* **meg-** *comb form* [Gk, fr. *megas* large, great, strong — more at MUCH] **1 a :** great **:** large ⟨*mega*bacterium⟩ ⟨*mega*spore⟩ **:** powerful ⟨*mega*scope⟩ **:** of the major order ⟨*mega*diastrophism⟩ ⟨*mega*mutation⟩ **:** enlarged ⟨*mega*type⟩ or abnormally enlarged ⟨*mega*duodenum⟩ ⟨*mega*esophagus⟩ **b :** having a (specified) part of large size ⟨*mega*dont⟩ ⟨*mega*gnathous⟩ **c :** capable of being distinguished or identified without the aid of the microscope ⟨*mega*breccia⟩ ⟨*mega*fossil⟩ ⟨*mega*phenocryst⟩ **2 :** a million of **:** multiplied by one million ⟨*meg*ohm⟩ ⟨*mega*lumen⟩ ⟨*meg*ampere⟩

megacaryocyte *var of* MEGAKARYOCYTE

mega·ce·phal·ic \ˌmegəsəˈfalik\ *also* **mega·ceph·a·lous** \ˌ≈≈ˈsefələs\ *adj* [*mega-* + *-cephalic, -cephalous*] **:** large-headed; *specif* **:** having a cranial capacity in excess of the mean **— mega·ceph·a·ly** \ˌ≈≈ˈsefəlē\ *n* -ES

me·gac·e·ros \məˈgasəˌräs\ [NL, fr. *mega-* + *-ceros* (fr. Gk *keras* horn) — more at HORN] *syn of* MEGALOCEROS

mega·chi·le \ˌmegəˈkī(ˌ)lē\ *n, cap* [NL, fr. *mega-* + *-chile* (fr. Gk *cheilos* lip) — more at GILL] **:** a genus (the type of the family Megachilidae) of leaf-cutting bees including some that are important pollinators of alfalfa and other legumes

[1]**mega·chi·lid** \ˌ≈≈ˈkīləd\ *adj* [NL *Megachilidae*] **:** of or relating to the Megachilidae

[2]**megachilid** \"\ *n* -s [NL *Megachilidae*] **:** a bee of the family Megachilidae

mega·chil·i·dae \ˌ≈≈ˈkiləˌdē\ *n pl, cap* [NL, fr. *Megachile*, type genus + *-idae*] **:** a family of bees comprising rather large usu. dark-colored solitary leaf-cutting and mason bees — see MEGACHILE

mega·chiroptera \ˌ≈≈+\ *n pl, cap* [NL, fr. *mega-* + *Chiroptera*] **:** a suborder of Chiroptera comprising the large powerful Old World fruit bats that are distinguished by smooth-crowned molars and a claw on the index finger **— mega·chiropteran** \"+\ *adj or n* **— mega·chiropterous** \"+\ *adj*

mega·colon \ˈ≈≈,-\ *n* [ISV *mega-* + *colon*] **:** great often congenital dilation of the colon — compare HIRSCHSPRUNG'S DISEASE

mega·cosm \ˈmegəˌkäzəm\ *n* -s [Gk *mega-* (fr. *megas* large, great) + E *-cosm* — more at MUCH] **:** MACROCOSM

mega·curie \ˈ≈≈+\ *n* [*mega-* + *curie*] **:** one million curies

mega·cycle \ˈ≈≈,-\ *n* [*mega-* + *cycle*] **:** one million cycles; *esp* **:** one million cycles per second used as a unit of radio frequency — abbr *mc*

mega·der·mat·i·dae \ˌ≈≈(ˌ)dərˈmad·əˌdē\ *n pl, cap* [NL, fr. *Megadermat-, Megaderma*, type genus (fr. *mega-* + *-derma*) + *idae*] **:** a family of tropical Old World carnivorous bats with large ears united across the forehead, a large nose leaf, and no external tail — see BIG-EARED BAT, FALSE VAMPIRE BAT

mega·der·mi·dae \ˌ≈≈ˈdərməˌdē\ [NL, fr. *Megaderma* + *-idae*] *syn of* MEGADERMATIDAE

mega·dont \ˈ≈≈ˌdänt\ *adj* [irreg. fr. *mega-* + *-odont*] **:** MACRODONT **— mega·dont·ism** \-nˌtizəm\ *n* -s **— mega·don·ty** \-ntē\ *n* -ES

mega·dri·li \ˌ≈≈ˈdrīˌlī\ *n pl, cap* [NL, fr. *mega-* + *-drili* (fr. Gk *drilos* earthworm)] *in some classifications* **:** a group of Oligochaeta comprising relatively large predominantly terrestrial worms that have a capillary network on the nephridium and being nearly coextensive with Neoligochaeta — compare MICRODRILI

mega·dynamics \ˌ≈≈+\ *n pl but often sing in constr* [*mega-* + *dynamics*] **:** the mechanics of major earth movements

mega·evolution \"+\ *n* [*mega-* + *evolution*] **:** MACROEVOLUTION **— mega·evolutionary** \"+\ *adj*

mega·fauna \"+\ *n* [NL, fr. *mega-* + *fauna*] **:** MACROFAUNA 2 — used chiefly in paleontology **— megafaunal** *adj*

mega·fossil \"+\ *n* [*mega-* + *fossil*] **:** MACROFOSSIL

mega·gamete \"+\ *n* [*mega-* + *gamete*] **:** MACROGAMETE — used esp. in botany

mega·gametophyte \"+\ *n* [*mega-* + *gametophyte*] **:** the female gametophyte produced by a megaspore — compare MICROGAMETOPHYTE

mega·hertz \ˈ≈≈,-\ *n* [*mega-* + *hertz*] **:** a unit of frequency equal to one million hertz — abbr. *MHz*

mega·karyoblast \ˌ≈≈+\ *n* [ISV *mega-* + *kary-* + *-blast*] **:** a large cell with large reticulate nucleus that gives rise to megakaryocytes

mega·karyocyte *also* **mega·caryocyte** \"+\ *n* -s [ISV *mega-* + *kary-, cary-* + *-cyte*] **:** a large cell that has a lobulated nucleus, is found esp. in the bone marrow, and is held to be the source of blood platelets **— mega·karyocytic** \"+\ *adj*

megal- *or* **megalo-** *comb form* [NL, fr. Gk, fr. *megal-, megas* large, great — more at MUCH] **:** large **:** great **:** of giant size ⟨*megalo*blast⟩ ⟨*megal*ops⟩ ⟨*Megalo*saurus⟩ **:** grand **:** grandiose ⟨*megalo*mania⟩ **:** capable of or used for enlarging ⟨*megalo*graph⟩ ⟨*megalo*scope⟩; *specif, med* **:** abnormally large ⟨*megalo*cardia⟩ ⟨*megalo*cornea⟩

meg·al·ad·a·pis \ˌmegəl+\ *n, cap* [NL, fr. *megal-* + *Adapis*] **:** a genus of Pleistocene lemurs of Madagascar

mega·lai·ma \ˌmegəˈlīmə, -ˈlāmə\ *n, cap* [NL, fr. *mega-* + *-laima* (fr. Gk *laimos* throat) — more at GYMNOLAEMATA] **:** a genus of scansorial barbets of southeastern Asia

mega·la·nia \ˌ≈≈ˈlānēə\ *n, cap* [NL, fr. *mega-* + *-lania* (fr. Gk *ēlainein* to wander about + NL *-ia*); fr. the terrestrial nature of such lizards] **:** a genus of extinct lizards related to but larger than the modern monitors and known from remains found in the Pleistocene of Queensland and the Asiatic Pliocene

meg·a·la·trac·tus \ˌ≈≈ləˈtraktəs\ *n, cap* [NL, fr. *megal-* + Gk *atraktos* spindle — more at TORTURE] **:** a genus of Australian marine snails (family Xancidae) including the largest known living gastropod

mega·lecithal \ˌmegə+\ *adj* [*mega-* + *lecithal*] *of an egg* **:** containing very large amounts of yolk **:** TELOLECITHAL, CENTROLECITHAL

meg·aleth·o·scope \ˌmegəˈlethəˌskōp\ *n* [*mega-* + *alethoscope*, a kind of stereoscope, fr. Gk *alētho-* (fr. *alēthēs* true) + E *-scope*] **:** a stereoscope having a large magnifying lens

mega·lith \ˈ≈≈ˌlith\ *n* -s [*mega-* + *-lith*] **1 :** one of the huge undressed stones used in various types of prehistoric monuments — compare MENHIR, MONOLITH, SARSEN **2 :** a prehistoric monument (as a dolmen) constructed of huge stones

mega·lith·ic \ˌ≈≈ˈlithik\ *adj* [*mega-* + *-lithic*] **1 :** of prehistoric megalith construction **:** constructed of large undressed stones **2 :** of or relating to a people who erected megaliths or to their culture

meg·a·lo·bat·ra·chus \ˌmegəlōˈba·trəkəs\ *n, cap* [NL, fr. *megal-* + *-batrachus*] **:** a genus that consists of the giant salamander and that is sometimes included in the genus *Cryptobranchus*

meg·a·lo·blast \ˈ≈≈≈ˌblast\ *n* [ISV *megal-* + *-blast*] **1 :** ERYTHROBLAST 1 **2 :** a large nucleated abnormal red blood cell appearing in the blood in pernicious anemia **— meg·a·lo·blas·tic** \ˌ≈≈≈ˈblastik\ *adj*

megaloblastic anemia *n* **:** any of several anemias (as pernicious anemia) in which megaloblasts are present in the circulating blood

meg·a·lo·ce·phal·ic \ˌ≈≈≈səˈfalik\ *or* **meg·a·lo·ceph·a·lous** \-ˈsefələs\ *adj* [*megal-* + *-cephalic, -cephalous*] **:** MEGACEPHALIC **— meg·a·lo·ceph·a·ly** \ˌ≈≈≈ˈsefəlē\ *n* -ES

meg·a·loc·e·ros \ˌ≈≈ˈläsəˌräs\ *n, cap* [NL, fr. Gk *megalokerōs* having large horns, fr. *megal-* + *-kerōs* (fr. *keras* horn) — more at HORN] **:** a genus of Pleistocene European cervid mammals including the gigantic Irish elk

meg·a·lo·cyte \ˈmegələˌsīt\ *n* -s [ISV *megal-* + *-cyte*] **:** MACROCYTE **— meg·a·lo·cyt·ic** \ˌ≈≈≈ˈsid·ik\ *adj*

meg·a·lo·mania \ˌmegəlō, -lə *also* -gl- +\ *n* [NL, fr. *megal-* + *mania*] **1 :** a mania for or for doing great or grandiose things ⟨an outburst of wildly extravagant commercial ~ —*Times Lit. Supp.*⟩ **2 :** infantile feelings of omnipotence esp. when retained in later life

[1]**meg·a·lo·maniac** \ˌ≈≈≈+\ *n* [*megal-* + *maniac*] **:** one affected with or exhibiting megalomania

[2]**megalomaniac** \"\ *or* **meg·a·lo·maniacal** \"+\ *or* **meg·a·lo·manic** \"+\ *adj* **:** belonging to, exhibiting, or affected with megalomania ⟨a once ~ motion picture industry —Cecil Beaton⟩

meg·al·on·yx \ˌmegəˈläniks\ *n, cap* [NL, fr. *megal-* + *-onyx*] **:** a genus of large extinct Pliocene and Pleistocene edentate mammals of No. America

meg·a·lo·pa \ˌ≈≈ˈlōpə\ *n* -s [NL, fr. Gk *megalōpē*, fem. of *megalōpos* having large eyes, fr. *megal-* + *-ōpos* (fr. *ōps* eye) — more at EYE] **:** MEGALOPS

meg·a·lop·ic \ˌ≈≈ˈläpik\ *adj* [NL *megalop-, megalops* + E *-ic*] **:** of, relating to, or being a megalops

[1]**meg·a·lo·pine** \ˈmegələˌpīn, məˈgaləˌ-\ *adj* [NL *megalop-, megalops* + E *-ine*] **1 :** of or relating to the megalops **2** [NL *Megalop-, Megalops* + E *-ine*] **:** of or relating to the genus *Megalops*

[2]**megalopine** \"\ *n* -s **1 :** a megalops larva **2 :** a fish of the genus *Megalops*

meg·a·lop·o·lis \ˌmegəˈläpələs\ *n* -ES [*megal-* + *-polis*] **1 :** a very large city **2 :** a thickly populated region centering around a metropolis ⟨the ~ including New York City and adjacent sections of New York, New Jersey, and Connecticut⟩

[1]**meg·a·lo·pol·i·tan** \ˌmegəlōˈpälətᵊn *also* -ətən *or* -əd·ən\ *adj* [fr. *megalopolis*, after such pairs as E *metropolis: metropolitan*] **:** of, relating to, or characterized by a megalopolis ⟨becoming a ~ people —B.I.Bell⟩ ⟨this immense ~ civilization —Kenneth Rexroth⟩

[2]**megalopolitan** \"\ *n* -s **:** one who lives in a megalopolis

meg·a·lo·pol·i·tan·ism \-ᵊnˌizəm, -əˌni-\ *n* -s **:** the quality or state of being megalopolitan **:** megalopolitan character

meg·a·lo·pore \ˈmegələˌpō(ə)r\ *n* [ISV *megal-* + *-pore*] **:** one of the large pores that are found in the dorsal shell of some chitons and that lead to photosensitive organs

meg·a·lops \ˈ≈≈ˌläps\ *n* [NL, fr. *megal-* + *-ops*] **1** *pl* **megalops** *or* **megalopses :** a larva or larval stage following the zoea in the development of most crabs in which the legs and abdominal appendages have appeared, the abdomen is relatively long, and the eyes are large — called also *megalopa* **2** *cap* **:** a genus of fishes that contains several East Indian and So. Pacific species closely related to and resembling the tarpon and is sometimes made the type of a separate family but is usu. considered to form a subfamily of the Elopidae

meg·a·lop·tera \ˌ≈≈ˈläptərə\ *n pl, cap* [NL, fr. *megal-* + *-ptera*] **:** a small order of usu. large insects that are often included in Neuroptera, have ample wings with a folded anal area in the hind pair, and develop from aquatic predacious larvae — compare ALDER FLY, DOBSON FLY **— meg·a·lop·ter·an** \-tərən\ *n* -s **— meg·a·lop·ter·ous** \ˌ≈≈≈t(ə)rəs\ *adj*

meg·a·lo·pyg·i·dae \ˌmegəlōˈpijəˌdē\ *n pl, cap* [NL, fr. *Megalopyge*, type genus (fr. *megal-* + Gk *pygē* buttocks) + *-idae* — more at FOG] **:** a family of chiefly So. American hirsute moths having larvae with stinging hairs

meg·a·lor·nis \ˌmegəˈlȯrnəs\ [NL, fr. *megal-* + *-ornis*] *syn of* GRUS

meg·a·lor·nith·i·dae \ˌ≈≈≈ˈnithəˌdē\ [NL, fr. *Megalornith-, Megalornis* + *-idae*] *syn of* GRUIDAE

meg·a·lo·saur \ˈmegələˌsȯ(ə)r\ *n* -s [NL *Megalosaurus*] **:** a dinosaur of the genus *Megalosaurus* or family Megalosauridae

meg·a·lo·sau·rus \ˌ≈≈≈ˈsȯrəs\ *n, cap* [NL, fr. *megal-* + *-saurus*] **:** a genus (the type of the family Megalosauridae) of gigantic carnivorous saurischian dinosaurs of the suborder Theropoda occurring in the European Jurassic and Lower Cretaceous

meg·a·lo·sphere \ˈ≈≈≈+,-\ *n* [*megal-* + *sphere*] **:** the large chambered initial shell of the sexual individuals of some dimorphic foraminiferans **— meg·a·lo·spher·ic** \ˌ≈≈≈ˈsferik\ *adj*

-meg·a·ly \ˈmegəlē, -li\ *also* **-me·ga·lia** \məˈgālyə\ *n comb form, pl* **-megalies** *also* **-megalias** [NL *-megalia*, fr. *megal-* + L *-ia* *-y*] **:** abnormal enlargement (of a specified part) ⟨acro*megaly*⟩ ⟨gastro*megaly*⟩ ⟨hepatosplено*megalia*⟩

mega·mere \ˈmegəˌmi(ə)r\ *n* -s [ISV *mega-* + *-mere*] **:** MACROMERE

mega·nephridium \ˌ≈≈+\ *n, pl* **meganephridia** [NL, fr. *mega-* + *nephridium*] **:** a relatively large nephridium usu. found one pair per segment in some annelid worms

mega·neu·ra \ˌ≈≈ˈn(y)u̇rə\ *n pl, cap* [NL, fr. *mega-* + *-neura*] **:** a genus of extinct insects (order Protodonata) that includes some with a wingspread of about three feet and that is known from the Upper Carboniferous of Commentry, France

me·gan·thro·pus \məˈgan(t)thrəpəs, ˌmeˌganˈthrōpəs\ *n, cap* [NL, fr. *mega-* + *-anthropus*] **:** a genus of large extinct primates of the Lower Pleistocene of Java known from fragmentary jawbones and held to be primitive men

mega·nucleus \ˌmegə+\ *n* [NL, fr. *mega-* + *nucleus*] **:** MACRONUCLEUS

mega·parsec \"+\ *n* [*mega-* + *parsec*] **:** one million parsecs

[1]**mega·phone** \ˈmegəˌfōn\ *n* [*mega-* + *-phone*] **1 :** a cone-shaped device used to intensify or direct the voice ⟨a cheerleader's ~⟩ ⟨power ~⟩ **2 :** one that expresses or publicizes others' opinions or ideas **:** MOUTHPIECE ⟨making herself the ~ of his suggestions —Nigel Dennis⟩

megaphone 1

[2]**megaphone** \"\ *vb* -ED/-ING/-S *vt* **1 :** to transmit through or as if through a megaphone **:** publicize widely ⟨~ an announcement to the crowd⟩ ⟨wouldn't care to ~ my career —*N.Y.Sun*⟩ ⟨~ the dictator's views⟩ **2 :** to address through or as if through a megaphone ⟨~ a passing ship⟩ ~ *vi* **:** to speak through or as if through a megaphone

mega·phon·ic \ˌ≈≈ˈfänik\ *adj* **1 :** of, relating to, or transmitted by a megaphone ⟨~ messages⟩ **2 :** suggestive of a megaphone or its effect ⟨a ~ voice⟩ **— mega·phon·i·cal·ly** \-nək(ə)lē\ *adv*

mega·phon·ist \ˈ≈≈ˌfōnəst\ *n* -s **:** one who uses a megaphone; *specif* **:** a motion-picture director

me·gaph·y·ton \məˈgafəˌtän\ *n, cap* [NL, fr. *mega-* + Gk *phyton* plant — more at PHYT-] **:** a form genus of fossil tree ferns based on trunks with distichous scars

mega·pode \ˈmegəˌpōd\ *also* **mega·pod** \-ˌpäd\ *n* -s [NL *Megapodiidae*] **:** a bird of the family Megapodiidae — called also *mound bird*

mega·po·di·idae \ˌ≈≈pəˈdīəˌdē\ *n pl, cap* [NL, fr. *Megapodius*, type genus + *-idae*] **:** a family of gallinaceous birds inhabiting Australia and neighboring islands north and east to the Philippines and Ladrones and known for their habit of heaping up a mass of vegetable debris in which their eggs are laid and hatched — compare BRUSH TURKEY, LEIPOA, MALEO

mega·po·di·us \ˌ≈≈ˈpōdēəs\ *n, cap* [NL, fr. *mega-* + *-podius* (fr. Gk *pod-, pous* foot) — more at FOOT] **:** a genus (the type of the family Megapodiidae) of gallinaceous birds

me·gap·o·lis \məˈgapələs\ *n* -ES [NL, fr. *mega-* + Gk *polis* city — more at POLICE] **:** MEGALOPOLIS

mega·pol·i·tan \ˌmegəˈpälətᵊn *also* -ətən *or* -əd·ən\ *adj* [fr. *megapolis*, after such pairs as E *metropolis: metropolitan*] **:** MEGALOPOLITAN ⟨rise of the ~ city —Howard M. Jones⟩

mega·pros·o·pous \ˌ≈≈ˈpräsəpəs\ *adj* [*mega-* + *prosop-* + *-ous*] **:** having a large face

me·gap·tera \mə'gaptərə\ *n, cap* [NL, fr. *mega-* + *-ptera*] **:** a cetacean genus comprising the humpback whale

mega·rhi·nus \ˌmegə'rīnəs\ *n, cap* [NL, fr. *mega-* + *-rhinus*] **:** a genus of very large nonbiting American mosquitoes with a curved beak, greenish or bluish coloration, and predaceous larvae

mega·rhyssa \ˌ==+\ *n, cap* [NL, fr. *mega-* + *Rhyssa*] **:** a genus of large ichneumon flies having an extremely long slender ovipositor and including a common species (*M. lunator*) of the eastern U. S. that is a parasite of the larva of the pigeon horntail

¹**me·gar·i·an** \me'ga(a)rēən, mə'-\ *also* **me·gar·e·an** \", ˌmegə'rēən\ *adj, usu cap* [*megarian* fr. *Megara*, city of ancient Greece (fr. L, fr. Gk) + E *-an*; *megarean* fr. L *megareus* Megarian (fr. *Megara*) + E *-an*] **1 :** of, relating to, or characteristic of the city of Megara **2 :** of or relating to a Socratic school of philosophy established by Euclid of Megara and best known for the use of logical paradoxes and subtle arguments bordering on the specious and for holding that the good is one and is the only true being

²**megarian** \"\ *also* **megarean** \"\ *n* -s **1** *cap* **:** a native or inhabitant of Megara, Greece **2** *usu cap* **:** a member of the Megarian school of philosophy

me·gar·ic \me'garik, mə'-\ *adj or n, usu cap* [L *megaricus*, fr. Gk *megarikos*, fr. *Megara*, Greece + Gk *-ikos* -ic] **:** MEGARIAN

meg·a·ron \'megəˌrän\ *n, pl* **mega·ra** \-rə\ [Gk, fr. *megas* large, great — more at MUCH] **1 :** the great central hall of an ancient Mycenaean house usu. containing a center hearth **2 :** CELLA

mega·sclere \'==+ˌ-\ *n* [*mega-* + *sclere*] **:** a large spicule; *specif* **:** one of the skeletal spicules of a sponge — **mega·scleric** \ˌ==¦sklirik, -ler-\ *or* **mega·scle·rous** \-¦sklirəs, -ler-\ *adj*

mega·sco·lec·i·dae \ˌ==skə'lesəˌdē\ *n pl, cap* [NL, fr. *Megascolec-, Megascolex*, type genus (fr. *mega-* + Gk *skōlēk-, skōlēx* worm) + *-idae*] **:** a very large family of earthworms chiefly of the southern hemisphere containing giant forms that include an Australian species (*Megascolides australis*) held to reach a length of 11 feet

mega·scop·ic \ˌ==¦skäpik\ *adj* [*mega-* + *-scopic*] **1 :** ENLARGED, MAGNIFIED **2 a :** visible to the unaided eye **:** MACROSCOPIC — used esp. of the physical features of rocks **b :** based on or relating to observations made with the unaided eye ⟨the ~ study of rocks⟩ — **mega·scop·i·cal·ly** \-pək(ə)lē\ *adv*

mega·se·cop·tera \ˌ==sə'käptərə\ *n pl, cap* [NL, prob. fr. *mega-* + Gk *sēkos* pen, fold, trunk of a tree + NL *-ptera*] **:** an order of extinct insects of the Upper Carboniferous and Permian that are related to the mayflies and dragonflies and have extremely long cerci

mega·seism \'megəˌsīzəm *sometimes* -sez- *or* -säz- *or* -sēz-\ *n* [ISV *mega-* + *seism*] **:** a violent earthquake — **mega·seis·mic** \ˌ==¦sīzmik *also* \|sm- *sometimes* -¦se| *or* -¦sä| *or* -¦sē|\ *adj*

mega·sporangium \ˌ==+\ *n* [NL, fr. *mega-* + *sporangium*] **:** a sporangium that develops only megaspores (as the nucellus in a seed plant) — called also *macrosporangium*; compare MICROSPORANGIUM

mega·spore \'==+ˌ-\ *n* [ISV *mega-* + *spore*] **1 :** one of the spores in heterosporous plants that give rise to female gametophytes and are generally larger than the microspores **2 :** MACROSPORE 2 — **mega·spor·ic** \ˌ==¦spōrik\ *adj*

megaspore mother cell *n* **:** a cell that produces megaspores by reduction usu. in tetrads or linear groups

megasporocyte \ˌ==+\ *n* [*mega-* + *sporocyte*] **:** MEGASPORE MOTHER CELL

mega·spo·ro·gen·e·sis \ˌ==ˌspōrə'jenəsəs\ *n* [NL, fr. ISV *megaspore* + L *genesis*] **:** the formation and maturation of a megaspore — compare MICROSPOROGENESIS

mega·sporophyll \ˌ==+\ *n* [*mega-* + *sporophyll*] **:** a sporophyll that develops only megasporangia

me·gass \mə'gaa(ə)s, -ais-, -äs\ *or* **megasse** *n, pl* **megasses** [modif. of F *bagasse* — more at BAGASSE] **:** BAGASSE

mega·synthetic \ˌmegə+\ *adj* [*mega-* + *synthetic*] **:** forming an extensive or ponderous synthesis ⟨~ American Indian languages⟩

mega·there \'megəˌthi(ə)r\ *n* -s [NL *Megatherium*] **:** a member of the genus *Megatherium*

mega·the·ri·an \ˌ==¦thirēən\ *adj* [NL *Megatherium* + E *-an*] **:** of, relating to, or characteristic of the genus *Megatherium* or the family Megatheriidae

mega·the·ri·um \ˌ=='thirēəm\ *n, cap* [NL, fr. *mega-* + *-therium*] **:** a genus (the type of the family Megatheriidae) of ground sloths found in the Pliocene and Pleistocene of America that are often of gigantic size and are related to the sloths and anteaters, the skull and dentition resembling those of the former and the vertebrae those of the latter

mega·therm \'megəˌthərm\ *n* [ISV *mega-* + *-therm*] **:** a plant that requires great heat combined with very abundant moisture for its successful growth — compare MESOTHERM, MICROTHERM — **mega·ther·mal** \ˌ==¦thərməl\ *or* **mega·ther·mic** \-mik\ *adj*

mega·thy·mi·dae \ˌ=='thīməˌdē\ *n pl, cap* [NL, fr. *Megathymus*, type genus (fr. *mega-* + Gk *thymos* warty excrescence, thymus) + *-idae*] **:** a family of strong-flying No. American skipper butterflies that is often considered a subfamily of Hesperiidae — see AGAVEWORM, GIANT SKIPPER

mega·ton \'megəˌtən, -ˌtän\ *n* [*mega-* + *ton*] **:** an explosive force equivalent to that of a million tons of TNT ⟨assume further that the pertinent energy release is 8 ~s —R.E.Lapp⟩ — **mega·ton·ic** \ˌ==¦tänik\ *adj*

mega·tron \'==ˌträn\ *n* -s [*mega-* + *-tron*] **:** LIGHTHOUSE TUBE

mega·var \'==+ˌ-\ *n* [*mega-* + *var*] **:** one million volt-amperes

mega·volt \"+ˌ-\ *n* [ISV *mega-* + *volt*] **:** one million volts

mega·watt \"+ˌ-\ *n* [ISV *mega-* + *watt*] **:** one million watts **:** one thousand kilowatts

mega·zooid \"+\ *n* [*mega-* + *zooid*] **:** a relatively large stalked vegetative individual of certain higher ciliates (as *Vorticella*) — compare MICROZOOID

mega·zoospore \'==+\ *n* [*mega-* + *zoospore*] **:** a large zoospore **:** MACROZOOSPORE

megged *past of* MEG

megging *pres part of* MEG

me·gilp *also* **ma·gilp** \mə'gilp\ *n* -s [origin unknown] **1 :** a gelatinous preparation commonly of linseed oil and mastic varnish used by artists as a vehicle for oil colors **2 :** a vehicle that facilitates a fluid application and prevents running of color

meg·nin·ia \meg'ninēə\ *n, cap* [NL, fr. Jean *Megnin* †1905 Fr. veterinarian + NL *-ia*] **:** a genus of analgesid mites common on the feathers of various domesticated birds

meg·ohm \'meˌgōm\ *n* [ISV *mega-* + *ohm*] **:** one million ohms

meg·ohm·me·ter \-ˌmēd·ə(r)\ *n* [*megohm* + *-meter*] **:** an instrument for the measurement of large electrical resistances

meg·rel \'megrəl\ *n, pl* **megrel** *or* **megrels** *usu cap* **:** MINGRELIAN

¹**me·grim** \'mēgrəm, 'māg-\ *n* -s [ME *migrene, migrein, migrime*, fr. MF *migraine* — more at MIGRAINE] **1 a :** MIGRAINE **b :** VERTIGO, DIZZINESS ⟨gives me the ~s to look down this way —Maxwell Anderson⟩ **2 a :** a random, furtive, or unbidden thought or feeling **:** FANCY, WHIM ⟨as though some lurking ~, some microbe of dissatisfaction with ourselves, was at work within us —John Galsworthy⟩ ⟨and with no ~ in my head of having been possessed by some great moral purpose —R.B.Cunninghame Graham⟩ **b megrims** *pl* **:** low spirits **:** DESPONDENCY, BLUES — usu. used with *the* ⟨fell victim to an attack of the combat flier's ~s —Paul Gallico⟩ **3 :** any of numerous diseases of animals marked by disturbance of equilibrium and abnormal gait and behavior — usu. used in pl.

²**megrim** \'mēgrəm\ *n* -s [origin unknown] **:** any of several small flatfishes: as **a :** a European flounder (*Arnoglossus laterna*) of the family Bothidae — called also *lantern flounder* **b :** a whiff (*Lepidorhombus megastoma*)

megs *pl of* MEG, *pres 3d sing of* MEG

me·ha·ri \mə'härē\ *n* -s [F *méhari*, fr. Ar *mahārīy*, pl. of *mahrīy* of Mahrah, fr. *Mahrah*, district on the southern coast of Arabia] **:** one of a breed of swift dromedaries used chiefly as saddle animals

me·ha·rist *or* **me·ha·riste** \-rəst\ *n* -s [F *méhariste*, fr. *méhari* + *-iste* -ist] **:** one mounted on a mehari

me·her·rin \mə'herən\ *n, pl* **meherrin** *or* **meherrins** *usu cap* [fr. the *Meherrin* river] **1 a :** an Iroquoian people of the Meherrin river valley in Virginia and North Carolina **b :** a member of such people **2 :** the language of the Meherrin people

meh·lis' gland \'māləs(əz)-\ *n, usu cap M* [fr. the name *Mehlis*] **:** one of the large unicellular glands surrounding the ootype of a flatworm and possibly playing a part in eggshell formation; *collectively* **:** the group of such glands in a worm

meh·man·dar \mə'mänˌdär\ *n* -s [Per *mihmāndār*, fr. *mihmān* guest (fr. MPer *mēhmān*) + *-dār* holder — more at BHUMIDAR] **:** an official in India, Persia, or Afghanistan appointed to escort an ambassador or traveler

meh·ri \'mārē\ *n, pl* **mehri** *or* **mehris** *usu cap* **:** MAHRI

meh·tar *also* **meh·ter** \'mād·ə(r)\ *n* -s [Per *mihtar* prince, greater, elder, fr. *mih* great (fr. MPer *meh, mas*) + *-tar*, comparative suffix (fr. MPer, fr. OPer *-tara-*)] **1 :** a groom or stable boy in Iran **2** *usu cap* **:** a member of a harijan caste of sweepers and scavengers in India

mei·bo·mian gland \(')mī¦bōmēən, -myən-\ *n, often cap M* [Heinrich *Meibom* †1700 Ger. physician + E *-ian*] **:** one of the long sebaceous glands of the eyelids that discharge a fatty secretion which lubricates the lids

mei·bos \'mēˌbäs\ *var of* MEBOS

meidan *var of* MAIDAN

mei·kle \'mēkəl\ *var of* MICKLE

meiny \'mānē, -ni\ *n* -ES [ME *meynie* (also, household, family) — more at MENIAL] **1** *archaic* **a :** a group of attendants or followers **:** RETINUE ⟨summoned up their ~, straight took horse —Shak.⟩ **b :** a group of associates **:** BAND, COMPANY ⟨the priest of Loyola's ~ —W.H.Gardner⟩ **2** *now chiefly Scot* **:** a great number **:** MULTITUDE

meio- — see MI-

meio·bar \'mīə+ˌ-\ *n* [ISV *mi-* + *bar*] **1 :** a region of low barometric pressure **2 :** an isobar of low pressure

meio·cyte \-ˌsīt\ *n* -s [*mi-* + *-cyte*] **:** a cell undergoing meiosis

mei·o·nite \'mīəˌnīt\ *n* -s [F *méionite*, fr. Gk *meiōn* less + F *-ite*] **:** a mineral $Ca_4Al_6Si_6O_{24}(SO_4,CO_3,Cl_2)$ consisting of an aluminosilicate of calcium with other anions (as sulfate, carbonate, and chloride) and being isomorphous with marialite — see SCAPOLITE

meio·phyl·ly \'==ˌfilē\ *n* -ES [*mi-* + *phyll-* + *-y*] **:** the suppression of one or more leaves in a whorl

mei·o·sis \mī'ōsəs\ *n, pl* **meioses** [NL, fr. Gk *meiōsis* diminution, fr. *meioun* to diminish (fr. *meiōn* less) + *-sis* — more at MINOR] **1 a :** representation of a thing so as to cause it to be taken as less than it really is **b :** LITOTES, UNDERSTATEMENT **2 :** the sequence of complex nuclear changes resulting in the production of cells (as gametes) with half the number of chromosomes present in the original cell and typically involving an actual reduction division in which the chromosomes without undergoing prior splitting join in pairs with homologous chromosomes of maternal and paternal origin associated and then separate so that one member of each pair enters each daughter nucleus and a second division not involving reduction — compare MATURATION, MITOSIS

meio·stoma·tous \ˌmīə¦stämədˌəs, -stōm-\ *adj* [*mi-* + *-stomatous*] *of a larval nematode* **:** having the oral structures reduced or simplified as compared with related forms

meio·stome \'mīəˌstōm\ *n* -s [*mi-* + *-stome*] **:** a meiostomatous nematode

meio·taxy \-ˌtaksē\ *n* -ES [*mi-* + *-taxy*] **:** the suppression of a complete whorl of leaves or sporophylls

mei·ot·ic \mī'äd·ik\ *adj* [Gk *meiōtikos* lowering, diminishing, fr. *meiōtos* capable of being lowered (fr. *meioun* to lower, diminish) + *-ikos* -ic — more at MEIOSIS] **:** of, relating to, or characterized by meiosis — **mei·ot·i·cal·ly** \-ək(ə)lē\ *adv*

meis·sen \'mīsᵊn\ *also* **meissen china** *or* **meissen ware** *n* -s *usu cap M* [fr. *Meissen*, Saxony, Germany] **:** ceramic ware made at Meissen near Dresden; *esp* **:** a European hard-paste porcelain developed under the patronage of the king of Saxony about 1715 and used for both ornamental and table wares

meiss·ner effect \'mīsnə(r)-\ *n, usu cap M* [after Alexander *Meissner* †1958 Austrian radio engineer] **:** the partial or complete absence of magnetic induction in metallic substances even in a magnetic field when cooled into the superconducting state

meissner's corpuscle *n, usu cap M* [after Georg *Meissner* †1905 Ger. physiologist] **:** any of the small elliptical tactile end organs in hairless skin containing numerous transversely placed tactile cells and fine flattened nerve terminations

meissner's plexus *n, usu cap M* [after Georg *Meissner*] **:** a plexus of gangliated nerve fibers lying between the muscular and mucous coats of the intestine — compare AUERBACH'S PLEXUS

mei·ster·ge·sang \'mīstə(r)gəˌzäŋ\ *n, pl* **meistergesän·ge** \-ˌzeŋə\ *often cap* [G, fr. MHG *meistersanc, meistergesanc*, fr. *meister* master + *sanc* song, singing (fr. OHG *sang*) *or gesanc* song, singing, fr. *ge-*, collective prefix (fr. OHG *gi-*) + *sanc* — more at CO-, SONG] **1 :** one of the songs of the meistersinger consisting of strophic mechanical verse usu. didactic or religious in nature and composed according to strict rules to fit a few traditional monophonic melodies **2 :** the songs of the meistersinger as a literary genre

mei·ster·lied \-ˌlēt\ *n, pl* **meisterlie·der** \-ˌlēdə(r)\ *often cap* [G, fr. *meister* master (fr. OHG *meistar*) + *lied* song, fr. OHG *liod* — more at LAUD] **:** MEISTERGESANG

mei·ster·sing·er \-ˌsiŋə(r), -ˌziŋ-\ *n, pl* **meistersinger** *or* **meistersingers** *usu cap* [G, fr. MHG, fr. *meister* master (fr. OHG *meistar*, fr. L *magister*) + *singer*, fr. *singen* to sing (fr. OHG *singan*) + *-er*, fr. OHG *-āri* -er — more at MASTER, SING] **:** a member of any of various German guilds esp. of the 15th and 16th centuries composed chiefly of middle-class workingmen and craftsmen and formed for the cultivation of poetry and music — see MEISTERGESANG

¹**meith** \'mēth\ *n* -s [of Scand origin; akin to ON *mith* middle, mark, fishing banks, *mithr*, adj., middle — more at MID] **1** *Scot* **:** LANDMARK; *esp* **:** a marker serving as a guide in navigation **2** *Scot* **:** MEASURE, MEASUREMENT

²**meith** \"\ *vt* -ED/-ING/-s [of Scand origin; akin to ON *mitha* to mark, fr. *mith* mark] *Scot* **:** to mark out

mei·thei \'māˌthā\ *n, pl* **meithei** *or* **meitheis** *usu cap* **1 a :** a people of Manipur, India **b :** a member of such people **2 :** the Tibeto-Burman language of the Meithei people

mejlis *also* **mejliss** *var of* MAJLIS

MEK *abbr* methyl ethyl ketone

me·ke \'mākē\ *n* -s [Fijian] **:** a Fijian dance accompanied by singing; *also* **:** a festival of these dances

mek·er burner \'mekə(r)-\ *n, usu cap M* [after George *Meker*, 20th cent. chemist] **:** a laboratory gas burner that differs from a typical Bunsen burner in having a constriction in the tube and a grid at the top of the burner causing the flame of burning gas to consist of a number of short blue inner cones and a large single outer cone and to be hotter generally than the Bunsen flame

Meker burner

mekh·i·tar·ist *or* **mech·i·tar·ist** \ˌmekə'tärəst\ *n* -s *usu cap* [fr. Peter M. *Mekhitar* †1749 Armenian religious reformer + E *-ist*] **:** one of an Armenian order of Roman Catholic monks founded in the 18th century at Constantinople and having congregations at Venice and Vienna

mekka *usu cap, var of* MECCA

mek·nes *or* **mek·nès** \mek'nes\ *adj, usu cap* [fr. *Meknes* (F *Meknès*), Morocco] **:** of or from the city of Meknes, Morocco **:** of the kind or style prevalent in Meknes

¹**mel** *or* **mell** \'mel\ *n* -s [L *mel* — more at MELLIFLUOUS] **:** HONEY ⟨sweet as the ~ of the bee —Samuel Bamford⟩

²**mel** \"\ *n* -s [prob. fr. *M* (1000) + *-el* (as in *bel*)] **:** a subjective unit of tone pitch equal to one thousandth of the pitch of a tone having a frequency of one thousand cycles — used esp. in audiology

¹**mel-** — *see* MELA-

²**mel-** *comb form* [NL, fr. Gk *melos* — more at MELODY] **:** limb ⟨*mel*algia⟩

³**mel-** *or* **melo-** *comb form* [NL, fr. Gk *mēla* cheeks, lit., apples, pl. of *mēlon* apple] **:** cheek ⟨*mel*itis⟩ ⟨*melo*plasty⟩

me·la \'mā(ˌ)lä\ *n* -s [Hindi *melā*, fr. Skt *melaka, melā* meeting, assembly — more at MILITATE] **:** an Indian religious festival or fair **:** a gathering of people

mela- *or* **mel-** *also* **melo-** *comb form* [ISV, fr. Gk *melas* black — more at MULLET] **:** black ⟨*mela*diorite⟩ ⟨*Melo*grammataceae⟩

me·lac·o·nite \mə'lakəˌnīt\ *n* -s [alter. (influenced by *-ite*) of earlier *melaconise*, fr. F *mélaconise*, fr. *méla-* mela- + *-conise* (fr. Gk *konis* ashes, dust) — more at INCINERATE] **:** an earthy black massive variety of tenorite

me·la·da \mə'lädə\ *n* -s [AmerSp, fr. Sp, fem. of *melado*, past part. of *melar* to boil sugarcane juice into syrup, fr. *miel* honey, fr. L *mel* — more at MELLIFLUOUS] **:** crude cane sugar as it comes mixed with molasses from the boiling of cane juice and prior to refining

melaena *var of* MELENA

me·lai·no·type \mə'līnəˌtīp, -lān-\ *n* -s [Gk *melaino-* black, fr. *melaina*, fem. of *melas* — more at MULLET] **:** FERROTYPE 1

mel·a·leu·ca \ˌmelə'lükə\ *n* [NL, fr. *mela-* + *-leuca* (fr. Gk *leukos* white); fr. the black trunk and white branches — more at LIGHT] **1** *cap* **:** a genus of Australian and East Indian shrubs and trees (family Myrtaceae) having numerous stamens in fascicles — see CAJEPUT, HONEYMYRTLE, TEA TREE 2 **2** -s **:** any plant of the genus *Melaleuca*

mel·am \'meˌlam\ *n* -s [G, fr. *mel-* (origin unknown) + *-am* (prob. fr. NL *ammonia*)] **:** an amorphous compound $C_6H_9N_{11}$ obtained by heating ammonium thiocyanate or as a by-product in the preparation of melamine

me·la·med *or* **me·lam·med** \mə'lämәd, me'l-, ˌmelə'mäd\ *n, pl* **melam·dim** \mə'lämdəm, me'l-\ [Heb *mĕlammēdh* teacher] **:** a teacher of Hebrew language and traditions esp. in a heder

mel·a·mine \'meləˌmēn, -ləmən\ *n* -s [G *melamin*, fr. *melam* + *-in* -ine] **1 :** a white crystalline high-melting organic base $C_3N_3(NH_2)_3$ that is a cyclic trimer of cyanamide but is usu. made by heating dicyandiamide to high temperatures and that is used chiefly in making melamine resins; 2, 4, 6-triamino-*s*-triazine — called also *cyanuramide* **2 :** a melamine resin or a plastic made from such a resin

melamine formaldehyde *n* **:** a condensation product, resin, or plastic made from melamine and formaldehyde

melamine resin *n* **:** any of a group of thermosetting resins made from melamine and an aldehyde (as formaldehyde), characterized by resistance to heat and water and good electrical resistance, and used chiefly in molded products, laminated products, adhesives, and coatings and in treating textiles (as for improving resistance to shrinkage and creasing) and paper (as for improving wet strength)

mel·amp·so·ra \ˌmelam(p)'sōrə\ *n, cap* [NL, fr. *melan-* + Gk *psōra* scab, mange — more at PSORIASIS] **:** a genus (the type of the family Melampsoraceae) of rusts that have sessile one-celled teliospores in a single layer — see FLAX RUST

mel·am·py·rum \ˌmeləm'pīrəm\ *n, cap* [NL, fr. Gk *melampyron* ball mustard, fr. *melan-* + *pyros* wheat — more at FURZE] **:** a small genus of branching annual herbs (family Scrophulariaceae) with opposite leaves and small irregular flowers with four stamens — see COWWHEAT

melan- *or* **melano-** *also* **melam-** *comb form* [*melan-* fr. ME, fr. MF, fr. LL, fr. Gk, fr. *melan-, melas*; *melano-* & *melam-* fr. NL, fr. Gk, fr. *melan-, melas* — more at MULLET] **1 :** black **:** dark ⟨*melan*ic⟩ ⟨*melan*in⟩ ⟨*melano*comous⟩ ⟨*Melam*psora⟩ **2 :** melanin **:** marked by the presence of melanin ⟨*melano*gen⟩ ⟨*melan*emia⟩ ⟨*melano*sarcoma⟩

mel·a·nau \'meləˌnaủ\ *also* **mil·a·nau** \'mil-\ *or* **mil·a·no** \'mīləˌnō\ *n, pl* **melanau** *or* **melanaus** *usu cap* **:** a member of a native people in Sarawak

mel·an·cho·lia \ˌmelən'kōlēə, -lyə\ *n, pl* **melancholi·as** \-ēəz, -yəz\ *also* **melancholi·ae** \-ōlēˌē, -ōlēˌī\ [NL, fr. LL, melancholy — more at MELANCHOLY] **:** a disordered mental condition characterized by extreme depression of spirits, bodily complaints, and often hallucinations and delusions; *specif* **:** a manic-depressive psychosis **syn** see SADNESS

mel·an·cho·li·ac \-lēˌak\ *n* -s [NL *melancholia* + E *-ac*] **:** one affected with melancholia

¹**mel·an·chol·ic** \ˌmelən¦kälik, -ālēk\ *adj* [ME *melancolik*, fr. MF *melancolique*, fr. L *melancholicus*, fr. Gk *melancholikos*, fr. *melancholia* melancholy + *-ikos* -ic — more at MELANCHOLY] **1** *obs* **a :** of, relating to, being, or associated with the presence or secretion of black bile **b :** causing or constituting the melancholy that is associated with disordered secretion of black bile **2 :** given to or affected with melancholy **:** subject to depression of spirits **:** DEPRESSED **3 :** affected with, like, or relating to melancholia **4 :** tending to depress the spirits **:** SADDENING ⟨this ~ view of our future⟩ — **mel·an·chol·i·cal·ly** \-äläk(ə)lē, -ālēk-, -li\ *adv*

²**melancholic** \"\ *n* -s **1** *obs* **a :** MELANCHOLY **b :** a melancholy person **2 :** MELANCHOLIAC

mel·an·chol·i·ly \ˌmelən¦kälәlē, -ōli, *chiefly Brit* '==ˌkələli *or* -eləŋk-\ *adv* **:** in a melancholy manner **:** with a show of melancholy

mel·an·choli·ness \ˌmelən¦kälēnəs, -ālin-, *chiefly Brit* '==ˌkəlinəs *or* -eləŋk-\ *n* -ES **:** the quality or state of being melancholy

mel·an·cho·lious \ˌ==¦kōlyəs, -lēəs\ *adj* [ME *melancolious*, fr. MF *melancolieus*, fr. *melancolie* melancholy + *-eus* -ous — more at MELANCHOLY] *archaic* **:** MELANCHOLY

mel·an·chol·ish \'==ˌkälish\ *adj* [¹*melancholy* + *-ish*] *archaic* **:** inclined to lowness of spirits

mel·an·chol·ist \-ləst\ *n* -s [¹*melancholy* + *-ist*] **1** *archaic* **:** a person in whom black bile is the predominant humor **2 :** MELANCHOLIAC

mel·an·chol·ize \ˌ==¦käˌlīz\ *vb* -ED/-ING/-s [²*melancholy* + *-ize*] *vi* **:** to indulge in melancholy ~ *vt* **:** to make melancholy or depict as melancholy

¹**mel·an·choly** \'melənˌkälē, -äli, *chiefly Brit* -ˌkəli *or* -eləŋk-\ *n* -ES [ME *malencolie*, fr. MF *melancolie*, fr. LL *melancholia*, fr. Gk, fr. *melan-* + *cholē, cholos* gall, bile + *-ia* -y — more at GALL] **1 a** *archaic* **:** a supposed abnormal state held to be due to the presence of an excess of black bile and characterized by sullen irascibility or gloomy mental depression **b** *archaic* **:** BLACK BILE **c :** MELANCHOLIA **2** *obs* **:** a condition of sullen ill-temper **:** ANGER, IRASCIBILITY **3 a :** depression of spirits **:** gloomy mood or condition **:** DEJECTION **b :** a pensive or moody condition **:** quietly serious thoughtfulness **4** *obs* **a :** a cause of melancholy **b :** an attack of melancholy **syn** see SADNESS

²**melancholy** \"\ *adj* **1** *obs* **a :** affected with or subject to melancholy **b :** of, relating to, or caused by black bile **2** *obs* **:** ILL-NATURED, SULLEN, IRASCIBLE **3 a :** depressed in spirits **:** DEJECTED, GLOOMY, DISMAL, MOURNFUL, SAD **b :** seriously thoughtful or meditative **:** PENSIVE **4 a :** suggestive or expressive of melancholy or dejection **:** DEPRESSING ⟨~ music⟩ **b :** producing sadness **:** causing dejection **:** LAMENTABLE, AFFLICTING ⟨a ~ event⟩ **c** *obs* **:** favorable to meditation **:** SOMBER

melancholy thistle *n* **:** a perennial stoloniferous Old World thistle (*Circium heterophyllum*) with lanceolate finely toothed basal leaves and usu. solitary heads of reddish purple florets

¹**mel·anch·tho·nian** \ˌmeˌlaŋ(k)¦thōnēən, mə¦la-, -ōnyən\ *adj, usu cap* [Philipp *Melanchthon* (Schwarzert) †1560 Ger. scholar and religious reformer + E *-ian*] **:** of or relating to the reformer Melanchthon or his theological teachings or views

²**melanchthonian** \"\ *n* -s *usu cap* **:** a follower of Melanchthon

mel·an·co·ni·a·ce·ae \ˌmelənˌkōnē'āsēˌē\ *n pl, cap* [NL, fr. *Melanconium*, type genus (fr. *melan-* + *-conium*, fr. *konis*, *konia* dust) + *-aceae* — more at INCINERATE] **:** a family of fungi coextensive with the order Melanconiales — see CORYNEUM, GLOEOSPORIUM — **mel·an·co·ni·a·ceous** \ˌ==ˌ==¦āshəs\ *adj*

mel·an·co·ni·a·les \ˌ==ˌ==ā(ˌ)lēz\ *n pl, cap* [NL, fr. *Melanconium* + *-ales*] **:** an order of imperfect fungi that have the conidia borne in acervuli which are either immersed or erumpent and that are parasites of higher plants — see ANTHRACNOSE, MELANCONIACEAE

-mel·ane \'meˌlān\ *n* -s *comb form* [Gk *melan-, melas* black — more at MULLET] **:** black substance **:** dark substance ⟨lepido*melane*⟩ ⟨sidero*melane*⟩

mel·a·nel·li·dae \ˌmelə'neləˌdē\ *n pl, cap* [NL, fr. *Melanella*, type genus + *-idae*] **:** a family of small spiral usu. white marine gastropod mollusks (order Pectinibranchia) including a number that are parasitic on various echinoderms

mel·an·emia \ˌmelən¦ēmēə\ *n* -s [NL, fr. *melan-* + *-emia*] **:** an abnormal condition in which the blood contains melanin

1mel·a·ne·sian \\,melə'nēzhən, -ēsh-\\ *n* -s *cap* [*Melanesia*, islands in the Pacific ocean northeast of Australia + E *-an*] **1 :** a member of the dominant native group of Melanesia who constitute a dark-skinned people with thick beards and frizzy often elaborately dressed hair and who are generally considered to be a cross between the Papuans and the Polynesians or the Malays **2 :** a language group of the Austronesian languages of Melanesia

2melanesian \\¦==¦==\\ *adj, usu cap* **:** of or relating to Melanesia, the Melanesians, or their Austronesian languages ⟨a *Melanesian* littoral fauna⟩

melanesian pidgin *n, usu cap M* **:** BÊCHE-DE-MER 2

mel·a·ne·sid \\,melə'nēsəd\\ *n* -s *usu cap* [*Melanes*ia + E *-id*] **:** MELANESIAN 1

mé·lange *also* **me·lange** \\(')mā¦länzh, -änj\\ *n* -s [F *mélange*, fr. MF *melange*, fr. *mesler, medler, meler* to mix — more at MEDDLE] **:** MIXTURE, COMMINGLING: as **a :** a mixture of heterogeneous and often incongruous elements ⟨this turgid ~ of pacification and threat⟩ ⟨the psychosis represents a bizarre ~ of behavioral normality and abnormality —Hudson Hoagland⟩ **b :** a former dress fabric of cotton and wool **c :** a yarn spun from stock printed in different colors **d :** a silken pillow lace made with a combination of Chantilly and Spanish designs **e :** a batch or sales lot of diamonds in assorted sizes **f :** coffee mixed with cream, served in a tall glass, and topped with whipped cream

me·lan·ger \\-zhə(r), -jə(r)\\ *n* -s **:** an operator of a melangeur

me·lan·geur \\,mā,län'zhər(·), -än'jər(·)\\ *n* -s [F *mélangeur*, fr. *mélanger* to mix, (fr. *mélange*) + *-eur* -or] **:** a power-driven machine in which chocolate paste is mixed with sugar and flavoring and reduced to a fine smooth consistency

me·la·nia \\mə'lānēə, -nyə\\ [NL, fr. *melan-* + *-ia*] *syn of* THIARA

me·la·nian \\-ēən,-yən\\ *adj* [F *mélanien*, fr. *mélan-* melan- + *-ien* -ian] **1 :** of dark or black pigmentation **2** *usu cap* **:** belonging to a stock characterized by dark pigmentation — used of various black-skinned or brown-skinned peoples or of such peoples collectively

1me·lan·ic \\mə'lanik\\ *adj* [*melan-* + *-ic*] **1 a :** MELANOTIC **b :** MELANISTIC **2 :** MELANIAN

2melanic \\"\\ *or* **mel·a·nist** \\'melənəst\\ *n* -s **:** a melanistic individual

mel·a·nif·er·ous \\¦melə¦nif(ə)rəs\\ *adj* [*melan-* + *-iferous*] *of a body structure* **:** containing black pigment

mel·a·ni·idae \\,melə'nīə,dē\\ [NL, fr. *Melania* + *-idae*] *syn of* THIARIDAE

mel·a·nin \\'melənən\\ *n* -s [ISV *melan-* + *-in*] **1 :** any of various dark brown or black pigments of animal or plant structures (as skin, hair, the choroid coat, or raw potato when exposed to air) **2 :** any of various pigments that are similar to the natural melanins, are obtained esp. by enzymatic oxidation of tyrosine or dopa, and are believed to be quinonoid polymers derived from indole

melaninlike \\'===,=\\ *adj* **:** resembling or chemically related to melanins

mel·an·irid·o·some \\,melə,nī'ridə,sōm\\ *n* -s [*melan*ophore + *irido*phore + *-some*] **:** a multiple or compound chromatophore with melanophore and iridophore components that is common in teleosts

mel·a·nism \\'melə,nizəm\\ *n* -s [*melan-* + *-ism*] **1 a :** an unusual development of black or nearly black color in the skin or in the plumage or pelage occurring either as a characteristic of a variety or as an individual variation esp. in mammals and birds **b :** a melanistic variety or individual **2 :** the character in man of having a high degree of pigmentation in skin, eyes, and hair **3 :** a surface browning or blackening of tissues (as of wheat) due to development of pigment in the outer layers

mel·a·nist \\'melənəst\\ *n* -s [*melan-* + *-ist*] **:** MELANIC

mel·a·nis·tic \\¦melə¦nistik\\ *adj* **:** affected with or characterized by melanism **:** constituting melanism

mel·a·nite \\'melə,nīt\\ *n* -s [G *melanit*, fr. *melan-* + *-it* -ite] **:** a black garnet of the variety andradite — **mel·a·nit·ic** \\¦melə¦nid·ik\\ *adj*

mel·a·ni·za·tion \\,melənə'zāshən, -,nī'z-\\ *n* -s **:** the quality or state of being or the process of becoming melanized

mel·a·nize \\'melə,nīz\\ *vt* -ED/-ING/-s [*melan-* + *-ize*] **1 :** to convert into or infiltrate with melanin ⟨*melanized* cell granules⟩ **2 :** to render dark or black

melanized soil *n* **:** a soil (as that of a mesophytic forest) that is darkened by incorporated humus

mel·a·no \\'melə,nō\\ *n* -s [*melan-*] **:** a melanistic individual — compare ALBINO

1melano- — see MELAN-

2melano- *comb form, usu cap* [*melan*ian + *-o-*] **:** Melanian and ⟨*Melano*-Papuan⟩

melano·blast \\'melənō,blast, mə'lanə,-\\ *n* [ISV *melan-* + *-blast*] **:** a cell that produces melanin — **melano·blas·tic** \\¦===¦blastik, =¦==-\\ *adj*

melano·blas·to·ma \\,===,bla'stōmə, =,==-\\ *n, pl* **melanoblastomas** \\-məz\\ *or* **melanoblastoma·ta** \\-məd·ə\\ [NL, fr. ISV *melanoblast* + NL *-oma*] **:** a malignant tumor derived from melanoblasts

mel·a·no·carcinoma \\¦melə(,)nō+\\ *n* [NL, fr. *melan-* + *carcinoma*] **:** a melanoma believed to be of epithelial origin

mel·a·no·cerite \\¦melənō+\\ *n* -s [G *melanozerit*, fr. *melan-* + *zerit* cerite] **:** a mineral consisting of a complex silicate, borate, tantalate, fluoride, or other compound of cerium, yttrium, calcium, and other metals and occurring in brown or black rhombohedral crystals

mel·a·noch·roi \\,melə'näkrə,wī\\ *n pl, sometimes cap* [NL, fr. *melan-* + Gk *ōchroi*, nom. pl. masc. of *ōchros* pale] **:** Caucasians having dark hair and pale complexion — **mel·a·no·chro·ic** \\¦melənō¦krōik\\ *also* **mel·a·noch·roid** \\-¦nä,kròid\\ *adj, sometimes cap*

mel·a·noch·ro·ous \\¦melə¦näkrəwəs\\ *adj* [Gk *melanochroos, melanochrous*, fr. *melan-* *-chroos, -chrous* (fr. *chroa, chroia* skin)] **:** having a dark or swarthy skin

mel·a·noc·o·mous \\-kəməs\\ *adj* [*melan-* + Gk *komē* hair + E *-ous*] **:** having dark or black hair

mel·a·no·crat·ic \\¦melənō¦krad·ik\\ *adj* [*melan-* + Gk *kratein* to be strong, rule (akin to Gk *kratos* strength) + E *-ic* — more at HARD] *of igneous rock* **:** having predominantly dark mineral constituents — compare LEUCOCRATIC, MESOCRATIC

melano·cyte \\'melənō,sīt, mə'lanə,-\\ *n* -s [ISV *melan-* + *-cyte*] **:** a cell producing or containing dark pigment — compare MELANOBLAST

melano·derm \\-,dərm\\ *n* -s [*melan-* + *-derm*] **:** a person with a dark skin; *specif* **:** a black-skinned or brown-skinned person — compare XANTHODERM

mel·a·no·der·ma \\,melənō'dərmə\\ *n* -s [NL, fr. *melan-* + *-derma*] **:** abnormally intense pigmentation of the skin — **mel·a·no·der·mic** \\¦===¦=mik\\ *adj*

mel·a·no·gas·ter \\'===,gastə(r), ,==='==\\ *n, cap* [NL, fr. *melan-* + *-gaster*] **:** a genus of hard-skinned puffballs of the family Sclerodermataceae — see RED TRUFFLE

mel·a·no·gen \\'melənō,jen; mə'lanəjən, -,jen\\ *n* -s [*melan-* + *-gen*] **:** a precursor of melanin

mel·a·no·genesis \\,melənō+\\ *n* [NL, fr. *melan-* + L *genesis*] **:** the formation of melanin

melanogenetic *adj* [*melan-* + *-genetic*] **:** of or relating to melanogenesis

mel·a·no·gen·ic \\¦===¦jenik\\ *adj* [*melan-* + *-genic*] **1 :** of, relating to, or characteristic of melanogenesis **2 :** producing melanin

1mel·a·noid \\'melə,nȯid\\ *adj* [ISV *melan-* + *-oid*] **1 :** characterized or darkened by melanins ⟨a ~ lesion⟩ **2 :** relating to or occurring in melanosis ⟨~ symptoms⟩

2melanoid \\"\\ *n* -s **1 :** a melanistic individual **2 :** a pigment (as one contributing esp. to the yellow color of the skin) that is a disintegration product of a melanin

mel·a·noi·din \\,melə'nȯidᵊn\\ *n* -s [*2melanoid* + *-in*] **:** any of various colored substances formed from proteins or amino acids (as in the presence of glucose) — compare HUMIN b

mel·a·no·ma \\,melə'nōmə\\ *n, pl* **melanomas** \\-ōməz\\ *also* **melanoma·ta** \\-ōməd·ə\\ [NL, fr. *melan-* + *-oma*] **1 :** a skin tumor containing dark pigment **2 :** a tumor of high malignancy that starts in a black mole and metastasizes rapidly and widely — called also *malignant melanoma*

mel·a·no·ma·to·sis \\,melə,nōmə'tōsəs\\ *n, pl* **melanomatoses** \\-ō,sēz\\ [NL, fr. *melanomat-, melanoma* + *-osis*] **:** the condition of having multiple melanomas in the body ⟨an advanced ~⟩

mel·a·noph·i·la \\,melə'näfələ\\ *n, cap* [NL, fr. *melan-* + *-phila*] **:** a genus of buprestid beetles that includes several destructive borers of forest trees

melano·phore \\'melənə,fō(ə)r, mə'lan-\\ *n* -s [*melan-* + *-phore*] **:** a chromatophore containing melanin **:** a black or brown pigment cell — **melano·phor·ic** \\¦===¦fȯrik, =¦==-\\ *adj*

me·lan·o·plus \\mə'lanəpləs\\ *n, cap* [NL, fr. *melan-* + *-oplus* (fr. Gk *hoplon* tool, implement) — more at HOPLITE] **:** a large American genus containing the migratory locusts of the western U. S. and other common American grasshoppers

mel·a·nor·rhoea \\,melənə'rēə\\ *n, cap* [NL, fr. *melan-* + *-rrhoea*] **:** a small genus of East Indian trees (family Anacardiaceae) with simple leaves, panicled flowers, and drupaceous fruit — see BLACK-VARNISH TREE

mel·a·no·sarcoma \\¦melə(,)nō+\\ *n* [NL, fr. *melan-* + *sarcoma*] **:** a sarcoma that is believed to be derived from melanoblasts

mel·a·nose \\'melə,nōs, -ōz\\ *n* -s [F *mélanose* melanosis, melanose, fr. NL *melanosis*] **1 :** a disease of the grapevine caused by a fungus (*Septoria ampelina*) that attacks the leaves causing them to fall **2 :** a disease of citrus trees and fruits caused by an imperfect fungus (*Diaporthe citri*) that produces hard brown raised and often gummy spots in the rind of the fruit and also on twigs and leaves

mel·a·no·sis \\,melə'nōsəs\\ *n, pl* **melano·ses** \\-ō,sēz\\ [NL, fr. *melan-* + *-osis*] **:** a condition characterized by abnormal deposition of melanins or sometimes other pigments in the tissues of the body

mel·a·no·sper·mous \\¦melənō¦spərməs\\ *adj* [*melan-* + *-spermous*] *of an alga* **:** having dark olivaceous spores

mel·a·no·stib·i·an \\,melənō'stibēən\\ *n* -s [G, fr. *melan-* + *stibium* + *-an*] **:** a black mineral approximately $(Mn,Fe)_6Sb_2O_9$ that is an oxide of iron, manganese, and antimony

mel·a·no·te·kite \\-nō'tē,kīt\\ *n* -s [Sw *melanotekit*, fr. *melan-* + Gk *tēkein* to melt + Sw *-it* -ite; fr. its fusing to a black glass — more at THAW] **:** a black or dark gray mineral $Pb_2Fe_2Si_2O_9$ that is a lead iron silicate

mel·a·not·ic \\¦melə¦näd·ik\\ *adj* [*melan-* + *-otic*] **:** having or characterized by black pigmentation ⟨a ~ tumor⟩ ⟨a ~ race⟩

mel·a·not·ri·chous \\¦melə¦nä·trəkəs\\ *adj* [*melan-* + *-trichous*] **:** MELANOCOMOUS

mel·a·no·tus \\,melə'nōd·əs\\ *n, cap* [NL, fr. *mela-* + *-notus*] **:** a widely distributed genus of small brown elaterid beetles whose larvae include several destructive wireworms

mel·a·nous \\'melənəs\\ *adj* [*melan-* + *-ous*] **:** having black hair and dark brown or blackish skin — used chiefly of the darker Melanochroi

mel·a·no·vanadite \\¦melə(,)nō+\\ *n* -s [*melan-* + *vanadite*] **:** a mineral $Ca_2V_{10}O_{25}$ that is a complex oxide of calcium and vanadium

me·lan·ter·ite \\mə'lantə,rīt\\ *n* -s [G *melanterit*, fr. F *mélantérie* melanterite (fr. NL *melanteria*, fr. Gk *melantēria* pigment used for blacking shoes, fr. *melan-* + *tērein* to watch, preserve, keep + *-ia* -y) + G *-it* -ite] **:** native copperas $FeSo_4.7H_2O$ that is isomorphous with kirovite and pisanite

mel·an·tha·ce·ae \\,melən'thāsē,ē, ,me,lan-\\ *n pl, cap* [NL, irreg. fr. *Melanthium*, type genus + *-aceae*] *in some classifications* **:** a family of monocotyledonous plants (order Liliales) distinguished from the Liliaceae by the septicidal capsule and by the absence of bulbs — see MELANTHIUM — **mel·an·tha·ceous** \\¦=(,)=¦thāshəs\\ *adj*

me·lan·thi·um \\mə'lan(t)thēəm\\ *n, cap* [NL, fr. *mela-* + *anth-* + *-ium;* fr. the dark color of the fading perianth] **:** a small No. American genus that is sometimes made type of the family Melanthaceae or now more usu. included among the Liliaceae and that comprises perennial herbs with heavy rootstocks and erect leafy stems bearing a terminal panicle of yellowish flowers having clawed perianth segments — see BUNCHFLOWER

mel·an·uria \\,melə'n(y)u̇rēə\\ *n* -s [NL, fr. *melan-* + *-uria*] **:** the presence of melanins in the urine — **mel·an·uric** \\¦==-¦=rik\\ *adj*

mel·a·phyre \\'melə,fī(ə)r\\ *n* -s [F *mélaphyre*, fr. *méla-* mela- + *-phyre*] **1 :** a porphyritic rock consisting of phenocrysts of feldspar in a dark groundmass; *broadly* **:** a porphyritic igneous rock with dark-colored aphanitic groundmass and phenocrysts of various kinds **2 :** a Mesozoic basalt

me·las·ma \\mə'lazmə\\ *n* -s [NL, fr. Gk, black spot, fr. *melas* black — more at MULLET] **:** a dark pigmentation of the skin (as in Addison's disease) — **me·las·mic** \\-zmik\\ *adj*

melasses *obs var of* MOLASSES

me·las·si·gen·ic \\mə¦lasə¦jenik\\ *adj* [*melass*es + *-i-* + *-genic*] **:** producing molasses **:** preventing or tending to restrict the crystallization of sugar — used esp. of certain inorganic salts

me·las·to·ma \\mə'lastəmə\\ *n, cap* [NL, fr. *mela-* + *-stoma;* fr. the staining property of the fruit] **:** the type genus of Melastomaceae comprising Asiatic shrubs that have coriaceous leaves and large purple flowers with several anthers of unequal lengths

me·las·to·ma·ce·ae \\mə,lastə'māsē,ē\\ *n pl, cap* [NL, fr. *Melastoma*, type genus + *-aceae*] **:** a family of trees, shrubs, or herbs (order Myrtales) that are characterized by opposite 3- to 9-nerved leaves, anthers with thickened connectives, and petals inserted on the throat of the calyx and that include numerous forms cultivated as ornamentals — see RHEXIA — **me·las·to·ma·ceous** \\=¦==¦māshəs\\ *adj*

me·las·to·ma·ta·ce·ae \\mə,lastəmə'tāsē,ē\\ [NL, fr. *Melastomat-, Melastoma* + *-aceae*] *syn of* MELASTOMACEAE

mel·a·stome \\'melə,stōm\\ *also* **me·las·to·mad** \\mə'lastə,mad\\ *n* -s [*melastome* fr. NL *Melastoma; melastomad* fr. NL *Melastoma* + E *-ad*] **:** a plant of the family Melastomaceae

mel·a·tope \\'melə,tōp\\ *n* -s [*mela-* + Gk *topos* place — more at TOPIC] **:** the point in an interference figure corresponding to the direction of an optic axis in the crystal section or grain producing the figure

me·la·veh mal·kah \\mə,lävə'mälkə\\ *n, pl* **melaveh malkahs** [Heb *mĕlweh malkāh*, lit., escorting the queen] **:** a traditional weekly ceremony observed chiefly by Hasidim on Saturday evening to bid farewell to the Queen Sabbath and marked by feasting, singing, dancing

mel·a·xu·ma \\,melə'kümə, -lək'sü-,-lə'zü-\\ *n* -s [NL, prob. irreg. (Gk χ being taken as E *x*) fr. *mela-* + Gk *chyma* fluid, fr. *chein* to pour — more at FOUND (melt)] **:** any of various plant diseases producing dark or black bark cankers; *esp* **:** a disease of the walnut caused by the imperfect fungus (*Dothiorella gregaria*)

mel·ba \\'melbə\\ *n* -s [after Madame Nellie *Melba* (Helen Porter Mitchell) †1931 Austral. operatic soprano] **:** fruit served with ice cream, raspberry sauce, and whipped cream ⟨ate and drank . . . sundaes, shakes, parfaits, whips, ~*s* —Elizabeth Taylor⟩ — see PÊCHE MELBA

melba sauce *n* [after Nellie *Melba*] **:** sauce made essentially of raspberries and sugar and served often with ice cream or whipped cream on fruit — compare PÊCHE MELBA

melba toast *n, sometimes cap M* [after Nellie *Melba*] **:** very thin bread toasted or rusked till crisp and well browned

mel·bourne \\'melbə(r)n *also* -,bōrn *or* -,bȯrn *or* -ōən *or* -ȯ(ə)n\\ *adj, usu cap* [fr. *Melbourne*, Australia] **:** of or from Melbourne, the capital of Victoria, Australia **:** of the kind or style prevalent in Melbourne

mel·bur·ni·an \\mel'bərnēən\\ *n* -s *cap* [*Melbourne*, Australia + E *-ian*] **:** a native or resident of Melbourne, Australia

melch \\'melch, -lsh\\ *adj* -ER/-EST [ME, prob. fr. OE *melsc* mellow; prob. akin to OE *melu* meal — more at MULCH] **1** *now dial Brit* **:** yielding easily to pressure **:** SOFT ⟨~ ground⟩ **2** *dial Brit* **:** MILD ⟨a ~ day⟩

1mel·chite *or* **mel·kite** \\'mel,kīt\\ *n* -s *usu cap* [ML *Melchita*, fr. MGk *Melchitēs*, lit., royalist, fr. Syr *malkā* king + Gk *-itēs* -ite] **1 :** a Christian in Egypt and Syria who accepted the decrees of the Council of Chalcedon in A.D. 451 against Nestorians and Monophysites **2 :** a Uniat of the Byzantine rite in Egypt, Syria, or Palestine

2melchite \\"\\ *adj, usu cap* **:** of or relating to the Melchites

melchite alphabet *n, usu cap M* **:** a Syriac alphabet at first uncial but becoming later cursive and the most deformed of Syriac scripts

mel·chiz·e·dek \\mel'kizə,dek\\ *adj, usu cap* [after *Melchizedek*, Biblical priest-king (Gen 14:18 ff.)] **:** being the greater or higher order of priesthood in the Mormon Church — compare AARONIC 2

1meld \\'meld\\ *vb* -ED/-ING/-S [G *melden* to announce, report, fr. OHG *meldōn;* akin to OE *meldian* to announce, reveal, inform on, *meld* proclamation, OS *meldon* to inform on, betray, OS & OHG *melda* betrayal, OSlav *moliti* to ask for, request, pray, Arm *malt'em* I request, Hitt *maltai, maldi* he prays; basic meaning: to pray] *vt* **:** to show or announce (a card or combination of cards that has scoring or other value in a game being played) usu. by placing face up on the table ⟨~*ing* four kings in pinochle⟩ ~ *vi* **:** to show or announce a card or combination of cards as a meld

2meld \\"\\ *n* -s **:** a card or combination of cards that is or can be melded in a card game

3meld \\"\\ *vb* -ED/-ING/-S [blend of *1melt* and *2weld*] **:** MERGE

mel·der \\'mel(d)ə(r)\\ *n* -s [ME *meltyre*, of Scand origin; akin to ON *meldr* flour or grain in the mill; akin to OS *maldar*, a measure for grain, OHG *maltar;* akin to OE *melu* flour — more at MEAL] *dial Brit* **:** the quantity of meal ground at one time **:** meal just ground; *also* **:** a grinding of grain

mel·do·la's blue \\'meldələz-\\ *or* **meldola blue** *n, usu cap M&B* [after Raphael *Meldola* †1915 Eng. chemist] **:** a basic dye — see DYE table I (under *Basic Blue 6*)

meld out *vi* **:** to meld the last card or cards of one's hand (as in canasta or rummy)

me·le \\'mā(,)lā\\ *n* -s [Hawaiian] **:** an Hawaiian song or chant

mele·agrid·i·dae \\,melēə'gridə,dē\\ *n pl, cap* [NL, fr. *Meleagrid-, Meleagris*, type genus + *-idae*] **:** a family of large No. American birds (order Galliformes) that comprise the turkeys and a few extinct related birds and are sometimes placed in a subfamily of Phasianidae

mele·agri·na \\-rīnə,-rēnə\\ [NL, fr. *Meleagris*, genus of mollusks in some former classifications (fr. L, guinea fowl) + *-ina;* fr. the spotted appearance of the mollusks] *syn of* PINCTADA

mele·agris \\,melē'agrəs, -'āg-\\ *n, cap* [NL, fr. L, guinea fowl, fr. Gk] **:** the type genus of Meleagrididae comprising the wild and domestic turkeys

m electron *n, usu cap M* **:** an electron in the M-shell

1me·lee \\'mā(,)lā, mā'lā *sometimes* mə'lā *or* me'lā *or* 'me(,)lā\\ *n* -s [F *mêlée*, fr. OF *meslee, medlee, melee* mixture, argument, fight — more at MEDLEY] **1 :** a fight or contest between individuals mingled in a confused mass **:** a confused struggle ⟨killed in a border ~⟩ ⟨this week's wrestling card includes two team ~*s*⟩ **2 :** a cavalry exercise in which two groups of riders try to cut paper plumes off the helmets of their opponents **3 :** a confused mingling together of often incongruous elements **:** MÉLANGE ⟨pushing their . . . way through a ~ of taxis, bicycles, and people —*Atlantic*⟩ **syn** see BRAWL

2melee \\"\\ *n* -s [origin unknown] **:** a small diamond cut from a fragment of a larger stone and usu. less than one-eighth carat in weight

mel·e·gue·ta pepper \\¦melə¦ged·ə-, -gād·ə-\\ *or* **mal·a·gue·ta pepper** *or* **mal·a·guet·ta pepper** *also* **mal·a·get·ta pepper** \\¦malə-\\ *n* [F & Sp; F *méléguette, maliguette*, fr. Sp *malagueta*] **:** GRAIN OF PARADISE 1

me·le·na *or* **me·lae·na** \\mə'lēnə\\ *n* -s [NL, fr. Gk *melaina*, fem. of *melas* black — more at MULLET] **:** the passage of dark tarry stools containing decomposing blood that is usu. an indication of bleeding in the upper part of the alimentary canal

mel·eng·ket \\¦meləŋ¦ket\\ *n* -s [native name in the Philippines] **:** a soft Manila copal gathered about two weeks after the trees have been tapped

me·les \\'mē(,)lēz\\ *n, cap* [NL, fr. L, badger, marten] **:** a genus of mustelid mammals comprising the typical Old World badgers

1me·le·tian \\mə'lēshən\\ *adj, usu cap* [*Meleti*us, 4th cent. A.D. bishop of Lycopolis + E *-an*] **:** of or relating to Meletius the bishop of Lycopolis

2meletian \\"\\ *n* -s *usu cap* **:** a member or supporter of a schismatic party upholding Meletius the bishop of Lycopolis in exercising episcopal functions in the see of Alexandria early in the 4th century A.D.

3meletian \\"\\ *adj, usu cap* [*Meleti*us †381 A.D. Greek ecclesiastic, bishop of Antioch + E *-an*] **:** of or relating to Meletius the bishop of Antioch in Syria

4meletian \\"\\ *n* -s *usu cap* **:** a member or supporter of a schism occasioned by dissensions over the opinions of Meletius the bishop of Antioch

me·lets·ki \\mə'letskē\\ *or* **me·liz·ki** \\-lit-\\ *n, pl* **meletski** *or* **meletskis** *or* **melizki** *or* **melizkis** *usu cap* **:** a member of a division of the Chulyma Tatars

me·lez·i·tose \\mə'lezə,tōs *also* -ōz\\ *n* -s [F *mélézitose*, fr. *mélèze* larch (fr. Prov *meleze*) + mél*itose* melitose] **:** a nonreducing trisaccharide sugar $C_{18}H_{32}O_{16}.2H_2O$ that is less sweet than sucrose, that is obtained esp. from exudations of various trees (as the larch or Douglas fir) or from honey made from such exudations, and that on partial hydrolysis yields glucose and turanose

meli- *comb form* [Gk *meli* — more at MELLIFLUOUS] **:** honey ⟨*meli*lite⟩

me·lia \\'mēlēə, -lyə\\ *n, cap* [NL, fr. Gk *melia, meliē* manna ash; fr. the resemblance of the leaves to those of the ash] **:** a genus (the type of the family Meliaceae) of East Indian and Australian deciduous trees with pinnate or bipinnate leaves resembling those of the ashes, fragrant white or lilac flowers in axillary panicles, and small drupaceous fruits containing hard bony seeds — see CHINABERRY 2, MARGOSA

-melia \\'mēlēə, 'mel-, -lyə\\ *n comb form* -s [NL, fr. Gk *melos* limb + NL *-ia* — more at MELODY] **:** condition of the limbs ⟨aniso*melia*⟩ ⟨schisto*melia*⟩ ⟨ectro*melia*⟩

me·li·a·ce·ae \\,mēlē'āsē,ē\\ *n pl, cap* [NL, fr. *Melia*, type genus + *-aceae*] **:** a family of tropical trees and shrubs (order Geraniales) that have monadelphous stamens and include various important timber and ornamental trees — see MAHOGANY, MELIA — **me·li·a·ceous** \\¦==¦āshəs\\ *adj*

1me·lian \\'mēlēən, -lyən\\ *adj, usu cap* [*Mel*os, one of the Cyclades islands in the southern Aegean sea + E *-ian*] **:** of or relating to the island of Melos

2melian \\"\\ *n* -s *cap* **:** a native or inhabitant of Melos

me·li·an·tha·ce·ae \\,mēlē,an'thāsē,ē\\ *n pl, cap* [NL, fr. *Melianthus*, type genus + *-aceae*] **:** a family of African trees and shrubs (order Sapindales) having irregular flowers and stipulate leaves — see MELIANTHUS — **me·li·an·tha·ceous** \\¦mēlē,an¦thāshəs\\ *adj*

me·li·an·thus \\,mēlē'an(t)thəs\\ *n, cap* [NL, fr. *meli-* + *-anthus*] **:** a small genus (the type of the family Melianthaceae) of southern African shrubs having odd-pinnate leaves and racemose flowers with unequal sepals and four stamens — see HONEYFLOWER

mel·i·bi·ose \\,melə'bī,ōs *also* -ōz\\ *n* -s [ISV *meli*tose + *bi-* + *-ose*] **:** a disaccharide sugar $C_{12}H_{22}O_{11}$ formed by partial hydrolysis of raffinose; 6-galactosyl-glucose

1mel·ic \\'melik\\ *adj* [L *melicus*, fr. Gk *melikos*, fr. *melos* song + *-ikos* -ic — more at MELODY] **1 :** of or belonging to song **:** designed to be sung **:** LYRIC **2 :** being or relating to Greek poetry essentially lyrical and musical in character following the elegiac and iambic poetry of the 7th and 6th centuries B.C. and including monodic poetry (as in Sappho) closely akin to the modern lyric and choral poetry (as in Pindar)

2melic \\"\\ *n* -s **:** melic poetry

mel·i·ca \\'meləkə\\ *n, cap* [NL, fr. It *melica, meliga* sorghum, modif. (influenced by L *mel* honey) of ML (*herba*) *medica*, lit., medical herb, fr. *herba* herb + *medica*, fem. of *medicus* medical — more at MELLIFLUOUS, MEDICAL] **:** a genus of perennial mostly woodland grasses somewhat resembling *Festuca* but having lemmas 2-lobed at the apex and the upper 2 or 3 lemmas empty and forming a club-shaped mass — see MELIC GRASS

mel·i·cer·ta \\,melə'sərd·ə\\ *n, cap* [NL, after *Melicerta*, a sea-god, fr. L, fr. Gk *Melikertēs*] **:** a genus of rotifers (order Monogononta) that are usu. tube-living and have a conspicuous lobed corona

mel·ic grass \\'melik-\\ *also* **melic** *or* **melick** *n* [NL *Melica*] **:** a grass of the genus *Melica*

mel·i·chrous \\'meləkrəs, me'likrəwəs\\ *adj* [Gk *melichroos, melichrous*, fr. *meli* honey + *-chroos, -chrous* -chrous — more at MELLIFLUOUS] **:** of the color honey yellow

mel·i·coc·ca \\,melə'käkə\\ *n, cap* [NL, fr. *meli-* + Gk *-cocca* (fr. *kokkos* kermes berry)] **:** a genus of tropical American trees and shrubs (family Sapindaceae) having pinnate leaflets, abruptly tetramerous flowers with a peltate stigma, and a one-seeded or two-seeded berry

mel·i·crate \'melə,krāt\ *n* -s [LL *melicratum*, fr. Gk *melikraton*, fr. *meli* honey + *-kraton* (fr. *kerannynai* to mix) — more at MELLIFLUOUS, CRATER] *archaic* **:** a fermented or unfermented beverage of honey and water **:** HYDROMEL

mel·i·lite \'melə,līt\ *n* -s [F *mélilite*, fr. *méli-* meli- + *-lite*] **:** an often honey-yellow mineral $(Ca,Na_2)(Mg,Fe,Al)(Si,Al)_2O_7$ occurring in small tetragonal crystals that is a silicate of sodium, calcium, aluminum, and iron; *esp* **:** a member of the series consisting of an isomorphous solid-solution series between gehlenite and akermanite

mel·i·lot \'melə,lät\ *n* -s [ME *mellilot*, fr. MF *melilot*, fr. L *melilotos*, fr. Gk *melilōtos*, fr. *meli* honey + *lōtos* clover, melilot, lotus — more at LOTUS] **:** a plant of the genus *Melilotus* **:** SWEET CLOVER; *esp* **:** YELLOW SWEET CLOVER 1 — compare BLUE MELILOT

mel·i·lo·tus \,melə'lōd·əs\ *n* [NL, fr. L *melilotos* melilot] **1** *cap* **:** a genus of annual or biennial erect Old World leguminous herbs that comprise the sweet clovers, have trifoliolate leaves, small white or yellow flowers in axillary racemes, and short straight one-seeded or two-seeded pods, and are widely cultivated and naturalized as escapes **2** -s **:** a plant of the genus *Melilotus*

¹meline \'mē,līn, 'me,-\ *adj* [L *melinus*, fr. *meles* marten, badger + *-inus* -ine] **:** made up of or resembling badgers ⟨the ~ mammals⟩

²meline \"\ *adj* [Gk *mēlinos* of a quince, quince-yellow, fr. *mēlon* apple, quince] **:** of the color quince yellow

mel·i·nite \'melə,nīt\ *n* -s [F *mélinite*, fr. Gk *mēlinos* quince-yellow + F *-ite*] **:** a high explosive similar to lyddite

mel·i·oi·do·sis \,melē,ȯi'dōsə̇s\ *n, pl* **melioido·ses** \-ō,sēz\ [NL, fr. Gk *melis*, a disease of equines, prob. glanders + ISV *-oid* + NL *-osis*] **:** a highly fatal bacterial disease closely related to glanders that occurs naturally in rodents of southeastern Asia but is readily transmitted to other mammals and man by the rat flea or under certain conditions by dissemination of the causative bacterium (*Pseudomonas pseudomallei*) in air

meli·o·la·les \,melēə'lā(,)lēz, mə̇,līə-\ *n pl, cap* [NL, fr. *Meliola* genus of fungi (fr. Gk *mēlon* apple + NL *-i-* + L *-ola*, dim. suffix) + *-ales*] **:** an order of fungi (subclass Euascomycetes) having a stroma that resembles a perithecium and is not noticeably flattened

me·lio·rate \'mēlyə,rāt, -lēə-\ *vb* -ED/-ING/-S [LL *melioratus*, past part. of *meliorare*, fr. L *melior* better; akin to L *multus* much, Gk *mala* very, Umbrian *mutu* penalty, fine, Latvian *milns* very much] *vt* **:** to make better or more tolerable **:** AMELIORATE, SOFTEN ~ *vi* **:** to become better or more tolerable

me·lio·ra·tion \,mēlyə'rāshən, -lēə-\ *n* -s [LL *melioration-*, *melioratio*, fr. *melioratus* + L *-ion-*, *-io* -ion] **:** the quality or state of being meliorated or an act of meliorating **:** BETTERMENT: as **a :** lasting or major improvement of land (as by a tenant) ⟨the effect of ~s was greater on height growth of fir and on soil flora and condition —*Biol. Abstracts*⟩ **b :** the historical process by which the semantic and connotative status of a word tends to rise ⟨the emergence of *steward* from *sty-ward* is an example of ~ in action⟩ — compare PEJORATION

me·lio·ra·tive \'=(=),rād·iv, -,rə|, \tiv, -ēv\ *adj* **:** tending to effect melioration **:** resulting in or leading toward betterment (as of status)

me·lio·rism \'mēlyə,rizəm, -lēə-\ *n* -s [L *melior* better + E *-ism*] **:** the belief or doctrine that the world tends to become better and that man has the power to aid its betterment ⟨~ seeks a compromise between both optimism and pessimism: the world is neither good nor evil, but can be improved on the condition that its parts do their best to improve it —Frank Thilly⟩ — compare DETERIORISM

¹me·lio·rist \-,rə̇st\ *n* -s [L *melior* + E *-ist*] **:** an advocate or adherent of meliorism

²meliorist \"\ *or* **me·lio·ris·tic** \¦=(=)=¦ristik\ *adj* **:** of or relating to meliorism

me·lior·i·ty \mēl'yȯrəd·ē, ,mēlē'ȯ-\ *n* -ES [ML *melioritas*, fr. L *melior* better + *-itas* -ity — more at MELIORATE] **:** the quality or state of being better

mel·i·phag·i·dae \,melə'fajə,dē\ *n pl, cap* [NL, fr. *Meliphaga*, type genus (fr. *meli-* + *-phaga*) + *-idae*] **:** a family of oscine birds that are almost entirely restricted to the Australian biogeographic region and have the tongue modified for taking nectar and insects from flowers — see HONEY EATER — **mel·i·phag·i·dan** \¦==¦fajədən\ *adj or n*

me·liph·a·gous *or* **mel·liph·a·gous** \(')me¦lifəgəs\ *adj* [*meli-* + *-phagous*] **:** feeding or living upon honey

mel·i·phane \'melə,fān\ *n* -s [*meli-* + Gk *phainesthai* to appear, pass. of *phainein* to show — more at FANCY] **:** MELIPHANITE

me·liph·a·nite \mə̇'lifə,nīt\ *n* -s [*meliphane* + *-ite*] **:** a mineral occurring as a fluosilicate of sodium, calcium, and beryllium in yellow crystals

me·lip·o·na \mə̇'lipənə\ *n, cap* [NL, fr. *meli-* + *-pona* (fr. Gk *ponein* to toil)] **:** a genus of honeybees of tropical America that comprises small bees with a vestigial but functionless sting — compare STINGLESS BEE — **me·lip·o·nine** \-pə,nīn\ *adj*

melis \'mēlə̇s, 'mel-\ *n* -ES [G, fr. Gk *meli* honey — more at MELLIFLUOUS] **:** a usu. slightly yellowish imperfectly refined sugar usu. prepared in loaf form

me·lis·ma \mə̇'lizmə\ *n, pl* **melisma·ta** \-zməd·ə\ [Gk, song, melody, fr. *melizein* to sing, fr. *melos* song — more at MELODY] **1 :** SONG, TUNE **2 :** a group of notes or tones sung to one syllable in plainsong **3 :** melodic embellishment or ornamentation **4 :** CADENZA

mel·is·mat·ic \¦meləz¦mad·ik\ *adj* [Gk *melismat-*, *melisma* + E *-ic*] *of music* **:** relating to or having melisma **:** FLORID

mel·is·mat·ics \-ks\ *n pl but sing or pl in constr* **:** the art of florid vocalization

me·lis·sa \mə̇'lisə\ *n* [NL, fr. Gk *melitta*, *melissa* bee, fr. *melit-*, *meli* honey — more at MELLIFLUOUS] **1** *cap* **:** a genus of Old World mints having axillary clusters of small white or yellowish flowers with a bilabiate calyx, exserted corolla, and divergent anther lobes — see BALM 3a, LEMON BALM **2** -s **:** a plant of the genus *Melissa*

me·lis·sic acid \mə̇'lisik-\ *n* [Gk *melissa* bee + E *-ic*] **:** a crystalline fatty acid $CH_3(CH_2)_{28}COOH$ found free or in the form of its ester with myricyl alcohol in beeswax and other waxes and also obtained by oxidation of myricyl alcohol — called also *triacontanoic acid*

me·lis·syl alcohol \-səl-\ *n* [*melissic* + *-yl*] **:** MYRICYL ALCOHOL

mel·i·ten·sis \¦melə¦ten(t)səs\ *adj* [NL (specific epithet of *Brucella melitensis*), fr. L *melitensis* of Malta, fr. *Melita* Malta, island in the Mediterranean + L *-ensis* -ese] **:** of, derived from, or caused by a bacterium (*Brucella melitensis*) ⟨~ proteins⟩ ⟨~ fever⟩

mel·i·tose \'melə,tōs *also* -ōz\ *n* -s [ISV *meli-* + connective *-t-* + *-ose*; prob. orig. formed as F *mélitose*] **:** RAFFINOSE

mel·it·tia \mə̇'lid·ēə\ *n, cap* [NL, fr. Gk *melitta*, *melissa* bee + NL *-ia*] **:** a large genus of chiefly tropical clearwings (family Aegeriidae) including some that mimic wasps — see SQUASH BORER

mel·it·tol·o·gist \,melə'täləjə̇st\ *n* -s [*melittology* study of bees (fr. Gk *melitta*, *melissa* bee + E *-o-* + *-logy*) + *-ist* — more at MELISSA] **:** an entomologist specializing in the study of bees

mel·i·tu·ria *or* **mel·li·tu·ria** \,melə'tu̇rēə, -lə'tyu̇-\ *n* -s [NL, fr. Gk *melit-*, *meli* honey + *-uria*] **:** the presence of any sugar in the urine

melizki *usu cap, var of* MELETSKI

melk·hout \'mel,kōt\ *n* -s [Afrik, fr. *melk* milk + *hout* wood] **:** MILKWOOD d

melkite *usu cap, var of* MELCHITE

¹mell \'mel\ *n* -s [ME — more at MAUL] **1** *dial Brit* **:** a hammer or mallet esp. of wood **2** *dial Brit* **a :** the prize (as a mallet) given to the participant who places last in a contest **b :** the participant who places last in a contest

²mell \"\ *vt* -ED/-ING/-S [ME *mellen*, fr. *mell*, n.] *dial Brit* **:** to strike with a mell **:** BEAT

³mell \"\ *vb* -ED/-ING/-S [ME *mellen*, fr. MF *mesler*, *medler*, *meller* — more at MEDDLE] *vt*, *dial Brit* **:** MIX, MINGLE ~ *vi* **1** *now dial Brit* **:** to join in combat — usu. used with *with* **2** *now dial Brit* **:** JOIN, ASSOCIATE — usu. used with *with* ⟨~ with bad company⟩ **3** *now dial Brit* **:** to interest or occupy oneself ⟨~ with war —C.L.Smith⟩ **:** MEDDLE — usu. used with *with* or *on*

⁴mell \"\ *var of* MEL

⁵mell \"\ *n* -s [origin unknown] **1** *dial chiefly Eng* **:** KIRN 2 **2** *dial chiefly Eng* **:** HARVEST HOME 2

mell- *or* **melli-** *comb form* [L — more at MELLIFLUOUS] **:** honey **:** like honey ⟨*mell*ite⟩ ⟨*melli*sugent⟩ ⟨*melli*sonant⟩

mel·lah \'melə\ *n* -s [origin unknown] **:** the Jewish quarter of a northern African city — compare MEDINA

mel·lay \mə'lā, me'lā, 'me(,)lā, 'melē\ *n* -s [ME *melle*, fr. MF *meslee*, *medlee*, *melee* mixture, quarrel, fight — more at MEDLEY] **:** MELEE 1, 3

mell-doll \'=,=\ *n* [⁵*mell*] *dial Eng* **:** HARVEST DOLL

mel·le·ous \'melēəs\ *adj* [L *melleus*, fr. *mell-* + *-eus* -eous — more at MELLIFLUOUS] **:** resembling or containing honey

mel·ler \'melə(r)\ *n* -s [by shortening and alter.] *slang* **:** MELODRAMA 2

mel·lif·er·ous \(')me¦lif(ə)rəs\ *adj* [L *mellifer* (fr. *mell-* + *-fer* -ferous) + E *-ous*] **:** producing or yielding honey

mel·lif·lu·ent \-fləwənt\ *adj* [LL *mellifluent-*, *mellifluens*, fr. L *melli-* mell- + *fluent-*, *fluens*, pres. part. of *fluere* to flow — more at FLUID] *archaic* **:** MELLIFLUOUS

mel·lif·lu·ous \mə'lifləwəs\ *adj* [LL *mellifluus*, fr. L *melli-* (fr. *mell-*, *mel* honey) + *-fluus* (fr. *fluere* to flow); akin to OE *milisc* sweet, mild, *mildēaw*, *melēdēaw* honeydew, OS *milidou* mildew, OHG *militou* mildew, Goth *milith* honey, Gk *melit-*, *meli*, OIr *mil*, Arm *melr*, Alb *mjal*, Hitt *milit*] **1 :** flowing or sweetened with or as if with honey ⟨~ confections⟩ **2 :** sweetly flowing **:** SMOOTH, HONEYED ⟨a ~ voice⟩ — **mel·lif·lu·ous·ly** *adv* — **mel·lif·lu·ous·ness** *n* -ES

mel·li·lite \'melə,līt\ *n* -s [*mell-* + *-lite*] **1 :** MELILITE **2 :** MELLITE

mel·lis·o·nant \(')me¦lis°nənt, mə'l-\ *adj* [*mell-* + L *sonant-*, *sonans*, pres. part. of *sonare* to sound — more at SOUND] **:** pleasing to the ear

mel·li·su·gent \,melə¦süjənt\ *adj* [*mell-* + L *sugent-*, *sugens*, pres. part. of *sugere* to suck — more at SUCK] **:** feeding by sucking up honey or nectar

mel·li·tate \'melə,tāt\ *n* -s [*mellitic* + *-ate*] **:** a salt or ester of mellitic acid

mel·lite \'me,līt\ *n* -s [NL *mellites*, fr. *mell-* + *-ites* -ite; trans. of G *honigstein*] **1 :** a honey-colored mineral $Al_2C_{12}O_{12}.18H_2O$ that is a hydrous aluminum mellitate found in brown coal and is in part a product of vegetable decomposition **2** [ISV *mell-* + *-ite*] **:** a medicinal preparation containing honey

mel·lit·ic acid \(')me¦lid·ik-, mə'l-\ *n* [*mellite* + *-ic*] **:** a crystalline acid $C_6(COOH)_6$ occurring in the form of its aluminum salt as the mineral mellite and also made synthetically (as by oxidation of coal or graphite); benzene-hexa-carboxylic acid

melliturία *var of* MELITURIA

mel·liv·o·ra \me'livərə, mə'l-\ *n, cap* [NL, fr. *mell-* + *-vora*] **:** a genus of mustelid mammals consisting of the ratel

mel·liv·o·rous \(')me¦livərəs, mə'l-\ *adj* [*mell-* + *-vorous*] **:** MELIPHAGOUS

mel·lon *or* **mel·on** \'me,län\ *n* -s [G *mellon*, irreg. fr. *melam* + *-on*, -one] **:** a yellow powder $C_6H_3N_9$ formed on heating various cyanogen compounds or as a by-product in the preparation of melamine

mel·lo·phan·ic acid \¦melə¦fanik-\ *n* [ISV *mellite* + *-o-* + Gk *phan-* (stem of *phainesthai* to appear, pass. of *phainein* to show) + ISV *-ic* — more at FANCY] **:** either of two isomeric acids derived from benzene: **a :** PREHNITIC ACID **b b :** a crystalline acid $C_6H_2(COOH)_4$ formed by oxidation of isodurene; 1,2,3,5-benzene-tetracarboxylic acid

mel·lo·phone \'melə,fōn\ *n* ['*mellow* + *-phone*] **:** an althorn in circular form sometimes used as a substitute for the French horn

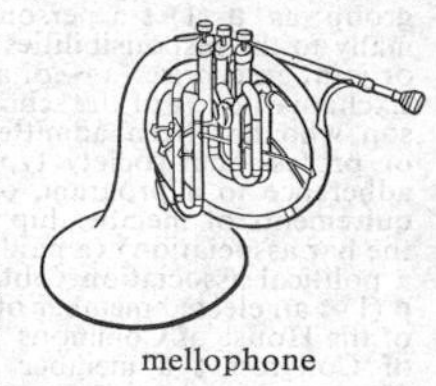

mellophone

¹mel·low \'me(,)lō, -lə; -ləw, -,lō+V\ *adj* -ER/-EST [ME *melwe*, *melowe*] **1 :** fully matured: as **a** *of a fruit* **:** having attained the flavor, sweetness, and softness of perfect ripeness **:** soft in substance and sweet in taste ⟨bit into a ~ peach⟩ **b** *of a wine* **:** adequately and properly aged so as to be free of harshness or acidity **:** mild and pleasing in flavor ⟨a ~ port⟩ **c :** having attained to softness, gentleness, or kindliness through aging and experience **:** freed from the rashness or harshness of youth ⟨~ wisdom⟩ ⟨the peace of ~ age⟩ **2 a** *of soil* **:** rich and easily worked **:** of soft and loamy consistency **b** (1) **:** free from coarseness, roughness, or harshness **:** rich and full but free from garishness or stridency — used esp. of sound, color, style ⟨the ~ tones of an old violin⟩ ⟨furnished the room with ~ old fabrics and richly polished woods⟩ (2) *of a speech sound* **:** characterized by no friction or by friction that is comparatively mild in that there is only one friction-producing component in the articulation ⟨\t\ is frictionless and ~; \th\, which has tongue-teeth friction only, is ~; but \sh\, which has both tongue-teeth and tongue-palate friction, is not⟩ — compare STRIDENT **c** *of livestock* **:** having a hide that is soft, sleek, and flexible to the touch **3 a :** somewhat intoxicated **:** warmed and relaxed by liquor **b :** relaxed and at ease **:** pleasantly convivial **:** GENIAL **4 a** *of a chemical solution* **:** weakened by use or materially altered in the course of time (as by bacterial action) **b** *of a process* **:** involving use of a mild solution to obtain mild results — **mel·low·ly** *adv* — **mel·low·ness** *n* -ES

²mellow \"\ *vb* -ED/-ING/-S *vt* **:** to make mellow ~ *vi* **:** to become mellow ⟨grapes ~*ing* in the sun⟩

mellow bug *n, chiefly South & Midland* **:** WHIRLIGIG BEETLE

mel·lowy \'meləw|ē, -lō|, |i\ *adj* [ME *melowy*, fr. *melwe*, *meluwe* + *-y*] *archaic* **:** MELLOW, SOFT

mells *pl of* MELL, *pres 3d sing of* MELL

mell supper *n* **:** HARVEST HOME 2

mel·ly \'melē\ *archaic var of* MELLAY

¹melo \'me(,)lō, 'me(-\ [NL, fr. LL, melon — more at MELON] *syn of* CYMBIUM

²melo \'me(,)lō, -,lə; -,ləw,-,lō+V\ *n* -s [by shortening] **:** MELODRAMA

¹melo- *comb form* [F *mélo-*, fr. Gk *melo-*, fr. *melos* limb, musical phrase, melody, song — more at MELODY] **:** song ⟨*melo*logue⟩ ⟨*melo*mania⟩

²melo- — see MEL-

mel·o·cactus \¦melə+\ *n, cap* [NL, fr. LL *melo* melon + NL *Cactus*] **:** a genus comprising tropical American strongly ribbed globose, spheroidal, or short cylindrical cacti with a terminal woolly or spiny cap that in many classifications are divided among several other genera — see CACTUS 1

mel·o·co·ton \¦meləkə¦tōn, -tän\ *also* **mel·o·co·toon** \-tün\ *n* -s [Sp *melocotón* melocoton, peach, fr. ML *melum cotonium* quince, alter. of L *malum cotonium*, fr. *malum* apple (fr. Gk *mēlon*) + *cotonium*, *cotoneum* quince — more at QUINCE] **:** a peach grafted on a quince rootstock and formerly supposed to have special qualities of excellence

me·lo·de·on \mə̇'lōdēən\ *n* -s [alter. of *melodion*] **1 :** AMERICAN ORGAN **2** *archaic* **:** MUSIC HALL

me·lo·dia \-ēə\ *n* -s [LL — more at MELODY] **1 :** MELODY, SONG **2 :** an 8-foot labial organ stop with wood pipes and tone of soft flute quality

me·lo·di·al \mə'lōdēəl, me'-\ *adj* **:** relating to melody — **me·lo·di·al·ly** \-ēəlē\ *adv*

me·lod·ic \mə̇'lädik, me'-, -dēk\ *adj* [LL *melodicus*, fr. Gk *melōidikos*, fr. *melōidia* melody + *-ikos* -ic — more at MELODY] **:** relating to, containing, constituting, or characterized by melody **:** MELODIOUS — **me·lod·i·cal·ly** \-dək(ə)lē, -dēk-, -li\ *adv*

melodic curve *n* **:** the curve described by the successive musical notes or tones of a melody

melodic minor scale *n* **:** a minor scale with the ascending intervals between the scale tones consisting of whole steps except those between two and three and seven and eight and with the descending intervals corresponding to the pattern of the natural minor scale with half steps between six and five and three and two

me·lod·i·con \-dəkən\ *n* -s [NL, fr. Gk *melōidikon*, neut. of *melōidikos* melodic] **:** a keyboard musical instrument invented about 1800 that gave its tones from tuning forks or steel bars

me·lo·di·on \-'lōdēən\ *n* -s [G, fr. *melodie* melody, fr. OF] **1 :** a keyboard musical instrument invented in 1806 consisting of graduated metal rods sounded by contact with a revolving cylinder **2 :** AMERICAN ORGAN

me·lo·di·ous \mə'lōdēəs, me'-\ *adj* [ME, fr. MF *melodieus*, fr. ML *melodiosus*, fr. LL *melodia* + L *-osus* -ous — more at MELODY] **1 :** agreeable to the ear by a sweet succession of sounds **2 :** producing or designed to produce melody ⟨a ~ instrument⟩ ⟨these ~ poets⟩ **3 a :** containing, constituting, or characterized by melody **b :** having a melody — **melodiously** *adv* — **melodiousness** *n* -ES

mel·o·dism \'melə,dizəm\ *n* -s **:** preferential use of melody

mel·o·dist \-,də̇st\ *n* -s **1 :** SINGER **2 :** a composer of melodies ⟨was not a really first-rate composer, only an agreeable ~ —Arnold Bennett⟩

mel·o·dize \-,dīz\ *vb* -ED/-ING/-S *vt* **:** to make melodious **:** set to melody ~ *vi* **:** to make melody **:** compose a melody — **mel·o·diz·er** \-zə(r)\ *n* -s

melo·drama \'melə+,-\ *n* [modif. (influenced by *drama*) of F *mélodrame*, fr. *mélo-* ¹melo- + *drame* drama, fr. LL *drama* — more at DRAMA] **1 a :** a romantic sensational stage play interspersed with songs and orchestral music **b :** a recitation of a dramatic or lyric text to a musical background — compare DUODRAMA, MONODRAMA **2 a :** a play characterized by extravagant theatricality, subordination of characterization to plot, and predominance of physical action **b :** the genre of dramatic literature constituted by such plays **3 :** something resembling a melodrama; *esp* **:** melodramatic events or behavior ⟨a monster of villainy whose life and death prove that the most lurid ~ still exists —Richard Watts⟩

melo·dramatic *also* **melo·dramatical** \¦melə+\ *adj* [*melodrama* + *-tic*, *-tical* (as in *dramatic*, *dramatical*)] **1 :** of, relating to, or characteristic of melodrama **2 :** suitable to melodrama esp. in being sensational in situation or action — **melo·dramatically** \"+\ *adv*

melo·dramatics \,melə+\ *n pl but sing or pl in constr* **:** melodramatic conduct or writing

melo·dramatist \"+\ *n* [*melodrama* + *-tist* (as in *dramatist*)] **:** a writer of melodramas

melo·dramatize \"+\ *vt* [*melodrama* + *-tize* (as in *dramatize*)] **1 :** to make melodramatic ⟨*melodramatizing* a situation⟩ **2 :** to make a melodrama of (as a novel)

mel·o·drame \'melə,dräm, -ram\ *n* -s [F *mélodrame* — more at MELODRAMA] *archaic* **:** MELODRAMA ⟨worn by the hero of a ~ —J.P.Kennedy †1870⟩

¹mel·o·dy \'melədē, -di\ *n* -ES [ME *melodie*, fr. OF, fr. LL *melodia*, fr. Gk *melōidia* chanting, singing, choral song, music, fr. *melos* limb, musical phrase, melody, song + *-ōidia* (fr. *aeidein* to sing); akin to Bret *mell* joint, articulation, Corn *mel*, W *cymal* joint, articulation, Toch A & Toch B *mälk* to fit together, Skt *marman* limb of the body — more at ODE] **1 :** a sweet or agreeable succession or arrangement of sounds **:** musical quality **:** TUNEFULNESS ⟨lulled with sound of sweetest ~ —Shak.⟩ **2 a** (1) **:** a rhythmically organized and meaningful succession of single musical notes or tones having a definite relationship one with the other and forming an esthetic whole (2) **:** the melodic unit so formed **b :** a musical line as it appears on the staff when viewed horizontally — compare HARMONY, RHYTHM **c :** the chief or principal part in a harmonic composition (as the cantus firmus) **3 :** something (as color in a painting) likened to or exhibiting a quality suggestive of musical melody

²melody \"\ *vb* -ED/-ING/-ES *vi* **:** to make melody **:** SING ~ *vt* **:** to make melody of

mel·o·dy·less \-ləs\ *adj* **:** lacking melody

mel·oe \'melə,wē\ *n* [NL] **1** *cap* **:** a widely distributed genus of beetles that is type of the family Meloidae and comprises the oil beetles **2** -s **:** OIL BEETLE

melo·farce \'melō+,-\ *n* [*melodrama* + *farce*] **:** melodrama of farcically exaggerated character

mel·o·gram·ma·ta·ce·ae \,melə,gramə'tāsē,ē\ *n pl, cap* [NL, fr. *Melogrammat-*, *Melogramma*, type genus (fr. *mela-* + Gk *grammat-*, *gramma* letter) + *-aceae* — more at GRAM] **:** a small family of fungi (order Sphaeriales) with perithecia sunken in pulvinate stromata and one-celled to many-celled ascospores

mel·o·graph \'melə,graf, -rȧf\ *n* [¹*melo-* + *-graph*] **:** a mechanical device for notating keyboard music through recording the action of the keys by stencil

¹mel·oid \'me,lōid, 'meləwəd\ *adj* [NL *Meloidae*] **:** of or relating to the Meloidae

²meloid \"\ *n* -s [NL *Meloidae*] **:** a beetle of the family Meloidae

me·loi·dae \mə̇'lōə,dē, -lȯi,-\ *n pl, cap* [NL, fr. *Meloe*, type genus + *-idae*] **:** a widely distributed family of moderate-sized usu. rather soft-bodied cylindrical beetles that exhibit a complex hypermetamorphosis during development, are often defoliators as adults, and include some whose larvae are beneficial predators on other insects — see BLISTER BEETLE, MELOE

me·loi·do·gyne \mə̇'lȯidə,jīn, -gīn\ *n, cap* [NL, fr. Gk *mēlon* apple, gourd + *-oeidēs* -oid + *gynē* woman — more at QUEEN] **:** a genus related to *Heterodera* and comprising the typical root-knot nematodes

mel·o·logue \'melə,lȯg *also* -läg\ *n* -s [¹*melo-* + *-logue*] **1 :** vocal and instrumental music interspersed with spoken declamation — compare MELODRAMA 1 **2 :** a spoken declamation with musical accompaniment

¹mel·o·lon·thid \¦melə¦län(t)thə̇d\ *adj* [NL *Melolonthidae*] **:** of or relating to the Melolonthidae

²melolonthid \"\ *n* -s [NL *Melolonthidae*] **:** a beetle of the family Melolonthidae

mel·o·lon·thi·dae \,melə'län(t)thə,dē\ *n pl, cap* [NL, fr. *Melolontha*, type genus (fr. Gk *mēlolonthē* cockchafer) + *-idae*] **:** a family of beetles closely related to and often included as a subfamily of Scarabaeidae — see COCKCHAFER — **mel·o·lon·thine** \¦==¦län(t)thən\ *adj*

mel·o·lon·thoid \¦==¦län,thȯid\ *adj* [NL *Melolonthidae* + E *-oid*] **:** resembling or like that of the Melolonthidae; *esp*, *of a beetle larva* **:** having a strongly curved body and small but definite thoracic legs

mel·o·mane \'melə,mān\ *adj* [F *mélomane*, fr. *mélo-* ¹melo- + *-mane* manic (back-formation fr. *manie* mania, fr. NL *mania*) — more at MANIA] **:** exhibiting melomania

melo·mania \,melə+\ *n* [NL, fr. *melo-* + *mania*] **:** an inordinate liking for music or melody **:** excessive or abnormal attraction to music

melo·maniac \"+\ *n* [¹*melo-* + *maniac*] **1 :** a musical enthusiast **:** one exhibiting melomania **2 :** an individual (as a person or dog) that is inordinately and abnormally affected by musical or other tones in certain ranges of sound

¹mel·on \'melən, *dial* 'milyən\ *n* -s *often attrib* [ME *meloun*, fr. MF *melon*, fr. LL *melon-*, *melo*, short for L *melopepon-*, *melopepo*, fr. Gk *mēlopepōn*, fr. *mēlon* apple + *pepōn*, a kind of edible gourd — more at PUMPKIN] **1 a :** either of two soft-fleshed sweet-flavored pepos that are usu. eaten raw as a fruit: (1) **:** MUSKMELON (2) **:** WATERMELON **b** *or* **melon vine :** a plant that bears melons **2 :** something suggesting a muskmelon or watermelon esp. in roundness ⟨graceful ~ sleeves⟩: as **a** *archaic* **:** STAPHYLOMA **b :** a rounded mass of blubber found between the blowhole and the end of the nose in the grampus and several other cetaceans **c** *slang* **:** an abdomen that protrudes (as from fat or pregnancy) **3 :** a strong yellowish pink that is redder and less strong than salmon pink, yellower and paler than peach red or madder scarlet, and redder and paler than average salmon **4 a :** a large surplus of profits available for distribution to stockholders ⟨the shareholders cut a ~ of nearly a million dollars⟩ **b :** an abundant and usu. nonrecurrent or irregular amount (as of profits or spoils) shared or available for sharing among various individuals — compare PLUM 4

²mel·on \'me,län\ *var of* MELLON

³mel·on \'melən\ *n* -s [by shortening] *Austral* **:** PADEMELON

melon aphid *n* **:** COTTON APHID

melon apple *n* **:** MANGO MELON

melon beetle *n* **:** either of two chrysomelid beetles (*Diabrotica vittata* and *D. duodecimpunctata*) injurious to melons

melon cactus *n* **:** a plant of the genus *Melocactus*

melon fly *n* **:** a small two-winged fly (*Dacus cucurbitae*) whose maggot is destructive to melons, other cucurbits, and tomatoes esp. in Hawaii
melon foot *n* **:** a ball foot carved with ridges
melon fruit *n* **:** PAPAYA
mel·on·ge·na \ˌmelənˈjēnə\ *n* [NL, fr. It dial. *melongiana, melangiana*, fr. Ar *bādhinjān* — more at BRINJAL] **1** -S **:** EGGPLANT **2 a** *cap* **:** a genus of tropical marine mollusks (family Xancidae) **b** -S **:** a mollusk of this genus; *esp* **:** a large edible Caribbean mollusk (*M. corona*) that resembles a whelk
mel·on·gene \ˈmelənˌjēn\ *n* -S [F *mélongène*, fr. NL *melongena*] *chiefly Brit* **:** EGGPLANT
melon hole *n* [³*melon*] **:** one of the shallow holes that honeycomb the soil of parts of interior Australia and are attributed esp. to the burrowing of pademelons

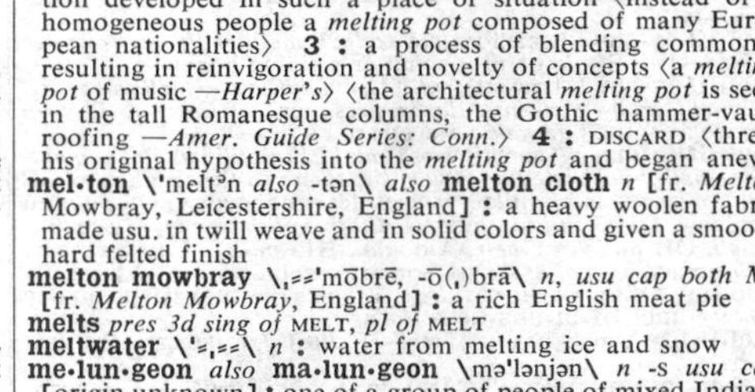
melon foot

mel·on·ist \ˈmelənə̇st\ *n* -S **:** a melon grower
mel·o·nite \ˈmeləˌnīt\ *n* -S [*Melones* mine, Calaveras county, Calif., its locality + E *-ite*] **:** a mineral $NiTe_2$ consisting of a nickel telluride and occurring in California
melon lo·co \ˌmelənˈlō(ˌ)kō, məˌlōn-\ *n* [MexSp *melón loco*, lit., crazy melon] **:** a rough creeping cucurbitaceous vine (*Apodanthera undulata*) of the southwestern U. S. and adjacent Mexico that has a small fruit resembling a gourd and containing seeds rich in oil
melon louse *n* **:** COTTON APHID
melon pear *n* **:** PEPINO
melon pink *n* **:** a vivid yellowish pink
mel·on·ry \ˈmelənrē\ *n* -ES **:** a place for growing melons
melon seed *n* **:** a small wide shallow-draft sailboat with centerboard and a single-boomed spritsail that was formerly built in New Jersey for use in choppy inshore waters
melon shell *n* **:** any of several very large ovoid and often lustrous and richly colored gastropod mollusks constituting the genus *Cymbium* and being widely distributed in the southwestern Pacific ocean — called also *bailer shell, boat shell*
melon tree *n* **:** PAPAYA 1
melonworm \ˈ=ˌ=ˌ=\ *n* **:** a small caterpillar that is the larva of a white and black pyralidid moth (*Diaphania hyalinata*) and that is destructive to melons and other cucurbits by feeding on the foliage and immature fruits
melon yellow *n* **:** a variable color averaging a light orange yellow
me·loph·a·gus \məˈläfəgəs\ *n, cap* [NL, fr. Gk *mēlon* sheep + NL *-phagus* — more at SMALL] **:** a genus of wingless hippoboscid flies that includes the sheep ked
mel·o·phon·ic \ˌmeləˈfänik\ *adj* [¹*melo-* + Gk *phōnē* sound, voice + E *-ic* — more at PHONE] **:** relating to music or to its performance
mel·o·pho·nist \ˈmeləˌfōnə̇st, məˈläfən-\ *n* -S [¹*melo-* + Gk *phōnē* + E *-ist*] **:** MELODIST
melo·piano \ˌmelō+\ *n* [¹*melo-* + *piano*] **:** a piano equipped with a pedal attachment for prolonging a tone at will by means of a series of rapidly striking supplementary hammers
mel·o·plas·ty \ˈmeləˌplastē\ *n* -ES [ISV ³*mel-* + *-plasty*] **:** the restoration of a cheek by plastic surgery
mel·o·poe·ia \ˌmeləˈpē(y)ə\ *n* -S [LL, fr. Gk *melopoiia*, fr. *melopoiein* to write a lyric poem, to set to music, fr. *melo-* ¹melo- + *poiein* to make — more at POET] **1 :** MELODY **2 :** the art or theory of inventing melody
mel·o·po·et·ic \ˌmeləpōˈedˌik\ *also* **mel·o·poe·ic** \-ləˈpēik\ *adj* [*melopoetic* fr. ¹*melo* + *poetic*; *melopoeic* fr. *melopoeia* + *-ic*] **:** of, relating to, or involving melopoeia — **mel·o·po·et·i·cal·ly** \-ləpōˈedə̇k(ə)lē\ *adv*
¹**melos** \ˈmeˌläs, ˈmēˌ-\ *n* -ES [Gk — more at MELODY] **:** SONG, MELODY; *esp* **:** characteristic tone succession considered apart from rhythm — compare ¹MODE 1
²**melos** *pl of* MELO
me·lo·sa \məˈlōsə\ *n* -S [AmerSp, fr. Sp, fem. of *meloso* of honey, resembling honey, fr. LL *mellosus*, fr. L *mell-* + *-osus* -ous] **:** a So. American herb (*Madia sativa*) with glandular viscid foliage
mel·o·spi·za \ˌmeləˈspīzə\ *n, cap* [NL, fr. ¹*melo-* + Gk *spiza* chaffinch — more at FINCH] **:** a genus of birds (family Fringillidae) containing the American song sparrow and swamp sparrow
me·lothria \məˈläthrēə, -lōth-\ *n, cap* [NL, fr. Gk *mēlōthron*, a kind of white grape + NL *-ia*] **:** a genus of chiefly tropical monoecious herbaceous vines (family Cucurbitaceae) with white or yellow flowers, an elongated ovary, and a fruit resembling a typical berry that are cultivated as ornamentals
mel·o·trope \ˈmeləˌtrōp\ *n* -S [¹*melo-* + *-trope*] **:** a piano having a mechanical device for playing music from a stencil previously recorded by a melograph
mels *pl of* MEL
melsh *var of* MELCH
¹**melt** \ˈmelt\ *vb* **melted** \-tə̇d\ **melted** \ˈ"\ *also* **mol·ten** \ˈmōltᵊn *also* -tən\ **melting; melts** [ME *melten*, fr. OE *meltan*, v.i., & *mieltan*, v.t., causative fr. the root of *meltan*; akin to ON *melta* to malt for brewing, to digest, Goth *gamalteins* departure, L *mollis* soft, Gk *meldein* to melt, Skt *mṛdnāti* he squeezes, rubs, L *molere* to grind — more at MEAL] *vi* **1 a :** to change from a solid to a liquid state usu. by the action of heat ⟨ice ~*ing* in the sun⟩ ⟨gold ~*s* at 1945°F⟩ **b :** to be or become extremely hot **:** run with perspiration ⟨~*ing* in heavy winter clothing⟩ **2 a :** DISSOLVE, DISINTEGRATE ⟨sugar ~*ing* in hot coffee⟩ **b :** to disappear as if dissolving **:** become dispersed, dissipated, or wholly consumed ⟨the morning fog usu. ~*s* as the sun rises in the sky⟩ ⟨their determination ~*ed* in the face of increasing hazards⟩ — often used with *away* ⟨their money ~*ed* away on unexpected expenses⟩ ⟨sometimes a tumor will ~ completely under adequate irradiation⟩ **3** *obs* **:** to become subdued, prostrated, or crushed (as by sorrow or remorse) **4 :** to become softened **:** become mild, tender, or gentle ⟨~*ed* at his kindly words⟩ **5 :** to become absorbed **6 :** to lose distinct individuality of outline **:** blend or blur by imperceptible degrees — usu. used with *into* ⟨the brown foothills ~*ing* into the steeper slopes⟩ ~ *vt* **1 a :** to reduce (as a metal) from a solid to a liquid state usu. by the action of heat ⟨~ wax over a flame⟩ — often used with *down* ⟨~*ed* down the family plate⟩ **b** *obs* **:** to form by melting **:** form from melted material **2 a** *archaic* **:** to cause to dissolve or disintegrate **b :** to cause to disappear or disperse ⟨the sun ~*ed* the clouds⟩ **3 a :** to make tender, gentle, or susceptible to mild influences **:** SOFTEN ⟨the child's tears ~*ed* his determination⟩ **b** *obs* **:** to take away the firmness of **:** WEAKEN, ENERVATE **4 :** to cause to merge insensibly (as colors, sounds, or outlines) **:** cause to fuse **:** BLEND **5** *slang Brit* **:** SPEND ⟨~*ing* his money⟩ **:** CASH ⟨~ a check⟩ — **melt in one's mouth :** to be of notable tenderness of texture or sometimes delicacy of flavor ⟨turns out pastry that *melts in your mouth*⟩
²**melt** \ˈ"\ *n* -S **1 a :** a melted substance **:** material in the molten state ⟨glass, being a ~ and not a crystal, has an immense range in both chemical composition and physical properties —G.F.H. Smith⟩ **b :** the mass melted at a single operation or the quantity melted during a certain period **2 a :** an act or process of melting **b :** the condition of being melted
³**melt** \ˈ"\ *also* **milt** \ˈmilt\ *n* -S [ME *milte*, fr. OE; akin to OHG *milzi* spleen, ON *milti*, and prob. to OE *meltan* to melt — more at ¹MELT] **:** SPLEEN; *esp* **:** spleen of slaughtered animals for use as food or feed ⟨use of hog ~ in mink rations⟩
⁴**melt** *var of* MILT
melt·abil·i·ty \ˌmeltəˈbilə̇d·ē\ *n* **:** the quality or state of being meltable
melt·able \ˈmeltəbəl\ *adj* **:** capable of or suitable for melting
melt·age \-tij\ *n* -S **:** the act, result, or amount of melting ⟨slow ~ of ice⟩
meltdown \ˈ=ˌ=\ *n* -S [fr. *melt down*, v.] **:** the process or course of melting something (as scrap metal or ice cream)
¹**melt·er** \ˈmeltə(r)\ *n* -S **1 :** one (as a melting pot) that melts or is used for melting **2 :** one whose work is melting: as **a :** one who melts metal in a foundry furnace; *esp* **:** a worker in charge of the melting and purifying of scrap iron in the production of steel **b :** one who melts and molds silver or gold for use in making jewelry **c :** one who refines magnesium crystals into pure magnesium in a crucible furnace

²**melt·er** \ˈ"\ *archaic var of* MILTER
melt·ers \-tə(r)z\ *n pl but sing or pl in constr* [¹*melt* + *-ers* (as in *glanders*)] **:** LEAK 3
mel·teth \ˈmelˌteth\ *or* **mel·tith** \-ˌtith\ *n* -S [ME *meltid* — more at MEALTIDE] *Scot* **:** MEALTIME
melt·ing·ly *adv* **:** so as to melt **:** in a melting manner **:** DELICATELY, TENDERLY ⟨a ~ flavored peach⟩ ⟨gazed at him ~⟩
melt·ing·ness *n* -ES **:** the quality or state of being melting
melting out *n* -S [fr. gerund of *melt out*, v.] **:** a disease of turf grasses caused by fungi of the genus *Helminthosporium* and characterized by a bluish cast of irregularly shaped areas which later turn yellow and die out
melting point *n* **:** the temperature at which a solid melts **:** FREEZING POINT ⟨the *melting point* of ice is 0°C or 32°F⟩
melting pot *n* **1 :** a vessel (as a crucible) in which something is melted **2 a :** a place or situation where racial amalgamation and sociocultural assimilation are taking place ⟨the United States, Israel, and Brazil are great *melting pots*⟩ **b :** a population developed in such a place or situation ⟨instead of a homogeneous people a *melting pot* composed of many European nationalities⟩ **3 :** a process of blending commonly resulting in reinvigoration and novelty of concepts ⟨a *melting pot* of music —*Harper's*⟩ ⟨the architectural *melting pot* is seen in the tall Romanesque columns, the Gothic hammer-vault roofing —*Amer. Guide Series: Conn.*⟩ **4 :** DISCARD ⟨threw his original hypothesis into the *melting pot* and began anew⟩
mel·ton \ˈmeltᵊn *also* -tən\ *also* **melton cloth** *n* [fr. *Melton* Mowbray, Leicestershire, England] **:** a heavy woolen fabric made usu. in twill weave and in solid colors and given a smooth hard felted finish
melton mowbray \ˌ==ˈmōbrē, -ō(ˌ)brā\ *n, usu cap both Ms* [fr. *Melton Mowbray*, England] **:** a rich English meat pie
melts *pres 3d sing of* MELT, *pl of* MELT
meltwater \ˈ=ˌ==\ *n* **:** water from melting ice and snow
me·lun·geon *also* **ma·lun·geon** \məˈlənjən\ *n* -S *usu cap* [origin unknown] **:** one of a group of people of mixed Indian, white, and Negro ancestry in the southern Appalachians esp. of eastern Tennessee
mel·ur·sus \meˈlərsəs\ *n, cap* [NL, fr. L *mel* honey + *ursus* bear — more at MELLIFLUOUS, ARCTIC] **:** a genus of large Asiatic mammals (family Ursidae) consisting of the sloth bear
-me·lus \ˌmələs\ *n comb form, pl* **-meli** [NL, fr. Gk *melos* limb — more at MELODY] **:** one having a (specified) abnormality of the limbs ⟨*anisomelus*⟩ ⟨*ectromelus*⟩
Mel·u·sine \ˌmel(y)əˈsēn\ *trademark* — used for a silky long-haired felt for hats
mel·vie \ˈmelvi\ *vt* [prob. alter. of *melwie*, fr. ME *melw-*, stem of *mele* meal — more at MEAL] *archaic Scot* **:** to cover with meal
¹**mem** \ˈmem\ *n* -S [Heb *mēm*, lit., water] **1 :** the 13th letter of the Hebrew alphabet — symbol מ; see ALPHABET table **2 :** the letter of the Phoenician or any of various other Semitic alphabets corresponding to Hebrew mem
²**mem** \ˈmem\ *n* -S [alter. of *ma'am*] **:** MADAM 1
mem *abbr* **1** member **2** memento **3** memoir **4** memorandum **5** memorial
mem·ber \ˈmembə(r)\ *n* -S *often attrib* [ME *membre*, fr. OF, fr. L *membrum*; akin to Goth *mimz* flesh, OIr *mīr* bite, Gk *mēninx* membrane, *mēros* thigh, Skt *māṁsa* flesh; basic meaning: flesh] **1 a :** a bodily part or organ ⟨a lolling, impudent tongue — a truly unruly ~ —E.J.Banfield⟩ ⟨the thyroid gland . . . may be the offending ~ —H.A.Overstreet⟩; *specif* **:** a part (as a limb) that projects from the main mass of the body ⟨a man with sandy hair and large bodily ~*s* —G.S.Perry⟩ **b :** PENIS ⟨let my ~ turn to dust —William Goyen⟩ **c :** a unit of structure in a plant body ⟨a vessel ~⟩ **2 :** one who forms part of a metaphorical or metaphysical body ⟨~*s* of Christ⟩ ⟨we are ~*s* one of another —Eph 4:25 (RSV)⟩ **3 :** one of the individuals composing a society, community, association, or other group: as **a** (1) **:** a person who has been admitted usu. formally to the responsibilities and privileges of some association or joint enterprise ⟨a ~ of a law firm⟩ ⟨a ~ of the N.Y. Stock Exchange⟩ ⟨a ~ of the school's governing board⟩ (2) **:** a person who has been admitted usu. formally into some social or professional society typically requiring payment of dues, adherence to a program, or compliance with some other requirements of membership ⟨a ~ of a women's club⟩ ⟨~*s* of the bar association⟩ ⟨a paid-up ~⟩ **b :** a branch or affiliate of a political association ⟨obtained the support of all ~ states⟩ **c** (1) **:** an elected member of the British Parliament **:** a member of the House of Commons (2) **:** a member of the lower house of Congress **:** a member of the House of Representatives (3) **:** a person having membership in any of numerous legislative bodies **d** *obs* **:** a participant or associate in an action or benefit **e :** a church communicant **:** a person baptized or enrolled in a church **f :** one of the persons composing a territorial, kinship, or sociological unit ⟨~*s* of the immediate family attended the funeral⟩ ⟨alert and responsible ~*s* of their communities —*Official Register of Harvard Univ.*⟩ ⟨~*s* of the middle class⟩ ⟨~*s* of a tribe⟩ **4 :** a constituent part of a whole: as **a :** a section or district of an estate, port, or other territorial unit **b** (1) **:** a syntactic or rhythmic unit of a sentence **:** CLAUSE (2) **:** one of the propositions of a syllogism **c :** one of the elements of which a mathematical aggregate is composed **d** (1) **:** a part of a building or other structure whether constructional (as a pier or lintel) or decorative (as a molding) (2) **:** an essential part of a framed structure, a machine, or a device ⟨the design of compression ~*s* of bridge trusses —*U.S. Nat'l Bureau of Standards Annual Report*⟩ **e :** a minor stratigraphic unit of a geologic formation **f :** something belonging to a class or category ⟨*x* is a ~ of *A*⟩ ⟨a ~ of a species⟩ ⟨one who philosophizes is a ~ of the class of philosophers⟩ **syn** see PART
member bank *n* **:** a bank having membership in the Federal Reserve System
mem·bered \ˈmembə(r)d\ *adj* [ME *membred*, fr. *membre* member + *-ed*] **1 :** consisting of or divided into members ⟨a ~ body⟩ **2** *heraldry* **:** depicted with legs of a specified tincture differing from that of the body — used chiefly of a bird
mem·ber·less \ˈmembə(r)ləs\ *adj* **:** having no member ⟨the organization is still ~⟩
mem·ber·ship \-)ˌship\ *n* **1 :** the state or status of being a member **2 :** the body of members (as of a society) **3 :** the relation between a member of a class and the class — contrasted with *inclusion*
membership star *n* **:** a small gilt star worn by brownie scouts and girl scouts for each year of troop membership

membership star

¹**mem·bra·cid** \ˈmembrəsə̇d, (ˈ)mem-ˈbras-\ *adj* [NL *Membracidae*] **:** of or relating to the Membracidae
²**membracid** \ˈ"\ *n* -S [NL *Membracidae*] **:** an insect of the family Membracidae **:** TREEHOPPER
mem·brac·i·dae \memˈbrasəˌdē\ *n pl, cap* [NL, fr. *Membracis*, type genus (fr. Gk *membrak-, membrax* cicada) + *-idae*] **:** a large family of Homoptera consisting of the treehoppers
¹**mem·bra·cine** \ˈmembrəˌsīn\ *adj* [NL *Membracis* + E *-ine*] **:** MEMBRACID
²**membracine** \ˈ"\ *n* -S **:** MEMBRACID
mem·bral \ˈmemb(ə)rəl\ *adj* [L *membrum* member + E *-al* — more at MEMBER] **:** of, relating to, or characteristic of a member — **mem·bral·ly** \-rəlē\ *adv*
membran- *or* **membrani-** *or* **membrano-** *comb form* [*membran-* fr. MF, fr. L, fr. *membrana* skin, membrane, parchment; *membrani-* & *membrano-* fr. NL, fr. L *membrana* — more at MEMBRANE] **1 :** membrane ⟨*membran*oid⟩ ⟨*membrani*ferous⟩ ⟨*Membrani*pora⟩ ⟨*membrano*genic⟩ **2** *usu* **membrano- :** membranous and ⟨*membrano*cartilaginous⟩ ⟨*membrano*nervous⟩
mem·bra·na \memˈbrānə, -rän-\ *n, pl* **mem·bra·nae** \-ˌā,nē, -ä,nī\ [L — more at MEMBRANE] **:** MEMBRANE
mem·bra·na·ceous \ˌmembrəˈnāshəs\ *adj* [L *membranaceus*, fr. *membran-* + *-aceus* -aceous] **:** MEMBRANOUS — **mem·bra·na·ceous·ly** *adv*
mem·bra·nate \ˈmembrəˌnāt, (ˈ)memˈbrānə̇t\ *adj* [*membran-* + *-ate*] **:** being, resembling, or having a membrane
mem·brane \ˈmemˌbrān *sometimes* -ˌbrən\ *n* -S [L *membrana* skin, membrane, parchment, fr. *membrum* member — more at MEMBER] **1 :** a thin soft pliable sheet or layer esp. of animal or vegetable origin **2 :** a limiting protoplasmic surface or interface — see CELL 5 **3 :** a piece of parchment forming part of a roll ⟨the pages in the . . . ~ usually were square and had two to four columns to the page —A.T.Robertson⟩
membrane bone *n* **:** a bone that ossifies directly in connective tissue without previous existence as cartilage
membrane curing *n* **:** a method of curing concrete usu. in pavements by which a material in liquid form is sprayed over the exposed surface shortly after the concrete is finished after which the material solidifies and becomes essentially impervious and thus holds the mixing water in the concrete so that it can hydrate the cement over a period of time
mem·braned \-nd\ *adj* **:** having a membrane
mem·brane·less \-nləs\ *adj* **:** being without a membrane
mem·bra·nel·lar \ˌmembrəˈnelə(r)\ *adj* **:** of, relating to, or constituting a membranelle
mem·bra·nelle \-l\ *also* **mem·bra·nel·la** \ˌ==ˈnelə\ *n, pl* **membra·nelles** \ˌ==ˈnelz\ *also* **membranel·lae** \ˌ==ˈne(ˌ)lē, -eˌlī\ [NL *membranella*, dim. of L *membrana* membrane — more at MEMBRANE] **:** a flattened vibrating organ like a membrane comprised of a row of fused cilia in various ciliates
membrane of cor·ti \-ˈkȯrd·ē, -ō(ə)rˌtē\ *usu cap C* [after Alfonso *Corti* †1876 Ital. anatomist] **:** a membrane overlying the organ of Corti
membrane of descemet *usu cap D* [after Jean *Descemet* †1810 Fr. anatomist] **:** DESCEMET'S MEMBRANE
membrane of hen·le \-ˈhenlē, -lə\ *usu cap H* [after Friedrich G. J. *Henle* †1885 Ger. pathologist and anatomist] **:** FENESTRATED MEMBRANE
membrane of krause *usu cap K* **:** KRAUSE'S MEMBRANE
mem·bra·ne·ous \(ˈ)memˈbrānēəs\ *adj* [L *membraneus* of parchment, fr. *membrana* membrane, parchment + *-eus* -eous — more at MEMBRANE] **:** MEMBRANOUS
membrani- — see MEMBRAN-
mem·bra·nip·o·ra \ˌmembrəˈnipərə\ *n, cap* [NL, fr. *membran-* + *-pora*] **:** a genus (the type of the family Membraniporidae) of colonial encrusting bryozoans (order Cheilostomata)
membrano- — see MEMBRAN-
mem·bra·noid \ˈmembrəˌnȯid\ *adj* [*membran-* + *-oid*] **:** like a membrane
mem·bra·no·phone \memˈbrānəˌfōn\ *n* [ISV *membran-* + *-phone*] **:** a musical instrument (as a drum or kazoo) having a tightly stretched membrane as a vibrator or resonator and made to vibrate by percussion or by friction — **mem·bra·no·phon·ic** \(ˌ)memˌbrānəˈfänik\ *adj*
mem·bra·nous \ˈmembrənəs, (ˈ)memˈbrān-\ *adj* [MF *membraneux*, fr. *membran-* + *-eux* -ous] **1 :** of, relating to, or resembling membrane ⟨a ~ lining⟩ **2 :** thin, pliable, and often somewhat transparent ⟨~ leaves⟩ **3 :** characterized or accompanied by the formation of a membrane or pseudomembrane ⟨~ croup⟩ ⟨~ gastritis⟩ — **mem·bra·nous·ly** *adv*
membranous labyrinth *n* **:** the sensory structures of the inner ear including the receptors of the labyrinthine sense and the cochlea — compare BONY LABYRINTH
mem·branu·la \memˈbrānyələ, -ran-\ *also* **mem·bra·nule** \ˈmembrəˌn(y)ül, memˈbrān(ˌ)yül\ *n* -S [NL, fr. L, small membrane, dim. of *membrana* membrane — more at MEMBRANE] **:** a fine structure like a membranelle formed by the fusion of a few long cilia (as in the posterior ciliary ring of vorticellids)
mem·brum \ˈmembrəm\ *n, pl* **mem·bra** \-rə\ [L, lit., member — more at MEMBER] **:** PENIS
me·men·to *also* **momento** \məˈmen(ˌ)tō, -n·(ˌ)tō\ *n, pl* **mementos** *or* **mementoes** [ME *memento*, fr. L, 2d sing. fut. imper. of *meminisse* to remember; akin to L *ment-, mens* mind — more at MIND] **1** *often cap* **:** either of two prayers in the canon of the Roman mass, one for the living and one for the dead, beginning with *memento* **2 a :** something that serves to warn or remind with regard to conduct or future events **b** *archaic* **:** REMINDER, WARNING **c** (1) **:** something that serves to remind or is a vestige (as of a past event or condition) **:** RELIC, TRACE ⟨covered with such ~*s* in several languages —Cyril Mango⟩ ⟨she was . . . a ~ of that era —Nancy Hale⟩ (2) **:** something that is kept in memory of a person or event **:** MEMORIAL, KEEPSAKE ⟨fond of carrying away ~*s* of so enjoyable an evening —Norman Douglas⟩ ⟨a state park contains ~*s* of early days —*Amer. Guide Series: Texas*⟩ **3 :** MEMORY, REMEMBRANCE ⟨the names of the streets . . . seem to fill you with terrible ~*s* —C.B.Fairbanks⟩
memento mo·ri \=ˌ=(ˌ)=ˈmȯr(ˌ)ē, -rˌī\ *n, pl* **memento mori** [L, remember that you must die] **1 :** a warning to be prepared for death ⟨that *memento mori* which it never ceases to din into the ears of the faithful —Paul Siwek⟩ **2 :** something that serves to remind of death ⟨the corpse of a bad philosophy is a powerful *memento mori* —J.H.Sledd⟩; *specif* **:** a death's head or other symbolic object used as a reminder of death ⟨two *memento mori* or mourning pieces —W.L.Warren⟩
meml *abbr* memorial
¹**memo** \ˈme(ˌ)mō *sometimes* ˈmē(-\ *n* -S [by shortening] **:** MEMORANDUM
²**memo** \ˈ"\ *vt* -ED/-ING/-S **1 :** to make a memorandum of or communicate in a memorandum ⟨~*ed* what she'd have to do —Bernard Malamud⟩ **2 :** to send a memorandum to ⟨we'll ~ you in the morning —A.C.Spectorsky⟩
mem·oir \ˈmemˌwär, -wä(r *also* -wȯ(ə)r *or* -wȯ(ə) *sometimes* ˈmem- *or* ˈmām- *or* -ˌmȯ- *or* -ˌmā- *or* -ˌmä- *or* =ˈ= *or* mamˈw- *or* məˈm-\ *n* -S [F *mémoire*, fr. *mémoire* memory, fr. L *memoria* — more at MEMORY] **1 :** an official note or report **:** MEMORANDUM, RECORD ⟨wrote a ~ on the subject for his royal master⟩ **2 a :** a history or narrative composed from or stressing personal experience and acquaintance with the events, scenes, or persons described ⟨a satirical ~ of the city of his birth —Saxe Commins⟩ — usu. used in pl. ⟨have written ~*s* of the event —Ruth McKenney⟩ **b :** an autobiographical account often anecdotal or intimate in tone whose focus of attention is usu. on the persons, events, or times known to the writer ⟨a best-selling ~ that a duke paid a fortune to keep unpublished —*N. Y. Herald Tribune*⟩ ⟨an autobiographical ~ by the dean of American literary historians —*Saturday Rev.*⟩ — usu. used in pl. ⟨in his ~*s* he describes the framework —*Amer. Guide Series: Minn.*⟩ ⟨a secret emergency fund . . . for the acquisition of just such ~*s* —S.H.Adams⟩ **c :** a biography or biographical sketch usu. based on personal acquaintance with the subject and sometimes having the character of a memorial ⟨a ~ of his brilliant pupil . . . who died early —Sarah G. Bowerman⟩ ⟨its spirit is so devout as to make it . . . more a ~ than a biography —A.J.Nock⟩ ⟨a ~ . . . by his colleague —Edmund Wilson⟩ **3 a :** an account of something regarded as noteworthy **:** a record of investigations of some subject **:** DISSERTATION, REPORT ⟨the work described and discussed in this ~ represents a first-class investigation —J.A.Steers⟩ **b memoirs** *pl* **:** the record of the proceedings of a learned society
mem·oir·ist \-ˌärə̇st, -ärə̇-, -ȯrə̇-\ *n* -S **:** a writer of a memoir
mem·o·ra·bilia \ˌmemərəˈbilēə, -bēl-, -lyə\ *n pl* [L, fr. neut. pl. of *memorabilis* memorable — more at MEMORABLE] **1 :** things remarkable and worthy of remembrance or record ⟨contains a . . . wealth of ~ of early Texas —*Amer. Guide Series: Texas*⟩; *also* **:** things that stir recollection **:** MEMENTOS ⟨more than twenty trunks of ~ —R.L.Taylor⟩ **2 :** a record of noteworthy things (as events)
mem·o·ra·bil·i·ty \ˌmem(ə)rəˈbilə̇d·ē, -lətē, -i\ *n* **:** the quality or state of being memorable
¹**mem·o·ra·ble** \ˈmem(ə)rəbəl, ˈmemərb-\ *adj* [ME, fr. L *memorabilis*, fr. *memorare* to remind (fr. *memor* mindful) + *-abilis* -able — more at MEMORY] **1 :** worthy of being remembered or noted **:** NOTABLE, DISTINGUISHED, IMPRESSIVE, SIGNIFICANT ⟨an early and ~ masterpiece —F.L.Mott⟩ ⟨considered his most ~ work —C.C.Walcutt⟩ ⟨the ~ winter of 1861⟩ ⟨the one ~ recording of the . . . sonata —Irving Kolodin⟩ **2 :** remembered or easy to remember — **mem·o·ra·ble·ness** \-bəlnə̇s\ *n* -ES — **mem·o·ra·bly** \-blē, -bli\ *adv*
²**memorable** \ˈ"\ *n* -S *archaic* **:** something that is memorable — usu. used in pl.
¹**mem·o·ran·dum** \ˌmeməˈrandəm, -raan-\ *n, pl* **memorandums** \-dəmz\ *or* **memoran·da** \-də\ [ME, fr. L, neut. of *memorandus* to be remembered, fut. pass. part. of *memorare* to remind — more at MEMORABLE] **1 a :** an informal record of something that one wishes to remember or preserve for future

use **:** a note to help or jog the memory **:** one of the notes in a diary ⟨this book . . . was assembled from his diaries, ~*s*, and letters —*New Yorker*⟩ **b :** MEMENTO, REMINDER **2 a** (1) **:** a brief or informal note in writing of some transaction or an outline of an intended instrument **:** an instrument drawn up in a brief and compendious form (2) **:** the clause beginning a record in the former Court of King's Bench in proceedings by bill (3) **:** MEMORANDUM OF ASSOCIATION (4) **:** the body of exceptions making up the clause in a marine insurance policy exempting the insurer wholly or partially from liability for loss on various articles **b** (1) **:** a statement by the shipper of the terms of a shipment sent with the privilege of return if not sold — used esp. in the jewelry trade (2) **:** the third or duplicate copy of a bill of lading **3 a :** an informal diplomatic communication; *specif* **:** a written statement from a department of state or a ministry of foreign affairs to an embassy or legation used esp. for routine transmissions or inquiries and never bearing a signature **b :** a usu. brief informal communication typically written for interoffice circulation on paper headed *memorandum* ⟨depend on countless *memoranda* for giving directions and for exchanging essential information —Milton Hall⟩ **c :** a routine publication by an authorized military headquarters containing directive, advisory, or informative matter

²**memorandum** \"\ *vt* -ED/-ING/-S **:** to make a memorandum of

memorandum decision *or* **memorandum opinion** *n* **1 :** a brief opinion of a court or a judge announcing the result of litigation without an extended discussion of the principles involved but sometimes with the citation of precedents — compare PER CURIAM DECISION **2 :** an opinion of the Tax Court of the U. S. that is ordered not to be published but that is authoritative as a precedent **3 :** an opinion of a court or a judge announcing the conclusions reached on the issues of fact and of law and giving directions as to the matters to be set forth in an order, judgment, or decree to be entered **4 :** an opinion of a court or a judge setting forth the conclusions reached on issues of fact and of law and containing the actual order, judgment, or decree of the court or judge

memorandum of association *Eng law* **:** a document resembling articles of association in the U. S. which in case of a company to be formed legally must be executed and filed to form the charter of the company

mem·o·ra·tive \ˈmeməˌrād·iv, ˈmem(ə)rəd·-\ *adj* [ME *memoratif*, fr. MF, fr. LL *memorativus*, fr. L *memoratus* (past part. of *memorare* to remind) + *-ivus* -ive — more at MEMORABLE] **1** *archaic* **:** COMMEMORATIVE **2 :** relating to the memory ⟨powers perfected by experience . . . estimative and ~ powers —G.P.Klubertanz⟩

¹**me·mo·ri·al** \məˈmōrēəl, -mȯr-\ *adj* [ME, fr. L *memorialis*, fr. *memoria* memory + *-alis* -al — more at MEMORY] **1 :** serving to preserve remembrance **:** COMMEMORATIVE ⟨a ~ building⟩ ⟨a ~ sketch⟩ ⟨a ~ showing of an artist's work⟩ **2 :** of or relating to memory **:** utilizing, caused by, or done from memory ⟨the scene had been gotten by shorthand or ~ method —C.A. Greer⟩ ⟨the bad quarto . . . is a ~ reconstruction —Leo Kirschbaum⟩ ⟨~ contamination of a manuscript⟩

²**memorial** \"\ *n* -S [ME, fr. LL *memoriale*, fr. L, neut. of *memorialis*, adj.] **1** *obs* **:** MEMORY, REMEMBRANCE, RECOLLECTION **2 a** (1) **:** something that serves to preserve memory or knowledge of an individual or event **:** RELIC, TRACE ⟨the form in which he expresses his emotion bears no ~ of any external form that may have provoked it —Clive Bell⟩ ⟨a ~ of those stormy feuds . . . is the thick oak door with its square hole —Brian Fitzgerald⟩ ⟨their bones remain . . . as ~*s* of a noble attempt —W.E.Swinton⟩ (2) **:** something that is kept to preserve the memory of a person or event **:** KEEPSAKE, MEMENTO ⟨carved walking stick, umbrella and best black hat still remained, sacred ~*s* —Rex Ingamells⟩ ⟨revive the liking for wearing ~*s* of the dead —Joan Evans⟩ (3) **:** something designed to commemorate or preserve the memory of a person or event ⟨his two-volume ~ to his father . . . was published —*Current Biog.*⟩ ⟨to visit this ~ to a former slave is a rewarding experience —Oscar Schisgall⟩ ⟨Walker *Memorial* is the student center —*Visitor's Guide to Mass. Inst. of Tech.*⟩ ⟨the mound . . . should be regarded as a ~ rather than an interment —F.M.Stanton⟩ ⟨the state's history is well recorded in 17 historic ~*s* —Melvin Beck⟩ **b :** COMMEMORATION 2 **3 a :** RECORD, MEMOIR ⟨the text of the ~ that accompanied the map —Marjorie S. Douglas⟩ **b :** MEMORANDUM, NOTE ⟨present a long ~ to the emperor —*Times Lit. Supp.*⟩; *specif* **:** a legal abstract **c** (1) **:** a statement of facts addressed to a government or some branch of it often accompanied with a petition or remonstrance ⟨submitted a ~ to Congress —Joseph Dorfman⟩; *also* **:** a similar statement presented to a nongovernmental body (2) **:** a pleading before the Permanent Court of International Justice in which a case is set forth including facts, law, and submissions

³**memorial** \"\ *vt* -ED/-ING/-S **:** MEMORIALIZE

memorial arch *n* **:** TRIUMPHAL ARCH

memorial day *n, usu cap M&D* **1 :** May 30 formerly observed as a legal holiday in most states of the U. S. in commemoration of dead servicemen — called also *Decoration Day* **2 :** the last Monday in May observed as a legal holiday in most states of the U.S. **3 :** CONFEDERATE MEMORIAL DAY **4 :** any of several days set aside for the public commemoration of war dead

me·mo·ri·al·ist \-ələst\ *n* -S **1 :** a person who writes or signs a memorial ⟨the ~*s* are not entitled to be heard —T.E.May⟩ **2 :** a writer of memorials or memoirs ⟨France's amplest secret ~ —Janet Flanner⟩; *specif* **:** one who writes a commemorative memoir ⟨critics of the work rather than ~*s* of the man —*Times Lit. Supp.*⟩

me·mo·ri·al·iza·tion \ˌ=ˌ==ələˈzāshən, -ˌlīˈz-\ *n* -S **:** the act or an instance of memorializing or the state of being memorialized ⟨won . . . glamour for future ~ —J.F.Dobie⟩

me·mo·ri·al·ize \=ˈ==əˌlīz\ *vt* -ED/-ING/-S **1 :** to address or petition by a memorial **:** present a memorial to ⟨~ the governors and legislatures of the several states —E.M.Carroll⟩ **2 :** COMMEMORATE ⟨*memorialized* by an avenue bearing his name —David Dempsey⟩ — **me·mo·ri·al·iz·er** \-zə(r)\ *n* -S

me·mo·ri·al·ly \-əlē\ *adv* **:** by memory **:** as a memorial

memorial mass *n, often cap both Ms* **:** a Roman Catholic requiem mass offered on specif. appointed days of the year for the repose of a dead person's soul

memorial park *n* **:** CEMETERY

memorial rose *n* **:** a vigorous prostrate or trailing evergreen rose (*Rosa wichuraiana*) of eastern Asia with large fragrant white flowers in clusters of few to many

memorial service *n* **:** a commemorative service of worship held for a dead person

memorial stamp *n* **:** a commemorative stamp

me·mo·ria tech·ni·ca \məˈmōrēəˈteknəkə\ *n* [NL, lit., artificial memory] **:** an artificial aid to the memory **:** a mnemonic aid ⟨evidence the survival of this primitive *memoria technica* —Edward Clodd⟩

mem·o·ried \ˈmem(ə)rēd, -rid\ *adj* [*memory* + *-ed*] **1 :** having a memory of a specified kind — usu. used in combination ⟨long-*memoried* men and women . . . were not deluded —Eden Phillpotts⟩ **2 a :** full of memories ⟨this serene and ~ village —*Amer. Guide Series: Vt.*⟩ **b :** REMEMBERED ⟨explosion of ~ happiness —Han Suyin⟩

¹**me·mo·ri·ter** \məˈmȯrəˌte(ə)r, -ərəd·ər\ *adv* [L, fr. *memor* mindful — more at MEMORY] **:** by or from memory **:** by heart ⟨learn ~ a series of propositions —*World Rev.*⟩

²**memoriter** \"\ *adj* **:** marked by emphasis on memorization ⟨there is little ~ work required —*Atlantic*⟩

mem·o·ri·za·tion \ˌmem(ə)rəˈzāshən, ˌmeməˌrīˈz-\ *n* -S **:** the act or an instance of memorizing

mem·o·rize \ˈmeməˌrīz\ *vb* -ED/-ING/-S [*memory* + *-ize*] *vt* **1 a** *archaic* **:** to commemorate in writing **:** RECORD, MENTION ⟨the great founders of the university are tactfully *memorized* —*Encyc. Britannica*⟩ **b** *archaic* **:** to cause to be remembered **:** COMMEMORATE ⟨entombed with a Northern spade and *memorized* with a Northern slab —H.R.Helper⟩ **c** *chiefly dial* **:** REMEMBER ⟨I ~ that egg —Earl Hamner⟩ ⟨wanted folk to ~ him —Stewart Toland⟩ ⟨for the first time in *memorized* history man was free to act —*Time*⟩ **2 :** to commit to memory **:** learn by heart ⟨dread to ~ a speech for fear they will forget it —Max Eastman⟩ ~ *vi* **:** to learn something by heart ⟨these children can . . . ~ easily —Gertrude H. Hildreth⟩

mem·o·riz·er \-zə(r)\ *n* -S **:** one that memorizes

mem·o·ry \ˈmem(ə)rē, -ri\ *n* -ES [ME *memorie*, fr. MF *memorie, memoire*, fr. L *memoria*, fr. *memor* mindful + *-ia* -y; akin to OE *gemimor* well-known, *mimorian* to remember, MD *mimeren* to muse, brood, L *mora* delay, OIr *airmert* prohibition, Gk *mermēra* trouble, Skt *smarati* he remembers; basic meaning: to remember] **1 a** *archaic* **:** a ceremony of commemoration **:** a service for the dead **b** *obs* **:** a historical or biographical record **c** *obs* **:** MEMORIAL, MEMENTO **2 a** (1) **:** the power or process of reproducing or recalling what has been learned and retained esp. through nonconscious associative mechanisms **:** conscious or unconscious evocation of things past ⟨semantic reception is associated with great use of ~ —Norbert Wiener⟩ ⟨seemed lost in thought or ~ —E.A. McCourt⟩ ⟨in ~, one images or reproduces his whole state of mind on the remembered occasion —Richard Taylor⟩ (2) **:** this power regarded as vested in an individual **:** an individual's capacity for reproducing or recalling what has been learned and retained ⟨has a good ~ for faces⟩ ⟨rely on the faulty ~ of a cross section of people —S.L.Payne⟩ ⟨his ~ annoyed him . . . it did not work willingly any more —Stuart Cloete⟩ (3) **:** the process of reproducing or recalling what has been learned as manifested in some special way or as associated with some bodily process ⟨visual ~⟩ ⟨muscular ~⟩ **b :** persistent modification of structure or of behavior resulting from an organism's activity or from its passively acquired experience **c** (1) **:** the totality of what has been learned and retained esp. as evidenced by recall and recognition ⟨drew on his ~ to supply the needed names⟩ ⟨even birds and animals have an ancestral ~ —*Horizon*⟩ (2) **:** the function of memory regarded as a compartment or chamber in which images, perceptions, or learning are stored ⟨filling their ~ with a lumber of words —R.L.Stevenson⟩ ⟨the invisible storehouse in nothingness, called ~ —Walter Sorell & Denver Lindley⟩ ⟨retain in their ~ the preceding movements —George Balanchine⟩ ⟨a richly stored ~⟩ **3 a** (1) **:** commemorative remembrance ⟨a statue erected in ~ of the hero⟩ ⟨has been held in ~ in Ireland —Maxwell Nurnberg & Morris Rosenblum⟩ ⟨a local museum dedicated to the ~ of the celebrity —*Amer. Guide Series: Maine*⟩ (2) **:** a person or thing held in commemorative remembrance ⟨his deeds are the country's proudest *memories*⟩ **b :** the fact or condition of being remembered ⟨~ of such upheavals goes back to remote antiquity⟩ ⟨persecutions which were of recent ~ —K.S.Latourette⟩ **4 a :** a particular act of recalling something learned or experienced **:** the fact or a condition of recalling **:** REMEMBRANCE, RECOLLECTION, RECALL ⟨woke with . . . complete ~ of where she had been —Pearl Buck⟩ ⟨have no ~ of that incident⟩ ⟨recited the poem from ~⟩ **b** (1) **:** an image, impression, or other mental trace of someone or something known or experienced **:** the content of something remembered ⟨my first ~ is one of being held up to a window —George Dangerfield⟩ ⟨the ~ of his voice as distinct in her mind as it ever had been in her ear —Glenway Wescott⟩ ⟨pleasant *memories* of an Italian summer⟩ ⟨the ~ of the captain's wife had not left him —Carson McCullers⟩ ⟨*memories* of the Japanese occupation . . . created a heritage of ill will —R.H.Fifield⟩ ⟨have written down their ~ . . . of one such occasion —F.I.Cobb⟩ ⟨made the town's isolation a ~ —*Amer. Guide Series: Texas*⟩ ⟨the course is a ~ and a mark is no longer even a ghost —Norman Nathan⟩ ⟨the depression is only a bad ~⟩ (2) **:** the total impression or generalized image of a person preserved in remembrance, history, or tradition **:** posthumous opinion ⟨this ruler left behind him golden *memories*⟩ ⟨a prince of glorious ~⟩ (3) **:** the character, personality, or achievements of a person as preserved in remembrance ⟨the man whose ~ the Royal Irish Academy honors —Gearoid O'Sullivan⟩ ⟨his ~ recalled the most wonderful and exciting . . . adventures —R.H.Davis⟩ ⟨hates her ~ and all other women —Lucy M. Montgomery⟩ **c :** the time within which past events can be or are remembered ⟨within the ~ of living men⟩ **5 :** CONCENTRATION 5 **6 a :** a component in an electronic computing machine (as a computer) in which information (as data or program instructions) may be inserted and stored and from which it may be extracted when wanted **b :** a device external to a computer for the insertion, storage, and extraction of information **7 a :** a capacity for showing effects recognized as the result of past treatment — used esp. of materials ⟨the wire begins to turn in the other direction corresponding to the first twisting — the ~ of the recent short-term handling has been obliterated by that of the more remote but longer lasting and therefore more impressive one —Bernhard Gross⟩ **b :** a capacity for returning to a former condition (as after being stretched) — used esp. of a material ⟨the ~ will cause the material to resume the shape it had when you purchased it —*Road Mag.*⟩

syn REMEMBRANCE, RECOLLECTION, REMINISCENCE, MIND, SOUVENIR: MEMORY applies both to the faculty of remembering and to what is remembered, sometimes remembered dearly or cherished ⟨a very good *memory*⟩ ⟨a *memory* training course⟩ ⟨it was the merest *memory* now, vague and a little sweet, like the remembrance of some exceptional spring day —John Galsworthy⟩ REMEMBRANCE can be the same as MEMORY but more often refers to the act of remembering and usu. to a particular act of remembering esp. something pleasant or cherished in memory, or it may apply to the state of being remembered ⟨the only moments I've lived my life to the full and that live in *remembrance* unfaded —W.W.Gibson⟩ ⟨the vivid *remembrance* of an almost identical setting one evening —Henry Miller⟩ ⟨the *remembrance* of things past —Shak.⟩ ⟨the *remembrance* of the event always brought a pang of regret⟩ RECOLLECTION is like REMEMBRANCE but carries a strong suggestion of more voluntary and sometimes effortful recalling to mind, and it may apply to the thing remembered in this way ⟨they have a tendency to forget the facts of the present in their fond *recollection* of the past —S.M.Crothers⟩ ⟨you ask me to put down a few *recollections* of your father —W.E.H. Lecky⟩ REMINISCENCE may refer to remembrance of something long past, esp. as remembered casually and accidentally; it is closely synonymous with RECOLLECTION in references to what is remembered ⟨would use all the techniques of modern psychology in his analyses of the subconscious; the phenomena of involuntary *reminiscence* fascinate him —B.M.Woodbridge⟩ ⟨the author's own *reminiscences* of childhood and youth are a good deal less pretentious and more amusing than this model —*Times Lit. Supp.*⟩ MIND in this sense commonly appears only in a few idiomatic phrases ⟨to keep in *mind*⟩ ⟨out of sight, out of *mind*⟩ SOUVENIR may still be used as a synonym of MEMORY ⟨then she carefully restored them, her mind full of *souvenirs* newly awakened —Arnold Bennett⟩

memory book *n* **1 :** SCRAPBOOK ⟨not so much a book of memoirs as a *memory book* —*New Yorker*⟩ **2 :** a small album for autographs

mem·o·ry·less \ˈmem(ə)rēləs, -ril-\ *adj* **:** devoid of memory

memory span *n* **:** the greatest amount (as the longest series of letters or digits) that can be perfectly reproduced by the subject after a single presentation by the experimenter

memory tube *n* **:** a vacuum tube (as a camera tube or electronic computer tube) that retains information for later use by having a receptive element on which an electron beam impresses signals

memory verse *n* **:** a brief passage of Scripture to be memorized in connection with a Sunday-school lesson — compare GOLDEN TEXT

memos *pl of* MEMO, *pres 3d sing of* MEMO

mem·phi·an \ˈmem(p)fēən\ *n* -S *cap* [*Memphis*, Egypt + E *-an*] **1 :** MEMPHITE; *also* **:** EGYPTIAN **2** [*Memphis*, Tenn. + E *-an*] **:** a native or resident of Memphis, Tenn.

mem·phis \-fəs\ *adj, usu cap* [fr. *Memphis*, Tenn.] **:** of or from the city of Memphis, Tenn. ⟨the *Memphis* cotton market⟩ **:** of the kind or style prevalent in Memphis

¹**mem·phite** \ˈmemˌfīt\ *n* -S *usu cap* [L *Memphites*, fr. Gk *Memphitēs*, fr. *Memphis*, Egypt + Gk *-itēs* -ite] **:** a native or resident of ancient Memphis in Egypt

²**memphite** \"\ *also* **mem·phit·ic** \(ˈ)memˈfid·ik\ *adj, usu cap* [*Memphite* fr. L *Memphites*, fr. *Memphites*, n.; *Memphitic* fr. Gk *Memphitikos*, fr. *Memphitēs* + *-ikos* -ic] **:** of or relating to ancient Memphis, its inhabitants, or the dynasties of Egyptian kings who made it their capital

mem·phit·ic \memˈfid·ik\ *n* -S *usu cap* [fr. *Memphitic*, adj.] **:** the Coptic dialect of Memphis and vicinity

mems *pl of* MEM

mem·sahib \ˈmem+,-\ *n* [Hindi *mem-sāhib*, fr. E ²*mem* + Hindi *ṣāhib* — more at SAHIB] **:** a foreign woman of the white race and some social status living in India ⟨growing up to be another nice infuriating superior English ~ —H.E.Bates⟩; *esp* **:** the wife of an English official or other white man of some social status in colonial India ⟨found the white ~*s* more violently intoxicated with . . . race poison than their men —Edmond Taylor⟩ ⟨this is a ~'*s* book, recalling . . . the last years of that ascendancy in India —*Times Lit. Supp.*⟩ ⟨houses designed for British officials and their ~*s* —Christopher Rand⟩

men *pl of* MAN

men- *or* **meno-** *comb form* [NL, fr. Gk *mēn* month — more at MOON] **:** menstruation ⟨*meno*pause⟩ ⟨*men*acme⟩

me·nac·can·ite \məˈnakəˌnīt\ *n* -S [irreg. fr. *Manaccan*, Cornwall, England + E *-ite*] **:** ILMENITE — **me·nac·can·it·ic** \ˌ=ˌ==ˈnid·ik\ *adj*

¹**men·ace** \ˈmenəs *also* -nis\ *n* -S [ME *manace, menasse*, fr. MF *manace, menace*, fr. L *minacia*, fr. *minac-, minax* projecting, threatening (fr. *minari* to project, threaten) + *-ia* -y — more at MOUNT] **1 a :** a show of intention to inflict harm **:** a threatening gesture, statement, or act ⟨~*s* of damnation —T.S.Eliot⟩ ⟨spitting angry ~*s* at her —Arnold Bennett⟩ ⟨would advance with simulated ~ —Osbert Lancaster⟩ ⟨exploding in ~*s* and threats of vengeance —George Meredith⟩ **b :** threatening import, character, or aspect **:** THREAT ⟨ominous silence of the woods held no ~ for her —Osbert Sitwell⟩ ⟨the ~ of the European war to American interests —C.B.Forcey⟩ ⟨the sky became leaden with vague ~ —Adrian Bell⟩ ⟨with a hysterical cry of ~ —C.G.D.Roberts⟩ **c :** the condition of being threatened **:** a threatening atmosphere or situation ⟨in the ~ and confusion of the . . . postwar period —Hans Weigel⟩ **:** impending evil ⟨a sense of ~, of unease, runs through their conversation —T.H.White b.1915⟩ **2 a :** someone or something that represents a threat **:** DANGER ⟨tuberculosis and syphilis were major ~*s* —T.H.Fielding⟩ ⟨the intoxicated motorist is a ~ to life and limb —Wayne Hughes⟩ ⟨the ~*s* of air, such as tornado and whirlwind —Osbert Sitwell⟩ **b :** a person whose actions or idiosyncrasies cause intense annoyance or discomfiture ⟨that boy's a ~⟩ ⟨her friends were beginning to find her a ~ —Guy McCrone⟩

²**menace** \"\ *vb* -ED/-ING/-S [ME *manacen, menacen*, fr. MF *manacer, menacer*, fr. *manace, menace*, n.] *vt* **1 a :** to make a show of intention to harm **:** make a threatening gesture, statement, or act against ⟨*menaced* him with immediate expulsion —G.B.Shaw⟩ **b :** to threaten the infliction of **:** offer threat of ⟨*menacing* the emperor's displeasure —S.T.Coleridge⟩ ⟨he *menaced* ruin —H.R.Trevor-Roper⟩ **2 :** to represent or pose a threat to **:** ENDANGER ⟨the ferries were *menaced* by floating mines —P.W.Thompson⟩ ⟨mature bolls are *menaced* by the army worm —*Amer. Guide Series: Ark.*⟩ ~ *vi* **:** to make a threatening gesture, statement, or act ⟨the few snakes that ~ with their mouths open —C.H.Curran & Carl Kauffeld⟩ **syn** see THREATEN

menacing *adj* [fr. pres. part. of ²*menace*] **:** presenting, suggesting, or constituting a menace **:** THREATENING ⟨unemployment reached ~ proportions —P.E.James⟩ ⟨his all-knowing and rather ~ smile —Louis Auchincloss⟩ ⟨the prospect of a third world war is so ~ —John Strachey⟩ ⟨chamber was somber and almost ~ —Dorothy Sayers⟩ — **men·ac·ing·ly** *adv*

men·acme \mən, (ˈ)mēn+\ *n* [*men-* + *acme*] **:** the portion of a woman's life during which menstruation occurs

menad *var of* MAENAD

men·a·di·one \ˌmenəˈdīˌōn\ *n* -S [*methyl* + *naphthoquinone* + *-dione*] **:** a yellow crystalline compound $C_{11}H_8O_2$ that is usu. made by oxidation of beta-methylnaphthalene, that has the biological activity of natural vitamin K to which it is chemically related, and that is often administered in the form of a water-soluble white crystalline addition compound with sodium bisulfite; 2-methyl-1,4-naphthoquinone — called also *vitamin* K_3

me·na·do·nese \məˌnädəˈnēz, -ēs\ *n, pl* **menadonese** *cap* [*Menado* (Manado) residency in Celebes, Indonesia + E *-nese* (as in *Japanese*)] **:** an Indonesian native or inhabitant of Manado in northeastern Celebes

mé·nage \(ˈ)māˈnäzh, -nàzh\ *n* -S [F *ménage*, fr. OF *mesnage* dwelling house, fr. (assumed) VL *mansionaticum*, fr. L *mansion-, mansio* habitation, dwelling — more at MANSION] **1 a :** a domestic establishment **:** HOUSEHOLD ⟨a respectable ~ —F.A.Swinnerton⟩ ⟨an unstable ~ —Harry Levin⟩ ⟨add one or two concubines to his ~ —John Blofeld⟩ **b :** a place in which a person keeps house or that is managed like a household **:** QUARTERS ⟨lunch with the young men at their mess — as all communal ~*s* appear to be called in the East —Evelyn Waugh⟩ ⟨apartment, an eight-room ~ on the fourteenth floor —E.J.Kahn⟩ ⟨very formal, and very well kept, whereas I had expected to find myself in an entirely Bohemian ~ —George Copeland⟩ **c :** domestic management **:** HOUSEKEEPING ⟨accommodates our democratic ~ to the taste of the richest and most extravagant plebeian among us —W.D.Howells⟩ **2 a :** a savings club organized in some Scottish and English communities so that each member pays in a set sum each week and the total sum is paid to a different member each week **b** *dial Brit* **:** the selling of goods (as cloth) on installments often by an itinerant vendor

ménage à trois \mānäzhä·trwä\ *n* [F, lit., household of three] **:** an arrangement in which three persons (as a married couple and the lover of one of the couple) share sexual relations esp. while they are living together ⟨leaves a feeble young husband to become part of a Bohemian *ménage à trois* —*Times Lit. Supp.*⟩ ⟨a more or less harmonious *ménage à trois* —Edmund Wilson⟩

me·nag·er·ie \məˈnaj(ə)rē, -ri *also* -azh-\ *n* -S [F *ménagerie*, fr. MF *menagerie* management of a household or a farm, place where animals are tended, fr. *menage* household + *-erie* -ery] **1 a :** a place where animals are kept and trained esp. for exhibition **b :** a collection of wild or foreign animals in cages or enclosures; *esp* **:** one kept for exhibition (as with a circus) **c** *obs* **:** AVIARY **2 :** a varied group or collection of persons or things that are strange, odd, or startling or foreign to one's experience ⟨a wonderful ~ of royal hangers-on —V.S.Pritchett⟩

me·nag·er·ist \-rəst\ *n* -S **:** the proprietor or manager of a menagerie

me·nai·on \məˈnāˌän\ *n, pl* **me·naia** \-āə\ [MGk *mēnaion*, fr. neut. of *mēnaios* monthly, fr. Gk *mēn* month — more at MOON] *usu cap* **:** a collection of hymns and collects for all days of the year in the Eastern Orthodox Church arranged in calendar order and usu. divided into 12 volumes each for a different month and each containing the proper of the immovable feasts of Christ or the saints for the month; *also* **:** any of these volumes

menald \ˈmenᵊld, ˈmēn-\ *adj* [origin unknown] **:** SPECKLED, VARIEGATED

me·naph·thone \məˈnafˌthōn\ *n* -S [*methyl* + *naphthaquinone*] **:** MENADIONE

men·ar·che \məˈnärˌ(ˌ)kē, meˈ-\ *n* -S [NL, fr. *men-* + Gk *archē* beginning — more at ARCHI-] **:** the initiation of menstruation **:** the first menstrual period of an individual — **men·ar·che·al** *also* **men·ar·chi·al** \-ˌkēəl\ *adj*

menat

men·as·pis \məˈnaspəs\ *n, cap* [NL, fr. Gk *mēnē* moon + NL *-aspis* — more at MOON] **:** a genus of Upper Permian cartilaginous fishes (subclass Holocephali) related to the chimaeras

me·nat \məˈnat\ *n* -S [Egypt *mnit*] **:** an amulet worn in ancient Egypt to secure divine protection

me·nav·e·lings \məˈnavələnz, -liŋz\ *var of* MANAVELINS

menck·en·ese \ˌmeŋkəˈnēz, -enk-, -ēs\ *n* -S *usu cap* [H. L. *Mencken* †1956 Amer. journalist and satirist + E *-ese*] **:** the peculiarly vigorous racy flamboyant and often caustic style characteristic of the journalist Mencken or a style patterned on or resembling that of Mencken ⟨difficult to read through a daily paper without finding a feature writer who employs *Menckenese* —George Mayberry⟩

1menc·ke·ni·an \(ˈ)meŋ¦kēnēən, -en¦-\ *adj, usu cap* [H. L. *Mencken* + E *-ian*] **:** of, relating to, resembling, or suggestive of the journalist Mencken or his writings **:** critical of philistinism and shams and generally iconoclastic in point of view ⟨when he attacks congressmen, he is very *Menckenian* —Saul Bellow⟩ ⟨the writing is so *Menckenian* in style that it is sometimes embarrassing —Charles Angoff⟩ ⟨free of the engaging *Menckenian* slapstick —*Newsweek*⟩

2menckenian \"\ *n* -s *usu cap* **:** a disciple or imitator of the journalist Mencken ⟨the literary world was full of *Menckenians* —J.T.Farrell⟩

1mend \ˈmend\ *vb* -ED/-ING/-S [ME *menden*, short for *amenden* — more at AMEND] *vt* **1 a** (1) **:** to improve in manners or morals **:** REFORM ⟨dear to their tender bosoms . . . is a bad man they are ~*ing* —George Meredith⟩ ⟨too late to ~ the nation —V.J.Ryan⟩ — usu. used in the phrases *mend one's ways* ⟨he could be counseled to ~ his ways —Ralph Linton⟩ and *mend one's manners* ⟨young man, you had better ~ your manners⟩ (2) **:** to remove or eliminate the defects of **:** set right **:** CORRECT ⟨~ a corrupt text⟩ (3) **:** to make right, improve, or remedy (a condition or state of affairs) **:** RECTIFY ⟨think I can do something to ~ all this —William Black⟩ ⟨an attempt was made to ~ matters by a law —C.L.Jones⟩ (4) **:** to improve or strengthen or consolidate by negotiation, maneuvering, or similar activity — used chiefly in the phrase *mend one's fences* ⟨spends the weekend ~*ing* political fences —E.O.Hauser⟩ ⟨went through Europe ~*ing* fences with assiduous alacrity —John Gunther⟩ **b** (1) **:** to put into good shape or working order again **:** patch up **:** REPAIR ⟨used to come in and ~ our car —Michael Davie⟩ ⟨the roads were never ~*ed* —Ellen Glasgow⟩ ⟨~ a torn sleeve⟩ (2) **:** to put in better order **:** READJUST — now used chiefly in the phrase *mend sail* (3) **:** to remove slack between a fishing rod tip and fly by flipping (the line) up-current so that the fly is not dragged downstream **c :** to restore to health **:** CURE ⟨before the bone was fully ~*ed* —*Current Biog.*⟩ ⟨learned to ~ his soul by going to sea —John Erskine †1951⟩ ⟨no sleep but one can ~ him —Herbert Gold⟩ **d** (1) **:** to improve the condition or quality of **:** make better **:** AMELIORATE ⟨the standards of marriage must be ~*ed* —F.S.Mitchell⟩ ⟨men who needed to ~ their fortunes —T.B.Costain⟩ (2) *obs* **:** to improve or better by adding to or increasing (as wages) (3) *dial* **:** to make up or add fuel to (a fire) (4) *obs* **:** to supply the deficiency or loss of **:** SUPPLEMENT (5) **:** to make more rapid **:** QUICKEN — usu. used in the phrase *mend one's pace* ⟨~*ed* his pace with suitable haste —Stephen Crane⟩ **2 :** to make amends or atonement for **:** atone for — now used only in the proverb *least said, soonest mended* ~ *vi* **1 :** to improve morally **:** REFORM — now used chiefly in the proverb *it's never too late to mend* **2 :** to grow better **:** become corrected or improved ⟨her troubles were beginning to ~ —Ellen Glasgow⟩ ⟨depression and lack of spirit ~*ed* visibly —Arnold Nicholson⟩ **3 a :** to improve in health **:** get well ⟨if he ~s in time to play again —Rogers Whitaker⟩ ⟨after that I began to ~ —Corra Harris⟩ **b :** HEAL ⟨waited for his injury to ~ —*Amer. Guide Series: Tenn.*⟩ **4** *chiefly dial* **:** to rise or gain in price, weight, or other respect **:** INCREASE

syn REPAIR, PATCH, REBUILD, REMODEL: MEND, often applying to any freeing from faults or defects, usu. suggests a making of something whole or sound that has been broken, torn, or injured ⟨*mend* a sock⟩ ⟨*mend* a worn shoe sole⟩ ⟨*mend* one's ways⟩ ⟨*mend* a broken marriage⟩ REPAIR, similar to MEND and often interchangeable with it in the sense of to make whole or sound, more commonly applies to more complex things or to a more extensive damage or dilapidation ⟨*repair* a ripped coat⟩ ⟨*repair* a broken bicycle⟩ ⟨the fault which must be *repaired* swiftly —S.L.A.Marshall⟩ ⟨*repaired* the irregularities of his teeth —John Buchan⟩ ⟨constantly *repairing* an old run-down house⟩ PATCH, often PATCH UP, implies a mending of a hole, rent, or weak spot by the application of a patch but can extend to cover several ideas suggestive of this, as (in the form *patch up*) to mend or repair temporarily in an obvious, hurried, careless, or clumsy way, or to fix something up expediently ⟨*patch* a punctured tire⟩ ⟨*patch* a road with asphalt⟩ ⟨*patch up* a hole in the roof⟩ ⟨each community might make a list of its strong and weak points and go to work to *patch up* the latter —Chester Bowles⟩ ⟨*patch up* a damaged ship in order to make port⟩ ⟨*patch up* an excuse⟩ REBUILD in this comparison has a currency in industry and business to imply a more thoroughgoing repair than usual, suggesting an almost complete renewing ⟨*rebuild* old typewriters⟩ ⟨shoe *rebuilding*⟩ REMODEL implies repairing with alterations, often extensive, in the structure or design ⟨forced the owners of 6000 houses and apartment buildings to repair or *remodel* —*Time*⟩ ⟨the house was enlarged and it has been subsequently *remodeled* and modernized —*Amer. Guide Series: N. C.*⟩

2mend \"\ *n* -s [ME, fr. *menden*, v.] **1 mends** *pl but usu sing in constr, chiefly dial Brit* **a :** compensation or atonement for a wrong, injury, or loss **:** AMENDS **b :** IMPROVEMENT, CURE **2 mends** *pl, obs* **:** means of getting reparation **:** REMEDY **3 a :** an act of mending **:** REPAIR **b :** a mended place — **on the mend** *adv* (*or adj*) **:** in the way of improvement ⟨his health is *on the mend*⟩ ⟨business . . . continues *on the mend* —*N.Y.Times*⟩

men·da·cious \(ˈ)men¦dāshəs\ *adj* [L *mendac-, mendax* lying, false + E *-ious* — more at AMEND] **:** given to deception or falsehood ⟨a ~ person⟩ **:** having a false or lying character ⟨the memoirs are ~ and uninteresting —E.A.Walker⟩ **syn** see DISHONEST

men·da·cious·ly *adv* **:** in a mendacious manner

men·da·cious·ness *n* -ES **:** MENDACITY

men·dac·i·ty \menˈdasəd-ē, -daas-, -sətē, -i\ *n* -ES [LL *mendacitas*, fr. L *mendac-, mendax* + *-itas* -ity] **:** the quality or state of being mendacious **:** the practice or an instance of lying **:** FALSEHOOD ⟨blushed . . . at his own ~ —J.D.Beresford⟩ ⟨man's peculiar type of ~ —Leo Stein⟩

men·de \ˈmendē\ *n, pl* **mende** *or* **mendes** *usu cap* **1 a :** a politically important people of Mandingo affiliation in Sierra Leone and Liberia, West Africa **b :** a member of such people **2 :** a Mande language of the Mende people

mended *past of* MEND

men·de·lé·eff's law *or* **men·de·le·ev's law** \ˌmendəˈlā(y)əfs-, -əvz-\ *n, usu cap M* [after Dmitri I. *Mendeleev* †1907 Russ. chemist] **:** PERIODIC LAW

men·de·le·vi·um \ˌmendəˈlēvēəm, -lāv-\ *n* -s [NL, fr. D. *Mendeleev* + NL *-ium*] **:** a radioactive element artificially produced (as by bombardment of einsteinium with high-energy alpha particles) — symbol *Md* or *Mv*; see ELEMENT table

1men·de·lian \(ˈ)men¦dēlēən, -lyən\ *adj, usu cap* [Gregor J. *Mendel* †1884 Austrian botanist + E *-ian*] **:** of or relating to Mendel **:** of, relating to, or in accordance with Mendel's laws

2mendelian \"\ *n* -s *usu cap* **:** an advocate or exponent of Mendelism

mendelian character *n, usu cap M* **:** a character inherited in accordance with Mendel's laws

mendelian factor *or* **mendelian unit** *n, usu cap M* **:** GENE

mendelian inheritance *n, usu cap M* **:** PARTICULATE INHERITANCE

men·de·lian·ism \-ˌnizəm\ *n* -s *usu cap* **:** MENDELISM

men·de·lian·ist \-ˌnəst\ *n* -s *usu cap* **:** MENDELIAN

mendelian ratio *n, usu cap M* **:** the ratio of occurrence of various phenotypes in any cross involving Mendelian characters; *esp* **:** the 3:1 ratio shown by the second filial generation of offspring from parents differing in respect to a single character

men·del·ism \ˈmendəˌlizəm\ *n* -s *usu cap* [Gregor J. *Mendel* + E *-ism*] **:** the principles or the operations of Mendel's laws; *also* **:** PARTICULATE INHERITANCE

1men·del·ist \-ˌləst\ *adj, usu cap* [Gregor J. *Mendel* + E *-ist*] **:** MENDELIAN

2mendelist \"\ *n* -s *usu cap* **:** MENDELIAN — **men·del·is·tic** \¦≈≈¦listik\ *adj, usu cap*

men·del·ize \ˈ≈≈ˌlīz\ *vb* -ED/-ING/-S *sometimes cap* [Gregor J. Mendel + E *-ize*] *vi* **:** to conform to Mendel's laws ~ *vt* **:** to cause to conform to Mendel's laws

men·del's law \ˈmendᵊlz-\ *n, usu cap M* [after Gregor J. *Mendel*, its formulator] **1 :** a principle in genetics: paired hereditary units representing alternate characters (as tallness or dwarfness) separate during the formation of gametes so that every gamete receives but one member of a pair — called also *law of segregation* **2 :** a principle in genetics limited and modified as a result of the subsequent discovery of the phenomenon of linkage: the corresponding hereditary units in a pair of gametes unite in the zygote to form new combinations and recombinations according to the laws of chance — called also *law of independent assortment* **3 :** a principle in genetics proved subsequently to be subject to many limitations: because one of each pair of hereditary units dominates the other in expression, characters are inherited alternatively on an all or nothing basis — called also *law of dominance*; compare BLENDING INHERITANCE

men·de·lye·ev·ite \ˌmendəlˈyā(y)əˌvīt, -dəˈlā-\ *n* -s [Dmitri I. Mendeleev (*Mendelyeev*) †1907 Russ. chemist + E *-ite*] **:** a calcium urano-titanio-niobate occurring in black isometric crystals and masses and being essentially a titanian and rare-earth-bearing betafite

mend·er \ˈmendə(r)\ *n* -s [ME, fr. *menden* to mend + *-er* — more at MEND] **:** one that mends or is used for mending; *specif* **:** a person whose work is mending for the purpose of repairing torn, worn, or defective parts (as of garments, textiles, parachutes, hats, straw goods, fishing nets)

men·di·can·cy \ˈmendəkənsē, -dēk-, -si\ *n* -ES **1 :** the condition of being a beggar ⟨reduced to ~⟩ **2 :** the practice or act of begging ⟨legal enactments against ~ —C.B.Fairbanks⟩

1men·di·cant \-nt\ *n* -s [L *mendicant-, mendicans*, pres. part. of *mendicare* to beg, fr. *mendicus* beggar — more at AMEND] **1 :** a person who begs; *esp* **:** one that lives by begging **2** *often cap* **:** a member of a mendicant order **:** FRIAR 1a

2mendicant \"\ *adj* [L *mendicant-, mendicans*, pres. part.] **1 :** practicing beggary **:** BEGGING ⟨~ friars⟩ **2 :** characteristic of a mendicant ⟨went about with a ~ air⟩

mendicant order *n* **:** any of various religious orders (as the Franciscans, Dominicans, Carmelites, or Augustinians) in which monastic life and outside religious activity are combined and in which neither personal nor community tenure of property is allowed under original regulations though less stringent regulations regarding the ownership and use of property now usu. prevail

men·di·cate \-dəˌkāt\ *vb* -ED/-ING/-S [L *mendicatus*, past part. of *mendicare*] *archaic* **:** BEG — **men·di·ca·tion** \ˌ≈≈ˈkāshən\ *n* -s *archaic*

men·dic·i·ty \menˈdisəd-ē, -sətē, -i\ *n* -ES [ME *mendicite*, fr. MF *mendicité*, fr. L *mendicitat-, mendicitas*, fr. *mendicus* indigent, beggar + *-itat-, -itas* -ity — more at AMEND] **:** the practice or habit of begging **:** the state or life of a beggar **:** MENDICANCY ⟨the vast increase in ~ —E.A.Peers⟩

mending *n* -s [ME, fr. gerund of *menden* to mend — more at MEND] **1 :** an accumulation of articles (as clothing) requiring repair **2 :** the act of one that mends **:** the process of repairing flaws or defects esp. in fabrics

men·dip·ite \ˈmendəˌpīt\ *n* -s [*Mendip* hills, Somersetshire, England + E *-ite*] **:** a mineral $Pb_3O_2Cl_2$ consisting of oxide and chloride of lead

men·do·za \(ˈ)men¦dōzə\ *adj, usu cap* [fr. *Mendoza*, Argentina] **:** of or from the city of Mendoza, Argentina **:** of the kind or style prevalent in Mendoza

men·do·zite \menˈdōˌzīt\ *n* -s [*Mendoza*, Argentina + E *-ite*] **:** a mineral $NaAl(SO_4)_2.11H_2O$ (?) consisting of a monoclinic hydrous sulfate of sodium and aluminum

mends *pl of* MEND, *pres 3d sing of* MEND

men·e·ghi·nite \ˌmenəˈgēˌnīt\ *n* -s [J. *Meneghini* †1889 It. mineralogist + E *-ite*] **:** a mineral $Pb_{13}Sb_7S_{23}$ consisting of dark lead-gray lead antimony sulfide

me·ne·hu·ne \ˌmenəˈhünē\ *n, pl* **menehune** *or* **menehunes** [Hawaiian] **:** a small mythical Polynesian being usu. pictured as a dwarf living in the mountains and working at night as a stone builder

me·nel \məˈnel\ *n* -s [by alter.] **:** MANILLE — used esp. of the nine of trumps in klaberjass

men·e·la·us' theorem \ˌmenə¦lāəs(əz)-\ *n, usu cap M* [after *Menelaus*, 1st cent. A.D. Greek geometer] **:** a theorem in geometry: if through a triangle ABC a transversal is drawn cutting the sides BC, AB, AC (produced if necessary) in the respective points p, q, r, then the product Aq×Bp×Cr is numerically equal to the product Bq×Cp×Ar

me·ne·vian \məˈnēvēən\ *adj, usu cap* [*Menevia*, ancient parish in Pembrokeshire, Wales (fr. LL) + E *-an*] **:** of or relating to the division of the European Cambrian between the Harlech and the Lingulella — see GEOLOGIC TIME table

menfolk *or* **menfolks** \ˈ≈ˌ≈\ *n pl* **1 :** the male sex **:** MEN **2 :** the men of a family, household, or community ⟨keep quiet when their ~ talk —Charles Angoff⟩

meng \ˈmeŋ\ *vb* -ED/-ING/-S [ME *mengen*, fr. OE *mengan* — more at MINGLE] *dial Brit* **:** MIX, MINGLE, BLEND

men·ha·den \(ˈ)men¦hādᵊn, mənˈh- *sometimes* -had-\ *n, pl* **menhaden** *also* **menhadens** [of Algonquian origin; prob. akin to Narraganset *munnawhatteaûg* menhaden, fr. *munnohquohteau* he fertilizes; fr. the use of menhaden as fertilizer] **:** a marine fish (*Brevoortia tyrannus*) of the family Clupeidae having a large head, deep compressed body, toothless jaws, and closely imbricated bluish silvery scales, attaining a length of 12 to 16 inches, and being by far the most abundant of fishes on the Atlantic coast of the U. S. where scores of millions are annually taken and used for bait or converted into oil and fertilizer — called also *mossbunker, pogy*

menhaden oil *n* **:** a drying fatty oil obtained from the body of the menhaden and used chiefly in paint, varnish, inks, and linoleum and in treating leather

men·hir \ˈmenˌhi(ə)r, ≈ˈ≈\ *n* -s [F, fr. Bret, fr. *men* stone + *hir* long; akin to W *maen* stone, Corn *mēn*, and to OIr *sīr* long — more at SINCE] **:** a single upright rude monolith usu. of prehistoric origin

1me·nial \ˈmēnēəl, -nyəl\ *adj* [ME *meynal, meynial*, fr. *meynie* household, family, retinue (fr. OF *mesnie, meinie*, fr. — assumed — VL *mansionata*, fr. L *mansion-, mansio* dwelling, habitation + *-ata* -ate) + *-al* — more at MANSION] **1 a** *archaic* **:** belonging to or constituting a retinue or train of servants **:** DOMESTIC ⟨stood knight and squire, and ~ train —S.T. Coleridge⟩ **b :** of or relating to the service of a household **:** appropriate to a domestic servant ⟨a few Indian women for ~ offices —W.H.Prescott⟩ **2 :** of, relating to, or being work or an occupation or position not requiring special skill or not calling into play the higher intellectual powers or ranking as low in some occupational or social scale and often regarded as lacking dignity, status, or interest **:** LOWLY, HUMBLE ⟨those who . . . regard translation as an uninspired and ~ occupation have never practiced it —*Times Lit. Supp.*⟩ ⟨~ occupations in hotels, laundries, cigar factories —*Amer. Guide Series: N. Y.*⟩ ⟨most ~ of stations in that aristocratic old Boston world —V.L.Parrington⟩ ⟨encouraged to rise from the ~ and mechanical operations of his craft —Lewis Mumford⟩ ⟨spread from the top down to the most ~ levels of the administration —*Economist*⟩ ⟨a relatively ~ category to which volunteers without degrees . . . are generally relegated —Robert Rice⟩ ⟨~ tasks⟩ **3 a :** appropriate to a menial **:** SERVILE ⟨the wealthy nation they had dared speak to only in ~ tones for so long —*Atlantic*⟩ **b :** lacking interest or dignity ⟨life for each man had become a ~ thing —Robert Lowry⟩ **syn** see SUBSERVIENT

2menial \"\ *n* -s [ME *meynal, meynial*, fr. *meynal, meynial*, adj.] **:** a domestic servant or retainer ⟨in the classic period the musician was generally looked upon as a ~ —A.E.Wier⟩

me·nial·ly \-ēəlē, -əli\ *adv* **:** in a menial manner

mé·ni·ère's disease *or* **mé·ni·ère's syndrome** \ˌmānē¦e(ə)rz, (ˈ)mān¦ye(-\ *n, usu cap M* [after Prosper *Ménière* †1862 Fr. physician] **:** a disorder of the membranous labyrinth of the ear that is marked by recurrent attacks of dizziness, tinnitus, and deafness, is often accompanied by nausea and vomiting, and is commonly attributed to increased pressure of the endolymphatic fluid though it is possibly of obscure allergic origin

men·i·lite \ˈmenᵊlˌīt\ *n* -s [F *ménilite*, fr. *Ménil*montant parish (now part of Paris), France + F *-ite*] **:** an impure opal in brown or dull grayish concretions

me·nin·die clover \məˈnindē-\ *n, usu cap M* [fr. *Menindie* county, New So. Wales, Australia] **:** a perennial fragrant plant (*Trigonella suavissima*) resembling clover and abundant in New South Wales

mening- *or* **meningo-** *also* **meningi-** *comb form* [NL, fr. *meninges*] **:** meninges ⟨*meningo*coccus⟩ ⟨*mening*ioma⟩ ⟨*meningitis*⟩ **:** meninges and ⟨*meningo*myelitis⟩ ⟨*meningo*vascular⟩

me·nin·ge·al \¦menən¦jēəl *sometimes* məˈninjē-\ *adj* [*meninges* + *-al*] **:** of, relating to, or affecting the meninges

meningeal artery *n* **:** any of three arteries supplying the meninges of the brain and neighboring structures

meninges *pl of* MENINX

me·nin·gi·o·ma \məˌninjēˈōmə\ *n, pl* **meningiomas** \-məz\ *or* **meningioma·ta** \-məd-ə\ [NL, fr. *mening-* + *-oma*] **:** a slow-growing encapsulated tumor arising from the meninges and often causing damage by pressing upon the brain or adjacent parts

men·in·gis·mus \ˌmenənˈjizməs\ *also* **me·nin·gism** \məˈninˌjizəm, ˈmenən-,-\ *n, pl* **men·in·gis·mi** \-ˈjizˌmī\ *also* **meningisms** \-ˌjizəmz\ [NL *meningismus*, fr. *mening-* + L *-ismus* -ism] **:** a state of meningeal irritation with symptoms suggesting meningitis that often occurs at the onset of acute febrile diseases esp. in children

men·in·git·ic \¦menən¦jid·ik\ *adj* [NL *meningitis* + E *-ic*] **:** of, relating to, or like that of meningitis

men·in·gi·tis \ˌmenənˈjīd·əs\ *n, pl* **meningit·i·des** \-ˈjid·əˌdēz\ [NL, fr. *mening-* + *-itis*] **1 :** inflammation of the meninges, esp. the pia mater and the arachnoid **2 :** a disease in which inflammation of the meninges occurs and which is caused by microorganisms (as the meningococcus, the tubercle bacillus, or a pneumococcus)

me·nin·go·cele *also* **me·nin·go·coele** \məˈniŋgəˌsēl, -injə-\ *n* -s [ISV *mening-* + *-cele, -coele*] **:** a protrusion of meninges through a defect in the skull or spinal column forming a cyst filled with cerebrospinal fluid

me·nin·go·coc·ce·mia *also* **me·nin·go·coc·cae·mia** \məˌniŋgōˌkäkˈsēmēə, -injō-, -äˈkēm-\ *n* -s [NL, fr. *meningococcus* + *-emia*] **:** the presence of meningococci in the circulating blood

me·nin·go·coc·cic \≈¦≈≈¦käk(s)ik\ *also* **me·nin·go·coc·cal** \-äkəl\ *adj* [NL *meningococcus* + E *-ic* or *-al*] **:** having or caused by meningococci ⟨~ infection⟩ ⟨~ meningitis⟩

me·nin·go·coc·cus \-¦käkəs\ *n, pl* **meningococ·ci** \-äˌkī, -ä(ˌ)kē, -äkˌsī, -äk(ˌ)sē\ [NL, fr. *mening-* + *-coccus*] **:** a bacterium (*Neisseria meningitidis*) that causes cerebrospinal meningitis

me·nin·go·encephalitis \mə¦niŋ(ˌ)gō, -in(ˌ)jō+\ *n* [NL, fr. *mening-* + *encephalitis*] **:** inflammation of the brain and the meninges

me·nin·go·encephalocele \"+\ *n* [ISV *mening-* + *encephalocele*] **:** a protrusion of meninges and brain through a defect in the skull

me·nin·go·encephalomyelitis \"+\ *n* [NL, fr. *mening-* + *encephalomyelitis*] **:** inflammation of the meninges, brain, and spinal cord

me·nin·go·myelocele \"+\ *n* [ISV *mening-* + *myelocele*] **:** a protrusion of meninges and spinal cord through a defect in the spinal column

menin·ting \məˈnintiŋ, ˈmenənˌt-\ *n* -s [native name in the East Indies] **:** an East Indian kingfisher (*Alcedo meninting*)

meninx \ˈmēniŋ(k)s, ˈmen-\ *n, pl* **me·nin·ges** \məˈnin(ˌ)jēz\ [NL, fr. Gk *mēninx* membrane — more at MEMBER] **1 :** any of the three membranes that envelop the brain and spinal cord — compare ARACHNOID, DURA MATER, PIA MATER **2 :** the solitary sheath of stout connective tissue enclosing the central nervous system of some lower vertebrates and embryos of higher forms — called also *primitive meninx*

me·nis·co·cyte \məˈniskəˌsīt\ *n* -s [Gk *mēniskos* crescent + E *-cyte*] **:** SICKLE CELL

me·nis·co·cy·to·sis \≈ˌ≈≈ˌsīˈtōsəs\ *n* [NL, fr. ISV *meniscocyte* + NL *-osis*] **:** SICKLE CELL ANEMIA

me·nis·coid \məˈniˌskȯid\ *adj* [NL *meniscus* + E *-oid*] **:** resembling a meniscus in shape

me·nis·co·ther·i·dae \məˌniskəˈtherəˌdē\ *n pl, cap* [NL, fr. *Meniscotherium*, type genus (fr. Gk *mēniskos* crescent + NL *-therium*) + *-idae*] **:** a family of American Eocene five-toed mammals (order Condylarthra)

me·nis·cus \məˈniskəs\ *n, pl* **menis·ci** \-iˌskī, -iˌsī\ *also* **meniscus·es** *often attrib* [NL, fr. Gk *mēniskos*, dim. of *mēnē* moon — more at MOON] **1 :** a crescent or crescent-shaped body **:** a crescent moon **2 :** a fibrocartilage within a joint esp. of the knee **3 :** a concavo-convex lens; *esp* **:** one of true crescent-shaped section **4 :** the curved upper surface of a liquid column that is concave when the containing walls are wetted by the liquid and convex when not

A B

meniscus 4: concave meniscus of water, *A;* convex meniscus of mercury, *B*

men·i·sper·ma·ce·ae \ˌmenə(ˌ)spərˈmāsēˌē\ *n pl, cap* [NL, fr. *Menispermum*, type genus + *-aceae*] **:** a family of herbaceous or woody climbers (order Ranales) having small 3-parted dioecious flowers and curved embryo — **men·i·sper·ma·ceous** \¦≈≈(ˌ)≈¦māshəs\ *adj*

men·i·sper·mum \ˌmenəˈspərməm\ *n, cap* [NL, fr. *meni-* (fr. Gk *mēnē* moon) + *-spermum* (fr. Gk *sperma* seed) — more at SPERM] **1 :** a genus (family Menispermaceae) of climbing herbs having numerous stamens and black drupaceous fruit — see MOONSEED **2** -s **:** YELLOW PARILLA

menkind \ˈ≈ˌ≈\ *n* **:** MENFOLK

1men·nist \ˈmenəst\ *n* -s *usu cap* [*Menno* Simons †1559 Frisian religious reformer + E *-ist*] **:** MENNONITE

2men·nist *adj, usu cap* **:** MENNONITE

men·no·nist \ˈmenənəst\ *n* -s *usu cap* [*Menno* Simons + connective *-n-* + E *-ist*] **:** MENNONITE

1men·no·nite \ˈmenəˌnīt, *usu* -īd.+V\ *n* -s *usu cap* [G *Mennonit*, fr. *Menno* Simons †1561 Frisian religious reformer + connective *-n-* + G *-it* -ite] **:** a member of a denomination of evangelical Protestant Christians formed from the Anabaptist movement of the 16th century and noted for belief in Scriptural authority, plainness of dress, rejection of oaths, adult baptism, aloofness from the state, exercise of excommunication, restriction of marriage to members of the group, and practice of the rite of foot washing

2mennonite \"\ *adj, usu cap* **:** of or relating to the Mennonites or to their doctrines or practices

men·no·nit·ism \-ˌīd-ˌizəm, -ˌīˌti-\ *n* -s *usu cap* **:** the doctrines and practices of Mennonites **:** the Mennonite Church or movement

me·no \ˈmā(ˌ)nō\ *adv* [It, fr. L *minus* — more at MINUS] **:** LESS — used as a direction in music

1meno- — see MEN-

2meno- *comb form* [NL, fr. Gk *menein* to remain — more at MANSION] **:** remaining **:** persisting ⟨*Meno*rhyncha⟩

men·o·dus \ˈmenədəs\ *n, cap* [NL, fr. Gk *mēnē* moon + NL *-odus* — more at MOON] **:** a genus of large Lower Oligocene horned perissodactyls (family Brontotheriidae) of No. America

me·nog·na·thous \(ˈ)meˈnägnəthəs\ *adj* [*2meno-* + *-gnathous*] **:** having biting mandibles during both the larval and imaginal stages — used of various insects having a complete metamorphosis; contrasted with *metagnathous*

me·no·lo·gion \ˌmēnəˈlō(ˌ)yän\ *n* -s *usu cap* [MGk *mēnologion*] **:** an ecclesiastical calendar and short martyrology of the Eastern Orthodox Church **:** an abbreviated version of the complete Menaion

me·nol·o·gy \məˈnäləjē, mēˈ-\ *n* -ES [MGk *mēnologion*, fr. Gk *mēn* month + *logos* word, account + *-ion*, dim. suffix — more at LEGEND] **1 :** an ecclesiastical calendar of festivals celebrated in honor of particular saints and martyrs; *also* **:** a register of saints or outstanding religious personages **2 :** MENOLOGION

meno·metrorrhagia \¦menō +\ *n* [NL, blend of *menorrhagia* and *metrorrhagia*] **:** a combination of menorrhagia and metrorrhagia

me·nom·i·nee whitefish \məˈnäməné-\ *n, often cap M* **:** a small whitefish (*Prosopium quadrilaterale*) occurring in lakes in Canada, Alaska, and parts of the northern U. S.

me·nom·i·ni *also* **me·nom·i·nee** \məˈnäməné\ *n, pl* **menomini** *or* **menominis** *also* **menominee** *or* **menominees** **1** *usu cap* **a :** an Indian people of the Upper Peninsula, Michigan, and northeastern Wisconsin **b :** a member of such people **c :** an Algonquian language of the Menomini people **2** *often cap* **:** MENOMINEE WHITEFISH

me·no mos·so \ˌmānōˈmȯ(s)(ˌ)sō\ *adj* (*or adv*) [It] **:** less lively **:** SLOWER — used as a direction in music

men·o·pau·sal \¦menə¦pȯzəl\ *adj* **:** of, relating to, or undergoing menopause ⟨~ disorders⟩ ⟨~ women⟩

men·o·pause \'menə,pȯz\ *n* [F *ménopause,* fr. *méno-* men- + *pause*] **1 :** the period of natural cessation of menstruation occurring usu. between the ages of 45 and 50 — called also *change of life* **2 :** the whole group of physical and physiological alterations that occur in the menopausal woman — see CLIMACTERIC 1

men·o·pon \'menə,pän\ *n, cap* [NL, perh. fr. ²*meno-* + Gk *ponos* pain] **:** a genus of bird lice that includes the shaft louse of poultry

me·no·rah \mə'nōrə, -nȯrə\ *n* -s [Heb *mĕnōrāh* candlestick] **1 :** a holy candelabrum with seven candlesticks of the ancient Jewish temple in Jerusalem **2 :** a candelabrum with any of various numbers of candlesticks used primarily in Jewish religious services; *esp* **:** one with nine candlesticks used in the celebration of Hanukkah

menorah 1

men·o·rhyn·cha \,menə'riŋkə\ *n pl, cap* [NL, fr. ²*meno-* + *-rhyncha* (fr. Gk *rhynchos* snout)] **:** a division of insects including those which take food by suction in both the larval and adult stages — **men·o·rhyn·chous** \¦menə¦riŋkəs\ *adj*

men·or·rha·gia \,menə'rāj(ē)ə\ *n* -s [NL, fr. *men-* + *-rrhagia*] **:** abnormally profuse menstrual flow — compare METRORRHAGIA — **men·or·rhag·ic** \¦menə¦rajik\ *adj*

men·or·rhea \,menə'rēə\ *n* -s [NL, fr. *men-* + *-rrhea*] **:** normal menstrual flow

men·o·typh·la \,menə'tiflə\ *n pl, cap* [NL, fr. ²*meno-* + *-typhla* (fr. Gk *typhlon* caecum) — more at TYPHL-] **:** a suborder of Insectivora comprising the elephant shrews and commonly the tree shrews in all of which the pubic symphysis is long and the postorbital process well developed — compare LIPOTYPHLA

men·o·typh·lic \¦menə¦tiflik\ *adj* [²*meno-* + *typhl-* + *-ic*] **1 :** having a cecum **2** [NL *Menotyphla* + E *-ic*] **:** of or relating to the Menotyphla

men·sa \'men(t)sə\ *n, pl* **mensas** \-səz\ *or* **men·sae** *in sense 1* -n(,)sā, *in sense 2* -n(,)sē, -n,sī *sometimes* -n(,)sä\ [ML, fr. L, table, fr. OL, flat cake offered to the gods, perh. fr. fem. of *mensus,* past part. of *metiri* to measure — more at MEASURE] **1** *Roman Catholicism* **:** the top of the altar; *esp* **:** the top or central slab upon which the eucharistic elements are placed **2** [NL, fr. L] **:** the grinding surface of a tooth

men·sal \'men(t)səl\ *adj* [LL *mensalis,* fr. L *mensa* table + *-alis* -al] **1 :** belonging to or used at the table **:** done or carried on at table ⟨pleasant ~ talk⟩ **2 a :** set aside for the maintenance of the table of an ancient Irish or Scotch prince or king ⟨~ land⟩ **b :** set aside for the support of a cleric of the Roman Catholic Church ⟨~ fund⟩

mensal line *n, usu cap M* **:** LINE OF HEART

¹**mense** \'men(t)s\ *n* -s [alter. of ME *menske, mensk,* fr. ON *mennska* humanity, fr. *mennskr* human — more at LUFT-MENSCH] **1** *dial Brit* **a :** mannerly or gracious behavior **:** PROPRIETY; *specif* **:** HOSPITALITY **b :** a large amount or number **2** *dial Brit* **:** a source of honor **:** HONOR, CREDIT **3** *dial Brit* **:** neatness or freshness in appearance **:** SPRUCENESS

²**mense** \"\ *vt* -ED/-ING/-S [alter. of ME *mensken,* fr. *menske, mensk,* n.] **1** *dial Brit* **:** to do honor to **:** DECORATE, GRACE **2** *dial Brit* **:** to make clean or orderly **:** dress up

mense·ful \-fəl\ *adj, dial Brit* **:** DECOROUS, DISCREET, CONSIDERATE; *also* **:** NEAT, TIDY

mense·less \-ləs\ *adj, dial Brit* **:** lacking manners, discretion, or neatness ⟨ye ~ coof —Theodore Bonnet⟩

menservants *pl of* MANSERVANT

men·ses \'men(,)sēz\ *n pl but sing or pl in constr* [L, lit., months, pl. of *mensis* month — more at MOON] **:** the flow characteristic of menstruation; *also* **:** MENSTRUATION

men·she·vik \'menchə,vik, -,vēk\ *n, pl* **mensheviks** \-ks\ *also* **men·she·viki** \-,vikē, -,vēkē\ *usu cap* [Russ *men'shevik,* fr. *men'she* less, smaller (comp. of *malo* little, few) + *-vik* (nominal suffix); fr. their forming the minority group of the Russian Social Democratic party in 1903; akin to Russ *malyĭ* small, L *malus* bad — more at SMALL] **:** a member of the wing of the Russian Social Democratic party before and during the Russian Revolution that believed in gradualism and relied on reformist methods and an alliance with the liberal bourgeoisie to achieve socialism and that after the establishment of the Soviet government assumed an attitude of vigorous opposition to the Communist regime — compare BOLSHEVIK

men·she·vism \-,vizəm\ *n* -s *usu cap* [*Menshevik* + *-ism*] **:** the doctrines, tactics, or practices of the Mensheviks

men·she·vist \-,vəst\ *adj, usu cap* **:** of or relating to Menshevism

men's house *n* **:** a building in a primitive community reserved for the exclusive use of males and serving as a bachelors' dormitory, a recreational center, a cult house, or as a center for some other communal male activity

mens rea \'menz'rēə, -n(t)s'rāə\ *n* [NL, lit., guilty mind] **:** the intent or state of mind accompanying an act, manifesting a purpose harmful to society, providing no justification for the act, and subjecting the perpetrator thereof to criminal punishment **:** criminal as distinguished from innocent intent

men's room *n* **:** a room equipped with lavatories, toilets, and usu. urinals that is for the exclusive use of men

men·stru·al \'menztr(əw)əl, -n(t)str-\ *adj* [ME *menstruall,* fr. L *menstrualis,* fr. *menstrua* menses (fr. neut. pl. of *menstruus* of a month, monthly, of menstruation, fr. *mensis* month) + *-alis* -al — more at MOON] **1 :** of or relating to menstruation **2** [L *menstrualis,* fr. *menstruus* + *-alis* -al] *archaic* **a :** occurring once a month **:** MONTHLY **b :** lasting for a month ⟨a ~ flower⟩

menstrual cycle *n* **:** the whole cycle of physiologic changes from the beginning of one menstrual period to the beginning of the next

menstrual epact *n* **:** EPACT 1b

men·stru·ate \'menztrə,wāt, -n(t)str-, ÷-nz,trāt ÷-n(t),strāt, *usu* -ād·+V\ *vi* -ED/-ING/-S [LL *menstruatus,* past part. of *menstruari,* fr. L *menstrua* menses] **:** to undergo menstruation

men·stru·a·tion \,menztrə'wāshən, ,men(t)str-, ÷menz'trā-, ÷men(t)'strā-\ *n* -s [LL *menstruatus* + E *-ion*] **:** a discharging of blood, secretions, and tissue debris associated with necrotic changes of the uterine mucosa that recurs in nonpregnant breeding-age females of various primates at intervals of 3½ to 5 weeks (as in women typically at 4 week intervals and lasting 3 to 5 days) and that is usu. held to represent a readjustment of the uterus to the nonpregnant state following proliferative changes accompanying the preceding ovulation; *also* **:** an instance of the occurrence of this discharging **:** PERIOD

menstruosity *n* -ES [fr. *menstruous,* after such pairs as E *curious: curiosity*] *obs* **:** menstruous state or discharge

men·stru·ous \'menztr(əw)əs, -n(t)str-\ *adj* [L *menstruus* of a month, monthly, of menstruation — more at MENSTRUAL] **1 :** undergoing menstruation **:** MENSTRUATING **2 :** of or relating to menstruation **:** MENSTRUAL

men·stru·um \'menztr(əw)əm, -n(t)str-\ *n, pl* **menstruums** \-)əmz\ *or* **mens·trua** \-)ə\ [ML, lit., menses, alter. of L *menstrua;* fr. the comparison made by alchemists of a base metal in a solvent undergoing transmutation into gold with an ovum in utero undergoing transformation by the menstrual blood — more at MENSTRUAL] **1 :** a substance that dissolves a solid or holds it in suspension **:** SOLVENT; *specif* **:** a solvent used to extract soluble principles from drugs esp. by percolation **2 :** a universal or general solvent in which other things are dissolved or disintegrated or lose their separate identities ⟨the sea . . . has been so well named the ~ of life —W.E. Swinton⟩ ⟨one unifying ~ of all the sciences — H.M.Kallen⟩

men·su·al \'menchəwəl\ *adj* [LL *mensualis,* irreg. fr. *mensis* month + *-alis* -al — more at MOON] **:** MONTHLY

mensur *abbr* mensuration

men·su·ra·bil·i·ty \,men(t)sərə'bilǝd·ē, -nchər-\ *n* **:** the quality or state of being mensurable

men·su·ra·ble \-rəbəl\ *adj* [LL *mensurabilis,* fr. *mensurare* to measure + L *-abilis* -able — more at MEASURE] **1 :** capable of being measured **:** MEASURABLE ⟨reducing to a ~ order . . . the process of life —Lewis Mumford⟩ **2 :** MENSURAL 1 — **men·su·ra·ble·ness** *n* -ES

men·su·ral \'men(t)sərəl, 'menchər-\ *adj* [LL *mensuralis,* fr. L *mensura* measure + *-alis* -al — more at MEASURE] **1 :** relating to mensural music or mensural notation **2 :** of or relating to measure

men·su·ral·ist \-əst\ *n* -s **:** a composer of mensural music

mensural music *also* **mensurable music** *n* [trans. of ML *musica mensurabilis*] **:** polyphonic music originating in the 13th century with each note having a definite and exact time value — compare GREGORIAN CHANT

mensural notation *n* **:** a musical notation originating in the 13th century consisting of single notes (as large, breve) and ligatures each with a definitely fixed time value and thereby making possible the combination of independent voice parts that led historically to the development of counterpoint and the modern notation

men·su·rate \-,rāt\ *vt* -ED/-ING/-S [LL *mensuratus,* past part. of *mensurare* — more at MEASURE] **:** MEASURE

men·su·ra·tion \,men(t)sə'rāshən, ,menchə'-\ *n* -s [LL *mensuration-, mensuratio,* fr. *mensuratus,* + L *-ion-, -io* -ion] **1 :** the act, process, art, or an instance of measuring **:** MEASUREMENT ⟨problems in ~ and rudimentary astronomy —*Times Lit. Supp.*⟩ **2 :** the application of geometry to the computation of lengths, areas, or volumes from given dimensions or angles **3 :** the temporal relationships between the note values in mensural notation comparable to the different meters of the modern system ⟨customary for those reading . . . notation to deduce the ~ from the context —*Score*⟩

men·su·ra·tion·al \¦==¦rāshən³l, -shnəl\ *adj* **:** of or relating to mensuration

men·su·ra·tive \'==,rād·iv, -,rəd-·\ *adj* **:** adapted for measuring

mens·wear *or* **men's wear** \'=,=\ *n* **1** *usu men's wear* **:** clothing for men **:** HABERDASHERY **2 :** a fabric (as worsted) suitable for men's clothing and also used for women's clothing

¹**-ment** \,mənt *sometimes* ,ment\ *n suffix* -s [ME, fr. OF, fr. L *-mentum,* fr. *-men,* n. suffix + *-tum* (akin to *-tus,* past. part. ending); akin to Gk *-ma,* n. suffix — more at -ED] **1 a :** concrete result, object, or agent of a (specified) action ⟨entangle*ment*⟩ ⟨incre*ment*⟩ ⟨attach*ment*⟩ ⟨frag*ment*⟩ **b :** concrete means or instrument of a (specified) action ⟨comple*ment*⟩ ⟨nutri*ment*⟩ ⟨orna*ment*⟩ **2 a :** action, process, art, or act of a (specified) kind ⟨encircle*ment*⟩ ⟨recruit*ment*⟩ ⟨state*ment*⟩ ⟨govern*ment*⟩ ⟨develop*ment*⟩ **b :** place or object of a (specified) action ⟨escarp*ment*⟩ ⟨canton*ment*⟩ **3 :** state or condition ⟨amaze*ment*⟩ ⟨embroil*ment*⟩ ⟨fulfill*ment*⟩ ⟨involve*ment*⟩

²**-ment** *when no syllable-increasing suffix (as -ed or -ing) follows,* ,ment *also* ,mənt; *when a syllable-increasing suffix follows,* ,ment *sometimes* ,mənt\ — as final syllable in verbs corresponding to nouns of identical spelling ending in *-ment* ⟨compli*ment*⟩ ⟨imple*ment*⟩

menta *pl of* MENTUM

¹**men·tal** \'ment³l\ *adj* [ME, fr. MF, fr. LL *mentalis,* fr. L *ment-, mens* mind + *-alis* -al — more at MIND] **1 :** of or relating to mind: as **a :** relating to the integrated activity of an organism; *specif* **:** relating to the total emotional and intellectual response of an organism to its environment ⟨the role played by the comics in the ~ life of the children —Winfred Overholser⟩ ⟨found him in a terrible ~ state — very depressed and even panicky⟩ ⟨the ~ set of an individual⟩ **b :** of or relating to intellectual as contrasted with emotional activity **:** of or relating to the process or mode of thought or capacity for thought ⟨free from any ~ defects⟩ ⟨racial explanations of the ~ character of the Greeks —Benjamin Farrington⟩ ⟨note what ~ level you are on with that person —W.J.Reilly⟩ ⟨~ exertions⟩ **c :** of, relating to, or being intellectual as contrasted with overt physical activity ⟨~ work⟩ ⟨made swift ~ calculations⟩ **d :** occurring or experienced in the mind **:** not voiced or given other sensory expression **:** INNER ⟨~ reservations⟩ ⟨filled it for him, under ~ protest —George Meredith⟩ ⟨refusal to shape either the words or the ~ images of prayer —Frank Yerby⟩ ⟨~ anguish⟩ **e :** relating to or concerned with mind, its activity, or its products as an object of study **:** relating to or concerned with ideology **:** IDEOLOGICAL ⟨exercised a great influence on the philosophy of history, the study of jurisprudence, politics, and indeed on all the ~ sciences —Frank Thilly⟩ ⟨the whole of ~ science —William James⟩ **f :** relating to or being spirit or idea as opposed to matter **:** IMMATERIAL, SPIRITUAL, IDEAL ⟨the distinction between physical things and ~ ideas —J.W.Yolton⟩ ⟨your mind is ~, but that which you perceive with your senses is also ~ —*Encore*⟩ **2 a** (1) **:** of, relating to, or affected by mental deficiency or any of a variety of psychiatric disorders ⟨a ~ patient⟩ ⟨a ~ case⟩ (2) **:** WACKY, CRAZY ⟨are ~ from birth . . . and every so often go quite round the bend —Rose Macaulay⟩ ⟨anyone who isn't ~ can see it's a bowl —Anthony West⟩ — often used in the phrase *go mental* ⟨was going a bit ~ from old age —Nevil Shute⟩ ⟨when people go ~ they nearly always turn against their nearest . . . relations —Rosamond Lehmann⟩ **b :** intended for or devoted to the care or treatment of persons affected by psychiatric disorders ⟨a ~ hospital⟩ ⟨the qualified psychiatric nurse in Britain is officially registered as a registered ~ nurse —*Trained Nurse & Hospital Rev.*⟩ **3 :** relating to or marked by possession or display of telepathic, mind-reading, or other occult powers ⟨set up the stage for the ~ act —W.L.Gresham⟩ ⟨the greatest ~ medium of all time —Hereward Carrington⟩

syn INTELLIGENT, INTELLECTUAL, CEREBRAL, PSYCHIC: MENTAL indicates a connection with or emphasis on the mind as a center of rational activity; it contrasts matters emotional or physical ⟨she writes straight from the emotions; nothing *mental* ever gets in her way —Anita Loos⟩ ⟨if from any bodily or *mental* defect the eldest son is disqualified for ruling —J.G.Frazer⟩ ⟨completed the banishment of natural appearances from the art of painting, substituting therefor a *mental* world of geometrical derivatives —F.J.Mather⟩ INTELLIGENT indicates a degree of mental power enabling a person or animal to appraise a situation and make a variety of sound or acceptable decisions; it often contrasts with *stupid* or *silly* ⟨*intelligent* self-interest should lead to a careful consideration of what the road is able to do without ruin —O.W.Holmes †1935⟩ ⟨friends who were a little more *intelligent* and would understand —John Hersey⟩ INTELLECTUAL may indicate connection with the higher powers of the mind; it may contrast with *emotional* and may suggest a noticeable scope, depth, or complexity ⟨words have an emotional and imaginative, as well as an *intellectual* context —J.L.Lowes⟩ ⟨a scientist is known not by his technical processes but by his *intellectual* processes —F.W.Peabody⟩ INTELLECTUAL may suggest an accustomed or lasting concern with higher challenges to the intellect rather than the acumen displayed in a particular decision ⟨less *intellectual* and therefore more *intelligent* in his approach —Edgar Smith⟩ CEREBRAL may suggest cold, analytic intellectual activity or inclination, to the exclusion of the emotional or sensuous ⟨wrote about Catholicism from the *cerebral* slant of the converted intelligentsia —*Book-of-the-Month Club News*⟩ PSYCHIC suggests reference to the psyche, the inner self, and guides the reader away from notions of the physical, physiological, or organic ⟨not materialist but *psychic* factors are the decisive forces of history —*Time*⟩ ⟨I don't accept the idea of *psychic* diseases analogous to mental diseases —Compton Mackenzie⟩

²**mental** \"\ *n* -s **:** a mentally disordered person ⟨no ~*s* had occurred for a hundred years or more —*Mag. of Fantasy & Science Fiction*⟩

³**mental** \"\ *adj* [L *mentum* chin + E *-al;* akin to W *mant* mouth, lip, L *mont-, mons* mountain — more at MOUNT] **:** of or relating to the chin, the median part of the lower jaw, or the mentum of an insect **:** GENIAL

⁴**mental** \"\ *n* -s **:** a plate, scale, or shield (of a fish or reptile) occurring in the mental area

mental age *n* **:** the level of a person's intellectual ability esp. as measured by an intelligence test and expressed as the numerical equivalent of the chronological age of the typical person having the same level of intellectual ability — abbr. *MA*

mental capacity *or* **mental competence** *n* **1 :** sufficient understanding and memory to comprehend in a general way the situation in which one finds himself and the nature, purpose, and consequence of any act or transaction into which one proposes to enter **2 :** the degree of understanding and memory the law requires to uphold the validity of or to charge one with responsibility for a particular act or transaction ⟨*mental capacity* to commit crime requires the accused to know right from wrong⟩

mental chemistry *n* **:** associationism by analogy with chemistry that forms mental compounds with qualities not inherent in the elements to be combined

mental cruelty *n* **1 :** a course of conduct by an offending spouse without physical cruelty evidencing personal indignities that wound the feelings of and show a lack of respect and affection for the complaining spouse and constituting a basis for separation **2 :** a course of conduct by an offending spouse without physical violence evidencing personal indignities calculated to endanger the mental and physical health of the complaining spouse in view of their aggravated character and the latter's sex and sensibilities and constituting a basis for divorce esp. if actual impairment results (as required in many courts)

mental deficiency *n* **:** failure in intellectual development resulting in social incompetence that is considered to be the result of defect in the central nervous system and to be accordingly incurable **:** FEEBLEMINDEDNESS — compare IDIOCY, IMBECILITY, MORONITY

mental disease *n* **:** a disease characterized esp. by mental symptoms **:** mental disorder **:** INSANITY

mental foramen *n* [³*mental*] **:** a foramen for the passage of blood vessels and a nerve on the outside of the lower jaw on each side near the chin

mental hygiene *n* **:** the science of maintaining mental health and preventing the development of psychosis, neurosis, or other personality disturbance

mental incapacity *or* **mental incompetence** *n* **1 :** an absence of mental capacity **2 :** an inability through mental illness or mental deficiency of any sort to carry on the everyday affairs of life or to care for one's person or property with reasonable discretion

men·ta·lis \men'taləs, -tāl-,-täl-\ *n, pl* **mentales** \-a(,)lēz, -ā(,)lēz, -ä(,)lās\ [NL, fr. L *mentum* chin + *-alis* -al — more at MENTAL] **:** a muscle that raises the chin and pushes up the lower lip

men·tal·ism \'ment³l,izəm\ *n* -s **1 a :** a doctrine that mind is the fundamental reality **:** BERKELEIANISM — compare IDEALISM, MATERIALISM **b :** a doctrine that distinguishes mental processes fundamentally from the accompanying brain activity **2 :** a view that conscious processes as revealed by introspection are the proper data of psychology — opposed to *behaviorism* **3 :** a hypothesis that special factors of mind must be assumed to analyze, classify, or explain some or all phenomena of language — compare MECHANISM

men·tal·ist \-əst\ *n* -s **1 :** an advocate of mentalism **2 :** a mind reader or fortune-teller ⟨how did the ~ know the birthdays of spectators —W.L.Gresham⟩

men·tal·is·tic \¦==¦istik\ *adj* **1 :** of or relating to mentalism ⟨commendably assaults ~ ways of thinking —J.R.Kantor⟩ **2 :** of or relating to mental phenomena **:** INTROSPECTIONISTIC ⟨such ~ sentences as "I remember to have seen this person before" —Arthur Pap⟩ — **men·tal·is·ti·cal·ly** \-tək(ə)lē\ *adv*

men·tal·i·ty \men'taləd·ē, -lətē, -i\ *n* -ES **1 :** mental power or capacity **:** learning ability **:** INTELLIGENCE ⟨a criminal whose ~ is low —B.N.Cardozo⟩ ⟨a man of keen ~ —S.H.Adams⟩ ⟨the ~ of apes⟩ **2 :** mode or way of thought, mental set, or disposition **:** OUTLOOK ⟨resent his Anglican curate ~ —Gordon Kent⟩ ⟨shunned attempting to depict the ~ of pregnancy —C.W.Cunnington⟩ ⟨a growing socialist ~ —A.R.Williams⟩ ⟨one of the most suggestive studies of the whole Eastern ~ —H.J.Laski⟩ ⟨the civilized Roman ~ —G.G.Coulton⟩

men·tal·ly \'ment³lē, -³li\ *adv* **1 :** without overt motor activity or sensory expression **:** in the mind **:** in thought **:** INWARDLY ⟨work a problem out ~⟩ ⟨~ reproached himself for his weakness⟩ ⟨~ cursed him and all his works⟩ **2 :** as concerns the mind or its operations **:** as concerns capacity for thought or reasoning ⟨a ~ deficient person⟩ ⟨vigorous both physically and ~⟩ **3 :** as concerns intellectual life **:** IDEOLOGICALLY, INTELLECTUALLY ⟨a ~ stimulating atmosphere⟩ ⟨one of the most ~ provocative books of our time⟩

mental philosophy *n* **:** psychology, logic, and metaphysics in a single discipline or area of study or instruction ⟨a professor of *mental philosophy* and moral philosophy —*Current Biog.*⟩ — compare MORAL PHILOSOPHY, NATURAL PHILOSOPHY

mental prominence *or* **mental process** *or* **mental protuberance** *n* **:** the bony prominence at the front of the lower jaw forming the chin

mental ratio *n* **:** INTELLIGENCE QUOTIENT

mentals *pl of* MENTAL

mental spine *or* **mental tubercle** *n* [³*mental*] **:** either of two small elevations on the inner side of the symphysis of the lower jaw providing attachment for the genioglossus and geniohyoid muscles

mental telepathist *n* **:** MIND READER

mental telepathy *n* **:** MIND READING

mental test *n* **:** any of various standardized procedures applied to an individual in order to ascertain his ability or evaluate his behavior in comparison with other individuals or with the average of any class of individuals

men·ta·tion \men'tāshən\ *n* -s [L *ment-, mens* mind + E *-ation* — more at MIND] **:** mental activity ⟨probe the innermost layers of ~ —Warren Beck⟩ ⟨~ is severely affected —*Seminar*⟩ ⟨aspects of unconscious ~ —*Times Lit. Supp.*⟩

men·ta·wei·an \,mentə'wīən\ *n, pl* **mentaweian** *or* **mentaweians** *usu cap* [*Mentawei* islands off the western coast of Sumatra + E *-an*] **1 a :** an Indonesian people inhabiting the Mentawei islands **b :** a member of such people **2 :** the Austronesian language of the Mentaweian people

mentd *abbr* mentioned

menth- *or* **mentho-** *comb form* [ISV, fr. *menthol*] **:** menthol ⟨*menth*one⟩ ⟨*menth*ane⟩

men·tha \'men(t)thə\ *n, cap* [NL, fr. L, mint — more at MINT] **:** a widely distributed genus of herbs comprising the common mints (family Labiatae), having small white or pink verticillate flowers with a nearly regular corolla and four equal stamens, and yielding aromatic volatile oils — see PEPPERMINT, SPEARMINT

men·tha·ce·ae \men'thāsē,ē\ *n pl, cap* [NL, fr. *Mentha,* type genus + *-aceae*] *in some classifications* **:** a family of plants coextensive with the Labiatae — **men·tha·ceous** \(')men¦thāshəs\ *adj*

men·tha·di·ene \,men(t)thə'dī,ēn\ *n* -s [*menthane* + *-diene*] **:** any of several terpenes $C_{10}H_{16}$ (as dipentene, limonene, terpinolene) of which the menthanes are the tetrahydrides

men·thane \'men,thān\ *n* -s [ISV *menth-* + *-ane*] **:** any of three isomeric liquid saturated cyclic hydrocarbons $C_{10}H_{20}$ that are hexahydro derivatives of the cymenes; *esp* **:** the para isomer that is the parent compound of many terpenoids (as carvone, menthol, terpineol) — compare STRUCTURAL FORMULA

para-menthane (*p*-menthane)

men·tha·nol \'men,thā,nōl, -nȯl\ *n* -s [ISV *menthane* + *-ol*] **:** a monohydroxy alcohol $C_{10}H_{19}OH$ (as menthol) derived from a menthane

men·thene \'men,thēn\ *n* -s [ISV *menth-* (fr. NL *Mentha*) + *-ene*] **1 :** an oily unsaturated hydrocarbon $C_{10}H_{18}$ that is a tetrahydro derivative of the para isomer of cymene obtained from menthol by dehydration **2 :** any of several tetrahydro derivatives $C_{10}H_{18}$ (as carvomenthene) of the cymenes

men·the·nol \'men,thē,nōl, -nȯl\ *n* -s [ISV *menthene* + *-ol*] **:** a monohydroxy alcohol $C_{10}H_{17}OH$ (as terpineol) derived from a menthene

men·the·none \'men(t)thə,nōn\ *n* -s [ISV *menthene* + *-one*] **:** a monoketone $C_{10}H_{16}O$ (as pulegone) derived from a menthene

men·thol \'men,thȯl, -thōl\ *n* -s [G, fr. NL *Mentha* + G *-ol*] **:** a secondary terpenoid alcohol $C_{10}H_{19}OH$ that is known in 12 optically isomeric forms including (1) a crystalline levorotatory form that has the odor and cooling properties of peppermint, that occurs naturally esp. in peppermint oil and Japanese mint oil as the principal constituent and is also made synthetically (as from citronellal), and that is used chiefly in medicine (as locally to relieve pain, itching, and nasal congestion) and in flavoring and (2) a crystalline racemic form made synthetically (as by reduction of thymol) and used similarly to the natural form; 3-*para*-menthanol — called also respectively (1) *levo-menthol*, *l-menthol*, *mint camphor*, *peppermint camphor* and (2) *dl-menthol*

men·tho·lat·ed \ˈmen(t)thəˌlād·əd, -ātəd\ *adj* **1 :** treated with menthol **2 :** containing or impregnated with menthol

men·thone \ˈmenˌthōn\ *n* -s [ISV *menth-* + *-one*] **:** a liquid ketone $C_{10}H_{18}O$ that occurs in a levorotatory form esp. in peppermint oil and pennyroyal oil and that can be made synthetically by oxidation of menthol

men·thyl \ˈmen(t)thəl\ *n* -s [ISV *menth-* + *-yl*] **1 :** the univalent radical $C_{10}H_{19}$ derived from menthol by removal of the hydroxyl group; 3-*para*-menthyl **2 :** any of the univalent radicals $C_{10}H_{19}$ derived from menthane by removal of one hydrogen atom

menti- *comb form* [L *ment-, mens* — more at MIND] **:** mind ⟨*menti*cide⟩

men·ti·cide \ˈmentəˌsīd\ *n* -s [*menti-* + *-cide*] **:** a systematic and intentional undermining of a person's conscious mind for the purpose of instilling doubt and replacing that doubt with ideas and attitudes directly inimical to his normal ideas and attitudes by subjecting him to mental and physical torture, extensive interrogation, suggestion, training, and narcotics — compare BRAINWASHING

men·ti·cir·rhus \ˌmentəˈsirəs\ *n, cap* [NL, fr. *menti-* (fr. L *mentum* chin) + *-cirrhus*; fr. the appendage on the lower jaw — more at MENTAL] **:** a genus of No. American food fishes (family Sciaenidae) comprising the whitings

[1]**men·tion** \ˈmenchən\ *n* -s [ME *mencioun*, fr. OF *mention*, fr. L *mention-, mentio*, fr. *ment-, mens* mind + *-ion-, -io* -ion — more at MIND] **1 a :** the act or an instance of citing, noting, or calling attention to someone or something esp. in a brief, casual, or incidental manner **:** reference or citation in speech or writing ⟨his is the earliest ~ of obstetric forceps —Harvey Graham⟩ ⟨so obvious that we ought perhaps to pass it over with only a ~ —H.A.Overstreet⟩ ⟨the wealth of ~ and keenness of observation —W.C.Ford⟩ ⟨the mere ~ of an . . . alliance at this stage is enough to dismiss the idea —*Atlantic*⟩ **b :** specific and usu. formal citation by name (as in a military dispatch or the report of a contest jury) in recognition of outstanding achievement or work well done ⟨his service . . . from 1916 to 1918 earned him a ~ —*Sydney (Australia) Bull.*⟩ ⟨honorable ~s went to the authors of two magazine articles⟩ ⟨many will receive special ~s and special awards —Celia E. Klotz⟩ **2** *obs* **:** INDICATION, VESTIGE, TRACE

[2]**mention** \"\ *vb* **mentioned; mentioned; mentioning** \-ch(ə)niŋ\ **mentions** [MF *mentionner*, fr. *mention*, n.] *vt* **:** to cite, note, or call attention to esp. in a brief, casual, or incidental manner **:** make mention of **:** refer to ⟨had not thought of it at all until she ~*ed* it —J.P.Marquand⟩ ⟨~*ed* as a possible choice for the post of secretary-general —*Current Biog.*⟩ ⟨~*s* that the addition of alkyds improves the flexibility —H.J. Wolfe⟩; *specif* **:** to cite usu. formally in recognition of outstanding achievement or work well done ⟨~*ed* in the dispatches —*Current Biog.*⟩ **~** *vi, obs* **:** to make mention **:** SPEAK — usu. used with *of*

syn NAME, INSTANCE, SPECIFY: MENTION indicates a calling attention to, usu. by name where possible, sometimes by a brief, cursory, or incidental reference ⟨I shall *mention* the accident which directed my curiosity originally into this channel —Charles Lamb⟩ ⟨intellectuals are such puritanical devils that they usually recoil with horror when prayer is *mentioned* —E.M.Forster⟩ ⟨usually the class is not directly *mentioned* in our statement; but there must be an implicit understanding, since otherwise the probability would be indeterminate —A.S. Eddington⟩ ⟨*mentioning* several minor figures in his lecture on Shakespeare⟩ NAME implies clear mention of a name and therefore may suggest greater explicitness ⟨*naming* Doe and Roe in the report and implicating their associates⟩ INSTANCE may indicate clear explicit reference or definite emphasis as a typical example or special case ⟨examples can be *instanced* from the first to the twentieth century —K.S.Latourette⟩ ⟨is it unfair to *instance* Marlowe, who died young —A.T.Quiller-Couch⟩ ⟨I have *instanced* his book because it was flagrant, not unique —Margaret Leech⟩ SPECIFY indicates statement explicit, detailed, and specific so that misunderstanding is impossible ⟨the standards *specify* the names under which these five varieties must be sold —*Americana Annual*⟩ ⟨as changes emerge from the storm of civil commotion, it is often just as hard to *specify* the exact day on which a government is born or dies —P.C.Jessup⟩

men·tion·able \-ch(ə)nəbəl\ *adj* **:** capable of being mentioned

men·tion·er \-ch(ə)nə(r)\ *n* -s **:** one that mentions

mento- *comb form* [NL, fr. L *mentum* — more at MENTAL] **:** chin **:** chin and ⟨*mento*anterior⟩ ⟨*mento*condyloid⟩

men·ton \ˈmenˌtän\ *n* -s [F, chin, fr. L *mentum*] **1 :** the lowest point in the median plane of the chin **2 :** GNATHION

men·tor \ˈmenˌtȯ(ə)r, -ō(ə), -ntə(r)\ *n* -s [after *Mentor*, tutor of Telemachus in the Odyssey of Homer, fr. L, fr. Gk *Mentōr*] **1 :** a close, trusted, and experienced counselor or guide ⟨every one of us needs a ~ who, because he is detached and disinterested, can hold up a mirror to us —P.W.Keve⟩ ⟨was much more than a ~; he supplied decisions —Hilaire Belloc⟩ ⟨has been my ~ since 1946 —Lalia P. Boone⟩ ⟨regarded by patrons . . . as a personal friend as well as fashion ~ —*N.Y. State Legislative Committee on Problems of the Aging*⟩ **2 :** TEACHER, TUTOR, COACH ⟨a writer of monographs, and a ~ of seminars —*Atlantic*⟩ ⟨although he had never accepted a pupil . . . she persuaded him to become her ~ —*Current Biog.*⟩ ⟨one of the game's most successful young ~s —*Official Basketball Guide*⟩

mentor barberry *n* **:** an upright half-evergreen barberry (*Berberis mentorensis*) used as an ornamental and having elliptic ovate subcoriaceous leaves, solitary or sparse yellowish flowers, and dark red fruit

men·tor·ship \-ˌship\ *n* **1 :** the quality or state of being a mentor **:** the office of a mentor **2 :** the influence, guidance, or direction exerted by a mentor ⟨its ~ has been mild enough —*Harper's*⟩ ⟨as it affects the power process, we call such influence ~ —H.D.Lasswell & Abraham Kaplan⟩

-ments *pl of* -MENT

men·tum \ˈmentəm\ *n, pl* **men·ta** \-tə\ [in sense 1, fr. L; in other senses, NL, fr. L — more at MENTAL] **1 :** CHIN **2 a :** a projection like a chin in some orchid flowers formed by the sepals and the base of the column **3 :** a median plate of the labium of an insect — see LABIAL PALPUS **4 :** a projection below the mouth of certain mollusks

ment·ze·lia \men(t)ˈsēlēə\ *n* [NL, fr. Christian *Mentzel* †1701 Ger. physician and botanist + NL *-ia*] **1** *cap* **:** a genus of scabrous and bristly western American herbs or undershrubs (family Loasaceae) with alternate leaves, yellow or white flowers, and a one-celled ovary with numerous ovules **2** -s **a :** any plant of the genus *Mentzelia* — called also *bartonia* **b :** a plant of the related genus *Nuttallia*

menu \ˈme(ˌ)nyü *also* ˈmā(- *sometimes* -nü\ *n* -s [F, fr. *menu*, adj., small, slender, detailed, fr. L *minutus* small — more at MINUTE (adj.)] **1 a** (1) *or* **menu card :** BILL OF FARE ⟨reading the ~s outside cafés —Elizabeth Taylor⟩ (2) **:** DIET, REGIMEN ⟨~s can be made up which will include a variety of foods —H.R.Litchfield & L. H. Dembo⟩ **b :** the dishes served at a meal or the meal itself ⟨serves an excellent ~⟩ ⟨the present trend is toward shorter ~s —Fannie M. Farmer⟩ **c :** the range or variety of food consumed ⟨improves his ~ with bass and bream caught within sight of his kitchen —Jackson Rivers⟩ ⟨the ~ of the rough-legged hawk —D.C.Peattie⟩ **2 :** a program of music, drama, or other entertainment or recreation ⟨the ~ was routine, the playing ditto —Virgil Thomson⟩ ⟨mastering the style of the varied ~ which the . . . company presents —Henry Hewes⟩ ⟨yachting is included in the summer fun ~ —*Springfield (Mass.) Daily News*⟩

menuet *or* **menuetto** *var of* MINUET

me·nu·ra \məˈn(y)u̇rə\ *n, cap* [NL, fr. Gk *mēnē* moon + NL *-ura* — more at MOON] **:** a genus (the type of the family Menuridae) consisting of the lyrebirds

me·nu·rae \-ü(ˌ)rē\ *n pl, cap* [NL, fr. pl. of *Menura*] **:** a suborder of birds (order Passeriformes) comprising the lyrebirds and scrubbirds

me·nus plai·sirs \m(ə)nēplāzēr\ *n pl* [F] **:** small pleasures ⟨spend her small income on her clothes and the *menus plaisirs* of the family —W.S.Maugham⟩

meny·an·tha·ce·ae \ˌmenēˌanˈthāsēˌē\ *n pl, cap* [NL, fr. *Menyanthes*, type genus + *-aceae*] **:** a widely distributed family of aquatic or bog plants (order Gentianales) having basal or alternate leaves and valvate corolla lobes — **menyanthaceous** *adj*

meny·an·thes \ˌmenēˈan(t)(ˌ)thēz\ *n, cap* [NL, fr. *meny-* (origin unknown) + *-anthes*] **:** a genus (the type of the family Menyanthaceae) of bog plants, having thickish creeping rootstocks and racemose flowers on a naked scape — see BUCKBEAN

men·yie *or* **men·zie** \ˈmen(y)i\ *now chiefly Scot var of* MEINY 2

men·zie·sia \menˈzēzh(ē)ə\ *n, cap* [NL, fr. Archibald *Menzies* †1842 Scot. botanist + NL *-ia*] **:** a genus of shrubs (family Ericaceae) of No. America and eastern Asia having small bell-shaped flowers and bluish tinged foliage — see FALSE AZALEA

men·zies larkspur \ˈmenzēz-, -eŋəs-, ˈmiŋəs-\ *n, usu cap M* [after Archibald *Menzies*] **:** a low larkspur (*Delphinium menziesii*) of western No. America, having brownish yellow flowers with blue veins on the petals and being poisonous to stock

menzies spruce *n, usu cap M* [after Archibald *Menzies*] **:** SITKA SPRUCE

meo *usu cap, var of* MIAO

[1]**me·ow** *or* **mi·aow** *also* **mi·aou** *or* **meaow** \mēˈau̇\ *n* -s [imit.] **1 :** the cry of a cat **2 :** a spiteful or malicious remark ⟨the ~ of the week —Walter Winchell⟩

[2]**meow** \"\ *vb* -ED/-ING/-S *vi* **1 :** to utter the characteristic cry of a cat **:** MEW ⟨gave me that long, baffled look of which cats are capable, and immediately ~*ed* to be let out —Paul Gallico⟩ **2 :** to make a catty remark **~** *vt* **:** to utter by or as if by meowing **:** MEW

MEP *abbr, often not cap* mean effective pressure

mep·a·crine \ˈmepəˌkrēn, -ˌkrən\ *n* -s [*meth*yl + *pa*ludism + *acridine*] *Brit* **:** QUINACRINE

me·per·i·dine \məˈperəˌdēn, -ˌdən\ *n* -s [*meth*yl + *piperidine*] **:** a synthetic narcotic drug $C_{15}H_{21}NO_2$ used in the form of its crystalline hydrochloride as an analgesic, sedative, and antispasmodic; ethyl 1-methyl-4-phenyl-piperidine-4-carboxylate

me·phen·e·sin \məˈfenəsən\ *n* -s [*methyl* + *phenol* + cresol + *-in*] **:** a crystalline compound $C_{10}H_{14}O_3$ used chiefly in the treatment of neuromuscular conditions; 3-*ortho*-toloxy-1,2-propane-diol

mephis·to·phe·lian \ˌmefəstəˈfēlyən, ˌmeˌfis-, məˈfis-, meˈfis-, -ēlēən\ *or* **mephis·tophe·lean** \", ˌmefəˌstäfəˈlēən\ *adj, usu cap* [*Mephistopheles*, the devil in various versions of the Faust legend, esp. that of Johann Wolfgang von Goethe †1832 Ger. poet + E *-ian* or *-an*] **:** having a devilish character or aspect **:** SATURNINE ⟨looked . . . slightly *Mephistophelian*, yet with human and lonely brown eyes —*Times Lit. Supp.*⟩

me·phit·ic \məˈfid·ik\ *also* **me·phit·i·cal** \-d·əkəl\ *adj* [F or LL; F *méphitique*, fr. LL *mephiticus*, *mefiticus*, fr. L *mephitis*, *mefitis* mephitis + *-icus* -ic] **:** of, relating to, or like mephitis **:** offensive to the sense of smell **:** NOXIOUS, PESTILENTIAL ⟨the ~ verdure of the Malay peninsula —Jean Stafford⟩ ⟨that purpose which is now hidden in a ~ cloud of love and romance and prudery and fastidiousness —G.B.Shaw⟩

mephitic air *or* **mephitic gas** *n* **1** *archaic* **:** CARBON DIOXIDE **2** *archaic* **:** air exhausted of oxygen and containing chiefly nitrogen

[1]**meph·i·tine** \ˈmefəˌtēn, -ətən\ *adj* [NL *Mephitis* + E *-ine*] **:** of or relating to skunks

[2]**mephitine** \"\ *n* -s **:** SKUNK

me·phi·tis \məˈfīd·əs\ *n* [L *mephitis*, *mefitis*, fr. Oscan] **1** -ES **a :** a noxious, pestilential, or foul exhalation from the earth **b :** an offensive or poisonous smell from any source **:** STENCH **2** *cap* [NL, fr. L] **:** a genus of mammals that includes the No. American striped skunks

mepho·barbital \ˌmefō+\ *n* [*methyl* + *pho-* (fr. *phenyl*) + *barbital*] **:** a crystalline barbiturate $C_{13}H_{14}N_2O_3$ used as a sedative and in the treatment of epilepsy

me·pro·ba·mate \məˈprōbəˌmāt, ˌmeprōˈbaˌmāt\ *n* -s [*methyl* + *propyl* + dicar*bamate*] **:** a bitter powder $CH_3(C_3H_7)C(CH_2OOCNH_2)_2$ that is an ester of carbamic acid and a derivative of propane-diol and is used as a tranquilizer

meq *abbr* milliequivalent

mer \ˈmər\ *n* -s [*-mer*] **:** a monomeric unit of a polymer

mer *abbr* **1** meridian **2** meridional

[1]**mer-** *comb form* [ME, fr. *mere* sea, lake, pond, fr. OE — more at MARINE] **:** sea ⟨*mer*maid⟩ ⟨*mer*man⟩ ⟨*mer*woman⟩

[2]**mer-** *or* **mero-** *comb form* [Gk *mēr-*, *mēro-*, fr. *mēros* — more at MEMBER] **:** thigh ⟨*mer*algia⟩ ⟨*mero*cele⟩

[3]**mer-** *or* **mero-** *comb form* [ISV, fr. Gk, fr. *meros* part — more at MERIT] **:** part **:** partial ⟨*mer*aspis⟩ ⟨*mero*hedral⟩ ⟨*mero*sporangium⟩

-mer \ˌmə(r)\ *n comb form* -s [ISV, fr. Gk *meros* part — more at MERIT] *chem* **:** member of a (specified) class ⟨iso*mer*⟩ ⟨meta*mer*⟩ ⟨poly*mer*⟩

me·ral·gia \məˈralj(ē)ə\ *n* -s [NL, fr. [2]*mer-* + *-algia*] **:** pain esp. of a neuralgic kind in the thigh

mer·al·lu·ride \məˈralyəˌrīd, -ˌrəd\ *n* -s [*mercury* + *all-* + [1]*ur-* + *-ide*] **:** a diuretic consisting of a chemical combination of an organic mercurial compound $C_9H_{16}HgN_2O_6$ and theophylline and administered chiefly by injection as an aqueous solution of its sodium salt

mer·a·mec \ˈmerəˌmak, -ˌmek\ *adj, usu cap* [fr. *Meramec* river, Mo.] **:** of or relating to the division of the Mississippian geologic period between the Osagian and the Chesterian — see GEOLOGIC TIME table

me·ran·ti \məˈrantē\ *n* -s [Malay *měranti*] **1 :** the soft weak light usu. pinkish to dark red wood of various trees of the genera *Hopea* and *Shorea* of Malaysia, Borneo, and the Philippines that is sometimes substituted for mahogany in cabinetwork, veneer, and interior finishes — compare LAUAN **2 :** a tree that yields meranti

me·ras·pis \məˈraspəs\ *n* -ES [NL, fr. [3]*mer-* + *aspis* shield — more at ASPID-] **:** a late larva of a trilobite in which the pygidium is beginning to form

me·ra·tia \məˈrāsh(ē)ə\ [NL, fr. François Victor *Mérat* †1851, Fr. physician and botanist + NL *-ia*] *syn of* CHIMONANTHUS

me·ra·wan \məˈräwən\ *n* -s [Malay *měrawan*] **:** the yellowish to brown usu. moderately heavy, hard, and durable wood of several Malayan trees of the genus *Hopea* that is used chiefly for furniture and construction work — compare MERANTI

mer·bro·min \ˌmərˈbrōmən\ *n* -s [*mer*curic acetate + di*bromo*-fluorescein] **:** an iridescent green crystalline mercurial compound $C_{20}H_8Br_2HgNa_2O_6$ made from dibromo-fluorescein and mercuric acetate and applied topically as an antiseptic and germicide in the form of its red solution having a yellow-green fluorescence

merc *abbr* **1** mercantile **2** mercurial; mercury

mer·cal·li scale \merˈkälē-, mər|\ *n, usu cap M* [after Giuseppe *Mercalli* †1914 Ital. priest and geologist] **:** an arbitrary scale of earthquake intensity ranging from I for an earthquake detected only by seismographs to XII for one causing total destruction of all buildings

mer·cal·lite \(ˌ)mərˈkaˌlīt\ *n* -s [G, *Mercalli* + E *-ite*] **:** a mineral $KHSO_4$ consisting of a bisulfate of potassium

mer·can·tile \ˈmərkənˌtēl, ˈmək-, ˈməik-, -nˌtīl *sometimes* -ntᵊl *or* -ntəl\ *adj* [F, fr. It, fr. *mercante* merchant (fr. L *mercant-, mercans*, fr. pres. part. of *mercari* to trade, deal in commodities) + *-ile* — more at MERCHANT] **1 :** of or relating to merchants or trading **:** appropriate to or characteristic of merchants **:** engaged in trade ⟨the ~ North was forging ahead —Van Wyck Brooks⟩ **2 :** of, relating to, or having the characteristics of mercantilism ⟨~ system⟩ ⟨~ theories⟩ **3 :** having or exhibiting the motives of a merchant **:** having gain as its objective **:** MERCENARY ⟨preached a ~ and militant patriotism —John Buchan⟩

mercantile agency *n* **1 :** the agency of a factor who in the customary course of his business has authority binding on his principal to buy or to sell goods, to consign goods for sale, or to raise money by pledging goods **2 :** an agency that collects credit information about businesses and businessmen and furnishes it to subscribers — called also *commercial agency*

mercantile agent *n* **1 :** one having the powers of mercantile agency **:** FACTOR 1a **2 :** the conductor of a mercantile agency

mercantile credit *n* **:** credit extended by one business to another — distinguished from *consumer credit*

mercantile law *n* **:** the laws that govern merchants in business dealings — compare COMMERCIAL LAW, LAW MERCHANT

mercantile marine *n* **:** MERCHANT MARINE

mercantile paper *n* **:** notes, bills, and acceptances based on business activity — compare COMMERCIAL PAPER

mer·can·til·ism \ˈmərkənˌtēˌlizəm, ˈmək-, ˈməik-, -nˌtīˌl- *sometimes* -ntᵊlˌizəm *or* -ntəˌlizəm\ *n* -s [F *mercantilisme*, fr. *mercantile* + *-isme* -ism] **1 :** the spirit, theory, or practice of mercantile pursuits **:** devotion to commercial enterprise **:** COMMERCIALISM **2 :** an economic system developing during the centralization of power accompanying the decay of feudalism and intended primarily to unify and increase the power and esp. the monetary wealth of a nation by a strict governmental regulation of the entire national economy usu. through policies designed to secure an accumulation of bullion, a favorable balance of trade, the development of agriculture and manufactures, and the establishment of foreign trading monopolies — compare AUTARKY, CAMERALISM, CAPITALISM, COMMUNISM, FREE ENTERPRISE, LAISSEZ-FAIRE, LIBERALISM, PLANNED ECONOMY, SOCIALISM

[1]**mer·can·til·ist** \-ˌləst\ *n* -s [*mercantile* + *-ist*] **:** an advocate or practitioner of mercantilism

[2]**mercantilist** \" *also* **mer·can·til·is·tic** \ˌ==(ˌ)=ˈlistik\ *adj* **:** of or relating to the theory or practice of mercantilism ⟨the monopoly chartered companies of the medieval and ~ periods —L.M.Hacker⟩

mercapt- *or* **mercapto-** *comb form* [ISV, fr. *mercaptan*] **:** derived from or related to a mercaptan ⟨*mercapt*al⟩ ⟨*mercapt*ide⟩

mer·cap·tal \(ˌ)mərˈkapˌtal\ *n* -s [ISV *mercapt-* + *-al*] **:** any of a class of compounds that are sulfur analogues of the acetals characterized by the group $>C(SR)_2$, that are formed by the reaction of mercaptans with aldehydes or ketones, and that in the case of the members of low molecular weight are oily liquids of unpleasant odor

mer·cap·tan \-ˌtan\ *n* -s [G, fr. Dan, fr. ML *mercurium captans*, lit., seizing mercury] **:** any of a class of compounds with the general formula RSH that are analogous to the alcohols and phenols but contain sulfur in place of oxygen and that in the case of those of low molecular weight have very disagreeable odors; *esp* **:** ETHYL MERCAPTAN — called also *thiol*; compare HYDROSULFIDE, THIOALCOHOL, THIOPHENOL

mer·cap·tide \-ˌtīd\ *n* -s [*mercapt-* + *-ide*] **:** a metallic derivative of a mercaptan

mer·cap·to \-ˌtō\ *adj* [*mercapt-*] *chem* **:** being or containing the group SH

mer·cap·to·acetic acid \(ˌ)=ˈ==+-\ *n* [*mercapt-* + *acetic*] **:** THIOGLYCOLIC ACID

mer·cap·to·benzothiazole \(ˌ)=ˈ==+\ *n* [*mercapt-* + *benz-* + *thiazole*] **:** a crystalline heterocyclic compound $C_7H_4NS(SH)$ made by heating aniline, sulfur, and carbon disulfide and used chiefly as an accelerator for the vulcanization of rubber — called also 2-*mercaptobenzothiazole*

mer·cap·tole \(ˌ)mərˈkapˌtōl\ *n* -s [ISV *mercapt-* + *-ole*] **:** a mercaptal formed from a ketone and analogous to a ketal

mer·cap·tom·er·in \(ˌ)mərˌkapˈtämərən\ *n* -s [*mercapt-* + *mercury* + *-in*] **:** a mercurial diuretic related chemically to mercurophylline and administered by injection of an aqueous solution of its sodium salt $C_{16}H_{25}HgNNa_2O_6S$

mer·cap·to·purine \(ˌ)=ˈkaptō+\ *n* [*mercapt-* + *purine*] **:** an antimetabolite $C_5H_4N_4S$ that is a sulfur analogue of hypoxanthine and adenine, that interferes esp. with the metabolism of purine bases and the biosynthesis of nucleic acids, and that is sometimes useful in the treatment of acute leukemia esp. in children; 6-purine-thiol

mer·cap·tu·ric acid \ˈmərˌkapˈt(y)u̇rik-\ *n* [ISV *mercapturic*, fr. *mercapt-* + *-uric*] **:** an acid $RSCH_2CH(NHCOCH_3)COOH$ formed from cysteine and an aromatic compound (as bromobenzene) in the body and usu. excreted in the urine (as in the form of a glucuronide); an *S*-aryl derivative of *N*-acetyl-cysteine

mer·ca·tor chart \ˌmərˈkād·ər-, merˈkä,tȯ(ə)r-\ *n, usu cap M* [after Gerhardus *Mercator* †1594 Flemish geographer] **:** a chart or map drawn on the Mercator projection

[1]**mer·ca·to·ri·al** \ˌmərkəˈtōrēəl, -tȯr-\ *adj* [L *mercatorius*, fr. *mercator* merchant, fr. *mercatus* (past part. of *mercari* to trade) + *-or* — more at MERCHANT] *archaic* **:** MERCANTILE

[2]**mercatorial** \"\ *adj, usu cap* [Gerhardus *Mercator* + E *-ial*] **:** of or relating to the geographer Mercator or his method of projection ⟨*Mercatorial* bearings⟩

mercator projection *n, usu cap M* [after Gerhardus *Mercator*]

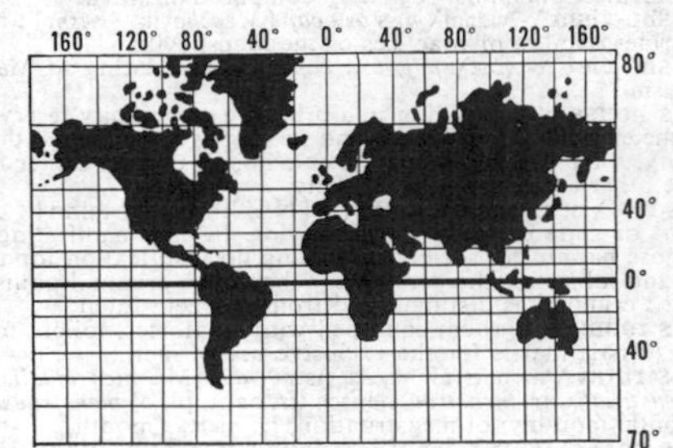

mercator projection

: a map projection in which the meridians are drawn parallel to each other and the parallels of latitude are straight lines whose distance from each other increases with their distance from the equator so that at all places the degrees of latitude and longitude have to each other the same ratio as on the sphere itself with resultant apparent enlargement of the polar regions but with great value in navigation since a rhumb line on a Mercator map is always a straight line

mer·ce·dar·i·an \ˌmərsəˈda(a)rēən\ *n* -s *usu cap* [ML *merced-, merces* mercy (in *Ordo Beatae Mariae de Mercede* Order of Our Lady of Mercy) + E *-arian* — more at MERCY] **:** a member of the Order of Our Lady of Mercy founded at Barcelona about 1218 by St. Peter Nolasco

mer·ce·nar·ia \ˌmərsəˈna(a)rēə\ *n, cap* [NL, fr. L, fem. of *mercenarius* mercenary; fr. the use of the shells of *Mercenaria mercenaria* as wampum beads by American Indians — more at MERCENARY] **:** a genus of clams (family Veneridae) including the quahog

mer·ce·nar·i·ly \ˈmərsᵊnˈerəlē, ˈməs-, ˈməis-, -li\ *adv* **:** in a mercenary manner

mer·ce·nar·i·ness \ˈ==ˌerēnəs, -rin-\ *n* -ES **:** the quality or state of being mercenary

[1]**mer·ce·nary** \ˈ==ˌerē, -ri\ *n* -ES [ME *mercenarie*, fr. L *mercenarius, mercennarius*, adj. & n., fr. *merced-, merces* wages, reward + *-arius* -ary — more at MERCY] **1 :** one that serves merely for wages **:** HIRELING ⟨half a dozen such *mercenaries* judiciously placed . . . may turn a cold audience into an enthusiastic one —A.T.Weaver⟩ **2 :** a person paid for his work; *esp* **:** a soldier hired into foreign service ⟨the kingdom was now supported . . . largely by foreign *mercenaries* and a made-to-order navy —A.L.Kroeber⟩

[2]**mercenary** \"\ *adj* [L *mercenarius, mercennarius*] **1 a :** serving merely for pay or gain **:** seeking sordid advantage **:** VENAL ⟨abandoned their high standards and disinterested motives in favor of a ~ concern over fees —W.T. & Barbara Fitts⟩ ⟨so thoroughly ~, so frankly greedy, that there's nothing disagreeable about it —Dashiell Hammett⟩ **b :** showing conspicuous lust for money **:** based on or marked by greed ⟨if a writer's attitude toward his characters and his scene is . . . as ~ as an auctioneer's, vulgar and meretricious will his product for ever remain —Willa Cather⟩ **2 a :** employed or engaged primarily on a wage basis — now used only of a soldier serving in the army of a country other than his own **b** *obs* **:** PAID, SALARIED **:** COMMERCIAL — used of an office or enterprise

mer·cer \ˈmərsə(r), ˈmə̄sə(r, ˈməis-\ *n* -s [ME, fr. OF *mersier, mercier* merchant, fr. *mers, merz* merchandise (fr. L *merc-, merx* ware, merchandise) + *-ier* -er — more at MARKET] *Brit* **:** a dealer in textile fabrics

mer·cer·i·za·tion \ˌ==səˈzāshən, -ˌrīˈz-\ *n* -s **:** the act or process of mercerizing

mer·cer·ize \ˈ==ˌrīz\ *vt* -ED/-ING/-S *see -ize in Explan Notes* [John *Mercer* †1866 English calico printer + E *-ize*] **1 :** to give (cotton yarn or cloth) luster, strength, and receptiveness to dyes by treatment under tension with caustic soda — compare CAUSTICIZE 2 **2 :** to steep (wood pulp) in a caustic soda solution during the manufacture of viscose rayon

mer·cer·iz·er \-ˌrīzə(r)\ *n* -s **1 :** a textile worker who mercerizes **2 :** a machine for mercerization

mer·cers·burg \ˈmərsərz,bərg\ *adj, usu cap* [fr. *Mercersburg*, Pa., the former site of the Theological Seminary of the German Reformed Church, where the doctrine was in part formulated] **:** of or relating to a system of American theology developed in the German Reformed Church in the middle and late 19th century and marked by Christocentrism, a Calvinist view of the Lord's Supper, and emphasis on the liturgical element in worship

mer·cery \ˈmərs(ə)rē, ˈmə̄s-,ˈməis-, -ri\ *n* -ES [ME *mercerie*, fr. OF *merserie, mercerie*, fr. *mers, merz* merchandise + *-erie* -ery] **1** *Brit* **:** a mercer's wares or shop **2** *Brit* **:** a mercer's occupation or dealings

merch *abbr* merchantable

mer·chan·dis·able \ˈmərchən,dīzəbəl, ˈmə̄ch-,ˈməich-, ˌ==-ˈ===\ *adj* [²*merchandise* + *-able*] **:** MERCHANTABLE

¹**mer·chan·dise** \ˈ==ˌdīz, -īs\ *n* -s [ME *marchaundise*, fr. OF *marcheandise*, fr. *marcheant* merchant — more at MERCHANT] **1 a :** the commodities or goods that are bought and sold in business **:** the wares of commerce **b** *obs* **:** an article of merchandise **2** *archaic* **:** the buying and selling of goods for profit **:** the occupation of a merchant **:** business activity

²**mer·chan·dise** *also* **mer·chan·dize** \-īz\ *vb* -ED/-ING/-S [ME *marchaundisen*, fr. *marchaundise*, n.] *vi* **:** to carry on commerce **:** TRADE, TRAFFIC ~ *vt* **1 :** to buy and sell **:** deal in **:** make merchandise of **2 :** to carry on sales promotion of **:** advertise, publicize, or present attractively or effectively — **mer·chan·dis·er** \-zə(r)\ *n* -s

merchandise freight *n* **:** goods in less than carload lots for expedited movement in merchandise trains

merchandising *n* -s [fr. gerund of ²*merchandise*] **:** sales promotion as a comprehensive function including market research, development of new products, coordination of manufacture and marketing, and effective advertising and selling

¹**mer·chant** \ˈmərchənt, ˈmə̄ch-,ˈməich-\ *n* -s [ME *marchaunt, marchaund, marchant*, fr. OF *marcheant*, fr. (assumed) VL *mercatant-, mercatans*, fr. pres. part. of (assumed) VL *mercatare*, fr. L *mercatus*, past part. of *mercari* to trade, deal in commodities, fr. *merc-, merx* ware, merchandise — more at MARKET] **1 a :** a buyer and seller of commodities for profit **:** TRADER **b :** the operator of a retail business **:** STOREKEEPER **2** *Scot* **:** CUSTOMER **3** *archaic* **:** FELLOW, GUY **4** *obs* **:** MERCHANTMAN **5 :** a person conspicuous for ideas or activities of a particular kind **:** PURVEYOR, SPECIALIST ⟨his guess is likely to be as accurate as that of the ~ of doom —Harrison Smith⟩ ⟨had been . . . acquiring among musical-comedy orchestrators a reputation as a speed ~ —H.W.Wind⟩

²**merchant** \"\ *adj* [ME *marchaund, marchant*, fr. *marchaunt, marchaund, marchant*, n.] **1 a :** of, relating to, or used in commerce **b :** of or relating to a merchant marine **c :** having a merchant's traits or qualities **2 a :** of ordinary or standard shape or size **:** not made to special order **:** STOCK — used of metal bars and ingots ⟨~ pig iron⟩ **b :** producing metal bars or ingots in standard shapes and sizes ⟨~ mill⟩

³**merchant** \"\ *vb* -ED/-ING/-S [ME *marchaunden*, fr. MF *marchander*, fr. OF *marcheandier*, fr. *marcheant* merchant] *vi, archaic* **:** to deal or trade as a merchant ~ *vt* **:** to buy and sell **:** deal or trade in ⟨something considerably superior to what Broadway usually ~*s* in these days —G.J.Nathan⟩

mer·chant·able \-təbəl\ *adj* [ME *merchandabull*, fr. *marchaunden* + *-abull*, *-able* -able] **:** of commercial quality **:** acceptable to buyers **:** SALABLE ⟨it is estimated that a thousand million tons of ~ coal are in reserve —*Canadian Mining Jour.*⟩ — **merchant·able·ness** *n* -ES

merchant adventurer *n, pl* **merchant adventurers** *or* **merchants adventurers** [ME *marchaunt adventurer*] **:** a merchant who establishes foreign trading stations and carries on business ventures abroad; *esp* **:** a member of one of the former English companies of merchant adventurers operating from the 14th to the 16th centuries

merchant banker *n* **:** an acceptance house that also does investment banking

merchant flag *n* **:** a flag flown by the merchant vessels of a country that is sometimes identical with the national flag

merchantlike \ˈ==ˌ=\ *adj* **1 :** like or proper to a merchant **2** *obs* **:** MERCANTILE

merchantly *adj, obs* **:** of or relating to merchants

mer·chant·man \ˈ==mən\ *n, pl* **merchantmen** [ME *marchand man*] **1** *archaic* **:** MERCHANT **2 :** a ship commercially operated to carry passengers or freight **:** a ship used in commerce — called also *merchant ship*

merchant marine *n* **1 :** the privately or publicly owned commercial vessels of a nation as distinguished from its navy **2 :** the personnel of a merchant marine

merchant middleman *n* **:** a middleman who takes title to goods purchased for resale

merchant navy *n, Brit* **:** MERCHANT MARINE

merchant prince *n* **:** a merchant of great wealth

mer·chant·ry \ˈmərchəntrē\ *n* -ES **:** a merchant's dealings **:** TRADE

merchant seaman *n* **:** a seaman employed on a merchant ship

merchant service *n* **:** MERCHANT MARINE

merchant ship *n* **:** MERCHANTMAN 2

merchant tailor *n* **:** a custom tailor who owns his business and supplies the fabrics he uses

merchant venturer *n, obs* **:** MERCHANT ADVENTURER

merchet *var of* MARCHET

¹**mer·cian** \ˈmərsh(ē)ən\ *adj, usu cap* [*Mercia*, ancient Anglian kingdom in central England + E *-an*] **1 a :** of, relating to, or characteristic of the Anglian kingdom of Mercia **b :** of, relating to, or characteristic of the Mercians **2 :** of, relating to, or constituting the Old English dialect of Mercia

²**mercian** \"\ *n* -s *cap* **1 :** a native or inhabitant of Mercia **2 :** the Old English dialect of Mercia

mercies *pl of* MERCY

mer·ci·ful \ˈmərsəfəl, ˈmə̄s-, ˈməis-, -sēf-\ *adj* [ME, fr. *merci, mercy* mercy + *-ful* — more at MERCY] **:** full of mercy **:** marked, exercising, or disposed to mercy **:** CLEMENT, COMPASSIONATE, LENIENT ⟨if tried by the manners of his age, Caesar was the most ~ of conquerors —J.A.Froude⟩ ⟨the ~ possibilities of the antibiotics —F.L.Allen⟩ **syn** see FORBEARING

mer·ci·ful·ly \-f(ə)lē, -li\ *adv* [ME, fr. *merciful* + *-ly*] **:** in a merciful manner **:** so as to be merciful ⟨struggles that were ~ brief⟩

mer·ci·ful·ness \-fəlnəs\ *n* -ES **:** the quality or state of being merciful

mer·ci·less \-sēləs, -sələs *sometimes* -sləs\ *adj* [ME *mercyles*, fr. *merci, mercy* mercy + *-les* -less] **:** having, extending, or showing no mercy **:** CRUEL, HARSH, PITILESS, REMORSELESS ⟨turns a ~ spotlight on the precocious technicians, the spiritual sophomores, and the hairy-chested muscle men of contemporary literature —Gilbert Highet⟩ — **mer·ci·less·ly** *adv* — **mer·ci·less·ness** *n* -ES

Mer·cu·hy·drin \ˌmərkyəˈhīdrən\ *trademark* — used for meralluride

mercur- *or* **mercuro-** *comb form* [ISV, fr. *mercury*] **:** mercury ⟨*mercuro*phylline⟩

¹**mer·cu·rate** \ˈmərkyərət, -ˌrāt, *usu* -d·+V\ *also* **mer·cu·ri·ate** \(ˌ)mərˈkyu̇rēət, -ēˌāt, *usu* -d·+V\ *n* -s [*mercur-* or *mercuri-* + *-ate* (n. suffix)] **:** any of various salts containing bivalent mercury in a complex anion — compare IODOMERCURATE

²**mer·cu·rate** \ˈmərkyəˌrāt, ˈmə̄k-, ˈməik-, *usu* -ād·+V\ *vt* -ED/-ING/-S [*mercur-* + *-ate* (v. suffix)] **:** to combine or treat with mercury or a mercury salt **:** introduce mercury into (as an organic compound) — **mer·cu·ra·tion** \ˌ==ˈrāshən\ *n* -s

mercuri- *comb form* [ISV, fr. *mercury*] *chem* **:** mercuric ⟨chloro*mercuri*phenol $ClHgC_6H_4OH$⟩

¹**mer·cu·ri·al** \ˌmərˈkyu̇rēəl, ˌmə(r)ˈk-, (ˈ)mə̄ˈk-, (ˈ)məiˈk-\ *adj* [L *mercurialis* of the god Mercury, of the planet Mercury, fr. *Mercurius* Mercury, ancient Roman god of commerce and messenger of the gods & *Mercurius* Mercury, the 1st planet from the sun (fr. *stella Mercurii*, lit., star of Mercury, after *Mercurius*, the god Mercury; trans. of Gk *astēr tou Hermou*, lit., star of Hermes, Greek messenger of the gods) + *-alis* -al] **1** *usu cap* **:** of, relating to, or like the ancient Roman god Mercury **2 a :** of or relating to the planet Mercury **b :** born under or influenced astrologically by the planet Mercury **3 :** having qualities of eloquence, ingenuity, sharp dealing, or thievishness attributed in myth to the god Mercury and in astrology to the influence of the planet Mercury ⟨more than ~ thievishness —*Sat. Rev.*⟩ **4 :** characterized by rapid and unpredictable changeableness or by quick-wittedness **:** SPRIGHTLY, TEMPERAMENTAL, VOLATILE ⟨a deeply ~ intuitive artist —Christopher Morley⟩ ⟨~ desponds —D.C.Peattie⟩ ⟨~ twists of temperament —T.B.Costain⟩ ⟨the Japanese are ~ — high-strung, touchy, ready to fly into a rage —D.G. Haring⟩ **5** [*Mercury* + *-al*] **a :** of, relating to, containing, or consisting of mercury ⟨~ preparations⟩ **b :** caused by or exhibiting the physiological effect of the use of mercury ⟨~ sore mouth⟩ **syn** see INCONSTANT

²**mercurial** \"\ *n* -s **1** *obs* **:** a person born under Mercury or having mercurial qualities **2** [L (*herba*) *mercurialis* dog's mercury, lit., Mercurial herb] *obs* **:** GOOD-KING-HENRY **3 :** a pharmaceutical preparation or chemical compound containing mercury ⟨the diuretic action of ~*s*⟩

mer·cu·ri·a·lis \(ˌ)mərˌkyu̇rēˈaləs, -ˈāl-, -ˈäl-\ *n* [NL, fr. L (*herba*) *mercurialis* dog's mercury] **1** *cap* **:** a small genus of slender herbs (family Euphorbiaceae) having opposite pinnately-veined leaves and apetalous flowers in interrupted axillary spikes — see BOYS-AND-GIRLS 2, DOG'S MERCURY **2** -ES **:** an herb (*Mercurialis annua*) formerly dried for use as a purgative, diuretic, and antisyphilitic

mer·cu·ri·al·ism \(ˌ)=ˈ==əˌlizəm\ *n* -s **:** chronic poisoning with mercury (as from excessive medication or industrial contacts with the metal or its fumes) — called also *hydrargyrism*

mercurialist *n* -s *obs* **:** MERCURIAL 1

mer·cu·ri·al·i·ty \(ˌ)=ˌ==ˈaləd·ē\ *n* -ES **:** the quality or state of being mercurial **:** VOLATILITY

mer·cu·ri·al·ly \ˌmərˈkyu̇rēəlē, ˌmə(r)ˈk-, (ˈ)mə̄ˈk-, (ˈ)məiˈk-, -li\ *adv* **:** in a mercurial manner

mercurial ointment *n* **:** an ointment containing about 50 percent of finely divided metallic mercury incorporated with wool fat, white wax, mercury oleate, and white petrolatum — compare BLUE OINTMENT

¹**mercurian** *adj* [*Mercury* (god & planet) + E *-an*] *obs* **:** MERCURIAL

²**mer·cu·ri·an** \(ˌ)mərˈkyu̇rēən\ *n* -s *usu cap* **1 :** one born under Mercury **2 :** one that has a well-developed Mount of Mercury and a long and large finger of Mercury and that is usu. held by palmists to be characterized by shrewdness, quickness, and energy

mercuriate *var of* MERCURATE

mer·cu·ric \ˌmərˈkyu̇rik, ˌmə(r)ˈk-, (ˈ)mə̄ˈk-, (ˈ)məiˈk-, -rēk\ *adj* [*mercur-* + *-ic*] **:** of, relating to, or containing mercury — used esp. of compounds in which this element is bivalent

mercuric chloride *n* **:** MERCURY CHLORIDE b

mercuric cyanide *n* **:** the mercury cyanide $Hg(CN)_2$

mercuric iodide *n* **:** MERCURY IODIDE b

mercuric oxide *n* **:** a slightly water-soluble crystalline poisonous compound HgO known in two forms (1) a yellow finely divided powder obtained usu. by precipitation from solutions of mercury chloride (sense b) and sodium hydroxide and used chiefly in medicine (as in antiseptic ointments), in antifouling paints, and in making other mercury compounds (2) a bright red coarse powder obtained by precipitation from hot solutions or by heating mercurous nitrate and used similarly to the yellow form and also in dry cells — called also *mercury(II) oxide*

mercuric sulfide *n* **:** an insoluble compound HgS occurring in nature as the red mineral cinnabar and the black mineral metacinnabar and also made synthetically in red and black forms — called also *mercury(II) sulfide;* see VERMILION 1a

mer·cu·ride \ˈmərkyəˌrīd, -rə̇d\ *n* -s [*mercur-* + *-ide*] **:** a binary compound of mercury with a more electropositive element or radical — compare AMALGAM

mer·cu·rize \-ˌrīz\ *vt* -ED/-ING/-S [*mercur-* + *-ize*] **:** MERCURATE

mercuro- — see MERCUR-

Mer·cu·ro·chrome \(ˌ)mərˈkyu̇rəˌkrōm\ *trademark* — used for merbromin

mer·cu·ro·phyl·line \ˌmərkyərōˈfiˌlēn, -ˌlən\ *n* -s [*mercur-* + *theophylline*] **:** a diuretic consisting of a chemical combination of an organic mercurial compound or its sodium salt $C_{14}H_{24}HgNNaO_5$ and theophylline

mer·cu·rous \(ˌ)mərˈkyu̇rəs, ˈmərkyər-\ *adj* [*mercur-* + *-ous*] **:** of, relating to, or containing mercury — used esp. of compounds in which this element is regarded as univalent ⟨the ~ ion . . . is $Hg:Hg^{++}$ rather than Hg^+ —E.S.Gould⟩

mercurous chloride *n* **:** CALOMEL

mercurous iodide *n* **:** MERCURY IODIDE a

mer·cu·ry \ˈmərkyərē, ˈmə̄k-, ˈməik-, -k(ə)rē, -ri\ *n* -ES **1** [ME *mercurie*, fr. ML *mercurius*, fr. L *Mercurius* Mercury, ancient Roman god of commerce and messenger of the gods; prob. fr. the comparison of the mobility of the metal to the traditional fleetfootedness of the god] **a :** a heavy silver-white univalent and bivalent poisonous metallic element that is the only metal liquid at ordinary temperatures, that occurs native and in cinnabar, calomel, and a few other minerals, that is prepared usu. by roasting cinnabar and condensing the vapors, and that is used chiefly in scientific instruments (as electrical apparatus, control devices, thermometers, barometers), mercury boilers, mercury pumps, and mercury-vapor lamps — symbol *Hg;* called also *quicksilver;* see AMALGAM, ELEMENT table **b :** the mercury in a thermometer or barometer ⟨in a climate where the ~ sports around 110 the whisky should be only of the best quality —D.D.Martin⟩ **c :** pressure (as in the manifold of an engine) measured in inches or millimeters of mercury ⟨pulling between forty-seven and fifty inches of ~ —J.M. Redding & H.I.Leyshon⟩ **d :** a pharmaceutical preparation containing the metal mercury or a compound of it **e** *often cap, obs* **:** mercurial quality **:** brilliance, inconstancy, or volatility of mood or attitude **f :** the principle of liquidity and volatility in alchemy **2** [ME *mercurie* fr. *Mercurie* the god *Mercury*, fr. L *Mercurius;* after L (*herba*) *mercurialis* dog's mercury] **:** any of several plants: as **a :** a plant of the genus *Mercurialis; esp* **:** DOG'S MERCURY **b :** GOOD-KING-HENRY **c :** POISON IVY **3** [after *Mercury*, messenger of the gods, fr. ME *Mercurie*] **a** *often cap, archaic* **:** a bearer of messages or news or a conductor of travelers **b** *usu cap, obs* (1) **:** a statue of Mercury (2) **:** SIGNPOST (3) **:** HERM **c** *usu cap, obs* **:** a hawker of pamphlets

mercury arc *n* **:** an electric discharge through mercury vapor in a glass or quartz tube emitting a blue-green light rich in actinic and ultraviolet rays and used for various purposes (as for water sterilization, in photography, and in a rectifier)

mercury-arc lamp *n* **:** MERCURY-VAPOR LAMP

mercury-arc rectifier *n* **:** an alternating-current rectifier consisting of a mercury arc esp. designed to utilize its rectifying action, one electrode being a pool of mercury with current flowing only during that part of the cycle in which the mercury acts as the cathode

mercury bichloride *n* **:** MERCURY CHLORIDE b — not used systematically

mercury chloride *n* **:** a chloride of mercury: as **a :** CALOMEL **b :** a heavy transparent crystalline poisonous compound $HgCl_2$ made usu. by heating mercury with gaseous chlorine or by subliming a mixture of mercury sulfate and common salt and used chiefly as a disinfectant and fungicide, in making other mercury compounds, and in photography — called also *corrosive sublimate, mercuric chloride, mercury(II) chloride*

mercury cyanide *n* **:** a cyanide of mercury; *esp* **:** the crystalline poisonous mercuric compound $Hg(CN)_2$ made usu. by reaction of mercuric oxide with hydrocyanic acid and used chiefly in medicine

mercury fulminate *n* **:** a crystalline compound $Hg(ONC)_2$ that when dry explodes violently on percussion or heating, that is usu. made by reaction of mercury, alcohol, and nitric acid, and that is used in blasting caps, percussion caps, and detonators — called also *fulminating mercury*

mercury glass *n* **:** thin glass blown with double walls and sealed after silvering of the enclosed surface of the inner wall to produce an ornamental ware — called also *silvered glass*

mercury iodide *n* **:** either of two iodides of mercury: **a :** a yellow amorphous powder Hg_2I_2 that turns greenish on exposure to light — called also *mercurous iodide* **b :** a red crystalline poisonous salt HgI_2 that changes to a yellow crystalline modification when heated above 126° C and that is used chiefly in medicine — called also *mercuric iodide*

mercury lamp *n* **:** MERCURY-VAPOR LAMP

mercury line *n, usu cap M* [after *Mercury*, Roman god of commerce, fr. L *Mercurius*] **:** LINE OF MERCURY

mercury oxide *n* **:** an oxide of mercury; *esp* **:** MERCURIC OXIDE

mercury red *n* **:** vermilion or a color resembling it

mercury's staff *n, usu cap M* **:** CADUCEUS 2

mercury sulfide *n* **:** a sulfide of mercury; *esp* **:** MERCURIC SULFIDE

mercury switch *n* **:** a switch in which an electric circuit is closed and opened by tilting a reservoir of liquid mercury

mercury thiocyanate *n* **:** a thiocyanate of mercury; *esp* **:** the crystalline poisonous mercuric compound $Hg(SCN)_2$ made by precipitation and used chiefly in fireworks — see PHARAOH'S SERPENT

mercury-vapor lamp \ˈ===ˌ==-\ *n* **:** a gas-discharge lamp in which the gaseous medium is mercury vapor

mercury weed *n* **:** THREE-SEEDED MERCURY

mer·cy \ˈmərsē, ˈmə̄s-, ˈməis-, -si\ *n* -ES [ME *merci, mercy*, fr. OF *mercit, merci*, fr. ML *merced-, merces*, fr. L, price paid for something, wages, reward, recompense, fr. *merc-, merx* ware, merchandise — more at MARKET] **1 a :** compassion or forbearance shown to an offender or subject **:** clemency or kindness extended to someone instead of strictness or severity **:** LENIENCY ⟨the illusion of omniscience . . . brings endless inhumanity when it leads us to shut the gates of ~ —M.R. Cohen⟩; *esp* **:** the mercy of God to man ⟨showing ~ unto thousands of them that love me and keep my commandments —Exod 20:6 (AV)⟩ **b :** a sentence of imprisonment rather than of death imposed in clemency on a person convicted of first-degree murder **2 a :** a blessing regarded as an act of divine favor or compassion ⟨seemed oblivious of all the many *mercies* of his daily life⟩ **b :** a fortunate event or circumstance ⟨the more open ground was a ~ —Fred Majdalany⟩ **3 :** relief of distress **:** compassion shown to victims of misfortune ⟨seek ways of performing acts of kindness and ~ abroad —Vera M. Dean⟩

syn CLEMENCY, LENITY, CHARITY, GRACE: MERCY, a word of much emotional force and hence one applicable to extreme situations, indicates a kindly refraining from inflicting punishment or pain, often a refraining brought about by genuinely felt compassion and sympathy, or a general disposition toward these latter characteristics ⟨earthly power doth then show likest God's when *mercy* season justice —Shak.⟩ ⟨the quality of brutality was not isolated in the Japanese, nor was the quality of *mercy* unknown to them —Agnes N. Keith⟩ CLEMENCY, a less emotionally colored word, indicates a tendency to be mild and compassionate, to administer or direct moderate punishment or treatment rather than drastically severe ⟨*clemency* . . . is the standing policy of constitutional governments, as severity is of despotism —Henry Hallam⟩ ⟨Cicero had prophesied so positively that Caesar would throw off the mask of *clemency* . . . that he was disappointed to find him persevere in the same gentleness —J.A.Froude⟩ LENITY may suggest absence of severity, may connote a clemency uninterrupted and unvaried and verging onto softness and careless leniency ⟨whether this indulgence comes from the wisdom and *lenity* of the government —Tobias Smollett⟩ ⟨not to be expected that they would show much *lenity* to one . . . regarded as the chief of the Rye House Plot —T.B.Macaulay⟩ CHARITY indicates clemency of judgment, a disposition to judge mildly or tolerantly ⟨marriage had begun where it so often ends happily, in *charity* of mind —Ellen Glasgow⟩ In other, more common uses it suggests a benevolent good will arising from a feeling of love of others ⟨with malice toward none, with *charity* for all —Abraham Lincoln⟩ In older usage GRACE may combine the associations of CLEMENCY and CHARITY ⟨his eyes upraised to sue for *grace* —William Wordsworth⟩ — **at the mercy of :** wholly in the power of ⟨their lives are *at the mercy of* the conqueror —John Locke⟩ ⟨farming was a risky business, *at the mercy of* weather, pests, limited markets —*Printers' Ink*⟩

mercy seat *n* [fr. *mercy seat*, gold covering over the ark of the covenant in the Bible (Exod 25:17); trans. of G *gnadenstuhl*, trans. of Heb *kappōreth*] **:** the throne of God regarded as a place of divine atonement, communion, or propitiation

merd *n* -s [ME, fr. MF *merde*, fr. L *merda* — more at IMMERD] *obs* **:** DUNG

mer·div·o·rous \(ˈ)mərˈdivərəs\ *adj* [L *merda* excrement + E *-i-* + *-vorous*] **:** COPROPHAGOUS

¹**mere** \ˈmi(ə)r, -iə\ *n* -s [ME, fr. OE — more at MARINE] **1** *obs* **a :** SEA **b :** an arm of the sea **:** CREEK, INLET **2 :** a sheet of standing water **:** LAKE, POOL ⟨had seen several boats on an inland ~ —*Yale Rev.*⟩ **3 :** FEN, MARSH

²**mere** \"\ *n* -s [ME, fr. OE *mǣre, gemǣre* — more at MUNITION] *archaic* **:** BOUNDARY **:** a mark or line defining a boundary **:** LANDMARK, LIMIT

³**mere** \"\ *vb* -ED/-ING/-S *vt, archaic* **:** to mark the boundaries of ~ *vi, obs* **:** to abut on

⁴**mere** \"\ *adj* -ER/-EST [ME, fr. L *merus* pure, bare — more at MORN] **1 a :** done or invoked without assistance or support — used chiefly in legal contexts in the phrases *mere motion, mere will* **b** *law* **:** having theoretical or legal but not practical reality ⟨~ right⟩ **2** *obs* **:** fully realized or developed **:** ABSOLUTE, TOTAL, UNDIMINISHED **3 :** exclusive of or considered apart from anything else **:** BARE ⟨if he does not want us to accept his theory of the good on his ~ authority, he needs to give us some rational ground for it —M.R.Cohen⟩ ⟨something above ~ politics —D.W.Brogan⟩ **4 :** having no admixture **:** PURE, UNDILUTED ⟨~ genius —Stanislaus Joyce⟩

⁵**mere** \ˈmerē\ *n* -s [Maori] **1** *Austral* **:** a Maori war club **2** *Austral* **:** a miniature Maori war club fashioned of greenstone and worn as an ornament

⁶**mere** \ˈmi(ə)r, -iə\ *n* -s [*-mere*] *zool* **:** SEGMENT, METAMERE

-mere \ˌmi(ə)r, -iə\ *n comb form* -s [F *-mère*, fr. Gk *meros* part — more at MERIT] **1** *biol* **:** part **:** segment ⟨*arthromere*⟩ ⟨*cytomere*⟩ **2** *chem* **:** -MER ⟨*isomere*⟩

¹**mer·e·dith·i·an** \ˌmerəˈdithēən\ *adj, usu cap* [George *Meredith* †1909 Eng. novelist & poet + E *-ian*] **:** of, relating to, or characteristic of George Meredith or his writings

²**meredithian** \"\ *n* -s *usu cap* **:** a follower of George Meredith or an enthusiast for his works, his style, or his attitudes

mer·els \ˈmerəlz\ *n pl but sing in constr* [ME, pl. of *merel*, counter in the game of merels, fr. MF *merel, marel* counter, token, fr. OF; akin to OF *merele, marele* counter] **:** ²MORRIS

mere·ly *adv* [⁴*mere* + *-ly*] **1** *obs* **:** without admixture **:** PURELY **2 :** to the full extent **:** ENTIRELY, QUITE, WHOLLY ⟨it becomes surprising that . . . one could have been so ~ engrossed —Oliver La Farge⟩ **3 :** no more than **:** BARELY, ONLY, SIMPLY, SOLELY ⟨went past the bounds of bohemianism to the verge of the ~ sordid —*New Yorker*⟩

me·ren·gue \məˈreŋ(ˌ)gā\ *also* **mé·ringue** \mäˈraŋ\ *n* -s [AmerSp *merengue* & Haitian Creole *méringue*] **:** a popular Dominican and Haitian ballroom dance with a limping step

me·re·ol·o·gy \ˌmirēˈäləjē\ *n* -ES [irreg. fr. ³*mer-* + *-logy*] *logic* **:** a theory of extended individuals in their relationships of parts to whole and of overlapping — compare CALCULUS OF INDIVIDUALS

meres·man \ˈmi(ə)rzmən\ *n, pl* **meresmen** [*meres* (gen. of ²*mere*) + *man*] *archaic* **:** a parish officer named to ascertain boundaries

mere·stone \ˈmi(ə)rˌstōn\ *n* [ME *merstane*, fr. OE *mǣrstān*, fr. *mǣre* ²boundary + *stān* stone — more at MUNITION, STONE] *archaic* **:** a stone indicating a boundary **:** LANDMARK

mer·e·tri·cious \ˌmerəˈtrishəs\ *adj* [L *meretricius*, fr. *meretric-, meretrix*] **1 :** of or relating to a prostitute **:** having a harlot's traits ⟨the Pennsylvania court . . . did not believe that there was a common-law marriage here, but merely a ~ relationship —Morris Ploscowe⟩ **2 :** exhibiting synthetic or spurious attractions **:** based on pretense or insincerity

: cheaply ornamental ⟨what counts in a boat is design and seaworthiness, not the ~ attractions of newness —*New Yorker*⟩ ⟨might have had fortune from the beginning if she had been willing to appear in ~ plays —E.C.Wagenknecht⟩ **syn** see GAUDY

mer·e·tri·cious·ly *adv* : in a meretricious manner

mer·e·tri·cious·ness *n* -ES : the quality or state of being meretricious

mer·e·trix \ˈmerə̇(ˌ)triks\ *n, pl* **meretri·ces** \ˌmerə̇ˈtrī(ˌ)sēz\ [L, fr. *merēre* to earn, gain — more at MERIT] : PROSTITUTE ⟨with my lamentable visits to the Ring at Blackfriars, or to my ~ in Holland Park —Cyril Connolly⟩

mer·folk \ˈmər, ˈmə̄+,-\ *n pl* [¹*mer-* + *folk*] : a legendary people of the sea having human head, trunk, and arms and the tail of a fish — compare MERMAID, MERMAN

mer·gan·ser \(ˌ)mərˈgan(t)sər, ˈ≈,≈≈\ *n* -S [NL, fr. L *mergus* diver (waterfowl) + *anser* goose — more at MERGUS, GOOSE] : any of various diving ducks of *Mergus* and related genera that constitute a distinct subfamily of Anatidae, have a slender bill hooked at the end and serrated along the margins, usu. a crested head, a long broad tail, and short somewhat clumsy wings, feed almost entirely on fish, and are considered inferior as food for man — see AMERICAN MERGANSER, GOOSANDER, HOODED MERGANSER, RED-BREASTED MERGANSER, SMEW; see BILL illustration

merge \ˈmərj, ˈmə̄j, ˈməij\ *vb* -ED/-ING/-S [L *mergere*; akin to Skt *majjati* he dives, Lith *mazgoti* to wash] *vt* **1** *obs* : to plunge or engulf in a medium that wholly surrounds or absorbs : IMMERSE **2** : to cause to be legally absorbed, sunk, or extinguished by merger **3** : to cause to combine, unite, or coalesce ⟨planned to ~ the two companies⟩ **4** : to blend gradually : alter by transitional stages : blunt or destroy the distinctness of ⟨individuality and uniqueness are *merged* and blurred —Norman Kelman⟩ ~ *vi* **1** : to become legally absorbed or extinguished by merger **2** : to become combined into one ⟨the two banks *merged* to form an institution that dwarfed its nearest competitor⟩ **3** : to blend or come together without abrupt change : lose identity by absorption or intermingling : pass gradually ⟨long slopes of alluvial material spread out from the base of the mountains and ~ into a plain —Samuel Van Valkenburg & Ellsworth Huntington⟩ ⟨two streams of traffic *merging* to form the base of a gigantic Y⟩ **syn** see MIX

mer·gence \ˈmərjən(t)s, ˈmə̄j-, ˈməij-\ *n* -S : the act or process of merging or the condition of being merged ⟨~ of colored blues and white crooning, itself a Negro derivative, reflects racial integration —H.F.Mooney⟩

merg·er \-jə(r)\ *n* -S [*merge* + -*er* (as in *waiver*)] **1** *law* **a** : the absorption of an estate, a contract, or an interest in another, of a minor offense in a greater, or of an obligation into a judgment **b** (1) *common law* : the vesting of a lesser estate and a greater one or a higher security, obligation, or interest and a lower one in one person in the same right without an intermediate estate (2) *equity* : the vesting in one person of two interests in the same right but subject to separate treatment according to equitable demands **2 a** : absorption by a corporation of one or more others — distinguished from *consolidation*; see AMALGAMATION **b** : any of various other methods of combining two or more business concerns **3** : the combination of two or more groups (as political organizations, churches, or government departments) on any of various terms or conditions **4** : MERGENCE

mergh \ˈmerk\ *Scot var of* ¹MARROW

merging *n* -S [fr. gerund of *merge*] : the act or process of blending, combining, joining, or uniting

mer·gus \ˈmərgəs\ *n, cap* [NL, fr. L, diver (waterfowl), fr. *mergere* to dip, plunge — more at MERGE] : a genus of highly aquatic diving ducks including several typical mergansers having males that are brightly marked and develop an eclipse plumage

meri- *comb form* [F *méri-*, fr. Gk *meris* part — more at MERIT] : part : partial ⟨*meri*clinous⟩ ⟨*meri*quinone⟩ ⟨*meri*stele⟩

mer·i·ah khond \ˈmerēə-\ *n, usu cap M&K* : a member of a Khond people of eastern India formerly engaging in human sacrifices

-mer·ic \ˌmerik, -rēk, *when there is a related noun form in* "*-mere*", ˈmer- *or* ˈmir-\ *adj comb form* [ISV ³*mer-* + -*ic*] **1** *biol* : having (such) parts or segments ⟨cyto*meric*⟩ **2** [ISV -*mer* + -*ic*] *chem* : having a (specified) association of substances in compounds ⟨poly*meric*⟩ ⟨tauto*meric*⟩

mer·i·carp \ˈmerə,kärp\ *n* -S [F *méricarpe*, fr. *méri-* + -*carpe* -carp] : one of the two carpels that resemble achenes and form the schizocarp of an umbelliferous plant

mer·i·cli·nal \ˌmerəˈklīnᵊl\ *or* **mer·i·cli·nous** \-nəs\ *adj* [*meri-* + -*clinal*, -*clinous*] *of a plant chimera* : incompletely periclinal : having tissue of one kind incompletely surrounded by tissue of another kind

mé·ri·da \ˈmerədə\ *adj, usu cap* [fr. *Mérida*, Mexico] : of or from the city of Mérida, Mexico : of the kind or style prevalent in Mérida

-mer·ide \ˌməˌrīd, -rə̇d\ *n comb form* -S [ISV -*mer* + -*ide*] : -MER ⟨iso*meride*⟩ ⟨poly*meride*⟩

¹**me·rid·i·an** \məˈridēən\ *n* -S [ME *meridien, meridian*, fr. MF *meridien*, fr. *meridien*, adj.] **1 a** *obs* : the hour of noon : MIDDAY **b** *Scot* : a midday dram **2** : a great circle of the celestial sphere passing through its poles and the zenith of a given place **3 a** *archaic* : the highest apparent point reached in the heavens by the sun or a star **b** : a high point (as of development or prosperity) ⟨the problem of the unmarried don after he had passed the ~ —H.J.Laski⟩ **4 a** (1) : a great circle on the surface of the earth passing through the poles and any given place (2) : the half of such a circle included between the poles with a plane coinciding with that of the astronomical meridian of the place — see PRIME MERIDIAN **b** : a representation of such a circle or half circle on a map or globe : any of a series of lines drawn at intervals due north and south or in the direction of the poles and numbered according to the degrees of longitude ⟨the 90th ~ east of Greenwich⟩ **c** : a graduated circle (as of brass) in which a globe is suspended and revolves **5** *archaic* : special tastes, capacities, or conditions ⟨suited the ~ of the . . . servants' hall —Washington Irving⟩ **6** : *or* **meridian curve** : the curve formed by the intersection of a surface of revolution and a plane passing through the axis of revolution **7** : a line or circle (as on the globular shell of some sea urchins) resembling a meridian of longitude

²**meridian** \ˈ"\ *adj* [ME *meridien*, fr. MF, fr. L *meridianus*, fr. *meridies* noon, south (fr. *meri-* — alter. of *medius* mid — + *dies* day) + -*anus* -an — more at MID, DEITY] **1** : being at or relating to midday : belonging to or passing through the highest point attained by a heavenly body in its diurnal course **2** : of or relating to a meridian **3 a** : of or relating to a high point, crest, or culmination ⟨the Roman people had arrived at their ~ glory —C.G.Bowers⟩ **b** *obs* : supremely excellent : CONSUMMATE, EXTREME

meridian altitude *n* **1** : the arc of the meridian intercepted between a celestial body at meridian transit and the south point of the horizon **2** : the altitude of a celestial body when it is on an observer's meridian

meridian angle *n* : the angle between the upper branch of the celestial meridian of an observer and the hour circle of a celestial object measured either westward or eastward from zero to 180 degrees — compare HOUR ANGLE

meridian circle *n* : an astronomical transit instrument having its vertical circle very accurately graduated for precise measurements of declination

meridian day *n* : the day on which a ship in the Pacific crosses the international date line losing a day going east and adding one going west

meridian instrument *n* : an astronomical transit instrument or meridian circle

meridian line *n* : a line running accurately north and south through any given point on or near the earth's surface

meridian mark *n* : a fixed mark due north or south of a meridian instrument to aid in adjusting or finding its azimuth error

meridian passage *n* : the passage of a celestial body across an observer's meridian

meridian sailing *n* : sailing north or south — opposed to *parallel sailing*

mé·ri·di·enne \məˌridēˈen\ *n* -S [F, lit., midday nap, fr. fem. of *méridien* meridian, of midday, fr. OF *meridien* — more at MERIDIAN] : a short sofa of the French Empire period having one arm higher than the other

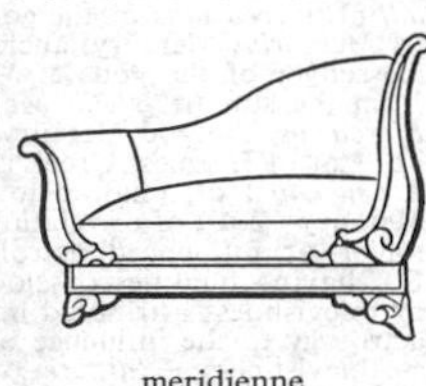
meridienne

me·rid·i·on \məˈridēˌän\ *n, cap* [NL, fr. Gk, dim. of *merid-*, *meris* part, portion — more at MERIT] : a genus (coextensive with the family Meridionaceae) of freshwater pennate diatoms having cuneate cells arranged in flat, fan-shaped, or spiral colonies and often causing odors in public water supplies

¹**me·rid·i·o·nal** \-ˈ≈ēənᵊl\ *adj* [ME, fr. MF *meridionel*, fr. LL *meridionalis*, irreg. fr. L *meridies* noon, south + -*alis* -al — more at MERIDIAN] **1** : of, relating to, or situated in the south : having a southern aspect : SOUTHERN, SOUTHERLY ⟨should attract ~ travelers weary of the big-business aspects of Continental tourism —Dore Ashton⟩ **2** : of, relating to, or characteristic of people living in the south esp. of France ⟨welcomed him with ~ hospitality, and filled his leisure hours with the noisy boisterous fun of Provence —Dorothy C. Fisher⟩ **3** *obs* **a** : of or relating to the position of the sun at noon **b** : of, relating to, or characteristic of noon or midday **4 a** : of or relating to a meridian : following a north-south direction ⟨a ~ circulation which transports poleward the excess energy received at tropical latitudes —Harry Wexler⟩ **b** : marked with lines in the plane of the axis **5** *of a map* : having a meridian as the vertical axis and bounded by the circle of a meridian — **me·rid·i·o·nal·ly** \-nᵊlē\ *adv*

²**meridional** \ˈ"\ *n* -S : an inhabitant of southern Europe and esp. southern France ⟨a typical ~ —Rosemary Benet⟩

meridional difference of latitude *or* **meridional distance** : the difference of the meridional parts for any two latitudes

meridionality *n* -ES *obs* : the quality or state of being meridional or on the meridian : position in the south

meridional part *n* : the linear length of one minute of longitude on a Mercator chart

meridional projection *n* : a projection of a sphere on a plane parallel to a meridian plane through the point of projection

me·rim·di·an *or* **me·rim·de·an** \məˈrimdēən\ *adj, usu cap* [*Merimdeh*, ruins on the western branch of the Nile in the Delta west of Ashmun, Egypt + E -*an*] : of or relating to an early Neolithic Egyptian culture of about 5000–4000 B.C. characterized by agriculture, animal husbandry, pottery, working in gold and silver, loom-weaving, coiled basketry, pit houses, and boats made of bundles of papyrus

mé·ri·mée's yellow \ˈmerēˌmāz-\ *n, usu cap M* [prob. after Jean-François *Mérimée* †1836 French painter and chemist] : a permanent yellow pigment prepared by fusing lead monoxide and ammonium chloride with a little bismuth antimonate — called also *antimony yellow*

mering *pres part of* MERE

¹**me·ringue** \məˈraŋ, -raiŋ\ *n* -S [F] **1** : a mixture of beaten egg whites and powdered sugar baked at low temperature and used as a topping (as on pies, puddings) **2** : a shell made of meringue and filled with fruit or ice cream

²**méringue** *var of* MERENGUE

me·ringu·er \məˈraŋə(r), -raiŋ-\ *n* -S : one that mixes or spreads meringue

me·ri·no \məˈrē(ˌ)nō\ *n* [Sp] **1 a** *usu cap* : a breed of fine-wooled white sheep originating in Spain, widely popular esp. on the ranges of America and Australia, and excelling all others in weight and quality of fleece although not ranking high as a mutton producer **b** *also* **merino sheep** -S *usu cap M* : a sheep of the Merino breed **2** -S **a** : a soft clothing fabric resembling cashmere, orig. of merino wool and now of any fine wool or wool and cotton **b** : a garment of this fabric; *esp* : a merino dress or loose dressing gown **3** -S : a fine wool and cotton yarn used for hosiery and knitwear

mer·i·on bluegrass \ˈmerēən-\ *n, usu cap M* [prob. fr. the name *Merion*] : a strain of Kentucky bluegrass that is low growing, rapid spreading, and resistant to leaf spot

me·ri·o·nes \məˈrīəˌnēz\ *n, cap* [NL, fr. Gk *mēria* thigh bones, fr. *mēros* thigh; fr. the formation of the hind legs — more at MEMBER] : a genus of gerbils

mer·i·on·eth·shire \ˌmerēˈänəth,shi(ə)r, -ˌshiə, -ˌshə(r)\ *or* **merioneth** *adj, usu cap* [fr. *Merionethshire* or *Merioneth* county, Wales] : of or from the county of Merioneth, Wales : of the kind or style prevalent in Merioneth

meri·quinone \ˌmerə+\ *n* [*meri-* + *quinone*] : a compound (as quinhydrone) that is partly quinonoid and partly benzenoid — compare SEMIQUINONE

meri·quinonoid \ˈ"+\ *or* **meri·quinoid** \ˈ"+\ *adj* [ISV *meri-* + *quinonoid* or *quinoid*; orig. formed as G *meriquinonoid*] : partly quinonoid : having the properties of a meriquinone — compare HEMIQUINONOID

-mer·is \ˌmərə̇s\ *n comb form* [NL, fr. Gk *meris* part — more at MERIT] : one having a (specified) part — in generic names ⟨*Pipto*meris⟩

mer·i·sis \ˈmerəsə̇s\ *n, pl* **merises** [NL, fr. *meri-* + -*sis*] *biol* : GROWTH; *specif* : growth by increase in cell number — compare AUXESIS

¹**mer·ism** \ˈme,rizəm\ *n* -S [³*mer-* + -*ism*] *biol* : a repetition of homologous parts — compare METAMERISM

²**merism** \ˈ"\ *n* -S [Gk *merismos*, lit., division, fr. *merizein* to divide, fr. *mer-* ³*mer-* + -*izein* -ize] : a synecdoche in which a totality is expressed by two contrasting parts ⟨*old and young, thick and thin, near and far* are typical ~*s*⟩

-mer·ism \ˌmə,rizəm\ *n comb form* -S [ISV -*mer* + -*ism*] **1** : possession of a (specified) association of substances in chemical compounds ⟨iso*merism*⟩ ⟨tauto*merism*⟩ **2** [ISV ³*mer-* + -*ism*] : possession of (such or so many) parts

mer·is·mat·ic \ˌmerə̇zˈmad·ik\ *adj* [Gk *merismat-*, *merisma* part (fr. *merizein* to divide) + E -*ic*] **1** *bot* : MERISTEMATIC **2** *zool* : dividing by formation of internal partitions

me·ris·moid \məˈriz,mȯid\ *or* **me·ris·ma·toid** \-zmə,tȯid\ *adj* [Gk *merisma* part, division + E -*oid*] *of a fungus* : having a branched pileus

meri·stele \ˌmerə+\ *n* [ISV *meri-* + *stele*] : one of the units of vascular tissue in a polystele — **meri·stelic** \ˈ"+\ *adj*

meri·stem \ˈmerə,stem\ *n* -S [Gk *meristos* divided, divisible (fr. *merizein* to divide) + E -*em* (as in *system*)] : a formative plant tissue made up typically of small essentially isodiametric cells lacking prominent vacuoles and capable of an indefinite number of divisions and giving rise to initiating cells that remain meristematic and to derivatives that undergo differentiation to produce the various tissues and organs of the plant, all postembryonic growth depending ultimately on the proliferation of meristematic cells — compare CAMBIUM

meri·ste·mat·ic \ˌ≈≈stəˈmad·ik\ *adj* [*meristem* + -*atic* (as in *systematic*)] : consisting of or having the qualities of meristem — **meri·ste·mat·i·cal·ly** \-ə̇k(ə)lē\ *adv*

me·ris·tic \məˈristik\ *adj* [Gk *meristos* divided, divisible + E -*ic* — more at MERISTEM] **1** : of, relating to, or divided into segments (as metameres) ⟨~ changes⟩ ⟨~ organization of body structures⟩ **2** : characterized by or involving modification in number or in geometrical relation of body parts ⟨~ variation⟩ ⟨~ characters⟩ — **me·ris·ti·cal·ly** \-tə̇k(ə)lē\ *adv*

meri·stog·e·nous \ˌmerəˈstäjənəs\ *adj* [Gk *meristos* divided, divisible + E -*genous*] : arising from a single hyphal cell or a group of adjacent hyphal cells by repeated cross and longitudinal divisions (as in the development of certain pycnidia) — compare SYMPHOGENOUS

¹**mer·it** \ˈmerə̇t, *usu* -ə̇d·+V\ *n* -S [ME *merite, merit*, fr. OF *merite*, fr. L *meritum*, fr. neut. of *meritus*, past part. of *merēre*, *merērī* to earn, deserve, merit; akin to Gk *meros* & *meris* part, share, *moros* fate, lot, L *mora* delay — more at MEMORY] **1 a** *obs* : reward or punishment earned or deserved : just deserts **b** : one's character regarded as the basis of his deserts : laudable or blameworthy traits or actions ⟨opinions of his ~ vary⟩ **c** : a praiseworthy quality : VIRTUE ⟨but originality, as it is one of the highest, is also one of the rarest, of ~*s* —E.A. Poe⟩ **d** : worth or excellence in quality or performance : character or conduct deserving reward, honor, or esteem ⟨she is handsome no longer, and she never had any other ~ —W.M. Thackeray⟩ ⟨composed a number of works of ~ —H.E.Starr⟩ **2** : spiritual credit or stored moral surplusage regarded as earned by performance of righteous acts and as ensuring future benefits ⟨"she has acquired ~," returned the lama. "Peradventure it was a nun" —Rudyard Kipling⟩ ⟨had thereby added to a surplus of ~ already enriched by what Christ had done —K.S.Latourette⟩ **3 a merits** *pl* : the intrinsic rights and wrongs of a legal case as determined by matters of substance in distinction from matters of form : the strict legal rights of the parties as distinguished from considerations depending on practice or jurisdiction ⟨the plaintiff . . . is entitled to have its claim decided here on its ~*s* —T.M.Maddes⟩ **b** : legal significance, standing, or importance ⟨the contention is without ~ —E.B.Denny⟩ **syn** see DUE, EXCELLENCE

²**merit** \ˈ"\ *vb* -ED/-ING/-S [MF *meriter*, fr. *merite*, n.] *vt* **1** *obs* : REWARD, REQUITE **2 a** : to be worthy of or entitled or liable to : EARN ⟨~*ed* the large sale which they obtained —E.S.Bates⟩ ⟨the man who owned both the lump and the abdomen ~*ed* as much consideration as either —Harvey Graham⟩ ⟨~ the penalty of expulsion —Virginia Murphy⟩ **b** : to have a claim on (divine mercy or reward) ⟨the supernatural life which Christ ~*ed* for us —J.J.Maher⟩ ~ *vi* **1** *obs* : to gain merit : acquire favor : be entitled to reward or honor ⟨if in my poor death fair France may ~ —Francis Beaumont & John Fletcher⟩ **2** : to be or become deserving of good or ill **syn** see DESERVE

mer·it·able \ˈmerəd·əbəl, -ətəb-\ *adj* [ME, fr. *merite, merit* merit + -*able* — more at MERIT] : MERITORIOUS

merited *adj* : that is properly earned or deserved ⟨often sharp in ~ criticism —G.L.Hendrickson⟩ ⟨a ~ success⟩ — **mer·it·ed·ly** *adv*

meriter *n* -S *obs* : one that merits

mer·it·less \ˈ≈≈lə̇s\ *adj* : lacking merit : WORTHLESS

meritmonger \ˈ≈≈,≈≈\ *n, archaic* : one who expects salvation as a recompense for good works

mer·i·to·ri·ous \ˌmerəˈtōrēəs, -tȯr-\ *adj* [ME, fr. ML *meritorius*, fr. L, that brings in money, fr. *meritus* (past part. of *merēre* to earn) + -*orius* -ory — more at MERIT] **1** : serving to win divine favor, blessing, or reward ⟨it is ~ to believe what cannot be demonstrated —Frank Thilly⟩ **2** : worthy of reward, gratitude, honor, or esteem ⟨made up for his lack of talent by ~ industry —W.M.Thackeray⟩ **3** *obs* : DESERVING — used with *of* — **mer·i·to·ri·ous·ly** *adv* — **mer·i·to·ri·ous·ness** *n* -ES

meritorious consideration *n* : GOOD CONSIDERATION

merit rating *n* **1** : computation of an insurance premium for a particular risk on the basis of its individual loss-causing characteristics — see EXPERIENCE RATING **2** : the rating of an employee by systematic evaluation of his proficiency in a job

merits *pl of* MERIT, *pres 3d sing of* MERIT

merit system *n* : the system of appointing employees to office in the civil service and of promoting them for competency only ⟨advocates of the *merit system* always concede that policy-determining posts should be political —D.D.McKean⟩ — opposed to *spoils system*

merk \ˈmerk\ *chiefly Scot var of* ³MARK 2b

mer·kel-ran·vier corpuscle \ˈmer|kəl|ränⁿ|vyā-, ˈmər|\ *n, usu cap M&R* [after Friedrich S. *Merkel* †1919 Ger. anatomist & Louis A. *Ranvier* †1922 Fr. histologist] : MERKEL'S CELL

merkel's cell *or* **merkel's corpuscle** *or* **merkel's disc** *n, usu cap M* [after Friedrich S. *Merkel*] : a touch receptor of the deep layers of the skin consisting of a flattened or cupped body associated peripherally with a large modified epithelial cell and centrally with an efferent nerve fiber

mer·ker grass \ˈmərkə(r)-\ *n, usu cap M* [prob. fr. the name *Merker*] : NAPIER GRASS

mer·kin \ˈmərkə̇n\ *n* -S [origin unknown] **1** *obs* : the hair of the female genitalia **2** : false hair for the female genitalia

merl *or* **merle** \ˈmər(-ə)l\ *n* -S [MF *merle*, fr. L *merulus*, *merula*, fr. (assumed) *misula*; akin to OE *ōsle* blackbird, OHG *amsla, amsala*, W *mwyalchen*] : BLACKBIRD 1a

merle \ˈ"\ *n* -S [origin unknown] **1** : a bluish gray color of the coats of some dogs **2** : AUSTRALIAN CATTLE DOG

mer·lin \ˈmərlə̇n\ *n* -S [ME *merilon*, fr. AF *merilun*, fr. OF *esmerillon*, aug. of *esmeril*, of Gmc origin; akin to MD *smerle, smeerle* merlin, OHG *smerlo, smiril*, ON *smyrill*] **1** : a small European falcon (*Falco aesalon*) related to the American pigeon hawk **2** : PIGEON HAWK a

mer·lin's-grass \ˈmərlə̇nz+,-\ *n, pl* **merlin's-grasses** *usu cap M* [prob. after *Merlin*, legendary 5th cent. Welsh wizard] : a common European quillwort (*Isoetes lacustris*)

mer·lon \ˈmərlən\ *n* -S [F, fr. It *merlone*, aug. of *merlo* battlement, fr. ML *merulus*, fr. L, blackbird — more at MERL] **1** : one of the solid intervals between embrasures of a battlemented parapet — see BATTLEMENT illustration **2** *archaic* : a part of a warship's bulwark resembling a merlon

mer·luc·ci·us \mərˈlüchēəs\ *n, cap* [NL, fr. ML *merlutius*, *merlucius* hake, fr. L *merula*, a sea fish, blackbird — more at MERL] : a genus of fishes related to the cods and included with them in Gadidae or now often isolated in a separate family — see HAKE

mer·maid \ˈmər, ˈmə̄+,-\ *n* [ME *mermaide*, fr. ¹*mer-* + *maide* maid — more at MAID] **1 a** : a fabled marine creature usu. represented as having the head, trunk, and arms of a woman and a lower part like the tail of a fish ⟨I have heard the ~*s* singing, each to each —T.S. Eliot⟩ — compare NIX **b** : a girl swimmer ⟨sat by the pool . . . and watched the ~*s* in the seventy-six-degree November sun —Horace Sutton⟩ **2** : a representation of a mermaid usu. holding a mirror in one hand and a comb in the other esp. as a heraldic emblem or the sign of an inn or tavern **3** *obs* **a** : SIREN 1a **b** : HARLOT **4** : a grayish yellow green that is yellower and paler than average sage green or palmetto and yellower and darker than celadon **5** : SIRENOMELUS **6** : SIRENIAN; *esp* : MANATEE

mermaid 2

mer·maiden \ˈ"+,-\ *n* [ME, fr. ¹*mer-* + *maiden*] : MERMAID 1

mermaid's-hair \ˈ≈,≈ˈ≈\ *n, pl* **mermaid's-hairs** : a common filamentous marine blue-green alga (*Lyngbya majuscula*) growing in long matted tufts on eelgrass and on larger algae

mermaid's purse *n* : the dark horny or leathery egg case of various skates or other elasmobranch fishes

mermaid weed *n* : any aquatic herb of the genus *Proserpinaca*

mer·man \ˈmər,man, ˈmə̄,m-, -,maa(ə)n, -,man\ *n, pl* **mermen** [¹*mer-* + *man*] **1** : a fabled marine male creature usu. represented as having the head, trunk, and arms of a man and a lower part like the tail of a fish — called also *manfish*; compare MERMAID **2** : a male swimmer

mer·mis \ˈmərmə̇s\ *n, cap* [NL, fr. Gk, cord, string, thread; akin to ON *merth* fish trap, OSw *mærthi* fish trap, MIr *braige, braiga* captive, Gk *brochos* noose, OSlav *mrěža* net; basic meaning: to plait, tie] : a genus (the type of the family Mermithidae) of very slender nematode worms that as adults live in damp earth often appearing on the ground in great numbers after rains and as larvae live in the bodies of insects

mer·mith·ergate \ˌmərməth+\ *n* [NL *Mermith-, Mermis* + E *ergate*] : a worker ant hypertrophied and altered in bodily form by parasitic nematodes — compare MERMITHIZED

¹**mer·mi·thid** \ˈmərməthə̇d\ *adj* [NL *Mermithidae*] : of or relating to the Mermithidae

²**mermithid** \ˈ"\ *n* -S : a worm of the family Mermithidae

mer·mith·i·dae \(ˌ)mərˈmithəˌdē\ *n pl, cap* [NL, fr. *Mermith-*, *Mermis*, type genus + -*idae*] : a family of elongated round-headed nematode worms (order Enoplida) having the digestive tract nonfunctional in the adult — see MERMIS

mer·mi·thi·za·tion \ˌ≈məthə̇ˈzāshən, -ˌthīˈz-\ *n* -S [NL *Mermithidae* + E -*ization*] : mermithid infestation

mer·mi·thized \ˈ≈≈,thīzd\ *adj* [NL *Mermithidae* + E -*ize* + -*ed*] : infested with mermithid worms — used esp. of ants

me·ro \ˈmā(ˌ)rō\ *n* -S [Sp] : any of several large groupers or jewfishes of warm seas

mero- — see MER-

mero·blas·tic \ˌmerəˈblastik\ *adj* [ISV ³*mer-* + -*blastic*] *of an egg* : undergoing incomplete cleavage as a result of the presence of an impeding mass of yolk material : lacking cleavage planes that divide the whole egg into distinct and separate blastomeres — opposed to *holoblastic* — **mero·blas·ti·cal·ly** \-tə̇k(ə)lē\ *adv*

me·roc·er·ite \mə'räsə,rīt\ *n* -s [³*mer-* + Gk *keras* horn, antenna + E *-ite* — more at HORN] : the fourth segment of the antenna of a crustacean — **me·roc·er·it·ic** \ˌ⁼ˌ⁼ˈrid·ik\ *adj*

mer·o·crine \'merəkrən, -əˌkrīn\ *adj* [ISV ³*mer-* + *-crine* (fr. Gk *krinein* to separate) — more at CERTAIN] : producing a secretion that is discharged without major damage to the secreting cells; *also* : produced by a merocrine gland — compare HOLOCRINE

mer·o·cyanine \ˌ⁼⁼+\ *or* **merocyanine dye** *n* [³*mer-* + *cyanine*] : any of a class of polymethine dyes that are used like the cyanine dyes as sensitizers in photography but differ from the cyanine dyes in containing an acidic heterocyclic nucleus (as rhodanine or pyrazolone) linked to a basic heterocyclic nucleus (as quinoline or benzothiazole) and in not being ionized

me·rog·a·my \mə'rägəmē\ *n* -ES [ISV ³*mer-* + *-gamy*] : MICROGAMY

mero·genesis \ˌmerə+\ *n* [NL, fr. ³*mer-* + *genesis*] : the production of segmental parts : SEGMENTATION

mero·genetic \"+\ *or* **mer·o·genic** \"+ ˈjenik\ *adj* [³*mer-* + *-genetic*] : of or relating to merogenesis : exhibiting merogenesis : SEGMENTED

me·rog·na·thite \mə'rägnəˌthīt\ *n* [³*mer-* + *gnathite*] : the fourth segment of a crustacean gnathite

mer·o·gon \'merəˌgän\ *also* **mer·o·gone** \-ˌgōn\ *n* -s [ISV, back-formation from *merogony*] : a product of merogony

mer·o·gon·ic \ˌ⁼⁼ˈgänik\ *or* **me·rog·o·nous** \mə'rägənəs\ *adj* [*merogony* + *-ic* or *-ous*] : of, relating to, or induced by merogony

me·rog·o·ny \mə'rägənē\ *n* -ES [ISV ³*mer-* + *-gony*; orig. formed as F *mérogonie*] : development of an embryo by a process that is genetically equivalent to male parthenogenesis and that involves segmentation and differentiation of an egg or egg fragment deprived of its own nucleus but having a functional male nucleus introduced

mer·o·he·dral \ˌmerəˈhēdrəl *sometimes chiefly Brit* -ˈhed-\ *or* **mer·o·he·dric** \-drik\ *adj* [³*mer-* + *-hedral* or *-hedric* (fr. Gk *hedra* seat + E *-ic*)] : marked by merohedrism

mer·o·he·drism \ˌ⁼⁼ˈhēˌdrizəm, -ˈheˌ-\ *n* -s [³*mer-* + Gk *hedra* seat + E *-ism*] : the conditioning of a crystal due to symmetrical suppression of half or three fourths of the faces of the holohedral form

mero·is·tic \ˌmerəˈwistik\ *adj* [³*mer-* + Gk *ōion* egg + E *-istic* — more at EGG] : producing nutritive cells as well as eggs from oocytes — used of the ovaries of various insects

mero·it·ic \ˌmerəˈwid·ik\ *n, usu cap* [*Meroë*, ancient city and kingdom in northern Sudan + E *-itic*] **1** : a language of northern Sudan of unknown relationship known from inscriptions from the period 700 B.C. to A.D. 350 **2** : a script derived from Egyptian hieroglyphics in which the Meroitic language was written

mer·o·mic·tic \ˌmerəˈmiktik\ *adj* [ISV ³*mer-* + *mict-* (fr. Gk *miktos* mixed, verbal of *mignynai* to mix) + *-ic* — more at MIX] *of a lake* : undergoing incomplete circulation at the fall overturn — compare HOLOMICTIC

mer·o·mix·is \-ˈmiksəs\ *n, pl* **meromix·es** \-kˌsēz\ [NL, fr. ³*mer-* + *-mixis*] : the condition of being meromictic

mero·mor·phic function \ˌmerəˈmȯrfik-, -ˈmō(ə)f-\ *n* [*meromorphic* fr. ³*mer-* + *-morphic*] : a function of a complex variable that is regular in a region except for a finite number of points at which it has infinity for limit

mero·my·ar·i·an \ˌmerōˌmīˈa(a)rēən\ *also* **mero·my·ar·i·al** \-ēəl\ *adj* [³*mer-* + Gk *mys* muscle, mouse + E *-arian* or *-arial* — more at MOUSE] : having few cells in each quadrant of a cross section — used of the arrangement of muscle cells in a nematode worm — **mero·my·ar·i·ty** \ˌ⁼⁼ˌmīˈard·ə·ē\ *n* -ES

me·ro·pia \mə'rōpēə\ *n* -s [NL, fr. ³*mer-* + *-opia*] : partial blindness

me·rop·i·dae \⁼ˈräpəˌdē\ *n pl, cap* [NL, fr. *Merop-*, *Merops*, type genus + *-idae*] : a family of chiefly tropical usu. brightly colored gregarious birds that nest in holes in the ground and constitute a distinct suborder of Coraciiformes — see BEE-EATER, MEROPS

mer·o·plankton \ˌmerə+\ *n* [NL, fr. ³*mer-* + *plankton*] : the portion of the plankton found only a part of the time at or near the surface — **mer·o·planktonic** \"+\ *adj*

me·rop·o·dite \mə'räpəˌdīt\ *n* -s [³*mer-* + *podite*] : the segment fourth from the base of some limbs of crustaceans (as the ambulatory limbs of decapods) — **me·rop·o·dit·ic** \ˌ⁼ˌ⁼ˈdid·ik\ *adj*

merops \'meˌräps, 'mē,-\ *n, cap* [NL, fr. Gk *merops* bee-eater] : the type genus of Meropidae comprising various Old World bee-eaters

me·ros \'mēˌräs\ *n* -ES [NL, fr. Gk *mēros* thigh — more at MEMBER] : the plain surface between the channels of a triglyph

mer·o·so·ma·ta \ˌmerəˈsōməd·ə\ *n, cap* [NL, fr. ³*mer-* + *-somata*] *in some classifications* : a group consisting of those compound ascidians that have zooids with the body divided into regions (as thorax and abdomen)

mer·o·spo·ran·gi·um \ˌ⁼⁼+\ *n* [NL, fr. ³*mer-* + *sporangium*] : one of the cylindrical outgrowths developing from the swollen sporangium tip in various fungi of the order Mucorales and having contents that divide to form a series of sporangiospores like a chain and simulate conidia upon breakdown of the sporangium wall

mer·o·spore \'⁼⁼ˌspō(ə)r\ *n* [³*mer-* + *-spore*] : a sporangiospore formed from a merosporangium

mer·o·sto·ma·ta \ˌ⁼ˈstōməd·ə\ *n pl, cap* [NL, fr. ²*mer-* + *-stomata*] *in some classifications* : a class or other category of chelicerate arthropods including the Xiphosura and Eurypterida and sometimes made a subdivision of Arachnida

mer·o·stomatous \ˌ⁼⁼ˈstäməd·əs, -stōm-\ *also* **me·ros·to·mous** \mə'rästəməs\ *adj* [NL *Merostomata* + E *-ous*] : of or relating to the Merostomata

mer·o·stome \'merəˌstōm\ *n* -s [NL *Merostomata*] : an arthropod of the class Merostomata

mer·o·symmetrical \ˌ⁼⁼+\ *adj* [³*mer-* + *symmetrical*] : MEROHEDRAL

mer·o·symmetry \"+\ *n* [³*mer-* + *symmetry*] : MEROHEDRISM

mer·o·systematic \"+\ *adj* [³*mer-* + *systematic*] : MEROHEDRAL

me·rot·o·mize \mə'räd·əˌmīz\ *vt* -ED/-ING/-S [*merotomy* + *-ize*] : to divide into parts

me·rot·o·my \-ˌmē\ *n* -ES [ISV ³*mer-* + *-tomy*; orig. formed as F *mérotomie*] : division into parts

me·rot·ro·py \mə'rä·trəpē\ *n* -ES [ISV ³*mer-* + *-tropy*] : TAUTOMERISM

-mer·ous \ˌmərəs\ *adj comb form* [NL *-merus*, fr. Gk *-merēs*, fr. *meros* part — more at MERIT] : having (such or so many) parts ⟨*homomerous*⟩ ⟨*pentamerous*⟩ ⟨*6-merous*⟩

¹**mer·o·vin·gian** \ˌmerəˈvinj(ē)ən\ *adj, usu cap* [F *mérovingien*, fr. ML *Merovingi* Merovingians (after *Merovaeus* — Merowig — †458 Frankish king, founder of the dynasty) + F *-ien* -ian] **1** : of or relating to the first Frankish dynasty reigning from about A.D. 500 to A.D. 751 **2** : of or relating to a narrow intricate court hand developed from the Roman cursive and found in Gaul from the 7th century

²**merovingian** \"\ *n -s usu cap* : a member of the Merovingian dynasty

me·rox·ene \mə'räkˌsēn\ *n* -s [G *meroxen*, fr. NL (*Astrites*) *meroxenus*; NL *meroxenus* fr. ³*mer-* + Gk *xenos* stranger, guest] : a mineral consisting of a biotite

mer·o·zoa \ˌmerəˈzōə\ [NL, fr. ³*mer-* + *-zoa*] *syn of* CESTODA

mer·o·zo·ite \-ˈzōˌīt\ *n* -s [ISV ³*mer-* + Gk *zōion* animal + ISV *-ite* — more at ZO-] : a small amoeboid trophozoite that is produced by schizogony in some sporozoans and that is capable of initiating either a new asexual or a sexual cycle of development

mer·peo·ple \'mər, 'mə+ˌ-\ *n pl* [¹*mer-* + *people*] : MERFOLK

mer·rie \'merē, -ri\ *archaic var of* MERRY

mer·ri·ly \'merəlē, -li\ *adv* [ME *merioure*, *mirily*, *merily*, fr. *mury*, *miry*, *mery* merry + *-ly*] : in a merry manner : GAILY

mer·ri·ment \-rēmənt, -rim-\ *n* s [¹*merry* + *-ment*] **1** *obs* : something that causes mirth : JEST, PRANK; *esp* : a brief comic presentation **2 a** : lighthearted gaiety or fun-making : laughing enjoyment : HILARITY, JUBILATION ⟨no one has painted the riotous ~ of a country fair . . . with such zest —Laurence Binyon⟩ ⟨it was now her turn to be overcome with ~ —Owen Wister⟩ **b** : a gay celebration or party : ENTERTAINMENT, FESTIVITY ⟨in the course of this million-dollar ~, the host passed out fifty-dollar bills to one and all —R.L. Taylor⟩ ⟨special ~ such as dances, parades, feasts of regional delicacies and similar gaiety —R. E. Meyer⟩

mer·ri·ness \-rēnəs, -rin-\ *n* -ES [ME *mirines*, *merines*, fr. *mury*, *miry*, *mery* merry + *-nes* -ness] : the quality or state of being merry : MIRTH

¹**mer·ry** \'merē, -ri\ *adj* -ER/-EST [ME *mury*, *miry*, *mery*, fr. OE *myrge*, *mirge*, *merge*; akin to OHG *murg*, *murgi* short, Goth *gamaurgian* to shorten — more at BRIEF] **1** *archaic* : giving pleasure or causing happiness : AGREEABLE, AMUSING, DELIGHTFUL, SWEET **2 a** : full of gaiety or high spirits : marked by animation or vivacity : CHEERFUL, HILARIOUS, JOYOUS, LAUGHING, MIRTHFUL ⟨happy as the ~ whistle of a schoolboy —John Burroughs⟩ ⟨spun yarns that are still ~ reading —*Amer. Guide Series: Va.*⟩ ⟨the windows were alight; signs of ~ life within —George Meredith⟩ **b** *obs* : HAPPY **c** : elated with drink : HIGH ⟨became ~ and befuddled —George Woodbury⟩ **d** *archaic* : MOCKING, TEASING **3** : marked by festive celebration and rejoicing ⟨a ~ holiday time⟩ **4** *of a dog* : snappy and attractive in action : ALERT, QUICK — used also of the tail **5** : BRISK, INTENSE, SHARP ⟨a major factor in keeping industrial wheels turning at a ~ clip —*Spokane (Wash.) Spokesman-Rev.*⟩ — often used as an intensive ⟨gave him ~ hell⟩

syn BLITHE, JOCUND, JOVIAL, JOLLY: MERRY suggests gay, cheerful, or joyous, uninhibited enjoyment ⟨very kind *merry* young people, disposed to take things as gaily as they might —W.M.Thackeray⟩ ⟨the song of the *merry* encounter of some clerk or cavalier with a mocking or complaisant shepherdess —H.O.Taylor⟩ BLITHE suggests a fresh lightheartedness lastingly glad, buoyant, and debonair ⟨then they both laughed together, and heard their own laughter returning in the echoes, and laughed again at the response, so that the ancient and solemn grove became full of merriment for these two *blithe* spirits —Nathaniel Hawthorne⟩ ⟨a *blithe* tale, and a pleasant solvent of anxiety and gloom —Amy Loveman⟩ JOCUND may suggest a habit of exhilaration, elation, good humor, cheer, or beaming complaisance ⟨this they appeared to regard rather as a *jocund* form of sport than a serious employment, and often the professor's arid chuckle echoed upon the chime of Shiloh's fiery laughter —Elinor Wylie⟩ ⟨the great rumbling, roaring, *jocund* tornado of a man, all masculine save sometimes a catlike glint, hardly a twinkle, in his merry eyes —W.A.White⟩ JOVIAL describes the convivially jolly, taking a high pleasure in good fellowship ⟨a *jovial*, full-stomached, portly government servant with a marvelous capacity for making bad puns in English —Rudyard Kipling⟩ ⟨as he roamed with his companions about Assisi singing *jovial* choruses and himself the leader of the frolic —H.O. Taylor⟩ JOLLY may suggest the abundant high spirits that go with laughing, bantering, and jesting ⟨the most colorful restaurants are those that cater to Swedish patronage, and here is often a *jolly* crowd made up mostly of workingmen with their wives or girls, with here and there a professor from the university, all sharing with gusto the beer, the lutefisk, and the occasional outburst of song —*Amer. Guide Series: Minn.*⟩ ⟨ebullient, *jolly*, big-bosomed hoydens, very clearly neither maids nor wives —W.B.Adams⟩

²**merry** \"\ *n* -ES [modif. of F *merise* (taken as pl.), prob. blend of *amer* bitter (fr. L *amarus*) and *cerise* cherry — more at AMAROID, CERISE] : GEAN 1b

mer·ry-an·drew \ˌ⁼⁼ˈan(ˌ)drü\ *n* -s *often cap M&A* [¹*merry* + the name *Andrew*] : one that clowns publicly : BUFFOON, MOUNTEBANK ⟨a *merry-andrew*, frivolous, vain, far too free and familiar —Van Wyck Brooks⟩

merrybell \'⁼⁼ˌ⁼\ *n* : BELLWORT 2 — usu. used in pl.

merry-go-round \'⁼⁼(ˌ)⁼ˌ⁼\ *n* -s **1 a** : a contrivance commonly found at amusement parks and carnivals that consists of a circular platform having seats often in the form of horses or other animals and rotating around a fixed center usu. to calliope music — called also *carrousel* **b** : a children's playground device that revolves about a fixed center **2** : a busy rapid round : WHIRL ⟨the high-pressure *merry-go-round* of big business administration —*Advertising Age*⟩ ⟨the weary *merry-go-round* of the commuting train —Scott Fitzgerald⟩ ⟨the familiar *merry-go-round* of fashion with its rapid alternations of season —Edward Sapir⟩

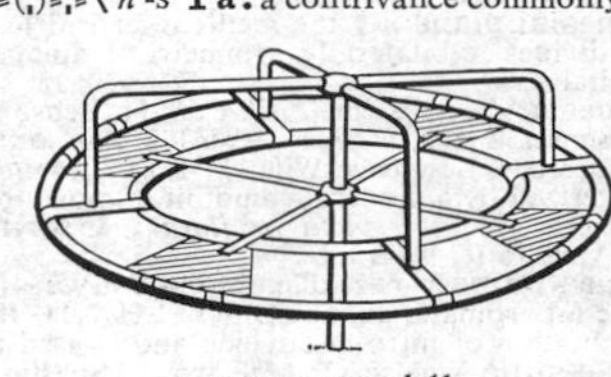

merry-go-round 1b

mer·ry·ing \'merēiŋ\ *n* -s [¹*merry* + *-ing*] *archaic* : FESTIVITY

¹**merrymake** \'⁼⁼ˌ⁼\ *n* [fr. the phrase *make merry*] *archaic* : MERRYMAKING

²**merrymake** \"\ *vi, archaic* : to make merry : be festive

merrymaker \'⁼⁼ˌ⁼⁼\ *n* : one that shares in festivity or gaiety : REVELLER

merrymaking \'⁼⁼ˌ⁼⁼\ *n* **1** : gay or festive activity : CONVIVIALITY, MERRIMENT **2** : a convivial occasion : FESTIVITY, PARTY

mer·ry·man \'⁼⁼mən\ *n, pl* **merrymen** *archaic* : BUFFOON, JESTER

merry-meeting \'⁼⁼ˌ⁼⁼\ *n, archaic* : a festive gathering

merry night *n, dial Eng* : an evening of entertainment and dancing

merrythought \'⁼⁼ˌ⁼\ *n, chiefly Brit* : WISHBONE

merrywing \'⁼⁼ˌ⁼\ *n* **1** : BUFFLEHEAD **2** : GOLDENEYE 1

mers *pl of* MER

-mers *pl of* -MER

mer·sal·yl \(ˌ)mər'saˌlil, -ˌlēl\ *also* **mersalyl sodium** *n* -s [*mercury* + *salicyl*] : an organic mercurial $C_{13}H_{16}HgNNaO_6$ administered by injection in combination with theophylline as a diuretic

merse \'mərs\ *chiefly Scot var of* MARSH

mer·ten·sia \(ˌ)mər'tench(ē)ə, -n(t)sēə\ *n, cap* [NL, fr. Franz K *Mertens*, †1831 Ger. botanist + NL *-ia*] : a large genus of herbs (family Boraginaceae) of temperate regions with funnel-shaped blue or purple flowers — see VIRGINIA COWSLIP

Mer·thi·o·late \(ˌ)mər'thīəˌlāt, -ˌlət\ *trademark* — used for thimerosal

mer·u·la \'mer(y)ələ\ [NL, fr. L, blackbird — more at MERL] *syn of* TURDUS

me·ru·li·us \mə'rülēəs\ *n, cap* [NL, fr. L *merula* blackbird; fr. the black color of the fungus] : a genus of fungi (family Polyporaceae) having resupinate sporophores on which the hymenium forms reticulate or sinuous folds — see HOUSE FUNGUS

me·rus \'mi(ə)rəs\ *n* -ES [NL, fr. Gk *mēros* thigh — more at MEMBER] : MEROPODITE; *esp* : the meropodite of a chela constituting the enlarged palm of the hand

-mer·us \ˌmərəs\ *n comb form* [NL, fr. Gk *mēros* thigh] : animal or insect having a (specified) type of thigh — in generic names in entomology ⟨*Tomicomerus*⟩ ⟨*Symmerus*⟩

mer·win·ite \'mərwəˌnīt\ *n* -s [Herbert E. *Merwin* b1878 Am. petrologist + E *-ite*] : a mineral $MgCa_3(SiO_4)_2$ consisting of a calcium magnesium silicate with monoclinic crystals

mer·woman \'mər, 'mə+ˌ-\ *n, pl* **merwomen** [¹*mer-* + *woman*] : MERMAID

-mery \ˌmərē, -ri\ *n comb form* -ES [ISV ³*mer-* + *-y*] : possession of (such or so many) parts ⟨*gonomery*⟩ ⟨*metamery*⟩

mer·yc·hip·pus \ˌmerēˈkipəs\ *n, cap* [NL, fr. Gk *mērykasthai* to ruminate + NL *-hippus*] : an American genus of extinct Miocene horses

mer·yc·oi·do·don \ˌ⁼⁼ˈkȯidəˌdän\ *n, cap* [NL, fr. Gk *mērykasthai* to ruminate + NL *-oides* -oid + *-odon*] : a genus (the type of the family Merycoidodontidae) of Oligocene four-toed artiodactyls of the size of a peccary and the form of a swine that are regarded as probably archaic ruminants living in No. America from the Eocene to the early Pliocene

mer·y·co·pot·a·mus \-ˌkōˈpäd·əməs\ *n, cap* [NL, fr. Gk *mērykasthai* + NL *-o-* + *potamos* river — more at HIPPOPOTAMUS] : a genus of Asiatic Pliocene and Pleistocene artiodactyls related to the genus *Anthracotherium* and sometimes made the type of a distinct family

-mer·yx \ˌməriks\ *n comb form* [NL, fr. Gk *mēryx*, a ruminating fish, fr. *mērykasthai* to ruminate] : ruminant — chiefly in generic names of extinct ruminating mammals ⟨*leptomeryx*⟩

MEs *pl of* ME

mes- *or* **meso-** *comb form* [L, fr. Gk, fr. *mesos* — more at MID] **1 a** : in the middle : intermediate (as in position, size, type, time, degree) ⟨*meso*derm⟩ ⟨*meso*dont⟩ ⟨*meso*nephroma⟩ ⟨*meso*plankton⟩ ⟨*meso*prosopic⟩ ⟨*Meso*zoa⟩ ⟨*meso*carp⟩ **b** : mesentery or membrane supporting a (specified) part ⟨*meso*caecum⟩ ⟨*meso*colon⟩ ⟨*mes*archium⟩ **c** : mesoderm : mesodermal and ⟨*mes*ameboid⟩ **2** *meso-* : a reduction product of a porphyrin or other pyrrole derivative in which one or more vinyl groups have been hydrogenated to ethyl ⟨*meso*hemin⟩ ⟨*meso*bilirubin⟩ **3** : an inorganic acid regarded as an intermediate hydrated form ⟨di*meso*periodic acid $H_4I_2O_9$⟩ **4** *meso-*, *usu ital* **a** : an optical isomer whose inactivity is attributed to the molecule's being internally compensated ⟨*meso*-tartaric acid⟩ **b** : a middle position or group esp. in a cyclic compound ⟨*meso*-chloro-anthracene is 9-chloro-anthracene⟩ ⟨*meso*-phenyl-imidazole is 2-phenyl-imidazole⟩ — abbr. *ms* or *μ* **5** : of late Paleozoic or of Mesozoic age — in names of igneous rocks

me·sa \'māsə *sometimes* -āzə\ *n* -s [Sp, lit., table, fr. L *mensa*] **1 a** : a usu. isolated hill or mountain having abrupt or steeply sloping sides and a level top that is composed of a resistant nearly horizontal stratum of rock and is usu. greater in area than that of a butte : a small isolated plateau **b** : a broad terrace (as along a river) with an abrupt slope or escarpment on one side : BENCH **2** : CARTOUCHE 6

me·sa·bite \mə'säˌbīt\ *n* -s [*Mesabi* range, Minn. + E *-ite*] : an ocherous goethite

mes·acon·ic acid \ˌme|zə|ˈkänik-, |mē|, |sə|\ *n* [prob. fr. ISV *mes-* + citr*aconic acid*] : a crystalline unsaturated acid $HOOCCH{=}C(CH_3)COOH$ made by thermal isomerization of citraconic acid; methyl-fumaric acid

mesad \'me|ˌzad, 'mē|, |ˌsad\ *also* **mesi·ad** \|ˌzēˌad, |sē-\ *adv* [*mesad* fr. *mesal* + *-ad* (adv. suffix); *mesiad* fr. *mesial* + *-ad*] : toward or on the side toward the mesial plane

mes·ade·nia \ˌme|zə'dēnēə, ˌmē|, |sə-\ *n, cap* [NL, fr. *mes-* + Gk *aden-*, *adēn* gland + NL *-ia*; fr. the central projection of the receptacle — more at ADEN-] *in some classifications* : a separate genus comprising the New World members of the genus *Cacalia*

mes·ade·ni·um \-nēəm\ *n, pl* **mesade·nia** \-nēə\ [NL, fr. *mes-* + Gk *aden-*, *adēn* gland + NL *-ium*] : one of the accessory glands of mesodermal origin of male insects — compare ECTADENIUM

mesa dropseed *n* : a tufted perennial No. American grass (*Sporobolus flexuosus*) having spreading or reflexed branches and usu. lead-colored spikelets

mesal *var of* MESIAL

més·al·liance \ˌmāˌzalˈyäⁿs; ˌmāzəˈlīən(t)s, ˌmezə-, ˌmesə-\ *n, pl* **mésal·liances** \-äⁿs(əz), -ənsəz\ [F, fr. *més-* mis- + *alliance* (fr. MF *alliance*, *aliance*)] : a marriage with a person of inferior social position : MISALLIANCE

mes·ameboid \ˌme|z, |mē|, |s +\ *n* -s [*mes-* + *ameboid* (adj.)] : a primitive amoeboid mesodermal cell that gives rise to the blood cells of the embryo : HEMATOBLAST

mé·sange \mā'zäⁿzh\ *n, pl* **mé·sanges** \-zh(əz)\ [F, titmouse, fr. MF, fr. OF *mesenge*, *masenghe*, of Gmc origin; akin to OHG *meisa* titmouse — more at TITMOUSE] : a pale green that is bluer and duller than celadon gray or spray green — called also *titmouse blue*

mes·aortitis \ˌme|z, |mē|, |s +\ *n* -ES [NL, fr. *mes-* + *aorta* + *-itis*] : inflammation of the middle layer of the aorta

¹**mes·a·ra·ic** \ˌmezəˈrāik, -esə-\ *adj* [alter. (influenced by Gk *mesaraikos*) of ME *miserak*, fr. MF *mesaraique*, fr. Gk *mesaraikos*, fr. *mesaraion* mesentery (fr. *mes-* mid, in the middle — fr. *mesos* — + *araia* belly, fr. fem. of *araios* thin, slender) + *-ikos* -ic — more at MID] *archaic* : MESENTERIC

²**mesaraic** \"\ *n -s archaic* : one of the mesenteric veins

mes·arch \'me|ˌzärk, 'mē|, |ˌsä-\ *adj* [*mes-* + *-arch*] **1** : having metaxylem developed both internal and external to the protoxylem **2** : originating in a mesic habitat — used of an ecological succession; compare HYDRARCH, XERARCH

mes·arteritis \ˌme|z, |mē|, |s +\ *n* [NL, fr. *mes-* + *arteri-* + *-itis*] : inflammation of the middle layer of an artery

mesati- *comb form* [Gk *mesatos* midmost, irreg. superl. of *mesos* mid, in the middle] : of medium or intermediate proportion

me·sati·ce·phal·ic \məˌsadˌəsəˈfalik, məˈsa-\ *also* **me·sati·ceph·a·lous** \-d·əˈsefələs\ *adj* [*mesaticephalism* + *-ic* or *-ous*] : having a head of medium proportion with a cephalic index of 76 to 81

me·sati·ceph·a·lism \ˌ⁼ˌ⁼⁼ˈsefəˌlizəm\ *or* **me·sati·ceph·a·ly** \-fəlē\ *n* [*mesaticephalism* fr. *mesati-* (fr. Gk *mesatos* midmost, irreg. superl. of *mesos* mid, in the middle) + *-cephalism*; *mesaticephaly*, ISV *mesati-* + *-cephaly*] : the quality or state of being mesaticephalic

me·sat·i·pel·lic \⁼ˌ⁼ˈpelik\ *adj* [*mesati-* + *-pellic* (fr. Gk *pella* wooden bowl + E *-ic*) — more at PELVIS] : having a pelvis of moderate size with a pelvic index of 90 to 95 — **me·sat·i·pel·ly** \⁼ˌ⁼ˌpelē\ *n* -ES

me·sati·skelic \⁼ˌ⁼⁼+\ *adj* [*mesati-* + *skelic*] : having limbs of moderate length in proportion to the trunk with a skelic index of 85 to 90

mes·ax·o·nia \ˌme|zakˈsōnēə, ˌmē|, |ˌsa-\ [NL, fr. *mes-* + Gk *axōn* axis + NL *-ia* — more at AXIS] *syn of* PERISSODACTYLA

mes·ax·on·ic \ˌ⁼⁼ˈsänik\ *adj* **1** [*mes-* + Gk *axōn* axis + E *-ic*] : having the axis of the foot formed by the middle digit **2** [NL *Mesaxonia* + E *-ic*] : of or relating to the Perissodactyla

mes·cal *also* **mez·cal** \(ˈ)meˈskal, məˈs-\ *n* -s [Sp *mescal*, *mezcal*, *mexcal*, fr. Nahuatl *mexcalli* mescal (liquor), fr. *metl* maguey + *xcalli*, short for *ixcalli* stew, decoction] **1** : a small cactus (*Lophophora williamsii*) with rounded stems covered with jointed tubercles that is used as a stimulant and antispasmodic esp. among the Mexican Indians who also employ it as a mild intoxicant in various ceremonies — see MESCAL BUTTON, PEYOTE **2 a** : a usu. colorless Mexican liquor distilled esp. from the central leaves of maguey plants after they have been roasted and fermented — compare SOTOL, TEQUILA; see PULQUE **b** : a plant from which mescal is produced; *esp* : MAGUEY

mescal bean *n* **1** : MESCAL BUTTON **2 a** : a leguminous shrub or small tree (*Sophora secundiflora*) with alternate pinnate leaves often poisonous to livestock, flowers in dense one-sided racemes, and bright red narcotic seeds that resemble beans — called also *coral bean* **b** : a seed of this plant

mescal button *n* : one of the dried disklike tops of the mescal

mes·ca·lero \ˌmeskəˈle(ˌ)rō\ *n, pl* **mescalero** *or* **mescaleros** *usu cap* [AmerSp, fr. Sp *mescal*, *mezcal*, *mexcal* mescal] **1 a** : an Apache people formerly ranging esp. through western and central Texas and eastern New Mexico **b** : a member of such people **2** : the language of the Mescalero people

mes·ca·line *also* **mez·ca·line** \'meskəˌlēn, -ˌlən\ *n* -s [*mescal* + *-ine*] : a crystalline alkaloid $C_{11}H_{17}NO_3$ that is the chief active principle in mescal buttons, produces hallucinations when administered, and is useful in experimental psychiatry for producing the symptoms of catalepsy; 3,4,5-trimethoxy-phenyl-ethylamine

mes·calism \meˈskaˌlizəm, məˈ-; ˈmeskəˌl-\ *n* -s : addiction to mescal

mescal maguey *n* **1** : MESCAL 2b **2** : a fiber obtained from a Mexican plant (*Agave pseudotequilana*)

¹**meschant** *adj* [ME *mischaunt*, fr. MF *meschant*, fr. OF *mescheant*, *mescheant* unlucky, miserable, fr. pres. part. of *mescheoir* to be unlucky, fr. *mes-* mis- + *cheoir* to happen, befall, fall — more at CHUTE] *obs* : WICKED, BASE — **meschantly** *adv, obs*

²**meschant** *n -s obs* : SCOUNDREL, WRETCH

mesdames *pl of* MADAM *or of* MADAME

mesdemoiselles *pl of* MADEMOISELLE

mes·ectoderm \(ˈ)me|z, (ˈ)mē|, |s +\ *n* [*mesoderm* + *ectoderm*] : an embryonic blastomere or cell layer not yet differentiated into mesoderm and ectoderm but destined to give rise to both — **mes·ectodermal** *adj* — **mes·ectodermic** \ˌme|z, |mē|, |s +\ *adj*

me·seems \məˈsēmz, mēˈ-\ *vb impersonal, past 3d sing* **me-**

seemed \-ēmd\ *pres 3d sing* **meseems** [*me* + *seems*, 3d sing. pres. indic. of *seem*] *archaic* : it seems to me ⟨~ that here is much discourtesy —Alfred Tennyson⟩

mesel *n* -s [ME, loathsome person, leper, fr. OF, leper, fr. ML *misellus*, fr. L, wretch, fr. *misellus*, adj., miserable, fr. *miser* miserable] *obs* : a loathsome person

me·self \mə̇, mē+\ *pron* [ME, fr. OE *meseolf*, fr. *me* + *seolf*, *self* self — more at SELF] *now dial* : MYSELF

me·sem \mə̇'zem\ *n* -s [by shortening] *Africa* : MESEMBRYANTHEMUM

me·sem·bry·an·the·mum \mə̇,zembrē'an(t)thəməm\ *n* [NL, fr. Gk *mesēmbria* midday, noon (fr. *mes-* + *hēmera* day) + NL *-anthemum* — more at HEMERA] **1** *cap* : a genus of chiefly southern African herbs or subshrubs (family Aizoaceae) having fleshy leaves and flowers with a gamosepalous calyx and a capsular fruit **2** -s : any plant of the genus *Mesembryanthemum*

mes·encephalic \(¦)me¦z, (¦)mē¦, ¦s +\ *adj* [NL *mesencephalon* + E *-ic*] : of or relating to the midbrain

mes·encephalon \¦me¦z, ¦mē¦, ¦s +\ *n* [NL, fr. *mes-* + *encephalon*] : the middle division of the brain : MIDBRAIN

me·sen·chy·ma \mə̇'zeŋkəmə, me¦, ¦'se-\ *n* -s [NL, fr. *mes-* + *-enchyma*] : MESENCHYME

mes·en·chy·mal \-məl; ¦mez°n¦kīməl, ¦mē¦, ¦s°n-\ *adj* [ISV *mesenchyme* + *-al*] : of, relating to, or being mesenchyme

mes·en·chym·a·tous \¦me¦z°n¦kimədəs, ¦mē¦, ¦s°n-\ *adj* [NL *mesenchymat-*, *mesenchyma* + E *-ous*] : resembling or consisting of mesoderm

mes·en·chyme \'me¦z°n,kīm, 'mē¦, ¦s°n-\ *also* **mesen·chym** \-,kim; mə̇'zeŋkə̇m, -'se-\ *n* -s [G *mesenchym*, fr. *mes-* + *-enchym* -enchyme] : a loosely organized mesodermal connective tissue comprising all the mesoblast except the mesothelium and the structures derived from it and giving rise to such structures as connective tissues, blood lymphatics, bone, and cartilage

mes·endoderm *also* **mes·entoderm** \(')me¦z, (')mē¦, ¦s +\ *n* [*mesoderm* + *endoderm* or *entoderm*] : an embryonic blastomere or cell layer not yet differentiated into mesoderm and endoderm but destined to give rise to both

mesene \'me¦,zēn, 'mē¦, ¦,sēn\ *adj* [G *mesen*, fr. *mes-* + *-en* as in *euryen* euryene — more at EURYENE] : having a forehead of moderate proportions with an upper facial index of 48 to 53 on the living or of 50 to 55 on the skull — **meseny** \-nē\ *n* -ES

me·sen·na \mə̇'zenə, -'se-\ *also* **mu·sen·na** \myü'-\ *or* **mous·sena** \mü'-\ *n* -s [Amharic *mĕsanna*] : the bark of an Ethiopian tree (*Albizzia anthelmintica*) used to expel tapeworms

mes·en·te·ri·al \¦mes°n¦tirēəl, -ez°n-\ *adj* [NL *mesenterium* mesentery + E *-al*] : MESENTERIC; *specif* : indicating certain threadlike glandular organs attached to the inner edge of the mesenteries of anthozoans

mes·en·ter·ic \-¦terik\ *adj* [F *mésentérique*, fr. MF *mesenterique*, fr. *mesentere* mesentery + *-ique* -ic] : of, relating to, or located in or near a mesentery

mesenteric artery *n* [trans. of F *artère mésentérique*] : an artery passing between the two layers of the mesentery to the intestine; *specif* : either a superior artery in man arising from the upper part of the aorta and distributed to the greater part of the small intestine, the cecum, and the colon or an inferior artery in man arising near the lower end of the aorta and distributed to the remainder of the large intestine

mesenteric gland *n* : one of the lymphatic glands of the mesentery

mesenteric plexus *n* : either of two sympathetic plexuses lying mostly in the mesentery in close proximity to and distributed to the same structures as the corresponding mesenteric arteries

mesenteric vein *n* [trans. of F *veine mésentérique*] : a branch of the portal vein leading from the intestine between the two layers of mesentery; *specif* : either a superior vein in man or an inferior vein in man corresponding to the two mesenteric arteries

mes·en·teri·o·lum \,≈≈,terē'ōləm, -,tə'rīələm\ *n*, *pl* **mesen·terio·la** \-lə\ [NL, dim. of *mesenterium* mesentery] : MESOAPPENDIX

mes·en·ter·i·tis \,≈≈,te'rīd·ə̇s, -,tə'r-\ *n* -ES [NL, fr. *mesenterium* mesentery + *-itis*] : inflammation of the mesentery

mes·enteron \(')me¦z, (')mē¦, ¦s +\ *n*, *pl* **mesentera** [NL, fr. *mes-* + *enteron*] **1** : the part of the alimentary canal that is developed from the archenteron and is lined with hypoblast — compare PROCTODAEUM, STOMODAEUM **2** : the central gastric cavity of an actinozoan as distinguished from the spaces between the mesenteries — compare METENTERON — **mes·en·ter·on·ic** \(¦)me¦z¦entə'rānik, (¦)mē¦, ¦,se-\ *adj*

mes·en·tery \'mes°n,terē, -ez°n-\ *n* -ES [NL *mesenterium*, fr. MF & Gk; MF *mesentere*, fr. Gk *mesenterion*, *mesenteron*, fr. *mes-* + *enteron* intestine] **1 a** : the membranes or one of the membranes that consist of a double fold of the peritoneum and enclosed tissues and that in a vertebrate animal invest the intestines and their appendages, connect them with the dorsal wall of the abdominal cavity, and serve to retain the organs in position and to support and convey to them blood vessels, nerves, and lymphatics; *specif* : these membranes connected with the jejunum and ileum in man — compare MESOCECUM, MESOCOLON, MESOGASTRIUM, MESORECTUM **b** : any comparable fold of membrane supporting a viscus (as the heart or an ovary) that is not a part of the digestive tract **c** : a membranous or muscular fold or septum connecting the intestine and body wall in an invertebrate **2** : one of the radial muscular partitions extending inward from the wall of the digestive cavity of actinozoans

mes·epimeron \¦me¦z, ¦mē¦, ¦s +\ *n* [NL, fr. *mes-* + *epimeron*] : the epimeron of the mesothorax of an insect

mes·episternum \"+\ *n* [NL, fr. *mes-* + *episternum*] : the episternum of the mesothorax of an insect

mes·epithelium \"+\ *n* [NL, fr. *mes-* + *epithelium*] : MESOTHELIUM

me·se·ta \mə̇'sād·ə, mā'-\ *n* -s [Sp, dim. of *mesa*] **1** : a small mesa **2** : an extensive upland or plateau often with an uneven surface and forming the central physical feature of a region ⟨the Spanish ~⟩

¹mes·ethmoid \(')me¦z, (')mē¦, ¦s +\ *adj* [*mes-* + *ethmoid*, adj.] : located in the middle of the ethmoid region : being or relating to a median cartilaginous or bony element of the ethmoidal region that generally forms the greater part of the nasal septum

²mesethmoid \"\ *n* [*mes-* + *ethmoid*, n.] : a mesethmoid bone or cartilage

¹mesh \'mesh\ *n* -ES *often attrib* [prob. fr. obs. D *maesche*, *masche*, fr. MD *maessce*; akin to OE *masc*, *max*, *mǣscre* mesh, OS & OHG *masca*, ON *mǫskvi* mesh, Lith *mazgas* knot, *megsti* to weave nets, knot] **1** : one of the openings between the threads or cords of a net; *also* : one of the similar spaces in any network ⟨the ~*es* of a sieve⟩ ⟨lock joint holds each ~ in true alignment —*Amer. Fence Catalog*⟩ ⟨steel ~ used for reinforcing concrete —*Dict. of Occupations*⟩ — often used to designate a size of screen or of the material passed by a screen in terms of the number of such openings per linear inch ⟨the ~ of the bolting wire —*Correspondence Course in Flour Milling*⟩ ⟨a 60-*mesh* screen⟩ ⟨30-*mesh* granulated zinc⟩ **2 a** : the cords, threads, or wires that produce the open spaces in a net or screen : the fabric of a net ⟨built a ramp out of wire ~ —W.B.Huie⟩ — often used in pl. ⟨a net with almost invisible ~*es*⟩ **b** : a woven, knit, or knotted fabric that has an open texture with evenly spaced small holes ⟨a ~ hose⟩ ⟨a ~ handbag⟩; *specif* : the net background fabric of many laces **c** : an arrangement of interlocking metal links used esp. for jewelry ⟨a ~ bracelet⟩ **d** : a flexible netting of fine wire used in surgery esp. in the repair of large hernias and other body defects **3 a** : an interlocking or intertwining arrangement or construction : NETWORK, WEB ⟨a ~ of narrow streets —John Buchan⟩ ⟨the ~ of irrigation canals —*Amer. Guide Series: Oregon*⟩ **b** : something that catches and holds or involves : TOILS, SNARE — usu. used in pl. ⟨took to panhandling, got detained in the ~*es* of the big city —Dixon Wecter⟩ ⟨diplomacy caught in its own ~*es*⟩ **c** : an intricate or inscrutable system or combination ⟨fixed in the ~ of the divine purpose —V.L.Parrington⟩ ⟨book is a gigantic dense ~ of complicated relations —Edmund Wilson⟩ ⟨a ~ of circumstance⟩ **4** : working contact (as of the teeth of gear wheels or of a slide fastener) — used esp. in the phrases *in mesh* and *out of mesh* **5** : a closed figure produced by joining electrical components in series ⟨~ connection⟩

²mesh \"\ *vb* -ED/-ING/-ES *vt* **1 a** : to catch in a mesh : NET ⟨nets . . . of such a mesh size that the fish are ~*ed* —*Australian Fisheries*⟩ **b** : ENMESH, ENTANGLE ⟨the unseen anchor ~*ed* in rock or bar —Spencer Brown⟩ ⟨become ~*ed* in thought⟩ **2 a** : to provide with a mesh **b** : to cause to resemble network ⟨the city was ~*ed* in haze —*New Yorker*⟩ ⟨trees ~*ed* with sunlight⟩ **3 a** : to come into or be in working contact with esp. by the fitting together of teeth : ENGAGE **b** : to cause to come into working contact esp. by the fitting together of teeth ⟨noiselessly he ~*ed* the gears —C.B.Kelland⟩ **c** : to coordinate closely (as in a satisfactory working arrangement) : INTERLOCK ⟨the idea is to ~ the know-how and experience of the regulars with the enthusiasm of the amateur volunteers —Raymond Moley⟩ : fit together properly ⟨learn to ~ layouts —*Mademoiselle*⟩ ~ *vi* **1** : to become entangled in or as if in meshes ⟨the fish will not ~ today⟩ **2** : to be in or come into proper working contact — used esp. of gears or other toothed working parts ⟨wooden-cogged wheels ~*ing* at an angle —A.L.Kroeber⟩ ⟨a slide fastener that will not ~⟩ **3** : to combine or fit together intricately, properly, or harmoniously : ACCORD, COORDINATE, HARMONIZE ⟨making the operations of the mind ~ with physical actuality —Aram Vartanian⟩ ⟨my plans are ~*ing* together smoothly —C.A.Lindbergh b. 1902⟩ ⟨two themes that do not quite ~ when they meet —Lisle Bell⟩ ⟨an integrating and ~*ing* of personalities —D.L.Cohn⟩

³mesh \"\ *dial var of* MARSH

⁴mesh \"\ *dial var of* MASH

me·shech \'mē,shek\ *n pl*, *usu cap* [Heb *Meshekh*] : MOSCHI

¹meshed \'mesht\ *adj* [¹*mesh* + *-ed*] **1** : having meshes ⟨~ tissues⟩ **2** : resembling meshes or network : RETICULATE, TANGLED ⟨a ~ road system⟩ **3** : fitting together and interacting : ENGAGED — used of toothed working parts ⟨~ gears⟩

²me·shed \mə'shed\ *adj*, *usu cap* [fr. *Meshed*, Iran] : of or from the city of Meshed, Iran : of the kind or style prevalent in Meshed

mesh knot *n* : SHEET BEND

meshrabiyeh *var of* MOUCHARABY

me·shug·ga *or* **me·shu·ga** *or* **me·shug·ge** *or* **me·shu·ge** \mə̇'shügə\ *adj* [*meshugga* or *meshuga* fr. Heb *mĕshuggā'*; *meshugge* or *meshuge* fr. Yiddish *meshuge*, fr. Heb *mĕshuggā'*] : mentally unbalanced : CRAZY

me·shug·gaas *or* **me·shu·gaas** \mə̇(,)shü'gäs\ *n*, *pl* **meshuggaas·en** *or* **meshugaas·en** \-äs°n\ [Yiddish *meshugaas*, fr. Heb *mĕshuggā'*, adj.] : NONSENSE, FOOLISHNESS

me·shul·lah *or* **me·shu·lah** *or* **me·shul·lach** *or* **me·shu·lach** \mə̇'shü,läk, -shü,-\ *n*, *pl* **meshulla·him** *or* **meshula·him** *or* **meshulla·chim** *or* **meshula·chim** \≈,≈'läkə̇m, -(,)kēm\ [Heb *mĕshūllāh*, lit., one who is sent] : an accredited itinerant collector sent out to raise funds esp. for the maintenance of orthodox Jewish religious and charitable institutions in Palestine — compare HALUKKAH

me·shum·mad \mə̇'shü,mäd\ *n*, *pl* **meshumma·dim** \≈,≈(,)mä'dēm\ [Heb *mĕshummādh*, lit., one who is destroyed] : an apostate from Judaism

meshwork \'≈,≈\ *n* : MESHES, NETWORK ⟨a complicated vascular ~ —*Biol. Abstracts*⟩

meshy \'meshē\ *adj* -ER/-EST : composed of meshes : NETTED

me·sia \'mēsh(ē)ə\ *n* -s [NL *Mesia*, genus of birds] : an Asiatic hill tit (*Leiothrix argentauris*) with the crown black, the ear coverts silvery gray, a red bar across the wing, and the remaining plumage yellow and olive green

mesiad *var of* MESAD

mesial \'mezēəl, 'mē¦, ¦sē-; 'mēzhəl, -ēsh-\ *also* **mesal** \¦zəl, ¦səl\ *adj* [*mes-* + *-ial* or *-al*] **1** : MIDDLE, MEDIAN ⟨the ~ aspect of the metacarpal head⟩ **2** : lying in, being in the region of, or directed toward the mesial plane ⟨the heart is ~ to the lungs⟩ — opposed to *distal* — **mesi·al·ly** \-əlē\ *also* **mesal·ly** \-əlē\ *adv*

mesial plane *n* : the median vertical longitudinal plane that divides a bilaterally symmetrical animal into right and left halves

mesic \'me¦zik, 'mē¦, ¦sik\ *adj* [in sense 1, fr. *meson* + *-ic*; in senses 2 & 3, fr. *mes-* + *-ic*] **1** : MESONIC ⟨the radii of the ~ orbits —Lawrence Wilets⟩ **2** *of a habitat* : having or characterized by a moderate amount of moisture : neither hydric nor xeric **3** *of a plant or flora* : MESOPHYTIC — **mesi·cal·ly** \¦zə̇k(ə)lē, ¦sə̇-\ *adv*

mes·i·dine \'mezə,dēn, -esə-, -,dən\ *n* -s [ISV *mesityl* + *-idine*] : an aromatic amine $(CH_3)_3C_6H_2NH_2$ that is obtained by reduction of nitro-mesitylene and is used as a dye intermediate

me·si·lla \mə̇'sē(y)ə, -'zē-\ *n* -s [Sp, dim. of *mesa*] *Southwest* : a small mesa

mesio- *comb form* [*mesial* + *-o-*] : mesial and ⟨*mesio*buccal⟩ ⟨*mesio*labial⟩ ⟨*mesio*occlusal⟩

mesio·clu·sion \¦me¦zēə'klüzhən, ¦mē¦, ¦sē-\ *also* **mesio·occlusion** \¦me¦zē(,)ō, ¦mē¦, ¦sē- +\ *n* [*mesio-* + *occlusion* or *occlusion*] : malocclusion characterized by mesial displacement of one or more of the lower teeth

me·si·tes \mə̇'sīd·(,)ēz\ [NL, fr. Gk *mesitēs* mediator, fr. *mesos* middle, mid + *-ites* -ite — more at MID] *syn of* MESITORNIS

mes·i·tite \'mezə,tīt, -esə-\ *or* **mes·i·tine** \-,tēn, -,tən\ *also* **mesitine spar** *n* -s [*mesitite* fr. G *mesitit*, fr. earlier *mesitinspath* mesitine spar (fr. Gk *mesitēs* mediator + G *-in* -ine + *spath*, *spat* spar) + *-it* -ite; *mesitine* fr. G *mesitin*, short for *mesitinspath*; *mesitine spar*, trans. of G *mesitinspath*; fr. its being intermediate between magnesite and siderite] : ferroan magnesite

mes·it·or·nis \,≈≈'tȯrnə̇s\ *n*, *cap* [NL, fr. Gk *mesitēs* + NL *-ornis*] : a genus that consists of two species (*M. variegata* and *M. unicolor*) of Madagascan birds related to the rails but resembling thrushes and that with the monotypic genus *Monias* forms the family Mesitornithidae

mes·it·or·nith·i·dae \-,tȯr'nithə,dē\ *n pl*, *cap* [NL, fr. *Mesitornith-*, *Mesitornis*, type genus + *-idae*] : a small family (coextensive with the suborder Mesitornithides of the order Gruiformes) of Madagascan birds

mes·i·tyl \'≈≈,til\ *n* -s [Gk *mesitēs* mediator + E *-yl*] **1** : a hypothetical radical C_3H_5 of which mesityl oxide was once regarded as the oxide and acetone as the hydroxide **2** : either of two univalent radicals C_9H_{11} derived from mesitylene by removal of one hydrogen atom: **a** : the substituted phenyl radical $(CH_3)_3C_6H_2$— **b** : the substituted benzyl radical $(CH_3)_2C_6H_3CH_2$—; 3,5-dimethyl-benzyl — called also *alpha-mesityl*

me·sit·y·lene \mə̇'sid·°l,ēn\ *n* -s [*mesityl* + *-ene*] : an oily hydrocarbon $C_6H_3(CH_3)_3$ occurring in coal tar and petroleum and also made synthetically (as by distilling acetone with sulfuric acid); 1,3,5-trimethylbenzene

mesityl oxide *n* : a fragrant liquid ketone $(CH_3)_2C{=}CHCOCH_3$ obtained by the dehydration of diacetone alcohol and used as a solvent and an intermediate in organic synthesis

meslin \'mezlə̇n\ *dial Brit var of* ²MASLIN

mes·mer·ic \(')mez'merik, -es¦m-\ *adj* **1** : of, relating to, or induced by mesmerism : that mesmerizes ⟨~ trance —E.A. Poe⟩ ⟨by his strange ~ powers held the listeners in the hollow of his hand —Agnes S. Turnbull⟩ **2** : FASCINATING, IRRESISTIBLE ⟨a ~, warm charm that emanated from her person —Mary McCarthy⟩ — **mes·mer·i·cal·ly** \-rə̇k(ə)lē\ *adv*

mes·mer·ism \'mezmə,rizəm, -esm-\ *n* -s [F. A. *Mesmer* †1815 Austrian physician + E *-ism*] **1** : hypnotic induction by Mesmer's method believed to involve animal magnetism; *broadly* : HYPNOTISM **2 a** : a state induced by hypnotic induction esp. by Mesmer's method **b** : hypnotic appeal : intense fascination

mes·mer·ist \-,rə̇st\ *n* -s : one who practices mesmerism

mes·mer·iza·tion \,≈≈rə̇'zāshən, -,rī'z-\ *n* -s **1** : the act of mesmerizing **2** : the state of being mesmerized

mes·mer·ize \'≈≈,rīz\ *vt* -ED/-ING/-S *see -ize in Explan Notes* [*mesmerism* + *-ize*] **1** : to hypnotize esp. by Mesmer's method **2** : SPELLBIND, FASCINATE — usu. used as a past participle ⟨his *mesmerized* immersion in small-town snobbery —C.J.Rolo⟩ ⟨*mesmerized*, the skipper . . . stands at his periscope watching for the success or failure of his approach —E.L.Beach⟩

mes·mer·iz·er \-zə(r)\ *n* -s : one that mesmerizes : HYPNOTIST

mes·nal·ty \'mēn°ltē\ *also* **mes·nal·i·ty** \mē'naləd·ē\ *n* -ES [*mesnalty* prob. fr. AF *mesnalté* (attested as *mesnatty*, *mesnattie*), fr. *mesne*, n. + *-alté* as in *comunalté* commonalty; *mesnality*, alter. (influenced by *-ity*) of *mesnalty*] : the estate or condition of a mesne lord

¹mesne \'mēn\ *adj* [AF, alter. of MF *meien* occupying a middle position — more at MEAN] *law* : MIDDLE, INTERVENING; *specif* : intermediate in time of occurrence or performance ⟨~ assignment⟩ ⟨~ encumbrance⟩

²mesne \"\ *n* -s **1** *archaic* : something that falls between extremes **2** [AF, fr. *mesne*, adj.] : MESNE LORD

mesne lord *n* [trans. of AF *seignior mesne*, *seignor mesne*] *Eng law* : a lord who holds land of a superior and is tenant to the superior but lord to his own tenant

mesne process *n* : all process issued after the commencement by original writ or any modern substitute therefor and before the termination of a lawsuit by a writ of execution

meso \'me¦(,)zō, 'mē¦, ¦(,)sō\ *adj* [*mes-*] *of a molecule or compound* : optically inactive because internally compensated

meso- — see MES-

meso·american \¦me¦(,)zō, ¦mē¦, ¦(,)sō +\ *adj*, *usu cap* [*Mesoamerica*, region extending from north central No. America to Nicaragua (fr. Sp *Mesoamérica*, fr. *meso-* mes- + *América* America) + E *-an*] : of, relating to, or characteristic of Mesoamerica or of the people of Mesoamerica ⟨general problems of *Mesoamerican* prehistory —*Amer. Antiquity*⟩ ⟨the classic period, which saw the full flowering of *Mesoamerican* civilization in Guatemala, Honduras, El Salvador, and Mexico —A.V. Kidder⟩ — compare CENTRAL AMERICAN, MIDDLE AMERICAN

meso·appendiceal \"+\ *adj* [NL *mesoappendic-*, *mesoappendix* + E *-eal* (after *appendiceal*)] : of or relating to the mesoappendix

meso·appendix \"+\ *n* [NL, fr. *mes-* + *appendix*] : the mesentery of the vermiform appendix

meso·benthos \"+\ *n* [NL, fr. *mes-* + *benthos*] : the fauna and flora of the sea bottom between 100 and 500 fathoms

meso·biotic \"+\ *adj* [*mes-* + *-biotic*] *of a seed* : surviving in the dormant state for a relatively long period usu. between 3 and 15 years — compare MACROBIOTIC, MICROBIOTIC

meso·blast \'me¦zō, 'mē¦, ¦sō +,-\ *n* [*mes-* + *-blast*] : the middle germ layer of an embryo; *also* : the undifferentiated presumptive mesoderm that makes up this layer

meso·blastema \¦≈≈+\ *n* -s [NL, fr. *mes-* + *blastema*] : MESOBLAST — **meso·blastemic** \"+\ *adj*

meso·blas·tic \¦≈≈¦blastik\ *adj* [*mesoblast* + *-ic*] : relating to, derived from, or made up of mesoblast

meso·car·dia \,me¦zō'kärdēə, ,mē¦, ¦sō-\ *n* -s [NL, fr. *mes-* + *-cardia*] : abnormal location of the heart in the central part of the thorax

meso·car·di·um \-dēəm\ *n* -s [NL, fr. *mes-* + *-cardium*] **1** : the transitory mesentery of the embryonic heart **2** : the portion of the epicardium enclosing the blood vessels that join the heart

meso·carp \'≈≈,kärp\ *n* -s [*mes-* + *-carp*] : the middle layer of a pericarp — compare ENDOCARP

meso·cecum \¦me¦zō, ¦mē¦, ¦sō + \ *n* [NL, fr. *mes-* + *cecum*] : the fold of peritoneum attached to the cecum

meso·cen·trous \"+ ¦sen·trəs\ *adj* [*mes-* + *centr-* + *-ous*] : having a median center of ossification

meso·ceph·al \'≈≈,sefəl\ *n* -s [NL *mesocephalus*, fr. *mes-* + *-cephalus*] : a mesaticephalic person

meso·ce·phal·ic \¦≈≈sə̇¦falik\ *adj* [*mes-* + *-cephalic*] **1** : MESATICEPHALIC **2** [F *mésocéphalique*, fr. *mésocéphale* mesencephalon (fr. *méso-* mes- + Gk *kephalē* head) + *-ique* -ic — more at CEPHALIC] : MESENCEPHALIC

meso·ceph·a·ly \¦≈≈'sefəlē\ *n* -ES [ISV *mesocephalic* + *-y*] : the quality or state of being mesocephalic

meso·ces·toi·des \,≈≈,se'stȯi,dēz\ *n*, *cap* [NL, fr. *mes-* + L *cestus* girdle + *-oides* -oid — more at CESTUS] : a genus (the type of the family Mesocestoididae) of atypical unarmed cyclophyllidean tapeworms having the adults parasitic in mammals and birds and a slender threadlike contractile larva free in cavities or encysted in tissues of mammals, birds, and sometimes reptiles

meso·chon·dri·um \,me¦zō'kändrēəm, ,mē¦, ¦sō-\ *n*, *pl* **meso·chon·dria** \-ēə\ [NL, fr. *mes-* + *chondr-* + *-ium*] : the matrix of cartilage

meso·chro·ic \¦≈≈¦krōik\ *adj* [*mes-* + *-chroic*] : having a complexion intermediate between light and dark

mesocne·mic \¦me¦zō¦nēmik, ¦mē¦, ¦sō¦n-, ¦,zäk¦n-, ¦,säk¦n-\ *adj* [*mes-* + *-cnemic*] *of a shinbone* : rounded with a platycnemic index of 63 to 70

meso·coele *also* **meso·coel** *or* **meso·cele** \'me¦zō,sēl, 'mē¦, ¦sō-\ *or* **meso·coe·lia** \¦≈≈'sēlēə\ *n* -s [*mesocoele* or *mesocele* fr. *mes-* + *-coele*; *mesocoel*, alter. of *mesocoele*; *mesocoelia*, NL, fr. *mes-* + *coelia*] : the ventricle of the mesencephalon — **meso·coe·li·an** \¦≈≈¦sēlēən\ *adj* — **meso·coe·lic** \-lik\ *adj*

meso·colon \¦≈≈+\ *n* [NL, fr. Gk *mesokōlon*, fr. *meso-* mes- + *kōlon* colon — more at COLON (intestine)] : a mesentery joining the colon to the dorsal abdominal wall

meso·conch \'≈≈+,-\ *also* **meso·chonchic** \¦≈≈+\ *adj* [*mesoconch* fr. *mes-* + *-conch* (fr. L *concha* conch, shell); *mesoconchic* fr. *mesoconch* + *-ic* — more at CONCH] : having the orbits moderately rounded with an orbital index of 83 to 89 — **meso·con·chy** \'≈≈,käŋkē\ *n*

¹meso·coracoid \¦≈≈+\ *adj* [*mes-* + *coracoid*, adj.] : of or relating to a median element of the coracoid arch in some teleost fishes

²mesocoracoid \"\ *n* [*mes-* + *coracoid*, n.] : a mesocoracoid bone

meso·cot·yl \'me¦zō,käd·°l, 'mē¦, ¦sō-\ *n* [*mes-* + *-cotyl*] : an elongated portion of the axis between the cotyledon and the coleoptile of a grass seedling

me·soc·ra·cy \mə̇'zäkrəsē, -'sä-\ *n* -ES [*mes-* + *-cracy*] : government by the middle classes

meso·cranial \¦me¦zō, ¦mē¦, ¦sō+\ *adj* [prob. fr. G *mesokran* mesocranial (fr. *meso-* mes- + Gk *kranion* cranium) + E *-ial* — more at CRANIUM] : having a skull of medium proportions with a cranial index of 75–80

meso·cra·ny \'≈≈,krānē\ *n* -ES [ISV *mesocranial* + *-y*] : the quality or state of being mesocranial

meso·crat·ic \¦≈≈¦krad·ik\ *adj* [*mes-* + *-cratic* (as in *leucocratic*)] *of igneous rock* : having nearly equal dark and light mineral constituents ⟨a ~ diorite⟩ — compare LEUCOCRATIC, MELANOCRATIC

mesode \'me¦,zōd, 'mē¦, ¦,sōd\ *n* [Gk *mesōidos*, fr. *mes-* + *ōidē* song — more at ODE] *in the Greek choral dance* : a portion of a choral ode between a strophe and its antistrophe — **mes·od·ic** \mə̇'zädik, -'sä-\ *adj*

meso·derm \'me¦zə,dərm, 'mē¦, ¦sə-\ *n* [ISV *mes-* + *-derm*] : the middle of the three primary germ layers of an embryo being the source of bone, muscle, connective tissue, inner layer of the skin, and other adult structures : MESOBLAST; *broadly* : tissue wherever located that is derived from this germ layer — **meso·der·mal** \¦≈≈¦dərməl\ *or* **meso·der·mic** \-mik\ *adj*

meso·des·ma \,me¦zō'dezmə, ,mē¦, ¦sō-\ *n*, *cap* [NL, fr. *mes-* + Gk *desma* band, bond — more at DESMA] : a genus of marine bivalves (suborder Tellinacea) living mostly in the sand in shallow water

meso·dont \'≈≈,dänt\ *adj* [*mes-* + *-odont*] : having medium-sized teeth — **meso·don·ty** \-tē\ *n* -ES

meso·duodenum \¦≈≈+\ *n* [NL, fr. *mes-* + E *duodenum*] : the mesentery of the duodenum usu. not persisting in adult life in man and other mammals in which the developing intestine undergoes a counterclockwise rotation

me·soe·nas \mə̇'zēnəs, -'sē-\ [NL, fr. *mes-* + Gk *oinas* wild pigeon] *syn of* MESITORNIS

mes·oe·nat·i·dae \,mezə'nad·ə,dē, -esə-\ [NL, fr. *Mesoenat-*, *Mesoenas*, type genus + *-idae*] *syn of* MESITORNITHIDAE

meso–esophagus \¦me¦zō, ¦mē¦, ¦sō+\ *n* [NL, fr. *mes-* + E *esophagus*] : the transitory mesentery of the embryonic esophagus that is later modified into the mediastinum

meso·fauna \"+\ *n* [NL, fr. *mes-* + *fauna*] : animals of intermediate size ranging from those barely visible with a hand lens to forms (as worms, mollusks, and arthropods) that are several centimeters in length — compare MACROFAUNA, MICROFAUNA

meso·furca \"+\ *n*, *pl* **mesofurcae** [NL, fr. *mes-* + *furca*] : the middle apodeme of the thorax of an insect projecting upward from the sternum into the body cavity — **meso·furcal** \"+\ *adj*

meso·gaster \'≈≈+,-\ *n* [NL, fr. *mes-* + *-gaster*] : MESOGASTRIUM

meso·gastric \¦≈≈+\ *adj* [NL *mesogastrium* + E *-ic*] **1** : of or relating to the mesogastrium **2** : of or relating to the middle gastric lobe of a crab's carapace

meso·gas·tri·um \ˌ=='gastrēəm\ *n, pl* **mesogas·tria** \-ēə\ [NL, fr. *mes-* + *gastr-* + *-ium*] **1 :** a ventral mesentery of the embryonic stomach that persists as the falciform ligament and the lesser omentum **2 :** a dorsal mesentery of the embryonic stomach that gives rise to ligaments between the stomach and spleen and kidney

meso·gastropoda \ˌme\|zō, ˈmē\|, \|sō+\ [NL, fr. *mes-* + *Gastropoda*] *syn of* TAENIOGLOSSA

meso·glea *or* **meso·gloea** \"+\ *n* [NL, fr. *mes-* + LGk *gloia* glue — more at GLOEA] **:** a gelatinous substance between the endoderm and ectoderm of sponges or coelenterates — **meso·gloeal** \"+\ *adj*

meso·gnathion \"+\ *n* [NL, fr. *mes-* + *gnathion*] **:** the lateral part of the premaxilla bearing the lateral incisor tooth on each side

me·sog·na·thous \mə'zägnəthəs, me'-,mē'-, -'sä-\ *also* **me·sognath·ic** \ˌme\|zə(g)ˈnathik, ˈmē\|, \|sə-\ *adj* **1** [*mes-* + *-gnathous* or *gnathic*] **:** having the jaws of medium size and slightly projecting with a gnathic index of 98 to 103 **2** [NL *mesognathion* + E *-ous* or *-ic*] **:** of or relating to the mesognathion

me·sog·na·thy \mə'zägnəthē, me'-,mē'-, -'sä-\ *n* -ES [ISV *mesognathous* + *-y*] **:** the state of being mesognathous **:** mesognathous character

meso·gyrate \ˌme\|zō, ˈmē\|, \|sō+\ *adj* [*mes-* + *gyrate*] **:** curving toward the center — used esp. of the umbones of a bivalve; compare PROSOGYRATE

meso·hippus \"+\ *n, cap* [NL, fr. *mes-* + *-hippus*] **:** a genus of No. American Oligocene 3-toed horses probably not on the direct ancestral line of the modern horses — see EQUIDAE illustration

meso·kur·tic \ˌ==ˈkərd·ik\ *adj* [*mes-* + Gk *kyrtos* bulging, convex, curved + E *-ic*; akin to L *curvus* bent, curved — more at CROWN] **:** closely resembling a normal frequency distribution **:** neither leptokurtic nor platykurtic

meso·lecithal \ˌme\|zō, ˈmē\|, \|sō+\ *adj* [*mes-* + *-lecithal* (as in *centrolecithal*)] **:** CENTROLECITHAL

meso·lim·net·ic \ˌ==ˈlim\|ned·ik\ *adj* [NL *mesolimnion* + E *-etic*] **:** of or relating to a thermocline

meso·lim·ni·on \-ˈlimnē,än, -ēən\ *n, pl* **mesolim·nia** \-ēə\ [NL, fr. *mes-* + *-limnion*] **:** THERMOCLINE

meso·lite \'==,līt\ *n* -s [G *mesolith*, fr. *meso-* mes- + *-lith*] **:** a zeolitic mineral $Na_2Ca_2Al_6Si_9O_{30}.8H_2O$ consisting of hydrous aluminosilicate of sodium and calcium

meso·lith·ic \ˌ==ˈlithik\ *adj, usu cap* [ISV *mes-* + *-lithic*] **:** of, relating to, or being a transitional period of the Stone Age between the Paleolithic and the Neolithic characterized by the appearance of the dog as the first domestic animal, of the bow and arrow, and of pottery and represented by several cultures of Europe — see ASTURIAN, AZILIAN, CAMPIGNIAN, ERTEBOLLE, MAGLEMOSIAN, TARDENOISIAN

mesome \ˈme,zōm, ˈmē\|, \|,sōm\ *n* -s [*mes-* + *telome*] **:** an internode between two forkings that was orig. a telome but was relegated to an internodal position by the growth of a new telome

meso·mere \ˈme\|zō,mi(ə)r, ˈmē\|, \|sō-\ *n* -s [*mes-* + *-mere*] **:** a blastomere of medium size; *also* **:** an intermediate part of the mesoderm

meso·mer·ic \ˌ==ˈmerik, -mir-\ *adj* [*mesomerism* + *-ic*] **:** of or relating to the resonance of a molecule, ion, or radical

me·som·er·ism \mə'zämə,rizəm, -'sä-\ *n* [*mes-* + *-merism*] **:** RESONANCE 5

meso·me·tri·al \ˌme\|zō\|mē·trēəl, ˈmē\|, \|sō-\ *or* **meso·me·tric** \-rik\ *adj* [*mesometrial* fr. NL *mesometrium* + E *-al*; *mesometric* fr. NL *mesometrium* + E *-ic*] **:** of or relating to the mesometrium — **meso·me·tri·al·ly** \-rēəlē\ *adv*

meso·me·tri·um \ˌ==ˈtrēəm\ *n, pl* **mesome·tria** \-ēə\ [NL, fr. *mes-* + Gk *mētra* womb + NL *-ium* — more at METRA] **:** a mesentery supporting the oviduct or uterus

meso·mitosis \ˌme\|zō, ˈmē\|, \|sō+\ *n* [NL, fr. *mes-* + *mitosis*] **:** nuclear division of essentially mitotic character that takes place within the intact nuclear membrane (as in various protozoa) — compare METAMITOSIS, PROMITOSIS

meso·morph \ˈ==,mȯrf\ *n* -s [*mes-* + *-morph*] **1 a :** an intermediate or average type of human body — distinguished from *hypomorph* and *hypermorph* **b :** a mesomorphic body or person — see MESOMORPHIC 2 **2 :** a plant having typically mesophytic morphology; *esp* **:** MESOPHYTE

meso·mor·phic \ˌ==ˈmȯrfik\ *adj* **1** *also* **meso·mor·phous** \-fəs\ [*mesomorphic* fr. *mes-* + *-morphic*; *mesomorphous* fr. *mesomorphic* + *-ous*] **:** relating to, existing in, or being an intermediate state (as of a semicrystalline condition characteristic of liquid crystals) — see NEMATIC, SMECTIC **2** [*mesomorph* + *-ic*] **:** characterized by predominance of the structures (as bone, muscle, and connective tissue) developed from the mesodermal layer of the embryo **:** of the muscular or athletic type of body-build — compare ECTOMORPHIC, ENDOMORPHIC **3** [*mesomorph* + *-ic*] **:** typical of a mesomorph ⟨~ leaves⟩

meso·mor·phism \ˌ==ˈ=,fizəm\ *n* -s [*mesomorphic* + *-ism*] **:** the quality or state of being mesomorphic

meso·mor·phy \ˈ==,=,fē\ *n* -ES [*mes-* + *-morphy*] **1 :** mesomorphic build or type **2 :** mesomorphic quality (as of a plant)

meso·my·o·di \ˌme\|zō\|mī'ō,dī, ˈmē\|, \|sō-\ *n pl, cap* [NL, fr. *mes-* + *-myodi* (fr. Gk *myōdēs* muscular, fr. *mys* mouse, muscle) — more at MOUSE] *in some classifications* **:** a group of passerine birds nearly equivalent to Clamatores having the syringeal muscles attached to the middle of the bronchial half rings — compare ACROMYODI — **meso·my·o·di·an** \ˌ==,=ˈōdēən\ *adj or n* — **meso·my·o·dous** \-dəs\ *adj*

meson \ˈme\|zän, ˈmē\|, ˈmā\|, \|,z°n, \|,sän, \|,s°n\ *n* -s [ISV *mes-* + *-on*] **:** any of a group of short-lived subatomic particles that have masses typically between those of the electron and the proton and that have zero or an integral number of quantum units of spin — called also *mesotron*; see MU-MESON, PI-MESON — **me·son·ic** \(ˈ)meˈzänik, (ˈ)mē\|, (ˈ)mā\|, mə\|, \|sä-\ *adj*

meso·nemertini \ˌme\|(,)zō, ˈmē\|, \|(,)sō+\ *n pl, cap* [NL, fr. *mes-* + *Nemertini*] *in some classifications* **:** an order of nemerteans comprising the members of Palaeonemertea that have the mouth far behind the anterior end of the body

meso·neph·ric \ˌme\|zō\|nefrik, ˈmē\|, \|sō-\ *adj* [*mes-* + *nephr-* + *-ic*] **:** of or relating to the mesonephros

mesonephric duct *n* **:** the efferent duct of the embryonic mesonephros persisting as a functional ureter in females and as a urinogenital duct in males of lower vertebrates in which the mesonephros is the definitive kidney and as the genital duct in males of higher forms — called also *wolffian duct*

meso·nephridium \ˌme\|(,)zō, ˈmē\|, \|(,)sō+\ *n* [NL, fr. *mes-* + *nephridium*] **:** a nephridium of mesodermal origin

meso·nephros *also* **meso·nephron** \ˌme\|zō, ˈmē\|, \|sō+\ *n, pl* **mesonephroi** *also* **mesonephra** [NL, fr. *mes-* + *-nephros*] **:** either member of the second and midmost of the three paired vertebrate renal organs that functions in adult fishes and amphibians but functions only in the embryo of reptiles, birds, and mammals in which it is replaced by a metanephros in the adult — called also *wolffian body*; compare PRONEPHROS

meso·notal \"+\ *adj* [NL *mesonotum* + E *-al*] **:** of or relating to the mesonotum

meso·notum \"+\ *n* [NL, fr. *mes-* + Gk *nōton* back — more at NATES] **:** the dorsal portion of the mesothoracic integument of insects

mes·onych·i·dae \ˌme,zō'nikə,dē, ˌmē\|, \|sō-\ *n pl, cap* [NL, fr. *Mesonych-*, *Mesonyx*, type genus + *-idae*] **:** a family of extinct creodont carnivorous mammals from the Paleocene and Eocene of No. America and Europe

mes·onyx \ˈ==,niks\ *n, cap* [NL, fr. *mes-* + *-onyx*] **:** a genus of extinct creodont mammals of the family Mesonychidae

meso·ontomorph \ˌme\|zō\|äntə,mȯrf, ˈmē\|, \|sō-\ *n* [*mes-* + *onto-* + *-morph*] **:** a body type characterized by a thickset robust powerful build; *also* **:** an individual of this type — opposed to *hyperontomorph*

meso·pause \ˈme\|zə,pȯz, ˈmē\|, \|sə-\ *n* [*mesosphere* + *pause*] **:** the upper boundary of the mesosphere where the temperature of the atmosphere reaches its lowest point

meso·perrhenic acid \ˌ==+...-\ *n* [*mes-* + *perrhenic*] **:** PERRHENIC ACID b

meso·phase \ˈ==,fāz\ *n* [*mes-* + *phase*] **:** a mesomorphic phase

meso·phile \-,fīl\ *also* **meso·phil** \-,fil\ *n* -s [prob. fr. *mesophile*, adj.] **:** an organism growing at a moderate temperature (as bacteria that grow best at about the temperature of the human body) — compare PSYCHROPHILE, THERMOPHILE

meso·phil·ic \ˌ==ˈfilik\ *also* **meso·phile** \ˈ==,fīl\ *or* **me·soph·i·lous** \mə'säfələs, (ˈ)me\|, (ˈ)mē\|, \|sä-\ *adj* [prob. fr. G *mesophil* mesophilic (fr. *meso-* mes- + *-phil* -phile) + E *-ic* or *-ous*] **:** growing or thriving best in an intermediate environment (as in one of moderate temperature)

meso·phragma \ˌme\|zō, ˈmē\|, \|sō+\ *n* [NL, fr. *mes-* + *phragma*] **1 :** a phragma of the mesothorax in various insects **2 :** a process of the endosternite forming an arch over the sternal canal in some crustaceans — **meso·phragmal** \"+\ *adj*

me·soph·ry·on \mə'zäfrēən, -'sä-, -ē,än\ *n, pl* **mesoph·rya** \-ēə\ [Gk, fr. *mes-* + *ophrys* eyebrow — more at BROW] **:** GLABELLA 1

meso·phyll \ˈme\|zō,fil, ˈmē\|, \|sō-\ *n* -s [NL *mesophyllum*] **:** the parenchyma between epidermal layers of a foliage leaf — **meso·phyl·lic** \ˌ==ˈfilik\ *or* **meso·phyl·lous** \-ləs\ *adj*

meso·phyllum \ˌme\|zō, ˈmē\|, \|sō+\ *n* [NL, fr. *mes-* + *-phyllum*] **:** MESOPHYLL

meso·phyte \ˈ==,fīt\ *n* -s [ISV *mes-* + *-phyte*] **:** a plant that grows under medium conditions of moisture — compare HYDROPHYTE, XEROPHYTE

meso·phyt·ic \ˌ==ˈfid·ik\ *adj* [ISV *mesophyte* + *-ic*] **1** *of a plant* **:** growing in or adapted to moderately moist environment **2** *of a habitat* **:** moderately moist

me·sopic \(ˈ)me\|zä\|pik, (ˈ)mē\|-, -\|s\|, \|ōp-\ *adj* [*mes-* + Gk *ōp-*, *ōps* face, eye + E *-ic* — more at EYE] **:** having a face on which the root of the nose and central line of the face project moderately

meso·plankton \ˌme\|zō, ˈmē\|, \|sō+\ *n* [ISV *mes-* + *plankton*] **1 :** the plankton of middle depths below the penetration of photosynthetically effective light **2 :** NET PLANKTON — **meso·planktonic** \"+\ *adj*

meso·plas·tral \ˌ==ˈplastrəl\ *adj* [*mesoplastron* + *-al*] **:** of or relating to a mesoplastron

meso·plastron \"+\ *n* [*mes-* + *plastron*] **:** one of a pair of bones in the plastron of various pleurodiran turtles situated one on each side between the hyoplastron and hypoplastron

meso·pleural \"+\ *adj* [NL *mesopleuron* + E *-al*] **:** of or relating to a mesopleuron

meso·pleuron \"+\ *n* [NL, fr. *mes-* + *pleuron*] **:** a pleuron of the mesothorax of an insect

me·sop·lo·don \mə'zäplə,dän\ *n, cap* [NL, fr. *mes-* + Gk *hoplon* weapon + NL *-odon* — more at HOPLITE] **:** a genus of nearly cosmopolitan small-toothed whales — **me·sop·lo·dont** \-nt\ *adj*

meso·po·di·al \ˌme\|zə\|pōdēəl, ˈmē\|, \|sə-\ *adj* [NL *mesopodium* + E *-al*] **:** of or relating to the mesopodium

meso·po·di·um \-dēəm\ *n* [NL, fr. *mes-* + *podium*] **:** the middle portion of the foot of a mollusk — compare PROPODIUM

mes·o·po·ta·mia \ˌmesəpə'tāmēə, -āmyə\ *n* -s [Gk, fr. fem. of *mesopotamios* between rivers, fr. *meso-* mes- + *potamos* river; akin to Gk *piptein* to fall — more at FEATHER] **:** a region between rivers

[1]**mes·o·po·ta·mian** \ˌ====ˈtāmēən, -myən\ *adj* **1** *usu cap* [*Mesopotamia*, region in southwest Asia between the Tigris and Euphrates rivers (fr. Gk) + E *-an*] **:** of, relating to, or characteristic of Mesopotamia ⟨*Mesopotamian* architecture⟩ **2** [Gk *mesopotamia* + E *-an*] **:** of, relating to, or characteristic of a mesopotamia

[2]**mesopotamian** \"\ *n* -s *cap* **:** a native or inhabitant of Mesopotamia

meso·prescutum \ˌme\|zō, ˈmē\|, \|sō+\ *n* [NL, fr. *mes-* + *prescutum*] **:** the prescutum of the mesothorax of an insect

meso·pro·sopic \ˌ==prə\|sōpik, -säp-\ *adj* [ISV *mes-* + *prosop-* + *-ic*] **:** having a face of average width with a facial index of 84 to 88 on the living or 85 to 90 on the skull — **meso·proso·py** \ˌ==ˈpräsəpē, -prə'sōpē\ *n* -ES

mesop·te·ryg·i·um \ˌme\|,zäptə'rijēəm, ˈmē\|, \|sä-\ *n* [NL, fr. *mes-* + Gk *pterygion* fin, lit., small wing — more at PTERYGIUM] **:** the middle one of the three principal basal cartilages in the pectoral fins of various fishes (as the sharks and rays) — compare BASIPTERYGIUM

[1]**meso·pterygoid** \ˌme\|(,)zō, ˈmē\|, \|(,)sō+\ *adj* [*mes-* + *pterygoid*, adj.] **:** oriented with respect to the pterygoids; *specif* **:** being or relating to a part or a process of the pterygoid bone of a bird, to a distinct pterygoid element of a bony fish articulating in front with the palatine, behind with the metapterygoid, and laterally with the pterygoid, or to the space in a mammal between the pterygoids of opposite sides

[2]**mesopterygoid** \"\ *n* [*mes-* + *pterygoid*, n.] **:** a mesopterygoid part (as a bone)

mesop·tile \(ˈ)me\|zäptəl, (ˈ)mē\|, \|sä-\ *n* -s [*mes-* + *-ptile*] **:** one of the second set of down feathers in a bird having two sets

me·sor·chi·um \mə'zȯ(r)kēəm, -'sȯ-\ *n, pl* **mesor·chia** \-ēə\ [NL, fr. *mes-* + *orchi-* + *-ium*] **:** the fold of peritoneum that attaches the testis to the dorsal wall in the fetus

meso·rectum \ˌme\|zō, ˈmē\|, \|sō+\ *n* [NL, fr. *mes-* + *rectum*] **:** the mesentery that supports the rectum

mes·oreodon \(ˌ)me\|z, (ˌ)mē\|, \|s+\ *n, cap* [NL, fr. *mes-* + *Oreodon*] **:** a genus of extinct artiodactyls (family Merycoidodontidae) from the Miocene of No. America

mesor·rhinal *or* **meso·rhinal** \ˌme\|zō, ˈmē\|, \|sō+\ *adj* **1** [NL *mesorrhinium*, *mesorhinium* + E *-al*] **:** of or relating to the mesorrhinium **2** [*mes-* + *rhinal*] **:** situated between the nostrils

[1]**mesor·rhine** \ˈ==,rīn\ *also* **mesor·rhin·ic** \ˌ==ˈrinik\ *or* **mesorhine** *adj* [*mesorrhine* or *mesorhine* fr. *mes-* + *-rrhine* or *-rhine*; *mesorrhinic* fr. *mesorrhine* + *-ic*] **:** having a nose of moderate size with a nasal index of 47 to 51 on the skull or of 70 to 85 on the living — **mesor·rhi·ny** \ˈ==,rīnē\ *n*

[2]**mesorrhine** *also* **mesorhine** \"\ *n* -s **:** a mesorrhine individual

mesor·rhin·i·um *or* **meso·rhin·i·um** \ˌ==ˈrinēəm\ *n, pl* **mesorrhin·ia** *or* **mesorhin·ia** \-ēə\ [NL, fr. *mes-* + *rhin-* + *-ium*] **:** the part of the base of the upper mandible of a bird that lies between the nostrils

meso·salpinx \ˌme\|zō, ˈmē\|, \|sō+\ *n* [NL, fr. *mes-* + *salpinx*] **:** a fold of the broad ligament investing and supporting the fallopian tube

meso·saprobe \"+\ *n* -s [ISV *meso-* + *saprobe*; prob. orig. formed as G *mesosaprobie*] **:** a mesosaprobic organism

meso·saprobic \"+\ *adj* [ISV *mes-* + *saprobic*; prob. orig. formed as G *mesosaprobisch*] **:** living in or being a moderately oxygenated environment in which considerable organic material and bacteria are present — compare KATHAROBIC, OLIGOSAPROBIC, SAPROBIC

meso·saur \ˈme\|zō,sȯ(ə)r, ˈmē\|, \|sō-\ *n* -s [NL *Mesosaurus*] **:** an extinct aquatic reptile of the genus *Mesosaurus*

meso·sau·ria \ˌ==ˈsȯrēə\ *n pl, cap* [NL, fr. *mes-* + *-sauria*] **:** an order of primitive aquatic and probably web-footed reptiles from the Permian of So. America and Africa that are distinguished by an elongate head with the nostrils near the eyes and are sometimes included in Pelycosauria as a suborder

meso·sau·rus \-rəs\ *n, cap* [NL, fr. *mes-* + *-saurus*] **:** a genus of small aquatic presumably fish-eating Permian reptiles of So. America and southern Africa

meso·scapula \ˌme\|zō, ˈmē\|, \|sō+\ *n* [NL, fr. *mes-* + *scapula*] **:** the spine of the scapula regarded as a distinct element — **meso·scapular** \"+\ *adj*

meso·scutal \"+\ *adj* [NL *mesoscutum* + E *-al*] **:** of or relating to the mesoscutum

meso·scutellar \"+\ *adj* [NL *mesoscutellum* + E *-ar*] **:** of or relating to the mesoscutellum

meso·scutellum \"+\ *n* [NL, fr. *mes-* + *scutellum*] **:** the scutellum of the mesothorax of insects

meso·scutum \"+\ *n* [NL, fr. *mes-* + *scutum*] **:** the scutum of the mesothorax of an insect

meso·seismal \"+\ *adj* [*mes-* + *seismal*] **:** of or relating to the center of an area of earthquake disturbance

meso·seme \ˈme\|zō,sēm, ˈmē\|, \|sō-\ *adj* [F *mésosème*, fr. *méso-* mes- + Gk *sēma* sign, mark — more at SEMANTICS] **:** MESOCONCH

meso·sere \-,si(ə)r\ *n* [*mes-* + *sere*] **:** an ecological sere originating in a mesic habitat or initiated by mesophytes

meso·sigmoid \ˌme\|zō, ˈmē\|, \|sō+\ *n* [*mes-* + *sigmoid*] **:** the mesentery of the sigmoid part of the descending colon

meso·soma \"+\ *n, pl* **mesosomata** [NL, fr. *mes-* + *-soma*] **:** the middle region of the body of various invertebrates esp. when this cannot readily be analyzed into its primitive segmentation (as in most mollusks and in arachnids) — **meso·somatic** \"+\ *adj*

meso·some \ˈ==+,sōm\ *n* -s **1** [NL *mesosoma*] **:** MESOSOMA **2** [*mes-* + *-some* (body)] **:** the intromittent organ of a dipterous insect **:** AEDEAGUS

meso·so·mic \ˌ==+ˈsōmik\ *adj* [in sense 1, fr. NL *mesosoma* + E *-ic*; in sense 2, fr. *mesosome* + *-ic*; in sense 3, fr. *mes-* + *-somic* (as in *leptosomic*)] **1 :** of or relating to the mesosoma **2 :** of or relating to a mesosome **3 :** having intermediate or average body-build

meso·sphere \ˈme\|zō, ˈmē\|, \|sō+,-\ *n* [*mes-* + *-sphere*] **:** a layer of the atmosphere extending from the top of the stratosphere to an altitude of about 55 miles — **mesospheric** *adj*

meso·spore \"+,-\ *also* **meso·spo·ri·um** \ˌ==ˈspōrēəm\ *n, pl* **mesospores** \-z\ *or* **mesospo·ria** \-ōrēə\ [*mesospore* fr. *mes-* + *-spore*; *mesosporium* fr. NL, fr. *mes-* + *-sporium*] **1 :** the middle coat of a spore that has three coats **2 :** a one-celled spore found among the compound teliospores of some rusts (as members of the genus *Puccinia*)

meso·staph·y·line \ˌme\|zō\|stafə,lin, ˈmē\|, \|sō-\ *adj* [*mes-* + Gk *staphylē* uvula + E *-ine* — more at STAPHYL-] **:** having a palate of moderate size with a palatal index of 80 to 85 — **meso·staph·y·li·ny** \-nē\ *n* -ES

meso·sternum \ˌme\|zō, ˈmē\|, \|sō+\ *n, pl* **mesosterna** [NL, fr. *mes-* + *sternum*] **1 :** GLADIOLUS 3 **2 :** the ventral piece of the mesothorax in insects

me·sos·to·ma \mə'zästəmə, -'sä-\ *n, cap* [NL, fr. *mes-* + *-stoma*] **:** a cosmopolitan genus of large transparent freshwater rhabdocoelous turbellarians — **me·sos·to·mid** \-məd\ *n* -s

meso·style \ˈme\|zō, ˈmē\|, \|sō+,-\ *n* [*mes-* + *style* (cusp)] **:** the small cusp between the metacone and paracone of a molar

meso·sty·lous \ˌ==ˈstīləs\ *adj* [*mes-* + *-stylous*] *of a flower* **:** having styles of intermediate length — compare MACROSTYLOUS, MICROSTYLOUS

meso·su·chia \ˌ==ˈsükēə\ *n pl, cap* [NL, fr. *mes-* + Gk *souchos* crocodile + NL *-ia*] *in some classifications* **:** a suborder of Loricata comprising variable and more or less archaic reptiles of the Jurassic and Lower Cretaceous — **meso·su·chi·an** \ˌ==ˈkēən\ *adj or n*

meso·tae·ni·a·ce·ae \ˌ==,tēnēˈāsē,ē\ *n pl, cap* [NL, fr. *Mesotaenium*, type genus (fr. *mes-* + *-taenium* — fr. L *taenia* ribbon, band, fillet) + *-aceae* — more at TAENIA] **:** a family of unicellular or colonial green algae (order Zygnematales) comprising the saccoderm desmids and differing from the Desmidiaceae in having the cell wall in a single piece and without pores — see DESMIDIALES

meso·tarsal \ˌme\|zō, ˈmē\|, \|sō+\ *adj* [*mes-* + *tarsal*] **:** of or relating to the median plane of the tarsus

meso·the·lae \ˌ=='thē(,)lē\ [NL, fr. *mes-* + Gk *thēlē* nipple — more at FEMININE] *syn of* LIPHISTIOMORPHAE

meso·the·li·al \ˌ==ˈthēlēəl\ *adj* [NL *mesothelium* + E *-al*] **:** of or relating to mesothelium

meso·the·li·o·ma \ˌ==,thēlēˈōmə\ *n, pl* **mesothe·liomas** \-məz\ *or* **mesothelioma·ta** \-məd·ə\ [NL, fr. *mesothelium* + *-oma*] **:** a tumor derived from mesothelial tissue (as that lining the peritoneum or pleura)

meso·the·li·um \-'thēlēəm\ *n, pl* **mesothe·lia** \-lēə\ [NL, fr. *mes-* + *epithelium*] **:** epithelium that is derived from mesoderm, that in vertebrate embryos lines the primordial body cavity, and that gives rise to the epithelium of the peritoneum, pericardium, and pleurae, the striated muscles, the heart muscle, the epithelium of the urogenital organs except the bladder and urethra, and several minor structures

meso·therm \ˈ==,thərm\ *n* -s [ISV *mes-* + *-therm*; prob. orig. formed as F *mésotherme*] **:** a plant that requires a moderate degree of heat for successful growth — compare MEGATHERM, MICROTHERM

meso·ther·mal \ˌ==ˈthərməl\ *adj* **1** [*mes-* + *thermal*] **:** deposited from warm waters at intermediate depth under conditions in the medium ranges of temperature and pressure — used of mineral veins and ore deposits; compare EPITHERMAL, HYPOTHERMAL **2** [*mesotherm* + *-al*] **:** of, relating to, or living as a mesotherm

me·soth·e·sis \mə'zäthəsəs, -'sä-\ *n, pl* **mesothe·ses** \-thə,sēz\ [NL, fr. *mes-* + Gk *thesis* setting, position — more at THESIS] **:** a mediating agency or principle

meso·thet·ic \ˌme\|zə\|thed·ik, ˈmē\|, \|sə-\ *adj* [*mes-* + Gk *thetikos* of placing, fr. *thetos* (verbal of *tithenai* to place) + *-ikos* -ic — more at DO] **:** being in a middle position **:** INTERMEDIATE

meso·thoracic \ˌ==+\ *adj* [NL *mesothorac-*, *mesothorax* + E *-ic*] **:** of or relating to the mesothorax

meso·thorax \ˌ==+\ *n* [NL, fr. *mes-* + *thorax*] **:** the middle of the three segments of the thorax of an insect — see INSECT illustration

meso·thorium \ˌme\|zō, ˈmē\|, \|sō+\ *n* [NL, fr. *mes-* + *thorium*] **:** either of two radioactive products intermediate between thorium and radiothorium in the thorium series or a mixture of the two products obtained usu. from thorium minerals (as monazite sand) and used as a substitute for radium esp. in luminous paints: **a :** an isotope of radium — called also *mesothorium 1*; symbol $MsTh_1$ or Ra^{228} **b :** an isotope of actinium — called also *mesothorium 2*; symbol $MsTh_2$ or Ac^{228}

meso·tonic system \ˌ==+...-\ *n* [*mes-* + *tonic*] **:** MEANTONE SYSTEM

meso·troch \ˈme\|zə,träk, ˈmē\|, \|sə-\ *n* -s [*mes-* + *-troch*] **:** a band of ciliated cells surrounding the middle of the body of a larval marine annelid — **me·sot·ro·chal** \mə'zä·trəkəl, -'sä-\ *or* **me·sot·ro·chous** \-kəs\ *adj*

me·sot·ro·cha \mə'zä·trəkə, -'sä-\ *n, pl* **mesotro·chae** \-,kē\ *also* **mesotrochas** [NL, fr. *mes-* + *-trocha*] **:** a mesotrochal larva

meso·tron \ˈme\|zə,trän, ˈmē\|, \|sə-\ *n* -s [*mes-* + *electron*] **:** MESON — **meso·tron·ic** \ˌ==ˈtränik\ *adj*

meso·troph \ˈ==,träf\ *n* -s [back-formation fr. *mesotrophic*] **:** a mesotrophic organism

meso·troph·ic \ˌ==ˈträfik\ *adj* [*mes-* + *-trophic*] **:** requiring either a single amino acid or ammonia and an organic acid as a source of metabolic nitrogen — compare METATROPHIC — **meso·trophy** \ˈ==,träfē\ *n* -ES

meso·trop·ic \-ˈträpik\ *adj* [*mes-* + *-tropic*] **:** turned or directed toward or located in the median plane of a cavity

mes·ovarium \ˌme\|z, ˈmē\|, \|s+\ *n, pl* **mesovaria** [NL, fr. *mes-* + *ovarium*] **:** the mesentery uniting the ovary with the body wall

meso·ve·li·id \ˌme\|zō'vēlēəd, ˌmē\|, \|sō-\ *n* -s [NL *Mesoveliidae*] **:** WATER TREADER

meso·ve·li·idae \-,vəˈlīə,dē\ *n pl, cap* [NL, fr. *Mesovelia*, type genus (fr. *mes-* + L *velum* veil, sail + NL *-ia*) + *-idae*] **:** a small widely distributed family of semiaquatic hemipterous insects that inhabit the surface of freshwater or the ground near water

meso·ventral \ˌme\|zō, ˈmē\|, \|sō+\ *adj* [*mes-* + *ventral*] **:** median and ventral — **meso·ventrally** \"+\ *adv*

mes·ox·al·ic acid \ˌme\|zäkˈsalik-, ˈmē\|, \|säkˈsalik-\ *n* [*mes-* + *oxalic acid*] **:** a crystalline acid $CO(COOH)_2$ or $C(OH)_2(COOH)_2$ made esp. by oxidation of amino-malonic acid

mes·ox·a·lyl \mə'zäksəlәl, -'sä-\ *n* [ISV *mesoxalic* + *-yl*] **:** the bivalent radical $CO(CO)_2$ or $C(OH)_2(CO)_2$ of mesoxalic acid

mes·ox·a·lyl·urea \-,===ˈ(y)ürēə\ *n* [NL, fr. ISV *mesoxalyl* + NL *urea*] **:** ALLOXAN

meso·zoa \ˌme\|zəˈzōə, ˌmē\|, \|sə-\ *n pl, cap* [NL, fr. *mes-* + *-zoa*] **:** a group of small wormlike parasitic animals that are typically comparable to a stereoblastula with an outer layer of somatic cells and an inner mass of reproductive cells and are often regarded as intermediate in organization between Protozoa and Metazoa though perhaps being degenerate descendants of more highly organized forms — see DICYEMIDA, ORTHONECTIDA — **meso·zo·an** \ˌ==ˈzōən\ *adj or n*

[1]**meso·zo·ic** \ˌ==ˈzōik\ *adj, usu cap* [*mes-* + *-zoic*] **:** of or relating to a grand division of geological history that includes the entire interval of time between the Permian and the Tertiary and is marked by the dinosaurs, marine and flying reptiles, ganoid fishes, cycads, and evergreen trees — see GEOLOGIC TIME table

[2]**mesozoic** \"\ *n* -s *usu cap* **:** the Mesozoic era or system of rocks

mes·pi·lus \ˈmespələs\ *n, cap* [NL, fr. L, medlar — more at MEDLAR] **:** a genus of Eurasian trees (family Rosaceae) having large solitary flowers, leafy calyx lobes, and a pomaceous fruit with an open top and five easily detached stones — see MEDLAR

mes·qui·tal \ˌmeskəˈtal\ *n* -s [Sp *mezquital,* fr. *mezquite* mesquite] **1** *Southwest* **:** an area on which mesquite is the dominant plant form **2** *Southwest* **:** a thicket of mesquite ⟨take the saddle off her and hide it in a ~ —J.F.Dobie⟩ — called also *mesquite;* compare CHAPARRAL 2

mes·quite *also* **mes·quit** *or* **mez·quit** *or* **mez·quite** \məˈskēt, meˈ-, *usu* -ēd·+V\ *n* -s [Sp *mezquite, mesquite,* fr. Nahuatl *mizquitl*] **1 :** a plant of the genus *Prosopis:* as **a :** a spiny deep-rooted tree or shrub (*P. juliflora*) of the southwestern U. S. and Mexico that bears pods which are rich in sugar and important as a livestock feed, that tends to form extensive thickets, and that is often the only woody vegetation on large areas — called also *algarroba* **b :** SCREW BEAN 2 **2 :** MESQUITAL

mesquite bean *n* **:** the pod of a mesquite (*Prosopis juliflora*) or its seed used for food by southwestern Indians — compare ALGARROBA 4

mesquite grass *n* **:** any of various pasture grasses (as *Bouteloua oligostachya* and other members of the genus *Bouteloua*) found associated with mesquite in the southwestern U.S.

mesquite gum *n* **:** a gum that is obtained from mesquite pods, resembles gum arabic, and yields L-arabinose on hydrolysis

mes·ro·pi·an alphabet \(ˈ)mesˌrōpēən-\ *n, usu cap M* [*Mesrob* †A.D.439 Armenian bishop and scholar, its reputed inventor + E *-an*] **:** ARMENIAN ALPHABET

¹mess \ˈmes\ *n* -ES *often attrib* [ME *mes,* fr. OF, fr. LL *missus* course at a meal, fr. *missus,* past part. of *mittere* to put, place, fr. L, to send] **1 :** a quantity of food: **a** *archaic* **:** food set on a table at one time **:** COURSE **b :** a prepared dish (as of soft or pulpy food) ⟨a ~ of milk, made by crumbling bread into it —G.E.Fussell⟩ **:** a mixture of ingredients cooked or eaten together ⟨a curious savory ~ of sweetbreads and chicken liver —Margery Allingham⟩ ⟨took a lot of cheese, a lot of hardtack, and a lot of bully beef, ground them up together, and then baked the ~ —*N.Y. Times*⟩ **c :** sufficient quantity (of a specified kind of food) for a dish or a meal ⟨picking a little ~ of red raspberries for her breakfast —Jean Stafford⟩ ⟨a ~ of string beans any time you wanted it —G.S.Perry⟩ **:** CATCH ⟨a ~ of trout⟩ **d** *dial* **:** the milk given by a cow at one milking **2 :** a quantity of any soft, moist, smeary, or pulpy substance often of an unpleasant nature ⟨cannot bear to be reminded that under the skin there is blood, ~, and entrails —F.R.Leavis⟩ **3 a** [ME *messe,* fr. *mes* course] **:** one of the small groups (as of four) into which companies at banquets were formerly divided for being served — now used only of parties of benchers or students in the Inns of Court **b :** a group of persons (as of military personnel) who regularly take their meals together ⟨every officer serving with a unit . . . is obliged to belong to a ~ —S.G.Maurice⟩ **c :** a meal so taken **d** (1) **:** a place (as a room or tent) where food or sometimes drink is served ⟨fresh fruit was a rarity in marine ~*es* —H.L. Merillat⟩ ⟨were at the wine ~ —Frederic Wakeman⟩ ⟨the field ~ is open —John Masters⟩ (2) **:** quarters comprising both kitchen and dining areas ⟨~ building⟩ ⟨~ steward⟩ ⟨~ officer⟩ **4** *dial* **:** AMOUNT, NUMBER ⟨a little ~ of eggs —Elizabeth M. Roberts⟩ ⟨substitute father to a ~ of newly orphaned children —*Newsweek*⟩ **:** a large quantity ⟨a ~ of preaching ain't going to alter her over —Sarah O. Jewett⟩ ⟨a bigg ~ of people⟩ **5 a :** a confused, untidy, dirty, unpleasant, or offensive state or condition **:** HODGEPODGE, JUMBLE, MUSS ⟨clear away the ~ left by the guests —Sherwood Anderson⟩ ⟨the apartment was a ~ — floors unswept —John & Ward Hawkins⟩ ⟨the falling tide had left us well caught in a great ~ of shoals —D.B.Putnam⟩ **b :** a disordered or unsavory situation, state, or condition resulting from misunderstanding, blundering, or misconduct ⟨the ~ he is making of his life —Carl Binger⟩ ⟨viewed realistically, the past is merely a series of ~*es* —E.M.Forster⟩ — often used with *in* or *into* ⟨get himself in a ~⟩

²mess \"\ *vb* -ED/-ING/-ES [ME *messen,* fr. *mes,* n.] *vt* **1** *now dial Brit* **:** to portion out (food) **:** deal out (as a meal) **:** SERVE **2 :** to assign to a mess ⟨personnel will be ~*ed* in the building —*Crowsnest*⟩ ⟨quarter and ~ them together at some distance from their places of normal duty —*Infantry Jour.*⟩ **3 a :** to make dirty or untidy **:** DISARRANGE ⟨his clothes are all ~*ed*⟩ — often used with *up* ⟨without getting ~*ed* up in the mud of the highroad —Richard Joseph⟩ **b :** to mix up **:** BOTCH, BUNGLE, MUDDLE ⟨unless his chance came in extraordinarily lucky guise, he would probably ~ it —*Scribner's*⟩ ⟨the schedule of appointments, carelessly ~*ed* for the day —Helen Howe⟩ — often used with *up* ⟨a variety of state standards ~*es* up national contracts —*N.Y. Times*⟩ ⟨when something happens that ~*es* up the girl's life —Evelyn M. Duvall⟩ **c :** DAMAGE, SPOIL — usu. used with *up* ⟨a frost which would have ~*ed* up the outdoor peaches —Nigel Balchin⟩ **d :** to interfere with — used with *up* ⟨magnetic storms that ~ up communications —*Time*⟩ **e :** to handle roughly **:** rough up **:** MANHANDLE — used with *up* **~** *vi* **1 :** to prepare food for and serve messes **2 :** to take meals with a mess **:** belong to a mess ⟨had marched and ~*ed* together through the war —Dixon Wecter⟩ ⟨granted the privilege of ~*ing* away from the naval activity —*Naval Reservist*⟩ ⟨will ~ only twice a day aboard ship —Alan Surgal⟩ ⟨~ together by tribes —C.S.Coon⟩ **3 :** to make a mess **:** DABBLE ⟨stop ~*ing* and eat your breakfast⟩ **4 a :** PUTTER, TINKER, TRIFLE, PLAY ⟨~*es* with motors in his spare time⟩ ⟨child ~*ing* with his fork and spoon⟩ **b :** to become involved esp. voluntarily **:** INTERFERE, MEDDLE — usu. used with *in* or *with* ⟨~*ing* in other people's affairs⟩ **c :** to act toward someone in a rough or annoying manner **:** TEASE — usu. used with *with* ⟨if he ever ~*es* with me any more —James Jones⟩ **d :** to become mixed up or confused **:** BLUNDER — usu. used with *up* ⟨her own life ~*es* up —H.C.Webster⟩

³mess \"\ *dial Brit var of* ¹MASS

mess about *vi, chiefly Brit* **:** to mess around ⟨those who like *messing about* in boats in quiet waters —S.P.B.Mais⟩ ⟨no *messing about* and wasting time —Arnold Bennett⟩

mes·sa di vo·ce \ˌmäsədēˈvō(ˌ)chā, ˌmes-\ *n, pl* **mes·se di voce** \-(ˌ)sād-\ [It, lit., placing of the voice] **:** the singing of a gradual crescendo and decrescendo on a long sustained tone — used of a vocal technique originating in 18th century bel canto

¹mes·sage \ˈmesij, -sēj\ *n* -s [ME, fr. OF, fr. ML *missaticum,* fr. L *missus* (past part. of *mittere* to send) + *-aticum* -age — more at SMITE] **1 :** a charge, service, or function of a messenger **:** MISSION ⟨murmuring her lesson to herself like a child sent on a ~ —Francis Hackett⟩ ⟨the girl will go on a ~ to the shop —Cahir Healy⟩ **2 :** a written or oral communication or other transmitted information sent by messenger or by some other means (as by signals) **3 a :** a divinely inspired or revealed communication (as of a prophet) **:** an inspired utterance **:** EVANGEL **b :** the basic teachings of a religious revelation ⟨the reader becomes aware of some subordinate aims which have left their mark on the form of the ~ —*Interpreter's Bible*⟩; *also* **:** an interpretation of such a revelation ⟨had preached a rather shallow ~ —J.C.Brauer⟩ **c :** a sermon or homiletical discourse forming part of a worship service or other religious meeting ⟨the pastor brought the ~⟩ **d :** a discourse or statement made to a gathering and intended esp. to inspire, encourage, or greet ⟨gave an appropriate blessing and also a ~ of goodwill for the absent members —Joseph Hitrec⟩ **4 :** an official communication (as from a sovereign to a parliament or from a chief executive to a legislature) often not made in person but delivered by messenger and read by an authorized person ⟨the presidential ~ has grown from a formal requirement of the Constitution to a recognized and influential source of legislative action —W.S. Sayre⟩ ⟨the ~*s* the president must work on are the State of the Union address, the budget, and the economic report —*N.Y. Times*⟩ **5 a :** a principle or basic purpose signified in one's life or lifework **:** a meaning (as of a work of art) that communicates itself **:** IMPORT, SIGNIFICANCE ⟨the ~ of a fine symphony or string quartet —Winthrop Sargeant⟩ ⟨the role of a work of art is to communicate its ~ to the spectator —Ladislas Segy⟩ **b :** an underlying or pervasive theme or idea intended to inspire, urge, advise, warn, or enlighten ⟨the ~ of a movie dealing with juvenile delinquency⟩ ⟨calls her novels fables with a ~ —W.S Campbell⟩ ⟨small size and population permits an energetic candidate to carry his ~ personally throughout the state —Douglass Cater⟩ **6 :** a group of words used to advertise or notify ⟨postcards with advertising ~*s* —*Nat'l Stamp News*⟩ ⟨the ~ of a radio commercial⟩ **7 :** a communication held to originate with a departed spirit, to be transmitted by a medium, and to be intended for a living person **8 a :** the substance of a telephone call **b :** the contents of a telegram, cablegram, or radiogram **9 :** a unit of information that is received by a sensory organ, is transmitted centrally in the nervous system, and functions as a stimulus ⟨certain definite and fixed ~*s* will be sent to the brain by the vestibular sense acting in coordination with sight and muscle sense —H.G.Armstrong⟩

²message \"\, *esp in pres part* -səj\ *vb* -ED/-ING/-S *vt* **:** to send as a message or by messenger ⟨the commander . . . *messaged* "well done" to his pilots —*Associated Press*⟩ ⟨the bill is *messaged* back to the house of origination, which house may then vote either to concur or nonconcur in the amendments —Rhoten Smith⟩ **:** order or instruct by message ⟨*messaged* the other PT to follow us into the attack —Dave Richardson⟩ **~** *vi* **:** to communicate by message ⟨after much *messaging* back and forth over the secret radio —Richard Thruelsen & Elliott Arnold⟩

message stick *n* **:** a carved stick serving as a mnemonic device and means of indentification for messengers among some primitive peoples (as in Australia and Africa)

mes·sa·lian \məˈsālyən, -lēən\ *n* -s *usu cap* [LGk *Messalianoi, Massalianoi,* pl., fr. Syr *mešallěyānē,* lit., those who pray] **:** EUCHITE 1

mes·sa·line \ˌmesəˈlēn\ *n* -s [F] **:** a lightweight silk dress fabric having a warp satin weave and characterized by a soft hand and high luster

mes·san \ˈmesᵊn\ *n* -s [ScGael *measan,* fr. MIr *messán, mesán,* dim. of *mess, mes* fosterling — more at MESTOME] *chiefly Scot* **:** LAPDOG

mess and mell *var of* MESS OR MELL

¹mes·sa·pi·an \məˈsāpēən\ *or* **mes·sapic** \-sāpik, -sap-\ *adj, usu cap* [L *Messapii* + E *-an* or *-ic*] **1 :** of, relating to, or characteristic of the Messapii **2 :** of, relating to, or characteristic of the Messapian language or the alphabet in which it was written

²messapian \"\ *or* **messapic** \"\ *n* -s *cap* **1 :** one of the Messapii **2 :** the ancient language of Messapia sometimes classed as Illyrian

mes·sa·pii \-sāpēˌī\ *n pl, cap* [L, fr. Gk *Messapioi*] **:** a people of Messapia, an ancient country of southeastern Italy

mess around *vi* **1 a :** DABBLE, PUTTER ⟨small boys and girls who like to *mess around* with paints —*New Yorker*⟩ **:** to work according to one's whim or mood ⟨busy *messing around* with cameras under water, in the air —Marya Mannes⟩ **b :** to waste time **:** DAWDLE, IDLE ⟨*mess around* on the beach most of the summer⟩ **2 :** INTERFERE, INTRUDE **3 a :** ASSOCIATE ⟨don't *mess around* with admirals much —K.M.Dodson⟩ **b :** FLIRT, PHILANDER ⟨reckon he *messes around* with some lady friend —Erskine Caldwell⟩ **~** *vt* **:** to treat roughly **:** MANHANDLE ⟨the hoodlums *messed* him *around* considerably⟩

mess beef *n* **:** barreled salt beef consisting of about 80 pounds of assorted cuts

messboy \ˈ=ˌ=\ *n* **:** one who takes care of the crew's messroom on a ship and waits on the tables

mess call *n* [¹*mess*] **:** a bugle call for meals

messcook \ˈ=ˌ=\ *n* **:** MESSMAN

messdeck \ˈ=ˌ=\ *n, Brit* **:** mess quarters on a ship

messed *past of* MESS

messe di voce *pl of* MESSA DI VOCE

mes·sen·ger \ˈmesᵊnjə(r)\ *n* -s [ME *messager, messangere, messengere,* fr. OF *messagier,* fr. *message,* fr. ML *missaticum,* fr. L *missus,* past part. of *mittere* to send — more at SMITE] **1 :** one who bears a message or does an errand **:** COURIER, EMISSARY, ENVOY: as **a** *archaic* **:** one who prepares the way **:** FORERUNNER, HARBINGER ⟨behold, I send my ~ to prepare the way before me —Mal 3:1 (RSV)⟩ **b :** a dispatch bearer (as for an official or a government body or in military service) ⟨queen's ~⟩ ⟨city ~⟩ ⟨~*s*, orderlies, and any other soldiers —F.V.W.Mason⟩ **c :** one employed by a business concern to do errands within or outside the establishment ⟨bank ~*s* empty the boxes once a week —L.H.Olsen⟩ **d** (1) **:** a postal employee who delivers special-delivery mail (2) **:** MAIL MESSENGER **e :** a delegate to a religious convention or meeting; *esp* **:** one sent from a local church within a denomination that adheres to a congregational polity **f :** a character esp. in a classical Greek play who comes onstage to make known an action that has occurred offstage ⟨all theatergoers now must have watched for the entrance of the breathless ~, who knows the result —John Masefield⟩ **2 a :** a rope or chain passed round a capstan and having its two ends lashed together to form an endless rope or chain **b :** a light line used in hauling a heavier line (as between ships) **c :** a device sliding on a line for operating a trip (as to release a target or close a net) **d :** MESSENGER CABLE

messenger-at-arms \ˌ=ˌ===ˈ=\ *n,* **messengers-at-arms :** an officer appointed by the Lyon king of arms and charged with executing summonses and warrants

messenger buoy *n* **:** a buoy that can be released by personnel inside a sunken submarine to aid rescue efforts

messenger cable *or* **messenger wire** *n* **:** a usu. steel cable supporting a telephone cable or other wires conducting electricity

messes *pl of* MESS, *pres 3d sing of* MESS

mes·set \ˈmesət\ *n* -s [prob. alter. (influenced by *-et*) of *messan*] *dial Brit* **:** LAPDOG

mess hall *n* **1 :** a dining room in which mess is served **2 :** a building (as in an army camp) serving chiefly as a dining hall

mess house *n, West* **:** MESS HALL

mes·si·ah \məˈsīə\ *n* -s [Heb *māshīaḥ* & Aram *mĕshīḥā* anointed, Messiah] **1 a :** an expected deliverer or savior **b** *usu cap* **:** the expected king and deliverer of the Jews **2 :** one accepted as or claiming to be a leader destined to bring about a desired state or condition ⟨security, which the political ~*s* promise —Vardis Fisher⟩ ⟨our self-appointed moral ~*s* —Asher Moore⟩

mes·si·ah·ship \-ˌship\ *n, sometimes cap* **:** the office, condition, profession, or state of being a messiah ⟨the mission and ~ of Jesus —*Interpreter's Bible*⟩

mes·si·an·ic \ˌmesēˈanik, -nēk\ *adj* [fr. (assumed) NL *Messianicus,* fr. LL *Messias* + L *-anicus* (as in L *Romanicus* Romanic)] **1** *often cap* **:** of, relating to, or being a messiah; as **a :** of or relating to the Messiah expected by the Hebrews **b :** of or relating to Jesus Christ as the Messiah **2** *sometimes cap* **:** of or relating to a nativistic religious cult (as one whose prophet professes salvation of the native population and destruction of foreign culture and influence) ⟨the ~ element common to the present sect and nonliterate nativistic efforts —L.C.May⟩ **3** *sometimes cap* **:** mystically idealistic in a manner suggestive of messiahship and often in an aggressive or crusading spirit ⟨sustained by a ~ hope of social perfection —T.E.Utley⟩ ⟨a ~ sense of historic mission —Edmond Taylor⟩ — **mes·si·an·i·cal·ly** \-nək(ə)lē, -nēk-, -li\ *adv, sometimes cap*

mes·si·a·nism \ˈmesēəˌnizəm, məˈsīə,-\ *n* -s *often cap* [*messianic* + *-ism*] **1 :** belief in a messiah; *specif* **:** an ideological movement or system of ideas that teaches the salvation of mankind through the enthroning of a messiah that may be an individual, a class, or an idea **2 :** the vocation of a messiah

mes·si·a·nist \-nəst\ *n* -s *often cap* **:** an advocate of messianism

mes·si·as \-īəs\ *n* -ES *cap* [ME, fr. LL, fr. Gk, fr. Aram *mĕshīḥā*] **:** MESSIAH 1 ⟨I know that *Messias* cometh, which is called Christ —Jn 4:25 (AV)⟩

messieurs *pl of* MONSIEUR

mess·i·ly \ˈmesəlē, -li\ *adv* **:** in a messy manner

messin *var of* MESSAN

mes·si·na \məˈsēnə\ *adj, usu cap* [fr. *Messina,* Italy] **:** of or from the city of Messina, Italy, in Sicily **:** of the kind or style prevalent in Messina

mes·si·nese \ˌmesəˈnēz, -ēs\ *n, pl* **messinese** *cap* [It, fr. *Messina* (fr. L & Gk; L *Messana,* fr. Gk *Messana, Messēnē*) + *-ese*] **:** a native or inhabitant of Messina, Italy, in Sicily

mess·i·ness \ˈmesēnəs, -sin-\ *n* -ES **:** the quality or state of being messy ⟨there is a certain ~ in the analysis in that he is forced from the start to assume multiple values —A.A.Hill⟩

mess jacket *n* **:** a man's semiformal tailless jacket for social or service wear, reaching just below the waistline, and worn open at the front with a vest or cummerbund — called also *monkey jacket, shell jacket*

mess jacket

mess kit *or* **mess gear** *n* **1 :** the cooking and table utensils of a mess together with the receptacle in which they are packed for transportation **2 :** a soldier's or camper's kit for cooking or holding food at mess

mess·man \ˈmesmən\ *n, pl* **messmen :** a navy enlisted man on temporary duty in the sailors' or officers' dining quarters who serves the food and clears the tables

messmate \ˈ=ˌ=\ *n* **1 :** an associate in a mess (as on a ship) **2 :** any of several Australian eucalypts (as *Eucalyptus amygdalina* and *E. obliqua*) **3 :** COMMENSAL 2

mess of pottage [ME *mes of potage;* fr. allusion to Esau's selling of his birthright to his twin brother Jacob for a mess of pottage (Gen 25:29–34)] **:** something valueless or trivial or of inferior value — used esp. of something accepted instead of a rightful thing of far greater value ⟨suspense is the *mess of pottage* for which the Shakespearean birthright has been sold —E.R.Bentley⟩

mess or mell *vi, Scot* **:** to have familiar intercourse **:** ASSOCIATE — used with *with*

mess pork *n* **:** barreled salt pork made from shoulders and sides of lightweight hogs cut in pieces of about 4 pounds each

messroom \ˈ=ˌ=\ *n* **:** a room (as on a ship) used for a mess **:** DINING ROOM

messrs. *usu cap* [*messieurs*] *pl of* MR.

mess·tin \ˈ=ˌ=\ *n* **:** an oval-shaped metal utensil having a bail and forming part of a soldier's mess equipment

mess traps *n pl, Brit* **:** MESS KIT

mes·suage \ˈmeswij\ *n* -s [ME, fr. AF, prob. alter. of OF *mesnage* — more at MÉNAGE] *law* **:** a dwelling house with the adjacent buildings and curtilage and the adjoining lands used in connection with the household

mess-up \ˈ=ˌ=\ *n* -s [fr. the phrase *mess up*] **:** a confused or disordered situation or condition **:** MIX-UP, MUDDLE

messy \ˈmesē, -si\ *adj* -ER/-EST [¹*mess* + *-y*] **1 :** in a confused, disordered, or dirty state or condition **:** UNTIDY ⟨a ~ room⟩ ⟨those ~ herbaceous borders —Osbert Lancaster⟩ **2 :** that causes or is likely to cause a confused, disordered, or dirty state or condition ⟨a ~ pen⟩ ⟨the ~ business of infant feeding —*New Yorker*⟩ **3 :** lacking neatness or precision **:** CARELESS, SLOVENLY ⟨~ thinking⟩ ⟨~ legislation⟩ ⟨cannot simply eliminate attitudes, emotions, values, desires, multiple and ~ meanings —H.J.Muller⟩ **4 :** unpleasantly or tryingly difficult of execution or settlement ⟨a ~ job⟩ ⟨~ lawsuits⟩ ⟨a ~ traffic problem⟩ ⟨scandal, crime, and ~ disasters sell newspapers —A.J.Liebling⟩ **5 :** effusive or sentimental to an excessive or embarrassing degree ⟨~ introductions⟩ ⟨the ~ rhetorical violence of the other speakers —Robert Lowell⟩ ⟨a certain ~ generosity of manner —Louis Auchincloss⟩

mes·ta \ˈmestə\ *n* -s [prob. fr. Hindi] **:** KENAF

mes·te·ño \məˈstān(ˌ)yō\ *n* -s [Sp, adj., wild, stray — more at MUSTANG] *West* **:** a horse or cow sometimes branded that has escaped from the owner and is running wild; *also* **:** any wild horse — compare MUSTANG

mes·ti·za \meˈstēzə, məˈ-\ *n* -s [Sp, fem. of *mestizo*] **:** a female mestizo

mes·ti·za·tion \ˌmestəˈzāshən\ *n* -s [*mestizo* + *-ation*] **:** the process or state of race mixture

mes·ti·zo \meˈstē(ˌ)zō, məˈ-\ *n, pl* **mestizos** *also* **mestizoes** [Sp, fr. *mestizo,* adj., mixed, fr. LL *misticius, mixticius,* fr. L *mixtus,* past part. of *miscēre* to mix, mingle — more at MIX] **1 :** MIXED-BLOOD: **a :** a person of mixed European and non-Caucasian stock; *specif* **:** one of European (as Spanish or Portuguese) and American Indian ancestry **b** *Philippines* **:** a person of foreign (as Chinese) and native ancestry **2 :** a completely acculturated Central or So. American Indian

¹me·sto \ˈme(ˌ)stō\ *adj* [It, fr. L *maestus* dejected, sad; akin to L *maerēre* to mourn, be sad] **:** sad and pensive — used as a direction in music

²mesto \"\ *n* -s **:** a musical composition of sad and pensive character

mes·tome \ˈmeˌstōm\ *also* **mes·tom** \-täm\ *n* -s [G *mestom,* fr. Gk *mestos* full + G *-om* -ome; akin to Gk *medea, mezea, mēdea,* pl., male genitals, MIr *mess* acorns, W *mes,* pl., acorns, and perh. to MIr *mess* fosterling] *of a vascular plant* **:** the conducting tissues comprising leptome and hadrome — compare STEREOME

me·sua \ˈmeshəwə\ *n, cap* [NL, fr. Johannes *Mesuë* (Ar Yūḥanna ibn-*Māsawayh*) †857 Persian Christian physician in the service of the Caliph] **:** a genus of tropical Asiatic trees (family Guttiferae) having large solitary flowers with a 2-celled ovary — see ROSE CHESTNUT

me·su·ran·ic \ˌmeshəˈranik\ *adj* [*mes-* + *uran-* + *-ic*] **:** having a maxillo-alveolar index of between 110.0 and 114.9 — **me·su·rany** \ˈ==ˌranē\ *n* -ES

mes·vin·ian \(ˈ)mesˈvinēən\ *adj, usu cap* [F *mesvinien,* fr. *Mesvin,* Belgium + F *-ien* -an] **:** of or relating to a middle paleolithic culture of Belgium contemporaneous with that of Levalloisian and Clactonian

mesyl \ˈmesəl, ˈmēs-\ *n* -s [*methane* + *sulfonyl*] **:** the univalent radical CH_3SO_2– of methane-sulfonic acid; methylsulfonyl

me·sym·ni·on \məˈsimnēˌän, -ēən\ *n* -s [Gk, fr. *mes-* + *hymnos* hymn] *classical prosody* **:** a short colon or rhythmic series interpolated in a stanza

met *past of* MEET

met *abbr* **1** metal **2** metallurgical; metallurgy **3** metaphor; metaphorical **4** metaphysical; metaphysics **5** meteorological; meteorology **6** metronome **7** metropolitan

meta \ˈmed·ə, -etə\ *adj* [*meta-*] **:** relating to, characterized by, or being two positions in the benzene ring that are separated by one carbon atom — compare META- 4 b

meta- *in pronunciations below,* ˌ==ˈmed·ə *or* ˌmetə\ *or* **met-** *prefix* [NL & ML, fr. LL or Gk; LL, fr. Gk, fr. Gk *meta* between, with, after; akin to OE *mid,* with, OS *mid, midi,* OHG *mit, miti* with, ON *meth* with, between, Goth *mith* with, and perh. to OE *midd* mid — more at MID] **1 a :** occurring later **:** in succession to **:** after ⟨*meta*chronism⟩ ⟨*meta*biosis⟩ ⟨*meta*genesis⟩ ⟨*meta*infective⟩ **b :** situated behind **:** posterior ⟨*meta*pore⟩ ⟨*meta*nephron⟩ **c :** later or more highly organized or specialized form of ⟨*Metazoa*⟩ ⟨*meta*phyte⟩ **d :** with **:** occurring with ⟨*meta*cinnabar⟩ **2 a** [MF & L; MF, fr. L, fr. Gk, fr. *meta*] **:** change in **:** transformation of ⟨*meta*morphosis⟩ ⟨*meta*plasia⟩ **b :** produced by metamorphism ⟨*meta*diorite⟩ ⟨*meta*sediment⟩ **3 a** [ME, fr. ML, fr. Gk *meta* after, as used in *ta meta ta physika* the (works) after the physics — more at METAPHYSICS] **:** beyond **:** transcending ⟨*meta*physics⟩ ⟨*meta*psychosis⟩ ⟨*meta*geometry⟩ ⟨*meta*biological⟩ ⟨*meta*mpirics⟩ **b :** of a higher logical type — in nouns formed from names of disciplines and designating new but related disciplines such as can deal critically with the nature, structure, or behavior of the original ones ⟨*meta*language⟩ ⟨*meta*theory⟩ ⟨*meta*system⟩ **4** [ISV, fr. Gk, with, after, fr. *meta*] **a :** one that is isomeric with, polymeric with, or otherwise closely related to ⟨*meta*ldehyde⟩ — in names of chemical compounds — compare ¹PARA- 2a **b** (1) **:** relation of two positions in the benzene ring that are separated by one carbon atom (2) *meta-, usu ital* **:** derivative that has two substituting groups occupying such positions — abbr. *m-* (*meta*-xylene or *m*-xylene is 1,3-dimethyl-benzene; compare ORTH- 3b, ¹PARA- 2b **c :** regarded as derived from (the ortho acid) by loss of water (as of one molecule of water from each molecule of acid) — in names of inorganic acids ⟨*meta*phosphoric acid⟩; compare ORTH- 3a, PYR- 2a **d :** derived from by removal or loss of some or all of the contained water — in names of minerals ⟨*meta*autunite⟩ ⟨*meta*halloysite⟩

meta·autunite \ˌ== *at* META-+\ *n* [*meta-* + *autunite*] **:** a mineral consisting of a partially dehydrated autunite

me·tab·a·sis \məˈtabəsəs\ *n, pl* **metaba·ses** \-bəˌsēz\ [Gk, fr. *metabainein* to change, fr. *meta-* + *bainein* to go, move — more at COME] **1 :** a shift from one subject, point, or division in a discourse to another; *specif* **:** the rhetorical device used to effect such a shift **2 :** a medical change (as of disease, symptoms, or treatment)

meta·biological \¦== *at* META- + \ *adj* **:** of or relating to metabiology

meta·biology \"+\ *n* [*meta-* + *biology*] **:** a system of knowledge or belief built around biological principles ⟨a faith which complied with the first condition of all religions that have ever taken hold of humanity: namely, that it must be . . . a science of ~ —G.B.Shaw⟩

meta·bi·o·sis \,==,bī'ōsəs\ *n* [NL, fr. *meta-* + *-biosis*] **:** a mode of life in which one organism so depends on another that it cannot flourish unless the latter precedes and influences the environment favorably

meta·bi·ot·ic \¦==,bī¦äd·ik, -ät\, \ēk *also* ,bē¦ä-\ *adj* [*meta-* + *-biotic*] **:** of, relating to, or marked by metabiosis — **meta·bi·ot·i·cal·ly** \¦ək(ə)lē, \ēk- *also* -li\ *adv*

meta·bisulfite \¦==+\ *n* [ISV *meta-* + *bisulfite*] **:** a salt containing the bivalent anion $S_2O_5^{--}$ obtained by heating a bisulfite — called also *pyrosulfite*

me·tab·o·la \mə'tabələ\ *n pl, cap* [NL, fr. neut. pl. of Gk *metabolos* changeable, fr. *metaballein* to change, fr. *meta-* + *ballein* to throw — more at DEVIL] *in some classifications* **:** a division of Insecta comprising insects that undergo a metamorphosis

me·tab·o·le \-(,)lē\ *also* **me·tab·o·la** \-_lə\ *n* -s [NL, fr. Gk *metabolē* change, fr. *metaballein*, v.] **1 :** METABASIS 2 **2 :** METAMORPHOSIS 2a

meta·bo·li·an \,med·ə'bōlēən\ *n* -s **:** an insect of the division Metabola

meta·bol·ic \¦== *at* META- +¦bälik, -lēk\ *also* **meta·bol·i·cal** \-ləkəl, -lēk-\ *adj* [*metabolic* fr. G *metabolisch*, fr. Gk *metabolikos* changing, fr. *metabolē* change + *-ikos* -ic; *metabolical* fr. *metabolic* + *-al*] **1 :** of, relating to, or worked by metabolism ⟨our feelings as well as our physical acts have an essentially ~ pattern —Susanne K. Langer⟩ **2 a :** undergoing metamorphosis **:** changeable in form **b** [NL *Metabola* + E *-ic* or *-ical*] **:** of or relating to the Metabola **3 :** VEGETATIVE 1a — used esp. of a cell nucleus that is not dividing; compare RESTING NUCLEUS — **meta·bol·i·cal·ly** \-lək(ə)lē, -lēk-, -li\ *adv*

metabolic heat *n* **:** ANIMAL HEAT

metabolic movement *n* **:** EUGLENOID MOVEMENT

metabolic water *n* **:** water produced by living cells as a by-product of oxidative metabolism; *sometimes* **:** water produced in plants as a consequence of respiration as distinguished from water of the transpiration stream

me·tab·o·lism \mə'tabə,lizəm\ *n* -s [ISV *metabol-* (fr. Gk *metabolē* change) + *-ism*] **1 a :** the sum of the processes concerned in the building up of protoplasm and its destruction incidental to life **:** the chemical changes in living cells by which energy is provided for the vital processes and activities and new material is assimilated to repair the waste ⟨basal ~⟩ ⟨methods of determining body and tissue ~ —*Bull. of the Univ. of Ky.*⟩ — see ANABOLISM, CATABOLISM; compare ASSIMILATION, FOOD 1a, NUTRITION, SECRETION **b :** the sum of the processes by which a particular substance is handled (as by assimilation and incorporation or by detoxification and excretion) in the living body ⟨the ~ of iodine in the thyroid⟩ ⟨vanadium ~ of tunicates⟩ **c :** the sum of the metabolic activities taking place in a particular habitat or environment ⟨the ~ of a lake⟩ ⟨complex processes of historical ~ involving the whole range of man's cultural, social, and economic existence —Walter Abell⟩ **2 :** METAMORPHOSIS 2 a — usu. used in combination ⟨*ametabolism*⟩ ⟨*holometabolism*⟩

me·tab·o·lite \-,līt\ *n* -s [*metabolism* + *-ite*] **1 :** a product of metabolism: **a :** a metabolic waste usu. more or less toxic to the organism producing it **:** EXCRETION **b :** a product of one metabolic process that is essential to another such process in the same organism **c :** a metabolic waste of one organism that is markedly toxic to another **:** ANTIBIOTIC **2 :** a substance essential to the metabolism of a particular organism or to a particular metabolic process

me·tab·o·liz·a·bil·i·ty \=,==,līzə'biləd·ē, -ətē, -i\ *n* **:** the quality or state of being metabolizable

me·tab·o·liz·able \=¦==¦līzəbəl\ *adj* [*metabolize* + *-able*] **1** *of a nutrient* **:** capable of being utilized in metabolism **2** *of energy* **:** producible or produced by metabolic processes

me·tab·o·lize \=' ==,līz\ *vb* -ED/-ING/-S *see -ize in Explan Notes* [*metabolism* + *-ize*] *vt* **:** to subject (as a chemical substance) to metabolism ~ *vi* **:** to perform metabolism

me·tab·o·lous \-ləs\ *adj* [Gk *metabolos* changeable + E *-ous* — more at METABOLA] **:** METABOLIC 2

me·tab·o·ly \-lē\ *n* -ES [Gk *metabolē*, *metabolia* change, fr. *metaballein* to change] **:** METAMORPHOSIS

meta·borate \¦== *at* META-+\ *n* [ISV *metabor-* (in *metaboric acid*) + *-ate*] **:** a salt or ester of a metaboric acid

meta·boric acid \¦==+-\ *n* [*metaboric* ISV *meta-* + *boric*] **:** an acid HBO_2 or $(HBO_2)_n$ formed as a glassy amorphous solid by heating orthoboric acid but usu. obtained in the form of its salts

meta·branchial \"+\ *adj* [*meta-* + *branchial*] **:** of or relating to a posterior lobe of the carapace of a crab

meta·can·tho·ceph·a·la \,==,kan(t)thə'sefələ\ *n pl, cap* [NL, fr. *meta-* + *Acanthocephala*] *in some classifications* **:** a class of Acanthocephala comprising the orders Archiacanthocephala and Palaeacanthocephala

[1]**meta·car·pal** \¦==¦kärpəl\ *adj* [NL *metacarpus* + E *-al*] **:** of or relating to the metacarpus

[2]**metacarpal** \"\ *n* **:** a metacarpal bone **:** any of the long bones that separate the carpus from the phalanges of the hand — see BAT illustration

meta·car·pa·le \,==+\ *n* [NL, fr. *metacarpus* + *-ale* (fr. neut. of L *-alis* -al, adj. suffix)] **:** METACARPAL

meta·car·po·phalangeal \¦==¦kärpə+\ *adj* [*metacarpo-* (fr. NL *metacarpus*) + *phalangeal*] **:** of, relating to, or involving both the metacarpus and the phalanges

meta·carpus \¦==+\ *n* [NL, fr. *meta-* + *carpus*] **:** the part of the hand or forefoot between the carpus and the phalanges that contains five more or less elongated bones when all the digits are present but is modified in many animals by the loss or reduction of some bones or the fusing of adjacent bones — compare CANNON BONE, SPLINT BONE

meta·center \'==+,-\ *n* [F *métacentre*, fr. *méta-* meta- + *centre* center] **:** the point of intersection of the vertical through the center of buoyancy of a floating body with the vertical through the new center of buoyancy when the body is displaced however little

metacenter: *1* center of gravity, *2* center of buoyancy, *3* new center of buoyancy when boat is displaced, *4* point of intersection

meta·centric \¦==+\ *adj* **1 :** of or relating to the metacenter **2** [*meta-* + *-centric*] *of a chromosome* **:** having two equal arms because of the median position of the centromere — compare TELOCENTRIC — **meta·centricity** \,==+\ *n*

metacentric height *n* **:** the distance of the metacenter above the center of gravity of a floating body

meta·cercaria \¦==+\ *n* [NL, fr. *meta-* + *cercaria*] **:** a late larva of a digenetic trematode that is tailless and encysted and usu. constitutes the form which is infective for the definitive host — compare ADOLESCARIA, CERCARIA, MARITA

meta·cestode \"+\ *n* -s [*meta-* + *cestode*] **:** a stage of a tapeworm occurring in an intermediate host **:** a larval tapeworm

meta·chemic \"+\ *or* **meta·chemical** \"+\ *adj* [*metachemistry* + *-ic* or *-ical*] **:** of or relating to metachemistry

meta·chemistry \"+\ *n* [*meta-* + *chemistry*] **1 :** chemistry beyond the bounds of chemistry proper (as in a nonmaterial sphere) **:** highly speculative chemistry **2 :** a branch of chemistry that deals with substances (as molecules in activated metastable states) capable of releasing abnormally large amounts of energy in comparison with their mass

meta·chla·myd·e·ae \,==klə'midē,ē\ *n pl, cap* [NL, fr. *meta-* + *-chlamydeae* (fr. Gk *chlamyd-*, *chlamys* cloak, mantle)] **:** a group of Dicotyledoneae comprising plants in which the petals of the flowers are united — compare ARCHICHLAMYDEAE — **meta·chla·myd·e·ous** \¦==+\ *adj*

meta·chro·ma·sia \,==krō'māzh(ē)ə\ *or* **meta·chro·ma·sy** \-'krōməsē\ *or* **meta·chro·ma·sis** \-əsəs\ *n, pl* **metachromasias** *or* **metachromasies** *or* **metachromasises** [NL *metachromasia* or *metachromasis*, fr. *meta-* + *-chromasia* or *-chromasis* (perh. alter. of *-chromasia*); *metachromasy*, ISV, fr. NL *metachromasia* or *metachromasis*] **1 :** the property of various tissues of staining in a different color (as when treatment with a blue aniline dye makes a cellular element red) **2 :** the property of various biologic stains that permits a single dye to stain different tissue elements in different colors

meta·chromatic \¦==+\ *adj* [NL *metachromasia* + E *-atic* (as in *chromatic*)] **:** of or relating to metachromasia ⟨vivid ~ color changes were noted —D.J.Hamerman⟩

meta·chromatin \,==+\ *n* [ISV *metachromatic* + *-in*] **1 :** VOLUTIN **2 :** a granular densely staining material in plant cell vacuoles that may be identical with volutin — **meta·chromatinic** \¦==+\ *adj*

meta·chromatism \,==+\ *n* [*meta-* + Gk *chrōmat-*, *chrōma* color + E *-ism* — more at CHROMATIC] **:** change of color; *specif* **:** a change of color due to a change in physical conditions (as in the temperature of a body)

[1]**meta·chrome** \'==,krōm\ *n* [ISV *meta-* + *-chrome* (n. suffix); orig. formed as F *métachrome*] **:** a metachromatic granule

[2]**metachrome** \"\ *adj, often cap* [ISV *meta-* + *-chrome* (adj. suffix)] **1 :** being any of a series of mordant azo dyes — see DYE table I (under *Mordant*) **2 :** relating to a one-bath method of dyeing by applying a chromium mordant and a dye simultaneously

[3]**metachrome** \"\ *vt* **:** to dye by the metachrome method

metachronism *n* -s [ML *metachronismus* chronological error, fr. Gk *metachronios*, *metachronos* out of date, anachronistic (fr. *meta-* after — fr. *meta* — + *chronos* time) + L *-ismus* -ism — more at META-] *obs* **:** an error in chronology committed by placing an event after its real date — compare PARACHRONISM

me·tach·ro·nous \mə'takrənəs\ *adj* [*meta-* + *-chronous*] *of a geological surface* **:** composed of several parts formed or developed at various times

meta·chro·sis \,== *at* META- + 'krōsəs\ *n, pl* **metachro·ses** \-,sēz\ [NL, fr. *meta-* + Gk *chrōsis* coloring, fr. *chrōs* color — more at CHROMATIC] **:** the power of some animals (as many fishes and reptiles) to change color voluntarily by the expansion of special pigment cells

meta·cinnabar \"+\ *also* **meta·cin·na·bar·ite** \,==+'sinəbə,rīt\ *n* [*metacinnabar* fr. *meta-* + *cinnabar*; *metacinnabarite*, ISV *meta-* + *cinnabar* + *-ite*; orig. formed as G *metacinnabarit*] **:** a mineral HgS that consists of a native black mercuric sulfide and is polymorphous with cinnabar

met·ac·neme \'me,tak,nēm\ *n* -s [NL, fr. *meta-* + Gk *knēmē* leg, shin] **:** a mesentery of any of the various secondary sets developed in most zoantharians

meta·cone \'== *at* META- +,-\ *n* [*meta-* + *cone*] **:** the posterior of the three cusps of a primitive upper molar **:** the posteroexternal cusp in higher forms

meta·co·nid \,=='kōnəd\ *n* -s [*meta-* + *con-* + *-id*] **:** the cusp of a lower molar corresponding to a metacone

meta·co·nule \"+'kōn(,)yül\ *n* -s [*meta-* + *con-* + *-ule*] **:** the posterior intermediate cusp of a mammalian upper molar between the hypocone and the metacone

meta·coracoid \¦==+\ *n* [*meta-* + *coracoid*] **:** one of the two elements forming the coracoid process

meta·cresol \"+\ *n* [*meta-* + *cresol*] **:** the meta isomer of cresol — written systematically with ital. *meta-* or *m-*

meta·cro·mi·on \"+krōmē,än, -ən\ *n* [NL, fr. *meta-* + *acromion*] **:** a process projecting backward and downward from the acromion of the scapula of some mammals

meta·cryptozoite \¦==+\ *n* [*meta-* + *cryptozoite*] **:** a member of a second or subsequent generation of tissue-dwelling forms of a malaria parasite derived from the sporozoite without intervening generations of blood parasites — compare CRYPTOZOITE

meta·cryst \'==,krist\ *n* -s [*meta-* + *phenocryst*] **:** a crystal of a secondary mineral embedded in metamorphic rock — called also *porphyroblast*

meta·cyclic \¦==+\ *adj* [*meta-* + *cyclic*] *of a trypanosome* **:** broad and stocky, produced in an intermediate host, and infective for the definitive host

me·tad \mə'täd\ *or* **metad rat** *n* -s [Telugu dial. *mettād*] **:** a small field rat (*Millardia meltada*)

meta·discoidal \"+\ *adj* [*meta-* + *discoidal*] *of a placenta* **:** orig. diffuse but becoming discoidal (as in man and some apes)

meta·dyne \'==,dīn\ *n* [*meta-* + *-dyne* (fr. Gk *dynamis* power) — more at DYNAMIC] **:** a direct-current generator used as an exciter and voltage control for larger machines

metaestrus *var of* METESTRUS

meta·ethical \¦== *at* META-+\ *adj* **:** of or relating to metaethics

meta·ethics \"+\ *n pl but usu sing in constr* [*meta-* + *ethics*] **:** a discipline dealing with the foundations of ethics specif. with the nature of normative utterances and ethical justification

meta·galactic \"+\ *adj* [ISV *meta-* + *galactic*] **:** of or relating to the metagalaxy

meta·galaxy \"+\ *n* [ISV *meta-* + *galaxy*] **:** the entire system of galaxies **:** UNIVERSE

meta·gastric \"+\ *adj* [*meta-* + *gastric*] **:** of or relating to the two posterior gastric lobes of the carapace of a crab

met·age \'mēd·ij, -ēt\, \ēj\ *n* -s ['*mete* + *-age*] **1 :** the official measuring of contents or weight (as of coal or grain) **2 :** the charge for metage

meta·gelatin *also* **meta·gelatine** \¦== *at* META- +\ *n* [ISV *meta-* + *gelatin* or *gelatine*] **:** gelatin so modified by heat or acids that it remains fluid

meta·genesis \"+\ *n* [NL, fr. *meta-* after (fr. Gk *meta*) + L *genesis* — more at META-] **:** ALTERNATION OF GENERATIONS; *esp* **:** regular alternation of a sexual and an asexual generation

meta·genetic \"+\ *adj* [*meta-* + *genetic*] **:** of, relating to, or produced by metagenesis — **meta·genetically** \"+\ *adv*

meta·gen·ic \¦==¦jenik\ *adj* [NL *metagenesis* + E *-ic*] **:** METAGENETIC

me·tag·na·thous \mə'tagnəthəs\ *adj* [*meta-* + *-gnathous*] **1** *of a bird* **:** having the tips of the mandibles crossed **2** *of an insect* **:** having biting mandibles in the larval stage and sucking mouth parts when adult — contrasted with *menognathous*

me·tag·no·my \-nəmē\ *n* -ES [F *métagnomie*, fr. *méta-* meta- + *-gnomie* -gnomy] **:** DIVINATION ⟨recent investigations . . . incline the student of psychic research toward a decidedly antispiritist explanation of ~ —H.H.U.Cross⟩

meta·gon·i·mus \,med·ə'gänəməs\ *n, cap* [NL, fr. *meta-* + Gk *gonimos* productive, creative — more at GONIMOBLAST] **:** a genus of small intestinal flukes (family Heterophyidae) that includes a species common in man, dog, and cat in parts of eastern Asia as a result of the eating of raw fish containing the larva

me·ta·gra·phy \mə'tagrəfē\ *n* -ES [*meta-* + *-graphy*] **:** TRANSLITERATION

meta·grob·o·lize \,med·ə'gräbə,līz\ *also* **meta·grab·o·lize** \-rab-\ *vt* -ED/-ING/-S [obs. F *matagraboulizer*, *matagraboliser*, fr. MF *matagraboliser*, *matagroboliser*] **:** PUZZLE, MYSTIFY ⟨all this duncical nonsense has my brains *metagrobolized* —*Wall Street Jour.*⟩

meta·halloysite \¦== *at* META-+\ *n* [*meta-* + *halloysite*] **:** a mineral consisting of a partially dehydrated halloysite

meta·hewettite \"+\ *n* [*meta-* + *hewettite*] **:** a mineral resembling hewettite but differing slightly from it in its behavior during hydration

meta·hohmannite \"+\ *n* [*meta-* + *hohmannite*] **:** a mineral consisting of a partially dehydrated hohmannite

me·tai \mə'tī\ *n, pl* **metai** *or* **metais** *usu cap* **1 :** a people of the Manipure valley of Assam in India **2 :** a member of the Metai people

meta·igneous \¦== *at* META-+\ *adj* [*meta-* + *igneous*] **:** of, relating to, or being metamorphosed igneous rock

meta·kamacite \"+\ *n* [*meta-* + *kamacite*] **:** a mineral α_2-(Fe,Ni) consisting of an unstable distorted body-centered cubic alloy of iron and about six percent nickel occurring in meteorites

meta·ken·trin \,==+'ken·trən\ *n* -s [*meta-* + Gk *kentron* sharp point, goad + E *-in* — more at CENTER] **:** LUTEINIZING HORMONE

meta·ki·ne·sis \¦==+\ *n* [NL, fr. *meta-* + *-kinesis*] **1 a :** METAPHASE **b :** PROMETAPHASE **2 :** dance movement with psychical overtones

meta·kinetic \"+\ *adj* **:** of, relating to, or characterized by metakinesis

[1]**met·al** \'med·ᵊl, -etᵊl\ *n* -s *often attrib* [ME, fr. OF *metal*, *metail*, fr. L *metallum* metal, mine, fr. Gk *metallon* mine (later, metal); prob. akin to Gk *metallan* to search after, inquire about] **1 a :** any of a large group of substances (as gold, bronze, steel) that typically show a characteristic luster, are good conductors of electricity and heat, are opaque, can be fused, and are usu. malleable or ductile — compare ALLOY **b :** any such substance without reference to special character ⟨a piece of ~⟩ **c :** one of more than three fourths of the known chemical elements that exhibit typical metallic properties and that except for rubidium, cesium, gallium, and mercury are crystalline solids at or near room temperature **:** an element that in general is characterized chemically by the ability to form cations by loss of one or more electrons from each atom and to form basic oxides and hydroxides — compare METALLOID 2b **2 :** something that is made of metal: as **a :** SWORD ⟨draw this ~ from my side —Shak.⟩ **b** (1) **:** the barrel of a gun; *specif* **:** the surface of the barrel between the two sights (2) **:** the aggregate mass or power of guns or armament ⟨the British ship, more than twice as powerful in men and ~, struck her colors —Edward Breck⟩ **c metals** *pl, Brit* **:** the rails of a railroad ⟨a night train roared along the ~s —Rudyard Kipling⟩ ⟨one coach . . . had left the ~s —F.A.Swinnerton⟩ **3 :** either of the heraldic tinctures or and argent **4 :** METTLE ⟨showed his ~ in dealing with such austere diplomats —Claude Pepper⟩ **5 :** the material usu. earthy substance out of which a person or thing is made ⟨here's ~ more attractive —Shak.⟩ ⟨the ~ of which American character has been built —F.D.Roosevelt⟩ **6 a :** the basic material of glass; *esp* **:** glass in its molten state **b :** the regulus in copper smelting containing about 60 percent of copper — called also *blue metal* **7 a :** ore from which a metal is derived **b :** country rock as distinguished from coal — used esp. in coal mining **8 a :** a specific metallic alloy used in an art or trade ⟨roofer's ~ of the cheapest kind⟩ **b** (1) **:** printing type metal ⟨~ rule is softer than brass rule⟩ (2) **:** set type matter ⟨the book is now in ~⟩ ⟨alterations made in the ~⟩ **9** *Brit* **:** ROAD METAL

[2]**metal** \"\ *vt* **metaled** *or* **metalled; metaled** *or* **metalled; metaling** *or* **metalling** \'med·ᵊliŋ, -et(ᵊ)l-\ **metals 1 :** to cover or furnish with metal ⟨~ a ship's bottom⟩ **2** *Brit* **:** to provide with road metal: **a :** MACADAMIZE, HARD-SURFACE ⟨a bright ~*ed* road —Laurence Irving⟩ **b :** BALLAST 4a

metal *abbr* metallurgical; metallurgy

metal age *or* **metallurgic age** *n, usu cap M&A* **:** the period of the Bronze Age and the Iron Age

meta·language \'== *at* META-+,-\ *n* [*meta-* + *language*] **:** a language used to express data about or discuss another language — compare OBJECT LANGUAGE

met·al·ate \'med·ᵊl,āt, -etᵊl-, *usu* -äd-+V\ *vt* -ED/-ING/-S [back-formation fr. *metalation*] **:** to bring about metalation in

met·al·a·tion \,=='āshən\ *n* -s ['*metal* + *-ation*] **:** the process of attaching a metal atom to a carbon atom of an organic molecule

meta·law \'med·ə+,-\ *n* [*meta-* + *law*] **:** law that governs the correlative rights and duties of intelligent beings on earth and those intelligent beings that may be found in outer space and that is based on the postulate that those on earth must treat the others as they desire to be treated

metal cloth *n* **:** LAMÉ

metal coloring *n* **:** BRONZING 1

metalcraft \'==,=\ *n* **:** the art of executing artistic designs in metal (as in repoussé work, chasing, inlaying)

met·al·de·hyde \mə'taldə,hīd, me'-\ *n* [*meta-* + *aldehyde*] **:** a crystalline compound $(CH_3CHO)_4$ that is a tetramer of acetaldehyde formed by cold acidic treatment of acetaldehyde and that is used as a solid fuel for portable stoves and as a lure and poison for snails — compare PARALDEHYDE

meta·lep·sis \,med·ᵊl'epsəs\ *n, pl* **metalep·ses** \-,sēz\ [L, fr. Gk *metalēpsis*, lit., alteration, participation, fr. *metalambanein* to exchange, participate in, fr. *meta-* + *lambanein* to take — more at LATCH] **:** a figure of speech consisting in the substitution by metonymy of one figurative sense for another

meta·lep·tic \¦med·ᵊl¦eptik\ *also* **meta·lep·ti·cal** \-təkəl\ *adj* [Gk *metalēptikos*, fr. (assumed) *metalēptos* (verbal of *metalambanein* to have a share of, exchange) + *-ikos* -ic, -ical] **:** of or relating to metalepsis — **meta·lep·ti·cal·ly** \-k(ə)lē\ *adv*

met·al·er *or* **met·al·ler** \'med·ᵊlə(r), -etᵊl-\ *n* -s **:** one that places metal sheets on sized work

meta·lim·net·ic \¦med·ə(,)lim¦ned·ik\ *adj* [NL *metalimnion* + E *-etic*] **:** of or relating to a thermocline

meta·lim·ni·on \,=='limnē,än, -ən\ *n, pl* **metalim·nia** \-nēə\ [NL, fr. *meta-* + *-limnion*] **:** THERMOCLINE

metaling *or* **metalling** *n* -s [fr. gerund of [2]*metal*] *Brit* **:** road metal for a road or railroad

meta·linguistic \¦== *at* META- +\ *adj* [*meta-* + *linguistic*] **1 :** of or relating to a metalanguage ⟨~ expressions⟩ **2 :** belonging to metalinguistics ⟨~ analysis⟩

meta·linguistics \"+\ *n pl but sing in constr* [*meta-* + *linguistics*] **:** a branch of linguistics that deals with the relation of language to the rest of culture-determined behavior

met·al·ist *or* **met·al·list** \,med·ᵊləst, -etᵊl-\ *n* -s **:** a worker in metals

metalize *var of* METALLIZE

metal·kase brick \'==,kās-\ *n* ['*metal* + *-kase* (alter. of *case*)] **:** magnesite or magnesite-chrome brick provided with thin steel casings

metall- *or* **metallo-** *comb form* [L or Gk; L *metallum*, fr. Gk *metallon* mine (later, metal) — more at METAL] **1 :** metal ⟨*metallurgy*⟩ ⟨*metallography*⟩ **2 :** containing a metal atom or ion in the molecule ⟨*metalloflavoprotein*⟩

metal leaf *n* **:** thin metal sheet

met·al·le·i·ty \,med·ᵊl'ēəd·ē, -ətē, -i\ *n* -ES [prob. fr. F *métalléité*, fr. (assumed) VL *metalleus* of metal (fr. L *metallum* metal) + F *-ité* -ity] **:** METALLICITY

metalli- *comb form* [L, fr. *metallum*] **:** metal ⟨*metalliform*⟩ ⟨*metallify*⟩

me·tal·lic *also* **me·tal·ic** \mə'talik, -lēk\ *adj* [F or L; F *métallique*, fr. L *metallicus*, fr. Gk *metallikos* metallic, of mines, fr. *metallon* mine, metal + *-ikos* -ic — more at METAL] **1 a :** of, relating to, or being a metal ⟨a ~ element⟩ ⟨metals and alloys form a distinct subdivision of the solid state of matter known as the ~ state —Marian Balicki⟩ **b :** made of or containing a metal ⟨~ salts⟩ ⟨~ ceiling⟩ **c :** having properties of a metal ⟨a ~ substance⟩; *esp* **:** exhibiting the characteristic properties of a metal in the free elemental state ⟨~ lead⟩ ⟨~ selenium⟩ **2 :** yielding metal **:** METALLIFEROUS **3 :** resembling metal: **a** *of a color* **:** having reflective and iridescent properties similar to those of a freshly cut surface of a metal ⟨~ gray finish⟩ ⟨the birds were . . . a brilliant ~ green and black —John Seago⟩ **b** *of a taste sensation* **:** resembling that produced by various metals esp. in mildly acrid unpleasant quality ⟨the tea had a ~ taste⟩ **c** *of a sound* **:** SHARP, HARSH, GRATING ⟨~ voice⟩ ⟨~ laughter⟩ ⟨the monotonous, ~ note of the bellbird —Llewelyn Powys⟩ **d** *of a literary style* **:** STARK ⟨minor poets . . . better employed in being brittle and bright and ~ than in being soft and opulently luscious —Elinor Wylie⟩ **e** *of a person* **:** cold, sharp, and hard **:** MECHANICAL ⟨hard-boiled businessmen, ~ women —Jacques Maritain⟩ — **me·tal·li·cal·ly** \-lək(ə)lē, -lēk-, -li\ *adv*

metallic bond *n* **:** the chemical bond typical of the metallic state and characterized by mobile valence electrons that hold the atoms together usu. in crystal lattices and are responsible for the good electrical and heat conductivity of metals

metallic brown *n* **1 :** any of various light reddish brown to dark purplish brown pigments that are made by calcining limonite or siderite ores and contain about 50 percent or more of ferric oxide **2 :** MINERAL BROWN

metallic cartridge *n* **:** a cartridge with a metal case — used esp. to distinguish a fixed load from a loose powder-and-ball load or a paper cartridge

metallic glaze *n* **:** a glaze with a metallic film on its surface formed as a result of the reduction of a metallic oxide by the kiln fire

metallic gray *n* **:** GRANITE 4

met·al·lic·i·ty \,med·ᵊl'isəd·ē\ *n* -ES **:** the quality or state of being metallic

me·tal·li·cize \mə'talə,sīz\ *vt* -ED/-ING/-S **:** to make (as a telephone line) fully metallic by adding another wire in place of a ground return

metallic luster *n* **:** a luster characteristic of metals in a compact state and shown also by other substances (as a mineral or dye)

metallic oxide *n* **:** an oxide of a metal

metallic paint *n* **1 :** a paint in which the pigment is chiefly iron oxide and which is used for painting metal surfaces **2 :** a paint in which the pigment is a metal (as bronze powder)

metallic paper *n* **1 :** paper so coated (as with lime, whiting, and size) that marks made on it with a metal point are indelible **2 :** paper coated with finely flaked metal to give the effect of a metallic surface **3 :** paper to which a metallic foil has been laminated — called also *foil, foil paper*

metallic red *n* **:** a pigment similar to metallic brown but containing a higher percentage of ferric oxide

me·tal·lics \mə'taliks, -lēks\ *n pl* **:** metallic substances

metallic soap *n* **:** a salt of a monocarboxylic acid (as a higher fatty acid, resin acid, naphthenic acid) and usu. a bivalent or trivalent metal (as calcium, cobalt, zinc, copper, lead, aluminum) that typically is insoluble in water but soluble in benzene and that is used chiefly in lubricants or driers, in thickening, waterproofing, or flatting, or in fungicides

met·al·lif·er·ous \ˌmed·ᵊl'if(ə)rəs, -etᵊl-\ *adj* [L *metallifer* metalliferous (fr. *metalli-* metal — fr. *metallum* — + *-fer* -ferous) + E *-ous*] **:** yielding or containing metal ⟨~ veins⟩ ⟨~ deposits⟩ ⟨a ~ compound whose very existence is still a geological enigma —J.D.Hillaby⟩

metallike \'==,=\ *adj* **:** resembling a metal in properties **:** METALLIC 1b

met·al·line \'med·ᵊl,īn, -ᵊl,ēn, -ᵊn\ *adj* [ME *metalline*, fr. MF or ML; MF *metaline*, fr. ML *metallinus* made of metal, fr. L *metallum* metal + *-inus* -ine] **1 :** METALLIC 1 **2 :** impregnated with metallic substances ⟨~ water⟩

metalling *var of* METALING

metallist *var of* METALIST

met·al·li·za·tion *also* **met·al·i·za·tion** \ˌmed·ᵊlə'zāshən, -etᵊl-, -ᵊl,ī'z-\ *n* -s **:** the process of metallizing

met·al·lize *also* **met·al·ize** \'med·ᵊl,īz, -etᵊl-\ *vt* -ED/-ING/-S [ˡmetal + -ize] **1 :** to treat with a metal: as **a :** to coat with a metal (as by spraying) ⟨~ filament lamps⟩ **b :** to impregnate with metal or a metallic compound **2 :** to combine (as an azo dye) with a metal

metallo- — see METALL-

me·tal·lo·genetic \məˌtalōjə'ned·ik\ *also* **me·tal·lo·genic** \-ˌjenik\ *adj* [*metall-* + *-genetic* or *-genic*] **:** relating to the origin of ores

me·tal·lo·graph \mə'==,graf\ *n* [*metall-* + *-graph*] **1 :** a metallurgical microscope equipped with a camera **2 :** a photomicrograph, microradiograph, or electronmicrograph of a metallic surface

met·al·log·ra·pher \ˌmed·ᵊl'ägrəfə(r), -etᵊl-\ *also* **met·al·log·ra·phist** \-fəst\ *n* -s [*metallography* + *-er* or *-ist*] **:** one that specializes in the visual study of the structure of metals and alloys

me·tal·lo·graph·ic \məˌtalə'grafik\ *also* **me·tal·lo·graph·i·cal** \-fəkəl\ *adj* [F *métallographique*, fr. *métallographie*, n. + *-ique* -ic, -ical] **:** of, relating to, or produced by means of metallography ⟨~ examination of sheet copper⟩ — **me·tal·lo·graph·i·cal·ly** \-fək(ə)lē\ *adv*

met·al·log·ra·phy \ˌmed·ᵊl'ägrəfē, -etᵊl-, -fi\ *n* -ES [F *métallographie*, fr. *métallo-* metall- + *-graphie* -graphy] **:** a study of the structure of metals and alloys; *esp* **:** study of such structure with the microscope

ˡmet·al·loid \'med·ᵊl,ȯid, -etᵊl-\ *n* -s [*metall-* + *-oid*] **1** *archaic* **:** an alkali metal (as sodium) or an alkaline-earth metal (as calcium) **2 a :** NONMETAL **b :** a nonmetal (as carbon or nitrogen) that can combine with a metal to form an alloy ⟨low ~ steel (almost pure iron) —*Steelways*⟩ **c :** an element (as boron, silicon, arsenic, or tellurium) intermediate in properties between the typical metals and nonmetals — compare SEMICONDUCTOR

²metalloid \"\ *also* **met·al·loi·dal** \ˌ==ˈȯidᵊl\ *adj* [*metalloid* fr. *metalloid*, n.; *metalloidal* fr. *metalloid* + *-al*] **1 :** resembling a metal **2 :** of, relating to, or being a metalloid

metallo-organic \məˌtalō+\ *also* **me·tall·or·gan·ic** \mə-ˌtal, ˌmed·ᵊl+\ *adj* [ISV *metall-* + *organic*] *of an organic compound* **:** containing a metal in the molecule; *esp* **:** ORGANOMETALLIC

me·tal·lo·phone \mə'talə,fōn\ *n* [ISV *metall-* + *-phone*] **:** a percussion musical instrument of definite pitch consisting of a series of graduated metal bars that are struck by hammers either manually or by a mechanical arrangement controlled from a keyboard

me·tal·lo·porphyrin \məˌtalō+\ *n* [*metall-* + *porphyrin*] **:** a compound (as heme) formed from a porphyrin and a metal ion

me·tal·lo·scope \mə'talə,skōp\ *n* [*metall-* + *-scope*] **:** an instrument for examining metal

met·al·los·co·py \ˌmed·ᵊl'äskəpē\ *n* -ES [*metall-* + *-scopy*] **:** the act or process of examining metal with a metalloscope

met·al·lur·gi·cal \ˌmed·ᵊl'ərjəkəl, -etᵊl-, -'ōj-, -əij-, -jēk-\ *also* **met·al·lur·gic** \-jik, -jēk\ *adj* **:** of or relating to metallurgy — **met·al·lur·gi·cal·ly** \-jək(ə)lē, -jēk-, -li\ *adv*

met·al·lur·gist \'med·ᵊl,ərjəst, -etᵊl-, -ōj-, -əij- *chiefly Brit* mə'talə(r)jəst\ *n* -s [NL *metallurgia* + E *-ist*] **:** a specialist in the science or application of metallurgy

met·al·lur·gy \-jē, -ji\ *n* -ES [NL *metallurgia*, fr. Gk *metallourgein* to work a mine (fr. *metallon* mine, metal + *ergon* work) + *-ia* -y — more at METAL, WORK] **:** a science and technology that deals with the extraction of metals from their ores, refining them, and preparing them for use and includes processes (as alloying, rolling, and heat-treating) and the study of the structure and properties of metals

metal man *n* **:** a worker who melts used type metal and casts it for reuse

metalmark \'==,=\ *n* [so called fr. the metallic spots or lines on its wings] **:** a butterfly of the family Riodinidae

meta·log·ic \ˌmed·ᵊl'äjik, -d·ə,lä-\ *n* [ML *Metalogicus*, title of a work on logic by John of Salisbury †1180 Eng. ecclesiastical leader and classical scholar] **:** a branch of analytic philosophy that deals with the critical examination of the basic concepts of logic abstracted from any meaning given them in the systems studied ⟨the ~ which grounds or justifies the logical system as a whole —R.L.Barber⟩

meta·log·i·cal \-jəkəl\ *adj* **1 a :** of or relating to metalogic ⟨~ investigations⟩ **b :** SYNTACTICAL **2 :** passing beyond the scope of logic ⟨not only in poetry are such ~ meanings found —Philip Wheelwright⟩ — **meta·logically** \~k(ə)lē, -li\ *adv*

meta·loph \'med·ə,läf\ *n* -s [*meta-* + *-loph*] **:** a crest on a lophodont molar extending from the ectoloph to the hypocone

metal-organic \ˌ==,=ˈ==\ *adj* **:** ORGANOMETALLIC

metals *pl of* METAL, *pres 3d sing of* METAL

metalsmith \'==,=\ *n* [ˡ*metal* + *smith*] **:** one skilled in metalworking

metalware \'==,=\ *n* **:** work or ware of metal; *esp* **:** metal utensils for household use ⟨table . . . loaded with a lot of shiny hotel ~ —John Dos Passos⟩

metalwork \'==,=\ *n* [ˡ*metal* + *work*] **:** a product of metalworking ⟨fine glass and ~ for export trade —Frances Rogers & Alice Beard⟩ ⟨sheet ~⟩ ⟨bench ~⟩

metalworker \'==,==\ *n* **:** one that is employed in metalworking

metalworking \'==,==\ *n* -s **:** the act or process of shaping things out of metal ⟨primitive ~⟩

metalworks \'==,=\ *n pl but usu sing in constr* [ˡ*metal* + *works*] **:** a workshop or factory where metal is treated, forged, or otherwise shaped

meta·mathematical \ˌ== *at* META-+\ *adj* [*meta-* + *mathematical*] **:** of or relating to metamathematics

meta·mathematician \"+\ *n* **:** a specialist in metamathematics

metamathematics \"+\ *n pl but usu sing in constr* [*meta-* + *mathematics*] **:** the philosophy of mathematics; *esp* **:** the logical syntax of mathematics ⟨~ . . . is the analysis of such mathematical concepts as "function", "variable", "real number" —Arthur Pap⟩

meta·mer \'med·əmə(r)\ *n* -s [*meta-* + *isomer*] **1 :** a chemical compound that is metameric with one or more others **2 :** either of two colors that appear identical to the eye but have different spectral composition

meta·mere \-,mi(ə)r\ *n* -s [ISV *meta-* + *-mere*] **:** any of a linear series of primitively similar segments into which the body of a higher invertebrate or vertebrate is divisible and which are usu. clearly distinguishable in the embryo, identifiable in somewhat modified form in various invertebrates (as annelid worms), and detectable in the adult higher vertebrate only in specialized segmentally arranged structures (as cranial and spinal nerves or vertebrae) **:** SOMITE — see ANTIMERE

meta·mer·ic \ˌ==ˈmerik\ *adj* [*meta-* + *mer-* (part) + *-ic*] **1 :** relating to or exhibiting chemical metamerism **:** ISOMERIC **2 a :** of, relating to, or exhibiting bodily metamerism ⟨a ~ animal⟩ **b :** of, relating to, or occurring in a metamere ⟨~ arrangement of blood vessels⟩ **:** SEGMENTAL — **meta·mer·i·cal·ly** \-rək(ə)lē\ *adv*

me·tam·er·ism \mə'tamə,rizəm\ *n* -s **1 :** isomerism esp. of chemical compounds of the same type (as butylamine and methyl-propyl-amine) **2 :** the condition of having or the stage of evolutionary development characterized by a body made up of metameres that is usu. held to be an essential prelude to the differentiation of the more highly organized animals (as arthropods and vertebrates) through the disproportionate development and elaboration of some segments together with the coalescence, reduction, or loss of others

met·a·mer·ization \ˌmed·əmərə'zāshən, məˌtamər-, -ˌrī'z-\ *n* -s [ISV *metamer-* (fr. *metamere*) + *-ization*] **:** the formation or differentiation of metameres

me·tam·er·ized \mə'tamə,rīzd, 'med·əmə,r-\ *adj* [*metamere* + *-ize* + *-ed*] **:** divided into metameres ⟨a ~ embryo⟩

me·tam·er·ous \mə'tamərəs\ *adj* [*metamerism* + *-ous*] **:** METAMERIC

me·tam·ery \-rē\ *n* -ES [*meta-* + *-mery*] **:** METAMERISM

meta·mict \'med·ə,mikt\ *adj* [*meta-* + Gk *miktos* mixed, compounded, verbal of *mignynai, meignynai* to mix — more at MIX] *of a mineral* **:** amorphous because of the disruption of the crystal structure by radiation from contained or nearby radioactive atoms

meta·mitosis \ˌ== *at* META- +\ *n* [NL, fr. *meta-* + *mitosis*] **:** mitosis involving both nuclear and cytoplasmic activities **:** EUMITOSIS

meta·mor·phic \ˌ==ˈmȯrfik, -ō(ə)f-\ *adj* [*metamorphosis* + *-ic*] **1 :** of or relating to metamorphosis ⟨a ~ stage⟩ **2** *of a rock* **:** of, relating to, or produced by metamorphism ⟨~ granite⟩

meta·mor·phism \ˌ==ˈ=,fizəm\ *n* -s [*metamorphosis* + *-ism*] **1 :** METAMORPHOSIS **2 :** a change in the constitution of rock; *specif* **:** a pronounced change usu. effected by action of pressure, heat, and water that results in a more compact and more highly crystalline condition of the rock — compare ANAMORPHISM 2, EPIGENESIS 2, KATAMORPHISM

meta·mor·phize \ˌ==ˈ=,fīz\ *vt* -ED/-ING/-S [L *metamorphosis* + E *-ize*] **:** METAMORPHOSE

ˡmeta·mor·phose \-,fōz, -ōs\ *vb* -ED/-ING/-S [prob. fr. MF *metamorphoser*, fr. *metamorphose*, n.] *vt* **1 a :** to change into a different physical form; *esp* **:** to effect such a change in, by, or as if by supernatural means ⟨men were by the force of that herb *metamorphosed* into swine —Richard Steele⟩ **b :** to change strikingly the appearance or character of **:** TRANSFORM ⟨you are so *metamorphosed* I can hardly think you my master —Shak.⟩ ⟨*metamorphosing* the most familiar things and endowing them with a sense of mystery —J.B.D.Cotter⟩ **2 :** to cause (rock) to undergo metamorphism ⟨the rocks had been baked and thereby *metamorphosed* —Arthur Holmes⟩ ~ *vi* **1 :** to undergo biological metamorphosis ⟨a tadpole ~s into a frog⟩ **2 :** to undergo a transformation ⟨the little song . . . later *metamorphosed* into one of the noblest chorales —P.L. Miller⟩ ⟨many humans never ~ into moral manhood —Weston La Barre⟩ **syn** see TRANSFORM

²meta·mor·phose \-,fōs\ *n* -s [prob. fr. MF *metamorphose*, fr. L *metamorphosis*] *archaic* **:** METAMORPHOSIS

meta·mor·pho·sis \ˌ==ˈmȯ(r)fəsəs *sometimes* -ˌmȯ(r)'fōs-\ *n* [L, fr. Gk *metamorphōsis*, fr. *metamorphoun* to transform, fr. *meta-* change, transformation (fr. *meta* with, between, after) + *morphē* form — more at META-, FORM] **1 a :** change of physical form or substance; *esp* **:** such a change brought about by or as if by supernatural means ⟨the ~ of men into animals⟩ **b :** a striking alteration (as in appearance, character, or circumstances) ⟨~ of the old house which he had inherited —Claud Phillimore⟩ ⟨the prospect of facing his . . . family and guests in this new ~ —David Walden⟩ **2 a :** a marked and more or less abrupt change in the form or structure of an animal during postembryonic development (as when the larva of an insect becomes a pupa or a tadpole changes into a frog) ⟨~ of a butterfly⟩ — compare EPIMORPHOSIS **b :** the sum of the various modifications whether phylogenetic or primarily ontogenetic through which a primitive plant structure may pass in the course of its development **c** *archaic* **:** evolutionary change or modification of form over the centuries **3 a :** transformation of one kind of tissue into another ⟨~ of cartilage into bone⟩ **b :** tissue degeneration marked by conversion of tissues or structures into other material ⟨fatty ~ of the liver⟩ **4 a :** a chemical change (as oxidation, reduction, hydrolysis, substitution) **b :** a changing of a chemical compound into an isomeric form **5 :** a transformation of a musical figure or idea into a rhythmically or melodically altered repetition of the original ⟨its continuity . . . relies upon the ~ of themes rather than the use of the leitmotiv —Norman Demuth⟩

meta·mor·phot·ic \ˌ==ˈfäd·ik\ *adj* [*metamorphosis* + *-otic* (as in *narcotic*)] **:** METAMORPHIC

meta·myelocyte \ˌ==+\ *n* [ISV *meta-* + *myelocyte*] **:** a granulocyte that is the least mature present in normal blood and is distinguished by typical cytoplasmic granulation in combination with a simple kidney-shaped nucleus

met·amyn·o·don \ˌmed·ə'minə,dän\ *n, cap* [NL, fr. *meta-* + *Amynodon*] **:** a genus of hornless rhinoceroses from the Oligocene of No. America and Asia

met·analysis \ˌmed·+\ *n* [*meta-* + *analysis*] **:** the analysis of words or groups of words into new elements (as *an apron* for *a napron*) — called also *affix-clipping*

meta·nauplius \ˌ== *at* META- +\ *n* [NL, fr. *meta-* + *nauplius*] **:** a crustacean larva of the stage after the nauplius that has about seven pairs of appendages

met·an·dric \mə'tandrik\ *adj* [*meta-* + *-andric* (as in *holandric*)] *of an annelid worm* **:** retaining only the posterior pair of the primitive two pairs of testes — compare HOLANDRIC, PROANDRIC

meta·nemertini \ˌ== *at* META- +\ *n pl, cap* [NL, fr. *meta-* + *Nemertini*] *in some classifications* **:** an order of Nemertea comprising forms in which the brain and lateral nerves lie within the somatic musculature

meta·nephric \"+\ *also* **meta·nephritic** \"+\ *adj* [*metanephric* fr. *meta-* + *nephr-* + *-ic*; *metanephritic* fr. *meta-* + *nephritic*] **:** of or relating to the metanephros

meta·ne·phrid·i·al \"+\ *adj* [NL *metanephridium* + E *-al*] **:** of, relating to, or having metanephridia

meta·nephridium \"+\ *n* [NL, fr. *meta-* + *nephridium*] **:** a nephridium that originates in a ciliated coelomic funnel — compare PROTONEPHRIDIUM

meta·neph·ro·gen·ic \ˌ==ˌnefrə'jenik\ *adj* [NL *metanephros* + E *-genic*] **:** producing the metanephroi

meta·neph·ros \ˌ=='ne,fräs\ *also* **meta·neph·ron** \-,frän\ *n, pl* **metaneph·roi** \-,frȯi\ *also* **metaneph·ra** \-,frə\ [NL, fr. *meta-* situated behind (fr. Gk *meta* after) + *-nephros* — more at META-] **:** one of the posterior of the three pairs of embryonic renal organs developed in higher vertebrates persisting in the adult as the definitive kidney — compare MESONEPHROS

meta·nepionic \ˌ==+\ *adj* [*meta-* + *nepionic*] **:** of, relating to, or being the median of the three nepionic stages in the development of an individual **:** late nepionic

met·a·nil·ic acid \ˌmed·ə;nilik-\ *n* [ISV *meta-* + *sulfanilic acid*] **:** a crystalline sulfonic acid $H_2NC_6H_4SO_3H$ that is isomeric with sulfanilic acid, is made by sulfonating nitrobenzene and then reducing, and is used as an intermediate for azo dyes; *meta*-amino-benzenesulfonic acid

met·a·nil yellow \'med·ə,nil-\ *n, often cap M&Y* [ISV *metanil*, fr. *metanilic (acid)*] **:** a yellow azo dye made from diazotized metanilic acid and diphenylamine — see DYE table I (under *Acid Yellow 36*)

meta·noia \ˌmed·ə'nȯi(y)ə\ *n* -s [Gk, fr. *metanoein* to change one's mind, repent, be converted (fr. *meta-* + *noein* to perceive, think) + *-ia* -y; akin to Gk *noos, nous* mind] **:** a fundamental transformation of mind or character; *specif* **:** a spiritual conversion

meta·no·tal \ˌ==ˈnōdᵊl\ *adj* [NL *metanotum* + E *-al*] **:** of, relating to, or situated on the metanotum

meta·no·tum \ˌ=='nōd·əm\ *n* [NL, fr. *meta-* + Gk *nōton* back — more at NATES] **:** the dorsal portion of the metathoracic integument of an insect

meta·nym \'med·ə,nim\ *n* -s [*meta-* + *-onym*] **:** a generic name rejected because based on a type species congeneric with the type of a previously published genus

metaperiodic acid *n* [*meta-* + *periodic*] **:** PERIODIC ACID b

metaperrhenic acid *n* [*meta-* + *perrhenic*] **:** PERRHENIC ACID a

metaph *abbr* **1** metaphor; metaphorical **2** metaphysical; metaphysics

meta·phase \'med·ə+,-\ *n* [ISV *meta-* + *phase*; orig. formed in G] **:** the stage of mitosis preceding the anaphase

metaphase plate *n* **:** the equatorial plane of the spindle with the chromosomes as oriented therein during metaphase

Met·a·phen \'med·əfən\ *trademark* — used for nitromersol

meta·phloem \ˌ== *at* META- +\ *n* [*meta-* + *phloem*] **:** the later-formed part of the primary phloem that consists of mature phloem elements and is differentiated mainly after elongation of the axis has ceased — compare PROTOPHLOEM

met·a·phone \'==,fōn\ *n* [*meta-* + *-phone*] **:** a free allophonic variant chosen in preference to another because regarded as more suitable to the style of speech being used

met·a·phon·ic \ˌ=='fänik\ *adj* [*meta-* + *-phonic*] **:** of or relating to umlaut **:** cognate in a manner explainable in terms of metaphony

me·taph·o·ny \mə'tafənē, me'-\ *n* -ES [ISV *meta-* + *-phony*] **:** UMLAUT

met·a·phor \'med·ə,fȯ(ə)r, 'metə-, -ō(ə) *also* -,fə(r) *sometimes* -,fō(ə)r *or* -ōə\ *n* -s [MF or L; MF *metaphore*, fr. L *metaphora*, fr. Gk, fr. *metapherein* to transfer, change, fr. *meta-* + *pherein* to bear — more at BEAR] **:** a figure of speech in which a word or phrase denoting one kind of object or action is used in place of another to suggest a likeness or analogy between them (as in *the ship plows the seas* or in *a volley of oaths*) **:** an implied comparison (as in *a marble brow*) in contrast to the explicit comparison of the simile (as in *a brow white as marble*) — compare TROPE

met·a·phor·i·cal \ˌ=='fȯrəkəl, -'fär-, -rēk-\ *also* **met·a·phor·ic** \-rik, -rēk\ *adj* [*metaphorical* fr. ML *metaphoricus* metaphorical (fr. Gk *metaphorikos*, fr. *metaphora* metaphor + *-ikos* -ic) + E *-al*; *metaphoric* fr. ML *metaphoricus*] **:** of, relating to, characteristic of, or comprising a metaphor ⟨a ~ expression⟩ — **met·a·phor·i·cal·ly** \-rək(ə)lē, -rēk-, -li\ *adv* — **met·a·phor·i·cal·ness** \-kəlnəs\ *n* -ES

met·a·phor·ist \'==,fȯrəst, -,fər-\ *n* -s **:** one who makes metaphors

met·a·phor·ize \-,fə,rīz, -,fō,-\ *vb* -ED/-ING/-S [F *métaphoriser*, fr. *métaphore* metaphor + *-iser* -ize] *vt* **:** to express metaphorically ~ *vi* **:** to make metaphors

meta·phosphate \ˌ== *at* META- +\ *n* [ISV *metaphosph-* (fr. *metaphosphoric acid*) + *-ate*] **1 :** a salt or ester of a metaphosphoric acid — see SODIUM METAPHOSPHATE, TETRAMETAPHOSPHATE, TRIMETAPHOSPHATE **2 :** any of various usu. glassy phosphates approximating a metaphosphate in composition — see SODIUM PHOSPHATE GLASS

meta·phosphoric acid \"+-\ *n* [*meta-* + *phosphoric acid*] **:** an acid HPO_3 or $(HPO_3)_n$ formed by heating orthophosphoric acid but usu. obtained in the form of salts

ˡmet·a·phrase \'med·ə,frāz\ *n* [NL *metaphrasis*, fr. Gk, fr. *metaphrazein* to translate (fr. *meta-* + *phrazein* to point out, show, tell) + *-sis*] **1** *archaic* **:** a translation esp. in verse **:** PARAPHRASE **2 :** a literal translation from one language into another — opposed to *paraphrase*

²metaphrase \"\ *vt* **1 :** to make a metaphrase of **2** *archaic* **:** to render into verse **3 :** to alter the wording of

me·taph·ra·sis \mə'tafrəsəs, me'-\ *n* -ES [NL] **:** METAPHRASE

met·a·phrast \'med·ə,frast\ *n* -s [MGk *metaphrastēs*, fr. Gk *metaphrazein* to translate] **:** TRANSLATOR; *specif* **:** one who turns verse into a different meter or prose into verse — **met·a·phras·tic** \ˌ=='frastik\ *or* **met·a·phras·ti·cal** \-tәkәl\ *adj* — **met·a·phras·ti·cal·ly** \-k(ə)lē\ *adv*

me·taph·y·se·al \məˌtafə'sēəl, -'zēəl *also* ˌmed·əˌfizē-\ *adj* [NL *metaphysis* + E *-eal* (as in *apophyseal*)] **:** of or relating to a metaphysis ⟨~ decalcification⟩

ˡmeta·phys·ic \ˌ== *at* META- + ˈfizik, -ēk\ *n* -s [ME *methaphesik, metaphesyk*, fr. ML *metaphysica*, fem. sing. & neut. pl. — more at METAPHYSICS] **1 a :** METAPHYSICS ⟨the most fantastic speculations of the later German ~ —Josiah Royce⟩ ⟨~ did not mean much to him —*Times Lit. Supp.*⟩ **b :** a particular system or theory of metaphysics ⟨this view of nature and man's place in nature is a ~ —W.H.Sheldon⟩ ⟨the three possible monistic ~s: materialism, idealism, and neutral monism —J.W.Smith⟩ **2 :** the system of first principles or philosophy underlying a particular study or subject of inquiry ⟨each injustice . . . rationalizes the claims it embodies by sheltering under a half-examined ~ of values —H.J.Laski⟩ ⟨the ~ of his love poems —George Haines⟩

²metaphysic \"\ *adj* [ML *metaphysicus*, after Gk *Ta meta ta Physika* (a work by Aristotle), lit., the (work) after the *Physics* (a work by Aristotle)] **:** METAPHYSICAL

meta·phys·i·cal \-zәkәl, -zēk-\ *adj* [ME, fr. ML *metaphysicalis*, fr. *metaphysica* metaphysics + L *-alis* -al] **1 :** of, relating to, or based on metaphysics ⟨~ truth⟩ ⟨the ~ assumption⟩ ⟨idealism which still remained ~ although no longer explicitly theistic —Emil Brunner⟩ **2 a :** of or relating to what is conceived as transcendent, supersensible, or transcendental ⟨fleeing from experience to a ~ realm —John Dewey⟩ **b :** PRETERNATURAL ⟨fate and ~ aid doth seem to have thee crown'd —Shak.⟩ **c** *archaic* **:** IMAGINARY, FANCIFUL ⟨those ~ persons . . . John Doe and Richard Roe —Sir Walter Scott⟩ **3 a :** showing an inclination toward or addiction to metaphysics ⟨a ~ man⟩ ⟨his ~ talent —Harriet B. Stowe⟩ **b :** highly abstract or abstruse ⟨~ reasoning⟩ ⟨the prohibition of ~ questions —*Social Research*⟩ **4 a :** synthetic a priori ⟨a ~ judgment⟩ **b :** neither analytic nor subject to empirical verification ⟨the view . . . that ~ statements are not, as scientific statements are, descriptions of real features of fact, but, at best, expressions of attitudes about which rational argument is impossible — W.H.Walsh⟩ **5 :** of, relating to, or producing metaphysical poetry ⟨~ school⟩ ⟨~ poem⟩ ⟨~ poet⟩

meta·phys·i·cal·ly \-zək(ə)lē, -zēk-, -li\ *adv* **1 :** in the manner of metaphysics or of a metaphysician ⟨the assimilation of men to machines, whatever may be thought of it ~, is hardly likely to give us a just standard of values —Bertrand Russell⟩ **2 :** in the mode of a metaphysical reality or existence ⟨the universal was more real ~, than the particular —John Dewey⟩

metaphysical poetry *n* **:** highly intellectualized poetry marked by bold and ingenious conceits, incongruous imagery, complexity and subtlety of thought, frequent use of paradox, and often by deliberate harshness or rigidity of expression

metaphysical truth *n* **:** the truth of ultimate reality as partly or wholly transcendent of perceived actuality and experience

meta·physician \ˌ==+\ *n* [prob. fr. MF *metaphysicien*, fr. *metaphysique* metaphysics (fr. ML *metaphysica*) + *-ien* -an] **:** one who is versed in or advocates metaphysics ⟨the ~ . . . is trying to provide for all possible classes of facts rather than to predict which will be actualized —Charles Hartshorne⟩ ⟨every significant artist is a ~, a propounder of beauty-truths and form-theories —Aldous Huxley⟩ ⟨the ~ of history pretends that every scene is what it is by virtue of its role in the play as a whole —Kurt Riezler⟩

meta·phys·i·cize \ˌ=='fizə,sīz\ *vi* -ED/-ING/-S [ˡ*metaphysic* + *-ize*] **:** to engage in metaphysical speculation

meta·phys·ics \ˌ=='fiziks, -zēks\ *n pl but usu sing in constr* [pl. of ˡ*metaphysic*; rendering of ML *metaphysica*, neut. pl., fr. Gk *(ta) meta (ta) physika* the (works) after the physics, the things after those relating to external nature; fr. the fact that this section of the collected works of Aristotle †322 B.C. Greek philosopher was reputedly so designated by the editor, Andronicus of Rhodes *fl* 1st cent. B.C. Greek philosopher in Rome, because it came after the physics] **1 a (1) :** a division of philosophy that includes ontology and cosmology ⟨~ . . . treats of the relations obtaining between the underlying reality and its manifestations —Fred Sommers⟩ ⟨~ . . . analyzes the generic traits manifested by existences of any kind —J.H. Randall⟩ ⟨~, or the attempt to conceive the world as a whole by means of thought, has been developed, from the first, by the union and conflict of two very different human impulses, the one urging men towards mysticism, the other urging them towards science —Bertrand Russell⟩ (2) **:** ontology and epistemology ⟨~ as a philosophic discipline . . . concerned with the nature of the real only so far as that problem is amenable to the reflective method —C.I.Lewis⟩ (3) **:** ONTOLOGY **b** (1) **:** something that deals with what is beyond the physical or the experiential (2) **:** the more abstruse philosophical sciences ⟨the mathematics and the ~, fall to them as you find your stomach serves you —Shak.⟩ **2 :** METAPHYSIC 2 ⟨differentiates between a theory of esthetic experience and a ~ of beauty —J.G.Brennan⟩ ⟨each language . . . conceals a unique ~ —B.L.Whorf⟩ ⟨erected a ~ on this fundamental antagonism of vitality or "Life" . . . and what he calls "Spirit" —V.C.Aldrich⟩ **3 :** the Christian Science system of mental healing

me·taph·y·sis \mə'tafəsəs\ *n, pl* **metaphy·ses** \-ə,sēz\ [NL, fr. *meta-* + *-physis* (as in NL *apophysis*)] **:** the transitional zone at which the diaphysis and epiphysis of a bone come together

meta·phyte \'⸗⸗ *at* META- + ,fīt\ *n* -S [ISV *meta-* + *-phyte;* orig. formed as G *metaphyt*] **:** a multicellular plant — compare PROTOPHYTE — **meta·phyt·ic** \¦⸗⸗¦fid·ik\ *adj*

meta·pla·sia \,⸗⸗'plāzh(ē)ə\ *n* -S [NL, fr. *meta-* + *-plasia*] **1 :** transformation of one tissue into another ⟨~ of cartilage into bone⟩ **2 :** abnormal replacement of cells of one type by cells of another

meta·plasm \'⸗⸗,plazəm\ *n* -S **1** [L *metaplasmus,* lit., transformation, fr. Gk *metaplasmos,* fr. *metaplassein* to remold, fr. *meta-* + *plassein* to mold — more at PLASTER] **:** alteration of regular verbal, grammatical, or rhetorical structure usu. by transposition of the letters or syllables of a word or of the words in a sentence **2** [ISV *meta-* + *-plasm;* orig. formed as G *metaplasma*] **:** material consisting of lifeless derivatives of protoplasm (as cell walls, starch grains) — **meta·plas·mic** \¦⸗⸗¦plazmik\ *adj*

meta·plast \'⸗⸗,plast\ *n* -S [*meta-* + *-plast*] **:** a metaplasmic body

meta·plastic \¦⸗⸗+\ *adj* [*meta-* + *-plastic*] **1 :** relating to or produced by metaplasia **2 :** of or relating to metaplasm

meta·pleural \"+\ *adj* [NL *metapleuron* + E *-al*] **:** of or relating to a metapleuron

meta·pleuron \¦⸗⸗+\ *n, pl* **metapleura** \"+\ [NL, fr. *meta-* + *pleuron*] **:** a pleuron of the metathorax of an insect

meta·pneumonic \"+\ *adj* [*meta-* + *pneumonic*] **:** secondary to pneumonia

met·ap·neus·tic \¦me,tap¦n(y)üstik\ *adj* [*meta-* + Gk *pneustikos* of or for breathing, fr. (assumed) Gk *pneustos* (verbal of Gk *pnein* to breathe) + Gk *-ikos* -ic — more at SNEEZE] *of an insect larva* **:** breathing through a single pair of posterior or anal spiracles

meta·po·di·al \¦⸗⸗ *at* META- + ¦pōdēəl\ *n* -S [NL *metapodium* metatarsus (fr. *meta-* + *-podium*) + E *-al* (n. suffix, fr. *-al,* adj. suffix)] **:** a metacarpal or metatarsal bone

meta·po·di·a·le \,⸗⸗,pōdē'ā(,)lē\ *n, pl* **metapodia·lia** \-ālēə\ [NL, fr. *metapodium* metatarsus + L *-ale* (fr. neut. of *-alis* -al, adj. suffix)] **:** METAPODIAL

meta·po·di·um \,⸗⸗'pōdēəm\ *n, pl* **metapo·dia** \-dēə\ [NL, fr. *meta-* + *-podium*] **:** the posterior division of the foot in mollusks

meta·political \¦⸗⸗ *at* META- +\ *adj* **:** of or relating to metapolitics

meta·politician \"+\ *n* [*metapolitics* + *-an*] **:** one who engages in abstract political theorizing

meta·politics \"+\ *n pl but sing in constr* [*meta-* + *politics*] **:** theoretical or philosophical political science

meta·poph·y·sis \,med·ə'päfəsəs\ *n* [NL, fr. *meta-* + *apophysis*] **:** a tubercle projecting from the anterior articular process of a vertebra esp. in the lumbar region

meta·postscutellar \¦⸗⸗ *at* META- +\ *adj* [NL *metapostscutellum* + E *-ar*] **:** of or relating to the metapostscutellum

meta·postscutellum \"+\ *n* [NL, fr. *meta-* + *postscutellum*] **:** the postnotum of the metathorax of an insect

meta·prescutal \¦⸗⸗+\ *adj* [NL *metaprescutum* + E *-al*] **:** of or relating to the metaprescutum

meta·prescutum \"+\ *n* [NL, fr. *meta-* + *prescutum*] **:** the prescutum of the metathorax of an insect

meta·protein \"+\ *n* [*meta-* + *protein*] **:** any of various products derived from proteins through the action of acids or alkalies by which the solubility and sometimes the composition of the proteins is changed — compare ALBUMINATE

meta·psychic \¦⸗⸗+\ *or* **meta·psychical** \"+\ *adj* [*metapsychic* fr. F *métapsychique,* fr. *méta-* + *psychique* psychic, fr. Gk *psychikos* of the soul, of life; *metapsychical* fr. F *métapsychique* + E *-al* — more at PSYCHIC] **:** of or relating to phenomena (as mediumistic) outside the range of orthodox psychology ⟨the existence of telepathic phenomena, as well as other ~ phenomena, is not accepted by most biologists and physicians —Alexis Carrel⟩

meta·psychological \"+\ *adj* **:** of or relating to metapsychology

meta·psychology \¦⸗⸗+\ *n* [ISV *meta-* + *psychology*] **1 :** a theory that aims to supplement the facts and empirical laws of psychology by speculations on the connection of mental and physical processes or on the place of mind in the universe; *specif* **:** the aspect of Freud's theory that aims to supplement his treatment of the conscious and unconscious and of the motivation of behavior by a theory of memories as charges of physical energy and of emotion as a process of discharge **2 :** PARAPSYCHOLOGY

me·tap·ter·yg·i·um \mə¦taptə¦rijēəm\ *n, pl* **metapteryg·ia** \-jēə\ [NL, fr. *meta-* + Gk *pterygion* fin, lit., small wing — more at PTERYGIUM] **:** the posterior of the three principal basal cartilages in the pectoral fins of some fishes (as sharks and rays) — compare BASIPTERYGIUM

¹met·ap·ter·y·goid \¦me,tap¦terə,gȯid\ *adj* [*meta-* + *pterygoid* (n.)] **:** situated behind the pterygoid

²metapterygoid \"\ *n* [*meta-* + *pterygoid*] **:** a metapterygoid part (as a bone)

meta·rossite \¦⸗⸗ *at* META- +\ *n* [*meta-* + *rossite*] **:** a mineral consisting of a hydrous calcium vanadate — compare ROSSITE

met·ar·rhi·zi·um \,med·ə'rīzēəm\ *n, cap* [NL, fr. *meta-* + Gk *rhizion* small root, dim. of *rhiza* root — more at WORT (herb)] **:** a genus of imperfect fungi (family Moniliaceae) closely related to *Penicillium* and of interest chiefly in biological control of various insects — see GREEN MUSCARDINE

met·ar·te·ri·ole \,med·,är'tirē,ōl\ *n* [*meta-* + *arteriole*] **:** a delicate blood vessel held to connect some arteries and veins and distinguished from a true capillary by the presence of smooth muscle in its walls

meta·science \¦⸗⸗ *at* META- +\ *n* [*meta-* + *science*] **:** a theory or science of science

meta·scientific \"+\ *adj* [*meta-* + *scientific*] **:** of, relating to, or based on metascience ⟨the richness of ~ speculation —L.S.Feuer⟩

meta·scope \'⸗⸗,skōp\ *n* [*meta-* + *-scope*] **1 :** a telescope that produces on a fluorescent screen by means of infrared light visible images of objects in total darkness **2 :** a device designed to locate the source of infrared rays by converting them to visible light

meta·scutal \¦⸗⸗¦skyüd·ᵊl\ *adj* [NL *metascutum* + E *-al*] **:** of or relating to the metascutum

meta·scutellar \"+\ *adj* [NL *metascutellum* + E *-ar*] **:** of or relating to the metascutellum

meta·scutellum \"+\ *n* [NL, fr. *meta-* + *scutellum*] **:** the scutellum of the metathorax of an insect

meta·scutum \"+\ *n* [NL, fr. *meta-* + *scutum*] **:** the scutum of the metathorax of an insect

meta·sediment \"+\ *n* [*meta-* + *sediment*] **:** a metamorphic rock of sedimentary origin — **meta·sedimentary** \"+\ *adj*

meta·sequoia \¦⸗⸗+\ *n* [NL,'fr. *meta-* + *Sequoia*] **1** *cap* **:** a genus of deciduous coniferous trees (family Pinaceae) comprising both fossil and living forms and having opposite arrangement of leaves, buds, and branches and only flat needlelike leaves **2 :** any tree or fossil of the genus *Metasequoia; esp* **:** DAWN REDWOOD

meta·sideronatrite \"+\ *n* [*meta-* + *sideronatrite*] **:** a mineral $Na_4Fe_2(SO_4)_4(OH)_2.3H_2O$, consisting of a basic hydrous sulfate of sodium and iron

meta·silicate \"+\ *n* [ISV *meta-* + *silicate*] **1 :** a silicate containing the anion SiO_3^{--} or $(SiO_3)_n^{2n-}$ in which the ratio of silicon to oxygen is 1 to 3 **2 :** INOSILICATE

meta·silicic acid \¦⸗⸗+-\ *n* [ISV *meta-* + *silicic acid*] **:** a hypothetical acid H_2SiO_3 or $(H_2SiO_3)_n$ from which the metasilicates may be regarded as derived

meta·so·ma \,⸗⸗'sōmə\ *n* [NL, fr. *meta-* + *-soma*] **:** the hind region of the body of some invertebrates; *esp* **:** such a region that cannot be readily analyzed into its primitive segmentation (as in some mollusks and arachnids) — **meta·so·mal** \¦⸗⸗¦sōməl\ *adj*

meta·somatic \¦⸗⸗+\ *adj* **1** [*metasomatism* + *-ic*] **:** of or relating to metasomatism **2** [NL *metasomat-, metasoma* + E *-ic*] **:** of or relating to a metasoma

meta·so·ma·tism \,⸗⸗'sōmə,tizəm\ *n* -S [*meta-* + Gk *sōmat-, sōma* body + E *-ism* — more at -SOME (body)] **:** metamorphism that usu. involves important changes in the chemical composition as well as in the mineral composition and texture of rock

meta·so·ma·to·sis \,⸗⸗,sōmə'tōsəs\ *n, pl* **metasomato·ses** \-ō,sēz\ [NL, fr. *meta-* + Gk *sōmat-, sōma* body + NL *-osis*] **1 :** METENSOMATOSIS **2 :** METASOMATISM

meta·some \'⸗⸗,sōm\ *n* -S **1** [NL *metasoma*] **:** METASOMA **2** [*meta-* + *-some*] **:** the replacing mineral where one mineral grows in size at the expense of another

meta·stability \¦⸗⸗+\ *n* **:** the quality or state of being metastable

meta·stable \"+\ *adj* [ISV *meta-* + *stable*] **:** marked by only a slight margin of stability — used esp. in chemistry and physics ⟨a supercooled liquid is ~⟩ ⟨many of the processes in the atmosphere are . . . ~: a slight action may initiate a very large-scale process —Roger Revelle⟩ ⟨life is fleeting, ~, a thing of delicate equilibrium of easily decomposed compounds —C.C. Furnas⟩

metastable state *n* **:** a state of precarious stability; *specif* **:** such a state of an atom which though excited cannot emit radiation without a further supply of energy

me·tas·ta·sis \mə'tastəsəs, -'taas-\ *n, pl* **metastases** [NL, fr. LL, transition, fr. Gk, fr. *methistanai* to change, fr. *meta-* + *histanai* to cause to stand, place — more at STAND] **:** change of position, state, or form: **a** (1) **:** transfer of a disease-producing agency (as cells or bacteria) from an original site of disease to another part of the body with development of a similar lesion in the new location ⟨~ in the lung usually occurs by way of the blood stream —J.B.Amberson⟩ ⟨*metastases* of breast cancer to bone —*Medical Physics*⟩ — compare CANCER, IMPLANTATION (2) **:** a secondary growth resulting from such transfer of cells of a malignant tumor **b :** METABOLISM 1 **c :** a paramorphic change in rock (as recrystallization of limestone or devitrification of glassy rock)

me·tas·ta·size \-,sīz\ *vi* -ED/-ING/-S [NL *metastasis* + E *-ize*] **:** to spread by metastasis — used chiefly of malignant tumors ⟨the lesion already had *metastasized* beyond the larynx before a diagnosis of carcinoma was made —*Amer. Practitioner*⟩

meta·static \¦⸗⸗ *at* META- +\ *adj* [fr. NL *metastasis,* after such pairs as LL *hypostasis:* E *hypostatic*] **:** of, relating to, or caused by metastasis ⟨~ lung cancer⟩ ⟨~ lesions⟩

meta·sternal \"+\ *adj* [NL *metasternum* + E *-al*] **:** of or relating to the metasternum

meta·sternum \"+\ *n* [NL, fr. *meta-* + *sternum*] **1 :** the ventral plate of the metathorax of an insect **2 :** XIPHISTERNUM

meta·sthenic \¦⸗⸗ *at* META- + ¦sthenik, -thēn-\ *adj* [*meta-* + Gk *sthenos* strength + E *-ic* — more at ASTHEN-] **:** strong in the hinder part of the body

me·tas·to·ma \mə'tastəmə, -'taas-\ *n, pl* **meta·sto·ma·ta** \,med·ə'stōməd·ə\ [NL, fr. *meta-* + Gk *stoma* mouth — more at STOMACH] **:** a median platelike process behind the mouth in crustaceans and related arthropods

meta·stome \'⸗⸗ *at* META- + ,stōm\ *n* -S [NL *metastoma*] **:** METASTOMA

meta·strengite \¦⸗⸗+\ *n* [*meta-* + *strengite*] **:** a mineral $FePO_4.2H_2O$ that consists of a hydrous phosphate of iron and is polymorphous with strengite and prob. isomorphous with metavariscite

meta·strongyle \"+\ *n* [NL *Metastrongylus*] **:** METASTRONGYLID

¹meta·strongylid \¦⸗⸗+\ *adj* [NL *Metastrongylidae*] **:** of or relating to the family Metastrongylidae

²metastrongylid \"\ *n* -S [NL *Metastrongylidae*] **:** a nematode worm of the family Metastrongylidae

meta·stron·gyl·i·dae \¦⸗⸗,strän'jilə,dē\ *n pl, cap* [NL, fr. *Metastrongylus,* type genus + *-idae*] **:** a large family of parasitic strongyloid nematode worms — see DICTYOCAULUS, METASTRONGYLUS, PROTOSTRONGYLUS

meta·strongylus \¦⸗⸗+\ *n, cap* [NL, fr. *meta-* + *Strongylus*] **:** a genus (the type of the family Metastrongylidae) of slender threadlike nematode worms that parasitize as adults the lungs and sometimes other organs of mammals and as larvae various earthworms

meta·style \'⸗⸗+,-\ *n* [*meta-* + *style* (cusp)] **:** a cusp posterior to the metacone of a molar tooth

meta·syndesis \¦⸗⸗+\ *n* [NL, fr. *meta-* + *syndesis*] **:** TELOSYNAPSIS

¹meta·tarsal \¦⸗⸗+\ *adj* [NL *metatarsus* + E *-al*] **:** of or relating to the metatarsus — **meta·tar·sal·ly** \-səlē\ *adv*

²metatarsal \"\ *n* -S **:** a metatarsal bone

metatarsale \¦⸗⸗+\ *n, pl* **metatarsalia** [NL, fr. *metatarsus* + L *-ale* (n. suffix, fr. neut. of *-alis* -al, adj. suffix)] **:** METATARSAL

meta·tar·sal·gia \,⸗⸗,tär'saljēə\ *n* -S [NL, fr. *metatarsus* + *-algia*] **:** a cramping burning pain below and between the metatarsal bones where they join the toe bones — called also *Morton's toe*

meta·tar·so·phalangeal \¦⸗⸗¦tär,sō+\ *adj* [*metatarso-* (fr. NL *metatarsus*) + *phalangeal*] **:** of, relating to, or involving both the metatarsus and the phalanges

meta·tarsus \¦⸗⸗+\ *n* [NL, fr. *meta-* + *tarsus*] **1 :** the part of the foot in man or of the hind foot in quadrupeds that is between the tarsus and phalanges, contains when all the digits are present five more or less elongated bones but is modified in many animals with loss or reduction of some bones or fusing of others, and forms in man the instep, in horses and cattle the part of the hind leg from the hock to the fetlock joint, and in birds the tarso-metatarsus **2 a :** the proximal segment of the tarsus of an insect **b :** the tarsus of the posterior pair of legs of an insect **c :** the proximal segment of the foot of a spider

me·ta·te \mə'täd·ē\ *n* -S [Sp, fr. Nahuatl *metlatl*] **:** a stone with a concave upper surface used as the nether millstone for grinding maize and other grains ⟨each woman in turn rose and knelt at the ~ and ground some of the corn grains —Gertrude Diamant⟩ — compare MANO

meta·thalamus \¦⸗⸗ *at* META- +\ *n* [NL, fr. *meta-* + *thalamus*] **:** the part of the diencephalon that contains the geniculate bodies

meta·thenardite \"+\ *n* [*meta-* + *thenardite*] **:** a mineral consisting of a high-temperature polymorph of thenardite occurring in fumaroles on Martinique Island

meta·theory \"+\ *n* [*meta-* + *theory*] **:** a theory concerned with the investigation, analysis, or description of theory itself ⟨if we investigate, analyze, and describe a language L_1 . . . the sum total of what can be known about L_1 and said in L_2 may be called the ~ of L_1 —Rudolf Carnap⟩

meta·the·ria \,⸗⸗'thirēə\ *n pl, cap* [NL, fr. *meta-* + *-theria*] **1 :** a hypothetical group ancestral to placental mammals postulated to have reached a stage of development equivalent to that of the marsupials **2** *in some classifications* **:** a group coextensive with Marsupialia

¹meta·the·ri·an \,med·ə¦thirēən\ *adj* [NL *Metatheria* + E *-an*] **:** of or relating to the Metatheria

²metatherian \"\ *n* -S **:** a mammal of the group Metatheria

me·tath·e·sis \mə'tathəsəs\ *n, pl* **metathe·ses** \-,sēz\ [LL transposition of letters, fr. Gk, fr. *metatithenai* to transpose, fr. *meta-* + *tithenai* to place, set — more at DO] **1 :** a change of place or condition **:** REVERSAL; *specif* **:** transposition of two phonemes in a word (as in Old English *wæsp, wæps*) **2 :** DOUBLE DECOMPOSITION

me·tath·e·size \-,sīz\ *vb* -ED/-ING/-S [*metathesis* + *-ize*] *vi* **:** to undergo metathesis ~ *vt* **:** to subject to metathesis

me·tath·e·tely \mə'tathə,telē\ *n* -ES [Gk *metathetos* changed, changeable (verbal of *metatithenai* to transpose, change) + *telos* end, completion, maturity + E *-y* — more at WHEEL] **1 :** retardation of development in insect larvae without retardation of growth (as that resulting from the presence of various parasitic worms) **2 :** HYSTEROTELY

meta·thet·i·cal \¦med·ə¦thed·əkəl\ *also* **meta·thet·ic** \-¦thed·ik\ *adj* [LGk *metathetikos* able to change, fr. Gk *metathetos* changed, changeable + *-ikos* -ic, -ical] **:** of or relating to metathesis — **meta·thet·i·cal·ly** \-ək(ə)lē\ *adv*

me·tath·e·tize \mə'tathə,tīz\ *vb* -ED/-ING/-S [*metathetical* + *-ize*] **:** METATHESIZE

meta·thoracic \¦⸗⸗ *at* META-+\ *adj* [NL *metathorac-, metathorax* + E *-ic*] **:** of or relating to the metathorax

meta·thorax \"+\ *n* [NL, fr. *meta-* + *thorax*] **:** the posterior segment of the thorax in an insect — see INSECT illustration

meta·torbernite \"+\ *n* [*meta-* + *torbernite*] **:** a mineral $Cu(UO_2)_2(PO_4)_2.8H_2O$ consisting of a hydrous phosphate of copper and uranium containing less water than torbernite

meta·tracheal \¦⸗⸗+\ *adj* [*meta-* + *tracheal*] **:** arranged in bands or laminae mostly having no association with vessels or vascular tracheids ⟨~ parenchyma⟩ — compare APOTRACHEAL, PARATRACHEAL, VASICENTRIC

meta·troph \'⸗⸗,träf, -rōf\ *n* -S [back-formation fr. *metatrophic*] **:** a metatrophic organism

meta·trophic \¦⸗⸗¦träfik, -rōf-\ *adj* [*meta-* + *-trophic*] **:** requiring complex organic sources of carbon and nitrogen for metabolic synthesis **:** HETEROTROPHIC — compare MESOTROPHIC — **me·tat·ro·phy** \mə'ta·trəfē\ *n* -ES

meta·tungstate \¦⸗⸗ *at* META- +\ *n* [ISV *metatungst-* (fr. *metatungstic acid*) + *-ate*] **:** a salt of metatungstic acid

meta·tungstic acid \¦⸗⸗+-\ *n* [ISV *meta-* + *tungstic acid*] **:** a yellow crystalline acid $H_8W_{12}O_{40}.xH_2O$ or $H_6[H_2(W_3O_{10})_4].24H_2O$ soluble in water

meta·type \'⸗⸗+,-\ *n* [*meta-* + *type*] **:** a topotype or homeotype determined by the original author of its species — **meta·typ·ic** \¦⸗⸗¦tipik\ *adj*

meta·uranopilite \¦⸗⸗+\ *n* **:** a mineral $(UO_2)_6(SO_6)(OH)_{10}.5H_2O$ consisting of a hydrous basic sulfate of uranyl with less water than uranopilite

meta·vanadate \"+\ *n* [ISV *metavanad-* (fr. *metavanadic acid*) + *-ate*] **:** a salt or ester of metavanadic acid

meta·vanadic acid \¦⸗⸗+-\ *n* [ISV *meta-* + *vanadic acid*] **:** an acid HVO_3 or $H_4V_4O_{12}$ obtained by precipitation from a solution of vanadium pentoxide in water

meta·variscite \¦⸗⸗+\ *n* [*meta-* + *variscite*] **:** a mineral $AlPO_4.2H_2O$ that consists of a hydrous phosphate of aluminum and is polymorphous with variscite and isomorphous with metastrengite

meta·vauxite \"+\ *n* [*meta-* + *vauxite*] **:** a mineral $FeAl_2(PO_4)_2(OH)_2.8H_2O$ consisting of a hydrous iron aluminum phosphate derived by alteration from vauxite

meta·voltine \"+\ *n* -S [ISV *meta-* + *volt-* (fr. *voltaite*) + *-ine*] **:** a mineral $(K, Na, Fe)_5Fe_3(SO_4)_6(OH)_2.9H_2O(?)$ consisting of a basic hydrous sulfate of iron, sodium, and potassium

meta·xenia \"+\ *n* [NL, fr. *meta-* + *xenia*] **:** the effect of a pollen parent on the developing maternal tissues of a seed or fruit outside the embryo and endosperm due to hormones produced by the embryo and endosperm after double fertilization — compare CARPOXENIA, XENIA

me·tax·ite \mə'tak,sīt\ *n* -S [G *metaxit,* fr. LGk *metaxa* raw silk + G *-it* -ite] **:** a mineral consisting of a fibrous serpentine

meta·xylem \¦⸗⸗ *at* META- +\ *n* [ISV *meta-* + *xylem*] **:** the part of the primary xylem that differentiates after the protoxylem and is typically distinguished by broader tracheids and vessels with pitted or reticulate walls

mé·ta·yage \¦med·ə¦yäzh, ¦mād-\ *n* -S [F, irreg. fr. *métayer* + *-age*] **:** the métayer system of farming land

mé·ta·yer \-¦yā\ *n* -S [F, fr. MF, fr. OF *meteer, meiteier,* fr. LL *medietat-, medietas* half + OF *-ier* -er — more at MOIETY] **:** one that cultivates land for a share of its yield usu. receiving stock, tools, and seed from the landlord

meta·zeunerite \¦⸗⸗ *at* META- +\ *n* [*meta-* + *zeunerite*] **:** a mineral $Cu(UO_2)_2(AsO_4)_2.8H_2O$ consisting of a hydrous arsenate of copper and uranium with less water than zeunerite

meta·zoa \,med·ə'zōə\ *n pl, cap* [NL, fr. *meta-* + *-zoa*] **:** a group that comprises all animals having the body when adult composed of numerous cells differentiated into tissues and organs and usu. a digestive cavity lined with specialized cells and that is used usu. to include the Coelenterata and all higher animals but sometimes is extended to include the Parazoa and Mesozoa — compare PROTOZOA

meta·zo·al \¦⸗⸗¦zōəl\ *or* **meta·zo·ic** \-ik\ *adj* [NL *Metazoa* + E *-al* or *-ic*] **:** METAZOAN

¹meta·zo·an \-ən\ *adj* [NL *Metazoa* + E *-an*] **:** of or relating to the Metazoa

²metazoan \"\ *n* -S **:** one of the Metazoa

met·a·zoea *also* **meta·zoaea** \¦⸗⸗+\ *n* [NL, fr. *meta-* + *zoea* or *zoaea*] **:** a larva of various higher crustaceans intermediate between the zoea and the megalops

meta·zo·on \,⸗⸗'zō,än\ *n, pl* **meta·zoa** \-ōə\ [NL, sing. of *Metazoa*] **:** one of the Metazoa

met·calfe bean \'met,kaf-, -,kəf-, -,kāf\ *n, usu cap M* [after J. K. *Metcalfe* who introduced it to the southwestern U. S. in the late 19th cent.] **1 :** a prostrate perennial bean (*Phaseolus metcalfei*) of the southwestern U. S. and adjacent Mexico that is sometimes cultivated for forage **2 :** the flat circular brownish black seed of the Metcalfe bean

¹mete \'mēt, *usu* -ēd·+V\ *vt* -ED/-ING/-S [ME *meten,* fr. OE *metan;* akin to OS *metan* to measure, OFris *meta,* MD *meten,* OHG *mezzan* to measure, ON *meta* to value, Goth *mitan* to measure, L *modus* measure, moderation, manner, *meditari* to meditate, *modestus* moderate, modest, *moderari* to moderate, OIr *midiur* I judge, Gk *medesthai* to be mindful of, *medimnos* grain measure; basic meaning: to measure] **1** *archaic* **a :** to find the quantity, dimensions, or capacity of by any rule or standard **:** MEASURE ⟨~*s* the thin air and weighs the flying sound —George Crabbe†1832⟩ **b :** to determine the value of **:** APPRAISE ⟨a pattern or a measure . . . by which his Grace must ~ the lives of others —Shak.⟩ **2 :** to assign by measure **:** deal out **:** ALLOT, APPORTION — usu. used with *out* ⟨~ out punishment⟩ ⟨so has my portion been *meted* out to me —Oscar Wilde⟩

²mete \"\ *n* -S **:** MEASURE ⟨sprinkled sugar over it with neither ~ nor measure —Della Lutes⟩

³mete \"\ *n* -S [AF, fr. L *meta* goal, boundary] **:** BOUNDARY — now used chiefly in the phrase *metes and bounds*

met·empiric \¦med·+\ *n* [*meta-* + *empiric* (adj. & n.)] **1 :** METEMPIRICS **2 :** METEMPIRICIST

met·empirical \"+\ *adj* [*meta-* + *empirical*] **:** of, relating to, or advocating metempirics — **met·empirically** \"+\ *adv*

met·empiricism \,med·+\ *n* [*metempiric* + *-ism*] **:** METEMPIRICS

met·empiricist \"+\ *n* [*meta-* + *empiricist*] **:** one who advocates or practices metempirics

met·empirics \"+\ *n pl but sing in constr* [pl. of *metempiric*] **:** the study of concepts and relationships conceived as beyond and yet related to knowledge gained empirically ⟨~ sweeps out of this region in search of the otherness of things —G.H. Lewes⟩

met·em·psy·chic \¦med·,em¦sīkik, -d·əm-\ *or* **metem·psy·cho·sic** \mə¦tem(p)sə¦kōsik, -d·əm,sī¦k-, -ōzik\ *also* **metem·psy·cho·si·cal** \-ōsəkəl, -ōzə-\ *adj* [*metempsychic* fr. LL *metempsychosis* + E *-ic; metempsychosic* or *metempsichosical* fr. LL *metempsychosis* + E *-ic* or *-ical*] **:** of or relating to metempsychosis

me·tem·psy·chose \mə'tem(p)sə,kōs, ,med·əm'sī,k-, -ōz\ *also* **metem·psy·cho·size** \mə,tem(p)sə'kō,sīz, ,med·əm,sī'k-\ *vt* -ED/-ING/-S [*metempsychose,* back-formation fr. LL *metempsychosis; metempsychosize* fr. LL *metempsychosis* + E *-ize*] **:** to translate or transfer (as the soul) from one body to another

metem·psy·cho·sis \mə,tem(p)sə'kōsəs, ,med·,em,sī'k-, -d·əm-,sī'k-\ *n* [LL, fr. Gk *metempsychōsis,* fr. *metempsychousthai* to undergo metempsychosis, fr. *meta-* + *empsychos* animate, fr. *em-* en- + *psychē* soul, spirit] **:** the passing of the soul at death into another body either human or animal **:** transmigration of souls ⟨could remember all the previous lives in his *metempsychoses* —Erwin Schrödinger⟩ — contrasted with *metensomatosis*

met·encephalic \ˌmed·+\ *adj* [NL *metencephalon* + E *-ic*] : of or relating to the metencephalon

met·encephalon \ˌmed·+\ *n* [NL, fr. *meta-* + *encephalon*] **1 a** : the anterior segment of the rhombencephalon **b** : the cerebellum and pons that evolve from this segment **2** : MYELENCEPHALON **b** — used only when the anterior segment is designated *epencephalon*

met·en·so·ma·to·sis \ˌmed·ˌen,sōmə'tōsəs\ *n, pl* **metensomatoses** [LL, fr. LGk *metensōmatōsis*, fr. Gk *meta-* + *en-* + *sōmat-, sōma* body + *-ōsis* -osis — more at -SOME (body)] : the migration into one body of different souls — contrasted with *metempsychosis*

met·en·ter·on *n* [NL, fr. *meta-* + *enteron*] **1** : the alimentary canal modified in any manner from the primitive archenteron **2** : one of the radial digestive chambers of an anthozoan — compare MESENTERON — **met·en·ter·on·ic** \ˌ=ˌ==ˈränik\ *adj*

me·teo·graph \'mēd·ēə,graf, -räf\ *n* [*meteo-* (fr. ¹*meteor*) + *-graph*] : METEOROGRAPH

¹me·te·or \'mēd·ēə(r), -ētē-, -ē,ó(ə)r, -ó(ə)\ *n* -s [ME, fr. MF *meteore*, fr. ML *meteorum*, fr. Gk *meteōron* astronomical phenomenon, thing in the heaven above, fr. neut. of *meteōros* high in air, raised off the ground, fr. *meta-* + *-eōros* (akin to Gk *aeirein* to lift, raise, *aiora* suspension) — more at AORTA] **1** : a phenomenon or appearance in the atmosphere (as lightning, whirlwind, rainbow, snowfall) ⟨all day the hoary ~ fell —J.G.Whittier⟩ ⟨the ~ of the ocean air shall sweep the clouds no more —O.W.Holmes †1894⟩ **2 a** : a streak of light in the night sky produced by the passage through the earth's atmosphere of one of the countless small particles of solid matter in the solar system **b** : the small particle itself or any physical phenomenon associated with it

²meteor \"\ *adj* : METEORIC 3

meteor- *or* **meteoro-** *comb form* [MF or Gk; MF, fr. Gk *meteōr-* high in air (fr. *meteōros*), *meteōro-* astronomical phenomenon, thing in the heaven above, fr. *meteōron*] **1** : meteor ⟨*meteor*oid⟩ **2** : weather and climate ⟨*meteoro*biology⟩

meteor *abbr* meteorological; meteorology

meteor crater *also* **meteorite crater** *n* : a depression in the earth's surface produced by the impact of a large meteorite

meteor echo *n* : a radar echo from the ionized cylinder of air made by the passage of a meteor through the atmosphere

me·te·or·ic \ˌmēd·ē'ȯrik, -ētē-, -'är-, -ēk\ *adj* [ML *meteoricus* elevated, fr. L *meteorus* high, exalted (fr. Gk *meteōros*) + *-icus* -ic — more at METEOR] **1 a** : of, relating to, or dependent on the earth's atmosphere ⟨~ phenomena⟩ ⟨~ flowers⟩ **b** : derived from the earth's atmosphere — used esp. of water ⟨water precipitated from the atmosphere, ~ water, which falls as rain or snow —P.G.Worcester⟩ — compare CONNATE 5, MAGMATIC **2** [¹*meteor* + *-ic*] : of, relating to or composed of meteors ⟨~ shower⟩ **3** : resembling a meteor in brilliance, rapidity, or short duration ⟨a young executive whose rise in his company has been ~ —*Modern Industry*⟩ ⟨the ~ rise, temporary supremacy, and abrupt fall of this liberal coalition —P.R.Levin⟩ ⟨the brief ~ career of a Negro jazz musician —Jerome Stone⟩ — **me·te·or·i·cal·ly** \-rək(ə)lē, -rēk-, -li\ *adv*

meteoric iron *n* : iron of meteoric origin — compare METEORITE

meteoric paper *n* : a paperlike substance consisting of the dried remains of filamentous green algae found floating in the air

me·te·or·ism \'mēd·ēə,rizəm, -ētē-\ *n* -s [F *météorisme*, fr. MF, fr. Gk *meteōrismos*, lit., act of lifting, fr. *meteōrizein* to lift, fr. *meteōr-* high in air, exalted (fr. *meteōros*) + *-izein* -ize] : gaseous distention of the stomach or intestine : TYMPANITES, BLOAT 2

me·te·or·ist \-ˌrəst\ *n* -s : a specialist in the study of meteors

me·te·or·it·al \ˌ=ˌ==ˈrīd·ᵊl\ *adj* [*meteorite* + *-al*] : METEORITIC

me·te·or·ite \'mēd·ēə,rīt, -ētē-\ *n* -s [¹*meteor* + *-ite*] : a solid particle from interplanetary space that survives the destructive effects of a flight through the earth's atmosphere and falls to the ground in one or more pieces

me·te·or·it·ic \ˌ=ˌ==ˈrid·ik\ *or* **me·te·or·it·i·cal** \-ə̇kəl\ *adj* : of, relating to, or caused by meteorites ⟨~ crater⟩ ⟨~ hypothesis⟩

me·te·or·it·i·cist \ˌ=ˌ==ˈrid·əsəst\ *n* -s : a specialist in meteoritics

me·te·or·it·ics \-'rid·iks\ *n pl but sing in constr* [*meteorite* + *-ics*] : a science that deals with meteors and meteorites

me·te·o·ro·biology \ˌmēd·ēə(ˌ)rō+\ *n* [*meteor-* + *biology*] : a science that deals with the effects of weather and climate on living beings

me·te·or·o·gram \ˌmēd·ē'ȯrə,gram\ *n* [ISV *meteor-* + *-gram*] : a record made by a meteorograph

me·te·or·o·graph \-,graf, -räf\ *n* [*meteor-* + *-graph*] : an autographic apparatus for recording simultaneously several meteorologic elements (as air pressure, temperature, moisture) — **me·te·or·o·graph·ic** \ˌ=ˌ=ˌ==ˈgrafik\ *adj* — **me·te·o·rog·ra·phy** \ˌmēd·ēə'rägrəfē\ *n* -ES

me·te·or·oid \'mēd·ēə,rȯid\ *n* -s [¹*meteor* + *-oid*] **1** : a meteor revolving around the sun **2** : a meteor particle itself without relation to the phenomena it produces when entering the earth's atmosphere

me·te·or·o·lite \ˌmēd·ē'ȯrə,līt\ *also* **me·te·or·o·lithe** \-lith\ *n* -s [partly fr. *meteor-* + *-lite* and partly fr. F *météorolithe*, fr. *météoro-* meteor- + *-lithe* -lith] : METEORITE — **me·te·or·o·lit·ic** \ˌ=ˌ=ˌ==ˈlid·ik\ *adj*

me·te·oro·log·i·cal \ˌmēd·ēˌȯrəˈläjəkəl, -ētˌ, ˌēˌär-, ˌēər-, ÷ ˌər(ə)ˈl-, ÷ ˌēərˈl-, -jēk-\ *also* **me·te·oro·log·ic** \-jik,-jēk\ *adj* [fr. MF *meteorologique* meteorological (fr. Gk *meteōrologikos*, fr. *meteōrologia* meteorology + *-ikos* -ic) or Gk *meteōrologikos* + E *-al; meteorologic* fr. F *météorologique* (fr. MF *meteorologique*) or Gk *meteōrologikos*] : of or relating to meteorology ⟨~ chart⟩ ⟨~ report⟩ ⟨~ factors⟩ — **me·te·oro·log·i·cal·ly** \-jək(ə)lē, -jēk-, -li\ *adv*

meteorological element *n* : any of the subjects of meteorological observation (as temperature, relative humidity, or barometric pressure)

meteorological tide *n* : tidal constituents resulting from variations in somewhat periodically recurring weather conditions

me·te·o·rol·o·gist \ˌmēd·ēəˈräləjəst, -ētˌ, ÷ ˌəˈr-\ *n* -s [Gk *meteōrologos* meteorologist (fr. *meteōro-* meteor- + *-logos* -logue) + E *-ist*] : a specialist in meteorology

me·te·o·rol·o·gy \-jē,-ji\ *n* -ES [F or Gk; F *météorologie*, fr. MF, fr. Gk *meteōrologia*, fr. *meteōro-* astronomical phenomenon, thing in the heaven above (fr. *meteōron*) + *-logia* -logy — more at METEOR] **1 a** : a science that deals with the atmosphere and its phenomena (as variations of heat, moisture, or winds) — compare CLIMATOLOGY **b** : a science that deals with weather and weather forecasting **2** : the atmospheric phenomena and weather of a region ⟨the ~ of the Gulf of Mexico⟩

me·te·o·rous \'mēd·ēərəs, mə'tē-\ *adj* [¹*meteor* + *-ous*] : METEORIC ⟨~ pleasures which dance before us and are dissipated —Samuel Johnson⟩

meteors *pl of* METEOR

meteor shower *also* **meteoric shower** *n* : the phenomenon observed when members of a meteor swarm encounter the earth's atmosphere and their luminous paths appear to diverge from a single point or radiant in the sky

meteor swarm *n* : a group of meteoroids that have closely similar orbits around the sun — see METEOR SHOWER

meteor trail *n* **1** : a bright streak in the sky of very short duration caused by the shining of a meteor during its passage through the atmosphere **2** : the track of a meteor

meteor train *n* : a persistent glow sometimes left by a meteor after the meteor trail has faded out and caused by luminous matter left in the meteoroid's wake

met·epimeral \ˌmed·+\ *adj* [NL *metepimeron* + E *-al*] : of or relating to a metepimeron

met·epimeron \ˌ=+\ *n* [NL, fr. *meta-* + *epimeron*] : the epimeron of the metathorax of an insect

met·episternal \ˌ=+\ *adj* [NL *metepisternum* + E *-al*] : of or relating to a metepisternum

met·episternum \ˌ=+\ *n* [NL, fr. *meta-* + *episternum*] : the episternum of the metathorax of an insect

¹me·ter \'mēd·ə(r), -ētə-\ *n* -s *see -er in Explan Notes* [ME *meter, metre*, fr. OE & MF; OE *mēter*, fr. L *metrum*, fr. Gk *metron* meter, measure; MF *metre*, fr. OF, fr. L *metrum* — more at MEASURE] **1 a** : systematically arranged and measured rhythm in verse ⟨the only strict antithesis to prose is ~ —William Wordsworth⟩: (1) : rhythm that continuously repeats a single basic pattern or rhythmic system ⟨iambic ~⟩ ⟨dactylic ~⟩ — compare CADENCE (2) : rhythm characterized by the regular recurrence of a systematic arrangement of such basic patterns or systems into larger figures ⟨a verse with sapphic ~⟩ **b** : a measure or unit of metrical verse : METRON — usu. used in combination ⟨di*meter*⟩ ⟨penta*meter*⟩; compare FOOT **c** : a fixed metrical pattern : verse form ⟨the heroic couplet was a favorite ~ of the neoclassic poets⟩ **d** *archaic* : a metrical composition : VERSE ⟨a pebble of the brook warbled out these ~s meet —William Blake⟩ **e** : rhythm in verse **2 a** : the part of rhythmical structure concerned with the division of a musical composition into measures by means of regularly recurring accents with each measure consisting of a uniform number of beats or time units the first of which has the strongest accent **b** : the distribution of long and short notes or tones within measures : TIME **syn** see RHYTHM

²meter \"\ *vb* **metered; metered; metering** \-əriŋ *also* 'mē·triŋ\ **meters** *see -er in Explan Notes* [ME *metren*, fr. *metre, meter*, n.] *vi* : to engage in poetic composition : VERSIFY ~ *vt* **1** : to put into meter : give metrical form to **2** : to analyze metrically : SCAN ⟨expansion of the liquid after it is ~ed —E.E.Reed⟩

³meter \"\ *n* -s [ME, fr. *meten* to mete, measure + *-er* — more at METE] : one that measures; *esp* : an official measurer of commodities

⁴meter \"\ *n* -s *see -er in Explan Notes* [F *mètre*, fr. Gk *metron* measure] : the basic metric unit of length that is equal to the distance between two lines on a platinum-iridium bar kept at the International Bureau of Weights and Measures near Paris, is approximately equal to 39.37 inches, and is equal to 1,650,-763.73 wavelengths of the orange-red light of excited krypton of mass number 86 — see METRIC SYSTEM table

⁵meter \"\ *n* -s *often attrib* [*-meter*] **1 a** : an instrument for measuring and recording the amount of something (as water, gas, electricity) as it flows **b** : a device (as a valve in a carburetor) that regulates the flow of a fluid **2 a** : an instrument for measuring and usu. recording distance, time, weight, speed, or intensity **b** : an instrument for measuring and recording the amount of a commodity or service consumed: as (1) : PARKING METER (2) : POSTAGE METER **3 a** : the impression made by a postage meter on a piece of mail **b** : a philatelic cover bearing such an impression

⁶meter \"\ *vb* **metered; metered; metering** \-əriŋ *also* 'mē·triŋ\ **meters** *vt* **1** : to measure by means of a meter ⟨water . . . is ~ed and charged for —Tom Marvel⟩ **2** : to supply (fuel, oil, or other fluid) in a measured or regulated amount ⟨fuel is then ~ed to the engine by the idle adjusting needle —H.F.Blanchard & Ralph Ritchen⟩ **3 a** : to print postal indicia on by means of a postage meter **b** : to imprint a revenue stamp on by means of a machine similar to a postage meter ~ *vi* : to meter a fluid (as fuel or oil) ⟨the drilled opening in the ~ing jet controls the amount of fuel that can pass through the main fuel supply system —William Landon⟩ ⟨a ~ing pump for molasses⟩

-me·ter \məd·ə(r), mətə-, *esp in words in which a letter other than "o" precedes the "m", alternatively or only* ˌmed·ə(r) *or* ˌmētə-\ *n comb form* -s [F *-mètre*, fr. Gk *metron* measure — more at MEASURE] : instrument or means for measuring ⟨baro*meter*⟩ ⟨calori*meter*⟩ ⟨volta*meter*⟩

meter angle *n* [⁴*meter*] : the angle between the visual axes and the median plane when the eyes are focused on a point at a distance of one meter in that plane

meter bar *n* [⁴*meter*] : a metal bar on which a meter length has been marked to serve as the standard length of a meter

meter boat *n* [⁴*meter*] : a racing sloop designed to the international rule of measurement expressed in meters

meter cancellation *n* [⁵*meter*] : an impression on mail by a postage meter indicating the amount of postage paid and usu. the place and date of mailing — compare CANCELLATION 2

meter-candle \'==ˌ==\ *n* [⁴*meter*] : LUX

meter-candle-second \'==ˌ==ˌ==\ *n* : a unit of exposure to light equivalent to an illumination of one lux for one second

metered mail *n* [fr. *metered*, past part. of ⁶*meter*] : prepaid mail requiring no postage stamps but marked by an electrical machine that is set and controlled by the post office

meter impression *n* [⁵*meter*] : the postal indicia printed on a piece of mail by a postage meter — called also *postage impression*

meter-kilogram \'==ˌ==ˌ=\ *n* [⁴*meter*] : KILOGRAM-METER

meter-kilogram-second \'==ˌ==ˌ==\ *adj* : of, relating to, or being a system of units based on the meter as the unit of length, the kilogram as the unit of mass, and the mean solar second as the unit of time — abbr. *mks*

meter mail *n* [⁵*meter*] : mail bearing a meter impression

meter·man \'==mən\ *n, pl* **metermen** [⁵*meter* + *man*] : a man trained to read and adjust meters (as gas meters)

meter mark *n* [⁵*meter*] : METER IMPRESSION

meter postage *n* [⁵*meter*] **1** : postage paid through use of a postage meter **2** : METER STAMP

meter rate *n* [⁵*meter*] : a utility service rate (as for water, gas, electricity) based on the number of units a customer consumes as measured by a meter

meters *pl of* METER, *pres 3d sing of* METER

meter slogan *n* [⁵*meter*] : an advertising slogan on metered mail imprinted along with the postal indicia

meter stamp *n* [⁵*meter*] : postal indicia printed by a postage meter

meterstick \'==ˌ=\ *n* [⁴*meter* + *stick*] : a measuring stick that is one meter long and is usu. marked off in centimeters and millimeters

metes *pres 3d sing of* METE, *pl of* METE

metes and bounds *n pl* [trans. of AF *metes et boundes*] **1** : the boundaries or limits of a tract of land; *specif* : the boundaries of land established by reference to natural or artificial monuments along it (as a stream, ditch, fence, road) as distinguished from those established by beginning at a fixed starting point and running therefrom by stated compass courses and stated distances — compare BUTTS AND BOUNDS **2** : established limits ⟨rules formulated by the Supreme Court in setting the *metes and bounds* of freedom of religion —E.S. Newman⟩

met·estrous *or* **met·oestrous** \(ˈ)med·+\ *adj* [NL *metestrus, metoestrus* + E *-ous*] : of or relating to metestrus

met·estrus *or* **met·oestrus** \(ˈ)med·+\ *also* **met·aestrus** \"\ *or* **met·estrum** *or* **met·oestrum** \(ˈ)med·+\ *n* [NL, fr. *meta-* + *estrus* or *oestrus* or *estrum* or *oestrum*] : the period of regression that follows estrus in the mammalian sexual cycle

metewand \'=ˌ=\ *or* **meteyard** \'=ˌ=\ *n* [ME *metwande* or *met yerde*, fr. *meten* to mete, measure + *wande* wand or *yerde* yard — more at METE] : a measuring rod

metgl *abbr* meteorological

meth- *or* **metho-** *comb form* [ISV, fr. *methyl*] : methyl ⟨*metha*crylic⟩ ⟨*metho*bromide⟩

meth *abbr* **1** method **2** methylated

metha·choline \ˌmethə+\ *n* [*meth-* + *acetylcholine*] : a parasympathomimetic drug $[(CH_3)_3NCH_2CH(CH_3)OOCCH_3]OH$ administered in the form of its crystalline chloride or bromide; acetyl-β-methyl-choline

meth·acrylate \(ˈ)meth +\ *n* [ISV *methacryl-* (fr. *methacrylic acid*) + *-ate*] **1** : a salt or ester of methacrylic acid **2** *or* **methacrylate resin** *or* **methacrylate plastic** : an acrylic resin or acrylic plastic made by polymerization of a derivative of methacrylic acid; *esp* : METHYL METHACRYLATE 2

meth·acrylic acid \ˌmeth+-\ *n* [ISV *meth-* + *acrylic*] : an unsaturated liquid or crystalline acid $CH_2{=}C(CH_3)COOH$ that is isomeric with crotonic acid, that occurs in Roman chamomile oil but is usu. obtained by reaction of acetone cyanohydrin and sulfuric acid, and that resembles acrylic acid in ease of polymerization; α-methyl-acrylic acid

metha·done \'methə,dōn\ *also* **metha·don** \-,dän\ *n* -s [*dimethylamino-* + ¹*diphenyl* + *heptanone*] : a narcotic drug $C_2H_5COC(C_6H_5)_2CH_2CH(CH_3)N(CH_3)_2$ administered usu. in the form of its bitter crystalline hydrochloride for the relief of pain; 6-dimethylamino-4,4-diphenyl-3-heptanone; *also* : the hydrochloride or other salt of this compound

meth·allyl \(ˈ)meth+\ *n* [*meth-* + *allyl*] : the beta- or 2-methyl-allyl radical $CH_2{=}C(CH_3)CH_2{-}$

meth·amphetamine \ˌ=+\ *n* [*meth-* + *amphetamine*] : an amine $C_6H_5CH_2CH(CH_3)NHCH_3$ used in the form of its crystalline hydrochloride as a stimulant for the central nervous system and in the treatment of obesity; *dextro-N-α-dimethyl-phenethyl-amine* — called also *deoxyephedrine*

meth·a·nal \'methə,nal\ *n* -s [ISV *methane* + *-al*] : FORMALDEHYDE

meth·a·na·tion \ˌmethə'nāshən\ *n* -s [*methane* + *-ation*] : METHANIZATION

meth·ane \'me,thān\ *n* -s [ISV *meth-* + *-ane*] : a colorless odorless flammable gaseous saturated hydrocarbon CH_4 that is lighter than air and forms explosive mixtures with air or oxygen, that occurs naturally as a product of decomposition of organic matter in marshes and mines and esp. in natural gas and is formed also in the carbonization of coal, and that is used chiefly as a fuel and as a raw material in the manufacture of carbon black and in chemical synthesis — see FIREDAMP; compare MARSH GAS

methane series *n* : the homologous series of saturated open-chain hydrocarbons C_nH_{2n+2} of which methane is the first and lowest member followed by ethane, propane, the butanes, the pentanes, the hexanes, and higher members — called also *paraffin series;* compare ¹PARAFFIN 2

meth·a·ni·za·tion \ˌmethənə'zāshən, -ˌnī'z-\ *n* -s : the process of methanizing

meth·a·nize \'==ˌnīz\ *vt* -ED/-ING/-S [*methane* + *-ize*] : to convert (as a mixture of carbon monoxide and hydrogen) to methane

methano- *comb form* [ISV, fr. *methane*] : methylene as a bridging group — in names of polycyclic chemical compounds ⟨1,4-*methano*naphthalene⟩

meth·a·no·ic acid \ˌmethə'nōik-\ *n* [ISV *methanal* + *-o-* + *-ic*] : FORMIC ACID

meth·a·nol \'methə,nōl, -nȯl\ *n* -s [ISV *methane* + *-ol*] : a light volatile pungent flammable poisonous liquid alcohol CH_3OH formed in the destructive distillation of wood but now usu. made synthetically (as by catalytic reaction of carbon monoxide and hydrogen under pressure) and used chiefly as a solvent, antifreeze, denaturant for ethyl alcohol, and raw material in the synthesis of formaldehyde and other chemicals — called also *methyl alcohol, wood alcohol;* see CARBINOL, PYROLIGNEOUS ACID

meth·a·no·lic \ˌ==ˈnōlik, -näl-\ *adj* : containing methanol usu. as solvent

meth·a·nol·y·sis \ˌ==ˈnäləsəs\ *n* [NL, irreg. fr. ISV *methanol* + NL *-lysis*] : alcoholysis with methanol

meth·a·no·mon·a·da·ce·ae \ˌmethə(ˌ)nō,mänə'dāsē,ē\ *n pl, cap* [NL, fr. *Methanomonad-, Methanomonas*, type genus (fr. ISV *methane* + NL *-o-* + *-monad-, -monas*) + *-aceae*] : a family of gram-negative rod-shaped soil and water bacteria (order Pseudomonadales) that obtain energy by oxidizing simple carbon and hydrogen compounds and are often motile by means of polar flagella

meth·an·the·line \me'than(t)thə,lēn, -ˌlən\ *n* -s [*meth-* + *xanthene* carboxylate + *-ine*] : an anticholinergic drug usu. administered in the form of its crystalline bromide $C_{21}H_{26}BrNO_3$ in the treatment of peptic ulcers

me·theg·lin \mə'theglən\ *n* -s [W *meddyglyn*, fr. *meddyg* physician (fr. L *medicus*) + *llyn* liquor, lake — more at MEDICAL, LINN] : a beverage usu. made of fermented honey and water and often spiced or medicated : MEAD

met·hem·albumin \ˌmet,hēm+\ *n* [*meta-* + *hem-* + *albumin*] : an albumin complex with hematin found in plasma during diseases (as blackwater fever) that are associated with extensive hemolysis

met·hemoglobin \(ˌ)met+\ *n* [ISV *meta-* + *hemoglobin*] : a soluble brown crystalline basic pigment that is found in normal blood in much smaller amounts than hemoglobin, that is formed from blood, hemoglobin, or oxyhemoglobin by oxidation (as by ozone, peroxide, ferricyanide, permanganate), and that differs from hemoglobin in containing ferric iron instead of ferrous iron and in being unable to combine reversibly with molecular oxygen — called also *ferrihemoglobin, hemiglobin*

met·hemoglobinemia \ˌmet+\ *n* -s [NL, fr. ISV *methemoglobin* + NL *-emia*] : the presence of methemoglobin in the blood due to conversion of part of the hemoglobin to this inactive form

met·hemoglobinuria \"+\ *n* -s [NL, fr. ISV *methemoglobin* + NL *-uria*] : the presence of methemoglobin in the urine

me·the·na·mine \mə'thēnə,mēn, -then-, -ˌmən\ *n* [*methene* + *amine*] : hexamethylenetetramine used as a urinary antiseptic

meth·ene \'me,thēn\ *n* -s [ISV *meth-* + *-ene*] **1** : METHYLENE **2** : a complex unsaturated derivative of methane of the general formula $R{-}CH{=}R'$ ⟨di-pyrryl-*methene* $HNC_4H_3{-}CH{=}C_4H_3N$⟩

meth·e·nyl \'methə,nil\ *n* -s [ISV *methene* + *-yl*] : METHYLIDYNE

mether *var of* MADDER

me·thex·is \mə'theksəs\ *n* -ES [Gk, fr. *metechein* to share in, fr. *meta-* + *echein* to have — more at SCHEME] : PARTICIPATION 2

meth·ide \'me,thīd\ *n* -s [*meth-* + *-ide*] **1** : a binary compound of methyl usu. with a metal ⟨mercuric ~ $Hg(CH_3)_2$⟩ **2** : a compound that contains a methylene group as part of a quinonoid structure and that is formed as an intermediate in the condensation of a phenol and formaldehyde to yield a resin ⟨quinone ~ $O{=}C_6H_4{=}CH_2$⟩

me·thig·lum \mə'thigləm\ *dial var of* METHEGLIN

meth·ine \'me,thēn, -ˌthən\ *n* -s [ISV *meth-* + *-ine*] : METHYLIDYNE — used esp. in names of classes of cyanine dyes and other polymethine dyes

methine basic orange G *n, usu cap M&B&O* : a basic dye — see DYE table I (under *Basic Orange 21*)

methine basic yellow 3G *n, usu cap M&B&Y* : a basic dye — see DYE table I (under *Basic Yellow 11*)

me·thinks \mə'thiŋ(k)s, mē'-\ *vb impersonal, past 3d sing* **me·thought** \-'thȯt\ *pres 3d sing* **methinks** [ME *me thinketh*, fr. OE *mē thyncth*, fr. *mē* (suppletive dat. of *ic* I) + *thyncth*, 3d sing. pres. indic. of *thyncan* to seem — more at ME, THINK] *archaic* : it seems to me ⟨~ that I have heard them echo back —William Wordsworth⟩ ⟨*methought* a star came down from heaven —P.B.Shelley⟩

meth·io·dal sodium \mə'thīə,dal\ *n* [*methiodal* fr. *meth-* + *iod-* + *-al*] : a crystalline salt CH_2ISO_3Na used as a radiopaque contrast medium in intravenous urography; sodium iodo-methane-sulfonate

meth·iodide \məth+\ *n* [*meth-* + *iodide*] : a compound with methyl iodide

meth·ion·ic acid \ˌmethīˌänik-\ *n* [*methionic* fr. *meth-* + *thionic*] : a deliquescent crystalline acid $CH_2(SO_3H)_2$ formed from acetylene or acetamide by the action of fuming sulfuric acid; methane-disulfonic acid

me·thi·o·nine \mə'thīə,nēn, -ˌnən\ *n* [ISV *me-* (fr. *methyl*) blend of *meth-* + *thion-* + *-ine*] : a crystalline essential amino acid $CH_3SCH_2CH_2CH(NH_2)COOH$ that occurs in the L-form as a constituent of many proteins (as casein and egg albumin), that is important esp. as a source of sulfur for the biosynthesis of cystine and as a source of methyl groups for transmethylation reactions (as in the biosynthesis of choline, creatine, and adrenaline), that is prepared synthetically in the racemic DL-form, and that is used as a dietary supplement for humans and their domestic mammals and poultry and in the treatment of fatty infiltration of the liver; α-amino-γ-methyl-mercapto-butyric acid

metho- — see METH-

metho·bromide \ˌmethō+\ *n* [*meth-* + *bromide*] : a compound with methyl bromide

meth·od \'methəd\ *n* -s [MF or L; MF *methode*, fr. L *methodus*, fr. Gk *methodos*, fr. *meta-* + *hodos* way — more at CEDE] **1** : a procedure or process for attaining an object: as **a** *obs* : the medical system of the methodists **b** (1) : a systematic procedure, technique, or set of rules employed in philosophical inquiry : a particular approach to problems of truth or knowledge ⟨the pragmatic ~ tries to interpret each notion by tracing its respective practical consequences —William James⟩ ⟨the dialectical ~ assumes the primacy of matter⟩ ⟨the ~ of the positivists applied to philosophy the procedures of the natural sciences⟩ (2) : a discipline or system sometimes considered a branch of logic that deals with the principles applicable to inquiry into or exposition of some subject (3) : a systematic procedure, technique, or mode of inquiry employed by or proper to a particular science, art, or discipline : METHODOLOGY ⟨the historical ~⟩ ⟨the ~ of logic⟩ ⟨exploring the broadest possibilities of iconographic ~ —Harry Bober⟩ (4) **:** a systematic plan followed in presenting material for instruction ⟨the lecture ~⟩ ⟨a course in ~s⟩ (5) **:** a particular way of viewing, organizing, and giving shape and significance to artistic materials ⟨hadn't found his ~, but he had definitely found his theme —Graham Greene⟩ ⟨~ . . . can be determined only from the work as a whole —M.K.Spears⟩ ⟨~ and sensibility ought never . . . to be kept long separate —R.P. Blackmur⟩ **c** (1) **:** a way, technique, or process of or for doing something ⟨there are three ~s of touring Britain by car —Richard Joseph⟩ ⟨found their respective working ~s congenial —*Current Biog.*⟩ ⟨often slow in their business ~s —T.R.Ybarra⟩ ⟨to whom she owed her excellent ~ —*Opera News*⟩ (2) **:** a body of skills or techniques ⟨deeply professional, learned in the art of the novel, heavily armed with ~ —J.D.Scott b.1917⟩ **2 a :** orderly arrangement, development, or classification **:** PLAN, DESIGN ⟨the book is completely lacking in ~⟩ **b** *obs* (1) **:** a methodical exposition (2) **:** a table of contents (3) **:** an arrangement that follows a plan or design **c :** orderliness and regularity or habitual practice of them in action ⟨thrift was as much in her nature as ~ —Sylvia T. Warner⟩ ⟨time enough to do everything if only you used ~ —Angela Thirkell⟩

syn METHOD, MODE, MANNER, WAY, FASHION, and SYSTEM can all indicate the means used or the procedure followed in doing a given kind of work or achieving a given end. METHOD can apply to any plan or procedure but usu. implies an orderly, logical, effective plan or procedure, connoting also regularity ⟨the crude *methods* of trial and error —Henry Suzzallo⟩ ⟨the *method* of this book is to present a series of successive scenes of English life —G.M.Trevelyan⟩ ⟨Marx's doctrine is not a system of scientific truths, it merely represents a *method* — one possible approach to social and historical reflection —Paolo Milano⟩ ⟨surely not to leave to fitful chance the things that *method* and system and science should order and adjust —B.N. Cardozo⟩ MODE, sometimes interchangeable with METHOD, seldom implies order or logic, suggesting rather custom, tradition, or personal preference ⟨a rational *mode* of dealing with the insane —W.R.Inge⟩ ⟨this intuition is essentially an aesthetic *mode* of apprehension —H.J.Muller⟩ ⟨the *mode* of reproduction of plants and animals, however, is fundamentally identical —*Encyc. Americana*⟩ MANNER usu. suggests a personal or peculiar course or procedure, often interchanging with MODE in this sense ⟨the *manner* by which the present pattern of land ownership in this country has evolved —A.F.Gustafson⟩ ⟨it is not consistent with his *manner* of writing Latin —G.C. Sellery⟩ ⟨bearing loaves of sweet bread and of cornbread made with yeast in the Portuguese *manner* —Dana Burnet⟩ WAY is general and interchangeable with METHOD, MODE, or MANNER ⟨a special *way* to raise orchids⟩ ⟨the *way* the machine works⟩ ⟨the town's *way* of life⟩ ⟨one's *way* of tying his tie⟩ FASHION, in this comparison, may be distinguished from WAY in often suggesting a more superficial origin or source as in a mere fashion or ephemeral style ⟨was so popular that his subjects took to wearing monocles, in his *fashion* —*Time*⟩ ⟨Harvard has stoutly and successfully resisted the *fashion* by which the grounds of an American college have come to be known as a campus —*Official Register of Harvard Univ.*⟩ ⟨who were poor in a *fashion* unknown to North America —Herbert Agar⟩ SYSTEM suggests a fully developed, often carefully formulated method, usu. emphasizing the idea of rational orderliness ⟨every new discovery claims to form an addition to the *system* of science as transmitted from the past —Michael Polanyi⟩ ⟨behavior which is not in accord with the individual's *system* elicits responses of fear —Ralph Linton⟩ ⟨an earnest plea for radical reformation of the *system* of assessment and taxation —C.A.Duniway⟩

¹me·thod·ic \mə'thädik, me'-, -dēk\ *adj* [MF *methodique*, fr. L *methodicus*, fr. Gk *methodikos*, fr. *methodos* + *-ikos* -ic] **1** *obs* **:** METHODICAL 2 **2 :** done or acting with method **:** of or relating to method **:** METHODICAL, SYSTEMATIC ⟨~ religious exercise —Cecil Sprigge⟩ ⟨an attitude of ~ doubt⟩

²methodic \"\ *n* -s **:** METHODIST 2

me·thod·i·cal \-dəkəl, -dēk-\ *adj* [MF *methodique* + E *-al*] **1 a :** arranged with regard to method **:** characterized by method or orderliness **:** disposed or performed with method or order ⟨~ arrangement⟩ **b :** habitually proceeding according to method **:** SYSTEMATIC ⟨in habits he was regular and ~ —A.W.Long⟩ **2 :** of, relating to, or constituting an ancient school of physicians — compare ¹METHODIST **3 :** of or relating to method ⟨meeting these ~ demands, it provides a theory of change —K.R.Popper⟩ **syn** see ORDERLY

me·thod·i·cal·ly \-k(ə)lē, -li\ *adv* **:** in a methodical manner **:** SYSTEMATICALLY ⟨chewing slowly and ~ —J.E.Macdonnell⟩

me·thod·i·cal·ness \-kəlnəs\ *n* -ES **:** the quality or state of being methodical

methodies *pl of* METHODY

meth·od·ism \'methə,dizəm\ *n* -s **1** *cap* **:** the doctrines, polity, and worship peculiar to Methodists **2 :** methodical procedure **:** excessive devotion to methods

¹meth·od·ist \-dəst\ *n* -s [*method* + *-ist*] **1 a :** a person devoted to some method or laying great stress on method ⟨the ~s are many and the men of vision very few —J.H.Randall⟩ **b** *archaic* **:** SYSTEMATIST 2 **2 :** a member of an ancient school of physicians basing its proceedings on theory and reasoning rather than observation of the patient's state and concentrating its attention esp. on the pores, an acute disease being indicative of their contraction and chronic disease being associated with their relaxation **3** *usu cap* **:** a member or adherent of a denomination of trinitarian Protestant Christians starting as a revival within the Church of England but later separating from that church, adopting a modified episcopacy as its form of polity in America, and emphasizing an Arminian rather than a Calvinist theology in the area of doctrine

²methodist \"\ *adj, usu cap* **:** of or relating to the Methodists or Methodism

meth·od·is·tic \¦==¦distik\ *adj, usu cap* **:** of, relating to, or characteristic of Methodists or Methodism **:** resembling a Methodist or Methodism ⟨the government was *Methodistic* —F.S. Mead⟩ — **meth·od·is·ti·cal** \-təkəl\ *adj, usu cap* — **meth·od·is·ti·cal·ly** \-k(ə)lē\ *adv, usu cap*

meth·od·ization \,methədə'zāshən, -,dī'z-\ *n* -s **:** the act or process of methodizing or the state of being methodized

meth·od·ize \'==,dīz\ *vb* -ED/-ING/-s [*method* + *-ize*] *vt* **1 :** to reduce to method **:** arrange in an orderly manner **:** SYSTEMATIZE ⟨developed specialized procedures . . . and *methodized* them —S.E.Hyman⟩ **2** *often cap* **:** to turn or make Methodist ~ *vi, often cap* **:** to talk or act as a Methodist **:** incline to Methodism **syn** see ORDER

meth·od·less \-dləs\ *adj* **:** lacking order or method

method of agreement : a method of scientific induction devised by J. S. Mill according to which if two or more instances of a phenomenon under investigation have only a single circumstance in common the circumstance in which all the instances agree is the cause or effect of the phenomenon

method of concomitant variations : a method of scientific induction devised by J. S. Mill according to which a phenomenon varying in any way whenever another phenomenon varies in some particular way is a cause or effect of that phenomenon or is related to it through some fact of causation

method of difference : a method of scientific induction devised by J. S. Mill according to which if an instance in which the phenomenon under investigation occurs and an instance in which it does not occur have each circumstance except one in common, that one occurring only in the former, the circumstance in which the two instances differ is the effect or cause or necessary part of the cause of the phenomenon — compare INDIRECT METHOD OF DIFFERENCE

method of exclusion : a method in scientific induction which proceeds by the progressive exclusion of the nonessential antecedents by comparison of cases to find the essential residue or real cause; *also* **:** a method that proceeds to the determination of the true principle by successive elimination as false of all the possible or plausible hypotheses except that one

method of least squares : LEAST SQUARES

method of residues : a method of scientific induction devised by J. S. Mill according to which if one subtracts from a phenomenon the part known by previous inductions to be the effect of certain antecedents the remaining part of the phenomenon is the effect of the remaining antecedents

meth·od·o·logical \¦methədə+\ *adj* **:** of or relating to method or methodology **:** of or relating to a guiding approach, procedure, or the working concepts or premises employed ⟨rejected the ~ axioms of the Greeks — the superiority of the heavenly bodies, the circularity of their bodies —S.F.Mason⟩ ⟨~ doubt is . . . an essential for scientific progress —L.J. McGinley⟩ ⟨in spite of its ~ attractiveness —G.D.Wiebe⟩ ⟨a useful enough ~ principle to begin with —Edward Sapir⟩ — **meth·od·o·logically** \"+\ *adv*

meth·od·ol·o·gist \,methə'däləjəst\ *n* -s **:** a person who treats method as an object of study or who is greatly concerned with method ⟨a controversy which . . . has split not only logicians and ~s —Alfred Schutz⟩

meth·od·ol·o·gy \-jē, -ji\ *n* -ES [NL *methodologia*, fr. L *methodus* method + *-o-* + *-logia* -logy — more at METHOD] **1 a :** a body of methods, procedures, working concepts, rules, and postulates employed by a science, art, or discipline ⟨the limitation of science arises from a feature of its ~ —Henry Margenau⟩ ⟨the statistical ~ is perhaps the most useful tool for controlling quality —N.C.Brown⟩ ⟨applying the . . . ~ of geology and soil science to the practical problems of mineral exploration —H.T.U.Smith⟩ **b :** the processes, techniques, or approaches employed in the solution of a problem or in doing something **:** a particular procedure or set of procedures ⟨attempts to teach students a ~ of reading — Hargis Westerfield⟩ ⟨the first stage of the research has been devoted to the development of a ~ —*Amer. Anthrop. Assoc. Bull.*⟩ ⟨the ~ of this study is outlined —*Jour. Amer. Med. Assoc.*⟩ **c :** the theoretical foundations of a philosophical doctrine **:** the basic premises, postulates, and concepts of a philosophy ⟨the ~ of Aristotelianism⟩ ⟨the ~ of dialectical materialism⟩ ⟨these *methodologies* . . . are so divergent as to render futile any effort at reconciliation —Murray Krieger⟩ **2 :** a science or the study of method ⟨graduate schools of education . . . are wholeheartedly devoted to ~ —M.B.Smith⟩; *specif* **:** a branch of logic that analyzes the principles or procedures that should guide inquiry in a particular field

methods *pl of* METHOD

methods engineer *n* **:** a person qualified by training, skill, or experience to engage in methods engineering

methods engineering *n* **1 :** a branch of industrial engineering specializing in the analysis of methods and the improvement and standardization of methods, equipment, and working conditions **2 :** the work of one who engages in the analysis, improvement, and standardization of industrial methods, equipment, and working conditions

methods man *n* **:** a clerical technician

meth·ody \'methədē, -di\ *n* -ES *usu cap* [by shortening & alteration] *dial* **:** METHODIST

meth·one \'me,thōn\ *n* -s [*meth-* + *-one*] **:** DIMEDON

me·th·o·ni·um \mə'thōnēəm\ *n* -s [NL, fr. *meth-* + *-onium*] **:** any of several bivalent doubled substituted ammonium ions (as decamethonium or hexamethonium) in which the two quaternary nitrogen atoms are separated by a polymethylene chain ⟨~ salts⟩

metho·sulfate \¦methō+\ *n* [*meth-* + *sulfate*] **:** a compound with methyl sulfate

methought *past 3d sing of* METHINKS

methoughts *obs var of* METHOUGHT

meth·oxide \(')meth+\ *n* [*meth-* + *oxide*] **:** a binary compound of methoxyl; *esp* **:** a base formed from methanol by replacement of the hydroxyl hydrogen with a metal ⟨sodium ~ $NaOCH_3$⟩

me·thoxy \mə'thäksē, me'-\ *adj* [*methoxy-*] **:** relating to or containing methoxyl

methoxy- *comb form* [ISV, fr. *methoxyl*] **:** containing methoxyl — in names of chemical compounds ⟨*methoxy*acetophenone⟩

me·thoxy·carbonyl \=¦==+\ *n* [*methoxy-* + *carbonyl*] **:** CARBOMETHOXYL

me·thoxy·chlor \='==,klō(ə)r\ *n* -s [*methoxy-* + *trichloroethane*] **:** a crystalline insecticide $(CH_3OC_6H_4)_2CHCCl_3$ said to be faster acting and less toxic to warm-blooded animals than DDT — called also *methoxy DDT*

meth·ox·yl \mə'thäksəl, me'-\ *n* [*meth-* + *ox-* + *-yl*] **:** a univalent radical CH_3O— composed of methyl united with oxygen

me·thu·se·lah \mə'th(y)üz(ə)lə *also* -üs(-\ *n* -s *usu cap* [after *Methuselah*, Biblical patriarch represented as having lived 969 years (Gen 5:27)] **1 :** a person of great age ⟨one of the other *Methuselahs*, reminded . . . of his own aches and miseries —Mary McCarthy⟩ **2 :** an oversize wine bottle holding about six and a half quarts

meth·yl \'methəl, *chiefly by Brit chemists* 'mē,thīl\ *n* -s [G *methyl* & F *méthyle*, back-formation fr. ISV *methylene*] **:** an alkyl radical CH_3 derived from methane by removal of one hydrogen atom that is known usu. in combination in many compounds but is also isolated momentarily in the free state as a gaseous fragmentation product of the pyrolysis of organic compounds

methyl acetate *n* **:** a volatile flammable fragrant liquid ester CH_3COOCH_3 made from methanol and acetic acid and used chiefly as a solvent (as for nitrocellulose and cellulose acetate)

methyl acetone *n* **:** a flammable mixture of solvents consisting usu. of about one half acetone and one half methyl acetate and methanol

meth·yl·acetylene \¦methəl+\ *n* [ISV *methyl* + *acetylene*] **:** an unpleasant-smelling gaseous hydrocarbon $CH_3C{\equiv}CH$ that burns with a smoky flame — called also *allylene*

meth·yl·al \,methə'lal, '==,=\ *n* -s [ISV *methyl* + *-al*] **1 :** a volatile flammable liquid acetal $CH_2(OCH_3)_2$ that has a pleasant ethereal odor, is made by reaction of formaldehyde and methanol or by partial oxidation of methanol, and is used chiefly as a solvent and in organic synthesis — called also *formal* **2 :** FORMAL 2

methyl alcohol *n* **:** the first in the series of simple aliphatic alcohols **:** METHANOL

meth·yl·amine \¦methələ¦mēn, -thə'lamən\ *n* [ISV *methyl* + *amine*] **1 :** a flammable explosive gaseous base CH_3NH_2 that has a strong ammoniacal odor, that is very soluble in water, and that is usu. made from methanol and ammonia and used chiefly in organic synthesis — called also *monomethylamine* **2 :** an amine containing methyl attached to amino nitrogen — see DIMETHYLAMINE, TRIMETHYLAMINE

meth·yl·aminophenol \¦methəl+\ *n* [ISV *methyl* + *aminophenol*] **:** a poisonous crystalline compound $CH_3NHC_6H_4OH$ used chiefly in the form of its sulfate as a photographic developer — called also *methyl-p-aminophenol*, *para-methylaminophenol*

meth·yl·aniline \"+\ *n* [ISV *methyl* + *aniline*] **:** a methyl derivative of aniline; *esp* **:** a colorless oily secondary amine $C_6H_5NHCH_3$ made usu. by heating aniline hydrochloride with methanol — compare TOLUIDINE

methyl anthranilate *n* **:** a fragrant liquid ester $NH_2C_6H_4COOCH_3$ found in various essential oils (as neroli oil) and in grape juice and used in perfumes and flavoring materials

¹meth·yl·ate \'methə,lāt, -,lət\ *n* -s [*methyl* + *-ate* (n. suffix)] **:** METHOXIDE

²meth·yl·ate \-,lāt, *usu* -ād·+V\ *vt* -ED/-ING/-s [*methyl* + *-ate* (v. suffix)] **1 :** to impregnate or mix with methanol **2 :** to introduce the methyl group into (a compound) — **meth·yl·a·tion** \,=='lāshən\ *n* -s — **meth·yl·a·tor** \'==,lād·ə(r), -ātə-\ *n* -s

methylated spirit *or* **methylated spirits** *n* **:** alcohol (sense 3) denatured with methanol

meth·yl·benzene \¦methəl+\ *n* [ISV *methyl* + *benzene*] **:** TOLUENE

methyl bromide *n* **:** a poisonous gaseous compound CH_3Br used chiefly as a fumigant against rodents, worms, and insects; bromo-methane

methyl cellulose *n* **:** any of various tasteless gummy substances that are made by methylating cellulose, have the property of swelling in water, and are used chiefly as emulsifiers, adhesives, and thickeners and in medicine as bulk laxatives

methyl chavicol *n* **:** ESTRAGOLE

methyl chloride *n* **:** a sweet-smelling gaseous compound CH_3Cl made usu. by the action of hydrochloric acid on methanol and used chiefly as a refrigerant and methylating agent — called also *chloromethane*

meth·yl·cholanthrene \¦methəl+\ *n* [ISV *methyl* + *cholanthrene*] **:** a potent carcinogenic hydrocarbon $C_{21}H_{16}$ obtained as yellow crystals from certain bile acids and cholesterol and also synthetically

methyl cotton blue *also* **methyl blue** *n, often cap M&C&B* **:** an acid triphenylmethane dye used chiefly in writing ink and as a biological stain — see DYE table I (under *Acid Blue 93*)

methyl cyanide *n* **:** ACETONITRILE

meth·yl·dihydromorphinone \¦methəl+\ *n* [*methyl* + *dihydr-* + *morphine* + *-one*] **:** METOPON

meth·yl·ene \'methə,lēn\ *n* -s [F *méthylène*, fr. Gk *methy* wine + *hylē* wood + *-ēnē* (fem. patronymic suffix) — more at MEAD] **:** a bivalent hydrocarbon radical $CH_2{=}$ or $-CH_2-$ derived from methane by removal of two hydrogen atoms — compare POLYMETHYLENE

methylene azure *n, sometimes cap M&A* **:** a dye obtained by oxidation of methylene blue and used in biological stains

methylene blue *n, sometimes cap M&B* **:** a basic dye of the thiazine class used as a biological stain, as an antidote esp. in cyanide poisoning, as an oxidation-reduction indicator, and in a test for the bacterial content of milk — see DYE table I (under *Basic Blue 9*)

methylene chloride *n* **:** a low-boiling nonflammable liquid CH_2Cl_2 used chiefly as a solvent, paint remover, refrigerant, and propellant in aerosols; dichloro-methane

methylenedioxy- *comb form* [*methylene* + *dioxy-*] **:** containing the group $-OCH_2O-$ — in names of organic compounds ⟨*methylenedioxy*benzaldehyde⟩

methylene green *n, sometimes cap M&G* **:** a basic dye obtained by nitrating methylene blue — see DYE table I (under *Basic Green 5*)

methylene iodide *n* **:** a yellowish liquid compound CH_2I_2 remarkable for its high specific gravity (3.325 at 20° C) and high index of refraction that make it useful in separating minerals and determining specific gravities and indexes of refraction — called also *diiodomethane*

methylene violet 3R *n, usu cap M&V* **:** a basic dye — see DYE table I (under *Basic Violet 5*)

meth·yl·en·imine \¦methə¦lēnə,mēn, -mən\ *n* [ISV *methylene* + *imine*] **:** a hypothetical compound $CH_2{=}NH$ known in the form of derivatives — called also *azomethine*

methyl ester *n* **:** an ester that yields methanol on hydrolysis ⟨*methyl esters* of carboxylic acids⟩

methyl ether *n* **1 :** a flammable easily condensable gas $(CH_3)_2O$ that has an agreeable odor and is usu. obtained by heating methanol with sulfuric acid — called also *dimethyl ether* **2 :** an ether in which one of the radicals united to oxygen is methyl ⟨the *methyl ether* of benzyl alcohol⟩

methyl ethyl ketone *n* **:** a flammable liquid compound $CH_3COC_2H_5$ resembling acetone made usu. by dehydrogenation of secondary butyl alcohol and used chiefly as a solvent — called also *2-butanone*

methylethylpyridine \¦==¦==¦==,=\ *n* [*methyl* + *ethyl* + *pyridine*] **:** a liquid base $C_5H_3N(CH_3)(C_2H_5)$ that has a penetrating odor, is usu. made by catalytic reaction of paraldehyde with ammonia, and is used chiefly in organic synthesis (as of nicotinic acid) — called also *aldehyde collidine*, *aldehydine*, *collidine*, *2-methyl-5-ethylpyridine*

meth·yl·glyoxal \¦methəl+\ *n* [ISV *methyl* + *glyoxal*] **:** PYRUVALDEHYDE

methyl green *n* **:** a basic triphenylmethane dye made by adding methyl chloride to crystal violet and used chiefly as a biological stain

methyl heptine carbonate *n* **:** an oily ester $CH_3(CH_2)_4C{\equiv}CCOOCH_3$ that has a strong odor like violets and is used in perfumes and cosmetics; methyl 2-octyn-oate — not used systematically

me·thyl·ic \(')me¦thilik\ *adj* [ISV *methyl*ene + *-ic*] **:** of, relating to, or containing methyl ⟨the ~ content⟩

me·thyl·i·dyne \me'thilə,dīn\ *n* -s [*meth-* + *-ylidyne*] **:** the trivalent radical $HC{\equiv}$ or $=CH-$ derived from methane — called also *methenyl*, *methine*

methyl iodide *n* **:** a volatile pungent flammable heavy liquid compound CH_3I that turns brown on exposure to light, that causes burning on contact with the skin and is poisonous on inhalation of the vapor, and that is made usu. by interaction of methanol, red phosphorus, and iodine and used chiefly in organic synthesis; iodo-methane

methyl isobutyl ketone *n* **:** a pleasant-smelling flammable liquid compound $CH_3COCH_2CH(CH_3)_2$ made usu. by catalytic hydrogenation of mesityl oxide and used chiefly as a solvent; 4-methyl-2-pentanone

methyl methacrylate *n* **1 :** a volatile flammable liquid ester $CH_2{=}C(CH_3)COOCH_3$ that polymerizes readily (as in the presence of a peroxide) **2** *or* **methyl methacrylate resin :** an acrylic resin made by polymerization of monomeric methyl methacrylate

meth·yl·morphine \¦methəl+\ *n* [ISV *methyl* + *morphine*] **:** CODEINE

meth·yl·naphthalene \"+\ *n* [*methyl* + *naphthalene*] **:** either of two isomeric hydrocarbons $C_{10}H_7CH_3$ occurring in coal tar and petroleum: **a :** an oily liquid used as a reference fuel in determining the cetane number — called also *alpha-* or *1-methylnaphthalene* **b :** a crystalline solid used chiefly in organic synthesis (as of menadione) — called also *beta-* or *2-methylnaphthalene*

methyl naphthyl ketone *n* **:** ACETONAPHTHONE

meth·yl·ol \'methə,lōl, -lȯl\ *n* -s [*methyl* + *-ol*] **:** HYDROXYMETHYL — used esp. in naming compounds in which hydroxymethyl is attached to nitrogen

methylolurea \¦==,==¦=\ *n* [*methylol* + *urea*] **:** either of two compounds formed as the first stage in making urea-formaldehyde resins: **a :** a crystalline compound $H_2NCONHCH_2OH$ obtainable from one mole each of urea and formaldehyde and used esp. for impregnating wood with which it forms hard resins — called also *monomethylolurea* **b :** DIMETHYLOLUREA

methyl orange *n, sometimes cap M&O* **:** a basic azo dye $(CH_3)_2NC_6H_4N{=}NC_6H_4SO_3Na$ which is made by coupling diazotized sulfanilic acid with dimethylaniline, is used chiefly as an acid-base indicator, and whose dilute solution is yellow when neutral and pink when acid — see DYE table I (under *Acid Orange 52*); compare HELIANTHIN

meth·yl·para·ben \,methəl'parə,ben\ *n* [*methyl* + *para-hydroxybenzoic (acid)*] **:** a crystalline compound $HOC_6H_4COOCH_3$ used as a preservative (as in pharmaceutical ointments and cosmetic creams and lotions); the methyl ester of *para*hydroxybenzoic acid

meth·yl·pentose \¦methəl+\ *n* [*methyl* + *pentose*] **:** a methyl derivative of a pentose **:** a deoxy-hexose; *esp* **:** such a derivative $CH_3(CHOH)_4CHO$ with a terminal methyl group on the carbon chain (as in fucose or rhamnose)

methyl phthalate *n* **:** a methyl ester of phthalic acid; *esp* **:** DIMETHYL PHTHALATE

meth·yl·propene \¦methəl+\ *n* [*methyl* + *propene*] **:** ISOBUTYLENE — used in the system of nomenclature adopted by the Internat. Union of Pure and Applied Chemistry

methyl propyl ketone *n* **:** PENTANONE a

methyl red *n, sometimes cap M&R* **:** a basic azo dye $(CH_3)_2NC_6H_4N{=}C_6H_4COOH$ used similarly to methyl orange as an acid-base indicator

meth·yl·rosaniline chloride \¦methəl+-\ *n* [*methyl* + *rosaniline*] **:** CRYSTAL VIOLET

methyl rubber *n* **:** a synthetic rubber made in Germany during World War I by polymerization of dimethyl-butadiene

methyls *pl of* METHYL

methyl salicylate *n* **:** a liquid ester $HOC_6H_4COOCH_3$ that has a strong odor of wintergreen, that is the principal constituent of wintergreen oil and sweet-birch oil but is usu. made synthetically, and that is used chiefly as a flavoring material, in perfumes, and in medicine as a counterirritant — called also *sweet-birch oil*, *wintergreen oil*

methyl sulfate *n* **:** a methyl ester of sulfuric acid; *esp* **:** the poisonous liquid dimethyl ester $(CH_3)_2SO_4$ used as a methylating agent

meth·yl·testosterone \¦methəl+\ *n* [*methyl* + *testosterone*] **:** a synthetically prepared crystalline compound $C_{20}H_{30}O_2$ administered orally in cases of male sex hormone deficiency

meth·yl·thiouracil \"+\ *n* -s [*methyl* + *thiouracil*] **:** a crystalline compound $C_5H_6N_2OS$ used in the suppression of hyperactivity of the thyroid — called also *6-methyl-2-thiouracil*

methyl violet *n, often cap M&V* : any of several basic dyes that are methyl derivatives of pararosaniline: as **a** *or* **methyl violet B** : a dye consisting essentially of pentamethyl-pararosaniline chloride and used chiefly in making organic pigments (as for printing inks) and as a biological stain — called also *gentian violet;* see DYE table I (under *Basic Violet 1, Pigment Violet 3,* and *Solvent Violet 8*) **b** : CRYSTAL VIOLET

methyl yellow *n* : OIL YELLOW 1b

met·ic \ˈmed·ik\ *n* -S [Gk *metoikos,* fr. *meta-* + *oikos* house — more at VICINITY] : an alien resident of an ancient Greek city who had some civil privileges

me·tic·u·los·i·ty \mə̇ˌtikyəˈläsəd·ē\ *n* -ES [fr. *meticulous,* after such pairs as E *curious: curiosity*] : the quality or state of being meticulous : METICULOUSNESS

me·tic·u·lous \-ˈ==ləs\ *adj* [L *meticulosus,* fr. *metus* fear + *-iculosus* (as in *periculosus* dangerous)] **1** *obs* : TIMID, FEARFUL **2** : marked by extreme painstaking care in the consideration or treatment of details: **a** : unduly fussy esp. through fear of error or censure ⟨if I seem rather ~ in my examination of this question —*World Report*⟩ ⟨in their work, they were rigid and overzealous, ~, overconscientious, inelastic —Harold Rosen & H.E.Kiene⟩ ⟨no longer interpret contracts with ~ adherence to the letter when in conflict with the spirit —B.N. Cardozo⟩ **b** : commendably thorough or precise : STRICT ⟨that fullness and ~ documentation which the scholar requires —G.W.Allen⟩ ⟨a ~ scholar, who has mastered the documents of the age —Reinhold Niebuhr⟩ ⟨using ~ intravascular injection techniques —N.M.Pusey⟩ ⟨had observed a ~ neutrality —Sir Winston Churchill⟩ ⟨a ~ regard for law and usage —C.G.Bowers⟩ **syn** see CAREFUL

me·tic·u·lous·ly *adv* : in a meticulous manner : with meticulousness ⟨behaved ~ toward the extremely suspicious government —Richard Watts⟩ ⟨the escape was planned ~ and executed boldly —Edmond Taylor⟩

me·tic·u·lous·ness *n* -ES : the quality of being meticulous ⟨dressed with almost stiff ~ —Harriet La Barre⟩ ⟨this ~ which prevents fields of knowledge from spilling over into each other —Dallas Finn⟩ ⟨the artist's ~, that fine intuitive eye for detail and relevance and comparisons —*Times Lit. Supp.*⟩

mé·tier \(ˈ)māˈtyā, (ˈ)me-\ *n* -S [F, fr. OF *mestier,* fr. (assumed) VL *misterium,* alter. of L *ministerium* work, occupation, ministry — more at MINISTRY] **1** : VOCATION, TRADE, BUSINESS ⟨to be a sailor, this is a lonely ~ —*Lamp*⟩ ⟨blue sweatshirt, with grease from the truck and the stains of his ~ marked on it —Kay Boyle⟩ ⟨the ~ of the engineer or the practical scientist —Bernard Wall⟩ **2 a** : a special line of activity ⟨exploration was at that time the principal ~ of British geography —O.J.R.Howarth⟩ **b** : an area of activity in which one is most expert, successful, or happy : FORTE ⟨his ~ seems to be rather the stage fabrication of rough-and-tumble popular entertainment —G.J.Nathan⟩ ⟨political oratory is not my ~ —Francis Younghusband⟩ **3** : the special techniques characteristic of an art or vocation : MODE, METHOD ⟨new writers who have something to say and try to say it with sincerity and a grasp of the ~ of the novelist —*Nation*⟩

me·tif \māˈtēf\ *n, pl* **metifs** \", -fs\ *sometimes cap* [F *métif,* alter. of *métis*] : MÉTIS

meting *pres part of* METE

mé·tis \māˈtē(s)\ *n, pl* **métis** \", -tēz\ *sometimes cap* [F (prob. influenced in meaning by Sp *mestizo*), fr. MF *metis* mongrel, of parents of different nations, fr. LL *misticius, mixticius* mixed — more at MESTIZO] : one that is of mixed blood: **a** : HALF-BREED; *specif* : one of French and Indian ancestry **b** : a crossbred animal (as a horse or a sheep)

mé·tisse \māˈtēs\ *n, pl* **métisses** \", -ēsəz\ [F, fem. of *métis*] : a female half-breed — compare MÉTIS

met·myoglobin \(ˌ)met+\ *n* [*meta-* + *myoglobin*] : a reddish brown crystalline pigment that is formed by oxidation of myoglobin

METO *abbr* maximum except take-off

met·obelus \(ˈ)med·+\ *n, pl* **metobeli** [NL, fr. *meta-* + *obelus*] : a symbol variously written (as by:) and used in ancient manuscripts (as of the Septuagint) to mark the end of a suspected or spurious passage — compare OBELUS

metoestrus *or* **metoestrum** *var of* METESTRUS

Me·tol \ˈmēˌtōl, -tōl\ *trademark* — used for a photographic developer

me·ton·ic cycle \meˈtänik-\ *n, usu cap M* [*Meton,* 5th cent. B.C. Greek astronomer + E *-ic*] : a period of 19 years after the lapse of which the phases of the moon return to a particular date in the calendar year: **a** : one of the 19-year periods reckoning from June 27, 432 B.C., that were used in determining lengths of years and the placing of the intercalary month in the ancient Greek calendar **b** : one of the 19-year periods reckoning from 1 B.C. that are used in determining the date of Easter in the Gregorian calendar

met·o·nym \ˈmed·əˌnim\ *n* -S [back-formation fr. *metonymy*] : a word used in metonymy

met·o·nym·ic \ˌ==ˈnimik\ *or* **met·o·nym·i·cal** \-mə̇kəl\ *adj* [*metonymic* fr. Gk *metōnymikos,* fr. *metōnymia* metonymy + *-ikos* -ic; *metonymical* fr. Gk *metōnymikos* + E *-al*] : of, relating to, or involving metonymy : used in metonymy — **met·o·nym·i·cal·ly** \-mə̇k(ə)lē\ *adv*

me·ton·y·my \mə̇ˈtänəmē, meˈ-, -əmi\ *n* -ES [L *metonymia,* fr. Gk *metōnymia,* fr. *meta-* + *-ōnymia* -onymy] : a figure of speech that consists in using the name of one thing for that of something else with which it is associated (as in "spent the evening reading *Shakespeare*", "lands belonging to the *crown*", "demanded action by *City Hall*", "ogling the heavily mascaraed *skirt* at the next table") : use of one word for another that it may be expected to suggest — compare TROPE

¹me-too \ˈ=ˈ=\ *adj* [fr. the phrase *me too*] : marked by similarity to or acceptance of something (as a political policy) that has proved successful or persuasive when promoted by an opponent or rival ⟨conducted a *me-too* campaign⟩ ⟨*me-too* candidates⟩ ⟨has been in the forefront of . . . the *me-too* faction —*N.Y.Times*⟩

²me-too \"\ *vt* -ED/-ING/-S : to agree with or adopt a successful or persuasive practice or policy of (a rival) ⟨*me-too* the president⟩

me-too·er \ˈ=ˈ=ə(r)\ *n* -S : one that adopts a me-too policy or principle

me-too·ism \ˈ=ˈ=ˌizəm\ *n* -S : the policies or principles of a me-tooer

met·ope \ˈmed·ˌōp, -e,tōp\ *n, pl* **metopes** \-ps\ *also* **met·o·pae** \-d·əˌpē\ [Gk *metopē,* fr. *meta-* + *opē* opening, hole; akin to Gk *osse* (two) eyes — more at EYE] : the space between two triglyphs of a Doric frieze often adorned with carved work

me·top·ic \meˈtäpik\ *adj* [Gk *metōpikos,* fr. *metōpon* forehead + *-ikos* -ic] : of or relating to the forehead : FRONTAL; *esp* : of, relating to, or being a suture uniting the frontal bones in the fetus and sometimes persistent after birth

met·o·pi·idae \ˌmed·əˈpīəˌdē\ [NL, fr. *Metopia,* type genus (fr. Gk *metōpion* forehead) + *-idae*] *syn of* SARCOPHAGIDAE

me·to·pi·on \məˈtōpēən\ *n* -S [NL, fr. Gk *metōpion* forehead, dim. of *metōpon,* fr. *meta-* + *-ōpon* (fr. *ōp-, ōps* face, eye) — more at EYE] : a point situated midway between the frontal eminences of the skull — see CRANIOMETRY illustration

met·o·pism \ˈmed·əˌpizəm\ *n* -S [ISV *metop-* (fr. Gk *metōpon* forehead) + *-ism*] : the condition of having a persistent metopic suture

me·to·pi·um \məˈtōpēəm\ *n* -S [NL, fr. *Metopium,* genus of trees including the black poison, fr. L, juice from a species of *Ferula,* fr. Gk *metōpion,* dim. of *metōpon,* a species of *Ferula,* prob. fr. *metōpon* forehead] : BLACK POISON

met·o·poc·e·ros \ˌmed·əˈpäsərəs\ *n, cap* [NL, fr. Gk *metōpon* forehead + *keras* horn — more at METOPION, HORN] : a genus of Iguanidae containing the horned iguana

met·o·pon \ˈmed·əˌpän\ *n* -S [*methyldihydromorphinone*] : a narcotic drug $C_{18}H_{21}NO_3$ derived from morphine that is usu. administered by mouth in the form of its crystalline hydrochloride and that is more effective than morphine in its analgesic action

met·o·pos·co·py \ˌmed·əˈpäskəpē\ *n* -ES [Gk *metōposkopos* observing the forehead (fr. *metōpon* forehead + *skopos* watcher) + E *-y* — more at METOPION, SCOPE] **1** : the art of reading character or telling fortunes from the markings of the forehead **2** : PHYSIOGNOMY

me·tox·e·nous \mə̇ˈtäksənəs\ *adj* [irreg. fr. *meta-* + Gk *xenos* stranger, guest + E *-ous*] : HETEROECIOUS — **me·tox·e·ny** \-nē\ *n* -ES

metr- *or* **metro-** *comb form* [NL, fr. Gk *mētr-,* fr. *mētra*] **1** : uterus ⟨*metritis*⟩ ⟨*metro*fibroma⟩ ⟨*metro*tome⟩ **2** : pith ⟨*Metro*sideros⟩ ⟨*Metro*xylon⟩

¹me·tra \ˈmē·trə\ *n, pl* **me·trae** \-ē,-trē\ [NL, fr. Gk *mētra,* fr. *mētr-, mētēr* mother — more at MOTHER] : UTERUS 1

²metra *pl of* METRON *or of* METRUM

-me·tra \ˈmē·trə\ *n comb form* -S [NL, fr. Gk *mētra* womb] : a (specified) condition of the uterus ⟨hemato*metra*⟩ ⟨hydro*metra*⟩

me·tra·term \ˈmē·trə+,-\ *n* [*metra* + L *terminus* boundary, limit, end — more at TERM] : the distal muscular portion of the uterus of a flatworm

Met·ra·zol \ˈme·trəˌzōl, -zōl\ *trademark* — used for pentylenetetrazol

me·tre \ˈmēd·ə(r), -ētə-\ *chiefly Brit var of* METER

metreme \ˈmeˌtrēm, ˈmē-\ *n* -S [prob. fr. F *métrème,* fr. *mètre* meter + *-ème* -eme — more at METER] : the minimal unit of metrical structure : FOOT

me·tri·al \ˈmē·trēəl\ *adj* [NL *metra* + E *-ial*] : of or relating to the uterus — often used in combination ⟨endo*metrial*⟩

¹met·ric \ˈme·trik, -rēk\ *n* -S [in sense 1, fr. Gk *metrikē,* fr. fem. of *metrikos;* in other senses, fr. *metric* (var. of *metrical*)] **1** : the part of prosody that deals with metrical structure ⟨the analytical study of ~ —T.S.Eliot⟩ — often used in pl. but sing. or pl. in constr. ⟨classical ~*s*⟩ **2** : a standard of measurement ⟨its scale or ~ is determined by a definition —E.H.Hutten⟩ ⟨it is fairly certain that no ~ exists that can be applied directly to happiness —*Scientific Monthly*⟩ — often used in pl. but sing. or pl. in constr. ⟨an integrated system of photography, interpretation, and ~*s* —G.T.McNeil⟩ ⟨the ~*s* of his trade —C.S. Spooner⟩ **3** *math* : a means of specifying values of a variable or positions of a point ⟨Euclidean ~⟩ ⟨Riemannian ~⟩

²met·ric \"\ *or* **met·ri·cal** \-rə̇kəl, -rēk-\ *adj* [*metric* fr. F *métrique,* fr. *mètre* meter + *-ique* -ic; *metrical* fr. F *métrique* + E *-al* — more at METER] : based on the meter as a standard of measurement : of or measured in terms belonging to the metric system ⟨~ equivalents⟩ — **met·ri·cal·ly** \-rə̇k(ə)lē, -rēk-, -li\ *adv*

-met·ric \ˈme·trik, -rēk\ *or* **-met·ri·cal** \-rə̇kəl, -rēk-\ *adj comb form* [*-metric* fr. F *-métrique,* fr. *métrique* metrical, fr. L *metricus; -metrical* fr. F *-métrique* + E *-al* — more at METRICAL] **1** : of, employing, or obtained by (such) a meter ⟨baro*metric*⟩ ⟨helio*metric*⟩ **2** : of or relating to (such) an art, process, or science of measuring ⟨chrono*metric*⟩ ⟨geo*metric*⟩ ⟨psycho*metric*⟩

met·ri·cal \ˈme·trə̇kəl, -rēk-\ *or* **met·ric** \-rik, -rēk\ *adj* [*metrical* fr. L *metricus* (fr. Gk *metrikos,* fr. *metron* measure, meter + *-ikos* -ic) + E *-al; metric* fr. L *metricus* — more at MEASURE] **1** : of, determined by, or in meter ⟨sent his mind ticking in a vague ~ rhythm —Joseph Hitrec⟩ ⟨anything ~ is rhythmical, but not all rhythms may be successfully reduced to meter —D.A.Stauffer⟩ ⟨even very irregular poems, which are generally included in anthologies as ~ rather than free verse —Evelyn H. Scholl⟩ ⟨not a ~ romanticist —Jonathan Daniels⟩ ⟨~ accent⟩ **2** : used in, involving, or relating to measurement ⟨the ~ properties of space —James Jeans⟩ ⟨science is nothing if it is not ~ —T.H.Savory⟩ **3** [¹*metric*] *math* : relating to or capable of being defined by a metric — **met·ri·cal·ly** \-rə̇k(ə)lē, -rēk-, -li\ *adv*

metrical signature *n* : TIME SIGNATURE

metric carat *n* : CARAT 1b

metric centner *n* : a centner of 220.46 pounds or 100 kilograms — called also *double centner*

metric geometry *n* : geometry that postulates a method of determining the distance between any two of its points and thence determines the size of geometrical magnitudes (as lengths, areas, volumes, angles)

metric horsepower *n* : a horsepower unit equal to 75 kilogram-meters per second

metric hundredweight *n* : a unit of weight equal to 50 kilograms or 110.23 pounds

me·tri·cian \meˈtrishən, mə̇ˈ-\ *n* -S [F *métricien,* fr. *mètre* (poetic) meter (fr. MF *metre*) + *-icien* -ician — more at METER] : a composer in or student of meter : METRIST

met·ri·cism \ˈme·trəˌsizəm\ *n* -S : the character or property of being metric or having a tendency to metricity

met·ri·cist \-ˌsə̇st\ *n* -S : METRIST

me·tric·i·ty \meˈtrisəd·ē, mə̇ˈ-\ *n* -ES : the character or property of being metrical or having meter

met·ri·cize \ˈme·trəˌsīz\ *vt* -ED/-ING/-S : to make metrical

metric system *n* : a decimal system of weights and measures orig. based entirely on the meter with the unit of capacity equal to the cubic decimeter and the unit of mass equal to one cubic centimeter of water at its maximum density but now having these units based on the kilogram

metric ton *n* : a unit of mass and weight equal to 1000 kilograms or 2,204.6 pounds avoirdupois — abbr. *MT;* see METRIC SYSTEM table

me·trid·i·um \məˈtridēəm\ *n, cap* [NL, fr. Gk *mētridios* having a womb, fruitful, fr. *mētra* womb — more at METRA] : a genus of sea anemones

-metries *pl of* -METRY

met·ri·fi·ca·tion \ˌme·trəfə̇ˈkāshən\ *n* -S [ML *metrificatus* (past part. of *metrificare*) + E *-ion*] : composition in metrical form : VERSIFICATION

met·ri·fy \ˈ==ˌfī\ *vt* -ED/-ING/-ES [MF *metrifier,* fr. ML *metrificare,* fr. L *metrum* meter + *-ificare* -ify — more at METER] : to compose in or put into meter : make a metrical version of

metring *var of* METERING

met·rio·cra·nic \ˌme·trēōˈkrānik\ *adj* [G *metriokran* metriocranic (fr. Gk *metrios* moderate — fr. *metron* measure — + *kranion* skull) + E *-ic* — more at MEASURE, CRANIUM] : having a skull of moderate height in proportion to its width with a breadth-height index of 92 to 98 — **met·rio·cra·ny** \ˈ===-ˌ=nē\ *n* -ES

met·rio·metopic \ˌ===+\ *adj* [Gk *metrios* + E *metopic*] : having a forehead moderately wide in relation to the brain case — **met·rio·met·o·py** \ˌ===ˈmed·əpē\ *n* -ES

metrist \ˈme·trə̇st, ˈmē-\ *n* -S [ML *metrista,* fr. L *metrum* meter + *-ista* -ist — more at METER] **1** : a maker of verses **2** : one skillful in handling meter **3** : a student of meter or metrics

me·tri·tis \məˈtrīd·ə̇s\ *n* -ES [NL, fr. *metr-* + *-itis*] : inflammation of the uterus

-me·tri·um \ˈmē·trēəm\ *n comb form, pl* **-me·tria** \-trēə\ [NL, fr. *metr-* + *-ium*] : part or layer of the uterus ⟨endo*metrium*⟩ ⟨myo*metrium*⟩

¹met·ro \ˈme·(ˌ)trō\ *n* -S [F *métro,* short for *métropolitain,* fr. (*chemin de fer*) *métropolitain* metropolitan railway] : SUBWAY

²metro \"\ *usu cap* — a communications code word for the letter *m*

metro- — see METR-

met·ro·logical \ˌme·trə+\ *adj* : of or relating to metrology ⟨~ services and laboratories —E.C.Crittenden⟩ — **met·ro·logically** \"+\ *adv*

me·trol·o·gist \məˈträləjə̇st\ *n* -S : one who specializes in metrology

me·trol·o·gy \-jē\ *n* -ES [F *métrologie,* fr. Gk *metrologia* theory of ratios, fr. *metron* measure + *-logia* -logy — more at MEASURE] **1** : the science of weights and measures : the science of measurement **2** : a system of weights and measures

met·ro·mania \ˌme·trō+\ *n* [NL, fr. Gk *metron* measure, meter + NL *mania*] : a mania for writing verses

met·ron \ˈmeˌträn\ *n, pl* **met·ra** \-ˌtrə\ [Gk, measure, meter — more at METER] : the minimal unit of measure in classical Greek verse constituting in certain meters (as the iambic, trochaic, anapestic, and the lyric forms of dactylic) a syzygy of two feet, in others (as hexameters of epic verse) a dipody and where necessary for analysis in the case of spondaic series a single foot, and in compound meters (as the ionic and choriambic) a foot of four syllables

met·ro·nome \ˈme·trəˌnōm\ *n* -S [Gk *metron* measure, meter + *nomos* law — more at NIMBLE] : an instrument that emits an audible repetitive tap regulated to mark rhythm (as for music, marching, sports, or industrial repetition)

met·ro·nom·ic \ˌ==ˈnämik\ *also* **met·ro·nom·i·cal** \-mə̇kəl\ *adj* **1** : of or relating to a metronome or the marking of time with it **2** : mechanically regular (as in tempo) ⟨an exactitude of rhythm that gets dangerously close to the ~ —Neville Cardus⟩ ⟨correct attitudes, ~ meters, dulled rhymes —*Publ's Mod. Lang. Assoc. of Amer.*⟩ ⟨the plane rose and fell with ~ monotony as we flew —Sumner Welles⟩ — **met·ro·nom·i·cal·ly** \-mə̇k(ə)lē\ *adv*

metronome

metronomic mark *or* **metronome mark** *n* : a mark at the beginning of a piece of music to show its tempo according to the metronome

metro·nym·ic \ˌmē·trəˈnimik, ˌme-\ *n* -S [MGk *mētrōnymikos,* adj., named after one's mother, fr. Gk *mētr-, mētēr* mother + *onyma, onoma* name + *-ikos* -ic — more at MOTHER, NAME] : MATRONYMIC

me·tron·y·my \məˈtränəmē\ *n* -ES [back-formation fr. *metronymic*] : the custom of using matronymics

met·ro·pole \ˈme·trəˌpōl\ *n* -S [F *métropole,* fr. LL *metropolis*] **1** : a chief town : METROPOLIS **2** : a metropolitan see : METROPOLIS **3** : a Salvation Army hostel **4** : MOTHER COUNTRY — compare METROPOLIS 2

me·trop·o·lis \mə̇ˈträp(ə)lə̇s, meˈ-\ *n* -ES [LL, mother city, fr. Gk *mētropolis,* fr. *mētr-, mētēr* mother + *-o-* + *polis* city — more at MOTHER, POLICE] **1** : a metropolitan see **2** : the

METRIC SYSTEM

LENGTH

unit	abbreviation	number of meters	approximate U.S. equivalent
myriameter	mym	10,000	6.2 miles
kilometer	km	1,000	0.62 mile
hectometer	hm	100	109.36 yards
decameter	dkm	10	32.81 feet
meter	m	1	39.37 inches
decimeter	dm	0.1	3.94 inches
centimeter	cm	0.01	0.39 inch
millimeter	mm	0.001	0.04 inch

AREA

unit	abbreviation	number of square meters	approximate U.S. equivalent
square kilometer	sq km *or* km²	1,000,000	0.3861 square mile
hectare	ha	10,000	2.47 acres
are	a	100	119.60 square yards
centare	ca	1	10.76 square feet
square centimeter	sq cm *or* cm²	0.0001	0.155 square inch

VOLUME

unit	abbreviation	number of cubic meters	approximate U.S. equivalent
decastere	dks	10	13.10 cubic yards
stere	s	1	1.31 cubic yards
decistere	ds	0.10	3.53 cubic feet
cubic centimeter	cu cm *or* cm³ *also* cc	0.000001	0.061 cubic inch

CAPACITY

unit	abbreviation	number of liters	approximate U.S. equivalent: *cubic*	*dry*	*liquid*
kiloliter	kl	1,000	1.31 cubic yards		
hectoliter	hl	100	3.53 cubic feet	2.84 bushels	
decaliter	dkl	10	0.35 cubic foot	1.14 pecks	2.64 gallons
liter	l	1	61.02 cubic inches	0.908 quart	1.057 quarts
deciliter	dl	0.10	6.1 cubic inches	0.18 pint	0.21 pint
centiliter	cl	0.01	0.6 cubic inch		0.338 fluidounce
milliliter	ml	0.001	0.06 cubic inch		0.27 fluidram

MASS AND WEIGHT

unit	abbreviation	number of grams	approximate U.S. equivalent
metric ton	MT *or* t	1,000,000	1.1 tons
quintal	q	100,000	220.46 pounds
kilogram	kg	1,000	2.2046 pounds
hectogram	hg	100	3.527 ounces
decagram	dkg	10	0.353 ounce
gram	g *or* gm	1	0.035 ounce
decigram	dg	0.10	1.543 grains
centigram	cg	0.01	0.154 grain
milligram	mg	0.001	0.015 grain

mother city or state of a colony (as of ancient Greece) : MOTHER COUNTRY **3 a** : the chief town or city of a country or other land area : CAPITAL ⟨the ~ of the valley⟩ **b** : a city regarded as the center of a particular activity ⟨a lumber ~⟩ ⟨a cattle ~⟩ **c** : CITY; *esp* : an important city ⟨the world's great ~*es* —P.E. James⟩ ⟨the boom spirit which saw in every village a future ~ —G.R.Stewart⟩ **4** : a region where a particular kind of organism (as a variety or species) is most abundant

¹met·ro·pol·i·tan \ˌme·trə¦pälət°n *also* -ətən *or* -əd·ən\ *n* -s [ME, fr. LL *metropolitanus*, fr. *metropolitanus*, adj.] **1** : the head of an ecclesiastical province: **a** : the head of an ecclesiastical province of the Eastern Orthodox Church who has his headquarters in a large city **b** : an archbishop of the Roman Catholic Church who presides over at least one suffragan see **c** : an archbishop of the Church of England **2** : one who lives in or has manners, customs, or ideas characteristic of a metropolis ⟨modern apartment-dwelling ~ —R.M.Weaver⟩

²metropolitan \"\ *adj* [LL *metropolitanus*, fr. *metropolita*, *metropolites* metropolite + L *-anus* -an — more at METROPOLITE] **1** : of or befitting a metropolitan or his see : being an ecclesiastical metropolitan ⟨~ authority⟩ ⟨~ bishops⟩ **2** : of, relating to, characteristic of, or constituting a city that is a metropolis ⟨~ markets⟩ ⟨~ newspapers⟩ **3** : evincing characteristics (as urbane manners or cosmopolitan ideas) regarded as typical of residents of a great city : not provincial ⟨our instinctive desire to be ~ rather than parochial, to be "in the know" rather than to be ignorant of the very latest idiom —G.W.Sherburn⟩ **4** : of, relating to, or constituting a mother country ⟨various ~ nations⟩ ⟨~ currency⟩ ⟨~ military forces⟩ ⟨~ France⟩ ⟨there was upon the Witwatersrand very largely the same crowd of ~ miners —C.W.de Kiewiet⟩ **5** : of, relating to, or constituting a region including a city and the densely populated surrounding areas that are socially and economically integrated with it ⟨~ area⟩ ⟨~ district⟩

met·ro·pol·i·tan·ate \-ˌāt\ *n* -s : the see or office of a metropolitan bishop

metropolitan borough *n* : any of numerous administrative divisions that with the City of London form Greater London

metropolitan cross *n* : CROSS-STAFF 1

met·ro·pol·i·tan·ism \ˌ==ˈ===ˌizəm\ *n* -s : the condition of being metropolitan : metropolitan character

met·ro·pol·i·tan·ize \-ˌīz\ *vt* -ED/-ING/-S : to make metropolitan

metropolitan round *n, often cap M* : a round in archery consisting for men of 30 arrows fired successively at 100 yards, 80 yards, 60 yards, 50 yards, and 40 yards and for women of 30 arrows fired successively at 60 yards, 50 yards, 40 yards, and 30 yards

met·ro·pol·i·tan·ship \ˌ==ˈ===ˌship\ *n* : METROPOLITANATE

me·trop·o·lite \mə'träpəˌlīt, me'-\ *n* -s [LL *metropolita*, *metropolites*, fr. LGk *mētropolitēs*, fr. *mētropolis* + *-itēs* -ite — more at METROPOLIS] **1** : METROPOLITAN 1 **2** : a resident of a metropolis ⟨most ~*s* feel at home only in their own block —Frederic Morton⟩

met·ro·political \ˌme·trō+\ *adj* [LL *metropoliticus* (fr. LGk *mētropolitikos*, fr. *mētropolitēs* metropolite + *-ikos* -ic) + E *-al*] **1** : METROPOLITAN 1 ⟨~ courts⟩ **2** *obs* : METROPOLITAN 2 — **met·ro·politically** \"+\ *adv*

me·trop·o·ly \mə'träpəlē, me'-\ *n* -ES [F *métropolie*, fr. *métropole* + *-ie* -y] : METROPOLITANATE

metror·rha·gia \ˌmē·trə'rāj(ē)ə, ˌme-\ *n* -s [NL, fr. *metr-* + *-rrhagia*] : profuse bleeding from the uterus esp. between menstrual periods — compare MENORRHAGIA — **metror·rhag·ic** \¦==¦rajik\ *adj*

metro·si·de·ros \ˌ==sə'dirəs\ *n, cap* [NL, fr. *metr-* + Gk *sideros* iron] : a genus of trees, shrubs, and vines (family Myrtaceae) chiefly of the Pacific islands that have hard dense heavy wood and large flowers borne in 2-forked or 3-forked cymes — see LEHUA, LIGNUM VITAE 3

me·trox·y·lon \mə'träksəˌlän\ *n, cap* [NL, fr. *metr-* + *-xylon*] : a genus of Indo-Malayan pinnate-leaved palms that flower and fruit once and then die — see SAGO PALM 1a

met·rum \'me·trəm\ *n, pl* **met·ra** \-rə\ [L, fr. Gk *metron* meter, measure — more at MEASURE] : METRON

-me·try \ˌmə·trē, -ri\ *n comb form* -ES [ME *-metrie*, fr. MF, fr. L *-metria*, fr. Gk, fr. *metrein* to measure (fr. *metron* measure) + *-ia* -y — more at MEASURE] : art, process, or science of measuring (something specified) ⟨chrono*metry*⟩ ⟨hygro*metry*⟩ ⟨hyper*metry*⟩ ⟨photo*metry*⟩ ⟨psycho*metry*⟩

met·ter·nich·i·an \ˌmed·ə(r)¦nikēən\ *adj, usu cap* [Prince Klemens W. N. L. von *Metternich* †1859 Austrian statesman and diplomatist + E *-ian*] : of, relating to, or suggestive of Metternich or his political ideas or diplomatic policies

¹met·tle \'med·°l, -et°l\ *n* -s [ME *metel* metal, mettle — more at METAL] **1** *archaic* : METAL **2** : quality of temperament or disposition : SPIRIT, SPIRITEDNESS, TEMPER ⟨a girl of ~ —Norman MacCaig⟩ ⟨but that poetry might be of finer ~ than prose he never apparently dreamed —S.T.Williams⟩ **3** : qualities (as ardor, courage, and stamina) and abilities in relation to a given situation ⟨those who try their ~ against the sea —Walter Hayward⟩ ⟨trucks had proved their ~ in army transport —*Pioneer & Pacemaker*⟩ ⟨spoke in Spanish later on, but at first tried my ~ by using only Yaqui —E.H.Spicer⟩ **syn** see COURAGE — **on one's mettle** *also* **upon one's mettle** : in a state of being challenged or aroused to make one's best efforts ⟨the family business failed and put him *on his mettle* as a writer —Van Wyck Brooks⟩ ⟨putting both major parties *on their mettle* —John Lodge⟩

²mettle \"\ *adj, archaic Scot* : SPIRITED, METTLESOME ⟨an honest and a ~ gentleman —R.L.Stevenson⟩

met·tled \ˌmed·°ld, -et°ld\ *adj* **1** *obs* : METTLESOME **2** : having (such) a mettle — usu. used in combination ⟨muddy-*mettled*⟩ ⟨high-*mettled*⟩

met·tle·some \'med·°lsəm, -et°l-\ *adj* : full of mettle : SPIRITED, HIGH-SPIRITED ⟨a ~ dramatic performer —Lee Rogow⟩ ⟨one of the watch, a ~ fellow who fought like a wildcat —T.B. Costain⟩ ⟨a ~ horse⟩ ⟨a ~ blend of nervous fancy and impromptu characterization —James Kelly⟩ ⟨~ intellectual climate —John Cheever⟩

mett sausage \'met-\ *n* [part trans. of G *mettwurst*] : METTWURST

mett·wurst \'met,=\ *n* -s [G, fr. LG *mettworst*, fr. MLG, fr. *mett* meat, pork + *worst* sausage; akin to OHG *maz* food — more at MEAT, WURST] : a sausage of lean beef and salt pork seasoned, dried, and smoked

met·u·la \'mechələ\ *n, pl* **metu·lae** \-ˌlē\ [NL, fr. L, small cone or pyramid, dim. of *meta* cone, pyramid, boundary mark; perh. akin to ON *meithr* tree, MIr *methas* boundary district, Skt *methī* post, L *munire* to fortify — more at MUNITION] : one of the outermost branches of a conidiophore from which flask-shaped phialides radiate (as in molds of the genera *Aspergillus* and *Penicillium*)

me·tur·ge·man \mə'tərgəmən\ *n, pl* **meturgemans** [Heb & Aram *mĕthurgĕmān*, *mĕthargĕmān*] : a religious official of the early Hebrew synagogue who orally translated the Scriptures from Hebrew into the vernacular

met·wand \'met,wänd\ *var of* **metewand**

Met·y·caine \'med·ə,kān\ *trademark* — used for hydrochloride of piperocaine

metzograph *var of* MEZZOGRAPH

meu·bles \mœbl(°), -b(lə)\ *n pl* [F, fr. MF, fr. pl. of *meuble* movable goods, fr. OF, fr. *meuble* movable, fr. L *mobilis* — more at MOBILE] : a class of property under French law that consists essentially of movables — compare IMMEUBLES

me·um \'mēəm\ *n, cap* [NL, fr. L, spicknel, fr. Gk *mēon*] : a genus of European aromatic perennial herbs (family Umbelliferae) with flowers in compound umbels — see SPICKNEL

meu·nière \ˌmə(r)n'ye(ə)r, mən-\ *adj* [F (*à la*) *meunière*, lit., in the manner of a miller's wife; F *meunière* miller's wife, fem. of *meunier* miller, fr. L *molinarius*, fr. *molina* mill + *-arius* -ary — more at MILL] : cooked in or served with browned butter

¹meuse \'myüs, -üz\ *n* -s [MF *muce*, *musse*, fr. *mucer*, *musser* to hide, conceal] **1** : a gap or hole (as in a hedge or wall) through which a wild animal is accustomed to pass **2** : something resembling a meuse in affording a means of escape : LOOPHOLE

²meuse \"\ *vi* -ED/-ING/-S : to go through a meuse

meute \'myüt\ *n* -s [by alter.] : ⁴MEW 1

MEV *abbr, often not cap* million electron volts

mev·a·lon·ic acid \¦mevə¦länik-\ *n* [*methyl* + *valerolactone* + *-ic*] : a branched dihydroxy acid ($HO_2C_5H_9COOH$ that is obtained by extraction of dried distillers' solubles with organic solvents or made synthetically and that is changed by enzymes in acid solution into squalene; 3,5-dihydroxy-3-methyl-valeric acid

¹mew \'myü\ *also* **mew gull** *n* -s [ME, fr. OE *mǣw*; akin to OS *mēw* gull, MD *meeuw*, ON *mār*; prob. of imit. origin] : GULL; *esp* : the common European gull (*Larus canus*)

²mew \"\ *vb* -ED/-ING/-S [ME *mewen*, of imit. origin] *vi* **1** : MEOW **2** : to make the natural noise of a gull ⟨gulls now swooped and ~*ed* round the ship —Ngaio Marsh⟩ ~ *vt* : to utter by mewing : MEOW ⟨~*ing* pitiful cries⟩

³mew \"\ *n* -s : MEOW ⟨gave a quick consolatory ~ of understanding —Hortense Calisher⟩

⁴mew \"\ *n* -s [ME *muwe*, *mewe*, fr. MF *mue*, fr. *muer* to molt — more at ⁶MEW] **1** : a cage for hawks esp. while molting **2 a** : a coop or cage for fattening animals; *esp* : a pen for fattening fowls **b** *dial chiefly Eng* : a breeding cage (as for canaries) **3 a** *obs* : CONFINEMENT : a place of confinement **b** : a secret place : a place of retirement : HIDEAWAY ⟨I've been three weeks shut within my ~ —Robert Browning⟩ **4 mews** *pl but usu sing in constr, chiefly Brit* **a** (1) : STABLES; *esp* : a range of stables usu. with carriage houses and living quarters built around a yard, court, or street (2) : living quarters or housing developed from such stables **b** : the court or street upon which such stables or the dwellings developed from them open : ALLEY, BACK STREET **c** : a row or group of garages

⁵mew \"\ *vt* -ED/-ING/-S [ME *muwen*, *mewen*, fr. *muwe mewe*, n.] **1 a** *obs* : to shut in or coop up for fattening — used esp. of fowl **b** : to shut or lock in : CONFINE — often used with *up* ⟨better . . . than sitting ~*ed* in a stuffy bedroom with a prayer book —Virginia Woolf⟩ ⟨a group of men ~*ed* up for years in a draughty barrack —Noel Coward⟩ **2** : to put or keep (a hawk) in a mew esp. in molting time

⁶mew \"\ *vb* -ED/-ING/-S [ME *muwen*, fr. MF *muer* to molt, change, fr. L *mutare* to change — more at MISS] *vt* **1** : to cast off (feathers) : MOLT **2** *obs* : to bring about a change in (as color or coat) : SHED **3 a** : to get rid of (the horns) : CAST — used of a stag **b** : to shed the horns from (the head) ~ *vi* **1** : to cast the feathers : MOLT **2** : to shed or cast horns

⁷mew \"\ *dial Brit var of* MOW

me·ward \'mēwə(r)d\ *adv* [*me* + *-ward*] : toward me ⟨for her hands have no kindness ~ —Ezra Pound⟩

me·wa·ri \mā'wärē\ *n* -s *usu cap* : the Rajasthani dialect of Mewar

mew·er \'myüə(r)\ *n* -s : one that mews

¹mewl \'myül\ *vi* -ED/-ING/-S [imit.] **1** : to cry weakly like a child : make whimpering sounds : WHINE **2** : MEOW

²mewl \"\ *n* -s : the act or sound of mewling

mewl·er \-lə(r)\ *n* -s : one that mewls

¹mex \'meks\ *adj, usu cap* [by shortening] : MEXICAN ⟨get my feet all mixed up in these *Mex* dances —Edwin Corle⟩ ⟨offering him for sale for ten *Mex* dollars —Richard Hallet⟩ ⟨cost four dollars *Mex*⟩

²mex \"\ *n, pl* **mex** *or* **mexes** [by shortening] **1** *cap* : MEXICAN ⟨some *Mex* he'd never seen before was behind the bar —Oakley Hall⟩ — often used disparagingly **2** *often cap* : MEXICAN DOLLAR ⟨paper money was so plentiful that . . . a ~ was the smallest that would buy anything —Upton Sinclair⟩

me·xi·ca \'mehē,kä, 'māh-\ *n* -s *usu cap* [Sp *méxica*, prob. fr. Nahuatl *Mexictli*, an Aztec war god] : NAHUATL

¹mex·i·can \'meksəkən, -sēk-\ *adj, usu cap* [Sp *mexicano*, *mejicano*, fr. *México*, *Méjico* Mexico, country in southern No. America + Sp *-ano* -an] **1 a** : of, relating to, or characteristic of Mexico **b** : of, relating to, or characteristic of the people of Mexico **2** : of, relating to, or characteristic of the Mexican language **3** : CENTRAL AMERICAN 2

²mexican \"\ *n* -s **1** *cap* **a** : a native or inhabitant of Mexico **b** : a person of Mexican descent **c** *Southwest* : a person of mixed Spanish and Indian descent **2 a** *usu cap* : NAHUATL **b** *cap* : Spanish as spoken in Mexico **3** *usu cap* : MEXICAN DOLLAR **4** *often cap* : FRENCH YELLOW

mexican asphalt *n, usu cap M* : the residuum obtained from the distillation of Mexican petroleum

mexican bamboo *n, usu cap M* : JAPANESE KNOTWEED

mexican bean beetle *n, usu cap M* : a spotted ladybug (*Epilachna varivestis*) that feeds on the leaves of various kinds of beans and is now an important pest in the U. S.

mexican blue oak *n, usu cap M* : an evergreen oak (*Quercus oblongifolia*) of the southwestern U.S. and adjacent Mexico that grows chiefly in dry sunny regions, varies from a thicket-forming shrub to a tall tree, and produces an annual crop of edible acorns which are locally important as wildlife food

mexican breadfruit *n, usu cap M* : a ceriman (*Monstera deliciosa*)

mexican broomroot *n, usu cap M* : BROOMROOT

mexican buckeye *n, usu cap M* : BUCKEYE 1c

mexican cedar *n, usu cap M* : SPANISH CEDAR

mexican chicken bug *n, usu cap M* : ADOBE BUG

mexican clover *n, usu cap M* : a tropical American herb (*Richardia scabra*) sometimes cultivated as a forage plant

mexican cypress *n, usu cap M* : an evergreen tree (*Cupressus lusitanica*) cultivated for its spreading habit and drooping branchlets

mexican devil-weed \-'==,=\ *n, usu cap M* : a large aster (*Aster spinosus*) having almost leafless often spiny stems and linear or subulate leaves and occurring as a weed in the southern and western U.S.

mexican dollar *n, usu cap M* : a Mexican silver peso

mexican eagle *n, usu cap M* : AUDUBON'S CARACARA

mexican elm *n, usu cap M* : a tropical American elm (*Ulmus mexicana*) that has heavy hard strong wood and is native to Mexico and Central America

mexican fever *n, usu cap M* : TEXAS FEVER

mexican fiber *n, usu cap M* : ISTLE b

mexican fire plant *n, usu cap M* **1** : a showy poinsettia (*Poinsettia heterophylla*) found from the southern U.S. to Peru **2** *also* **mexican fireweed** : SUMMER CYPRESS

mexican fruit fly *n, usu cap M* : a small trypetid fly (*Anastrepha ludens*) having a maggot that feeds in and damages various fruits (as citruses and mangoes)

mexican hairless *n* **1** *usu cap M&H* : an old breed of dogs of unknown origin that are found in Mexico, are of about the size of a fox terrier, and are hairless except for a tuft on the skull and a fuzz on the lower half of the long tail **2** *usu cap M* : a dog of the Mexican Hairless breed

mexican hog *n, usu cap M* : PECCARY

mex·i·can·ism \'meksəkə,nizəm, -sēk-\ *n* -s *usu cap* [Sp *mexicanismo*, *mejicanismo*, fr. *mexicano*, *mejicano* Mexican + *-ismo* -ism — more at MEXICAN] : a word, phrase, or mode of expression distinctive of Spanish as spoken in Mexico ⟨language seasoned with *Mexicanisms*⟩

mex·i·can·ist \-nəst\ *n* -s *usu cap* : an authority on the history or civilization of Mexico

mex·i·can·ization \ˌ==kənə'zāshən, -ˌnī'z-\ *n* -s *usu cap* **1** : the action of mexicanizing **2** : the state (in industry or farming) of having or being supplied with a large number of Mexican personnel or laborers ⟨the *Mexicanization* of farm work in the southwest⟩

mex·i·can·ize \'==kə,nīz\ *vt* -ED/-ING/-S *often cap* [¹*mexican* + *-ize*] : to make Mexican in quality, traits, customs, or modes of conduct

mexican jumping bean *n, usu cap M* : JUMPING BEAN

me·xi·ca·no \ˌmehē'kä(ˌ)nō, ˌmāh-\ *n* -s [Sp *mexicano*, *mejicano* — more at MEXICAN] **1** *cap* : MEXICAN 1 **2** *usu cap* : NAHUATL

mexican onyx *n, usu cap M* : ALABASTER 1

mexican orange *n, usu cap M* : a round-headed evergreen Mexican shrub (*Choisya ternata*) of the family Rutaceae that has opposite trifoliolate leaves with entire obovate leaflets stippled with pellucid dots and fragrant white pentamerous flowers in axillary and terminal cymes and that is widely cultivated in mild and moderate climates as a hedge or specimen plant

mexican persimmon *n, usu cap M* : a persimmon tree (*Diospyros texana*) of Texas and Mexico having small cuneate leaves and black fruit

mexican piñon *also* **mexican piñon pine** *n, usu cap M* : a bush or low tree (*Pinus cembroides*) of the southern U.S. and Mexico having usu. three needles in each fascicle and globular cones

mexican poppy *n, usu cap M* : PRICKLY POPPY

mexican red *n, often cap M* : RAW SIENNA 2

mexican rose *n, usu cap M* : a portulaca (*Portulaca grandiflora*)

mexican rubber *n, usu cap M* : GUAYULE

mexican scammony *n, usu cap M* : IPOMOEA 3

mexican sisal *n, usu cap M* : HENEQUEN 1

mexican skipjack *n, usu cap M* : FRIGATE MACKEREL

mexican snapper *n, usu cap M* : RED SNAPPER a

mexican spanish *n, cap M&S* : the Spanish used in Mexico

mexican standoff *n, usu cap M* : DRAW 3b, DEADLOCK

mexican star *or* **mexican star-of-bethlehem** *n, usu cap M&B* : FROST FLOWER 1a

mexican stud *n, usu cap M* : a variety of five-card stud poker in which all cards are dealt face down but each player must turn up one card before a round of betting begins

mexican sunflower *n, usu cap M* : TITHONIA 2

mexican tea *n, usu cap M* : a rank-scented tropical American pigweed (*Chenopodium ambrosioides*)

mexican tiger *n, usu cap M* : JAGUAR

mexican tulip poppy *n, usu cap M* : GOLDEN CUP 2

mexican weed *n, usu cap M* : BIRDEYE

mexican whisk *n, usu cap M* : BROOMROOT

mexican white pine *n, usu cap M* : AYACAHUITE

mex·i·co \'meksə,kō, -sē,-\ *adj, usu cap* [fr. *Mexico*, country in southern No. America] **1** : of or from Mexico : of the kind or style prevalent in Mexico **2** *or* **mexico city** *usu cap M&C* [fr. *Mexico City*, Mexico] : of or from Mexico City, the capital of Mexico : of the kind or style prevalent in Mexico City

mey·er·hoff·er·ite \'mī(ə)r,häfə,rīt\ *n* -s [Wilhelm *Meyerhoffer* †1906 Ger. chemist + E *-ite*] : a mineral $Ca_2B_6O_{11}.7H_2O$ consisting of a hydrous calcium borate

¹mezcal *var of* MESCAL

²mez·cal \'me¦skäl, mə's-\ *n* -s [AmerSp (El Salvador) *mescal*, *mezcal*, *mexcal*, fr. Sp, mescal] : MEXICAN ELM

mezcaline *var of* MESCALINE

me·ze·re·on \mə'zirēən, -zer-\ *n* -s [ME *mizerion*, fr. ML *mezereon*, fr. Ar *māzariyūn*, fr. Per] **1** : a small European shrub (*Daphne mezereum*) with fragrant lilac purple flowers that appear before the leaves, an acrid bark used in medicine, and a scarlet fruit sometimes used as an adulterant of black pepper **2** : MEZEREUM

mezereon family *n* : THYMELAEACEAE

me·ze·re·um \-ēəm\ *n* -s [NL, alter. of ML *mezereon*] **1** : MEZEREON 1 **2** : the dried bark of mezereon or other European shrubs (genus *Daphne*) used externally as a vesicatory and irritant

mezquit *or* **mezquite** *var of* MESQUITE

me·zu·zah *or* **me·zu·za** \mə'zůzə\ *n, pl* **me·zu·zoth** *or* **me·zu·zot** \-ˌzō̇t(h)\ *or* **mezuzahs** *or* **mezuzas** [Heb *mĕzūzāh*, lit., doorpost] : a piece of parchment inscribed on one side with the scriptural passages Deut 6:4–9 and 11:13–21 written in 22 lines and on the other with the name Shaddai, rolled up in a scroll, and placed in a small wooden, metal, or glass case or tube that is affixed to the doorpost of some Jewish homes as a symbol of Jewishness and a reminder of faith in God

mez·za majolica \¦metsə-, -edzə-,-ezə-\ *n* [It *mezza maiòlica*, lit., half majolica] : early Italian earthenware resembling majolica but whitened with a clay slip under a lead glaze and partly decorated with sgraffito

mez·za·nine \¦mez°n¦ēn\ *also* **mezzanine floor** *or* **mezzanine story** *n* -s [F, fr. It *mezzanino*, fr. *mezzano* middle, intermediate (fr. L *medianus*) + *-ino* (dim. suffix) — more at MEDIAN] **1 a** : a low-ceilinged story between two main stories of a building; *esp* : an intermediate or fractional story that projects in the form of a balcony over the ground story **b** (1) : the lowest balcony in a theater (2) : the first few rows of such a balcony **2** : a flooring laid over a floor to bring it up to a desired height or level **3** *Brit* : the floor beneath the stage of a theater from which trapdoors and other pieces of stage machinery are worked

mezza or·ches·tra \-ȯr¦kestrə, -¦ȯrkəstrə\ *adv* [It, lit., half orchestra] : with but half the orchestra

¹mez·za vo·ce \¦metsə¦vō(ˌ)chā, -edzə-\ *adv (or adj)* [It, lit., half voice] : with medium or half volume of tone — used as a direction in music

²mezza voce \"\ *n* : a medium or half volume of tone ⟨the quality of her voice in *mezza voce* was warm and expressive —Winthrop Sargeant⟩

mez·zo \'met(ˌ)sō, -ed(ˌ)zō, -e(ˌ)zō\ *n* -s [by shortening] **1** : MEZZO-SOPRANO **2** : MEZZOTINT

mezzo forte \¦=(ˌ)=¦=(ˌ)=\ *adj (or adv)* [It] : moderately loud — used as a direction in music

mezzo-forte \"\ *n* [*mezzo forte*] : a moderately loud tone ⟨one of those quiet atmospheric moods that never rise above a *mezzo-forte* —Julian Herbage⟩

mez·zo·graph *also* **metzo·graph** \'metsə,graf, -räf\ *n* [It *mezzo* half (fr. L *medius* middle) + E *-graph* (as in *photograph*) — more at MID] : a halftone made with a grain screen and having a grained surface instead of crossline screen dots

mezzo legato *adv (or adj)* [It, lit., half legato] : in a manner intermediate between legato and staccato — used as a direction in music

mezzo piano *adj (or adv)* [It] : moderately soft — used as a direction in music

mezzo-re·lie·vo *or* **mezzo-ri·lie·vo** \¦=(ˌ)rē'lē(ˌ)vō, -rēl'yā-, -yē\ *n, pl* **mezzo-relievos** \-vōz\ *or* **mezzo-rilie·vi** \-rēl'yā(ˌ)vē, -ye-\ [It *mezzorilievo*, fr. *mezzo* half + *rilievo* relief — more at RELIEF] : sculptural relief that is intermediate in degree of projection between bas-relief and high relief with approximately half of the natural circumference of the modeled form projecting from the surrounding surface

mezzo-soprano \¦=(ˌ)=+\ *n* [It *mezzosoprano*, fr. *mezzo* half + *soprano* — more at SOPRANO] : a woman's voice of medium compass (as a to f″) between that of the soprano and contralto; *also* : a singer having a voice of such compass

mezzo-soprano clef *n* : the C clef placed on the second line of the staff

¹mez·zo·tint \'==,=\ *also* **mez·zo·tin·to** \¦=¦tin·(ˌ)tō\ *n* -s [modif. of It *mezzatinta*, fr. *mezza* (fem. of *mezzo* half) + *tinta* tint — more at TINT] **1** *archaic* : DEMITINT **2 a** : a manner of engraving on copper or steel by working on a surface previously roughened with a rocker or cradle and removing the roughness in places by burnishing to produce the requisite light and shade **b** : an engraving produced in this manner

²mezzotint \"\ *also* **mezzotinto** \"\ *vt* -ED/-ING/-S : to engrave in or represent as if in mezzotint

mez·zo·tint·er \'=,=,tintə(r)\ *n* : one skilled in mezzotint

mf *abbr* **1** manufacture **2** microfarad **3** millifarad

MF *abbr* **1** machine finish **2** *often not cap* medium frequency **3** *often not cap* mezzo forte **4** mill finish **5** motor freight

MFBM *abbr* [L *mille* thousand] thousand feet board measure

mfd *abbr* **1** manufactured **2** microfarad

mfg *abbr* manufacturing

MFH *abbr* master of foxhounds

MFN *abbr* most favored nation

MFP *abbr* mean free path

mfr *abbr* manufacture; manufacturer

mg *abbr* **1** margin **2** meaning **3** milligram **4** morning

MG *abbr* **1** machine-glazed **2** machine gun **3** [F *main gauche*] left hand **4** major general **5** make good **6** military government **7** mill glazed **8** mixed grain **9** motor generator

Mg *symbol* magnesium

MGB *abbr* motor gunboat

MGC *abbr* machine-gun company; machine-gun corps

MGD *abbr, often not cap* million gallons per day

mgm *abbr* milligram

MGO *abbr* military government officer

mgr *abbr* **1** manager **2** monseigneur **3** monsignor

mgrm *abbr* milligram

mgt *abbr* management

mh *abbr* millihenry

MH *abbr* **1** magnetic heading **2** maleic hydrazide **3** most honorable

MHCP *abbr, often not cap* mean horizontal candlepower

MHD *abbr* minimum hemolytic dose

mho \'mō\ *n* -s [backward spelling of *ohm*] : the practical unit of conductance equal to the reciprocal of the ohm

mho·me·ter \ˈ=ˌmēd·ə(r), -ētə-\ *n* [*mho* + *-meter*] **:** an instrument for measuring conductance

mhorr *var of* MOHR

MHSCP *abbr* mean hemispherical candlepower

MHT *abbr* mean high tide

MHW *abbr* mean high water

MHWN *abbr* mean high water neaps

MHWS *abbr* mean high water springs

MHz *abbr* megahertz

mi \ˈmē\ *n* -s [ML, fr. L *mira* wonders, a word sung to this note in a medieval hymn to St. John the Baptist] **1 :** the third tone of the diatonic scale in solmization **2 :** the tone *E* in the fixed-do system

mi- *or* **mio-** *also* **meio-** *comb form* [prob. fr. NL *meio-*, fr. Gk, fr. *meiōn* — more at MINOR] **1 a :** less ⟨*Mio*cene⟩ **:** smaller ⟨*Mio*hippus⟩ **b :** slightly ⟨*mi*concave⟩ **2 :** fewer ⟨*meio*phylly⟩

mi *abbr* **1** mile **2** mill **3** minor **4** minute

MI *abbr* **1** malleable iron **2** medical inspection **3** memorial inscription **4** metabolic index **5** military intelligence

MIA *abbr* missing in action

mi·ac·i·dae \mīˈasəˌdē\ *n pl, cap* [NL, fr. *Miacis*, type genus + *-idae*] **:** a family of primitive generalized carnivorous mammals widely distributed from the Palaeocene through the lower Oligocene, sometimes classed with the creodonts, but probably being early ancestral types of the Fissipeda

mi·a·cis \ˈmīəsəs, mīˈās-\ *n, cap* [NL] **:** the type genus of Miacidae comprising short-legged long-tailed arboreal carnivores comparable in form to the civets and prob. ancestral to *Cynodictis*

¹mi·ami \mīˈamē, -amə\ *n, pl* **miami** *or* **miamis** *usu cap* **1 a :** an Indian people of northern Indiana **b :** a member of such people **2 :** a dialect of the Illinois language

²miami \ˈ"\ *adj, usu cap* [fr. *Miami*, city in southeast Florida] **:** of or from the city of Miami, Fla. ⟨*Miami* hotels⟩ **:** of the kind or style prevalent in Miami

mia–mia \ˈmīəˌmīə\ *n* -s [native name in Australia] **:** a rude usu. temporary hut of the Australian aborigines

mi·am·i·an \mīˈamēən\ *n* -s *cap* [*Miami*, Florida + E *-an*] **:** a native or resident of Miami, Fla.

mi·a·na bug \ˈmēəˌnä-\ *n, often cap M* [fr. *Mianeh*, town in Azerbaijan, Iran] **:** CHICKEN TICK; *also* **:** a closely related Asiatic tick (*Argas mianensis*) that has been implicated as a vector of relapsing fever

mi·ang \mēˈäŋ\ *n* -s [Thai] **:** a wild tea (*Thea sinensis*) of Thailand

mi·ao *also* **meo** *or* **maeo** \mēˈau̇\ *n, pl* **miao** *or* **miaos** *usu cap* [Chin (Pek) *Miao*²] **1 a :** an aboriginal people of China inhabiting southwestern China and the northern parts of Vietnam, Laos, and Thailand **b :** a member of such people **2 :** a language of the Miao people

miao–tse *also* **miao–tze** *or* **miao–tzu** \mēˈau̇dzə\ *n, pl* **miao-tse** *or* **miao-tses** *usu cap* [Chin (Pek) *Miao*² *-tzu*³, fr. *Miao*² + *tzu*³ son, child] **:** MIAO

miaow *also* **miaou** *var of* MEOW

mi·ao–yao \mēˈau̇ˈyau̇\ *n, usu cap M&Y* **:** a language group containing the Miao and Yao languages of uncertain wider relationship

mi·ar·gy·rite \(ˌ)mīˈärjəˌrīt\ *n* [G *miargyrit*, fr. *mi-* + *argyr-* + *-it* -ite] **:** a mineral $AgSbS_2$ consisting of a silver antimony sulfide and occurring in iron-black to steel-gray crystals or masses whose powder is cherry red

mi·a·ro·lit·ic \ˌmēərōˈlid·ik\ *adj* [ISV *miaro-* (fr. It dial. *miarolo* granite with small cavities) + *-litic*] **1** *of igneous rock* **:** characterized by irregular cavities into which well-formed crystals project ⟨~ structure⟩ ⟨~ granites⟩ **2** *of a cavity* **:** having an irregular form into which such crystals project

mi·as \ˈmīəs\ *n* -ES [Iban *mayas*] **:** ORANGUTAN

mi·as·ma \mīˈazmə, mēˈ-\ *also* **mi·asm** \ˈmīˌazəm\ *n, pl* **mias·mas** \mīˈazməz, mēˈ-\ *or* **mias·ma·ta** \ˈ=ˈ=məd·ə\ *also* **miasms** [NL *miasma*, fr. Gk, defilement; akin to Gk *miainein* to defile — more at MOLE] **1 :** a vaporous exhalation (as of a marshy region or of putrescent matter) formerly believed to contain a substance causing disease (as malaria) ⟨the ~s of Matto Grosso —Jean Stafford⟩; *broadly* **:** a heavy vaporous emanation or atmosphere ⟨a ~ of tobacco smoke⟩ ⟨seems to be more than a scent that emanates from the hops: it is almost a visible ~, sweet yet agreeably acrid —Jan Struther⟩ **2 :** a pervasive influence or atmosphere that tends to deplete or corrupt ⟨abandoned its task in a ~ of words —J.K.Galbraith⟩ ⟨from its pages flow that same ~ of dread suspense, that same air of dissolution, decay, and death —Margaret B. Hexter⟩

mi·as·mal \(ˈ)mīˈazməl, (ˈ)mēˈ-\ *adj* [*miasma* + *-al*] **:** MIASMIC ⟨blinding flashes of newspaper cameras and the ~ air of the closed, unventilated room —C.M.Smith⟩

mi·as·mat·ic \ˌmīəzˈmad·ik, ˌmēə-\ *adj* [F *miasmatique*, fr. NL *miasmat-*, *miasma* + F *-ique* -ic] **:** MIASMIC ⟨the ~ northern and northeastern coast —*Encyc. Americana*⟩

mi·as·mic \(ˈ)mīˈazmik,(ˈ)mēˈ-\ *adj* [*miasma* + *-ic*] **1 :** of, relating to, or like a miasma **:** caused by miasma **:** producing a miasma **:** characterized by miasma ⟨rubber plantations of the ~ jungle —Robert Littell⟩ **2 :** foully contagious **:** NOXIOUS, MEPHITIC ⟨a clamorous square mile of plants and pens that spread a ~ stench —*Newsweek*⟩

mi·as·tor \mīˈastə(r)\ *n, cap* [NL, fr. Gk *miastōr* one that defiles; akin to Gk *miainein* to defile] **:** a genus of flies (family Cecidomyiidae) that are remarkable for their parthenogenetic and paedogenetic reproduction by which the larva on hatching from the egg develops internally a brood of similar larvae that on escaping may repeat the process for several generations before pupation and development of mature individuals

mi·aul \mēˈau̇l, -ˈōl\ *vi* -ED/-ING/-S [F *miauler*, of imit. origin] **1 :** MEW, MEOW **2 :** CATERWAUL

mib \ˈmib\ *n* -s [prob. by shortening & alter. fr. *marble*] **1** *dial* **:** MIG **2 mibs** *pl but sing in constr, dial* **:** the game of marbles

mi·ca \ˈmīkə\ *n* -s *often attrib* [NL (prob. influenced by L *micare* to flash, sparkle), fr. L *mica* grain, crumb; akin to Gk *mikros* small, short — more at DIMICATION, MICR-] **:** any of a group of minerals that crystallize in forms apparently orthorhombic or hexagonal but really monoclinic and characterized by highly perfect cleavage, readily separating into very thin somewhat elastic leaves, that are all silicates although differing widely in composition and varying in color from colorless, pale brown, or yellow to green or black, that are prominent constituents of many igneous and metamorphic rocks, and that form a division including the brittle micas and chlorites as well as the micas proper — see BIOTITE, LEPIDOLITE, LEPIDOMELANE, MUSCOVITE, PARAGONITE, PHLOGOPITE, ZINNWALDITE; compare DAMOURITE

mi·ca·ceous \(ˈ)mīˈkāshəs\ *adj* [prob. fr. (assumed) NL *micaceus*, fr. NL *mica* + L *-aceus* -aceous] **1 :** consisting of or containing mica ⟨~ sandstone⟩ **2 :** resembling mica (as in foliation or luster)

micaceous iron ore *n* **:** hematite having a micaceous structure

micalike \ˈ=ˌ=ˌ=\ *adj* **:** resembling mica

Mi·car·ta \mīˈkärd·ə\ *trademark* — used for any of various laminated products made by bonding layers of paper or cloth with a resin under heat and pressure and used in the form of sheets, rods, tubes, or other molded shapes

mi·caw·ber \məˈkȯbə(r)\ *n* -s *usu cap* [fr. Wilkins *Micawber*, character in the novel *David Copperfield* (1849–50) by Charles Dickens †1870 Eng. author] **:** an improvident person who lives in expectation of an upturn in his fortunes

mi·caw·ber·ish \-b(ə)rish\ *adj, usu cap* **:** of, relating to, or characteristic of a Micawber (as in being habitually expectant of an upturn in one's fortunes) ⟨home production continued to lag, but the Government went on its *Micawberish* way, waiting for something to turn up —*Economist*⟩

mi·caw·ber·ism \-bəˌrizəm\ *n* -s *usu cap* **:** the improvident state or habitually optimistic point of view of a Micawber

mice [ME *mys*, fr. OE *mȳs*] *pl of* MOUSE

mi·cel·lar \(ˈ)mīˈselə(r), məˈ-\ *adj* [ISV *micelle* + *-ar*] **:** of, relating to, or characterized by a micelle or micelles — **mi·cel·lar·ly** *adv*

micellar theory *or* **micellar hypothesis** *n* **:** a theory in cytology: protoplasm and some of its products (as the plant cell wall) exist primarily as or are largely made up of micelles

mi·celle \mīˈsel, məˈ-\ *also* **mi·cel·la** \-elə\ *or* **mi·cell** \-el\ *n, pl* **micelles** \-lz\ *also* **micel·lae** \-ˌlē\ *or* **micells** [NL *micella*, fr. L *mica* crumb + *-ella*] **:** a unit of structure built up from polymeric molecules or ions: as **a :** an ordered region in a natural or synthetic fiber (as of cellulose, silk, or viscose rayon) — compare CRYSTALLITE 2, FIBRIL **b :** a highly associated particle of a colloidal solution ⟨colloidal ~s of soaps and detergents —J.W.McBain⟩ **c :** an organic colloidal particle ranging in size from one micron to one millimicron and found in coal and some shales

mice pink *n* **:** DEPTFORD PINK

mich \ˈmich, ˈmēch\ *var of* MEECH

mich·ael·mas \ˈmikəlməs\ *n* -ES *usu cap* [ME *mychelmesse*, fr. OE *Michaeles mæsse*, fr. *Michaeles* (gen. of *Michael*, archangel identified as patron of the Jewish nation in Dan 10:21 and as leader in a war against the devil in Rev 12:7–9) + OE *mæsse* mass, feast day — more at MASS] **:** the feast of the archangel Michael that is a church festival celebrated on September 29 and is one of the four quarter days in England

michaelmas blackbird *n, usu cap M* **:** RING OUZEL

michaelmas daisy *n, usu cap M* **1 :** any of several wild asters; *esp* **:** one blooming about Michaelmas **2 :** any of various hybrid asters developed from the heath aster, the New England aster, and other asters of No. America

michaelmas term *n, usu cap M* **1 :** the term from November 2 to 25 during which the superior courts of England were formerly open — compare EASTER TERM, HILARY TERM, TRINITY TERM **2 :** the first or fall term of the academic year lasting from the beginning of October until Christmas — used at British universities

michaelmastide \ˈ=ˌ=ˌ=ˌ=\ *n, usu cap* **:** the season of Michaelmas

mi·chael reaction \ˈmīkəl-\ *or* **michael condensation** *n, usu cap M* [after Arthur *Michael* †1942 Am. chemist] **:** the addition of a sodium enolate (as the sodium derivative of ethyl malonate) to the double bond of an alpha,beta-unsaturated ester (as ethyl cinnamate) or ketone

mi·chel·an·ge·lesque \ˌmīkəˌlanjəˈlesk\ *adj, usu cap* [*Michelangelo* Buonarroti †1564 Ital. sculptor, painter, architect, and poet + E *-esque*] **:** characteristic of or resembling Michelangelo or his work which is preeminent for grandeur of conception, dramatic action, and technical mastery of execution ⟨*Michelangelesque* statuary⟩

mi·che·lia \mīˈkēlēə, -lyə\ *n* [NL, fr. Piero Antonio *Micheli* †1737 Ital. botanist + NL *-ia*] **1** *cap* **:** a genus of Asiatic shrubs and trees (family Magnoliaceae) having introrse anthers and the pistil-bearing receptacle stalked within the flower — see BANANA SHRUB, CHAMPAC **2** -s **:** any plant of the genus *Michelia*

mi·chel·son–mor·ley experiment \ˌmīkəlsənˈmȯrlē-\ *n, usu cap both Ms* [after Albert A. *Michelson* †1931 Am. physicist and Edward W. *Morley* †1923 Am. chemist and physicist] **:** an experiment that shows that the two parts of a divided ray of light travel at the same speed over paths perpendicular to each other (as over east-west and north-south paths) and that leads to the deductions that the motion of the earth through space has no effect upon the velocity of light and the absolute motion of the earth is not measurable

mich·er \ˈmichə(r), ˈmēch-\ *var of* MEECHER

¹mich·i·gan \ˈmishəgən, -shēg-\ *adj, usu cap* [fr. *Michigan*, state in the north central U.S., fr. Lake *Michigan*, of Algonquian origin; akin to Fox *mešikami* large lake] **:** of or from the state of Michigan ⟨the *Michigan* automotive industry⟩ **:** of the kind or style prevalent in Michigan **:** MICHIGANIAN

²michigan \ˈ"\ *n* -s *usu cap* [fr. *Michigan*, state in the north central U.S.] **:** a card game in which players put chips on a layout of ace, king, queen, and jack of different suits taken from another pack, in which all cards are dealt out with an extra hand that may be taken by the dealer or sold by him to the highest bidder, in which starting with the lowest card of a suit in the hand of the player who selects and starts the suit each suit is played in sequence until it has been stopped, in which a player who plays a card matching a card of the layout takes all the chips on that card, and in which the player who first plays the last of his cards wins the deal — called also *boodle, Chicago, Newmarket, stops*

michigan bankroll *n, usu cap M, slang* **:** a roll of paper money consisting of a bill of large denomination on the outside of small-denomination or counterfeit bills

mich·i·gan·der \ˌmishəˈgandə(r), -gaan-\ *n* -s *cap* [fr. *Michigander* (derogatory nickname of Lewis Cass †1866 Am. lawyer and political figure), blend of *Michigan* and E *gander*] **:** a native or resident of Michigan

michigan grayling *n, usu cap M* **:** a fish that is a variety (*Thymallus signifer tricolor*) of the arctic grayling and that occurs only in northern Michigan

¹mich·i·ga·ni·an \ˌmishəˈgānēən, -gan-\ *n* -s *cap* [*Michigan* + E *-an*, n. suffix] **:** MICHIGANDER

²michiganian \ˈ"\ *adj, usu cap* [*Michigan* + E *-an*, adj. suffix] **1 :** of, relating to, or characteristic of the state of Michigan **2 :** of, relating to, or characteristic of the people of Michigan

mich·i·gan·ite \ˈmishəgəˌnīt, -shēg-\ *n* -s *cap* [*Michigan* + E *-ite*] **:** MICHIGANDER

michigan rummy *n, usu cap M* **:** a form of five hundred rum in which each hand is a completed game

mich·ing \ˈmiching, ˈmēch-\ *var of* MEECHING

mich·ler's ketone \ˈmiklə(r)z-\ *n, usu cap M* [after Wilhelm T. *Michler* †1889 Ger. chemist] **:** a crystalline amino ketone $[(CH_3)_2NC_6H_4]_2CO$ made by treating dimethylaniline with phosgene and used in the manufacture of triphenylmethane dyes

micht \ˈmikt\ *Scot var of* MIGHT

mich·tam \ˈmikˌtam\ *usu cap* [Heb *mikhtām*] — used in the Bible in the headings of Psalm 16 and Psalms 56 to 60 (AV) possibly to suggest atonement

mi·chu·rin·ism \məˈchu̇rəˌnizəm\ *n* -s *usu cap* [Ivan V. *Michurin* †1935 Russ. horticulturist + E *-ism*] **:** LYSENKOISM — **mi·chu·rin·ist** \-nəst\ *or* **mi·chu·rin·ite** \-ˌnīt\ *adj or n, usu cap*

¹mick \ˈmik\ *also* **mike** \ˈmīk\ *n* -s *sometimes cap* [prob. fr. *Mick*, *Mike*, nicknames fr. the name *Michael*] **:** IRISHMAN — often taken to be offensive

²mick \ˈmik\ *n* -s [origin unknown] *Austral* **:** the head of a penny

mick·ery \ˈmik(ə)rē\ *n* -ES [origin unknown] *Austral* **:** ²SOAK 2

mick·ey *also* **micky** \ˈmikē, -ki\ *n, pl* **mickeys** *also* **mickies** [prob. fr. *Mickey*, nickname fr. the name *Michael*] **1** *sometimes cap* **:** IRISHMAN — often taken to be offensive **2** *pl usu* *mickies* **:** POTATO 2a(2) ⟨roast *mickies* in the gutter fires —Joseph Mitchell⟩ **3** *usu cap* **:** MICKEY FINN ⟨as soon slip you a *Mickey* as look at you —Merle Miller⟩

mickey finn \-ˈfin\ *n, usu cap M&F* [prob. fr. the name *Mickey Finn*] **1 :** a drink of liquor doctored with a drastic purgative or a stupefying drug **2 :** an anglers' streamer fly with silver body and red and yellow wings

¹mick·le \ˈmikəl\ *adj* -ER/-EST [ME *mikel, muchel*, fr. OE *micel, mycel* — more at MUCH] *chiefly Scot* **:** GREAT, MUCH

²mickle \ˈ"\ *adv* [ME *mikel, muchel*, fr. OE *micel, mycel* (fr. accus. sing. neut. of *micel, mycel*, adj.) and *micle, mycle* (fr. instrumental sing. neut. of *micel, mycel*, adj.) and *miclum, myclum* (fr. dat. pl. of *micel, mycel*, adj.)] *chiefly Scot* **:** to a great degree

³mickle \ˈ"\ *n* -s [ME *mikel*, fr. *mikel, muchel*, adj.] *chiefly Scot* **:** a great amount or sum

mick·le·mote \-ˌmōt\ *or* **mick·le·gemote** \ˈ=ˌ=+\ *n* -s *usu cap* [OE *mycel gemōt*, fr. *mycel* large, great + *gemōt* gemot — more at GEMOT] **:** the great council under an Anglo-Saxon king — compare GEMOT, WITENAGEMOT

mickle–mouthed \ˈ=ˌ=ˈ=\ *adj, Scot* **:** having a big mouth

mic·mac \ˈmikˌmak\ *n, pl* **micmac** *or* **micmacs** *usu cap* [Micmac *Migmac*, lit., allies] **1 a :** an Indian people of the Maritime Provinces and Newfoundland, Canada **b :** a member of such people **2 :** an Algonquian language of the Micmac people

¹mi·co \ˈmē(ˌ)kō\ *n* -s [Muskogee *miko*] **:** a Muskogean chief

²mico \ˈ"\ *n* -s [Sp, of Cariban origin; akin to Galibi *méku* marmoset] **:** MARMOSET; *esp* **:** a black-tailed marmoset (*Callithrix melanurus*) of tropical So. America

mi·concave \(ˈ)mī+\ *adj* [*mi-* + *concave*] **:** slightly curved — used esp. of a type of crystal commonly used in open-faced watches

mi·co·nia \mīˈkōnēə\ *n, cap* [NL, fr. Francisco *Micó* (*Micón*) 16th cent. Span. physician and botanist + NL *-ia*] **:** a large genus of tropical American shrubs or trees (family Melastomaceae) with small flowers in showy terminal inflorescences

mi con·tra fa \ˌmēˌkänˌtrəˈfä, -kōn-, -kȯn-\ *n* [ML, lit., mi against fa] **:** TRITONE — used in early contrapuntal music as an expression of caution to the musician against the use of dangerous intervals

mi·co·qui·an \mēˈkōkēən\ *also* **mi·coque·an** \ˈ", -ōkən\ *adj, usu cap* [La *Micoque*, site near Les Eyzies, commune in southwest central France, where remains of the culture were found + E *-an*] **:** of or relating to a late Acheulean culture of England and southern France characterized by biface hand axes having very narrow points and thin cross section and by a developed flake industry

micr- *or* **micro-** *comb form* [ME *micro-*, fr. L, fr. Gk *mikr-, mikro-*, fr. *mikros, smikros* small, short; akin to OE *smēalīc* careful, exquisite, OHG *smāhi* small, low, ON *smār* small, and perh. to OE *smītan* to smear — more at SMITE] **1 a :** small **:** minute **:** petty ⟨*micro*cyst⟩ — often used to contrast with *macr-* **b :** enlarging **:** magnifying or amplifying — in names of instruments ⟨*micro*phone⟩ ⟨*micro*scope⟩ **c :** used for small or minute size, quantities, intensities, or variations ⟨*micro*barograph⟩ ⟨*micro*calorimeter⟩ ⟨*micro*graph⟩ **d :** minutely ⟨*micro*level⟩ **2 :** one millionth part of (a specified unit) ⟨*micro*second⟩ — esp. in terms used in the metric system ⟨*micro*gram⟩ and in electricity ⟨*micro*farad⟩ ⟨*micro*ohm⟩ **3 :** microscopic: as **a :** dealing with, employing, or used in microscopy ⟨*micro*paleontology⟩ ⟨*micro*tome⟩ **b :** revealed by or having its structure discernible only by microscopical examination ⟨*micro*fossil⟩ **c :** prepared for microscopical examination ⟨*micro*section⟩ **4 :** abnormally small ⟨*micro*dactylous⟩ — chiefly in nouns denoting a condition of a specified part of the body ⟨*micro*gnathia⟩ **5 :** of, involving, or for very small or minute quantities of material **:** on a small or minute scale of chemical operation **:** microchemical **:** microanalytical ⟨*micro*balance⟩ ⟨*micro*sublimation⟩ — compare SEMIMICRO-, ULTRAMICRO- **6 :** of very fine grain — in names of rocks ⟨*micro*granite⟩ **7 :** of or relating to a small area ⟨*micro*climate⟩ ⟨*micro*economics⟩ ⟨*micro*habitat⟩ **8 :** microphotographed or microfilmed ⟨*micro*copy⟩ **:** employed in or relating to microphotographing or microfilming ⟨*micro*reader⟩

micra *pl of* MICRON

mi·cra·ner \ˈmīkrəˌne(ə)r, mīˈkrānər\ *n* -s [NL, fr. *micr-* + Gk *anēr* man, male animal — more at ANDR-] **:** a male ant of unusually small stature

mi·cras·ter \mīˈkrastə(r)\ *n, cap* [NL, fr. *micr-* + *-aster*] **:** a genus of extinct heart urchins (order Exocycloida) with ambulacral furrows arranged in a small star on the dorsal surface

mi·cren·ceph·a·lon \ˌmīˌkr+\ *n, pl* **micrencephala** [NL, fr. *micr-* + *encephalon*] **:** CEREBELLUM

mi·cren·ceph·a·lous \ˌmīˌkrenˈsefələs\ *adj* [*micr-* + *-encephalous*] **:** having an abnormally small brain

mi·cren·ceph·a·ly \-lē\ *n* -ES [NL *micrencephalia*, fr. *micr-* + *-encephalia* -encephaly] **:** the condition of having an abnormally small brain

mi·crer·gate \mīˈkrərˌgāt\ *also* **mi·cro·er·gate** \ˌmīkrōˈər,-\ *n* -s [*micr-* + Gk *ergatēs* worker — more at ERGAT-] **:** a member of a caste of small workers among various ants

mi·cri·nite \ˈmīkrəˌnīt\ *n* -s [*micr-* + *-inite* (as in *fusinite*)] **:** an opaque structureless material that is the dominant constituent of durain

¹mi·cro \ˈmīˌkrō\ *n* -s [NL *micro-* (as in *Microlepidoptera*)] **:** a very small moth

²micro \ˈ"\ *adj* [*micr-*] **:** small or minute in size **:** MICROSCOPIC ⟨the chemistry of ~ quantities of transuranium and radioactive materials —*Chem. & Engineering News*⟩ ⟨placed in a ~ fractionating apparatus —*Jour. of Biological Chem.*⟩ ⟨whether the pests be plants or animals, macro or ~ in size —R.N. Shreve⟩ — see MACR-

micro- — see MICR-

mi·cro·aerophile \ˈmīkrō+\ *n* -s [*microaero-* (fr. *micr-* + *aer-*) + *-phile*] **:** an organism requiring very little free oxygen

mi·cro·aero·phil·ic \ˌ=ˌ=ˌ(=)=ˈfilik\ *also* **mi·cro·aerophile** \ˈ=ˌ=+\ *or* **mi·cro·aer·oph·i·lous** \ˈ"+ˌ=(=)ˈräfələs\ *adj* [*microaerophilic* fr. *microaerophile*, n. + *-ic*; *microaerophile*, *microaerophilous* fr. *microaero-* + *-phile* or *-philous*] **:** requiring very little free oxygen — **mi·cro·aero·phil·i·cal·ly** \ˈ"+ˌ=(=)ˈ=filək(ə)lē\ *adv*

mi·cro·ammeter \ˈ=ˌ=+\ *n* [*micr-* + *ammeter*] **:** an instrument for measuring electric current in microamperes — compare AMMETER

mi·cro·ampere \ˈ"+\ *n* [ISV *micr-* + *ampere*] **:** one millionth of an ampere

mi·cro·analysis \ˌ=(ˌ)=+\ *n* [ISV *micr-* + *analysis*] **:** chemical analysis on a small or minute scale that usu. requires special, very sensitive, or small-scale apparatus **:** qualitative or quantitative analysis dealing with quantities usu. of the order of milligrams (as in the vicinity of 1 mg.) or smaller — opposed to *macroanalysis*; compare CHEMICAL MICROSCOPY, SEMIMICROANALYSIS, ULTRAMICROANALYSIS — **mi·cro·analyst** \ˈ=ˌ=+\ *n* — **mi·cro·analytic** \ˈ"+\ *or* **mi·cro·analytical** \ˈ"+\ *adj*

mi·cro·anatomy \ˌ=(ˌ)=+\ *n* [*micr-* + *anatomy*] **:** HISTOLOGY

mi·cro·atoll \ˈ=ˌ=+\ *n* [*micr-* + *atoll*] **:** a coralline growth resembling a miniature atoll

mi·cro·bacterium \ˌ=(ˌ)=+\ *n* [NL, fr. *micr-* + *bacterium*] **1** *cap* **:** a genus of minute nonmotile gram-positive thermoduric lactobacteria that are common in dairy products and the mammalian intestinal tract **2** *pl* **microbacteria :** any of numerous minute heat-resistant bacteria; *specif* **:** one of the genus *Microbacterium*

mi·cro·bal \(ˈ)mīˈkrōbəl\ *adj* [*microbe* + *-al*] **:** MICROBIAL

mi·cro·balance \ˈmīkrō+\ *n* [ISV *micr-* + *balance*] **:** a balance designed to measure very small weights with great precision

mi·cro·bar \ˈmīkrə+ˌ-\ *n* [*micr-* + *bar*] **:** a unit of pressure equal to one dyne per square centimeter — used esp. in acoustics and meteorology

mi·cro·barograph \ˈmīkrō+\ *n* [ISV *micr-* + *barograph*] **:** a barograph for recording small and rapid changes

mi·crobe \ˈmīˌkrōb\ *n* -s [ISV *micr-* + *-be* (fr. Gk *bios* mode of life); orig. formed in F — more at QUICK] **:** a very minute organism **:** MICROORGANISM, GERM — used esp. of pathogenic bacteria **syn** see MICROORGANISM

mi·crobe·less \-ləs\ *adj* **:** being without microbes **:** free from microbes

mi·cro·bi·al \(ˈ)mīˈkrōbēəl\ *adj* [*microbe* + *-ial*] **:** being of or between microbes ⟨~ physiology⟩ ⟨~ antagonism⟩ **:** done by or by the use of microbes ⟨~ fermentation⟩ ⟨~ warfare⟩ **:** developed from microbes ⟨~ purification of milk⟩ **:** involving microbes ⟨the ~ concept of infection⟩ **:** that are the ~ enemies of man⟩

mi·cro·bi·an \-bēən\ *or* **mi·cro·bic** \-ˈkrōbik, -ˈkräb-\ *adj* [*microbian* ISV *microbe* + *-an*; *microbic* fr. *microbe* + *-ic*] **:** MICROBIAL

mi·cro·bi·ci·dal \mīˌkrōbəˈsīdᵊl\ *adj* [*microbe* + *-i-* + *-cidal*] **:** destructive to microbes

mi·cro·bi·cide \-ˈkrōbəˌsīd\ *n* -s [ISV *microbe* + *-i-* + *-cide*] **:** an agent that destroys microbes

mi·cro·biological \ˌmīkrō+\ *also* **mi·cro·biologic** \ˈ"+\ *adj* [*microbiological* fr. *microbiology* + *-ical*; *microbiologic* ISV *microbiology* + *-ic*] **:** of or relating to microbiology — **mi·cro·biologically** \ˈ"+\ *adv*

mi·cro·biologist \ˌ=(ˌ)=+\ *n* [ISV *microbiology* + *-ist*] **:** a specialist in microbiology

mi·cro·biology \ˈ"+\ *n* [ISV *micr-* + *biology*] **:** a branch of biology dealing esp. with microscopic forms of life (as bacteria, protozoa, viruses, and fungi)

mi·cro·bi·on \-ˈkrōbēˌän\ *n, pl* **micro·bia** \-bēə\ [NL, fr. F *microbe* — more at MICROBE] **:** MICROBE

mi·cro·bi·o·sis \ˌmīkrōˌbīˈōsəs\ *n* -ES [NL, fr. *microbion* + *-osis*] **:** infection by microbes

mi·cro·biota \ˌmīkrō+\ *n* [NL, fr. *micr-* + *biota*] **:** the microscopic flora and fauna of a region

mi·cro·biotic \ˈ"+\ *adj* [NL *microbiota* + E *-ic*] **1 :** of, relating to, or constituting a microbiota **2** [*micr-* + *-biotic*] *of a seed* **:** surviving in the dormant state for a relatively brief period usu. not exceeding three years — compare MACROBIOTIC, MESOBIOTIC

mi·cro·bism \ˈmīˌkrōˌbizəm\ *n* -s [ISV *microbe* + *-ism*] **:** the state of being infested with microbes

mi·cro·bi·um \mīˈkrōbēəm\ *n* -s [NL, fr. F *microbe*] : MICROBE

mi·cro·blast \ˈmīkrōˌblast\ *n* -s [ISV *micr-* + *-blast*] : an erythroblast destined to produce an atypically small erythrocyte

mi·cro·burette *or* **mi·cro·buret** \¦mī(ˌ)krō+\ *n* [*micr-* + *burette*] : a burette (as one with a capacity of 10 milliliters or less) for use esp. in microanalysis

mi·cro·burner \¦÷÷+\ *n* [*micr-* + *burner*] : a burner giving a very small flame for use esp. in microanalysis

mi·cro·bus \ˈmīkrōˌbəs\ *n* [AmerSp *microbús*, fr. *micr-* + *-bús* (fr. Sp *autobús* motor bus, fr. F *autobus*, fr. *auto-* — fr. *automobile* — + *-bus* — fr. *omnibus*) — more at OMNIBUS] : a small motor bus

mi·cro·calorimeter \¦mīkrō+\ *n* [*micr-* + *calorimeter*] : an instrument for measuring very small quantities of heat — **micro·calorimetric** \"+\ *adj* — **mi·cro·calorimetry** \"+\ *n*

mi·cro·camera \"+\ *n* [*micr-* + *camera*] : a camera used for photomicrography

Mi·cro·card \ˈmīkrōˌkärd\ *trademark* — used for a sensitized card approximately 3 in. x 5 in. on which printed matter is reproduced photographically in greatly reduced form

mi·cro·cebus \"+\ *n, cap* [NL, fr. *micr-* + Gk *kēbos* long-tailed monkey — more at CEBUS] : a genus of Madagascar lemurs consisting of the dwarf lemurs

mi·cro·centrosome \"+\ *n* [ISV *micr-* + *centrosome*] : CENTRIOLE 1

mi·cro·centrum \"+\ *n* [NL, fr. *micr-* + L *centrum* center — more at CENTER] : a centrosome or a group of centrioles functioning as a centrosome — compare CENTRAL APPARATUS

[1]**mi·cro·cephalic** \¦÷(ˌ)÷+\ *also* **mi·cro·ceph·a·lous** \¦÷÷¦sefələs\ *adj* [*microcephalic* prob. fr. NL *microcephalus* microcephalous + E *-ic*; *microcephalous* fr. NL *microcephalus*, fr. Gk *mikrokephalos* having a small head, fr. *mikr-* micr- + *-kephalos* -cephalous] : having a small head; *specif* : having an abnormally small head — **mi·cro·ceph·a·lism** \ˌ÷÷ˈsefəˌlizəm\ *n* -s

[2]**mi·cro·cephalic** \¦÷(ˌ)÷+\ *n* -s : an individual with an abnormally small head

mi·cro·ceph·a·lus \ˌ÷÷ˈsefələs\ *n, pl* **microcepha·li** \-ˌlī\ [NL, fr. Gk *mikrokephalos* having a small head] : MICROCEPHALY; *also* : a microcephalic individual

mi·cro·ceph·a·ly \-lē, -li\ *n* -ES [NL *microcephalia*, fr. *microcephalus* microcephalous + *-ia*] : a condition of abnormal smallness of head usu. associated with mental defects

mi·cro·cer·a·tous \¦÷÷¦serəd·əs\ *adj* [*micr-* + *cerat-* + *-ous*] : having short antennae ⟨a ~ insect⟩

mi·cro·cer·cous \¦÷÷¦sərkəs\ *adj* [*micr-* + *cerc-* + *-ous*] *of a cercaria* : having a short broad tail

[1]**mi·cro·chae·ta** \ˌ÷÷ˈkēd·ə\ *n, cap* [NL, fr. *micr-* + *-chaeta*] : a genus of earthworms of which one southern African form (*M. rappi*) reaches a length of five feet

[2]**microchaeta** \"\ *n, pl* **microchae·tae** \-ēd·(ˌ)ē\ [NL, fr. *micr-* + *chaeta*] : a small bristle on the body of some insects (as many two-winged flies) — distinguished from *macrochaeta*

mi·cro·chemical \¦÷÷+\ *adj* [ISV *micr-* + *chemical*] : of, relating to, or using the methods of microchemistry

mi·cro·chemistry \"+\ *n* [ISV *micr-* + *chemistry*] : chemistry dealing with the manipulation of very small quantities for purposes of preparation, characterization, or analysis — contrasted with *macrochemistry*

mi·cro·chiroptera \¦÷(ˌ)÷+\ *n pl, cap* [NL, fr. *micr-* + *Chiroptera*] : a suborder of Chiroptera including all bats except the fruit bats — **mi·cro·chiropteran** \"+\ *adj or n* — **mi·cro·chiropterous** \"+\ *adj*

mi·cro·chronometer \"+\ *n* [ISV *micr-* + *chronometer*] : an instrument for measuring very small intervals of time : CHRONOSCOPE

mi·cro·cinematographic \¦÷÷+\ *adj* [ISV *micr-* + *cinematographic*] : made by means of or relating to cinephotomicrography

mi·cro·cinematography \"+\ *also* **mi·cro·kinematography** \"+\ *n* [ISV *micr-* + *cinematography*] : CINEPHOTOMICROGRAPHY

mi·cro·citrus \"+\ *n, cap* [NL, fr. *micr-* + *Citrus*] : a small genus of Australian shrubs or trees (family Rutaceae) having fingerlike fruit

mi·cro·climate \"+\ *n* [ISV *micr-* + *climate*] : the local climate of a given site or habitat varying in size from a tiny crevice to a large land area but being usu. characterized by considerable uniformity of climate over the site involved and relatively local as compared with its enveloping macroclimate from which it differs because of local climatic factors (as elevation and exposure)

mi·cro·climatic \"+\ *adj* [*microclimate* + *-ic*] : of or relating to a microclimate

mi·cro·climatologic \"+\ *or* **mi·cro·climatological** \"+\ *adj* [*microclimatology* + *-ic* or *-ical*] : of or relating to microclimatology

mi·cro·climatology \"+\ *n* [ISV *microclimate* + *-o-* + *-logy*; orig. formed as G *mikroklimatologie*] : the study of microclimates : climatology of restricted areas

mi·cro·cline \ˈmīkrəˌklīn\ *n* -s [G *mikroklin*, fr. *mikr-* micr- + *-klin* (fr. Gk *klinein* to lean) — more at LEAN] : a mineral of the feldspar group that is like orthoclase in composition but is triclinic though approaching orthoclase in crystal habit and crystal angles and that is white to pale yellow, red, or green in color

microcline green *n* : a very pale green that is yellower, lighter, and slightly less strong than tourmaline, bluer and duller than emerald tint, and bluer and slightly stronger than celadon tint

mi·cro·coccaceae \¦mīˌkrō+\ *n pl, cap* [NL, fr. *Micrococcus*, type genus + *-aceae*] : a family of heterotrophic spherical or elliptical eubacteria that usu. lack endospores, divide in two or three planes forming pairs, tetrads, or masses of cells, prefer an aerobic environment, and produce yellow, orange, or red pigment and that include pathogenic toxin-producing forms (as *Staphylococcus aureus* syn. *Micrococcus pyogenes* var. *aureus*) as well as numerous harmless commensals and saprophytes

mi·cro·coc·cus \ˌ÷÷ˈkäkəs\ *n* [NL, fr. *micr-* + *-coccus*] **1** *cap* : a large genus (the type of the family Micrococcaceae) of spherical bacteria occurring in plates or irregular groups rather than in packets or chains and now usu. including numerous forms formerly placed in the genus *Staphylococcus* **2** *pl* **micrococci** : a small spherical bacterium; *esp* : a member of the genus *Micrococcus*

mi·cro·coleoptera \¦÷÷+\ *n pl* [NL, fr. *micr-* + *Coleoptera*] : the smaller beetles

mi·cro·colony \"+\ *n* [*micr-* + *colony*] : a minute colony; *specif* : a minute colony made up of L-forms

mi·cro·colorimeter \"+\ *n* [*micr-* + *colorimeter*] : a colorimeter designed for use with small quantities of material — **mi·cro·colorimetric** \"+\ *adj* — **mi·cro·colorimetry** \"+\ *n*

mi·cro·community \¦÷(ˌ)÷+\ *n* [*micr-* + *community*] : the community occupying a microhabitat

mi·cro·conidial \"+\ *adj* [*microconidium* + *-al*] : of or relating to a microconidium

mi·cro·conidium \"+\ *n* [NL, fr. *micr-* + *conidium*] : a small conidium as contrasted with a larger conidium both frequently being produced by the same species and differing often in shape (as in members of the genus *Fusarium*) — compare MACROCONIDIUM

mi·cro·conjugant \¦÷÷+\ *n* [*micr-* + *conjugant*] : the smaller member of a pair of conjugating protozoans or anisogamous gametes

mi·cro·con·o·don \ˌ÷÷ˈkänəˌdän\ *n, cap* [NL, fr. *micr-* + [2]*con-* + *-odon*] : a genus of small American Triassic reptiles (order Ictidosauria) long believed to be one of the most ancient mammals

mi·cro·constituent \¦÷(ˌ)÷+\ *n* [*micr-* + *constituent*] : a microscopic constituent ⟨~*s* in high-temperature alloys⟩

mi·cro·copier \¦÷÷+\ *n* [[2]*microcopy* + *-er*] : an apparatus for making microcopies

[1]**mi·cro·copy** \"+\ *n* [ISV *micr-* + *copy*, n.] : a photographic copy in which printed or other graphic matter is reduced in size (as on microfilm)

[2]**microcopy** \"\ [ISV, fr. [1]*microcopy*] *vt* : to reproduce by means of a microcopy ~ *vi* : to make microcopies

mi·cro·cosm \ˈmīkrəˌkäzəm\ *n* -s [ME *microcosme*, *mycrocossmos*, *microcosmus*, fr. ML *microcosmus*, alter. (influenced by L *micro-* micr-) of Gk *mikros kosmos*, fr. *mikros* small — *kosmos* order, universe — more at MICR-] **1** : a little world : a miniature universe ⟨the ~ of the atom grows constantly richer in content and interest —*Scientific American Reader*⟩ **2** : man or human nature believed to be an epitome of the world or the universe ⟨man is a ~, not in the natural sense, but in the historical sense, a compendium of universal history —*Encore*⟩ — contrasted with *macrocosm* **3** : a community, institution, or other unity believed to be an epitome of a larger unity (as a nation or the world) ⟨a set of characters, from all levels of the town's ~ —Anthony Boucher⟩ ⟨the boardinghouse was a ~ of a larger world —Van Wyck Brooks⟩ ⟨poetry is a discovery of ~*s*, of representative worlds —C.S.Kilby⟩ ⟨when the battle is a ~ of the entire conflict —T.C.Chubb⟩ ⟨a sunken ship is a ~ of the civilization that launched it —A.C.Clarke⟩ — **in microcosm** : in miniature ⟨the camp became a city *in microcosm*⟩

mi·cro·cos·mic \¦mīkrō¦käzmik, -mēk\ *adj* [NL *microcosmicus*, fr. ML *microcosmus* microcosm + L *-icus* -ic] : of, relating to, or characteristic of a microcosm ⟨the ~ world of business —*Amer. Fabrics*⟩ — **mi·cro·cos·mi·cal·ly** \-mək(ə)lē, -mēk-, -li\ *adv*

microcosmic salt *n* [trans. of NL *sal microcosmicus*; fr. the fact that it was originally obtained from human urine] : a white crystalline salt $NaNH_4HPO_4.4H_2O$ that is obtained by mixing solutions of sodium phosphate and ammonium phosphate or chloride, that is changed to a sodium phosphate glass on heating, and that is used as a flux like borax in beads for testing for metallic oxides and salts; sodium ammonium hydrogen phosphate

mi·cro·cosmos \¦÷÷+\ *n* [ME *mycrocossmos*] **1** : MICROCOSM ⟨a little world of life, a ~ of great intimacy —William Beebe⟩ ⟨the ~ of the atomic nuclei —*Science News Letter*⟩ **2** : the world below the threshold of visibility by the naked eye

mi·cro·cos·mus \ˌ÷÷ˈkäzməs\ *n, cap* [NL, fr. ML, microcosm] : a widely distributed genus of large simple ascidians including a Mediterranean form (*M. sulcatus*) that is sometimes used for food in southern Europe

mi·cro·cra·nous \¦÷÷¦krānəs\ *adj* [*micr-* + *cran-* (fr. *cranium*) + *-ous*] : having a skull of small volume or capacity

mi·cro·crustacean \¦÷÷+\ *n* [*micr-* + *crustacean*] : a minute crustacean

mi·cro·crystal \"+\ *n* [ISV *micr-* + *crystal*] : a crystal visible only under the microscope

mi·cro·crystalline \"+\ *adj* [ISV *micr-* + *crystalline*] : of or relating to crystallinity that is visible only under the microscope ⟨was able to show that the halides are always ~ —C.E.K. Mees⟩ ⟨chalcedony . . . is a natural, ~ fibrous silica —F.J. Pettijohn⟩ — **mi·cro·crystallinity** \"+\ *n*

microcrystalline wax *n* : any of various plastic materials that are obtained from petroleum (as by refining of tank bottoms from crude oil or by removal with a solvent of oil from crude petrolatum), that differ in general from paraffin waxes in having higher melting points and viscosities and much finer and less distinct crystals, and that are used chiefly in laminated paper, in coatings and liners, in adhesives and sealing compositions, and in polishes — compare PETROLEUM WAX

mi·cro·curie \¦÷÷+\ *n* [*micr-* + *curie*] : one millionth of a curie

mi·cro·cyclic \"+\ *adj* [*micr-* + *cyclic*] : SHORT-CYCLED

mi·cro·cy·pri·ni \ˌ÷(ˌ)÷səˈprīˌnī, -rēˌnī\ *n pl, cap* [NL, fr. *micr-* + L *cyprini*, pl. of *cyprinus* carp — more at CYPRINUS] : an order or other division of small teleost fishes resembling but somewhat more advanced than the Haplomi and including the killifishes and topminnows and various related families of chiefly freshwater and brackish-water fishes

mi·cro·cyst \ˈmīkrə+ˌ-\ *n* [ISV *micr-* + *cyst*] **1 a** : a small cyst or spore (as a chlamydospore or a resting cell formed from a slime-mold swarm spore) — compare MACROCYST **b** : a minute resistant body in some higher bacteria that is thought to be a haploid spore **2** : a very small pathological cyst; *esp* : one arising from another cyst

mi·cro·cys·tis \ˌ÷÷ˈsistəs\ *n, cap* [NL, fr. *micr-* + *-cystis*] : a genus of unicellular blue-green algae (family Chroococcaceae) forming irregularly shaped colonies within a common gelatinous envelope and including at least one species (*M. aeruginosa*) that is poisonous and may become abundant and troublesome in lakes esp. where much organic matter is present

mi·cro·cyte \ˈmīkrəˌsīt\ *n* -s [ISV *micr-* + *-cyte*] : a red blood cell of exceptionally small size present esp. in some anemias

mi·cro·cy·the·mia \ˌmī(ˌ)krōsīˈthēmēə\ *also* **mi·cro·cy·te·mia** \-ˈtē-\ *n* -s [NL, fr. ISV *microcyte* + NL *-emia*] : the presence of abnormally small red blood cells in the blood — **mi·cro·cy·the·mic** \¦÷÷¦thēmik\ *adj*

mi·cro·cyt·ic \¦÷÷¦sid·ik\ *adj* [ISV *microcyte* + *-ic*] : of, relating to, or characterized by the presence of microcytes

microcytic anemia *n* : anemia characterized by the presence of microcytes in the blood

mi·cro·cy·to·sis \ˌ÷÷sīˈtōsəs\ *n, pl* **microcyto·ses** \-ˌsēz\ [NL, fr. ISV *microcyte* + NL *-osis*] : decrease in the size of red blood cells

mi·cro·densitometer \¦÷÷+\ *n* [*micr-* + *densitometer*] : a densitometer for measuring the density of very small areas of a photographic plate or film — **mi·cro·densitometry** \"+\ *n*

mi·cro·determination \¦÷(ˌ)÷+\ *n* [*micr-* + *determination*] : determination by microanalysis or by the microscope

mi·cro·dissection \"+\ *n* [*micr-* + *dissection*] : dissection under the microscope; *specif* : dissection of cells or tissues by means of fine needles operated through a precise system of levers

mi·cro·distillation \¦÷÷+\ *n* [*micr-* + *distillation*] : the distillation of minute quantities of material

mi·cro·dont \ˈmīkrəˌdänt\ *adj* [ISV *micr-* + *-odont*] : having small teeth — **mi·cro·dont·ism** \-nˌtizəm\ *n* -s — **mi·cro·don·tous** \¦÷÷¦däntəs\ *adj* — **mi·cro·don·ty** \ˈ÷÷ˌdäntē\ *n* -ES

mi·cro·drawing \¦mīkrō+\ *n* [*micr-* + *drawing*] : a drawing made to exhibit microscopic structures or other very small details

mi·cro·dri·li \ˌ÷÷ˈdrīˌlī\ *n pl, cap* [NL, fr. *micr-* + *-drili* (fr. Gk *drilos* earthworm)] *in some classifications* : a group of Oligochaeta that comprises slender elongated predominantly aquatic worms lacking a capillary network on the nephridium and that is nearly coextensive with Archioligochaeta — compare MEGADRILI

mi·cro·drop \ˈmīkrə+ˌ\ *n* [*micr-* + *drop*] : a very small drop or minute droplet (as 0.1 to 0.01 of a drop)

mi·cro·economics \¦mīkrō+\ *n pl but usu sing in constr* [*micr-* + *economics*] : a study of economics in terms of individual areas of activity (as a firm, household, prices) — opposed to *macroeconomics*

mi·cro·electrode \¦÷(ˌ)÷+\ *n* [*micr-* + *electrode*] : a minute electrode or one used in microelectrolysis

mi·cro·electrolysis \"+\ *n* [*micr-* + *electrolysis*] : electrolysis on a very small scale using small quantities of material — **mi·cro·electrolytic** \"+\ *adj*

mi·cro·electrophoresis \"+\ *n* [*micr-* + *electrophoresis*] : electrophoresis in which the movement of single particles is observed in a microscope or ultramicroscope — **mi·cro·electrophoretic** \"+\ *or* **mi·cro·electrophoretical** \"+\ *adj* — **mi·cro·electrophoretically** \"+\ *adv*

mi·cro·element \¦÷÷+\ *n* [*micr-* + *element*] : TRACE ELEMENT

mi·cro·environment \¦÷(ˌ)÷+\ *n* [*micr-* + *environment*] : MICROHABITAT — **mi·cro·environmental** \"+\ *adj*

microergate *var of* MICRERGATE

mi·cro·estimation \¦mīkrō+\ *n* [*micr-* + *estimation*] : estimation (as by microanalysis) involving minute quantities of material : MICRODETERMINATION

mi·cro·evolution \"+\ *n* [*micr-* + *evolution*] : evolutionary change resulting from selective accumulation of minute variations held by many biologists to be chiefly responsible for evolutionary differentiation — distinguished from *macroevolution* — **mi·cro·evolutionary** \"+\ *adj*

mi·cro·examination \¦÷(ˌ)÷+\ *n* [*micr-* + *examination*] : examination by means of the microscope

mi·cro·facsimile \"+\ *n* [*micr-* + *facsimile*] : MICROCOPY

mi·cro·farad \¦÷÷+\ *n* [ISV *micr-* + *farad*] : one millionth of a farad

mi·cro·fauna \"+\ *n* [NL, fr. *micr-* + *fauna*] **1** : a small or strictly localized fauna : the fauna of a microhabitat **2** : minute animals; *esp* : those invisible to the naked eye ⟨the soil ~⟩ — compare MACROFAUNA, MESOFAUNA — **mi·cro·faunal** \"+\ *adj*

micro-feeder \"+\ *n* [*micr-* + *feeder*] : a microphagous organism

mi·cro·fibril \"+\ *n* [ISV *micr-* + *fibril*] : a fine fibril; *esp* : one of the submicroscopic elongated bundles of cellulose of the plant cell wall — **mi·cro·fibrillar** \"+\ *adj*

mi·cro·fiche \ˈmīkrəˌfēsh\ *n, pl* **microfiche** *or* **microfiches** [F, fr. *micr-* + *fiche* index card, slip of paper, peg, fr. OF, point, fr. *ficher*, *fichier* to drive in, pin, fasten — more at FICHU] : a sheet of microfilm; *esp* : one containing several rows of images

mi·cro·fil·a·re·mia *also* **mi·cro·fil·a·rae·mia** \ˌ÷÷ˌfiləˈrēmēə\ *n* -s [NL, fr. *microfilaria* + *-emia*] : the presence of microfilariae in the blood of one affected with some forms of filariasis

mi·cro·filaria \¦÷(ˌ)÷+\ *n* [NL, fr. *micr-* + *filaria*] : a minute larval filaria — **mi·cro·filarial** \"+\ *adj*

[1]**mi·cro·film** \ˈmīkrə+ˌ-\ *n* [ISV *micr-* + *film*] : a film often in the form of a strip 16 millimeters or 35 millimeters wide bearing a photographic record on a reduced scale of printed or other graphic matter (as for storage or transmission in small space) that is enlarged for reading or viewing

[2]**microfilm** \"\ *vt* : to photograph on microfilm ~ *vi* : to take microfilms

mi·cro·filmer \"+\ *n* : one that microfilms; *esp* : an apparatus for producing microfilms

mi·cro·fine \¦mīkrō+\ *adj* [*micr-* + *fine*] : consisting of or being particles of minute size : MICROCRYSTALLINE

mi·cro·flash \"+\ *adj* [*micr-* + *flash*] : producing or produced by means of a high-intensity light flash of extremely short duration ⟨a ~ lamp⟩ ⟨a ~ picture⟩

mi·cro·flora \"+\ *n* [NL, fr. *micr-* + *flora*] **1** : a small or strictly localized flora : the flora of a microhabitat **2** : minute plants; *esp* : those invisible to the naked eye ⟨aquatic ~⟩ — **mi·cro·floral** \"+\ *adj*

mi·cro·form \ˈmīkrəˌfȯrm\ *n* [*micr-* + *form*] **1** : MICROORGANISM **2** : a rust which lacks aecia, uredinia, and usu. pycnia and in which the teliospores undergo a resting stage prior to germination — compare LEPTOFORM

mi·cro·fossil \¦mīkrō+\ *n* [*micr-* + *fossil*] : a fossil whether a fragment of a larger organism or the entire remains of a minute organism that can be studied only microscopically — compare MACROFOSSIL

mi·cro·gadus \"+\ *n, cap* [NL, fr. *micr-* + *Gadus*] : a genus of gadoid fishes consisting of the tomcods

mi·cro·gamete \¦÷(ˌ)÷+\ *n* [ISV *micr-* + *gamete*] : the smaller or male gamete of an organism or species producing differentiated gametes — compare MACROGAMETE

mi·cro·gametocyte \"+\ *n* [ISV *micr-* + *gametocyte*] : a gametocyte producing microgametes

mi·cro·gametophyte \"+\ *n* [*micr-* + *gametophyte*] : the male gametophyte produced by a microspore — compare MEGAGAMETOPHYTE

mi·crog·a·my \mīˈkrägəmē\ *n* -ES [*micr-* + *-gamy*] : syngamy between gametes much smaller than the vegetative cells occurring in protozoans and various algae — compare MACROGAMY

mi·cro·gas·ter \ˌmīkrōˈgastə(r)\ *n, cap* [NL, fr. *micr-* + *-gaster*] : a genus of small braconid wasps whose larvae are parasitic on various caterpillars

mi·cro·geographic \¦÷÷+\ *also* **mi·cro·geographical** \"+\ *adj* [*micr-* + *geographic*] : geographically localized : involving or concerned with strict geographic localization ⟨~ diversification⟩ ⟨*microgeographical* researches⟩ — **mi·cro·geography** \¦÷(ˌ)÷+\ *n*

microgeographic race *n* : a highly localized and distinguishably differentiated population within a natural species

mi·crog·lia \mīˈkräglēə\ *n* -s [NL, fr. *micr-* + *-glia*] : a sustentacular and presumably phagocytic tissue element scattered through the central nervous system and made up of small cells that resemble lymphocytes and are now usu. considered to be of mesodermal origin and to arise from cells of the blood vessels — compare NEUROGLIA — **mi·crog·li·al** \(ˈ)÷¦÷÷əl\ *adj*

mi·cro·gnathia \ˌmīkrōˈnāthēə, -nath-, -ˌkräg'n-\ *n* -s [NL, fr. *micr-* + *gnath-* + *-ia*] : abnormal shortening of one or both jaws

mi·cro·graft \ˈmīkrə+ˌ-\ *n* [*micr-* + *graft*, n.] : a composite plant produced by micrografting

mi·cro·grafting \¦÷÷+\ *n* -s [*micr-* + *grafting*, gerund of *graft*, v.] : the operation of engrafting a weak plant (as a hybrid embryo) on a related but more vigorous stock

mi·cro·gram \ˈ÷÷+ˌ-\ *n* [ISV *micr-* + *gram*] **1** : one millionth of a gram **2** [*micr-* + *-gram*] : MICROGRAPH 2

mi·cro·granite \¦mīkrō+\ *n* [ISV *micr-* + *granite*; orig. formed as G *mikrogranit*] : an igneous rock composed of minute crystals of quartz and alkalic feldspar

mi·cro·granular \"+\ *adj* [*micr-* + *granular*] : minutely granular ⟨~ dolomite⟩

[1]**mi·cro·graph** \ˈmīkrəˌgraf, -ˌräf\ *n* [ISV *micr-* + *-graph*] **1** : an instrument for executing minute writing or engraving **2** : a graphic reproduction of the image of an object or part of an object formed by a microscope **3** : an instrument for measuring minute movements by the magnified record of movements of a diaphragm

[2]**micrograph** \"\ *vt* : to make a micrograph of — **mi·crog·ra·pher** \mīˈkrägrəfə(r)\ *n* -s

mi·cro·graph·ic \¦mīkrə¦grafik\ *adj* [ISV *micrography*, *micrograph* + *-ic*] **1** : of or relating to micrography **2** : relating to or disclosed by micrographs or by the making of micrographs — **mi·cro·graph·i·cal·ly** \-fək(ə)lē\ *adv*

mi·crog·ra·phy \mīˈkrägrəfē, -fi\ *n* -ES [*micr-* + *-graphy*] **1** : examination or study with the microscope : MICROSCOPY — opposed to *macrography* **2** : the art or process of producing micrographs

mi·cro·groove \ˈmīkrə+ˌ-\ *n* [*micr-* + *groove*] : a minute closely spaced V-shaped groove used on long-playing and extended-play phonograph records

mi·cro·gyne \-ˌjīn\ *n* -s [ISV *micr-* + *-gyne*] : a dwarf female ant

mi·cro·habitat \¦mīkrō+\ *n* [*micr-* + *habitat*] : a small usu. distinctly specialized and effectively isolated habitat (as a decaying stump, a pat of dung, or the rhizosphere of a plant)

mi·cro·hardness \"+\ *n* [*micr-* + *hardness*] : hardness of a substance (as an alloy) measured by an indenter (as a diamond point) that penetrates microscopic areas

mi·cro·henry \"+\ *n* [*micr-* + *henry*] : one millionth of a henry

mi·crohm \ˈmīˌkrōm\ *n* [ISV *micr-* + *ohm*] : one millionth of an ohm

mi·crohm·me·ter \ˈmīˌkrōmˌmēd·ə(r)\ *n* [ISV *microhm* + *-meter*] : a sensitive ohmmeter for measuring very small resistances

[1]**mi·cro·hydra** \¦mīkrō+\ [NL, fr. *micr-* + *hydra*] *syn of* CRASPEDACUSTA

[2]**microhydra** \"\ *n* [NL, fr. [1]*Microhydra*] : a minute freshwater hydroid without tentacles that is the polyp of medusae of the genus *Craspedacusta*

[1]**mi·cro·hy·lid** \-¦hīləd\ *adj* [NL *Microhylidae*] : of or relating to the Microhylidae

[2]**microhylid** \"\ *n* [NL *Microhylidae*] : one of the Microhylidae

mi·cro·hy·li·dae \ˌ÷÷ˈhīləˌdē\ *n pl, cap* [NL, fr. *Microhyla*, type genus (fr. *micr-* + *Hyla*) + *-idae*] *in some classifications* : a family of chiefly tropical frogs closely related to the Brevicipitidae to which they are more commonly assigned

mi·cro·hymenopteron \¦÷÷+\ *n* [NL, fr. *micr-* + *Hymenopteron*] : any of numerous minute and often parasitoid insects of the order Hymenoptera — used chiefly in pl. as if a taxon and then capitalized — **mi·cro·hymenopterous** \"+\ *adj*

mi·cro·inch \"+ˌ-\ *n* [*micr-* + *inch*] : a unit of length equal to one millionth of an inch

mi·cro·incineration \¦÷(ˌ)÷+\ *n* [*micr-* + *incineration*] : a technique employing high temperatures (as 600–650°C) for driving off the organic constituents of cells or tissue fragments leaving the inorganic matter for chemical identification

mi·cro·injection \"+\ *n* [*micr-* + *injection*] : injection under the microscope; *specif* : injection into cells or tissues by means of a fine mechanically controlled capillary tube

microkinematography *var of* MICROCINEMATOGRAPHY

mi·cro·lecithal \¦mīkrō+\ *adj* [*micr-* + *lecithal*] : having little yolk : ALECITHAL ⟨echinoderm eggs are ∼⟩

mi·cro·lepidoptera \"+\ *n pl, cap* [NL, fr. *micr-* + *Lepidoptera*] *in some classifications* : a major division of Lepidoptera comprising the smaller moths and a few closely related larger moths (as of the families Tineidae, Tortricidae, Pyralididae, Psychidae, and Eucleidae) — usu. used descriptively without taxonomic implications and often uncapitalized; compare MACROLEPIDOPTERA — **mi·cro·lepidopterous** \"+\ *adj*

mi·cro·lepidopterist \"+\ *n* [NL *Microlepidoptera* + E *-ist*] : a student of the Microlepidoptera

mi·cro·level \"+\ *vt* [*micr-* + *level*] : to bring (an elevator) close to an exact level by automatic means

mi·cro·lite \'mīkrə,līt\ *n* -s [*micr-* + *-lite*] **1** : a mineral $(Na,Ca)_2Ta_2O_6(O,OH,F)$ that consists of an oxide of sodium, calcium, and tantalum with small amounts of fluorine and hydroxyl and that is isomorphous with pyrochlore **2** [G *mikrolith*, fr. *mikr-* micr- + *-lith* -lite] : a minute crystal that is visible only under the microscope and usu. affects polarized light : MICROCRYSTAL — **mi·cro·lit·ic** \¦==¦lid·ik\ *adj*

mi·cro·liter \¦mīkrō+\ *n* [ISV *micr-* + *liter*] : a unit of capacity equal to one millionth of a liter

mi·cro·lith \'mīkrə,lith\ *n* -s [ISV *micr-* + *-lith*] : a tiny blade tool of the late Paleolithic usu. in the form of a triangle or other geometric figure and often set in a bone or wooden haft

mi·cro·lith·ic \¦==¦lithik\ *adj* [*microlith* + *-ic*] **1** : being or resembling a microlith **2** : of or relating to the people who produced microliths

mi·cro·logical \-¦läjə̇kəl\ *or* **mi·cro·log·ic** \-jik\ *adj* [*micrological* fr. *micrology* + *-ical*; *micrologic* ISV *micrology* + *-ic*] : of or relating to micrology

mi·crol·o·gist \mī'krälə̇jə̇st\ *n* -s [²*micrology* + *-ist*] : a specialist in micrology

¹mi·crol·o·gy \-jē, -ji\ *n* -ES [Gk *mikrologia*, fr. *mikr-* micr- + *-logia* (fr. *logos* speech) — more at LEGEND] : attention to petty items or differences

²micrology \"\ *n* -ES [*micr-* + *-logy*] : a science dealing with the handling and preparation of microscopic objects for study

mi·cro·lux \'mīkrə+,-\ *n* [*micr-* + *lux*] : one millionth of a lux

mi·cro·manipulation \¦mī(,)krō+\ *n* [ISV *micr-* + *manipulation*] : the technique or practice of microdissection and microinjection — compare MICRURGY

mi·cro·manipulator \"+\ *n* [ISV *micr-* + *manipulator*] : an instrument for micromanipulation

mi·cro·manometer \"+\ *n* [ISV *micr-* + *manometer*] : a manometer specially designed to measure minute differences of pressure

mi·cro·mas·tia \,==¦mastēə\ *n* -s [NL, fr. *micr-* + *-mastia*] : postpubertal immaturity and abnormal smallness of the breasts

mi·cro·me·lia \-'mēlēə\ *n* -s [NL, fr. *micr-* + *-melia*] : a condition characterized by abnormally small and imperfectly developed extremities — **mi·cro·melic** \¦==¦melik, -mēl-\ *adj*

mi·cro·membrane \¦==+\ *n* [*micr-* + *membrane*] : a very thin semipermeable membrane

mi·cro·mer·al \¦mīkrə¦mirəl\ *or* **mi·cro·mer·ic** \-¦merik, -¦mir-\ *adj* [*micromere* + *-al* or *-ic*] : of or relating to a micromere

mi·cro·mere \'mīkrə,mi(ə)r\ *n* -s [ISV *micr-* + *-mere*] : one of the smaller blastomeres resulting from the unequal segmentation of an egg — opposed to *macromere*; see BLASTULA illustration

mi·cro·me·ria \,==¦mirēə\ *n, cap* [NL, fr. *micr-* + Gk *meros* part, portion + NL *-ia* — more at MERIT] : a large genus of fragrant chiefly Old World herbs (family Labiatae) having a calyx chiefly 13-veined, a small corolla barely exserted, and four unequal anthers — see YERBA BUENA

mi·cro·me·rit·ics \,=(,)krōmə'rid·iks\ *n pl but sing in constr* [prob. fr. *micr-* + *mer-* (fr. Gk *meros* part) + *-ite* + *-ics*] : a science that treats of small particles and that is applied esp. in soil physics

mi·cro·mesentery \¦mīkrō+\ *n* [*micr-* + *mesentery*] : an incomplete secondary mesentery in an anthozoan

mi·cro·meteorite \"+\ *n* [*micr-* + *meteorite*] : a meteorite so small that it penetrates through the earth's atmosphere without becoming intensely heated and hence without disintegration

mi·cro·meteorological \"+\ *adj* : of or relating to micrometeorology

mi·cro·meteorology \"+\ *n* [*micr-* + *meteorology*] : the study of the meteorological characteristics of a local site that is usu. small and often is confined to a shallow layer of air next to the ground

¹mi·crom·e·ter \mī'krämədˑə(r), -ətə-\ *n* [F *micromètre*, fr. *micr-* + *-mètre* -meter] **1** : an instrument used with a telescope or microscope for measuring minute distances or the apparent diameters of objects which subtend minute angles **2** : MICROMETER CALIPER

²micrometer \"\ *vt* : to measure by means of a micrometer

³mi·cro·me·ter \'mīkrō,mēd·ə(r), -krə,-, -ētə-\ *n* [ISV *micr-* + *meter*] : a unit of length equal to one millionth of a meter

micrometer caliper *n* : a caliper for making precise measurements having a spindle moved by a finely threaded screw

micrometer eyepiece *n* : an eyepiece fitted with a filar micrometer the lines of which are in the focal plane of the eyepiece and so coincide with the objective image when the microscope or telescope is in focus — called also *ocular micrometer*

micrometer caliper: *1* anvil, *2* spindle, *3* frame, *4* sleeve, *5* thimble

micrometer microscope *n* : a microscope fitted with a micrometer eyepiece

mi·cro·method \¦mīkrō+\ *n* [*micr-* + *method*] : a method (as of microanalysis) involving very small quantities of material or the use of the microscope — opposed to *macromethod*

mi·cro·metrical \"+\ *also* **mi·cro·metric** \"+\ *adj* [*micrometrical* fr. *micrometer* + *-ical*; *micrometric* ISV *micrometer* + *-ic*] : relating to or made by a micrometer — **mi·cro·metrically** \"+\ *adv*

mi·crom·e·try \mī'krämə·trē, -ri\ *n* -ES [ISV *micr-* + *-metry*] : measurement with a micrometer

mi·cro·mho \'mīkrə+,-\ *n* [*micr-* + *mho*] : one millionth of a mho

mi·cro·microfarad \¦mīkrō+\ *n* [*micr-* + *microfarad*] : one millionth of a microfarad

mi·cro·micron \"+\ *n* [*micr-* + *micron*] : one millionth of a micron

mi·cro·millimeter \"+\ *n* [ISV *micr-* + *millimeter*] : one millionth of a millimeter — called also *millimicron*

mi·cro·modification \"+\ *n* [*micr-* + *modification*] : a modification of a method or procedure for use on a small scale (as in microanalysis)

mi·cro·mole \'mīkrə+,-\ *n* [*micr-* + *mole*] : one millionth of a mole

mi·cro·motion \¦mīkrō+\ *n* [*micr-* + *motion*] : the technique in time and motion study of making a pictorial elapsed-time study of the elements or subdivisions of an operation by means of a high-speed motion-picture camera and a specialized timing device

mi·cro·mount \'mīkrə+,-\ *n* [*micr-* + *mount*] : a small often beautifully crystallized mineral specimen usu. suitable only for examination with a microscope

mi·cro·mutation \¦mī(,)krō+\ *n* [*micr-* + *mutation*] : a small-scale or highly localized mutation; *esp* : one involving alteration at a single gene locus

mi·cro·mycete \¦=='mī,sēt, -,mī'sēt\ *n* [ISV *micr-* + *-mycete*] : a fungus (as a rust) that does not produce a large fleshy fruiting body

mi·cro·mys \'mīkrə,mis\ *n, cap* [NL, fr. *micr-* + *-mys*] : a genus of myomorph rodents comprising the tiny Old World harvest mice

mi·cron \'mī,krän *sometimes* 'mi- *or* ,krən\ *n, pl* **microns** \-nz\ *also* **mi·cra** \-krə\ [NL, fr. Gk *mikron*, neut. of *mikros* small — more at MICR-] **1** : a unit of length equal to one thousandth of a millimeter or about 0.000039 inch — symbol μ **2** : a unit of low pressure (as in a vacuum tube) equal to the pressure of a column of mercury one micron high

mi·cro·needle \¦mīkrō+\ *n* [*micr-* + *needle*] : a needle for micromanipulation

mi·cro·nephridium \¦=(,)=+\ *n* [NL, fr. *micr-* + *nephridium*] : a small nephridium usu. numerous in each segment of various annelid worms

¹mi·cro·ne·sian \¦mīkrə¦nēzh|ən *also* -ēsh| *or* -ēzē|\ *adj, usu cap* [ISV, fr. NL *Micronesia*, islands of the western Pacific ocean east of the Philippines + ISV *-an*, adj. suffix] **1 a** : of, relating to, or characteristic of Micronesia **b** : of, relating to, or characteristic of the Micronesians **2** : of, relating to, or characteristic of the Micronesian languages

²micronesian \"\ *n* -s *cap* [ISV, fr. ¹*micronesian*] **1** : a native or inhabitant of Micronesia **2** : a group of Austronesian languages spoken in the Micronesian islands

mi·cron·ize \'mīkrə,nīz\ *vt* [*micron* + *-ize*] : to pulverize extremely fine; *esp* : to pulverize into particles a few microns in diameter ⟨*micronized* graphite⟩ ⟨*micronized* penicillin⟩

mi·cro·nuclear \¦mīkrō+\ *adj* [*micronucleus* + *-ar*] : of or relating to a micronucleus

mi·cro·nucleate \"+\ *adj* [*micronucleus* + *-ate*] : having a micronucleus

mi·cro·nucleus \"+\ *n* [NL, fr. *micr-* + *nucleus*] : a minute nucleus; *specif* : one regarded as primarily concerned with reproductive and genetic functions in most ciliated protozoans — distinguished from *macronucleus*

¹mi·cro·nutrient \"+\ *n* [*micr-* + *nutrient*] **1** : TRACE ELEMENT **2** : an organic compound (as a vitamin) essential in minute amounts only to the growth and welfare of an animal — compare MACRONUTRIENT

²micronutrient \"\ *adj* : of, relating to, or being a micronutrient ⟨∼ deficiency⟩ : required for nutrition only in minute amounts ⟨∼ elements such as manganese and zinc —*Science*⟩

mi·cro·organic \"+\ *adj* [*micr-* + *organic*] : of, relating to, or characteristic of microorganisms

mi·cro·organism \"+\ *n* [ISV *micr-* + *organism*] : an organism of microscopic or ultramicroscopic size — used esp. of bacteria and protozoa ⟨soil-inhabiting ∼*s* —S.A.Waksman⟩

syn GERM, MICROBE, BACTERIUM, BACILLUS, VIRUS, PATHOGEN: MICROORGANISM is the general term for any organism of microscopic or ultramicroscopic size. GERM and MICROBE are early nonscientific synonyms for MICROORGANISM. GERM often refers to microorganisms regarded as a source or origin (as of a disease) ⟨typhus *germs*⟩ It is often used to indicate a rudimentary beginning or embryo capable of evolving or developing ⟨*germs* of the doctrine of which he is the founder may be traced to much earlier, even ancient periods —*Encyc. Americana*⟩ MICROBE may be somewhat more awesome than GERM and is rarely used with pleasing suggestion ⟨the late stage of true invasion of the tissues around the brain and spinal cord by the deadly *microbes* —F.G.Slaughter⟩ BACTERIUM is now the common scientific designation for a large group of microscopic plants with single-celled or acellular bodies of various forms that affect the life of man in various ways. BACTERIA is sometimes used to designate rod-shaped bacteria that do not form endospores and is contrasted with BACILLUS in its narrow sense. BACILLUS in science refers to any straight rod-shaped bacterium or to any straight aerobic rod-shaped bacterium that forms endospores; popularly it refers to various disease-causing bacteria ⟨the *bacilli* of diphtheria⟩ VIRUS technically indicates a submicroscopic infective agent sometimes considered as composed of complex protein molecules capable of growth in living cells ⟨polio *virus*⟩ VIRUS is applicable to any dread, insidious, inexorable agent ⟨right in claiming that the *virus* of Pan-Germanism and Nazism was present in the speeches —*Times Lit. Supp.*⟩ PATHOGEN is applicable to any living agent that causes disease (as a bacterium, virus, fungus, or worm); it stresses this aspect and implies nothing about relative size, being freely applied to agencies that are not microorganisms ⟨many *pathogens* attack a vigorous host most readily —*Science*⟩

mi·cro·organismal \"+\ *adj* : MICROORGANIC

mi·cro·paleontological \"+\ *also* **mi·cro·paleontologic** \"+\ *adj* [*micropaleontology* + *-ical* or *-ic*] : of or relating to micropaleontology

mi·cro·paleontologist \"+\ *n* [*micropaleontology* + *-ist*] : a paleontologist specializing in the identification and study of microfossils

mi·cro·paleontology \"+\ *n* [ISV *micr-* + *paleontology*] : the study of microfossils

mi·cro·pantograph \"+\ *n* [*micr-* + *pantograph*] : a pantograph that produces microscopic copies

mi·cro·parasite \"+\ *n* [*micr-* + *parasite*] : a parasitic microorganism — **mi·cro·parasitic** \"+\ *adj*

mi·cro·pedology \¦=(,)=+\ *n* [*micr-* + *pedology*] : a science dealing with the microscopic phenomena of soils

mi·cro·pegmatite \¦==+\ *n* [*micr-* + *pegmatite*] : microcrystalline graphic granite — **mi·cro·pegmatitic** \"+\ *adj*

mi·cro·perthite \"+\ *n* [G *mikroperthit*, fr. *mikr-* micr- + *perthit* perthite, fr. E *perthite*] : a perthite the structure of which can be discerned only with the microscope — compare CRYPTOPERTHITE — **mi·cro·perthitic** \"+\ *adj*

mi·cro·phage \'mīkrə,fāj\ *n* -s [ISV *micr-* + *-phage*; orig. formed in F] : a small phagocyte; *specif* : a polymorphonuclear leukocyte

mi·croph·a·gous \(')mī¦kräfəgəs\ *adj* [*micr-* + *-phagous*] : feeding on minute particles (as bacteria) ⟨∼ ciliates⟩ ⟨∼ habit⟩ — compare MACROPHAGOUS — **mi·croph·a·gy** \=¦==jē\ *n* -ES

mi·cro·pha·kia \,mīkrō'fākēə\ *n* -s [NL, fr. *micr-* + *phac-* + *-ia*] : abnormal smallness of the lens of the eye

¹mi·cro·phone \'mīkrə,fōn\ *n* [ISV *micr-* + *-phone*] : an instrument whereby sound waves are caused to generate or modulate an electric current usu. for the purpose of transmitting or recording speech or music

²microphone \"\ *vt* : to transmit by microphone

mi·cro·phon·ic \¦==¦fänik\ *adj* [¹*microphone* + *-ic*] **1** : of or relating to a microphone : serving to intensify sounds **2** : having the effect of a microphone because of faulty construction or design — used of amplifier tubes or other circuit elements **3** : of or relating to microphonics of the cochlea

mi·cro·phon·ics \,=='fäniks\ *n pl but sing in constr* [¹*microphone* + *-ics*] **1** : a science treating of the microphone or of the means of increasing the intensity of low or weak sounds **2** : noises in a loudspeaker resulting from unwanted variations of current in the circuit or mechanical movement of tubes or other parts **3** *often* **microphonic** [*micr-* + *phon-* + *-ics* or *-ic*] : an electrical potential arising in the cochlea when the mechanical energy of a sound stimulus is transformed to electrical energy as the action potential of the transmitting nerve

mi·cro·phon·ing \'==,fōniŋ\ *n* -s [¹*microphone* + *-ing*] : the positioning of microphones or performers so as to produce desired effects in sound reproduction

¹mi·cro·photograph \¦mīkrō+\ *n* [ISV *micr-* + *photograph*] **1** : a small photograph that is normally magnified for reading or viewing : MICROCOPY **2** : PHOTOMICROGRAPH — not used technically — **mi·cro·photographic** \"+\ *adj* — **mi·cro·photography** \¦=(,)=+\ *n*

²microphotograph \"\ *vt* : to make a microphotograph of

¹mi·cro·photometer \¦mī(,)krō+\ *n* [ISV *micr-* + *photometer*] : an instrument for measuring the amount of light transmitted or reflected by small areas or for measuring the relative densities of spectrum lines on a photographic plate — **mi·cro·photometric** \"+\ *adj* — **mi·cro·photometrically** \"+\ *adv* — **mi·cro·photometry** \¦=(,)=+\ *n*

²microphotometer \"\ *vt* : to measure or examine with a microphotometer

mi·croph·thal·mia \,mī,kräf'thalmēə, ÷-kräp¦th-\ *n* -s [NL, fr. *micr-* + *ophthalmia*] : abnormal smallness of the eye usu. occurring as a congenital anomaly

mi·croph·thal·mic \,=,='=mik\ *adj* [*microphthalmia* + *-ic*] : exhibiting microphthalmia : having small eyes

mi·croph·thal·mus \,=,='=məs\ *or* **mi·croph·thal·mos** \-məs, -mäs\ *n, pl* **microphthal·mi** \-,mī\ *or* **microphthal·moi** \-,mȯi\ [*microphthalmus* fr. NL, fr. *micr-* + *-ophthalmus*; *microphthalmos* fr. NL, fr. *micr-* + Gk *ophthalmos* eye] : MICROPHTHALMIA

mi·cro·phyll \'mīkrə,fil\ *n* -s [ISV *micr-* + *-phyll*] **1** : a small leaf **2** : a plant (as a xerophyte) having small leaves

mi·cro·phyl·lous \¦==¦filəs\ *adj* [*micr-* + *-phyllous*] **1** : having small leaves ⟨the ∼ plants of desert regions⟩ **2** : having leaves with a single unbranched vein ⟨a ∼ lycopod⟩ — compare MACROPHYLLOUS

mi·cro·physical \¦mīkrō+\ *adj* [fr. *microphysics*, after E *physics*: *physical*] : of or relating to microphysics ⟨events in the ∼ world —*Time*⟩

mi·cro·physics \"+\ *n pl but sing in constr* [*micr-* + *physics*] : the physics of molecules, atoms, and elementary particles

mi·cro·phyte \'mīkrə,fīt\ *n* -s [ISV *micr-* + *-phyte*; prob. orig. formed in F] : a minute plant: as **a** : BACTERIUM **b** : a dwarfed plant occurring under unfavorable environmental conditions and consisting typically of an abbreviated stem, a single reduced leaf, and a single minute floral unit — **mi·cro·phyt·ic** \¦==¦fid·ik\ *adj*

mi·cro·pipette *or* **mi·cro·pipet** \¦mī(,)krō+\ *n* [*micr-* + *pipette*] **1** : a pipette for the measurement or transferring of very small volumes **2** : a small and extremely fine-pointed pipette used in microdissection and microinjection

mi·cro·plankton \¦==+\ *n* [ISV *micr-* + *plankton*] : microscopic plankton; *esp* : NANNOPLANKTON

mi·crop·o·dal \(')mī¦kräpədᵊl\ *also* **mi·crop·o·dous** \-dəs\ *adj* [*micropodal* fr. NL *micropodus* + E *-al*; *micropodous* fr. NL *micropodus*, fr. *micr-* + *-podus* -podous] : having abnormally small feet

mi·cro·pod·i·dae \,mīkrō'pädə,dē\ [NL, fr. *Micropod-*, *Micropus* + *-idae* — more at MICROPUS] *syn of* APODIDAE

mi·cro·pod·i·for·mes \,mīkrə,pädə'fȯr,mēz\ [NL, fr. *Micropod-*, *Micropus* + *-iformes*] *syn of* APODIFORMES

mi·cro·polariscope \¦mī(,)krō+\ *n* [*micr-* + *polariscope*] : a microscope with polarizer and analyzer attached (as for use in crystallography)

mi·cro·pore \'mīkrə+,-\ *n* [ISV *micr-* + *pore*] **1** : one of the small pores in the shell of some chitons **2** : a very fine pore (as one not easily visible to the naked eye)

mi·cro·porosity \¦mī(,)krō+\ *n* [*micr-* + *porosity*] : extremely fine porosity (as in metal castings)

mi·cro·porous \¦==+\ *adj* [*micr-* + *porous*] : full of or characterized by very fine pores ⟨∼ synthetic rubber⟩

mi·cro·potentiometer \¦=(,)=+\ *n* [*micr-* + *potentiometer*] : a potentiometer for the accurate measurement of potential differences of only a few microvolts

¹mi·cro·print \'mīkrə+,-\ *n* [*micr-* + *print*] : a photographic or photomechanical print of printed or other graphic matter in reduced size usu. viewed with an enlarging device

²microprint \"\ *vt* : to make a microprint of ⟨material ∼*ed* on cards⟩

mi·cro·procedure \¦mī(,)krō+\ *n* [*micr-* + *procedure*] : a procedure (as for microanalysis) involving very small quantities of material — opposed to *macroprocedure*

mi·cro·projection \"+\ *n* [*micr-* + *projection*] : the process of projecting microscope images on a screen by means of a microprojector

mi·cro·projector \"+\ *n* [*micr-* + *projector*] : a projector utilizing a compound microscope for projecting on a screen a greatly enlarged image of a microscopic object

mi·crop·sia \mī'kräpsēə\ *also* **mi·crop·sy** \'=,=sē\ *n, pl* **micropsias** *also* **micropsies** [NL *micropsia*, fr. *micr-* + *-opsia*] : a pathological condition in which objects appear to be smaller than they are in reality — opposed to *macropsia*

mi·crop·ter·ism \¦'==tə,rizəm\ *n* -s [*micropterous* + *-ism*] : the state or condition of being micropterous

mi·crop·ter·ous \(')mī¦kräpt(ə)rəs\ *adj* [prob. fr. (assumed) NL *micropterus*, fr. NL *micr-* + *-pterus* -pterous] : having small or rudimentary wings or fins

mi·crop·ter·us \='=tərəs\ *n, cap* [NL, fr. *micr-* + *-pterus*; fr. the fact that the specimen on which the name was based had a mutilated dorsal fin and the author of the name consequently believed its fins were small] : a genus of sunfishes (family Centrarchidae) to which the American freshwater black basses belong

¹mi·crop·ter·y·gid \¦mī(,)kräp¦terə̇jə̇d\ *adj* [NL *Micropterygidae*] : of or relating to the Micropterygidae

²micropterygid \"\ *n* -s : a moth of the family Micropterygidae

mi·crop·te·ryg·i·dae \=,=tə'rijə,dē\ *n pl, cap* [NL, fr. *Micropteryg-*, *Micropteryx*, type genus (fr. *micr-* + *-pteryg-*, *-pteryx*) + *-idae* — more at -PTERYX] : a family of tiny very primitive moths sometimes made a separate order Zeugloptera that have functional mandibles

mi·crop·tic \(')mī¦kräptik\ *adj* [*micr-* + *optic*] : of, relating to, or affected with micropsia

mi·cro·puccinia \¦mī(,)krō+\ *n* -s *usu cap P* [NL, fr. *micr-* + *Puccinia*] : a parasitic fungus of the genus *Puccinia* producing only teliospores

mi·cro·pus \mī'krōpəs\ [NL, fr. MGk *mikropod-*, *mikropous* having small feet, fr. Gk *mikr-* micr- + *pod-*, *pous* foot — more at FOOT] *syn of* APUS

mi·cro·py·lar \¦mīkrə¦pīlə(r)\ *adj* [ISV *micropyle* + *-ar*] : of, relating to, or adjacent to a micropyle ⟨eggs . . . somewhat flattened with a conical ∼ knob —E.O.Essig⟩

mi·cro·pyle \'==,pīl\ *n* -s [ISV *micr-* + *-pyle* (fr. Gk *pylē* gate); prob. orig. formed in F — more at PYLON] **1 a** : a differentiated area of surface in many eggs through which a sperm enters **b** : an opening in various spores through which enclosed protoplasts escape **2** : a minute opening in the integument of an ovule of a seed plant through which the pollen tube normally penetrates to the embryo sac and which often persists in the seed as an opening or superficial scar — called also *foramen*

mi·cro·pyrometer \¦mī(,)krō+\ *n* [*micr-* + *pyrometer*] : an instrument used for the optical determination of the temperature or emissivity of microscopic glowing bodies and having a minute glow lamp mounted in the eyepiece of a microscope so that the image of the filament is superimposed upon that of the observed glowing particle

mi·cro·radiograph \¦==+\ *n* [*micr-* + *radiograph*] : an X-ray photograph showing the minute internal structure (as of a metal or wood in thin section) — **mi·cro·radiographic** \"+\ *adj* — **mi·cro·radiography** \"+\ *n*

mi·cro·reader \"+\ *n* [*micr-* + *reader*] : an apparatus that gives an enlarged image of a microphotograph suitable for reading or viewing

mi·cro·relief \¦=(,)=+\ *n* [*micr-* + *relief*] : slight irregularities of a land surface causing variations in elevation amounting to no more than a few feet

mi·cro·reproduction \¦==+\ *n* [*micr-* + *reproduction*] **1** : microphotographic reproduction **2** : MICROCOPY

mi·cro·respirometer \"+\ *n* [*micr-* + *respirometer*] : an apparatus for the quantitative study of the respiratory activity of minute amounts of living material (as individual cells or protozoans) — **mi·cro·respirometry** \"+\ *n*

mi·cro·rhabdus \"+\ *n* [NL, fr. *micr-* + *rhabdus*] : a rod-shaped sponge spicule

mi·cro·rho·pi·as \,=='rōpēəs\ *n, cap* [NL, perh. irreg. fr. *micr-* + Gk *rhōpeia* bushes] : a genus of typical ant wrens

mi·cro·saur \'mīkrə,sȯ(ə)r\ *n* -s [NL *Microsauria*] : one of the Microsauria

mi·cro·sau·ria \,=='sȯrēə\ *n pl, cap* [NL, fr. *micr-* + *-sauria*] **1** : an order of extinct amphibians (suborder Lepospondyli) of the Pennsylvanian and Lower Permian that resemble salamanders, are sometimes considered ancestral to modern apodal and caudate amphibians, or are placed among the primitive reptiles **2** *in some classifications* : an order or other group of amphibians equivalent to Lepospondyli (sense a)

mi·cro·scale \'mīkrə+,-\ *n* [*micr-* + *scale*] : a grade, standard, or extent suited to the handling of minute quantities or measurements — often used with *on* ⟨development of clinical methods on a ∼ —*Postwar Research in Mellon Inst.*⟩

mi·cro·sclere \"+,-\ *n* [*micr-* + *sclere*] : a minute sponge spicule usu. supporting a single cell — **mi·cro·scleric** \¦==+\ *or* **mi·cro·sclerous** \"+\ *adj*

mi·cro·scolex \,=='skō,leks\ *n, cap* [NL, fr. *micr-* + *-scolex*] : a genus of earthworms containing a species (*M. phosphoreus*) native to So. America but now widely distributed that is sometimes highly luminescent and gives a greenish yellow light resembling that of a glowworm

¹mi·cro·scope \ˈmīkrə,skōp\ *n* [NL *microscopium*, fr. *micr-* + *-scopium* -scope] **1 :** an optical instrument consisting of a lens or combination of lenses for making enlarged images of minute objects; *esp* **:** COMPOUND MICROSCOPE — see PHASE MICROSCOPE, POLARIZING MICROSCOPE, ULTRAMICROSCOPE **2 :** an instrument using radiations other than light (as electrons, ultraviolet, or X rays) for making enlarged images of minute objects ⟨electron ~⟩

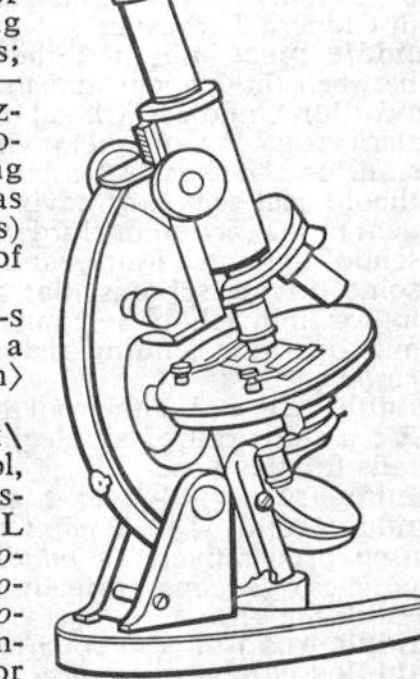

microscope 1

²microscope \"\ *vt* -ED/-ING/-S **1 :** to look at with or as if with a microscope ⟨~ a new program⟩ **2 :** MAGNIFY ⟨~ a minor failing⟩

mi·cro·scop·ic \ˌ==ˈskäpik, -pēk\ *or* **mi·cro·scop·i·cal** \-pəkəl, -pēk-\ *adj* [*microscopic* fr. (assumed) NL *microscopicus*, fr. NL *microscopium* + L *icus* -ic; *microscopical* fr. (assumed) NL *microscopicus* + E *-al*] **1 a** *usu microscopical* **:** of, relating to, or conducted with the microscope or microscopy ⟨*microscopical* examination⟩ **b :** attainable by use of the microscope ⟨~ accuracy⟩ **2 :** resembling a microscope **:** able to see very minute objects ⟨the ~ eye of the engraver —*Amer. Guide Series: N.J.*⟩ **3 a :** so small or fine as to be invisible or not clearly distinguished without the use of a microscope ⟨~ plants⟩ ⟨~ crystallization⟩ — often distinguished from *submicroscopic* and *ultramicroscopic;* opposed to *macroscopic* **b :** very small or fine ⟨a ~ dog⟩ ⟨no matter how ~ his wage —Irving Stone⟩ ⟨~ division of labor —P.M.Mazur⟩ **c :** extremely accurate or meticulous ⟨examined the object with ~ care⟩ **syn** see SMALL

mi·cro·scop·i·cal·ly \-pək(ə)lē, -li\ *adv* **1 :** by means of the microscope ⟨a fact that can be demonstrated ~⟩ **2 :** to a microscopic degree ⟨took great care to get the surface ~ level —G.R.Gilbert⟩ ⟨contribute ~ to the appreciation of art —Vincent Starrett⟩ **3 :** in a microscopic manner **:** with extreme accuracy or meticulousness ⟨studying ~ the statistics of trade and industry —G.G.Coulton⟩

microscopic anatomy *n* **:** HISTOLOGY

mi·cros·co·pist \mīˈkräskəpəst, ˈmīkrə,skōpəst\ *n* -S [ISV ¹*microscope* + *-ist*] **:** a specialist in microscopy

mi·cros·co·py \-pē, -pi\ *n* -ES [¹*microscope* + *-y*] **:** the use of the microscope **:** investigation with the microscope

mi·cro·second \ˈmīkrō+\ *n* [ISV *micr-* + *second*] **:** a unit of time equal to one millionth of a second

mi·cro·section \"+\ *n* [*micr-* + *section*] **:** a thin section (as of rock or of animal or vegetable tissue) prepared for microscopic examination

mi·cro·seism \ˈmīkrə,sīzəm *sometimes* -sez- *or* -sāz- *or* -sēz-\ *n* -S [ISV *micr-* + *-seism*] **:** a feeble rhythmically recurring earth tremor that is not directly perceptible, that is detected only by means of specially constructed apparatus, and that is caused by an earthquake or by a storm at sea — compare MACROSEISM — **mi·cro·seis·mic** \ˌ==ˈsīzmik *also* |sm- *sometimes* -ˈse| *or* -ˈsā| *or* -ˈsē|\ *adj*

mi·cro·seismograph \ˈmīkrō+\ *n* [ISV *microseism* + *-o-* + *-graph*] **:** MICROSEISMOMETER

mi·cro·seismology \ˌ=(ˌ)=+\ *n* [*microseism* + *-o-* + *-logy*] **:** a science dealing with microseisms

mi·cro·seismometer \"+\ *n* [*microseism* + *-o-* + *-meter*] **:** a seismometer for measuring microseisms — **mi·cro·seis·mometry** \"+\ *n*

mi·cro·septum \ˌ==+\ *n* [NL, fr. *micr-* + *septum*] **:** a narrow or imperfect mesentery in anthozoans

mi·cro·ser·al \ˌ==ˈsirəl\ *adj* [*microsere* + *-al*] **:** of or relating to a microsere

mi·cro·sere \ˌ==+,-\ *n* [*micr-* + *sere*] **:** the sere of a microhabitat usu. terminating by the loss of identity of the habitat and without the development of a climax

mi·cro·sheet \"+,-\ *n* [*micr-* + *sheet*] **:** MICROFICHE

mi·cro·slide \"+,-\ *n* [*micr-* + *slide*] **:** a slip of glass on which a preparation is mounted for microscopic examination

mi·cros·mat·ic \ˌmī,kräzˈmad·ik\ *adj* [*micr-* + *osmatic*] **:** having the sense of smell feebly developed

mi·cro–sociology \ˈmīkrō+\ *n* [*micr-* + *sociology*] **:** the study of small systems of social behavior

mi·cro·so·ma \ˌmīkrəˈsōmə\ *n, pl* **microsoma·ta** \-məd·ə\ [NL, fr. G *mikrosom*] **:** MICROSOME

mi·cro·som·al \ˌ==ˈsōməl\ *adj* [*microsome* + *-al*] **:** of or relating to microsomes

mi·cro·so·ma·tous \ˌ==ˈsōməd·əs\ *adj* [*micr-* + *-somatous*] **:** having a small body **:** DWARFISH

mi·cro·some \ˈmīkrə,sōm\ *n* -S [G *mikrosom*, fr. *mikr-* micr- + *-som* -some] **1 :** any of various minute structures of the cell esp. as observed at the limit of resolution of the light microscope **2 :** a particle in a particulate fraction that is obtained by heavy centrifugation of broken cells and consists of various amounts of ribosomes, fragmented endoplasmic reticulum, and mitochondrial cristae

mi·cro·sorex \ˈmīkrō+\ *n, cap* [NL, fr. *micr-* + *Sorex*] **:** a genus formerly considered a subgenus of *Sorex* comprising the pygmy shrews

mi·cro·species \"+\ *n, pl* **microspecies** [*micr-* + *species*] **:** a small usu. localized population slightly but effectively differentiated from related forms — compare MACROSPECIES

mi·cro·spectrophotometer \"+\ *n* [*micr-* + *spectrophotometer*] **:** a spectrophotometer adapted to the examination of light transmitted by very small specimens (as a single organic cell) — **mi·cro·spectrophotometric** \"+\ *also* **mi·cro·spectrophotometrical** \"+\ *adj* — **mi·cro·spectrophotometrically** \"+\ *adv* — **mi·cro·spectrophotometry** \"+\ *n*

mi·cro·spectroscope \"+\ *n* [*micr-* + *spectroscope*] **:** a spectroscope arranged for attachment to a microscope for observation of the spectrum of light from minute portions of an object — **mi·cro·spectroscopic** \"+\ *adj* — **mi·cro·spectros·copy** \"+\ *n*

mi·cro·sper·mae \ˌ==ˈspər(ˌ)mē\ [NL, fr. *micr-* + *-spermae*] *syn of* ORCHIDALES

mi·cro·sper·mop·ter·is \-(ˌ)spərˈmäptərəs\ *n, cap* [NL, fr. *micr-* + *sperm-* + *-pteris*] **:** a genus of Carboniferous seed ferns exhibiting features in common with the genera *Lyginopteris* and *Heterangium* and being of special interest because of the evidence it provides concerning the origin of seed plants from the Psilophytales

mi·cro·sphae·ra \-ˈsfirə\ *n, cap* [NL, fr. *micr-* + *-sphaera*] **:** a genus of powdery mildews (family Erysiphaceae) having several asci in each perithecium and the appendages once or more dichotomously branched — see LILAC MILDEW

mi·cro·sphere \ˈmīkrə+,-\ *n* [*micr-* + *sphere*] **:** a very small primordial shell of the asexual individuals of various dimorphic Foraminifera — **mi·cro·spher·ic** \-ˈsfirik, -fer-\ *adj*

mi·cro·splanchnic \ˈmīkrō+\ *adj* [ISV *micr-* + *splanchnic;* orig. formed as It *microsplancnico*] **:** ECTOMORPHIC — opposed to *macrosplanchnic;* compare NORMOSPLANCHNIC

mi·cro·spo·range \ˈmīkrōspə,ranj, -krə,spōr,anj\ *n* [NL *microsporangium*] **:** MICROSPORANGIUM

mi·cro·sporangium \ˈmīkrō+\ *n* [NL, fr. *micr-* + *sporangium*] **:** a sporangium bearing microspores (as the pollen sac of the anther in a seed plant) — compare MEGASPORANGIUM

mi·cro·spore \ˈmīkrə+,-\ *n* [ISV *micr-* + *spore*] **1 :** one of the spores of a heterosporous plant (as the pollen grain of a seed plant) that gives rise to male gametophytes and that is generally smaller than the megaspore **2 :** the smaller of two forms of spores produced by various protozoans (as Radiolaria) — **mi·cro·spor·ic** \ˌ==ˈspōrik\ *or* **mi·cro·spor·ous** \ˌ==ˈspōrəs,(ˈ)mīˈkräspərəs\ *adj*

mi·cro·spo·rid·ia \ˌmīkrəspəˈridēə\ *n pl, cap* [NL, fr. *micr-* + *-sporidia*] **:** an order of Cnidosporidia comprising protozoan parasites of arthropods and fishes that typically invade and destroy host cells — see NOSEMA — **mi·cro·spo·rid·i·an** \ˌ==ˈridēən\ *adj or n*

mi·cro·spo·ri·di·ida \ˌ==ˌspōrəˈdīədə\ [NL, fr. *micr-* + *sporidium* + *-ida*] *syn of* MICROSPORIDIA

mi·cro·spo·ro·cyte \ˌ==ˈspōrə,sīt\ *n* [*microspore* + *-o-* + *-cyte*] **:** a microspore mother cell

mi·cro·spo·ro·gen·e·sis \ˌ==ˌ==+\ *n* [NL, fr. *microsporo-* (fr. ISV *microspore*) + L *genesis*] **:** the formation and maturation of a microspore — compare MEGASPOROGENESIS

mi·cros·po·ron \mīˈkräspə,rän\ *syn of* MICROSPORUM

mi·cro·sporophyll \ˈmīkrō+\ *n* [*micr-* + *sporophyll*] **:** a sporophyll (as a stamen) bearing microsporangia

mi·cro·spo·ro·sis \ˌmīkrō,spəˈrōsəs\ *n, pl* **microsporo·ses** \-,sēz\ [NL, fr. *Microsporum* + *-osis*] **:** ringworm caused by fungi of the genus *Microsporum* — compare TINEA CAPITIS

mi·cros·po·rum \mīˈkräspərəm\ *n, cap* [NL, fr. *micr-* + *-sporum* (fr. Gk *spora* seed) — more at SPORE] **:** a genus of fungi (family Moniliaceae) producing both small, nearly oval single-celled spores and large spindle-shaped multicellular spores with a usu. rough outer wall — see RINGWORM

mi·cro·sthene \ˈmīkrəs,thēn\ *n* -S [NL *Microsthenes*] **:** one of the Microsthenes

mi·cros·the·nes \mīˈkrästhə(ˌ)nēz\ *n pl, cap* [NL, fr. *micr-* + *-sthenes* (fr. Gk *sthenos* strength) — more at ASTHEN-] *in former classifications* **:** a division of eutherian mammals approximately equal to the orders Insectivora, Chiroptera, Rodentia, and Edentata — **microsthenic** *adj*

mi·cro·stoma·tous \ˌmīkrəˈstäməd·əs, -stōm-\ *adj* [*micr-* + *-stomatous*] **:** having a small mouth ⟨a ~ shell⟩

mi·cro·stome \ˈmīkrə,stōm\ *n* -S [*micr-* + *-stome*] **:** a small orifice

mi·cro·sto·mia \ˌ==ˈstōmēə\ *also* **mi·cros·to·mus** \mīˈkrästəməs\ *n, pl* **microstomi·as** \-tōmēəz\ *also* **microsto·mi** \-tə,mī\ [NL, fr. *micr-* + *-stomia* or *-stomus*] **:** an abnormally small mouth

mi·cros·to·mous \(ˈ)mīˈkrästəməs\ *adj* [*micr-* + *-stomous*] **:** MICROSTOMATOUS

mi·cro·strongyle \ˈmīkrō+\ *n* [*micr-* + *strongyle*] **:** a microsclere having the form of a strongyle

mi·cro·structural \"+\ *adj* **:** of or relating to microstructure

mi·cro·structure \"+\ *n* [ISV *micr-* + *structure*] **:** the structure of a material (as an alloy or other crystalline mass) on a minute scale as revealed by the microscope or other means

mi·cro·sty·lous \ˌ==ˈstīləs\ *adj* [*micr-* + *-stylous*] *of a flower* **:** having short styles; *specif* **:** having short styles and long filaments — compare MACROSTYLOUS, MESOSTYLOUS

mi·cro·sublimation \"+\ *n* [*micr-* + *sublimation*] **:** sublimation of a minute quantity of a material for microscopic examination

mi·cro·switch \ˈmīkrə+,-\ *n* [*micr-* + *switch*] **:** a small and highly sensitive switch in which minute motion establishes contact and which is used esp. in automatic-control devices

mi·cro·symbiote \ˈmīkrō+\ *n* [*micr-* + *symbiote*] **:** a microorganism living in symbiosis with a more advanced organism ⟨the ~s of many insects⟩ — compare MYCETOCYTE

mi·cro·technic \"+\ *or* **mi·cro·technique** \"+\ *n* [ISV *micr-* + *technic* or *technique*] **:** microscopic technic **:** MICROLOGY

mi·cro·text \ˈmīkrə+,-\ *n* [*micr-* + *text*] **:** a microfilmed or microphotographed text

mi·cro·thel·y·phon·i·da \ˌmīkrō,theləˈfänədə\ *n pl, cap* [NL, fr. *micr-* + *Thelyphonus* genus of whip scorpions + *-ida* — more at THELYPHONIDAE] **:** an order of Arachnida including minute arthropods with a whiplash at the tip of the abdomen

mi·cro·therm \ˈmīkrə,thərm\ *n* [ISV *micr-* + *-therm*] **:** a plant requiring a mean annual temperature between 0° and 14° C for full growth — compare MEGATHERM, MESOTHERM — **mi·cro·ther·mic** \ˌ==ˈthərmik\ *adj*

mi·cro·thermal \ˌ==+\ *adj* [*micr-* + *thermal*] **:** of, involving, or relating to very small quantities of heat or changes of temperature ⟨~ measurements⟩

mi·cro·thorax \ˈmīkrō+\ *n* [NL, fr. *micr-* + *thorax*] **:** a membranous section in the neck region of an insect consisting of a number of small sclerites

mi·cro·thy·ri·a·ce·ae \ˌmīkrə,thīrēˈāsē,ē\ *n pl, cap* [NL, fr. *Microthyrium*, type genus (fr. *micr-* + Gk *thyrion*, dim. of *thyra* door) + *-aceae* — more at DOOR] **:** a family of ascomycetous fungi (order Microthyriales) with shield-shaped or radiate perithecia

mi·cro·thy·ri·a·les \-ˈā(ˌ)lēz\ *n pl, cap* [NL, fr. *Microthyrium* + *-ales*] **:** an order of fungi (subclass Euascomycetes) that have peltate fructifications and develop asci on ascogenous hyphae arising from among the pseudoparenchymatous stroma

mi·crot·i·dae \mīˈkräd·ə,dē\ [NL, fr. *Microtus* + *-idae*] *syn of* CRICETIDAE

mi·cro·time \ˈmīkrə+,-\ *n* [*micr-* + *time*] **:** a very short interval of time (as 0.01 millionth of a second) ⟨~ photography⟩

mi·cro·titration \ˈmī(ˌ)krō+\ *n* [*micr-* + *titration*] **:** microanalytical titration

¹mi·cro·tome \ˈmīkrə,tōm\ *n* -S [ISV *micr-* + *-tome*] **:** an instrument for cutting sections (as of organic tissues) for microscopic examination

²microtome \"\ *vt* -ED/-ING/-S **:** to cut in sections with a microtome

mi·cro·tomic \ˌ==ˈtämik\ *also* **mi·cro·tom·i·cal** \-məkəl\ *adj* [*microtome* + *-ic* or *-ical*] **:** of or relating to the microtome or microtomy **:** that cuts thin slices

mi·crot·o·my \mīˈkräd·əmē\ *n* -ES [*microtome* + *-y*] **:** the technique of using the microtome or of preparing with its aid objects for microscopic study

mi·cro·ton·al \ˌmīkrəˈtōnᵊl\ *adj* [*microtone* + *-al*] **:** relating to or characterized by music containing microtones — **mi·cro·ton·al·ly** \-ᵊlē\ *adv*

mi·cro·to·nal·i·ty \-tōˈnaləd·ē\ *n* [*microtonal* + *-ity*] **:** the quality or state of being microtonal

mi·cro·tone \ˈmīkrə+,-\ *n* [*micr-* + *tone*] **:** a musical interval smaller than a half tone

mi·cro·trich·i·um \ˌ==ˈtrikēəm\ *n, pl* **microtrich·ia** \-ēə\ [NL, fr. *micr-* + Gk *trich-, thrix* hair + NL *-ium* — more at TRICHINA] **:** one of the minute fixed hairs on the integument (as the wings) of various insects — compare MACROTRICHIUM

mi·cro·tron \ˈmīkrə,trän\ *n* -S [*micr-* + *-tron*] **:** a device for accelerating electrons in the same manner as the cyclotron accelerates heavier particles

mi·cro·tus \mīˈkrōd·əs\ *n, cap* [NL, fr. *micr-* + *-otus* (fr. Gk *ōt-, ous* ear) — more at EAR] **:** a genus of myomorph rodents (family Cricetidae) comprising the voles of the northern hemisphere

mi·cro·tylote \ˈmīkrō+\ *n* [*micr-* + *tylote*] **:** a microsclere having the form of a tylote

mi·cro·type \ˈmīkrə+,-\ *n* [*micr-* + *type*] **:** MICROSPECIES — **mi·cro·typical** \ˌ==+\ *adj*

mi·cro·volt \"+,-\ *n* [ISV *micr-* + *volt*] **:** one millionth of a volt

mi·cro·watt \"+,-\ *n* [*micr-* + *watt*] **:** one millionth of a watt

¹mi·cro·wave \"+,-\ *n* [*micr-* + *wave*] **:** a very short electromagnetic wave: as **a :** a wave of less than ten meters in wavelength **b :** a wave between 100 centimeters and one centimeter in wavelength

²microwave \"\ *vt* **:** to transmit by means of microwaves

microwave relay *n* **:** a combination of receiving, amplifying, and transmitting equipment that is used to pick up, amplify, and retransmit a microwave signal

microwave spectroscope *n* **:** an apparatus for observing and measuring the absorption of different substances for microwaves as a function of wavelength and thus obtaining the microwave spectra of the substances — **microwave spectroscopy** *n*

microwave spectrum *n* **:** an absorption spectrum in the microwave wavelength range; *esp* **:** one in the range between about 15 centimeters and 0.25 centimeters

mi·crox·ea \mīˈkräksēə\ *n* [NL, fr. *micr-* + *oxea*] **:** a microsclere having the form of an oxea

¹mi·cro·zo·an \ˌmīkrəˈzōən\ *or* **mi·cro·zo·ic** \-ik\ *adj* [NL *microzoon* + E *-an* or *-ic*] **:** of or relating to the microzoa

²microzoan \"\ *n* -S **:** MICROZOON 1

mi·cro·zooid \ˌ==+\ *n* [*micr-* + *zooid*] **:** a minute free-swimming individual supposed to be budded from the megazooid of various higher ciliates

mi·cro·zo·on \ˌ==ˈzō,än\ *n, pl* **micro·zoa** \-ˈzōə\ [NL, fr. *micr-* + *-zoon*] **1 :** a microscopic animal; *esp* **:** PROTOZOAN **2** *microzoa pl, sometimes cap* **:** microscopic animal life

mi·cro·zoospore \ˈmīkrō+\ *n* [*micr-* + *zoospore*] **:** a small zoospore — compare MACROZOOSPORE

mi·crur·gi·cal \(ˈ)mīˈkrərjəkəl\ *or* **mi·crur·gic** \-jik\ *adj* [*micrurgy* + *-ical* or *-ic*] **:** of or relating to micrurgy

mi·crur·gist \ˈ=(ˌ)=jəst\ *n* -S [*micrurgy* + *-ist*] **:** a specialist in micrurgy

mi·crur·gy \-jē\ *n* -ES [ISV *micr-* + *-urgy*] **:** MICROMANIPULATION; *broadly* **:** the practice of using minute tools in a magnified field

mi·cru·ri·dae \mīˈkru̇rə,dē\ [NL, fr. *Micrurus* + *-idae*] *syn of* ELAPIDAE

mi·cru·rus \-rəs\ *n, cap* [NL, fr. *micr-* + *-urus*] **:** a genus of small venomous elapid snakes comprising the American coral snakes

mic·tic \ˈmiktik\ *adj* [Gk *miktos* mixed (verbal of *mignynai* to mix) + E *-ic* — more at MIX] **1 :** requiring, involving, or produced by sexual reproduction or union of germ cells **:** exhibiting mixis **2 a** *of a female rotifer* **:** producing eggs that without fertilization develop into males or with fertilization form resting eggs that later develop into amictic females **b :** being or relating to the egg of such a female

mic·tion \-kshən\ *n* -S [LL *miction-, mictio*, fr. L *mictus* (past part. of *mingere* to urinate) + *-ion-, -io* -ion] **:** URINATION

mic·tu·rate \ˈmikchə,rāt, *usu* -ād.+V\ *vi* -ED/-ING/-S [L *micturire* + E *-ate*] **:** URINATE

mic·tu·ri·tion \ˌ==ˈrishən\ *n* -S [prob. fr. (assumed) NL *micturition-, micturitio*, fr. (assumed) L *micturitus* (past part. of L *micturire* to urinate, want to urinate, fr. *mictus*, past part. of *mingere* to urinate) + L *-ion-, -io* -ion — more at MIXEN] **:** URINATION

¹mid \ˈmid\ *adj* [ME *mid, midde*, fr. OE *midd, midde;* akin to OHG *mitti* mid, middle, ON *mithr*, Goth *midjis*, L *medius*, Gk *mesos*, Skt *madhya*] **1 :** being the part in the middle or midst ⟨in ~ ocean⟩ — often used in combination ⟨*mid*-August⟩ ⟨*mid*-1950s⟩ ⟨*mid*-Renaissance⟩ **2 :** occupying a middle position **:** MIDDLE 1a ⟨the ~ finger⟩ — often used in combination ⟨*mid*-incisor⟩ ⟨*mid*-pillar⟩ **3** *of a vowel* **:** articulated with the arch of the tongue midway between its highest and its lowest elevation — compare CLOSE, OPEN

²mid \"\ *n* -S [ME *mid, midde*, fr. *mid, midde*, adj.] *archaic* **:** MIDDLE

³mid \"\ *adv* [ME *mid, midde*, fr. *mid, midde*, adj.] **:** in the middle

⁴mid \"\ *prep* [by shortening] **:** AMID

⁵mid \"\ *n* -S [by shortening] **:** MIDSHIPMAN

mid *abbr* **1** middle **2** midland **3** midnight **4** midshipman

MID *abbr* **1** military intelligence department **2** military intelligence division **3** minimum infective dose

midafternoon \ˈ=ˌ=ˈ=\ *n* **:** the middle part of the afternoon

mid-age \ˈ=ˌ=\ *n* [ME *myd-age*, fr. *myd, mid, midde* mid + *age*] **:** MIDDLE AGE

mid-aged \ˈ=ˈ=\ *adj* **:** MIDDLE-AGED

midair \ˈ=ˈ=\ *n* **1** *obs* **:** the intermediate of the three regions into which the air was formerly distinguished including the level of the clouds **2 :** any point or region in the air not immediately adjacent to the ground or other solid or liquid surface beneath it ⟨colliding in ~⟩ ⟨hovering in ~⟩ ⟨suspended in ~⟩ ⟨sat staring at ~ —Charles Dickens⟩

mid-american \ˌ==ˈ===\ *adj, sometimes cap M & usu cap A* **:** of, relating to, or characteristic of the central section of the U.S. or its inhabitants

mi·das \ˈmīdəs\ [NL, after *Midas* legendary king of Phrygia whose touch turned everything to gold and whose ears were turned by Apollo into ass's ears, fr. L, fr. Gk] *syn of* LEONTOCEBUS

midas fly *var of* MYDAS FLY

mi·das's–ear \ˈmīdəsəˈzi(ə)r\ *n, pl* **midas's–ears** *usu cap* [after King *Midas*] **:** an Old World snail (*Ellobium aurismidae*)

midas touch *n, usu cap M* [after King *Midas*] **:** the talent for making wealth out of any activity one turns one's hands to

mid-back \ˈ=ˈ=\ *adj, of a vowel* **:** articulated with the tongue arched at the back midway between its highest and its lowest elevation

midbrain \ˈ=ˌ=\ *n* **1 :** the middle division of the embryonic vertebrate brain that gives rise to the corpora quadrigemina, cerebral peduncles, and tegmentum and encloses the aqueduct of Sylvius **2 :** the parts of the definitive brain that develop from the embryonic midbrain

midcapacity \ˈ==ˈ===\ *n* **:** the pulmonary volume when the lungs are in the state of contraction characteristic of the end of a normal quiet exhalation equal to the sum of the volumes occupied by the residual air, supplemental air, and dead space

midcarpal \ˈ=ˈ==\ *adj* **:** being between the proximal and distal carpals — used esp. of an anatomical articulation

mid-central \ˈ=ˈ==\ *adj, of a vowel* **:** articulated with the tongue arched in the middle midway between its highest and its lowest elevation

mid·day \ˈmidˈdā\ *n, often attrib* [ME, fr. OE *middæg*, fr. *middle* mid + *dæg* day — more at MID, DAY] **1 :** the middle part of the day **:** NOON **2 :** SEXT 1

mid·den \ˈmidᵊn\ *n* -S [ME *midding*, of Scand origin; akin to Dan *mødding, møgdynge* dunghill, fr. *møg* dung, muck + *dynge* heap; akin to ON *myki* dung and to ON *dyngja* manure pile — more at MUCUS, DUNG] **1 :** DUNGHILL **2 a :** an accumulation of refuse about a dwelling place **:** a refuse heap **b :** KITCHEN MIDDEN **3 :** one of the masses of highly organic soil deposited by an earthworm about its burrow; *sometimes* **:** organic debris left on the soil by various other animals

middenhead \ˈ==,=\ *n, Brit* **:** the top of a dunghill

middenstead \ˈ==,=\ *n* **1** *Brit* **:** the site of a dunghill **:** LAYSTALL **2** *Brit* **:** DUNGHILL

¹mid·dest \ˈmidəst\ *adj* [¹*mid* + *-est*] *archaic* **:** MIDMOST

²middest *obs var of* MIDST

middie *var of* MIDDY

¹mid·dle \ˈmidᵊl\ *adj* [ME *middel*, fr. OE; akin to OFris *middel* middle, OS *middil*, OHG *mittil* middle, ON *methal* among, between, OE *midde* mid — more at MID] **1 a :** equally distant (as reckoned by number, space, or other particular) from the extremes **:** MEAN ⟨lived in the ~ house in a row⟩ ⟨a ~ rank in life⟩ ⟨the ~ portion⟩ **b :** halfway between the bid and asked prices ⟨the ~ price⟩ ⟨87 ~⟩ — used of prices on the London stock exchange **2** *archaic* **:** constituting or occupying the middle ⟨through ~ empire of the freezing air —John Milton⟩ **3 a :** being at neither extreme **:** INTERMEDIATE, INTERVENING ⟨filled up the ~ space⟩ ⟨of ~ size⟩ ⟨a ~ opinion⟩ ⟨a ~ line of action⟩ **b** *archaic* **:** acting as an intermediary **4 :** of middle size or volume — now used only of wool of medium-length staple **5** *archaic* **:** being the middle part **:** MID 1 **6 a** *often cap* **:** constituting a division intermediate between those prior and later or upper and lower ⟨the ~ ages⟩ ⟨*Middle* Jurassic⟩ ⟨*Middle* Paleozoic⟩ **b** *usu cap* **:** constituting a period of a language or literature that is intermediate between a period called *Old* and a period called *New* or *Modern* ⟨~ English⟩ ⟨~ High German⟩ **c** *of management* **:** responsible for the administration and supervision of policies and practices — distinguished from *top* **7** *of a verb form or voice* **:** typically asserting that the person or thing represented by the grammatical subject both performs and is subjected to or affected by the action represented by the verb ⟨Greek *louomai* "I wash myself" is in the ~ voice⟩ — used esp. in the grammar of Greek and Sanskrit; compare ACTIVE **8** *of a mute in ancient Greek* **:** MEDIAL **9** *usu cap* **:** of or relating to the earliest known culture of Mexico

²middle \"\ *n* -S [ME *middel*, fr. OE, fr. *middel*, adj.] **1 a :** a portion or part separated by equal or approximately equal substantial distances from the ends or the opposite sides (as of a line, surface, solid) or from the limits of anything regarded as extending between two extremities (as a period of time, an event, process, or condition continuing over a certain period of time, a series, or a range or compass) ⟨the ~ of the street was unpaved⟩ ⟨apples from the ~ of the barrel⟩ ⟨rain during the ~ of April⟩ ⟨the ~ of the war⟩ ⟨a voice strong in the ~⟩ ⟨in the ~ of the social scale⟩ ⟨the beginning, ~, and end of a list —R.S.Woodworth⟩ **b :** a midpoint (as of a line), median line (as of a surface), or median plane (as of a solid) or a point (as in time or other measurable entity) midway between two limits ⟨a sheet of paper folded down the ~⟩ **c :** all except the two terminal segments or units of something consisting of a series of segments or units **:** INTERIOR ⟨remove a link from the ~ of the chain⟩ ⟨the small circle joins easily to other consonant strokes at the beginning, in the ~, or at the end of a word —*New Standard Course in Pitman Shorthand*⟩

2 : an area or space at or near the center and separated by substantial distances from the exterior limits (as of a larger area or space) **:** central part ⟨a small bird . . . which they release . . . in the ~ of their fields —J.G.Frazer⟩ **3 :** the position of being among or surrounded by others **:** MIDST 2 **4 :** the mid-part of the human body **:** WAIST **5 :** something intermediate between extremes ⟨in this, as in most questions of state, there is a ~ —Edmund Burke⟩ **6 a :** a range of points of view held or of policies advocated or practiced (as in the realm of politics) intermediate between those points of view and policies commonly regarded as reactionary and conservative and those commonly regarded as liberal and radical **b :** those persons or groups (as political parties) collectively that hold points of view or advocate or practice policies that fall in such a middle **7 :** the body proper of an animal; *specif* **:** either of the pieces forming a dressed side between the shoulder and rump or ham **8 :** the large intestine of beef used as casing for bologna **9** *chiefly South* **:** the strip or ridge of earth left between two rows of a crop (as corn or cotton) during the growing season **10 :** the middle voice of a verb or a form in this voice **11 :** MIDDLE TERM **12 :** MIDDLE GROUND 1 **13 middles** *pl but sometimes sing in constr* **:** usu. low-grade material forming the middle or internal layer or layers of pasteboard or combination board **14 :** the guard covering the middle stump in cricket **15** *Canadian football* **:** TACKLE **16 :** MIDDLE ARTICLE **17 :** MIDDLEWEIGHT **syn** see CENTER — **in the middle** *adv (or adj)* **:** in a position between two sources of difficulty **:** in a tight spot ⟨whatever you do, you're sure to be caught *in the middle*⟩ — **in the middle of 1 :** during ⟨interrupted *in the middle of* his speech⟩ **2 :** deeply involved in **:** in the thick of ⟨whose father was *in the* very *middle of* the Boulangist movement —Arnold Bennett⟩

³**middle** \"\ *vt* **middled; middled; middling** \-d(ᵊ)liŋ\ **middles 1 :** to put in the middle **2** *naut* **:** to fold in the middle **:** DOUBLE ⟨~ a hawser⟩ ⟨~ a sail⟩ — **middle the cable :** to let out the cables of a ship having two anchors out in such a way as to have the same amount of cable to each anchor

middle age *n* [ME *middel age*] **:** the period of life between youth and old age ⟨that increasingly elastic expanse called *middle age* —Harrison Smith⟩

middle-age \ˌ==ˈ=\ *adj* **1** [fr. the *middle age* or the *middle ages* (trans. of NL *Medium Aevum*), the period of European history from about A.D. 500 to about 1500] **:** MEDIEVAL **2** [*middle age*] **:** MIDDLE-AGED

middle-aged \ˌ==ˈ=\ *adj* **1 a :** being at an age beyond youth and below old age **b :** of, relating to, or characteristic of middle-aged persons ⟨*middle-aged* love —Michael Arlen⟩ **2 a** *of a thing* **:** having existed longer than things of the same type and group commonly or conventionally regarded as new **b :** of, relating to, or characteristic of such things **3** [the *middle age* + E *-ed*] *obs* **:** MEDIEVAL — **mid·dle-aged·ly** \ˌ==ˈājədlē, -jd-\ *adv* — **mid·dle-aged·ness** \-jədnəs, -j(d)n-\ *n* -ES

mid·dle-ag·er \ˈ==ˈājə(r)\ *n* [*middle age* + *-er*] **:** one that is middle-aged

mid·dle-ag·ing \ˌ==ˈājiŋ\ *adj* [*middle age* + *-ing*] **:** entering upon middle age

middle-aisle \ˈ==ˌ=\ *vt* **middle-aisled; middle-aisled; middle-aisling; middle-aisles** [so called fr. the traditional bridal procession down the middle aisle of a church] *slang* **:** MARRY — usu. used with *it* ⟨are expected to *middle-aisle* it in August⟩

middle american *adj, usu cap M&A* [*Middle America*, the region including Mexico, Central America, and sometimes the Caribbean islands + E *-an*] **:** of or relating to Middle America

middle americanist *n, usu cap M&A* **:** a specialist in Middle American studies

middle and leg *n* **:** the guard covering the middle and leg stumps in cricket

middle and off *n* **:** the guard covering the middle and off stumps in cricket

middle angle *n* **:** THIRD ANGLE

middle article *n, Brit* **:** a popular or light literary essay or article of less immediate current significance than an editorial printed in or suitable for printing in a newspaper or weekly

middle assyrian *adj, usu cap M&A* **:** of, relating to, or characteristic of the middle period of the Assyrian civilization

middle babylonian *n, usu cap M&B* **:** the dialect of Akkadian used in Babylonia between 2000 and 1500 B.C.

middle base point *n* **:** the lower middle part of the field of an escutcheon — see POINT illustration

middle belt *n, usu cap M&B* [fr. *Middle Belt*, the central section of the area where tobacco is grown in the U. S., consisting principally of the Piedmont area of Va. and No. Car.] **:** a flue-cured tobacco produced in No. Carolina

middle body *n* **:** the part of a ship's body amidships having a uniform or nearly uniform cross section — compare AFTERBODY, FOREBODY

middlebreaker \ˈ==ˌ==\ *n* **:** LISTER 1

¹**middlebrow** \ˈ==ˌ=\ *n* [¹*middle* + *brow*] **1 :** a person who is moderately but not highly cultivated ⟨Mozart is everyone's tea, pleasing to highbrows, ~*s* and lowbrows alike —Rose Macaulay⟩ **2 :** a person who possesses or has pretensions to intellectual interests but who dislikes works of art and literature that are original or unconventional in nature or that require effort for comprehension **:** PHILISTINE ⟨the ~*s* have become more intransigent in their opposition to everything that is serious and creative in our culture —Irving Howe⟩

²**middlebrow** \"\ *adj* **:** of, relating to, characteristic of, or suitable for a middlebrow ⟨the safe and comforting patterns of ~ feeling —Irving Howe⟩ ⟨~ culture attacks distinctions as such and insinuates itself everywhere, devaluating the precious, infecting the healthy, corrupting the honest, and stultifying the wise —Clement Greenberg⟩

middlebrowed \ˌ==ˈ=\ *adj* **:** MIDDLEBROW

mid·dle·brow·ism \ˈmidᵊlˌbrau̇ˌizəm\ *n* -S **:** the state of mind or quality of culture characteristic of a middlebrow

middle brunswick green *n, often cap B* **:** a green that is duller and slightly yellower than holly green (sense 1), bluer, stronger, and slightly lighter than deep chrome green, yellower than average hunter green, and yellower, lighter, and stronger than deep Brunswick green

middle-burster \ˈ==ˌ==\ *n* **:** LISTER 1

middlebuster \ˈ==ˌ==\ *n* **:** LISTER 1

middle C *n* **1 :** the musical note or tone *c′* — see PITCH illustration **2 :** the key of a keyboard sounding *c′*

middle chief point *n* **:** the upper middle part of the field of an escutcheon — called also *chief point;* see POINT illustration

middle chrome yellow *n* **:** DEEP CHROME YELLOW

middle class *n* **1 :** a social class occupying a position between the upper class and the lower class: as **a :** a class achieving prominence in modern times during the transition from a medieval to a modern economy and constituting a grouping of people (as artisans, independent farmers, tradesmen, and lesser officials) between the hereditary nobility on the one hand and the laborers and peasants on the other **b :** a class occupying a position (as in England) between the aristocracy and the working class **c :** a fluid heterogeneous socio-economic grouping (as in the U. S.) having a status intermediate between the upper and lower classes and composed principally of business and professional people, bureaucrats, and some farmers and skilled workers sharing common social characteristics and values **2 middle classes** *pl* **:** an aggregate of social groupings that includes the upper middle class and the lower middle class

middle-class \ˌ==ˈ=\ *adj* [*middle class*] **1 :** of or relating to the middle class ⟨his unrecognized claim to *middle-class* status —Ray Gold⟩ ⟨the traditional *middle-class* basis of American politics —Samuel Lubell⟩ ⟨*middle-class* women attach more importance to social approval —P.M.Gregory⟩ **2 :** belonging to or associated with the middle class and its possession of or inclination toward a diversified social morality that includes such traits as a desire for stability and a high material standard of living, a respect for convention and the proprieties, and high ideals of education, professional competence, and personal ambition ⟨a proper air of *middle-class* gentility —Gene Baro⟩ ⟨her rebellion against *middle-class* conventions —*Current Biog.*⟩ ⟨live up to *middle-class* standards of cleanliness —T.M.Newcomb⟩ — compare LOWER-CLASS, UPPER-CLASS

mid·dled \ˈmidᵊld\ *adj* [²*middle* + *-ed*] *of an animal* **:** having a middle or middles — used with a qualifying term ⟨a trim ~ lamb⟩

middle distance *n* **1 :** a part of a pictorial representation or scene that is between the foreground and the background — called also *middle ground;* compare PERSPECTIVE **2 :** any footrace distance from 400 meters and 440 yards to and sometimes including 1500 meters and one mile

middle dutch *n, cap M&D* **:** the Dutch in use from about 1100 to about 1500 — see INDO-EUROPEAN LANGUAGES table

middle ear *n* **:** the intermediate portion of the ear of higher vertebrates consisting typically of a small air-filled membrane-lined chamber in the temporal bone continuous with the nasopharynx through the eustachian tube, separated from the external ear by the tympanic membrane and from the inner ear by fenestrae, and containing a chain of three ossicles that extends from the tympanic membrane to the vestibular fenestra and transmits vibrations to the inner ear — compare INCUS, MALLEUS, STAPES

middle-earth \ˈ==ˌ=\ *n* [ME *middelerthe*, alter. (influenced by *erthe* earth) of *midelerde, midelert*, alter. (influenced by *middel* middle) of *middenerd*, fr. OE *middaneard*, alter. (influenced by *eard* region, dwelling-place) of *middangeard;* akin to OS *middilgard* middle-earth, OHG *mittelgart, mittingart*, ON *mithgarthr*, Goth *midjungards;* all fr. a prehistoric Gmc compound whose first constituent is akin to OE *midde* mid and whose second constituent is akin to OE *geard* yard, dwelling, land, world — more at MID, YARD] **:** the earth regarded as situated between the upper and lower regions or as occupying the center of the universe

middle eastern *adj, usu cap M&E* [*Middle East* + E *-ern* (as in *eastern*)] **:** of, relating to, or concerned with the Middle East — used orig. esp. of the region included in the Ottoman Empire but now usu. of southwestern Asia and northeastern Africa extending from Libya to Afghanistan or often from Morocco to Pakistan — compare FAR EASTERN, NEAR EASTERN

middle egyptian *n, cap M&E* **:** the language of Egypt under the 11th to 17th dynasties

middle english *n, cap M&E* **:** English as exhibited in manuscripts of the 12th to 15th centuries — distinguished from *Old English;* see INDO-EUROPEAN LANGUAGES table

middle-erd *n* [ME *midelerde, middelert* — more at MIDDLE-EARTH] *obs* **:** MIDDLE-EARTH

middle-european \ˌ==ˌ==ˈ==\ *adj, usu cap M&E* [*Middle Europe* + E *-an* (as in *European*)] **:** of, relating to, or characteristic of Middle Europe — used of a vaguely defined region generally conceived of as comprising some or all of the countries east of France and west of the Soviet Union

middle finger *n* **:** the midmost of the five fingers of the hand

middle french *n, cap M&F* **:** French as exhibited in manuscripts of the 14th to 16th centuries — see INDO-EUROPEAN LANGUAGES table

middle finger

middle game *n* **:** the middle phase of a board game; *specif* **:** the part of a chess game during which players work out combinations — compare END GAME, OPENING

middle greek *n, cap M&G* **:** the Greek language as used in the 7th to 15th centuries

middle ground *n* **1** *naut* **:** a shoal in a fairway having a channel on either side **2 :** MIDDLE DISTANCE 1 **3 :** a standpoint midway between extremes ⟨a *middle ground* between firmness and appeasement —*Wall Street Jour.*⟩ ⟨a characterless *middle ground* between the academic and the avant-garde —Sidney Alexander⟩

middle-grounder \ˈmidᵊlˈgrau̇ndə(r)\ *n* [*middle ground* + *-er*] **:** one that maintains a stand between extremes

middlehand \ˈ==ˌ=\ *n* [trans. of G *mittelhand*] **:** the second player in turn to bid in skat

middle high german *n, cap M&H&G* **:** the High German in use from 1100 to about 1500 — see INDO-EUROPEAN LANGUAGES table

middle horde *n, usu cap M&H* **:** a subdivision of the Kirghiz living chiefly in Turkestan and Tashkent

middle indic *n, cap M&I* **:** the Prakrit languages

middle indo-aryan *n, cap M&I&A* **:** PRAKRITS

middle initial *n* **:** the initial of a middle name

middle iranian *n, cap M&I* **:** the Iranian languages between the ancient and modern tongues comprising Middle Persian, Sogdian, and Sakian

middle irish *n, cap M&I* **:** the form of Irish employed between the 11th and 15th centuries — see INDO-EUROPEAN LANGUAGES table

middle lamella *n* **:** a layer of intercellular material that as seen by conventional staining and microscopic techniques lies between the apparent walls of adjacent plant cells

middle latin *n, cap M&L* **:** MEDIEVAL LATIN

middle latitude *n* **:** the latitude of the point situated midway on a north-and-south line between two parallels

middle life *n* **1 :** MIDDLE AGE **2** *Brit* **:** the life lived by the middle classes

middle low german *n, cap M&L&G* **:** the Low German in use from about 1100 to about 1500 — see INDO-EUROPEAN LANGUAGES table

mid·dle·man \ˈmidᵊlˌman, -aa(ə)n\ *n, pl* **middlemen 1** *obs* **:** a soldier at the middle of a file **2 :** one that adopts or follows a middle course **3 :** an intermediary or agent between two parties (as in business dealings, management, administration, or negotiations): as **a :** a dealer or agent intermediate between the producer of goods and the retailer or consumer; *specif* **:** a person or business firm that performs functions or services in the transfer of title to goods in their flow from producers (as farmers and manufacturers) to industrial users and ultimate consumers — see AGENT MIDDLEMAN, MERCHANT MIDDLEMAN **b :** an intermediary between landlord and tenant (as for collection of rents or management of property) **:** BAILIFF **c :** an agent for one (as a professional entertainer or the owner of a patent or copyright) that seeks to sell services or an intangible commodity **4 :** one leasing land in Ireland in large tracts and subletting it in small portions **5 :** one that transmits ideas, cultural standards, or similar intangibles ⟨the perfect ~ for this new movement of ideas —Van Wyck Brooks⟩ ⟨a kind of ~ of taste between the experimenters and the general public —F.O.Matthiessen⟩ **6 :** a performer in a minstrel show who occupies the middle seat

mid·dle·man·ism \-ˌmaˌnizəm, -ˌmaa,-\ *n* -S **:** a system of using middlemen (as in business dealings)

mid·dle·most \ˈ==ˌmōst *also chiefly Brit* -ˌməst\ *adj* [ME *middelmast*, fr. *middel* middle + *-mast* -most] **:** being in the middle or nearest the middle **:** MIDMOST

middle name *n* **1 :** a name between one's first name and surname; *esp* **:** the second of two forenames ⟨the use of *middle names* is a modern invention —Bruce Bliven b. 1889⟩ **2 :** an associated or characteristic personification ⟨trouble is our *middle name* —Joseph Driscoll⟩

middle of the road 1 : a course of action or program for action midway between extremes **2 :** a standpoint midway between extremes

middle-of-the-road \ˌ====ˈ=\ *adj* [*middle of the road*] **1 :** following a course of action or advocating a program for action that is midway between extremes ⟨a *middle-of-the-road* government⟩ ⟨a *middle-of-the-road* candidate⟩ **2 :** characterized by action or advocacy of action that is midway between extremes ⟨a *middle-of-the-road* course⟩ ⟨a *middle-of-the-road* political philosophy⟩ **3 :** standing between extremes ⟨the paintings illustrated are mostly *middle-of-the-road* subject pictures —J.T.Soby⟩

middle-of-the-road·er \ˈ====ˈrōdə(r)\ *n* -S [*middle of the road* + *-er*] **1 :** one that takes or advocates a course of action midway between extremes **2 :** one that stands midway between extremes (as in opinions)

middle oil *n* **:** CARBOLIC OIL

middle passage *n, often cap M&P* **:** the middle part of the journey of a slave from Africa to America; *specif* **:** the trip across the Atlantic ocean ⟨half died on the way to the ships, and a quarter in the *Middle Passage* —G.S.Mitchell⟩

middle path *n, usu cap M&P* **:** the eightfold path of Buddhism regarded as a golden mean between self-indulgence and self-mortification — called also *middle way*

middle persian *n, cap M&P* **:** Persian between Old Persian and Modern Persian including chiefly Pahlavi and the language of Christian and Manichaean documents recently discovered in Chinese Turkestan

middle piece *n, zool* **:** the portion of a sperm cell that lies between the nucleus and the flagellum

mid·dler \ˈmidlə(r)\ *n* -S [¹*middle* + *-er*] **1** *obs* **:** INTERAGENT, MEDIATOR **2 :** one belonging to an intermediate group, division, or class: as **a :** a student in the second year class of a theological seminary having a three-year program **b :** a student in the second or third year class in some private secondary schools having a four-year course **c :** a student in a division in some private schools that corresponds approximately to the junior high school — compare MIDDLE SCHOOL **3 :** a rolling-mill operator tending the middle set of rolls — called also *plateman*

middle rail *n* **1 :** the rail of a door above the bottom rail **2 :** a third rail of an electric railway when it is between the rails for the wheels

middle-rate \ˌ==ˈ=\ *adj* **:** MEDIOCRE

middle-road \ˌ==ˈ=\ *adj* **:** MIDDLE-OF-THE-ROAD — not often used predicatively ⟨a *middle-road* government⟩ ⟨*middle-road* policies⟩ ⟨a comparatively popular, *middle-road* jazz pianist —Bill Simon⟩

middle-road·er \ˈ==ˈrōdə(r)\ *n* -S **:** MIDDLE-OF-THE-ROADER

middles *pl of* MIDDLE, *pres 3d sing of* MIDDLE

mid·dles·brough \ˈmidᵊlzbrə\ *adj, usu cap* [fr. *Middlesbrough*, Eng.] **:** of or from the county borough of Middlesbrough, England **:** of the kind or style prevalent in Middlesbrough

middle school *n* **1** *obs* **:** a school in England intended esp. for children from middle-class families **2 :** a school or a division in the school system in any of various foreign countries embracing class levels that correspond approximately to those of the American junior and senior high schools and in some countries also class levels that correspond approximately to the upper grades of the American elementary school **3 a :** a division in some private schools embracing class levels that correspond approximately to those of the junior high school **b :** a school or a division in the school system in any of various foreign countries embracing class levels that correspond approximately to those of the American junior high school **4 :** a division in some private or public schools embracing or approximately embracing the upper elementary grades

middle scots *n, cap M&S* **1 :** the Scots language in use between the latter half of the 15th and the early decades of the 17th centuries **2 :** the form of Scots spoken in central Scotland

middle semitic *n, cap M&S* **:** ²CANAANITIC

mid·dle·sex \ˈmidᵊlˌseks\ *adj, usu cap* [fr. *Middlesex* county, Eng.] **:** of or from the county of Middlesex, England **:** of the kind or style prevalent in Middlesex

middle-sized \ˌ==ˈ=\ *adj* **:** of medium size ⟨the small and *middle-sized* powers made a little progress —*Time*⟩ — **middle-sized·ness** \ˌ==ˈsīzədnəs, -z(d)n-\ *n* -ES

middlesplitter \ˈ==ˌ==\ *n* **:** LISTER 1

middle stone *n* **:** HONEY 6

middle stump *n* **:** the stump between the leg stump and the off stump of a cricket wicket

middle-temperature error *n* **:** irregularity of rate in a watch or chronometer due to unequal progression of expansion and elasticity factors at average temperatures

middle term *n* **:** the term of a syllogism that occurs in both premises

middle tint *n* **:** a subdued or neutral tint or tone

middletone \ˈ==ˌ=\ *n* **:** HALFTONE

middletown \ˈ==ˌ=\ *n, usu cap* [fr. *Middletown*, arbitrary name given to a midwestern town studied in *Middletown — a Study in Contemporary American Culture* (1929) by Robert S. Lynd *b*1892 and Helen M. Lynd *b*1897 Amer. sociologists] **:** a community typically representative of middle-class American life and culture

middle wall *n* [ME *midelwalle*] **:** a partition wall

middle watch *n* **:** MIDWATCH

middleway \ˌ==ˈ=\ *adv* **:** MIDWAY, HALFWAY

middle way *n* **1 :** a course of action, mode of conduct, or policy for action or conduct between two extremes: as **a** *usu cap M&W* **:** MIDDLE PATH **b :** a system of democratic economy between individualism and socialism **2** *obs* **:** the middle of one's way

middleweight \ˈ==ˌ=\ *n* **:** one of average weight: as **a :** a boxer weighing more than 147 but not over 160 pounds **b :** a wrestler weighing more than 158 but not over 174 pounds

middle welsh *n, cap M&W* **:** the Welsh in use from about 1150 to 1500

middle west *n, usu cap M&W* **:** MIDWEST

middle western *adj, often cap M&W* [*Middle West* + *-ern* (as in *western*)] **:** MIDWESTERN

middle westerner *n, usu cap M&W* **:** MIDWESTERNER

middle white *n* **1** *usu cap M&W* **:** a British breed of medium-sized white swine used esp. for production of small quick-maturing porkers — compare YORKSHIRE **2** *often cap M&W* **:** an animal of the Middle White breed

middlewoman \ˈ==ˌ==\ *n, pl* **middlewomen** *Brit* **:** a woman who acts as intermediary between homeworkers and a lace warehouse

¹**mid·dling** \ˈmidliŋ, -lēŋ\ *adj* [ME (Sc) *mydlyn*, prob. fr. *mid, midde* mid + *-ling*] **1 :** falling between two extremes **:** constituting a mean **:** INTERMEDIATE ⟨the extreme school of innovators had wanted a people's republic, not a national monarchy, and protested noisily against the ~ solution —Cecil Sprigge⟩ **2 :** of middle, medium, or moderate size or degree ⟨the harbor was no wider than a ~ American river —Christopher Rand⟩ **3 a :** of middle or medium quality **:** falling in a middle range of quality **b :** producing a yield (as of crops) or creating works (as of art or literature) falling in a middle range of quality or value ⟨the ~ lands —*Time*⟩ ⟨whether eventually I proved first-class or merely ~ — I should at least strive for consistent standards —Rex Ingamells⟩ **4 :** MEDIOCRE, SECOND-RATE ⟨the ~ performance of a vulgar artist —Edmund Burke⟩ **5** *dial* **a :** in moderately good health **b :** not very well **:** in rather poor health **6 :** of, relating to, or constituting a middle class

²**middling** \"\ *adv* **:** MODERATELY, RATHER, FAIRLY ⟨the extremely successful, the ~ successful, and the least successful —*New Yorker*⟩

³**middling** \"\ *n* -S **1 middlings** *pl but sometimes sing in constr* **a :** the medium-sized particles separated in the sifting of ground grain **b :** a by-product of flour milling comprising several grades of granular particles containing different proportions of endosperm, bran, germ, and crude fiber and used as animal feed **2 a :** FLITCH 1b **b** *or* **middling meat** *chiefly South & Midland* **:** SALT PORK — often used in pl. **3 :** the basic grade of cotton on which market quotations are based **4 middlings** *pl but sing or pl in constr* **:** a product of ore dressing intermediate between concentrate and tailings and containing enough of the valuable mineral to make re-treatment of it profitable **5 middlings** *pl* **:** an inferior refined oil from petroleum

mid·dling·ly *adv* **:** INDIFFERENTLY, TOLERABLY ⟨I dare say I thought but ~ of them —Thomas Moore⟩

middorsal \ˈ=ˈ==\ *adj* **:** situated in the middle part or median line of the back

mid·dy *also* **mid·die** \ˈmidē, -di\ *n, pl* **middies** [by shortening and alter.] **1 :** MIDSHIPMAN **2** *or* **middy blouse :** a loose overblouse with a sailor collar worn by women and children

middy 2

mi·de *or* **mi·dé** \ˈmē(ˌ)dā\ *n* -S [Ojibwa *midē*] **:** MIDEWIWIN

mid-earth \ˈ=ˌ=\ *n* [¹*mid* + *earth*] *archaic* **:** MIDDLE-EARTH

mideastern \ˈ=ˈ==\ *adj, usu cap* **:** MIDDLE EASTERN

midevening \ˈ=ˈ==\ *n* **:** the middle of the evening

mi·de·wi·win \məˈdāwəˌwin\ *also* **mi·de·win** \məˈdāˌwin\ *n* -S [Ojibwa *midēwiwin*] **:** a once powerful secret society among the Ojibwa and neighboring Indians which aimed at the prolongation of life by herbal, magical, and ritual techniques

midfeather \'ˌ=ˌ==\ *n* [¹*mid* + *feather* (projecting strip)] **:** a longitudinal partition or division: as **a :** a brick partition wall in a salt furnace **b :** a vertical baffle in a beater or other papermaking machine of similar function **c :** a support between adjacent mine tunnels

midfield \'=ˌ=\ *n* **1 :** the middle portion of a field; *esp* **:** the middle portion of the field on which any of various sports (as football and lacrosse) is played **2 :** the second attack, center, and second defense of a lacrosse team

mid·field·er \'mid,fēldə(r)\ *n* **:** a member of the midfield of a lacrosse team

mid-front \'=¦=\ *adj, of a vowel* **:** articulated with the tongue arched at the front midway between its highest and its lowest elevation

midge \'mij\ *n* -s [ME *migge*, fr. OE *mycg;* akin to OS *myggia* midge, OHG *mucka*, ON *mȳ* midge, Gk *myia* fly, L *musca*, OSlav *mucha*] **1 :** any of numerous tiny two-winged flies chiefly of the families Ceratopogonidae, Cecidomyiidae, and Chironomidae, many of which are capable of giving painful bites and some of which are vectors or intermediate hosts of parasites of man and various other vertebrates — compare BITING MIDGE **2 a :** a diminutive person **b :** a very small fish

¹**midg·et** \'mijət, *usu* -əd.+V\ *n* -s [*midge* + *-et*] **1 :** BITING MIDGE, PUNKIE **2 :** a very small person; *specif* **:** a person of unusually small size who is physically well-proportioned — compare DWARF 1a **3 :** any creature or thing that is much smaller than the usual, the typical, or the average for its kind ⟨a ~ among the industries in its field⟩ ⟨all squids live in the sea, and there are many species of diverse forms and sizes from ~s to the giant squid —R.E.Coker⟩ **4 :** a member of a midget variety, type, or arbitrarily defined class: as **a :** a racing automobile of a class restricted to vehicles substantially smaller and lighter and of less piston displacement than standard automobiles **b :** MIDGET SUBMARINE

²**midget** \"\ *adj* **1 :** much smaller than the usual or the typical **:** MINIATURE, DIMINUTIVE ⟨the ~ nation of Andorra⟩ ⟨a miniature locomotive with ~ cars —W.L.Gresham⟩ **2 a :** belonging to a variety or type whose members are conspicuously smaller than what are regarded as the typical, normal, or standard or to an arbitrarily defined class in which the maximum permitted size is considerably less than the size that is usual or typical when no maximum is imposed ⟨~ beans⟩ ⟨~ racing auto⟩ ⟨a race for ~ planes⟩ **b :** of, relating to, or constituting an organization or an activity (as an organized sport) for children who are usu. the youngest eligible to belong or the smallest or lightest eligible to participate ⟨~ football⟩ ⟨*midget*-league baseball⟩

midget golf *n* **:** MINIATURE GOLF

midg·et·ism \-jəd.ˌizəm\ *n* -s **:** the state of being a midget

midget submarine *n* **:** a small submarine usu. having a crew of only two and carrying a single torpedo for use in surprise attacks

midgrass \'=ˌ=\ *n* **:** any of various grasses that are characterized by moderate stature, form the dominant feature of undisturbed prairie, and include the majority of economically important forage grasses of temperate regions — compare SHORTGRASS

mid-gray \'=¦=\ *n* **:** MEDIAN GRAY

midgut \'=ˌ=\ *n* **1 :** the middle part of the alimentary canal of a vertebrate embryo between the foregut and hindgut **2 :** the mesodermal intermediate part of the intestine of an invertebrate animal

midheaven \'=¦==\ *n* **1** *archaic* **:** the point of the ecliptic on the meridian **2 :** the middle part of the sky **3 :** the midst of heaven

¹**mid·i·an·ite** \'midēə,nīt\ *n* -s *usu cap* [*Midian*, son of Abraham and Keturah (Gen 25:2), the eponymous ancestor of the Midianites + E *-ite*] **:** a member of an ancient northern Arabian tribe mentioned in the Bible

²**midianite** \"\ *adj, usu cap* **:** of, relating to, or characteristic of the Midianites

mid·i·an·it·ish \-īd·ish\ *adj, usu cap* [¹*Midianite* + *-ish*] **:** MIDIANITE

mid·i·dae \'midə,dē\ [NL, fr. *Midas* + *-idae*] *syn of* CALLITHRICIDAE

mid·i·nette \ˌmidᵊn'et, ˌmēdē'net\ *n* -s [F, prob. blend of *midi* noon (fr. OF, fr. *mi* mid, middle — fr. L *medius* — + *di* day, fr. L *dies*) and *dinette* light lunch, fr. *dîner* to dine, breakfast + *-ette;* fr. the traditional light lunches eaten at noon by the midinettes — more at MID, DEITY, DINE] **:** a Parisian shopgirl; *esp* **:** a Parisian seamstress

midiron \'=ˌ==\ *n* **:** an iron golf club with more loft than a driving iron and less than a mashie used typically for medium distance shots on the fairway and long approach shots from the fairway — called also *number two iron;* see IRON illustration

mid-kidney \'=¦==\ *n* **:** MESONEPHROS

¹**mid·land** \'midlənd, -d,land, -aa(ə)nd\ *n* [¹*mid* + *land*] **1 :** the interior or central region of a country (as the central counties of England or central part of the U.S.) **2** *or* **midland dialect** *usu cap M* **a :** the dialect of English spoken in the midland counties of England **b :** the dialect of English spoken in the part of the U. S. that lies between the southern boundary of Northern and a line running from central Delaware through Maryland, southwest along the Blue Ridge, east to include part of the North Carolina Piedmont, and then west through northern Georgia and Alabama and that includes parts of New Jersey and Delaware, northern Maryland, central and southern Pennsylvania, Ohio, Indiana, and Illinois, the Appalachian Mountain area, West Virginia, Kentucky, and most of Tennessee

²**midland** \"\ *adj* **1 :** being or situated in the interior country **:** distant from the coast or seashore **:** INLAND **2 a :** of, relating to, or characteristic of the midlands **b** *usu cap* **:** of, relating to, or characteristic of Midland dialect **3 :** surrounded or nearly surrounded by land **:** MEDITERRANEAN

mid·lan·der \-də(r)\ *n, often cap* **:** a native or inhabitant of the interior or central region of a country

mid-latitude \'=¦===\ *adj* **:** of, relating to, or characteristic of the mid-latitudes

mid-latitudes \'=¦==ˌ=\ *n pl* **:** latitudes of the temperate zones or from about 30 to 60 degrees north or south of the equator

¹**midleg** \'=ˌ=\ *n* [¹*mid* + *leg*] **:** the middle of the leg

²**midleg** \'=¦=\ *adv* **1 :** at the middle of the leg **2 :** to the middle of the leg

mid·lent·ing \'mid,lentiŋ\ *n* -s [*Mid-Lent (Sunday)* + *-ing*] **:** MOTHERING

mid-lent sunday *n, usu cap M&L&S* [ME *mydlent Sonday*] **:** the 4th Sunday in Lent

mid-life \'=ˌ=\ *n* **:** MIDDLE AGE

midline \'=ˌ=\ *n* **:** a median line; *esp* **:** the median line or median plane of the body or some part of the body

mid·lo·thi·an \(')mid¦lōthēən, -thyən\ *adj, usu cap* [fr. *Midlothian* county, Scot.] **:** of or from the county of Midlothian, Scotland **:** of the kind or style prevalent in Midlothian

mid-mashie \'=¦==\ *n* **:** an iron golf club with less loft than a mashie iron — called also *number three iron;* see IRON illustration

mid-mixed \'=¦=\ *adj, of a vowel* **:** MID-CENTRAL

midmorn \'=¦=\ *n, archaic* **:** MIDMORNING

midmorning \'=¦==\ *n* **:** the middle of the period from sunrise to noon or from rising to noon or from the beginning of the ordinary time of daily activities to noon ⟨the torrid ~ sun —Linton Wells⟩ ⟨the ~ coffee break⟩

¹**mid·most** \'mid,mōst *also chiefly Brit* -,məst\ *adj* [ME *midmest*, fr. OE *midmest*, *middemest*, fr. *midd*, *midde* mid + *-mest* -most — more at MID] **1 :** being in the exact middle **:** MIDDLEMOST **2 :** the middle of **3 :** most intimate **:** INNERMOST

²**midmost** \"\ *n* [ME *midmest*, fr. *midmest*, adj.] **:** the midmost part

³**midmost** \"\ *adv* [¹*midmost*] **:** in the very midst or middle

⁴**midmost** \"\ *prep* [¹*midmost*] **:** in the very middle of

midn *abbr* **1** midnight **2** midshipman

¹**midnight** \'=ˌ=\ *n* [ME *midnight*, *midniht*, fr. OE *midniht*, fr. *midd*, *midde* mid + *niht* night — more at MID, NIGHT] **1 :** the middle of the night; *specif* **:** twelve o'clock at night **2 a :** deep darkness or gloom **b :** a period of deep darkness or gloom **3** *or* **midnight blue :** a variable color averaging a blackish blue that is greener and stronger than Romany

²**midnight** \"\ *adj* **1 :** of, relating to, occurring at, like, or suggestive of midnight **2 a :** being in the middle of the night ⟨~ studies⟩ **b :** characteristic of the middle of the night ⟨~ gloom⟩

midnight appointment *n* **:** an appointment to political office made during the last hours of the term of office of the person in whom the right of making such appointment is vested

midnight line *n* **:** a hypothetical line imagined as circling the earth so as to pass over every locality exactly at midnight

¹**mid·night·ly** \'mid,nītlē, -li\ *adv* [¹*midnight* + *-ly* (adv. suffix)] **:** every midnight **:** regularly at midnight

²**midnightly** \"\ *adj* [¹*midnight* + *-ly* (adv. suffix)] **1 :** occurring at midnight **2 :** occurring every midnight

midnight oil *n* **:** diligent effort expended late at night or as if late at night — compare BURN THE MIDNIGHT OIL

midnight sun *n* **1 :** the sun above the horizon at midnight in the arctic or antarctic summer **2 :** CHROME SCARLET

midnoon \'=¦=\ *n* **:** MIDDAY, NOON

mid off *n, cricket* **:** a fielding position on the off side of the field nearer to the batsman than long off; *also* **:** a player fielding in this position — see CRICKET illustration

mid on *n, cricket* **:** a fielding position on the on side of the field nearer to the batsman than long on; *also* **:** a player fielding in this position

midpalatal \'=¦===\ *adj* **:** MEDIOPALATAL

midparent \'=¦==\ *n* **:** a hypothetical single parent occupying an intermediate position between the two parents — **mid·parentage** \'=¦===\ *n* — **midparental** \¦=¦==¦=\ *adj*

midpassage \'=¦==\ *n* **1 :** the midst of the act or state of passing **2 :** the midst of a passage

midplane \'=ˌ=\ *n* **:** a plane passing through something in such a way as to divide it into symmetrical halves

midpoint \'=ˌ=\ *n* **1 :** a point at or approximately at the center of an area or midway between the extremities of a line **2 a :** the point of time midway between the extremities of a period of time or of an event, process, or condition continuing over a given period of time **b :** a point of time assumed to be midway or approximately midway between the beginning and the probable time of termination of an event, process, or condition whose end lies at some future and not precisely determinate point of time **3 a :** a point on a line segment or an arc of a curve whose distances from the end points measured along the segment or arc are equal **b :** the arithmetic mean of the upper and lower limits of a class interval

midportion *n* **:** a middle part

midrange \'=ˌ=\ *n* **1 :** a range of medium length **2 :** the midrange of a range (as of distance or time) **3 :** a middle portion (as of a range of musical pitch) **4 :** the arithmetic mean of the largest and smallest observations of a group

midrange trajectory *n* **:** the height of a bullet's trajectory measured at a point falling midway between the muzzle of the piece and the target

mid·rash \'mi,drăsh\ *n, pl* **mid·rash·im** \mi'drăshəm, ˌ=drä'shēm\ *also* **mid·rash·oth** *or* **mid·rash·ot** \ˌ=ˌdrä'shōt(h)\ [Heb *midhrāsh* exposition, explanation] **1 a** *sometimes cap* **:** an ancient Jewish exposition of a passage of the Scriptures that may be either halakic or haggadic in type **b** *often cap* **:** a collection of midrashim **2** *sometimes cap* **:** Jewish religious exposition by means of midrashim **3** *usu cap* **:** the body of midrashic literature **4 :** an ancient Jewish narrative that has the form characteristic of a midrash and the purpose of setting forth or illustrating a religious teaching

mid·rash·ic \(')mi¦drashik\ *adj, often cap* **1 :** of, relating to, characteristic of, or constituting a midrash or the Midrash **2 :** resembling midrashim

midrib \'=ˌ=\ *n* **1 :** the central vein of a leaf **2 :** a dividing line, depression, or ridge analogous or similar to the midrib of a leaf

midribbed \'=¦=\ *adj* **:** having a midrib

mid·riff \'mi,drif\ *n* -s [ME *midrif*, fr. OE *midhrif* (akin to OFris *midhrif*, *midhref* midriff), fr. *midd*, *midde* mid + *hrif* belly, womb; akin to OFris *href*, *hrif* belly, OHG *href* body, lower body, womb, L *corpus* body, MIr *crí* body, Gk *prapides* diaphragm, Skt *kṛp* shape, beautiful appearance] **1 :** DIAPHRAGM 1 **2 :** the mid-region of the human torso; *esp* **:** its external ventral aspect **3 a :** a section of a woman's garment that is fitted across the midriff **b :** a woman's garment similar to a halter that exposes the midriff

¹**mids** *pl of* MID

²**mids** \'midz\ *n, pl* **mids** [ME *middes* — more at MIDST] **1** *now Scot* **:** MIDST, MIDDLE **2** *obs* **:** MEANS, METHOD **3** *now Scot* **:** a middle course **:** MEAN

midsagittal \'=¦===\ *adj* **:** median and sagittal

midsection \'=¦==\ *n* **:** a section midway or about midway between the extremes: as **a :** MIDRIFF 2 **b :** MIDRIFF 3

midsemester \'=¦=¦==\ *n* **1 :** the end of the first half of an academic semester that is often a time for examinations and reports on students' progress — compare MIDTERM **2 :** a midsemester examination

midship \'=ˌ=\ *n* **1 :** the portion of a ship between the bow and the stern **2 :** the vertical line in a ship midway between the forward and aft perpendiculars

midship beam *n* **:** the beam in the deck in the midship section of a ship or boat

midship bend *n* **:** the frame in a ship or boat at the dead flat

midship frame *n* **:** the frame at the greatest breadth in a ship or boat

midship line *n* **:** the center line of the body plan of a ship or boat

mid·ship·man \(')mid¦shipmən\ *n, pl* **midshipmen** **1 a :** a naval cadet in old-time deep-waisted ships of war **b :** a commissioned officer of the lowest rank in the British navy formerly completing training at sea but now undergoing a final period of shore training **c :** a student naval officer ranking above a master chief petty officer and below a warrant officer and orig. educated principally at sea but since 1845 usu. at the Naval Academy or other college or university — see NAVAL CADET **d :** a student officer of any nation who is comparable to a British or American midshipman **2 :** any of several American toadfishes that constitute the genus *Porichthys* and have rows of luminous organs on the under surface; *esp* **:** a common fish (*P. notatus*) of the Pacific coast from Lower California to Puget Sound that is coppery brown above shading to bright yellow below and that produces a humming sound with its air bladder — called also *singing fish*

midshipman's-butter \(')=¦==ˌ==\ *n, pl* **midshipman's-butters :** AVOCADO

mid·ship·man·ship \(')=¦==,ship\ *n* **:** the position of a midshipman

midshipman's hitch *n* **:** a hitch used esp. for mooring and lifesaving and made by tying a rolling hitch with the end of a line to the standing part

midshipman's hitch

midshipman's nuts *also* **midshipmen's nuts** *n pl* **:** pieces of broken sea biscuit ⟨sailors . . . pick up their broken biscuits, or *midshipman's nuts* —Herman Melville⟩

mid·ship·mite \'mid,ship,mīt\ *n* [blend of *midshipman* and *mite*] *nonstand* **:** MIDSHIPMAN; *esp* **:** a small or very young midshipman

¹**mid·ships** \'mid,ships\ *n pl* [prob. fr. pl. of ¹*midship*] **:** the middle part of a ship or boat

²**midships** \"\ *adv* [short for ¹*amidships*] **1 :** AMIDSHIPS 1a **2 a :** midway between the stem and stern of the hull of a ship or boat **b :** midway between the sides of the hull of a ship or boat

midship section *n* **:** a drawing of the cross section of a ship amidships showing details of frames, beams, and other structural parts

midship spoke *n* **:** the spoke of a steering wheel that is up when the rudder is amidships

mid-shot \'=ˌ=\ *n* **:** MEDIUM SHOT

mid-side \'=ˌ=\ *n* [ME *mid side*] **:** the middle of the side

midsole \'=ˌ=\ *n* **:** a layer of leather, rubber, or other material placed between the insole and the outsole of a shoe

¹**midst** \'midzt, 'midst, 'mitst\ *n* -s [ME *middest*, alter. of *middes*, back-formation fr. *amiddes* amid — more at AMID] **1 :** the interior or central part or point **:** MIDDLE, INTERIOR — preceded by *the* or occas. a possessive and now usu. only in prepositional phrases ⟨the trees in the ~ of the forest⟩ ⟨fine early houses set in the ~ of a region of fine farms —*Amer. Guide Series: N.H.*⟩ ⟨passing through the ~ of some great inland sea —Carl Van Vechten⟩ ⟨sooner or later India would seek to wipe out this enclave in its ~ —*Collier's Yr. Bk.*⟩ **2 :** position among the members of a group, company, or society — preceded by *the* or a possessive and used only in prepositional phrases ⟨a visitor in our ~⟩ ⟨dangerous criminals in their ~⟩ ⟨they saw him in their ~ like an avenging Marius —J.A.Froude⟩ ⟨why it was he should feel in the ~ of all these people so utterly detached and so lonely —Louis Bromfield⟩ ⟨missionaries in the ~ of the unbelieving —W.H. Whyte⟩ ⟨a cluster of three or four villages . . . in the ~ of irrigated rice fields —Francis Kingdon-Ward⟩ **3 a :** the condition of being figuratively surrounded ⟨grew up in the ~ of farm influences —H.W.Wiley⟩ or beset ⟨nor should he ever forget, in the ~ of his problems, that there are large if circumscribed powers that lie within himself —Weston La Barre⟩ **b :** a period of time approximately about the middle of the duration or embracing all except the extreme beginning and end of the duration (as of an event, state, or action) ⟨in the ~ of a long reign⟩ ⟨the model which he was in the ~ of building —Marcia Davenport⟩ ⟨in the ~ of life we are in death —*Bk. of Com. Prayer*⟩ **4** *obs* **:** a middle course **:** MEAN, MEDIUM **syn** see CENTER

²**midst** \"\ *adv* **1** *archaic* **:** in the middle place **2 :** in the midst

³**midst** \"\ *prep* [prob. short for *amidst*] **:** in the midst of **:** AMIDST ⟨heads down the harbor ~ the cheers —Helen Henley⟩

¹**midstream** \'=ˌ=\ *n* [¹*mid* + *stream*] **1 a :** the portion of a stream well removed from both sides ⟨keep the boat in ~⟩ ⟨the political axiom of not changing horses in ~⟩ **b :** the center line of a stream **:** a line of which the course is midway or what is considered to be midway between the sides of a stream ⟨the ~ is the boundary⟩ **2 :** the portion of a stream well removed from both source and mouth ⟨in the ~ of his career —Arthur Berger⟩ ⟨in ~ both as writer and in his profession —R.C.Beatty⟩

²**midstream** \"\ *adv* **:** in midstream

midsummer \'=¦==\ *n* [ME *midsumer*, *midsomer*, fr. OE *midsumer*, fr. *midd*, *midde* mid + *sumer* summer — more at MID, SUMMER] **1 :** the middle of summer **2 :** the period about the summer solstice

midsummer day *n, usu cap M&D* [ME *midsomer day*, fr. OE *midsumer dæg*] **:** June 24 **:** SAINT JOHN THE BAPTIST'S DAY

midsummer eve *or* **midsummer night** *n, usu cap M&E&N* **:** the eve of Midsummer Day ⟨in Brittany treasure-seekers gather fern seed at midnight on *Midsummer Eve* —J.G. Frazer⟩

midsummer madness *n* **:** extreme folly **:** emotional extravagance and absurdity

mid·sum·mery \'mid¦səmərē\ *adj* **:** like or characteristic of midsummer

midterm \'=ˌ=\ *n* **1 :** the midpoint, the approximate midpoint, or an approximate midpoint of a term of time: as **a :** the end of the first half of an academic term that is often a time for examinations and reports on students' progress **b :** a midterm examination ⟨the student who normally studies only before a ~ —Hargis Westerfield⟩ **2 :** the approximate middle of a term of office; *specif* **:** the date midway between quadrennial presidential elections when congressional and many local elections are held ⟨opposition gains at ~⟩ — compare OFF YEAR

mid-to-four watch \'==¦=-\ *n* [*midnight to four*] **:** MIDWATCH

mid-totality \'=='===\ *n* **:** the middle of the period during which an eclipse is total

midtown \'=ˌ=\ *n* **:** a section of a city situated between other sections conventionally called *downtown* and *uptown* or between the main business section and an outlying section

midvein \'=ˌ=\ *n* **:** MIDRIB 1

¹**mid-victorian** \¦==¦===\ *adj, often cap M & usu cap V* [³*mid* + *Victorian*] **1 :** of, relating to, or characteristic of the middle period of the reign (1837–1901) of Queen Victoria ⟨*mid-Victorian* furniture⟩ **2 a :** like one of the mid-Victorian period — often used disparagingly ⟨has a *mid-Victorian* taste in art⟩ and in this use usu. stronger than *Victorian* **b :** OLD-FASHIONED, ANTIQUATED ⟨your attitude is *mid-Victorian*⟩

²**mid-victorian** \"\ *n, often cap M & cap V* **1 :** one belonging to the mid-Victorian period **2 :** one having the moral or aesthetic standards characteristic or supposedly characteristic of the mid-Victorian period

mid-victorianism \'=='===ˌ==\ *n, often cap M & usu cap V* **:** the actual or supposed moral or aesthetic standards of the mid-Victorian period

mid-wall column *or* **mid-wall shaft** *n* **:** a column or shaft carrying a wall thicker than its own diameter and standing about midway between the front and back of the wall

midwatch \'=ˌ=\ *n* **:** a watch on a ship from midnight to 4 A.M. — called also MIDDLE WATCH, MID-TO-FOUR WATCH

mid-water \'=ˌ==\ *n* **:** the middle portion vertically of a body of water **:** water substantially below the surface and substantially above the bottom

¹**mid·way** \'mid,wā\ *n* [ME, fr. OE *midweg*, fr. *midd*, *midde* mid + *weg* way — more at MID, WAY] **1** *obs* **:** the middle of the way or distance ⟨paths indirect, or in the ~ faint —John Milton⟩ **2** *archaic* **:** a middle way or course ⟨all good things keep the ~ of the eternal deep —R.W.Emerson⟩ **3** [fr. the *Midway* (*Plaisance*), a section of a park in Chicago which became the site of the amusement section of the Columbian Exposition of 1893] **a :** an avenue or area at a fair, exposition, carnival, or amusement park along which or in which are concessions for exhibitions of curiosities, games of chance, scenes from foreign life, merry-go-rounds and other rides, and other light amusements **b :** the amusements in a midway that constitute one of the divisions into which the attractions of a fair, exposition, or amusement park are grouped **c :** the buildings, tents, enclosures, and other structures in a midway with the exhibits and amusement devices contained in them **4 :** a place (as a street or highway) likened to a midway on account of bright lights (as of advertising signs) or of the nature of the places of business or amusement along its course

²**midway** \'=¦=\ *adv* **:** in the middle of the way or distance **:** HALFWAY ⟨~ between reform and revolution —John Strachey⟩ ⟨~ up the mountain —Rafael Sabatini⟩ ⟨stopped ~ for a light meal⟩

³**midway** \"\ *adj* **1 a :** occupying an intermediate position **:** situated between those parts or those things or beings of the same class that are at or near the extremes ⟨the ~ air —Shak.⟩ **b :** being in the middle of the way or distance **2 :** intermediate between extremes

⁴**midway** \'=¦=\ *prep* **1 :** in the middle of **:** about halfway along **2 :** about halfway between

midweek \'=¦=\ *n* **:** the middle of the week ⟨a holiday in ~⟩

mid·week·ly \(')mid¦wēklē\ *adj* **:** occurring, appearing, or being held during the middle of the week ⟨held a ~ prayer meeting⟩

midwest \'=¦=\ *n, usu cap* **1 :** regions lying somewhat to the west of a specified or implied point of orientation ⟨the farmlands of the *Midwest*⟩ **2 :** something (as people, culture, or institutions) characteristic of the Midwest ⟨the *Midwest* strongly favored the new policies⟩

midwestern \(')=¦==\ *adj, often cap* **:** of, relating to, or characteristic of the Midwest

midwesterner \'=¦===\ *n, usu cap* **:** a native or resident of the Midwest

¹**mid·wife** \'mid,wīf\ *n, pl* **mid·wives** \-īvz\ [ME *midwif*, fr. *mid* with (fr. OE) + *wif* woman, wife — more at META-, WIFE] **1 a :** a woman not qualified as a physician who assists other women in childbirth esp. habitually or as a means of livelihood **b :** an accoucheur of either sex **2 :** one that helps to produce or bring forth something ⟨thou art the ~ of my woe —Shak.⟩ ⟨what Engels had meant by describing war as the ~ of social change —E.R.Bentley⟩

²**midwife** \"\ *vt* **midwifed** \-īft\ *or* **midwived** \-īvd\ **midwifed** *or* **midwived; midwifing** \-īfiŋ\ *or* **midwiving** \-īviŋ\ **midwifes** \-īfs\ *or* **midwives** \-īvz\ **1 :** to assist in bringing (a child) to birth **2 :** to assist in producing, bringing forth, or bringing about ⟨probably the first time in history that a bank *midwived* a successful biographical novel —Irving Stone⟩

midwife frog *or* **midwife toad** *n* **:** OBSTETRICAL TOAD

mid·wife·ry \-f(ə)rē, -ri\ *n, pl* **midwiferies** [ME *medewifry,* fr. *medewif, midwif* midwife + *-ry*] **1 :** the art or act of assisting at childbirth; *also* **:** OBSTETRICS **2 :** the art, act, or process of producing or bringing forth or bringing about ⟨would have been a sorry failure but for the ~ of the director⟩

midwing monoplane \ˈ=ˌ=-\ *n* **:** a monoplane in which the wing is mounted midway between the top and bottom of the fuselage

mid·win·ter \ˈmidˈwintə(r)\ *n* [ME, fr. OE, fr. *midd, midde* mid + *winter* — more at MID, WINTER] **:** the middle of winter

midwinter day *n, usu cap M&D archaic* **:** CHRISTMAS

mid·win·ter·ly \-(r)lē\ *adj* **:** MIDWINTRY

mid·win·try \-n·trē\ *adj* **:** of, relating to, or characteristic of midwinter

mid-world \ˈ=ˌ=\ *n* **1** *obs* **:** MIDDLE-EARTH **2 a :** an intermediate realm ⟨neither beast nor bird, it inhabits an anomalous *mid-world* —*Saturday Rev.*⟩ **b :** a body (as of persons) occupying an intermediate position (as between two attitudes or opinions) ⟨this *mid-world* of persons, no longer hostile or indifferent to religion, though not as yet ecclesiastically or theologically minded —W.L.Sperry⟩

¹midyear \ˈ=ˌ=\ *n* [¹*mid* + *year*] **1 a :** the middle or middle portion of a calendar year ⟨the warm weather in ~⟩ **b :** the middle of an academic year ⟨changes of courses at ~⟩ **2 a :** a midyear examination **b midyears** *pl* **:** the set of examinations at midyear or the period of midyear examinations ⟨looking forward with apprehension to the ~*s*⟩

²midyear \ˈ=ˌ=\ *adj* **1 :** occurring in the middle of a civil year ⟨a proposed ~ holiday⟩ **2 :** occurring in the middle of an academic year ⟨~ examinations⟩ ⟨the ~ vacation⟩

mien \ˈmēn\ *n* -S [by shortening & alter. (influenced by F *mine* appearance, perh. fr. Bret *min* beak, snout) fr. ²*demean*] **1 :** the air or bearing of a person esp. as expressive of mood or personality **:** MANNER, EXPRESSION ⟨that ~ of a commercial traveler who has been everywhere and through everything —Arnold Bennett⟩ ⟨his ~ of settled woe —Robertson Davies⟩ ⟨usually presents a ~ of solemnity —*Current Biog.*⟩ **2 :** APPEARANCE, ASPECT ⟨dresses of fairly formal ~ —Lois Long⟩ ⟨a monster of most ferocious ~ —G.W.Johnson⟩ **3** *archaic* **:** SHOW, PRETENSE — usu. used in the phrase *make mien* ⟨foreigners who . . . made ~ to stay —F.B.Gummere⟩

mierkat *var of* MEERKAT

miers·ite \ˈmirˌzīt\ *n* -S [Sir Henry A. *Miers* †1942 Eng. mineralogist + E *-ite*] **:** a mineral (Ag, Cu)I consisting of silver copper iodide

¹miff \ˈmif\ *n* -S [origin unknown] **1 :** a fit of ill humor or bad temper **2 :** a petty or trivial quarrel or argument

²miff \"\ *vt* -ED/-ING/-S **:** to put into an ill humor **:** make peevish **:** OFFEND, DISPLEASE ⟨~*ed* by this refutation of his diagnosis —F.G.Slaughter⟩ ⟨~ a few . . . musical sophisticates —*Time*⟩

miffed *adj* [fr. past part. of ²*miff*] put out **:** OFFENDED, HURT ⟨he looks thoroughly ~ —Jacob Hay⟩ ⟨still ~ because he wasn't . . . honored with the assignment —Joseph Wechsberg⟩ ⟨~ that my arrival did not rate a more formal reception —Mohamed Mehdevi⟩

miffy \ˈmifē, -fi\ *adj* -ER/-EST **1 :** inclined to take offense **:** TOUCHY ⟨next afternoon the ~ matron was back —*Tuscaloosa (Ala.) News*⟩ **2 :** requiring favorable conditions for growth ⟨the saxifrage plants were ~⟩

mig *or* **migg** \ˈmig\ *n* -S [origin unknown] **:** a playing marble; *esp* **:** one used as an object to be shot at (as in ringer)

mig·gle \ˈmigəl\ *n* -S [*mig* + *-le*] **1** *dial* **:** MIG **2 miggles** *pl but sing in constr, dial* **:** MIB 2

¹might \ˈmīt, *usu* -īd.+V\ *archaic 2d sing* **might·est** \-īd·əst\ *or* **mightst** \-ītst\ [ME *mighte,* fr. OE *meahte, mihte;* akin to OHG *mahta, mohta* could, was able, ON *mātti,* Goth *mahta* — more at MAY] *past of* MAY — used in auxiliary function to express permission, liberty, probability, possibility in the past ⟨the king ~ do nothing without parliament's consent⟩ or a present condition contrary to fact ⟨if he were older he ~ understand⟩ or less probability or possibility than *may* ⟨~ get there before it rains⟩ ⟨~ be a good idea to wait and see⟩ or as a polite alternative to *may* ⟨~ I ask who is calling⟩ or to *ought* or *should* ⟨you ~ at least apologize⟩

²might \"\ *n* -S [ME, fr. OE *miht;* akin to OS & OHG *maht* might, power, ON *māttr,* Goth *mahts* might, OE *magan* to be able — more at MAY] **1 a** (1) **:** the power, authority, or collective resources wielded by an individual, group, or other entity ⟨the fading ~ of Spain⟩ ⟨the growing ~ of the middle class⟩ ⟨the ~ of three great states was arrayed against the republic⟩ ⟨sought to weaken the ~ of the barons⟩; *specif* **:** the power of such an entity given a concrete form or embodiment ⟨resisting the power of the German armed ~ —D.W.Brogan⟩ ⟨our growing ~ in the air⟩ (2) **:** power or supreme power regarded as the attribute of a divine being, as an abstraction, or as a personalized force or idea ⟨'tis ~ half-slumbering on its own right arm —John Keats⟩ (3) **:** the power or force of an inanimate, incorporeal, or intangible thing or agency ⟨the ocean's ~⟩ ⟨the ~ of winter's icy blasts⟩ ⟨the ~ of a redeeming love⟩ **b** (1) **:** power to effect a desired object **:** MEANS, RESOURCES, CAPACITY ⟨not zeal or goodwill were lacking, but the ~⟩ (2) **:** physical or bodily strength ⟨with a man's will and a man's ~ —Robert Browning⟩ (3) *archaic* **:** active property **:** VIRTUE, EFFICACY (4) **:** the power, energy, or intensity of purpose, feeling, or action of which one is capable ⟨watched a wren . . . singing with all its ~ —Stuart Chase⟩ ⟨save ourselves by the ~ of our minds —L.M.Chamberlain⟩ ⟨began to strain with all his ~ toward his own left —A.C. Whitehead⟩ ⟨ran with all his ~⟩ — often used in the intensive phrase *with might and main* ⟨were staring with ~ and main —William Black⟩ **c :** naked material power or superiority of strength regarded as the ultimate arbiter of disputes or conflicts of interest ⟨~ makes right⟩ **2** *dial* **:** a considerable amount **:** a great deal **syn** see POWER

might and main *adv* **:** with might and main **:** VIGOROUSLY ⟨such as any sage practical politician would strive *might and main* to avoid —G.E.G.Catlin⟩

mightest *archaic past 2d sing of* MAY

might·ful \-tfəl\ *adj* [ME, fr. *might* + *-ful*] *archaic* **:** MIGHTY

might-have-been \ˈmīd·ə(v),bin, -ītə-\ *n, pl* **might-have-beens 1 :** something that might have happened ⟨who can calculate the *might-have-beens* —W.M.Thackeray⟩ ⟨reconstructs the *might-have-beens* of English and French elections —H.C.Mansfield⟩ **2 :** a person who might have amounted to something or to more

might·i·ly \ˈmīd·ᵊl|ē -īt|, |əl|, |i\ *adv* [ME, fr. OE *mihtiglīce,* fr. *mihtig* mighty + *-līce* -ly — more at MIGHTY] **1 :** in a mighty manner **:** EARNESTLY, VIGOROUSLY, POWERFULLY ⟨strove ~ to impress a customer with the book's merits —Bennett Cerf⟩ **2 :** to a great degree **:** very much ⟨can help you ~ in all your relations with others —W.J.Reilly⟩ ⟨~ important was the sex of a child in the imperial family —P.I.Wellman⟩

might·i·ness \ˈmīd·ēnəs, -īt|, |in-\ *n* -ES [ME *mihtinesse,* fr. *mihty, mighty* + *-nesse* -ness] **1 :** the quality or state of being mighty **:** possession of might **:** POWER **2 :** HIGHNESS, EXCELLENCY — used as a title of dignity ⟨Your *Mightiness*⟩ ⟨their High *Mightinesses*⟩

might·less \ˈmītləs\ *adj* [ME *mightles,* fr. *might* + *-les* -less] **:** lacking might **:** POWERLESS

might·n't \ˈmītᵊnt\ [by contr.] **:** might not

¹mighty \ˈmīd·|ē, -īt|, |i\ *adj* -ER/-EST [ME, fr. OE *mihtig,* fr. *miht* might + *-ig* -y — more at MIGHT] **1 a :** having or wielding great power or authority **:** strong in material resources or social position **:** POWERFUL ⟨the mismanagement and dishonesty of those once ~ in finance —Oscar Handlin⟩ ⟨knowing the well-heeled and the ~ rather than the poor and the unimportant —John Mason Brown⟩ **b :** marked by or reflecting intellectual or artistic ability of a high order **:** immensely gifted or effective **:** GREAT, NOTABLE, EXTRAORDINARY ⟨soon recognized as the *mightiest* preacher in New England —*Amer. Guide Series: Mass.*⟩ ⟨master of a ~ line⟩ ⟨one of the *mightiest* poets of our time⟩ **c** (1) **:** strong in body or valor ⟨repeated the exploits of the ~ logger —*Amer. Guide Series: Wash.*⟩ ⟨this ~ man of small stature —*Boy Scout Handbook*⟩ (2) **:** exerting or made with great force **:** STRENUOUS, VIOLENT ⟨swing ~ blows to sharpen a dull bit —*Lamp*⟩ ⟨a ~ tempest⟩ ⟨a ~ thrust⟩ ⟨a ~ wind⟩ (3) **:** doing or engaging in something intensively, on a large or massive scale, or with notable success ⟨were ~ wanderers in those days —Meridel Le Sueur⟩ ⟨a ~ drinker⟩ ⟨the Egyptian cat was a ~ hunter —Agnes Repplier⟩ (4) **:** very favorable **:** HIGH ⟨has a ~ opinion of his work⟩ **d :** potent or effective in action **:** EFFICACIOUS, EFFICIENT ⟨essayed such tasks with no *mightier* tools than picks or shovels —O.S.Nock⟩ ⟨cast a ~ spell upon her⟩ ⟨the bullet was *mightier* than the ballot —Hessell Tiltman⟩ **2 :** great or imposing in size, amount, extent, or degree ⟨periods of high ideals and ~ achievement —Mary D. Anderson⟩ ⟨the great country and ~ river he had explored —Tom Marvel⟩ ⟨one of the *mightiest* ruins in the world —Kennett Love⟩ ⟨the designer of a ~ bridge —B.N. Cardozo⟩

²mighty \"\ *adv* **:** in a great degree **:** EXTREMELY, VERY ⟨a ~ fine record⟩ ⟨~ proud of you —Gerald Beaumont⟩ ⟨a few had it ~ good —James Street⟩

³mighty \"\ *n* -ES **:** a person of might

mig·ma·tite \ˈmigməˌtīt\ *n* -S [LL *migmat-, migma* mixture (fr. Gk, fr. *meignynai, mignynai* to mix) + E *-ite* — more at MIX] **:** a gneiss produced by the injection of igneous material between the laminae of a schistose formation — called also *injection gneiss*

mignard *adj* [F *mignard,* fr. *mignon* darling + *-ard* — more at MINION] *obs* **:** DAINTY, DELICATE, MINCING

mig·niar·dise \ˈminyə(r)dəs\ *n* -S [F *mignardise,* fr. *mignard*] *archaic* **:** delicate fondling **:** migniard appearance or behavior

mi·gnon \ˈminˌyän, *in sense 2* mēnˈyōⁿ *or* ˈmēnˌyōⁿ\ *n* -S [F, lit., darling] **1 :** a moderate purple that is duller and slightly bluer than heliotrope (sense 4a), bluer and paler than average amethyst, bluer and less strong than manganese violet or cobalt violet, and bluer and duller than average lilac (sense 3a) **2** [by shortening] **:** FILET MIGNON

mi·gnon·ette \ˌminyəˈnet, *usu* -ed.+V\ *n* -S [F *mignonnette,* fr. obs. F, fem. of *mignonnet* dainty, fr. MF, fr. *mignon* — more at MINION] **1 :** an herb of the genus *Reseda; esp* **:** an annual (*R. odorata*) that is native to northern Africa and is widely cultivated for its long racemes of fragrant greenish yellow or greenish white flowers **2 :** a narrow bobbin lace having scattered small designs on a ground somewhat like tulle and made esp. by the French and Flemish in the 16th through the 19th centuries **3 :** *or* **mignonette green :** RESEDA 2a

mignonette

mignonette family *n* **:** RESEDACEAE

mignonette pepper *n* **:** coarsely ground pepper

mignonette tree *n* **:** HENNA 1

mignonette vine *n* **:** MADEIRA VINE

mi·gnonne \mēnˈyōⁿ\ *adj* [F, fem. of *mignon*] **:** daintily small **:** PETITE

mi·graine \ˈmīˌgrān\ *n* -S [F, fr. LL *hemicrania* pain in one side of the head, fr. Gk *hēmikrania,* fr. *hēmi-* hemi- + *kranion* skull — more at CRANIUM] **1 :** a condition that is marked by recurrent usu. unilateral severe headache often accompanied by nausea and vomiting and followed by sleep, that tends to occur in more than one member of a family, and that is of uncertain origin though attacks appear to be precipitated by dilatation of intracranial blood vessels **2 :** an episode or attack of migraine ⟨suffered from ~*s* all her life⟩

mi·grain·oid \(ˈ)mīˈgrāˌnȯid\ *adj* **:** resembling migraine

mi·grain·ous \-ānəs\ *adj* **:** of, relating to, or suffering from migraine

mi·gran·cy \ˈmīgrənsē\ *n* -ES **:** the fact, condition, or phenomenon of habitual movement from one place of residence to another; *specif* **:** habitual migration from one area to another in search of seasonal work ⟨the large extent of ~ is not in doubt —Wilfred Whiteley⟩ ⟨the social and economic evils of ~⟩

mi·grans \ˈmīˌgranz\ *n, pl* **mi·gran·tes** \mīˈgranˌtēz\ [NL, fr. L, pres. part. of *migrare* to migrate — more at MIGRATE] **:** a winged parthenogenetic viviparous female aphid produced by a fundatrigenia and serving to spread the colony either to new primary host plants or to secondary hosts

¹mi·grant \ˈmīgrənt\ *adj* [L *migrant-, migrans,* pres. part. of *migrare* to migrate] **:** of, relating to, or being a migrant ⟨~ birds⟩ ⟨the economic and social conditions of ~ life⟩

²migrant \"\ *n* -S **:** one that migrates: as **a :** a person who moves into another area in order to find work esp. seasonal labor ⟨full of pluck—as most ~*s* are when they first take to the road —*Amer. Child*⟩ **b :** an animal that shifts from one habitat to another whether by chance, as a normal phase of a life cycle, or as part of a population expansion ⟨appearance of coyotes as ~*s* in New York⟩

migrant shrike *n* **:** a shrike (*Lanius ludovicianus migrans*) of central No. America that winters in the southern Mississippi valley and Texas and is distinguished by black eye bands that meet above the bill

mi·grate \ˈmīˌgrāt, *usu* -ād.+V\ *vb* -ED/-ING/-S [L *migratus,* past part. of *migrare;* akin to Gk *ameibein* to change, and perh. to Skt *mayate* he exchanges — more at MEAN] *vi* **:** to move from one place to another: as **a** (1) **:** to leave one country, region, or place in order to settle in another ⟨pretty lucky to have *migrated* to this country —Victor Boesen⟩ (2) **:** to move from one area to another in search of work (as seasonal labor) ⟨*migrating* with the alternation of crops through field after field of the West —Oscar Handlin⟩ (3) **:** TRANSFER; *specif* **:** to transfer from one college to another at a university in the British Isles ⟨designing to ~ presently to a theological college —John Buchan⟩ ⟨*migrated* to Emmanuel . . . probably to be at his elder brother's college —A.J.Shirren⟩ **b** (1) **:** to pass periodically from one region or climate to another for feeding or breeding ⟨birds that ~ only at night —F.A.Geldard⟩ (2) **:** to extend the habitat gradually from an old or into a new region ⟨some plants failed to ~ into their old ranges as the glaciation diminished⟩ (3) **:** to move from one site to another in a host organism esp. as part of a life cycle ⟨filiarial worms ~ within the human body⟩ (4) **:** to alter position in the course of embryologic development or other organic process ⟨one eye gradually ~*s* across the top the head, until both are on the same side —R.E.Coker⟩ **c** (1) **:** to move or undergo removal from one locality to another as a result of the operation of natural forces ⟨the dunes usually ~ inland —W.W.Atwood b.1906⟩ (2) *of an atom or group* **:** to shift position within a molecule (3) *of an ion* **:** to move toward an electrode (4) *of a chemical substance* **:** to move or diffuse into an environing medium ⟨plasticizers that ~ into the adhesive film —*Product Engineering*⟩ ⟨retard the development of rancidity when oxidable oils . . . ~ into it —J.J.Aid⟩ **d :** to change locale or center of gravity **:** SHIFT ⟨the coal-mining centers . . . have *migrated* eastward —L.D. Stamp⟩ ⟨industry, having *migrated* from the manor to the craft guild of the town —Stringfellow Barr⟩ **~** *vt* **:** to cause to migrate ⟨~ a silicon atom —J.R.Goldsmith⟩

mi·gra·tet·ic \ˌmīgrəˈted·ik\ *adj* [prob. fr. *migrate* + *-etic*] **:** of or relating to electronography

mi·gra·tet·ics \ˌ==ˈted·iks\ *n pl but usu sing in constr* **:** ELECTRONOGRAPHY

mi·gra·tion \mīˈgrāshən\ *n* -S [F or L; F, fr. L *migration-, migratio,* fr. *migratus* (past part. of *migrare* to migrate) + *-ion-, -io* -ion — more at MIGRATE] **1 :** the act, process, or an instance of migrating: as **a** (1) **:** the act or an instance of moving from one country, region, or place to settle in another ⟨for the first time, the U.S. counted a net deficit by ~ —Oscar Handlin⟩ ⟨~ to the suburbs —C.B.Palmer b. 1910⟩ (2) **:** the act or an instance of moving from one area to another in search of work (as seasonal labor) ⟨the circle of their ~*s* reached as far north as the beet fields of Michigan —Oscar Handlin⟩ **b :** periodic movement from one region or climate to another for feeding or breeding ⟨the ~*s* of birds⟩ **c** (1) **:** a shifting of an atom or atoms from one part of the molecule to another (2) **:** a movement or drift of ions toward one or the other electrode under the influence of electromotive force **d :** an underground movement of oil, gas, or water not occasioned by artificial means **2 :** the individuals taking part in a migratory movement or those migrating during a given period — **mi·gra·tion·al** \(ˈ)mīˈgrāshənᵊl, -shnəl\ *adj*

mi·gra·tion·ist \mīˈgrāsh(ə)nəst\ *n* -S **:** a person who assigns primary importance to migration in the diffusion of culture or the distribution of species

migration route *n* **:** a well-defined subdivision of a flyway

mi·gra·tive \ˈmīgrəd·iv\ *adj* [*migrate* + *-ive*] **:** MIGRATORY

mi·gra·tor \ˈmīˌgrād·ə(r)\ *n* -S [LL, fr. L *migratus* + *-or*] **:** one that migrates; *specif* **:** a migratory bird

mi·gra·to·ri·al \ˌmīgrəˈtōrēəl, -tȯr-\ *adj* **:** MIGRATORY

¹mi·gra·to·ry \ˈmīgrəˌtōrē, -tȯr-, -ri\ *adj* [NL *migratorius,* fr. L *migratus* (past part. of *migrare* to migrate) + *-orius* -ory — more at MIGRATE] **1 a :** making a migration **:** moving habitually or occasionally from one region or climate to another ⟨~ birds⟩ ⟨~ tribes⟩ **b** (1) **:** moving in response to the demand for seasonal labor ⟨a ~ worker⟩ (2) **:** of or relating to migrant laborers ⟨the ~ shacks in the valley —Thurston Scott⟩ **2 :** ROVING, WANDERING ⟨a ~ cocktail set —Edmund Wilson⟩ ⟨a history of ~ joint pain —C.F. McKhann⟩ **3 :** of or relating to migration ⟨~ movements⟩

²migratory \"\ *n* -ES **:** MIGRATOR, MIGRANT ⟨you know how . . . all of us feel about these *migratories* —Rachel Field⟩

migratory ant *n* **:** ARMY ANT

migratory divorce *n* **:** a divorce granted to one party in a state other than that where the other party resides or is domiciled or in a state where neither party in fact resides or is domiciled

migratory grasshopper *n* **:** any of several migratory locusts of the genus *Melanoplus,* including serious pests of grain-growing and range areas of the central and western U.S.

migratory locust *n* **:** a locust that engages in group migrations; *esp* **:** a very destructive Old World locust (*Locusta migratoria*)

migratory thrush *n* **:** ROBIN 1c

mi·grule \ˈmīˌgrül\ *n* -S [*migrate* + *-ule*] **:** a disseminule by which a plant spreads into new areas **:** DIASPORE

migs *pl of* MIG

miguelet *var of* MIQUELET

MIH *abbr, often not cap* miles in the hour

mih·rab \ˈmērəb\ *n* -S [Ar *miḥrāb*] **:** a niche or chamber in a mosque indicating the direction of Mecca and usu. containing a copy of the Koran; *sometimes* **:** a slab only, used to indicate the direction — compare KAABA

mi·ka·do \məˈkä(ˌ)dō, -kā(-\ *n* -S [Jap, fr. *mi-* (honorific prefix) + *kado* door] **1 :** an emperor of Japan — compare TENNO **2 :** a strong to vivid reddish orange

mikado brown *n* **:** a moderate brown that is yellower, lighter, and stronger than auburn, lighter, stronger, and slightly redder than chestnut brown, and yellower and stronger than toast brown — called also *stroller tan*

mikado orange *n* **1 :** a moderate orange that is yellower and stronger than honeydew, yellower, stronger, and slightly lighter than Persian orange, and stronger and slightly redder and darker than average apricot **2** *often cap M&O* **:** a direct dye — see DYE table I (under *Direct Orange 15*)

mikado yellow G *n, often cap M&Y* **:** a direct dye — see DYE table I (under *Direct Yellow 6*)

mi·ka·nia \məˈkānēə\ *n, cap* [NL, fr. J.G. *Mikan* †1814 Czech botanist + NL *-ia*] **:** a large genus of mostly tropical American herbaceous or woody vines (family Compositae) with opposite leaves and small discoid heads in panicled clusters — see CLIMBING HEMPWEED

mik·a·su·ki \ˌmikəˈsükē\ *n, pl* **mikasuki** *or* **mikasukis** *usu cap* **1 a :** a Muskogean people of northwestern Florida orig. members of the Creek Confederacy but later largely absorbed into the Seminole people **b :** a member of such people **2 :** the language of the Mikasuki people and of part of the Seminole people

¹mike \ˈmīk\ *n* -S [origin unknown] *slang Brit* **:** an act or instance of miking — used esp. in the phrases *do a mike* and *have a mike*

²mike \"\ *vi* -ED/-ING/-S *slang Brit* **:** LOAF, LOITER

³mike *var of* MICK

⁴mike \ˈmīk\ *n* -S [by shortening & alter.] **1 :** MICROPHONE **2 :** MICROMETER CALIPER

⁵mike \"\ *vb* -ED/-ING/-S *vi* **:** to have a dimension indicated by a micrometer caliper ⟨the diameter ~*s* at 0.534 inch⟩ **~** *vt* **:** to measure with a micrometer caliper

⁶mike \"\ *usu cap* — a communications code word for the letter *m*

mike fright *n* [⁴*mike*] **:** intense fright or nervousness experienced by a person on having to broadcast into a microphone ⟨suffered *mike fright* and lost his voice completely —*Psychological Abstracts*⟩

mi·kir \ˈmēˈki(ə)r\ *n, pl* **mikir** *or* **mikirs** *usu cap* **1 a :** a hill people of Assam — called also *Arleng* **b :** a member of such people **2 :** the Tibeto-Burman language of the Mikir people

mikra *var of* MIQRA

mik·vah *or* **mik·veh** \ˈmikvə\ *n* -S [Heb *miqwāh*] **:** a ritual bath or bathing place for purification in accordance with Jewish law

mil \ˈmil\ *n* -S [L *mille* thousand — more at MILE] **1 :** a unit of length equal to ¹⁄₁₀₀₀ inch or 0.0254 millimeter used esp. for the diameter of wire **2 :** a unit of angular measurement used in artillery and equal to ¹⁄₆₄₀₀ of the circumference of a circle or approximately the angle subtended by one yard at 1000 yards range **3 :** a monetary unit formerly used in Palestine equal to ¹⁄₁₀₀₀ pound; *also* **:** a bronze coin representing this unit

mil *abbr* **1** mileage **2** military **3** militia **4** millieme **5** million

mil·acre \ˈmilˌākə(r)\ *n* [*mil-* (fr. L *mille* thousand) + *acre*] **:** a plot of ground having an area of ¹⁄₁₀₀₀ acre used as a test or sample area esp. for vegetational studies

mi·la·dy *also* **mi·la·di** \məˈlādē, mīˈ-, -di\ *n, pl* **miladies** *also* **miladis** [F *milady,* fr. E *my lady*] **1 :** an Englishwoman of noble or gentle birth — often used as an appellation **2** a woman of fashion ⟨hats designed for ~⟩

milage *var of* MILEAGE

¹mi·lan \məˈlan, -aa(ə)n, -lăn\ *adj, usu cap* [fr. *Milan,* city in northern Italy] **1 :** of or from the city of Milan, Italy **:** of the kind or style prevalent in Milan **2** *of lace or needlepoint* **:** having a usu. scroll or floral pattern formed of braid or tape

²milan \"\ *n, often cap, often attrib* [fr. *Milan,* Italy] **:** a fine straw braid made from Italian wheat straw used chiefly for hats

mil·a·naise \ˌmiləˈnāz\ *adj* [F, fem. of *milanais* of Milan, fr. *Milan,* Italy] **:** garnished with spaghetti or macaroni with Parmesan cheese in a tomato sauce containing truffles and mushrooms ⟨veal cutlet ~⟩

milanau *or* **milano** *usu cap, var of* MELANAU

milan cabbage *n* **:** SAVOY CABBAGE

¹mil·a·nese \ˌmiləˈnēz, -ēs\ *n, pl* **milanese** [It, fr. *Milano* Milan + It *-ese,* n. suffix] **1** *cap* **:** a native or resident of Milan, Italy **2** *cap* **:** the Italian dialect of Milan **3 :** a fine lightweight warp-knitted fabric usu. of silk, rayon, or nylon for women's wear characterized by interlocked stitches, resistance to runs, fine diagonal lines

²milanese \ˌ==ˈ=\ *adj, usu cap* [It, fr. *Milano* Milan + It *-ese,* adj. suffix] **:** of or relating to Milan, Italy or its inhabitants

milanese mandolin *n, usu cap 1st M* **:** a mandolin having five or six pairs of strings

mi·lan·ji cedar *also* **mlan·je cedar** \məˈlänjē-\ *n, often cap M* [after Mt. *Milanji* or *Mlange,* Nyasaland, Africa] **:** a tall coniferous tree (*Widdringtonia whytei*) of the uplands of southern and eastern Africa that is closely related to the cypresses but much resembles a typical cedar

mi·lar·ite \ˈmēˌläˌrīt, ˈmilə,r-\ *n* -S [G *milarit,* fr. Val *Milar,* Switzerland + G *-it* -ite] **:** a mineral $K_2Ca_4Be_4Al_2Si_{24}O_{62}·H_2O$ consisting of a hydrous silicate of potassium, calcium, beryllium, and aluminum occurring in glassy hexagonal crystals

milch \ˈmilk, ˈmilch, ˈmilks\ *adj* [ME *milche* giving milk, fr. OE *-milce* (in *thrimilce* month of May when cows can be milked three times daily); akin to OHG *melch* giving milk, ON *mjolkr* giving milk, OE *melcan* to milk — more at MILK] **1** *of a domestic animal* **:** giving milk; *specif* **:** bred for or suitable for milk production as distinct from other uses (as meat or wool production or draft) ⟨~ goat⟩ ⟨~ cattle⟩ **2** *obs* **:** flowing as if with milk **:** WEEPING ⟨would have made ~ the burning eyes of heaven —Shak.⟩

milch cow *n* [ME *milche cow,* fr. *milche* milch + *cow*] **1 :** a cow in milk or kept for her milk **2 :** a source of easily acquired gain ⟨the tobacco . . . industry is regarded as one of the best . . . *milch cows* of national revenue —*Canadian Horticulture & Home*⟩

milch·er \ˈmilkə(r), ˈmilchə(r)\ *n* -s **:** a milch animal

milch glass *n* **:** MILK GLASS

mil·chig \ˈmilkik\ *adj* [Yiddish, fr. *milch* milk (fr. MHG, fr. OHG *miluh*) + *-ig* -y (fr. MHG *-ic*, fr. OHG *-ig*) — more at MILK] *Jewish cookery* **:** made of or derived from milk or dairy products ⟨menus for ~ meals⟩

mil·chigs \-ks\ *n pl* **:** milk or dairy products

¹mild \ˈmīld, *esp before pause or consonant* -īəld\ *adj* -ER/-EST [ME *mild, milde*, fr. OE *milde*; akin to OHG *milti* kind, gracious, ON *mildr* gentle, Goth *mildiths* affection, Gk *malthakos* soft, Skt *mardhati* it is moist, OE *melu* meal — more at MEAL] **1 a** *archaic* **:** KIND, GRACIOUS, CONSIDERATE ⟨peace on earth and mercy ~ —Charles Wesley⟩ **b :** gentle in nature or behavior **:** not harsh or vehement **:** not giving offense ⟨~ disposition⟩ ⟨~ manners⟩ **2 a :** moderate in action or sensuous effect ⟨~ drug⟩ ⟨~ cigar⟩ **:** of moderate strength or intensity **:** not sharp or bitter ⟨~ oath⟩ ⟨~ humus⟩ ⟨~ slope⟩ ⟨~ reproof⟩ **:** BLAND ⟨~ as milk⟩ ⟨~ cheese⟩ **b** *of ale or beer* **:** not strongly flavored with hops **c** *of disease* **:** not severe or dangerous **:** BENIGN ⟨~ case of whooping cough⟩ **3 a** *archaic* **:** not wild **:** TAME ⟨wild beasts . . . at his sight grew ~ —John Milton⟩ **b :** of less than normal or expected vigor, boldness, or severity ⟨~ sarcasm⟩ ⟨~ game of bridge⟩ ⟨~ punishment⟩ ⟨~ exercise⟩ **c :** characterized by absence of extremes in temperature **:** TEMPERATE ⟨~ climate⟩ **d :** not cold **:** pleasantly warm ⟨~ spring day⟩ ⟨~ spell in February⟩ **syn** see SOFT

²mild \"\ *adv*, *archaic* **:** MILDLY

³mild \"\ *n* -s **1** *Brit* **:** mild ale or beer **2** *usu cap* **:** coffee of fine quality **:** coffee other than Brazil — usu. used in pl.

mild alkali *n* **:** a weak alkali (as sodium carbonate) — distinguished from *caustic alkali*

mild-and-bitter \ˈ==ˈ==\ *n* -s *Brit* **:** a drink consisting of a mixture of mild and bitter draft beers or ales

mild·en \ˈmīldən\ *vb* -ED/-ING/-S *vt* **:** to make mild or milder ⟨did what little they could to ~ their evil governments —*Foreign Affairs*⟩ ~ *vi* **:** to become mild or milder ⟨if the weather ~s, the river will thaw⟩

¹mil·dew \ˈmil,d(y)ü\ *n* -s [ME, fr. OE *meledēaw, mildēaw*; akin to OHG *militou* honeydew; both fr. a prehistoric WGmc compound whose original first constituent, prob. represented by Goth *milith* honey, was influenced by the word represented by OE *melu* meal, and whose second constituent is represented by OE *dēaw* dew — more at MELLIFLUOUS, MEAL, DEW] **1** *obs* **:** HONEYDEW 1 **2 a :** a superficial usu. whitish growth produced on various forms of organic matter and on living plants by fungi (as of the families Erysiphaceae and Peronosporaceae) **b :** a fungus producing such growth — compare DOWNY MILDEW, ⁵MOLD, POWDERY MILDEW **3 :** a discoloration (as on cloth, leather, paper) caused by parasitic fungi

²mildew \"\ *vt* -ED/-ING/-S **:** to affect with or as if with mildew ⟨prejudices that ~ attempts at social interpretation —Harlow Shapley⟩ ~ *vi* **:** to become affected with mildew ⟨prevent books from ~*ing*⟩

mil·dew·cide \-ti,sīd\ *n* -s **:** an agent that destroys mildew

mildewed *adj* [fr. past part. of ²*mildew*] **1 :** covered with or ruined by mildew ⟨~ wheat⟩ **2 :** decaying from age or disuse **:** gone bad from keeping too long ⟨~ jokes⟩ ⟨~ notion⟩ ⟨~ old butler⟩

¹mildewproof \ˈ=,=,=\ *adj* [¹*mildew* + *proof*] **:** resistant to mildew

²mildewproof \"\ *vt* **:** to make resistant to mildew ⟨~*ing* sails⟩

mil·dewy \ˈmil,d(y)üē\ *adj* **1 :** affected with mildew **2 :** like mildew

mildhearted \ˈ=ˈ==\ *adj* [ME *mildherted*, fr. ¹*mild* + *herted* hearted] *archaic* **:** MERCIFUL

mild·ish \ˈmīldish\ *adj* **:** somewhat mild ⟨~ weather⟩ **:** somewhat lacking in sharpness or vigor ⟨~ wit⟩

mild·ly *adv* [ME *mildely*, fr. OE *mildelīce*, fr. *milde* mild + *-līce* -ly] **:** in a mild manner **:** to a moderate degree or extent ⟨protested ~⟩ ⟨~ successful⟩ ⟨~ cynical⟩

mild mercurous chloride *or* **mild mercury chloride** *n* **:** CALOMEL

mild·ness *n* -ES [ME *mildenesse*, fr. *milde* mild + *-nesse* -ness] **:** the quality or state of being mild ⟨surprised at the ~ of his reply⟩

mild steel *n* **:** low-carbon steel that contains usu. 0.05 to 0.20 percent carbon, is soft and easily worked, and is used for structural purposes

mild streak *n* **:** BROWN BERRY

mile \ˈmīl, *esp before pause or consonant* -īəl\ *n*, *pl* **miles** *also* **mile** *often attrib* [ME, fr. OE *mīl*; akin to OHG *mīla, mīlla* mile; both fr. a prehistoric WGmc word borrowed fr. L *milia* miles (fr. *milia passuum*, lit., thousands of paces), pl. of *mille* mile, fr. *mille passus*, lit., thousand paces, fr. *mille* thousand + *passus*, pl. of *passus* step, pace; L *mille* thousand perh. fr. a prehistoric compound whose first constituent is represented by Gk *hen-, heis* one and whose second constituent is akin to Gk *chilioi* thousand, Skt *sahasra* — more at SAME] **1 :** any of various units of distance derived from an ancient Roman unit equal to 1620 English yards or 1482 meters: as **a :** a unit equal to 5280 ft. ⟨a distance of six ~*s*⟩ ⟨a ~ race⟩ — called also *statute mile*; see MEASURE table **b :** NAUTICAL MILE **2 :** a race of a mile ⟨has achieved a four minute ~⟩ **3 :** a relatively great distance or interval ⟨missed the target by a ~⟩ ⟨thoughts ~*s* away⟩ ⟨his guilt stuck out a ~⟩

mile·age *also* **mil·age** \ˈmīlij, -lēj\ *n* -s **1 :** an allowance for traveling expenses at a certain rate per mile **2 :** aggregate length or distance in miles: as **a :** the track of a railroad company or wire of a telegraph company **b :** the total miles traveled in a day or other period of time; *also* **:** rate of travel in miles **c :** the amount of service which something (as an automobile tire) will yield expressed in terms of miles of travel **3 :** a charge per mile (as for the use of the cars of a railroad) **4 :** USEFULNESS, ADVANTAGE, PROFIT ⟨greater press ~ from printing plates⟩ ⟨get more ~ out of school buildings by operating them all year round⟩ ⟨political ~ in promising tax cuts⟩

mile of line *or* **mile of road :** a unit for expressing the distance between points connected by railroad line as distinct from the amount of trackage composing the line

milepost \ˈ=,=\ *n* **1 :** a post placed at a distance of a mile from a similar post or showing the distance in miles from a certain point **2 :** a significant point in a line of progress or development ⟨~*s* in the chronological development around which this brief discussion may be centered —W.B.Graves⟩

mil·er \ˈmīlə(r)\ *n* -s **:** a man or a horse that competes in races at the mile distance

mi·les glo·ri·o·sus \ˈmē,lāz,glōrēˈō,süs\ *n*, *pl* **mi·li·tes glo·ri·o·si** \ˈmēlē,täz,glōrēˈō,sē\ [L] **:** a boastful soldier; *esp* **:** a stock comic character of this type in Roman and Renaissance comedy

¹mi·le·sian \məˈlēzhən, (ˈ)mī¦l-, -ēshən\ *adj*, *usu cap* [L *milesius* Milesian (fr. Gk *milēsios*, fr. *Milētus* Miletus) + E *-an*] **1 :** of or belonging to the ancient city of Miletus, Asia Minor, or to its residents **2 :** belonging or relating to a Milesian school of nature philosophers of the 6th century B.C. who were mainly concerned with the basal stuff of which the world is made — compare ANAXIMANDRIAN, THALESIAN

²milesian \"\ *n* -s *usu cap* **1 :** a native or resident of ancient Miletus **2 :** a member of the Milesian school

³milesian \"\ *adj*, *usu cap* [*Milesius* (*Miledh*), mythical Spanish king whose followers are supposed to have conquered Ireland about 1300 B.C. and are regarded as the ancestors of most of the Irish + E *-an*] **:** belonging or relating to the legendary earliest Celts of Ireland; *broadly* **:** IRISH ⟨the banshee haunts only members of the high *Milesian* race —Padraic Colum⟩

⁴milesian \"\ *n* -s *usu cap* **:** one of a legendary early Celtic people of Ireland said to have come from Spain; *broadly* **:** IRISHMAN ⟨a true *Milesian*, pious Catholic, and descendant of King Somebody —Anthony Trollope⟩

milesian tale *n*, *usu cap M* [¹*milesian*] **:** one of a class of short salacious tales current in Greek and Roman antiquity

¹milestone \ˈ=,=\ *n* **1 :** a stone serving as a milepost **2 :** a significant point in any progress or development

²milestone \"\ *vt* **:** to furnish or mark with or as if with a milestone ⟨life pathetically *milestoned* with fragments . . . frustrated hopes —W.H.Gardner⟩

BOSTON 20 MILES

milestone 1

mile-ton \ˈ=ˈ=\ *n* **:** TON-MILE

mil·foil \ˈmil,fȯil\ *n* -s [ME, fr. OF, fr. L *millifolium, millefolium*, fr. *mille* thousand + *folium* leaf — more at MILE, BLOW] **1 :** YARROW **2 :** WATER MILFOIL

mil-foot \ˈ=ˈ=\ *n* **:** a unit of electrical conducting material equal to material having a length of one foot and a cross section of one circular mil

milia *pl of* MILIUM

mil·i·a·ceous \ˌmilēˈāshəs\ *adj* [L *miliaceus* consisting of millet, fr. *milium* millet + *-aceus* -aceous] **:** MILIARY

mil·ia·ren·sis \ˌmilyəˈren(t)səs\ *n*, *pl* **miliaren·ses** \-(t),sēz\ [LL, fr. L *mille* thousand] **:** a Byzantine silver coin introduced by Constantine the Great equal to 1/1000 pound or 1/14 solidus or after the reign of Justinian I 1/12 solidus

mil·i·a·ria \ˌmilēˈa(a)rēə, -ˈer-, -ˈär-\ *n* -s [NL, fr. L, fem. of *miliarius* of millet] **:** an inflammatory disorder of the skin that involves the sweat glands, is characterized by redness, eruption, and burning, itching, or pricking sensations, and is associated with excessive sweating and retention of sweat in sweat glands with occluded ducts; *esp* **:** PRICKLY HEAT

mil·i·ary \ˈmilē,erē, -lyər-, -ri\ *adj* [L *miliarius* of millet, fr. *milium* millet + *-arius* -ary — more at MILLET] **1 :** accompanied or marked by an eruption or formation of lesions the size of millet seeds **2 :** small and numerous **:** made up of many small projections ⟨~ tubercles⟩ ⟨~ granulation⟩

miliary fever *n* **:** an epidemic disease characterized by fever, excessive sweating, and eruption of military vesicles in the skin

miliary tuberculosis *n* **:** acute tuberculosis in which minute tubercles are formed in one or more organs of the body by tubercle bacilli usu. spread by way of the blood

mi·lieu \mēlˈyə̄, -ˈyü, -ˈyə(r)\ *n*, *pl* **mi·lieus** \-z\ *also* **mi·lieux** \-(z)\ [F, environment, center, midst, fr. OF, center, midst, fr. *mi* middle (fr. L *medius*) + *lieu* place, fr. L *locus* — more at MID, STALL] **1 :** ENVIRONMENT, SETTING ⟨historical ~ of a novel⟩ ⟨stylistic and dialectical speech ~*s* —B.H.Smeaton⟩ **2 a :** the numbers in the middle column of the layout in roulette when a bet is placed on them **b :** the numbers 13 to 24 in the roulette layout **:** the second dozen

milieu therapy *n* **:** the manipulation of the environment of a mental patient as an aid toward the patient's recovery

mil·inch \ˈmi,linch\ *n* [*mil-* (fr. L *mille* thousand) + *inch*] **:** a unit of length equal to 1/1000 inch

mi·li·o·la \məˈlīələ, ,milēˈōlə\ *n*, *cap* [NL, dim. of L *milium* millet; fr. the resemblance of shells of animals of this genus to millet seed] **:** a genus of Foraminifera (the type of a large family Miliolidae) including forms that have existed since the Triassic and have contributed largely to the formation of various limestones

mil·i·o·lid \ˈmilēōləd\ *n* -s [NL *Miliolidae*, fr. *Miliola*, type genus + *-idae*] **:** a foraminiferan of the genus *Miliola* or the family Miliolidae

mil·i·o·line \-ō,līn, -lən\ *adj* [NL *Miliola* + E *-ine*] **:** relating or belonging to the genus *Miliola* or the family Miliolidae

mil·i·o·lite \-ō,līt\ *n* -s [NL *Miliola* + E *-ite*] **:** a fossil shell of or similar to one of the genus *Miliola*

mil·i·o·lit·ic \ˌmilēō¦lid·ik\ *adj* [*miliolite* + *-ic*] **:** of or relating to the genus *Miliola* **:** containing miliolites

mil·i·tance \ˈmiləd·ən(t)s, -lətən- *also* -lətˀn-\ *n* -s [fr. ¹*militant*, after such pairs as E *attendant: attendance*] **:** MILITANCY

mil·i·tan·cy \-nsē, -si\ *n* -ES [¹*militant* + *-cy*] **:** the quality or state of being militant

¹mil·i·tant \-nt\ *adj* [ME, fr. MF, fr. L *militant-, militans*, pres. part. of *militare* to engage in warfare — more at MILITATE] **1 :** engaged in warfare or conflict **:** FIGHTING ⟨~ powers⟩ **2 :** given to fighting **:** COMBATIVE **3 :** aggressively active in a cause ⟨~ suffragist⟩ ⟨~ trade unionism⟩ **4** *obs* **:** MILITARY ⟨banners ~ —William Wordsworth⟩ **syn** see AGGRESSIVE

²militant \"\ *n* -s **:** a militant person ⟨~*s* of the radical party⟩

mil·i·tant·ly *adv* **:** in a militant manner ⟨~ vociferous . . . sectarian minority —C.I.Glicksberg⟩

mil·i·tant·ness *n* -ES **:** the quality or state of being militant

militar *adj* [MF *militaire*] *obs* **:** MILITARY

mil·i·tar·i·ly \ˌmilə¦terəlē, -li\ *adv* **:** in a military manner ⟨intervene ~⟩ **:** from a military standpoint ⟨it is ~ stupid to criticize your allies —*Short Guide to Great Britain*⟩

mil·i·tar·i·ness \ˈ==,terēnəs\ *n* -ES **:** the quality or state of being military

mil·i·ta·rism \ˈmiləd·ə,rizəm, -lətə,-\ *n* -s [F *militarisme*, fr. *militaire* + *-isme* -ism] **:** predominance of the military class or prevalence of their ideals **:** subordination of the civil ideals or policies of a government to the military **:** a spirit which exalts military virtues and ideals **:** a policy of aggressive military preparedness

¹mil·i·ta·rist \-,rəst\ *n* -s [¹*military* + *-ist*] **1** *archaic* **:** an expert in military matters **2 :** one imbued with militarism

²militarist \"\ *adj* **:** characterized by militarism ⟨~ faction⟩ **:** dominated by military aims and ideals ⟨~ dictator⟩ — **mil·i·ta·ris·tic** \ˌmiləd·ə¦ristik, -lətə¦-, -tēk\ *adj* — **mil·i·ta·ris·ti·cal·ly** \-tək(ə)lē, -tēk-, -li\ *adv*

mil·i·ta·ri·za·tion \ˌmiləd·ərəˈzāshən, -lətər-, -rīˈ-\ *n* -s **:** the act of imbuing with a military character or converting to military status ⟨~ of youth organizations⟩

mil·i·ta·rize \ˈmiləd·ə,rīz, -lətə,-\ *vt* -ED/-ING/-S *see -ize in Explan Notes* [F *militariser*, fr. *militaire* military + *-iser* -ize] **1 :** to arm or equip with military forces and defenses **:** prepare for military purposes ⟨a *militarized* frontier⟩ **2 :** to give (an individual or a civilian organization) a military character ⟨a merger between maintenance workers and *militarized* plant guards⟩ **:** subject to military methods ⟨~ labor⟩

¹mil·i·tary \ˈmilə,terē, -ri\ *adj* [MF *militaire*, fr. L *militaris*, fr. *milit-, miles* soldier + *-aris* -ar — more at MILITATE] **1 :** of or relating to soldiers, arms, or war **:** ⟨the country's ~ needs⟩ ⟨~ draft⟩ **:** belonging to, engaged in, or appropriate to the affairs of war ⟨~ parade⟩ **:** according to the methods and customs of war or of organized fighting men ⟨~ discipline⟩ — distinguished from *civil* **2 a :** performed or made by armed forces ⟨~ expedition⟩ **b :** supported by armed force ⟨~ government⟩ **3 :** of or relating to the army — distinguished from *naval*

²military \"\ *n*, *pl* **military** *also* **militaries** **1 :** ARMED FORCES **:** military branches of government ⟨permit the ~ to control scientific research⟩ ⟨different branches of the ~⟩ ⟨alarmed the *militaries* of both countries⟩ ⟨coronation procession overweighted by ~ though it was —*Manchester Guardian Weekly*⟩ **2 :** military persons; *esp* **:** army officers ⟨the ~ in the car gave . . . no salute as they drove off —William Sansom⟩

military academy *n* **1 :** a military school for the training of army officers ⟨U. S. *Military Academy* at West Point⟩ **2 :** a preparatory school for boys where the students habitually wear uniforms and follow military routine

military band *n* **1 :** a musical wind band attached to a military establishment **2 :** a band consisting of brass, woodwind, and percussion instruments

military brush *n* **:** one of a pair of hairbrushes without handles

military college *n* **:** a civilian college where the students habitually wear uniforms and follow military routine

military commission *n* **:** a court organized in time of war or suspension of the civil power to try offenses by persons (as civilians) not subject to trial by a court martial

military crest *n* **:** a line or position often below the topographical crest and on the slope toward the enemy from which maximum observation of the remainder of the slope can be obtained

military engineering *n* **:** the art and practice of designing and building offensive and defensive military works and of building and maintaining lines of military transport

military government *n* **:** the government established by a military commander in conquered territory to administer the military law declared by him under military authority applicable to all persons in the conquered territory and superseding any incompatible local law — compare MILITARY LAW

military governor *n* **:** a military officer serving as chief political executive of an area under military government ⟨German . . . actions were subject to the veto of the United States *military governor* —E.H.Litchfield⟩

military heel *n* **:** a woman's shoe heel like the Cuban heel but lower and thicker

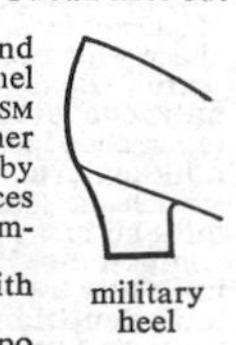

military heel

military hospital *n* **:** a hospital for the care and treatment of sick and wounded military personnel

mil·i·tary·ism \ˈmilə,terē,izəm\ *n* -s **:** MILITARISM

military law *n* **:** law enforced by military rather than civil authority; *specif* **:** law prescribed by statute for the government of the armed forces and of the civilians accompanying them — compare MARTIAL LAW, MILITARY GOVERNMENT

military macaw *n* **:** a macaw (*Ara militaris*) with red and green coloring

military march *n* **:** a march esp. of lively tempo intended for performance by a military band

military necessity *n* **:** the necessity attending belligerent military operations that is held to justify all measures necessary to bring an enemy to complete submission excluding those (as cruelty, torture, poison, perfidy, wanton destruction) that are forbidden by modern laws and customs of war

military occupation *n* **:** control and possession of hostile territory that enables an invading nation to establish military government against an enemy or martial law against rebels or insurrectionists in its own territory

military occupational specialty *n* **:** the duty or related group of duties that a soldier by training, skill, and experience is best qualified to perform and that is a basis for the classification, assignment, and advancement of enlisted personnel — abbr. *MOS*

military order *n* **:** an association of military persons under certain rules membership in which confers some distinction

military ordinariate *n* **:** a body of Roman Catholic chaplains serving the military forces of a particular country and subject to the jurisdiction of an appointed bishop of that country

military police *n* **1 :** an organized part of an army or command that exercises the functions of police among the soldiers and those attached to the troops, arrests stragglers, takes charge of prisoners **2 :** police organized on military lines — abbr. *MP*

military policeman *n* **:** a member of the military police

military press *n* **:** PRESS 9a

military psychology *n* **:** the application of methods and principles of psychology to problems of military training, discipline, combat behavior

military salvage *n* **:** rescue of property from the enemy in time of war that gives the rescuer a right to demand a reward in the prize court

military school *n* **:** MILITARY ACADEMY 2

military science *n* **:** the known principles underlying military conflict; *specif* **:** a course in military training offered (as by a college) as part of an educational program

military service *n* **1 :** service in arms rendered by a feudal tenant holding by military tenure **2 :** active duty in a branch of the armed forces

military tenure *n* **:** feudal tenure of land on condition of performing military service — compare KNIGHT SERVICE, GRAND SERGEANTY

military testament *or* **military will** *n* **:** NUNCUPATIVE WILL

military time *n* **:** time measured in hours numbered to twenty-four (as 0100, 0800, 1600, 2300) from one midnight to the next — compare TIME illustration

mil·i·tate \ˈmilə,tāt, *usu* -ād·+V\ *vi* -ED/-ING/-S [L *militatus*, past part. of *militare*, fr. *milit-, miles* soldier; perh. akin to Gk *homilos* assembly, Skt *melā*] **1** *obs* **a :** to serve as a soldier **:** engage in warfare **b :** to fight for a cause or a principle **2 :** to have weight or effect ⟨facts ~ against this opinion⟩ ⟨cultural unity has tended to ~ . . . in favor of political independence —G.T.Rowles⟩

militation *n* -s [*militate* + *-ion*] *obs* **:** CONFLICT, CONTRADICTION

milites gloriosi *pl of* MILES GLORIOSUS

mi·li·tia \məˈlishə\ *n* -s [L, military service, warfare, fr. *milit-, miles* soldier + *-ia* -y] **1** *obs* **a :** military practice or system **b :** military service **c :** ARMAMENT **2** *obs* **:** a particular military force **3 :** HOME RESERVE **4 :** the whole body of able-bodied male citizens declared by law as being subject to call to military service

mi·li·tia·man \-shəmən\ *n*, *pl* **militiamen :** a member of an organized militia

mil·i·um \ˈmilēəm\ *n*, *pl* **mil·ia** \-ēə\ [ME, fr. L — more at MILLET] **1** *pl* **milia**, *obs* **:** MILLET **2** *cap* [NL, fr. L, millet] **:** a widely distributed genus of grasses having flat leaves, large compound panicles, one-flowered spikelets, and an awnless lemma — see MILLET GRASS **3** *pl* **milia** [NL, fr. L, millet] **:** a small pearly firm noninflammatory elevation of the skin (as of the face) due to retention of oil gland secretion in a gland duct blocked by a thin layer of epithelium — compare COMEDO

mil·jee \ˈmil,jē\ *n* -s [native name in Australia] **:** UMBRELLA BUSH

¹milk \ˈmilk, ˈmiu̇k\ *n* -s [ME, fr. OE *milc, meolc, meoluc*; akin to OHG *miluh* milk, ON *mjolk*, Goth *miluks*; all fr. a prehistoric Gmc noun prob. influenced by the prehistoric Gmc verb represented by OE *melcan* to milk but itself prob. akin to Gk *galakt-, gala* milk; OE *melcan* to milk akin to OHG *melchan*, L *mulgēre*, Gk *amelgein* to milk, Skt *mrjati* he wipes, strokes — more at GALAXY] **1 :** a white or yellowish fluid secreted by the mammary glands of female mammals for the nourishment of their young and holding in suspension fat, protein, sugar, and inorganic salts in varying proportions **2 a :** something that is mild or bland ⟨this drink goes down like ~⟩ ⟨the new general, lanky and amiable, seemed a man of ~ —A.J.Liebling⟩ **b :** something that suggests the relation of mother and child ⟨thy nature . . . too full of the ~ of human kindness —Shak.⟩ **c :** something that suggests an abundance of goodness or blessings ⟨a land flowing with ~ and honey —Josh 5:6 (RSV)⟩ ⟨drunk the ~ of Paradise —S.T.Coleridge⟩ **3 :** a liquid like milk in appearance: as **a :** the latex of a plant **b :** the juice of the coconut **c :** the contents of an unripe kernel of grain **d :** the ripe undischarged spat of an oyster **e :** MILT **f :** an emulsion made by bruising seeds **g :** a suspension of starch or other white powder in water — **in milk :** LACTATING — **in the milk** *of grain* **:** of a milky consistency because of incomplete maturity

²milk \"\ *vb* -ED/-ING/-S [ME *milken, melken*, fr. OE *milcian, meolcian*, fr. *milc, meolc, meoluc*, n.] *vt* **1 :** to press or draw milk from the breasts or udder of by the hand or by a mechanical device **:** withdraw the milk of **2 :** to draw (milk) from the breast or udder ⟨~ wholesome milk from healthy cows⟩ **3 a** *obs* **:** to suck milk from the breast ⟨love the babe that ~*s* me —Shak.⟩ **b :** SUCKLE — now used only of animals ⟨ewe unable to ~ her lamb⟩ **4 :** to draw something from as if by milking: as **a :** to compel or persuade to yield profit or advantage illicitly or to an unreasonable degree ⟨lawyers ~*ing* an estate⟩ **:** EXPLOIT, BLEED ⟨~ an enterprise⟩ ⟨comedian ~*ing* a joke for the last possible laugh⟩ ⟨~ a scene⟩ **b :** to draw out (as information) **:** ELICIT ⟨~ news from a source of information⟩ **c :** to draw venom from (a snake) by inducing to strike **d :** to draw (sap, turpentine) from a tree **5 :** to handle or manipulate in a manner like that of drawing milk from a teat ⟨~ blood along the tube in a blood transfusion⟩ ⟨nervously ~*ing* the fringe of the tablecloth⟩ **6 :** to put milk into ⟨cans of tea, already ~*ed* and sugared —Flora Thompson⟩ **7 :** to shuffle (cards) by drawing one from the top and one from the bottom simultaneously allowing them to fall on the table face down ~ *vi* **1 :** to draw or yield milk ⟨return in time for ~*ing*⟩ ⟨when a cow is ~*ing* heavily⟩ **2 :** to become cloudy or foggy — used with *up* ⟨weather began to ~ up⟩

³milk \"\ *adj* [¹*milk*] **1 :** of, from, or made with milk ⟨~ chowder⟩ **:** producing or dealing with milk ⟨~ route⟩ **2 :** milk-fed ⟨~ animal⟩

milk adder *n* **:** MILK SNAKE

milk-and-water \ˈ=ˈ=ˈ==\ *adj* **:** lacking in vigor and richness **:** WEAK, INSIPID, WISHY-WASHY ⟨*milk-and-water* poetry⟩

milk-and-wine lily \ˈ==ˈ=ˈ==\ *n* **:** a crinum (*Crinum sanderianum*) of tropical western Africa that has narrow leaves and white flowers in umbels of three or four with lanceolate red-

banded recurved petals and that is often cultivated as an ornamental
milk bar *n* **:** a counter or a room having a counter where milk drinks and ice cream are served
milk brother *n* **:** a foster brother
milkbush \ˈ⸗,⸗\ *n* **1 :** an Australian shrub (*Wrightia saligna*) of the family Apocynaceae **2 :** a southern African spurge (*Euphorbia tirucalli*) that resembles a cactus and has milky juice which is used locally to treat syphilis **3** *West Indies* **:** a shrub (*Rauwolfia tetraphylla*) with milky juice
milk chocolate *n* **:** chocolate to which sugar and milk have been added in processing
milk cistern *n* **:** the space at the base of a teat or nipple into which the lactiferous ducts of a mammary gland discharge
milk colic *n* **:** pulpy kidney disease of nursing lambs and kids on pasture
milk cow *n* **:** MILCH COW
milk dentition *n* **:** the set of milk teeth
milk·en \ˈmilkən\ *adj, archaic* **:** MILKY, FOGGY
milk·er \ˈmilkə(r)\ *n* -s [ME, fr. *milken* to milk + *-er*] **1 a :** one that milks **b :** MILKING MACHINE **2 a :** one (as a cow) that gives milk **b :** one (as a tree) that gives a fluid resembling milk
milker's nodules *n pl but sing in constr* **:** a mild virus infection characterized by reddish blue nodules on the hands, arms, face, or neck acquired by direct contact with the udders of cows affected with cowpox
milk fat *n* **:** BUTTERFAT
milk fever *n* **1 :** any of various febrile disorders (as puerperal fever) that follow parturition and are popularly associated with the establishment of lactation **2 a :** a disease of recently calved cows or occasionally sheep or goats that is closely related to or identical with grass tetany and caused by excessive drain on the body mineral reserves during the establishment of the milk flow **b :** ketosis of domestic animals
milkfish \ˈ⸗,⸗\ *n* **1 :** a large active silvery herbivorous food fish (*Chanos chanos*) that is widely distributed in the warm parts of the Pacific and Indian oceans and is the sole living representative of the family Chanidae **2 :** a silvery gray or dusky small-scaled percoid fish (*Parascorpis typus*) of the southern African coastal waters
milk-float \ˈ⸗,⸗\ *n, Brit* **:** a light two-wheeled horse-drawn milk cart
milk fungus *n* **:** a mushroom of the genus *Lactarius*
milk gap *or* **milking gap** *n, South & Midland* **:** an enclosure where cows are milked **:** COW PEN
milk glass *n* **:** opaque glass orig. milky white but later made in many colors
milkgrass \ˈ⸗,⸗\ *n* **:** CORN SALAD
milk gravy *n* **:** gravy made by thickening milk with a blend of flour and fat typically from fried salt pork
milk hedge *n* **:** MILK BUSH 2
milk house *n* **:** a building for cooling, handling, or bottling milk
milkier *comparative of* MILKY
milkiest *superlative of* MILKY
milk ill *n* **:** indigestion and scouring of young lambs associated with unclean housing
milk·i·ly \ˈmilkəlē\ *adv* **:** in a milky manner
milk·i·ness \-kēnəs\ *n* -ES **:** the quality or state of being milky
milking *pres part of* MILK
milking machine *n* **:** a mechanical suction apparatus for milking cows
milking parlor *n* **:** an isolated room or separate building to which cows kept on a loose-housing system are taken for milking
milking shorthorn *n, usu cap M&S* **:** a breed of Shorthorn cattle developed esp. for milk-producing qualities
milking stool *n* **:** a three-legged stool with a half-round shaped seat
milk ipecac *n* **1 :** FLOWERING SPURGE **2 :** SPREADING DOGBANE
milk lamb *n* **:** a lamb fat and ready for market before weaning **:** a milk-fed lamb
milk leg *n* **1 :** postpartum thrombophlebitis of a femoral vein **2 :** a chronic general swelling of the leg of a horse following an attack of lymphangitis

milking stool

milk·less \ˈ⸗ləs\ *adj* **:** having or yielding no milk ⟨~ breasts⟩ **:** having no milky juice ⟨~ fungus⟩
milklike \ˈ⸗,⸗\ *adj* **:** resembling milk **:** MILKY
milk line *n* **:** the line of modified glandular tissue appearing on either side of the body of a mammalian embryo between the base of the front and rear limb buds and giving rise to the mammary glands
milk-livered \ˈ⸗¦⸗⸗\ *adj* **:** COWARDLY, TIMOROUS ⟨*milk-livered* man, that bear'st a cheek for blows —Shak.⟩
milkmaid \ˈ⸗,⸗\ *n* **:** DAIRYMAID
milk·man \ˈ⸗,man, -aa(ə)n, -,mən\ *n, pl* **milkmen 1 :** a man who sells milk or milk products or delivers them to customers **2 :** a man who milks cows
milkman's syndrome *n, usu cap M* [after L. A. *Milkman* b1895 Am. roentgenologist] **:** an abnormal condition marked by porosity of bone and tendency to spontaneous often symmetrical fractures
milk molar *n* **:** one of the deciduous molar teeth of mammals that are shed and replaced by the premolars
milk mushroom *n* **:** MILK FUNGUS
milk·ness *n* -ES [ME, fr. ¹*milk* + *-ness*] *chiefly Scot* **:** yield of milk
milk of almonds : ALMOND MILK
milk of bismuth : a thick white suspension of bismuth hydroxide and bismuth subcarbonate in water used esp. in the treatment of diarrhea
milk of lime : a suspension of calcium hydroxide or hydrated lime in water — compare LIMEWATER
milk of magnesia : a milk-white suspension of magnesium hydroxide in water used as an antacid and laxative
milk of sulfur : PRECIPITATED SULFUR
milk parsley *n* **:** a Eurasian herb (*Peucedanum palustre*) having an acrid milky juice
milk pea *n* **:** a leguminous plant of the genus *Galactia* (esp. *G. regularis*)
milk plant *n* **:** CAUSTIC CREEPER
milk plasma *n* **:** the fluid part of milk comprising the dissolved casein, proteins, and minerals and excluding the suspended butterfat
milk powder *n* **:** DRIED MILK
milk punch *n* **:** a mixed drink consisting of an alcoholic liquor (as rum, whiskey), milk, and sugar served iced and flavored with nutmeg
milk purslane *n* **:** any of several spurges of the genus *Euphorbia*
milk run *n* [so called fr. the resemblance in regularity and uneventfulness to the morning delivery of milk] **:** a regularly recurrent aerial bombing or search mission orig. of the early morning and expected to be without danger
milks *pl of* MILK, *pres 3d sing of* MILK
milk safe *n* **:** a cupboard with pierced tin panels formerly used for storing milk
milk shake *n* **:** milk and a flavoring syrup sometimes with added ice cream shaken up and down in a hand shaker or blended in an electric mixer
milkshed \ˈ⸗,⸗\ *n* [¹*milk* + *shed* (divide)] **:** a region furnishing milk to a particular community
milksick \ˈ⸗,⸗\ *n* **:** MILK SICKNESS
milk sickness *n* **1 :** an acute disease characterized by weakness, vomiting, and constipation and caused by eating the dairy products or meat of cattle poisoned by various plants — compare TREMBLE 3 **2 :** TREMBLE 3
milk snail *n* **:** a pulmonate snail (*Helix lactea* or *Otala lactea*) with a pure white shell native to the dry parts of the Mediterranean region but introduced to several parts of the New World where it is sometimes a serious pest of cultivated plants
milk snake *n* **:** KING SNAKE; *esp* **:** a common harmless snake (*Lampropeltis triangulum*) that is grayish or tan with black-bordered brown blotches and an arrow-shaped occipital spot, occurs from Canada to Mexico, and is popularly believed to frequent milk houses to drink milk though in fact it preys upon the mice infesting such places
milk·sop \ˈ⸗,säp\ *n* [ME, fr. ¹*milk* + *sop*] **1 :** a piece of bread sopped in milk **2 :** an effeminate or unmanly man **:** MOLLYCODDLE ⟨that our writers are a lot of school-marmish ~s —*Times Lit. Supp.*⟩
milk·sop·ping \-piŋ\ *adj* **:** MILKSOPPY
milk·sop·py \-pē\ *adj* **:** resembling or of the nature of a milksop **:** WEAK, VAPID
milkstone \ˈ⸗,⸗\ *n* **1 a :** a stone (as galactite) believed to increase milk secretion **b :** any of various white stones (as a flint pebble) **2 :** a hard body that forms in the bovine udder **3 :** a hard deposit of milk residues that accumulates on imperfectly cleansed dairy utensils and serves as a substrate for bacteria and contributes off-flavors to milk
milk sugar *n* **:** LACTOSE
milk thistle *n* [ME *mylkthystel*, fr. *mylk*, *milk* milk + *thystel*, *thistel* thistle] **1 :** a tall thistle (*Silybum marianum*) that has large clasping white-blotched leaves and large purple flower heads with bristly receptacles and is native to southern Europe but adventive or naturalized in No. America and many other areas **2 :** MILKWEED e(2)
milk toast *n* **:** hot usu. buttered toast served in hot milk and sweetened with sugar or seasoned with salt and pepper
milk-toast \ˈ⸗,⸗\ *adj* [*milk toast*] **:** lacking in boldness or vigor **:** MILD, INOFFENSIVE ⟨~ policy of dealing with criminals⟩
milk tooth *n* **:** a temporary deciduous tooth of a mammal; *esp* **:** one of man's set of temporary deciduous teeth consisting of four incisors, two canines, and four molars in each jaw
milk train *n* **1 :** a local train that stops at all or most points benefiting principally the dairy farmers who make daily shipments of milk **2 :** a slow train making numerous stops
milk tree *n* **:** any of several trees esp. of *Brosimum*, *Mimusops*, and *Couma* having abundant latex; *specif* **:** COW TREE 1
milk vein *n* **:** a large subcutaneous vein that extends along the lower side of the abdomen of a cow and returns blood from the udder and is often supposed to be an index of milking qualities — see COW illustration
milk vetch *n* **1 :** a bright green prostrate perennial Old World herb (*Astragalus glycyphyllos*) that has sulfur yellow flowers in dense spikes and is popularly supposed to increase the milk yield of goats **2 :** any of various plants (as members of the genera *Astragalus*, *Geoprumnon*, and *Phaca*) that are related to the common milk vetch and that include some which are highly poisonous to livestock — compare LOCOWEED
milk-warm \ˈ⸗¦⸗\ *adj* [ME *mylke warme*, fr. *mylke*, *milk* milk + *warme*, *warm* warm] **:** as warm as fresh-drawn milk **:** LUKEWARM
milkweed \ˈ⸗,⸗\ *n* **:** any of several plants that secrete latex: as **a :** a plant of the family Asclepiadaceae; *specif* **:** one of the genus *Asclepias* **b :** a plant of the genus *Euphorbia* **c :** a plant of the genus *Lactuca* **d :** DOGBANE 1 **e** *Brit* (1) **:** MILK PARSLEY (2) **:** an annual sow thistle (*Sonchus oleraceus*) having leaves with soft spiny teeth
milkweed bug *n* **:** a bug feeding on milkweed; *esp* **:** a large black red-marked bug (*Oncopeltus fasciatus*) now cultured widely as a research organism
milkweed butterfly *n* **:** MONARCH 3
milkweed family *n* **:** ASCLEPIADACEAE
milk well *n* **:** one of the passages through the abdominal wall of a cow by which the milk veins pass into the abdomen
milk white *n* [ME *milc-whit*, fr. OE *meolchwīt*, fr. *meolc* milk + *hwīt* white] **:** a yellowish white that is less strong and slightly greener and lighter than average shell tint — compare SKIMMED-MILK WHITE
milk willow herb *n* **1 :** either of two loosestrifes (*Lythrum salicaria* and *L. alatum*) **2 :** SWAMP LOOSESTRIFE
milkwood \ˈ⸗,⸗\ *n* **:** any of several trees or shrubs having abundant latex: as **a :** a moraceous tree (*Pseudolmedia spuria*) of tropical America **b :** a tree (*Sapium laurofolium*) of Jamaica that resembles a cactus — called also *Jamaica milkwood* **c :** a West Indian poisonous shrub (*Rauwolfia canescens*) **d :** a timber tree (*Sideroxylon inerme*) of southern Africa **e** *Austral* **:** PAPERBARK
milkwort \ˈ⸗,⸗\ *n* **1 :** a plant of the genus *Polygala; esp* **:** a European plant (*P. vulgaris*) formerly reputed to promote human lactation **2 :** a plant of the genus *Campanula* **3 :** SEA MILKWORT
milkwort family *n* **:** POLYGALACEAE
milky \ˈmilkē, -ki\ *adj* -ER/-EST [ME, fr. ¹*milk* + *-y*] **1 :** like or suggestive of milk in color or consistency ⟨~ skin⟩ ⟨~ sap of a cactus⟩; *specif* **:** whitish and turbid ⟨~ water of a mountain torrent⟩ ⟨~ quartz⟩ **2 :** MILD, GENTLE, TAME, SPIRITLESS, EFFEMINATE, TIMOROUS ⟨has friendship such a faint and ~ heart —Shak.⟩ **3 a :** consisting of, containing, or abounding in milk ⟨pails high foaming with a ~ flood —Alexander Pope⟩ **b :** yielding milk; *specif* **:** having the characteristics of a good milk producer **4** *of an oyster* **:** SPAWNING
milky disease *n* **:** a highly fatal disease of Japanese beetle larvae and other scarabaeid grubs due to bacilli (*Bacillus popilliae* and related species) that invade the circulation, multiply, and sporulate in great numbers to give a characteristic opaque milky look to the infected larva
milky mangrove *n* **:** BLIND-YOUR-EYES
milky way *n* [ME, trans. of L *via lactea*] **1** *usu cap M&W* **:** a broad luminous irregular band of light stretching completely around the celestial sphere, visible only at night, and caused by the light of myriads of faint stars; *specif* **:** MILKY WAY GALAXY **2 :** GALAXY
milky way galaxy *also* **milky way system** *n, usu cap M&W* **:** the galaxy of which the sun and the solar system are a part and which contains the myriads of stars that comprise the Milky Way together with all the individual stars, clusters, bright and dark nebulosities seen in the sky
¹**mill** \ˈmil\ *n* -s *often attrib* [ME *mille*, fr. OE *mylen;* akin to OHG *muli*, *mulin* mill, ON *mylna;* all fr. a prehistoric NGmc-WGmc word borrowed fr. LL *molina*, *molinum* mill, fr. fem. and neut. of *molinus* of a mill, of a millstone, fr. L *mola* mill, millstone + *-inus* -ine; akin to L *molere* to grind — more at MEAL] **1 :** a building provided with machinery for grinding grain into flour ⟨the never-failing brook, the busy ~ —Oliver Goldsmith⟩ ⟨~ sluice⟩ ⟨the ~ cannot grind with water that is past⟩ **2 a :** a machine for grinding grain **:** QUERN ⟨two shall be grinding at the ~ —Mt 24:41 (RSV)⟩ **b :** a machine for crushing or comminuting some substance ⟨coffee ~⟩ ⟨bone ~⟩ ⟨curd ~⟩ **c :** machinery for the hulling, cleaning, scouring, and polishing of rice kernels **d :** a factory or a machine for reducing hay to meal suitable for poultry and other stock **3 :** a machine that manufactures by the continuous repetition of some simple action ⟨operating a stamp ~⟩ ⟨a pulverizing ~⟩ **4 :** a building or collection of buildings with machinery by which the processes of manufacturing are carried on ⟨textile ~⟩ ⟨fulling ~⟩ ⟨paper ~⟩ ⟨~ hands were laid off⟩ **5 a :** a screw press formerly used for stamping coins that raised and marked or serrated the edge as it struck the coin **b :** a machine for expelling juice from vegetable tissues by pressure or grinding ⟨cider ~⟩ ⟨cane ~⟩ **c :** a machine for polishing ⟨a lapidary ~⟩ **6 :** an institution or office that turns out products in the manner of a factory or machine ⟨diploma ~⟩ ⟨propaganda ~⟩ **7** [²*mill*] **a :** a mass of people or animals moving in a circle or without clear direction ⟨turned the leaders of the stampede so as to form a ~⟩ **b :** a boxing match **c :** a folk-dance design usu. formed by two couples in which each dancer joins right or left hands with the one diagonally opposite and all move in a circle to right or left — called also *star, wagon wheel* **8 :** TREADMILL **9** *Scot* **:** a snuffbox esp. with apparatus for pulverizing tobacco **10 a :** a slow or laborious process or routine ⟨legislative ~⟩ **b :** an experience or process that has a marked effect (as of hardening, disciplining, disillusioning) on the character or personality — usu. used in the phrase *through the mill* ⟨through the ~ of higher education⟩ **11 a :** a hardened steel roller having a design in relief used for imprinting a reversed copy of the design in a softer metal (as copper) **b :** MILLING MACHINE, MILLING CUTTER **12 :** ²MORRIS — used with *the* **13** *slang* **a :** the engine of an automobile or boat **b :** TYPEWRITER
²**mill** \"\ *vb* -ED/-ING/-S *vt* **1 :** to subject to some operation or process in a mill **:** shape or finish by means of a mill or machine: as **a :** to full (cloth) in a fulling mill **b :** to grind into flour, meal, or powder **c :** to hull (seeds) by using a mill **d :** to shape or dress (as metal) by means of a rotary cutter **:** to make (as a key seat) with such a cutter **e :** to stamp (a coin) in a screw press **f :** to pass (soap chips) through a roller mill in the manufacture of toilet soap or soap flakes ⟨French ~*ed* soap⟩ **g :** to mix and condition (as rubber) by passing between rotating rolls **h :** to roll (as steel) into bars **i :** to crush or grind (ore) in a mill **2 :** to give a raised rim to (a coin) by a machine operation on the coin blank before striking **3 :** to make frothy by churning or whipping ⟨~ chocolate⟩ **4 :** to beat with the fists **:** THRASH, SLUG **5 :** to turn or guide (as cattle) into a circular course **6 a :** to make ridges or corrugations on the edge of (a coin) by pressure against a corrugated collar at the time of striking **b :** to cut grooves or crosshatching in the metal surface of (a knob or a finger nut) to aid gripping **:** KNURL **7 :** to saw and dress (timber) in a sawmill ~ *vi* **1 :** to hit out with the fists; *esp* **:** to slug furiously ⟨the match was mostly rough-and-tumble ~*ing*⟩ **2 a** *of cattle* **:** to move or stampede in a circle **b :** to move in an eddying or disorderly mass ⟨rioters ~*ing* about in the streets⟩ ⟨crowd ~*ing* in the theater lobby⟩ **3** *of a whale* **:** to swim suddenly in a new direction **4 :** to undergo milling or hulling ⟨seeds was too wet to ~ properly⟩
³**mill** \"\ *vt* -ED/-ING/-S [perh. fr. ²*mill*] *archaic* **:** to break into or rob (a house)
⁴**mill** \"\ *n* -s [L *mille* thousand — more at MILE] **:** a unit of monetary value equal to $\frac{1}{1000}$ U.S. dollar or $\frac{1}{10}$ cent
mill *abbr* million
mil·la \ˈmilə, ˈmē(y)ə\ *n, cap* [NL, fr. J. *Milla*, 18th cent. Span. horticulturist] **:** a small genus of tropical American cormose herbs (family Liliaceae) that are sometimes cultivated for their showy flowers — see FROST FLOWER
mill·able \ˈmiləbəl\ *adj* **:** suitable for cutting up in a sawmill ⟨acres of ~ forest⟩
mill addition *n* **:** insoluble materials added to frit before grinding in the preparation of a slip for glaze or enamel — called also *mill material*
mill·age \ˈmilij, -lēj\ *n* -s **:** a rate (as of taxation) expressed in mills per dollar
mill agent *n* **:** the responsible local executive at a mill controlled by absentee ownership
mill bill *n* **:** an adz for dressing millstones
mill blank *n* **:** a combination paperboard typically with liners of good grade and cheap filler
millboard \ˈ⸗,⸗\ *n* [alter. of *milled board*, fr. milled (past part. of ²*mill*) + *board*] **:** strong heavy hard paperboard suitable for lining book covers and for paneling in furniture
mill cake *n* **1 :** the incorporated materials for gunpowder in the form of a dense mass or cake **2 :** oil cake obtained by milling
mill construction *n* **:** wooden building construction designed to procure the greatest possible protection against fire without actual fireproofing by disposing of the timberwork in solid masses without boxed-up hollow places and by supporting the flooring directly on girders and brick walls
millcourse \ˈ⸗,⸗\ *n* **:** MILLRACE
milldam \ˈ⸗,⸗\ *n* [ME *milndam*, fr. *miln*, *mille* mill + *dam*] **:** a dam to make a millpond; *also* **:** MILLPOND
mill drop *n* **:** a textile product of a discontinued pattern
mil·le \ˈmi(,)lē\ *n* -s [L — more at MILE] **:** THOUSAND — used chiefly in *per mille* ⟨a ratio of 1068 females per ~ males⟩
mill edge *n* **:** an edge of a sheet of paper or a book page cut by the slitting machine but not evenly trimmed
mille-feuille \mēlfœy\ *n, pl* **mille-feuilles** \"\ [F, fr. *mille* thousand (fr. L) + *feuille* leaf, fr. L *folia*, pl. of *folium* leaf — more at BLOW] **:** NAPOLEON 4
mil·le·fi·o·ri *also* **mil·le·fi·o·re** \,miləfēˈōrē\ *n* -s [It, fr. *mille* thousand (fr. L) + *fiori* flowers, pl. of *fiore*, fr. L *flor-*, *flos* flower — more at BLOW] **:** ornamental glass usu. of a floral pattern produced by cutting cross sections of fused bundles of glass rods of various colors and sizes and often embedding them in clear glass
mille·fleur *or* **mille·fleurs** \(ˈ)mēl¦flər-, -flü(ə)r\ *adj* [F *mille-fleurs*] **:** having an allover pattern of small flowers and plants ⟨~ tapestry⟩
mille fleur \"\ *n, usu cap M&F* [F *mille-fleurs*] **1 :** a breed of bantam chickens with compact body, feathered shanks, and large ear muffs **2** *pl* **mille fleurs :** a bird of the Mille Fleur breed
mille·fleurs \"\ *n pl but sing in constr* [F *mille-fleurs*, fr. *mille* thousand (fr. L) + *fleurs* flowers, pl. of *fleur*, fr. L *flor-*, *flos* flower] **:** a perfume made from extracts of several flowers
mille·grain \ˈmil,grān\ *adj* [F *mille* + *grain*] *of a gem setting* **:** having the edge shaped into a fine beading
¹**mil·le·nar·i·an** \¦milə¦na(a)rēən\ *adj* [LL *millenarius* of a thousand + E *-an*] **1 :** of or relating to 1000 years **2 a :** relating to the millennium, millenarianism, or the millenarians **b :** believing in the millennium
²**millenarian** \"\ *n* -s **:** one that believes in a millennium **:** CHILIAST
mil·le·nar·ian·ism \-,nizəm\ *n* -s **:** belief in the millennium of Christian prophecy
mil·le·nar·ist \ˈ⸗⸗,nerəst\ *n* -s [¹*millenary* + *-ist*] **:** MILLENARIAN
¹**mil·le·nary** \ˈmilə,nerē, məˈlenərē, -ri\ *n* -ES [LL *millenarium* millennium, fr. neut. of *millenarius* of a thousand] **1 a :** a group of 1000 units or things **b :** 1000 years **:** MILLENNIUM **2** [ML *millenarius*, fr. LL *millenarius*, adj.] **:** MILLENARIAN **3 :** a 1000th anniversary or its celebration
²**millenary** \"\ *adj* [LL *millenarius* of a thousand, fr. L *milleni* one thousand each (fr. *mille* thousand) + *-arius* -ary] **1 a :** relating to or consisting of 1000 (as 1000 years) **b :** being in command of 1000 men **2 :** relating to the millennium or millenarians **:** MILLENNIAL
mill end *n* **:** a mill remnant of cloth
¹**mil·len·ni·al** \məˈlenēəl\ *adj* [*millennium* + *-al*] **1 :** relating to a millennium **2 :** of, belonging to, or relating to the millennium of Christian prophecy
²**millennial** \"\ *n* -s **:** a 1000th anniversary or its celebration
millennial church *n, usu cap M&C* **:** the church of the Shakers
millennial dawn·ist \-ˈdȯnəst, -ˈdän-\ *n, usu cap M&D* [*Millennial Dawn* (1886), book by Charles T. Russell †1916 Am. religious leader + E *-ist*] **:** RUSSELLITE
mil·len·ni·al·ism \məˈlenēə,lizəm\ *n* -s **:** a doctrine that the prophecy in the book of Revelation will be fulfilled with an earthly millennium of universal peace and the triumph of righteousness
mil·len·ni·al·ist \-,ləst\ *n* -s **:** MILLENARIAN
mil·len·ni·al·ly \-əlē, -li\ *adv* **1 :** during 1000 years **:** in terms of thousands of years ⟨~ old customs⟩ **2 :** in a manner of or suggesting the millennium
¹**mil·len·ni·an** \-ēən\ *n* -s [*millennium* + *-an*, n. suffix] **:** MILLENARIAN
²**millennian** \"\ *adj* [*millennium* + *-an*, adj. suffix] **:** of or relating to a millennium
mil·len·ni·ary \-,erē, -ri\ *adj* [*millennium* + *-ary*] **:** MILLENNIAL
mil·len·ni·um \məˈlenēəm\ *n, pl* **millen·nia** \-ēə\ *or* **millenniums** [NL, fr. L *mille* thousand + *-ennium* (as in *biennium* period of two years) — more at BIENNIAL] **1 a :** a period of 1000 years ⟨records dating back several *millennia*⟩ **b :** a 1000th anniversary or its celebration **2 a :** the thousand years mentioned in Revelation 20 during which holiness is to be triumphant and Christ is to reign on earth **b :** a period of prevailing virtue or great happiness or perfect government or freedom from familiar ills and imperfections of human existence
millepede *also* **milleped** *var of* MILLIPEDE
mil·le·po·ra \,miləˈpōrə, məˈlepərə\ *n, cap* [NL, fr. L *mille* thousand + NL *-pora*] **:** a genus of corals comprising the recent millepores
mil·le·pore \ˈmilə,pō(ə)r\ *n* [NL *Millepora*] **:** any of the stony hydrozoan reef-building corals comprising the order Milleporina with the single recent genus *Millepora* and like the madrepores with which they constitute the major reef-building corals assuming a variety of branching, encrusting, or massive forms though differing from the madrepores in passing through a free-swimming medusoid stage
mil·le·po·ri·na \,miləpəˈrīnə, -rēnə\ *n pl, cap* [NL, fr. *Millepora* + *-ina*] **:** an order of Hydrozoa comprising reef-building stony corals — see MILLEPORE
mil·le·po·rite \ˈ⸗⸗,pȯr,īt, ,⸗⸗ˈ⸗,⸗\ *n* -s [ISV *millepore* + *-ite*] **:** a fossil millepore
mill·er \ˈmilə(r)\ *n* -s [ME *millere*, fr. *mille* mill + *-ere* -er]

1 : one that operates a mill; *specif* **:** one that grinds grain into flour **2 a :** any of various moths having powdery wings **b :** EAGLE RAY **c :** the male hen harrier **d** *dial Eng* **:** a young spotted flycatcher **e** *dial Eng* **:** WHITETHROAT 1 **3 a :** MILLING MACHINE **b :** a tool for use in a milling machine **4 :** SOIL MILLER

mil·ler-ab·bott tube \ˈmilə(r)ˈabət-\ *n, usu cap M&A* [after Thomas Grier *Miller* †1886 Am. physician and William Osler *Abbott* †1943 Am. physician] **:** a double-lumen balloon-tipped rubber tube used for the purpose of decompression in treating intestinal obstruction

miller index *n, usu cap M* [after William Hallowes *Miller* †1880 Eng. mineralogist] **:** any of a set of three numbers or letters used to indicate the position of a face or internal plane of a crystal and determined on the basis of the reciprocal of the intercept of the face or plane on the crystallographic axes

mil·ler·ing \ˈmiləriŋ, -rēŋ\ *n* -s **:** the occupation or business of a miller

mil·ler·ism \-,rizəm\ *n* -s *usu cap* [William *Miller* †1849 Am. sectarian leader + E *-ism*] **:** the doctrines of the Millerites

¹mil·ler·ite \-,rīt\ *n* -s *usu cap* [William *Miller* †1849 + E *-ite*] **:** a believer in the doctrine of the American preacher William Miller who taught that the end of the world and the second coming of Christ were at hand and who specif. predicted that this would occur in 1843

²millerite \"\ *n* -s [G *millerit*, fr. William Hallowes *Miller* †1880 Eng. mineralogist + G *-it* -ite] **:** sulfide of nickel NiS generally occurring in capillary crystals

miller's itch *n* **:** GROCER'S ITCH

miller's-thumb \ˈ==,=\ *n, pl* **miller's-thumbs** [ME *myllarys thowmbe*, fr. *myllarys, milleres* (gen. of *myllar, millere* miller) + *thowmbe, thombe* thumb] **1 :** any of several small fresh-water spiny-finned sculpins (genus *Cottus*) of Europe (as *C. gobio*) and No. America **2** *dial Eng* **:** any of several small birds (as the goldcrest or the willow warbler)

milles *pl of* MILLE

¹mil·les·i·mal \məˈlesəməl\ *n* -s [L *millesimus*, adj., thousandth + E *-al* (as in *decimal*, n.)] **:** THOUSANDTH

²millesimal \"\ *adj* [L *millesimus*, adj., thousandth (fr. *mille* thousand) + E *-al*, adj. suffix — more at MILE] **:** consisting of or concerned with thousandths ⟨~ fractions⟩ — **mil·les·i·mal·ly** \-məlē\ *adv*

¹mil·let \ˈmilət, *usu* -əd·+V\ *n* -s [ME *milet*, fr. MF, fr. *mil* millet (fr. L *milium*) + *-et*; akin to Gk *melinē* millet and prob. to OE *melu* meal — more at MEAL] **1 :** any of various small-seeded annual cereal and forage grasses that produce abundant foliage and fibrous root systems: **a :** a grass (*Panicum miliaceum*) extensively cultivated in Europe and Asia for its grain which is used both as an article of diet for man and as a food for birds and in the U.S. sometimes grown for hay **b :** any of several grasses of genera closely related to *Panicum* (as *Echinochloa, Setaria, Pennisetum, Eleusine*, and *Sorghum*) **2 :** the seed or grain of any of these grasses

²mil·let \məˈlet\ *n* -s [Turk, nation, people, body of coreligionists, fr. Ar *millah* religion] **:** a non-Muslim group or community in Turkey organized under a religious head of its own who also exercises civil functions of importance

millet disease *n* **:** a chronic disease resembling osteoporosis of the bones of horses largely fed with millet

millet grass *n* **1 :** a grass of the genus *Milium*; *esp* **:** a tall woodland grass (*M. effusum*) found throughout the north temperate zone **2 :** AUSTRALIAN MILLET

millet-seed sand \ˈ==,=-\ *n* **:** sand that consists of smoothly rounded grains about the size of a millet seed and is generally indicative of prolonged eolian action

mil·let·tia \məˈled·ēə\ *n, cap* [NL, fr. Charles *Millett*, 19th cent. Eng. official in the Far East + NL *-ia*] **:** a genus of trees and shrubs (family Leguminosae) found in the Old World tropics and having showy streaked dark reddish or chocolate-colored wood

millfeed \ˈ=,=\ *n* **:** the by-products (as bran, shorts, middlings) of the milling of wheat flour used for feeding livestock

mill fever *n* [¹*mill*] **:** BYSSINOSIS

mill file *n* [¹*mill* + *file*; fr. its use for filing the saws of a cotton gin] **:** a single-cut tapered or blunt file

mill files

mill finish *n* **:** MACHINE FINISH — abbr. *MF*

mill head *n* **:** the head of water employed to turn a mill wheel

mill-headed \ˈ=ˈ==\ *also* **mill-head** \ˈ=ˈ=\ *adj* **:** having a milled head ⟨*mill-headed* watch stem⟩

mill hole *n* **1 :** GLORY HOLE 4 **2 :** an excavation adjacent to mine workings to obtain waste rock for filling stopes

millhouse \ˈ=,=\ *n* [ME *myllehowse*, fr. *mylle, mille* mill + *howse, hous* house] **:** a building that houses milling machinery

milli- *comb form* [F *milli-*, fr. L *milli-, mili-* thousand, fr. *mille* — more at MILE] **:** thousandth — esp. in terms belonging to the metric system ⟨*millig*ram⟩ ⟨*milli*bar⟩ ⟨*milli*meter⟩

mil·li·ammeter \ˈmilē+\ *n* [short for earlier *milliamperemeter* (ISV *milliampere* + *-meter*)] **:** an instrument for measuring electric currents in milliamperes — compare AMMETER

mil·li·amp \"+,-\ *n* [by shortening] **:** MILLIAMPERE

mil·li·ampere \"+\ *n* [ISV *milli-* + *ampere*] **:** one thousandth of an ampere

mil·li·angstrom \"+\ *n* [*milli-* + *angstrom*] **:** one thousandth of an angstrom

mil·liard \ˈmil,yärd, -lē,ärd\ *n* -s *often attrib* [F, fr. MF *miliart*, fr. *mili-* (fr. *milion, million* million) + *-ard, -art* -ard] *Brit* **:** a thousand millions — see NUMBER table

mil·li·ary \ˈmilē,erē\ *adj* [L *milliarius, miliarius* consisting of a thousand, one mile long, fr. *milli-, mili-* (fr. *mille* thousand) + *-arius* -ary — more at MILE] **:** marking the distance of a mile

mil·li·bar \ˈmilə+,-\ *n* [ISV *milli-* + *bar*; orig. formed in G] **:** a unit of atmospheric pressure equal to $\frac{1}{1000}$ bar or 1000 dynes per square centimeter

mil·li·barn \"+,-\ *n* [*milli-* + *barn*] **:** a unit of nuclear cross section equal to $\frac{1}{1000}$ barn

mil·li·cron \ˈmilə,krän, -krən\ *n* -s [*milli-* + *micron*] **:** MILLIMICRON

mil·li·curie \ˈmilə+\ *n* [ISV *milli-* + *curie*] **:** one thousandth of a curie

mil·li·darcy \"+\ *n* [*milli-* + *darcy*] **:** a unit of porous permeability equal to $\frac{1}{1000}$ darcy

mil·li·degree \"+\ *n* [*milli-* + *degree*] **:** a unit of temperature equal to $\frac{1}{1000}$ degree

mil·lieme \(ˈ)mē(l)ˈyem\ *n* -s [F *millième* thousandth, fr. MF *millieme*, fr. *mille* thousand, fr. L] **1 :** a unit of value equal to one thousandth of a basic monetary unit (as in Egypt and Sudan and formerly in Libya $\frac{1}{1000}$ pound) **2 :** an Egyptian or Libyan coin representing one millieme

mil·li·equivalent \ˈmilē+\ *n* [*milli-* + *equivalent*] **:** one thousandth of an equivalent of a chemical element, radical, or compound

mil·li·farad \ˈmilə+\ *n* [*milli-* + *farad*] **:** one thousandth of a farad

mil·li·gal \ˈmilə+,-\ *n* [ISV *milli-* + *gal*] **:** a unit of acceleration equivalent to $\frac{1}{1000}$ gal or 10 microns per second per second that is approximately one millionth of normal acceleration of gravity at the earth's surface

mil·li·gram \ˈmilə,gram, -aa(ə)m\ *n* [F *milligramme*, fr. *milli-* + *gramme* gram — more at GRAM] **:** a metric unit of mass and weight equal to $\frac{1}{1000}$ gram — see METRIC SYSTEM table

milligram-hour \ˈ==,=ˈ=\ *n* **:** a unit in which the therapeutic dosage of radium is expressed and which consists in exposure to the action of one milligram of radium for one hour

mil·li·henry \ˈmilə+\ *n* [ISV *milli-* + *henry*] **:** one thousandth of a henry

mil·li·lambert \"+\ *n* [*milli-* + *lambert*] **:** one thousandth of a lambert

mil·li·liter \"+\ *n* [F *millilitre*, fr. *milli-* + *litre* liter — more at LITER] **:** a metric unit of capacity equal to $\frac{1}{1000}$ liter — see METRIC SYSTEM table

mil·li·lux \ˈ==+,-\ *n* [*milli-* + *lux*] **:** one thousandth of a lux

mil·lime \məˈlēm\ *n* -s [modif. (influenced by F *millième* thousandth) of Ar *mallīm*, fr. F *millième* — more at MILLIEME] **1 :** a Tunisian monetary unit equal to $\frac{1}{1000}$ dinar — see MONEY table **2 :** a coin representing one millime

mil·li·meter \ˈmilə,+\ *n* [F *millimètre*, fr. *milli-* + *mètre* meter — more at METER] **:** a metric unit of length equal to $\frac{1}{1000}$ meter — abbr. *mm.*; see METRIC SYSTEM table

mil·li·met·ric \ˌ==ˈme·trik\ *adj* [ISV *millimeter* + *-ic*] **:** of a magnitude measured in millimeters **:** MINUTE ⟨~ distinctions⟩

mil·li·micron \"+\ *n* [ISV *milli-* + *micron*] **:** a unit of length (as for light waves) equal to one thousandth of a micron or one millionth of a millimeter **:** MICROMILLIMETER — symbol *mμ*

mil·li·microsecond \"+\ *n* [*milli-* + *microsecond*] **:** one thousandth of a microsecond or one billionth of a second

mil·li·mol·ar \ˌmiləˈmōlə(r)\ *adj* [*millimole* + *-ar*] **:** of, relating to, or containing a millimole — **mil·li·mo·lar·i·ty** \-məˈlarəd·ē\ *n*

mil·li·mole \ˈmilə,mōl\ *n* [ISV *milli-* + *mole*] **:** one thousandth of a mole

mil·line \ˈmilˈlīn\ *n* [blend of *million* and *line*] **1 :** a unit of space and circulation equivalent to one agate line appearing in one million copies of a publication **2** *or* **milline rate :** the cost of one milline figured by multiplying the actual cost of one line by a million and dividing by the circulation

mil·li·ner \ˈmilənə(r)\ *n* -s [irreg. fr. *Milan*, city in northern Italy + E *-er*; fr. the importation of women's finery into England from Italy in the 16th century] **:** one who designs, makes, trims, or sells women's hats

mil·li·nery \-,nerē, -ri\ *n* -ES [*milliner* + *-y*] **1 :** the articles made or sold by milliners; *esp* **:** women's headwear **2 :** the business or work of a milliner

milling *n* -s [fr. gerund of ²*mill*] **:** a corrugated edge on a coin

milling cutter *n* **:** a rotary tool-steel cutter used in a milling machine for shaping and dressing metal surfaces

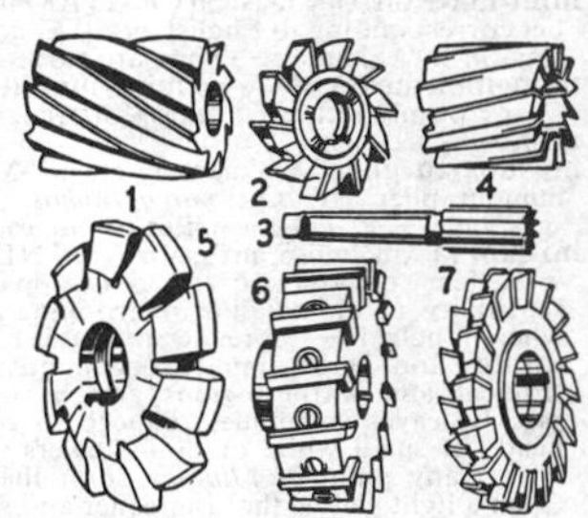

milling cutters: *1* plain, *2* side, *3* end mill, *4* spiral shell end mill, *5* gear, *6* face with inserted teeth, *7* interlocking

milling dye *or* **milling acid dye** *n* **:** an acid dye that is fast to fulling on wool — see DYE table I

milling-in-transit *n* \ˈ===ˈ==\ **:** an arrangement by which a through shipment may be detained at an intermediate point usu. for the application of some manufacturing process (as conversion of wheat into flour) with or without increase of freight charge by the carrier — compare FABRICATION-IN-TRANSIT

milling machine *n* **:** a machine tool on which work usu. of metal secured to a carriage is shaped by being fed against rotating milling cutters — called also *miller*

mil·li·normal \ˌmilə+\ *adj* [*milli-* + *normal*] **:** thousandth normal ⟨~ solution⟩

¹mil·lion \ˈmilyən, ˈmiy-\ *n, pl* **millions** *or* **million** [ME *million, milioun*, fr. MF *milion*, fr. OIt *milione*, aug. of *mille* thousand, fr. L — more at MILE] **1 :** 1000 thousand **:** 100,000 times 10 — see NUMBER table **2 a :** one million units or objects ⟨a total of a ~⟩ **b :** a group or set of a million **3 :** the numerable quantity symbolized by the arabic numerals 1,000,000 **4 :** a very large or indefinitely great number ⟨~*s* of mosquitoes poured into the tent⟩ **5 :** the mass of common people

²million \"\ *adj* **1 :** being one million in number ⟨a ~ years⟩ **2 :** being very great in number ⟨a ~ questions⟩ — usu. preceded by *a* or a numeral (as *one, four*)

mil·lion·aire \ˌmilyəˈna(a)(ə)r, ˌmiy-, -ne(ə)r, -na(a)ə, -neə, ˈ==,=\ *n* -s [F *millionnaire*, fr. *million*, fr. MF *milion*] **:** one whose wealth is estimated at a million or millions (as of dollars)

mil·lion·aire·dom \-dəm\ *n* -s **:** the state of being a millionaire; *collectively* **:** the millionaires of a society or of the world **:** the world of the very rich

mil·lion·air·ess \-rəs\ *n* -ES **:** a female who is a millionaire or the wife of a millionaire

mil·lion·air·ism \-,rizəm\ *n* -s **:** existence or dominating influence of millionaires

¹mil·lion·ary \ˈmilyə,nerē, ˈmiy-\ *adj* [¹*million* + *-ary*] **:** having a million or millions of money

²millionary \"\ *n* -ES **:** MILLIONAIRE

mil·lioned \ˈmilyənd, ˈmiy-\ *adj* **1 :** numbered by millions **:** INNUMERABLE **2 :** having a million or millions of money

mil·lion·fold \ˌmilyənˈfōld, ˌmiy-\ *adv* [¹*million* + *-fold*] **:** by 1,000,000 times — usu. preceded by *a* or a numeral

mil·lion·ism \ˈmilyə,nizəm, ˈmiy-\ *n* -s **:** MILLIONAIRISM

mil·lions \ˈmilyənz, ˈmiy-\ *also* **millions fish** *or* **million fish** *n pl but sing or pl in constr* [so called fr. the rapidity with which it reproduces] **:** GUPPY

¹mil·lionth \ˈmilyən(t)th, ˈmiy-\ *adj* **1 a :** being number one million in a countable series — see NUMBER table **b :** being one of a million equal parts into which something is divisible **2 :** constructed or drawn on a scale of one millionth of the natural size ⟨a ~ map⟩ ⟨a ~ globe⟩

²millionth \"\ *n, pl* **millionths** \-yən(t)s, -yən(t)ths\ **1 :** number one million in a countable series **2 :** the quotient of a unit divided by one million **:** one of a million equal parts of something

mil·li·pede *or* **mil·le·pede** \ˈmilə,pēd\ *also* **mil·li·ped** \-ped\ *n* -s [L *millepeda*, a small crawling animal, perh. the wood louse, fr. *mille* thousand + *-peda* (fr. *ped-, pes* foot) — more at MILE, FOOT] **:** any of numerous myriopods constituting the class Diplopoda having usu. a more or less cylindrical body covered with hard integument and composed of numerous segments with two pairs of legs on most apparent segments, feeding largely on vegetable matter, and having no poison fangs — compare CENTIPEDE

mil·li·phot \ˈmilə+,-\ *n* [*milli-* + *phot*] **:** one thousandth of a phot

mil·li·poise \"+,-\ *n* [*milli-* + *poise*] **:** one thousandth of a poise

mil·li·roentgen \ˌ==+\ *n* [*milli-* + *roentgen*] **:** one thousandth of a roentgen

mil·li·second \"+\ *n* [ISV *milli-* + *second*] **:** one thousandth of a second

mil·lis·ite \ˈmilə,sīt\ *n* -s [F. T. *Millis*, 20th cent. Am. mineral collector + E *-ite*] **:** a mineral $(Na,K)CaAl_6(PO_4)_4(OH)_9\cdot 3H_2O$ consisting of a basic hydrous phosphate of sodium, potassium, calcium, and aluminum

mil·li·thrum \ˈmilə,thrəm\ *n* -s [prob. alter. of *miller's-thumb*] **:** LONG-TAILED TIT

mil·li·volt \ˈmilə+,-\ *n* [ISV *milli-* + *volt*] **:** one thousandth of a volt

mil·li·volt·me·ter \-,mēd·ə(r), -ētə-\ *n* [ISV *millivolt* + *-meter*] **:** an instrument for measuring potential differences in millivolts

mil·li·watt \ˈmilə+,-\ *n* [*milli-* + *watt*] **:** one thousandth of a watt

millken *n* -s [³*mill* + *ken*] *obs* **:** HOUSEBREAKER

mill leat *n, Brit* **:** MILLRACE

mill·man \ˈmilmən\ *n, pl* **millmen 1 :** one that owns, runs, operates, or works in a mill **2 :** one who performs all the hand-tool and machine operations in the making of furniture parts, window and door frames, or other lumber products

mill material *n* **:** MILL ADDITION

mill moth *n, Brit* **:** MEDITERRANEAN FLOUR MOTH

mil·lon's reagent \(ˈ)mēˈlōⁿz-\ *or* **millon reagent** *n, usu cap M* [after Eugène *Millon* †1865 Fr. chemist] **:** a solution that is usu. made by dissolving mercury in concentrated nitric acid and diluting with water and that when heated with phenolic compounds gives a red coloration used as a test esp. for tyrosine and proteins containing tyrosine

mill outlet *n* **:** COMPANY STORE b

millowner \ˈ=,==\ *n* **:** one who owns a mill

mill pick *n* [ME *milnpik*, fr. *miln, mille* mill + *pik* pick] **:** MILL BILL

millpond \ˈ=,=\ *n* **:** a pond produced by damming a stream to produce a head of water for operating a mill

millpool \ˈ=,=\ *n* **:** MILLPOND

millpost \ˈ=,=\ *n* [ME *milnepost*, fr. *milne, mille* mill + *post*] **1 :** a large post supporting a windmill **2 :** a post on which the cap of a smock mill turns

millrace \ˈ=,=\ *n* [ME *milnras*, fr. *miln, mille* mill + *ras* race, current] **:** a canal in which water flows to and from a mill wheel; *also* **:** the current that drives the wheel

mill ream *n* **:** a 472-sheet ream of handmade or moldmade paper composed of 18 inside 24-sheet quires and 2 outside 20-sheet quires

millrind *or* **millrynd** \ˈ=,=\ *n* **1 :** an iron support fixed across the hole in the upper millstone of a grist mill **2** *heraldry* **:** a conventional or stylized representation of the millrind of a millstone: as **a** *or* **millrind cross :** CROSS MOLINE **b :** a rectangle, square, or lozenge, voided or pierced, with two projections angling or curving out from the upper side and two from the lower side

millrind 2b

mill roll *n* **:** a roll of paper of the width made on a paper machine

mill run *n* **1 :** a test of the mineral contents of rock or ore by actual milling **2 :** MILLRACE **3 :** the salable lumber output of a sawmill **4 :** the common run of an article passing through a mill **5 :** something or someone average, ordinary, or mediocre ⟨an unpredictable kind of man, very different from the *mill run* of us down here —Angus Mowat⟩

¹mill-run \ˈ=ˈ=\ *adj* [*mill run*] **:** being in the state in which it comes from a run in a mill **:** ungraded and usu. uninspected ⟨*mill-run* steel⟩ ⟨*mill-run* cloth⟩

²mill-run \ˈ=,=\ *vt* [*mill run*] **:** to yield (so much weight or worth of precious metal per ton of ore) at a mill run

mill saw *n* **:** SASH SAW

mill scale *n* **:** a black scale of magnetic oxide of iron formed on iron and steel when heated for rolling, forging, or other processing **:** ⁵SCALE 4a(1)

mill's canons \ˈmilz-\ *or* **mill's methods** *n pl, usu cap 1st M* [after John Stuart *Mill* †1873 Eng. philosopher and economist] **:** the five canons of logical induction formulated by J. S. Mill — compare INDIRECT METHOD OF DIFFERENCE, METHOD OF AGREEMENT, METHOD OF CONCOMITANT VARIATIONS, METHOD OF DIFFERENCE, METHOD OF RESIDUES

millsite \ˈ=,=\ *n* **:** a site for a mill; *specif* **:** a portion of the public lands acquired under federal law to be used for the erection of a mill or reduction plant in connection with a patent for mineral lands or rights

mill soke *n, Anglo-Saxon & early Eng law* **:** the duty of the tenants of land (as a manor) or of others to have their grain ground at a mill; *also* **:** the franchise of receiving the fees for such grinding — compare THIRLAGE

mill spindle *n* [ME *mylle spyndelle*, fr. *mylle, mille* mill + *spyndelle, spindel* spindle] **:** a vertical shaft supporting the upper millstone of a grist mill

millstone \ˈ=,=\ *n* [ME *mulleston, mylneston*, fr. *mulle, mylne, mille* mill + *ston* stone] **1 :** either of two circular stones often built up of several pieces and used for grinding grain or other substance fed through a center hole in the upper stone — see MILLRIND, MILL SPINDLE **2 :** BUHRSTONE 1 **3 a :** something that grinds or crushes ⟨caught between the ~*s* of high prices and low wages⟩ **b :** a heavy or crushing burden (as of guilt)

millstone bridge *n* **:** MILLRIND

mill store *n* **:** COMPANY STORE b

millstream \ˈ=,=\ *n* **1 :** a stream whose flow is utilized to run a mill **2 :** MILLRACE

milltail \ˈ=,=\ *n* **:** the water that flows from a mill wheel after turning it or the channel in which the water flows

mill tax *n* **:** a tax of one or more tenths of a cent on each dollar of assessed valuation

mill tooth *n* **1** *obs* **:** MOLAR **2 :** a saw tooth having a perpendicular leading edge and a curving after edge

mill wheel *n* [ME *myln whele*, fr. OE *mylenhwēol*, fr. *mylen* mill + *hwēol* wheel] **:** a water wheel that drives a mill

mill white *n* **:** an interior white paint usu. made with a varnish or bodied oil liquid and generally drying with a glossy or semigloss appearance

millwork \ˈ=,=\ *n* **1 a :** the setting up or operating of mill machinery **b :** the shafting, gearing, and other driving machinery of mills **2 :** woodwork (as doors, sashes, trim) that has been machined at a planing mill — compare CABINETWORK

millwright \ˈ=,=\ *n* [ME *mylle wryte*, fr. *mylle, mille* mill + *wryte, wrighte* wright] **1 :** one whose occupation is to plan and build mills or to set up their machinery **2 :** a workman who erects the shafting, moves machinery, and cares for the mechanical equipment in a workshop, mill, or plant **3 :** MILLMAN 2

miln \ˈmiln\ *now dial var of* MILL

mil·ner \ˈmilnə(r)\ *n* -s [ME *mylner*, fr. *mylne, mille* mill + *-er*] **1** *dial Eng* **:** MILLER 1 **2** *dial Eng* **:** MILLMAN 1

mi·lo \ˈmī(,)lō\ *also* **milo maize** *n* -s [Sotho *maili*] **:** any of various rather small usu. early and drought-resistant grain sorghums with compact bearded heads of large yellow or whitish seeds — compare DURRA, FETERITA, KAFFIR

milo disease *n* **:** a root and crown rot of milo and sometimes other sorghums caused esp. by a fungus (*Periconia circinata*)

mi·lon·ga \mēˈlōŋgə\ *n* -s [AmerSp] **:** an Argentine ballroom dance that preceded the tango early in the 20th century

mi·lord \məˈlȯ(ə)r(d), mēˈ-, -ō(ə)(d)\ *n* [F, fr. MF *millour, milourd*, fr. ME *my lord*] **:** an English lord or any well-to-do Englishman ⟨the ~, owner of the handsome yacht —George Eliot⟩

mi·lo·ri blue \məˈlōrē-\ *n, often cap M* [after A. *Milori*, 19th cent. Fr. color maker] **:** PRUSSIAN BLUE 2

milori green *n, often cap M* **:** DEEP CHROME GREEN

mil·pa \ˈmilpə\ *n* -s [MexSp, fr. Nahuatl, fr. *milli* cultivated plot + *pa* in, on] **1 a :** a small field esp. in Mexico or Central America that is cleared from the jungle, cropped for a few seasons, and then abandoned for a fresh clearing — compare SWIDDEN **b :** a maize field in Mexico or Central America **2 :** the maize plant

milque·toast \ˈmilk,tōst\ *n* -s *often cap* [after Caspar *Milquetoast*, comic strip character created by H. T. Webster †1952 Am. cartoonist, fr. *milk toast*] **:** a timid, meek, or apologetic person **:** one who is habitually afraid to assert himself **:** one readily intimidated by aggression or authority

mil·reis \(ˈ)milˈrās(h), -āz(h)\ *n, pl* **milreis** \"\ [Pg *mil-réis*, fr. *mil* thousand (fr. L *mille*) + *réis*, pl. of *real* — more at MILE, REAL] **1 a :** a Portuguese unit of value equal before 1911 to 1000 reis; *also* **:** a coin representing this value **2 :** the basic monetary unit of Brazil until 1942; *also* **:** a coin representing this unit

mils *pl of* MIL

mil·sey *or* **mil·sie** \ˈmilsē, -si\ *n* -s [alter. of E dial. *milk-sye*, fr. ME *mylke syhe*, fr. *mylke, milk* milk + *syhe* sieve, fr. *sien, syen* to strain — more at SIE] *chiefly Scot* **:** a milk strainer

¹milt *var of* MELT

²milt \ˈmilt\ *also* **melt** \ˈmelt\ *n* -s [prob. fr. MD *milte* milt of fish, spleen; akin to OE *milte* spleen — more at MELT] **:** the male reproductive glands of fishes in breeding condition when filled with secretion ⟨a ~ shad⟩; *also* **:** the secretion itself

³milt \"\ *vt* -ED/-ING/-S **:** to impregnate (roe) with milt

milt·er \ˈmiltə(r)\ *n* -s [prob. fr. ²*milt* + *-er*] **:** a male fish in breeding condition

mil·to·nia \milˈtōnēə\ *n* [NL, fr. Charles W.W.Fitzwilliam, Viscount *Milton* †1857 Eng. statesman + NL *-ia*] **1** *cap* **:** a genus of tropical American orchids having flowers with a large unlobed labellum and flat spreading perianth — see PANSY ORCHID **2** -s **:** a plant or flower of the genus *Miltonia*

¹mil·to·nian \(ˈ)milˈtōnēən\ *adj, usu cap* [John *Milton* †1674 Eng. poet + E *-an*] **:** MILTONIC

²miltonian \"\ *n* -s *usu cap* **:** a specialist in the life or works of John Milton

mil·ton·ic \=ˈtänik\ *adj, usu cap* **1 :** characteristic of or relating to John Milton or his work ⟨a reading of those critics who have . . . ventured a comment on the *Miltonic* simile reveals a complete and far-reaching difference of opinion —L.D.Lerner⟩ **2 :** marked by sustained sublimity of style

mil·ton·ism \ˈmiltə,nizəm\ *n* -s *usu cap* **:** a Miltonic expression
mil·ton·ist \-,nəst\ *n* -s *usu cap* **:** MILTONIAN
mil·ton·ize \-,nīz\ *vi* -ED/-ING/-S *sometimes cap* **:** to write in imitation of John Milton's poetic style ~ *vt* **:** to make Miltonic in style
milty \ˈmiltē\ *adj* -ER/-EST [²*milt* + -*y*] **:** like, resembling, or full of milt ⟨~ trout⟩
mi-lu \ˈmēˈlü\ *n* -s [Chin (Pek) *mi²* *lu⁴*, fr. *mi²* tailed deer + *lu⁴* deer] **:** PÈRE DAVID'S DEER
mil·va·go \milˈvā,gō\ *n, cap* [NL, irreg. fr. L *milvus* kite] **:** a genus of brown and white So. American caracaras
mil·vus \ˈmilvəs\ *n, cap* [NL, fr. L, kite] **:** a genus of birds (family Falconidae) including the common European kite
mil·wau·kee \(ˈ)milˈwȯkē\ *adj, usu cap* [fr. *Milwaukee*, city in southeast Wisconsin] **:** of or from the city of Milwaukee, Wis. ⟨a *Milwaukee* industry⟩ **:** of the kind or style prevalent in Milwaukee
mil·wau·kee·an \-ēən\ *n* -s *cap* **:** a native or resident of Milwaukee, Wis.
milwaukee brick *n, often cap M* **:** a pale orange yellow to yellow
milz·brand \ˈmilts,bränt\ *n* [G, fr. *milz* spleen (fr. OHG *milzi*) + G *brand* fire, burning, fr. OHG *brant* brand, fire — more at MILT, BRAND] **:** ANTHRAX 2
mim \ˈmim\ *adj* [imit.] *dial* **:** affectedly shy or modest **:** RETICENT, RETIRING **:** PRIM
mim *abbr* mimeograph
mim- *or* **mimo-** *comb form* [L, fr. Gk, fr. *mimos* mime] **:** mime **:** mimic ⟨*mimo*type⟩
mim·al·lon·i·dae \,miməˈlänə,dē\ *n pl, cap* [NL, fr. *Mimallon-, Mimallo*, type genus (fr. Gk *mimallon-, mimallōn* bacchante) + -*idae*] **:** a family of stout hairy medium-sized diurnal American moths — see SACK-BEARER
mi·mam·sa \mēˈmämⁿsə\ *n* -s *usu cap* [Skt *mīmāṁsā*, lit., reflection, investigation, fr. *manyate* he thinks — more at MIND] **:** an orthodox Hindu philosophy concerned with the interpretation of Vedic texts and literature and comprising one part dealing with the earlier writings concerned with right practice and another part dealing with the later writings concerned with right thought — called also respectively *Purva Mimamsa, Uttara Mimamsa;* compare VEDANTA
mimbar *var of* MINBAR
mim·bre·ño \mēmˈbrān(,)yō\ *n, pl* **mimbreño** *or* **mimbreños** *usu cap* [AmerSp, fr. *Mimbres* mountains, southwestern New Mexico + Sp -*eño* (suffix added to place names to form names of inhabitants)] **1 :** an American Indian people constituting a subdivision of the Gileño **2 :** a member of the Mimbreño people
mim·bres \ˈmimbrəs\ *adj, usu cap* [*Mimbres* river, southwestern New Mexico] **:** of or belonging to a culture in southern New Mexico characterized by dominant Anasazi traits introduced into the Mogollon culture
¹mime \ˈmīm *also* ˈmēm\ *n* -s [L *mimus*, fr. Gk *mimos;* akin to Gk *mimeisthai* to imitate, represent] **1 a :** an actor in a mime **b :** one that practices the modern art of mime **2 :** one (as a jester, mimic, clown, or buffoon) that performs in ways resembling or held to resemble a performer in a mime **3 a :** a Greek and Roman dramatic entertainment representing scenes from life usu. in a ridiculous manner **b :** a modern form of dramatic entertainment resembling or held to resemble the Greek and Roman mime **4 :** an imitation done in or as if in a mime ⟨a perfect ~ of his performance⟩ **5 :** the art of creating and portraying a character or of narration by body movement (as by realistic and symbolic gestures) ⟨the use of ~ to tell out a story is not uncommon in Polynesia —*Amer. Anthropologist*⟩ ⟨almost entirely musical on the sound track, the action being in ~ —John Huntley⟩ **6 :** a performance of mime
²mime \"\ *vb* -ED/-ING/-S *vi* **:** to act as a mime **:** play a part with mimic gesture and action usu. without words ⟨*mimed* with all his well-known sensitiveness and power —Phyllis W. Manchester & Iris Morley⟩ ~ *vt* **1 :** MIMIC ⟨his peons loyally *mimed* extreme fright —Kenneth Tynan⟩ ⟨he *mimed* outrage, batting his . . . hands together and stamping like a wrestler —A.J.Liebling⟩ **2 :** to act out in the manner of a mime ⟨the warrior ~s the slaying of an enemy —H.B.Alexander⟩ ⟨dancers ~ the stories of the ancient myths while singers chant —*Atlantic*⟩
¹mim·e·o·graph \ˈmimēə,graf, -raa(ə)f, -raif, -räf\ *n* [fr. *Mimeograph*, a trademark] **1 :** a duplicator for making many copies that consists of a frame in which the stencil is stretched and an inking roller for pressing ink through the porous lines of the stencil onto paper **2 :** a copy made on a mimeograph
²mimeograph \"\ *vb* -ED/-ING/-S *vt* **1 :** to produce with a mimeograph ⟨~ copies of a report⟩ **2 :** to copy with a mimeograph ⟨~ a letter⟩ ~ *vi* **:** to use a mimeograph
mim·er \ˈmīmə(r) *also* ˈmēm-\ *n* -s [²*mime* + -*er*] **:** MIME, MIMIC
mi·me·sis \məˈmēsəs, mīˈ-\ *n* -ES [LL, fr. Gk *mimēsis*, fr. *mimeisthai* to imitate] **:** IMITATION, MIMICRY
mim·e·tene \ˈmimə,tēn\ *also* **mi·met·e·site** \məˈmed·ə,sīt, mīˈ-\ *n* -s [*mimetene* modif. of F *mimétèse* mimetite; *mimetesite* fr. G *mimetesit*, fr. F *mimétèse* + G -*it* -ite] **:** MIMETITE
mi·met·ic \məˈmed·|ik, (ˈ)mī|m-, -et|, |ēk\ *adj* [LL *mimeticus*, fr. Gk *mimētikos*, fr. *mimētēs* imitator (fr. *mimeisthai* to imitate) + -*ikos* -ic] **1 :** having an aptitude for or a tendency toward mimicry **:** IMITATIVE ⟨~ tendency of infancy —R.W. Hamilton⟩ **2 :** of, relating to, or characterized by mimicry **3 :** MIMIC 3 ⟨a whole copse of ~ fir trees was being felled —Christopher Morley⟩ **4 a :** characterized by or exhibiting biological mimicry ⟨sometimes an animal develops ~ coloring —A.M.Woodbury⟩ ⟨~ type⟩ **b :** simulating the action or effect of — usu. used in combination ⟨sympatho*mimetic* drugs⟩ ⟨adrenocortico*mimetic* activity⟩ **5 :** characterized by resemblance to other forms — used of crystals ⟨a ~ growth of parallel feldspar crystals produces a comblike structure —G.E. Goodspeed⟩ **6 :** representing an emotion by imitative gestures and expressions ⟨a ~ dance⟩ ⟨a ballet is a series of solo and concerted dances with ~ actions —Mark Perugini⟩ **7 a :** ONOMATOPOEIC ⟨*hiss* is a ~ word⟩ **b :** resulting from analogy — used of change in a word form
mi·met·i·cal·ly \|ək(ə)lē, |ēk-, -li\ *adv* **:** in a mimetic manner **:** by mime ⟨such dialogue as can be clearly expressed ~ —*Wisconsin Idea Theatre Quarterly*⟩
mim·e·tism \ˈmimə,tizəm, ˈmīm-\ *n* -s [ISV *mimet-* (fr. Gk *mimētēs* imitator) + -*ism*] **:** MIMICRY
mim·e·tite \ˈmimə,tīt, ˈmīm-\ *n* -s [G *mimetit*, fr. F *mimétèse* mimetite (fr. Gk *mimētēs* imitator, fr. *mimeisthai* to imitate) + G -*it* -ite; fr. its resemblance to pyromorphite] **:** a lead arsenate and chloride $Pb_5Cl(AsO_4)_3$ isomorphous with pyromorphite
mi·mi·am·bi \,mīmēˈam,bī, ,mim-\ *n pl* [L, fr. Gk *mimiamboi*, fr. *mimos* mime + *iamboi*, pl. of *iambos* iamb] **:** mimes in iambic or choliambic verse
¹mim·ic \ˈmimik, -mēk\ *n* -s [L *mimicus*, adj.] **1 a :** a performer in mimes **:** MIME 1 **b :** one that mimics (as for amusement) **2 :** a cheap or servile imitator **3 :** a feeble or poor imitation **4 :** a usu. edible and harmless animal that escapes predation by being mistaken by potential predators for a distasteful or venomous animal
²mimic \"\ *adj* [L *mimicus*, fr. Gk *mimikos*, fr. *mimos* mime + -*ikos* -ic] **1 a :** of, acting as, or resembling a mime **b :** having an aptitude for or practicing mimicry **2 :** befitting or having the characteristics of a mime or mimicry ⟨explained them with great detail and ~ illustration —Ernest Beaglehole⟩ **3 :** constituting a copy or imitation of something, often for amusement ⟨the ~ warfare of the opera stage —Archibald Alison⟩ ⟨throwing ~ spears formed of fern stalks —Sacheverell Sitwell⟩ **4 :** MIMETIC 5
³mimic \"\ *vb* **mimicked; mimicked; mimicking; mimics** [¹*mimic*] *vt* **1 :** to copy or imitate very closely esp. in external characteristics (as voice, gesture, or manner) ⟨~s their manners with dexterity —Francis Fergusson⟩ ⟨learned Spanish by . . . *mimicking* the speech of the natives —M.B.Smith⟩ ⟨the Communist and Socialist politicians ~ Soviet policy —*Western Political Quarterly*⟩ **2 :** to ridicule by imitation **:** make sport of by copying or imitating ⟨jumped about the platform, *mimicked* the tight, unseeing capitalists of his . . . imagination —Adria Langley⟩ **3 :** to imitate by representation **:** represent by imitation **:** SIMULATE ⟨how closely he could ~ marble on paper —Charles Reade⟩ ⟨yellow cretonnes *mimicked* the sunshine that never shone through the . . . windows —Aldous Huxley⟩ **4 :** to exhibit biological mimicry with **:** resemble by biological mimicry ~ *vi* **:** to perform the action of a mimic ⟨chanting and gesturing, painting and *mimicking* and shedding blood —Emma Hawkridge⟩ **syn** see COPY
mim·i·cal \-məkəl\ *adj* [²*mimic* + -*al*] **:** MIMIC — **mim·i·cal·ly** \-mək(ə)lē\ *adv*
mimic gene *n* **:** any of two or more nonallelic genes that have the same effect
mim·ic·ry \ˈmimikrē, -mēk-, -ri\ *n* -ES [*mimic* + -*ry*] **1 :** an instance of mimicking **2 a :** the action, practice, or art of mimicking **b :** imitation less creative than mime **3 :** a superficial resemblance that some organisms exhibit to other organisms or to the natural objects among which they live and thereby secure concealment, protection, or some other advantage — compare AGGRESSIVE 3a, APOSEMATIC, CRYPTIC 4
mimic thrush *n* **:** MOCKING THRUSH; *esp* **:** MOCKINGBIRD
mim·i·dae \ˈmimə,dē\ *n pl, cap* [NL, fr. *Mimus*, type genus + -*idae*] **:** a family of American passerine birds that includes the catbird, mockingbirds, and thrashers and is sometimes considered to constitute a subfamily of Troglodytidae
mi·mine \ˈmī,mīn, ˈmi,, -,mən\ *adj* [NL *Miminae*, subfamily in some classifications coextensive with the Mimidae, fr. *Mimus*, type genus + -*inae*] **:** of or relating to the Mimidae
miming *pres part of* MIME
mim·i·ny-pim·i·ny \ˌmimənēˌpimənē\ *adj* [prob. alter. (influenced by *mim*) of *niminy-piminy*] **:** absurdly nice **:** ridiculously delicate ⟨a *miminy-piminy* . . . young man —W.S.Gilbert⟩ **:** FINICAL
mim·ma·tion \məˈmāshən\ *n* -s [Ar *mīm* (letter of the alphabet corresponding to English *m*) + E -*ation*] **:** the addition of a final *m* in Akkadian — compare NUNNATION
mim-mouthed \ˈ≈ˌ≈\ *or* **mim-mou'd** \ˈ≈ˌmüd\ *adj, chiefly Scot* **:** primly reticent **:** CLOSEMOUTHED
mimo- — see MIM-
mi·mog·ra·pher \məˈmägrəfə(r), mīˈ-\ *n* -s [L *mimographus* mimographer (fr. Gk *mimographos*, fr. *mim-* + -*graphos* -grapher) + E -*er*] **:** a writer of mimes
mi·mo·sa \məˈmōsə, mīˈ-, -ōzə\ *n* [NL, fr. L *mimus* mime + -*osa*, fem. of -*osus* -ose; fr. its apparent imitation of the sensitivity of animal life in drooping and closing its leaves when touched — more at MIME] **1** *cap* **:** a genus of trees, shrubs, and herbs (family Leguminosae) that are native to tropical and warm regions and have usu. bipinnate often prickly leaves sometimes reduced to phyllodes and globular heads of small white or pink flowers — see SENSITIVE PLANT **2** -s **:** any plant of *Mimosa* or of the related genus *Acacia* **3** -s **:** a light yellow that is greener and slightly less strong than average maize, greener and duller than jasmine, and greener than popcorn — called also *queen's yellow, turmeric*
mim·o·sa·ceae \,mimə'sāsē,ē, ,mīm-\ *n pl, cap* [NL, fr. *Mimosa*, type genus + -*aceae*] *in some classifications* **:** a family of plants (order Rosales) that are commonly included in the family Leguminosae and that have pinnate leaves and small regular flowers in heads or spikes — **mim·o·sa·ceous** \ˌ≈≈ˈsāshəs\ *adj*
mimosa webworm *n* **:** a small brown webworm that is the larva of a silvery gray black-spotted moth (*Homadaula albizziae*) and that has recently become prominent as a defoliator of mimosa and honey locust esp. in the southeastern U.S.
mimosa yellow *n* **:** a variable color averaging a brilliant greenish yellow that is redder and paler than strontian yellow
mi·mo·sine \məˈmō,sēn, mīˈ-, -ōsən\ *n* -s [G *mimosin*, fr. NL *Mimosa* + G -*in* -ine] **:** a crystalline amino acid $C_8H_{10}N_2O_4$ (OH)$CH_2CH(NH_2)$COOH that is a derivative of alanine and a hydroxy pyridone and is found esp. in the common sensitive plant and the lead tree
mim·o·type \ˈmimə,tīp\ *n* [*mim-* + *type*] **:** a plant or animal resembling in many respects another from which it is systematically distinct and geographically isolated ⟨the New World hummingbirds are ~s of the Old World sunbirds⟩ — **mim·o·typ·ic** \ˌ≈≈ˈtipik\ *adj*
mim·u·lus \ˈmimyələs\ *n* [NL, fr. LL, comic actor, fr. L *mimus* mime + -*ulus*; prob. fr. the resemblance of the flower bud to a mask] **1** *cap* **:** a genus of American herbs (family Scrophulariaceae) having a tubular 5-angled calyx and an irregular 2-lipped corolla — see MONKEY FLOWER **2** -ES **:** any plant of the genus *Mimulus*
mi·mus \ˈmīməs\ *n, cap* [NL, fr. L, mime — more at MIME] **:** a genus of birds containing the mockingbirds and being the type of the family Mimidae
-mi·mus \"\ *n comb form* [NL, fr. L *mimus* mime] **:** mimic **:** imitator — in generic names of animals ⟨*Ceto*mimus⟩
mi·mu·sops \məˈmyü,säps\ *n, cap* [NL, fr. MGk *mimous* (gen. of *mimō* ape, prob. fr. Gk *mimeisthai* to imitate) + NL -*ops*] **:** a genus of Old World tropical trees (family Sapotaceae) having abundant milky juice, coriaceous leaves, and small hexamerous or octamerous flowers with as many staminodia as stamens — see BANSALAGUIN, MANILKARA
min \ˈmin\ *n, pl* **min** *usu cap* [Chin (Pek) *Min³* Fukien, province in southeast China] **:** any of the Chinese dialects of Fukien province
min *abbr* **1** mineral **2** mineralogical; mineralogy **3** minim **4** minimum **5** mining **6** minister; ministry **7** minor **8** minute
¹mi·na \ˈmīnə\ *n, pl* **minas** \-əz\ *also* **mi·nae** \-ī,nē\ [L, fr. Gk *mna*, of Sem origin; akin to Heb *māneh* mina] **:** an ancient unit of weight of the Babylonians, Hebrews, Greeks, and others varying around one and two pounds
²mina \"\ *n* -s [Hindi *mainā* — more at MYNA] **:** MYNA; *esp* **:** HILL MYNA
min·able *or* **mine·able** \ˈmīnəbəl\ *adj* **:** capable of being mined ⟨~ coal⟩ ⟨~ graphite⟩ ⟨~ waters⟩
mi·na·cious \məˈnāshəs\ *adj* [L *minac-, minax* threatening + E -*ious* — more at MENACE] **:** of a menacing or threatening character
¹mi·nae·an \məˈnēən\ *adj, usu cap* [L *Minaeus* Minaean (fr. Gk *Minaios*, fr. Ar *Maʿān, Maʿīn*) + E -*an*, adj. suffix] **:** of, relating to, or being an ancient kingdom of southwestern Arabia
²minaean \"\ *n* -s *usu cap* [L *Minaeus* Minaean + E -*an*, n. suffix] **1 :** a member of the Minaean people **2 :** the Semitic language of the Minaean people
mi·na·hasa \,mēnəˈhäsə\ *or* **mi·na·has·san** \-sən\ *n, pl* **minahasa** *or* **minahassans** *usu cap* **1 :** an Indonesian people inhabiting the Minahasa peninsula of northeast Celebes **2 :** a member of the Minahasa people
mi·nang·ka·bau \,mēnäŋkəˈbaù\ *n, pl* **minangkabau** *also* **minangkabaus** *usu cap* [Malay] **1 :** an Indonesian people in central Sumatra **2 :** a member of the Minangkabau people
mi·nar \məˈnär\ *n* -s [Ar *manār*] **:** a tower or turret found esp. in India
min·a·ret \ˌminəˈret, *usu* -ed·+V\ *n* -s [F, fr. Turk *minare*, fr. Ar *manārah* lighthouse, lamp] **1 :** a slender lofty tower attached to a mosque and surrounded by one or more projecting balconies from which the summons to prayer is cried by the muezzin **2 :** a structure resembling a minaret ⟨the Town Hall . . . , an ornate cream and white building with ~s —*Amer. Guide Series: Maine*⟩
min·a·ret·ed \-ed·əd\ *adj* **:** having or characterized by minarets ⟨the great ~ . . . mosque —Robert Sherrod⟩ ⟨fanciful cities, bright colored and mildly ~ —R.M.Coates⟩
mi·nas·rag·rite \,mēnäsˈrä,grīt\ *n* -s [*Minasragra*, near Cerro de Pasco, Peru + E -*ite*] **:** a hydrous acid vanadyl sulfate $(VO)_2H_2(SO_4)_3.15H_2O$ occurring as a blue efflorescent crust
mina·tory \ˈminə,tōrē, -tȯr-, -ri *also* ˈmīn-\ *adj* [LL *minatorius*, fr. L *minatus* (past part. of *minari* to threaten) + -*orius* -ory — more at MOUNT] **:** having a menacing quality **:** expressive of or conveying a threat ⟨thrusting out a ~ forefinger —Lionel Hale⟩ ⟨the law was ~ and repressive —G.B.Sansom⟩ ⟨their conversation is in the decisive and ~ tone —Earl of Chesterfield⟩
mi·nau·de·rie \mēˈnōdrē\ *n* -s [F, fr. MF, fr. (assumed) MF *minauder* to simper (whence F *minauder*) (fr. MF *mine* appearance, look) + MF -*erie* -ery — more at MIEN] **:** a coquettish air — usu. used in pl. ⟨the ~s of the young ladies in the ballrooms —W.M.Thackeray⟩
minaul *var of* MONAL
min·a·way \ˈminə,wā\ *n* -s [F *menuet* — more at MINUET] *archaic Scot* **:** MINUET
min·bar \ˈmin,bär\ *or* **mim·bar** \-im,-\ *n* -s [Ar *minbar*] **:** a Muslim pulpit

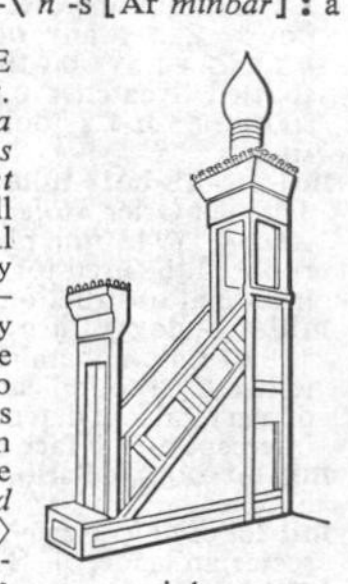
minbar

¹mince \ˈmin(t)s\ *vb* -ED/-ING/-S [ME *mincen*, fr. MF *mincer, mincier*, fr. (assumed) VL *minutiare*, fr. L *minutia* smallness, minuteness, fr. *minutus* minute + -*ia* -y — more at MINUTE] *vt* **1 a :** to cut or chop into very small pieces ⟨~ ham⟩ ⟨~ glands in medical research⟩ **b :** to subdivide minutely ⟨his days . . . were *minced* into hours —Van Wyck Brooks⟩; *esp* **:** to damage by cutting up ⟨the director *minced* up the play⟩ **2 :** to cut up (a plover) **3 :** to utter or pronounce with affectation (as of refinement or elegance) **:** clip in pronunciation ⟨*minced* the word in the manner of the old lady⟩ ⟨who *minced* his mother tongue —Leslie Stephen⟩ **4** *archaic* **:** to diminish in representation **:** tell in part or by degrees **:** weaken the force of **:** make little of **:** EXTENUATE, MINIMIZE ⟨I do not ~ the truth —P.J.Bailey⟩ **5 a :** to moderate or restrain (words) within the bounds of politeness and decorum ⟨*minced* no words in stating his dislike —J.T.Farrell⟩ ⟨a typical old-school editor who never *minced* words with his enemies —*Amer. Guide Series: Pa.*⟩ **b :** EUPHEMIZE ⟨such *minced* words as *heck, darn, durn, danged* —Thomas Pyles⟩ **6 :** to do or perform (something) in an affected way ~ *vi* **1 :** to walk with short steps or in a prim affected manner ⟨a painted woman . . . *minced* up to them —T.B.Costain⟩ ⟨a slender, small, dapper man *minced* over the threshold —C.B. Kelland⟩ ⟨while the birds . . . ~ on the pavement at their feet —Constance Carrier⟩ **2 :** to speak with affected nicety or elegance **3 :** to chop food materials fine — **mince matters** *or* **mince the matter :** to speak in a restrained or subtle manner **:** avoid speaking frankly or bluntly — used in the negative ⟨he thought she was wrong and did not *mince matters* in telling her so⟩
²mince \"\ *n* -s **:** small bits or pieces into which something is chopped ⟨a ~ of mushrooms⟩; *specif* **:** MINCEMEAT
mincemeat \ˈ≈,≈\ *n* [alter. of *minced meat*, fr. *minced* (past part. of ¹*mince*) + *meat*] **1 :** minced meat **2 :** a finely chopped and usu. cooked mixture of raisins, apples, spices, and other ingredients with or without meat and suet **3 :** something felt to resemble finely chopped meat; *specif* **:** a state of destruction or annihilation — used in the phrase *make mincemeat of* ⟨science making ~ of the old-time religion —F.L. Allen⟩ ⟨making ~ of the inhabitants —Richard Joseph⟩
mince pie *also* **minced pie** *n* **:** a pie made of mincemeat
minc·er \ˈmin(t)sə(r)\ *n* -s **:** one that minces ⟨a dozen golden-haired languishers and ~s —Max Peacock⟩ ⟨the bone is . . . ground in a ~ under sterile conditions —*Yr. Bk. of Orthopedics & Traumatic Surgery*⟩
mincha *var of* MINHAH
min·chen \ˈminchən\ *n* -s [ME *mynchoun*, fr. OE *mynecen, mynecenu*, fem. of *munuc* monk — more at MONK] *archaic* **:** NUN
min·chery \-chərē\ *n* -ES [*minchen* + -*ery*] *archaic* **:** NUNNERY
min-chia \ˈminjēˈä, -nˈjä\ *n, pl* **min-chia** *usu cap* M [Chin (Pek) *Min²* -*chia²*, fr. *min²* people + *chia²* family] **1 a :** a people constituting a sinicized remnant of the Tai of southwest China **b :** a member of such people **2 :** the language of the Min-chia people
min·chia·te \mēnˈkyätā\ *n* -s [It] **:** an early form of tarok
mincing *adj* [fr. pres. part. of ¹*mince*] **1 a :** characterized by or expressive of affected daintiness and elegance ⟨trying to speak in a small ~ treble —George Eliot⟩ ⟨the ~ step of old-fashioned Chinese ladies —Harold Seymour⟩ **b :** affectedly dainty or delicate (as in speech, manner of walking, or behavior) ⟨a ~ lady . . . pushed a streamlined pram —Earle Birney⟩ **2** *archaic* **:** characterized by an attempt to minimize or extenuate ⟨those ~ names designed only to palliate wrong actions —John Doran⟩ **3** [fr. gerund of ¹*mince*] **:** used or designed for cutting (something) into small pieces ⟨a ~ machine⟩ ⟨a ~ knife⟩
minc·ing·ly *adv* **:** in a mincing manner ⟨the movies are bright in dialogue but ~ polite in physical action —Gilbert Seldes⟩ ⟨had to step ~ to keep from crushing bantam-size eggs —Howell Walker⟩
min·co·pie *also* **min·co·pi** *or* **min·kop·i** \ˈminkəpē\ *n* -s *usu cap* **:** ANDAMANESE 1
mincy \ˈmin(t)sē\ *adj* -ER/-EST [¹*mince* + -*y*] *dial* **:** overly particular or delicate ⟨he's hard to cook for — so ~ about his food⟩
¹mind \ˈmīnd\ *n* -s *often attrib* [ME *minde, mynde*, fr. OE *gemynd;* akin to OHG *gimunt* memory, Goth *gamunds* commemoration, mention; all fr. a prehistoric Gmc compound whose first constituent is represented by OE *ge-* (perfective, associative, and collective prefix) and whose second constituent is akin to L *ment-, mens* mind, *monēre* to warn, Gk *menos* spirit, intent, *mnasthai* to remember, *mimnēskein* to remind, Skt *manas* mind, *manyate* he thinks — more at CO-] **1 :** the state of remembering or being remembered **:** MEMORY, RECOLLECTION — used chiefly in phrases ⟨important to keep in ~ the purpose for which the council was summoned —Vernon Bartlett⟩ ⟨hunting, fishing, and other sports . . . come to ~ —E.L.Ullman⟩ ⟨rattle it off out of ~ —*Stamps*⟩ ⟨put me in ~ of an old story —E.G.Bulwer-Lytton⟩ **2 :** the commemoration of a deceased person esp. by a requiem just a month or a year after the funeral — see MONTH'S MIND, YEAR'S MIND **3 a :** that which reasons **:** the doer of intellectual work — usu. distinguished from *will* and *emotion* ⟨formulas toward which her meditating ~ ran —R.P.Blackmur⟩ **b** (1) **:** an organized group of events in neural tissue occurring mediately in response to antecedent intrapsychic or extrapsychic events which it perceives, classifies, transforms, and coordinates prior to initiating action whose consequences are foreseeable to the extent of available information (2) **:** the aspect of a biological organism that is not organic in nature ⟨in man ~ is experienced as emotions, imagination, or will⟩ **c :** the sum total of the conscious states of an individual **d :** the sum total of the individual's adaptive activity considered as an organized whole though also capable of being split into dissociated parts ⟨as the conscious and the unconscious ~⟩ **e :** one's capacity for mental activity **:** one's available stock of mental and adaptive responses **4 :** INCLINATION, INTENTION, DESIRE, WISH, PURPOSE — used chiefly in phrases ⟨of a ~ to listen to reason —T.B.Costain⟩ ⟨one of my crack stockmen when he has a ~ to work —Rex Ingamells⟩ ⟨anyone who was of a ~ to ransacked the floors above him —Andy Logan⟩ ⟨know one's own ~⟩ ⟨changed her ~⟩ **5 :** the normal or healthy condition of the mental faculties ⟨out of his ~⟩ ⟨lost her ~⟩ **6 :** the bent or fixed direction of one's thoughts, inclinations, or desires ⟨kept his ~ on one sole aim —Alfred Tennyson⟩ ⟨a wife to his ~⟩ **7 :** that which one thinks regarding something **:** OPINION, VIEW ⟨the governor desired every member of the board would deliver his ~ —*Colonial Records of Penn.*⟩ ⟨a fool uttereth all his ~ —Prov 29:11 (AV)⟩ ⟨unwilling to speak his ~⟩ **8 :** the state of one's spirits **:** mental disposition **:** cast of thought or feeling **:** MOOD **9 a :** a person who is the embodiment of mental qualities (as thought, feelings, or disposition) ⟨the artistic ~⟩ ⟨the scientific ~⟩ ⟨the work of . . . the world's best ~s —*advt*⟩ **b :** a group of people or the inhabitants of an area who are the embodiment of such qualities ⟨the European ~⟩ ⟨the public ~⟩ **10 :** intellectual quality **:** mental power ⟨the works of men of ~ —Alfred Tennyson⟩ **11** *cap* **a :** DEITY 1b ⟨haunted forever by the eternal *Mind* —William Wordsworth⟩ **b** *Christian Science* **:** ²GOD b(6) **12 a :** the conscious element or factor in the universe that in dualistic metaphysical systems is contrasted with matter and in monistic idealistic systems is held to be the only ultimate reality **:** SPIRIT, NOUS, INTELLIGENCE **b :** the quality, relatedness, or temporal organization exhibited by a spatial extensity and related to it in a manner analogous to the relation of consciousness to a conscious organism **c :** the objectification of consciousness or awareness **:** that which attends **13** *dial* **:** ATTENTION — usu. used with negative ⟨don't pay him any ~⟩
syn INTELLECT, SOUL, PSYCHE, BRAIN, BRAINS, INTELLIGENCE, WIT (OR WITS): MIND indicates the complex of man's faculties involved in perceiving, remembering, considering, evaluating,

and deciding; it contrasts variously with *body, heart, soul,* and *spirit* ⟨the *mind* must have its share in deciding these important matters, not merely the emotions and desires —Rose Macaulay⟩ MIND may indicate the peculiar complex of a particular individual as differing from all others ⟨the *mind* of a dreamer joined to the temperament of a soldier —John Buchan⟩ INTELLECT, sometimes interchangeable with MIND, may focus attention on knowing and thinking powers, those by which one may know, comprehend, consider, and conclude — more coldly analytic powers independent of and discrete from willing and feeling ⟨the emotionalist steeps himself or herself in luxurious feeling and pathetic imagination, which makes no severe call upon either the will or the *intellect* —W.R.Inge⟩ ⟨now the significance of Sir Thomas Browne lies in the fact that he was at once by *intellect* a force in the forward movement and by temperament a reactionary —P.E.More⟩ SOUL, used with considerable variation in meaning and suggestion, may indicate that principle which vitalizes, directs, selects, or inspires in matters emotional and volitional as well as mental ⟨my inner existence, that consciousness which is called the *soul* —Richard Jefferies⟩ ⟨the *soul* is an intelligent, sensitive, and vital principle, a trinity which forms and moves the body predisposed to such action, as well as feels, thinks, and wills — Frank Thilly⟩ PSYCHE may refer to the totality of self composed of all attributes, powers, and activities not purely bodily or somatic but definitely including the unconscious or subconscious ⟨by the *psyche* I understand the totality of all the psychic processes, both conscious as well as unconscious; whereas by soul, I understand a definitely demarcated function-complex that is best characterized as a "personality" — H.G.Baynes⟩ BRAIN or BRAINS in the sense here considered may more forcefully than INTELLECT focus attention on powers of individual comprehension or independent thought ⟨it requires *brains* and education to follow the argument —W.R. Inge⟩ ⟨have I ever even felt inclined to write anything, until my emotions had been unduly excited, my *brain* immoderately stirred, my senses unusually quickened, or my spirit extravagantly roused? —John Galsworthy⟩ INTELLIGENCE is likely to apply specific ability to cope with problems and situations or to exhibition of the play of powers of the intellect or comparable ones ⟨has turned capable men into mere machines doing their work without *intelligence* —G.B.Shaw⟩ ⟨wild animals are not automata — they have *intelligence* if they lack intellect —J.S.Clarke⟩ WIT and WITS may refer to a mind marked by inborn capacity, strong common sense, bright perception, or ready intelligence ⟨had the *wit* to look for him at the Federation meeting —Arnold Bennett⟩ ⟨everyone had to be a jack-of-all-trades, everyone had to live by his *wits* —Van Wyck Brooks⟩ **syn** see in addition MEMORY

— **be a mind** *dial* : WISH, INTEND : be inclined — usu. used with the infinitive ⟨I'll do what *I'm a mind* to⟩ — **in two minds** : irresolute between two choices — **on one's mind** : occupying one's thoughts and often causing anxiety ⟨too many problems *on her mind*⟩

²**mind** \"\ *vb* -ED/-ING/-S [ME *minden, mynden,* fr. *minde, mynde* mind, memory — more at ¹MIND] *vt* **1 a** *chiefly dial* : to put (one) in mind of something : REMIND ⟨fight valiantly today; and yet I do thee wrong to ~ thee of it —Shak.⟩ ⟨~ the boy to perform his tasks⟩ ⟨the noise ~*ed* them of their danger⟩ **b** : to serve as a reminder of ⟨that as a sacred symbol it may dwell in her son's flesh, to ~ revengement — Edmund Spenser⟩ **2** *chiefly dial* : to recall and bear in mind : have in mind : REMEMBER ⟨the lads you leave will ~ you — A.E.Housman⟩ ⟨I ~ me how . . . from my Sunday coat I brushed off the burrs —J.G.Whittier⟩ ⟨I ~*ed* how easy her delicacy had been startled —R.L.Stevenson⟩ ⟨~ tomorrow's early meeting —Robert Browning⟩ **3 a** : to occupy oneself with : attend to (something) closely : direct one's attention or energies upon ⟨~*s* his own business⟩ ⟨~*s* her work and is never heard gossiping⟩ **b** *chiefly dial* : to have a liking for ⟨~*ed* nothing but eating and sleeping⟩ **4** *obs* : to remember in prayers or a will ⟨~ us when at the throne of grace —Michael Shields⟩ **5** : to become aware of : NOTICE, PERCEIVE ⟨I'll fall flat. Perchance he will not ~ me —Shak.⟩ **6 a** *obs* : to have (something) in view : contemplate with the intention of taking action ⟨that noble prince began . . . to ~ the reformation of things there run amiss —Edmund Spenser⟩ **b** *chiefly dial* : to have as a wish, inclination, or intention : PURPOSE — usu. used with an infinitive phrase ⟨I ~ to tell him plainly what I think —Shak.⟩ **7 a** : to give heed to attentively in order to obey ⟨~ the instructions that are about to be issued⟩ **b** : to follow the orders or directions of : OBEY ⟨his aunt could not make the child ~ her⟩ ⟨~ your mother⟩ **8 a** : to be concerned or troubled about : become vexed or angered over ⟨I did not ~ his being a little out of humor —Richard Steele⟩ ⟨never ~ your unfortunate mistake⟩ **b** : to object to : DISLIKE ⟨would you ~ answering a few questions⟩ ⟨another man who does not ~ the cold —Geoffrey Boumphrey⟩ **9** : to bear in mind and take care : SEE — usu. used with a clause ⟨~ that you don't forget to mail the letters⟩ ⟨~ you finish the work today⟩ ⟨~ you beat down his prices a bit —Christopher Isherwood⟩ **10 a** : to be cautious or wary about : be on guard against ⟨~ the broken rung on the ladder⟩ **b** : to be careful or attentive about ⟨I wish either . . . had ~*ed* what they were about — Laurence Sterne⟩ **11** : to take care of : have the charge or oversight of : guard from harm or injury : watch over : TEND ⟨women who ~ the child for a small fee —*Social Services in Brit.*⟩ ⟨the man who ~*s* a machine in a factory —J.M. Richards⟩ ⟨the shepherd ~*s* his sheep⟩ **12** : to regard with attention : treat as of consequence : consider or note (something) as having importance ⟨we ~ such ideas as justice and liberty; we know that they matter —H.J.Muller⟩ ⟨and this, ~ you, from a man who voted for woman suffrage —W.A. White⟩ ~ *vi* **1** *chiefly dial* : REMEMBER — often used with *of, on, upon* ⟨I ~ of what he was saying last week⟩ ⟨he could ~ when that tone first crept into Pa's voice —Minnie H. Moody⟩ **2** : to be attentive or wary : be on guard **3** : to become concerned or troubled : feel agitated or angry : CARE, WORRY ⟨never ~ about the matter⟩ ⟨we thought he would be angry but he did not ~⟩ ⟨when the weather stays dry . . . nobody ~*s* about petty irritations —Hilary Phillips⟩ ⟨if nobody ~*s*, I shall go straight to bed —Nigel Balchin⟩ **4** : to pay heed or attention; *esp* : OBEY ⟨a teacher must make the children ~⟩ ⟨the dog ~*s* well⟩ ⟨assigned them extra homework if they didn't ~⟩ **syn** see OBEY, REMEMBER

³**mind** \'mīnd\ *or* **minn** \'min\ *n* -S [OIr *mind*] : a thin semi-oval gold plate believed to have been used by the ancient Celts as an ornament and esp. as a diadem

mind cure *n* : a method or act of healing disease (as the neuroses) by mental procedures : PSYCHOTHERAPY — used esp. in nonmedical practice

mind doctor *n* : PSYCHIATRIST

mind·ed \'mīndəd\ *adj* [¹*mind* + *-ed*] **1** : having an intention, inclination, or disposition (to do something) ⟨many young couples are ~ to marry —F.S.Mitchell⟩ ⟨are further ~ to make fresh provision for the government of our colony —*Nigeria Letters Patent*⟩ ⟨was ever ~ to side with the heretic —Sidney Lovett⟩ ⟨one might query if so ~ —A.L.Kroeber⟩ **2** : having or characterized by a mind of a specified character — usu. used in combination ⟨an open-*minded* examination —J.G.Palfrey⟩ ⟨how small-*minded* a few of them can be —H.H.Martin⟩ ⟨the hospitable and open-*minded* attitude —*Saturday Rev.*⟩ ⟨absent-*minded*⟩ **3** *obs* : having a specified disposition toward someone or something **4** : having one's thoughts, tastes, or interests inclined in a specified direction (as toward a particular object) ⟨viewing by a statistically ~ . . . group yielded the following data —Walter Goodman⟩ ⟨moral religious-*minded* communities —*Amer. Guide Series: Texas*⟩ ⟨philanthropically ~ individuals and organizations —Thomas Woody⟩ ⟨to vacation-*minded* . . . buyers —Warren Winstanley⟩ ⟨a woman who is society-*minded* —H.A.Overstreet⟩ **5** : possessing a mind ⟨predispositions of the ~ organism —H.J.McLendon⟩ **6** : having the status of an immediate object of consciousness ⟨with us human folk there is probably little that is cognitively ~ which is not in some measure conceptualized —C.L.Morgan⟩

mind·ed·ness *n* -ES : the quality or state of being minded — usu. used in combination ⟨those who pride themselves on their tough-*mindedness* —A.G.N.Flew⟩ ⟨this word-*mindedness* . . . distinguishes writers from scholars —Malcolm Cowley⟩ ⟨the self-*mindedness* of children⟩

min·del \'mindᵊl\ *n* -S *usu cap* [*Mindel* river, southwest Bavaria, Germany] : the second stage of glaciation in Europe during the Pleistocene

mindel-riss \ˈ≈≈ˌ≈\ *n, usu cap M&R* : the second interglacial stage of the European Pleistocene between the Mindel and Riss stages of the ice advance

mind·er \'mīndə(r)\ *n* -S **1** *chiefly Brit* : one that minds: as **a** : one that tends or watches something — often used in combination ⟨the housewife who has to get a baby-*minder* in when she is acting as school manager —Barbara Wootton⟩ **b** : PRESSMAN 1 **2** *Brit* : a child entrusted to the care of a private person

mind·ful \'mīn(d)fəl\ *adj* [ME *myndeful,* fr. *minde, mynde* mind, memory + *-ful* — more at MIND] **1 a** : bearing or keeping in mind : AWARE — often used with *of* ⟨the whites, ~ of the vagaries of natives' directions, paid little heed —Tom Marvel⟩ ⟨~ of the unhonored dead —Thomas Gray⟩ ⟨~ that . . . this newspaper has opposed protectionism —*Wall Street Jour.*⟩ **b** : inclined to be aware (as of events occurring around one) ⟨a stirring and important book for all ~ Americans —*New Republic*⟩ **2** *obs* : having an intention or inclination (to do something) ⟨tired and ~ to rest —James Chetham⟩ — **mind·ful·ly** \-lē, -li\ *adv* — **mind·ful·ness** *n* -ES

mind-healer \ˈ≈ˌ≈≈\ *n* : one who endeavors to cure physical ills by exclusively mental processes

minding *pres part of* MIND

mind·less \'mīndləs, *rapid* -nl-\ *adj* [ME *myndles,* fr. OE *gemyndlēas* foolish, senseless, fr. *gemynd* mind, memory + *-lēas* -less — more at MIND] **1 a** : destitute of mind or consciousness : characterized by or exhibiting a lack of consciousness ⟨hatred toward the sea as though it were not a ~ force but a conscious one —C.B.Nordhoff & J.N.Hall⟩ ⟨fell into a ~ sleep —Mary Austin⟩ **b** : lacking or held to be without intellectual powers : STUPID, UNINTELLIGENT ⟨become more than friendly with . . . a gorgeous ~ creature who teaches riding —*New Yorker*⟩ ⟨his white hair crested like a wave over his ~ face —Edith Sitwell⟩ **c** : characterized by or displaying no use of the powers of the intellect : UNTHINKING ⟨that deep ~ sympathy —Douglas Stewart⟩ **d** : out of one's mind : MAD **2** : unattentive to : having no concern or interest for — usu. used with *of* ⟨empiricism . . . ~ of what has been painfully learned about Communist behavior in the past —Sidney Hook⟩ ⟨the younger men . . . dive for sixpences ~ of sharks —Joseph Crowe⟩ — **mind·less·ly** *adv* — **mind·less·ness** *n* -ES

mind out *vi, dial* : to watch out

mind reader *n* : one that professes or is held to have ability in mind reading

mind reading *n* : the art or faculty of perceiving another's thought without normal means of communication

minds *pres 3d sing of* MIND, *pl of* MIND

mind-set \ˈ≈ˌ≈\ *n* **1** : the direction of one's thinking ⟨our educational system has been the most powerful influence in determining the *mind-set* . . . of our youth —C.C.Morrison⟩ **2** : a fixed state of mind

mind's eye *n* [ME *myndes ye,* fr. *mindes, mindes* (gen. of *minde, mynde* mind, memory) + *ye, eie, eye* eye] : the faculty held capable of seeing a mental vision consisting of an imaginary or recollected sight as opposed to one actually seen at the time ⟨in my *mind's eye* I could still see the fields covered with tanks, guns, and tents —G.S.Patton⟩ ⟨a hundred times, in his *mind's eye,* his car stopped at their little gate —D.D.Lloyd⟩

mind stuff *n* : the elemental material held to be the basis of reality and to consist internally of the constituent substance of mind and to appear externally in the form of matter — compare MONISM 1a

¹**mine** [ME *min,* fr. OE *mīn,* suppletive gen. of *ic* I; OE *mīn* akin to OHG *mīn* (suppletive gen. of *ih* I), ON *mīn* (suppletive gen. of *ek* I), Goth *meina* (suppletive gen. of *ik* I); all fr. a prehistoric Gmc inflectional form derived fr. the root of OE *mē* me — more at ME] *obs possessive of* ²I

²**mine** \'mīn\ *adj* [ME *min,* fr. OE *mīn* — more at MY] *archaic* : MY — used as modifier of a following noun esp. when it immediately precedes a word beginning with a vowel or *h* ⟨~ eyes⟩ ⟨~ own true love⟩ ⟨~ host⟩ ⟨~ hour is not yet come —Jn 2:4 (AV)⟩ or sometimes as a modifier of a preceding noun ⟨mother ~⟩ or as the first of two possessive adjectives modifying the same following noun ⟨~ and your ticket —Sydney Smith⟩

³**mine** \"\ *pron, sing or pl in constr* [ME *min,* fr. OE *mīn,* fr. *mīn,* adj., my — more at MY] **1** : my one or my ones — used without a following noun as a pronoun equivalent in meaning to the adjective *my* ⟨your dog is large and ~ is small⟩ ⟨your eyes are blue and ~ are brown⟩; often used after *of* to single out one or more members of a class belonging to or connected with the one speaking or writing ⟨a friend of ~⟩ ⟨four or five books of ~⟩ or merely to identify something or someone as belonging to or connected with one speaking or writing without any implication of membership in a more extensive class ⟨those big feet of ~⟩ ⟨that preoccupied manner of ~⟩ **2** : something belonging to me : what belongs to me ⟨vengeance is ~, I will repay, says the Lord —Rom 12:19 (RSV)⟩

⁴**mine** \"\ *n* -S *often attrib* [ME, fr. MF, fr. (assumed) VL *mina,* prob. of Celt origin; akin to W *mwyn* ore] **1 a** (1) : a pit or excavation in the earth from which mineral substances (as ores, precious stones, or coal) are taken by digging or by some other method of extraction ⟨a gold ~⟩ ⟨an asphalt ~⟩ — compare OPENCUT, QUARRY (2) : such a pit or excavation together with the land, buildings, and machinery belonging to it **b** : an ore deposit ⟨newly discovered ~⟩ **2** *Brit* : something that is mined : MINERAL ORE; *esp* : iron ore **3 a** : a subterranean passage excavated under the wall of a besieged fortress and designed to give access to the besiegers or to cause the wall to fall as a result of the removal of its foundation **b** (1) : a cavity or excavation in the earth under an enemy position and containing an explosive charge for destroying enemy personnel, material, or works (2) : the explosive charge placed in such a cavity or excavation **c** : an encased explosive anchored or floating in water or placed on or under the earth that may be detonated by contact, the passage of time, magnetic force, sound waves, or controlled means and designed to destroy or damage personnel or an object (as a boat, airplane, or vehicle) — compare ACOUSTIC 1c, AERIAL MINE, ANTIPERSONNEL, ³CONTACT 1, LAND MINE, MAGNETIC MINE, SONIC MINE **4** : a rich source of supply : an abundant store from which something may be obtained in plenty ⟨this book . . . is a ~ of curious and interesting information —R.S. Churchill⟩ ⟨intellectually he was an inexhaustible ~ of sympathy —W.J.Locke⟩ ⟨the window is a favorite ~ of motives for artists to exploit —Henry Adams⟩ **5** : a place where ore, metals, or precious stones are obtained by digging or washing the soil ⟨a placer ~⟩ **6** : a pyrotechnic piece comprising various small fireworks (as stars) that are scattered into the air with a loud report **7** : a gallery made by an insect esp. between the surfaces of a leaf

⁵**mine** \"\ *vb* -ED/-ING/-S [ME *minen,* fr. MF *miner,* fr. OF, fr. *mine,* n. — more at ⁴MINE] *vi* **1** : to dig in the earth esp. for the purpose of constructing a mine under an enemy fortification ⟨they began to ~ under the castle —Richard Grafton⟩ **2** : to dig a mine : to get ore, metals, coal, or precious stones out of the earth : to work in a mine ~ *vt* **1 a** : to dig under for the purpose of gaining access through or causing the collapse of (as the walls of an enemy fortification) **b** : to attack, ruin, or destroy by slow and secret means : UNDERMINE **2 a** : to get (as ore, metal, or other natural constituent) from the earth (as by digging, blasting, or pumping) ⟨to ~ oil shale⟩ ⟨to ~ ground water⟩ ⟨to ~ gold⟩ **b** : to extract from a usu. rich source of supply ⟨novels . . . from which more skillful dramatizers have been able to ~ good theatrical plays —*London Calling*⟩ **3** : to dig or make a hollow in : burrow beneath the surface of ⟨a larva that ~*s* leaves⟩ **4 a** : to place an explosive charge in or under for the purpose of destroying (as an enemy fortification) **b** : to lay military mines in (as water) : place mines in or under (as land) **5** : to furnish with underground passages : make subterranean passages under **6 a** : to dig into (as the ground) for ore or metal **b** : to process for obtaining a natural constituent ⟨~ the air for nitrogen⟩ ⟨~ sea water for magnesium⟩ **c** : to dig into (a usu. rich source of supply) for the purpose of obtaining items of use or value ⟨the many historical novels that have *mined* the rich vein of history in upstate New York —*Amer. Guide Series: N.Y.*⟩ ⟨so far *mined* only a fraction of the cultural treasures of those times —*Saturday Rev.*⟩ **7 a** : to crop (as land) repeatedly without applying fertilizer **b** *or* **mine out** : to deplete the riches or resources from (a source of supply) without making any provision for replenishment ⟨a system . . . which will increase its productivity instead of *mining* its wealth —Elspeth Huxley⟩ ⟨has . . . scholarship at last *mined out* the field —T.H.Williams⟩

mineable *var of* MINABLE

minecraft \ˈ≈ˌ≈\ *n* : warships of various types whose primary mission is laying or sweeping mines ⟨commander of ~ in the Pacific Fleet —Walter Karig & Welbourn Kelley⟩

mine detector *n* : a device for locating buried or concealed mines usu. by indicating the presence of metal or by giving a signal when it is passed over something different from the ground in the vicinity

minefield \ˈ≈ˌ≈\ *n* : an area occupied by mines anchored or sunk in water or buried in the ground for offensive or defensive purposes ⟨tanks could pass through the ~*s* and engage the enemy —Walter Nash⟩ ⟨~*s* are swept by flotillas —F.E. Dodman⟩

minehead \ˈ≈ˌ≈\ *n* : PITHEAD

mine inspector *n* : one that checks mines to determine the safety condition of working areas, equipment, ventilation, and electricity and to detect fire and dust hazards

minelayer \ˈ≈ˌ≈≈\ *n* : a naval vessel especially equipped for or engaged in the laying of underwater mines

mineowner \ˈ≈ˌ≈≈\ *n* : a whole or part owner of a mine

mine pig *n* : pig iron made wholly from ore

mine planter *n* : a small ship resembling a minelayer and formerly used by the U. S. Army to lay mines as part of harbor defense operations

min·er \'mīnə(r)\ *n* -S [ME *miner, minere,* alter. (influenced by *-er, -ere* -er) of *minour,* fr. OF *mineor,* fr. *miner* to mine + *-eor* -or — more at MINE] **1** : one that mines: as **a** : one that constructs or lays military mines; *esp* : a soldier having such duties **b** : one engaged in the business or occupation of getting ore, coal, precious substances, or other natural substances out of the earth **c** : a machine for automatic mining (as of coal) **d** : a worker on the construction of underground tunnels and shafts (as for roads, railways, waterways) **2 a** : any of numerous insects that in the larval state excavate galleries in the parenchyma of leaves **b** : any of several honey eaters of Australia and Tasmania (as *Myzantha melanocephala*)

min·er·ag·ra·phy \ˌminəˈragrəfē\ *or* **min·er·al·og·ra·phy** \ˌminərəˈlägrəfē\ *n* -ES [*mineragraphy* fr. *mineral* + *-graphy; mineralography* fr. *mineral* + *-o-* + *-graphy*] : the technique of studying polished surfaces of minerals with the reflecting microscope

¹**min·er·al** \'min(ə)rəl\ *n* -S [ME, fr. ML *minerale,* fr. neut. of *mineralis,* adj.] **1 a** : a solid homogeneous crystalline chemical element or compound (as diamond or quartz) that results from the inorganic processes of nature and that has a characteristic crystal structure and chemical composition or range of compositions — compare METAMICT, MINERALOID **b** : any of various naturally occurring homogeneous or apparently homogeneous and usu. but not necessarily solid substances (as ore, coal, asbestos, asphalt, borax, clay, fuller's earth, pigments, precious stones, rock phosphate, salt, soapstone, sulfur, building stone, cement rock, peat, sand, gravel, slate, salts extracted from river, lake, and ocean waters, petroleum, water, natural gas, air, and gases extracted from the air) obtained for man's use usu. from the ground **c** : a synthetic substance having the chemical composition and crystalline form and other physical properties of a naturally occurring mineral ⟨compounds made in the laboratory or in the smelting furnace are at best called artificial ~*s* —E.S.Dana⟩ **2** *obs* : MINE ⟨like some ore among a ~ of metals base —Shak.⟩ **3** : something that is neither animal nor vegetable (as in the old general classification of things into three kingdoms: animal, vegetable, and mineral) **4** : ORE — used esp. in the mining industry **5** : an inorganic substance; *esp* : a mineral element whether in the form of an ion, compound, or complex — compare ³ASH 1b ⟨the ~*s* or the contents of the ash from the body —K.F.Maxcy⟩ **6 minerals** *pl, Brit* : MINERAL WATER; *esp* : an artificially carbonated water sometimes flavored (as ginger ale) ⟨~*s* were served . . . as well as morning coffee and afternoon teas —Sylvia T. Warner⟩

²**mineral** \"\ *adj* [ME, fr. ML *mineralis,* fr. *minera* ore, mine (fr. OF *miniere* mine, fr. *mine*) + L *-alis* -al — more at MINE] **1** *obs* **a** : of or relating to mines **b** : skilled in or well informed about mining **2** : of or relating to minerals : consisting of or of the nature of a mineral ⟨~ ores⟩ : INORGANIC ⟨~ deposits in the water passages surrounding the valve seats —H.F. Blanchard & Ralph Ritchen⟩ **3** : impregnated with mineral substances (as salts) ⟨~ waters⟩

mineral acid *n* : an inorganic acid ⟨the strong *mineral acids,* such as nitric, sulfuric, and hydrochloric —W.C.Tobie⟩

mineral bister *n* : SHERRY 2

mineral black *n* : a black pigment: as **a** : one made by grinding carbonaceous shale or slate **b** : a natural pigment containing graphite **c** : black iron oxide

mineral blue *n* **1** : a blue pigment: as **a** : a natural pigment made by grinding the mineral azurite or a synthetic pigment of similar composition — called also *mountain blue;* compare BLUE VERDITER **b** : BREMEN BLUE 2 **c** : an iron blue usu. lightened by admixture (as with white clay) **2 a** : AZURITE BLUE **b** : ANTWERP BLUE 2

mineral brown *n* **1** : any of several colors of native earths colored with iron oxide that average the color negro — called also *iron, metallic brown* **2** : any of several pigments (as metallic brown) from natural sources

mineral caoutchouc *n* : ELATERITE

mineral charcoal *n* : a substance resembling charcoal that is interlaminated in silky fibrous layers in beds of ordinary bituminous coal — called also *mother of coal*

mineral coal *n* : COAL 3a

mineral color *n* : an inorganic pigment usu. of natural origin

mineral dressing *n* : the mechanical preparation of a mineral (as ore) either for direct use or for further processing

mineral element *n* : a chemical element usu. other than carbon, hydrogen, oxygen, or nitrogen that is a constituent of plant or animal tissue and in most cases is found in the ash remaining after incineration of the tissue ⟨specific roles of the *mineral elements* in plants —B.S.Meyer & D.B.Anderson⟩ — compare MACRONUTRIENT, TRACE ELEMENT

mineral gray *n* : a light greenish gray that is yellower, lighter, and stronger than French gray and darker than ash gray

mineral green *n* **1** : a green pigment: as **a** : MALACHITE GREEN 1a **b** : SCHEELE'S GREEN **2** : MALACHITE GREEN 3

min·er·al·ist \'min(ə)rələst\ *n* -S [¹*mineral* + *-ist*] *archaic* : MINERALOGIST ⟨the mountain . . . has several of the appearances described by ~*s* —Jedidiah Morse⟩

min·er·al·iza·tion \ˌmin(ə)rələˈzāshən, -lī'-\ *n* -S **1** : the action of mineralizing : the state of being mineralized ⟨~ of soil nitrogen⟩ ⟨~ of bone⟩ **2 a** : the process of change or metamorphism whereby minerals are secondarily developed in a rock; *esp* : the formation or introduction of ore minerals into previously existing rock masses : METALLIZATION **b** : the state resulting from such a process of change **3** : deposition in the cell wall of inorganic salts

min·er·al·ize \'min(ə)rəˌlīz\ *vb* -ED/-ING/-S *vt* **1** : to transform (a metal) into an ore **2** : to impregnate or supply with minerals or any inorganic compound ⟨*mineralized* water⟩ ⟨~ organic matter⟩ : convert into mineral or inorganic form ⟨*mineralized* nitrogen in soils⟩ **3** : PETRIFY ~ *vi* : to promote the formation of minerals

min·er·al·ized \-zd\ *adj* : having or characterized by a usu. abundant supply of ore ⟨the red stains that signalize ~ land —*Science Illustrated*⟩ ⟨the most richly ~ district in the world —C.O.Dunbar⟩

min·er·al·iz·er \-zə(r)\ *n* -S **1** : an element that in combination with a metal forms an ore ⟨in galena sulfur is a ~⟩ **2** : a dissolved gas or vapor (as water or fluorine) that promotes the crystallization of minerals in a molten magma, in adjacent rock, or in veins genetically related to the intrusion of the magma

mineral jelly *n* : a semisolid substance from petroleum that is similar to but cruder than petrolatum and that is used as a stabilizer in explosives

mineral kingdom *n* : the one of the three basic groups of natural objects that comprises inorganic objects — compare ANIMAL KINGDOM, PLANT KINGDOM

mineral lands *n pl* **:** lands usu. held by a federal government as public lands and valuable for deposits of metals and other minerals (as marble, slate, petroleum, asphalt, and guano)

mineral lease *n* **:** MINING LEASE

min·er·alo·corticoid \ˌmin(ə)rəlō+\ *n* [ISV [1]*mineral* + *-o-* + *corticoid*] **:** a corticoid (as deoxycorticosterone) that affects chiefly the electrolyte and fluid balance in the body

min·er·al·og·i·cal \ˌmin(ə)rəˈläjəkəl, -jēk-\ *also* **min·er·al·og·ic** \-jik, -jēk\ *adj* [*mineralogical* fr. *mineralogy* + *-ical*; *mineralogic* prob. fr. F *minéralogique*, fr. *minéralogie* (prob. fr. E *mineralogy*) + *-ique* -ic] **:** of or relating to mineralogy ⟨a ~ table⟩ ⟨~ chemistry⟩ ⟨~ changes⟩

min·er·al·o·gist \÷ˌminəˈräləjəst, -ral-\ *n* -s [prob. fr. (assumed) NL *mineralogia* mineralogy + E *-ist*] **:** a specialist in mineralogy

mineralography *var of* MINERAGRAPHY

min·er·al·o·gy \÷ˌminəˈräləjē, -ral-, -ji\ *n* -ES [prob. fr. (assumed) NL *mineralogia*, irreg. fr. ML *minerale* mineral + L *-logia* -logy] **1 :** the science of minerals that deals with their crystallography and their physical and chemical properties in general, their classification, and the ways of finding and distinguishing them **2 :** the materials of the science of mineralogy (as minerals or the attributes of minerals or mineral formations) ⟨the ~ of the Black Hills⟩ **3 :** a treatise of the science of mineralogy

min·er·al·oid \ˈmin(ə)rəˌlȯid\ *n* -s [ISV [1]*mineral* + *-oid*; prob. orig. formed in G] **:** an amorphous substance that would otherwise have the attributes of a mineral; *esp* **:** a metamict substance derived from a mineral — compare GEL MINERAL

mineral oil *n* **:** a liquid product of mineral origin that is within the viscosity limits recognized for oils (as petroleum, shale oil, or any oil obtained from them by refining); *esp* **:** LIQUID PETROLATUM — compare HYDROCARBON OIL, PARAFFIN OIL

mineral orange *n* **1 :** ORANGE MINERAL **2 :** FIRE RED 1

mineral pigment *n* **:** an inorganic pigment whether natural or synthetic — distinguished from *organic pigment*

mineral pitch *n* **:** [1]ASPHALT 1

mineral pulp *n* **:** a fibrous variety of talc used as a filler in paper manufacture

mineral purple *n* **1 :** a dark red pigment consisting of iron oxide **2 :** PURPLE OF CASSIUS

mineral red *n* **:** a grayish red that is bluer and duller than Pompeian red or bois de rose and yellower and duller than appleblossom

mineral resin *n* **:** any of a group of resinous usu. fossilized deposits found in various rocks **:** BITUMEN **:** ASPHALT

mineral right *n* **:** the legal right or title to all or to specified minerals in a given tract **:** the right to explore for and extract such minerals or to receive a royalty for them

mineral rod *n* **:** DIVINING ROD

mineral rubber *n* **1 :** any of various rubbery substances of mineral origin (as asphalt) **2 :** an artificial asphalt obtained usu. by blowing petroleum residues with air and used in compounding rubber and in insulation — compare BLOWN OIL 2

mineral salt *n* **1 :** a salt of an inorganic acid **2 :** a salt occurring as a mineral (as rock salt)

mineral seal oil *n* **:** a distillate of petroleum that boils higher than kerosine and is used as an illuminant and as a solvent oil

mineral soil *n* **:** a soil derived from minerals or rocks and containing little humus or organic matter

mineral spirit *n* **:** PETROLEUM SPIRIT

mineral spring *n* **:** a spring with water containing much mineral matter in solution that is usu. enough and of such kinds as to be noticeable to the taste

mineral surveyor *n* **:** a surveyor appointed under federal law and authorized to make official surveys of mineral lands — called also *deputy surveyor*

mineral tallow *n* **:** HATCHETTINE

mineral tanning *n* **:** the process of tanning (an animal skin) by impregnating with metallic salts — compare CHROME TANNING, TAW

mineral tar *n* **:** MALTHA

mineral violet *n* **:** MANGANESE VIOLET

mineral water *n* **:** water naturally or artificially impregnated with mineral salts or gases (as carbon dioxide) — compare SALINE WATER, SODA WATER 2a, SULFUR WATER

mineral wax *n* **:** a wax of mineral origin; *esp* **:** OZOKERITE

mineral white *n* **1 :** BLANC FIXE **2 :** gypsum ground and used in pigments

mineral wool *n* **:** any of various light-weight vitreous materials produced in the form of fibers that resemble wool fibers or glass fibers and that are used as such or after conversion into granular form, felted form (as in batts, blankets, or boards), or molded form chiefly in heat and sound insulation, in insulating cements, and as filter media: as **a :** SLAG WOOL **b :** ROCK WOOL **c :** GLASS WOOL

mineral yellow *n* **1 a :** YELLOW OCHER **b :** ORPIMENT 2 **2 :** CASSEL YELLOW 1

miner's anemia *n* **:** HOOKWORM DISEASE

miner's asthma *or* **miner's consumption** *n* **:** PNEUMOCONIOSIS

miner's cramps *n pl* **:** HEAT CRAMPS

miner's inch *n* **:** a unit of water flow that varies with locality; *esp* **:** a flow equal to 1.5 cubic feet per minute

miner's phthisis *n* **:** a disease of miners: as **a :** ANTHRACOSIS **b :** ANTHRACOSILICOSIS **c :** PNEUMOCONIOSIS

miner's right *n* **:** a license given to Australian miners to explore for and extract a mineral (as gold)

miner's tent *n* **:** a usu. triangular tent that is suspended from a tree or set up with one center pole

miner's worm *n* **:** the hookworm (*Ancylostoma duodenale*) that often infests miners and tunnel workers

mine–run \ˈ≈ˌ≈\ *n* **1 :** the unsorted product of a mine **2 :** a product of common or average grade ⟨the *mine-run* of commercial breads pall with continued eating —Lee Anderson⟩

min·ery \ˈmīnərē\ *n* -ES [ML *mineria, minaria*, fr. OF *miniere* mine — more at MINERAL] *archaic* **:** a place where mining is carried on

mi·nes·tra \məˈnestrə\ *n* -s [It, fr. *minestrare* to serve minestra, dish up, fr. L *ministrare* to serve, dish up — more at MINISTER] **:** Italian vegetable soup **:** MINESTRONE

min·e·stro·ne \ˌminəˈstrōnē, ÷-ōn\ *n* -s [It, aug. of *minestra*] **:** a rich thick vegetable soup with dried beans, macaroni, vermicelli, or similar ingredients sometimes topped with grated cheese

minesweeper \ˈ≈ˌ≈≈\ *n* **:** a warship designed for sweeping or neutralizing mines

minesweeping \ˈ≈ˌ≈≈\ *n* **:** the action of dragging a body of water for submarine or floating mines in order to remove, neutralize, explode, or otherwise make them harmless

mi·nette \məˈnet\ *n* -s [G, fr. F, oolitic iron ore, fr. F *mine* ore, mine + *-ette* — more at MINE] **1 :** a dark igneous rock composed chiefly of biotite and orthoclase that occurs usu. in narrow dikes and sheets and that constitutes one of the lamprophyres **2** [F] **:** an oolitic iron ore containing as a rule 28 to 48 percent of iron and 1.5 to 2 percent of phosphorus that is plentiful in Luxemburg and Lorraine and is adapted for the basic Bessemer process

minever *var of* MINIVER

mine worker *n* **:** a workman in a mine

[1]**ming** *vt* -ED/-ING/-S [ME *mingen* to mention, remind, fr. OE *myngian, myndgian, mynegian*; akin to OE *gemynd* mind, memory — more at MIND] *obs* **:** MENTION

[2]**ming** \ˈmiŋ\ *var of* MENG

[3]**Ming** \"\ *adj, usu cap* [*Ming*, Chin. dynasty (1368–1644), fr. Chin (Pek) *ming*[2] bright, clear, luminous] **:** of, relating to, or having the characteristics of the period of the Ming dynasty and esp. the art forms developed during that period ⟨a *Ming* bowl⟩ ⟨ordinary *Ming* porcelain is apt to be heavy —Bernard Leach⟩

minge \ˈminj\ *n* -s [prob. alter. of *midge*] **:** MIDGE; *esp* **:** BITING MIDGE

[1]**min·gle** \ˈmiŋgəl\ *vb* **mingled; mingled; mingling** \-g(ə)liŋ\ **mingles** [ME *menglen*, freq. of *mengen* to mix, mingle, fr. OE *mengan*; akin to MD *mengen* to mix, mingle, MHG *mengen* to mix, mingle, Gk *massein, mattein* to knead, Russ *myagkiĭ* soft] *vt* **1 :** to bring or combine together or with something else so that the components remain distinguishable in the combination **:** INTERMIX, MIX ⟨its designer . . . has *mingled* type, photographs and contemporary prints to make a book —J.K.Bettersworth⟩ ⟨these questions of . . . economic behavior clearly ~ the fields of economics and law —G.B. Hurff⟩ **2 :** to mix so that the components become physically united or form a new combination ⟨the two rivers ~ their waters to form a lake⟩ **3 :** to make or prepare by mixing ingredients **:** CONCOCT ⟨~ a sleeping draft⟩ **~** *vi* **1 :** to become combined or brought together or with something else — used esp. of things ⟨three major state highways all meet, ~, and marvellously disengage themselves —*New Yorker*⟩ ⟨beguiling byways where fact and fancy ~ —Drew Middleton⟩ ⟨apple and peach orchards along the route ~ with farms and vineyards —*Amer. Guide Series: Va.*⟩ ⟨the muddy water of the river ~*s* with the green of the Gulf —*Amer. Guide Series: La.*⟩ **2 a :** to associate or come in contact — used esp. of people ⟨as communication expands and races ~ —A.W.Hummel⟩ ⟨on the streets three classes ~ but do not mix —*Amer. Guide Series: Texas*⟩ ⟨he ~*s* only with millionaires —H.J.Laski⟩ **b :** to move about (as in a group) ⟨~ occasionally in society —Sir Walter Scott⟩ ⟨newspaper spies who were able to ~ among politicians —W.A.Swanberg⟩ **syn** see MIX

[2]**mingle** \"\ *n* -s **1** *archaic* **:** the action of mingling or the state of being mingled **2** *archaic* **:** something that is mingled **:** MIXTURE

[1]**min·gle–man·gle** \ˈ≈≈ˌmaŋgəl\ *n* -s [redupl. of [2]*mingle*] **:** a usu. confused mixture or medley **:** HODGEPODGE

[2]**mingle–mangle** *vt, obs* **:** to make a mingle-mangle of

min·gle·ment \ˈmiŋgəlmənt\ *n* -s **:** the action or an instance of mingling ⟨a close ~ of Egyptian and Babylonian culture—*Times Lit. Supp.*⟩

min·go \ˈmiŋ(ˌ)gō\ *n, pl* **mingoes** *or* **mingos** *usu cap* [of Algonquian origin; akin to Del *Mingwe* Iroquois, lit., stealthy, treacherous] **:** IROQUOIS 1b

min·gre·li·an \minˈgrēlēən, miŋˈ-\ *also* **min·grel** \ˈmiŋgrəl, ˈmiŋg-\ *n, pl* **mingrelian** *or* **mingrelians** *also* **mingrel** *or* **mingrels** *usu cap* **1 a :** a people of the Kutais region of the Caucasus related to the Georgians whose physical beauty they share **b :** a member of such people **2 :** the South Caucasic language of the Mingrelian people

ming tree *n* [perh. fr. *Ming*, Chin. dynasty (1368–1644) — more at MING] **1 :** a dwarfed evergreen conifer grown in a container or pot **2 :** an artificial plant patterned after bonsai and made by wiring or otherwise attaching flattened pads of prostrate alpine buckwheat (*Eriogonum ovalifolium*) left natural gray, dyed, or painted to one or more twiggy branches usu. of manzanita — called also *Peruvian cypress* **3 a :** BONSAI **b :** an ornamental arrangement patterned after the bonsai

min·gy \ˈminjē\ *adj* -ER/-EST [perh. blend of [1]*mean* and *stingy*] **:** STINGY, MEAN

min·hag \ˈminˈhäg, ˈ≈ˌ≈\ *n, pl* **min·ha·gim** \minˈhäˌgēm, ˌ≈≈ˈ≈\ [Heb *minhāgh* custom] **1 :** Jewish religious custom **2 :** the form of Hebrew liturgy prevailing in a particular community **3 :** local Jewish religious practices not specified in the Talmud or medieval rabbinical codes but having authority through long observance

min·hah *or* **min·chah** *also* **min·ha** *or* **min·cha** \minˈkä, ˈminkə\ *n* -s [Heb *minḥāh*, lit., gift, offering] **:** a daily afternoon liturgy of the Jews — compare MAARIB, SHAHARITH

min·i·a·ceous \ˌminēˈāshəs\ *adj* [L *miniaceus*, fr. *minium* cinnabar, red lead + *-aceus* -aceous — more at MINIUM] **:** of the color of minium or red lead

min·i·a·scape \ˈminēəˌskāp\ *n* [[2]*miniature* + *-scape*] **:** a dish garden made with dry or other plants and materials that do not require water — compare BONSAI

min·i·ate \ˈminēˌāt\ *vt* -ED/-ING/-S [L *miniatus*, past part. of *miniare* to color with cinnabar or red lead, fr. *minium* cinnabar, red lead] **1 :** to paint with red lead or vermilion **2 a :** to decorate (as a manuscript) with letters or the like painted red **:** RUBRICATE **b :** ILLUMINATE 4

[1]**min·i·a·ture** \ˈmin(ē)əˌchu̇(ə)r, -ùə, -ˌchə(r), -nichə(r), -nēchə(r) *also* -ˌtù-, -ˌtyù- *sometimes* -nyəˌ-\ *n* -s [It *miniatura* picture on a small scale, art of manuscript illumination, fr. *miniato* (past part. of *miniare* to illuminate a manuscript) (fr. L *miniatus*, past part. of *miniare* to color with cinnabar or red lead) + *-ura* -ure] **1 :** a representation on a much reduced scale **:** a small copy or image ⟨turned the valley into a lush ~ of the Imperial Valley across the border —Marion Wilhelm⟩ ⟨a ~ of the . . . headquarters store in its capacity to meet every grade of customer —McKenzie Porter⟩ **2 :** a drawing or painting included in a book or manuscript esp. of the medieval period **:** ILLUMINATION **3 :** the art of painting miniatures **4 :** a portrait or other painting done on a very small scale (as on ivory or metal) ⟨the art of portrait ~*s* was orginated in England —Louise H. Burchfield⟩ **5 :** a chess problem with few (as seven or fewer) chessmen **6 :** a set or model built on a reduced scale that appears to be of normal size when photographed (as in the movies or television) **7 :** a small camera **8 :** MINIATURE SHEET **9** *also* **miniature rose :** FAIRY ROSE **10 :** a production (as in literature or music) of short length or restricted scope — **in miniature :** in a greatly diminished size, form, or scale **:** in microcosm ⟨imitating *in miniature* the elaborate programmes of the state universities —W.L.Sperry⟩ ⟨a . . . carnival which is a sort of Mardi Gras fiesta *in miniature* —Green Peyton⟩

[2]**miniature** \"\ *adj* **1 :** being or represented on a small scale ⟨~ reproductions⟩ ⟨a ~ book⟩ ⟨a ~ war⟩ **2 :** of or relating to still photography in which film 35 millimeters wide or smaller is used ⟨a ~ camera⟩ ⟨a ~ negative⟩ **syn** see SMALL

[3]**miniature** \"\ *vt* -ED/-ING/-S **:** to represent in a small compass or on a small scale ⟨this round orb . . . ~*s* the world —*New Monthly Mag.*⟩

miniature golf *n* **:** a novelty golf game played with a putter on a miniature course having tunnels, bridges, sharp corners, and other obstacles over which the ball must be guided

miniature pink *n* **:** a pale to grayish yellowish pink — called also *reveree*

miniature sheet *n* **1 :** a small sheet of postage stamps (as of 25 stamps) with gum and perforations that is printed as a souvenir and bears in the margins lettering identifying some notable event being commemorated **2 :** SOUVENIR SHEET 1 **3 :** a set of mounted postage stamps displaying all of the plate numbers (as four) from an original sheet in their correct relative positions

min·i·a·tur·ist \-chu̇rəst, -chər-\ *n* -s [F *miniaturiste*, fr. *miniature* picture on a small scale (fr. It *miniatura*) + *-iste* -ist] **:** a maker of miniatures

min·i·a·tur·iza·tion \ˌ≈(≈)≈ˌchu̇rəˈzāshən, -ˌchər-\ *n* -s **:** the action or process of miniaturizing ⟨heat is a major problem in ~ of . . . many electrical instruments —Annesta R. Gardner⟩ ⟨the recent trend toward ~ in the . . . field of electronics —*Materials & Methods*⟩

min·i·a·tur·ize \ˈ≈(≈)≈ˌchu̇ˌrīz, -ˌchəˌ-\ *vt* -ED/-ING/-S **:** to design or construct in small size esp. for economy of space or weight ⟨an all-out campaign to ~ electronic equipment —*advt*⟩

min·i·bus \ˈminəbəs\ *n* [prob. blend of [2]*miniature* and *omnibus*] **:** a light carriage usu. having a rear door and seats for four passengers and formerly used as a cab — compare OMNIBUS

min·i·cam \ˈminəˌkam\ *also* **mini·camera** \ˈminə+ˌ-\ *n* -s [by shortening fr. *miniature camera*] **:** a miniature camera

mini·car \ˈminə+ˌ-\ *n* [[2]*miniature* + *car*] **:** a small automobile

min·i·con·jou \ˌminəˈkän(ˌ)jü\ *n, pl* **miniconjou** *or* **miniconjous** *usu cap* **:** a people of the western plains constituting a division of the Teton Dakota

min·ié ball \ˈminē-, -ē,ā-\ *n, sometimes cap M* [after Claude Étienne *Minié* †1879 Fr. army officer] **:** a rifle bullet having a cylindrical body, conical head, and hollow base and much used in the middle of the 19th century

min·i·fer \ˈminəfə(r)\ *dial var of* MINIVER

min·i·fi·ca·tion \ˌminəfəˈkāshən\ *n* -s [fr. *minify*, after such pairs as E *magnify*: *magnification*] **:** the action or process of minifying

min·i·fy \ˈminəˌfī\ *vt* -ED/-ING/-S [L *minimus* smallest + E *-fy*] **:** to make small or smaller **:** LESSEN

[1]**min·i·kin** \ˈminəkən, -nēk-\ *n* -s [obs. D *minneken* darling, fr. MD *minnekijn*, fr. *minne* love, beloved + *-kijn* -kin; akin to OHG *minna* love, ON *minni* memory, Goth *gaminthi* remembrance, OE *gemynd* mind, memory — more at MIND] **1** *obs* **a :** a thin gut treble string of a viol or lute **b :** LUTE, VIOL **2** *obs* **:** DARLING 1a **3** *archaic* **:** a small creature **:** a diminutive or insignificant thing ⟨prepared to harry some whitebait threading the tide but . . . the ~*s* escaped —Hugh McCrae⟩

[2]**minikin** \"\ *adj* **1** *archaic* **:** dainty in manner or appearance; *esp* **:** AFFECTED **3** ⟨the pettiness, the ~ finical effect of this little man —Nathaniel Hawthorne⟩ **2 :** very small in size or form **:** DIMINUTIVE, MINIATURE, TINY ⟨the ~ little dribble that I called a canal —S.H.Adams⟩ ⟨a ~ fraction of history⟩ **3** *obs* **:** SHRILL — used of a voice ⟨one blast of thy ~ mouth —Shak.⟩

[1]**min·im** \ˈminəm\ *n* -s [in sense 1, fr. ME *mynym*, fr. ML *minima*, fr. L, fem. of *minimus* smallest, least; in sense 2, fr. ML *minimus*, fr. L, smallest, least; in other senses, fr. L *minimus* smallest, least — more at MINIMUM] **1 a** (1) **:** the note in mensural notation formerly equaling one half or one third the value of the semibreve depending upon whether imperfect or perfect time respectively and constituting sometimes the shortest note in use (2) **:** HALF NOTE **b :** HALF REST **2** *usu cap* **:** a member of an austere order of mendicant hermits or friars founded in the 15th century by St. Francis of Paola **3 :** something very minute: as **a :** a creature or thing of the least size or consequence **b :** the smallest or least possible part or particle **:** JOT **4 :** a single downstroke in penmanship (as any of the three in the letter *m*) **5 :** either of two units of liquid capacity equal to $\frac{1}{60}$ fluid dram: **a :** a U. S. unit equivalent to 0.003759 cubic inches — see MEASURE table **b :** a British unit equivalent to 0.003612 cubic inches — see MEASURE table **6 :** a small worker ant among ants having polymorphic workers — compare MAXIM

[2]**minim** \"\ *adj* **:** of the smallest size **:** MINUTE ⟨a ~ mammal which you might imprison in the finger of your glove —George Eliot⟩

[3]**minim** \"\ *n* -s [alter. (prob. influenced by [1]*minim*) of *minnow*] *dial* **:** a small fish; *esp* **:** MINNOW

min·i·mal \ˈminəməl\ *adj* [*minimum* + *-al*] **1 :** of, being, or having the character of a minimum **:** constituting the least possible in size, number, or degree **:** extremely minute ⟨a ~ charge for materials⟩ ⟨a willingness to accept ~ terms —Oscar Handlin⟩ ⟨the number required for even ~ defense —Denis Healey⟩ ⟨required . . . to enforce ~ standards —M.W. Straight⟩ **2 :** incapable of being further distinguished significantly **:** depending upon a single articulatory difference ⟨~ distinctions —Daniel Jones⟩

min·i·mal·ist \-ləst\ *n* -s [F *minimaliste*, fr. *minimal* (prob. fr. E) + *-iste* -ist; intended as trans. of Russ *men'shevik* Menshevik] **:** one that favors restricting something (as the functions and powers of a political organization or the achievement of a set of goals) to a minimum — compare MAXIMALIST

minimal lineage *n* **:** a small kinship group usu. comprising the children of one man — contrasted with *maximal lineage*; compare LINEAGE

min·i·mal·ly \-lē\ *adv* **:** in a minimal amount or degree ⟨the program that is to make us . . . ~ secure —Richard Parke⟩

minimal pair *n* **:** two spoken-language items that are identical in all constituents except one (as |ˈded: ˈdad|) and that are often used in demonstrating or testing the phonemicness of the differing constituents

min·i·mi·za·tion \ˌminəməˈzāshən\ *n* -s **:** the action or process of minimizing ⟨interested primarily in the ~ of governmental activity —E.E.Schattschneider⟩

min·i·mize \ˈminəˌmīz\ *vt* -ED/-ING/-S *see -ize in Explan Notes* [*minimum* + *-ize*] **1 :** to reduce to the smallest possible number, degree, or extent ⟨centuries of cultivation have *minimized* the distinctions between the various regions —Jacquetta & Christopher Hawkes⟩ ⟨new operating methods have helped to ~ delays —C.F.Craig⟩ **2 :** to estimate in the least possible terms, number, or proportion; *esp* **:** DEPRECIATE **2** ⟨the navy . . . was inclined to ~ its own losses —E.L.Jones⟩ ⟨will ~ and conceal the impact of this experience —*New Republic*⟩ ⟨inclined to ~ the dangers of her underwater research —*Current Biog.*⟩ **syn** see DECRY

[1]**min·i·mum** \ˈminəməm\ *n, pl* **mini·ma** \-nəmə\ *also* **minimums** [L, neut. of *minimus* smallest, least, superl. fr. the root of L *minor* smaller — more at MINOR] **1** *archaic* **:** a portion (as of matter) so small as to be incapable of further division **2 :** the least quantity assignable, admissible, or possible in a given case — opposed to *maximum* ⟨economic stabilization with a ~ of government regulation —Gerhard Colm⟩ ⟨designed for a maximum of comfort and ~ of clutter —*Technical Education News*⟩ ⟨the cost per page is reduced to a ~ —*Scientific Monthly*⟩ ⟨rigid legal *minima* for bank reserves —E.W.Kemmerer⟩ **3 a :** a number not greater than any other number of a finite set of numbers **b :** a value of a mathematical function of one or more independent variables such that either increasing or decreasing any one of the independent variables by a sufficiently small amount results in an increase in the function **4 :** the lowest degree or amount of variation (as of temperature) reached or recorded **5 a :** the time of least brightness or the magnitude at this time in a variable star **b :** the time when sunspots are least numerous in the 11-year cycle **6 :** MINIM 5

[2]**minimum** \"\ *adj* **:** of, relating to, or constituting a minimum **:** least attainable or possible ⟨the book contains a ~ discussion of the dynamics of British politics —R.R.Hackford⟩ ⟨having achieved the highest ~ wage —H.R.Northrup⟩ ⟨types of taxation . . . administered with ~ possibility of revenue loss —Matthew Woll⟩

minimum dose *n* **:** the smallest dose of a medicine or drug that will produce an effect

minimum lethal dose *n* **:** the smallest dose experimentally found to kill any one animal of a test group

minimum premium *n* **:** the smallest single charge for which an insurer will write a particular policy having a specified period

minimum rate *n* **1 :** an insurance rate applied uniformly to all risks within a given group or class regardless of possible differences in hazards **2 :** the lowest permissible rate at which traffic may be handled by a carrier **3 :** the lowest wage rate assigned for a given task or to a given class of employees — compare MINIMUM WAGE

minimum separable *n* **:** the least separation at which two parallel lines are recognized by the eye as separate — compare MINIMUM VISIBLE, VISUAL ACUITY

minimum visible *n* **:** the least area that can be perceived as distinct by the eye — compare MINIMUM SEPARABLE, VISUAL ACUITY

minimum wage *n* **1 :** LIVING WAGE **2 :** a wage fixed by legal authority or by contract as the least that will provide the minimum standard of living necessary for the health, efficiency, and well-being of designated employees — compare MINIMUM RATE

minimum weight *n* **:** the least weight at which goods or commodities will be transported by a carrier at a specified rate usu. applied to large quantities (as barge load, carload, or truckload)

[1]**min·i·mus** \ˈminəməs\ *n, pl* **mini·mi** \-nəˌmī\ [L, smallest, least] **1 :** a being of the smallest size **:** a tiny creature **2** [NL, fr. L] **:** the little finger or toe **:** the fifth digit

[2]**minimus** \"\ *adj* [L] **:** LEAST: as **a :** the youngest or lowest in standing of several pupils in an English public school who have the same surname **b :** SMALLEST

mining *n* -s [fr. gerund of [5]*mine*] **:** the process or business of making or of working mines

mining claim *n* **:** a tract of land having access to a vein or lode of valuable minerals supposed to exist below and definitely located on its surface by a miner with the right to occupy and mine in the manner and under the conditions prescribed by law usu. involving discovery and the filing of legal notice

mining engineer *n* **:** an engineer whose training or occupation is in mining engineering

mining engineering *n* **:** a branch of engineering concerned primarily with the location and evaluation of mineral deposits, the survey of mining areas, the layout and equipment of mines, and the supervision of mining operations

mining geology *n* **:** a branch of economic geology that deals with the application of geology to mining

mining lease *n* **:** a legal contract for the right to work a mine and extract the mineral or other valuable deposits from it under prescribed conditions of time, price, rental, or royalties — called also *mineral lease*

mining partnership *n* **:** a legal partnership in which the partners agree to conduct mining operations and to share profits and losses, which is recognized in many states as having the character of an ordinary partnership except that it exists only during the existence of actual mining operations, which upon the death or bankruptcy of a partner is not dissolved, and in which upon the sale of a partner's interest his assignee becomes a partner regardless of the consent of the other partners

[1]**min·ion** \'minyən\ *n* -s [MF *mignon* darling, fr. *mignot* dainty, wanton, fr. OF, perh. of Celt origin; akin to OIr *mīn* smooth, gentle — more at MITIGATE] **1 :** an obsequious or servile dependent **:** CREATURE 3a ⟨the inability of a dictator's ∼*s* to tell him the truth —Reinhold Niebuhr⟩ **2 :** a piece of light artillery of about 3-inch caliber and 125 paces range used in the 16th and 17th centuries **3 :** one highly esteemed and favored **:** FAVORITE, IDOL ⟨his great charity to the poor renders him the ∼ of the people —Jonas Hanway⟩ **4** [F *mignonne*, fem. of *mignon*] **:** an old size of type of approximately 7-point and between nonpareil and brevier **5 :** a subordinate (as an agent, deputy, or follower) of an individual or organization; *esp* **:** one having an official status ⟨the masters, not the ∼*s* of the state —Russell Davenport⟩ ⟨a little fat director . . . was dispatching ∼*s* to chivvy and silence the gaping natives —Jeremy Potter⟩ ⟨invasion of their homes by governmental ∼*s* —*Books of the Month*⟩

[2]**minion** \"\ *adj* [MF *mignon*, fr. *mignot* dainty, wanton] *archaic* **:** DELICATE, DAINTY, PRETTY ⟨made . . . a downward crescent of her ∼ mouth —Alfred Tennyson⟩

[3]**minion** *var of* MUNNION

min·ion·ette \,minyə'net\ *n* -s [F *mignonnette*, fr. obs. F, fem. of *mignonnet* dainty, fr. MF, fr. *mignon*] **:** an old size of type of approximately 6 ½-point and between nonpareil and minion

miniscule *var of* MINUSCULE

min·ish \'minish\ *vt* -ED/-ING/-ES [ME *menusen, minishen*, fr. MF *menusier, menuiser* to lessen, mince, fr. (assumed) VL *minutiare* to mince, fr. L *minutia* smallness, minuteness, fr. *minutus* minute + -*ia* -y — more at MINUTE] *archaic* **:** to make less (as in size, amount, or degree) **:** make fewer in number **:** diminish in power or influence **:** LESSEN ⟨have ∼*ed* their numbers —Sir Walter Scott⟩ ⟨would not . . . ∼ by a tittle the respect due to the Magistrate —J.R.Lowell⟩ ⟨without . . . muddling it up with myths which simply ∼ its interest —George Saintsbury⟩

[1]**min·is·ter** \'minəstə(r)\ *n* -s [ME *ministre*, fr. OF, fr. L *minister* servant; akin to L *minor* smaller — more at MINOR] **1 :** one that acts under the orders or authority of another **:** one employed by another for the execution of purposes **:** AGENT ⟨the angels are ∼*s* of the divine will —H.P.Liddon⟩ ⟨a principle to which time is the ∼ and not the master —P.E.More⟩ **2 a :** one duly authorized (as by ordination) to conduct Christian worship, preach the gospel, and administer the sacraments: as (1) **:** a priest who officiates at an altar in the conduct of a service of worship (as a mass) (2) **:** a deacon or subdeacon at solemn services (3) **:** a clergyman of a Protestant church (4) **:** PREACHER (5) *chiefly Eng* **:** a member of the clergy of a nonconformist church **b :** one who performs the duties of a clergyman during his customary vocation but who has never been formally licensed or ordained as a minister **3** *archaic* **:** one that waits upon or serves **:** ATTENDANT, SERVANT ⟨cooks and other inferior ∼*s* employed in the . . . kitchens —Edward Gibbon⟩ **4 :** one exercising non-Christian clerical functions **5 a** *or* **minister-general :** the superior of one of several religious orders **b :** the assistant to the rector or the bursar of a Jesuit house **6 :** a high officer of state entrusted by the chief of state or the executive head of a government with the management of a division of governmental activities ⟨British . . . ∼*s* who exercise the powers of government derive their formal authority from the king —J.A.Corry⟩ ⟨Canadian . . . ∼*s* carry the political responsibility for their departments —Alexander Brady⟩ — see FOREIGN MINISTER, PRIME MINISTER; compare COMMISSAR 2 **7 a :** a diplomatic representative (as an ambassador) accredited by a sovereign or government to the court or seat of government of a foreign state ⟨shall appoint ambassadors, other public ∼*s* and consuls —*U.S.Constitution*⟩ **b :** a diplomatic representative ranking below an ambassador and usu. accredited to states of less importance ⟨send ambassadors to most countries and ∼*s* to the less important ones —F.A.Magruder⟩ — compare MINISTER PLENIPOTENTIARY, MINISTER RESIDENT

[2]**minister** \"\ *vb* **ministered; ministered; ministering** \-t(ə)riŋ\ **ministers** [ME *ministren*, fr. MF *ministrer*, fr. L *ministrare* to serve, dish up, fr. *minister* servant] *vi* **1 :** to serve or officiate in worship **:** act in the capacity of or perform the functions of a minister of religion — often used with *to* ⟨became rector of a small parish where he ∼*ed* for several years⟩ ⟨after a rabbi has ∼*ed* to a congregation for . . . fifteen years —B.Z.Bokser⟩ **2 :** to attend to the wants and comforts of someone **:** give aid **:** SERVE — usu. used with *to* ⟨happily he . . . had ∼*ed* to this man —Louis Auchincloss⟩ ⟨during the plague he ∼*ed* to the sick⟩ **3 :** to do things needful or helpful **:** be serviceable or conducive — usu. used with *to* ⟨a tract for the times . . . ∼*ed* to the needs of the moment —R.W.Southern⟩ ⟨this conclusion ∼*ed* to complacency —R.H.Bainton⟩ ∼ *vt* **1** *archaic* **:** FURNISH, SUPPLY, AFFORD ⟨limbs . . . made to ∼ delight —P.J.Bailey⟩ ⟨neither give heed to fables . . . which ∼ questions —1 Tim 1:4 (AV)⟩ **2** *archaic* **:** ADMINISTER, DISPENSE ⟨I thither went to ∼ the sacrament —John Wilson †1854⟩ ⟨that he might ∼ the Gospel to the Gentiles —R.M. Benson⟩

[1]**min·is·te·ri·al** \¦minə¦stirēəl, -tēr-\ *adj* [LL *ministerialis*, lit., that functions as a servant, fr. L *ministerium* service (fr. *minister* servant) + -*alis* -al] **1 a :** of, being, or having the characteristics of a minister of religion ⟨those serving in a ∼ capacity are trained in a Bible training school —F.S.Mead⟩ ⟨a ∼ habit of mind —M.A.D.Howe⟩ **b :** of, relating to, or preparing to enter the clerical ministry ⟨examine ∼ candidates —J.C.Brauer⟩ ⟨a code of ∼ ethics —P.H.Furfey⟩ **2 a :** of, being, or having the characteristics of an act or duty belonging to the administration of the executive function in government and specifically prescribed by law as part of the official duties of an office **b :** of, relating to, or being an act that a person after ascertaining the existence of a specified state of facts performs in obedience to a mandate of legal authority without the exercise of personal judgment upon the propriety of the act and usu. without discretion in its performance — opposed to *judicial* ⟨action by public officials can be compelled only if the act is a purely ∼ one —B.F.Tucker⟩ ⟨the controversy turns . . . on whether the function is discretionary or ∼ —G.W. Folta⟩ **3 :** acting or active as an agent, instrument, or means **:** INSTRUMENTAL ⟨those uses of conversation which are ∼ to intellectual culture —Thomas De Quincey⟩ **4 a :** of, relating to, or having the status of a governmental minister ⟨representatives of the political parties . . . were given ∼ posts —W.S. Vucinich⟩ ⟨jobs below the ∼ level —H.M.Somers⟩ ⟨promotion . . . to the office of paymaster general, a ∼ appointment —*Current Biog.*⟩ **b** *often cap* **:** of, relating to, or supporting the ministry as opposed to the opposition in a parliamentary system ⟨the situation was . . . saved by a *Ministerial* crisis —*Peace Handbooks*⟩ ⟨∼ benches in the House of Commons⟩ ⟨the principle of ∼ responsibility under a parliamentary system —Taylor Cole⟩

[2]**ministerial** \"\ *n* -s [LL *ministerialis* imperial household officer, fr. *ministerialis*, adj.] **:** an administrative household officer under the feudal system

min·is·te·ri·al·ist \,==¦=rēələst\ *n* -s **:** a supporter of the ministry in office ⟨enrolled himself . . . in the ranks of the ∼*s* —G.O.Trevelyan⟩

min·is·te·ri·al·ly \¦==¦=rēəlē\ *adv* **:** in the manner or capacity of a minister ⟨called on to visit ∼ one . . . lying on his deathbed —C.A.Johns⟩ ⟨acting judicially and ∼ —*Law Times*⟩

min·is·te·ri·um \,minə'stirēəm\ *n* -s [G, fr. L, service] **1 :** a body in the Lutheran Church: **a :** one composed of ordained ministers and charged with the examination, licensure, and ordination of candidates for the ministry and with the trial for heresy of ministers and also laymen on appeal from a church council **b :** a representative body of ministers and laymen meeting periodically to attend to the interests of the churches represented **2 :** a regional group or association of ministers in the Evangelical and Reformed Church meeting periodically for fellowship and attending to problems of common interest

minister of music : a director of music in a church or synagogue usu. responsible for training the choir and often for service as an organist

minister of state *n, pl* **ministers of state :** a British governmental official having a status between a minister and a parliamentary secretary and usu. appointed to relieve a minister of portions of his departmental work ⟨promoted *Minister of State* at the Foreign Office —Herbert Morrison⟩

minister plenipotentiary *n, pl* **ministers plenipotentiary :** a principal diplomatic agent ranking below an ambassador but possessing full power and authority as the representative of his government at a foreign court or seat of government — see [2]ENVOY 1a; compare MINISTER 7b

minister–president \'==='=(=)=\ *n, pl* **ministers–president** *or* **minister–presidents** [trans. of G *ministerpräsident*] **:** the principal governmental minister usu. chosen by the legislature in a number of German länder and resembling a prime minister in power and status ⟨the *minister-president* . . . appoints and heads a cabinet responsible to the legislature —R.H.Wells⟩

minister resident *n, pl* **ministers resident 1 :** a diplomatic agent resident at a foreign court or seat of government and ranking below a minister plenipotentiary — compare MINISTER 7b **2 :** a member of the British ministry appointed to reside and handle special governmental functions in a location outside the United Kingdom ⟨a *minister resident* in West Africa was appointed to coordinate the war effort of the four dependencies —Martin Wight⟩

ministers *pl of* MINISTER, *pres 3d sing of* MINISTER

minister's face *n, dial* **:** the upper half of a hog's head with jowls, eyes, and usu. ears and nose removed

min·is·ter·ship \'minəstə(r),ship\ *n* **:** the office of minister

minister without portfolio *n, pl* **ministers without portfolios :** a member of a ministry to whom no special department is assigned

min·is·tra·ble \'minəstrəbəl\ *n* -s [F, fr. *ministrable* suitable for appointment as a cabinet minister, fr. *ministre* minister + -*able*] **:** a recurrent member of successive ministries ⟨the ∼*s* were usually seasoned parliamentarians⟩

[1]**min·is·trant** \'minəstrənt\ *adj* [L *ministrant-, ministrans*, pres. part. of *ministrare* to serve, dish up — more at MINISTER] **:** performing service as a minister ⟨the angels ∼ sang —Bayard Taylor⟩

[2]**ministrant** \"\ *n* -s **:** one that ministers ⟨orgies of dissipation . . . were ∼*s* to the clear, springing life of the imagination —Rose Macaulay⟩ ⟨∼*s* at the altar —*Liverpool Daily Post*⟩

min·is·tra·tion \,minə'strāshən\ *n* -s [ME *ministracioun*, fr. L *ministration-, ministratio*, fr. *ministratus* (past part. of *ministrare* to serve, dish up) + -*ion-*, -*io* -ion] **1 :** the action of giving aid, service, or comfort ⟨under the tender ∼*s* of this fair sister of mercy, the young warrior revived —Cedomilj Mijatovic⟩ **2 :** the action of ministering in religious matters **:** MINISTRY 2 ⟨all the baptized were to come under the disciplinary ∼*s* of the Church —K.S.Latourette⟩ ⟨worshiping . . . under the ∼*s* of a missionary —*Amer. Anthropologist*⟩

min·is·tress \'minəstrəs\ *n* -ES [MF *ministresse*, fr. *ministre* minister + -*esse* -ess] **:** a female minister ⟨come . . . to be ∼ at London —Thomas Gray⟩ ⟨the lovely ∼ of truth and good in this dark world —Mark Akenside⟩

min·is·try \'minəstrē, -ri\ *n* -ES [ME *ministerie*, fr. L *ministerium* service, fr. *minister* servant — more at MINISTER] **1 :** the action of ministering **:** the performance of any service or function for another **:** MINISTRATION ⟨the ∼ of books is at least threefold —T.V.Smith⟩ ⟨the ingenuity of destruction . . . had outrun the ∼ of healing —Dixon Wecter⟩ ⟨the Gospels . . . become part of the present saving ∼ of the Redeemer —H.H. Farmer⟩ **2 :** the office, duties, or functions of a minister of religion ⟨prepared for the ∼ —A.E.Bailey⟩ ⟨the true missionary is . . . occupied with the vital aspects of his ∼ —E.A. Nida⟩ ⟨answered the call to the ∼ —Wayne Hooper⟩ **3** *obs* **:** a specific kind of service **:** FUNCTION, OFFICE ⟨to sever the wheat from the tares . . . must be the angel's ∼ —John Milton⟩ **4 :** the body of ordained ministers of religion **:** CLERGY ⟨insistence on a highly trained ∼ —R.T.Handy⟩ **5 :** a person or thing through which something is accomplished **:** AGENCY 2, INSTRUMENTALITY ⟨heroic believers become such by the ∼ of heroic pains —Austin Phelps⟩ **6 a :** the period of service of a minister of religion **b :** the total life of service of a religious figure ⟨an outline account of the ∼ of our Lord —*Times Lit. Supp.*⟩ **7** *often cap* **a** (1) **:** the whole body of ministers entrusted with the government of a nation or state and from which a smaller cabinet is sometimes selected ⟨when a cabinet goes out of office, it . . . carries the entire ∼ with it —F.A.Ogg & Harold Zink⟩ ⟨the crown is the supreme executive . . . in all the dominions but it acts on the advice of different *ministries* —Robert Borden⟩ ⟨a responsible ∼⟩ (2) **:** the usu. smaller group of ministers constituting a cabinet **b :** the whole body of ministers or the cabinet currently holding office **8 a :** a government department presided over by a minister ⟨*ministries* of justice have been the spearhead in promoting the recurrent great codifications of Continental law —C.J.Friedrich⟩ ⟨the Communists received the three *ministries* they . . . wanted —W.S.Vucinich⟩ ⟨∼ of foreign affairs⟩ ⟨∼ of transport⟩ **b :** the building in which the business of a ministry is transacted ⟨whether he had noticed any other member . . . entering the ∼ —C.D.Lewis⟩ **9 :** the term of office held by an individual minister or by a body of ministers ⟨the Tory ∼ lasted for fifteen years⟩

minitari *var of* MINNETAREE

min·i·track \'minə,trak\ *n, sometimes cap* [*mini*ature + *track*] **:** an electronic system for tracking an earth satellite or rocket by radio waves transmitted from it to a chain of ground stations

min·i·um \'minēəm\ *n* -s [ME, fr. L, cinnabar, red lead, of Iberian origin; akin to Basque *armineá* cinnabar] **1 a :** GOYA **b :** FIERY RED **2 a :** red lead oxide Pb_3O_4 sometimes found as a mineral but usu. prepared synthetically; tri-lead tetroxide **b :** RED LEAD

min·i·ver *also* **min·e·ver** \'minəvə(r)\ *n* -s [ME *meniver*, fr. OF *menu vair*, fr. *menu* small (fr. L *minutus*) + *vair* — more at MINUTE, VAIR] **1 :** a white or whitish fur probably from the vair and more recently from ermine or rabbit used in the medieval period esp. for the clothing of noble and wealthy persons and now chiefly for robes of state ⟨parliament robes are of crimson cloth furred with ∼ —Dorothy M. Stuart⟩ **2** *dial Eng* **:** an ermine in its white winter coat

min·i·vet \'minə,vet\ *n* -s [origin unknown] **:** any of several cuckoo shrikes that belong to the Asiatic genus *Pericrocotus* and that are brilliantly colored with the males chiefly black and scarlet and the females usu. gray and yellow

mink \'miŋk\ *n, pl* **mink** *or* **minks** *often attrib* [ME *mynk*] **1 a :** the fur or pelt of the mink varying in color from white to dark brown ⟨an elbow-length cape of cerulean ∼ —*New Yorker*⟩ **b :** an article of clothing (as a coat) made of this fur ⟨the girl was wearing a ∼ —Eric Greywood⟩ **2 :** any of several slender-bodied semi-aquatic carnivorous mammals that resemble and are closely related to the weasels, comprise a subgenus of *Mustela*, and have partially webbed feet, a thick soft usu. dark brown coat, and a rather short bushy tail

mink

mink·ery \-kərē\ *n* -ES **:** a place where minks are bred usu. for commercial purposes

mink frog *n* **:** a black-spotted frog (*Rana septentrionalis*) of the northern U. S. having a strong musky odor

minkopi *usu cap, var of* MINCOPIE

minn *var of* MIND

min·ne·ap·o·lis \¦minē¦ap(ə)ləs\ *adj, usu cap* [fr. *Minneapolis*, city in southeast central Minnesota] **:** of or from Minneapolis, Minn. ⟨*Minneapolis* mills⟩ **:** of the kind or style prevalent in Minneapolis

min·ne·a·pol·i·tan \,minēə'pälətᵊn, -lədᵊn\ *n* -s *cap* [fr. *Minneapolis*, after E *metropolis*: *metropolitan*] **:** a native or resident of Minneapolis, Minn.

min·ne·lied \'minə,lēt\ *n, pl* **minnelie·der** \-ēdə(r)\ *often cap* [G, fr. MHG *minneliet*, fr. *minne* love + *liet* song, fr. OHG *liod* — more at LAUD] **1 :** a song of or in the style of the minnesingers **2 :** LOVE SONG

min·ne·sing·er \'minē,siŋə(r), -nə,-\ *also* **min·ne·säng·er** \'minə,zeŋ-\ *n, pl* **minnesingers** *also* **minnesänger** [G, fr. MHG *minnesinger, minnesenger*, fr. *minne* love (fr. OHG *minna*) + *singer* (fr. *singen* to sing — fr. OHG *singan* — + -*er*, fr. OHG -*āri* -er) *or senger* singer, fr. *sanc* song, singing (fr. OHG *sang*) + -*er* — more at MINIKIN, SING, SONG] **:** one of a class of aristocratic German lyric poets and musicians of the 12th to the 14th centuries inspired by the French troubadors and characterized by having love and beauty as the subject of their songs — compare MEISTERSINGER

min·ne·song \'minē,sȯŋ, -nə,-, -säŋ\ *or* **min·ne·sang** \'minə,zäŋ\ *n* [in sense 1, *minnesong* part trans. of G *minnelied*; in sense 1, *minnesang* alter. (influenced by G *minnesang*) of *minnesong*; in sense 2, *minnesong* part trans. of G *minnesang*; in sense 2, *minnesang* fr. G, fr. MHG *minnesanc*, fr. *minne* love + *sanc* song, singing] **1 :** a song of a minnesinger **2 :** the whole body of minnesongs constituting a musical form ⟨another characteristic shared in common by English music and German ∼ —Gilbert Reaney⟩

[1]**min·ne·so·ta** \¦minə¦sōd·ə, -ōtə\ *adj, usu cap* [fr. *Minnesota*, state in the north central U. S., fr. *Minnesota* river, southern Minnesota, fr. Dakota *minisota* white water] **:** of or from the state of Minnesota ⟨a *Minnesota* lake⟩ **:** of the kind or style prevalent in Minnesota **:** MINNESOTAN

[2]**minnesota** \"\ *n* -s *usu cap* **:** either of two breeds of swine developed in Minnesota: **a** *or* **minnesota number one** *usu cap M&N&O* **:** a breed of red meat type swine developed by selection from crosses between Tamworths and Danish Landrace **b** *or* **minnesota number two** *usu cap M&N&T* **:** a breed of white black-spotted swine similarly developed from Large Whites and Poland Chinas

min·ne·so·ta·ite \,==='sōd·ə,īt\ *n* -s [*Minnesota* (state) + E -*ite*] **:** a hydrous silicate of iron $Fe_3Si_4O_{10}(OH)_2$ probably isomorphous with talc

[1]**min·ne·so·tan** \,minə'sōtᵊn\ *also* **min·ne·so·ti·an** \-ōd·ēən\ *n* -s *cap* [*Minnesota* (state) + E -*an*, n. suffix] **:** a native or resident of the state of Minnesota

[2]**minnesotan** \¦==¦==\ *also* **minnesotian** \¦==¦===\ *adj, usu cap* [*Minnesota* (state) + E -*an*, adj. suffix] **1 :** of, relating to, or characteristic of the state of Minnesota **2 :** of, relating to, or characteristic of the people of Minnesota

min·ne·ta·ree \,minə'tärē\ *n* -s *usu cap* [Mandan *minitari* they crossed the water] **:** HIDATSA

min·ni \'minē\ *n, pl* **minni** *or* **minnis** *usu cap* **1 :** a primitive Mongol people inhabiting the foothill region of the southern Caucasus during pre-Babylonian times — compare KASSITE **2 :** a member of the Minni people

[1]**min·nie** *or* **min·ny** \'mini\ *n, pl* **minnies** [prob. baby-talk alter. of *mother*] *chiefly Scot* **:** MOTHER — a childish or informal term

[2]**min·nie** \'minē\ *n* -s [by shortening & alter. fr. [1]*minimum*] **1 :** a hand barely strong enough for an opening bid in bridge **2 :** the lowest possible hand that wins in lowball or high-low poker

min·nie·bush \'minē,bu̇sh\ *n* [*minnie-* (irreg. fr. Archibald *Menzies* †1842 Scot. botanist) + *bush*] **:** a low shrub (*Menziesia pilosa*) of eastern No. America with greenish purple flowers

min·now \'mi(,)nō, -nə\ *n, pl* **minnows** *also* **minnow** *often attrib* [ME *menawe*; akin to OE *myne* minnow, OHG *munewa*, a fish, Russ *men'* eelpout, and perh. to Gk *manos* sparse — more at MONK] **1 a :** a small European cyprinid fish (*Phoxinus phoxinus*) common in gravelly streams and attaining a length of about three inches maximum; *broadly* **:** any of the usu. small fishes constituting the family Cyprinidae **b :** a small killifish or topminnow — see MUDMINNOW **c :** a fish of the family Galaxiidae **2 :** a small fish not specified as a sport fish or game fish esp. in game laws **3 :** a small or insignificant person or thing **4 :** a live or artificial minnow used as bait in fishing — see LURE illustration

min·ny \'minē\ *n* -ES [by alter.] *dial* **:** MINNOW

mi·no·an \mə'nōən, (ˈ)mī¦n-\ *adj, usu cap* [L *minous* Cretan, of Minos (fr. Gk *minōios*, fr. *Minōs* Minos, legendary king of Crete) + E -*an*] **1 :** of or relating to the Bronze Age culture of Crete (3000 B.C.–1100 B.C.) and being in its latest phase virtually identical with Mycenaean — compare AEGEAN, CYCLADIC, ETEOCRETAN, HELLADIC **2 a :** of, relating to, or being the language of ancient Crete **b :** of or relating to inscriptions and documents in the Minoan language or to the hieroglyphic and esp. the linear script in which they were written — compare JAPHETIC

[2]**minoan** \"\ *n* -s *usu cap* **1 :** a native or inhabitant of ancient Crete **2 :** the language of the ancient Cretan civilization — compare ETEOCRETAN, MYCENAEAN

mi·no bird \'mī(,)nō-\ *n* [*mino* alter. of *myna*] **:** MYNA

mi·nom·e·ter \mə'nämədə(r), mī'-\ *n* [[3]*minute* + -*o-* + -*meter*] **:** an instrument for the detection and measurement of stray radiations from X-ray generators and radioactive materials

[1]**mi·nor** \'mīnə(r)\ *n* -s [in sense 1, fr. ME, fr. ML, fr. L *minor*, adj.; in sense 2, fr. LL, fr. L *minor*, adj.; in other senses, fr. [2]*minor*] **1 a :** the premise in logic that contains the minor term: (1) **:** the second proposition of a regular syllogism (2) **:** the categorical premise in a hypothetical syllogism **b :** MINOR TERM **2 a :** a person of either sex under full age or majority **:** one who has not attained the age at which full civil rights are accorded **:** one who in England and generally in the U.S. is under 21 years of age — compare [1]AGE 1d(2), INFANT **b :** a person in Scots law who has exceeded the age of pupillarity by being over 14 if a boy or over 12 if a girl but who has not attained the majority age of 21 years **3 :** a minor musical interval, scale, key, or mode ⟨listened . . . to the pulsating sweet ∼*s* of the hymns —Irwin Shaw⟩ **4** *or* **minor determinant :** a mathematical determinant obtained by deleting the same number of rows and columns from the given determinant **5 a :** a minor academic course **b :** a minor academic subject ⟨degree in history with a ∼ in school administration —*Current Biog.*⟩ **6 :** MINOR LEAGUE — usu. used in pl. with *the* ⟨an old pitcher retired to the ∼*s* —Vincent McHugh⟩ **7 :** MINOR SUIT

[2]**minor** \"\ *adj* [ME, fr. L, smaller, less, inferior; akin to OHG *minniro* smaller, ON *minni* smaller, Goth *minniza* least, younger, inferior, L *minuere* to lessen, Gk *meiōn* less, Skt *mināti* he lessens] **1 a :** inferior in importance **:** comparatively unimportant **:** lower in standing or reputation than others of the same kind ⟨these hardy adventurers were ∼ noblemen —R.A.Billington⟩ ⟨back roads which serve as bridle paths —*Amer. Guide Series: Mass.*⟩ ⟨a ∼ poet⟩ **b :** being the less important of two things ⟨a ∼ canon⟩ ⟨a ∼ piece in chess⟩ **2 :** having the status of a legal minor not having reached the age of majority or full legal age ⟨∼ children follow the nationality of the parents —William Samore⟩ **3** *archaic* **:** being in or constituting a numerical minority ⟨another person had the ∼ vote in the election —Thomas Hutchinson⟩ **4 a** (1) *of a scale* **:** having half steps between the second and third, fifth and sixth, and sometimes seventh and eighth degrees — see HARMONIC MINOR SCALE, MELODIC MINOR SCALE, NATURAL MINOR SCALE (2) *of a key* **:** based (as in harmonic relations) on such a scale — opposed to *major*; used after the name of a keynote ⟨fugue in D ∼⟩ ⟨in the key of B ∼⟩ **b** *of an interval* (1) **:** less by a half step than the corresponding major interval **:** of a size equal to the distance between the keynote and a (specified) degree of the minor scale — used of the second, third, sixth, and seventh (2) **:** less by a comma — used of one whole step in an untempered scale compared with another ⟨D to E is a ∼ whole step, smaller by a comma than C to D⟩ **c** *of a mode in measurable music* **:** having the long divided into breves **5 :** being the second in age or school standing of two or more boys with the same surname in an English public school ⟨Smith ∼⟩ **6** *med* **:** not serious or involving risk to life ⟨a ∼ illness⟩ ⟨a ∼ operation⟩ — compare MAJOR **7 :** of, relating to, or being a branch of the judiciary having jurisdiction limited to a specified local area and to cases usu. involving matters of lesser importance ⟨∼ courts . . . deal with such cases as breaches of the traffic laws, petty theft, and minor domestic cases —*Canadian Citizenship Series*⟩ **8 a :** of, relating to, or being an academic course usu. having fewer class hours than a major course **b :** of, relating to, or being an

academic subject usu. requiring fewer courses or hours than a major subject and given secondary emphasis in a student's schedule ⟨his ~ subjects for his M.A. were plant ecology and entomology —*Current Biog.*⟩

3minor \"\ *vi* -ED/-ING/-S [1*minor*] **:** to take courses in a specified field of study as one's minor ⟨will major in . . . literature and ~ in theater work —*Goucher Alumnae Quarterly*⟩

mi·nor·ate \'mīnə,rāt\ *vt* -ED/-ING/-S [LL *minoratus*, past part. of *minorare*, fr. L *minor* smaller] *archaic* **:** to make less in estimation or value **:** DIMINISH

minoration *n* -S [LL *minoration-*, *minoratio*, fr. *minoratus* + L *-ion-*, *-io* -ion] *obs* **:** DIMINUTION ⟨the excuse and ~ of our actual impieties —Jeremy Taylor⟩

minor axis *n* **:** the chord of an ellipse passing through the center perpendicular to the major axis

mi·nor·ca \mə̇'nȯrkə, -nȯ(ə)kə\ *n* [*Minorca*, second largest of the Balearic islands off the east coast of Spain] **1** *usu cap* **:** a breed of domestic fowls of the Mediterranean class resembling the Leghorns but larger **2** -S *often cap* **:** any bird of the Minorca breed

minor cadence *n* **:** a musical cadence ending on a minor chord

1mi·nor·can \mə̇'nȯrkən, -nȯ(ə)k-\ *adj, usu cap* [*Minorca*, Balearic islands + E *-an*] **1 :** of, relating to, or characteristic of Minorca **2 :** of, relating to, or characteristic of the people of Minorca

2minorcan \"\ *n* -S *cap* **:** a native or resident of Minorca

minor canon *n* **1 :** a canon who receives no prebend **2 :** a canon in the Church of England who has no vote in the chapter to which he belongs but who receives a stipend — compare MAJOR CANON

minor coin *n* **:** a base-metal coin (as a nickel or cent) of a denomination smaller than the basic monetary unit — compare SUBSIDIARY COIN

minor diameter *n* **:** the smallest diameter of a screw thread

minor element *n* **:** TRACE ELEMENT

minor excommunication *n* **:** separation or suspension from the sacraments but not absolute exclusion from the Roman Catholic Church — distinguished from *major excommunication*

1mi·nor·i·ty \mə̇'nȯrəd·ē, mī'-, -när-, -ətē, -i\ *n* -ES [ML *minoritat-*, *minoritas*, fr. L *minor* smaller + *-itat-*, *-itas* -ity] **1 :** the state of being a legal minor **:** the period of being under full legal age — compare INFANCY **2 a :** the smaller in number of two aggregates that together constitute a whole ⟨barred from all but a tiny ~ of cinemas —Roger Manvell⟩ ⟨ten of our presidents have had only a ~ of the popular vote behind them —F.A.Ogg & P.O.Ray⟩ **b :** the smaller in number of two groups that together constitute a larger entity ⟨only a small ~ of students is majoring in a basic subject —W.H.Whyte⟩; *specif* **:** a group (as in a legislative body) having less than the number of votes necessary for control ⟨dividing each constituency . . . into two halves, the majority to govern and the ~ to criticize —C.J.Friedrich⟩ **3** *or* **minority group :** a group characterized by a sense of separate identity and awareness of status apart from a usu. larger group of which it forms or is held to form a part: as **a :** a body of nationals of a state forming a small but appreciable part of the population of another and usu. neighboring state ⟨peasants in eastern Europe . . . wanting a guarantee that the evicted German *minorities* shall never return —A.J.Toynbee⟩ **b :** a group differing from the predominant section of a larger group in one or more characteristics (as ethnic background, language, culture, or religion) and as a result often subjected to differential treatment and esp. discrimination ⟨the constitution protects the rights of individuals and of *minorities* —Luis Muñoz Marín⟩ **c :** a group numerically smaller than other groups or a combination of other groups in a community but constituting the predominant element ⟨whites have frequently been dominant *minorities* —H.O.Dahlke⟩

2minority \"\ *adj* **:** of, relating to, or being a minority ⟨an advisory committee on ~ housing —*Springfield* (*Mass.*) *Union*⟩ ⟨each committee is . . . composed of majority and ~ members —F.A.Ogg & P.O.Ray⟩ ⟨~ races⟩ ⟨~ rule⟩

minority leader *n* **:** the leader of the minority party in a legislative body — compare MAJORITY LEADER

minority report *n* **:** a separate report prepared by a group constituting or representing a numerical minority (as of a committee) ⟨if any members of a committee disagree . . . they may submit a *minority report* —Alice F. Sturgis⟩ ⟨the majority and *minority reports* of this inquiry —*Current Biog.*⟩

minor key *n* **1 :** a musical key or tonality in the minor mode **2 :** a mood of melancholy or pathos **3 :** a restrained manner **:** a small or limited scale ⟨the high moments of social life on the farm . . . are in a decidedly *minor key* —Don Murray⟩ ⟨art in Australia . . . reflected English traditions in a *minor key* —Bernard Smith⟩

minor league *n* **:** a league or association of professional clubs in a particular sport (as baseball or ice hockey) other than the recognized major leagues

minor-league \¦==¦=\ *adj* [*minor league*] **1 :** of, relating to, or having the characteristics of a minor league in sports ⟨a *minor-league* baseball club⟩ **2 :** of, relating to, or being of relatively small stature or importance ⟨a *minor-league* official in one of the Hollywood studios —L.M.Uris⟩ ⟨a simple, fascinating, *minor-league* tragedy —Mel Heimer⟩ ⟨a *minor-league* hero⟩

minor mode *n* **1 :** the arrangement or grouping of musical notes or tones as found in the minor scale **2 :** a scale in the minor mode

minor order *n, often cap M&O* **1 :** the grade of acolyte, exorcist, lector, or doorkeeper in the Roman Catholic Church — compare MAJOR ORDER **2 :** the grade of subdeacon, lector, or singer in the Eastern Orthodox Church

minor party *n* **:** a political party whose electoral strength is so small as to prevent its gaining control of a government except in rare and exceptional circumstances — compare MAJOR PARTY, THIRD PARTY

minor penalty *n* **:** a two-minute suspension of a player in ice hockey with no substitute allowed — compare MAJOR PENALTY

minor piece *n* **:** a bishop or knight in chess — compare MAJOR PIECE

minor planet *n* **:** ASTEROID 1

minor premise *n* **:** the premise of a syllogism that contains the minor term

minor prophets *n pl, usu cap M&P* **1 :** the group of Old Testament prophets from Hosea to Malachi whose biblical writings are relatively brief **2 :** the books of the Bible written by the Minor Prophets

minor seminary *n* **:** PREPARATORY SEMINARY

minor sentence *n* **:** a word, phrase, or clause functioning as a sentence and having in speech an intonation characteristic of a sentence but lacking the grammatical completeness and independence of a full sentence (as *Yes, indeed*)

minor seventh chord *n* **:** a chord consisting of a minor triad and a minor seventh — see SEVENTH CHORD illustration

minor socratic *n, usu cap S* **:** SOCRATIC 2

minor suit *n* **:** clubs or diamonds in bridge — compare MAJOR SUIT

minor surgery *n* **:** surgery involving little risk to the life of the patient; *specif* **:** an operation on the superficial structures of the body or a manipulative procedure that does not involve a serious risk — compare MAJOR SURGERY

minor tenace *n* **:** a tenace in bridge and other card games consisting of the king and jack — compare MAJOR TENACE

minor term *n* **:** the term of a syllogism that forms the subject of the conclusion

minor triad *n* **1 :** a triad whose frequencies are in the proportions 10:12:15 **2 :** a musical triad consisting of a fundamental tone and its minor third and perfect fifth — see TRIAD illustration

mi·not \mē'nō\ *n* -S [MF, fr. OF, fr. *mine*, a unit of measure of volume, fr. L *hemina*, fr. Gk *hēmina*, fr. *hēmi-* hemi- — more at SEMI-] **:** any of several old French units of dry measure; *esp* **:** the Paris unit for grain equal to about 39 liters

minsk \'minsk\ *adj, usu cap* [fr. *Minsk*, city in western U.S.S.R.] **:** of or from the city of Minsk, U.S.S.R. **:** of the kind or style prevalent in Minsk

min·ster \'min(t)stə(r)\ *n* -S [ME, fr. OE *mynster*, fr. (assumed) VL *monisterium*, fr. LL *monasterium* — more at MONASTERY] **1** *obs* **:** MONASTERY **2 a** (1) **:** a church of a monastery (2) **:** a church orig. belonging to a monastery but remaining after the monastery has ceased to exist **b :** a cathedral or a church of large size or importance that has never been monastic

minsteryard \'==,=\ *n* **:** the close of a cathedral or other minster

1min·strel \'min(t)strəl\ *n* -S *often attrib* [ME *minstrale*, *menestrel*, fr. OF *menestrel* minstrel, official, servant, fr. LL *ministerialis* imperial household officer — more at MINISTERIAL] **1 :** one of a class of medieval professional musical entertainers; *esp* **:** a singer of verses to the accompaniment of a harp or other instrument — compare GLEEMAN, JONGLEUR **2 :** one (as a musician or poet) felt to resemble a medieval minstrel **3 a :** one of a troupe of musical performers and comedians of a kind originating early in the 19th century in the U.S. and typically giving a program of Negro melodies, jokes, and impersonations and usu. blacked in imitation of Negroes ⟨small troupes of blackface ~*s* were among the earliest . . . traveling companies —*Amer. Guide Series: Wash.*⟩ **b :** MINSTREL SHOW ⟨the first full-scale ~ staged by the church —*Springfield* (*Mass.*) *Union*⟩

2minstrel \"\ *vt* -ED/-ING/-S **:** to celebrate in song esp. in the style of a minstrel

minstrel gallery *n* **:** a small interior balcony over the entrance doors in a church, castle, or similar public building

minstrel show *n* **:** a performance by blackface minstrels

min·strel·sy \-lsē\ *n* -ES [ME *minstralcie*, fr. MF *menestralsie*, fr. *menestral*, *menestrel* minstrel] **1 :** the arts and occupation of minstrels; *specif* **:** the singing and playing of a minstrel **2 :** a body of minstrels **3 :** a group of songs; *esp* **:** one of minstrel's songs

1mint \'mint\ *n* -S [ME *mynt*, fr. OE *mynet;* akin to OHG *munizza* coin; both fr. a prehistoric WGmc word borrowed fr. L *moneta* mint, coin, money, fr. *Moneta*, epithet of Juno, ancient Italian goddess, wife of Jupiter; fr. the fact that the Romans coined money in the temple of Juno Moneta] **1** *obs* **:** COIN, MONEY **2 a :** a place (as a factory) where coins are made ⟨coinage by private ~*s* was born of necessity —Abraham Kosoff⟩ ⟨the abbot . . . owned the one-man ~ of that town —John Craig⟩ **b** *usu cap* **:** a government agency charged with making coins ⟨the Royal *Mint*⟩ ⟨Director of the U.S. *Mint*⟩ **3 :** a place where anything is manufactured or fabricated **:** a source of invention ⟨a man . . . that hath a ~ of phrases in his brain —Shak.⟩ **4 :** a vast sum (as of money) **:** a great amount or supply ⟨some of the scarce items cost a ~ —T.H.Fielding⟩ ⟨you save a ~ of money —*advt*⟩ ⟨he had a ~ of faith in himself —Rosalind Duforet⟩ **5** [3*mint*] **:** a coin or stamp in mint condition ⟨20th century ~*s* —*advt*⟩

2mint \"\ *vb* -ED/-ING/-S *vt* **1 :** to make (as coins or money) out of metal usu. by a special manufacturing process **:** create in or by the authority of a mint **:** COIN 1 ⟨a patent . . . to ~ copper coinage for Ireland —J.H.Plumb⟩ ⟨trade dollars . . . continued to be ~*ed* in proof —E.G.Bradfield⟩ ⟨Anglo-Saxon coins were ~*ed* by individuals commissioned by the rulers —C.V.Kappen⟩ **2 :** to convert (a metal) into coins ⟨this copper was to be ~*ed* into . . . 9d. pieces —R.T.Hoober⟩ ⟨the silver which was mined there was ~*ed* into coins —J.W.M.Decker⟩ **3 :** to manufacture or create as if in a mint **:** COIN 3 ⟨a phrase newly ~*ed* here —R.H.Rovere⟩ ⟨the language is freshly ~*ed* —Alfred Kreymborg⟩ ⟨new ideas . . . are ~*ed* in a few months —*Times Lit. Supp.*⟩ ~ *vi* **:** to conduct the operations of a mint **:** make coins ⟨the Romans . . . learned to ~ from the Greeks —John Craig⟩

3mint \"\ *adj* **1 :** of or relating to a mint **2 :** in the original condition as if fresh from a mint **:** absolutely unmarred and unused ⟨a collection of ~ and used stamps —*Nat'l Stamp News*⟩ ⟨the coins are . . . all in ~ condition —*Numismatist*⟩ ⟨his copy . . . still ~ in dust jacket, precisely as it came from the publisher —Charles Rosner⟩

4mint \"\ *n* -S *often attrib* [ME *minte*, fr. OE; akin to OHG *minza* mint; both fr. a prehistoric WGmc word borrowed fr. L *mentha*, *menta* mint, of non-IE origin; akin to the source of Gk *minthē* mint] **1 :** any of various aromatic plants constituting the family Labiatae; *esp* **:** a member of the genus *Mentha* — see PEPPERMINT, SPEARMINT **2 :** a soft or hard confection flavored with peppermint or spearmint and often served after dinner

5mint \"\ *vt* -ED/-ING/-S **:** to flavor or season with mint

6mint \"\ *vb* -ED/-ING/-S [ME *minten*, fr. OE *myntan;* akin to OE ge*mynd* mind, memory — more at MIND] *vt* **1** *chiefly Scot* **:** INTEND, PURPOSE ⟨~*s* to go tomorrow⟩ **2** *chiefly Scot* **:** ATTEMPT, VENTURE, DARE ⟨cleave to the brisket the first man that ~*s* another stroke —Sir Walter Scott⟩ **3** *chiefly Scot* **:** INSINUATE, SUGGEST ~ *vi* **1** *chiefly Scot* **:** to make a feint **:** FEIGN ⟨don't just ~ at it; do it⟩ **2** *chiefly Scot* **:** ASPIRE — used with *at* ⟨they that ~ at a gown of gold —Sir Walter Scott⟩ **3** *chiefly Scot* **:** HINT ⟨cannot understand what we ~ at, unless we speak it out —Sir Walter Scott⟩

7mint \"\ *n* -S [ME, fr. *minten* to intend] *now chiefly Scot* **:** ATTEMPT, EFFORT ⟨make a ~ at it⟩

mint·age \-tij, -tēj\ *n* -S **1 a :** the action or process of minting coins ⟨a seigniorage . . . might be charged for the service of ~ —J.M.Keynes⟩ ⟨assign the varieties to their place of ~ —*Numismatist*⟩ **b :** the privilege of minting coins ⟨~ has long been a prerogative of the rulers of the country —Ludwig Von Mises⟩ **2 :** the production or fabrication of something as if by minting ⟨literary theories of modern ~ —H.J.S.Maine⟩ ⟨those achievements . . . were not of intellectual ~ —W.C.Mason⟩ **3 :** an impression or stamp resembling one placed upon a coin ⟨became stamped with the common ~ of their colleagues' manners —*London Times*⟩ **4 :** the coins produced by minting; *esp* **:** coins produced by a particular mint or minter or at a particular time ⟨the silver coinage now current . . . will be gradually replaced by the new ~ —*U.S. Treasury Report*⟩ **5 a :** the cost of manufacturing coins **b :** a charge made for coining — compare BRASSAGE

mintbush \'=,=\ *n* **:** any of several low shrubs of the genus *Prostanthera* and the family Labiatae having resinous opposite leaves and 2-lipped flowers

mint camphor *n* **:** MENTHOL

mint charge *n* **:** MINTAGE 5b ⟨a *mint charge* for coining gold . . . should be reimposed —John Craig⟩

mint·er \'mintə(r)\ *n* -S [ME *mynter*, fr. OE *mynetere;* akin to MD *munter* minter, MHG *münzære;* all fr. a prehistoric WGmc word borrowed fr. LL *monetarius* minter, fr. L *moneta* mint, coin + *-arius* -ary] **:** one that mints money ⟨pioneer gold coins of private ~*s* —Roy Hill⟩ ⟨if a ~ be convicted of striking bad money —F.M.Stenton⟩

mint family *n* **:** LABIATAE

mint geranium *n* **:** COSTMARY 1

mint green *n* **:** a variable color averaging a light green that is bluer and stronger than variscite green and paler and very slightly yellower than serpentine

minting *n* -S [fr. gerund of 2*mint*] **:** MINTAGE 4 ⟨this British ~ had lasted . . . for a century —John Craig⟩

mint julep *n* **:** JULEP 2b

mintleaf \'=,=\ *n* **1 :** a variable color averaging a strong green that is very slightly yellower than pepper green, yellower and less strong than primitive green, and yellower, lighter, and slightly stronger than viridian **2** *of textiles* **:** a strong yellowish green

1mintmark \'=,=\ *n* **:** a special letter or mark placed upon a coin at the time of coinage to identify the mint

2mintmark \"\ *vt* **:** to place a mintmark upon (as a coin)

mintmaster \'=,==\ *n* **1 :** the official in charge of a mint **2** *obs* **:** one apt in or given to coining words ⟨custom, the sole ~ of current words —Thomas Fuller⟩

min·ton ware \'mintᵊn-\ *n, usu cap M* [after Thomas *Minton* †1836 and Herbert *Minton* †1858 Eng. pottery manufacturers] **:** ceramic tableware produced in the Minton factory in Stoke-on-Trent, Staffordshire, England

mint par of exchange : PAR 1a

mintplace \'=,=\ *n* **:** a place where a mint is located ⟨old German towns that were once ~*s*⟩

mint price *n* **:** the price at which a mint buys metal for coining ⟨a considerable difference between the market and *mint prices* of gold —Louis Infield⟩

mintweed \'=,=\ *n* **:** a salvia (*Salvia reflexa*) that is troublesome as a weed and stock-poisoning plant in Australia

minty \'mintē\ *adj* -ER/-EST [4*mint* + *-y*] **:** having the flavor of mint

min·u·end \'minyə,wend\ *n* -S [L *minuendum* something to be lessened, neut. of *minuendus*, gerundive of *minuere* to lessen — more at MINOR] **:** a quantity in mathematics from which another quantity is to be subtracted — compare SUBTRAHEND

1min·u·et \,minyə'wet, *usu* -ed·+V\ *or* **men·u·et** \,men-\ *also* **min·u·et·to** \,minyə'wed·(,)ō\ *or* **men·u·et·to** \,men-\ *n* -S [*minuet*, *menuet* fr. F *menuet*, fr. obs. F *menuet* tiny, delicate, fr. OF, fr. *menu* small, fr. L *minutus; minuetto*, *menuetto* fr. It *minuetto*, fr. F *menuet;* fr. the short steps of the dance — more at MINUTE] **1 :** a slow graceful dance fashionable in 17th and 18th century France and England and consisting of forward balancing, bowing, crossing, grapevines, and toe pointing **2 :** a piece of music written for or in the rhythm and spirit of a minuet and usu. in $\frac{3}{4}$ time — compare SCHERZO **3 :** a dance movement retained from the Baroque suite and incorporated into the larger musical compositions (as symphony, sonata, quartet) of the 18th century usu. as one of the two middle movements

2minuet \"\ *vi* -ED/-ING/-S **:** to dance the minuet

1mi·nus \'mīnəs\ *prep* [ME *mynus*, fr. L *minus*, neut. of *minor* smaller, less — more at MINOR] **1 :** diminished by **:** with the subtraction or deduction of **:** LESS ⟨seven ~ four equals three⟩ ⟨list price ~ the discount⟩ ⟨his ideas added up to Communism ~ violence —Hallam Tennyson⟩ — compare PLUS **2 :** deprived of **:** having lost **:** WANTING **:** WITHOUT ⟨came out of the army ~ a hand —Drew Middleton⟩ ⟨she met him, ~ the book, but carrying a . . . balloon —Phil Stong⟩

2minus \"\ *n* -ES **1 :** MINUS SIGN ⟨rendered quantitative by the use of pluses, ~*es*, and marks denoting extreme degrees of the behavior in question —F.H.Allport⟩ **2 :** a negative quantity ⟨an overdose of philosophical . . . conclusions and a ~ of historical or other data —J.B.Mason⟩ **3 :** something (as a deficiency or defect) held to resemble a negative quantity ⟨over against these advantages outside critics set a great ~ —*New Republic*⟩

3minus \"\ *adj* **1 a :** requiring subtraction ⟨the ~ sign⟩ **b :** algebraically negative ⟨a ~ quantity⟩ **2 :** having negative qualities or characteristics ⟨a boy . . . might live in a ~ neighborhood but not be a delinquent —Edwin Powers & Helen Witmer⟩ ⟨plus or ~ reactions to women . . . or men with beards —Jerome Frank⟩ **3 a :** reacting sexually to a morphologically indistinguishable but physiologically separable plus form — used of lower fungi in which maleness and femaleness are indeterminable as such; compare HETEROTHALLIC, MATING TYPE **b :** of, relating to, or exhibiting such a sexual character **4 :** of lesser quality than — used postpositively ⟨hesitated to give it a grade so high as C ~ —*Amer. Literature*⟩ **5 :** smaller than a specified size ⟨stocks of ~ 2-inch stone —*Pit & Quarry*⟩ ⟨all powders were ~ 200 mesh —*Amer. Jour. of Veterinary Research*⟩ **6 :** absorbing principally light of its own hue — used of subtractive color primaries

mi·nus·cu·lar \mə̇'nəskyələ(r)\ *adj* [1*minuscule* + *-ar*] **:** MINUSCULE 2 ⟨tiny white flowers with ~ yellow centers —Victoria Lincoln⟩

1minus·cule \'minə,skyül *sometimes* mə̇'nə- *or* 'minyə-\ *n* -S [F, n. & adj.] **1 a :** one of several styles of ancient and medieval writing developed from the cursive hand and differing from majuscule in having simplified and smaller forms — see CAROLINE MINUSCULE illustration; compare BOOK HAND, CAPITAL 2b **b :** a letter in this style **c :** a manuscript written in minuscule **2 :** a lowercase letter in printing

2minuscule \"\ *or* **miniscule** \'minə,-, mə̇'ni,-\ *adj* [F, fr. L *minusculus* rather small, fr. *minus-*, stem of *minor* smaller, less] **1 :** written in or in the size or style of minuscules ⟨adapted the Greek ~ letters into an alphabet —R.M.French⟩ ⟨~ script⟩ **2 :** very small in size or importance **:** DIMINUTIVE, INSIGNIFICANT, PETTY ⟨this ~ investment . . . paid astronomical dividends —L.S.Kuter⟩ ⟨miserable creatures on ~ salaries —John Gunther⟩ ⟨~ sculptured panels in the doors —Lewis Mumford⟩ ⟨a ~ kitchen⟩

mi·nus la·ti·um \¦mī(,)nü'släd·ē,üm\ *n* [L, lit., lesser Latium, fr. *minus* smaller, lesser (neut. of *minor*) + *Latium*, ancient country of Italy] **:** the right of Roman citizenship conferred upon the holder of a magistracy in a territorial unit (as a colony) outside Rome but applying only to the magistrate himself as an individual and not to his children and other relatives — compare JUS LATII, MAJUS LATIUM

minus lens *n* **:** a lens having a virtual focus for parallel rays

minus sight *n* **:** FORESIGHT 5

minus sign *n* **1 :** a sign — used in mathematics to require subtraction (as in 8−6=2) or designate a negative quantity (as in −10°) — compare PLUS SIGN **2 :** a sign — used in logic to indicate exception or exclusion (as in *a*−*b* to indicate the class of A's excepting the B's) or abstraction among concepts (as in "human−rational" to indicate those attributes that man has in common with other animals)

1min·ute \'minə̇t, *usu* -ə̇d·+V\ *n* -S *often attrib* [ME, fr. MF, fr. ML *minuta* minute, 60th part of an hour, brief note, fr. LL, 60th part of a degree, fr. L, fem. of *minutus* small — more at 3MINUTE] **1 a :** a unit of time equal to the 60th part of an hour and containing 60 seconds **b :** a point or short space of time **:** MOMENT ⟨these letters didn't get here a ~ too soon —Kenneth Roberts⟩ ⟨the train will be starting in a ~ —Florence Montgomery⟩ **c :** a particular instant of time ⟨wash . . . all sieves the ~ you are through using them —June Platt⟩ ⟨my plan is but this ~ come into my head —Charles Lamb⟩ **d :** the distance that can be traversed in a minute ⟨five ~*s* across the park . . . are Spanish-speaking slums —Irwin Edman⟩ **2** [ME, fr. LL *minuta*] *or* **minute of arc :** a unit of angular measure equal to the 60th part of a degree and containing 60 seconds of arc **3** [ML *minuta*] **a :** a usu. brief note of instructions, recommendations, or record in the form of an annotation on an existing document or of a separate memorandum **b :** an official memorandum drafted (as by an individual or a governmental agency) usu. to authorize or recommend a course of action or to analyze a particular situation ⟨the position of civil servants . . . was previously regulated by a Treasury ~ —T.E.May⟩ ⟨the governor . . . forwarded a ministerial ~, expressing alarm —Ethel Drus⟩ ⟨the whole question was reviewed . . . in a masterly ~ by the Viceroy —L.J.L.Dundas⟩ **c** (1) **:** a brief summary of events or transactions ⟨began to take their sense in ~ as right as I could —W.S.Perry⟩ ⟨unity of judgment enough to warrant a ~ of conclusion —Rufus Jones⟩ (2) **minutes** *pl* **:** a series of brief notes taken to provide a record of proceedings (as of an assembly or conference) or of transactions (as of the directors of a corporation); *specif* **:** an official record composed of such notes ⟨the ~*s* of the . . . conference are not available to the public —Vera M. Dean⟩ ⟨a complete copy of the ~*s* of the . . . presbytery —*Amer. Guide Series: Tenn.*⟩ **d :** a rough draft usu. constituting a preliminary stage of a more elaborate project ⟨the ~ of a letter . . . was submitted to the ambassador —J.L.Motley⟩ **e** (1) **:** a written statement addressed to a court under Scots law referring to some interlocutory matter (as a defect in pleading or a point of law) (2) **:** an answer to such a statement embodying the court's order and the grounds of the order **4** [LL *minutum*, fr. L, neut. of *minutus* small] *obs* **:** a very small or insignificant thing **:** a minute detail **5 :** a fixed part (as 1/12, 1/18, 1/30, 1/60) of a module — **up to the minute :** up to date in the highest degree ⟨bringing navy vessels *up to the minute* in radio equipment by replacing old sets with the newest modern apparatus —*N.Y. Times*⟩ ⟨additions calculated to give the impression of being *up to the minute* —*Saturday Rev.*⟩

2minute \"\ *vt* -ED/-ING/-S **1 :** to determine to the minute **:** ascertain or note exactly the time, speed, or duration of **:** TIME ⟨*minuted* the speed of the train —Samuel Smiles⟩ **2 a :** to write (something) in or in the form of a minute ⟨the Empress . . . *minuted* an edict for universal tolerance —George Bancroft⟩ **b :** to make a note (as of instructions, comment, or record) on ⟨~ a dispatch⟩ **c :** to make notes or a brief summary of **:** record in the form of minutes ⟨in conversations . . . duly *minuted* on both sides —M.O.Hudson⟩ ⟨~*s* the proceedings of the meeting —James Bryce⟩

3mi·nute \(')mī¦n(y)üt, mə̇'n-, *usu* -üd·+V\ *adj, usu* -ER/-EST [L *minutus* small, minute, past part. of *minuere* to lessen — more at MINOR] **1 :** very small in size **:** TINY, INFINITESIMAL ⟨two ~, whiplike threads of protoplasm —W.E.Swinton⟩

⟨irrigation ... could be applied only to ~ areas —P.E.James⟩ ⟨~ amounts of ... impurities are introduced into chemically pure silicon —*Wall Street Jour.*⟩ **2 :** of very small importance or consequence **:** TRIFLING, PETTY ⟨the law ... may extend to the *minutest* phases of the life of the individual —C.L.Jones⟩ ⟨small-scale ... almost one might say ~ capitalists —J.H.Plumb⟩ ⟨explaining all the ~ happenings of the ranch —Mary Austin⟩ **3 :** marked by close attention to and meticulous exactness in the treatment of very small parts or details ⟨made a ~ scientific examination of the bullets —W.H.Wright⟩ ⟨the land is ... cultivated with ~ care —Owen & Eleanor Lattimore⟩ ⟨a division in the tapestry so artfully constructed as to defy the *minutest* inspection —Jane Austen⟩ **syn** see CIRCUMSTANTIAL, SMALL

minute book *see* 1MINUTE\\ *n* **1 :** a book in which written minutes or other records are entered **2 :** the official written record of the transactions of the stockholders and directors of a corporation

minute gun *see* 1MINUTE\\ *n* **:** a discharge of a cannon repeated at intervals of a minute usu. in connection with the funeral of a general or flag officer

minute hand *see* 1MINUTE\\ *n* **:** the long hand that marks the minutes on a watch or clock — compare SECOND HAND

1mi·nute·ly \\(ˈ)mī¦n(y)ütlē, məˈn-, -li\\ *adv* [3*minute* + *-ly*] **1 :** into very small pieces ⟨~ fragmented and scattered holdings —George Kuriyan⟩ **2 :** in a minute manner or degree **:** with precision **:** EXACTLY ⟨~ measured and studied —*Amer. Guide Series: Minn.*⟩ ⟨study their personalities and their work ~ —H.H.Arnold & I.C.Eaker⟩

2min·ute·ly \\ˈminətlē\\ *adv* [1*minute* + *-ly,* adv. suffix] **:** every minute **:** from minute to minute ⟨two daughters ... played daily, hourly, ~ —Samuel Wilberforce⟩ ⟨~ proclaimed in thunder from heaven —Henry Hammond⟩

3minutely \\"\\ *adj* [1*minute* + *-ly,* adj. suffix] **:** happening every minute **:** CONTINUAL **:** UNCEASING ⟨our ~ conduct toward each other —S.T.Coleridge⟩ ⟨God's ~ providence —Henry Hammond⟩

min·ute·man \\ˈ==,man, -aa(ə)n\\ *n, pl* **minutemen 1 :** a member of a group of armed men pledged to take the field at a minute's notice during and immediately before the American Revolution **2 :** one who resembles a Revolutionary minuteman esp. in qualities of vigilance and readiness to take prompt action ⟨participation by political *minutemen,* excited by the issues of the day —Hubert Humphrey⟩ ⟨its vigilant lobbyists are so many *minutemen* —*Tomorrow*⟩

minute mark *see* 1MINUTE\\ *n* **:** the mark ′ used to express chronological, geographical, or mathematical minutes

mi·nute·ness *pronunc at* 3MINUTE + nəs\\ *n* -ES **:** the quality or state of being minute: **a :** attention to or extreme precision in small details ⟨that he would peruse with ~ and attention —F.M.Ford⟩ **b :** extreme smallness (as in size or degree) ⟨the ~ of the parts formed a great hindrance to my speed —Mary W. Shelley⟩

minute of arc : 1MINUTE 2

minute pudding *n* [1*minute*] **:** flour stirred into boiling milk

minute repeater *see* 1MINUTE\\ *n* **:** a repeater watch that strikes minutes

minutes *pl of* MINUTE, *pres 3d sing of* MINUTE

minute steak *n* [1*minute*] **:** a small thin steak that can be quickly cooked

minute wheel *n* [1*minute*] **:** a wheel in the dial train of a timepiece that is driven by the cannon pinion and that drives the hour wheel by means of an attached pinion

mi·nu·tia \\məˈn(y)üsh(ē)ə, mīˈ-\\ *n, pl* **minuti·ae** \\-shē,ē\\ *also* **minutia** [L, smallness, fr. *minutus* small, minute + *-ia* -y — more at MINUTE] **:** a minute or precise detail **:** a minor particular **:** a petty matter **:** a small thing — usu. used in pl. ⟨specialized lingo and technical *minutiae* —H.B.Hough⟩ ⟨a printer caring greatly for the *minutiae* of his craft —*Countryman*⟩ ⟨even the ~ of combat cannot be ignored —H.W.Baldwin⟩

mi·nu·tial \\məˈn(y)üshəl, (ˈ)mī¦n-\\ *adj* [L *minutia* + E *-al*] *archaic* **:** of or relating to or being minutiae ⟨~ matters⟩

mi·nu·ti·ose \\-shē,ōs\\ *or* **mi·nu·ti·ous** \\-shēəs\\ *adj* [*minutiose* alter. (influenced by *-ose*) of *minutious,* fr. F *minutieux,* fr. *minutie* minutia (fr. L *minutia*) + *-eux* -ous] **:** attentive to or dealing with minutiae ⟨precision of ~ observation —J.A.Thomson⟩ ⟨~ and troublesome attentions —*Metropolis*⟩

minx \\ˈmiŋks\\ *n* -ES [origin unknown] **1 :** a pert girl **:** a saucy jade **:** HUSSY ⟨never make a wife out of the ~ he had seen coquetting on the opera-house stage —Marcia Davenport⟩ **2** *obs* **:** a lewd or wanton woman ⟨a couple of alluring wanton ~*es* —John Dryden⟩

minx·ish \\-sish\\ *adj* **:** resembling or having the character of a minx

miny \\ˈmīnē\\ *adj* [4*mine* + *-y*] *archaic* **:** of, resembling, or having the characteristics of a mine ⟨a ~ cavern⟩

min·y·ad·i·dae \\,minēˈadə,dē\\ *n pl, cap* [NL, fr. *Minyad-, Minyas,* type genus (fr. Gk *Minyas,* legendary founder of the city Orchomenus in northwest Boeotia) + *-idae*] **:** a family of pelagic sea anemones of southern oceans

1min·yan \\ˈminyən\\ *n, pl* **min·ya·nim** \\,minyəˈnēm\\ *or* **minyans** [Heb *minyān,* lit., number, count] **:** a quorum or number necessary for conducting Jewish public worship consisting by the rules of Mishnah of not less than 10 males above the age of 13

2min·y·an \\ˈminēən, -nyən\\ *adj, usu cap* [Gk *Minyai,* ancient people of Boeotia (fr. *Minyas,* legendary founder of Orchomenus) + E *-an*] **:** of, relating to, or having the characteristics of a prehistoric Greek civilization noted for its pottery

min·yu·lite \\ˈminyə,līt\\ *n* -S [*Minyulo* Well, Dandaragan, Western Australia + E *-ite*] **:** a mineral $KAl_2(PO_4).4H_2O$(?) consisting of a hydrous basic phosphate of potassium and aluminum found in Australia

mio- — see MI-

1mi·o·cene \\ˈmīə,sēn\\ *also* **mi·o·cen·ic** \\¦==¦senik\\ *adj, usu cap* [*miocene* fr. *mi-* + *-cene; miocenic* prob. fr. 2*miocene* + *-ic*] **:** of, relating to, or characterizing an epoch of the Tertiary preceding the Pliocene and succeeding the Oligocene — see GEOLOGIC TIME table

2miocene \\"\\ *n* -S *usu cap* [1*miocene*] **:** the Miocene epoch or series

mio·geosynclinal \\"+\\ *adj* **:** of or relating to a miogeosyncline

mio·geosyncline \\¦mī(,)ō+\\ *n* [ISV *mi-* + *geosyncline*] **:** a comparatively stable geosyncline in which sediments accumulate without contemporaneous volcanism — compare EUGEOSYNCLINE

mi·o·hip·pus \\,mīōˈhipəs\\ *n, cap* [NL, fr. *mi-* + *-hippus*] **:** a genus of very small extinct horses from the Oligocene of No. America

mio·lecithal \\¦mīō+\\ *adj* [*mi-* + *lecithal*] **:** MICROLECITHAL

mi·o·lith·ic \\¦mīō¦lithik\\ *adj, usu cap* [*mi-* + *-lithic*] **:** MESOLITHIC

mi·om·bo \\mīˈäm(,)bō\\ *n* -S [native name in East Africa] **:** a sparse open deciduous woodland characteristic of dry parts of eastern Africa

mi·o·sis *also* **my·o·sis** \\mīˈōsəs\\ *n, pl* **mio·ses** *also* **myo·ses** \\-ō,sēz\\ [NL, fr. *mi-, my-* (fr. Gk *myein* to close, be shut, shut the eyes) + *-osis* — more at MYSTERY] **:** excessive smallness or contraction of the pupil of the eye

mio·thermic \\¦mīō+\\ *adj* [*mi-* + *thermic*] **:** relating to or characterized by temperature conditions on the earth that now prevail as opposed to warmer or colder periods

1mi·ot·ic *or* **my·ot·ic** \\(ˈ)mī¦ädik\\ *adj* [ISV, fr. NL *miosis, myosis,* after such pairs as E *narcosis: narcotic*] **:** relating to or characterized by miosis

2miotic *or* **myotic** \\"\\ *n* -S [ISV, fr. 1*miotic*] **:** an agent that causes contraction of the pupil of the eye

MIP *abbr* **1 :** marine insurance policy **2** *often not cap* **:** mean indicated pressure

miq·ra *also* **mik·ra** \\ˈmikrə\\ *n* -S [Heb *miqrā'*] **1 :** the Hebrew text of the Bible **2 :** a liturgical reading of the miqra

miq·ue·let \\ˈmikə,let\\ *or* **mig·ue·let** \\-igə,-\\ *n* -S [Sp *miquelete, miguelete,* fr. Catal *miquelet,* prob. fr. the name *Miquel*] **1** *obs* **:** a bandit of the Pyrenees **2 a :** an irregular or partisan soldier during the Peninsular War **b :** a soldier of various Spanish local infantry regiments frequently used as escorts **3 :** a flintlock developed in Spain and distinguished by external mounting of mainspring and hammer

1mir \\ˈmi(ə)r\\ *n* -S [Russ, mir, world, peace; akin to L *mitis* soft, mild — more at MITIGATE] **:** a village community common in Russia before the collectivization of agriculture under the Communist regime and characterized by joint ownership of the land by the peasants and cultivation by individual families on a rotational basis

2mir \\"\\ *n* -S *often cap* [Per *mīr,* alter. of *amīr,* fr. Ar] **:** CHIEF, LEADER — used as a title applied esp. in India to descendants of Muhammad; compare SAYYID

mir·a·belle \\ˈmirə¦bel\\ *n* -S [F] **1 :** a small hardy European plum tree (*Prunus domestica institia*) with finely toothed leaves and small cherry-shaped fruit **2 :** the fruit of the mirabelle tree used esp. for preserves and for making a liqueur **3 :** a usu. colorless brandy distilled from the fermented juice of the mirabelle plum

mi·ra·bi·le dic·tu \\məˈräbə(,)lāˈdik(,)tü, -rabə(,)lē'-\\ [L] **:** wonderful to relate ⟨has managed *mirabile dictu* to combine baby-sitting with his grandson and writing an article —F.H.Herrick⟩

mi·rab·i·lis \\məˈrabələs\\ *n, cap* [NL, fr. L, wonderful — more at MARVEL] **:** a genus of American perennial herbs (family Nyctaginaceae) having a tubular-campanulate brightly colored calyx subtended by an involucre that resembles a calyx — see FOUR-O'CLOCK

mi·rab·i·lite \\məˈrabə,līt\\ *n* -S [G *mirabilit,* fr. NL *mirabile* (in *sal mirabile* Glauber's salt, lit., wonderful salt) (fr. L, neut. of *mirabilis* wonderful) + G *-it* -ite] **:** a mineral $Na_2SO_4.10H_2O$ consisting of hydrous sodium sulfate occurring as a deposit from saline lakes, playas, and springs and as an efflorescence

mira·ble *adj* [ME, fr. L *mirabilis*] **:** WONDERFUL

mi·ra·cid·i·al \\¦mīrə¦sidēəl\\ *adj* [*miracidium* + *-al*] **:** of or relating to a miracidium

mi·ra·cid·i·um \\,==ˈsidēəm\\ *n, pl* **miracid·ia** \\-ēə\\ [NL, fr. Gk *meirak-, meirax* girl, boy + NL *-idium* — more at MARRY] **:** the free-swimming ciliated first larva of a digenetic trematode that seeks out and penetrates a suitable snail intermediate host in which it develops into a sporocyst

mir·a·cil D \\ˈmirə,sil-\\ *n* [origin unknown] **:** a yellow crystalline compound $C_{20}H_{24}N_2OS.HCl$ that is a derivative of thioxanthone and is effective in the treatment of some types of schistosomiasis

mir·a·cle \\ˈmirəkəl, -rēk-\\ *n* -S [ME, fr. OF, fr. L *miraculum,* fr. *mirari* to wonder at — more at SMILE] **1 a :** an extraordinary event taken to manifest the supernatural power of God fulfilling his purposes ⟨perform the healing ~*s* described in the Gospels⟩ **b :** an event or effect in the physical world deviating from the laws of nature **2 a :** an accomplishment or occurrence so outstanding or unusual as to seem beyond human capability or endeavor ⟨test if man can produce, through his will and faith, the ~ of peace —B.M.Baruch⟩ ⟨economic ~⟩ **b :** a wonderful thing worthy of admiration **:** a truly superb representative of its kind ⟨became a ~ of learning —H.O.Taylor⟩ ⟨the story is a little ~ —Willa Cather⟩ **3 :** MIRACLE PLAY **4** *Christian Science* **:** a divinely natural occurrence that must be learned humanly **syn** see WONDER — **to a miracle** *adv* **:** marvelously well ⟨I understand my part *to a miracle* —R.L.Stevenson⟩

miracle drug *n* **:** a drug usu. newly discovered that elicits a dramatic response in a patient's condition (as an antibiotic, sulfonamide, or hormone)

miracle man *n* **:** one who works or seems to work miracles

miracle play *n* **1 :** one of a medieval type of dramatic representation showing a sequence of episodes from the life of a wonder-working saint or martyr **2 :** a dramatic composition similar to the miracle play in character — compare 2MYSTERY 3

mi·rac·u·lar \\məˈrakyələ(r)\\ *adj* [L *miraculum* miracle + E *-ar*] **:** relating to or of the nature of a miracle

mi·rac·u·lism \\-yə,lizəm\\ *n* -S [L *miraculum* + E *-ism*] **:** belief in miracles

mi·rac·u·list \\-ləst\\ *n* -S [L *miraculum* + E *-ist*] **:** a maker of or believer in miracles

mi·rac·u·lize \\-yə,līz\\ *vt* -ED/-ING/-S [L *miraculum* + E *-ize*] **:** to cause to seem to be or to treat as a miracle

mi·rac·u·lous \\məˈrakyələs\\ *adj* [MF *miraculeux,* fr. ML *miraculosus,* fr. L *miraculum* + *-osus* -ose] **1 :** of the nature of a miracle **:** interpreted as performed by supernatural power or effected by the direct agency of an almighty power and not by natural causes **:** SUPERNATURAL **2 :** resembling a miracle **:** possessing such unusual qualities as to seem supernatural **:** MARVELOUS, WONDERFUL ⟨the ~ thing about the airplane was speed —*Harper's*⟩ ⟨the book appeared to have met an almost ~ response —C.B.Forcey⟩ ⟨gave proof of a ~ memory —*Time*⟩ **3 :** working or having the power to work miracles ⟨wore a ~ medal —Jean Stafford⟩

miraculous fruit *or* **miraculous berry** *n* **1 :** either of two tropical African fruits that have a lingering sweetish aftertaste that causes indifferent or acid foods eaten after them to taste sweet **2 :** a plant yielding miraculous fruit: **a :** a small shrubby tree (*Synsepalum dulcificum*) of the family Sapotaceae having a fruit that is a fleshy single-seeded berry **b :** an herb (*Thaumatococcus daniellii*) of the family Marantaceae whose edible fruit is the jellylike aril surrounding the seeds

mi·rac·u·lous·ly *adv* **:** in a miraculous manner **:** by or as if by a miracle ⟨countryside through which the little train chugs its way is ~ beautiful —Arthur Knight⟩ ⟨a few parts might ~ be salvaged —Bryan Morgan⟩

mi·rac·u·lous·ness *n* -ES **:** the quality or state of being miraculous

mir·a·dor \\¦mirə¦dō(ə)r, -dȯ(ə)r\\ *n* -S [Sp, fr. Catal, fr. *mirar* to look at, fr. L *mirari* to wonder at] **1 a :** WATCHTOWER **b :** a turret or a bay window, oriel window, loggia, or enclosed balcony designed to command an extensive outlook — used chiefly of Spanish architecture **2 :** ART BROWN

1mi·rage \\məˈräzh, -räl *sometimes* ¦j\\ *n* -S [F, fr. *mirer* to look at, aim at (*se mirer* to look at oneself, be reflected), fr. L *mirari* to wonder at — more at SMILE] **1 a :** an optical phenomenon that is often observed on still days over deserts or hot pavements, that has the mirrorlike appearance of a quiet lake or pool in which distant objects are seen inverted by reflection though usu. distorted, and that is due to a layer of air which has been heated and therefore rarefied by contact with the ground and which has a density distribution such as to cause rays falling obliquely upon it to curve back upward — see FATA MORGANA, LOOMING **b :** an atmospheric phenomenon in which the air appears to move in ascending waves like those above heated metal **2 :** something illusory like a mirage **:** something visionary and unattainable ⟨if one is to write one must have at least the ~ of an audience —F.M.Ford⟩ ⟨explorers, attracted by the ~ of a Northwest passage, pushed through the wilderness —*Amer. Guide Series: Minn.*⟩

2mirage \\"\\ *vt* -ED/-ING/-S **:** to present as a mirage ⟨on the horizon level, we could see *miraged* several small islands —*Australian Museum Mag.*⟩

mi·ra·nya *or* **mi·ra·nha** \\məˈrānyə\\ *n, pl* **miranya** *or* **miranyas** *or* **miranha** *or* **miranhas** *usu cap* **:** an Indian people of the Putumayo River region of Brazil and Colombia — often used to designate any little known people of the region

mi·rate \\ˈmī,rāt\\ *vi* -ED/-ING/-S [prob. back-formation fr. *miration*] *Midland* **:** to feel or express surprise or admiration — used with *about, at, on, over* ⟨*mirated* at the size of the potatoes⟩

mi·ra·tion \\mīˈrāshən\\ *n* -S [prob. short for *admiration*] *chiefly South & Midland* **:** the act of mirating ⟨made a great ~ about the fish he caught⟩

mir·bane oil *also* **myr·bane oil** \\ˈmər,bān-\\ *n* [origin unknown] **:** NITROBENZENE

mird \\ˈmird\\ *vb* -ED/-ING/-S [origin unknown] *vi, Scot* **:** to make amorous advances usu. in a light or trifling manner ~ *vt, Scot* **:** ATTEMPT

1mire \\ˈmī(ə)r, -īə\\ *n* -S [ME, fr. ON *mȳrr;* akin to OE *mōs* marsh, bog — more at MOSS] **1 a :** wet spongy earth **:** MARSH, SWAMP, BOG ⟨the ~ is relieved only by small stretches of open dry forest —*Saturday Rev.*⟩ **b :** something resembling a mire ⟨stuck fast in the ~ of debt —Adrian Bell⟩ ⟨wallowed continuously in an emotional ~ —Lucius Garvin⟩ ⟨sink deeper in the ~ of conflict —Joseph Alsop⟩ **2 :** heavy often deep mud, slush, or dirt ⟨played on a football field that was thick with ~⟩

2mire \\"\\ *vb* -ED/-ING/-S [ME *myren,* fr. *myre, mire,* n.] *vt* **1 a :** to cause to stick fast in or as if in mire **:** plunge or fix in mire ⟨many cattle were lost in the swamps where ... they were *mired* down —W.M.Kollmorgen⟩ ⟨the advent of a thaw which will ~ roads and fields —*N. Y. Herald Tribune*⟩ **b :** ENTANGLE, INVOLVE ⟨the people ... are no more *mired* in the past —Louis Kronenberger⟩ ⟨the most brilliant leadership can be *mired* in detail and confusion —Clinton Rossiter⟩ **2 :** to soil with mud, slush, or dirt ⟨my *mired* boots played havoc with the neatly sanded floor —A.T.Quiller-Couch⟩ ⟨furious because she *mired* the car⟩ ~ *vi* **:** to stick or sink in mire ⟨a road in which horses and wagons *mired* regularly —Edmund Arnold⟩

mire crow *n, dial Eng* **:** BLACK-HEADED GULL

mire–drum \\ˈmī(ə)r,drəm\\ *n* [so called fr. its booming cry] *dial Eng* **:** the European bittern (*Botaurus stellaris*)

mire duck *n, dial Brit* **:** MALLARD

mire·poix *also* **mire·pois** \\mirˈpwä\\ *n, pl* **mirepoix** *also* **mirepois** \\"\\ [F, prob. fr. Charles Pierre Gaston François de Lévis, duc de *Mirepoix* †1757 Fr. diplomat and general] **:** a foundation of ham or bacon, vegetables, herbs, and seasonings used chiefly under meat in braising

mire·snipe \\ˈmī(ə)r,snīp\\ *n, Scot* **:** the common European snipe (*Capella gallinago*)

mirey *var of* MIRY

mir·gil \\ˈmi(ə)rgəl\\ *also* **mir·ga** \\mirˈgä\\ *or* **mir·gal** \\ˈmi(ə)rgəl\\ *n* -S [Bengali *mirgala* & Oriya *mirgā*] **:** a large Indian cyprinid food or sport fish (*Cirrhina mirgala*) having a very small mouth located well under the head

1mi·rid \\ˈmīrəd, ˈmir-\\ *adj* [NL *Miridae*] **:** of or relating to the Miridae

2mirid \\"\\ *n* -S **:** CAPSID

mi·ri·dae \\ˈmīrə,dē, ˈmir-\\ *n pl, cap* [NL, fr. *Miris,* type genus + *-idae*] **:** a large family of small often brightly colored leaf bugs (order Hemiptera) which feed chiefly on the juices of plants

mi·rif·ic \\(ˈ)mī¦rifik\\ *also* **mi·rif·i·cal** \\-fəkəl\\ *adj* [*mirific* fr. MF *mirifique* marvelous, fr. L *mirificus,* fr. *mirus* wonderful + *-ficus* -fic; akin to L *mirari* to wonder at; *mirifical* fr. *mirific* + *-al*] **:** working wonders **:** MARVELOUS ⟨his ~ adventures —W.J.Locke⟩

mi·ri·ki \\,mērēˈkē\\ *n* -S [native name in Brazil] **:** WOOLLY SPIDER MONKEY

mir·i·ness \\ˈmīrēnəs\\ *n* -ES **:** the quality or state of being miry

mir·i·ti palm *or* **mir·i·ty palm** \\ˈmirəd·ē-\\ *n* [*miriti, mirity* fr. Pg *muriti* muriti palm, miriti palm — more at MURITI PALM] **:** a lofty pinnate-leaved So. American palm (*Mauritia flexuosa*) having edible fruits and buds and yielding wine from the sap, a sago from the stem, and a cordage fiber from the leaf sheaths

mirk *var of* MURK

mirky *var of* MURKY

mirled \\ˈmirld, ˈmər-\\ *or* **mir·ly** \\-li\\ *adj* [*mirled* alter. of *marled; mirly* alter. of 2*marly*] *Scot* **:** MARBLED 2

mir·li·goes \\ˈmərli,gōz\\ *n pl* [origin unknown] *Scot* **:** DIZZINESS, VERTIGO

mir·li·ton \\,mirlə¦tōⁿ\\ *n* -S [F, perh. of imit. origin] **1 :** KAZOO **2 :** CHAYOTE

mi·ro \\ˈmē(,)rō\\ *n* -S [Maori] **1 :** a New Zealand timber tree (*Podocarpus ferruginea*) the brown wood of which is used in interior carpentry **2** *Tahiti* **:** PORTIA TREE

mi·roun·ga \\məˈraüŋgə\\ *n, cap* [NL, fr. Australian *miouroung* elephant seal] **:** a genus of Phocidae consisting of the elephant seal

1mir·ror \\ˈmirə(r)\\ *n* -S [ME *mirour,* fr. OF *mireor, mireour,* fr. *mirer* to look at, fr. L *mirari* to wonder at — more at SMILE] **1 a** (1) **:** a polished or smooth substance that forms images by the reflection of light ⟨the burnished ~ of his shield⟩ ⟨the mountain reflected in the ~ of the lake⟩ (2) **:** LOOKING GLASS ⟨picked up the ~ on her dressing table⟩ **b** (1) **:** something that resembles or acts as a mirror **:** something which gives a true representation or in which a true image may be visualized ⟨art is a ~ whose facets reflect all kinds of current trends —Alan McCulloch⟩ ⟨each life is the ~ of many others —Malcolm Cowley⟩ ⟨the press as a ~ of public opinion —C.G.Bowers⟩ (2) **:** something esp. exemplary that may serve as a model ⟨no modern building could act as a better ~ of functional needs ... than this seventeenth-century Spanish mission —*Liturgical Arts*⟩ **2 :** the speculum of a bird's wing **syn** see MODEL — **with mirrors** *adv* **:** by or as if by magic ⟨problem could have only been solved *with mirrors* —*Newsweek*⟩ ⟨for something done *with mirrors,* it looked pretty good —Wright Morris⟩

2mirror \\"\\ *vt* -ED/-ING/-S **1 :** to reflect or behold as in a mirror ⟨its clear waters ~*ing* the dense swamp foliage —*Amer. Guide Series: Fla.*⟩ ⟨the students' moods ~*ed* the weather —*Better Homes & Gardens*⟩ **2 :** to serve as a model for **:** REPRESENT ⟨a single city that ~*s* so clearly the development and character of the Scottish community —R.E.Dickinson⟩ ⟨the President ~*s* the nation —Max Ascoli⟩

mirror canon *n* **:** a musical canon capable of being played in retrograde or inversion as if read in a reflection of a mirror

mirror carp *n* **:** a fish that is a domesticated variety of the carp distinguished by few large scattered shining scales

mir·rored \\ˈmirə(r)d\\ *adj* [1*mirror* + *-ed*] **1 :** fitted with or used as a mirror ⟨buildings of ~ surfaces, expanses of plate glass, and chromium trim —*Amer. Guide Series: N.C.*⟩ **2** [fr. past part. of 2*mirror*] **:** reflected as in a mirror ⟨the brook ... forms ~ pools of beauty —*Amer. Guide Series: Conn.*⟩

mirror fugue *n* **:** a musical fugue capable of being played in retrograde as if read in a mirror placed at the end of the composition or capable of being played in inversion as if read in a mirror placed underneath the music

mirror image *n* **:** something that has its parts so arranged as to present a reversal of the arrangement in another essentially similar thing regarded as a model or that is reversed with reference to an intervening axis or plane

mirror–image relationship *n* **:** the relationship of an object to its mirror image; *specif* **:** the relationship exhibited by two similar but nonsuperimposable crystals or molecular structures — see ASYMMETRIC CARBON ATOM illustration, ENANTIOMORPHISM

mirror iron *n* [trans. of G *spiegeleisen*] **:** SPIEGELEISEN

mirrorlike \\ˈ==,=\\ *adj* **:** resembling a mirror

mirror plate *n* **1 :** a flat glass mirror without a frame **2 :** flat glass suitable for making mirrors

mir·ror·scope \\ˈmirə(r),skōp\\ *n* [*mirror* + *-scope*] **:** an apparatus resembling a camera used in rapid field sketching or painting

mirror writing *n* **:** backward writing that produces manuscript resembling in slant and order of letters the reflection of ordinary writing in a mirror

mir·rory \\ˈmirərē\\ *adj* **:** of, relating to, or resembling a mirror

mirs *pl of* MIR

mirth \\ˈmərth, ˈmə̄th\\ *n* -S [ME *mirthe, myrthe,* fr. OE *myrgth,* fr. *myrge* merry + *-th* — more at MERRY] **1 :** rejoicing esp. as shown in merrymaking ⟨Christmas which ... lights up the fireside of home with ~ —Washington Irving⟩ **2** *obs* **:** joyous sport or entertainment ⟨not amiss ... to give a kingdom for a ~ —Shak.⟩ **3 a :** gladness or gaiety as shown by or accompanied with laughter **:** JOLLITY, MERRIMENT ⟨they broke into laughter, and she thought this shared ~ drew them closer —B.A.Williams⟩ **b** *obs* **:** an object of merriment ⟨he's all my exercise, my ~, my matter —Shak.⟩

mirth·ful \\-thfəl\\ *adj* [ME, fr. *mirth, mirthe, myrthe* mirth + *-ful*] **1 :** full of mirth or merriment **2 :** characterized by, expressing, or indicating, mirth — **mirth·ful·ly** \\-fəlē, -li\\ *adv* — **mirth·ful·ness** *n* -ES

mirth·less \\-thləs\\ *adj* [ME *myrtheles,* fr. *mirthe, myrthe* mirth + *-les* -less] **:** containing no gaiety or joy ⟨gave a ~ laugh —W.H.Wright⟩ — **mirth·less·ly** *adv* — **mirth·less·ness** *n* -ES

miry *also* **mir·ey** \\ˈmīrē, -ri\\ *adj* **mirier; miriest** [ME *myry,* fr. *myre, mire* mire + *-y*] **1 :** resembling a mire **:** characterized by swampy ground **:** BOGGY ⟨~ ground and a matted, marshy vegetation —R.L.Stevenson⟩ **2 :** characterized by heavy often deep mud or slush ⟨a ~ waste of paddy fields —George Orwell⟩ **3 :** stained or spattered with mire ⟨~ shoes⟩

mir·za \\ˈmirzə\\ *n* -S [Per *mīrzā, mirzā,* lit., son of a lord, fr. *mīr* lord, chief + *zā* born, son, fr. *zād, zāda,* fr. *zādan* to be born, fr. MPer *zātan;* akin to Av *zāta-* born, L *gignere* to beget — more at MIR, KIN] **:** a common title of honor in Persia prefixed to the surname of a person of distinction

mis \ˈmis\ *n* -ES [Afrik, fr. MD *mist, mest* — more at MIXEN] *Africa* : DUNG; *specif* : dried dung used as fuel

1mis- *prefix* [partly fr. ME, fr. OE; partly fr. ME *mes-, mis-*, fr. OF *mes-*, of Gmc origin; akin to OE *mis-*; akin to OHG *missa-, missi-* mis-, OS & ON *mis-*, Goth *missa-* mis-, OE *missan* to miss — more at MISS] **1 a** : in an incorrect or improper manner : badly : mistakenly : wrongly ⟨*mis*advise⟩ ⟨*mis*classify⟩ ⟨*mis*judge⟩ ⟨*mis*cooked⟩ ⟨*mis*copied⟩ **b** : unfavorably ⟨*mis*deem⟩ **c** : in a fearful or suspicious manner ⟨*mis*doubt⟩ **2** : incorrect : improper : bad : mistaken : wrong ⟨*mis*deed⟩ ⟨*mis*impression⟩ ⟨*mis*reliance⟩ **3 a** : opposite of ⟨*mis*advantage⟩ ⟨*mis*thrift⟩ **b** : lack of ⟨*mis*adjustment⟩ ⟨*mis*ease⟩ **4** : not ⟨*mis*constitutional⟩ ⟨*mis*convenient⟩

2mis- or **miso-** *comb form* [Gk, fr. *misein* to hate & *misos* hatred] : hatred ⟨*miso*gynic⟩ ⟨*miso*neism⟩ ⟨*miso*sophy⟩

mis·address \ˌmis+\ *vt* [*1mis-* + *address*] : to address incorrectly or improperly ⟨~*ed* the letter⟩ ⟨~*ed* his remarks to the previous speaker instead of to the chairman⟩

mis·adjustment \"+\ *n* [*1mis-* + *adjustment*] : wrong adjustment or agreement ⟨corrected the ~ which had caused the watch to run slow⟩

mis·adventure \"+\ *n* [ME *mesaventure, mesadventure, misaventure*, fr. OF *mesaventure*, fr. *mesavenir* to chance badly, happen badly (fr. *mes-* 1mis- + *avenir* to chance, happen, fr. L *advenire* to come to), after OF *avenir: aventure* adventure — more at ADVENE, ADVENTURE] **1 a** : calamitous misfortune : DISASTER ⟨a record of ~ by shipwreck —*Times Lit. Supp.*⟩; *esp* : a piece of bad luck : MISHAP ⟨his marital ~*s* (his first wife was a prostitute, his second a shrew) —G.N. Ray⟩ **b** *law* : an accident that causes serious injury or death to a human being and that does not involve negligence, wrongful purpose, or unlawful conduct ⟨a verdict of death by ~⟩ **2** : a minor and sometimes ridiculous mishap : BLUNDER ⟨this happy-souled and sometimes uproarious book . . . belongs to the domestic ~ school —*Time*⟩ ⟨his ~*s* as a young immigrant in search of an unknown uncle —Wallace Markfield⟩

misadventured *adj, obs* : UNFORTUNATE ⟨whose ~ piteous overthrows doth with their death bury their parents' strife —Shak.⟩

mis·adventurous \ˌmis +\ *adj* : UNFORTUNATE, UNLUCKY

mis·advise \"+\ *vt* [*1mis-* + *advise*] : to give wrong advice to ⟨had fatally *misadvised* his countrymen —George Grote⟩

mis·aim \(ˈ)mis+\ *vt* [*1mis-* + *aim*] *archaic* : to aim wrongly ⟨missing the mark of his ~*ed* sight —Edmund Spenser⟩

mis·aligned \"+\ *adj* [*1mis-* + *aligned*] : not properly aligned

mis·alignment \ˌ=+\ *n* [*1mis-* + *alignment*] : the condition of being out of line or improperly adjusted

mis·alliance \"+\ *n* [modif. (influenced by E *1mis-*) of F *mésalliance* — more at MÉSALLIANCE] **1** : an improper alliance or combination ⟨the linking of farce and tragedy is usually a ~⟩ **2** : a marriage between persons unsuited to each other ⟨so far apart in age that marriage between them would almost certainly be a ~⟩

mis·ally \"+\ *vt* [*1mis-* + *ally*] : to ally wrongly or unsuitably

mis·an·dry \ˈmiˌsandrē, -aan-, -ri\ *n* -ES [Gk *misandria*, fr. *misandros* hating men (fr. *mis-* 2mis- + *-andros*, fr. *andr-, anēr* man) + *-ia* -y — more at ANDR-] : a hatred of men ⟨her bitter experiences with men led her to bring up her daughter in a spirit of ~⟩ — opposed to *misogyny*

mis·an·thrope \ˈmisᵊnˌthrōp, ˈmiz'ᵊn-\ *n* -S [Gk *misanthrōpos* hating mankind, fr. *mis-* 2mis- + *anthrōpos* man, human being — more at ANTHROP-] : one who hates or despises mankind ⟨a ~, whose only strong emotions are those of disgust, rage, occasional sex hunger —Richard Plant⟩

mis·an·throp·ic \ˌ==ˈthräpik, -pēk\ *also* **mis·an·throp·i·cal** \-pəkəl, -pēk-\ *adj* **1** : of, relating to, or characteristic of a misanthrope ⟨their ~ natures gave a tartness to their observation and their wit —John Cournos⟩ **2** : marked by a hatred or contempt for mankind ⟨the moral corruption he saw around him made him ~⟩ **3** : avoiding the company of others : SOLITARY ⟨a ~ hermit⟩ ⟨claw marks fourteen feet high on a tree trunk, left there by some ~ monarch as a warning to other bears: don't trespass here —Corey Ford⟩ **syn** see CYNICAL

mis·an·throp·i·cal·ly \-pək(ə)lē, -pēk-\ *adv* : in a misanthropic manner

mis·an·thro·pism \məˈs|an(t)thrəˌpizəm, -ˈz|, |aan-\ *n* -S : MISANTHROPY

mis·an·thro·pist \-pəst\ *n* -S : MISANTHROPE

mis·an·thro·pize \-ˌpīz\ *vi* -ED/-ING/-S : to hate mankind

mis·an·thro·py \-pē, -pi\ *n* -ES [Gk *misanthrōpia*, fr. *misanthrōpein* to be misanthropic (fr. *misanthrōpos* hating mankind) + *-ia* -y — more at MISANTHROPE] : a hatred of mankind : distrust of human nature ⟨now that he has revealed so much tenderness, we cannot talk of his ~ —Granville Hicks⟩ — contrasted with *philanthropy*

mis·application \(ˌ)mis+\ *n* [*1mis-* + *application*] **1** : the action of misapplying ⟨language develops by a felicitous ~ of words —J.B.Greenough & G.L.Kittredge⟩ **2** : a misuse or embezzlement of usu. public money

mis·applier \ˌ=+\ *n* : one that misapplies

mis·apply \"+\ *vt* [*1mis-* + *apply*] **1** : to apply wrongly ⟨virtue itself turns vice, being *misapplied* —Shak.⟩ ⟨legal points in the ruling are *misapplied* to the transaction as it actually occurred —D.C.Alexander⟩ **2** : to misuse or spend (as public money) without proper authority ⟨while the handling of the relief fund was irregular . . . he could not say that any part of it had been *misapplied* or embezzled —*Ohio State Jour.*⟩

mis·appreciate \"+\ *vt* [*1mis-* + *appreciate*] : to appreciate or estimate wrongly or improperly — **mis·appreciation** \"+\ *n*

mis·apprehend \(ˌ)mis+\ *vt* [*1mis-* + *apprehend*] : to understand incorrectly : take the wrong meaning of ⟨the real point at issue continues to be ~*ed* by almost everyone who writes upon the question —Richard Garnett †1906⟩

mis·ap·pre·hend·ing·ly *adv* : by misapprehension

mis·apprehension \"+\ *n* [*1mis-* + *apprehension*] **1** : the action of misapprehending ⟨changed certain equivocal passages to prevent further ~ of his views —S.P.Chase & J.K. Snyder⟩ **2** : the state of being misapprehended ⟨an attempt to eliminate some of the common ~*s* and confusions which have traditionally haunted aesthetic thought —Hunter Mead⟩

mis·apprehensive \"+\ *adj* [*1mis-* + *apprehensive*] : inclined to misapprehend ⟨though he seemed to listen carefully, he was inattentive and ~⟩ — **mis·apprehensively** \"+\ *adv* — **mis·apprehensiveness** \"+\ *n*

mis·appropriate \ˌ=+\ *vt* [*1mis-* + *appropriate*] **1 a** : to apply to illegal purposes ⟨the directors *misappropriated* the company's funds for speculation⟩ **b** : to appropriate dishonestly for one's own use : EMBEZZLE ⟨*misappropriated* these funds for his own use —Hamilton Basso⟩ **2** : to appropriate wrongly or misapply in use ⟨the social scientist's techniques can be easily *misappropriated* —W.H.Whyte⟩ — **mis·appropriation** \"+\ *n*

mis·arranged \"+\ *adj* [*1mis-* + *arranged*] : arranged in a wrong order or manner ⟨the books were ~ on the shelf⟩ ⟨badly ~ tools⟩

mis·arrangement \"+\ *n* [*1mis-* + *arrangement*] : a wrong or bad arrangement ⟨the ~ of the clothes was evidence of hurried packing⟩

mis·array \"+\ *n* [*1mis-* + *array*] *archaic* : DISARRAY

mis·ascription \"+\ *n* [*1mis-* + *ascription*] : a wrong ascription ⟨the ~ of witticisms to well-known writers⟩

mis·assignment \"+\ *n* [*1mis-* + *assignment*] : an assignment of a person to a particular job or duty for which he is not equipped or trained ⟨psychological tests are widely used to prevent ~ of personnel⟩

mis·attribution \(ˌ)=+\ *n* [*1mis-* + *attribution*] : a wrong attribution (as of a book or painting) ⟨collectors of old masters have been the victims of many ~*s*⟩

mis·be·come \ˌmisbəˈkəm, -spə-\ *vt* [*1mis-* + *become*] : to suit badly : to be inappropriate or unbecoming to ⟨what I have done that *misbecame* my place —Shak.⟩ ⟨such personal antagonism ~*s* a scholar⟩

misbecoming *adj* [*1mis-* + *becoming*] *archaic* : UNBECOMING

mis·be·get \ˌmisbəˈget, -spə-\ *vt* [ME *misbegeten*, fr. *1mis-* + *begeten* to beget — more at BEGET] : to beget wrongly or unlawfully

mis·be·got·ten \-ˈgätᵊn\ *adj* [fr. past part. of *misbeget*] **1** : unlawfully conceived : ILLEGITIMATE ⟨never acknowledged his ~ child⟩ **2 a** : having a disreputable or improper origin : ill-conceived ⟨some of our antiquated and ~ tax laws —R.M. Blough⟩ **b** : DEFORMED, CONTEMPTIBLE ⟨a scrawny ~ tree⟩ ⟨a ~ scoundrel⟩

mis·be·had·den \ˌmisbəˈhadᵊn, -spə-\ *Scot var of* MISBEHOLDEN

mis·be·have \ˌmisbəˈhāv, -spə-\ *vb* [ME *misbehaven*, fr. *1mis-* + *behaven* to behave — more at BEHAVE] *vt* : to conduct (oneself) badly or improperly ⟨*misbehaved* herself in school⟩ ⟨*misbehaved* herself with several men⟩ ~ *vi* **1 a** : to behave with disregard for accepted moral standards esp. in sexual relations ⟨invited a man to her room and *misbehaved* with him —*Time*⟩ **b** : to behave with disregard for good manners or courtesy ⟨ran through the train, shouting and *misbehaving*⟩ **c** : to behave in a cowardly or unmilitary manner ⟨convicted . . . of *misbehaving* in the face of the enemy —*Associated Press*⟩ **2** : to behave in an unexpected or unwelcome way ⟨does the water you use in processing or as a raw material *misbehave* —*Chem. Engineering News*⟩ **3** : to act as if not housebroken ⟨a pigeon ~*s* itself on his shoulder —H.J.Laski⟩ — **mis·be·hav·er** \-və(r)\ *n* -S

mis·be·hav·ior \-vyə(r)\ *n, see -or in Explan Notes* [ME *misbehaviour*, fr. *1mis* + *behaviour*] **1** : bad, improper, or rude behavior : ill conduct ⟨the irresponsible ~ of a drunken driver resulted in an accident⟩ ⟨the trial court's power to hold prosecuting attorneys in contempt for ~ in official transactions committed out of court —*Harvard Law Rev.*⟩ **2** *U. S. military law* : any conduct by a member of the armed forces before or in the presence of the enemy that does not conform to the standard of behavior established by the custom of U. S. arms for such a situation ⟨~ before the enemy on the same day, by making an unnecessary and disorderly retreat —H.E.Scudder⟩

mis·be·hold·en \ˌmisbəˈhōldən, -spə-\ *adj* [*1mis-* + *beholden*] *dial Brit* : UNBECOMING, DISOBLIGING, OFFENSIVE

mis·be·lief \ˌmisbəˈlēf, -spə-\ *n* [alter. of ME *misbileve, misbileave*, fr. *1mis-* + *beleve, beleave* belief — more at BELIEF] **1** : religious belief regarded as false or unorthodox : HERESY ⟨tried to convert him from his ~⟩ **2** : opinion or doctrine thought to be false ⟨the ~*s* and unscientific notions of prehistoric man⟩

mis·be·lieve \-ēv\ *vb* [ME *misbileven, misbeleven*, fr. *1mis-* + *bileven, beleven* to believe — more at BELIEVE] *vi, obs* : to hold a belief or doctrine thought to be false or unorthodox ⟨chide at him that made her ~ —Edmund Spenser⟩ ~ *vt, archaic* : DISBELIEVE ⟨some people . . . ~ I was ever married —Robert Grant †1940⟩

mis·be·liev·er \-və(r)\ *n* : one who holds a doctrine or religious belief thought to be false : HERETIC, UNBELIEVER ⟨call me ~, cut-throat dog —Shak.⟩

misbelieving *adj* : holding a belief regarded as false or heretical ⟨called for a crusade against the ~ Saracens⟩ — **mis·be·liev·ing·ly** *adv*

mis·be·seem \ˌmisbəˈsēm, -spə-\ *vt* [*1mis-* + *beseem*] : MISBECOME

mis·be·stow \ˌmisbəˈstō, -spə-\ *vt* [*1mis-* + *bestow*] : to bestow wrongly ⟨had ~*ed* her wealth on a scoundrel⟩

mis·birth \(ˈ)misˈbərth, -iˈspə-\ *n* [*1mis-* + *birth*] : ABORTION

mis·brand \(ˈ)misˈbrand, -ˈspr-\ *vt* [*1mis-* + *brand*] : to brand falsely or in a misleading way; *specif* : to brand (as containers of drugs or foodstuffs) in violation of statutory requirements ⟨took steps to stop the ~*ing* of dangerous drugs⟩

misc *abbr* **1** miscellaneous **2** miscellany

mis·ca *or* **mis·ca'** \(ˈ)misˈkȯ, -ˈkä\ *Scot var of* MISCALL

miscal *var of* MISKAL

mis·calculate \(ˌ)mis+\ *vb* [*1mis-* + *calculate*] *vt* : to calculate wrongly ⟨*miscalculated* his dive into the canal . . . and scored his chest into one mass of wounds —D.H.Lawrence⟩ ⟨*miscalculated* the state of the tide —W.F.Hambly⟩ ~ *vi* : to make a mistake in calculation ⟨either elation or depression tends to make you ~ when you're driving a car —*Better Homes & Gardens*⟩

mis·calculation \"+\ *n* [*1mis-* + *calculation*] : a mistake in calculation : wrong calculation ⟨a glaring ~ or oversight —J.S.Weiner⟩ ⟨an instance of political ~ —Walter Millis⟩

mis·calculator \"+\ *n* : one that miscalculates

mis·call \(ˈ)=+\ *vt* [ME *miscallen*, fr. *1mis-* + *callen* to call — more at CALL] **1** : to call by a wrong name : MISNAME ⟨a public whose concept of a book is the ~*ed* "comics" —G.W. Johnson⟩ ⟨a situation which I will not ~, which I dare not name —Edmund Burke⟩ **2** *chiefly dial* : to call by a bad name : ABUSE, REVILE ⟨you're not to ~ . . . the best man alive —Sheila Kaye-Smith⟩ ⟨~*ing* the wind and the cold and the wet lunch basket —Alec Robertson⟩ — **mis·caller** \"+\ *n*

mis·carriage \məs+\ *n* [*1mis-* + *carriage*] **1 a** : mismanagement or bad administration ⟨the immense disorganization and ~ of life that is taking place —Lewis Mumford⟩ **b** : a blunder or failure esp. in the administration of justice ⟨these various ~*s* cannot all be ascribed to ill fortune, since some were due to defective organization and staff work —Russell Grenfell⟩ ⟨by a grave ~ of justice, was acquitted, though admitting the crime —A.F.Harlow⟩ **2** *archaic* : an error of behavior : MISDEED ⟨conducted themselves with such loyalty . . . as might justly wipe off all memory of former ~*s* —Sir Walter Scott⟩ **3 a** : a failure (as of a letter) to arrive at its destination **b** : a failure (as of goods) to carry properly **4 a** : expulsion of a human fetus before it is viable esp. between the 12th and 28th weeks of gestation — compare ABORTION, PREMATURE DELIVERY **b** : abortion esp. when due to natural causes **5** *archaic* : MISCHANCE, DISASTER **syn** see FAILURE

mis·carry \(ˌ)mis+\ *vi* [ME *miscarien*, fr. *1mis-* + *carien* to carry — more at CARRY] **1** *obs* : to come to harm : become lost or destroyed : DIE, PERISH ⟨the great soldier who *miscarried* at sea —Shak.⟩ ⟨my ships have all *miscarried*, my creditors grow cruel —Shak.⟩ **2** : to suffer miscarriage : become delivered of an abortion ⟨*miscarried* several times before her first child was born⟩ **3 a** : to go wrong : fail of an effect : come to nothing ⟨an election conducted by means of paper ballots can ~ —Allen Walker⟩ ⟨instances, all too many, in which justice has *miscarried* —B.N.Cardozo⟩ **b** : to fail in one's intention : be unsuccessful ⟨even the most gifted actor will ~ if he neglects to take direction⟩ **4** : to fail to reach the intended destination : go to the wrong destination ⟨decided that the letter must have *miscarried*⟩

mis·cast \(ˈ)=+\ *vt* [*1mis-* + *cast*] **1** : to place in an unsuitable occupation; *esp* : to give an unsuitable acting part to ⟨a journalist without such faith is ~ —F.L.Mott⟩ ⟨life had ~ her in the role of wife and mother —Edna Ferber⟩ ⟨the actress who plays the lead is grotesquely ~⟩ **2** : to make an unsuitable assignment of acting parts in ⟨the play is ~⟩ ⟨the leading roles are ~⟩

mis·cege·na·tion \məˌsejəˈnāshən *also* ˌmiˌsej- *or* ˌmisəj-\ *n* -S [L *miscēre* to mix + *genus* race + E *-ation* — more at MIX, KIN] : a mixture of races; *esp* : marriage or cohabitation between a white person and a member of another race

mis·cel·la \məˈselə\ *n* -S [NL, fr. L, fem. of *miscellus* mixed — more at MISCELLANEOUS] : a solution or mixture containing an extracted oil or grease ⟨~ from soybeans obtained by extraction with a hydrocarbon solvent —P.L.Julian & H.T. Iveson⟩

mis·cel·la·nea \ˌmisəˈlānēə\ *n pl* [L, fr. neut. pl. of *miscellaneus*] **1** : a collection of miscellaneous writings or notes ⟨a batch of ~ including a number of verses —*Times Lit. Supp.*⟩ **2** : a collection of miscellaneous objects ⟨the Japanese influence has been joined by early Chinese furniture and Hawaiian ~ —T.H.Robsjohn-Gibbings⟩

mis·cel·la·ne·i·ty \-ˌləˈnēəd·ē, -ətē, -i\ *n* -ES [*miscellaneous* + *-ity*] : the quality or state of being miscellaneous ⟨its appearance of ~ in the absence of any general idea —Raymond Williams⟩

mis·cel·la·neous \ˌmisəˈlānēəs, -nyəs\ *adj* [L *miscellaneus*, fr. *miscellus* mixed, prob. fr. *miscēre* to mix — more at MIX] **1** : comprising members or items of different kinds : grouped together without system : ASSORTED : HETEROGENEOUS ⟨special areas where tiger, rhino, and ~ smaller game were produced in abundance —Dillon Ripley⟩ ⟨did a vast amount of ~ reading —Martin Gardner⟩ **2 a** : having various traits : dealing with or interested in unrelated topics or subjects ⟨a formal work would not have suited him; he had a ~ talent —John Derby⟩ ⟨as a writer I was too ~ —George Santayana⟩ **b** : lacking in unity : having the characteristics of a patchwork ⟨the French pavilion has been severely criticized . . . for being excessively ~ —David Sylvester⟩ ⟨the large white wooden structure stands in its heroic proportions with a kind of ~ nobility —*Amer. Guide Series: Vt.*⟩ — **mis·cel·la·neous·ly** *adv* — **mis·cel·la·neous·ness** *n* -ES

mis·cel·la·nist \ˈmisəˌlānəst, ˌ==ˈ==, *chiefly Brit* ˈmisələn- *or* məˈselən-\ *n* -S [*miscellany* + *-ist*] : a writer of miscellanies

1mis·cel·la·ny \ˈmisəˌlānē, -ni, *chiefly Brit* ˈmisələn- *or* məˈselən-\ *n* -ES [prob. modif. of F *miscellanées*, pl., fr. L *miscellanea* — more at MISCELLANEA] **1** : a mixture of various things : HODGEPODGE : MEDLEY ⟨a ~ of lumber, fish, dairy products —*Amer. Guide Series: Minn.*⟩ ⟨ranged along the walls were a ~ of violin backs, viola bellies, and whole but unvarnished cellos —Joseph Wechsberg⟩ **2 a miscellanies** *pl* : separate studies or writings collected in one volume ⟨a book of ~⟩ **b** : a collection of writings on various subjects ⟨the newspaper serves all classes of readers and must always be a highly composite ~ —F.L.Mott⟩ ⟨its haphazard compilation leaves a doubt whether a fiction magazine, a critical journal, or a general ~ is intended —*Times Lit. Supp.*⟩

2miscellany \"\ *adj* [L *miscellaneus* — more at MISCELLANEOUS] *archaic* : MISCELLANEOUS

1mis·chance \(ˈ)mis(h), məs(h)+\ *n* [ME *meschaunce, mischaunce*, fr. OF *meschance, mescheance*, fr. *mes-* 1mis- + *chance, cheance* chance — more at CHANCE] **1** : bad luck : MISFORTUNE ⟨the fears and disorders of today are a passing phase, the results of political ~ rather than of political incompetence —*Times Lit. Supp.*⟩ **2** : a piece of bad luck : an unfortunate accident : MISHAP ⟨similar ~*s* are frequently recorded at wrestlings —G.G.Coulton⟩

2mischance \"\ *vi, archaic* : to come about by mischance

mis·chance·ful \-fəl\ *adj* [ME *mischaunceful*, fr. *mischaunce* + *-ful*] *archaic* : UNLUCKY

mis·chancy \"+\ *adj* [*1mischance* + *-y*] *dial chiefly Brit* : RISKY, UNLUCKY

mischan·ter \məs(h)ˈchantər, məˈsha-\ *var of* MISHANTER

1mis·chief \ˈmis(h)chəf\ *n* -S [ME *meschief, mischef*, fr. OF *meschief* calamity, misfortune, fr. *mes-* 1mis- + *chef, chief* end, head — more at CHIEF] **1** *obs* : CALAMITY : MISFORTUNE ⟨to mourn a ~ that is past and gone is the next way to draw new ~ on —Shak.⟩ **2 a** : a specific injury or damage caused by a person or other agency ⟨will never forget the ~*s* they have done to us⟩ ⟨the polished floor . . . often causes ~ — bruises, sprains, dislocations —Herbert Spencer⟩ **b** : harm, evil, or damage that results from a particular agency or cause ⟨one failure led to another, suspicion became general, and the ~ was done —J.A.Todd⟩ ⟨the concealment of a truth, with its resultant false beliefs, must produce ~ —G.B.Shaw⟩ **3** : a diseased condition : a cause of sickness ⟨the ~ is out of your system, and all you have to do is to build your system up —John Buchan⟩ **4 a** : a cause or source of harm, evil, or irritation; *esp* : a person who causes mischief ⟨housing in rocks, of mariners the ~ —Robert Browning⟩ ⟨he's a real ~ to his family⟩ **b** : the aspect of a situation or the quality of a thing that produces harm or causes irritation ⟨the ~ of snow is that it turns to slush⟩ ⟨the ~ is that people . . . do not confine themselves to one cocktail —Arnold Bennett⟩ **5** : DEVIL ⟨an accident that played the ~ with his plans⟩ ⟨can't see why in the ~ you ever got mixed up with that reform gang —Willa Cather⟩ **6 a** : action or conduct that annoys or irritates without causing or meaning to cause serious harm ⟨little wretches, always up to some ~ . . . all bedraggled from some roguery —Virginia Woolf⟩ ⟨a seasonal ritual among Rochester's youth, like today's Halloween ~*s* —S.H.Adams⟩ **b** : MISCHIEVOUSNESS ⟨inclined to ~ rather than malice —*Amer. Guide Series: Ariz.*⟩ ⟨a defiance, offered from sheer, youthful, wanton ~ —Arnold Bennett⟩ **7** : DISCORD, DISSENSION ⟨has often made ~ between husband and wife⟩ ⟨stirred up ~ between the young people⟩ **syn** see INJURY

2mischief \"\ *vt* -ED/-ING/-S [ME *mischefen*, fr. *mischef*, n.] : to do harm to : INJURE ⟨that . . . tyrant that ~*s* the world with his mines of Ophir —John Milton⟩ ⟨any of the other boys . . . they would have ~*ed*, but they just tweaked Peter's nose —J.M.Barrie⟩

mis·chief·ful \-ə(f)fəl\ *adj* [*1mischief* + *-ful*] *dial* : MISCHIEVOUS

mischief-maker \ˈ==ˌ==\ *n* : one that makes mischief : one who excites or instigates quarrels or enmity ⟨their reconciliation defeated the efforts of the *mischief-makers*⟩

mis·chieve \məs(h)ˈchēv\ *vt* -ED/-ING/-S [ME *mischeven*, fr. MF *meschever* to come to misfortune, fr. OF, fr. *mes-* 1mis + *-chever* (fr. *chef, chief* end, head) — more at CHIEF] **1** *archaic* : MISCHIEF **2** *archaic* : ABUSE, REVILE

mis·chie·vous \ˈmis(h)chəvəs, *chiefly in substand speech* məs(h)ˈchēvəs *or* -ˈchēvēəs\ *adj* [ME *mischevous*, fr. *mischef* + *-ous*] **1 a** : involving or productive of harm or injury : HARMFUL, INJURIOUS ⟨a thing which is excellent in moderation and only ~ in excess —A.C.Benson⟩ ⟨this ~ separation of the logic from the practice of science —Benjamin Farrington⟩ **b** : able to do harm or engaged in doing harm ⟨the solid foundations of church and state were threatened by ~ men —V.L. Parrington⟩ ⟨a ~ fanatic who was trying to destroy liberty of contract —*Times Lit. Supp.*⟩ **2 a** : capable of causing or tending to cause annoyance, trouble, or minor injury or damage to others ⟨windows broken by ~ children⟩ ⟨the younger animals are most ~, and I have known bags of flour ripped open and the contents scattered about —James Stevenson-Hamilton⟩ **b** : having or expressing a spirit of irresponsible fun or playfulness ⟨this same stimulating and occasionally ~ style —W.C.Brice⟩ ⟨her eyes . . . had a sharp and ~ glitter in them —T.B.Costain⟩ — **mis·chie·vous·ly** *adv* — **mis·chie·vous·ness** *n* -ES

mischmasch *var of* MISHMASH

misch metal \ˈmish-\ *n* [G *mischmetall*, fr. *mischen* to mix (fr. OHG *miskan*, fr. L *miscēre*) + *metall* metal, fr. MHG *metalle*, fr. L *metallum* — more at MIX, METAL] : a pyrophoric alloy that consists of a crude mixture of cerium, lanthanum, neodymium, and other rare-earth metals in the approximate ratio in which they occur in monazite sand and that is obtained usu. by electrolysis of the fused mixed chlorides of the metals

mis·choice \(ˈ)mis(h), məs(h)+\ *n* [*1mis-* + *choice*] : a wrong or improper choice

mis·choose \"+\ *vb* [ME *mischesen*, fr. *1mis-* + *chesen* to choose — more at CHOOSE] *vi* : to choose wrongly ⟨~*s* because he does not stop to think⟩ ~ *vt* : to make a wrong choice of ⟨~*s* the showy instead of the beautiful⟩

misch·spra·che \ˈmish,shpräkə\ *n, pl* **mischspra·chen** \-kən\ *usu cap* [G, fr. *mischen* to mix + *sprache* language] : a language alleged to have arisen from a mixture of two or more previously existing languages

mis·ci·bil·i·ty \ˌmisəˈbiləd·ē, -ətē, -i\ *n* -ES [fr. *miscible*, after such pairs as E *possible: possibility*] : the property of being able to mix or become homogeneous

mis·ci·ble \ˈmisəbəl\ *adj* [ML *miscibilis*, fr. L *miscēre* to mix + *-ibilis* -ible — more at MIX] : capable of being mixed : MIXABLE; *specif* : capable of mixing in any ratio without separation of two phases — used esp. of fluids; compare COMPATIBLE 2f ⟨two ~ liquids, such as water and alcohol, or oil and kerosene —George M. Sutheim⟩ ⟨gases are completely ~ —F.H. Getman & Farrington Daniels⟩

miscible oil *n* : a hydrocarbon oil that contains emulsifiers, forms a milky emulsion with water, and is suitable for use esp. as a dormant spray

mis·cite \(ˈ)mis+\ *vt* [*1mis-* + *cite*] : MISQUOTE

miscl *abbr* miscellaneous

mis·classification \(ˌ)mis+\ *n* [*1mis-* + *classification*] : a wrong classification

mis·color \(ˈ)mis+\ *vt* [*1mis-* + *color*] : to give a wrong color to : MISREPRESENT ⟨~*ed* the facts in order to win the jury's sympathy⟩

mis·comprehend \(ˌ)=+\ *vt* [*1mis-* + *comprehend*] : to get a wrong idea of or about : MISUNDERSTAND ⟨~*ed* the point of the lecture⟩

mis·comprehension \"+\ *n* [*1mis-* + *comprehension*] : MISUNDERSTANDING

1mis·conceit \ˌ=+\ *n* [*1mis-* + *conceit* (n.)] : MISCONCEPTION

2misconceit \"\ *vt* [*1mis-* + *conceit* (v.)] : MISCONCEIVE

mis·conceive \"+\ *vb* [ME *misconceiven*, fr. *1mis-* + *conceiven* to conceive — more at CONCEIVE] *vi* : to conceive wrongly ⟨~*s*, if he thinks acting is all fun and no work⟩ ~ *vt* : to form a wrong idea of : mistake the meaning of ⟨*misconceived* the size of the continent⟩ ⟨*misconceived* the nature of the problem⟩ — **mis·con·ceiv·er** \-və(r)\ *n*

mis·conception \"+\ *n* [1*mis-* + *conception*] **:** the act or result of misconceiving **:** a wrong or inaccurate conception ⟨such popular ~*s* as the belief that interplanetary space is of a sub-zero frigidity —J.F.McComas⟩

1**mis·conduct** \(')=+\ *n* [1*mis-* + *conduct* (n.)] **1 :** mismanagement esp. of governmental or military responsibilities ⟨was charged with ~ of the war⟩ **2 :** intentional wrongdoing **:** deliberate violation of a rule of law or standard of behavior esp. by a government official **:** MALFEASANCE ⟨one of his district judges has been removed from the bench . . . for official ~ —H.H.Martin⟩ ⟨indicted on two counts of bribe taking and three of ~ —*Time*⟩ **3 a :** bad conduct **:** improper behavior ⟨was fined for ~ on the field⟩ **b :** sexual immorality; *esp* **:** ADULTERY ⟨charged her husband with ~⟩

2**mis·conduct** \¦=+\ *vt* [1*mis-* + *conduct* (v.)] **1 :** to manage badly **:** MISMANAGE ⟨~*ed* the expedition, losing half his supplies⟩ **2 :** to behave (oneself) improperly ⟨~*ed* himself in office⟩

mis·construct \"+\ *vt* [1*mis-* + *construct*] *archaic* **:** MISCONSTRUE

mis·construction \"+\ *n* [1*mis-* + *construction*] **1 :** the action of misconstruing **:** wrong interpretation (as of words, intentions, or actions) ⟨avowal would inevitably lead to ~ of motive —W.J.Locke⟩ ⟨~ of his words has made him seem to advocate what he opposes⟩ **2 :** a bad or wrong construction ⟨this is correct in Latin, but a ~ in English⟩

mis·construe \¦mis=¦=, (')mis¦==, məs'=,=\ *vt* [ME *misconstruen*, fr. 1*mis-* + *construen* to construe — more at CONSTRUE] **1 :** to interpret wrongly **:** MISINTERPRET ⟨*misconstrued* his abruptness of manner . . . found him assertive and inflexible —Arnold Bennett⟩ ⟨the reader should be on guard against *misconstruing* the intention of a given passage —Carlos Baker⟩ **2 :** to misinterpret the meaning or intention of ⟨~*s* me if he thinks I will give up my support of the plan⟩

1**mis·content** \¦mis+\ *adj* [ME, fr. 1*mis-* + *content*] *archaic* **:** DISCONTENTED

2**mis·content** \"\ *vt* [ME *miscontenten*, prob. fr. MF *mescontenter*, fr. *mes-* 1mis- + *contenter* to satisfy, make content — more at CONTENT] *archaic* **:** DISPLEASE

mis·contentment \"+\ *n* [1*mis-* + *contentment*] *archaic* **:** DISCONTENT

mis·cook \(')=+\ *vt* [1*mis-* + *cook*] **1 :** to ruin in cooking ⟨simple dishes almost impossible to ~⟩ **2** *chiefly Scot* **:** to manage badly **:** SPOIL

mis·copy \"+\ *vt* [1*mis-* + *copy*] **:** to copy wrongly ⟨the typist *miscopied* the letter⟩

mis·correct \¦=+\ *vt* [1*mis-* + *correct*] **:** to make a mistake in an attempt to correct ⟨"the reason I think you're silly is that — is because —" she ~*ed* herself —Philip Wylie⟩

mis·counsel \(')=+\ *vt* [ME *misconselen*, prob. fr. MF *mesconseillier*, fr. OF, fr. *mes-* 1mis- + *conseillier*, *conseiller* to give counsel — more at COUNSEL] **:** to advise wrongly ⟨~*ed* him to refuse a job that would have suited him perfectly⟩

1**mis·count** \"+\ *vb* [ME *misconten*, fr. MF *mesconter* to count falsely, cheat in counting, fr. *mes-* 1mis- + *conter* to count — more at COUNT] *vt* **:** to count wrongly **:** MISCALCULATE ⟨~*ed* the money twice⟩ **~** *vi* **:** to make a wrong count ⟨often ~*s* in figuring the number of hours he has worked⟩

2**miscount** \"\ *n* [1*mis-* + *count* (n.)] **:** a wrong count **:** MISCALCULATION ⟨lost the fight as a result of a ~ by the referee⟩

mis·cre·ance \'miskrēən(t)s\ *n* -s [ME *mescreaunce*, fr. MF *mescreance*, fr. *mes-* 1mis- + *creance* belief, trust, confidence — more at CREANCE] **:** MISBELIEF

mis·cre·an·cy \-nsē, -si\ *n* -ES **1** *archaic* **:** MISBELIEF **2 :** VILLAINY ⟨embittered by the ~ of those who had cheated them⟩

1**mis·creant** \-nt\ *adj* [ME *miscreaunt* unbelieving, fr. MF *mescreant*, pres. part. of *mescroire* to disbelieve, fr. *mes-* 1mis- + *croire* to believe, fr. L *credere* — more at CREED] **1 :** holding a religious faith or doctrine regarded as false **:** UNBELIEVING, HERETICAL ⟨either weakminded or ~ for holding that we are incapable of any rational knowledge of God —James Collins⟩ **2 :** DEPRAVED, VICIOUS, VILLAINOUS ⟨a ~ gang⟩

2**miscreant** \"\ *n* -s [ME *miscreaunt* unbeliever, fr. *miscreaunt*, adj.] **1 :** one who holds a religious faith or doctrine regarded as false **:** INFIDEL, HERETIC ⟨called upon to show that he is not a pagan or a ~ —Thomas DeQuincey⟩ **2 :** one who behaves criminally or viciously ⟨understanding of the ~ here involved will not, of itself, necessarily solve painful administrative decisions —*Group Psychotherapy*⟩ **syn** see VILLAIN

1**mis·create** \'miskrēˌāt, ¦==¦āt\ *adj* [1*mis-* + *create* (adj.)] **:** created or shaped badly or unnaturally ⟨a ~ monstrosity of a building⟩

2**mis·create** \(¦)=+\ *vt* [1*mis-* + *create* (v.)] **:** to create misshapen or amiss ⟨we ~ our evils —R.W.Emerson⟩

mis·creation \¦=+\ *n* [1*mis-* + *creation*] **1 :** the action of miscreating **2 :** a miscreated person or thing

mis·creative \(¦)=+\ *adj* [1*mis-* + *creative*] **:** creating or shaping badly

mis·creator \"+\ *n* **:** one that miscreates

mis·creed \(')=+\ *n* [1*mis-* + *creed*] *archaic* **:** a false creed

1**mis·cue** \"+\ *n* [1*mis-* + *cue* (n.)] **1 a :** a faulty stroke in billiards in which the cue tip slips off the cue ball ⟨nearly ruins a billiard table with a ~ —Hamilton Basso⟩ **b :** an error or misplay in other games (as baseball) ⟨has learned to bottle up his anger over a strikeout or a ~ —*Time*⟩ **2 :** MISTAKE **:** SLIP ⟨the slightest ~ hurtling him down six stories to the back yard —E.D.Radin⟩ ⟨a few ~*s* in the landing of certain units —*Infantry Jour.*⟩

2**miscue** \"\ *vi* **1 a :** to make a miscue in billiards ⟨got the off-the-cushion cannon but then *miscued* —*Billiard Player*⟩ **b :** to make an error or mistake ⟨typical of official *miscuing* were the statements . . . made throughout the week —*Time*⟩ **2 :** to miss a stage cue **:** to answer a wrong cue ⟨*miscued* and collided with an actor entering from the right⟩

mis·date \(')mis¦dāt, -i¦stā-\ *vt* [1*mis-* + *date*] **:** to date wrongly ⟨carelessly *misdated* the letter⟩ ⟨~*s* several of the plays he discusses by as much as five years⟩

1**mis·deal** \(')mis¦dē(ə)l, -i¦stē-\ *vb* [1*mis-* + *deal* (v.)] *vi* **:** to deal cards incorrectly ⟨*misdealt*, and the cards had to be dealt again⟩ **~** *vt* **:** to deal incorrectly ⟨*misdealt* the hand and it had to be played over⟩

2**misdeal** \"\ *n* [1*mis-* + *deal* (n.)] **:** a mistake in dealing cards: as **a :** a dealer's error that causes him to lose his turn to deal **b :** an irregularity in a bridge hand that requires a new deal by the same dealer

misdealing *n* **:** wrong conduct **:** false dealing ⟨exposed his ~ in the awarding of contracts⟩

mis·deed \(')mis¦dēd, -i¦stēd\ *n* [ME *misdede*, fr. OE *misdǣd*, (akin to OHG *missitāt* misdeed, OFris *misdēde*, Goth *missadeths*), fr. *mis-* 1mis + *dǣd* deed — more at DEED] **:** a wrong deed **:** an immoral or criminal action ⟨the wickedness and ~*s* of the Borgia and his family are world-famous —R.A.Hall b.1911⟩

mis·deem \(')mis¦dēm, -i¦stēm\ *vb* [ME *misdemen*, fr. 1*mis-* + *demen* to deem — more at DEEM] *vt* **1** *archaic* **:** to judge unfavorably **:** think badly of ⟨made him to ~ my loyalty —Edmund Spenser⟩ **2 a :** to have a mistaken opinion of **:** MISJUDGE ⟨~*ed* the power of the opposition⟩ ⟨a gruffness that led us to ~ their true intentions⟩ **b :** to think or suppose wrongly ⟨but he ~*s* that he is wise —P.B.Shelley⟩ **3 :** to mistake for something or someone else ⟨~ fantasy for reality⟩ **~** *vi* **:** to be mistaken **:** hold a wrong opinion ⟨farther on, if I ~ not —H.F.Cary⟩

mis·de·liv·er \¦misdə¦livə(r), -stə-\ *vt* [1*mis-* + *deliver*] **:** to deliver wrongly ⟨~*ed* the letter to the wrong address⟩ — **mis·de·liv·ery** \-v(ə)rē, -ri\ *n*

1**mis·de·mean** \¦misdə¦mēn, -stə-\ *vt* [1*mis-* + *demean* (v.)] *archaic* **:** to behave (oneself) badly ⟨you that best should teach us, have ~*ed* yourself —Shak.⟩

2**misdemean** \"\ *n* [1*mis-* + *demean* (n.)] *archaic* **:** an act of misbehavior ⟨if any convict shall . . . commit any ~ —S.J. Barrows⟩

mis·de·mean·ant \-nənt\ *n* -s [1*misdemean* + *-ant*] **1 :** a person guilty of or convicted of a misdemeanor ⟨an administrator in a fairly large court handling ~*s* exclusively —Edmond FitzGerald⟩ **2 :** a person guilty of misconduct ⟨though he has never been jailed, he is a confirmed drunkard and ~⟩

mis·de·mean·or \-nə(r)\ *n, see -or in Explan Notes* [1*mis-* + *demeanor*] **1 :** a crime less than a felony; *specif* **:** a crime that is not punishable by death or imprisonment in a state penitentiary **2 a** *archaic* **:** evil conduct **:** MISBEHAVIOR ⟨the whole town . . . is distressed for the ~ of a few —Samuel Johnson⟩ **b :** an act of bad conduct **:** MISDEED, OFFENSE ⟨the failure of the family, a being of incalculable ~*s* —H.G.Wells⟩ ⟨leads to such ~*s* in literary criticism as the too facile relating of a writer's entire working life to an unhappy childhood —Miriam Allott⟩

mis·de·scribe \¦misdə¦skrīb, -stə-\ *vt* [1*mis-* + *describe*] **:** to describe wrongly ⟨seem not so much to be describing something with which I am not acquainted as to be *misdescribing* something with which I am all too well acquainted —J.H. Muirhead⟩

mis·de·scrip·tion \-¦skripshən\ *n* [1*mis-* + *description*] **:** an inaccurate description ⟨dangerously misleading ~ —A.G.N. Flew⟩

mis·de·scrip·tive \-ptiv, -tēv *also* -təv\ *adj* [1*mis-* + *descriptive*] **:** serving to describe incorrectly ⟨ruled that the label was ~ and could not be used⟩

mis·di·rect \¦misdə¦rekt, -stə-\ *vt* [1*mis-* + *direct*] **1 a :** to give a wrong direction to ⟨~*ed* a stranger asking the way to the station⟩ **b :** to put a wrong direction or address on ⟨~*ed* the letter⟩ **2 :** to charge (a jury) erroneously as to the law applicable to a case ⟨the prisoner is entitled, however, to contend that the judge ~*ed* the jury —Ronald Rubinstein⟩

mis·di·rec·tion \-kshən\ *n* [1*mis-* + *direction*] **1 a :** the action of misdirecting ⟨~ of the audience's attention is the secret of a magician's success⟩ **b :** the state of being misdirected ⟨accomplished little because of the ~ of his energies⟩ **2 a :** a wrong direction ⟨gave him a ~ that wasted an hour of his time⟩ **b :** an error of a judge in charging a jury on a matter of law

mis·di·vi·sion \¦misdə¦vizhən, -stə-\ *n* [1*mis-* + *division*] **1 :** wrong or incorrect division (as of a word) **2 :** an abnormal transverse division of a centromere that results in the formation of two telocentric chromosomes from a single metacentric chromosome

mis·do \(')mis¦dü, -i¦stü\ *vb* [ME *misdon*, fr. OE *misdōn*, fr. 1*mis-* + *dōn* to do — more at DO] *vi, obs* **:** to do wrong ⟨not willfully ~*ing*, but unware misled —John Milton⟩ **~** *vt* **:** to do wrongly or improperly ⟨~ even a simple assignment⟩

mis·do·er \-üə(r), -ü(ə)r, -üə\ *n* [ME, fr. *misdon* to misdo + *-er*] **:** one who does wrong ⟨watching for pickpockets and other ~*s* —*N.Y. Times*⟩

misdoing *n* [ME, fr. gerund of *misdon* to misdo] **:** WRONGDOING ⟨the grievances . . . were due to the ~*s* of royal officers —J.G.Edwards⟩

1**mis·doubt** \(')mis¦dau̇t, -i¦stau̇t\ *vb* [1*mis-* + *doubt* (v.)] *vt* **1 a :** to doubt the reality or truth of ⟨~*ing* his own executive ability —C.S.Forester⟩ — often used with a noun clause as object ⟨he took to his bed yesterday, but I ~ he is very ill —T.B.Costain⟩ **b :** to regard with suspicion or distrust **:** SUSPECT ⟨he was extremely presentable . . . you could not ~ him —George Meredith⟩ **2** *chiefly dial* **:** to be apprehensive of **:** suspect or fear as an evil ⟨the prisoner ~*ed* him to be an apparition of his own imagining —Charles Dickens⟩ **~** *vi, chiefly dial* **:** to have doubt or suspicion

2**misdoubt** \"\ *n* [1*mis-* + *doubt* (n.)] **:** SUSPICION, DISTRUST ⟨had some ~ regarding the truth of the story⟩ ⟨could not overcome his ~⟩

mise \'mēz, 'mīz\ *n* -s [MF, lit., action of putting or setting, fr. fem. of *mis*, past part. of *mettre* to put, set, fr. L *mittere* to send — more at SMITE] **:** the issue in a legal proceeding upon a writ of right; *also* **:** the writ itself

mis·ease \(')mis+\ *n* [ME *meseise, misese*, fr. OF *mesaise*, fr. *mes-* 1mis- + *aise* comfort, ease — more at EASE] **:** lack of ease **:** DISCOMFORT, DISTRESS

mis·educated \(¦)=+\ *adj* [1*mis-* + *educated*] **:** educated in the wrong way **:** badly educated ⟨people who have been ~ in the towns —Robert Gibbings⟩ ⟨millions were uneducated, millions more ~ —Benjamin Fine⟩

mis·education \"+\ *n* [1*mis-* + *education*] **:** education regarded as wrong and harmful in purpose, content, or method ⟨~ of the public in scientific matters —Irene T. Jones⟩

mise-en-scène \¦mē,zäⁿ'sen, -sän\ *n, pl* **mise-en-scènes** [F *mise en scène*, lit., (action of) putting onto the stage] **1 a :** the process of putting a play or other theatrical production on the stage **:** the arrangement of the scenery, properties, and actors onstage ⟨the *mise-en-scène* suggested that nobody had had much rehearsal —Winthrop Sargeant⟩ ⟨a *mise-en-scène* that included eight horses galloping onstage in the last act —John Briggs⟩ **b :** STAGE SETTING ⟨a shabby, down-at-the-heels *mise-en-scène* that scarcely could be called decor —*Saturday Rev.*⟩ ⟨spectacle plays attempted a more realistic, three-dimensional *mise-en-scène* —A.N.Vardac⟩ **2 a :** the physical setting of an action ⟨gaze on this ordinary house that became the *mise-en-scène* of an extraordinary drama —E.M.Lustgarten⟩ **b :** ENVIRONMENT, MILIEU ⟨the books of chivalry . . . were part of the Spanish *mise-en-scène* —*New Yorker*⟩

mis·emphasis \(')mis+\ *n* [1*mis-* + *emphasis*] **:** misplaced emphasis ⟨faith has been diverted to ~ on guilt —*Saturday Rev.*⟩

mis·emphasize \"+\ *vt* [1*mis-* + *emphasize*] **:** to give a misplaced or wrong emphasis to ⟨a theory of direction, interesting in itself, had run away with a performance and *misemphasized* a play —*Theatre Arts*⟩

mis·employ \¦=+\ *vt* [1*mis-* + *employ*] **:** to use improperly ⟨~ his talents⟩ — **mis·employment** \"+\ *n*

mi·senite \mə'ze,nīt, -zā,-\ *n* -s [It, fr. *Miseno*, locality near Naples, Italy + It *-ite*] **:** a mineral $K_8H_6(SO_4)_7$ consisting of a native acid potassium sulfate

mi·ser \'mīzə(r)\ *n* -s [L, fr. *miser* wretched, miserable] **1** *archaic* **:** a wretched person ⟨~*s* in the hospital —Sir Walter Scott⟩ **2 :** a mean grasping person; *esp* **:** a person who lives miserably in order to hoard his wealth ⟨the unenjoying ~'*s* treasures —S.T.Coleridge⟩ ⟨a ~ who inherited a fortune but lives in a shanty⟩

mis·er·a·bi·lism \'mizərbə,lizəm, -iz(ə)rəb-\ *n* -s [L *miserabilis* miserable + E *-ism*] **:** a philosophy of pessimism

1**mis·er·a·ble** \'mizərbəl, -z(ə)rəb-\ *adj* [ME, fr. MF, fr. L *miserabilis* wretched, pitiable, fr. *miserari* to lament, pity (fr. *miser* wretched) + *-abilis* -able] **1** *chiefly dial Eng* **:** STINGY, MISERLY **2 a :** wretchedly deficient or meager **:** having little value **:** CONTEMPTIBLE **:** WORTHLESS ⟨the squalor of mean and ~ streets —Laurence Binyon⟩ ⟨a bitter sort of acorns, from which a ~ flour is ground —J.G.Frazer⟩ ⟨read the ~ newspapers which the censors plus the paper shortage permitted —Upton Sinclair⟩ **b :** marked by or productive of extreme discomfort or unhappiness ⟨spent a wet and ~ weekend — their medicine gone and their food running low —*Amer. Guide Series: Calif.*⟩ ⟨no pressure of opinion forces him to raise their ~ standard of living above the bare necessities —P.E.James⟩ **3 :** existing in a state of extreme poverty or unhappiness **:** WRETCHED ⟨a confused, uprooted mass of ~ human beings —R.E.Crist⟩ ⟨for five thousand years had been among the most ~ people on earth —Claire Sterling⟩ **4 :** SHAMEFUL, DISCREDITABLE ⟨a ~ abdication of the rights of a friend —Herbert Read⟩ ⟨it's downright ~ of you to make fun of it —Robertson Davies⟩ ⟨his ~ treatment of his family⟩

syn WRETCHED: in reference to a person's feelings, MISERABLE suggests acute discomfort or distress; in reference to things it may describe what is deplorably or contemptibly poor, mean, meager, or deficient ⟨I should like him to die *miserable*, poor, and starving, without a friend. I hope he'll rot with some loathsome disease —W.S.Maugham⟩ ⟨the witch's cabin seemed only somewhat more *miserable* than that of other old women. The floor was mud, the rafters unceiled; the stars shone through the turf roof —Charles Kingsley⟩ In reference to a person's feelings or condition, *wretched* suggests extreme despondence and misery because of affliction, oppression, or destitution; in reference to things, it indicates extreme badness or deplorable poorness ⟨our *wretched* captive, shivering and cowering in the grasp of the detective —A. Conan Doyle⟩ ⟨the youth was *wretched*. His home life was obviously hellish —Dorothy Thompson⟩ ⟨the ruin wrought by the most *wretched* type of slum which seems infinitely uglier and crueller than the vilest railroad tenements —Marcia Davenport⟩

2**miserable** \"\ *n* -s **:** one who is miserable; *esp* **:** one who is extremely poor ⟨a ~ without a shirt to his back⟩

mis·er·a·ble·ness *n* -ES **:** the quality or state of being miserable

mis·er·a·bly \-blē, -li\ *adv* [ME, fr. 1*miserable* + *-ly*] **1 :** in a miserable manner **:** UNCOMFORTABLY, UNHAPPILY **:** WRETCHEDLY ⟨conscious that her feet were ~ wet —J.C.Powys⟩ ⟨~ eking out his existence as a hack writer —R.A.Hall b.1911⟩ **2 :** MEANLY, POORLY ⟨men so ~ paid —Kenneth Roberts⟩ ⟨well fed but ~ housed⟩ **3 :** in a deplorable manner or to a deplorable extent **:** PITIABLY ⟨tried so hard and often failed so ~ to bring order out of financial chaos —*Current Biog.*⟩ ⟨~ deluded by what they take to be realism —W.L.Sullivan⟩

mi·sère \mə'ze(ə)r\ *n* -s [F, lit., poverty, misery, fr. MF *misere* — more at MISERY] **:** a declaration (as in the game of Boston) by which a card player engages to lose every trick

mi·se·re·re \,mizə'rerē, -'rire; ,mēzə'rā(,)rā, ,mēsə-\ *n* -s [L, be merciful, 2d sing. pres. imp. of *misereri* to be merciful, fr. *miser* wretched, miserable; fr. the first word of the 50th Psalm in the Vulgate] **1** *usu cap* **:** a musical setting of the 50th Psalm in the Vulgate **2 :** a prayer, exclamation, or speech that asks for mercy ⟨settled back to feeding him beer and cigarettes and listening to his windy ~ —Paul Moor⟩ **3 :** MISERICORD 2

mi·ser·i·cord *or* **mi·ser·i·corde** \mə'zerə,kȯrd, 'mizər-\ *n* -s [ME *misericorde*, fr. MF, lit., mercy, fr. L *misericordia* mercy, compassion, fr. *misericord-*, *misericors* merciful, compassionate (fr. *miser* + *-i-* + *cord-*, *cor* heart) + *-ia* -y — more at HEART] **1 :** a thin-bladed medieval dagger used to give the coup de grace **2 :** a small projection on the bottom of a hinged church seat that gives support to a standing worshiper when the seat is turned up; *also* **:** the seat itself — called also *miserere* **3 :** a small hall in some medieval monasteries for use as a refectory by monks temporarily dispensed from monastic fast or abstinence

mi·ser·i·cor·dia \mə,zerə'kȯrdēə, mə,ser-, ,mizər-\ *n* -s [ML, fr. L, mercy, compassion] **:** AMERCEMENT

mi·ser·li·ness \'mīzə(r)lēnəs, -lin-\ *n* -ES **:** the quality or state of being miserly

mi·ser·ly \-lē, -li\ *adj* [*miser* + *-ly*] **:** of, relating to, or characteristic of a miser **:** GRASPING, MEAN ⟨the difference between a ~ man who hoards money out of avarice and a thrifty man who saves money out of prudence —William Empson⟩ **syn** see STINGY

mis·ery \'miz(ə)rē, -ri\ *n* -ES [ME *miserie, misere*, fr. MF, fr. L *miseria*, fr. *miser* wretched, miserable + *-ia* -y] **1 :** a state of suffering and want that is the result of poverty or other external conditions ⟨the flood brought ~ to hundreds whom it made homeless⟩ ⟨living in overcrowded slums in conditions of great ~⟩ **2 :** a circumstance, thing, or place that causes suffering or discomfort **:** CALAMITY, MISFORTUNE ⟨primitive societies in process of disappearance are therefore usu. full of maladjustments, *miseries*, and unsolved problems —A.L.Kroeber⟩ ⟨a thin ~ of rain, chilling and spiteful —T.H.Jones⟩ ⟨it was a terrible country . . . tamarack swamps, and spruce thickets, and windfalls, and all kinds of ~ —Henry van Dyke⟩ **3 :** a state of great unhappiness and emotional distress ⟨had killed her father, cheated and shamed herself with a remorse horribly spurious, exchanged content for ~ —Arnold Bennett⟩ ⟨had ~ and loneliness in their eyes —Bruce Marshall⟩ **4** *dial* **:** PAIN, ACHE ⟨had a ~ in his back, it bothered him so much there were days when he couldn't ride —Ross Santee⟩ **5 :** a wretched person or animal ⟨we want to see our weaned foals nice and round and solid, and we do not want to see any dull-coated, potbellied little *miseries* —Henry Wynmalen⟩ **6 :** MISÈRE **syn** see DISTRESS

mises *pl of* MISE *or of* MIS

1**mis·esteem** \¦mis+\ *vt* [1*mis-* + *esteem* (v.)] **:** to esteem wrongly **:** to hold in too little regard ⟨the public ~*s* him, though he has done valuable scientific research⟩

2**misesteem** \"\ *n* [1*mis-* + *esteem* (n.)] **:** a lack of esteem or respect **:** DISRESPECT ⟨the ~ of the newspaper press by the government —J.M.Murry⟩

mis·estimate \(')=+\ *vt* [1*mis-* + *estimate*] **:** to estimate falsely **:** make a wrong estimate of ⟨*misestimated* his character and underestimated his ability⟩ — **mis·estimation** \(¦)=+\ *n*

mis·evaluation \¦=+\ *n* [1*mis-* + *evaluation*] **:** a wrong evaluation **:** a false or confused view of reality ⟨lead not only to confusions and perplexities in discourse and discussion, but also to ~*s* in everyday life —S.I.Hayakawa⟩

mis·explain \"+\ *vt* [1*mis-* + *explain*] **:** to explain badly or incorrectly ⟨argued that earlier interpreters had ~*ed* the text⟩

mis·fea·sance \mis'fēzᵊn(t)s\ *n* -s [MF *mesfaisance*, fr. *mesfais-* (stem of *mesfaire* to do wrong, fr. *mes-* 1mis- + *faire* to make, do, fr. L *facere*) + *-ance* — more at DO] **:** a wrong action **:** TRESPASS: as **a :** the performance of a lawful action in an illegal or improper manner **b :** wrong or improper conduct in public office — compare MALFEASANCE

mis·fea·sor \-zə(r)\ *n* -s [AF *mesfesor, mesfeisour*, fr. OF *mesfais-* (stem of *mesfaire*) + *-or, -our* -or] **:** one who is guilty of misfeasance or trespass

mis·feature \(')mis+\ *n* [1*mis-* + *feature*] *archaic* **:** a bad or distorted feature

mis·featured \"+\ *adj, archaic* **:** having bad or distorted features

1**mis·field** \"+\ *vt* [1*mis-* + *field*] **:** to field (a ball) badly **:** FUMBLE

2**misfield** \"\ *n* **:** an error in fielding a ball (as in cricket or rugby)

mis·file \"+\ *vt* [1*mis-* + *file* (v.)] **:** to file in the wrong place

1**mis·fire** \"+\ *vi* [1*mis-* + *fire* (v.)] **1 :** to have the explosive or propulsive charge fail to ignite at the proper time or ignite intermittently — used of an internal-combustion engine or rocket engine **2 :** to fail to fire — used of a gun or mine **3 :** to miss its intended effect ⟨as criticism, this essay ~*s* —Stephen Spender⟩ ⟨some of it is, without doubt, magnificent, and a good deal of it ~*s* painfully and embarrassingly —Hollis Alpert⟩

2**misfire** \"\ *n* **1 a :** a failure to fire **b :** a cartridge that fails to fire when the primer is struck by the firing pin **2 :** something that misfires ⟨made the scapegoats for the ~ of the recent currency conversion —*Current History*⟩

1**mis·fit** \"+\ *n* [1*mis-* + *fit* (n.)] **1 :** something (as an article of clothing) that fails to fit or fits badly **2 :** a person who is poorly adjusted to his environment ⟨took refuge in queer and original behavior, the customary retreat of the social ~ —E.J.Simmons⟩ ⟨today's homeless youngsters are frequently tomorrow's ~*s* and delinquents —Alice Lake⟩

2**misfit** \"\ *vb* [1*mis-* + *fit* (v.)] *vt* **:** to fail to fit or to fit badly ⟨hobbling about in shoes that *misfitted* him⟩ **~** *vi* **:** to be a misfit ⟨nothing could better illustrate the world of that day; and it is small wonder that the Brontë family *misfitted* —*Times Lit. Supp.*⟩

mis·formed \(')mis+\ *adj* [1*mis-* + *formed*] **:** MISSHAPEN

mis·fortunate \"+\ *adj* [1*mis-* + *fortunate*] **:** UNFORTUNATE ⟨not so . . . holy that I can look down on a ~ girl —Joseph Hergesheimer⟩ — **mis·fortunately** \"+\ *adv*

mis·fortune \"+\ *n* [1*mis-* + *fortune*] **1 a :** bad fortune **:** ADVERSITY ⟨it seemed to him that the tie between husband and wife, even if breakable in prosperity, should be indissoluble in ~ —Edith Wharton⟩ **b :** an instance of bad luck **:** MISHAP ⟨had the ~ to break his leg during his first season in the major leagues⟩ ⟨has the ~ to be situated between two opposing powers⟩ ⟨~*s* never come singly⟩ **2** *dial* **:** the bearing of an illegitimate child; *also* **:** an illegitimate child

mis·for·tuned \"+d\ *adj* **:** UNFORTUNATE

mis·give \(')mis¦giv, -i¦skiv\ *vb* [1*mis-* + *give*] *vt* **:** to suggest doubt or fear to **:** make suspicious or apprehensive ⟨I began to dread that she might not be coming, that her heart might ~ her —Llewelyn Powys⟩ ⟨his mind *misgave* him that his own indiscretion had been inexcusable —Margaret Kennedy⟩ **~** *vi* **1 :** to be fearful or apprehensive **:** have misgivings ⟨fetch me the handkerchief: my mind ~*s* —Shak.⟩ **2** *chiefly Scot* **a :** to go wrong **:** MISCARRY **b** *of a gun* **:** MISFIRE

misgiving *n* [fr. gerund of *misgive*] **:** a feeling of doubt or suspicion **:** a lack of confidence and trust ⟨in the midst of suspicion a sudden ~ chilled me — had I told them about this goat before —L.P.Smith⟩ ⟨those doubts and ~*s* which are ever the result of a lack of decision —Theodore Dreiser⟩ **syn** see APPREHENSION

mis·giv·ing·ly *adv* **:** in a misgiving manner

mis·go \(')mis¦gō, -i¦skō\ *vi* [ME *misgon, misgoon*, fr. 1*mis-* + *gon, goon* to go — more at GO] *chiefly dial* **:** to take the wrong route : go astray in conduct or action : go wrong : MISCARRY

mis·got·ten \(ˈ)misˈgätᵊn, -iˈskä-\ *adj* [ME *misgoten*, fr. ¹*mis-* + *goten*, past part. of *geten* to get — more at GET] **1** : ILL-GOTTEN ⟨~ treasure⟩ **2** : MISBEGOTTEN

mis·gov·ern \(ˈ)misˈgəvə(r)n, -iˈskə-\ *vt* [ME *misgovernen*, fr. ¹*mis-* + *governen* to govern — more at GOVERN] : to rule or govern badly ⟨if people were forbidden to ~ themselves they must be satisfied that they were being well governed —John Buchan⟩ ⟨the most ~*ed* corner of Europe —C.S. Forester⟩

mis·gov·ern·ance \-nən(t)s\ *n* [ME *misgovernaunce*, fr. ¹*mis-* + *governaunce* governance — more at GOVERNANCE] **1** *obs* **a** : MISCONDUCT **b** : MISUSE **2** : bad government

mis·gov·ern·ment \(ˈ)mis+*pronunc at* GOVERNMENT, *or* -sk- *instead of* -sg-\ *n* [¹*mis-* + *government*] : bad or corrupt government ⟨been brought into a diseased state by prolonged ~ —J.M.Synge⟩

mis·gov·er·nor \(ˈ)mis+*pronunc at* GOVERNOR, *or* -sk- *instead of* -sg-\ *n* [¹*mis-* + *governor*] : one who governs badly : an inept or corrupt ruler ⟨a ~ who was forced to abdicate and leave the country⟩

misgraffed *adj* [¹*mis-* + *graffed* (fr. past part. of *graff*)] *obs* : wrongly grafted : badly matched

mis·growth \(ˈ)misˈgrōth, -iˈskrō-\ *n* [¹*mis-* + *growth*] : distorted or abnormal growth

mis·gug·gle \(ˈ)misˈgəgəl, -iˈskə-\ *vt* [¹*mis-* + Sc *guggle*, *gruggle* to crumple, rumple, prob. fr. D *kreukelen*, fr. MD *krokelen*, fr. *kroke* wrinkle, fold; akin to OE *crycc* crutch — more at CRUTCH] *Scot* : to handle roughly or clumsily : MAUL, MAR, BUNGLE

mis·guid·ance \(ˈ)misˈgīdᵊn(t)s, -iˈskī-\ *n* [¹*mis-* + *guidance*] : wrong guidance : MISDIRECTION ⟨his young wife . . . being left to her own ~ —Nathaniel Hawthorne⟩

mis·guide \(ˈ)misˈgīd, -iˈskīd\ *vt* [¹*mis-* + *guide*] **1** *Scot* : to treat badly : SPOIL, INJURE, ABUSE **2** : to lead astray : MISDIRECT, MISLEAD ⟨see wherein we have been *misguided* in the past and so shape our future course for the better —*N.Y. Times*⟩ — **mis·guid·er** \-də(r)\ *n*

misguided *adj* **1** : directed by mistaken ideas, principles, or motives ⟨this ~ man who had doomed nineteen others to hardships and sufferings —J.N.Hall & C.B.Nordhoff⟩ ⟨well-meaning but ~ professors and teachers —*Irish Digest*⟩ **2** : marked by or resulting from mistaken ideas, principles, or motives : MISDIRECTED ⟨victim of her own ~ kindness —*Newsweek*⟩ ⟨~ management actions in connection with training —Bruce Payne⟩ — **mis·guid·ed·ly** *adv* — **mis·guid·ed·ness** *n* -ES

mis·handle \(ˈ)mis+\ *vt* [ME *mishandelen*, fr. ¹*mis-* + *handelen* to handle — more at HANDLE] **1** : to treat roughly or cruelly : MALTREAT ⟨dragged her out and *mishandled* her —Polly Adler⟩ ⟨tormented, *mishandled*, shamefully cast away peoples —Sir Winston Churchill⟩ **2** : to manage wrongly or ignorantly ⟨many of them also ~ or totally ignore some of the basic philosophic problems of materialism —Eliseo Vivas⟩ ⟨*mishandled* the car and burned out a bearing⟩

mi·shan·ter \mə̇ˈshantər\ *n* -S [by alter.] *chiefly Scot* : MISADVENTURE

mis·hap \(ˈ)mis+\ *n* [ME, fr. ¹*mis-* + *hap*] **1** *archaic* : bad luck : MISFORTUNE ⟨either my good fortune or ~, to be keenly susceptible to the influence of the atmosphere —Washington Irving⟩ **2** : an unfortunate accident ⟨any great ~, such as the rolling down of huge masses of rocks, or a landslide —W.D.Wallis⟩ ⟨directed the concert without any of the ~*s* expected of a twenty-year-old's performance —*Current Biog.*⟩

mis·hear \"+\ *vb* [ME *misheren*, fr. OE *mishȳran*, fr. ¹*mis-* + *hȳran* to hear — more at HEAR] *vt* : to hear wrongly ⟨he often ~*s* the southern Englishman —Sidney Baker⟩ ~ *vi* : to misunderstand what is heard ⟨if we are given a sentence pair which is distinguished by a juncture, we often ~ or are uncertain —Z.S.Harris⟩

mi·shi·ma \ˈmēshəmə\ *n* -S *often cap* [fr. *Mishima*, city in Honshu, Japan] : a Korean method of decorating pottery by carving the raw body and filling the cuts with clay of a different fired color

mis·hit \(ˈ)mis+\ *n* [¹*mis-* + *hit*] : a poor hit in cricket

mish·mash *also* **misch·masch** \ˈmish,mash, -,mäsh, -,maa(ə)sh, -,maish, -,mȧsh\ *n* [redupl. of ¹*mash*] : a mixture thrown together without coherence : HODGEPODGE ⟨a soggy ~ of sentimentality and half-digested social consciousness —John Woodburn⟩ ⟨a pretentious ~ of primitive rhythms, pop tunes, and sensuality —*Time*⟩

mish·mi \ˈmishmē\ *n*, *pl* **mishmi** *or* **mishmis** *usu cap* **1 a** : a primitive Mongoloid hill people of the upper Brahmaputra and a branch of the Naga **b** : a member of such people **2** : the Tibeto-Burman language of the Mishmi people

mish·nah *also* **mish·na** \ˈmishnə\ *n*, *pl* **mish·na·yoth** \,mishnäˈyōt(h)\ *usu cap* [Heb *mishnāh* instruction, oral law, fr. *shānāh* to repeat, learn] **1** : the traditional doctrine of the Jews as represented and developed chiefly in the decisions of the rabbis before A.D. 200 **2 a** : a single rabbinical tenet **b** : a collection of such tenets — **mish·na·ic** \(ˈ)mishˈnāik\ *adj*, *usu cap*

mi·shong·no·vi \məˈshäŋnəvē\ *n*, *pl* **mishongnovi** *or* **mishongnovis** *usu cap* **1 a** : a Shoshonean people of Arizona **b** : a member of such people **2** : the language of the Mishongnovi people

mish·pa·chah \mə̇shˈpäkə, -pȯkə\ *or* **mish·po·cha** \-pȯkə\ *n* -S [*mishpachah* fr. Heb *mishpāhāh* family, clan; *mishpocha* fr. Yiddish *mishpokhe*, fr. Heb *mishpāhāh*] : a Jewish family or social unit including close and distant relatives ⟨invited the whole ~⟩

mis·impression \ˌmis+\ *n* [¹*mis-* + *impression*] : a mistaken impression ⟨was under a ~ as to the purpose of the meeting⟩

mis·improve \"+\ *vt* [¹*mis-* + *improve*] **1** : to use wrongly : make an improper use of : ABUSE ⟨has *misimproved* and wasted his talents⟩ **2** *archaic* : to make worse in an attempt to improve — **mis·improvement** \"+\ *n*

mis·inform \"+\ *vt* [ME *misenfourmen*, fr. ¹*mis-* + *enfourmen* to inform — more at INFORM] : to give incorrect, untrue, or misleading information to ⟨~*ed* his partner as to the extent of the firm's liabilities⟩ ⟨had been ~*ed* about the time of the meeting⟩ — **mis·information** \(ˌ)mis+\ *n*

mis·informative \ˌmis+\ *adj* [¹*mis-* + *informative*] : serving to misinform ⟨some good common sense, some information, some ~ gossip —*New Republic*⟩

mis·intelligence \"+\ *n* [in sense 1, prob. fr. F *mésintelligence*, fr. MF, fr. *més-* ¹*mis-* + *intelligence*; in sense 2, fr. ¹*mis-* + *intelligence*] **1** : a mistaken impression : MISUNDERSTANDING ⟨a glaring ~ of the facts of the case⟩ **2** : lack of intelligence ⟨a poor showing that might have been a sign of miseducation rather than ~⟩

mis·interpret \"+\ *vt* [¹*mis-* + *interpret*] **1** : to understand wrongly ⟨causes the pilot to ~ level ground as tipping laterally —H.G.Armstrong⟩ **2** : to give an incorrect interpretation to : explain wrongly ⟨his note on this passage ~*s* the author's meaning⟩ — **mis·interpreter** \"+\ *n*

mis·interpretable \"+\ *adj* : capable of being misinterpreted

mis·interpretation \"+\ *n* [¹*mis-* + *interpretation*] : incorrect interpretation ⟨attributed to ~ of conventional objects, to mass hysteria, or to simple hoaxes —*Current Biog.*⟩

mis·joinder \(ˈ)mis+\ *n* [¹*mis-* + *joinder*] : an incorrect union of parties or of causes of action in a single legal proceeding

mis·judge \"+\ *vb* [¹*mis-* + *judge*] *vt* **1** : to judge wrongly : have a mistaken estimation of ⟨will inject himself into his books, misread them, and so ~ them —H.A.Overstreet⟩ **2** : to have an unjust opinion of ⟨if you think him capable of such an action, you ~ him⟩ ~ *vi* : to be mistaken in judgment ⟨we have *misjudged*, and owe him an apology⟩ — **mis·judger** \"+\ *n*

mis·judg·ing·ly *adv* : in a misjudging manner : so as to make a misjudgment

mis·judgment *or* **mis·judgement** \(ˈ)mis+\ *n* [¹*mis-* + *judgment*] : incorrect or distorted judgment ⟨the accident was caused by his ~ of the sharpness of the curve⟩ ⟨his prejudices have led him into a serious ~ of his opponent⟩

mis·kal *also* **mis·cal** *or* **mith·kal** \miˈskäl, mithˈkäl\ *n* -S [Turk, Per, & Ar; Turk *miskal*, fr. Per *misqāl*, fr. colloq. Ar *misqāl* (Ar *mithqāl*)] **1** : any of various units of weight of Muslim countries: as **a** : a Persian unit equal to about 71 grains **b** : a Turkish unit equal to 74.2 grains **2 a** : a silver 10-dirhem piece of Morocco **b** : a unit of value of Chinese Turkestan ⟨5, 4, 3, and 2 ~ silver coins struck 1900–11⟩

mis·ken \(ˈ)mis+\ *vt* [ME (Sc) *miskennen*, fr. ¹*mis-* + *kennen* to ken — more at KEN] **1** *chiefly Scot* **a** : to have incorrect ideas about : MISUNDERSTAND **b** : to have a false estimation of (oneself) **2** *chiefly Scot* : MISKNOW 1 **3** *chiefly Scot* : to pretend not to know : IGNORE

mis·kenning \"+\ *n* [ME, fr. ¹*mis-* + *kenning*] *old Eng law* : a mistake or variance in pleading or argument in court

miskin *var of* MIXEN

mi·ski·to \məˈskēd·(,)ō\ *n*, *pl* **miskito** *or* **miskitos** *usu cap* **1 a** : a people of the Atlantic coast of Nicaragua and Honduras **b** : a member of such people **2** : a language of the Miskito people — called also *Mosquito*

mis·know \(ˈ)mis+\ *vt* [ME *misknowen*, fr. ¹*mis-* + *knowen* to know — more at KNOW] **1** : to fail to recognize ⟨welcome our enemies and ~ our friends⟩ **2** : to know incorrectly : MISUNDERSTAND ⟨he who knows something quickly, often ~*s* it⟩

mis·knowledge \"+\ *n* [¹*mis-* + *knowledge*] : false knowledge : MISUNDERSTANDING ⟨might have augmented the already great ~ of the Arctic had I published everything I imagined I had seen —Vilhjalmur Stefansson⟩

mis·kolc \ˈmish,kōlts\ *adj*, *usu cap* [fr. *Miskolc*, Hungary] : of or from the city of Miskolc, Hungary : of the kind or style prevalent in Miskolc

misky \ˈmiskē, -ki\ *adj*, *usu* -ER/-EST [alter. of *misty*] *dial chiefly Eng* : MISTY : FOGGY

mis·label \(ˈ)mis+\ *vt* [¹*mis-* + *label*] : to label incorrectly or falsely ⟨charged that the company had ~*ed* its products⟩

mis·lay \"+\ *vt* [ME *mysse layen*, fr. *mysse-*, *mis-* ¹*mis-* + *layen* to lay — more at LAY] **1** : to lay, place, or set incorrectly ⟨*mislaid* the tiles so that the pattern was ruined⟩ ⟨~ the table for the usual four persons instead of six⟩ ⟨~ a stair carpet⟩ **2 a** : to put in an unremembered place ⟨~ a book⟩ ⟨~ a pair of gloves⟩ **b** : put aside : LOSE ⟨*mislaid* his principles in the drive for success⟩

mis·lead \"+\ *vb* [ME *misleden*, fr. OE *mislǣdan*, fr. ¹*mis-* + *lǣdan* to lead — more at LEAD] *vt* : to lead in a wrong direction or into a mistaken action or belief : DECEIVE ⟨had been much opposed by women, crossed, balked, wronged, *misled* —Francis Hackett⟩ ⟨the persons who have first deceived themselves are most effective in ~*ing* others —John Dewey⟩ ~ *vi* : to lead astray ⟨exciting as they are, they ~ —E.M. Forster⟩ **syn** see DECEIVE

mis·leader \"+\ *n* [ME *misleder*, fr. *misleden* + *-er*] : one that misleads ⟨have called him a ~ of youth, a debaser of traditional values and a corrupter of historical verities —C.V. Woodward⟩

misleading *adj* : tending to mislead : DECEIVING ⟨so vague as to be really meaningless, if not inaccurate and ~ —Havelock Ellis⟩ — **mis·lead·ing·ly** *adv* — **mis·lead·ing·ness** *n* -ES

mis·lear \(ˈ)misˈli(ə)r, -lēr\ *vt* [ME *misleren*, fr. OE *mislǣran*, fr. ¹*mis-* + *lǣran* to teach — more at LERE] *dial Brit* : MISLEAD

mis·leared \-rd\ *adj*, *chiefly Scot* : UNMANNERLY, ILL-BRED

misled *past of* MISLEAD

mis·lest \məˈslest\ *or* **mis·list** \-list\ *vt* -ED/-ING/-S [by alter. (influence of ¹*mis-*)] *dial* : MOLEST

¹**mis·like** \(ˈ)mis+\ *vt* [ME *misliken*, fr. OE *mislīcian*, fr. ¹*mis-* + *līcian* to be pleasing — more at LIKE] **1** *archaic* : to be displeasing to : DISPLEASE ⟨if my best wines ~ thy taste —T.B.Aldrich⟩ **2** : to have an aversion to : disapprove of : DISLIKE ⟨no one, least of all his father, could ~ the bearing of the youth —Francis Hackett⟩ — **mis·liker** \"+\ *n*

²**mislike** \"\ *n* : DISLIKE ⟨his ~ of pomp and ceremony⟩

mis·line \"+\ *vt* [¹*mis-* + *line*] : to arrange or divide (poetry) into lines incorrectly in copying or printing

mis·lippen \"+\ *vt* -ED/-ING/-S [¹*mis-* + *lippen*] **1** *dial Brit* : DECEIVE, DISAPPOINT **2** *dial Brit* : NEGLECT, OVERLOOK **3** *chiefly Scot* : DOUBT, SUSPECT

mis·locate \(ˈ)mis, ˌmis+\ *vt* [¹*mis-* + *locate*] : MISPLACE ⟨that is why his commercialized elation seems so *mislocated* —C.W.Mills⟩ — **mis·location** \ˌ+\ *n*

¹**mis·luck** \(ˈ)mis+\ *n* [¹*mis-* + *luck* (n.)] *chiefly Scot* : bad luck : MISFORTUNE

²**misluck** \"\ *vi* [¹*mis-* + *luck* (v.)] *chiefly Scot* : to experience misfortune

mis·machine \ˌmis+\ *vt* [¹*mis-* + *machine*] : to machine to faulty dimensions ⟨resize a *mismachined* part⟩

mis·made \(ˈ)mis+\ *adj* [ME *mismad*, fr. ¹*mis-* + *mad* made — more at MADE] : badly or improperly made ⟨limping possibilities of ~ human nature —Elizabeth B. Browning⟩

mis·manage \"+\ *vt* [¹*mis-* + *manage*] : to manage wrongly or incompetently ⟨*mismanaging* an allowance intended for their maintenance —Margaret Kennedy⟩ ⟨a *mismanaged* household⟩ — **mis·manager** \"+\ *n*

mis·management \"+\ *n* [¹*mis-* + *management*] : corrupt or improper management ⟨an early history of scandal or ~ —*Amer. Guide Series: N.Y. City*⟩ ⟨the bankruptcy of the business was directly due to ~⟩

mis·mannered \"+\ *adj* [¹*mis-* + *mannered*] *dial Brit* : ILL-MANNERED

mis·marriage \"+\ *n* [¹*mis-* + *marriage*] : an unsuitable marriage ⟨the trap of poverty and ~ —G.N.Ray⟩

¹**mis·match** \"+\ *vt* [¹*mis-* + *match* (v.)] : to match wrongly or unsuitably ⟨a ~*ed* couple, who are always quarreling⟩ ⟨~*ed* him with a much better fighter⟩

²**mismatch** \"\ *n* : a faulty or unsuitable match ⟨a poor job of wallpapering, with many ~*es*⟩ ⟨the contest between the two teams was an obvious ~⟩

mis·mate \"+\ *vb* [¹*mis-* + *mate*] *vt* : to mate unsuitably ⟨*mismated* myself for love of you —Thomas Hardy⟩ ⟨the awful internal bleeding of *mismated* lives —*Time*⟩ ⟨a style that ~*s* Gothic and modern⟩ ~ *vi* : to become wrongly or unsuitably mated ⟨pious men who ~ with the daughters of him "who slew his brother" —*Modern Language Notes*⟩

mis·mother \"+\ *vt* [¹*mis-* + *mother*] *of a ewe* : to fail to own and care for (her lamb)

mis·move \"+\ *n* [¹*mis-* + *move*] : a wrong move : MISPLAY ⟨scared for fear she would make a ~ and there the trout would go flashing off —Helen Rich⟩

misn *abbr* misnumbered

misnagid *often cap*, *var of* MITNAGGED

mis·name \(ˈ)mis+\ *vt* [¹*mis-* + *name*] **1** : to call by a bad name : ABUSE ⟨let none, therefore, in our country and Commonwealth or in the outside world ~ or traduce our motives —Sir Winston Churchill⟩ **2** : to name incorrectly : MISCALL ⟨*misnamed* him a primitive painter⟩

mis·nomed \məˈsnōmd\ *adj* [*misnomer* + *-ed*] *archaic* : MISNOMERED

mis·nomer \məˈsnōmə(r)\ *n* -S [ME *misnoumer*, fr. AF *misnomer* to call by a wrong name, fr. MF *mesnommer* to call by a bad name, fr. *mes-* ¹*mis-* + *nommer* to name, fr. L *nominare* to name — more at NOMINATE] **1** : the misnaming of a person in a legal instrument or proceeding (as in a complaint or indictment) **2 a** : a use of a wrong name ⟨it is a ~ to call such works of fiction biographies⟩ **b** : a wrong name : an incorrect designation or term ⟨"fruit," as used to describe potatoes, is a ~ —Jackson Rivers⟩ ⟨found to his great pleasure that the name Green Lanes was no ~ for the village —Compton Mackenzie⟩

mis·no·mered \-(r)d\ *adj* : wrongly called or designated ⟨a patch of burned grass ~ a lawn⟩

mi·so \ˈmē(,)sō\ *n* -S [Jap] : a paste used in preparing soups and other foods that is made by grinding a mixture of steamed rice, cooked soybeans, and salt and fermenting it in brine

miso- — see MIS-

miso·cai·nea \,misōˈkīnēə, ,mīs-, -kān-\ *n* -S [NL, fr. ²*mis-* + *-cainea* (fr. Gk *kainos* new, recent) — more at RECENT] : an abnormal hatred of new ideas

miso·gam·ic \ˌmisəˈgamik, ˌmīs-\ *adj* [*misogamy* + *-ic*] : having a hatred of marriage

mi·sog·a·mist \məˈsägəməst, mīˈ-\ *n* -S [*misogamy* + *-ist*] : one who hates marriage

mi·sog·a·my \-mē\ *n* -ES [²*mis-* + *-gamy*] : a hatred of marriage ⟨remained a bachelor because of his ingrained ~, not for lack of opportunity to marry⟩

miso·gyn·ic \ˌmisəˈjinik, ˌmīs-\ *also* **mi·sog·y·nous** \məˈsäjənəs, mīˈ-\ *adj* [*misogyny* + *-ic* or *-ous*] : having or showing a hatred and distrust of women ⟨a ~ writer who portrays all women as scheming and selfish⟩ **syn** see CYNICAL

mi·sog·y·nism \məˈsäjə,nizəm, mīˈ-\ *n* -S [*misogyny* + *-ism*] : MISOGYNY

mi·sog·y·nist \-nəst\ *n* -S [Gk *misogynēs* misogynist (fr. *miso-* ²*mis-* + *gynē* woman) + E *-ist* — more at QUEEN] : one who hates women ⟨the fulfillment of a suffragette's dream and a *misogynist's* nightmare —*Newsweek*⟩ ⟨an early and unfortunate love affair which had made of him a ~ —*Cosmopolitan*⟩ — **mi·sog·y·nis·tic** \ˌ==ˈnistik\ *adj*

mi·sog·y·ny \məˈsäjənē, mīˈ-, -ni\ *n* -ES [Gk *misogynia*, fr. *miso-* ²*mis-* + *gynē* woman + *-ia* -y] : a hatred of women ⟨his ~ vanished under the influence of her beauty and charm⟩ — opposed to *misandry*

mi·sol·o·gist \məˈsäləjəst, mīˈ-\ *n* -S : one given to misology ⟨~*s* who like to pose as hardheaded men of action⟩

mi·sol·o·gy \-jē\ *n* -ES [Gk *misologia*, fr. *miso-* ²*mis-* + *logos* word, reason, speech, account + *-ia* -y — more at LEGEND] : a dislike, distrust, or hatred of argument, reasoning, or enlightenment ⟨must keep away both from ~ . . . and from the magical attitude of those who make an idol of wisdom —K.R.Popper⟩

miso·ne·ism \,misōˈnē,izəm, ,mīs-\ *n* -S [It *misoneismo*, fr. *miso-* ²*mis-* + Gk *neos* new + It *-ismo* -ism — more at NEW] : a hatred or intolerance of something new or changed ⟨there is developed more and more as the years go on a true ~, so that the patient will positively not tolerate any change in the usual order of things —W.A.White⟩

miso·ne·ist \-ēəst\ *n* -S [*misoneism* + *-ist*] : one who is subject to misoneism — **miso·ne·is·tic** \ˌ==nēˈistik\ *adj*

miso·pe·dia \,misəˈpēdēə, ,mīs-\ *n* -S [NL, fr. ²*mis-* + Gk *paid-*, *pais* child + NL *-ia* — more at FEW] : a hatred of children

miso·pe·dist \-dəst\ *n* -S [NL *misopedia* + E *-ist*] : one who hates children

misophobia *var of* MYSOPHOBIA

¹**mis·order** \(ˈ)mis+\ *n* [ME, fr. ¹*mis-* + *order* (n.)] : DISORDER

²**misorder** \"\ *vt* [¹*mis-* + *order* (v.)] **1** : to put in disorder or confusion (as through mismanagement) **2** *obs* : to behave (oneself) badly

mis·orderly \"+\ *adj* [¹*mis-* + *orderly*] : DISORDERLY

misos *pl of* MISO

mis·pel \ˈmispəl\ *n* -S [Afrik, fr. MD *mispele*, *mespele* medlar, fr. L *mespila* — more at MEDLAR] : MEDLAR 3

mis·perception \ˌmis+\ *n* [¹*mis-* + *perception*] : a false perception ⟨that any of the perennial human preoccupations should be mere illusion or a ~ of something else is . . . repugnant to common sense —J.V.L.Casserley⟩

mis·perform \"+\ *vt* [¹*mis-* + *perform*] : to perform wrongly or improperly ⟨the ship ~*ed* the maneuver and almost collided with the pier⟩ — **mis·performance** \"+\ *n*

mis·pick \(ˈ)mis+\ *n* [¹*mis-* + *pick* (n.)] : an improperly meshed pick in textile machinery; *also* : a defect resulting from such improper meshing

mis·pick·el \ˈmi,spikəl\ *n* -S [G *mispickel*, *misspickel*] : ARSENOPYRITE

mis·place \(ˈ)mis+\ *vt* [¹*mis-* + *place*] **1 a** : to put in a wrong place or position ⟨the sign at the western end of the bridge is *misplaced* —*Amer. Guide Series: La.*⟩ **b** : to put in an unaccustomed or forgotten place : MISLAY ⟨*misplaced* his hat⟩ ⟨*misplaced* the tickets⟩ **2** : to set (as one's hopes or confidence) on a wrong object or eventuality ⟨the barrage of good wishes with which the assembly had opened had not been *misplaced* —Guthrie Moir⟩ ⟨a sad example of trust that was *misplaced*⟩ **3** : to set aside : LOSE ⟨we are granted some insight into what has caused him to ~ his will to live —John Mason Brown⟩ ⟨this useful piece of wisdom was sadly *misplaced* in later American epochs —Van Wyck Brooks⟩ — **mis·placement** \"+\ *n*

¹**mis·play** \"+\ *n* [¹*mis-* + *play* (n.)] : a wrong or unskillful play : ERROR ⟨was charged with a ~ when he fumbled the ball⟩ ⟨one ~ caused them to lose the rubber⟩

²**misplay** \"\ *vt* [¹*mis-* + *play* (v.)] : to play wrongly or unskillfully ⟨the shortstop ~*ed* the ball and it went past him⟩ ⟨~*ed* her hand and was set two tricks⟩ ⟨~*ed* his return of service⟩

mis·pleading \(ˈ)mis+\ *n* [¹*mis-* + *pleading*] : an error in pleading : a wrong pleading or omission

mis·point \"+\ *vt* [¹*mis-* + *point*] *archaic* : to punctuate wrongly

mis·praise \"+\ *vb* [ME *mispraisen*, fr. ¹*mis-* + *praisen* to praise — more at PRAISE] *vt* **1** : DISPRAISE **2** : to praise wrongly ~ *vi* : to give expression to improper or unwise praise

¹**mis·print** \"+\ *vb* [¹*mis-* + *print* (v.)] *vt* : to print incorrectly ~ *vi*, *of horned game* : to walk in an uneven manner : leave irregular footprints

²**misprint** \"\ *n* : a mistake in printed matter (as a deviation from copy or a typographical error) ⟨a book full of ~*s*⟩

¹**misprise** *var of* MISPRIZE

²**mis·prise** *or* **mis·prize** \məˈsprīz\ *n* -S [MF *mespris*, fr. *mespriser* to despise, scorn — more at MISPRIZE] : ²MISPRISION

³**misprise** *or* **misprize** *vt* -ED/-ING/-S [MF *mespris*, past part. of *mesprendre*] *obs* : MISTAKE, MISUNDERSTAND ⟨you spend your passion on a *mispris'd* mood —Shak.⟩

¹**mis·pri·sion** \məˈsprizhən\ *n* -S [ME, fr. MF *mesprison* error, wrongdoing, fr. OF, fr. *mespris*, past part. of *mesprendre* to make a mistake, do wrong, fr. *mes-* ¹*mis-* + *prendre* to take, fr. L *prehendere* to seize, grasp — more at GET] **1 a** : neglect or wrong performance of official duty : misconduct or maladministration by a public official : MISDEMEANOR **b** : a clerical error in a legal proceeding that can be corrected in a summary manner as distinguished from judicial error for the correction of which formal appellate or other procedure is required **c** : the active or passive concealment of treason or felony from the prosecuting authorities by one not guilty of those crimes ⟨~ of treason⟩ ⟨~ of felony⟩ **d** : a contempt against the government, the sovereign, or the courts (as lese majesty or disloyal or seditious conduct) **2** : a misunderstanding in which one thing is taken for another : MISTAKE ⟨more than ~ of the fact —Robert Browning⟩

²**misprision** \"\ *n* -S [¹*misprise* + *-ion* (as in ¹*misprision*)] : CONTEMPT, SCORN : DEPRECIATION, DISPARAGEMENT ⟨expressed his evident ~ of realism and other modern modes of literature —J.P.Bishop⟩ ⟨with a refined ~ of her country . . . lived in exile —Ellery Sedgwick⟩

mis·priz·al *also* **mis·pris·al** \-ˈsprīzᵊl\ *n* -S [¹*misprise* + *-al*] : ²MISPRISION ⟨a broken engagement added to her ~ of herself —Ernestine Evans⟩

¹**mis·prize** *also* **mis·prise** \məˈsprīz\ *vt* [MF *mesprisier*, fr. *mes-* ¹*mis-* + *prisier* to value, appraise — more at PRIZE] **1** : to hold in contempt : DESPISE ⟨do not ~ that body of just and patriotic men —S.H.Adams⟩ **2** : NEGLECT, UNDERVALUE ⟨it will acclaim foreign talent and ~ its own —W.B.Adams⟩ ⟨nor did he ~ the Spanish factor in Peru —Waldo Frank⟩ — **mis·priz·er** \-zə(r)\ *n* -S

²**misprize** *var of* MISPRISE

mis·pronounce \ˌmis+\ *vb* [¹*mis-* + *pronounce*] *vt* **1** : to pronounce incorrectly ⟨a name almost invariably *mispronounced* by newcomers to the town⟩ ⟨had picked up a certain fluency in French, though he *mispronounced* the language ludicrously⟩ **2** : to pronounce in a way regarded as incorrect because of variations from some stated or implied criterion (as the practice of educated speakers, a regional speech assumed to be standard, spelling, or a pronunciation prescribed as correct by accepted authority) ⟨a list of words commonly *mispronounced*⟩ ⟨told him he would never be a gentleman until he stopped *mispronouncing* so many words⟩ ⟨guessed he would go to his grave *mispronouncing* "February" as "Febuary"⟩ ~ *vi* : to make a mispronunciation — **mis·pronouncer** \"+\ *n*

mis·pronunciation \"+\ *n* [¹*mis-* + *pronunciation*] **1** : the act of mispronouncing ⟨~ is often the result of affectation and a striving for elegance⟩ **2** : an instance of mispronouncing ⟨~ of this word is comparatively rare⟩

mis·proud \(ˈ)mis+\ *adj* [ME, fr. ¹*mis-* + *proud*] **:** wrongly or unreasonably proud **:** ARROGANT

mis·punctuate \"+\ *vt* [¹*mis-* + *punctuate*] **:** to punctuate in a way regarded as incorrect — **mis·punctuation** \(ˌ)mis+\ *n*

mis·put \(ˈ)mis+\ *vt* [¹*mis-* + *put*] *dial* **1 :** MISPLACE **2 :** DISCONCERT

mis·quotation \ˌ=+\ *n* [¹*mis-* + *quotation*] **1 :** the act of misquoting ⟨he is given to ~ and distortion of what people say⟩ **2 :** an instance of misquoting ⟨this is a flagrant ~ of what he wrote⟩

¹mis·quote \(ˈ)mis+\ *vb* [¹*mis-* + *quote* (v.)] *vt* **:** to quote incorrectly ⟨people commonly ~ some of the most famous lines in English poetry⟩ ~ *vi* **:** to give quotations incorrectly ⟨loves to quote, but usually ~*s*⟩ — **mis·quoter** \"+\ *n* -s

²misquote \"\ *n* **:** an incorrect quotation

mis·read \"+\ *vt* [¹*mis-* + *read*] **1 :** to read incorrectly or misinterpret in reading ⟨the driver . . . ~ an important signal —O.S.Nock⟩ ⟨suspect that this book has been ~ by a whole generation —Caroline Gordon⟩ **2 :** to interpret incorrectly ⟨totally ~ the lesson of history —Christopher Hollis⟩ ⟨Ingres' paintings still are ~ in terms of nineteenth century stereotypes —T.B.Hess⟩ — **mis·reader** \"+\ *n*

mis·reckon \"+\ *vi* [¹*mis-* + *reckon*] **:** to reckon wrongly **:** make an incorrect calculation ⟨unless I ~, the bill comes due tomorrow⟩

mis·recollect \(ˌ)mis+\ *vi* [¹*mis-* + *recollect*] **:** to recollect wrongly ⟨I put the book on the second shelf, if I do not ~⟩ — **mis·recollection** \"+\ *n*

mis·register \(ˈ)mis+\ *n* [¹*mis-* + *register*] *printing* **:** inaccurate register esp. of a second or subsequent color

mis·remember \ˌmis+\ *vb* [¹*mis-* + *remember*] *vt* **1 :** to remember incorrectly ⟨in some of the essays the facts seem to have been wrenched or ~*ed* to fit the theory —*Times Lit. Supp.*⟩ ⟨asked an expert about it, but misunderstood or ~*ed* the answer —*Time*⟩ **2** *chiefly dial* **:** FORGET ~ *vi, chiefly dial* **:** to be unable to remember

¹mis·report \"+\ *vt* [ME *misreporten*, fr. ¹*mis-* + *reporten* to report — more at REPORT] **1 :** to report falsely **:** to give an incorrect account of ⟨~*ed* the results of the hearing⟩ **2 :** to give an incorrect report of the words or opinions of ⟨~*ed* him as favoring the bill when he had spoken against it⟩

²misreport \"\ *n* [¹*mis-* + *report* (n.)] **:** a false or incorrect account

mis·represent \(ˌ)mis+\ *vb* [¹*mis-* + *represent*] *vt* **1 :** to represent incorrectly **:** to give a false, imperfect, or misleading representation of ⟨they all ~*ed* the past in the same prescribed way —R.B.Merriman⟩ **2 :** to serve badly or improperly as a representative of ⟨the principal lobbyists . . . were absolutely representative of those societies —F.D.Roosevelt⟩ ~*ing* the membership of those societies —F.D.Roosevelt⟩ ~ *vi* **:** to make an assertion or give an impression not in accord with the facts ⟨~*s* when he says that he was driving carefully⟩ ⟨presents much from a partisan point of view; yet he never intentionally ~*s* —W.H.Allison⟩

syn MISREPRESENT and BELIE can mean, in common, to represent falsely. MISREPRESENT usu. implies intent, suggesting deliberate falsification, injustice, bias, or prejudice ⟨a biography completely *misrepresenting* his true character⟩ ⟨*misrepresent* a case before a jury⟩ BELIE, in this connection, implies merely to give an impression at variance with the facts ⟨nothing she saw or touched gave token of even its own reality: even her wrist watch seemed to *belie* time —Elizabeth Bowen⟩ ⟨the brevity and cheerfulness of the study *belie* the importance of its subject —*Times Lit. Supp.*⟩

mis·representation \"+\ *n* [¹*mis-* + *representation*] **:** an untrue, incorrect, or misleading representation (as of a fact, event, or person); *specif* **:** a representation by words or other means that under the existing circumstances amounts to an assertion not in accordance with the facts ⟨his duty to further the interest of his client does not require him to employ any sort of trickery, chicane, deceit, or ~ —H.S.Drinker⟩

¹mis·representative \"+\ *adj* [¹*mis-* + *representative*] **:** serving to misrepresent ⟨the production is ~ of the spirit of the play⟩

²misrepresentative \"\ *n* **:** one who is not a proper representative ⟨a ~ of the people of his state⟩

mis·representer \"+\ *n* **:** one that misrepresents ⟨a ~, or calumniator, or what they will —J.G.Lockhart⟩

mis·route \(ˈ)mis+\ *vt* [¹*mis-* + *route*] **:** to route incorrectly or improperly (as by a longer or more expensive route) ⟨*misrouted* freight⟩

¹mis·rule \"+\ *vt* [ME *misreulen*, fr. ¹*mis-* + *reulen* to rule — more at RULE] **:** to rule badly **:** MISGOVERN ⟨*misruled* and impoverished his people⟩ — **mis·ruler** \"+\ *n*

²misrule \(ˈ)mis+\ *n* [ME *misreule*, fr. ¹*mis-* + *reule* rule — more at RULE] **1 :** the action of misruling or the condition of being misruled ⟨not the result of a single specific grievance but a reaction to a long period of ~⟩ **2 :** a condition of disorder and confusion **:** ANARCHY ⟨the loud ~ of Chaos —John Milton⟩ ⟨in the absence of a stable government, the country fell into a state of ~⟩

mis·run \"+\ *n* [¹*mis-* + *run*] **:** a metal casting not fully formed

¹miss \ˈmis\ *vb* -ED/-ING/-ES [ME *missen*, fr. OE *missan*; akin to OHG *missan* to miss, ON *missa* to miss, be lacking, Goth *maidjan* to change, L *mutare* to change, Latvian *mitu̧ôt* to exchange, Skt *methati, mithati* he changes] *vt* **1 :** to fail to hit, reach, or make contact with ⟨~*ed* the target by a good two feet⟩ ⟨swung at the ball with great power but ~*ed* it⟩ ⟨~*ed* the step and fell to the ground⟩ ⟨~*ed* each other by seconds at the railroad station⟩ ⟨~*ed* his way⟩ **2 a :** to discover the absence or omission of ⟨~*ed* his watch almost as soon as the stranger had left⟩ ⟨cut out half of the third act knowing it would never be ~*ed*⟩ **b :** to feel the lack of **:** be unhappy because of the loss or absence of ⟨~*ed* his wife terribly⟩ ⟨~*ed* his old room and familiar surroundings⟩ **3 a :** to fail to obtain or receive ⟨ignorance ~*es* the best things in this life —W.R.Inge⟩ ⟨it is, no doubt, true that remarkable men . . . ~*ed* the presidency when contemporaries of far less ability attained it —H.J. Laski⟩ **b** *archaic* **:** to fail to do ⟨lest I should ~ to bid thee a good-morrow —John Keats⟩ **4 :** ESCAPE, AVOID ⟨~*ed* being killed by a few feet⟩ ⟨just ~*ed* hitting the other car⟩ **5 a :** to leave out **:** OMIT ⟨in such a hurry that he ~*ed* his breakfast⟩ ⟨not only is there an occasional beat ~*ed* at the wrist but there is no sound over the heart —H.G.Armstrong⟩ ⟨has not ~*ed* a dividend in 39 years —*Time*⟩ **b :** to let slip **:** OVERLOOK ⟨~*ed* a bet in failing to see the possibilities of his discovery⟩ ⟨book publishers are ~*ing* a trick in not making a wider practice of including their old titles in current book lists —J. D. Adams⟩ **6 a :** to fail to perceive or understand ⟨were delighted with its merciless exposure of aristocratic attitudes but ~*ed* its attack on the businessmen and the middle class —Max Lerner⟩ ⟨to put the orthodox value on it is to expose an inappreciation of his most vital criticism, to ~ its force —F.R.Leavis⟩ ⟨~ the point⟩ **b :** to fail to see, hear, or experience ⟨~*ed* some of the softer passages⟩ ⟨a picture not to be ~*ed*⟩ ⟨though it was a frightening experience, he would not have ~*ed* it⟩ **7 :** to neglect the performance of or attendance at ⟨hasn't ~*ed* a day's work in years⟩ ⟨~*ed* school all week because of illness⟩ ⟨seldom ~*ed* a major military operation —Ed Cunningham⟩ **8 :** to be too late for ⟨~*ed* his train⟩ ⟨~*ed* his appointment by five minutes⟩ ~ *vi* **1** *archaic* **:** to fail to get or secure something **:** fail to find or reach someone or something **:** fail to do something — used with *of* ⟨had very narrowly ~*ed* of success —T.B. Macaulay⟩ **2 :** to fail to hit something ⟨took three shots and ~*ed* each time⟩ ⟨took another cut at the ball but ~*ed* again⟩ **3** *archaic* **:** to be lacking or absent **4 a :** to be unsuccessful **:** FAIL — sometimes used with *out* ⟨such a fine prospect that he can't ~⟩ ⟨a play which ~*ed* on Broadway —William Barrett⟩ ⟨this is his big chance and he can't afford to ~ out⟩ **b** *dial Brit* **:** to fail to germinate or grow **c** *of a domestic animal* **:** to fail to become pregnant when bred **d :** MISFIRE — used of an internal-combustion engine **e :** to lose as caster of the dice; *specif* **:** to lose by throwing a point and then a seven rather than by throwing craps — **miss fire 1 :** to fail to go off — used of firearms **2 :** to fail to have the expected or planned result ⟨his speech was carefully planned, but it *missed fire*⟩ — **miss stays** *of a ship* **:** to fail in the attempt to go about — **miss the boat :** to blunder badly by failing to grasp an opportunity in time or by making a false judgment ⟨waiting until after the candidates are nominated is waiting until you have *missed the boat* —Marguerite J. Fisher & D.G.Bishop⟩ — **miss the bus :** to waste an opportunity **:** throw away one's chances

²miss \"\ *n* -ES [ME *mis, misse*, fr. *missen*, v.] **1** *chiefly dial* **:** WANT, LOSS, LACK; *also* **:** disadvantage, harm, or regret resulting from loss or deprivation **2 a :** a failure to hit something struck at or aimed at ⟨hit the nail on the head every time without a single ~⟩ ⟨hit the target five times without a ~⟩ ⟨whatever truth you contribute to the world will be one lucky shot in a thousand ~*es* —Walter Lippman⟩ **b :** a failure to attain a desired or planned result ⟨the picture is a pathetic ~ —*Time*⟩ **3 a :** MISCARRIAGE ⟨the time she thought she was going to have a baby and only had a ~ —Robert Fawcett⟩ **b** *of a domestic animal* **:** a failure to become pregnant after breeding **4 :** a deliberate avoidance of something **:** GO-BY ⟨felt so tired that she decided to give the dance a ~⟩ ⟨give dessert a ~⟩ **5 :** MISFIRE ⟨will pick up from there to a fast acceleration without a ~ —*Car Life*⟩ **6 :** an impression of a printing press when no sheet has been fed in ⟨print a ~ on the tympan as a base for makeready⟩ **7 :** MISSOUT

³miss \(ˌ)mis, ˌməs\ *n* -ES [short for ¹*mistress*] **1** *archaic* **a :** PROSTITUTE **b :** a kept woman **:** MISTRESS **2 a** — used as a conventional title of courtesy before the name of an unmarried woman or girl ⟨*Miss* Ann Brown⟩ ⟨*Miss* Smith⟩ or sometimes before the given name of a married woman ⟨*Miss* Mary, the wife of Mr. Green⟩ **b** — used before the name of a place (as a country, city) or of a profession or other line of activity (as a sport) or before some epithet to form a title applied to a usu. young unmarried female viewed or recognized as esp. outstanding in or as representative of the thing indicated ⟨was chosen as *Miss* America⟩ ⟨well now, *Miss* High-and-Mighty⟩ **3 :** young lady **:** GIRL — used in direct address and not followed by the given name or surname of the young woman addressed and used typically as a generalized term of conventional politeness in addressing a young woman that is a stranger ⟨may I have the menu, ~⟩ **4 :** a young unmarried woman or girl ⟨a New England ~ engaged to tutor his children —*Amer. Guide Series: Fla.*⟩ ⟨no stage-struck ~ has ever been quite so fortunate —*Irish Digest*⟩

⁴miss \ˈmis\ *vt* -ED/-ING/-ES **:** to address as miss

miss *abbr* missionary

¹mis·sal \ˈmisəl\ *n* -s *sometimes cap* [ME *messel, missall*, fr. MF & ML; MF *messel*, fr. ML *missale*, fr. neut. of *missalis* of mass, fr. LL *missa* mass + L *-alis* -al — more at MASS] **1 :** a book containing all that is said or sung at mass during the entire year and including with the ordinary, proper, and common votive masses and supplementary prayers and masses for certain localities or orders **2 :** a book of devotions

²missal \"\ *adj* [ML *missalis*] *archaic* **:** of or relating to the mass or a missal

missal initial *also* **missal letter** *or* **missal capital** *n* **:** a decorative initial fashioned after those used in old missals

missal stand *n* **:** a lectern used to support a missal

missal stand

mis·say \(ˈ)mi(s)+\ *vb* [ME *mis-seyen, missayen*, fr. ¹*mis-* + *seyen, sayen* to say — more at SAY] *vt* **:** to speak evil of **:** SLANDER ⟨rebuked, reviled, *missaid* thee —Alfred Tennyson⟩ ~ *vi* **:** to say something wrong or incorrect ⟨knew . . . what the press . . . would ~, misunderstand, understate, and exaggerate about him —H.S.Canby⟩

missed *past of* MISS

missed abortion *n* **:** an intrauterine death of a fetus that is not followed by its immediate expulsion

missed labor *n* **:** a retention of a fetus in the uterus beyond the normal period of pregnancy

mis·seem \(ˈ)mi(s)+\ *vt* [ME *missemen*, fr. ¹*mis-* + *semen* to seem — more at SEEM] **:** MISBECOME

missel thrush *var of* MISTLE THRUSH

mis·send \(ˈ)mi(s)+\ *vt* [¹*mis-* + *send*] **:** to send or forward incorrectly ⟨containing what little mail was *missent* to our train —B.A.Long & W.J.Dennis⟩

¹misses *pres 3d sing of* MISS, *pl of* MISS

²miss·es \ˈmisəz\ *n pl* [fr. pl. of ³*miss*] **:** a clothing size for women and girls with average figures

mis·set \(ˈ)mi(s)+\ *vt* [ME *missetten*, fr. ¹*mis-* + *setten* to set — more at SET] **1 :** to set or place wrongly **:** MISPLACE **2** *Scot* **:** to put out of sorts **:** DISPLEASE

mis·sey-moo·sey \ˈmisēˈmüsē\ *n* -s [alter. of *moosemise*] **:** AMERICAN MOUNTAIN ASH

¹mis·shape \(ˈ)mis(h)+\ *vt* [ME *misshapen*, fr. ¹*mis-* + *shapen* to shape — more at SHAPE] **:** to shape badly **:** give an unnatural form to **:** DEFORM ⟨may tend seriously to ~ the cakes of butter —*Scientific American*⟩ ⟨the book that has most shaped and *misshaped* our conceptions —A.L.Kroeber⟩

²misshape \"\ *n* [ME, fr. ¹*mis-* + *shap, shape* shape — more at SHAPE] **:** DEFORMITY

mis·shapen \"+\ *adj* [ME, fr. ¹*mis-* + *shapen*, past part. of *shapen* to shape] **1 :** having an ugly or deformed shape ⟨the tree . . . dwarfed and ~ by repeated stripping of its branches —*Amer. Guide Series: N.J.*⟩ ⟨a very little oldish, spinsterish, thin, ~, stooping woman —Arnold Bennett⟩ **2 :** morally or intellectually deformed or distorted ⟨the system of representation had become so ~ that a new theory had arisen to give constitutional sanction to existing methods —V.L.Parrington⟩ ⟨~ ideas of justice⟩ — **mis·shap·en·ly** *adv* — **mis·shap·en·ness** *n* -ES

missies *pl of* MISSY

¹mis·sile \ˈmisəl *sometimes* -izəl, *chiefly Brit* -iˌsīl\ *adj* [L *missilis*, fr. *missus* (past part. of *mittere* to throw, send) + *-ilis* -ile — more at SMITE] **1 :** capable of being thrown or projected to strike an object at a distance **2 :** adapted for throwing or hurling missiles

²missile \"\ *n* -s [L, fr. neut. of *missilis*] **1 :** a weapon or other object thrown or projected (as a stone, bullet, or artillery shell) ⟨spears are still used as ~*s* in some parts of the world⟩ ⟨open head wounds due to ~*s* —*Jour. Amer. Med. Assoc.*⟩ **2 :** a self-propelling unmanned weapon (as a rocket or a robot bomb) — compare GUIDED MISSILE

mis·sil·eer \ˌmisəˈli(ə)r *sometimes* -izə-\ *n* -s [²*missile* + *-eer*] **:** MISSILEMAN

mis·sile·man *pronunc at* MISSILE + mən\ *n, pl* **missilemen :** one who helps to design, build, or operate guided missiles

mis·sile·ry \-lrē\ *also* **mis·sil·ry** \-isəlrē\ *n* -ES [²*missile* + *-ry*] **1 :** MISSILES; *esp* **:** GUIDED MISSILES **2 :** the science dealing with the design, manufacture, and use of guided missiles

missing *adj* [fr. pres. part. of ¹*miss*] **1 :** not able to be found **:** not present **:** ABSENT ⟨~ in action⟩ ⟨the ~ part of the machine⟩ ⟨an understanding of character is ~ from the book⟩ **2 :** absent without explanation from one's home or usual or expected place of resort ⟨turned up ~ in the morning and hasn't been seen since⟩ ⟨the common-law principle that anyone who has been declared a ~ person may, after seven years, be presumed dead —*Time*⟩

missing link *n* **1 :** an absent thing or member needed to complete a series ⟨modern technology and capital are the only major *missing links* in the underdeveloped areas —J.K.Rose⟩ **2 :** a hypothetical intermediate form between man and his presumed simian progenitors ⟨supposed by some people to be the nearest thing to the *missing link*, and thus the most primitive human being in existence —Alan Moorehead⟩ — compare APE-MAN, PREHOMINID

missing movement *n* **:** an offense under the U.S. Uniform Code of Military Justice that consists of missing through neglect or design the movement of a ship, aircraft, or unit with which a person is required in the course of duty to move

mis·sio·log·i·cal \ˌmisēəˈläjəkəl\ *adj* **:** of or relating to missiology ⟨a ~ classic⟩

mis·si·ol·o·gy \ˌmisēˈäləjē\ *n* -ES [¹*mission* + *-logy*] **:** the study of the church's mission esp. with respect to the nature, purpose, and methods of its missionary activity

¹mis·sion \ˈmishən\ *n* -s *often attrib* [NL, ML & L; NL *mission-, missio* ministry commissioned by a religious organization, fr. ML, task with which one is charged, fr. L, act of sending, fr. *missus* (past part. of *mittere* to throw, send) + *-ion-, -io* -ion — more at SMITE] **1** *obs* **:** the act or an instance of sending **2 a :** a ministry (as preaching or educational or medical work) commissioned by a church or some other religious organization for the purpose of propagating its faith or carrying on humanitarian work ⟨organized a ~ to the Indians⟩ ⟨conducted a ~ among the refugees⟩ — compare FOREIGN MISSION, HOME MISSION, RESCUE MISSION **b :** assignment to or work in a field of missionary enterprise ⟨go on ~ as an unprofessed sister⟩ **c** (1) **:** a mission institution (as a church, school, or hospital) or establishment (as a compound or a community and its lands) or a building ⟨~ hall⟩ (2) **:** a local church that is not self-supporting and that relies upon its denomination or larger religious organization for financial support **d :** the body of missionaries or the administrative organization of a missionary territory working under a church or religious organization **e missions** *pl* **:** organized missionary work ⟨the seminary's professor of ~*s*⟩ ⟨give more to local expenses than to ~*s*⟩ **f :** the administrative division of a Roman Catholic vicariate or apostolic prefecture corresponding to a parish **g :** a course of sermons and services at a particular place and time for the special purpose of quickening the faith and zeal of Christians and of converting unbelievers ⟨to conduct a preaching ~⟩ **3 :** a body of persons appointed to go somewhere to perform a service or carry on an activity: as **a :** a group of persons sent to a foreign country to conduct diplomatic or political negotiations ⟨the ill-fated Grey ~ to the United States in the latter part of 1919 —*Times Lit. Supp.*⟩ **b :** a permanent embassy or legation in a foreign country ⟨reopen diplomatic ~*s* in those countries . . . in which it had been previously authorized to establish consular offices —John Hay b. 1910⟩ **c :** a team of scientific or technical specialists sent to a foreign country (as to aid in the development of industry or natural resources) ⟨served on a ~ to help improve agricultural methods⟩ **d :** a group of leaders in culture or education unofficially representing their country in a foreign country ⟨step up the exchange of cultural ~*s*⟩ **e :** a team of military specialists sent to a foreign country to assist in the training of its armed forces ⟨military ~*s* sent by its allies have helped greatly to modernize its army⟩ **4 a :** a specific task with which a person or group is charged; *esp* **:** an assignment given to a person or group in an official capacity ⟨given the difficult and dangerous ~ of exploring the newly acquired territory⟩ ⟨by patient negotiation succeeded in his ~ of averting a strike⟩ ⟨hero of a rescue ~⟩ **b :** the chief function or responsibility of an organization or institution ⟨the Erie's principal ~, however, is freight service —*Trains*⟩ ⟨the ~ of that school was to make distant times . . . intelligible and acceptable to a society issuing from the eighteenth century —J.E.E.Dalberg-Acton⟩ **5 :** a continuing task or responsibility that one is destined or fitted to do or specially called upon to undertake **:** LIFEWORK, VOCATION ⟨took upon himself the ~ of bettering the school system⟩ ⟨his ~ was to preserve the Union⟩ ⟨gave sense and direction to a young life seeking a ~ —P.H. Vieth⟩ **6 a :** a major continuing duty assigned to a military service or command as a part of its function in the national military establishment ⟨the wartime ~ of a Navy is to gain and maintain control of the seas —R.A.Ofstie⟩ **b :** a definite military or naval task assigned to an individual or unit usu. for performance in a combat area or enemy territory ⟨the patrol successfully carried out its ~ of bringing back two enemy prisoners⟩ ⟨~ accomplished⟩ **c :** a flight operation of a single airplane or a group of airplanes charged with the performance of a specific task ⟨flew nineteen ~*s* during the war⟩ ⟨a weather ~⟩

²mission \"\ *vb* **missioned; missioned; missioning** \-sh(ə)niŋ\ **missions** *vt* **1 :** to send on or entrust with a mission ⟨~*ed* her . . . servants to enrich the fretted splendor of each nook and niche —John Keats⟩ ⟨for the last several years, she had been ~*ed* at St. Mary's Convent —*Springfield (Mass.) Union*⟩ **2 :** to carry on a religious mission among or in ⟨~*ed* a territory larger than the state of Texas⟩ ~ *vi* **:** to carry on a mission **:** to act as a missionary ⟨now ~*ing* in Argentina for the Midland Bank —*Time*⟩

mission architecture *n* **:** a Spanish colonial architectural style used for the early Spanish mission buildings of the southwestern U.S.

¹mis·sion·ary \ˈmishəˌnerē, -ri\ *adj* [NL *missionarius*, fr. *mission-, missio* mission + L *-arius* -ary — more at MISSION] **1 a :** of or relating to missions ⟨a ~ undertaking⟩ ⟨the ~ hospital⟩ **b :** engaged in or devoted to mission work ⟨a ~ religion⟩ ⟨~ priests⟩ **2 :** suitable to or characteristic of a person sent on or undertaking a mission ⟨a generous composer with ~ instincts . . . who will attempt to lead other composers —Robert Evett⟩ ⟨threw himself into the campaign with ~ zeal⟩ **3** *Roman Catholicism* **:** not having a canonically established hierarchy and subject immediately to Rome as a mission or prefecture or vicariate apostolic ⟨a ~ territory⟩

²missionary \"\ *n* -ES **1 a :** one sent to propagate the faith, doctrine, and principles of a religion or a religious group among nonbelievers ⟨sent *missionaries* into those regions in the early part of the 19th century —*Amer. Guide Series: Pa.*⟩ **b :** one who undertakes a special religious or humanitarian mission among those of his own faith or country ⟨the ~ can . . . put the fear of the Lord into complacent souls that is necessary for their return to grace and salvation —D.J.Corrigan⟩ ⟨became a city ~ devoting his life to helping the down-and-out⟩ **c :** one who attempts to convert others to a specific way of life, set of ideas, or course of action ⟨these early *missionaries* of a new and boundless materialism —M.D. Geismar⟩ ⟨the pressures brought directly or indirectly by the *missionaries* of home ownership —J.P.Dean⟩ ⟨has become an enthusiastic ~ for vitamin E —Eric Hutton⟩ **2 :** one who undertakes a political or diplomatic mission **:** AGENT, EMISSARY ⟨the administration's most-traveled diplomatic ~ —*Newsweek*⟩ **3 :** one who acts to undermine the morale of workers on strike

³missionary \"\ *vi* -ED/-ING/-ES [²*missionary*] **:** to work as a missionary ⟨in her wildest dreams of ~*ing* . . . had never looked forward to anything quite like her new home —R.L. Taylor⟩

missionary apostolic *n, pl* **missionaries apostolic :** a Roman Catholic missionary sent by commission from the pope

missionary bishop *n* **:** a Protestant Episcopal bishop serving in a state, territory, or foreign field not organized into dioceses

missionary district *n* **:** an area presided over by a missionary bishop

missionary rector *n* **:** a Roman Catholic priest in charge of an important mission or quasi parish

missionary salesman *n* **:** a manufacturer's sales representative sent into a territory to stimulate sales of a product (as through special promotions, public-relations work)

missionary society *n* **:** a local, denominational, or interdenominational religious organization dedicated to the support of Christian missionary work

mis·sion·ate \ˈmishəˌnāt\ *vb* -ED/-ING/-S [¹*mission* + *-ate*] **:** MISSIONIZE

mission bells *n pl but sing or pl in constr* **:** either of two herbs (*Fritillaria lanceolata* or *F. mutica*) with purple yellowish mottled flowers

mission church *n* **:** a church that is not locally self-supporting but that depends at least partially upon the support of mission funds from the larger religious organization that established it

mis·sion·er \ˈmish(ə)nə(r)\ *n* -s [¹*mission* + *-er*] **:** MISSIONARY

mission furniture *n* [so called fr. the occurrence of this style in the Spanish missions of the U. S. Southwest] **:** plain, dark, heavy furniture of a style characterized by straight lines and square sections

mission home *n* **:** a benevolent institution (as for the care of the indigent or the aged) maintained by a religious organization

mission indians *n pl, usu cap M&I* **:** members of Indian tribes Christianized by Spanish Franciscan missionaries in California

mis·sion·ization \ˌmishənəˈzāshən, -ˌnīˈz-\ *n* -s **:** the act or process of conducting a mission

mis·sion·ize \ˈmishəˌnīz\ *vb* -ED/-ING/-S [¹*mission* + *-ize*] *vi* **:** to carry on missionary work ⟨was *missionizing* in distant China —*Times Lit. Supp.*⟩ ~ *vt* **:** to conduct a mission or do missionary work among ⟨enable Christians to take heathens from barbaric conditions in order to civilize and ~ them —J. C.Brauer⟩ ⟨were visited, *missionized*, colonized, and civilized from India —A.L.Kroeber⟩ — **mis·sion·iz·er** \-zə(r)\ *n* -s

missions *pl of* MISSION

mission station *n* **:** a place of missionary residence in or from which missionary activity in a given area is carried on

missis *var of* MISSUS

miss·ish \'misish\ *adj* [³*miss* + *-ish*] **:** appropriate to or characteristic of a young girl **:** PRIM, AFFECTED ⟨a maudlin, ~, namby-pamby sentimentality —Anthony Trollope⟩ — **miss·ish·ness** *n* -ES

¹**mis·sis·sip·pi** \ˌmisəˈsipē, (ˈ)misˈsi-, -pi *sometimes* ˈmizəˈsi- *or* (ˈ)mizˈsi-\ *adj, usu cap* [*Mississippi* river, central U. S., of Algonquian origin; akin to Ojibwa *Misisipi* Mississippi river, fr. *misi* big + *sipi* river] **1 :** of or relating to the Mississippi river **2** [*Mississippi*, state in the southern U. S., fr. the *Mississippi* river] **:** of or from the state of Mississippi **:** of the kind or style prevalent in Mississippi **3 :** of, relating to, or constituting a culture pattern in the region of the Mississippi drainage system dating A.D.1300–1700 and characterized by the village-state composed of scattered hamlets dominated by a village that is the ceremonial center and has large pyramidal structures around a plaza

²**mississippi** \"\ *n* -S *usu cap* **:** a game resembling bagatelle in which the balls are played against the side cushions and through numbered arches at the end of the table

¹**mis·sis·sip·pi·an** \-pēən\ *adj, usu cap* [*Mississippi* state & river + E *-an*] **1 :** of, relating to, or characteristic of the state of Mississippi or the Mississippi river **2 :** of, relating to, or characteristic of the people of Mississippi or of the Mississippi river region **3 :** of, relating to, or constituting the division of the Paleozoic era or system in No. America following the Devonian and preceding the Pennsylvanian — see GEOLOGIC TIME table

²**mississippian** \"\ *n* -S **1** *cap* **:** a native or resident of Mississippi or of the Mississippi river region **2** *usu cap* **:** the Mississippian period or system of rocks

mississippi catfish *also* **mississippi cat** *n, usu cap M* **1 :** BLUE CAT **2 :** FLATHEAD CATFISH

mississippi kite *n, usu cap M* **:** a small kite (*Ictinia mississippiensis*) that has chiefly lead-colored plumage with a blackish tail and that is found from southern Illinois to Central America

¹**mis·sive** \'misiv, -sēv *also* -səv\ *adj* [ME, fr. MF or ML; MF *missif*, fr. ML *missivus*, fr. L *missus* (past part. of *mittere* to send) + *-ivus* -ive — more at SMITE] **1 :** specially sent or prepared to be sent — see LETTER MISSIVE **2 :** MISSILE

²**missive** \"\ *n* -S [MF (*lettre*) *missive*, fr. *lettre* letter + *missive*, fem. of *missif*] **1 :** a written communication **:** LETTER ⟨many of their ~s were illiterate, and the more violent of them were unsigned —R.B.Merriman⟩; *often* **:** a formal or official letter ⟨the driver delivered the ~ at the embassy door —Upton Sinclair⟩ **2** *Scots law* **:** a formal authenticated document in the style of a letter by which a party to a contract submits to the other contracting party his own offer or acceptance **3** *obs* **:** MESSENGER ⟨came ~s from the king, who all-hail'd me thane of Cawdor —Shak.⟩ **4 :** something that is thrown or used as a weapon **:** MISSILE ⟨making use of any ~, even a proverb, that came ready to hand —Aldous Huxley⟩

miss nan·cy \-ˈnan(t)sē, -aan-, -ain-, -si\ *n, pl* **miss nancys** *usu cap M&N* [fr. the name *Miss Nancy*] **:** an effeminate boy or man **:** SISSY ⟨"ain't he brave?" he says in a *Miss Nancy* voice, and the rest of them laughed —Helen Eustis⟩ ⟨often mocked as *Miss Nancys* by the more emancipated —Dixon Wecter⟩ — **miss-nancy·ish** \ˌ;ˌ;=(t)sēish\ *adj*

miss-nancy·ism \=ˈ==ˌizəm\ *n* -S **:** EFFEMINACY

¹**mis·sort** \(ˈ)mi(s)+\ *vt* [¹*mis-* + *sort*] **:** to sort badly or incorrectly

²**missort** \"\ *n* -S **:** an item (as a letter or check) that is incorrectly sorted

¹**mis·sou·ri** \məˈzu̇rə, -zu̇r-, -rē, -ri\ *adj, usu cap* [*Missouri*, state in the central U. S., fr. the *Missouri* river, fr. F, fr. *Missouri* (people)] **:** of or from the state of Missouri ⟨a *Missouri* mule⟩ **:** of the kind or style prevalent in Missouri **:** MISSOURIAN — **from missouri** *usu cap M* [*Missouri* (state)] **:** not easily fooled **:** hard to convince **:** SKEPTICAL ⟨in social dealings with foreigners, the Englishman is *from Missouri;* he has got to be shown —D.W.Brogan⟩

²**missouri** \"\ *n, pl* **missouri** *or* **missouris** *usu cap* [F, fr. Illinois, lit., owners of big canoes] **1 a :** a Siouan people of the Missouri river valley, Missouri **b :** a member of such people **2 :** a dialect of Chiwere

¹**mis·sou·ri·an** \-rēən\ *adj, usu cap* [*Missouri* (state & people) + E *-an*] **1 :** of, relating to, or characteristic of the state of Missouri **2 :** of, relating to, or characteristic of Missourians **3 :** of or relating to the subdivision of the Pennsylvanian geologic period between the Desmoinesian and the Virgilian — see GEOLOGIC TIME table

²**missourian** \"\ *n* -S *cap* **:** a native or resident of Missouri

missouri currant *n, usu cap M* **:** BUFFALO CURRANT 1

missouri gooseberry *n, usu cap M* **1 :** a slender spiny shrub (*Ribes missouriense*) of the central U. S. that has greenish white flowers **2 :** the large edible brown or purplish berry of the Missouri gooseberry

missouri gourd *n, usu cap M* **:** PRAIRIE GOURD

missouri grape *n, usu cap M* **1 :** a woody vine (*Vitis palmata*) of the central and southern U. S. **2 :** the fruit of the Missouri grape

missouri skylark *n, usu cap M* **:** SPRAGUE'S PIPIT

miss·out \(ˈ)mis+\ *n* -S [fr. *miss out*, v.] **1 :** a loss by the caster of the dice in craps usu. by the throwing of a point and then a seven **2 :** the casting of a 2, 3, or 12 on the first throw — compare ⁵CRAP 2

mis·speak \(ˈ)mi(s)+\ *vt* [¹*mis-* + *speak*] **1 :** to speak incorrectly ⟨he uses long words, but he ~s them⟩ **2 :** to express (oneself) badly or imperfectly ⟨*misspoke* himself because he didn't take time to think⟩

mis·spell \"+\ *vt* [¹*mis-* + *spell*] **:** to spell incorrectly ⟨~s many words through carelessness⟩

mis·spelling \"+\ *n* [¹*mis-* + *spelling*] **:** an incorrect spelling ⟨the occasional ~s and faulty grammar of one more at home in Chinese than in his mother tongue —Vincent Cronin⟩

mis·spend \"+\ *vt* [ME *misspenden*, fr. ¹*mis-* + *spenden* to spend — more at SPEND] **:** to spend wrongly **:** SQUANDER, WASTE ⟨a vacation without books would be grievously *misspent* —Orville Prescott⟩ ⟨*misspent* a fortune on fake old masters⟩ — **mis·spender** \"+\ *n*

mis·state \"+\ *vt* [¹*mis-* + *state* (v.)] **:** to state wrongly **:** give a false account of ⟨~s the facts to make it appear that he was the injured party⟩ — **mis·stater** \"+\ *n*

mis·statement \"+\ *n* [¹*mis-* + *statement*] **:** a false or incorrect statement

mis·step \"+\ *n* [¹*mis-* + *step* (n.)] **1 :** a wrong step ⟨made a ~ and fell down the stairs⟩ **2 a :** a mistake in judgment or action **:** BLUNDER ⟨a ~ that could lead to disaster⟩ **b :** a lapse in sexual behavior by a girl or woman; *esp* **:** the bearing of an illegitimate child ⟨a ~ of her youth that she tried to keep a secret⟩

mis·strike \"+\ *n* [¹*mis-* + *strike* (n.)] **:** a coin whose design is off center

mis·sus *or* **mis·sis** \'misəz, -isəs, -izəz, -izəs\ *n* -ES [alter. of *mistress*] **1 :** WIFE — not in formal use ⟨be sure to bring the ~⟩ **2** *dial* **:** MISTRESS 2

¹**missy** \'misē, -si\ *n* -ES [³*miss* + *-y* (n. suffix)] **:** a young girl **:** MISS ⟨the pious little ~, stiff as a board —Irving Howe⟩

²**missy** \"\ *adj* [³*miss* + *-y* (adj. suffix)] **:** relating to, resembling, or characteristic of a young girl ⟨despite her attempt to seem grown-up, she has a ~ primness of manner⟩

missy *abbr* missionary

¹**mist** \'mist\ *n* -S [ME, fr. OE; akin to MD *mist, mest* mist, fog, Icel *mistur* mist, haze, Gk *omichlē* mist, fog, Arm *meg*, Lith *migla*, Skt *mih* mist, *megha* cloud] **1 :** water in the form of particles suspended in the atmosphere at or near the surface of the earth **:** small water droplets floating or falling, approaching the form of rain, and sometimes distinguished from fog as being more transparent or as having particles perceptibly moving downward ⟨heavy ~s hung in the valley and obscured the mountains —Willa Cather⟩ ⟨still summerlike except for the ~ on the lawn as dusk fell —Kathleen Freeman⟩ **2 :** something that hides or blurs objects or concepts **:** something that dims or obscures one's perceptions or understanding ⟨its origins are lost in the ~s of antiquity —G.G.Coulton⟩ ⟨a revelation of the world of nature that had lain so long under the ~ of erroneous medieval geography —*Saturday Rev.*⟩ ⟨heard through the ~ of sleep the voice . . . praying in her room —Louis Bromfield⟩ **3 :** a dimness of vision **:** a haze or film before the eyes ⟨a ~ seemed to come before her eyes —Gilbert Parker⟩ **4 a :** a cloud of small particles or objects resembling or suggestive of a mist ⟨the thick ~ of smoke and unescaped vapors which filled the room —Liam O'Flaherty⟩ ⟨saw it all in a wondrous light, in the ~ of leaves, in the flash of the river —Van Wyck Brooks⟩ **b :** a suspension of a finely divided liquid in a gas **:** FOG 2c — compare FUME 1b **c :** a fine spray **:** FOG 3b ⟨spraying with insecticidal ~s —*Atlantic*⟩ **5** *or* **mist gray :** a reddish gray that is bluer and paler than evenglow and bluer, lighter, and stronger than opal gray

²**mist** \"\ *vb* -ED/-ING/-S [ME *misten*, fr. OE *mistian*, fr. *mist*, n.] *vi* **1 :** to be or become misty **:** form a mist ⟨it's ~*ing* from the marshes or fogging from the sea —T.H.Fielding⟩ ⟨it was still only ~*ing* when they took their seats —*Pasadena (Calif.) Independent*⟩ **2 :** to become dim or blurred ⟨old eyes ~*ed* as he recalled the most important and tragic day of his life —Barnaby Conrad⟩ **~** *vt* **:** to cover with or as if with mist **:** CLOUD, DIM ⟨damp ~s her glasses —R.P.Warren⟩

mist *abbr* [L *mistura*] mixture

mis·tak·able \məˈstākəbəl\ *adj* **:** capable of being misunderstood or mistaken ⟨the twins are easily ~ for each other⟩ — **mis·tak·ably** \-blē, -li\ *adv*

¹**mis·take** \məˈstāk\ *vb* **mis·took** \məˈstu̇k, (ˈ)miˈs-\ **mis·tak·en** \məˈstākən\ **mistaking; mistakes** [ME *mistaken*, fr. ON *mistaka* to take by mistake, make a slip, fr. *mis-* ¹mis- + *taka* to take — more at TAKE] *vt* **1 :** to choose wrongly **:** blunder in the choice of ⟨ambition quite ~s her road —Edward Young⟩ ⟨*mistook* the track across the moors, and led the army into boggy ground —T.B.Macaulay⟩ **2 a :** to take in a wrong sense **:** misunderstand the meaning or intention of ⟨don't ~ me; I will do exactly as I say⟩ ⟨had *mistaken* the meaning of her question —Carson McCullers⟩ **b :** to be wrong in the estimation or understanding of **:** MISINTERPRET ⟨*mistook* the class structure and ownership distribution of developed capitalism —Peter Wiles⟩ **c :** to make a wrong judgment of the character or ability of **:** UNDERESTIMATE ⟨they ~ their man if they think they can frighten me⟩ **3 a :** to fail to recognize or to identify wrongly ⟨there's no *mistaking* him⟩ ⟨there's no *mistaking* that house⟩ **b :** to substitute incorrectly in thought or perception **:** take wrongly for someone or something else ⟨~ gush for vigor and substitute rhetoric for imagination —C.D.Lewis⟩ ⟨could be and often was *mistaken* for a farmer —H.S.Canby⟩ **4 :** to be wrong in regard to (time) ⟨somehow *mistook* the hour . . . I had told her nine o'clock, and she came at ten —Mary R. Rinehart⟩ **~** *vi* **:** to be wrong **:** be under a misapprehension ⟨you *mistook* when you thought I laughed at you —Thomas Hardy⟩ ⟨if I ~ not . . . the entire import of the illustration changes —John Dewey⟩ — **mis·tak·er** \-kə(r)\ *n*

²**mistake** \"\ *n* **1 :** a misunderstanding of the meaning or implication of something ⟨it is a ~ to think that the supreme or legislative power of a commonwealth can do what it will —John Locke⟩ ⟨it is a great ~ to think that the bare scientific idea is the required invention —A.N.Whitehead⟩ **2 :** a wrong action or statement proceeding from faulty judgment, inadequate knowledge, or inattention **:** an unintentional error ⟨it would be a ~, however, to drain all bogs —*Boy Scout Handbook*⟩ ⟨gave him a ten-dollar bill in ~ for a one⟩ **3** *law* **:** an erroneous belief **:** a state of mind not in accordance with the facts **syn** see ERROR — **and no mistake :** SURELY, UNDOUBTEDLY ⟨he's the one I saw, *and no mistake*⟩

mistaken *adj* [fr. past part. of ¹*mistake*] **1 :** MISUNDERSTOOD, MISCONCEIVED ⟨a case of ~ identity⟩ **2 :** having a wrong opinion or incorrect information ⟨is ~ in his ideas about education⟩ ⟨it is both unfair and immoral to charge perjury against a man who is only ~ —L.P.Stryker⟩ **3 :** wrong in action or thought **:** ERRONEOUS, MISGUIDED ⟨the psychologist is as much interested in ~ behavior as in correct behavior —G.A.Miller⟩ ⟨his ~ venture into poetic drama —H.V. Gregory⟩ ⟨correct some of the ~ ideas about farming —C.R. Hope⟩ — **mis·tak·en·ly** *adv* — **mis·tak·en·ness** \-kən(n)əs\ *n* -ES

mistake of fact *law* **:** a mistake other than a mistake of law

mistake of law : a mistake as to the legal consequences or significance of an act, transaction, or state of affairs

mis·tak·ing·ly *adv* **:** in a mistaking manner

mis·tal \'mistᵊl\ *n* -S [prob. of Scand origin; akin to Norw *melkestøl* milking shed in a saeter, fr. *melk* milk (fr. ON *mjolk*) + *støl* milking shed, fr. ON *stöthull* — more at MILK, STADDLE] *dial Eng* **:** a shed for cows

mis·tas·si·ni \ˌmistəˈsēnē\ *n* -S [fr. Lake *Mistassini*, Quebec, Canada] **:** a dwarf primrose (*Primula mistassinica*) of northern and alpine America

mist blower *n* **:** a machine for the application of insecticides or fungicides in the form of a mist — compare HYDRAULIC SPRAYER

mist blue *n* **1 :** DUSTY BLUE **2 :** CAMEO GREEN

mist board *n* **:** a paperboard with an outside liner of two fibers of different color typically black and white

mistbow \ˈ=ˌ=\ *n* **:** FOGBOW

mist brown *n* **:** BEIGE BROWN

mist concentrate sprayer *n* **:** CONCENTRATE SPRAYER

mis·teach \(ˈ)miˈstēch\ *vt* [ME *mistechen*, fr. OE *mistǣcan*, fr. ¹*mis-* + *tǣcan* to teach — more at TEACH] **:** to teach wrongly or badly — **mis·teach·er** \-chə(r)\ *n*

mist·ed \'mistəd\ *adj* [¹*mist* + *-ed*] **:** covered with or enveloped by or as if by mist ⟨a ~ pitcher of lemonade on the table —John & Ward Hawkins⟩ **:** FOGGED ⟨a mind that was ~ through fatigue⟩

mis·telle \məˈstel\ *n* -S [F, fr. Sp *mistela*, fr. *misto, mixto* mixed (fr. L *mixtus*, past part. of *miscēre* to mix) + *-ela* (dim. suffix) — more at MIX] **:** grape juice or slightly fermented white wine to which brandy has been added that is used in the production of other wines (as some vermouths and Malaga)

mis·tempered \(ˈ)miˈstempə(r)d\ *adj* [¹*mis-* + *tempered*] **1** *archaic* **:** DERANGED **2** *obs* **:** tempered for a bad purpose ⟨throw your ~ weapons to the ground —Shak.⟩

¹**mis·ter** \'mistə(r)\ *n* -S [ME, occupation, kind, need, fr. OF *mestier* — more at MÉTIER] **1** *archaic* **:** CLASS, KIND, SORT ⟨what ~ word is that —Francis Quarles⟩ **2** *chiefly Scot* **:** a case or condition of need

²**mister** \"\ *n* -S [alter. of ¹*master*] **1** — used sometimes in writing instead of the usual *Mr.* **2 :** SIR — used in direct address and not followed by the given name or surname of the man addressed and typically expressing abject deference (as of a beggar) ⟨can you let me have a dime, ~⟩ or stiff formality tinged with displeasure or with anger ⟨try that again, ~, and you'll be sorry⟩ or used simply as a generalized term of direct address of a man that is a stranger esp. by younger persons ⟨hey, ~, do you want to buy a paper⟩ **3 :** a man not entitled to a title of rank or an honorific or professional title ⟨though he was only a ~, he was a greater scholar in his field than any Ph.D.⟩ **4 :** HUSBAND ⟨maybe your *Mister* likes herbs, but then again, he mayn't —Alice Ross⟩

³**mister** \"\ *vt* **mistered; mistered; mistering** \-t(ə)riŋ\ **misters :** to address or refer to as *mister* or *Mr.* ⟨I ~*ed* him and sirred him no longer —*Century Mag.*⟩

mi·ste·ri·o·so \məˌstirēˈō(ˌ)sō, (ˌ)miˌs-, -)zō\ *adv (or adj)* [It, mysterious, fr. *mistèrio, mistèro* mystery (fr. L *mysterium*) + *-oso* -ose (fr. L *-osus*) — more at MYSTERY] **:** in a mysterious manner — used as a direction in music

mis·term \(ˈ)miˈstərm\ *vt* [¹*mis-* + *term*] **:** to apply a wrong name or designation to **:** term incorrectly ⟨fly-by-night schools that ~ themselves colleges⟩

mistery *var of* MYSTERY

mis·tetch \(ˈ)miˈstech\ *vt* -ED/-ING/-ES [alter. of *misteach*] *dial Eng* **:** to teach bad habits to

mistflower \ˈ=ˌ==\ *n* **:** an American herb (*Eupatorium coelestinum*) with violet heads — called also *blue boneset*

mist·ful \'mistfəl\ *adj* [¹*mist* + *-ful*] **:** MISTY

mist gray *n* **:** MIST 5

mist green *n* **:** a variable color averaging a light yellowish green that is lighter and much less strong than apple green (sense 1), greener and paler than pistachio, and greener and duller than ocean green

mis·think \(ˈ)mis+\ *vb* [¹*mis-* + *think*] *vi, archaic* **:** to think wrongly, mistakenly, or unfavorably **~** *vt, archaic* **:** to think badly or unfavorably of

misti *pl of* MISTUS

mis·ti·blu \ˌmistēˌblü\ *n* -S [alter. of *misty blue*] **:** a grayish blue that is redder and paler than electric, greener and paler than copenhagen or old china, and redder and lighter than Gobelin

mis·tic \'mistik\ *also* **mis·ti·co** \-təˌkō\ *n* -S [Sp *mistico*, perh. fr. Ar *musaṭṭah*, an armed ship] **:** a small lateen-rigged sailing ship used in the Mediterranean

mistier *comparative of* MISTY

mistiest *superlative of* MISTY

mis·ti·gris \'mistēˌgris\ *n* -ES [F *mistigri* pussycat, jack of clubs, card game played with the jack of clubs wild, prob. irreg. fr. *miste, mite* pussycat (prob. of imit. origin) + *gris* gray — more at GRIZZLE] **1 :** a joker or blank card that the holder can play as any card **2 :** poker as played with a mistigris

mist·i·ly \'mistəlē, -li\ *adv* [ME, fr. *misty* + *-ly*] **:** in a misty manner **:** OBSCURELY, VAGUELY ⟨the summits of the most distant mountains . . . were dark and ~ purple —Robert Hichens⟩ ⟨explains it somewhat ~ —*Newsweek*⟩

mis·time \(ˈ)miˈstīm\ *vt* [ME *mistimen*, fr. ¹*mis-* + *timen* to time — more at TIME] **1 :** to time wrongly or improperly ⟨*mistimed* his arrival⟩ ⟨*mistimed* his swing and struck out⟩ **2 :** to reckon or state the time of incorrectly ⟨~s the accession of Queen Victoria by five years⟩

mis·timed \-md\ *adj, chiefly dial Eng* **:** disturbed in regular routine or habits esp. of eating and sleeping

mist·i·ness \'mistēnəs, -tin-\ *n* -ES [ME, *mistines*, fr. *misty* + *-nes* -ness] **:** the quality or state of being misty ⟨the vagueness and ~ . . . in his early poems —H.H.Clark⟩

misting *pres part of* MIST

mis·tis \'mistəs\ *n* -ES [by alter.] *South* **:** MISTRESS

mist·less \'mistləs\ *adj* [¹*mist* + *-less*] **:** not misty

mis·tle thrush *also* **mis·sel thrush** \'misəl-\ *n* [obs. E *mistle, missel* mistletoe, fr. ME *mistel*, fr. OE — more at MISTLETOE] **:** a large European thrush (*Turdus viscivorus*) that has closely spotted underparts and feeds on mistletoe berries — called also *mistletoe thrush*

mis·tle·toe \'misəlˌtō, *chiefly Brit also* 'mizə-\ *n* -S [ME *mistilto* (attested only in the meaning "basil"), fr. OE *mistel-tān*, fr. *mistel* mistletoe, basil + *tān* twig; OE *mistel* akin to OHG & OS *mistil* mistletoe, ON *mistilteinn* mistletoe and perh. to OHG *mist* dung; OE *tān* akin to OHG *zein* twig, ON *teinn*, Goth *tains;* fr. the seeds being planted in the droppings of birds that have eaten the berries — more at MIXEN] **1 :** a Eurasian hemiparasitic shrub (*Viscum album*) that has dichotomously branching greenish stems, thick persistent leathery leaves, small yellowish flowers, and waxy-white glutinous berries and that grows pendent from various usu. deciduous trees (as the apple) **2 :** any of numerous plants of the family Loranthaceae that are felt to resemble the typical Old World mistletoe: as **a :** any of various American plants of the genus *Phoradendron* that grow on deciduous trees **b :** any of various Old World plants of the genus *Viscum* **c** *Austral* (1) **:** FLAME TREE a(2) (2) **:** a plant of the genus *Loranthus* (3) **:** a plant (*Notothixos incana*) that is parasitic on other mistletoes **d :** AMERICAN MISTLETOE 1 **3** *Austral* **:** DODDER LAUREL

mistletoe bird *n* **:** an Australian flower-pecker (*Dicaeum hirundinaceum*)

mistletoe cactus *n* **:** a plant of the genus *Rhipsalis*

mistletoe family *n* **:** LORANTHACEAE

mistletoe fig *n* **:** a shrub or small tree (*Ficus diversifolia*) sometimes grown as a pot plant that has foliage resembling that of the mistletoe and globose to pyriform fruit

mistletoe gray *n* **:** a variable color averaging a grayish yellow green that is yellower and paler than average sage green or palmetto and greener and duller than mermaid

mistletoe green *n* **:** a variable color averaging a grayish yellow green that is yellower, less strong, and slightly lighter than average sage green and yellower, lighter, and stronger than palmetto

mistletoe thrush *n* **:** MISTLE THRUSH

mist maiden *n* **:** either of two alpine or arctic perennial herbs (*Romanzoffia sitchensis* or *R. unalaschkensis*) of the family Hydrophyllaceae of western No. America with rounded crenate basal leaves and white funnelform flowers in a loose raceme

mis·to·nusk \'mistəˌnəsk\ *n* -S [Cree *mīstanask*, lit., broad, fr. *mist* much + *anâsk* spread out] **:** AMERICAN BADGER

mistook *past of* MISTAKE

mis·train \(ˈ)miˈstrān\ *vt* [¹*mis-* + *train*] **:** to train badly or incorrectly

mis·tral \'mistrəl, məˈsträl\ *n* -S [F, fr. Prov *mistral, mistrau*, fr. *mistral, mistrau* masterful, fr. OProv *maystral*, fr. L *magistralis* — more at MAGISTRAL] **:** a violent cold dry northerly wind of the Mediterranean provinces of France ⟨the ~ blew viciously —Horace Sutton⟩

mis·transcription \ˌmis+\ *n* [¹*mis-* + *transcription*] **:** a mistake in transcription **:** an incorrect copy ⟨some errors, ~s and mistranslations impair confidence —*Listener*⟩

mis·translate \"+\ *vt* [¹*mis-* + *translate*] **:** to translate incorrectly — **mis·translation** \"+\ *n*

mis·treat \(ˈ)miˈstrēt\ *vt* [ME *mistreten*, prob. fr. MF *mestreitier, mestraitier*, fr. OF, fr. *mes-* ¹mis- + *treitier, traitier* to treat — more at TREAT] **:** to treat badly **:** ABUSE ⟨administered a public thrashing to the landlord who had ~*ed* his brother —C.V.Woodward⟩ — **mis·treatment** \"+\ *n*

¹**mis·tress** \'mistrəs; *preceding a name as a title, pronounced like* MRS.\ *n* -ES [ME *maistresse*, fr. MF, fr. OF, fem. of *maistre* master — more at MASTER] **1** *obs* **:** a woman or something personified or venerated as a woman regarded as a guide or protector ⟨conjuring the moon to stand auspicious ~ —Shak.⟩ **2 :** a woman who has power, authority, or ownership: as **a :** the female head of a family or household ⟨having her here as ~ of this house — as your father's wife —Kathleen Freeman⟩ ⟨presided as ~ of the White House during the closing scenes of the administration —T.P.Abernethy⟩ **b :** a woman who employs or supervises servants ⟨the . . . kitchen maid, whose pleasure during the week is in the thought of vying with her ~ on Sunday —Herbert Spencer⟩ **c :** a woman who possesses, owns, or controls something ⟨though she was angry, she was still ~ of her temper⟩ ⟨~ of a large fortune⟩ ⟨a dog whose ~ devoted hours a day to its care⟩ ⟨determined to get a job and become her own ~⟩ **d :** a woman who is in charge of a school or other establishment or group ⟨this guidance is given by a ~ of postulants and the ~ of novices —Mary Augustine⟩ **e :** a woman of the Scottish nobility who holds in her own right a status comparable to that of a master; *specif* **:** the eldest daughter and heiress presumptive of a Scottish peer **3 a** *chiefly Brit* **:** a female teacher or tutor ⟨while classics *mistress* in an East Anglian college —*Irish Digest*⟩ ⟨when I pointed this out to the drawing ~ she rebuked me and told me that the "feeling" was wonderful —Ralph Vaughan Williams⟩ **b :** a woman who is skilled in something or who has achieved mastery in some field ⟨shows herself ~ of almost every conceivable type of fairy lore —Polly Goodwin⟩ ⟨~ of the art of portraiture⟩ ⟨~ of the science of medicine⟩ **4 :** a country or state regarded as having supremacy or control over others ⟨when Rome was ~ of the world⟩ ⟨became undisputed ~ of the continent⟩ **5 :** something personified as female that rules or directs ⟨Mother and *Mistress* of all the churches —William Leonard & Bernard Orchard⟩ ⟨the sea is a stern ~ and an unyielding disciplinarian —Bill Redgrave⟩ **6 a :** a woman with whom a man habitually fornicates ⟨leaving his wife, an actress, behind, he travels with his ~ —Bernice Matlowsky⟩ **b** *archaic* **:** a beloved woman **:** SWEETHEART **7 a** *archaic* **:** MADAM 1 **b** — used archaically as a conventional title of courtesy before the given name or surname or before both names of an unmarried woman **c** *chiefly South & Midland* **:** MRS. 1a **8** *dial chiefly Brit* **:** WIFE

²**mistress** \"\ *vt* -ED/-ING/-ES **1 :** to address as mistress **2 :** to achieve mastery of (an art) — used of a woman **3 :** to rule or control as a mistress **:** DOMINATE — **mistress it :** play the mistress

mis·tress·ly *adj* [¹*mistress* + *-ly*] **:** resembling or characteristic of a woman who has a mastery of something ⟨a ~ demonstration of acting⟩

mistress of ceremonies : a woman who presides at a public ceremony or who acts as hostess of a stage, radio, or television show

mistress of the robes *usu cap M&R* **:** a duchess who is ap-

pointed nominally in the British royal household to have charge of the queen's robes and who attends the queen at all state ceremonies
mistress-ship \'⸗⸗,ship\ *n* **:** the condition or position of a mistress ⟨she was looking forward to her *mistress-ship* of the robes —Israel Zangwill⟩ ⟨achieved the *mistress-ship* of the seas⟩ ⟨appointed to the mathematics *mistress-ship*⟩
mis·trial \(')mi¦strīəl\ *n* [¹*mis-* + *trial*] **1 :** a trial that has no legal effect by reason of some error in the proceedings **2 :** a trial not resulting or not likely to result in a lawful decision or verdict because of serious prejudicial misconduct or error
¹**mis·trust** \(')mi¦strəst\ *n* [ME, fr. ¹*mis-* + *trust*, n.] **:** a lack of confidence **:** DISTRUST, SUSPICION ⟨a certain unbreakable core of ~, suspicion, and disbelief —A.R.Marcus⟩ ⟨realize how weak the love of truth is in the majority and how widespread the ~ of reason —W.R.Inge⟩ **syn** see UNCERTAINTY
²**mistrust** \"\ *vb* [ME *mistrusten*, fr. ¹*mis-* + *trusten* to trust — more at TRUST] *vt* **1 :** to regard with suspicion **:** have no trust or confidence in **:** SUSPECT ⟨~ me and are forever questioning me about my personal life —Isaac Rosenfeld⟩ ⟨she feared an argument; she ~*ed* herself —Arnold Bennett⟩ **2 :** to have doubts about the truth, validity, or effectiveness of ⟨calculated to make the weak-willed reader ~ his own judgment —B.R.Redman⟩ ⟨who ~ the investment of U.S. money, technical and military aid —Adrienne Koch⟩ **3 :** to have a foreboding of the existence or occurrence of **:** feel or believe to be likely **:** SURMISE — often used with noun clause as object ⟨your mind ~*ed* there was something wrong —Robert Frost⟩ ~ *vi* **:** to lack confidence **:** be suspicious ⟨a place so wild that a man less accustomed to these things might have ~*ed* and feared for his life —Willa Cather⟩ — **mis·trust·er** \-tə(r)\ *n*
mis·trust·ful \-fəl\ *adj* **1 :** given to mistrust **:** SUSPICIOUS ⟨so ~ of everybody that they never know what to believe —Upton Sinclair⟩ **2 :** full of mistrust **:** marked by mistrust ⟨the ~ atmosphere of dubious peace —J.W.Aldridge⟩ — **mis·trust·ful·ly** *adv* — **mis·trust·ful·ness** *n*
mis·trust·ing·ly *adv* **:** in a mistrusting manner
mis·trust·less \-ləs\ *adj* **:** having no mistrust **:** UNSUSPECTING
mis·tryst \(')mi¦strīst\ *vb* [¹*mis-* + *tryst*] *vt*, *chiefly Scot* **:** to break an agreement with; *esp* **:** to fail to keep an engagement with ~ *vi*, *chiefly Scot* **:** to fail to keep an agreement (as an engagement or an appointed meeting)
mistrysted *adj*, *chiefly Scot* **:** PERPLEXED, FRIGHTENED ⟨they are sore ~ yonder in their parliament house about this robbery —Sir Walter Scott⟩
mists *pl of* MIST, *pres 3d sing of* MIST
mis·tune \(')mi¦stün\ *vt* [¹*mis-* + *tune*] **:** to tune incorrectly **:** render discordant ⟨like a pleasant air when performed on a *mistuned* instrument —Sir Walter Scott⟩
mis·tus \'mistəs\ *n*, *pl* **mis·ti** \-,stī\ *also* **mistuses** [NL, fr L, past part. of *miscēre* to mix — more at MIX] **:** an intraspecific hybrid plant
misty \'mistē, -ti\ *adj*, *usu* -ER/-EST [ME, fr. OE *mistig* misty, fr. *mist* + *-ig* -y — more at MIST] **1 a :** obscured by or covered with mist or something resembling mist ⟨westward the ~ summits of the Coast range —*Amer. Guide Series: Oregon*⟩ ⟨the ~ sheen of the moonlight —O.E.Rölvaag⟩ ⟨was barely heated and ~ with dust —Arthur Miller⟩ **b :** consisting of or marked by mist ⟨the darkness of sky and water was streaked with a long, ~ line of foam —Herman Melville⟩ **c :** unclear in shape or outline **:** INDISTINCT ⟨could perceive the outlines of land, blue and ~ in the distance —C.B.Nordhoff & J.N.Hall⟩ **2 a :** clouded as if by mist **:** DIM, OBSCURE ⟨through the safe and rather ~ glass of ready-made dogmas —Mary Webb⟩ **b :** vague or confused in thought or style ⟨poetry which was essentially vague, ~ and dim —Delmore Schwartz⟩ ⟨a ~ nostalgia for a royalist authoritarianism —Gordon Merrick⟩
misty blue *n* **:** DUSTY BLUE
misty-eyed \¦⸗⸗¦⸗\ *adj* **:** DREAMY, SENTIMENTAL ⟨a *misty-eyed* young lover⟩ ⟨*misty-eyed* recollections⟩
misty morn *n* **:** a light grayish brown to reddish brown that is less strong and slightly lighter than sandstone
mis·understand \(¦)mis+\ *vt* [ME *misunderstanden*, fr. ¹*mis-* + *understanden* to understand — more at UNDERSTAND] **1 :** to fail to understand **:** miss the true meaning of ⟨~ a poem⟩ ⟨*misunderstood* the idea the lecturer was trying to develop⟩ ⟨*misunderstood* the potentialities of colonization —Albert Hyma⟩ **2 :** to interpret (as something said or done) incorrectly **:** attach a wrong meaning to ⟨the women who blacken your character and ~ your wife's amusements —Rudyard Kipling⟩ — **mis·under·stander** \"+\ *n*
mis·understanding \"+\ *n* [ME *misundirstonding*, fr. ¹*mis-* + *undirstonding*, *understanding* understanding] **1 :** a failure to understand **:** MISINTERPRETATION ⟨the ~ which arose from reports of these golden palaces fired the imagination of Columbus —G.F.Hudson⟩ **2 :** DISAGREEMENT, QUARREL ⟨the ~*s* between the two territories have grown during the emergency —Vernon Bartlett⟩
mis·un·der·stand·ing·ly *adv* **:** in a misunderstanding manner **:** so as to misunderstand or as a result of misunderstanding
mis·under·stood \(¦)mis+\ *adj* [fr. past part. of *misunderstand*] **1 :** wrongly or imperfectly understood ⟨a ~ question⟩ ⟨a ~ criticism⟩ **2 :** not sympathetically appreciated ⟨claimed to be a much ~ husband⟩
mis·usage \(')mi¦shü . . ., (')mis¦yü . . .— *see* USAGE\ *n* [MF *mesusage*, fr. *mes-* ¹*mis-* + *usage* — more at USAGE] **1 :** bad treatment **:** ABUSE ⟨charged ~ of patients by one of the attendants⟩ **2 :** wrong or improper use (as of words) ⟨an instance of what he regarded as ~ appeared in a conservative publication —Kathryn A. McEuen⟩
¹**mis·use** \(')mi¦shüz, (')mis¦yüz\ *vt* [ME *misusen*, partly fr. ¹*mis-* + *usen* to use; partly fr. MF *mesuser* to abuse, use wrongly, fr. OF, fr. *mes-* ¹*mis-* + *user* to use — more at USE] **1 :** to use incorrectly or carelessly **:** MISAPPLY ⟨~*s* words in such number that it is impossible to understand him⟩ **2 :** to use for a wrong or improper purpose ⟨~*s* his talents⟩ ⟨possibility that the members would ~ the organization for inhumane and selfish purposes —Raphael Demos⟩ ⟨regards a battle as a major occasion for *misusing* his social position —William Empson⟩ **3 :** to do harm to **:** ABUSE, MISTREAT ⟨the intent of this regulation is highly commendable, namely to keep the Indians from being *misused* —C.B.Hitchcock⟩
²**mis·use** \(')mi¦shüs, (')mis¦yüs\ *n* [ME, partly fr. ¹*mis-* + *use*; partly fr. MF *mesus* abuse, wrong use, fr. *mes-* ¹*mis-* + *us* use — more at USE] **1 :** incorrect or careless use **:** MISAPPLICATION ⟨the first statement involves a ~ of the verb "to create" —Arthur Pap⟩ ⟨the ~ of words which are actually in the language —Barrett Wendell⟩ **2 :** wrong or improper use ⟨intended to keep their secret until adequate controls against its ~ had been devised —Vera M. Dean⟩
misuse of patents : an attempt of a patent owner to extend his monopoly beyond the express terms of the patent grant resulting in the denial by the courts of protection to the patent
¹**mis·us·er** \(')mi¦shüzə(r), (')mis¦yüz-\ *n* [¹*misuse* + *-er*] **:** one that misuses ⟨these wretched ~*s* of language —S.T. Coleridge⟩
²**misuser** \"\ *n* [AF, fr. OF *mesuser* to misuse] **:** an unlawful use of a right; *esp* **:** an unlawful use of a public office or grant of authority
mis·value \(')mis+\ *vt* [¹*mis-* + *value*] **:** to value wrongly; *esp* **:** UNDERVALUE ⟨neglected and *misvalued* his work for many years⟩
mis·venture \"+\ *n* [¹*mis-* + *venture*] **:** an unlucky venture **:** MISADVENTURE
mis·word \"+\ *n* [¹*mis-* + *word*] *dial chiefly Brit* **:** a word wrongly spoken **:** a cross word
mis·write \"+\ *vt* [ME *miswriten*, fr. OE *miswrītan*, fr. ¹*mis-* + *wrītan* to write — more at WRITE] **:** to write incorrectly **:** make a mistake in writing ⟨*miswrote* the title of the poem he was quoting⟩ ⟨carelessly ~*s* common words⟩
mis·writing \"+\ *n* [fr. gerund of *miswrite*] **:** a mistake in writing ⟨the inclusion of many ~*s* mislabeled misspelling helps to invalidate the investigator's conclusions about spelling —Hall Swain⟩
mit *var of* MITT
mit- *or* **mito-** *comb form* [NL, fr. Gk, fr. *mitos* — more at DIMITY] **1 :** thread ⟨*mito*plast⟩ **2 :** mitosis ⟨*mito*clastic⟩ ⟨*mito*depressive⟩ ⟨*mit*ogenetic⟩
mit *abbr* [L *mitte*, 2nd pers. sing. imper. of *mittere* to send — more at SMITE] send

MIT *abbr* milled in transit; milling in transit
mi·ta \'mēd·ə\ *n* -s [AmerSp, fr. Quechua *mit'a*, lit., turn, time] **:** a forced-labor draft imposed by the Spaniards on the Indians of Peru
mi·tan·ni \mə'tanē\ *n*, *pl* **mitanni** *or* **mitannis** *usu cap* **1 a :** an ancient Subaraean people with an Indo-Iranian ruling class having a kingdom in northern Mesopotamia that was dominant in Mesopotamia and northern Syria from the end of the 15th to the middle of the 14th century B.C. **b :** a member of these people **2 :** the language of the Mitanni people that was of uncertain relationship
mi·tan·nian \-nēən, -nyən\ *n* -s *usu cap* [*Mitanni* + E *-an*] **:** MITANNI 1b, 2
¹**mitch** \'mich\ *dial Eng var of* MUCH
²**mitch** \", 'mēch\ *var of* MEECH
mitch·board \'mich+,⸗\ *n* [*mitch* (origin unknown) + *board*] **:** an upright timber on the deck of a ship forming a crutch for the mast to rest on when lowered
mitch·el·la \mi'chelə\ *n* [NL, fr. John *Mitchell* †1768 Am. botanist born in England] **1** *cap* **:** a genus of creeping evergreen herbs (family Rubiaceae) having shiny evergreen leaves and fragrant white tubular flowers growing in pairs — see PARTRIDGEBERRY **2** -s **:** any plant of the genus *Mitchella* **3** -s **:** the dried plant of the partridgeberry formerly used as a diuretic, tonic, and astringent
mitch·ell grass \'michəl-\ *n*, *usu cap M* [prob. after Thomas L. *Mitchell* †1855 Scot. explorer in Australia] **:** any of several Australian grasses of the genus *Astrebla* with flowering spikes resembling wheat
mitchell movement *n*, *usu cap 1st M* [after John T. *Mitchell* 20th cent. bridge expert, its originator] **:** a method of conducting a game of duplicate bridge or whist so that the North-South pairs play only against the East-West pairs — compare HOWELL SYSTEM
¹**mite** \'mīt, *usu* -īd.+V\ *n* -s [ME, fr. OE *mīte* mite (small insect); akin to MD *mite* mite, small copper coin, OHG *mīza* mite (insect), *meizan* to cut, ON *meita* to cut, Goth *maitan* to hew, cut, and to OE *gemād* silly, mad — more at MAD] **1 :** any of numerous small to very minute arachnids of the order Acarina that have a body without a constriction between the cephalothorax and abdomen, mandibles generally chelate or adapted for piercing, usu. four pairs of short legs in the adult and but three in the young larvae, and often breathing organs in the form of tracheae and that include parasites of insects and vertebrates some of which are important disease vectors, parasites of plants in which they frequently cause gall formation, pests of various stored products, and completely innocuous free-living aquatic and terrestrial forms — see BLISTER MITE, CHEESE MITE, CLOVER MITE, ITCH MITE **2** [ME, fr. MF or MD; MF, small Flemish copper coin, fr. MD] **a** (1) **:** LEPTON 2 ⟨a certain poor widow . . . threw in two ~*s* —Mk 12:42 (AV)⟩ (2) **:** half a farthing **b :** a very small theoretical unit of value or coin; *specif* **:** a unit of value in England about 1600 worth usu. ¹⁄₂₄ penny **3 :** an old moneyers' unit of weight equal to ¹⁄₂₀ grain that is no longer used **4 a :** a very little **:** BIT, JOT ⟨only a ~ of what it could have taught was seen and learned —Tom Fitzsimmons⟩ — often used adverbially with *a* ⟨his voice is a ~ less luscious than formerly —R.C.Bagar⟩ **b :** a very small object, creature, or person ⟨a little kindergarten . . . ~ —Marie Imelda⟩
²**mite** \"\ *vt* -ED/-ING/-S [prob. fr. G *meiden* to shun, avoid, fr. OHG *mīdan*; akin to OE *mīthan* to hide, conceal, avoid, shun, MD *mīden* to avoid, shun, and to OE *missan* to miss — more at MISS] **:** to impose an Amish mite on ⟨was *mited* by church officials for using an automobile⟩
³**mite** \"\ *n* -s **:** a social and economic boycott applied to a member by an Amish congregation for transgressing church law
mite box *n* [¹*mite*] **:** a small box distributed individually to the members of a church or Sunday school for the collection of a special offering ⟨lenten *mite boxes*⟩
mi·tel·la \mə'telə\ *n*, *cap* [NL, fr. L, headband, turban, dim. of *mitra*] **:** a genus of low slender Asiatic and No. American herbs (family Saxifragaceae) having opposite leaves and flowers with trifid or pinnatifid petals and a superior one-celled ovary — see MITERWORT
¹**mi·ter** *also* **mi·tre** \'mīd·ə(r), 'mītə-\ *n* -s [ME *mitre*, fr.

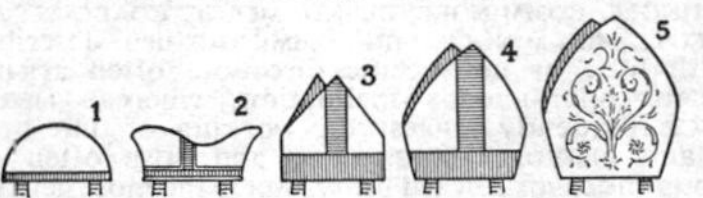

miter 1c: *1* 11th century, *2* 12th century, *3* 15th century, *4* 18th century, *5* 20th century

MF, fr. OF, fr. L *mitra* headband, turban, fr. Gk *mitra*, *mitrē*; akin to Skt *mitra* friend, Av *mithra* friend, treaty, OPer *Mithra* Mithras, god of light and defender of truth] **1 :** any of various turbans, tall caps, or other pieces of headgear: as **a :** a headband worn by women of ancient Greece **b :** the official headdress of the ancient Jewish high priest consisting of a linen turban having attached at the front a gold plate with the inscription "Holy to the Lord" **c :** a liturgical headdress that is worn by bishops and abbots and usu. has high stiff back and front pieces curving to a point and two lappets hanging from the back, is made of white silk or linen or of cloth of gold, and may be plain, orphreyed, or richly ornamented **2** [perh. fr. *miter* turban] **a** (1) **:** a surface forming the beveled end or edge of a piece where a miter joint is made (2) **:** MITER JOINT (3) **:** MITER SQUARE **b :** a corner or angle joining made by seaming on a diagonal line from the inside angle to the outside point and used esp. in fitting facings or hems and in matching stripes in sewing **3** *or* **miter shell a** *usu mitre* **:** a snail of the genus *Mitra* or family Mitridae **b :** the shell of such a snail **4 :** a piece (as of eaves trough or pipe insulation) made with a right angle bend to fit a corner or elbow ⟨install an inside ~ below the valley⟩
²**miter** *also* **mitre** \"\ *vb* **mitered** *also* **mitred; mitered** *also* **mitred; mitering** *also* **mitring** \-īd·əriŋ, -ītər-, -ī·tr-\ **miters** *also* **mitres** [ME *mitren*, fr. ML *mitrare*, fr. *mitra* liturgical miter, fr. L] *vt* **1 :** to raise to a rank privileged to wear a miter **:** confer a miter on ⟨~*ed* some of the less radical Protestant leaders —George Willison⟩ **2** [¹*miter* (joint)] **a :** to match together in a miter joint ⟨~ the ends of the boards⟩ **:** bevel the ends of for the purpose of matching together at an angle ⟨~ the side pieces⟩ **:** bring together at an angle without overlapping ⟨~ the cover materials at the inside corner of the book⟩ **b :** to join (lines of a cover decoration) accurately without overrunning at corners or crosslines **c :** to sew together in a miter ⟨stripes are ~*ed* to the waist —*Women's Wear Daily*⟩ **d :** to square off (a bottom corner of a bed sheet) by making a triangular fold and tucking it under ~ *vi* **:** to form a miter joint **:** meet in a miter joint
miter box *n* **:** a device for guiding a handsaw at the proper angle in making a miter joint and often in the form of a wooden or metal trough with fixed or adjustable vertical slots in its upright sides

miter box (with saw)

miter brad *n* **:** CORRUGATED FASTENER
miter cap *n* **:** a molded cushion of a newel post into which the handrail is mitered
miter clamp *or* **miter cramp** *n* **:** a clamp for holding together a glued miter joint while the glue sets
mi·tered \'mīd·ə(r)d, 'mītə-\ *adj* [ME *mitred*, fr. *mitre* + *-ed*; trans. of ML *mitratus*, fr. L, wearing a turban — more at MITRATE] **1 :** wearing a miter ⟨stood robed and ~ before the altar⟩ **2 :** having an upper part shaped like a miter ⟨the ~ headgear of the knight's lady⟩
mitered abbey *n* **:** an abbey under a mitered abbot
mitered abbot *n* **:** an abbot papally privileged to wear a miter and in pre-Reformation England entitled to sit and vote in the House of Lords
mi·ter·er \'mīd·ərə(r), 'mītə-\ *n* -s **:** one that miters; *esp* **:** a tool or machine for forming miters or bevels
miter gage *n* **:** a tool with graduations used to set a saw at any desired angle for a miter joint

miter gate *n* **:** one of a pair of canal lock gates that swing out from the side walls and meet at an angle pointing toward the upper level
miter gear *n* **:** one of a pair of interchangeable bevel gears with axes at right angles
miter joint *n* **:** a joint made by fastening together usu. perpendicularly parts with the ends cut at an angle **:** a butt joint with beveled ends

miter joints: *1* plain, *2* milled, *3* rabbeted

miter mushroom *n* [so called fr. the shape of the pileus] **:** a mushroom of the genus *Helvella* (esp. *H. crispa*)
miter plane *n* **:** a plane for general use in making angle and butt joints
miter post *n* **:** the vertical member at the free edge of a miter gate
miter rod *n* **:** a smooth flat plate of steel with one end cut back at a 45 degree angle used by a plasterer in finishing a reentrant corner
miter saw *or* **miter box saw** *n* **:** a saw similar to a backsaw but usu. with a longer blade for cutting miter joints in a miter box
miter shell *n* **:** MITER 3
miter sill *n* **:** a raised step against which a canal lock gate shuts
miter square *n* **1 :** a bevel with an immovable arm at an angle of 45 degrees for striking miter lines **2 a :** a square with an arm adjustable to any angle **b :** a rigid square with a 45 degree bevel on the end of the stock
miter valve *n* **:** a valve consisting of a disk fitting in a conical seat faced at 45 degrees to the valve axis
miterwort *also* **mitrewort** \'⸗⸗,⸗\ *n* -s **1 :** any of various rhizomatous perennial herbs that constitute the genus *Mitella* and have a capsule resembling a bishop's miter — called also *bishop's cap*; see FAIRY CAP **2 :** any of various white-flowered annual herbs constituting a genus (*Cynoctonum*) of the family Loganiaceae; *esp* **:** a plant (*C. mitreola*) of the southeastern U.S.
mites *pl of* MITE, *pres 3d sing of* MITE
mith \'mith\ *chiefly Scot var of* ¹MIGHT
mith·an *also* **mith·un** \'mithən\ *n*, *pl* **mithan** *also* **mithun** [native name in Assam and Chittagong] **:** an Indian bison or wild ox related to the gaur
¹**mith·er** \'mithər\ *Scot var of* MOTHER
²**mi·ther** \'mīthə(r)\ *dial Eng var of* MOIDER
mithkal *var of* MISKAL
mith·rae·um \mi'thrēəm\ *n*, *pl* **mith·raea** \-ēə\ *also* **mithraeums** *usu cap* [NL, fr. Gk *Mithraion* shrine of Mithras, fr. *Mithras*, Persian god of light and defender of truth, fr. OPer *Mithra* — more at MITER] **:** an underground room simulating a cave used for mithraic rites (as initiations)
mith·ra·ic \mi'thrāik\ *adj*, *usu cap* [LGk *mithraikos* of Mithras, fr. Gk *Mithras* + *-ikos* -ic] **:** of or relating to Mithraism or its god ⟨acolyte of the *Mithraic* cult —Stuart Cloete⟩
mith·ra·ism \'mithrə,izəm\ *n* -s *usu cap* [*Mithras*, Persian god of light (fr. L, fr. Gk) + E *-ism*] **:** an oriental mystery cult incorporating elements from Zoroastrianism, the primitive religions of Asia Minor, and Hellenism, having as its deity Mithras, the savior hero of Persian myth, admitting only men to its seven degrees of initiation, and constituting a serious rival of Christianity in the Roman Empire between the second and fourth centuries A.D.
mith·ra·ist \-əst\ *n* -s *usu cap* **:** an adherent of Mithraism — **mith·ra·is·tic** \¦⸗⸗¦istik\ *adj*, *usu cap*
mith·ri·date \'mithrə,dāt\ *also* **mith·ri·da·tum** \,⸗⸗'dād·əm\ *n* -s [ML *mithridatum*, fr. LL *mithridatium* antidote, fr. L, dogtooth violet (used as an antidote) fr. Gk *mithridation*, fr. *Mithridatēs* Mithridates] **:** an antidote against poison **:** ALEXIPHARMIC; *specif* **:** an electuary supposed to be a remedy or a protection against poison
mithridate mustard *n* **:** PENNYCRESS
mith·ri·dat·ic *or* **mith·ra·dat·ic** \¦mithrə¦dad·ik\ *adj* [*mithridatic* fr. L *Mithridaticus*, fr. *Mithridates* + *-icus* -ic; *mithradatic*, alter. (influenced by Gk *Mithradatēs* Mithridates) of *mithridatic*] **1** *usu cap* **:** of or relating to Mithridates VI of ancient Pontus **2 :** of or relating to mithridatism
mith·ri·da·tism \,⸗⸗'dād·,izəm\ *n* -s [*Mithridates* VI †63 B.C. king of ancient Pontus (fr. L *Mithridates*, fr. Gk *Mithridatēs*, *Mithradatēs*) + E *-ism*; fr. the fact that he reputedly produced this condition in himself] **:** tolerance to a poison acquired by taking gradually increased doses of it
mith·ri·da·tize \-ād·,īz\ *vt* -ED/-ING/-S **:** to produce mithridatism in
mit·i·ci·dal \¦mīd·ə¦sīdᵊl\ *adj* [¹*mite* + *-icidal* (as in *insecticidal*)] **:** ACARICIDAL
mit·i·cide \'⸗⸗,sīd\ *n* -s [¹*mite* + *-icide* (as in *insecticide*)] **:** ACARICIDE
mitier *comparative of* MITY
mitiest *superlative of* MITY
mit·i·ga·ble \'mid·əgəbəl, -itə-\ *adj* **:** that can be mitigated
mit·i·gant \-gənt\ *n* -s [obs. *mitigant*, adj., mitigative, fr. L *mitigant-*, *mitigans*, pres. part. of *mitigare* to mitigate] **:** something mitigating
mit·i·gate \'mid·ə,gāt, -itə-, *usu* -ād.+V\ *vt* -ED/-ING/-S [ME *mitigaten*, fr. L *mitigatus*, past part. of *mitigare* to soften, mitigate, fr. *mitis* soft, mild + *agere* to drive; akin to OIr *mōith* soft, *mīn* smooth, gentle, Skt *mayas* enjoyment, pleasure, Lith *mielas*, *mylas* dear — more at AGENT] **1 :** to cause (a person) to become more gentle or less hostile **:** MOLLIFY **2 :** to make less severe, violent, cruel, intense, painful **:** SOFTEN, ALLEVIATE ⟨used opium to ~ the horrors to which condemned criminals were subjected —*Science*⟩ ⟨disasters can be, if not prevented, at least *mitigated* —K.S.Davis⟩ **:** TEMPER ⟨in the summer the altitude tempers the heat, and in the winter the latitude ~*s* the cold —C.W.DeKiewiet⟩ **:** LESSEN ⟨a sentence of 20 days solitary confinement may be *mitigated* to 10 days —*Naval Orientation*⟩ ⟨tends to increase rather than to ~ these differences in students —*General Education in a Free Society*⟩ ⟨~ the sincerity of what I said —Mary Austin⟩ **syn** see RELIEVE
mit·i·gat·ed·ly *adv* [*mitigated*, past part. of *mitigate* + *-ly*] **:** in a mitigated degree
mit·i·ga·tion \,⸗⸗'gāshən\ *n* -s [ME *mitigacioun*, fr. AF & L; AF *mitigation*, fr. L *mitigation-*, *mitigatio*, fr. *mitigatus* (past part.) + *-ion-*, *-io* -ion] **1 :** the act of mitigating or state of being mitigated: **a :** abatement or diminution of something painful, harsh, severe, afflictive, or calamitous **:** ALLEVIATION, MODERATION, PALLIATION ⟨the cure, prevention, or ~ of disease —*Encyc. Americana*⟩ ⟨prison in ~ of the death sentence —Melitta Schmideberg⟩ **b** *obs* **:** QUALIFICATION, LIMITATION **2 :** a mitigating thing or fact ⟨a large number of drugs and ~*s* . . . at the clinic —*Jour. Amer. Med. Assoc.*⟩
mit·i·ga·tive \'⸗⸗,gād·iv\ *adj* [ME *mitigatif*, fr. MF, fr. LL *mitigativus*, fr. L *mitigatus* (past part.) + *-ivus* -ive] **:** tending to mitigate **:** ALLEVIATING, LENITIVE ⟨an air of being a trifle apologetic; and this ~, tentative quality shows . . . in their stance —*Time*⟩
mit·i·ga·tor \-,gād·ə(r)\ *n* -s **:** one that mitigates
mit·i·ga·to·ry \'mid·əgə,tōrē, -itə-\ *adj* [L *mitigatorius*, fr. *mitigatus* (past part. of *mitigare* to mitigate) + *-orius* -ory] **:** MITIGATIVE
mit·i·mae \,mid·ə'mä,ā\ *n* -s [AmerSp (Peru), fr. Quechua *mitma*, lit., foreigner, stranger] **1 :** a member of a part of a conquered Indian people forced by the Incas to settle in a distant area **2 :** compulsory transplantation and colonization of conquered peoples under the Incas
miting *pres part of* MITE
mi·tis \'mīd·əs\ *adj* [L, mild — more at MITIGATE] **:** tending to be less than averagely virulent — used esp. of strains of diphtheria bacilli; compare GRAVIS, INTERMEDIUS
mi·tis green \¦mēd·əs-\ *n* [part trans. of G *mitisgrün*, fr. Ignatz *Mitis* †1842 Ger. manufacturer + G *grün* green] **1** *usu cap M* **:** Paris green used as a pigment **2** *often cap M* **:** EMERALD 2a
mit·nag·ged \,mitnä'ged, mi'snägəd\ *or* **mis·na·gid** \mi'snägəd\ *n*, *pl* **mit·nag·ge·dim** *or* **mit·nag·dim** \,mitnäg(ə)'dēm, mi'snägdəm\ *or* **mis·nag·dim** \mi'snägdəm\ *often cap*

[NHeb *mithnăggēd* & Yiddish *misnaged*, fr. Heb *mithnăggēd* opposing, opponent] **1 :** an orthodox Jew esp. in eastern Europe opposed to the teachings of the Hasidim **2 :** a non-Hasid

mito- — see MIT-

mito·chon·dri·al \ˌmīd·ə¦kändrēəl, ¦mid·ə-\ *adj* [NL *mitochondrion* + E *-al*] **:** of, relating to, or being mitochondria

mito·chondriome \ˌ==+\ *n* [NL *mitochondrion* + E *-ome*] **:** CHONDRIOME

mito·chon·dri·on \ˌ==ˈ=drēən\ *n, pl* **mitochon·dria** \-ēə\ [NL, fr. *mit-* + Gk *chondrion* small grain — more at CHONDRI-] **:** any of various round or long cellular organelles that are found outside the nucleus, produce energy for the cell through cellular respiration, and are rich in fats, proteins, and enzymes — see CELL illustration

mito·cla·sic \ˌ==¦kläsik\ *or* **mito·clas·tic** \-¦klastik\ *adj* [*mitoclasic* fr. F *mitoclasique*, fr. *mito-* mit- + *-clasique* (fr. Gk *klasis* act of breaking + F *-ique* -ic); *mitoclastic*, prob. modif. (influenced by E *-clastic*) of F *mitoclasique* — more at -CLASIA] **:** interrupting the normal course of mitosis ⟨~ chemicals⟩

mito·ge·net·ic \ˌmīd·ō, ¦mid·ō+\ *adj* [*mit-* + *-genetic*] **:** producing mitosis ⟨the ~ effect⟩ ⟨~ radiation⟩

mitogenetic ray *n* **:** an ultraviolet ray said to be given off by physiologically active cells and to stimulate mitotic activity of adjacent cells — usu. used in pl.

mito·inhibitory \ˌ==+\ *adj* [*mit-* + *inhibitory*] **:** retarding or inhibiting mitosis

mi·tome \ˈmīd·ˌōm\ *n* -s [G *mitom*, fr. *mit-* + *-om* -ome] **:** the supposed fibrillar reticulum of protoplasm — compare PARAMITOME

mito·plast \ˈmīd·ə,plast, ˈmid-\ *n* -s [ISV *mit-* + *-plast;* prob. orig. formed as F *mitoplaste*] **:** a filamentous plastid

mi·to·sis \mīˈtōsə̇s\ *n, pl* **mito·ses** \-ˌsēz\ [NL, fr. *mit-* + *-osis*] **1 :** cell division in which complex nuclear division usu. involving differentiation and halving of chromosomes precedes cytoplasmic fission and which involves typically a series of steps consisting of the prophase, metaphase, anaphase, and telophase **:** indirect cell division — called also *karyokinesis;* opposed to *amitosis;* compare MEIOSIS 2 **2 :** KARYOKINESIS 1

mito·some \ˈmīd·ə,sōm, ˈmid-\ *n* -s [ISV *mit-* + *-some* (body)] **1 :** a threadlike cytoplasmic inclusion; *esp* **:** one that is held to be derived from the preceding mitotic spindle **2 :** NEBENKERN

mi·to·te \mə̇ˈtōd·ē\ *n* -s [Sp, fr. Nahuatl *mitotiqui* dancer] **:** an ancient and modern secular round dance of the Aztecs and other tribes in the Sierra Madre Occidental

mi·tot·ic \(ˈ)mī¦täd·ik, -ätik, -ēk\ *adj* [fr. NL *mitosis*, after such pairs as NL *hypnosis:* E *hypnotic*] **:** of or relating to mitosis **:** KARYOKINETIC — **mi·tot·i·cal·ly** \-ə̇k(ə)lē, -ēk-, -li\ *adv*

mitotic figure *n* **:** the spindle-shaped figure presented (as by the chromosomes, asters) during mitosis

mitotic index *n* **:** the number of cells per thousand cells actively dividing at a particular time

mi·tra \ˈmī·trə\ *n* [NL, fr. L, headband, turban; fr. the shape of the shell — more at MITER] **1** *cap* **:** a genus (the type of the family Mitridae) of chiefly East Indian marine snails having a slender acutely pointed often brightly colored shell **2** -s [NL, fr. L] **a :** GALEA **b :** the thick rounded pileus of various mushroom fungi

mi·traille \mēˈtrī\ *n* -s [F, fr. MF, old iron, pieces of metal, small coins, change, alter. of OF *mitaille*, fr. *mite* small copper coin — more at MITE (coin)] **1 :** small missiles (as bits of iron grape) for loading cannon **2 :** SMOKED PEARL

mi·trail·leuse \ˌmē·trə¦yə(r)z, -¦yə̄z\ *n* -s [F, fr. *mitrailler* to fire mitraille, fr. *mitraille*] **1 :** a breech-loading machine gun using small projectiles and consisting of a number of barrels fitted together and so arranged that the barrels can be fired simultaneously or successively and rapidly and first used by the French army in the war of 1870 with Germany **2 :** MACHINE GUN

mi·tral \ˈmī·trəl\ *adj* [¹*miter* + *-al*] **1 :** resembling a miter **2 :** of, relating to, indicating, or adjoining a mitral valve or the mitral orifice

mitral cell *n* **:** any of the pyramidal cells of the olfactory bulb about which terminate numerous fibers from the olfactory cells of the nasal mucosa

mitral insufficiency *also* **mitral incompetence** *n* **:** inability of the mitral valve to close perfectly permitting blood to flow back into the auricle and leading to varying degrees of heart failure

mitral orifice *n* **:** the left auriculoventricular orifice

mitral stenosis *n* **:** a condition usu. the result of disease in which the mitral valve is abnormally narrow

mitral valve *n* [trans. of NL *mitralis valvula*] **:** a valve in the heart that guards the opening between the left atrium and the left ventricle, prevents the blood in the ventricle from returning to the atrium, and consists of two triangular flaps attached at their bases to the fibrous ring which surrounds the opening and connected at their margins with the ventricular walls by the chordae tendineae and papillary muscles

mi·trate \ˈmī·ˌtrāt\ *adj* [L *mitratus* wearing a turban, turbaned, fr. *mitra* turban + *-atus* -ate — more at MITER] **:** suggestive of a miter or bonnet in shape

mitre *var of* MITER

mit·ri·dae \ˈmi·trə,dē\ *n pl, cap* [NL, fr. *Mitra*, type genus + *-idae*] **:** a family of marine snails (suborder Stenoglossa) comprising the miters — see MITRA

mi·tri·form \ˈmī·trə,fȯrm\ *adj* [NL *mitriformis*, fr. L *mitra* turban + *-iformis* -iform] **:** shaped like a bishop's miter

mits *pl of* MIT

mitsch·er·lich·ite \ˈmichə(r)lə̇,kīt\ *n* -s [Eilhardt *Mitscherlich* †1863 Ger. chemist, who first produced it + E *-ite*] **:** a mineral $K_2CuCl_4.2H_2O$ consisting of hydrous chloride of copper and potassium

mitsch·er·lich's law \ˈmichə(r)(ˌ)liks-\ *n, usu cap M* [after E. *Mitscherlich*] **:** a statement in crystallography and chemistry: isomorphous substances have similar chemical compositions and analogous formulas

mit·su·ku·ri·na \ˌmitsəkəˈrīnə, -rēnə\ *n* [NL, fr. Kakichi *Mitsukuri* †1909 Jap. zoologist + NL *-ina*] *syn of* SCAPANORHYNCHUS

mit·su·ma·ta \ˌmitsəˈmäd·ə\ *n* -s [Jap, lit., three-pronged fork, fr. *mitsu* three + *mata* forked] **:** a low shrub (*Edgeworthia papyrifera*) of the family Thymelaeaceae of temperate Asia that is cultivated in Japan for its bark used in papermaking

mitt *also* **mit** \ˈmit, *usu* -id·+V\ *n* -s [short for *mitten*] **1 a :** a woman's dress glove leaving the fingers uncovered, often extending to or above the elbow, and made of a dressy material (as lace, net, silk) **b :** MITTEN 1 ⟨wearing thick Arctic ~s⟩ **c** (1) **:** a baseball catcher's glove with heavy padding and a separate section only for the thumb (2) **:** a first baseman's glove with a padded palm, thumb, and one or two finger sections (3) **:** a protective mitten used in punching bag practice **d :** a device of cloth or similar material shaped (as for household dusting or car washing) to wear over the hand ⟨dust ~⟩ ⟨wash ~⟩ ⟨oven ~⟩ **2** *slang* **:** HAND ⟨dinner pail in his hardened ~ —Sinclair Lewis⟩ ⟨get your ~s out of my desk drawer⟩

mitt 1a

mit·tel·hand \ˈmid·ᵊl,hänt\ *n* [G, lit., middle hand, fr. *mittel* middle + *hand*] **:** MIDDLEHAND

mit·tel·schmerz \-,shmerts\ *n* -ES *sometimes cap* [G, lit., middle pain, fr. *mittel* middle + *schmerz* pain] **:** pain occurring between the menstrual periods and usu. considered to be associated with ovulation

mit·ten \ˈmitᵊn\ *n* -s [ME *mitain, mitein*, fr. MF *mitaine*, fr. OF, fr. *mite*] **1 :** a covering for the hand and wrist having a separate section for the thumb only and made in various designs and materials for warmth and protection — distinguished from *glove* **2** *chiefly Scot* **:** a thick worsted glove **3 :** MITT 1a **4** *slang* **:** REFUSAL, REJECTION, DISMISSAL; *esp* **:** the jilting of a suitor — usu. used in the phrases *get the mitten, give (someone) the mitten, send (someone) the mitten* **5** *slang* **:** BOXING GLOVE — usu. used in pl.

mitten 1

mit·ti·mus \ˈmid·əməs\ *n* -ES [L, we send, 1st pers. pl. pres. indic. of *mittere* to send — more at SMITE] **1 a :** a writ formerly used in England for directing the trial of a cause in a county palatine **b :** a warrant of commitment to prison **c :** a writ for removing records from one court to another **2** *Brit* **:** DISCHARGE, DISMISSAL **3** *Brit* **:** MAGISTRATE

mit·tle \ˈmitᵊl\ *vt* -ED/-ING/-S [perh. fr. F *mutiler*, fr. MF, fr. L *mutilare* — more at MUTILATE] *Scot* **:** MUTILATE, HURT

mit·tler's green \ˈmitlə(r)z-\ *n* [prob. part trans. of G *mittlers grün*, fr. *mittlers* (prob. fr. the name *Mittler*) + *grün* green] **1** *usu cap M* **:** Guignet's green often mixed with barium sulfate **2** *often cap M* **:** GUIGNET'S GREEN 2

mi·tu \ˈmēd·(ˌ)ü\ *n* [AmerSp (Argentina) *mitú*, fr. Guarani] **1** -s *archaic* **:** an unidentifiable but prob. gallinaceous Brazilian bird **2** [NL, fr. AmerSp *mitú*] **a** *cap* **:** a genus of curassows **b** -s **:** any curassow of the genus *Mitu*

mi·tua \ˈmichəwə\ [NL, fr. *Mitu*] *syn of* MITU

mity \ˈmīd·ē, -ītē\ *adj* -ER/-EST [¹*mite* + *-y*] **:** infested with mites

mitz·vah *also* **mits·vah** \ˈmitsvə, -(ˌ)vä\ *n, pl* **mitz·voth** *or* **mitz·vot** \-ˌvōt(h), -ōs\ *or* **mitz·vahs** \-ˌvəz, -(ˌ)väz\ *also* **mits·voth** *or* **mits·vot** \-ˌvōt(h), -ōs\ *or* **mits·vahs** [Heb *miṣwāh* commandment] **1** *Jewish relig* **:** a biblical or rabbinic commandment **2** *Jewish relig* **:** a meritorious performance (as of a religious or civic duty or a humanitarian or charitable act) **:** a good deed **3 :** a privilege of assisting in the ritual in a synagogue

mi·u·rus \mīˈyu̇rəs\ *n* -ES [LL, adj., being a miurus, fr. Gk *meiouros*, lit., tapering, prob. alter. of *myouros*, fr. *my-* + *-ouros* -urous] **:** a dactylic hexameter having its last foot an iamb or pyrrhic instead of a spondee or trochee — compare DOLICHURUS

mi·wok \ˈmē,wäk\ *n, pl* **miwok** *or* **miwoks** *usu cap* [Miwok, people] **1 a :** an Indian people of central California **b :** a member of such people **2 :** a Moquelumnan language of the Miwok people **3 :** MOQUELUMNAN

¹**mix** \ˈmiks\ *vb* **mixed** *also* **mixt** \ˈmikst\ **mixed** *also* **mixt; mixing; mixes** [ME *mixen*, fr. *mixte*, adj., mixed, fr. MF, fr. L *mixtus*, past part. of *miscēre* to mix; akin to Gk *misgein*, *mignynai, meignynai* to mix, Skt *miśra* mixed, OIr *mescaim* I mix] *vt* **1 a :** to stir, shake, or otherwise bring together (different substances) with a loss of separateness or identity **:** cause to be scattered or diffused throughout **:** combine (as the ingredients of smokeless powder) in one mass **:** intermingle thoroughly ⟨~ the flour with a little water⟩ ⟨~ the ingredients to a thick paste⟩ ⟨~ sand, clay, and humus⟩ ⟨~ colors to get the right shade⟩ **:** put as an ingredient ⟨~ an egg into the batter⟩ **:** combine with or introduce into a mass already formed **:** put in disorder **:** JUMBLE ⟨~ the slips well in the hat and draw one⟩ **b :** to bring together (as different kinds of people or things) in close association ⟨a party that ~*ed* people of all ages and interests⟩ ⟨~ business with pleasure⟩ ⟨charter granting was ~*ed* with politics —J.D.Magee⟩ ⟨told in a style that ~*es* erudition and bawdiness —*Saturday Rev.*⟩ **2 :** to prepare or form by mixing different components ⟨~ a drink at the bar⟩ ⟨the principals of integrated schools have been making conscious efforts . . . to ~ their classes —Walter Goodman⟩ **3 :** CONFUSE ⟨~*ed* his dates and arrived a week late⟩ ~ *vi* **1 a :** to become mixed **:** enter into combination **:** be capable of mixing ⟨a medicine which will ~ with water⟩ ⟨manual and intellectual labor seldom ~ well —H.S.Canby⟩ **b :** to be compatible — usu. used in negative constructions ⟨insecticides and geese won't ~ —*Springfield (Mass.) Daily News*⟩ **2 :** to enter into relations **:** ASSOCIATE ⟨on the streets three classes mingle but do not ~ —*Amer. Guide Series: Texas*⟩ ⟨learned to ~ with sons of lawyers, doctors, manufacturers —D.W.Brogan⟩ **3 :** CROSSBREED **4 a :** to enter as a participant ⟨a high-priced lawyer . . . ~*ing* into a case like this —Erle Stanley Gardner⟩ sometimes in an interfering manner ⟨the political crowd ~*ed* in and took over —*Springfield (Mass.) Union*⟩ **:** become involved **:** take part ⟨not in keeping with his position as a judge to ~ in politics —*Amer. Guide Series: Nev.*⟩ **b :** to become involved in a struggle or fight **:** TANGLE ⟨hesitated to ~ with someone bigger than he was⟩

syn MINGLE, COMMINGLE, BLEND, MERGE, COALESCE, AMALGAMATE, FUSE: MIX, MINGLE, and COMMINGLE usu. describe activities with little or no specific direction, often arising from chance or spontaneous inclination, whereas MERGE and COALESCE frequently suggest the working of time or natural force, and BLEND, AMALGAMATE, and FUSE often imply a conscious endeavor toward unity. MIX is the most general term; it usu. applies to elements which, though different, are capable of forming a stable and homogeneous product; sometimes MIX implies a loss of identity in the elements ⟨to *mix* colors in painting⟩, but more often the elements are distinguishable in the combination ⟨to *mix* pepper and salt⟩ ⟨to *mix* a drink⟩ ⟨a building of *mixed* architectural styles⟩ MINGLE implies that the elements are distinguishable both before and after combining; the combination is looser and the interpenetration less thorough than with MIX ⟨a *mixed* marriage⟩ ⟨*mixed* company⟩ but ⟨*mingled* sensations⟩ ⟨*mingled* emotions⟩ ⟨a street displaying *mingled* architectural styles⟩ COMMINGLE is almost interchangeable with MINGLE, but somewhat more intensive ⟨he has brains, wit, humanity, and a delicate acerbity *commingled* with a robust and refreshing ribaldry —*Times Lit. Supp.*⟩ BLEND implies a mixing of like or harmonious things in an intimate union which partakes of the qualities of each of its components, while absorbing their individualities ⟨various kinds of coffee may be *blended*, but coffee is *mixed* with chicory⟩ ⟨kinship with the land . . . she knew that this transfigured instinct was *blended* of pity, memory, and passion —Ellen Glasgow⟩ MERGE emphasizes still more the loss of the constituents in the whole, or the complete absorption of one element into another ⟨still had doubts as to the morality of his procedure, but . . . these doubts would soon be *merged* in . . . admiration of the tactical advantages of his approach —Louis Auchincloss⟩ COALESCE suggests a natural and gradual growing of kindred things into an organic whole ⟨the lips of a wound *coalesce*⟩ ⟨the small white clouds of early morning had swollen and *coalesced* —Osbert Lancaster⟩ ⟨touch and smell and sight and hearing come together and *coalesce* in the commonsense notion of an object —Bertrand Russell⟩ AMALGAMATE implies a union by assimilation, adaptation, or integration without complete loss of individual identity ⟨immigrants of various nationalities are constantly being *amalgamated* with the native American population⟩ ⟨thesis and plot are carefully *amalgamated* —F.B. Millet⟩ FUSE, more than any of the foregoing, stresses the oneness and indissolubility of the resulting product; yet each component plays a necessary and observable part in the whole ⟨one is conscious of the intellectuality and compacted thought which he *fuses* in emotional expression —H.O.Taylor⟩ ⟨in our daily lives we *fuse* our identities as Jew, as American, and as Israeli —Carl Alpert⟩ ⟨what I have done is to *fuse* together in this book all my ideas past and present on freedom of speech —Zechariah Chafee⟩

— **mix it** *or* **mix it up** *slang* **:** to engage in a fight **:** exchange blows aggressively ⟨the two boxers stopped stalling and *mixed it up*⟩ ⟨battle groups were *mixing it* with German tanks —Russell Hill⟩ ⟨hate to see the day when men were afraid to *mix it up* for pretty girls —J.A.Michener⟩

²**mix** \"\ *n* -ES **1 :** an act or process of mixing ⟨arming themselves for a big ~⟩ **2 :** a product of mixing **:** MIXTURE: as **a :** a commercially prepared mixture of dry ingredients for a food usu. requiring the addition of only water or sometimes eggs and cooking or baking ⟨roll ~⟩ ⟨soup ~⟩ ⟨cake made from a packaged ~⟩ ⟨an instant pudding ~ that needs only milk and mixing⟩ **b :** a mixture of materials to form a concrete, mortar, or asphaltic batch **c :** MIXTURE 2d **3 :** a state of confusion ⟨so tired he was in a ~⟩ **4 :** the ratio of different constituents going into a product; *specif* **:** an often empirical formula giving the proportions and constituents of a mixture (as of scrap, charcoal, ferroalloy) for making steel **5 :** DISSOLVE

mix·a·bil·i·ty \ˌmiksəˈbiləd·ē, -ətē, -i\ *n* **:** the quality or state of being mixable

mix·able *also* **mix·ible** \ˈmiksəbəl\ *adj* [¹*mix* + *-able* or *-ible*] **:** capable of being mixed **:** MISCIBLE — **mix·able·ness** *n* -ES

mixblood \ˈ=,=\ *n* [by alter.] **:** MIXED-BLOOD

mix-crystal \ˈ=,==\ *or* **mixed crystal** *n* [*mix-crystal*, alter. of *mixed crystal*, trans. of G *mischkristall*, fr. *mischen* to mix + *kristall* crystal] **:** SOLID SOLUTION

mi·xe \ˈmē,hā\ *n, pl* **mixe** *or* **mixes** *usu cap* [AmerSp, fr. Mixe, lit., people of the clouds] **1 a :** a Zoquean people of Oaxaca, Veracruz, and Chiapas, Mexico **b :** a member of such people **2 :** the language of the Mixe people

mixed \ˈmikst\ *adj* [alter. (influenced by *mixed*, past part. of ¹*mix*) of ME *mixte* — more at MIX] **1 :** combining the characteristics of more than one kind or class **:** not conforming to a single type ⟨~ grain in lumber⟩ ⟨a horse with a ~ gait⟩: as **a :** having the legal attributes of two or more classes ⟨a personal, real, or ~ action⟩ **b :** uniting features of two or more of the recognized systems of government (as aristocracy, democracy, monarchy) ⟨gave to ~ government the form of a system of checks and balances —G.H.Sabine⟩ ⟨a ~ state⟩ ⟨a ~ constitution, in which King, Lords, and Commons all played their historical part —Ernest Barker⟩ **c :** combining features or exhibiting symptoms of more than one condition or disease ⟨a ~ tumor⟩ **d** *of a hand* **:** having the fingers and palm of more than one type and usu. held by palmists to indicate versatility and ease of comprehension and creativity often combined with erratic behavior and a lack of concentration — compare CONIC, PHILOSOPHIC, PSYCHIC, SPATULATE, SQUARE **e** *of an inflorescence* **:** combining racemose and cymose formations ⟨the ~ thyrsus of the lilac⟩ **f :** involving joint ownership by both government and private individuals or business organizations ⟨a ~ corporation⟩ **g :** of or constituting a life-insurance company having a paid-up capital in addition to its accumulated assets and awarding a small portion of its profits to the proprietors or shareholders and the remainder to the assured (as in the mutual plan) ⟨the ~ plan⟩ ⟨a ~ company⟩ **h** *of a chemical compound* **:** characterized by different groups, radicals, or ions of similar type ⟨~ glycerides⟩ — opposed to *simple* **2 :** made up of or involving individuals or items of more than one kind ⟨a ~ carload⟩ ⟨a highway open to ~ traffic⟩ ⟨a ~ repertory of music old and new —Virgil Thomson⟩ ⟨go to town in fatigues, ~ uniforms and practically anything we want —Glen Carlsen⟩: as **a** (1) **:** made up of or involving persons differing in race, national origin, religion, or class ⟨a ~ trade union with Negroes and whites in the same local⟩ ⟨the ~ group of Alsatians, French, Swiss, Germans . . . who founded and developed the community —*Amer. Guide Series: Texas*⟩ ⟨the religion of children in ~ households⟩ (2) **:** including persons of dubious social status or moral character **:** not select ⟨admit that the early Christians were a very ~ lot —G.B.Shaw⟩ (3) **:** made up of representatives of both sides (as of a matter in dispute) and often one or more neutral members ⟨settle their frontier disputes by means of ~ frontier commissions —*UN Dept. of Public Information*⟩ — compare JOINT (4) **:** constituted by native and foreign judges for the administration of justice between persons of different nationalities ⟨the jurisdiction of the ~ courts extends over all civil cases between Europeans and Egyptians —Evelyn Baring⟩ ⟨set up a ~ tribunal for the suppression of the slave trade —R.E.Crist⟩ **b** (1) **:** made up of or involving individuals of both sexes ⟨a story considered unfit for ~ company⟩ ⟨~ socials⟩ ⟨the couple who sang soprano and bass in the ~ quartet⟩ ⟨a contract bridge contest for ~ pairs⟩ (2) **:** of both men and women performing in combination ⟨a work for ~ voices sung by the men's and women's glee clubs⟩ ⟨a ~ chorus⟩ **c** *of a stable natural community* **:** containing two or more kinds of organism in abundance ⟨a ~ prairie including both short grasses and midgrasses⟩ **d** *of a canasta* **:** containing one or more wild cards **3 a :** including or accompanied by inconsistent or incompatible elements ⟨considered technical advance a ~ blessing⟩ ⟨got a ~ reaction from the family⟩ — often used with plural nouns ⟨acted from ~ motives when money was involved⟩ ⟨~ feelings toward a writer close to him in expression but alien in temperament —Irving Howe⟩ ⟨~ reviews, ranging from "a sound musical drama" to "a very tasteless and pointless production" —*Current Biog.*⟩ **b** *of a market* **:** characterized by price movements in both directions **:** IRREGULAR ⟨the bond market was ~⟩ **4 :** that derives from two or more recognized races or breeds ⟨a person of ~ blood⟩ ⟨a dog of ~ breed⟩ **5** *of a vowel* **:** CENTRAL 7

mixed account *n* **:** an account that combines the features of a real account and a nominal account (as in showing a trial balance representing both supplies used and supplies on hand)

mixed acid *n* **:** a mixture of acids; *esp* **:** a mixture of nitric acid and sulfuric acid used in nitration

mixed alphabet *n* **:** an alphabet that has been rearranged or disordered either systematically or at random

mixed arch *n* **:** an architectural arch that is struck from several centers

mixed bag *n* **:** a miscellaneous collection **:** ASSORTMENT ⟨a *mixed bag* of stocks and bonds⟩ ⟨a prissy individual . . . and a *mixed bag* of other characters —John McCarten⟩

mixed-blood \ˈ=¦=\ *n* **:** a person whose ancestors belonged to two or more races — compare PUREBLOOD

mixed bud *n* **:** a bud (as of an apple, pear, or blackberry) that produces a branch and leaves as well as flowers — compare FLOWER BUD, LEAF BUD, SIMPLE BUD

mixed chalice *n* **:** the practice traditional in nearly all ancient Christian rites of adding a few drops of water to the wine in the eucharistic chalice — compare KRASIS

mixed cropping *n* **:** the growing of two crops (as corn and soybeans) intermingled together in the same field

mixed decimal *n* **:** a mixed number whose fractional part is a decimal fraction (as in 7.238)

mixed doubles *n pl* **:** a doubles contest (as in tennis) in which each team is composed of a male and a female player

mixed drink *n* **:** an alcoholic beverage prepared from a recipe calling for two or more ingredients stirred or shaken before serving

mixed economy *n* **:** an economy in which both publicly and privately owned enterprises operate simultaneously

mixed ether *n* **:** an ether (as methyl ethyl ether $CH_3OC_2H_5$) in which the radicals united to oxygen are different

mixed farming *n* **:** the growing of food or cash crops, feed crops, and livestock on the same farm ⟨planned to do *mixed farming*, keep a cow, enjoy the black duck —E.A.Weeks⟩ — compare SUBSISTENCE FARMING

mixed feed *n* **:** a feed for livestock that consists of a mixture of wheat particles, bran, middlings, shorts, and other material in various proportions and is a by-product of flour milling

mixed-flow \(ˈ)=¦=\ *adj* [¹*mixed* + *flow* (n.)] **:** combining or utilizing in succession two or more different types of flow (as axial and radial) — used esp. of turbines and pumps

mixed forest *n* **:** a forest with two or more predominant kinds of trees and with at least 20 percent of the stand consisting of other than the most common tree

mixed foursome *n* **:** a foursome in which each side consists of a man and a woman

mixed franking *n* **:** a franking on a postal cover including stamps of more than one country

mixed gland *n* **:** a gland producing more than one kind of secretion; *esp* **:** a mucoserous gland

mixed grill *n* **:** several broiled meats and vegetables (as a lamb chop, kidney, bacon, mushroom, and tomato) served on one plate

mixed larceny *n* **1 :** a larceny that includes the aggravation of a taking from another's house or person with or without violence and putting that other in fear — compare ROBBERY **2 :** a larceny deemed to be aggravated under circumstances set out in a statute

mixed·ly \ˈmiksə̇dlē, -kstlē, -li\ *adv* **:** in a mixed manner ⟨annuals and perennials growing ~ in the bed⟩ ⟨reacted ~ to his going⟩

mixed marriage *n* **:** a marriage between persons of different races or religions

mixed melting point *n* [¹*mixed* + *melting point*] **:** the fusion temperature of a mixture of two components that in the case of two different substances is usu. lower than that of either component or that in the case of a mixture of two samples of the same substance prepared by different methods as a check on their identity is not lower than that of either sample

mixed metaphor *n* **:** a figure of speech combining two or more inconsistent or incongruous metaphors (as in Shakespeare's "to take arms against a sea of troubles")

mixed mode *n* **1 :** an ecclesiastical mode whose ambitus extends through the combined range of an authentic and its related plagal mode **2** *Lockeanism* **:** a mode (as beauty) resulting from the combination of simple ideas of different kinds — contrasted with *simple mode*

mixed nerve *n* **:** a nerve containing both sensory and motor fibers

mixed·ness \ˈmiksədnəs, -ks(t)n-\ *n* -ES **:** the quality or state of being mixed

mixed nuisance *n* **:** a public nuisance that also causes harm or annoyance to a person in the exercise of his private rights as distinct from those common to the public generally

mixed number *n* **:** a number that is composed of an integer and a proper fraction and is their sum ⟨5⅔ is a *mixed number*⟩

mixed planting *n* **:** a combination of woody and herbaceous plants

mixed proportion *n* **:** proportion by addition and subtraction

mixed salt *n* **:** a salt (as a double salt) derived from more than one base or more than one acid

mixed tithe *n* **:** a tithe arising from animals nourished by the immediate products of the soil (as wool, milk or cheese, or honey and wax) — compare PERSONAL TITHE, PRAEDIAL TITHE

mixed train *n* **:** a train made up of both passenger cars and freight cars and used mainly on branch lines

mixed-up \(ˈ)=¦=\ *adj* [fr. *mixed up*, past part. of *mix up*] **:** marked by bewilderment, perplexity, or disorder **:** CONFUSED ⟨a *mixed-up* character ripe for the analyst —Lucy Crockett⟩ ⟨is only one reflective part of a *mixed-up* age —Norman Cousins⟩

mix·en \ˈmiksən\ *n* -S [ME, fr. OE, dung, dunghill; akin to OE *meox* dung, filth, *mīgan* to urinate, MD *mist*, *mest* dung, OS & OHG *mist* dung, ON *mīga* to urinate, Goth *maihstus* dung, L *mingere*, *meiere* to urinate, Gk *omichein*, *omeichein* to urinate, Skt *mehati* he urinates] *dial chiefly Eng* **:** a pile of dung or refuse **:** a manure heap

mix·er \ˈmiksə(r)\ *n* -S [1*mix* + -er] **1 :** one that mixes: **a** (1) **:** one whose work is weighing or measuring and mixing the ingredients of a product (as paint, a drug, bread, pottery, cement, glass, fertilizer) (2) **:** one who balances and controls the dialogue, music, and sound effects to be recorded for or with a motion picture or television **b :** a container, device, or machine for mixing: as (1) **:** a valve or burner in which fuel is mixed with air for combustion (2) **:** a storage tank from which molten pig iron drawn from blast furnaces can be transferred to an open-hearth or electric furnace or a converter (3) **:** any of various types of stationary or portable equipment (as an agitator, emulsifier, homogenizer, or pug mill) used for mixing gases, liquids, or solids in industry or in the laboratory (4) **:** an electrical circuit in a sound-recording or broadcasting system for combining the signals from several sources (as microphones, turntables, or wire lines) in any desired proportion (5) **:** MIXING FAUCET (6) **:** MIXING VALVE (7) **:** a stationary or portable kitchen utensil equipped with one or more beaters for mixing, beating, creaming, or whipping a variety of foods (as batters, cream, whites of eggs, boiled potatoes) ⟨electric ~⟩ (8) **:** a revolving drum with paddles attached for mixing concrete and mortar or a hopper with revolving paddles for mixing asphaltic concretes (9) **:** a composing or photocomposing machine in which matrices from more than one magazine can be automatically keyboarded into a single line **c :** a game, stunt, or dance used at a get-together to give members of the group an opportunity to meet one another in a friendly, informal atmosphere — called also *icebreaker* **2 :** one that mixes with others or in combinations: as **a** (1) **:** a person considered as to his casual sociability ⟨was shy and a poor ~⟩ (2) **:** a person marked by easy sociability ⟨the genial extroversion of the salesman, the . . . good ~ —Aldous Huxley⟩ **b :** a nonalcoholic beverage (as ginger ale) used to thin a mixed drink

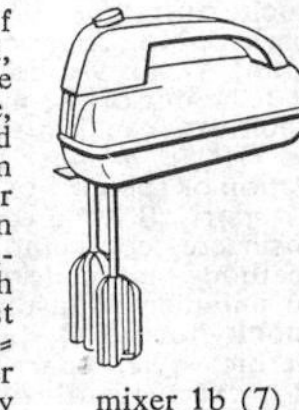
mixer 1b (7)

mixer tube *n* **:** an electron tube used for heterodyne operation

mixes *pres 3d sing of* MIX, *pl of* MIX *or of* MIXE

mix-hellene \ˈ=¦=,=\ *n*, *usu cap H* [Gk *mixellēn*, fr. *mix-* mixed (fr. *mixis* act of mixing) + *Hellēn* Hellene] **:** a person of mixed Hellenic and barbarian descent

mix·hill \ˈmiks+,-\ *n* [ME *mix* dung, filth (fr. OE *meox*) + E *hill* — more at MIXEN] *dial Eng* **:** MIXEN

mixible *var of* MIXABLE

mixing *n* -S [fr. gerund of 1*mix*] **:** the process of operating a mixer in sound recording or broadcasting

mixing faucet *n* **:** a faucet that mixes hot and cold water as they pass through the spout in proportions controlled by separate handles

mixing valve *n* **:** a device composed of a chamber with a sliding valve controlled often thermostatically by a handle and used to regulate water temperature in a shower or tub

mix·is \ˈmiksəs\ *n* -ES [Gk, act of mixing, fr. *mignynai* to mix — more at MIX] **:** the state characteristic of those organisms in which fertilization and related processes result in the existence of well-marked, alternating, diploid and haploid phases — compare APOMIXIS

-mix·is \ˈmiksəs\ *n comb form*, *pl* **-mixes** [NL *-mixis*, fr. Gk, act of mingling, act of mixing, fr. *mixis*] **:** an intermingling in reproduction ⟨apo*mixis*⟩ ⟨endo*mixis*⟩ ⟨pseudo*mixis*⟩ ⟨partheno*mixis*⟩ — compare -GAMY

mix·ite \ˈmik,sīt\ *n* -S [G *mixit*, fr. A. *Mixa*, 19th cent. Czech mine inspector + G *-it* -ite] **:** a mineral $Cu_{11}Bi(AsO_4)_5(OH)_{10}.6H_2O$ consisting of green to whitish hydrous basic copper bismuth arsenate

mixo- *comb form* [Gk, fr. *mixis* act of mingling or mixing] **1 :** mixed ⟨*mixo*trophic⟩ ⟨*mixo*chimaera⟩ **2 :** mixture of isomers of (a specified compound) ⟨*mixo*octane⟩ — compare IS-

mixo·biosis \,miksō+\ *n*, *pl* **mixobioses** [NL, fr. *mixo-* + *-biosis*] **:** a form of mutualism in which organisms (as ants) of different species live together in composite colonies

mixo·biotic \¦==+\ *adj* [fr. NL *mixobiosis*, after such pairs as NL *hypnosis:* E *hypnotic*] **:** of, relating to, or living in mixobiosis

mixo·chromosome \¦==+\ *n* [*mixo-* + *chromosome*] **:** a chromosome supposed to be formed by the fusion of all or part of two or more chromosomes

mixo·dec·tes \,=='dek,tēz\ *n*, *cap* [NL, fr. *mixo-* + *-dectes*] **:** a genus (the type of the family Mixodectidae) of extinct insectivores having very large incisors from the lower Eocene of the U.S.

mixo·gram \ˈmiksə,gram\ *n* [*mixo-* + *-gram*] **:** a graphic record of flour mixes from various wheats as related to the qualities of resultant dough mixes

mixo·graph \-,graf\ *n* [*mixo-* + *-graph*] **:** a graphic chart that provides supplementary baking data on dough mixes from various wheats

mix·ol·o·gist \mik'säləjəst\ *n* -S [1*mix* + *-ologist* (as in *psychologist*)] **:** a bartender skilled in preparing mixed drinks

mix·ol·o·gy \-jē, -ji\ *n* -ES [*mixologist* + *-y*] **:** the art or skill of preparing mixed drinks

mixo·lyd·i·an mode \¦miksə¦lidēən-\ *n* [*mixolydian* fr. Gk *mixolydios* mixolydian (fr. *mixo-* + *lydios* Lydian) + E *-an;* *mixolydian mode* trans. of Gk *mixolydios harmonia*] **1 :** a Greek mode consisting of two disjunct tetrachords represented on the white keys of the piano by a descending diatonic scale from B to B — see GREEK MODE illustration **2 :** an authentic ecclesiastical mode consisting of a pentachord and an upper conjunct tetrachord represented on the white keys of the piano by an ascending diatonic scale from G to G — see MODE illustration

mixo·ploid \ˈmiksə,plȯid\ *n* -S [ISV *mixo-* + *-ploid;* prob. orig. formed in G] **:** an organism having different numbers of genomes in different cells **:** CHIMERA — **mixo·ploi·dy** \-,plȯidē\ *n* -ES

mixo·sau·rus \,miksə'sȯrəs\ *n*, *cap* [NL, fr. *mixo-* + *-saurus*] **:** a genus of reptiles of Triassic age similar to *Ichthyosaurus* but with less fully developed paddles

mixo·troph·ic \¦miksə¦träfik, -trōf-\ *adj* [*mixo-* + *-trophic*] **:** deriving nourishment from both autotrophic and heterotrophic mechanisms — used esp. of symbionts and partial parasites

mixt \ˈmikst\ *n* -S [ML *mixtum* motley, mixed material, fr. L, neut. of *mixtus*, past part. of *miscēre* to mix — more at MIX] *archaic* **:** COMPOUND 2a

mix·tec \ˈmē,stek\ *or* **mix·te·co** \mē'stā(,)kō, -te(-\ *also* **mix·te·ca** \-_kə\ *n*, *pl* **mixtec** *or* **mixtecs** *or* **mixteco** *or* **mixtecos** *usu cap* [AmerSp *mixteca*, *mixteco*, of AmerInd origin] **1 a :** a people of the states of Oaxaca, Guerrero, and Puebla, Mexico, speaking languages of the Mixtecan family **b :** a member of such people **2 :** the language of the Mixtec people

mix·te·can \(ˈ)mē¦stākən, -tek-\ *n* -S *usu cap* **:** a language family of the states of Oaxaca, Guerrero, and Puebla, Mexico, including Amusgo, Cuicatec, and Mixtec

1**mix·tie-max·tie** *or* **mix·ty-max·ty** \¦mikstē¦makstē, -ti\ *adj* [alter. & redupl. of *mixt*, obs. var. of 1*mixed*] *chiefly Scot* **:** jumbled together **:** CONFUSED

2**mixtie-maxtie** *or* **mixty-maxty** \"\ *also* **mix·ter-max·ter** \ˈmikstər¦makstər\ *n* [*mixter-maxter*, alter. of *mixtie-maxtie*] *chiefly Scot* **:** a heterogeneous mixture

mixtion *n* -S [ME *mixcioun*, fr. MF or L; MF *mixtion*, fr. OF *mistion*, fr. L *mixtion-*, *mixtio*, *mistion-*, *mistio* act or process of mixing, fr. *mixtus*, *mistus* (past part.) + *-ion-*, *-io* -ion] **1** *obs* **:** the state of being mixed **2** *obs* **:** the process of mixing **3** *obs* **:** a product of mixing

mix·ture \ˈmikschə(r)\ *n* -S [MF, fr. OF *misture*, fr. L *mixtura*, *mistura*, fr. *mixtus*, *mistus* (past part. of *miscēre* to mix) + *-ura* -ure — more at MIX] **1 a :** an act, process, or instance of mixing ⟨a gradual ~ of languages⟩ ⟨a paste made by the ~ of flour and water⟩ ⟨one of those slight ~*s* in the stock which . . . provides a variant —Lucien Price⟩ **b** (1) **:** the state of being mixed (2) **:** the relative proportions of constituents **:** PROPORTION, RATIO ⟨youngsters do go through phases but with varied timing and in varied ~*s* —Dorothy Barclay⟩; *specif* **:** the fuel-to-air proportions of the charge produced in the carburetor for combustion in an engine or turbine **2** [ME, fr. L *mixtura*, *mistura* (also, act of mixing)] **:** a product of mixing **:** COMBINATION ⟨beat milk into the dry ingredients until the ~ thickens⟩ ⟨the interior . . . is a ~ of forest and grassland —P.E.James⟩ ⟨a unique ~ of sentimentality and toughness —J.A.Morris b.1904⟩: as **a :** a portion of matter consisting of two or more components that do not bear a fixed proportion to one another and that however thoroughly commingled are regarded as retaining a separate existence — usu. distinguished from *complex* and *compound;* compare ALLOY, MECHANICAL MIXTURE, SOLID SOLUTION, SYSTEM 8 **b :** an aqueous liquid medicine **:** POTION; *specif* **:** a preparation in which insoluble substances are suspended in watery fluids by the addition of a viscid material (as gum, sugar, glycerol) **c :** a combination of several different kinds of some article of consumption (as tea or tobacco) ⟨a smoking ~⟩ **d** (1) **:** a yarn spun from two or more fibers or from a fiber dyed two or more colors (2) **:** a fabric made from such yarn or woven with different yarns in the warp and the weft **e :** a batch or packet of postage stamps sold by weight and usu. comprising stamps gathered by a nonphilatelic agency (as a bank, a government bureau, or a missionary society) — compare KILOWARE

mixture stop *also* **mixture** \"\ *n* -S **:** a pipe-organ stop having more than one pipe for each digital — compare PARTIAL STOP

mix up *vt* **:** CONFUSE ⟨an explanation that *mixed* me *up* even more⟩ ⟨*mixed up* two similar words⟩

mix-up \ˈ=,=\ *n* -S [*mix up*] **1 :** a state or instance of confusion ⟨further the *mix-up* in terminology we have been attempting to correct —Thomas Munro⟩ ⟨sent to the wrong base through a *mix-up* in orders⟩ **2 :** MIXTURE ⟨such a general *mix-up* that our most distinctive . . . endowments disappear —Norman Goodall⟩ ⟨the man is a *mix-up* of cheerful schoolboy and devout elder —Paul Holt⟩ **3 :** MELEE

mi·ya·ga·wa·nel·la \,mēyə,gäwə'nelə\ *n*, *cap* [NL, fr. Yoneji *Miyagawa* b1885 Jap. bacteriologist + connective *-n-* + NL *-ella*] **:** a genus of coccoid to spherical microorganisms (family Chlamydiaceae) usu. placed among the rickettsias and including a number of important parasites (as *M. lymphogranulomatis*, the cause of venereal lymphogranuloma, and *M. psittaci*, the cause of psittacosis)

miz·maze \ˈmiz,māz\ *n* [redupl. and alter. of 1*maze*] **1 :** MAZE ⟨the way lies through . . . an intricate ~ of tracks —S.P.B. Mais⟩ **2** *dial Eng* **:** a state of confusion or bewilderment **:** WHIRL ⟨so surprised he was all of a ~⟩

miz·pah \ˈmizpə\ *adj* [*Mizpah*, place in ancient Palestine where Jacob and Laban erected a heap of stones as a sign of covenant between them (Gen 31:44–49), fr. Heb *Miṣpah*] **:** worn (as by lovers) to signify remembrance ⟨a ~ ring⟩ ⟨~ half coins⟩

miz·rach *also* **miz·rah** \ˈmiz,räk\ *n* -S [NHeb *mizrāḥ*, fr. Heb, east, place of sunrise, fr. *zāraḥ* to rise, come forth] **1 :** an ornamental or sacred picture hung on the east wall of a house or synagogue in the direction of Jerusalem toward which Jews face when in prayer **2 :** the eastern wall of a synagogue

miz·ra·chi *also* **miz·ra·hi** \miz'räkē\ *adj*, *usu cap* [*Mizrachi*, movement in Zionism founded in 1902, fr. Heb *Mizrāḥī*, lit., of the east, fr. *mizrāḥ* east] **:** of or relating to a movement in Zionism supported by strictly orthodox Jews

1**miz·zen** *or* **miz·en** \ˈmizᵊn\ *n* -S [ME *mesein*, *meson*, prob. fr. MF *misaine*, alter. (influenced by OIt *mezzana*) of *migenne*, fr. OCatal *mitjana;* OIt *mezzana* & OCatal *mitjana*, fr. Ar *mazzān* mast] **1 :** a fore-and-aft sail set on the mizzenmast — see SAIL illustration **2 :** MIZZENMAST **3 :** the aftermast and sail of a yawl

2**mizzen** *or* **mizen** \"\ *adj* [ME *meson*, fr. *meson*, n.] **:** of or relating to the mizzenmast ⟨~ shrouds⟩ ⟨the ~ peak halyards⟩

miz·zen·mast \-,mast, -,maa(ə)st, -,maist,-,måst, -_məst\ *n* [ME *meson mast*, fr. *meson* (n.) + *mast*] **:** the mast aft or next aft of the mainmast in a ship — see SHIP illustration

1**miz·zle** \ˈmizəl\ *vi* **mizzled; mizzled; mizzling** \-z(ə)liŋ\ **mizzles** [ME *misellen;* akin to D dial. *miezelen* to drizzle, MD *misel* mist, dew, drizzle, Flem *mijzelen*, *mizzelen* to drizzle, LG *mis* foggy weather, MD *mist*, *mest* mist, fog — more at MIST] *chiefly dial* **:** to rain in very fine drops

2**mizzle** \"\ *n* -S [fr. earlier *mysell*, *misle*, prob. fr. MD *misel*] *chiefly dial* **:** a fine rain **:** DRIZZLE

3**mizzle** \"\ *vt* -ED/-ING/-S [origin unknown] *chiefly dial* **:** CONFUSE, MUDDLE, MISINFORM

4**mizzle** \"\ *vi* -ED/-ING/-S [origin unknown] *slang chiefly Brit* **:** to take oneself off **:** disappear suddenly **:** slink away **:** DECAMP ⟨gone an' *mizzled* to the war —C.J.Dennis⟩

5**mizzle** \"\ *vt* -ED/-ING/-S [perh. alter. of obs. E *measle* to cover with or as if with measles, fr. *measle*, sing. of *measles*] *Scot* **:** to make spotted **:** SPECKLE

miz·zly \ˈmiz(ə)lē, -li\ *adj* [1*mizzle* + *-y*] *chiefly dial* **:** characterized by or consisting of mizzle

miz·zo·nite \ˈmizᵊn,īt\ *n* -S [G *mizzonit*, fr. Gk *meizōn* greater + G *-it* -ite] **:** a mineral of the scapolite group intermediate between meionite and marialite and containing 54 to 57 percent of silica; *specif* **:** a volcanic mizzonite occurring in clear crystals

mk *abbr* **1** mark **2** markka

mkd *abbr* marked

mkm *abbr* marksman

MKS *abbr*, *usu not cap* meter-kilogram-second

mkt *abbr* market

ml *abbr* **1** mail **2** milliliter

mL *abbr* millilambert

ML \(ˈ)e¦mel\ *abbr or n* -S [L *magister legum*] **:** a master of laws

ML *abbr* **1** mean level **2** mine layer **3** mixed lengths **4** mold line **5** motor launch **6** muzzle-loading

mlanje cedar *often cap M*, *var of* MILANJI CEDAR

mld *abbr* **1** mild **2** mold; molded; molding

MLD *abbr*, *often not cap* mininum lethal dose

mldg *abbr* molding

mldr *abbr* molder

mlech·chha \mə'lechə\ *n* -S [Skt *mleccha*] *chiefly India* **:** one who does not practice Hinduism; *specif* **:** FOREIGNER

m level *n*, *usu cap M* **:** the energy level of an electron in an M-shell

mlle *abbr*, *often cap* [F] mademoiselle

mlnr *abbr* milliner

MLR *abbr* **1** main line of resistance **2** muzzle-loading rifle

MLS *abbr* microwave landing system

MLT *abbr* mean low tide

MLW *abbr* mean low water

MLWN *abbr* mean low water neaps

MLWS *abbr* mean low water springs

mm *abbr* millimeter

mM *abbr* millimole

MM *abbr* **1** machinist's mate **2** made merchantable **3** Maelzel's metronome **4** [L *magistri*] masters **5** Majesties **6** [L, *martyres*] martyrs **7** master mechanic **8** mercantile marine; merchant marine **9** [F] messieurs **10** methyl methacrylate **11** middle marker **12** *often not cap* [L] mutatis mutandis

mme *abbr*, *often cap* [F] madame

mmf *abbr* micromicrofarad

MMF *abbr*, *often not cap* magnetomotive force

mmfd *abbr* micromicrofarad

mmm *abbr* micromillimeter

MN *abbr* **1** magnetic north **2** merchant navy

Mn *symbol* manganese

mnem- *or* **mnemo-** *comb form* [*mnem-*, NL, fr. Gk *mnēm-*, fr. *mnēmē;* *mnemo-* prob. fr. F *mnémo-*, fr. Gk *mnēmo-*, fr. Gk *mnēmē*] **:** memory ⟨*mnemo*genic⟩ ⟨*mnemo*technical⟩

mne·me \ˈnē(,)mē\ *n* -S [NL, fr Gk *mnēmē* memory; akin to Gk *mnasthai* to remember — more at MIND] **:** the persistent or recurrent effect of past experience of the individual or of the race — **mne·mic** \-_mik\ *adj*

1**mne·mon·ic** \nē'mänik, nə'-, ne'-\ *also* **mne·mon·i·cal** \-änəkəl\ *adj* [Gk *mnēmonikos*, fr. *mnēmon-*, *mnēmōn* mindful + *-ikos* -ic, -ical; akin to Gk *mnasthai* to remember] **1 :** assisting or intended to assist memory ⟨some ~ device like a string tied around the finger⟩ **:** of or relating to mnemonics **2 :** of or relating to memory ⟨~ skill⟩ — **mne·mon·i·cal·ly** \-änək(ə)lē\ *adv*

2**mnemonic** \"\ *n* -S **1 :** a mnemonic device ⟨made up a word from the initials of the successive steps for a ~⟩ **2 :** MNEMONICS

mne·mon·ics \-äniks\ *also* **mne·mon·ic** \-k\ *n pl but usu sing in constr* [*mnemonics* modif. (influenced by E *-ics*) of NL *mnemonica*, fr. Gk *mnēmonika*, fr. neut. pl. of *mnēmonikos* mnemonic; *mnemonic* sing. of *mnemonics*] **:** a technique of improving the efficiency of the memory

mne·mo·technical \¦nēmō+-\ *or* **mne·mo·technic** \"+-\ *adj* [*mnemotechnica* fr. *mnemotechnic* (prob. fr. F *mnémotechnique*, fr. *mnémotechnie* mnemonics — fr. *mnémo-* mnem- + *-technie* -techny — + *-ique* -ic) + *-al*] **:** MNEMONIC — **mne·mo·technically** \"+-\ *adv*

-mne·sia \(m)ˈnēzh(ē)ə\ *n comb form* -S [NL, fr. *amnesia*] **:** a (specified) type or condition of memory ⟨crypto*mnesia*⟩ ⟨pan*mnesia*⟩

mnes·tic \ˈnestik\ *adj* [ISV *mnest-* (fr. Gk *mnēstis* memory) + *-ic;* prob. formed as G *mnestisch;* akin to Gk *mnasthai* to remember] **:** of or relating to memory or mneme

mng *abbr* managing

mngr *abbr* **1** manager **2** monseigneur **3** monsignor

mni·a·ce·ae \nī'āsē,ē\ *n pl*, *cap* [NL, fr *Mnium*, type genus + *-aceae*] **:** a family of erect mosses (order Eubryales) that is sometimes treated as a subfamily of the Bryaceae but distinguished by the club-shaped paraphyses and the hexagonal cells of the upper leaf surfaces

mni·oid \ˈnī,ȯid\ *adj* [NL *Mnium* + E *-oid*] **:** resembling a moss of the genus *Mnium*

mnio·til·ti·dae \,nīə'tiltə,dē\ [NL, fr. *Mniotilta*, genus of warblers (fr. Gk *mnion* moss, seaweed + *tiltos* plucked, verbal of *tillein* to pluck) + *-idae*] *syn of* PARULIDAE

mni·um \ˈnīəm\ *n*, *cap* [NL, fr. Gk *mnion* moss, seaweed; akin to Gk *mnoos*, *mnous* soft down, *mateisai*, fem. pl., walking, stepping, MIr *men* meal, W *mathru* to trample, Skt carn*amna* tanner, Lith *miniava* close turf, *minti* to step] **:** a genus of mosses (family Mniaceae) resembling *Bryum* but larger and with usu. horizontal capsules

MNT *abbr* mononitrotoluene

mntn *abbr* maintenance

1**mo** \ˈmō\ *adj or adv or n* [ME — more at MORE] *chiefly dial* **:** MORE

2**mo** \"\ *n* -S [by shortening] *slang* **:** MOMENT

-mo \,mō\ *n suffix* -S [duodeci*mo*] — after numerals or their names to indicate the number of leaves made by folding a sheet of paper ⟨sixteen*mo*⟩ ⟨16*mo*⟩ ⟨eighteen*mo*⟩ ⟨18*mo*⟩

mo *abbr* month; monthly

MO *abbr* **1** mail order **2** manually operated **3** mass observation **4** medical officer **5** [NL] modus operandi **6** money order **7** mustered out

Mo *symbol* molybdenum

moa \ˈmōə\ *n* -S [Maori] **:** any of various extinct flightless ratite birds of New Zealand constituting the family Dinornithidae and including numerous forms that range in size from one (*Dinornis giganteus*) which is about 12 feet in height to one (*Anomolopteryx oweni*) which is about the size of a turkey

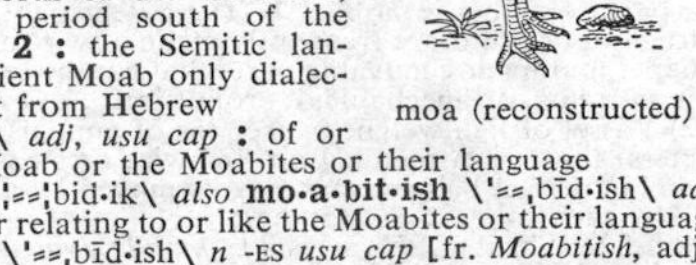
moa (reconstructed)

1**mo·ab·ite** \ˈmōə,bīt\ *n* -S *usu cap* [ME, fr LL *Moabita*, *Moabites*, fr. Gk *Mōabitēs*, fr. *Mōab* Moab, ancient kingdom in Syria + *-itēs* -ite] **1 :** a member of a people living in Old Testament times east of the Dead sea, north of the Edomites, and at one period south of the Ammonites **2 :** the Semitic language of ancient Moab only dialectally different from Hebrew

2**moabite** \"\ *adj*, *usu cap* **:** of or relating to Moab or the Moabites or their language

mo·a·bit·ic \¦==¦bid·ik\ *also* **mo·a·bit·ish** \ˈ==,bīd·ish\ *adj*, *usu cap* **:** of or relating to or like the Moabites or their language

mo·a·bit·ish \ˈ==,bīd·ish\ *n* -ES *usu cap* [fr. *Moabitish*, adj.] **:** MOABITE 2

1**moan** \ˈmōn\ *n* -S [ME *mone*, *man*, *mane*, *moon*, fr. (assumed) OE *mān* lamentation, moan; perh. akin to OE *mǣnan* to have in mind, purpose — more at MEAN] **1 :** LAMENTATION, COMPLAINT ⟨made a great ~ if he had to work —D.H.Lawrence⟩ **2 a :** a low prolonged sound indicative of pain or of grief **b :** any similar low mournful or murmuring sound **3** *obs* **:** a state of lamentation **:** SORROW, GRIEF

2**moan** \"\ *vb* -ED/-ING/-S *vt* **1 :** to bewail audibly **:** LAMENT, BEMOAN ⟨~*ed* that their absence accounted for the low state of learning —Joseph Dorfman⟩ **2 :** to utter wailingly or with lamentation ⟨~ and warble the latest cowboy songs —D.B. Davis⟩ ~ *vi* **1 :** LAMENT, COMPLAIN ⟨~*ing* over the inadequate proofs of the existence of God —W.L.Sullivan⟩ **2 a :** to make a low prolonged sound of grief or pain **:** groan softly **b :** to emit a sound like a moan ⟨the wind ~*ed* in the trees⟩

moan·ful \-fəl\ *adj* [1*moan* + *-ful*] **:** full of moaning **:** expressing sorrow or grief **:** PLAINTIVE, SAD ⟨a ~ song⟩ — **moan·ful·ly** \-fəlē\ *adv*

moan·ing·ly *adv* [fr. *moaning*, pres. part. of 2*moan* + *-ly*] **:** in a moaning manner **:** with a moan

mo·a·no \mō'ä(,)nō\ *or* **mo·a·na** \-_nə\ *n* -S [Hawaiian, Tahitian, Maori, & Samoan] **:** either of two important Hawaiian food fishes: **a :** a Pacific goatfish (*Pseudupeneus multifasciatus*) banded in light and dark red **b :** a closely related fish (*P. bifasciatus*)

mo·ar·i·an \(ˈ)mō¦a(a)rēən\ *adj*, *usu cap* [NL *Moaria*, a hypothetical continental area (fr. E *moa* + L *-aria*, fem. of *-arius* -ary) + E *-an*] **:** of, relating to, or constituting a hypothetical continental area now represented only by New Zealand and adjacent parts of Polynesia

1**moat** \ˈmōt, *usu* -ōd·+V\ *n* -S [ME *mot*, *mote*, prob. fr. MF *motte* hill, bank, mound, fr. OF *mote*] **1 :** a deep and wide trench around the rampart of a castle or other fortified place that is usu. filled with water — see CASTLE illustration **2 a :** an artificial channel resembling a moat (as for confinement of animals in a zoo or for landscaping) **b :** a natural feature resembling a moat (as at the margin of a receding glacier, around the inner cone of a volcano, or on the sea floor at the base of a seamount or beside a coral reef)

2**moat** \"\ *vt* -ED/-ING/-S [ME *moten*, fr. *mote*, n.] **:** to surround with or as if with a moat

mo·a·za·gotl cloud \mō'ätsə,gäd·ᵊl\ *n*, *usu cap M* [*moazagotl* fr. G dial. (Switzerland)] **:** one or more cloud banks formed on the lee side of a mountain under foehn conditions

¹mob \'mäb\ *n* -s **1** [origin unknown] *obs* **:** UNDRESS, DISHABILLE **2** [perh. modif. of obs. D *mop* woman's cap] **:** MOBCAP

²mob \"\ *vb* **mobbed; mobbed; mobbing; mobs** *vt* **1** [perh. back-formation fr. *moble*] *archaic* **:** to muffle the head of (as in a hood) **2** [¹*mob*] *archaic* **:** to dress (oneself) negligently ~ *vi, archaic* **:** to go to an unfashionable place disguised or so dressed as to avoid recognition

³mob \"\ *n* -s *often attrib* [short for ³*mobile*] **1 :** the lower classes of a community **:** the populace or the lower part of it **:** MASSES ⟨the use of superstition for the purpose of policing the ~ —Benjamin Farrington⟩ ⟨political spellbinding to appeal to the ~ mind⟩ **2 a :** a large and disorderly collection of people tending to acts of violence ⟨windows smashed and police beaten by the angry ~⟩ ⟨a fear of ~ rule⟩ **b** *obs* **:** people in a large disorderly group — used without an article ⟨the lane was full of ~ and the house so full we could not get in —Horace Walpole⟩ **3** *chiefly Austral* **:** a flock, drove, or herd of animals **4 a :** a criminal set or organization (as of pickpockets or gangsters) **:** GANG **b :** CLIQUE, SET **syn** see CROWD

⁴mob \"\ *vb* **mobbed; mobbed; mobbing; mobs** *vt* **1 a :** to crowd about and attack or annoy ⟨*mobbed* by autograph hunters before he could enter the theater⟩ **:** attack in a mob ⟨a crowd tried to ~ him and he ran for safety into the superintendent's office —H.S.Warner⟩ **b :** to crowd into or around ⟨bargain hunters that ~ the stores on sale days⟩ **2** *dial Eng* **:** to rail at **:** SCOLD, ABUSE **3 :** to hunt (as a fox) in such a way as to allow the quarry no chance to escape (as by surrounding it) ~ *vi* **:** to form a disorderly mob **:** crowd or riot in a mob ⟨the waiting newsmen *mobbed* forward —*Newsweek*⟩

mob *abbr* **1** mobile **2** mobilization; mobilized

MOB *abbr* money-order business

mob·ber \'mäbə(r)\ *n* -s [⁴*mob* + *-er*] **:** one that mobs

mob·bish \-bish\ *adj* [³*mob* + *-ish*] **:** characteristic of a mob **:** LAWLESS ⟨fanned mounting tension into ~ terrorizing —*Time*⟩ — **mob·bish·ly** *adv* — **mob·bish·ness** *n* -ES

mob·bism \-,bizəm\ *n* -s **:** mobbish conduct

mob·bist \-bəst\ *n* -s **:** one who advocates mobbism **:** MOBBER

mobcap \'=,=\ *n* [¹*mob* + *cap*; perh. intended as rendering of obs. D *mopmuts*, fr. *mop* woman's cap, mobcap + *muts* cap] **:** a woman's indoor cap; *esp* **:** a fancy cap made of sheer material with a high full crown and often tied under the chin

mo·bed *also* **mo·bad** \'mōbəd\ *n* -s [Per *maubad, mūbad, mūbid*] **:** a Parsi priest of the second rank

¹mo·bile \'mōbəl, -,bēl *also* -,bīl *or* -(,)bil *sometimes* mō-'bē(ə)l\ *adj* [MF, fr. L *mobilis*, fr. (assumed) L *movibilis*, fr. L *movēre* to move + *-ibilis* -ible — more at MOVE] **1 :** capable of moving or being moved from one place to another **:** MOVABLE: as **a :** capable of moving or being moved about readily ⟨globular proteins that are ~ and rod-shaped proteins that form solid structures⟩ ⟨the tongue . . . is clearly the most ~ articulator —G.A.Miller⟩; *specif* **:** characterized by an extreme degree of fluidity ⟨ether and mercury are ~ liquids⟩ — compare VISCOUS **b :** organized and equipped for ready movement (as by truck or air transport) ⟨~ fighting forces⟩ ⟨~ television units for on-the-spot reporting⟩ **c :** free for use or service anywhere **:** not restricted or committed ⟨~ dollars to be used where they can best advance the welfare of the whole institution —*Saturday Rev.*⟩ ⟨~ labor . . . could be sent anywhere in England —Henry Green⟩ **d :** designed as a vehicle or mounted on a vehicle or easily placed on or in a vehicle (as a trailer or truck) ⟨~ loudspeakers carrying the campaign speeches into the streets⟩ ⟨a ~ missile launcher⟩ ⟨~ homes⟩ **2 :** capable of or tending to change **:** CHANGEABLE: as **a :** changing readily in appearance and expression under the influence of mind or feeling ⟨his ~ face mirrors every feeling from bitter sadness to ecstasy —Eleanor Harris⟩ **b :** easily swayed in feeling, purpose, or direction ⟨a mind adventurously flexible but not frivolously ~ —Cecil Sprigge⟩ **c :** marked by ready adaptability ⟨industrial resources so ~ that they could be quickly switched from producing for export to producing for home demand⟩ **:** alert and flexible in the use of resources ⟨a ~ imagination⟩ ⟨an organization ~ enough to cope with any emergency⟩ **3 :** characterized by frequent or continuous movement ⟨the wind in ~ grasses⟩; *specif* **:** tending to travel or migrate from place to place ⟨we began as explorers, empire builders, pilgrims, and refugees, . . . and we are still today the most ~ people on the face of the earth —G.W.Pierson⟩ ⟨the Indians of the Great Plains were ~ bison hunters —Clark Wissler⟩ **4 a :** characterized by the mixing of social groups ⟨the general confusion in moral standards which characterizes ~ societies —E.R.Mowrer⟩ **:** affording opportunity for a shift in social status ⟨American society, though highly ~ . . . is not classless —*Times Lit. Supp.*⟩ **b :** having the opportunity for or undergoing a shift in status within the hierarchical social levels of a society ⟨a society in which women are more ~ than men⟩ ⟨born of upward ~ middle-class . . . parents —*Newsweek*⟩ **5 :** marked by the use of vehicles for transportation ⟨~ defense⟩ ⟨~ warfare⟩ ⟨took to their cars for a ~ holiday⟩ **6 :** of, relating to, or having the characteristics of a mobile

²mo·bile \'mō,bēl *sometimes* -,bīl *or* -,bil *or* mō'bē(ə)l; *in sense 3* mō'bē(ə)l *or* 'mō,bēl\ *n* -s [MF (*premier*) *mobile* primum mobile, part trans. of ML (*primum*) *mobile*, fr. neut. of L *mobilis*, adj.] **1 :** something that occasions movement or action — see PRIMUM MOBILE **2 a :** a movable or moving body or part **:** one that is mobile **b** (1) **:** a delicately balanced construction or sculpture frequently made of wire and sheet metal shapes and having movable parts that can be set in motion by air currents or mechanical propulsion — compare STABILE (2) **:** a set of lightweight figures (as of animals or story characters) that are suspended on fine wire or string so that they hang in perfect balance and may be moved by a current of air **3** [by shortening] **:** AUTOMOBILE

³mob·i·le \'mäbə(,)lē\ *n* -s [L *mobile* (*vulgus*) changeable crowd, the movable common people, neut. of *mobilis*, adj.] **:** ³MOB 1

⁴mo·bile \(')mō¦bē(ə)l\ *adj, usu cap* [fr. *Mobile*, Ala.] **:** of or from the city of Mobile, Ala. ⟨*Mobile* gardens⟩ **:** of the kind or style prevalent in Mobile

-mo·bile \mō,bēl, mə,- *sometimes* -,bil\ *n comb form* -s [*automobile*] **:** vehicle ⟨club*mobile*⟩ ⟨book*mobile*⟩ ⟨blood*mobile*⟩

mobile gate *n* **:** a starting gate affixed to the rear of an automobile and consisting of two metal arms that extend one to each side and fold and swing forward to facilitate a fair start of a harness race

mobile library *n* **:** BOOKMOBILE

mobile station *n* **:** a radio transmitting station on a ship, airplane, or other vehicle

mobile terrapin *n, usu cap M* [⁴*mobile*; fr. its locality] **:** an edible terrapin (*Pseudemys concinna mobilensis*) of the southern U.S. distinguished by a broad scarlet band on each side of the head

mobile unit *n* **:** an establishment on wheels (as an automobile or trailer) equipped for some special service (as a traveling library, an ambulance, an X-ray clinic, or television pickup)

mo·bil·ian \mō'bēlēən, -lyən\ *n* -s *cap* **1** [*Mobile*, Ala. + E *-ian*] **:** a native or resident of Mobile, Alabama **2 :** a pidgin language based on Choctaw and formerly a lingua franca in the southeastern U.S.

mo·bil·iary \mō'bilē,erē, -lyərē\ *adj* [F *mobiliaire*, fr. MF, fr. *mobile* movable property (fr. ML, fr. L *mobilia*, pl., fr. neut. pl. of *mobilis* movable, mobile) + MF *-aire* -ary] **1 :** of or relating to movable property **2 :** of or relating to household furniture

mo·bil·i·ty \mō'bilәd-ē, -ətē, -i\ *n* -ES [MF *mobilité*, fr. OF, fr. L *mobilitat-, mobilitas*, fr. *mobilis* mobile + *-itat-, -itas* -ity — more at MOBILE] **1 :** the quality or state of being mobile **:** the capacity or facility of movement **:** MOVABILITY ⟨the ~ of a liquid⟩ ⟨factors of birth, income, and education affecting social ~⟩ ⟨the high ~ of modern labor⟩ **2 :** the measure of the rate at which a solid is deformed under stress after the yield point has been exceeded **3 a :** the average speed at which either gaseous or electrolytic ions move under the influence of a unit potential gradient **b :** the average speed with which molecules in solution diffuse under the influence of a unit osmotic pressure gradient

mo·bi·liz·able \¦mōbə¦līzəbəl\ *adj* **:** capable of being mobilized

mo·bi·li·za·tion \,mōbələ'zāshən, -,lī'z-\ *n* -s [partly fr. ¹*mobile* + *-ization* and partly fr. F *mobilisation*, fr. *mobiliser* (v.) + *-ation*] **:** the act or process of mobilizing ⟨~ of wealth⟩ ⟨~ of glycogen⟩ ⟨prompt ~ of all national resources⟩

mo·bi·lize \'==,līz\ *vb* -ED/-ING/-S *see -ize in Explan Notes* [F *mobiliser*, fr. *mobile* (adj.) + *-iser* -ize] *vt* **1 :** to put into movement or circulation **:** make mobile ⟨mortgages may be *mobilized* like every other instrument of credit and . . . invade the bond market —J.A.Schumpeter⟩; *specif* **:** to release (something stored in the body) for body use ⟨the body ~*s* its antibodies⟩ **2 a :** to assemble (as an army corps or a fleet) and put in a state of readiness for active service in war ⟨~ all reserve forces for overseas duty⟩ ⟨~ industry for the defense effort⟩ **b :** to assemble (as resources) and make ready for use or action **:** ORGANIZE, MARSHAL, RALLY ⟨~ support for the proposal⟩ ⟨the sympathetic nervous system . . . ~*s* the bodily resources as a means of preparing for fight or flight —H.G. Armstrong⟩ **3 :** to separate (an organ or part) from associated structures so as to make more accessible for operative procedures ⟨~ the sigmoid colon⟩ **4 :** to develop to a state of acute activity ⟨ego feeling and ego attitude . . . ~ hostile feelings toward others —Abram Kardiner⟩ ~ *vi* **:** to undergo mobilization **:** assemble and organize for action ⟨in disasters . . . scouts have *mobilized* to give aid —*Boy Scout Handbook*⟩

mo·bi·liz·er \-zə(r)\ *n* -s **:** one that mobilizes persons or things

mo·bil·om·e·ter \,mōbə'lämәd-ə(r)\ *n* [*mobility* + *-o-* + *-meter*] **:** an apparatus for determining the consistency of plastic materials

mö·bi·us band \'mər|bēəs-, 'mə|, 'mā|, 'mē|\ *or* **möbius strip** *n, usu cap M* [after August F. *Möbius* †1868 Ger. mathematician] **:** a one-sided surface formed by holding one end of a rectangle fixed, rotating the opposite end through 180 degrees, and then applying it to the first end

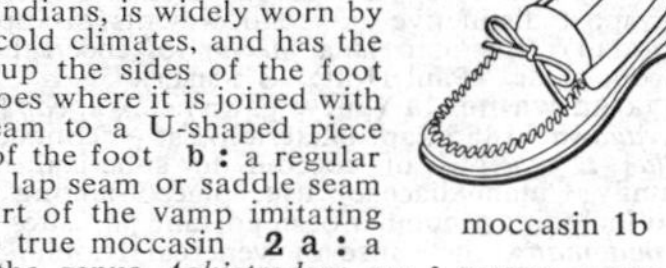

Möbius band

mo·ble \'mäbəl\ *vt* -ED/-ING/-S [prob. alter. of ¹*muffle*] *archaic* **:** to wrap or muffle the head of (as in a hood)

mob·oc·ra·cy \mä'bäkrəsē\ *n* -ES [³*mob* + *-o-* + *-cracy*] **1 :** the rule of the mob **2 :** the mob as a ruling class **:** a ruling or governing mob **3 :** rule by mobsters or gangsters

mob·o·crat \'mäbə,krat\ *n* -s [fr. *mobocracy*, after such pairs as E *democracy: democrat*] **1 :** one who favors mobocracy **2 :** mob leader — **mob·o·crat·ic** \¦==¦krad·ik\ *adj*

mobs *pl of* MOB, *pres 3d sing of* MOB

mobs·man \'mäbzmən\ *n, pl* **mobsmen** [*mobs* (gen. of ³*mob*) + *man*] **1 :** a member of a mob **2** *Brit* **:** SWELL-MOBSMAN

mob·ster \'mäbztə(r), -bst-\ *n* -s [³*mob* + *-ster*] **:** a member of a criminal gang

mob·u·la \'mäbyələ\ *n, cap* [NL] **:** a genus of large rays that contains imperfectly known fishes of warm seas and is the type of the family Mobulidae

mo·bu·li·dae \mə'byülə,dē\ *n pl, cap* [NL, fr. *Mobula*, type genus + *-idae*] **:** a family of rays that includes the genera *Mobula* and *Manta* — see DEVILFISH

moc \'mäk\ *n* -s [by shortening] **:** MOCCASIN 1

moc·ca·sin *also* **moc·as·sin** \'mäkəsən\ *n* -s [of Algonquian origin; akin to Natick *mokkussin* shoe, Narraganset *mocussin*, Ojibwa *makisin*] **1 a :** a heelless shoe or boot of soft leather that is the distinctive footwear of American Indians, is widely worn by aborigines of cold climates, and has the sole brought up the sides of the foot and over the toes where it is joined with a puckered seam to a U-shaped piece lying on top of the foot **b :** a regular shoe having a lap seam or saddle seam on the forepart of the vamp imitating the seam of a true moccasin **2 a :** a pit viper of the genus *Agkistrodon*; *esp* **:** WATER MOCCASIN **b :** any snake resembling or thought to resemble a moccasin (as a water snake of the genus *Natrix*) **3 :** ARGUS BROWN

moccasin 1b

moccasin flower *n* **:** any of several lady's slippers of the genus *Cypripedium*; *esp* **:** a once common woodland orchid (*C. acaule*) of eastern No. America that has usu. solitary pink or white moccasin-shaped flowers — called also *nerveroot*

moccasin telegraph *n* **:** GRAPEVINE 2b

moch \'mäk, 'mōk\ *n* -s [alter. of ¹*moth*] *Scot* **:** MOTH

mo·cha \'mōkə\ *n* -s [fr. *Mocha*, Arabia, seaport near which the coffee was orig. grown and from which it was orig. exported] **1 a** *or* **mocha coffee** (1) **:** arabica coffee that is grown in Arabia, is characterized by small irregular green or yellowish beans, and produces a superior beverage (2) **:** a coffee of superior quality **b :** a flavoring made of a strong coffee infusion or of a mixture of cocoa or chocolate with coffee **2 :** a soft pliable glove leather made by frizzing off the grain and then suede finishing the grain side of sheepskins from Africa **3** *often cap* **:** ³BARK 3

mocha bisque *n* **:** a light to moderate brown that is slightly redder than suede and very slightly yellower than tanbark

mocha stone *n, usu cap M* [prob. fr. *Mocha*, Arabia] **:** MOSS AGATE

mocha ware *also* **mocha** *n, usu cap M* **:** a coarse English earthenware with colored bands and brush patterns (as of seaweed, earthworms, and tree silhouettes) and made esp. in Staffordshire from the late 18th to the early 20th century

mo·chi·ca \mō'chēkə\ *adj, usu cap* [after *Mochica*, a pre-Inca people of high cultural achievement living on the northern coast of Peru (of AmerInd origin)] **:** of or relating to a culture period in the valleys of the northern Peruvian coast A.D. 600–700 characterized by fine red and white modeled pottery for grave offerings and ceremonial use predominantly in the form of a container with a stirrup spout

mo·chi·la \mō'chēlə\ *also* **mo·chil·la** \-chilə\ *n* -s [Sp *mochila*, prob. fr. *mochil* errand boy, fr. Basque *mutil, motil* youth, servant, fr. L *mutilus* maimed, mutilated — more at MUTILATE] **1 :** KNAPSACK, HAVERSACK; *specif* **:** a saddle pouch **2 :** a square leather saddle covering having openings for the horn and cantle and sometimes equipped with saddlebags ⟨many riders and even more ponies carried the mail, but only the ~ made the entire trip —J.T.Adams⟩

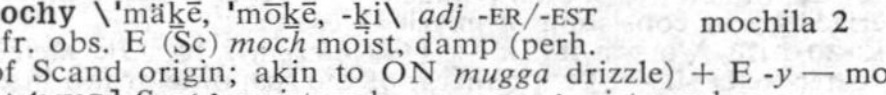

mochila 2

mochy \'mäkē, 'mōkē, -ki\ *adj* -ER/-EST [fr. obs. E (Sc) *moch* moist, damp (perh. of Scand origin; akin to ON *mugga* drizzle) + E *-y* — more at ⁴MUG] *Scot* **:** moist and warm; *esp* **:** misty and muggy

¹mock \'mäk, 'mȯk\ *vb* -ED/-ING/-S [ME *mocken, mokken*, fr. MF *mocquer*, fr. OF *moquier*] *vt* **1 :** to treat with scorn or contempt or ridicule **:** DERIDE ⟨~*ed* him for showing fear⟩ ⟨insolently ~*ing* the poor⟩ **2 :** to disappoint the hopes of **:** DECEIVE, DELUDE ⟨for any government to ~ men's hopes with mere words and promises and gestures —D.D.Eisenhower⟩ **3 :** DEFY, DISREGARD ⟨it's ~*ing* Heaven to run away and want to earn your own living —Israel Zangwill⟩ **4 a :** IMITATE, MIMIC ⟨a mockingbird was ~*ing* a cardinal —Nelson Hayes⟩ **b :** to mimic in sport or derision **:** ridicule by mimicry ⟨followed the old man along the street ~*ing* his gait⟩ **5** *obs* **:** PRETEND, FEIGN, SIMULATE ⟨~*ing* marriage with a dame of France —Shak.⟩ **6 :** to make a sham of ⟨the presence of the Red Army ~*ed* the concessions and vitiated the propaganda —*New Republic*⟩ ~ *vi* **:** to treat a person or thing with scorn, contempt, or ridicule — often used with *at* ⟨was ~*ed* at by the others⟩ **syn** see COPY, RIDICULE

²mock \"\ *n* -s [ME *mokk*, fr. *mokken*, v.] **1 :** an act of ridicule or derision **:** SNEER, GIBE ⟨make a ~ of him⟩ **2 :** one that is an object of or is deserving of ridicule, derision, or scorn **3 :** MOCKERY, RIDICULE ⟨take to heart what was said in ~⟩ **4 a :** an act of imitation **b :** something made as an imitation

³mock \"\ *adj* **:** of the character of an imitation, parody, or semblance **:** SIMULATED ⟨houses in a variety of styles from ~ Moorish to ~ Tudor —Peter Ustinov⟩ ⟨~ seam⟩ ⟨~ marriage⟩ ⟨~ oyster⟩ ⟨~ epic⟩ **:** SHAM ⟨a custom of appointing a . . . ~ king to represent the real king for a time —J.G.Frazer⟩ **:** FALSE, PSEUDO, QUASI ⟨the curious ~ daylight which even a light fall of snow gives to a morning —Mary Webb⟩ **:** FEIGNED **:** MIMICKED ⟨the ~ solemnity of the parody⟩

⁴mock \"\ *adv* **:** in an insincere or counterfeit manner — usu. used in combination ⟨a gabbing, ambitious, *mock*-tough, pretentious young man —Dylan Thomas⟩ ⟨a fawn trench coat *mock*-modestly covering a neat green uniform —Sean O'Casey⟩

⁵mock \"\ *n* -s [origin unknown] **1** *dial Eng* **:** the stump and root of a tree **2** *dial Eng* **:** a large block or stick; *specif* **:** a piece of wood usu. burned at Christmas

mock·able \-kəbəl\ *adj* **:** that can be mocked

mock·a·do \mə'kä(,)dō\ *n* -ES [modif. of obs. It *mocaiardo, mocaiarro* fabric of camel's or goat's hair, mohair — more at MOHAIR] **1 :** a fabric made chiefly in the 16th and 17th centuries usu. of wool and in imitation of velvet **2** *obs* **:** inferior stuff **:** TRUMPERY

mock·age \'mäkij, 'mȯk-, -kēj\ *n* -s [ME, fr. *mocken* (v.) + *-age*] **:** MOCKERY

mock apple *n* **:** WILD CUCUMBER c

mockbird \'=,=\ *n* **1** *dial* **:** a bird that mocks; *esp* **:** MOCKINGBIRD **2 a :** SEDGE WARBLER **b :** BLACKCAP

mock bishop's-weed *or* **mock bishop-weed** *n* **:** a plant of the genus *Ptilimnium*; *esp* **:** a slender American marsh herb (*P. capillaceum*)

mock brawn *n* **:** HEADCHEESE

mock chicken *n* **:** meat other than chicken (as veal) cooked or shaped to resemble chicken

mock cucumber *n* **:** WILD CUCUMBER c

mock cypress *n* **:** SUMMER CYPRESS

mock-dominance \(')=¦===\ *n* **:** PSEUDODOMINANCE

mock duck *n* **:** a shoulder of lamb shaped to resemble a duck with the boned foreshank forming the head and neck and the remainder after removal of the blade bones forming the body

mocked *past of* MOCK

mock·er \'mäkə(r), 'mȯk-\ *n* -s **:** one that mocks; *specif* **:** MOCKINGBIRD

mockernut \'==,=\ *also* **mockernut hickory** *n* **:** a smooth-barked No. American hickory (*Carya tomentosa*) with fragrant 7- to 9-foliolate leaves — called also *black hickory* **2 :** the nut of the mockernut tree

mock·ery \'mäk(ə)rē, 'mȯk-, -ri\ *n* -ES [ME *moquerie*, fr. MF, fr. OF, fr. *moquier* to mock] **1 :** insulting or contemptuous action or speech **:** DERISION **2 :** a subject of laughter, derision, or sport **3 a :** a counterfeit appearance **:** IMITATION **b :** an insincere, contemptible, or impertinent imitation ⟨arbitrary methods that made a ~ of justice⟩ **4 :** something ridiculously or impudently unsuitable

¹mock–heroic \¦==¦==\ *adj* **1 :** ridiculing or burlesquing the heroic style, character, or action ⟨a *mock-heroic* poem⟩ **2 :** extravagantly imitating the grand or heroic manner — **mock–heroically** \¦==¦==(=)=\ *adv*

²mock–heroic *n* [*mock-heroic*] **:** a mock-heroic composition

mocking *pres part of* MOCK

mockingbird \'==,=\ *n* **:** a common bird (*Mimus polyglottos*) of the southern U.S. that is remarkable for its exact imitations of the notes of other birds, has the back gray, the underparts grayish white, and the tail and wings blackish marked with white, and is represented by subspecies in Mexico, Central America, and the West Indies

mock·ing·ly *adv* **:** in a mocking manner ⟨smiled ~ at his unaccustomed helplessness⟩

mocking thrush *n* **:** a bird of the family Mimidae; *esp* **:** THRASHER

mocking wren *n* **:** an American wren of the genus *Thryothorus* or of *Thryomanes* — compare CAROLINA WREN

mock knee *n* **:** a large pedunculate fibrous tumor in front of the knee esp. in cattle

mock locust *n* **:** a fetid false indigo (*Amorpha californica*) with dark purple racemose flowers

mock moon *n* **:** PARASELENE

mock olive *n* **:** AXBREAKER 1

mock orange *n* **1 :** a shrub of the genus *Philadelphus* — called also *syringa* **2 :** any of several American shrubs or trees: as **a :** CHERRY LAUREL **b :** OSAGE ORANGE **c :** SOUTHERN BUCKTHORN **3 :** a gourd resembling an orange **4 :** WILD CUCUMBER c **5** *Austral* **:** NATIVE LAUREL 1

mock ore *n* **:** SPHALERITE

mock pennyroyal *n* **:** HEDEOMA 2

mock regent bird *n* [³*mock* + *regent bird*] **:** FLYING COACHMAN

mocks *pres 3d sing of* MOCK, *pl of* MOCK

mock–strawberry \'=;=. . .\ *n* **:** a plant of the genus *Duchesnea*; *esp* **:** INDIAN STRAWBERRY

mock sun *n* **:** PARHELION

mock thrush *n* **:** MOCKING THRUSH

mock turtle soup *n* **:** a soup made of calf's head, veal, or other meat and condiments in imitation of green turtle soup

mock–up \'=,=\ *n* -s [¹*mock* (imitate) + *up*] **:** a structural model built accurately to scale (as out of plywood, cardboard, canvas, clay) chiefly for study, testing, or display ⟨a *mock-up* of an airplane⟩

mock up *vt* [*mock-up*] **:** to make a mock-up of

mock willow *n* **:** MEADOWSWEET 1

mocky *also* **mock·ie** \'mäkē, -ki\ *n, pl* **mockies** [prob. fr. Yiddish *makeh* sore, pest, plague, fr. Heb *makāh* blow, wound, plague] **:** JEW — usu. used disparagingly

mo·co \mə'kō\ *n* -s [Pg *mocó*, fr. Tupi] **:** a large semiamphibious So. American histricomorph rodent (*Kerodon rupestris*) closely related to the cavies

mo·coa \mə'kōə\ *n* -s *usu cap* [Sp, of AmerInd origin] **:** COCHE

mo·cock \mə'käk\ *also* **mo·cuck** \-kək\ *n* -s [of Algonquian origin; akin to Ojibwa *makak* box] **:** a box or basket (as of birch bark) for keeping food

mocock

mo·co·ri·to \,mōkə'rēd·(,)ō\ *n, pl* **mocorito** *or* **mocoritos** *usu cap* [prob. fr. MexSp, of AmerInd origin] **1 :** a Taracahitian people of Sinaloa, Mexico **2 :** a member of the Mocorito people

moco·ví \mōkə¦vē, ¦mäk-\ *n* -s *usu cap* [AmerSp *mocoví, mocobí*, of AmerInd origin] **1 a :** a Guaicuruan people of Mato Grosso, Brazil **b :** a member of such people **2 :** the language of the Mocoví people

mocs *pl of* MOC

mod \'mōd\ *n* -s *usu cap* [ScGael *mōd*, fr. ON *mōt* meeting; akin to OE *mōt* meeting, assembly — more at MEET] **:** a meeting or gathering for the study and performance of Gaelic arts — compare EISTEDDFOD, FEIS

mod *abbr* **1** model **2** moderate **3** moderato **4** moderator **5** modern **6** modification; modified; modify **7** modulator

MOD *abbr* **1** mail-order department **2** money-order department

mod·acrylic fiber \¦mäd+. . .-\ *n* [*modified acrylic* (n.)] **:** any of various synthetic textile fibers that are long-chain polymers composed of 35 to 85 percent by weight of acrylonitrile units

¹mod·al \'mōdᵊl\ *adj* [ML *modalis*, fr. L *modus* measure, manner + *-alis* -al — more at METE] **1 :** of or relating to mode or modality in logic **2 :** containing provisions as to the mode of procedure or the manner of taking effect — used of a contract or legacy **3 :** of or relating to a musical mode; *specif* **:** written in one of the ecclesiastical modes ⟨uses diatonic harmonies with a ~ flavor —Humphrey Searle⟩ **4 :** of or relating to form as opposed to substance **:** having form without reality **5 a :** of, relating to, or constituting a grammatical form or category characteristically indicating predication of an action or state in some manner other than as a simple fact **b :** of, relating to, or constituting a grammatical case that denotes manner **6 :** of or relating to a statistical mode **:** most common **:** TYPICAL ⟨the anthropologist's ~ concept of culture pattern which is based upon observations of what most people seem to be doing —Jacob Fried⟩ ⟨has produced his first novel at the age of sixty . . . approximately thirty years after the ~ American novelist reaches his peak —J.K.Galbraith⟩ **7 :** of or relating to modalism — **mod·al·ly** \-ᵊlē, -li\ *adv*

²modal \"\ *n* -s **1 :** a modal proposition or statement in logic **2 :** a grammatical form belonging to a class of words or inflectional affixes with a modal function; *specif* **:** a modal auxiliary in English grammar

modal auxiliary *n* **:** a verb or a grammatical form resembling a verb that is characteristically used with a verb of predication and expresses a modal modification (as *can, shall, will, must, might, ought, could, should, would, may, need, dare*) and that in English differs formally from other verbs in lacking *-s, -ing,* and past-tense forms and shares with other auxiliaries the affixing of negative *-n't*

mod·al·ism \-ᵊl,izəm\ *n* -s [¹*modal* + *-ism*] **:** the theological doctrine that the members of the Trinity are not three distinct persons but rather three modes or forms of activity (the Father, Son, and Holy Spirit) under which God manifests himself

mod·al·ist \-ᵊləst\ *n* -s [¹*modal* + *-ist*] **:** an adherent of modalism — **mod·al·is·tic** \ˌmōdᵊlˈistik\ *adj*

modalistic monarchian *n, usu cap both Ms* **:** an adherent of Modalistic Monarchianism

modalistic monarchianism *n, usu cap both Ms* **:** Monarchianism holding that Jesus Christ was not a distinct person of the Trinity but was rather one of three successive modes or manifestations of God

mo·dal·i·ty \mōˈdaləd·ē, -ətē, -i\ *n* -ES [F *modalité,* fr. MF, fr. *modal* (fr. ML *modalis*) + *-ité* -ity] **1 a :** the quality or state of being modal ⟨the ~ of his music⟩ ⟨~ of a circle⟩ **b :** a modal quality, attribute, or circumstance **:** FORM, PATTERN ⟨as the varying subject matter requires, the narrative and style take on the *modalities* of comedy, romance, tragedy, or tragicomedy —J.W.Beach⟩ **2 :** that qualification of logical propositions according to which they are distinguished as asserting or denying the possibility, impossibility, contingency, or necessity of their content — see CATEGORY 1b **3 :** one of the main avenues of sensation (as vision or audition) **4 a :** any of several agencies used in physical therapy (as diathermy, high-frequency currents, or massage) **b :** an apparatus for applying such agencies **5 :** a tendency to conform to a pattern or type ⟨the greater ~ of the male in this regard is indicated by a smaller representation of males than females in the category "Miscellaneous" —Eleanor Smith & J.H. Greenberg Monane⟩

modal value *n* **:** MODE 8

¹**mode** \ˈmōd\ *n* -s [ME *moede,* fr. L *modus* measure, manner,

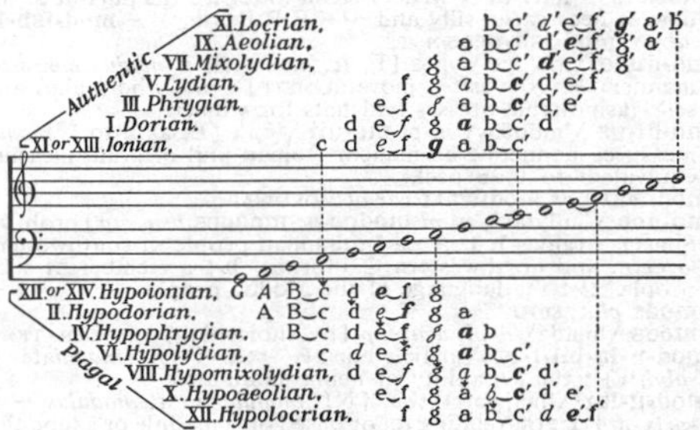

mode 1a : ecclesiastical modes

musical mode — more at METE] **1 a :** a musical arrangement of the eight diatonic notes or tones of an octave according to one of various fixed schemes of their intervals — see ECCLESIASTICAL MODE, GREEK MODE **b :** a rhythmical scheme; *specif* **:** one of the six metrical patterns in 13th and 14th century music corresponding to the feet (as trochee or dactyl) in classical poetry and expressed in triple time **2 :** ²MOOD 2b ⟨the indicative ~ of flat assertion alone —Weston La Barre⟩ **3** [LL *modus,* fr. L, measure, manner] **a :** ²MOOD 1a **b :** the manner in which a logical proposition is asserted or denied esp. as being possible, impossible, necessary, or contingent **4 a :** a particular form or variety of something ⟨a large and overpowering set of brothers and sisters, who were ~s or replicas of the same type —Henry Adams⟩ ⟨her anguish of the night before was in another ~ —Josephine Pinckney⟩ ⟨separating movement on foot from other ~s of traffic —Lewis Mumford⟩ **b :** a form, pattern, or manner of expression **:** STYLE ⟨the only English poet who has adapted it to his needs as a regular poetic ~ —W.H.Gardner⟩ ⟨his romanticism (his first literary ~) —Austin Warren⟩ ⟨perhaps the major expressive ~ of his day, the ~ of the liberal Emersonian sermon —R.P.Blackmur⟩ **5 :** a manner of doing something or of performing a particular function or activity ⟨as the one or the other ~ of ratification may be proposed by the Congress —*U.S. Constitution*⟩ ⟨new ~s of experimentation had to be developed —J.B.Conant⟩ ⟨the Renaissance ~ of thinking in symbols —Michael Kitson⟩ **6 :** a condition or state of being **:** a manifestation, form, or manner of arrangement; *specif* **:** a particular form or manifestation of some underlying substance, or of some permanent aspect or attribute of such a substance — compare MIXED MODE, SIMPLE MODE **7 :** a state or manner of living **:** CUSTOM ⟨a homogeneous population that departs reluctantly from long-accepted institutions and ~s —*Amer. Guide Series: Pa.*⟩ ⟨bound up with regional ~s of feeling and local traditions —Van Wyck Brooks⟩ ⟨a sedentary agricultural-hunting ~ of life —R.W. Murray⟩ **8 :** the value of the variable in a statistical distribution for which the frequency is a maximum **:** the value that occurs most frequently **:** the most common value ⟨whenever the talk is of Americans the image is always one of the ~ or average person —*Saturday Rev.*⟩ **9 :** any of various stationary-vibration patterns of which an elastic body or an oscillatory system is capable ⟨the vibration ~s and frequencies of the airplane were computed —Wilhemina Kroll⟩; *specif* **:** the vibration pattern of electromagnetic waves (as in lines or wave guides) ⟨in the field of radar theory the various ~s in which waves are propagated are designated by different symbols —*Television & Radar Encyc.*⟩ **10 :** the actual mineral composition of a rock as distinguished from the norm **11** *crystallog* **:** the type of lattice (as primitive or body-centered) ⟨lattice-*mode*⟩ **syn** see METHOD, STATE

²**mode** \"\ *n* -s [F, fr. L *modus* measure, manner — more at METE] **1 :** a prevailing fashion or style of dress or behavior ⟨harbored the cultural backwash of Europe and looked to its stale romanticism as the ~ —H.F.Mooney⟩ ⟨sleeping on top of television sets is the ~ of the day for cats —*New Yorker*⟩ ⟨the contemporary ~⟩ ⟨the newest ~ in dresses⟩ ⟨all the ~⟩ **2 :** ALAMODE **syn** see FASHION

mode beige *n* [²*mode*] **:** DRAB 2a

mo·dec·ca flower \mōˈdekə-\ *n* [*modecca* fr. NL *Modecca* (syn. of *Adenia,* genus name of the killer plant *Adenia sinensis*)] **:** KILLER PLANT

¹**mod·el** \ˈmädᵊl\ *n* -s [MF *modelle,* fr. OIt *modello,* fr. (assumed) VL *modellus,* fr. L *modulus* small measure, fr. *modus* measure, manner + *-ulus*] **1** *obs* **:** a set of plans for a building to be erected or of drawings to scale for a structure already built; *also* **:** a ground plan esp. of a garden ⟨we first survey the plot, then draw the ~ —Shak.⟩ **2** *dial Brit* **:** a person or thing that exactly resembles another **:** COPY, IMAGE ⟨had my father's signet in my purse, which was the ~ of that Danish seal —Shak.⟩ **3** *obs* **:** something that encases or wraps around **:** MOLD ⟨~ to thy inward greatness, like little body with a mighty heart —Shak.⟩ **4 :** structural design **:** PATTERN ⟨built his home on the ~ of an old farmhouse⟩ ⟨began his teaching by organizing a seminar on the German ~ —J.S. Bassett⟩ ⟨providing for the founding of New Jersey towns on the New England ~ —*Amer. Guide Series: N.J.*⟩ **5** *archaic* **:** an abstract or summary of a written work **:** EPITOME **6 a :** a usu. miniature three-dimensional representation of something existing in nature or constructed or to be constructed ⟨a mile-long concrete ~ of the Mississippi valley —*Time*⟩ ⟨a 15-foot ~ of a full-rigged ship —*Amer. Guide Series: Md.*⟩ ⟨miniature, like some exquisite ~ seen through a glass case —Osbert Sitwell⟩ **b :** a representation in relief or three dimensions in plaster, papier-mâché, wood, plastic, or other material of a surface or solid **7 :** something made in a usu. pliable material (as clay or wax) and intended to serve as a pattern of an object or figure to be made in a more permanent material ⟨made many ~s of the coin before he was satisfied with one⟩ **8 :** a person or thing regarded as worthy of imitation **:** something perfect of its kind ⟨brevity that renders both writers such valuable ~s to an age whose worst literary fault is diffuseness —Richard Garnett †1906⟩ ⟨still remains a ~ of scientific argument —B.W.Bacon⟩ ⟨his written addresses are ~s of clearness, logical order, and style —A.B. Noble⟩ **9 :** a person or thing that serves as a pattern or source of inspiration for an artist or writer ⟨his father was the ~ for one of the most famous characters in literature⟩; *esp* **:** one who poses for an artist ⟨his wife served as the ~ for many of his early paintings⟩ **10 :** ARCHETYPE **11 :** an organism whose appearance a mimic imitates — compare MIMICRY **12 :** one who is employed to display clothes or to appear in displays of other merchandise (as in a fashion show, in a photograph, or on television) ⟨left school to go to work as a dress ~ in the garment district —*Current Biog.*⟩ ⟨he has appeared as a ~ in advertisements for cigars⟩ **13 a** (1) **:** a specific type or design of clothing ⟨favors the Alaskan-trapper ~ with a high guard at the toe —R.L.Neuberger⟩ (2) **:** an article of clothing (as a dress with a distinctive design) ⟨girls, self-conscious in their Paris ~s —Paul Bowles⟩ **b :** a specific type or design of car ⟨offers eight new ~s for next year, including a completely restyled convertible⟩ **c :** a modification or variation of a general type or mark of military equipment **14 a :** a description, a collection of statistical data, or an analogy used to help visualize often in a simplified way something that cannot be directly observed (as an atom) **b :** a theoretical projection in detail of a possible system of human relationships (as in economics, politics, or psychology) **:** BLUEPRINT ⟨his ~ of an election procedure based on permanent personal registration reveals some of the problems to be solved⟩ ⟨constructed the first of the world ~s of the present century —S.F.Mason⟩

syn EXAMPLE, PATTERN, EXEMPLAR, PARADIGM, IDEAL, BEAU IDEAL, STANDARD, MIRROR: MODEL applies to something set up or held out as worthy of imitation, sometimes preeminently so ⟨a workmen's compensation law which is still considered a *model* piece of legislation —*Current Biog.*⟩ ⟨*models* for the development of his own habitual responses to various situations —Ralph Linton⟩ ⟨the very *model* of a modern major general —W.S.Gilbert⟩ EXAMPLE applies chiefly to a person to be imitated or, in some contexts, emphatically not to be imitated since his case serves not as an inducement but as a warning ⟨one of the immortal *examples* of a true man in a world of bounders, cowards, and squeaking specters —W.L. Sullivan⟩ ⟨presents an *example* in modern department store designing —*Retailing Daily*⟩ ⟨making the mutineers *examples* for the rest of the crew⟩ PATTERN may suggest a clear or detailed archetype or prototype ⟨many hymns that set the *pattern* for the stately hymnology of the American Protestant Church —*Amer. Guide Series: N.J.*⟩ ⟨the ancient *pattern* of life had been woven continuously for so many centuries that even illiterate farmers knew how to be courtly and dignified at family celebrations or at the great yearly festivals —John Blofeld⟩ EXEMPLAR indicates either a faultless example to be emulated or a perfect typification ⟨Christianity was primarily an ethical system; Christ was its great teacher and *exemplar;* and to be a Christian meant to conduct one's life in accordance with the principles which governed Him —A.C. McGiffert⟩ ⟨the living *exemplar* of tragedy as the human lot —V.S.Pritchett⟩ PARADIGM, now rare in this sense, may suggest an exemplar of a perfection impossible or unusual in reality ⟨a love worthy of being a *paradigm* of the cosmic relation of universal matter and universal form, this all-comprising power, cannot be a vague feeling —F.P.Bargebuhr⟩ IDEAL indicates the best possible exemplification either in reality or in a mental conception ⟨he had the courage and rebelliousness of his . . . cousins too much on his mind; they were his *ideal* —Glenway Wescott⟩ ⟨a multitude of stories and traditions grew up around his name, to be interpreted according to the hearers' own *ideals* of personality and education —D.E.Smith⟩ BEAU IDEAL sometimes is taken to mean "beautiful ideal" ⟨the very *beau ideal* of a perfect government is the government of a majority, acting through a representative body —J.C.Calhoun⟩ STANDARD may indicate that which embodies criteria for excellence and sets a high example for emulation ⟨the ideal of general cultivation has been one of the *standards* in education —C.W.Eliot⟩ ⟨human life on earth cannot continue unless we ordinary men and women can manage to practice these virtues up to a far higher *standard* —A.J.Toynbee⟩ MIRROR was once often used to mean a model of perfection ⟨bounteous Buckingham, the *mirror* of all courtesy —Shak.⟩

²**model** \"\ *vb* **modeled** *or* **modelled; modeled** *or* **modelled; modeling** *or* **modelling** \-d(ᵊ)liŋ\ **models** *vt* **1 :** to plan or form after a pattern **:** FRAME, SHAPE ⟨~*ed* a double-decked steamboat —Waldemar Kaempffert⟩ **2** *archaic* **:** to make into an organization (as an army, government, or parish) **3 a :** to shape or fashion in a pliable material (as clay, wax, or dampened leather) ⟨a file of plasticene animals ~*ed* by the little girls —Elizabeth Bowen⟩ **b :** to give a three-dimensional appearance to in painting or drawing esp. by means of chiaroscuro ⟨~*s* the head so that it seems to stand out from the canvas⟩ **c :** to emphasize the three-dimensional qualities of (a photographic subject) by means of highlights and shadows ⟨a ~*ing* light for portraiture⟩ ⟨use shadows to lend interest to the scene, to ~ it, give it emphasis —Aaron Sussman⟩ **4 :** to construct or fashion in imitation of a particular model ⟨~*ed* its constitution on that of the U.S.⟩ ⟨as for the speeches to Congress, they were palpably ~*ed* upon the speeches from the throne of the English kings —H.L.Mencken⟩ **5 :** to display by wearing, using, or posing with ⟨~*ed* her inaugural gowns at a fashion show —*N.Y.Times*⟩ ⟨famous for ~*ing* refrigerators and other appliances⟩ ~ *vi* **1 :** to design or imitate forms **:** make a pattern ⟨she enjoys ~*ing* in clay⟩ **2 :** to work or act as a model ⟨asked each contestant . . . to ~ before the judges' enclosure —Lillian Ross⟩

³**model** \"\ *adj* **:** serving as or capable of serving as a model ⟨a ~ house⟩ ⟨a ~ husband⟩ ⟨a ~ farm⟩

model basin *or* **model tank** *n* **:** a tank in which ship models are tested (as for inertia) by being towed at various speeds

mod·el·er *or* **mod·el·ler** \ˈmäd(ᵊ)lə(r)\ *n* -s **:** one that models: as **a :** a carver of leather shoe vamps and uppers **b :** one who molds in a plastic material designs to be copied for decorative tile or statuary

mod·el·ist \-dᵊləst\ *n* -s **:** a maker of models

mod·el·ize \-dᵊl,īz\ *vt, archaic* **:** to give a particular form to **:** SHAPE

model school *n* **:** a graded school usu. connected with a normal school or teachers' training college and used as a model in organization and methods of teaching

model t *adj, usu cap M&T* [fr. *Model T,* early type of motor car having only two speeds forward and a hand gasoline feed that was manufactured by the Ford Motor Co. between 1909 and 1927] **1 :** belonging to an initial or rudimentary phase of development ⟨when nuclear weapons were in the *Model T* stage of development —*N.Y.Times*⟩ **2 :** OLD-FASHIONED, OUTMODED ⟨a *Model T* plot⟩ ⟨a *Model T* school plant⟩

¹**mo·de·na** \ˈmōdᵊnə, -ᵊn,ä\ *adj, usu cap* [fr. *Modena,* city in northern Italy, capital of the province of Modena] **:** of or from the city of Modena, Italy **:** of the kind or style prevalent in Modena

²**modena** \"\ *n* [fr. *Modena,* province or its capital city in northern Italy] **1** *usu cap* **:** an Italian breed of small hen pigeons that have an erect carriage and varicolored plumage with the head and wings often of a color different from that of the body **2** -s *often cap* **:** any pigeon of the Modena breed

mod·e·nese \ˌmōdᵊnˈēz, -ēs\ *n, pl* **modenese** \"\ *cap* [It *modenese,* fr. *Modena,* Italy + It *-ese*] **:** a native or resident of Modena

mod·er·ant \ˈmädərənt\ *n* -s [²*moderate* + *-ant,* n. suffix] **:** something that moderates

mod·er·ant·ism \-n,tizəm\ *n* -s [F *modérantisme,* fr. *modérant* (pres. part. of *modérer* to moderate, fr. L *moderare*) + *-isme* -ism] **:** a policy of moderation esp. in politics

mod·er·ant·ist \-,təst\ *n* -s [F *modérantiste,* fr. *modérant* + *-iste* -ist] **:** an adherent of moderantism

¹**mod·er·ate** \ˈmäd(ə)rət, *usu* -əd·+V\ *adj* [ME, fr. L *moderatus,* past part. of *moderare, moderari* to moderate, fr. *modus* measure, manner — more at METE] **1 a :** characterized by an avoidance of extremes of behavior **:** observing reasonable limits **:** showing discretion and self-control ⟨a ~ drinker⟩ ⟨a ~ eater⟩ ⟨a person of ~ habits⟩ **b :** free from passion or excitement **:** CALM, REASONABLE ⟨though very much in favor of the measure, he expressed himself in ~ language⟩ ⟨his demands were very ~⟩ **2 a :** tending toward the mean or average: as (1) **:** neither small nor large ⟨a family of ~ income⟩ ⟨a room of ~ size⟩ ⟨a ~ crop⟩ (2) **:** neither short nor long ⟨a book of ~ length⟩ ⟨a ~ distance⟩ **b :** having an average or less than average quality **:** MEDIOCRE ⟨cheesecakes very ~ indeed —H.E. Bates⟩ ⟨wrote ~ poetry to the end of his life —Carl Van Doren⟩ **3 :** not violent or rigorous **:** TEMPERATE ⟨a ~ winter⟩ ⟨a ~ wind⟩ ⟨a ~ climate⟩ **4 :** of or relating to a political or social philosophy or program that avoids extreme measures and violent or partisan tactics ⟨has no interest in leading a party that goes off to extremes, that the party direction must be ~ and yet progressive and dynamic —*N.Y. Times*⟩ ⟨all left-wing and some ~ and right-wing groups had boycotted the election —*Collier's Yr. Bk.*⟩ **5 a :** limited in scope or effect ⟨made a ~ change in the bill which failed to satisfy its critics⟩ ⟨his new wealth had only a ~ effect on his way of life⟩ **b :** not severe in effect **:** not seriously or permanently disabling or incapacitating ⟨a few days of ~ illness accompanied by chilly sensations and loss of appetite —Morris Fishbein⟩ ⟨of the 18 cases in which whooping cough developed . . . 13.3 percent were very mild, 4.8 percent were mild and 3.7 percent were ~ —*Jour. Amer. Med. Assoc.*⟩ **6 :** not expensive **:** reasonable or low in price ⟨how to be well dressed at a ~ cost —*Current Biog.*⟩ ⟨a ~ price for a new house⟩ **7** *of a color* **:** of medium lightness and medium chroma

²**mod·er·ate** \ˈmädə,rāt, *usu* -ād·+V\ *vb* -ED/-ING/-S [ME *moderaten,* fr. L *moderatus,* past part. of *moderare, moderari* to moderate] *vt* **1 a :** to lessen the intensity or extremeness of **:** make less violent or excessive **:** keep within bounds **:** make moderate or temperate ⟨considerations of logic and analogy and history and tradition which ~ and temper the promptings of policy and justice —B.N.Cardozo⟩ ⟨*moderated* the harshness of their initial demands⟩ ⟨a quick and efficient job of snow removal *moderated* the effect of the storm⟩ **b :** to lower or soften the tone of (a voice) ⟨*moderated* his voice as they approached the sickroom⟩ ⟨~ your voice if you expect to be listened to⟩ **2** *archaic* **:** to exercise control over **:** REGULATE, RULE **3 :** to preside over or act as chairman at ⟨*moderated* the debate with perfect fairness⟩ ⟨*moderated* a small local variety show —Gladwin Hill⟩ **4 :** to reduce the speed or energy of (neutrons) ~ *vi* **1 :** to act as a moderator ⟨became famous when he *moderated* on a weekly panel show⟩ **2** *archaic* **:** to act as a mediator **3 :** to become less violent, severe, rigorous, or intense ⟨the wind has *moderated*⟩ ⟨loitering a little because the night had *moderated* —Kay Boyle⟩

syn QUALIFY, TEMPER, ATTEMPER: MODERATE indicates abating extremes or excesses in keeping within reasonable or due limits ⟨*moderating* his big voice to the dimensions of the room —Clifton Daniel⟩ ⟨if the new poets can bring themselves to *moderate* their attitude of somewhat sensitive resentment towards those who call their art in question —J.L.Lowes⟩ QUALIFY may indicate addition of restriction or precise definition to make a comment less sweeping, inclusive, or open to objection; it may be a close synonym for MODERATE ⟨the neat craftsman has means of *qualifying* or abating his own perilous air of arrant omniscience —C.E.Montague⟩ ⟨but this simple and bare outline of the procedure must be supplemented and *qualified* —Samuel Alexander⟩ ⟨*qualified* his reports in the *Boston News-Letter* according to the demands of the royal governor —F.L.Mott⟩ TEMPER may suggest an alleviating or mitigating of the severe or a modifying to accommodate to a situation ⟨always a cool breeze *tempered* the sunshine —A.B. Osborne⟩ ⟨close to being a major work in war fiction, and only my caution *tempers* my admiration —M.D.Geismar⟩ ⟨the catalogue of one Virginia seminary was promising to *temper* the severities of arithmetic to the delicacy of the female mind —*Amer. Guide Series: Va.*⟩ ATTEMPER is a close but now rarely used synonym for TEMPER in the sense of lessening ⟨the shadow . . . *attempered* the cheery western sunshine —Nathaniel Hawthorne⟩

³**mod·er·ate** \ˈmäd(ə)rət, *usu* -əd·+V\ *n* -s [¹*moderate;* intended as trans. of F *modéré*] **1 :** one who holds moderate views esp. in politics or religion ⟨the middle-of-the-road ~s in the world . . . who wanted both stability and liberalism —W.G. Carleton⟩ ⟨always a ~, he deprecated extremists of both sections —H.K.Beale⟩ **2** *often cap* **:** a member or adherent of a political party or group favoring a moderate program ⟨second term as the candidate of the *Moderates* —*Rev. of Reviews*⟩

moderate breeze *n* **:** wind having a speed of 13 to 18 miles per hour — see BEAUFORT SCALE table

moderate gale *n* **:** wind having a speed of 32 to 38 miles per hour — see BEAUFORT SCALE table

mod·er·ate·ly \ˈmädər(ə)tlē, -drət-, -li\ *adv* [ME *moderatly,* fr. *moderat, moderate* moderate + *-ly*] **:** in a moderate manner or to a moderate extent **:** FAIRLY, TEMPERATELY ⟨lived ~⟩ ⟨a ~ hot day⟩

mod·er·ate·ness *n* -ES **:** the quality or state of being moderate

moderate oven *n* **:** an oven heated to a temperature between 325° and 400° F

mod·er·a·tion \ˌmädəˈrāshən\ *n* -s [ME *moderacion,* fr. L *moderation-, moderatio,* fr. *moderatus* (past part. of *moderare, moderari* to moderate) + *-ion-, -io* -ion] **1 :** the quality or state of being moderate **:** an avoidance of extremes **:** TEMPERATENESS ⟨a man who knew no ~ in his requests and impulses —Thomas Hardy⟩ ⟨a ~ of speech and of outward attitude which gave conservative constituents a sense of security and radical constituents a gleam of hope —Jeannette P. Nichols⟩ **2 :** the action of moderating; *specif* **:** a lessening of severity or intensity ⟨international policy with respect to the control or ~ of depressions —A.H.Hansen⟩ **3 moderations** *pl* **:** the first public examination for the B.A. in classics or mathematics at Oxford university following responsions — called also *mods* — **in moderation** *adv* **:** without excess **:** TEMPERATELY

mod·er·a·tion·ist \-nəst\ *n* -s **:** an advocate of moderation

mod·er·at·ism \ˈmäd(ə)rəd·,izəm, -ə,tiz-\ *n* -s **:** moderation in doctrines or opinions; *specif* **:** the opinions or policy of a moderate party or group in politics or religion

mod·er·at·ist \-əd·əst, -ətəst\ *n* -s **:** an adherent of moderatism

mod·er·a·to \ˌmädəˈräd·(,)ō\ *adj (or adv)* [It (past part. of *moderare* to moderate), fr. L *moderatus,* past part. of *moderare, moderari* to moderate — more at MODERATE] **:** MODERATE — used as a direction in music to indicate tempo

mod·er·a·tor \ˈmädə,rād·ə(r), -rātə-\ *n* -s [ME *moderatour,* fr. L *moderator,* fr. *moderatus* (past part. of *moderare, moderari* to moderate) + *-or*] **1 :** one that rules or directs **:** GOVERNOR ⟨act in his name as ~ of the Western realm —E.A.Freeman⟩ **2 :** one who arbitrates **:** MEDIATOR ⟨the governor persuaded both sides to continue their talks with the ~ —*Springfield (Mass.) Union*⟩ **3 :** one who presides over an assembly, meeting, or discussion: as **a :** a presiding officer of any of various church meetings or assemblies within Protestant Christianity; *esp* **:** the presiding officer elected within a Presbyterian polity to preside over a general assembly or over a smaller regional meeting **b :** an official presiding over the exercises formerly prescribed for candidates for an academic degree — now used of an examiner for moderations at Oxford as well as of one of the two officers presiding over the mathematical tripos at Cambridge **c :** the nonpartisan presiding officer of a town meeting **d :** a person who acts as chairman of a discussion group (as on radio or television) **4** *archaic* **:** a person or thing that moderates or calms ⟨angling was . . . a ~ of passions —Izaak Walton⟩ **5 a :** a member of a group opposed to the violent methods of the regulators in No. Carolina about 1770 **b :** a member of one of numerous illegal bands active esp. in Texas about the middle of the 19th century **6 :** a candidate for the B.A. at Dublin taking first or second honors **7 :** a substance (as graphite, deuterium in heavy water, or beryllium) used for slowing down neutrons in a nuclear reactor

mod·er·a·to·ri·al \ˌmädərəˈtōrēəl, -tȯr-\ *adj* **:** of, relating to, or characteristic of a moderator

moderator lamp *n* **:** a 19th century oil lamp burning colza oil and having a special regulator for the oil supply to the wick

mod·er·a·tor·ship \ˈmädə,rād·ə(r),ship, -rātə(-\ *n* **:** the position or duties of a moderator

1mod·ern \R 'mädərn, — R -dən or -dᵊn; R & — R also ÷ -d(ə)rən\ *adj, often* -ER/-EST [LL *modernus*, fr. L *modo*, adv., just now, fr. abl. of *modus* measure, manner — more at METE] **1 a :** of, relating to, or characteristic of a period extending from the more or less remote past to the present time ⟨totem poles, therefore, are ~ rather than prehistoric —R.W.Murray⟩ ⟨the difference between the classic and the ~ notion of experience —John Dewey⟩ ⟨links ancient and ~ in many ways —W.H. Ingrams⟩ ⟨~ thought . . . is a very recent affair, dating back only to the seventeenth century —Josiah Royce⟩; *specif* **:** of or relating to the historical period extending from about A.D. 1500 to the present day — compare ANCIENT, MEDIEVAL **b :** of, relating to, or characteristic of the present time or the immediate past **:** CONTEMPORARY, PRESENT-DAY ⟨bipartisanship in foreign policy is a ~ development in American politics —Arthur Krock⟩ ⟨instruments available to ~ government for the wider extension of wealth and well-being —Barbara Ward⟩ **c :** suitable to or expressive of the present time ⟨a ~ look⟩ ⟨~ furnishings⟩ ⟨the second house is even more ~ in appearance —*Springfield (Mass.) Daily News*⟩ **2 :** produced by or embodying the most recent techniques, methods, or ideas **:** UP-TO-DATE ⟨going to include in this addition and in this renovation ~ electric wiring and ~ plumbing and ~ means of keeping the offices cool —F.D.Roosevelt⟩ ⟨a very ~ and well-graded surface —L.D. Stamp⟩ **3** *obs* **:** COMMONPLACE, ORDINARY, TRITE ⟨full of wise saws and ~ instances —Shak.⟩ **4** *usu cap, of a language* **:** of, relating to, or having the characteristics of the present or most recent period of development as contrasted with earlier periods — compare MIDDLE, OLD **5 :** of, relating to, or having the characteristics of a movement or style in the arts marked by a break with traditional esp. academic forms and techniques of expression, an emphasis upon experimentation, boldness, and creative originality, and an attempt to deal with modern themes — compare ABSTRACT, ACADEMIC **syn** see NEW

2modern \"\ *n* -S **1 a :** a person of modern times ⟨the first ~ to state in human terms the principles of democracy —John Dewey⟩ **b :** a person alive at present ⟨the hurried ~ learns to speed quickly down a page, taking in a sentence or paragraph at a glance —Thomas Munro⟩ ⟨the threat of atomic warfare has prompted a mood of hysteria among many ~*s* —Reinhold Niebuhr⟩ **2 :** a person with modern ideas, tastes, or attitudes ⟨a complete ~, university educated, and trained as an administrator along European lines —Colin Wills⟩ ⟨furniture designed for young ~*s*⟩ **3 :** a practitioner of modern art ⟨was making a name for himself as one of the ~*s* —Shirley A. Grau⟩ ⟨turned from his Provençal models except as he continued at times to translate them; he became a ~ —Yvor Winters⟩ **4 :** a style of printing type based on an 18th century design of Giambattista Bodoni and distinguished esp. as contrasted with old style by regularity of shape, precise curves, straight hairline serifs, and heavy downstrokes ⟨this is an example of ~⟩

mo·derne \mə'de(ə)rn\ *adj* [F, modern, fr. LL *modernus*] **:** tastelessly or pretentiously modern ⟨a ~ front attached to an old late eighteenth century house —Anthony West⟩

modern figure *n* **:** LINING FIGURE

modern game *n, usu cap M&G* **:** the class or breed of game fowls that is characterized by sparse feathering, tall upright carriage, and long neck — see EXHIBITION GAME FOWL, PIT GAME FOWL; compare OLD ENGLISH GAME

modern greats *n pl, usu cap M&G* **:** an honor school of philosophy, politics, and economics at Oxford University

modern hebrew *n, usu cap M&H* **:** Hebrew as used in present-day Israel

mod·ern·ish *pronunc at* MODERN + ish\ *adj* **:** suggestive of modern style **:** somewhat modern

mod·ern·ism *pronunc at* MODERN + ,izəm\ *n* -S [1*modern* + -*ism*] **1 a :** a practice, usage, or expression peculiar to or characteristic of modern times ⟨there is not a house in Warsaw that is not lousy — to use a ~ — with secret passages —Gerald Kelly⟩ **b :** a way of living or thinking characteristic of modern times ⟨opposed to electricity in homes as a concession to ~ —G.P.Musselman⟩ **2 a** *often cap* **:** a movement in Protestant Christianity originating in the latter half of the 19th century and continuing to the present that seeks to establish the meaning and validity of the Christian faith in relation to present human experience and to reconcile and unify traditional theological concepts with the requirements of modern knowledge — compare LIBERALISM 2a **b** *usu cap, Anglicanism* **:** the position that all knowledge by which religion can be affected necessarily reaffirms the fundamental truths of Christianity but necessitates their official restatement by the Church in the language relevant to the intellectual conditions of the age **c** *often cap, Roman Catholicism* **:** a system of interpretation of Christian doctrine developed at the end of the 19th century and condemned by Pope Pius X in 1907 that denied the objective truth of revelation and the whole supernatural world and maintained that the only vital element in any religion and Catholicism in particular was its power to preserve and communicate to others the best religious experiences of the race **3 :** the philosophy and practices of modern art; *esp* **:** a self-conscious and deliberate break with the past and a search for new forms of expression in any of the arts ⟨an outraged press and public pounced on it as the very model of loathsome ~ —A.L.Chanin⟩

1mod·ern·ist \-,nəst\ *n* -S [1*modern* + -*ist*] **1 :** an admirer of modern ways or things **:** one who asserts the superiority of modern times ⟨its subject is the perennial conflict between conservative and ~ —Moses Hadas⟩ **2 :** an adherent of modernism in religion **3 :** one who practices, advocates, or admires modernism in the arts

2modernist \"\ *adj* **:** of, relating to, or characteristic of modernism or modernists

mod·ern·is·tic \¦==¦nistik, -tēk\ *adj* [1*modernist* + -*ic*] **1 :** MODERNIST ⟨his stimulating, ~ conception of what should be the aims and methods of education —*N.Y. Times*⟩ ⟨lays bare the emptiness of the ~ substitutes for the ancient certitudes —*Va. Quarterly Rev.*⟩ **2 :** having the superficial mannerisms or surface characteristics of modern style **:** falsely modern ⟨his tight suit and stiff hat all angles, like a ~ lampstand —William Faulkner⟩ **syn** see NEW

mo·der·ni·ty \mä'dərnəd·ē, mə'-, -dēn-, -dəin-, -nətē, -i\ *n* -ES [ML *modernitat-, modernitas*, fr. LL *modernus* modern + -*itat-, -itas* -ity] **:** the quality or state of being modern **:** MODERNISM ⟨this sleepy little city . . . is waiting for a motor speedway to breathe new life and a spirit of ~ into it —Arnaldo Cortesi⟩

mod·ern·iza·tion \R ,mädərnə'zāshən, —R -dən- *or* -dᵊn-; R & —R *also* ÷ -d(ə)rən-; -,nī'z-\ *n* -S **1 :** the act of modernizing or the state of being modernized ⟨careful consideration to the ~ of the federal tax structure —H.S.Truman⟩ ⟨only as ~ takes place can countries make their full contribution to the world's wealth —Eugene Mayer⟩ **2 :** a modernized version (as of a play) ⟨produced ~*s* of a number of Shakespeare's plays⟩

mod·ern·ize *pronunc at* MODERN +,īz\ *vb* -ED/-ING/-S *vt* **:** to make modern **:** adapt to modern needs, taste, or usage ⟨a determination to ~ poetry, and bring it closer to life —F.R.Leavis⟩ ⟨the method of lumbering has been *modernized* —*Amer. Guide Series: Maine*⟩: as **a :** REMODEL, REPAIR ⟨~ the theater⟩ ⟨the curse of many downtown districts . . . is the owner who refuses to ~ his building —Hal Burton⟩ **b :** to change (a text) to make conform to modern usage in spelling and language ⟨has *modernized* it quite considerably, printing proper names in their modern form, correcting grammatical lapses, and inserting the equivalent of obsolete words in brackets —G.R.Crone⟩ **~** *vi* **:** to adopt modern ways **:** act, write, or speak in a modern manner ⟨it is natural . . . for scribes to ~ and for poets to archaize —C.A.Lynch⟩ — **mod·ern·iz·er** \-zə(r)\ *n* -S

modern languages *n pl but sing or pl in constr* **:** the living literary languages esp. of Europe considered as a department of study or teaching

mod·ern·ly *adv* **1 :** in modern times **:** NOW ⟨society as ~ organized cannot tolerate so broad an area of official irresponsibility —R.H.Jackson⟩ **2 :** in a modern manner ⟨a ~ designed house⟩ ⟨a ~ run office⟩

mod·ern·ness \-(n)nəs\ *n* -ES **:** MODERNITY ⟨the ~ or antiquity of an action . . . has nothing to do with its fitness for poetical representation —Matthew Arnold⟩

modern pentathlon *n* **:** a 5-event athletic contest; *specif* **:** a composite contest that consists of the 300-meter freestyle swim, the 4000-meter cross-country run, the 5000-meter 30-jump steeplechase, fencing with the épée, and target shooting at 25 meters

modern school *n* **:** SECONDARY MODERN SCHOOL

mod·est \'mädəst\ *adj, sometimes* -ER/-EST [L *modestus* moderate, modest — more at METE] **1 a :** having a limited and not exaggerated estimate of one's abilities or worth **:** lacking in vanity or conceit **:** not bold or self-assertive ⟨the well-bred man . . . is ~ without being bashful, and steady without being impudent —Earl of Chesterfield⟩ ⟨was entirely natural, ~, and unaffected in manner —Eliot Clark⟩ ⟨was so certain he was right he could be rather charmingly simple and ~ —T.R.Ybarra⟩ **b :** diffident and retiring in manner **:** SHY ⟨the most ~, silent, sheepfaced and meek of little men —W.M. Thackeray⟩ **2 :** arising from or showing a self-effacing and unassertive attitude **:** free from exaggeration or overstatement **:** REASONABLE, MODERATE ⟨the reply seems calm, ~ and highly persuasive —R.K.Carr⟩ ⟨what nearly all newsmen were actually doing was a ~ job of explaining the bald facts —F.L.Mott⟩ ⟨his emotions he records in the plain and ~ language of the eighteenth century —Theodore Baird⟩ **3 :** observing conventional standards of proper dress and behavior **:** free from coarseness or indecency **:** chaste in thought and conduct ⟨all the females of our family have been perfectly ~ and delicate —Margaret Deland⟩ ⟨the pure bashful maiden was too ~, too tender, too trustful —W.M.Thackeray⟩ **4 a :** limited in size or amount **:** not excessive ⟨a quietly prosperous rural society, in which landownership, opportunity and ~ wealth were widely distributed —G.M.Trevelyan⟩ ⟨while their means were always ~ there was no trace of dire poverty —J.T.Ellis⟩ ⟨the galaxy of which our sun is a ~ member —B.J.Bok⟩ **b :** limited in extent or aim **:** not showy or ostentatious **:** UNPRETENTIOUS ⟨the day-to-day work of the scientist depends on ~ working hypotheses rather than on broad sweeping theories —Eric Ashby⟩ ⟨press agent for a ~ nightclub —*Newsweek*⟩ ⟨quite famous in a ~ sort of way —Robertson Davies⟩ **syn** see CHASTE, HUMBLE, SHY

mod·est·ly *adv* **:** in a modest manner or to a modest extent ⟨a book, whose authorship he ~ professed —Sidney Lovett⟩

mod·es·ty \'mädəstē, -ti\ *n* -ES [L *modestia*, fr. *modestus* moderate, modest + -*ia* -y] **1 a** *archaic* **:** freedom from excess or exaggeration **:** MODERATION ⟨an excellent play . . . set down with as much ~ as cunning —Shak.⟩ **b :** freedom from conceit or vanity **:** an awareness of one's limitations ⟨has great natural ~, with a stronger dependence on my judgment than on his own —Jane Austen⟩ ⟨~ . . . is essential to anyone who deals successfully with nature, since the ego must be capable of awe —L.J.Halle⟩ **c :** freedom from coarseness, indelicacy, or indecency **:** a regard for propriety in dress, speech, or conduct ⟨while retaining all her ~, had lost all her shyness —Arnold Bennett⟩ ⟨that affectation of extreme shyness, silence, and reserve, which misses in their teens are apt to take for an amiable ~ —Sir Walter Scott⟩ **2 :** a plain or decorative fill-in for a low neckline esp. of a dress **3 :** limitation in size, amount, or extent ⟨operates on a budget appropriate to the ~ of its quarters —*Report: (Canadian) Royal Commission on Nat'l Development*⟩ **4 a :** HARE'S-EAR 1 **b :** FLOWER-OF-AN-HOUR

modi *pl of* MODUS

mo·dic·i·ty \mō'disəd·ē, -ətē, -i\ *n* -ES [F *modicité*, fr. LL *modicitat-, modicitas*, fr. L *modicus* moderate + -*itat-, -itas* -ity] *archaic* **:** MODERATENESS ⟨found compensation for the darkness of her frontage in the ~ of her rent —Henry James †1916⟩

mod·i·cum \'mädəkəm, 'mōd-\ *n* -S [ME, fr. L, neut. of *modicus* moderate, small, fr. *modus* measure, manner + -*icus* -ic — more at METE] **:** a small portion **:** a limited quantity or amount ⟨a falsehood without even a ~ of truth in it⟩

mod·i·fi·a·bil·i·ty \,mädə,fīə¦biləd·ē, -lətē, -i\ *n* **:** the capability of being modified ⟨this ~ is one of the intrinsic qualities of living protoplasm —J.S.Shrike⟩

mod·i·fi·able \,mädə¦fīəbəl\ *adj* **:** capable of being modified ⟨the rhythm of physiological time is not ~ except by interference with certain fundamental processes —Alexis Carrel⟩ — **mod·i·fi·able·ness** *n* -ES

mod·i·fi·cand \¦==fə¦kand\ *n* -S [L *modificandum* something to be moderated, neut. of *modificandus*, gerundive of *modificare, modificari*] **:** a term having a grammatical qualifier

mod·i·fi·ca·tion \,==fə'kāshən\ *n* -S [MF, fr. ML *modification-, modificatio*, fr. L, measure, measuring, fr. *modificatus* (past part. of *modificare, modificari* to measure, moderate) + -*ion-, -io* -ion] **1 :** the act of limiting the meaning or application of a concept or statement **:** QUALIFICATION, RESTRICTION ⟨with some ~*s* this statement is true today —J.B.Conant⟩ **2 :** 1MODE 6 **3 a** (1) **:** the act or action of changing something without fundamentally altering it ⟨making the exactly minimum degree of ~ to her institutions necessary to fit them to new conditions —John Strachey⟩ (2) **:** the state of being so changed **b :** a result of such partial change **:** a modified form ⟨a ~ of last year's hardtop⟩ ⟨a ~ of a European breed⟩ ⟨a ~ of his batting style⟩ **c :** a noninheritable change in an organism caused by the influence of its environment **4 a :** a limitation or qualification of the meaning of a word by another word, by an affix, or by internal change **b :** INFLECTION 4a **c :** a change that a linguistic form undergoes when borrowed from one language into another **5 a :** an alteration by environmental influence of the articulatory components of a word or other speech item ⟨the alteration of *has* to \z\ in \hē stäpt\ (*he's stopped*) is a phonetic ~⟩ **b :** UMLAUT 1 **6** *Scots law* **:** the action of awarding or decreeing something done or paid in settlement (as the award of a minister's stipend against his parish)

1mod·i·fi·ca·tive \'===,kād·iv\ *n* -S [L *modificatus* + E -*ive*, n. suffix] **:** something that modifies

2modificative \"\ *adj* [L *modificatus* + E -*ive*, adj. suffix] **:** serving to modify

mod·i·fi·ca·tor \-,kād·ə(r)\ *n* -S [L *modificatus* + E -*or*] **:** MODIFIER

mod·i·fi·ca·to·ry \'mädəfəkə,tōrē, ,mädə'fik-, mä'difək- *chiefly Brit* ¦mädəfə¦kātəri *or* -ā·tri\ *adj* [L *modificatus* + E -*ory*] **:** serving to modify

modified basket maker *n, usu cap M&B&M* **:** an ancient culture of the plateau area of southwestern U.S. characterized by fired pottery, permanent pithouses, grooved hammers, notched axes, bows and arrows, the cultivation of beans and corn, and the domesticated turkey

modified life policy *n* **:** a life insurance policy providing for low premiums during an initial period of three or five years

modified milk *n* **:** milk altered in composition (as by the addition of lactose) esp. for use in infant feeding

modified soda *n* **:** a mixture of soda ash and sodium bicarbonate in various proportions for use esp. in laundering

mod·i·fier \'mädə,fī(ə)r, -īə\ *n* -S **1 :** one that modifies **2 a :** a grammatical qualifier **:** a subordinate constituent of a grammatical construction **b :** a phonetic symbol of defined meaning that alters the value or provides a more exact description of the symbol to which it is attached (as \ⁿ\ in \äⁿ\ representing a nasalized \ä\) **:** DIACRITIC **3 a :** a gene known only by its effect on the expression of another gene occupying a different locus **b :** a gene that modifies the effect of another **4 :** a substance added during a process or operation to bring about a desired effect or impart desired qualities (as in polymerization processes for controlling cross-linking or in ore flotation for decreasing the tendency of flotation of the undesired particles of gangue)

mod·i·fy \-,fī\ *vb* -ED/-ING/-ES [ME *modifien*, fr. MF *modifier*, fr. L *modificare, modificari* to measure, moderate, fr. *modus* measure, manner + -*ficare, -ficari* -fy — more at METE] *vt* **1 :** to make more temperate and less extreme **:** lessen the severity of **:** MODERATE ⟨the proximity of the ocean *modifies* the temperature —*Amer. Guide Series: R.I.*⟩ ⟨traffic rules were *modified* to let him pass —Van Wyck Brooks⟩ **2** *Scots law* **:** to award or decree as something to be done or paid (as a minister's stipend against his parish) **3 a :** to limit or restrict the meaning of **:** be subordinate to in a grammatical construction **:** QUALIFY **b :** to change (a vowel) by umlaut **4 :** to make minor changes in the form or structure of **:** alter without transforming ⟨the *aeroplane* — as it was called for many years before the word was *modified* to *airplane* —A.F.Harlow⟩ ⟨represents a type already partly *modified* by domestication —P.C.Mangelsdorf⟩ **b :** to make a basic or important change in **:** ALTER ⟨the older view that laws ~ conduct and that punishment effectively limits crime —Alex Comfort⟩ ⟨the weakening of the geographical factor in social organization must . . . profoundly ~ our attitude toward the meaning of personal relations —Edward Sapir⟩ ⟨have *modified* my views of conduct to conform with what seem to me the implications of my beliefs —T.S.Eliot⟩ **5 :** to change the form or properties of for a definite purpose ⟨the equipment was *modified* to produce locomotives —*Amer. Guide Series: Va.*⟩ ⟨a Navy trainer . . . was *modified* . . . for flight study of the system of boundary-layer control by blowing —*Report: Nat'l Advisory Committee for Aeronautics*⟩ ⟨starch is *modified* by heating to produce British gum⟩ **~** *vi* **:** to undergo change **syn** see CHANGE

mo·dil·lion \mō'dilyən\ *n* -S [It *modiglione*, fr. (assumed) VL *mutilion-, mutilio*, fr. L *mutulus* modillion, mutule] **:** an enriched block or horizontal bracket generally found under the corona of the cornice of the Corinthian and Composite entablature and sometimes in a plainer form in other orders

modillion

mo·di·nha \mə'dēnyə\ *n* -S [Pg, dim. of *moda* mode, fr. F *mode*] **:** a Portuguese art song typically romantic and sentimental

mo·di·o·lar \mə'dīələ(r)\ *adj* [prob. fr. (assumed) NL *modiolaris*, fr. NL 2*modiolus* + L -*aris* -ar] **:** of or relating to the modiolus of the ear

1mo·di·o·lus \-ləs\ *n, cap* [NL, fr. L, nave of a wheel, cylinder of a pump, dim. of *modius*] **:** a genus of sea mussels (family Mytilidae) including the horse mussels

2modiolus \"\ *n, pl* **modio·li** \-,lī\ [NL, fr. L] **:** a central bony column in the cochlea of the ear

mod·ish \'mōdish, -dēsh\ *adj* **:** being in the mode **:** FASHIONABLE ⟨a ~ hat⟩ ⟨a ~ writer⟩ ⟨tend to regard the pursuit of the new as necessarily silly and ~ —E.R.Bentley⟩ — **mod·ish·ly** *adv* — **mod·ish·ness** *n* -ES

mo·diste \mō'dēst\ *n* -S [F, fr. *mode* (fr. L *modus* measure, manner) + -*iste* -ist — more at METE] **:** one who makes and sells fashionable dresses and hats for women

mo·di·us \'mōdēəs\ *n, pl* **mo·dii** \-ē,ī\ [L; akin to L *modus* measure, manner] **:** an ancient Roman unit of grain measure equivalent to 0.96 peck

modiwarp *or* **modiwart** *var of* MOLDWARP

mo·doc \'mō,däk\ *n, pl* **modoc** *or* **modocs** *usu cap* [prob. fr. Shasta, stranger] **1 a :** a Lutuamian people of southwestern Oregon and northwestern California **b :** a member of such people **2 :** the language of the Modoc people

1mods *pl of* MOD

2mods \'mädz\ *n pl, usu cap* [by shortening] **:** MODERATIONS

mod·u·la·bil·i·ty \,mäjələ'biləd·ē, -ətē, -i\ *n* [*modulate* + -*ability*] **:** the capability of being modulated

mod·u·lar \'mäjələ(r)\ *adj* [NL *modularis*, fr. *modulus* + L -*aris* -ar] **1 :** of, relating to, or based on a module or a modulus **2** [*module* + -*ar*] **:** planned or constructed on the basis of a standard pattern or standard dimensions **:** capable of being easily joined to or arranged with other parts or units ⟨~ furniture⟩ ⟨a ~ wall unit⟩

mod·u·late \-,lāt, *usu* -ād·+V\ *vb* -ED/-ING/-S [L *modulatus*, past part. of *modulari* to measure, modulate, fr. *modulus* small measure, meter, melody, module, fr. *modus* measure + -*ulus* — more at METE] *vt* **1 :** INTONE, SING ⟨~ a prayer⟩ ⟨~ a song⟩ **2 a :** to tune to a key or pitch **:** vary in tone **:** make tuneful or pleasing in sound ⟨the radio engineers do not try to ~ his voice —*Current Biog.*⟩ ⟨did not scream or roar . . . she was old enough to ~ her voice and conserve her energies —John Mason Brown⟩ **b :** to adjust to or keep in proper measure or proportion **:** soften or tone down **:** TEMPER ⟨*modulated* his thunders according to the tree, shrub, or weed to be blasted —T.S.Eliot⟩ ⟨the humor is either *modulated* or relegated to the background —Marc Slonim⟩ **3 :** to vary a characteristic (as amplitude, frequency, phase) of (a carrier wave or signal) in a periodic or intermittent manner for the transmission of intelligence **~** *vi* **1 :** to play or sing with modulation **2 a :** to pass by regular chord progression from one musical key or tonality into another or from one mode to another **b :** to pass by regular melodic progression from one key to another **3 :** to pass gradually from one state to another ⟨had a fierce quality that had *modulated*, but not softened, to authority —Lionel Trilling⟩

modulated continuous waves *n pl* **:** CONTINUOUS WAVES 2

mod·u·la·tion \,==ˈlāshən\ *n* -S [ME *modulacion*, fr. L *modulation-, modulatio*, fr. *modulatus* (past part. of *modulari* to modulate) + -*ion-, -io* -ion] **1** *archaic* **:** a singing or making of music **:** musical sound **:** MELODY **2 :** a fitting or regulating according to a certain measure or proportion **:** a tempering or toning down ⟨appetites so vigorous and senses so vivid do not lend themselves to temperance, to tolerance, to ~ —Francis Hackett⟩ **3 a :** an inflection or varying of the tone or pitch of the voice ⟨that singularly individual voice . . . mature, confident, seldom varying in pitch, but full of slight, very moving ~*s* —Willa Cather⟩ **b :** a particular intonation or inflection of the voice ⟨told us, in rich nasal ~ —E.V.Lucas⟩ ⟨the soft ~ of her voice soothed the infant⟩ **c** (1) **:** the use of stress or pitch to convey meaning (2) **:** an instance of such modulation **4 :** the determination of proportions in a classic architectural order by means of the module or unit of length **5 a :** one of four tones (final, dominant, mediant, participant) of an ecclesiastical mode on which a phrase may begin or end **b :** the act or process of changing from one tonality to another without a break in the melody or the chord succession **6 :** a melodious use of language esp. by variations of rhythm and tone **:** verbal harmony ⟨we read it as much for its pleasing rendition of a state of mind . . . as for the ~ of its prose rhythms —David Daiches⟩ ⟨the metrical mastery which catches so naturally, yet with so true a ~, the faltering accents of the supplicant —Edmund Wilson⟩ **7 :** the variation of a characteristic (as amplitude, frequency, or phase) of a carrier or signal in a periodic or intermittent manner for the transmission of intelligence (as in telegraphy, telephony, radio, television) **8 :** a reversible change in histological structure due to physiological factors

modulation index *n* **:** a measure of the degree of frequency modulation expressed numerically for a pure tone modulation as the ratio of the frequency deviation to the frequency of the modulating signal

mod·u·la·tor \'mäjə,lād·ə(r), -ātə-\ *n* -S [L, fr. *modulatus* (past part. of *modulari* to modulate) + -*or*] **1 :** one that modulates: as **a :** a device (as an electron tube) for modulating a carrier wave or signal for the transmission of intelligence (as in telegraphy, telephony, radio, television) **b :** LIGHT VALVE — called also *light modulator* **2 :** any of the nerve fibers that carry impulses from single retinal cones and are believed to be responsible for the transmission of discrete sensations of color

mod·u·la·to·ry \-,lə,tōrē, -tōr-, -ri\ *adj* **:** of or relating to modulation (as in music) **:** serving to modulate ⟨a ~ passage⟩

mod·ule \'mä(,)jül\ *n* -S [L *modulus* small measure, meter, module in architecture, fr. *modus* measure + -*ulus* — more at METE] **1 a** *archaic* **:** something that serves as a model or pattern **:** EXEMPLAR ⟨the text ~ is a sentence from . . . Thoreau —William Beebe⟩ **b** *obs* **:** a counterfeit image ⟨but a clod and ~ of confounded royalty —Shak.⟩ **2 :** a standard or unit of measurement **3 a** [F, fr. L *modulus*] **:** the size of some one part (as the diameter or semidiameter of the base of a shaft) taken as a unit of measure by which the proportions of the other parts of a classical or nonclassical architectural composition are regulated **b :** a unit of size used as a basis for standardizing the design and construction of building parts and materials or articles of furniture ⟨use of dimensional coordination on the four-inch ~ —R.T.Liddicoat⟩ ⟨fabricated for assembly on a 2-foot ~ —S.D.Sturgis⟩ **4 a :** a device used for measuring the flow of water or for delivering a fixed volume of water (as in irrigation systems) **b :** the volume discharged by such a device

5 : the diameter of a coin, token, or medal **6 :** a ratio equal to the pitch diameter of a gear in millimeters divided by the number of teeth in the gear

mod·u·lo \ˈmäjə,lō\ *prep* [NL, abl. of *modulus*] **:** with respect to a modulus of

mod·u·lus \-ləs\ *n, pl* **moduli** \-,lī\ [NL, fr. L, small measure] **1 :** a constant or coefficient that expresses numerically the degree in which a property is possessed by a substance or body **2 a :** the absolute value of a complex number **b :** a number (as a positive integer) or other mathematical entity (as a polynomial) that in a congruence divides the difference of the two congruent members without leaving a remainder **3** *cap* **:** a genus (the type of the family Modulidae) of thin-shelled, bulbous, operculate marine snails of tropical seas

modulus of a logarithm : the factor by which the logarithm to a given base of any number must be multiplied to obtain the logarithm of the same number

modulus of elasticity : the ratio of the stress in a body to the corresponding strain (as in bulk modulus, shear modulus, and Young's modulus) — called also *coefficient of elasticity, elastic modulus*

modulus of rigidity : SHEAR MODULUS

modulus of rupture : an ultimate strength pertaining to the failure of beams by flexure equal to the bending moment at rupture divided by the section modulus of the beam

mo·dus \ˈmōdəs\ *n, pl* **mo·di** *see sense 2* \-,dī\ [L, measure, manner — more at METE] **1 :** the immediate manner in which property may be acquired (as by occupation or prescription) or the particular tenure by which it is held **2** *pl* **moduses :** a customary mode of tithing by composition instead of by payment in kind ⟨still took his tithe pig or his ~ —George Eliot⟩ **3 :** a mode of procedure **:** a way of doing something ⟨no ~ of accomplishing this desired result —Ezra Pound⟩ **4 :** MODE

modus op·e·ran·di \-,äpəˈrandē, -,dī\ *n, pl* **modi operandi** [NL] **1 :** a manner of operating or working ⟨their *modus operandi* is the old Indian art of tracking —Frank Cameron⟩ ⟨the *modus operandi* of a particularly nasty type of middle-class woman —John Nerber⟩ **2 :** a distinct pattern or method of procedure thought to be characteristic of an individual criminal and habitually followed by him ⟨got her picture identified, discovered her *modus operandi*, and put a stakeout on her neighborhood —*Time*⟩ — abbr. *M.O.*

modus po·nens \-ˈpō,nenz\ *n, pl* **modi po·nen·tes** \-,pōˈnen,tēz\ [NL, proposing mode] **:** a mode of reasoning from a hypothetical proposition according to which if the antecedent be affirmed the consequent is affirmed (as, if A is true, B is true; but A is true; therefore, B is true)

modus tol·lens \-ˈtä,lenz\ *n, pl* **modi tol·len·tes** \-(,)täˈlen,tēz\ [NL, removing mode] **:** a mode of reasoning from a hypothetical proposition according to which if the consequent be denied the antecedent is denied (as, if A is true, B is true; but B is false; therefore A is false)

modus vi·ven·di \-vəˈvendē, -,dī\ *n, pl* **modi vivendi** [NL, manner of living] **1 :** an arrangement between two nations or groups that effects a workable compromise on issues in dispute without permanently settling them ⟨essential that a *modus vivendi* be set up if conflict is to be avoided —Donald Davidson⟩ ⟨a *modus vivendi* which both worlds could accept and which would provide to each physical security against military attack —*Newsweek*⟩ **2 :** a manner of living **:** a way of life ⟨after many spiritual fits and starts, he found himself and worked out a satisfactory *modus vivendi* —*New Yorker*⟩ ⟨cocktail parties were a *modus vivendi* in themselves —Jean Stafford⟩

mody \ˈmōdē\ *adj* [²*mode* + *-y*] *archaic* **:** MODISH

moe \ˈmō\ *adj or adv or n* [ME *mo* — more at MORE] *chiefly dial* **:** MORE

moeh·rin·gia \mōˈrinjēə\ *n, cap* [NL, fr. P. H. G. *Moehring* †1792 Ger. naturalist + NL *-ia*] **:** a genus of low herbs (family Caryophyllaceae) growing in the north temperate regions and having opposite entire leaves, small white flowers, and few-seeded capsules — see SANDWORT

moel·lon \(ˈ)mweˈlōⁿ\ *or* **moellon de·gras** \,==dāˈgrä\ *n, pl* **moellons** \-ōⁿ(z)\ *or* **moellons degras** [*moellon* fr. F, prob. fr. *moelle* marrow, fr. OF *moele*, alter. of *meole*, fr. L *medulla* marrow, pith; *moellon degras* fr. *moellon* + *degras* — more at MEDULLA] **:** DEGRAS 1a

moeri·there \ˈmirə,thi(ə)r, ˈmer-\ *n* -S [NL *Moeritherium*] **:** an animal or fossil of the genus *Moeritherium*

moeri·the·ri·um \,==ˈthirēəm\ *n, cap* [NL, fr. Lake *Moeris*, ancient lake in Faiyûm province, northern Upper Egypt where remains of the genus were found + NL *-therium*] **:** a genus of Upper Eocene and Oligocene northern African mammals (order Proboscidea) that are about as large as tapirs and have a short proboscis and mastodont teeth including enlarged second incisors which are considered precursors of the tusks of later related forms (as mastodons and elephants)

moe·so·goth \ˈmēsə,-ēzə+,-\ *n, usu cap* [NL *Moeso-Gothi* (pl.), fr. L *Moesi* inhabitants of Moesia, ancient country south of the Danube river and extending from the Drina river to the Black sea + LL *Gothi* Goths — more at GOTH] **:** a Goth of the ancient Roman province of the middle Danube or Moesia

¹moe·so·gothic \;==+\ *adj, usu cap* [NL *Moeso-Gothicus*, fr. *Moeso-Gothi* + L *-icus* -ic] **:** of or relating to the Moesogoths or their language

²moesogothic \"\ *n, usu cap* **:** the form of Gothic spoken by the Moesogoths

mo·fette *also* **mof·fette** \mōˈfet\ *n* -S [F *mofette* gaseous exhalation, mofette, fr. It *mofeta*, of Gmc origin; akin to MHG *müffeln* to smell moldy] **:** a vent from which carbon dioxide and some nitrogen and oxygen issue from the earth in a last stage of volcanic activity

mof·fle \ˈmäfəl\ *var of* MAFFLE

mo·fus·sil \mōˈfəsəl\ *n* -S [Hindi *mufaṣṣal, mufaṣṣil*, fr. Ar *mufaṣṣal* separated] **:** the provincial or rural districts of India **:** COUNTRYSIDE ⟨an urgent need for more teachers who can get out to the farming areas in the ~ —*India Internat'l*⟩

mo·fus·sil·ite \-,lit\ *n* -S **:** one who lives in the mofussil

mog \ˈmäg, ˈmōg\ *vb* **mogged; mogged; mogging; mogs** [origin unknown] *vi* **1** *dial* **:** to move away **:** DEPART — usu. used with *off* or *on* **2** *chiefly dial* **:** to walk slowly and steadily **:** JOG ⟨all the men go *mogging* gloomily along —Ralph Knight⟩ ~ *vt, dial Eng* **:** to move or cause to move from one place to another

mog·a·di·shu \-di(,)shü\ *or* **mog·a·di·scio** \,mägəˈdi(,)shō, -dē(-, -dishē,ō\ *adj, usu cap* [fr. *Mogadishu* or *Mogadiscio*, Somalia] **:** of or from Mogadishu, the capital of Somalia **:** of the kind or style prevalent in Mogadishu

mog·a·dor *also* **mog·a·dore** \,mägəˈdō(ə)r, -dò(ə)r\ *n* -S [*Mogador*, seaport city in southwestern Morocco] **:** a silk or rayon fabric that is similar to fine faille and is usu. made in colorful stripes for neckties and sportswear

mogador gum *or* **mogadore gum** *n* **:** MOROCCO GUM

mog·dad coffee \(ˈ)mägˈdad-\ *n, often cap M* [*mogdad* fr. native name in Senegal, western Africa] **:** COFFEE SENNA

mogen david *usu cap M&D, var of* MAGEN DAVID

mog·gan \ˈmägən\ *n* -S [origin unknown] *Scot* **:** STOCKING; *esp* **:** a long stocking without a foot

mog·gy \ˈmägē, -gi\ *n* -ES [prob. fr. *Moggy*, fr. *Mog* (nickname fr. the name *Margaret*) + *-y*] **1** *dial Brit* **a :** COW, CALF — used as a pet name **b :** HOUSE CAT **2** *dial Eng* **:** SLATTERN

moghul *cap, var of* MOGUL

mogi- *comb form* [NL, fr. Gk, fr. *mogis* barely, with effort; akin to Gk *mogos* exertion, labor, Latvian *smags* burdensome] **:** with difficulty ⟨*mogiphonia*⟩

mo·go \ˈmō,gō\ *n* -S [native name in New South Wales, Australia] **:** an Australian stone-hatchet

¹mo·go·llon \,mōgəˈyōn, ,mägə,yōn\ *n, pl* **mogollon** *or* **mogollons** *usu cap* [*Mogollon* Mesa, tableland in central Arizona, and *Mogollon* mountains, range in western New Mexico] **1 :** an American Indian people constituting a subdivision of the Gileños **2 :** a member of the Mogollon people

²mogollon \"\ *adj, usu cap* **:** of or relating to an ancient culture of west central New Mexico and adjacent Arizona characterized in its earlier stages by polished brown or red ceramic ware, the equal importance of hunting and agriculture, deep pit houses, notched bone awls, and heavy corner-notched projectile points

mo·go·te \məˈgōdē\ *n* -S [AmerSp, fr. Sp, conical pile of fagots, knoll, budding antler, prob. fr. Basque *moko* point] *Southwest* **:** a patch of brush or thickly grown shrubbery

¹mo·gul \ˈmōgəl, (ˈ)mōˈgəl\ *n* -S [Per *Mughul*, fr. Mongolian *Mongol*] **1** *also* **mo·ghul** \"\ *or* **mu·ghal** *or* **mu·ghul** \ˈmügəl\ *cap* **:** an Indian Muslim of or descended from one of several conquering groups of Mongol, Turkish, and Persian origin; *esp* **:** GREAT MOGUL **2 :** a dominant person in a particular business or field ⟨the supposedly omnipotent ~*s* of the dress trade and the advertising trade —F.L.Allen⟩ ⟨found the party ~*s* still canvassing the poor pick of availables —S.H. Adams⟩ ⟨movie ~*s*⟩ ⟨literary ~*s*⟩

²mogul \"\ *adj, usu cap* **:** of or relating to the Moguls or their empire

mogul base *n* **:** an electric lamp base of larger than standard residential size

MOH *abbr* **1** master of otterhounds **2** medical officer of health

mo·hair \ˈmō,ha(a)(ə)r, -,he|, |ə\ *n* -S [by folk etymology (influence of ¹*hair*) fr. earlier *mocayare*, fr. obs. It *mocaiarro*, fr. Ar *mukhayyar*, lit., choice, select] **1 :** any of various fabrics or yarns made wholly or in part of the hair of the Angora goat: as **a :** a camlet of mohair **b :** a wiry lustrous clothing fabric of mohair and cotton made in plain or twill weaves **c :** a cut-pile upholstery fabric with a mohair pile and a cotton or wool back **2 :** the long silky hair of the Angora goat

mohammedan *usu cap, var of* MUHAMMADAN

mohammedan blue *n, often cap M* **:** a dark violet cobalt blue used as an underglaze color on certain Chinese porcelains of the Ming dynasty

mo·har \ˈmōhə(r)\ *n* -S [Nepali *mohar, mohor*, fr. Hindi *muhur, muhr* mohur — more at MOHUR] **:** a silver coin of Nepal; *also* **:** a corresponding unit of value ⟨½-*mohar* coins⟩

moharra *var of* MOJARRA

moharram *usu cap, var of* MUHARRAM

mo·ha·ve *also* **mo·ja·ve** \mōˈhävē, -hāv-, -vi\ *n, pl* **mohave** *or* **mohaves** *also* **mojave** *or* **mojaves** *usu cap* [Mohave *hamakhava* three mountains; fr. the peaks near Needles, California, regarded by the Mohave as the center of their territory] **1 a :** an Indian people of the Colorado river valley in Arizona, California, and Nevada **b :** a member of such people **2 :** a Yuman language of the Mohave people

mo·hawk \ˈmō,hȯk\ *n* -S *see sense 1* [of Algonquian origin; akin to Narraganset *Mohowaùuck* Mohawk, lit., they eat animate things] **1** *or pl* **mohawk** *usu cap* **a :** an Iroquoian people of the Mohawk river valley, New York **b :** a member of such people **2** *usu cap* **:** the language of the Mohawk people **3** *often cap* **:** TUSCAN BROWN **4** *sometimes cap, in fancy skating* **:** a stroke forward on either edge of either skate followed by a stroke backward on the corresponding edge of the other skate

mohawk weed *n* **:** a bellwort (*Uvularia perfoliata*) of eastern No. America — called also *mealy bellwort*

mo·he·gan \mōˈhēgən\ *or* **mo·hi·can** \-ēkən\ *n, pl* **mohegan** *or* **mohegans** *or* **mohican** *or* **mohicans** *usu cap* **1 :** an Indian people of southeastern Connecticut **2 :** a member of the Mohegan people

mo·hel \ˈmō(h)el\ *n* -S [Heb *mōhēl*] **:** a person who circumcises male infants in accordance with Jewish ritual

mohican *usu cap, var of* MAHICAN

moh·ism \ˈmō,izəm\ *n* -S *usu cap* [*Mo Ti fl* 400 B.C. Chin. philosopher + connective *-h-* + E *-ism*] **:** the teachings of Mo Ti characterized by an emphasis on equalitarian universal love and opposition to traditionalism and Confucianism

¹moh·ist \ˈmōəst\ *n* -S *usu cap* [*Mo* Ti + connective *-h-* + E *-ist*] **:** an adherent of Mohism

²mohist \"\ *adj, usu cap* **:** of or relating to Mo Ti or his teachings or followers

moh·mand \ˈmōmənd\ *n, pl* **mohmand** *or* **mohmands** *usu cap* **1 :** a people of eastern Afghanistan related to the Persians and Afghans **2 :** a member of the Mohmand people

mohn·seed \ˈmōn,sēd\ *n* [part trans. of G *mohnsame*, fr. *mohn* poppy (fr. MHG *mān, māhen*, fr. OHG *māho*) + *same* seed; akin to OHG *mago* poppy — more at MAW] **:** POPPY SEED

¹mo·ho \ˈmō(,)hō\ *n* [Hawaiian] **1 a** -S **:** any of several Hawaiian honey eaters that have pectoral tufts of yellow feathers **b** *cap* [NL, fr. Hawaiian] **:** a genus comprising such birds **2** -S **:** a small flightless extinct Hawaiian rail (*Pennula millsi*)

²mo·ho \"\ *or* **mo·ho·ro·vi·cic discontinuity** \,mōhōˈrōvə,chich-\ *n* -S *usu cap M* [*moho* short for *mohorovicic discontinuity*, after Andrija Mohorovičić †1936 Yugoslav geologist] **:** a point at depths ranging from about three miles beneath the ocean basin floor to about 25 miles beneath the continental surface at which seismological and other studies indicate a change in earth materials from those of the earth's crust to those of the subjacent mantle

mo·hock \ˈmō,häk\ *n* -S *usu cap* [alter. of *Mohawk*] **:** one of a gang of aristocratic ruffians who assaulted and otherwise maltreated people in London streets in the early 18th century

mo·hock·ism \-,kizəm\ *n* -S *usu cap* **:** the practices of the Mohocks or behavior resembling that of the Mohocks

mo·ho·li lemur \məˈhōlē-\ *n* [*moholi* fr. Tswana *mogwêlê*] **:** a common active gregarious arboreal lemur (*Galago senegalensis*) of tropical Africa

mohr *also* **mhorr** \ˈmō(ə)r, ˈmȯ(ə)r\ *n* -S [Ar *muhr, muhr* colt] **:** a gazelle of northern Africa (*Gazella dama mhorr*) having horns on which are 11 or 12 prominent rings — compare ADDRA

mohr balance \ˈmō(ə)r-\ *n, usu cap M* [after Karl F. *Mohr* †1879 Ger. pharmacist] **:** WESTPHAL BALANCE

mohr pinchcock *n, usu cap M* **:** a pinchcock consisting of a wire spring

Mohr pinchcock

mohr's salt *n, usu cap M* **:** a light green crystalline salt $FeSO_4.(NH_4)_2SO_4.6H_2O$ used chiefly in iron plating, in photography, and in chemical analysis; ferrous ammonium sulfate

mohs' scale \ˈmōz-, -ōs(əz)-\ *n, usu cap M* [after Friedrich *Mohs* †1839 Ger. mineralogist] **1 :** a scale of hardness for minerals ranging from 1 for the softest to 10 for the hardest in which 1 represents the hardness of talc; 2, gypsum; 3, calcite; 4, fluorite; 5, apatite; 6, orthoclase; 7, quartz; 8, topaz; 9, corundum; and 10, diamond **2 :** a revised and expanded version of the original Mohs' scale in which 1 represents the hardness of talc; 2, gypsum; 3, calcite; 4, fluorite; 5, apatite; 6, orthoclase; 7, vitreous pure silica; 8, quartz; 9, topaz; 10, garnet; 11, fused zirconia; 12, fused alumina; 13, silicon carbide; 14, boron carbide; and 15, diamond

mo·hur \ˈmōhə(r)\ *n* -S [Hindi *muhur, muhr* gold coin, seal, fr. Per *muhr*; akin to Skt *mudrā* seal, sign, token] **1 :** an old gold coin of the Moguls that circulated in India from the 16th century **2 :** a gold coin of British India equivalent to 15 rupees last issued in 1918 **3 :** any one of several gold coins formerly issued by Indian states (as Bikaner, Gwalior, Hyderabad) and by Nepal and Tibet **4 :** a unit of value equivalent to one mohur coin

mohurrum *usu cap, var of* MUHARRAM

mohwa *var of* MAHUA

¹moi \ˈmȯē\ *n, pl* **moi** *or* **mois** *usu cap* [Annamese] **1 :** a group of Veddoid or Indo-Australoid peoples living in the mountain uplands of Annam **2 :** a member of a Moi people

²moi \ˈmōˈē\ *n* -S [Hawaiian *moʻī*] **:** a Hawaiian ruling chief or sovereign

moi·der \ˈmȯidə(r)\ *or* **moi·ther** \-ōit̲hə-\ *vb* -ED/-ING/-S [origin unknown] *vt* **1** *dial Brit* **:** to throw into disorder or an unsettled state **:** PERPLEX, BEWILDER ⟨had me so ~*ed*, with his talk about securities —*Irish Digest*⟩ **2** *dial Brit* **:** DISTRACT, BOTHER ⟨~ one so with their chatter —Gerald O'Donovan⟩ ~ *vi* **1** *dial Brit* **:** to talk incoherently **:** be delirious **2** *dial Brit* **:** to wander about aimlessly or in a confused manner

moi·dore \ˈmȯi,dō(ə)r\ *n* -S [modif. of Pg *moeda de ouro*, lit., coin of gold] **1 a :** a gold coin of Portugal and Brazil from about 1540 to 1732 containing 4.93 grams of fine gold **b :** a corresponding unit of value **2 :** a gold 2-moidore piece or double moidore

moi·e·ty \ˈmȯiəd-ē, -ətē, -i\ *n* -ES [ME *moite*, fr. MF *moité*, fr. LL *medietat-, medietas*, fr. *medie-* (fr. L *medius* middle) + *-tat-, -tas* -ty — more at MID] **1 a :** one of two equal portions **:** HALF ⟨the site was conveyed in lease in two distinct *moieties* —E.K.Chambers⟩ **b :** one of two approximately equal portions ⟨war, pestilence, and famine had consumed . . . the ~ of the human species —Edward Gibbon⟩ **2 a :** one of the portions into which something is divided **:** COMPONENT, PART ⟨the psychopathic ~ of the personality —*Brit. Jour. of Delinquency*⟩ ⟨the hemoglobin molecule contains four heme *moieties* —Lionel Whitby⟩; *specif* **:** a share paid by the government to an informer out of duties and penalties collected because of his help ⟨the ~ paid to an informer must be 25 percent of the value of the amount recovered —*Chicago Tribune*⟩ **b** *obs* **:** a small portion **:** FRACTION ⟨thine being but a ~ of my grief —Shak.⟩ **3 :** one of two basic complementary tribal subdivisions; *esp* **:** one (as a phratry) of two unilateral usu. exogamous groups

¹moil \ˈmȯil, *esp before pause or consonant* ˈmȯiəl\ *vb* -ED/-ING/-S [ME *moillen*, fr. MF *moillier*, fr. (assumed) VL *molliare*, fr. L *mollis* soft — more at MELT] *vt* **1** *chiefly dial* **:** to make wet or dirty **:** DAMPEN, SMEAR ⟨letters ~*ed* with my kisses —Elizabeth B. Browning⟩ **2** *chiefly dial* **:** to make distraught **:** TORMENT, WORRY ~ *vi* **1 :** to work with grueling persistence **:** DRUDGE, GRUB ⟨piles of earth . . . are evidence that here a scant hundred years ago thousands ~*ed* for gold —F.W. Taber⟩ **2** *dial Eng* **:** to be fidgety or restless **:** WORRY **3 a :** to be in continuous agitation **:** CHURN, SWIRL ⟨a crowd of men and women ~*ed* like nightmare figures in the smoke-green haze —Ralph Ellison⟩ ⟨caused all the wrongs of his past life to ~ up inside of him and sear his brain —*True Police Cases*⟩ **b :** to become involved in discussion **:** CHAFFER, WRANGLE ⟨last week's diplomatic ~*ing* in Europe —*Life*⟩

²moil \"\ *n* -S **1 :** hard work **:** DRUDGERY, LABOR ⟨escape from the ~ . . . and money-grubbing of ordinary life —*Times Lit. Supp.*⟩ ⟨the drab . . . toil and ~ of a collier's existence —Harry Lauder⟩ **2 a** *dial Eng* **:** MUD, MIRE **b :** BLEMISH, TAINT ⟨undefiled . . . by ~ of printed word —F.L.Gwynn⟩ **3 a :** a jumble of sound or motion **:** UPROAR, TURBULENCE ⟨lost in a vast ~ of noise —Norman Mailer⟩ ⟨the ~ and brine of the sea —D.C.Peattie⟩ **b :** a state of confusion **:** TURMOIL ⟨the ~ of events is . . . unintelligible —H.B.Alexander⟩

³moil \"\ *n* -S [IrGael *maol* bald & W *moel* — more at MULEY] *dial Brit* **:** a hornless ox or cow

⁴moil \"\ *n* -S [perh. fr. F *meule*, lit., haystack, fr. L *metula* small cone or pyramid — more at METULA] **1 :** excess glass left at the end of an article in contact with the blowing mechanism during the manufacture of blown glass and usu. removed in finishing the article **2 :** a coating of glass on the gathering iron to prevent it from scaling off into the molten glass

⁵moil \"\ *n* -S [origin unknown] **:** a steel bar sharpened to a point or a chisel end for hand use (as in mining) — compare ¹GAD 1c

moil·er \-lə(r)\ *n* -S [¹*moil* + *-er*] **:** one that moils **:** DRUDGE

moil·ey \ˈmȯilī\ *Irish & Scot var of* MULEY

moiling *adj* [fr. pres. part. of ¹*moil*] **1 a :** requiring hard work **:** TOILSOME ⟨~ job⟩ **b :** HARDWORKING, INDUSTRIOUS ⟨~ worker⟩ **2 :** violently agitated **:** NOISY, TURBULENT ⟨the earth a roaring, ~ mass of tanks —*Fortune*⟩ ⟨~ life beyond the quiet close —O.S.J.Gogarty⟩ — **moil·ing·ly** *adv*

moine \ˈmȯin\ *adj, usu cap* [prob. fr. *Moin*, moorland in Sutherland, northern Scotland] **:** of or relating to an epoch of the Precambrian era — see GEOLOGIC TIME table

moi·ra \ˈmȯirə\ *n, pl* **moi·rai** \-ȯi,rī\ *often cap* [Gk; akin to Gk *meros* part — more at MERIT] **:** individual destiny **:** the will of the gods **:** FATE

¹moire *in sense 2 like* MOIRÉ *or sometimes* ˈmō(ə)r *or* ˈmwär *or* ˈmȯ(ə) *or* ˈmwȧ(r; *in sense 1 prob one-syllabled*\ *n* -S [F, fr. E *mohair*] **1** *archaic* **:** a watered mohair **2 :** ²MOIRÉ 2

²moi·ré \(ˈ)mōˈrā, (ˈ)mwäˈrā\ *or* **moire** *see* ¹MOIRE\ *n* -S [F *moiré*, fr. *moiré*, adj.] **1 a :** an irregular wavy finish usu. produced on a fabric by pressing between engraved rollers **b :** a wavy pattern in fur (as Persian lamb) **c :** a ripple pattern on the face or back of a stamp as a protection against forgery — compare BURELAGE **d :** a dot formation in a halftone print that consists often of geometric figures or wavy lines, is usu. considered an imperfection, and occurs typically in work done from a cut made by rescreening a halftone print or in superimposed impressions in bad register from two or more cuts **2** [alter. (influenced by ³*moiré*) of ¹*moire*] **:** a fabric (as a corded silk or rayon) having a wavy watered appearance ⟨a satchel lined with navy blue ~ —*New Yorker*⟩

³moiré *or* **moire** \"\ *adj* [F *moiré*, fr. *moire* + *-é* (fr. L *-atus* -ate)] **:** having a wavy or watery appearance

⁴moiré *or* **moire** \"\ *vt* **moiréd** *or* **moired; moiréing** *or* **moireing; moirés** *or* **moires :** to produce a watered pattern on (a fabric)

mois *pl of* MOI

mois·san·ite \ˈmȯisᵊn,īt\ *n* -S [Henri *Moissan* †1907 Fr. chemist + E *-ite*] **:** a silicon carbide SiC found in the Diablo Canyon meteoric iron — compare CARBORUNDUM

¹moist \ˈmȯist\ *adj* -ER/-EST [ME *moiste*, fr. MF, fr. (assumed) VL *muscidus*, alter. (prob. influenced by L *musteus* resembling new wine, fr. *mustum* new wine) of L *mucidus* slimy — more at MUST, MUCID] **1 a** *obs* **:** consisting of water **:** LIQUID ⟨tears, the ~ impediments unto my speech —Shak.⟩ **b** *obs* **:** characterized by succulence **:** LUSH, JUICY ⟨these ~ trees —Shak.⟩ ⟨eat ~ grapes —Num 6: 3 (AV)⟩ **c :** naturally or constitutionally wet — used in ancient and medieval sciences to describe one of the qualities of the four elements; opposed to *dry* **d** *of a sign of the zodiac* **:** having a moist complexion **e** *obs* **:** containing or bringing moisture ⟨the vapors of a ~ pot . . . soar up into the open air —*Return from Parnassus: Part II*⟩ ⟨the ~ daughters of huge Atlas —Edmund Spenser⟩ **2 a :** full of tears **:** WATERY ⟨the eyes of both of us . . . were ~ with the joy of success —Jack London⟩ **b** (1) **:** slightly or moderately wet **:** DAMP ⟨the gravel paths were ~ . . . with dew —Ernest Hemingway⟩ (2) **:** saturated with moisture **:** HUMID, SOGGY ⟨air which was still warmer and more ~ moved in —G.R. Stewart⟩ ⟨the lush, ~, rice and cotton lands —*Amer. Guide Series: Texas*⟩ **c :** characterized by humidity and frequent precipitation ⟨jungles thrive in warm ~ regions⟩ **3 :** employing or accompanied by moisture: as **a** (1) **:** accompanied by tears **:** TEARFUL ⟨the urgent ~ look in his eyes —Ethel Wilson⟩ (2) **:** emotionally sentimental **:** MAUDLIN ⟨emotionally very ~ about nationalism —A.F.Rolle⟩ **b :** utilizing a washing process ⟨copper, zinc, and silver . . . extracted in the ~ way —William Crookes⟩ **c** (1) **:** marked by a discharge or exudation of liquid ⟨~ eczema⟩ (2) **:** suggestive of the presence of liquid — used of sounds heard in auscultation ⟨~ rales⟩ **syn** see WET

²moist *n* -S [ME *moiste*, fr. *moiste*, adj.] *obs* **:** MOISTURE ⟨myrtles and bays for want of ~ grew wan —Josuah Sylvester⟩

³moist *vt* -ED/-ING/-S [ME *moisten*, fr. *moiste*, adj.] *obs* **:** MOISTEN ⟨no more the juice of Egypt's grape shall ~ this lip —Shak.⟩

moist color *n* **:** a watercolor pigment in the form of paste

moist·en \ˈmȯisᵊn\ *vb* **moistened; moistened; moistening** \-s(ᵊ)niŋ\ **moistens** [¹*moist* + *-en*] *vt* **:** to make moist **:** DAMPEN, SATURATE ⟨~*ed* her lips in anticipation —Beverley Nichols⟩ ⟨broad alluvial plain . . . plentifully ~*ed* by rain-bearing winds —R.S.Billington⟩; *specif* **:** to make moist by immersing in a liquid ⟨passed the cup to his wounded neighbor, without stopping even to ~ his own lips —Andrew Combe⟩ ~ *vi* **:** to become moist ⟨heard a catch in his voice and saw his eyes ~⟩

moist·en·er \-s(ᵊ)nə(r)\ *n* -S **:** one that moistens; *specif* **:** a device for moistening gummed surfaces (as stamps, envelopes, labels)

moist·ful \ˈmȯistfəl\ *adj* [²*moist* + *-ful*] *archaic* **:** MOIST

moist gangrene *n* **:** gangrene that develops in the presence of combined arterial and venous obstruction, is usu. accompanied by a superimposed infection, and is characterized by a watery discharge usu. of foul odor

moisteners

moist·i·fy \ˈmȯistə,fī\ *vt* -ED/-ING/-ES [¹*moist* + *-ify*] *archaic* **:** MOISTEN

moist·ish \-tish\ *adj* **:** somewhat moist

moist·less \-tləs\ *adj, archaic* **:** lacking moisture **:** DRY

moist·ly *adv* **:** in a moist manner

moist·ness *n* -ES [ME *moistnes*, fr. *moiste* moist + *-nes* -ness — more at MOIST] **:** the quality or state of being moist

mois·ture \ˈmȯis(h)chə(r)\ *n* -S [ME, modif. (influenced by *-ure*) of MF *moistour*, fr. *moiste* moist — more at MOIST]

1 a : liquid (as water) diffused or condensed in relatively small quantity and dispersed through a gas as invisible vapor or as fog or in or on a solid body in insensible form or as sensible dampness or condensed on a cool surface as visible dew; *specif* **:** atmospheric water vapor ⟨the dew point is a reliable indication of the amount of ~ in the air⟩ **b** *obs* **:** the watery component of an object or an individual ⟨all my body's ~ scarce serves to quench my furnace-burning heart —*Shak.*⟩ **c :** TEARFULNESS ⟨a ~ of the eye —H.S.Scott⟩ **2 :** a liquid substance (as water) ⟨rubbing the ~ out of the coat of a . . . fox terrier —Arnold Bennett⟩; *specif* **:** PRECIPITATION ⟨69 percent of the annual ~ occurred during the growing season —R.H. Brown⟩

moisture equivalent *n* **:** the water content expressed as a percentage of the dry weight that a soil can retain against a centrifugal force one thousand times the force of gravity and used as a convenient laboratory measure of soil moisture conditions

mois·ture·less \-(r)ləs\ *adj* **:** lacking moisture ⟨the most ~ piece of cake⟩

moisture meter *n* **:** an instrument for determining the percentage of moisture in a material (as timber, flour, soil, or tobacco) commonly by measuring its electrical resistivity

¹moistureproof \ˈ;==;=\ *adj* [*moisture* + *proof*] **:** impervious to water vapor ⟨store the bread in a ~ container⟩ — compare WATERPROOF

²moistureproof \"\ *vt* -ED/-ING/-S **:** to make impervious to water vapor

moisty \ˈmȯistē\ *adj* -ER/-EST [ME *moisty*, fr. *moiste* moist + -*y*] **:** DAMP, WET ⟨a misty ~ morning⟩

¹moit \ˈmȯit\ *n* -S [alter. of *²mote*] **:** a fragment of stick or other foreign matter found in wool

²moit \"\ *vb* -ED/-ING/-S **:** ³MOTE

moither *var of* MOIDER

moity \ˈmȯid·ē\ *adj* -ER/-EST **:** full of moits

mo·jar·ra *also* **mo·har·ra** \mōˈhärə\ *n* -S [AmerSp, fr. Sp, lance head, a small flat fish found off the coast of Spain, prob. fr. Ar *muḥarrab* pointed, fr. *ḥarrab* to sharpen, point] **1 :** a fish of the family Gerridae **2 :** any of various fishes somewhat similar to the mojarras; *esp* **:** any of numerous small So. American fishes of the family Cichlidae

mojave *usu cap, var of* MOHAVE

mo·ji \ˈmōjē\ *adj, usu cap* [fr. *Moji*, Japan] **:** of or from the city of Moji, Japan **:** of the kind or style prevalent in Moji

¹mo·jo \ˈmō,hō\ *n, pl* **mojo** *or* **mojos** *usu cap* [Sp, of AmerInd origin] **1 a :** an Arawakan people of northern Bolivia **b :** a member of such people **2 :** the language of the Mojo people

²mo·jo \ˈmō(,)jō\ *n, pl* **mojos** *or* **mojoes** [prob. of African origin; akin to Gullah *moco* witchcraft, magic, Fulani *moco'o* medicine man] *chiefly South* **:** a voodoo spell or amulet

mo·ka *Brit var of* MOCHA

moke \ˈmōk\ *n* -S [origin unknown] **1 a** *slang Brit* **:** DONKEY, ASS **b** *slang Austral* **:** a horse esp. of poor appearance **2** *slang* **:** NEGRO — usu. used disparagingly

¹mo·ki *also* **mo·qui** \ˈmōkē\ *n, pl* **moki** *or* **mokis** *usu cap* **:** HOPI

²moki \"\ *or* **mo·ki·hi** \-ē,hē\ *n, pl* **moki** *or* **mokis** *or* **mokihi** *or* **mokihis** [Maori] **1** *NewZeal* **:** a trumpeter fish (*Latridopsis ciliaris*) **2 :** a Maori raft made of bundles of flags, rushes, or dry flower stalks of flax

mo·ki·ha·na \,mōkēˈhänə\ *n* -S [Hawaiian] **:** a Hawaiian tree (*Pelea anisata*) of the family Rutaceae growing only on the Island of Kauai and having fragrant fruits that are strung in leis and represent Kauai in the leis of the Islands

mo·ko \ˈmō(,)kō\ *n* -S [Maori] **1 :** the Maori system of tattooing **2 :** a Maori tattoo consisting of pigment rubbed into spiral grooves made in the skin with a small implement resembling an adz

moko-moko \;mō(,)kō;mō(,)kō\ *n* -S [Maori] **:** a common small lizard (*Lygosoma moco*) of New Zealand

mok·po \ˈmäk(,)pō\ *adj, usu cap* [fr. *Mokpo* (*Moppo*), Korea] **:** of or from the city of Mokpo, Korea **:** of the kind or style prevalent in Mokpo

mo·ksha *also* **mo·ksa** \ˈmōkshə\ *n* -S [Skt *mokṣa*; akin to Skt *muñcati* he releases — more at MUCUS] *Hinduism & Jainism* **:** release from samsara and liberation from karma together with the attainment of Nirvana for the Hindu or kaivalya for the Jain **:** salvation from the bondage of finite existence — compare DHARMA, KAMA

mo·kum *or* **mo·kume** \ˈmōkəm\ *n* -S [Jap *mokume*, lit., wood grain] **:** a Japanese alloy used in decorative work on gold and silver

mol *var of* ⁷MOLE

mol *abbr* molecular; molecule

mo·la \ˈmōlə\ *n* [NL, fr. L, millstone; fr. its shape and rough skin — more at MILL] **1** *cap* **:** the type genus of the family Molidae including solely a large widely distributed ocean sunfish (*M. mola*) **2** *pl* **mola** *or* **molas :** any fish of the genus *Mola*; *broadly* **:** OCEAN SUNFISH

mo·lal \ˈmōləl\ *adj* [⁷*mole* + -*al*] *chem* **:** of, relating to, or containing a mole ⟨the ~ volume of a gas is 22.4 liters at standard conditions⟩; *esp* **:** containing one mole of solute per 1000 grams of solvent ⟨a ~ solution⟩ — compare MOLAR

mo·la·la \məˈläla\ *n, pl* **molala** *or* **molalas** *usu cap* **1 a :** a Waiilatpuan people of the Molala and Santiam river valleys in northwestern Oregon **b :** a member of such people **2 :** the language of the Molala people

mo·lal·i·ty \mōˈlaləd·ē\ *n* -ES **:** molal concentration

¹mo·lar \ˈmōlə(r)\ *n* -S [L *molaris*, fr. *molaris* of a mill, grinding, fr. *mola* mill, millstone + -*aris* -ar — more at MILL] **1** *also* **molar tooth :** a tooth adapted for grinding by having a broad rounded or flattened though often ridged or tuberculated surface; *specif* **:** one of the cheek teeth in mammals behind the incisors and canines sometimes including the premolars but more exactly restricted to the three posterior pairs in each jaw on each side in adult man which are not preceded by deciduous teeth — see DENTAL FORMULA, DENTITION illustration **2 :** a process with a grinding surface on the inner aspect of the mandible of an insect or crustacean

²molar \"\ *adj* [L *molaris* of a mill, grinding] **1 a :** pulverizing by friction **:** GRINDING ⟨~ teeth⟩ ⟨waves, wind, and sand are ~ agents⟩ **b :** of, relating to, or located near the molar teeth ⟨~ gland⟩ **2** [⁶*mole* + -*ar*] **:** of, relating to, possessing the qualities of, or characterized by a uterine mole ⟨~ pregnancy⟩

³molar \"\ *adj* [L *moles* mass + E -*ar* — more at MOLE (mound)] **1 :** of or relating to a mass of matter as distinguished from the properties or motions of molecules or atoms **2** [⁷*mole* + -*ar*] **:** of, relating to or containing a mole or molecules **:** MOLECULAR; *esp* **:** containing one mole of solute in 1000 milliliters of solution — compare MOLAL **3 :** of or relating to larger units of behavior esp. as relatable to a prior deprivation or motivational pattern of the organism ⟨interest in such ~ problems of personality as the ego functions —R.R. Holt⟩ — opposed to *molecular*

mo·lar·i·form \mōˈlarə,fȯrm\ *adj* [¹*molar* + -*iform*] **:** resembling a molar tooth esp. in shape

mo·lar·i·ty \-rəd·ē\ *n* -ES [³*molar* + -*ity*] **:** molar concentration

mo·lar·iza·tion \,mōlərəˈzāshən\ *n* -S [¹*molar* + -*ization*] **:** the evolution of less specialized teeth into molars

mo·la·ry \ˈmōlərē\ *adj* [L *molarius* of a mill, fr. *mola* mill, millstone + -*arius* -ary — more at MILL] **:** adapted for grinding food **:** MOLAR

mo·lasse \məˈläs\ *n* -S *usu cap* [F, perh. alter. of *mollasse* soft, fr. *mou* (after It *mollaccio* soft: *molle* soft, fr. L *mollis*), fr. L *mollis* — more at MELT] **:** a series of fossiliferous sedimentary deposits in and near Switzerland that are chiefly of Miocene age but include some Upper Oligocene beds

mo·las·sed \məˈlasəd\ *also* **mo·las·sied** \-sēd\ *adj* **:** impregnated with molasses ⟨~ silage⟩

mo·las·ses \məˈlasəz, -laas-, -ˈlais *sometimes* -lás-, *dial* ˈl-\ *n* -ES *often attrib* [Pg *melaço*, fr. LL *mellaceum* must, fr. neut. of (assumed) *mellaceus* resembling honey, fr. L *mell-*, *mel* honey + -*aceus* -aceous — more at MELLIFLUOUS] **1 :** the thick dark to light brown viscid syrup that is separated from raw sugar in the successive processes of sugar manufacture and graded according to its quality — compare BLACKSTRAP 3, TREACLE **2 :** a syrup made by boiling down sweet vegetable or fruit juice or sap ⟨citrus ~⟩ ⟨wood ~⟩

molasses grass *n* **:** a valuable perennial forage grass (*Melinis minutiflora*) native to tropical Africa but widely cultivated and covered with hairs which secrete a sweet substance having the odor of molasses — called also *candy grass*

mo·la·ve \mōˈlä(,)vā\ *n* -S [Sp, fr. Tag *mulavin*] **1 :** a large Philippine timber tree (*Vitex littoralis*) **2 :** the valuable durable heavy hard yellow wood of the molave tree

¹mold *or* **mould** \ˈmōld\ *n* -S [ME *mold*, *molde*, fr. OE *molde* sand, dust, soil; akin to OHG *molta* dust, soil, ON *mold*, Goth *mulde* dust, soil, OHG *malan* to grind — more at MEAL] **1 :** crumbling soft friable earth suited to plant growth **:** SOIL; *esp* **:** soil rich in humus — see LEAF MOLD **2** *dial Brit* **a :** the surface of the earth **:** GROUND ⟨the fairest knight on Scottish ~ —Sir Walter Scott⟩ **b :** the earth of the burying ground ⟨calling his ghost to the ~ —A.P.Graves⟩ — often used in pl. ⟨were baith in the ~s —Sir Walter Scott⟩ **3** *archaic* **:** earth that is the substance of the human body ⟨leprous sin will melt from human ~ —John Milton⟩ ⟨be merciful great Duke to men of ~ —*Shak.*⟩

²mold *also* **mould** \"\ *vb* -ED/-ING/-S *vi* **:** MOLDER ⟨it was closed for ages, ~*ing* away —Angus Mowat⟩ ~ *vt* **:** to cover with soil or mold **:** hill up ⟨potatoes . . . should be kept weed-free and ~*ed* —*New Zealand Jour. of Agric.*⟩

³mold *or* **mould** \"\ *n* -S *often attrib* [ME *molde*, *mold*, fr. OF *modle*, *molle*, *moule*, fr. L *modulus*, dim. of *modus* measure — more at MODE] **1 :** distinctive nature or character **:** TYPE, STAMP ⟨a philosopher of the grand ~ —D.C.Williams⟩ **2 a :** a pattern or template that serves as a guide for construction; *specif* **:** a thin wood or paper pattern for part of a ship made in a mold loft **b** (1) **:** the frame on or around which an object is constructed ⟨laid the dome on a ~ of packed earth —Green Peyton⟩ (2) **:** a wire-covered frame for forming sheets of paper; *esp* **:** one of the cylinders covered with wire cloth that forms the sheet on a cylinder machine **3 a :** a cavity in which a fluid or malleable substance is given form: as (1) **:** a container (as of gypsum, rubber, metal, or wood) in which a piece of ceramic ware is formed (2) **:** a form for making bricks (3) **:** a metal form for casting cement, mortar, or concrete test specimens (4) **:** a matrix in which an article (as of metal, glass, or plastic) is shaped by casting or pressure molding; *specif* **:** a recessed matrix from which a relief printing surface (as type or a stereotype or electrotype) is cast (5) **:** a cooking utensil in which a dish (as a pudding or jelly) is given a decorative shape (6) **:** a carved wooden block by means of which a design is pressed into a soft food (as cookie dough or butter) **b :** a molded object ⟨plaster ~⟩ ⟨fill the center of the ring ~ with cottage cheese⟩ **4 a :** MOLDING **b :** a group of moldings **5 a** *obs* **:** an example to be followed ⟨the glass of fashion and the ~ of form —*Shak.*⟩ **b :** a prototype from which an idea or individual is derived ⟨thou all-shaking thunder . . . crack nature's ~s—*Shak.*⟩ ⟨an integral part of the team and cut from the same heroic ~ —A.J.Daley⟩ **c :** a fixed pattern or contour **:** DESIGN, CAST ⟨compresses all these characters into the relentless ~ of the story —E.B.Garside⟩ ⟨settling in the ~ of a dignified, permanent community —Mabel R. Gillis⟩ **d** *obs* **:** a fashionable style **:** MODE ⟨houses of the new ~ in London —Peter Heylin⟩ **6 :** a package of goldbeater's skin usu. consisting of about 900 pieces **7 a :** an impression made in earth or rock by the outside of a fossil shell or other organic form **b :** a cast of the inner surface of such a fossil — compare ²CAST 7a(2) **8 :** a grained copper photoengraving plate with the gelatin image on it ready for etching

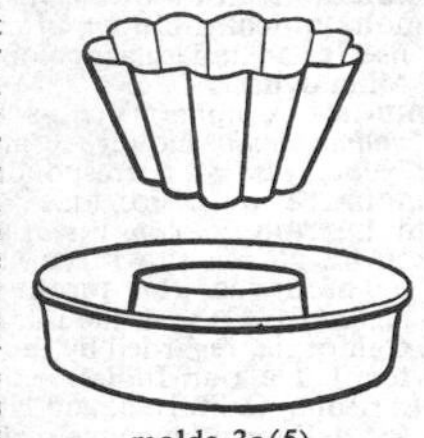

molds 3a(5)

⁴mold *or* **mould** \"\ *vb* -ED/-ING/-S [ME *molden*, fr. *molde*, *mold*, n.] *vt* **1 a** *archaic* **:** to knead (dough) into a desired consistency or shape **b :** to give shape to (as a fluid or malleable substance) ⟨the wind ~s the waves⟩ ⟨his long hands ~*ing* the air —*Time*⟩ ⟨chemical processes that . . . are now ~*ing* the earth's crust —W.H.Bucher⟩ **c** *obs* **:** to be a component of **:** help to build ⟨all princely graces that ~ up such a mighty piece as this —*Shak.*⟩ **2 a** (1) **:** to form by pouring or pressing into a mold ⟨~ a glass bottle⟩ ⟨to attain a flare in design it is necessary to ~ the plywood into shape —R.J.Whittier⟩ ⟨~ a stereotype⟩ (2) **:** to make a mold from ⟨~ a type form⟩ **b :** to form a foundry mold of (as in sand) **c :** to exert influence on **:** determine the ultimate quality or nature of ⟨~ public opinion⟩ ⟨environmental factors which ~ the minds and emotions of youngsters —R.H.Wittcoff⟩ ⟨the culture of the Western world has been ~*ed* by the Bible —I.M.Price⟩ ⟨a great scholar who has ~*ed* his taste and judgment through reflective reading —E.S.McCastney⟩ **3 :** to fit the contours of **:** HUG ⟨~*ed* hipline⟩ ⟨silhouettes that ~ the body —*New Yorker*⟩ **4 :** to ornament by molding or carving the material of ⟨ceilings . . . with ~*ed* or precast ornamental patterns —H.S.Morrison⟩ ~ *vi* **1 :** to become formed **:** take shape ⟨the Norman man-at-arms had begun to ~ into the English country gentleman —*Ecclesiologist*⟩ **2 :** to become fitted to a contour **:** ADAPT ⟨cloche . . . so flexible it ~s to any head size —*N.Y.Times*⟩ ⟨the river ran, leaped, ~*ed* to rocks and leaped again —Philip Murray b.1924⟩ **3 :** to make or use a mold ⟨the outstanding development in ~*ing* —*Technical News Bull.*⟩

⁵mold *also* **mould** \"\ *n* -S [ME *mowlde*, perh. alter. (influenced by *molde* soil) of *mowle*, fr. *moulen* to grow moldy; akin to ON *mygla* to grow moldy — more at ¹MOLD] **1 :** a superficial often woolly growth produced on various forms of organic matter esp. when damp or decaying and on living organisms **2 :** a fungus esp. of the order Mucorales that produces mold — compare BLACK MOLD, BLUE MOLD, MILDEW

⁶mold *or* **mould** \"\ *vb* -ED/-ING/-S [ME *mouleden*, fr. *mowlde*, n.] *vt, obs* **:** to allow to become moldy ⟨hoarding housewives that do ~ their food —William Browne⟩ ~ *vi* **1 :** to become moldy ⟨bread tends to ~ in damp weather⟩ **2** *obs* **:** to deteriorate for lack of use ⟨the man that ~s in idle cell —Edmund Spenser⟩

mold·abil·i·ty *or* **mould·abil·i·ty** \,mōldəˈbiləd·ē\ *n* **:** the property of being moldable

mold·able *or* **mould·able** \ˈmōldəbəl\ *adj* [⁴*mold*, *mould* + -*able*] **:** capable of being molded ⟨clays are plastic and ~ when sufficiently finely pulverized and wet, rigid when dry —R.N.Shreve⟩

¹mol·da·vi·an \mälˈdāvēən, -vyən\ *n* -S *cap* [*Moldavia*, province of Romania + E -*an*] **1 :** a native or inhabitant of Moldavia **2 :** Romanian as spoken in Moldavia

²moldavian \(ˈ)=;=(=)=\ *adj, usu cap* **:** of or relating to the province of Moldavia or to its people

moldboard *or* **mouldboard** \ˈ=,=\ *n* [¹*mold*, *mould* + *board*] **1 a :** a curved iron plate attached above a plowshare that lifts and turns the soil — called also *breast board* **b :** the flat or curved blade (as of a snowplow or bulldozer) that pushes material to one side as the machine advances **2** [³*mold*, *mould* + *board*] **:** one of the boards forming a mold for concrete

moldboard plow *n* **:** a plow equipped with a moldboard; *esp* **:** a general-purpose plow having a moldboard of intermediate length and curvature — called also *turnplow*; compare ¹BREAKER 2b, LISTER, SWIVEL PLOW; see PLOW illustration

molded *or* **moulded** *adj* [fr. past part. of ⁴*mold*, *mould*] **1 :** decorated or finished with a molding ⟨~ panel⟩ **2 a :** formed in or on a mold ⟨~ pottery⟩ ⟨~ plywood⟩; *specif* **:** blown in a mold ⟨~ glass is usually called blown-molded by most collectors —G.S. & Helen McKearin⟩ — compare BLOWING 4, PRESSED GLASS **b :** determined by or cut to specifications prepared in a mold loft — used of the parts of a ship ⟨~ line⟩ ⟨~ keel⟩ **3 :** CLOSE-FITTING ⟨~ bodice⟩

molded breadth *n* **:** the greatest breadth of a ship's hull exclusive of the outside plating

molded brick *n* **1 :** brick made in a mold as distinguished from wire-cut brick **2 :** brick molded into special shapes for use in ornamental brickwork

molded depth *n* **:** the vertical distance from the top of the keel to the top of the upper deck beams amidships at the gunwale

molded pulp *n* **:** wood pulp formed into protective packaging (as containers for eggs or sleeves for liquor bottles)

¹mold·er *or* **mould·er** \ˈmōldə(r)\ *n* -S [ME *molder*, fr. *molden* to mold + -*er* (n. suffix) — more at MOLD (knead)] **1 :** a kneader of bread dough **2 a :** a worker that makes molds or produces molded articles: as (1) **:** a maker of foundry molds (2) **:** BRICKMAKER 2 (3) **:** an operator of a machine with abrasive wheels for cutting decorative designs on stone and concrete products **b :** MOLDING MACHINE **c** (1) **:** ³MOLD 3a (2) *or* **molder plate :** CASTER 1b **d :** a firm that makes a business of molding ⟨the sale of . . . plastic material to commercial ~s —Milo Perkins⟩ **3 :** one that exerts a determining influence on an attitude or course of development ⟨~ of public opinion⟩ ⟨~ of talent⟩ ⟨~s of western monasticism —Helen Sullivan⟩

²molder *or* **moulder** \"\ *vb* **moldered** *or* **mouldered; moldered** *or* **mouldered; moldering** *or* **mouldering** \-d(ə)riŋ\ **molders** *or* **moulders** [freq. of ⁶*mold*, *mould*] *vi* **1 a :** to crumble away **:** DISINTEGRATE, DECAY ⟨the leaves . . . ~*ed* and went back to the earth —Margaret Kennedy⟩ ⟨body lies a-~*ing* in the grave —*John Brown's Body*⟩ ⟨left the final habitations to ~ into dust —W.E.Swinton⟩ **b :** to deteriorate for lack of exercise ⟨long periods of solitary confinement caused his mental faculties to ~⟩ ⟨air crews ~*ed* in the barracks⟩ **2** *archaic* **:** to decrease in size **:** DWINDLE ⟨the Christian army . . . was ~*ing* away with disease —John Lingard⟩ ~ *vt* **1 :** to cause to disintegrate ⟨time's . . . gradual touch has ~*ed* into beauty many a tower —William Mason⟩ **2 :** to fritter away **:** WASTE ⟨they have ~*ed* away their time in inactivity —M.G.J. de Crèvecoeur⟩

mold·i·ness *or* **mould·i·ness** \ˈmōldēnəs\ *n* -ES **:** the quality or state of being moldy

mold·ing *or* **mould·ing** \ˈmōldiŋ, -dēŋ\ *n* -S [ME *molding*, fr. gerund of *molden* to mold, shape] **1 a :** an act or process of molding ⟨dry sand ~⟩ ⟨opinion ~⟩; *specif* **:** the shaping of the fetal head to allow it to pass through the birth canal during parturition **b :** an object produced by molding ⟨bronze ~s cast in antique forms⟩ **c :** the art or occupation of a molder **2 :** the dimensions of a ship's timber measured from inside the plating to the center line — opposed to *siding*; compare MOLDED BREADTH, MOLDED DEPTH **3 a :** a continuous narrow contoured surface either recessed or projecting used singly or in groups for the decorative effect created by the play of light and shadow over it ⟨the piers were short and crowned with square blocks of stone, the ~s being ax-hewn —E.H.Short⟩ **b :** a decorative plane or curved strip (as of wood or metal) used for ornamentation or finishing ⟨carved ~s applied on doors . . . to form panels —J.E.Gloag⟩ ⟨baseboard ~⟩ ⟨~s are designed to meet typical building conditions —*Sweet's Catalog Service*⟩

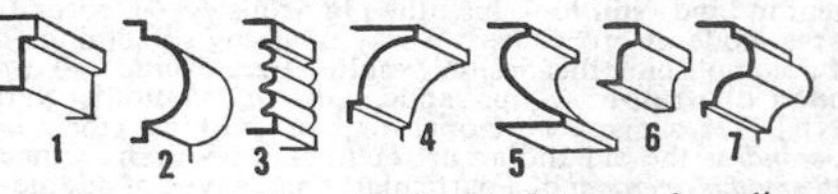

moldings 3a : *1* fillet and fascia, *2* torus, *3* reeding, *4* cavetto, *5* scotia, *6* congé, *7* beak

molding book *n* **:** a book prepared in the mold loft giving the dimensions of the structural members of a ship

molding machine *n* **1 :** a planing machine for cutting moldings **2 :** a foundry machine to assist in making molds; *esp* **:** a machine to pack the sand

molding plaster *n* **:** a finely ground retarded gypsum plaster for use in molds and for cast ornaments (as rosettes, medallions, friezes)

molding sand *n* **:** a mixture of sand and clay suitable for making foundry molds

mold loft *n* [³*mold*] **:** a large building or floor in a building where the lines of a ship or plane are laid down full size and molds and templates made from them for structural units

mold loftsman *n* **:** a worker in a mold loft

moldmade paper \ˈ=,=-\ *n* **:** a machine-made deckle-edged imitation of handmade paper

mold·man \ˈ=,man\ *n, pl* **moldmen 1 :** a worker who cleans and readies ingot molds to receive molten metal **2 :** an operator of a molding machine

moldo- *comb form, usu cap* [²*moldavian*] **:** Moldavian and ⟨*Moldo*-Wallachian⟩

moldproof \ˈ=;=\ *adj* [⁵*mold*] **:** impervious to mildew

molds *pl of* MOLD, *pres 3d sing of* MOLD

mold·warp \ˈmōl,dwȯrp\ *or* **mold·i·warp** \-ldi,w-\ *n* -S [ME *moldewerp*, *moldewarp*, *moldywarp*, *molwarp*; akin to OS *moldwerp* mole, MD *moldewerp*, MHG *multwerf*, *multwerf*; all fr. a prehistoric WGmc compound whose 1st constituent is represented by E ¹*mold* and whose 2d constituent is akin to OE *weorpan* to throw — more at WARP] **1** *dial Brit* **:** a European mole (*Talpa europaea*) **2** *dial* **:** a stupid or shiftless person ⟨the old man . . . a shambling ~ —Maristan Chapman⟩

moldy *or* **mouldy** \ˈmōldē, -di\ *adj* -ER/-EST [⁵*mold*, *mould* + -*y*] **1 a :** old and moldering **:** ANCIENT, CRUMBLING ⟨a dark ~ courtyard on a side street —P.E.Deutschman⟩ **b :** old and outmoded **:** ANTIQUATED, FUSTY ⟨~ tradition⟩ ⟨helping ~ professors to teach grubby students —Oliver La Farge⟩ **c** *slang* **:** DISREPUTABLE, MISERABLE ⟨wearing a ~ sport shirt —J.W.Ellison b.1929⟩ **2 :** of, resembling, or covered with a mold-producing fungus ⟨~ moss⟩ ⟨~ feed⟩ ⟨~ bread⟩

moldy corn poisoning *n* **:** CORNSTALK DISEASE 2

moldy nose *n* **:** WHITE ROT 2c

moldy rot *n* **:** a disease of the tapping panels of the Para rubber tree caused by a fungus (*Ceratostomella fruibriata*)

¹mole \ˈmōl\ *n* -S [ME *mool*, *mole*, fr. OE *māl* spot, blemish; akin to OHG *meil* spot, Goth *mail* wrinkle, and perh. to Gk *miainein* to pollute, defile, Lith *maiva* swamp] **1** *archaic* **:** a discolored spot in cloth **:** STAIN **2 a :** a congenital spot, mark, or small permanent protuberance on the human body; *esp* **:** a pigmented nevus **b** *obs* **:** an identifying mark or blemish ⟨a ~ in the fair face of church government —Nathaniel Bacon⟩

²mole \"\ *vt* -ED/-ING/-S [ME *molen*, fr. *mool*, *mole*, n.] *archaic* **:** STAIN, DISCOLOR

³mole \"\ *n* -S *often attrib* [ME; akin to MD *mol* mole, MLG *mul*, *mol* mole, and prob. to OE *molde* soil — more at MOLD] **1 a :** any of numerous burrowing mammals chiefly of the family Talpidae living mainly in temperate parts of Europe, Asia, and No. America and having minute eyes often covered with skin, small concealed ears, very soft and often iridescent fur, and strong fossorial feet **b :** MOLE CRICKET **c :** MOLE RAT **d :** the short dense velvety pelt of the mole used as a fur — called also *moleskin* **2** *archaic* **:** a blind man or one who works in a dark place ⟨well said, old ~! canst work in the earth so fast —*Shak.*⟩ **3 a :** the borer of a mole plow **b :** MOLE PLOW **4** *or* **mole gray a :** a nearly neutral, slightly bluish, dark gray that is lighter and slightly greener than pewter — called also *moleskin* **b :** TAUPE 1

⁴mole \"\ *vi* **moled; moled; moling; moles :** to make or traverse an underground passage **:** BURROW, TUNNEL ⟨enemy remnants . . . had *moled* in under the wreckage —*Infantry Jour.*⟩ ⟨the diversion tunnel *moled* 1161 feet through an almost solid rock canyon wall —*Civil Engineering*⟩; *specif* **:** to make a mole drain

⁵mole \"\ *n* -S [MF, fr. OIt *molo*, fr. LGk *mōlos*, fr. L *moles*, lit., mass, exertion; akin to OE *mēthe* weary, OHG *muodi*, ON *mōthr* weary, Goth *afmauiths* exhausted, Gk *mōlos* exertion, Russ *mayat'* to fatigue, torment, annoy] **1 a :** a mound or massive work formed of masonry and large stones or earth laid in the sea as a pier or breakwater **b :** the harbor formed by such a work **2** [L *moles*] *obs* **:** a large piece **:** MASS, BULK **3** [L *moles*, lit., mass, exertion] **:** an ancient Roman tomb or mausoleum

⁶mole \"\ *n* -S [F *môle*, fr. L *mola* mooncalf, mole (lit., mill, millstone); trans. of Gk *mylē* (lit., millstone) — more at MILL] **:** an abnormal mass in the uterus: **a :** a blood clot containing a degenerated fetus and its membranes **b :** HYDATIDIFORM MOLE

⁷mole *also* **mol** \"\ *n* -S [G *mol*, short for *molekulargewicht* molecular weight, fr. *molekular* molecular + *gewicht* weight] **:** the quantity of a chemical substance that has a weight in mass units (as grams or pounds) numerically equal to the molecular weight or that in the case of a gas has a volume occupied by such a weight under specified conditions (as 22.4 liters at 0°C and a pressure of 760 millimeters of mercury);

esp : GRAM MOLECULE ⟨a ~ of any substance contains the same number of molecules —Farrington Daniels & R.A.Alberty⟩

⁸mo·le \'mō(,)lā\ *n, usu cap* : MOSSI

⁹mo·le \'mōlē\ *n* -S [MexSp, fr. Nahuatl *mulli, molli* sauce, stew] : a highly spiced sauce made principally of chile and chocolate but containing numerous other ingredients and served with meat (as beef or turkey)

molecast \'ˌˌ\ *n* [³*mole* + *cast*] : MOLEHILL

mole catcher *n* : one that catches moles; *specif* : BROWN KING SNAKE

mole crab *n* : BAIT BUG

mole cricket *n* : an insect of the widespread family Gryllotalpidae (order Orthoptera) having large fossorial front legs adapted for digging in moist soil and feeding largely on the roots of plants

mo·lec·u·la \mə'lekyələ\ *n, pl* **molecu·lae** \-yə,lē\ [NL — more at MOLECULE] *archaic* : MOLECULE

mo·lec·u·lar \mə'lekyələ(r)\ *adj* [ISV *molecule* + *-ar*] **1** : relating to, connected with, produced by, or consisting of molecules : MOLAR, MOLAL ⟨~ structure⟩ ⟨~ rearrangement⟩ ⟨~ oxygen⟩ **2** : consisting of two or more atomic statements related by logical connectives ⟨~ proposition⟩ — see ¹ATOMIC 4 **3** : relating to or emphasizing individual responses or structures of behavior ⟨proceed by more and more detailed analysis to the ~ facts of perception —G.A.Miller⟩ — opposed to *molar* — **mo·lec·u·lar·ly** *adv*

molecular beam *n* : a stream of molecules that escape at thermal speeds from a heated enclosure, that are controlled by slits so as to move in nearly parallel paths, and that are used in determining the electric and magnetic properties of atoms, atomic nuclei, and molecules

molecular biology *n* : a branch of biology dealing with the ultimate physicochemical organization of living matter

molecular compound *n* : a compound regarded as a union of molecules retaining their identities (as in boron trifluoride-ethyl ether $BF_3.(C_2H_5)_2O$) — called also *addition compound;* compare DOUBLE SALT 2

molecular distillation *n* : distillation that is carried out under a high vacuum in an apparatus so designed as to permit molecules escaping from the warm liquid to reach the cooled surface of the condenser before colliding with other molecules and consequently returning to the liquid and that is used in the purification of substances of low volatility (as in the separation of vitamin A and vitamin E from fish-liver oils)

molecular film *n* : a monomolecular film or layer : MONOLAYER

molecular formula *n* : a chemical formula based on both analysis and molecular weight ⟨$C_2H_4O_2$ and $C_6H_{12}O_6$ are the *molecular formulas* of acetic acid and glucose respectively or twice and six times the empirical formulas respectively⟩ — compare STRUCTURAL FORMULA

molecular heat *n* : the heat capacity per gram molecule of any pure substance : the specific heat in calories per degree per gram multiplied by the molecular weight — compare ATOMIC HEAT

mo·lec·u·lar·i·ty \mə,lekyə'larəd·ē *also* -'ler-\ *n* -ES : the quality, state, or degree of being molecular; *esp* : the number of molecules or atoms involved in a chemical reaction ⟨there is no necessary correlation between the ~ and the order — Farrington Daniels & R.A.Alberty⟩

molecular layer *n* **1** : the outer layer of the cortex of the cerebellum and cerebrum consisting of a mass of unmedullated fibers rich in synapses **2** : either of the two plexiform layers of the retina

molecular model *n* : a scale model showing the arrangement of

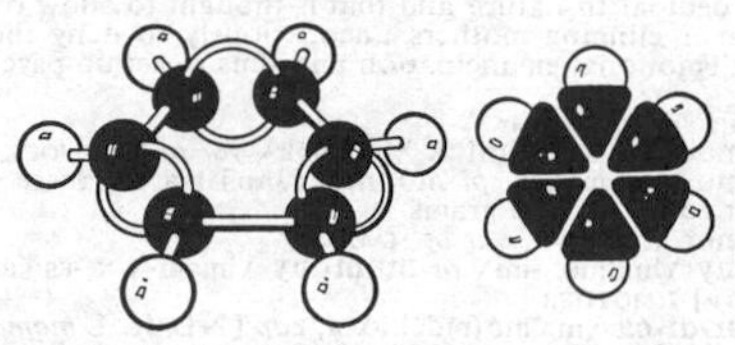

two molecular models of benzene, in which carbon atoms are represented by dark balls and quasi tetrahedrons, and hydrogen atoms by light balls and half spheres

atoms in a molecule (as of an organic compound)

molecular pump *n* : a vacuum pump that depends for its action on the adhesion of the gas or vapor molecules to a rapidly moving metal disk or cylinder by which they are carried away

molecular rotation *n* : a value obtained by multiplying the specific rotation by the molecular weight

molecular sieve *n* : a crystalline substance (as a zeolite) that is characterized by pores of molecular dimensions and uniform size formed by heating to drive off the water of hydration and that by its ability to adsorb small molecules but not large ones can be used esp. in separations (as of gases or liquids) based on differences in sizes of molecules or as a carrier (as of accelerators in rubber vulcanization)

molecular silver *n* : a gray powdery active form of silver obtained by reducing silver chloride with zinc

molecular spectrum *n* : a spectrum of radiation due to electron transitions and other quantum energy changes within molecules and consisting of series of characteristic spectrum bands which are found upon high dispersion to be made up of very fine lines

molecular still *n* : an apparatus for carrying out a molecular distillation

molecular volume *n* : the quotient obtained by dividing the molecular weight by the specific gravity — compare ATOMIC VOLUME

molecular weight *n* : the weight of a molecule that may be calculated as the sum of the atomic weights of its constituent atoms

mol·e·cule \'mälə,kyül, -lē,-\ *n* -S [F *molécule,* fr. NL *molecula,* dim. of L *moles* mass — more at MOLE (structure)] **1 a** : a unit of matter that is the smallest particle of an element or chemical combination of atoms (as a compound) capable of retaining chemical identity with the substance in mass ⟨a few elements (as helium and neon) have monatomic ~*s*⟩ ⟨the viruses are one kind of giant ~*s* —Linus Pauling⟩ — see AVOGADRO'S LAW; compare ION, RADICAL **5 b** : a quantity proportional to the molecular weight; *esp* : ⁷MOLE **2** : a tiny bit : FRACTION, FRAGMENT ⟨every tone . . . is a ~ of music — Henry Miller⟩ ⟨a ~ of political honesty —*Time*⟩

moled *past of* MOLE

mole drain *n* [³*mole*] : an underground channel made by a mole plow and used esp. for draining heavy farm soils of more or less uniform slope

mole drainage *or* **mole draining** *n* : an act, instance, or system of drawing off water from farmland by mole drains

mole fraction *n* [⁷*mole*] : the ratio of the number of moles of one component of a solution or other mixture to the total number of moles representing all of the components

mole gray *n* : ³MOLE 4

molehill \'ˌˌ\ *n* [ME, fr. *mole* + *hill*] **1** : a little ridge of earth thrown up by a mole working close to the surface — called also *molecast* **2** : an insignificant obstacle or difficulty : TRIFLE ⟨make a mountain out of a ~⟩

mole mouse *n* : SOKHOR

mole plant *also* **mole tree** *n* : CAPER SPURGE

mole plow *or* **mole drainer** *n* [³*mole*] : a subsoil plow having a vertical knife behind the tooth of which is drawn a round or tapered metal ball that opens an underground channel

mole rat *n* : any of various rodents resembling true moles in habit or appearance: as **a** : SOKHOR **b** : a member of the family Spalacidae of the eastern Mediterranean region **c** : a member of the family Bathyergidae and esp. of the African genus *Bathyergus* **d** : a member of the East Indian murid genus *Nesokia*

moles *pl of* MOLE, *pres 3d sing of* MOLE

mole salamander *n* : a brownish black burrowing salamander (*Ambystoma talpoideum*) of the southeastern U.S.

mole shrew *n* **1 a** : an American short-tailed shrew of the genus *Blarina* **b** : any of several shrews of the genus *Anourosorex* that resemble moles, have the ears and eyes greatly reduced, have slate-colored glossy fur, and live in the high mountains of Burma, China, and Siam **2** : SHREW MOLE

moleskin \'ˌˌ\ *n* **1** : ³MOLE 1d **2 a** : a heavy durable cotton fabric made in satin weave for industrial, medical, and clothing uses and usu. with a smooth twilled surface on one side and a short thick velvety nap on the other **b** : a garment (as trousers) made of moleskin — usu. used in pl. ⟨got on their boots and ~*s* —Mary S. Broome⟩ **3** : ³MOLE 4a

mole snake *n* **1** : a valuable colubrid snake (*Pseudaspis cana*) that is common in South and East Africa and feeds on rats and mice **2** : BROWN KING SNAKE

¹mo·lest \mə'lest\ *vt* -ED/-ING/-S [ME *molesten,* fr. MF *molester,* fr. L *molestare,* fr. *molestus* burdensome, annoying, irreg. fr. *moles* mass — more at MOLE (structure)] **1** *obs* **a** : INCONVENIENCE, HARASS, PLAGUE ⟨the heats of summer are . . . incapable of ~*ing* you —Joseph Addison⟩ **b** : to affect injuriously : AFFLICT ⟨they were generally ~*ed* with . . . sciatica —Sir Thomas Browne⟩ **2 a** : ANNOY, PERSECUTE, DISTURB, TORMENT ⟨painted in a loft, drawing up the ladder after him that he might not be ~*ed* by his family —Laurence Binyon⟩ ⟨leaders . . . should not be ~*ed* in any way nor should their party be outlawed —Sidney Hook⟩; *specif* : RAID ⟨traders turn to ~*ing* the Spanish borderlands —R.A.Billington⟩ **b** : to meddle or interfere with unjustifiably often as a result of abnormal sexual motivation ⟨charges of being drunk and ~*ing* a woman —Frank Yerby⟩ ⟨~*ing* small boys in the washroom of a moving picture house —Wenzell Brown⟩

²molest \"\ *n* -S [ME, fr. MF *moleste,* irreg. fr. L *molestia* trouble, fr. *molestus* + *-ia* -y] : MOLESTATION ⟨within his walls, secure from all ~ —W.J.Linton⟩

mo·les·ta·tion \,mō,le'stāshən, -lə'-\ *n* -S [ME *molestacioun,* fr. MF *molestation,* fr. LL *molestation-, molestatio,* fr. L *molestatus* (past part. of *molestare*) + *-ion-, -io* -ion] **1 a** *archaic* : a cause or state of harassment : VEXATION ⟨all the ~*s* of marriage are abundantly recompensed with other comforts —Thomas Fuller⟩ **b** : an act or instance of molesting : ANNOYANCE, OBSTRUCTION ⟨liberty to . . . worship without ~ — William Sewel⟩ ⟨seas upon which our ships and planes can travel without ~ —*U.S.Code*⟩ **2 a** *Scots law* : interference with or troubling another in his possession of land **b** : willful injury inflicted upon another by interference with his user of rights as to person, character, social position, or property

mo·lest·er \mə'lestə(r)\ *n* -S : one that molests

mo·lest·ful \-tfəl\ *adj, archaic* : TROUBLESOME, ANNOYING ⟨~ battle with carnal vices —Thomas Wright⟩

molet *var of* MULLET

mo·le·ta \mə'lād·ə\ *n* -S [Pg *moleta, muleta,* fr. *muleta* crutch, fr. Sp — more at MULETA] : a short-masted Portuguese fishing boat having a large lateen sail, two outriggers and a bowsprit that carry up to six sails, and an outrigger at the stern with two triangular sails

moleta

mole·warp \'mōl,wȯrp\ *var of* MOLDWARP

mol·ge \'mōljē\ [NL, fr. G *molch* salamander, fr. OHG *mol, molm, molt;* akin to OS & MLG *mol* salamander, and perh. to Arm *molēz* lizard] *syn of* TRITURUS

mol·gu·la \'mälgyələ\ *n, cap* [NL, fr. Gk *molgos* hide, skin + NL *-ula;* perh. akin to OHG *malaha* leather bag, ON *malr* bag] : a cosmopolitan genus (the type of the family Molgulidae) of almost spherical ascidians with long siphons and a thin somewhat transparent tunic — **mol·gu·lid** \-ləd\ *adj or n*

¹mo·lid \'mōləd\ *adj* [NL *Molidae*] : of or relating to the Molidae

²molid \"\ *n* -S : a fish of the family Molidae

mol·i·dae \'mälə,dē\ *n pl, cap* [NL, fr. *Mola,* type genus + *-idae*] : a family of large pelagic marine fishes (order Plectognathi) that have very large heads, short compact bodies, and teeth fused to form a beak and that lack a dorsal fin — see MOLA

mo·li·men \mə'līmən\ *n, pl* **mo·lim·i·na** \-limənə\ [NL, fr. L, exertion, fr. *moliri* to struggle, fr. *moles* mass, burden — more at MOLE (structure)] : discomfort or sensations of tension preceding or accompanying menstruation

moliminous *adj* [L *molimin-, molimen* + E *-ous*] *obs* : CUMBERSOME, WEIGHTY

mol·i·nary \'mälə,nerē, 'mōl-\ *adj* [LL *molina* mill + E *-ary* — more at MILL] : of or relating to a mill or the process of grinding

mo·line \'mōlən, mō'līn\ *adj* [fr. (assumed) AF *moliné,* fr. OF *molin* mill, fr. LL *molinum* — more at MILL] *of a cross* : having the end of each arm forked and recurved — compare ANCRÉE, CROSS MOLINE, FOURCHÉE, PATY, RECERCELÉE; see CROSS illustration

molinet *n* -S [F *moulinet,* fr. MF *molinet,* dim. of *molin* mill] **1** *obs* : a stick for whipping chocolate **2** *obs* : a small grinding mill

moling *pres part of* MOLE

mo·lin·ia \mə'linēə\ *n, cap* [NL, fr. Juan Ignacio *Molina* †1829, Chilean naturalist + NL *-ia*] : a small genus of Eurasian grasses having narrow flat leaves, slender panicles, and awnless glumes — see MOOR GRASS 2

¹mo·li·nism \'mōlə,nizəm, 'mäl-\ *n* -S *usu cap* [Sp *molinismo,* fr. Luis *Molina* †1600 Span. Jesuit and theologian + Sp *-ismo* -ism] : a doctrine that it is man's free cooperation which makes it possible for him to perform a good act with God's helping grace — compare CONGRUISM, THOMISM

²molinism \"\ *n* -S *usu cap* [Sp *molinismo,* fr. Miguel de *Molinos* †*ab*1697 Span. priest and mystic + Sp *-ismo* -ism] : QUIETISM

¹mo·li·nist \-,nəst\ *n* -S *usu cap* [Sp *molinista,* fr. Luis *Molina* †1600 + Sp *-ista* -ist] : an advocate or follower of the doctrine of Luis Molina

²molinist \"\ *n* -S *usu cap* [Sp *molinista,* fr. Miguel de *Molinos* + Sp *-ista* -ist] : an advocate or follower of the quietism of Miguel de Molinos

mo·lisch reaction \'mōlish-\ *or* **molisch test** *n, usu cap M* [after Hans *Molisch* †1937 Ger. botanist] : a test for carbohydrate in which a reddish violet color is formed by reaction with alpha-naphthol in the presence of concentrated sulfuric acid

¹moll \'mȯl\ *adj* [G, fr. ML (*b*) *molle* b flat; fr. *b* + L *molle,* neut. of *mollis* soft, weak — more at MELT] : composed in the minor mode : MINOR ⟨G ~⟩

²moll \'mäl, 'mȯl\ *n* -S [prob. fr. *Moll,* nickname for *Mary*] **1** : PROSTITUTE **2 a** : DOLL 2 ⟨a sailor and his ~⟩ **b** : a gangster's girl friend — called also *gun moll* ⟨frequented by gangsters and their ~*s* —W.S.Maugham⟩

mollah *var of* MULLAH

moll–buzzer \'ˌˌ\ *n* [²*moll*] *slang* : a pickpocket whose victims are women

mo·lle \'mō(,)yā\ *n* -S [AmerSp, fr. Quechua *mulli*] : PEPPER TREE 1

mollemock *var of* MALLEMUCK

mol·li·crush \'mäli,krəsh, -rəsh\ *vt* [perh. fr. E dial. *mully* powdery (fr. E ¹*mull* + *-y*) + E *crush*] *dial Eng* : to beat to jelly : CRUSH, PULVERIZE

¹mollie *var of* MOLLY

²mol·lie *also* **mol·ly** \'mälē\ *n, pl* **mollies** [by shortening] : MOLLIENISIA 2

mol·li·e·nis·ia \,mälēə'nisēə\ *n* [NL, irreg. after Comte François N. *Mollien* †1850 Fr. statesman] **1** *cap* : a genus of brightly colored topminnows of the family Poeciliidae highly valued as aquarium fishes — see SAILFIN **2** -S : any fish of the genus *Mollienisia*

mol·lier diagram \'mȯl(,)yā-\ *or* **mollier chart** *n, usu cap M* [after Richard *Mollier* †1935 Ger. mechanical engineer] : a diagram showing thermodynamic properties of a substance with various quantities (as temperature and pressure) constant esp. in terms of entropy and enthalpy as coordinates

mollies *pl of* MOLLY

mol·li·fi·able \'mälə,fīəbəl, ˌˌ'ˌˌˌ\ *adj* : capable of being mollified

mol·li·fi·ca·tion \,mäləfə'kāshən\ *n* -S [ME *mollificacioun,* fr. MF *mollification,* fr. ML *mollification-, mollificatio,* fr. LL *mollificatus* (past part. of *mollificare* to soften) + *-ion-, -io* -ion — more at MOLLIFY] **1** : an act or instance of tempering : AMELIORATION, APPEASEMENT **2** : the quality or state of being mollified

mollifier *n* -S : one that mollifies ⟨vinegar . . . is itself a prime corrector and ~ —Thomas Fuller⟩

mol·li·fy \'mälə,fī\ *vb* -ED/-ING/-ES [ME *mollefien, mollifien;* fr. MF *mollifier,* fr. LL *mollificare,* fr. L *mollis* soft + *-ficare* -fy — more at MELT] *vt* **1** : to soothe in temper or disposition : CONCILIATE, PACIFY ⟨*mollified* by her flattery⟩ ⟨should have *mollified* their artistic critics —Hunter Mead⟩ ⟨eager to ~ his own . . . nationalists —Claire Sterling⟩ **2** : to reduce the stiffness or rigidity of : SOFTEN ⟨shaving cream *mollifies* the beard⟩ ⟨they have riddled and *mollified* the rocks —D.C. Peattie⟩ ⟨plump cushions with bright covers ~ the lounges —Blanche E. Baughan⟩ **3 a** : to reduce in intensity or violence : ASSUAGE, AMELIORATE ⟨their solicitude *mollifies* his pique⟩ ⟨the behavior was not only *mollified* but improvement continued to recovery —*Diseases of the Nervous System*⟩ **b** : to make more agreeable : TEMPER ⟨prevailed on him to ~ his demands⟩ ⟨nor can the social necessity for the product ~ the process —Lewis Mumford⟩ ~ *vi, archaic* : to become less angry or obstinate : SOFTEN, RELENT ⟨the father *mollifies* and is reconciled to the marriage —*Examiner*⟩ **syn** see PACIFY

mol·li·fy·ing·ly *adv* : in a mollifying manner

mol·li·grant \'mäli,grant\ *n* -S [origin unknown] *Scot* : a wailing lamentation : COMPLAINT

mol·lis·i·a·ce·ae \mə,lisē'āsē,ē\ *n pl* [NL, fr. *Mollisia,* type genus (irreg. fr. L *mollis* soft + NL *-ia*) + *-aceae*] : a family of fungi (order Helotiales having the hymenium of the apothecium surrounded by a pseudoparenchymatous rim of dark mostly thick-walled cells

mol·lis·i·ose \mə'lisē,ōs\ *n* -S [NL *Mollisia* + E *-ose*] : LEAF SCORCH b

mol·li·sol \'mälə,säl\ *n* -S [L *mollis* soft + *solum* ground — more at MELT, SOIL] : the surface layer of permanently frozen ground in which the ice melts during the summer

mol·lu·go \mə'lü(,)gō\ *n, cap* [NL, fr. L, stickseed, fr. *mollis* soft] : a genus of low chiefly tropical American herbs (family Aizoaceae) having whorled leaves and pedicellate flowers — see CARPETWEED

mol·lus·ca \mə'ləskə\ *n pl, cap* [NL, fr. L, neut. pl. of *molluscus* soft, fr. *mollis* — more at MELT] : a large phylum of invertebrate animals that include the chitons, tooth shells, snails, mussels and other bivalves, octopuses, and related forms and that have a soft unsegmented body lacking segmented appendages and commonly protected by a calcareous shell secreted by a mantle which extends from the body wall usu. as an enveloping fold; a muscular foot which is formed from part of the ventral surface of the body and is variously modified for creeping, digging, or swimming; a well-developed heart and vascular system and usu. one or more pairs of gills; a complex nervous system with several pairs of ganglia and longitudinal and transverse commissures; and frequently more or less complex eyes and otocysts — compare AMPHINEURA, CEPHALOPODA, GASTROPODA, LAMELLIBRANCHIA, SCAPHOPODA

mol·lus·can *also* **mol·lus·kan** \-kən\ *adj* [NL *Mollusca* + E *-an*] : of or relating to the Mollusca

mol·lus·ci·ci·dal \mə,ləs(k)ə'sīdᵊl\ *also* **mol·lus·ca·ci·dal** \-skə-\ *adj* : of, relating to, or being a molluscicide ⟨~ action⟩

mol·lus·ci·cide \mə'ləs(k)ə,sīd\ *or* **mol·lus·ca·cide** \-skə-\ *n* -S [*molluscicide* fr. NL *Mollusca* + E *-i-* + *-cide; mollus-cacide* fr. NL *Mollusca* + E *-cide*] : an agent for destroying mollusks (as snails)

mol·lus·civ·o·rous \,mälə's(k)iv(ə)rəs\ *adj* [NL *Mollusca* + E *-i-* + *-vorous*] : feeding upon mollusks

¹mol·lus·coid \mə'lə,skȯid\ *also* **mol·lus·coi·dal** \,mälə'skȯidᵊl\ *adj* [*molluscoid* fr. NL *Molluscoidea*; *molluscoidal* fr. NL *Molluscoidea* + E *-al*] : of, like, or relating to the Molluscoidea

²molluscoid \"\ *n* -S : one of the Molluscoidea

mol·lus·coi·da \,mälə'skȯidə\ [NL, fr. *Mollusca* + *-oida*] *syn of* MOLLUSCOIDEA

mol·lus·coi·dea \-dēə\ *n pl, cap* [NL, fr. *Mollusca* + *-oidea*] *in some classifications* : a phylum of invertebrate animals distinguished by possession of a lophophore and typically including the present groups Brachiopoda, Bryozoa, Entoprocta, and Phoronidea — **mol·lus·coi·de·an** \ˌˌˌ'skȯidēən\ *adj or n*

¹mol·lus·cous \mə'ləskəs\ *adj* [NL *Mollusca* + E *-ous*] : MOLLUSCAN

²molluscous \"\ *adj* [NL *molluscum* + E *-ous*] : of, relating to, or having the properties of a molluscum

mol·lus·cum \mə'ləskəm\ *n, pl* **mollus·ca** \-kə\ [NL, fr. L *molluscum,* a fungus, fr. neut. of *molluscus* soft — more at MOLLUSCA] : any of several skin diseases marked by soft pulpy nodules — see MOLLUSCUM CONTAGIOSUM

molluscum con·ta·gi·o·sum \-kən,tajē'ōsəm\ *n, pl* **mollusca contagio·sa** \-sə\ [NL, lit., contagious molluscum] : a mild chronic viral disease of the skin characterized by the formation of small nodules with a central opening and contents resembling curd

mol·lusk *or* **mol·lusc** \'mäləsk\ *n* -S [F *mollusque,* fr. NL *Mollusca*] : one of the Mollusca : SHELLFISH

moll·wei·de projection \'mȯl,vīdə-\ *n, usu cap M* [after Karl B. *Mollweide* †1825 Ger. mathematician and astronomer] : an equal-area map projection capable of showing the entire surface of the earth in the form of an ellipse with all parallels as straight lines more widely spaced at the equator than at the poles, with the central meridian as one half the length of the equator, and with all other meridians ellipses equally spaced

¹mol·ly *or* **mol·lie** \'mälē, -li\ *n, pl* **mollies** [fr. *Molly, Mollie,* nickname for *Mary*] **1** *slang* : ²MOLL **2** *slang* : MOLLYCODDLE

²molly *or* **mollie** \"\ *n, pl* **mollies** [by shortening and alter.] : MALLEMUCK

³molly *var of* MALI

⁴molly *var of* MOLLIE

¹mollycoddle \'ˌˌˌˌ\ *n* [¹*molly* + *coddle*] **1** : a pampered darling : a spineless weakling ⟨his mother might turn him into a ~ —Aldous Huxley⟩ ⟨catch those ~*s* getting away from the steam heaters —*Everybody's Mag.*⟩; *specif* : an effeminate man ⟨the men . . . were ~*s,* and the women were sexually unemployed —Francis Hackett⟩ **2** : GOODY-GOODY ⟨these are the words not of a ~ or a sentimentalist, but of a veteran soldier —*Nation*⟩

²mollycoddle \"\ *vt* : to treat with fond indulgence : protect and cater to : PAMPER, SPOIL ⟨believes we have *mollycoddled* women too much —*N. Y. Times*⟩ ⟨judges ~ these young hoods —James McGlincy⟩ **syn** see INDULGE

mol·ly·cod·dler \'ˌˌ,käd(ᵊ)lə(r)\ *n* : one that mollycoddles

mol·ly·cot \'mäli,kät\ *n* [¹*molly* + obs. *cot* man who does women's work, short for *cotquean*] *dial Eng* : one unduly concerned with housekeeping; *esp* : a man who takes an interest in or does housework usu. performed by women

mol·ly·grubs \'mäli,grəbz\ *var of* MULLIGRUBS

mol·ly·hawk \'mälē,hȯk\ *n* -S [by folk etymology fr. *mallemuck*] : MALLEMUCK

mollymawk *var of* MALLEMUCK

mol·man \'mälmən\ *n, pl* **molmen** [ME, fr. *mol-* (fr. OE *māl* terms, agreement, pay) + *man* — more at MAIL] : one of a class of tenants in feudal England released from most of their service on condition of paying certain rents for their land

mo·loch \'mō,läk, 'mä,läk\ *n* [LL, an ancient Semitic deity, fr. Gk, fr. Heb *Mōlekh*] **1** -S *usu cap* : a tyrannical power to be propitiated by human subservience or sacrifice ⟨duty has become the *Moloch* of modern life —Norman Douglas⟩ ⟨began . . . to suspend members of his staff as a human sacrifice to propitiate the *Moloch* of fear and hysteria —*New Republic*⟩ **2** [NL, fr. LL] **a** *cap* : a genus of small spiny Australian desert lizards **b** -S : any lizard of the genus *Moloch*

moloch 2b

1mo·loid \'mō,lȯid\ *adj* [NL *Mola* + E *-oid*] **:** of, relating to, or resembling a mola or the Molidae

2moloid \"\ *n* -s **:** an ocean sunfish **:** MOLA

mol·o·kan \,mälə'kän\ *n, pl* **molokans** \-nz\ *also* **moloka·ni** \-nē\ *usu cap* [Russ, fr. *moloko* milk; prob. fr. the dietary laws of the sect that permit milk drinking during Lent] **:** a member of a religious sect originating in Russia as an offshoot of the Doukhobors, becoming an antiritualistic group stressing the authority of the Bible, and calling themselves Spiritual Christians

1mo·los·si·an \mə'läsh(ē)ən, -läsēən, -äsyən\ *n* -s *usu cap* [*Molossis*, district in northwestern Greece + E *-an*] **1 :** a native or inhabitant of Molossis, a district of ancient Epirus famous for its dogs **2 :** a large dog of ancient times resembling a mastiff

2molossian \"\ *adj, usu cap* **:** of, relating to, or characteristic of Molossis or Molossians

1mo·los·sic \mə'läsik\ *adj* [*molossus* + *-ic*] **:** of or relating to a molossus

2molossic \"\ *n* -s **1 :** MOLOSSUS 1 **2 :** a word whose syllables form a molossus

mo·los·sid \mə'läsə̇d\ *adj* [NL *Molossidae*] **:** of or relating to the Molossidae or to mastiff bats

mo·los·si·dae \-sə,dē\ *n pl, cap* [NL, fr. *Molossus*, type genus + *-idae*] **:** a family of Microchiroptera comprising the typical mastiff bats

mo·los·sus \mə'läsəs\ *n* [L, fr. Gk *molossos*, fr. *Molossos* Molossian] **1** *pl* **molos·si** \-ä,sī\ *classical prosody* **:** a foot of three long syllables **2** *cap* [NL, fr. L, Molossian, fr. Gk (*kyōn*) *Molossos*, lit., Molossian dog] **:** a genus of mastiff bats that is the type of the family Molossidae

mol·o·thrus \'mäləthrəs\ *n, cap* [NL, prob. modif. of Gk *molobros* greedy fellow] **:** a genus of Icteridae consisting of the cowbirds

mo·lo·tov \'mälə,tȯf, 'mȯl-, 'mōl-\ *adj, usu cap* [*Molotov*, former name (1940–58) of Perm, city near the Ural mountains U.S.S.R.] **:** PERM

molotov cocktail *n, usu cap M* [after Vyacheslav M. *Molotov* *b*1890 Russ. statesman] **:** a crude hand grenade made of a bottle filled with a flammable liquid (as gasoline) and fitted with a wick or saturated rag taped to the bottom and ignited at the moment of hurling

mol·pa·dia \mäl'pādēə\ *n, cap* [NL, prob. after *Molpadia*, a minor goddess of Greek mythology, fr. Gk] **:** a widely distributed genus (the type of the family Molpadiidae) comprising smooth-bodied burrowing sea cucumbers having a well-developed respiratory tree and a distinct caudal prolongation of a body — **mol·pa·did** \'mälpədə̇d\ *n or adj*

1molt *or* **moult** \'mōlt\ *vb* -ED/-ING/-S [alter. of ME *mouten*, fr. (assumed) OE *mūtian* to change (as in *bemūtian* to exchange), fr. L *mutare* — more at MUTABLE] *vi* **:** to shed or cast off hair, feathers, shell, horns, or an outer layer of skin in a process of growth or periodic renewal with the cast-off parts being replaced by new growth ⟨birds ~ once or twice a year⟩ ⟨a mature lobster ~*s* . . . in the spring or early summer —Joe McCarthy⟩ **~** *vt* **1 :** to cast off (an outer covering) in a periodic process of growth or renewal ⟨~*ed* its wing feathers —*Nat'l Geographic*⟩ ⟨the crab ~*s* its shell⟩; *specif* **:** to throw off (the old cuticle) — used of an arthropod ⟨a spider, like a lobster, ~*s* its covering as it grows —Eugene Kinkead⟩ **2 :** to free oneself from **:** CHANGE ⟨~ his old notions in a transition period⟩ **syn** see DISCARD

2molt *or* **moult** \"\ *n* -s **1 :** the act or process of molting ⟨helps hens to lay right through the ~ —*Poultry Tribune*⟩; *specif* **:** ECDYSIS **2 :** a cast-off covering ⟨bare ground . . . heavily besprinkled with the whitish aphid skins or ~*s* —*Jour. of Agric. Research*⟩ — compare EXUVIAE

mol·ten \'mōltᵊn *also* -ltən\ *adj* [ME, fr. past part. of *melten* to melt — more at MELT] **1 a** *obs* **:** formed in a mold **:** CAST **b :** fused or liquefied by heat **:** MELTED ⟨~ lead was poured drop by drop from the top of the tower and . . . solidified as lead shot —*Linguaphone Mag.*⟩ ⟨volcanoes pour forth . . . ~ basalt —R.W.Murray⟩ ⟨~ Parmesan cheese —C.S.Forester⟩ **2 :** having warmth or brilliance **:** HEATED, GLOWING ⟨seething . . . he set himself to compose a ~ political pamphlet —Edgar Johnson⟩ ⟨the ~ sunlight of warm skies —T.B.Costain⟩ — **mol·ten·ly** *adv*

mol·te·no disease \mäl'tē(,)nō-\ *n, usu cap M* [after *Molteno* Farmers' Assoc., Union of So. Africa, that first investigated it] **:** a frequently fatal intoxication of southern African cattle marked by liver injury and extreme emaciation due to feeding on a groundsel (*Senecio burchellii*) — compare WINTON DISEASE

molt·er *or* **moult·er** \'mōltə(r)\ *n* -s [ME *mowtare*, fr. *mowtan, mouten* to molt + *-are, -er* -er] **:** one that molts or is molting

mol·to \'mōl(,)tō\ *adv* [It, fr. L *multum*, fr. neut. of *multus* much — more at MELIORATE] **:** MUCH, VERY — used in musical directions ⟨~ adagio⟩ ⟨~ sostenuto⟩

mo·luc·ca \mə'ləkə\ *also* **mo·luc·can** \-kən\ *adj, usu cap* [*Molucca* fr. *Molucca* islands, Indonesia; *Moluccan* fr. *Molucca* islands + E *-an*] **:** of or relating to the Moluccas or Spice islands of the Malay archipelago

molucca balm *n, usu cap M* **:** an annual herb (*Moluccella laevis*) with a greenish calyx resembling a bell surrounding the shorter whitish corolla — called also *bells of Ireland, shellflower*

molucca bean *n, usu cap M* **:** NICKER NUT

molucca grains *n pl, usu cap M* **:** seeds of a tree (*Croton tiglium*) that yield croton oil

mol·uc·cel·la \,mälək'selə\ *n, cap* [NL, fr. *Molucca* islands, + NL *-ella*] **:** a small genus of mints found in the Mediterranean region, cultivated widely, and usu. having small white pink-tipped flowers in whorls

1mo·ly \'mōlē\ *n* -ES [L, fr. Gk *mōly*; akin to Skt *mūla* root] **1 :** a mythical herb described by Homer as having a black root and milk-white blossoms, being possessed of magical powers, and being given by Hermes to Odysseus to counteract the spells of Circe **2 :** a European wild garlic (*Allium moly*) cultivated for its bright yellow flowers

2moly \'mälē\ *n* -ES [by shortening] **:** MOLYBDENUM

molybd- *or* **molybdo-** *comb form* [L *molybd-*, fr. Gk *molybd-*, *molybdo-*, fr. *molybdos* — more at PLUMB] **1 :** lead ⟨*molybdo*phyllite⟩ **2** [NL *molybdena & molybdenum*] **:** molybdenum **:** molybdous ⟨*molybdo*phosphate⟩ ⟨*molybdo*cyanide⟩

mo·lyb·date \mə'lib,dāt\ *n* -s [*molybd-* + *-ate*] **:** a salt of a molybdic acid; *esp* **:** a normal salt derived from the acid H_2MoO_4

molybdate orange *also* **molybdated orange** *n* **:** a strong brilliant orange pigment made by coprecipitation of lead chromate and lead molybdate often in the presence of lead sulfate and used in protective coatings and printing inks — called also *molybdenum orange*

mo·lyb·de·na \mə'libdənə\ *n* -s [NL, fr. L *molybdaena* galena, fr. Gk *molybdaina*, fr. *molybdos* lead] **1** *obs* **a :** MOLYBDENITE **b :** MOLYBDENUM **2 :** an oxide of molybdenum of uncertain structure that is used in catalysis frequently supported on alumina

mo·lyb·de·nite \-də,nīt\ *n* -s [NL *molybdena* + E *-ite*] **:** a mineral MoS_2 consisting of molybdenum disulfide that is valued as a source of molybdenum and its compounds and occurs in foliated masses or scales resembling graphite but differing from the latter in its bluer color, in giving a greenish streak on porcelain, and in yielding a sulfurous odor before the blowpipe (hardness 1.5, sp. gr. 4.7–4.8)

mo·lyb·de·num \-dənəm\ *n* -s [NL, fr. *molybdena*] **:** a difficultly fusible polyvalent metallic element that resembles chromium and tungsten in many of its properties, that is obtained as a dark gray powder or hard silver-white metal usu. from its principal ore molybdenite by roasting to molybdenum trioxide and reducing, that is used chiefly in strengthening and hardening steel, and that is a trace element in plant and animal metabolism — symbol *Mo;* see FERROMOLYBDENUM; ELEMENT table

molybdenum blue *n* **:** a blue complex substance that is obtained usu. in colloidal form by mild reduction of a molybdate in acid solution and that serves as the basis of some methods of colorimetric analysis

molybdenum orange *n* **:** MOLYBDATE ORANGE

molybdenum steel *n* **:** steel containing molybdenum whose presence in a percentage of 10 to 15 percent produces a steel similar to tungsten steel

molybdenum trioxide *n* **:** a crystalline compound MoO_3 made usu. by roasting molybdenite or by heating ammonium molybdate and used chiefly in making other molybdenum compounds and metallic molybdenum and as a catalyst — called also *molybdic oxide*

mo·lyb·dic \mə'libdik\ *adj* [*molybd-* + *-ic*] **:** of, relating to, or containing molybdenum — used esp. of compounds in which this element has one of its higher valences (as six)

molybdic acid *n* **1 :** any of various acids derived from molybdenum trioxide; *esp* **:** the simplest acid H_2MoO_4 obtained as white crystals or as the yellow crystalline monohydrate $H_2MoO_4.H_2O$ but known chiefly in the form of salts many of which are unstable and readily form polymolybdates — compare HETEROPOLY ACID, PHOSPHOMOLYBDIC ACID **2 a :** MOLYBDENUM TRIOXIDE — not used systematically **b :** ammonium molybdate containing added molybdenum trioxide — called also *molybdic acid 85 percent;* not used systematically

molybdic ocher *n* **:** FERRIMOLYBDITE

molybdic oxide *n* **:** MOLYBDENUM TRIOXIDE

mo·lyb·dite \mə'lib,dīt\ *n* -s [G *molybdit*, modif. (influenced by *-it* -ite) of E *molybdine*, fr. *molybd-* + *-ine*] **:** FERRIMOLYBDITE — called also *molybdic ocher*

mo·lyb·do·me·nite \mə,libdō'mē,nīt\ *n* -s [F, fr. *molybd-* + Gk *mēnē* moon + F *-ite* — more at MOON] **:** a mineral $PbSeO_3$ consisting of native lead selenite

mo·lyb·do·phosphate \mə¦lib(,)dō+\ *n* [*molybd-* + *phosphate*] **:** PHOSPHOMOLYBDATE — used in the system of nomenclature adopted by the International Union or Pure and Applied Chemistry

mo·lyb·do·phosphoric acid \"+ . . . -\ *n* [ISV *molybd-* + *phosphoric*] **:** PHOSPHOMOLYBDIC ACID

mo·lyb·do·phyl·lite \mə,libdō'fi,līt\ *n* -s [ISV *molybd-* + *phyll-* + *-ite*, fr. its occurrence in foliated masses] **:** a mineral $(Pb,Mg)_2SiO_4.H_2O(?)$ consisting of a hydrous lead magnesium silicate

mo·lyb·dous \mə'libdəs\ *adj* [*molybd-* + *-ous*] **:** of, relating to, or containing molybdenum — used esp. of compounds in which this element has a lower valence than in molybdic compounds

mol·y·site \'mälə,sīt\ *n* -s [It *molisite*, fr. Gk *mōlysis* action of parboiling, simmering (fr. *mōlyein* to parboil + *-sis*) + It *-ite*] **:** a mineral $FeCl_3$ consisting of native ferric chloride found in Vesuvian lava

mom \'mäm, 'məm\ *n* -s [short for *momma*] **:** MOTHER ⟨approximately 6000 youngsters, ~*s* and pops watched the two shows —*Springfield (Mass.) Union*⟩

MOM *abbr* middle of month

mom·bin \mōm'bēn\ *n* -s [AmerSp *mombin*, fr. Carib] **1 :** a common tropical American shrub or small tree (*Spondias purpurea*) with compound leaves and purple paniculate flowers — called also *jocote;* compare HOG PLUM **2 :** the edible purplish fruit of the mombin

1mom·ble \'mäm(b)əl\ *vt* -ED/-ING/-S [alter. of *1mumble*] **1** *dial Eng* **:** to treat roughly **:** ABUSE, BUNGLE **2** *dial Eng* **:** to wrap or conceal in a disordered condition **3** *dial Eng* **:** CONFUSE, BEWILDER ⟨he was so *mombled* he couldn't speak⟩

2momble \"\ *n* -s *dial Eng* **:** a state of confusion or untidiness **:** a bungling job

mombuttoo *var of* MANGBETU

1mome \'mōm\ *n* -s [origin unknown] *archaic* **:** a dull doltish person **:** BLOCKHEAD, FOOL

2mome *n* -s [prob. fr. NL *momus*] *obs* **:** a caviling critic

mo·ment \'mōmənt\ *n* -s [ME, fr. MF, fr. L *momentum* movement, motion, moment, influence, fr. earlier (assumed) *movimentum*, fr. *movēre* to move + *-mentum* -ment — more at MOVE] **1 a :** a minute portion of time ⟨the ~ stretched out to a minute, the minute to an hour —Hesketh Pearson⟩ ⟨a ~ of dreadful suspense —Graham Greene⟩ **b :** a point of time **:** INSTANT ⟨to us . . . the ~ 8:17 a.m. means something —Aldous Huxley⟩ ⟨at this very ~ of his life's lowest ebb —Osbert Sitwell⟩ ⟨if the great famine had not come along at that particular ~ —Paul Blanshard⟩ **c :** a comparatively brief period of time ⟨this whole ~ of thought hardly lasted five minutes —Carl Jonas⟩ ⟨in ~*s* of solitude when I was milking the cows —David Fairchild⟩ ⟨a presidential candidate . . . must symbolize the forces seeking expression during his ~ in history —V.L.Albjerg⟩ **d :** the present time — usu. used with *the* ⟨at the ~ she is at work on her fourth novel —*Holiday*⟩ ⟨the . . . flavor so much in fashion at the ~ —Kenneth Hince⟩ ⟨a catchword of the ~ —J.A.R.Pimlott⟩ **e :** a particular period (as of importance, significance, or pleasure) ⟨all had their ~*s* when their subject . . . made them greater than their normal selves —R.E.Priestley⟩ ⟨sailors have their ~*s* as in any seaboard town —*Amer. Guide Series: N.H.*⟩ **2** *obs* **:** a minute portion or part **:** PARTICLE ⟨every little ~ of the earth —Thomas Blundeville⟩ **3 :** importance in influence or effect **:** CONSEQUENCE, CONSIDERATION, WEIGHT ⟨decisions of ~ must be made by our government —L.H.Evans⟩ ⟨meanings which are . . . of no ~ to the student —Edward Sapir⟩ ⟨taught men to reckon virtue of more ~ than security —W.F.Hambly⟩ ⟨the political issues of their day seemed . . . of enormous ~ —Christopher Hollis⟩ **4** *obs* **:** a cause or motive of action **:** an influential point or consideration **:** a deciding factor ⟨I have seen her die twenty times upon far poorer ~ —Shak.⟩ **5 :** a definite period or point in a course of events: as **a :** a stage in historical development (as of an institution) ⟨a document of one ~ in the history of thought and sensibility in the nineteenth century —T.S.Eliot⟩ **b :** a stage in logical development, in cognition, or in the growing adequacy of thought **c :** a phase, aspect, or partial apprehension of a subject or thing **d** *in existentialist theology* **:** a timeless point of decision within the inner subjectivity of a person when he freely enacts his relationship to eternity **6 a :** tendency or measure of tendency to produce motion esp. about a point or axis **b :** the product of quantity (as a force) and the distance to a particular axis or point — see MOMENT OF A COUPLE, MOMENT OF A FORCE, MOMENT OF INERTIA **7 :** an essential or constituent element (as of a complex conceptual entity) ⟨the understanding is a necessary ~ in the reason —Bernard Bosanquet⟩ **8 :** the average or sum of the deviations or some power of the deviations of the elements of a frequency distribution from a specified norm **syn** see IMPORTANCE

momenta *pl of* MOMENTUM

mo·men·tal \mō'mentᵊl\ *adj* [prob. fr. F, fr. ML *momentalis* momentary, fr. (assumed) LL (attested as *momentaliter*, adv., in a moment), fr. L *momentum* moment + *-alis* -al] **1** *obs* **:** MOMENTARY 1a ⟨not one ~ minute doth she swerve —Nicholas Breton⟩ **2 :** of or relating to moment or momentum

mo·men·ta·ne·ous \,mōmən¦tānēəs\ *adj* [LL *momentaneus*, fr. L *momentum* moment + *-aneus* (as in *subterraneus* subterranean)] **1 :** MOMENTARY 1a ⟨the rapid ~ association of things which meet and pass —D.H.Lawrence⟩ **2** *archaic* **:** INSTANTANEOUS ⟨in which ~ explosion of the whole quantity all the force consists —William Clarke⟩ **3** *of an aspect or form of a verb* **:** of, relating to, or characterizing action begun and terminated in an instant — **mo·men·ta·ne·ous·ly** *adv* — **mo·men·ta·ne·ous·ness** *n* -ES

momentany *adj* [MF *momentané*, fr. LL *momentaneus*] *obs* **:** MOMENTARY 1a ⟨~ as a sound —Shak.⟩

mo·men·tar·i·ly \,mōmən¦terəlē, -li\ *adv* **1 :** for a moment ⟨television serials that ~ distract suburban housewives from their ironing —Wolcott Gibbs⟩ ⟨only ~ troubled by such reports —*Publishers' Weekly*⟩ **2 :** INSTANTLY ⟨the friar groaned, but almost ~ recovered his emotion —Elizabeth Helme⟩ **3 :** at any moment **:** from moment to moment ⟨~ expected his coming —Charlotte Brontë⟩ ⟨when some draperies ~ expected . . . are hung —R.H.Rovere⟩ **4 :** in a few minutes ⟨I'll be there ~⟩

mo·men·tar·i·ness \'mōmən,terēnə̇s\ *n* -ES **:** the quality or state of being momentary ⟨the freshness and ~ of intense life —C.E.Montague⟩

mo·men·tary \-rē, -ri\ *adj* [L *momentarius*, fr. *momentum* moment + *-arius* -ary — more at MOMENT] **1 a :** continuing only a moment **:** lasting a very short time **:** TRANSITORY ⟨makes all human trouble appear but a ~ annoyance —Nathaniel Hawthorne⟩ ⟨law and order have reigned with only one ~ breakdown —J.H.Huizinga⟩ **b :** having a very brief life **:** EPHEMERAL — used of a living being ⟨truth more complete than the parcel of truth any ~ individual can seize —Matthew Arnold⟩ **2 :** operative or recurring at every moment ⟨in ~ terror of being hurled headlong down a precipice —T.L. Peacock⟩ **3 :** MOMENTANEOUS 3 **syn** see TRANSIENT

mo·ment·ly *adv* **1 :** from moment to moment **:** every moment ⟨amid the ~ increasing confusion —E.A.Poe⟩ ⟨the bill . . . grew ~ larger and larger —Aldous Huxley⟩ **2 :** at any moment ⟨~ expecting death from heart disease —*Time*⟩ **3 :** for a moment ⟨a bedlamite speeds to thy parapets, tilting there ~ —Hart Crane⟩

momento *var of* MEMENTO

moment of a couple : the product of either of the forces of a couple by the perpendicular distance between them

moment of a force 1 *of a point* **:** the product of the distance from the point to the point of application of the force and the component of the force perpendicular to the line of the distance **2** *of a line* **:** the product of the perpendicular distance from the axis to the point of application of the force and the component of the force perpendicular to the line of the distance and in a plane perpendicular to the axis

moment of inertia 1 *of a mass* **:** the ratio of the torque applied to a rigid body free to rotate about a given axis to the angular acceleration thus produced about that axis and equal to the sum of the products of each element of mass by the square of its distance from the given axis — called also *rotational inertia* **2** *of an area* **:** the sum of the products of each element of a plane area by the square of its distance from a given axis in the plane of the area

moment of momentum : ANGULAR MOMENTUM

mo·men·tous \mō'mentəs *also* mə'-\ *adj* [*moment* + *-ous*] **1 :** having moment **:** of moment or consequence **:** very important **:** WEIGHTY ⟨on the eve of another ~ election —*N.Y. Times*⟩ ⟨the ~ character of the choice —M.R.Cohen⟩ ⟨brought about the ~ changes that affect us all —W.S.Maugham⟩ **2 :** having importance or influence — used of a person ⟨made a ~ captive, an Indian . . . prisoner —Bernard DeVoto⟩ — **mo·men·tous·ly** *adv*

mo·men·tous·ness *n* -ES **:** the quality or state of being momentous ⟨impress his visitors with the ~ . . . of all he had to say —H.V.Gregory⟩

mo·men·tum \mō'mentəm *also* mə'-\ *n, pl* **momen·ta** \-tə\ *also* **momentums** [L, motion — more at MOMENT] **1 :** a property of a moving body that determines the length of time required to bring it to rest when under the action of a constant force or moment — see ANGULAR MOMENTUM, LINEAR MOMENTUM **2 :** MOMENT 7 ⟨a ~ in the spiritual relations of him and God —A.B.Davidson⟩ **3 a :** the force of motion acquired by a moving body as a result of the continuance of its motion **:** IMPETUS — not used technically ⟨steps took him to the door . . . so neatly that he was able to seize the handle and enter without losing ~ —Robertson Davies⟩ ⟨still he galloped, and with a velocity and ~ continually increasing —William Cowper⟩ **b :** something held to resemble such force of motion of a moving body ⟨the . . . music not only lacks passion; it even lacks ~ of any sort —Winthrop Sargeant⟩ ⟨the conspiracy gained ~ and direction —R.C.Doty⟩ ⟨moved along by the ~ of events —Norman Cousins⟩

momes *pl of* MOME

momie cloth \'mōmē-, 'məmē-\ *n* [prob. alter. (influenced by F *momie* mummy) of *mummy cloth*] **:** a pebble-surfaced crepe with a cotton, rayon, or silk warp and a wool filling that is used for dresses, curtains, and upholstery

mom·ism \'mä,mizəm\ *n* -s [*mom* + *-ism*] **:** an excessive popular adoration and oversentimentalizing of mothers that is held to be oedipal in nature and that is thought to allow overprotective or clinging mothers unconsciously to deny their offspring emotional emancipation and thus to set up psychoneuroses

momma *var of* MAMMA

mom·mack *or* **mom·mick** \'mämə̇k\ *var of* MAMMOCK

mom·me \'mämē\ *n, pl* **momme** [Jap] **:** a Japanese unit of weight equal to 3.75 grams

mom·met \'mämə̇t\ *var of* MAUMET

mom·my \'mämē, -mi\ *or* **mum·my** \'məm-\ *n* -ES [alter. of *mammy*] **:** MOTHER

mo·mor·di·ca \mə'mȯ(r)də̇kə\ *n, cap* [NL, fr. L *momordisse*, perf. inf. of *mordēre* to bite; fr. the fact that the seeds appear to have been bitten — more at SMART] **:** a genus of tropical Old World herbaceous vines (family Cucurbitaceae) having a campanulate corolla and a warty fruit — see BALSAM APPLE

momot *var of* MOTMOT

mo·mot·i·dae \mə'mäd·ə,dē\ *n pl, cap* [NL, fr. *Momotus*, type genus + *-idae*] **:** a family of tropical American birds (order Coraciiformes) related to the rollers and kingfishers and consisting of the motmots and in some classifications also the todies

mo·mo·tus \mə'mōd·əs\ *n, cap* [NL, fr. *momot*] **:** the type genus of Momotidae

momser *or* **momzer** *var of* MAMZER

mo·mus \'mōməs\ *n, pl* **momuses** \-səz\ *or* **mo·mi** \-ō,mī\ [NL, fr. *Momus*, god of ridicule in Greek mythology, fr. Gk *Mōmos*, lit., blame, ridicule; perh. akin to Gk *mōkos* mocker] **:** a carping critic **:** FAULTFINDER

1mon \'män\ *n, chiefly dial Brit var of* MAN

2mon \"\ *n* -s [Jap] **:** the usu. circular badge of a Japanese family esp. of the ancient feudal nobility consisting typically of conventionalized forms from nature (as flowers, birds, insects, lightning, waves of the sea) or geometric symbolic figures and used on lacquer, pottery, and fabrics — compare CHRYSANTHEMUM 3

mon of the Tokugawa family

3mon \'mōn\ *n, pl* **mon** *or* **mons** *usu cap* **1 a :** the dominant native people of Pegu in Burma **b :** a member of such people **2 :** the Mon-Khmer language of the Mon people

4mon \'män\ *n, pl* **mon** [native name in the Solomon islands] **:** a usu. large plank boat resembling a canoe and common in Melanesia

mon- *or* **mono-** *comb form* [ME, fr. MF & L; MF, fr. OF, fr. L, fr. Gk, fr. *monos* alone, single — more at MONK] **1 a :** consisting of or having only one **:** single ⟨*mon*arch⟩ ⟨*mono*plane⟩ **b :** by or from one only ⟨*mono*genic⟩ ⟨*mono*drama⟩ **c :** restricted to only one ⟨*mono*gamy⟩ ⟨*mono*logue⟩ **d :** only one at a time ⟨*mono*tocous⟩ **e :** alone ⟨*mono*phobia⟩ **2 a :** containing one atom, radical, or group (of a specified kind) ⟨*mon*oxide⟩ ⟨*mono*ether⟩ ⟨*mono*bromide⟩ — usu. omitted in names of specific compounds as being understood ⟨*mono*bromoacetone *or* bromoacetone⟩ **b :** monomolecular ⟨*mono*film⟩ ⟨*mono*layer⟩ **3 a :** affecting a single part ⟨*mono*plegia⟩ **b :** due to a single cause ⟨*mono*bacillary⟩ **c :** monomeric ⟨*mono*styrene⟩

mon *abbr* **1** monastery **2** monetary **3** monitor **4** monsieur **5** monsignor **6** monument

mo·na \'mōnə\ *n* -s [NL, prob. fr. Sp or It, monkey, ape — more at MONKEY] **:** a small West African guenon monkey (*Cercopithecus mona*)

1mona·can \'mänəkən, mə'nak-, 'mänēk-, mə'nȧk- *sometimes* 'mōn- *or* mə'nak-\ *adj, usu cap* [*Monaco*, principality of southern Europe + E *-an*] **:** MONEGASQUE

2monacan \"\ *n, cap* **:** MONEGASQUE

3mon·a·can \'mänəkən\ *n, pl* **monacan** *or* **monacans** *usu cap* **1 :** an extinct Siouan people in the upper James river valley of Virginia **2 :** a member of the Monacan people

1mon·a·can·thid \¦mänə¦kan(t)thə̇d\ *also* **mon·a·can·thine** \-thən, -n,thīn\ *adj* [*monacanthid* fr. NL *Monacanthidae; monacanthine* fr. NL *Monacanthus*, genus of fishes + E *-ine*] **:** of or relating to the Monacanthidae

2monacanthid \"\ *also* **monacanthine** \"\ *n* -s **:** a monacanthid fish

mon·a·can·thi·dae \,==ˈkan(t)thə,dē\ *n pl, cap* [NL, fr. *Monacanthus*, type genus (fr. *mon-* + *-acanthus*) + *-idae*] **:** a family of bony fishes (order Plectognathi) including the filefishes

monacetin var of MONOACETIN
mon·a·cha \'mänəkə\ [NL, fr. LL, nun, fr. Gk *monachē*, fem. of *monachos*, adj., single — more at MONK] *syn of* MONASA
mon·a·chal *or* **mon·a·cal** \'mänəkəl\ *adj* [*monachal* fr. MF or LL; MF, fr. LL *monachalis*, fr. *monachus* monk + L *-alis* -al; *monacal* prob. fr. F, fr. MF *monachal* — more at MONK] **:** of, relating to, or having the characteristics of monks or monastic life **:** MONASTIC
mon·a·chism \-nə,kizəm\ *n* -s [prob. fr. MF *monachisme*, fr. ML *monachismus*, fr. LGk *monachismos*, fr. Gk *monachos* monk + Gk *-ismos* -ism — more at MONK] **:** MONASTICISM ⟨set itself . . . to reform European ~ —G.G.Coulton⟩
mon·a·chist \-,kəst\ *adj* **:** MONKISH ⟨lived a life that was essentially ~ in tone —*Times Lit. Supp.*⟩
monacid *var of* MONOACID
mona·co \'mänə,kō, mə'nä(,)kō, 'mänē,-, mə'nä(- *sometimes* 'mōn- *or* mə'na(-\ *adj, usu cap* [fr. *Monaco*, principality in southern Europe] **:** of or from the principality of Monaco **:** of the kind or style prevalent in Monaco **:** MONACAN, MONEGASQUE
mon·act \mä'nakt\ *n* -s [*mon-* + *-act* (fr. Gk *aktis* ray) — more at ACTIN-] **:** a monactine sponge spicule
1**mon·ac·tine** \mä'naktən, -k,tīn\ *also* **mon·ac·ti·nal** \-tənᵊl, ¦mä,nak¦tīnᵊl\ *adj* [*mon-* + *-actine* or *-actinal*] **:** having a single ray — used of a sponge spicule
2**monactine** \"\ *n* -s **:** MONACT
1**mon·ac·ti·nel·lid** \mä¦naktə¦neləd\ *or* **mon·ac·ti·nel·li·dan** \-lədən\ *adj* [*monactinellid* fr. NL *Monactinellida*; *monactinellidan* fr. NL *Monactinellida* + E *-an*] **:** MONAXONID
2**monactinellid** \"\ *n* -s **:** MONAXONID
mon·ac·ti·nel·li·da \⸗,⸗⸗'nelədə\ [NL, fr. *mon-* + *actin-* + *-ella* + *-ida*] *syn of* MONAXONIDA
1**mo·nad** \'mō,nad *sometimes* 'mä,-\ *n* -s [LL *monad-, monas* unit, monad, fr. Gk, fr. *monos* sole, lone, single + *-ad-, -as* -ad — more at MONK] **1 a :** a unit in Greek philosophy constituting the number one or an individual; *specif* **:** a metaphysical entity (as the One or an atom) **b :** a metaphysical entity in the philosophy of Giordano Bruno that differs from the Democritean atom in being spatially extended and psychically sensitive **c :** a spiritual being, substance, or soul in Leibnizian philosophy that is unextended, indivisible, indestructible, and impenetrable and a center of force from which property all the physical properties of matter are derived — see MONADISM **d :** a similar hypothetical indivisible unit possessing both physical and mental characteristics of various kinds **2 :** a minute simple organism or organic unit: as **a :** ZOOSPORE **b :** a flagellate protozoan; *esp* **:** a member of *Monas* or a related genus **3 :** a univalent element, atom, or radical
2**monad** \"\ *adj* **:** of the nature of a monad
mo·nad·al \(')mō¦nadᵊl, (')mä¦-\ *adj* [1*monad* + *-al*] **:** MONADIC 1b
monadelph *var of* MONODELPH
mon·a·del·phous \¦mänə¦delfəs\ *adj* [*mon-* + *-adelphous*] *of stamens* **:** united by the filaments into one group usu. forming a tube around the gynoecium — compare DIADELPHOUS, POLYADELPHOUS
monades *pl of* MONAS
monadi- *comb form* [1*monad*] **:** monad ⟨*monadi*form⟩ ⟨*monadi*gerous⟩
mo·nad·ic \(')mō¦nadik, (')mä¦-\ *adj* [Gk *monadikos*, fr. *monad-, monas* monad + *-ikos* -ic] **1 a :** consisting of monads **b :** of, relating to, or like monads **:** ATOMISTIC, INDIVIDUAL, UNITARY **c :** of or relating to monadism **2 :** having only a single argument — used of a predicate or propositional function ⟨*x is red* is ~, while *x loves y* is not⟩
mo·nad·i·cal \-dəkəl\ *adj* [Gk *monadikos* monadic + E *-al*] *archaic* **:** MONADIC 1b
mo·nad·i·dae \mə'nadə,dē\ *n pl, cap* [NL, fr. *Monad-, Monas*, type genus + *-idae*] **:** a family of free-living flagellates (order Protomonadina) that may be active or attached and that often form colonies
mon·a·di·na \,mänə'dīnə\ *n pl, cap* [NL, fr. LL *monad-, monas* unit, monad + NL *-ina* — more at MONAD] *in some esp former classifications* **:** a group nearly equivalent to Mastigophora
mo·nad·ism \'mō,na,dizəm, 'mä,n-, -,nə,d-\ *n* -s [prob. fr. F *monadisme*, fr. *monade* monad + *-isme* -ism] **:** a theory based upon a conception of monads; *specif* **:** the Leibnizian theory that the universe is composed of a hierarchy of monads each of which is a microcosm reflecting the world with differing degrees of clarity from its particular point of view without external stimulation in a system of harmony preestablished by God
mo·nad·is·tic \¦⸗,⸗¦distik, -,nə¦-\ *adj* [1*monad* + *-istic*] **:** of or relating to monadism ⟨~ idealism⟩
mo·nad·nock \mə'nad,näk\ *n* -s [fr. Mt. *Monadnock*, N.H.] **:** a hill or mountain of residual rock surmounting a peneplain
mo·nad·o·log·i·cal \,mō,nadə¦läjəkəl, ¦mä,-, -,nəd-\ *adj* [*monadology* + *-ical*; trans. of G *monadologisch*] **:** of, relating to, or based on monadology **:** MONADIC 1b ⟨culminated in a ~ pluralism —W.A.Kaufmann⟩
mo·nad·ol·o·gy \,mō,na'däləjē, ,mä,-, -,nə'-\ *n* -ES [F *monadologie*, fr. *monade* monad (fr. LL *monad-, monas*) + *-o-* + *-logie* -logy] **:** a philosophical theory about monads; *specif* **:** Leibnizian monadism
mon·a·ghan \'mänəgən, -nəhən, -nəkən\ *adj, usu cap* [fr. *Monaghan*, county in Ireland] **:** of or from County Monaghan, Ireland **:** of the kind or style prevalent in County Monaghan
mon·a·ker *var of* MONIKER
mo·nal *also* **mo·naul** *or* **moo·nal** *or* **moo·naul** *or* **mi·naul** \mə'nȯl, -näl\ *n* -s [Nepali *munāl, monāl*] **:** any of various large pheasants of India; *esp* **:** any of several large showy pheasants of the genus *Lophophorus* found at high altitudes in northern India — see IMPEYAN PHEASANT
monamide *var of* MONOAMIDE
monamine *var of* MONOAMINE
mon·an·day \'mənən,de\ *usu cap, Scot var of* MONDAY
mon·an·der \mə'nandə(r)\ *n* -s [*mon-* + *-ander*] **:** a monandrous plant
mo·nan·dria \-drēə\ *n pl, cap* [NL, fr. *mon-* + *-andria*] *in former classifications* **:** a class of flowering plants comprising those with flowers that have a single stamen
mo·nan·dri·an \-ēən\ *adj* [NL *Monandria* + E *-an*] **:** of or relating to the Monandria
mo·nan·drous \-rəs\ *adj* **1** [*mon-* + *-androus*] **a** *of a plant* **:** having flowers with a single stamen ⟨many orchids are ~⟩ **b** *of a flower* **:** having a single stamen **2** [Gk *monandros*, fr. *mon-* + *-andros* having (such or so many) men — more at -ANDROUS] **:** of, relating to, or characterized by monandry ⟨a ~ family system⟩
mo·nan·dry \-rē\ *n* -ES [*monandrous* + *-y*] **1 :** a marriage form or custom in which a woman has only one husband at a time — compare POLYANDRY **2 :** a monandrous condition of a plant or flower
mo·nan·tha vetch \mə'nan(t)thə-\ *n* [NL *monantha* (specific epithet of *Vicia monantha*), fr. *mon-* + *-antha* (fem. of *-anthus* -anthous)] **:** a weak-stemmed viny vetch (*Vicia articulata*) of southern Europe used for forage and hay in parts of the U.S. having mild winters
mon·ap·sal \(')mä¦napsəl, (')mō¦-\ *adj* [mon- + *-apsal* (as in *triapsal*)] **:** having only one apse ⟨a ~ church⟩
1**mon·arch** \'mänə(r)k, -ä,närk, -,nák\ *n* -s [LL *monarcha*, fr. Gk *monarchēs, monarchos*, fr. *mon-* + *-archēs, -archos* -arch (n. comb. form)] **1 :** a person who reigns over a major territorial unit (as a kingdom or empire) usu. for life and by hereditary succession: as **a :** one invested with sovereign power and exercising direct and effective control over the functions of government ⟨an absolute ~⟩ **b :** one acting primarily as chief of state and carrying out political functions limited in nature and extent (as by custom or a written constitution) ⟨a constitutional ~⟩ — compare CZAR, EMPEROR, KAISER, KING, QUEEN **2 :** one held to resemble a monarch in sovereign power or preeminent position ⟨the live oak is the ~ of the Texas low forests —*Amer. Guide Series: Texas*⟩ ⟨of as much interest to them as the business of any money ~ is to him —H.R.Penniman⟩ ⟨cotton, ~ of the textile world —*Wall Street Jour.*⟩ **3** *also* **monarch butterfly :** a large American butterfly (*Danaus plexippus*) having orange-brown wings with black veins and borders and characterized by larvae that feed on milkweed and by an annual two-way migration — compare VICEROY 2
2**monarch** \"\ *vi* -ED/-ING/-S **:** to play the monarch — often used with *it* ⟨~s it in his own closet —*Common Sense*⟩
3**monarch** \"\ *adj* [*mon-* + *-arch* (adj. comb. form)] **:** having only one xylem strand or group — used esp. of roots
mo·nar·chal \mə'närkəl, -nák-\ *adj* [1*monarch* + *-al*] **1** *archaic* **:** MONARCHICAL 2 ⟨~ government⟩ **2** *archaic* **:** having the status or exercising the functions of a monarch **3 :** of, having the characteristics of, or befitting a monarch ⟨the golden age of ~ splendor —Joseph Wechsberg⟩ ⟨an impression of trees, very dark and ~ —H.E.Bates⟩
mon·arch·ess \'mänə(r)kəs, -ä,närk-\ *n* -ES [1*monarch* + *-ess*] **:** a female monarch
mo·nar·chi·al \mə'närkēəl, -nák-\ *adj* [*monarchy* + *-al*] **:** MONARCHICAL ⟨the ~ institution⟩ ⟨man's subjection to a ~ God —N.A.Ford⟩ ⟨a country that was ~ in tradition —Beverley Baxter⟩
1**mo·nar·chi·an** \-ēən\ *n* -s *usu cap* [LL *monarchianus*, fr. *monarchia* monarchy, individual rule + L *-anus* -an — more at MONARCHY] **:** an adherent of Monarchianism
2**monarchian** \"\ *adj, usu cap* **:** of or relating to Monarchianism
mo·nar·chi·an·ism \-ēə,nizəm\ *n* -s *usu cap* **:** an anti-Trinitarian doctrine or theory current in the Christian church of the 2d and 3d centuries A.D. in several forms and having as a common principle a belief that God is a single person as well as a single being — see DYNAMIC MONARCHIANISM, MODALISTIC MONARCHIANISM; compare PATRIPASSIANISM
mo·nar·chi·cal \-kəkəl, -kēk-\ *or* **mo·nar·chic** \-(r)kik, -kēk\ *adj* [MF *monarchique*, fr. Gk *monarchikos*, fr. *monarchos* monarch + *-ikos* -ical, -ic — more at MONARCH] **1 :** MONARCHAL 3 ⟨reconciled to ~ rule —C.G.Bowers⟩ ⟨~ gestures⟩ **2 :** of, possessing, or having the form of a monarchy ⟨~ systems⟩ ⟨a ~ government⟩ **3 :** having the power and functions of a monarch and esp. of one having absolute power ⟨from being primus inter pares he came to be a ~ bishop —C.T. Craig⟩ **4 :** of, relating to, or favoring monarchism ⟨win him over to the ~ side —*Times Lit. Supp.*⟩ ⟨~ candidates⟩
mo·nar·chi·cal·ly \-(r)kək(ə)lē, -kēk-, -li\ *adv* **:** in a monarchical form or manner ⟨nor are those provinces . . . aristocratically governed but ~ —Thomas Hobbes⟩
mon·ar·chism \'mänə(r),kizəm\ *n* -s [F *monarchisme*, fr. *monarchie* monarchy + *-isme* -ism] **1 :** the principles of monarchical government **2 :** belief in or advocacy of the principles of monarchical government
1**mon·ar·chist** \-,kəst\ *n* -s [*monarchy* + *-ist*] **:** one that advocates or believes in monarchy as a form of government
2**monarchist** \"\ *adj* **:** of, relating to, or favoring monarchism
mon·arch·ize \-(r),kīz\ *vb* -ED/-ING/-S [1*monarch* + *-ize*] *vi, archaic* **:** to act or rule as a monarch ⟨vice . . . in every land doth ~ —Thomas Dekker⟩ ~ *vt* **1** *obs* **:** to rule over as a monarch **2** *archaic* **:** to make a monarchy of ⟨efforts to ~ a government⟩
mo·nar·cho·mach \mə'närkə,mak\ *n* -s [NL *monarchomachus*, fr. *monarcho-* (fr. LL *monarcha* monarch) + L *-machus* one who fights (fr. Gk *-machos*); akin to Gk *machesthai* to fight — more at MONARCH] **:** one of a group of 16th century political theorists advocating resistance or rebellion against a monarch guilty of acts held to be unlawful
mo·nar·cho·mach·ic \⸗¦⸗⸗¦makik\ *adj* **:** of, relating to, or favoring the doctrines of the monarchomachs ⟨the right of revolution implicitly set forth in . . . ~ pronouncements —H.E.Barnes & H.P.Becker⟩
mon·ar·chy \'mänə(r)kē, -ki *sometimes* -ä,närk- *or* -,nák-\ *n* -ES [ME *monarchie*, fr. MF, fr. LL *monarchia*, fr. Gk, fr. *monarchēs, monarchos* monarch + *-ia* -y — more at MONARCH] **1 :** undivided rule or absolute sovereignty by a single person ⟨if one man be the sole landlord of a territory . . . his empire is absolute ~ —James Harrington⟩ **2 a :** a territorial unit (as a nation or state) having a monarch as chief of state ⟨Morocco is a sovereign independent ~ —*Statesman's Yr. Bk.*⟩ **b :** such a territorial unit having a monarchical government without a monarch as chief of state ⟨officially Spain has been a ~ without a king —*Springfield (Mass.) Union*⟩ **3 a :** a form of government having a single usu. hereditary chief of state with life tenure who may exercise governmental powers varying from nominal to absolute ⟨the constitution of Libya provided for a hereditary ~ —*Statesman's Yr. Bk.*⟩ — compare 1ABSOLUTE 3, 1CONSTITUTIONAL 4, LIMITED 2, MIXED 1b **b :** a specific government or governmental institution headed by a monarch ⟨the Russian ~ was never so popular —Malcolm Muggeridge⟩
mo·nar·da \mə'närdə\ *n* [NL, after N. *Monardes* †1588 Span. physician and botanist] **1** *cap* **:** a genus of coarse No. American mints having a tubular many-nerved calyx and whorls of variously colored flowers — see HORSEMINT 2, OSWEGO TEA, WILD BERGAMOT **2** -s **:** any plant of the genus *Monarda*
mon·ar·del·la \,mänə(r)'delə\ *n, cap* [NL, fr. N. *Monardes* + NL *-ella*] **:** a genus of fragrant herbs (family Labiatae) of the western U.S. having flowers in terminal heads and a 10- to 13-nerved calyx — see MUSTANG MINT
mon·articular \¦män, ¦mōn+\ *adj* [*mon-* + *articular*] **:** affecting one body joint only ⟨tuberculous arthritis is usually ~ —*Jour. Amer. Med. Assoc.*⟩
mo·nas \'mō,nas, 'mä,-\ *n* [LL & Gk; LL, fr. Gk — more at MONAD] **1** *pl* **mon·a·des** \'mänə,dēz\ **:** MONAD **2** *cap* [NL, fr. LL, unit, monad] **:** a genus of small aquatic flagellates that is the type of the family Monadidae
-mo·nas \mənəs\ *n comb form* [NL, fr. LL *monas*] **:** unit **:** simple organism of a (specified) kind — in generic names ⟨Chlamydo*monas*⟩ ⟨Cellulo*monas*⟩ ⟨Lepto*monas*⟩
mo·na·sa \'mänəsə\ *n, cap* [NL] **:** a genus of So. American puffbirds — see NUN BIRD
1**mon·as·cid·i·an** \¦mänə¦sidēən\ *adj* [NL *Monascidiae*, suborder of tunicates (fr. *mon-* + *Ascidiae*) + E *-an*] **:** of or relating to the simple ascidians
2**monascidian** \"\ *n* -s **:** a simple ascidian
mon·ase \'mänəs\ *n* -s [NL *Monasa*] **:** NUN BIRD
mon·aster \(')män, (')mōn+\ *n* [NL, fr. *mon-* + *-aster*] **:** a single aster formed in an aberrant type of mitosis
mon·as·te·ri·al \¦mänə¦stirēəl\ *adj* [ME, fr. LL *monasterialis*, fr. *monasterium* monastery + L *-alis* -al] **:** of, relating to, or having the characteristics of a monastery or monastic life
mon·as·tery \'mänə,sterē, -ri\ *n* -ES [ME *monasterie*, fr. LL *monasterium*, fr. LGk *monastērion*, fr. Gk, hermit's cell, fr. *monazein* to live alone, fr. *monos* lone, sole, single — more at MONK] **:** a house of religious retirement or of seclusion from the world for persons under religious vows **:** CONVENT 3
1**mo·nas·tic** \mə'nastik, mō'-, -naas-, -tēk\ *adj* [F & LL; F *monastique*, fr. MF, fr. LL *monasticus*, fr. LGk *monastikos*, fr. (assumed) Gk *monastos* (verbal of *monazein* to live alone) + *-ikos* -ic] **1 a :** of, relating to, or connected with a monastery ⟨bishop of a ~ cathedral —F.M.Stenton⟩ ⟨great ~ establishments —G.E.Fussell⟩ ⟨wholesale pillage of ~ assets —M.W.Baldwin⟩ **b :** of, relating to, or having the characteristics of occupants of monasteries ⟨a ~ congregation⟩ ⟨~ vows⟩ **2 :** having or held to have characteristics of life in a monastery ⟨the colleges . . . were still ~ in regimen and spirit —George Willison⟩; *specif* **:** secluded from temporal concerns and devoted to religion ⟨devout Christians . . . not fully embracing the ~ life —Norman Goodall⟩
2**monastic** \"\ *n* -s **:** a member of a monastic order; *specif* **:** MONK
mo·nas·ti·cal \-təkəl, -tēk-\ *adj* [ME, fr. LL *monasticus* monastic + ME *-al*] *archaic* **:** MONASTIC ⟨one of the first founders of the ~ orders —William Aglionby⟩
mo·nas·ti·cal·ly \-tək(ə)lē, -tēk-, -li\ *adv* **:** in a monastic style or manner ⟨the chairs and table were ~ plain —T.B. Costain⟩
mo·nas·ti·cism \-tə,sizəm\ *n* -s **:** the monastic life, system, or condition; *specif* **:** organized asceticism as practiced in a monastery
mon·atomic \¦män, ¦mōn+\ *adj* [*mon-* + *atomic*] **1 a :** consisting of one atom **:** having one atom in the molecule **:** ATOMIC 5 ⟨helium is a ~ gas⟩ ⟨~ metals⟩ **b :** having a thickness equal to the diameter of a constituent atom ⟨a ~ layer of cesium⟩ **2 :** UNIVALENT **3 :** having one replaceable atom or radical ⟨~ alcohols⟩
monaul *var of* MONAL
mon·au·lic \(')mä¦nȯlik\ *adj* [*mon-* + Gk *aulos* pipe, tube, reed instrument like an oboe + E *-ic* — more at ALVEOLUS] **:** having a single common genital opening — used of an hermaphroditic animal
mon·aural \(')män, (')mōn+\ *adj* [*mon-* + *aural*] **1 :** of, relating to, affecting, or designed for use with one ear ⟨~ deafness⟩ **2 :** MONOPHONIC 3 — **mon·aurally** \"+\ *adv*
mon·axial \(')män, (')mōn+\ *adj* [*mon-* + *axial*] **:** having or based on a single axis **:** UNIAXIAL ⟨~ symmetry⟩ — compare PLURIAXIAL
1**mon·ax·on** \(')mä¦nak,sän, (')mō¦-\ *adj* [*mon-* + Gk *axōn* axis — more at AXIS] **1 :** developed by growth along a single axis — used esp. of a sponge spicule **2 :** having monaxon spicules
2**monaxon** \"\ *n* -s **:** something distinguished by a single axis or axial process (as a nerve cell); *specif* **:** a monaxon sponge spicule
mon·ax·o·nia \,mä,nak'sōnēə\ [NL, fr. *mon-* + Gk *axōn* axis + NL *-ia*] *syn of* MONAXONIDA
mon·ax·on·ic \¦mä,nak¦sänik, ¦mō,-\ *adj* [*mon-* + Gk *axōn* axis + E *-ic*] **:** having but one axis
1**mon·ax·on·id** \¦mä,nak¦sänəd\ *adj* [NL *Monaxonida*] **:** of or relating to the Monaxonida
2**monaxonid** \"\ *n* -s **:** a monaxonid sponge
mon·ax·on·i·da \,⸗,⸗'sänədə\ *n pl, cap* [NL, fr. *mon-* + Gk *axōn* axis + NL *-ida*] *in some classifications* **:** a subclass or order of Demospongiae that comprises sponges with siliceous monaxonic megascleres and with or without spongin
mon·a·zite \'mänə,zīt\ *n* -s [G *monazit*, fr. Gk *monazein* to be alone, live alone + G *-it* -ite; fr. its rarity — more at MONASTERY] **:** a mineral $(Ce,La,Md,Pr,Th)PO_4$ consisting of a yellow, red, or brown phosphate of the cerium metals and thorium and occurring often in sand and gravel deposits (as in the Carolinas and Brazil)
mond *var of* MOUND
1**mon·daine** \mōn'dān\ *n* -s [F, fr. fem. of *mondain*, adj.] **:** a woman belonging to fashionable society **:** woman of the world **:** SOPHISTICATE ⟨all the barbershop roués and millinery-parlor ~s —Sinclair Lewis⟩
2**mondaine** *or* **mon·dain** \"\ *adj* [F *mondaine*, fem., & *mondain*, masc., fr. L *mundanus* of the world — more at MUNDANE] **:** WORLDLY, SOPHISTICATED, FASHIONABLE ⟨a comedy, very corrupt and ~, with a continental background —Margaret Kennedy⟩ ⟨the perfectly coiffed, ~ woman —May Sarton⟩
mon·day \'məndē, -di *also* -n(,)dā\ *n* -s, *usu cap* [ME, fr. OE *mōnandæg, mōndæg*; akin to OFris *monendei* Monday, MD *maendach, manendach*, MLG *māndach, mānendach*, OHG *mānatag*; all fr. a prehistoric WGmc compound formed from components represented by OE *mōna* moon and *dæg* day; trans. of L *dies Lunae*, trans. of Gk *hēmera Selēnēs* — more at MOON, DAY] **:** the second day of the week **:** the day following Sunday
monday disease *or* **monday-morning disease** *n, usu cap Monday* **:** azoturia of horses
monday fever *n, usu cap M* **:** BYSSINOSIS
mon·day·ish \'məndēish, -di,ish *also* -n,dāish\ *adj, usu cap* **:** characteristic of Monday; *specif* **:** fagged out after Sunday — **mon·day·ish·ness** *n* -ES *usu cap*
monday morning quarterback *also* **monday quarterback** *n, usu cap Monday* [so called fr. the fact that most American football games are played on weekends] **:** a person who using hindsight criticizes what others have done ⟨easy to be a *Monday morning quarterback* . . . and to be omniscient after the event, to expect superhuman deeds from human beings —H.W.Baldwin⟩
mon·days \'məndēz, -diz *also* -n,dāz\ *adv, usu cap* **:** on Monday repeatedly **:** on any Monday
mond gas \'mänd-, 'mōnt-\ *n, usu cap M* [after Ludwig *Mond* †1900 Ger. chemist] **:** a producer gas made by using a large proportion of steam to air at a relatively low temperature so that large amounts of ammonia can be recovered as a by-product
mon·di·al \'mändēəl\ *adj* [F, fr. LL *mundialis*, fr. L *mundus* world + *-ialis* -ial — more at MUNDANE] **:** of or involving a large part of the world **:** WORLD ⟨in this day, so distraught with ~ events and characters —J.T.Adams⟩
mon·do \män'dō\ *n* -s [Jap *mondō*] **:** a rapid question and answer technique employed in Zen Buddhism by a master seeking to lead a pupil into transcending the limitations of conceptual thought
m-1 \'em'wən\ *or* **m-1 rifle** *n, pl* **m-1's** *or* **m-1 rifles** *usu cap M* **:** a gas-operated semiautomatic .30 caliber rifle fed from a magazine containing a clip of eight rounds, mechanically capable of firing 16 to 32 rounds a minute, having an effective range of 500 yards, and weighing 9½ pounds — called also *Garand rifle*
monecious *var of* MONOECIOUS
1**mon·e·gasque** \¦mänə¦gask\ *adj, usu cap* [F *monégasque*, adj. & n., fr. Prov *mounegasc*, fr. *Mounegue* Monaco] **:** of or relating to the principality of Monaco **:** MONACAN
2**monegasque** \"\ *n* -s *cap* [F *Monégasque*] **:** a native or inhabitant of Monaco
Monel Metal \mō,nel-\ *trademark* — used for an alloy of approximately 67 percent nickel, 28 percent copper, and 5 percent other elements that is made by direct reduction from ore in which the constituent metals occur in these proportions
mon·embryonic \(¦)män+\ *also* **mono·embryonic** \¦mänō+\ *adj* **:** characterized by monembryony
mon·em·bry·o·ny \mä'nembrēənē, ,mänem'brīə-\ *also* **mono·em·bry·ony** \,mänō'embrēənē, ,mänōem'brīə-\ *n* [*mon-* + *embryony*] **1 :** the condition of having but a single embryo **2 :** production of a single embryo from a single egg
mon·ep·ic \(')mä¦nepik, (')mō¦-\ *adj* [*mon-* + Gk *epos* word + E *-ic* — more at VOICE] **:** consisting of one word or of sentences of one word
mon·episcopacy \,män+\ *n* [*mon-* + *episcopacy*] **:** church government by monarchical bishops **:** monarchical episcopacy — **mon·episcopal** \¦män+\ *adj*
mon·e·pis·co·pus \,mänə'piskəpəs\ *n* -ES [NL, fr. *mon-* + LL *episkopus* bishop — more at BISHOP] **:** a monarchical bishop
1**monera** *pl of* MONERON
2**mo·ne·ra** \mə'nirə\ *n pl, cap* [NL, fr. pl. of *moneron*] *in some classifications* **a :** a taxon of variable rank comprising the monera **b :** a kingdom or other major division of living beings comprising those (as bacteria and blue-green algae) that lack organized condensed nuclei
mo·ne·ral \mə'nirəl\ *or* **mo·ne·ric** \-rik, -ner-\ *adj* [NL *moneron* & 2*Monera* + E *-al* or *-ic*] **:** of or relating to the monera
1**mo·ne·ran** \-nirən\ *adj* [NL 2*Monera* + E *-an*] **:** of or relating to the Monera
2**moneran** \"\ *or* **mo·ner** \'mōnə(r)\ *n* -s **:** a moneran organism
monergic *var of* MONOERGIC
mon·er·gism \'mänə(r),jizəm\ *n* -s [*mon-* + *erg-* + *-ism*] **:** the theological doctrine that regeneration is exclusively the work of the Holy Spirit — compare SYNERGISM
mon·er·gist \-,jəst\ *n* -s [*mon-* + *erg-* + *-ist*] **:** one who accepts or supports the doctrine of monergism
mon·er·gis·tic \¦⸗⸗¦jistik\ *adj* **:** of or relating to monergism
mo·ne·ron \mə'ni,rän\ *n, pl* **mone·ra** \-irə\ [NL, modif. of Gk *monērēs* solitary, singular, fr. *monos* single, alone — more at MONK] **:** a postulated primitive ancestral mass of protoplasm lacking a nucleus
mo·ne·ro·zoa \mə,nirə'zōə\ [NL, fr. *moneron* + *-zoa*] *syn of* MONERA
mo·ne·sia \mə'nēzhə\ *n* -s [AmerSp] **:** an astringent vegetable extract derived from the bark of a So. American tree (*Pradosia lactescens*) of the family Sapotaceae
mon·estrous *also* **mon·oestrous** \(')män+\ *adj* [*mon-* + *estrous, oestrous*] **:** experiencing estrus once each year **:** having a single annual breeding period ⟨most wild carnivorous mammals are ~⟩
mon·e·tar·i·ly \¦mänə¦terəlē, ¦mən-, -li *also* ¦mōn-\ *adv* **:** with respect to money **:** from a monetary standpoint ⟨was incorruptible, both ethically and ~ —R.H.Ferrell⟩
mon·e·tary \'⸗⸗,terē, -ri\ *adj* [LL *monetarius* of a mint, of money, fr. L *moneta* mint, coin, money, + *-arius* -ary — more

at MINT] **:** of or relating to money or to the instrumentalities and organizations by which money is supplied to the economy **:** PECUNIARY ⟨~ stocks of gold and silver⟩ ⟨~ reserves⟩ ⟨a ~ system⟩ ⟨~ inflation⟩ ⟨the ~ authorities⟩

monetary policy *or* **monetary management** *n* **:** measures taken by the central bank and treasury to strengthen the economy and minimize cyclical fluctuations through the availability and cost of credit, budgetary and tax policies, and other financial factors and comprising credit control and fiscal policy

monetary unit *n* **1 :** the standard unit of value of a national currency (as dollar, pound, franc) — called also *currency unit* **2 :** any unit of monetary value ⟨bundles of twenty cotton threads were the *monetary unit* for inexpensive articles —Phares Sigler⟩

mon·e·tite \ˈmänə,tīt\ *n* -S [*Moneta* island, near Puerto Rico + E *-ite*] **:** a mineral $CaHPO_4$ consisting of an acid calcium hydrogen phosphate and occurring in yellowish white crystals

mon·e·ti·za·tion \,mänəd·ə̇ˈzāshən *sometimes* ,mən-\ *n* -S **:** the act or process of monetizing (as silver) ⟨~ of credit⟩

mon·e·tize \ˈmänə,tīz *sometimes* ˈmən-\ *vt* -ED/-ING/-S [L *moneta* mint, coin, money + E *-ize* — more at MINT] **1 a :** to establish as the standard of a national currency ⟨demonetize gold and ~ silver⟩ **b :** to establish as legal tender **:** authorize for use as national currency with a fixed value in relation to the standard monetary unit **2 a :** to coin into money ⟨the Treasury merely ~*s* the gold that comes in —A.H.Hansen⟩ **b :** to convert (assets or debt instruments) into time deposits in the banking system ⟨~ national debts⟩

¹**mon·ey** \ˈmənē, -ni\ *n, pl* **moneys** *or* **monies** *often attrib* [ME *moneye*, fr. MF *moneie*, fr. L *moneta* mint, coin, money — more at MINT] **1 :** something generally accepted as a medium of exchange, a measure of value, or a means of payment ⟨have used gold, copper, wampum, or cattle for ~⟩: as **a :** officially coined or stamped metal currency **b :** MONEY OF ACCOUNT ⟨a coin worth less than a penny in our ~⟩ **c :** coinage or negotiable paper issued as legal tender by a recognized authority (as a government) ⟨took some ~ from her purse to pay him⟩ ⟨storekeepers who would accept foreign ~⟩ **2 a** (1) **:** assets or compensation in the form of or readily convertible to cash **:** monetary possessions ⟨can lose or make a lot of ~ in that business⟩ ⟨allowed to accept ~ for their services⟩ **:** pecuniary gain ⟨do the job for love or ~⟩ **:** PAY ⟨gets good ~ in that job⟩ (2) **:** property valued in terms of money ⟨died and left all his ~ to charity⟩ **b :** an amount of money ⟨raised the ~ for the new dormitory⟩ ⟨returned the ~ you lent him⟩ ⟨spent all the food ~ before payday⟩ **:** price paid ⟨got his ~'*s* worth⟩ **c :** capital dealt in as a commodity to be loaned or invested ⟨this year . . . mortgage ~ is much more plentiful⟩ ⟨the ~ supply in the country today⟩ ⟨~'*s* cheap these days, particularly on the security we'd be able to offer —John Morrison⟩ **d** *monies or moneys pl* **:** sums of money **:** FUNDS ⟨the collection of tax *monies*⟩ ⟨the servants brawled and stole the royal ~*s* —*Life*⟩ ⟨taking interest for ~*s* lent —G.G.Coulton⟩ **3 a :** a particular form or denomination of coin or paper money — usu. used in pl. ⟨copying the patterns of the ~*s* . . . current at the time of the Roman evacuation —John Craig⟩ **b :** a monetary value (as the silver dollar, pound sterling) taken as the basis of a system of monetary units **4 a :** the group receiving prize money in a contest; *specif* **:** the group finishing first, second, or third in a horse or dog race — used esp. in the phrase *in the money* or *out of the money* **b :** PRIZE MONEY — usu. used with *first*, *second*, or *third* ⟨his horse took third ~⟩ **5 :** persons or interests possessing or controlling great wealth regarded as a group or class **:** moneyed people ⟨there's a lot of ~ in that town⟩ ⟨politicians at the beck and call of ~⟩ — **for money** *adv* **:** for cash — used on the London stock exchange — **for one's money :** according to one's preference or opinion ⟨*for my money*, the play . . . is extraordinarily good fun —C.J. Rolo⟩ — **in the money** *adv* (*or adj*) **:** in an affluent state **:** with an ample supply of funds ⟨*in the money* and not worried about costs —Alva Johnston⟩ — **money for jam** *Brit* **:** something of advantage or profit gained with little or no investment or effort **:** EASY MONEY ⟨production grants . . . are *money for jam*, for they mostly benefit farmers who would in any event do the jobs —Clyde Higgs⟩

²**money** \"\ *vt* **moneyed**; **moneyed**; **moneying**; **moneys** **1 :** COIN **2 :** to convert into money by sale **3 :** to supply with money

moneybags \ˈ==,=\ *n pl but sing or pl in constr* **1 :** WEALTH 2 ⟨are fighting for the rich and their ~ —Bruce Marshall⟩ **2 :** a person having or believed to have considerable wealth ⟨that fleeting and uneasy dictatorship of the ~ —A.L.Guérard⟩

money belt *n* **:** a belt with pockets for carrying money that is usu. worn concealed

money belt

money bill *n* **:** a bill for raising revenue for general public purposes (as for imposing a tax on the people or transferring money or property from the people to the state) as distinguished from one providing a specific service for a fee or charge

money broker *n* **:** an intermediary who arranges short-term loans usu. in large amounts for borrowers and who in the U.S. also arranges the sale of excess bank reserve balances to banks short of reserves

money changer \ˈ==,==\ *n* [ME *moneye chaunger*] **1 :** one whose occupation is the exchanging of kinds or denominations of currency **2 :** a device for holding and dispensing sorted change

money changer 2

money changing *n* **:** the act or occupation of exchanging kinds or denominations of currency

money chest *n* **:** a metal container for valuables (as cash or gems) designed to resist burglary

money cowrie *n* **:** a cowrie used as money; *specif* **:** a yellow-shelled or white-shelled cowrie (*Cypraea moneta*) of the western Pacific and Indian oceans — see COWRIE illustration

money crop *n* **:** CASH CROP

money economy *n* **:** a system or stage of economic life in which money replaces barter in the exchange of goods

mon·eyed *also* **mon·ied** \ˈmənēd, -nid\ *adj* [ME *moneyed*, fr. *moneye* + *-ed*] **1 :** supplied with money **:** having money **:** WEALTHY ⟨the ~ tourist from abroad⟩ **2 :** consisting in or composed of money **:** derived from or due to money ⟨the ~ power of the landed gentry —J.W.Beach⟩

moneyed capital *n* **:** capital that consists in money or represents money that is used or invested and reinvested from time to time for the sake of making a profit on it as money (as by a bank or investment company)

moneyed corporation *n* **:** a corporation authorized to engage in the investment of moneyed capital

mon·ey·er \ˈmənēə(r)\ *n* -S [ME *moneyer*, *moneyour*, fr. OF *monier*, fr. LL *monetarius* master of a mint, coiner, fr. L *moneta* mint, coin, money + *-arius* -ary — more at MINT] **:** an authorized coiner of money **:** MINTER; *specif* **:** a craftsman formerly employed in England to cut and size blanks and strike coins

money grass *n* **:** RATTLE 3a

moneygrubber \ˈ==,==\ *n* **:** a person bent on accumulating money

money illusion *n* **:** the illusion that the face value of money is representative of its purchasing power **:** preoccupation (as of a wage earner) with wages rather than with real income or prices

moneylender \ˈ==,==\ *n* **:** one whose business is lending money; *specif* **:** PAWNBROKER

moneylending \ˈ==,==\ *n* **:** the act or occupation of lending money at interest

mon·ey·less \ˈmənēlə̇s\ *adj* **:** having no money ⟨virtually ~ rural regions —*Atlantic*⟩

money-maker \ˈ==,==\ *n* [ME *moneyemaker*, fr. *moneye* + *maker*] **1** *obs* **:** one who coins or prints money **:** MINTER; *also* **:** a counterfeiter of money **2 :** one who accumulates money or

MONEY

NAME	SYMBOL	SUBDIVISION	COUNTRY
afghani	Af	100 puls	Afghanistan
austral[1]		100 pesos	Argentina
baht *or* tical	B *or* Tc	100 satang	Thailand
balboa	B	100 centesimos	Panama
birr	E$ *or* EB	100 cents	Ethiopia
bolivar	B	100 centimos	Venezuela
boliviano	$b	100 centavos	Bolivia
cedi	₵	100 pesewas	Ghana
colon	₡	100 centimos	Costa Rica
colon	₡	100 centavos	El Salvador
cordoba	C$	100 centavos	Nicaragua
cruzeiro[2]		100 centavos	Brazil
dalasi	D	100 bututs	Gambia
deutsche mark[3]	DM	100 pfennig	Germany
dinar	DA	100 centimes	Algeria
dinar	BD	1000 fils	Bahrain
dinar	ID	1000 fils	Iraq
dinar	JD	1000 fils	Jordan
dinar	KD	1000 fils	Kuwait
dinar	LD	1000 dirhams	Libya
dinar[4]	£SY	1000 fils	Southern Yemen
dinar	D	1000 millimes	Tunisia
dinar	Din	100 paras	Yugoslavia
dirham	DH	100 centimes *or* francs[5]	Morocco
dirham	UD	1000 fils[6]	United Arab Emirates
dobra	Db	100 centavos[7]	Sao Tome and Principe
dollar	EC$[8]	100 cents	Antigua and Barbuda
dollar	$A	100 cents	Australia
dollar	B$	100 cents	Bahamas
dollar	Bds$	100 cents	Barbados
dollar	$	100 cents	Belize
dollar	$	100 cents	Bermuda
dollar	B$	100 sen *or* cents	Brunei
dollar	$	100 cents	Canada
dollar *or* yuan	NT$	100 cents	China (Taiwan)
dollar	EC$[8]	100 cents	Dominica
dollar	F$	100 cents	Fiji
dollar	EC$[8]	100 cents	Grenada
dollar	G$	100 cents	Guyana
dollar	HK$	100 cents	Hong Kong
dollar	J$	100 cents	Jamaica
dollar	$	100 cents	Liberia
dollar	N$	100 cents	Namibia
dollar	NZ$	100 cents	New Zealand
dollar	EC$[8]	100 cents	Saint Kitts-Nevis
dollar	EC$[8]	100 cents	Saint Lucia
dollar	EC$[8]	100 cents	Saint Vincent and the Grenadines
dollar	S$	100 cents	Singapore
dollar	TT$	100 cents	Trinidad and Tobago
dollar	$	100 cents	United States
dollar	Z$	100 cents	Zimbabwe
dong	D	100 xu	Vietnam
drachma[3]	Dr	100 lepta	Greece
escudo	Esc	100 centavos	Cape Verde
escudo[3]	$ *or* Esc	100 centavos	Portugal
euro[9]	€	100 cents	Austria, Belgium, Finland, France, Germany, Greece, Ireland, Italy, Luxembourg, Netherlands, Portugal, Spain
florin see GULDEN, below			
forint	F *or* Ft	100 filler	Hungary
franc[3]	FR *or* F *or* BF	100 centimes	Belgium
franc	CFAF[10]	100 centimes	Benin
franc	CFAF[10]	100 centimes	Burkina Faso
franc	FBu	100 centimes	Burundi
franc	CFAF[10]	100 centimes	Cameroon
franc	CFAF[10]	100 centimes	Central African Republic
franc	CFAF[10]	100 centimes	Chad
franc	CFAF[10]	100 centimes	Congo
franc	DjFr	100 centimes	Djibouti
franc *or* franco	CFAF[10]	100 centimes	Equatorial Guinea
franc[3]	Fr *or* F	100 centimes	France
franc	CFAF[10]	100 centimes	Gabon
franc	GF	100 centimes	Guinea
franc	CFAF[10]	100 centimes	Ivory Coast
franc[3]	Fr *or* F	100 centimes	Luxembourg
franc	Fr *or* F *or* FMG	100 centimes	Madagascar
franc	CFAF[10]	100 centimes	Mali
franc		100 centimes	Monaco
franc	CFAF[10]	100 centimes	Niger
franc	RWF	100 centimes[11]	Rwanda
franc	CFAF[10]	100 centimes	Senegal
franc	Fr *or* FR *or* SF	100 centimes *or* rappen	Switzerland
franc	CFAF[10]	100 centimes	Togo
gourde	Gde *or* G	100 centimes	Haiti

NAME	SYMBOL	SUBDIVISION	COUNTRY
guarani	G	100 centimos	Paraguay
gulden *or* guilder *or* florin[3]	F *or* fl *or* G	100 cents	Netherlands
gulden *or* guilder *or* florin	Sf	100 cents	Suriname
kina	K	100 toea	Papua New Guinea
kip	K	100 at	Laos
koruna[12]	Kčs	100 halers	Czechoslovakia
krona	Kr	100 aurar	Iceland
krona	SKr	100 öre	Sweden
krone	DKr	100 öre	Denmark
krone	Nkr	100 öre	Norway
kuna		100 lipa	Croatia
kwacha	K	100 tambala	Malawi
kwacha	K	100 ngwee	Zambia
kwanza		100 lwei	Angola
kyat	K	100 pyas	Burma (Myanmar)
lek	L	100 qintar	Albania
lempira	L	100 centavos	Honduras
leone	Le	100 cents	Sierra Leone
leu	L	100 bani	Romania
lev	Lv	100 stotinki	Bulgaria
lilangeni (*plural* emalangeni)	E *or* L	100 cents	Swaziland
lira[3]	L *or* Lit	100 centesimi	Italy
lira *or* pound		100 pence	Malta
lira *or* pound	TL	100 kurus *or* piasters	Turkey
lira see POUND, below			
loti (*plural* maloti)	M	100 licente *or* lisente (*sing* sente)	Lesotho
manat		100 gopik	Azerbaijan
manat		100 tennesi	Turkmenistan
mark *or* ostmark[13]	M *or* OM	100 pfennigs	East Germany
mark see DEUTSCHE MARK, above			
markka[3]	Mk *or* Fmk	100 pennia	Finland
metical		100 centavos	Mozambique
naira	₦	100 kobo	Nigeria
ngultrum	N	100 chetrums	Bhutan
ostmark see MARK, above			
ouguiya	UM	5 khoums	Mauritania
pa'anga	T$	100 seniti	Tonga
pataca	P *or* $	100 avos	Macao
peseta[3]	Pta *or* P (*pl.* Pts)	100 centimos	Spain
peso		100 centavos	Chile
peso	$	100 centavos	Colombia
peso	$	100 centavos	Cuba
peso	RD$	100 centavos	Dominican Republic
peso		100 centavos	Guinea-Bissau
peso	$	100 centavos	Mexico
peso	P	100 sentimos *or* centavos	Philippines
peso	$	100 centesimos	Uruguay
pound	£	1000 mils[14]	Cyprus
pound	£E	100 piasters	Egypt
pound[3]	£	100 pence	Ireland
pound	L£ *or* LL	100 piasters	Lebanon
pound	£S *or* LSd	100 piasters	Sudan
pound *or* lira	£S *or* LS	100 piasters	Syria
pound	£	100 pence	United Kingdom
pound see LIRA, above			
pula	P	100 thebe	Botswana
quetzal	Q	100 centavos	Guatemala
rand	R	100 cents	So. Africa
real		100 centavos	Brazil
rial	R *or* Rl	100 dinars	Iran
rial	R	1000 baizas	Oman
rial *or* riyal[4]	YR	40 buqshas	Yemen Arab Republic
riel	CR	100 sen	Cambodia
ringgit	$	100 sen	Malaysia
riyal		100 dirhams	Qatar
riyal	R	100 halala	Saudi Arabia
ruble[15]	R *or* Rub	100 kopecks	U.S.S.R.
rupee	Re (*pl.* Rs)	100 paise	India
rupee	Re (*pl.* Rs)	100 cents	Mauritius
rupee	Re (*pl.* Rs)	100 paisa	Nepal
rupee	Re (*pl.* Rs)	100 paisa	Pakistan
rupee	Re (*pl.* Rs)	100 cents	Seychelles
rupee	Re (*pl.* Rs)	100 cents	Sri Lanka
rupiah	Rp	100 sen	Indonesia
schilling[3]	S *or* Sch	100 groschen	Austria
shekel		100 agorot	Israel
shilling	KSh	100 cents	Kenya
shilling *or* shilingi	TSh	100 cents *or* senti	Tanzania
shilling	USh	100 cents	Uganda
sol	S/ *or* $	100 centavos[16]	Peru
som		100 tyiyn	Kyrgyzstan
Somali shilling *also* somalo	SomSh	100 cents	Somalia
sucre	S/	100 centavos	Ecuador
syli		100 cauris	Guinea
taka	Tk	100 paisa	Bangladesh

continued

wealth **3 :** something (as a plan, device, product) that produces money or profit

[1]**moneymaking** \ˈ⁼⁼,⁼⁼\ *adj* **1 :** affording profitable returns ⟨~ investments⟩ **2 :** engaged or successful in gaining money ⟨the ~ members of the family⟩

[2]**moneymaking** \"\ *n* **:** the act or process of making money **:** the acquisition and accumulation of wealth

moneyman \ˈ⁼⁼,⁼\ *n, pl* **moneymen :** FINANCIER

money market *n* **1 :** the lenders and borrowers of short-term funds and the intermediaries who bring them together **2 :** a financial center where institutions comprising the money market are well developed

mon·ey·ness *n* -ES **:** the quality or state of being readily convertible to cash **:** LIQUIDITY

money of account : a denominator of value or basis of exchange which is used in keeping accounts and for which there may or may not be an equivalent in coin or paper money

money of necessity : NECESSITY MONEY

money order *n* **:** an order for the payment of money; *specif* **:** an order issued at a post office upon application by a person making a remittance and payable at another post office

money plant *n* **1 :** HONESTY 3 **2 :** MONEYWORT

money player *n* **:** a participant in competition (as a sports match) who performs best under pressure

money-purchase \ˈ⁼⁼,⁼⁼\ *adj* **:** of, relating to, or being a plan for retirement income in which contributions are at a fixed rate and benefits are determined by what the money thus set aside will buy

moneys *pl of* MONEY, *pres 3d sing of* MONEY

money scrivener *n* **:** a person engaged in the business of arranging for the loan of money to others

money spider *n* **:** a spider popularly supposed to indicate that the person upon whom it crawls will gain money

money spinner *n, chiefly Brit* **:** a moneymaking person, product, or activity **:** MONEY-MAKER ⟨in the western province the *money spinner* is cocoa —Wynford Vaughan-Thomas⟩

money supply *n* **:** the stock of money consisting of coin, currency, and bank demand deposits — called also *money stock*

money weight *n* **:** COIN WEIGHT

moneywort \ˈ⁼⁼,⁼\ *n* **:** a trailing European herb of the genus *Lysimachia* (*L. nummularia*) introduced into No. America and having shiny rounded opposite leaves and yellow flowers on slender separate stalks with one in each axil of each pair of opposite leaves

[1]**mong** \ˈməŋ\ *n* [ME *mong* mixture, short for *ymong*, fr. OE *gemong*, *gemang* mingling, crowd — more at AMONG] *dial Eng* **:** a mixture of meal for domestic animals

[2]**mong** \"\ *n* -S [short for *mongrel*] *Austral* **:** a mongrel dog

[1]**monger** \ˈməŋgə(r), ˈmäŋ- *sometimes* -ŋə-\ *n* -S [ME *mongere*, fr. OE *mangere*, fr. L *mangon-*, *mango* dealer in furbished wares, slave dealer, horse trader (of Gk origin; akin to Gk *manganon* charm, ballista) + OE *-ere* -er — more at MANGONEL] **1 :** one engaged in the sale of a commodity **:** DEALER — usu. used in combination ⟨ale*monger*⟩ ⟨cheese*monger*⟩ ⟨pear*monger*⟩ **2 :** a person engaged in petty or discreditable dealings ⟨a ~ of . . . clichés —L.A.Fiedler⟩ ⟨~*s* of class warfare —M.H.Stans⟩ — usu. used in combination ⟨victims of the local slander*mongers* —*New Yorker*⟩ ⟨a patronage-*monger*⟩

[2]**monger** \"\ *vt* **mongered; mongered; mongering** \-ŋ(g)(ə)riŋ\ **mongers :** to act as a monger in purveying **:** PEDDLE, SPREAD ⟨no use ~*ing* words unless we know what stands behind them —L.Baralt⟩

monger·er \-ŋ(g)ərə(r)\ *n* -S [[2]*monger* + *-er*] **:** MONGER

mongering *n* -S [[1]*monger* + *-ing*] **:** the activity of a monger **:** SELLING, TRAFFICKING — usu. used in combination ⟨sensation-*mongering*⟩ ⟨hate*mongering*⟩ ⟨peace*mongering*⟩

mon·gler \ˈməŋglə(r), ˈmäŋ-\ *n* -S [alter. of [1]*mongrel*] *dial* **:** STILT SANDPIPER

mongo *or* **mongoe** *var of* MUNGO

[1]**mon·gol** \ˈmäŋgəl, -äŋ,gōl, -än,gōl\ *n* -S [Mongolian *Mongol*] **1** *cap* **:** a member of one of the chiefly pastoral peoples of Mongolia that physically typify the Mongoloid race, conquered much of Asia and eastern Europe in the 12th and 13th centuries, are prevailingly Lamaistic in religion, and include as important tribal groups the Kalmucks to the west, the Khalkhas of the Mongolian People's Republic, the Buryats to the north, and the true Mongols to the east **2** *usu cap* **:** MONGOLIAN 2 **3** *usu cap* **:** MONGOLOID 1 **4** *sometimes cap* **:** MONGOLIAN 3

[2]**mongol** \"\ *adj, usu cap* **:** MONGOLIAN

mongolfier *var of* MONTGOLFIER

mongol-galchic alphabet *n, usu cap M&G* **:** an alphabet consisting of the Uighur alphabet supplemented by five letters from the Tibetan added to adapt it to the Mongolic speech

mon·go·lia \(ˈ)mäŋ¦gōlēə, -äŋ¦-, -lyə\ *adj, usu cap* [fr. *Mongolia*, vast territory with indefinite boundaries in east-central Asia] **:** of or from Mongolia **:** of the kind or style prevalent in Mongolia **:** MONGOLIAN

[1]**mon·go·li·an** \-ən\ *adj* [*Mongolia*, territory in Asia + E *-an*] **1** *usu cap* **:** of or relating to Mongolia or the Mongolian People's Republic or to the Mongols or their language ⟨a *Mongolian* pony⟩ ⟨the *Mongolian* embassy⟩ **2** *usu cap* **:** MONGOLOID 1 **3** *sometimes cap* **:** of, relating to, or affected with mongolism

[2]**mongolian** \"\ *n* -S **1** *cap* **a :** MONGOL 1 **b :** MONGOLOID 1 **c :** a native or inhabitant of the Mongolian People's Republic **2** *usu cap* **:** the Mongolic language of the Mongol people **3** *sometimes cap* **:** one affected with mongolism

mongolian bluebeard *n, usu cap M* **:** a bluebeard (*Caryopteris mongholica*) of China and Mongolia having linear nearly entire leaves and blue flowers in few-flowered clusters

mongolian fold *or* **mongoloid fold** *or* **mongolic fold** *n, usu cap M* **:** EPICANTHIC FOLD

mongolian pheasant *n, usu cap M* **1 :** a large pheasant (*Phasianus colchicus mongolicus*) native to the colder part of China and similar to the ring-necked pheasant but with the wing coverts almost entirely white **2 :** RING-NECKED PHEASANT

mongolian release *n, usu cap M* **:** an arrow release in which the bowstring is drawn by the bent thumb with overlocked forefinger and the arrow held in the hollow at the base of finger and thumb

mongolian spot *or* **mongol spot** *n, often cap M* **:** BLUE SPOT

[1]**mon·gol·ic** \(ˈ)mäŋ¦gälik, -än¦-\ *adj, usu cap* [[1]*Mongol* + *-ic*] **:** MONGOLOID 1

[2]**mongolic** \"\ *n* -S *usu cap* **:** a group of Altaic languages including Mongolian, Buryat, and Kalmuck

mon·gol·ism \ˈmäŋgə,lizəm\ *or* **mon·go·li·an·ism** \mäŋˈgōlēə,nizəm, mänˈ-, -lyə,-\ *n* -S *sometimes cap* [[2]*Mongol* or [1]*Mongolian* + *-ism*] **:** a congenital condition which is characterized by moderate to severe mental deficiency, by slanting eyes, by a broad short skull, by broad hands with short fingers, and by trisomy of the chromosome numbered 21 in man — called also *Down's syndrome*

mon·gol·iza·tion \,mäŋgələˈzāshən\ *n* -S *usu cap* **:** the act or process of mongolizing

mon·gol·ize \ˈmäŋgə,līz\ *vt* -ED/-ING/-S *often cap* [[2]*Mongol* + *-ize*] **1 :** to make Mongolian in racial relationship or characteristics by an admixture of Mongolian blood ⟨*mongolized* Tartars⟩ **2 :** to furnish (a country) with or allow a significant increase in population belonging to the Mongolian race

mongolo- *comb form, usu cap* [[2]*Mongol*] **:** Mongolian and ⟨*Mongolo*-Manchurian⟩ ⟨*Mongolo*-Tatar⟩ ⟨*Mongolo*-Turkic⟩

mon·golo-dravidian \¦mäŋgə,lō+\ *adj, usu cap M&D* [*Mongolo-* + *Dravidian*] **:** of, relating to, or constituting a mixed ethnological type of Bengal and Orissa, India, marked by a broad head, dark complexion, medium stature, somewhat broad nose, and plentiful beard

[1]**mon·gol·oid** \ˈmäŋgə,lȯid\ *adj* [[1]*Mongol* + *-oid*] **1** *usu cap* **:** of, constituting, or characteristic of a racial stock that is native to Asia, that is commonly distinguished as one of the major racial divisions of mankind and considered to comprise peoples prevalent in northern and eastern Asia, Malaysians, Eskimos, and often American Indians, and that has as typical features a yellowish complexion, coarse straight black hair and scant beard, short stature, a round head, and a broad flat face with small nose and prominent cheekbones and with eyes having an epicanthic fold **2** *sometimes cap* **:** MONGOLIAN 3

[2]**mongoloid** \"\ *n* -S **1** *cap* **:** a person of Mongoloid racial stock **2** *sometimes cap* **:** MONGOLIAN 3

MONEY—*concluded*

NAME	SYMBOL	SUBDIVISION	COUNTRY
tala	WS$	100 sene	Western Samoa (Samoa)
tical see BAHT, above			
tolar		100 stotinov	Slovenia
tugrik	Tug	100 mongo	Mongolian People's Republic (Mongolia)
won	W	100 jun	No. Korea
won	W	100 chon	So. Korea
yen	Y	100 sen[11]	Japan
yuan	Y	100 cents	China
yuan see DOLLAR, above			
zaire	Z	100 makuta (*sing.* likuta)	Zaire (Democratic Republic of the Congo)
zloty	Zl *or* Z	100 groszy	Poland

[1]Replaced by the peso in 1991.
[2]Replaced by the real in 1993.
[3]Replaced by the euro in 2002.
[4]Southern Yemen and Yemen Arab Republic became united as Yemen in 1990 with the rial of 100 fils as its currency.
[5]Until 1974.
[6]Since 1988 revaluation there have been 100 fils to the United Arab Emirates dirham.
[7]Replaced by centimos in 1977.
[8]Dollars issued by the *Eastern Caribbean Central Bank*, established to promote economic cooperation among the member nations.
[9]Came into use by 12 of the 15 European Union nations Jan. 1, 2002.
[10]Francs issued by the African Financial Community (*Communauté Financière Africaine*), established to promote economic cooperation among the member nations.
[11]Now a subdivision in name only.
[12]Since 1993 the koruna of 100 halers has been the currency of the Czech Republic.
[13]In 1990 Germany was reunified with the deutsche mark of 100 pfennigs as its currency. That was replaced by the euro of 100 cents in 2002.
[14]Replaced by 100 cents in 1983.
[15]Since 1991 the ruble of 100 kopecks has been the currency of Russia.
[16]Replaced by centimos in 1996.

mongoloid idiocy *n, sometimes cap M* : MONGOLISM

mongols *pl of* MONGOL

mon·goose \'mäŋ,güs, ǀn,- *sometimes* 'mäŋ\ *n, pl* **mongooses**

mongoose 1a

[Hindi *mūgūs, māgūs*, fr. Prakrit *maṅguso*, perh. of Dravidian origin; akin to Tamil *mūṅkā* mongoose] **1 a** : an agile keen-sighted grizzled brown and black viverrine mammal (*Herpestes nyula*) of India that is about the size of a ferret, has a sharp snout and a long heavy tail, captures and feeds on snakes including the most venomous and on rodents, and is often domesticated **b** : any other member of the genus *Herpestes* or of various related genera native to Asia and Africa — compare ICHNEUMON 1 **2** *or* **mongoose lemur** : a Madagascan lemur (*Lemur mongoz*)

mongos *pl of* MONGO

[1]**mon·grel** \'məŋgrəl, 'mäŋ-\ *n* -s [prob. fr. [1]*mong*] **1** : an animal or plant resulting from the interbreeding of two or more breeds or strains; *esp* : an individual of unknown ancestry but not necessarily of inferior quality — contrasted with *crossbred* and *grade;* distinguished from *scrub* **2 a** : a person of mixed birth or tendencies or of undefined status **b** : a cross between types of persons or things **3** *dial* : STILT SANDPIPER

[2]**mongrel** \"\ *adj* **1** : of mixed breeding : being a mongrel ⟨a ~ dog⟩ **2** : of or being a mixed race or nationality — sometimes used disparagingly **3** : of mixed origin, character, or kinds : assignable to no definite class or type ⟨a ~ mixture, including some grass, more weeds, patches of moss —R.M. Yoder⟩

mongrel buffalo *n* : BLACK BUFFALO

mon·grel·ism \-rə,lizəm\ *n* -s : the quality or state of being mongrel

mon·grel·iza·tion \,məŋgrələ'zāshən, ,mäŋ-, -lī'-\ *n* -s **1** : the process of mongrelizing ⟨pledged to fight . . . the ~ of the white race —Cabell Phillips⟩ **2** : the quality or state of being mongrelized ⟨the use of crossbreds . . . will not mean the reversion to the ~ of the fowl —L.M.Winters⟩

mon·grel·ize \'məŋgrə,līz, 'mäŋ-\ *vt* -ED/-ING/-S [[1]*mongrel* + *-ize*] : to cause to become mongrel — **mon·grel·iz·er** \-zə(r)\ *n* -s

mon·grel·ly \-rəlē\ *adj* : having the character of a mongrel

mon·grel·ness *n* -ES : the quality or state of being mongrel

mongrel skate *n, dial* : a monkfish (*Squatina squatina*)

mongs *pl of* MONG

mon·guor \'mäŋ,gwȯ(ə)r, -äŋ,-\ *n, pl* **monguor** *or* **monguors** *usu cap* **1** : a sinicized group of Mongol peoples inhabiting the Kansu-Tsinghai provincial borders in the northeast Tibetan highlands **2** : a member of a Monguor people

mon·hys·ter·i·na \,män,histə'rīnə\ [NL, fr. *mon-* + *hyster-* + *-ina*] *syn of* CHROMADORIDA

mo·ni·al \'mōnēəl\ *n* -s [ME *moynel, moniel*, fr. MF *moinel*, perh. fr. *moyen* middle, fr. L *medianus* — more at MEDIAN] : MULLION 1

mo·ni·as \'mōnēəs\ *n, cap* [NL, fr. Gk, solitary, fr. *monos* alone, single — more at MONK] : a monotypic genus of Madagascan birds (family Mesitornithidae) having a longer bill and tail than members of the closely related genus *Mesitornis*

mon·ie \'məni\ *chiefly Scot var of* MANY

monied *var of* MONEYED

monies *pl of* MONEY

mo·nie·zia \mə'nezh(ē)ə\ *n* [NL, fr. Romain-Louis *Moniez* †1936 Fr. physician + NL *-ia*] **1** *cap* : a genus of cyclophyllidean tapeworms (family Anoplocephalidae) parasitizing the intestine of various ruminants and having a cysticercoid larva in oribatid mites **2** -s : any worm of the genus *Moniezia*

mon·i·ker *or* **mon·ick·er** \'mänəkə(r), -nēk-\ *n* -s [origin unknown] *slang* : NAME, NICKNAME ⟨might have preferred a substantial ~ like Patrick —*Brentano's Bk. Chat*⟩ ⟨earned him the ~ "Iron-jawed George" —*Pittsfield (Mass.) News*⟩

mo·nil·e·thrix *or* **mo·nil·i·thrix** \mə'nilə,thriks\ *n, pl* **mon·i·let·ri·ches** \,mänə'le·trə,kēz\ *or* **mon·i·lit·ri·ches** \-li-\ [NL, fr. L *monili-, monile* necklace + NL *-thrix* — more at MANE] : a disease of the hair in which each hair appears as if strung with small beads or nodes

mo·nil·ia \mə'nilēə\ *n* [NL, fr. L *monile* necklace; fr. the chain of spores] **1** *cap* : the type genus of Moniliaceae comprising imperfect fungi with hyaline or colored oval to short cylindric conidia borne in branched chains that resemble the vegetative hyphae and including in some classifications various fungi that are now usu. placed in other genera (as *Candida*) **2** *pl* **monilias** *or* **monilia** : any fungus of the genus *Monilia* **3** *or* **monilia disease** -s : BROWN ROT 1a

mo·nil·i·a·ce·ae \mə,nilē'āsē,ē\ *n pl, cap* [NL, fr. *Monilia*, type genus + *-aceae*] : a family of imperfect fungi (order Moniliales) having white or brightly colored hyphae and similarly colored spores that are produced directly on the mycelium and not aggregated in fruiting bodies

mo·nil·i·al \mə'nilēəl\ *adj* [NL *Monilia* + E *-al*] : of, relating to, or caused by a fungus of the genus *Candida*

mo·nil·i·a·les \mə,nilē'ā(,)lēz\ *n pl, cap* [NL, fr. *Monilia* + *-ales*] : an order of imperfect fungi lacking conidiophores or having conidiophores that are superficial and free or gathered in tufts or pulvinate masses but never enclosed in an acervulus or pycnidium

mon·i·li·a·sis \,mänə'līəsəs\ *n, pl* **monilia·ses** \-ī ə,sēz\ [NL, fr. *Monilia* + *-iasis*] : infection with or disease caused by yeastlike fungi of the family Moniliaceae; *specif* : THRUSH

mo·nil·i·form \mə'nilə,fȯrm\ *adj* [L *monili-, monile* necklace + E *-form* — more at MANE] : jointed or constricted at regular intervals so as to resemble a string of beads ⟨a ~ root⟩ ⟨an insect with ~ antennae⟩ — see ANTENNA illustration, ROOT illustration — **mo·nil·i·form·ly** *adv*

mo·nil·i·for·mis \mə,nilə'fȯrməs\ *n, cap* [NL, fr. L *monili-, monile* necklace + L *-formis* -form] : a genus of acanthocephalan worms usu. parasitic in rodents but occas. found in dogs, cats, or rarely man

mo·nil·iid \mə'nilēəd\ *n* -s [NL *Monilia* + E *-id*] : a secondary commonly generalized dermatitis resulting from hypersensitivity developed in response to a primary focus of infection with a fungus of the genus *Candida*

mo·nil·i·oid \mə'nilē,ȯid\ *adj* [L *monili-, monile* necklace + E *-oid*] : MONILIFORM

mon·i·ment \'mänimənt\ *n* -s [alter. of *monument*] *Scot* : a person whose behavior and actions provoke ridicule

mo·nim·ia \mə'nimēə\ *n, cap* [NL, fr. L *Monima* (fr. L, fr. Gk *Monimē*), the wife of Mithridates VI †63B.C. king of ancient Pontus after whom a related genus (*Mithridatea*) had been named + NL *-ia*] : a genus (the type of the family Monimiaceae) of shrubs native to the Mascarene islands having opposite leaves and small diclinous flowers

mo·nim·i·a·ce·ae \mə,nimē'āsē,ē\ *n pl, cap* [NL, fr. *Monimia*, type genus + *-aceae*] : a family of chiefly tropical American trees and shrubs (order Ranales) having evergreen usu. opposite leaves and insignificant generally unisexual flowers

mo·nim·o·lite \mə'nimə,līt\ *n* -s [Sw *monimolit*, fr. Gk *monimos* stable, steady (fr. *menein* to remain) + Sw *-lit* -lite — more at MANSION] : a yellowish or brownish green mineral $(Pb,Ca)_3Sb_2O_8$(?) consisting of an oxide of lead, calcium, and antimony

mon·i·mo·sty·lic \,mänəmō'stīlik\ *adj* [Gk *monimos* + E *-stylic*] *of a reptile* : having the quadrate bone united to the skull by a suture

mon·i·plies \'mäni,plīz\ *Scot var of* MANYPLIES

mon·ish \'mänish\ *vt* -ED/-ING/-ES [ME *monesen, monisshen* alter. (*monest-* being taken as past & past part.) of *monesten*, fr. OF *monester*, fr. (assumed) VL *monestare*, fr. L *monēre* to warn — more at MIND] : ADMONISH

mon·ism \'mō,nizəm, 'mä,-\ *n* -s [G *monismus*, fr. *mon-* + *-ismus* -ism] **1 a** (1) : the metaphysical view that there is only one kind of substance or ultimate reality — compare DUALISM, PLURALISM (2) : the metaphysical view that reality is one unitary organic whole with no independent parts — contrasted with *pluralism* **b** : an epistemological theory that proclaims the identity of the object and datum of knowledge — contrasted with *dualism* **2** : MONOGENESIS **3** : a viewpoint, theory, or methodology that reduces either all phenomena or those within its particular domain to one fundamental principle **4** : a sociological doctrine that the laws of man and nature are united in one single harmonious force

mon·ist \-,nəst\ *n* -s [G, fr. *mon-* + *-ist*] : an advocate of monism

mo·nis·tic \mə'nistik, mō'-, -tēk\ *also* **mo·nis·ti·cal** \-təkəl, -tēk-\ *adj* **1** : of, relating to, or involving monism : relying on one factor or method in explanation ⟨the ~ school would regard national law and international law as an integrated whole —J.S.Roucek⟩ — distinguished from *dualistic* and *pluralistic* **2** : of one type or character ⟨that American culture is a ~, unified, homogeneous culture —David Golovensky⟩

monistic idealism *n* : a system of philosophical idealism emphasizing the primacy of the One (as the Absolute or Nature) rather than of the many — contrasted with *pluralistic idealism;* compare HEGELIANISM, SPINOZISM

mo·ni·tion \mə'nishən\ *n* -s [ME *monicioun*, fr. MF *monition*, fr. L *monition-, monitio*, fr. *monitus* (past part. of *monēre* to remind, warn) + *-ion-, -io* -ion — more at MIND] **1** : instruction or advice given by way of caution : ADMONITION, WARNING, CAUTION **2** : an intimation, indication, or notice of something esp. of a dangerous kind present or impending **3 a** : a legal process in the nature of a summons or citation to appear and answer (as in default of performing some certain act) **b** : an order from a bishop or ecclesiastical court to desist from a specified offense

[1]**mon·i·tor** \'mänəd·ə(r), -ətə(r) *sometimes* -ə,tȯ(ə)r *or* -ȯ(ə)\ *n* -s [L, one that reminds or warns, overseer, fr. *monitus* + *-or*] **1 a** : a student appointed to assist a teacher (as by keeping order, performing routine duties, or in some educational systems teaching younger students) **b** : a person or thing that gives advice (as of caution) or instruction regarding conduct : one that reproves, reminds, or instructs : ADMONISHER, ADVISER ⟨enough practical experience on the fighting line to serve as ~s and instructors for troops green in the game of war —*N. Y. Times*⟩ : REMINDER ⟨observed the customary stack of documents on this busy man's reading table, and . . . took it as a silent ~ —Upton Sinclair⟩ **c** (1) : one that monitors something ⟨learned from a broadcast heard by a U. S. ~⟩ ⟨an electronic ~⟩ (2) : an observer responsible for reporting misdeeds ⟨the correspondents put fresh vigor into their classic role as people's ~ over the Government —*Time*⟩ (3) : an instrument that measures (as vital signs during surgery) or gives warning (as of excessive radiation) (4) : a cathode-ray tube used for display (as of television pictures or computer information) **2** *archaic* : a board worn or fastened across the back to give erectness to the figure **3** *also* **monitor lizard** [so called fr. the belief that such lizards give warning of the presence of crocodiles] : any of various large tropical Old World pleurodont lizards closely related to the iguanas and constituting the genus *Varanus* and the family Varanidae and including an African lizard (*V. niloticus*) that destroys crocodile eggs — compare KOMODO DRAGON **4** [fr. the *Monitor*, the first ship of this type, designed in 1862 for the U. S. Navy by John Ericsson †1889 Am. engineer and inventor born in Sweden] **a** : a heavily armored warship formerly used in coastal operations, having a very low freeboard and one or more revolving turrets with heavy guns, and sacrificing speed and coal capacity to steadiness as gun platforms and to thickness of armor **b** : a small modern warship with shallow draft and two 15-inch guns for coastal bombardment **5** *also* **monitor top** : a raised central portion of a roof (as along the ridge of a gable roof) having low windows or louvers along its sides and used to provide light and air **6** *or* **monitor nozzle** : a nozzle capable of turning completely round in a horizontal plane with a limited play in a vertical plane and used in hydraulic mining and fire fighting **7** : a tool-holding turret on a machine

[2]**monitor** \"\ *vb* **monitored; monitored; monitoring** \-d·əriŋ, -tər-, -ôr-, -nə·triŋ\ **monitors** *vt* **1 a** : to check and sometimes to adjust (as a radio or television signal, channel, or program) for quality or fidelity to a band by means of a receiver during or sometimes before transmission ⟨the frequency must be exact, constant, and carefully ~*ed* —M.H. Aronson⟩ ⟨gradually introducing automatic ~*ing* of the aural quality of its programs —*Times Rev. of Industry*⟩ **b** : to check (as a radio or television broadcast or a telephone conversation) for military, political, or criminal significance by means of a receiver ⟨~ radiotelephone messages out of Hawaii —*New Republic*⟩ **2** : to test (as air, a surface, a beam of radiation, clothing, personnel) for intensity of radiation (as from radioactivity) to determine whether the intensity comes within specified limits ⟨~ the upper air to collect telltale evidence of atomic explosions —*Time*⟩ **3** : to watch, observe, or check esp. for a special purpose ⟨had to ~ every word and thought —Polly Adler⟩ ⟨crew chiefs ~*ed* engines and the array of dials, switches and lights that told them how each item of equipment was functioning —Gordon Williams⟩ ⟨~ political gossip⟩ **4** : to keep track of, regulate, or control (as a process or the operation of a machine) ⟨personnel . . . involved in ~*ing* the work of this contract —A.A.Campbell⟩ — used esp. of an automatic electronic device ⟨the line is ~*ed* by a new instrument called the quality control indicator —*Science News Letter*⟩; *specif* : to keep track of (aircraft in flight) by means of radar ⟨radar stations ~*ing* all our heavy bombers —W.R. Frye⟩ **5** : to check or regulate the volume or quality of (sound) in preparation for recording or during recording ⟨sound is ~*ed* and the correct effect is introduced; it would obviously be ludicrous to have close-up sound in a long shot —O.B.Hanson⟩ ~ *vi* : to act as a monitor

monitor bug *n* : CONENOSE

mon·i·to·ri·al \,mänə'tōrēəl, -tȯr-\ *adj* [L *monitorius* monitory + E *-al* — more at MONITORY] **1** : MONITORY ⟨always teaching the public something, an editorial, ~ urge crowding his brain —H.R.Warfel⟩ **2** : of, relating to, done by, or in charge of a monitor ⟨~ instruction⟩ — **mon·i·to·ri·al·ly** \-ēəlē, -li\ *adv*

monitorial system *n* : an educational system formerly in use by many charity schools that consisted in employing older pupils to teach the younger ones — see LANCASTERIAN

monitor lizard *n* : MONITOR 3

mon·i·tor·ship \'mänəd·ə(r),ship\ *n* : the position or function of a monitor : SUPERVISION

[1]**mon·i·to·ry** \'mänə,tōrē, -tȯr-, -ri\ *adj* [L *monitorius*, fr. *monitus* (past part. of *monēre* to warn) + *-orius* -ory — more at MIND] : giving admonition : WARNING ⟨a ~ proverb⟩

[2]**monitory** \"\ *n* -ES : a monitory letter ⟨exhortations, decrees, and *monitories* of the popes —D.H.Wiest⟩

mon·i·tress \'mänə·trəs\ *n* -ES [[1]*monitor* + *-ess*] **1** : a woman that admonishes **2** : a girl that is a monitor in a school

[1]**monk** \'məŋk\ *n* -s [ME *munk, monk*, fr. OE *munuc*, fr. LL *monachus*, fr. LGk *monachos*, fr. Gk, adj., single, fr. *monos* single, alone; akin to OHG *mangolōn, mengen* to lack, be without, OIr *mēn* smooth, soft, *menb* small, Toch B *menki* less, Gk *manos* sparse, Skt *manāk* a little; basic meaning: small] **1** : a man who is a member of a monastic order; *also* : a man who has retired from the world to devote himself to asceticism as a solitary or cenobite — compare HERMIT **2 a** : a So. American saki (*Pithecia monachus*) **b** *dial Brit* : the European bullfinch **c** : ANGLER 2 **3** *archaic* : a blotch or dark spot on a printed sheet caused by excessive deposition of ink — compare FRIAR **4** : MONK SHOE

[2]**monk** \"\ *n* -s [by shortening] : MONKEY

monk bat *n* : any of several bats in which the males live in communities; *esp* : a bat (*Molossus tropidorhynchus*) of the West Indies

monkbird \'⸗,⸗\ *n* : FRIARBIRD

monk·ery \'məŋkərē, -ri\ *n* -ES **1** : the state, life, or profession of monks : MONASTICISM **2** : a body or community of monks : MONASTERY **3** : monastic usage, custom, or practice **4** *Brit* **a** : the country as distinguished from the city **b** : the world of tramps : TRAMPS **c** : tramping as a practice

[1]**mon·key** \'məŋkē, -ki\ *n* -s [prob. of LG, D, or Flem origin; akin to MFlem *Monnekin*, nickname for a monkey, MLG *Moneke*, name of an ape in the epic *Reynard the Fox;* both prob. diminutives of a word of Romance origin; akin to OSp *mona* monkey, prob. short for *maimón, maimona*, prob. fr. Ar *maymūn*, lit., happy] **1 a** : a member of the order Primates excepting man and usu. also the lemurs and tarsiers **b** : any of the smaller longer-tailed primates (as members of the New World family Cebidae) as contrasted with the larger nearly or quite tailless apes — see CAPUCHIN, GUEREZA, LANGUR, SPIDER MONKEY **2 a** : a person resembling a monkey in appearance or behavior (as a mimic or a performer of antics) **b** : a ludicrous figure : DUPE ⟨made a ~ of him⟩ **3** : an unusually active and mischievous child **4 a** : a heavy weight or tup slung from the roof of an ironworks and used in upsetting the end of a piece too long to be treated by the forging hammer **b** : a falling weight used for driving something by percussion (as the falling weight of a pile driver or of a drop hammer) **5 a** : a small pot or crucible used for melting small quantities of glass **b** : MONKEY POT **6** *slang* : the sum of 500 pounds or 500 dollars **7** *Brit* : TEMPER, ANGER, DANDER ⟨got his ~ up⟩ **8** *Brit* : a mortgage on a building **9** : CINDER NOTCH **10** : an airway in an anthracite mine **11** : a desperate desire for or addiction to drugs regarded as an intolerable burden — often used in the phrase *monkey on one's back*

[2]**monkey** \"\ *adj* **1** : of, relating to, or having the characteristics of a monkey : resembling that of a monkey **2** : being of small size ⟨a ~ chute in a mine⟩ **3** : being something small or odd in location, arrangement, or use on a ship ⟨~ rudder⟩

[3]**monkey** \"\ *vb* **monkeyed; monkeyed; monkeying; monkeys** [[1]*monkey*] *vi* **1** : to act in a grotesque, mischievous, or meddlesome manner **2 a** : FOOL, TRIFLE — often used with *around* **b** : TAMPER — usu. used with *with* ⟨warned not to ~ with the controls⟩ ~ *vt* : to treat as a monkey does : MIMIC

monkey apple *n* **1** : POND APPLE **2** : WILD FIG 3 **3** : a tropical Old World tree (*Anisophyllea laurina*) of the family Rhizophoraceae having an edible fruit resembling a plum

monkey bass *n* : PIASSAVA 2

monkey bear *n* : KOALA

monkey block *n* : a small single block strapped with a swivel

monkeyboard \'⸗⸗,⸗\ *n, Brit* : a footboard at the back of a vehicle (as for a footman or on an omnibus for the conductor)

monkey boat *n, Brit* : a small usu. half-decked boat used in docks and on the Thames river

monkey bread *n* **1** : the fruit of the baobab **2** *also* **monkey-bread tree** : BAOBAB

monkey bridge *n* : a high narrow platform above a deck or in an engine room or boiler room

monkey business *n* : mischievous or questionable activity : FOOLING ⟨told the boys to quit their *monkey business*⟩

monkey cap *n* **:** a small pillbox equipped with a chin strap
monkey–faced owl \ˈ⁼⁼ˌ⁼-\ *n* **:** BARN OWL
monkey fist *or* **monkey's fist** *n* **:** a large heavy knot resembling a Turk's head used to weight the end of a messenger or heaving line
monkey flower *n* **1 :** a plant of the genus *Mimulus* **2 :** TOADFLAX
monkey flush *n* **:** three cards of the same suit in poker
monkey foresail *n* **:** a square foresail on a sloop or schooner
mon•key•fy \ˈməŋkēˌfī\ *vt* -ED/-ING/-ES [*monkey* + *-fy*] **:** to make like or suggestive of a monkey **:** cause to be ridiculous in appearance

monkey cap

monkey gaff *n* **:** a light gaff on a mizzenmast above the spanker gaff for the better display of signals
monkey grass *n* **:** piassava fiber
monkey hammer *or* **monkey press** *n* **:** DROP HAMMER
mon•key•hood \ˈməŋkēˌhu̇d\ *n* **:** the state of being a monkey
mon•key•ish \-ˌish\ *adj* **:** having the characteristics of a monkey — **mon•key•ish•ly** *adv* — **mon•key•ish•ness** *n* -ES
monkey island *n* **:** the top of the pilothouse on a ship

monkey fist

monkey jack *n* **:** a jack for pushing over tree trunks and stumps after the lateral roots have been cut
monkey jacket *n* **:** MESS JACKET
monkey ladder *n* **:** a light ship's ladder (as to the monkey bridge)
monkey line *n* **:** a line used in lowering a boat
monkey–nut \ˈ⁼⁼ˌ⁼\ *n* **1 :** PEANUT **2 :** the fruit of a European basswood (*Tilia glabra*)
monkey orange *n* **1 :** either of two deciduous African shrubs or small trees (*Strychnos inocua* and *Strychnos spinosa*) having a hard globose fruit with edible pulp **2 :** the fruit of a monkey orange
monkeypod \ˈ⁼⁼ˌ⁼\ *n* **:** RAIN TREE
monkey pot *n* **1 a :** a large woody urn-shaped operculate fruit characteristic of the sapucaias and various closely related trees (as the manbarklaks) **b :** SAPUCAIA; *also* **:** MANBARKLAK **2 :** a pot used in glassmaking; *specif* **:** any of several round-topped oval cylinders enclosed in firebrick arches at the base of a chimney and used as melting pots in the making of flint glass
monkey puzzle *also* **monkey puzzler** *n* **:** a tall Chilean evergreen tree (*Araucaria araucana*) having intertwined branches and stiff sharp-pointed leaves and bearing large edible nuts — called also *Chile pine*
monkey rail *n* **:** a second and lighter rail raised a little above the quarter rail of a ship
monkey–rope \ˈ⁼⁼ˌ⁼\ *n* **1 :** LIANA **2 :** a safety rope secured to a sailor's waist (as when he is working over the ship's side)
monkey rum *n, South & Midland* **:** the distilled syrup of sugarcane or sorghum cane
monkeys *pl of* MONKEY, *pres 3d sing of* MONKEY
monkeyshine \ˈ⁼⁼ˌ⁼\ *n* **:** a mischievous or questionable trick or prank **:** a piece of monkey business — usu. used in pl. ⟨the ~*s* of some political candidates⟩
monkey skin *n* **:** a light reddish brown that is redder, lighter, and slightly stronger than copper tan, redder and duller than peach tan, and lighter than peach bisque
monkey spar *n* **:** a mast or yard of reduced size (as on a ship on which boys are trained as seamen)
monkey suit *n* **1 :** any of various uniforms ⟨difference between the . . . uniforms of other navies and the makeshift *monkey suits* our sailors wear —*Amer. Mercury*⟩ **2 :** TUXEDO
monkeytail \ˈ⁼⁼ˌ⁼\ *n* **1 :** a piece of rope attached to the bend of a hook to aid in handling it without risk of jamming the hand **2 :** a vertical scroll terminating a handrail
monkey vine *n* **:** a tropical Old World morning glory (*Ipomoea nil*) that has large showy often fringed or double flowers and is the source of many cultivated forms
monkey way *n* **:** MONKEY 10
monkeywood \ˈ⁼⁼ˌ⁼\ *n* **:** QUIRA 2
monkey wrench *n* **1 :** a wrench with one fixed and one adjustable jaw at right angles to a straight handle **2 :** something disrupting ⟨a speech on foreign policy . . . threw a *monkey wrench* into our foreign relations at a critical time —*Kiplinger Washington Letter*⟩

monkey wrench 1

monkfish \ˈ⁼ˌ⁼\ *n* **1 :** any of several small bottom-dwelling squaloid sharks (genus *Squatina*) having the pectoral and ventral fins large and lateral in position so that the outline when viewed from above resembles that of a skate or ray rather than a typical shark **2 :** ANGLER 2
mon–khmer \ˈ⁼ˌ⁼\ *n, usu cap M&K* [³*Mon* + *Khmer*] **1 :** a language family containing Mon, Khmer, Palaung, Wa, Jakun, Sakai, Khasi **2 :** a branch of the Mon-Khmer family containing Mon, Khmer, and a few other closely related languages of southeast Asia
monk•hood \ˈməŋkˌhu̇d, -ŋˌku̇d\ *n* [¹*monk* + *-hood*] **1 :** the character, condition, or profession of a monk **:** MONASTICISM **2 :** monks as a body or a class
monk•ish \ˈməŋkish, -kēsh\ *adj* **1 :** of or relating to monks **:** MONASTIC ⟨the ~ church . . . often included three bays of the nave —E.H.Short⟩ **2 :** characteristic of or befitting monks ⟨the poem is thoroughly medieval and ~ in conception —A.E.Bailey⟩ ⟨brooding and moiling in ~ seclusion —A.M.Schlesinger b.1888⟩ **3 a :** being or resembling a monk ⟨working with much of the patient thoroughness of his ~ predecessors —G.W.Eve⟩ **:** ASCETIC ⟨I esteem even more a man who puts poverty and a shelf of books above profiteering and evenings of jazz; I am naturally ~ —H.L.Mencken⟩ **b :** resembling that of or attributed to a monk or having features attributed to monasticism ⟨a ~ robe⟩ ⟨it is ~, parsimonious, and timid to despise the lavish and complex beauty of life —D.C.Peattie⟩ **4 :** made or used by monks ⟨flesh begins to appear on the bones of these ~ annals —B.R.Redman⟩ ⟨~ Latin⟩ — **monk•ish•ly** *adv* — **monk•ish•ness** *n* -ES
monk•ism \-ŋˌkizəm\ *n* -S **:** MONASTICISM
monk•ist \-kəst\ *adj* **:** MONASTIC ⟨the ~ vows included chastity —J.H.Robinson †1936⟩
monk•ly *adj* **:** of or relating to a monk **:** MONASTIC ⟨many illuminations made by patient ~ hands —T.B.Costain⟩
monk parrot *or* **monk parrakeet** *n* **:** a common So. American green and gray parrot (*Myiopsitta monachus*)
monk saki *n* **:** a saki (*Pithecia monachus*) of which the ruff suggests a monastic tonsure
monk's cloth *n* **:** a coarse heavy fabric in basket weave made orig. of worsted and used for monk's habits but now chiefly of cotton or linen and used for draperies
monk seal *n* **:** any of several hair seals (genus *Monachus*) known from the Mediterranean, the Caribbean, and Hawaii but once so extensively hunted for hides and oil that they are now rare in much of their former range
monk•ship \ˈməŋkˌship\ *n* **:** MONKHOOD
monk shoe *n* **:** a low shoe having two quarters and a vamp and held to the foot by a strap passing over the instep and usu. buckled at the side — compare MONK STRAP
monks•hood \ˈməŋksˌhu̇d\ *n* [*monk's* (gen. of ¹*monk*) + *hood*] **:** ACONITE 1; *esp* **:** a widely distributed Eurasian herb (*Aconitum napellus*) with a thickened or tuberous rootstock and finely palmate leaves that is often cultivated for its showy terminal racemes of cucullate white or purplish flowers and that is extremely poisonous in all its parts — see ACONITE 2; compare WOLFSBANE 1
monkshood–vine \ˈ⁼ˌ⁼\ *n* **:** a slender Chinese tendril climber (*Ampelopsis aconitifolia*) used as an ornamental vine and having digitately 3- to 5-parted leaves, inconspicuous flowers, and orange-colored berries

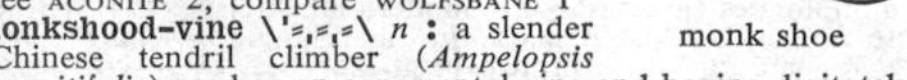

monk shoe

monk's pepper tree *n* **:** AGNUS CASTUS
monk's seam *or* **monk seam** *n* **:** an extra middle seam made at the junction of two breadths of canvas ordinarily joined by only two rows of stitches
monk's tale stanza *n, usu cap M&T* [fr. the *Monk's Tale* in *The Canterbury Tales* (1386–1400) by Geoffrey Chaucer †1400 Eng. poet, where such stanzas are used] **:** a stanza of eight five-stress lines with the rhyme scheme *ababbcbc*
monk strap *n* **1 :** a strap passing over the instep of a monk shoe and holding the shoe to the foot **2 :** MONK SHOE
monmouth cap *n, usu cap M* [fr. *Monmouth*, England] **:** a flat round cap formerly worn by soldiers and sailors ⟨did good service . . . wearing leeks in their *Monmouth caps* which your Majesty know to this hour is an honourable badge of the service —Shak.⟩
mon•mouth•shire \ˈmənməthˌshi(ə)r, ˈmän-, -ˌshiə, -ˌshə(r)\ *or* **mon•mouth** *adj, usu cap* [fr. *Monmouthshire* or *Monmouth* county, England] **:** of or from the county of Monmouth, England **:** of the kind or style prevalent in Monmouth
¹**mo•no** \ˈmō(ˌ)nō\ *n, pl* **mono** *or* **monos** *usu cap* [Sp, of AmerInd origin] **1 a :** a Shoshonean people of southeastern California **b :** a member of such people **2 :** the language of the Mono people
²**mono** \ˈmä(ˌ)nō, ˈmō(ˌ)-\ *adj* [*mon-*] **:** containing one atom, radical, or group of a particular kind in the molecule
³**mo•no** \ˈmō(ˌ)nō\ *n* -S [Sp, monkey, prob. alter. of *mona* — more at MONKEY] **:** a black howler monkey (*Alouatta villosa*) of Central America
⁴**mono** \"\ *n* -S [by shortening] **:** MONOSABIO
⁵**mono** \ˈmä(ˌ)nō, ˈmō(ˌ)-\ *n* -S [by shortening fr. *Monotype*] **:** a typesetting machine
mono- *in pronunciations below*, ¦⁼⁼ = ¦mä(ˌ)nō *also* ¦mō(ˌ)nō *or* -nə\ — see MON-
mono•acetate \¦⁼⁼ *at* MONO-+\ *n* [ISV *mon-* + *acetate*] **:** a salt, ester, or acylal containing only one acetate group
mono•acetin \"+\ *also* **mon•acetin** \(ˈ)män, (ˈ)mōn+\ *n* [ISV *mon-* + *acetin*] **:** ACETIN a
¹**mono•acid** \¦⁼⁼ *at* MONO-+\ *or* **mono•acidic** \"+\ *also* **mon•acid** \(ˈ)män, (ˈ)mōn+\ *adj* [*mon-* + *acid* or *acidic*] **1 :** able to react with only one molecule of a monobasic acid to form a salt or ester **:** characterized by one hydroxyl group — used of bases and sometimes of alcohols **2 :** containing only one hydrogen atom replaceable by a basic atom or radical — used esp. of acid salts
²**monoacid** \"\ *also* **monacid** \"\ *n* **:** an acid (as hydrochloric acid) having only one acid hydrogen atom
mono•alphabetic substitution \¦⁼⁼ *at* MONO-+-\ *n* [*mon-* + *alphabetic*] **:** substitution in cryptography that uses a single substitution alphabet so that each plaintext letter always has the same cipher equivalent — compare POLYALPHABETIC
mono•amide \"+\ *also* **mon•amide** \(¦)män, (¦)mōn+\ *n* [ISV *mon-* + *amide*] **:** an amide containing only one amido group
mono•amine \¦⁼⁼ *at* MONO-+\ *also* **mon•amine** \(¦)män, (¦)mōn+\ *n* [ISV *mon-* + *amine*] **:** an amine containing only one amino group — **mono•amino** \¦⁼⁼ *at* MONO-+\ *adj*
mono•ammonium phosphate \¦⁼⁼ *at* MONO-+-\ *n* [*mon-* + *ammonium*] **:** AMMONIUM PHOSPHATE
mono•azo \"+\ *adj* [ISV *monaz-*, *monazo-*, fr. *mon-* + *az-*] **:** containing one azo group in the molecule ⟨~ dyes⟩
mono•basic \"+\ *adj* [ISV *mon-* + *basic*] **1 a :** having only one hydrogen atom replaceable by a basic atom or radical — used of acids (as hydrochloric acid) **b :** containing only one atom of a univalent metal or its equivalent ⟨~ sodium phosphate NaH_2PO_4⟩ **c :** having only one basic hydroxyl group **:** able to react with only one molecule of a monobasic acid — used of bases and basic salts **2 :** based orig. upon a single species — used of taxonomic genera; compare MONOTYPIC — **mono•basicity** \"+\ *n*
mono•bath \¦⁼⁼+ˌ-\ *n* [*mon-* + *bath*] **:** a single solution including ingredients for more than one photographic process (as for developing and fixing)
mono•blast \-ˌblast\ *n* [ISV *mon-* + *-blast*] **:** a motile cell of the spleen and bone marrow that gives rise to the monocyte of the circulating blood
mono•blastic \¦⁼⁼+\ *adj* [*mon-* + *blastic*] **:** having or derived from a single germ layer
mono•bleph•a•ri•da•les \ˌ⁼⁼+ˌblefərəˈdā(ˌ)lēz\ *n pl, cap* [NL, fr. *Monoblepharid-*, *Monoblepharis* genus of fungi (fr. *mon-* + Gk *blepharid-*, *blepharis* eyelash) + *-ales*] **:** an order of fungi (subclass Oomycetes) that are distinguished from related forms by possession of a large nonmotile egg which is fertilized by a small uniflagellate motile sperm
mono•bloc \ˈ⁼⁼ˌ⁼\ *adj* [fr. *mon-* + *bloc*, alter. of *block*] **:** made in one block or casting ⟨a ~ cylinder casting⟩
mono•branchiate \¦⁼⁼ *at* MONO-+\ *adj* [*mon-* + *branchiate*] **:** having one gill or set of gills
monobrom- *or* **monobromo-** *comb form* [ISV *mon-* + *brom-*] **:** containing one atom of bromine — in names of chemical compounds ⟨*monobromo*naphthalene⟩; compare BROM-
mono•bromate \¦⁼⁼ *at* MONO-+\ *vt* [*mon-* + *bromate*] **:** MONOBROMINATE ⟨*monobromated* camphor⟩
mono•brominate \"+\ *vt* [*mon-* + *brominate*] **:** to introduce one bromine atom into (as an organic compound) ⟨~ benzene⟩ — **mono•bromination** \"+\ *n*
Mono•caine \ˈ⁼⁼ˌkān\ *trademark* — used for a crystalline local anesthetic that is an ester of the *para*-aminobenzoic acid
mono•calcium \¦⁼⁼ *at* MONO-+\ *adj* [*mon-* + *calcium*] **:** containing one atom or equivalent of calcium in the molecule
monocalcium phosphate *n* **:** CALCIUM PHOSPHATE 1a(1)
mon•o•can•thi•dae \ˌmänəˈkan(t)thəˌdē\ *syn of* MONACANTHIDAE
mono•carboxylic \¦⁼⁼ *at* MONO-+\ *adj* [*mon-* + *carboxylic*] **:** containing one carboxyl group
¹**mono•car•di•an** \"+¦kärdēən\ *adj* [*mon-* + Gk *kardia* heart + E *-an* — more at HEART] **:** having a single auricle and ventricle to the heart
²**monocardian** \"\ *n* -S **:** an animal having a monocardian heart
mono•carp \ˈ⁼⁼ˌkärp\ *n* -S [F *monocarpe*, fr. *mon-* + Gk *karpos* fruit — more at HARVEST] **:** a monocarpic plant — **mono•car•pal** \¦⁼⁼¦kärpəl\ *adj*
mono•carpellary \¦⁼⁼+\ *adj* [*mon-* + *carpellary*] **:** consisting of a single carpel — compare POLYCARPELLARY
mono•car•pi•an \¦⁼⁼¦kärpēən\ *adj* **:** MONOCARPIC
mono•car•pic \-pik\ *adj* [prob. fr. (assumed) NL *monocarpicus*, fr. NL *mon-* + *-carpicus* -carpic] **:** bearing fruit but once and dying — used esp. of annual and biennial flowering plants; compare CENTURY PLANT
mon•o•car•pous \-pəs\ *adj* [NL *monocarpus*, fr. *mon-* + *-carpus* -carpous] **:** having a single ovary ⟨a ~ gynoecium⟩; *esp* **:** MONOCARPELLARY
mono•cau•lus \ˌ⁼⁼ˈkȯləs\ *n, cap* [NL, fr. *mon-* + Gk *kaulos* stalk, stem — more at HOLE] **:** a genus of giant hydroids that may attain a length of eight feet
mono•cellular \¦⁼⁼ *at* MONO-+\ *adj* [*mon-* + *cellular*] **:** having or involving a single kind of cell
mono•centric \"+\ *adj* [*mon-* + *-centric*] **:** having a single center — compare POLYCENTRIC
mono•ceph•a•lous \¦sefələs\ *adj* [*mon-* + *-cephalous*] **:** having a solitary head or capitulum ⟨a ~ aster⟩
mo•noc•er•os \məˈnäsərəs\ *n* -ES [ME, fr. MF, fr. L, fr. Gk *monokerōs*, fr. *mon-* + *-kerōs* (fr. *keras* horn) — more at HORN] **1** *obs* **:** UNICORN 1a(1) **2 :** a fish (as the swordfish or sawfish) with one hornlike process
mono•cha•sium \ˌ⁼⁼ *at* MONO-+ˈkāzh(ē)əm\ *n, pl* **monochasia** \-zh(ē)ə\ [NL, fr. *mon-* + *-chasium* (as in *dichasium*)] **:** a cymose inflorescence that produces only one main axis — compare DICHASIUM, POLYCHASIUM
mono•chla•myd•e•ae \-kləˈmidēˌē\ *n pl cap* [NL, fr. *mon-* + *-chlamydeae* (fr. Gk *chlamyd-*, *chlamys* cloak, mantle)] *in some classifications* **:** a group of Archichlamydeae nearly coextensive with Apetalae and comprising plants with flowers that lack petals or sepals but not both
mono•chla•myd•e•ous \¦⁼⁼+\ *adj* **:** of or relating to the Monochlamydeae
monochlor- *or* **monochloro-** *comb form* [ISV *mon-* + *chlor-*] **:** containing one atom of chlorine — in names of chemical compounds ⟨*monochloro*benzene⟩
mono•chloramine \¦⁼⁼ *at* MONO- +\ *n* [ISV *monochlor-* + *amine*] **:** the chloramine NH_2Cl
mono•chloride \"+\ *n* [*monochlor-* + *-ide*] **:** a compound containing one atom of chlorine combined with an element or radical
mono•chlorinate \"+\ *vt* [*mon-* + *chlorinate*] **:** to combine with one atom of chlorine either by substitution or addition
mono•chloro \"+\ *adj* [*monochlor-*] **:** containing one atom of chlorine in the molecule
mono•chloroacetic acid \"+-\ *n* [*monochlor-* + *acetic*] **:** CHLOROACETIC ACID
mono•chlorobenzene \"+\ *n* [*monochlor-* + *benzene*] **:** CHLOROBENZENE
mono•chlorosilane \"+\ *n* [*monochlor-* + *silane*] **:** CHLOROSILANE 1
mono•chord \ˈmänəˌkȯrd, -ō(ə)d\ *n* [ME *monocorde*, fr. MF, fr. ML *monochordum*, fr. Gk *monochordon*, fr. *mon-* + *-chordon* -chord] **1 :** an instrument of ancient origin for measuring and demonstrating the mathematical relations of musical tones that consists of a single string stretched over a sounding board and a movable bridge set on a graduated scale — called also *sonometer* **2 :** an instrument of the late middle ages similar to the single-string monochord but having added strings for sounding chords **3 :** TRUMPET MARINE
mono•chorial \¦⁼⁼ *at* MONO- +\ *also* **mono•chorionic** \"+\ *adj* [*mon-* + *chorial* or *chorionic*] *of twins* **:** sharing or developed with a common chorion
mono•chro•ic \"+¦krōik\ *adj* [*mon-* + *-chroic*] **:** MONOCHROMATIC
mono•chro•mat \¦⁼⁼¦krōˌmat, ˈ⁼⁼krōˌmat\ *n* -S [L *monochromatos* consisting of one color, fr. Gk *monochrōmatos*, fr. *mon-* + *chrōmat-*, *chrōma* color — more at CHROMATIC] **1 :** one unable to perceive colors **:** one who responds only to brilliance and sees all colors as tones of gray **:** a completely color-blind individual — compare DICHROMAT, TRICHROMAT **2 :** an optical part (as a microscope objective) that is used only in a limited wavelength range **3 :** a monochromatic filter
mono•chromatic \"+\ *adj* [L *monochromatos* + E *-ic*] **1 :** having or consisting of one color or hue **2 :** consisting of radiation of a single wavelength or of a very small range of wave lengths **3 a :** of, relating to, or exhibiting monochromatism **b :** having the characteristics of a monochromat — **mono•chromatically** \"+\ *adv* — **mono•chromaticity** \"+\ *n* -ES
monochromatic illuminator *n* **:** MONOCHROMATOR
mono•chromatism \"+\ *also* **mono•chro•ma•sy** \ˌ⁼⁼+ˈkrōməsē\ *n, pl* **monochromatisms** *also* **monochromasies** **:** complete color blindness in which all colors appear as shades of gray — compare TRICHROMATISM
mono•chromatize \¦⁼⁼ *at* MONO- +\ *vt* [*monochromatic* + *-ize*] **:** to make monochromatic
mono•chro•ma•tor \¦⁼⁼+¦krōˌmād·ə(r)\ *n* -S [*monochromatic* *illuminator*] **:** a spectroscope modified by replacing the eyepiece with a narrow slit parallel to the original slit of the instrument in order to isolate for use a narrow portion of the spectrum
¹**mono•chrome** \ˈ⁼⁼ˌkrōm\ *n* [ML *monochroma*, fr. L, fem. of *monochromos* of one color, fr. Gk *monochrōmos*, fr. *mon-* + *-chrōmos* -chrome] **1 :** a painting or drawing in a single hue **2 :** a photograph made with a single hue **3 :** MONOCHROMY
²**monochrome** \"\ *adj* **1 :** of, relating to, or made with a single color or hue **2** *of pottery* **:** painted a usu. dark color that contrasts with the usu. light color of the body clay — compare POLYCHROME **3 :** METACHROME 2
mono•chro•mic \¦⁼⁼¦krōmik\ *also* **mono•chro•mi•cal** \-məkəl\ *adj* [¹*monochrome* + *-ic*, *-ical*] **:** MONOCHROME 1 — **mono•chro•mi•cal•ly** \-mək(ə)lē\ *adv*
mono•chrom•ist \ˈ⁼⁼ˌkrōməst\ *n* -S **:** an artist in monochrome; *also* **:** an advocate of its use
mono•chro•mous \¦⁼⁼¦krōməs\ *adj* [L *monochromos* consisting of one color — more at MONOCHROME] **:** MONOCHROME 1
mono•chro•my \ˈ⁼⁼ˌkrōmē\ *n* -ES [¹*monochrome* + *-y*] **:** the art or process of producing monochromes
mo•noch•ro•nous \məˈnäkrənəs\ *adj* [LL *monochronos*, fr. Gk, fr. *mon-* + *-chronos* -chronous] **:** MONOSEMIC
mono•ciliated \¦⁼⁼ *at* MONO- +\ *adj* [*mon-* + *ciliated*] **:** UNIFLAGELLATE
mon•o•cle \ˈmänəkəl, -nēk-\ *n* -S [F, fr. LL *monoculus* having one eye, fr. *mon-* + *oculus* eye — more at EYE] **:** an eyeglass for one eye
mon•o•cled \-kəld\ *adj* **:** wearing a monocle
mono•cleid *also* **mono•cleide** \ˈmänəˌklīd, ˈmōn-\ *n* -S [*mon-* + Gk *kleid-*, *kleis* key — more at CLOSE] **:** a cabinet or desk in which all the drawers are locked simultaneously by one key
¹**mono•cli•nal** \¦⁼⁼ *at* MONO- +¦klīnᵊl\ *adj* [*mon-* + *-clinal*] **:** of or relating to a monocline **:** having a single oblique inclination ⟨~ fold⟩ ⟨~ flexure⟩

monocle

²**monoclinal** \"\ *n* -S **:** a monoclinal fold
mono•cli•nal•ly \-nᵊlē, -lī\ *adv* **:** in a monoclinal manner **:** so as to be monoclinal
mono•cline \ˈ⁼⁼ˌklīn\ *n* -S [*mon-* + *-cline*] **:** a geologic structure in which the strata are all inclined in the same direction at a uniform angle of dip — compare HOMOCLINE
mono•clin•ic \¦⁼⁼¦klinik\ *adj* [ISV *mon-* + *-clinic*] *crystallog* **:** having one oblique intersection of the axes
monoclinic system *n* **:** a crystal system characterized by three unequal axes with one oblique intersection — see CRYSTAL SYSTEM illustration
mono•clin•ism \ˈ⁼⁼ˌklīˌnizəm\ *n* -S [ISV *mon-* + *-clinism*] **:** the condition of being monoclinous
mono•cli•no•met•ric \¦⁼⁼¦klīnə¦me·trik\ *adj* [*monocline* + *-o-* + *-metric*] **:** MONOCLINIC
mono•cli•nous \¦⁼⁼¦klīnəs\ *adj* [NL *monoclinus*, fr. *mon-* + *-clinus* -clinous] **:** having the stamens and pistils in the same flower — compare DICLINOUS
mono•clo•ni•us \ˌ⁼⁼ˈklōnēəs\ *n, cap* [NL, fr. *mon-* + *-clonius* (fr. Gk *klōnion*, dim. of *klōn* twig); akin to Gk *klan* to break — more at HALT] **:** a genus of ceratopsian dinosaurs with a large nasal horn found in the Upper Cretaceous of No. America
mono•coque \ˈ⁼⁼ˌkōk, -ˌkäk\ *n* -S *often attrib* [F *monocoque*, fr. *mon-* + *coque* shell, fr. L *coccum* excrescence on a tree — more at COAK] **1 :** an aircraft structure in which the stressed outer skin (as of metal or plywood) carries all or a major portion of the torsional and bending stresses ⟨~ fuselage⟩ **2 :** the structure of a vehicle (as a motor truck, trailer, or railroad car) in which the body is integral with and shares the stresses with the chassis ⟨~ construction⟩
mono•cot \ˈ⁼⁼ˌkät\ *or* **mono•cot•yl** \¦⁼⁼+\ *n* -S [by shortening] **:** MONOCOTYLEDON
mon•o•cot•y•le•don \¦⁼⁼+\ *n* [NL *Monocotyledoneae*] **:** a plant of the subclass Monocotyledoneae — compare DICOTYLEDON
mono•cot•y•le•do•ne•ae \ˌ⁼⁼ˌkäd·ᵊlˈdōnēˌē\ *n pl, cap* [NL, alter. of *Monocotyledones*, fr. *mon-* + *cotyledones*, pl. of *cotyledon*] **:** a subclass of Angiospermae comprising seed plants (as grasses and lilies) that produce an embryo with a single cotyledon and have usu. parallel-veined leaves, stems without central pith or annual rings and with the vascular strands scattered throughout the ground tissue, and floral organs usu. arranged in cycles of three or six, including some chiefly tropical arborescent plants (as the palms), but being chiefly herbaceous in habit — compare DICOTYLEDONEAE
mono•cot•y•le•do•nes \-ˌkäd·ᵊlˈēdᵊnˌēz\ *syn of* MONOCOTYLEDONEAE
mono•cotyledonous \¦⁼⁼+\ *adj* [NL *Monocotyledoneae* + E *-ous*] **:** of, relating to, or characteristic of the Monocotyledoneae; *often* **:** having a single cotyledon — contrasted with *dicotyledonous*; compare POLYCOTYLEDONOUS
mo•noc•ra•cy \məˈnäkrəsē, -si\ *n* -ES [*mon-* + *-cracy*] **:** government by a single person **:** undivided rule **:** AUTOCRACY
mono•crat \ˈ⁼⁼ *at* MONO- + ˌkrat\ *n* -S [*mon-* + *-crat*] **1 :** one who governs alone **:** AUTOCRAT **2 :** one who favors monocracy — **mono•crat•ic** \¦⁼⁼¦krad·ik\ *adj*

mono·crotaline \¦⸗⸗+\ *n* -s [*mon-* + NL *Crotalaria* + E *-ine*] **:** a poisonous crystalline alkaloid $C_{16}H_{23}NO_6$ found in some plants of the genus *Crotalaria* (as *C. spectabilis*)

mono·crot·ic \¦⸗⸗¦krädik\ *adj* [*mon-* + *-crotic*] *of the pulse* **:** having a simple beat and forming a smooth single-crested curve on a sphygmogram — compare DICROTIC, POLYCROTIC

¹mo·noc·u·lar \məˈnäkyələ(r)\ *adj* [LL *monoculus* having one eye + E *-ar* — more at MONOCLE] **1 :** of, involving, or affecting a single eye ⟨a ~ cataract⟩ **2 :** relating or adapted to the use of only one eye ⟨~ vision⟩ ⟨a ~ microscope⟩ — **mo·noc·u·lar·ly** *adv*

²monocular \"\ *n* **:** a monocular device (as a microscope or a field glass)

mo·noc·u·lous \-ləs\ *adj* [LL *monoculus* having one eye] **:** MONOCULAR

mono·cultural \¦⸗⸗ *at* MONO-+\ *adj* **:** of or relating to monoculture

mono·culture \"+\ *n* [*mon-* + *culture*] **:** the cultivation of a single product (as wheat or wool) to the exclusion of other possible uses of the land

mono·cycle \ˈ⸗⸗+ˌsīkəl\ *n* [*mon-* + *-cycle* (as in *bicycle*)] **:** a one-wheeled vehicle propelled by its rider — compare UNICYCLE

monocular

mono·cyclic \¦⸗⸗+\ *adj* [ISV *mon-* + *cyclic*] **1 :** arranged in or consisting of one whorl or circle ⟨the floral organs of many plants are ~⟩ **2 :** containing one ring in the molecular structure ⟨a ~ terpene⟩ **3 :** having a single annual maximum of population — used chiefly of planktonic organisms — **mono·cy·cly** \ˈ⸗⸗ˌsīklē\ *n* -ES

mono·cy·cli·ca \ˌ⸗⸗+ˈsīklәkə\ *n pl, cap* [NL, fr. *mon-* + L *cyclica*, neut. pl. of *cyclicus* cyclic — more at CYCLIC] *in some classifications* **:** a division of Crinoidea comprising forms in which the cup of the calyx has a single basal series of ossicles

mono·cystic \¦⸗⸗ *at* MONO-+\ *adj* [*mon-* + *cystic*] **1 :** consisting of or having a single cyst **2 :** of or relating to the genus *Monocystis*

mono·cys·tid \ˌ⸗⸗ˈsistəd\ *adj* [NL *Monocystid-*, *Monocystis* & *Monocystidae*] **:** of or relating to the genus *Monocystis* or the family Monocystidae

mono·cys·tid·ea \-(ˌ)siˈstidēə\ [NL, fr. *Monocystid-*, *Monocystis*] *syn of* ACEPHALINA

mono·cys·tis \-ˈsistəs\ *n, cap* [NL, fr. *mon-* + *-cystis*] **:** a genus (the type of the family Monocystidae) of acephaline gregarines not having the protoplasm divided into segments by septa and including internal parasites of invertebrates (as *M. agilis* of the reproductive system of earthworms)

mono·cyte \ˈ⸗⸗ˌsīt\ *n* -s [ISV *mon-* + *-cyte*] **:** a large sluggish phagocytic leukocyte with an oval or horseshoe-shaped nucleus having a chromatin network and with basophilic cytoplasm containing faint eosinophile granulations — **mono·cyt·ic** \¦⸗⸗¦sidik\ *adj* — **mono·cy·toid** \-¦sīˌtȯid\ *adj*

monocytic leukemia *n* **:** leukemia characterized by the presence of large numbers of monocytes in the circulating blood

mono·cy·to·pe·nia \ˌ⸗⸗ˌsīd-əˈpēnēə\ *n* -s [NL, fr. ISV *monocyte* + NL *-o-* + *-penia*] **:** a deficiency in circulating monocytes

mono·cy·to·poi·e·sis \-ˌpȯiˈēsəs\ *n* [NL, fr. ISV *monocyte* + NL *-o-* + *-poiesis*] **:** formation of monocytes

mono·cy·to·poi·et·ic \¦⸗⸗¦⸗⸗ˌ⸗⸗¦ed·ik\ *adj* [*monocyte* + *-o-* + *-poietic*] **:** of or relating to monocytopoiesis

mono·cy·to·sis \ˌ⸗⸗ˌsīˈtōsəs\ *n, pl* **monocyto·ses** \-ˌsēz\ [NL, fr. ISV *monocyte* + NL *-osis*] **:** an abnormal increase in the number of monocytes in the circulating blood; *specif* **:** BLUE COMB — compare GRANULOCYTOSIS, LYMPHOCYTOSIS

mono·dac·tyle \¦⸗⸗ˈdaktəl\ *adj* [F, fr. Gk *monodaktylos* having one toe] **:** MONODACTYLOUS

mono·dac·tyl·ism \ˌ⸗⸗ˈdaktəˌlizəm\ *or* **mono·dac·ty·ly** \-lē\ *n, pl* **monodactylisms** *or* **monodactylies :** the condition of being monodactylous

mono·dac·ty·lous \¦⸗⸗¦daktələs\ *adj* [Gk *monodaktylos* having one toe, fr. *mon-* + *daktylos* finger, toe] **1 :** having one digit or claw **2 :** SUBCHELATE 2

mono·delph *or* **mona·delph** \ˈ⸗⸗ˌdelf\ *n* -s [*monodelph* fr. NL *Monodelphia*; *monadelph* alter. of *monodelph*] **:** EUTHERIAN

mono·del·phia \ˌ⸗⸗ˈdelfēə\ *or* **mono·del·phes** \-ˌfēz\ [NL, fr. *mon-* + *-delphia* or *-delphes* (fr. Gk *delphys* womb) — more at DOLPHIN] *syn of* EUTHERIA

mono·del·phi·an *or* **mona·del·phi·an** \¦⸗⸗¦delfēən\ *adj or n* [*monodelphian* fr. NL *Monodelphia* + E *-an*; *monadelphian* alter. of *monodelphian*] **:** EUTHERIAN

mono·del·phic \-fik\ *also* **monodel·phous** \-fəs\ *adj* [*mon-* + Gk *delphys* womb + E *-ic* or *-ous*] **1 :** having a single female genital tract **2** [NL *Monodelphia* + E *-ic* or *-ous*] **:** EUTHERIAN

mono·dermic \¦⸗⸗ *at* MONO- +\ *adj* [*mon-* + *dermic*] **:** of or relating to a single layer of cells

mo·nod·ic \məˈnädik, -dēk\ *also* **mo·nod·i·cal** \-dəkəl, -dēk-\ *adj* [Gk or LGk *monōidikos*, fr. Gk *monōidia* monody + *-ikos* -ic, -ical — more at MONODY] **:** of, relating to, or of the nature of monody ⟨the beautiful Hindu melodies, built upon various scales . . . are of course all ~ —Harold Brown⟩ — **mo·nod·i·cal·ly** \-dək(ə)lē, -dēk-, -li\ *adv*

mono·dimetric \¦⸗⸗ *at* MONO-+\ *adj* [ISV *mon-* + *dimetric*] **:** TETRAGONAL

mono·disk *or* **mono·disc** \¦⸗⸗+\ *adj* [*mon-* + *disk, disc*] *of a scyphistoma* **:** producing but one ephyra at a time — compare POLYDISK

mono·disperse \"+\ *also* **mono·dispersed** \"+\ *adj* [*mon-* + *disperse* (adj.) or *dispersed*, past part. of *disperse*, v.] **:** characterized by particles of uniform size in a dispersed phase ⟨~ aerosols⟩

mon·o·dist \ˈmänədəst\ *n* -s [*monody* + *-ist*] **:** a writer, singer, or composer of monody

mo·nod·o·mous \məˈnädəməs\ *adj* [*mon-* + Gk *domos* house — more at TIMBER] **:** inhabiting a single nest — used of ant colonies; compare POLYDOMOUS

mon·odon \ˈmänəˌdän, ˈmōn-\ *n, cap* [NL, fr. *mon-* + *-odon*] **:** a genus (the type of the family Monodontidae) of arctic cetaceans comprising the narwhal

mon·odont \ˈ⸗⸗ˌdänt\ *adj* [Gk *monodont-*, *monodous*, fr. *mon-* single + *odont-*, *odous* tooth — more at TOOTH] **1** *or* **mon·odon·tal** \¦⸗⸗¦dänt³l\ [*monodontal* fr. Gk *monodontos* + E *-al*] **:** having only one tooth **2** *or* **monodontid** [NL *Monodont-*, *Monodon* & *Monodontidae*] **:** of or relating to the genus *Monodon* or the family Monodontidae

mono·drama \¦⸗⸗ *at* MONO- +\ *n* [*mon-* + *drama*] **1 :** a drama acted or designed as if to be acted by a single person **2 :** a dramatic representation of what passes in an individual mind **3 :** a musical drama for a solo performer — **mono·dramatic** \"+\ *adj*

mono·dramatist \"+\ *n* [*monodrama* + *-tist* (as in *dramatist*)] **:** a writer or composer of a monodrama

mon·o·dy \ˈmänədē, -di\ *n* -ES [ML *monodia*, fr. Gk *monōidia*, fr. *monōidos* singing alone (fr. *mon-* alone + *ōidē* song) + *-ia* -y — more at ODE] **1 a :** an ode sung by one voice (as by one of the actors in a Greek tragedy) **b :** a funeral song or oration **2 :** an elegy or a dirge in which a single mourner laments **3 :** an unaccompanied chant sung in unison **4 a :** the style of musical composition in which but one voice part carries a melody; *specif* **:** the solo style of the earliest operas and oratorios **b :** a melody or monodic composition; *specif* **:** a composition with but a single voice part

mono·dynamism \¦⸗⸗ *at* MONO- +\ *n* [*mon-* + *dynamism*] **:** the theory that a single force causes the various forms of activity in nature

mo·noe·cia \məˈnēs(h)ēə\ *n pl, cap* [NL, fr. *mon-* + *-oecia*] *in former classifications* **:** a class of plants comprising all monoecious flowering plants — **mo·noe·cian** \-s(h)ēən, -shən\ *adj*

¹mo·noe·cious *or* **mo·ne·cious** \-shəs\ *adj* [NL *Monoecia* + E *-ous*] **1 :** having male and female sex organs in the same individual **:** HERMAPHRODITIC **2 :** having pistillate and staminate flowers on the same plant — **mo·noe·cious·ly** \-lē\ *adv*

²monoecious *var of* MONOICOUS

mo·noe·cism \məˈnēˌsizəm\ *or* **monoe·cy** \ˈmäˌnēsē, ˈmō,-\ *n, pl* **monoecisms** *or* **monoecies** [NL *Monoecia* + E *-ism* or *-y*] **:** the condition of being monoecious

mono·embryony \¦⸗⸗ *at* MONO- +\ *var of* MONEMBRYONY

mono·energetic \"+\ *adj* [*mon-* + *energetic*] **1 :** having equal energy — used of particles or radiation quanta **2 :** composed of monoenergetic particles or radiation quanta

mono·er·gic \"+¦ərjik\ *also* **mon·er·gic** \(ˈ)män, (ˈ)mōn+\ *adj* [*mon-* + *-ergic* (fr. *-ergy* + *-ic*)] **:** MONOENERGETIC

mono·ester \¦⸗⸗ *at* MONO- +\ *n* [*mon-* + *ester*] **:** an ester (as of a dibasic acid) containing only one ester group ⟨salts of ~s of sulfuric acid⟩

monoestrous *var of* MONESTROUS

mono·ethanolamine \¦⸗⸗ *at* MONO- +\ *n* [*mon-* + *ethanolamine*] **:** ETHANOLAMINE 1

mono·ethyl \"+\ *adj* [*mon-* + *ethyl*] **:** containing one ethyl group esp. in place of hydrogen

mono·ethylamine \"+\ *n* [*mon-* + *ethylamine*] **:** ETHYLAMINE 1

mono·factorial \"+\ *adj* [*mon-* + *factorial*] **:** MONOGENIC 1b(2)

mono·fil \ˈ⸗⸗+ˌfil\ *n* -s [by shortening] **:** MONOFILAMENT

mono·filament \¦⸗⸗ *at* MONO- +\ *n* [*mon-* + *filament*] **:** a single untwisted synthetic filament (as of nylon) made in varying diameters for use in textiles, hosiery, and screens or as bristles, fishing lines, and sutures — compare MULTIFILAMENT

mono·flagellate \"+\ *adj* [*mon-* + *flagellate*] **:** UNIFLAGELLATE

mono·fuel \"+\ *n* [*mon-* + *fuel*] **:** a substance (as nitromethane) that contains an oxidizer (as the nitro group) capable of burning the remainder of the substance without recourse to an external oxidizer **:** MONOPROPELLANT

mono·gamic \"+¦gamik\ *adj* [*monogamy* + *-ic*] **:** MONOGAMOUS

mo·nog·a·mist \məˈnägəməst\ *n* -s [*monogamy* + *-ist*] **:** one who practices or upholds monogamy

mo·nog·a·mis·tic \¦⸗⸗¦mistik\ *adj* **:** of or relating to monogamists or monogamy **:** upholding monogamy

mo·nog·a·mous \məˈnägəməs\ *adj* [LL *monogamus* marrying once, fr. Gk *monogamos*, fr. *mon-* + *gamos* marriage — more at BIGAMY] **:** of or relating to monogamy **:** upholding or practicing monogamy ⟨a ~ community⟩ ⟨~ doctrines⟩ — **mo·nog·a·mous·ly** *adv* — **mo·nog·a·mous·ness** *n* -ES

mo·nog·a·my \-mē, -mi\ *n* -ES [F *monogamie*, fr. LL *monogamia*, fr. Gk, fr. *monogamos* + *-ia* -y] **1 :** single marriage: **a :** one marriage only during life — compare DIGAMY **b :** marriage with but one person at a time — compare BIGAMY, POLYGAMY **2 :** the condition of having a single mate at any one time

mono·ganglionic \¦⸗⸗ *at* MONO- +\ *adj* [*mon-* + *ganglionic*] **:** having one ganglion

mono·gastric \"+\ *adj* [F *monogastrique*, fr. *mon-* + *gastrique* gastric, fr. E *gastric*] **1 :** having one digestive cavity **2** *of a muscle* **:** having but one venter

mo·nog·e·na \məˈnäjənə\ *syn of* MONOGENEA

mono·gene \¦⸗⸗ *at* MONO- + ¦jēn\ *adj* [ISV *mon-* + Gk *-genēs* born; prob. orig. formed as G *monogen* — more at -GEN] *geol* **:** built up by a single eruption or by an uninterrupted succession of eruptions

mono·ge·nea \ˌ⸗⸗ˈjēnēə\ *n pl, cap* [NL, fr. *mon-* + Gk *genea* race, descent — more at KIN] **:** a subclass of Trematoda comprising worms having a direct life cycle and ordinarily living as ectoparasites on a single fish host throughout the entire cycle — compare ASPIDOGASTREA, DIGENEA — **mono·ge·nean** \¦⸗⸗¦nēən, -nyən\ *adj or n*

mono·ge·ne·i·ty \ˌ⸗⸗jəˈnēəd·ē, -ətē, -i\ *n* -ES [*monogeneous* + *-ity*] **:** the quality or state of being monogeneous

mono·ge·neous \¦⸗⸗ *at* MONO- + ¦jēnēəs, -nyəs\ *adj* [*mon-* + Gk *genea* + E *-ous*] **:** developing without cyclic change of form — used esp. of the Monogenea **2 :** MONOGENOUS

mono·genesis \"+\ *n* [NL, fr. *mon-* + L *genesis*] **:** unity of origin; *specif* **:** the presumed origin of all life from one original entity or cell

mono·gen·e·sy \ˌ⸗⸗ˈjenəsē\ *n* -ES [NL *monogenesia*, fr. *mon-* + *-genesia*] **:** MONOGENISM

mono·genetic \¦⸗⸗ *at* MONO- +\ *adj* [*mon-* + *-genetic*] **1 :** relating to or involving monogenesis **2 :** resulting from one process of formation — used of a mountain range **3 :** of or relating to the Monogenea **:** MONOGENEAN **4** *of a dye* **:** yielding only one color or shade under any conditions of application

mono·ge·net·i·ca \ˌ⸗⸗jəˈned·əkə\ *n* [NL, fr. ISV *monogenetic*] *syn of* MONOGENEA

mono·gen·ic \¦⸗⸗¦jenik\ *adj* [ISV *mon-* + *-genic*] **1 :** having a single or a common origin: as **a :** relating to an igneous rock composed of but a single mineral species — compare MONOMICT **b** (1) **:** of or relating to monogenesis **:** MONOGENETIC (2) **:** of, relating to, or controlled by a single gene or by either of an allelic pair of genes **:** of or relating to a unit character **c :** descended from one pair **:** characterized by monogenism — compare POLYGENIC **2 :** producing offspring of one sex only — **mono·gen·i·cal·ly** \-nək(ə)lē\ *adv*

mo·nog·e·nism \məˈnäjəˌnizəm\ *n* -s [ISV *mon-* + *-gen* + *-ism*] **:** the doctrine or belief that all human races have descended from a single created pair or from a common ancestral type — compare POLYGENISM

mo·nog·e·nist \-nəst\ *n* -s [ISV *mon-* + *-gen* + *-ist*] **:** one who accepts the doctrine of monogenism

mo·nog·e·nis·tic \¦⸗⸗¦nistik\ *adj* **:** of or relating to monogenism or monogenists

mo·nog·e·nous \məˈnäjənəs\ *adj* [ISV *mon-* + *-genous*] **:** of or relating to monogenesis

mo·nog·e·ny \-nē, -ni\ *n* -ES [ISV *mon-* + *-geny*] **1 a :** the descent of man from a single created pair — compare POLYGENY **b :** MONOGENISM **2** [G *monogenie*, fr. *mono-* mon- + *-genie* -geny] **:** MONOGONY

¹mono·glot \ˈmänəˌglät, *usu* -läd·+V\ *adj* [*mon-* + *-glot*] **:** familiar with, making use of, or written in a single language — compare POLYGLOT

²monoglot \"\ *n* -s **:** a person familiar with only one language **:** MONOLINGUAL

mono·glyceride \¦⸗⸗ *at* MONO- +\ *n* [*mon-* + *-glyceride*] **:** an ester of glycerol in which only one of the three hydroxyl groups is esterified either in the alpha- or 1-position or in the beta- or 2-position

mono·go·nad·ic \¦⸗⸗gō¦nadik\ *adj* [*mon-* + *gonad* + *-ic*] *of a tapeworm* **:** having a single set of reproductive organs in each segment

mono·go·neu·tic \¦⸗⸗gōˈn(y)üd·ik\ *adj* [*mon-* + (assumed) Gk *goneutos* (verbal of Gk *goneuein* to produce, beget, fr. *goneus* one that begets, progenitor, father, fr. *gonos* offspring) + E *-ic* — more at GON-] **:** having only one brood in a year

mono·go·non·ta \ˌ⸗⸗gōˈnäntə\ *n pl, cap* [NL, fr. *mon-* + *gon-* + Gk *-onta* (neut. pl. part. ending)] **:** a large order of Rotifera comprising forms with a single ovary and lateral antennae

mono·gono·por·ic \¦⸗⸗¦gänəˈpȯrik\ *or* **mono·go·nop·o·rous** \-ˌgəˈnäpərəs\ *adj* [*mon-* + *gon-* + Gk *poros* passage + E *-ic* or *-ous*] **:** having a single genital opening for both male and female organs

mo·nog·o·ny \məˈnägənē, -ni\ *n* -ES [*mon-* + *-gony*] **:** asexual reproduction

¹mono·gram \ˈmänəˌgram, -aa(ə)m\ *n* [LL *monogrammus*, fr. L, adj., consisting of lines only, sketched, fr. *mon-* + *-grammus* (fr. Gk *grammē* line, fr. *graphein* to write) — more at CARVE] *archaic* **:** a picture in lines only **:** OUTLINE, SKETCH

²monogram \"\ *n* [LL *monogramma*, fr. Gk *mon-* + Gk *gramma* letter — more at GRAM] **:** a character or cipher usu. composed of two or more letters interwoven or combined, usu. representing a name or a part of it, and often used (as on seals, ornamental pins and rings, linens) to show personal ownership — compare CALLIGRAM

monograms

³monogram \"\ *vt* **monogrammed; monogrammed; monogramming; monograms :** to mark with a monogram ⟨always *monogrammed* her own handkerchiefs⟩

mono·gram·mat·ic \¦⸗⸗ˌgrəˈmad·ik\ *also* **mono·gram·mat·i·cal** \-d·əkəl\ *adj* [LL *monogrammat-*, *monogramma* + E *-ic*] **:** of, relating to, or resembling a monogram

mono·gram·mic \¦⸗⸗¦gramik\ *adj* [²*monogram* + *-ic*] **:** MONOGRAMMATIC

¹mono·graph \ˈ⸗⸗ˌgraf, -aa(ə)f, -aif, -äf\ *n* [*mon-* + *-graph*] **1 a :** a special treatise on a particular subject in natural history **b :** a learned detailed thoroughly documented treatise covering exhaustively a small area of a field of learning ⟨this ~ covers the development of intravenous anesthesia from 1872 —*Jour. Amer. Med. Assoc.*⟩ ⟨his ~ comprises an essay analyzing Irish bookbinding —*Times Lit. Supp.*⟩ **2 :** a written account of a single thing: as **a :** a biographical study ⟨in every language of Europe there are ~s . . . of the man who so affected Christendom and remade it —Hilaire Belloc⟩ **b :** a collection of plates (as reproductions of paintings) showing the work of a single artist and usu. accompanied by biographical or critical text **syn** see DISCOURSE

²monograph \"\ *vt* **:** to make a monograph on **:** discuss in a monograph

mo·nog·ra·pher \məˈnägrəfə(r)\ *n* -s [NL *monographus* monographer (fr. *mon-* + *-graphus*, fr. Gk *graphein* to write) + E *-er*] **:** one who prepares a monograph

mono·graph·ic \ˌmänəˈgrafik\ *also* **mono·graph·i·cal** \-fəkəl\ *adj* [*monograph* + *-ic*, *-ical*] **1 :** of, relating to, or characteristic of a monograph ⟨the eruditely written ~ volume —M.M.Willey⟩ ⟨~ studies of narrowly specialized topics —A.T.Cutler⟩ **2** [*mon-* + *-graphic*] *in cryptography* **:** involving one letter at a time ⟨~ substitution⟩ — **mono·graph·i·cal·ly** \-fək(ə)lē\ *adv*

mo·nog·ra·phist \məˈnägrəfəst\ *n* -s [*monograph* & *monography* + *-ist*] **:** MONOGRAPHER ⟨the historical ~ —F.T.Marsh⟩

mo·nog·ra·phy \-fē\ *n* -ES [NL *monographia*, fr. *mon-* + *-graphia* -graphy] **:** MONOGRAPH ⟨*monographies* on the great educators —*Amer. Council of Learned Soc. Newsletter*⟩

¹mono·grap·tid \¦⸗⸗ *at* MONO- + ¦graptəd\ *adj* [NL *Monograptus* + E *-id*] **:** of or relating to the genus *Monograptus* or the family Monograptidae

²monograptid \"\ *n* -s **:** a graptolite of the genus *Monograptus* or the family Monograptidae

mono·grap·tus \ˌ⸗⸗ˈ⸗təs\ *n, cap* [NL, fr. *mon-* + Gk *graptos* engraved, written, fr. *graphein* to write — more at CARVE] **:** a genus (the type of the family Monograptidae) of graptolites with a single row of overlapping thecae

mono·gyn·ic \¦⸗⸗¦jinik\ *also* **mono·gyn·i·ous** \-nēəs\ *adj* [*monogyny* + *-ic* or *-ous*] **:** MONOGYNOUS

mo·nog·y·nist \məˈnäjənəst\ *n* -s [*monogyny* + *-ist*] **:** one who believes in or practices monogyny

mono·gy·noe·cial \¦⸗⸗ *at* MONO- + jə¦nēshəl, gə¦-\ *adj* [*mon-* + NL *gynoecium* + E *-al*] **:** formed from a single pistil

mo·nog·y·nous \məˈnäjənəs\ *adj* [*mon-* + *-gynous*] **1 :** having one pistil **2 a :** of, relating to, or living in monogyny **:** having but one wife **b :** having only one female mate **3 :** having a single functional female in the colony — used of social insects ⟨the honeybee is a typical ~ insect⟩

mo·nog·y·ny \-nē, -ni\ *n* -ES [ISV *mon-* + *-gyny*] **1 :** the quality or state of being monogynous; *specif* **:** the state or custom of having only one wife at a time — compare POLYGYNY **2 :** the state or custom of having only one chief, head, or jural wife together with other consorts

mono·haploid \¦⸗⸗ *at* MONO- +\ *adj* [*mon-* + *haploid*] **:** having a haploid chromosome number containing a single genome — used of a diploid; compare POLYHAPLOID

¹mono·hybrid \"+\ *n* [*mon-* + *hybrid*] **:** an individual or strain heterozygous for one specified factor or gene

²monohybrid \"\ *adj* **:** of or relating to a monohybrid

mono·hydrate \"+\ *n* [ISV *mon-* + *hydrate*] **:** a hydrate containing one molecule of water — **mono·hydrated** \"+\ *adj*

mono·hy·dric \"+¦hīdrik\ *adj* [*mon-* + *-hydric*] **1** *archaic* **:** containing one atom of acid hydrogen **2 :** MONOHYDROXY — used esp. of alcohols and phenols

mono·hydroxy \"+\ *adj* [ISV *monohydroxy-*, fr. *mon-* + *hydroxy-*] **:** containing one hydroxyl group in the molecule

mo·noi·cous \məˈnȯikəs\ *also* **mono·noe·cious** \-nēshəs\ *adj* [*mon-* + *-oicous* (fr. Gk *oikos* house + E *-ous*) — more at VICINITY] **:** having archegonia and antheridia on different branches of the same plant — compare AUTOICOUS, DIOICOUS, HETEROICOUS, PAROICOUS, POLYOICOUS, SYNOICOUS

mono·ide·ism \¦⸗⸗ *at* MONO- + ˈīdēˌizəm\ *n* -s [ISV *mon-* + *idea* + *-ism*] **:** a state of prolonged absorption in a single idea (as in mental depression, trance, hypnosis) — opposed to *polyideism*

mono·ide·is·tic \¦⸗⸗¦⸗⸗¦istik\ *adj* [ISV *mon-* + *idea* + *-istic*] **:** of, relating to, or characterized by monoideism

mono·ion \¦⸗⸗ *at* MONO- +\ *n* [*mon-* + *ion*] **:** an ion having only one charge

mono·isotopic \"+\ *adj* [*mon-* + *isotopic*] **:** consisting of a single isotope — used of an element

mono·ketone \"+\ *n* [*mon-* + *ketone*] **:** a chemical compound containing one ketonic carbonyl group

mo·nol·a·ter \məˈnäləd·ə(r)\ *also* **mo·nol·a·trist** \-lə·trəst\ *n* -s [*monolatry* + *-er* or *-ist*] **:** one whose religious practices are typified by monolatry

mo·nol·a·trous \-ə·trəs\ *adj* [*monolatry* + *-ous*] **:** of or relating to monolatry

mo·nol·a·try \-ə·trē\ *n* -s [*mon-* + *-latry*] **:** HENOTHEISM

mono·layer \¦⸗⸗ *at* MONO- +\ *n* [*mon-* + *layer*] **:** a single continuous layer or film that is one cell or molecule in thickness

¹mono·line \"+\ *adj* [*mon-* + *line* (n.)] **:** having or relating to a single line: as **a :** writing only one main branch of insurance — compare MULTIPLE-LINE **b :** MONORAIL

²monoline \"\ *n* [*mon-* + *line*] **:** MONORAIL

¹mono·lingual \¦⸗⸗ *at* MONO- +\ *adj* [*mon-* + *lingual*] **:** expressed in or knowing or using only one language

²monolingual \"\ *n* -s **:** a person who understands and speaks only one language

mono·literal \"+\ *adj* [*mon-* + *literal*] **1 :** consisting of one letter **2 a :** using single letters as cipher equivalents **b :** MONOGRAPHIC — **mono·literally** \"+\ *adv*

¹mono·lith \ˈmän³lˌith, ˈmōn-\ *n* -s [F *monolithe*, fr. *monolithe*, adj., monolithic, fr. L *monolithus*, fr. Gk *monolithos*, fr. *mon-* + *lithos* stone] **1 a** (1) **:** a single great stone often in the form of an obelisk or column ⟨the 120-ton ~s on three sides of the choir altar —*Amer. Guide Series: Maine*⟩ — compare MEGALITH (2) **:** something resembling a monolith and usu. having tremendous size or strength **:** COLOSSUS ⟨weld together even more tightly the parallel ~s of party and state —*Time*⟩ ⟨his friends see him as a pillar of determination; his enemies consider him a thick-skinned ~ —*Newsweek*⟩ **b** (1) **:** a single large block of concrete serving a specific purpose (2) **:** one of many large blocks cast in place to form gravity-type concrete dams **2 :** a mountain or large hill apparently composed of one kind of rock usu. of a coarse-grained igneous rock **3 :** a column of soil several feet deep removed as a unit

²monolith \"\ *adj* [F *monolithe*] **:** MONOLITHIC

mono·lith·ic \¦⸗⸗¦ithik, -thēk\ *adj* [F *monolithe* or L *monolithus* monolithic + E *-ic*] **1 a :** formed or carved from a single block of stone **b :** made up of monoliths ⟨Stonehenge is a ~ monument⟩ **2 a :** consisting of one stone — used of the shaft of a column not built up of drums **b :** having a type of architecture or construction depending upon rock cutting or excavation from the solid rock **3 a** *of a concrete structure* **:** cast as a single piece **b** *of a concrete floor or pavement* **:** having a special quality surface layer which is applied while the bottom layer is still green so that both layers harden to form an integral unit **4 :** constituting one massive undifferentiated whole exhibiting solid uniformity often without diversity or variability ⟨have rejected the idea of the domination of the single ~ party —John Dewey⟩ ⟨a ~ commercial enterprise —*Atlantic*⟩

mono·lith·ism \ˈ⸗⸗ˌiˌthizəm\ *n* -s [F *monolithisme*, fr. *monolithe* + *-isme* -ism] **:** the quality or state of being monolithic ⟨where political ~ inevitably leads —*Saturday Rev.*⟩

mono·lithologic \¦⸗⸗ *at* MONO- +\ *adj* [*mon-* + *lithologic*] **:** composed of but one kind of rock

mono·lobular \"+\ *adj* [*mon-* + *lobular*] **:** having one lobe

mono·locular \"+\ *adj* [ISV *mon-* + *locular*] **:** UNILOCULAR

mono·log·ic \ˌmän³l¦äjik\ *or* **mono·log·i·cal** \-jəkəl\ *adj* [*monology* + *-ic*, *-ical*] **:** of, relating to, or characteristic of a monologue ⟨voice . . . mounted from a ~ mutter to a high-tensioned harangue —L.C.Douglas⟩

mo·nol·o·gist \məˈnäləjəst, *in sense 3* " *also* ˈmän³lˌȯgə- *or* -³lˌäg- *sometimes* ˈmōn³l-,-\ *n* -s **1 :** one who soliloquizes **2 :** one who monopolizes conversation **3 :** a performer of monologues ⟨greatest ~s in modern minstrelsy —C.F.Withe⟩

mo·nol·o·gize \məˈnäləˌjīz *also* ˈmän³lˌōˌgīz *or* -³lˌäg- *sometimes* ˈmōn³l-,-\ *also* **mon·o·logu·ize** \ˈ⸗⸗ˌ⸗ˌ⸗\ *vi* -ED/-ING/-s [*monology* + *-ize*] **:** to utter a monologue **:** SOLILOQUIZE

¹mon·o·logue *also* **mon·o·log** \'män°l,ȯg *also* -°l,äg *sometimes* 'mōn°l,-\ *n* -s [F *monologue*, fr. *mon-* + *-logue* (as in *dialogue*) — more at DIALOGUE] **1 a :** a dramatic scene in which one person soliloquizes ⟨such passages as the ~ at the beginning of the second scene —*Manchester Guardian Weekly*⟩ **b :** a dramatic sketch performed by one actor **2 :** a literary composition written in the form of a soliloquy ⟨early poems are the ~s of a young man very isolated . . . in his genius —Stephen Spender⟩ **3 :** a long speech uttered by one person while in company with others ⟨habit of lecturing his friends in ~ —H.S.Canby⟩

²monologue \"\ *vi* -ED/-ING/-S **:** MONOLOGIZE ⟨at once took charge of the meeting and began to ~ —W.A.White⟩

mon·o·logu·ist \-gəst\ *n* -s [¹*monologue* + *-ist*] **:** MONOLOGIST

mon·o·logu·ize \-,gīz\ *vi* -ED/-ING/-S [¹*monologue* + *-ize*] **:** MONOLOGIZE

mo·nol·o·gy \mə'näləjē\ *n* -ES [*mon-* + *-logy*] **1** *obs* **:** MONOLOGUE **2 :** the habit of soliloquizing

mo·nom·a·chy \mə'näməkē\ *n* -ES [MF *monomachie*, fr. L *monomachia*, fr. Gk, fr. *mon-* + *-machia* -machy] **:** a combat between two persons **:** DUEL

mono·mania \¦== *at* MONO- +\ *n* [NL, fr. *mon-* + *mania*] **1 :** mental derangement restricted to one idea or group of ideas **:** true paranoia **2 :** such concentration on a single object or idea as to suggest mental derangement

¹mono·maniac \"+\ *n* [*mon-* + *maniac* (n.)] **1 :** a person affected by monomania **2 :** one who has a craze ⟨a complete ~ about his beloved rockets —*Times Lit. Supp.*⟩

²monomaniac \"\ *or* **mono·maniacal** \"+\ *adj* [*mon-* + *maniac, maniacal* (adj.)] **:** relating to, characterized by, or affected with monomania

Mono·mark \'mänō,märk, -mák\ *trademark* — used for a system employed chiefly in England by which an individual or a firm may register a combination of letters or figures as an identification mark

mono·mastigote \¦== *at* MONO- +\ *adj* [alter. of earlier *monomastigate*, fr. *mon-* + *mastig-* + *-ate*] **:** UNIFLAGELLATE

mono·me·nis·cous \"+mə¦niskəs\ *adj* [*mon-* + NL *meniscus* + E *-ous*] **:** having but one lens — used of a simple eye

mono·mer \'mänəmə(r), 'mōn-\ *n* -s [ISV *mon-* + *-mer*] **:** the simple unpolymerized form of a chemical compound having relatively low molecular weight ⟨styrene, methyl methacrylate, and other ~s are polymerized in this manner —H.F.Mark⟩ — compare DIMER, POLYMER

mono·mer·ic \¦==¦merik\ *adj* **:** of, relating to, or consisting of a monomer ⟨a ~ unit . . . contains the same kinds and number of atoms as the real or hypothetical monomer —*Rubber & Rubber-Like Materials*⟩

mo·nom·er·ous \mə'nämərəs\ *adj* [Gk *monomerēs* of one part, fr. *mon-* + *meros* part — more at MERIT] **1 a** *of a flower* **:** having a single member in each whorl **b :** MONOCARPELLARY **2 :** having or characterized by one-jointed tarsi

mono·metallic \¦== *at* MONO- +\ *adj* [*mon-* + *metallic*] **1 :** consisting of or employing one metal **:** of or relating to monometallism **2 :** containing one atom of metal in the molecule ⟨~ carbonyls⟩

monometallic balance *n* **:** a watch or chronometer balance of nickel, steel, or alloy with an uncut rim — compare COMPENSATION BALANCE

mono·met·al·lism \¦== *at* MONO- + ¦med·°l,izəm, -et°l-\ *n* -s [ISV *mon-* + *-metallism* (as in *bimetallism*)] **1 :** the legalized use of one metal only (as gold or silver) in the standard currency of a country or as the standard of money values **2 :** the theory, belief, or practice favoring or employing a single metallic standard — compare BIMETALLISM

mono·met·al·list \-°ləst\ *n* -s [ISV *mon-* + *-metallist* (as in *bimetallist*)] **:** an advocate of monometallism

mo·nom·e·ter \mə'nämədə(r)\ *n* [LL, fr. Gk *monometros*, fr. *mon-* + *metron* measure — more at MEASURE] **:** a verse consisting of a single metrical unit (as a foot or dipody)

mono·methine \¦== *at* MONO- +\ *n* [*mon-* + *methine*] **:** CYANINE 2

mono·methyl \"+\ *adj* [*mon-* + *methyl*] **:** containing one methyl group esp. in place of hydrogen

mono·methylamine \"+\ *n* [*monomethyl* + *amine*] **:** METHYLAMINE 1

mono·methylolurea \"+\ *n* [NL, fr. *mon-* + ISV *methylol* + NL *-urea*] **:** METHYLOLUREA a

mono·metric \"+\ *adj* [*mon-* + Gk *metron* measure + E *-ic* — more at MEASURE] **:** EQUIGRANULAR

mono·metrical \"+\ *or* **mono·metric** \"+\ *adj* [*mon-* + *metrical, metric*] **:** relating to or consisting of a monometer

¹mo·no·mi·al \mə'nōmēəl\ *n* -s [*mon-* + *-omial* (as in *binomial*)] **:** a mathematical expression consisting of a single term

²monomial \"\ *adj* **1 :** of or relating to monomials **2 :** consisting of a single word or term — used of the technical name of a plant or animal

mono·mict \¦== *at* MONO- + ,mikt\ *adj* [Ger *monomikt*, fr. *mon-* + Gk *miktos* mixed, blended, fr. *misgein* to mix — more at MIX] **:** relating to a sedimentary rock composed of but a single mineral species — compare MONOGENIC 1a

mono·mineral \"+\ *or* **mono·min·er·al·ic** \"+¦minə¦ralik\ *adj* [ISV *mon-* + *mineral, mineralic* (fr. ¹*mineral* + *-ic*); orig. formed as Ger *monomineralisch*] **:** composed wholly or almost wholly of a single mineral species

mono·molecular \¦== *at* MONO- +\ *adj* [*mon-* + *molecular*] **:** relating to or consisting of a single or simple molecule ⟨a ~ compound⟩ **:** being only one molecule thick ⟨a ~ film⟩ ⟨a ~ layer⟩ **:** UNIMOLECULAR — **mono·molecularly** \"+\ *adv*

mono·mo·ri·um \,==¦mōrēəm\ *n, cap* [NL, fr. *mon-* + Gk *morion* part, portion, dim. of *moros* lot, fate — more at MERIT] **:** a large widely distributed genus of ants including important household pests — see LITTLE BLACK ANT, PHARAOH ANT

mono·morphemic \¦== *at* MONO- +\ *adj* [*mon-* + *morphemic*] **:** consisting of only one morpheme ⟨*raise* is ~ but *rays* is not⟩

mono·mor·phic \¦==¦mȯrfik\ *or* **mono·mor·phous** \-fəs\ *adj* [*mon-* + *-morphic, -morphous*] **1 :** having but a single form **:** exhibiting the same or essentially similar structure in all members — used esp. of a taxonomic group **2 a :** retaining the same form throughout various stages of development — used of an ametabolic insect **b :** having but one structural pattern — used of a primitive worker ant; compare POLYMORPHIC **3 :** producing spores of one form or kind — used of a plant

mono·mor·phism \,==¦=,fizəm\ *n* -s **:** the quality or state of being monomorphic

mono·my·ar·ia \,==,mī'a(a)rēə\ *or* **mono·mya** \,=='mīə\ *n pl, cap* [*Monomyaria*, NL, fr. *mon-* + *my-* + *-aria*; *Monomya*, NL, fr. *mon-* + *-mya*] *in some classifications* **:** a division of Lamellibranchia comprising bivalve mollusks (as the oysters, pearl oysters, and scallops) having but one adductor muscle — compare DIMYARIA — **mono·my·ar·i·an** \¦==,=¦a(a)rēən\ *adj or n*

mon·onch \'mä,näŋk, 'mō,-\ *n* -s [NL *Mononchus*] **:** a worm of the genus *Mononchus*

mo·non·chus \mə'näŋkəs\ *n, cap* [NL, fr. *mon-* + *-onchus* (modif. of Gk *onkos* barbed hook) — more at ANGLE] **:** a genus of predatory nematodes (order Chromadorida) usu. having a single pharyngeal tooth and living in fresh water and in soil where they have been estimated to number up to 300,000,000 to the acre

mono·neural \¦== *at* MONO- +\ *adj* [*mon-* + *neural*] *of a muscle* **:** receiving branches from but one nerve

mo·non·ga·he·la \mə,näŋgə'hēlə, -äŋg-, -hālə\ *n* -s *usu cap* [fr. *Monongahela* river valley in southwestern Pennsylvania and northern West Virginia where it was first produced] **:** American whiskey; *specif* **:** rye whiskey made in western Pennsylvania

mono·nitrate \¦== *at* MONO- +\ *n* [*mon-* + *nitrate*] **:** a compound containing a single nitrate group ⟨glycol ~ $HOCH_2CH_2ONO_2$⟩

mono·nitrated \"+\ *adj* [*mon-* + *nitrated*, past part. of *nitrate*, v.] **:** modified by the introduction of one nitro group or one nitrate group

mono·nitration \"+\ *n* [*mon-* + *nitration*] **:** the act or process of modifying by the introduction of one nitro group or one nitrate group

mono·nitro \"+\ *adj* [ISV *mononitro-*, fr. *mon-* + *nitr-*] **:** containing one nitro group in the molecule

mon·ont \'mä,nänt, 'mō,-\ *n* -s [*mon-* + *-ont*] **:** SCHIZONT

¹mono·nuclear \¦== *at* MONO- +\ *adj* [ISV *mon-* + *nuclear*] **1 :** having only one nucleus **2 :** MONOCYCLIC 2 ⟨~ aromatic compounds⟩

²mononuclear \"\ *n* -s [ISV, fr. ¹*mononuclear*] **:** a mononuclear cell; *esp* **:** MONOCYTE

mono·nucleated \"+\ *adj* [*mon-* + *nucleated*] **:** MONONUCLEAR

mono·nu·cle·o·sis \,==,n(y)üklē'ōsəs\ *n, pl* **mononucleo·ses** \-,sēz\ [NL, fr. ISV ²*mononuclear* + NL *-osis*] **1 :** an abnormal increase in the number of agranulocytes in the circulating blood; *specif* **:** INFECTIOUS MONONUCLEOSIS **2 :** MONOCYTOSIS

mono·nucleotide \¦== *at* MONO- +\ *n* [*mon-* + *nucleotide*] **:** a nucleotide derived from one molecule each of a nitrogen base, a sugar, and phosphoric acid

mon·on·y·chous \mə'nänəkəs, (')mä¦nä-, (')mō¦nä-; ¦mänə¦nikəs, ¦mōn-\ *adj* [*mon-* + *onych-* + *-ous*] **:** having an uncleft claw — used of an insect

mono·olefin \¦== *at* MONO- +\ *n* [*mon-* + *olefin*] **:** ALKENE — **mono·olefinic** \"+\ *adj*

mono·ou·sian \¦== *at* MONO- + ¦üzēən, -üsēən, -üzh(ē)ən, -üsh(ē)ən\ *or* **mono·ou·sious** \-əs\ *adj* [*monoousian* fr. LGk *monoousios* monoousian (fr. Gk *mon-* + *ousia* substance, essence) + E *-an*; *monoousious* fr. LGk *monoousios* — more at OUSIA] *relig* **:** of one substance or essence

mono·pack \'==+,-\ *n* [*mon-* + *pack*] **:** INTEGRAL TRIPACK

mono·parental \¦==+\ *adj* [*mon-* + *parental*] **:** having or derived from a single parent

mono·pectinate \"+\ *adj* [*mon-* + *pectinate*] **:** pectinate along one side

mono·persulfuric acid \"+-\ *n* [*mon-* + *persulfuric*] **:** PERMONOSULFURIC ACID

mono·petalous \"+\ *adj* [NL *monopetalus*, fr. *mon-* + *-petalus* -petalous] **1 :** GAMOPETALOUS 1 **2 :** having a solitary petal

mo·noph·a·gous \mə'näfəgəs\ *adj* [*mon-* + *-phagous*] **1 :** feeding on or utilizing a single kind of food **:** feeding on a single kind of plant or animal — used esp. of an insect; compare OLIGOPHAGOUS **2 :** entering only a single host cell — used esp. of the thallus of parasitic fungi; compare POLYPHAGOUS

mo·noph·a·gy \-jē\ *n* -ES [*mon-* + *-phagy*] **:** a monophagous character or condition

mono·phase \¦== *at* MONO- +\ *adj* [*mon-* + *phase*] **:** SINGLE-PHASE

mono·pha·sia \,==¦fāzh(ē)ə\ *n* -s [NL, fr. *mon-* + *-phasia*] **:** aphasia marked by repeated utterance of one word or phrase

mono·pha·sic \¦==¦fāzik\ *adj* [*mon-* + *phasic*] **1 :** SINGLE-PHASE ⟨a ~ electric current⟩ **2** *of an animal* **:** having a single period of activity followed by a period of rest in each 24 hours ⟨man may be considered a naturally ~ being⟩ — compare POLYPHASIC

mono·pho·bia \,==¦fōbēə\ *n* [NL, fr. *mon-* + *-phobia*] **:** a morbid dread of being alone

mono·phonemic \¦==+\ *adj* [*mon-* + *phonemic*] **:** constituting, consisting of, or standing for a single phoneme

mono·phon·ic \"+¦fänik\ *also* **mo·noph·o·nous** \mə'näfənəs\ *adj* [*mon-* + *-phonic, -phonous*] **1 :** consisting of a solo voice with accompaniment **2 :** having a single melodic line with little or no accompaniment — compare HOMOPHONIC 3, POLYPHONIC **3 :** of or relating to sound transmission, recording, or reproduction by techniques that provide a single transmission path — compare BINAURAL, STEREOPHONIC

mo·noph·o·ny \mə'näfənē\ *n* -ES [*mon-* + *-phony*] **:** melody for one voice esp. if unaccompanied

mon·oph·thal·mic \,mä,näf¦thalmik, ¦mō,n-, ÷ -näp¦th-\ *adj* [Gk *monophthalmos* one-eyed (fr. *mon-* + *ophthalmos* eye) + E *-ic* — more at OPHTHALMIA] **:** having one eye

mon·oph·thong \'mänəf,thȯŋ, -nə,th- *also* -thäŋ\ *n* -s [LGk *monophthongos* single vowel, fr. Gk *mon-* + *phthongos* sound] **:** a vowel sound that throughout its duration has a single constant articulatory position and acoustic structure and whose boundary on either side is a consonant or a syllable boundary — compare DIPHTHONG, TRIPHTHONG — **mon·oph·thon·gal** \¦==¦=¦=(g)əl\ *adj*

mon·oph·thong·ization \,==,=(g)ə'zāshən, -,(g)ī'z-\ *n* -s **:** the process of monophthongizing

mon·oph·thong·ize \'==,=(g)īz\ *vt* -ED/-ING/-S **:** to change into a monophthong **:** reduce (a diphthong or triphthong) to a simple vowel sound

mono·phyletic \¦== *at* MONO- +\ *adj* [ISV *mon-* + *phyletic*] **:** of or relating to a single stock **:** developed from a single common parent form — opposed to *polyphyletic*

monophyletic theory *n* **:** a theory in physiology: all the cellular elements of the blood derive from a common stem cell — compare POLYPHYLETIC THEORY

mono·phyle·tism \,==¦fīlə,tizəm, -'fil-\ *or* **mono·phyle·ty** \-lədē\ *n, pl* **monophyletisms** *or* **monophyleties** [*monophyletism* ISV *monophyletic* + *-ism*; *monophylety* fr. *monophyletic* + *-y*] **:** the quality or state of being monophyletic **:** shared descent from a single common stemform

mono·phy·odont \¦==¦fīə,dänt\ *adj* [Gk *monophyēs* single (fr. *mon-* + *-phyēs*, fr. *phyein* to bring forth) + *odont-*, *odous* tooth — more at BE, TOOTH] **:** having but one set of teeth of which none are replaced at a later stage of growth — opposed to *diphyodont*; distinguished from *polyphyodont*

mo·noph·y·sism \mə'näfə,sizəm, mä'-, mō'-\ *n* -s *usu cap* [F *monophysisme*, fr. *monophysite* (fr. ML *Monophysita*) + *-isme* -ism] **:** MONOPHYSITISM

¹mo·noph·y·site \-,sīt\ *n* -s *usu cap* [ML *Monophysita*, fr. MGk *Monophysitēs*, fr. Gk *mon-* + *physis* nature + *-itēs* -ite — more at PHYSICS] **:** one who maintains the anti-Chalcedonian doctrine that the human and divine in the person of Jesus Christ constitute only one nature which is regarded either as thoroughly unified or as composite — compare ARMENIAN, DYOPHYSITE

²monophysite \"\ *adj, usu cap* **:** MONOPHYSITIC

mo·noph·y·sit·ic \=¦==¦sid·ik\ *adj, usu cap* [¹*Monophysite* + *-ic*] **:** of or relating to the Monophysites or Monophysitism **:** supporting Monophysitism

mo·noph·y·sit·ism \='==,sīd·,izəm\ *n* -s *usu cap* [¹*Monophysite* + *-ism*] **:** the doctrines of the Monophysites

mono·placula \¦== *at* MONO- +\ *n* [NL, fr. *mon-* + *placula*] **:** a placula consisting of a single layer of cells — **mono·placular** \"+\ *adj* — **mono·placulate** \"+\ *adj*

mono·plane \'mänə,plān\ *n* [*mon-* + *plane*] **:** an airplane with only one main supporting surface

mono·pla·net·ic \¦== *at* MONO- + plə¦ned·ik\ *adj* [*mon-* + Gk *planētikos* migratory — more at DIPLANETIC] *of a fungus* **:** having but a single swarming period — compare DIPLANETIC

mono·plan·et·ism \,==¦planəd·,izəm\ *n* -s [*monoplanetic* + *-ism*] **:** the quality or state of being monoplanetic

mono·plasmatic \¦== *at* MONO- +\ *adj* [*mon-* + *plasmatic*] **:** composed of but one substance

mono·plast \'==,plast\ *n* -s [*mon-* + *-plast*] **:** a single-celled organism or a simple structural element

mono·plas·tic \¦==¦plastik\ *adj* [*mon-* + *-plastic*] **:** retaining a primary form **:** UNDIFFERENTIATED, UNIFORM

mono·ple·gia \,=='plēj(ē)ə\ *n* -s [NL, fr. *mon-* + *-plegia*] **:** paralysis affecting a single limb, body part, or group of muscles — **mono·ple·gic** \¦==¦=jik\ *adj*

¹mono·ploid \'==,plȯid\ *adj* [ISV *mon-* + *-ploid*] **:** having or being a chromosome set comprising a single genome — compare HAPLOID

²monoploid \"\ *n* -s **:** a monoploid individual

mono·pneu·mo·na \,=='n(y)ümənə, ,==näp'n-\ *also* **mono·pneu·mo·nes** \-,nēz\ *n pl, cap* [NL, fr. *mon-* + *-pneumona* (fr. Gk *pneumon-*, *pneumōn* lungs) — more at PNEUMONIA] *in some classifications* **:** an order including the genus *Ceratodus* — **mono·pneu·mo·ni·an** \¦==¦mōnēən\ *adj or n* — **mono·pneu·mo·nous** \¦==¦n(y)ümənəs\ *adj*

mo·nop·o·dal \mə'näpəd°l\ *adj* [*mon-* + *-pod* + *-al*] **:** forming a single pseudopodium at any one time

¹mono·pode \'== *at* MONO- + ,pōd\ *n* [LL *monopodius*] **1 :** a one-footed creature; *specif* **:** a fabulous one-footed Ethiopian that uses his foot as a sunshade **2** [NL *monopodium*] **:** MONOPODIUM

²monopode \"\ *adj* [LL *monopodius*, fr. Gk *monopod-*, *monopous*, fr. *mon-* + *pod-*, *pous* foot — more at FOOT] **:** having only one foot

mono·po·di·al \¦==¦pōdēəl\ *adj* [NL *monopodium* + E *-al*] **1 :** of or relating to a monopodium **:** having or involving the formation of offshoots from a main axis ⟨~ theories of evolution⟩ **2 :** RACEMOSE — **mono·po·di·al·ly** \-ēlē\ *adv*

mono·pod·ic \¦==¦pädik\ *adj* [*monopody* + *-ic*] **:** consisting of or relating to a single metrical foot

mono·po·di·um \,=='pōdēəm\ *n, pl* **monopo·dia** \-ēə\ [NL, fr. *mon-* + *-podium*] **:** a main or primary axis that continues its original line of growth giving off successive axes or lateral branches (as in the excurrent trunk of some coniferous tree) — compare SYMPODIUM

mo·nop·o·dy \mə'näpədē\ *n* -ES [Gk or LGk *monopodia* measurement by single feet, fr. Gk *mon-* + *pod-*, *pous* foot + *-ia* -y — more at FOOT] **:** a measure of a single metrical foot

mono·polar \¦== *at* MONO- +\ *adj* [*mon-* + *polar*] **:** UNIPOLAR — **mono·polarity** \"+\ *n*

monopole *n* -s [MF, fr. L *monopolium* — more at MONOPOLY] *obs* **:** MONOPOLY

monopoler *n* -s [MF *monopolier*, fr. *monopole* + *-ier* -er] *obs* **:** MONOPOLIST

mo·nop·o·lism \mə'näpə,lizəm\ *n* -s [*monopoly* + *-ism*] **:** the system, policy, or practices of monopolies or monopolists

mo·nop·o·list \-,ləst\ *n* -s [*monopoly* + *-ist*] **:** one who monopolizes **:** one who has a monopoly or favors monopoly ⟨a ~ controlling a limited supply of goods —R.W.Firth⟩

mo·nop·o·lis·tic \=¦==¦listik, -tēk\ *adj* **:** of, relating to, or characteristic of a monopoly or a monopolist ⟨a ~ conspiracy to determine freight rates —*New Republic*⟩ — **mo·nop·o·lis·ti·cal·ly** \-tək(ə)lē, -tēk-, -lī\ *adv*

monopolistic competition *n* **:** competition that is used among sellers whose products are similar but not identical and that takes the form of product differentiation and advertising with less emphasis upon price — compare IMPERFECT COMPETITION

mo·nop·o·li·za·tion \mə,näpələ'zāshən, -,lī'z-\ *n* -s **:** the quality or state of being monopolized; *also* **:** the process of being monopolized

mo·nop·o·lize \mə'näpə,līz\ *vt* -ED/-ING/-S *see -ize in Explan Notes* [*monopoly* + *-ize*] **:** to acquire a monopoly of **:** have or get the exclusive privilege of the means of dealing in or the exclusive possession of **:** engross the whole of

syn ENGROSS, ABSORB, CONSUME: MONOPOLIZE implies the exclusive, often overbearingly exclusive, possession or control of something which more generally would be distributed, publicly available, or more publicly controlled ⟨*monopolize* the auto market in the area⟩ ⟨*monopolize* the attention of a guest⟩ ⟨*monopolize* a family car⟩ ENGROSS applies usu. to an unprotested monopolizing of attention, interest, or time, as of one charmed or held irresistibly ⟨a group of boys sprawl, teen-age fashion, on couches and chairs, *engrossed* in a drama that blares from a television set —*Lamp*⟩ ⟨they were so *engrossed* in each other that she didn't see me until I was five feet away —Scott Fitzgerald⟩ ⟨an *engrossing* novel⟩ ABSORB is often interchangeable with ENGROSS but usu. has a nonpersonal subject and suggests a monopolizing more often against the will of the one acted upon than does ENGROSS ⟨crammed with ideas, projects, hobbies — enough to keep you *absorbed* and fascinated for the next five hundred years —Glynne Hiller⟩ ⟨petty cares and vexations that *absorb* life's energies —M.R.Cohen⟩ CONSUME, in the somewhat extended sense pertinent here, stresses the monopolizing of the total attention, interest, or time which is its usual object ⟨a *consuming* interest⟩ ⟨a *consuming* curiosity⟩ ⟨the guilt which *consumed* Lawrence during those treacherous moments —H.M.Sachar⟩

mo·nop·o·liz·er \-zə(r)\ *n* -s **:** one that monopolizes

mo·nop·o·loid \-,lȯid\ *adj* [*monopoly* + *-oid*] **:** of, relating to, or resembling a monopoly ⟨~ corporate and financial gigantism —*New Republic*⟩

mo·nop·o·ly \mə'näp(ə)lē, -li\ *n* -ES *see sense 6* [L *monopolium*, fr. Gk *monopōlion*, *monopōlia*, fr. *mon-* + *-pōlion*, *-pōlia* (fr. *pōlein* to sell); prob. akin to MLG *vēle* for sale, MD *veile*, *veil*, OHG *fāli*, *feili*, ON *falr* for sale, Sk *paṇate* he barters, trades] **1 :** ownership or control that permits domination of the means of production or the market in a business or occupation usu. for controlling prices and that is achieved through an exclusive legal privilege (as a governmental grant, charter, patent, or copyright) or by control of the source of supply (as ownership of a mine) or by engrossing a particular article or commodity (as in cornering the market) or by combination or concert of action — compare DUOPOLY, OLIGOPOLY **2 :** exclusive possession ⟨no country has a ~ on morality or truth —Helen M. Lynd⟩ **3 :** the exclusive legal privilege of a monopoly **4 :** the commodity to which the monopoly relates **5 :** a company or combination having a monopoly

Monopoly \"\ *trademark* — used for a board game in which players pretend to buy, rent, and sell real estate

mono·poly·logue \,== *at* MONO- + 'pälə,lȯg *also* -läg\ *n* -s [*mon-* + *poly-* + *-logue*] **:** an entertainment in which one actor plays many characters

mono·potassium \¦==+\ *adj* [*mon-* + *potassium*] **:** containing one atom of potassium in the molecule

mono·print \'==+,-\ *n* [*mon-* + *print*] **1 :** an impression made on paper from glass or some equally smooth material (as celluloid or oilcloth) to which oil paint has been applied **2 :** the art or process of making monoprints

mono·pri·on \¦==¦prīən\ *or* **mono·pri·o·nid** \-ənəd\ *or* **mono·pri·o·nid·i·an** \-¦nidēən\ *adj* [*monoprion* fr. *mon-* + Gk *priōn* saw; *monoprionid* fr. *mon-* + Gk *priōn* + E *-id*; *monoprionidian* fr. *mon-* + Gk *priōn* + E *-id* + *-ian* — more at PRIOR] **:** of, relating to, or being graptolites that have cells on one side of the stem only

¹mono·propellant \¦==+\ *n* [*mon-* + *propellant*] **:** a rocket propellant in which both the fuel and the oxidizer are contained in a single substance — compare BIPROPELLANT

²monopropellant \"\ *adj* **:** of, relating to, or employing a monopropellant

mo·nop·so·nist \mə'näpsənəst\ *n* -s [*monopsony* + *-ist*] **:** one who is a single buyer for a product or service of many sellers

mo·nop·so·nis·tic \=¦==¦nistik\ *adj* **:** of, relating to, or characteristic of monopsony

mo·nop·so·ny \='==nē\ *n* -ES [*mon-* + Gk *opsōnia* purchase of victuals, catering — more at DUOPSONY] **:** a market situation in which there is a single buyer for a given product or service from a large number of sellers — compare DUOPSONY, OLIGOPSONY

mono·psychism \¦== *at* MONO- +\ *n* [*mon-* + Gk *psychē* soul + E *-ism* — more at PSYCHIC] **:** a doctrine that there is but one immortal soul of which individual souls are manifestations

mo·nop·ter·al \(')mä¦näptərəl, (')mō¦-\ *adj* [L *monopteros* having a single row of columns (fr. Gk, fr. *mon-* + *pteron* wing) + E *-al* — more at FEATHER] *in circular buildings* **:** marked by columniation consisting of a single ring of supporting columns without a cella — see COLUMNIATION illustration

mo·nop·te·ron \-,rän\ *also* **mo·nop·te·ros** \-,räs\ *n, pl* **mo·nop·tera** \-,rə\ [L, fr. Gk *monopteron* (neut. of *monopteros*) & *monopteros*, adj.] **:** a monopteral structure

mon·optic \(')män, (')mōn+\ *also* **mon·optical** \"+\ *adj* [*mon-* + *optic, optical*] **:** having one eye

mono·py·laea \,== *at* MONO- + pī'lēə\ *or* **mono·py·lar·ia** -'la(a)rēə\ [NL, fr. *mon-* + *-pylaea* (fr. Gk *pylē* gate) or *-pylaria* (fr. *pyl-* + *-aria*) — more at PYLON] *syn of* MONOPYLEA

mono·py·lea \-pī'lēə\ *n pl, cap* [NL, fr. *mon-* + *-pylea* (fr. Gk *pylē* gate)] **:** a suborder of Radiolaria comprising protozoans with or without spiculate skeletons and with the central capsule interrupted by a single perforated plate — **mono·py·le·an** \¦==¦=¦lēən\ *adj or n*

¹mono·rail \'== *at* MONO- + ,-\ *n* [*mon-* + *rail*] **1 :** a single rail serving as a track for a wheeled conveyance **2 :** a single rail mounted on trestles constituting the track for railway cars that usu. sit astraddle over it or hang suspended from it

²monorail \"\ *adj* **:** operated by or involving a monorail

¹mon·or·chid \(')mä¦nȯrkəd\ *adj* [irreg. fr. Gk *monorchis*, fr. *mon-* + *orchis* testicle — more at ORCHIS] **:** having but one testis or but one descended into the scrotum — compare CRYPTORCHID

²monorchid \"\ *n* -s **:** a monorchid individual

mon·or·chid·ism \-kə,dizəm\ *also* **mon·or·chism** \-,kizəm\ *n* -s **:** the quality or state of being monorchid

mon·or·chis \mä'nȯrkəs\ *n, pl* **monorchi·des** \-kə,dēz\ [NL, fr. Gk *monorchis*, adj.] **:** MONORCHID

mon·organic \¦män, ¦mōn+\ *adj* [*mon-* + *organic*] **:** of, relating to, or affecting a single organ or set of organs

mono·rhi·na *or* **mon·or·rhi·na** \,mänə'rīnə, ,mōn-, -rēnə\

[NL, fr. mon- + -rhina, -rrhina (fr. Gk rhin-, rhis nose); akin to Gk rhein to flow — more at STREAM] syn of CYCLOSTOMI
mono·rhi·nal \¦== at MONO- + ¦rīnᵊl\ or **mono·rhine** \-¦rīn\ adj [mon- + -rhinal (fr. rhin- + -al) or -rhine] : having a single nostril ⟨a ~ cyclostome⟩
mono·rhin·ic \¦==¦rinik\ adj [mono- + rhin- + -ic] : affecting only one nostril ⟨~ stimulation shows that many individuals have keener smell on one side than the other —R.S.Woodworth⟩
mono·rhyme also **mono·rime** \'==+,-\ n [F monorime, fr. mon- + rime rhyme — more at RHYME] 1 : a strophe or poem in which all the lines have the same end rhyme 2 **monorhymes** pl : the lines of a monorhyme — **mono·rhymed** \¦==+\ adj
monos pl of MONO
mo·no·sa·bio \,mänə'säbē,ō, ,mōn-\ n -s [Sp, fr. mono monkey + sabio wise, fr. LL sapidus, fr. L, savory — more at SAPID] : a bullring attendant
mono·saccharide \¦== at MONO- +\ n [ISV mon- + sacchar- + -ide; prob. orig. formed as G monosaccharid] : any of the class of simple sugars that contain in each molecule one or more alcoholic hydroxyl groups and one carbonyl group of aldehyde or ketone character or its equivalent as a cyclic hemiacetal and that are classed as aldoses or ketoses and further according to the number of carbon atoms present with pentoses and hexoses the most common : GLYCOSE 2
mono·saccharose \"+\ n [mon- + saccharose] : MONOSACCHARIDE
mono·scope \'==+,skōp\ n [mon- + -scope] : a cathode-ray tube designed to produce for test purposes a video signal of a stationary pattern which has been printed in black foil ink on the aluminum-coated signal plate and sealed in the tube
mon·ose \'mä,nōs, 'mō,-, -ōz\ n -s [mon- + -ose] : MONOSACCHARIDE
mono·se·mic \¦== at MONO- + ¦sēmik\ adj [mon- + -semic] : consisting of or equal in duration to one mora ⟨a ~ syllable⟩
mono·sep·al·ous \"+¦sepələs\ adj [mon- + -sepalous] 1 : GAMOSEPALOUS 2 : having a single sepal
mono·silane \"+\ n [mon- + silane] : a colorless gas SiH_4 that is spontaneously flammable in air, is liquefiable only at a low temperature, and is formed by the action of hydrochloric acid on magnesium silicide
mono·siphonic \"+\ or **mono·siphonous** \"+\ adj [mon- + siphon- + -ic or -ous] : consisting of a single tube or row of cells (as the thallus of various red algae or the hydrocaulus of some hydrozoans) — compare POLYSIPHONIC
mono·ski \'==+\ n [mon- + ski] 1 : a single ski on which a person can stand with both feet and which is equipped with a handle bar that also serves as a brake 2 : a sled with a single runner in the center
mon·osmatic \(¦)män, (')mōn+\ adj [mon- + osmatic] : lacking a Jacobson's organ — used of a lower vertebrate in which this typical reptilian structure is absent
mono·sodium \¦== at MONO- +\ adj [mon- + sodium] : containing one atom of sodium in the molecule
mon·o·so·di·um glu·ta·mate n : a crystalline salt NaOOC-$CH_2CH_2CH(NH_2)COOH$ used for enhancing the flavor of foods (as meat or soup)
monosodium phosphate n : SODIUM PHOSPHATE 1a
mono·some \'==+,sōm\ n -s [mon- + -some] 1 : an unpaired X chromosome 2 : a chromosome lacking a synaptic mate 3 : an individual or cell lacking one or more chromosomes
¹**mono·so·mic** \¦==¦sōmik\ adj [mon- + -somic] : having one less than the diploid number of chromosomes
²**monosomic** \"\ n -s : a monosomic individual
mono·sperm \'==+,-\ n [mon- + sperm] : a monospermous plant
mono·sper·mic \¦==¦spərmik\ adj [NL monospermicus, fr. mon- + -spermicus -spermic] : involving or resulting from a single sperm cell ⟨~ fertilization⟩
mono·sper·mous \-məs\ adj [NL monospermus, fr. monomon- + -spermus -spermous] : having or producing a single seed
mono·sper·my \'==,spərmē\ n -ES [ISV mon- + -spermy] : the entry of a single fertilizing sperm into an egg — compare DISPERMY, POLYSPERMY
mono·spherical \¦==+\ adj [mon- + spherical] : having or consisting of one sphere only
mono·spondylic \"+\ adj [mon- + spondylic] : having no well-developed intercentra alternating with the true centra of the vertebrae
mono·spo·ran·gi·um \,==+spə'ranjēəm\ n [NL, fr. ISV monospore + NL -angium] : a sporangium which bears monospores
mono·spore \'==+,-\ n [ISV mon- + spore] : a simple nonmotile asexual spore in some algae exhibiting alternation of generations that is produced by a plant of the diploid generation and germinates to form another diploid plant — called also neutral spore; contrasted with tetraspore
mono·spored \¦==¦spō(ə)rd\ adj [mon- + spore + -ed] : MONOSPOROUS
mono·sporidial \"+\ adj [mon- + sporidial] : of, from, or relating to a single sporidium
mono·spor·ous \¦==¦spōrəs, mə'näspərəs\ adj [mon- + -sporous] 1 : having a single spore 2 or **monosporiferous** \¦== at MONO- +\ : reproducing by means of monospores
mono·stele \'==,stēl also ¦==¦stēlē\ n [mon- + stele] : PROTOSTELE — **mono·ste·ly** \'==,stēlē\ n -ES
¹**mono·stich** \'==,stik\ n [LL monostichum, fr. Gk monostichon, fr. neut. of monostichos consisting of one verse, fr. mon- + stichos line, verse — more at STICH] : a single verse; also : a poem of one verse
²**monostich** \"\ adj [Gk monostichos] : consisting of a single verse
mono·stich·ic \¦==¦stikik\ adj [¹monostich + -ic] : of or relating to a single verse or monostich
mo·nos·ti·chous \mə'nästəkəs\ adj [mon- + -stichous] 1 : arranged in a single row on one side of an axis 2 : consisting of a single layer or series
mono·sto·ma·ta \,== at MONO- + 'stōmədə\ n pl, cap [NL, fr. mon- + -stomata] in some classifications : a suborder of Digenea comprising trematode worms lacking a ventral sucker — **mono·sto·mate** \¦==+\ adj
¹**mono·stome** \'==,stōm\ adj [Gk monostomos, fr. mon- + -stomos -stomous] 1 : having one mouth or sucker 2 [NL Monostomata] : of or relating to the Monostomata
²**monostome** \"\ n -s : a trematode worm of the suborder Monostomata
mo·nos·to·mous \mə'nästəməs\ adj [Gk monostomos] : MONOSTOME 1
mono·stot·ic \¦== at MONO- + ¦städ·ik\ adj [mon- + Gk osteon bone + E -otic] : relating to or affecting a single bone
mono·stro·mat·ic \"+strō¦mad·ik\ adj [mon- + Gk strōmat-, strōma couch, bed + E -ic — more at STROMA] : having the cells in a single layer — used of the leaf of mosses and the thallus of algae
mono·strophe \'mänə,strōf(ē)\ n [Gk monostrophos consisting of a single strophe, fr. mon- + strophē strophe — more at STROPHE] 1 : a poem of one stanza 2 : a poem in which all the stanzas are of the same metric form
mono·strophic \¦==¦sträfik, -rōf-\ adj [Gk monostrophikos, fr. mon- + strophikos strophic — more at STROPHIC] : consisting of monostrophes
mono·stroph·ics \-ks\ n pl : monostrophic verses
mono·sty·lous \"+¦stīləs\ adj [mon- + -stylous] : having a single style
mono·substituted \"+\ adj [mon- + substituted] : having one substituent atom or group in the molecule ⟨~ acetylenes⟩ — **mono·substitution** \"+\ n
mono·sulfide \"+\ n [mon- + sulfide] : a sulfide containing one atom of sulfur in the molecule
mono·sulfonic acid \"+-\ n [mon- + sulfonic] : a compound containing one sulfonic acid group
mono·syllabic \"+\ adj [prob. fr. F monosyllabique, fr. monosyllabe + -ique -ic] 1 : having only one syllable : composed of monosyllables 2 a : using or speaking only monosyllables b : conspicuously brief in answering or commenting : pointedly terse ⟨merry where he was grave, talkative where he was ~ —Dorothy Sayers⟩ — **mono·syllabically** \"+\ adv — **mono·syllabicity** \"+\ n -ES

monosyllabic language n : a language all or nearly all of whose words are monosyllables
mono·syllable \¦== at MONO- +\ n [modif. (influenced by syllable) of MF or LL; MF monosyllabe, fr. LL monosyllabon, fr. Gk, fr. neut. of monosyllabos having one syllable, fr. mon- + syllabē syllable — more at SYLLABLE] : a word or other grammatical unit of one syllable
monosyllabon n, pl **monosyllaba** [L, fr. Gk, neut. of monosyllabos monosyllabic, fr. mon- + syllabē syllable — more at SYLLABLE] obs : MONOSYLLABLE
mono·symmetric \¦== at MONO- +\ or **mono·symmetrical** \"+\ adj [mon- + symmetric, symmetrical] 1 : MONOCLINIC 2 : symmetrical bilaterally with reference to a single plane : ZYGOMORPHIC — **mono·symmetrically** \"+\ adv — **mono·symmetry** \"+\ n
mono·symptomatic \"+\ adj [mon- + symptomatic] : exhibiting or manifested by a single principal symptom
mono·synaptic \"+\ adj [mon- + synaptic] : having or involving a single neural synapse
mono·terpene \"+\ n [mon- + terpene] : any of a class of terpenes $C_{10}H_{16}$ (as myrcene or limonene) containing two isoprene units in the molecule; also : a derivative of such a terpene
mono·thal·a·mous \"+¦thaləməs\ also **mono·thalamic** \"+\ adj [mon- + thalam- + -ous or -ic] : having one chamber : UNILOCULAR
mono·the·cal \-¦thēkəl\ adj [mon- + Gk thēkē box, case + E -al — more at TICK] : UNILOCULAR
mono·the·ism \'==(,)thē,izəm sometimes mə'näthē-\ n [mon- + -theism] : the doctrine or belief that there is but one God ⟨Christianity and the other ~s —S.E.Hyman⟩
mono·the·ist \'==,thēəst sometimes mə'näthē-\ n [mon- + -theist] : one who believes in monotheism
mono·the·is·tic \¦==(,)thē¦istik sometimes mə¦näthē¦-, -tēk\ also **mono·the·is·ti·cal** \-təkəl, -tēk\ adj : of, relating to, or characterized by monotheism — **mono·the·is·ti·cal·ly** \-tək(ə)lē, -tēk-, -li\ adv
mo·noth·e·lism \mə'näthə,lizəm\ n -s usu cap [Monothelite + -ism] : MONOTHELITISM
mo·noth·e·lite \-,līt\ also **mo·noth·e·lete** \-,lēt\ n -s usu cap [Monothelite fr. ML Monothelita, modif. (influenced by L -ita -ite) of MGk Monothelētēs, fr. Gk mon- + thelētēs one that wills, fr. thelein, ethelein to will, wish; Monothelete fr. MGk Monothelētēs — more at GILDER] : an adherent of Monothelitism
mo·noth·e·lit·ic \=¦==¦lid·ik\ also **mo·noth·e·let·ic** \-¦led·ik\ adj, usu cap : of or relating to the Monothelites or Monothelitism
mo·noth·e·lit·ism \=¦==,līd-,izəm\ also **mo·noth·e·let·ism** \-,lēd-,-\ n -s usu cap : the theological doctrine that in Christ there is but one will though two natures — opposed to Dyothelitism
mono·thematic \¦== at MONO- +\ adj [mon- + thematic] : having a single dominating theme; esp : having a theme continuing through more than one movement of a musical composition
mono·thet·ic \"+¦thed·ik\ adj [mon- + Gk thetikos fit for placing, fr. thetos placed, set (fr. tithenai to place, set) + -ikos -ic — more at DO] : positing but one essential element
mono·tint \'== at MONO- + ,-\ n [mon- + tint] 1 : a single tint or color 2 : a picture wholly or chiefly of a single color : MONOCHROME
mo·noto·car·dia \mə,näd·ə'kärdēə\ [NL, fr. mon- + Gk ōtoear, auricle (fr. ōt-, ous) + NL -cardia — more at EAR] syn of PECTINIBRANCHIA
mo·noto·car·di·ac \=¦==¦==,ak\ adj [NL Monotocardia + E -ac (as in cardiac)] : of or relating to the Pectinibranchia
¹**mo·noto·car·di·an** \-ēən\ adj [NL Monotocardia + E -an] : of or relating to the Pectinibranchia
²**monotocardian** \"\ n -s : a mollusk of the order Pectinibranchia
mo·not·o·cous \mə'näd·əkəs\ adj [mon- + Gk tokos birth, offspring — more at TOCO-] : producing a single egg or young at one time — compare POLYTOCOUS
monotomous adj [mon- + -tomous] obs : having a distinct cleavage in one direction only — used of a mineral
¹**mono·tone** \'mänə,-\ n [mon- + tone] 1 a : a succession of syllables, words, or sentences in one unvaried key or pitch ⟨speaking in an old man's ~, just too loud for ordinary conversation —G.R.Clay⟩ — compare POLYTONE b : a sound resembling a monotone ⟨the brook's ~⟩ ⟨a ~ of street noises filtered through⟩ 2 a : a single unvaried musical tone b : recitation esp. of liturgy in such a tone : INTONING c : a person not able to properly produce or distinguish between musical intervals 3 : a monotonous reiteration or recurrence : tedious repetition ⟨a ~ of flat fields watered by numerous creeks —Amer. Guide Series: Pa.⟩ 4 : uniformity of style usu. characterized by a lack of brilliance esp. in writing ⟨an odd, unconvincing, and regrettably sketchy story, told in a ~ —Brendan Gill⟩ 5 : uniformity of color ⟨the land itself is often a gray ~ —G.R.Stewart⟩
²**monotone** \"\ adj [prob. fr. F, fr. Gk monotonos — more at MONOTONOUS] 1 : MONOTONOUS ⟨the ~ sound of the sea⟩ 2 : having a uniform color ⟨her ~ suit⟩ 3 : MONOTONIC 3
³**monotone** \"\ vb [¹monotone] vt : to talk, recite, or chant in an unvaried tone : INTONE ⟨ponderous professors had monotoned us through modern literature —Ellen Hanford⟩ ~ vi : to recite or chant something in an unvaried tone ⟨listened to the choir monotoning⟩
mono·ton·ic \¦==¦tänik\ adj [¹monotone + -ic] 1 : of, relating to, or uttered in a monotone ⟨the ~ buzzing of the voices carried —James Jones⟩ 2 : producing only one musical tone 3 : being a mathematical function that either never decreases or never increases as the independent variable increases — **mono·ton·i·cal·ly** \-nək(ə)lē\ adv
mo·not·o·nist \mə'nätᵊnəst also -tn-\ n -s [monotony + -ist] : one who speaks in a monotonous manner : one addicted to or preferring monotony
mo·not·o·nize \-tᵊn,īz also -t,nīz\ vt -ED/-ING/-S [monotony + -ize] : to make monotonic or monotonous
mo·not·o·nous \-tᵊnəs also -tn-\ adj [Gk monotonos, fr. mon- + tonos tone — more at TONE] 1 : uttered or sounded in one unvarying tone : marked by a sameness of pitch and intensity ⟨an owl kept up a faint ~ hooting —Louis Bromfield⟩ ⟨tried to keep his voice calm and ~ as he spoke —Elinor Wylie⟩ 2 : having no change or variety : wearisomely uniform : REPETITIOUS ⟨the trim ~ cottages —W.F.Jenkins⟩ ⟨this waste of mud, water and ~ vegetation —Wilfred Thesiger⟩
mo·not·o·nous·ly adv : in a monotonous manner ⟨all men here looked ~ alike —Oscar Handlin⟩ ⟨the theme of rags to riches, exploited ~ but with singular success . . . runs like a bright thread through American folklore —R.B.Morris⟩
mo·not·o·nous·ness n -ES : the quality or state of being monotonous ⟨there is a profound ~ about its facts —Mark Twain⟩
mo·not·o·ny \-tᵊnē also -tn-, -i\ n -ES [Gk monotonia, fr. monotonos + -ia -y] 1 : sameness that produces boredom : lack of the variety that provides interest and stimulation : the same thing over and over : depressing uniformity ⟨the desire for change, for novelty, for a relief from the ~ of every day —Aldous Huxley⟩ ⟨the little shows and sports and wellmeant activities that relieve the ~ of toil —G.B.Shaw⟩ ⟨the ~ of the brush plains to the eastward —Kenneth Roberts⟩ 2 : sameness or uniformity of tone or sound or the utterance or use of one unvarying tone or sound ⟨a dominant rhythm persists above loose phrasing and verbal ~ —H.V.Gregory⟩
mono·top·ic \¦== at MONO- + ¦täpik\ adj [mon- + top- + -ic] : of, relating to, or characterized by monotopism
monoto·pism \'mōnə,tō,pizəm, 'mänə,-, mə'näd·ə,p-\ n -s [mon- + top- + -ism] : origin of a systematic group only once (as by mutation) or at a single location — compare POLYTOPISM
mono·tre·mal \¦== at MONO- + -¦trēməl\ or **mono·tre·mous** \-məs\ adj [monotreme + -al or -ous] : MONOTREMATOUS
mono·trema·ta \,==·'treməd·ə, -rēm-\ n pl, cap [NL, fr. mon- + -tremata] : the lowest order of Mammalia consisting of the only surviving representatives of the subclass Prototheria — see ECHIDNA, PLATYPUS
mono·trema·tous \¦==·¦tremədəs, -rēm-\ or **mono·tremate** \-māt, -,māt\ adj [monotrematous fr. NL Monotremata + E -ous; monotremate fr. NL Monotremata] : of or relating to the order Monotremata
mono·treme \'==,trēm\ n -s [NL Monotremata] : one of the Monotremata
mo·not·ri·chous \mə'nä·trəkəs\ also **mono·trich·ic** \¦== at MONO- + -¦trikik\ or **mo·not·ri·chate** \mə'nä·trəkət\ adj [mon- + -trichous or -trichate (fr. trich- + -ate) or -trichic (fr. trich- + -ic)] : having a single flagellum at one pole — used of bacteria
mono·triglyph \¦== at MONO- +\ n [L monotriglyphus monotriglyphic, fr. Gk monotriglyphos, fr. mon- + triglyphos triglyph — more at TRIGLYPH] : monotriglyphic intercolumniation
mono·triglyphic \"+\ adj : having only one triglyph over the space between two columns
mono·troch \'mänə,träk, 'mōn-\ or **mono·troche** \-rōk\ n -s [Gk monotrochos wheelbarrow, fr. mon- + trochos wheel — more at TROCHE] archaic : a one-wheeled vehicle
mo·no·tro·cha \mə'nä·trəkə\ n -s [NL, fr. mon- + -trocha] : a monotrochal larva
mo·not·ro·chal \-kəl\ adj [NL monotrocha + E -al] : having a prototroch only — used of annelid larvae
mono·tron hardness test \'mänə·,trän-, 'mō\ n [fr. Monotron, a trademark] : an indentation test that measures the load required to produce a definite penetration of steel by a standard spherical penetrator
mo·not·ro·pa \mə'nä·trəpə\ n, cap [NL, fr. Gk monotropē, fem. of monotropos living alone, fr. mon- + tropos turn, way, fr. trepein to turn — more at TROPE] : a genus of leafless fleshy saprophytic herbs (family Pyrolaceae) with solitary polypetalous flowers or with trimerous to pentamerous flowers in racemes — see HYPOPITYS, MONOTROPACEAE; INDIAN PIPE, PINESAP
mo·not·ro·pa·ce·ae \mə,nä·trə'pāsē,ē\ n pl, cap [NL, fr. Monotropa, type genus + -aceae] in some classifications : a family of saprophytic herbs of which Monotropa is the type genus
mono·troph·ic \¦== at MONO- + ¦träfik, -rōf-\ adj [mon- + -trophic] : feeding only on one kind of food
mono·trop·ic \-¦träpik\ adj [mon- + -tropic] 1 : relating to or exhibiting monotropy 2 : visiting only a single kind of flower for nectar — used of an insect; compare OLIGOTROPIC, POLYTROPIC — **mono·trop·i·cal·ly** \-pək(ə)lē\ adv
mono·trop·sis \,==·'träpsəs\ n, cap [NL, blend of Monotropa and -opsis; fr. its resemblance to Monotropa] : a genus of herbs (family Pyrolaceae) that is native to the southeastern U.S. — see CAROLINA BEECHDROPS
mo·not·ro·py \mə'nä·trəpē\ n -ES [ISV mon- + -tropy; prob. orig. formed as Ger monotropie] : the relation of two different forms of the same substance (as white and red phosphorus) that have no definite transition point since only one form (as red phosphorus) is stable and the change from the unstable form to the stable form is irreversible
mono·typ·al \¦== at MONO- + ¦tīpəl\ adj [monotype + -al] : MONOTYPIC
mono·type \'==+,-\ n [mon- + type] 1 a : the only representative of its group (as a single species constituting a genus) b : a holotype when there are no paratypes c : the type species of a monobasic genus 2 : an impression on paper of a design that has been painted usu. with the finger or a brush on a metal, glass, or similar surface
Mono·type \"\ trademark 1 — used for a typesetting apparatus consisting of a keyboard whose operation produces perforations on a roll of paper and a caster which casts and assembles individual pieces of type in justified lines in the order determined by the perforations 2 : matter produced by a Monotype machine or printing done from such matter
monotype paper n : KEYBOARD PAPER
mono·typ·ic \¦== at MONO- + ¦tipik\ adj [mon- + -typic] 1 : including a single representative — used esp. of a genus with only one species — opposed to polytypic 2 : of or relating to a Monotype machine
¹**mono·valent** \"+\ adj [ISV mon- + valent] 1 : UNIVALENT 2 : containing antibodies specific for or antigens of a single strain of an organism
²**monovalent** \"\ n -s : a univalent chromosome or individual
monovalent antibody n : BLOCKING ANTIBODY
mono·variant \"+\ adj [mon- + variant] : UNIVARIANT
mono·verticillate \"+\ adj [mon- + verticillate] : having a single whorl ⟨a ~ shell⟩
mon·ovular \(')män, (')mōn+\ adj [mon- + ovular] : derived from a single ovum — used of identical twins or their characteristic state; compare BIOVULAR
mo·nox·e·nous \mə'näksənəs\ adj [mon- + -xenous] of a parasite : living on only one kind of host
mon·oxide \mə'n, mä'n+,-\ n [ISV mon- + oxide] : an oxide containing one atom of oxygen in the molecule
mon·oxime \"+,-\ n [mon- + oxime] : a compound containing one oxime grouping
mon·o·zoa \,mänə'zōə, ,mōn-\ [NL, fr. mon- + -zoa] syn of CESTODARIA
mon·o·zo·an \¦==¦zōən\ adj [NL Monozoa + E -an] : of or relating to the Cestodaria
mono·zo·ic \¦== at MONO- + ¦zōik\ adj [mon- + -zoic] 1 : MONOZOOTIC 2 of a spore : producing one sporozoite
mono·zootic \"+\ adj [mon- + zo- + -otic] : consisting of a single zooid or individual; specif : consisting of a single differentiated unit — used of cestodarians; distinguished from polyzootic — **mono·zo·o·ty** \,==·əd·ē\ n -ES
mono·zygotic \¦==+\ adj [mon- + zygotic] of twins : produced from a single zygote : MONOVULAR
monozy·gous \"+¦zīgəs, (')mä¦näzəgəs\ adj [mon- + -zygous] : MONOZYGOTIC
mon·roe doctrine \mən'rō, 'mən,rō-\ n, usu cap M&D [fr. the Monroe Doctrine, a statement proclaimed Dec. 2, 1823 by James Monroe †1831, 5th U. S. president, to the effect that the U. S. would not brook any interference in the western hemisphere by European powers] : a foreign policy opposed to the extension of outside political, economic, and ideological systems into a nation's existing sphere of influence ⟨the Australians had already proclaimed, in their own hearts, a Monroe Doctrine for the South Pacific —W.K.Hancock⟩
mon·ro·lite \mən'rō,līt\ n -s [Monroe, town in Orange county, N. Y. + E -lite] : SILLIMANITE
mon·ro·via \mən'rōvēə\ adj, usu cap [fr. Monrovia, Liberia] : of or from Monrovia, the capital of Liberia : of the kind or style prevalent in Monrovia
¹**mons** \'mänz\ n, pl **mon·tes** \-n-,tēz\ [NL, fr. L, mountain — more at MOUNT] : a body part or area raised above or demarcated from surrounding structures (as the papilla of mucosa through which the ureter enters the bladder)
²**mons** pl of MON
³**mons** abbr, often cap monsieur
mon·sei·gneur \,män,sān¦yər(·)\ n, pl **mes·sei·gneurs** \¦mā-,sān¦yər(·), -rz\ [F, fr. OF, lit., my lord] : a French dignitary (as a prince or prelate) — used as a title of honor preceding a title of office or rank ⟨Monseigneur the Archbishop⟩ ⟨Monseigneur the Dauphin⟩; abbr. Msgr.
mon·sieur \məs(h)'yə, -yər(·), -yə; mə'si(ə)r, -iə; məs(h)'yü(ə)r, -üə, mə'shü-; as a title both syllables may be without stress or the first two sounds may be mi with secondary stress and there may or may not be secondary stress on the second syllable\ n, pl **mes·sieurs** \" or with mā or me as the first two sounds or with z at end\ [MF, lit., my lord] 1 a : a Frenchman of high rank or station ⟨would pray our ~s to think an English courtier may be wise —Shak.⟩ b : the next collateral heir to the French throne; specif : the second son or the oldest brother of the king of France 2 : MISTER — used as a title of courtesy prefixed to the name of a Frenchman; abbr. M.
mon·si·gnor \(')män¦sēnyə(r), also mən'sē- sometimes -ēn-,yō(ə)r or -ēn,yō(ə) or ¦män,sēn¦yō- or in rapid speech prob by n dissimilation mə'sē-\ n, pl **monsignors** or **monsigno·ri** \¦män,sēn¦yōrē\ [It monsignore, monsignor (when used as a title) fr. F monseigneur] 1 : a prelate of the Roman Catholic Church — used as a title of honor; abbr. Msgr. 2 : a strong purple that is redder and deeper than mauve — **mon·si·gno·ri·al** \¦män,sēn¦yōrēəl\ adj
mon·so·ni \män'sōnē\ n, pl **monsoni** or **monsonis** usu cap 1 : a Cree people of the Moose river region, northeastern Ontario, Canada 2 : a member of the Monsoni people
mon·soon \(')män¦sün\ n -s [obs. D monssoen, fr. Pg monção, alter. of moução, fr. Ar mawsim time, season] 1 : a wind blow-

ing part of the year from one direction alternating with a wind from the opposite direction **2 a :** a periodic wind in various latitudes in the Indian ocean and southern Asia generally which blows from the southwest from the latter part of April to the middle of October and from the northeast from about the middle of October to April **b :** the season of the southwest monsoon in India and adjacent countries which is a season of heavy rainfall **:** rainy season — **mon·soon·al** \-nᵊl\ *adj*

monsoon forest *n* **:** open deciduous or partially deciduous forest of tropical regions that develops in areas with alternating seasons of heavy rainfall and prolonged drought

¹mon·ster \ˈmänztə(r), -n(t)st-\ *n* -S [ME *monstre*, fr. MF, fr. L *monstrum* evil omen, monster, monstrosity, prob. fr. *monēre* to remind, warn — more at MIND] **1** *obs* **:** something unnaturally marvelous **:** PRODIGY **2 a :** an animal or plant departing greatly in form or structure from the usual type of its species — compare TERATOLOGY 2 **b :** one who shows a deviation from the normal in behavior or character ⟨at the heart of the legends the researcher too often discovers a stuffed shirt, a faker, or a moral ~ —DeLancey Ferguson⟩ **3 a :** a legendary animal usu. of great size and ferocity that has a form either partly brute and partly human or compounded of elements from several brute forms **b :** a threatening force **:** an engulfing power ⟨the same ~ —Destiny . . . that rolls every civilization to doom —W.L.Sullivan⟩ ⟨that ~ of a forest fire threatening the town⟩ ⟨the swollen rivers . . . are ~*s* —Gordon Cuyler⟩ **4 a :** an animal of strange and often terrifying shape ⟨visualize this scaleless ~, eight or nine feet long, sprawling in the shade by the side of the mud pools —W.E.Swinton⟩ **b :** a living thing unusually large for its kind ⟨a ~ of nine pounds . . . was said to be the largest weakfish —Hamilton Basso⟩ **c :** something huge and often of unmanageable proportions ⟨better a variety of different sandwiches than one ~ which may prove unwieldy —Al Hine⟩ ⟨a great ~ of a book —*New Yorker*⟩ **5 :** something monstrous; *esp* **:** a person of unnatural or excessive ugliness, deformity, wickedness, or cruelty ⟨the woman is a ~ of egoism —Sylvia T.Warner⟩

²monster \"\ *vt* -ED/-ING/-S **1** *obs* **:** to make a monster of ⟨sure her offense must be of such unnatural degree that ~*s* it —Shak.⟩ **2 :** to exhibit as unusual or wonderful

³monster \"\ *adj* **:** enormous in size, extent, or numbers ⟨the shiny black back of a ~ sperm whale —H.A.Chippendale⟩ ⟨new ~ construction is announced —Flora Lewis⟩ ⟨~ entertainment proves a colossal bore —*Saturday Rev.*⟩ ⟨drew up a ~ petition —James Leasor⟩

mon·stera \ˈmänztərə, -n(t)st-\ *n* [NL, perh. irreg. fr. L *monstrum* monster — more at MONSTER] **1** *cap* **:** a genus of tropical American climbing plants (family Araceae) having deeply incised and perforated leaves and a spadix enclosed in a yellow concave spathe — see CERIMAN **2** -S **:** any plant of the genus *Monstera*

monsterlike \ˈ≈≈,≈\ *adj* **:** having the appearance or qualities of a monster ⟨most ~ be shown —Shak.⟩

mon·strance \ˈmänztrən(t)s, -n(t)st-\ *n* -S [MF, fr. ML *monstrantia*, fr. L *monstrant-*, *monstrans* (pres. part. of *monstrare* to show, instruct) + *-ia* -y — more at MUSTER] **1 :** a vessel in which the consecrated Host is exposed to receive the adoration of the faithful **2 :** a receptacle holding sacred relics when exposed to view

monstrance 1

mon·stros·i·ty \mänzˈträsəd·ē, -n(t)ˈst-, -ətē, -i\ *n* -ES [LL *monstrositas*, fr. L *monstrosus*, *monstruosus* monstrous (fr. *monstrum* monster + *-osus* -ous) + *-itas* -ity — more at MONSTER] **1 a :** a malformation of a plant or animal **b :** something showing deviation from the normal ⟨whatever a woman has of intelligence and worth . . . is to be excised as a superfluous growth, a ~ —Mary Austin⟩ **:** FREAK 3b **2** *obs* **:** MONSTER 3a **3 :** the quality or state of being monstrous ⟨to be lost . . . does not imply any uncommonness of vice or ~ of wickedness —A.B.Davidson⟩ **4 a :** an object of terrifying size or force or complexity ⟨at night, we steamed through a lane of . . . *monstrosities* of ice —H.A.Chippendale⟩ ⟨the invention of the atomic bomb and the moral issues in . . . creating this ~ —Harrison Smith⟩ ⟨an effective start was made in cleaning up the political and economic ~ which passes as our federal tax system —D.A.Reed⟩ **b :** an excessively bad or shocking example **:** a hideous thing ⟨the day of bigness . . . resulted in some real *monstrosities* of landscape art —R.M. Coates⟩ ⟨a ~ of a Victorian chaise longue —M.R.Ridley⟩

¹mon·strous \ˈmänztrəs, -n(t)st-\ *adj* [ME *monstrous*, fr. MF *monstrueux*, fr. L *monstruosus*, fr. *monstrum* monster + *-osus* -ous — more at MONSTER] **1** *obs* **:** STRANGE, UNNATURAL ⟨this ingrateful seat of ~ friends —Shak.⟩ **2 :** having extraordinary often overwhelming size **:** unusually and often unpleasantly big **:** HUGE, GIGANTIC, MAMMOTH ⟨the moon like a ~ crystal —G.K.Chesterton⟩ ⟨a ~ precipice —Thomas Gray⟩ ⟨clad in ~ coat and huge shoes —C.F.Wittke⟩ ⟨the task may well appear ~ —C.W.Shumaker⟩ ⟨he seemed of ~ bulk and significance —G.D.Brown⟩ **3 a :** having the qualities or appearance of a monster ⟨the subtle, ~ horror that broke forth last night and went prowling about the old hallways —W.H.Wright⟩ ⟨hate, a ~ sun that dissolves the bones in the body —Edith Sitwell⟩ **b** *obs* **:** teeming with monsters ⟨under the whelming tide visit'st the bottom of the ~ world —John Milton⟩ **4 a :** extraordinary because of ugliness or viciousness **:** ATROCIOUS, HORRIBLE ⟨the ~ gang who were bringing his country to ruins —Harrison Smith⟩ ⟨a ~ joke, a deception of matchless cruelty —B.R.Redman⟩ **b :** shockingly wrong or ridiculous ⟨the legend assumed ~ proportions —Louis Untermeyer⟩ ⟨the search for truth was largely diverted . . . into a ~ and deadening discussion —P.E.More⟩ **5 :** deviating greatly from the natural form or character **:** ABNORMAL, MALFORMED ⟨a ~ fetus⟩ ⟨a ~ melon⟩ **6 :** very great — used as an intensive ⟨the ~ agnostic —Alistair Cooke⟩ ⟨awakened . . . by a ~ hammering on his door —G.D.Brown⟩

syn PRODIGIOUS, TREMENDOUS, STUPENDOUS, MONUMENTAL: MONSTROUS applies to what is like a monster usu. in being abnormally large or often in being deformed or fabulously formed ⟨a procession of some of the most obese and *monstrous* types of humanity. Almost naked, they wandered around the arena, mountains of flesh glistening in the electric light —Hugh Walpole⟩ ⟨*monstrous*, like a doll that is alive and bigger than the child who tries to hold it —Babette Deutsch⟩ ⟨a *monstrous* kind of a creature who had never had but one leg, and that in the middle of his body —R.L.Stevenson⟩ PRODIGIOUS describes what is extraordinarily vast or immense often unexpectedly or disproportionately ⟨notice his *prodigious* strength. His hand actually seemed like a steel vice that could have crushed mine —Bram Stoker⟩ ⟨the demand was *prodigious*. Almost unimaginably huge quantities of cotton were consumed in its manufacture and virtual armies of men were engaged in making it —A.C.Morrison⟩ TREMENDOUS may apply to the huge or gigantic that arouses dread or awe ⟨the forces that tie an atom together are *tremendous* —Waldemar Kaempffert⟩ ⟨the younger rock slips from time to time, as some earth movement takes place, and the resultant *tremendous* jar is felt throughout the region —*Amer. Guide Series: Wash.*⟩ STUPENDOUS describes what stuns or amazes, usu. because of great size or number, vast complexity, or awesome force ⟨mountain ranges, the most *stupendous* in the world —Faubion Bowers⟩ ⟨a ray of light tells us of a *stupendous* catastrophe that occurred in the constellation —Waldemar Kaempffert⟩ MONUMENTAL refers to that which is impressive or massive enough to serve as a monument — often used figuratively ⟨statues are most successful when they are massive, *monumental*, and have something approaching an architectural context —John Dewey⟩ ⟨the *monumental* character demanded by Americans in their public buildings is achieved by the huge 32-story tower —*Amer. Guide Series: N.Y.*⟩ **syn** see in addition OUTRAGEOUS

²monstrous \"\ *adv*, *chiefly dial* **:** EXCEEDINGLY, VERY ⟨~ pretty girl she was too —Archibald Marshall⟩ ⟨she thought it ~ vulgar —Harrietta Wilson⟩

mon·strous·ly *adv* **:** in a monstrous manner ⟨so ~ inept a job of reasoning —Irving Brant⟩ ⟨whales . . . seem quite ~ and impossibly large —Alan Moorehead⟩

mon·strous·ness *n* -ES **:** the quality or state of being monstrous ⟨the ~ of the man he plays is kept in bounds — he is scary, but not too scary —*Saturday Rev.*⟩

mon·stru·os·i·ty \,mänztrəˈwäsəd·ē, -n(t)st-, -ətē, -i\ *n* -ES [ME *monstruosite*, modif. of LL *monstrositas* — more at MONSTROSITY] *archaic* **:** MONSTROSITY

mon·stru·ous \ˈmänztrəwəs, -n(t)st-\ *adj* [ME, fr. L *monstruosus* — more at MONSTROUS] *archaic* **:** MONSTROUS

mons ve·ne·ris \-ˈvenərə̇s\ *n*, *pl* **montes veneris** [NL, lit., eminence of Venus or of venery] **:** a rounded eminence of fatty tissue upon the pubic symphysis of the human female

mon·ta·dale \ˈmäntə,dāl\ *n* [*Montana* state + *dale* (valley)] **1** *usu cap* **:** an American breed of white-faced hornless sheep developed by crossing Cheviot and Columbia sheep and noted for its efficient production of a heavy fleece on a body of good meat conformation **2** -S *often cap* **:** a sheep of the Montadale breed

¹mon·tage \(ˈ)män¦täzh, -tȧzh\ *n* -S [F *montage*, fr. *monter* to mount + *-age* — more at MOUNT] **1 a :** the act or photographic process of combining several distinct pictures so that they often blend with or into each other to produce a composite picture which may or may not appear to be made up of separate pictures **b :** a picture made by montage **2 :** an artistic composition made by combining heterogeneous elements **3 a :** a style of film editing in which contrasting shots or sequences are juxtaposed for the purpose of suggesting a total idea or impression **b :** an impressionistic sequence of images linked usu. by dissolves or superimpositions and introduced into a film or television program to develop a single theme, suggest a state of mind, or bridge a time lapse **4 :** a musical composite of heterogeneous themes or fragments usu. played in quick succession and used to represent or bridge a gap in the sequence of time **5 :** a quick succession of snatches of dialogue, music, and sound effects used as a technique in radio writing **6 a :** a literary technique in which heterogeneous images, themes, or fragments of ideas are juxtaposed to produce a single total effect **b :** a literary composite made by means of such technique **7 :** something felt to resemble a montage ⟨for a few seconds his mind held in ~ all the wrecked towns —Norman Mailer⟩ ⟨recalls this phase of his childhood as a dizzy ~ of whistles, intermeshing gears, ladles spilling ore —R.L.Taylor⟩

²montage \"\ *vt* -ED/-ING/-S **:** to combine into or depict in a montage

mon·ta·gnais \¦mäntən¦yā\ *n*, *pl* **montagnais** \-ā(z)\ *also* **monta·gnaises** \-āz\ *usu cap* [F, fr. *montagne* mountain, fr. OF *montaigne* — more at MOUNTAIN] **1 :** CHIPEWYAN **2 a :** an Indian people of northern Quebec, Canada **b :** a member of such people **3 :** a dialect of Cree

mon·ta·gnard \-¦yär(d)\ *n*, *pl* **montagnard** \"\ *or* **montagnards** \", -r(d)z\ *usu cap* [F, lit., mountaineer, fr. *montagne* + *-ard*] **1 :** one of several Athapaskan peoples (as the Sekani and Kaska) in the Rocky mountains of Canada **2 :** a member of the Montagnard people **3 :** SEKANI 2

mon·taign·esque \¦män·,tā¦nesk\ *adj*, *usu cap* [F, fr. Michel Eyquem de *Montaigne* †1592 Fr. essayist + F *-esque*] **:** of, relating to, or having the characteristics of the essayist Montaigne, his literary style, or his thought

¹mon·tana \(ˈ)män·¦tanə\ *adj*, *usu cap* [*Montana*, state in the northwestern U. S., fr. L *montana* mountainous regions, fr. neut. pl. of *montanus* of a mountain, mountainous — more at MOUNTAIN] **1 :** of or from the state of Montana ⟨a *Montana* dude ranch⟩ **:** of the kind or style prevalent in Montana **:** MONTANAN **2 :** of or relating to the subdivision of the No. American Cretaceous between the Colorado and the Laramie — see GEOLOGIC TIME table

²montana \"\ *n* **1** -S *often cap* **:** a sheep bred or raised in Montana **2 a** *or* **montana number one** *usu cap M&N&O* **:** a breed of productive meat-type hogs developed by crossing Hampshires with Danish Landrace — called also *Hamprace* **b** -S *often cap* **:** an animal of this breed

³mon·ta·ña \män·ˈtanyə\ *n* -S [AmerSp, fr. Sp, mountain, fr. (assumed) VL *montanea* — more at MOUNTAIN] **:** a forested region of the eastern slopes of the Andes

montana grayling *n*, *usu cap M* **:** a fish of a variety (*Thymallus signifer montanus*) of the Arctic grayling that is restricted to various tributaries of the Missouri river

¹mon·tan·an \(ˈ)män·¦tanən\ *or* **mon·tan·ian** \-anēən, -anyən\ *adj*, *usu cap* [*Montana* state + E *-an*, *-ian*] **:** of, relating to, or characteristic of Montana or Montanans

²montanan \"\ *or* **montanian** \"\ *n* -S *cap* **:** a native or resident of the state of Montana

mon·tane \(ˈ)män¦tān\ *adj* [L *montanus* of a mountain, mountainous — more at MOUNTAIN] **1 a :** of, relating to, or being the biogeographic zone made up of relatively moist cool upland slopes below timberline and characterized by the presence of large evergreen trees as a dominant life form — compare ALPINE, SUBALPINE **b :** growing in this zone ⟨~ evergreens⟩ **2 :** of, relating to, or made up of montane plants or animals ⟨a ~ flora⟩

mon·tan·ic acid \(ˈ)män·¦tanik-\ *n* [*montan* (*wax*) + *-ic*] **:** a crystalline fatty acid $C_{27}H_{55}COOH$ or $C_{28}H_{57}COOH$ found free or in the form of esters in montan wax, beeswax, and other natural waxes

mon·ta·nism \ˈmäntə,nizəm\ *n* -S *usu cap* [*Montanus* + E *-ism*] **:** the doctrines of Montanists

¹mon·ta·nist \-nəst\ *n* -S *usu cap* [*Montanus*, 2d cent. A.D. Christian schismatic of Phrygia in Asia Minor + E *-ist*] **:** a follower of Montanus who claimed that the Holy Spirit dwelt in him

²montanist \"\ *or* **mon·ta·nis·tic** \¦≈≈¦nistik\ *adj*, *usu cap* **:** of or relating to Montanists or their doctrines **:** embracing Montanism

mon·tan·ite \mänˈ·ta,nīt\ *n* -S [*Montana* state + E *-ite*] **:** a mineral $Bi_2(OH)_4TeO_6$ consisting of a basic bismuth tellurate

mon·ta·nize \ˈmäntə,nīz\ *vi* -ED/-ING/-S *usu cap* [*Montanus* + E *-ize*] **:** to adhere to Montanism

mon·tan wax \ˈmän·,tan-\ *n* [L *montanus* of a mountain — more at MOUNTAIN] **:** a hard brittle high-melting mineral wax that is brown when crude but yellow to white after refining, that is obtained usu. from lignites by extraction with solvents, and that is used chiefly in polishes, carbon paper, and insulating compositions

mont blanc ruby \(ˈ)mōⁿ¦bläⁿ-\ *n*, *usu cap M&B* [fr. *Mont Blanc*, mountain in southeastern France] **:** RUBASSE

mont·bray·ite \mäntˈbrā,īt, mōⁿ ˈ-\ *n* -S [*Montbray*, Quebec province, Canada, its locality + E *-ite*] **:** a mineral Au_2Te_3 consisting of telluride of gold

¹mont·bre·tia \mäntˈbrēsh(ē)ə\ *n* -S [NL, fr. A. F. E. Coquebert de *Montbret* †1801 French naturalist + NL *-ia*] **:** a plant of *Tritonia* or the closely related genus *Crocosmia*; *esp* **:** a hybrid cormose plant (*Crocosmia* × *crocosmiiflora*) that is widely cultivated for its spikes of showy yellow or orange flowers

²montbretia \"\ [NL, fr. A. F. E. C. de *Montbret* + NL *-ia*] *syn of* TRITONIA

mont-de-pié·té \mōⁿd(ə)pyāˈtā\ *n*, *pl* **monts-de-piété** \"\ [F, fr. It *monte di pietà*, lit., bank of pity] **:** a public pawnbroker's office for lending money at reasonable rates

mon·te \ˈmäntē\ *n* -S [Sp, lit., bank, fr. It, mountain, heap, bank, fr. L *mont-*, *mons* mountain — more at MOUNT] **1 a** *or* **monte bank :** a card game in which players select any two of four cards faced in a layout and bet that one of them will be matched before the other as cards are dealt one at a time from the pack **b :** THREE-CARD MONTE **2** [MexSp, fr. Sp] *Southwest* **:** an uncultivated area covered usu. densely with spiny shrubs or small trees (as mesquite) **:** CHAPARRAL — compare PAMPA

mon·te·bra·site \,mäntēˈbrä,zīt\ *n* -S [F, fr. *Montebras*, France, its locality + F *-ite*] **:** a mineral $LiAlPO_4(OH)$ consisting of a basic phosphate of aluminum and lithium isomorphous with amblygonite and natromontebrasite

mon·teith \(ˈ)män·¦tēth, mən·ˈ-\ *also* **mon·teth** \", -teth\ *n* -S [after *Monteith* (*Monteigh*), 17th cent. Scotchman who wore a cloak scalloped at the bottom] **:** a large usu. silver punch bowl that has a scalloped rim

monteith

monte–jus \(ˈ)mänt¦jüs, (ˈ)mōⁿ ¦zhü\ *n* [F, fr. *monter* to mount, raise + *jus* juice — more at MOUNT, JUICE] **:** an apparatus for raising a liquid by pressure of air or steam in a reservoir containing the liquid — compare ACID EGG

¹mon·te·ne·grin \¦mäntə¦nēgrən\ *adj*, *usu cap* [*Montenegro*, region in southwestern Yugoslavia + E *-in*] **1 :** of, relating to, or characteristic of Montenegro **2 :** of, relating to, or characteristic of the people of Montenegro

²montenegrin \"\ *also* **mon·te·ne·grine** \"\ *n* -S *cap* **:** a native or inhabitant of Montenegro

mon·te·ra \män·ˈterə\ *n* -S [Sp, fr. *montero* hunter, fr. *monte* mountain, forested region + *-ero* (fr. L *-arius* -ary) — more at MONTE] **:** a cloth cap or hat; *specif* **:** the soft black bicorne hat worn by bullfighters

mon·te·rey cheese \¦mäntə¦rā-\ *also* **monterey** *or* **monterey jack** *n*, *usu cap M&J* [fr. *Monterey* county, Calif.] **:** jack cheese of low moisture content

monterey cypress *n*, *usu cap M* [fr. *Monterey* Bay, Calif.] **:** a tall California cypress (*Cupressus macrocarpa*) endemic on Monterey Bay and now widely used for ornament, reforestation, and shelterbelt planting

monterey halibut *n*, *usu cap M* [fr. *Monterey* Bay, Calif.] **:** CALIFORNIA HALIBUT

monterey pine *n*, *usu cap M* [fr. *Monterey* county Calif.] **:** a southern California pine (*Pinus radiata*) that is often 90 feet high and has leaves in fascicles of two or three, cones lopsided, and cone scales with minute prickles

monterey spanish mackerel *n*, *usu cap M&S* [fr. *Monterey* Bay, Calif.] **:** an unspotted mackerel (*Scomberomorus concolor*) that is found off the California coast and is related to the Spanish mackerel

mon·te·ro \män·ˈte(,)rō\ *n* -S [Sp — more at MONTERA] **1 :** HUNTSMAN **2 :** a round cap with a flap worn by huntsmen **3 :** a forester or ranger in the Philippines

mon·ter·rey \¦mäntə¦rā\ *adj*, *usu cap* [fr. *Monterrey*, Mexico] **:** of or from the city of Monterrey, Mexico **:** of the kind or style prevalent in Monterrey

montes *pl of* MONS

mon·tes·so·ri·an \¦mäntə¦sōrēən\ *adj*, *usu cap M* [Maria *Montessori* †1952 Ital. physician & educator + E *-an*] **:** of, following, or relating to a system for training young children emphasizing free physical activity, informal and individual instruction, early development of writing and reading, and extended sensory motor training

mon·te·video \¦mäntəvə¦dā,ō *also* -¦vidē,ō\ *adj*, *usu cap* [fr. *Montevideo*, Uruguay] **:** of or from Montevideo, the capital of Uruguay **:** of the kind or style prevalent in Montevideo

mon·te·zu·ma cypress \¦mäntə¦zümə-\ *n*, *usu cap M* [prob. after *Montezuma* II †1520 Aztec ruler at the time of the Spanish conquest of Mexico] **:** AHUEHUETE

mont·gol·fi·er *or* **mon·gol·fi·er** \män(t)ˈgälfēə(r), mōⁿˈgälfē,ā\ *n* -S [after Joseph M. *Montgolfier* †1810 and Jacques E. *Montgolfier* †1799 French inventors who built the first practical fire balloon] **:** FIRE BALLOON 1

¹mont·gom·ery \-mən(t)ˈgəmrē, (ˈ)män(t)ˈgəm-, -ri *also* (ˈ)män(t)¦gäm- *sometimes* ¦mən(t)¦gəm- *or* -mər-\ *adj*, *usu cap* [fr. *Montgomery*, Alabama] **:** of or from Montgomery, the capital of Alabama **:** of the kind or style prevalent in Montgomery

²montgomery \"\ *n*, *usu cap* [fr. *Montgomery*, district in Pakistan where the breed originated] **:** SAHIWAL

mont·gom·ery·ite \-¦,īt\ *n* -S [Arthur *Montgomery* *b*1909 Am. geologist + E *-ite*] **:** a mineral $Ca_4Al_5(PO_4)_6(OH)_5.11H_2O$ consisting of a hydrous basic phosphate of calcium and aluminum

mont·gom·ery·shire \mən(t)ˈ≈(≈)≈,shi(ə)r, -,shər, män(t)- *sometimes* ,mən(t)-\ *adj*, *usu cap* [fr. *Montgomeryshire* or *Montgomery*, county in Wales] **:** of or from the county of Montgomery, Wales **:** of the kind or style prevalent in Montgomery

month \ˈmən(t)th\ *n*, *pl* **months** \ˈmən(t)s, -n(t)ths\ [ME

MONTHS OF THE PRINCIPAL CALENDARS

GREGORIAN[1] name	number of days	JEWISH name	number of days	MUHAMMADAN name	number of days	HINDU[5] name
January begins 10 days after winter solstice	31	Tishri	30	Muharram[4] in A.H. 1391 began February 27, 1971	30	Chait[6] (March-April)
February in leap years	28 29	Heshvan	29 or 30	Safar	29	Baisakh (April-May)
March	31	Kislev	29 or 30	Rabi I	30	Jeth (May-June)
April	30	Tebet	29	Rabi II	29	Asarh (June-July)
May	31	Shebat	30	Jumada I	30	Sawan (July-August)
June	30	Adar[2]	29 or 30	Jumada II	29	Bhadon (August-September)
July	31	Nisan[3]	30	Rajab	30	Asin (September-October)
August	31	Iyar	29	Sha'ban	29	Kartik (October-November)
September	30	Sivan	30	Ramadan	30	Aghan (November-December)
October	31	Tammuz	29	Shawwal	29	Pus (December-January)
November	30	Ab	30	Dhu'l-Qa'dah	30	Magh (January-February)
December	31	Elul	29	Dhu'l-Hijja in leap years	29 30	Phagun (February-March)

[1]The equinoxes occur on March 21 and September 23, the solstices on June 22 and December 22.

[2]In leap years Adar is followed by Veadar or Adar Sheni, an intercalary month of 29 days.

[3]Anciently called Abib; the first month of the postexilic calendar; sometimes called the first month of the ecclesiastical year.

[4]Retrogresses through the seasons; the Muhammadan year is lunar and each month begins at the approximate new moon; the year 1 A.H. began on Friday, July 16, A.D. 622.

[5]An extra month is inserted after every month in which two new moons occur (once in three years). The intercalary month has the name of the one that precedes it.

[6]Baisakh is sometimes considered the first month of the Hindu year.

moneth, month, fr. OE *mōnath;* akin to OHG *mānōd* month, ON *mānathr,* Goth *menoths* month, *mena* moon — more at MOON] **1** : a measure of time corresponding or nearly corresponding to the period of the moon's revolution: as **a** : a period of approximately four weeks, 30 days, or 1/12 of a year based primarily on the period of the moon's revolution and cycle of phase changes — see ANOMALISTIC MONTH, NODICAL MONTH, SIDEREAL MONTH, SYNODIC MONTH, TROPICAL MONTH **b** : one of the twelve portions into which the year is divided in the Gregorian calendar; *also* : a similar portion of a year in any calendar **c** : a period of time about the length of a lunar month but not necessarily coinciding with a calendar month **d** : *months, pl* : an indefinite usu. extended period of time ⟨been asking you to come forward for ~s —Graham Greene⟩ **2 a** *archaic* : a lunar month in common law **b** : a period of time presumed by statute in the U. S. and Great Britain to mean a calendar month **3** : one ninth of the typical duration of human pregnancy ⟨she was in her eighth ~⟩ — **month of sundays** *usu cap S* : an indefinitely long time ⟨hadn't been anywhere for a *month of Sundays*⟩

¹month·ly \ˈmən(t)thlē, -li\ *adv* [*month* + *-ly* (adv. suffix)] : once a month : by the month ⟨the annuity is payable semiannually, quarterly, or ~ —J.B.Maclean⟩

²monthly \"\ *adj* [*month* + *-ly* (adj. suffix)] **1** : of or relating to a month: as **a** : payable every month ⟨~ allowances to parents for the maintenance . . . of the child —*Current Biog.*⟩ **b** : reckoned by the month ⟨an average ~ wage⟩ **c** : based on a month ⟨a ~ rate⟩ ⟨~ statistics⟩ **2** : having a duration of one month : completed in a month ⟨the ~ revolution of the moon⟩ **3** : occurring, appearing, or being made, done, or acted upon every month or once a month ⟨produces a ~ television show⟩ ⟨a ~ magazine⟩

³monthly \"\ *n* -ES **1** : a periodical that is published regularly once a month **2 monthlies** *pl* : a menstrual period

monthly concert *n* : a monthly meeting formerly held in some Protestant Christian churches for the purpose of offering concerted prayer for missions

monthly epact *n* : EPACT 1b

monthly meeting *n, usu cap both Ms* **1** : an organizational unit of the Society of Friends made up of one or several local congregations — see QUARTERLY MEETING **2** : a session of a Monthly Meeting

month's mind *n* [ME *moneth mynde,* fr. *moneth* month + *mynde* mind] **1** *Roman Catholicism* : a requiem mass for a person a month after his death **2** *Brit* : strong desire : INCLINATION ⟨I see you have a *month's mind* to them —Shak.⟩

mon·tia \ˈmäntēə\ *n, cap* [NL, fr. Giuseppe *Monti* †1760 Ital. botanist & NL *-ia*] : a small genus of densely tufted annual herbs (family Portulacaceae) having opposite fleshy leaves, flowers with two sepals and three white petals, and a three-seeded capsule — see BLINKS, TOAD LILY, WATER CHICKWEED

mon·ti·cel·lite \ˌmäntəˈseˌlīt, -ˈche-\ *n* -S [Teodoro *Monticelli* †1845 Ital. naturalist + E *-ite*] : a mineral $CaMgSiO_4$ consisting of a colorless or gray calcium magnesium silicate related to olivine

mon·ti·cle \ˈmäntəkəl\ *n* -S [F *monticule* — more at MONTICULE] : a little hill

mon·tic·u·late \mänˈtikyələt\ *adj* [*monticule* + *-ate*] : having monticules

mon·ti·cule \ˈmäntəˌkyül\ *n* -S [F, fr. LL *monticulus,* dim. of L *mont-, mons* mountain — more at MOUNT] **1** : a little mount : a small elevation or prominence : HILLOCK **2** : a subordinate cone of a volcano

mon·ti·cu·lip·ora \ˌmäntəkyəˈlipərə\ *n, cap* [NL, fr. LL *monticulus* + NL *-pora*] : a genus of fossil bryozoans forming massive zoaria similar to coral and composed of polygonal mostly thin-walled zooecia and represented by numerous species in the Ordovician and extending into the Silurian — **mon·ti·cu·lip·o·rid·e·an** \ˌ≈≈≈ˌ≈≈ˈridēən\ *adj or n* — **mon·ti·cu·lip·o·roid** \ˌ≈≈≈ˈ≈≈ˌrȯid\ *adj or n*

mon·tic·u·lose \mänˈtikyəˌlōs\ *adj* [LL *monticulus* + E *-ose*] : covered with small eminences

mon·tic·u·lous \-ləs\ *adj* [ML *monticulosus,* fr. LL *monticulus* + L *-osus* -ous] : MONTICULATE

mon·tic·u·lus \-ləs\ *n* -ES [LL — more at MONTICULE] **1** : MONTICULE **2** [NL, fr. LL] : the median dorsal projection of the cerebellum

mon·til·la \mänˈtilə\ *n* -S [Sp, fr. *Montilla,* town in Spain] : a very pale dry sherry

mont·mar·trite \mäntˈmärˌtrīt\ *n* -S [F, fr. *Montmartre,* section of Paris, France, its locality + F *-ite*] : gypsum from Montmartre

mont·mo·ril·lon·ite \ˌmäntməˈriləˌnīt\ *n* -S [F, fr. *Montmorillon,* Dept. Vienne, France + F *-ite*] : a soft clay mineral $RMgAl_5Si_{12}O_{30}(OH)_6 \cdot nH_2O$ with R representing exchangeable bases that is usu. white, grayish, pale red, or blue and that consists of a hydrous aluminum silicate with considerable capacity for exchanging part of the aluminum for magnesium, alkalies, and other bases — compare HECTORITE — **mont·mo·ril·lon·it·ic** \ˌ≈≈ˌ≈≈ˈnid·ik\ *adj*

mont·pe·lier \(ˈ)mäntˈpēlyə(r), -ˈpil-\ *adj, usu cap* [fr. *Montpelier,* Vt.] : of or from Montpelier, the capital of Vermont ⟨*Montpelier* granite⟩ : of the kind or style prevalent in Montpelier

mont·pel·lier green \ˌmōⁿpelˈyā-\ *n, often cap M* [prob. fr. *Montpellier,* city in southern France] : VERDIGRIS 4

montpellier yellow *n* **1** *usu cap M* : CASSEL YELLOW 1 **2** *often cap M* : ORPIMENT 2

mon·tra·chet \ˌmōⁿträˈshā\ *n* -S *usu cap* [F, fr. *Montrachet,* vineyard in Dept. Côte-d'Or, France] : a white Burgundy wine

mon·tre \ˈmōⁿtrə\ *n* -S [F, lit., show, display, fr. MF, fr. *montrer* to show, fr. L *monstrare* — more at MUSTER] **1** : an open diapason or other pipe-organ stop having its pipes displayed as a part of the organ case **2** : PYROMETRIC CONE

mon·tre·al \ˌmän·trēˈȯl, ˌmən-\ *adj, usu cap* [fr. *Montreal,* Canada] : of or from the city of Montreal, Quebec : of the kind or style prevalent in Montreal

mon·tre·al·er \-lə(r)\ *n* -S *cap* [*Montreal,* Canada + E *-er*] : a native or inhabitant of Montreal

mon·troy·dite \mänˈtrȯiˌdīt\ *n* -S [*Montroyd* Sharpe, 20th cent. Am. mine owner + E *-ite*] : a mineral HgO consisting of mercuric oxide

monts-de-piété *pl of* MONT-DE-PIÉTÉ

mon·ture \ˈmänchə(r)\ *n* -S [F, fr. MF, fr. *monter* to mount + *-ure* — more at MOUNT] **1** : a frame or setting esp. for a jewel **2** : a manner of mounting or setting (as a jewel)

mon·tu·vio \mänˈtüvēˌō\ *also* **mon·tu·bio** \-bēˌō\ *n* -S [AmerSp, fr. Sp *monte* mountain, forested region — more at MONTE] : an Ecuadorian of mixed white, Indian, and Negro descent

¹mon·u·ment \ˈmänyəmənt\ *n* -S [ME, fr. L *monumentum, monimentum,* fr. *monēre* to remind + *-mentum* -ment — more at MIND] **1** *obs* : a burial vault : SEPULCHER ⟨her body sleeps in Capel's~, and her immortal part with angels lives —Shak.⟩ **2** *archaic* : a written legal document or record : TREATISE ⟨the critical study of the ~s of Roman and feudal law —Mark Pattison⟩ **3 a** : something that by surviving represents or testifies to the greatness or achievement esp. of an individual or an age ⟨visible ~s to the early struggles of the pioneers . . . are the old forts —*Amer. Guide Series: Maine*⟩ ⟨the circular world map drawn on a single skein of vellum . . . is one of the great cartographic ~s —*Brit. Book News*⟩ ⟨whose life work was a ~ to pure science —H.J.Muller⟩ **b** (1) : a conspicuous instance : a notable example ⟨the great Connecticut dictionary stood as a ~ of New England learning —Van Wyck Brooks⟩ ⟨that speech . . . was a model, or rather a ~, of beautiful English utterance —George Sampson⟩ ⟨that ~ of dignity would never connive at anything —Margery Allingham⟩ (2) : one of unusual prominence : a distinguished figure ⟨the answer must be sought in the period before the man became a ~ —G.W.Johnson⟩ ⟨made himself into a ~ within his own lifetime —Walter Millis⟩ **4** : a structure (as a pillar, stone, or building) erected or maintained in memory of the dead or to preserve the remembrance of a person, event, or action ⟨the Lincoln Memorial is a ~ to a great president⟩ ⟨~s celebrating the victories of war —R.B.Fosdick⟩ ⟨the first ~ in Italy to depict Christ as a worker —*Time*⟩ **5** *archaic* : an identifying mark : EVIDENCE; *also* : PORTENT, SIGN ⟨gaze . . . as if they saw some wondrous ~, some comet or unusual prodigy —Shak.⟩ **6** *obs* : a carved statue : EFFIGY ⟨if the quick fire of youth light not your mind, you are no maiden but a ~ —Shak.⟩ **7** : a natural or artificial but permanent object serving to indicate a limit or to mark a boundary (as a lake, stream, blazed tree, iron pip) **8** : a natural feature (as a mountain or canyon) or an area of special historic or scientific interest (as a battle site or fossil remains) that is set aside by a local or national government as public property **9** : a rock pinnacle or column resulting from erosion and resembling a man-made monument — compare HOODOO **10** : a written tribute : TESTIMONIAL ⟨a model of appreciative biography, a charming ~ to a great man —T.F.Hamlin⟩

²mon·u·ment \-ˌment, -ˌmənt — see ²-MENT\ *vt* -ED/-ING/-S **1** : to erect a monument to : signalize the memory of : COMMEMORATE **2** : to place or set up monuments on ⟨erected chapels and altars there, and ~*ed* the places of sacred scenes and associations —Hezekiah Butterworth⟩ **3** : to mark with monuments in surveying ⟨in locating, ~*ing,* and mapping the boundary, extensive use has been made of the geodetic maps of North America —*U.S.Daily*⟩

mon·u·men·tal \ˌmänyəˈmentᵊl\ *adj* [LL *monumentalis,* fr. L *monumentum* monument + *-alis* -al] **1 a** *obs* : of or relating to a sepulcher ⟨that whiter skin of hers than snow, and smooth as ~ alabaster —Shak.⟩ **b** : serving as a monument ⟨~ chapels of this style —Thomas Rickman⟩ **2** : resembling a monument: as **a** : having impressive bulk or size : IMMENSE, MASSIVE ⟨the entrance on this side is vigorously indicated . . . by a great ~ carriageway —*Amer. Guide Series: N.Y.City*⟩ ⟨the steps are flanked by ~ sculptures —*Amer. Guide Series: La.*⟩ ⟨he could paint superbly on a ~ scale —Herbert Read⟩ **b** : marked by outstanding quality : highly significant : INESTIMABLE ⟨in this ~ work the entire storehouse of the world's art is surveyed —*advt*⟩ ⟨he was too modest, and had too varied tastes . . . to care to be the ~ critic —T.S.Eliot⟩ **3** : of, relating to, or belonging to a monument : occurring on a monument ⟨failed to carry the use of the arch into ~ architecture —A.L.Kroeber⟩ ⟨a ~ script —Maurice Vieyra⟩ **4** : very great — used as an intensive ⟨notable for their ~ respectability —John Kobler⟩ ⟨~ failures of the past —W.E.Swinton⟩ ⟨their inertia is as ~ as their grief —John Mason Brown⟩

syn see MASSIVE, MONSTROUS

mon·u·men·tal·ism \ˌ≈≈ˈmentᵊlˌizəm\ *n* -S : a monumental style

mon·u·men·tal·i·ty \ˌ≈≈mənˈtalədē, -ˌmen-, -lətē, -i\ *n* -ES : the quality or state of being monumental ⟨differentiates modern design from the immobile and ponderous ~ of the past —Lewis Mumford⟩

mon·u·men·tal·ize \ˌ≈≈ˈmentᵊlˌīz\ *vt* -ED/-ING/-S : to record or memorialize lastingly by or as if by a monument : to make monumental

mon·u·men·tal·ly \ˌmänyəˈmentᵊlē, -ᵊli\ *adv* : in a monumental manner ⟨~ shy —Robert Henderson⟩ ⟨built mostly of sandstone . . . it rises ~ —Christopher Rand⟩

mon·u·ment·less *adj* : having no monuments

monument plant *n* : AMERICAN COLUMBO

mony \ˈmänē, -ni\ *chiefly Scot var of* MANY

mon·zo·nite \ˈmänzəˌnīt, ˈmōn-\ *n* -S [F, fr. Mt. *Monzoni,* northeast Italy + F *-ite*] **1** : a granular igneous rock composed of plagioclase and orthoclase in about equal quantities together with augite and a little biotite **2** : any of a large group of rocks intermediate between the syenite group and the diorite-gabbro group — **mon·zo·nit·ic** \ˌ≈≈ˈnid·ik\ *adj*

¹moo \ˈmü\ *vb* -ED/-ING/-S [imit.] *vi* : to make the natural throat noise of a cow : LOW ~ *vt* : to utter with a sound resembling the lowing of a cow ⟨meltingly ~ a religious ballad —*Punch*⟩

²moo \"\ *n* -S **1** : the lowing of a cow **2** : a sound that resembles a moo

moo·cah \ˈmükə\ *n* -S [prob. by alter.] : MARIJUANA

¹mooch \ˈmüch\ *vb* -ED/-ING/-ES [prob. fr. F dial. *muchier* to hide, lurk] *vi* **1** *dial chiefly Brit* : to absent oneself : play truant **2** : to move slowly or apathetically : wander aimlessly : AMBLE, SAUNTER ⟨the crowd ~*ed* away in sullen disinterest —Bruce Marshall⟩ ⟨hateful to be without a garden; there is nowhere to sit or ~ —Gladys B. Stern⟩ ⟨~*ed* forward on to the grass where he sat down . . . and emitted two short, gruff barks —Mervyn Wall⟩ ⟨the destroyer ~*ed* around all over the channel for two weeks —Irwin Shaw⟩; *specif* : SLINK ⟨heard I had been ~*ing* round his house and spying —John Buchan⟩ **3** : to take without giving : impose on another's hospitality or generosity : SPONGE, CADGE ⟨~*ed* on relatives for a living so he could devote full time to his art⟩ ⟨a rich young man addicted to ~*ing* from his friends —*Newsweek*⟩ **4** *West* : to troll (as for salmon) with a spinner or spoon ⟨the angler may spin or ~ on the same trip, as fancy dictates —*Fisherman's Encyc.*⟩ ~ *vt* **1** : to take surreptitiously : make off with : SNEAK, STEAL ⟨~ an apple when the huckster isn't looking⟩ **2** : to get by coaxing or wheedling : CADGE, BEG ⟨a dark-eyed urchin came up and tried to ~ a cigarette —*Newsweek*⟩ ⟨forest ponies . . . line the roads on Sundays to ~ tea buns from picnickers —A.J. Liebling⟩

²mooch \"\ *n* -ES **1** *slang* : an act or instance of mooching : PROWL, SLOUCH; *specif* : a jazz dance of the 1920s characterized by sensuous hip jerking and knee shivering **2** *slang* **a** : MOOCHER **b** : a customer looking for bargains; *specif* : an inexperienced stock speculator ⟨suckers or ~*es* . . . who have in the past bought blue-sky stocks —*Industrial Digest*⟩

moo·cha \ˈmüchə\ *n* -S [Zulu *umutsha*] : a loincloth of animals' tails or strips of animal skin worn by native peoples of So. Africa

mooch·er \ˈmüchə(r)\ *n* -S **1 a** *slang* : one that loiters or snoops **b** : an inspector of rivets and welded joints and seams of steel structures **2** *slang* : one that begs or takes surreptitiously : CADGER, GRAFTER **3** *West* : one that trolls for salmon with a spinner or spoon

¹mood \ˈmüd\ *n* -S [ME *mod, mood,* fr. OE *mōd;* akin to OHG *muot* emotion, mood, mind, purpose, ON *mōthr* wrath, moodiness, Goth *mōths* courage, anger, L *mos* custom, Gk *maiesthai* to strive, and perh. to Lith *matyti* to see, OSlav *motriti* to look] **1 a** : a conscious subjective state of mind : predominant emotion : FEELING, TEMPER ⟨it had taken possession of him again — that indomitable, conquering ~ which seemed to give him the right of way wherever he went —O.E.Rölvaag⟩ ⟨sometimes the ~ of one player may cause him to change some detail of interpretation —S.E.Wier⟩ ⟨the ox was his companion . . . and he had walked behind and praised it and cursed it as his ~ was —Pearl Buck⟩ **b** : a particular state of mind predisposing to action : receptive spirit ⟨in the ~ to listen to her —Mary Webb⟩ ⟨The House was, at that time, in no giving ~ —T.B.Macaulay⟩ **2** *archaic* : a fit of anger : RAGE ⟨who, in my ~, I stabbed unto the heart —Shak.⟩ **3 a** : a prevailing attitude : general spirit : DISPOSITION ⟨our national ~ has changed with our fortunes in battle —J.K. Little⟩ ⟨the Indians betrayed their ~ by accepting only rifles . . . and hatchets in payment for their furs —John Mason Brown⟩ **b** : a distinctive atmosphere or emotional context : tonal quality : AURA ⟨a large open room that had the ~ of a French commercial outpost somewhere in the tropics —D.W. Dresden⟩ ⟨the emotional ~ of the play —H.F.Helvenston⟩ ⟨the ~ of the landscape, achieved by the beauty of the evening light —Kenneth Clark⟩ ⟨in this book his ~ is doggedly elegiac —Anthony Quinton⟩ **c** : a degree of activity or gradation of illumination : ASPECT ⟨the sea in all its ~s —W.H.Taylor⟩ ⟨watching land and water, rocks and trees, and their ever-changing hues and ~s —Richard Semon⟩

syn HUMOR, TEMPER, VEIN: MOOD is the comprehensive term for any state of mind in which one emotion or desire or set of them is ascendant, stressing possibly more than the other terms a pervasiveness and compelling quality ⟨the tense limbs of a body possessed by a single *mood* of rapt exaltation —Laurence Binyon⟩ ⟨everything was going along smoothly and the men were in a happy *mood* —H.A.Chippendale⟩ ⟨the disgustingly bilious *mood* which a nasty night at sea never fails to produce —David Fairchild⟩ ⟨practicality was the prevailing *mood* after the war —Dixon Wecter⟩ ⟨the normally sedate neighborhood relaxes in holiday *mood* —*Amer. Guide Series: Md.*⟩ HUMOR in this context applies chiefly to a mood resulting from one's special temperament or physical or mental condition at the moment, suggesting a capriciousness or whimsicality ⟨in no *humor* to be trifled with⟩ ⟨a man of violent *humors* and yet touching affection⟩ ⟨I would not only consult the interest of the people, but I would cheerfully gratify their *humors* —Edmund Burke⟩ TEMPER can apply to a mood dominated by a single strong emotion, usu. anger when the term is unmodified; when modified by an adjective indicating the controlling emotion, the term indicates any humor manifest in a display of feeling ⟨found his friend in quite a *temper*⟩ ⟨wake up in a foul *temper*⟩ ⟨find his boss in a pleasant *temper*⟩ VEIN is often used in the sense of MOOD, usu. suggesting greater transitoriness, or of HUMOR but almost devoid of any implication of physical or temperamental cause ⟨the whole is written in a *vein* of ironic seriousness — H.J.Laski⟩ ⟨be in a jubilant *vein* after a small triumph⟩ ⟨make a request of a man while he is in an affable and generous *vein*⟩

²mood \"\ *n* -S [alter. (influenced by ¹*mood*) of ¹*mode*] **1 a** : the form of a syllogism classified according to the quantity and quality of the constituent propositions and traditionally shown by a sequence formed from the letters A, E, I, O such that the first letter indicates the major premise, the second the minor, and the third the conclusion — compare FIGURE 10, OPPOSITION 2a(2) **b** : MODE 3b **2 a** : distinction of form in a verb to express whether the action or state it denotes is conceived as fact or in some other manner (as command, possibility, or wish) ⟨the Latin verb has person, tense, number, ~, and voice⟩ **b** : a set of inflectional forms of a verb that express whether the action or state it denotes is conceived as fact or in some other manner ⟨the indicative ~⟩ ⟨the imperative ~⟩ ⟨the subjunctive ~⟩ ⟨the optative ~⟩ **c** : the part of the meaning of a verb form that consists of the expression of whether the action or state it denotes is conceived as fact or in some other manner **3** : MODE 1b

mood·i·ly \ˈmüdᵊlē, -dəl, |i\ *adv* : in a moody manner : DISMALLY, GLOOMILY

mood·i·ness \-dēnəs, -din-\ *n* -ES : the quality or state of being moody : MELANCHOLY, GLOOM

mood swing *n* [¹*mood*] : a marked change in mood esp. to elation or depression (as in cyclothymia) ⟨certain personality characteristics . . . such as *mood swings,* paranoid features and self-punishment drives —E.F.Kerman⟩

¹moody \ˈmüdē, -di\ *adj* -ER/-EST [ME *mody,* fr. OE *mōdig,* fr. *mōd* mood, courage + *-ig* -y — more at MOOD] **1** *obs* : full of wrath : ANGRY **2 a** : subject to or characterized by depression or discontent : SULLEN, GLOOMY ⟨mental depression made him . . . morose, ~, and at times childish —C.N.Boyd⟩ ⟨grew ~ and petulant and would not eat —Pearl Buck⟩ **b** : subject to moods : TEMPERAMENTAL ⟨~ artist⟩ ⟨outscheming the ~ winds —K.D.Curtis⟩ **c** : expressive of a mood ⟨the meanings come through as a result of some fine ~ direction —Hollis Alpert⟩

²moody \ˈmüdi\ *var of* MOUDIE

mooed *past of* MOO

mooing *n* -S [fr. gerund of ¹*moo*] : ²MOO

mool \ˈmül\ *n* -S [by alter.] **1** *dial Brit* : ¹MOLD **1** **2** *dial Brit* : ¹MOLD 2b

moo·la *or* **moo·lah** \ˈmülə\ *n* -S [origin unknown] *slang* : MONEY ⟨ninety grand is a lot of ~ —Harold Robbins⟩

mool·ey \ˈmüli\ *chiefly dial var of* MULEY

mool·ings \ˈmülənz, -liŋz\ *n pl* [pl. of *mooling,* gerund of Sc *mool* to crumble, fr. *mool,* n.] *Scot* : CRUMB

moolvee *var of* MAULVI

¹moon \ˈmün\ *n* -S *often attrib* [ME *mone, moone,* fr. OE *mōna;* akin to OHG *māno* moon, ON *māni,* Goth *mena* moon, L *mensis* month, Gk *mēn* month, *mēnē* moon, Skt *mās, māsa* moon, month, and perh. to Skt *māti* he measures — more at MEASURE] **1 a** : the earth's only known natural satellite and next to the sun the most conspicuous object in the heavens shining by the sun's reflected light, revolving about the earth from west to east in about 29½ days with reference to the sun or about 27⅓ days with reference to the stars, having a diameter of 2160 miles and a mean distance from the earth of about 238,857 miles, a mass about one eightieth that of the earth and a volume about one forty-ninth, and rotating as it revolves so that it always presents nearly the same face to the earth **b** : one complete moon cycle consisting of four phases ⟨the old ~ in the arms of the new⟩ — see FULL MOON, NEW MOON; compare ECLIPSE, GIBBOUS, LIBRATION, TIDE **c** : any satellite in the sky ⟨observing the ~s of Jupiter or Saturn⟩ ⟨launching of a man-made ~ —L.V.Berkner⟩ **2** : the time of a synodic month ⟨labored for many ~s to complete this unusual work of primitive art —*Amer. Guide Series: Conn.*⟩ **3** : MOONLIGHT ⟨keep out of the ~ or it may turn your head —H.R. Haggard⟩ **4** : something that resembles a moon: as **a** : a disk on the face of a clock showing the phases of the moon ⟨the plate that carries the ~ —James Ferguson⟩ **b** : a globe surrounding a light ⟨a green ~ of porcelain over a naked electric bulb —Frances Towers⟩ **c** : a slice bar with a nearly circular blade perforated in the middle and used in tending a brickkiln fire **d** : a highly translucent spot in old porcelain **e** : LUNULE a **f** : MOON KNIFE **5** : something impossible or inaccessible ⟨reach for the ~⟩ **6** *slang* : ¹MOONSHINE 3 ⟨five or six good stiff drinks of ~ —Sherwood Anderson⟩ **7** : PLATY

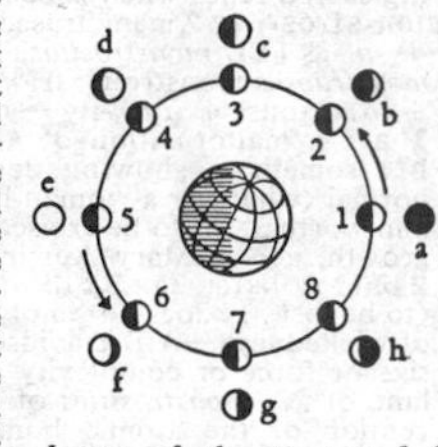

phases of the moon: *1–8* showing the moon in orbit around the earth; *a–h* corresponding phases as seen from the earth; *1* new moon, *3* first quarter, *5* full moon, *7* last quarter; *a* new moon, *b* waxing crescent, *c* half-moon, *d* gibbous, *e* full moon, *f* gibbous, *g* half-moon, *h* waning crescent

²moon \"\ *vb* -ED/-ING/-S *vt* **1** *archaic* : to expose to moonlight ⟨the huge man . . . not sunning, but ~*ing* himself —Thomas De Quincey⟩ **2** : to spend in idle reverie : DREAM — used with *away* ⟨~ the afternoon away⟩ **3** : to locate by sighting against the moon ⟨a ~ a possum⟩ ⟨darted along . . . till I could ~ the house with the old stack —Joseph Furphy⟩ **4** : to scrape (a skin or hide) with a moon knife ~ *vi* : to behave in an abstracted way : move or gaze dreamily or absentmindedly : DAWDLE, GAPE ⟨~*ed* around the house all day in a dream —Patrick Campbell⟩ ⟨got to ~*ing* over her dead father —Grace Metalious⟩ ⟨~*ing* up into his eyes —Jack Slater⟩ ⟨~s over tape-recorded music —Gilbert Millstein⟩ ⟨~*ing* over a silken phrase and relaxing the flow of melody to a point where the tempo becomes obscured —Roland Gelatt⟩

moonal *or* **moonaul** *var of* MONAL

moonbeam \ˈ≈ˌ≈\ *n* **1** : a ray of light from the moon **2** : PEARL 6b

moonbill \ˈ≈ˌ≈\ *n, South* : RING-NECKED DUCK

¹moon-blind \ˈ≈ˌ≈\ *adj* [¹*moon* + *blind*] : afflicted with moon blindness

²moon-blind \ˈ≈ˌ≈\ *n* : MOON BLINDNESS

moon blindness *n* : a periodic ophthalmia or recurrent inflammation of the eye of the horse resulting ultimately in corneal opacity and blindness that has been attributed to genetic factors and to infection but is now usu. considered to be due to a deficiency of riboflavin in the diet

moon·bow \ˈ≈ˌbō\ *n* [¹*moon* + *rainbow*] : a rainbow formed by light from the moon

moon cake *n* : a small pastry filled with a mixture of meat and other ingredients traditionally associated with the Chinese harvest festival

mooncalf \ˈ≈ˌ≈\ *n* **1 a** *obs* : uterine mole **b** : MONSTER 2a **2** : a foolish or absentminded person : DOLT, SIMPLETON

moon daisy *n, Brit* : DAISY 1b

moondial \ˈ≈ˌ≈≈\ *n* : NIGHT DIAL 1

moon dog *n* : PARASELENE

moondown \ˈ≈ˌ≈\ *n* [*moon* + *-down* (as in *sundown*)] : MOONSET

¹mooned *past of* MOON

²mooned \ˈmün(ə)d\ *adj, archaic* [¹*moon* + *-ed*] : ornamented with or shaped like the moon esp. in the shape of a crescent ⟨with his ~ train the strutting peacock . . . flutters into the Ark —Michael Drayton⟩ ⟨the angelic squadron . . . sharpening in ~ horns their phalanx —John Milton⟩

moon·er \ˈmünə(r)\ *n* -S [²*moon* + *-er*] : one that moons; *specif* : one that moons skins or hides

mooney *var of* MOONY

mooneye \'=,=\ *n* **1 a :** an eye affected with moon blindness **b :** MOON BLINDNESS **2 a :** any of three American freshwater fishes constituting the genus *Hiodon* that are closely related to the goldeye, resemble the shad, but are inferior as food; *esp* **:** a fish (*H. tergisus*) of the Great Lakes and Mississippi valley **b :** ³BLOATER 2

mooneye cisco *n* **:** ³BLOATER 2

moon–eyed \'=;=\ *adj* **1 :** MOON-BLIND **2 a :** SQUINT-EYED **b :** ROUND-EYED **3** *archaic* **:** able to see well at night

moonfaced \'=,=\ *adj* **:** having a face as round as a full moon

moon fern *n* **:** MOONWORT 1

moonfish \'=,=\ *n, pl* **moonfish** *or* **moonfishes :** any of a number of compressed often short deep-bodied silvery or yellowish marine fishes: as **a :** LOOKDOWN FISH; *also* **:** any of several closely related fishes (genus *Vomer*) widely distributed in warm parts of the Atlantic **b :** OPAH **c :** a spadefish (*Chaetodipterus faber*) **d :** an ocean sunfish (*Mola mola*) **e :** PLATY

moonflower \'=,=\ *n* **1** *Brit* **:** DAISY 1b **2 a :** a tropical American night-blooming morning glory (*Calonyction aculeatum*) with fragrant white or purple flowers **b :** any of several plants of the related genera *Ipomoea* and *Quamoclit* **3** *dial Eng* **:** a European wood anemone (*Anemone nemorosa*) **4** *Africa* **:** ANGEL'S-TRUMPET

moon gate *n* **:** a circular opening used in Chinese architecture to afford passage through a wall

moonglow \'=,=\ *n* **:** MOONLIGHT

moon·ie *or* **moony** \'münē\ *n, pl* **moonies** [*moon* + *-ie, -y*] **:** a little ball cut from translucent stone and used in playing marbles

moonier *comparative of* MOONY

mooniest *superlative of* MOONY

moon gate

moon·i·ly \'münᵊlē, -nəlē\ *adv* **:** in a moony manner **:** ABSTRACTEDLY, DREAMILY

moon·i·ness \-nēnəs\ *n* -ES **:** the quality or state of being moony **:** DREAMINESS, INATTENTION

mooning *n* -S [fr. gerund of ²*moon*] **1 :** aimless reverie or vacuous contemplation **2** [¹*moon* + *-ing*] **:** an occurrence of small translucent spots in the paste of porcelains (as in Chelsea china of about 1758)

moon·ish \'münish\ *adj* **:** DOLTISH, CAPRICIOUS — **moon·ish·ly** *adv*

moon jelly *n* **:** a flat white or bluish jellyfish (*Aurelia aurita*) common along both coasts of No. America

moon knife *n* **:** a crescent-shaped knife with a handle across the center used in leather finishing

moon·less \'münləs\ *adj* **1 :** having no satellite ⟨~ planet⟩ **2 :** lacking the light of or as if of the moon ⟨~ night⟩ ⟨lone is the empty dark, and the ~ heart —Walter de la Mare⟩

moon·let \'münlət\ *n* -S **:** a small natural or artificial satellite of the earth or other celestial body ⟨the particles that compose the rings of Saturn are ~s⟩

moon letter *n* [trans. of Ar *alhurūf alqamarīyah;* fr. the fact that the *l* of the Ar definite article *al* is not assimilated to the initial *q* of *qamar* moon, used as a type word] **:** an Arabic consonant to which the *l* of a preceding definite article *al* is not assimilated in pronunciation — called also *lunar letter;* opposed to *sun letter*

¹**moonlight** \'=,=\ *n, often attrib* [ME *monelight,* fr. *mone* moon + *light* — more at MOON, LIGHT] **1 :** the light of the moon **2 :** sunlight reflected by the moon **2 :** FLESH 6

²**moonlight** \"\ *vi* -ED/-ING/-S **:** to engage in moonlighting **:** carry on the activities of a moonlighter

moonlight blue *n* **:** a grayish blue that is greener and paler than electric or copenhagen and lighter and slightly greener than Gobelin — called also *infantry*

moonlighted \'=,==\ *adj* **:** MOONLIT

moon·light·er \'mün,līd·ə(r), -ītə-\ *n* **:** one that engages in activity by or as if by the light of the moon: as **a :** a participant in a night raid **b :** MOONSHINER **c :** a person holding two jobs at the same time

moonlight flit *or* **moonlight flitting** *n, slang Brit* **:** a departure by night with one's possessions to avoid paying rent

moon·light·ing \-īd·|iŋ, -īt|, |ēŋ\ *n* **:** carrying on activity by or as if by the light of the moon: as **a :** night raiding **b :** holding two jobs at once

moonlight school *n* **:** an evening session for adult illiterates esp. in country school districts of the South

moon·lit \'mün,lit\ *adj* [*moon* + *lit*] **:** lighted by or as if by the moon ⟨~ path⟩ ⟨his face . . . remained ~ in its pallor —John Mason Brown⟩

moonmist \'=,=\ *n* **:** a yellowish gray that is redder and slightly paler than sand and redder and duller than natural

moon month *n* **:** a month determined only and directly by observation of the moon's phase (as in the Hebrew calendar)

moonpath \'=,=\ *n* **:** a lengthened reflection of the moon from slightly agitated water

moonpenny \'=,==\ *n* **:** DAISY 1b

moon pillar *n* **:** a light pillar extending vertically above and below the moon

moon plant *n* **:** an East Indian vine (*Sarcostemma brevistigma*) of the family Asclepiadaceae whose milky juice yields an intoxicating beverage

moonproof \'=;=\ *adj, archaic* **:** proof against the light or influence of the moon

moonquake \'=,=\ *n* **:** an agitation of the moon's surface that is analogous to a terrestrial earthquake

moonraker \'=,==\ *n* **1** *chiefly Brit* **:** a stupid fellow **:** SIMPLETON **2 :** MOONSAIL

moonraking \'=,==\ *n, archaic* **:** WOOLGATHERING

moonrat \'=,=\ *n* **:** a whitish insectivore (*Echinosorex gymnurus*) of southeastern Asia having a long snout and a long naked tail

moonrise \'=,=\ *n* **1 :** the rising of the moon above the horizon **2 :** the time of the moon's rising

moons *pl of* MOON, *pres 3d sing of* MOON

moon·sail \'münsəl (usual nautical pronunciation), -n,sāl\ *n* **:** a light square sail set above a skysail and carried by some clipper ships in light winds

moon·scape \'mün,skāp\ *n* [¹*moon* + *-scape*] **:** the surface of the moon as seen or as depicted

moonseed \'=,=\ *n* **:** a plant of the genus *Menispermum* having crescent-shaped seeds and bluish black fruits — see CAROLINA MOONSEED

moonseed family *n* **:** MENISPERMACEAE

moonset \'=,=\ *n* **1 :** the descent of the moon below the horizon **2 :** the time of the moon's setting

moonshee *var of* MUNSHI

moon shell *n* **:** a globose smooth-shelled carnivorous marine snail of the family Naticidae

¹**moon·shine** \'mün,shīn\ *n, often attrib* [¹*moon* + *shine*] **1 :** MOONLIGHT ⟨the world looked very beautiful in the ~ —Fanny K. Wister⟩ **2 :** airy fabrication or empty talk **:** ridiculous chatter **:** NONSENSE ⟨nothing ensues but ~ and mere sentimentality —George Santayana⟩ **3 :** intoxicating liquor; *esp* **:** illegally distilled corn whiskey ⟨charged with possession of ~ —*Tallahassee (Fla.) Democrat*⟩ **4 a :** PEARLY EVERLASTING **b :** a balsamweed (*Gnaphalium obtusifolium*)

²**moonshine** \"\ *vb* -ED/-ING/-S *vi* **:** to operate an illicit still ⟨the Treasury reports an alarming increase in *moonshining* and bootlegging —Howard Brubaker⟩ ~ *vt* **:** to distill illegally ⟨the best of it . . . was *moonshined* during prohibition —J.C. Furnas⟩

moon·shin·er \-nə(r)\ *n* **:** one that makes or sells illicit whiskey ⟨married to a convicted ~ —Jacob Hay⟩

moon·shiny \-nē\ *adj* **1 :** MOONLIT **2 :** insubstantial or unreal **:** VISIONARY, NONSENSICAL

moon sight *n* **:** an observation of the altitude of the moon made for navigational purposes

moon's man *n* **:** HOMO SIGNORUM

moon snail *n* **:** MOON SHELL

moon snake *n* **:** QUEEN SNAKE

moonstone \'=,=\ *n* **:** a transparent or translucent gemstone of pearly or opaline luster that is a feldspar classed according to specimens under orthoclase or under plagioclase

moonstone blue *n* **:** a pale purplish blue that is redder and paler than hydrangea blue and redder than starlight blue

moonstruck \'=,=\ *adj* **1 :** affected by or as if by the moon: as **a :** marked by or as if by mental unbalance ⟨to hand over those rights to be interpreted away by lawyers, seemed to him ~ madness —V.L.Parrington⟩ **b :** romantically sentimental ⟨the proper witchery of ~ love —Sinclair Lewis⟩ **2 :** MOONLIT

moon tide *n* **:** LUNAR TIDE

moon type *n, usu cap M* [after William *Moon* †1894 Eng. inventor] **:** a system of large embossed letters used in printing for the blind and esp. for those blinded late in life that requires less finger sensitivity than braille, consists of nine characters derived from Roman capital letters and used in varying positions to denote the whole alphabet, and is used with full orthography, the lines being printed alternately from left to right and right to left

Moon type

moonvine \'=,=\ *n* **:** MOONFLOWER

moon·ward \'münwə(r)d\ *or* **moon·wards** \-dz\ *adv* [*moon* + *-ward, -wards*] **:** toward the moon ⟨hurl a rocket ~⟩

moonwatcher \'=,==\ *n* **:** one that tracks the course of a man-made satellite

moonwort \'=,=\ *n* **1 :** a fern of the genus *Botrychium* (esp. *B. lunarium*) **2 :** HONESTY 3

¹**moony** *also* **moon·ey** \'münē, -ni\ *adj* **moonier; mooniest** [¹*moon* + *-y*] **1 :** of or relating to the moon **2 :** shaped like the moon: **a :** resembling or ornamented with the crescent moon ⟨snakes . . . put a trailing, ~ division between weed and weed —Eudora Welty⟩ ⟨the ~ standards of proud Ottoman —Josuah Sylvester⟩ **b :** resembling the full moon **:** ROUND **3 :** MOONLIT ⟨~ night⟩ **4 :** ABSTRACTED, DREAMY ⟨a rather ~ . . . brat, interested mostly in mathematics, with a trick of standing with those goggle eyes gazing bluely at you —F.M. Ford⟩ ⟨conductors are likely to keep these movements low in dynamics and to get ~ over them —Virgil Thomson⟩; *esp* **:** MOONSTRUCK ⟨I always was ~ over you —Zane Grey⟩

²**moony** *var of* MOONIE

moop \'müp\ *vi* -ED/-ING/-S [origin unknown] *Scot* **:** to keep company **:** associate closely

¹**moor** \'mu̇(ə)r, -üə *sometimes* 'mō(ə)r *or* 'mȯ(ə)r *or* 'mōə *or* 'mȯ(ə)\ *n* -S *often attrib* [ME *mor,* fr. OE *mōr;* akin to MD *moer* mire, swamp, OHG *muor* swamp, sea, ON *mœrr* land, *marr* sea — more at MARINE] **1 a** *chiefly Brit* **:** an extensive area of open rolling infertile land consisting of sand, rock, or peat usu. covered with heather, bracken, coarse grass, and sphagnum moss **:** HIGH MOOR ⟨an empty desolation of ~s, hill and mountain stretching to the Scottish border —G.E. Fussell⟩ — compare HEATH 2 **b :** a boggy area of wasteland usu. dominated by grasses and sedges growing in a thick layer of peat **:** FEN ⟨boggy ~s are favorite sites for gull colonies —*Brit. Birds in Colour*⟩ ⟨bicycle across the Nantucket ~s — a broad, flat expanse of cranberry bogs . . . and Scotch heather —*Look at America: New England*⟩ — compare LOW MOOR, MUSKEG **2** *Brit* **a :** moorland soil **:** PEAT **b :** moorland vegetation (as heather) ⟨the natural vegetation is largely ~s . . . with a great amount of heather —Samuel Van Valkenburg & Ellsworth Huntington⟩ **c :** a game preserve consisting of moorland

²**moor** \"\ *n* -S *usu cap* [ME *More,* fr. MF, fr. L *Maurus,* prob. of Berber origin] **1 a :** a member of a dark-skinned people of mixed Arab and Berber ancestry inhabiting ancient Mauretania in No. Africa and conquering Spain in the 8th century A.D. **:** MOROCCAN **b :** BERBER **2 :** MUSLIM; *esp* **:** ¹MOORMAN — compare MORO **3 a** *archaic* **:** BLACKAMOOR **b :** one of a group of people of mixed Indian, white, and Negro ancestry in central Delaware — compare NANTICOKE **4 :** a goldfish similar to the fringetail but velvety black

³**moor** \"\ *vb* -ED/-ING/-S [ME *moren;* akin to OE *mǣrels-rāp* ship's rope, MD *maren, meren* to tie, moor, OFris *mere* thong, strap, OHG *marawen* to tie together, connect, LG *vermoren* to moor, and perh. to Gk *mēryesthai* to roll up, *mermis* cord, thread — more at MERMIS] *vt* **1 :** to make fast with cables and lines or with more than one anchor ⟨a motorboat, ~*ed* after dark to a buoy in the harbor —H.M.Parshley⟩ ⟨down went the second anchor, and there we were doubly ~*ed* —Jack London⟩ ⟨~ a dirigible to a mast⟩ ⟨~ an airplane to the ground⟩ **2 :** to attach firmly **:** tie on ⟨suitcases . . . having handles can be more firmly ~*ed* to a bucking vehicle than some other kinds of luggage —E.J.Kahn⟩ ~ *vi* **1 :** to secure a boat by mooring **:** ANCHOR ⟨brought her in through Long Island Sound and ~*ed* off Throgs Neck —James Dugan⟩ **2 :** to be made fast ⟨enables small vessels to ~ close to land —J.H. Bennet⟩

⁴**moor** \"\ *n* -S **:** the act or process of mooring

moor·age \'mu̇rij, -rēj *sometimes* 'mōr- *or* 'mȯr-\ *n* -S [*moor* + *-age*] **1 :** an act of mooring **2 :** a charge for mooring

moorball \'=,=\ *n* [¹*moor* + *ball*] **:** a globular mass of filaments of a green alga (*Cladophora holsatica*) often found in lakes and ponds

moor besom *n* **:** a heather (*Calluna vulgaris*)

moorbird \'=,=\ *n* **:** RED GROUSE

moor blackbird *n, dial Brit* **:** RING OUZEL

moor·burn \'mu̇(ə)r,bərn\ *n* [ME(Sc) *murburn,* fr. *mur, mor* moor + *burn*] **1** *Scot* **:** the burning over of a moor to improve the pasturage **2** *Scot* **:** an outburst of temper

moor buzzard *n, dial Brit* **:** MARSH HARRIER

moorcock \'=,=\ *n* **1 :** the male of the red grouse **2 :** BLACKCOCK

moor coot *n* **:** MOORHEN 2

moore·ite \'mu̇,rīt, 'mō,, 'mȯ,-\ *n* -S [Gideon E. *Moore* †1895 Am. chemist + E *-ite*] **:** a mineral $(Mg,Zn,Mn)_8(SO_4)(OH)_{14}{\cdot}4H_2O$ consisting of a hydrous basic sulfate of magnesium, zinc, and manganese

moor evil *n* [¹*moor*] *dial Eng* **:** dysentery in sheep and cattle

moorfowl \'=,=\ *n* **:** RED GROUSE

moor game *n* **:** RED GROUSE

moor grass *n* **1 :** HEATH GRASS **2 :** a coarse perennial mountain grass (*Molinia coerulea*) of Europe that is considered a good forage grass — called also *flying bent* **3 :** a common cotton grass (*Eriophorum angustifolium*) of the north temperate zone **4 :** a grass growing on a moor

moor hag *n* **:** rough moorland

moor harrier *n* **:** MARSH HARRIER

moor hawk *n, dial Brit* **:** MARSH HARRIER

moorhen \'=,=\ *n* [ME *morhen,* fr. *mor* moor + *hen*] **1 :** the female of the red grouse **2 :** GALLINULE; *esp* **:** the common European gallinule (*Gallinula chloropus*) **3 :** an Australian rail (*Tribonyx ventralis*)

moorier *comparative of* MOORY

mooriest *superlative of* MOORY

moor ill *n, dial Brit* **:** dysentery in cattle

moor·ing \'mu̇riŋ, -rēŋ *sometimes* 'mōr- *or* 'mȯr-\ *n* -S [ME *moring,* fr. gerund of *moren* to moor — more at MOOR] **1 :** an act of making fast a boat or aircraft by means of chains, lines, anchors, or other devices **2 a :** a place where or an object to which a craft can be made fast ⟨the lake provides ~ for 166 planes —Elsie M. B. Grosvenor⟩ ⟨yacht clubs . . . of the sort that maintains neither docks nor ~*s* —M.M.Hunt⟩ **b :** a chain, line, or other device by which an object (as a boat) is secured in place ⟨one of the best tests of a seaman is to let him pick up a ~ under varying conditions of wind, sea and tide —W.P. Moore⟩ **3 :** an established practice or stabilizing influence **:** ANCHORAGE 4 — usu. used in pl. ⟨modern man has been torn from his spiritual ~*s* —F.L.Baumer⟩ ⟨this shift from normal political ~*s* —Arthur Krock⟩

mooring anchor *n* **:** a mushroom anchor or an anchor with only one fluke used for holding a mooring buoy or channel marker in place

mooring bitt *n* **:** BITT

mooring board *n* **:** MANEUVERING BOARD

mooring buoy *n* **:** an anchored buoy fitted to receive a ship's mooring chain or hawser

mooring dog *n* **:** a heavy iron bar on the side of a boat near the waterline to which a mooring line can be secured — called also *mooring staple*

mooring anchor

mooring mast *or* **mooring tower** *n* **:** a mast on shore or on a ship with a fitting at the top to receive the mooring device of a rigid dirigible airship

mooring pipe *n* **:** an oval or round casting fitted in the bulwark through which mooring lines are passed

mooring shackle *n* **:** MOORING SWIVEL

mooring staple *n* **:** MOORING DOG

mooring swivel *n* **:** a swivel joining the two chain cables of a moored ship near the bow in such a way as to keep them from becoming twisted or entangled — called also *mooring shackle*

¹**moor·ish** \'mu̇rish, -rēsh *sometimes* 'mōr- *or* 'mȯr-\ *adj, usu cap* [ME *morys,* fr. *More* Moor + *-ys, -ish* — more at MOOR] **1 :** of, relating to, or in a style characteristic of the Moors **2** *archaic* **a :** of or relating to the Moormen of India **:** MUHAMMADAN **b :** HINDUSTANI, URDU

²**moorish** \"\ *adj* [ME *morish,* fr. *mor* moor + *-ish*] **1** *obs* **:** MARSHY, SWAMPY — used of soil ⟨it was upon low ~ ground near the sea and I believed it would not be wholesome —Daniel Defoe⟩ **2** *archaic* **a :** abounding in moors ⟨the land is mountainous and ~ —R.G.Preston⟩ **b :** of, relating to, or characteristic of a moor ⟨a . . . ~ place, on the banks of the Poole —Robert Burns⟩

moorish arch *n, usu cap M* **:** a horseshoe arch

moorish architecture *n, usu cap M* **:** the style developed by the Moors in the later middle ages esp. in No. Africa and Spain — compare ALHAMBRESQUE, HISPANO-MORESQUE, SARACENIC ARCHITECTURE

moorish idol *n, usu cap M* **:** a brightly colored fish (*Zanclus cornutus*) or a related form (*Z. canescens*) both widely distributed in the tropical Indo-Pacific from the east coast of Africa to Japan and the west coast of Mexico

moorish red *n* **:** a strong orange that is yellower and lighter than pumpkin, yellower and less strong than cadmium orange, and yellower and lighter than mandarin orange

moor·land \'=lənd, -,land, -aa(ə)nd\ *n, often attrib* **:** land consisting of moors **:** a stretch of moor ⟨wild ~, bleak and treeless except in the valleys —A.E.Trueman⟩

moor macaque *or* **moor monkey** *n* [²*Moor*] **:** a large gray-legged black macaque (*Macaca maura*) of Celebes

¹**moor·man** \'=,man, -aa(ə)n, -mən\ *n, pl* **moormen** *usu cap* [²*Moor* + *man*] *India & Ceylon* **:** MUHAMMADAN; *esp* **:** a Muhammadan of mixed Arab and Indian ancestry

²**moorman** \"\ *n, pl* **moormen** [¹*moor* + *man*] **:** an inhabitant of a moor ⟨on Dartmoor . . . there was an old ~'*s* granite cottage —G.E.Fussell⟩

moor·mi bhotiah \'mu̇(ə)rmē'bōd·ēə\ *n, pl* **moormi bhotiah** *or* **moormi bhotiahs** *usu cap M&B* **1 :** a non-Tibetan people of Nepal adhering to Lamaism **2 :** a member of the Moormi Bhotiah people

moor pout *or* **moor poot** *n* [¹*moor*] *chiefly Scot* **:** a young grouse

moor·pun·ky \mȯ(r)'pəŋkē\ *n* -ES [Hindi *morpākhī,* fr. *morpākhī* of a peacock wing, fr. *mor* peacock (fr. Skt *mayūra*) + *pākh* wing, feather (fr. Skt *pakṣa*); fr. its peacock-shaped sternpiece] **:** a large long ornamental pleasure craft propelled by paddles and formerly used as a state barge in India

moors *pl of* MOOR, *pres 3d sing of* MOOR

moor's head *n, pl* **moor's heads** *or* **moors' heads** *usu cap M* [²*Moor*] **1 a :** a representation of a human head with features characteristic or formerly supposed to be characteristic of a Moor **b :** a heraldic representation of a head usu. with the features and color of a Negro depicted in profile with a band about the forehead unless a different position or a different headdress is specified **2 :** something likened to the head of a Moor: as **a** *obs* **:** a dark or black head usu. occurring on a roan horse **b** *archaic* **:** a globular copper or glass condenser for the top of a still

moors·man \'mu̇rzmən\ *n, pl* **moorsmen 1 :** one who lives on a moor **:** MOORMAN **2 :** one who frequents moors

moor·stone \'mu̇(ə)r,stōn\ *n* [¹*moor* + *stone*] *dial Eng* **:** granite found esp. in Cornwall

moor·tet·ter \'=,ted·ə(r)\ *n* -S **:** MOOR TIT

moor tit *or* **moor titling** *n* **1 :** a European stonechat (*Saxicola torquata*) **2 :** MEADOW PIPIT

moo·rup *or* **mu·rup** \mü'ru̇p\ *also* **moo·ruk** \-u̇k\ *n, pl* **moorup** *or* **murup** *also* **mooruk** [imit.] **:** a cassowary (*Casuarius bennetti*) with rather small stout legs found on the island of New Britain

moorva *var of* MURVA

moorwort \'=,=\ *n* [¹*moor* + *wort*] **:** BOG ROSEMARY

moory \'mu̇rē *sometimes* 'mōrē *or* 'mȯrē\ *adj* -ER/-EST [¹*moor* + *-y*] **:** of, relating to, or of the nature of a moor **:** MARSHY, SWAMPY

moos *pres 3d sing of* MOO, *pl of* MOO

moose \'müs\ *n, pl* **moose** *often attrib* [of Algonquian origin; akin to Natick *moos* moose, fr. *moos-u* he trims, shaves; fr. the animal's habit of stripping bark and lower branches off trees] **1 a :** a large ruminant mammal (*Alces americana*) of the family Cervidae that inhabits forested parts of Canada and the northern U. S., is closely related to the European elk but slightly larger standing about seven feet high at the humped shoulders and often weighing over 1000 pounds, and has an ungainly form with the legs long, the tail short, and the head large with a thick overhanging snout and broadly palmated antlers with many points **b :** ELK 1a **2** *cap* **:** a member of one of the major benevolent and fraternal orders **3** *sometimes cap* **:** BULL MOOSE

moose 1a

moose·berry \'müs- *see* BERRY\ *n* **1 a :** HOBBLEBUSH **b :** the fruit of the hobblebush **2 :** CRANBERRY BUSH 2

moosebird \'=,=\ *n* **:** CANADA JAY

moosebush \'=,=\ *n* **:** HOBBLEBUSH

moosecall \'=,=\ *n* **:** an instrument (as a piece of birch bark rolled like a horn) used by hunters in calling moose

moose elm *n* **:** SLIPPERY ELM

mooseflower \'=,==\ *n* **:** TRILLIUM

moose fly *n* **:** a tabanid fly **:** HORSEFLY

moose maple *n* **:** MOUNTAIN MAPLE a

moose·mise \'mü,smīs\ *or* **moose–misse** \-mis\ *n* -S [of Algonquian origin; akin to Chippewa & Nipissing *monsomish* hobblebush] **:** MOUNTAIN ASH 1b

moose tick *n* : WINTER TICK
moosetongue \'⸗,⸗\ *n* : WILLOW HERB
moosewood \'⸗,⸗\ *n* **1** : STRIPED MAPLE **2** : LEATHERWOOD 1a **3** : HOBBLEBUSH
¹moot \'müt, *usu* -üd·+V\ *n* -s [ME *mot, moot,* fr. OE *mōt* assembly, meeting, encounter; akin to OFris *mōtlik* legal, OS *mōt* meeting, encounter, MHG *muoze* encounter, ON *mōt* meeting, assembly, OE *mētan* to meet — more at MEET] **1 a** : a meeting for discussion and deliberation; *esp* : a meeting of freemen (as of a town, city, or shire in early England) or their representatives to administer justice or for administrative purposes — compare FOLKMOOT, GEMOT, HUNDRED, WITENAGEMOT **b** : a place for holding such a meeting **2** *obs* : ARGUMENT, DISCOURSE, DISCUSSION ⟨but to end this ~ —John Milton⟩ **3** : a hypothetical case argued or practice hearing held by law students ⟨elected by his classmates as prosecutor for the weekly ~⟩
²moot \"\ *vb* -ED/-ING/-S [ME *moten,* fr. OE *mōtian,* fr. *mōt,* n.] *vi, obs* : to argue a case at law (as a hypothetical case) as a student in a law school ⟨~*ed* seven years in the Inns of Court —John Earle⟩ ~ *vt* **1** *archaic* : to discuss from a legal standpoint : ARGUE ⟨to ~ cases on the . . . ruin of the constitution —Edmund Burke⟩ **2 a** : to bring up for discussion : ²BROACH 6, SUGGEST ⟨condemned such a step when it was first ~*ed* a year before —Ethel Drus⟩ ⟨plans have been ~*ed* for altering the general system of criminal procedure —Ernest Barker⟩ **b** : DISCUSS, DEBATE ⟨the question, so often ~*ed* and never solved, of church unity —*Commonweal*⟩ ⟨the diction of poetry is now, as it has always been, a vigorously ~*ed* point —J.L.Lowes⟩ **3** : to deprive of practical significance : make academic ⟨the case was ~*ed* by unwillingness of the complainant to prosecute⟩
³moot \"\ *adj* [¹*moot*] **1 a** : open to question : subject to discussion : DEBATABLE, UNSETTLED ⟨it is a ~ question what might have happened —O.D.Tolischus⟩ ⟨words of ~ etymology —A.H.Marckwardt⟩ ⟨fill in gaps . . . and to check ~ points —Leslie Spier⟩ **b** : subjected to discussion : CONTROVERSIAL, DISPUTED ⟨with a ~ point of law cleared up —John LaFarge⟩ ⟨extract . . . his views on the then ~ subject of a second front —Henry Cassidy⟩ **2** : deprived of practical significance : made abstract or purely academic ⟨thought that the Supreme Court would drop the case as a ~ question, if the bill should become law —*Time*⟩ ⟨appeal does not become ~ when the alien leaves the country, since the possibility of a criminal prosecution for attempted re-entry . . . remains —*Harvard Law Rev.*⟩ **3** : concerned with a hypothetical situation ⟨~ court⟩ ⟨student participation in a ~ . . . case —*Bulletin of Information: Academy of Advanced Traffic*⟩
⁴moot \'müt\ *vt* -ED/-ING/-S [ME *moten*] *dial Eng* : to grub out (as a tree root) or unearth (as an otter)
moot·able \'müd·əbəl\ *adj* [²*moot* + *-able*] : DEBATABLE
moot court *n* : a mock court in which students of law argue hypothetical cases for practice
mooth \'müth\ *dial Brit var of* MOUTH
moot hall *n* [ME *mothalle, moothalle,* fr. *mot, moot* moot + *halle* hall — more at MOOT, HALL] : a room or building in which a moot is held; *specif* : TOWN HALL
moot hill *n* : a hill used as the meeting place of a moot in early England ⟨each little village-commonwealth . . . had its *moot hill* or sacred tree as a center —J.R.Green⟩
mooting *n* -s [fr. gerund of ²*moot*] : DISCUSSION, DEBATE; *specif* : participation in a moot court
moot·man \'mütmən\ *n, pl* **mootmen** *Brit* : a student arguing a moot case in the Inns of Court
moot·ness *n* -ES : the quality or state of being moot — used of an issue, question, or case before a court
moot-stow \'⸗,stō\ *n* [OE *mōtstōw,* fr. *mōt* assembly, meeting + *stōw* place — more at MOOT, STOW] : a town or borough serving as the seat of a moot
mootworthy \'⸗,⸗⸗\ *adj* [¹*moot* + *worthy*] *Anglo-Saxon law* : qualified to attend a moot as a member : FREE
¹mop \'mäp\ *n* -s *often attrib* [ME *mappe,* short for *mappel,* prob. fr. ML *mappula* handkerchief, towel, fr. LL, dim. of L *mappa* napkin — more at MAP] **1 a** : a household implement consisting of a mass of absorbent material (as coarse yarn, cellulose, or rags) fastened to a long handle and used typically for cleaning floors — compare DISHMOP, DRY MOP **b** : a cloth or wad of material for absorbing moisture : SWAB ⟨a surgical ~ of absorbent cotton⟩ **2** *dial Eng* : STATUTE FAIR **3** : something that resembles a mop: as **a** : a thick often unruly mass of hair ⟨his hair was a disorderly yellow ~ —T.B.Costain⟩ ⟨grizzled ~s of the elderly Fiji chieftains —Mollie Panter-Downes⟩ ⟨perambulating ~s known as Yorkshire terriers —*Time*⟩; *specif* : the matted forelock of a buffalo ⟨gathered the ~s from the heads that were left unskinned on the prairie —Mari Sandoz⟩ **b** : a dauber for applying a liquid ⟨dip this ~ into the barbecue sauce and slap the roasting meat with it —Sheila Hibben⟩ ⟨poisoned syrup was applied to the tops of plants with a ~ —*Amer. Guide Series: Fla.*⟩ **c** : STAR-MOP

mops 1a

²mop \"\ *vb* **mopped; mopped; mopping; mops** *vt* **1** : to use a mop on: as **a** : to clean by mopping ⟨~ a floor⟩ — often used with *up* ⟨strained to ~ up the debris left by the . . . flood —*N. Y. Times*⟩ **b** : to wipe or polish with a mop ⟨a pitcher . . . should be well *mopped* out, taking care to scrub the whole interior surface —Emily Holt⟩ ⟨*mopped* his brow with a silk handkerchief —Waldo Frank⟩ ⟨*mopped* an imaginary tear from her eye —David Garnett⟩ ⟨*mopping* his plate with a limp piece of new bread —Kenneth Roberts⟩ — often used with *up* ⟨~s up his plate with a tortilla folded twice —M.M. Liberman⟩ **c** : to apply (a liquid) with a mop ⟨*mopping* . . . astringents over that area will shorten the period of discomfort —H.G.Armstrong⟩ ⟨built-up roof coverings shall consist of two or more layers of saturated felt sheets . . . thoroughly *mopped* with a hot bituminous cement —*Code for Dwelling Construction*⟩ **2** *slang Brit* : to consume eagerly : GOBBLE, GUZZLE — usu. used with *up* ⟨swam round with great vigor and *mopped up* his worms greedily —*Irish Digest*⟩ ⟨*mopping up* gin and looking a bit glazed —Anton Vogt⟩ **3** : to overcome decisively : polish off : TROUNCE ⟨sent its superb team of oarsmen . . . to ~ the field in the Henley Royal Regatta —David Dodge⟩ — used esp. in the slang phrase *mop the floor with* ⟨the king of Spain *mopped* his floor with him —*London Daily News*⟩; often used with *up* ⟨just let me at him — I'll ~ him up⟩ ⟨a raiding battleship could ~ up any and every convoy . . . guarded only by cruisers —*U. S. Naval Inst. Proceedings*⟩ ~ *vi* : to clean a surface (as a floor) with a mop ⟨first she dusted, then she *mopped*⟩ — often used with *up* ⟨residents and workers *mopped* up after a Sunday night flood —*Springfield (Mass.) Daily News*⟩
³mop \"\ *vi* **mopped; mopped; mopping; mops** [perh. fr. obs. *mop* fool — more at MOPPET] : to make a face ⟨a shaggy creature . . . came and danced along with her, *mopping* and mowing —Mary Webb⟩
⁴mop \"\ *n* -s *archaic* : GRIMACE, FACE ⟨the ~s and mows of the old witch —R.L.Stevenson⟩
MOP *abbr* **1** manuscript on paper **2** *often not cap* mother-of-pearl **3** mustering-out pay
mo·pan \mō'pän\ *n, pl* **mopan** *or* **mopans** *usu cap* [Sp *mopán* of AmerInd origin] **1 a** : an Indian people of northeastern Guatemala **b** : a member of such people **2** : a Mayan language of the Mopan people closely related to or a dialect of Yucatec
mo·pa·ni \mō'pänē\ *or* **mo·pa·ne** \-nə\ *n, pl* **mopanies** *or* **mopanes** [Sechuana] : a tropical African ironwood (*Copaifera mopane*) yielding hard durable timber
mopboard \'⸗,⸗\ *n* [¹*mop* + *board*] : BASEBOARD
¹mope \'mōp\ *vb* -ED/-ING/-S [prob. fr. obs. *mope* fool, alter. of *mop* — more at MOPPET] *vi* **1** *chiefly dial Brit* : to act in a distracted, bewildered, or stupid manner ⟨a wretched and peevish fellow . . . to ~ with his fat-brained followers so far out of his knowledge —Shak.⟩ **2** : to give oneself up to brooding : become dull, dejected, or listless ⟨doesn't pretend he is glad to be retired but he is not *moping* about it —Katharine Hamill⟩ ⟨the *moping* owl does to the moon complain —Thomas Gray⟩ **3** : to move slowly or aimlessly : DAWDLE ⟨even when the little woman does ~ along in traffic —Paul Jones⟩ ⟨sadly turned his back on us, *moped* into the sea, and took to swimming —*Harper's*⟩ ~ *vt* **1** : to make dull, dejected, or listless : cause to brood ⟨you must come about with me and not ~ yourself —Thomas Hughes⟩ **2** : to pass (as a period of time) in a dull, dejected, or listless state ⟨directs him not to shut himself up in a cloister alone, there to ~ . . . away his life —George Horne †1792⟩
²mope \"\ *n* -s **1** : one that mopes : a dull or gloomy person ⟨meager, muse-rid ~, adust and thin —Alexander Pope⟩ **2 mopes** *pl* : a fit of depression : ²BLUES ⟨he's got the ~s because she's mad at him⟩
mope-eyed \'⸗,⸗\ *adj* [¹*mope* + *eyed*] *archaic* : NEARSIGHTED
mop·er \'mōpə(r)\ *n* -s : one that mopes; *esp* : a slow driver
mop·ery \-p(ə)rē\ *n* -ES [¹*mope* + *-ery*] *slang* : an act of moping : DAWDLING, VAGRANCY
mop·ey *also* **mopy** \-pē\ *adj* **mopier; mopiest** [¹*mope* + *-y*] : DEPRESSED, DROOPY ⟨sad songs make her ~⟩ ⟨infested fowls are in a ~ drowsy condition —R.L.Metcalf⟩ — **mop·i·ness** \-pēnəs\ *n* -ES
mophead \'⸗,⸗\ *n* **1** : the mass of material at the end of a mop ⟨fluffy nylon ~ collects dirt and dust —*advt*⟩ **2** : a thick or bushy head of hair or the individual possessing it
mop-headed \'⸗'⸗⸗\ *adj* : having a bushy top — used esp. of a tree without a leader ⟨*mop-headed* cabbage palms —*Amer. Guide Series: Fla.*⟩
mop·ish \'mōpish\ *adj* [¹*mope* + *-ish*] : given to or characterized by moping
mop·ish·ness *n* -ES : the quality or state of being mopish
mopoke *var of* MOREPORK
mop·per \'mäpə(r)\ *n* -s : one that mops; *specif* : one that wipes or polishes
mopper-up \'⸗⸗'⸗\ *n, pl* **moppers-up** [*mop up* + *-er*] : one that mops up; *specif* : one that follows in the wake of a military attack to eliminate remaining pockets of enemy resistance and dispose of debris
mop·pet \'mäpət, *usu* -əd·+V\ *n* -s [obs. E *mop* fool, child (fr. ME) + *-et*; prob. akin to LG *mops* simpleton, pugnosed dog, D *mop, mops* pugnosed dog, obs. D *moppen* to pout, grumble] **1** : CHILD, YOUNGSTER ⟨a production that will wow the ~s and their parents —*Billboard*⟩ ⟨a jury of ~s aged from about four through twelve render opinions on the problems of other children —*Pasadena (Calif.) Independent*⟩ **2** *archaic* **a** : a young woman : DAMSEL ⟨lustily calling to the landlubbers and to the fair ~s about her —*Pall Mall Mag.*⟩; *esp* : one given to frivolity **b** : an effeminate man : FOP ⟨several times dismissed such manikins as ~s —I.J.C.Brown⟩
mopping *n* -s [fr. gerund of ²*mop*] : a liquid coating applied with a mop ⟨embed each board firmly in the bituminous ~ —P.D.Close⟩
mop·py \'mäpē\ *adj, usu* -ER/-EST [¹*mop* + *-y*] : resembling a mop : BUSHY ⟨shaking their ~ heads —Christopher Rand⟩ ⟨his ~ black hair —George Moore⟩
mops *pl of* MOP, *pres 3d sing of* MOP
mopstick \'⸗,⸗\ *n* **1** : the long thin handle of a mop **2** *or* **mopstick rail** : a handrail of nearly round section
mop·sy *or* **mop·sey** \'mäpsē\ *n, pl* **mopsies** *or* **mopseys** [obs. E *mop* child, fool + *-sy* — more at MOPPET] **1** *obs* : a pretty child : DARLING, SWEETHEART — used as a term of endearment or deprecation **2** [influenced in meaning by ¹*mop*] *archaic* : a slovenly woman : SLATTERN
mop up *vt* **1** : to dispose of : clean up ⟨have heard much less of Brighton's race gangs since the war, so let us hope that they have been *mopped up* —S.P.B.Mais⟩; *specif* : to follow in the wake of an attacking military force and clear (an area) of remaining pockets of resistance ⟨the bulk of the troops were still needed to guard and *mop up* the captured territory —*Infantry Jour.*⟩ ⟨it was left to Australians to *mop up* the bypassed Japanese —D.L.Oliver⟩ **2** : to take up or assimilate : GARNER, ABSORB ⟨urchins are abundant in nearby waters and are . . . *mopped up* by the tubful —W.C.Allee⟩ ⟨added seventeen swimming and diving gold medals to the 56 they had *mopped up* in other events —*Newsweek*⟩ ⟨contributes to anti-inflation . . . in that it *mops up* funds that might otherwise be paid out in higher wages and dividends —W.H.Anderson⟩ ⟨sales of assets will serve to *mop up* surplus credit —W.M. Dacey⟩ ~ *vi* : to complete a project or transaction : clean up ⟨most of the East Cambridge apparatus was *mopping up* at the two engine house fires —*Springfield (Mass.) Union*⟩ ⟨quick-freezers, whose products were not rationed, *mopped up* on the home front —*Harper's*⟩; *specif* : to carry out a military cleanup ⟨behind it would come truck-borne infantry and mobile guns to *mop up* and to widen the breach —Tom Wintringham⟩
mop-up \'⸗,⸗\ *n* -s [*mop up*] : an act of concluding or final disposal : CLEANUP: as **a** : the clearance of enemy stragglers from a captured area by troops assigned to the task ⟨after the decisive battles come the *mop-ups* —*Time*⟩ **b** : the carrying out of safety measures after a forest fire is brought under control ⟨there was still an endless amount of *mop-up* . . . and some crews would have to be kept on the fire for a week or two —G.R.Stewart⟩
mo·pus \'mōpəs\ *n, pl* **mopuses** *or* **mopusses** [origin unknown] *slang* : MONEY, CASH; *esp* : ready money — usu. used in pl.
mo·que·lum·nan \,mōkə'ləmnən\ *n* -s *usu cap* : a language family of Penutian stock in California comprising three languages all known as Miwok — called also *Miwok*
mo·quette \mō'ket\ *n* -s [F, alter. of *moucade*] **1** : a usu. machine-made pile carpet resembling Axminster but less expensive **2** : an upholstery fabric similar to the moquette carpeting made with a cut or uncut pile of mohair or wool and a cotton foundation usu. in solid colors or small jacquard patterns
mo·qui \'mōkē\ *usu cap, var of* MOKI
mor \'mō(ə)r\ *n* -s [Dan, lit., humus] : forest humus that consists characteristically of a layer of largely organic matter abruptly distinct from the mineral soil beneath — compare DUFF, ⁸MULL
mor *abbr* **1** morendo **2** morocco **3** mortar
¹mo·ra \'mōrə, 'mȯrə\ *n, pl* **mo·rae** \-,rē\ *or* **moras** [L, lit., delay — more at MORATORY] **1** *Roman & civil law* : delay in the performance of an obligation; *esp* : culpable delay **2 a** : the minimal unit of quantitative measure in temporal prosodic systems equivalent in the time value to an average short syllable **b** : such a unit used in linguistic analysis esp. with reference to vowel quantity
²mo·ra *or* **mor·ra** \'mȯrə\ *n* -s [It] : an Italian game in which a player extends a number of fingers of his hand in an attempt to match the number of fingers simultaneously extended by his opponent ⟨the little singing girls playing ~ —Joseph Hergesheimer⟩
³mo·ra \mō'rä\ *n* -s [Hindi *moṛhā*] *India* : a low wicker stool or footstool
⁴mo·ra \'mōrə, 'mȯrə\ *n* [NL, perh. modif. of Tupi *moiratinga,* fr. *moira* tree + *tinga* white] **1 a** *cap* : a small genus of tall half-evergreen forest trees (family Leguminosae) of northern So. America that are often included in a closely related genus (*Dimorphandra*) **b** -s : any tree of the genus *Mora*; *esp* : a tall buttressed tree (*Mora excelsa* or *Dimorphandra mora*) that often grows in nearly pure stands on alluvial lands chiefly of British Guiana and Trinidad and that yields a strong heavy wood which is highly resistant to dry rot and to termite injury and is used extensively for railway ties, heavy construction, and in shipbuilding **c** -s : the wood of the British Guiana mora **2** -s : FUSTIC 1
mor·a·buk·ea *also* **mor·a·buc·quea** \,mōrə'bəkēə\ *n* -s [native name in British Guiana] : a leguminous tree (*Mora gonggrijpii* or *Dimorphandra gonggrijpii*) of British Guiana and Surinam that is closely related to the mora, that often grows in dense pure stands, and that yields hard heavy strong often streaked reddish brown wood very resistant to decay
mo·ra·ce·ae \mə'rāsē,ē\ *n pl, cap* [NL, fr. *Morus,* type genus + *-aceae*] : a family of trees or shrubs (order Urticales) that have a milky juice and small diclinous flowers with a one-celled ovary — see ARTOCARPUS, FICUS, MORUS — **mo·ra·ceous** \-āshəs\ *adj*
mo·ra·da \mə'rädə\ *n* -s [AmerSp, fr. Sp, house, dwelling, fr. *morar* to live, dwell, fr. L *morari* to delay, remain — more at MORATORY] : a meetinghouse or chapel of the Penitentes ⟨knees growing numb on the stone floor of the ~ —R.V.Hunter⟩
mo·rad·a·bad \mə'rädə,bäd, -radə,bad\ *adj, usu cap* [fr. *Moradabad,* city in northern India] : of or from the city of Moradabad, India : of the kind or style prevalent in Moradabad
mo·raea \mə'rēə\ *n* [NL, irreg. fr. Robert *More* †1780 Eng. collector of exotic plants] **1** *cap* : a genus of southern African or Australian bulbous or tuberous plants (family Iridaceae) with a divided perianth and petaloid style branches **2** -s : any plant of the genus *Moraea*
mora hair *n* [perh. fr. ⁴*mora*] : SPANISH MOSS
mo·rain·al \mə'rānᵊl, mō'-, mȯ'-\ *adj* : of or relating to a moraine
mo·raine \-ān\ *n* -s [F, fr. F dial. (Savoy) *morêna*] : an accumulation of earth and stones carried and finally deposited by a glacier — see END MORAINE, GROUND MORAINE, LATERAL MORAINE, MEDIAL MORAINE, PUSH MORAINE, RECESSIONAL MORAINE, TERMINAL MORAINE; compare ABLATION
mo·rain·ic \-nik, -nēk\ *adj* [ISV *moraine* + *-ic*] : of or relating to a moraine
¹mor·al \'mȯrəl, 'märəl\ *adj* [ME, fr. MF, fr. L *moralis,* fr. *mor-, mos* custom + *-alis* -al — more at MOOD] **1 a** : of or relating to principles or considerations of right and wrong action or good and bad character : ETHICAL ⟨~ values⟩ ⟨~ distinctions⟩ ⟨~ conduct⟩ ⟨~ convictions⟩ ⟨a ~ monster⟩ **b** : of or relating to the study of such principles or considerations **2** : expressing or teaching a conception of right behavior : DIDACTIC, MORALIZING ⟨a ~ lesson⟩ ⟨a ~ poem⟩ ⟨a ~ story⟩ **3 a** : capable of being judged as good or evil or in terms of principles of right and wrong action : resulting from or belonging to human character, conduct, or intentions ⟨the use of science is a ~ question, that is to say, a human question —Irwin Edman⟩ ⟨a ~ act, the result of a choice —Norman Podhoretz⟩ **b** : capable of right and wrong action or of being governed by a sense of right ⟨a ~ agent⟩ **4** : of, relating to, or acting upon the mind, character, or will : PSYCHOLOGICAL ⟨a whole series of political, organizational, military and . . . ~ triumphs —Joseph Alsop⟩ ⟨gone to the dinner party determined to make a success . . . understanding the ~ importance to herself of this initial contact with society —I.V. Morris⟩ **5 a** : conforming to or proceeding from a standard of what is good and right : PRINCIPLED ⟨not exactly a religious man, though a highly ~ one —Katharine F. Gerould⟩ ⟨a ~ life⟩ ⟨took a ~ position on the issue though it cost him the nomination⟩ ⟨show ~ courage⟩ **b** *Hegelianism* : relating to virtuous conduct or natural excellence as distinguished from civic or legal righteousness **6 a** : based upon inner conviction ⟨have a ~ certainty that my will is free⟩ **b** : virtual rather than actual, immediate, or completely demonstrable ⟨have a ~ certainty that the prisoner is guilty⟩ **7** : sanctioned by or operating upon one's conscience or ethical judgment ⟨the ranch was legally all Mother's, except that Grampa . . . had a ~ claim upon it —Mary Austin⟩ ⟨felt under a sort of ~ obligation not to be indifferent —Joseph Conrad⟩ **8 a** : of or relating to the accepted customs or patterns of social or personal relations ⟨a reflection of the ~ imperatives of the community —Kingsley Davis⟩ ⟨the enormous importance of ~ conformity to the stability of society —Talcott Parsons⟩ **b** : sexually virtuous : not adulterous or promiscuous ⟨middle-aged and cautious and monogamic and ~ —Sinclair Lewis⟩ **c** : conforming to generally accepted standards of correct behavior ⟨appeared ~, self-controlled, well-bathed, and literate —Jean Stafford⟩ ⟨the teacher had to be more ~ — which usually meant more conventional —J.M.Barzun⟩ **d** : expecting or exacting a strict adherence to conventional standards of speech or conduct : PROPER ⟨a highly ~ man who was outraged by the rowdy language of his fellow soldiers⟩
syn ETHICAL, VIRTUOUS, RIGHTEOUS, NOBLE: in describing persons and their actions and conduct, MORAL, opposed to *immoral,* may designate conformity to established sanctioned codes or accepted notions of right and wrong, now particularly in sexual conduct ⟨living a *moral* life⟩ ⟨the right thinker, the great *moral* statesman, the perfect model of the Christian cad —H.L.Mencken⟩ ⟨there were black marketeers, but they were not seen as products of the *moral* deficiencies of the ruling class —Edward Shils⟩ ETHICAL may suggest conformity to a code or to the conclusions of other considerations of right, fair, equitable conduct ⟨an *ethical* decision⟩ ⟨an *ethical* solution to the problem —Edward Shils⟩ VIRTUOUS may still indicate blended rectitude and integrity; often it implies abstinence from illicit sex ⟨pacifists assume that other people are as reasonable and *virtuous* as they are themselves —Harold Nicolson⟩ ⟨a man might grind the faces of the poor; but so long as he refrained from caressing his neighbors' wives and daughters, he was regarded as *virtuous* —Aldous Huxley⟩ ⟨all *virtuous* persons . . . whose lives are chaste and placid —Elinor Wylie⟩ RIGHTEOUS suggests freedom from guilt, culpability, or questionability; it may suggest religious or sectarian sanction or sanctimoniousness ⟨persecution seemed justified in reason; it was very logical; broad reasons of Christian statecraft seemed to make for it; and often a *righteous* zeal wielded the weapon —H.O.Taylor⟩ ⟨our wits are much more alert when engaged in wrongdoing (in which one mustn't be found out) than in a *righteous* occupation —Joseph Conrad⟩ ⟨a republic admirable in justice and *righteous* in all its ways —V.L. Parrington⟩ NOBLE may indicate moral eminence with lack of any taint of the petty or dubious ⟨a *noble* ideal, worthy of a Christian —V.L.Parrington⟩ ⟨behavior . . . when the crisis actually came was simple, dignified, and even *noble* —P.E. More⟩ ⟨the true task of man is to create for himself a *noble* memory, a mind filled with grandeur, forgiveness, restless ideals, and the dynamic ethical ferment preached by all religions at their best —J.L.Liebman⟩
²moral \", *in sense 7 like* MORALE\ *n* -s **1 a** : the moral significance or practical lesson taught by or capable of being derived from a story, event, experience, or object ⟨love makes gentlemen even of boors . . . is the constant ~ of medieval story —Henry Adams⟩ ⟨the ~ of his life⟩ ⟨the ~ of recent history⟩ **b** : a passage pointing out usu. in conclusion the lesson to be drawn from a story : MAXIM ⟨the view . . . that highly serious art is didactic, ending with a ~ —G.K.Chalmers⟩ **2** : MORALITY PLAY **3 morals** *pl* **a** : the moral practices of an individual or culture : habits of life or modes of conduct ⟨as principal, he maintained a high standard of ~s and manners in the school —L.M.Crosbie⟩ ⟨losing touch with the ordinary patterns and ~s of life —Alan Moorehead⟩ **b** : sexual conduct ⟨provoked a long and thoughtful discussion of the mores and ~s of American womanhood —T.O.Heggen⟩ ⟨a person of loose ~s⟩ **4 morals** *pl* : the study dealing with the principles of conduct : ETHICS ⟨the science of ~s endeavors to divide men into the good and the bad —J.W.Krutch⟩ **5 morals** *pl* : moral teachings : the moral principles of an individual or culture ⟨the Greek dramatists moralize only because ~s are woven through and through the texture of their tragic idea —T.S.Eliot⟩ ⟨an authoritative code of ~s has force and effect when it expresses the settled customs of a stable society —Walter Lippmann⟩ **6** *archaic* : COUNTERPART, IMAGE ⟨the long chin . . . is the very ~ of the governor's —Tobias Smollett⟩ **7** [F, morale, moral nature, fr. *moral,* adj.] : MORALE ⟨the ~ of the nation is therefore likely to be as important a factor in war as the ~ of armies has always been —*Atlantic*⟩
³moral *like* ¹MORAL\ *vb, archaic* : MORALIZE
mo·rale \mə'ral, mō'-, mȯ'-\ *n* -s [in sense 1, fr. F, fr. fem. of *moral,* adj.; in other senses, modif. (influenced by E *morale,* sense 1) of F *moral* morale, moral nature, fr. *moral,* adj. — more at MORAL] **1** : moral principles, teachings, or conduct : MORALITY ⟨conversations which American law and ~ consider privileged —A.F.Westin⟩ ⟨a ~ of fair-mindedness, intellectual integrity —John Dewey⟩ **2 a** : a confident, resolute, willing, often self-sacrificing and courageous attitude of an individual to the function or tasks demanded or expected of him by a group of which he is a part that is based upon such factors as pride in the achievements and aims of the group, faith in its leadership and ultimate success, a sense of fruitful personal participation in its work, and a devotion and loyalty to the other members of the group ⟨high ~ and personal pride are at least barely possible in large firms —Peter Wiles⟩ ⟨whatever happened, ~ meant to them resistance, and capitulation was a proof that they had lost their nerve —Ruth Benedict⟩

b : a sense of common purpose or a degree of dedication to a common task regarded as characteristic of or dominant in a particular group or organization **:** ESPRIT DE CORPS ⟨the ~ of the ship improved after two days of shore leave⟩ ⟨the ~ of the faculty was high⟩ ⟨the ~ of the reform group suffered a severe blow when their candidate was defeated⟩ **3 :** a state of individual psychological well-being and buoyancy based upon such factors as physical or mental health, a sense of purpose and usefulness, and confidence in the future ⟨a long period of unemployment had weakened his ~⟩ ⟨the failure of his play did not affect his ~⟩

mo·ral·er *n* -s [³*moral* + *-er*] *obs* **:** MORALIZER ⟨you are too severe a ~ —Shak.⟩

moral hazard *n* **:** the possibility of loss to an insurance company arising from the character, habits, or circumstances of the insured

moral insanity *also* **moral imbecility** *n* **:** PSYCHOPATHIC PERSONALITY

mor·al·ism \ˈmȯrəˌlizəm, ˈmär-\ *n* -s **1 a :** the habit or practice of moralizing ⟨before he had slipped into transcendentalism and ~ and complacency in mediocrity —George Santayana⟩ **b :** an instance of moralizing **:** a conventional moral attitude or saying ⟨the traditional ~ of melodrama — the idea of Virtue Triumphant —E.R.Bentley⟩ ⟨his brain was clogged with ~*s*, inchoate poetry, and unclear ambitions —H.S.Canby⟩ **2 :** the practice of morality as distinct from religion **:** the doctrine or practice of religion reduced to morality ⟨make out a case for activism and ~ as the fundamental American heresy —*Rev. of Religion*⟩

mor·al·ist \-ləst\ *n* -s **1 :** one who leads a moral life ⟨a ~ who practices what he preaches⟩ **2 :** a teacher or student of morals **:** a thinker or writer concerned with moral principles and problems ⟨was attracted particularly by the great classical ~*s*, and found in their ethical teaching inspiration and instruction —A.C.McGiffert⟩ ⟨nowadays it is . . . far harder to be a ~ of any true simplicity of spirit —Lionel Trilling⟩ ⟨like all good writers, a ~ at bottom —Bernard Kalb⟩ **3 :** one who is concerned to regulate the morals of others ⟨~*s* looked upon it as a lewd distraction that would take the mind off work —Lewis Mumford⟩ ⟨once the ~ . . . becomes the censor of art, with power to enforce his judgments, art is seriously jeopardized —Hunter Mead⟩

mor·al·is·tic \ˌ≈≈ˈlistik, -tēk\ *adj* **1 :** characterized by or expressive of a concern with morality ⟨when man developed, when he became more scientific and more ~ —Havelock Ellis⟩ ⟨~ wit, or the joke that teaches a lesson —Ernst Simon⟩ **2 :** characterized by or expressive of a narrow and conventional moral attitude ⟨the conventional and ~ prettifications of life then in vogue —R.M.Coates⟩ ⟨the ponderous and ~ style of the early nineteenth century —*Amer. Guide Series: Tenn.*⟩ — **mor·al·is·ti·cal·ly** \-tək(ə)lē, -tēk-, -li\ *adv*

mo·ral·i·ty \məˈralədē, mȯ'-, mō'-, -ətē, -i\ *n* -ES [ME *moralitee*, fr. MF *moralité*, fr. LL *moralitat-, moralitas*, fr. L *moralis* moral + *-tat-, -tas* -ty — more at MORAL] **1 moralities** *pl*, *archaic* **:** moral traits ⟨a saint . . . in her *moralities* —Lord Byron⟩ **2 a :** a moral discourse, statement, or lesson **:** a piece of moralizing ⟨a poem full of commonplace *moralities*⟩ ⟨ended his lecture with a trite ~⟩ **b :** a literary or other imaginative work conceived as a moral allegory and teaching a moral lesson ⟨the book's undeniable power as a ~ is diminished by . . . a style of bright impersonal smartness —*Times Lit. Supp.*⟩ ⟨has managed to turn out a ~ in which he spares his readers any moralizing —*Time*⟩ **c :** MORALITY PLAY ⟨increased use of the comic element marked the development of the *moralities* as popular plays —F.H.O'Hara & Marguerite Bro⟩ **3 a :** a doctrine or system of ideas concerned with conduct ⟨the basic law which an adequate ~ ought to state —Marjorie Grene⟩ ⟨the object of systems of ~ is to take possession of human life —Matthew Arnold⟩ **b moralities** *pl* **:** particular moral principles or rules of conduct ⟨we were all brought up on one of these *moralities* —*Psychiatry*⟩ ⟨instruction in the fundamental *moralities* of life . . . and its decent amenities —W.A. White⟩ **4 :** the quality or fact of conforming to or deriving from right ideals of human conduct ⟨admitted the expediency of the law but questioned its ~⟩ **5 a :** moral conduct **:** goodness and uprightness of behavior **:** VIRTUE ⟨~ consists in the aims at the ideal —A.N.Whitehead⟩ ⟨a new low in public ~ —*Current History*⟩ ⟨a person of strict ~⟩ ⟨~ today involves a responsible relationship toward the laws of the natural world —P.B.Sears⟩ **b :** conduct conforming to the customs or accepted standards of a particular culture or group ⟨in Christian love and forgiveness lay some reversal of Saxon ~ —H.O. Taylor⟩ ⟨the ~ of a world plunging itself into chaos —G.P. Musselman⟩ ⟨an abyss separated the domestic and business ~ of the Victorian world —F.B.Millett⟩ ⟨customs, *moralities*, scenes, and quaint observances of the time —Joseph Hudnut⟩

morality play *n* **:** an allegorical play popular esp. in the 15th and 16th centuries in which the characters personify moral qualities (as charity or vice) or abstractions (as death or youth) and in which moral lessons are specifically taught

mor·al·iza·tion \ˌmȯrələˈzāshən, ˌmär-, -līˈ-\ *n* -s [ME *moralizacion*, fr. ML *moralization-, moralizatio*, fr. *moralizatus* (past part. of *moralizare* to moralize) + L *-ion-, -io* -ion] **1 a :** the giving of a moral interpretation to something **:** an explanation in moral terms ⟨his criticism of the play is simply a ~ of it⟩ **b :** the act of moralizing **:** a moral reflection or discourse ⟨~*s* . . . were the beginnings of thought, feelings, perceptions, which led him to write the novels —J.T.Farrell⟩ **2 a :** the act of making moral ⟨the best government it had ever known, with ~ of public offices —Hubert Herring⟩ **b :** the process of becoming moral ⟨progressive ~ of the idea of holiness in the Old Testament —R.C.Dentan⟩

mor·al·ize \ˈmȯrəˌlīz, ˈmär-\ *vb* -ED/-ING/-S *see -ize in Explan Notes* [ME *moralysen*, fr. MF *moraliser*, prob. fr. ML *moralizare*, fr. L *moralis* moral + LL *-izare* -ize] *vt* **1 :** to explain or interpret morally **:** draw a moral from or furnish with a moral meaning ⟨always posed an insoluble problem for those who would ~ the play —D.P.Harding⟩ **2 a :** to give a moral quality or direction to **:** make aware of or subject to the influence of moral values ⟨the sentiments and force of will are neutral . . . and may become antisocial unless they are *moralized* —*General Education in a Free Society*⟩ ⟨has always felt strongly the compulsion to ~ his fellowmen —Asher Moore⟩ **b :** to make more moral **:** improve the morals or moral conduct of ⟨modern efforts to ~ business and to subordinate profit seeking to humane ends —Walter Lippmann⟩ **3** *archaic* **:** to make more tolerable **:** bring into a better state of mind by moral speech or reflection **~** *vi* **:** to make moral reflections **:** talk, write, or think in moral terms ⟨the tendency to ~ upon the relations of beauty to conduct —Bliss Perry⟩ ⟨never descends to the sermonizing and *moralizing* that filled so many pages in Victorian histories —*Saturday Rev.*⟩

mor·al·iz·er \-zə(r)\ *n* -s **:** one that moralizes

moralizing *adj* **:** that moralizes **:** painting a moral ⟨this trite ~ way of regarding natural phenomena —L.P.Smith⟩ — **mor·al·iz·ing·ly** *adv*

moral law *n* **:** a general rule of right living; *esp* **:** such a rule or group of rules conceived as universal and unchanging and as having the sanction of God's will, of conscience, of man's moral nature, or of natural justice as revealed to human reason ⟨the basic protection of rights is the *moral law* based on man's dignity —*Time*⟩

moraller *var of* MORALER

mor·al·less \ˈmȯrəlləs, ˈmär-\ *adj* **:** having no moral significance ⟨a ~ story⟩ ⟨regards art as a ~ activity⟩

mor·al·ly \-rəlē, -li\ *adv* [ME, fr. ¹*moral* + *-ly*] **1 :** from the point of view of moral rules or principles **:** in terms of accepted moral standards ⟨if public administration is ~ bad but legally sound —*Sydney (Australia) Bull.*⟩ **2 :** according to reason or probability **:** VIRTUALLY ⟨there is precise record of so many East Asiatic junks reaching the Pacific coast . . . during the past hundred years that its having happened again and again in preceding centuries is ~ certain —A.L.Kroeber⟩ **3 :** with respect to the mental and psychological as distinguished from the physical ⟨helped her, ~ rather than physically, to rise —Arnold Bennett⟩ ⟨~ and physically exhausted⟩

moral philosophy *or* **moral science** *n* **:** a study of the motivations and principles of human conduct; *esp* **:** such study formerly prominent as a distinct subject in institutions of higher education and including subjects (as psychology) now separately studied — compare MENTAL PHILOSOPHY, NATURAL PHILOSOPHY

moral re-armament *n*, *often cap M&R&A* **:** a movement developing out of the Oxford Group movement and applying its doctrine and techniques esp. to the problems of international relations

morals *pl of* MORAL

moral sense *n* **:** a feeling of the rightness or wrongness of an action or the ability to have such feelings

moral theology *n* **:** a branch of theology that treats of morals; *also* **:** theology or theological doctrines developed as inferences from moral grounds or reasons

moral theory *or* **moral influence theory** *n* **:** a theory of the atonement introduced by Peter Abelard in the 12th century and common in modern liberal theology holding that the life and death of Jesus Christ reconcile man to God by so revealing the holiness and love of God as to win man to repentence and faith — called also *subjective theory;* compare SATISFACTION THEORY

moral turpitude *n* **1 :** an act or behavior that gravely violates the moral sentiment or accepted moral standards of the community; *esp* **:** sexual immorality ⟨was considered unfit to hold office because of *moral turpitude*⟩ **2 :** the morally culpable quality held to be present in some criminal offenses as distinguished from others ⟨permits may be denied for bad moral character . . . or conviction for an offense involving *moral turpitude* —David Fellman⟩ — compare MALUM PROHIBITUM

moral victory *n* **:** an actual defeat regarded as a virtual victory because of the narrowness of the margin or because of some circumstance that gives satisfaction or hope

moral virtue *n*, *Aristotelianism* **:** a virtue concerned with the practical life (as liberality or gentleness) or with the vegetative and appetitive (as temperance or self-control) — contrasted with *intellectual virtue*

morant hutch \məˈrant-\ *n* [after Major G. F. *Morant*, 19th cent. Eng. agriculturist, its designer] **:** a rabbit hutch with a wire mesh floor used on grassland

moras *pl of* MORA

mo·rass \məˈras, mȯ'-, mō'-, -raa(ə)s-, -rais\ *n* -ES [D *moeras*, alter. (influenced by obs. D *moer* mire, swamp, fr. MD) of MD *maras, marasch*, fr. OF *mareis, maresc*, of Gmc origin; akin to OE *mersc, merisc* marsh — more at MARSH, MOOR] **1 :** a tract of soft, swampy, or boggy ground **:** MARSH, SWAMP **2 :** something that traps, confuses, or impedes **:** a state of confusion or entanglement ⟨a ~ of clumsy exposition and preposterous dialogue —Bruce Bliven b.1916⟩ ⟨guides her out of her ~ of insecurity —*Newsweek*⟩ — **mo·rassy** \-sē\ *adj*

morass ore *n* [trans. of G *morasterz*] **:** BOG IRON ORE

mo·rat \ˈmōˌrat\ *n* -s [ML *moratum*, fr. L *morum* mulberry — more at MULBERRY] **:** a medieval drink of wine flavored with mulberries

mor·a·to·ri·um \ˌmȯrəˈtōrēəm, ˌmär-, -tȯr-\ *n*, *pl* **moratoriums** \-mz\ *or* **moratoria** \-ēə\ [NL, fr. LL, neut. of *moratorius* dilatory, retarding] **1 a :** a legally authorized period of delay in the performance of a legal obligation or the payment of a debt ⟨asked the legislature for a ~ of one year on farm mortgage payments⟩ **b :** waiting period set by some authority **:** a delay officially required or granted ⟨usually there was at least one day's ~ on news coming out of such background briefings —Douglass Cater⟩ — compare INDULGENCE 3c **2 :** a suspension of activity **:** a temporary ban on the use or production of something ⟨so thorough was the ~ on brains that nobody in power dared do any primary thinking —J.R. Chamberlain⟩ ⟨a ~ on new systems —C.W.Thornthwaite⟩

mor·a·tory \ˈ≈≈ˌtōrē, -tȯr-, -ri\ *adj* [F *moratoire*, fr. LL *moratorius* dilatory, retarding, fr. L *moratus* (past part. of *morari* to delay, remain, fr. *mora* delay) + *-orius* -ory — more at MEMORY] **:** of, relating to, or authorizing delay in payment of an obligation ⟨~ interest⟩ ⟨a ~ law⟩

¹mo·ra·vi·an \məˈrāvēən, mȯ'-, mō'-, -vyən\ *n* -s *cap* [ML *Moravia* Moray, region in northern Scotland including the present county of Moray + E *-an*, n. suffix] **:** a native or inhabitant of Moray, Scotland

²moravian \"\ *adj*, *usu cap* [ML *Moravia* Moray + E *-an*, adj. suffix] **1 :** of, relating to, or characteristic of Moray, Scotland **2 :** of, relating to, or characteristic of the people of Moray

³moravian \"\ *adj*, *usu cap* [*Moravia*, former province in central Czechoslovakia + E *-an*, adj. suffix] **1 a :** of, relating to, or characteristic of Moravia **b :** of, relating to, or characteristic of the people of Moravia **2 :** of, relating to, or characteristic of the Moravian Church

⁴moravian \"\ *n* -s **1** *usu cap* **:** a member of a Christian denomination that traces its history back through the evangelical movement in Moravia and Bohemia stemming from the efforts of the reformer John Hus and that accepts the Bible as the sole rule of faith and practice — called also *Herrnhuter* **2** *cap* **a :** a native or inhabitant of Moravia; *esp* **:** a descendant of the Slavic people who ruled Moravia in medieval times **b :** the group of dialects spoken by the Moravian people and transitional between Slovak and Czech

moravian brethren *n pl*, *usu cap M&B* **:** members of the Moravian Church

mo·ra·vi·an·ism \-ēəˌnizəm\ *n* -s *usu cap* **:** the doctrines and practices of Moravians

mo·ra·vite \məˈrāˌvīt, ˈmȯrə,-\ *n* -s [*Moravia*, former province in central Czechoslovakia + E *-ite*] **:** a mineral $Fe_2N_2Fe)_4Si_7O_{20}(OH)_4$ consisting of a fine scaly black basic silicate of iron and aluminum of the chlorite group

mo·rav·ska os·tra·va \ˈmȯrəfskəˈȯstrəvə\ *adj*, *usu cap M&O* [fr. *Moravska Ostrava*, city in central Czechoslovakia] **:** of or from the city of Moravska Ostrava, Czechoslovakia **:** of the kind or style prevalent in Moravska Ostrava

¹mo·ray \məˈrā, ˈmȯ(ˌ)rā\ *or* **moray eel** *n* -s [*moray* fr. Pg *moréia*, fr. L *murena, muraena*, fr. Gk *myraina;* perh. akin to Gk *smyrid-, smyris* powdered emery — more at SMEAR] **:** any of numerous often brightly colored savage voracious eels constituting the family Muraenidae, having small round gill openings, no pectoral or pelvic fins, and usu. narrow jaws with strong knifelike teeth and no tongue, occurring in all warm seas esp. in crevices about coral reefs, and including a Mediterranean eel (*Muraena helena*) valued as a food fish

²mor·ay \ˈmər·|ē, ˈmə·r|, |i\ *or* **mor·ay·shire** \ˈ≈≈ˌshi(ə)r, -ˌshiə, -ˌsh(ə)r\ *adj*, *usu cap* [fr. *Moray, Morayshire*, county in northeast Scotland] **:** of or from the county of Moray, Scotland **:** of the kind or style prevalent in Moray

mor·bid \ˈmȯrbəd, ˈmȯ(ə)b-\ *adj* [L *morbidus* diseased, unwholesome, fr. *morbus* disease; akin to Gk *marainein* to waste away — more at SMART] **1 a :** of, relating to, or characteristic of disease ⟨~ anatomy⟩ **b :** affected with or induced by disease **:** not sound and healthful ⟨only the sick in mind crave cleverness, as a ~ body turns to drink —H.M.Tomlinson⟩ ⟨a ~ state⟩ ⟨~ alteration of tissues⟩ **c :** productive of disease ⟨introduction into the blood of ~ substances from without —Robert Chawner⟩ **2 :** abnormally susceptible to or characterized by gloomy or unwholesome feelings ⟨a ~, frustrated, sensitive and prophetic man —William Phillips b.1878⟩ ⟨a career of ~ introspection and self-pity —*Times Lit. Supp.*⟩ ⟨an almost ~ sense of guilt about the uses to which their discoveries have been put —Reinhold Niebuhr⟩ **3 :** GRISLY, GRUESOME ⟨a day for ~ joys and gruesome delights —Gertrude Diamant⟩ ⟨war has a ~ fascination for many men and women —D.L.Cohn⟩ **syn** see UNWHOLESOME

mor·bi·dez·za \ˌmȯ(r)bəˈdetsə\ *n* -s [It, fr. *morbido* tender, delicate, fr. L *morbidus* diseased, unwholesome] **1 :** an extreme delicacy and softness ⟨marveled at the ~ of the Italian women —Francis Hackett⟩ ⟨had too heroic a style for the ~ of the music he played⟩ **2 :** a sensual delicacy of flesh-coloring in painting ⟨~ in his treatment of flesh —Edward McCurdy⟩

mor·bid·i·ty \mȯ(r)ˈbidədē, -ətē, -i\ *n* -ES **1 :** an abnormal or unhealthy state of mind; *esp* **:** one marked by excessive gloom ⟨his very ~ of mind . . . drove him into company as the only refuge from his haunting fears —Robert Lynd⟩ ⟨their passion for privacy verges on ~ —Green Peyton⟩ **2 :** a diseased state or symptom **:** fever up to 100.4°F ⟨lumbar puncture, if improperly performed, may be followed by a significant ~ —*Jour. Amer. Med. Assoc.*⟩ ⟨puerperal ~⟩ **3 :** the incidence of disease **:** the rate of sickness (as in a specified community or group) ⟨while TB mortality has declined fairly steadily, ~ has been rising —*Time*⟩ ⟨the collection of statistics on mental illness ~ —G.N.Raines⟩

mor·bid·ly *adv* **:** in a morbid manner or to a morbid extent ⟨~ sensitive⟩ ⟨~ fearful⟩ ⟨~ shy⟩

mor·bid·ness *n* -ES **:** the quality or state of being morbid

mor·bif·ic \(ˈ)mȯ(r)ˈbifik\ *adj* [prob. fr. (assumed) NL *morbificus*, fr. L *morbus* disease + *-ficus* -fic] **1 :** causing disease **:** generating a sickly state **2** *archaic* **:** DISEASED

mor·bil·li \mȯ(r)ˈbiˌlī\ *n pl* [ML, pl. of *morbillus* spot on skin, pustule, dim. of L *morbus* disease] **:** MEASLES 1

mor·bil·li·form \(ˈ)mȯrˈbiləˌfȯrm\ *adj* [ISV *morbilli-* (fr. ML *morbilli*) + *-form*] **:** resembling the eruption of measles

mor·bose \(ˈ)mȯrˈbōs\ *adj* [L *morbosus*, fr. *morbus* disease + *-osus* -ose] **:** DISEASED, MORBID

mor·bus \ˈmȯrbəs\ *n*, *pl* **mor·bi** \-ˌbī\ [L] **:** DISEASE

morbus gal·li·cus \-ˈgaləkəs\ *n*, *usu cap G* [NL, lit., Gallic disease] *archaic* **:** SYPHILIS

mor·ceau \mȯrˈsō\ *n*, *pl* **mor·ceaux** \-ō(z)\ *also* **morceaus** \-ōz\ [F, fr. OF *morsel* — more at MORSEL] **:** a short literary or musical piece

mor·cel·la·tion \ˌmȯ(r)səˈlāshən\ *n* -s [F *morceler* to divide into small pieces (fr. *morceau* morsel) + E *-ation*] **:** division and removal in small pieces (as of a tumor)

mor·celle·ment \ˌmȯ(r)selˈmäⁿ\ *n* -s [F, fr. *morceler* to divide into small pieces + *-ment*] **1 :** division into small pieces **2 :** MORCELLATION

mor·chel·la \mȯ(r)ˈkelə\ *n*, *cap* [NL, fr. G *morchel* morel, fr. OHG *morhila* — more at MOREL] **:** a genus of edible fungi (family Helvellaceae) having an irregularly folded and pitted apothecium grown around the upper part of the stalk — see MOREL — **mor·chel·loid** \-eˌlȯid\ *adj*

mor·da·cious \(ˈ)mȯ(r)ˈdāshəs\ *adj* [L *mordac-, mordax* biting, given to biting (fr. *mordēre* to bite) + E *-ious* — more at SMART] **1 :** biting or given to biting ⟨bitten in as with ~ acid —*Times Lit. Supp.*⟩ **2 :** biting or sharp in manner or style **:** CAUSTIC ⟨the lady's ~ look showed plainly that she hated us all —Pauline R. Fadiman⟩ — **mor·da·cious·ly** *adv*

mor·dac·i·ty \mȯ(r)ˈdasədē, -aas-, -ətē, -i\ *n* -ES [L *mordacitat-, mordacitas*, fr. *mordac-, mordax* + *-itat-, -itas* -ity] **1** *archaic* **:** a readiness to bite **2 :** a biting quality of speech

mor·dan·cy \ˈmȯ(r)dᵊnsē, -si\ *n* -ES [¹*mordant* + *-cy*] **1 :** a biting and caustic quality of style **:** INCISIVENESS ⟨the ~ of his comments made his opponent wince⟩ **2 :** a sharply critical or bitter quality of thought or feeling **:** HARSHNESS ⟨marked by a deepening note of grimness and ~ —J.E.M.White⟩ ⟨forceful criticisms of the maladjustments of life, bitterness, ~, and despair —Leslie Rees⟩

¹mor·dant \-ᵊnt\ *adj* [MF, pres. part. of *mordre* to bite, fr. L *mordēre*] **1 :** biting and caustic in thought, manner, or style **:** INCISIVE, KEEN ⟨fun ranging from slapstick clowning to . . . savage ~ wit —Robert Bendiner⟩ ⟨the ~ things you try to say to listeners, cruelties invariably regarded as merely gently whimsical —Irwin Edman⟩ ⟨a ~ analyst and remorseless judge of snobbery —*Time*⟩ **2 a :** acting as a mordant (as in dyeing) **b :** of, relating to, or subject to application by means of a mordant **3 :** BURNING, PUNGENT ⟨~ pain⟩ **4 :** prone to biting ⟨a ~ dog⟩ — **mor·dant·ly** *adv*

²mordant \"\ *n* -s [F, fr. *mordant*, pres. part. of *mordre* to bite] **1 :** a chemical (as a salt or hydroxide of chromium or aluminum or tin) that serves to fix a dye in or on a substance (as a textile fiber, fur, or microscopic preparation of cells or tissues) by combining with the dye to form an insoluble compound **2 :** any sticky matter used to cause leaf metal to adhere **3 :** a corroding substance (as an acid solution) used in etching

³mordant \"\ *vt* -ED/-ING/-S **1 :** to subject (as a textile fabric) to the action of or treat with a mordant or similar chemical ⟨with the old dyewoods, cotton . . . was first ~*ed* with a metallic salt —C.M.Whittaker & C.C.Wilcock⟩ **2 :** to treat (an emulsion or other photographic material) with a chemical that confers the ability to combine with dyes

⁴mordant *var of* MORDENT

mordant acid dye *n* **:** a mordant dye (as a chrome dye) that dyes in an acid bath — see DYE table I

mordant dye *n* **:** a dye (as most natural dyes and many anthraquinone dyes) that becomes fixed on a fiber by forming an insoluble compound with a mordant — see DYE table I

mordant rouge *n* **:** RED LIQUOR 2

mor·del·la \mȯ(r)ˈdelə\ *n*, *cap* [NL, fr. L *mordēre* to bite + NL *-ella*] **:** the type genus of the family Mordellidae

¹mor·del·lid \(ˈ)mȯ(r)ˈdeləd\ *adj* [NL *Mordellidae*] **:** of or relating to the Mordellidae

²mordellid \"\ *n* -s [NL *Mordellidae*] **:** a beetle of the family Mordellidae

mor·del·li·dae \mȯ(r)ˈdeləˌdē\ *n pl*, *cap* [NL, fr. *Mordella*, type genus + *-idae*] **:** a widespread family of small pubescent beetles that have the body strongly arched and tapered to a sharp tip and that are usu. found on flowers

mor·den·ite \ˈmȯ(r)dᵊnˌīt\ *n* -s [*Morden*, Nova Scotia + E *-ite*] **:** a zeolite approximately $(Ca,Na_2,K_2)_4Al_8Si_{40}O_{96}\cdot 28H_2O$ found in minute crystals or fibrous concretions

mor·dent *also* **mor·dant** \ˈmȯrdᵊnt, ˈmȯ(ə)d-\ *n* -s [It *mordente*, fr. L *mordent-, mordens*, pres. part. of *mordēre* to bite] **1 :** a melodic musical grace made by a quick alternation of a principal tone with an auxiliary tone usu. a half step lower **2 :** ACCIACCATURA

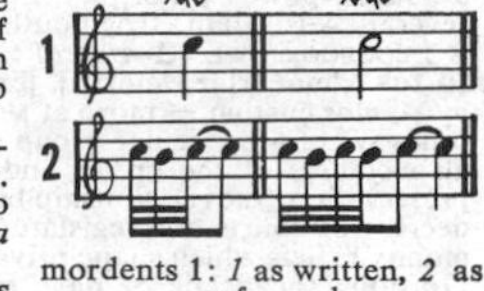

mordents 1: *1* as written, *2* as performed

mor·di·sheen \ˌmȯ(r)dəˈshēn\ *n* -s [Pg *mordexim*, fr. Marathi *modśī*, fr. *modnē* to break, fail, lose health] *India* **:** ASIATIC CHOLERA

mor·do·ré \ˌmȯ(r)dəˈrā\ *n* -s [F, fr. *More, Maure* Moor (fr. L *Maurus*) + *doré* gilded, past part. of *dorer* to gild, fr. LL *deaurare* — more at MOOR, DORADO] **:** PENCILWOOD

mor·do·vi·an \mȯ(r)ˈdōvēən\ *n* -s *cap* **:** MORDVIN

mord·va \(ˈ)mȯrdˈvä\ *n pl*, *cap* **:** MORDVINS

mord·vin \-vin\ *or* **mord·vin·i·an** \mȯrdˈvinēən\ *n*, *pl* **mordvin** *or* **mordvins** *or* **mordvinian** *or* **mordvinians** *cap* **1 a :** an agricultural people of the middle Volga provinces of European Russia **b :** a member of such people **2 :** a Finno-Ugric language of the Mordvin people — see URALIC LANGUAGES table

mord·wil·ko·ja \ˌmȯ(r)dwəlˈkōjə, mȯ(r)dˈwilkəjə\ *n*, *cap* [NL, fr. Aleksandr K. *Mordvilko* †1938 Russ. entomologist] **:** a genus of aphids that cause disfiguring galls on cottonwood in western No. America

¹more \ˈmō(ə)r, ˈmȯ(ə)r, -ōə, -ō(ə)\ *adj* [ME *more, moore, mo*, fr. OE *māra* (adj.), *mā* (adj. & adv. & n.); OE *māra* akin to OHG *mēro* larger, ON *meiri* larger, more, Goth *maiza* greater, elder; OE *mā* akin to OHG *mēr* more, ON *meirr*, Goth *mais;* both OE *māra* and OE *mā* akin to OIr *mōr*, *mār* large, Gk *enchesimōros* fighting with a spear, OPruss *muisieson* more] **1 a** *archaic* **:** superior in kind or degree ⟨proceed in their coaches through the city for the ~ solemnity of it —John Evelyn⟩ **b :** superior in quality or intensity ⟨the ~ fool you⟩ ⟨made for something ~ than a guerilla chieftain —H.E. Scudder⟩ **c :** superior in age **:** OLDER ⟨never seemed ~ in years than one of her own . . . brood —Della Lutes⟩ **2 :** ADDITIONAL, FURTHER ⟨offered him ~ coffee⟩ ⟨are going to stake ~ billions on the future —C.F.Craig⟩ ⟨one ~ word and you'll go straight to your room⟩ **3 :** of a larger size or extent ⟨for the ~ part . . . did not talk of ephemerae —Lucien Price⟩ **4 a :** of a larger quantity or amount ⟨the average high school senior does a lot ~ and a lot deeper thinking than his temperamental ways . . . suggest —Milton Lomask⟩ ⟨better democracy is more important than ~ democracy —Francis Biddle⟩ **b :** of a larger number ⟨there are ~ ways than one to skin a cat⟩ ⟨the ~ students who need instruction . . . the greater the demand for my services —H.A.Burton⟩

²more \"\ *adv* [ME *more, moore, mo*, fr. OE *māre* (fr. neut. of *māra*, adj.), *mā* (adj. & adv. & n.)] **1 a :** beyond a previously indicated number, amount, or length of time **:** in addition ⟨went to England a couple of times ~ —Maddy Vegtel⟩ ⟨what ~ could a speaker ask —B.F.Fairless⟩ ⟨the poor man's tired and old . . . and he hasn't much ~ to go —Lenard Kaufman⟩ **b :** in addition to points already enumerated **:** BESIDES, MOREOVER ⟨~, Jefferson failed to anticipate the gigantic changes —J.P.Boyd⟩ **2 a :** to a greater extent or degree ⟨~ as a measure of desperation than as one calculated to achieve victory

—C.E.Black & E.C.Helmreich⟩ — often used with adjectives and adverbs to form the comparative ⟨some of her ~ remarkable sons and visitors —J.P.Marquand⟩ ⟨the ~ learned the writer . . . the harder it is —W.T.Jones⟩ ⟨ostensibly to guard the trains but ~ probably to relieve the fears of Washington —Eben Swift⟩ **b :** to a closer degree **:** NEARER ⟨the plover has ~ a lark's habits —Alwyn Lee⟩ ⟨the real rates are . . . ~ like 18 per thousand —B.K.Sandwell⟩

³**more** \"\ *n* -s [ME *more, moore, mo,* fr. OE *māre* (fr. neut. of *māra,* adj.), *mā* (adj. & adv. & n.)] **1 :** a larger portion or number ⟨the ~ the merrier⟩ ⟨climb the ~ than four hundred steps —Budd Schulberg⟩ — often used with singular verb ⟨~ than one charge of discrimination was involved —*N.Y.Times*⟩ **2 a :** an additional number, amount, or length of time ⟨it costs a little ~ but it's worth it⟩ **b :** something in addition to what has already been mentioned ⟨what is ~ the gadget can be made to do lovely embossed patterns —Bertram Mycock⟩ **c :** further discussion ⟨~ on this topic later —G.A.Miller⟩ **3** *obs* **:** one that is of superior rank ⟨both ~ and less have given him the revolt —Shak.⟩ **4 :** something different or additional ⟨water is no ~ than ice thawed by heat —Tobias Smollett⟩

⁴**more** \"\ *pron* [¹*more*] **1 a :** something superior or above average ⟨~ is expected of you⟩ **b :** something of greater importance or significance ⟨his book is ~ than a guide —*Geog. Jour.*⟩ ⟨there is ~ to prophecy than the knack of accurate forecasting —D.R.Weimer⟩ **2** *pl in constr* **:** additional persons or things ⟨~ were found as the search continued⟩

⁵**more** \ˈmä(r)\ *n* -s [ME, fr. OE *more, moru* carrot, parsnip; akin to OHG *moraha* carrot, Gk *brakana* wild vegetables, Russ *morkov'* carrot] *dial Eng* **:** ROOT, STUMP

⁶**more** \ˈmō(ə)r\ *archaic var of* MOOR

⁷**mo·ré** \məˈrā\ *n* -s *usu cap* **:** MOSSI

more and more *adv* [ME] **:** to a progressively increasing extent ⟨his interest turned *more and more* to meteorology —W.J. Humphreys⟩

mo·reen \məˈrēn\ *n* -s [prob. irreg. fr. ¹*moire* + *-een*] **1 :** a strong cross-ribbed upholstery fabric of wool or wool and cotton with a plain glossy or moiré finish **2 :** a cotton imitation of moreen with vertical ribs that is used for clothing

more·ish \ˈmōrish, ˈmȯr-\ *adj* [¹*more* + *-ish*] **:** causing a desire for more **:** PALATABLE

¹**mo·rel** *also* **mo·relle** \məˈrel\ *n* -s [ME, fr. OF *morele,* fr. (assumed) VL *maurella,* fr. L *Maurus* Moor + *-ella* — more at MOOR] **:** any of various nightshades; *esp* **:** BLACK NIGHTSHADE

²**morel** \", ˈmȯrəl, ˈmär-\ *n* -s [F *morille,* of Gmc origin; akin to OHG *morhila* morel, dim. of *moraha* carrot] **1 :** an edible fungus of the genus *Morchella* (esp. *M. esculenta*) **2 :** a fungus of any of several genera closely related to *Morchella*

mo·relles \məˈrelz\ *n pl* [F *morelles, marelles, mérelles* (pl.), fr. MF *merelles,* fr. pl. of *merelle* counter, disk used in a board game, fr. OF *merele, marele* — more at MERELS] **:** ²MORRIS

mo·rel·lo \məˈre(ˌ)lō\ *n* -s [prob. modif. of Flem *marelle,* short for *amarelle,* fr. ML *amarellum* sour cultivated cherry — more at AMARELLE] **1** *or* **morello cherry** *also* **morel** \məˈrel\ **:** any of several cultivated cherries derived from the sour cherry and distinguished from the amarelles by their dark-colored skin and juice **2 :** MULBERRY 2b

mo·re·los orange worm \məˈrā lōs-\ *n, usu cap M* [*Morelos,* state in south central Mexico] **:** the maggot of the Mexican fruit fly

mo·ren·cite \məˈren(t)ˌsīt\ *n* -s [*Morenci,* Arizona + E *-ite*] **:** a hydrated ferric silicate clay mineral in yellow fibrous forms related to chloropal

mo·ren·do \məˈren(ˌ)dō\ *adj (or adv)* [It, fr. L *moriendum,* gerund of *mori* to die — more at MURDER] **:** dying away **:** with a gradual softening of tone and slowing of movement — used as a direction in music

more·ness *n* -ES **:** the quality or state of being more

mo·ren·o·site \məˈrenəˌsīt\ *n* -s [Sp *morenosita,* fr. *Moreno,* 19th cent. Spaniard + connective *-s-* + Sp *-ita* -ite] **:** a mineral $NiSO_4.7H_2O$ consisting of nickel sulfate and occurring in light green crystals or fibrous crusts

more or less *adv* [ME *moore or lesse*] **1 :** to a varying or undetermined extent or degree **:** SOMEWHAT, RATHER ⟨men who are all *more or less* expert in their knowledge —L.M.Judd⟩ ⟨stabilizing the . . . *more or less* arbitrary exchange rates —Jacob Viner⟩ ⟨*more or less* economical⟩ ⟨a copious supply of remedies, *more or less* drastic —W.G.Constable⟩ **2 :** with small variations **:** APPROXIMATELY, SUBSTANTIALLY ⟨birds . . . looking *more or less* in one direction —James Stevenson-Hamilton⟩ ⟨*more or less* what this article will examine —N.A. Luyten⟩ — used in legal documents to cover trivial differences usu. overlooked when bargaining in good faith ⟨comprising an area of 6600 square feet *more or less*⟩

more·over \mōrˈō-, mȯrˈō-, ˈ=ˌ== *sometimes* məˈrō-\ *adv* [ME, fr. ²*more* + *over,* adv.] **:** in addition to what has been said **:** BESIDES, FURTHER ⟨~, the method has obvious limitations —T.H.Savory⟩ ⟨has therefore an extensive range, and is ~ found in large numbers throughout a considerable portion of it —James Stevenson-Hamilton⟩

more·pork \ˈmōrˌpȯrk, ˈmȯrˌpȯrk\ *also* **mo·poke** \ˈmōˌpōk\ *or* **more·poke** \ˈmōrˌpōk, ˈmȯr-\ *n* [imit.] **1 :** any of several Australian frogmouths (esp. *Podargus strigoides*) **2 :** BOOBOOK OWL **3** *Austral* **:** a dull-witted person

mo·res \ˈmō(ˌ)rˌāz, ˈmȯ(ˌ)r, |ēz *sometimes* |ās\ *n pl* [L, pl. of *mor-, mos* custom — more at MOOD] **1 :** the fixed customs or folkways of a particular group that are morally binding upon all members of the group and necessary to its welfare and preservation ⟨the relationship between law and ~, between the decrees of courts and legislatures and the vast body of community beliefs which shape private action —J.P.Roche & M.M. Gordon⟩ ⟨academic ~ have frowned upon the invasion of another man's craft —J.R.Butler⟩ ⟨have tended to withdraw and develop a self-sufficient society of their own, with distinct and rigid ~ —James Stirling⟩ **2 :** moral attitudes ⟨conformity to the evershifting ~ of the moment —Havelock Ellis⟩ ⟨some knowledge of the environment and the dominant ~ of the author —G.W.Sherburn⟩ **3 :** HABITS, MANNERS ⟨her uncanny familiarity with the ~ of feline life —*New Yorker*⟩ ⟨in rural New England, organized dancing developed a whole set of ~ and practices of its own —R.L.Taylor⟩

¹**mo·res·co** \məˈres(ˌ)kō\ *adj, usu cap* [It, fr. *Moro* Moor (fr. L *Maurus*) + *-esco* -esque — more at MOOR] *archaic* **:** of or relating to the Moors **:** MOORISH

²**moresco** \"\ *n* -ES *usu cap, archaic* **:** MOOR; *esp* **:** a Moorish resident of Spain

¹**mo·resque** *also* **mau·resque** \məˈresk\ *adj, often cap* [F, fr. Sp *morisco,* fr. *Moro* Moor, fr. L *Maurus*] **:** having the characteristics of Moorish art, architecture, or decoration

²**moresque** *also* **mauresque** \"\ *n* -s *often cap* **:** an ornament or decorative motif in Moorish style

more·ton bay ash \ˈmōrtᵊn-\ *n, usu cap M&B* [*Moreton Bay,* Queensland, Australia] **:** an Australian tree (*Eucalyptus tessellaris*) with tough durable wood and gum rich in tannin

moreton bay chestnut *n, usu cap M&B* **:** BEAN TREE a

moreton bay fig *n, usu cap M&B* **:** an Australian fig tree (*Ficus macrophylla*) often planted for shade

moreton bay pine *n, usu cap M&B* **:** HOOP PINE

mor·frey \ˈmȯrfrī\ *n* -s [alter. of ¹*hermaphrodite*] *dial Eng* **:** a farmer's 2-wheeled cart that can be converted to a 4-wheeled wagon

morgagni's crypt *n, usu cap M* **:** CRYPT OF MORGAGNI

¹**mor·gan** \ˈmȯgən\ *n* -s [perh. alter. of E dial. *marg,* perh. short for obs. E *margaret* daisy, fr. ME *margarete,* fr. MF *margarite* daisy, pearl — more at MARGARITE] *dial Eng* **:** any of various plants of the genus *Anthemis*

²**morgan** \ˈmȯrgən, ˈmȯ(ə)g-\ *n* [after Justin *Morgan* †1798 Am. teacher who owned the stallion that became the progenitor of the breed] **1** *usu cap* **:** an American breed of light horses originated in Vermont from the progeny of one prepotent stallion of uncertain ancestry and various native mares **2** -s *often cap* **:** a horse of the Morgan breed

mor·ga·nat·ic \ˌmȯ(r)gəˈnad·ik\ *adj* [NL *morganatica* morning gift (in the term *matrimonium ad morganaticam* morganatic marriage), prob. alter. of ML *morganaticum,* fr. MHG *morgen* morning (fr. OHG *morgan*) + L *-aticum* -age — more at MORN] **:** of, relating to, or being a form of valid marriage contracted by a member of a European royal or noble family with a person of inferior rank on the understanding that the rank of the inferior partner remains unchanged and that the children of the marriage though legitimate do not succeed to the titles, fiefs, or entailed property of the parent of higher rank — compare LEFT-HANDED 5 — **mor·ga·nat·i·cal·ly** \-d·ək(ə)lē\ *adv*

mor·gan·ite \ˈmȯ(r)gəˌnīt\ *n* -s [J. P. *Morgan* †1913 Am. financier + E *-ite*] **:** a rose-colored gem variety of beryl

mor·gan·ize \ˈmȯ(r)gəˌnīz\ *vt* -ED/-ING/-S [William *Morgan* †1826? Am. Freemason allegedly murdered by Freemasons for threatening to publish the secrets of Freemasonry + E *-ize*] **:** to assassinate or do away with secretly in order to prevent or punish disclosure of secrets

mor·gen \ˈmȯrgən\ *n, pl* **morgen** [D, fr. MD, fr. *morgen* morning; akin to OHG *morgan* morning] **:** an old Dutch unit of land area equal to 2.116 acres that is now used in southern Africa

mor·gen·age \-nij\ *n* -s **:** area in morgen

¹**morgue** \ˈmȯrg, ˈmȯ(ə)g\ *n* -s [F] **:** an air of pride and superiority **:** HAUGHTINESS ⟨had gathered his dignity around him and put on the most terrific ~ as he always did when he had to get into a public vehicle in uniform —Ion Braby⟩ ⟨rigid with caste, insolent with ineffable ~ —*Times Lit. Supp.*⟩

²**morgue** \"\ *n* -s [F, perh. fr. *morgue* haughtiness] **1 :** a place where the bodies of unidentified persons or those who have died of violence or unknown causes are kept until released for burial **2 a :** a collection of reference works and files of reference material (as newspaper clippings and photographs) in the editorial offices of a newspaper or news periodical **:** a newspaper library **b :** a filing cabinet or storage place (as in a library or office) where material only occas. in use is kept

¹**mor·i·bund** \ˈmȯrə(ˌ)bənd, ˈmär-\ *adj* [L *moribundus,* fr. *mori* to die — more at MURDER] **1 :** being in a dying state **:** approaching death ⟨in the ~ patient deepening stupor and coma are the usual preludes to death —Norman Cameron⟩ ⟨convinced that their textile mills are ~, many weavers are quitting their looms —*Time*⟩ **2 :** being in a state of suspended activity or arrested growth **:** DORMANT ⟨after being more or less ~ for years, interest in electrolytic diffusion suddenly revived —A.R.Gordon⟩ ⟨a dull ~ form of the faith dozes on in the monasteries and monastic shrines of these secluded highlands —Ellen Semple⟩ — **mor·i·bun·di·ty** \ˌ==ˈbəndəd·ē, -dətē, -i\ *n* -ES

²**moribund** \"\ *n* -s **:** a dying person ⟨the poor ~ was delirious and knew not what he said —Rafael Sabatini⟩

mo·ri·che \məˈrēchā\ *or* **moriche palm** *n* -s [Sp *moriche,* fr. Tupi *muriti*] **:** MIRITI PALM

mo·rig·er·ate \məˈrijəˌrāt\ *adj* [L *morigeratus,* past part. of *morigerari* to comply with, gratify, fr. *morigerus*] *archaic* **:** MORIGEROUS

mo·rig·er·a·tion \=ˌ==ˈrāshən\ *n* -s [L *morigeration-, morigeratio,* fr. *morigeratus* + *-ion-, -io* -ion] **:** servile obedience **:** OBSEQUIOUSNESS ⟨a much more contemptible form of ~ than that of courtiers to princes —*Fortnightly Rev.*⟩

mo·rig·er·ous \məˈrijərəs\ *adj* [L *morigerus,* fr. *mor-, mos* custom + *-i-* + *-gerus* (fr. *gerere* to bear) — more at MOOD, CAST] *archaic* **:** OBEDIENT, SUBMISSIVE

mo·ril·lon \məˈrilən\ *n* -s [F, duck with dark plumage, dark-colored grape fr. OF *morillon, moreillon,* fr. *morel* dark brown, fr. (assumed) VL *maurellus,* fr. L *Maurus* Moor — more at MOOR] **1 :** any of several European ducks; *esp* **:** a female or immature male goldeneye **2 :** a light olive that is greener, stronger, and slightly darker than citrine, greener and deeper than grape green, and greener than old moss green

mo·rin \ˈmōrən, ˈmȯr-\ *n* -s [F *morine,* fr. NL *Morus* + F *-ine;* fr. the former belief that the fustic tree belonged to the genus *Morus* — more at MORUS] **:** a pale yellow crystalline flavono pigment $C_{15}H_{10}O_7$ found in old fustic and osage orange

mo·rin·da \məˈrində\ *n, cap* [NL, fr. *mor-* (fr. L *morus* mulberry tree) + L *inda,* fem. of *indus* of or connected with India, fr. Gk *indos* — more at MULBERRY, IND-] **:** a large genus of chiefly East Indian tropical trees and shrubs (family Rubiaceae) having small heads of confluent flowers that form an aggregate pulpy fruit and including several that yield yellow dyes

mo·rin·din \-dən\ *n* -s [NL *Morinda* + E *-in*] **:** any of several crystalline glycosides extracted from the bark of rubiaceous trees of the genera *Morinda* and *Coprosma*

mo·rin·done \-inˌdōn\ *n* -s [NL *Morinda* + E *-one*] **:** an orange-red crystalline dye $CH_3C_{14}H_4O_2(OH)_3$ derived from anthraquinone and obtained from morindin by hydrolysis

mor·i·nel \ˈmȯrəˌnel, ˈmär-\ *n* -s [NL *morinellus,* partly fr. L *Morini,* people inhabiting the part of Gaul nearest to Britain, partly fr. Gk *mōros* stupid; fr. its commonness in northern France and fr. its stupidity — more at MORON] **:** DOTTEREL

mo·rin·ga \məˈriŋgə\ *n, cap* [NL, prob. fr. Malayalam *muriṅṅa*] **:** a genus of East Indian and African trees constituting the family Moringaceae and having pinnate leaves and irregular flowers with 10 stamens and a 3-valved capsular fruit — see HORSERADISH TREE

mo·rin·ga·ce·ae \ˌmōriŋˈgāsēˌē, ˌmȯr-\ *n pl, cap* [NL, fr. *Moringa,* type genus + *-aceae*] **:** a family of trees (order Rhoeadales) coextensive with the genus *Moringa* — **mo·rin·ga·ceous** \ˌ==ˈgāshəs\ *adj*

mo·rin·gad \məˈriŋˌgad\ *n* -s [NL *Moringa* + E *-ad*] **:** a tree of the family Moringaceae

mo·rin·gu·i·dae \ˌmōriŋˈg(y)üəˌdē, ˌmȯr-\ *n pl, cap* [NL, fr. *Moringua,* type genus (perh. fr. Tamil *malaṅku* eel) + *-idae*] **:** a family of eels comprising the very slender wormlike whip eels

mo·rin·ite \ˈmōrəˌnīt, ˈmȯr-\ *n* -s [F, fr. *Morineau,* 19th cent. Fr. mine director + F *-ite*] **:** a mineral $Na_2Ca_4Al_4(PO_4)_4O_2F_6 \cdot 5H_2O$ that consists of a basic aluminum calcium sodium fluophosphate occurring in colorless to white or pale pink monoclinic crystals (hardness 4.5, sp. gr. 2.9) — called also *jezekite*

mo·ri·o·ka \ˌmōrēˈōkə, ˌmȯrēˈōkə\ *adj, usu cap* [fr. *Morioka,* city in northern Honshu, Japan] **:** of or from the city of Morioka, Japan **:** of the kind or style prevalent in Morioka

¹**mo·ri·on** \ˈmōrēˌän, ˈmȯr-\ *n* -s [MF] **:** a visorless high-crested helmet of Spanish origin worn by foot soldiers in the 16th and 17th centuries ⟨a battered ~ on his brow —Sir Walter Scott⟩

morion

²**morion** \"\ *n* -s [misreading in early editions of Pliny for L *mormorion*] **:** a nearly black variety of smoky quartz or cairngorm

mo·ri·o·ri \ˌmōrēˈōrē, ˌmȯrēˈōrē\ *n, pl* **moriori** *or* **morioris** *usu cap* **1 a :** an extinct people surviving until very recent times in the Chatham islands, east of New Zealand **b :** a member of such people **2 :** the Austronesian language of the Moriori

mo·ris·ca \məˈriskə\ *or* **mo·ris·co** \-i(ˌ)skō\ *n* -s [modif. (prob. influenced by ¹*morisco*) of It *moresca,* fr. fem. of *moresco* moorish — more at MORESCO] **:** a battle dance symbolizing the victory of the Christians over the Moors that developed during the Crusades, varied in different periods and countries, and is still popular at fiestas of the Iberian peninsula and Latin America

¹**mo·ris·co** \məˈri(ˌ)skō\ *adj, usu cap* [Sp, fr. *Moro* Moor, fr. L *Maurus* — more at MOOR] **:** MOORISH

²**morisco** \"\ *n, pl* **moriscos** *or* **moriscoes** *usu cap* [Sp, fr. *morisco,* adj.] **:** MOOR; *esp* **:** one of the Moorish people in Spain

mor·lop \ˈmȯrˌläp\ *n* -s [origin unknown] **:** a variety of jasper found in Australia

mor·ma·er *or* **mor·ma·or** \märˈmāər\ *n* -s [ScGael *mōrmhaor,* fr. *mōr* great (fr. OIr *mōr, mār* large, great) + *maor* steward, fr. L *major* larger, greater — more at MORE, MAJOR] **:** the ruler of one of the seven provinces into which medieval Scotland was divided — **mor·ma·er·ship** *or* **mor·ma·or·ship** \-ərˌship\ *n*

mor·mal \ˈmȯrməl\ *n* -s [ME, fr. MF *mormal, mortmal,* fr. *mort* dead (fr. L *mortuus,* past part. of *mori* to die) + *mal* disease — more at MURDER, MAL] *archaic* **:** a bad sore or ulcer

¹**mor·mon** \ˈmȯrmən, ˈmȯ(ə)m-\ *n* -s *usu cap* [after *The Book of Mormon* (first published 1830), sacred scriptures of the Latter-day Saints] **:** LATTER-DAY SAINT; *esp* **:** a member of the Church of Jesus Christ of Latter-day Saints

²**mormon** \"\ *adj, usu cap* **:** of or relating to the Mormons

³**mormon** \"\ *n* -s [NL (specific epithet of the mandrill *Mandrillus mormon*), fr. Gk *mormōn, mormō* she-monster, bugbear — more at FORMIDABLE] **:** MANDRILL

mormon cricket *n, usu cap M* **:** a large dark wingless katydid (*Anabrus simplex*) that resembles a cricket and is found in the arid parts of western U.S. where it occas. occurs in great numbers and damages crop plants

mor·mon·dom \-ndəm\ *n* -s *usu cap* **:** the community of the Mormons or the region inhabited by them

mor·mon·ess \-nəs\ *n* -ES *usu cap* **:** a female Mormon

mor·mon·ism \-məˌnizəm\ *n* -s *cap* **:** the doctrines and practices of Mormons

mor·mon·ist \-ˌnəst\ *n* -s *usu cap* **:** MORMON

mor·mon·ite \-məˌnīt\ *n* -s *usu cap* **:** MORMON

mormon tea *n, usu cap M* [so called fr. its use in the treatment of gonorrhea, with allusion to the former Mormon practice of polygamy] **1 :** a plant of the genus *Ephedra* **2 :** a drink made from a plant of the genus *Ephedra*

mor·mon·weed \ˈ==ˌ=\ *n, usu cap* **:** INDIAN MALLOW 1

mor·mo·ops \mȯ(r)ˈmōˌäps\ *n, cap* [NL, fr. Gk *mormō* she-monster, bugbear + NL *-ops*] **:** a genus of bats (family Phyllostomatidae) comprising the tropical American cinnamon bats

mor·mo·ran·do \ˌmȯ(r)məˈrän(ˌ)dō\ *adj (or adv)* [It, murmuring, fr. L *murmurandum,* gerund of *murmurare* to murmur — more at MURMUR] **:** in a murmuring manner **:** MURMURING — used as a direction in music

¹**mor·my·rid** \(ˈ)mȯ(r)ˈmīrəd\ *adj* [NL *Mormyridae*] **:** of or relating to the Mormyridae

²**mormyrid** \"\ *also* **mor·myr** \ˈmȯrmər\ *n* -s [*mormyrid* fr. NL *Mormyridae; mormyr* fr. NL *Mormyrus*] **:** a fish of the family Mormyridae

mor·myr·i·dae \mȯ(r)ˈmirəˌdē\ *n pl, cap* [NL, fr. *Mormyrus,* type genus + *-idae*] **:** a family of African freshwater fishes (order Isospondyli) that have the gill openings reduced to small slits, small eyes usu. covered with skin, and the mouth small and often situated at the end of a tubular projection — see MORMYRUS

mor·my·rus \mȯ(r)ˈmīrəs\ *n, cap* [NL, fr. Gk *mormyros,* a sea fish] **:** the type genus of the family Mormyridae comprising oily fleshed edible fishes and including the sacred fishes of ancient Egypt

¹**morn** \ˈmȯ(ə)rn, ˈmȯ(ə)n\ *n* -s [ME *morn, morwen* dawn, morning, fr. OE *morgen;* akin to OHG *morgan* morning, ON *morginn,* Goth *maurgins* morning, L *merus* pure, unmixed, Gk *marmairein* to flash, sparkle, Skt *marīci* ray of light] **1 a :** the beginning of the day **:** DAWN, SUNRISE ⟨it was the lark, the herald of the ~ —Shak.⟩ ⟨a certain ~ broke beautiful and blue —Robert Browning⟩ **b :** the first or early part of the day **:** MORNING ⟨been on the go since ~ —G.W.Brace⟩ ⟨working from ~ to night, he had no time for frills —John Buchan⟩ **2** *chiefly dial Brit* **:** TOMORROW — used with *the* ⟨the ~'s the Sabbath —J.M.Barrie⟩ **3 :** EAST ⟨the bugle that blows in lands of ~ —A.E.Housman⟩

²**morn** \"\ *adj* **:** MORNING

mor·nay \(ˈ)mȯrˈnā\ *also* **mornay sauce** *n* -s *usu cap M* [perh. after Philippe de *Mornay* †1623 Fr. Huguenot leader] **:** a cheese-flavored cream sauce

¹**morne** \ˈmȯ(ə)rn\ *n* -s [ME *moorne,* fr. MF *morne* cap to cover the head of a tilting lance, fr. *morner* to blunt, fr. OF, of Gmc origin; akin to OHG *mornēn* to grieve, mourn — more at MOURN] **:** the head of a lance blunted for tilting

²**mor·né** \(ˈ)mȯrˈnā\ *adj* [F, fr. past part. of *morner* to blunt] **:** of or relating to a heraldic representation of a lion without teeth, tongue, or claws

³**morne** \ˈmȯ(ə)rn\ *adj* [F, fr. OF, fr. *morner* to blunt] **:** having a dismal quality or effect **:** GLOOMY ⟨the ~ cliffs, the dead cities, the desolate shores of a leaden sea —Boris von Anrep⟩

¹**morn·ing** \ˈmȯrniŋ, ˈmȯ(ə)n-, -nēŋ\ *n* -s [ME *morning, morwening,* fr. *morn, morwen* + *-ing* (as in ME *evening*)] **1 a :** the break of day **:** DAWN ⟨upon their path the ~ broke —P.B.Shelley⟩ ⟨the red ~ touched him with its light —R.W. Emerson⟩ ⟨tossed and turned all night until ~ finally came⟩ **b :** the early hours of light **:** the time from rising to noon ⟨uses the ~s for calling on his customers⟩ ⟨does his best work in the ~⟩ **c :** the time from midnight to noon ⟨there was a full moon, and about two o'clock in the ~ a great concourse assembled —John Buchan⟩ ⟨it was then eleven o'clock in the ~ —Nevil Shute⟩ **2 :** the beginning of something **:** a period of first development or of freshness and vigor ⟨a steamship five times the size of the biggest vessel afloat then, in the ~ of steamers — James Dugan⟩ ⟨the ~ of the world, when life seemed simpler if no less cruel —Herbert Agar⟩ ⟨the ~ of life⟩ **3** *chiefly Scot* **a :** an alcoholic drink taken before breakfast **b :** a light meal eaten before breakfast

²**morning** \"\ *adj* **:** of, belonging to, or intended primarily for use in the morning ⟨~ coffee⟩ ⟨~ freshness⟩ ⟨~ tabloids have a heavy sale among homeward bound theatergoers —Bruce Westley⟩ ⟨once more I was my ~ self, tough, hearty, and invulnerable —Nancy Hale⟩

morning after *n, pl* **mornings after 1 :** HANGOVER 2a ⟨illusions, headaches, *mornings after* —Carl Sandburg⟩ **2 :** a time when the effects of overindulgence are felt

morning campion *n* **:** RED CAMPION

morning coat *n* **:** CUTAWAY ⟨in *morning coat,* striped trousers, and, very likely, with a carnation in his buttonhole —Frances Towers⟩

morning dress *n* **1 :** a woman's dress suitable for wear around the home; *esp* **:** an informal dress for housework **2 :** the conventional attire for men for highly formal daytime wear including a cutaway coat, striped trousers, and a silk hat all in shades of gray and black — compare EVENING DRESS

morning gift *n* **:** a gift made by a husband to his wife on the morning after the consummation of marriage

morning glory *n* **1 a :** a plant of the genus *Ipomoea* (esp. *I. purpurea*) — see JAPANESE MORNING GLORY **b :** a plant of a related genus (as *Convolvulus*) — compare FIELD BINDWEED, HEDGE BINDWEED **2 :** HOODED MERGANSER **3 a :** someone or something that starts out impressively but fades quickly ⟨was a brilliant student as a freshman, but turned out to be only a *morning glory*⟩ **b** *slang* **:** a racehorse that performs well in morning workouts but runs poorly in races

morning glory 1a

morning-glory family *n* **:** CONVOLVULACEAE

morning gown *n* **:** an informal dress for wear at home; *esp* **:** an elaborate dressing gown ⟨caught by unexpected guests one day when still in her *morning gown* —Elizabeth Coatsworth⟩

morning gun *n* **:** the firing of a gun at the first note of reveille or of a preceding march at military installations

morning hour *n* **:** a period of the day devoted by the U.S. Senate and the House of Representatives to routine business (as the introduction of bills)

morning line *n* **:** a bookmaker's published list of entries and the probable odds on each for a race meet to be held later in the day

morning loan *n* **:** DAY LOAN

morning prayer *n, usu cap M&P* **:** a morning service of liturgical prayer in Anglican churches — called also *matins*

morning report *n* **:** a daily military report for permanent record made by each company, troop, battery, or higher headquarters and giving its daily history (as strength, movements, or changes in status of individuals)

morning room *n* **:** a sitting room for general family use esp. during the day — compare DRAWING ROOM

morn·ings \ˈmȯrniŋz, ˈmȯ(ə)n-, -nēŋz\ *adv* **:** in the morning repeatedly **:** on any morning ⟨goes to the office ~⟩

morning sickness *n* **:** nausea and vomiting on rising in the morning occurring esp. during the earlier months of pregnancy

morning star *n* **1 a :** a bright planet (as Venus) seen in the eastern sky before sunrise **b :** any of the five planets that may be seen with the naked eye if in the sky at sunrise ⟨Venus, Jupiter, Mars, Mercury, and Saturn may be *morning stars*⟩ **c :** a planet that sets after midnight **2** [trans. of G *morgenstern*] **:** a weapon consisting of a heavy ball set with spikes and either attached to a staff or suspended from one by a chain — called also *holy-water sprinkler* **3 :** an annual California herb (*Mentzelia aurea*) with showy yellow flowers

morningtide \ˈ⸗⸗,⸗\ *n, archaic* **:** morning time **:** MORNING

morning watch *n* **:** the watch on a ship from 4 a.m. to 8 a.m.

morns *pl of* MORN

mo·ro \ˈmō(,)rō, ˈmȯ(,)-\ *n, pl* **moro** *or* **moros** *usu cap* [Sp, lit., Moor, fr. L *Maurus* — more at MOOR] **1 a :** any of several Muslim peoples of the southern Philippines chiefly of the Sulu archipelago and parts of Mindanao — see MAGINDANAO, MARANAO, SAMAL, TAW-SUG **b :** a member of any of these peoples **2 :** any of the Austronesian languages of the Moro peoples

mor·oc \ˈmä,räk\ *n* -s [prob. fr. Tigré *marāḥ* guide] **:** HONEY GUIDE

mor·o·cain \¦mȯrə¦kān\ *n* -s [prob. modif. of F *marocain* Moroccan, fr. *Maroc* Morocco] **:** MOROCCO RED

¹mo·roc·can \məˈräkən\ *adj, usu cap* [*Morocco*, sultanate in northwest Africa + E *-an*] **1 :** of, relating to, or characteristic of Morocco **2 :** of, relating to, or characteristic of the people of Morocco

²moroccan \"\ *n* -s **1** *cap* **:** a native or inhabitant of Morocco **2** *often cap* **:** a dark red to reddish orange that is slightly bluer and less strong than autumn glory

¹mo·roc·co \-ä(,)kō\ *n* -s [fr. *Morocco*, sultanate in northwest Africa] **1** *or* **morocco leather a :** a fine very firm flexible leather prepared from goatskin tanned with sumac and having a distinctive pebbly grain brought out by graining or boarding **b :** an imitation made from sheepskin or lambskin **2** *often cap* **:** MOROCCO RED

²morocco \"\ *adj, usu cap* [fr. *Morocco*, sultanate in northwest Africa] **:** of or from Morocco **:** of the kind or style prevalent in Morocco **:** MOROCCAN

morocco gum *n, usu cap M* **:** gum arabic exported from Morocco and believed to be obtained from any of several acacias (as *Acacia gummifera*) other than those that are usual sources of gum arabic

morocco–head \⸗ˈ⸗(,)⸗,⸗\ *n, usu cap, dial* **:** AMERICAN MERGANSER

morocco–jaw \⸗ˈ⸗(,)⸗,⸗\ *n, usu cap, dial* **:** SURF SCOTER

morocco millet *n, usu cap 1st M* **:** JOHNSON GRASS

morocco red *n, often cap M* **:** a strong reddish brown that is redder, less strong, and slightly lighter than Sierra — called also *caldron, marocain, morocain, Morocco*

moro crab *n* [part trans. of Sp *cangrejo moro*, fr. *cangrejo* crab + *moro* Moorish, fr. *Moro* Moor, fr. L *Maurus* — more at MOOR] **:** STONE CRAB 1

mo·ron \ˈmō,rän, ˈmȯ,-\ *n* -s [irreg. fr. Gk *mōros* sluggish, dull, stupid; akin to Skt *mūra* dull, stupid] **1 :** a feebleminded person or mental defective with a potential mental age of between eight and twelve years who is capable of doing routine work under supervision **2 :** a stupid or boorish individual ⟨if it is well-adjusted ~*s* that we must have, then by all means let us encourage dating and going steady —G.A.Panichas⟩ ⟨these ~*s* . . . laugh loudly when a player on the screen is dying, they titter at love scenes —*Auckland (New Zealand) Star*⟩ **3 :** SEXUAL PERVERT ⟨turned and gaped at her with a ~*'s* excited eyes —J.T.Farrell⟩ **syn** see FOOL

mo·ro·ne \məˈrōnē\ *n, cap* [NL] **:** a genus of carnivorous fresh and salt water percoid fishes (family Serranidae) including several sport and food fishes — see MORONIDAE, WHITE PERCH, YELLOW BASS

mo·ron·ic \məˈränik, (ˈ)mō¦r-, (ˈ)mȯ¦r-, -nēk\ *adj* **1 :** consisting of or having the characteristics of morons ⟨have no difficulty making the ~ millions laugh at ancient jokes —John Dolman⟩ ⟨the sinking of the academic mind to the level of the ~ mob —*Christian Century*⟩ **2 :** like a moron **:** mentally retarded **:** DULL ⟨this ~ but devastating nitwit —*Variety*⟩ **3 :** characteristic of or suitable for morons **:** BRUTISH, STUPID ⟨all the ~ delight of a gangster trying out his first machine gun —Raymond Chandler⟩ ⟨intelligent enough not to fall for such a ~ form of pastime —*Springfield (Mass.) Union*⟩ ⟨an orgy of ~ vulgarity —*No. Amer. Rev.*⟩ — **mo·ron·i·cal·ly** \-nək(ə)lē, -nēk-, -li\ *adv*

mo·ron·i·dae \məˈränə,dē\ *n pl, cap* [NL, fr. *Morone*, type genus + *-idae*] *in some classifications* **:** an important family of carnivorous spiny-finned fishes of northeastern No. America, Russia, and Siberia that comprises numerous food and sport fishes and is now usu. included in the family Serranidae

mo·ron·ism \ˈmō,rä,nizəm, ˈmȯ,rä-\ *n* -s **:** MORONITY

mo·ron·i·ty \məˈränəd·ē\ *n* -ES **1 :** a mild degree of feeblemindedness or mental deficiency **2 :** STUPIDITY

mor·o·pus \ˈmȯrəpəs, ˈmär-\ *n, cap* [NL, fr. Gk *mōros* sluggish, dull + NL *-pus*; fr. its suggested affinities to the sloth] **:** a genus of American Miocene clawed perissodactyls (family Chalicotheriidae) attaining the size of modern horses

moror *var of* MAROR

moros *pl of* MORO

mo·rose \məˈrōs, (ˈ)mō¦r-, (ˈ)mȯ¦r-\ *adj* [L *morosus*, fr. *mor-, mos* custom, habit + *-osus* -ose — more at MOOD] **1 :** having a sullen and gloomy disposition **:** not friendly or sociable ⟨always found her silent even to the pitch of appearing ~ —Compton Mackenzie⟩ ⟨when deprived of spirits, he became gloomy, ~, and irritable —C.B.Nordhoff & J.N.Hall⟩ **2 :** marked by or expressive of gloom ⟨a ~ little essay on the low state of the short story —James Kelly⟩ ⟨a long, ~ dressing gown grotesquely capped with a derby —Brooks Atkinson⟩ **syn** see SULLEN

mo·rose·ly *adv* **:** in a morose manner **:** SULLENLY ⟨ate stoically, ~, saying hardly a word —Harold Sinclair⟩

mo·rose·ness *n* -ES **:** the quality or state of being morose ⟨the ~ of age and infirmity never touched him, and he never quarreled with a friend or lost one —Matthew Arnold⟩

mo·ros·i·ty \məˈräsəd·ē\ *n* -ES [L *morositat-, morositas*, fr. *morosus* + *-itat-, -itas* -ity] **:** MOROSENESS

mor·o·soph \ˈmȯrə,säf, ˈmōr-\ *or* **mo·ros·o·phist** \məˈräsəfəst\ *n* -s [*morosoph* fr. obs. F *morosophe*, fr. Gk *mōrosophos*, fr. *mōros* dull, stupid + *sophos* wise; *morosophist* fr. obs. F *morosophe* + E *-ist*] **:** a learned fool

mo·ro·to·co \,mōrōˈtō(,)kō\ *n, usu cap* **:** a dialect of the Zamuco people

mo·rox·ite \məˈräk,sīt\ *n* -s [G *moroxit*, fr. Gk *moroxos* pipe clay, fuller's earth + G *-it* -ite] **:** a greenish blue or bluish variety of apatite

morph \ˈmȯ(ə)rf, ˈmȯ(ə)f\ *n* -s [back-formation fr. *morpheme*] **1 :** ²ALLOMORPH **2 :** a phoneme or sequence of phonemes that is presumably an allomorph but that is not considered as assigned to any particular morpheme ⟨the *slep-* \slep\ of *slept* is considered a ~ by a linguist analyzing English who has not yet encountered the *sleep* \slēp\ of *sleep well*⟩ — compare ²ALLOMORPH, MORPHEME 2

morph- *or* **morpho-** *comb form* [G *morpho-* form, fr. Gk *morph-, morpho-*, fr. *morphē* — more at FORM] **:** form **:** shape **:** structure **:** type ⟨*morphic*⟩ ⟨*morpho*differentiation⟩

-morph \,mȯrf, ,mȯ(ə)f\ *n comb form* -s [ISV, fr. *-morphous*] **:** one having (such) a form ⟨*isomorph*⟩

morph *abbr* morphological; morphology

-mor·pha \ˈmȯrfə, ˈmȯ(ə)fə\ *n comb form, pl* **-morpha** [NL, fr. fem. sing. & neut. pl. of *-morphus* -morphous, fr. Gk *-morphos* — more at -MORPHOUS] **:** one or ones having (such) a form ⟨Entero*morpha*⟩ — esp. in names of zoological taxa larger than a genus ⟨Cyno*morpha*⟩ ⟨Hystrico*morpha*⟩

mor·pha·dite *also* **mor·phi·dite** *or* **mor·pho·dite** \ˈmȯ(r)fə,dīt\ *n* -s [by shortening & alter.] **:** HERMAPHRODITE

-mor·phae \ˈmȯr,fē, ˈmȯ(ə)-,\ *n pl comb form* [NL, fr. fem. pl. of *-morphus* -morphous] **:** ones having (such) a form — in names of zoological taxa, esp. of birds, larger than a genus ⟨Psittaco*morphae*⟩

mor·phal·lax·is \¦mȯrfə¦laksəs\ *n, pl* **morphallax·es** \-k,sēz\ [NL, fr. *morph-* + Gk *allaxis* exchange, fr. *allassein, allattein* to change, exchange, fr. *allos* other — more at ELSE] **:** regeneration on a reduced scale of a part or organism from a fragment by reorganization without cell proliferation — compare EPIMORPHOSIS

mor·phea *also* **mor·phoea** \mȯ(r)ˈfēə\ *n, pl* **morphe·ae** *or* **morphoe·ae** \-ē,ē\ [ML *morphea*] **:** localized scleroderma

mor·phe·an \ˈmȯ(r)fēən\ *adj, usu cap* [*Morpheus* + E *-an*] *archaic* **:** of, relating to, or producing sleep ⟨some drowsy *Morphean* amulet —John Keats⟩

mor·pheme \ˈmȯr,fēm, ˈmȯ(ə),-\ *n* -s [F *morphème*, fr. *morph-* + *-ème* -eme] **1 :** a feature of language showing the relations between nouns, verbs, adjectives, and concrete adverbs (as an affix, reduplication, preposition, conjunction, auxiliary verb, copulative verb, intonation, accentuation, ablaut variation, or order of words) — now little used by linguists; distinguished from *semanteme* **2 :** a meaningful linguistic unit whether a free form (as *pin, child, load, pray*) or a bound form (as the *-s* of *pins*, the *-hood* of *childhood*, the *un-* and *-er* of *unloader*, and the *-ed* of *prayed*) that contains no smaller meaningful parts — compare ²ALLOMORPH, MORPH — **mor·phe·mic** \(ˈ)mȯ(r)¦fēmik, -mēk\ *adj* — **mor·phe·mi·cal·ly** \-mək(ə)lē, -mēk-, -li\ *adv*

morpheme alternant *or* **morphemic alternant** *n* **:** ²ALLOMORPH

mor·phe·mics \mȯ(r)ˈfēmiks, -mēks\ *n pl but sing in constr* **1 :** a branch of linguistic analysis that consists of the study of morphemes (sense 2) **2** *of a language* **:** the structure in terms of morphemes (sense 2) **:** a statement of the structure in terms of morphemes

mor·pheus \ˈmȯrfēəs, -,fyüs\ *n, usu cap* [after *Morpheus*, deity represented by Ovid as causing dreams in which a human being appears] **:** something that induces or prolongs sleep ⟨awoke from a deep sleep, jerked from the grip of *Morpheus* —H.A.Smith⟩ ⟨overcome by *Morpheus*⟩

mor·phew \ˈmȯr,fyü\ *n* -s [ME *morphue, morphe*, fr. ML *morphea*] *archaic* **:** MORPHEA

mor·phewed \-üd\ *adj, archaic* **:** covered with or as if with a morphea ⟨the windows blank and sightless, the walls ~ with scaling —John Masefield⟩

-mor·phi \ˈmȯr,fī, ˈmȯ(ə),-\ *n pl comb form* [NL, fr. pl. of *-morphus* -morphous] **:** ones having (such) a form — in names of fish taxa larger than a genus ⟨Haleco*morphi*⟩

mor·phia \ˈmȯ(r)fēə\ *n* -s [NL, fr. *Morpheus*] **:** MORPHINE

mor·phic \ˈmȯrfik\ *adj* [*morph-* + *-ic*] **:** of or relating to form **:** MORPHOLOGICAL — **mor·phi·cal·ly** \-fək(ə)lē\ *adv*

-mor·phic \¦mȯrfik, ¦mȯ(ə)f-, -fēk\ *adj comb form* [prob. fr. F *-morphique*, fr. Gk *morphē* form + F *-ique* -ic — more at FORM] **:** having (such) a form ⟨dolicho*morphic*⟩

morphic effect *n* **:** a type of effect on the physical properties of a crystal due to the change of symmetry that occurs when a crystal is strained

-morphies *pl of* -MORPHY

mor·phine \ˈmȯr,fēn, ˈmȯ(ə),- *sometimes* ⸗ˈ⸗\ *n* -s [F, fr. *Morpheus* + F *-ine*] **:** a bitter crystalline narcotic habit-forming base $C_{17}H_{19}NO_3$ that is the principal alkaloid of opium occurring in amounts up to 15 percent, that chemically is a complex derivative of phenanthrene, that produces powerful complex physiological and psychic effects similar in some respects to those of opium, and that is used in the form of a soluble salt (as the hydrochloride or sulfate) chiefly as an analgesic and sedative — **mor·phin·ic** \(ˈ)mȯ(r)¦finik\ *adj*

morphine meconate *n* **:** the morphine salt of meconic acid that occurs naturally in opium

mor·phin·ism \ˈmȯ(r)fə,nizəm\ *n* -s [ISV *morphine* + *-ism*] **:** a condition produced by the habitual use of morphine **:** the morphine habit

mor·phin·ist \-,nəst\ *n* -s [ISV *morphine* + *-ist*] **:** one addicted to the use of morphine

mor·phin·ize \-fə,nīz\ *vt* -ED/-ING/-s **:** to treat with or subject to the influence of morphine

mor·phi·no·ma·nia \,mȯ(r)fənōˈmānēə\ *also* **mor·phi·o·ma·nia** \-fēō'-\ *n* [*morphinomania* fr. NL, fr. *morphino-* (fr. ISV *morphine*) + LL *mania*; *morphiomania* fr. NL, fr. *morphio-* (fr. *morphia*) + LL *mania*] **:** an habitual and uncontrollable craving for morphine

mor·phi·no·ma·ni·ac \-fənōˈmānē,ak\ *also* **mor·phi·o·ma·ni·ac** \-fēō'-\ *n* [fr. NL *morphinomania, morphiomania*, after E *manic*: *maniac*] **:** one who is afflicted with morphinomania

-mor·phism \¦mȯ(r),fizəm\ *n comb form* -s [LL *-morphus* -morphous (fr. Gk *-morphos*) + E *-ism* — more at -MORPHOUS] **1 :** quality or state of having (such) a form ⟨hetero*morphism*⟩ ⟨iso*morphism*⟩ **2 :** conceptualization in (such) a form ⟨physico*morphism*⟩

mor·pho \ˈmȯr(,)fō\ *n* [NL, fr. Gk *Morphō* (epithet of Aphrodite in Sparta)] **1** *cap* **:** a genus (the type of the family Morphoidae) of large showy tropical American butterflies noted for the very brilliant bright blue metallic luster of the upper surface of the wings of some forms **2** -s **:** any butterfly of the genus *Morpho*

morpho- — see MORPH-

mor·pho·differentiation \¦mȯ(r)(,)fō+\ *n* [*morph-* + *differentiation*] **:** structure or organ differentiation (as in tooth development)

morphodite *var of* MORPHADITE

morphoea *var of* MORPHEA

mor·pho·gen·e·sis \,mȯ(r)fəˈjenəsəs\ *n* [NL, fr. *morph-* + L *genesis*] **1 :** BIOGENESIS 2 **2 :** the formation and differentiation of tissues and organs **:** ORGANOGENESIS

mor·pho·ge·net·ic \,mȯ(r)fōjə¦ned·ik\ *adj* [*morph-* + *-genetic*] **:** concerned with or tending to the development of normal organic form ⟨~ movements of early embryonic cells⟩

mor·pho·gen·ic \,mȯ(r)fəˈjenik\ *adj* [*morph-* + *-genic*] **:** MORPHOGENETIC

mor·phog·e·ny \mȯ(r)ˈfäjənē\ *n* -ES [ISV *morph-* + *-geny*] **:** MORPHOGENESIS

mor·pho·graph·ic \¦mȯ(r)fə¦grafik\ *adj* [NL *morphographicus*, fr. *morphographia* morphography + L *-icus* -ic] **:** of or relating to morphography

mor·phog·ra·phy \mȯ(r)ˈfägrəfē\ *n* -ES [NL *morphographia*, fr. *morph-* + *-graphia* -graphy] **1 :** descriptive morphology **2 :** the phenomena or aspect (as of a region) described by morphography

mor·pho·lide \ˈmȯ(r)fə,līd\ *n* -s [*morpholine* + *-ide*] **:** an amide derived from morpholine as the amine

mor·pho·line \-,lēn, -,lən\ *n* -s [ISV *morphol-* (ISV *morphine* + *-ol*) + *-ine*; fr. a former belief that its molecular structure was similar to that of morphine] **:** an oily cyclic secondary amine $O(CH_2CH_2)_2NH$ made from ethylene oxide and ammonia and used chiefly as a solvent and emulsifying agent; tetrahydro-1,4-oxazine

mor·pho·log·i·cal \¦mȯ(r)fə¦läjəkəl, -jēk-\ *also* **mor·pho·log·ic** \-jik, -jēk\ *adj* [*morphological* fr. *morphology* + *-ical*; *morphologic* fr. F *morphologique*, fr. *morphologie* morphology + *-ique* -ic] **1 :** of, relating to, or concerned with form or structure ⟨pre-Darwinian classifications of living things were ~ rather than genetic, the attempt being made to classify according to similarities of fundamental characteristics —W.P. Kent⟩ **2 :** of or relating to points for taking measurements that are present on the skeleton as well as on the living person or the cadaver — compare PHYSIOGNOMIC — **mor·pho·log·i·cal·ly** \-jək(ə)lē, -jēk-, -li\ *adv*

morphological construction *or* **morphologic construction** *n* **:** a sequence of morphemes forming a complex or compound word (as *unlike, baseball*) — compare SYNTACTIC CONSTRUCTION

morphological index *n* **:** the ratio of the volume of the human trunk to the sum of the lengths of one arm and one leg multiplied by 100

mor·phol·o·gist \mȯ(r)ˈfäləjəst\ *n* -s [*morphology* + *-ist*] **:** one who concerns himself with morphology or carries on morphological studies

mor·phol·o·gy \-jē, -ji\ *n* -ES [G *morphologie*, fr. Gk *morph-* (fr. *morphē* form) + G *-logie* -logy — more at FORM] **1 a :** a branch of biology that deals with the form and structure of animals and plants **:** a study of the forms, relations, metamorphoses, and phylogenetic development of organs apart from their functions — see ANATOMY; compare PHYSIOLOGY **b :** the features comprised in the form and structure of an organism or any of its parts **2 a :** a study and description of word-formation in a language including inflection, derivation, and compounding — distinguished from *syntax* **b :** the system of word-forming elements and processes in a language **3 a :** a study of the structure or form of something ⟨no one had attempted to sketch out a ~ of the political party as such —*Times Lit. Supp.*⟩ ⟨social ~⟩ **b :** the structure or form of something **:** MAKEUP ⟨the evidence speaks in favor of a number of common genetic factors in the ~ of gamblers —R.M. Lindner⟩ ⟨in general ~ the later Dutch settlements bore a strong resemblance to those of New England —G.T.Trewartha⟩ ⟨the unique ~ of the city —H.J.Nelson⟩ **4 :** the external structure of rocks in relation to the development of erosional forms or topographic features **:** GEOMORPHOLOGY **5 a :** the study of the development of the forms of crystals **b :** the assemblage of forms on a crystal

mor·pho·ma·ni·ac \,mȯ(r)fəˈmānē,ak\ *n* [by alter.] **:** MORPHINOMANIAC

mor·phome \ˈmȯr,fōm\ *n* -s [alter. (influenced by Gk *morphōma* form, fr. *morphē*) of *morpheme*] **:** MORPHEME 2

mor·pho·met·ric \¦mȯ(r)fə¦me·trik\ *also* **mor·pho·met·ri·cal** \-rəkəl\ *adj* **:** of, relating to, or involving morphometry ⟨~ studies of the Pacific salmons⟩ — **mor·pho·met·ri·cal·ly** \-rək(ə)lē\ *adv*

mor·phom·e·try \mȯ(r)ˈfämə·trē\ *n* -ES [*morph-* + *-metry*] **:** measurement of external form; *esp* **:** a branch of limnology that deals with morphologic measurements of a lake and its basin

mor·pho·phoneme \¦mȯ(r)fō+\ *n* [*morpho-* (fr. *morpheme*) + *phoneme*] **:** a class of phonemes that belong to the same morpheme (as the \-s, -z, -əz\ plural suffix of *kits, kids, kisses*; \f, v\ in *knife, knives*); *also* **:** an arbitrarily selected member of such a class as its representative in grammatical description (as the plural suffix -s, or the F in \nīF\) ⟨group together into one ~ the phonemes which replace each other in corresponding parts of the various members of a morpheme —Z.S. Harris⟩

mor·pho·phonemic \¦mȯ(r)(,)fō+\ *adj* [*morpho-* (fr. *morpheme*) + *phonemic*] **:** of or relating to a class of phonemes that belong to the same morpheme or to the relations among them and the conditions that determine their occurrences ⟨a ~ alteration of long vowel in open syllable and short vowel in closed syllable —J.H.Greenberg⟩ — **mor·pho·phonemi·cally** \"+\ *adv*

mor·pho·phonemics \"+\ *n pl but sing in constr* [*morpho-* (fr. *morpheme*) + *phonemics*] **1 :** a study of the phonemic differences between allomorphs of the same morpheme (as the ē, e difference in slēp, slep ⟨~ thus concerns the phonemic shape of morphemes —J.B.Carroll⟩ **2 :** the distribution in one morpheme of alternants (as the *ed* of *played*, the *o* in *wrote* as distinguished from *write*, the *t* in *built* as distinguished from *build*) and of zero features (as the zero suffix of *let*, past) regardless of whether the assigned members have any phonemes in common **3 :** the structure of a language in terms of morphophonemics or a statement of this ⟨the total class of these differences so described, classified, and compared is called the ~ of the language in question —R.S.Wells⟩

mor·pho·plasm \ˈmȯ(r)fə,plazəm\ *n* -s [ISV *morph-* + *-plasm*] **1 :** KINOPLASM **2 :** TROPHOPLASM — **mor·pho·plasmic** \¦⸗⸗¦plazmik\ *adj*

mor·pho·sis \mȯ(r)ˈfōsəs\ *n, pl* **morpho·ses** \-ō,sēz\ [NL, fr. Gk *morphōsis* action or process of forming, fr. *morphoun* to form, fr. *morphē* form] **1 :** the mode of development of an organism or one of its parts **2 :** a nonadaptive structural modification

-mor·pho·sis \ˈmȯ(r)fəsəs *sometimes* ,mȯ(r)ˈfōsəs\ *n comb form, pl* **-morpho·ses** \ˈ⸗fə,sēz, ,⸗ˈfō,sēz\ [L, fr. Gk *-morphōsis*, fr. *morphōsis*] **1 :** development or change of form of a (specified) thing ⟨cyto*morphosis*⟩ **2 :** development or change of form in a (specified) manner ⟨hetero*morphosis*⟩

mor·pho·species \¦mȯ(r)(,)fō+\ *n* [*morph-* + *species*] **:** a taxonomic species based wholly on morphological differences from related species

mor·phot·ic \mȯ(r)ˈfäd·ik\ *adj* [fr. *morphosis*, after such pairs as E *narcosis*: *narcotic*] **:** of or relating to morphosis

mor·phot·o·my \mȯ(r)ˈfäd·əmē\ *n* -ES [ISV *morph-* + *-tomy*] **:** ANATOMY 3

-mor·phous \¦mȯrfəs, ¦mȯ(ə)f-\ *adj comb form* [Gk *-morphos*, fr. *morphē* form — more at FORM] **:** having (such) a form ⟨iso*morphous*⟩

mor·phrey \ˈmȯrfri\ *var of* MORFREY

morphs *pl of* MORPH

-morphs *pl of* -MORPH

-mor·phy \,mȯrfē, ,mȯ(ə)fē, -fi\ *n comb form* -ES [ISV *-morph* + *-y*] **:** quality or state of having (such) a form ⟨hetero*morphy*⟩ ⟨iso*morphy*⟩

mor·phy caliper \ˈmȯrfē-\ *n* [by shortening & alter.] **:** HERMAPHRODITE CALIPER

mor·pi·on \ˈmȯ(r)pēən\ *n* -s [MF, fr. *mordre* to bite (fr. L *mordēre*) + *pion, peon* foot soldier, fr. ML *pedon-, pedo* — more at SMART, PAWN] **:** CRAB LOUSE

morra *var of* MORA

mor·ral \məˈral, -rȧl\ *n, pl* **morrals** \-lz\ *or* **morra·les** \-ä,läs\ [Sp, fr. *morro* protruding lips] *West* **:** a fiber bag usu. used as a food bag for horses **:** NOSE BAG ⟨the provisions were in a ~ hung on a tree —J.F.Dobie⟩

mor·rhua \ˈmȯrəwə, ˈmär-\ [NL, fr. ML *morua* cod] *syn of* GADUS

mor·rhu·ate \-rə,wāt\ *n* -s [*morrhuic* (in *morrhuic acid*) + *-ate*] **:** a salt or ester of morrhuic acid

mor·rhu·ic acid \-rəwik-\ *n* [*morrhuic* fr. NL *Morrhua* + E *-ic*] **:** a mixture of fatty acids obtained from cod-liver oil

mor·rice *or* **mor·ris** \ˈmȯrəs, ˈmär-\ *vi* **morriced** *or* **morrised; morricing** *or* **morrising; morrices** *or* **morrises** [¹*morris*] *archaic* **:** to move off quickly **:** DECAMP

¹mor·ris *or* **mor·rice** \ˈmȯrəs, ˈmär-\ *also* **morris dance** *n, pl* **morrises** *or* **morrices** [ME *moreys daunce*, fr. *moreys, morys* Moorish + *daunce* dance — more at MOORISH] **1 :** a vigorous dance done by men wearing costumes and bells and carrying sticks or handkerchiefs and performed as a traditional part of English pageants, processions, and May Day games, often by a group of six men plus solo dancers who represent traditional characters **2 :** a lively and rhythmic movement suggestive of a morris

²morris \"\ *n* -ES [alter. of *merels*] **:** an ancient game for two in which each player has from 3 to 12 counters placed at the angles of a figure consisting of three concentric squares and tries to be first to secure a row of 3 on any line — called also *merels, mill, morelles*

morris chair *n* [after William *Morris* †1896 Eng. poet and artist] **:** an easy chair of simple design with adjustable back and removable cushions in the seat and back

morris chair

mor·ris·ite \ˈmȯrə,sīt, ˈmär-\ *n* -s *usu cap* [Joseph *Morris* *fl*1860 Am. leader of a dissenting group of Mormons + E *-ite*] **:** one of a schismatic group that broke off from the Mormon Church in 1861

morris–pike \ˈ⸗⸗,⸗\ *n* [ME *marespike*, fr. *mares, morys* Moorish + *pike*] **:** a large pike used by foot soldiers esp. in the 15th and early 16th centuries

morris style *n, usu cap M* [after William *Morris* †1896] **:** a simple style of furniture developed in the late 19th century as a protest against overdecoration

¹mor·row \ˈmä(,)rō, -rə *also* ˈmȯ(,)-; *often* ⸗+V\ *n* -s [ME *morwe, morwen* — more at MORN] *archaic* **:** MORNING ⟨I shall say good night till it be ~ —Shak.⟩ **2 :** the next following day **:** the day after any day specified or understood ⟨had expected to go back on the following morning, but instead it looked as if they were going to spend the ~ and a few other morrows in the trenches —Patrick McGill⟩ ⟨told us that the task force would sortie on the ~ —F.J.Bell⟩ **3 :** the time immediately after a specified event ⟨on the ~ of their triumph, jealousy stepped in —*Encyc. Americana*⟩ ⟨has made haste on the ~ of his subject's death to bring out this supplement —*New Yorker*⟩

²morrow \"\ *adj, archaic* **:** of or relating to the next day ⟨a sadder and a wiser man he rose the ~ morn —S.T.Coleridge⟩

mor·row·an \ˈmärəwən *also* ˈmȯr-\ *adj, usu cap* [*Morrow* county, Ohio + E *-an*] **:** of, relating to, or constituting a subdivision of the Pennsylvanian — see GEOLOGIC TIME table

mor·row·ing \ˈmärəwiŋ\ *n* -s [prob. alter. of *marrowing*, gerund of ³*marrow* in its dial. sense (Northern Ireland) of "to exchange aid with a neighbor"] *Irish* **:** an exchange of aid among farmers

morrowmass *n* [ME *morwemasse*, fr. *morwe* morning + *masse* mass] *obs* **:** a mass said early in the morning **:** daily mass

mors *pl of* MOR

mor·sal \ˈmȯrsəl\ *adj* [L *morsus* bite + E *-al*] **:** OCCLUSAL

[1]**morse** \ˈmȯ(ə)rs, ˈmȯ(ə)s\ *n* -s [ME *mors*, fr. MF, morse, bite, fr. OF, bite] **:** a clasp or brooch used to fasten a cope

[2]**morse** \"\ *n* -s [Lapp *morša*] **:** WALRUS

[3]**morse** \"\ *n* -s *often cap* [after Samuel F. B. *Morse* †1872] **:** MORSE CODE

[4]**morse** \"\ *vb* -ED/-ING/-S *vi* **:** to send Morse code **:** communicate by means of Morse code ~ *vt* **:** to signal to by means of Morse code **:** TELEGRAPH

morse code *n, usu cap M* [after Samuel F. B. *Morse* †1872 Am. artist and inventor] **:** either of two codes in which letters of the alphabet, numbers, and other symbols are represented by

MORSE CODE

AMERICAN MORSE CODE[1]

A •–	K –•–	U ••–	5 –––
B –•••	L —	V •••–	6 ••••••
C •• •	M ––	W •––	7 ––••
D –••	N –•	X •–••	8 –••••
E •	O • •	Y •• ••	9 –••–
F •–•	P •••••	Z ••• •	0 —
G ––•	Q ••–•	1 •––•	, (comma) •–•–
H ••••	R • ••	2 ••–••	. ••––••
I ••	S •••	3 •••–•	& • •••
J –•–•	T –	4 ••••–	

INTERNATIONAL CODE[2]

A •–	N –•	Á •––•–	8 –––••
B –•••	O –––	Ä •–•–	9 ––––•
C –•–•	P •––•	É ••–••	0 –––––
D –••	Q ––•–	Ñ ––•––	, (comma) ––••––
E •	R •–•	Ö –––•	. •–•–•–
F ••–•	S •••	Ü ••––	? ••––••
G ––•	T –	1 •––––	; –•–•–•
H ••••	U ••–	2 ••–––	: –––•••
I ••	V •••–	3 •••––	' (apostrophe) •––––•
J •–––	W •––	4 ••••–	- (hyphen) –••••–
K –•–	X –••–	5 •••••	/ –••–•
L •–••	Y –•––	6 –••••	parenthesis –•––•–
M ––	Z ––••	7 ––•••	underline ••––•–

[1]Formerly used on landlines in the U.S. and Canada; now largely out of use.

[2]Often called the continental code; a modification of this code, with dots only, is used on ocean cables.

dots and dashes or long and short sounds and used for transmitting messages by audible or visual signals (as by telegraphy, wigwag, or light flashes)

[1]**mor·sel** \ˈmȯrsəl, ˈmȯ(ə)s-\ *n* -s [ME, fr. OF, fr. *mors* bite (fr. L *morsus*, fr. *morsus*, past part. of *mordēre* to bite) + *-el* — more at SMART] **1 a :** a small piece or quantity of food **:** BITE ⟨the multitude was kept quiet by the ~*s* of meat which were flung to it —J.A.Froude⟩ ⟨deftly ladled a spoonful of this and a ~ of that into the . . . skillet —Elinor Wylie⟩ ⟨a bitter ~ to swallow⟩ **b :** a small meal **:** SNACK ⟨came home, ate his ~ quickly, and left⟩ **2 :** a small quantity of something **:** a little piece or portion **:** FRAGMENT ⟨that ~ of information lay dormant for over a hundred years —C.C.Furnas⟩ ⟨his last remaining ~ of self-respect⟩ ⟨a tiny ~ of land lost in the ocean⟩ **3 a :** a tasty dish **:** TIDBIT ⟨such exotic ~*s* as Japanese frog legs, Alaskan king crabs, Indian pompano —*Time*⟩ ⟨sitting apart munching his own delectable ~*s* —C.S.Kilby⟩ **b :** something delectable and pleasing ⟨the girl . . . is young and very pretty . . . a ~ worth a little lordly condescension —Eric Blom⟩ ⟨his shorter piano pieces include some choice ~*s*⟩ **4 :** a small or negligible person ⟨this ancient ~ —Shak.⟩

[2]**morsel** \"\ *vt* **morseled** *or* **morselled; morseled** *or* **morselled; morseling** *or* **morselling; morsels :** to divide into or apportion in small pieces

morse lamp *n, usu cap M* **:** a lamp used for signaling by flashes corresponding to the dashes and dots of the Morse code

mor·sing \ˈmȯrsiŋ\ *n* -s [fr. gerund of obs. Sc *mors* to grease, prime (a firearm), modif. of MF *amorcer, amorsser* to prime (a firearm), bait, fr. *amorce, amorse* bait, fr. OF, fr. *amorse*, fem. of *amors*, past part. of *amordre* to bite, fr. L *admordēre*, fr. *ad-* + *mordēre* to bite] *archaic Scot* **:** PRIMING

mor·sure \ˈmȯr,shu̇r\ *n* -s [ME, fr. MF, fr. LL *morsura*, fr. L *morsus*, past part. of *mordēre* to bite] *archaic* **:** BITE

[1]**mort** \ˈmȯ(ə)rt, ˈmȯ(ə)t, *usu* -d·+V\ *n* -s [prob. alter. (influenced by MF *mort* death, fr. L *mort-, mors*) of ME *mot* note of a horn, fr. MF, note of a horn, word, saying — more at MOT] **1 :** a note sounded on a hunting horn when a deer is killed ⟨the hunters, with their horns and voices, whooping and blowing a ~ —Sir Walter Scott⟩ **2 :** the act of putting to death **:** KILLING ⟨~ of the English stag —Glenway Wescott⟩

[2]**mort** \"\ *n* -s [origin unknown] **1** *archaic* **:** GIRL, WOMAN ⟨male gypsies all, not a ~ among them —Ben Jonson⟩ **2** *archaic* **:** MISTRESS, SWEETHEART

[3]**mort** \ˈmȯrt\ *n* -s [prob. alter. of obs. E *morkin* animal that has died a natural death, fr. ME *mortkyn*, prob. modif. (influenced by ME *-kyn, -kin* -kin) of MF *morticine* carrion, fr. LL *morticina*, fr. L, fem. of *morticinus* dead of natural causes, fr. *mort-, mors* death] *chiefly Scot* **:** the skin or fleece of a sheep that has died a natural death

[4]**mort** \"\ *n* -s [origin unknown] *dial Eng* **:** the fat of a hog from which lard is made **:** LARD

[5]**mort** \ˈmȯ(ə)rt, ˈmȯ(ə)t, *usu* -d·+V\ *n* -s [F or L; F, fr. *mort*, adj., dead, fr. L *mortuus*, past part. of *mori* to die] **:** a dead body **:** CORPSE ⟨unburied ~ —Henry James †1916⟩

[6]**mort** \"\ *n* -s [prob. back-formation fr. [1]*mortal*] **:** a great quantity or number **:** a great deal **:** ABUNDANCE ⟨had a ~ of things to be thankful for —Ellen Glasgow⟩ ⟨after the ~ of trouble I took —James Still⟩

mor·ta·cious \mȯrˈtāshəs\ *adv* [prob. fr. [6]*mort* + *-acious* (as in *audacious*)] *dial Eng* **:** EXTREMELY, TERRIBLY

mor·ta·del·la \,mȯ(r)d·əˈdelə\ *n* -s [It, irreg. fr. L *murtatum* sausage seasoned with myrtle berries, fr. *murtus* myrtle + *-atum* -ate — more at MYRTLE] **:** a sausage made of chopped beef, pork, and pork fat, seasoned with pepper and garlic, stuffed into large casings, cooked, and smoked

[1]**mor·tal** \ˈmȯr|d·ᵊl, ˈmȯ(ə)|, |tᵊl\ *adj* [ME, mortal, deadly, subject to death, fr. MF *mortel, mortal*, fr. L *mortalis* subject to death, mortal, fr. *mort-, mors* death + *-alis* -al; akin to L *mori* to die — more at MURDER] **1 :** destructive to life **:** causing or capable of causing death **:** FATAL ⟨a ~ disease⟩ ⟨a ~ blow⟩ ⟨a ~ wound⟩ ⟨~ danger⟩ ⟨a new fact that was ~ to his theory⟩ **2 :** subject to death **:** destined to die ⟨all men are ~⟩ ⟨attended all that was ~ of their benefactor to the funeral pyre —J.G. Frazer⟩ ⟨these pictures have a very ~ look, but the poems refuse to fade —*N. Y. Herald Tribune Bk. Rev.*⟩ **3 a :** aiming at extermination **:** fought to the death ⟨living in one of those periods of history when wars are frequent and ~ —John Strachey⟩ ⟨won a ~ contest against a totalitarian system which denied all the values of freedom —Alan Barth⟩ **b :** having or marked by an unrelenting hostility **:** IMPLACABLE ⟨a ~ enemy⟩ ⟨a ~ aversion⟩ ⟨a ~ hatred⟩ **4 a :** existing in the greatest degree **:** marked by great intensity or severity **:** EXTREME, OVERPOWERING ⟨was no longer in ~ dread of her job collapsing under her —J.W.Vandercook⟩ ⟨the underworld that was in ~ terror of him —Richard Watts⟩ **b :** very great **:** AWFUL ⟨it's a ~ shame —Ellen Glasgow⟩ ⟨made a ~ mess of things⟩ **5 :** of or relating to man or mankind **:** HUMAN ⟨attempting to thwart me with ~ morals —Sidney Howard⟩ ⟨a nobody with an all too ~ longing to be a somebody —*Time*⟩ ⟨the most marvelous work of ~ genius —W.L.Sullivan⟩ **6 :** not able to be forgiven or condoned **:** deserving or entailing death ⟨a weakening in our purpose, and therefore in our unity . . . is the ~ crime —Sir Winston Churchill⟩ — see MORTAL SIN **7 :** of, relating to, or connected with death ⟨the ~ moment when the bombers, committed to their target, are locked defenseless in their courses —*Time*⟩ ⟨fell with a scream of ~ agony —F.V.W.Mason⟩ **8 :** humanly conceivable or possible **:** EARTHLY ⟨every ~ thing the heart could wish for —A.E. Coppard⟩ ⟨done all you asked — every ~ thing —Michael McLaverty⟩ **9** *archaic* **:** marked by many deaths ⟨a very sickly and ~ autumn —John Evelyn⟩ **10 :** long and wearisome **:** TEDIOUS ⟨here they lay for four ~ hours, their faces close to the muddy water —E.T.Brown⟩ ⟨three ~ hours — a hundred and eighty minutes — ticked off with jerky precision —Ida Treat⟩ **11** *chiefly Scot* **:** DEAD-DRUNK **syn** see DEADLY

[2]**mortal** \"\ *adv* [ME, fr. *mortal*, adj.] *chiefly dial* **:** MORTALLY

[3]**mortal** \"\ *n* -s [[1]*mortal*] **1** *obs* **:** something that is mortal **:** a mortal substance ⟨this corruptible must put on incorruption, and this ~ must put on immortality —1 Cor 15:53 (AV)⟩ **2 :** one who is mortal **:** a human being ⟨what fools these ~*s* be —Shak.⟩ ⟨parallels are risky matters between ~*s* —Claudia Cassidy⟩ **3 :** INDIVIDUAL, PERSON ⟨just the same careless ~ as to small properties that he used to be —Rachel Henning⟩

mor·tal·ism \-ᵊl,izəm\ *n* -s *usu cap* **:** the doctrine that the soul is mortal

mor·tal·ist \-ᵊləst\ *n* -s *usu cap* **:** one who holds the soul to be mortal; *specif* **:** a member of a 17th century English sect believing that the soul and body perished together at death and would be resurrected together

mor·tal·i·ty \mȯ(r)ˈtaləd·ē, -ətē, -i\ *n* -ES [ME *mortalitee*, fr. MF *mortalité*, fr. L *mortalitat-, mortalitas*, fr. *mortalis* mortal + *-tat-, -tas* -ty] **1 :** the quality or state of being mortal ⟨salvation is the rescue of men from the ~ which sin has brought upon them —K.S.Latourette⟩ **2 :** the death of large numbers **:** a heavy loss of life (as by war or disease) ⟨the Black Death of 1348 caused a terrible ~ throughout Europe⟩ ⟨those rabbits, frogs, hedgehogs and caterpillars which suffer such ~ on our country roads —*Punch*⟩ **3** *archaic* **:** DEATH ⟨here on my knee I beg ~ —Shak.⟩ **4 :** the human race **:** MANKIND ⟨take these tears, ~*'s* relief —Alexander Pope⟩ **5 a :** the whole sum or number of deaths in a given time or a given community ⟨many died and the ~ among the children mounted daily —*Amer. Guide Series: Minn.*⟩ **b :** the proportion of deaths to population or to a specific number of the population **:** DEATH RATE ⟨for years has had the lowest general ~ and infant death rates —V.G.Heiser⟩ — opposed to *fertility* **c :** the number lost or the rate of loss or failure in a field of human endeavor (as business or education) ⟨the ~ among college students⟩ ⟨the ~ rate of small businesses⟩

mortality table *n* **:** an actuarial table based upon statistical records of mortality over a number of years (as a decade) giving the rate of death per 1000 in each age group — called also *life table;* see COMBINED EXPERIENCE TABLE, COMMISSIONERS STANDARD ORDINARY TABLE

mor·tal·ize \ˈmȯ(r)d·ᵊl,īz\ *vt* -ED/-ING/-S **:** to make mortal **:** treat as mortal ⟨contemporary art ~*s* the immortals, stripping them of everything divine and noble —P.A.Sorokin⟩

mor·tal·ly \ˈmȯ(r)d·ᵊlē, -(r)tᵊl-, -ᵊli\ *adv* [ME, fr. [1]*mortal* + *-ly*] **1 :** in a deadly or fatal manner **:** to the point of death ⟨his colonel and lieutenant colonel were both ~ wounded —J.D.Hicks⟩ **2 :** to an extreme degree **:** GRIEVOUSLY, INTENSELY ⟨millions have come out of the war lost souls . . . still ~ afraid —F.S.Kinney⟩ ⟨~ hates and fears a fall in farm income —*Time*⟩ **3 :** by way of mortal sin ⟨the souls of those who have sinned ~ —R.M.French⟩ **4 :** AWFULLY, EXTREMELY ⟨all novelists and dramatists without genius . . . are usually being ~ serious about middle-class people entangled by Fate —F.A.Swinnerton⟩

mortal mind *n, Christian Science* **:** a belief that life, substance, and intelligence are in and of matter **:** ILLUSION — opposed to *Spirit*

mortal sin *n* [ME *mortal synne*] *Roman Catholicism* **:** a serious sin or a lesser sin aggravated by circumstances committed willfully and viewed as involving spiritual death and loss of divine grace — contrasted with *venial sin*

[1]**mor·tar** \ˈmȯrd·ər, ˈmȯ(ə)|d·ə(r, |tə-\ *n* -s [ME *morter*, fr. OE *mortere* & MF *mortier*, fr. L *mortarium* mortar, vessel in which substances are pounded or rubbed, plastic building material that hardens and is used in masonry, trough in which mortar is mixed; akin to Gk *marainein* to waste away — more at SMART] **1 a :** a small usu. bowl-shaped vessel made of a hard material (as porcelain or brass) in which substances are pounded or rubbed with a pestle **b :** a large cast-iron receptacle in which ore is crushed in a stamp mill **2** *archaic* **a :** a bowl of oil with a floating wick **b :** a thick candle **3** [MF *mortier* muzzle-loading cannon having a tube short in relation to its caliber, vessel in which substances are pounded or rubbed] **a :** a muzzle-loading cannon having either a rifled or smooth bore and a tube short in relation to its caliber that is used to throw projectiles with low muzzle velocities at high angles **b :** any of several similar firing devices used for various purposes (as to throw a lifeline or to fire pyrotechnic bombs or shells)

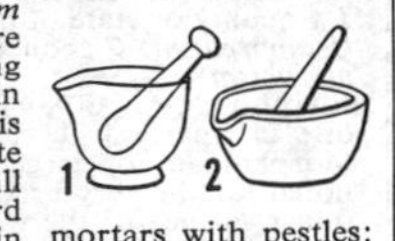

mortars with pestles: *1* glass, *2* porcelain

[2]**mortar** \"\ *vb* -ED/-ING/-S *vt* **:** to direct mortar fire upon or to hit with mortar shells ⟨the enemy . . . was ~*ing* a crossroads behind our lines and interfering with our movements —C.C.Wertenbaker⟩ ⟨the leading tank . . . radioed it had been ~*ed* —*Life*⟩ ~ *vi* **:** to fire mortars ⟨can expect the ~*ing* to begin any minute —Ned Calmer⟩

[3]**mortar** \"\ *n* -s [ME *morter*, fr. OF *mortier*, fr. L *mortarium*] **1 :** a plastic building material that hardens and is used in masonry or plastering; *esp* **:** a mixture of cement, lime, or gypsum plaster with sand and water that is used in either the plastic or hardened state ⟨the masons are calling for ~ —Walt Whitman⟩ **2 :** something that binds or holds together ⟨our dreams are built solidly with the ~ of our toil and blood —Stuart Cloete⟩ ⟨moral and spiritual values . . . the ~ which holds together the other educational ingredients —*Educational and Psychological Measurement*⟩

[4]**mor·tar** \ˈmȯrtər\ *vb* -ED/-ING/-S [ME *morteren*, fr. *morter*, n.] *vt* **:** to plaster or make fast with mortar ~ *vi, dial Eng* **:** to tramp about esp. with mud or dirt on one's feet ⟨keep ~*in'* in and out, in and out, for everlastin' trampin' through —H.E. Bates⟩

mortar bed *n* **1 :** a shallow box or receptacle in which mortar is mixed **2 :** a layer of sand or gravel cemented by calcium carbonate and resembling hardened mortar

mortarboard \ˈ⸗⸗,⸗\ *n* **1 a :** HAWK 3 **b :** a board or platform about 3 feet square for holding mortar **2 :** an academic cap consisting of a closely fitting headpiece surmounted by a broad flat projecting square top ⟨the shape of the hat as stiff and uncoquettish as a ~ —Frances G. Patton⟩ ⟨the candidates for honorary degrees, now sitting fussing nervously with their gowns and ~ hats —*Harper's*⟩

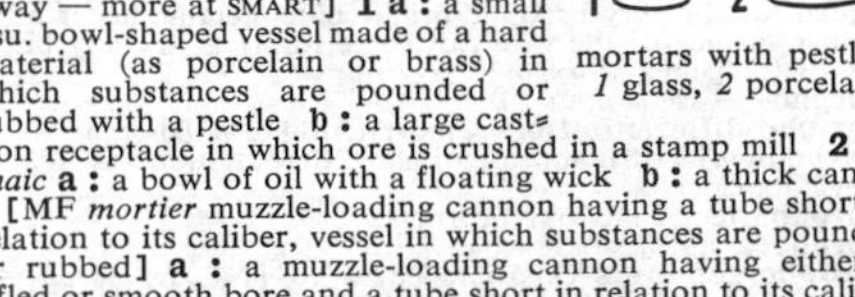

mortarboard 2

mortar boat *n* **:** a boat adapted to carrying a mortar or mortars for bombarding

mor·tar·less \ˈmȯ(r)d·ə(r)ləs\ *adj* **:** having or using no mortar ⟨a ~ stone foundation⟩

mor·tar·man \ˈ⸗⸗mən\ *n, pl* **mortarmen :** a member of a crew that fires a mortar

mortarware \ˈ⸗⸗,⸗\ *n* [[1]*mortar* + *ware*] **:** a hard stoneware first made by Wedgwood and used in the manufacture of mortars

mor·tary \ˈmȯ(r)d·ərē\ *adj* [[3]*mortar* + *-y*] **:** consisting of, containing, or resembling mortar

mort·cloth \ˈmȯrt,klȯth\ *n* [obs. E *mort* death (fr. MF, fr. L *mort-, mors*) + E cloth — more at MORTAL] **1** *chiefly Scot* **:** a funeral pall ⟨let the bedclothes, for a ~, drop into great laps and folds of sculptor's work —Robert Browning⟩ **2** *Scot* **:** money paid for the use of a pall

mort d'an·ces·tor \mär'dan,sestər\ *n* [AF, death of the ancestor] **:** an obsolete writ or brieve in English and Scots law for the recovery by an heir from an abator of a tenement which his deceased ancestor held in seisin at his death

mor·ter·sheen \ˈmȯ(r)tə(r),shēn\ *n* -s [prob. modif. of (assumed) obs. F *mort d'échine*, lit., death of the spine, fr. MF *mort de eschine*] *Scot* **:** GLANDERS

[1]**mort·gage** \ˈmȯrgij, ˈmȯ(ə)g-, -gēj\ *n* -s [ME *morgage*, fr. MF, fr. OF, fr. *mort* dead (fr. L *mortuus*, past part. of *mori* to die) + *gage* security, gage — more at MURDER, GAGE] **1 a :** a conveyance of property upon condition (as security for the payment of a debt or the performance of a duty) that operates as a lien or charge securing the payment of the money or the performance of an obligation so that the mortgagee may under certain conditions take possession and may foreclose the property upon default, that becomes void upon payment or performance according to stipulated terms, and that leaves possession with the mortgagor and subjects the mortgagee's defeasible estate in the land to the equity of redemption and foreclosure rules of the equity courts — see CHATTEL MORTGAGE, EQUITABLE MORTGAGE, FIRST MORTGAGE, INSTALLMENT MORTGAGE, JUNIOR MORTGAGE, LEASEHOLD MORTGAGE, PARTICIPATING MORTGAGE, PURCHASE-MONEY MORTGAGE, SECOND MORTGAGE, TRUST MORTGAGE; compare ANTICHRESIS, EQUITY OF REDEMPTION, GAGE, HYPOTHEC, LIVING PLEDGE, PLEDGE **b :** the instrument by which a mortgage conveyance is made, the state of the property so conveyed, or the interest of the mortgagee in it **2 :** a binding obligation ⟨however stridently the American writer may protest his Americanism . . . he can never pay off his ~ to the past —*Times Lit. Supp.*⟩ ⟨the first president . . . to feel unencumbered by any ~ to Congress —W.E. Binkley⟩

[2]**mortgage** \", *esp in pres part* -gəj\ *vt* -ED/-ING/-S **1 :** to grant or convey by a mortgage **:** make a mortgage conveyance of **2 :** to subject to a claim or obligation **:** PLEDGE ⟨found myself *mortgaged* to my father for about one hundred and fifty dollars —Roger Eddy⟩ ⟨a view of life . . . in which the individual is *mortgaged* to society —David Riesman⟩

mortgage bond *n* **:** a bond secured by a mortgage on property — distinguished from *debenture bond*

mortgage clause *or* **mortgagee clause** *n* **:** a clause endorsed on a mortgagor's insurance policy whereby the insurance company agrees to protect the mortgagee's interest regardless of any violation of the policy terms by the mortgagor

mortgage deed *n* **:** a deed embodying a mortgage

mort·ga·gee \¦mȯ(r)gə¦jē\ *n* -s [[2]*mortgage* + *-ee*] **:** a person who takes a mortgage on another's property as security for a debt or obligation

mortgage guarantee bond *n* **:** insurance against loss due to default in payments of interest or principal by a mortgagor

mortgage insurance *n* **:** insurance that protects a mortgagee against loss because of default in payments by a mortgagor

mortgage loan *n* **:** a loan secured by a mortgage on real property

mortgage redemption insurance *n* **:** insurance upon the life of a mortgagor providing for payment of any unpaid balance of the mortgage loan at the insured's death

mort·ga·gor \¦mȯrgi¦jȯ(ə)r, ¦mȯgi¦jȯ(ə), ˈ⸗⸗jə(r)\ *also* **mort·gag·er** \ˈ⸗⸗jə(r)\ *n* -s [[2]*mortgage* + *-or* or *-er*] **:** a person who gives a mortgage on his property as security for a loan he receives or other obligation

mor·tial \ˈmȯrshəl\ *dial var of* MORTAL

mortice *var of* MORTISE

mor·ti·cian \mȯ(r)ˈtishən\ *n* -s [L *mort-, mors* death + E *-ician* — more at MORTAL] **:** FUNERAL DIRECTOR ⟨saw the old Victorian houses taken over by ~*s* and auto showrooms —*Time*⟩ ⟨on the scene appears a solemn ~ —Robert Frost⟩

mor·tier \mȯrˈtyā\ *n* -s [F, mortier, vessel in which substances are pounded or rubbed — more at MORTAR] **:** a headdress formerly worn by certain high functionaries of the law in France

mor·tif·er·ous \(ˈ)mȯ(r)¦tif(ə)rəs\ *adj* [L *mortifer, mortiferus*, fr. *morti-* (fr. *mort-, mors* death) + *-fer, -ferus* -fer, -ferous] **:** DEADLY, FATAL — **mor·tif·er·ous·ly** *adv* — **mor·tif·er·ous·ness** *n* -ES

mor·tif·ic \(ˈ)mȯ(r)¦tifik\ *adj* [LL *mortificus*, fr. L *morti-* (fr. *mort-, mors* death) + *-ficus* -fic] *archaic* **:** producing death

mor·ti·fi·ca·tion \,mȯ(r)d·əfəˈkāshən, -(r)tə-\ *n* -s [ME *mortificacion*, fr. MF *mortification*, fr. LL *mortification-, mortificatio* mortification, killing, fr. *mortificatus* (past part. of *mortificare* to mortify, kill) + L *-ion-, -io* -ion] **1 a :** the subjection and denial of bodily passions and appetites by abstinence or self-inflicted pain or discomfort ⟨fasted for the day as a ~⟩ **b :** something that mortifies **:** a cause of humiliation or chagrin **2** *Scots law* **:** a gift for religious, charitable, or public uses corresponding to mortmain **3** *archaic* **:** a numbing of the vital faculties **:** a loss of consciousness at the approach of death **:** INSENSIBILITY **4 :** local death of tissue in the animal body **:** GANGRENE **5 :** a sense of humiliation and shame caused by something that wounds one's pride or self-respect (as a slight, a deep disappointment, or a personal failure) **:** CHAGRIN ⟨the ~ of being jilted by a little boarding-school girl —Washington Irving⟩ ⟨felt deep ~ at the plight of his invincible fleet —J.L.Motley⟩ ⟨in real life she suffered such bitter ~ in the company of her fellow creatures —Robert Cantwell⟩

mortification root *n* **:** MARSHMALLOW 1a

mortified *adj* [fr. past part. of *mortify*] **1 :** insensible to worldly or sensual pleasures **:** having the appetites in subjection **:** ASCETIC, AUSTERE ⟨the fame of his ~ life and supernatural gift of counsel —C.M.Rooney⟩ ⟨could be no gainsaying his brilliant intellectual gifts or his ~ daily life —*Times Lit. Supp.*⟩ **2 :** affected by gangrene **:** GANGRENOUS **3** *obs* **:** being without feeling **:** DEADENED ⟨strike in their numbed and ~ bare arms pins, wooden pricks, nails —Shak.⟩ **4** *archaic* **:** DECAYED, ROTTEN ⟨in such a ~ condition, that no other people . . . would feed upon it —Tobias Smollett⟩ **5 :** deeply embarrassed or humiliated ⟨terribly ~ to find that his host had forgotten about him⟩ **syn** see ASHAMED

mor·ti·fied·ly *adv* **:** in a mortified manner

mor·ti·fi·er \ˈmȯrd·ə,fī(ə)r\ *n* -s **:** one that mortifies

mor·ti·fy \ˈmȯ(r)d·ə,fī, -(r)tə-\ *vb* -ED/-ING/-ES [ME *mortifien*, fr. MF *mortifier*, fr. LL *mortificare* to mortify, kill, fr. L *morti-* (fr. *mort-, mors* death) + *-ficare* -fy] *vt* **1** *obs* **a :** to put to death **:** DESTROY ⟨if ye through the spirit do ~ the deeds of the body, ye shall live —Rom 8:13 (AV)⟩ **b :** to destroy the strength, vitality, or functioning of **:** deaden the effect of ⟨the tendons were *mortified* and . . . he could never have the use of his leg —Daniel Defoe⟩ ⟨the knowledge of future evils *mortifies* present felicities —Sir Thomas Browne⟩ **2 :** to subdue or deaden (as the body or bodily appetites) by abstinence, self-discipline, or self-inflicted pain or discomfort ⟨the flesh tended to corruption, and to achieve the pious ends of life one must ~ it . . . lessening its appetites by fasting and abstention —Lewis Mumford⟩ ⟨one is taught in the novitiate to ~ one's palate at least once during every meal —Monica Baldwin⟩ **3** *Scots law* **:** to grant in mortmain for religious, charitable, or public uses ⟨to administer and manage the whole revenue and property of the University including funds *mortified* for bursaries and other purposes —*Edinburgh Univ. Cal.*⟩ **4** *obs* **:** to make (meat) tender by aging **5 :** to subject to or cause to feel embarrassment, chagrin, or vexation **:** HUMILIATE ⟨it would ~ me that you shouldn't be perfectly dressed —W.S. Maugham⟩ ⟨was no longer *mortified* by comparisons between her sisters' beauty and her own —Jane Austen⟩ ~ *vi* **1 :** to practice mortification **:** lead an ascetic life ⟨a sort of mammoth lay monastery relieved of the obligation to ~ —James Binder⟩ **2 :** to lose organic structure **:** become gangrenous **:** DECAY

mor·ti·fy·ing·ly *adv* **:** in a mortifying manner

mor·tis cau·sa \ˈmȯrd·ə'skau̇sə, -kȯl, |zə\ *adj* [L, because of death] **:** made by reason of or in contemplation of impending death ⟨her last will and testament, or rather her *mortis causa* settlement —Sir Walter Scott⟩

[1]**mor·tise** *also* **mor·tice** \ˈmȯr|d·əs, ˈmȯ(ə)|, |təs\ *n* -s [ME *mortays, morteys*, fr. MF *mortaise*] **1 :** a hole, groove, or slot into or through which some other part of any arrangement of parts fits or passes; *specif* **:** a usu. rectangular cavity cut into a piece of timber or other material to receive a tenon **2 :** a hole in a printing plate or cut into which other matter (as type) can be inserted

[2]**mortise** *also* **mortice** \"\ *vt* -ED/-ING/-S [ME *morteysen*, fr. *mortays, morteys*, n.] **1 :** to join or fasten securely; *specif* **:** to join or fasten by a tenon and mortise ⟨a thin strip of beech is nailed across each corner instead of being *mortised* —Joseph Downs⟩ ⟨this loyalty and this courage, like all virtues not *mortised* in philosophy, are limited —Clifton Fadiman⟩ ⟨a

tightly *mortised*, exciting plot —E.J.Fitzgerald⟩ **2 a :** to cut or make a mortise in **b :** to cut away part of the body of (a printing character) to obtain a closer fit

mortise gage *n* **:** a carpenter's tool for scribing parallel lines for mortises

mortise joint *n* **:** a joint made by a mortise and tenon

mortise lock *n* **:** a door lock inserted in a mortise

mortise pin *n* **:** a tapered wooden pin driven either through both members of a mortised joint or through the extended tenon in order to lock and tighten the joint

mortise joint

mor·tis·er \-sə(r)\ *n* -s **1 :** one that mortises by hand or by machine **2 :** a woodworking machine for cutting mortises

mortise wheel *n* **:** a cast-iron wheel with wooden teeth inserted in mortises

mort·lake \ˈmȯrt,lāk\ *n* [prob. fr. *Mortlake*, parish in Barnes municipal borough, southwestern suburb of London, England] *Brit* **:** OXBOW LAKE

mort·ling \ˈmȯrtliŋ\ *n* -s [ME *morlyng*, prob. modif. (influenced by ME *-lyng*, *-ling* -ling) of MF *morticine* carrion — more at MORT] **:** wool taken from a dead sheep

mort·main \ˈmȯrt,mān, ˈmȯ(ə)t-\ *n* -s [ME *morte-mayne*, fr. MF *mortemain*, fr. OF (trans. of ML *mortua manus*), fr. *morte* (fem. of *mort* dead, fr. L *mortuus*, past part. of *mori* to die) + *main* hand, fr. L *manus* — more at MURDER, MANUAL] **1 a :** an inalienable possession or tenure of lands or buildings by an ecclesiastical or other corporation — see STATUTES OF MORTMAIN **b :** the condition of property or other gifts left to a corporation in perpetuity esp. for religious, charitable, or public purposes **2 :** the influence of the past regarded as controlling or restricting the present ⟨the tradition . . . has become a deadweight, a ~ hanging evilly over the school —John Raymond⟩ ⟨in the grip of ~, under thrall of a fascinating past —*Saturday Rev.*⟩

mor·ton mains disease \ˈmȯrtᵊn'mānz-\ *n*, *usu cap both Ms* [perh. fr. a name *Morton Mains*] **:** cobalt deficiency disease of sheep and cattle in New Zealand — compare ¹PINE 3

mor·ton's toe *also* **morton's disease** \ˈmȯrtᵊnz-\ *n*, *usu cap M* [after Thomas G. *Morton* †1903 Am. surgeon] **:** METATARSALGIA

morts *pl of* MORT

¹**mor·tu·ary** \ˈmȯ(r)chə,werē, -ri\ *n* -ES [ME *mortuarie*, fr. ML *mortuarium*, fr. L, neut. of *mortuarius*, adj.] **1 :** CORSEPRESENT **2 :** a place in which dead bodies are kept until burial; *esp* **:** FUNERAL HOME

²**mortuary** \"\ *adj* [L *mortuarius* of the dead, fr. *mortuus* dead (past part. of *mori* to die) + *-arius* -ary] **1 :** of or relating to the burial of the dead ⟨ropes, palls, velvet, ostrich feathers, and other ~ properties —W.M.Thackeray⟩ ⟨~ arrangements⟩ **2 :** of, relating to, or characteristic of death ⟨it continues to receive a kind of ~ tribute in the schoolroom —Clifton Fadiman⟩ ⟨an embalmed darkness, a darkness at once soothing and ~ —R.M.Adams⟩

mor·tu·um va·di·um \ˈmȯrchəwəm'vādēəm\ *n* [ML, lit., dead pledge] **:** a mortgage agreement in early English law that gave possession of the mortgaged land and the use of its rents and profits to the mortgagee until such time as the mortgage was paid — compare VIVUM VADIUM

mort·warp *or* **mort·worp** \ˈmȯr,twȯrp\ *var of* MOLDWARP

mo·ru \ˈmō(,)rü, ˈmȯ(,)-\ *n*, *pl* **moru** *or* **morus** *usu cap* **1 a :** a people of the Sudan **b :** a member of such people **2 :** a Central Sudanic language of the Moru people

mor·u·la \ˈmȯrələ, ˈmär-\ *n*, *pl* **moru·lae** \-rə,lē\ [NL, fr. L *morum* mulberry + *-ula*] **1 :** a globular mass of blastomeres formed by cleavage of the egg of many animals in its early development and distinguished from a typical blastula which may arise from it by the absence of any trace of a central cavity — compare GASTRULA **2 :** a cluster of developing male germ cells esp. in certain annelids in which final development of spermatozoa occurs outside the testis — **mor·u·lar** \-lə(r)\ *adj*

mor·u·la·tion \,ˌ=ˈlāshən\ *n* -s [NL *morula* + E *-ation*] **:** formation of a morula

mo·rus \ˈmōrəs, ˈmȯr-\ *n*, *cap* [NL, fr. L, mulberry tree, fr. *morum* mulberry — more at MULBERRY] **:** a widely distributed genus of trees that is the type of the family Moraceae and that comprises the mulberries which have usu. dentate or lobed leaves, spicate flowers, and edible multiple fruits consisting of aggregates of juicy one-seeded drupes

mor·wong \ˈmȯr,wäŋ\ *n* -s [native name in New South Wales, Australia] **:** any of several important Australian food fishes of the family Cheilodactylidae — called also *sea carp*

mos *pl of* MO

-mos *pl of* -MO

MOS *abbr or n* -s military occupational specialty ⟨had an ~ of clerk typist⟩

¹**mo·sa·ic** \mō'zāik, -āek, mə'-\ *n* -s [ME *musycke*, fr. MF *mosaique*, fr. OIt *mosaico*, fr. ML *musaicum*, alter. of LL *musivum*, fr. neut. of *musivus* of a muse, artistic, fr. L *musa* muse + *-ivus* -ive] **1 a :** a surface decoration made by inlaying small pieces of variously colored material (as tile, marble, or glass) to form patterns or pictures **b :** the process of making such a decoration **2 a :** a picture or design made in mosaic **b :** an article decorated in mosaic **3 :** something resembling a mosaic ⟨passages that are ~*s* of quotations —Malcolm Cowley⟩ ⟨a ~ of colorful bits from history —*College English*⟩ ⟨great cities turn out . . . to be a ~ of segregated peoples —R.E.Park⟩ **4 :** a mosaic individual **:** CHIMERA **5 a :** LEAF MOSAIC 1 **b** *also* **mosaic disease :** any of several virus diseases of plants characterized esp. by more or less diffuse light and dark green or yellow and green mottling or spotting of the foliage and sometimes by pronounced curling, dwarfing, and narrowing of the leaves **6 :** a composite photographic map formed by matching a series of overlapping photographs of adjoining areas of the earth's surface taken vertically from the air at a constant height **7 :** the photosensitive element in a television camera tube consisting of a layer of many minute photoelectric particles that convert light to an electric charge

²**mosaic** \"\ *adj* **1 a** *also* **mosaical** \-āəkəl\ **:** of, relating to, or produced by mosaic ⟨a ~ floor⟩ ⟨bright ~ tile⟩ **b :** resembling mosaic esp. in pattern, variegation, or composition ⟨a ~ compilation⟩ **2 :** exhibiting mosaicism: **a :** CHIMERAL **b :** of, relating to, or constituting a mosaic hybrid or mosaic inheritance **3** *of a plant* **:** affected with mosaic **4 :** GRANOBLASTIC **5 :** DETERMINATE 6 **6 :** of or relating to the mosaic of a television camera tube — **mo·sa·i·cal·ly** \-āək(ə)lē\ *adv*

³**mosaic** \"\ *vt* **mosaicked** *also* **mosaiced** \-ikt,-ēkt\ **mosaicked** *also* **mosaiced; mosaicking** *also* **mosaicing** \-āəkiŋ\ **mosaics** [¹*mosaic*] **1 :** to decorate with or as if with mosaics ⟨doors and roofs were carved and sculptured and painted and *mosaicked* —Rose Macaulay⟩ **2 :** to form into or as if into a mosaic ⟨an artificial patchwork . . . *mosaicked* out of bought, stolen, and plundered provinces —J.L.Motley⟩

⁴**mosaic** \"\ *also* **mo·sa·i·cal** \-āəkəl\ *adj*, *usu cap* [*Mosaic* fr. NL *Mosaicus*, fr. *Moses* Biblical prophet and lawgiver + L *-icus* -ic; *Mosaical* fr. NL *Mosaicus* + E *-al* — more at MOSES] **:** of or relating to Moses or the institutions or writings attributed to him ⟨the *Mosaic* code⟩

mosaic binding *n* **:** a full-leather bookbinding with inlaid colored designs — called also *inlaid binding*

mosaic dwarf *n* **:** CURLY DWARF

mosaic glass *n* **:** MILLEFIORI

mosaic gold *n* **1 :** a yellow scaly crystalline pigment consisting essentially of stannic sulfide **2 :** ORMOLU 2

mosaic hybrid *n* **1 :** CHIMERA **2 :** an individual exhibiting mosaic inheritance

mosaic image *n* **:** the image formed by a compound eye (as of an insect) in which each visual facet receives independently a small portion of the image and the total visual impression is a composite of the various unit images

mosaic inheritance *n* **1 :** supposed inheritance of both of a pair of contrasted parental characters one or the other of which is manifested in pure form at any given point (as in variegated flowers) — compare MOSAICISM **2 :** typical Mendelian inheritance of alternate parental characters

mo·sa·i·cism \mō'zāə,sizəm\ *n* -s **:** a condition in which patches of tissue of unlike genetic constitution are mingled in an organism owing esp. to abnormalities of chromosome separation during mitosis

mo·sa·i·cist \-səst\ *n* -s **1 a :** a designer of mosaics **b :** a workman who makes mosaics **2 :** a dealer in mosaics

mosaic law *n*, *usu cap M* [⁴*Mosaic*] **:** the ancient Hebrew moral and ceremonial law attributed to Moses

mosaic rhyme *n* **:** BROKEN RHYME

mosaics *pl of* MOSAIC, *pres 3d sing of* MOSAIC

mosaic screen *n* **:** a flat transparent light filter composed of minute colored elements through which the exposure is made on a panchromatic emulsion layer and through which the image is viewed in the screen process of additive color photography

mosaic structure *n* **:** irregularity of orientation of small blocks of varying sizes in a crystal

mosaic-tailed rat \=ˌ==ˌ=-\ *n* **:** any of various large rats (genus *Uromys*) of northern Australia and adjacent islands distinguished by tail scales that do not overlap but meet in a mosaic pattern

mosaic theory *n* **:** a theory in embryology: each part of the protoplasm of an egg has its function in forming a special part of the embryo

mo·sa·ism \ˈmōzā,izəm\ *n* -s *usu cap* [⁴*Mosaic* + *-ism*] **1 :** the ancient Hebrew religious and legal system attributed to Moses **2 :** attachment to the Mosaic system or doctrines

mo·sa·ist \ˈmō(,)zāəst, mō'z-\ *n* -s [¹*mosaic* + *-ist*] **:** MOSAICIST

mo·san \ˈmōsᵊn\ *n* -s *usu cap* [*mos-* (fr. *mōs*, *bōs* "four" in various Chemakuan, Wakashan & Salishan languages) + E *-an*] **:** a language phylum of British Columbia and Washington comprising the Salishan, Wakashan, and Chemakuan stocks

mo·san·drite \mō'san,drīt\ *n* -s [G *mosandrit*, fr. Carl G. *Mosander* †1858 Swed. chemist + G *-it* -ite] **:** a mineral approximately $NaCa_6Ce_2(Ti,Zr)_2Si_7O_{24}(OH,F)_7$ consisting of a silicate of sodium, calcium, titanium, zirconium, and the cerium metals

mo·sa·saur \ˈmōsə,sȯ(ə)r\ *n* -s [NL *Mosasaurus*] **:** a reptile of the genus *Mosasaurus* or the family Mosasauridae

mo·sa·sau·ria \,==ˈsȯrēə\ *or* **mo·sa·sau·ri** \-ó,rī\ [NL, fr. *Mosasaurus* + *-ia*] *syn of* PYTHONOMORPHA

¹**mo·sa·sau·ri·an** \,==ˈsȯrēən\ *adj* [NL *Mosasaurus* + E *-ian*] **:** of or relating to the genus *Mosasaurus* or the family Mosasauridae

²**mosasaurian** \"\ *n* -s **:** MOSASAUR

mo·sa·sau·rus \,==ˈsȯrəs\ *n*, *cap* [NL, fr. L *Mosa* the river Meuse (near which the first known species was discovered) + NL *-saurus*] **:** a genus (the type of the family Mosasauridae) of large extinct aquatic Cretaceous fish-eating lizards related to the recent monitors but having the limbs modified into swimming paddles

mos·cha·tel \,mäskə'tel\ *n* -s [modif. (influenced by NL *moschatellina* — specific epithet of *Adoxa moschatellina* — fr. F *moscatelle* or It *moscatella* + NL *-ina*) of F *moscatelle*, fr. It *moscatella*, fr. *moscato* musk (fr. LL *muscus* musk + It *-ato*, fr. L *-atus* -ate) + *-ella* (dim. suffix) — more at MUSK] **:** a small herb (*Adoxa moschatellina*) of the north temperate zone with greenish white musk-scented flowers

mo·schel·lands·berg·ite \,mōshə'lan(d)zbə(r),gīt\ *n* -s [*Moschellandsberg*, town in Bavaria, Germany + E *-ite*] **:** a mineral Ag_2Hg_3 consisting of a natural alloy or amalgam of silver and mercury

mos·chi \ˈmä,skī\ *n pl*, *usu cap* [L, fr. Gk *Moschoi*] **:** one of numerous ancient peoples in Armenia associated with ironworking

mos·chus \ˈmäskəs\ *n*, *cap* [NL, fr. ML, musk — more at MUSK] **:** a genus comprising the Asiatic musk deer usu. segregated in a subfamily of Cervidae but formerly placed in a separate family

moscovite *var of* MUSCOVITE

mos·cow \ˈmä,skaü, -ä(,)skō\ *adj*, *usu cap* [fr. *Moscow*, U.S.S.R.] **:** of or from Moscow, capital of the U.S.S.R. **:** of the kind or style prevalent in Moscow

mo·selle \mō'zel\ *n* -s *usu cap* [G *moselwein*, fr. *Mosel* (Moselle) river in southwestern Germany + G *wein* wine] **1 :** a white usu. still but sometimes sparkling table wine made from grapes grown in the valley of the Moselle from Trier to Coblenz and in the valleys of its tributaries, the Saar and the Ruwer **2 :** a wine resembling Moselle ⟨California *Moselle*⟩

moses \ˈmōzəz, -zəs\ *n* -ES [after *Moses*, biblical prophet and lawgiver who led the Israelites from Egypt to Canaan *ab* 1200 B.C. (Exod 12 ff.), fr. LL *Moses*, *Moyses*, fr. Gk *Mōsēs*, *Mōysēs*, fr. Heb *Mōsheh*] **1** *usu cap* **:** LEADER ⟨theatregoers may have found a *Moses* who will lead them out of their wilderness —*Theatre Arts*⟩ **2** *or* **moses boat :** a broad flat-bottomed ship's boat formerly used in the West Indies esp. for lightering hogsheads of sugar

mo·ses·ite \ˈmōzə,zīt, -,sīt\ *n* -s [Alfred J. *Moses* †1920 Am. mineralogist + E *-ite*] **:** a mineral $Hg_2N(X).H_2O$ consisting of a hydrous nitride of mercury with other anions and water exchangeable within wide limits

moses-on-a-raft \ˈ====ˈ=\ *also* **moses-in-the-bulrushes** \ˈ====ˈ=,=\ *n*, *usu cap* [so called fr. the infant Moses' having been placed by his mother in an ark made of bulrushes on the edge of a river to escape death by the Egyptians (Exod 2:3)] **:** OYSTER PLANT 3

mo·se·te·ne \,mōsə'tā(,)nā\ *or* **mo·se·te·no** \-nō\ *n*, *pl* **mosetene** \-nā\ *or* **mosete·nes** \-nās\ *or* **moseteno** \-nō\ *or* **mosete·nos** \-nōs\ *usu cap* **a :** an Amerind people of eastern Bolivia **b :** a member of such people **2 :** the language of the Mosetene people

¹**mo·sey** \ˈmōzi\ *adj* [ME *mosy*, fr. *mos* moss + *-y* — more at MOSS] **1** *dial Brit* **:** HAIRY; *esp* **:** having soft downy hair **2** *dial Brit* **:** MOLDY, ROTTEN — used esp. of overripe fruit

²**mo·sey** \ˈmōzē, -zi\ *vi* **moseyed; moseyed; moseying; moseys** [origin unknown] **1 :** to hurry away **:** DECAMP, SCRAM ⟨vamoose, skedaddle, ~ —S.V.Benét⟩ **2 a :** to move in a leisurely, shuffling, or aimless manner **:** SAUNTER, AMBLE ⟨just ~*ed* along, mostly traveling by shanks' mare —Helen Eustis⟩ ⟨~*ed* into position to sneak a look at the owner of the rough voice —Joel Sayre⟩ ⟨a mild river that ~*ed* at will through parks and plowland —W.H.Auden⟩ **b :** to move slowly while observing or inspecting ⟨spend three or four weeks . . . just ~*ing* about, discovering lesser-known museums, galleries, and places of historic interest —Richard Joseph⟩ ⟨~*ed* around the general store, testing the cheese straight off the round —Eric Sevareid⟩

mosgu *usu cap*, *var of* MUSGU

mo·shav \mō'shäv\ *n*, *pl* **mo·sha·vim** \,mōshə'vēm\ [NHeb *mōshābh*, fr. Heb, dwelling] **:** a cooperative small holders' settlement of individual farms in Israel

mo·sha·va \,mōshə'vä\ *n*, *pl* **mosha·voth** *or* **mosha·vot** \-vōt(h)\ [NHeb *mōshābhāh*, fem. of *mōshābh*] **:** a settlement or colony of independent farmers in Israel who own and work their own land

moshav ov·dim \-ōv'dēm\ *n*, *pl* **mosh·vei ovdim** \mōsh'vā-\ [NHeb *mōshābh 'obhēdhīm*, lit., settlement of workers] **:** a workers' settlement of small holders in Israel with independent but cooperatively worked farm units

moshav shi·tu·fi \-,shi,tü'fē\ *n*, *pl* **moshavim shitu·fim** \-'fēm\ [NHeb *mōshābh shittūphī*, lit., partnership settlement] **:** a collective small holders' settlement in Israel

mos·ke·neer \,mäskə'niə\ *vt* -ED/-ING/-S [Yiddish *mashken* pledge, pawn (fr. Heb *mashkōn*) + E *-eer* (as in *profiteer*, v.)] *Brit* **:** to pawn for more than the value of the article

¹**mosk·er** \ˈmäskə(r)\ *vi* -ED/-ING/-S [origin unknown] *dial chiefly Eng* **:** DECAY, MOLDER

²**mosk·er** \ˈmäskə(r\ *n* -s [*moskeneer* + *-er*] *Brit* **:** one that moskeneers

moslem *usu cap*, *var of* MUSLIM

mos·lem·ize \ˈmäzlə,mīz, ˈmäs-\ *vt* -ED/-ING/-S *often cap* **:** to make Muslim in religion or culture ⟨~ a region⟩ ⟨*moslemized* Christians⟩

mo·so \ˈmō(,)sō\ *also* **mos·so** \ˈmȯ(-\ *n*, *pl* **moso** *or* **mosos** *also* **mosso** *or* **mossos** *usu cap* **:** NA-KHI

mo·so·sau·rus \,mōsə'sȯrəs\ [NL, alter. of *Mosasaurus*] *syn of* MOSASAURUS

mosque \ˈmäsk\ *n* -s [fr. earlier *moschee*, *muskie*, fr. MF *musquee*, *mosquee*, fr. OIt *moschea*, alter. of *mosqueta*, *meschita*, fr. OSp *mezquita*, fr. Ar *masjid* temple, fr. *sajada* to prostrate oneself] **:** an Islamic place of public religious worship — called also MASJID

mosque swallow *n* **:** any of numerous Asian and northern African swallows that commonly nest about buildings

¹**mos·qui·to** \mə'skēd·(,)ō, -ē(,)tō, -ēd·ə, -ētə\ *n*, *pl* **mosquitoes** *also* **mosquitos** *often attrib* [Sp, dim. of *mosca* fly, fr. L *musca* — more at MIDGE] **:** any of numerous two-winged flies of the family Culicidae that have a rather narrow abdomen, usu. a long slender rigid proboscis, and narrow wings with a fringe of scales on the margin and usu. on each side of the wing veins, that have in the male broad feathery antennae and mouthparts not fitted for piercing and in the female slender antennae and a set of needlelike organs in the proboscis with which they puncture the skin of animals to suck the blood, that have the eggs laid on the surface of stagnant water, that in many species pass through several generations in the course of a year and hibernate as adults and in others winter in the egg state, and that in some species are the only vectors of certain diseases — see AEDES, ANOPHELES, CULEX; compare GNAT

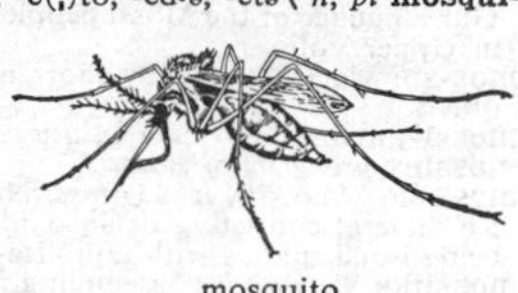

mosquito

²**mosquito** \"\ *n*, *pl* **mosquito** *or* **mosquitos** *usu cap* [by alter.] **:** MISKITO

mosquito bar *n* **:** MOSQUITO NET ⟨slept in hammocks . . . protected by *mosquito bars* —Ralph Watson⟩

mosquito bee *n* **:** STINGLESS BEE

mosquitobill \=ˈ=(,)=,=\ *n* **:** a California shooting star (*Dodecatheon hendersonii*)

mosquito blight *n* **1 :** TEA MOSQUITO **2 :** the disease of tea produced by the punctures of the tea mosquito

mosquito boat *n* **:** MOTOR TORPEDO BOAT

mosquito boot *n* **:** a high shoe or low boot worn in the tropics ⟨don trousers and, very often, *mosquito boots* in the evening —K.L.Little⟩

mos·qui·to·ey \mə'skēd·|ōē, -ēt|, |əwē, -i\ *adj* [*mosquito* + *-y*] **:** full of mosquitoes ⟨the screened porch where one might sit in peace during the ~ seasons —Thomas Barbour⟩

mosquito fern *n* **:** a water fern of the genus *Azolla*

mosquito fish *n* **:** any of numerous small fishes used to exterminate mosquito larvae; *esp* **:** either of two No. American live-bearers (*Gambusia affinis* and *Heterandria formosa*)

mosquito fleet *n* **:** a fleet of comparatively small ships ⟨fast= moving light tanks, agile weaving fighter planes, and high= powered boats of the *mosquito fleet* all operate on the same principles —J.R.Newman⟩

mosquito hawk *n* **1 :** NIGHTHAWK **2** *South & Midland* **:** DRAGONFLY

mosquito net *n* **:** a net or screen for keeping out mosquitoes; *specif* **:** one suspended from a frame so as to surround a bed

mosquito netting *n* **:** netting used for mosquito nets

mosquito plant *n* **1** *or* **mosquito trap :** an Asian vine (*Cynanchum acuminatifolium*) whose flowers sometimes entrap small insects **2 :** a plant (as basil mint or pennyroyal) believed to be efficacious in driving away mosquitoes **3 :** MOSQUITO FERN

¹**moss** \ˈmȯs *also* ˈmäs\ *n* -ES *often attrib* [ME *mos*, *moss*, fr. OE *mōs*; akin to OE *mēos* moss, OHG *mos* moss, swamp, *mios* moss, ON *mosi* moss, swamp, L *mundus* clean, neat, *muscus* moss, Gk *myzein* to suck, *mydan* to be damp, Skt *mūtra* urine, *mudira* cloud; basic meaning: wet] **1 a** *dial chiefly Brit* **:** BOG, MORASS, SWAMP; *esp* **:** PEAT BOG — often used in pl. with *the* ⟨the ~*es* of the English-Scottish border⟩ **b :** spongy soil ⟨the ~ came nearly to the knee —R.L.Stevenson⟩ **2 a :** a plant of the class Musci **b :** a mat, clump, or sward made up of moss plants **3 :** any of various plants more or less like moss in appearance or habit of growth — often used in combination **4 :** a mossy outgrowth or covering (as on the moss rose) **5 :** a fracture or other imperfection (as in a gemstone) having the appearance of moss; *specif* **:** such a fracture in an emerald **6 :** OLD MOSS

²**moss** \"\ *vb* -ED/-ING/-ES [ME *mosen*, *mossen*, fr. *mos*, *moss*, n.] *vt* **:** to cover, overgrow, or fill in with moss ⟨an oak whose boughs were ~*ed* with age —Shak.⟩ ⟨frames were ~*ed* in the baggage cars en route —*Florists Exchange*⟩; *specif* **:** to cover (the stems of a cinchona tree) with a layer of moss to increase the yield of alkaloids ~ *vi* **:** to gather moss

moss agate *n* **:** a mineral consisting of agate containing brown, black, or green mosslike or dendritic markings due in part to oxide of manganese — called also *Mocha stone*

moss animal *or* **moss animalcule** *n* **:** BRYOZOAN

mossback \ˈ=,=\ *also* **mossyback** \ˈ=,=,=\ *n* **1 a :** an old turtle with a mosslike growth on its back ⟨a little clearing where a ~ lived —*McClure's*⟩ **b :** a large sluggish fish (as a muskellunge) ⟨the old ~*s* . . . big 30 and 40 pound muskies —F.R. Steel⟩; *esp* **:** LARGEMOUTH BLACK BASS **c :** a wild range steer or cow that has evaded many roundups ⟨the old ~ would let us get no closer —*Hunting & Fishing*⟩ **2 a :** a person who lives in the backwoods **:** RUSTIC ⟨an old ~ . . . preaching about some herd of horses —H.L.Davis⟩ **b :** one who is far behind the times **:** an extremely conservative person **:** FOGY ⟨turn-of= the-century ~*s* —*New Republic*⟩

moss-backed \ˈ=ˈ=\ *also* **mossy-backed** \ˈ=ˈ=ˈ=\ *adj* **1 :** having a mosslike growth on the back **:** overgrown with moss **2 :** marked by sluggishness of thought or life **:** behind the times ⟨*moss-backed* architectural traditions —*Newsweek*⟩ ⟨a *moss-backed* judge —*Nation*⟩

moss-berry \ˈ=- — *see* BERRY\ *n* **:** EUROPEAN CRANBERRY

moss-bound \ˈ=,=\ *adj* **:** BOGGY

mossbunker *also* **mossbanker** *or* **marshbanker** \ˈ=,=,=\ *n* **:** MENHADEN

moss bush *n* **:** MOSS PLANT 2

moss campion *n* **:** a low growing perennial herb (*Silene acaulis*) that has small linear leaves and solitary terminal purplish flowers and forms dense mosslike tussocks on barren cliffs and mountains of the northern hemisphere — called also *carpet pink*, *cushion pink*

moss cheeper *n* **1 :** MEADOW PIPIT **2** *dial Brit* **:** REED BUNTING

moss coral *n* **:** BRYOZOAN

moss crab *n* **:** a large sluggish hairy shallow-water crab (*Loxorhynchus crispatus*) of the California coast

moss crop *n*, *dial Brit* **:** COTTON GRASS

moss duck *n*, *dial Brit* **:** MALLARD

mossed \ˈmȯst *also* ˈmäst\ *adj* **:** overgrown with moss

mossed bark *n* **:** the bark and bare trunk of a cinchona that remain after alternate strips of bark have been removed and that are covered with moss until the new bark appears — compare NATURAL BARK, RENEWED BARK

moss·er \-sə(r)\ *n* -s [¹*moss* + *-er*] **:** one that gathers or works with moss

moss·ery \-s(ə)rē\ *n* -ES [¹*moss* + *-ery*] **:** a place where mosses are grown

mosses *pl of* MOSS, *pres 3d sing of* MOSS

moss fern *n* **:** POLYPODY

moss fiber *n* **:** one of the complexly ramifying nerve fibers that surround some nerve cells of the cerebellar cortex

moss forest *n* **:** wet tropical upland forest characterized by the presence of abundant epiphytic mosses and ferns

moss fringe *n* **:** a heavy pile trim used as a decorative cording in upholstery

moss fruit *n* **:** SPOROGONIUM

moss gold *n* **:** gold in dendritic forms

moss gray *n* **:** a grayish green that is bluer and duller than average bayberry, bluer and paler than slate green, and yellower and duller than average blue spruce

moss green *n* **:** a variable color averaging a moderate yellow green that is yellower and duller than average pea green or spring green, yellower, lighter, and slightly less strong than spinach green, and less strong and slightly greener and lighter than mosstone — called also *mousse*

moss-grown \ˈ=,=\ *adj* **1 :** overgrown with moss ⟨steeples and *moss-grown* towers —Shak.⟩ **2 :** ANTIQUATED ⟨the family was noble without being . . . moss-grown —Francis Hackett⟩ ⟨moss-grown regimental traditions —Ralph Thompson⟩

moss hag *n, chiefly Scot* : a pit or slough in a marshy place; *esp* : a place where peat has been cut

moss hammer *n* : the European bittern

mosshead \'=,=\ *n* : HOODED MERGANSER

mosshorn \'=,=\ *or* **mossyhorn** \'==,=\ *n, chiefly West* : a longhorn steer so old that its horns have become scaly

mos·si \'mäsē\ *n, pl* **mossi** *or* **mossis** *usu cap* **1 a** : a people of the west central Sudan **b** : a member of such people **2** : a Gur language of the Mossi people and of several other peoples in Upper Volta

mos·sie \'mäsē\ *n* -s [by shortening & alter.] *Austral* : MOSQUITO

mossi-gurunsi \¦===¦==\ *n, usu cap M&G* : GUR

mossing *pres part of* MOSS

moss·ite \'mȯ,sīt\ *n* -s [*Moss*, Norway, its locality + E *-ite*] : a mineral consisting of an oxide of iron and tantalum and being isomorphous with tapiolite

mosslike \'=,=\ *adj* : resembling moss ⟨~ plants⟩ ⟨patches of ~ matter . . . in the field of the microscope —John Tyndall⟩

moss locust *or* **mossy locust** *n* : BRISTLY LOCUST

moss·man fever \'mȯsmən-\ *n, usu cap M* [fr. *Mossman* district, northern Queensland, Australia] *Austral* : TSUTSUGAMUSHI DISEASE

1**mos·so** \'mō(,)sō\ *adj (or adv)* [It, fr. past part. of *muovere* to move, fr. L *movēre* — more at MOVE] : ANIMATED, RAPID — used as a direction in music

2**mosso** *usu cap, var of* MOSO

moss owl *n, chiefly Scot* : SHORT-EARED OWL

moss phlox *n* : MOSS PINK

moss pink *n* : a low tufted perennial phlox (*Phlox subulata*) with needlelike evergreen leaves that is native to the eastern U. S. and is widely cultivated as a ground cover and for its abundant usu. pink or white flowers — called also *dwarf phlox*

moss plant *n* **1** : MOSS; *esp* : the leafy gametophyte of the moss **2** : a small mosslike arctic heath (*Cassiope hypnoides*) of the family Ericaceae having delicate bell-shaped white flowers

moss polyp *n* : BRYOZOAN

moss rose *n* **1 a** : a rose that forms a variety of the cabbage rose and is distinguished by a glandular mossy calyx and flower stalk **b** : a false mallow (*Malvastrum coccineum*) of the western U. S. with racemose red flowers **c** : ROSE MOSS **2** : a deep to dark pink

moss rose 1a

moss silver *n* : silver in dendritic or filiform shapes

moss stitch *n* : a knitting stitch that is made by alternating knit and purl stitches and that produces a small check pattern

mosstone \'=,=\ *n* : a moderate yellow green that is yellower and deeper than average moss green, yellower and darker than average pea green, yellower and duller than apple green (sense 1), and yellower, lighter, and slightly stronger than spinach green

moss-trooper \'=,==\ *n* **1** : one of a class of 17th century raiders in the marshy border country between England and Scotland **2** : FREEBOOTER

moss-trooping \'=,==\ *adj* : having the characteristics of or suggesting the practices of moss-troopers

mossy \'mȯsē, -si *also* 'mäs-\ *adj* -ER/-EST [1*moss* + *-y*] **1** *dial Brit* : BOGGY **2** : overgrown with or covered with moss or something like moss : DOWNY ⟨some ~ gravestone —Nathaniel Hawthorne⟩ ⟨exposing his round throat, ~ chest —Herman Melville⟩ **3** : resembling moss ⟨~ green⟩ ⟨~ carpets —Earle Birney⟩ **4** : ANTIQUATED, MOSS-BACKED ⟨~ ideas that had hung on —*Women's Wear Daily*⟩ ⟨~ old parson —M.L.Bach⟩

mossyback *var of* MOSSBACK

mossy cell *n* : one of the typical astrocytes of the gray matter distinguished by much-branched cytoplasmic processes — see SPIDER CELL

mossy-cup oak *n* : BUR OAK

mossyhorn *var of* MOSSHORN

mossy saxifrage *n* : a low tufted perennial herb (*Saxifrage hypnoides*) of the mountains of Europe often cultivated for its white flowers

mossy stonecrop *n* : a European stonecrop (*Sedum acre*)

mossy zinc *n* : a granulated modification of zinc made by pouring melted zinc into water

1**most** \'mōst\ *adj* [ME *mest, mast, most*, fr. OE *mǣst, māst;* akin to OHG *meist* most, ON *mestr*, Goth *maists;* superlative fr. the root of OE *mā* more — more at MORE] **1** : the greatest number of : the majority of ⟨~ men⟩ ⟨~ problems⟩ ⟨~ eligible voters went to the polls⟩ — used with the noun in the pl. **2 a** : greatest in quantity, extent, or degree ⟨owning the ~ land⟩ ⟨the car with the ~ speed⟩ ⟨he has the ~ ability⟩ ⟨she has the ~ need of it⟩ — used with the noun in the sing. **b** *obs* : in the highest degree : GREATEST ⟨these politicians . . . are our ~ fools —George Chapman⟩ **3** *chiefly dial* : CHIEF, MAIN ⟨the ~ place where you will be safe —Augusta Gregory⟩ — **for the most part** : in most cases : MAINLY

2**most** \"\ *adv* [ME *mest, mast, most*, fr. OE *mǣst, māst;* akin to OHG *meist* most, ON *mest*, Goth *maist*, adv., *maists*, adj. — more at 1MOST] **1 a** : to the greatest or highest degree : to the greatest extent ⟨the book that pleased him ~⟩ — often used with adjectives or adverbs to form the superlative ⟨the ~ beautiful woman there⟩ ⟨writes ~ beautifully of all⟩ **b** : to a very great degree ⟨the argument was ~ persuasive⟩ ⟨a ~ careful workman⟩ **2** *obs* : for the most part : MOSTLY ⟨states are ~ collected into monarchies —Francis Bacon⟩ — **most an end** *adv, dial Eng* : GENERALLY, CONTINUALLY

3**most** \"\ *n* -s [ME *mest, mast, most*, fr. OE *mǣst, māst*, fr. *mǣst, māst*, adj. — more at 1MOST] : the greatest amount or quantity ⟨the ~ I can give you⟩ ⟨the ~ we can say for him⟩ — **at most** *or* **at the most** *adv* : at the maximum ⟨take a little "recess" every two hours *at most* —Arnold Bennett⟩

4**most** \"\ *pron, sing or pl in constr* [1*most*] : the greatest number or part : MAJORITY ⟨some of the people stayed behind but ~ went⟩ ⟨~ who were present⟩ ⟨~ of it is out of sight⟩

5**most** \"\ *adv* [by shortening] : ALMOST ⟨~ anywhere in Europe —*N. Y. Herald Tribune*⟩ ⟨you feel the way ~ everybody else has felt —Gwethalyn Graham⟩

-most \,mōst *also chiefly Brit* məst\ *adj suffix* [ME *-mast, -most*, alter. (influenced by *mast, most* most) of *-mest* (as in *formest* foremost)] : most ⟨inner*most*⟩ : most toward ⟨head*most*⟩

moste [ME, fr. OE *mōste* — more at MUST] *past of* MOTE

most-favored-nation \'='=='==\ *adj* : of or relating to a nation that is the beneficiary of a most-favored-nation clause ⟨*most-favored-nation* treatment⟩ — abbr. *MFN*

most-favored-nation clause *n* : a clause often inserted in treaties by which a nation binds itself to grant to another nation in certain stipulated matters the same terms as are then or may be thereafter granted to any other nation

most high *n, cap M&H* : GOD — usu. used with *the* ⟨the *Most High* rules the kingdom of men —Dan 4: 17 (RSV)⟩

most honorable — used as a courtesy title for marquesses and also applied to certain distinguished bodies (as the Order of the Bath and the Privy Council)

mostlike \'=,=\ *adv, dial* : very likely

most·lings \'mōstlənz, -liŋz\ *adv* [1*most* + *-lings*] *dial Brit* : for the most part

most·ly *adv* [1*most* + *-ly*] **1 a** : for the most part ⟨the sky was ~ overcast —Elyne Mitchell⟩ **b** : USUALLY, GENERALLY ⟨it is then that decay ~ sets in —*Punch*⟩ **2** : MOST ⟨the person whose society she ~ prized —Jane Austen⟩ **3** *dial chiefly Scot* : ALMOST ⟨~ blinded both his eyes —D.M.Moir⟩

most reverend — used as a courtesy title for various high ecclesiastical officials (as Anglican archbishops, Roman Catholic archbishops and bishops, the presiding bishop of the Protestant Episcopal Church)

1**mo·sul** \mō'sül, 'mōsəl\ *adj, usu cap* [fr. *Mosul*, Iraq] : of or from the city of Mosul, Iraq : of the kind or style prevalent in Mosul

2**mosul** \"\ *n, often cap* : a light brown to moderate yellowish brown that is very slightly yellower than dogwood

1**mot** *n* -s [MF, word, saying, fr. L *muttum* grunt — more at MOTTO] **1** *obs* : MOTTO, DEVICE ⟨eye may read the ~ afar —Shak.⟩ **2** \'mō, *pl* -ō(z)\ [F, fr. MF] : a pithy or witty saying ⟨the poet . . . delivers three ~*s* in rapid succession —Peter De Vries⟩ ⟨such ~*s* as "Chivalry is the most delicate form of contempt" —*New Yorker*⟩

2**mot** \'mät\ *n* -s [F *motte* mound, hillock — more at MOTTE] **1** *dial Brit* : MARK, TARGET; *esp* : the mark in a game of quoits **2** : 1MOTTE

mot *abbr* motor; motorized

mo·ta·cil·la \,mōd·ə'silə\ *n* [NL, fr. L *motacilla* wagtail] **1** *cap* : a genus (the type of the family Motacillidae) of oscine birds comprising the wagtails **2** -s : any bird of the genus *Motacilla*

1**mo·ta·cil·lid** \¦==¦siləd\ *adj* [NL *Motacillidae*] : of or relating to the Motacillidae

2**motacillid** \"\ *n* -s : a bird of the family Motacillidae

mo·ta·cil·li·dae \,=='silə,dē\ *n pl, cap* [NL, fr. *Motacilla*, type genus + *-idae*] : a family of oscine birds comprising the wagtails and the pipits

1**mote** \'mōt\ *verbal auxiliary, past* **moste** \'mōst\ [ME *moten*, fr. OE *mōtan* to be allowed to, be able to, have to — more at MUST] *archaic* : MAY, MIGHT

2**mote** \'mōt, *usu* -ōd·+V\ *n* -s [ME *mot, moot*, fr. OE *mot;* akin to MD & Fris *mot* earth, sand, Norw *mutt* speck] **1 a** : a small particle (as of floating dust) : SPECK ⟨~*s* danced in the shafts of sunlight —Margaret Kennedy⟩ **b** *archaic* : a bit of foreign matter in food or drink **c** *obs* : something extremely minute : TRIFLE, JOT, TITTLE **2** *dial Brit* : STRAW, STALK **3 a** : a small undeveloped seed or fragment that has not been removed in cotton ginning **b** : a black spot in yarn or cloth due to such an impurity — **mote in the eye** : a comparatively slight fault noted in another person by one who fails to see a greater fault in himself ⟨why beholdest thou the ~ that is in thy brother's eye, but considerest not the beam that is in thine own eye —Mt 7: 3 (AV)⟩

3**mote** \"\ *vt* -ED/-ING/-S : to remove motes from (cotton)

4**mote** \"\ *n* -s [ME, fr. OF *mote, motte* mound, hillock, mote — more at MOTTE] **1** *or* **mote hill** : HEIGHT, HILL; *esp* : an elevated place used as a fortification **2** : BARROW, TUMULUS

mot·ed \-ōd·əd\ *adj* [2*mote* + *-ed*] : filled with motes ⟨~ sunbeam —Alfred Tennyson⟩

mo·tel \(')mō¦tel\ *n* -s [blend of *motor* and *hotel*] : an establishment which provides lodging and parking and in which the rooms are usu. accessible from an outdoor parking area ⟨an endless row of . . . two-story ~*s* —Bennett Cerf⟩

mo·tet \mō'tet, *usu* -ed·+V\ *n* -s [ME, fr. MF, dim. of *mot* word — more at MOT] **1 a** : a polyphonic choral musical composition of a kind originated in the 13th century, based on a sacred Latin text, designed for church performance, and usu. sung unaccompanied — compare MADRIGAL 2a **b** : the English anthem **2** : a polyphonic instrumental composition intended for church performance

mo·te·tus \mō'tēd·əs\ *n* -ES [ML *motetus, motetum*, fr. MF *motet*] **1** : the middle voice or the voice above the tenor in medieval motets **2** : MOTET 1a

motey \'mōd·ē\ *adj* [2*mote* + *-y*] : full of motes

1**moth** \'mȯ|th *also* 'mä|\ *n, pl* **moths** \|t͟hz, |ths, |z\ *often attrib* [ME *mothe*, fr. OE *moththe;* akin to MD & MLG *motte, mutte* moth, MHG *motte*, ON *motti*, and perh. to OE *matha* worm, maggot — more at MAGGOT] **1 a** (1) : CLOTHES MOTH (2) : an insect that feeds on materials (as woolens and furs) — compare CARPET BEETLE, DERMESTES **b** *obs* : any obnoxious insect (as a mosquito, roach, or maggot) **c** : any of various insects that constitute a major division (Heterocera) of the order Lepidoptera, are usu. nocturnal or crepuscular, have antennae which are often feathery and rarely clubbed, are typically stouter-bodied, less brilliantly colored, and proportionately smaller winged than the butterflies, and have larvae which are caterpillars and feed often very destructively on vegetation — see GYPSY MOTH, SILK MOTH **2** *archaic* : a thing or a person that gradually eats away, wastes, or consumes something **3** : MOTH GRAY **4** : a class of racing sailboat of varying design but having an overall length of 11 ft. and 73 sq. ft. of sail area; *also* : a boat in this class

2**moth** \"\ *vi* -ED/-ING/-S : to hunt for moths

1**mothball** \'=,=\ *n* [1*moth* + *ball*] **1** : a ball of the size of a marble made formerly of camphor but now of naphthalene and used to keep moths from clothing **2 mothballs** *pl* : the condition of being put into protective storage or relegated to a reserve, standby, or caretaker status ⟨the warships in ~*s* at the Puget Sound Naval shipyard —*N.Y.Times*⟩ ⟨a million-dollar aluminum powder plant . . . is being taken out of ~*s* Monday —*Wall Street Jour.*⟩ ⟨then the war ended and ~*s* took over —E.L.Beach⟩; *also* : a state of having been rejected for further use or dismissed from further consideration ⟨you can put that idea into ~*s* and forget it⟩

2**mothball** \"\ *vt* -ED/-ING/-S : to inactivate and preserve (as a ship) chiefly by dehumidification ⟨plastic . . . is sprayed over the gun mount of a ship being ~*ed* —*All Hands*⟩ ⟨our sick bay had been ~*ed* —J.J.Micka⟩ ⟨the packing plant ~*ed* for five years —*Newsweek*⟩

3**mothball** \"\ *adj* : PRESERVED, INACTIVATED ⟨~ ships⟩

mothball fleet *n* : an aggregate of inactivated preserved warships that can be commissioned and made ready for war in a few months; *specif* : the U.S. Navy Reserve Fleet ⟨the entrance of the battleship . . . into the *mothball fleet* —*All Hands*⟩

moth bean *also* **moth** *n* -s [*moth* prob. by folk etymology (influence of 1*moth*) fr. Marathi *maṭh* moth bean, fr. Skt *makuṣṭa*] **1** : an East Indian bean (*Phaseolus aconitifolius*) that is used esp. in India as a forage and soil-conditioning crop and has hairy foliage, small yellow flowers, and cylindrical pods **2** : the small yellowish brown seed of the moth bean used as food in India

moth borer *n, chiefly Brit* : a moth whose larva is a borer

moth-eaten \'=,==\ *adj* **1 a** : eaten into by moths ⟨*moth-eaten* cloth⟩ **b** : having the appearance of something eaten into by moths ⟨a *moth-eaten* horse ready for the glue factory —C.V. Little⟩ : PATCHY, RAGGEDY, UNKEMPT ⟨a little man . . . with *moth-eaten* hair —W.A.White⟩ **2 a** : DILAPIDATED ⟨the town had one *moth-eaten* old museum —C.W.Thayer⟩ ⟨a lot of *moth-eaten* barges —John Buchan⟩ **b** : ANTIQUATED, OUTMODED ⟨the *moth-eaten* motto of some of the . . . aristocracy —W.H.Stevenson⟩ ⟨*moth-eaten* . . . theories about race —Dwight Macdonald⟩

1**moth·er** \'mət͟hə(r)\ *n* -s [ME *moder*, fr. OE *mōdor;* akin to OHG *muoter* mother, ON *mōthir*, L *mater*, Gk *mētēr*, Skt *mātṛ*] **1 a** : a woman who has given birth to a child : a female parent ⟨a ~ of five⟩ ⟨food for the nursing ~⟩ ⟨in the union of the sexual cells the chromosomes coming from the ~ —S.F. Mason⟩ ⟨in chimpanzees the female's functions as ~ and mate alternate in stretches of time —Weston La Barre⟩ **b** : one related to another in a way paralleling or suggesting the relation of mother to child: as (1) : one to whom a filial affection and respect are usu. due : adoptive mother : STEPMOTHER, MOTHER-IN-LAW (2) : a woman having authority or dignity like that of a mother ⟨because these class ~*s* proved so helpful —Gertrude H. Hildreth⟩ **c** : an elderly woman — often used preceding the surname ⟨*Mother* Hubbard⟩ **2 a** : one that has produced or nurtured something : parent stock : SOURCE ⟨although nature is our ~, she is not a complete guide to human conduct —Brooks Atkinson⟩ ⟨the fertile ~ of . . . civilizations —Edward Clodd⟩ ⟨Hebrew was considered the ~ of European languages —R.W.Weiman⟩ ⟨the free press is the ~ of all our liberties —A.E.Stevenson †1965⟩ **b** : PROTOTYPE ⟨huge ~ of ocean liners, she was five times the size of the largest vessel then afloat —C.V.Woodward⟩ **3 a** *obs* : WOMB ⟨diseases of the ~ —William Coles⟩ **b** *archaic* : HYSTERIA ⟨the particular diseases of this sign are . . . hardness of the spleen, ~, hypochondriac melancholy —Ebenezer Sibly⟩ **4** : feeling (as tenderness or affection) inherited from or characteristic of a mother ⟨all my ~ came into mine eyes and gave me up to tears —Shak.⟩ ⟨all the ~ in her soul awakes —Alexander Pope⟩ **5** : MOTHER LIQUOR — usu. used in pl. with *the* **6** : a device for sheltering chickens after incubation — called also *artificial mother* **7** : MATRIX 4f

2**mother** \"\ *vt* **mothered**; **mothered**; **mothering** \-t͟h(ə)riŋ\ **mothers** **1 a** : to give birth to ⟨she ~*ed* five sons but no daughters⟩ **b** : to give rise to as if by birth : PRODUCE ⟨this . . . unexplored country has ~*ed* many legends —V.W.Von Hagen⟩ **2** : to care for, cherish, or protect in the manner of a mother ⟨all his life . . . he had to be ~*ed* by somebody —Van Wyck Brooks⟩ **3 a** : to acknowledge that one is the mother or author of **b** : to attribute the maternity or origin of to a particular person **4** : to act as a protective-fire cover or escort for in a military or naval operation ⟨the low-flying contact machines . . . ~*ing* the infantry —*Airman's Outings*⟩ ⟨~*ing* subs off the Grand Banks —*Atlantic*⟩

3**mother** \"\ *adj* **1 a** : of, relating to, or being a mother ⟨~ love⟩ ⟨~ pains⟩ **b** : bearing a relationship to others that is parallel to or suggestive of that of a mother ⟨~ lodge⟩ ⟨~ stream⟩ **2** : derived from or as if from one's mother ⟨~ dialect⟩ **3** : acting as or providing parental stock — used without reference to sex ⟨~ plant⟩ ⟨~ tubercle⟩ ⟨pollen ~ cells —*Americana Annual*⟩

4**mother** \"\ *n* -s [akin to MD *modder, moeder* mud, swamp, dregs, lees, MLG *moder, modder* putrid body, swampland, *mudde* thick mud — more at MUD] **1** *archaic* : LEES, DREGS **2** *or* **mother of vinegar** : a slimy membrane that develops on the surface of alcoholic liquids undergoing acetous fermentation, that is composed of yeast cells and bacteria of the genus *Acetobacter* (esp. *A. acetus* syn. *Mycoderma aceti*) which produce the fermentation, and that is added to wine or cider as a starter to produce vinegar

5**mother** \"\ *vi* -ED/-ING/-S : to become mothery ⟨her wines sour and pickles ~ —Samuel Johnson⟩

mother aircraft *n* **1** : an aircraft electronically equipped to direct the flight of a drone **2** : a large aircraft modified to carry piloted or unpiloted aircraft that can be launched and recovered in flight

mother bed *or* **mother block** *n* : an area that is devoted to plants known to be free from diseases and true to type and that is used as a source of stock for propagation

mother bulb *n* : a bulb (as of a narcissus) that produces several offsets

mother car·ey's chicken \-'ka(a)rēz-\ *n, usu cap M&1stC* [origin unknown] : any of several small petrels; *esp* : STORM PETREL

mother carey's goose *n, usu cap M&C* : GIANT PETREL

mother carey's hen *n, usu cap M&C* : a petrel of medium size

mother cell *n* : a cell from which another usu. of a different sort is formed ⟨a sperm *mother cell*⟩

mother church *n* **1** *archaic* : a parish church ⟨the *mother churches* . . . and rural chapels in the late Saxon and early Norman periods —*Bull. of Inst. of Historical Research*⟩ **2** : the principal church of a locality or land; *specif* : a cathedral or a metropolitan church ⟨the *mother church* . . . which no visitor to these parts should fail to see —T.I.Ellis⟩ **3** : the original church from which others have sprung ⟨the *mother church* of Unitarianism in America —Leo Pfeffer⟩ **4** : the original church or communion in which a person has been nurtured ⟨returning to his *mother church*, he died in obscurity —K.S.Latourette⟩

mother-city \'==,==\ *n* : METROPOLIS ⟨they still kept in touch with the *mother-city* —E.R.Bevan⟩

mother cloves *n pl* : the dried fruits of the clove tree that resemble the true cloves but are less aromatic

mother country *n* **1** : the country of one's parents or ancestors ⟨a sentimental journey back to the *mother country*⟩ **2** : the country from which the people of a colony derive their origin ⟨a *mother country* . . . in its relationships with its overseas possessions —C.A.Buss⟩ **3** : a country that is the origin of something ⟨the *mother country* of social graces —*Newsweek*⟩

mothercraft \'==,=\ *n* : knowledge and skill required for the care of babies and young children ⟨courses in ~ for prospective mothers —*N.Y.Times*⟩

mother earth *n* **1** : the mother of everything animate or inanimate upon the earth **2** : SOIL, GROUND

mother goose rhyme *n, usu cap M&G* [after *Mother Goose*, pretended author of *Mother Goose's Melodies*, a collection of nursery rhymes published in London, England, about 1760] : NURSERY RHYME

moth·er·hood \'mət͟hə(r),hu̇d\ *n* : the quality or state of being a mother : MATERNITY ⟨~ and childhood are entitled to special care and assistance —*U. N. Declaration of Human Rights*⟩

motherhouse \'==,=\ *n* **1** : the monastery or convent in which the superior general or the provincial of a religious community resides **2** : the original monastery or convent of a religious community

mother hubbard \-'həbə(r)d\ *n, pl* **mother hubbards** *often cap M&H* [prob. after *Mother Hubbard*, character in a nursery rhyme (1805) by Sarah C. Martin †1826 Eng. writer; fr. the garb worn by Mother Hubbard in old illustrations] : a woman's loose usu. shapeless dress ⟨she had an old *mother hubbard* wrapped loosely about her —Bill Ballinger⟩

mother·ing *n* -s : a rural custom in England of visiting one's parents on Mid-Lent Sunday and presenting a gift

mother-in-law \'mət͟hə(r)ən,lȯ, -t͟hrən-, -t͟hə(r)n-\ *n, pl* **mothers-in-law** \-t͟hə(r)zən-\ [ME *moder in lawe*] **1** : the mother of one's spouse **2** : STEPMOTHER

mother-in-law plant *n* : DUMB CANE

motherland \'==,=\ *n* **1** : the land of origin of something ⟨Germany . . . the ~ of philology —René Wellek⟩ **2** : the home country of colonies or former colonies ⟨ballads brought into this country from the ~ —*Dial*⟩ **3** : one's native land or country : the country to which one claims native allegiance : FATHERLAND ⟨nurture our children in affectionate regard for the ~ —J.L.Childs⟩

moth·er·less \'mət͟hə(r)ləs\ *adj* [ME *moderles*, fr. OE *mōdorlēas*, fr. *mōdor* mother + *-lēas* -less — more at MOTHER] : having no mother; *esp* : having no mother living ⟨a ~ child⟩ — **moth·er·less·ly** *adv* — **moth·er·less·ness** *n* -ES

moth·er·li·ness \-lēnəs, -lin-\ *n* -ES : maternal quality : the tenderness, warmth, or affection of or befitting a mother ⟨her ~ made her invaluable in caring for the twins —Elizabeth Goudge⟩

mother liquor *also* **mother liquid** *n* : a residual liquid resulting from crystallization and remaining after the substances that readily or regularly crystallize have been removed — called also *mother water*

mother lode *n* : the principal vein or lode of a region (as of gold-bearing quartz along the western foothills of the Sierra Nevada, Calif.)

1**moth·er·ly** \-lē, -li\ *adj* [ME *moderly* fr. OE *mōdorlīc*, fr. *mōdor* mother + *-līc* -ly] **1** : of, befitting, or proper to a mother ⟨her ~ instincts had been aroused —Hervey Allen⟩ ⟨~ tenderness —A. Conan Doyle⟩ ⟨in a ~ tone —Ellen Glasgow⟩ **2** : resembling a mother in love, protectiveness, or conduct : maternally soft, warm, or sympathetic : MATERNAL ⟨a handsome and ~ young woman —Floyd Dell⟩

2**motherly** \"\ *adv* [ME *moderly*, fr. *moderly*, adj.] *archaic* : in a motherly manner

mother mark *var of* MOTHER'S MARK

mother-naked \¦==¦==\ *adj* [ME *moder naked*, fr. *moder* mother + *naked*] : naked as at birth : stark naked ⟨caught *mother-naked* in the full glare of a searchlight —Campbell Nairne⟩ — **mother-na·ked·ness** *n*

mother of coal : MINERAL CHARCOAL

mother-of-millions \'==='==\ *n pl but usu sing in constr* : KENILWORTH IVY

1**mother-of-pearl** \'==='=\ *n* -s : the hard pearly iridescent internal layer of various mollusk shells (as of pearl oysters, river mussels, abalones) that is extensively used for making small articles (as buttons) and inlays : NACRE; *sometimes* : a shell or a shellfish having such a pearly layer

2**mother-of-pearl** \"\ *adj* [1*mother-of-pearl*] : IRIDESCENT — used esp. of the luster of a glaze or enamel

mother-of-pearl cloud *n* : NACREOUS CLOUD

mother-of-thousands \'==='==\ *n pl but usu sing in constr* **1** : KENILWORTH IVY **2** : STRAWBERRY GERANIUM **3** : DAISY 1

mother-of-thyme \'==='=\ *n* -s **1** : WILD THYME **2** : BASIL BALM 2

mother of vinegar [4*mother*] : 4MOTHER 2

mother-of-wheat \'==='=\ *n* -s **1** : COWWHEAT **2** : IVY-LEAVED SPEEDWELL

mother plane *or* **mother ship** *n* : an airplane that carries, launches, or controls another aircraft

mother right *n* [prob. trans. of G *mutterrecht*] : the matriarchal principle or custom : MATRIARCHY 2

mothers *pl of* MOTHER, *pres 3d sing of* MOTHER

mother's boy *n* : a boy or young man who is excessively attached to his mother; *esp* : one who as a result of such an attachment is disinclined to follow masculine pursuits or assume masculine responsibilities ⟨his grandfather . . . fearing that the youth was on his way to becoming a *mother's boy*, taught him to swim at an early age —E.J.Kahn⟩ — compare MAMA'S BOY

mother's day *n, usu cap M&D* **:** a day (as the second Sunday in May) appointed for the special honoring of mothers by their children

mother's–heart \ˈ⸗⸗ˌ⸗\ *n, pl* **mother's–hearts :** SHEPHERD'S PURSE

mother ship *n* **1** *chiefly Brit* **:** a naval vessel escorting or guarding smaller craft (as torpedo boats or submarines) **2 :** a ship serving several smaller craft **:** TENDER

mother–sib \ˈ⸗⸗ˌ⸗\ *n* **:** sib based on matrilineal descent

mother's mark *or* **mother mark** *n* **:** BIRTHMARK

mother superior *n, pl* **mother superiors** *also* **mothers superior :** a nun who is the head of a religious house

mother tongue *n* **1 :** the language of one's mother **:** the language naturally acquired in infancy and childhood **:** one's first language **2 :** a language from which another language originates

mother tree *n* **:** SEED TREE

moth·er·um·bung \ˌmət͟hə'rəm,bəŋ\ *or* **moth·er·um·bah** \-mbə\ *n* -s [native name in Australia] **:** a shrub or small tree (*Acacia cheelii*) of Australia having the flowers in pairs or threes and in spikes and the fruit narrow and flat with a thickened margin

mother water *n* **:** MOTHER LIQUOR

mother wit *n* **:** natural or native wit or intelligence

motherwort \ˈ⸗⸗ˌ⸗\ *n* -s [ME *moderwort*, fr. *moder* mother + *wort* — more at MOTHER, WORT] **1 :** a plant of the genus *Leonurus*; *esp* **:** a bitter Old World mint (*L. cardiaca*) with dentate wedge-shaped leaves and axillary whorls of small purple flowers **2 :** MUGWORT 1 **3 :** FEVERFEW **4 :** MARSH MILKWEED **5 :** MONEYWORT

moth·ery \ˈmət͟h(ə)rē\ *adj* [⁴*mother* + *-y*] **:** consisting of, containing, or resembling mother ⟨~ vinegar⟩ ⟨~ mold⟩

mother yaw *n* **:** the initial superficial lesion of yaws appearing at the site of inoculation after an incubation period of several weeks

moth fly *or* **moth gnat** *or* **moth–midge** \ˈ⸗ˌ⸗\ *n* **:** a small two-winged fly of the family Psychodidae having hairy or scaly wings

moth gray *n* **:** a grayish yellow that is paler and slightly redder than chamois, redder and paler than old ivory, and redder and lighter than crash — called also *sheepskin*

moth hawk *or* **moth hunter** *n* **:** GOATSUCKER

mothing *pres part of* MOTH

moth miller *n* **:** MILLER 2a

moth mullein *n* **:** a European mullein (*Verbascum blattaria*) that is naturalized as a weed in America and that has smooth leaves and large yellow or purplish flowers

moth orchid *or* **moth plant** *n* **:** an orchid of the genus *Phalaenopsis* (esp. *P. amabilis*)

¹**mothproof** \ˈ⸗ˌ⸗\ *adj* [¹*moth* + *proof*] **:** impervious to penetration by moths ⟨~ wool⟩

²**mothproof** \"\ *vt* -ED/-ING/-S **:** to make mothproof ⟨~*ing* textile fabrics —*Chem. Abstracts*⟩ — **mothproofer** *n* -s

moths *pl of* MOTH, *pres 3d sing of* MOTH

mothy \ˈmȯthē\ *adj* -ER/-EST **:** full of moths

mo·tif \mōˈtēf\ *n* -s [F, motive, motif — more at MOTIVE] **1 a :** a usu. recurring salient thematic element or feature (as in a work of art); *esp* **:** a dominant idea or central theme ⟨the isles of the blest, the mandrake, the stone monster . . . there is enough material from comparative religion to elucidate these ~*s* —G.L.Anderson⟩ ⟨ran like a ~ through his letters of those years —*Atlantic*⟩ ⟨the ~ of disillusion —G.R.Hamilton⟩ ⟨an excellent ~ for a novel —*Times Lit. Supp.*⟩ **b :** a single or repeated design or color (as in interior decoration or clothes designing) ⟨mulberry and silver form the color ~ of the decorations —*N.Y.Times*⟩ ⟨a brown necktie tastily done out in a skyscraper ~ —Pierce Fredericks⟩ **c :** MOTIVE 5 ⟨flute ~⟩ ⟨the familiar device of development by reiteration of short simple ~*s* with chromatic ornamentation —Henry Cowell⟩ **2 :** an influence or stimulus prompting to action ⟨the proselyting ~ was not forgotten —*Atlantic*⟩ ⟨the profit ~ —*Saturday Rev.*⟩ ⟨the ~ of the new measure is reformation —*Spectator*⟩

¹**mo·tile** \ˈmōd·ᵊl, -ōtᵊl, -ō,tīl, -ō(,)til\ *adj* [L *motus* (past part. of *movēre* to move) + E *-ile* — more at MOVE] **:** exhibiting or capable of movement ⟨~ cilia⟩ ⟨~ spores⟩

²**motile** \"\ *n* -s **:** one whose prevailing mental imagery is motor rather than visual or auditory and takes the form of inner feelings of action (as incipient pronunciation of words, muscular movements) — compare AUDILE, TACTILE, VISUALIZER

mo·til·i·ty \mōˈtiləd·ē, -ətē, -i\ *n* -ES **:** the quality or state of being motile **:** CONTRACTILITY ⟨gastrointestinal ~ —*Science*⟩

mo·ti·lón \ˌmōd·əˈlōn\ *n, pl* **motilón** \"\ *or* **motilo·nes** \-lō,nās\ *usu cap* [Sp, of AmerInd origin] **1 a :** a Cariban people of northern Colombia and Venezuela **b :** a member of such people **2 :** the language of the Motilón people

moting *pres part of* MOTE

¹**mo·tion** \ˈmōshən\ *n* -s [ME *mocioun*, fr. MF *motion*, fr. L *motion-, motio* movement, fr. *motus* (past part. of *movēre* to move) + *-ion-, -io* -ion — more at MOVE] **1 a** *obs* **:** PROMPTING, SUGGESTION ⟨give ear to his ~*s* —Shak.⟩ **b :** a formal proposal made in a deliberative assembly ⟨a ~ of censure⟩ ⟨a ~ to adjourn⟩ ⟨the ~ has been seconded⟩ ⟨the ~*s* to discharge and to table may be filed at the same time —Don Irwin⟩ **c :** an application made to a court or judge orally in open court or in written form to obtain an order, ruling, or direction in favor of the applicant usu. to advance the case toward trial or hearing, obtain some interlocutory advantage, or relieve from some injustice but sometimes to obtain for the applicant a final decree or judgment on some matter of law after a hearing or trial on pleadings or after evidence is taken ⟨on ~ of the defendant's lawyer⟩ ⟨~ to quash the indictment⟩ ⟨the ~ for a new trial was denied —Max & Edna A. Lerner⟩ **2 :** an irregular stirring, shaking, or oscillating movement **:** AGITATION ⟨the ~ of the water⟩ ⟨the swaying ~ of the train⟩ ⟨there was no ~ in the heavy sultry atmosphere —W.H.Hudson †1922⟩ **3 a :** the action or process of a body passing from one place or position to another ⟨the ~ of the planets⟩ ⟨a pendulum in ~⟩ **b :** such action or process conceived in terms of one of its characteristics (as direction, course, velocity) ⟨linear ~⟩ ⟨angular ~⟩ ⟨rotational ~⟩ ⟨the earth, according to the Copernican scheme . . . has three ~*s* —G.C.Sellery⟩ ⟨learned in the valuing of ~ . . . I saw that we were now running thirteen miles an hour —Thomas DeQuincey⟩ **c** *obs* **:** a constant moving from place to place ⟨my perpetual ~*s* . . . between Wotton and London —John Evelyn⟩ **d :** a process of change — used chiefly in philosophy ⟨four kinds of ~: substantial (origin and decay); quantitative (change in the size of a body by addition and subtraction); qualitative (transformation of one thing into another); and local (change of place) —Frank Thilly⟩ **4 :** an impulse or inclination of the mind, will, or desires **:** MOVEMENT 2a(1) ⟨between the acting of a dreadful thing and the first ~ —Shak.⟩ ⟨those obscure ~*s* of the mind —J.C. Powys⟩ ⟨the fundamental ~*s* of humanity to good or evil —T.S.Eliot⟩ ⟨studied navigation of his own ~ —*Times Lit. Supp.*⟩ **5 a :** an act or instance of moving the body or any of its members **:** GESTURE ⟨every ~ in the old dances had meaning —Reginald & Gladys Laubin⟩ ⟨every . . . ~ of her head —H.M.Reichard⟩ ⟨signaled with a ~ of his arm⟩ ⟨a sucking ~⟩ **b :** style of moving **:** CARRIAGE 2b ⟨personal habits, such as vocalization . . . ~, and address —William James⟩ **c** *obs* **:** power of moving ⟨devoid of sense and ~ —John Milton⟩ **d :** a conventionalized bodily movement (as a step, gait, athletic movement) ⟨the standard ~*s* of a show horse⟩ **e** *obs* **:** bodily exercise ⟨when in your ~ you are hot and dry —Shak.⟩ **f** *archaic* **:** ACTIVITY — usu. used in pl. ⟨taking advantage of the night to conceal his ~*s* —George Stanhope⟩ **g :** the change or prospective change (as of attitude or position) suggested by the posture of an artistic figure ⟨the expressive ~ of the statue⟩ **6** *obs* **a :** PUPPET SHOW ⟨a ~ of the Prodigal Son —Shak.⟩ **b :** PUPPET ⟨did you think you had married a ~ —Ben Jonson⟩ **7 a :** an evacuation of the bowels ⟨has no control over . . . urine or ~*s* —*Farmer's Weekly (So. Africa)*⟩ **b :** the matter evacuated — often used in the pl. ⟨blood in the ~*s* —*Lancet*⟩ **8 a :** the wheelwork of a watch **:** MOVEMENT 3 **b :** MECHANISM ⟨a straight-line ~⟩ ⟨link ~⟩ ⟨loosen lower ~ . . . and turn —*Civil Engineering*⟩ **9 a :** melodic change of pitch in the successive musical tones of a voice part ⟨note repetitions and scalewise ~ quite foreign to characteristic twelve-tone practice —Arthur Berger⟩ **b :** melodic progression of two or more voice parts relatively considered ⟨transition is by way of a passage in contrary ~ for the woodwinds —A.K. Holland⟩

²**motion** \"\ *vb* **motioned; motioned; motioning** \-sh(ə)niŋ\ **motions** *vt* **1** *archaic* **:** PROPOSE, RECOMMEND ⟨what I ~*ed* was of God —John Milton⟩ **2 :** to direct by a motion (as of the hand or head) ⟨~*ed* them to come quietly —Jean Stafford⟩ ⟨~*ed* me to a seat —L.C.Douglas⟩ ~ *vi* **1** *archaic* **:** to propose or suggest a plan or action ⟨well hast thou ~'*d* —John Milton⟩ **2** *archaic* **:** to move in such a way as to suggest an intended action ⟨this he declined, ~*ing* at the same time to go away —Helena Wells⟩ **3 :** to signal by a movement or gesture (as of the hand) ⟨the pitcher ~*ed* to the catcher⟩ **4 :** to vibrate in angular rotation — used of a watch balance ⟨a mainspring should . . . make the watch ~ properly —*Watchmakers' Handbook*⟩

mo·tion·al \-shənᵊl, -shnəl\ *adj* **:** of, relating to, or characterized by motion **:** KINETIC

motional impedance *n* **:** the part of the electrical impedance in a telephone receiver or loudspeaker that is due to the motion of the diaphragm

motion and time study *n* **:** TIME AND MOTION STUDY

motioner *n* -s *obs* **:** one that proposes or instigates

mo·tion·less \-shənləs\ *adj* **:** being without motion **:** STILL — **mo·tion·less·ly** *adv* — **mo·tion·less·ness** *n* -ES

motion picture *n* **1 :** a series of pictures (as photographs taken with a special camera) presented to the eye in very rapid succession with some or all of the objects in the scene represented in successive positions slightly changed so as to produce because of persistence of vision the optical effect of a continuous picture in which the objects move — see SOUND MOTION PICTURE **2 :** a representation of a story or other subject matter by means of motion pictures

motion–picture camera *n* **:** a camera adapted to make rapid exposure of moving objects on a strip of film perforated along the edges to ensure accurate registration

motion–picture projector *n* **:** a machine that projects and shows motion pictures on a screen and that is usu. fitted with suitable electrical or mechanical attachments for reproducing sound in synchronism with the picture — compare SOUND PROJECTOR

motion plate *n, Brit* **:** a transverse plate usu. of annealed cast steel which is situated between the cylinders and driving axle of an inside-cylinder locomotive and to which the slide bars and intermediate valve-rod guides are attached

motion sickness *n* **:** sickness induced by motion (as in travel by air, car, or ship) and characterized by nausea

motion study *n* **:** TIME AND MOTION STUDY

motion work *n* **:** the wheelwork controlling the relative motions of the hour and minute hands of a timepiece

mo·ti·ta·tion \ˌmōd·əˈtāshən\ *n* -s [L *motitatus* (past part. of *motitare* to move often, move about, freq. of *motare* to keep moving, move about, fr. *motus*, past part. of *movēre* to move) + E *-ion* — more at MOVE] **:** a quivering movement

mo·ti·vate \ˈmōd·ə,vāt, -ōtə-, *usu* -ād·+V\ *vt* -ED/-ING/-S [¹*motive* + *-ate*] **1 :** to provide with a motive **:** IMPEL, INCITE ⟨the deep unconscious and subconscious factors that ~ people —Vance Packard⟩ ⟨the novelist has adequately *motivated* his hero⟩ **2 a :** to stimulate the active interest of in a study through appeal to associated interests or by special devices ⟨the ingenious teacher can ferret out a thousand methods of *motivating* the child to learn new words —*Education Digest*⟩ **b :** to make (a study) interesting or otherwise appealing to students ⟨program . . . is thoroughly *motivated* —D.H.Patton⟩

mo·ti·va·tion \ˌ⸗⸗ˈvāshən\ *n* -s [¹*motive* + *-ation*] **1 :** the act or process of motivating ⟨Shakespeare . . . neglected ~ when it was already supplied in his sources —Muriel C. Bradbrook⟩ ⟨in the secondary school ~ involves many types of activities —D.G.Tarbet⟩ **2 :** a motivating force or influence **:** DRIVE, INCENTIVE ⟨sex as the ~ of animal behavior —E.A.Armstrong⟩ ⟨economic ~⟩ ⟨the most intrinsic ~ for learning is the child's spontaneous interests —Bernice Neugarten & Nelle Wright⟩ **3 :** the condition of being motivated ⟨found to have good ~ and high morale —*Jour. Amer. Med. Assoc.*⟩ ⟨~ was at a very high level, and the students did not have to be prodded —Haym Kruglak⟩

mo·ti·va·tion·al \ˌ⸗⸗ˈvāshənᵊl, -shnəl\ *adj* **:** of or relating to motivation ⟨~ research⟩ ⟨~ approach⟩ ⟨~ factors⟩

mo·ti·va·tive \-ād·iv\ *adj* **:** of, relating to, or providing motivation ⟨it may well be that ethical language has primarily a ~ function —Arthur Pap⟩

¹**mo·tive** \ˈmōd·|iv, -ōt|, |ēv *also* |əv; *in senses 4 and 5* " *or* mōˈtēv\ *n* -s [ME, fr. MF *motif*, fr. *motif*, adj., moving, causing to move, fr. ML *motivus*, fr. L *motus* (past part. of *movēre* to move) + *-ivus* -ive — more at MOVE] **1 a :** something within a person (as need, idea, organic state, or emotion) that incites him to action ⟨ordinarily his ~ is a wish to . . . avoid unfavorable notice and comment —Thorstein Veblen⟩ **b :** the consideration or object influencing a choice or prompting an action ⟨the principal ~ of American policy —C.E.Black & E.C.Helmreich⟩ ⟨the ~ for the crime⟩ **2** *obs* **a :** a prompting force or incitement working on a person to influence volition or action **:** MOVER, INSTIGATOR, CAUSE ⟨nature, whose ~ in this case should stir me most —Shak.⟩ ⟨am I the ~ of these tears —Shak.⟩ **3** *obs* **:** a part of the body capable of movement ⟨her wanton spirits look out at every joint and ~ of her body —Shak.⟩ **4** [F, fr. MF, motive] **a :** the guiding or controlling idea in an artistic work or in one of its parts **b :** MOTIF 1b **5** [G *motiv*, fr. F *motif*] **:** THEME, SUBJECT; *specif* **:** a leading phrase or figure that is reproduced and varied through the course of a musical composition or movement — compare LEITMOTIV

syn MOTIVE, SPRING, IMPULSE, INCENTIVE, INDUCEMENT, SPUR, and GOAD can mean, in common, a stimulus prompting a person to act in a particular way. MOTIVE can apply to any emotion, desire, or appetite operating on the will of a person and moving him to act ⟨the habit so prevalent with us of always seeking the *motive* of everyone's speech or behavior —W.C. Brownell⟩ ⟨shielding her husband's murderer, from whatever *motives* of pity or friendship —Rose Macaulay⟩ ⟨it was the deepest *motive* of her soul, this self mistrust —D.H.Lawrence⟩ SPRING, usu. in the plural, is usu. interchangeable with MOTIVE, possibly more precisely applying to a hidden or not fully recognized stimulus to action ⟨the *springs* and consequences of international policy —David Mitrany⟩ ⟨the mysteriously working emotional *springs* of human action⟩ IMPULSE stresses impetus or driving power rather than an effect; in a general sense, it can apply to any strong incitement to activity, esp. one deriving from personal temperament or constitution ⟨the religious *impulse* and the scientific *impulse* —Havelock Ellis⟩ ⟨one strong *impulse* that bound them together — their common love of fine horses —Sherwood Anderson⟩ ⟨the extraordinary vitality of the critical *impulse* in American letters —C.I.Glicksberg⟩ ⟨the *impulse* that led to the evolution of man —Joshua Whatmough⟩ but in a more special use it applies to a spontaneous, often irrational urge to do something ⟨the first *impulse* of a child in a garden is to pick every attractive flower —Bertrand Russell⟩ ⟨suffered an odd *impulse* to get up and kick his chair over —Mary Austin⟩ INCENTIVE applies chiefly to a cause inciting or encouraging to action, applying commonly to some external reward ⟨his love for the family was a strong *incentive* to continued effort in their behalf⟩ ⟨money is not the only *incentive* to work, nor the strongest —G.B.Shaw⟩ ⟨the only *incentive* to travel . . . was the luxury of the accommodation —O.S.Nock⟩ INDUCEMENT implies an external influence and often a purposeful attempt to entice to action ⟨the chief *inducements* to serve were the pension and the right of citizenship which awaited a soldier on his discharge —John Buchan⟩ ⟨a community that . . . holds young people and offers *inducements* to them to stay and help build a greater home town —J.C.Penney⟩ ⟨free gas was offered to factories as an *inducement* for locating in towns —*Amer. Guide Series: Ind.*⟩ SPUR applies to any impetus which can stir to action or increase energy or ardor in an action already undertaken ⟨fear or despair may be a temporary *spur* to action —*Saturday Rev.*⟩ ⟨under the *spur* of his annoyance —Hamilton Basso⟩ ⟨Russia with its drive for warm water ports, China with its inexorable pressure of population — they, too, have a physical *spur* to expansive policies —Barbara Ward⟩ GOAD can apply to anything that strongly incites to action or keeps one in action against one's will or desire ⟨the threat of . . . aggression was a standing *goad* to the defense effort —*N.Y.Times*⟩ ⟨was . . . a *goad* for an indolent writer —Van Wyck Brooks⟩

²**mo·tive** \ˈmōd·|iv, -ōt|, |ēv *also* |əv\ *adj* [MF or ML; MF *motif*, fr. ML *motivus* — more at ¹MOTIVE] **1 :** moving or tending to move to action ⟨~ arguments⟩ **2 :** having or concerned with the function of initiating action ⟨the ~ nerves⟩ **3 :** of or relating to motion or the causing of motion ⟨~ energy⟩

³**motive** \"\ *vt* -ED/-ING/-S [¹*motive*] **:** MOTIVATE 1

mo·tive·less \|əvləs\ *adj* **:** lacking a motive ⟨~ malignity —S.T.Coleridge⟩ — **mo·tive·less·ly** *adv* — **mo·tive·less·ness** *n* -ES

motive power *n* **1 :** an agency (as water, steam, wind, electricity) used to impart motion to machinery **:** MOTOR, MOVER **2 :** the locomotives of a railroad

mo·ti·vic \ˈmōd·əvik\ *also* **mo·ti·val** \-vəl\ *adj* [¹*motive* + *-ic* or *-al*] **:** of or relating to a musical motive ⟨~ variation . . . through which the composer is able to create areas of tension and relaxation —Virgil Thomson⟩

mo·tiv·i·ty \mōˈtivəd·ē\ *n* -ES [²*motive* + *-ity*] **:** the power of moving or producing motion **:** available energy

mot juste \mōzhüst\ *n, pl* **mots justes** \mōzhüst(s)\ [F] **:** the exactly right word **:** precisely expressive phrasing ⟨pride in having found the *mot juste* —Angela Thirkell⟩

¹**mot·ley** \ˈmätlē, -li\ *adj, sometimes* **motleyer** *or* **motlier;** *sometimes* **motleyest** *or* **motliest** [ME *motteley, motley*, perh. fr. *mot* speck — more at MOTE] **1 :** marked by a mixture of usu. startlingly diverse or haphazardly arranged colors **:** PARTI-COLORED ⟨Swiss guardsmen in the strange ~ garb . . . contrived for them —Nathaniel Hawthorne⟩ ⟨clad in a ~ coat with red-and-yellow scarf —J.P.O'Donnell⟩ **2** *obs* **:** made of motley ⟨a leather bag, a ~ jacket —Richard Brathwaite⟩ **3 a :** DIVERSE, HETEROGENEOUS ⟨how ~ are the qualities that go to make up a human being—W.S.Maugham⟩ ⟨these ~ elements of skepticism and reform —Felix Frankfurter⟩ **b :** composed of a haphazard and incongruous mixture of heterogeneous elements ⟨lived in varied cities and very ~ societies —G.K. Chesterton⟩ ⟨the ~ speakers of late provincial Latin —Yakov Malkiel⟩ ⟨a ~ crowd⟩ ⟨a ~ crew⟩ ⟨a ~ scene⟩ **syn** see VARIEGATED

²**motley** \"\ *n* -s [ME *motteley, motley*, prob. fr. *motteley, motley*, adj.] **1 :** a varicolored woolen fabric woven of mixed threads in 14th to 17th century England and used esp. for clothing and cloth bags **2 a :** a garment of this fabric; *esp* **:** the characteristic dress of the professional fool ⟨~'s the only wear —Shak.⟩ **b :** the guise or character of a comedian ⟨no circus clown . . . when he has put aside the makeup and the ~ —Emmett Kelly⟩ ⟨a reign where even tragedy was expected to wear ~ —Frances Winwar⟩ **3 a :** a professional fool **:** JESTER ⟨all the ~*s* with their caps and bells —W.H.Dixon⟩ **b :** a person who by overfamiliarity or clowning cuts a ludicrous figure in company ⟨made myself a ~ to the view —Shak.⟩ ⟨making herself a ~ to the view with all fresh acquaintances —Angela Thirkell⟩ **4 :** a heterogeneous collection or mixture of incongruous elements **:** MEDLEY ⟨a ~ of borrowed or invented raiment —Ellen Glasgow⟩ ⟨a ~ of hand-me-downs, baggy generalities, and shabby prejudices —H.J.Muller⟩ ⟨a ~ of nations . . . thrown together —A.L.Kroeber⟩

³**motley** \"\ *vt* **motleyed; motleyed; motleying; motleys** [ME *motleyen*, fr. *motteley, motley*, adj.] **:** to make motley or variegated

mot·mot \ˈmät,mät\ *also* **mo·mot** \ˈmō,-\ *n* -s [AmerSp *mot-mot*, of imit. origin] **:** any of numerous birds of the family Momotidae confined to tropical forests from Mexico to Brazil that resemble jays in form, are colored chiefly green with blue, black, and rufous markings, and have long peculiarly shaped tails

motmot blue *n* **:** a moderate to strong greenish blue

motmot green *n* **:** a moderate yellowish green to light green

mo·to \ˈmōd·(,)ō, ˈmō(,)tō\ *n* -s [It, movement, motion, fr. L *motus*, fr. *motus*, past part. of *movēre* to move — more at MOVE] **:** movement with regard to musical tempo

moto- *comb form* [¹*motion* & ²*motor*] **:** motion **:** motor ⟨*motofacient*⟩ ⟨*motoneuron*⟩

mo·to·neuron *also* **mo·to·neurone** \ˌmōd·ō+\ *n* [*moto-* + *neuron, neurone*] **:** a motor nerve cell with its processes

moto per·pe·tuo \-perˈped·ə,wō\ *n* [It] **:** PERPETUUM MOBILE

¹**mo·tor** \ˈmōd·ə(r), -ōtə-\ *n* -s [L, fr. *motus* (past part. of *movēre* to move) + *-or* — more at MOVE] **1 :** one that imparts motion **:** a source of mechanical power ⟨in the medieval world view . . . the heavenly spheres and their angelic ~*s* —S.F. Mason⟩ **2 a :** PRIME MOVER 2a(1) **b :** a small compact engine ⟨can take twelve exposures in 5 seconds on 35 mm film, with one winding of the clockwork ~ —*Eastman Kodak Monthly Abstract Bull.*⟩ ⟨~*s* powered by compressed air are used in wagon drill feeds, in hoists, and in many other machines which operate near a supply of compressed air —H.L.Nichols⟩ **c :** a gasoline engine (as for an automotive vehicle or motorboat) ⟨internal-combustion type ~ is universally called an engine in the aircraft industry —W.W.Stout⟩ **d :** INTERNAL-COMBUSTION ENGINE **3 a :** AUTOMOBILE ⟨bought the fastest ~ on the market —Victoria Sackville-West⟩ **b :** MOTOR VEHICLE ⟨a cycle and ~ dealer —Christopher Lynch-Robinson⟩ **4 :** a rotating machine that transforms electrical energy into mechanical energy and that consists mainly of a field-magnet winding or a distributed-stator winding which produces a magnetic field and a rotating armature or rotor in whose conductors flow currents which are acted upon by the magnetic field and cause rotation, some of these machines being capable of use as either motors or generators

²**motor** \"\ *adj* **1 a :** causing or imparting motion ⟨~ power⟩ **b :** of, relating to, or being a nerve or nerve fiber that passes from the central nervous system or a ganglion to a muscle and conducts an impulse that causes movement **:** EFFERENT ⟨the normal spinal ~ nerve cell —*Physical Therapy Rev.*⟩ **c :** of, relating to, or involving muscular movement ⟨~ activity⟩ ⟨~ response⟩ ⟨~ behavior patterns⟩ ⟨violent ~ reactions . . . convulsions and shakings —E.T.Clark⟩ ⟨the mental and ~ skills of effective speaking —*Quarterly Jour. of Speech*⟩ **2 a :** equipped with or driven by a motor ⟨a two-man ~ toboggan —R.M.Grant⟩ **b :** of, in, or relating to an automobile ⟨~ trip⟩ ⟨~ industry⟩ **c :** designed for motor vehicles or motorists ⟨~ road⟩ ⟨~ fuels⟩ ⟨~ hotel⟩

³**motor** \"\ *vb* -ED/-ING/-S *vi* **:** to travel by automobile **:** go by car **:** DRIVE ⟨often ~*ed* down from London —Susan Ertz⟩ ~ *vt* **1 :** to convey or transport by motorcar **:** DRIVE ⟨whose parents ~ them to many places of historic . . . interest —*Brit. Book News*⟩ **2 :** to set or keep in motion (as by a motor) ⟨it was not possible to ~ engines connected to the induction-type dynamometer —M.A.Elliott⟩

mo·tor·able \-ərəbᵊl\ *adj* [²*motor* + *-able*] *chiefly Brit* **:** usable by motor vehicles **:** PASSABLE ⟨~ roads⟩

motor aphasia *n* **:** the inability to speak or to organize the muscular movements of speech — compare APHASIA

motor area *n* **:** any of various areas of cerebral cortex believed to be associated with the initiation, coordination, and transmission of motor impulses to lower centers; *specif* **:** a region immediately anterior to the central sulcus having an unusually thick zone of cortical gray matter, including the giant pyramidal cells, and communicating with lower centers chiefly through the pyramidal tracts

motor automatism *n* **1 :** the performance without intent of actions (as speaking or writing) normally under strictly voluntary control **2 :** a product of motor automatism

motor barrel *n* **:** the mainspring unit in watches that have the main wheel detached from the barrel but turning as a unit with the barrel arbor to eliminate strain on the main wheel teeth if the mainspring should break — compare GOING BARREL

motor bicycle \ˈ⸗⸗ˈ⸗(,)⸗⸗\ *or* **motorbike** \ˈ⸗⸗,⸗\ *n* **1 :** MOTORCYCLE **2 a :** a light motorcycle resembling a bicycle in design and structure **b :** a bicycle to which a motor for propulsion is attached

¹**motorboat** \ˈ⸗⸗,⸗\ *n* [¹*motor* + *boat*] **1 :** a boat or small ship propelled by an internal-combustion engine or an electric motor **2 :** any of certain classes of boats according to statute (as a boat not more than 65 feet long propelled by machinery) except steam-propelled tugboats and towboats

2motorboat \"\ *vi* **1 :** to ride in or drive a motorboat **2 :** to make sounds resembling the exhaust of a motorboat
motorboating \'==,==\ *n* **:** an inherent low frequency instability in electronic circuits characterized when heard on a telephone receiver or loudspeaker by a noise similar to the exhaust of a motorboat
motor boss *n* **:** one who directs and records mine haulage operations underground or at the surface — called also *dispatcher*
motor bus *n* **:** an automotive omnibus **:** MOTOR COACH
mo·tor·cade \ˌmōd·ə(r)ˌkād, -ōtə-\ *n* -S [¹*motor* + *-cade*] **:** a procession of automobiles ⟨the prime minister's ~ passed —*St. John (New Brunswick) Telegraph-Jour.*⟩ ⟨taken in a twenty-five-car ~ to City Hall —Fendall Yerxa⟩
motorcar \'==,=\ *n* **1 :** AUTOMOBILE **2** *usu* **motor car a :** a railroad car containing motors for propulsion ⟨several railroads operate electric *motor cars* in suburban passenger train service —*Stories Behind the Pictures*⟩ **b :** a motor-propelled inspection or work car on a railroad
motor cargo insurance *n* **:** insurance against loss resulting from damage to goods in transit by motor truck
motor carriage *n* **:** a self-propelled mount for a weapon
motor carrier *n* **:** a highway passenger and freight carrier regulated by the federal government
motor cell *n* **:** BULLIFORM CELL
motor center *n* **:** a nervous center that controls or modifies (as by inhibiting or reinforcing) a motor impulse — compare MOTOR AREA
motor coach *n* **:** an automotive omnibus **:** MOTOR BUS ⟨a fleet of *motor coaches* —*Motor (London)*⟩
motor converter *n* **:** a machine consisting of an induction motor and a synchronous converter mounted on a common shaft with their rotor windings in series with each other
motor cortex *n* **:** the cortex of a motor area; *also* **:** the motor areas as a functional whole
motor court *n* **:** MOTEL ⟨*motor courts* with swimming pools and finely furnished bungalows —*N.Y.Times*⟩
1motorcycle \'==,==\ *n* [fr. earlier *motor bicycle*] **:** a 2-wheeled tandem automotive vehicle having 1 or 2 riding saddles and sometimes having a 3d wheel for the support of a sidecar
2motorcycle \"\ *vi* **:** to ride a motorcycle or go by motorcycle
motorcyclist \'==,==\ *n* **:** one that rides a motorcycle
motor drive *n* **:** an electric motor and auxiliaries for driving a machine or group of machines
mo·tor·drome \'mōd·ə(r),drōm\ *n* [¹*motor* + *-drome*] **:** a track or course usu. enclosed and furnished with seats for spectators at races or tests of automobiles or motorcycles
mo·tored \'mōd·ə(r)d\ *adj* [¹*motor* + *-ed*] **:** equipped with a motor — often used in combination ⟨a four-*motored* airplane⟩
motor end plate *n* **:** the terminal arborization of a motor axon on a muscle fiber
motor fiber *n* **:** a nerve fiber whose stimulation causes muscular contraction
motor generator *or* **motor-generator set** *n* **:** one or more motors mechanically coupled to one or more generators for transforming or converting electric currents
motor horn *n* **:** a warning horn used on a motor vehicle
mo·to·ri·al \mō'tōrēəl\ *adj* [L *motorius* moving + E *-al* — more at MOTORY] **:** MOTOR 1
mo·tor·ic \mō'tōrik, -tär-\ *adj* [¹*motor* + *-ic*] **:** MOTOR 1c — **mo·tor·i·cal·ly** \-rək(ə)lē\ *adv*
1motoring *n* -S [fr. gerund of ³*motor*] **:** the act or recreation of riding in or driving an automobile
2motor·ing *adj, chiefly Brit* **:** of or relating to automobiles, the driving of automobiles, or the people who drive automobiles ⟨the design has been virtually dictated by American ~ opinion —Bertram Wycock⟩ ⟨~ offences⟩
mo·tor·ism \'mōd·ə,rizəm\ *n* -S [¹*motor* + *-ism*] **:** addiction to or practice of motoring
mo·tor·ist \'mōd·ərəst, -ōtə-\ *n* -S **:** one who makes a practice of driving a car or traveling by car
mo·to·ri·um \mō'tōrēəm\ *n, pl* **moto·ria** \-ēə\ [NL, fr. LL, neut. of *motorius* moving — more at MOTORY] **1 :** the part of an organism (as of its nervous system) that is concerned in movement as distinguished from that concerned in sensation **2 :** a differentiated cytoplasmic area in certain protozoans that acts as a coordinating center analogous to the brain of higher animals
mo·tor·iza·tion \ˌmōd·ərə'zāshən, -ōtər-, -rī'-\ *n* -S **:** the act or process of motorizing
mo·tor·ize \'mōd·ə,rīz, -ōtə-\ *vt* -ED/-ING/-S *see -ize in Explan Notes* [¹*motor* + *-ize*] **:** to equip with a motor ⟨a *motorized* wheelchair⟩: as **a :** to equip with motor-driven vehicles in substitution for those otherwise propelled ⟨~ a fire department⟩ ⟨~ a farm⟩ **b :** to equip (as ground-fighting troops) with motor-driven vehicles for transportation — distinguished from *mechanize* **c :** to equip with automobiles ⟨the population is becoming increasingly *motorized* —Harold Callender⟩ ⟨~ the police⟩ **d :** to design or adapt (as a machine or a tool) for direct operation esp. by an electric motor ⟨~ a lathe⟩
motor launch *n* **:** a launch propelled by an internal-combustion engine
mo·tor·less \-ə(r)ləs\ *adj* **:** having no motor
motor liner *n* **:** a motor-driven ocean liner
motor-lorry \'==,==\ *n, Brit* **:** MOTORTRUCK
mo·tor·man \'mōd·ə(r)mən\ *n, pl* **motormen 1 :** an operator of a motor-driven vehicle; *esp* **:** an operator of a street railway car, subway or elevated train, dinkey, or other haulage engine **2 :** one who operates the sound and camera motors used in the making of motion pictures
motor-minded \'==,'==\ *adj* **:** inclined to think of things in terms of the muscular movements they involve — compare EYE-MINDED — **mo·tor-mind·ed·ness** *n* -ES
motor paralysis *n* **:** paralysis of the voluntary muscles
motor pendulum *n* **:** a pendulum that is used to drive the wheelwork and hands of a turret clock and is maintained in motion by electromagnetic impulses applied at regular intervals
motor phrase *n* **:** a precisely timed movement division in dancing
motor point *n* **:** a small area on a muscle at which electrical or other stimulation is most effective
motor pool *n* **:** a group of motor vehicles controlled by a single governmental agency whether or not assembled in one place and dispatched for use as needed by different organizations or individuals
motor pumper *n* **:** a unit of automotive fire apparatus with fire pump driven by the engine — compare FIRE ENGINE b
motor root *n* **:** a nerve root containing only motor fibers; *specif* **:** the ventral root of a spinal nerve
motors *pl of* MOTOR, *pres 3d sing of* MOTOR
motor sailer *n* **:** a motorboat with sailing equipment
motor scooter *n* **:** a low 2- or 3-wheeled automotive vehicle resembling a child's scooter, having a seat so that the rider does not straddle the engine, sometimes having a parcel compartment, but having smaller wheels and being less powerful than a motorcycle

motor scooter

motor scythe *n* **:** a mower with a short reciprocating knife attached to a garden tractor mechanism
motorship \'==,=\ *n* **:** a seagoing ship propelled by a motor; *esp* **:** one propelled by an internal-combustion engine
motor spirit *n, chiefly Brit* **:** a volatile liquid used as a fuel in internal-combustion engines; *specif* **:** GASOLINE, PETROL
motor torpedo boat *n* **:** a high-speed 60 to 100 ft. motorboat mounting two or four torpedo tubes and antiaircraft and machine guns and equipped with depth charges and smoke-making apparatus — called also *mosquito boat, PT boat*
motor transport *n* **:** commercial transport (as trucks) on streets and highways
motortruck \'==,=\ *n* **:** an automotive truck for transporting freight
motor unit *n* **:** a motor neuron together with the muscle fibers on which it acts
motor vehicle *n* **:** an automotive vehicle not operated on rails; *esp* **:** one with rubber tires for use on highways
motor vessel *n* **:** an inland waterway boat or ocean ship propelled by one or more diesel engines
motorway \'==,=\ *n, Brit* **:** a motor highway; *esp* **:** SUPERHIGHWAY
mo·to·ry \'mōd·ərē\ *adj* [LL *motorius* moving, fr. L *motus* (past part. of *movēre* to move) + *-orius* -ory — more at MOVE] **:** MOTOR 1
mo·to·zin·tlec \ˌmōd·əsənt'lek\ *n, pl* **motozintlec** *or* **motozintlecs** *usu cap* [Sp *motozintleca,* fr. *Motozintla,* town in Chiapas state, Mexico] **1 a :** an Indian people of southeastern Mexico **b :** a member of such people **2 :** a Mayan language of the Motozintlec people
mots *pl of* MOT
1motte *or* **mott** \'mät\ *n* -S [MexSp *mata,* fr. Sp, bush, shrub, orchard, prob. fr. LL *matta* mat — more at MAT] *chiefly Southwest* **:** a grove or clump of trees; *esp* **:** a shrubby copse in open prairie country ⟨a thick oak ~⟩
2motte \"\ *n* -S [F, fr. OF *mote,* motte mound, hillock, fr. OProv *mota*] **:** MOTE 1; *specif* **:** a palisaded mound common in prehistoric Europe
mot·tet·to \mō'ted·(ˌ)ō\ *n, pl* **mottettos** *or* **mottet·ti** \-d·ē\ [It, fr. F *motet* — more at MOTET] **:** MOTET
1mot·tle \'mäd·ᵊl, -ätᵊl\ *n* -S [prob. back-formation fr. ¹*motley*] **1 :** a colored spot ⟨streaks and ~*s*⟩ **2 a :** a surface having colored spots, blotchings, or cloudings ⟨his chest and flanks were a ~ of bruises —Arthur Morrison⟩ **b :** the arrangement of such markings on a surface ⟨available in a variety of opaque colors or ~*s* —*Modern Plastics Catalog*⟩ **3 :** MOSAIC 5b
2mottle \"\ *adj* **:** MOTTLED
3mottle \"\ *vt* **mottled; mottled; mottling** \-d·ᵊliŋ, -t(ᵊ)liŋ\ **mottles :** to mark with spots or blotches of different color or shades of color as if stained **:** SPOT, BLOTCH ⟨drifting clouds *mottled* the sea —J.A.Michener⟩
mottled *adj* **:** marked with spots of different colors **:** DAPPLED, SPOTTED ⟨~ wood⟩ ⟨a ~ complexion⟩ ⟨~ linoleum⟩ ⟨hills . . . some mantled in green, some ~ with the hues of red clay and white granite —Mabel R. Gillis⟩ ⟨his face was ~ with embarrassment —Mary Austin⟩
mottled brant *or* **mottled goose** *n* **:** WHITE-FRONTED GOOSE
mottled duck *n* **:** a Louisiana and Texas variety (*Anas fulvigula maculosa*) of the Florida duck
mottled enamel *n* **:** a spotted condition of the enamel of teeth caused by continual use of drinking water containing excessive amounts of fluorides during the time the teeth are calcifying
mottled iron *n* **:** cast or pig iron that is intermediate between white and gray iron and shows a mottled surface on fracture
mottled owl *n* **:** an American screech owl in the gray phase of plumage
mottle-leaf \'==,=\ *also* **mottled leaf** *n* **1 :** a zinc deficiency disease of citrus plants characterized by a partial chlorosis, reduced size of leaves and fruits, and stunting **2 :** a virus disease of cherry characterized by chlorotic mottling, puckering, distortion, and wrinkling of the leaves
mot·tle·ment \'mäd·ᵊlmənt\ *n* -S **:** mottled condition or appearance
mot·tler \'mäd·ᵊlə(r), -ät(ᵊ)l-\ *n* -S **:** one that mottles (as in dyeing or ceramics); *specif* **:** a brush for producing a mottled surface
mottling *n* -S **1 :** MOTTLE 2 ⟨inhabitants of certain districts had a curious ~ of their teeth —*Irish Digest*⟩; *specif* **:** a mingling of other-colored spots with the normal green in foliage (as in many variegated plants and in mosaic diseases) **2 :** the act or process of producing mottle
mot·to \'mäd·(ˌ)ō, -ä(ˌ)tō\ *n, pl* **mottoes** *also* **mottos** [It, fr. L *muttum* grunt, mumble, fr. *muttire* to mutter, mumble — more at MUTE] **1 :** a sentence, phrase, or word accompanying a heraldic achievement ⟨two bends with the owner's word, reason, or ~ —W.H.St.John Hope⟩ **2 a :** a sentence, phrase, or word inscribed on something as appropriate to or indicative of its character or use ⟨"Cry Aloud and Spare Not", the belligerent ~ of the paper —*Amer. Guide Series: Tenn.*⟩ **b :** a short suggestive expression of a guiding principle **:** MAXIM ⟨the Boy Scout ~ "Be Prepared"⟩ **c :** a short usu. quoted passage prefixed to a literary work (as a novel, essay, or poem) or to one of its divisions (as a chapter or canto) and intended to suggest the subject matter that follows **d** (1) *or* **motto kiss :** a piece of candy in a paper wrapper inscribed with or enclosing a saying or verse (2) **:** a party novelty consisting of a fancy wrapper containing usu. a paper printed with a sentimental or humorous verse, a paper hat, and a small toy or charm — compare CRACKER 2c, FAVOR 4b **3** *also* **motto theme :** a recurring phrase or musical figure possibly varied and usu. alluding to a specific idea
mot·toed \-ōd\ *adj* **:** bearing or having a motto
mot·tram·ite \'mä·trəˌmīt\ *n* -S [*Mottram* St. Andrew, Cheshire, England + E *-ite*] **:** a mineral $(Cu,Zn)Pb(VO_4)(OH)$ that consists of a basic vanadate of lead, copper, and zinc with more copper than zinc and that is isomorphous with descloizite
mot·ty *also* **mot·tie** \'mätī\ *adj* [*mot* (Sc. var. of ²*mote*) + *-y*] *Scot* **:** full of motes **:** DUSTY
1mo·tu \'mō(ˌ)tü\ *n, pl* **motu** *or* **motus** *usu cap* **1 a :** a Melanesian people in New Guinea **b :** a member of such people **2 :** the language of the Motu people used in trade on the southeast coast of Papua New Guinea
2motu \"\ *n, pl* **motu** *or* **motus** [Maori, Tahitian, Tuamotuan, Marquesan, Samoan, & Tongan] **:** a Polynesian reef islet with vegetation
mo·tu pro·prio \ˌmō(ˌ)tü'prōprēˌō\ *n* [L, by one's own impulse] **:** a rescript initiated and issued by the pope of his own accord and apart from the advice of others
1mou \'mü\ *Scot var of* MOUTH
2mou \'maů, 'mü\ *or* **mow** \'maů\ *also* **mu** \'mü\ *n, pl* **mou** *or* **mow** [Chin (Pek) *mou*³, *mu*³] **:** any of various Chinese units of land area; *esp* **:** one equal to 0.1518 acre
mouch *chiefly Brit var of* MOOCH
mou·char·a·by \mü'sharəbē\ *or* **mouch·ra·bi·eh** \ˌmüshrə'bē(y)ə\ *or* **mesh·ra·bi·yeh** \ˌmeshrə'bē(y)ə\ *also* **mush·re·bi·yeh** \ˌmüshrə'bē(y)ə\ *n, pl* **moucharabies** *or* **mouchrabiehs** *or* **meshrabiyehs** [F & Ar; F *moucharaby, moucharabièh,* fr. Ar *mushrabīyah*] **:** a Moorish projecting oriel window or enclosed balcony of which the enclosure is largely made up of carved wooden latticework
mou·choir \(')mü'shwär\ *n* -S [F, fr. *moucher* to blow the nose, fr. (assumed) VL *muccare,* fr. L *muccus, mucus* mucus — more at MUCUS] **:** HANDKERCHIEF
mou·die *or* **mou·dy** \'mōdi, 'müdi\ *n, pl* **moudies** [short for *moudiewarp*] *chiefly Scot* **:** ³MOLE 1a
mou·die·warp \-ˌwórp\ *or* **mou·die·wort** \-rt\ *Scot var of* MOLDWARP
moue \'mü\ *n* -S [F — more at MOW] **:** a little grimace (as of distaste or playful impudence) **:** POUT, MOW ⟨made a ~, to show that he didn't expect to enjoy the occasion —Upton Sinclair⟩ ⟨his ~ of comic disdain permitted their laughter —L.A.Fiedler⟩
mouf·lon *or* **mouf·flon** *also* **muf·lon** *or* **muf·flon** \'müflən\ *n, pl* **mouflon** *or* **mouflons** *or* **moufflon** *or* **moufflons** [F *mouflon,* fr. It dial. (Corsica) *mufrone, muvrone* & Sardinian *muvrone,* fr. LL *mufron-, mufro*] **1 :** a wild sheep (*Ovis musimon*) inhabiting the mountains of Sardinia and Corsica and having large curling horns that in the male have a triangular base, a reddish brown coat with a grayish buff patch on the sides, and white on the legs, belly, and buttocks **2 :** a wild sheep with large horns

mouflon 1

mought *US* 'maůt, *Brit* 'mōt *or* 'müt\ [ME *moghte*] *chiefly dial past of* MAY
mouil·la·tion \mü'yāshən\ *n* -S [*mouillé* + *-ation*] **:** mouillé pronunciation
mouil·lé \(')mü'yā\ *adj* [F, fr. past part. of *mouiller* to wet, moisten, palatalize, fr. (assumed) VL *molliare* to soften with water, fr. L *mollis* soft — more at MELT] **:** pronounced palatally — used esp. in *l mouillé* and with reference to the sound \lʸ\ in Old French and certain dialects of Modern French or rarely with reference to its counterpart \y\ in standard Modern French
mouil·lure \mü'yü(ə)r\ *n* -S [F, fr. *mouiller* + *-ure*] **:** MOUILLATION
moujik *var of* MUZHIK
moul \'mül\ *var of* MOOL
mou·lage \(')mü'läzh\ *n* -S [F, molding, casting, fr. MF, fr. *mouler* to mold (fr. OF, fr. *modle, molle, moule* mold) + *-age* — more at MOLD] **1 a :** the taking of an impression (as of a tire mark or tooth print) for use as evidence in a criminal investigation **b :** an impression or cast made for use as evidence in a criminal investigation **:** MOLDING **2 :** a mold of a lesion or defect used as a guide in applying medical treatment (as in radiation therapy) or in performing reconstructive surgery esp. on the face
1mould *var of* MOLD
2mould \'mōld\ *n* -S [ME *molde,* fr. OE *molda* or *molde* — more at -BLAST] **1** *archaic* **:** the top of the head **2 :** FONTANEL
mouldboard *var of* MOLDBOARD
mould·warp \'mōld,wórp\ *archaic var of* MOLDWARP
moulder *var of* MOLDER
mou·lin \(')mü'laⁿ\ *n* -S [F, lit., mill, fr. LL *molinum* — more at MILL] **:** a nearly cylindrical vertical shaft in a glacier scoured out by meltwater and rock debris pouring into it
moul·mein cedar \(')mül'mān-, (')mōl-, -'mīn-\ *n, usu cap M* [fr. *Moulmein,* Burma] **:** TOON
moult *var of* MOLT
moulten *adj* [*moult* + *-en*] *obs* **:** MOLTED **:** having lost its plumage ⟨a ~ raven —Shak.⟩
1moulter *var of* MOLTER
2moul·ter \'mō(l)tə(r)\ *chiefly dial var of* ²MOLDER
moulvi *var of* MAULVI
1mound \'maůnd\ *vb* -ED/-ING/-S [origin unknown] *vt* **1** *archaic* **a :** to surround with a barrier **:** FENCE ⟨to ~ over the hill would require double the rails —Jethro Tull⟩ **b :** to enclose or fortify with a ridge of earth ⟨heaped hills that ~ the sea —Alfred Tennyson⟩ **2 a :** to gather into a heap **:** PILE ⟨snow ~*ed* in high white cones above the pillars —Josephine Johnson⟩ **b :** to surround or cover with a raised heap **:** BANK, HILL ⟨roses are ~*ed* for winter protection⟩ ⟨the ~*ed* grave of a British Tommy —T.O.Heggen⟩ ⟨spotted the wreck, which the silt of 22 centuries had ~*ed* up —*Nat'l Geographic*⟩ ~ *vi* **:** to become a mound **:** pile up ⟨thunderheads are ~*ing* in the west⟩
2mound \"\ *n* -S *often attrib* [origin unknown] **1 a** *dial chiefly Eng* **:** an encompassing hedge or fence **b** *obs* **:** a line of demarcation **:** BOUNDARY ⟨stars, whose whirling courses . . . mark the true ~*s* of years, and months, and days —Josuah Sylvester⟩ **2 a :** an earthwork used as a fortification **:** RAMPART **b :** a prehistoric earthwork constructed by Indian mound builders of No. America over a burial or sacrificial altar or as a foundation or fortification or for ceremonial purposes **3 a :** an accumulated mass or artificially produced heap **:** PILE ⟨~*s* of oyster shells surround the weathered frame shacks —*Amer. Guide Series: Fla.*⟩ ⟨began to process ~*s* of orders —M.E.Harvey⟩ ⟨fluffy ~*s* of mashed potatoes —Jack Alexander⟩ **b :** the slightly elevated area in which a baseball pitcher's plate is set **c :** a natural elevation **:** HILL, KNOLL ⟨~*s* and dunes of loose sand —Willa Cather⟩ ⟨hurricanes . . . dragging in their centers a ~ of seawater —Marjory S. Douglas⟩; *specif* **:** HUMP ⟨under his left eye was a ~ of bluish flesh —G.B.Shaw⟩
3mound \"\ *also* **mond** \'mänd\ *n* -S [MF *monde,* lit., world, fr. L *mundus*] **:** ORB 1c(3)
mound ant *n, Austral* **:** MEAT ANT
mound bird *n* **:** MEGAPODE
mound builder *n* **1** *usu cap M&B* **:** a member of one of the prehistoric Indian peoples of central No. America whose extensive earthworks are found esp. around the Great Lakes and in the Mississippi valley region and many of whom were skilled craftsmen in pottery, stone, or copper — compare EFFIGY MOUND, HOPEWELL, MOUND 2b **2 :** MEGAPODE
mound burial *n* **:** the practice of laying a corpse on the surface and covering it with earth or stones or of heaping up a mound of soil and sinking a grave into it — compare ¹BARROW 2
mound layer *n* **:** a new shoot of a woody plant (as a currant bush) that has been mounded with earth to induce it to root
mound layering *also* **mound layerage** *n* **:** a method of propagation in which various woody-stemmed plants (as currants, gooseberries, quinces) are cut back to the ground in early spring and the new shoots that they develop are covered with soil to a depth of six to eight inches to induce root growth which forms individual plants that can be removed in the fall — called also *stool layering*
mound lily *or* **mound lily yucca** *n* **:** SPANISH DAGGER 1
mound maker *n* **:** MEGAPODE
mounds·man \'maůn(d)zmən\ *n, pl* **moundsmen :** ²PITCHER 1a
mound turkey *n* **:** any of several of the larger megapodes: as **a :** BRUSH TURKEY **b :** JUNGLE FOWL 2a
moun·seer \maůn'si(ə)r, -iə\ *n* -S [by alter.] *archaic* **:** MONSIEUR
1mount \'maůnt\ *n* -S [ME *munt, mont, mount,* partly fr. OE *munt,* fr. L *mont-, mons;* partly fr. OF *mont,* fr. L *mont-, mons;* akin to ON *mœnir* ridgepole, *mœna* to project, L *minari* to project, threaten, W *mynydd* mountain, Av *framanyente* they get a head start, *mati-* promontory; basic meaning: mountain] **1 a :** a lofty promontory **:** MOUNTAIN; *specif* **:** a high usu. more or less conical detached hill rising from a landscape ⟨*Mount* Vesuvius⟩ **b :** a lofty position **:** VANTAGE POINT ⟨mystics . . . returned from the ~ of vision —J.S.Bixler⟩ **c** *heraldry* **:** a hill proper vert in base **2 a** *archaic* **:** a protective earthwork **:** RAMPART **b** *obs* **:** CAVALIER 1 **3 a :** an artificial elevation **:** MOUND ⟨~ in the background is the icehouse —*Nat'l Geographic*⟩ **b** *obs* **:** an elevated area in a garden that affords a view of the surrounding countryside ⟨have a ~ of some pretty height . . . to look abroad into the fields —Francis Bacon⟩ **4** *obs* **:** a lending agency **:** BANK, PAWNBROKER — compare MONT-DE-PIÉTÉ **5** *usu cap* **:** a small protrusion of flesh on the palm of the hand esp. at the base of a finger that is held by palmists to indicate predominant traits and degrees of temperament ⟨the absence of *Mounts* . . . indicates the lack of the virtues represented by that *Mount* —Josef Ranald⟩ — see LOWER MARS, MOUNT OF APOLLO, MOUNT OF JUPITER, MOUNT OF LUNA, MOUNT OF MERCURY, MOUNT OF SATURN, MOUNT OF VENUS, UPPER MARS
2mount \"\ *vb* -ED/-ING/-S [ME *mounten,* fr. MF *monter,* fr. (assumed) VL *montare,* fr. L *mont-, mons* mountain] *vi* **1 a :** to become greater in amount or extent **:** INCREASE ⟨weekends when passenger volume ~*s* sharply —W.A.Howe⟩ ⟨costs of operation . . . are continually ~*ing* —C.F.Robinson⟩ ⟨you know how those storage bills ~ up —Berton Roueché⟩ **b :** to reach an ultimate amount or extent **:** TOTAL ⟨the cost of champagne . . . is liable to ~ up to a couple of pounds per head —*English Digest*⟩ **2 a :** to wing upward **:** SOAR ⟨the lark . . . ~*ing* from the lea —William Allingham⟩ ⟨the soul ~*ing* toward the eternal forms —Bernard DeVoto⟩ **b :** to make or appear to make a steep ascent **:** CLIMB ⟨~*ing* ivy⟩ ⟨the narrow road ~*s* to higher levels —*Amer. Guide Series: Fla.*⟩ ⟨astride these promontories are . . . residential sections, and even some of the business areas have ~*ed* partway —*Amer. Guide Series: Minn.*⟩ **c :** to reach upward **:** TOWER ⟨the skyscraper ~*s* through the dusk to a winking red light on top⟩ **d :** to move upward **:** RISE ⟨hid her face on the bounteous breast that ~*ed* to her —George Meredith⟩ **e :** to surge up and suffuse the face ⟨blushes ~ to her cheeks —Upton Sinclair⟩ **f :** to attain greater height or magnitude **:** GROW ⟨a vine, remarkable for its tendency . . . to mass and ~ —Willa Cather⟩ ⟨a ~*ing* economic and political problem —Gordon Walker⟩ **g :** to become aroused or amplified **:** KINDLE, INTENSIFY ⟨~ to high moral indignation —M.R. Cohen⟩ ⟨a sense of ~*ing* excitement —T.B.Costain⟩ **h :** ¹COUPLE 1 ⟨meet and ~ like stray dogs in the street —George Barker⟩ **3 a :** to become promoted **:** ADVANCE ⟨younger brother . . . proposed to ~ over the head of the elder by marrying the late King's widow —Edith Sitwell⟩ **b** *archaic* **:** to reach back through the years ⟨an antiquity which ~*s* up to the eighth century of our era —J.M.Jephson⟩ **4 a :** to seat oneself upon a means of conveyance (as a horse) ⟨puts his foot in the stirrup and ~*s*⟩ ⟨~*ed* and rode off in a cloud of dust⟩ **b :** to become elevated by or secured to a support ⟨~ on French heels when

you go to the ball —*London Magazine*⟩ ⟨the transmission ~s crosswise in the vehicle —*Principles of Automotive Vehicles*⟩ **5** *slang* **:** to ascend the witness stand **:** TESTIFY ⟨their price is five shillings for what they call ~*ing* —George Parker⟩ ~ *vt* **1 a :** to climb or appear to climb **:** ASCEND ⟨~*ed* a short flight of steps —W.B.Furlong⟩ ⟨the town ~s the hills —Claudia Cassidy⟩; *specif* **:** to take one's place on a raised structure ⟨~ a pulpit⟩ ⟨~ the judicial bench⟩ **b** *obs* **:** to soar into ⟨did He . . . not only ~ the firmament but ascend the heaven of heavens —James Hervey⟩ **c** *archaic* **:** to scale for the purpose of assault ⟨first to ~ the breach —Sir Walter Scott⟩ **2 a :** to lift up **:** ELEVATE ⟨hedgehogs . . . ~ their pricks at my footfall —Shak.⟩ ⟨had the brilliant idea of ~*ing* enormous masts . . . down the center of the roadway —H.V.Morton⟩ ⟨clouds . . . ~*ing* thunderheads in the north —Norman Mailer⟩; *specif* **:** to raise (a shotgun) to the shoulder preparatory to firing **b :** to set on something that elevates ⟨a cluster of outbuildings . . . each ~*ed* on poles —Mary Kingsley⟩ **c** *archaic* **:** to raise in esteem or spirituality **:** EXALT ⟨whom his tenth epic ~s to fame —Edward Young⟩ ⟨this ~s my soul with more heroic fires —Francis Quarles⟩ **3 a :** to dispose in battle array **:** POSITION ⟨on this rampart he ~*ed* his little train of artillery —W.H. Prescott⟩ **b :** to be equipped with or have in position ⟨a war canoe ~*ing* 40 or more oars⟩ ⟨a wooden stockade ~*ing* cannon —P.M.Angle⟩ ⟨vehicles . . . which can ~ 105 mm. recoilless weapons —*Combat Forces Jour.*⟩ **c** (1) **:** to post for defense or observation ⟨~*ed* some guards⟩ (2) **:** to take up (a post of protective custody) ⟨~ guard over the person of the emperor —A.M.Young⟩ **d** (1) **:** to organize and equip (an attacking force) ⟨the logistical support . . . to ~ and support the operation —H.A.Jordan⟩ (2) **:** to launch and carry out (an assault or campaign) ⟨first ship specially designed for ~*ing* helicopter assaults —A.W.Jessup⟩ ⟨~*ed* 1525 effective sorties during the period —*N. Y. Times*⟩ ⟨is ~*ing* a successful trade offensive —D.L.Cohn⟩ **4 :** [1]COVER 10a ⟨crouching like a domestic hen that wants to be ~*ed* —T.H.White b. 1906⟩ **5 a :** to get on (a means of conveyance) ⟨~ a horse⟩ ⟨went running to ~ the motorcycle —Richard Llewellyn⟩ ⟨clouds ~ the wind —Russell Lord⟩ **b :** to sit or be set upon (a means of conveyance) ⟨~*ed* the tractor and rode into the barnyard⟩ ⟨a horse would be led out and I would be ~*ed* . . . upon it —O.S.J.Gogarty⟩ **c :** to furnish with a means of conveyance ⟨wanted horses to ~ his dragoons —*Amer. Guide Series: Vt.*⟩ **6 a** (1) **:** to attach to a support or assemble for use ⟨after the final polishing . . . the blade is ready to be ~*ed* —L.D.Bement⟩ ⟨the pulley shaft is ~*ed* on large capacity ball bearings —*Whitin Rev.*⟩; *specif* **:** to attach to a base (as of metal or wood) and make type high (a printing plate or cut) (2) **:** to attach to a backing for reinforcement or display ⟨old Roman filet . . . ~*ed* on a net foundation that would give almost invisible support to its fragile threads —*advt*⟩ ⟨black satin motifs ~*ed* on white felt —*Women's Wear Daily*⟩; *specif* **:** to glue or paste (as a sheet of paper) upon firm material in bookbinding **b :** to prepare for display: as (1) **:** to frame or provide with an appropriate setting ⟨classifying, ~*ing*, and labeling specimens —G.O.Blough⟩ ⟨the jeweler ~s a pearl in a ring⟩ ⟨~ a statue on a pedestal⟩; *specif* **:** to place (an object) on a slide for microscopic examination (2) **:** to stuff or arrange (the skin or skeleton of an animal) for exhibition esp. in a natural position or attitude — compare TAXIDERMY ⟨~*ed* a group of orangutans, and then a habitat group of muskrats —Clyde Fisher⟩ (3) **:** to fasten (a stamp) on the page of an album esp. by use of a hinge or on a sheet of paper or cardboard for display **c** (1) **:** to put on view **:** EXHIBIT ⟨one of the finest shows the museum has ever ~*ed* —*Time*⟩; *specif* **:** to arrange (a slide) under a microscope for examination (2) *archaic* **:** to don esp. for display ⟨~*ed* a fashionable greatcoat —*Sporting Mag.*⟩ **d :** to provide with scenery, costumes, lighting, and properties **:** equip for public presentation ⟨the manner in which a play is composed, ~*ed* and performed —Samuel Selden⟩ ⟨a tastefully ~*ed* television show⟩ ⟨a beautifully ~*ed* circus, meaning it had luster and snap and dazzle —T.W.Duncan⟩; *specif* **:** PRODUCE ⟨the manager's stubborn determination to ~ a Wagner opera although he had only a few leading singers to put into it —Marcia Davenport⟩ **syn** see ASCEND, RISE

[3]**mount** \"\ *n* -S **1 a :** an act or instance of mounting ⟨the circus rider leaped to the horse's back in a flying ~⟩ ⟨took pride in the spread and ~ of his fame —J.L.Davis⟩; *specif* **:** a gymnastic maneuver consisting of a spring from the floor to a position on the apparatus **b :** COUPLING 1 ⟨the copulatory behavior of macaques . . . consists of a series of ~s —C.S. Ford & F.A.Beach⟩ **2 :** FRAME, SUPPORT: as **a :** the strips (as of wood or ivory) constituting the framework of a fan **b :** a mat that serves as a background for a picture ⟨salon ~⟩ **c :** a jewelry setting ⟨flexible platinum ~ set with 68 round diamonds —*Precious-Stone Jewelry*⟩ **d :** a decorative border or detail applied to objects (as furniture, clocks, saddles); *also* **:** protective or functional hardware (as escutcheons or drawer pulls) of furniture — usu. used in pl. ⟨a clock with ormolu ~s⟩ **e :** an undercarriage or part that fits a device for use or serves to attach an accessory ⟨engine ~⟩ ⟨weapons on towed or self-propelled ~s —*U. S. War Dept. Technical Manual*⟩ ⟨invented a ~ for a telescopic gunsight⟩ ⟨a good lens in focusing ~ —R.C.Holslag⟩; *specif* **:** the base upon which a printing plate or cut is mounted to make it type high **f :** a hinge, card, or acetate envelope for mounting a stamp for display (as in an album) **g** (1) **:** a glass slide with its accessories on which objects are placed for examination with a microscope (2) **:** a specimen mounted on a slide for microscopic examination **h :** a piece of material used for reinforcement or backing ⟨~ for a book cover⟩ **3 a :** a means of conveyance ⟨a cavalry action, with jeeps as ~s —Blair Clark⟩; *specif* **:** SADDLE HORSE ⟨too many officers' ~s and not enough draft animals —F.V.W.Mason⟩ **b :** a supply of saddle horses ⟨told me the color and the brand on every horse that was in my ~ —Ross Santee⟩ — compare [1]STRING 11c **c** (1) **:** an opportunity to ride ⟨offering an unsuspecting person a ~ on a savage horse —Robert Lynd⟩; *specif* **:** an assignment to ride as a jockey in a race ⟨phone is always ringing, with owners and trainers offering ~s —Allen Andrews⟩ (2) **:** a horse entered in a competition

mount·able \ˈmau̇ntəbəl\ *adj* **:** capable of being mounted

[1]**moun·tain** \ˈmau̇nt³n, -tᵊn\ *n* -S [ME *mountaine*, fr. OF *montaigne*, fr. (assumed) VL *montanea*, fr. fem. of *montaneus* of a mountain, alter. of L *montanus*, fr. *mont-, mons* mountain + *-anus* -an — more at MOUNT] **1 a :** a steep elevation with a restricted summit area projecting 1000 feet or more above the surrounding land surface ⟨a volcanic ~⟩ **b :** a high landmass culminating in several peaks or forming an elongated ridge **c :** any conspicuous hill in an area of low relief; *esp* **:** one that is rounded at the base and has comparatively steep sides ⟨we were in what a Mississippian would call ~s but which New Englanders call hills —William Faulkner⟩ **2 a :** an enormous mass or bulk **:** HEAP, HUNK ⟨beaches crowded with ~s of supplies —H.L.Merillat⟩ ⟨a ~ of a man —E.K.Brown⟩ **b :** a vast number or quantity **:** PILE, SLEW ⟨the ~ of personnel records accumulated by the armed forces —Seth King⟩ ⟨found a ~ of work awaiting him when he got back from vacation⟩ ⟨crushed by . . . ~s of throbbing, elemental sound —*Christian Science Monitor*⟩ **c :** a major obstacle or difficulty **:** CRISIS ⟨make a ~ out of a molehill⟩ **3 :** a region characterized by mountains — usu. used in pl. ⟨preferred the ~s to the seashore⟩ **4 a** *archaic* **:** [1]MOUNT 4 **b :** [1]MOUNT 5 **5** *or* **mountain wine :** a sweet white Malaga wine made from grapes picked when thoroughly ripe

[2]**mountain** \"\ *adj* **1 :** consisting of mountains ⟨~ range⟩ ⟨~ country⟩ **2 a :** situated on a mountain or in or among mountains ⟨~ stream⟩ ⟨~ cabin⟩ ⟨a ~ republic⟩ **b :** characteristic of mountains or a mountain region ⟨~ music⟩ **c :** MONTANE ⟨~ sheep⟩ **3** *archaic* **:** HUGE, MOUNTAINOUS ⟨thy lakes and ~ hills —S.T.Coleridge⟩ **4** *usu cap* **:** ROCKY MOUNTAIN ⟨the *Mountain* states of the U. S.⟩

mountain accentor *n* **:** a Siberian oscine bird (*Prunella montanella*) related to the hedge sparrow

mountain adder *n* **:** BERG ADDER

mountain alder *n* **1 :** any of several trees of the genus *Alnus; esp* **:** a tree (*A. rhombifolia*) that is native to upland regions of the western U. S. **2 :** MOUNTAIN MAPLE

mountain andromeda *n* **:** MOUNTAIN FETTERBUSH

mountain antelope *n* **:** GOAT ANTELOPE

mountain apple *n, Hawaii* **:** MALAY APPLE

mountain ash *n* **1 :** any of various trees of the genus *Sorbus:* as **a :** ROWAN TREE 1 **b :** AMERICAN MOUNTAIN ASH **c :** WESTERN MOUNTAIN ASH **2 :** any of several Australian eucalypts (esp. *Eucalyptus sieberiana* and *E. regnans*) with deeply furrowed bark suggesting that of old trees of the genus *Fraxinus* — see AUSTRALIAN OAK **3 :** a low-growing Texas ash (*Fraxinus texensis*) having leaves with mostly five leaflets

mountain-ash sawfly *n* **:** a European sawfly (*Pristiphora geniculata*) that defoliates mountain ash in the northeastern U. S.

mountain asp *n* **:** AMERICAN ASPEN

mountain avens *n* **:** a plant of the genus *Dryas; esp* **:** an arctic or alpine plant (*D. octopetala*) having large white flowers

mountain badger *n* **:** HOARY MARMOT

mountain balm *n* **:** either of two yerba santas (*Eriodictyon californicum* or *E. angustifolium*)

mountain balsam *n* **:** any of several American firs: as **a :** a tree (*Abies fraseri*) of the Allegheníes **b :** either of two trees (*A. amabilis* or *A. lasiocarpa*) in the mountains of western U. S.

mountain banana *n* **:** FEI

mountain barometer *n* **:** a portable barometer used in measuring the heights of mountains

mountain battery *n* **:** a battery of mountain artillery

mountain beaver *n* **:** a bulky fossorial nocturnal rodent (*Aplodontia rufa*) of the uplands of the Pacific coast of No. America having small ears and eyes and a rudimentary tail and superficially resembling the ground squirrels to which it is actually but distantly related being the sole recent survivor of a once extensive group (Aplodontoidea of the Sciuromorpha), of primitive rodents that first appeared in the Paleocene

mountain beech *n, Austral & NewZeal* **:** a tree of the genus *Nothofagus*

mountain bindweed *n* **:** SOLDANELLA 2

mountain birch *n* **:** WESTERN PAPER BIRCH

mountain black snake *n* **:** PILOT BLACK SNAKE

mountain blue *n* **1 :** MINERAL BLUE 1a **2 :** AZURITE BLUE

mountain bluebird *n* **:** a bluebird (*Sialia currucoides*) of western No. America having a blue rather than a red breast

mountain bluet *n* **:** a European perennial herb (*Centaurea montana*) often cultivated for its blue flowers

mountain bobcat *n* **:** LYNX CAT

mountain boomer *n* **1 :** COLLARED LIZARD **2** *South & Midland* **:** RED SQUIRREL 1 **3** *chiefly Midland* **:** MOUNTAINEER 1

mountain box *n* **:** a common New Zealand shrub (*Veronica buxifolia*) with white flowers and leaves resembling heath

mountain breeze *n* **:** MOUNTAIN WIND

mountain brome *also* **mountain bromegrass** *n* **:** a western bromegrass (*Bromus carinatus* or *B. marginatus*) with large heavy heads that is used as a range grass

mountain bunch grass *n* **:** a forage grass (*Festuca viridula*) of the western U. S.

mountain cabbage *n* **:** a cabbage palm (*Roystonea oleracea*)

mountain caribou *n* **:** a large dark caribou (*Rangifer montanus*) found from British Columbia to Alaska and being the largest of the American caribous

mountain cat *n* **1 a :** COUGAR **b :** BAY LYNX **2 :** CACOMISTLE

mountain cedar *n* **1 :** any of various junipers; *esp* **:** ROCK CEDAR **2 :** MOUNTAIN PINE 3b

mountain cherry *n* **:** any of various trees or shrubs of the genus *Prunus; esp* **:** CHICKASAW PLUM

mountain chickadee *n* **:** a chickadee (*Penthestes gambeli*) of western No. America that resembles the black-capped chickadee but has a white line over the eye

mountain clematis *n* **:** a trailing or climbing vine (*Clematis verticellata*) of northeastern No. America having flowers with thin blue sepals and the outermost stamens usu. altered into prominently veined staminodia that resemble petals

mountain cock *n* **:** CAPERCAILLIE

mountain cork *n* **:** an asbestos resembling cork in texture and lightness — called also *rock cork*

mountain crab *n* **:** BLACK CRAB

mountain cranberry *n* **:** a low evergreen shrub (*Vaccinium vitis-idaea*) of high north temperate regions having thick oval leaves, white nodding bell-shaped flowers, and dark red berries — called also *cowberry, foxberry, lingonberry*

mountain crystal *n* **:** ROCK CRYSTAL

mountain curassow *n* **:** a curassow (*Oreophasis derbianus*) of the high mountains of Guatemala that is greenish black with white underparts and has a white tail band, red feet, and a red casque on the head

mountain currant *n* **:** ALPINE CURRANT

mountain daisy *n* **:** MOUNTAIN SANDWORT

mountain damson *n* **:** PARADISE TREE 1a

mountain devil *n* **:** MOLOCH 2b

mountain dew *n* **:** MOONSHINE 3

mountain duck *n* **1 :** HARLEQUIN DUCK **2** *Austral* **:** a sheldrake (*Casarca tadornoides*)

mountain eagle *n* **:** GOLDEN EAGLE

mountain ebony *n* **:** a small East Indian tree (*Bauhinia variegata*) having hard dark wood and bark used in tanning

moun·tained \ˈmau̇nt³nd, -tᵊnd\ *adj* [[1]*mountain* + *-ed*] *archaic* **:** heaped as high as a mountain ⟨the ~ sea —William Falconer⟩

[1]**moun·tain·eer** \ˌmau̇nt³nˈi(ə)r, -tᵊnˈi-, -iə\ *n* -S [[1]*mountain* + *-eer*] **1 a :** a native or inhabitant of a mountainous region ⟨encouraging some of these isolated ~s to come down and live in more compact settlements —B.M.Bowie⟩; *specif* **:** HILLBILLY ⟨critical of the rural . . . ~s —A.N.Votaw⟩ **b :** MOUNTAIN MAN 2 **2 :** one who climbs mountains for sport

[2]**mountaineer** \"\ *vi* -ED/-ING/-S **:** to climb mountains for sport

mountaineering *n* -S **:** the sport or technique of scaling mountains

mountain fern *n* **:** either of two common shield ferns (*Dryopteris oreopteris* or *D. phegopteris*)

mountain fetterbush *n* **:** an ornamental evergreen shrub (*Pieris floribunda*) of the southeastern U. S. with small white bell-shaped flowers — called also *mountain andromeda*

mountain fever *n* **1 :** any of various febrile diseases occurring in mountainous regions: as **a :** COLORADO TICK FEVER **b :** ROCKY MOUNTAIN SPOTTED FEVER **2 :** INFECTIOUS ANEMIA

mountain finch *n* **:** BRAMBLING

mountain flax *n* **1 a :** PURGING FLAX **b :** SENEGA ROOT **c :** a centaury (*Centaurium umbellatum*) **d :** QUAKING GRASS 1 **e :** CORN SPURRY **f :** a New Zealand herb (*Phormium cookianum*) **2 :** ASBESTOS 1,2

mountain flower *n* **:** a common Eurasian cranesbill (*Geranium sylvaticum*)

mountain fly honeysuckle *n* **:** a common erect shrub (*Lonicera villosa*) of the north temperate zone with yellow flowers and bluish black berries

mountain fringe *n* **1 :** CLIMBING FUMITORY **2 :** a wormwood (*Artemisia frigida*) of Colorado

mountain geranium *n* **:** HERB ROBERT

mountain glacier *n* **:** ALPINE GLACIER

mountain goat *n* **1 :** a goatlike animal (*Oreamnos montanus*) related to the Old World chamois being widely but sparsely distributed in the mountainous parts of northwestern No. America and having a thickset body, small black polished horns present in both sexes, a tufted chin, short legs, and a thick hairy pure white coat — called also *Rocky Mountain goat* **2 :** GOAT ANTELOPE

mountain goat 1

mountain gorilla *n* **:** a dark hairy gorilla of the mountain forests of the eastern Congo distinguished from the coast gorilla by a narrower skull and longer palate and separated as a subspecies (*Gorilla gorilla beringeri*) or sometimes as a full species (*G. beringeri*)

mountain grape *n* **1 :** SAND GRAPE **2 :** OREGON GRAPE

mountain green *n* **1 a :** MALACHITE **b :** GREEN EARTH **2 c :** CHRYSOCOLLA **d :** Paris green mixed with gypsum or barite **2 :** MALACHITE GREEN 3

mountain gum *n* **:** either of two Australian eucalypts (*Eucalyptus goniocalyx* or *E. dalrympleana*)

mountain gun *n* **:** a gun used by mountain artillery and capable of being transported on muleback

mountain hare *n* **1 a :** the American varying hare (*Lepus americanus*) **b :** the large common hare (*Lepus saxatilis*) of southern Africa **2 :** JUMPING HARE

mountain heath *n* **:** a small shrub (*Phyllodoce caerulea*) found in cool regions of the north and having tiny evergreen leaves and pink or purple flowers

mountain hemlock *n* **:** a hemlock (*Tsuga mertensiana*) of the western U. S. that attains large size and has wood much harder than that of Canadian hemlock — called also *black hemlock*

mountain hickory *n* **:** a large Australian timber tree (*Acacia penninervis*) with hard wood similar to blackwood

mountain holly *n* **1 :** a shrub (*Nemopanthus mucronata*) of the family Aquifoliaceae of eastern No. America with smooth obovate leaves and scarlet drupes — called also *Canadian holly* **2 :** an upland holly (*Ilex montana*) of the eastern U. S.

mountain holly fern *n* **:** HOLLY FERN a

mountain indigo *or* **mountain indigo bush** *n* **:** a glabrous shrub (*Amorpha glabra*) of the southeastern U. S. with broad leaflets and clustered racemes of purple flowers

mountain ivy *n, chiefly NewEng* **:** MOUNTAIN LAUREL

mountain juniper *n* **:** a depressed or trailing juniper that is a variety (*Juniperus communis saxatilis*) of the common juniper, occurs in exposed places and mountains chiefly in northeastern No. America, and has short broad curved pointed leaves with a broad white stripe

mountain laurel *n* **1 :** a No. American evergreen shrub (*Kalmia latifolia*) having glossy mostly alternate leaves and umbels of rose-colored or white flowers — called also *American laurel, calico bush* **2 :** CALIFORNIA LAUREL

mountain leather *n* **:** an absorbent asbestos occurring in thin tough flexible sheets **:** PALYGORSKITE

moun·tain·less \ˈmau̇nt³nləs, -tᵊn-\ *adj* **:** lacking mountains

mountain lilac *n* **:** a Californian shrub of the genus *Ceanothus*

mountain lily *n* **1 :** a Japanese lily (*Lilium auratum*) with showy crimson-spotted yellow-banded white flowers **2 :** a showy white-flowered buttercup (*Ranunculus lyallii*) of New Zealand **3 :** SAND LILY

mountain limestone *n* **:** a carboniferous limestone occurring in the hills and mountains of England and generally equivalent to the Mississippian of the No. American section

mountain lion *n* **:** COUGAR

mountain lover *n* **1 :** a small trailing evergreen shrub (*Pachistima canbyi*) of the southeastern U. S. **2 :** OREGON BOX

mountain magnolia *n* **:** any of several upland American magnolias (esp. *Magnolia acuminata* and *M. fraseri*)

mountain magpie *n* **1 :** GREEN WOODPECKER **2** *dial Eng* **:** a European butcher-bird (*Lanius exubitor*)

mountain mahoe *n* **:** a West Indian tree (*Hibiscus tiliaceus*) related to the majagua and having flowers that change from pale pink in the morning to deep red in the evening — compare CUBAN BAST

mountain mahogany *n* **1 :** any of several shrubs or small shrubby trees of western No. America that constitute the genus *Cercocarpus* of the family Rosaceae and are often important browse or forage plants; *esp* **:** an evergreen tree (*C. ledifolius*) with cherry red to chocolate brown very hard strong heartwood that is sometimes used for turnery and carving — see FEATHER TREE 2, HARDTACK 2 **2 :** SWEET BIRCH **3 :** a yew (*Taxus brevifolia*) of the Pacific coast of the U. S.

mountain-making \ˈ==ˌ==\ *adj* **:** causing the upthrust of mountains

mountain man *n* **1 :** MOUNTAINEER 1a **2 :** a pioneering frontiersman (as a trapper or trader) at home in wilderness country ⟨trappers, traders, scouts, hunters, guides — whatever they were . . . they were all *mountain men* —Frank Waters⟩ ⟨all the way across the continent there would be an advance screen of long hunters and *mountain men* —Bernard DeVoto⟩

mountain maple *n* **:** any of various American shrubby maples found in mountain regions: as **a :** a tall shrub or bushy tree (*Acer spicatum*) of the eastern U. S. with flaky or furrowed bark and slender cylindrical panicles of greenish flowers — called also *moose maple, mountain alder* **b :** DWARF MAPLE **c :** VINE MAPLE

mountain mint *n* **1 :** an American mint of the genus *Pycnanthemum; esp* **:** BASIL MINT **2 :** CALAMINT **3 :** OSWEGO TEA

mountain misery *n* **:** a California undershrub (*Chamaebatia foliolosa*) having dark green fernlike leaves and a fragrant gummy exudate — called also *bear clover, bear mat*

mountain oak *n* **:** a chestnut oak (*Quercus montana*)

mountain of venus *usu cap V* [trans. of NL *mons Veneris*] **:** MONS VENERIS

moun·tain·ous \ˈmau̇nt(³)nəs, -tᵊn-\ *adj* [[1]*mountain* + *-ous*] **1 :** characterized by mountains ⟨turn eastward into the ~ Vermont wilderness —Budd Schulberg⟩ **2 :** resembling a mountain **:** HUGE, GIGANTIC ⟨rescued from the ~ seas —*News from New Zealand*⟩ ⟨seemed slender beside that ~ woman —Ann Bridge⟩ **3** *obs* **:** leading a primitive life in an inaccessible mountain region ⟨this wild ~ people —Samuel Purchas⟩ **4** *archaic* **:** MOUNTAIN 2a ⟨the ash and other ~ trees —Richard Warner⟩ — **moun·tain·ous·ly** *adv*

moun·tain·ous·ness *n* -ES **:** the quality or state of being mountainous

mountain oyster *n* **:** the testis of a bull calf, sheep, boar, or other animal used as food — called also *Rocky Mountain oyster*

mountain paca *n* **:** any of several rodents of the mountains of western So. America that constitute a genus (*Stictomys*) closely related to *Dasyprocta*

mountain panther *n* **1 :** SNOW LEOPARD **2 :** COUGAR

mountain paper *n* **:** an asbestos resembling mountain leather

mountain parrot *n* **:** KEA

mountain parsley *n* **1 :** a European herb (*Peucedanum oreoselinum*) having an aromatic seed and root **2 :** PARSLEY FERN b(2)

mountain partridge *n* **1 :** PARTRIDGE DOVE **2 :** MOUNTAIN QUAIL

mountain pheasant *n, South* **:** RUFFED GROUSE

mountain phlox *n* **1 :** a common mountain herb (*Phlox ovata*) of the southeastern U. S. having showy pink or red flowers **2 :** MOSS PINK

mountain pine *n* **1 a :** any of several pines of the U. S.; *esp* **:** a tall western timber tree (*Pinus monticola*) resembling the white pine **b** (1) **:** SWISS MOUNTAIN PINE (2) **:** MUGHO PINE **2 :** any of several Australian upland cypress pines (as black cypress pine or white cypress pine) **3 :** either of two New Zealand trees: **a :** a tree of the genus *Dacrydium* having tough wood and foliage that resembles cedar **b :** an evergreen tree (*Libocedrus bidwillii*) resembling the kawaka — called also *kaikawaka*

mountain pine beetle *n* **:** a bark beetle (*Dendroctonus ponderosae*) of the western U. S. that is extremely destructive to stands of lodgepole and sugar pines

mountain pink *n* **:** MOSS PINK

mountain plover *n* **:** a small plover (*Eupoda montana*) of the plains of the western U. S.

mountain plum *n* **:** the false sandalwood or its fruit

mountain pride *n* **:** a pentstemon (*Pentstemon newberryi*) of the mountains of California having pinkish to lavender open-mouthed flowers

mountain quail *n* **:** a partridge (*Oreortyx picta palmeri*) of California slightly larger than the California quail

mountain railroad *or* **mountain railway** *n* **:** a railroad employing special devices (as cables, racks and pinions, central rails) to hold the cars on the steep track — compare FUNICULAR

mountain range *n* **:** a series of mountains or mountain ridges closely related in position and direction — compare OROGEN

mountain raspberry *n* **:** CLOUDBERRY

mountain rat *n* **:** a bushy-tailed wood rat (*Neotoma cinerea*) of the western U. S.

mountain rice *n* **:** BUNCHGRASS; *esp* **:** a valuable forage grass (*Oryzopsis hymenoides*) that is widely distributed in dry upland areas and plains of western No. America

mountain rimu *n* **:** a prostrate or suberect shrub (*Dacrydium laxifolium*) of New Zealand with slender trailing branches
mountain rose *n* **1 :** a European alpine rose (*Rosa pendulina*) with crimson flowers **2 :** CORALVINE **3 :** CATAWBA RHODODENDRON
mountain rosebay *n* **:** CATAWBA RHODODENDRON
mountains *pl of* MOUNTAIN
mountain sage *n* **1 :** any of several plants of the genus *Artemisia* **2 :** WOOD SAGE 1
mountain sandwort *or* **mountain starwort** *n* **:** a boreal or alpine sandwort (*Arenaria groenlandica*) with subulate or filiform leaf blades and small white flowers — called also *mountain daisy*
mountain sheep *n* **:** any of various wild sheep inhabiting high mountains in different parts of the world — compare AOUDAD, ARGALI, BIGHORN, DALL SHEEP
mountain sickness *n* **:** altitude sickness experienced by mountain climbers or by those ascending or living above 10,000 feet elevation and caused by insufficient oxygen in the air breathed
mountainside \ˈ⸗⸗,⸗\ *n* **:** a part of a mountain between the summit and the foot ⟨from every ~ let freedom ring —S.F. Smith⟩
mountain snow *n* **:** SNOW-ON-THE-MOUNTAIN
mountain soap *n* **:** SAPONITE
mountain sorrel *n* **:** a low perennial herb (*Oxyria digyna*) found in northern latitudes in both hemispheres and having kidney-shaped leaves and greenish flowers
mountain sparrow *n* **:** TREE SPARROW 1
mountain specter *n* **:** BROCKEN SPECTER
mountain spinach *n* **:** GARDEN ORACHE
mountain spleenwort *n* **:** a spleenwort (*Asplenium montanum*) of eastern No. America
mountain spruce *n* **:** ENGELMANN SPRUCE
mountain sucker *n* **:** any of several small suckers of the genus *Pantosteus* widely distributed in upland areas of the western U.S.
mountain sumac *n* **1 :** DWARF SUMAC **2 :** AMERICAN MOUNTAIN ASH
mountain tea *n* **1 :** WINTERGREEN 2a **2 :** an infusion of wintergreen leaves
mountain tent *n* **:** a lightweight usu. wedge-shaped tent having a floor and zippered doorway
mountain thrush *n* **1** *dial Eng* **:** RING OUZEL **2 :** an Australian thrush (*Zoothera dauma lunulata*)
mountain time *or* **mountain standard time** *n, often cap M* **:** the time of the 7th time zone west of Greenwich that is based on the 105th meridian, is used in the west central Canada and the U.S., and is two hours slower than eastern time — abbr. *MT* or *MST*
mountain timothy *n* **:** a north temperate perennial grass (*Phleum alpinum*) with ovoid or short cylindrical panicles
mountaintop \ˈ⸗⸗,⸗\ *n* **:** the summit of a mountain
mountain trout *n* **1 :** BROOK TROUT **2 :** an Australian upland minnow (*Galaxias coxi*)
mountain vizcacha *n* **:** any of several vizcachas constituting the genus *Lagidium* and living in mountainous parts of western So. America
mountain wall *n* **:** a steep mountainside
moun·tain·ward \ˈmau̇ntᵊnwə(r)d, -tᵊn-\ *or* **moun·tain·wards** \-dz\ *adv* **:** toward the mountains
mountain watercress *n* **:** a bitter cress (*Cardamine rotundifolia*) of streams and damp places of the mountains of eastern No. America having diffuse reclining or trailing stems and simple rounded leaves
mountain white *n* **:** a white person inhabiting a mountain region esp. in the southeastern U.S. ⟨the poor *mountain whites,* primitive, rugged, proud —*Amer. Guide Series: Va.*⟩
mountain willow *n* **1 :** a much-branched shrubby willow (*Salix planifolia*) of Europe and northeastern No. America **2 :** a tree willow (*Salix scouleriana*) of uplands in the western U.S.
mountain wind *n* **:** a breeze of diurnal period depending on the unevenness of land surfaces and blowing down the slope by night — called also *mountain breeze;* compare VALLEY WIND
mountain winterberry *n* **:** MOUNTAIN HOLLY 2
mountain witch *n* **:** a quail dove (*Geotrygon versicolor*) of the West Indies
mountain wood *n* **:** compact fibrous asbestos resembling dry wood in appearance
moun·tainy \ˈmau̇nt(ᵊ)nē, -tᵊnē, -ni\ *adj* **1 a :** full of mountains **:** MOUNTAINOUS ⟨~ mass —Rose Macaulay⟩ **b :** of, relating to, or characteristic of mountainous regions **:** MOUNTAIN ⟨worked on a ~ farm —F.M.Ford⟩ ⟨passed from ~ foothills, through green slopes, lush flatlands, and desert —A.J. Liebling⟩ **2 :** living in or associated with the mountains ⟨an old ~ man that had a shirt and trousers of unbleached flannel —W.B.Yeats⟩ ⟨a ~ man and not used to horses —B.T. Cleeve⟩
mountain zebra *n* **:** a narrow-striped now nearly extinct zebra (*Equus zebra zebra*) of southern Africa
moun·tant \ˈmau̇ntᵊnt\ *n* -s [²*mount* + *-ant*] **1 :** an adhesive used for fastening a print or drawing to a mount **2 :** any substance in which a specimen is suspended between a slide and a cover glass for microscopic examination
¹**moun·te·bank** \ˈmau̇ntə,baŋk, -aiŋk\ *n* -s [It *montambanco, montimbanco,* fr. *montare* to mount, climb (fr. — assumed — VL) + *in* in, on (fr. L) + *banco, banca* bench — more at MOUNT, IN, BANK] **1 a :** an itinerant hawker of pills and patent medicines **:** PITCHMAN, QUACK ⟨bought an unction of a ~ —Shak.⟩ **b :** an entertainer (as a juggler or magician) employed by a quack to attract a crowd ⟨three or four ~*s* . . . manipulated their blue and yellow lion —Nora Waln⟩ **2 :** a pretender to competence or knowledge **:** CHARLATAN, SWINDLER ⟨almost all politicians were frauds and ~*s* —J.T.Farrell⟩
²**mountebank** *vt, obs* **:** to beguile or transform by trickery ⟨I'll ~ their loves —Shak.⟩ ⟨amazed to see their money ~*ed* to mercury —Daniel Defoe⟩ ~ *vi* **:** to play the mountebank ⟨you'd better stop ~*ing* round this town —J.B.Priestley⟩
moun·te·bank·ery \-ŋk(ə)rē\ *n* -ES **1 :** CHARLATANRY, HOCUS-POCUS **2 :** an action characteristic of a mountebank ⟨this is wonderful ~ . . . at once pathetic and uproarious —*N.Y. Times*⟩
mounted *adj* [fr. past part. of ²*mount*] **1** *archaic* **:** piled high **:** heaped up ⟨the farthest bourn of ~ eastern cloud —George Meredith⟩ **2 a :** seated or riding on a horse **:** serving on horseback ⟨~ police⟩ **b :** provided with a means of transportation ⟨a ~ messenger shall record the actual number of times he stops his vehicle to make a delivery —*U.S. Post Office Manual*⟩ **c :** performed with the aid of a means of transportation ⟨no ~ patrol⟩ ⟨no ~ collection is needed in strictly residential territory —*U.S. Post Office Manual*⟩ **3 :** being in working order or placed in position for firing ⟨a completely ~ rifle⟩ ⟨the quarter-deck guns all adrift, and not even ~ —Frederick Marryat⟩ **4 a :** assembled or equipped for use esp. by being attached to a support ⟨tractors with ~ implements —Roy Lewis & Angus Maude⟩ **b :** prepared for display esp. by being furnished with an appropriate frame or setting ⟨~ engraving⟩ ⟨thousands of ~ specimens of tiger beetles —R.K.Plumb⟩; *specif* **:** decorated with applied ornamentation ⟨spied the trim, brass ~ carbine of the ranger —F.V.W. Mason⟩ **c** *of a gemstone* **:** backed with enamel, foil, or dye in order to improve the color **d :** having the pipes displayed as part of the organ case or otherwise specially set up — used of a pipe-organ stop **5 :** equipped with scenery, lighting, costumes, and properties ⟨learn what she is thinking through an impressionistically ~ sound flashback —Lewis Jacobs⟩
mounted delivery *n* **:** mail delivery by uniformed carriers using mail trucks in a suburban area too heavily populated for rural free delivery
mounted route *n* **:** a postal route served by mounted delivery
mounted work *n* **:** silverware with ornaments soldered on
mount·er \ˈmau̇ntə(r)\ *n* -s **:** one that mounts: as **a :** a jewelry worker who fashions settings **b :** a worker who mounts optical lenses in frames **c :** a setter of watch jewels **d :** an assembler of radios or radio tubes **e :** a craftsman who attaches carvings and other decorations to furniture **f :** a machine for attaching or inserting small pieces of paper or film in or to a punched card
mount·ie *also* **mounty** \ˈmau̇ntē, -ti\ *n, pl* **mounties** *usu cap* [*mounted* policeman + *-ie, -y*] **:** a member of the Royal Canadian Mounted Police ⟨a *Mountie* always gets his man⟩
¹**mount·ing** \ˈmau̇ntiŋ, -tēŋ\ *n* -s [ME, fr. gerund of *mounten* to mount — more at MOUNT] **1 :** an act or instance of mounting; *specif* **:** getting on a horse ⟨one method of ~ is to place the left foot in the stirrup and swing the right leg over the saddle⟩ **2 :** FRAME, SUPPORT, EMBELLISHMENT: as **a :** a jewelry setting ⟨bought a ~ for the pearl —Lynn Groh⟩ **b :** a handle, mount, or coupling for a mechanical device ⟨the ~ of the sword was encrusted with jewels⟩ ⟨guns . . . on portable carriages or stationary ~*s* —*Notes & Queries on Anthropology*⟩ ⟨engines . . . attached to the frame at two, three, or four points according to the type of ~ —Joseph Heitner⟩ **c :** MOUNT 2b ⟨an interesting picture enhanced by an artistic ~⟩ **d :** the harness of a loom **e :** the nonoptical parts of a telescope (as the pier, axes, circles, and tubes); *specif* **:** the standard or support of a telescope ⟨an equatorial ~⟩ **3 :** the decor and lighting of a theatrical production as distinguished from its performance **:** STAGING ⟨technicolor gives the picture a fairly handsome ~ —*Time*⟩
²**moun·ting** \"\ *dial var of* MOUNTAIN
mounting medium *n* **:** a medium in which a biological specimen is mounted for preservation or display
mount of apollo *usu cap M&A* [after *Apollo,* Greco-Roman god associated with the sun] **:** a mount located at the base of the third finger that when well developed is usu. held by palmists to indicate a love for all things beautiful and artistic — called also *Mount of Brilliancy, Mount of the Sun;* see PALMISTRY illustration
mount of brilliancy *usu cap M&B* **:** MOUNT OF APOLLO
mount of jupiter *usu cap M&J* [after *Jupiter,* Roman god of the sky, fr. L *Juppiter* — more at DEITY] **:** a mount located at the base of the first finger that when well developed is usu. held by palmists to indicate ambition, pride, enthusiasm, and desire for power — see PALMISTRY illustration
mount of luna *usu cap M&L* [*luna* fr. L, moon — more at LUNAR] **:** a mount located on the side of the hand below lower Mars and across the palm from the Mount of Venus that when well developed is usu. held by palmists to indicate refinement, imagination, idealism, and a taste for things romantic and beautiful — called also *Mount of the Moon;* see PALMISTRY illustration
mount of mars *usu cap both Ms* [after *Mars,* Roman god of war and agriculture, fr. L *Mart-, Mars*] **1 :** UPPER MARS **2 :** LOWER MARS
mount of melody *usu cap both Ms* **:** MOUNT OF VENUS
mount of mercury *usu cap both Ms* [after *Mercury,* Roman god of commerce, fr. L *Mercurius*] **:** a mount located at the base of the little finger that when well developed is usu. held by palmists to indicate a predominance of practical qualities (as shrewdness, diplomacy, and adaptability) that often lead to success in business and politics — see PALMISTRY illustration
mount of saturn *usu cap M&S* [after *Saturn,* Roman god connected with the sowing of seed, fr. L *Saturnus*] **:** a mount located at the base of the second finger that when well developed is usu. held by palmists to indicate seriousness, prudence, and often a love of quiet and solitude — see PALMISTRY illustration
mount of the moon *usu cap both Ms* **:** MOUNT OF LUNA
mount of the sun *usu cap M&S* **:** MOUNT OF APOLLO
mount of venus *usu cap M&V* [after *Venus,* Roman goddess of love — more at VENUS] **:** a mount constituted by the large development of the hand at the base of the thumb that when well developed is held by palmists to indicate affection, sympathy, sexual attraction, and love of beauty, color, and melody — called also *Mount of Melody;* see PALMISTRY illustration
mounts *pl of* MOUNT, *pres 3d sing of* MOUNT
mounture *n* -s [²*mount* + *-ure*] *obs* **:** the angle of a gun when raised for firing
mounty *usu cap, var of* MOUNTIE
mourn \ˈmō(ə)rn, ˈmȯ(ə)rn, ˈmōən, ˈmȯ(ə)n\ *vb* -ED/-ING/-S [ME *mournen, mornen,* fr. OE *murnan;* akin to OHG *mornēn* to mourn, sorrow, ON *morna,* Goth *maurnan* to mourn, sorrow, Gk *mermeros* anxious — more at MEMORY] *vi* **1 a :** to be sorry **:** feel or express deep regret ⟨announced his resignation and everybody ~*ed*⟩ **b** *archaic* **:** to look or act unhappy **:** DROOP, PINE ⟨flowers . . . rejoice at the presence of the sun; and ~ at the absence thereof —Francis Bacon⟩ ⟨cattle ~*ed* for want of milkers —Samuel Purchas⟩ **2 a :** to be sorrowful over a death **:** GRIEVE ⟨time is the great solace of those who ~⟩ ⟨a service which seems spoken by the dead man himself to those who ~ —Walter Besant & James Rice⟩ **b :** to exhibit the conventional signs of mourning; *esp* **:** to wear black ⟨grieve for an hour, perhaps, then ~ a year —Alexander Pope⟩ **3 a :** to murmur mournfully — used esp. of doves **b** *dial* **:** MOAN ~ *vt* **1 :** to be distressed over **:** BEWAIL, PROTEST ⟨led a funeral procession up . . . Fifth Avenue to ~ pogroms —*Time*⟩ ⟨hair-splitting statesmen . . . may ~ the passing of our subjunctive —Weston La Barre⟩ **2 :** to grieve for (someone who has died) ⟨she was ~*ed* by thousands of persons whose lives she had touched —A.J.Kennedy⟩ **3 :** to utter mournfully ⟨let the whirlwind ~ its requiem —W.S.Gilbert⟩ **syn** see GRIEVE
mourn·er \-nə(r)\ *n* -s [ME *morener,* fr. *mournen, mornen* to mourn + *-er*] **1 a :** one that mourns ⟨the book business has outlived most of its ~*s* —Aaron Sussman⟩; *esp* **:** one who attends a funeral out of respect or affection for the deceased ⟨when he died, the wayward boys he had befriended were among his chief ~*s*⟩ **b :** one hired to attend a funeral or wail for the dead ⟨~*s* were provided to attend the funeral —Roger L'Estrange⟩ **2 :** one that publicly repents of his sins at a revival meeting ⟨asks for ~*s* to come up and be saved —J.H. Stuart⟩
mourners' bench *n* **:** ANXIOUS BENCH 1
mourn·ful \-nfəl\ *adj, sometimes* **mournfuller;** *sometimes* **mournfullest 1 a :** full of sorrow **:** SAD ⟨stared with ~ eyes at a daydream of her lost husband —Eric Linklater⟩ **b :** causing sorrow **:** SADDENING ⟨~ news⟩ **2 a :** of a melancholy nature **:** DOLEFUL, DISPIRITED ⟨took a ~ view of human affairs —Ellen Glasgow⟩ ⟨in a ~ rehearsal in Philadelphia I read to my dancers . . . and they took heart —Agnes de Mille⟩ **b :** having a gloomy sound or aspect **:** DISMAL, SOMBER ⟨a long, ~ howl —Lyle Saxon⟩ ⟨the ~ tolling of a bell —Jack London⟩ ⟨a country of ~ cedar thickets —*Amer. Guide Series: Tenn.*⟩ **3 :** causing disappointment **:** REGRETTABLE ⟨a ~ obtuseness of moral feeling in regard to the crimes of military and political life —W.E. Channing⟩ — **mourn·ful·ly** \-fəlē, -li\ *adv*
mourn·ful·ness \-lnəs\ *n* -ES **:** the quality or state of being mournful
mourn·ing \ˈmō(ə)rniŋ, ˈmȯ(ə)rn-, ˈmōən-, ˈmȯ(ə)n-, -nēŋ\ *n* -s [ME *mourning, morning,* fr. gerund of *mournen, mornen,* to mourn — more at MOURN] **1 :** an act or instance of feeling or expressing sorrow ⟨general ~ over loss of the championship⟩; *specif* **:** grief caused by bereavement ⟨a sound of ~ came from the dead man's room⟩ **2 a :** the ritual observances accompanying a death ⟨~ is repeated for all those who have died during the last few years —*Drums and Shadows*⟩; *specif* **:** the wearing of black ⟨~ is traditional for pallbearers⟩ **b :** the black clothing, draperies, or emblems symbolic of grief esp. among western nations ⟨didn't believe in old-fashioned ~ . . . nobody wore it any longer —Margaret A. Barnes⟩ ⟨lots of people there, and only one man in full ~ —Arnold Bennett⟩ ⟨the room had been cleaned and the ~ pinned up again in newspapers —Ellen Glasgow⟩ — compare CRAPE 3a, ³WEED 2 **c :** the period during which black is worn by a mourner ⟨after a long ~, resume their ordinary dresses —Henry Reed †1854⟩
mourning bride *n* **:** a plant of the genus *Scabiosa; esp* **:** a half-hardy annual (*S. atropurpurea*)
mourning cloak *or* **mourning cloak butterfly** *n* **:** a blackish brown butterfly (*Nymphalis antiopa*) with a broad yellow border on the wings found in Europe and No. America and having dark spiny larvae that live in clusters esp. on elm, willow and hackberry — called also *Camberwell beauty*
mourning dove *n* **:** a wild dove (*Zenaidura macroura carolinensis*) of the U.S. resembling the passenger pigeon in form and plumage though much smaller, having a plaintive note and being represented by distinct subspecies in Cuba and western No. America
mourn·ing·ly *adv* **:** MOURNFULLY
mourning of the chine [by folk etymology fr. MF *mort de eschine,* lit., death of the spine] *obs* **:** GLANDERS
mourning warbler *n* **:** a warbler (*Oporornis philadelphia*) of eastern No. America, the male having the head, neck, and chest deep ash gray mixed with black on the throat and chest with the lower parts pure yellow
mour·ni·val \ˈmōrnəvəl\ *n* -s [MF *mornifle*] **1** *archaic* **:** a set of four aces, kings, queens, or knaves in one hand in the game of gleek **2** *obs* **:** a group of four ⟨a ~ of protests; or a gleek at least —Ben Jonson⟩
mourns *pres 3d sing of* MOURN
mous *pl of* MOU
¹**mouse** \ˈmau̇s\ *n, pl* **mice** \ˈmīs\ *often attrib* [ME *mous,* fr. OE *mūs;* akin to OHG & ON *mūs* mouse, L *mus,* Gk *mys,* Skt *mūs* mouse, and perh. to L *movēre* to move — more at MOVE] **1 a :** any of numerous small rodents typically resembling diminutive rats with pointed snout, rather small ears, elongated body, and slender hairless or sparsely haired tail, including all the smaller members of the genus *Mus* and many members of other rodent genera and families having little more in common than their relatively small size — see HARVEST MOUSE, HOUSE MOUSE, JUMPING MOUSE, POCKET MOUSE, WHITE-FOOTED MOUSE **b :** a young muskrat **2 a** *slang* **:** WOMAN, GIRL FRIEND ⟨in the role of . . . the rich Chicago ~ —*Playbill*⟩ ⟨the ~ he was shackin' up with —Earle Birney⟩ **b :** a timid or diffident person ⟨he might be a lion, but in . . . public affairs he must remain a ~ —W.H.Hale⟩ **c :** something trivial or insignificant ⟨labors over a mountain of the chaff of experience to bring forth a poor ~ of reflection —Edward Sapir⟩ **3 :** something that resembles a mouse: as **a** *archaic* **:** a small lump of muscle meat **b (1)** *archaic* **:** a knot on a ship's stays to prevent a rope from slipping **(2) :** MOUSING **c :** a dark-colored swelling caused by a blow ⟨a heavy right to the cheekbone . . . raised a ~ —*New South Wales Bull.*⟩; *specif* **:** BLACK EYE 1a ⟨began the voyage by hanging a ~ on the steward's eye —*Time*⟩ **d :** RAT 3 **e (1) :** a small lead weight fastened to a string and used to pull window sash cords into place over pulleys in the jambs of the frame **(2) :** a similar weight used by plumbers to clear a stoppage in a pipe **(3) :** a loose-fitting plug that is forced through a conduit by compressed air and carries with it wires to be drawn into place **4 a :** an olive gray — called also *beige gray* **b :** MOUSE GRAY

mouse 1a

²**mouse** \ˈmau̇z, ˈmau̇s\ *vb* -ED/-ING/-S [ME *mousen,* fr. *mous,* n.] *vi* **1 :** to hunt for or catch mice ⟨the large white owl . . . *moused* in the long grass —Charlotte Yonge⟩ **2 a :** to poke around or make a curious inspection **:** EXPLORE, SNOOP ⟨go *mousing* around libraries . . . looking for dead facts —Garrett Mattingly⟩ ⟨*mousing* politicians —Telford Taylor⟩ **b :** to move stealthily or slowly **:** CREEP, SAUNTER ⟨walked eastward, *mousing* doggedly along on the shady side —John Galsworthy⟩ ⟨just ~ along, putting one sadde shoe in front of the other —Peg Bracken⟩ ~ *vt* **1** *obs* **a :** NIBBLE, GNAW ⟨death . . . feasts, *mousing* the flesh of men —Shak.⟩ **b :** to harass playfully **:** toy with — used chiefly in the phrase *touse and mouse* ⟨none but naughty women sat there, whom they toused and *moused* —William Wycherley⟩ **2 :** to apply a mousing to (a hook) **3 :** to discover by painstaking search — usu. used with *out* ⟨~ out a neighborhood scandal⟩
mousebane \ˈ⸗,⸗\ *n* **:** a common European monkshood (*Aconitum napellus*) with poisonous foliage
mouse barley *n* **:** WALL BARLEY
mousebird \ˈ⸗,⸗\ *n* **1 :** COLY **2 :** WHITE-RUMPED SHRIKE
mouse bloodwort *n* **:** MOUSE-EAR 1a
mouse bur *n* **:** UNICORN PLANT
mouse-colored \ˈ⸗¦⸗⸗\ *adj* **:** of the color mouse-gray
mouse deer *n* **:** CHEVROTAIN
mouse-ear \ˈ⸗,⸗\ *n* [ME *mousere,* fr. *mous* mouse + *ere* ear — more at EAR] **1 a** *or* **mouse-ear hawkweed :** a European hawkweed (*Hieracium pilosella*) having soft hairy leaves — called also *felon herb, mouse bloodwort* **b** *or* **mouse-ear everlasting** *or* **mouse-ear plantain :** an everlasting (*Antennaria plantaginifolia*) with soft gray leaves — called also *cat's-foot* **c :** MARSH CUDWEED **2 :** FORGET-ME-NOT 1a
mouse-ear chickweed *or* **mouse-eared chickweed** *also* **mouse-ear** *n* **:** any of several hairy chickweeds of the genus *Cerastium* (esp. *C. vulgatum* and *C. viscosum*) — called also *clammy chickweed*
mouse-ear cress *also* **mouse-ear** *n* **:** a Eurasian herb (*Arabidopsis thaliana*) naturalized as a weed in the U.S.
mouse-eared \ˈ⸗¦⸗\ *adj* **:** having an appendage suggestive of the ear of a mouse
mousefish \ˈ⸗,⸗\ *n* **:** a common sargassum fish (*Histrio pictus*)
mouse galago *n* **:** a West African galago (*Galago demidoffi*)
mouse gray *or* **mouse dun** *n* **:** a brownish gray that is lighter, stronger, and slightly yellower than taupe, yellower and lighter than chocolate, and lighter and slightly redder and stronger than castor — called also *boulevard, murinus, Sakkara, sparrow*
mouse hare *n* **:** PIKA
mousehawk \ˈ⸗,⸗\ *n* **1** *dial* **:** OWL **2** *dial* **:** any of several hawks (as the marsh hawk or the rough-legged hawk)
mousehole \ˈ⸗,⸗\ *n* [ME *mousholе,* fr. *mous* mouse + *hole*] **1 a :** a mouse's burrow **b :** a small hole (as in a baseboard) gnawed by a mouse **2 a :** a small opening or passageway **b :** a small space used for storage or for living quarters **:** CUBBY
mousehunt \ˈ⸗,⸗\ *n, dial chiefly Eng* **:** WEASEL
mouse·kin \ˈmau̇skən\ *n* -s [¹*mouse* + *-kin*] **:** a little mouse
mouse lemur *n* **:** any of several small lemurs (as a dwarf lemur or a member of the genus *Cheirogaleus*)
mouse·let \ˈmau̇slət\ *or* **mouse·ling** \-liŋ, -lēŋ\ *n* -s **:** a small or baby mouse
mouselike \ˈ⸗,⸗\ *adj* **1 :** of, relating to, or characteristic of a mouse ⟨~ tail⟩ **2 :** resembling a mouse in nondescript coloring or timidity of behavior ⟨~ clerk⟩ ⟨a nervous, nondescript, ~ little man⟩
mouse opossum *n* **1 :** an opossum of the genus *Marmosa* **2 :** DORMOUSE OPOSSUM
mouse owl *n* **:** SHORT-EARED OWL
mousepox \ˈ⸗,⸗\ *n* **:** a virus disease of mice that is related to smallpox — called also *ectromelia, infectious ectromelia*
mouseproof \ˈ⸗¦⸗\ *adj* **:** proof against mice ⟨store grain in a ~ shed⟩
mous·er \ˈmau̇zə(r), -au̇sə-\ *n* -s [ME *mowsare,* fr. *mowsen, mousen* to mouse + *-are, -er* -er — more at MOUSE] **:** one that catches mice and rats; *esp* **:** a cat or other animal that habitually catches mice
mous·ery \ˈmau̇s(ə)rē, -ri\ *n* -ES **1 :** a place inhabited by a colony of mice or voles **2 :** a place where mice are bred and reared in captivity
mousetail \ˈ⸗,⸗\ *n* **1 :** a plant of the genus *Myosurus; esp* **:** a plant (*M. minimus*) with a flower whose receptacle looks like a tail **2 :** any of various plants with an inflorescence resembling a tail
mouse-tailed bat \ˈ⸗¦⸗-\ *n* **:** any of several rather small insectivorous bats (genus *Rhinopoma*) having a long tail, a reduced interfemoral membrane, and two joints to the index finger and being widely distributed in northern Africa and southern Asia
¹**mousetrap** \ˈ⸗,⸗\ *n* [ME *mowse trape,* fr. *mowse, mous* mouse + *trape, trappe* trap — more at TRAP] **1 a :** a trap for mice **b :** a sharp cheese of the type used for baiting a mousetrap ⟨that wonderful uniform cheddar we call . . . ~ —R.W.Howard⟩ **2 :** something that resembles a mousetrap: as **a :** a stratagem that lures one to defeat or destruction; *specif* **:** a football play in which a defensive player is allowed to cross the line of scrimmage and is unexpectedly blocked from the side while the ball carrier advances through the spot he has vacated — called also *trap, trap play* **b :** a small place **:** HOLE-IN-THE-WALL ⟨this pitiable young man shutting himself up in a ~ —Rebecca West⟩ **c :** a fishing tool for removing small objects from a drilled well **d :** a new or improved product that attracts attention in a highly competi-

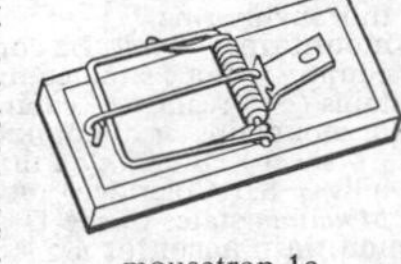
mousetrap 1a

tive market ⟨current experiments amount to attempts at building a better ~ —Paul Haney⟩

²mousetrap \"\ *vt* **:** to snare in or as if in a mousetrap ⟨two prize motorized armor divisions . . . had been *mousetrapped*, and subsequently destroyed —P.W.Thompson⟩ ⟨~ a politician into a damaging statement⟩; *specif* **:** to block out (a defensive lineman) in a football game by means of the mousetrap play

mouse·web \ˈmü,sweb, ˈmüz,w-\ *n, chiefly Scot* **:** COBWEB

mousey *var of* MOUSY

mousier *comparative of* MOUSY

mousiest *superlative of* MOUSY

mous·i·ly \ˈmau̇səlē, -au̇zə-, -li\ *adv* **:** in a mousy manner **:** QUIETLY, TIMIDLY

mous·i·ness \-sēnəs, -sin-, -zēn-, -zin-\ *n* -ES **:** the quality or state of being mousy **:** DRABNESS, TIMIDITY

mousing *n* -s [fr. gerund of ²*mouse*] **1 :** the pursuit or extermination of mice and rats ⟨cats were used for ~ —G.B.Saul⟩ **2 :** a turn or lashing (as of rope yarn) used by seamen esp. across the open end of a hook to prevent the load carried from slipping off

mousle *vt* [freq. of ²*mouse*] *obs* **:** MOUSE 1b

mous·que·taire \ˌmüskəˈta(a)(ə)r, -te(ə)r, -ta(a)ə, -teə\ *n* -s [F — more at MUSKETEER] **1** *usu cap* **:** a French musketeer; *esp* **:** one of the royal musketeers of the 17th and 18th centuries conspicuous for their daring and their dandified dress **2** *usu* **mousquetaire glove :** a woman's long gauntlet glove often made with a lengthwise buttoned opening at the wrist

mousse \ˈmüs\ *n* -s [F, lit., froth, fr. LL *mulsa* hydromel, fr. L, fem. of *mulsus* mixed with honey, sweet as honey — more at MULSE] **1 a :** a frothy dessert; *esp* **:** a dessert of sweetened and flavored whipped cream, or thin cream and gelatin, frozen without stirring **b :** a purée of meat or fish lightened with gelatin or whipped cream or both ⟨chicken ~⟩ **c** *also* **mousse·line** \ˌmüsˈlēn, -üsəˈl-\ **:** a food so prepared as to be light, spongy, or creamy in texture and usu. containing gelatin, cream, or whites of eggs ⟨broccoli ~⟩ — compare SOUFFLÉ **2 :** MOSS GREEN

mousse·line \(ˈ)müsˈlēn, -üsəˈl-\ *n* -s [F, lit., muslin — more at MUSLIN] **1 :** a fine sheer clothing fabric of silk, rayon, wool, or cotton that resembles muslin and has a crisp finish **2 a** *or* **mousseline sauce :** a frothy sauce or purée made so by the addition of whipped cream or beaten egg whites; *specif* **:** hollandaise sauce to which whipped cream or beaten egg whites have been added **b :** MOUSSE 1c ⟨a fluffy ~ of potatoes —*Mag. of Books*⟩

mousseline de laine \-dəˈlān\ *n* [F, lit., woolen muslin] **:** DELAINE 1

mousseline de soie \-də̇ˈswä\ *n, pl* **mousselines de soie** [F, lit., silk muslin] **:** a silk muslin resembling chiffon but having a crisp finish and used esp. for evening dresses and trimmings

moussena *var of* MESENNA

mous·tache *or* **mus·tache** \ˈməˌstash, ˌməˈs-, -taa(ə)sh, -taish *also* ˌməˈs- *or* -täsh\ *n* -s [MF *moustache*, fr. OIt *mustaccio*, *mostaccio*, *mostacchio*, fr. MGk *moustaki*, fr. Gk (Doric) *mystak-*, *mystax* upper lip, moustache; akin to Gk (Attic) *mastax* mouth, jaws — more at MOUTH] **1 :** the hair growing on a man's or a woman's upper lip or that on either side of the upper lip ⟨a pair of ~s⟩ **2 :** something that resembles a moustache: as **a :** hair or bristles growing around the mouth of an animal **b :** a conspicuous stripe of color on the side of the head beneath the eye of a bird

moustache cup *n* **:** a cup having a guard to keep the moustache out of the liquid while one is drinking

moustache cup

mous·tached *or* **mus·tached** \(ˈ)məˈ-stasht, -taa(ə)sht, -taisht *also* -täsht *or* ˌməˈs-\ *adj* **:** having a moustache

moustache monkey *also* **moustache** *n* -s **:** a guenon of western Africa (*Cercopithecus cephus*) having a bluish face with a white stripe on the upper lip

mous·tach·ial *pronunc at* MOUSTACHE +ēəl\ *adj* **:** having or being a color marking suggesting a moustache — used of a bird

moustachio *var of* MUSTACHIO

mous·te·ri·an *or* **mous·tie·ri·an** \(ˈ)müˈsti(ə)rēən\ *adj, usu cap* [F *moustérien, moustiérien*, fr. Le Moustier, cave in Dordogne dept. in southwestern France where archeological finds were made + F *-ien* -ian] **:** of, relating to, or being a late lower Paleolithic period characterized by tools which were primarily flakes with retouched edges but sometimes biface core tools

mousy *or* **mousey** \ˈmau̇sē, -au̇zē, -i\ *adj* **mous·i·er; mous·i·est 1 a :** of, relating to, or characteristic of a mouse ⟨~ color⟩ ⟨~ smell⟩ **b :** infested with or smelling of mice ⟨~ cellar⟩ **2 a :** lacking in boldness or definition **:** COLORLESS, TIMID ⟨a ~, respectable novel —*New Yorker*⟩ ⟨the ~, competent little countryman —W.A.White⟩ **b :** making no noise **:** QUIET, STEALTHY ⟨slipped out in the ~ way . . . she so disliked —*Cosmopolitan*⟩ **c :** MOUSE-COLORED ⟨little girls with ~ pigtails —Winifred Bambrick⟩

¹mout \ˈmüt\ *dial Brit var of* MOLT

²mout \ˈmōt, ˈmau̇t\ [ME *moghte* — more at MAY] *chiefly dial past of* MAY

mou·tan \ˈmüˈtan\ *also* **moutan peony** *n* [Chin (Pek) *mou³⁻ tan¹, mu³-tan¹*] **:** TREE PEONY

¹mouth \ˈmau̇th\ *n, pl* **mouths** \ˈmau̇thz *also* -au̇z *sometimes* -au̇ths; -au̇ths *esp. in compounds whose meaning is "something having a certain kind of mouth," as "blabbermouth"*\ *often attrib* [ME, fr. OE *mūth*; akin to OHG *mund* mouth, ON *munnr, muthr*, Goth *munths* mouth, L *mandere* to chew, Gk *masasthai* to chew, *mastax* mouth, jaws] **1 a :** the opening through which food passes into the body of an animal; *specif* **:** the orifice in the head of higher vertebrates bounded by the lips or jaws **b :** the cavity bounded externally by the lips or jaws and internally by the pharynx or gullet that encloses in the typical vertebrate the tongue, gums, and teeth **:** the buccal cavity **c :** the structures enclosing or lying within the mouth cavity regarded as a whole ⟨the dog seized the bone in his ~⟩ ⟨my ~ is sore⟩ **2 a :** the lips as a feature of the face ⟨kissed her on the ~⟩ **b :** GRIMACE 1 ⟨make a ~⟩ **c :** response to guiding pressure on the bit — used of a horse ⟨a well-trained horse has a good ~⟩ **d :** an individual requiring food ⟨carnivora . . . keep down the number of useless ~s by killing off practically all the weak and aged —James Stevenson-Hamilton⟩ **e** (1) **:** the salivary glands ⟨pastry that makes one's ~ water⟩ (2) **:** the organs of taste **:** PALATE ⟨had my ~ all set for oysters⟩ **f** *obs* **:** a threatening vicinity ⟨we unawares run into danger's ~ —John Milton⟩ **3 a** *archaic* **:** oral communication **:** TONGUE ⟨learned . . . his faith from the ~ of the Roman priest —Mark Pattison⟩ **b** *obs* **:** a means of utterance ⟨the midnight bell did with his . . . brazen ~ sound on —Shak.⟩ **c :** the baying of a dog ⟨the musical ~ of a hound on the scent⟩ **4 a :** one that speaks **:** VOICE ⟨with all the ~s of Rome to second you —Joseph Addison⟩ ⟨through the ~ of his chancellor . . . made an unusual demand —R.W.Southern⟩ **b** *archaic* **:** an oral interchange **:** CONVERSATION ⟨the names . . . were in many ~s —T.B.Macaulay⟩ **c** (1) **:** a pronouncement attributed to someone ⟨artificial speeches placed in the ~s of historical figures —R.A.Hall b.1911⟩ (2) **:** expression in words **:** SPEECH ⟨names came up . . . and she might remember them in her father's ~ —Padraic Fallon⟩ **d** (1) **:** MOUTHPIECE 3a ⟨he is the ~ . . . of the House in its relations with the Crown —T.E. May⟩ (2) *archaic* **:** a gullible person **:** DUPE ⟨the whole gang will be . . . watching an opportunity to make a ~ of you —Charles Cotton⟩ **e** *archaic* (1) **:** a frame of reference **:** VIEW ⟨in a Roman ~, the graceful name of prophet and of poet was the same —William Cowper⟩ (2) **:** a sphere of authority **:** PROVINCE ⟨does it lie in the ~ of members of that government to taunt the . . . party with having no policy —Randolph Churchill⟩ **f** (1) **:** a tendency to excessive talk **:** VOLUBILITY ⟨he is not all ~ . . . he gets results —*Time*⟩ — often modified by *big* ⟨now you've spilled the beans, you and your big ~⟩ (2) **:** saucy or disrespectful language **:** IMPUDENCE, BACK TALK ⟨just don't take any ~ from him —Jackson Burgess⟩ **5 :** something that resembles a mouth: as **a** (1) **:** the place where a tributary enters a larger stream or body of water (2) **:** the entrance to a harbor (3) **:** the place where a valley or gorge begins (4) **:** the place where a side street enters a main thoroughfare **b :** the surface outlet of an underground shaft or passageway ⟨~ of a well⟩ ⟨~ of a mine⟩ ⟨~ of a volcano⟩ ⟨~s of all underdrains should be looked to —Adrian Bell⟩ ⟨arriving at the ~ of the burrow he lay down —J.T.McNish⟩ **c :** the opening at the receiving end of a container ⟨~ of a pocket⟩ ⟨~ of a bottle⟩ ⟨~ of a fisherman's trawl⟩; *specif* **:** the curved portion of a hook between the bill and the shank **d** (1) **:** the opening in a metallurgical furnace through which it is charged (2) **:** TAPHOLE (3) **:** any of several furnaces in a pottery kiln each connected by a flue to a central opening in the oven (4) **:** the opening in a covered glass pot **e :** the space between the cutting or gripping edges of a tool (as a vise) **f :** the muzzle of a piece of ordnance ⟨charged right up into the ~s of those cannon —F.B.Gipson⟩ ⟨the ~ of the automatic pressed closer against the back in the light overcoat —Kay Boyle⟩ **g :** the space in front of the cutter of a carpenter's plane through which the shavings pass **h** (1) **:** the open end of a wind instrument (as a horn) (2) **:** an opening (as in a flute) across which the player blows (3) **:** the opening between the lips of an organ flue pipe **i :** the summit of the tube of a corolla **j :** the opening of a univalve shell **k** *archit* **:** SCOTIA — **a poor mouth :** a plea of poverty ⟨I've got the millionaire tag because I always pay my bills within seven days and never put on *a poor mouth* —Sam Edgar⟩ ⟨some people put on *a poor mouth* over circumstances less unfortunate than those with more serious problems who accept them in a dignified manner⟩ — **down in the mouth :** sad or sulky in expression **:** DEJECTED, DISGRUNTLED ⟨came home with an empty creel, looking *down in the mouth*⟩ — **from mouth to mouth :** from person to person by word of mouth ⟨the news spread like wildfire *from mouth to mouth*⟩ — **full mouth** *obs* **:** with unrestrained voice **:** LOUDLY ⟨she was coming *full mouth* upon me with her contract —George Farquhar⟩ — **on the wrong side of one's mouth :** RUEFULLY ⟨we shall be laughing *on the wrong side of our mouths* before the day is over —W.E.Norris⟩

²mouth \ˈmau̇th\ *vb* -ED/-ING/-S [ME *mouthen*, fr. *mouth*, n.] *vt* **1 a :** to give utterance to **:** SPEAK, PRONOUNCE ⟨taught to ~ the word *cow* —Don Murray⟩ ⟨glibly ~*ed* by so many people —Edna Ferber⟩ ⟨only ~s words in talking about the need for faith —R.W.Flint⟩ **b :** to utter sententiously or bombastically ⟨~*ing* big phrases to hide little thought —Bruce Marshall⟩ ⟨~*ing* sonorous Virgil —Robert Keable⟩ **c :** to form soundlessly with the lips ⟨~*ing* the words, "this is what she thinks is tea" —Jean Stafford⟩ **2 a :** to take into the mouth ⟨he keeps them . . . in the corner of his jaw, first ~*ed* to be last swallowed —Shak.⟩; *esp* **:** EAT ⟨~*ed* down a square of cheese —Norman Mailer⟩ **b :** to work over with the mouth or teeth ⟨~*ing* the eggs and young for oxygenation purposes —L.P.Schultz⟩; *specif* **:** MANGLE ⟨a crooked . . . little man who had been ~*ed* by a whale —R.M.Lovett **3 a :** to accustom (a horse) to the bridle and bit ⟨a horse must be carefully ~*ed* before he is taught to jump⟩ **b :** to examine the teeth of (a horse or sheep) esp. as a means of estimating age ⟨sheepmen always ~ . . . sheep they are about to buy, to see if the age is as represented —*Lamb Production*⟩ **4 :** to swage the top of (a metal can) to receive the cover ~ *vi* **1 a :** to express oneself in speech **:** TALK, RECITE ⟨go around annoying people by ~*ing* to yourself —W. R.Benét⟩ ⟨juvenile ~*ing* of the multiplication tables⟩ **b :** to speak bombastically or angrily **:** DECLAIM, RAIL ⟨the bad old tradition of ~*ing* and ranting to bring . . . characters to life —Vernon Jarratt⟩ **c :** to divulge information **:** TELL ⟨wasn't going to have him ~ around the countryside that I had the stove for my own personal comfort —Michael McLaverty⟩ **2** *obs* **:** to caress with the lips **:** KISS ⟨the duke . . . would ~ with a beggar, though she smelt brown bread and garlic —Shak.⟩ **3 a :** to make faces **:** GRIMACE ⟨the children were giggling, bubbling, ~*ing* —Alexander Saxton⟩ **b :** to move the lips silently ⟨the octopus roped down from his hand, suckers still faintly ~*ing* —Norman Lewis⟩ **4 :** to issue into a larger body of water **:** DEBOUCH — used of a tributary ⟨where does this creek ~⟩

mouth bet *n* **:** a bet which a player announces but for which he does not put up the stake

mouth breather *n* **:** a person who habitually inhales and exhales through the mouth rather than through the nose

mouthbreeder \ˈ=,==\ *n* **1 :** any of several small fishes (family Cichlidae) that carry their eggs and young in the mouth; *esp* **:** a No. African fish (*Haplochromes multicolor*) often kept in a tropical aquarium **2 :** any of several marine catfishes that carry the eggs and young in the mouth

mouthed \ˈmau̇thd, -au̇tht\ *adj* [¹*mouth* + *-ed*] **1 :** having a mouth ⟨sat me down and took a ~ shell —John Keats⟩ — often used in combination ⟨wide-*mouthed* jar⟩ ⟨large-*mouthed* bass⟩ ⟨many-*mouthed* delta⟩ ⟨gentle-*mouthed* horse⟩ ⟨bull-*mouthed* siren⟩ **2** *obs* **a :** having a mouth of similar shape ⟨beaver . . . ~ like a cony —Thomas Morton⟩ **b :** GAPING, YAWNING ⟨~ graves will give thee memory —Shak.⟩

mouth·er \ˈmau̇thə(r)\ *n* -s **:** one that mouths; *esp* **:** a declamatory speaker ⟨a benevolent ~ of platitudes —John Mason Brown⟩

mouth-filling \ˈ=,==\ *adj* **:** of notable length or sonority ⟨an impressive, *mouth-filling* sentence —J.N.Hook⟩ ⟨a *mouth-filling* and rather clumsy phrase —Lister Hill⟩

mouth footed *adj* **:** having maxillipeds

mouth·ful \ˈmau̇th,fu̇l\ *n, pl* **mouthfuls** \-,fu̇lz\ **1 a :** a quantity that fills the mouth ⟨was submerged by a wave and got a ~ of seawater⟩ **b :** the quantity usu. taken into the mouth at one time **:** BITE ⟨assuagement of their hunger by a few more ~s —Glenway Wescott⟩ **2 :** a small quantity **:** MORSEL ⟨take a ~ of sweet country air —John Dryden⟩ **3 a :** a mouth-filling word or phrase ⟨the description of his new duties as "administrative coordination of developmental foreign investments" was a ~⟩ **b** *slang* **:** a comment or remark rich in meaning or substance ⟨you said a ~⟩

mouthier *comparative of* MOUTHY

mouthiest *superlative of* MOUTHY

mouth·i·ness \ˈmau̇thēnəs, -thin-, -thēn-, -thin-\ *n* -ES **:** the quality or state of being mouthy

mouthing *n* -s [fr. pres. part. of ²*mouth*] **1 :** a movement of the lips; *esp* **:** GRIMACE ⟨outward signs of repentance . . . groanings, ~s, and eyes upturned —Edith Sitwell⟩ **2 a :** an act or instance of speaking ⟨no matters . . . worth any labor in the ~ —George Barker⟩; *specif* **:** ORATION ⟨listened to the ~s of demagogues —*Saturday Rev.*⟩ **b :** a bombastic speech or phrase ⟨let them keep their sanctimonious ~s —Farley Mowat⟩ ⟨idealism and spirituality when separated from . . . concrete social situations are vague semantic ~s —Agnes Meyer⟩ **3 :** the process of accustoming a horse to a bridle and bit ⟨~ can be begun on the third day when the animal is . . . less inclined to resent gear and fitting —J.A.Miller⟩

mouthing-bit \ˈ=,=,=\ *n* **:** a bit used in mouthing a horse

mouth·less \ˈmau̇thləs\ *adj* **:** lacking or appearing to lack a mouth

mouthless crab *n* **:** a large hairy-legged land crab (*Cardisoma crassum*) of the western coast of Central and So. America

mouth-made *adj, obs* **:** coming from the mouth rather than the heart **:** INSINCERE ⟨those *mouth-made* vows which break themselves in swearing —Shak.⟩

mouth mirror *n* **:** a long-handled dental mirror for inspecting the teeth and gums

mouth organ *n* **1 a :** PANPIPE **b** *or* **mouth harp :** HARMONICA 3 **2 :** MOUTHPART

mouthpart \ˈ=,=\ *n* **:** a structure or appendage near the mouth (as of an insect) — usu. used in pl.; see TROPHI

mouthpiece \ˈ=,=\ *n* **1 :** a structure or appendage that serves as a mouth ⟨~ of a reed organ pipe⟩; *specif* **:** an appendage to an inlet or outlet of a pipe or container that controls the flow of a fluid or other material (as of coal into a coal gas retort) **2 a :** a part that goes in the mouth ⟨~ of a respirator⟩ ⟨~ of a saxophone⟩ ⟨~ of a briar pipe⟩ ⟨the entire action of the bit should be concentrated in the ~ —W.H.Carter⟩; *specif* **:** a cigar or cigarette holder **b :** a part to which the mouth is applied ⟨~ of a trumpet⟩ ⟨~ of a telephone⟩ **c :** a protective device for the mouth; *specif* **:** a guard worn in the mouth over the upper teeth by a boxer to protect the teeth and reduce the hazard of cut lips **3 a :** one that expresses or interprets another's views ⟨accept her as the conventional ~ for all the discontents the author wishes to discharge —G.J.Becker⟩ ⟨government, as the ~ and executive instrument of the people —A.J.Bruwer⟩; *specif* **:** an official spokesman ⟨his assistants, ~s, and messengers . . . carried out his orders —S.G.Morley⟩ ⟨virtually every newspaper was the bought-and-paid-for ~ of a party or clique —W.A.Swanberg⟩ ⟨could create the sense in all who listened to him that he was the ~ of destiny —J.H.Plumb⟩ **b** *slang* **:** CRIMINAL LAWYER

mouthpiece for tobacco pipe

mouthpipe \ˈ=,=\ *n* **1 :** an organ flue pipe **2 :** the section of a musical wind instrument into which the mouthpiece is inserted

mouthroot \ˈ=,=\ *n* **:** GOLDTHREAD 1

mouthrot \ˈ=,=\ *n* **:** a usu. fatal bacterial disease marked by severe necrotic changes of the mouth tissues of snakes esp. in captivity

mouths *pl of* MOUTH, *pres 3d sing of* MOUTH

mouth-to-airway method \ˌ=,=ˈ=,=-\ *n* **:** a variation of the mouth-to-mouth method of artificial respiration in which a rescuer blows through an airway inserted in the victim's mouth over the tongue

mouth-to-mouth method \ˌ==ˈ=-\ *n* **:** a method of artificial respiration in which a rescuer's mouth is placed tightly over the victim's mouth in order to force air into his lungs by blowing forcefully enough every few seconds to inflate them — called also *rescue breathing*

mouthwash \ˈ=,=\ *n* **:** a liquid preparation (as an antiseptic solution) for cleansing the mouth and teeth — called also *collutorium*

mouth-watering \ˈ=ˈ===\ *adj* **:** causing a flow of saliva into the mouth **:** APPETIZING ⟨a *mouth-watering* odor came from the kitchen⟩

mouthy \ˈmau̇thē, -au̇thē, -i\ *adj* -ER/-EST [¹*mouth* + *-y*] **:** excessively talkative or clamorous **:** GARRULOUS ⟨a ~ character who couldn't stay off the telephone —John & Ward Hawkins⟩; *specif* **:** BOMBASTIC ⟨strides about with many a ~ speech —Washington Irving⟩

mou·ton \ˈmü,tän, =ˈ=\ *n* -s [ME *motoun*, fr. MF *mouton*, lit., ram — more at MUTTON] **1 :** AGNEL **2** [F, lit., sheep, fr. MF, ram] **:** a spy planted in a prison cell to obtain incriminating evidence **3** [F, sheep, sheepskin] **:** processed sheepskin that has been sheared and dyed to resemble beaver or seal and is used esp. for women's coats

mou·ton·née \ˌmütᵊnˈā\ *n* -s [by shortening] **:** ROCHE MOUTONNÉE

MOV *abbr* manuscript on vellum

mov·a·bil·i·ty *or* **move·a·bil·i·ty** \ˌmüvəˈbilədē, -lətē, -i\ *n* **:** the quality or state of being movable

¹mov·able *or* **move·able** \ˈmüvəbəl\ *adj* [ME *mevable*, *movable*, fr. *meven, moven* to move + *-able* — more at MOVE] **1** *obs* **a :** FICKLE, INCONSTANT **b :** inclined to move or quick in movement **2 a :** capable of being moved **:** not fixed **:** not stationary ⟨a device with a ~ attachment⟩ **:** not restricted to one position or location ⟨~ hexachord⟩ ⟨~ clef sign⟩ **b** *of property* (1) **:** that can be removed or displaced and that is thus usu. personal rather than real ⟨~ wealth⟩ ⟨~ goods⟩ (2) *Scots law* **:** that does not descend to an heir by inheritance **:** that is not heritable **3 :** that varies chronologically; *specif* **:** that varies in calendar date from one year to the next ⟨a ~ holiday⟩ **4 :** alternating with zero morphophonemically or in etymologies **5** *of a letter or sound* **:** that in some forms or in some verbal environments is sometimes present (as for euphony) and sometimes absent — compare NU MOVABLE, QUIESCENT **6 :** pronounced as distinguished from quiescent ⟨~ consonants and syllables in Hebrew⟩

²movable *or* **moveable** \"\ *n* -s [ME *mevable*, fr. *mevable*, *movable*, adj.] **1 :** a piece of property (as an article of furniture) that can be removed or displaced **:** a movable piece of property **2** *Scots law* **:** a piece of property that is not heritable

movable-do system \ˈ=ˌ==ˈdō-\ *n* **:** a system of solmization in which the sol-fa syllables may be transposed to any key — compare FIXED-DO SYSTEM

movable exchange *n* **:** INDIRECT EXCHANGE 2

movable finger *n* **:** the dactylopodite of a chela

movable fixture *n* **:** FIXTURE 2c(2)

movable kidney *n* **:** NEPHROPTOSIS

mov·able·ness *n* -ES [ME *mevablenes*, fr. *mevable*, *movable* + *-nes* -ness] **:** MOVABILITY

movable type *n* **:** printing type made up of individual pieces each carrying usu. a single letter or other character so that the pieces can be freely assembled or reassembled for printing any desired combination or line

mov·ably \ˈmüvəblē, -li\ *adv* **:** so as to be movable ⟨a rod that is attached ~ to the device⟩

mov·ant *also* **mov·ent** \ˈmüvənt\ *n* -s [¹*move* + *-ant* or *-ent*] **:** one that makes an application or petition to a court of law or to a judge with the intention of obtaining a favorable ruling

¹move \ˈmüv\ *vb* **moved; moved; moving** *with speakers who "drop the g" of present participles, often* ˈmübᵊm, *often satirized by the spelling "moom pictures"*\ **moves** [ME *meven*, *moven*, fr. MF *mouvoir*, *movoir*, fr. L *movēre*; prob. akin to Gk *ameusasthai* to surpass, *amynein* to ward off, Skt *mīvati* he pushes, shoves, Lith *mauti* to pull (a garment) on or off; basic meaning: to push] *vi* **1 a** (1) **:** to go continuously from one point or place to another ⟨the weary band of travelers *moved* slowly along the road⟩ (2) **:** to go forward **:** get along **:** make progress **:** PROCEED, ADVANCE ⟨wanted to keep *moving*, no matter what the obstacles⟩; *specif* **:** MARCH ⟨a victorious army *moving* through the countryside⟩ (3) **:** to become more fully worked out through the addition or accretion of successive details or greater elaboration or some other form of further development ⟨the plot of the drama ~s swiftly⟩ ⟨a novel that hardly seems to ~⟩ (4) **:** to go along from one note or group of notes of music to the next in the course of the development or performance of a musical composition ⟨a melody that ~s smoothly⟩ ⟨at this point the tenor part ~s upward⟩ **b** (1) **:** to leave one point or place and go on to a new one ⟨remained outside the town for about one day and then *moved* inside and began the campaign⟩ (2) **:** to start away from some point or place **:** be on one's way **:** DEPART ⟨it was getting late and I thought it was time to be *moving*⟩ **c** (1) **:** to become transferred from one position to another in the course of play — used of pieces used in some games (as checkers, chess) ⟨in chess the bishop ~s diagonally⟩ (2) **:** to transfer a piece used in some games (as checkers, chess) from one position to another ⟨his turn to ~⟩ **d :** to settle in a new or different place (as of residence, business) usu. abandoning a former one **:** change one's abode or location ⟨did not like small towns and decided to ~ to the city⟩ **e** (1) **:** to become disposed of or to change hands by being sold or rented ⟨had a line of goods that was *moving* very slowly⟩ (2) **:** to become distributed through being borrowed by readers ⟨find readers ⟨some books in public libraries hardly ever seem to ~⟩ **2 a** (1) **:** to change position or posture or otherwise exhibit outward activity **:** cause or allow the self or a part of the self to change position or posture **:** STIR ⟨so frightened that she stood rigid and didn't ~⟩ ⟨told him not to ~ or he would shoot⟩ (2) **:** to indicate recognition by some outward act (as inclining the head) ⟨thought she *moved* slightly when we were introduced, but it was impossible to be sure⟩ **b** (1) **:** to produce outwardly noticeable changes in position or in alignment of parts through being subjected to some external force ⟨the boat *moved* slowly from side to side at its mooring as the wind rose⟩ ⟨the trees *moved* gently in the breeze⟩ (2) **:** to become activated into operating or functioning or working in a designed or usual or expected way ⟨pushed and pushed but the door wouldn't ~⟩ ⟨pressed a button and the machine began *moving*⟩ **c :** to show marked activity **:** be very busy **:** snap into or maintain lively activity **:** HUM ⟨for a while there was not much to do, but suddenly things really began to ~⟩ **3 a :** to have life **:** EXIST ⟨in him we live, and ~, and have our being —Acts 17: 28 (AV)⟩ **b :** to live one's life in a specified environment **:** pass one's life or carry on one's activities in everyday acquaintance or familiarity with something indicated ⟨now ~s in only the best of circles⟩ **c :** to comport oneself in a specified way **:** behave in a particular manner ⟨must ~ very carefully so as not to offend her⟩ **4 :** to go ahead and do something **:** take action or begin to take action **:** ACT ⟨the time has come for us to make up our mind and ~⟩ **5 :** to make a formal request or proposal or application or appeal — used with *for* ⟨the delegate *moved* for a reconsideration of the suggestion⟩ ⟨the plaintiff *moved* for a rehearing⟩ **6** *of the bowels* **:** to eject fecal matter **:** EVACUATE, VOID ~ *vt* **1 a** (1) **:** to change the place or position of **:** cause to be shifted or removed from one place or position to another ⟨*moved* the chair to a different part of the room⟩ (2) **:** to dislodge or displace from a fixed position **:** force loose or out **:** BUDGE ⟨the knife had sunk deeply into the wood and couldn't be *moved*⟩ ⟨was unable to ~ him from his obstinate convictions⟩ **b :** to transfer (a piece used in some games, as checkers or chess) from one position to another **c :** to take off or lift or tip (one's hat, cap) in salutation ⟨*moved* his hat politely when he saw her⟩ **d :** to cause to be disposed of or cause to change hands through sale or rent — usu. used in passive ⟨the new cars were *moved* very quickly⟩ **2 a** (1) **:** to cause to go or cause to keep on going continuously from one point or place to another ⟨*moved* the flag slowly up and down as a signal⟩ (2) **:** to cause to advance or cause to keep on advancing ⟨*moving* the troops farther into enemy territory⟩ **b** (1) **:** to activate into operating or functioning or working in a designed or usual or expected way **:** ACTUATE ⟨this button ~*s* the whole mechanism⟩ (2) **:** to cause (as an implement) to go or act or be driven or agitated in a direction or manner designed to produce a particular result ⟨*moved* the handle first to the left and then to the right and the door finally opened⟩ **c :** to put into activity or cause to continue in activity **:** rouse up from inactivity **:** cause not to remain at rest ⟨the breeze *moved* the branches of the trees⟩ ⟨news that *moved* them from their torpor⟩ **3 :** to cause (the self or a part of the self) to change position or posture or otherwise exhibit outward activity ⟨*moved* his lips but not a sound could be heard⟩ **4 :** to prompt or impel or rouse to the doing of something by reason of being a motive or incentive or similar influence **:** serve as an influence on the mind or will of **:** PERSUADE ⟨the happiness that could be his *moved* him to acting swiftly⟩ ⟨the logic and sanity of the argument *moved* them to reconsider the plan⟩ **5 a** (1) **:** to stir the emotions of **:** affect emotionally **:** rouse the feelings or passions of ⟨was greatly *moved* by such kindness⟩; *esp* **:** to cause to experience emotions of tenderness or compassion or sympathy ⟨her grief deeply *moved* them⟩ (2) **:** to affect in such a way as to lead to an indicated manifestation of emotion or passion ⟨a story that *moved* them to tears⟩ ⟨ingratitude that *moved* him to anger⟩ **b** *archaic* **:** to bring forth or excite or evoke (an indicated reaction) ⟨the exaggerations of both the great parties in the state *moved* his scorn —T.B.Macaulay⟩ **6 a** *obs* **:** to make an appeal to **:** earnestly solicit **:** BEG **b :** to make a formal application to (as a legislative body) — used with *for* ⟨*moved* the assembled delegates for reconsideration of the bill⟩ **7 :** to propose (as a question, resolution) formally in a deliberative assembly for consideration and determination ⟨*moved* that the meeting adjourn⟩ **8 :** to cause (the bowels) to eject fecal matter

syn ACTUATE, DRIVE, IMPEL: MOVE indicates simply the fact of altering position or place of setting or keeping going or in motion ⟨*move* furniture about the room⟩ ⟨the car *moves* slowly in low gear⟩ ⟨a plane *moved* across the sky⟩ ⟨retail prices *moved* steadily upward —*Americana Annual*⟩ ACTUATE, generally used in connection with machinery or mechanisms, lays stress upon the communication of the power to work or set in action; in application to persons the activation is usu. a specified motive ⟨as you entered a driveway you could throw out a short electrical impulse which would *actuate* equipment installed in the garage to open the doors mechanically —*Science Yr. Bk.*⟩ ⟨figurines which once performed amusing antics *actuated* by power from a waterwheel —*Amer. Guide Series: Conn.*⟩ ⟨*actuated* by altruistic motives⟩ ⟨*actuated* by jealousy⟩ DRIVE often signifies providing or communicating the power to set and keep in action ⟨a small turbine engine *drives* the wheel⟩ generally stresses the movement imparted, often suggesting the effect of speed or force ⟨the engine *drives* the crane back and forth across the short elevated track⟩ ⟨a propeller-*driven* plane⟩ ⟨a blade *driven* at a terrific speed by a small engine sliced the material into small strips⟩ ⟨*drive* a rod through a wall⟩ IMPEL, usu. used in figurative applications, is to drive with a great impetus ⟨he was *impelled* down the stairs by a pair of powerful arms⟩ ⟨*impelled* by a sense of duty —R.M.Lovett⟩ ⟨the motives which *impelled* him to take up and carry forward so difficult and thankless a work —V.L.Parrington⟩

syn MOVE, REMOVE, SHIFT, TRANSFER can mean, in common, to change or cause to change from one place to another. MOVE in itself implies no more than the motion or activity except in the special sense of to move one's habitation ⟨*move* along a street⟩ ⟨*move* a chair back⟩ ⟨*move* into a new house⟩ REMOVE usu. adds to MOVE the implication of a change from a normal, original, or usual location, station, or occupation; it is preferred to MOVE when the idea of eradicating is stressed ⟨*remove* a box from a shelf⟩ ⟨*remove* a wart from a finger⟩ ⟨*remove* faults by effort of will⟩ SHIFT throws emphasis on the change of location or direction, often suggesting unrest or instability ⟨*shift* from job to job⟩ ⟨*shift* from foot to foot⟩ ⟨the wind *shifted* to the east⟩ ⟨help a man *shift* a bureau to one side⟩ TRANSFER commonly implies a change from hand to hand, from one mode of conveyance to another, from one depository to another ⟨*transfer* a heavy package from one hand to the other⟩ ⟨*transfer* from the train to the bus⟩ ⟨*transfer* property from a man to his son⟩ ⟨*transfer* one's affection from person to person easily⟩

[2]**move** \"\ *n* -s **1 a** (1) **:** the action of moving a piece (as in checkers, chess) (2) **:** the turn of a player to move a piece (as in checkers, chess) **b :** advantage in end play in checkers or chess depending on which player must move in a given position — used with *the* ⟨after the exchange White has the ~ and wins⟩ — compare OPPOSITION 4b **2 a :** a step taken so as to gain some objective **:** a calculated procedure **:** MANEUVER ⟨made a clever ~ that outwitted all his rivals⟩ ⟨what's our next ~⟩ **b** (1) **:** the action of moving from a motionless position **:** the action of becoming active after previously being stationary or otherwise inactive ⟨the silence was appalling and no one dared to make a ~⟩ (2) **:** the action of rising from table ⟨sat there politely, waiting for someone else to make the first ~⟩ (3) **:** an incipient or initial action of moving esp. out of or away from a place ⟨was bored with their company, but no one seemed ready to make a ~⟩ **c :** a change of abode or location ⟨will make their ~ to the city next week⟩ **3 a :** a nominal period of time during which a certain amount of work can on the average be done or produced and which is sometimes used as a basis for paying a worker in proportion to the work actually done or produced **b :** the amount of work theoretically capable of being done or produced in the course of such a period of time — **on the move** *adv* (*or adj*) **1 :** in a state or process of moving about from place to place ⟨is a salesman and is constantly *on the move*⟩ **2 a :** in a state or process of moving ahead or making progress ⟨said that civilization is always *on the move*⟩ **b :** in a state of marked activity or distinct motion ⟨was not content to twiddle his thumbs but wanted to be *on the move*⟩

moveable *var of* MOVABLE

moved *past of* MOVE

move·less \'müvləs\ *adj* **:** that is without movement **:** MOTIONLESS, FIXED, IMMOBILE ⟨banks of ~ cloud hung about the horizon —George Meredith⟩ ⟨a crowd of quite 200 persons, standing ~ —Arnold Bennett⟩ — **move·less·ly** *adv* — **move·less·ness** *n* -ES

move·man \-ˌman, -mən\ *n, pl* **movemen :** a worker in an industrial plant who keeps materials or products moving on schedule from one operation or processing job to the next

move·ment \-vmənt, *in rapid speech sometimes* -bm-\ *n* -s [ME *movement, mevement,* fr. MF *movement, mouvement,* fr. *movoir, mouvoir* to move + *-ment* — more at MOVE] **1 a** (1) **:** the action or process of moving; *esp* **:** change of place or position or posture ⟨the ~ of pioneers to the West⟩ ⟨studying the ~ of planets⟩ (2) **:** a particular instance or manner of such moving ⟨made an impatient ~⟩ ⟨was entranced with her graceful ~*s*⟩ **b** (1) **:** a tactical or strategic shifting of a military unit (as an army division) **:** MANEUVER (2) **:** the orderly advance or progress of a military unit toward some point or in the course of some maneuver ⟨a steady ~ of troops over the border⟩ **c :** ACTION, ACTIVITY — usu. used in pl. ⟨carefully watched the ~*s* of the crowd⟩ **d :** a change or marked direction in the price of a commodity or stock ⟨an upward ~ in the price of coffee⟩ **2 a** (1) **:** a particular impulse or inclination (as of the will) ⟨had some good ~*s* in him —W.M.Thackeray⟩ ⟨a ~ of the will toward what appears good⟩ (2) **:** TENDENCY, TREND ⟨an age marked by a strong ~ toward materialism⟩ (3) **:** a progression in a particular direction or toward a particular objective ⟨was not sure toward what conclusion the ~ of the argument was leading⟩ **b** (1) **:** a series of actions taken by a body of persons to achieve an objective (2) **:** the body of persons taking part in such a series of actions **3 :** the moving parts of a mechanism that transmit a definite motion or transform motion; *esp* **:** a delicate train of wheelwork (as in a watch) **4 a :** MOTION 9 **b :** the rhythmic character or quality of a musical composition ⟨a dance ~⟩ **c :** TIME 7c **d :** TEMPO **e :** a distinct structural unit or division complete in its own key, rhythmic structure, and themes, and forming part of an extended musical composition ⟨a ~ of a suite⟩ ⟨the largo ~⟩ **5 a** (1) **:** a quality in a fine arts work (as a piece of sculpture, a painting) of representing or suggesting motion (2) **:** a quality in a fine arts work of dynamic rhythm and of harmonious variation and progression and of freedom from incongruity and from monotony **b** (1) **:** the quality in a piece of prose or poetry of being vibrant and alive through having a quickly moving plot or an abundance of interesting incidents or through having a fresh smooth stimulating style or through some other device that engages the constant interest of the reader (2) **:** the particular rhythmic flow of a piece of poetry **:** CADENCE **6 a :** an act of evacuation of the bowels **b :** matter evacuated from the bowels at one passage **:** STOOL

movent *var of* MOVANT

mov·er \'müvə(r)\ *n* -s [ME *mover, mever,* fr. *moven, meven* to move + *-er* — more at MOVE] **:** one that moves: as **a** (1) **:** one that sets something into motion **:** ACTUATOR ⟨viewing God as the ~ of the universe⟩ (2) **:** one that incites or instigates to action or that promotes an action that has been begun ⟨hotheaded ~*s* of rebellion⟩ (3) **:** one that proposes something in a deliberative assembly ⟨the ~ of a resolution⟩ (4) **:** one whose business or occupation is the moving of household goods from one residence to another **b** (1) **:** one that is in motion or that is capable of motion ⟨a deer is a fast ~⟩ (2) **:** MIGRANT; *specif* **:** one participating in the extensive 19th century migration to the West of the U. S.

moves *pres 3d sing of* MOVE, *pl of* MOVE

mov·ie \'müvē, -vi\ *n* -s [*mov*ing picture + *-ie*] **1 a :** MOTION PICTURE ⟨saw her favorite star in a new ~⟩ **b :** material or method suitable for motion pictures ⟨a novel with a plot that is good ~⟩ ⟨a style of direction that was authentic ~⟩ **2 :** a theater designed or used for the presentation of motion pictures ⟨dropped in at a neighborhood ~⟩ **3 movies** *pl* **a** (1) **:** motion pictures considered esp. as a source of entertainment or as an art form — usu. used with *the* ⟨liked nothing better than the ~*s*⟩ (2) **:** the motion-picture industry ⟨worked for years in the ~*s*⟩ **b :** a showing of a motion picture — used with *the* ⟨felt like going to the ~*s*⟩

mov·ie·dom \'⸗⸗dəm\ *n* -s **:** FILMDOM

moviegoer \'⸗⸗ˌ⸗⸗\ *n* **:** one that goes to see motion pictures esp. frequently

moviegoing \'⸗⸗ˌ⸗⸗\ *n* **:** the act or habit of going to see motion pictures

movie house *n* **:** an indoor theater designed for the public presentation of motion pictures

movieland \'⸗⸗ˌ⸗\ *n* **:** FILMDOM

moviemaker \'⸗⸗ˌ⸗⸗\ *n* **:** one engaged in the production of motion pictures **:** a motion-picture magnate

mo·vi·men·to \ˌmōvə'men·(ˌ)tō\ *n* -s [It, lit., movement, fr. *movere* to move (fr. L *movēre*) + *-mento* -ment — more at MOVE] **:** TEMPO

mov·ing *see pres part at* [1]MOVE\ *adj* [ME, fr. pres. part. of *moven* to move — more at MOVE] **1 a :** that is marked by or capable of movement **:** that is not fixed or stationary ⟨a device with ~ parts⟩ **b :** that advances or progresses ⟨living in a ~ world⟩ **2 a** (1) **:** that causes or produces or carries on motion or action or change **:** ACTUATING ⟨the ~ force of a machine⟩ (2) **:** that originates or instigates or promotes something ⟨was one of the ~ spirits behind the plan⟩ **b :** that stirs up or arouses or plays upon the emotions **:** that affects one's feelings or influences the mental outlook emotionally **:** that affects the sensibilities ⟨a ~ plea for justice⟩ ⟨a ~ tale of heroism⟩ **c :** that excites interest and discussion and controversy **:** VITAL ⟨one of the ~ questions of the day⟩

syn IMPRESSIVE, POIGNANT, AFFECTING, TOUCHING, PATHETIC: MOVING applies to any strong emotional excitation, including thrilling, entrancing, saddening, or calling forth pity and sympathy ⟨a modern version of the hero who for the good of mankind exposed himself to the agonies of the damned. It is always a *moving* subject —W.S.Maugham⟩ ⟨a *moving* revelation of child life in an orphanage —Mary MacColl⟩ IMPRESSIVE may describe that which forcibly commands attention, respect, admiration, awe, wonder, or conviction ⟨he was especially *impressive* before a court or jury and on account of his masterly arguments and effective oratorical powers the courtroom was always filled when it was known that he would speak —Marie B. Owen⟩ ⟨the southern entrance is *impressive*, with great rock walls rising abruptly on each side of the river bed in barren and forbidding grandeur —*Amer. Guide Series: Texas*⟩ POIGNANT refers to whatever keenly or sharply affects one's sensitivities, now esp. to whatever compels pity ⟨the most *poignant* of all perfumes: that which rises from a meadow on a July night —Kenneth Roberts⟩ ⟨that tenderness became sometimes so *poignant* that perhaps neither of us knew whether it was joy or pain —Havelock Ellis⟩ ⟨is anything in the world more *poignant* than youth and love —Virgil Thomson⟩ AFFECTING applies to whatever deeply moves the emotions; it is less specific than others in this list but is commonly used in situations involving pathos ⟨funeral the next day was a more *affecting* spectacle than anything ever seen in his theater —Green Peyton⟩ TOUCHING may describe that which calls forth tenderness or compassion ⟨a clean sober little maid, with a very *touching* upward look of trust —John Galsworthy⟩ ⟨when an aging man begins to cry in front of his colleagues, he presents a *touching* spectacle —Francis Hackett⟩ PATHETIC suggests pity for sorrow and distress, but unlike others in this group and like the word *pitiful* it may connote blended pity and amusement or contempt for weakness, inadequacy, and futility ⟨infant mortality, as the *pathetic* little cemeteries bore witness, was cruelly high —Allan Nevins & H.S.Commager⟩ ⟨her death has all the *pathetic* uselessness of martyrdom —Oscar Wilde⟩ ⟨staged the *pathetic* little rebellion of 1798 against England. It ended in quick disaster —Paul Blanshard⟩ ⟨this southern tradition was *pathetic* because it was but a remnant of an old aristocratic society —Reinhold Niebuhr⟩

moving average *n* **:** the average of statistical data (as in a time series) computed over a progressively shifting interval

moving cluster *n* **1 :** a cluster of stars that have common motions in space **2 :** an open cluster comparatively near the sun whose individual proper motions may be measured

moving–coil \¦⸗⸗¦⸗\ *adj* **1 :** operated by the force exerted upon a movable electric-current-carrying coil suspended in a magnetic field ⟨a *moving-coil* galvanometer⟩ **2 :** operating by means of an electric-current-carrying coil or a single conductor that moves in a magnetic field (as in a dynamic loudspeaker or a dynamic pickup)

moving–iron meter \¦⸗⸗¦⸗(⸗)-\ *n* **:** an instrument in which a vane or plunger of soft iron is moved by the magnetic field set up by a coil carrying the current to be measured — called also *iron-vane meter*

mov·ing·ly *adv* **:** in a moving manner **:** in such a way as to touch one's feelings or sensibilities **:** TOUCHINGLY, AFFECTINGLY ⟨spoke ~ of the country's glorious past⟩ ⟨writes ~ of his disappointment —Jay Walz⟩

moving picture *see pres part at* [1]MOVE\ *n* **:** MOTION PICTURE

moving sidewalk *n* **:** a sidewalk constructed on the principle of an endless belt or a series of such belts side by side and moving at different gradated speeds so that a person stepping on it will be carried along

moving staircase *or* **moving stairway** *n* **:** a set of stairs arranged like an endless belt and power driven so that the steps or treads may be made to ascend or descend continuously —called also *escalator*

mo·vin·gui *or* **mo·vin·gue** \mō'viŋgē\ *n* -s [native name in western Africa] **1 :** a West African leguminous tree (*Distemonanthus benthamianus*) having straw-colored wood with evident pores **2 :** the wood of the movingui used esp. for veneers

[1]**mow** \'mau̇\ *n* -s [ME *mowe, mow, mough,* fr. OE *mūga, mūha, mūwa;* akin to MHG *mūche* disease of a horse's foot, *mocke* lump, ON *mūgi, mūgr* crowd, heap, Gk *mykōn* heap] **1 :** a stack or heap of hay or straw or grain or similar produce esp. when stored in a barn **2 :** the part of a barn where hay, straw, or grain is stored

[2]**mow** \"\ *vt* -ED/-ING/-S [ME *mowen,* fr. *mowe,* n.] **:** to stack or store in or as if in a haymow — usu. used with *away*

[3]**mow** \'mō\ *vb* **mowed; mowed** *or* **mown; mowing; mows** [ME *mowen,* fr. OE *māwan;* akin to OHG *māen* to mow, MLG *meien, meigen,* MD *maeyen* to mow, L *metere* to reap, mow, W *medi* to reap, Gk *aman* to cut, mow, reap] *vt* **1 a :** to cut down (as standing grass, grain) with a scythe or sickle or machine; *esp* **:** to crop (relatively short standing grass) close to the ground with a lawn mower ⟨agreed to ~ the grass once a week⟩ **b :** to cut the standing grass or grain or similar produce of with a scythe or sickle or machine ⟨~*ed* the field so as to provide the cattle with fodder⟩; *esp* **:** to crop close to the ground the relatively short standing grass of with a lawn mower ⟨~*ed* the lawn regularly⟩ **2 a** (1) **:** to kill or destroy in rapid succession and in great numbers and indiscriminately ⟨~*ed* down with machine-gun fire⟩ (2) **:** to kill or destroy with sudden savage swiftness and without mercy or concern ⟨was ~*ed* down by gunmen after being lured from his home —Len Arthur⟩ (3) **:** to cause to fall from a standing position with sudden impetuous force **:** cause to tumble from an upright position **:** bowl over **:** knock over **:** knock down ⟨burst through the revolving door and ~*ed* down a couple of shoppers⟩ **b :** to meet and overcome swiftly and completely and decisively **:** make short work of **:** utterly crush **:** ROUT, SMASH ⟨~ down the opposition —Ira Wolfert⟩ ~ *vi* **:** to cut down standing grass or grain or similar produce with a scythe or sickle or machine

[4]**mow** *also* **mowe** \'mau̇, 'mō\ *n* -s [ME *mowe,* fr. MF *moue,* of Gmc origin; akin to MD *mouwe* thick or protruding lip] **:** a contortion of the face or lips; *esp* **:** a mocking or derisive grimace ⟨watched the monkeys making ~*s* at us⟩

[5]**mow** \"\ *vi* -ED/-ING/-S [ME *mowen,* fr. *mowe,* n.] **1 :** to contort the face esp. so as to produce a mocking or derisive expression **:** make faces ⟨when the unintelligent brute force that lies at the bottom of society is made to growl and ~ —R.W.Emerson⟩ **2 :** to keep the lips constantly moving and contorting without actually speaking ⟨then he jabbers and ~*s* and trembles —Rudyard Kipling⟩

[6]**mow** *var of* MOU

mowburnt \'⸗¦⸗\ *adj* **:** fermented or moldy through being stored in a mow while still damp ⟨~ hay⟩

mow·die \'mōdi\ *var of* MOUDIE

mow·er \'mō(ə)r, -ōə\ *n* -s [[3]*mow* + *-er*] **1** *also* **mowing machine :** an agricultural implement for cutting standing grass or grain or similar produce consisting of a reciprocating knife or sickle operated through guards or fingers and driven by a connecting rod from a crank and of gearing governing the speed of the crank and of dividers to divide the cut produce from the standing produce **2 :** LAWN MOWER

mow·ha \'mau̇hə\ *n* -s [Hindi *mahūā* — more at MAHUA] **:** MAHUA

mowhay \'⸗ˌ⸗\ *n* [[1]*mow* + *hay*] *dial Eng* **:** STACKYARD

mowing *n* -s [fr. gerund of [3]*mow*] **1 :** the amount of produce (as grass or grain) mowed at one time **2 :** HAYFIELD

mowle \'mōl\ *var of* MOOL

mown *past part of* MOW

mow·ra *or* **mow·rah** \'mau̇rə\ *n* -s [Hindi *mahūā* — more at MAHUA] **:** MAHUA

mowrah butter *or* **mowrah oil** *also* **mahua butter** *n* **:** a bitter-tasting white or yellow soft fat obtained from the seeds of various East Indian trees of the genus *Madhuca* (as *M. latifolia* and *M. longifolia*) and used in soap, candles, and foods — compare INDIAN BUTTER

mowrah meal *n* **:** a meal produced as a by-product of mowrah butter and used to kill earthworms in lawns and other fine turfs and in greenhouses

mows \'mōz\ *n pl* [fr. pl. of obs. *mow* jest, fr. ME *mowe* grimace, jest — more at MOW] *chiefly Scot* **:** something that causes laughter **:** a laughing matter ⟨it's not ~ to be out at such a time —J.M.Barrie⟩

mowt \'mōt, 'mau̇t\ [ME *moghte*] *chiefly dial past of* MAY

moxa \'mäksə\ *n* -s [NL, fr. Jap *mogusa*] **1 :** a soft woolly mass prepared from the young leaves of various wormwoods of eastern Asia and used esp. in Japanese popular medicine as a cautery by being ignited on the skin **2 :** any of various substances applied and ignited like moxa as a counterirritant

mox·ie \'mäksē, -si\ *n* -s [fr. *Moxie,* a trademark for a soft drink] **1** *slang* **:** ENERGY, PEP, LIFE ⟨he shook out of my grip, but there wasn't much ~ in it —P.W. Denzer⟩ **2** *slang* **a** (1) **:** COURAGE, PLUCK ⟨had plenty of ~ and was afraid of nothing⟩ (2) **:** AUDACITY, NERVE ⟨only in the outposts of the British Empire do males have the ~ to regularly wear shorts in mixed company —*Fortnight*⟩ **b :** STAMINA, BACKBONE, GUTS ⟨show that mob in the stadium that you've got the old ~ —*Saturday Rev.*⟩

mox·ie·ber·ry \'⸗⸗- — *see* BERRY\ *also* **mox·ie** \'⸗⸗\ *or* **mox·ie·plum** \'⸗⸗ˌ⸗\ *n* [origin unknown] **:** CREEPING SNOWBERRY

moy *abbr* money

moy·en \'mȯi(y)ən\ *n* -s [ME, fr. MF *meien, moien, moyen* — more at MEAN] **1 a** *chiefly Scot* **:** a means of doing something **b** *obs* **:** MEDIATION, INTERCESSION **2** *chiefly Scot* **:** a course of action

moyen–âge \¦mwäyə¦näzh\ *adj, often cap M&A* [F *moyen âge* middle ages; trans. of NL *Medium Aevum* — more at MIDDLE-AGE] **:** of, relating to, or suggestive of medieval times **:** MIDDLE-AGE ⟨a *moyen-âge* costume⟩

mo·zab·ite \mō'zaˌbīt, 'mōzəˌ-\ *n* -s *cap* [F, fr. *Mzab* (*M'zab*), group of oases in Ghardaïa territory, Algeria + F *-ite*] **:** a Berber of the Ibadite sect holding to a literal interpretation of the Koran

mo·zam·bi·can \¦mōzəm¦bēkən, -ˌzam-\ *adj, usu cap* [*Mozambique,* colony in southeastern Africa + E *-an*] **:** of or relating to Mozambique or its inhabitants

mo·zam·bique \¦mōzəm¦bēk -ˌzam-\ *n* -s [fr. *Mozambique,* colony in southeastern Africa] **:** a lightweight dress fabric in small fancy patterns that is loosely woven with a cotton warp and a mohair weft

moz·ar·ab \mō'zarəb *also* -zer-\ *n, usu cap* [Sp *mozárabe,* fr. Ar *Musta'rib* would-be Arab, fr. *'Arab* Arab] **:** a Spanish Christian in the period of Muslim domination of Spain from about the 9th century to the 15th century

moz·ar·a·bic \(')mō¦zarəbik\ *adj, usu cap* [F *mozarabique,* fr. Sp *mozárabe* + F *-ique* -ic] **:** of, relating to, or used by Mozarabs ⟨*Mozarabic* poetry⟩ ⟨the *Mozarabic* liturgy⟩

mo·zar·te·an *also* **mo·zar·ti·an** \(')mōt¦särd·ēən\ *adj, usu cap* [Wolfgang A. *Mozart* †1791 Austrian composer + E *-ean, -ian*] **:** of, relating to, or characteristic of Mozart or his music

mozca *usu cap, var of* MUISCA

mo·zo \'mō(ˌ)sō\ *n* -s [Sp, lit., boy, fr. OSp *moço*] **1** *chiefly Southwest* **a :** a male hired to assist with household work or to attend to various small jobs or to do chiefly manual work of a usu. somewhat heavy or menial kind: as (1) **:** a male servant **:** male domestic (2) **:** HANDYMAN (3) **:** a luggage porter (4) **:** LABORER **b :** a waiter in a restaurant or other dining room **2** *chiefly Southwest* **:** a male hired to assist with a train of pack animals

moz·za·rel·la \ˌmätsə'relə, ˌmȯt-\ *n* -s [It, dim. of *mozza,* a kind of cheese, fr. *mozzare* to cut off] **:** a moist white rubbery unsalted cheese that has a somewhat acid flavor

moz·zet·ta *also* **mo·zet·ta** \mōt'sed·ə, mō'ze-\ *n* -s [It, short for *almozzetta,* irreg. fr. ML *almutia* amice + It *-etta,* dim. suffix] **:** a short cape with a small ornamental hood worn on occasion over the rochet by some ecclesiastics

moz·zie \'mäzē\ *var of* MOSSIE

MP \(')em¦pē\ *abbr or n* -s **1 :** a member of Parliament **2 :** a group of military police **3 :** a member of a group of military police **:** a military policeman

mp *abbr* melting point

MP *abbr* **1** mail payment **2** meeting point **3** memorandum of partnership **4** metropolitan police **5** mezzo piano **6** milepost **7** minister plenipotentiary **8** morning prayer **9** motion picture **10** mounted police **11** multipole **12** municipal police

m paper *n, usu cap M* **:** paper containing minor imperfections and graded second quality — compare N PAPER, P PAPER

MPB *abbr* missing persons bureau

MPG *abbr, often not cap* miles per gallon

MPH *abbr, often not cap* miles per hour
MPHPS *abbr, often not cap* miles per hour per second
MPI *abbr, often not cap* mean point of impact
MPM *abbr* **1** *often not cap* meters per minute **2** multipurpose meal
MPO *abbr* military post office
mpon·do \əm'pän(,)dō\ *n, pl* **mpondo** *or* **mpondos** *usu cap* : PONDO
mpong·we \əm'päŋ(,)wā\ *n, pl* **mpongwe** *or* **mpongwes** *usu cap* **1 a** : a people of the southern part of French Equatorial Africa just north of the equator and distributed chiefly about the estuary of the Gabon river **b** : a member of such people **2** : a Bantu language of the Mpongwe people
MPS *abbr* **1** marbled paper sides **2** *often not cap* meters per second
m-q developer *n, usu cap M&Q* [Metol (trademark applied to *N*-methyl-*para*-aminophenol) + quinol] : a photographic developer containing the developing agents *para*-methylaminophenol sulfate and hydroquinone and usu. a preservative, an activator, and an antifoggant
mr. \'mistə(r), *in rapid speech sometimes* (')mist\ *n, pl* **messrs.** \'mesə(r)z *sometimes* -eshə- *or* -es(h)yə- *or* -ezə- *or* -ezhə- *or* -ez(h)yə-\ *usu cap* [ME *Mr*, abbr. of *maister* master — more at MASTER] **1 a** — used as a conventional title of courtesy except when usage requires the substitution of a title of rank or the substitution of an honorific or professional title before a man's surname ⟨spoke to *Mr.* Doe⟩ ⟨may I have a word with you, *Mr.* Doe⟩ or sometimes before a man's given name and surname when the two are used together ⟨a *Mr.* John Doe has left a message for you⟩ **b** — used in direct address as a conventional title of respect before a man's title of office now usu. only when the title of office is not followed by the surname ⟨may I ask one more question, *Mr.* President⟩ **c** — used before the name of a place (as a country, city) or of a profession or other line of activity (as a sport) or before some epithet (as *clever*) to form a title applied to a male viewed or recognized as esp. outstanding in or as representative of the thing indicated ⟨was *Mr.* Baseball to many for a number of years⟩ ⟨was elected *Mr.* America⟩ **2** *obs* : MASTER ⟨refused the title of *Mr.* of Arts —Robert Godfrey⟩ **3** : ²MISTER
mr *abbr* milliroentgen
MR *abbr* **1** map reference **2** master of the rolls **3** mate's receipt **4** mill run **5** mineral rubber **6** mine-run **7** minister resident **8** missionary rector
MRA *abbr* moral rearmament
MRC *abbr* medical reserve corps
MRD *abbr* minimum reacting dose
mrg *or* **mrgn** *abbr* margin; marginal
mrkr *abbr* marker
mrng *abbr* morning
MRO *abbr* maintenance, repair, and operation
m roof *n, cap M* : a roof formed by the junction of two common gable roofs with a valley between them — compare SAWTOOTH ROOF

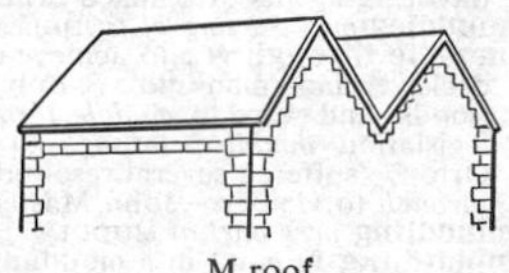
M roof

mrs. \'misəz, 'misəs, 'mizəz, 'mizəs, (')mis, -məs (*in the southern U S these last two forms occur chiefly before a Christian name*), (')miz, -məz *sometimes chiefly in substand speech or in the speech of older persons* 'misərz *or* 'misrəs *or* 'mizərz *or* 'mizrəs *or* 'mizrəz; *the forms with z immediately following the first or only vowel occur chiefly in the southern U S*\ *n, pl* **mrs.** *any of the preceding two-syllable pronunciations*\ *or* **mes·dames** \(')mā'däm, -dam, -daa(ə)m, -dām\ *usu cap* [fr. abbr. of ¹*mistress*] **1 a** — used as a conventional title of courtesy except when usage requires the substitution of a title of rank or the substitution of an honorific or professional title before a married woman's surname ⟨spoke to *Mrs.* Doe⟩ ⟨may I have a word with you, *Mrs.* Doe⟩ or sometimes before a married woman's surname with the given name of her husband or her own given name intervening ⟨a *Mrs.* John Doe has left a message for you⟩ **b** — used before the name of a place (as a country, city) or of a profession or other line of activity (as a sport) or before some epithet (as *clever*) to form a title applied to a married female viewed or recognized as esp. outstanding in or as representative of the thing indicated ⟨was elected *Mrs.* Homemaker⟩ **2** *obs* : MISTRESS **3** *obs* — used as a conventional title of courtesy before the surname or before the given name and surname of an unmarried woman **4** : WIFE ⟨pick up the *Mrs.* at the five-and-dime —Alan Kapelner⟩
MRS *abbr* medical receiving station
mrs. grun·dy \-'grəndē, -di\ *n, pl* **mrs. grundys** *also* **mrs. grundies** *usu cap M&G* [fr. *Mrs. Grundy*, character alluded to in the play *Speed the Plough* (1798) by Thomas Morton †1838 Eng. playwright] : a person marked by a narrowly conventional outlook or by prudishness or by stiff intolerance of any breach of propriety
mrtm *abbr* maritime
mru \mə'rü\ *n, pl* **mru** *or* **mrus** *usu cap* **1 a** : an Indo-Chinese people of the hill districts of Chittagong and Arakan in the western part of Burma **b** : a member of such people **2** : the Tibeto-Burman language of the Mru people
MS \(')e'mes\ *abbr or n* -s Master of Science
ms *abbr* **1** *often cap M&S* manuscript **2** *usu ital* meso- **3** millisecond
MS *abbr* **1** machinery survey **2** mail steamer **3** main switch **4** [It *mano sinistra*] left hand **5** margin of safety **6** master sergeant **7** maximum stress **8** mean square **9** medium shot **10** medium steel **11** [L *memoriae sacrum*] sacred to the memory **12** meters per second **13** metric system **14** mild steel **15** minesweeper **16** mint state **17** months after sight; month's sight **18** morphine sulfate **19** motor ship **20** multiple sclerosis
m's *or* **ms** *pl of* M
msa·sa \əm'säsə\ *n* -s [native name in southern Rhodesia] : any of various African trees of the genus *Brachystegia*
MSc \'e,me(s)'sē\ *abbr or n* -s Master of Science
msc *abbr* **1** millisecond **2** miscellaneous; miscellany
MSC *abbr* **1** mile of standard cable **2** moved, seconded, and carried
MSCP *abbr, often not cap* mean spherical candlepower
msec *abbr* millisecond
MSF *abbr* muscle shock factor
msg *abbr* message
MSG *abbr* monosodium glutamate
msgr *abbr* **1** messenger **2** *often cap* monseigneur **3** *often cap* monsignor
MSH *abbr* master of staghounds
m-shell \'=,=\ *n, usu cap M* : the third innermost shell of electrons surrounding an atomic nucleus — compare K-SHELL, L-SHELL
MSL *abbr, often not cap* mean sea level
MSM *abbr* [L *mille* thousand] thousand feet surface measure
msn *abbr* mission
msngr *abbr* messenger
mss *abbr, often cap M & both Ss* manuscripts
mst *abbr* measurement
MST *abbr* **1** mean solar time **2** mountain standard time
m star *n, usu cap M* : a star of spectral type M — see SPECTRAL TYPE table
MsTh₁ *symbol* mesothorium a
MsTh₂ *symbol* mesothorium b
mstr *abbr* **1** master **2** moisture
mt *abbr* **1** empty **2** might **3** most **4** mount; mountain
MT *abbr* **1** mail transfer **2** mandated territory **3** mean tide **4** mean time **5** measurement ton **6** mechanical transport **7** metric ton **8** military training **9** motor transport **10** mountain time
MTB *abbr or n* -s motor torpedo boat
MTC *abbr* **1** mechanical transport corps **2** motor transport corps
mtd *abbr* mounted
MTD *abbr* mean temperature difference
MTF *abbr* mechanical time fuse
mtg *abbr* **1** meeting **2** mortgage **3** mounting
mtgd *abbr* mortgaged
mtge *abbr* mortgage
mtgee *abbr* mortgagee
mtgor *abbr* mortgagor
mth *abbr* month
MTI *abbr* moving target indicator
mtl *abbr* material
MTL *abbr* mean tidal level
mtn *abbr* mountain
mtr *abbr* motor
MTR *abbr* **1** materials testing reactor **2** multiple track radar
mtrl *abbr* material
¹**mu** \'myü, 'mü, *in sense 1 sometimes* 'mē\ *n* -s [Gk *my*] **1** : the 12th letter of the Greek alphabet — symbol M or *μ*; see ALPHABET table **2** *or* **mu factor** : the amplification factor in an electron tube ⟨the tube oscillates as a low ~ tube —*Radio Corp. of Amer. Rev.*⟩ **3** : MICRON **4** : a bridging position or group joining two or more central atoms or ions in a polynuclear coordination complex — symbol *μ* ⟨tetraethyl-*μ*-dibromo-di-gold⟩
²**mu** *var of* MOU
³**mu** \'mü\ *n* -s [Hawaiian] : MAMAMU
MU *abbr* **1** maintenance unit **2** mobile unit **3** motor union
muazzin *also* **mu'adhdhin** *var of* MUEZZIN
muc- *or* **muci-** *or* **muco-** *comb form* [L *muc-*, fr. *mucus* nasal mucus — more at MUCUS] **1** : mucus : mucous ⟨*mucific*⟩ ⟨*mucocele*⟩ ⟨*mucoid*⟩ **2** : mucous and ⟨*mucopurulent*⟩
muc *abbr* mucilage
mu·ced·i·na·ceous \(')myü'sedᵊn'āshəs\ *adj* [NL *Mucedinaceae*, family of mold fungi in some classifications (fr. L *mucedin-*, *mucedo* nasal mucus — fr. *mucus* — + NL *-aceae*) + E *-ous*] : MUCEDINOUS
mu·ce·dine \'myüsə,dēn, -,dən\ *n* -s [NL *Mucedineae*, family of mold fungi in some classifications, fr. L *mucedin-*, *mucedo* + NL *-eae*] : a mold fungus
mu·ced·i·nous \(')myü'sedᵊnəs\ *or* **mu·ce·din·e·ous** \'myüsə'dinēəs\ *adj* [*mucedinous* fr. L *mucedin-*, *mucedo* + E *-ous*; *mucedineous* prob. fr. NL *Mucedineae* + E *-ous*] : having the nature of or resembling mold or mildew
¹**much** \'məch\ *adj* **more** \(')mō(ə)r, -ō(ə)r, -ōə, -ō(ə)\ **most** \(')mōst\ [ME *muche, miche*, fr. *muchel, michel* great, large, much, fr. OE *micel, mycel*; akin to OHG *mihhil* great, large, ON *mikill*, Goth *mikils*, L *magnus*, Gk *megas*, Skt *mahat*] **1 a** : that exists or is present in a great quantity or amount or to a considerable extent or degree ⟨has ~ money⟩ ⟨spent ~ time⟩ ⟨there is ~ truth in what you say⟩ **b** : that exists or is present in an indicated relative quantity or amount or to an indicated relative extent or degree — used with a qualifying adverb ⟨how ~ money have you got⟩ ⟨has taken too ~ time⟩ ⟨there is as ~ validity in the one theory as in the other⟩ **2** : MANY ⟨~ thanks⟩ ⟨came out against him with ~ people —Num 20:20 (AV)⟩ **3** : very good ⟨wouldn't think I was ~ on literature —C.B.Kelland⟩ ⟨he's not so ~ on looks, but he really is charming —*Atlantic*⟩
²**much** \"\ *adv* **more** \"\ **most** \"\ [ME *muche, miche*, fr. *muche, miche*, adj.] **1 a (1)** : to a great degree or extent : very considerably or notably : GREATLY ⟨is ~ happier now⟩ **(2)** : VERY — usu. used with adjectival past participles ⟨~ interested⟩ ⟨~ pleased by the compliment⟩ ⟨~ gratified⟩ and in negative constructions ⟨not ~ good at all⟩ **b (1)** : FREQUENTLY, OFTEN ⟨went ~ to the theater⟩ **(2)** : for a considerable length of time ⟨was with her ~, but didn't find out anything⟩ : LONG ⟨didn't get there ~ before midnight **2 a** : just about : APPROXIMATELY ⟨the patient was ~ the same as he had been earlier⟩ ⟨comes to ~ the same thing —George Sampson⟩ ⟨the two writers, who are ~ of an age —*Times Lit. Supp.*⟩ **b** : NEARLY ⟨speaks and thinks very ~ as his father used to⟩
³**much** \'məch\ *n* -ES [ME *muche, miche*, fr. *muche, miche*, adj.] **1** : a great quantity or amount or extent or degree : a great deal ⟨learned ~ from this experience⟩ ⟨gave away ~ of what he owned⟩ — often used in negative or interrogative constructions with a following dependent specifying phrase consisting of a generalized category introduced by *of a* and used typically to belittle or query the extent to which something exists in the indicated category ⟨wasn't ~ of a teacher⟩ **2** : something considerable or important or significant or impressive ⟨the evidence didn't amount to ~⟩ ⟨thought it ~ to have made even a little progress⟩ ⟨was not ~ to look at⟩
⁴**much** \"\ *vt* -ED/-ING/-ES *dial* : to make much of : **a** : to show affection for (as by petting or caressing) ⟨~ that dog and see won't he come along —Horace Kephart⟩ **b** : CODDLE ⟨my mother shielded me and ~*ed* me —W.A.White⟩
mu·cha·cha \mü'chächə\ *n* -s [Sp, fem. of *muchacho*] **1** *chiefly Southwest* : a young woman : GIRL **2** *chiefly Southwest* : a female servant
mu·cha·cho \-(,)chō\ *n* -s [Sp, fr. obs. Sp *mochacho*, fr. Sp *mocho* cropped, shorn] **1** *chiefly Southwest* : a young man : BOY **2** *chiefly Southwest* : a male servant
much as *conj* : however much : even though ⟨when a person's afraid — *much as* he might wish to blame his fear on others . . . he's really afraid of himself —W.J.Reilly⟩
much-hunger \'=,==\ *n* : a plant of the genus *Trillium*
much·ly *adv* : MUCH — now not often in formal use ⟨wore a voluminous navy-blue cotton print wrapper, ~ patched —Willie S. Ethridge⟩
much·ness *n* -ES [ME *mochenes*, fr. *moche, muche, miche* much + *-nes* -ness] *archaic* : the quality or state of being great in quantity or amount or extensive in degree — **much of a muchness** : very much the same : just about the same ⟨when we grow a little older we discover we're all very *much of a muchness* —W.S.Maugham⟩
mu·cic acid \'myüsik-\ *n* [*mucic* ISV *muc-* + *-ic*] : an optically inactive crystalline acid HOOC(CHOH)₄COOH obtained from galactose or lactose by oxidation with nitric acid
mu·cid \'myüsəd\ *adj* [L *mucidus*, fr. *mucēre* to be moldy or musty — more at MUCUS] *archaic* : MOLDY, MUSTY
mu·cif·er·ous \(')myü'sif(ə)rəs\ *adj* [*muc-* + *-ferous*] : containing or producing or filled with mucus ⟨~ ducts⟩ ⟨~ glands⟩
mu·cif·ic \-fik\ *adj* [*muc-* + *-fic*] : secreting mucus ⟨a ~ gland⟩
mu·ci·fi·ca·tion \,myüsəfə'kāshən\ *n* -s [*mucific* + *-ation*] : acquisition by epithelial cells of the capacity to form and secrete mucus
mu·ci·fy \'==,fī\ *vi* -ED/-ING/-ES [*muc-* + *-fy*] : to produce or cause the production of mucus
mu·ci·gen \-,jən, -,jen\ *n* -s [ISV *mucin* + *-gen*] : MUCINOGEN
mu·ci·lage \'myüs(ə)lij, -lēj\ *n* -s [ME *mucilage*, fr. LL *mucilago* musty juice, fr. L *mucus* nasal mucus — more at MUCUS] **1** : a gelatinous substance that contains protein and polysaccharides and usu. uronides and that is obtained esp. from the seed coats of various plants (as fucoid seaweeds, marshmallows, flaxes, quinces) and that is similar to plant gums (as gum arabic) but that swells in water without dissolving and forms a slimy mass **2 a** : an aqueous usu. viscid solution of a gum or of some other substance resembling a gum that is used as an adhesive and that is used specif. in pharmacy as an excipient and in medicine as a demulcent — compare PASTE 2 **b** : a similar liquid adhesive of low bonding strength
mucilage cell *n* : a plant cell that secretes mucilage (sense 1) usu. by disorganization of its wall
mu·ci·lag·i·nous \,myüsə'lajənəs\ *adj* [LL *mucilaginosus*, fr. *mucilagin-*, *mucilago* mucilage + L *-osus* -ose] **1 a** : relating to mucilage or the secretion of mucilage ⟨~ disorganization in a plant cell⟩ **b** : resembling mucilage: as **(1)** : viscid and moist **(2)** : slimily sticky **2** : containing or secreting mucilage ⟨a ~ plant cell⟩ — **mu·ci·lag·i·nous·ly** *adv*
mu·cin \'myüsən\ *n* -s [ISV *muc-* + *-in*] : any of a group of mucoproteins that are found in various secretions and tissues of man and lower animals (as in saliva, lining of the stomach, skin) and that are white or yellowish powders when dry and that are viscid when moist ⟨gastric ~⟩
mu·cin·o·gen \myü'sinəjən, -,jen\ *n* -s [ISV *mucin* + *-o-* + *-gen*] : any of various substances easily converted into mucins (as by the action of alkalies)
mu·cin·oid \'myüsᵊn,ȯid\ *adj* [ISV *mucin* + *-oid*] : resembling mucin
mu·ci·no·lyt·ic \,myüsᵊnō'lid·ik\ *adj* [*mucin* + *-o-* + *-lytic*] : able or tending to break down or lower the viscosity of mucin-containing body secretions or components ⟨a ~ enzyme⟩
mu·ci·nous \'myüsᵊnəs\ *adj* [*mucin* + *-ous*] : relating to or containing mucin : MUCOID
¹**muck** \'mək\ *n* -s [ME *muk*, perh. fr. OE *-moc*; akin to ON *myki* dung — more at MUCUS] **1** : soft moist farmyard manure esp. when mixed with decomposing vegetable material and used as a fertilizer **2** *obs* : MONEY **3 a (1)** : wet clinging slimy dirt or filth ⟨spattered with ~ from the pigpen⟩ **(2)** : something (as defamatory remarks) that injures or tends to injure the reputation or standing of another ⟨throwing as much ~ as possible at her rivals⟩ **b (1)** *chiefly dial* : RUBBISH, TRASH, JUNK **(2)** : idle remarks or observations : NONSENSE, GUFF ⟨recall some ~ about chucking someone out —Ernest Hemingway⟩ ⟨the usual ~ of old-timers and loafers —S.E.White⟩ **4 a** : an untidy or messy condition ⟨was all in a ~ of sweat⟩ **b** : a state of confusion, uncertainty, or disorganization : a fouled-up condition ⟨has made such a ~ of things —Agatha Christie⟩ ⟨we're all in a ~, and we're to do the best we can —Richard Llewellyn⟩ **5 a (1)** : a dark usu. black earth that is capable of absorbing much water, that is usu. moist or wet so as to have a consistency like that of moist or wet loam or humus, that is marked by the presence of organic usu. plant matter in an advanced state of decomposition and in a proportion of usu. less than 50 percent, that is rich in nitrogen and relatively low in mineral content (as potash) and that is very fertile **(2)** : earth resembling such muck in wetness or sogginess : soft wet mud : MIRE ⟨floundering through the wet black ~ —Marjory S. Douglas⟩ **b** : something that is oozy, viscid, or sticky like such muck : GOO, GUNK ⟨was given some kind of ~ to use as a salve⟩ **c** : a heavy soggy, slushy, or slimy deposit or mass of sedimentation or some similar heavy wet mass : SLUDGE ⟨oily ~ on the floor of a garage⟩ ⟨pushed through the ~ of dirty snow and half-thawed ice⟩ ⟨~ at the bottom of the drainpipe⟩ **6** : material removed in the process of excavating or mining: as **a** : the total mass of material (as soft earth, hardpan, gravel, rock) so removed **b** : ore or rock in a loose heap as first broken in the process of mining **c** : the material removed by hydraulic mining
²**muck** \"\ *vb* -ED/-ING/-S [ME *mukken*, fr. *muk*, n.] *vt* **1 a** : to clean up; *esp* : to clear of manure or filth ⟨an old pair of boots with rubber feet and felt tops that were used for ~*ing* out the corrals and the pigpen —W.V.T.Clark⟩ **b (1)** : to clear of material (as soft earth, gravel, rock) in the process of excavating or mining ⟨~*ing* an excavation⟩ **(2)** : to dig out or otherwise remove (as soft earth, gravel, rock) in the process of excavating or mining ⟨after each blast they ~*ed* out the rock⟩ **2** : to cover with manure or some other fertilizing muck ⟨~*ing* the orchards each year⟩ **3 a** : to dirty with or as if with muck : SOIL ⟨you can't touch pitch and not be ~*ed* —R.L.Stevenson⟩ **b** : to dirty by tracking or littering : make untidy or messy ⟨~*ed* up the floor⟩ **4** *chiefly Brit* **a** : to make a mess of : BOTCH, BUNGLE ⟨was afraid of ~*ing* up the experiment⟩ **b** : to throw into a state of confusion or disorganization : foul up : SNARL, TANGLE ⟨acting ~*s* up childhood —Clemence Dane⟩ ⟨~*ed* up every plan⟩ **5** *chiefly Brit* : to push around : SHOVE ⟨still ~*ing* the salt about —Richard Llewellyn⟩ ⟨~*ed* about by the last war, by inflations and depressions —*Time*⟩ ~ *vi* **1** *dial Eng* : to work energetically or slavishly : TOIL, DRUDGE **2** *chiefly Brit* **a (1)** : to move about aimlessly or idly : WANDER, LOITER ⟨the country was full of people ~*ing* about the fields —A.J.Liebling⟩ **(2)** : to waste time in trivial or altogether useless activities : DAWDLE, PUTTER ⟨~*ing* about in the affairs of other peoples —A.J. Nock⟩ **b** : to play around : mess around : FOOL, TRIFLE ⟨hadn't ~*ed* around with boys since the time when she was little —Ruth Park⟩ ⟨~*ing* about with some sort of occultism —Ngaio Marsh⟩
³**muck** \"\ *n* -s [alter. of *amuck* (initial vowel taken as indefinite article *a*)] *archaic* : the act of running amok
¹**muck·a·muck** \'məkə,mək\ *vb* [Chinook jargon] *Northwest* : EAT
²**muckamuck** \"\ *n* [Chinook jargon] *Northwest* : FOOD
³**muckamuck** \"\ *also* **muck·ety-muck** \'məkəd·ē,mək\ *n* [short for *high-muck-a-muck, high-muckety-muck*] : an individual of great importance or consequence : BIG SHOT
muck·en·der \'məkəndə(r), 'mük-\ *n* -s [alter. of ME *mokadour*, prob. fr. (assumed) OProv *mocador* (whence Prov *moucadou*), fr. OProv *mocar* to blow or wipe the nose, fr. *moc* nasal mucus, fr. L *mucus* — more at MUCUS] *dial Eng* : HANDKERCHIEF
¹**muck·er** \'məkə(r)\ *vb* -ED/-ING/-S [freq. of ²*muck*] *vt* : BOTCH, BUNGLE, SNARL, TANGLE ~ *vi* : WANDER, LOITER, DAWDLE, PUTTER, FOOL, TRIFLE
²**mucker** \"\ *n* -s *chiefly Brit* : MUCK 4
³**mucker** \"\ *n* -s [¹*muck* + *-er*] **1** *chiefly Brit* : ³CROPPER **2 a (1)** : a coarse boorish person : OAF, PHILISTINE **(2)** : CAD **(3)** : one that lacks the qualities of a good sportsman **(4)** : BASTARD 7 **b** : a tough sometimes vicious individual : ROUGHNECK — **muck·er·ish** \-k(ə)rish\ *adj*
⁴**muck·er** \'məkə(r)\ *n* -s [²*muck* + *-er*] : one that clears away material (as earth, gravel, rock) from a working area: as **a** : a mine worker who scrapes up the chippings left in the channels made by a coal-cutting machine **b** : one that clears bark and debris from a log landing
muck·er·ism \'məkə,rizəm\ *n* -s : behavior characteristic of a mucker
muck·et \'məkət, *usu* -əd·+V\ *n* -s [origin unknown] : any of several freshwater mussels; *esp* : the common mussel (*Actinonaias carinata*) with a lustrous nacreous shell that is used in button manufacture
muck grower *also* **muck farmer** *n* : one who grows vegetables on a muck soil
muckhill \'=,=\ *or* **muckheap** \'=,=\ *n* [*muckhill* fr. ME *mukhill*, fr. *muk* muck + *hill*; *muckheap* fr. ME *mukhepe*, fr. *muk* muck + *hepe* heap] : a pile of manure
muck in *vi* **1** *slang* : to share rations **2** *slang* : to share the burden of some work or project
mucking *adj* [fr. pres. part. of ²*muck*] : DAMNED 2 ⟨if I ever hit you I'll break your ~ jaw —Ernest Hemingway⟩
muck·ite \'mə,kīt, 'mu̇,k-\ *n* -s [G *muckit*, fr. H. *Muck*, 19th cent. Ger. mineralogist, its discoverer + G *-it* -ite] : a yellow resinous hydrocarbon that is a variety of retinite and that is found in a region of central Europe about the upper valley of the Oder river
muck·land \'mə,kland\ *n* : a land area marked by the occurrence of extensive tracts of fertile muck soil
muck·le \'məkəl\ *var of* MICKLE
muck·le·shoot \'məkəl,shüt\ *n, pl* **muckleshoot** *or* **muckleshoots** *usu cap* **1 a** : a Salishan people of the White river valley, Washington **b** : a member of such people **2** : a dialect related to Skagit
muckluck *also* **mucluc** *var of* MUKLUK
muck·ment \'məkmənt, 'mük-\ *n* -s [²*muck* + *-ment*] *dial Eng* : MUCK
muckmidden \'=,==\ *n, chiefly Scot* : MUCKHILL
¹**muck·rake** \'mək,rāk\ *vb* [fr. obs. E *muckrake*, n., rake for gathering dung into a heap, fr. ¹*muck* + *rake*] *vi* : to search out and charge with and seek to expose publicly real or apparent misconduct or vice or corruption on the part of prominent individuals (as public officials) ⟨a politician that ~*s* at every opportunity⟩ : dig up scandal ⟨would enjoy himself if he could ~ in his own backyard —Reginald Reynolds⟩ ~ *vt* **1** : to subject to muckraking ⟨*muckraked* his rivals with great relish⟩ **2** : to investigate or go over assiduously with the purpose of digging up scandal or of incriminating ⟨~*s* his subject with pious zeal —*Time*⟩
²**muckrake** \"\ *n* [fr. obs. E *muckrake*, n.] **1 a** : MUCKRAKING — used with *the* ⟨jeered at me and my colleagues of the ~ —Lincoln Steffens⟩ ⟨such a bold defender of the people, if it be necessary, will use the much dreaded ~ —A.M.Grussi⟩ **b** : a book, article, speech, or other medium used as a vehicle for a muckraking disclosure ⟨will publish his newest ~ later this year⟩ **2** : MUCKRAKER ⟨a confirmed holier-than-thou ~⟩
muck·rak·er \-kə(r)\ *n* : one marked by or given to muckraking ⟨had no patience with ~*s*⟩
¹**muckraking** *adj* [fr. pres. part. of ¹*muckrake*] : marked by preoccupation with or inclination toward muckraking ⟨had grown famous for its ~ articles —Ben Riker⟩ ⟨the ~ magazines and those novelists with similar reformist zeal —W.V.O'Connor⟩ ⟨~ journalism⟩ ⟨a ~ political campaign⟩
²**muckraking** *n* [fr. gerund of ¹*muckrake*] : the action or prac-

tice of one that muckrakes ⟨~ and other sad substitutes for an intelligent policy⟩

muck rolls *n pl* [¹*muck*] **:** the first pair of a train of rolls for rolling wrought iron

mucks *pl of* MUCK, *pres 3d sing of* MUCK

muck soil *n* **:** soil consisting wholly or nearly wholly of muck

muckstick \ˈ=,=\ *n* **:** SHOVEL

muck·sy \ˈməksi, ˈmu̇k-\ *adj* [prob. by alter. (influence of *mixen*)] *dial Eng* **:** MUCKY

muckworm \ˈ=,=\ *n* **1 a :** MISER **b :** GUTTERSNIPE **2 :** WORM; *specif* **:** a worm found in mucky soil or manure — not used technically

¹**mucky** \ˈməkē, -ki\ *adj, usu* -ER/-EST [¹*muck* + -*y*] **1 a :** DIRTY, MESSY, FILTHY ⟨a ~ stable⟩ **b** *chiefly Brit* (1) **:** DISGUSTING, CONTEMPTIBLE ⟨a ~ way of doing things⟩ (2) **:** UNPLEASANT, DISAGREEABLE ⟨an embarrassing and altogether ~ situation⟩ (3) **:** MEAN, CHEAP, UNDERHANDED ⟨had played a ~ trick on him —Mary Deasy⟩ (4) **:** revoltingly fulsome **:** STICKY ⟨his ~ flattery —Samuel Butler †1902⟩ **c** (1) **:** MUGGY, HUMID ⟨~ weather⟩ (2) **:** MURKY, CLOUDED ⟨the slow ~ water of the creek⟩ **2 :** consisting of, marked by, or full of muck ⟨the ~ bottom of a pond⟩ **:** MIRY, MUDDY ⟨a ~ ditch⟩ ⟨a ~ road⟩

²**mucky** \ˈməki, ˈmu̇ki\ *vt* -ED/-ING/-ES *dial Eng* **:** to make dirty

muco- — see MUC-

mu·co·cele *also* **mu·co·coele** \ˈmyükə,sēl\ *n* -s [*muc-* + -*cele* or -*coele*] **:** a swelling like a sac that is due to distention of a hollow organ or cavity with mucus ⟨a ~ of the appendix⟩; *specif* **:** a dilated lacrimal sac

mu·co·cutaneous \ˌmyü(ˌ)kō+\ *adj* [*muc-* + *cutaneous*] **:** made up of, affecting, or involving both typical skin and mucous membrane ⟨the ~ junction of the mouth⟩ ⟨~ syphilis⟩

mu·co·flocculent \ˌ==+\ *adj* [*muc-* + *flocculent*] **:** consisting of or containing flaky shreds of mucus

¹**mu·coid** \ˈmyü,kȯid\ *also* **mu·coi·dal** \(ˈ)myüˈkȯidᵊl\ *adj* [*mucoid* ISV *muc-* + -*oid*; *mucoidal* fr. *mucoid* + -*al*] **1 :** resembling mucus **2 :** forming large moist sticky colonies — used of dissociated strains of bacteria; contrasted with *rough* and *smooth*

²**mu·coid** \ˈmyü,kȯid\ *n* -s [ISV *mucin* + -*oid*] **1 :** any of a group of complex proteins similar to mucins or mucoproteins but occurring esp. in connective tissue and in cysts **:** ²COLLOID 2 **2 :** MUCOPROTEIN

mucoid degeneration *n* [¹*mucoid*] **:** tissue degeneration marked by conversion of cell substance into a glutinous substance like mucin

mucoid tissue *n* **:** MUCOUS TISSUE

mu·co·i·tin·sulfuric acid *also* **mucoitin sulfate** \(ˈ)myü-ˈkōətən+-\ *n* [*mucoitin* ISV *muc-* + -*itin* (as in *chondroitin*)] **:** an acidic mucopolysaccharide that is found esp. in the cornea of the eye and in gastric mucosa and that is a derivative of glucosamine and glucuronic acid; an ester of hyaluronic acid and sulfuric acid

mu·co·lyt·ic \ˌmyükəˈlid·ik\ *adj* [ISV *muc-* + -*lytic*] **:** that hydrolyzes mucopolysaccharides **:** MUCINOLYTIC ⟨a ~ enzyme⟩

mu·con·ic acid \(ˈ)myüˈkänik-\ *n* [*muconic* ISV *muc-* + *itaconic*] **:** a crystalline unsaturated acid $(CHCHCOOH)_2$ obtained indirectly from mucic acid and formed by oxidation of benzene in the animal body; 1,3-butadiene-1,4-dicarboxylic acid

mu·co·periosteal \ˌmyükō+\ *adj* [NL *mucoperiosteum* + E -*al*] **:** of or relating to the mucoperiosteum

mu·co·periosteum \"+\ *n* [NL, fr. *muc-* + *periosteum*] **:** a periosteum backed with mucous membrane (as that of the palatine surface of the mouth)

mu·co·polysaccharide \"+\ *n* [ISV *muc-* + *polysaccharide*] **:** any of a class of polysaccharides (as chondroitinsulfuric acid, mucoitinsulfuric acid, or heparin) that are widely distributed in the body, that bind water to form thick gelatinous material serving to cement cells together and to lubricate joints and bursas, that are derived from a hexosamine (as glucosamine), a uronic acid, and often sulfuric acid, and that are constituents of mucoproteins, glycoproteins, and blood-group substances

mu·co·protein \"+\ *n* [*muc-* + *protein*] **:** any of a group of complex compounds (as mucins) containing mucopolysaccharides (as chondroitinsulfuric acid or mucoitinsulfuric acid) combined with amino acid units or polypeptides and occurring in body fluids and tissues — called also *mucoid*; compare GLYCOPROTEIN

mu·co·purulent \"+\ *adj* [ISV *muc-* + *purulent*] **:** containing both mucus and pus

mu·co·pus \ˌmyükō+\ *n* [ISV *muc-* + *pus*] **:** mucus mingled with pus

mu·cor \ˈmyükə(r), -,kȯ(ə)r\ *n* [NL, fr. L, mold, moldiness, fr. *mucēre* to be moldy or musty — more at MUCUS] **1** *cap* **:** a genus (the type of the family Mucoraceae) of molds that are distinguished from molds of the genus *Rhizopus* through having round usu. cylindrical or pear-shaped sporangia not clustered and not limited in location to the points where rhizoids develop **2** -s **:** any mold of the genus *Mucor*

mu·co·ra·ce·ae \ˌmyükəˈrāsē,ē\ *n pl, cap* [NL, fr. *Mucor*, type genus + -*aceae*] **:** a large family of chiefly saprophytic molds (order Mucorales) having a well-developed branching mycelium that lacks septa and including many molds (as members of the genera *Rhizopus* and *Mucor*) that are destructive to food products (as bread, fruits, or vegetables) — **mu·co·ra·ceous** \ˌ==ˈrāshəs\ *adj*

mu·co·ra·les \ˌ==ˈrā(ˌ)lēz\ *n pl, cap* [NL, fr. *Mucor* + -*ales*] **:** an order of mostly saprophytic fungi (subclass Zygomycetes) that reproduce asexually by spores borne within sporangia and sexually by homothallic or heterothallic zygospores and that include many common domestic molds

mu·cor·my·co·sis \ˌmyükə(r)+\ *n* [NL, fr. *Mucor* + *mycosis*] **:** mycosis caused by fungi of the genus *Mucor* usu. primarily involving the lungs and invading other tissues by means of metastatic lesions

mu·cor·rhea *or* **mu·cor·rhoea** \ˌmyükəˈrēə\ *n* -s [NL, fr. *muc-* + -*rrhea*, -*rrhoea*] **:** discharge of mucus esp. when excessive

mu·co·sa \myüˈkōsə, -ōzə\ *n, pl* **muco·sae** \-,sē, -,zē\ *or* **mucosa** *or* **mucosas** [NL, fr. L, fem. of *mucosus* mucous] **:** MUCOUS MEMBRANE — **mu·co·sal** \(ˈ)=ˈ=səl, -zəl\ *adj*

mu·co·sanguineous \ˌmyü(ˌ)kō+\ *adj* [*muc-* + *sanguineous*] **:** containing mucus and blood ⟨~ feces⟩

mu·cose \ˈmyü,kōs\ *adj* [L *mucosus*] **:** MUCOUS

mu·co·serous \ˌmyükō+\ *adj* [*muc-* + *serous*] **:** containing both mucous and serous matter ⟨a ~ discharge⟩; *esp* **:** producing both mucus and a serous secretion ⟨a ~ cell⟩ ⟨a ~ gland⟩

mu·cos·i·ty \myüˈkäsəd·ē, -ətē, -i\ *n* -ES [F *mucosité*, fr. L *mucosus* mucous + F -*ité* -ity] **:** the quality or state of being mucous

mucoso- *comb form* [L *mucosus* mucous] **:** mucous and ⟨*mucoso*purulent⟩ ⟨*mucoso*saccharine⟩

mu·cous \ˈmyükəs\ *adj* [L *mucosus*, fr. *mucus* nasal mucus + -*osus* -ose] **1 :** covered with mucus or similar viscous matter **:** SLIMY ⟨a ~ surface⟩ **2 :** of, relating to, or resembling mucus ⟨a ~ secretion⟩ **3 :** secreting or containing mucus ⟨~ glands of the intestine⟩

mucous colitis *n* **:** a functional commonly psychosomatic disorder of the colon characterized by the secretion and passage of large amounts of mucus, constipation alternating with diarrhea, and cramping abdominal pain

mucous membrane *n* **:** a membrane rich in mucous glands; *specif* **:** the membrane that lines the passages and cavities of the body which communicate directly or indirectly with the exterior (as the alimentary, respiratory, and genitourinary tracts) and that consists of two chief layers of which one is a deep vascular connective-tissue stroma which in many parts of the alimentary canal contains a thin but definite layer of nonstriated muscle and the other is a superficial epithelium varying in kind and thickness but always soft and smooth and kept lubricated by the secretions of the cells and numerous glands embedded in the membrane

mucous patch *n* **:** a broad flat syphilitic condyloma that is often marked by a yellowish discharge and that occurs on moist skin or mucous membranes

mucous tissue *n* **:** a gelatinous connective tissue containing stellate cells with long processes in a soft matrix that occurs in the umbilical cord and in the embryo and in myxomas

mu·co·vis·ci·do·sis \ˌmyükō,visəˈdōsəs\ *n, pl* **mucoviscidoses** \-,sēz\ [NL, fr. *muc-* + LL *viscidus* viscid + NL -*osis*] **:** an hereditary disease of infants and young children characterized by the presence of cysts and excessive fibrous tissue in glandular organs (as the pancreas and lungs), by excess mucous secretion which causes a blocking of respiratory passages and pancreatic ducts, and by resulting malnutrition, diarrhea, cough, and wheezing respiration — called also *cystic fibrosis, pancreatic fibrosis*

mu·cro \ˈmyü(ˌ)krō\ *n, pl* **mu·cro·nes** \=ˈ=,nēz\ *also* **mucros** [NL, fr. L, point, edge; akin to Gk *amyssein* to scratch, sting and prob. to Lith *mušti* to strike] **:** an abrupt sharp terminal point or tip or process of an animal part or a plant part: as **a :** the terminal segment of the springing appendage of an arthropod of the order Collembola **b :** the terminal point or tip of some leaves

mu·cro·nate \ˈmyükrənət, -,nāt, *usu* -d·+V\ *also* **mu·cro·nat·ed** \-,nād·əd\ *adj* [*mucronate* fr. L *mucronatus*, fr. *mucron-*, *mucro* point + -*atus* -ate; *mucronated* fr. L *mucronatus* + E -*ed*] **:** ending in an abrupt sharp terminal point or tip or process **:** marked by a mucro ⟨a ~ leaf⟩

mu·cro·na·tion \ˌ==ˈnāshən\ *n* -s [*mucronate* + -*ion*] **1 :** the quality or state of being mucronate **2 :** a mucronate point, tip, or process

mu·cu·lent \ˈmyükyələnt\ *adj* [LL *muculentus* sniveling, fr. L *mucus* nasal mucus + -*ulentus* -ulent] **:** MUCOID

mu·cu·na \myüˈkyünə\ *n, cap* [NL, fr. Pg *mucunã*, *mucuna* fr. Tupi *mucunán*, *mucuná*] **:** a genus of tropical herbs and woody vines (family Leguminosae) with trifoliolate leaves and showy flowers in axillary stalked clusters — see COWAGE

mu·cus \ˈmyükəs\ *n* -ES [L, nasal mucus; akin to ON *myki* dung, *mjūkr* soft, gentle, Goth *muka-* gentle, L *mucēre* to be moldy or musty, Gk *myxa* lamp wick, nasal mucus, Skt *muñcati* he releases, lets loose; basic meaning: slippery] **1 :** a viscid slippery secretion rich in mucins that is produced by mucous membranes and that serves to moisten and protect such membranes **2 :** a viscid animal secretion (as from the external body surface of snails) that resembles mucus

¹**mud** \ˈməd\ *n* -s *often attrib* [ME *mode, mudde*, prob. fr. MLG, thick mud; akin to MHG *mot* mud, morass, Sw *modd* dirty snow, OE *mōs* bog, swamp — more at MOSS] **1 :** a slimy sticky fluid-to-plastic mixture of finely divided particles of solid material and water ⟨a drizzling rain . . . turned the dust of the roads into ~ —George Borrow⟩ **2 a :** the worst part of a thing **:** DREGS ⟨the ~ of the earth . . . remains bespattering his spirit —Havelock Ellis⟩ **b :** the lowest place **:** DEPTHS ⟨that you should have been dragged down into the ~ —Christopher Isherwood⟩ **3 :** abusive and malicious remarks or charges ⟨a sorely bedeviled body of men who have had much ~ thrown at and around them —Roy Lewis & Angus Maude⟩ **4 :** a geological deposit having the physical character of mud ⟨sands and ~s . . . have been transformed by the stresses of millions of years into white marble —*Amer. Guide Series: Md.*⟩ **5 :** DRILLING FLUID **6 :** ²ANATHEMA 2b — used esp. in the phrase *name is mud* ⟨don't know what his right name is . . . but his name's ~ with me —S.V.Benét⟩ **7** *slang* **:** OPIUM

²**mud** \"\ *vb* **mudded; mudded; mudding; muds** *vt* **1 :** to make muddy or turbid ⟨the dog scampered through the brook, *mudding* it⟩ **2 :** to spread or plaster with mud ⟨these tanks were *mudded* up for camouflage —*Infantry Jour.*⟩ ⟨choose deliberately the path well-*mudded* —Roland Mathias⟩ ⟨~ the chinks in his cabin⟩ **3 :** to introduce mud into; *esp* **:** to introduce artificial muds containing a heavy constituent (as barite) into (an oil well) to seal against natural gas or water during drilling — often used with *off* ~ *vi* **:** to burrow or hide in mud ⟨a place where the eels ~⟩

³**mud** *var of* MUID

mu·dar *also* **mud·dar** *or* **ma·dar** \məˈdär, -dä(r\ *n* -s [Hindi *madār*] **:** either of two East Indian shrubs (*Calotropis gigantea* and *C. procera*) whose fine bast fiber resembles flax in strength but is too short to be of great commercial value

mud-baby \ˈ=,==\ *n* **:** BURHEAD 2

mudbank \ˈ=,=\ *n* **:** a submerged or partly submerged bank of mud along a shore or in a river ⟨an old dismantled steamer he had seen years ago rotting on a ~ —Joseph Conrad⟩

mud bass *n* **1 :** a small freshwater sunfish (*Acantharchus pomotis*) of the eastern U.S. **2 :** WARMOUTH

mud bath *n* **:** an immersion of the body or a part of it in mud (as for the alleviation of rheumatism or gout)

mud-blister worm \ˈ=ˈ==-\ *n* **:** a polychaete worm (*Polydora ciliata*) that lives in a mud-walled tube with which it lines U-shaped borings in chalky formations or in the shells of oysters on which it may be a destructive pest

mud boat *n* **1 :** a large flatboat used in dredging to carry off the mud and silt to deep water or elsewhere **2 :** a low sled with broad runners on which logs are hauled in swamps

¹**mudcap** \ˈ=,=\ *n* [¹*mud* + *cap*] **:** a blasting method in which explosive is placed on the surface of a rock fragment and covered with mud or clay — called also *adobe*

²**mudcap** \"\ *vt* **:** to blast by the mudcap process

mud cat *also* **mud catfish** *n* [¹*mud*] **1 :** FLATHEAD CATFISH **2 :** a large freshwater catfish of the Mississippi valley and adjoining regions

mudcat \ˈ=,=\ *n, usu cap* **:** MISSISSIPPIAN — used as a nickname

mud clerk *n* **:** the assistant to the purser of a river steamboat ⟨even her two *mud clerks* . . . wore uniforms —I.S.Cobb⟩

mud coot *n* **:** AMERICAN COOT

mud crab *n* **1 :** any of numerous marine crabs (family Xanthidae) dwelling on muddy bottoms; *esp* **:** one of a widely distributed genus (*Panopeus*) found along both coasts of No. and So. America and near western Africa **2 :** YELLOW SHORE CRAB

mud crack *n* **:** one of a system of cracks by which drying mud is divided; *specif* **:** one of the cracks after it has been filled and the mud and filling material changed to rock

mud dab *n* **1 :** WINTER FLOUNDER **2 :** any of several flounders (family Pleuronectidae) of the genus *Limanda*; *esp* **:** a flounder (*L. limanda*) of northern Europe resembling the winter flounder

mud dabbler *n* **:** a killifish (*Fundulus heteroclitus*) of the U.S.

mud dauber *n* **:** any of various wasps of the families Sphecidae and sometimes Eumenidae that construct mud cells on a solid base (as stone or woodwork of buildings) in which the female places an egg with spiders or insects paralyzed by a sting to serve as food for the larva

mud·der \ˈmədə(r)\ *n* -s [¹*mud* + -*er*] **1 :** a race horse that runs well on a wet or muddy track **2 :** a player or a team (as in football) that performs well on a wet field

mud devil *n* **:** HELLBENDER 1

muddied *past of* MUDDY

muddier *comparative of* MUDDY

muddies *pres 3d sing of* MUDDY

muddiest *superlative of* MUDDY

mud·di·ly \ˈmədəlē, -li\ *adv* **:** in a muddy manner

mud·di·ness \-dēnəs, -din-\ *n* -ES **:** the quality or state of being muddy ⟨the language is pure and correct, free from ~ —T.S. Eliot⟩

mudding *pres part of* MUD

mud dipper *n* **:** RUDDY DUCK

¹**mud·dle** \ˈmədᵊl\ *vb* **muddled; muddled; muddling** \-d(ᵊ)liŋ\ **muddles** [prob. fr. obs. D *moddelen* to make muddy or turbid, fr. MD, freq. of *modden* to make muddy or turbid, fr. *modde* mud; akin to MLG *mode, mudde* thick mud — more at MUD] *vt* **1 :** to spoil the clearness of (colors) ⟨the transparent freshness of watercolor drawings when the washes are not *muddled* —E.V.Neale⟩ **2 :** to make turbid or muddy ⟨*muddled* the brook with his splashings⟩ **3 :** to make (one's brain) cloudy or foggy **:** make stupid esp. with liquor ⟨the drink *muddled* him and his voice became loud and domineering⟩ **4 :** to make indistinct (as speech) **:** MUMBLE ⟨the unforgivable sin in a pupil is not ungrammatical speech but *muddled* speech —George Sampson⟩ **5 :** to waste or squander without purpose — usu. used with *away* ⟨~ away a fortune⟩ ⟨~ away the hours until train time⟩ **6 :** to mix confusedly **:** jumble together without purpose ⟨two worlds of discourse become *muddled* together in the same language and become nonsense —F.S.C.Northrop⟩ **7 :** to make a mess of **:** BUNGLE ⟨*muddled* themselves into the most indefensible positions —A.N.Whitehead⟩ ⟨too much is at stake in government for them to be permitted to ~ policies —V.L.Parrington⟩ **8** *of mixed drinks* **:** to crush and mix (as mint and sugar) by working a spoon or similar utensil on the bottom of a glass or mixer ~ *vi* **1 a :** to dabble or wallow in mud or dirt ⟨cats and dogs *muddling* round a fire —E.M.Forster⟩ **b** *archaic* **:** to do hard often dirty work **:** GRUB **2 :** to think, act, or go in a confused aimless way or in a way that tends to make a mess of things ⟨the story . . . is one of *muddling* and halfheartedness —R.C.K. Ensor⟩ ⟨~ around a house for a week —Peggy Durdin⟩ ⟨let her ~ along thinking she is getting ready —Marcia Davenport⟩

²**muddle** \"\ *n* -s **1 :** a state of confusion: as **a :** thinking that lacks clarity and precision **:** intellectual cloudiness **:** VACUITY ⟨the ~ in the argument —John Holloway⟩ ⟨surrounded by a vast ~ of hearsay —Janet Flanner⟩ **b :** a condition marked by bungling, uncertainty, and lack of clear procedure or aim ⟨dislike of the ~ and the misdirection of our institutions —*Times Lit. Supp.*⟩ ⟨the world's been confused and poor, a thorough ~ —H.G.Wells⟩ ⟨saw what faulty coordination and general ~ can do to an army —G.A.Craig⟩ **c :** an untidy litter of heterogeneous things out of place or order ⟨I'll move these newspapers, excuse the *muddle* —Janet Frame⟩ ⟨a mixture of Gothic and Renaissance, a ~ of gables and projections —S.P.B.Mais⟩ ⟨the shelves in ascending degrees of ~ covered the wall —John Updike⟩ **2 a :** a fish stew **b :** a gathering where muddle is served **syn** see CONFUSION

muddlebrained \ˈ==ˈ=\ *adj* **:** MUDDLEHEADED

mud·dled \ˈmədᵊld\ *adj* [fr. past part. of ¹*muddle*] **:** characterized by a confused state: as **a :** dull of mind **:** slightly stupid; *also* **:** INTOXICATED ⟨being at the same time slightly ~ with liquor —Charles Dickens⟩ **b :** having little reality **:** CLOUDY, VAGUE ⟨in a ~ platonic way he feels some affection for the girl —*Sydney (Australia) Bull.*⟩ ⟨the mixed and ~ skepticism of the Renaissance —T.S.Eliot⟩ ⟨~ thinking as ignoble as dirty conduct —H.G.Wells⟩ ⟨her ~ yearnings and dreamings dissolved into storms of furious tears —Ruth Park⟩ **c :** MIXED-UP, JUMBLED ⟨the gigantic growth of government expenditures, the ~ tax situation —E.B.George⟩ ⟨much of the information he gives is ~ —H.P.Stern⟩

mud·dled·ness *n* -ES **:** the quality or state of being muddled ⟨~ in the activities of the world —S.C.Pepper⟩

mud·dle·dom \ˈmədᵊldəm\ *n* -s **1 :** thinking or acting in an aimless or confused manner ⟨in a constant state of ~⟩ **2 :** a realm of unintelligible confusion ⟨a spiritual ~ is set up —E.M. Forster⟩

muddlehead \ˈ==,=\ *n* **:** a stupid person **:** BLOCKHEAD

muddleheaded \ˈ==ˈ==\ *adj* **:** characterized by a state of confused thought or by bungling and ineptitude ⟨such a confused, puddingheaded, ~ fellow —Laurence Sterne⟩ — **mud·dle·head·ed·ness** *n* -ES

mud·dle·ment \ˈmədᵊlmənt\ *n* -s **:** MUDDLEDNESS ⟨made her feel remote from the usual ~ of her thoughts —Ruth Park⟩

muddle-minded \ˈ==ˈ==\ *adj* **:** MUDDLEHEADED

mud·dler \ˈməd(ᵊ)lə(r)\ *n* -s **1 :** one that muddles; *specif* **:** a utensil usu. shaped like a pestle for crushing and mixing (as the flavoring agents of a mixed drink) **2 :** MILLER'S-THUMB 1

muddles *pres 3d sing of* MUDDLE, *pl of* MUDDLE

muddle through *vi* **:** to achieve a degree of success without a decisive plan ⟨mankind . . . only learns enough from glaciers, floods, and wars to *muddle through* —Henry Hewes⟩ ⟨social legislation *muddled through* in the right direction —W.A. Orton⟩ ⟨suffered several resounding disasters before *muddling through* to victory —John Masters⟩

muddling *pres part of* MUDDLE

mud·dling·ly *adv* **:** in a muddling manner

¹**mud·dy** \ˈmədē, -di\ *adj* -ER/-EST [ME *moddy*, fr. *mode, mudde* mud + -*y*] **1 :** morally impure **:** BASE ⟨has avoided any off-color ~ humor —*Newsweek*⟩ ⟨graft-ridden and ~ regime —D.M.Friedenberg⟩ **2 a :** having a great deal of mud **:** covered with mud ⟨clambering on the divan with ~ shoes —Lucius Garvin⟩ ⟨waded through the ~ water —Robert Hichens⟩ ⟨eyes were fixed on the ~ coastline —T.B.Costain⟩ **b :** characteristic of or resembling mud ⟨a ~ flavor in freshwater fish caught in a *muddy*-bottomed lake —Jane Nickerson⟩ ⟨a sky that had a ~ color⟩ **c :** turbid with sediment ⟨quaff ~ ale in the bar —Max Peacock⟩ ⟨the horrible ~ coffee⟩ **3 :** cloudy in color **:** having no brightness or clarity **:** DULL ⟨eyes a little wild, ~ with anger and lack of sleep —John & Ward Hawkins⟩ ⟨colors . . . are subdued, hinting thus at the ~ monotony of his later paintings —R.M.Coates⟩ **4 :** living naturally close to or in mud ⟨the coot is a ~ bird⟩ **5 a :** cloudy in mind **:** MUDDLED ⟨are you able to reconstruct happenings clearly . . . in your mind, or do they come ~ and distorted —Charles Yerkow⟩ ⟨a ~ thinker, but a superb artist —J.D.Adams⟩ **b :** obscure in meaning **:** CONFUSED ⟨his style is never ~ —W.J.M.Rankine⟩ **6 :** DEJECTED, GLOOMY ⟨the glandular, torpid, ~ stare —George Biddle⟩ **7** *of musical tones* **:** run together **:** not clearly defined or articulated **:** INDISTINCT **syn** see TURBID

²**muddy** \"\ *vb* -ED/-ING/-ES *vt* **1 :** to soil or stain with or as if with mud ⟨*muddied* and weary horsemen —S.H.Adams⟩ ⟨~ and cheapen the quality of our actual everyday life —Thomas Wolfe⟩ **2 :** to make turbid ⟨what are you doing in my well, ~*ing* it up like that —Erskine Caldwell⟩ **3 :** to make cloudy or dull in color ⟨a common admonition of the instructors is . . . "~ your colors" —*Amer. Fabrics*⟩ **4 :** to produce confusion in ⟨exhaustion broke him down . . . and *muddied* his mind —Norman Mailer⟩ ⟨emotionalism which has *muddied* discussion —C.J.Rolo⟩ ~ *vi* **:** to become muddy

muddybreast \ˈ==,=\ *n* **:** GOLDEN PLOVER

muddyheaded \ˈ==ˈ==\ *adj* **:** MUDDLEHEADED

muddy-mettled \ˈ==ˈ==\ *adj* **:** having a dull spirit ⟨a dull and *muddy-mettled* rascal —Shak.⟩

muddy-minded \ˈ==ˈ==\ *adj* **:** MUDDLEHEADED ⟨the expression of a *muddy-minded* humanitarianism —Raymond Moley⟩

mud eel *n* **:** a siren (*Siren lacertina*) that is lead gray in color, attains a length of about two feet, and inhabits the swamps and ditches of the southern U.S.

¹**mu·de·jar** \müˈt͟heˌhär\ *n, pl* **mudeja·res** \-ˌhä(ˌ)rās\ *usu cap* [Sp *mudéjar*, fr. Ar *mudajjan*, lit., allowed to remain] **:** a Muslim living under a Christian king esp. during the 8th to 11th centuries but retaining his religion, laws, and customs

²**mudejar** \"\ *adj, usu cap* **:** of, relating to, or characteristic of the Mudejars and esp. of their architecture ⟨cloisters separated from green gardens and fountains by delicate Gothic tracery or *Mudejar* colonnades —S.E.Morison⟩

mud fever *n* **1 :** a chapped inflamed condition of the skin of the legs and belly of a horse due to irritation from mud or drying resulting from washing off mud-spatters and closely related or identical in nature to grease heel **2 :** a severe enteritis of turkeys **3 :** a mild leptospirosis that occurs chiefly in European agricultural and other workers in wet soil, is caused by infection with an organism (*Leptospira grippotyphosa*) present in native field mice, and is marked by fever and headache without accompanying jaundice

mudfish \ˈ=,=\ *n* **:** any of several fishes that frequent muddy water or burrow in the mud: as **a :** BOWFIN **b :** MUD MINNOW **c :** a New Zealand fish (*Neochanna apoda*) of the family Galaxiidae that lives in burrows like a crayfish

mud flap *n* **:** a sheet of thin material suspended behind each rear wheel of a motor vehicle to intercept spattered mud and water

mud flat *n* **:** ²FLAT 1a(2)

mudflow \ˈ=,=\ *n* **1 a :** a mass of mingled volcanic particles and water which flows like lava from a volcano **b :** a body of rock formed in this manner **2 :** an eruption of mud from a mud volcano or mud spring **3 :** a moving mass of soil made fluid by rain or melting snow **:** a mud avalanche — compare EARTHFLOW **4 :** a minor structure present in various fine-grained sedimentary rocks and indicative of local flowage while the material was still soft

¹**mudge** \ˈməj\ *vi* -ED/-ING/-S [perh. alter. (influenced by ¹*move*) of ²*budge*] *chiefly Scot* **:** BUDGE, MOVE

²**mudge** \"\ *n* -s *Scot* **:** MOVEMENT

mud goose *n* **:** HUTCHINS'S GOOSE

mudguard \ˈ=,=\ *n* **1 :** FENDER 1d(1) **2 :** a strip of material (as of leather or rubber) applied to a shoe upper just above the sole intended as a protection against dampness or as an ornament — see SHOE illustration

mud gun *n* **:** a device for forcibly applying stiff mud or clay (as to the taphole of a blast furnace for closing it)

mudhead \ˈ=,=\ *n* **:** one of a Zuñi ceremonial clown fraternity appearing in tribal rites in mud-daubed masks symbolizing an early stage in the development of man

mud hen *n* : MARSH HEN 1
mudhole \ˈ⸗,⸗\ *n* **1** : a hole or hollow place containing much mud ⟨his swimming pool was nothing but a ~⟩ ⟨a dirt road full of ~*s*⟩ **2** : a very small town ⟨drifted into some rural ~ and set up shop —*Amer. Mercury*⟩
mudhook \ˈ⸗,⸗\ *n* : the anchor of a ship ⟨dropped his ~ . . . and ran up the American flag —*Nat'l Geographic*⟩
mudhopper \ˈ⸗,⸗⸗\ *n* : MUDSKIPPER
mu·dir \mü'di(ə)r\ *n* -s [Ar *mudīr*] : the governor of a mudiria
mu·di·ria *also* **mu·di·ri·eh** \,müdə'rē(y)ə\ *n* -s [Ar *mudīrīyah*] : a province in Egypt, the Sudan, and the Zanzibar protectorate
mud jacking *n* [*jacking* fr. gerund of ²*jack*] : the raising of a pavement or railroad subgrade by means of mud pumped under it through drilled holes
mud lark *n* **1** : a person who grubs in mud (as in search of stray bits of coal, iron, rope); *specif* : an urchin who grubs for a living along the tide flats of the English Thames **2 a** *dial Eng* : PIPIT **b** : any of various birds (as the meadowlark or the shoveler) that live in moist places **c** : the Australian magpie lark (*Grallina cyanoleuca*) that makes mud nests
mudlark \ˈ⸗,⸗\ *vi* [*mud lark*] : to play, dig, or search in mud or on muddy ground ⟨had been out all the morning sailing cork boats and ~*ing* in the marshes —Crosbie Garstin⟩
mud lava *n* : MUD 4
mud·less \ˈmədləs\ *adj* : having no mud
mud lump *n* : a broad low mound of clay or silt on a delta usu. near its outer margin (as on the delta of the Mississippi river)
mud mark *n* : MUDFLOW 4
mudminnow \ˈ⸗,⸗(,)⸗\ *n* : a small fish of the genus *Umbra* (order Haplomi); *esp* : a common small fish (*U. limi*) of the Mississippi valley
mudpack \ˈ⸗,⸗\ *n* **1** : a cosmetic paste for the face composed chiefly of fuller's earth, bleaches, and astringents **2** : the powder from which this paste is prepared
mud peep *n* : LEAST SANDPIPER
mud pickerel *n* : GRASS PICKEREL 1
mud plantain *n* **1** : a plant of the genus *Heteranthera; esp* : a No. American marsh or water plant (*H. dubia*) **2** : WATER PLANTAIN
mud plover *n* : BLACK-BELLIED PLOVER
mud puddle *n* : a small pool of dirty water usu. left by a rain storm ⟨*mud puddles* and ragged weeds by the road —Sinclair Lewis⟩
mud puppy *n* : any of various mostly large American salamanders: as **a** : HELLBENDER **b** : AXOLOTL **c** : a member of the genus *Necturus*
mud purslane *n* : a plant of the genus *Elatine*
mud puss·er \-,pu̇sə(r)\ *n* -s [¹*mud* + *pusser* (of unknown origin)] : the native mollienisia (*Mollienisia latipinna*) of Florida
mu·dra \məˈdrä\ *n* -s [Skt *mudrā* seal, sign, token] : symbolic hand gestures of India's natya dance crystallized by ancient sages from descriptive and expressive movements into an elaborate code
mud ring *n* : the ring or frame forming the bottom of a water leg in a steam boiler
mud-runner \ˈ⸗,⸗⸗\ *n* : MUDDER
muds *pl of* MUD, *pres 3d sing of* MUD
mud saw *n* : a cutting tool for very hard materials (as gems) consisting of a metal disk that dips into a semifluid abrasive mixture as it revolves and carries it to the point of cutting
mud shark *n* : any of several sluggish bottom-dwelling sharks esp. of the family Hexanchidae
mudsill \ˈ⸗,⸗\ *n* **1** : the lowest sill of a structure (as of a house, bridge, dam) usu. embedded in soil or mud **2** : a person of the lowest stratum of society ⟨a ~ like me trying to push in and help —Mark Twain⟩ ⟨all classes and conditions of society from the millionaire to the ~ —D.D.Martin⟩
mudskipper \ˈ⸗,⸗⸗\ *n* : any of several small Asiatic and Polynesian gobies (genera *Periophthalmus* and *Boleophthalmus*) that are able to leave the water and skip about actively over wet mud and sand and even to climb the roots of mangroves by means of fleshy modified pectoral fins
mudslinger \ˈ⸗,⸗⸗\ *n* : one that employs mudslinging
mudslinging \ˈ⸗,⸗⸗\ *n* : the use of offensive epithets and invective against an individual esp. during a political campaign ⟨acrimonious debate and ~ —*Amer. Guide Series: Ind.*⟩
mud snail *n* **1** : BASKET SHELL 2 **2** : a common Old World pond snail (*Lymnaea truncatella*) that is the English intermediate host of the sheep liver fluke
mud snake *n* : HOOP SNAKE 2a
mud snipe *n* : WOODCOCK 1a(2)
mudspate \ˈ⸗,⸗\ *n* : MUDFLOW 3
mudspringer \ˈ⸗,⸗⸗\ *n* : MUDSKIPPER
mud-star \ˈ⸗,⸗\ *n* : any of various active bottom-dwelling starfishes that constitute the genus *Luidia*
mudstone \ˈ⸗,⸗\ *n* : an indurated shale produced by the consolidation of mud
mudsucker \ˈ⸗,⸗⸗\ *n* **1** : any bird that thrusts its bill into mud in search of food (as the woodcock and certain ducks) **2** : a common goby (*Gillichthys mirabilis*) of muddy bays and sloughs of the southern California and Lower California coast that is much used as a baitfish
mud sunfish *n* : MUD BASS
mud swallow *n* : CLIFF SWALLOW
mud time *n, NewEng* : the muddy season in spring
mud turtle *or* **mud terrapin** *or* **mud tortoise** *n* : any bottom-dwelling freshwater turtle: as **a** : a musk turtle (genus *Kinosternon*) **b** : the Pacific mud turtle (*Clemmys marmorata*) **c** : SOFT SHELLED TURTLE
mu·du·ga \məˈdügə\ *n, pl* **muduga** *or* **mudugas** *usu cap* **1** : one of several peoples in the Nilgiri hills of southwest India with hereditary ties of friendship with the Toda people of this area **2** : a member of any of the Muduga peoples
mud volcano *n* : an orifice in the earth from which gas or vapor issues either through a pool of mud or with the ejection of mud which may accumulate in a conical mound — compare AIR VOLCANO
mud wagon *n* : a stagecoach lighter and smaller than the Concord coach with flat sides and simpler joinery
mud wasp *n* : a wasp that builds a nest of mud for its young; *esp* : MUD DAUBER
mudweed \ˈ⸗,⸗\ *n* : MUDWORT
mud whelk *n* : HERCULES CLUB
mudworm \ˈ⸗,⸗\ *n* **1** *NewEng* : EARTHWORM **2** : MUD-BLISTER WORM
mudwort \ˈ⸗,⸗\ *n* : an herb of the genus *Limosella* (esp. *L. aquatica*)

mud wagon

mueh·len·beck·ia \,myülən-ˈbekēə\ *n, cap* [NL, fr. H. G. *Mühlenbeck* †1845 Alsatian physician + NL *-ia*] : a genus of somewhat woody erect or climbing plants (family Polygonaceae) that are native to temperate parts of the southern hemisphere, have small opposite leaves or leaves replaced by cladophylls, and are sometimes grown as ornamentals or ground covers in mild regions
muelheim *usu cap, var of* MÜLHEIM
muellerian *sometimes cap, var of* MÜLLERIAN
muel·le·ri·us \myüˈlirēəs\ *n, cap* [NL, prob. fr. Fritz *Müller* †1897 Ger. zoologist] : a genus of lungworms (family Metastrongylidae) that are nearly cosmopolitan in sheep and goats and have larval stages in various snails and slugs
muenchen-gladbach *usu cap M&G, var of* MÜNCHEN-GLADBACH
¹**muenster** *usu cap, var of* MÜNSTER
²**muen·ster** *or* **muenster cheese** *also* **mun·ster** \ˈm(y)ün-stə(r), ˈmu̇n-,ˈmən-,ˈmin-,ˈmœn-, -n(t)st-\ *n, usu cap M* [*Münster, Munster*, city in Haut-Rhin department, northeastern France] : a semisoft cheese that may be bland or sharp in flavor depending upon the length of cure
muer·mo \ˈmwer(,)mō\ *n* -s [AmerSp, fr. Araucan] **1** : a tall Chilean timber tree (*Eucryphia cordifolia*) **2** : the hard wood of the muermo tree
muet \mwᵊe\ *or* **muette** \-et\ *adj* [*muet* fr. F, lit., mute, fr. MF; *muette* fr. F, fem. of *muet* — more at MUTE] **1** *of e in French* : silent or sometimes silent and sometimes pronounced **2** *of h in French* : initial in the orthography of a word before which elision and liaison occur — compare ASPIRÉ
mu·ez·zin *or* **mu·az·zin** *also* **mu'·adh·dhin** \m(y)üˈez°n, -ˈaz-; ˈmüəzən, -,zēn\ *n* -s [Ar *mu'adhdhin*] : a Muslim crier who calls the hour of daily prayers from the minaret of a mosque
MUF *abbr, often not cap* maximum usable frequency
¹**muff** *n* -s [D *mof* German, fr. G *muff* grumbler, sulky person, of imit. origin] *obs* : GERMAN, SWISS — usu. used disparagingly
²**muff** \ˈməf\ *n* -s [D *mof*, fr. MD *moffe, moffel, muffel* mitten, thick glove, muff, fr. MF *moufle* mitten, fr. ML *muffula*] **1** : a warm tubular covering with open ends into which the hands may be thrust that is usu. made of cloth or fur, usu. lined and padded, and used by men in the 18th century and now only by women and children **2 a** (1) : a cluster of feathers on the side of the face of domestic fowls of certain breeds (2) : feathering on the feet and shanks of some pigeons **b** : a protective pad or covering for the natural spurs of a cock worn during training fights — usu. used in pl. **3** : a blown cylinder of glass which is afterward flattened out to make a sheet **4** : a short hollow cylinder surrounding an object or used to connect two abutting objects (as pipes or shafts)
³**muff** \"\ *n* -s [prob. fr. ²*muff*] **1 a** : a bungling performance : a clumsy failure **b** : a failure to hold a ball in attempting to catch it **2 a** : an awkward person; *esp* : one who is poor in an athletic sport ⟨a complete ~ at cricket —G.M.Trevelyan⟩ **b** : a poor-spirited person : DUFFER
⁴**muff** \"\ *vb* -ED/-ING/-S *vt* **1** : to handle awkwardly : do awkwardly : BUNGLE, FLUFF ⟨gave me another chance to make good on a job I once ~*ed* —Agnes M. Cleaveland⟩ **2** : to fail to hold (a ball) when attempting a catch : FUMBLE ~ *vi* **1** : to act or do something stupidly or clumsily : BUNGLE, FLUFF **2** : to muff a ball — compare FUMBLE
muffed \ˈməft\ *adj* [²*muff* + *-ed*] **1** : having or wearing a muff : CRESTED **2** [fr. past part. of ⁴*muff*] : poorly executed ⟨a ~ pass⟩ ⟨a ~ play⟩
muff·et \ˈməfət, *usu* -fəd.+V\ *n* -s [prob. fr. ²*muff* + *-et;* fr. the ring of feathers around its neck] *Brit* : WHITETHROAT
muf·fe·tee *also* **muf·fa·tee** \¦məfə¦tē, ¦mu̇f-\ *n* -s [irreg. fr. ²*muff*] *dial chiefly Brit* **1** : a scarf or muffler worn around the neck **2** : WRISTLET
muf·fin \ˈməfən\ *n* -s [prob. fr. LG *muffen*, pl. of *muffe* cake] **1 a** : a quick bread made of batter containing egg and baked in a small cup-shaped pan **b** : a similarly shaped biscuit made from yeast dough — see ENGLISH MUFFIN **2** : a small-sized plate (as of clay or glass) **3** : HAZEL 4
muf·fin·eer \,məfəˈni(ə)r, -niə\ *n* -s : a shaker for sifting sugar on muffins
muffin pan *n* : a baking pan formed of a group of connecting cups usu. used for muffins or cupcakes
muffin ring *n* : a metal ring in which English muffins are baked
muffin stand *n* : a small three-tiered table for holding food (as sandwiches or cakes)

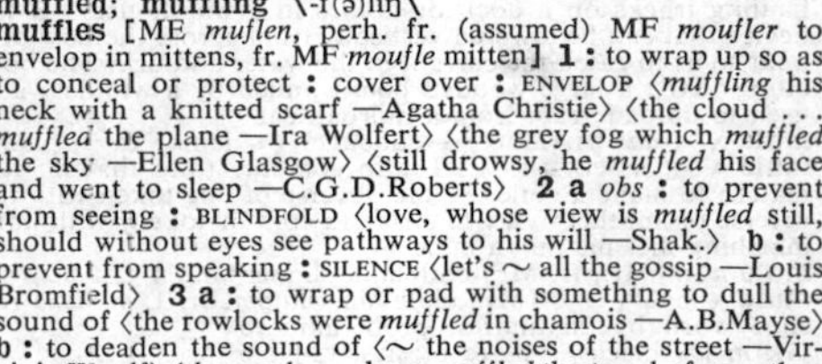

muffin pan

¹**muf·fle** \ˈməfəl\ *vt* **muffled; muffled; muffling** \-f(ə)liŋ\ **muffles** [ME *muflen*, perh. fr. (assumed) MF *moufler* to envelop in mittens, fr. MF *moufle* mitten] **1** : to wrap up so as to conceal or protect : cover over : ENVELOP ⟨*muffling* his neck with a knitted scarf —Agatha Christie⟩ ⟨the cloud . . . *muffled* the plane —Ira Wolfert⟩ ⟨the grey fog which *muffled* the sky —Ellen Glasgow⟩ ⟨still drowsy, he *muffled* his face and went to sleep —C.G.D.Roberts⟩ **2 a** *obs* : to prevent from seeing : BLINDFOLD ⟨love, whose view is *muffled* still, should without eyes see pathways to his will —Shak.⟩ **b** : to prevent from speaking : SILENCE ⟨let's ~ all the gossip —Louis Bromfield⟩ **3 a** : to wrap or pad with something to dull the sound of ⟨the rowlocks were *muffled* in chamois —A.B.Mayse⟩ **b** : to deaden the sound of ⟨~ the noises of the street —Virginia Woolf⟩ ⟨the sands . . . have *muffled* the tread of countless armies —Rex Keating⟩ **4** : to keep down : SUPPRESS ⟨the abrupt, bony, closemouthed prose . . . ~*s* his social comment —John Woodburn⟩ ⟨made an admirable effort to ~ his feelings —*Time*⟩
²**muffle** \"\ *n* -s **1 a** *archaic* : something that covers the neck or face : MUFFLER **b** : something resembling a muffle ⟨it had a soothing . . . influence, that ~ of snow —*Harper's*⟩ **2** [F *moufle*, lit., mitten, fr. MF] : a compartment or oven used in a furnace in firing wares (as those decorated over the glaze) that must be protected from flame — see MUFFLE FURNACE **3** : something that deadens sound; *also* : the sound deadened ⟨the ~ of distant thunder⟩ ⟨~ of marching feet⟩ **4** [F *moufle* mitten, fr. MF] *archaic* : BOXING GLOVE ⟨sometimes we must box without a ~ —Lord Byron⟩ **5** [F, lit., mitten, fr. MF] : a pulley block with several sheaves
³**muffle** \"\ *n* -s [F *mufle*, fr. MF, alter. (prob. influenced by MF *museau* muzzle, fr. OF *musel*) of *moufle* fat coarse face, fr. G *muffel* short snout, sulky person, of imit. origin — more at MUZZLE] : the rhinarium of mammals in which it is heavy and flabby
muf·fled \ˈməfəld\ *adj* **1** : wrapped up closely : COVERED ⟨the house itself ~ in ramblers and ivy —Edmund Wilson⟩ ⟨they were ~ figures deep in thick coats —John Steinbeck⟩ **2 a** : sounding as if from a distance : deadened in intensity : FAINT ⟨with the ~ roar of London around them —George Meredith⟩ ⟨the ~ footsteps of innumerable pilgrims —L.P. Smith⟩ **b** : said under the breath : MUTTERED ⟨made a ~ sound of disgust —Kenneth Roberts⟩ **3** : decorated or painted and treated in a muffle furnace to fix the color **4** : SUPPRESSED ⟨~ fighting —*Atlantic*⟩ — **muf·fled·ly** *adv*
muffle furnace *n* : a furnace having its charge inside a muffle and the source of heat outside so that the charge has no contact with the flame
muffle-jaw \ˈ⸗⸗,⸗\ *n* [³*muffle*] : MILLER'S-THUMB 1
¹**muf·fler** \ˈməflə(r)\ *n* -s **1 a** : a covering (as a veil or scarf) worn as a protection or disguise ⟨some awkwardness in her management of the ~ . . . a principal accomplishment of the coquettes of the time —Sir Walter Scott⟩ **b** *obs* : a bandage placed over the eyes ⟨fortune is painted . . . with a ~ afore her eyes —Shak.⟩ **c** : a scarf worn around the neck ⟨the outlandish sports coats and garish ~*s* —Bennett Cerf⟩ **d** : something that hides or disguises ⟨the mask and ~ of allegoric rhapsody —A.C.Swinburne⟩ **2** : a cushion for terminating or softening the tones made by a musical instrument (as the piano or drum) **3 a** : any of various devices to deaden the noise of escaping gases or vapors; *specif* : a tube filled with baffles through which the exhaust gases of an internal-combustion engine are passed **b** : something that silences ⟨nobody had ever put a ~ on him yet —S.H.Adams⟩
²**muffler** \"\ *adj* : relating to a device or a stage of amplification used with a radiating receiving set to suppress the radiation
muf·flin \-lən\ *n* -s [perh. irreg. fr. ¹*muffle*] *Brit* : LONG-TAILED TIT
mufflon *or* **muflon** *var of* MOUFLON
muffs *pl of* MUFF, *pres 3d sing of* MUFF
muffy \ˈməfē\ *adj* [²*muff* + *-y*] : of, relating to, or resembling a muff
¹**muf·ti** \ˈməftē, ˈmu̇f-, -ti\ *n* -s [Ar *muftī*] **1** : a professional jurist who interprets Muslim religious law **2** : the chief mufti of a district — called also *grand mufti*
²**muf·ti** \ˈməftē, -ti\ *n* -s [prob. fr. ¹*mufti*] : ordinary dress as distinguished from that denoting a calling or station; *esp* : civilian dress when worn by one in military service
¹**mug** \ˈməg\ *n* -s [origin unknown] **1 a** : a drinking cup usu. of metal or earthenware and usu. cylindrical with no lip but with a handle **b** : the quantity that a mug will hold : MUGFUL **2 a** (1) : the face or mouth of a person ⟨the sagebrush hero with the vacant ~ —Walker Gibson⟩ ⟨that lovable, ugly ~ of his —D.G.Peattie⟩ (2) *slang* : MUG SHOT **b** : a grotesque facial gesture : GRIMACE ⟨started making faces, pulling wide, ill-mannered ~*s* —*Picture Post*⟩ **3 a** (1) : an extremely stupid person : BLOCKHEAD, FOOL ⟨he knew he might look a ~ standing there just looking —Richard Llewellyn⟩ (2) *Brit* : a gullible person; *specif* : the victim of a swindle or fraud **b** : one of a criminal element : PUNK, THUG ⟨that hooey about what good guys the ~*s* are at heart —John Byron⟩ **syn** see FACE

mug 1a

²**mug** \"\ *vb* **mugged; mugged; mugging; mugs** *vi* : to make faces; *esp* : to call attention to oneself by grimacing or exaggerated gestures usu. on the stage or before a camera frequently for comic effect ⟨the technique of the ham actor *mugging* to the audience —Edward Montgomery⟩ ⟨students were on hand to ~ for TV cameras —*Newsweek*⟩ ~ *vt* **1** : to display by grimacing ⟨*mugged* displeasure at the offer —James Dugan⟩ **2** : PHOTOGRAPH ⟨he ~*s* criminals⟩
³**mug** \"\ *n* -s [origin unknown] *archaic Scot* : a breed of sheep with wool over the face
⁴**mug** \", ˈmu̇g\ *n* -s [prob. of Scand origin; akin to ON *mugga* drizzle; akin to ON *mjūkr* soft — more at MUCUS] *dial Eng* : DRIZZLE
⁵**mug** \ˈməg\ *vb* **mugged; mugged; mugging; mugs** [origin unknown] *vi, Brit* : to study (as for an examination) often with little understanding or spontaneous interest : CRAM — often used with *up* ⟨~ up on this assault engineering —*Springfield (Mass.) Republican*⟩ ~ *vt, Brit* : STUDY — often used with *up* ⟨been *mugging* up Greek —Thomas Wood †1950⟩ ⟨~ up other people's judgments and repeat them mechanically —Aldous Huxley⟩
⁶**mug** \"\ *vb* **mugged; mugged; mugging; mugs** [back-formation fr. ³*mugger*] *vi* : to assault someone esp. by garroting usu. with intent to rob ⟨supported themselves by *mugging* —*Sat. Eve. Post*⟩ ~ *vt* : to assault esp. by garroting usu. with intent to rob ⟨was *mugged* from behind and forced into a hallway —*N.Y. Times*⟩
mu·ga \ˈmügə\ *n* -s [Bengali *mūgā*] **1** : a silk from the cocoon of an Indian moth (*Antheraea assamensis*) **2** : the caterpillar producing muga
mug·ful \ˈməg,fu̇l\ *n, pl* **mugfuls** *also* **mugs·ful** \-g,fu̇lz, -gz,fu̇l\ [¹*mug* + *-ful*] : the amount that a mug will hold ⟨making slow progress with my ~ —Adrian Bell⟩
mug·ga \ˈməgə\ *n* -s [native name in New South Wales, Australia] : RED IRONBARK
¹**mug·ger** \ˈmu̇gər, ˈməg-\ *n* -s [¹*mug* + *-er*] *chiefly Scot* : a peddler of earthenware : TINKER
²**mug·ger** \ˈməgə(r)\ *n* -s [Hindi *magar*, fr. Skt *makara* water monster] : the common freshwater crocodile (*Crocodylus palustris*) of southeastern Asia that is usu. harmless to man although it may attain a length of 16 feet
³**mugger** \"\ *n* -s [prob. fr. obs. E *mug* to punch in the face (fr. E ¹*mug*) + E *-er*] : one who attacks usu. from behind with intent to rob
⁴**mugger** \"\ *n* -s [²*mug* + *-er*] : one that mugs; *esp* : an actor who depends on grimaces and exaggerated gestures for audience response
mug·get \ˈməgət\ *n* -s [origin unknown] *dial Eng* : entrails of a sheep or calf esp. when used as food
mug·gi·ly \ˈməgəlē\ *adv* : in a muggy manner
mug·gi·ness \-gēnəs, -gin-\ *n* -ES : the quality or state of being muggy
mugging *n* -s [in sense 1, fr. gerund of ²*mug;* in sense 2, fr. gerund of ⁶*mug*] **1** : the exaggerated action of an actor used to get audience response **2** : the act of strong-arming a robbery victim from behind; *also* : a street assault or beating esp. when robbery is involved
mug·gins \ˈməgənz\ *n, pl* **muggins** *often cap* [prob. fr. the name *Muggins*] **1 a** : a provision in many games played in England that if a player fails to record an earned score promptly his opponent may say *muggins* and claim that score — used esp. in cribbage and dominoes **b** : a dominoes game identical with sniff except that the muggins provision is included **c** : any of various card games in which a score overlooked may be claimed by saying *muggins* or in which the player with the worst score is called *muggins* — used esp. in children's games **2** : SIMPLETON ⟨had seen too many ~ come bowing and smiling —Enid Bagnold⟩
mug·gles \ˈməgəlz\ *n, pl* **muggles** [origin unknown] *slang* : ²REEFER
mug·gle·to·nian \,məgəlˈtōnēən, -nyən\ *n* -s *usu cap* [Lodowicke *Muggleton* †1698 Eng. Puritan tailor, one of the founders + E *-an*] : one of a British sect identifying its two founders with the witnesses of Revelation 11:3–6, rejecting the doctrine of the Trinity, condemning preaching and prayer, and believing matter to be eternal and reason the creation of the devil
¹**mug·gy** \ˈməgē, -gi\ *adj* -ER/-EST [⁴*mug* + *-y*] : marked by warm dampness : HUMID ⟨horribly ~ weather⟩
²**mug·gy** \ˈmu̇gi, ˈməgi\ *n* -ES [perh. alter. of *Maggie*, feminine name, dim. of *Mag*, nickname fr. the name *Margaret*] *dial Eng* : WHITETHROAT
mughal *or* **mughul** *cap, var of* MOGUL
mu·gho pine *or* **mu·go pine** \ˈm(y)ü(,)gō-\ *n* [*mugho* prob. fr. F, mugho pine, fr. It *mugo*] : a shrubby spreading pine (*Pinus mugo mughus*) that is a variety of the Swiss mountain pine and is widely cultivated as an ornamental
mughouse \ˈ⸗,⸗\ *n* : ALEHOUSE ⟨shrouded in the fumes of taverns and ~*s* —*Time*⟩
mu·gi·ent \ˈmyüjēənt\ *adj* [L *mugient-, mugiens*, pres. part. of *mugire* to bellow, moo; akin to Gk *myzein* to moan, Skt *muñjati, mojati* he emits a sound, L *mutus* mute — more at MUTE] : making a lowing sound : BELLOWING ⟨the ~ herds are turned out to pasture —Richard Amper⟩
mu·gil·i·dae \myüˈjiləˌdē\ *n pl, cap* [NL, fr. *Mugil*, type genus (fr. L *mugil* mullet) + *-idae;* akin to L *mucus* nasal mucus — more at MUCUS] : a family of fishes (suborder Mugiloidea) consisting of the gray mullets
¹**mu·gi·loid** \ˈmyüjə,lȯid\ *adj* [NL *Mugiloidea*] **1** : of or relating to the Mugiloidea **2** : resembling a gray mullet
²**mugiloid** \"\ *n* -s [NL *Mugiloidea*] : a fish of the suborder Mugiloidea
mu·gi·loi·dea \,⸗⸗ˈlȯidēə\ *n pl, cap* [NL, fr. *Mugil* + *-oidea*] : a suborder of the order Percomorphi that is distinguished by abdominal pelvic fins and includes the families Mugilidae, Atherinidae, and Sphyraenidae
mu·gon·go \müˈgäŋ(,)gō, -ˈgȯŋ-\ *n* -s [origin unknown] **1** : either of two African trees (*Ricinodendron rautanenii* and *R. africanum*) of the family Euphorbiaceae having extremely light wood **2** : the wood of the mugongo tree
mugs *pl of* MUG, *pres 3d sing of* MUG
mugsful *pl of* MUGFUL
mug shot *n* : a photograph of a person's face — usu. used of official police photographs
mu·guet \mᵊgā\ *n* -s [F, lily-of-the-valley, woodruff, fr. OF, fr. *muguete, muguede* (in *nois muguete, nois muguede* nutmeg); fr. the odor — more at NUTMEG] : LILY OF THE VALLEY 1
mug-up \ˈ⸗,⸗\ *n* -s [fr. E dial. *mug up*, v., to have a snack, prob. fr. E ¹*mug* + *up*] : a cup of coffee or tea and sometimes a snack between meals
mugweed \ˈ⸗,⸗\ *n* [ME *mugwed*, fr. *mug-* (in *mugwort*) + *wed, weed* weed] : MUGWORT 1
mug-wet \ˈmə,gwet\ *n* [by folk etymology fr. earlier *muguet*, fr. MF, fr. OF] **1** : SWEET WOODRUFF **2** : GUELDER ROSE
mug·wort \ˈməg+,-\ *n* [ME, fr. OE *mucgwyrt*, fr. *mucg-* (perh. akin to OE *mycg* midge) + *wyrt* wort — more at MIDGE, WORT] **1** : any of several wormwoods; *esp* : a Eurasian perennial herb (*Artemisia vulgaris*) **2** : BASTARD FEVERFEW **3** : CROSSWORT C
¹**mug·wump** \ˈmə,gwəmp\ *n* -s [Natick *mugquomp, mugwomp* captain, prob. fr. *mogki* great + *-omp* man] **1** : a person of importance : CHIEF 2a — often a generalized expression of disapproval **2 a** *often cap* : a bolter from the Republican party in the presidential election of 1884 **b** : one that withdraws his support from a political group or organization : a regular member who bolts a party and adopts an independent position **3** : one who is undecided or neutral (as in politics) often as a result of an inability to make up his mind : FENCE-SITTER ⟨too much of a ~ to be a politician —Bernard Kalb⟩ ⟨was at twenty still a restless mental ~ —D.C.Peattie⟩ ⟨a party question with the partisans lined up pro and contra and the ~*s* sorely perplexed —*Century Mag.*⟩
²**mugwump** \"\ *vi* -ED/-ING/-S : to act as or adopt the position of a mugwump
mug·wump·ery \ˈ⸗ˌgwəmp(ə)rē\ *n* -ES : the views and practices of mugwumps ⟨endeavoring to put a respectable front on his ~ —George Barker⟩

mug·wump·i·an \(')=¦gwəmpēən\ *adj* **:** of, suggesting, or being a mugwump ⟨tainted with a certain New England ~ independence —W.A.White⟩ ⟨a ~ Democrat —*Boston Jour.*⟩
mug·wump·ish \-pish\ *adj* **:** suggesting or having the characteristics of mugwumpery ⟨a ~ policy⟩
mug·wump·ism \-,pizəm\ *n* -s **:** independent action in politics; *esp* **:** MUGWUMPERY ⟨an inveterate organization Republican intolerant of ~ —Robert White⟩
mu·ha·ji·run \(,)mü,häjə'rün, =¦==¦=\ *n pl, often cap* [Ar *muhājirūna*] **:** fellow emigrants who fled with Muhammad during the Hegira
¹**mu·ham·mad·an** *or* **mo·ham·med·an** \mō'hamədᵊn, -häm-, -hàm-, -dən *sometimes* mə'- *or* mü'-\ *adj, usu cap* [*Muhammad, Mohammed* †A.D. 632 Arabian prophet and founder of Islam + E *-an*, adj. suffix] **:** of or relating to Muhammad or the religion and institutions founded by Muhammad
²**muhammadan** \"\ *or* **mohammedan** \"\ *n* -s *usu cap* [*Muhammad, Mohammed* †A.D. 632 + E *-an*, n. suffix] **:** MUSLIM — used predominantly by those outside the faith of Islam and usu. taken to be offensive by the Islamic believer
muhammadan era *n, usu cap M* **:** the era in use in Muhammadan countries for numbering Muhammadan calendar years since the hegira
mu·ham·mad·an·ism *or* **mo·ham·med·an·ism** \-dᵊn,izəm, -də,ni-\ *n* -s *usu cap* **:** ISLAM
mu·har·ram \mü'harəm\ *or* **mo·har·ram** \mō'-\ *or* **mo·hur·rum** \-'hərəm\ *n* -s *usu cap* [Ar *muḥarram*, lit., sacred, forbidden] **1 :** the first month of the Muhammadan year — see MONTH table **2 :** a Muslim festival held during the first ten days of the month of Muharram
muh·len·ber·gia \,myülən'bərjēə\ *n, cap* [NL, fr. Gotthilf H. E. *Mühlenberg* †1815 Am. clergyman and botanist + NL *-ia*] **:** a genus of slender often wiry perennial American and Asiatic grasses with small spikelets and capillary awns of some importance in the western U. S. as forage
muh·len·berg's turtle \'myülən,bərgs-\ *n, usu cap M* [prob. after Gotthilf H. E. *Mühlenberg* †1815] **:** a small American freshwater turtle (*Clemmys muhlenbergii*)
muhly \'myülē\ *also* **muhly grass** *n* -s [*muhly* fr. *muhl-* (fr. NL *Muhlenbergia*) + *-y*] **:** a grass of the genus *Muhlenbergia*
mu·hu·hu \mə'hü(,)hü\ *also* **mu·hu·gu** \-gü\ *or* **mu·hu·ga** \-gə\ *n* -s [native name in East Africa] **1 :** an East African tree (*Brachylaena hutchinsii*) of the family Compositae with strongly aromatic hard heavy durable wood similar to sandalwood **2 :** the wood of the muhuhu tree
muid *or* **mud** \'mə(r)d, 'məd\ *n* -s [Afrik *mud*, fr. D, fr. MD *mud, mudde;* akin to OE *mydd* bushel, OHG *mutti;* all fr. a prehistoric WGmc word borrowed fr. L *modius* — more at MODIUS] **:** a Dutch unit of capacity used in southern Africa equal to about three bushels
mu·il·la \myü'ilə\ *n, cap* [NL, backward spelling of *Allium* — more at ALLIUM] **:** a genus of bulbous California herbs (family Liliaceae) with greenish white flowers and foliage that resembles the onion but is odorless
muir \'myü(ə)r\ *n* -s [ME (Sc) *mur*, alter. of ME *mor* — more at MOOR] *chiefly Scot* **:** ¹MOOR
mu·i·ra·pi·ran·ga \,müə,räpə'raŋgə\ *n* -s [Pg, prob. fr. Tupi, fr. *muirá* wood, stick + *piranga* red] **:** SATINÉ
muir·burn \'myü(ə)r,bərn\ *n* [ME (Sc) *murbyrn*, fr. *mur* moor + *-byrn* (fr. ME *birnen* to burn) — more at BURN] *Scot* **:** the burning of the heath and stubble on a moor
muircock \'=,=\ *n* [ME (Sc) *mur cok*, fr. *mur* + ME *cok* cock] *Scot* **:** MOORCOCK
muirfowl \'=,=\ *n* [*muir* + *fowl*] *Scot* **:** RED GROUSE
muis·ca \'mwēskə\ *or* **moz·ca** \'möskə\ *n, pl* **muisca** *or* **muiscas** *or* **mozca** *or* **mozcas** *usu cap* **:** CHIBCHA
muis·hond \'mīs,hänt, 'mās-\ *n* -s [Afrik, fr. D, cat, weasel, fr. MD *muushont*, fr. *muus* mouse + *hont* dog; akin to OE *mūs* mouse and to OE *hund* dog — more at MOUSE, HOUND] **:** either of two southern African weasels that are black with white stripes and that emit a fetid odor when disturbed — see SNAKE MUISHOND, STRIPED MUISHOND
mui-tsai \¦müē¦jī\ *n, pl* **mui-tsai** [Chin (Cant) *moo¹-tsai*, fr. *moo¹* younger sister + *tsai* little; akin to Chin (Pek) *mei⁴-tsai³* little younger sister, fr. *mei⁴* younger sister + *tsai³* child] **1 :** a young slave girl in South China **2 :** a system of girl slavery in South China
mujik *var of* MUZHIK
muj·ta·hid \müj'tä,hid\ *n* -s [Ar, one who exerts himself] **:** an authoritative interpreter of the religious law of Islam; *esp* **:** a living religious teacher that is recognized by the Shi'a as competent to exercise private judgment in formulating authoritative answers to legal questions
muk·den \'mùkdən, 'mək-; (')mùk¦den, (')mük-\ *adj, usu cap* [fr. *Mukden*, city in southern Manchuria, northeast China] **:** of or from Mukden, Manchuria **:** of the kind or style prevalent in Mukden
mukh·tar \(')mùk¦tär\ *n* -s [Ar *mukhtār*, lit., chosen] **:** the head of the local government of a town
muk·luk *also* **muck·luck** *or* **muc·luc** \'mə,klək\ *n* -s [Esk *muklok* large seal] **1 :** a sealskin or reindeer-skin boot worn by Eskimos **2 :** a boot similar in style to the Eskimo mukluk often made of duck with a soft leather sole and worn over several pairs of socks
muk·ri \'mùkrē\ *n, pl* **mukri** *or* **mukris** *usu cap* **1 a :** an ancient Kurdish people of Persia **b :** a member of such people **2 :** the Kurdish dialect of the Mukri people
muk·ti \'mùktē, -tī\ *n* -s [Skt, fr. *muñcati* he releases — more at MUCUS] **:** MOKSHA
muk·tuk \'mək,tək\ *n* -s [Esk] **:** whale skin used for food
mu·la·da \mü'lädə\ *n* -s [Sp, fr. *mulo* mule] *Southwest* **:** a drove of mules
mu·la·dí \,mülə'thē\ *n, pl* **muladí·es** \-(,)ās\ [Sp, fr. Ar *muwalladīn* adopted ones] **:** a Spaniard who adopted the Muslim religion during the Moorish occupation — compare MOZARAB
mu·lat·ta \mə'ladə, myə'-, myü'-, -atə\ *n* -s [Sp *mulata*, fem. of *mulato*] **:** MULATTRESS
¹**mu·lat·to** \-ad·(,)ō, -adə, -a(,)tō, -atə\ *n, pl* **mulattoes** *also* **mulattos** [Sp *mulato*, fr. *mulo* mule, fr. L *mulus* — more at MULE] **1 :** the first-generation offspring of a Negro and a white **2 :** a person of mixed Caucasian and Negro ancestry
²**mulatto** \"\ *adj* **1 :** of or relating to a mulatto; *esp* **:** having the color of a mulatto **2** *South* **:** composed of or characterized by brown clay ⟨~ soil⟩ ⟨~ land⟩
mulatto land crab *n* [so called fr. its grayish color] **:** GREAT LAND CRAB
mulatto-wood \=¦=(,)=,=\ *n* **:** the wood of any of several Mexican timber trees (as of the genera *Celtis, Bursera*, and *Zanthoxylum*)
mu·lat·tress \=¦la·trəs\ *n* -ES [F *mulâtresse*, fr. *mulâtre* mulatto (modif. of Sp *mulato*) + *-esse* -ess] **:** a female mulatto
mulay saw *var of* MULEY SAW
mul·ber·ry \'məl,berē, -b(ə)rē, -ri — *see* BERRY\ *n* [ME *mulberie, murberie*, fr. OF *moure, meure* mulberry (fruit), (fr. — assumed — VL *mora*, fr. L, pl. of *morum* mulberry — fruit —, fr. Gk *moron* mulberry — fruit —, blackberry) + ME *berie, berye* berry; prob. akin to Arm *mor* blackberry] **1 a :** a tree of the genus *Morus* — compare PAPER MULBERRY **b :** the edible pleasantly acid berrylike usu. dark purple fruit of the mulberry tree **c :** THIMBLEBERRY **d :** any of several blackberries **e :** any of several other plants (as dodder and whitebeam) **2 a :** a dark purple that is bluer, lighter, and stronger than average prune or plum (sense 6b) and redder and paler than mulberry purple **b :** a purplish black that is bluer and stronger than black plum — called also *morello, murrey*

mulberry

mulberry bird *n* **:** ROSE-COLORED STARLING
mulberry family *n* **:** MORACEAE
mulberry fig *n* **:** SYCAMORE 1
mulberry fruit *n* **:** a very dark red that is slightly redder than port
mulberry purple *n* **:** a dark purple that is bluer, lighter, and stronger than average prune, bluer and deeper than mulberry (sense 2a), and bluer and stronger than plum (sense 6b)
mulberry whelk *n* **:** a boring mollusk (*Morula uva*) having a bluish white shell with black tubercles and a violet aperture and being sometimes a serious pest of Australian oyster beds
¹**mulch** \'məlch\ *n* -ES [perh. irreg. fr. *melch*] **1 :** rotting straw strewn over the ground and often mixed with mud or manure ⟨maids walking in pattens . . . to keep their shoes above the ~ —Thomas Hardy⟩ **2 :** a protective covering (as of sawdust, moss, compost, gravel, or paper) spread or left upon the ground to reduce evaporation, maintain even soil temperature, prevent erosion, control weeds, or enrich the soil **:** LITTER, TOPDRESSING — compare STUBBLE MULCH **3 :** DUST MULCH
²**mulch** \"\ *vt* -ED/-ING/-ES **1 :** to cover or dress with mulch ⟨~ an orchard⟩ **2 :** to make a layer of dry mulch on ⟨plow under green manure and ~ the ground afterward —*Farmer's Irrigation Guide*⟩
mulch·er \-chə(r)\ *n* -s **:** a device for applying mulch
¹**mulct** \'məlkt\ *n* -s [L *multa, mulcta*] **1 :** FINE, PENALTY, AMERCEMENT **2 :** an arbitrary exaction esp. of money ⟨a bill requiring bookmakers to buy a fifty-dollar tax stamp and then pay a ~ of 10 percent on their gross business —A.J.Liebling⟩
²**mulct** \"\ *vt* **mulcted; mulcted** *or* **mulct; mulcting; mulcts** [L *multare, mulctare*, fr. *multa, mulcta*, n.] **1 :** to punish or penalize by imposing a usu. pecuniary fine or forfeiture **:** exact a mulct from **:** FINE ⟨be ~*ed* or expelled by the stock exchange committee —G.B.Shaw⟩ **2 a :** to defraud esp. of money (as by extortion) **:** BLEED, MILK, SWINDLE ⟨aid the claimants in ~*ing* the insurance company —B.C.Dawkins⟩ ⟨~*ed* of their meager savings by thieves and swindlers —*Amer. Guide Series: N.Y.*⟩ **b :** to obtain (as money) from someone in an excessive amount or by fraud, duress, or theft ⟨mail fraud in ~*ing* $60,000 from clients —*Time*⟩ ⟨had ~*ed* an object of no value —S.J.Perelman⟩
mul·der \'məldə(r), 'məl-\ *dial Brit var of* MOLDER
¹**mule** \'myül\ *n* -s [ME, fr. OF *mul*, fr. L *mulus*, prob. of non-IE origin; akin to the source of LGk dial. (Phocian) *mychlos* male ass] **1 :** a hybrid between the horse and the ass: as **a :** the usu. sterile offspring of a male ass and a mare having the large head, long ears, and small hoofs of the ass and the form and size of the horse and being valued as a draft and pack animal because of its endurance and surefootedness **b :** HINNY **2 :** a very stubborn person **3 :** a plant that is self-sterile because of either infertile pollen or rudimentary pistils; *usu* **:** a hybrid that is self-sterile and cross-sterile **4 :** HYBRID; *esp* **:** one that is sterile — used esp. of hybrids between the canary and related birds **5** [prob. so called fr. its being regarded as combining the principles of two earlier machines] **:** a machine having a moving carriage for simultaneously drawing and twisting a sliver into yarn or thread and winding it into cops and used orig. for cotton but now limited largely to wool — called also *mule-jenny* **6 :** a sharp-sterned coble used on the northeast coast of England **7 :** a coin or token struck from dies belonging to two different issues (as the obverse die of a cent and the reverse die of a halfpenny) **8 a :** a small usu. electric locomotive (as for towing ships through a lock or pulling mine cars) **b :** a light tractor (as for hauling trucks on a dock or dollies in a warehouse) **9 :** a device that can be lowered vertically from across the bow of a boat so as to catch the current in the water and draw the boat along **10 :** a large wooden board pulled by a windlass and used to unload grain from a railroad car
²**mule** \"\ *adj* **:** HYBRID ⟨~ cabbage⟩ ⟨~ lamb⟩ ⟨a ~ plant⟩
³**mule** \"\ *vt* -ED/-ING/-S **1 :** to combine (dies that do not match) to make a mule ⟨~ the obverse of one token with the reverse of another⟩ **2 :** to strike (a coin or token) with nonmatching dies making a mule
⁴**mule** *n* -s [ME, fr. MF, chilblain, slipper] *obs* **:** CHILBLAIN
⁵**mule** \'myül\ *n* -s [MF, chilblain, slipper, fr. L *mulleus* red shoe worn by dignitaries; prob. akin to Gk *melas* black — more at MULLET] **:** a shoe or house slipper without quarter and often with a low heel

mule

mule armadillo *n* [¹*mule*] **:** a So. American armadillo (*Dasypus septemcinctus*)
¹**muleback** \'=,=\ *n* **:** the back of a mule
²**muleback** \"\ *adv* **:** on the back of a mule
mule chest *n* [¹*mule*] **:** BLANKET CHEST
mule deer *n* **:** a long-eared deer of western No. America (*Odocoileus hemionus* syn. *Cariacus macrotis*) that is larger and more heavily built than the Virginia deer — called also *black-tailed deer*
mule-ears \'=,=\ *n pl but sing in constr* **:** a plant of the genus *Wyethia*
mule fat *n* **:** a California composite shrub (*Baccharis viminea*) with slender leafy branching shoots that are an important browse for mule deer
¹**mule-foot** \'=¦=\ *or* **mule-footed** \'=¦==\ *adj* [¹*mule* + *foot* or *footed*] **1** *of a cloven-hoofed animal* **:** having a solid rather than a cleft hoof ⟨a *mule-foot* hog⟩ ⟨a *mule-foot* calf⟩ **2** *of a horse* **:** having a foot with small frog, upright hoof wall, and in hoof like that of a mule
²**mule-foot** \'=¦=\ *n* **1** *pl* **mule-feet :** a mule-foot hoof **2** *pl* **mule-foots :** a mule-foot animal
mule foot *n, pl* **mule foots** [¹*mule* + *foot;* fr. the shape of the shell] *South* **:** BOX TORTOISE
muleheaded \'=¦==\ *adj* **:** STUBBORN, PIGHEADED — **mule·head·ed·ly** \'=¦===\ *adv*
mule-jenny \'=,==\ *n* **:** MULE 5
mule killer *n, chiefly South* **:** any of several arthropods: **a :** WHIP SCORPION **b :** STICK INSECT **c :** MANTIS **d :** WHEEL BUG **e :** a mutillid wasp
mule·man \'=mən\ *n, pl* **mulemen :** one who tends mules
mule mark *n* **:** a dark dorsal stripe (as on a mule)
mule pulley *n* **:** an adjustable idler pulley for a belt; *esp* **:** one making an angle turn
mules \'myülz\ *vt* -ED/-ING/-ES [after J. H. W. *Mules*] **:** to perform the Mules operation on
mule skinner *n* **:** MULETEER
mules operation *n, usu cap M* [after J. H. W. *Mules*, 20th cent. Australian grazier who first suggested it] **:** removal of excess loose skin from either side of the crutch of a sheep to reduce the incidence of blowfly strike
mu·le·ta \mü'lād·ə, -ledə\ *n* -s [Sp, muleta, crutch, dim. of *mula* she-mule, fr. L, fem. of *mulus* mule — more at MULE] **:** a small cloth attached to a short tapered stick and used by a matador during the faena in place of the large fighting cape
mu·le·teer \,myülə¦ti(ə)r, -iə\ *n* -s [MF *muletier*, fr. *mulet* mule (fr. OF, fr. *mul* mule + *-et*) + *-ier* -eer — more at MULE] **:** one who drives a mule or team of mules
mu·let·ta \m(y)ü'ledə\ *n* -s [Pg *muleta*, prob. dim. of *mula* she-mule, fr. L] **:** a Portuguese coasting ship that is similar to a tartan, has a large lateen sail, uses a jumble of sails when fishing, and has a pointed bow painted with a human eye
¹**mu·ley** *also* **mul·ley** \'myülē, 'mùl-, 'mül-, -li\ *n* -s [IrGael & ScGael *maol* bald, hornless & W *moel* bald, hornless + E *-y*, n. suffix; IrGael & ScGael *maol* & W *moel* akin to each other and prob. to ON *meitha* to hurt, mutilate — more at MAD] **1 :** a polled or hornless animal; *esp* **:** a muley cow **2 :** COW — used as a pet name
²**muley** *also* **mulley** \"\ *adj* **:** POLLED, HORNLESS, DEHORNED; *esp* **:** naturally hornless ⟨occasionally a male deer will be ~ —Lyle St. Amant & Carrol Perkins⟩ — used esp. of cattle ⟨a ~ cow⟩ ⟨a big brindle, ~ ox —Andy Adams⟩
³**muley** \'myülē, -lī\ *adj* [¹*mule* + *-y*, adj. suffix] **:** MULISH
muley axle *n* [²*muley*] **:** a railroad car axle without collars at the outer ends of the journals
muley saw *also* **mu·lay saw** *pronunc at* ¹MULEY +\ *n* [²*muley*] **:** a stiff saw with vertical reciprocating motion used in sawmills
mul·ga \'məlgə\ *n, pl* **mulgas** *or* **mulga** [native name in Australia] **1 a :** a widely distributed irregular and often shrubby Australian acacia (*Acacia aneura*) that has usu. linear grayish green phyllodes, yields a very hard tough heavy wood, and is an important forage plant in much of the drier part of Australia **b :** any of several other Australian acacias that resemble mulga; *broadly* **:** any Australian tree of scrubby growth and notably hard wood **2 :** the wood of a mulga **3** *or* **mulga scrub** *or* **mulga country :** arid land of Australia on which the mulga (*Acacia aneura*) is the dominant form of vegetation
mül·heim *or* **mul·heim** *or* **muel·heim** \'m(y)ül,hīm, 'mēl-\ *adj, usu cap* [fr. *Mülheim* an der Ruhr, city in western Germany] **:** of or from the city of Mülheim an der Ruhr, Germany **:** of the kind or style prevalent in Mülheim an der Ruhr
mul·house \mə'lüz, mē'-\ *adj, usu cap* [fr. *Mulhouse*, city in northeast France] **:** of or from the city of Mulhouse, France **:** of the kind or style prevalent in Mulhouse
mu·li·ebral \¦myülē¦ebrəl, -lē¦ēb-\ *adj* [L *muliebris* + E *-al*] **:** of, relating to, or characteristic of women **:** FEMININE ⟨the sheer ~ warmth of her —Richard Llewellyn⟩
mu·li·ebria \,==='ebrēə, -'ēb-\ *n pl* [L, fr. neut. pl. of *muliebris*] **:** the female genitalia
mu·li·eb·ri·ty \,=='ebrəd·ē\ *n* -ES [LL *muliebritat-, muliebritas*, fr. L *muliebris* of a woman (fr. *mulier* woman) + *-itat-, -itas* -ity; prob. akin to L *mollis* soft — more at MELT] **1 :** the state of being a woman or of possessing full womanly powers **:** WOMANHOOD — compare VIRILITY **2 a :** WOMANLINESS, FEMININITY **b :** EFFEMINACY
mu·li·er puis·ne \¦myülēə(r)'pyünē\ *or* **mulier younger** *n, pl* **muliers puisne** *or* **muliers younger** [*mulier puisne* fr. (assumed) AF *mulieré puisné*, fr. AF *mulieré* legitimate son (fr. *mulier* wife, fr. L, woman, wife) + MF *puisné* younger; *mulier younger* part trans. of (assumed) AF *mulieré puisné* — more at PUNY] **:** a younger legitimate son of a married woman who prior to her marriage has had an older illegitimate son by the father of her legitimate child — compare BASTARD EIGNE
muling *n* -s [fr. gerund of ³*mule*] **:** ¹MULE 7
mul·ish \'myülish, -lēsh\ *adj* [¹*mule* + *-ish*] **:** STUBBORN, INFLEXIBLE, UNCOMPROMISING, UNYIELDING ⟨that expression of ~ obstinacy which no one can better assume at will than the French peasant —Dorothy Sayers⟩ **syn** see OBSTINATE
mul·ish·ly \-lәshlē, -lēsh-, -shli\ *adv* **:** in a mulish manner **:** STUBBORNLY, OBSTINATELY
mul·ish·ness \-lishnəs, -lēsh-\ *n* -ES **:** STUBBORNNESS, OBSTINACY
mu·li·ta \mü'lēd·ə\ *n* -s [AmerSp, dim. of Sp *mula* she-mule — more at MULETA] **:** MULE ARMADILLO
¹**mull** \'məl, *dial Brit* " *or* 'mùl\ *n* -s [ME *mul, mol*, prob. fr. MD; akin to OE *myl* dust, *melu* meal — more at MEAL] **1 a** *chiefly dial Brit* **:** DUST **:** dry mold **b** *chiefly dial Brit* **:** PEAT **2** [prob. fr. ²*mull*] **:** MIXTURE, MESS, MUDDLE ⟨~ of subtly flavored shrimps-of-the-sea heaped on a snowy hillock of rice —Jean Austen⟩ ⟨made a ~ of things up to now —Marguerite Steen⟩
²**mull** \'məl\ *vb* -ED/-ING/-S [ME *mullen*, fr. *mul, mol*, n.] *vt* **1 :** to grind or mix thoroughly (as in a mortar) **:** PULVERIZE, CRUMBLE, STIR ⟨~ a portion of the pigment with the oil —H.J. Wolfe⟩ ⟨the alloy, after removal from the amalgamator, was ~*ed* in the palm of the hand —*Jour. of Amer. Dental Assoc.*⟩ ⟨~ tobacco in making snuff⟩ **2 a** *Brit* **:** to make a mess of **:** BOTCH, FUMBLE, MUFF ⟨~ a catch in cricket⟩ **b** (1) **:** BLUNT, DULL, DEADEN ⟨walls were red brick, not a bright, brawling color, but sufficient to ~ the edge of a bitter day —Audrey Barker⟩ (2) **:** BEFUDDLE, BEMUSE ⟨pleasantly ~*ed* by the martinis —C.O.Gorham⟩ ⟨nerves dulled and ~*ed* by copious wine —Francis Hackett⟩ **3 :** to consider or talk over the aspects of (as a problem) at length or at leisure **:** go over in one's mind **:** PONDER ⟨tax experts, ~*ing* how to keep on a pay-as-you-go basis —*Time*⟩ ⟨aides ~ a batch of overseas disposal plans —*Wall Street Jour.*⟩ — often used with *over* ⟨the idea he was ~*ing* over that spring —Virginia D. Dawson & Betty D. Wilson⟩ ⟨sat ~*ing* over what she had said —Cortland Fitzsimmons⟩ ⟨~*ing* over a new quilt pattern —Julian Dana⟩ ⟨~*ed* the book over in his mind —Henry Giniger⟩ **4 :** TEMPER 3e ~ *vi* **1 :** MEDITATE, PONDER, THINK ⟨~ about for words that will convey suspicions as well as impressions —*Everybody's Mag.*⟩ ⟨all his talk of ~*ing* and weighing and balancing was vacillation —J.P.Marquand⟩ **2 :** MESS, MUDDLE, DAWDLE ⟨don't ~ over your breakfast —Lionel Shapiro⟩ ⟨spend two hours after dinner ~*ing* around with your agent —Niven Busch⟩
³**mull** \"\ *n* -s [ME (Sc) *mole*, prob. fr. ON *mūli* projecting crag, snout, muzzle; akin to OHG *mūla, mūl* mouth (of an animal), Goth *faurmūljan* to muzzle, Gk *myllon* lip, L *mutus* mute — more at MUTE] *Scot* **:** HEADLAND, PENINSULA ⟨the *Mull* of Galloway⟩ ⟨the *Mull* of Kintyre⟩
⁴**mull** \"\ *vt* -ED/-ING/-S [origin unknown] **:** to heat, sweeten, and flavor (as wine or cider) with spices
⁵**mull** \"\ *n* -s **:** a mulled beverage (as wine)
⁶**mull** \"\ *chiefly Scot var of* MILL
⁷**mull** \"\ *n* -s [by shortening & alter. fr. *mulmul*] **1 :** a soft fine sheer fabric in plain weave made of cotton, silk, or rayon singly or in combination and used with or without special finishes for clothing and in bookbinding **2 :** an ointment of high melting point intended to be spread on muslin or mull and used like a plaster ⟨zinc ~⟩
⁸**mull** \"\ *n* -s [G, fr. Dan *muld*, fr. ON *mold* dust, soil — more at MOLD] **:** granular forest humus consisting characteristically of a layer of mixed organic matter and mineral soil merging gradually into the mineral soil beneath — compare DUFF, MULCH
⁹**mull** \"\ *n* -s [by shortening] **:** MULLION
mull *abbr* mullion
mullagatawny *var of* MULLIGATAWNY
mul·lah *or* **mul·la** \'mələ, 'mùlə, 'mülə\ *or* **mol·lah** \'mōlə\ *n* -s [Turk *molla* & Per & Hindi *mulla*, fr. Ar *mawlā*] **:** a learned teacher or expounder of the religious law and doctrines of Islam
mul·lar \'mələ(r)\ *n* -s [perh. alter. of ¹*muller*] **:** a die cut in intaglio for stamping an ornament in relief (as upon metal)
mul·lein *also* **mul·len** \'mələn\ *n* -s [ME *moleyne*, fr. AF *moleine*, prob. fr. OF *mol* soft, fr. L *mollis* — more at MELT] **:** an herb of the genus *Verbascum* (*esp. V. thapsus*) **:** GREAT MULLEIN — see MOTH MULLEIN
mullein foxglove *n* **:** an American herb (*Seymeria macrophylla*) with coarse leaves and yellow tubular flowers
mullein pink *n* **:** a European herb (*Lychnis coronaria*) often cultivated for its attractive white woolly herbage and showy crimson flowers — called also *gardener's-delight, rose campion*
Mul·len Tester \'mələn-\ *trademark* — used for a machine for testing the bursting strength of paper
¹**mull·er** \'mələ(r)\ *n* -s [alter. (influenced by *-er*) of ME *molour*, prob. fr. *mullen* to pulverize, grind as in a mortar + *-our, -or* -or — more at MULL] **1 :** a stone or piece of wood, metal, or glass having a usu. flat base and often a handle and held in the hand to pound, grind, or mix a material (as grain, pigments, or drugs) or to polish a surface (as of glass) **:** MANO, PESTLE **2 :** any of several rotating shoes bearing against the bottom of a cylindrical pan used for agitating, mixing, and grinding molding sand; *also* **:** the whole of such apparatus **3 :** a heavy wheel rolling in the flat-bottomed cylindrical pan of a grinding wheel; *also* **:** the mill employing such a wheel **4 :** BUCKING HAMMER
²**muller** \"\ *n* -s [⁴*mull* + *-er*] **:** a vessel in which a beverage (as wine) is mulled over a fire
³**muller** \"\ *n* -s [²*mull* + *-er*] **1 :** a worker who moistens hat bodies for blocking **2 :** DAMPENER b(1)
mül·le·ri·an *also* **muel·le·ri·an** \'myü'lirēən, mi'-, mù'-, ,mə'-, mɛ'-\ *adj, sometimes cap* [Johannes Peter *Müller* †1858 Ger. physiologist and comparative anatomist, Heinrich M. *Müller* †1864 Ger. anatomist, & Fritz *Müller* †1897 Ger. zoologist + E *-an*] **1 :** discovered by or named after the German physiologist Johannes Peter Müller **2 :** discovered by or named after the German anatomist Heinrich M. Müller **3 :** discovered by or named after the German zoologist Fritz Müller
müllerian body *n, sometimes cap M* [*müllerian* prob. fr. the name *Müller* + E *-an*] **:** one of the minute nitrogenous and oily glands on the leaves of a myrmecophyte (*Cecropia adenopus*) serving as food for the symbiotic ants that inhabit the plant
müllerian duct *n, sometimes cap M* [*müllerian* fr. Johannes Peter *Müller* + E *-an*] **:** either of a pair of ducts parallel to the wolffian ducts in vertebrate animals and giving rise in the female to the oviducts
müllerian fiber *n, usu cap M* **:** FIBER OF MÜLLER
müllerian mimicry *n, sometimes cap 1st M* [*müllerian* fr.

Fritz *Müller* + E *-an*] **:** mimicry between two distasteful or dangerous species (as of butterflies)
mül·ler's larva \'myülə(r)z-, 'mil-, 'mul-, 'məl-, 'mœl-\ *n, usu cap M* [after Johannes Peter *Müller*] **:** a ciliated larva that resembles a modified ctenophore and is characteristic of various polyclad turbellarians
müller's muscle *n, usu cap 1st M* [after Heinrich M. *Müller*] **:** the circular fibers of the ciliary muscle of the eye
¹mul·let \'mələt\ *or* **mol·et** \'mäl-\ *n* -s [ME *molet*, fr. MF *molette* mullet, rowel of a spur] *heraldry* **:** a figure of a usu. 5-pointed star that is often used as a cadency mark to distinguish a third son — compare ESTOILE
²mul·let \'mələt, *usu* -əd.+V\ *n, pl* **mullet** *or* **mullets** [ME *molet*, fr. MF *mulet*, fr. L *mullus* red mullet, fr. Gk *myllos*; akin to Gk *melas* black, Skt *malina* dirty, black] **1 :** a fish of the family Mugilidae occurring in streams and most seas, living chiefly near the shore, reaching a length of from one to two feet, and being valued as food — called also *gray mullet*; see STRIPED MULLET, WHITE MULLET **2 :** any of various fishes that constitute the family Mullidae, are of moderate size with a small mouth, large scales, and two long barbels on the chin and of brilliant usu. red or golden color, and include many excellent food fishes as well as several reputed to have a powerful neurotoxin in the brain — called also *goatfish, red mullet, surmullet* **3 :** any of various other fishes; *esp* **:** any of several American suckers (family Catostomidae)
³mullet \"\ *n* -s [origin unknown] *Brit* **:** PUFFIN
mullet hawk *n* [²*mullet*] *dial Eng* **:** OSPREY
mulley *var of* MULEY
mul·lid \'mələd\ *n* -s [NL *Mullidae*] **:** a fish of the family Mullidae
mul·li·dae \-lə,dē\ *n pl, cap* [NL, fr. *Mullus*, type genus + *-idae*] **:** a family of percoid fishes consisting of the red mullets
¹mul·li·gan \'mələgən, -lēg-\ *also* **mulligan stew** *n* -s [prob. fr. the name *Mulligan*] **:** a stew made basically of vegetables and meat or fish
²mulligan \"\ *n* -s [prob. fr. the name *Mulligan*] **:** a free shot sometimes awarded a golfer in nontournament play when the preceding shot has been poorly played
mul·li·ga·taw·ny *also* **mul·la·ga·taw·ny** \ˌmələgə¦tȯnē, -ni\ *n* -ES [Tamil *milakutaṇṇi* a strongly seasoned soup, fr. *milaku* pepper + Tamil (colloquial) *taṇṇi* water, fr. Tamil *taṇṇir*, fr. *taṇ* cold + *nīr* water] **:** a soup usu. of chicken stock strongly seasoned with curry
mul·li·grubs *or* **mul·ly·grubs** \'mələ,grəbz\ *also* **mol·ly·grubs** \'mäl-\ *n pl* [alter. (prob. influenced by *grub*) of earlier *mulliegrums*, perh. alter. (perh. influenced by obs. E *mully* dusty, moldy, fr. E ¹*mull* + *-y*) of *megrims*, pl. of ¹*megrim*] **1 :** a despondent, sullen, or ill-tempered mood **:** SULKS, BLUES **2 :** a griping of the intestines **:** COLIC
mulling *pres part of* MULL
¹mul·lion \'məlyən\ *n* -s [prob. alter. of *monial*] **1 :** a slender vertical usu. nonstructural bar or pier forming a division between lights of windows, doors, or screens — distinguished from *transom*; compare MUNTIN; see DOOR illustration **2 :** an upright member of a framing (as of panels in wainscoting) — compare STILE **3 :** a pattern or structure found on some faulted rock surfaces consisting of rounded grooves or small stepped irregularities — compare SLICKENSIDE

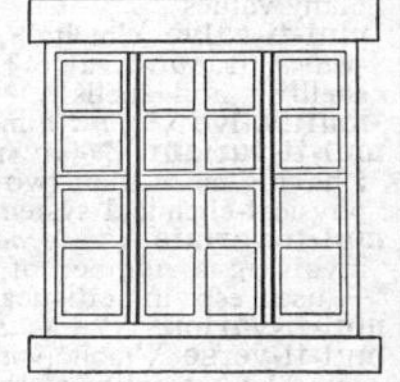

mullions 1

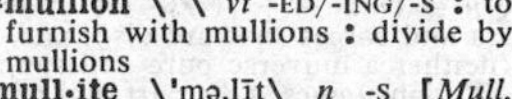

²mullion \"\ *vt* -ED/-ING/-S **:** to furnish with mullions **:** divide by mullions
mull·ite \'mə,līt\ *n* -s [*Mull*, island off the west coast of Scotland + E *-ite*] **:** a mineral $Al_6Si_2O_{13}$ consisting of a silicate of aluminum that is orthorhombic in form and resistant to corrosion and heat and is found naturally and also made synthetically for use as a refractory
mull·i·ti·za·tion \ˌmə,līd·ə'zāshən\ *n* -s **:** the formation of mullite in a fireclay body or from minerals of the sillimanite group by heating
¹mul·lock \'mələk, 'mul-\ *n* -s [ME *mullok*, fr. *mul, mol* dust, dry mold — more at MULL] **1** *chiefly dial Brit* **:** RUBBISH, REFUSE, DIRT **2** *dial* **:** a state of confusion **:** MUDDLE, MESS **3** *Austral* **a :** refuse earth or rock from a mine **b :** earth or rock bearing no gold
²mullock \"\ *vb* -ED/-ING/-S *vi, dial Brit* **:** to work in a slipshod way ~ *vt, dial Brit* **:** MESS, WASTE, SPOIL
mul·lock·er \-kə(r)\ *n* -s *Austral* **:** a mucker who shovels waste material for removal from a mine
mul·locky \-kē\ *adj* [¹*mullock* + *-y*] *Austral* **:** consisting or having the quality of mullock
mul·lo·way \'mələ,wā\ *n* -s [origin unknown] **:** a large Australian marine sciaenid fish (*Sciaena antarctica*) that is scarcely distinguishable from the European maigre and is a leading food fish of southern and eastern Australia — called also *jewfish*
mulls *pl of* MULL, *pres 3d sing of* MULL
mul·lus \'mələs\ *n, cap* [NL, fr. L, red mullet — more at MULLET] **:** a genus of percoid fishes that is the type of the family Mullidae
mulm \'məlm\ *n* -s [origin unknown] **:** organic sediment that accumulates in an aquarium
mul·mul \'məl,məl\ *n* -s [Hindi *malmal*, fr. Per] *India* **:** MUSLIN
mulse *n* -s [L *mulsum*, fr. neut. of *mulsus* mixed with honey, sweet as honey; akin to L *mel* honey — more at MELLIFLUOUS] *obs* **:** a beverage of honey mixed with wine or water
mult *abbr* multiple
mul·tan \(')mul'tän\ *adj, usu cap* [fr. *Multan*, Pakistan] **:** of or from the city of Multan, Pakistan **:** of the kind or style prevalent in Multan ⟨a *Multan* rug⟩
mult·angular \ˌməl¦t+-\ *adj* [NL *multangularis*, fr. *multangulum* polygon (fr. L, neut. of *multangulus* having many angles, fr. *multus* much, many + *angulus* angle) + L *-aris* -ar — more at ANGLE] **:** having many angles
mult·an·gu·lum \ˌməl'taŋgyələm, -taiŋ-\ *n, pl* **multangu·la** \-lə\ [NL, multangulum, polygon] **:** either the greater wrist bone articulating with the first metacarpal or the lesser wrist bone articulating with the second metacarpal
mul·ta·ni \mul'tänē\ *n* -s *cap* **:** the Lahnda dialect of Multan and vicinity
mul·te·i·ty \ˌməl'tēəd·ē, -ətē, -i\ *n* -ES [L *multus* much, many + E *-eity* (as in *spontaneity*)] **:** MULTIPLICITY
mul·ti- *in pronunciations below*, ¦==¦məltə *or* -tē *or* -l,tī\ *comb form* [ME, fr. MF or L; MF, fr. L, fr. *multus* much, many — more at MELIORATE] **1 a :** many **:** multiple **:** much ⟨*multi*coupler⟩ ⟨*multi*dimensional⟩ ⟨*multi*perforated⟩ **b :** consisting of, containing, or having more than two ⟨*multi*cuspid⟩ ⟨*multi*level⟩ **c :** consisting of, containing, or having more than one ⟨*multi*family⟩ **2 :** many times over ⟨*multi*millionaire⟩ **:** in many respects ⟨*multi*specialist⟩ **3 :** affecting many parts ⟨*multi*glandular⟩
mul·ti·angular \¦== *at* MULTI- +\ *adj* [by alter. (influenced by *multi-*)] **:** MULTANGULAR
mul·ti·axial \"+\ *adj* [*multi-* + *axial*] **:** having more than one axis
mul·ti·blade \"+\ *or* **mul·ti·blad·ed** \"+¦blādəd\ *adj* [*multi-* + *blade* or *bladed*] **:** having more than two blades
mul·ti·break \'məltə,brāk\ *adj* [*multi-* + *break*, n.] **:** being an electrical switch that breaks the circuit at two or more points at the same time
mul·ti·brood·ed \¦== *at* MULTI- +¦brüdəd\ *adj* [*multi-* + *brood*, n. + *-ed*] **:** having several batches of young in a season — used chiefly of parasitic insects
mul·ti·cellular \"+\ *adj* [ISV *multi-* + *cellular*] **:** having or consisting of many cells — **mul·ti·cellularity** \"+\ *n*
mul·ti·ceps \'məltə,seps\ *n* [NL, fr. L *multi-* + *-ceps* (as in *biceps* two-headed) — more at BICEPS] **1** *cap* **:** a genus of cyclophyllidean tapeworms (family Taeniidae) having a coenurus larva that is parasitic in ruminants, rodents, and rarely man including the parasite of gid (*M. multiceps*) and other worms that are typically parasites of carnivores **2** -ES **:** COENURUS
mul·ti·channel \¦== *at* MULTI- +\ *adj* **:** using two or more channels
¹mul·ti·color \'məltə, -tē+,-\ *adj* [L, fr. *multi-* + *color*, n.] **1 :** MULTICOLORED **2 :** that prints in several colors at one operation ⟨~ press⟩
²multicolor \"\ *n* **:** a combination of several colors **:** a color scheme using more than two colors ⟨a postage stamp in ~⟩
mul·ti·colored \"+,-\ *adj* [*multi-* + *colored*] **:** having more than two colors **:** of various colors **:** PARTI-COLORED
mul·ti·component \¦== *at* MULTI- +\ *adj* [*multi-* + *component*, n.] **:** having or consisting of two or more components ⟨vapor-liquid equilibria of ~ systems⟩
mul·ti·coupler \'məltə+,-\ *n* [*multi-* + *coupler*] **:** a device to permit a number of radio or television receivers to operate efficiently from a single antenna
mul·ti·cylinder \¦== *at* MULTI- +\ *adj* [*multi-* + *cylinder*] **:** marked by several or many cylinders
mul·ti·dimensional \"+\ *adj* [*multi-* + *dimensional*] **:** of, relating to, or marked by several dimensions ⟨a ~ problem⟩ ⟨~ calculus⟩ — **mul·ti·dimensionality** \"+\ *n*
mul·ti·disciplinary \"+\ *adj* [*multi-* + *disciplinary*] **:** combining several specialized disciplines (as those in the field of applied social science) for a common purpose ⟨use of a ~ approach by a child guidance clinic⟩
mul·ti·engine \"+\ *adj* [*multi-* + *engine*, n.] **:** having several engines
mul·ti·factorial \"+\ *adj* [*multi-* + *factorial*] **:** having characters or a mode of inheritance dependent on the interaction of a number of genes at different loci — compare MULTIPLE FACTOR — **mul·ti·factorially** \"+\ *adv*
mul·ti·far·i·ous \ˌməltə'fa(a)rēəs, -fer-, -far-\ *adj* [L *multifarius*, fr. *multifariam* on many sides, in many places, fr. *multi-* + *-fariam* (as in *bifariam* in two ways) — more at BIFARIOUS] **1 :** having multiplicity **:** having great diversity or variety **:** of various kinds ⟨the ~ activities of a farm —Kenneth Roberts⟩ ⟨~ noise of a great city —A.L.Kroeber⟩ **2** *of a pleading in law* **:** improperly uniting distinct and independent matters and thereby confounding them whether against one or several defendants — **mul·ti·far·i·ous·ly** *adv* — **mul·ti·far·ious·ness** *n* -ES
mul·ti·fid \'məltə,fid\ *adj* [L *multifidus*, fr. *multi-* + *-fidus* -fid] **:** cleft into several or many parts ⟨a ~ leaf⟩ — **mul·ti·fid·ly** *adv*
mul·tif·i·dus \ˌməl'tifədəs\ *n, pl* **multifi·di** \-fə,dī\ [NL, fr. L, multifid] **:** a muscle of the fifth and deepest layer of the back filling up the groove on each side of the spinous processes of the vertebrae from the sacrum to the skull and consisting of many fasciculi that pass upward and inward to the spinous processes and help to erect and rotate the spine
mul·ti·fil \'məltə,fil\ *n* -s [by shortening] **:** MULTIFILAMENT
mul·ti·filament \¦== *at* MULTI- +\ *n* [*multi-* + *filament*] **:** yarn composed of many individual filaments — compare MONOFILAMENT
mul·ti·flash \'məltə+,-\ *adj* [*multi-* + *flash*, n.] **:** employing or made with two or more photoflash lamps in synchronization with the shutter ⟨a ~ photograph⟩
mul·ti·flo·ra bean \ˌməltə¦flōrə-\ *n* [NL *multiflora* (specific epithet of *Lipusa multiflora*, syn. of *Phaseolus coccineus*, species name of the scarlet runner), fr. ML, fem. of *multiflorus* having many flowers, fr. L *multi-* + LL *-florus* -florous] **:** SCARLET RUNNER
multiflora rose *or* **multiflora** *n* -s [NL *multiflora* (specific epithet of *Rosa multiflora*), fr. ML, fem. of *multiflorus* having many flowers] **:** a rose (*Rosa multiflora*) characterized by clusters of numerous small flowers and used because of its vigorous growth as a grafting stock and for wildlife shelter and hedges — called also *Japanese rose*
¹mul·ti·foil \'məltə+,-\ *n* [*multi-* + *foil*] **:** a foil of more than five divisions — used esp. of a window foil
²multifoil \"\ *adj* **:** composed of or ornamented with many foils **:** SCALLOPED ⟨a coin having a ~ border⟩; *specif* **:** having an intrados composed of more than five foils ⟨a ~ arch⟩
mul·ti·fold \'məltə,fōld\ *adj* [*multi-* + *-fold*] **:** many times doubled **:** MANIFOLD, NUMEROUS ⟨regulate ~ and complex economic and social relationships —F.A.Ogg & P.O.Ray⟩
¹mul·ti·form \'məltə,fȯrm, -ō(ə)m\ *adj* [F *multiforme*, fr. L *multiformis*, fr. *multi-* + *-formis* -form] **:** having many forms, shapes, or appearances ⟨the ~ universe of nature and man —John Dewey⟩ ⟨a protean and ~ ego —J.L.Lowes⟩
²multiform \"\ *n* **:** something that is multiform ⟨the ~s of Christianity —F.S.Kinney⟩
mul·ti·formed \-md\ *adj* [*multi-* + *formed*] **:** MULTIFORM
mul·ti·form·i·ty \ˌməltə'fȯ(r)məd·ē\ *n* -ES [LL *multiformitat-*, *multiformitas*, fr. L *multiformis* multiform + *-tat-*, *-tas* -ty] **:** the state of being multiform **:** DIVERSITY ⟨the ~ and at the same time the regularity of the shapes in the structure of plants and animals —M.M.Novikoff⟩
mul·ti·gen·ic \ˌməltə¦jenik\ *adj* [*multi-* + *genic*] **:** MULTIFACTORIAL ⟨~ chromosomal blocks —*Advances in Genetics*⟩
mul·ti·graph \'məltə,graf, -räf\ *vt* **:** to print on a Multigraph machine
Mul·ti·graph \"\ *trademark* — used for a machine consisting essentially of a cylinder with grooves into which type or electrotypes are inserted
mul·ti·grav·i·da \ˌməltə'gravədə\ *n* [NL, fr. *multi-* + L *gravida*] **:** a woman who has been pregnant more than once — compare MULTIPARA
mul·ti·hued \¦== *at* MULTI- +\ *adj* [*multi-* + *hued*] **:** MULTICOLORED
mul·ti·lacunar \"+\ *adj* [*multi-* + *lacunar*] **:** having more than three leaf gaps — compare UNILACUNAR
mul·ti·lane \'məltə,lān\ *adj* [*multi-* + *lane*, n.] **:** having two or more lanes for traffic in one direction or four or more lanes for traffic in two directions ⟨a ~ divided highway⟩
mul·ti·lateral \¦== *at* MULTI- +\ *adj* [*multi-* + *lateral*] **1 :** having many sides **:** MANY-SIDED **2 a :** participated in by or involving more than two states ⟨~ treaty⟩ ⟨~ guarantees⟩ ⟨~ trade⟩ **b** *of a contract* **:** having three or more parties **3** *of a secondary school* **:** offering several distinct curricula — compare COMPREHENSIVE 3b — **mul·ti·laterally** \"+\ *adv*
mul·ti·lat·er·al·ism \ˌməltə'lad·ərə,lizəm\ *n* -s **:** freedom of international trade and currency transfers so as to achieve for each country a trading balance with the total trading area but not necessarily with any one particular country — contrasted with *bilateralism*
¹mul·ti·layer \¦== *at* MULTI- +\ *adj* [*multi-* + *layer*, n.] **:** having or relating to two or more layers of sensitive emulsion of differing color characteristics coated in superposition on a single support — used of a photographic material or process
²mul·ti·layer \'==+,-\ *n* [*multi-* + *layer*, n.] **:** a layer (as a polymolecular layer) built up of two or more layers and esp. monolayers
¹mul·ti·lingual \¦== *at* MULTI- +\ *adj* [*multi-* + *lingual*] **1 :** containing or expressed in several languages ⟨a ~ signboard⟩ **2 :** versed in or using several languages
²multilingual *n* -s **:** one who speaks and understands several languages
mul·ti·linguist \"+\ *n* [*multi-* + *linguist*] **:** MULTILINGUAL
mul·ti·lith \'məltə,lith\ *vt* -ED/-ING/-S **:** to print on a Multilith machine
Mul·ti·lith \"\ *trademark* — used for a small offset press used typically for duplicating office forms
mul·ti·lobed \ˌməltə¦lōbd\ *adj* **:** having two or more lobes
mul·ti·locular \¦== *at* MULTI- +\ *adj* [ISV *multi-* + *locular*] **:** having or divided into many small chambers or vesicles ⟨a ~ cyst⟩
mul·ti·loculate \"+\ *adj* [*multi-* + *loculate*] **:** MULTILOCULAR
mul·til·o·quence \ˌməl'tiləkwən(t)s\ *n* -s [LL *multiloquentia*, fr. L *multi-* + *-loquentia* (as in *eloquentia* eloquence)] **:** GARRULOUSNESS, TALKATIVENESS
mul·til·o·quent \-nt\ *adj* [*multi-* + *loquent*] **:** GARRULOUS, TALKATIVE — **mul·til·o·quent·ly** *adv*
mul·ti·lo·qui·ous \ˌməltə¦lōkwēəs\ *adj* [obs. E *multiloquy* garrulousness (fr. L *multiloquium*, fr. *multi-* + *-loquium* — as in *colloquium* colloquy) + E *-ous*] **:** MULTILOQUENT
mul·ti·mammate mouse *or* **mul·ti·mammate rat** \¦== *at* MULTI- + . . . -\ *n* [*multimammate* fr. *multi-* + *mammate*] **:** any of several common African rodents (genus *Rattus*) having 12 rather than the usual 5 or 6 mammae on each side
mul·ti·member district \'məltə+,- . . . -\ *n* [*multimember* fr *multi-* + *member*, n.] **:** an electoral district from which two or more members are sent to the legislature
Mul·tim·e·ter \ˌməl'timəd·ə(r)\ *trademark* — used for an electric meter
mul·ti·million \¦== *at* MULTI- +\ *n* [back-formation fr. *multimillionaire*] **:** many millions (as of dollars) — usu. used in pl. ⟨~s in almost pure silver and lead —J.A.Michener⟩
mul·ti·millionaire \"+\ *n* [*multi-* + *millionaire*] **:** one worth many millions (as of dollars, pounds, francs) ⟨an oil ~⟩
mul·ti·modal \"+\ *adj* [*multi-* + *modal*] **:** having several modes: as **a :** having several regions of maximum frequency ⟨~ distribution⟩ **b :** composed of several distinct types of activity ⟨a ~ conception of intelligence⟩ — **mul·ti·modality** \"+\ *n*
mul·ti·no·mi·al \ˌməltə¦nōmēəl\ *adj or n* [*multi-* + *-nomial* (as in *binomial*)] **:** POLYNOMIAL
mul·ti·nucleate *also* **mul·ti·nucleated** *or* **mul·ti·nuclear** \¦== *at* MULTI- +\ *adj* [ISV *multi-* + *nucleate* or *nuclear*] **:** having more than two nuclei — compare BINUCLEATE, UNINUCLEATE
mul·tip·a·ra \ˌməl'tipərə\ *n* [NL, fr. *multi-* + *-para*] **:** a woman who has borne more than one child — compare MULTIGRAVIDA
mul·ti·par·i·ty \ˌməltə'parəd·ē\ *n* [prob. fr. (assumed) NL *multiparitat-*, *multiparitas*, fr. NL *multiparus* multiparous + L *-itat-*, *-itas* -ity] **1 :** the production of two or more young at a birth **2 :** the condition of having borne a number of children
mul·tip·a·rous \ˌməl'tipərəs\ *adj* [NL *multiparus*, fr. *multi-* + L *-parus* -parous] **1 :** producing many or more than one at a birth **2 a :** of or relating to multiparity **b :** having experienced one or more previous parturitions ⟨a ~ heifer⟩ — compare PRIMIPAROUS **3 :** producing several lateral axes ⟨a ~ cyme⟩
mul·ti·par·tite \ˌməltə'pär,tīt\ *adj* [L *multipartitus*, fr. *multi-* + *partitus*, past part. of *partire* to divide, fr. *part-*, *pars* part — more at PART] **:** divided into several or many parts **:** having numerous members or signatories ⟨~ curve⟩ ⟨~ treaty⟩
mul·ti·path \'məltə+,-\ *adj* [*multi-* + *path*, n.] **:** of, relating to, or resulting from the propagation of electric waves over a number of different paths ⟨~ transmission⟩ ⟨~ phenomena⟩
¹mul·ti·ped \'məltə,ped\ *n* -s [L *multipeda* & LL *multiped-*, *multipes*; L *multipeda* fr. *multi-* + *-peda* (fr. *ped-*, *pes* foot); LL *multiped-*, *multipes* fr. L *multiped-*, *multipes*, adj. — more at FOOT] **:** a multiped animal
²multiped \"\ *adj* [L *multiped-*, *multipes*, fr. *multi-* + *ped-*, *pes* foot] **:** having many feet; *sometimes* **:** having more than four feet
mul·ti·phase \'məltə+,-\ *adj* [*multi-* + *phase*, n.] **:** having many phases; *specif* **:** POLYPHASE ⟨a ~ electrical system⟩
mul·ti·phasic \¦== *at* MULTI- +\ *adj* [*multi-* + *phasic*] **:** having many phases or aspects ⟨the ~ nature of speech —O.W. Nelson⟩ ⟨~ mass screening technique —E.R.Weinerman⟩
mul·ti·phyletic \"+\ *adj* [*multi-* + *phyletic*] **:** of multiple or complex origin ⟨the complexity and ~ nature of Southwestern cultures —W.W.Taylor⟩
mul·ti·plane \'məltə+,-\ *n* [ISV *multi-* + *plane*] **:** an airplane with two or more main supporting surfaces placed one above another
¹mul·ti·ple \'məltəpəl\ *adj* [F, fr. L *multiplex*, fr. *multi-* + *-plex* -fold — more at SIMPLE] **1 :** consisting of, including, or involving more than one ⟨~ birth⟩ ⟨~ burial of plague victims⟩ ⟨~ cable⟩ ⟨~ corolla⟩ ⟨~ drill⟩ ⟨~ rate⟩ ⟨~ skin eruption⟩ **2 :** MANY, MANIFOLD, SEVERAL ⟨~ achievements in politics and public life —B.H.Wall⟩ ⟨~ minds functioning together —*Amer. Scholar*⟩ ⟨plants were on a *multiple*-shift basis —*Annual Report General Motors Corp.*⟩ ⟨~ copies of a speech⟩ ⟨*multiple*-restaurant chain⟩ ⟨*multiple*-party system⟩ **3 :** occurring more than once or in higher degree than the first **:** REPEATED ⟨~ roots⟩ **4 :** belonging to or divided among several or many ⟨~ ownership⟩ ⟨~ responsibility⟩ **5 :** having numerous aspects or functions **:** VARIOUS, COMPLEX ⟨life is very ~; full of movements, facts, and news —John Galsworthy⟩ ⟨the ~ executive has been widely used in business and in government —Harold Koontz & Cyril O'Donnell⟩ **6 a :** being a circuit with a number of conductors in parallel **b :** being a group of terminals which make a circuit available at a number of points **7 :** developed by coalescence of the ripening ovaries of several distinct flowers (as in the mulberry and the pineapple) **:** COLLECTIVE — distinguished from *aggregate*; see FRUIT illustration **8 :** having a value equal to some multiple of a single unit ⟨~ dollars from 2- to 20-dollar pieces⟩ ⟨~ thaler⟩
²multiple \"\ *n* -s **1 a :** the product of a quantity by an integer ⟨35 is a ~ of 7⟩ ⟨gases . . . associated in ~s of the molecular weight —F.H.Getman⟩ **b :** an assemblage with respect to any of its divisions or parts ⟨lay mines in ~⟩ ⟨four road switchers running in ~ —*Trains*⟩ **2 :** PARALLEL 4b ⟨connected in ~⟩ **3 :** a multiple coin
multiple allele *or* **multiple allelomorph** *n* **:** any of more than two allelic factors located at one chromosome locus
multiple allelism *n* **:** the state of having more than two alternative contrasting characters controlled from a single gene locus
multiple-alphabet cipher *n* **:** polyalphabetic substitution in which the choice of alphabets is limited (as by a key word) — compare PROGRESSIVE-ALPHABET CIPHER
multiple-choice *adj* **:** having several answers given from which the correct or most commonly selected is to be chosen ⟨a *multiple-choice* question⟩ ⟨*multiple-choice* tests⟩
multiple correlation *n* **:** correlation involving two or more independent mathematical variables
multiple cropping *n* -s **:** the taking of two or more crops from the same field in one year
multiple-die press *n* **:** a punch press that operates two or more identical dies at a single stroke — called also *gang press*
multiple dwelling *n* **:** a residential structure to house three or more families
multiple-effect \'====,=\ *adj* **:** relating to or consisting of a series of evaporators in which the pressure decreases progressively from one to the next so that the vapor from each unit except the last heats the liquid in the next unit
multiple factor *n* **1 :** MULTIPLE ALLELE **2 :** one of a group of nonallelic genes that according to the multiple-factor hypothesis control various quantitative hereditary characters (as size and skin color) — compare POLYGENE, QUANTITATIVE INHERITANCE
multiple fission *n* **:** division of a cell into more than two parts — compare BINARY FISSION
multiple-line \'===,=\ *adj* **:** writing all or many kinds of insurance ⟨a *multiple-line* insurance company⟩ — compare MONOLINE
multiple listing *n* **:** a system of listing all properties for sale or rent by each real estate broker with a central bureau or on a list available to all brokers participating who may then sell or rent the properties with the commissions being split in agreed proportions between the brokers listing the properties and the brokers selling them — compare OPEN LISTING
multiple management *n* **:** a plan of management that permits employee participation in the formulation of policy
multiple myeloma *n* **:** a disease of bone marrow characterized by the presence of numerous myelomas in various bones of the body
multiple-party \'===,==\ *adj* **:** consisting of three or more political parties with no single party having a majority ⟨the *multiple-party* system prevailing in some European countries⟩
multiple personality *n* **:** an hysterical neurosis in which the personality becomes dissociated into two or more distinct but complex and socially and behaviorally integrated parts each of which becomes dominant and controls behavior from time to time to the exclusion of the others — see ALTERNATING PERSONALITY; compare SPLIT PERSONALITY, SCHIZOPHRENIA
multiplepoinding \'===¦==\ *n* [¹*multiple* + *poinding*] *Scots law* **:** a proceeding brought by one having in his possession money or goods belonging to another to which two or more persons make claim
multiple point *n* **1 :** a point on a curve through which two or more branches of the curve pass **:** a point on a surface through which three or more nappes of the surface pass **2 :** a point representing a set of conditions under which two or more phases can exist together
multiple press *n* **:** MULTIPLE-DIE PRESS
multiples *pl of* MULTIPLE

multiple sclerosis *n* **:** a chronic progressive disease of the central nervous system marked by patchy demyelination and hardening of nerve tissue and associated with varied motor and psychic changes depending upon the location of the lesions
multiple shop *or* **multiple store** *n, Brit* **:** CHAIN STORE
multiple-speed transmission *n* **:** transmission that provides a choice of gear ratios between the motor and the shaft or axle finally driven
multiple standard *n* **:** TABULAR STANDARD
multiple star *n* **:** several stars in close proximity that appear to form a single system
multiple switchboard *n* **:** a manual telephone switchboard in the jack field of which some or all subscriber lines appear more than once so as to be within reach of all operators
multiple synchronous telegraph *n* **:** a multiplex telegraph in which at the receiving station apparatus is maintained in exact synchronism with corresponding apparatus at the sending station
mul·ti·plet \ˈməltəplə̇t\ *n* -S [ISV [1]*multiple* + *-et*] **:** a spectrum line having several components
multiple thread *n* **:** a screw thread composed of two or more distinct parallel intertwined threads or helices
multiple-tuned \ˌ≈≈ˈ≈\ *adj* **:** tuned to more than one frequency or by more than one circuit or element — usu. used of antennas or electrical networks
multiple-unit \ˈ≈≈ˌ≈\ *adj* **:** of or relating to a system of electric traction in which two or more cars controlled from a single car are used to propel a train (as in commuter service)
multiple voting *n* **1 :** voting by the same individual at the same election in various places in each of which he possesses the legal qualifications **2 :** unauthorized and illegal voting by one person in two or more constituencies (as voting by floaters)
multiple watermark *n* **:** a watermark on a stamp that consists of more than one or portions of more than one unit of design
[1]**mul·ti·plex** \ˈməltəˌpleks\ *adj* [L *multiplex* — more at MULTIPLE] **1 :** having numerous parts or elements **:** MANIFOLD, MULTIPLE ⟨the ~ moods of our human nature —Herbert Read⟩ ⟨giants and the genii, ~ of wing and eye —G.K. Chesterton⟩ **2 :** being or relating to a system of transmitting several messages or signals simultaneously on the same circuit (as in telephony or telegraphy) or on the same channel (as in radio or television) ⟨favored the development and use of ~ sound and facsimile broadcasting —*Proceedings of the Institute of Radio Engineers*⟩
[2]**multiplex** \"\ *vb* -ED/-ING/-ES *vt* **:** to send (several messages or signals) by a multiplex system ~ *vi* **:** to multiplex messages or signals ⟨granted permission for FM stations to test stereo ~*ing*, a system that sends the two separate signals over a single radio frequency —*Time*⟩
[3]**multiplex** \"\ *n* -ES **1 :** a multiplex system **2 :** a stereoscopic instrument used in preparing topographic maps by projecting aerial photographs onto a surface so that the projected images when viewed with anaglyphic spectacles give a three-dimensional effect
mul·ti·plex·er *or* **mul·ti·plex·or** \-sə(r)\ *n* -S [[2]*multiplex* + *-er*] **:** a device for multiplex transmission of signals
mul·ti·pli·able \ˈməltəˌplīəbəl, ˌ≈≈ˈ≈≈≈\ *adj* [F, fr. OF, fr. *multiplier* to multiply + *-able* — more at MULTIPLY] **:** capable of being multiplied
mul·ti·plic·a·ble \ˌməltəˈplikəbəl\ *adj* [ME, fr. ML *multiplicabilis*, fr. L *multiplicare* to multiply + *-abilis* -able] **:** MULTIPLIABLE
mul·ti·pli·cand \ˌməltəplə̇ˈkand, -aa(ə)nd\ *n* -S [L *multiplicandum* something to be multiplied, neut. of *multiplicandus*, gerundive of *multiplicare* to multiply] **:** the number that is to be multiplied by another number — compare MULTIPLIER
[1]**mul·ti·pli·cate** \ˈməltəplə̇ˌkāt\ *adj* [ME, fr. L *multiplicatus*, past part. of *multiplicare* to multiply] **1 :** consisting of many or of more than one **:** MULTIPLE, MULTIFOLD ⟨~ forms⟩ **2 :** having many folds ⟨~ shells⟩
[2]**multiplicate** \"\ *n* -S **:** the form or condition of being exactly reproduced in many copies ⟨have copies made in ~⟩
mul·ti·pli·ca·tion \ˌməltəplə̇ˈkāshən\ *n* -S [ME *multiplicacioun*, fr. MF *multiplication*, fr. L *multiplication-, multiplicatio*, fr. *multiplicatus* (past part. of *multiplicare* to multiply) + *-ion-, -io* -ion — more at MULTIPLY] **1 a :** the act or process of multiplying ⟨combat the weevil and prevent its ~ —*Encyc. Americana*⟩ ⟨the ~ and distribution of a printed and bound message —B.L.Stratton⟩ **b :** the state of being multiplied ⟨this ~ of security investigations is institutionalized —H.J.Morgenthau⟩ ⟨when the converter is developing its greatest torque ~ —Joseph Heitner⟩ **2 a :** a mathematical operation commonly indicated by *ab*, *a·b*, or *a*×*b* and having various significances according to the type of numbers involved, the simplest being in the case of positive integers where the process is that of repeating *b* as many times as there are units in *a* or vice versa **b :** the mathematical process involving an operand and an operator each of which may consist of various kinds of numbers, symbols, expressions, assemblages, or magnitudes and in which the operand is affected by the operator in a manner governed by defined laws some of which are usu. the same as those that apply to the multiplication of numbers even when numbers are not involved ⟨the ~ of derivatives to yield derivatives of derivatives⟩ **3 :** the logical operation of forming a conjunction or product — rarely used outside the algebra of classes
multiplication dance *n* **:** a mixer in American social dances starting with one couple and multiplying by continual choice of new partners
multiplication factor *n* **:** the ratio of the number of neutrons produced in a nuclear pile to the number disappearing that must equal or exceed unity for a chain reaction to take place — called also *reproduction constant, reproduction factor*
multiplication table *n* **:** a table of the products of a set of numbers multiplied in some regular order; *usu* **:** a table of the products of the first 10 or 12 integers multiplied successively by 1, 2, 3, etc., up to 10 or 12

MULTIPLICATION TABLE

1	2	3	4	5	6	7	8	9	10	11	12
2	4	6	8	10	12	14	16	18	20	22	24
3	6	9	12	15	18	21	24	27	30	33	36
4	8	12	16	20	24	28	32	36	40	44	48
5	10	15	20	25	30	35	40	45	50	55	60
6	12	18	24	30	36	42	48	54	60	66	72
7	14	21	28	35	42	49	56	63	70	77	84
8	16	24	32	40	48	56	64	72	80	88	96
9	18	27	36	45	54	63	72	81	90	99	108
10	20	30	40	50	60	70	80	90	100	110	120
11	22	33	44	55	66	77	88	99	110	121	132
12	24	36	48	60	72	84	96	108	120	132	144

[1]**mul·ti·pli·ca·tive** \ˌməltəˈplikədˌ|iv, -ət|; ˈməltəplə̇ˌkād·|, -āt|; |ēv *also* |əv\ *adj* [LL *multiplicativus*, fr. L *multiplicatus* (past part. of *multiplicare* to multiply) + *-ivus* -ive] **:** tending or having the power to multiply numbers ⟨the ~ tendency of proportional representation —Barbara & Robert North⟩ ⟨a ~ scale of monetary weight units —A.L.Kroeber⟩ — **mul·ti·pli·ca·tive·ly** \|əvlē, -li\ *adv*
[2]**multiplicative** *n* -S **:** a numeral adjective (as *single, treble, twofold*) denoting how many times something is taken
mul·ti·pli·ca·tor \ˈməltəplə̇ˌkād·ə(r)\ *n* -S [LL, fr. L *multiplicatus* (past part. of *multiplicare* to multiply) + *-or*] **:** MULTIPLIER ⟨provides the necessary circulation in a ~ circuit —Anna Akeley⟩
multiplicious *adj* [L *multiplic-, multiplex* multiple + E *-ious*] *obs* **:** MULTIPLEX, MANIFOLD
mul·ti·plic·i·ty \ˌməltəˈplisəd·ē, -ətē, -i\ *n* -ES [MF *multiplicité*, fr. LL *multiplicitat-, multiplicitas*, fr. L *multiplic-, multiplex* multiple + *-itat-, -itas* -ity] **1 :** the quality or state of being multiple, manifold, or various **:** multiple or multiform character **:** MULTIFARIOUSNESS ⟨try to reduce the incomprehensible ~ of the universe to a comprehensible simplicity —F.L.Mott⟩ ⟨the ~ and heterogeneity of our environment —Hunter Mead⟩ ⟨there is a vast ~ of duty for the squadron commander —H.H.Arnold & I.C.Eaker⟩ **2 :** a great number ⟨a ~ of interesting paths crossed the featureless land —E.E. Shipton⟩ ⟨booklet is unfortunately marred by a ~ of minor errors —R.S.Churchill⟩ **3 a :** the number of components or sublevels in a given electronic multiple-energy state **b :** the number of components of a multiplet
mul·ti·pli·er \ˈməltəˌplī(ə)r, -īə\ *n* -S [ME, fr. *multiplien* to multiply + *-er*] **:** one that multiplies: as **a :** a number by which another number is multiplied — compare MULTIPLICAND **b** (1) **:** an instrument or device for multiplying or intensifying some effect ⟨~ phototube⟩ — compare VOLTAGE MULTIPLIER (2) **:** MULTIPLYING COIL **c** (1) **:** a set of gears causing the spool of a fishing reel to revolve faster than the crank thereby accelerating the speed at which the fishing line is reeled in (2) *or* **multiplier reel** *or* **multiplying reel :** a reel so equipped **d :** a key-operated machine or a key-operated mechanism or circuit on a machine (as on a calculating machine) that multiplies figures and records the products **e** (1) **:** one of the underground bulbils or offsets by which a multiplier onion increases — compare TOP ONION (2) *chiefly NewEng* **:** WINTER ONION; *esp* **:** MULTIPLIER ONION **f :** a factor in the game of skat that is derived by adding 1 for each matador held by the bidder or his opponents, 1 for fulfilling or failing to fulfill the contract, and 1 each for schneider or schwarz and predation thereof and that is used by multiplying by the base value of a game to determine the total score **g :** the ratio of the income held to result from an addition to investment to the amount of such addition ⟨the ~, which began as an analysis of the effects of public spending, has thus broadened into a general concept of income formation⟩ — compare ACCELERATOR
multiplier onion *n* **:** any of several perennial garden onions that constitute a variety (*Allium cepa* var. *aggregatum*) of the common onion and are grown chiefly for salad onions
[1]**mul·ti·ply** \ˈməltəˌplī\ *vb* -ED/-ING/-ES [ME *multiplien*, fr. OF *multiplier*, fr. L *multiplicare*, fr. *multiplic-, multiplex* multiple — more at MULTIPLE] *vt* **1 :** to increase in number esp. greatly or in multiples **:** make more numerous **:** add quantity to **:** AMPLIFY, AUGMENT ⟨the spread of such a prejudice may ~ readers —R.P.Blackmur⟩ ⟨no organized attempt to ~ good writings —G.G.Coulton⟩ ⟨when an original manuscript could only be *multiplied* by handwritten copies —G.F.Hudson⟩ ⟨inspiring other property owners to ~ their prices —Louise Levitas⟩ ⟨ask you not to ~ those errors into misfortunes for all of us —Irving Stone⟩ ⟨commerce *multiplied* wealth and comfort —Stringfellow Barr⟩ **2 a :** to find the product of **:** perform multiplication on **b :** to combine with (another number) by multiplication **3** *obs* **:** MAGNIFY ~ *vi* **1 a :** to become greater in number **:** increase in extent **:** SPREAD ⟨as time passed, the forges and the furnaces *multiplied* —Desmond Sprague⟩ ⟨the natural secrecy in which errors breed and ~ —Norman Cousins⟩ **b :** BREED, PROPAGATE ⟨every species of animals naturally *multiplies* in proportion to the means of their subsistence, and no species can ever ~ beyond it —Adam Smith⟩ ⟨allows virus to ~ more than a millionfold —*Monsanto Mag.*⟩ **2 :** to perform the mathematical operation of multiplication **syn** SEE INCREASE — **multiply the earth :** to add to the world's population ⟨front soldiers who have just returned from killing and destruction now begin calmly to *multiply the earth* as though nothing had happened —Lawrence Thompson⟩ — **multiply words :** to be verbose or garrulous ⟨a fool *multiplies words* —Eccles. 10: 14 (RSV)⟩
[2]**mul·ti·ply** \ˈməltə̇plē, -li\ *adv* [[1]*multiple* + *-ly*] **:** in a multiple manner **:** in several or many ways **:** in multiple ⟨the use of ~ applicable names —A.I.Melden⟩ ⟨that physical objects are ~ accessible to different people —J.W.Yolton⟩
mul·ti-ply \ˈməltə̇ˌplī\ *adj* [*multi-* + *ply*, n.] **:** composed of several or many plies ⟨*multi-ply* nylon⟩ ⟨*multi-ply* glass⟩
mul·ti·ply·ing \ˈməltəˌplīiŋ\ *adj* [ME *multeplyinge*, fr. pres. part. of *multeplien, multiplien* to multiply] **:** that multiplies ⟨the ~ train in a timepiece⟩ ⟨~ camera⟩
multiplying coil *n* **:** a resistor connected in parallel with an ammeter or in series with a voltmeter and so adjusted that the readings of the instrument must be multiplied in a fixed ratio (as 10: 1) to give the correct value — called also *multiplier*
multiplying reel *n* **:** MULTIPLIER c(2)
mul·ti·polar \ˌ≈≈ *at* MULTI- +\ *adj* [ISV *multi-* + *polar*] **:** having several poles: as **a :** having several dendrites ⟨~ nerve cells⟩ **b :** having a number of pairs of magnetic poles of alternate north and south polarity ⟨a ~ electric machine⟩ — **mul·ti·polarity** \"+\ *n*
[1]**mul·ti·pole** \ˈməltə̇ˌpōl\ *adj* [*multi-* + *pole*, n.] **:** MULTIPOLAR ⟨~ radiation field⟩
[2]**multipole** \"\ *n* [ISV *multi-* + *pole*] **:** a system (as a molecule) involving two or more pairs of electric or magnetic dipoles and having an electric or a magnetic moment
mul·tip·o·tent \ˌməlˈtipəd·ənt\ *adj* [L *multipotent-, multipotens*, fr. *multi-* + *potent-, potens* potent — more at POTENT] **:** having power to do many things ⟨~ goblins gyrated in a danse macabre —Saul Carson⟩ ⟨the synthesis of new ~ derivatives —*Jour. Amer. Med. Assoc.*⟩
mul·ti·purpose \ˌməltə̇+ˌ-\ *adj* [*multi-* + *purpose*, n.] **:** having several purposes ⟨~ dam⟩ ⟨~ furniture⟩
mul·ti·racial \ˌ≈≈ *at* MULTI- +\ *adj* [*multi-* + *racial*] **:** of, relating to, or representing various races ⟨~ government⟩
mul·ti·seriate \"+\ *adj* [prob. fr. (assumed) NL *multiseriatus*, fr. NL *multi-* + (assumed) NL *seriatus* seriate] **:** consisting of or arranged in several or many series
mul·ti·spiral \"+\ *adj* **:** having several whorls
mul·ti·stage \ˈməltə̇ˌstāj\ *adj* [*multi-* + *stage*, n.] **1 :** having successive operating stages ⟨~ compressor⟩ ⟨~ pump⟩ ⟨~ turbine⟩; *specif* **:** having two or more propulsion units that operate in turn ⟨~ rocket⟩ **2 :** conducted by stages ⟨~ amplification⟩ ⟨~ milling⟩ ⟨a ~ investigation⟩ ⟨~ sampling⟩
mul·ti·story \ˈməltə̇+ˌ-\ *adj* [*multi-* + *story*, n.] **:** having a number of stories ⟨a ~ parking garage⟩; *esp* **:** having a floor plan that is repeated on levels above the ground floor ⟨a ~ hotel⟩
mul·ti·syllabic \ˌ≈≈ *at* MULTI- +\ *adj* [*multi-* + *-syllabic*] **:** POLYSYLLABIC
mul·ti·syllability \ˌməltə̇ˌsiləˈbiləd·ē\ *n* [*multisyllable* + *-ity*] **:** the quality or state of being multisyllabic
mul·ti·syllable \ˈməltə̇+ˌ-\ *n* [*multi-* + *syllable*] **:** a word of many syllables
mul·ti·tentacled \"+\ *adj* [*multi-* + *tentacled*] **:** having several tentacles
mul·ti·tubercular \ˌ≈≈ *at* MULTI- +\ *adj* [*multi-* + *tubercular*] **:** MULTITUBERCULATE
mul·ti·tu·ber·cu·la·ta \ˌməltə̇təˌbərkyəˈlädə, -ˈlād·ə\ *n pl, cap* [NL, fr. neut. pl. of *multituberculatus* multituberculate] **:** an order of relatively small Mesozoic and Eocene mammals with multituberculate teeth coextensive with the subclass Allotheria and resembling the rodents although not considered ancestral to any recent mammals
[1]**mul·ti·tuberculate** \ˌ≈≈ *at* MULTI- +\ *adj* [NL *multituberculatus*, fr. *multi-* + *tuberculatus* tuberculate] **1** *of teeth* **:** having many simple conical cusps **2 :** of or relating to the Multituberculata **3 :** of or relating to multituberculy
[2]**multituberculate** *n* -S **:** a mammal of the order Multituberculata
mul·ti·tu·ber·cu·lism \ˌməltə̇təˈbərkyəˌlizəm\ *n* -S [*multituberculate* + *-ism*] **:** MULTITUBERCULY
mul·ti·tu·ber·cu·ly \-ˌlē\ *n* -ES [*multituberculate* + *-y*] **:** the state of having many tubercles — used esp. in ref. to a theory of the origin of mammalian teeth; compare TRITUBERCULY
mul·ti·tude \ˈməltəˌtüd, -təˌtyüd\ *n* -S [ME, fr. MF or L; MF, fr. L *multitudo*, fr. *multi-* + *-tudo* -tude] **1 :** the state of being many **:** NUMEROUSNESS ⟨whereas you were as the stars of heaven for ~ —Deut. 28:62 (RSV)⟩ ⟨the mind falters, confused by the ~ and yet the harmony of the detail —Theodore Dreiser⟩ ⟨of large numbers, note whether they are used precisely, or merely to express ~ —*Notes & Queries on Anthropology*⟩ **2 :** a great number **:** HOST ⟨~*s* in the valley of decision —Joel 3:14 (RSV)⟩ ⟨love covers a ~ of sins —1 Pet 4:8 (RSV)⟩ ⟨a language in which the same sound has to stand for a ~ of ideas —Edward Clodd⟩ ⟨a ~ of stories and traditions grew up around his name —D.E.Smith⟩ **3 :** a great number of persons collected together **:** CROWD, THRONG ⟨all the ~ was astonished —Mk 11:18 (RSV)⟩ ⟨the tourist buses disgorged their ~*s* —Mollie Panter-Downes⟩ **4 :** POPULACE, PUBLIC ⟨both scorns and seeks the understanding and approbation of the ~ —Arthur Knight⟩ ⟨does not like his defeat in a matter of the heart to be known, and needs must dissemble to the ~ —Rex Ingamells⟩
mul·ti·tu·di·nal \ˌməltəˈtüdᵊnəl, -təˈtyü-\ *adj* [L *multitudin-, multitudo* multitude + E *-al*] **:** MULTITUDINOUS
mul·ti·tu·di·nism \ˌ≈≈ˈtüdᵊnˌizəm, -ˈtyü-\ *n* -S [L *multitudin-, multitudo* multitude + E *-ism*] **:** a doctrine or policy giving primary importance to the interests of the multitude as opposed to the individual
mul·ti·tu·di·nous \ˌməltəˈtüdᵊnəs, -təˈtyü-\ *adj* [L *multitudin-, multitudo* multitude + E *-ous*] **1 :** including a multitude of individuals **:** POPULOUS ⟨the invasion of nature by ~ man —H.S.Canby⟩ ⟨in the ~ city —W.S.Maugham⟩ **2 :** existing in a great multitude **:** MYRIAD ⟨the mosquitoes were ~ and fierce —Claud Cockburn⟩ ⟨evaluates the ~ happenings of the day —F.L.Mott⟩ ⟨lunch of ~ hors d'oeuvres —Jean Stafford⟩ **3 :** existing in or consisting of innumerable forms, particles, elements, or aspects ⟨filling the air with a ~ musical clamor —John Burroughs⟩ ⟨urgent demand upon my attention made by the ~ world around me —Richard Church⟩ ⟨the long ~ rain —Carl Sandburg⟩
mul·ti·tu·di·nous·ly *adv* **:** in a multitudinous manner
mul·ti·tu·di·nous·ness *n* -ES **:** the state or quality of being multitudinous ⟨the ~ of their wants —Douglas Rimmer⟩
mul·ti-unit tube \ˈməltə̇+ˌ- . . . -\ *n* [*multi-unit* fr. *multi-* + *unit*, n.] **:** a single electron tube that contains in one envelope elements enabling it to perform the functions of two or more separate tubes
mul·ti·va·lence \ˌməltə̇ˈvālən(t)s\ *n* -S [fr. [1]*multivalent*, after such pairs as E *absent: absence*] **1** *or* **mul·ti·va·len·cy** \-nsē\ **:** POLYVALENCE **2 :** the quality or state of having many values, meanings, or appeals ⟨while ~ in the sense of appeal to different periods can not be demonstrated —*Western Rev.*⟩ ⟨the admission of relativity and ~ does not make value illusory or judgment futile —H.J.Muller⟩ ⟨the ~ of his imagery —James Burnham⟩
[1]**mul·ti·va·lent** \ˌ≈≈ *at* MULTI- +\ *adj* [ISV *multi-* + *valent*] **1 :** POLYVALENT **2 :** MULTIPLE — used of homologous chromosomes when more than two are present and associate in synapsis **3 :** having many values, meanings, or appeals ⟨even in the field of the terminal values of form, a work of art is ~ —George Boas⟩ ⟨as great and ~ a poet —Ramon Guthrie⟩
[2]**multivalent** \"\ *n* -S **:** one that is multivalent; *esp* **:** a multivalent chromosome group
mul·ti·valued \"+\ *adj* [*multi-* + *valued*] **:** having several or many values
[1]**mul·ti·valve** \ˈməltə̇+ˌ-\ *adj* [NL *multivalvis*, fr. *multi-* + *-valvis* (fr. *valva* valve)] **:** having many valves — used esp. of shellfish and shells
[2]**multivalve** \"\ *n* **:** a multivalve shellfish or shell
mul·ti·variant \ˌ≈≈ *at* MULTI- +\ *adj* [*multi-* + *variant*, adj.] **:** having more than two degrees of freedom — used esp. of a physical-chemical system; compare PHASE RULE
mul·ti·variate \"+\ *adj* [*multi-* + *variate*, n.] **:** having or involving a number of independent mathematical variables — used esp. in statistical analysis
mul·ti·various \"+\ *adj* [*multi-* + *various*] **:** widely diverse
mul·ti·verse \ˈməltə̇ˌvərs\ *n* -S [*multi-* + *-verse* (as in *universe*)] **:** a totality of things and forces that are disparate or lacking in ultimate unity ⟨neither a universe pure and simple nor a ~ pure and simple —William James⟩ ⟨the part that mind plays in changing individuals and their ~ —Maynard Whitlow⟩ — compare PLURIVERSE
mul·ti·vibrator \ˌməltə̇+\ *n* [ISV *multi-* + *vibrator*] **:** a radio-frequency oscillator that produces a controlled fundamental frequency but distributes its energy chiefly among several harmonic or subharmonic frequencies
mul·ti·vin·cu·lar \ˌməltə̇ˈviŋkyələ(r)\ *adj* [*multi-* + *vinculum* + *-ar*] **:** having several small separate ligaments — used of the hinge of various bivalves
mul·tiv·i·ous \ˌməlˈtivēəs\ *adj* [L *multivius*, fr. *multi-* + *-vius* (fr. *via* way, road) — more at VIA] **:** having many ways or roads
[1]**mul·ti·vitamin** \ˌ≈≈ *at* MULTI- +\ *adj* [*multi-* + *vitamin*, n.] **:** containing or employing several vitamins
[2]**multivitamin** \"\ *n* **:** a multivitamin preparation
mul·tiv·o·cal \ˌməlˈtivəkəl\ *adj* [*multi-* + *-vocal* (as in *equivocal*)] **1 :** signifying many things **:** of manifold meanings **:** EQUIVOCAL ⟨meet with an ambiguous or ~ word —S.T. Coleridge⟩ **2** [*multi-* + *vocal*] **:** VOCIFEROUS ⟨so bustling and ~ in pacifism —F.L.Paxson⟩ ⟨scandals and horrors of the moment in ~ . . . clamor —S.H.Adams⟩
mul·ti·vol·tine \ˌməltə̇ˈvōlˌtēn, -ˌtᵊn\ *adj* [*multi-* + *-voltine* (as in *bivoltine*)] **:** having several broods in a season — used esp. of an insect
mul·ti·volume \ˌ≈≈ *at* MULTI- +\ *or* **mul·ti·volumed** *adj* [*multi-* + *volume* (n.) *or volumed*] **:** comprising several volumes ⟨a ~ atlas⟩
[1]**mul·ti·wall** \ˈməltə̇ˌwȯl\ *adj* [*multi-* + *wall*, n.] **:** having a wall made up of several layers ⟨moisture-resistant ~ bags⟩
[2]**multiwall** \"\ *n* **:** a multiwall bag
mul·ture \ˈmyüchə(r)\ *n* -S [ME *multyr, multer*, fr. OF *molture*, lit., grinding, fr. (assumed) VL *molitura*, fr. L *molitus* (past part. of *molere* to grind) + *-ura* -ure — more at MEAL] *chiefly Scot* **:** a fee in the form of money, grain, or meal paid to a land proprietor or a tenant miller for the grinding of grain
mul·tur·er \-tərə(r)\ *n* -S **1** *chiefly Scot* **:** one who has grain ground at a mill **2** *chiefly Scot* **:** a miller to whom multure is paid
[1]**mum** \ˈməm\ *adj* [prob. imit. of a sound made with closed lips] **:** having no speech **:** SILENT ⟨to all of which I listened, ~ as an oyster —Carleton Beals⟩ ⟨officially he is still ~ on the subject —*Newsweek*⟩ — often used interjectionally to express a desire or need for silence
[2]**mum** \"\ *n* -S **:** abstention from speaking **:** SILENCE — often used in the expression *mum's the word*
[3]**mum** \"\ *vb* **mummed; mummed; mumming; mums** [ME *mommen*, fr. MF *momer* to go masked] *vi* **1 :** to act or play (as in a pantomime) usu. in mask or disguise ⟨miserable *mumming* on the stage —Donn Byrne⟩ **2 :** to go about merrymaking in disguise esp. during festivals ⟨the crowds *mumming* in the streets at Mardi Gras⟩ ~ *vt* **:** to make (one's way) esp. in disguise during festivals ⟨with soot-blackened faces and grotesque attire, *mumming* their way . . . singing for sixpences —A.J.Cronin⟩
[4]**mum** \"\ *n* -S [G *mumme*] **:** a strong ale or beer orig. made in Brunswick, Germany
[5]**mum** \"\ *chiefly Brit var of* MOM
[6]**mum** \", ˌməm, -əm\ *n* -S [alter. of *ma'am*] **:** MADAM
[7]**mum** \ˈməm\ *n* -S [by shortening] **:** CHRYSANTHEMUM
[1]**mum·ble** \ˈməmbəl\ *vb* **mumbled; mumbled; mumbling** \-b(ə)liŋ\ **mumbles** [ME *momelen*, of imit. origin] *vi* **1** *archaic* **:** to chew something gently with closed lips or with little use of the teeth **2 :** to make speech sounds that are hard to understand because of minimal displacement of the speech organs from their rest position **:** utter words in a low confused indistinct manner **:** MUTTER ⟨he lay . . . gray and limp, with a parson *mumbling* over him —Francis Yeats-Brown⟩ ~ *vt* **1 :** to utter with a low inarticulate voice ⟨*mumbled* something about not having a license —George Meredith⟩ **2 :** to chew or bite with or as if with toothless gums ⟨the old women *mumbling* soft sandwiches —A.P.Gaskell⟩ **3 :** to press or caress with the lips ⟨she *mumbled* his cheek and called him "lovey" —Robertson Davies⟩ **4** *chiefly dial Eng* **:** MOMBLE
[2]**mumble** \"\ *n* -S **:** a low confused indistinct utterance **:** MUTTERING ⟨the ~ of his voice vanished —Gwyn Thomas⟩
mumblebee \ˈ≈≈ˌ≈\ *n* -S [origin unknown] **:** a sloop-rigged Devonshire fishing boat with a mast stepped far aft, a large foresail, and a jib
mumblenews \ˈ≈≈ˌ≈\ *n pl but sing or pl in constr* **:** TALEBEARER
mum·bler \ˈməmb(ə)lə(r)\ *n* -S **1 :** one that mumbles **2** *Brit* **:** GLASSBLOWER

mum·ble·ty-peg \'məmbəltē,peg, -pāg\ *or* **mumble-the-peg** \'=⸗⸗,=\ *or* **mumble peg** *also* **mum·ble·de·peg** \'məmbəldē-,peg, -pāg\ *or* **mum·bly-peg** \-blē-\ *n* [fr. the phrase *mumble the peg;* fr. the loser's originally having to pull out with his teeth a peg driven into the ground] **:** a game in which the players try to flip or throw a knife from various positions so that the blade will stick into the ground

mum·bling·ly *adv* **:** in a mumbling manner

mum·bo jum·bo \'məm(,)bō'jəm(,)bō\ *n, pl* **mumbo jumbos** [perh. fr. Mandingo *mama dyumbo,* fr. *mama* ancestor + *dyumbo* pompon, wearer of a pompon] **1** *usu cap M&J* **a :** an idol or deity held to have been worshiped by various African peoples **b :** an object of superstitious homage and fear **2 a :** a complicated observance that is often ritualistic and accompanied by elaborate trappings ⟨spell woven by the *mumbo jumbo* of a ritual and the glamour of regalia —C.W. Ferguson⟩ ⟨the *mumbo jumbo* of the . . . coronation —Victoria Sackville-West⟩ **b :** complicated and sometimes purposeless activity intended to obscure and confuse ⟨the exchange of notes is not mere diplomatic *mumbo jumbo* —*Time*⟩ ⟨personal combat is not *mumbo jumbo* —J.V.Grombach⟩ **3 :** language that is unnecessarily involved and difficult to understand **:** GIBBERISH ⟨created a *mumbo jumbo* beyond . . . many a lawyer to translate —Stuart Chase⟩ ⟨professional *mumbo jumbo* of much of our scholarly writing —P.G.Hoffman⟩

[1]**mumbudget** *n* [prob. fr. [1]*mum* + *budget*] *obs* **:** SILENCE

[2]**mumbudget** *adj, obs* **:** SILENT

[3]**mumbudget** \,=ʹ=⸗\ *vi, obs* **:** to be silent

[1]**mum·chance** \'məm,chan(t)s, -cha(a)n-, -chain-, -chȧn-\ *n* [LG *mummenschanze* throw in a dice game played by masked revelers, fr. MLG, fr. *mummen* dice game played by masked revelers (fr. *mummen* to go masked, perh. fr. MF *momer*) + (assumed) MLG *schanze* throw of dice, fr. MF *chance* throw of dice, chance — more at CHANCE] **1 :** an old dice game in which the caster is not permitted to choose the player with whom he contests the stake — compare HAZARD **2** [influenced in meaning by [1]*mum*] *dial Eng* **:** a silent stupid person

[2]**mumchance** \"\ *vi* **1 :** MASQUERADE **2** *chiefly dial* **:** to be silent out of caution or stupidity

[3]**mumchance** \"\ *adj, chiefly dial* **:** SILENT

[4]**mumchance** \"\ *adv* [[3]*mumchance*] *chiefly Brit* **:** SILENTLY ⟨peering down ~ at its reflection in the river —Richard Llewellyn⟩

mu·me \'mümē\ *n* -s [Jap] **:** JAPANESE APRICOT

mu–meson \'=ʹ=,=\ *n* [[1]*mu* + *meson*] **:** a meson having a mass approximately 200 times that of the electron

mum·mer \'məmə(r)\ *n* -s [MF *mommeur, momeur* masker, fr. OF *momeor,* fr. *momer* to go masked + *-eor* -or] **1 a :** an actor in a pantomime **b :** a theatrical performer **2 :** one who goes merrymaking in disguise esp. during festivals ⟨this first of May morning when ~*s* were dancing in the fields —Winifred Bryher⟩

mum·mery \'məmərē\ *n* -ES [MF *momerie* masquerade, fr. *momer*] **1 :** a performance given by mummers **2 :** a ridiculous, hypocritical, or pretentious ceremony, observance, or performance ⟨practices . . . commonly regarded as superstitious *mummeries* were revived —T.B.Macaulay⟩ ⟨the ~ and ceremonial of modern life —W.P.Webb⟩

mummia *n* -s [ME *momyan,* fr. ML *mumia* — more at MUMMY] *obs* **:** MUMMY 1

mum·mi·chog *also* **mum·ma·chog** \'məmə,chäg\ *or* **mum·my·chog** \-mē,-\ *n* -s [Narraganset *moamitteaûg,* lit., they go in great numbers] **:** any of various killifishes; *esp* **:** a common American killifish (*Fundulus heteroclitus*)

mum·mick \'məmik\ *var of* MAMMOCK

mum·mi·fi·ca·tion \,məməfə'kāshən\ *n* -s [fr. *mummify,* after such pairs as E *amplify: amplification*] **1 a :** the process of mummifying or the state of being mummified **b :** a condition resembling mummification ⟨no time for empty formalities . . . or ~ in bandages of red tape —*Newsweek*⟩ **2 :** the devitalization of a tooth pulp followed by amputation of the coronal portion leaving the remainder of the devitalized tissue in the tooth canal **3 :** DRY GANGRENE

mum·mi·form \'məmə,fȯrm\ *adj* [[1]*mummy* + *-form*] **:** resembling or suggestive of a mummy in appearance

mum·mi·fy \'məmə,fī\ *vb* -ED/-ING/-ES [[1]*mummy* + *-fy*] *vt* **1 :** to embalm and dry (as the body of an animal) ⟨cats and other sacred animals of Egypt were *mummified* like kings —Emma Hawkridge⟩ **2 a :** to make into or like a mummy ⟨dead love affairs, *mummified* and bound in a book —C.W. Cunnington⟩ ⟨Arab women . . . bundled up and *mummified,* white shadows scurrying —Vincent Sheean⟩ ⟨*mummified* customs that have long outlasted their usefulness —W.R.Inge⟩ **b :** to cause to dry up and shrivel ⟨brown rot not only causes decay of fruits but *mummifies* many of them —Raymond Bush⟩ **3 :** to wrap (a body) in sheets to restrain movement ~ *vi* **:** to dry up and shrivel like a mummy

mum·ming \'məmiŋ\ *n* -s [ME *mommyng,* fr. gerund of *mommen* to mum — more at MUM] **:** participation in mummery **:** MASKING

mum·mock \'məmək\ *dial Eng var of* MAMMOCK

[1]**mum·my** \'məmē, -mi\ *n* -ES [ME *mummie,* fr. MF *momie,* fr. ML *mumia,* fr. Ar *mūmiyah* mummy, bitumen, fr. Per *mūm* wax] **1 :** a concoction formerly used as a medicament or drug containing powdered parts of a human or animal body **2 a** *obs* **:** lifeless flesh ⟨should have a mountain of ~ —Shak.⟩ **b** *chiefly dial* **:** a soft pulpy mass **3 a** (1) **:** a body of a human being or other animal embalmed or treated for burial with preservatives after the manner of the ancient Egyptians (2) **:** a body unusually well preserved owing to the manner of its burial or to some special preparation for burial ⟨a Peruvian ~⟩ (3) **:** a carcass fortuitously preserved (as by being sun-dried) **b :** one resembling a mummy; *esp* **:** a person whose energies have withered ⟨sat like a couple of *mummies* ever since we left home —Richard Blaker⟩ **4 :** a brown bituminous artists' pigment of varying properties (as made by grinding the bones of mummies) **5 a :** CONGO 4 **b :** MUMMY BROWN 2b **c :** a moderate yellowish brown that is redder and very slightly darker than Bismarck brown and darker and slightly redder than maple sugar **6 :** a dried-up or shriveled fruit first rotted by a fungus ⟨the brown-rot *mummies* of stone fruits⟩

[2]**mummy** \"\ *vb* -ED/-ING/-ES **:** MUMMIFY ⟨the *mummied* heath-bells of the past summer —Thomas Hardy⟩

[3]**mummy** *var of* MOMMY

mummy apple *n* [alter. of *mammee*] **:** PAPAYA

mummy bag *n* **:** a sleeping bag tapered at the feet and sometimes enclosed at the head with an opening for the face

mummy berry *n* **:** a disease of blueberries caused by a fungus (*Sclerotinia vaccinii*) characterized mainly by cream colored or brown shriveled fruit

mummy brown *n* **1 :** MUMMY 4 **2 a :** [2]BAY 2 **b :** a grayish brown to yellowish brown that is slightly paler than soot brown and slightly paler than gold bronze — called also *chukker brown, snuff, tamarack*

mummy case *n* **:** a case fitted closely to a swathed mummy usu. having the face modeled and the body covered with ritualistic emblems

mummy case

mummychog *var of* MUMMICHOG

mummy cloth *n* **1 :** a fabric used to wrap mummies **2 :** a heavy unbleached linen or cotton fabric in plain weave used as a foundation for embroidery **3 :** MOMIE CLOTH

mummy pot *n* **:** a vase used by the ancient Egyptians for keeping the mummies of small animals — compare CANOPIC JAR

mummy wheat *n* [so called fr. its having been found in Egyptian mummy cases] **:** POULARD WHEAT

[1]**mump** \'məmp, *dial Eng* " *or* 'mu̇mp\ *vb* -ED/-ING/-S [prob. of imit. origin] *vt, chiefly dial* **:** MUMBLE ⟨ladies who ~ their passion —Oliver Goldsmith⟩ ~ *vi* **1** *dial Eng* **:** to grimace with the mouth **:** GRIN **2** *dial Eng* **:** MUMBLE **3** *dial Eng* **:** to be sullen or sulky ⟨make a shift at bearing yourself like a man, not ~*ing,* not moping —J.G.Cozzens⟩

[2]**mump** \'məmp\ *n* -s **1** *obs* **:** GRIMACE, GRIN **2 mumps** *pl* **:** SULLENNESS **:** silent displeasure

[3]**mump** \'məmp, *dial Eng* " *or* 'mu̇mp\ *vb* -ED/-ING/-S [obs. D *mompen*] *vt, chiefly dial* **:** CHEAT ⟨some debauched person who will ~ you of your daughter —William Wycherley⟩ ~ *vi* **1** *dial Eng* **:** BEG, SPONGE ⟨one prince came ~*ing* to them annually —T.B.Macaulay⟩ **2** *dial Eng* **:** CHEAT

[1]**mump·er** \'məmpə(r), 'mu̇m-\ *n* -s [[3]*mump* + *-er*] *dial Eng* **:** a begging impostor **:** BEGGAR

[2]**mumper** \"\ *n* -s [[1]*mump* + *-er*] *dial Eng* **:** one that sulks

mump·ish \'məmpish\ *adj* [[2]*mump* + *-ish*] **:** SULLEN, SULKY

mumps \'məmps\ *n pl but sing in constr* [fr. pl. of [2]*mump*] **:** an acute contagious viral disease marked by fever and by swelling of the parotid gland and sometimes other salivary glands and ovaries or testes **:** PAROTITIS

mump·si·mus \'məmpsəməs\ *n* -ES [error for L *sumpsimus* we have taken, 1st pl. perf. ind. of *sumere* to take; fr. a familiar story in which this error was made in the ritual of the mass by an illiterate priest who when corrected replied that he would not change his old *mumpsimus* for his critic's new *sumpsimus* — more at ASSUME] **1 :** a bigoted adherent to exposed but customary error **2 :** a custom or tenet adhered to by a mumpsimus

mum·ruf·fin \'mūm,ru̇fin, 'məm,rəf-\ *n* -s [origin unknown] *dial Eng* **:** LONG-TAILED TIT

mums *pl of* MUM, *pres 3d sing of* MUM

mu·mu \'mü(,)mü\ *n* -s [Samoan, lit., red] **:** BANCROFTIAN FILARIASIS

[1]**mun** \'mu̇n, ,mən\ *verbal auxiliary* [ME *mun, mon,* must, shall, fr. ON *mon* shall (1st & 3d sing. pres indic; infin. *munu, monu*); akin to OE *man, mon* he remembers, thinks of (infin. *munan*) Goth *man* he thinks, believes, intends (infin. *munan*), L *ment- mens* mind — more at MIND] **1** *dial Brit* **:** MUST **2** *dial Eng* **:** MAY

[2]**mun** \'mu̇n, 'mən\ *n* -s [of Scand origin; akin to ON *munnr* mouth — more at MOUTH] *dial Eng* **:** MOUTH

[3]**mun** \,mən\ *pron* [ME, by shortening & alter. fr. *hemen*] **1** *dial Eng* **:** THEM **2** *dial Eng* **a :** HIM **b :** IT

[4]**mun** \'mən\ *n* -s [origin unknown] **:** one of a class of London street roisterers of the mid-seventeenth century

[5]**mun** *n* -s [alter. of [1]*man*] *chiefly dial* **:** MAN, FELLOW

mun *abbr* **1** municipal; municipality **2** munitions

mun·ce·ri·an \,mən'sirēən\ *n* -s *usu cap* [NL *Muncerianus,* fr. Thomas *Muncerus* (Münzer) †1525 Ger. religious leader + L *-ianus* -ian] **:** a follower of Thomas Münzer the Anabaptist

[1]**munch** \'mənch\ *vb* -ED/-ING/-ES [ME *monchen,* prob. of imit. origin] *vt* **1 :** to chew with a crunching sound **:** eat with relish ⟨a cow ~*ing* clover in a field —J.P.McGranery⟩ ⟨one of the most toothsome chicken dinners you'll ever ~ —Gelston Hardy⟩ **2 :** to move (the jaws) up and down as if chewing ⟨~*ed* her feeble old toothless jaws —Samuel Butler †1902⟩ ~ *vi* **1 :** to chew food with a crunching sound **:** eat food with relish **2 :** to move the jaws as if chewing

[2]**munch** \"\ *n* -ES **1 :** the act or sound of munching ⟨the ~ and stamp of work stock —A.B.Guthrie⟩ **2 :** a bite to munch ⟨between ~*es* of the big red apple —*Century Mag.*⟩

mun·chau·sen \'mən,chau̇zᵊn, 'mu̇n- *also* 'mən,chōz- *or* ,mən'- *or* mu̇n'-\ *adj, usu cap* [after Baron Karl Friedrich Hieronymus von *Münchhausen* †1797 Ger. huntsman and soldier famous for his tall tales] **:** of, relating to, or resembling the fabulous stories of his exploits told by Baron Munchausen ⟨mystify people by making them swallow as many of his more or less *Munchausen* stories as possible —C.D.Ley⟩

mun·chau·sen·ism \-ᵊn,izəm\ *n* -s *usu cap* [Baron von *Münchausen* + E *-ism*] **:** a tall tale ⟨it sounds like a *Munchausenism* but it's the truth —A.F.Collins⟩

mun·cheel \,mən'chē(ə)l\ *n* -s [Malayalam *manjīl*] **:** a litter used in India

mün·chen-glad·bach *or* **mun·chen-glad·bach** *or* **muen·chen-glad·bach** \'mu̇nkən'glät,bäk\ *adj, usu cap M&G* [fr. *München-Gladbach,* Germany] **:** of or from the city of München-Gladbach, Germany **:** of the kind or style prevalent in München-Gladbach

munch·er \'mənchə(r)\ *n* -s **:** one that munches

mun·chi \'mu̇nchē\ *or* **mun·shi** \-nshē\ *n, pl* **munchi** *or* **munchis** *or* **munshi** *or* **munshis** *usu cap* **:** TIV

mund \'mənd\ *n* -s [ME, fr. OE, protection, hand — more at MANUAL] **1** *early Eng law* **:** right of protection or guardianship (as over the person and property of a wife, a widow, an orphan, or the members of one's household or dependents) **2 :** GRITH 1b

mun·da \'mu̇ndə\ *n* -s *usu cap* **1 :** a member of any of various peoples representing an ancient pre-Aryan stock of India pushed back or nearly absorbed by incoming Caucasians or Mongolians **2 :** a language family restricted to central India including Asuri, Gadaba, Ho, Juang, Kharia, Korwa, Korku, Mundari, Santali, and Savara and included by some in the Austroasiatic family

mun·dane \,mən'dān\ *adj* [ME *mondeyne,* fr. MF *mondain,* fr. LL *mundanus,* fr. L *mundus* world + *-anus* -an] **1 a :** of, relating to, or characteristic of the world **:** characterized by human affairs, concerns, and activities that are often practical, immediate, transitory, and ordinary ⟨a reviewer is not expected to mention anything so ~ as the price of books —A.J.P.Taylor⟩ ⟨nothing but ~ businessmen —T.H.Fielding⟩ ⟨the occupations and distractions of ~ life —Harold Nicolson⟩ **b :** belonging to the world and having no concern for the ideal or the heavenly ⟨the trend which marks distinguished art from the more ~ —Carlyle Burrows⟩ ⟨a fairy palace, no: but a ~ wonder of a quite unimagined kind —R.A.W. Hughes⟩ **2 :** of or relating to the cosmos **:** COSMIC **syn** see EARTHLY

mundane astrology *n* **:** JUDICIAL ASTROLOGY

mundane house *n* **:** one of the twelve equal sectors in which the celestial sphere is divided in judicial astrology by six great circles intersecting at the north and south points of the horizon and which are regarded as fixed with respect to the horizon, the stars and planets passing through them each 24 hours — see HOROSCOPE

mun·dane·ly *adv* **:** in a mundane manner ⟨he spoke so ~ of university life⟩

mun·dane·ness \-ānnəs\ *n* -ES **:** the quality or state of being mundane

mun·dan·i·ty \,mən'danəd·ē\ *n* -ES [MF or ML; MF *mondanité,* fr. ML *mundanitat-, mundanitas,* fr. LL *mundanus* mundane + L *-itat-, -itas* -ity] **1 :** the quality or state of being mundane **:** WORLDLINESS ⟨an ideal opposed to ~⟩ **2 :** worldly inclinations — often used in pl. ⟨charm and graciousness, — her appreciation of fine clothes and houses — these are all *mundanities* —*Harper's Bazaar*⟩

mun·da·ri \,mən'därē\ *n* -s *usu cap* **:** a Munda dialect of the Kol people

mun·da·tory \'məndə,tōrē\ *n* -ES [LL *mundatorius* of cleaning, fr. L *mundatus* (past part. of *mundare* to clean, fr. *mundus* clean) + *-orius* -ory — more at MOSS] **:** a towel or cloth used to cleanse ecclesiastical vessels used in Holy Communion

mun·dic \'məndik\ *n* -s [perh. fr. Corn *mēn tēk,* fr. *mēn* stone + *tēk* pretty; akin to W *teg* pretty, OIr *ētig* ugly, ON *thægr* pleasant, *thiggja* to take, receive — more at MENHIR, THIG] *Cornwall* **:** PYRITE

mun·di·fy \'məndə,fī\ *vt* -ED/-ING/-ES [MF or LL; MF *mondifier* to cleanse, fr. LL *mundificare,* fr. L *mundus* clean + *-ificare* -ify — more at MOSS] **:** to wash thoroughly **:** DETERGE

mun·div·a·gant \,mən'divəgənt\ *adj* [L *mundus* world + *-i-* + *vagant- vagans* wandering, fr. pres. part. of *vagari* to wander — more at VAGARY] *archaic* **:** wandering over the world

mun·dle \'mu̇ndᵊl\ *n* -s [of Scand origin; akin to ON *möndull* handle; akin to (assumed) Oscan *manfur,* a part of a turner's lathe (whence L *mamphur*), Gk *mothos* din of battle, Skt *manthati* it swirls] *dial Eng* **:** a stick that is used for stirring

mun·du·gu·mor \,mən'dügə,mō(ə)r\ *n, pl* **mundugumor** *or* **mundugumors** *usu cap* **1 :** a Papuan people in the Sepik district, Territory of New Guinea **2 :** a member of the Mundugumor people

mun·dun·gus \,mən'dəŋgəs\ *n* -ES [modif. of Sp *mondongo* tripe] **1** *archaic* **:** REFUSE, TRASH **2 :** tobacco having an offensive smell

mun·du·ru·cú \,mündürü'kü\ *n, pl* **mundurucú** *or* **mundurucús** *usu cap* [Pg *mundurucú,* of AmerInd origin] **1 a :** a Tupian people of the upper Tapajoz river valley of Brazil **b :** a member of such people **2 :** the language of the Mundurucú people

mune \ mün\ *dial var of* MOON

mung *slang Austral var of* MONG

mun·ga \ məŋgə\ *n* -s [Kanarese *maṅga,* fr. Skt *marka*] **:** BONNET MONKEY

mung bean \'məŋ-\ *also* **mung** *n* -s [short for [3]*mungo*] **:** an erect bushy annual bean (*Phaseolus aureus*) that is probably native to India, is widely cultivated in warm regions for its edible usu. green or yellow seeds, for green manure, or for forage, and is the chief source of the bean sprouts used in Chinese cookery — called also *green gram;* see URD

[1]**munge** \'mu̇nzh, 'mənzh\ *vb* -ED/-ING/-S [perh. alter. (influenced by [1]*munch*) of obs. *mange* to eat, fr. ME *mangen,* fr. MF *mangier* — more at MANGE] *dial Brit* **:** MUNCH

[2]**munge** \"\ *vi* -ED/-ING/-S [origin unknown] *dial Brit* **:** GRUMBLE, MOAN

mungeet *var of* MUNJEET

[1]**mun·go** \'məŋ(,)gō\ *n* -s [prob. after *Mungo,* a Negro slave in the farce *The Padlock* (1768) by Isaac Bickerstaffe †*ab*1812 Ir. playwright] *archaic* **:** NEGRO

[2]**mungo** \"\ *also* **mon·go** *or* **mon·goe** \'mäŋ-\ *n* -s [origin unknown] **:** wool of poor quality and very short staple recovered from heavily felted wool goods and wastes — see SHODDY 1

[3]**mun·go** \'məŋ(,)gō\ *also* **mungo bean** *n* -s [Tamil *mūṅgu,* fr. Hindi *mūg,* fr. Skt *mudga*] **1 :** MUNG BEAN **2 :** URD

mun·goos *or* **mun·goose** \'məŋ,güs\ *archaic var of* MONGOOSE

mun·gu·ba \,məŋ'gübə\ *n* -s [Pg *munguba, monguba,* fr. Tupi] **:** a Brazilian silk-cotton tree (*Bombax munguba*)

mu·ni \'münē\ *n* -s [Skt — more at MANTIS] **:** a Hindu hermit sage

[1]**mu·nich** \'myünik, -nēk\ *adj, usu cap* [fr. *Munich,* Germany] **:** of or from the city of Munich, Germany **:** of the kind or style prevalent in Munich

[2]**munich** \"\ *n* -s *usu cap* [fr. *Munich,* Germany, the site of a 1938 agreement among England, France, and Italy that approved the dismemberment of Czechoslovakia by Hitler] **:** an instance of unresisting compliance with and capitulation to the demands of an aggressor nation ⟨the truce . . . was another *Munich* —R.T.Oliver⟩ ⟨do not think that a modus vivendi to save what can be saved . . . is necessarily a *Munich* —Frank Gorrell⟩

mu·nich·ism \-ni,kizəm\ *n* -s *usu cap* [[2]*munich* + *-ism*] **:** an attitude favoring appeasement ⟨the principal conservative critic of *Munichism* —*New Republic*⟩

munich lake *n, often cap M* **:** CARMINE 2

[1]**mu·nic·i·pal** \myü'nisəpəl, myə'-, ÷mə'- *or* ÷,myünə'sipəl\ *adj* [L *municipalis,* fr. *municip- municeps* inhabitant of a municipium, lit., undertaker of duties (fr. *munus* duty, service, gift + *-cip-, -ceps,* fr. *capere* to take) + *-alis* -al — more at MEAN, HEAVE] **1 :** of or relating to the internal affairs as distinguished from the foreign relations of a nation or other major political unit ⟨international law . . . only authorizes a belligerent to punish a spy under its ~ law —J.L.Kunz⟩ ⟨~ legislation . . . enacted for the fulfillment of the treaties —*U. S. Stat. 750*⟩ — compare INTERNAL LAW, INTERNATIONAL LAW **2 a :** of or relating to a municipality ⟨~ reform acts⟩ ⟨a ~ golf course⟩ ⟨~ university⟩ ⟨~ government⟩ ⟨~ architecture⟩ **b :** appointed, elected, or empowered by a municipality **:** functioning in a municipality ⟨~ council⟩ ⟨~ officer⟩ ⟨~ police⟩ **c :** issued by or under the authority of a municipality ⟨~ bond⟩ ⟨~ regulation⟩ **3 :** of, relating to, or having the characteristics of a municipium **4 :** restricted to one locality **:** having narrow limits ⟨a new very ~ variety of dwarf sweet pea —Osbert Sitwell⟩ ⟨the sacredness of human life is a purely ~ ideal of no validity outside the jurisdiction —O.W.Holmes †1935⟩

[2]**municipal** \"\ *n* -s **1 :** an inhabitant of a municipium **2 :** a member of the municipal guard of Paris **3 :** a security issued by a state or local government or by an authority set up by such a government — usu. used in pl. ⟨prospects . . . seemed better in low interest rate corporation issues than in ~*s* —*World's Work*⟩

municipal borough *n* **:** a borough in England or Wales having powers of self-government limited by its inclusion in an administrative county

municipal corporation *n* **:** a political unit (as a town, city, or borough) created and given quasi-independent status by a nation, state, or other major governing authority and usu. endowed with powers of local self-government **:** a public corporation created by law to act as an agency of administration and local self-government

municipal district *n* **:** a chiefly rural unit of local government in Canada and in some parts of Australia

municipal engineer *n* **:** one whose training or occupation is in municipal engineering

municipal engineering *n* **:** a branch of engineering that deals with the operation and problems (as laying out additions and parks, and constructing and maintaining sewer systems, waterworks, and pavements) peculiar to urban life

mu·nic·i·pal·i·ty \myü,nisə'paləd·ē, myə,-, -lətē, -i ÷mə,-\ *n* -ES [F *municipalité,* fr. *municipal* (fr. L *municipalis*) + *-ité* -ity — more at MUNICIPAL] **1 a :** a primarily urban political unit (as a town or city) having corporate status and usu. powers of self-government ⟨a ~ . . . has no powers save those conferred upon it by the laws of the state —S.J.Ervin⟩ **b :** the governing body of such a unit **2 :** an administrative area into which Philippine provinces are divided, comprising a number of barrios — compare POBLACIÓN

mu·nic·i·pal·iza·tion \myü,nisəpələ'zāshən, myə,-, ÷mə,-\ *n* -s **:** the action or result of municipalizing ⟨the ~ of a gas supply is not . . . a way of cheapening the public service —W.H.Y.Webber⟩

mu·nic·i·pal·ize \=ʹ=⸗pə,līz\ *vt* -ED/-ING/-S **:** to bring under municipal ownership, control, or supervision ⟨water and gas supply in practically all German towns . . . had been *municipalized* —G.M.Harris⟩

mu·nic·i·pal·ly \-p(ə)lē\ *adv* **:** by or in terms of a municipality ⟨the club . . . had grown into a ~ sponsored organization —*Amer. Guide Series: Ark.*⟩

municipal security *n* **:** a security (as a bond) issued by the government or a governmental agency of a municipality — usu. used in pl.

mu·ni·cip·i·um \,myünə'sipēəm\ *n, pl* **municip·ia** \-ēə\ [L, fr. *municip-, municeps* inhabitant of a municipium — more at MUNICIPAL] **:** a Roman municipality; *esp* **:** one giving its citizens the privileges of Roman citizenship and often the right of living according to their own laws and customs

mu·nif·i·cence \myü'nifəsən(t)s, myə'-, ÷mə'-\ *n* -s [MF, fr. L *munificentia,* fr. *munificus* generous (fr. *munus* service, gift + *-ficus* -fic) + *-entia* -ence — more at MEAN] **:** the quality or state of being munificent **:** a giving or bestowing with extraordinary liberality **:** lavish generosity ⟨the ~ of princes made possible the painting and sculpture of the Renaissance —Curt Stern⟩

munificency *n* -ES [L *munificentia*] *obs* **:** MUNIFICENCE

mu·nif·i·cent \-nt\ *adj* [fr. *munificence,* after such pairs as E *magnificence: magnificent*] **1 :** very liberal in giving or bestowing **:** LAVISH ⟨my father gave me ten shillings and my mother five and I thought them ~ —Samuel Butler †1902⟩ **2 :** characterized by great liberality or generosity ⟨a handful of fruit which in her system was a ~ gift —William Beebe⟩ ⟨~ endowment of $22,000,000 —*Amer. Guide Series: Va.*⟩ **syn** see LIBERAL

mu·nif·i·cent·ly *adv* **:** in a munificent manner

mu·nif·i·cent·ness *n* -ES **:** the quality or state of being munificent

mu·ni·fy \'myünə,fī\ *vt* -ED/-ING/-ES [irreg. fr. L *munire* to fortify + E *-fy* — more at MUNITION] **:** to provide defenses for **:** FORTIFY

mu·ni·ment \'myünəmənt\ *n* -s [MF, fr. L *munimentum,* fr. *munire* to fortify + *-mentum* -ment] **1 muniments** *pl* **a :** the evidences or writings that enable one to defend the title to an estate or maintain a claim to rights and privileges; *also* **:** title deeds and papers, statutory grants, charters, and judgments **b** *archaic* **:** things provided as furnishings ⟨bedrooms contain little beyond the ~*s* necessary for sitting and lying —G.C. Munday⟩ **2** *archaic* **:** something that supports or defends **:** a means of defense ⟨we cannot spare the coarsest ~ of virtue —R.W.Emerson⟩

muniment room *n* **:** a storage room for preservation of family or sometimes official or parochial records, papers, notebooks ⟨old manuscript treasures accumulated during the centuries in the *muniment rooms* of most of the noble and ancient families of Britain —St. Vincent Troubridge⟩ ⟨cobwebby old *muniment rooms* —R.D.Altick⟩

munite *vt* -ED/-ING/-S [ME *munyten*, fr. L *munitus*, past part. of *munire*] *obs* : to strengthen usu. by fortifying

¹**mu·ni·tion** \myü'nishən, myə'-\ *n* -S [MF, fr. L *munition-, munitio*, fr. *munitus* (past part. of *munire* to fortify, fr. *moenia* walls) + *-ion-, -io* -ion; akin to OE *mǣre, gemǣre* boundary, MD *mere* stake, ON *landamæri* borderland, L *murus* wall, *meta* pyramid, boundary mark, Skt *minoti* he fixes in the earth, builds; basic meaning: stake] **1 a** *obs* : RAMPART, FORTIFICATION, FORTRESS, STRONGHOLD ⟨his place of defense shall be the ~s of rocks —Isa. 33:16 (AV)⟩ **b** *archaic* : something that serves as a defense ⟨whose might, the chief ~ is of all our host —William Cowper⟩ **2 a** : material used in war for defense or attack : ammunition and all supplies for direct military action : ARMAMENT 2b **b** : necessary equipment or provision — usu. used in pl. ⟨~s for a political campaign⟩

²**munition** \"\ *vt* -ED/-ING/-S : to provide with munitions ⟨they were ~ed and ready for the campaign⟩

mu·ni·tion·eer \myü¦nishə¦ni(ə)r, myə¦-\ *n* -S **1** : MUNITIONER **2** : a profiteer in the sale of munitions

mu·ni·tion·er \-'shənə(r)\ *n* -S : one who is engaged in the manufacture of munitions

mu·ni·tion·ment \-nmənt\ *n* -S : a munition supply ⟨the army faced the problem of ~ for its forces⟩

mu·ni·ty \'myünəd·ē\ *n* -ES [ME *munitie*, short for *immunitie* exemption from duty, privilege of exemption — more at IMMUNITY] : a privilege that is granted

munj \'münj, 'mənj\ *also* **mun·ja** \-jə\ *n, pl* **munjes** *also* **munjas** [Hindi & Skt; Hindi *mūj, mū̃j*, fr. Skt *muñja*] : a tough Asiatic grass (*Saccharum munja*) whose tenacious culms are used for ropes, twine, and baskets

mun·jeet *or* **mun·geet** \,man'jēt\ *n* -S [Hindi *mājīṭh*, fr. Skt *mañjiṣṭhā*, fem. of *mañjiṣṭha* bright red] : INDIAN MADDER 1

mun·jis·tin \,mən'jistən\ *n* -S [NL *munjista* Indian madder (fr. Skt *mañjiṣṭhā*) + E *-in*] : a yellow crystalline compound $C_{15}H_8O_6$ obtained from the Indian madder; purpuroxanthin-carboxylic acid

mun·nion *also* **mun·ion** \'mənyən\ *or* **min·ion** \'min-\ *n* -S [alter. of *monial*] : MULLION

mun·nop·sis \,mə'näpsəs\ *n, cap* [NL, fr. *Munna*, genus of isopods + *-opsis*] : a genus of eyeless marine isopods that somewhat resemble shrimps and have greatly enlarged antennae

mun·roe effect \mən'rō-\ *n, usu cap M* [after Charles E. *Munroe* †1938 Am. chemist and inventor] : the greatly increased penetration of an explosive into a surface (as of metal or concrete) that is caused by shaping a conical or hemispherical hollow in the forward end of an explosive cartridge

mun·see \'mən(t)sē\ *n, pl* **munsee** *or* **munsees** *usu cap* [Delaware *Min-asin-ink*, lit., at the place where stones are gathered together] **1** : a Delaware Indian people of northern New Jersey and neighboring parts of New York west of the Hudson **2** : a member of the Munsee people

¹**mun·shi** *or* **moon·shee** \'münshē\ *n* -S [Hindi *munshī*, fr. Ar *munshi'*] **1** : a Hindu secretary or clerk **2** : a Hindu interpreter or language teacher

²**munshi** *usu cap, var of* MUNCHI

mun·son system \'mən(t)sən-\ *n, usu cap M* [after T. V. *Munson* †1913 Amer. viticulturist] : a system for training grape vines in which double wires spaced 18 to 24 inches apart with a third single wire between them are attached to posts about 6 feet in height

¹**mun·ster** \'mənztə(r), -n(t)st-\ *adj, usu cap* [fr. *Munster*, province in southern Ireland] : of or from the province of Munster, Ireland : of the kind or style prevalent in Munster

²**mün·ster** *or* **mun·ster** *or* **muen·ster** \'minztə(r), 'mœn-, 'm(y)ün-, 'mu̇n-, 'mən-, -n(t)st-\ *adj, usu cap* [fr. *Münster*, city in northwest Germany] : of or from the city of Münster, Germany : of the kind or style prevalent in Münster

³**munster** *usu cap, var of* MUENSTER

mun·ti·a·cus \,mən·'tīəkəs\ *n, cap* [NL, fr. E *muntjac*] : a genus of mammals consisting of the muntjacs

mun·tin \'mənt³n\ *or* **mun·ting** \-tiŋ\ *n* -S [alter. of earlier *montant* vertical dividing bar or timber, fr. F, fr. pres. part. of *monter* to rise — more at MOUNT] : a strip member separating panes of glass with a sash — compare MULLION

munt·jac *also* **munt·jak** \'mənt,jak\ *or* **mun·jak** \-n,-\ *n* -S [prob. modif. of Jav *mindjangan* deer] **1** : any of various small deer (genus *Muntiacus*) of southeastern Asia and the East Indies having the male distinguished by sharp exposed canine tusks and small upright antlers — called also *barking deer* **2** : a Tibetan deer (*Elaphodus cephalophus*) closely related to the muntjac and with it and various extinct related forms constituting a subfamily of the Cervidae

muntshi *var of* MUNCHI

muntz metal \'mən(t)s-\ *n, usu cap 1st M* [after George F. *Muntz* †1857 Eng. metal manufacturer] : an alloy of copper and zinc that contains 60 percent of copper, can be rolled hot, and is used esp. for sheathing and bolts

mu·on \'myü,än, 'mü-\ *n* -S [by contr.] : MU-MESON

muong \'mwäŋ\ *n, pl* **muong** *or* **muongs** *usu cap* **1 a** : an Indo-Chinese people of Tonkin and northern Annam **b** : a member of such people **2** : the language of the Muong people that is related to Vietnamese

¹**mu·ra** \'mürə\ *n, pl* **mura** *or* **muras** *usu cap* [Pg, of AmerInd origin] **1 a** : an Indian people of northwestern Brazil **b** : a member of such people **2** : the language of the Mura people that constitutes the Muran language family

²**mu·ra** \'mu̇rə\ *n* -S [Jap, village, hamlet] : a rural community in Japan

mura·bit \'mürə,bit\ *n* -S [Ar *murābiṭ* hermit, ascetic] : MARABOUT

mu·rae·na *or* **mu·re·na** \myü'rēnə\ *n* [NL, fr. L *muraena, murena* moray — more at MORAY] **1** *cap* : the type genus of Muraenidae **2** -S : MORAY

mu·rae·ni·dae \-rēnə,dē, -ren-\ *n pl, cap* [NL, fr. *Muraena*, type genus + *-idae*] : a family of eels comprising the morays

¹**mu·rae·noid** \-rē,nȯid\ *adj* [ISV *muraen-* (fr. NL *Muraena*) + *-oid*] : of, relating to, or resembling the Muraenidae

²**muraenoid** \"\ *n* -S : MORAY

mu·rage \'myu̇rij\ *n* -S [ME, fr. MF, fr. *murer* to enclose with a wall + *-age* — more at MURE] *Brit* : a tax paid for building or repairing the walls of a fortified town

¹**mu·ral** \'myu̇rəl, 'myür-\ *adj* [L *muralis*, fr. *murus* wall + *-alis* -al — more at MUNITION] **1** : of, relating to, or resembling a wall ⟨a margin of lofty unbroken ~ precipices —Samuel Haughton⟩ **2** : applied to and made integral with a wall surface ⟨paused to read the carved ~ tablet⟩ **3** : attached to and limited to a wall or a cavity ⟨~ thrombus⟩ ⟨~ abscess⟩

²**mural** \"\ *n* -S : a painting or other work applied to and made integral with a wall surface

mural arch *or* **mural arc** *n* : the wall or arch in the plane of the meridian formerly used for the attachment of an astronomical circle

mural crown *n* [trans. of L *corona muralis*] **1** : an open crown of gold having the upper rim indented to resemble a battlement bestowed among the ancient Romans on one that first mounted the wall of a besieged place and lodged a standard there **2** *or* **mural coronet** : a representation of an embattled open crown in heraldry

mural crown 2

mu·ral·ist \-ləst\ *n* -S : a painter of mural pictures or decorations

mu·ral·ly \-rəlē\ *adv* : with a mural crown

mu·ran \'mürən\ *adj, usu cap* [¹*Mura* + *-an*] : relating to or being the language family consisting of the language of the Mura people of Brazil

mu·ra·no glass \mü'rä(,)nō-\ *n, usu cap M* [fr. *Murano*, Italy] : glassware made at Murano, Italy

mu·rar·i·um \myü'ra(a)rēəm\ *n* -S [L *mur-, mus* mouse + E *-arium* — more at MOUSE] : a place for rearing mice or rats under controlled conditions

mu·ra·to·ri·an \¦myu̇rə¦tōrēən\ *adj, usu cap* [Lodovico Antonio *Muratori* †1750 Ital. antiquary and historian + E *-an*] : of or relating to the antiquary Muratori

mur·cia \'mərsh(ē)ə\ *adj, usu cap* [fr. *Murcia*, Spain] : of or from the city of Murcia, Spain : of the kind or style prevalent in Murcia

mur·ci·a·na \,mərshē'änə\ *n* -S [Sp, fr. fem. of *murciano* of Murcia, fr. *Murcia* + *-ano* -an] : a fandango of Murcia, Spain

¹**mur·der** \'mərdər, 'mədə(r, 'məidə(r\ *n* -S [partly fr. ME *murther*, fr. OE *morthor*; partly fr. ME *mordre, murdre*, fr. OF *murdre, murtre*, of Gmc origin; akin to OE *morthor;* akin to OE *morth* death, murder, Goth *maurthr* murder, OHG *mord*, ON *morth* murder, L *mort-, mors* death, *mori* to die, Gk *brotos, mortos* mortal, Skt *mṛta* death, *marate, mriyate* he dies] **1** *early Eng law* : the killing of a person secretly or with concealment as opposed to an open killing **2** : the crime of killing a person under circumstances precisely defined by statute: as **a** : first-degree murder that deserves either capital or severe punishment because of being willful and premeditated, being committed with atrocity or cruelty (as by poisoning, starvation, mayhem, or torture), being committed in the course of the commission of a serious felony (as arson, burglary, or kidnapping), or being committed after lying in wait for the purpose of killing the victim **b** : second-degree murder that in most states is all other murder not classified as first-degree murder **3** : the killing of people in war ⟨war is mass ~⟩ **4** : something extraordinarily difficult or dangerous ⟨it'll be ~ on those roads up in the Sierras —G.A.Wagner⟩ ⟨in the more modest cafeteria . . . the crush is ~ —Herbert Kubly⟩ **5** : a parlor game in which after a mock murder has been committed in the dark the lights are turned on and one player as the detective questions the others to try to find out who is the criminal

²**murder** \"\ *vb* **murdered; murdered; murdering** \-d(ə)riŋ\ **murders** [partly fr. ME *murthren*, fr. *murther*, n.; partly fr. ME *mordren, murdren*, fr. MF *mordrir, murdrir*, fr. OF, fr. *murdre, murtre*, n.] *vt* **1** : to kill (a human being) unlawfully and with premeditated malice or willfully, deliberately, and unlawfully **2** : to slaughter in a brutal manner esp. in war ⟨bombs ~ed people as they stood in the street⟩ **3 a** : to put an end to : DESTROY ⟨if ever he were in power would . . . ~ truth, freedom, and art —*Saturday Rev.*⟩ **b** : to harass or depress grievously : TEASE, TORMENT ⟨~ed this poor heart of mine —Shak.⟩ **c** : to mutilate, spoil, or deform by wretched performance : MANGLE ⟨someone's difficult sonata was ~ed on the piano —Anne Green⟩ ⟨the average British traveler leads the world in ~ing the French tongue —*Times Lit. Supp.*⟩ ~ *vi* : to commit murder **syn** see KILL

mur·der·ee \,mərdə'rē\ *n* -S [²*murder* + *-ee*] : the victim or intended victim of a murderer ⟨played the ~ in the . . . crime picture —Speed Lamkin⟩

mur·der·er \'mərdərər, 'mədərə(r, 'məidərə(r\ *n* -S [partly fr. ME *murtherer*, fr. *murthren* + *-er;* partly fr. ME *mordrour*, fr. MF *mordreur, murdreur*, fr. OF, fr. *mordrir, murdrir* + *-eur* -or] **1 a** : one legally guilty of committing murder **b** : one who slays a living creature **2** *obs* : a cannon used esp. for clearing a ship's decks **3** : a metal bar carrying several hooks for cod

mur·der·ess \-dərəs\ *n* -ES [*murderer* + *-ess*] : a female murderer

murdering *adj* [fr. pres. part. of ²*murder*] **1** : characterized by murder or the commitment of murder ⟨his ~ guns —John Dryden⟩ **2** : characterized by an intent or ability to injure or harm ⟨a ~ tongue⟩

murdering piece *n, obs* : MURDERER 2

mur·der·ous \'mərd(ə)rəs, 'məd-, 'məid-\ *adj* **1** : having the purpose or capability of murder : characterized by or causing murder or bloodshed ⟨the charge . . . was covered at a disciplined trot under ~ fire —Al Newman⟩ ⟨the ~ inadequacy of lifeboats and rafts —F.L.Paxson⟩ ⟨some uncontrollable impulse . . . may have driven the defendant to the commission of the ~ act —B.N.Cardozo⟩ ⟨the anger . . . crystallized in his demented brain into a cold, ~ fury —J.C.Powys⟩ **2** : having the ability or power to overwhelm : DEVASTATING ⟨the ~ heat that attended the opening —Wolcott Gibbs⟩ ⟨a hard-hitting and exhilarating book . . . full of quietly ~ thrusts —C.J.Rolo⟩ **3** : characterized by extreme difficulty ⟨the exams . . . are ~ —E.O.Hauser⟩ ⟨those unmanageable verbs, those ~ moods and tenses —*Times Lit. Supp.*⟩

mur·der·ous·ly *adv* : in a murderous manner ⟨a . . . schnauzer tore down from the garden barking ~ —Jean Stafford⟩

mur·der·ous·ness *n* -ES : the quality or state of being murderous

mur·drum \'mərdrəm\ *n* -S [ML, murder, fine for murder, fr. OF *murdre* murder — more at MURDER] *early Eng law* **1** : MURDER; *esp* : a killing in secret **2** : a fine exacted under the Norman kings from the hundred in which a person was slain unless the slayer was produced or proof was given that the slain person was not a Franco-Norman

¹**mure** \'myu̇(ə)r\ *vt* -ED/-ING/-S [ME *muren*, fr. MF *murer*, fr. LL *murare*, fr. L *murus* wall — more at MUNITION] **1** : IMMURE **2** : THRUST, SQUEEZE ⟨~ against a wall⟩

²**mure** *n* -S [MF *mur*, fr. L *murus*] *obs* : WALL : something resembling a wall

³**mure** \'myu̇(ə)r\ *adj* [ME, fr. MF *meur*, lit., ripe, fr. L *maturus* — more at MATURE] *dial Brit* : HUMBLE, MEEK

⁴**mure** \"\ *dial Eng var of* MOOR

murena *syn of* MURAENA

mu·ren·ger \'myu̇rənjə(r)\ *n* -S [alter. of earlier *murager*, fr. ME, fr. *murage* + *-er*] : one in charge of the wall of a town and its repairs

mu·rex \'myu̇,reks\ *n* [NL, fr. L, purple shell; akin to Gk *myak-, myax* sea-mussel, and prob. to L *mur-, mus* mouse — more at MOUSE] **1 a** *cap* : a genus (the type of the family Muricidae) of marine gastropods having a rough and often spinose shell and abounding in tropical seas **b** *pl* **mu·ri·ces** \-ürə,sēz\ *or* **murexes** : any mollusk of this genus or of the family Muricidae formerly much valued as the chief source of Tyrian purple dye **2** *pl* **murices** *or* **murexes** : a shell used as a trumpet

mu·rex·an \myu̇'rek,san\ *n* -S [*murexide* + *-an*] : URAMIL

mu·rex·ide \-,sīd, -səd\ *n* -S [G *murexid*, fr. NL *Murex* + G *-id* -ide] : a red crystalline compound $C_8H_8N_6O_6$ having a green luster, forming purple-red solutions with water, and formerly used as a dye; the ammonium salt of purpuric acid

murexide reaction *or* **murexide test** *n* : a reaction giving rise to murexide when uric acid or a related compound is heated with nitric acid and the product is treated with ammonia

mur·geon \'mərjən\ *n* -S [origin unknown] **1** *Scot* **a** : a wry face : GRIMACE **b** : a body contortion **2** *Scot* : GRUMBLINGS — usu. used in pl.

mu·ria \'mu̇rēə\ *n, pl* **muria** *or* **murias** *usu cap* : one of a Gond hill people of India inhabiting the Bastar region of Madhya Pradesh

mu·ri·ate \'myu̇rē,āt\ *n* -S [F, back-formation fr. *muriatique* (in *acide muriatique* muriatic acid), fr. L *muriaticus* pickled in brine, fr. *muria* brine; akin to L *muscus* moss — more at MOSS] : CHLORIDE — used chiefly commercially

mu·ri·at·ed \-ād·əd\ *adj* [fr. past part. of obs. *muriate* to pickle in brine, fr. L *muria* + E *-ate*, v. suffix] : combined or impregnated with a chloride or chlorides: as **a** : put in brine : PICKLED **b** : containing much salt : BRINY ⟨~ waters⟩

muriate of potash : POTASSIUM CHLORIDE — used chiefly of fertilizer grades

mu·ri·at·ic acid \¦myu̇rē¦ad·ik-, -at|, |ēk-|\ *n* [F *muriatique*] : HYDROCHLORIC ACID — now used esp. of commercial grades

mu·ri·cate \'myu̇rə,kāt, -kət\ *also* **mu·ri·cat·ed** \-,kād·əd\ *adj* [*muricate* fr. L *muricatus* pointed like a purple fish, fr. *muric-, murex* purple shell + *-atus* -ate; *muricated* fr. L *muricatus* + E *-ed* — more at MUREX] : roughened with sharp hard points — compare ECHINATE

mu·ri·cid \'myu̇rəsəd, myu̇'ris-\ *adj* [NL *Muricidae*] : of or relating to the Muricidae

²**muricid** \"\ *n* -S : a mollusk of the family Muricidae : MUREX 1b

mu·ric·i·dae \myu̇'risə,dē\ *n pl, cap* [NL, fr. *Muric-, Murex*, type genus + *-idae*] : a large family of gastropod mollusks (suborder Stenoglossa) marked by elongated sculptured shells often with rows of protuberances or spines, long siphon canal, and sessile eyes — **mu·ric·i·form** \-,fȯrm\ *adj* — **mu·ri·cine** \-rə,sīn, -sən\ *adj* — **mu·ri·coid** \-rə,kȯid\ *adj*

mu·ric·u·late \myu̇'rikyə,lāt, -lət\ *adj* [L *muriculus*, dim. of *muric-, murex* purple shell + E *-ate*] : minutely muricate

¹**mu·rid** \mu̇'rēd\ *n* -S [Ar *murīd*] *Islam* : DISCIPLE; *esp* : a Sufi disciple

²**mu·rid** \'myu̇rəd\ *adj* [NL *Muridae*] : of or relating to the Muridae

³**murid** \"\ *n* -S : a rodent of the family Muridae

mu·ri·dae \'myu̇rə,dē\ *n pl, cap* [NL, fr. *Mur-, Mus*, type genus + *-idae*] : a very large family of relatively small rodents (superfamily Muroidea) that include various orig. Old World rodents (as the house mouse and the common rats) that are now cosmopolitan in distribution and that are distinguished from the related cricetid rodents by complete absence of cheek pouches

¹**mu·ri·form** \'myu̇rə,fȯrm\ *adj* [L *murus* wall + E *-iform* — more at MUNITION] : resembling courses of bricks in arrangement; *esp* : having both horizontal and vertical septa ⟨~ spores⟩ — **mu·ri·form·ly** *adv*

²**muriform** \"\ *adj* [L *mur-, mus* mouse + E *-iform* — more at MOUSE] : resembling a mouse or rat in form or appearance

mu·ril·lo \myü'ri(,)lō, mə'rē(,)(y)ō\ *n, often cap* [after Bartolomé E. *Murillo* †1682 Span. painter] : a moderate blue that is greener and duller than average copen, redder and deeper than azurite blue, and greener and darker than Dresden blue

murillo bark *n* : SOAPBARK

¹**mu·rine** \'myu̇,rīn, -rən, myü'rēn\ *adj* [L *murinus* of mice, fr. *mur-, mus* mouse + *-inus* -ine — more at MOUSE] **1 a** : of or relating to the genus *Mus* or to the subfamily of Muridae that includes it and contains most of the rats and mice which habitually live in intimate association with man ⟨~ rodents⟩ **b** : of, relating to, or produced by the common house mouse ⟨a ~ odor⟩ **2** : affecting or transmitted by rats or mice ⟨~ rickettsial diseases⟩

²**murine** \"\ *n* -S : a murine animal

murine opossum *n* : any of several small arboreal opossums (genus *Marmosa*) widely distributed in So. and Central America

murine typhus *n* : a mild febrile disease marked by headache and rash, caused by a rickettsia (*Rickettsia mooseri*) widespread in nature in rodents, and transmitted to man by the common rat flea

mu·ri·nus \myü'rīnəs\ *n* -ES [L, of mice] : MOUSE GRAY

mu·ri·ti palm \¦mu̇rə¦tē-\ *n* [Pg *muriti, buriti* muriti palm, miriti palm, fr. Tupi] : a large Brazilian fan palm (*Mauritia vinifera*) yielding edible nuts and a useful fiber

mu·ri·um \'myu̇rēəm\ *n* -S [NL, back-formation fr. ISV *muriatic* (acid) + NL *-ium*] : a hypothetical element having muriatic acid as the oxide

mur·ji'·ite \'mərjē,īt\ *or* **murj·ite** \-r,jīt\ *n* -S *usu cap* [Ar *murji'ah* believers in suspension of judgment + E *-ite*] **1** : an early Muslim sect emphasizing a suspension of judgment against erring believers and the unfailing efficacy of faith over works **2** : a member of the Murji'ite sect

¹**murk** *or* **mirk** \'mərk, 'mək, 'məik\ *adj* -ER/-EST [ME *mirke*, prob. fr. ON *myrkr*; akin to OE *mirce* dark, & prob. to *morgen* morn — more at MORN] **1** *archaic* : having little or no light : dark and gloomy ⟨the heavens are ~ as the midnight —William Morris⟩ **2** *archaic* : obscured by or as if by mist : FOGGY

²**murk** *or* **mirk** \"\ *n* -S [ME *mirke*, prob. fr. ON *myrkr*, fr. *myrkr*, adj.] : DARKNESS, GLOOM; *also* : thick heavy air : FOG ⟨~ without, and leaden dusk in the huts —O.E.Rölvaag⟩ ⟨an early gull rose from the water . . . and soared away into the ~ —Nevil Shute⟩ ⟨out in the ~ and rain —H.W.Longfellow⟩

³**murk** *or* **mirk** \"\ *vt* -ED/-ING/-S [ME *mirken*, fr. *mirke*, adj.] : to make dark, dim, or gloomy; *also* : SOIL

murk·i·ly *or* **mirk·i·ly** \-kəlē\ *adv* : in a murky manner : DARKLY ⟨can imagine that ~ passionate nature —H.J. Laski⟩

murk·i·ness *or* **mirk·i·ness** \-kēnəs\ *n* -ES : the quality or state of being murky ⟨her abiding sense of the ~ of human life —Thomas Hardy⟩

murk·ness *n* -ES [ME *mirknesse*, fr. *mirke*, adj. + *-nesse* -ness] : MURKINESS

murk·some *or* **mirk·some** \-ksəm\ *adj* [²*murk, mirk* + *-some*] : quite murky

¹**murky** *or* **mirky** \'mərkē, 'məkē, 'məikē, -ki\ *adj* -ER/-EST [²*murk, mirk* + *-y*] **1 a** : characterized by intense darkness or gloominess ⟨a brown adobe structure with . . . no window to shed light in its ~ depths —Tom Marvel⟩ ⟨the ~ bayous that are the highways of the marsh country —*Lamp*⟩ **b** : difficult to understand : CLOUDY, OBSCURE ⟨however ~ the subject matter may be, the language is always crystal clear —James Yaffe⟩ ⟨the ~ field of politics —P.H.Douglas⟩ ⟨the ~ depths of public opinion —M.W.Childs⟩ **2** : characterized by thickness and heaviness of air : FOGGY, MISTY ⟨rain poured down from ~ skies —*Newsweek*⟩ ⟨the air was ~ with the smoke of brush fires —Christopher Rand⟩ **3** : dark or dull in color ⟨her tweeds are soft and ~ —Lois Long⟩ ⟨nighthawks sheer the gloom, the white bar just visible on the . . . ~ plumage —D.C.Peattie⟩ ⟨a rather wiry and very dark animal, with a ~ brooding eye —J.B.Priestley⟩ **4** : covered with dirt and grime ⟨dimly saw the ~ fanlight over the door —A. Conan Doyle⟩ **syn** see DARK

²**murky** \"\ *n* -ES [origin unknown] : a musical composition for keyboard instruments with a bass in broken octaves

murky bass *n* : an accompanying bass in broken octaves

murl \'mərl\ *vb* -ED/-ING/-S [perh. of Celt origin; akin to IrGael *muirlim* I crumble] *dial Brit* : CRUMBLE, MOLDER

mur·lin \'mərlən\ *n* -S [origin unknown] *Irish* : BADDERLOCKS

murly \'mərli\ *adj* [*murl* + *-y*] *dial Eng* : CRUMBLY — used esp. of soil

mur·mansk \(')mu̇r¦man(t)sk\ *adj, usu cap* [fr. *Murmansk*, U.S.S.R.] : of or from the city of Murmansk, U.S.S.R. : of the kind or style prevalent in Murmansk

mur·mi \'mu̇rmē\ *n, pl* **murmi** *or* **murmis** *usu cap* **1** : a member of a people that live on the border between Nepal and Sikkim, that are a pastoral division of the Bhutanese, and that have Mongolian features **2** : the Tibeto-Burman language of the Murmi people

¹**mur·mur** \'mərmər, 'məmə(r, 'məimə(r\ *n* -S [ME *murmure*, fr. MF, fr. L *murmur* murmur, grumbling, roar; akin to OHG *murmurōn, murmulōn* to murmur, ON *murra* to murmur, Gk *mormyrein* to roar and boil (of water), Skt *marmara* murmuring, rustling; of imit. origin] **1** : a complaint half suppressed or uttered in a low muttering voice : GRUMBLING ⟨the tax on chimneys . . . raised far louder ~s —T.B.Macaulay⟩ ⟨devices . . . which writers use confidently and readers accept without a ~ —Robert Humphrey⟩ ⟨a ~ of impatience in the crowd —G.B.Shaw⟩ **2 a** : a low indistinct but often continuous sound ⟨the ~ of voices in the street —Sherwood Anderson⟩ ⟨the ~ of the waves along the shore⟩ **b** : a soft-spoken word : gentle speech ⟨her ~ was a comforting word⟩ ⟨there was a ~, "Yes, Yes" —Millen Brand⟩ ⟨amid a ~ of salaams we seated ourselves —William Beebe⟩ **3** : RUMOR, WHISPER ⟨was fresh in ~ . . . that he did seek the love of fair Olivia —Shak.⟩ **4** : an abnormal sound of the heart heard through the chest wall indicating a functional abnormality or the site of a structural abnormality **5** *also* **murmur vowel** : the unstressed voiced or voiceless vowel \ə\ when morphemically incidental to the articulation of a consonant

²**murmur** \"\ *vb* **murmured; murmured; murmuring** \-m(ə)riŋ\ **murmurs** [ME *murmuren*, fr. MF *murmurer*, fr. L *murmurare*, fr. *murmur*] *vi* **1** : to make a low continuous sound ⟨the brook ~ed under the ice —Elliott Merrick⟩ ⟨a breeze ~ed in the trees —Wilfrid Campbell⟩ **2** : to utter complaints in a low half-articulated voice : express discontent : GRUMBLE ⟨no one dares ~ in public —*Time*⟩ ⟨the ignorant and ungrateful nation ~ed against its deliverers —T.B. Macaulay⟩ ~ *vt* **1 a** *Scot* : to murmur against : ACCUSE **b** : to utter with dissatisfaction : COMPLAIN ⟨critics . . . ~ today that it lacks a forward looking concept —M.W.Straight⟩ **2** : to utter or give forth in low or indistinct sounds or words ⟨the sentences men ~ again and again for years —W.B.Yeats⟩ ⟨she would be ~ing into the telephone important secrets —Elizabeth Headley⟩

mur·mu·ra·tion \,mərmə'rāshən\ *n* -S [ME *murmuracioun*, fr. MF *murmuration*, fr. L *murmuration-, murmuratio*, fr. *murmuratus* (past part. of *murmurare*) + *-ion-, -io* -ion] **1** : the act of murmuring : the utterance of low continuous sounds or complaining noises ⟨the ~ of the crowds —A.E. Richardson⟩ ⟨ceaseless, inarticulate ~ of prayer —Frederic Prokosch⟩ **2** *of starlings* : FLOCK ⟨in the stackyard there was a great ~ of starlings —Mary Webb⟩

murmur diphthong *n* **:** a falling diphthong whose ending position is that of \ə\ **:** a centering diphthong

mur·mur·er \'mərmərər, 'mōmərə(r, 'mәimərə(r\ *n* -S **:** one that murmurs

mur·mur·ing·ly *adv* **:** in a murmuring manner

mur·mur·less \'mərmərlə̇s\ *adj* **:** having no murmur — **mur·mur·less·ly** *adv*

mur·mur·ous \'mərm(ə)rəs, 'mōm-, 'mәim-\ *adj* **1 :** filled with murmurs **:** characterized by low indistinct but often continuous sound ⟨the empty chimneys became so alive with swallows that the whole place was faintly ~ —Ellen Glasgow⟩ ⟨the garden is ~ with bees —Booth Tarkington⟩ **2 :** spoken softly and gently **:** low and sometimes indistinct ⟨his voice . . . was of a ~ character, soft, attractive —Nathaniel Hawthorne⟩

mur·mur·ous·ly *adv* **:** in a murmurous manner ⟨palm trees . . . wave ~ —Sam Boal⟩

murn·gin \'mərnjə̇n\ *n, pl* **murngin** *or* **murngins** *usu cap* **:** an Australian people of Arnhemland

¹mu·roid \'myu̇,rȯid\ *adj* [NL *Muroidea*] **:** of or relating to the Muroidea

²muroid \"\ *n* -S **:** a rodent of the superfamily Muroidea

mu·roi·dea \myu̇'rȯidēə\ *n pl, cap* [NL, fr. *Mur-, Mus* + *-oidea*] **:** a superfamily of rodents approximately equal to Myomorpha with the Dipodidae excluded

mu·ro·mon·tite \,myu̇rə'män‚tīt\ *n* -S [G *muromontit*, fr. *Muromontium* (Mauersberg) in Saxony, Germany, its locality + G *-it* -ite] **:** a mineral $Be_2FeY_2(SiO_4)_3$(?) consisting of a silicate of yttrium, iron, and beryllium that is perhaps identical with gadolinite or is a variant of clinozoisite

muron *var of* MYRON

mur·phy \'mərfē\ *n* -ES [fr. *Murphy*, a common Irish surname; fr. the potato's being regarded as the staple food of Ireland] **:** POTATO

murphy bed *n, usu cap M* [after William L. *Murphy*, 20th cent. Amer. inventor] **:** a bed that may be folded or swung into a closet when not in use

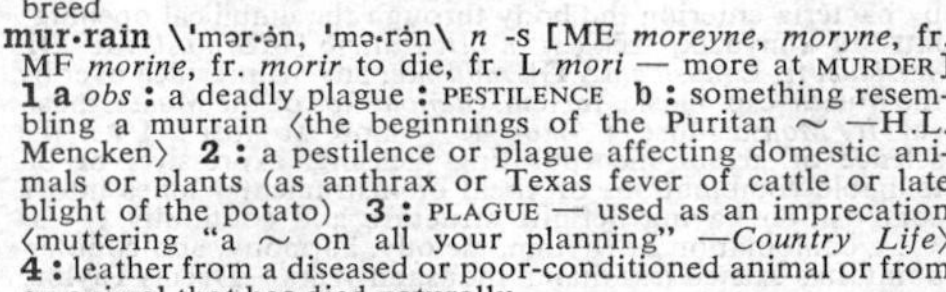
Murphy bed

murr *n* -S [ME *murre*] *obs* **:** a cold with hoarseness **:** CATARRH

mur·ra *or* **mur·rha** \'mərə\ *n* -S [L, prob. of Iranian origin like Gk *morrhia* murra; akin to Per *mori, muri* little glass ball] **:** a material thought to be of semiprecious stone or porcelain used to make costly vessels in ancient Rome

mur·rah \'mərə\ *n* [native name in India] **1** *usu cap* **:** an Indian breed of dairy type buffaloes with distinctive coiled horns **2** -S *often cap* **:** an animal of the Murrah breed

mur·rain \'mər·ən, 'mə·rən\ *n* -S [ME *moreyne, moryne*, fr. MF *morine*, fr. *morir* to die, fr. L *mori* — more at MURDER] **1 a** *obs* **:** a deadly plague **:** PESTILENCE **b :** something resembling a murrain ⟨the beginnings of the Puritan ~ —H.L. Mencken⟩ **2 :** a pestilence or plague affecting domestic animals or plants (as anthrax or Texas fever of cattle or late blight of the potato) **3 :** PLAGUE — used as an imprecation ⟨muttering "a ~ on all your planning" —*Country Life*⟩ **4 :** leather from a diseased or poor-conditioned animal or from an animal that has died naturally

mur·ral *or* **mur·rel** \'mərəl\ *n* -S [Skt *murala*] **:** a common freshwater snakehead (*Ophiocephalus striatus*) of southeast Asia and the Philippines that is an important food fish

mur·raya \'mərēə\ *n, cap* [NL, after Johan A. *Murray* †1791 Swed. botanist] **:** a genus of tropical Asiatic and Australian trees (family Rutaceae) having pinnate leaves and flowers with imbricated petals — see ORANGE JESSAMINE

mur·ray cod \'mərē-\ *n, usu cap M* [fr. *Murray* river, southeastern Australia] **:** a large serranid fish (*Oligorus macquariensis*) that is a leading freshwater food fish of Australia

murray crayfish *or* **murray lobster** *n, usu cap M* [fr. *Murray* river] **:** a large light-colored Australian crayfish (*Astacopsis serratus*) that is sought as a delicacy

murray down *n, usu cap M* [fr. *Murray* river] **:** the floss from the inflorescence of the carbungi

mur·ray·ian *or* **mur·ray·an** *also* **mur·ri·an** \'mərēən\ *n* -S *usu cap* [*Murray* river + E *-an*] **:** a member of an almost extinct ethnic group of southeastern Australia — compare CARPENTARIAN

murray pine *n, usu cap M* [in sense 1 after Andrew *Murray* †1878 Scot. naturalist; in sense 2 fr. *Murray* river] **1 :** LODGEPOLE PINE **b 2** *or* **murray river pine :** a spreading Australian cypress pine (*Callitris glauca*) with dark green foliage

murray red gum *n, usu cap M* [fr. *Murray* river] **:** a gum tree (*Eucalyptus camaldulensis*) that is native to Australia but is grown elsewhere in warm regions for ornament and shade and that has smooth gray bark, red wood, and umbellate flowers

murre \'mər(·)\ *n* -S [origin unknown] **1 :** any of several guillemots of the genus *Uria:* as **a :** FOOLISH GUILLEMOT **b :** THICK-BILLED MURRE **2 :** RAZORBILL

murree *usu cap, var of* MARI

murre·let \'mərlə̇t\ *n* -S [*murre* + *-let*] **:** any of several small sea birds (family Alcidae) found chiefly on islands of the north Pacific

mur·rey \'mərē\ *n* -S [ME *murrey, murreye*, fr. MF *moré, morée*, fr. ML *moratum, morata*, fr. neut. and fem. respectively of *moratus* mulberry-colored, fr. L *morum* mulberry + *-atus* -ate — more at MULBERRY] **1 :** MULBERRY 2b **2** *obs* **:** a fabric colored murrey

murrha *var of* MURRA

¹mur·rhine *also* **myr·rhine** \'mərə̇n, 'mə,rīn\ *adj* [L *murrinus, murrhinus, myrrhinus*, fr. *murra, murrha* + *-inus* -ine] **:** of, relating to, or made of murra ⟨sent him the poison to drink in a ~ cup —*Time*⟩

²murrhine *also* **myrrhine** \"\ *n* -S [L *murrinum, murrhinum, myrrhinum*, fr. neut. of *murrinus, murrhinus*] **:** a murrhine vase

mur·ri·na \mə'rīnə\ *n* -S [Sp *morriña*] **:** a disease of Central American horses and mules attributed to a protozoan blood parasite (*Trypanosoma hippicum*), characterized by emaciation, anemia, edema, conjunctivitis, fever, and paralysis of the hind legs, and often considered identical to surra

murr·nong \'mər,näŋ\ *n* -S [native name in Australia] **:** an Australian herb (*Microseris forsteri*) of the family Compositae having leaves all radical, flower heads solitary, and pappus bristles dilated at the base

mur·ry \'məri\ *dial Brit var of* MERRY

mur·shid \'mu̇rshēd\ *n* -S [Ar] **:** a Muslim religious teacher; *also* **:** the head of a religious order

mur·ther \'mərthər\ *chiefly dial var of* MURDER

mu·ru·mu·ru \mə¦rümə'rü\ *n* -S [Pg *murumurú, murumuru*, fr. Tupi] **:** a palm tree of Brazil (*Astrocaryum murumuru*) with small pear-shaped spiny fruits that turn yellow when ripe

murumuru fat *or* **murumuru oil** *n* **:** a fat obtained from the nuts of the murumuru and used chiefly in making soap

murup *var of* MOORUP

mu·rut \'mü,rüt\ *n, pl* **murut** *or* **muruts** *usu cap* **1 a :** any of several Dayak peoples in Sarawak and British No. Borneo sometimes considered to be a subdivision of the Klamantan people **b :** a member of any of the Murut peoples **2 :** the Austronesian language of the Murut people

mur·va *also* **moor·va** \'mu̇rvə\ *n* -S [Skt *mūrvā*] **1 :** an Asiatic bowstring hemp (*Sansevieria roxburghiana*) widely cultivated in India for its soft silky leaf fiber **2 :** the fiber yielded by the murva

¹mus *pl of* MU

²mus \'məs\ *n, cap* [NL, fr. L, mouse — more at MOUSE] **:** a genus (the type of the family Muridae) of rodents including the common house mouse and a few related small forms distinguished by the square-notched tip of the upper incisors as seen in profile

mus *abbr* **1** museum **2** music; musical; musician

mu·sa \'myüzə\ *n, cap* [NL, fr. Ar *mawzah* banana] **:** a genus of perennial herbs (family Musaceae) that resemble trees, and have huge sheathing leaves, flower clusters subtended by bright-colored bracts, and a fleshy baccate fruit — see ABACA, BANANA, PLANTAIN

MUSA *abbr* multiple-unit steerable antenna

mu·sa·ce·ae \myü'zāsē,ē\ *n pl, cap* [NL, fr. *Musa*, type genus + *-aceae*] **:** a family of trees or arborescent herbs (order Musales) that have clustered flowers subtended by spathaceous bracts, a perianth of two petaloid series, five anthers with one staminodium, and a baccate or capsular fruit — **mu·sa·ceous** \-āshəs\ *adj*

mu·saf *or* **mu·saph** \'müsəf\ *n* -S [Heb *mūsāph* addition] **:** an additional morning service on the Sabbath and on festivals in the liturgy of the Jews — compare SHAHARITH

mu·sa·har \'müsə¦här\ *n* -S *usu cap* [Bengali] **:** a member of a caste of hinduized jungle people of India who perform tasks such as crop watching and the bearing of palanquins

mu·sa·les \myü'zā(,)lēz\ *n pl, cap* [NL, fr. *Musa* + *-ales*] **:** an order of monocotyledonous tropical plants characterized by the cyclic flowers often with irregular perianth and one or more of the stamens suppressed

musalman *var of* MUSSULMAN

mu·sang \mü'säŋ, myü'saŋ\ *n* -S [Malay] **:** an East Indian palm civet (*Paradoxurus hermaphroditus*) with long shaggy fur obscurely patterned with spots and stripes

¹mu·sar \'myü,zär\ *n* -S [F *musard*, fr. OProv *musart, muzart*, lit., idler, fr. *musar, muzar* to gape, idle, loiter (fr. *mus* mouth of an animal, fr. ML *musus*) + *-art* -ard] **:** a 12th century ballad singer of Provence

²mu·sar \'mü,sär\ *n* -S [NHeb *mūsār*, fr. Heb, discipline, fr. *yōser* to discipline, punish] **:** a 19th century Jewish religio-ethical movement stressing strict moral discipline and piety

musc- *or* **musci-** *also* **musco-** *comb form* [L *musc-*, fr. *muscus* — more at MOSS] **:** moss ⟨*Musc*ites⟩ ⟨*musc*oid⟩ ⟨*musci*colous⟩ ⟨*musco*logy⟩

mus·ca \'məskə\ *n, cap* [NL, fr. L, fly — more at MIDGE] **:** a genus (the type of the family Muscidae) of flies now restricted to the common housefly (*M. domestica*) and closely related flies

mus·cade \,məs'kād\ *n* -S [F, nutmeg, fr. MF (*nois*) *muscade*, fr. OF — more at NUTMEG] **:** a light brown that is stronger and slightly yellower than blush and redder, lighter, and stronger than cork — called also *woodland rose*

mus·ca·din \'məskədə̇n\ *n* -S [F, lit., musk-scented lozenge — more at *muscardinus*] **:** a young French fop; *esp* **:** one of royalist sympathies during the French Revolution

mus·ca·dine \'məskə,dīn, -,dən\ *n* -S [prob. alter. (influenced by F *muscade* nutmeg & E *-ine*) of *muscatel*] **1** *archaic* **:** MUSCATEL **2** *or* **muscadine grape :** a tall-growing grape (*Vitis rotundifolia*) of the southern U.S. having rounded leaves and thick-skinned somewhat musky fruits in small clusters and being the source of several cultivated grapes (as the scuppernong)

mus·ca·din·ia \,məskə'dinēə\ *n, cap* [NL, fr. E *muscadine* + NL *-ia*] *in some esp former classifications* **:** a small genus of woody vines (family Vitaceae) having simple tendrils and a continuous pith

mus·cae vo·li·tan·tes \'mu̇,skī,wōlə'tän‚täs\ *n pl* [NL, lit., flying flies] **:** spots before the eyes, usu. in the form of dots, threads, beads, or circles, due to cells and cell fragments in the vitreous humor and lens

mus·car·dine \'məskə(r)də̇n, -(r),dēn\ *also* **muscardine disease** *n* -S [F *muscardine*] **:** any of various fungus diseases of insects caused by imperfect fungi that proliferate and ramify throughout the body of the host; *esp* **:** CALCINO — see GREEN MUSCARDINE

mus·car·di·ni·dae \,məskə(r)'dinə,dē\ [NL, fr. *Muscardinus*, type genus *-idae*] *syn of* GLIRIDAE

mus·car·di·nus \-dīnəs\ *n, cap* [NL, fr. F *muscardin*, *muscadin* musk-scented lozenge, hazel mouse, fr. *muscat* musky, fr. Prov — more at MUSCAT] **:** a genus of dormice (family Gliridae) comprising the hazel mouse and related small mice

mus·ca·ri \'məskə,rī\ *n, cap* [NL, fr. (assumed) obs. NGk *moschari* grape hyacinth, fr. Gk *moschos* musk — more at MUSK] **:** a genus of Old World bulbous herbs (family Liliaceae) having narrow fleshy leaves and racemes or spikes of urn-shaped flowers with the lower portion of the perianth segments united — see GRAPE HYACINTH

mus·ca·rine \'məskə,rēn, -,rə̇n\ *n* -S [G *muskarin*, fr. NL *muscaria* (specific epithet of *Amanita muscaria*, fr. L, fem. of *muscarius* of a fly, fr. *musca* fly + *-arius* -ary) + G *-in* -ine — more at MIDGE] **:** a quaternary ammonium base $C_8H_{19}NO_3$ that is chemically related to choline, was first found in the fly agaric, stimulates smooth muscle, and when ingested produces profuse salivation and sweating, abdominal colic with evacuation of bowels and bladder, contracted pupils and blurring of vision, excessive bronchial secretion, bradycardia, and respiratory depression

mus·ca·rin·ic \¦==¦rinik\ *adj* **:** of, resembling, or characteristic of muscarine ⟨a ~ drug⟩; *esp* **:** producing direct stimulation of smooth muscle ⟨~ physiologic effects⟩

mus·cat *also* **mus·kat** \'mə,skat, -,skət, *usu* -d·+V\ *n* -S [F *muscat*, fr. MF, fr. OProv, fr. *muscat* musky, fr. *musc* musk (fr. LL *muscus*) + *-at* -ate (fr. L *-atus*) — more at MUSK] **1 :** any of several cultivated vinifera grapes used esp. in making wine and raisins **2 :** MUSCATEL 1, 2

mus·cat and oman \'məs,kad·ən(d)ō'män, -,kəd-·\ *adj, usu cap* [fr. *Muscat and Oman*, country in southeast Arabia] **:** of or relating to Muscat and Oman **:** of the kind or style prevalent in Muscat and Oman

mus·ca·tel \¦məskə¦tel\ *also* **mus·ca·del** *or* **mus·ca·dell** *or* **mus·ca·delle** \-¦del\ *n* -S [ME *muskadelle*, fr. MF *muscadel*, *muscatel*, fr. OProv *muscadel*, fr. *muscadel* resembling musk, fr. *muscat* musky] **1 :** a sweet dessert wine that is golden to dark amber in color with a flavor and aroma peculiar to the muscat grapes from which it is made **2 :** a raisin produced from muscat grapes **3 :** MUSCAT 1

muscavado *var of* MUSCOVADO

mu·schel·kalk \'müshəl,kälk\ *adj, usu cap* [G, shell lime, fr. *muschel* mussel, shell + *kalk* lime] **:** of, relating to, or constituting a subdivision of the European Triassic — see GEOLOGIC TIME table

mus·ci \'mə,sī\ *n pl, cap* [NL, fr. pl. of L *muscus* moss — more at MOSS] **:** a class of Bryophyta comprising the mosses and being characterized by a well-developed leafy gametophyte that arises by budding from a protonema and bears sex organs among the leaves at its tip and by a sporophyte that develops from the fertilized egg, remains attached to the tip of the gametophyte, and is a naked usu. stalked and operculate capsule in which asexual spores are borne — see ANDREAEALIS, BRYALES, SPHAGNALES; compare EUBRYALES, HEPATICAE

¹musci- *comb form* [NL, fr. L *musca* — more at MIDGE] **:** fly ⟨*Musci*capidae⟩

²musci- — see MUSC-

mus·cic·a·pa \mə'sikəpə\ *n, cap* [NL, fr. ¹*musci-* + *-capa* (fr. L *capere* to take, seize) — more at HEAVE] **:** a genus of flycatchers including the common European spotted flycatcher (*Muscicapa striata* syn. *M. grisola*) and being the type of the family Muscicapidae — compare SYLVIIDAE

mus·ci·cap·i·dae \,məsə'kapə,dē\ *n pl, cap* [NL, fr. *Muscicapa*, type genus + *-idae*] **:** a very large family of oscine passerine birds consisting of the Old World or true flycatchers and sometimes including also the thrushes, warblers, and babblers

mus·cic·a·pine \mə'sikə,pīn, -,pə̇n\ *adj* [NL *Muscicapa* + E *-ine*] **:** of or relating to the Muscicapidae

mus·cic·o·lous \mə'sikələs\ *adj* [*musc-* + *-colous*] **:** growing on decaying mosses or hepatics

¹mus·cid \'məsə̇d\ *adj* [NL *Muscidae*] **:** of or relating to the Muscidae

²muscid \"\ *n* -S [NL *Muscidae*] **:** a fly of the family Muscidae

mus·ci·dae \'məsə,dē\ *n pl, cap* [NL, fr. *Musca*, type genus + *-idae*] **:** a family of two-winged flies (order Diptera) including the housefly (*Musca domestica*)

¹mus·ci·form \'məsə,fȯrm\ *adj* [*musc-* + *-form*] **:** resembling moss in form or appearance

²musciform \"\ *adj* [ISV ¹*musci-* + *-form*] **:** having the form or structure of an insect of the family Muscidae

mus·ci·ne·ae \mə'sinē,ē\ [NL, fr. *musc-* + *-ineae*] *syn of* BRYOPHYTA

mus·ci·tes \'məsə,tēz\ *n, cap* [NL, fr. *musc-* + L *-ites* -ite] **:** a form genus of fossil plants that resemble present-day tree mosses and may belong to the class Musci

¹muscle *var of* MUSSEL

²mus·cle \'məsəl\ *n* -S *often attrib* [MF, fr. L *musculus*, fr. dim. of *mus* mouse — more at MOUSE] **1 a :** a tissue that functions to produce motion and is made up of variously modified elongated cells capable of contracting when stimulated — see CARDIAC MUSCLE, SMOOTH MUSCLE, STRIATED MUSCLE **b :** an organ that contracts to produce, enhance, or check a particular movement and is made up of usu. striated muscle tissue enclosed in a perimysium and firmly attached at either end to a bone or other fixed point — see AGONIST, ANTAGONIST, SYNERGIST **2 a :** something that resembles or is likened to a muscle ⟨electronic circuits . . . are the ~s which carry out its orders —*Boeing Mag.*⟩ ⟨the ~s of England . . . the factories —Richard Joseph⟩ ⟨limbered his mental and moral ~s —Janet Whitney⟩ **b** (1) **:** muscular strength **:** BRAWN ⟨got the nerve for anything, only he hasn't got the ~ —Joseph Conrad⟩ (2) **:** effective strength or authority **:** FORCE, POWER ⟨put military ~ into the mutual defense pact —*N. Y. Herald Tribune*⟩ ⟨chosen less for polish and background, more for economic and executive ~ —*Time*⟩ ⟨a cup of . . . coffee that really has some ~ —R.M.Hodesh⟩ **c :** an essential item or service **:** NECESSITY ⟨economies that would cut out fat rather than ~ —D.W.Mitchell⟩ **3 a :** muscular tissue **b :** lean meat

³muscle \"\ *vb* **muscled; muscled; muscling** \-s(ə)liŋ\ **muscles** *vt* **1** *dial* **:** to move by muscular effort ⟨needed men to ~ chairs and tables —Linnell Jones⟩ **2 :** to use strength or influence on **:** achieve by coercion **:** FORCE, SHOVE ⟨was suddenly *muscled* aside as a swarm of his fellows rushed out —*Sydney (Australia) Bull.*⟩ ⟨a plane ~s its way through the . . . sound barrier —*Springfield (Mass.) Daily News*⟩ ⟨dreamers were *muscled* out of patent rights —Scott Fitzgerald⟩ **3 :** to furnish with strength or muscle **:** REINFORCE, CONDITION ⟨even the years of ballet exercises . . . had not *muscled* them into hardness —Winifred Bambrick⟩ ⟨~ up our diplomatic approach —*Newsweek*⟩ ⟨*muscling* their minds to strike —Rose Thurburn⟩ **~ vi 1 a :** to make one's way by brute strength ⟨slowly *muscled* up the cliff⟩ **b :** to overcome opposition by force — usu. used with *in* or *into* ⟨*muscled* into the queue —Bruce Marshall⟩ **2 :** to force one's way in (as by trickery or intimidation) against hostility or opposition esp. for fraudulent gain — usu. used with *in* ⟨some competing journalist would ~ in on my exclusive story —*N.Y.Times*⟩ ⟨*muscling* in on his territory —Green Peyton⟩ ⟨would ~ in on the racket⟩

muscle-bound \'==,=\ *adj* **1 :** having some of the muscles tense and enlarged and of impaired elasticity sometimes as a result of excessive exercise **2 :** lacking in flexibility **:** RIGID, STIFF ⟨suffers from *muscle-bound* doctrinaire inflexibility —Mollie Panter-Downes⟩ ⟨television is becoming *muscle-bound*, repetitious, unenterprising —*Saturday Rev.*⟩

muscled *adj* **:** furnished with muscles — often used in combination ⟨hard-*muscled* arms⟩

muscle fiber *n* **:** one of the cells of muscle

mus·cle·less \'məsəllə̇s\ *adj* **:** lacking muscle

muscleman \'==,=\ *n, pl* **musclemen :** a man hired (as by a gangster) to enforce compliance by strong-arm methods **:** GOON 1, ENFORCER ⟨ran the gambling games, acted as . . . *musclemen*, fixers, thugs —G.A.Hamid⟩

muscle plate *n* **:** a differentiated part of a primitive segment in a vertebrate embryo that forms voluntary muscle tissue

muscle reading *n* **:** a technique practiced by some magicians of detecting slight involuntary movements of a subject's muscles that furnish clues to the solution of problems or the finding of hidden objects

muscle scar *also* **muscle mark** *n* **:** one of the differentiated usu. depressed areas on the inner surface of a bivalve shell to which a muscle is fixed

muscle segment *n* **:** MYOCOMMA

muscle sense *n* **:** sensations arising from proprioceptors in the muscles and including those that are usu. held to give rise to awareness of the position in space of body parts

muscle spasm *n* **:** persistent involuntary hypertonicity of one or more muscles usu. of central origin and commonly associated with pain and excessive irritability

muscle spindle *n* **:** a proprioceptive sensory end organ in a muscle consisting of small striated muscle fibers richly supplied with nerve endings and enclosed in a connective tissue sheath

muscle sugar *n* **:** INOSITOL

mus·cling \'məs(ə)liŋ\ *n* -S [²*muscle* + *-ing*] **1 :** the distribution and state of development of muscles ⟨a heifer with splendid rump ~⟩ **2 :** MUSCULATURE 3

mus·cly \-lē\ *adj* **:** constituted of muscle ⟨the ~ mass from neck to shoulder blade —Robert Browning⟩

musco- — see MUSC-

¹mus·coid \'mə,skȯid\ *adj* [ISV *musc-* + *-oid*] **:** of, relating to, or resembling moss

²muscoid \"\ *adj* [NL *Muscoidea*] **:** of or relating to the superfamily Muscoidea; *specif* **:** resembling the muscoid fly maggot esp. in being headless, posteriorly truncate, and cylindrical to spindle-shaped

mus·coi·dea \,mə'skȯidēə\ *n pl, cap* [NL, fr. *Musca* + *-oidea*] **:** a superfamily of two-winged flies (suborder Brachycera) including the houseflies and many related flies (as of the families Muscidae, Gasterophilidae, Calliphoridae, Tachinidae) that have the head freely movable and the abdomen usu. oval and bristly

mus·co·log·ic \¦məskə¦läjik\ *or* **mus·co·log·i·cal** \-jə̇kəl\ *adj* **:** of or relating to muscology **:** BRYOLOGICAL

mus·col·o·gist \,mə'skäləjə̇st\ *n* -S [ISV *muscology* + *-ist*] **:** a specialist in muscology

mus·col·o·gy \-jē\ *n* -ES [NL *muscologia*, fr. *musc-* + *-logia* -logy] **:** BRYOLOGY; *esp* **:** a part of bryology that deals with the mosses — compare HEPATICOLOGY

mus·cone *or* **mus·kone** \'mə,skōn\ *n* -S [ISV ¹*musk* + *-one*] **:** an oily macrocyclic ketone $C_{16}H_{30}O$ that is the chief odoriferous constituent of musk and is used similarly in perfumes; 3-methyl-cyclo-pentadecan-one

mus·cose \'mə,skōs\ *adj* [L *muscosus*, fr. *musc-* + *-osus* -ose] **:** MOSSY

mus·co·va·do *also* **mus·ca·va·do** \,məskə'vā(,)dō, -vä(,)-\ *n* -S [Sp or Pg; Sp (*azúcar*) *mascabado*, fr. Pg (*açúcar*) *mascavado*, fr. *açúcar* sugar + *mascavado*, past part. of *mascavar* to adulterate, separate raw sugar (from molasses), fr. (assumed) VL *minuscapare*, fr. L *minus* less + *caput* head — more at MINUS, HEAD] **:** unrefined or raw sugar obtained from the juice of the sugarcane by evaporation and draining off the molasses

muscovian *adj, cap* [NL *Moscovia* + E *-an*] *obs* **:** MUSCOVITE

¹mus·co·vite \'məskə,vīt, *usu* -īd·+V\ *also* **mos·co·vite** \'mäskō,-\ *n* -S [ML or NL *Muscovia*, *Moscovia* Moscow (fr. ORuss *Moskovŭ*) + E *-ite*] **1** *cap* **a :** a native or resident of the ancient principality of Moscow or of the city of Moscow **b :** RUSSIAN **2** [*muscovy (glass)* + E *-ite*] **:** a mineral essentially $KAl_3Si_3O_{10}(OH)_2$ consisting of common or potassium mica that is usu. colorless or pale brown — see MICA **3 :** a dark greenish gray that is bluer and lighter than sagebrush green and bluer and stronger than castor gray

²muscovite \"\ *adj, usu cap* **1 :** of, belonging to, or characteristic of the ancient principality of Moscow, the city of Moscow, or Muscovites **2 :** RUSSIAN

mus·co·vit·iza·tion \,məskə,vīd·ə'zāshən\ *n* -S **:** conversion of a rock or mineral into muscovite

mus·co·vit·ize \'məskə,vīd,īz\ *vt* -ED/-ING/-S **:** to convert (a rock or mineral) wholly or partially into muscovite

mus·co·vy duck \'məs,kōvē-, (,)mə'skōvē-\ *also* **muscovy** *n* -ES *usu cap M* [fr. *Muscovy* principality of Moscow, Russia, fr. ML or NL *Muscovia*] **:** a duck (*Cairina moschata*) native from Mexico to southern Brazil but widely kept in domestication that is larger than the mallard and has a small crest and red caruncles about the eyes and forehead — called also *musk duck*

muscul- *or* **musculo-** *comb form* [LL *muscul-*, fr. L *musculus* — more at MUSCLE] **1 :** muscle ⟨*muscul*ar⟩ ⟨*muscul*in⟩ ⟨*musculo*spiral⟩ **2** *usu* **musculo- :** muscular and ⟨*musculo*epithelial⟩ ⟨*musculo*fibrous⟩

mus·cu·lar \'məskyələ(r)\ *adj* [*muscul-* + *-ar*] **1 a :** constituting or consisting of muscle ⟨~ fiber⟩ ⟨~ tissue⟩ **b :** of, relating to, or performed by the muscles ⟨~ energy⟩ ⟨~ activity⟩ **2 :** affecting the muscles ⟨~ fatigue⟩ ⟨~ atrophy⟩ **3 :** characterized by good musculature **:** SINEWY ⟨a ~ young man⟩ ⟨the swordfish is very ~ and a very rapid swimmer

—S.W.Tinker⟩ **4 a :** of or relating to physical strength **:** having actual or potential power **:** BRAWNY, MIGHTY ⟨~ rivers of the Rockies —J.H.Bradley⟩ ⟨white yawls, ~ with sail —George Loveridge⟩ **b :** of or relating to strength of expression or character **:** VIGOROUS, FORCEFUL ⟨capable of writing intensely ~ dramatic prose —Kenneth Tynan⟩ ⟨brings a fine resounding voice to the singing that fits the ~ music of the . . . fisherfolk —Oscar Brand⟩ ⟨for all its . . . ~ decisiveness, it is a calm and reasoned performance —H.S.Commager⟩ **c :** expressed in physical works or healthy activity ⟨~ Christianity⟩ — **mus·cu·lar·ly** *adv*

muscular dystrophy *n* **:** a hereditary disease characterized by progressive wasting of muscles

mus·cu·la·ris \ˌməskyəˈla(a)rəs\ *n* -ES [NL, fr. *muscul-* + *-aris* -ar] **1 :** the smooth muscular layer of the wall of various more or less contractile organs (as the bladder) — called also *muscularis propria* **2 :** the thin layer of smooth muscle that forms part of a mucous membrane — called also *muscularis mucosae*

mus·cu·lar·i·ty \ˌməskyəˈlarəd·ē, -ətē, -i *also* -ler-\ *n* -ES **:** the quality or state of being muscular **:** VIGOR, BRAWN

muscular rheumatism *n* **:** FIBROSITIS

muscular stomach *n* **:** GIZZARD 1

mus·cu·la·tion \ˌməskyəˈlāshən\ *n* -S [ISV *muscul-* + *-ation*] **:** MUSCULATURE

mus·cu·la·ture \ˈməskyələˌchu̇(ə)r, -u̇ə, -ˌchə(r) *sometimes* -lə-ˌtyu̇-\ *n* -S [F, fr. *muscul-* + L *-atus* -ate + F *-ure*] **1 :** the muscles of an animal or of any part of it that are related to each other and function together ⟨~ of the leg⟩ ⟨~ of the heart⟩ **2 :** the muscular system ⟨tensions are transferred . . . across the footlights and into the ~ of every spectator —John Martin⟩ **3 :** a well-developed underlying structure of or as if of muscles ⟨elaborate ~ of the male figures —J.T.Soby⟩ ⟨a sustaining pulse for the whole musical ~ —Virgil Thomson⟩

mus·cu·lo·cutaneous nerve \ˌməskyəlō+ . . . -\ *n* [ISV *muscul-* + *cutaneous*] **1 :** a large branch of the brachial plexus supplying various parts of the upper arm (as flexor muscles) and forearm (as the skin) **2 :** the superficial peroneal nerve

mus·cu·lo·epithelial \"+\ *adj* [*muscul-* + *epithelial*] **:** having both an epithelial and a muscular function — used of ectodermal cells of invertebrates (as hydra) that cover the body surface and contract the body

mus·cu·lo·membranous \"+\ *adj* [*muscul-* + *membranous*] **:** composed of both muscle and membrane

mus·cu·lo·phrenic \"+\ *adj* [*muscul-* + *phrenic*] **:** supplying the muscles of the body wall and the diaphragm ⟨~ nerve⟩ ⟨~ blood vessel⟩

mus·cu·lo·skeletal \"+\ *adj* [*muscul-* + *skeletal*] **:** of, relating to, or involving both musculature and skeleton ⟨~ defects⟩ ⟨the ~ organization of the arm⟩

mus·cu·lo·spiral \"+\ *adj* [*muscul-* + *spiral*] **:** of, relating to, or characterizing muscles having a spiral direction or structures having a spiral arrangement in relation to muscles

musculospiral groove *n* **:** a long shallow oblique groove in the shaft of the humerus that lodges the radial nerve

mus·cu·lo·trop·ic \ˌməskyələˈträpik\ *adj* [*muscul-* + *-tropic*] **:** having a direct usu. stimulatory effect on muscle

musculous *adj* [MF *musculeux*, fr. L *musculosus*, fr. *muscul-* + *-osus* -ous] *obs* **:** MUSCULAR

mus·cu·lus \ˈməskyələs\ *n, pl* **muscu·li** \-yəˌlī\ [L — more at MUSCLE] **:** MUSCLE

[1]**muse** \ˈmyüz\ *vb* -ED/-ING/-S [ME *musen*, fr. MF *muser* to idle, loiter, muse (prob. orig., "to gape, stare"), fr. *muse* mouth of an animal, snout, fr. ML *musus*] *vi* **1 a :** to become absorbed in thought **:** RUMINATE ⟨~ upon the continuity and the tragic finality of life —Irving Howe⟩ ⟨its suggestions set the imagination *musing* —Irwin Edman⟩ **b** *archaic* **:** to look reflectively ⟨the mind is left to ~ upon the solemn scene —William Wordsworth⟩ **2** *archaic* **:** to become astonished **:** WONDER, MARVEL ⟨do not ~ at me my most worthy friends —Shak.⟩ ~ *vt* **1** *archaic* **:** to ask oneself **:** WONDER ⟨~ what this young fox may mean —Matthew Arnold⟩ **2 a :** to ruminate on ⟨*mused* the question considerably once more —*Harper's*⟩ **b :** to say or think reflectively ⟨I could sell the house, she *mused*, but then where would I go⟩ **3** *obs* **:** to puzzle over (a fact or occurrence) **:** be surprised that ⟨I ~ my Lord of Gloucester is not come —Shak.⟩ **syn** see PONDER

[2]**muse** \"\ *n* -S [ME, fr. *musen*, v.] **:** a state of deep thought or dreamy abstraction **:** BROWN STUDY ⟨thrown into a ~ by the book she was reading⟩

[3]**muse** \"\ *n* -S [ME, fr. MF, fr. L *Musa*, fr. Gk *Mousa*; prob. akin to Gk *mnasthai* to remember — more at MIND] **1 a** *usu cap* **:** any of nine sister goddesses associated with the Graces in Greek mythology and regarded as presiding over learning and the creative arts (as poetry and music) — usu. used in pl. ⟨the *Muses* . . . gave the poet his song and sang it through his lips —T.B.L.Webster⟩ **b** *sometimes cap* **:** the personification of a guiding genius or principal source of inspiration ⟨an atmosphere in which the ~ of serendipity is most likely to be wooed and won —*Lamp*⟩ **2** *sometimes cap* **:** the creative spirit of an individual ⟨the situations that tempt his dramatic ~ are strained, acute situations —Leslie Rees⟩ ⟨pay the writing schools hard cash to liberate their ~ —Edward Uhlan⟩ **3 a :** a composer of songs or verse **:** POET ⟨so may some gentle ~ with lucky words favor my destined urn —John Milton⟩ **b** *archaic* **:** LIBERAL ARTS; *esp* **:** the creative arts — usu. used in pl. ⟨his retirement . . . was to the last devoted to the ~*s* —Connop Thirlwall⟩

[4]**muse** \"\ *n* -S [ME, fr. MF, fr. *muser* to muse, play the bagpipe — more at [1]MUSE] **1 :** BAGPIPE **2 :** the mouthpiece of a bagpipe

[5]**muse** \ˈmyüs, -üz\ *dial Eng var of* MEUSE

muse·ful \ˈmyüzfəl\ *adj* [[2]*muse* + *-ful*] *archaic* **:** BEMUSED, MEDITATIVE — **muse·ful·ly** \-fəlē\ *adv*

mu·se·ist \(ˈ)myüˈzēəst, ˈ=ˌ==\ *n* -S [*museum* + *-ist*] **:** MUSEOLOGIST

muse·less \ˈmyüzləs\ *adj* [[3]*muse* + *-less*] *archaic* **:** ILLITERATE, UNCULTURED

musenna *var of* MESENNA

museo- *comb form* [*museum*] **:** museum ⟨*museology*⟩

mu·se·og·ra·phy \ˌmyüzēˈägrəfē\ *n* -ES [F *muséographie*, fr. *muséo-* museo- + *-graphie* -graphy] **:** museum methods of classification and display

mu·seo·log·i·cal \ˌmyüzēəˈläjəkəl\ *adj* **:** of or relating to museology

mu·se·ol·o·gist \ˌ==ˈäləjəst\ *n* -S **:** a specialist in museum work

mu·se·ol·o·gy \-jē\ *n* -ES [*museo-* + *-logy*] **:** the science or profession of museum organization, equipment, and management

mus·er \ˈmyüzə(r)\ *n* -S [ME, fr. *musen* to muse + *-er* — more at MUSE] **:** one that muses

muset *n* -S [MF *musette*, *mucette*, dim. of *musse*, *muce* — more at MEUSE] *obs* **:** MEUSE

mu·sette \myüˈzet\ *n* -S [F, fr. MF, dim. of *muse* bagpipe — more at MUSE] **1 a :** a small bellows-filled bagpipe popular in France esp. in the 18th century and having a soft sweet tone **b** *also* **musette pipe :** a small simple oboe **c :** a reed stop of 4-foot or 8-foot pitch with a bright pleasing tone **2 a :** a quiet pastoral air that often has a drone bass, is adapted to the musette, and often constitutes the middle or trio of a group of three gavottes in which the first and third are the same **b :** a gavotte danced to the tune of a musette **3** *or* **musette bag :** a small canvas or leather knapsack suspended by a strap from the shoulder and used esp. by members of the armed forces for carrying provisions and personal belongings

mu·se·um \(ˈ)myüˈzēəm, ÷ ˈ=ˌ==\ *n* -S [L *Museum*, fr. Gk *Mouseion*, fr. neut. of *Mouseios* of the Muses, fr. *Mousa* Muse — more at MUSE] **1** *obs* **:** a scholar's library **:** STUDY ⟨admitted to an audience in his ~ —Charles Johnstone⟩ **2 a :** an institution devoted to the procurement, care, study, and display of objects of lasting interest or value ⟨British *Museum*⟩ ⟨American *Museum* of Natural History⟩ ⟨National Air and Space *Museum*⟩ **b :** a room, building, or locale where a collection of objects is put on exhibition ⟨art ~⟩ ⟨science ~⟩ ⟨striking outdoor ~, two hundred acres of it —Bernard De Voto⟩ **c :** EXHIBIT, COLLECTION ⟨the little ~ of . . . lore assembled in the foyer —Claudia Cassidy⟩ **3 :** something that resembles a museum ⟨the parlor was a ~ of Victorian bric-a-brac⟩ ⟨codes are maintained as no mere ~*s* of legal rules and principles —F.A.Ogg & Harold Zink⟩

museum beetle *n* **:** any of several beetles (esp. of the genera *Anthrenus* and *Dermestes*) that feed as larvae esp. on dried animal products (as skins or insect specimens)

mu·se·um·ist \-məst\ *n* -S **:** MUSEOLOGIST

museum jar *n* **:** a glass or pottery container capable of being tightly closed or sealed and used esp. for the storage or display of preserved organisms or dissections

museum piece *n* **1 :** an object of lasting interest or value (as an antique) suitable for or preserved in a museum ⟨early pie plates, now *museum pieces* —*Amer. Guide Series: Conn.*⟩ ⟨a *museum piece* volume —Claudia Cassidy⟩ ⟨some classics, no longer appropriate for daily use, become . . . *museum pieces* periodically dusted off by the critics —Waldo Frank⟩ **2 :** something antiquated or obsolete **:** a thing of the past ⟨tended to regard the old clerk of courts as a *museum piece*⟩ ⟨the taxicabs . . . are early-century *museum pieces* —E.O.Hauser⟩ ⟨contains the substance of lectures . . . which now are almost dated *museum pieces* —Irwin Edman⟩

mus·gu \ˈməsˌgü\ *also* **mos·gu** \ˈmäs-\ *n, pl* **musgu** *or* **musgus** *also* **mosgu** *or* **mosgus** *usu cap* **1 a :** a Negro people of the central Sudan in the Logone valley south of Lake Chad **b :** a member of such people **2 :** the language of the Musgu people

[1]**mush** \ˈməsh, *chiefly dial* ˈmu̇sh\ *n* -ES [prob. alter. of *mash*] **1 :** cornmeal boiled in water, eaten hot as a cereal or pudding, fried as cakes, or molded until cold and then sliced and fried — compare HASTY PUDDING **2 :** something having the consistency of cornmeal mush ⟨perspired so much the cast under his armpits . . . turned to ~ —Earle Birney⟩ **3 :** something soft and spongy or shapeless: as **a :** a formless mass **b :** weak sentimentality or mawkish amorousness **:** DRIVEL ⟨oratorical ~⟩ ⟨the tenderness never becomes ~ —Coulton Waugh⟩ ⟨it isn't youthful romance, it's the ~ of senility —Erle Stanley Gardner⟩ **c** *slang* **:** MOUTH, FACE ⟨slammed him in the ~ with the ball, and his eyes watered —J.T.Farrell⟩

[2]**mush** \"\ *vb* -ED/-ING/-ES *vt* **1** *chiefly dial* **:** to reduce to or mix up in a crumbly mass **:** CRUSH, PULVERIZE — often used with *up* ⟨~ up papier-mâché animals —R.L.Shayon⟩ **2** *slang* **:** to make amorously sentimental — used with *up* ⟨he would ~ it up and . . . we would sway sweet and slow —R.P.Warren⟩ ~ *vi* **1 :** to give way **:** CRUMBLE, SQUASH ⟨does not ~ down —*advt*⟩ ⟨the top of the pile sank, the lower logs ~*ing* out toward the water —*Mich. Log Marks*⟩ **2** *of an airplane* **a :** to fly in a half-stalled condition with controls ineffective ⟨throttled back and ~*ed* in —Walt Sheldon⟩ **b :** to fail to gain altitude or to lose it when the angle of attack would normally indicate a gain ⟨he was miles high, ~*ing*, nearly slumping, in the rare air —J.G.Cozzens⟩ **3** *slang* **:** to be effusive **:** GUSH; *esp* **:** to make love in public

[3]**mush** \ˈməsh\ *n* -ES [short for *mushroom*] *slang* **:** UMBRELLA

[4]**mush** \ˈməsh, *chiefly dial* ˈmu̇sh\ *vb* -ED/-ING/-ES [prob. fr. AmerF *moucher* to go fast, fr. F *mouche* fly, fr. L *musca* — more at MIDGE] *vi* **:** to hike or travel esp. over snow with a dogsled ⟨~ over a wilderness that no sled track has ever crossed before —Klondy Nelson⟩ ⟨huskies bark excitedly as they ~ across the ice and snow —Robert Meyer⟩ — often used in the imperative as a command to a dog team ⟨snapped the long lash of his whip . . . cried ~ —Frederick Palmer⟩ ~ *vt* **:** to urge (a dog team) forward ⟨the driver ~*ed* the dogs —Nan Dorland⟩ **:** transport by means of a dog team

[5]**mush** \"\ *n* -ES **:** a hike esp. across snow with a dog team

musha \ˈmu̇shə\ *interj* [IrGael *māiseadh*, fr. *mā* if + *is* is + *eadh* it] *Irish* — used esp. to express surprise or annoyance

mus·haa \müsˈhä\ *n* -S [Ar *mushāʻ* common] *Islam* **:** undivided common property

mush·a·roon *also* **mush·er·oon** \ˌməshəˈrün\ *dial var of* MUSHROOM

mushball \ˈ=ˌ=\ *n* [[1]*mush* + *ball*] **:** SOFTBALL

mush·er \ˈməshə(r), *chiefly dial* ˈmu̇sh-\ *n* -S [[4]*mush* + *-er*] **:** one that mushes; *esp* **:** the driver of a dog team

mush·et steel \ˈməshət-\ *or* **mushet's steel** *n, usu cap M* [after Robert F. *Mushet* †1891 Eng. metallurgist] **:** the first self-hardening steel

mushier *comparative of* MUSHY

mushiest *superlative of* MUSHY

mush·i·ly \ˈməshəlē, -li, *chiefly dial* ˈmu̇sh-\ *adv* **:** in a mawkish or mushy manner

mush·i·ness \-shēnəs, -shin-\ *n* -ES **:** the quality or state of being mushy or mawkishly sentimental

mush·mel·on \ˈməshˌmelən\ *n* [by alter.] *dial var of* MUSKMELON

mushquash *var of* MUSQUASH

mush·rat \ˈməshˌrat\ *dial var of* MUSKRAT

mushrebiyeh *var of* MOUCHARABY

[1]**mush·room** \ˈməˌshrüm, -ru̇m, *chiefly dial* |n\ *n* -S *often attrib* [ME *musseroun*, *muscheron*, fr. MF *mousseron*, fr. OF *meisseron*, fr. LL *mussirion-*, *mussirio*] **1 a** (1) **:** any of various enlarged complex aerial fleshy fruiting bodies of fungi (as most members of the class Basidiomycetes) that are technically sporophores, arise from an underground mycelium, and consist typically of a stem bearing a flattened pileus with spores developing in the folds or pores of a hymenium on its undersurface (2) **:** such a fruiting body that is edible; *esp* **:** MEADOW MUSHROOM — compare TOADSTOOL **b :** FUNGUS 1 **2** *archaic* **:** UPSTART 1 **3** *slang* **:** UMBRELLA **4 :** a woman's low-crowned hat with a convex brim **5 a :** MUSHROOM ANCHOR **b :** the head of a mushroom anchor without the shank **6 :** a metal traffic guide about 18 inches in diameter fixed in the pavement surface at an intersection **7 :** a bullet with a soft or hollow point that flattens on impact **8 :** an obturator for a cannon **9 :** a lateral and radial extension of reinforcing rods into the slab at the top of each column in a system of reinforced-concrete construction permitting the weight of the floors to be borne by the columns rather than by external walls **10 :** a spreading cloud (as of smoke or debris) ⟨~ of exploding five-inch shells —K.M.Dodson⟩ ⟨radioactive ~ from an atom-bomb explosion⟩ ⟨the stem of the ~ caused by the intense heat sucking up . . . debris —E.P.Boland⟩ **11 :** BEAVER 6

mushroom 1a(1)

[2]**mushroom** \"\ *vb* -ED/-ING/-S *vi* **1 :** to spring up suddenly or multiply rapidly ⟨towns . . . ~*ed* about factories near water power —R.H.Brown⟩ ⟨accidents ~*ed* so prodigiously . . . that it was evident some basic factor had been overlooked —Stanley Frank⟩ — often used with *up* ⟨stools and benches decorated with her handiwork had ~*ed* up all over the house —Virginia D. Dawson & Betty D. Wilson⟩ **2 a :** to flatten at the end due to impact — used esp. of a bullet ⟨bullets ~*ed* well, so the animal did not go far —W.Z.Bradley⟩ **b :** to puff out or spread ⟨the cloud of radioactive ash . . . ~*s* from the bomb —*Newsweek*⟩ ⟨the homely aroma . . . came ~*ing* over us —William Sansom⟩; *esp* **:** to well up and spread out laterally from a central source ⟨the fire was ~*ing* under the ceiling when fire fighters . . . arrived —*Springfield (Mass.) Union*⟩ **c :** to become enlarged or extended **:** EXPAND, GROW ⟨expenditures ~ on the trail —Joyce R. Muench⟩ ⟨from a sleepy little rural community . . . it has ~*ed* into a fast-growing center —Martha Alexander⟩ ⟨the vast ~*ing* of air travel —*Fortune*⟩ **d :** EXPLODE ⟨an enemy plane . . . ~*s* in your gunsight —R.L.Scott⟩ **3 :** to gather mushrooms ~ *vt* **1 :** to cause to spread or flatten out ⟨hamming can . . . ~ the end of the handle —H.D.Burghardt & Aaron Axelrod⟩ **2 :** to cause to extend or multiply suddenly or rapidly **:** EXPAND ⟨a city swollen with a ~*ed* population —Earl Brown⟩ ⟨~*ed* his interests over three quarters of the U.S. —*Time*⟩

mushroom anchor *n* **:** an anchor that has a bowl-shaped head with the shank welded to its center, is capable of grasping the ground however it falls, and is used chiefly for permanent moorings

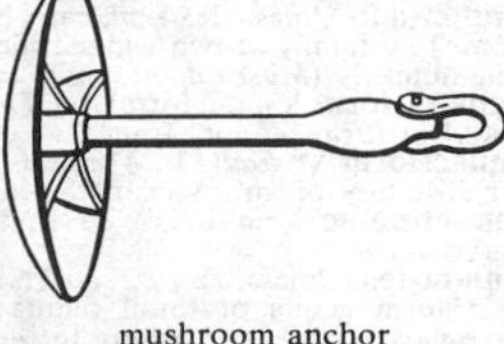
mushroom anchor

mushroom body *n* **:** any of various neural centers in the insect brain that are esp. well developed in social insects and are thought to be possible integration or association centers

mushroom chair *n* **:** a turned chair of the 17th and early 18th centuries having enlarged and usu. flattened balls topping and made in one piece with the front posts

mushroom coral *n* **:** any of various flattened disk-shaped stony corals of *Fungia* or related genera that are usu. solitary and in the adult stage completely free from the substrate

mushroom jellyfish *n* **:** a nearly globular brownish scyphozoan jellyfish (*Stomolophus meleagris*) having a greatly reduced mouth and often occurring in swarms many miles in extent

mushroomlike \ˈ=ˌ=ˌ=\ *adj* **1 :** resembling a mushroom in appearance **2 :** springing up suddenly

mushroom mite *n* **:** an Australian tarsonemid mite (*Tyrophagus putrescentiae*) or a related mite that infests fungi and is sometimes a house pest

mushroom pin *n* **:** SPOOL PIN

mushroom root rot *n* **:** a root rot caused by an agaric, esp. by the oak fungus (*Armillaria mellea*)

mushrooms *pl of* MUSHROOM, *pres 3d sing of* MUSHROOM

mushroom steamer *n* **:** TRAMP STEAMER

mushroom valve *n* **:** a lift valve resembling a mushroom in shape

mushroom ventilator *n* **:** a ship's ventilator with a curved hood that may be raised or lowered to regulate the air in cabins below deck

mush·roomy \ˈməˌshrümē, -ru̇m-\ *adj* **:** resembling a mushroom

mushroon *dial var of* MUSHROOM

mush rot *n* [[1]*mush*] **:** LEAK 3

mushsquash *var of* MUSQUASH

mushy \ˈməshē, -shi, *chiefly dial* ˈmu̇sh-\ *adj* -ER/-EST [[1]*mush* + *-y*] **1 a :** having the consistency of mush **:** SOFT, SPONGY ⟨concrete mix should be ~ but not soupy —*Building, Estimating & Contracting*⟩ ⟨the ground is covered with a soft, ~ tundra carpet —W.W.Atwood b. 1906⟩ **b :** lacking in definition **:** HAZY, BLURRED ⟨with more and more ~ effects, "artistic" photographers made imitation paintings —T.H.Benton †1975⟩ ⟨you . . . hear the pings faintly through a voice tube and they sound ~ —H.S.Pease⟩ **c :** lacking precision of performance **:** SLUGGISH ⟨the plane became ~ and controls lost efficiency —John Lewellen⟩ ⟨at low speeds, aileron movements feel ~ and light —*Flying*⟩ **2 :** excessively tender or emotional **:** SENTIMENTAL, EFFUSIVE ⟨~ handling of crime —*Emporia (Kans.) Gazette*⟩ ⟨a ~ sentiment, unstable and only half-sincere —William McFee⟩; *esp* **:** mawkishly amorous ⟨find a love story in that bunch of old magazines — a nice ~ one —*Lippincott's Mag.*⟩ **syn** see SENTIMENTAL

mushy chick *or* **mushy chick disease** *n* **:** a nonspecific and highly fatal infection of newly hatched chickens or turkeys marked by a soft swollen abdomen and foul odors and caused by bacteria entering the body through the umbilical opening

[1]**mu·sic** \ˈmyüzik, -zēk\ *n* -S *often attrib* [ME *musik*, fr. OF *musique*, fr. L *musica*, fr. Gk *mousikē*, any art presided over by the Muses, esp. music, fr. fem. of *mousikos* of the Muses, musical, fr. *Mousa* Muse + *-ikos* -ic — more at MUSE] **1 a :** the science or art of incorporating pleasing, expressive, or intelligible combinations of vocal or instrumental tones into a composition having definite structure and continuity ⟨~ as . . . a combination of rhythm, melody, harmony, and counterpoint, has existed less than a thousand years —Deems Taylor⟩ **b :** vocal or instrumental sounds having rhythm, melody, or harmony ⟨~ of a choir⟩ ⟨~ of a hurdy-gurdy⟩ **2 a :** an agreeable sound that is likened to a musical composition **:** EUPHONY ⟨~ of the nightingale⟩ ⟨the morning on the water has sharpened our appetites, and the sizzling and spluttering below is ~ in our ears —T.C.Roughley⟩; *specif* **:** the cry of hounds at sight of the game **b :** an unpleasant medley of sound **:** RACKET, DIN ⟨the stairwell echoed the ~ of clashing swords⟩; *esp* **:** a reprimand or legal prosecution for a misdeed ⟨urged the hunted man to give himself up and face the ~⟩ **c :** a quality of expression or movement characterized by tonal harmony or rhythmical grace ⟨to him two blending thoughts give a ~ perceptible as two blending notes of a lute —Ezra Pound⟩ ⟨the ~ of lovingly orchestrated words —*Saturday Rev.*⟩ ⟨a purely abstract language of form — a visual ~ —Roger Fry⟩ ⟨women with . . . waists of agile ~ —Dudley Fitts⟩ **d :** spiritual impulse or animation ⟨that sad and universal ~ which stirs when we look back upon our youth —V.S.Pritchett⟩ ⟨the ~ of her own happiness —Helen Howe⟩ ⟨the sweet ~ of free institutions —A.E.Stevenson †1965⟩ **3 a** *obs* **:** a piece of music composed or performed ⟨I have assailed her with ~*s* —Shak.⟩ **b :** a musical accompaniment ⟨a play set to ~⟩ **4 a :** a musical ensemble — now used chiefly of a military band ⟨another field ~, equipped with drums, cymbals, horns . . . played with great abandon —G.S.Patton⟩ **b** *chiefly dial* **:** a musical instrument ⟨fetch your ~ into the house —Vance Randolph & G.P.Wilson⟩ **5 a :** the score of a musical composition set down on paper ⟨leafed through the ~⟩ **b :** a recorded performance of a musical composition ⟨stacked the hi-fi with soft ~⟩

[2]**music** \"\ *vb* **musicked; musicked; musicking; musics** *vi* **:** to compose or perform music ⟨the man could talk in Latin, ~, mime —J.C.Ransom⟩ ~ *vt* **1** *archaic* **:** to instruct in music **2 :** to express in or set to music ⟨~*s* every jingle and clash and call —John Collier b.1901⟩

mu·si·ca fal·sa \ˌmyüzəkəˈfȯl(t)sə\ *n* [ML, lit., false music] **:** MUSICA FICTA

musica fic·ta \-ˈfiktə\ *n* [ML, lit., feigned music] **:** contrapuntal music in which accidentals or notes foreign to the mode are introduced — called also *false music*

[1]**mu·si·cal** \ˈmyüzəkəl, -zēk-\ *adj* [ME, fr. MF, fr. ML *musicalis*, fr. L *musica* music + *-alis* -al — more at MUSIC] **1 a :** of or relating to music or to its notation or performance ⟨~ form⟩ ⟨~ instrument⟩ **b :** having the pleasing harmonious qualities of music **:** MELODIOUS ⟨~ voice⟩ ⟨~ name⟩ ⟨the piano sonata is an . . . exquisitely ~ piece —Edward Sackville-West & Desmond Shawe-Taylor⟩ ⟨the little frogs are ~ —John Burroughs⟩ **2 a :** having an interest in or talent for music ⟨comes from a ~ family⟩ **b :** versed in music ⟨a galaxy of ~ artists⟩ **3 :** set to or accompanied by music ⟨~ extravaganza⟩ **4 :** of or relating to musicians or to music lovers ⟨~ organization⟩ — **mu·si·cal·ly** \-zək(ə)lē, -zēk-, -li\ *adv*

[2]**musical** \"\ *n* -S **1** *archaic* **:** MUSICALE **2 :** a film or theatrical production typically of a sentimental or humorous nature and consisting of musical numbers and dialogue based upon a unifying plot — called also *musical comedy*

musical accent *n* **:** PITCH ACCENT 2, INTONATION

musical box *n, chiefly Brit* **:** MUSIC BOX

musical chairs *n pl but sing in constr* **1 :** a game in which players march to music in single file around a row of chairs numbering one less than the players and scramble for seats when the music stops, one player and one chair being eliminated each time until one of the last two marchers claims the only remaining seat — called also *going to Jerusalem* **2 :** manipulating resources or maneuvering for advantage ⟨it was the game of *musical chairs* in Washington last month as . . . aviation leaders all moved up a notch —*Aero Digest*⟩ ⟨motorists played *musical chairs* while parking lot owners did a land-office business —*Springfield (Mass.) Union*⟩

musical clock *n* **:** a clock that plays a tune at set intervals or as desired

musical comedy *n* **:** MUSICAL

mu·si·cale \ˌmyüzəˈkal, -zēˈ- *sometimes* -käl *or* -kȧl\ *n* -S [F (*soirée*) *musicale*, lit., musical evening] **:** a usu. private concert of music typically comprising a social entertainment

musical flame *n* **:** a flame that produces a musical note by setting in vibration the air in an open tube held over it

musical glasses *n pl* **1 :** GLASS HARMONICA, HARMONICA b **2 :** a set of drinking glasses tuned to the scale and played by rubbing their brims with moistened fingers

mu·si·cal·i·ty \ˌmyüzəˈkaləd·ē, -zēˈ-, -lətē, -i\ *n* -ES **1 :** the quality or state of being musical **:** MELODIOUSNESS ⟨the supreme ~ of Verdi's opera —Herbert Kupferberg⟩ ⟨~ of her words —*Saturday Rev.*⟩ **2 :** sensitivity to, knowledge of, or talent for producing music ⟨an audience of genuine ~ —*Saturday Rev.*⟩ ⟨enabled his ~ to flower —Virgil Thomson⟩

mu·si·cal·ization \ˌmyüzəkələˈzāshən, -zēk-, -ˌlīˈz-\ *n* -S **:** an act or instance of setting to music ⟨the film is a ~ of the novel⟩

mu·si·cal·ize \ˈ==kəˌlīz\ *vt* -ED/-ING/-S [[1]*musical* + *-ize*] **:** to set to music ⟨refused to let them ~ his play⟩

mu·si·cal·ness *n* -ES : MUSICALITY
musical prawn *n* : a rather small prawn (*Penaeopsis novaeguineae*) both sexes of which possess stridulating organs on the thorax
musical sand *n* : sand that emits a musical note when stirred or trodden on
musical saw *n* : a handsaw made to produce melody by bending the blade with varying tension while sounding it with a small hammer or a violin bow
mu·si·ca men·su·ra·ta \ˌmyüzəkə,menchəˈrād·ə, -ˌmen(t)səˈ-, -rād·ə\ *n* [NL, lit., measured music] : MENSURAL MUSIC
music box *n* **1** : a container enclosing an apparatus capable of mechanically reproducing music esp. activated by clockwork ⟨Swiss *music box*⟩ **2** : JUKEBOX ⟨more nickels were shoved into the mechanical *music box* —Robert Hazel⟩
music director *n* : one in charge of musical activities (as in a school)
music drama *n* : an opera in which the action is not interrupted by formal song divisions (as recitatives or arias) and the music is determined solely by dramatic appropriateness — compare LEITMOTIV
music gallery *n* : MINSTREL GALLERY
music hall *n* : a vaudeville theater or variety show ⟨a song-and-dance man famous in London *music halls*⟩
mu·si·cian \myüˈzishən\ *n* -S [ME *musicien*, fr. MF, fr. L *musica* + MF *-ien* -ian — more at MUSIC] : one skilled in music; *esp* : a composer, conductor, or professional performer of music
mu·si·cian·er \-sh(ə)nə(r)\ *n* -S : MUSICIAN
mu·si·cian·ly \-shənlē, -li\ *adj* : having or exhibiting the taste or artistry appropriate to a skilled musician ⟨a ~ interpretation⟩ ⟨the tenor's wife is his ~ accompanist —Roland Gelatt⟩
mu·si·cian·ship \-,ship\ *n* : artistry and insight displayed in the interpretation or rendition of music ⟨the finesse, the virtuosity and the ~ of this performance —Robert Donington⟩
musicked *past of* MUSIC
mu·sick·er \ˈmyüzəkə(r)\ *n* -S [²*music* + *-er*] *chiefly dial* : MUSICIAN
musicking *pres part of* MUSIC
mu·sic·less \ˈmyüzikləs, -zēk-\ *adj* : lacking in harmony or melodious quality ⟨~ instruments⟩ ⟨this ~ biography of a musician —P.H.Lang⟩
music lyre *n* : a lyriform spring clamp on a stem that is used to hold the music book of a player in a marching band and is attachable to the instrument or the player's arm
mu·si·co \ˈmyüzə,kō\ *n* -S [It, fr. L *musicus*, fr. *musicus*, adj., of music, fr. Gk *mousikos* of the Muses, musical — more at MUSIC] : MUSICIAN
musico- *comb form* [¹*music*] **1** : music ⟨*musicography*⟩ ⟨*musicotherapy*⟩ **2** : musical and ⟨*musicodramatic*⟩ ⟨*musicoliturgical*⟩
music of the spheres : an ethereal harmony supposed by the Pythagoreans to be produced by the vibration of the celestial spheres upon which the stars and planets were thought to move — compare HARMONY OF THE SPHERES
mu·si·cog·ra·phy \ˌmyüzəˈkägrəfē, -zēˈ-, -fi\ *n* -ES [*musico-* + *-graphy*] : the art or science of writing music
mu·si·co·log·i·cal \ˌmyüzəkəˈläjəkəl\ *adj* : of or relating to musicology
mu·si·col·o·gist \,==ˈkäləjəst\ *n* -S : a specialist in musicology

music lyre

mu·si·col·o·gy \-jē, -ji\ *n* -ES [It *musicologia*, fr. *musico-* + *-logia* -logy] : a study of music as a branch of knowledge or field of research; *esp* : the historical and theoretical investigation and analysis of specific types of music
mu·si·co·therapy \ˌmyüzə(ˌ)kō+\ *n* [*musico-* + *therapy*] : the treatment of disease (as mental disease) by means of music
music roll *n* : a roll of paper on which music for a player piano is recorded in perforations that actuate the keys by regulating the flow of air from a bellows
musics *pl of* MUSIC, *pres 3d sing of* MUSIC
music shell *n* : a marine gastropod shell (esp. *Voluta musica* of the East Indies or a related species) having color markings suggesting printed music
music supervisor *n* : one who has general oversight of musical instruction in a school system or in some division of it
music visualization *n* **1** : the creation of a modern or ballet dance entirely from designs suggested by musical accompaniment **2** : a dance that constitutes a direct translation of music into motion
music wire *n* : steel wire used for the strings of musical instruments or for helical springs; *specif* : PIANO WIRE
mus·i·mon \ˈmasə,män\ *n* -S [L *musimon-*, *musimo*, *musmon-*, *musmo*] : MOUFLON
¹**musine** \ˈmyü,sīn, ˈmə,s-\ *adj* [irreg. fr. L *mus* mouse + E *-ine* — more at MOUSE] : of or relating to mice : MURINE : resembling a mouse : MOUSY
²**musine** \"\ *n* -S : MURINE
¹**mus·ing** \ˈmyüziŋ, -zēŋ\ *n* -S [ME, fr. gerund of *musen* to muse — more at MUSE] : MEDITATION
²**musing** \"\ *adj* [ME, fr. pres. part. of *musen* to muse] : thoughtfully abstracted : MEDITATIVE — **mus·ing·ly** *adv*
mu·sique con·crète \mᵫzēkkōⁿkret\ *n* [F, lit., concrete music] : the composition by tape-recording of freely selected and treated sounds and natural noises into an artistically ordered continuum
mu·sive \ˈmyüsiv, -uziv\ *adj* [fr. obs. E *musive*, n., mosaic, fr. LL *musivum* — more at MOSAIC] *archaic* : MOSAIC
¹**musk** \ˈməsk\ *n* -S [ME *muske*, fr. MF *musc*, fr. LL *muscus*, fr. Gk *moschos*, fr. Per *mushk* castoreum, musk, fr. Skt *muṣka* testicle, scrotum, vulva, dim. of *mūṣ*, mouse — more at MOUSE] **1 a** : a substance that has a penetrating persistent odor, that is obtained from a sac situated under the skin of the abdomen of the male musk deer, that when fresh in the pods is brown and unctuous and when dried is a grainy powder, that varies in quality according to the season and age of the animal, and that is used chiefly in the form of a tincture as a fixative in perfumes **b** : any of various strong-smelling substances obtained from other animals (as the musk-ox, muskrat, or civet cat) **c** : any of various synthetic compounds (as muscone, civetone, or musk ambrette) having musky odors and used similarly to natural musk **2** : the musk deer or a similar animal **3 a** : MUSK PLANT **b** : MUSK MALLOW **c** : MUSK CLOVER **d** : GRAPE HYACINTH **e** *Austral* : any of several shrubs of the genus *Olearia* **4** : a dark grayish yellowish brown that is stronger, slightly yellower, and lighter than seal brown, slightly redder and lighter than sepia brown, lighter and stronger than otter brown, and very slightly redder and deeper than lama or bison — called also *café noir, cattail* **5 a** : the odor of musk **b** : an odor (as an animal scent) that resembles musk ⟨~ of mignonette —Elizabeth S. Hardy⟩ ⟨the ~ where a polecat had passed —Edwin Granberry⟩
²**musk** \"\ *vt* -ED/-ING/-S : to perfume with musk
muskadel *var of* MUSCATEL
musk ambrette *n* : a white to yellow powdery synthetic musk $C_{12}H_{16}N_2O_5$ made from *meta*-cresol; methyl-*tert*-butyldinitro-anisole
muskat *var of* MUSCAT
muskat nut *n* : any of several nuts yielded by trees of the genus *Myristica* that resemble nutmegs and are used for oil
musk bag *n* : an odor-producing gland; *esp* : the preputial odor-bearing gland of the male musk deer — called also *musk gland*
musk beaver *n* : MUSKRAT
musk beetle *n* : a European longicorn beetle (*Aromia moschata*) having an odor suggesting that of attar of roses
musk buffalo *n* : MUSK-OX
musk cat *n* **1** : an animal producing musk: as **a** : CIVET CAT **b** : GENET **2** *obs* **a** : COURTESAN **b** : FOP
musk cattle *n* : MUSK-OXEN
musk cavy *n* : HUTIA
musk clover *n* : a low annual European herb (*Erodium moschatum*) resembling alfilaria — called also *muskus grass*
musk cow *n* : a female musk-ox
musk cucumber *n* : CASSABANANA
musk deer *n* **1** : a small heavy-limbed deer (*Moschus moschiferus*) of the central Asiatic uplands valued for the musk bag of the male and unique among the deers in the possession of a gall-bladder **2** : CHEVROTAIN

musk deer 1

musk duck *n* **1** [alter. of *muscovy duck*] : MUSCOVY DUCK **2** [so called fr. its characteristic odor during the breeding season] : an Australian duck (*Biziura lobata*) having a disk-shaped leathery chin lobe and exuding a musky odor during the breeding season
mus·keg \ˈmə,skeg\ *also* **mas·keg** \ˈma,skeg\ *n* -S [of Algonquian origin; akin to Ojibwa *mūskeg* grassy bog, Cree *maskek*, Fox *maskyägi*] **1** : BOG; *esp* : a sphagnum bog of northern No. America often with tussocks — compare ¹MOOR 1b **2** : an often very thick usu. imperfectly consolidated deposit of partially decayed vegetable matter characteristic of wet boreal regions
muskeg moss *n* : any of various mosses (as of the genera *Sphagnum* or *Hypnum*) that thrive on muskeg
mus·kel·lunge *or* **mus·kal·lunge** \ˈməskə,lənj\ *or* **mas·ki·nonge** \ˈmaskə,nänj\ *also* **mus·kal·longe** \ˈməskə,länj\ *or* **mas·ka·longe** \ˈmas-\ *n, pl* **muskellunge** *or* **muskellunges** *or* **muskallunge** *or* **muskallunges** *or* **maskinonge** *or* **maskinonges** [of Algonquian origin; akin to Ojibwa & Cree *maskinonge*, *mashkinonge* muskellunge, prob. lit., big fish] : a large No. American pike (*Esox masquinongy*) which may exceed six feet in length with a weight of 60 to 80 pounds and is highly prized as a game fish, the typical form occurring in the Great Lakes and being brownish green spotted with black — see CHAUTAUQUA MUSKELLUNGE
¹**mus·ket** \ˈməskət, *usu* -əd·+V\ *n* -S [ME *muskett*, fr. ONF *mousquet*, dim. of *mousque* fly, fr. L *musca* — more at MIDGE] : the male of the sparrow hawk
²**musket** \"\ *n* -S [MF *mousquet*, *mousquette*, fr. OIt *moschetto*, *moschetta* arrow for a crossbow, musket, dim. of *mosca* fly, fr. L *musca*] : a large-caliber usu. muzzle-loading and smooth-bore military shoulder firearm superseded by the rifle
musket arrow *n* : a feathered wooden arrow fired from a musket or other firearm of the 16th century
mus·ke·teer \ˌməskəˈti(ə)r, -iə\ *n* -S [modif. (influenced by *-eer*) of MF *mousquetaire*, fr. *mousquet* + *-aire* -ary] **1** : a soldier armed with a musket **2** [so called fr. the loyal friendship of the musketeers who are principal characters in the novel *Les Trois Mousquetaires* (1844) by Alexandre Dumas †1870 Fr. novelist] : a boon companion
mus·ke·toon \ˌməskəˈtün\ *n* -S [MF *mousqueton*, fr. OIt *moschettone*, aug. of *moschetto* musket — more at MUSKET] : a short musket with a large bore
musketproof \ˈ==ˌ=\ *adj, archaic* : capable of resisting penetration by a musket ball
mus·ket·ry \ˈməskətrē\ *n* -ES [F *mousqueterie*, fr. *mousquet* musket + *-erie* -ery — more at MUSKET] **1** : MUSKETS **2** : MUSKETEERS **3 a** : musket or rifle fire ⟨rattle of ~⟩ **b** : the technique of using small arms or of concentrating the collective fire of rifle and automatic rifle-fire units ⟨had not had enough training in . . . ~ —J.H.Michaelis⟩
muskflower \ˈ=ˌ==\ *n* : MUSK PLANT
musk gland *n* : MUSK BAG
muskgrass \ˈ=ˌ=\ *n* : CHARA 2
musk hog *n* : PECCARY
mus·kie *or* **mus·ky** \ˈməskē\ *n, pl* **muskies** [by shortening & alter.] : MUSKELLUNGE
muskier *comparative of* MUSKY
muskiest *superlative of* MUSKY
muskie weed *n* : an aquatic plant of the genus *Potamogeton*; *esp* : a large-leaved pondweed (*P. praelongus*)
musk·i·ness \ˈməskēnəs\ *n* -ES [¹*musky* + *-ness*] : the quality or state of being musky
musking *pres part of* MUSK
musk·ish \-kish\ *adj* : somewhat musky
musk kangaroo *n* : a small kangaroo (*Hypsiprymnodon moschatus*) of northeastern Australia characterized by a musky odor and closely related to the rat kangaroos — called also *muskrat*
musk ketone *n* : a white to yellow crystalline synthetic musk $C_{14}H_{18}N_2O_5$; *tert*-butyl-dinitro-xylyl methyl ketone
musk lorikeet *or* **musk parakeet** *n* : a green Australian lorikeet (*Glossopsitta concinna*) with bright red ear coverts and forehead
musk mallow *n* **1** : a European mallow (*Malva moschata*) adventive in No. America and having faintly musk-scented foliage — called also *musk rose* **2** : ABELMOSK
musk·melon \ˈməsk, *chiefly in dial or substand speech* ˈməsh+,-\ *n* : a usu. sweet musky-odored edible melon that is the fruit of a trailing or climbing Asiatic herbaceous vine (*Cucumis melo*): as **a** : any of various green-fleshed or orange-fleshed melons of small or moderate size with superficially netted skin and often fluted surface that constitute a distinct variety (*C. melo reticulatus*) and include most of the muskmelons cultivated in No. America — distinguished from *cantaloupe* (sense 1) **b** : CANTALOUPE 1 **c** : WINTER MELON
musk mole *n* : a grayish brown mole (*Scaptochirus moschatus*) of Siberia and northeastern China
mus·ko·ge·an *or* **mus·kho·ge·an** *also* **mus·ko·gi·an** \ˌməˈskōgēən\ *n, usu cap* **1** : a language family of southeastern U. S. that forms with the Natchesan the Natchez-Muskogean stock and includes Alabama, Choctaw, Hitchiti, Koasati, Muskogee, and Apalachee **2** : the peoples speaking Muskogean languages
mus·ko·gee \ˌməˈskōgē\ *n, pl* **muskogee** *or* **muskogees** *usu cap* **1 a** : a Muskogean people of Georgia and eastern Alabama constituting the nucleus of the Creek Confederacy **b** : a member of such people **2** : the language of the Muskogee people and of part of the Seminole people
muskone *var of* MUSCONE
musk orchis *or* **musk orchid** *n* : a European orchid (*Herminium monorchis*) having a musky scent
musk-ox \ˈ=,=\ *n, pl* **musk-oxen** : a heavy-set bovid mammal (*Ovibos moschatus*) circumpolar in distribution during the Pleistocene period but now confined to Greenland and the barren northern lands of No. America, being between the sheep and the oxen in size and in many characters but having a thick long shaggy pelage that is dark grayish brown or blackish with a light saddle marking — called also *musk sheep*

musk-ox

musk parrot *n* **1** : a large brightly colored Fijian parrot (*Prosopeia tabuensis*) with a pronounced musky odor that is readily domesticated and trained to speak **2** : any of several parrots related to the musk parrot
musk plant *n* **1** : a yellow-flowered No. American herb (*Mimulus moschatus*) with hairy foliage formerly of musky odor — called also *muskflower* **2** : MUSK MALLOW

muskrat 1a

musk·rat \ˈmə,skrat, *usu* -ad·+V\ *n, pl* **muskrat** *or* **muskrats** [prob. by folk etymology fr. a word of Algonquian origin — more at MUSQUASH] **1 a** *or* **muskrat beaver** : an abundant aquatic rodent (*Ondatra zibethica* syn. *Fiber zibethica*) found throughout the U. S. and Canada living in holes in the banks of ponds or streams or in dome-shaped houses of rushes and mud, being as large as a small cat with the tail long, scaly, and laterally compressed, the hind feet webbed, the fur dark glossy brown, and having small glands that emit a musky odor — called also *musquash* **b** : the fur or pelt of the muskrat **2** : any of various other musky-smelling or musk-producing animals (as the musk kangaroo, hutia, So. African genet, or musk shrew)
muskrat potato *n* : WAPATOO
muskrat weed *n* : TALL MEADOW RUE
muskroot \ˈ=,=\ *n* **1** : any of several plants having strong-scented roots: as **a** : MOSCHATEL **b** : an umbelliferous plant (*Ferula sumbul*) of central Asia whose musky aromatic roots constitute the chief sumbul of commerce **2** : SUMBUL 1
musk rose *n* **1** : a rose (*Rosa moschata*) of the Mediterranean region with curved or somewhat climbing branches and flowers having a musky odor **2** : MUSK MALLOW
musks *pl of* MUSK, *pres 3d sing of* MUSK
musk seed *n* : AMBER SEED
musk sheep *n* : MUSK-OX
musk shrew *n* **1** : any of various East Indian shrews having a powerful musky odor; *esp* : CROCIDURA 2 **2** : DESMAN
musk thistle *n* : a Eurasian thistle (*Carduus nutans*) naturalized in eastern No. America with nodding musky flower heads — called also *nodding thistle*
musk tree *n* : any of several Australasian musk-scented trees (as *Olearia argophylla*) — see MUSKWOOD 2
musk turtle *also* **musk terrapin** *or* **musk tortoise** *n* : any of several small American freshwater turtles of the genera *Sternotherus* and *Kinosternon*; *esp* : a turtle (*S. odoratus*) having a strong musky odor
mus·kus grass \ˈməskəs-\ *n* [D *muskus* musk, fr. L *muscus* — more at MUSK] : MUSK CLOVER
muskwood \ˈ=,=\ *n* **1 a** : a usu. small to medium-sized widely distributed tropical American musky-odored tree (*Guarea trichilioides*) **b** : the reddish brown rather light straight-grained wood of this tree used esp. formerly in the West Indies as a substitute for mahogany **2 a** : a musk tree (*Olearia argophylla*) **b** : the hard white wood of the musk tree used for cabinetwork
musk xylene *n* : a white to yellow crystalline synthetic musk $C_{12}H_{15}N_3O_6$ used esp. in perfumes for soaps; *tert*-butyltrinitro-xylene
¹**musky** \ˈməskē\ *adj* -ER/-EST [¹*musk* + *-y*] : having an odor of or resembling musk
²**musky** *var of* MUSKIE
¹**mus·lim** \ˈməzləm, ˈmüz-, ˈmüs- *sometimes* ˈməsləm\ *or* **mos·lem** \ˈmäzləm *sometimes* ˈmäsl-\ *also* **mus·lem** *like* MUSLIM\ *n, pl* **muslim** *or* **muslims** *or* **moslem** *or* **moslems** *usu cap* [Ar *muslim*, fr. *aslama* to surrender (to God)] : an adherent of or believer in Islam : one who submits to the will of Allah
²**muslim** \"\ *or* **moslem** \"\ *also* **muslem** \"\ *adj, usu cap* : of or relating to the religion, believers, or the institutions of Islam
mus·lim·ism \-lə,mizəm\ *n* -S *cap* : ISLAM
mus·lin \ˈməzlən\ *n* -S *often attrib* [F *mousseline*, fr. It *mussolina*, fr. Ar *mawṣilīy* of Mosul, fr. al-*Mawṣil* Mosul, city in northern Iraq where it was formerly made] **1 a** : a plainwoven cotton fabric that is produced in various qualities from sheer to coarse, used bleached or unbleached for sheeting, embroidery, or other purposes, given special finishes for industrial purposes (as in bookbinding), and dyed or printed for clothing — see BOOK MUSLIN, ORGANDY **b** : a garment (as a gown) made of muslin **2 a** : a trial model of a garment or manufactured article (as a handbag) worked out in muslin for preliminary showing or fitting and then used as a pattern **b** : a frame or backing (as for a fur coat) ⟨~*s* . . . are made in Paris and befurred over here —Lois Long⟩ — **in muslin** : covered with muslin and sold with or without upholstering in decorator fabrics of the buyer's choosing — used of upholstered furniture
muslin delaine *n* : DELAINE 1
mus·lin·et *or* **mus·lin·ette** \ˌməzləˈnet\ *n* -S [*muslin* + *-et* or *-ette*] *archaic* : a heavy muslin
muslin house *n* : CLOTH HOUSE
muslin kail *n, Scot* : broth of barley and greens
mus·nud \ˈmə,snəd\ *n* -S [Hindi *masnad*, fr. Ar] : a cushioned seat used as a throne by native princes of India
mu·soph·a·ga \myüˈsäfəgə\ *n, cap* [NL *muso-* (fr. *Musa*) + *-phaga*] : the type genus of the family Musophagidae comprising various typical touracos
mu·so·phag·i·dae \ˌmyüsəˈfajə,dē\ *n pl, cap* [NL, fr. *Musophaga*, type genus + *-idae*] : a family of African birds (order Cuculiformes) consisting of the touracos
mu·soph·a·gine \myüˈsäfə,jīn, -jən\ *adj* [NL *Musophaginae*, subfamily of African birds, fr. *Musophaga*, type genus + *-inae*] : of or relating to the Musophagidae
mus·quash \ˈmə,skwäsh, -wȯsh\ *also* **mush·squash** \ˈməsh-k-\ *n* -ES [of Algonquian origin; akin to Natick *musquash*] **1** : MUSKRAT 1a **2** *chiefly Brit* : MUSKRAT 1b
musquash root *n* : SPOTTED COWBANE
musquashweed \ˈ=,=,=\ *n* : TALL MEADOW RUE
mus·quaw \ˈmə,skwȯ\ *n* -S [of Algonquian origin; akin to Cree *maskwa* black bear, Natick *mosq*, *masq*, Delaware *machk*, Mohegan *muquh*] : BLACK BEAR 1
mus·rol \ˈməz,rōl\ *n* -S [MF *muserole*, fr. It *museruola*, *musarola*, fr. *muso* muzzle, snout, fr. ML *musus*] *archaic* : the noseband of a horse's bridle
¹**muss** \ˈməs\ *n* -ES [origin unknown] **1** *obs* **a** : a game in which players at a given signal scramble for small objects that have been thrown to the ground ⟨when I cried ho, like boys unto a ~, kings would start forth —Shak.⟩ **b** : SCRAMBLE ⟨bauble and cap no sooner are thrown down, but there's a ~ of more than half the town —John Dryden⟩ **2** *slang* : a confused conflict : DISTURBANCE, BRAWL, FIGHT ⟨kick up a ~⟩ **3** : a state of confusion or disorder : MESS ⟨can be quickly installed, without ~ or fuss⟩
²**muss** \"\ *vt* -ED/-ING/-ES : to make untidy : WRINKLE, DISARRANGE, RUMPLE, DISHEVEL ⟨if these fabrics are very ~*ed*, use dry press cloth —Mary B. Picken⟩ ⟨most of the new hats manage to ~ the hairdos —Lois Long⟩ — often used with *up* ⟨a hard apartment to ~ up and easy to straighten out —Dorothy Baker⟩
mus·saen·da \məˈsendə\ *n, cap* [NL, fr. Singhalese *mussænda*, a species of this genus] : a large genus of herbs or shrubs (family Rubiaceae) found in the Old World tropics and having an ornamental calyx with one sepal that is much enlarged and showy
mussaenda coffee *n* : the seeds of a tree (*Gaertnera vaginata*) of the family Loganiaceae that contain no caffeine but are used as a coffee substitute
mus·sal \məˈsäl\ *n* -S [Hindi *masāl*, *mashāl*, fr. Ar *mash'al*] *India* : a torch usu. of oil-soaked rags
mus·sal·chee \-l,chē\ *n* -S [Hindi *mash'alcī*, fr. Per, fr. Ar *mash'al* torch + Turk *-ci* (suffix denoting an agent)] *India* **1** : one that tends or carries a mussal : TORCHBEARER **2** : a kitchen servant : SCULLION — used by Europeans
mus·sel *also* **mus·cle** \ˈməsəl\ *n* -S *often attrib* [ME *muscle*, fr. OE *muscelle*, *muscle*, *musle*; akin to OS & OHG *muscula* mussel, MD *mosschele*; all fr. a prehistoric WGmc word borrowed fr. (assumed) VL *muscula*, alter. of L *musculus* small mouse, muscle, mussel — more at MUSCLE] **1** : a marine bivalve mollusk of *Mytilus* or a related genus usu. having an oval or elongated shell with a dark horny periostracum and being attached to the substrate by a byssus of fine threads secreted by the animal **2** : a freshwater bivalve mollusk of *Unio*, *Anodonta*, or related genera that is esp. abundant in rivers of the central U.S. and has a shell with a lustrous nacreous lining much used in making buttons — called also *freshwater clam, freshwater mussel*
mussel bill *n* : SURF SCOTER
mussel crab *n* **1** : a small American commensal crab (*Pinnotheres maculatus*) sometimes found in the mantle cavity of the mussel and other bivalves **2** : any of various crabs of the family Pinnotheridae — compare OYSTER CRAB
musselcracker *or* **musselcrusher** \ˈ==,==\ *n* [so called fr. its large incisors] : BISKOP

mussel digger *n* [so called fr. its habit of digging in the mud] **:** GRAY WHALE

mussel duck *n* **1 :** SCAUP DUCK **2 :** SCOTER

mussel poisoning *n* **:** a toxic reaction following the eating of mussels; *esp* **:** a severe often fatal intoxication following the consumption of mussels that have fed on gonyaulax or other red tide flagellates and stored up a dangerous alkaloid in their tissues

mussel scale *n* **:** any of numerous scale insects (as of the genus *Lepidosaphes*) shaped like a mussel shell

mussel–shrimp \ˈ≈≈,≈\ *n* **:** OSTRACOD

mus·si·dae \ˈməsə,dē\ *n pl, cap* [NL, fr. *Mussa*, type genus + *-idae*] **:** a family of imperforate corals that includes massive reef-building corals with compound polyps — see CACTUS CORAL

muss·i·ly \ˈməsəlē\ *adv* **:** in a mussy manner

muss·i·ness \-sēnəs\ *n* -ES **:** the quality or state of being mussy

mussitate *vi* -ED/-ING/-S [L *mussitatus*, past part. of *mussitare* to mutter, be silent, fr. *mussare*, prob. of imit. origin] *obs* **:** MUTTER

mus·si·ta·tion \,məsəˈtāshən\ *n* -S [L *mussitation-, mussitatio* action of muttering, fr. *mussitatus* + *-ion-, -io* -ion] **:** movement of the lips as if in speech but without accompanying sound

mus·so \ˈmə(,)sō\ *n, pl* **musso** *or* **mussos** *usu cap* **:** LAHU

mus·sul·man *or* **mus·sal·man** *also* **mus·ul·man** *or* **mus·al·man** \ˈməsəlmən\ *n, pl* **mussulmen** *or* **musalmen** *usu cap* [Turk *müslüman* & Per *musulmān*, modif. of Ar *muslim* (pl. *muslimūn*)] **:** MUSLIM

muss up *vt* **1 :** to batter or handle roughly **:** BEAT, MAUL ⟨wanted to get there in time to *muss* him *up* a bit —J.F. Fishman⟩ **2 :** to make chaotic or incoherent **:** CONFUSE ⟨sold them liquor, and generally *mussed up* the situation —William Kent⟩

mus·su·ra·na \,müsəˈränə\ *n* -S [Pg *muçurana* fr. Tupi, lit., cord] **:** a large harmless colubrid snake (*Cloelia cloelia* syn. *Pseudoboa cloelia*) of the West Indies and tropical America which constricts and swallows poisonous snakes

mussy \ˈməsē, -si\ *adj* -ER/-EST [¹*muss* + *-y*] **:** characterized by clutter or muss **:** MESSY, SLOVENLY

¹**must** \(ˈ)məs(t)\ *vb, pres & past all persons* **must** [ME *moste* (past ind. & subj. of *moten* to be allowed to, be able to, have to), fr. OE *mōste*, past ind. & subj. of *mōtan* to be allowed to, be able to, have to; akin to OS *mōtan* to have cause for, be obliged to, have to, OHG *muozan* to be allowed to, be able to, have to, Goth *gamotan* to have room, fit; basic meaning: to have allotted to one; derivative fr. the stem of OE *metan* to measure — more at METE] *verbal auxiliary* **1 a :** is commanded or requested to ⟨you ~ stop that noise⟩ ⟨you ~ hear my side of the story⟩ ⟨he ~ be made to obey⟩ ⟨I told him what he ~ do⟩ **b :** is urged to **:** ought by all means to ⟨you ~ read that book⟩ ⟨you ~ come to visit us soon⟩ **2 :** is compelled by physical necessity to ⟨man ~ eat to live⟩ **:** is required by immediate or future need or purpose to ⟨we ~ hurry if we want to catch the bus⟩ ⟨~ you take all that luggage along⟩ ⟨if you wished to see it you ~ queue —Leslie Eytle⟩ **3 :** is obliged to **:** is compelled by social considerations to ⟨I ~ say you're looking much better⟩ ⟨I ~ admit your plane's safer⟩ ⟨realized that he ~ say nothing about it⟩ **4 :** is required by law, custom, or moral conscience to ⟨we ~ obey the rules⟩ ⟨you ~ respect your father's wishes⟩ ⟨the present government ~ go . . . for it is too gross a scandal —John Buchan⟩ **5 a :** is compelled by resolve **:** is determined to ⟨if you ~ go at least wait till the storm is over⟩ **b :** is unreasonably or perversely compelled to ⟨I was planning a surprise for you, if you ~ know⟩ ⟨why ~ you be so stubborn⟩ ⟨why ~ it always rain on weekends⟩ **6 :** is logically inferred or supposed to ⟨he ~ be out of his mind to say that⟩ ⟨it ~ be nearly dinner time⟩ ⟨he ~ have done it, no one else was there⟩ ⟨it ~ have been the coffee that kept me awake⟩ **7 :** is compelled by fate or by natural law to ⟨what ~ be will be⟩ ⟨the innocent ~ suffer with the guilty⟩ ⟨three men who ~ leave their Queen on her death bed —Edith Sitwell⟩ ⟨a woman ~ have children to love —Edith Wharton⟩ **8 :** was presumably certain to **:** would surely or necessarily **:** was bound to ⟨if he had really been there I ~ have seen him⟩ ⟨buffalo . . . beat out a track where human beings ~ have measurably failed —S.C.Williams⟩ ⟨~ have fallen had the railing not been there⟩ ⟨my rifle was slung on my back . . . else I ~ have lost it —Lea MacNally⟩ **9** *dial* **:** MAY, SHALL — used chiefly in questions ⟨~ I bring in the soup now⟩ ~ *vi* **1 :** is obliged or compelled ⟨when Duty whispers low "thou ~" the youth replies "I can" —R.W.Emerson⟩ ⟨shoot if you ~ this old gray head —J.G. Whittier⟩ **2** *archaic* **:** ought to go **:** is obliged to go — used with adverb or adverbial phrase ⟨I ~ to Coventry —Shak.⟩ ⟨I ~ now to breakfast —John Buchan⟩ **syn** see OUGHT

²**must** \ˈməst\ *n* -S *often attrib* **1 a :** an imperative need or duty **:** OBLIGATION, REQUIREMENT ⟨in highly competitive modern industry, technological progress is a ~ —*Annual Report General Motors Corp.*⟩ ⟨told Republican leadership that the bill was a ~ —*N. Y. Times*⟩ ⟨less plagued . . . by rigid ~s —Walter de la Mare⟩ **b :** an indispensable item **:** ESSENTIAL, NECESSITY ⟨a raincoat is an absolute ~ —Richard Joseph⟩ ⟨facility, capacity and dependability of project equipment are ~s —*Military Engineer*⟩; *specif* **:** a priority item marked for inclusion without fail in a particular edition of a newspaper **2 :** something that deserves attention because of its outstanding merit ⟨this is a lovely place, a real ~ for visitors —Richard Joseph⟩ ⟨for the thrill of being close to the original . . . the volume is a ~ —Louis Marder⟩

³**must** \"\ *n* -S [ME, fr. OE, fr. L *mustum*, fr. neut. of *mustus* young, fresh, new; perh. akin to Gk *mysos* spot, stain, defect, OIr *mossach* dirty, OE *mos* moss — more at MOSS] **1 a :** the juice of grapes or other fruit before and during fermentation **b :** the juice in combination with the pulp and skins of the crushed fruit **2** *dial Eng* **:** the pomace of apples or pears often used as fodder for livestock

⁴**must** \"\ *n* -S [MF, alter. of *musc* — more at MUSK] **1 :** MUSK **2 :** MUSTINESS, MOLD ⟨the dust and ~ of a decade —Marcia Davenport⟩

⁵**must** \"\ *vi* **:** to become musty or moldy ~ *vt, archaic* **:** to powder (the hair) with musk

⁶**must** *var of* MUSTH

mustache *var of* MOUSTACHE

mus·ta·chio *or* **mous·ta·chio** \məˈstä‖shē,ō, -taǀ, ǀ(,)shō\ *n* -S [Sp & It; Sp *mostacho*, fr. It *mustaccio, mostaccio* — more at MOUSTACHE] **:** MOUSTACHE; *esp* **:** a large moustache

mus·ta·chioed *or* **mous·ta·chioed** \-ōd\ *adj* **:** having mustachios

mus·ta·fi·na \,məstəˈfēnə\ *also* **mus·tee·fi·no** \-tēˈfē(,)nō\ *n* -S [perh. fr. *mustee* + Sp *fino* fine — more at FINO] **:** the offspring of a white person and a mustee

¹**mus·tang** \ˈmə,staŋ\ *n* -S [MexSp *mesteño, mestengo*, fr. Sp, animal without an owner, stray, fr. *mesteño, mestengo*, adj., ownerless, strayed, fr. *mesta*, annual roundup of cattle formerly held in Spain, annual meeting of the owners of such cattle that disposed of strays, fr. ML (*animalia*) *mixta* mixed animals, fr. L *animalia* animals + *mixta*, neut. pl. of *mixtus*, past part. of *miscēre* to mix — more at MIX] **1 a :** the small hardy naturalized horse of the western plains directly descended from horses brought in by the Spaniards — compare CAYUSE 3, INDIAN PONY **b :** BRONCO **2** *slang* **:** a commissioned officer (as in the U. S. Navy) who has risen from the ranks **3 :** SPHINX 4

²**mustang** \"\ *vi* -ED/-ING/-S **:** to hunt wild horses

mus·tang·er \-ŋə(r)\ *n* -S **:** one who rounds up wild horses on the open range and sells them esp. for horsemeat

mustang grape *n* **:** a woody vine (*Vitis candicans*) of the southwestern U. S. having light-colored berries with a pungent pulp

mustang mint *n* **:** a fragrant California annual herb (*Monardella lanceolata*) with rose-purple flowers in bracted clusters

mus·tard \ˈməstə(r)d\ *n* -S *often attrib* [ME *mostard, mustard*, fr. OF *mostarde, moustarde* condiment made from mustard seed and must, mustard, fr. *moust* must, fr. L *mustum* — more at MUST] **1 a :** a pungent yellow condiment consisting of the pulverized seeds of the black mustard or sometimes the white mustard either dry or made into a paste (as with water or vinegar) and sometimes adulterated with other substances (as turmeric) or mixed with spices and serving as a stimulant and diuretic or in large doses as an emetic and as a counterirritant when applied to the skin as a poultice **b** *slang* **:** something that adds strength or piquancy **:** ENTHUSIASM, ZEST ⟨kick a lot of ~ out of . . . 'em —J.T.Farrell⟩ ⟨a lot of muscle and ~ —*Time*⟩ **2 a** (1) **:** any of several plants of the genus *Brassica* that have lyrately lobed leaves, yellow flowers, and linear beaked pods and that include some which are cultivated for their pungent seed or for their edible foliage — see BLACK MUSTARD, INDIAN MUSTARD, WHITE MUSTARD (2) **:** any of various other plants of the family Cruciferae — used chiefly in combination; see HEDGE MUSTARD, WORMSEED MUSTARD **b :** TOOTHBRUSH TREE **3 a :** a dark yellow **b :** a moderate yellow — compare MUSTARD YELLOW **4 a :** MUSTARD GAS **b :** NITROGEN MUSTARD

mustard beetle *n* **:** a small black European leaf beetle (*Phaedon cochleariae*) destructive to mustard and other cruciferous plants

mustard brown *n* **1 :** a variable color averaging a moderate olive brown that is greener and deeper than old olive **2 :** a moderate brown that is lighter, stronger, and slightly redder than chestnut brown, and yellower, lighter, and stronger than auburn

mus·tard·er \-tə(r)dər, -tədə(r)\ *n* -S **:** a maker or seller of mustard

mustard family *n* **:** CRUCIFERAE

mustard gas *n* [so called fr. its odor] **:** a vesicant war gas $(ClCH_2CH_2)_2S$ that also attacks the eyes and lungs and is a systemic poison, that is a high-boiling oily liquid with a pungent odor only when impure, and that is obtained by treating thiodiglycol with gaseous hydrogen chloride or ethylene with sulfur monochloride; bis-(2-chloroethyl) sulfide — called also *dichloroethyl sulfide, sulfur mustard*

mustard gold *n* **:** a variable color averaging a light olive brown that is much stronger and slightly lighter than drab or sponge

mustard oil *n* **1 :** an oil from mustard: as **a** *or* **mustard–seed oil :** a greenish yellow bland semidrying fatty oil that is expressed from the seeds usu. of black mustard and is used chiefly in soapmaking and as a salad oil **b :** a colorless to pale yellow pungent irritating essential oil that is obtained by distillation from the seeds usu. of black mustard after expression of the fatty oil and maceration with water, that consists largely of allyl isothiocyanate, and that is used esp. in liniments and medicinal plasters — compare SINIGRIN **2 a :** ALLYL ISOTHIOCYANATE **b :** an isothiocyanate ester ⟨phenyl *mustard oil* C_6H_5NCS⟩

mustard plaster *n* **1 :** a poultice made by spreading a paste of mustard, flour, and cold water on cloth **2** *or* **mustard paper :** a counterirritant and rubefacient plaster prepared by spreading a mixture of powdered black mustard and a rubber solution on fabric

mustard seed *n* **1** *or* **mustard–seed shot :** DUST SHOT **2** *also* **mustard–seed coal :** the smallest size of buckwheat coal

mustard spinach *n* **:** INDIAN MUSTARD

mustard tan *n* **:** a variable color averaging a light olive brown that is stronger and slightly greener than drab or sponge and deeper and slightly greener than dust

mustard yellow *n* **:** a moderate yellow that is duller than colonial yellow, greener and paler than brass, and redder and less strong than quince yellow — compare MUSTARD 3

mus·tee \,məˈstē, ˈ≈≈\ *n* -S [modif. & shortening of Sp *mestizo* — more at MESTIZO] **1 :** OCTOROON **2 :** HALF-BREED

musteefino *var of* MUSTAFINA

mus·te·la \,məˈstēlə\ *n, cap* [NL, fr. L, weasel, prob. fr. *mus* mouse + *-tela* (origin unknown) — more at MOUSE] **:** a genus of carnivorous mammals (the type of the family Mustelidae) comprising active predators and valuable furbearers

¹**mus·te·lid** \ˈməstələd\ *adj* [NL *Mustelidae*] **:** of or relating to the Mustelidae

²**mustelid** \"\ *n* -S **:** a mammal of the family Mustelidae

mus·tel·i·dae \,məˈstelə,dē\ *n pl, cap* [NL, fr. *Mustela*, type genus + *-idae*] **:** a large widely distributed family (superfamily Arctoidea) of rather small lithe active carnivorous mammals including many important furbearers (as the mink, fisher, and otter) and some destructive predators (as the weasels and polecats) and varying greatly in appearance and habits from the tiniest slender bloodthirsty weasel to the relatively large stocky slow-moving skunk or the burly wolverine

mus·te·line \ˈməstə,līn, -lən\ *adj* [NL *Mustela* + E *-ine*] **:** of or relating to weasels **:** like or related to weasels

mus·te·lus \,məˈstēləs\ *n, cap* [NL, fr. L *mustela* weasel, a fish — more at MUSTELA] **:** a genus of dogfishes of the family Triakidae including the smooth hound

¹**mus·ter** \ˈməstə(r)\ *vb* **mustered; mustered; mustering** \-t(ə)riŋ\ **musters** [ME *mostren, mustren* to show, muster, fr. OF *mostrer, monstrer, moustrer*, fr. L *monstrare* to show, point out, fr. *monstrum* evil omen, monster, monstrosity, marvel — more at MONSTER] *vt* **1 a :** ENLIST, ENROLL ⟨had been . . . ~*ed* as surgeon's mate —Tobias Smollett⟩ — used chiefly with *in* or *into* ⟨the army ~*s* in recruits⟩ ⟨a businessman recently ~*ed* into government service —*New Yorker*⟩ **b** (1) **:** to cause to gather **:** CONVENE, ASSEMBLE ⟨all hands were ~*ed* aft for watches to be told off —H.A.Chippendale⟩ ⟨~*ed* the ladies together and urged them into another room —Maurice Cranston⟩ ⟨did not ~ much of a crowd —Ben Riker⟩ (2) *Austral* **:** ROUND UP ⟨went up into the reserve to ~ our stock —F.S.Anthony⟩ **c :** to call the roll of ⟨fell out on deck and the mate ~*ed* the ship's company⟩ **2 a :** to bring together **:** COLLECT, ACCUMULATE ⟨~ a few pounds to buy some seed corn —Adrian Bell⟩ ⟨~*ed* shirts and socks and neckties from his chest of drawers —Richard Blaker⟩ ⟨could only ~ . . . two hundred votes —E.H.Collis⟩ **b :** to call forth **:** DEVELOP, INVOKE **:** work up ⟨couldn't ~ courage to pop the question —Agnes S. Turnbull⟩ ⟨have to ~ the right words as well as the midnight courage —E.B.White⟩ ⟨as soon as sufficient public support can be ~*ed* —Chester Bowles⟩ — often used with *up* ⟨cannot ~ up much sympathy for the . . . privations which he endured —W.E.Channing⟩ **3 :** to amount to **:** COMPRISE, INCLUDE, NUMBER ⟨the book-reading public ~*s* 55 percent of the population —J.D.Adams⟩ ⟨the senior program . . . ~*ed* 123,299 students —*Americana Annual*⟩ ~ *vi* **1 a :** to come together **:** CONGREGATE, FORGATHER ⟨thirty thousand men . . . were to ~ in the disguise of pilgrims —T.B. Macaulay⟩ **b** *obs* **:** GATHER ⟨vapors . . . drawn from the sea to ~ in the skies —Richard Blackmore⟩ **2** *Austral* **:** to conduct a roundup of livestock ⟨~*ed* in March this year on account of the late season and drove the stock down . . . in April —Nevil Shute⟩

²**muster** \"\ *n* -S [ME *mustre, moustre*, fr. MF *mostre, monstre, moustre*, fr. *mostrer, monstrer, moustrer*, v.] **1 :** a representative specimen **:** SAMPLE ⟨~*s* of goods for sale, in reasonable quantities —*Tariffs of Foreign Countries*⟩ **2** *obs* **:** PRESENTATION, DISPLAY ⟨begin to make some ~ and show of their learning —Richard Mulcaster⟩ **3 a** (1) **:** an act of assembling for enumeration or inspection ⟨the boys in the squad room sat around between ~*s* —Seymour Ettman⟩ (2) **:** an act or process of critical examination ⟨slipshod work that would never pass ~⟩; *specif* **:** formal military inspection ⟨call out the troops to stand ~⟩ **b :** a competitive demonstration ⟨eleven hand tub fire pumpers . . . have entered the Riverside Park Championship Fireman's ~ —*Springfield (Mass.) Daily News*⟩ **c** *Austral* **:** ROUNDUP — compare CAMP 1d **d** (1) **:** an assembled group **:** ACCUMULATION, GATHERING ⟨a ~ of biographical facts —*Time*⟩ ⟨last week's ~ of the heads of . . . governments —R.H.Rovere⟩ (2) *of peacocks* **:** FLOCK **e :** INVENTORY, ROSTER; *esp* **:** MUSTER ROLL ⟨were sent . . . to take the ~*s* of this expedition —G.R.Elton⟩

mus·ter·er \-tərə(r)\ *n* -S **1 :** one that musters **2** *Austral* **:** a ranch hand who rounds up livestock

mustering *n* -S [ME, fr. gerund of *mustren* to muster] **1 :** an act or instance of assembling **2** *Austral* **:** ROUNDUP

muster–master \ˈ≈≈,≈≈\ *n* **:** an officer or official charged with keeping a muster roll

muster out *vt* **:** to discharge from service (as military) ⟨at the end of the war was *mustered out* as an ensign —E.P.Snow⟩ ⟨tired liberals . . . *mustered* themselves *out* —Bruce Bliven b.1889⟩

muster–out \ˈ≈≈ˈ≈\ *n, pl* **musters–out** [*muster out*] **:** an act or process of mustering out **:** DISCHARGE ⟨the first great commands to complete their *musters-out* —Dixon Wecter⟩ ⟨ordered the *muster-out* of all troops not needed for occupation duties⟩

muster roll *n* **:** INVENTORY, ROSTER; *specif* **:** a register of all the officers and men in a military unit or ship's company

musth *or* **must** \ˈməst\ *n* -S [Hindi *mast* intoxicated, ruttish, fr. Per *mast*; akin to Skt *madati* he rejoices, is drunk — more at MEAT] **:** a periodic state of murderous frenzy of the bull elephant usu. connected with the rutting season and marked by the exudation of a dark brown odorous ichor from tiny holes above the eyes — **on must** *also* **in must :** in a state of belligerent fury — used of the bull elephant

must·i·ly \ˈməstəlē\ *adv* **:** in a musty manner

must·i·ness \-tēnəs\ *n* -ES **:** the quality or state of being musty

mustn't \ˈməsᵊnt\ [by contr.] **:** must not

musts *pl of* MUST

¹**musty** \ˈməstē, -ti\ *adj* -ER/-EST [⁴*must* + *-y*] **1 a :** impaired by damp or mildew **:** MOLDY ⟨~ relic⟩ **b :** tasting of mold ⟨~ wine⟩ **c :** smelling of damp and decay **:** FUSTY ⟨a pathetic air of dilapidation . . . and a ~, shut-up smell —George du Maurier⟩ **2 a :** TRITE, DULL, STALE ⟨the proverb is something ~ —Shak.⟩ **b :** ANTIQUATED, SUPERANNUATED ⟨~ statute⟩ ⟨a ~ clerk on a high stool⟩

²**musty** *vi* -ED/-ING/-ES *obs* **:** to become musty

musulman *usu cap, var of* MUSSULMAN

mut *var of* MUTT

mut *abbr* **1** mutilated **2** mutual

¹**mu·ta** \ˈmü(,)tä, -üd·ə\ *n* -S [It, fr. *mutare* to change, fr. L] **:** CHANGE — used as a direction in ensemble music for various instruments (as timpani) to change tuning preparatory to a change in key

²**muta** \"\ *n* -S [Ar *mut'ah* enjoyment] **:** a form of Muslim usufruct marriage for a specified period — compare BEENA MARRIAGE

mu·ta·bil·ia \,myüd·əˈbilēə, -lyə\ *n pl, cap* [NL, fr. L, neut. pl. of *mutabilis*] **1** *in former classifications* **:** a suborder of Caudata comprising all salamanders that normally undergo metamorphosis **2** *in some classifications* **:** a suborder of Caudata including all true salamanders as opposed to the Proteida and Meantes

mu·ta·bil·i·ty \,myüd·əˈbiləd·ē, -ütə-, -lətē, -i\ *n* -ES [ME *mutabilite*, fr. MF *mutabilité*, fr. L *mutabilitat-, mutabilitas*, fr. *mutabilis* + *-itat-, -itas* -ity] **1 :** the quality or state of being mutable or capable of mutation **2 :** an instance of being mutable

¹**mu·ta·ble** \ˈmyüd·əbəl, -ütəb-\ *adj* [L *mutabilis*, fr. *mutare* to change + *-abilis* -able — more at MISS] **1 :** prone or liable to change **:** INCONSTANT, FICKLE ⟨a ~ mind⟩ ⟨a ~ foreign policy⟩ **2 a :** capable of change or of being changed in form, quality, or nature ⟨a ~ substance⟩ **b :** subject to or capable of mutation **:** liable to mutate ⟨~ vowels⟩ — **mu·ta·ble·ness** *n* -ES

²**mutable** *n* -S **:** a mutable sound or grammatical form

mu·ta·bly \-blē, -li\ *adv* **:** in a mutable manner

mu·ta·fa·cient \,myüd·ə,fāshənt\ *adj* [*mutation* + *-facient*] **:** capable of inducing biological mutation — used chiefly of intracellular agents; compare MUTAGENIC

mu·tage \ˈmyüd·ij\ *n* -S [F, fr. *muter* to check fermentation (prob. fr. *muet* mute) + *-age* — more at MUTE] **:** the checking of fermentation (as by adding alcohol) in the must of grapes

mu·ta·gen \ˈmyüd·əjən, -,jen\ *n* -S [ISV *mutation* + *-gen*] **:** an agent (as mustard gas, various radiations, or possibly some viruses) that tends to increase the occurrence or extent of mutation

mu·ta·gen·e·sis \,myüd·əˈjenəsəs\ *n* [NL, fr. ISV *mutation* + NL *genesis*] **:** the occurrence or induction of mutation

mu·ta·gen·ic \ˈ≈≈ˈjenik\ *adj* **:** capable of inducing mutation — used chiefly of extracellular agents (as chemicals or X ray); compare MUTAFACIENT — **mu·ta·gen·i·cal·ly** \-nək(ə)lē\ *adv*

mu·ta·kal·li·mun \mü,tä,kaləˈmün\ *n pl* [Ar *mutakallimūna*] **:** scholastic theologians of Islam — compare KALAM

mu·tan·kiang \ˈmü,dänjēˈäŋ\ *adj, usu cap* [fr. *Mutankiang*, Manchuria] **:** of or from the city of Mutankiang, Manchuria **:** of the kind or style prevalent in Mutankiang

¹**mu·tant** \ˈmyütᵊnt\ *adj* [L *mutant-, mutans*, pres. part. of *mutare* to change — more at MISS] **:** of, relating to, or produced by mutation ⟨a ~ gene⟩

²**mutant** \"\ *n* -S **:** a mutant individual

mu·ta·rotate \ˈmyüd·ə+\ *vi* [back-formation fr. *mutarotation*] **:** to undergo mutarotation

mu·ta·rotation \"+\ *n* [L *mutare* to change + E *rotation*] **:** a change in optical rotation shown by various solutions on standing as a result of chemical change (as of alpha-D-glucose into an equilibrium mixture containing both alpha- and beta-D-glucose)

mutasarrif *var of* MUTESSARIF

mu·tase \ˈmyü,tās, -āz\ *n* -S [ISV *mut-* (fr. L *mutare* to change) + *-ase*] **1 :** an enzyme regarded as able to catalyze a dismutation (as of acetaldehyde to alcohol and acetic acid) **2 :** any of various enzymes (as phosphoglucomutase) that catalyze molecular rearrangements — compare ISOMERASE

¹**mu·tate** \ˈmyü,tāt, ≈ˈ≈\ *vb* [L *mutatus*, past part. of *mutare* to change — more at MISS] **:** to undergo or cause to undergo mutation

²**mutate** *n* -S **1 :** MUTANT **2 :** a word form with mutated vowel

mu·ta·tion \myüˈtāshən\ *n* -S [ME *mutacioun*, fr. MF *mutation*, fr. L *mutation-, mutatio*, fr. *mutatus* + *-ion-, -io* -ion] **1 :** a major change **:** a significant and basic alteration ⟨changes are not all gradual; they culminate in sudden ~*s* —John Dewey⟩ **2 a** *in medieval solmization* **:** the change from one hexachord to another involving a change of syllable for a given musical tone **b :** MUTATION STOP **3 a** (1) **:** any of several changes undergone by stops in Celtic languages because of their phonetic surroundings (2) **:** the phonetic changes that some initial consonants in Celtic languages undergo under certain sandhi conditions **b :** UMLAUT **4 a :** a hypothetical sudden fundamental change in heredity believed to result in the production of new individuals that are basically unlike their parents and that can be acted upon by natural selection to fix desirable changes and establish new species — compare DARWINISM, EVOLUTION, MACROEVOLUTION, SALTATION **b :** a relatively permanent change in hereditary material other than one brought about by Mendelian recombination of factors involving either a physical change in chromosome relations (as in polyploidy, nondisjunction, or deficiency) or a fundamental change in genes and occurring either in germ cells or in somatic cells but with only those in germ cells being capable of perpetuation by sexual reproduction — see GENE MUTATION, SOMATIC MUTATION **c** (1) **:** an individual or strain resulting from mutation — compare FREAK 3b (2) **:** an animal (as a mink) of a domesticated strain which differs esp. in coat color from typical animals of the wild type and whose difference is maintained by selective breeding; *also* **:** the coat color of such an animal — compare COLOR PHASE **5 :** one of a series of palaeontologic stages that are comparable to subspecies and that occur in the temporal succession of a line of fossils in successive horizons

mu·ta·tion·al \(ˈ)myüˈtāshənᵊl, -shnəl\ *adj* **:** of or relating to mutation — **mu·ta·tion·al·ly** \-ᵊlē, -əl|, |i\ *adv*

mu·ta·tion·ism \≈ˈ≈shə,nizəm\ *n* -S **:** the theory that mutation is a fundamental factor in evolution

mu·ta·tion·ist \-,nəst\ *n* -S **:** a believer in or upholder of mutationism

mutation plural *n* **:** a plural form differing from the singular by a vowel (as in *teeth, mice*)

mutation pressure *n* **:** a hypothetical tendency for biological mutation in one direction to occur disproportionately

mutation stop *n* **:** a pipe-organ stop sounding pitches other than those indicated by the notes or one of their octaves (as a fifth, a twelfth) — compare FOUNDATION STOP

mu·ta·tis mu·tan·dis \mü,täd·əsmüˈtändəs, myü,tad·əsmyüˈtan-\ *adv* [L] **1 :** with the necessary changes having been made **2 :** with the respective differences having been considered

mu·ta·tive \ˈmyüd·əd·iv\ *adj* [L *mutatus* + E *-ive*] **1 :** of, relating to, or marked by mutation **2 :** expressive of change **:** passing from one place or state into another **:** FACTIVE ⟨~ verbs like *fall, rise, melt*⟩

mu·ta·wal·li \ˈmüd·əwəˈlē\ *n* -S [Ar *mutawallī* one entrusted with something] **:** the trustee of a waqf (as a religious building)

mu·'ta·zi·la *also* **mu·'ta·zi·lah** \mü'tälzələ\ *n* -s *usu cap* [Ar *mu'tazilah* body of seceders] **:** the Mu'tazilite school
mu·'ta·zi·lism *or* **mu·ta·zi·lism** \-ˌlizəm\ *n* -s *usu cap* **:** the theological doctrines and methods of the Mu'tazilites
mu·'ta·zi·lite *or* **mu·ta·zi·lite** \-ˌlīt\ *n* -s *usu cap* [Ar *mu'tazilah* + E *-ite*] **1 :** a Muslim philosophical school founded in the 8th century A.D. emphasizing reason in religious interpretation, free will in opposition to predestination, and the unity and justice of Allah **2 :** a member of the Mu'tazilite school
mutch \'məch\ *n* -ES [ME (Sc dial.) *much*, fr. MD *mutse* cap, fr. ML *almutia* amice] *chiefly Scot* **:** a close-fitting cap (as of linen or muslin) often worn by old women or babies
mutch·kin \-kən\ *n* -s [ME (Sc) *muchekyn*] **:** a Scotch unit of liquid capacity equal to 0.90 pint
¹mute \'myüt, *usu* -üd·+V\ *adj* -ER/-EST [alter. (influenced by L *mutus*) of ME *muet, mewet*, fr. MF *muet*, fr. OF *mu*, fr. L *mutus;* akin to OHG *māwen* to cry out, shriek, Norw *mua* to be silent, Gk *mykos, mytis* mute, Skt *mūka;* basic meaning: inarticulate sound] **1 :** characterized by the inability to speak; *specif* **:** unable to utter articulate sounds as a result of never having heard speech sounds **2 :** characterized by absence of speech: as **a :** unable for a limited time to speak (as from astonishment, grief, shock, or other strong emotion) **b :** felt or experienced but not expressed ⟨gave him her hand with ~ thanks —George Meredith⟩ **c** *of a person arraigned by law* **:** making no answer, maintaining silence, or refusing to plead directly or stand trial — usu. used with *stand* **3 :** not giving tongue when hunting **:** SILENT — used of a hound **4 a** *of a coin* **:** devoid of inscription or means of identification other than heraldic or symbolical devices **b** *of a mineral* **:** not giving a ringing sound when struck **5 a** *of a written or printed character* (1) **:** contributing nothing to the pronunciation of a word (as *b* in *plumb* or the second *e* in *every* as it is usu. pronounced) (2) **:** contributing to the pronunciation of a word but not representing the nucleus of a syllable (as the *e* in *mate* which produces \māt\ instead of \mat\) **b** *of the e in French* **:** having no counterpart in the pronunciation in some environments or styles of utterance but pronounced \ə\ in other environments or styles of utterance (as *e* in *cheval* which is sometimes pronounced \shvȧl\ and sometimes \shəvȧl\) **syn** see DUMB
²mute \"\ *n* -s **1 a :** one that does not speak (as from physical inability or unwillingness) **b** *archaic* **:** a person whose part in a play does not require him to speak **c :** one hired to attend a funeral as a mourner **2 :** STOP 9 — used esp. in the study of Greek and Latin **3 :** a device on a musical instrument serving to reduce, soften, or muffle its tone: as **a :** a metal, ivory, or wood clamp that can be attached to the bridge of a bowed stringed instrument **b :** a cone or cylinder or pad inserted in the bell of a wind instrument — compare SORDINE **c :** one of the dampers of a piano action

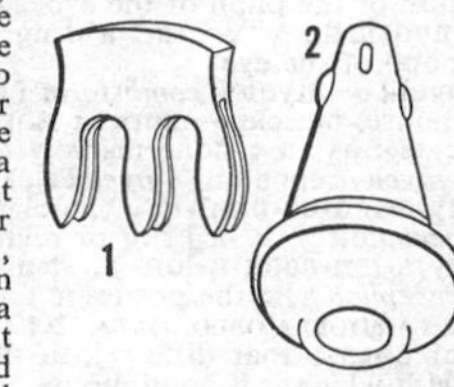

mutes 3: *1* for violin, *2* for trumpet

³mute \"\ *vt* -ED/-ING/-S **1 :** to muffle or reduce the sound of (as by a mute) **2 :** to subdue or tone down (a color)
⁴mute \"\ *vi* -ED/-ING/-S [ME *muten*, fr. MF *meutir*, short for *esmeutir*, fr. OF *esmeltir*, of Gmc origin; akin to MD *smelten* to melt, defecate (used of birds)] *of a bird* **:** DEFECATE
⁵mute \"\ *n* -s **:** the excrement of a bird
⁶mute *vi* -ED/-ING/-S [prob. fr. L *muttire* to mutter — more at MUTTER] *obs Scot* **:** COMPLAIN
mut·ed \'myüd·əd, -ütəd\ *adj* **1 :** being mute **:** SPEECHLESS, SILENT **2 :** provided with, produced by means of, or modified through the presence of a mute
mut·ed·ly *adv* **:** in a muted manner
mute·ly *adv* [¹*mute* + *-ly*] **:** in a mute manner
mute·ness *n* -ES **:** the quality or state of being mute
mute of malice *Eng law* **:** the silence assumed by a prisoner able to plead a felony but refusing to do so and thereby formerly exposing himself to the penalty of torture and death
¹muter *comparative of* MUTE
²mu·ter \mü'ter\ *n, pl* **muter** *or* **muters** *usu cap* **1 :** a nomadic Bedouin people in Arabia **2 :** a member of the Muter people
mu·tes·sar·if *also* **mu·ta·sar·rif** \ˌmüd·ə'sarəf\ *n* -s [Turk *mutasarrif*, fr. Ar *mutaṣarrif*] **:** an administrative authority of various sanjaks (as in the Ottoman Empire or in Iraq)
mutest *superlative of* MUTE
mute swan *n* **:** the common white swan (*Cygnus olor*) of Europe and western Asia that produces no loud notes
muth *var of* MATH
muth·mann·ite \'müt(h)məˌnīt\ *n* -s [G *muthmannit*, fr. F. W. *Muthmann* †1913 Ger. chemist + G *-it* -ite] **:** a silver gold telluride (Ag, Au)Te
mu·ti \'müd·ē, 'müd·ē\ *n* -s [Zulu *umu ti* tree, shrub, herb, medicine] *Africa* **:** MEDICINE
mu·tic \'myüd·ik\ *adj* [L *muticus* curtailed, docked — more at MUTILATE] **1 :** lacking the usu. defensive parts (as teeth or claws) **2 :** MUTICATE
mu·ti·ca \'myüd·əkə\ [NL, fr. L, neut. pl. of *muticus* docked] *syn of* CETACEA
mu·ti·cate \-d·əˌkāt, -d·əkət\ *also* **mu·ti·cous** \-d·əkəs\ *adj* [*muticate* fr. L *muticus* docked + E *-ate; muticous* fr. L *muticus*] **:** growing without an awn or point
¹mu·ti·late \'myüd·ᵊlˌāt, -ütᵊl,-, *usu* -ād·+V\ *adj* [L *mutilatus*, past part.] **1 :** MUTILATED **2 a :** having no hind limbs ⟨a ~ cetacean⟩ **b :** ABBREVIATED — used of the elytra of an insect
²mutilate \"\ *vt* -ED/-ING/-S [L *mutilatus*, past part. of *mutilare*, fr. *mutilus* mutilated, maimed; akin to L *muticus* docked, OIr *mut* short] **1 :** to cut off or permanently destroy a limb or essential part of ⟨a ~ a body⟩ ⟨~ a statue⟩; *sometimes* **:** CASTRATE **2 :** to cut up or alter radically so as to make imperfect ⟨~ a medieval manuscript⟩ **syn** see MAIM
³mutilate *n* -s [NL *Mutilata*, a former group of mammals comprising the whales and sirenians, fr. L, neut. pl. of *mutilatus*] *obs* **:** CETACEAN, SIRENIAN
mu·ti·la·tion \ˌmyüd·ᵊl'āshən, -ütᵊl'-\ *n* -s [LL *mutilation-, mutilatio*, fr. L *mutilatus* + *-ion-, -io* -ion] **1 :** deprivation of a limb or essential part esp. by excision ⟨the ~ of a body⟩ **2 :** an instance of mutilating
mu·ti·la·tive \'myüd·ᵊlˌād·iv\ *also* **mu·ti·la·to·ry** \-ᵊlə,tōrē\ *adj* **:** of or relating to mutilation ⟨a ~ deed⟩
mu·ti·la·tor \'myüd·ᵊlˌād·ə(r), -ütᵊl,-, -ātə-\ *n* -s **:** one that mutilates
mu·til·la \myü'tilə\ *n, cap* [NL, irreg. fr. L *mutilus* mutilated — more at MUTILATE] **:** a genus of parasitic wasps having wingless females — compare VELVET ANT
¹mu·til·lid \-ləd\ *adj* [NL *Mutillidae*] **:** of or relating to the Mutillidae
²mutillid \"\ *n* -s **:** a wasp of the family Mutillidae **:** VELVET ANT
mu·til·li·dae \-ləˌdē\ *n pl, cap* [NL, fr. *Mutilla*, type genus + *-idae*] **:** a family of wasps of which *Mutilla* is the type genus
mutilous *adj* [L *mutilus* — more at MUTILATE] *obs* **:** MUTILATED, DEFECTIVE, IMPERFECT
¹mutine *vb* -ED/-ING/-S [MF *(se) mutiner* to rebel, *mutiner* to incite to rebellion, fr. *mutin* insubordinate, mutinous, fr. *meute* revolt, fr. (assumed) VL *movita*, fr. fem. of *movitus*, alter. of L *motus*, past part. of *movēre* to move — more at MOVE] *vi, obs* **:** REBEL, MUTINY ~ *vt, obs* **:** to urge to rebel
²mutine *n* -s [MF *mutin*, fr. *mutin*, adj.] **1** *obs* **:** MUTINY **2** *obs* **:** MUTINEER
¹mu·ti·neer \ˌmyütᵊn'iə(r), -iə\ *n* -s [MF *mutinier*, fr. *mutin* mutiny + *-ier* -eer] **:** one that mutinies
²mutineer \"\ *vi* -ED/-ING/-S *archaic* **:** MUTINY
muting *pres part of* MUTE
muting switch *n* **:** a record changer switch which shuts off the phonograph pickup during the record changing cycle
mu·ti·nize \'myütᵊnˌīz\ *vi* -ED/-ING/-S [²*mutine* + *-ize*] *archaic* **:** MUTINY
mu·ti·nous \-ᵊnəs\ *adj* [²*mutine* + *-ous*] **1 a :** disposed to or in a state of mutiny **:** REBELLIOUS ⟨a ~ crew⟩ **b :** TURBULENT, UNRULY ⟨~ passions⟩ **2 :** constituting or characterized by mutiny ⟨~ acts⟩ **:** expressive of an inclination or readiness to mutiny ⟨~ thoughts⟩ **:** inciting mutiny ⟨a ~ speech⟩ **syn** see INSUBORDINATE
mu·ti·nous·ly *adv* **:** in a mutinous manner
mu·ti·nous·ness *n* -ES **:** the quality or state of being mutinous
¹mu·ti·ny \'myüt(ᵊ)nē, -ni\ *n* -ES [¹*mutine* + *-y*] **1** *obs* **:** violent commotion **:** TUMULT, STRIFE **2 :** insurrection against or willful refusal to obey constituted, recognized, or traditional authority **:** forcible or passive resistance to existing authority ⟨a colonial ~⟩; *specif* **:** concerted revolt against the rules of discipline or the lawful commands of a superior officer **syn** see REBELLION
²mutiny \"\ *vb* -ED/-ING/-S *vi* **1 a :** to rise against or refuse to obey or observe authority; *specif* **:** to rebel against military authority **b :** to be guilty of mutiny **2 :** to turn against one's group without warning ⟨the extreme left wing *mutinied* just before the election⟩ ~ *vt, archaic* **:** to incite to mutiny
mu·ti·sia \myü'tizh(ē)ə\ *n, cap* [NL, fr. José C. *Mutis* †1808 Sp. naturalist + NL *-ia*] **:** a large genus of So. American often climbing shrubs (family Compositae) having large heads of pistillate flowers with plumose pappus
mut·ism \'myüd·ˌizəm\ *n* -s [F *mutisme*, fr. L *mutus* mute, + F *-isme* -ism — more at MUTE] **:** the condition of being mute: as **a :** inability to speak whether from physical or functional cause **b :** a condition of persistent failure to speak in the absence of evident direct cause (as in mental disease)
mu·trie yellow \'mü·trē-\ *n, often cap M* [prob. fr. the name *Mutrie*] **:** CADMIUM LEMON
muts *pl of* MUT
mut·sud·dy \(')mùt'sədi\ *n* -ES [Hindi *mutaṣaddī*, fr. Ar] **:** a native accountant or clerk in British India
mutt *also* **mut** \'mət, *usu* -əd·+V\ *n* -s [short for *muttonhead*] **1 :** a stupid or commonplace person **2 :** a mongrel dog **:** CUR
¹mut·ter \'məd·ə(r), -ətə-\ *vb* **muttered; muttered; muttering** \-əd·əriŋ, -ətər-, -ə·tr-\ **mutters** [ME *muteren;* akin to Norw dial. *mutra* to mutter, OHG *mutilōn* to murmer, ON *muthla*, L *muttire* to mutter, *mutus* mute — more at MUTE] *vi* **1 :** to utter indistinctly or with a low voice and lips partly closed ⟨~s just before dying⟩ **2 :** to murmur complainingly or angrily **:** GRUMBLE, GROWL ⟨a ~*ing* group of workers⟩ **3 :** to make a low rumbling sound **:** murmur continuously or rumblingly ⟨forest noises ~*ing*⟩ ~ *vt* **1 :** to utter esp. in a low or imperfectly articulated manner ⟨~ an answer⟩ **2 :** to sound reverberatingly ⟨a fog horn ~*ing* danger⟩
²mutter \"\ *n* -s **1 :** a subdued scarcely audible utterance ⟨the ~ of an audience⟩ **2 :** a low continuous sound ⟨the ~ of surf⟩
mut·ter·er \-ərə(r)\ *n* -s **:** one that mutters
mut·ter·ing·ly *adv* **:** in a muttering manner
mut·ton \'mətᵊn\ *n* -s [ME *motoun*, fr. OF *moton, mouton* ram, wether, agnel, of Celt origin; akin to MIr *molt* wether, MBret *mout*, W *mollt:* prob. akin to L *molere* to grind — more at MEAL] **1 a :** the flesh of a mature ovine animal when killed for food **b :** the dressed carcass of a sheep usu. one year of age or older characterized by the dark red color of the flesh, whiteness of the fat, and hardness of the bone **2 :** AGNEL **3 :** the matter at hand **:** the central issue — usu. used in pl. ⟨now I must get to my ~s and write —H.J.Laski⟩
muttonbird \'==,=\ *n* **:** any of several Australasian sea birds often used (as by the Maori) for their meat, oil, and feathers: as **a** (1) **:** a short-tailed shearwater (*Puffinus tenuirostris*) of Australia and New Zealand (2) **:** a sooty shearwater (*Puffinus griseus*) of New Zealand **b :** any of several petrels (as *Pterodroma macroptera, P. lessoni*, and *P. neglecta*)
muttonchops \'==,=\ *also* **muttonchop whiskers** *n pl* [so called fr. the shape] **:** side-whiskers that are narrow at the temple and broad and round by the lower jaws

muttonchops

mutton corn *n, chiefly South* **:** sweet corn that is just ripe enough to be eaten **:** ROASTING EARS
muttonfish \'==,=\ *n* [so called fr. its flavor] **1 :** a snapper (*Lutjanus analis*) of the warmer parts of the western Atlantic that is usu. olive green and sometimes nearly white or tinged with rosy red and that is an excellent food and sport fish **2 :** an eelpout (*Zoarces anguillaris*) of the northerly eastern coastal waters of No. America **3** *also* **mutton shell** *Austral* **:** ABALONE
mutton fist *n* **1 :** a large brawny fist or hand **2** *archaic* **:** FIST-NOTE
mutton grass *also* **mutton bluegrass** *n* **:** a bluegrass (*Poa fendleriana*) of drier parts of the western U.S. used as forage
mutton ham *n* **1** *chiefly Scot* **:** a leg of mutton cured like a ham **2** *Midland* **:** a large sail on a fishing boat
muttonhead \'==,=\ *n* **:** a dull-witted person **:** OAF — **mut·ton·head·ed** \'==|==\ *adj*
mutton quad *n* [*mutton* so called fr. its use as a code word to distinguish pronounced *em quad* fr. *en quad*] **:** EM QUAD
mutton snapper *n* **:** MUTTONFISH 1
mut·tony \'mət(ᵊ)nē, -ni\ *adj* **1 :** suggesting mutton ⟨a ~ taste⟩ **2 a** *of a sheep* **:** having conformation suitable for production of meat **b** *of lamb meat* **:** coarse in texture and flavor
mutua *pl of* MUTUUM
mu·tu·al \'myüch(ə)wəl, -chəl\ *adj* [ME *mutuall*, fr. MF *mutuel*, fr. L *mutuus* lent, borrowed, reciprocal, mutual + MF *-el* -al; akin to L *mutare* to change — more at MISS] **1 a :** entertained, proffered, or exerted by each with respect to the other of two or to each of the others of a group **:** given and received in equal amount ⟨~ love⟩ **b :** having the same feelings one for the other ⟨~ enemies⟩ ⟨~ lovers⟩ **c :** shared in common **:** enjoyed by each **:** COMMON ⟨a ~ friend⟩ ⟨a ~ hobby⟩ **d :** possessed, experienced, or done by two or more persons or things at the same time **:** JOINT ⟨~ effort⟩ ⟨~ advantage⟩ **2 :** characterized by or suggestive of intimacy or familiarity ⟨~ contacts⟩ **3 :** belonging to each of two or more associates **:** RESPECTIVE ⟨~ property⟩ **4 :** of or relating to a plan whereby the members of an organization share in the profits, benefits, expenses, and liabilities; *specif* **:** of, relating to, or taking the form of a method or plan in insurance in which the policyholders constitute the members of the insuring company or association, elect their own managers or directors, and share in the profits and in which assessments may or may not be provided for — compare INSURANCE 2b **syn** see RECIPROCAL
mutual aid *n* **:** reciprocal aid and cooperation as among men in social groups
mutual aid association *n* **1 :** an organization whose purpose is not primarily to distribute earnings to its members but to assist, benefit, or protect them in some common matters or objectives **:** a beneficial association **2 :** BENEFIT SOCIETY
mutual benefit society *n* **:** BENEFIT SOCIETY
mutual conductance *n* **:** the quotient of a change in plate current in an electron tube by the change in grid voltage producing it, the plate voltage remaining unchanged
mutual fund *n* **:** an open-end investment company that invests money of its shareholders in a usu. diversified group of securities of other corporations
mutual gable *or* **mutual wall** *n, Scots law* **:** PARTY WALL
mutual inductance *n* **:** the measure of the inductance between two circuits or parts thereof
mutual induction *n* **:** the induction produced on each other by two adjacent circuits **:** the induction produced in charged conductors adjacent to each other
mutual inductor *n* **:** a device providing mutual inductance and usu. consisting of two inductance coils not connected by conductors
mutual investment company *or* **mutual investment trust** *n* **:** an investment company that has a variable number of shares outstanding and that is ready at any time to issue or redeem shares at or near current liquidating value
mu·tu·al·ism \'myüch(ə)wəˌlizəm, -chəˌl-\ *n* -s **1 a :** the doctrine or practice of mutual dependence as the condition of individual and social welfare **b :** a socialistic theory advocating a social organization based on common ownership, effort, and control and regulated by sentiments of mutual help and brotherhood **2 a :** mutually beneficial association between different kinds of organisms (as between various ants and aphids); *esp* **:** interaction between organisms of two kinds whereby a shared way of life becomes obligatory for both if the population of each is to increase — compare PREDATION **b :** the supposed factor or principle of mutual aid and cooperation among men and the lower animals
mu·tu·al·ist \-ləst\ *n* -s **1 :** an advocate of mutualism **2 :** one (as a commensal animal) that exists in a state of mutualism — **mu·tu·al·is·tic** \¦=(=)=¦listik\ *adj*
mu·tu·al·i·ty \ˌmyüchə'waləd·ē, -lətē, -i\ *n* -ES **1 :** the quality or state of being mutual **:** quality of reciprocity **:** INTERCHANGE, INTERACTION, INTERDEPENDENCE **2 a :** a sharing of sentiments between persons **:** interchange of kind acts or expressions
mu·tu·al·ization \ˌmyüch(ə)wələ'zāshən, -chəl-, -ˌlī'z-\ *n* -s **:** the act or action of making or becoming mutual
mu·tu·al·ize \'=(=)=ˌlīz\ *vt* -ED/-ING/-S [*mutual* + *-ize*] **1 :** to make mutual **2 :** to convert (a corporation) into a mutual plan by purchase and retirement of its stocks
mutual loan association *n* **:** SAVINGS AND LOAN ASSOCIATION
mu·tu·al·ly \'myüchəlē, -ch(ə)wəlē, -li\ *adv* **:** in a mutual manner
mu·tu·al·ness *pronunc at* MUTUAL + nəs\ *n* -ES **:** the quality or state of being mutual
mutual savings bank *n* **:** a bank organized without stock which receives savings deposits and whose earnings accrue entirely to the benefit of its depositors
mutual wills *n pl* **:** wills pursuant to agreement between and made by two or more persons that contain similar or identical testamentary provisions in favor of each other or of the same beneficiary — called also *reciprocal wills*
mu·tu·ary \'myüchəˌwerē\ *n* -ES [L *mutuarius* mutual, in exchange, fr. *mutuus* borrowed, lent + *-arius* -ary — more at MUTUAL] *Roman & civil law* **:** the borrower in a contract of mutuum
mutuate *vt* -ED/-ING/-S [L *mutuatus*, past part. of *mutuari* to borrow, fr. *mutuus* borrowed, lent] *obs* **:** BORROW — **mutuation** *n* -s *obs*
mu·tu·a·ti·tious \ˌmyüchəwə'tishəs\ *adj* [L *mutuaticius*, fr. *mutuatus* + *-icius* -itious — more at MUTUATE] *archaic* **:** BORROWED
mu·tu·el \'myüch(ə)wəl, -chəl\ *n* -s *often attrib* [by shortening] **:** PARI-MUTUEL
mu·tu·lar \'myüchələ(r)\ *or* **mu·tu·lary** \-ˌlerē\ *adj* **:** of or relating to the Doric order whose cornices bear mutules rather than dentils
mu·tule \-(ˌ)chül\ *n* -s [L *mutulus*] **:** a flat block projecting under the corona of the Doric cornice in the same position as the modillion of other orders — compare GUTTA
mu·tu·um \-ˌchəwəm\ *n, pl* **mu·tua** \-wə\ [ME, fr. L, fr. neut. of *mutuus* borrowed, lent — more at MUTUAL] **:** a loan in Roman and civil law of fungible things to be restored in similar property of the same quantity and quality; *also* **:** a contract in which movables are so loaned
muu·muu \'mü(ˌ)mü\ *n* -s [Hawaiian *mu'u mu'u*, lit., cut-off; fr. the yoke's having formerly been omitted] **:** a loose dress worn chiefly in Hawaii, having gay colors and patterns, and adapted from the dresses orig. distributed by missionaries to the native women
mu·vu·le *also* **mu·vu·li** *or* **mvu·le** *or* **mvu·li** \mə'vü(ˌ)lē\ *n* -s [native name in Africa] **:** IROKO
¹mux \'məks\ *vt* -ED/-ING/-ES [prob. back-formation fr. *mucksy*] *chiefly NewEng* **:** to put in disorder **:** make a mess of
²mux \"\ *n* -ES *chiefly NewEng* **:** a state of disorder **:** MESS
mu·yu·sa \mü'yüsə\ *n* -s [AmerSp] **:** the white-fleshed edible fruit of a stout cylindrical cactus (*Borzicactus sepium*) of Ecuador
mu·zhik *or* **mu·zjik** *or* **mu·jik** *or* **mou·jik** \(')mü¦zhik, -zhēk\ *n* -s [Russ *muzhik* peasant, dim. of *muzh* man, husband; fr. the fact that under old Russian law peasants were regarded as minors; akin to OSlav *mǫžĭ* man, OE *man* — more at MAN] **:** a Russian peasant
¹muzz \'məz\ *vt* -ED/-ING/-ES [back-formation fr. *muzzy*] *Brit* **:** to make muzzy
²muzz \"\ *n* -ES *Brit* **:** MUDDLE
muz·zi·ly \'məzəlē, -li\ *adv* **:** in a muzzy manner
muz·zi·ness \-zēnəs, -zin-\ *n* -ES **:** the quality or state of being muzzy
¹muz·zle \'məzəl\ *n* -s [ME *musell, mosel*, fr. MF *musel*, dim. of *muse* snout, muzzle, mouth of an animal, fr. ML *musus*] **1 a :** the projecting jaws and nose of an animal (as a horse or dog) **:** SNOUT — see COW illustration **b :** the human face or mouth **2 a :** a fastening or covering (as a band or cage) for the mouth of an animal used to prevent eating or biting **b :** something that restricts, censors, or otherwise circumscribes natural or normal expression ⟨a dictator's ~ on the popular press⟩ **3 :** the open end of an implement; *esp* **:** the end of a weapon from which the projectile emerges — see CANNON illustration **4** *archaic* **:** the clevis of a plow

muzzle 2a

²muzzle \"\ *vb* **muzzled; muzzled; muzzling** \-z(ə)liŋ\ **muzzles** *vi, dial chiefly Eng* **:** to push or root about with the muzzle ~ *vt* **1 :** to bind the muzzle of ⟨~ a dog⟩ **2 :** to restrain from expression (as by speech or action) **:** GAG ⟨~ freedom of speech⟩ **3 :** to press or rub with the muzzle or snout **:** NUZZLE **4 :** to take in (sail)
muzzlebag \'==,=\ *n* **:** a cover for the muzzle (as of a naval gun) used to keep out rain and spray and made usu. of canvas
muzzle blast *n* **:** an excessively loud report produced by a gun often having a barrel shorter than standard or using a powder charge greater than standard and usu. attributed to powder exploding both within and without the barrel as well as to the impact of gases on the outside atmosphere; *also* **:** the flash or flame at the muzzle accompanying such a report
muzzle brake *n* **:** a device attached to the muzzle of a gun tube that utilizes escaping gases to reduce the force of recoil — compare COMPENSATOR
muzzle device *n* **:** a device fixed to the muzzle of a shotgun to act as a muzzle brake and usu. to allow a selection of chokes
muzzle energy *n* **:** the energy of impact of a bullet at the velocity developed at the muzzle of the piece and calculated according to the formula

$$ME = \frac{V^2}{7000} \div 2g \times w$$

where ME represents muzzle energy in foot-pounds, V^2 the square of the muzzle velocity in feet per second, g the acceleration due to gravity, and w the weight of the bullet in grains avoirdupois
muzzle–loader \'==¦==\ *n* **:** a muzzle-loading firearm
muzzle–loading \'==¦==\ *adj, of a firearm* **:** receiving the cartridge or projectile at the muzzle
muz·zler \'məz(ə)lə(r)\ *n* -s **1 :** one that muzzles **2 :** a head-on wind
muzzle ring *n* **:** a ring or ringlike projection near the muzzle of a piece
muzzle velocity *n* **:** the speed of a projectile at the moment of leaving the muzzle of a gun
muzzlewood \'==,=\ *n* **:** BLACK SALLY
muz·zy \'məzē, -zi\ *adj* -ER/-EST [perh. blend of *muddled* and *fuzzy*] **1 :** muddled or confused in mind **:** DULL ⟨men ~ with drink⟩ **2 :** DULL, DEPRESSING ⟨a ~ day⟩; *also* **:** BLURRED ⟨a ~ brain⟩
mv *abbr* millivolt
MV *abbr* **1** main verb **2** market value **3** mean variation **4** medium voltage **5** merchant vessel **6** methyl violet **7** million volts **8** motor vessel **9** muzzle velocity
Mv *symbol* mendelevium
MVC *abbr* manual volume control
mvt *abbr* movement
mw *abbr* milliwatt
MW *abbr* **1** mixed widths **2** most worshipful **3** most worthy **4** music wire
Mw *abbr* megawatt
mwa·mi \mə'wämē\ *n* -s [native name in Africa] **:** the native ruler or king of Ruanda-Urundi, Africa
MWG *abbr* music-wire gauge
mwh *abbr* megawatt-hour
MWP *abbr* maximum working pressure
mx *abbr* **1** maxwell **2** multiplex
mxd *abbr* mixed
¹my [ME *my, mi, min*, fr. OE *mīn*, suppletive gen. of *ic* I] *obs possessive of* ²I
²my \(ˈ)mī, ˌmə\ *adj* [ME *my, mi, min*, fr. OE *mīn*, fr. *mīn*, suppletive gen. of *ic* I — more at MINE] **1 a :** of or belonging

to me or myself as possessor : due to me : inherent in me : associated or connected with me ⟨bumped ~ head⟩ ⟨defending ~ rights⟩ ⟨all ~ relatives⟩ **b** : of or relating to me or myself as author, doer, giver, or agent : effected by me : experienced by me as subject : that I am capable of ⟨criticized all ~ words and actions⟩ ⟨kept ~ promise⟩ ⟨was angry because of ~ being late⟩ ⟨did ~ very best⟩ **c** : of or relating to me as object of an action : experienced by me as object ⟨expected ~ election as secretary⟩ ⟨~ injuries didn't amount to much⟩ **d** : that I have to do with or am believed to possess or to have knowledge or a share of or some special interest in ⟨I like golf and I know ~ game⟩ **e** : that is esp. significant for me : that brings me good fortune or prominence — used with *day* or sometimes with other words indicating a division of time ⟨today was really ~ day: everything went fine⟩ **2 a** — used with a noun of address to express endearment ⟨tell me, ~ little sister⟩ or jocularity ⟨I see you're stepping out, ~ boy⟩ or familiarity ⟨come along, ~ man⟩ or compassion ⟨~ poor fellow⟩ **b** — used esp. with *lord* or *lady* functioning as a noun of address to express special deference or submission ⟨I'll obey your command, ~ lord⟩ **c** — used interjectionally to express surprise and sometimes reduplicated ⟨~, ~⟩ ⟨~ oh ~⟩; used also interjectionally with names of various parts of the body to express doubt or disapproval ⟨~ foot⟩ ⟨~ eye⟩; used also as an intensive in oaths ⟨oh ~ lord⟩

my- *or* **myo-** *comb form* [NL, fr. Gk, fr. *mys* — more at MOUSE] **1** : mouse ⟨*myo*morpha⟩ **2 a** : muscle ⟨*my*ology⟩ : muscle and ⟨*myo*elastic⟩ **b** : myoma and — with words ending in *-oma* ⟨*myo*fibroma⟩

my *abbr* **1** muddy **2** myopia

MY *abbr* motor yacht

mya \ˈmīə\ *n, cap* [NL, fr. L, mussel, irreg. fr. Gk *myax* — more at MUREX] : a genus (the type of the family Myacidae) of bivalve mollusks including the common soft-shell clam — see MYACEA

-mya \ˈmīə\ *n pl comb form* [NL, fr. Gk *mys* mouse, muscle] : creatures having such, so many, or so arranged musculature — in higher taxa of mollusks ⟨*Dimya*⟩ ⟨*Heteromya*⟩

my·a·cea \mīˈāshēə\ *n pl, cap* [NL, fr. *Mya* + *-acea*] : a suborder of Eulamellibranchia that comprises bivalve mollusks with well-developed siphons, gaping valves, and a pallial sinus and includes various economically important edible mollusks (as of the genus *Mya*) — see MYACIDAE

my·ac·i·dae \mīˈasəˌdē\ *n pl, cap* [NL, fr. *Myac-, Mya*, type genus + *-idae*] : a family of marine bivalve mollusks (suborder Myacea) comprising the soft-shell clams

my·al \ˈmīəl\ *adj* [origin unknown] : of or relating to myalism

my·al·gia \mīˈalj(ē)ə\ *n* -s [NL, fr. *my-* + *-algia*] : pain in one or more muscles

my·al·gic \-jik\ *adj* [NL *myalgia* + E *-ic*] : characteristic of or affected with myalgia

my·al·ism \ˈmīəˌlizəm\ *n* -s : a cult among West Indian Negroes akin to obeah and prob. of West African origin

¹my·all \ˈmīˌȯl\ *adj* [native name in Australia] *Austral* : WILD, UNCIVILIZED

²myall \"\ *n* -s *often attrib* : an Australian aborigine

³myall \"\ *n* -s [native name in Australia] **1** : any of various Australian acacias with hard fragrant wood: as **a** : WEEPING MYALL **b** : YARRAN 2 **c** : BASTARD MYALL **2** *also* **myall wood** : the hard heavy fine-grained wood of a myall that is used esp. for carving and small articles of fine woodworking

my·an·e·sin \mīˈanəsən\ *n* -s [fr. *Myanesin*, a trademark] : MEPHENESIN

my·ar·ia \mīˈa(a)rēə\ *n pl, cap* [NL, fr. *Mya* + *-aria*] *in some classifications* : a group of marine bivalves nearly equivalent to Myacea

-my·ar·ia \ˌmīˈa(a)rēə, -ˈer-, -ˈār-\ *n pl comb form* [NL, fr. *my-* + *-aria*] : -MYA

my·as·the·nia \ˌmīəsˈthēnēə\ *n* -s [NL, fr. *my-* + *asthenia*] : muscular debility

myasthenia gravis *n* [NL, lit., grave myasthenia] : a disease characterized by progressive weakness and exhaustibility of voluntary muscles without atrophy or sensory disturbance

my·as·then·ic \ˌ≈≈ˈthenik\ *adj* [NL *myasthenia* + E *-ic*] : of, relating to, or characterized by myasthenia

my·a·to·nia \ˌmīəˈtōnēə\ *n* -s [NL, fr. *my-* + LL *atonia* atony — more at ATONY] : lack of muscle tone : muscular flabbiness

myc- *or* **myco-** *comb form* [NL, irreg. fr. Gk *mykēs* fungus, mushroom; akin to Gk *myxa* lampwick, nasal mucus — more at MUCUS] : fungus ⟨*myc*elium⟩ ⟨*myco*biota⟩ ⟨*myco*genetic⟩ ⟨*myc*ology⟩ ⟨*myco*sis⟩; *specif* : mushroom ⟨*myco*phile⟩

my·ce·li·al \mīˈsēlēəl\ *adj* [NL *mycelium* + E *-al*] : of, relating to, or characterized by mycelium

my·ce·lia ste·ri·lia \mīˌsēlēəstəˈrilēə\ *n pl, cap M&S* [NL, lit., sterile mycelia] : a group that is usu. considered more or less equivalent to an order and that comprises genera of imperfect fungi having no known spore stage and producing sclerotia, rhizomorphs, or simply mycelial masses — see OZONIUM, RHIZOCTONIA, SCLEROTIUM

my·ce·li·oid \mīˈsēlēˌȯid\ *adj* [NL *mycelium* + E *-oid*] : resembling mycelium

my·ce·li·um \-lēəm\ *n, pl* **myce·lia** \-ēə\ [NL, fr. *myc-* + Gk *hēlos* nail, wart, callus + NL *-ium*; perh akin to Gk *eilyein* to fold — more at VOLUBLE] : the mass of interwoven hyphae that forms esp. the vegetative portion of the thallus of a fungus and that in the larger forms (as the mushrooms) forms cobwebby filaments penetrating the substrate but in many smaller fungi (as most parasitic forms) is invisible to the naked eye but ramifies through the substrate or tissues of the host usu. producing its spore fruits on the surface; *also* : a similar mass of filaments formed by a higher bacterium

¹my·ce·nae·an \ˌmīsəˈnēən\ *also* **my·ce·ni·an** \mīˈsēnēən\ *adj, usu cap* [*Mycenae*, ancient city of Greece (fr. L, fr. Gk *Mykēnai*) + E *-an* or *-ian*] **1 a** : of, relating to, or characteristic of the ancient city of Mycenae **b** : of, relating to, or characteristic of the people of Mycenae **2 a** : AEGEAN **b** (1) : of, relating to, or characteristic of the period of Mycenae's political ascendancy extending from about 1400 to 1100 B.C. (2) : of, relating to, or characteristic of the Bronze Age culture of the eastern Mediterranean area characterized by objects of Mycenaean style

²mycenaean \"\ *also* **mycenian** \"\ *n* -s *cap* **1** : a native or inhabitant of ancient Mycenae **2** : the early Greek language of the Mycenaeans known from inscriptions

-my·ces \ˈmīˌsēz\ *n comb form* [NL, fr. Gk *mykēs*] : fungus ⟨Actino*myces*⟩ ⟨Phyco*myces*⟩

mycet- *or* **myceto-** *comb form* [ISV, fr. Gk *mykēt-, mykēs* — more at MYC-] : fungus ⟨*myceto*colous⟩ ⟨*myceto*genetic⟩ ⟨*mycet*oma⟩ ⟨*Myceto*zoa⟩

-my·cete \ˈmīˌsēt, ˌmīˈsēt, *usu* -ēd·+V\ *n comb form* -s [NL *-mycetes*] : fungus ⟨micro*mycete*⟩

my·ce·tes \mīˈsēd·ēz\ [NL, fr. Gk *myketēs* one that bellows, fr. *mykasthai* to bellow; akin to MHG *mühen, mügen, müwen* to roar, bellow, L *mutus* mute — more at MUTE] *syn of* ALOUATTA

-my·ce·tes \ˌmīˈsēd·ēz, -ētēz\ *n pl comb form* [NL, fr. Gk *mykētes*, pl. of *mykēt-, mykēs* fungus, mushroom — more at MYC-] : fungi — chiefly in names of classes and subclasses ⟨Asco*mycetes*⟩ ⟨Schizo*mycetes*⟩

my·ce·tism \ˈmīsəˌtizəm\ *n* -s [*mycet-* + *-ism*] : MYCETISMUS

my·ce·tis·mus \ˌmīsəˈtizməs\ *n, pl* **mycetis·mi** \-zˌmī\ [NL, fr. *mycet-* + L *-ismus* -ism] : mushroom poisoning

my·ce·to·cyte \mīˈsēd·əˌsīt\ *n* -s [*mycet-* + *-cyte*] : a cell in various insects (as most true bugs) of a type that contains unicellular and prob. symbiotic fungi and is usu. clustered with others of its kind into paired mycetomes

my·ce·toid \mīˈsēˌtȯid\ *adj* [ISV *mycet-* + *-oid*] : of, relating to, or resembling a fungus : FUNGOID

my·ce·to·ma \ˌmīsəˈtōmə\ *n, pl* **mycetomas** \-məz\ *or* **mycetoma·ta** \-məd·ə\ [NL, fr. *mycet-* + *-oma*] : a condition marked by invasion of the deep subcutaneous tissues with fungi or actinomycetes: **a** : MADUROMYCOSIS **b** : NOCARDIOSIS — **my·ce·tom·a·tous** \ˌ≈≈ˈtäməd·əs, -ˈtōm-\ *adj*

my·ce·tome \ˈmīsəˌtōm\ *n* -s [*mycet-* + *-ome*] : either of a pair of organs in an insect (as a true bug) that consist of a cellular mass of mycetocytes and are located one in either fat body

my·ce·tom·ic \ˌmīsəˈtämik\ *adj* : of, relating to, or occurring in a mycetome ⟨~ yeasts⟩

my·ce·to·phag·i·dae \mīˌsēd·əˈfajəˌdē\ *n pl, cap* [NL, fr. *Mycetophagus*, type genus (fr. *mycet-* + *-phagus*, fr. Gk *phagein* to eat) + *-idae* — more at BAKSHEESH] : a family of small oval usu. hairy beetles having 5-jointed tarsi and generally feeding on fungi

my·ce·toph·a·gous \ˌmīsəˈtäfəgəs\ *adj* [*mycet-* + *-phagous*] : feeding on fungi : FUNGIVOROUS ⟨~ insects are themselves fed upon —Orlando Park⟩

¹my·ce·toph·i·lid \ˌmīsəˈtäfəlˌəd\ *adj* [NL *Mycetophilidae*] : of or relating to the family Mycetophilidae

²mycetophilid \"\ *n* -s [NL *Mycetophilidae*] : a fungus gnat of the family Mycetophilidae

my·ce·to·phil·i·dae \mīˌsēd·əˈfiləˌdē\ *n pl, cap* [NL, fr. *Mycetophila*, type genus (fr. *mycet-* + *-phila*) + *-idae*] : a large widely distributed family of small nematocerous two-winged flies that includes the majority of the fungus gnats — compare SCIARIDAE

my·ce·tous \mīˈsēd·əs\ *adj* [*mycet-* + *-ous*] : of, relating to, or resembling a fungus

my·ce·to·zoa \mīˌsēd·əˈzōə\ *n pl, cap* [NL, fr. *mycet-* + *-zoa*] : the Myxomycetes regarded as an order of rhizopod protozoans

¹my·ce·to·zo·an \-ˌ≈≈ˈzōən\ *adj* [NL *Mycetozoa* + E *-an*] : of or relating to the Mycetozoa

²mycetozoan \"\ *n* -s : MYXOMYCETE

my·ce·to·zo·on \≈ˌ≈≈ˈzōˌän\ *n, pl* **myceto·zoa** \-ōə\ [NL, fr. *mycet-* + *-zoon*] : MYXOMYCETE

-my·cin \ˈmīsᵊn\ *n comb form* -s [ISV *myc-* + *-in*] : substance obtained from a fungus ⟨carbo*mycin*⟩ ⟨erythro*mycin*⟩

myco- — see MYC-

my·co·bac·te·ri·a \ˌmīkōˌbakˈtirēə\ [NL, fr. *myc-* + *bacteria*] *syn of* ACTINOMYCETALES

my·co·bac·te·ri·a·ce·ae \ˌ≈≈ˌtirēˈāsēˌē\ *n pl, cap* [NL, fr. *Mycobacterium*, type genus + *-aceae*] : a family of rod-shaped bacteria (order Actinomycetales) rarely filamentous and with only occasional slight branching

my·co·bac·te·ri·al \ˌ≈≈ˌ≈ˈtirēəl\ *adj* [NL *Mycobacteria* + E *-al*] : of, relating to, or caused by mycobacteria

my·co·bacterium \ˌ≈≈ˌ≈ˈtirēəm\ *n* [NL, fr. *myc-* + *Bacterium*] **1** *cap* : a genus of nonmotile acid-fast aerobic bacteria (family Mycobacteriaceae) that are usu. slender and difficult to stain and that include forms causing tuberculosis and leprosy as well as numerous purely saprophytic forms **2** : any bacterium of *Mycobacterium* or a closely related genus

my·co·cecidium \ˌmīkō+\ *n* [NL, fr. *myc-* + *cecidium*] : a gall produced by the attacks of a parasitic fungus

my·co·cide \ˈmīkəˌsīd\ *n* -s [*myc-* + *-cide*] : a fungicide that destroys molds

my·co·der·ma \ˌmīkəˈdərmə\ *n* [NL, fr. *myc-* + *-derma*] **1** -s **a** : ⁴MOTHER 2 **b** *or* **my·co·derm** \ˈmīkəˌdərm\ : a bacterium or yeast that is a constituent of a mother or flor **2** *cap* : a genus of microorganisms recovered from mothers or flors orig. including a varied assortment of yeasts and acetobacters but now usu. restricted to various yeasts of the family Pseudosaccharomycetaceae that do not form ascospores but grow vegetatively in the presence of air producing a scum on the surface of alcoholic solutions (as wine and beer) — **my·co·der·ma·toid** \ˌmīkəˈdərməˌtȯid\ *adj* — **my·co·der·ma·tous** \-məd·əs\ *adj*

my·co·der·mic \-mik\ *adj* : of or relating to a mycoderm

my·co·flora \ˌmīkō+\ *n* [NL, fr. *myc-* + *flora*] : a flora of fungi — **my·co·floral** \"+\ *adj*

my·co·gone \ˈmīkəˌgōn\ *n, cap* [NL, fr. *myc-* + Gk *gonē* offspring, race, seed, womb, fr. the stem of *gignesthai* to be born — more at KIN] : a form genus of imperfect fungi (family Moniliaceae) having unequally two-celled conidia on short lateral conidiophores — see BUBBLE DISEASE

my·col·ic acid \(ˈ)mīˈkälik-\ *n* [*myc-* + L *oleum* oil + E *-ic* — more at OIL] : any of several hydroxy fatty acids that have very long branched chains and are obtained esp. from the wax of tubercle bacilli

my·co·log·ic \ˌmīkəˈläjik\ *or* **my·co·log·i·cal** \-jəkəl\ *adj* : of or relating to mycology — **my·co·log·i·cal·ly** \-jək(ə)lē\ *adv*

my·col·o·gist \mīˈkäləjəst\ *n* -s : a specialist in mycology

my·col·o·gize \-ləˌjīz\ *vi* -ED/-ING/-S : to study fungi

my·col·o·gy \-jē, -ji\ *n* -ES [NL *mycologia*, fr. *myc-* + L *-logia* -logy] **1** : a branch of botany dealing with fungi **2** : fungal life (as of a region) ⟨the ~ of a swamp⟩ **3** : the properties and life phenomena exhibited by a fungus, fungus type, or fungus group **4** : a treatise on fungi

my·co·my·cete \ˌmīkōˈmīˌsēt, ˌ≈≈ˌ≈ˈ≈\ *n* -s [NL *Mycomycetes*] : one of the Mycomycetes

my·co·my·ce·tes \ˌmīkōˌmīˈsēd·ēz\ *n pl, cap* [NL, fr. *myc-* + *-mycetes*] *in some classifications* : a class of fungi including the Ascomycetes and Basidiomycetes — compare PHYCOMYCETES — **my·co·my·ce·tous** \ˌ≈≈ˌ≈ˈsēd·əs\ *adj*

my·co·mycin \ˌmīkəˈmīsᵊn\ *n* -s [ISV *myc-* + *-mycin*] : a highly unsaturated antibiotic acid $C_{12}H_9COOH$ obtained from an actinomycete (*Nocardia acidophilus*)

my·coph·a·gist \mīˈkäfəjəst\ *n* -s [*mycophagy* + *-ist*] : one that eats fungi (as mushrooms)

my·coph·a·gous \-fəgəs\ *adj* [*myc-* + *-phagous*] : feeding on fungi : eating mushrooms ⟨a ~ coccinellid —*Biol. Abstracts*⟩

my·coph·a·gy \-fəjē\ *n* -ES [*myc-* + *-phagy*] : the eating of fungi (as mushrooms)

my·co·phenolic acid \ˌmīkō+ . . .-\ *n* [ISV *myc-* + *phenolic*] : a crystalline antibiotic $C_{17}H_{20}O_6$ obtained from fungi of the genus *Penicillium*

my·coph·tho·rous \mīˈkäfthərəs\ *adj* [*myc-* + Gk *phthor-* (stem of *phtheirein* to destroy, corrupt) + *-ous* — more at PHTHIRIASIS] *of a fungus* : parasitizing a fungus

my·co·plasm \ˈmīkəˌplazəm\ *also* **my·co·plas·ma** \ˌ≈≈ˈplazmə\ *n* [NL *mycoplasma*, fr. *myc-* + *-plasma*] : a hypothetical hibernating form of various fungi (as rusts) in which the fungus protoplasm is intimately fused with that of dormant structures (as seeds) of the host plant

my·co·plas·ma \ˌ≈≈ˈplazmə\ *n, cap* [NL *Mycoplasmat-, Mycoplasma*, fr. *myc-* + *-plasmat-, -plasma* -plasma] : the type and usu. sole genus of the family Mycoplasmataceae

my·co·plas·ma·ta·ce·ae \ˌmīkəˌplazməˈtāsēˌē\ *n pl, cap* [NL, fr. *Mycoplasmat-, Mycoplasma*, type genus + *-aceae*] : a family (coextensive with the order Mycoplasmatales) of minute pleomorphic gram-negative nonmotile microorganisms that are intermediate in some respects between viruses and bacteria, are reported to have complex life cycles, and are mostly parasitic usu. in mammals — compare PLEUROPNEUMONIA; *see* BORRELOMYCETACEAE

my·cor·rhi·za *also* **my·co·rhi·za** \ˌmīkəˈrīzə\ *n, pl* **my·corrhi·zae** \-ˌrīˌzē\ *or* **mycorrhizas** [NL, fr. *myc-* + *-rhiza*] : the symbiotic association of the mycelium of a fungus (as various basidiomycetes and ascomycetes) with the roots of a seed plant (as various conifers, beeches, heaths, and orchids) in which the hyphae form an interwoven mass investing the root tips or penetrate the parenchyma of the root — compare ECTOTROPHIC, ENDOTROPHIC — **my·cor·rhi·zal** *also* **my·co·rhi·zal** \ˌ≈≈ˈrīzəl\ *adj*

my·co·sis \mīˈkōsəs\ *n, pl* **myco·ses** \-ōˌsēz\ [NL, fr. *myc-* + *-osis*] : infection with or disease caused by a fungus

mycosis fun·goi·des \fəŋˈgȯidēz\ *n* [NL, lit., fungoid mycosis] : a chronic progressive disease possibly related to leukemia and marked by the development of reddish tumors esp. upon the scalp, face, and chest and sometimes by cellular infiltration of various visceral organs

my·co·sphaerella \ˌmīkō+\ *n, cap* [NL, fr. *myc-* + *Sphaerella*] : a genus (the type of the family Mycosphaerellaceae) of fungi of the order Sphaeriales having 2-celled ascospores borne in perithecia that are immersed in dead portions of the host — see CURRANT LEAF SPOT

my·co·stat \ˈmīkəˌstat\ *n* -s [*myc-* + *-stat*] : an agent that inhibits the growth of molds

my·co·stat·ic \ˌ≈≈ˈstad·ik\ *adj* : of or relating to a mycostat ⟨~ vapors⟩

my·cos·ter·ol \mīˈkästəˌrōl, -rȯl\ *n* [*myc-* + *sterol*] : any of a class of sterols obtained from fungi

my·co·symbiosis \ˌmīkō+\ *n* [NL, fr. *myc-* + *symbiosis*] : symbiosis in which a fungus participates

my·cot·ic \(ˈ)mīˈkäd·ik\ *adj* [G *mykotisch*, fr. *mykose* mycosis (fr. NL *mycosis*), after such pairs as G *hypnotisch* hypnotic: *hypnose* hypnosis, fr. NL *hypnosis*] : of, relating to, or characterized by mycosis ⟨~ dermatitis⟩

mycotic pneumonia *n* : brooder pneumonia of the chicken

mycotic stomatitis *n* : thrush of cattle and other ruminants

my·co·troph·ic \ˌmīkəˈträfik\ *adj* [ISV *myc-* + *-trophic*] : obtaining food by association with a fungus — **my·cot·ro·phy** \mīˈkä·trəfē\ *n* -ES

myc·te·ria \mikˈtirēə\ *n, cap* [NL, fr. Gk *myktēr* nostril, nose + NL *-ia*; akin to Gk *myxa* lampwick, nasal mucus — more at MUCUS] : a genus of storks now consisting only of the American wood ibis (*M. americana*)

myc·ter·ic \(ˈ)mikˈterik\ *adj* [Gk *myktēr* + E *-ic*] : of or relating to the nasal cavities

myc·ter·o·per·ca \ˌmiktərōˈpərkə\ *n, cap* [NL, fr. Gk *myktēr* + L *perca* perch — more at PERCH] : a widely distributed genus of groupers

myc·to·de·ra \ˌmiktəˈdirə\ [NL, fr. *mycto-* (fr. Gk *myktēr* nostril, nose) + L *-dera* (fr. Gk *derē, deirē* neck) — more at DER-] *syn of* MUTABILIA

myc·to·phid \ˈmiktəfəd\ *n* -s [NL *Myctophidae*] : one of the Myctophidae

myc·toph·i·dae \mikˈtäfəˌdē\ *n pl, cap* [NL, fr. *Myctophum*, type genus + *-idae*] : a family of marine fishes (order Isospondyli) comprising the true lantern fishes

myc·to·phum \mikˈtōfəm\ *n, cap* [NL, fr. Gk *myktēr* nose, nostril + *-ophum* (fr. Gk *ophis* snake) — more at ANGUIS] : a genus (the type of the family Myctophidae) of lantern fishes

my·da·i·dae \mīˈdāəˌdē\ *n pl, cap* [NL, fr. *Mydas*, type genus (irreg. fr. Gk *midax*, an insect destructive to beans) + *-idae*] : a small family of American and Australian dipterous insects containing the largest known two-winged flies

my·das fly *or* **mi·das fly** \ˈmīdəs-\ *n* [NL *Mydas*, genus of dipterous insects] : a fly of the family Mydaidae

myd·a·us \ˈmidāəs\ *n, cap* [NL, fr. Gk *mydan* to be damp — more at MOSS] : a genus of mammals (family Viverridae) consisting of the teledu

my·dri·a·sine \məˈdrīəˌsēn, mīˈ-, -ˌsən\ *n* -s [ISV *mydriasis* (fr. L *mydriasis*) + *-ine*] : a white crystalline compound $C_{17}H_{23}NO_3.CH_3Br$ used like atropine; atropine methobromide

my·dri·a·sis \məˈdrīəsəs, mīˈ-\ *n, pl* **mydria·ses** \-əˌsēz\ [L, fr. Gk] : dilatation of the pupil of the eye esp. when prolonged (as from the effect of drugs) or excessive

¹myd·ri·at·ic \ˌmidrēˈad·ik\ *adj* [fr. *mydriasis*, after such pairs as E *hypostatic: hypostasis*] : causing or involving dilatation of the pupil of the eye

²mydriatic \"\ *n* -s : a drug that produces dilatation of the pupil of the eye

myel- *or* **myelo-** *comb form* [NL, fr. Gk, fr. *myelos*, fr. *mys* mouse, muscle — more at MOUSE] : marrow ⟨*myelin*⟩ ⟨*myelocyte*⟩: as **a** : bone marrow ⟨*myelo*genous⟩ **b** : spinal cord ⟨*myel*encephalon⟩ ⟨*myelo*cele⟩

my·e·len·ce·phal·ic \ˌmīəˌlensəˈfalik\ *adj* [NL *myelencephalon* + E *-ic*] : of or relating to the myelencephalon

my·e·len·ceph·a·lon \ˌ≈≈lənˈsefəˌlän\ *n* [NL, fr. *myel-* + *encephalon*] : the posterior portion of the rhombencephalon: **a** : MEDULLA OBLONGATA **b** : the posterior part of the medulla oblongata that differs little in structure from the spinal cord with which it is continuous

-my·e·lia \ˌmīˈēlēə\ *n comb form* -s [NL, fr. *myel-* + *-ia*] : a (specified) condition of the spinal cord ⟨hemato*myelia*⟩

my·el·ic \(ˈ)mīˈelik\ *adj* [*myel-* + *-ic*] : of or relating to the spinal cord

my·e·lin \ˈmīələn\ *also* **my·e·line** \", -əˌlēn\ *n* -s [ISV *myel-* + *-in, -ine*; orig. formed as G *myelin*] : a soft white somewhat fatty material that in medullated nerve fibers forms a thick medullary sheath about the axis cylinder and contains lipids (as lecithin and cerebrosides) and proteins usu. combined with lipids — **my·e·lin·ic** \ˌmīəˈlinik\ *adj*

my·e·li·nat·ed \ˈmīələˌnād·əd\ *adj, of a nerve* : having a medullary sheath

my·e·li·na·tion \ˌ≈≈≈ˈnāshən\ *or* **my·e·lin·iza·tion** \ˌmīələnəˈzāshən\ *n* -s **1** : the process of acquiring a medullary sheath **2** : the condition of being myelinated

myelino- *comb form* [NL, fr. ISV *myelin*] : myelin ⟨*myelino*clasis⟩ ⟨*myelino*clastic⟩ ⟨*myelino*genesis⟩ ⟨*myelino*genetic⟩

myelin sheath *n* : MEDULLARY SHEATH 1

my·e·lit·ic \ˌmīəˈlid·ik\ *adj* [*myel-* + *-itic*] : of, relating to, or causing myelitis ⟨~ viruses⟩

my·e·li·tis \ˌmīəˈlīd·əs\ *n, pl* **myelit·i·des** \-lid·əˌdēz\ [NL, fr. *myel-* + *-itis*] : inflammation of the spinal cord or of the bone marrow

my·e·lo·blast \ˈmīəlōˌblast\ *n* [ISV *myel-* + *-blast*] **1** : HEMOCYTOBLAST **2** : a cell derived from the hemocytoblast and serving as precursor for the blood granulocytes — **my·e·lo·blas·tic** \ˌ≈≈≈ˈblastik\ *adj*

my·e·lo·blas·te·mia \ˌ≈≈≈ˌblaˈstēmēə\ *n* -s [NL, fr. ISV *myeloblast* + NL *-emia*] : the presence of myeloblasts in the circulating blood (as in myelogenous leukemia)

myeloblastic leukemia *n* : MYELOGENOUS LEUKEMIA

my·e·lo·blas·to·ma \ˌ≈≈≈ˌblaˈstōmə\ *n, pl* **myeloblastomas** \-məz\ *or* **myeloblastoma·ta** \-məd·ə\ [NL, fr. ISV *myeloblast* + NL *-oma*] **1** : a myeloma consisting of myeloblasts **2** : MYELOGENOUS LEUKEMIA

my·e·lo·brachium \ˌmīəlō+\ *n* [NL, fr. *myel-* + *brachium*] : RESTIFORM BODY

my·e·lo·cele \ˈmīəlōˌsēl\ *n* -s [ISV *myel-* + ¹*-cele*] : spina bifida in which the neural tissue of the spinal cord is exposed

my·e·lo·coele \ˈmīəlōˌsēl\ *n* -s [ISV *myel-* + *-coele*] : the central canal of the spinal cord

my·e·lo·cerebellar \ˌmīəlō+\ *adj* [*myel-* + *cerebellar*] : of or relating to the spinal cord and cerebellum

my·e·lo·cyte \ˈmīəlōˌsīt\ *n* -s [ISV *myel-* + *-cyte*] **1** : a bone-marrow cell; *esp* : a motile cell with cytoplasmic granules that gives rise to the granulocytes of the blood but is not itself present in normal blood **2** : a nerve cell of the gray matter of the central nervous system — **my·e·lo·cyt·ic** \ˌ≈≈≈ˈsid·ik\ *adj*

my·e·lo·cy·to·ma \ˌmīəlōˌsīˈtōmə\ *n, pl* **myelocytomas** \-məz\ *or* **myelocytoma·ta** \-məd·ə\ [NL, fr. ISV *myelocyte* + NL *-oma*] : a tumor of which the typical cellular element is a myelocyte or a cell of similar differentiation — **my·e·lo·cy·to·ma·to·sis** \ˌ≈≈≈ˌ≈ˌtōməˈtōsəs\ *n, pl* **myelocytomato·ses** \-ˈtōˌsēz\

my·e·lo·cy·to·sis \ˌmīəlōˌsīˈtōsəs\ *n, pl* **myelocyto·ses** \-tōˌsēz\ [NL, fr. ISV *myelocyte* + NL *-osis*] : the presence of excess numbers of myelocytes in blood, bone marrow, or other parts of the body

my·e·log·e·nous \ˌmīəˈläjənəs\ *also* **my·e·lo·gen·ic** \ˌmīəlōˈjenik\ *adj* [ISV *myel-* + *-genous, -genic*] : of, relating to, originating in, or produced by the bone marrow ⟨~ sarcoma⟩

myelogenous leukemia *n* : leukemia characterized by proliferation of myeloid tissue (as of the bone marrow and spleen) and an abnormal increase in the number of granulocytes, myelocytes, and myeloblasts in the circulating blood

my·e·lo·gram \ˈmīələˌgram\ *n* [ISV *myel-* + *-gram*] **1** : a differential study of the cellular elements present in bone marrow usu. made on material obtained by sternal biopsy **2** : a roentgenogram of the spinal cord made by myelography

my·e·lo·graph·ic \ˌ≈≈≈ˈgrafik\ *adj* [*myel-* + *-graphic*] : of, relating to, or by means of a myelogram or myelography — **my·e·lo·graph·i·cal·ly** \-fək(ə)lē\ *adv*

my·e·log·ra·phy \ˌmīəˈlägrəfē\ *n* -ES [ISV *myel-* + *-graphy*] : roentgenographic visualization of the spinal subarachnoid space after the injection of a contrast medium

my·e·loid \ˈmīəˌlȯid\ *adj* [ISV *myel-* + *-oid*] **1** : of or relating to the spinal cord **2** : of, relating to, arising from, or like the bone marrow; *esp* : of or relating to myeloblasts or to cells derived from them ⟨the ~ series consists of myeloblasts, myelocytes, and true granulocytes⟩ — compare ERYTHROID

myeloid leukemia *n* : MYELOGENOUS LEUKEMIA

my·e·lo·ma \ˌmīəˈlōmə\ *n, pl* **myelomas** \-məz\ *or* **myeloma·ta** \-məd·ə\ [NL, fr. *myel-* + *-oma*] : a primary tumor of the bone marrow formed of any one of the bone-marrow cells (as myelocytes or plasma cells) and usu. involving several different bones at the same time — see MULTIPLE MYELOMA

my·e·lo·ma·to·sis \ˌmīəˌlōməˈtōsəs\ *n, pl* **myelomato·ses** \-tōˌsēz\ [NL, fr. *myelomat-, myeloma* + *-osis*] : MULTIPLE MYELOMA

my·e·lom·a·tous \ˌmīəˈläməd·əs, -lōm-\ *adj* [NL *myelomat-, myeloma* + E *-ous*] : of or relating to a myeloma or to myelomatosis

my·e·lo·mere \ˈmīələ̄,mi(ə)r\ *n* -s [ISV *myel-* + *-mere*] **:** any of the segments of the developing central nervous system corresponding with a mesoblastic somite on either side
my·e·lon·ic \ˌmīəˈlänik\ *adj* [NL *myelon* spinal cord (fr. Gk *myelos* marrow) + E *-ic* — more at MYEL-] **:** of or relating to the spinal cord
my·e·lo·path·ic \ˌmīələ̄ˈpathik\ *adj* [ISV *myel-* + *-pathic*] **:** of or relating to a myelopathy **:** resulting from abnormality of the spinal cord or the bone marrow ⟨~ anemia⟩
my·e·lop·a·thy \ˌmīəˈläpəthē\ *n* -ES [ISV *myel-* + *-pathy*] **:** a disease or disorder of the spinal cord or the bone marrow
my·e·lo·phthisic anemia \ˌmīələ̄+ . . . -\ *n* [ISV *myel-* + *phthisic*] **:** anemia in which the blood-forming elements of the bone marrow are unable to reproduce normal blood cells and which is commonly caused by specific toxins or by overgrowth of tumor cells
my·e·lo·phthisis \"+\ *n* [NL, fr. *myel-* + *phthisis*] **:** MYELOPHTHISIC ANEMIA
my·el·o·plax \mīˈelə,plaks\ *n, pl* **myeloplaxes** \-sə̇z\ *or* **my·e·lop·la·ces** \ˌmīəˈläplə,sēz\ [NL, fr. *myel-* + Gk *plax* flat object — more at PLEASE] **:** one of the large multinucleate cells in bone marrow **:** MEGAKARYOCYTE, OSTEOCLAST
my·e·lo·poi·e·sis \ˌmīələ̄,pȯiˈēsə̇s\ *n, pl* **myelopoieses** \-ē,sēz\ [NL, fr. *myel-* + *-poiesis*] **1 :** production of marrow or marrow cells **2 :** production of blood cells in bone marrow; *esp* **:** formation of blood granulocytes
my·e·lo·poi·et·ic \ˌ≈≈,≈ˈed·ik\ *adj* [*myel-* + Gk *poiētikos* capable of making — more at POETIC] **:** of or relating to myelopoiesis
my·e·lo·sclerosis \ˌmīələ̄+\ *n* [NL, fr. *myel-* + *sclerosis*] **:** abnormal hardening of the bone marrow commonly associated with splenic disorder and constitutional symptoms
my·e·lo·sis \ˌmīəˈlōsə̇s\ *n, pl* **myelo·ses** \-ō,sēz\ [NL, fr. *myel-* + *-osis*] **1 a :** the proliferation of marrow tissue to produce the changes in cell distribution typical of myelogenous leukemia **b :** LEUKEMIA; *esp* **:** MYELOGENOUS LEUKEMIA **2 :** the formation of a tumor of the spinal cord
my·e·lo·spon·gi·um \ˌmīələ̄ˈspənjēəm\ *n, pl* **myelospongia** \-ēə\ [NL, fr. *myel-* + *-spongium*] **:** a network in the embryonic central nervous system derived from the spongioblasts and giving rise to the neuroglia
my·e·lo·toxic \ˌmīələ̄+\ *adj* [*myel-* + *toxic*] **:** destructive to bone marrow or any of its elements
my·e·lo·zoa \ˌmīələ̄ˈzōə\ [NL, fr. *myel-* + *-zoa*] *syn of* LEPTOCARDII
my·en·ter·ic \ˌmīənˈterik\ *adj* [*my-* + *enteric*] **:** of or relating to the muscular coat of the intestinal wall
myenteric plexus *n* **:** AUERBACH'S PLEXUS
my·en·ter·on \mīˈentə,rän\ *n* [NL, fr. *my-* + *enteron*] **:** the muscular coat of the intestine
1myg·a·le \ˈmigəlē\ *n* -s [L, fr. Gk *mygalē*] **:** SHREWMOUSE
2mygale \"\ [NL, fr. L, shrewmouse] *syn of* AVICULARIA
myg·a·lo·morph \ˈmigələ̄,mȯrf\ *n* [NL *Mygalomorphae*] **:** one of the Mygalomorphae
myg·a·lo·mor·phae \ˌ≈≈≈ˈmȯr,fē\ *n pl, cap* [NL, fr. *mygale* + *-morphae*] **:** a suborder of spiders comprising those in which the fangs move more vertically and four book lungs are present — see TARANTULA
myi- *or* **myio-** *comb form* [NL, fr. Gk, fr. *myia* — more at MIDGE] **:** fly ⟨*Myi*archus⟩
-my·ia \ˈmī(y)ə\ *n comb form* -s [NL, fr. Gk *myia*] **:** fly ⟨antho*myia*⟩ ⟨Cephenomyia⟩
myi·ar·chus \mīˈyärkəs\ *n, cap* [NL, fr. *myi-* + Gk *archos* ruler] **:** a genus of large plainly colored tyrant flycatchers widely distributed in America
my·ia·sis \ˈmī(y)əsə̇s\ *n, pl* **myia·ses** \-ə,sēz\ [NL, fr. *myi-* + *-iasis*] **:** infestation with or disease caused by fly maggots
my·i·dae \ˈmīə,dē\ [NL, fr. *Mya* + *-idae*] *syn of* MYACIDAE
my·if·er·ous \(ˈ)mīˈif(ə)rəs\ *adj* [*my-* + *-ferous*] **:** MYOPHOROUS
my·io·sis \mīˈyōsə̇s\ *n, pl* **myio·ses** \-ō,sēz\ [NL, fr. *myi-* + *-osis*] **:** MYIASIS
myl- *or* **mylo-** *comb form* [NL, fr. Gk, mill, molar, fr. *mylē* — more at MEAL] **:** molar ⟨*mylo*hyoid⟩
1myl·i·ob·a·tid \ˌmilēˈäbəd·ə̇d\ *adj* [NL *Myliobatidae*] **:** of or relating to the Myliobatidae
2myliobatid \"\ *n* -s [NL *Myliobatidae*] **:** one of the Myliobatidae
myl·i·o·bat·i·dae \ˌmilēō'bad·ə,dē\ *n pl, cap* [NL, fr. *Myliobatis*, type genus (fr. Gk *mylias, mylios* of a mill — fr. *mylē* mill, molar — + *batis*, a flat fish, prob. a skate or ray) + *-idae*] **:** a family of large flattened chiefly tropical sting rays — see EAGLE RAY
my·lo·don \ˈmīlə,dän\ *n* [NL, fr. *myl-* + *-odon*] **1** *cap* **:** a genus (the type of the family Mylodontidae) of large edentates of the Pleistocene of So. America **2** -s **:** a mammal of the genus *Mylodon*
1my·lo·dont \-nt\ *adj* [NL *Mylodont-, Mylodon*] **:** of or relating to the genus *Mylodon* or the family Mylodontidae
2mylodont \"\ *n* -s [NL *Mylodont-, Mylodon*] **:** a mammal of the genus *Mylodon* or the family Mylodontidae
1my·lo·hy·oid \ˌmīlō'hī,ȯid\ *also* **my·lo·hy·oi·de·an** \ˌ≈≈,hīˈȯidēən\ *adj* [*mylohyoid* fr. NL *mylohyoideus*, fr. *myl-* + *hyoides* hyoid bone; *mylohyoidean* fr. NL *mylohyoideus* + E *-an* — more at HYOID BONE] **:** of, indicating, or adjoining a muscle that extends from the inner surface of the mandible to the hyoid and forms the floor of the mouth
2mylohyoid \"\ *or* **my·lo·hy·oi·de·us** \ˌ≈≈,≈ˈȯidēəs\ *n, pl* **mylohyoids** \-dz\ *or* **mylohyoi·dei** \-dē,ī\ [NL *mylohyoideus*, fr. *mylohyoideus*, adj.] **:** a mylohyoid muscle
my·lo·nite \ˈmīlə,nīt, ˈmil-\ *n* -s [Gk *mylōn* mill (fr. *mylē* mill) + E *-ite* — more at MEAL] **:** a siliceous schist geologically produced by intense crushing of rocks
my·lo·nit·ic \ˌ≈≈ˈnid·ik\ *adj* **:** CATACLASTIC
my·lo·nit·i·za·tion \ˌ≈≈,nīd·əˈzāshən\ *also* **my·lo·ni·za·tion** \ˌ≈≈nəˈzāshən\ *n* -s **:** the process of producing mylonite
my·lo·nit·ize \ˈ≈≈,nī,tīz\ *also* **my·lo·nize** \ˈ≈≈,nīz\ *vt* -ED/-ING/-S *see -ize in Explan Notes* **:** to form by or subject to the process of mylonitization ⟨*mylonitized* dunite —*Jour. of Geol.*⟩
mym *abbr* myriameter
1my·mar·id \(ˈ)mīˈmarə̇d\ *adj* [NL *Mymaridae*] **:** of or relating to the Mymaridae
2mymarid \"\ *n* -s [NL *Mymaridae*] **:** a chalcid fly of the family Mymaridae
my·mar·i·dae \mīˈmarə,dē\ *n pl, cap* [NL, fr. *Mymar*, type genus (fr. Gk *mymar, mōmar, mōmos* blame, blemish) + *-idae*] **:** a family of minute chalcid flies that are parasitic in the larval state living principally in the eggs of other insects
my·na *or* **my·nah** \ˈmīnə\ *n* -s [Hindi *mainā*, fr. Skt *madana, madanaka*] **:** any of various Asiatic starlings esp. of the genera *Acridotheres, Gracula*, and *Sturnus*: as **a :** a dark brown slightly crested bird (*A. tristis*) of southeastern Asia that has white tail tip and wing markings and bright yellow bill and feet, is semigregarious and very aggressive, and has when introduced to other areas often replaced native birds and proved very destructive to crops (as small grains and some fruits) **b :** HILL MYNA
myn·heer \mīnˈhe(ə)r, -hi(ə)r\ *n* -s [D *mijnheer* (formerly spelled also *mynheer*), fr. *mijn* my + *heer* sir] **1 a :** MISTER — used as a title prefixed to the name of a male Netherlander or Dutch-speaking man **b :** SIR — used as a form of respectful or polite address to a male Netherlander or Dutch-speaking man **2 a :** GENTLEMAN — used esp. of a Netherlander of good birth **b :** DUTCHMAN ⟨the ~s of New Amsterdam⟩
myn·pacht \ˈmīn,päkt\ *n* -s [Afrik, fr. *myn* mine + *pacht* lease] **1** *southern Africa* **:** a mining concession; *esp* **:** one by the government to the owner of the surface concerned **2** *southern Africa* **:** a landowner's mining location covering one tenth of the surface leased to the government
myo- — see MY-
my·o·blast \ˈmīə,blast\ *n* [ISV *my-* + *-blast*] **:** an undifferentiated cell capable of giving rise to muscle cells
my·o·car·di·al \ˌmīəˈkärdēəl\ *adj* [NL *myocardium* + E *-al*] **:** of, relating to, or involving the myocardium
myocardial infarction *n* **:** infarction of the myocardium, typically resulting from coronary occlusion
myo·cardiograph \ˌmīō+\ *n* [*my-* + *cardiograph*] **:** a recording instrument for making a tracing of the action of the heart
my·o·car·di·tis \ˌmīə,kärˈdīd·ə̇s\ *n* [NL, fr. *myocardium* + *-itis*] **:** inflammation of the myocardium
my·o·car·di·um \ˌmīəˈkärdēəm\ *n, pl* **myocar·dia** \-ēə\ [NL, fr. *my-* + *-cardium*] **:** the middle muscular layer of the heart wall
my·o·cas·tor \ˈmīə,kastə(r)\ *n, cap* [NL, fr. *my-* + L *castor* beaver — more at CASTOR] **:** a genus of hystricomorph rodents comprising the coypu
my·o·clo·nia \ˌmīəˈklōnēə\ *n* -s [NL, fr. *myoclonus* + *-ia*] **1 :** a disturbance marked by myoclonus **2 :** MYOCLONUS — **my·o·clon·ic** \ˌ≈≈ˈklänik\ *adj*
my·oc·lo·nus \mīˈäklənəs\ *n* [NL, fr. *my-* + *clonus*] **:** irregular involuntary contraction of a muscle usu. resulting from functional disorder of controlling motoneurons
my·o·coel *also* **my·o·coele** \ˈmīə,sēl\ *n* -s [*my-* + *-coel, -coele*] **:** the cavity of a myotome
my·o·com·ma \ˌmīəˈkämə\ *n, pl* **myocomma·ta** \-məd·ə\ *also* **myocommas** [NL, fr. *my-* + *comma*] **1 :** one of the segments into which the muscles of the body or trunk of vertebrates are separated by connective-tissue septa **2 :** MYOSEPTUM
my·o·cyte \ˈmīə,sīt\ *n* -s [*my-* + *-cyte*] **:** a contractile cell; *specif* **:** a muscle cell
my·o·dar·ia \ˌmīəˈda(a)rēə\ *n pl, cap* [NL, irreg. fr. Gk *myia* fly + *-ōdēs* -ode + NL *-aria* — more at MIDGE] **:** a very large section of the suborder Brachycera that comprises typical two-winged flies having 3-jointed antennae with an arista on the third segment, a distinctly segmented abdomen, leg bases near together on each segment, and modified wing venation — **my·o·dar·i·an** \ˌ≈≈ˈda(a)rēən\ *adj or n*
my·o·des \mīˈōdēz\ [NL, fr. Gk *myōdēs* mouselike, fr. *my-* + *-ōdēs* -ode] *syn of* LEMMUS
myo·dynamics \ˌmīō+\ *n pl but often sing in constr* [*my-* + *dynamics*] **:** the physiology of muscular contraction
myo·elastic \"+\ *adj* [*my-* + *elastic*] **:** made up of muscular and elastic tissues ⟨a ~ junction⟩
myo·epicardial layer \"+. . . -\ *n* [*my-* + *epicardial*] **:** the layer of mesocardium that enters into the formation of the muscular and epicardial walls of the heart
myo·epithelial \"+\ *adj* [*my-* + *epithelial*] **:** of, relating to, or being large stellate cells that are associated with the secretory cells of the salivary glands or the alveolae of some other glands and are believed to play a mechanical role in expressing secretion
myo·fibril *also* **myo·fibrilla** \"+\ *n* [NL *myofibrilla*, fr. *my-* + *fibrilla*] **1 :** a bundle of contractile micelles of a muscle cell **2 :** MYONEME — **myo·fibrillar** \"+\ *adj*
myo·fibroma \"+\ *n* [NL, fr. *my-* + *fibroma*] **:** a tumor composed of fibrous and muscular tissue
my·o·gen \ˈmīəjən, -,jen\ *n* -s [ISV *my-* + *-gen*] **:** a mixture of albumins obtained by extracting muscle with cold water
my·o·gen·ic \ˌ≈≈ˈjenik\ *adj* [ISV *my-* + *-genic*] **1 :** originating in muscle ⟨~ pain⟩ **2** *of cardiac muscular contraction* **:** taking place in ordered rhythmic fashion because of inherent properties of cardiac muscle rather than by reason of specific neural stimuli — compare NEUROGENIC 2b — **my·o·ge·nic·i·ty** \ˌ≈≈jəˈnisəd·ē\ *n* -ES
myo·globin \ˌmīə+\ *n* [ISV *my-* + *globin*] **:** a red iron-containing protein pigment in muscles that is similar to hemoglobin but differs in the globin portion of its molecule, in the smaller size of its molecule (as in the mammalian heart muscle which has only one fourth the molecular weight of the hemoglobin in the blood of the same animal), in its greater tendency to combine with oxygen, and in its absorption of light at longer wavelengths — called also *myohemoglobin*
my·o·glo·bin·uria \ˌmīə,glōbə'n(y)u̇rēə\ *n* -s [NL, fr. ISV *myoglobin* + NL *-uria*] **:** the presence of myoglobin in the urine
my·o·gram \ˈmīə,gram\ *n* [*my-* + *-gram*] **:** a graphic representation of the phenomena (as velocity and intensity) of muscular contractions
my·o·graph \-raf, -räf\ *n* [*my-* + *-graph*] **:** an apparatus for producing myograms usu. consisting essentially of a series of transmitting levers and a revolving recording surface (as a kymograph) — **my·o·graph·ic** \ˌ≈≈ˈgrafik\ *adj* — **my·o·graph·i·cal·ly** \-fə̇k(ə)lē\ *adv*
my·og·ra·phy \mīˈägrəfē\ *n* -ES [ISV *my-* + *-graphy*] **:** use of the myograph
myo·hematin \ˌmīō+\ *n* [*my-* + *hematin*] **:** CYTOCHROME
myo·hemoglobin \"+\ *n* [ISV *my-* + *hemoglobin*] **:** MYOGLOBIN
myo·he·mo·glo·bin·uria \ˌmīō,hēmə,glōbə'n(y)u̇rēə\ *n* -s [NL, fr. ISV *myohemoglobin* + NL *-uria*] **:** MYOGLOBINURIA
my·oid \ˈmī,ȯid\ *adj* [ISV *my-* + *-oid*] **:** resembling muscle
my·oi·dea \mīˈȯidēə\ [NL, fr. *my-* + *-oidea*] *syn of* MUROIDEA
myo·inositol \ˌmīō+\ *n* [*my-* + *inositol*] **:** INOSITOL a
myo·kinase \"+\ *n* [*my-* + *kinase*] **:** a crystallizable enzyme that promotes the reversible transfer of phosphate groups in adenosine diphosphate with the formation of adenosine triphosphate and adenylic acid and that occurs in muscle and other tissues
my·o·lemma \ˌmīəˈlemə\ *n* -s [NL, fr. *my-* + *-lemma*] **:** SARCOLEMMA
my·o·log·ic \ˌmīəˈläjik\ *or* **my·o·log·i·cal** \-jə̇kəl\ *adj* **:** of or relating to myology
my·ol·o·gy \mīˈäləjē\ *n* -ES [F or NL; F *myologie*, fr. NL *myologia*, fr. *my-* + L *-logia* -logy] **1 :** a scientific study of muscles **2 :** the muscular makeup of an animal or part
myom- *or* **myomo-** *comb form* [NL *myoma*] **:** myoma ⟨*myom*ectomy⟩ ⟨*myomo*hysterectomy⟩ ⟨*myomo*tomy⟩
my·o·ma \mīˈōmə\ *n, pl* **myomas** \-məz\ *or* **myoma·ta** \-məd·ə\ [NL, fr. *my-* + *-oma*] **:** a tumor consisting of muscle tissue — **my·om·a·tous** \(ˈ)mīˈämədəs, -ˈōm-\ *adj*
my·o·mec·to·my \ˌmīəˈmektəmē\ *n* -ES [ISV *myom-* + *-ectomy*] **:** excision of a myoma
my·o·mere \ˈmīə,mi(ə)r\ *n* -s [ISV *my-* + *-mere*] **:** a muscle segment — compare METAMERE, MYOCOMMA — **my·o·mer·ic** \ˌ≈≈ˈmerik\ *adj*
my·o·me·tri·al \ˌmīəˈmē·trēəl\ *adj* [NL *myometrium* + E *-al*] **:** of, relating to, or affecting the myometrium
my·o·me·tri·um \ˌ≈≈ˈmē·trēəm\ *n* -s [NL, fr. *my-* + *metr-* + *-ium*] **:** the muscular layer of the wall of the uterus
1my·o·morph \ˈmīə,mȯrf\ *adj* [NL *Myomorpha*] **:** of or relating to the Myomorpha
2myomorph \"\ *n* -s [NL *Myomorpha*] **:** a rodent of the suborder Myomorpha
my·o·mor·pha \ˌ≈≈ˈmȯrfə\ *n pl, cap* [NL, fr. *my-* + *-morpha*] **:** the largest suborder of Rodentia comprising the true rats, mice, and related rodents — compare HYSTRICOMORPHA, SCIUROMORPHA — **my·o·mor·phic** \ˌ≈≈ˈmȯrfik\ *adj*
my·o·neme \ˈmīə,nēm\ *also* **my·o·ne·ma** \ˌ≈≈ˈnēmə\ *n* -s [NL *myonema*, fr. *my-* + *-nema*] **:** a contractile fibril in the body of a protozoan
myo·neural \ˌmīō+\ *adj* [*my-* + *-neural*] **:** of or relating to both muscle and nerve
myoneural junction *n* **:** the modified point of contact between muscle and motor nerve usu. considered to consist of specialized receptive matter of muscular origin, specialized transmitting matter of nervous origin, and intervening substance that is neither nerve nor muscle
my·o·path·ic \ˌmīəˈpathik\ *adj* [ISV *my-* + *-pathic*] **:** involving abnormality of the muscles ⟨~ syndrome⟩ **:** of or relating to myopathy
my·op·a·thy \mīˈäpəthē\ *n* -ES [ISV *my-* + *-pathy*] **:** a disorder of muscle tissue or muscles
my·ope \ˈmī,ōp\ *n* -s [F, fr. LL *myops* myopic, fr. Gk *myōps*, fr. *myein* to close (used of the lips and eyes) + *ōps* eye, face — more at MYSTERY, EYE] **:** a myopic person ⟨could be dangerous for ~s to drive without corrective lenses⟩ ⟨intellectual ~s⟩
my·o·phan \ˈmīə,fan\ *n* -s [*my-* + Gk *phan-*, stem of *phainein* to show — more at FANCY] **:** MYONEME
my·o·phore \ˈmīə,fō(ə)r, -fȯ(ə)r\ *n* -s [*my-* + *-phore*] **:** a part or process of a shell (as of a clam) adapted for the attachment of a muscle — **my·oph·o·rous** \(ˈ)mīˈäf(ə)rəs\ *adj*
my·o·phrisk \ˈmīə,frisk\ *n* -s [NL *myophrisca*, prob. irreg. fr. *my-* + *phor-* + *-isca* (fr. Gk *-iskos*, dim. suffix) — more at -ISH] **:** MYONEME
myo·physics \ˌmīō+\ *n pl but sing or pl in constr* [*my-* + *physics*] **:** the physics of muscular action
my·o·pia \mīˈōpēə\ *n* -s [NL, fr. Gk *myōpia*, fr. *myōp-*, *myōps* myopic + *-ia* -y — more at MYOPE] **1 :** a condition in which the visual images come to a focus in front of the retina of the eye because of defects in the refractive media of the eye or of abnormal length of the eyeball resulting esp. in defective vision of distant objects — called also *nearsightedness, shortsightedness;* compare EMMETROPIA **2 :** deficiency or lack of foresight, discernment, or liberality esp. in a particular field ⟨the ~ of the single mind is corrected through the perspectives of other minds —F.K.Davis⟩ ⟨the ~ of contemporary opinion —J.T.Soby⟩ ⟨a persistent emotional ~ —D.M.Friedenberg⟩ ⟨political ~⟩
my·o·pic \(ˈ)mīˈōpik, -ˈäp-\ *adj* [E *myope* & NL *myopia* + E *-ic*] **1 :** affected by myopia **:** of, relating to, or exhibiting myopia **2 :** lacking in foresight, discernment, or liberality ⟨the ~ perspective of the specialist —Erwin Schrödinger⟩ ⟨policies which are dangerously self-centered and ~ —N.D. Palmer⟩ — **my·o·pi·cal·ly** \-pə̇k(ə)lē, -li\ *adv*
myo·polar \ˌmīō+\ *adj* [*my-* + *polar*] **:** of or relating to muscular polarity
my·op·o·ra·ce·ae \mī,äpəˈrāsē,ē\ *n pl, cap* [NL, fr. *Myoporum*, type genus + *-aceae*] **:** a family of chiefly Australian shrubs and trees (order Polemoniales) having an irregular or bilabiate corolla, didynamous stamens, and berrylike fruit — **my·op·o·ra·ceous** \ˌ≈≈≈ˈrāshəs\ *adj* — **my·op·o·rad** \ˈ≈≈≈,rad\ *n* -s
my·op·o·rum \mīˈäpərəm\ *n, cap* [NL, fr. *myo-* (fr. Gk *myein* to close — used of the lips and eyes) + *-porum* (fr. Gk *poros* pore) — more at MYSTERY, PORE] **:** a genus (the type of the family Myoporaceae) of mostly Australasian shrubs or trees that have small axillary white flowers with a 5-parted bell-shaped calyx — see BASTARD SANDALWOOD
my·o·pus \ˈmīəpəs\ *n, cap* [NL, fr. *my-* + *-pus*] **:** a genus of rodents comprising the Old World red-backed lemmings
myo·sarcoma \ˌmīō+\ *n* [NL, fr. *my-* + *sarcoma*] **:** sarcomatous myoma
myo·septum \"+\ *n* [NL, fr. *my-* + *septum*] **:** the septum between adjacent myotomes
my·o·sin \ˈmīəsən\ *n* -s [ISV *myos-* (fr. Gk *myos*, gen. of *mys* mouse, muscle) + *-in* — more at MOUSE] **:** either of two proteins that are extracted from muscle by salt solutions and that are thought to constitute the chief components of the contractile mechanism: **a :** ACTOMYOSIN **b :** a fibrous globulin that interreacts with actin and adenosine triphosphate with resulting enzymatic hydrolysis of the triphosphate to adenosine diphosphate and inorganic phosphate
myosis *var of* MIOSIS
my·o·si·tis \ˌmīəˈsīd·ə̇s\ *n* -ES [NL, fr. Gk *myos* (gen. of *mys* mouse, muscle) + NL *-itis*] **:** muscular discomfort or pain from infection or an unknown cause
my·os·mine \mīˈäs,mēn, ˌäz, ˌmən\ *n* -s [*my-* + *osm-* + *-ine;* fr. the mouselike odor] **:** a heterocyclic liquid base $C_9H_{10}N_2$ formed during smoking of tobacco and obtained by pyrolysis of nicotine; 3-(dihydro-pyrryl)-pyridine
my·o·sote \ˈmīə,sōt\ *n* -s [NL *Myosotis*] **:** MYOSOTIS 2
my·o·so·tis \ˌ≈≈ˈsōd·ə̇s\ *n* [NL, fr. L, mouse ear, fr. Gk *myosōtis*, fr. *myos* (gen. of *mys* mouse) + *-ōtis* (fr. *ōt-, ous* ear) — more at MOUSE, EAR] **1** *cap* **:** a large genus of herbs (family Boraginaceae) with racemose flowers having a salverform or funnelform corolla, the lobes rounded, and basally attached nutlets — see FORGET-ME-NOT **2** -ES **:** any plant of the genus *Myosotis* — called also *myosote*
myosotis blue *n* **:** FORGET-ME-NOT 2b
my·o·su·rus \ˌmīəˈs(h)u̇rəs, -ˈsəˈyü-\ *n, cap* [NL, fr. Gk *myos* (gen. of *mys* mouse) + NL *-urus* — more at MOUSE] **:** a genus of small annual herbs (family Ranunculaceae) found in temperate regions and having tufted linear-spatulate radical leaves and flowers with the receptacle slender and elongated in fruit — see MOUSETAIL
my·o·tat·ic \ˌmīəˈtad·ik\ *adj* [ISV *my-* + Gk *tatikos* exerting tension, fr. *tatos* stretchable (fr. *teinein* to stretch) + *-ikos* -ic — more at THIN] *of muscular contraction* **:** resulting from stretching — used chiefly of reflexes (as the knee jerk) in which stretching of the associated tendon is followed by a sharp reflex contraction of a muscle
myotic *var of* MIOTIC
my·o·tis \mīˈōd·ə̇s\ *n, cap* [NL, fr. *my-* + *-otis* (fr. Gk *ōt-, -ous* ear) — more at EAR] **:** a very large cosmopolitan genus of vespertilionid bats comprising the common brown bats and numerous related forms
my·o·tome \ˈmīə,tōm\ *n* -s [ISV *my-* + *-tome*] **1 a :** the portion of an embryonic somite from which skeletal musculature is produced **b :** MYOCOMMA **c :** the muscles of a metamere esp. in a segmented invertebrate **2 :** an instrument for myotomy
my·ot·o·my \mīˈäd·əmē\ *n* -ES [ISV *my-* + *-tomy*] **:** incision or division of a muscle
my·o·to·nia \ˌmīəˈtōnēə\ *n* -s [NL, fr. *my-* + *-tonia*] **:** tonic spasm of one or more muscles; *also* **:** a condition characterized by such spasms
my·o·ton·ic \ˌ≈≈ˈtänik\ *adj* [NL *myotonia* + E *-ic*] **:** of, relating to, or exhibiting myotonia
my·o·trop·ic \ˌmīəˈträpik\ *adj* [*my-* + *-tropic*] **:** affecting or tending to invade muscles ⟨a ~ infection⟩
my·ox·ine \mīˈäk,sīn, -sən\ *adj* [LGk *myōxos* dormouse + E *-ine*] **:** of or relating to dormice
my·ox·us \mīˈäksəs\ [NL, fr. LGk *myōxos* dormouse] *syn of* GLIS
myr·a·bal·a·nus \ˌmirəˈbalənəs\ *n* -ES [NL, alter. of L *myrobalanum* — more at MYROBALAN] **:** MYROBALAN
myrabolam *var of* MYROBALAN
myrabolan *var of* MYROBALAN
myrbane oil *var of* MIRBANE OIL
myr·cene \ˈmər,sēn, -sən\ *n* -s [ISV *myrcia (oil)* + *-ene*] **:** a liquid acyclic terpene hydrocarbon $C_{10}H_{16}$ that is isomeric with ocimene, occurs in bay oil, hop oil, and other essential oils, and polymerizes readily
myr·cia \ˈmərsh(ē)ə\ *n, cap* [NL, alter. of L *myrtus* myrtle + NL *-ia* — more at MYRTLE] **:** a large genus of tropical American trees and shrubs (family Myrtaceae) distinguished by their few-seeded berries
myrcia oil *n* **:** BAY OIL
myri- *or* **myrio-** *comb form* [Gk, fr. *myrios* — more at MYRIAD] **:** indefinitely numerous **:** countless ⟨*myrio*phyllous⟩ ⟨*Myrio*phyllum⟩ ⟨*myrio*sporous⟩
myria- *comb form* [F, fr. Gk *myrios* — more at MYRIAD] **1 :** ten thousand ⟨*myria*coulomb⟩ — esp. in terms belonging to the metric system ⟨*myria*gram⟩ ⟨*myria*liter⟩ **2 :** MYRI- ⟨*Myria*poda⟩
myr·i·a·can·thous \ˌmirēəˈkan(t)thəs\ *adj* [*myri-* + *acanthous*] *biol* **:** having numerous spines or prickles
1myr·i·ad \ˈmirēəd\ *n* -s [Gk *myriad-, myrias*, fr. *myrios* countless, *myrioi* (its pl.) ten thousand; perh. akin to MIr *mūr* abundance] **1 :** the number of ten thousand **:** ten thousand persons or things — used esp. in translations from the Greek and Latin **2 :** an immense number **:** an indefinitely large number **:** a great multitude — usu. used with *of* and often used in pl. ⟨beset with a ~ of profound emotional stresses —H.G.Armstrong⟩ ⟨a ~ of mathematical possibilities —John Haverstick⟩ ⟨~s of insects, flying before north winds —R.A. Billington⟩ ⟨~s of freshman texts —W.N.Francis⟩
2myriad \"\ *adj* **1 :** consisting of a very great but indefinite number **:** INNUMERABLE, MULTITUDINOUS ⟨the involved and ~ events which fill the world's past —Edward Clodd⟩ ⟨the intricacies of human action are ~ —F.A.Geldard⟩ ⟨the faces ~ yet curiously identical in their lack of individual identity —William Faulkner⟩ **2 :** having innumerable aspects or elements ⟨the ~ activity of the new land —Meridel Le Sueur⟩ ⟨a ~ murmur of insects —Hamilton Basso⟩ ⟨the soft ~ darkness of a May night —William Faulkner⟩
1myr·i·ad·fold \ˈ≈≈≈ˈfōld\ *adj* **1 :** having myriad parts or aspects **2 :** being a myriad times as large, as great, or as many as some understood size, degree, or amount
2myriadfold \"\ *adv* **:** to a myriad times as much or as many **:** by a myriad times
myr·i·ad·ly *adv* **:** a myriad times **:** to a myriad degree **:** INNUMERABLY
myriad-minded \ˈ≈≈≈ˈ≈≈\ *adj* **:** having a mind versatility and power
myr·ia·me·ter \ˈmirēə,mēd·ə(r)\ *n* [F *myriamètre* + *-mètre* -meter] **:** a metric unit of length equa meters — see METRIC SYSTEM table

myr·i·an·gi·a·les \ˌmirēˌanjēˈā(ˌ)lēz\ *n pl, cap* [NL, fr. *Myriangium* + *-ales*] : an order of fungi (subclass Euascomycetes) having a single ascus in each chamber of the well-developed and often gelatinous stroma

myr·i·an·gi·um \ˌmirēˈanjēəm\ *n, cap* [NL, fr. *myri-* + *-angium*] : a genus of ascomycetous fungi (order Myriangiales) having asci borne at different levels in the stroma and including several forms that are parasitic on insects (as scales)

myr·i·an·i·da \ˌmirēˈanədə\ *n, cap* [NL, fr. Gk *myrios* countless — more at MYRIAD] : a genus of annelid worms related to *Autolytus* and reproducing similarly

myr·i·a·pod \ˈmirēəˌpäd\ *adj or n* [NL *Myriapoda*] : MYRIOPOD

myr·i·ap·o·da \ˌmirēˈapədə\ [NL, fr. *myria-* + *-poda*] *syn of* MYRIOPODA

myr·i·arch \ˈmirēˌärk\ *n* -s [Gk *myriarchēs, myriarchos*, fr. *myrioi* ten thousand + *-archēs, archos* -arch — more at MYRIAD] : a commander of ten thousand men in ancient Greece — **myr·i·archy** \-kē\ *n* -ES

my·ri·ca \məˈrīkə\ *n, cap* [NL, fr. L, tamarisk, fr. Gk *myrikē*, prob. of Sem origin; akin to the source of Gk *myrrha* myrrh — more at MYRRH] : a large widely distributed genus (the type of a family Myricaceae) of aromatic shrubs having exstipulate leaves and ovary with 2 to 4 bractlets

myr·i·ca·ce·ae \ˌmirəˈkāsēˌē\ *n pl, cap* [NL, fr. *Myrica*, type genus + *-aceae*] : a family of shrubs constituting an order Myricales having simple alternate mostly coriaceous leaves with small diclinous flowers borne in aments in the axils of bracts and infruit forming a small drupe or nut — **myr·i·ca·ceous** \ˌ;==ˈkāshəs\ *adj*

myr·i·ca·les \ˌ==ˈkā(ˌ)lēz\ *n pl, cap* [NL, fr. *Myrica* + *-ales*] : an order of dicotyledonous plants coextensive with the family Myricaceae

myrica tallow *n* : BAYBERRY WAX

my·ric·e·tin \məˈrisəd·ən\ *n* -s [ISV *myric-* (fr. NL *Myrica*) + *-et-* + *-in*] : a yellow crystalline flavone dye $C_{15}H_{10}O_8$ obtained from many plants (as from the bark of the box myrtle and the leaves of sumacs)

my·ric·i·trin \məˈrisəˌtrən\ *n* -s [ISV *myric-* (fr. NL *Myrica*) + *-itrin* (as in *quercitrin*)] : a crystalline glycoside $C_{21}H_{20}O_{12}$ obtained esp. from the bark of the box myrtle and yielding myricetin and rhamnose on hydrolysis

myr·i·cyl alcohol \ˈmirəˌsil-\ *n* [ISV *myric-* (fr. NL *Myrica*) + *-yl*] : a crystalline alcohol $CH_3(CH_2)_{29}OH$ occurring in the form of esters (as the palmitate) in beeswax and other waxes — called also *melissyl alcohol*

myr·i·en·to·ma·ta \ˌmirēən·ˈtōməd·ə\ *n pl, cap* [NL, fr. *Myriopoda* + *entom-* + *-ata*] *in some classifications* : a class of Arthropoda comprising the order Protura — used when the order is excluded from Insecta

myring- *or* **myringo-** *comb form* [NL, fr. *myringa*] : myringa ⟨*myringo*dermatitis⟩ ⟨*myringo*scope⟩ ⟨*myringo*tomy⟩

my·rin·ga \məˈriŋgə\ *n* -s [NL, alter. of ML *miringa* membrane, alter. of LL *mininga, meninga*, fr. Gk *mēning-, mēninx* — more at MEMBER] : TYMPANIC MEMBRANE

myr·in·gi·tis \ˌmirənˈjīd·əs\ *n* -ES [NL, fr. *myring-* + *-itis*] : inflammation of the tympanic membrane

myr·in·got·o·my \ˌmirənˈgäd·əmē\ *n* -ES [ISV *myring-* + *-tomy*] : incision of the tympanic membrane

myrio- — see MYRI-

myr·i·o·ne·ma \ˌmirēōˈnēmə\ *n, cap* [NL, fr. *myri-* + *-nema*] : a genus (the type of the family Myrionemataceae) of the order Chordariales of brown algae having a minute thallus consisting of a parenchymatous disk made up of radiating filaments and growing epiphytically on other algae (as the sea lettuces) — **myr·i·o·ne·moid** \ˌ;==;ˈnēˌmȯid\ *adj*

myr·i·o·phyl·lum \ˌmirēōˈfiləm\ *n, cap* [NL, fr. L *myriophyllon* water milfoil, fr. Gk, fr. *myrio-* myri- + *phyllon* leaf — more at BLADE] : a widely distributed genus of submerged aquatic plants (family Haloragaceae) having much-divided whorled or alternate leaves and emersed wind-pollinated flowers — see WATER MILFOIL

¹**myr·i·o·pod** \ˈmirēəˌpäd\ *adj* [NL *Myriopoda*] : of or relating to the Myriopoda

²**myriopod** \ˈ"\ *n* -s [NL *Myriopoda*] : an arthropod of the group Myriopoda

myr·i·op·o·da \ˌmirēˈäpədə\ *n pl, cap* [NL, fr. *myri-* + *-poda*] *in some classifications* : a diverse group formerly regarded as a class of arthropods that have a more or less elongated segmented body, one pair of antennae, and several to many pairs of segmentally arranged legs and that in current classification make up the classes Diplopoda, Pauropoda, Chilopoda, and Symphyla

myr·i·o·ra·ma \ˌmirēəˈramə, -rämə\ *n* -s [*myri-* + *-orama* (as in *panorama*)] : a picture made of several sections combinable in different ways so as to produce a variety of scenes

my·ris·tate \məˈriˌstāt\ *n* -s [ISV *myristic* + *-ate*] : a salt or ester of myristic acid

my·ris·ti·ca \-stəkə\ *n, cap* [NL, fr. LGk *myristikē*, fem. of *myristikos* fragrant, fr. Gk *myron* unguent, perfume + *-istikos* -istic — more at SMEAR] : a large genus of tropical trees (the type of a family Myristicaceae) with entire leaves and small white or yellow flowers succeeded by fleshy fruits — see NUTMEG

my·ris·ti·ca·ce·ae \məˌristəˈkāsēˌē\ *n pl, cap* [NL, fr. *Myristica*, type genus + *-aceae*] : a family of trees (order Ranales) having unisexual flowers, monadelphous stamens, and arillate seeds — see BECUIBA, NUTMEG — **my·ris·ti·ca·ceous** \ˌ;=;==ˈkāshəs\ *adj*

my·ris·tic acid \məˈristik-, (ˈ)mīˈristik-\ *n* [ISV *myristic*, fr. NL *Myristica*] : a crystalline fatty acid $CH_3(CH_2)_{12}COOH$ occurring esp. in the form of glycerides in most fats (as in nutmeg butter, sperm oil, coconut oil) — called also *tetradecanoic acid*

myristica oil *n* : NUTMEG OIL a

my·ris·ti·cin \məˈristəsən\ *n* -s [ISV *myristic* + *-in*] : a crystalline phenolic ether $C_{11}H_{12}O_3$ that has a strong odor and occurs in various essential oils (as nutmeg oil, mace oil, parsley oil)

my·ris·ti·civ·o·ra \məˌristəˈsiv(ə)rə\ *n, cap* [NL, fr. *Myristica* + *-vora*] *in some classifications* : a genus consisting of the nutmeg pigeons and now usu. included in the genus *Ducula*

my·ris·tin \məˈristən, mī'-\ *n* -s [ISV *myristic* + *-in*] : a glycerol ester of myristic acid; *esp* : TRIMYRISTIN

myrmec- *or* **myrmeco-** *comb form* [NL, fr. Gk *myrmēk-, myrmēko-*, fr. *myrmēk-, myrmēx* — more at PISMIRE] : ant ⟨*Myrmecia*⟩ ⟨*Myrmecophyte*⟩ ⟨*myrmecology*⟩ ⟨*myrmecophobic*⟩

myr·me·cia \mərˈmēsh(ē)ə, -ēsēə\ *n, cap* [NL, fr. *myrmec-* + *-ia*] : a genus containing the bulldog ant

myr·me·co·bi·ine \ˌmərməˈkōbēˌīn, -ēən\ *adj* [NL *Myrmecobius* + E *-ine*] : of or relating to the genus *Myrmecobius*

myr·me·co·bi·us \ˌ==ˈkōbēəs\ *n, cap* [NL, fr. *myrmec-* + *-bius*] : a genus of insectivorous marsupials including a single species (*M. fasciatus*) that is rufous gray banded with white on the back and has a long extensile tongue and 50 to 56 small teeth — see BANDED ANTEATER

myr·me·co·cho·rous \ˌmərməkōˈkōrəs\ *adj* [*myrmec-* + *-chorous*] : dispersed by ants ⟨~ seeds⟩ — **myr·me·co·cho·ry** \ˌ===ˈkōrē\ *n* -ES

¹**myr·me·coid** \ˈmərməˌkȯid\ *adj* [G or LGk *myrmēkoeidēs*, fr. Gk *myrmēk-* myrmec- + *-oeidēs* -oid] : resembling an ant

²**myrmecoid** \ˈ"\ *n* -s : a myrmecoid insect or spider

myr·me·coidy \-dē\ *n* -ES [²*myrmecoid* + *-y*] : the mimicking of ants by other insects

myr·me·co·log·i·cal \ˌmərməkəˈläjəkəl\ *adj* : of or relating to myrmecology

myr·me·col·o·gist \ˌmərməˈkäləjəst\ *n* -s : a specialist in myrmecology

myr·me·col·o·gy \-jē\ *n* -ES [ISV *myrmec-* + *-logy*] : a scientific study of ants

myr·me·coph·a·ga \ˌmərməˈkäfəgə\ *n, cap* [NL, fr. *myrmec-* + *-phaga*] : a genus (the type of a family Myrmecophagidae) of edentate mammals comprising the So. American ant bear — **myr·me·coph·a·gid** \-fəjəd\ *n or adj* — **myr·me·coph·a·gine** \-fəˌjīn, -jən\ *n or adj* — **myr·me·coph·a·goid** \-fəˌgȯid\ *n or adj*

myr·me·co·phag·i·dae \ˌmərməkōˈfajəˌdē\ *n pl, cap* [NL, fr. *Myrmecophaga*, type genus + *-idae*] : a family of edentate mammals including the So. American ant bear, the tamandua, and the silky anteater

myr·me·coph·a·gous \ˌ;mərməˈkäfəgəs\ *adj* [*myrmec-* + *-phagous*] : feeding on ants — used esp. of organisms that prey on but do not live with ants

myr·me·co·phile \ˈmərməkōˌfīl\ *n* -s [ISV *myrmec-* + *-phile*] : an organism (as an insect) that habitually shares the nest of a species of ant — **myr·me·coph·i·ly** \ˌmərməˈkäfəlē\ *n* -ES

myr·me·coph·i·lism \ˌmərməˈkäfəˌlizəm\ *n* -s : the practice or characteristic of habitually sharing the nest of a species of ant

myr·me·coph·i·lous \ˌ;==ˈkäfələs\ *adj* [*myrmec-* + *-philous*] : fond of or benefited by ants — used esp. of an insect

myr·me·co·pho·bic \ˌ;mərməkōˈfōbik *also* -fäb-\ *adj* [*myrmec-* + *-phobic*] : having a repulsion for ants — used of a plant that repels ants (as by hairs or glands)

myr·me·co·phyte \ˈmərməkōˌfīt\ *n* -s [ISV *myrmec-* + *-phyte*] : a plant that affords shelter or food or both to ants that live in symbiotic relations with it — **myr·me·co·phyt·ic** \ˌ;===ˈfid·ik\ *adj*

myr·me·cox·ene \ˌmərməˈkäkˌsēn\ *n* -s [*myrmec-* + *-xene*] : SYMPHILE

myr·me·kite \ˈmərməˌkīt\ *n* -s [G *myrmekit*, fr. Gk *myrmēkia* anthill, wart (fr. *myrmēk-* myrmec-) + G *-it* -ite] : an intergrowth of vermicular quartz and feldspar (as oligoclase) formed during the later stages in the consolidation of an igneous rock — **myr·me·kit·ic** \ˌ;==ˈkid·ik\ *adj*

myr·me·le·on \mərˈmēlēən\ *n, cap* [NL, modif. of Gk *myrmekoleōn* ant lion, fr. *myrmēk-* myrmec- + *leōn* lion — more at LION] : a genus (the type of the family Myrmeleontidae) of ant lions

myr·me·le·on·i·dae \ˌmərˌmēlēˈänəˌdē\ [NL, fr. *Myrmeleon* + *-idae*] *syn of* MYRMELEONTIDAE

myr·me·le·ont·i·dae \-ntə-\ *n pl, cap* [NL, fr. *Myrmeleont-, Myrmeleon*, type genus + *-idae*] : a family of insects (order Neuroptera) comprising the ant lions

myr·mi·cine \ˈmərməˌsīn, -ˌsən\ *n* -s [NL *Myrmicinae*, subfamily of ants, fr. NL *Myrmica*, type genus (irreg. fr. Gk *myrmēk-, myrmēx* ant) + *-inae*] : any of a large subfamily of ants having the pedicel of the abdomen in two well-marked segments and including many of the commonly encountered forms (as the little black ant, leaf-cutting ants, and the pavement ant)

myr·mi·don \ˈmərməˌdän, -ˌdən\ *n* -s [L *Myrmidon-, Myrmido*, fr. Gk *Myrmidon-, Myrmidōn*] **1** *usu cap* : one of a legendary Thessalian people accompanying Achilles to the Trojan War **2 a** : a loyal retainer or attendant **b** : a follower or subordinate who unquestioningly or pitilessly executes orders : HIRELING

myr·mo·the·rine \ˌmərməˈthēˌrīn, -rən\ *adj* [Gk *myrmos* ant + *thēran* to hunt (fr. *thēr* wild animal) + E *-ine* — more at PISMIRE, FIERCE] : MYRMECOPHAGOUS

my·rob·a·lan \mīˈräbələn, mə'-\ *also* **my·rob·a·lam** \-ləm\ *or* **my·rab·o·lam** \-rabələm\ *or* **my·rab·o·lan** \-lən\ *or* **my·rob·o·lan** \-räbələn\ *n* -s [MF *mirobolan, mirabolan*, fr. L *myrobalanus, myrobalanum*, fr. Gk *myrobalanos*, fr. *myron* unguent, perfume + *balanos* acorn — more at SMEAR, GLAND] **1 a** : the dried astringent fruit of any of several East Indian trees of the genus *Terminalia* (as *T. chebula* and *T. bellerica*) used chiefly in tanning and in inks **b** : a tree producing myrobalans **2 a** : CHERRY PLUM 1 **b** : EMBLIC

myrobalan family *n* : COMBRETACEAE

myrobalan plum *n* : CHERRY PLUM

my·ron *or* **mu·ron** \ˈmēˌrȯn\ *n* -s [Gk *myron* ointment — more at SMEAR] *Eastern Church* : CHRISM

myr·o·sin \ˈmirəsən, ˈmīr-\ *n* -s [alter. of earlier *myrosyne*, fr. F, fr. Gk *myron* unguent + connective *-s-* + *-yne* — more at SMEAR] : an enzyme occurring in various brassicaceous plants (as mustard) that hydrolyzes the glucoside sinigrin

myr·o·sin·ase \-səˌnās\ *n* -s [*myrosin* + *-ase*] : MYROSIN

my·ro·tham·na·ce·ae \ˌmīrəˌthamˈnāsēˌē\ *n pl, cap* [NL, fr. *Myrothamnus*, type genus + *-aceae*] : a family of plants (order Rosales) coextensive with the genus *Myrothamnus*

my·ro·tham·nus \ˌ==ˈthamnəs\ *n, cap* [NL, fr. Gk *myron* unguent, perfume + *thamnos* shrub] : a small genus of xerophytic southern African shrubs constituting a family (Myrothamnaceae) having small dioecious apetalous spicate flowers

my·rox·y·lon \mīˈräksəˌlän\ *n, cap* [NL, fr. Gk *myron* + NL *-xylon*] : a genus of tropical American trees (family Leguminosae) having pinnate leaves, white papilionaceous flowers, and one-seeded winged pods

myrrh \ˈmər, ˈmə̄\ *n* -s [ME *myrre, mirre*, fr. OE *myrre, myrra*, fr. L *murra, murrha, myrrha*, fr. Gk *myrrha*, of Sem origin; akin to Heb *mōr* myrrh, *mar* bitter, Ar *murr* myrrh, bitter] **1** : a yellow to reddish brown aromatic bitter gum resin that is obtained from various trees of the genus *Commiphora* esp. of East Africa and Arabia (as *C. myrrha* or *C. abyssinica*), that was used by the ancients as an ingredient of incense and perfumes and as a remedy for local application, and that is used today chiefly in the manufacture of dentifrices and perfumes and as a stimulating tonic — see BISABOL, HERABOL MYRRH; compare BDELLIUM **2** : labdanum or a mixture of myrrh and labdanum ⟨they offered him gifts, gold and frankincense and ~—Mt 2:11(RSV)⟩ **3** : the European sweet cicely

myrrhed \ˈmərd\ *adj* [ME *myrred*, fr. *myrre* + *-ed*] : containing myrrh

myrrh·ic \ˈmərik, ˈmir-\ *adj* : of or relating to myrrh

myrrhine *var of* MURRHINE

myr·rhis \ˈmirəs\ *n, cap* [NL, fr. L, sweet cicely, fr. Gk] : a genus of European pubescent perennial herbs (family Umbelliferae) having pinnate leaves, compound umbels of white flowers, and linear oblong beaked fruit — see SWEET CICELY

myr·rho·phore \ˈmirəˌfō(ə)r\ *n* -s *usu cap* [modif. (influenced by *myrrh*) of LGk *myrophoros*, fr. Gk, fem. of *myrophoros* bearing unguent, fr. *myron* unguent + *-phoros* -phore — more at SMEAR] : one of the women bearing spices to the sepulcher of Christ

myr·si·na·ce·ae \ˌmərsəˈnāsēˌē\ *n pl, cap* [NL, fr. *Myrsine*, type genus (fr. Gk *myrsinē* myrtle, prob. of Sem origin; akin to the source of Gk *myrrha* myrrh) + *-aceae* — more at MYRRH] : a family of tropical trees and shrubs (order Primulales) of which some occur in Florida and which have alternate glandular leaves, white or pink tetramerous flowers, and one-celled indehiscent fruit — see ARDISIA — **myr·si·na·ceous** \ˌ;==ˈnāshəs\ *adj*

myr·si·ne family \ˈmərsənē-\ *n* [NL *Myrsine*, genus of shrubs] : MYRSINACEAE

myr·si·phyl·lum \ˌmərsəˈfiləm\ *n, cap* [NL, fr. Gk *myrsinē* myrtle + NL *-phyllum*] *in some classifications* : a genus of plants comprising the smilax of the florist's trade that is now usu. included in the genus *Asparagus*

myr·ta·ce·ae \mərˈtāsēˌē\ *n pl, cap* [NL, fr. *Myrtus*, type genus + *-aceae*] : a family of trees and shrubs (order Myrtales) characterized by numerous stamens, cymose flowers with inferior ovary, and opposite exstipulate leaves that yield a fragrant oil — **myr·ta·ceous** \-āshəs\ *adj*

myr·ta·les \mərˈtā(ˌ)lēz\ *n pl, cap* [NL, fr. *Myrtus* + *-ales*] : an order of dicotyledonous herbs, shrubs, or trees including among others the Myrtaceae, Melastomaceae, Lythraceae, Rhizophoraceae, and Onagraceae and having simple leaves, flowers with inferior compound ovary and numerous ovules, and capsular or baccate fruit

myr·ti·flo·rae \ˌmərd·əˈflōˌrē\ [NL, fr. L *myrtus* myrtle + *-i-* + NL *-florae* (fr. LL, fem. pl. of *-florus* -florous)] *syn of* MYRTALES

myr·ti·form \ˈmərd·əˌfȯrm\ *adj* [L *myrtus* myrtle + E *-iform*] : resembling myrtle or myrtle berries

myr·tle \ˈmərd·əl, ˈmə̄l, ˈ|tᵊl\ *n* -s *often attrib* [ME *mirtille*, fr. MF *mirtille, myrtille*, fr. ML *myrtillus*, fr. L *myrtus, murtus*, fr. Gk *myrtos*, prob. of Sem origin; akin to the source of Gk *myrrha* myrrh — more at MYRRH] **1** : any of various plants of the family Myrtaceae; *esp* : a European shrub (*Myrtus communis*) having ovate or lanceolate evergreen leaves and solitary axillary white or rosy flowers followed by black berries **2 a** : PERIWINKLE 1a **b** : CALIFORNIA LAUREL **c** : MONEYWORT **3** *or* **myrtle green a** : a variable color averaging a moderate green that is yellower and deeper than sea green (sense 1a) or laurel green (sense 1) **b** : a dark grayish green to dark bluish green — called also *Baltic*

myrtle

myrtle beech *n* : an Australian and Tasmanian evergreen beech (*Nothofagus cunninghamii*)

myrtle family *n* : MYRTACEAE

myrtle oak *n* : a small shrubby oak (*Quercus myrtifolia*) of the southeastern U.S. that has stiff much-branched stems and small glossy oval to oblong dark green leaves and that often forms nearly impenetrable thickets in sandy coastal areas

myrtle oil *n* : a yellow to greenish fragrant essential oil obtained from the leaves and flowers of the European myrtle and formerly used in medicine

myrtle spurge *n* : CAPER SPURGE

myrtle tree *n* **1** : MYRTLE **2** : a wax myrtle (as *Myrica carolinensis* and *M. cerifera*) **3** : MYRTLE BEECH

myrtle warbler *or* **myrtle bird** *n* : a No. American warbler (*Dendroica coronata*) of which the male in full plumage is bluish gray streaked with black above and largely white below with a yellow patch on the crown, rump, and each side of the breast

myrtle wax *n* : BAYBERRY WAX

myr·tus \ˈmərd·əs\ *n, cap* [NL, fr. L, myrtle — more at MYRTLE] : a genus of chiefly So. American shrubs (the type of the family Myrtaceae) having flowers with numerous ovules — see MYRTLE

-mys \ˌmis\ *n comb form* [NL, fr. Gk *mys* — more at MOUSE] : mouse : mouselike creature — in generic names in zoology ⟨*Cynomys*⟩ ⟨Phascolo*mys*⟩

my·sel *or* **my·sell** \məˈsel\ *or* **my·sen** \-en\ *dial var of* MYSELF

my·self \mīˈself, mə'-, -eůf\ *pron* [ME, alter. (influenced by *my* & *herself*) of *meself*, fr. OE *mē selfum* & *mē selfne*, dat. & acc. respectively of *ic self* I myself — more at I, ME, SELF] **1** : that identical one that is I : the self that belongs to me : the self that is mine — used (1) reflexively as object of a preposition or direct or indirect object of a verb ⟨I'm doing it solely for ~⟩ ⟨busying ~ only with what concerns me⟩ ⟨I'm going to get ~ a new suit⟩; (2) for emphasis in apposition with *I* or *who* ⟨I ~ will go⟩ ⟨I told him so ~⟩ ⟨I can sympathize with you, I who have ~ had to go through the same thing⟩; (3) for emphasis instead of nonreflexive *me* as object of a preposition or direct or indirect object of a verb ⟨my income supports my wife and ~⟩; (4) for emphasis instead of *I* or instead of *I myself* as predicate nominative ⟨there is only one that wants to do it and that's ~⟩ or in comparisons after *than* or *as* ⟨no one knows more about it than ~⟩ or as part of a compound subject ⟨my brother and ~ will be glad to come⟩ or archaically or dialectally as only subject of a verb ⟨~ when young did eagerly frequent Doctor and Saint —Edward FitzGerald⟩; (5) in absolute constructions ⟨~ without a care in the world, I'll do it whenever I choose⟩ **2** : my normal, healthy, or sane condition ⟨the bewilderment passed quickly and I again came to ~⟩ : my normal, healthy, or sane self ⟨I had been somewhat unwell, but that day I was once more ~⟩

¹**my·si·an** \ˈmishēən\ *adj, usu cap* [*Mysia*, ancient country in northwestern Asia Minor + E *-an*] : of or relating to Mysia or to its inhabitants

²**mysian** \ˈ"\ *n* -s *cap* **1** : a native or inhabitant of Mysia **2** : the language of the Mysian people that is prob. related to Phrygian

¹**my·sid** \ˈmīsəd\ *adj* [NL *Mysidae*] **1** : of or relating to the Mysidae **2** : resembling a crustacean of the family Mysidae : of or relating to a mysis

²**mysid** \ˈ"\ *n* -s [NL *Mysidae*] **1** : a crustacean of the family Mysidae **2** : MYSIS

my·si·da·cea \ˌmisəˈdāshēə\ *n pl, cap* [NL, fr. *Mysid-, Mysis*, + *-acea*] : an order of Crustacea including the Mysidae and related families and formerly with the Euphausiacea constituting the Schizopoda — see OPOSSUM SHRIMP

mys·i·dae \ˈmisəˌdē\ *n pl, cap* [NL, fr. *Mysis*, type genus + *-idae*] : a family of small crustaceans (order Mysidacea) that resemble shrimps, have stalked eyes and 6 pairs of leglike appendages each bearing an exopodite, occur in both fresh and salt water, and form an important food supply of valuable fishes and whales

my·sis \ˈmīsəs\ *n* [NL, fr. Gk *mysis* action of closing (used of the lips or eyes), fr. *myein* to close (used of the lips or eyes), close the eyes + *-sis* — more at MYSTERY] **1** *cap* : the type genus of the family Mysidae **2** *or* **mysis stage** -ES : a larva of higher crustaceans (as macrurans and peneids) having all the thoracic appendages biramous

my·so·phil·ia \ˌmīsəˈfilēə\ *n* -s [NL, fr. Gk *mysos* uncleanness + NL *-philia*; akin to Gk *mydan* to be damp — more at MOSS] : abnormal attraction to filth

my·so·pho·bia *also* **mi·so·pho·bia** \-fōbēə\ *n* [NL, fr. Gk *mysos* uncleanness + NL *-phobia*] : abnormal fear of or distaste for uncleanliness or contamination — **my·so·pho·bic** \ˌ;==ˈfōbik *also* -fäb-\ *adj*

my·sore \(ˈ)mīˈsō(ə)r, -sȯ(ə)r\ *adj, usu cap* [fr. *Mysore*, India] : of or from the city of Mysore, India : of the kind or style prevalent in Mysore

mysore thorn *n, usu cap M* : a spreading thorny leguminous shrub (*Caesalpinia sepiaria*) that bears large erect racemes of red-marked yellow flowers, is native to India where it is used for hedging, and is often cultivated in the greenhouse for its showy flowers

my·sost \ˈmīˌsäst\ *n* -s [Norw *myseost, mysost*, fr. *myse* whey + *ost* cheese] : a hard brown cheese of mild flavor made from whey esp. of goat's milk

myst \ˈmist\ *n* -s [L *mystes*, fr. Gk *mystēs* — more at MYSTES] : MYSTES

myst *abbr* mysteries; mystery

mys·ta·ci·al \məˈstāsh(ē)əl\ *also* **mys·ta·cal** \ˈmistəkəl\ *or* **mys·ta·cine** \-təˌsīn, -ˌsən\ *or* **mys·ta·ci·nous** \ˌ;mistəˈsīnəs\ *adj* [Gk (Doric) *mystak-, mystax* moustache + E *-ial* or *-al* or *-ine* or *-inous* (fr. L *-inus*) — more at MOUSTACHE] : having a stripe or fringe of hairs suggestive of a moustache

mys·ta·co·car·i·da \ˌmistəkōˈkarədə\ *n pl, cap* [NL, fr. Gk (Doric) *mystak-, mystax* upper lip, moustache + NL *Carida*] : an order of obscure microscopic crustaceans living in intertidal sands and considered to be related to the copepods

mys·ta·co·ce·te \ˌmistəkōˈsēˌtē\ *or* **mys·ta·co·ce·ti** \-ˌtī\ [NL, by alter.] *syn of* MYSTICETI

mystae *or* **mystai** *pl of* MYSTES

mys·ta·gog·ic \ˌmistəˌgäjik\ *also* **mys·ta·gog·i·cal** \-jəkəl\ *adj* : of or relating to a mystagogue or mystagogy — **mys·ta·gog·i·cal·ly** \-jək(ə)lē\ *adv*

mys·ta·gogue \ˈmistəˌgäg *sometimes* -gōg\ *n* -s [L *mystagogus*, fr. Gk *mystagōgos*, fr. *mystēs* initiate + *agōgos* leader, fr. *agein* to lead — more at MYSTERY, AGENT] : one who initiates into or interprets mysteries (as the Eleusinian mysteries) : a teacher or disseminator of mystical doctrines

mys·ta·go·gy \-ˌgōjē\ *n* -ES [Gk *mystagōgia*, fr. *mystagōgein* to initiate (fr. *mystagōgos*) + *-ia* -y] : the doctrines, principles, or practice of a mystagogue : interpretation of mysteries

mys·tax \ˈmiˌstaks\ *n* -ES [NL, fr. Gk (Doric) *mystax* upper lip, moustache — more at MOUSTACHE] : a cluster or row of hairs above the mouth of insects (as various two-winged flies)

mys·te·ri·al \məˈstirēəl, -tēr-\ *adj* [LL *mysterialis*, fr. L *mysterium* mystery + *-alis* -al — more at MYSTERY] : MYSTIC, MYSTERIOUS

mys·te·ri·arch \-rēˌärk\ *n* -s [LL *mysteriarches*, fr. LGk *mystēriarchēs*, fr. Gk *mystērion* mystery + *-archēs* -arch — more at MYSTERY] : one that presides over mysteries

mys·te·ri·os·o·phy \məˌstirēˈäsəfē\ *n* -ES [Gk *mystērion* mystery + E *-sophy*] : esoteric doctrine concerning the ancient mysteries

mys·te·ri·ous \məˈstirēəs, -tēr-\ *adj* [MF *mysterieux*, fr. *mystere* mystery (fr. L *mysterium*) + *-ieux* -ious] **1** : of or relating to mystery : containing, conveying, intimating, or implying a mystery : difficult or impossible to understand : OBSCURE, ENIGMATICAL ⟨a ~ event⟩ ⟨these ~ changes⟩ **2 a** : proper to or characteristic of a mystery or solemn rite **b** : stirred by or attracted to the inexplicable — **mys·te·ri·ous·ly** *adv* — **mys·te·ri·ous·ness** *n* -ES

mysterious plant *n* : MEZEREON 1

mys·ter·ize \ˈmistəˌrīz\ *vi* -ED/-ING/-S : to cultivate mystery or a mysterious air

¹mys·tery \ˈmist(ə)rē, -ri\ *n* -ES [ME *misterie, mysterie*, fr. L *mysterium*, fr. Gk *mystērion*, fr. (assumed) *mystos*, verbal of *myein* to initiate into religious rites, fr. *myein* to close (used of the eyes and lips), close the eyes; perh. akin to Norw *mysa* to wink, Latvian *musinât* to whisper, murmur, L *mutus* mute — more at MUTE] **1 a** *obs* **:** a purely spiritual form or interpretation **b :** a religious truth revealed by God that man cannot know by reason alone and that once it has been revealed cannot be completely understood **c** *usu cap* **:** a Christian religious rite or sacrament: as (1) **:** EUCHARIST 1 (2) **mysteries** *pl* **:** HOLY MYSTERIES (3) **:** any of the 15 meditations on the events of the life of Christ forming the major part of the rosary devotion **d** (1) **:** a secret non-Christian religious rite marked by the showing of sacred objects to duly initiated worshipers, the pronouncing of formulas, and the performing of ritual acts (as washing, eating and drinking, sacrificing) with a view to bettering the worshipers in this life and assuring them of life after death through union with the god thus worshiped (2) *or* **mystery cult** *or* **mystery religion** *often cap M* **:** a cult chiefly among ancient Mediterranean peoples characterized by such rites — often used in pl. ⟨the Eleusinian *mysteries* of the Greeks and the Mithras *mysteries* of Persia⟩ **2 :** something that has not been or cannot be explained, that is unknown to all or concealed from some and therefore exciting curiosity or wonder, or that is incomprehensible or uncomprehended ⟨the ~ of his disappearance has never been solved⟩ ⟨it's a ~ to me⟩ ⟨why are they making such a ~ of their troubles⟩: as **a** *obs* **:** a private secret **b** (1) **:** the secret or specialized operations or processes peculiar to an occupation or accomplishment ⟨learned the *mysteries* of his trade as an apprentice⟩ ⟨baffled by the *mysteries* of his wife's toilette⟩ — usu. used in pl. (2) **:** a ritual or the practices or doctrines peculiar to some body of people (as a fraternal order or a primitive community) that are revealed only to members or initiates of that body — usu. used in pl. **c** *archaic* **:** a state or political secret **d :** something that is incomprehensible at a particular period or under particular circumstances but that is not normally so to people in general ⟨the thrilling *mysteries* of childhood, so soon outgrown⟩ **e** *or* **mystery story :** a piece of fiction in which the evidence relating to a crime or occasionally to another mysterious event is so presented that the reader has an opportunity to solve the problem, the author's solution being the final phase of the piece **3** *obs* **:** a mystical or recondite cause or significance **4 a :** profound and inexplicable quality or character **:** INCOMPREHENSIBILITY ⟨the *mysteries* and beauties of nature⟩ **:** the quality or state of defying solution or analysis ⟨puzzled by the ~ of her sly glance⟩ **b :** a tendency to surround things with puzzling circumstances or to make them obscure **:** an affectation of needless or excessive secrecy ⟨despising ~ in their rulers⟩ ⟨wrapped in ~ as in a cloak⟩
syn PROBLEM, PUZZLE, ENIGMA, RIDDLE, CONUNDRUM: MYSTERY refers to a matter inexplicable, one that defies attempts at explanation, or to something kept secret but intriguing and compelling speculation ⟨this *mystery* of growth of life —Richard Jefferies⟩ ⟨the veil of *mystery* that shrouds human sleep —Webb Garrison⟩ ⟨the disappearance of the Erebus and Terror in the Arctic was one of the great mid-Victorian *mysteries* —*Times Lit. Supp.*⟩ PROBLEM, more commonplace in its suggestions, refers to any question calling for solution or answer or to any factor causing perplexity and concern ⟨the *problem* of spontaneous generation —J.B. Conant⟩ ⟨with the shipping *problem* resolved by the allocation of ships to France —*Current Biog.*⟩ ⟨the withdrawn child or adolescent is, in the long run, more likely to become a serious psychological *problem* than is the mildly aggressive child —Paul Woodring⟩ PUZZLE applies to any problem notably baffling and challenging one's ingenuity or skill ⟨there are few things in the world so difficult to explain as real change; it appears to me that most scientists are far from realising the complexity of this metaphysical *puzzle* —W.R.Inge⟩ ENIGMA applies to whatever is quite obscure or inscrutable and challenges one's ingenuity for an answer ⟨he became an *enigma*. One side or the other of his nature was perfectly comprehensible; but both sides together were bewildering —Jack London⟩ ⟨just what his objectives are is an *enigma*, for he has been extremely adept in refusing to commit himself too far —Vance Johnson⟩ RIDDLE indicates a question or problem involving paradox or contradictions, often light, and usu. proposed for solution as an indication of wit or intellect ⟨I've got a brand-new *riddle* for you . . . what's the difference between a cat and a comma? . . . a comma's a pause at the end of a clause, and a cat's got claws at the end of its paws —J.W.Ellison b.1929⟩ CONUNDRUM may apply to punning riddles or to unsolvable problems inviting speculation ⟨Octavius — he was not for nothing the scion of banking stock — looked beyond the political *conundrum* to the economic problems of the land —John Buchan⟩

²mystery *or* **mis·tery** \"\ *n* -ES [LL *mysterium, misterium*, alter. (influenced by L *mysterium* mystery) of L *ministerium* work, occupation, ministry — more at MINISTRY] **1** *archaic* **:** one's occupation or calling **:** TRADE, CRAFT, HANDICRAFT, ART **2** *archaic* **:** a body of persons engaged in a particular trade, business, or profession **:** GUILD ⟨fie upon him, he will discredit our ~ —Shak.⟩ **3** *or* **mystery play** [ML *misterium, mysterium*, fr. LL] **a :** one of a class of medieval religious dramas based on Scriptural incidents and usu. centering in the life, death, and resurrection of Christ **b :** this type of drama — compare MIRACLE PLAY, MORALITY PLAY

mystery clock *n* **:** a clock so constructed as to run without gears or a visible source of power

mystery grass *n* **:** DEATH CAMAS

mystery ship *or* **mystery boat** *n* **:** Q-BOAT — first used of one of a class of ships built in England during World War I

mystery snail *n* **:** an apple snail (*Ampullaria cuprina*) often kept as a scavenger in aquariums

mys·tes \ˈmistēz\ *n, pl* **mys·tae** \-ˌstē\ *or* **mys·tai** \-ˌstī\ [L, fr. Gk *mystēs*, fr. *myein* to initiate into religious rites — more at MYSTERY] **:** an initiate in a mystery (as in the Eleusinian mysteries)

¹mys·tic \ˈmistik, -tēk\ *adj* [ME *mistik*, fr. L *mysticus*, fr. Gk *mystikos*, fr. (assumed) *mystos* (verbal of *myein* to initiate into religious rites) + *-ikos* -ic — more at MYSTERY] **1 :** MYSTICAL 1 **2 a :** of or relating to ancient mysteries (as the Eleusinian) **b :** constituting or belonging to something occult or esoteric — used of rites, observances, religions, and comparable matters **c** *of a fraternal order* **:** having a ritual known or practiced only by initiates **3 :** of or relating to mysticism, mystics, the mystical experience ⟨~ state⟩ ⟨the ~ way⟩ **4 a :** baffling or incomprehensible to the understanding **:** MYSTERIOUS ⟨the ~ gulf from God to man —R.W.Emerson⟩ **b :** ENIGMATIC, OBSCURE, MYSTIFYING, VAGUE ⟨the ~ words of the stranger⟩ **c :** inducing a feeling of awe, wonder, or similar response ⟨the ~ beauty of the night⟩ **d :** having magical properties or associations ⟨~ numbers⟩ **5** *obs* **:** SECRET, HIDDEN, COVERT, DISGUISED

²mystic \"\ *n* -S **1 :** a person subject to mystical experiences **:** a follower or an expounder of a mystical way of life **2 :** an initiate of a mystery **3 :** a holder or advocate of a theory of mysticism

mys·ti·cal \-tәkәl, -tēk-\ *adj* [L *mysticus* + E *-al*] **1 :** having a spiritual meaning, existence, reality, or comparable value that is neither apparent to the senses nor obvious to the intelligence **:** relating to such a value **:** SYMBOLICAL, ANAGOGIC ⟨the church is the ~ body of Christ⟩ ⟨the ~ interpretation of Scriptures⟩ ⟨the ~ style of Blake⟩ **2 a :** of, resulting from, or manifesting an individual's direct or intimate knowledge of or communion with God (as through contemplation, vision, an inner light) ⟨~ rapture⟩ ⟨~ experience⟩ **:** concerned with or relating to such experience ⟨a ~ artist⟩ **b :** derived immediately rather than mediately **:** based upon intuition, insight, or similar subjective experience ⟨the ~ character of Neoplatonism⟩ ⟨the ~ religions of the East⟩ **3 a :** remote from ordinary human knowledge or comprehension **:** UNINTELLIGIBLE, CRYPTIC, ENIGMATIC, OBSCURE **b :** FURTIVE, SECRET **4 :** ¹MYSTIC 2

mys·ti·cal·i·ty \ˌmistәˈkalәd·ē, -әtē, -i\ *n* -ES **:** mystical quality

mys·ti·cal·ly \ˈmistәk(ә)lē, -tēk-, -li\ *adv* **:** in a mystic or mystical manner **:** so as to produce a mystic or mystical effect

mys·ti·cal·ness *n* -ES **:** MYSTICALITY

mystic cross *n, sometimes cap M&C* **:** a mark resembling a cross that is sometimes found on the center of the palm between the line of Heart and the line of Head and under the Mount of Saturn and that is usu. held by palmists to indicate a great interest in mysticism and occult subjects

¹mys·ti·ce·te \ˌmistәˈsēˌtē\ *syn of* MYSTICETI

²mys·ti·cete \ˈmistәˌsēt\ *n* -S [NL *Mysticeti*] **:** WHALEBONE WHALE

mys·ti·ce·ti \ˌmistәˈsēˌtī\ *n pl, cap* [NL, pl. of *mysticetus* Greenland whale, fr. Gk *mystikētos*, a whale (dubious reading in some early editions of Aristotle where some recent editions read *ho mys to ketos* and interpret as "the 'mouse' — that is, the whale so called")] **:** a suborder of Cetacea consisting of the whalebone whales — compare ODONTOCETI — **mys·ti·ce·tous** \ˌ==ˈsēd·әs\ *adj*

mys·ti·cism \ˈmistәˌsizәm\ *n* -S [¹*mystic* + *-ism*] **1 :** the experience of mystical union or direct communion with ultimate reality reported by mystics **2 :** a theory of mystical knowledge **:** the doctrine or belief that direct knowledge of God, of spiritual truth, of ultimate reality, or comparable matters is attainable through immediate intuition, insight, or illumination and in a way differing from ordinary sense perception or ratiocination ⟨nature ~⟩ **3 a :** vague speculation **:** VAGARY **:** a belief without foundation **b :** any theory postulating or based on the possibility of direct and intuitive acquisition of ineffable knowledge or power

mys·tic·i·ty \mәˈstisәd·ē\ *n* -ES [F *mysticité*, fr. L *mysticus* mystic + F *-ité* -ity — more at MYSTIC] **:** mystic quality or state

mys·ti·cize \ˈmistәˌsīz\ *vb* -ED/-ING/-S [¹*mystic* + *-ize*] **:** to make mystic or mystical

mys·tic·ly *adv* **:** in a mystic manner **:** so as to produce a mystic effect

mystico- *comb form* [¹*mystic*] **:** mystical and ⟨*mystico*allegoric⟩

mystic will *or* **mystic testament** *n* **:** a will prepared by or at the instance of a testator, sealed up in an envelope, acknowledged on the outside of the envelope, and executed in accordance with required formalities before a notary

mys·tif·ic \mәˈstifik\ *n* -S [back-formation fr. *mystification*] **:** MYSTIFICATOR

mys·ti·fi·ca·tion \ˌmistәfәˈkāshәn\ *n* -S [F, fr. *mystifier* to mystify, after such pairs as F *falsifier* to falsify: *falsification* — more at MYSTIFY] **1 :** an act or instance of mystifying **2 :** the quality or state of being mystified **3 :** something that is designed to or that does mystify

mys·ti·fi·ca·tor \-ˌād·ә(r)\ *n* -S [F *mystificateur*, fr. *mystifier*, after such pairs as F *falsifier: falsificateur* falsifier] **:** one that mystifies

mys·tif·i·ca·to·ry \mәˈstifәkәˌtōrē\ *adj* **:** MYSTIFYING

mys·ti·fied·ly *adv* **:** in a mystified manner

mys·ti·fi·er \ˈmistәˌfī(ә)r\ *n* -S **:** one that mystifies

mys·ti·fy \-ˌfī\ *vt* -ED/-ING/-ES [F *mystifier*, fr. *mystère* mystery + *-ifier* -ify — more at MYSTERIOUS] **1 :** to intentionally perplex the mind of **:** impose upon the credulity of **:** BEWILDER ⟨caught trying to confuse and ~ his opponent⟩ **2 a :** to involve in mystery **:** make obscure or difficult to understand ⟨~ a passage of Scripture⟩ **b :** to embellish (as fact) mystically or fancifully **syn** see PUZZLE

mys·ti·fy·ing·ly *adv* **:** in a mystifying manner **:** so as to cause mystification

mys·tique \miˈstēk\ *n* -S [F, fr. *mystique*, adj., mystic, fr. L *mysticus* — more at MYSTIC] **1 a :** a complex of transcendental or semimystical beliefs and attitudes directed toward or developing around an object (as a person, institution, idea, or pursuit) and enhancing the value or significance of the object by endueing it with an esoteric truth or meaning ⟨the ~ of the leader⟩ ⟨a ~ of mountain climbing⟩ **b :** an object of a mystique or of the veneration characteristic of a mystique **:** a mystic symbol **2 :** the special esoteric skill or mysterious faculty essential in a calling or activity ⟨a dozen handicrafts each with its own ~⟩ **3 :** a mystical or metaphysical interpretation of reality or a real situation, usu. expressed in a creed or credo, often served by a cult, and serving or intended to serve as a guide to action (as of a religious or a political group)

my·ta·cism \ˈmīd·әˌsizәm\ *n* -S [Gk *mytakismos*, irreg. fr. *my* mu (the letter) + *-ismos* -ism] **:** excessive or wrong use of the letter *m* or of the sound it represents (as in writing or in defective speech)

myth \ˈmith\ *n* -S [Gk *mythos* tale, speech, myth; perh. akin to Goth *maudjan* to remind, OIr *smuainim* I think, OSlav *mysli* thought, Lith *maũsti* to desire ardently] **1 :** a story that is usu. of unknown origin and at least partially traditional, that ostensibly relates historical events usu. of such character as to serve to explain some practice, belief, institution, or natural phenomenon, and that is esp. associated with religious rites and beliefs — compare EUHEMERISM, FABLE, FOLKTALE **2 a :** a story invented as a veiled explanation of a truth **:** PARABLE, ALLEGORY; *esp* **:** one of Plato's philosophical allegories **b :** the theme or plot of a mythical tale occurring in forms differing only in detail **3 :** a person or thing existing only in imagination or whose actuality is not verifiable: as **a :** a belief given uncritical acceptance by the members of a group esp. in support of existing or traditional practices and institutions ⟨a ~ of racial superiority used to justify discrimination⟩ **b :** a belief or concept that embodies a visionary ideal (as of some future utopian state or condition) ⟨the Marxian-fostered ~ of a classless society⟩ **4 :** mythical matter **:** the whole body of myths ⟨features distinguishing modern fiction from ~⟩
syn LEGEND, SAGA: MYTH varies considerably in its denotation and connotation depending on the persuasion of the user. Often the word is used to designate a story, usu. fanciful and imaginative, that explains a natural phenomenon or a social practice, institution, or belief ⟨the old *myth*, imported hazily from the East, which represented the cat-moon devouring the gray mice of twilight —Agnes Repplier⟩ It is also used to designate a story, belief, or notion commonly held to be true but utterly without factual basis ⟨the doubts that women have about themselves are man-made, and most women are so enslaved to the *myths* of their own inferiority they are unable to see the truth for the *myth* —M.F.A.Montagu⟩ The word may be used with wide comprehensiveness in general writing or with narrow exclusiveness and specificity in more limited use ⟨*myths* may be subdivided into such classifications as origin *myths*, ritual *myths*, incidents involving the lives of the gods, stories of culture heroes, trickster tales, journeys to the other world, human and animal marriages, adaptations of old world *myths*, and retellings of biblical stories —L.J.Davidson⟩ ⟨*myths* are said to be expressions or objectifications of "collective wishes" which are personified in the "leader" who is endowed by a given society with powers of social magic to fulfill the collective wishes —A.L.Kroeber⟩ LEGEND is likewise used with latitude: it is likely to indicate a story, incident, or notion often fanciful, fabulous, or incredible, attached to a particular person or place ⟨the medieval *legends* of the saints⟩ ⟨the wrecking of the Palatine which, according to *legend*, did not sink but rose flaming into the sky —Fred Zimmer⟩ ⟨the violent deaths of several slaves quartered in them gave rise to a *legend* that this part of the house is haunted —*Amer. Guide Series: Md.*⟩ SAGA may refer to a long, continued, heroic story that is action-packed but not especially romantic, that deals with a person or group, and that is historical or legendary or both ⟨the *Saga* of Burnt Njal⟩ ⟨the building of the railroad in the Northwest was one of the great *sagas* of man's enterprise —Meridel Le Sueur⟩ **syn** see in addition ALLEGORY

mythi *pl of* MYTHUS

myth·i·cal \ˈmithәkәl, -thēk-\ *or* **myth·ic** \-thik, -thēk\ *adj* [*mythical* fr. LL *mythicus* (fr. Gk *mythikos*, fr. *mythos* myth + *-ikos* -ic) + E *-al*; *mythic* fr. LL *mythicus*] **1 a :** based on or described in a myth esp. as contrasted with factual history **:** imaginary, fancied, and existent only in myths ⟨the founder of the sacred grove . . . is clearly the ~ predecessor or archetype of the line of priests who served Diana —J.G.Frazer⟩ **b :** fabricated, invented, or imagined in a consciously arbitrary way ⟨a ~ all-star team⟩ or ignorantly and willfully without facts or in defiance of facts ⟨history . . . shows that the claim to purity of race on the part of any civilized people is entirely ~ —M.R.Cohen⟩ **c :** characterized by qualities suitable to myth esp. by fantastic or bizarre characteristics ⟨a ~ monster⟩ **d :** constituting myth ⟨~ accounts⟩ **2 a :** characterized by or using myths or mythical matter ⟨~ writers⟩ **b :** construing religious or other narratives about supernatural events to have originated as or to be based on myth ⟨the ~ theory of the Gospels⟩ **syn** see FICTITIOUS

myth·i·cal·ly \-thәk(ә)lē, -thēk-, -li\ *adv* **:** in a mythical manner **:** so as to constitute or give the effect of myth

myth·i·cal·ness *n* -ES **:** the quality or state of being mythical

myth·i·cist \ˈmithәsәst\ *n* -S **1 :** a student or interpreter of myths **2 :** an adherent of the view that apparently supernatural persons or events have their origin in human imagination esp. as revealed in myth

myth·i·cize \ˈmithәˌsīz\ *vt* -ED/-ING/-S **1 :** to make mythical **:** envelop or obscure in myths ⟨*mythicizing* the scanty historic remains of the earlier saints⟩ **2 :** to treat or represent as mythical or fabricated as a myth — **myth·i·ciz·er** \-zә(r)\ *n* -S

mythico- *comb form* [*mythical*] **:** mythical and ⟨*mythico*historical⟩ ⟨*mythico*romantic⟩

mythier *comparative of* MYTHY

mythiest *superlative of* MYTHY

myth·i·fy \ˈmithәˌfī\ *vt* -ED/-ING/-ES [*myth* + *-ify*] **:** to make myth of **:** give a mythical cast to

mythmaker \ˈ=ˌ==\ *n* **:** a creator of myths or of mythical situations or lore

mythmaking \ˈ=ˌ==\ *n* **:** the creation of myths or of mythical situations or lore

myth·o·clast \ˈmithәˌklast\ *n* -S [*myth* + *-o-* + *-clast*] **:** a decrier of myths — **myth·o·clas·tic** \ˌ==ˈklastik\ *adj*

mytho·genesis \ˌmithō+\ *n, also* **my·thog·e·ny** \mәˈthäjәnē\ *n, pl* **mythogeneses** *also* **mythogenies** [*myth* + *-o-* + *genesis* or *-geny*] **1 :** formation or production of myths **2 :** the tendency to make myths or to give mythical status to something (as a tradition or belief)

my·thog·ra·pher \mәˈthägrәfә(r)\ *n* -S [Gk *mythographos* mythographer (fr. *mythos* myth + *graphein* to write) + E *-e* — more at MYTH, CARVE] **:** a compiler of or writer about myths

my·thog·ra·phy \-fē\ *n* -ES [Gk *mythographia*, fr. *mythos* + *-graphia* -graphy] **1 :** the representation of mythical subjects in art **2 a :** descriptive mythology **b :** a critical compilation of myths

mytho green \ˈmi(ˌ)thō-\ *n* [*mytho* of unknown origin] **:** a grayish to moderate yellow green that is greener and lighter than sage green or pois green

mytho·heroic \ˌmithō+\ *adj* [*myth* + *-o-* + *heroic*] **:** celebrating the deeds of heroes of myths ⟨~ poetry⟩

mythoi *pl of* MYTHOS

my·tho·lo·gem \mәˈthälәjәm\ *n* -S [Gk *mythologēma* mythical narrative, fr. *mythologein* to narrate mythical tales — more at MYTHOLOGY] **:** a basic or recurrent theme of myth ⟨the universal flood and the fire bringer are ~s of diverse times and races⟩

my·thol·o·ger \mәˈthälәjә(r)\ *n* -S [Gk *mythologos* teller of myths or legends + E *-er* — more at MYTHOLOGIST] **:** MYTHOLOGIST

myth·o·log·i·cal \ˌmithәˈläjәkәl, -jēk-\ *also* **myth·o·log·ic** \-jik, -jēk\ *adj* [LL *mythologicus*, fr. Gk *mythologikos*, fr. *mythologia* legend, story-telling + *-ikos* -ic, -ical] **1 :** of or relating to mythology or myths **:** dealt with in mythology **2 :** lacking factual basis or historical validity **:** MYTHICAL, FABULOUS — **myth·o·log·i·cal·ly** \-jәk(ә)lē, -jēk-, -li\ *adv*

my·thol·o·gist \mәˈthälәjәst\ *n* -S [Gk *mythologos* teller of myths or legends (fr. *mythos* myth + *-logos*, fr. *logos* word, speech, account) + E *-ist* — more at MYTH, LEGEND] **1 :** a student of mythology or myths **2 :** MYTHMAKER

my·thol·o·gi·za·tion \mәˌthälәjәˈzāshәn\ *n* -S **:** the act or practice of mythologizing **:** the imparting of a mythical quality to something

my·thol·o·gize \mәˈthäləˌjīz\ *vb* -ED/-ING/-S *see -ize in Explan Notes* [F *mythologiser*, fr. *mythologie* mythology (fr. LL *mythologia* interpretation of myths) + *-iser* -ize] *vt* **1** *obs* **:** to explain the mythological references or the symbolical significance of **2 a :** to build a myth round **:** make the subject of mythical treatment **b :** to represent mythologically or as mythological **:** MYTHICIZE ~ *vi* **1 :** to relate, classify, and explain or attempt to explain myths **:** write about myths **2 :** to construct and propagate myths — **my·thol·o·giz·er** \-zә(r)\ *n* -S

my·thol·o·gy \mәˈthälәjē, -ji\ *n* -ES [F or LL; F *mythologie*, fr. LL *mythologia* interpretation of myths, fr. Gk, legend, myth, storytelling, fr. *mythologein* to narrate mythical tales (fr. *mythos* myth + *-logein*, fr. *logos* word, speech, account) + *-ia* -y — more at MYTH, LEGEND] **1** *obs* **:** the symbolical significance of something (as a name or a fable) **2 a :** an allegorical narrative **:** MYTH, PARABLE **b :** a body of myths: as (1) **:** the myths dealing with the gods, demigods, and legendary heroes of a particular people in stories that involve supernatural elements ⟨the ~ of ancient Greece⟩ (2) **:** a body of myths arising from a situation (as an activity or a historical event) or more or less consciously propagated by an agency (as a group or political party) ⟨the ~ that emerged out of World War II⟩ ⟨the ~ of Fascism⟩ **3 a :** a branch of knowledge that deals with myth **b :** a treatise on myths

myth·o·ma·nia \ˌmithәˈmānēә\ *n* [NL, fr. Gk *mythos* myth + NL *-mania*] **:** an abnormal propensity for lying and exaggerating — **myth·o·ma·ni·ac** \ˌ==ˈmānēˌak\ *n or adj*

myth·o·poe·ia \ˌmithәˈpēә\ *n* -S [LL, fr. Gk *mythopoiia*, fr. *mythopoiein* to make a myth (fr. *mythos* myth + *poiein* to make) + *-ia* -y — more at POEM] **:** a creating of myth or a giving rise to myths

myth·o·poe·ic \ˌ==ˈpēik\ *adj* [Gk *mythopoios* teller of legends or myths (fr. *mythopoiein*) + E *-ic*] **1 a :** creating or tending to create myth or myths ⟨the ~ stage of human culture⟩ **b :** preoccupied with mythological matters ⟨the ~ mind of the savage —David Bidney⟩ **2 :** giving rise to myths ⟨some great ~ event —J.C.Powys⟩

mytho·poem \ˌmithә+\ *n* [*myth-* + *-o-* + *poem*] **:** a mythological poem

myth·o·po·e·sis \ˌmithәpōˈēsәs\ *n* -ES [NL, fr. Gk *mythopoiēsis*, fr. *mythopoiein* + *-sis*] **:** the making of myths

mytho·poet \ˌmithә+\ *n* [*myth-* + *-o-* + *poet*] **:** MYTHMAKER

myth·o·po·et·ic \ˌmithәpōˈed·ik\ *adj* [*myth* + *-o-* + Gk *poiētikos* able to make, poetic — more at POETIC] **:** MYTHOPOEIC 1a

myth·o·po·et·i·cal \-d·әkәl\ *adj* [*myth* + *-o-* + Gk *poiētikos* able to make + E *-al*] **:** MYTHOPOEIC 2

mytho·poetry \ˌmithә+\ *n* [*myth* + *-o-* + *poetry*] **:** mythological poetry

my·thos \ˈmīˌthäs\ *n, pl* **my·thoi** \-thȯi\ [Gk — more at MYTH] **1 a :** MYTH 1 **b :** MYTHOLOGY 2b **2 :** the pattern of meaning and valuation expressive of the basic truths and enduring apprehensions of a people's historic experience characteristically expressed through a medium of high symbolism (as poetry, art, or drama) **3 :** the underlying theme or symbolic meaning of a creative work; *sometimes* **:** PLOT 4

myths *pl of* MYTH

my·thus \ˈmīthәs\ *n, pl* **mythi** [NL, fr. Gk *mythos*] **1 :** MYTH 1 **2 :** MYTHOS 2

mythy \ˈmithē\ *adj* -ER/-EST [*myth* + *-y*] **:** resembling, concerned with, or a subject for myth ⟨a ~ mind⟩ ⟨a ~ theme⟩

myt·i·la·cea \ˌmid·әˈlāshēә\ *n pl, cap* [NL, fr. *Mytilus* + *-acea*] **:** a suborder of Filibranchia including the family Mytilidae and sometimes related families (as Pteriidae) — **myt·i·la·cean** \ˌ==ˈlāshәn\ *adj or n* — **myt·i·la·ceous** \-shәs\ *adj*

¹myt·i·lid \ˈmid·ᵊlәd\ *adj* [NL *Mytilidae*] **:** of or relating to the Mytilidae

²mytilid \"\ *n* -S [NL *Mytilidae*] **:** a mollusk of the family Mytilidae **:** MUSSEL

my·til·i·dae \mīˈtilәˌdē\ *n pl, cap* [NL, fr. *Mytilus*, type genus + *-idae*] **:** a family of marine bivalve mollusks (order Filibranchia) having the shell elongated and equivalve with a large narrow internal ligament and a byssus for attachment to the substrate — compare MUSSEL

my·til·i·form \-ˌfȯrm\ *adj* [L *mytilus* + E *-iform*] **:** shaped like a mussel shell

myt·i·lus \ˈmid·ᵊlәs\ *n, cap* [NL, fr. L *mytilus, mutulus, mitulus*, a mussel, fr. Gk *mytilos, mitylos*] **:** the type genus of Mytilidae comprising usu. smooth-shelled marine mussels that live attached to solid objects chiefly in the intertidal zone and include the common edible mussel (*M. edulis*)

myx- *or* **myxo-** *comb form* [NL, fr. Gk, fr. *myxa* lampwick, nasal slime — more at MUCUS] **1 :** mucus **:** slime ⟨*myx*adenitis⟩ ⟨*myxo*cyte⟩ ⟨*myxo*ma⟩ ⟨*Myxo*mycetes⟩ **2 :** myxoma ⟨*myxo*fibroma⟩ ⟨*myxo*sarcoma⟩

-myxa \ˈmiksə\ *n comb form, pl* **-myxa** [NL, fr. Gk *myxa* lampwick, nasal slime] **:** one or ones consisting of or resembling slime — in taxonomic names esp. in protozoology ⟨Chlamydo*myxa*⟩ ⟨Proteo*myxa*⟩

myx·amoe·ba \ˌmiks+\ *n* [NL, fr. *myx-* + *amoeba*] **:** a naked amoeboid uninucleate protoplast that lacks both cilia and flagella, is a characteristic stage in the life cycle of slime molds and some other fungi, arises from a haploid derivative of a swarm spore or by fusion of two haploid zoospores, and typically develops into a plasmodium either by repeated nuclear fission or by fusion of individual myxamoebas

myx·ede·ma \ˌmiksəˈdēmə\ *n* -s [NL, fr. *myx-* + *edema*] **:** severe hypothyroidism characterized by firm inelastic edema, dry skin and hair, and loss of mental and physical vigor — **myx·edem·a·tous** \¦==¦demad·əs, -dēm-\ *adj*

myx·i·ne \mikˈsīnē\ *n, cap* [NL, fr. Gk *myxinos*, a kind of mullet, fr. *myxa* lampwick, nasal mucus + *-inos* -ine — more at MUCUS] **:** a genus (the type of the family Myxinidae) of cyclostomes containing the typical hagfishes that have on each side only a single external gill opening

myx·i·noid \ˈmiksəˌnȯid\ *adj or n* [NL *Myxine* + E *-oid*] **:** HYPEROTRETAN

myx·i·noi·dei \ˌ==ˈnȯidēˌī\ [NL, fr. *Myxine* + *-oidei*] *syn of* HYPEROTRETA

myx·o·bac·ter \ˈmiksəˌbaktə(r)\ *n* -s [NL *Myxobacter*, former genus of bacteria, fr. *myx-* + *-bacter*] **:** a bacterium of the order Myxobacterales

myx·o·bac·ter·a·les \ˌmiksəˌbaktəˈrā(ˌ)lēz\ *n pl, cap* [NL, fr. *Myxobacter* + *-ales*] **:** an order of higher bacteria having long slender nonflagellated vegetative cells that form colonies capable of creeping slowly over a layer of slime secreted by the cells, forming spores usu. in distinct fruiting bodies, and living chiefly as saprophytes on substrates rich in carbohydrates

myxo·bac·te·ria \ˌmiksəˌbakˈtirēə\ [NL, fr. *myx-* + *bacteria*, pl. of *bacterium*] *syn of* MYXOBACTERALES

1myx·o·bac·te·ri·a·ce·ae \ˌ==ˌ=ˌtirēˈāsēˌē\ [NL, fr. *Myxobacterium* + *-aceae*] *syn of* MYXOBACTERALES

2myxobacteriaceae \"\ [NL, fr. *Myxobacterium* + *-aceae*] *syn of* POLYANGIACEAE

myx·o·bac·te·ri·al \¦==ˌ=¦tirēəl\ *adj* [NL *Myxobacteriales*] **1 :** of or relating to the Myxobacterales **2 :** like or like that of a myxobacter

myx·o·bac·te·ri·a·les \ˌ==ˌ=ˌtirēˈā(ˌ)lēz\ [NL, fr. *Myxobacterium* + *-ales*] *syn of* MYXOBACTERALES

myxo·bac·te·ri·um \ˌmiksəˌbakˈtirēəm\ *n* [NL, former genus of bacteria, fr. *Myx-* + *bacterium*] **:** a bacterium of the order Myxobacterales

myx·ob·o·lus \mikˈsäbələs\ *n, cap* [NL, fr. *myx-* + Gk *bōlos* lump — more at BOLE] **:** a genus of cnidosporidian protozoans that includes the causative organism of boil disease of fishes

myx·o·coc·cus \ˌmiksəˈkäkəs\ *n* [NL, fr. *Myx-* + *-coccus*] **1** *cap* **:** a genus of myxobacteria in which the rod-shaped vegetative cells are transformed into ovoidal to spherical spores **2** *pl* **myxococ·ci** \-äˌkī, -ä(ˌ)kē, -äkˌsī, -äk(ˌ)sē\ **:** an organism of the genus *Myxococcus*

myx·o·coel \ˈmiksəˌsēl\ *n* -s [*myx-* + Gk *koilos* hollow, concave — more at CAVE] **:** a body cavity that is only partly of coelomic origin

myx·o·cyte \ˈmiksəˌsīt\ *n* -s [*myx-* + *-cyte*] **:** a stellate cell that is characteristic of mucous tissue

myx·o·flag·el·late \ˌmiksəˈflajəˌlāt\ *n* [*myx-* + *flagellate*] **:** a flagellated zoospore that follows the myxamoeba in various myxomycetes

myx·o·gas·ter \ˈmiksəˌgastə(r), ˌ==ˈ==\ *n* -s [NL, former genus of slime molds, fr. *myx-* + *-gaster*] **:** MYXOMYCETE

myx·o·gas·te·res \ˌ==ˈgastəˌrēz\ [NL, fr. pl. of *Myxogaster*] *syn of* MYXOGASTRES

myx·o·gas·tra·les \ˌ==ˌgaˈstrā(ˌ)lēz\ *n pl, cap* [NL, fr. *Myxogastr-, Myxogaster* + *-ales*] *in some classifications* **:** an order equivalent to the subclass Myxogastres

myx·o·gas·tres \ˌ==ˈgaˌstrēz\ *n pl, cap* [NL, fr. pl. of *Myxogaster*] **:** a subclass of Myxomycetes comprising those typical slime molds that develop definite fruiting bodies in which are produced spores which on germinating release one, two, or rarely several swarm spores — compare EXOSPOREAE — **myx·o·gas·tric** \¦==¦gastrik\ *or* **myx·o·gas·trous** \-rəs\ *adj*

myx·oid \ˈmikˌsȯid\ *adj* [*myx-* + *-oid*] **:** like mucus

myx·o·ma \mikˈsōmə\ *n, pl* **myxomas** \-məz\ *or* **myxoma·ta** \-məd·ə\ [NL, fr. *myx-* + *-oma*] **:** a soft tumor made up of gelatinous connective tissue resembling that found in the umbilical cord — **myx·om·a·tous** \(ˈ)mik¦sämәd·əs, -sōm-\ *adj*

myx·o·ma·to·sis \mikˌsōməˈtōsə̇s\ *n, pl* **myxomato·ses** \-tōˌsēz\ [NL, fr. *myxomat-, myxoma* + *-osis*] **1 :** a condition characterized by the presence of myxomas in the body; *specif* **:** a severe virus disease of rabbits that is marked by fever, swelling and inflammation, and myxomatous subcutaneous tumors tending to become necrotic, is transmitted by mosquitoes, and has been used in biological control of rabbits in plague areas **2 :** mucoid degeneration

myx·o·my·ce·tae \ˌmiksəˌmīˈsē(ˌ)d·ē\ [NL] *syn of* MYXOMYCETES

myx·o·my·cete \ˌmiksəˈmīˌsēt, ¦==ˌ=¦= *sometimes* mikˈsäməˌsēt\ *n* -s [NL *Myxomycetes*] **:** an organism of the class Myxomycetes

myx·o·my·ce·tes \ˌmiksəˌmīˈsēd·ēz\ *n pl, cap* [NL, fr. *Myx-* + *-mycetes*] **:** a class of organisms of uncertain systematic position that are sometimes considered to be protozoans but are now usu. regarded as plants and associated with the fungi or placed in a separate division, that exist vegetatively as complex mobile plasmodia, reproduce by means of spores which in almost all cases are borne in characteristic fruiting bodies, and have complex variable life cycles — see EXOSPOREAE, MYXOGASTRES; MYCETOZOA, MYXOPHYTA; SLIME MOLD — **myx·o·my·ce·tous** \¦==ˌ=¦sēd·əs *sometimes* mik¦säm¦s-\ *adj*

myx·o·my·ce·ti·dae \ˌ==ˌ=ˈsēd·əˌdē\ [NL, fr. *Myxomycetes* + *-idae*] *syn of* MYXOGASTRES

myx·o·my·coph·y·ta \ˌmiksəˌmīˈkäfəd·ə\ [NL, fr. *myx-* + *myc-* + *-phyta*] *syn of* MYXOPHYTA

myx·o·phy·ce·ae \ˌmiksəˈfisēˌē\ *n pl, cap* [NL, fr. *myx-* + *-phyceae*] **:** a class of unicellular or filamentous algae of simple structure that comprise the blue-green algae, have the chlorophyll masked by bluish green pigments, lack a condensed nucleus and chloroplasts, reproduce only by simple fission, and have been sometimes considered related to the bacteria — compare NOSTOC, OSCILLATORIA — **myx·o·phy·ce·an** \¦==¦fisēən\ *adj or n*

myx·oph·y·ta \mikˈsäfəd·ə\ *n pl, cap* [NL, fr. *myx-* + *-phyta*] *in some esp former classifications* **:** a division of plants coextensive with the class Myxomycetes — used when the myxomycetes are considered to constitute a group independent of Fungi

myx·op·o·da \mikˈsäpədə\ [NL, fr. *myx-* + *-poda*] *syn of* RHIZOPODA

myx·o·po·di·um \ˌmiksəˈpōdēəm\ *n, pl* **myxopo·dia** \-ēə\ [NL, fr. *myx-* + *-podium*] **:** a pseudopodium that tends to branch or anastomose like the foraminiferans, radiolarians, and myxomycetes

myx·op·o·dous \mikˈsäpədəs\ *adj* [NL *myxopod*ium + E *-ous*] **:** having myxopodia

myxo·pterygium \ˌmiksə+\ *n* [NL, fr. *myx-* + *pterygium*] **:** a clasper of an elasmobranch fish

myxo·sarcoma \¦miksō+\ *n* [NL, fr. *myx-* + *sarcoma*] **:** a sarcoma with myxomatous elements — **myxo·sarcomatous** \"+\ *adj*

myx·o·spon·gia \ˌmiksəˈspänjēə\ *or* **myx·o·spon·gi·ae** \-ēˌē\ [NL, fr. *myx-* + *-spongia, -spongiae*] *syn of* MYXOSPONGIDA

myxo·spongida \ˌmiksə+\ *n pl, cap* [NL, fr. *myx-* + *Spongida*] **:** an order of Demospongiae comprising sponges without either spicules or horny fibers

myx·o·spo·rid·ia \ˌmiksəspəˈridēə\ *n pl, cap* [NL, fr. *myx-* + *-sporidia*] **:** an order of cnidosporidian protozoans that are mostly parasitic in fishes and include various serious pathogens — compare BOIL DISEASE, TWIST DISEASE, WORMY HALIBUT — **myx·o·spo·rid·i·an** \¦===¦ridēən\ *adj or n*

myx·o·spo·ri·di·ida \ˌmiksəˌspōrəˈdīədə\ [NL, fr. *myx-* + *sporidium* + *-ida*] *syn of* MYXOSPORIDIA

myx·os·to·ma \mikˈsästəmə\ *n, cap* [NL, fr. *myx-* + *-stoma*] **:** a genus of cnidosporidian protozoans containing the organism causing twist disease

myxo·thallophyta \ˌmiksə+\ [NL, fr. *myx-* + *Thallophyta*] *syn of* MYXOPHYTA

myx·o·the·ca \ˌmiksəˈthēkə\ *n, pl* **myxothe·cae** \-ē(ˌ)sē\ [NL, fr. *myx-* + *-theca*] **:** the horny sheath of the end of a bird's lower mandible

myxo·xanthin \ˌmiksə+\ *n* [*myx-* + *xanthin*] **:** a violet crystalline carotenoid ketone $C_{40}H_{54}O$ that occurs in blue-green algae and is a provitamin A

-my·za \ˈmīzə\ *or* **-my·zon** \ˈmīˌzän\ *n comb form* [NL, fr. Gk *myzein, myzan* to suck; akin to Gk *mydan* to be damp — more at MOSS] **:** one that sucks or feeds by suction — in generic names in zoology ⟨Petro*myzon*⟩ ⟨Agro*myza*⟩

myzo- *comb form* [NL, fr. Gk *myzan, myzein* to suck] **:** sucking **:** sucker ⟨*myzo*dendron⟩ ⟨*Myzo*rhynchus⟩

my·zo·den·dron \ˌmīzəˈdendrən\ *n, cap* [NL, fr. *myzo-* + *-dendron*] **:** a genus (coextensive with the family Myzodendraceae) of semiparasitic plants of the order Santalales that usu. have unisexual flowers with the small perianth parts opposite the aduate stamens and 3-angled fruits with a greatly elongated hairy process projecting from each angle

my·zon·tes \mīˈzän·ˌtēz\ [NL, fr. Gk, nom. masc. pl. of *myzōn*, pres. part. of *myzein* to suck] *syn of* CYCLOSTOMI

my·zop·o·da \mīˈzäpədə\ *n, cap* [NL, fr. Gk *myzo-* + *-poda*] **:** a genus of bats including solely the sucker-footed bat

my·zo·rhyn·chus \ˌmīzəˈriŋkəs\ *n, pl* **myzorhyn·chi** \-ŋˌkī\ [NL, fr. *myzo-* + *-rhynchus*] **:** an apical sucker on the scolex of various tapeworms that is often stalked

my·zo·sto·mar·ia \ˌmīzəstəˈma(a)rēə\ *n pl, cap* [NL, fr. *Myzostomum*, type genus (fr. *myzo-* + *-stomum*) + *-aria*] **:** a class or other division of aberrant annelid worms that are probably related to the polychaetes, are parasites of echinoderms, have the form as an adult of an unsegmented disk with ventrally located parapodia, adhesive suckers, distinctive marginal cirri, a coelom obscured by connective tissue, no vascular system, and a single pair of nephridia opening into the posterior intestine, develop indirectly, and have a typical trochophore

my·zos·tome \mīˈzäˌstōm\ *n* -s [NL *Myzostomum*] **:** a worm of the class Myzostomaria

my·zus \ˈmīzəs\ *n, cap* [NL, fr. Gk *myzei* to suck — more at -MYZA] **:** a large widely distributed genus of aphids that includes several economically important plant pests — see GREEN PEACH APHID

mza·bite \emˈzäˌbīt\ *n* -s *cap* [*Mzab*, oasis in Algeria + E *-ite*] **:** a member of a Berber people of the Ghardaia oasis in the Algerian Sahara

[1]n \'en\ *n, pl* **n's** *or* **ns** \'enz\ *often cap, often attrib* **1 a :** the 14th letter of the English alphabet **b :** an instance of this letter printed, written, or otherwise represented **c :** a speech counterpart of orthographic *n* (as *n* in *nine, snow,* or Spanish *nuevo*) **2 :** a printer's type, a stamp, or some other instrument for reproducing the letter *n* **3 a :** someone or something arbitrarily or conveniently designated *n* esp. as the 13th or when j is used for the 10th the 14th in order or class **b :** an indefinite number; *esp* **:** a constant integer or a variable taking on integral values (as in an equation, curve, or algebraic expression) ⟨the rules for the permutations of ~ things taken *r* at a time —D.E.Smith⟩ — see NTH **c** (1) **:** the gametic number of chromosomes (2) **:** the basic number of chromosomes (as of a species or species group) — compare X **4 :** something having the shape of the capital letter N **5 :** EN 2 **6 :** an antigen of human blood that shares a common genetic locus with the M antigen

[2]n *abbr, often cap* **1** nail **2** name **3** nasal **4** national; nationalist **5** [L *natus*] born **6** naval **7** navigate; navigating; navigation **8** navy **9** Negro **10** nephew **11** net **12** neuter **13** new **14** newspaper **15** newton **16** night **17** night stop **18** [L *nocte*] at night **19** [L] nomen **20** nominative **21** none **22** noon **23** normal **24** *usu ital* normal (sense 10a) — used of solutions ⟨0.1 *N* hydrochloric acid⟩; normal (sense 10e) — with names of aliphatic hydrocarbons, their derivatives, or alkyl radicals ⟨*n*-butyl⟩ **25** north; northern **26** note **27** noun **28** [F *nous*] we; us **29** November **30** [L *novus*] new **31** number

[3]n *symbol* **1** *cap* **a** place for the insertion of the given name of a bride or of a female person — compare [3]M 1 **b** place for the insertion of the given name of a person (as in a ceremonial statement) — compare NN **2** *usu ital* neutron **3** *cap* nitrogen **4** *usu ital* index of refraction **5** *cap, ital* Avogadro number **6** *cap* knight

[1]'n *or* 'n' \ən, *usu* [a]n *after* t, d, s *or* z\ *conj* [by alter.] **:** AND ⟨sugar 'n spice⟩ — not often in formal use

[2]'n \"\ *conj* [by shortening] **:** THAN ⟨hotter'n blazes⟩ — not often in formal use

[3]'n \"\ *prep* [by shortening] **:** IN ⟨where'n blazes is he⟩ — not often in formal use

-n — see -EN

[1]**na** \nə\ *adv* [ME (northern dial.), fr. OE *nā* — more at NO] *chiefly Scot* **:** by no means **:** NO, NOT — often combined with a preceding verb ⟨a wooer like me mau*na* hope to come speed —Robert Burns⟩

[2]**na** \"\ *conj* **1** [ME, fr. OE *nā*, fr. *nā*, adv.] *chiefly Scot* **:** NOR **2** *chiefly Scot* **:** THAN

na *abbr* **1** nadir **2** nail

NA *abbr* **1** national academician; national academy **2** national association **3** nautical almanac **4** naval academy **5** naval architect **6** naval attaché **7** naval aviator **8** no account **9** no advice **10** nonacceptance **11** numerical aperture **12** nursing auxiliary

Na *symbol* [NL *natrium*] sodium

NAA *abbr, often not cap* not always afloat

naam *or* **nam** \'näm\ *n* -s [ME, fr. OE *nām*, fr. ON, action of taking or seizing (attested only in compounds such as *landnām* act of taking possession of land), learning; akin to OE *nǣm* action of taking, OHG *nāma* robbery; derivative fr. the stem of ON *nema* to take — more at NIMBLE] **1** *early Eng law* **:** distraint of chattels **2** *early Eng law* **:** things distrained

naart·je \'närchə\ *or* **naart·jie** \-chē\ *n* -s [Afrik, fr. Tamil *nārattai*, fr. *nāram* lemon] *southern Africa* **:** TANGERINE 2

na·as·sene \nā'a,sēn\ *n* -s *usu cap* [LGk *naassēnos*, fr. *naas* snake, fr. Heb *naḥash*] **:** a member of one of the Ophite group of Gnostic sects noted for its worship of the serpent as the principle of generation

[1]**nab** \'nab\ *n* -s [ME *nabb*, of Scand origin; akin to Norw *nabbe* crag, ON *nabbi* small conical protuberance; akin to ON *nef* beak — more at NEB] **1** *Scot* **:** a projecting part of an eminence (as a peak or promontory) **2 a** *obs slang* **:** HEAD **b** *archaic slang* **:** HAT **3 a :** the shoulder of the bolt of a lock on which the key acts to shoot the bolt **b :** the keeper of a door lock

[2]**nab** \'nab, 'naa(ə)b\ *vt* **nabbed; nabbed; nabbing; nabs** [perh. alter. of [5]*nap*] **1 :** to catch or seize in arrest **:** take into custody **:** APPREHEND **2 :** to seize or catch suddenly **:** lay hold of **:** obtain possession of usu. by some improper or irregular method ⟨*nabbed* the best seats in the house⟩; *esp* **:** STEAL

[3]**nab** \"\ *n* -s **1** *slang* **:** POLICEMAN **2** *slang* **:** ARREST

[4]**nab** \'nab\ *Scot var of* [3]NOB

NAB *abbr* **1** national aircraft beacon **2** naval air base

na·bal \'nābəl\ *n* -s *usu cap* [after *Nabal*, wealthy sheep owner who refused to pay tribute to King David for protecting his flocks (1 Sam 25:2), fr. Heb *Nābhāl*] **:** a churlish or niggardly man **:** MISER

na·ba·loi \,näbä'lōi\ *n, pl* **nabaloi** *or* **nabalois** *usu cap* **1 a :** a people inhabiting northern Luzon, Philippines — compare IGOROT 1a **b :** a member of such people **2 :** an Austronesian language of the Nabaloi people

na·bam \'nā,bam\ *n* -s [*Na* (symbol) + dithio*carbamate*] **:** a crystalline fungicide ($-CH_2NHCSSNa)_2$; disodium ethylene-bis-dithiocarbamate

nab·a·tae·an *also* **nab·a·te·an** \,nabə'tēən\ *n* -s *usu cap* [L *nabataeus, nabathaeus*, Nabataean (fr. *Nabataea, Nabathaea*, ancient Arab kingdom to the east and southeast of Palestine, fr. Ar *Nebāṭu*) + E -*an*] **1 :** an Arab of an ancient kingdom of Palestine that lasted from about 312 B.C. to A.D.106 when it was made a Roman province **2 :** a dialect of Aramaic spoken by the Nabataeans as shown in their inscriptions

nab·ber \'nabə(r)\ *n* -s [[2]*nab* + -*er*] **:** one that nabs

nab·by \'nabē\ *n* -ES [origin unknown] **:** an open sailboat with a lug rig and jib and a raking mast that is used esp. for fishing off the eastern coast of Scotland

nabby

nabcheat *n* [[1]*nab* (hat) + *cheat* (thing)] *obs slang* **:** HAT

nabe \'nāb\ *n* -s [by shortening & alter. fr. *neighborhood (theater)*] **:** a neighborhood theater

na·bel *or* **na·ble** \'nābəl\ *dial var of* NAVEL

na·be·shi·ma ware \'näbə'shēmə-\ *n, usu cap N* [after the *Nabeshima*, 15th–19th cent. feudal lords of Hizen, Japan] **:** a Hizen ware noted for its clean design and brilliant coloring

na·bes·na \nə'beznə\ *n, pl* **nabesna** *or* **nabesnas** *usu cap* [fr. the *Nabesna* river, southeastern Alaska] **1 :** an Athapaskan people of southeastern Alaska **2 :** a member of the Nabesna people

na·bi \'näbē\ *n* -s *often cap* [F, fr. Heb *nābhī* prophet] **:** a member of a group of French artists that was active about 1890 and followed a synthetic direction — compare SYNTHETISM

[1]**nab·id** \'nabəd, 'nāb-\ *adj* [NL *Nabidae*] **:** of or relating to the Nabidae

[2]**nabid** \"\ *n* -s [NL *Nabidae*] **:** a bug of the family Nabidae

nab·i·dae \'nabə,dē\ *n pl, cap* [NL, fr. *Nabis*, type genus (fr. L, giraffe) + -*idae*] **:** a widely distributed family of predaceous bugs that are related to the assassin bugs and typically have a four-segmented rostrum through which they suck the blood of soft-bodied insects

nab·la \'nablə\ *n* -s [Gk, of Sem origin; akin to Heb *nēbhel* harp] **1 :** an ancient stringed instrument probably like a Hebrew harp of 10 or 12 strings — called also *nebel* **2** [prob. so called fr. the resemblance of its symbol, the inverted Greek delta, to a harp] **:** DEL

na·bob \'nā,bäb\ *n* -s [Hindi *nawwāb, nawāb, nabāb*, fr. Ar *nuwwāb*, pl. of *nā'ib* vice-regent, governor] **1 :** a native deputy or viceroy in India **:** a governor of a province of the Mogul empire **2 a :** one who returns to Europe from the East with great riches **b :** man of great wealth **c :** a man of unusual prominence in a particular field ⟨these scientific ~*s*⟩ — sometimes a generalized expression of disapproval

na·bob·ess \-äbəs\ *n* -ES **1 :** a female nabob **2 :** a woman of a nabob's family

na·boom \'nä,bōm\ *n* -s [Afrik, fr. Hottentot *ngha* naboom + Afrik *boom* tree, fr. MD — more at BOOM] **:** a small tree (*Euphorbia ingens*) of dry open parts of southern Africa that has erect 4-angled branches which form a broad head suggesting a candelabra

na·bo·thi·an cyst *or* **na·bo·thi·an follicle** \nə'bōthēən-\ *n, sometimes cap N* [Martin *Naboth* †1721 Ger. anatomist + E -*ian*] **:** a mucous gland of the uterine cervix esp. when occluded and dilated

[1]**nabs** *pl of* NAB, *pres 3d sing of* NAB

[2]**nabs** \'nabz\ *n pl but sing or pl in constr* [origin unknown] *slang* **:** FELLOW, PERSON, CHAP — used with *my* and chiefly in nonspecific identification or as a mode of address ⟨my ~ of an officer⟩ ⟨well, my ~, shall we get along⟩; compare NIBS

nac *abbr* nacelle

NAC *abbr* **1** national advisory committee; national advisory council **2** naval aircraftsman **3** non-airline-carrier

nac·a·rat \'nakə,rat\ *n* -s [F, fr. MF *nacarade*, fr. OSp *nacarado*, fr. *nácar* nacre (fr. Ar *naqqārah* drum) + -*ado* (fr. L -*atus* -ate)] **:** GERANIUM LAKE 2

na·celle \nə'sel\ *n* -s [F, fr. lit., small boat, fr. LL *navicella*, dim. of L *navis* ship — more at NAVE] **:** an enclosed shelter on an aircraft for an engine or sometimes for the crew

nach·i·ku·fu \'nachə'kü(,)fü\ *also* **nach·i·ku·fan** \-küfən\ *adj, usu cap* [*Nachikufu* fr. *Nachikuḟu*, locality in Zambia; *Nachikuḟan* fr. *Nachikufu*, Zambia + E -*an*] **:** of or relating to a late Stone-Age culture of northeastern Zambia characterized by tranchet-type microliths, bored stones, and scrapers of the Smithfield type

nach·schlag \'näk,shläk\ *n, pl* **nachschlä·ge** \-lāgə\ *or* **nachschlags** [G, lit., afterstroke, fr. MHG *nāchslac* blow struck from behind, fr. *nāch* after, behind (fr. OHG *nāh*) + *slac* blow (fr. OHG *slag*); akin to OHG *slahan* to beat, strike — more at NIGH, SLAY] **1 :** a musical ornament consisting of one or several short unaccented grace notes attached to and played in the time of the preceding main note or tone **2 :** the auxiliary closing note or notes usu. played at the end of a trill

nacht·horn \'näkt,hȯrn\ *n, pl* **nachthör·ner** \-hərnər\ *or* **nachthorns** [G, fr. *nacht* night (fr. OHG *naht*) + *horn* (fr. OHG) — more at NIGHT, HORN] **:** COR-DE-NUIT

nacht·mu·sik \'näktmü,zēk\ *n, pl* **nachtmusi·ken** \-kən\ *or* **nachtmusiks** [G, fr. *nacht* night + *musik* music, fr. F *musique* — more at NIGHT, MUSIC] **:** SERENADE

[1]**nack·et** \'nakət\ *n* -s [obs. Sc *nacket* caddie at tennis, fr. MF *naquet* valet, caddie at tennis, prob. fr. *naquer* to bite, gnaw, cheat, of imit. origin] *Scot* **:** a mischievous or brattish boy

[2]**nacket** \"\ *n* -s [perh. contr. of *noon cate*] **1** *Scot* **:** a light lunch **2** *Scot* **:** a small cake resembling a pasty

[1]**nacre** \'nākə(r)\ *n* -s [MF, fr. OIt *naccara, nacchera* nacre, drum, fr. Ar *naqqārah* drum] **1** *archaic* **:** a shellfish that yields mother-of-pearl **2 :** the iridescent inner layer of various mollusk shells consisting chiefly of calcium carbonate deposited in thin overlapping sheets with some organic matter (as conchiolin) **:** MOTHER-OF-PEARL

[2]**na·cré** \nə'krā\ *also* **na·cre** \'nākə(r)\ *adj* [F *nacré*, fr. *nacre*, n.] **:** resembling nacre esp. in pearly iridescent luster: as **a** *of a fabric* **:** having a changeable iridescent luster produced usu. by use of a warp of one color and a filling of another ⟨~ taffeta⟩ **b** *of a plant sieve element* **:** having a thickened hydrated wall that appears pearly in section

na·cred \'nākə(r)d\ *adj* **:** lined with or like nacre

na·cre·ous \'nākrēəs\ *also* **na·crous** \-krəs\ *adj* **:** consisting of or resembling nacre **:** PEARLY

nacreous cloud *n* **:** a luminous iridescent cloud that occurs at altitudes of about 85,000 feet — called also *mother-of-pearl cloud*

na·crite \'nā,krīt\ *n* -s [F, fr. *nacre* + -*ite*; fr. its pearly scales] **:** a clay mineral $Al_2Si_2O_5(OH)_4$ consisting of hydrous silicate of aluminum and being polymorphous with kaolinite

NAD *abbr* **1** no appreciable disease **2** nothing abnormal discovered

na·da \'nädə, 'näthə\ *n* -s [Sp, nothing, fr. L (*res*) *nata* lit., thing born, small, insignificant thing (only attested in sense of "the question on hand"), fr. *res* thing + *nata*, fem. of *natus* born, past part. of *nasci* to be born — more at NATION] **:** a state of or as if of nonexistence **:** NOTHINGNESS ⟨the typical situation is love, with despair, against the background of ~ — of civilization gone to pot, or war, or death —R.P. Warren⟩

nad·der \'nadə(r)\ *n* -s [ME *naddre* — more at ADDER] *dial* **:** ADDER

na-de·ne *also* **na-dé·né** \'nädā'nā\ *n, pl* **na-dene** *usu cap N & sometimes cap D* [*na*- (fr. an Athapaskan word stem akin to Haida *na* to dwell, house, Tlingit *na* people) + *Déné*] **:** a language phylum comprising the Athapaskan, Eyak, Haida, and Tlingit stocks

[1]**na·dir** \'nādə(r), -ā,di(ə)r, -iə\ *n* -s [ME, fr. MF, fr. Ar *naẓīr* opposite (in the phrase *naẓīr as-samt* opposite the zenith)] **1 :** the point of the celestial sphere that is directly opposite the zenith and vertically downward from the observer **2 :** the lowest point ⟨the novel's ~ of degradation —Robert Hunting⟩ **:** the time of greatest depression

[2]**na·dir** \'nā,di(ə)r\ *n* -s [Malay] **:** a Malayan light-draft fishing boat

na·dir·al \'nādərəl\ *adj* [F, fr. *nadir* + -*al*] **:** relating to or constituting a nadir

nad·or·ite \'nadə,rīt, 'nād-\ *n* -s [F, fr. Jebel *Nador*, locality in northern Algeria + F -*ite*] **:** a mineral $PbSbO_2Cl$ consisting of a brownish yellow lead chloride and stibnite

nae \'nā\ *dial Brit var of* NA

nae·body \'nābədi\ *Scot var of* NOBODY

nae·ge·lia \nā'gēlēə\ *n* [NL, fr. Karl Wilhelm von *Naegeli* †1891 Ger. botanist + NL -*ia*] **1** *cap* **:** a small tropical American genus of rhizomatous perennial herbs (family Gesneriaceae) that are often cultivated for their showy tubular flowers and their velvety foliage **2** -s **:** any plant of the genus *Naegelia*

naem·o·rhe·dus \,nemə'rēdəs\ *n, cap* [NL, irreg. fr. L *nemor-, nemus* grove + *haedus* kid — more at NEMORAL, GOAT] **:** a genus of ruminant mammals comprising the Asiatic gorals

nae·thing \'nāthiŋ\ *Scot var of* NOTHING

naeve *n* -s [LL *naevus*, fr. L, mole, birthmark — more at NEVUS] *obs* **:** FLAW, SPOT, BLEMISH

naevus *var of* NEVUS

[1]**nag** \'nag, 'naa(ə)g, 'naig\ *n* -s [ME *nagge;* akin to D *negge* small horse and prob. to OE *hnǣgan* to neigh — more at NEIGH] **1 a** *archaic* **:** a small light saddle horse **:** a riding pony **b :** an inferior or aged and unsound horse **c** *slang* **:** RACEHORSE **2** *obs* **:** PROSTITUTE

[2]**nag** \"\ *vb* **nagged; nagged; nagging; nags** [prob. of Scand origin; akin to Sw & Norw dial. *nagga* to gnaw, bite, hurt, ON *gnaga* to gnaw — more at GNAW] *vi* **1 :** to engage in persistent petty faultfinding, scolding, or urging ⟨a good wife but she does ~ so⟩ **2 :** to cause distress by persistent small assaults (as of pain or words) — usu. used with *at* ⟨this tooth has been *nagging* at me for days⟩ ~ *vt* **1 :** to annoy by persistent petty faultfinding, scolding, or urging ⟨*nagged* her husband at every opportunity⟩ **2 :** to affect with recurrent awareness, uncertainty, need for consideration, or concern **:** make recurrently conscious of something (as a problem, solution, situation) ⟨a possible solution *nagged* the back of my mind⟩ ⟨that tattoo *nagged* my memory⟩ **syn** see WORRY

[3]**nag** \"\ *n* -s **1 :** an act of nagging **:** nagging conduct or speech **2 :** a person who nags habitually

[1]**na·ga** \'nägə\ *n, pl* **naga** *or* **nagas** *usu cap* **1 a :** one of a group of Tibeto-Burman peoples in the Naga hills, Assam, and in adjoining parts of Burma east of the Chindwin river and the Hukawng valley **b :** a member of any such group **2 :** any of the Tibeto-Burman languages of the Naga peoples

[2]**naga** \"\ *n* -s [Skt *nāga* serpent] **1 :** a member of a race of spirits recognized in Hinduism and Buddhism that have mingled superhuman and serpent qualities, are genii of waters and rain, and live in a subaqueous kingdom **2 :** a Hindu mendicant of any of various sects **3** *also* **nag** \'näg\ [nag fr. Hindi *nāg*, fr. Skt *nāga*] **:** SNAKE; *esp* **:** COBRA

na·gaed wood \'nägəd-\ *n* [*nagaed* prob. fr. Tag & Bisayan *naga* Honduras rosewood + E -*ed*] **:** HONDURAS ROSEWOOD

na·gai·ka \nə'gīkə\ *n* -s [Russ, of Turkic origin; akin to Kirghiz *nogai* Kazan Tatar] **:** a thick tightly twisted whip used by Cossacks

na·ga·mi kumquat \nə'gämē-\ *or* **nagami** *n* -s [*nagami* of unknown origin] **:** a kumquat (*Fortunella margarita*) having oval fruit and a persistent style base — compare MARUMI KUMQUAT

na·ga·na *or* **n'ga·na** \nə'gänə\ *n* -s [Zulu *u-nakane, ulu-nakane*] **:** a highly fatal disease of domestic animals in tropical Africa caused by a trypanosome (*Trypanosoma brucei*), marked by fluctuating fever, inappetence, edematous swelling, and sluggishness, and transmitted by tsetse and possibly other biting flies; *broadly* **:** trypanosomiasis of domestic animals

na·ga·ri \'nägərē\ *n* -s *usu cap, often attrib* [Skt *nāgarī*, lit., (writing) of the city, fr. *nagara* city, of Dravidian origin; akin to Tamil *nakar* dwelling, city, Telugu *nagaru* palace] **1 :** DEVANAGARI **2 :** the family of related alphabets of the Indian subcontinent of which Devanagari is a member

na·ga·sa·ki \'nägə'säkē, 'nag- 'nagə'sakē\ *adj, usu cap* [fr. *Nagasaki*, Japan] **:** of or from the city of Nagasaki, Japan **:** of the kind or style prevalent in Nagasaki

naga sore *n, usu cap N* [fr. *Naga* hills, region in Assam and Burma] **:** TROPICAL ULCER 2

na·ga·tel·ite \,nagə'te,līt\ *n* -s [*Nagate*jima, headland on the Noto peninsula, Japan + E -*lite*] **:** a rare mineral $Ca_2(Ce,La)_2Al_4Fe_2(Si,P)_6O_{25}(OH)$(?) that consists of phosphosilicate of aluminum, the rare earths, calcium, and iron, that is related to clinozoisite, and that occurs in black tabular masses

na·gel·fluh \'nägəl,flü\ *n* -s [G, fr. *nagel* nail (fr. OHG *nagal*) + G dial. (Switzerland) *fluh* cliff, mass of rock, fr. OHG *fluoh* cliff — more at NAIL, PLEASE] **:** a massive variegated conglomerate forming a prominent member of the Miocene series in the Alps

nag·gar \nə'gär\ *n* -s [Ar *nuqqār*] **:** a cargo boat used on the upper Nile river

nag·ger \'nagə(r)\ *n* -s [[2]*nag* + -*er*] **:** one that nags

naggin *var of* NOGGIN

nagging *adj* [fr. pres. part. of [2]*nag*] **1 :** persistently annoying, irritating, or faultfinding⟨a ~ husband⟩ **2 :** characterized by nagging ⟨a ~ fear⟩ — **nag·ging·ly** *adv* — **nag·ging·ness** *n* -ES

[1]**nag·gish** \'nagish\ *adj* [[1]*nag* + -*ish*] **:** having the quality of a nag **:** SMALL, INFERIOR

[2]**naggish** \"\ *adj* [[2]*nag* + -*ish*] **:** somewhat nagging

nag·gle \'nagəl\ *vi* -ED/-ING/-S [freq. of [2]*nag*] **:** to haggle or dispute pettily

nag·gly \'nag(ə)lē\ *adj*, -ER/-EST [*naggle* + -*y*] **:** of a naggling nature **:** petty and contentious ⟨~ arguments⟩

[1]**nag·gy** \'nagē\ *n* -ES [[1]*nag* + -*y* (dim. suffix)] **:** a little nag **:** PONY

[2]**naggy** \"\ *adj* -ER/-EST [[1]*nag* + -*y* (adj. suffix)] **:** [1]NAGGISH

[3]**naggy** \"\ *adj* -ER/-EST [[2]*nag* + -*y* (adj. suffix)] **1 :** given to or characterized by nagging **2** *dial Eng* **:** IRRITABLE, CROSS

na·gid \nä'gēd\ *n, pl* **na·gi·dim** \,nägē'dēm\ *also* **ne·gi·dim** \nəgē'dēm\ *n* -s [Heb *nāgīd*] **:** a Jewish ruler and religious authority presiding over Jewish communities esp. in medieval Spain and Egypt

nag·kassar \näg'kasə(r)\ *also* **nag·kes·ar** \-kes-\ *n* -s [Marathi & Hindi *nāgkesar*, fr. Skt *nāgakesara*, fr. *nāga* snake + *kesara* hair, nagkassar (*Mesua ferrea*); akin to L *caesaries* hair of the head] **:** either of two East Indian trees (*Mesua ferrea* and *Ochrocarpus longifolius*) of the family Guttiferae from whose flower buds a red or orange dye is obtained

nag·maal \'näk,mäl\ *n* -s [Afrik, fr. MD *nachtmael*, fr. *nacht* night + *mael* meal; akin to OE *niht* night and to OE *mǣl* appointed time, mealtime, meal — more at NIGHT, MEAL] **1** *Africa* **:** evening meal **2** *Africa* **:** COMMUNION 2

nag·nag \'nag,nag\ *vb* [by redupl.] **:** NAG

na·go \'nä(,)gō\ *n, pl* **nago** *or* **nagoes** *usu cap* **:** YORUBA

na·gor \'nā,gȯ(ə)r\ *n* -s [F, alter. of *nanguer* nanger — more at NANGER] **:** a reddish brown reedbuck (*Redunca redunca*) of western Africa

na·go·ya \nə'gȯyə\ *adj, usu cap* [fr. *Nagoya*, Japan] **:** of or from the city of Nagoya, Japan **:** of the kind or style prevalent in Nagoya

nag·pur \'näg,pu̇(ə)r\ *adj, usu cap* [fr. *Nagpur*, India] **:** of or from the city of Nagpur, India **:** of the kind or style prevalent in Nagpur

nags *pl of* NAG, *pres 3d sing of* NAG

nags·man \'nagzmən\ *n, pl* **nagsmen** [*nags* (pl. of [1]*nag*) + *man*] **:** a man employed to ride and show horses esp. in a sales ring

na·gual \nə'(g)wäl\ *also* **na·hual** \nə'(h)wäl\ *n, pl* **naguals** \-älz\ *or* **nagua·les** \-ä,lās\ *also* **nahuals** [Sp, fr. Nahuatl *nahualli, naualli*, fr. *nahua* to dance with tied hands] **1 a :** a personal guardian spirit or protective alter ego assumed by various Middle American Indians to reside in an animal or less frequently in some other embodiment — compare HUACA **b :** the animal double or guardian itself **2 :** a sorcerer believed by various Middle American Indians to be capable of transforming himself into animal form

na·gual·ism \-ä,lizəm\ *n* -s **:** belief in naguals

nag·ya·gite \'nagyə,gīt, 'najə,-\ *n* -s [G *nagyagit*, fr. *Nagyág* (*Săcărâmbu*), Romania + G -*it* -ite] **:** a mineral $Pb_5Au(Te,Sb)_4S_{5-8}$ that is a sulfide of lead, gold, tellurium, and antimony

nah *substand var of* NO

na·hal \nə'häl\ *n, pl* **nahal** *or* **nahals** *usu cap* **1 :** one of a group of peoples of the hill land of central India **2 :** a member of such people

na·ha·ne *or* **na·ha·ni** \nə'hänē\ *n, pl* **nahane** *or* **nahanes** *or* **nahani** *or* **nahanis** *usu cap* **:** KASKA

nah·co·lite \'nakə,līt\ *n* -s [*NaHCO* (in $NaHCO_3$, formula for sodium bicarbonate) + E -*lite*] **:** a mineral consisting of natural sodium bicarbonate

na·he·carida \,näə'karədə\ *n pl, cap* [NL, fr. *Nahecaris*, genus of crustaceans in some classifications (prob. fr. *Nahe*, river in western Germany + NL -*caris*) + -*ida*] **:** a subdivision of Malacostraca comprising extinct crustaceans that are similar in some respects to members of Phyllocarida

na·hoor \nə'hu̇(ə)r\ *n* -s [prob. fr. Nepali *nahūr*] **:** BHARAL

na·hua \'näwə\ *n, pl* **nahua** *or* **nahuas** *usu cap* [Sp, fr. Nahuatl (n. pl.)] **:** NAHUATL

na·huan \-ən\ *adj, usu cap* [*Nahua* + -*an*] **:** NAHUATLAN

na·hua·tl \'nä,wäd·[a]l, -wät[a]l\ *n, pl* **nahuatl** *or* **nahuatls** *usu cap* [Sp, fr. Nahuatl, sing. of *Nahua*] **1 a :** a group of peoples of southern Mexico and Central America including the Aztec **b :** a member of any such people **2 :** the Uto-Aztecan language of the Nahuatl people

[1]**na·huat·lan** \-wätlən\ *adj, usu cap* [*Nahuatl* + -*an*] **:** of or relating to the Nahuatl or to Nahuatlan

[2]**nahuatlan** \"\ *n, pl* **nahuatlan** *or* **nahuatlans** *usu cap* **1 :** NAHUATL **2 :** a language family of the Uto-Aztecan phylum comprising Nahuatl and Pipil

na·hys·san \nə'hisən\ *n, pl* **nahyssan** *usu cap* **1 a :** a Siouan people in the James river valley, Virginia **b :** a member of such people **2 :** the language of the Nahyssan people

nai \'näē\ *n* -s *usu cap* [Hindi *nāī*, fr. Skt *nāpita;* akin to Skt *snāti* he bathes — more at NOURISH] **:** a member of a barber caste of Hindus in India that grooms the living and the dead and thus is intimately associated with Hindu ceremonial life including the contraction of marriages

na·ia \'nāə\ *syn of* NAJA

na·iad \'nāəd, 'nī, |,ad\ *n, pl* **naiads** \-dz\ *or* **naia·des** \|ə,dēz\ [F or L; F *naiade*, fr. L *naiad-, naias*, fr. Gk, fr. *nan* to flow — more at NOURISH] **1 :** one of the nymphs believed by the ancient Greeks and Romans to live in and give life and perpetuity to lakes, rivers, springs, and fountains **2 :** one of the distinctive aquatic young of mayflies, dragonflies, damselflies, and stone-flies that differ markedly from the corresponding adults **3** [NL *Naiad-, Naias*] **:** a plant of the genus *Naias* or family Naiadaceae **4** [NL *Naiades*] **:** a mollusk of the tribe Naiades **:** a freshwater mussel

na·ia·da·ce·ae \,nāə'dāsē,ē, ,nīə-\ *n pl, cap* [NL, fr. *Naiad-, Naias*, type genus + -*aceae*] **:** a monotypic family of aquatic plants (order Naiadales) — see NAIAS — **na·ia·da·ceous** \¦==¦dāshəs\ *adj*

na·ia·da·les \,==¦dā(,)lēz\ *n pl, cap* [NL, fr. *Naiad-, Naias* + -*ales*] **:** an order of aquatic monocotyledonous herbaceous plants that have flowers either with or without perianth, apocarpous ovaries, and seeds without endosperm — see HYDROCHARITACEAE, JUNCAGINACEAE, NAIADACEAE

na·ia·des \'nāə,dēz, 'nīə-\ *n pl, cap* [NL, fr. L, pl. of *naiad-, naias* naiad] *in former classifications* **:** a tribe of mollusks that is practically equivalent to the family Unionidae and includes the freshwater mussels

na·iant \'nāənt\ *adj* [modif. of MF *noiant*, pres. part. of *noier* to swim, fr. L *natare* — more at NATANT] *heraldry* **:** represented in a horizontal position as if swimming ⟨a roach ∼⟩ ⟨a sea horse ∼ in waves⟩

na·ias \'nā|əs, 'nī|, |,as\ *n, cap* [NL *Naiad-, Naias*, fr. L *naiad-, naias* naiad] **:** a genus (coextensive with the family Naiadaceae) of submerged aquatic plants that have filiform stems, sheathing leaves, and minute diclinous flowers with a double perianth

na·ib *or* **na·ibe** \'nä,ēb\ *n* -S [It *naibi* playing cards, tarot, fr. Sp *naipes*, pl. of *naipe* playing card, perh. fr. Ar *nā'ib* vice-regent, governor] **:** TAROT 1

na·id \'nāəd\ *n* -S [L *naid-, nais*, fr. Gk, fr. *nan* to flow + *-id-, -is* -id] **1** *obs* **:** NAIAD **2** [NL *Naid-, Nais* genus of annelids fr. L, naiad] **:** any of numerous small freshwater annelids constituting *Nais* and related genera of the order Oligochaeta

na·i·dae \'nāə,dē\ [NL, fr. pl. of *Nais*] *syn of* NAIDIDAE

naides *pl of* NAIS

na·id·i·dae \nā'idə,dē\ *n pl, cap* [NL, fr. *Naid-, Nais*, type genus + *-idae*] **:** a family of small aquatic oligochaete worms that commonly reproduce by vegetative transverse segmentation and form chains of worms in various stages of development

na·i·do·mor·pha \,nāədō'mȯrfə\ *n pl, cap* [NL, fr. *Naid-, Nais* + *-o-* + *-morpha*] *in some classifications* **:** a group of aquatic worms nearly coextensive with Archioligochaeta

[1]**na·if** *or* **na·ïf** \nä'ēf\ *adj* [MF *naif*, — more at NAÏVE] **1 :** NAÏVE **2** *or* **na·ife** \"\ **:** having a true luster when uncut — used of precious stones

[2]**naïf** *or* **naif** \"\ *n* -S [F *naïf*, fr. *naïf*, adj.] **:** a naïve person

naig \'nāg\ *chiefly Scot var of* NAG 1

na·ik \'nä|ik\ *also* **na·ig** \|ig\ *or* **na·igue** \|,ēg\ *or* **na·ique** \|,ēk\ *or* **na·yak** \|yək\ *n* -S [Hindi *nāyak*, fr. Skt *nāyaka*, lit., leader, fr. *nayati* he leads; akin to MIr *nē, nīa* warrior, hero, Av *nayeiti* he leads, brings, Hitt *nāi-* to control, lead] **1 :** a leader, chief, or governor in India — used as a title of authority or form of address **2 :** a native subordinate officer in the British India army; *specif* **:** CORPORAL

na·ik·pod \'näik,päd\ *n* -S *usu cap* **1 :** one of various peoples that inhabit the jungle of Central India and practice shifting agriculture with the use of a digging stick **2 :** a member of any of such peoples

[1]**nail** \'nāl, *esp before pause or consonant* 'nāəl\ *n* -S *often attrib* [ME, fr. OE *nægl, nægel*; akin to OS & OHG *nagal* nail, fingernail, ON *nagl* fingernail, L *unguis* nail of the finger or toe, claw, Gk *onyx*, Lith *nagas*, Skt *nakha*] **1 a :** the horny plate of thickened and condensed epithelial stratum lucidum that grows out from a vascular matrix of cutis and sheathes the upper surface of the end of each finger and toe of man and most other primates and that is strictly homologous with the hoof or claw of other mammals from which it differs chiefly in shape and size **b :** a corresponding structure (as a claw or talon) terminating a digit **c :** a terminal horny process not associated with a digit: as (1) **:** a plate at the end of the bill of ducks and related birds (2) **:** a horny spur on the end of the tail of a few vertebrates — compare NAIL-TAILED WALLABY **2 a :** a slender and usu. pointed and headed fastener designed for impact insertion — see TREENAIL, WIRE NAIL; compare BRAD, SPIKE, TACK **b :** DATING NAIL **c :** a rod (as of metal) used to fix the parts of a broken bone in normal relation ⟨medullary ∼⟩ **3 :** something resembling a nail (as in shape or color) **4 a :** [3]CLOVE **b :** an English unit of length once used esp. for cloth equal to 1/16 yard or 2¼ inches — **nail in one's coffin :** something regarded as likely to shorten one's life — **on the nail** *adv (or adj)* **:** on the spot **:** immediately when due **:** at once ⟨paid his bills *on the nail*⟩ — **to the nail** *adv (or adj)* **:** to the last degree **:** PERFECTLY ⟨finished *to the nail*⟩

[2]**nail** \"\ *vt* -ED/-ING/-S [ME *nailen*, fr. OE *næglian*; akin to OHG *negilen* to nail, ON *negla*, Goth *ganagljan* to nail to, attach; denominative fr. the root of E [1]*nail*] **1 a :** to attach with a nail ⟨∼*ed* the proclamation to the church door⟩ **b** *archaic* **:** to pierce with a nail **c :** to put together with nails ⟨∼*ed* the timbers into a sturdy frame⟩ **d** *obs* **:** to stud with or as if with nails **e :** to close or make secure with nails — usu. used with adverbs expressive of direction or condition ⟨∼*ed* the box up⟩ ⟨∼ down the windows⟩ **f** *archaic* **:** [2]SPIKE 2a **g :** to fix in position with a nail ⟨∼*ed* the vines to the wall⟩ **h :** to block (fur garments) by dampening and attaching to a pattern board with nails **i :** to unite (parts of a broken bone) with a nail **2 a** *archaic* **:** to make fast as if with nails **b :** to secure or fasten to something ⟨∼*ed* to the tree by an Indian's arrow⟩ **c :** to be unalterably fixed to or associated with something (as a profession, a course of action) ⟨the clerk ∼*ed* to his counter⟩ **d :** to fix in steady attention ⟨∼*ing* his eyes on the crack⟩ **3 a :** CATCH, TRAP; *esp* **:** to detect and expose (as a lie or scandal) so as to stop currency or circulation ⟨∼*ed* the source of the story and forced a retraction⟩ **b** *slang* **:** to get hold of **:** SNATCH, STEAL ⟨∼ an apple⟩ **c** *slang* **:** CHECK, ARREST **d** *of a bird dog* **:** to point (as a covey) quickly, sharply, and accurately **4 a** *slang* **:** STRIKE, HIT ⟨∼*ed* him in the head with a rock⟩ **b :** to put out (a runner) in baseball — **nail one's colors to the mast :** to assume and manifest an inflexible attitude (as of determination not to acknowledge defeat)

nail·abil·i·ty \,nālə'bilədē\ *n* **:** suitability for being nailed ⟨a sheathing of superior ∼⟩

nail apron *n* **:** a coarse work apron with pockets for nails or similar small articles

nail bed *n* **:** MATRIX 1c

nail bit *n* **:** a wood-boring tool used for cutting across the grain

nail–biting \'⸗,⸗⸗\ *n* **1 a :** habitual biting at the fingernails usu. being symptomatic of emotional tensions and frustrations **b :** an act or instance of this behavior **2 :** a hopelessly or helplessly frustrated condition or activity ⟨their critical work has become largely a kind of ethical *nail-biting* —S.E.Hyman⟩

nail bone *n* **1 :** LACRIMAL BONE **2 :** the terminal phalanx of a digit

nail brush *n* **:** a small firm-bristled brush for cleaning the fingernails

nail down *vt* **:** to settle or establish clearly and unmistakably ⟨*nailed* his argument *down* with a quotation from the Bible⟩ ⟨called its 400 local drivers to a meeting . . . to *nail down* final strategy for the walkout —*Sacramento (Calif.) Bee*⟩

nailed shoe *n* **:** a shoe in which the upper is attached to the sole by means of nails

nail enamel *n* **:** nail polish in the form of a plastic liquid that forms a usu. colored coating on the nails

nail·er \'nālə(r)\ *n* -S [ME, fr. *nailen* to nail + *-er*] **1 :** a nail maker **2 :** one that drives nails or fastens together with nails: as **a :** a maker or lidder of wooden boxes **b :** a machine for automatic nailing **c :** an operator of such a machine **3** *slang* **:** something highly superior of its kind **:** one that is extremely capable at something

nail·ery \'nāl(ə)rē\ *n* -ES **:** a place where nails are made

nail fiddle *n* **:** NAIL VIOLIN

nail file *n* **:** [1]FILE 1b

nail fold *n* **:** the fold of the cutis at the margin of a fingernail or toenail

nail harmonica *n* **:** NAIL VIOLIN

nailhead \'⸗,⸗\ *n, often attrib* **1 a :** the usu. flattened boss that forms the end of a nail opposite to the point **b :** an ornament suggesting a nailhead ⟨a belt studded with enamel ∼*s*⟩ ⟨∼ taffeta⟩ **2 :** NAIL-HEADED MOLDING; *also* **:** one of the pyramids forming such molding

nail–headed \'⸗¦⸗⸗\ *adj* **:** having a head like that of a nail **:** formed so as to resemble the head of a nail

nail–headed molding *or* **nailhead molding** *n* **:** an architectural ornament consisting of a series of low four-sided pyramids suggestive of nailheads

nailhead rust *n* **:** LEPROSIS

nailhead spar *n* **:** calcite that crystallizes in nail-headed forms

nailhead spot *n* **:** a rot of the tomato that is caused by an imperfect fungus (*Alternaria tomato*) and is characterized by small sunken brown to black fruit spots resembling the head of a nail

nailing strip *n* **:** a strip of wood made fast (as by bolting) to a surface (as of concrete or metal) unsuitable for nailing in order to provide a means of attaching something (as flooring or lathing) by nailing

nail·less \'nā(ə)lləs\ *adj* **1 :** having no nails ⟨∼ fingers⟩ **2 :** requiring no nails for fastening ⟨a ∼ horseshoe⟩

naillike \'⸗,⸗\ *adj* **:** resembling a nail: as **a :** CORNEOUS ⟨a hard ∼ layer of tissue⟩ **b :** shaped like a fingernail or toenail ⟨a ∼ bone⟩ **c :** slender and tapered or pointed ⟨developed a ∼ colony in agar⟩

nail plate *n* **1 :** NAIL 1a; *also* **:** the homologous hard sheath of a claw **2 :** a sheet of iron from which cut nails are made

nail polish *n* **:** a dry or liquid preparation for giving a sheen to fingernails and toenails; *usu* **:** a lacquer or enamel that may be clear or opaque and colored or colorless and that forms a substantial covering over the surface of the nail

nail puller *n* **:** a device (as a bar with a notched end) for gripping and drawing a nail

nail puller

nailrod \'⸗,⸗\ *n* **1 a :** iron in rods or strips for cutting into nails **b :** a rod or strip of such iron **2** *Brit* **:** hard-pressed and usu. very dark tobacco made up in short rods or sticks

nails *pl of* NAIL, *pres 3d sing of* NAIL

nail–scissors \'⸗,⸗⸗\ *n pl* **:** small scissors with slender shaft and brief curved blades that are used chiefly for shaping and trimming the fingernails

nail·sea glass \'nā(ə)l,sē-\ *n, usu cap N* [fr. *Nailsea*, England] **:** glassware produced at Nailsea, England during the 18th and 19th centuries and typically ornamented with latticinio striping

nail set *n* **:** [3]PUNCH 1a(3)

nailsick \'⸗,⸗\ *adj* **1 :** weakened by repeated nailing ⟨patched the roof with ∼ boards⟩ **2 :** leaking at the nail holes ⟨a ∼ boat⟩

nail–tailed wallaby *also* **nail–tailed kangaroo** \'⸗,⸗-\ *or* **nail–tail** \'⸗,⸗\ *n* **:** any of a genus (*Onychogalea*) of small kangaroos with brightly marked silky fur and a horny nail on the tip of the tail

nail violin *n* **:** an 18th century musical instrument that consists of a semicircular sounding board with nails or iron pins of graduated size driven along its edge and that is played with a violin bow

nailwort \'⸗,⸗\ *n* **1 :** either of two whitlow grasses (*Draba verna* and *Saxifraga tridactylites*) **2 :** a plant of the genus *Paronychia*

naily \'nālē\ *adj* **:** full of nails ⟨a ∼ board⟩

nain \'nān\ *adj* [alter. (resulting from incorrect division of *mine ain*) of [2]*ain*] *Scot* **:** OWN

nain·sel *or* **nain·sell** \nān'sel\ *pron* [*nain* + *sel, sell*] **1** *Scot* **:** own self **2** *Scot* **:** a Scottish Highlander

nain·sook \'nān,sůk\ *n* -S [Hindi *nainsukh*, fr. *nain* eye (fr. Skt *nayana*, fr. *nayati* he leads) + *sukh* delight, fr. Skt *sukha* — more at NAIK] **:** a soft lightweight cotton fabric in plain weave and various finishes that is used esp. for clothing and curtains

naio \'nī(,)ō\ *n* -S [Hawaiian] **:** any of several trees of the genus *Myoporum*: as **a :** NGAIO **b :** BASTARD SANDALWOOD 2a (1) **c :** a tall Hawaiian tree (*M. sandwicense*) that has rough gray bark and pink or white flowers in terminal clusters and that yields a lumber which is sometimes substituted for sandalwood

nai·pa·li \nä'p-,nī'p-\ *cap, var of* NEPALI

naique *var of* NAIK

[1]**nair** *usu cap, var of* NAYAR

[2]**na·ir** \'nä,i(ə)r\ *n* -S [native name in India] **:** BEGTI

[3]**nair** \"\ *n* -S [native name in India] **:** the common Indian otter (*Lutra nair*)

nairn·shire \'naa(ə)rn,shi(ə)r, 'ne(ə)rn-, 'närn-, -shər\ *or* **nairn** *adj, usu cap* [fr. *Nairnshire* or *Nairn* county, Scotland] **:** of or from the county of Nairn, Scotland **:** of the kind or style prevalent in Nairn

nai·ro·bi \(')nī¦rōbē\ *adj, usu cap* [fr. *Nairobi*, Kenya] **:** of or from Nairobi, the capital of Kenya **:** of the kind or style prevalent in Nairobi

nairobi disease *n, usu cap N* **:** a severe and frequently fatal gastroenteritis of sheep or sometimes goats that occurs in parts of Kenya and is considered due to a virus transmitted by the bite of the brown tick

nairy *dial var of* NARY

na·is \'nāəs\ *n* [L — more at NAID] **1** *pl* **naises** \-səz\ *or* **na·i·des** \'nāə,dēz\ **:** a river nymph **:** NAIAD **2** *cap* [NL, fr. L, naiad] **:** a large genus of small aquatic oligochaete worms that is the type of the family Naididae

naish \'nāsh\ *var of* NESH

nais·sance \'nās[ə]n(t)s\ *n* -S [F, birth, origin, fr. MF, fr. *nais-* (stem of *naitre* to be born) + *-ance*] **:** an original issue or growth ⟨educational broadcasting, now in its crisis of ∼ —R.L.Shayon⟩ — sometimes distinguished from *renaissance*

nais·sant \-[ə]nt\ *adj* [MF, pres. part. of *naitre* to be born, fr. L *nascere*, fr. *nasci* — more at NATION] **1** *heraldry* **a :** ISSUANT **b :** rising or issuing from the middle of an ordinary (as a fess) in the instance of an animal with only the upper part visible **2 :** NASCENT

[1]**na·ive** *also* **na·ïve** \(')nä¦ēv, (')nä¦-, (')nī¦-\ *adj, sometimes* -ER/-EST [F *naïve*, fem. of *naïf*, fr. OF *naif* inborn, native, natural, fr. L *nativus* native — more at NATIVE] **1 :** marked by simplicity, ingenuousness, artlessness: **a :** showing candor, freshness, and spontaneity unchecked by convention, social diffidence, or guile ⟨when the experienced man speaks simply and wisely to the ∼ girl —Gilbert Highet⟩ **b :** showing lack of worldly experience **:** INNOCENT, SIMPLE ⟨their ∼ ignorance of life, hers and his, when they were first married —Arnold Bennett⟩ ⟨the same ∼ belief in an anthropomorphic Creator —H.L.Mencken⟩ ⟨the *naivest* person imaginable⟩ **c :** unsuspecting, credulous, and unwary about duplicity or distortion ⟨the work exhibits a ∼ acceptance of every kind of miracle —H.O.Taylor⟩ **2 :** marked by lack of instruction, experience, perception, learning **:** exhibiting lack of analysis, subtlety, or depth by ready acceptance without consideration **:** UNPHILOSOPHIC ⟨a little ∼ to suppose that when really vital differences emerge, one nation or another is likely to abandon its position on the first interchange of views —J.F.Byrnes⟩ **syn** see NATURAL

[2]**naïve** *also* **naive** \"\ *n* -S **:** a naïve person

na·ïve·ly *also* **na·ive·ly** *adv* **:** in a naïve manner **:** with naïveté

na·ïve·ness *n* -ES **:** NAÏVETÉ

naïve realism *n* **:** the commonsense viewpoint that our perception of the external world is a direct copy of it

na·ïve·té *also* **na·ive·té** \(,)nä,ēvə'tā, (,)nä,-, (,)nī,-, ⸗'⸗⸗,⸗, '⸗,ēv¦tā\ *n* -S [F *naïveté*, fr. OF *naiveté* inborn character, fr. *naif* inborn, native, natural + *-ité* -ity] **1 :** the quality or state of being naïve **:** native simplicity or unaffected naturalness **:** INGENUOUSNESS, ARTLESSNESS **2 :** a naive act

na·ïve·ty \nä'ēvətē, nā'-, -v(ə)tē, -i\ *n* -ES [modif. of F *naïveté*] **:** NAÏVETÉ

na·ja \'näjə\ *n, cap* [NL, fr. Skt *nāga* serpent] **:** a genus of elapid snakes comprising the true cobras

na·ja·da·ce·ae \,näjə'dāsē,ē\ *syn of* NAIADACEAE

na·ja·da·les \,näjə'dā(,)lēz\ *syn of* NAIADALES

naj·di \'najdē\ *n, pl* **najdi** *or* **najdis** *usu cap* **:** one of a major Arab people in the Kuwait region of Arabia

nak \'nak\ *n* -S [perh. fr. Hindi *nāk* nose; akin to Skt *nāsā* nose — more at NOSE] **:** the stigmatic point of the fruit of the mango (*Mangifera indica*)

nake \'nāk\ *vt* [ME *naken*, back-formation fr. *naked* (taken as past part.)] *archaic* **:** to make naked **:** lay bare **:** STRIP

[1]**na·ked** \'nākəd, *chiefly in southern US* 'nek-\ *adj, sometimes* -ER/-EST [ME, fr. OE *nacod, nacud, naced*; akin to OHG *nackot, nackut* naked, ON *nökkvithr*, Goth *naqaths*, L *nudus*, Gk *gymnos*, Skt *nagna*] **1 :** lacking covering **:** UNCOVERED: as **a** (1) **:** not wearing, covered by, or protected with clothing **:** NUDE ⟨the man and his wife were both ∼, and were not ashamed —Gen 2:25 (RSV)⟩ — used of a person, the body, or one of its parts ⟨∼ arms plunged into the dough⟩ ⟨never saw a colder ∼*er* man⟩ (2) **:** inadequately or partially clothed esp. so as to be socially unacceptable ⟨that blouse is a disgrace, the girl is simply ∼⟩ **b** *of a saddle or draft animal* **:** lacking the usual harness or trappings **c** (1) *of a sword or similar weapon* **:** free from its sheath **:** unsheathed and ready for immediate use ⟨advancing, ∼ sword in hand⟩ (2) **:** freed from or not provided with a protective enclosure ⟨a ∼ light⟩ **d** *of a plant or one of its parts* (1) **:** lacking pubescence ⟨smooth ∼ stems⟩ (2) **:** lacking some enveloping or subtending structure (as leaves, hulls, scales) ⟨a ∼ bud⟩ **e** *of an animal or one of its parts* **:** lacking some natural external covering (as of hair, feathers, or shell) ⟨a ∼ rhizopod⟩ ⟨the Transylvanian *naked*⸗necked fowl⟩ **f :** not clothed in substance or flesh — used esp. of personified concepts or unembodied entities ⟨the ∼ spirits of the air⟩ **g :** lacking a final covering layer ⟨a ∼ wall is one fully lathed but not yet plastered⟩ **2 a :** unprovided with needful or adequate clothing or other necessities of life **:** poverty-stricken **:** DESTITUTE ⟨∼ of comfort⟩ **b :** empty and barren **:** seeming bare by reason of the lack of usual covering, adornment, or furnishings ⟨glanced about the drab ∼ room⟩: as (1) **:** devoid of ornaments or embellishments ⟨hands ∼ of rings⟩ (2) **:** lacking foliage ⟨wintry trees spreading their gray ∼ arms⟩ (3) **:** devoid of or sparsely furnished with vegetation ⟨a ∼ desert⟩ ⟨the ∼ hills towering above⟩ **c :** lacking weapons or means of defense or offense **:** UNARMED, DEFENSELESS ⟨unwilling to slay a ∼ man⟩ **3 a :** devoid of anything that strengthens, supports, or confirms **:** lacking evident or proven authority or authoritativeness **:** MERE, SIMPLE ⟨a ∼ command⟩ ⟨∼ belief⟩ **b :** lacking in some material matter, or having nothing to validate, confirm, or support it ⟨a ∼ title⟩ ⟨such ∼ contracts are difficult to enforce⟩ **c :** lacking estimable qualities (as of worth, dignity, adequacy) **:** BALD, MEAGER, SCANTY ⟨a ∼ account of the conference⟩ **4 :** devoid of concealment or disguise ⟨confront ∼ realities at their source —Richard Eberhart⟩: as **a :** outspoken and straightforward **:** presented without reserve or embellishment ⟨a ∼ confession⟩ ⟨the ∼ truth⟩ **b :** open to view **:** plainly manifest **:** CLEAR, OBVIOUS ⟨the ∼ facts of the case⟩ ⟨an act of ∼ aggression⟩ **5** *chiefly dial* **a :** of full strength **:** UNDILUTED ⟨∼ spirits⟩ **b :** free from contamination or admixture **:** PURE ⟨∼ water⟩ **syn** see BARE

[2]**naked** *n* -S **1** *archaic* **:** NUDE ⟨covered the ∼ with a garment —Ezek 18:7 (AV)⟩ **2 :** the inadequately clothed ⟨clothes for the ∼⟩

naked bat *n* **:** a large Indo-Malayan bat (*Cheiromeles torquatus*) hairless except for a thin half collar

naked bed *n* [ME] *archaic* **:** a bed in which one sleeps unclothed

naked boys *n pl but sing or pl in constr* **:** MEADOW SAFFRON

naked broom rape *n* **:** a cancer root (*Orobanche uniflora*) that occurs chiefly in eastern No. America and has broad minutely ciliolate corolla lobes

naked bulb *n* **:** a plant bulb consisting of scales as distinguished from a tunicate bulb

naked catfish *n* **:** a catfish lacking dermal bony plates — distinguished from *armored catfish*

naked eye *n* **:** the eye unaided by any instrument that changes the apparent size or distance of an object or otherwise alters visual powers ⟨just visible to the *naked eye*⟩

naked fallow *n* **:** a fallow in which land is kept bare (as by repeated cultivation) rather than fallowed under a green manure or cover crop

naked floor *n* **1 :** a floor completely framed but as yet uncovered by flooring **2 :** a floor in which the joists extend unbroken from wall to wall

naked flower *n* **:** a flower lacking floral leaves

naked heeler *n* **:** a gamecock that is fought with natural spurs only

na·ked·ize \'nākə,dīz\ *vi* -ED/-ING/-S [[1]*naked* + *-ize*] **:** to be or go naked

naked lady *n* **:** MEADOW SAFFRON

na·ked·ly *adv* [ME, fr. *naked* + *-ly*] **:** in a naked manner: as **a :** without covering, disguise, or addition **:** MANIFESTLY, OPENLY, SIMPLY, BARELY **b :** as standing by or considered by itself alone ⟨a question discussed ∼⟩ **c :** in an unclothed, exposed, defenseless, or unprotected manner **d :** in a deficient or imperfect manner **:** POORLY, INADEQUATELY

naked mollusk *n* **:** a nudibranch mollusk

naked neck *n, usu cap both Ns* **:** a breed or strain of the domestic fowl having the neck bright red and wholly free from feathers

na·ked·ness *n* -ES [ME *nakednesse*, fr. OE *nacednisse*, fr. *nacod, nacud, naced* naked + *-nisse* -ness — more at NAKED] **1 a :** the quality or state of being naked **b :** one that is naked **2 :** something that should be covered; *esp* **:** PRIVATES

naked oat *n* **:** an oat (*Avena nuda*) that has multiple-flowered spikelets and naked mature kernels and that is sometimes cultivated esp. in interior Asia as a cereal grain

naked power *n* **:** COLLATERAL POWER **:** a power in gross as distinguished from one coupled with an interest

naked reverse *n* **:** a reverse play in football in which the ball is handed off to a player who runs without interference as though covering up a fake until he is outside the end and then goes downfield

naked smut *n* **:** a smut fungus (as *Ustilago nuda* or *U. tritici*) that converts the entire inflorescence of the host into a loose powdery mass of spores — compare COVERED SMUT

naked stopper *n* **:** any of several tropical American trees and shrubs constituting a genus (*Anamomis*) of the family Myrtaceae

naked trust *n* **:** PASSIVE TRUST

nakedwood \'⸗⸗,⸗\ *n* **1 :** any of several small or medium⸗sized trees (genus *Colubrina*) of Florida and the West Indies with thin scaly bark and strong hard heavy heartwood — see MABI **2 :** a stopper (*Eugenia dicrana*) of extreme southern Florida and the West Indies with thin scaly bark, aromatic fruits and fragrant seeds, and hard heavy close-grained wood **3 :** WILD CINNAMON 1

na·ker \'nākə(r)\ *n* -S [ME, fr. MF *nacaire*, fr. OIt *nacchera* kettledrum, nacre — more at NACRE] **:** KETTLEDRUM

na–khi \'nä'kē\ *also* **na·shi** \'näshē\ *n* -S *usu cap N&K* **:** one of a people closely related to the northern Lolo and found mainly in the high plateaus and mountains of the Yunnan-Szechwan borderlands of southwest China

na·kho·da \'nakə,dä\ *or* **nuc·que·dah** \'nək-\ *n* -S [Per *nākhudā*, fr. *nāv* boat (fr. OPer) + *khudā* master, fr. MPer *khutāī*; akin to Skt *nau* ship — more at NAVE] **:** a master of a native Indian vessel

na·kong \nə'käŋ\ *n* -S [Sechuana] **:** a western African antelope that is a variety (*Strepsiceros spekei gratus*) of the sitatunga

naks *pl of* NAK

nak·sha·tra \'nəkshə·trə\ *n* -S *usu cap* [Skt *nakṣatra*, lit., dominion over the night, fr. *nakt* night + *kṣatra* dominion — more at NIGHT, KSHATRIYA] **:** one of the asterisms in the moon's path or one of its celestial houses in Hindu astrology

na·ku·ru·i·tis \nə,kü,rü'īd·əs\ *n* -ES [NL, prob. fr. *Nakuru*, town in central Kenya + NL *-itis*] *eastern Africa* **:** a cobalt deficiency disease of sheep and cattle **:** PINE

nal \'nəl\ *n* -S [Hindi *nal*, fr. [Skt *nala* reed] *India* **:** GIANT REED 1

nall \'nȯl\ *dial Eng var of* AWL

nallah *or* **nalla** *or* **nala** *var of* NULLAH

nal·or·phine \'nalə(r),fēn\ *n* -S [*N-allylnormorphine*] **:** ALLYLNORMORPHINE

nam *var of* NAAM

[1]**na·ma** \'nämə\ *n, pl* **nama** *or* **namas** *usu cap* **1** *also* **na·man** \-ən\ **:** one of a Hottentot people of Great Namaqualand in South-West Africa **2 :** a dialect of Hottentot

[2]**na·ma** \'nämə\ [NL, fr. Gk, stream; akin to Gk *nan* to flow — more at NOURISH] *syn of* HYDROLEA

namable *var of* NAMEABLE

namad *var of* NUMDAH

na·ma·ma·hay \,nämə'mä'hī\ *n* -S [Tag] **:** a member of a former Philippine group or caste of serfs who were chiefly employed in agriculture

[1]**na·ma·qua** \nə'mäkwə\ *n* -S [fr. *Namaqua*land, coast region

in southwestern Africa] : a long-tailed African dove (*Oena capensis*)
²namaqua \"\ *or* **na·ma·quan** \-wən\ *n* -s *usu cap* : ¹NAMA
nam·ay·cush \'namē,kəsh, -mə,-\ *n* -ES [of Algonquian origin; akin to Cree *namekus* lake trout] : LAKE TROUT
na·maz \nə'mäz\ *n, pl* **namaz** [Pers *namāz;* akin to Skt *namas* obeisance — more at NEMORAL] : Islamic worship or prayer
nam·be \näm'bā\ *n, pl* **nambe** *or* **nambes** *usu cap* **1** : a Tanoan people occupying a pueblo in New Mexico **2** : a member of the Nambe people
nam·bi·cua·ra *or* **nam·bi·kua·ra** \,nambē'kwärə\ *or* **nham·bi·qua·ra** *or* **nham·bi·cua·ra** *n* -s *usu cap* [Pg *nambicuara, nhambicuara,* fr. Tupi, lit., long-eared] **1 a** : a people of Mato Grosso, Brazil **b** : a member of such people **2** : the language of the Nambicuara people
nam·by \'nambē\ *adj or n* [by shortening] : NAMBY-PAMBY
nam·by-pam·bi·ness \¦nambē¦pambēnəs\ *n* -ES : the quality or state of being namby-pamby
¹nam·by-pam·by \¦nambē¦pambē, ¦naam . . . aambē, -bi . . . bi\ *adj* [fr. *Namby Pamby,* nickname given to *Ambrose Philips* †1749 Eng. poet by some satirists of his time to ridicule the style of his verses] **1** : characterized by feeble sentimentality or insipid and artificial prettiness or elegance ⟨*namby-pamby* rhymes⟩ **2 a** *of a person* : lacking in vigor or manliness : weak, trifling, or childish in character or behavior ⟨*namby-pamby* boys afraid to leave their mothers' apron strings⟩ **b** : lacking in real worth, substance, or quality : unduly lax, soft, or conciliatory ⟨the *namby-pamby* handling of juvenile delinquents⟩ ⟨*namby-pamby* educational standards⟩
²namby-pamby \"\ *n* -ES : something (as talk, writing, or a person) that is namby-pamby
nam·by-pam·by·ism \"+,izəm\ *n* -s : NAMBY-PAMBINESS
¹name \'nām\ *n* -s [ME, fr. OE *nama;* akin to OHG & Goth *namo* name, ON *nafn,* L *nomen,* Gk *onyma, onoma,* Skt *nāma*] **1 a** : a word or sound or a combination of words or sounds by which an individual or a class of individuals (as persons or things) is regularly known or designated : a distinctive and specific appellation ⟨the ~ of the boy is Mark⟩ ⟨the ~ of this fruit is apple⟩ ⟨metal is the ~ of a class of substances each of which has an individual ~ (as gold, silver, lead, copper, iron)⟩ — see LEGAL NAME **b** (1) : a word usu. with little or no connotation that can serve as the subject of a sentence; *also* : the symbolic equivalent of such a word (2) : a designating or identifying expression ⟨"the smallest prime" and "the proposition that all men are equal" may be construed as ~s⟩ **2** *usu cap* : a symbol of divinity or an actual vehicle of divine attributes ⟨the ascetics testify that this *Name* has in itself the power of the presence of God —Elizabeth Cram⟩ ⟨*Name* — may mean either character, or manifestations of Jehovah, or Jehovah himself —W.A.Shelton⟩ **3 a** : a descriptive or qualifying appellation based on character, attributes, or acts ⟨his ~ shall be called Wonderful —Isa 9:6 (AV)⟩ **b** : an unpleasant, vulgar, or offensive appellation often based on some attribute ⟨it is wrong to call ~s⟩ **4 a** : reputed character : good or bad reputation ⟨had the ~ of a miser⟩ **b** : honorable reputation or illustrious fame ⟨had a ~ for learning⟩ ⟨a ~ to conjure with⟩ **5 a** : the designation of an individual regarded as his individuality or character ⟨one of the most detested ~s in history⟩ ⟨polio and cancer are among the most dread ~s today⟩ **b** : individuals sharing a name : RACE, FAMILY, CLAN **c** : a person or thing that is outstanding in importance, prominence, or interest ⟨tried to get several ~s to give glamor to the party⟩ **6** : the appellation of a thing in distinction to the reality : mere seeming ⟨the place was a town in ~ only⟩ ⟨a poet in ~ but scarcely in production⟩ ⟨gradual attrition reduced it to an empty ~⟩ **7** : the mystic essence, character, or spiritual attribute of a person — **by name** *adv* **1** : with specific personal designation : with the according of individual recognition ⟨mentioned each student *by name*⟩ **2 a** : as individuals : INDIVIDUALLY ⟨knew them all *by name*⟩ **b** : by reputation rather than by personal acquaintance or appearance ⟨knew the new supervisor *by name* only⟩ — **to one's name** : as one's property : among one's possessions
²name \"\ *vt* -ED/-ING/-S [ME *namen,* fr. OE *namian,* fr. *nama,* n.] **1** : to give a distinctive name or appellation to : ENTITLE, DENOMINATE, STYLE, CALL ⟨*named* the child after her grandmother⟩ **2** : to mention or identify by name : utter or publish the name of ⟨~ one person who would do such a thing⟩ ⟨everyone *named* him with praise⟩: as **a** : to introduce (as oneself) by name ⟨may I ~ these gentlemen⟩ **b** (1) : to mention the name of (a member of a legislative body) in formal reprimand — used of the speaker of the house (2) : to accuse by name ⟨~ the villain if you can⟩ **c** : to identify by naming ⟨~ that tree⟩ : tell over the names of : recognize or recount by name ⟨can ~ the books of the Bible in perfect order⟩ **3** : to appoint specif. or by name : assign to some purpose : NOMINATE ⟨the king *named* his eldest son to succeed him⟩ ⟨let's ~ an early day for the wedding⟩ **4 a** : to speak about : MENTION, STIPULATE, CITE, STATE, QUOTE ⟨will he ~ a price⟩ ⟨refused to ~ the source of the story⟩ **b** : to bring up in conversation : INDICATE, SUGGEST — usu. used with an indefinite *it* as object ⟨if you don't see what you want, ~ it⟩ ⟨I'll ~ it to him the next time we meet⟩ **syn** see DESIGNATE, MENTION
³name \"\ *adj* [¹*name*] **1** : bearing or intended for a name or names ⟨leather ~ tag⟩ ⟨ornately painted ~ signs⟩ **2 a** : named in honor or remembrance of another ⟨~ child⟩ **b** : being the person for whom another is named ⟨~ ancestor⟩ **3** : giving its or the name to a collection or composition ⟨the anthology opens with the ~ article⟩ **4** : accorded top rank for preeminence in performance under a distinctive name recognized as a mark of celebrity ⟨a ~ band⟩ ⟨a ~ writer⟩ ⟨a ~ train⟩ **5** : bearing a name (as a trade name) accepted by a widely distributed public as the mark of approved or quality products supplied by a particular enterprise ⟨insisting on ~ brands⟩ ⟨sales of ~ merchandise⟩
name·abil·i·ty *also* **nam·abil·i·ty** \,nāmə'biləd·ē\ *n* : the quality or state of being nameable
name·able *also* **nam·able** \'nāməbəl\ *adj* **1** : capable of being named : IDENTIFIABLE ⟨pick any ~ item⟩ **2** : worthy of being recalled or mentioned : MEMORABLE, NOTEWORTHY
nameboard \'=,=\ *n* : an identifying signboard (as for a station, a shop, or a ship); *also* : an identifying name displayed (as on the side of a ship) other than on a board — see SHIP illustration
name-caller \'=,==\ *n* : one that habitually engages in name-calling
name-calling \'=,==\ *n* : the use of opprobrious designations esp. to win an argument or to induce rejection or condemnation (as of a person or project) without due and unimpassioned consideration of relevant facts ⟨the campaign degenerated into mere scurrilous *name-calling*⟩ ⟨not above *name-calling* when it served his purposes⟩
named \'nāmd\ *adj* [ME *namyd,* fr. past part. of *namen* to name] **1** : mentioned by name : SPECIFIED ⟨arrived on the ~ date⟩ **2** : having a well-known name : NOTABLE ⟨this highly ~ philosopher⟩ **3** : having or known by a distinctive name ⟨there are hundreds of ~ roses that are no longer planted⟩
name day *n* **1** : the day of the saint whose name one bears **2** : the day under London stock exchange rules on which a ticket giving the name of the buyer of securities and the consideration is issued by the purchasing broker to the seller to be passed through the hands of all the parties to the transaction to the original seller so that the middlemen may settle differences and the actual transfer be made between the final holder of the ticket and the issuing broker
named insured *n* : a person specif. named in an insurance contract as the insured as distinguished from one protected under a policy whether so named or not
name-drop \'=,=\ *vi* [back-formation fr. *name-dropper* & *name-dropping*] : to engage in name-dropping ⟨we *name-drop* in order to establish some contact with a tradition more acceptable than our own —Clifton Fadiman⟩
name-dropper \'=,==\ *n* [¹*name* + *dropper*] : one who engages in name-dropping
name-dropping \'=,==\ *n* [¹*name* + *dropping*] : the practice of seeking to impress others by studied but apparently casual mention of prominent or powerful persons as friends or associates ⟨cultivate an air of Broadway knowingness largely by means of *name-dropping* —Henry Hewes⟩
name·less \'nāmləs\ *adj* [ME *nameles,* fr. ¹*name* + *-les* -less — more at NAME] **1** : lacking a distinguished name : not noted : OBSCURE ⟨understood the ~ men who fought and swore . . . and won a war —Merle Miller⟩ **2** : not known, specified, or mentioned by name often to avoid giving offense ⟨the hero of this tale must remain ~⟩ **3** : having no legal right to a name (as by reason of illegitimacy) : BASTARD **4** : having no name : not having been given a name ⟨discovered several ~ species of moss⟩ **5** : not marked with any name ⟨a ~ grave⟩ **6 a** : impossible to identify precisely or by name ⟨the ~ ills of old age⟩ : being such as to defy description usu. by reason of indefiniteness ⟨troubled by ~ fears and uncertainties⟩ **b** : too horrible, repulsive, or distressing to be mentioned ⟨this ~ abomination⟩ ⟨their ~ sensualities⟩ — **name·less·ly** *adv* — **name·less·ness** *n* -ES
¹namely *adv* [ME, fr. ¹*name* + *-ly* (adv. suffix)] **1** *obs* : SPECIFICALLY, ESPECIALLY, EXPRESSLY **2** : that is to say : to wit ⟨dropping one preconception, ~ the qualitative distinction between the heavens and the earth —S.F.Mason⟩
²name·ly \'nāmli\ *adj* [ME, fr. ¹*name* + *-ly* (adj. suffix)] *Scot* : FAMOUS ⟨~ for witches⟩ ⟨to be a ~ piper it was necessary to study for 7 years —Seton Gordon⟩
name part *n* : the title role in a play
nameplate \'=,=\ *n* **1** : a plate or plaque bearing or designed to bear a name (as of a resident, proprietor, or manufacturer) **2** : the name of a newspaper or periodical as it is regularly displayed usu. on the top of the first page of the newspaper or on the front cover or title page of the periodical
name prefix *n* : a patronymic prefix
nam·er \'nāmə(r)\ *n* -s : one that bestows a name or calls by name
names *pl of* NAME, *pres 3d sing of* NAME
namesake \'=,=\ *n* [prob. fr. *name's sake* (i.e., one named for the sake of another's name)] : one that has the same name as another; *esp* : one named after another
name tape *n* : firmly woven cotton tape with the name of a person interwoven or printed in linear series to be divided into single name-bearing segments for attachment to items (as garments) likely to require identification; *also* : one name-bearing section of such tape ⟨sewed *name tapes* on all her underwear⟩
naming *pres part of* NAME
nammad *var of* NUMDAH
nams *pl of* NAM
na·mu·ri·an \nə'm(y)u̇rēən\ *adj, usu cap* [*Namur,* town and province in Belgium + E *-ian*] : of or relating to a division of the Upper Carboniferous — see GEOLOGIC TIME table
nan \'nan, -aa(ə)-\ *usu cap* [fr. *Nan,* nickname fr. the name *Nancy*] — a communications code word for the letter *n*
NAN *abbr* [L *nisi aliter notetur*] unless otherwise noted
nan- *or* **nano-** *comb form* [F, fr. L *nanus* dwarf, fr. Gk *nanos, nannos;* prob. akin to Gk *nanna, nenna* female relative, aunt — more at NUN] : dwarf ⟨*nanocephaly*⟩ ⟨*nanoid*⟩ ⟨*nanosomia*⟩
¹na·na \'nanə, 'nänə, 'nänə\ *n* -s [prob. of baby-talk origin] : a child's nurse or nursemaid
²na·na \nə'nä\ *n* -s [Pg *naná,* fr. Guarani & Tupi] : PINEAPPLE
³nana \"\ *n* -s [Ar *na'nā'*] : MINT
⁴na·na \'nānə\ *adj* [NL, fr. LL, female dwarf, fem. of L *nanus* dwarf — more at NAN-] : DWARF, DWARFISH — used esp. of genetic variants of economic plants ⟨a ~ strain of corn⟩
na·nai·mo \nə'nī(,)mō\ *n, pl* **nanaimo** *usu cap* [Nanaimo *Sananaimux,* lit., people of Nanoose bay] **1 a** : a Salishan people of the east coast of Vancouver Island, British Columbia **b** : a member of such people **2** : a Salishan language of the Nanaimo people
na·nak·pan·thi \,nänək'pən(t)thē\ *n* -s *usu cap* [Hindi *nānakpanthī,* fr. Guru *Nanak* †1538 Indian religious leader who founded Sikhism + Skt *panthan, patha* way, path, course — more at FIND] : a member of a major Sikh party distinguished by its primary emphasis on the peaceful tenets of Guru Nanak — compare KHALSA
na·nan·der \nə'nandə(r)\ *n* -s [*nan-* + *-ander*] : NANNANDER
na·na·wood \'nänə'wu̇d\ *n* [Marathi *nānā* ben-teak (prob. fr. Skt *nandin,* any of various plants) + E *wood*] : BEN-TEAK
¹nan·ce \'nän(t)sā\ *also* **nan·che** \-nchā\ *n* -s [AmerSp, fr. Nahuatl *nantzi*] **1** : a tree of the genus *Byrsonima* **2** : the fruit of a nance and esp. of the golden spoon (*Byrsonima crassifolia*)
²nance \'nan(t)s\ *n* -s [short for ²*nancy*] *slang* : an effeminate male : HOMOSEXUAL
nan·chang \'nän'chäŋ\ *adj, usu cap* [fr. *Nanchang,* China] : of or from the city of Nanchang, China : of the kind or style prevalent in Nanchang
¹nan·cy \'nan(t)sē\ *adj, usu cap* [fr. *Nancy,* France] : of or from the city of Nancy, France : of the kind or style prevalent in Nancy
²nancy \"\ *n* -ES *sometimes cap* [fr. the female name *Nancy*] : ²NANCE
nancy-story \'=,==\ *also* **nancy** *n* [*nancy* by folk etymology (influence of name *Nancy*) fr. a West African word akin to Twi *a³na¹nse¹* spider, Ewe *a¹na³nse³*] : a folktale of the Negroes of the African Gold Coast or their West Indian descendants
¹nan·di \'nän,dē\ *n, pl* **nandi** *usu cap* **1 a** : a pastoral people on the Uganda-Kenya frontier **b** : a member of such people **2** : a Nilotic language of the Nandi people — called also *Kipsigis*
²nandi \"\ *n* -s [Skt *nāndī* joy, vigor, freshness] : a benediction or invocation spoken at the beginning of an Indian drama and usu. addressed to Vishnu or Siva but sometimes to Buddha
³nandi \"\ *n* -s [Telugu, prob. fr. Skt *nandin,* any of various plants] : BEN-TEAK
nan·di bear \'nandē-\ *n, often cap N* [prob. fr. *Nandi,* town in Kenya] : a large carnivorous animal that is said to resemble a bear and has been reported repeatedly from parts of southern and eastern Africa
¹nan·did \'nandəd\ *adj* [NL *Nandidae*] : of or relating to the Nandidae
²nandid \"\ *n* -s [NL *Nandidae*] : a fish of the family Nandidae
nan·di·dae \'nandə,dē\ *n pl, cap* [NL, fr. *Nandus,* type genus (perh. fr. Skt *nāndī* joy) + *-idae*] : a family of small deep-bodied percoid fishes of warm fresh and salt waters of the southern hemisphere — compare LEAF FISH
nan·di·na \nan'dīnə, -dēnə\ *n* [NL, fr. Jap *nandin* nandina] **1** *cap* : a monotypic genus of Chinese and Japanese evergreen shrubs (family Berberidaceae) having decompound leaves and small white paniculate flowers with numerous sepals that are followed by bright red or purplish fruits and being grown in warm regions as an ornamental **2** *also* **nan·din** \'nandən\ -s : any shrub of the genus *Nandina* — called also *sacred bamboo*
nan·dine \'nandən\ *n* -s [native name in Africa] : either of two spotted ring-tailed African palm civets (*Nandinia binotata* and *N. gerrardi*)
nan·du *also* **nan·dow** \'nan(,)dü\ *n* -s [Pg *nandu, nandú, nhandu, nhandú* & Sp *nandú, ñandú,* fr. Guarani & Tupi] : RHEA
nan·du·bay \¦nyändə¦bī\ *n* -s [Sp *ñandubay,* fr. Guarani] : a So. American tree or shrub (*Prosopis nandubay*) with rough hard bark and durable wood that is sometimes used for fence posts
nan·du·ti *or* **nan·du·ty** \¦nyändü¦tē\ *n* -ES [AmerSp *ñandutí,* fr. Guarani, web] : a delicate intricately patterned lace made in Paraguay from cotton or other fine vegetable fibers
¹nane \'nān\ *chiefly dial var of* NONE
²nane \"\ *var of* NAIN
nang·ca *or* **nang·ka** \näŋ'kä, 'näŋkə\ *n* -s [Tag] *Philippines* : the jackfruit tree or its fruit
nan·ger \'naŋgə(r)\ *n* -s [F *nanguer,* fr. a native name in Senegal] : ADDRA
na·ni·go \'nyänyē,gō\ *n* -s *sometimes cap* [AmerSp *ñáñigo*] : a men's secret society among Cuban Negroes; *also* : a member of this society
na·nism \'nā,nizəm, 'na,-\ *n* -s [F *nanisme,* fr. *nan-* + *-isme* -ism] : the condition of being abnormally or exceptionally small in stature : DWARFISHNESS — opposed to *gigantism* ⟨the ~ of the early generations of nonsexual castes of many social insects results from food shortage in a new or weak colony⟩
na·nit·ic \nā'nid·ik, nə'-\ *adj* [*nan-* + *-itic*] : exhibiting or affected with nanism : atypically small ⟨~ worker ants⟩
na·ni·za·tion \,nanə'zāshən, ,nan-\ *n* -s [F *naniser* to dwarf (fr. *nan-* + *-iser* -ize) + E *-ation*] : artificial dwarfing (as of trees by horticulturists)
nan·keen \(')nan¦kēn\ *also* **nan·kin** \-kin\ *or* **nan·king** \-kiŋ\ *n* -s [fr. *Nanking,* China, where it was first manufactured] **1 a** : a durable fabric handloomed in China from local cottons that had naturally a yellowish color; *also* : a firm twilled cotton fabric dyed to imitate the Chinese fabric **b** *or* **nankeen cotton** : a tree cotton (*Gossypium religiosum*) used for weaving the original nankeen fabric **2 nankeens** *pl* : trousers made of nankeen **3** *or* **nankeen yellow** *often cap N* : NAPLES YELLOW 2 **4** *usu cap* : NANKEEN PORCELAIN
nankeen bird *or* **nankeen night heron** *n* : an Australian night heron (*Nycticorax caledonicus*)
nankeen hawk *or* **nankeen kestrel** *n* : a pale yellowish Australian kestrel (*Falco cenchroides* syn. *Cerchneis cenchroides*)
nankeen lily *n* : a hybrid garden lily (*Lilium* × *testaceum*) with fragrant yellow flowers
nankeen porcelain *n, usu cap N* : chinese porcelain painted in blue on white — used esp. by dealers of all except the roughest sorts both ancient and modern
nankin *n* -s : NAPLES YELLOW 2
nan·king \(')nan¦kiŋ\ *adj, usu cap* [fr. *Nanking,* China] : of or from the city of Nanking, China : of the kind or style prevalent in Nanking
nanking cherry *n, usu cap N* : a large spreading hardy shrub or small compact tree (*Prunus tomentosa*) that has nearly sessile flowers, leaves tomentose on the under surface, and globular light red edible fruit and that is native to Asia but widely cultivated as an ornamental and for its fruit in regions of rigorous climate — called also *Manchu cherry*
nan·mu \'nan(,)mü\ *n* -s [Chin (Pek) *nan² mu⁴*] : a durable fragrant close-grained brown lumber obtained in western China from a lauraceous tree (esp. *Machilis namu*) and used by the Chinese esp. for fine framing and architectural adjuncts (as pillars)
nann- *or* **nanno-** *comb form* [NL, fr. Gk *nann-,* fr. *nannos, nanos* — more at NAN-] : dwarf ⟨*Nannippus*⟩ ⟨*nannocephaly*⟩
nan·nan·der \nə'nandə(r)\ *or* **nan·nan·dri·um** \-drēəm\ *n, pl* **nannanders** \-(r)z\ *or* **nannan·dria** \-ēə\ [*nannander* fr. *nann-* + *-ander; nannandrium,* NL, fr. *nann-* + *andr-* + *-ium*] : DWARF MALE 1
nan·nan·drous \-drəs\ *adj* [*nann-* + *-androus*] : having oogonia borne on normal-sized plants and antheridia borne on greatly reduced plants or filaments — used of green algae of the family Oedogoniaceae; compare MACRANDROUS
nan·nie *or* **nan·ny** \'nanē, -ni\ *n, pl* **nannies** [prob. of baby-talk origin] *chiefly Brit* : a child's nurse : NURSEMAID
nan·ning \(')nän¦niŋ\ *adj, usu cap* [fr. *Nanning,* China] : of or from the city of Nanning, China : of the kind or style prevalent in Nanning
nan·ni·nose \'nanə,nōs\ *n* -s [alter. of earlier *maninose, mananosay* — more at MANANOSAY] *dial* : SOFT-SHELL CLAM
nan·nip·pus \na'nipəs\ *n, cap* [NL, fr. *nann-* + *-hippus*] : a genus of tiny extinct three-toed American Pliocene horses
nan·no·plankton \¦nanō+\ *n* [NL, fr. *nann-* + *plankton*] : the smallest plankton comprising those organisms (as various flagellates, algae, bacteria) that pass through nets of number 25 mesh silk bolting cloth — compare NET PLANKTON — **nan·no·planktonic** \"+¦=¦==\ *adj*
nan·ny \'nanē, -ni\ *or* **nanny goat** *n* -ES [fr. *Nanny,* nickname for *Anne*] : a female domestic goat : a goat doe
nan·ny·berry \'nanē- *see* BERRY\ *n* **1** *or* **nannybush** : SHEEPBERRY 1a **2** : SHEEPBERRY 1b
nan·ny·gai \'nanē,gī\ *n* -s [native name in New So. Wales, Australia] : a red iridescent Australian food fish (*Trachichthodes affinis*) of the family Berycidae
nanny plum *n* : SHEEPBERRY 1
nanny tea *n* : a folk remedy for many ailments that consists of a hot infusion of sheep manure in water often with sugar
¹nano- — see NAN-
²nano- *comb form* [ISV, fr. L *nanus* dwarf — more at NAN-] : one billionth (10^{-9}) part of ⟨*nanosecond*⟩
na·no·gram \'nānə,gram, 'nan-\ *n* [*nan-* + *gram*] : a unit of mass equal to one billionth of a gram
na·noid \'nā,nȯid, 'na,-\ *adj* [*nan-* + *-oid*] : having an abnormally small body : DWARFISH
na·no·phy·e·tus \,nānə,fī'ēd·əs, ,nan-\ *or* **na·no·phy·es** \,=='fīēz\ [NL, fr. *nan-* + *-phyetus, -phyes* (fr. Gk *phyein* to bring forth) — more at BE] *syn of* TROGLOTREMA
na·no·plankton \¦nanō, ¦nanō+\ *n* [NL, fr. *nan-* + *plankton*] : NANNOPLANKTON
na·no·so·mia \,nānə'sōmēə, ,nan-\ *n* -s [NL, fr. *nan-* + *-somia*] : DWARFISM
na·no·so·mus \-məs\ *n* -ES [NL, fr. *nan-* + *-somus*] : DWARF
nan·pie \'nan,pī\ *n* [*Nan* (nickname fr. *Anne*) + *pie*] *dial Eng* : MAGPIE
nan·sen bottle \'nan(t)sən-\ *n, usu cap N* [after Fridtjof *Nansen* †1930 Norw. explorer and statesman] : an apparatus used in oceanographic studies for collecting water samples at predetermined depths
nansen passport *n, usu cap N* [after Fridtjof *Nansen*] : a passport issued through the agency of the League of Nations to a person without a home government
nantes \'nan(t)s\ *adj, usu cap* [fr. *Nantes,* France] : of or from the city of Nantes, France : of the kind or style prevalent in Nantes
nan·ti·coke \'nantə,kōk\ *n, pl* **nanticoke** *or* **nanticokes** *usu cap* [Nanticoke *Naitaquok,* lit., tidewater people] **1 a** : an Indian people of eastern Maryland and southern Delaware **b** : a member of such people **2** : an Algonquian language of the Nanticoke and Conoy peoples **3** : one of a group of people of mixed Indian, white, Negro ancestry in southern Delaware
nan·to·kite \'nantə,kīt\ *n* -s [Sp *nantoquita,* fr. *Nantoco,* village north of Copiapó, Chile + Sp *-ita* -ite] : a native cuprous chloride CuCl
nan·tuck·et·er \nan-'təkəd·ə(r)\ *n* -s *cap* [*Nantucket* Island, Mass. + E *-er*] : a native or resident of Nantucket Island
nan·tuck·et pine tip moth \(')nan-¦təkət-\ *n, usu cap N* [fr. *Nantucket* Island] : a small reddish brown silver-marked olethreutid moth (*Rhyacionia frustrana*) of the eastern and central U.S. with yellowish brown larva that feeds in and damages the new growth of various pines
nantucket sleighride *n, usu cap N* [fr. *Nantucket* Island] : a run in a whaling boat fast to a harpooned whale
nan·tung \(')nän¦tu̇ŋ\ *adj, usu cap* [fr. *Nantung,* China] : of or from the city of Nantung, China : of the kind or style prevalent in Nantung
nan·yu·ki·an \(')nän¦yükēən\ *adj, usu cap* [*Nanyuki,* town in Kenya + E *-an*] : of or belonging to an Upper Pleistocene culture of Kenya, East Africa, typified by a slightly modified Acheulean industry
nao \'nau̇\ *n* -s [Sp, fr. Catal *nau,* fr. L *navis* ship — more at NAVE] : a medium-sized sailing ship of the late middle ages
na·ol·o·gy \nā'äləjē\ *n* -ES [Gk *naos* temple + E *-logy*] : a study of sacred edifices
na·os \'nā,äs\ *n, pl* **na·oi** \-,ȯi\ [Gk, temple; akin to Gk *nostos* return home — more at NOSTALGIA] **1** : an ancient temple or shrine **2** : CELLA
¹nap \'nap\ *vi* **napped; napped; napping; naps** [ME *nappen,* fr. OE *hnappian;* akin to OHG *hnaffezen* to doze, nap, Norw *napp* nap] **1** : to sleep briefly esp. during the day : DOZE, SNOOZE **2** : to be in a careless unguarded state : NOD — often used with *catch* ⟨was caught *napping*⟩ **syn** see SLEEP
²nap \"\ *n* -s [ME *nap, nappe,* fr. *nappen,* v.] : a short sleep esp. during the day ⟨take a ~⟩ : DOZE, SIESTA, SNOOZE
³nap \"\ *n* -s [ME *noppe,* fr. MD, flock of wool, nap; akin to OE *hnoppian* to pluck, *āhnēopan* to pluck off, MLG *noppe* flock of wool, OSw *niupa* to pinch, Goth *dishniupan* to tear apart, Gk *konis, konia* ashes, dust — more at INCINERATE] **1** : a soft fuzzy fibrous surface (as on yarn and cloth) usu. raised by brushing against a rough surface (as by a cylinder covered with wire) : COVER — compare PILE **2** : a downy, shaggy, or tufted surface (as of fur) resembling the nap of a fabric ⟨hills with a mottled ~ of gray-green sagebrush —*Amer. Guide Series: Wash.*⟩

[4]nap \"\ *vt* **napped; napped; napping; naps :** to raise a nap on (fabric or leather)

[5]nap \"\ *vt* **napped; napped; napping; naps** [prob. of Scand origin; akin to Sw *nappa* to snatch, pinch, pluck, Dan & Norw *nappe* to snatch, pinch, & prob. to OSw *niupa* to pinch — more at [3]NAP] *chiefly dial Eng* **:** GRAB, NAB

[6]nap \"\ *var of* KNAP

[7]nap \"\ *n* -s [by shortening] **1 :** NAPOLEON 1 **2 :** NAPOLEON 3

[8]nap *chiefly dial var of* NAPE

[9]nap \'nap\ *n* -s [by shortening & alter.] *Austral* **:** KNAPSACK

NAP *abbr* naval aviation pilot

napa leather \'napə-\ *or* **napa** *n* -s [fr. *Napa*, Calif.] **1 :** a glove leather made in Napa, Calif., by tawing sheepskins with a soap-and-oil mixture **2 :** a leather resembling the original Napa leather in softness

[1]na·palm \'nā,pȧm, -pȧm, *also* -pälm\ *n* -s [*naphthenate* + *palmitate*] **1 :** a thickener consisting of a mixture of aluminum soaps used in jellying gasoline esp. for incendiary bombs and flamethrowers **2 :** the jellied fuel made by the addition of napalm to gasoline ⟨~ bomb⟩

[2]napalm \"\ *vt* -ED/-ING/-S **:** to attack with napalm bombs or flamethrowers

napa thistle *n, often cap N* [fr. *Napa*, Calif.] **:** TOCALOTE

nap-at-noon \'==,'=\ *n* [so called fr. the fact that its flowers close during the morning] **:** STAR-OF-BETHLEHEM

nape \'nāp, 'nap\ *n* -s [ME] **:** the back part of the neck — often used in the phrase *nape of the neck*

napecrest \'=,=\ *n* [*nape* + *crest*] **:** an African bird of the genus *Crinifer* related to the plantain eaters

na·per·er \'nāpərə(r)\ *n* -s [*napery* + *-er*] **:** an officer in a royal household having charge of the table linen

naperian *usu cap, var of* NAPIERIAN

na·pery \'nāp(ə)rē\ *n* -ES [ME, fr. MF *naperie, napperie*, fr. *nape, nappe* tablecloth + *-erie* -ery — more at NAPKIN] **:** household linen; *esp* **:** TABLE LINEN

napf·kuchen \'näpf+,-\ *n* [G, fr. *napf* bowl, drinking vessel (fr. OHG *hnapf*) + *kuchen* cake — more at HANAP, KUCHEN] **:** GUGELHUPF

nap hand *n* [[7]*nap*] **:** a favorable chance that invites the taking of risks

na·phaz·o·line \nə'fazə,lēn\ *n* -s [*naphthalene* + imid*azoline*] **:** a base $C_{14}H_{14}N_2$ derived from naphthalene and imidazoline and used locally in the form of its bitter crystalline hydrochloride esp. to relieve nasal congestion

naph·ta·lite \'naftə,līt\ *n* -s *usu cap* [*Naphtali*, second son of Jacob and ancestor of the tribe (fr. LL, fr. Heb *Naphtālī*) + E *-ite*] **:** a member of the Hebrew tribe of Naphtali

naphth- *or* **naphtho-** *also* **naphtha-** *comb form* [ISV, fr. *naphtha & naphthaline*] **1 :** naphtha ⟨*naphth*ene⟩ ⟨*naphth*yl⟩ **2 a :** related to naphthalene **:** naphthoic acid ⟨*naphtho*quinone⟩ ⟨*naphth*amide⟩ — sometimes in names of compounds in which a benzene nucleus has been replaced by a naphthalene nucleus ⟨*naphtho*resorcinol $C_{10}H_6(OH)_2$⟩ **b :** naphthol ⟨*naphth*oxide⟩ **3 a :** containing a naphthalene nucleus fused on one or two sides to one or two other rings ⟨*naphth*acridine⟩ ⟨*naphtho*pyran⟩ ⟨*naphtha*diazine⟩ **b :** BENZ- 2 — not used systematically ⟨*naphth*anthracene⟩

naph·tha \'nafthə, ÷ 'nap-\ *n* -s [L, fr. Gk, of Iranian origin; akin to Av *napta* moist, Pers *neft* naphtha; perh. akin to Gk *nephos* cloud, mist — more at NEBULA] **1 :** petroleum esp. when occurring in any of its more volatile varieties **2** *archaic* **:** any of various volatile strong-smelling flammable liquids (as ether or ethyl acetate) **3 :** any of various volatile often flammable liquid hydrocarbon mixtures used chiefly as solvents and diluents and as raw materials for conversion to gasoline: as **a :** a petroleum distillate containing principally aliphatic hydrocarbons and boiling usu. higher than gasoline and lower than kerosene — called also *petroleum naphtha;* see LIGROIN, STODDARD SOLVENT **b :** SOLVENT NAPHTHA

naph·tha·cene \'nafthə,sēn, ÷ 'napth-\ *n* -s [ISV *naphth-* + *-acene*] **:** an orange crystalline tetracyclic hydrocarbon $C_{18}H_{12}$ isomeric with chrysene and benzanthracene and present in small amounts in coal tar

naph·tha·late \'nafthə,lāt, ÷ 'napth-\ *n* -s [ISV *naphthalic* + *-ate*] **:** a salt or ester of naphthalic acid

naph·tha·lat·ed \'nafthə,lād·əd, ÷ napth-\ *adj* [*naphthalene* + *-ate* + *-ed*] **:** cleaned with naphtha to preserve its strength and resiliency ⟨~ wool⟩

naph·tha·lene \'nafthə,lēn, ÷ 'napth-\ *n* -s [alter. (influenced by *-ene*) of earlier *naphthaline*, fr. *naphtha* + connective *-l-* + *-ine*] **:** a crystalline aromatic hydrocarbon $C_{10}H_8$ that has a characteristic odor, that is the most abundant component of coal tar and is usu. obtained by distillation of tar and by recovery from coke-oven gas, that is constituted of two fused benzene rings and yields two varieties of monosubstitution products by substitution in the alpha or 1- and beta or 2-positions, and that is used chiefly as a raw material in organic syntheses (as of phthalic anhydride and many dye intermediates) and as a fumigant (as in moth balls) — see DECAHYDRONAPHTHALENE, TETRAHYDRONAPHTHALENE; compare STRUCTURAL FORMULA

naphthalene

naph·tha·lene·acetic acid \'==,=+ . . . -\ *n* [*naphthalene* + *acetic*] **:** either of two crystalline naphthyl derivatives $C_{10}H_7CH_2COOH$ of acetic acid; *esp* **:** the alpha or 1-compound used as a growth regulator for plants (as for preventing drop of apples before normal harvest time)

naph·tha·lene·disulfonic acid \" + . . . -\ *n* [*naphthalene* + *disulfonic*] **:** any of several disulfonic acids $C_{10}H_6(SO_3H)_2$ derived from naphthalene and used esp. in the form of hydroxy and amino derivatives (as chromotropic acid, H acid, G acid, R acid) as dye intermediates

naphthalene green V *n, usu cap N&G* **:** an acid dye — see DYE table I (under *Acid Green 16*)

naph·tha·lene·sulfonic acid \'==,=+ . . . -\ *n* [ISV *naphthalene* + *sulfonic*] **1 :** either of two crystalline monosulfonic acids $C_{10}H_7SO_3H$ obtained by sulfonation of naphthalene and used in the synthesis of dyes and naphthols **2 :** any of numerous sulfonic acids derived from naphthalene

naph·tha·lene·trisulfonic acid \" + . . . -\ *n* [*naphthalene* + *trisulfonic*] **:** any of several trisulfonic acids $C_{10}H_5(SO_3H)_3$ that are derived from naphthalene and that in some cases are used as dye intermediates

naph·tha·len·ic \,nafthə'lenik, ÷ ,napth-\ *adj* [ISV *naphthalene* + *-ic*] **:** of, relating to, or derived from naphthalene

naph·tha·len·oid \'==,lē,nȯid\ *adj* [*naphthalene* + *-oid*] **:** like naphthalene esp. in structure — sometimes contrasted with *benzenoid*

naph·thal·ic acid \(')naf'thalik-, ÷ (')nap\ *n* [ISV *naphthaline* + *-ic* + *acid*; prob. orig. formed as F *acide naphtalique*] **1 :** a crystalline acid $C_{10}H_6(COOH)_2$ formed by oxidation of acenaphthene; 1,8-naphthalene-dicarboxylic acid **2** *obs* **:** PHTHALIC ACID

naph·tha·mine dye \'naf|thə,mēn-, ÷ 'nap|, -mən-\ *n* [ISV *naphth-* + *amine*] **:** any of several direct azo dyes — see DYE table I (under *Direct Yellow 9* and *Direct Black 19*)

naphthaquinone *var of* NAPHTHOQUINONE

naphthas *pl of* NAPHTHA

naph·the·nate \'nafthə,nāt, ÷ 'napth-\ *n* -s [*naphthene* + *-ate*] **:** a salt or ester of a naphthenic acid ⟨~ drier⟩

naph·thene \'naf,thēn, ÷ 'nap,-\ *n* -s [ISV *naphth-* + *-ene*] **:** any of a series of saturated cyclic hydrocarbons of the general formula C_nH_{2n} **:** CYCLOPARAFFIN — used esp. of those members (as cyclopentane and cyclohexane and their alkyl derivatives) that occur in various kinds of petroleum, in shale, and in tar oil, and that yield useful aromatic hydrocarbons on dehydrogenation

naphthene-base \'=,=\ *adj* **:** containing relatively large amounts of various cyclic hydrocarbons (as naphthenes) — used esp. of crude petroleum; compare ASPHALT-BASE, PARAFFIN-BASE

naph·the·nic \-thēnik, -then-\ *adj* [ISV *naphthene* + *-ic*] **:** of, relating to, containing, or being a naphthene ⟨~ hydrocarbons⟩

naphthenic acid *n* **:** any of numerous chiefly monocarboxylic acids derived from naphthenes and obtained from naphthene-base and asphalt-base petroleums; *usu* **:** a commercial viscous liquid mixture of such acids used esp. in the form of salts (as copper naphthenate) as paint driers and preservatives for wood and textiles — see METALLIC SOAP

naph·thi·o·nate \'nafthēə,nāt, ÷'napth-\ *n* -s [ISV *naphthionic* + *-ate*] **:** a salt of naphthionic acid

naph·thi·on·ic acid \;==;änik-\ *n* [ISV, fr. *naphthylaminesulfonic*] **:** a crystalline naphthylaminesulfonic acid made by baking a mixture of alpha-naphthylamine and sulfuric acid and used in the preparation of Congo red and other dyes; 4-amino-1-naphthalenesulfonic acid

naphtho- — see NAPHTH-

naph·tho·ate \'nafthə,wāt, ÷'napth-\ *n* -s [ISV *naphth-* (in *naphthoic acid*) + *-oate*] **:** a salt or ester of a naphthoic acid

naph·tho·chrome violet R \'naf|thə,krōm-, ÷'nap|t\ *n, usu cap N&V* [*naphth-* + *-chrome*] **:** a mordant dye — see DYE table I (under *Mordant Violet 1*)

naph·tho·ic acid \(')naf|'thōik-, ÷(')nap|\ *n* [ISV *naphth-* + *-oic*] **:** either of two crystalline monocarboxylic acids $C_{10}H_7COOH$ derived from naphthalene

naph·thol \'naf,thȯl, ÷'nap,-, -thōl\ *n* -s [ISV *naphth-* + *-ol*] **1 :** either of two crystalline monohydroxy derivatives $C_{10}H_7OH$ of naphthalene found in small amounts in coal tar: **a :** the compound made usu. by hydrolysis of alpha-naphthylamine and used chiefly as a dye intermediate — called also *alpha-naphthol, 1-naphthol* **b :** the compound made usu. by alkali fusion of beta-naphthalenesulfonic acid and used chiefly as an intermediate (as for dyes, pharmaceuticals, and antioxidants for rubber) and esp. formerly in medicine as an antiseptic and parasiticide — called also *beta-naphthol, 2-naphthol;* see DYE table I (under *Developer 5*) **2 :** any of various hydroxy derivatives of naphthalene that resemble the simpler phenols but are in general more reactive **3** *often cap* **:** any of a series of compounds (as Naphthol AS) derived esp. from beta-naphthol and used as coupling components for azoic dyes

naphthol AS *n, usu cap N* [G *naphthol AS*, fr. *naphthol* + *AS*, fr. *a*nilid *s*äure *a*nilid + *s*äure acid] **1 :** a crystalline phenolic anilide $HOC_{10}H_6CONHC_6H_5$ used as a coupling component for azoic dyes; the anilide of 3-hydroxy-2-naphthoic acid — see DYE table I (under *Azoic Coupler 2*) **2 :** any of a series of arylides of either *ortho*-hydroxy aromatic carboxylic acids (as 3-hydroxy-2-naphthoic acid) or acyl derivatives (as acetoacetic acid) of acetic acid used as coupling components for azoic dyes — see DYE table I (under *Azoic Coupler*)

naphthol blue black *n, usu cap N & both Bs* **:** either of two acid dyes — see DYE table I (under *Acid Black 1 & 41*)

naphthol green B *n, usu cap N&G* **:** an acid dye — see DYE table I (under *Acid Green 1*)

naphthol NEL *n, usu cap 1st N* **:** a coupling agent for azoic dyes — see DYE table I (under *Azoic Coupler 34*)

naph·thol·sulfonic acid \;=,=+ . . . -\ *n* [ISV *naphthol* + *sulfonic*] **:** any of several sulfonic acids derived from the naphthols and used as dye intermediates: as **a :** NEVILE AND WINTHER'S ACID **b :** SCHAEFFER'S ACID **c :** CROCEIN ACID

naphthol yellow S *n, usu cap N&Y* **:** an acid dye — see DYE table I (under *Acid Yellow 1*)

naph·tho·quinone *also* **naph·tha·quinone** \;naftho, ÷;naptho+\ *n* [ISV *naphth-* + *quinone*] **:** any of three isomeric yellow to red crystalline compounds $C_{10}H_6O_2$ derived from naphthalene; *esp* **:** the alpha or 1, 4-compound that occurs naturally in the form of derivatives (as juglone, lawsone, vitamin K)

naph·thox·ide \naf'thäk,sīd, ÷ nap'-, -səd\ *n* [*naphth-* + *oxide*] **:** a derivative of naphthol formed by replacing its phenolic hydrogen by a metal or other cation (as sodium naphthoxide $C_{10}H_7ONa$)

naphthoxy- *comb form* [*naphthyl* + *oxy-*] **:** containing the univalent radical $C_{10}H_7O$– composed of naphthyl united with oxygen; naphthyl-oxy- ⟨*β-naphthoxy*acetic acid $C_{10}H_7OCH_2COOH$⟩

naph·tho·yl \'nafthə,wil, ÷'napth-\ *n* -s [ISV *naphth-* + *-yl*] **:** either of the radicals $C_{10}H_7CO$– of the naphthoic acids

naph·thyl \'naf,thil, ÷'nap,-\ *n* -s [ISV *naphth-* + *-yl*] **:** either of two univalent hydrocarbon radicals $C_{10}H_7$ derived from naphthalene: **a :** the radical derived by removal of a hydrogen atom in the alpha or 1-position — called also *alpha-naphthyl, 1-naphthyl* **b :** the radical derived by removal of a hydrogen atom in the beta or 2-position — called also *beta-naphthyl, 2-naphthyl*

naph·thyl·acetic acid \;=,=+ . . . -\ *n* [*naphthyl* + *acetic*] **:** NAPHTHALENEACETIC ACID

naph·thyl·amine \"+\ *n* [ISV *naphthyl* + *amine*] **:** either of two crystalline bases $C_{10}H_7NH_2$ that are amino derivatives of naphthalene and are used chiefly as dye intermediates: **a :** the alpha or 1-derivative made usu. by reduction of alpha-nitronaphthalene **b :** the carcinogenic beta or 2-derivative made usu. from beta-naphthol, ammonia, and ammonium sulfite

naphthylamine black *n, usu cap N&B* **:** either of two acid dyes — see DYE table I (under *Acid Black 1 and 7*)

naph·thyl·amine·sulfonic acid \" + . . . -\ *n* [ISV *naphthylamine* + *sulfonic*] **:** any of several amino sulfonic acids that are derived from the naphthylamines, have the properties of inner salts, and are used as dye intermediates: as **a :** BRÖNNER'S ACID **b :** CLEVE'S ACID **c :** LAURENT'S ACID **d :** NAPHTHIONIC ACID **e :** TOBIAS ACID

naph·thy·lene \'nafthə,lēn, ÷'napth-\ *n* -s [ISV *naphthyl* + *-ene*] **:** any of several bivalent radicals $-C_{10}H_6-$ derived from naphthalene

naph·thyl·ic \(')naf|thilik, ÷(')nap|-\ *adj* [ISV *naphthyl* + *-ic*] **:** of or relating to naphthyl

naphthyl methyl ketone *n* **:** ACETONAPHTHONE

naph·thyl·thiourea \;=,=+\ *n* [NL, fr. ISV *naphthyl* + NL *thiourea*] **:** either of two crystalline compounds $C_{10}H_7NHCSNH_2$ derived from thiourea — see ANTU

na·pi·er grass \'nāpēə(r)-\ *also* **napier** *or* **napier fodder** *n, often cap N* [fr. *Napier*, town in Cape Province, Union of So. Africa] **:** a tall stout perennial grass (*Pennisetum purpureum*) resembling sugarcane and first cultivated in Rhodesia but now grown in many countries for forage — called also *elephant grass*

na·pier·i·an *or* **na·per·i·an** \nə'pirēən\ *adj, usu cap N* [John *Napier*, Laird of Merchiston †1617 Scot. mathematician + E *-ian*] **:** of, relating to, or discovered by Napier

napierian logarithm *n, usu cap N* [John *Napier* + E *-ian*] **:** NATURAL LOGARITHM

na·pi·er's analogies \'nāpēə(r)z-\ *n pl, usu cap N* [after John *Napier*] **:** four formulas giving the tangent of half the sum or difference of two of the angles or sides of a spherical triangle in terms of the others

napier's bones *or* **napier's rods** *n pl, usu cap N* [after John *Napier*] **:** a set of 11 rods (as of wood) invented by Napier for the purpose of making numerical calculations

napier's circular parts *n pl, usu cap N* [after John *Napier*] **:** five parts of a right spherical triangle including the two legs and the complements of their opposite angles and of the hypotenuse

napier's rule *n, usu cap N* [after John *Napier*] **:** either of two rules in spherical trigonometry: the sine of any part is equal to the product of the tangents of the adjacent parts and the sine of any part is equal to the product of the cosines of the opposite parts

na·pi·form \'nāpə,fȯrm\ *adj* [ISV *nap-* (fr. L *napus* turnip, fr. Gk *napy* mustard) + *-iform*; akin to Gk *sinapy* mustard] *of roots* **:** shaped like a turnip **:** large and round above and tapering abruptly below — see ROOT illustration

[1]nap·kin \'napkən\ *n* -s [ME *napekin, nappekin*, fr. *nappe* tablecloth (fr. MF *nape, nappe*, fr. L *mappa* napkin) + ME *-kin* — more at MAP] **1 :** a usu. square piece of woven fabric or paper of variable size that is used to wipe the lips or the fingers ⟨cocktail ~⟩ ⟨dinner ~⟩ **2 :** a small cloth or towel ⟨the soul is sometimes shown borne upwards by angels in a ~ —Mary D. Anderson⟩: as **a** *dial Brit* **:** HANDKERCHIEF **b** *chiefly Scot* **:** KERCHIEF, NECKERCHIEF **c** *chiefly Brit* **:** DIAPER 2 b **3 :** SANITARY NAPKIN

[2]napkin \"\ *vt* -ED/-ING/-S **1 :** to cover, provide, serve, or wipe with a napkin ⟨after a most meticulous ~*ing* of his mouth —Alan Kapelner⟩ ⟨a ~*ed* tray⟩ **2** *archaic* **:** to conceal as if by hiding under a napkin ⟨a golden talent ~*ed* and hid away —*Saturday Rev.*⟩

napkin pattern *n* **:** LINENFOLD

napkin ring *n* **:** a usu. ring-shaped device used to enclose a folded table napkin

napkin ring

na·ples \'nāpəlz\ *adj, usu cap* [fr. *Naples*, Italy] **:** of or from the city of Naples, Italy **:** of the kind or style prevalent in Naples **:** NEAPOLITAN

naples biscuit *n, usu cap N* **:** LADYFINGER 2

nap·less \'napləs\ *adj* [[3]*nap* + *-less*] **:** being without nap **:** THREADBARE — **nap·less·ness** *n* -ES

naples yellow *n* **1** *usu cap N* **a :** a poisonous pigment consisting essentially of a basic lead antimonate used as an enamel color and in oil painting — called also *antimony yellow* **b :** any of several yellow pigments (as a mixture of chrome yellow and zinc white) substituted for Naples yellow **2** *often cap N* **:** a pale to grayish yellow that is redder and stronger than wine yellow and slightly redder than cream buff — called also *Nankeen, Nankin, Neapolitan Yellow*

na·po·leon \nə'pōlyən, -lēən\ *n* -s [after *Napoleon* I (Napoléon Bonaparte or Napoleone Buonaparte) †1821 Fr. emperor] **1** [F *napoléon (d'or)*, lit., Napoleon of gold, after *Napoléon* I] **:** a French 20-franc gold coin first issued in 1805 by Napoleon I but not in general circulation since World War I **2** *or* **napoleon boot :** a man's high boot worn esp. in the 19th century **3 a :** a card game played with hands of five cards in which the highest bidder having named the number of tricks he will try to take collects from each player the number of chips of the bid if he makes it or pays out that number if he fails; *also* **:** a bid to win all five tricks for a double premium **b :** any of various forms of solitaire **4 :** a rich pastry consisting of several oblong layers of puff paste with a filling of cream, custard, or jelly **5 a :** CRIMSON CLOVER **b :** CYPRESS SPURGE **6** *usu cap* **:** one like Napoleon I (as in ambition, discipline, strategy, or power) ⟨a *Napoleon* in the management of men —Cy Warman⟩ ⟨the little *Napoleon* of an automaking empire —*Time*⟩ ⟨a *Napoleon* of finance⟩

napoleon blue *n, often cap N* [after *Napoleon* I] **:** a deep blue that is greener and very slightly deeper than Yale blue and greener, lighter, and stronger than royal (sense 8b) — called also *Helvetia blue*

na·po·le·on·ic \nə,pōlē;änik, -nēk\ *adj, usu cap* [*Napoleon* I †1821 + E *-ic*] **:** of, relating to, or resembling Napoleon I ⟨*Napoleonic* Wars⟩ ⟨*Napoleonic* in loyalty to his family and early acquaintances —E.S.Bates⟩ ⟨*Napoleonic* ambitions⟩ — **na·po·le·on·i·cal·ly** \-nək(ə)lē, -nēk-, -li\ *adv, often cap*

na·po·leon·ism \nə'pōlyə,nizəm, -lēə,-\ *n* -s *usu cap* [*Napoleon* I + E *-ism*] **1 :** the policy of Napoleon I or the Napoleons **2 :** attachment to or advocacy of the Napoleonic dynasty — compare BONAPARTISM

na·po·leon·ist \-,nəst\ *n* -s *usu cap* [*Napoleon* I + E *-ist*] **:** a supporter of Napoleon I or the Napoleons **:** an advocate of Napoleonism

napoleon's-bell \=;=(=)=;=\ *n, pl* **napoleon's-bells** *usu cap N* [after *Napoleon* I; fr. the fact that the genus to which it belongs was named after the Empress Josephine (Joséphine de la Pagerie) †1814 Napoleon's consort] **:** a climbing plant (*Lapageria rosea*) having large leaves similar to smilax and rose-colored flowers

napoleon's-willow \=;=(=)=;=(,)=\ *n, pl* **napoleon's-willows** *usu cap N* [after *Napoleon* I; fr. the fact that his tomb at Saint Helena is overshadowed by a tree of this species] **:** WEEPING WILLOW

na·po·li·ta·na *also* **na·po·le·ta·na** \nə,pōlə'tänə\ *n* -s [It, fr. fem. of *napolitano, napoletano* Neapolitan, fr. L *Neapolitanus* — more at NEAPOLITAN] **:** a simple madrigal originating in 16th century Naples and similar to the villanella in style

[1]na·poo *or* **na·pooh** \nə'pü\ *interj* [modif. of F *il n'y en a plus* there is no more, it's over] *Brit* — used to indicate that something is finished, incapacitated, dead, all gone, or nonexistent or that the answer is no

[2]napoo *or* **napooh** \"\ *adj, slang Brit* **:** all gone **:** no more **:** FINISHED, INCAPACITATED, NONEXISTENT, DEAD

[3]napoo *or* **napooh** \"\ *vb* -ED/-ING/-S *vt, slang Brit* **:** to put an end to **:** STOP, FINISH, INCAPACITATE, EXHAUST, KILL ⟨the corporal's right arm being ~*ed* —*N. Y. Herald Tribune*⟩ ~ *vi, slang Brit* **:** to come to an end **:** DIE

nappe \'nap\ *n* -s [F, tablecloth, cover, sheet — more at NAPKIN] **1** [F *nappe (d'eau)*, lit., sheet of water] **:** a sheet of water falling from the crest of a weir **2 :** a large mass thrust over other rocks by a recumbent anticlinal fold, by thrust faulting, or by a combination of both **3 a :** SHEET 6 **b :** one of the two sheets that lie on opposite sides of the vertex and together make up a cone

napped \'napt\ *adj* [ME *noppyd*, fr. *noppe* nap (of cloth) + *-yd* -ed — more at NAP] **:** having a nap ⟨~ cloth⟩ ⟨~ leather⟩

[1]nap·per \'napə(r)\ *n* -s [[1]*nap* + *-er*] **1 :** one that takes a nap **:** one given to napping **2** *slang Brit* **:** HEAD ⟨had come within an ace of copping me on the ~ —P.G.Wodehouse⟩ ⟨nearly laughed his ~ off —Emlyn Williams⟩ ⟨gone off his ~ at last —William Sansom⟩

[2]napper \"\ *n* -s [[4]*nap* + *-er*] **:** one that naps cloth

[3]napper \"\ *var of* KNAPPER

nappe structure *n* **:** a mass of rocks that includes parts of one or more nappes

[1]nap·pi·ness \'napēnəs\ *n* -ES [[1]*nappy* + *-ness*] **:** the quality of having a nap **:** abundance of nap (as on cloth)

[2]nappiness \"\ *n* -ES [[1]*nappy* + *-ness*] *of a horse* **:** STUBBORNNESS, BALKINESS

napping *n* -s [fr. gerund of [4]*nap*] **:** the process of raising a nap (as on a textile)

napping hammer *var of* KNAPPING HAMMER

[1]nap·py \'napē, -pi\ *adj* -ER/-EST [ME *noppy*, fr. ME *noppe* nap (of cloth) + *-y* — more at NAP] **1 :** having a nap **:** DOWNY, SHAGGY **2 :** KINKY — used esp. of Negroes' hair ⟨carried on his ~ heads —J.P.Bishop⟩ ⟨~ hair —Richard Wright⟩ **3 a** *of liquor* **:** FOAMING, STRONG, HEADY ⟨~ ale⟩ **b** *archaic* **:** somewhat intoxicated **4** *of a horse* **:** given to sudden tricks or starts **:** STUBBORN, BALKY

[2]nap·py \'napi\ *n* -ES *chiefly Scot* **:** LIQUOR; *specif* **:** ALE

[3]nap·py \'napē\ *n* -ES [E dial. *nap* bowl (fr. ME, fr. OE *hnæpp* bowl, drinking vessel) + *-y* — more at HANAP] **:** a shallow open serving dish sometimes having one handle

[4]nap·py *or* **nap·pie** \'napi\ *n, pl* **nappies** [[1]*napkin* + *-y, -ie*] *chiefly Brit* **:** DIAPER 2b

nappies

nap·ra·path \'naprə,path\ *n* -s [Czech *naprava* correction + E *-path*] **:** a practitioner of naprapathy

na·prap·a·thy \nə'prapəthē\ *n* -ES [Czech *naprava* correction + E *-pathy*] **:** a therapeutic system of drugless treatment by manipulation depending on the theory that disease symptoms result from disorder in the ligaments and connective tissues

naps *pres 3d sing of* NAP, *pl of* NAP

na·pu \'nä(,)pü\ *n* -s [Malay *napoh*] **:** any of several Indo-Malayan chevrotains resembling but larger than the kanchils and probably all varieties of a single species (*Tragulus javanicus*)

nar \'när\ *chiefly dial var of* NEAR

nar *abbr* narrow

na·ra \'närə\ *adj, usu cap* [fr. *Nara*, city in Honshu, Japan, that was the chief Buddhist center of early Japan] **:** of or relating to the eighth century Buddhistic renaissance in Japan or the art that flourished during that time

na·ran·ji·lla \,närən'hēlyə\ *n* -s [Sp, dim. of *naranja* orange, fr. Ar *nāranj* — more at ORANGE] **1 :** a shrubby perennial herb (*Solanum quitoense*) cultivated in the uplands of northern So. America for its tomentose bright orange fruits that resemble tomatoes or small oranges **2 :** the richly flavored acid fruit of the naranjilla; *also* **:** a beverage made from this fruit

nar·as \'narəs\ *n* -ES [Hottentot (Nama dial.) *ǂnarab*] **:** a spiny southern African desert shrub (*Acanthosicyos horrida*) of the family Cucurbitaceae having a fruit resembling a melon and oily edible seeds

nar·bonne vetch \(')när;bän- *or* **nar·bo·nus vetch** \(')när;bōnəs-\ *n* [*narbonne* fr. *Narbonne*, France; *narbonus* NL, fr. L *Narbon-, Narbo* Narbonne] **:** an annual vetch (*Vicia* *narbonensis*) that is native to southern Europe but used elsewhere as a forage crop and that has leafy stipules and leaves ¾ inch or more broad

narc- *or* **narco-** *comb form* [ME *nark-*, fr. MF *narc-*, fr. ML, fr. Gk *nark-*, fr. *narkoun* to benumb — more at NARCOTIC] **1 :** numbness : stupor ⟨*narco*hypnia⟩ **2 :** narcosis : narcotic ⟨*narc*oma⟩ ⟨*narco*hypnosis⟩ ⟨*narco*anesthesia⟩ : narcotic and ⟨*narco*stimulant⟩ **3 :** deep sleep ⟨*narco*lepsy⟩ **4 :** electric ray ⟨*Narc*acion⟩ ⟨*Narco*batus⟩

nar·ca·ci·on·tes \ˌnärˌkāshēˈänˌtēz\ [NL, fr. pl. of *Narcacion*, genus of electric rays in some classifications, irreg. fr. *narc-* + Gk *akē* point + *-ōn*, pres. part. ending — more at EDGE] *syn of* NARCOBATOIDEA

nar·ce·ine \ˈnärsēˌēn, -sēən\ *n* -S [F *narcéine*, fr. Gk *narkē* numbness + F *-ine* — more at SNARE] **:** a bitter crystalline narcotic amphoteric alkaloid $C_{23}H_{27}NO_8$ found in opium and also obtainable from narcotine

nar·cism \ˈnärˌsizəm\ *n* -S [G *narzissmus* (formerly spelled *narcismus*), fr. *Narziss* Narcissus (fr. L *Narcissus*) + G *-ismus* -ism] **:** NARCISSISM

nar·cis·san \(ˈ)närˈsisᵊn\ *adj, often cap* [*Narcissus*, beautiful youth of Greco-Roman mythology who fell in love with his own image, died of unrequited love and was turned into the flower narcissus (fr. L, fr. Gk *Narkissos*) + E *-an*] **1 :** of or relating to the mythological Narcissus **2 :** NARCISSISTIC

nar·cis·sine \ˈ", -iˌsīn\ *adj, often cap* [L *Narcissus* + E *-ine*] **:** NARCISSAN

nar·cis·sism \ˈnärsəˌsizəm, ˈnäs-\ *n* -S [G *narzissismus*, fr. *Narziss* Narcissus (fr. L *Narcissus*) + *-ismus* -ism] **1 a :** EGOISM, EGOCENTRISM **b :** overevaluation of one's own attributes or achievements or of those of one's group **2 :** love of or sexual desire for one's own body **3 :** the state or stage of development in which there is a heavy investment of libido in one's own ego and which in abnormal forms persists through fixation or reappears through regression

nar·cis·sist \-səst\ *n* -S [G *narzissist*, fr. *Narziss* + G *-ist* (fr. L *-ista*)] **:** one showing symptoms of or suffering from narcissism

nar·cis·sis·tic \ˌnärsəˈsistik, ˌnäs-, -tēk\ *also* **narcissist** *adj* [*narcissistic* fr. G *narzisstisch*, fr. *narzissist* narcissist + *-isch* -ic (fr. OHG *-isc*, *-isk* -ish); *narcissist* fr. *narcissist*, n.] **:** of or relating to narcissism — **nar·cis·sis·ti·cal·ly** \-tək(ə)lē, -tēk-, -li\ *adv*

nar·cis·sus \närˈsisəs, näˈ-\ *n* [NL, fr. L, any of various plants of the genus Narcissus, fr. Gk *narkissos*, prob. by folk etymology (influence of *narkē* numbness) fr. a word of non-IE origin; fr. the plant's narcotic properties — more at NARCOTIC] **1** *cap* **:** a genus of Old World bulbous herbs (family Amaryllidaceae) having erect linear leaves and showy yellow or white or bicolor flowers with a large cup-shaped corona — see DAFFODIL 1, JONQUIL 1 **2** *pl* **narcissus** \ˈ"\ *or* **narcissuses** \-ˈsisəsəz\ *or* **narcis·si** \-ˈsiˌsī\ **:** any plant of the genus *Narcissus*; *esp* **:** any of numerous such plants (as from the species *N. poeticus*) of which the flowers have a short corona and are usu. borne separately — compare DAFFODIL, JONQUIL

narcissus 2

narcissus bulb fly *n* **1 :** a large yellow and black hairy syrphid fly (*Merodon equestris*) that resembles a small bumblebee, is native to Europe but now widespread in the U. S., and has a yellowish or whitish larva that bores in and destroys the bulbs of various plants (as narcissus, amaryllis, hyacinth) — called also *greater bulb fly* **2 :** LESSER BULB FLY

nar·cist \ˈnärsəst\ *n* -S [G *narzisst*, irreg. fr. *Narziss* Narcissus + G *-ist*] **:** NARCISSIST

nar·cis·tic \(ˈ)närˈsistik\ *adj* [G *narzisstisch*, fr. *narzisst* narcist + *-isch* -ic] **:** NARCISSISTIC

nar·co·analysis \ˌnärkō+\ *n* [NL, fr. *narc-* + *analysis*] **:** psychotherapy under sedation for the recovery of repressed memories together with the emotion accompanying the experience which is designed to facilitate an acceptable integration of the experience in the patient's personality

nar·co·anesthesia *also* **nar·co·anaesthesia** \ˈ"+\ *n* [NL, fr. *narc-* + *anesthesia*, *anaesthesia*] **:** anesthesia produced by a narcotic drug (as morphine)

nar·co·bat·i·dae \ˌnärkōˈbadəˌdē\ [NL, fr. *Narcobatus*, genus of electric rays in some classifications (fr. *narc-* + Gk *batos*, a skate) + *-idae*] *syn of* TORPEDINIDAE

nar·co·ba·toi·dea \ˌnärkōbəˈtȯidēə\ *n pl, cap* [NL, fr. *Narcobatus* + *-oidea*] **:** a suborder of Hypotremata coextensive with the family Torpedinidae comprising the electric rays

nar·co·diagnosis \ˌnärkō+\ *n* [NL, fr. *narc-* + *diagnosis*] **:** the use of sedative or hypnotic drugs for diagnostic purposes (as in psychiatry)

nar·co·hyp·nia \ˌnärkəˈhipnēə\ *n* -S [NL, fr. *narc-* + *hypn-* + *-ia*] **:** numbness felt on awaking from sleep

nar·co·hypnosis \ˌnärkō+\ *n* [NL, fr. *narc-* + *hypnosis*] **:** a hypnotic state produced by drugs and sometimes used in psychotherapy — compare NARCOANALYSIS, NARCOSYNTHESIS

nar·co·lep·sy \ˈnärkəˌlepsē\ *n* -ES [ISV *narc-* + *-lepsy*; orig. formed as F *narcolepsie*] **:** a condition characterized by a transient compulsive tendency to attacks of deep sleep usu. of unknown cause

¹nar·co·lep·tic \ˌ==ˈleptik\ *adj* [fr. *narcolepsy*, after such pairs as E *epilepsy*: *epileptic*] **:** of, relating to, or affected with narcolepsy

²narcoleptic \ˈ"\ *n* -S **:** a person subject to attacks of narcolepsy

nar·co·ma \närˈkōmə\ *n, pl* **narcomas** \-məz\ *also* **nar·coma·ta** \-mədə\ [NL, fr. Gk *narkoun* to benumb] **:** the stuporous state produced by narcotics

nar·co·mania \ˌnärkə+\ *n* [NL, fr. *narc-* + *mania*] **:** uncontrollable desire for narcotics

nar·co·medusae \ˈ"+\ *n pl, cap* [NL, fr. *narc-* + *medusae*] **:** a suborder of trachyline medusae sometimes regarded as an independent order — **nar·co·medusan** \ˌ==+\ *adj or n*

nar·cose \ˈnärˌkōs\ *also* **nar·cous** \-rkəs\ *adj* [ISV *narc-* + *-ose* or *-ous*] **:** marked by stupor

nar·co·sis \närˈkōsəs, näˈ-\ *n, pl* **narco·ses** \-ōˌsēz\ [NL, fr. Gk *narkōsis*, action of benumbing, fr. *narkoun* to benumb + *-sis* — more at NARCOTIC] **1 :** a state of stupor, insensibility, or unconsciousness from which recovery is possible produced by the influence of narcotics or other chemicals **2 :** a reversible state of arrested activity of various protoplasmic structures under the influence of various concentrations of some chemicals (as carbon dioxide, alcohols, or magnesium salts)

nar·co·stimulant \ˌnärkō+\ *n* [*narc-* + *stimulant*] **:** a substance possessing both narcotic and stimulant properties

nar·co·suggestion \ˈ"+\ *n* [*narc-* + *suggestion*] **:** the psychoanalytic use of suggestion in subjects who have received sedative or hypnotic drugs

nar·co·synthesis \ˈ"+\ *n* [NL, fr. *narc-* + *synthesis*] **:** narcoanalysis which has as its goal a reintegration of the patient's personality

nar·co·therapy \ˈ"+\ *n* [ISV *narc-* + *therapy*] **:** psychotherapy carried out with the aid of sedating or hypnotic drugs

¹nar·cot·ic \närˈkädˌik, -kät|, |ēk\ *n* -S [ME *narkotik*, fr. MF *narcotique*, fr. *narcotique*, adj., fr. ML *narcoticus*, fr. Gk *narkōtikos* benumbing, narcotic, fr. (assumed) *narkōtos* (verbal of *narkoun* to benumb, fr. *narkē* numbness, cramp, electric ray) + *-ikos* -ic — more at SNARE] **1 :** a drug (as of the opium, belladonna, or alcohol groups) that in moderate doses allays sensibility, relieves pain, and produces profound sleep but that in poisonous doses produces stupor, coma, or convulsions — often used in the pl. in attributive position ⟨~*s* addiction⟩ **2 :** something that soothes, relieves, or lulls ⟨a public comforted by the ~ of military supremacy⟩

²narcotic \(ˈ)==ˈ==\ *adj* [F or ML; F *narcotique*, fr. ML *narcoticus*] **1 :** having the properties of or yielding a narcotic; *sometimes* **:** inducing mental lethargy **:** SOPORIFEROUS ⟨a ~ speech⟩ **2 :** of, induced by, or concerned with narcotics **3 :** of, involving, or for narcotic addicts or their care

nar·cot·i·cal·ly \|ək(ə)lē\ *adv* **:** in a narcotic manner

nar·cot·i·cism \närˈkädəˌsizəm\ *n* -S [¹*narcotic* + *-ism*] **:** addiction to habit-forming drugs

nar·cot·ic·ness *n* -ES **:** the quality or state of being narcotic or a narcotic

nar·co·tine \ˈnärkəˌtēn, -tᵊn\ *n* -S [F, fr. *narcotique* narcotic + *-ine*] **:** a crystalline alkaloid $C_{22}H_{23}NO_7$ that is found in opium and possesses antispasmodic but no narcotic properties **:** a methoxy derivative of hydrastine

nar·co·tism \ˈnärkəˌtizəm\ *n* -S [F *narcotisme*, fr. *narcotique* narcotic + *-isme* -ism] **:** NARCOSIS, NARCOTICISM

nar·co·ti·za·tion \ˌnärkədəˈzāshən\ *n* -S **:** the act or process of inducing narcosis

nar·co·tize \ˈnärkəˌtīz\ *vt* -ED/-ING/-S [ISV *narcotic* + *-ize*] **1 :** to imbue with or subject to the influence of a narcotic **:** put into a state of narcosis **2 :** to soothe to unconsciousness or unawareness ⟨*narcotizing* the pains of confusion and soothing the fevers of frustration —D.L.Cohn⟩

nar·co·tol·ine \ˈnärkəˌtōˌlēn, -tō-, -lən\ *n* -S [ISV, blend of *narcotine* and *-ol*] **:** a crystalline alkaloid $C_{21}H_{21}NO_7$ found in the seed capsules of the opium poppy

narcous *var of* NARCOSE

¹nard \ˈnärd, ˈnäd\ *n* -S [ME *narde*, fr. MF or L; MF, fr. L *nardus*, fr. Gk *nardos*, fr. a Sem word (akin to Heb *nērd* nard) prob. derived fr. Skt *nalada* Indian spikenard] **1 a :** SPIKENARD 1b **b :** MATGRASS 1b **2 :** an ointment made partly from nard **:** SPIKENARD 1a **3 :** the rhizomes of any of several pharmaceutically useful plants of the genus *Valeriana* (as *V. celtica*, *V. tuberosa*) or of the related plant (*Nardostachys jatamansi*)

²nard \ˈ"\ *vt* -ED/-ING/-S **:** to anoint with nard

nar·dine \ˈnärdən, -rˌdīn\ *adj* [ME, fr. L *nardinus*, fr. Gk *nardinos*, fr. *nardos* nard + *-inos* -ine] **:** of or relating to nard **:** having the qualities of nard

nar·doo \närˈdü\ *or* **nar·do** \-dō\ *n* -S [native name in Australia] **1 :** an Australian clover fern (*Marsilea drummondii*) **2** *India* **:** a plant (*Sesbania aculeata*) whose seeds are ground into meal — compare DAINCHA

nar·dus \ˈnärdəs\ *n, cap* [NL, fr. L, nard — more at NARD] **:** a genus of grasses having spikelets forming a one-sided spike with each spikelet having a single flower — see MATGRASS

nar·gil \ˈnärˌgēl\ *n* -S [Per *nārgīl*] **:** the Indian coconut

nar·gi·leh \ˈnärgəˌle\ *also* **nar·ghi·le** \ˈnärgəlē\ *n* -S [Per *nārgīla*, fr. *nārgīl* coconut (of which the bowls were orig. made), of Indic origin; akin to Skt *nārikela*, *nādikela* coconut, Hindi *nāriyal*] **:** a pipe used chiefly in the Near East that cools the tobacco smoke by passing it through a reservoir of water and that is provided with long flexible stems resembling tubes — compare HOOKAH

nargileh

nar·i·al \ˈna(a)rēəl\ *also* **nar·ic** \ˈnarik\ *adj* [*naris* nostril + *-al* or *-ic*] **:** of or relating to the nares ⟨the ~ septum⟩

nar·i·ca \ˈnarəkə\ *n* -S [NL, fr. L *naris* + *-ica* (fem. of *-icus* -ic)] **:** BROWN COATI

nar·i·corn \ˈna(a)rəˌkȯrn\ *n* [L *naris* nostril + *cornu* horn — more at HORN] **:** the horny segment of the rhinotheca covering the nostrils of albatrosses and some other birds

nar·in·gen·in \ˌnarənˈjenən, -ˈge-, nəˈrinjən-\ *n* -S [ISV, blend of *naringin* and *-ene*] **:** a crystalline flavanone $C_{15}H_{12}O_5$ obtainable esp. by hydrolysis of naringin

na·rin·gin \nəˈrinjən, -iŋən\ *n* -S [ISV *naring-* (fr. Skt *nāraṅga*, *nāriṅga* orange tree) + *-in*; orig. formed in G] **:** a bitter crystalline glycoside $C_{27}H_{32}O_{14}$ that is found in the blossoms or fruit of the grapefruit and that on hydrolysis yields naringenin and a disaccharide constituted of D-glucose and L-rhamnose

naris \ˈna(a)rəs, ˈne|, ˈnā|\ *n, pl* **nares** \|(ˌ)rēz\ [L; akin to L *nasus* nose — more at NOSE] **:** the opening of the nose or nasal cavity of a vertebrate; *esp* **:** either of the actual orifices internal or external of the nasal cavity

¹nark \ˈnäk\ *n* -S [perh. fr. Romany *nok*, *nak* nose; akin to Skt *nāsā* nose — more at NOSE] *Brit* **:** a spy employed by the police **:** INFORMER, STOOL PIGEON

²nark \ˈ"\ *vb* -ED/-ING/-S *vt, Brit* **:** to inform or spy on ~ *vi, Brit* **:** to act as an informer

³nark \ˈ"\ *vt* -ED/-ING/-S [origin unknown] *Brit* **:** IRRITATE, ANNOY ⟨hope you aren't ~*ed* with me —Norman Lindsay⟩

⁴nark \ˈ"\ *n* -S **1** *chiefly Austral* **:** KILLJOY, WET BLANKET **2** *chiefly Austral* **:** an unpleasant irritating person

⁵nark \ˈ"\ *v imper* [origin unknown] *Brit* — sometimes used with *it* as a command or entreaty to cease ⟨~ it⟩

narky \-ki\ *adj* [³*nark* + *-y*] *Brit* **:** marked by ill temper and irritability ⟨a great deal of ~ petulance —*Listener*⟩

narr \ˈnär\ *n* -S [ML *narratio*, fr. L, narration — more at NARRATION] *archaic* **:** a declaration in legal pleading

nar·ra \ˈnärə\ *n* -S [Tag & Bisayan] **1 :** any of several timber trees of the genus *Pterocarpus* **2** *also* **narrawood** \ˈ==ˌ=\ **:** the hard wood of narra noted for its ability to take a high polish — called also *Philippine mahogany*

nar·ra·gan·set \ˌnarəˈgan(t)sət, -gaan- *also* ˌner-, *usu* -əd-+V\ *n, pl* **narraganset** *or* **narragansets** *usu cap* [prob. modif. of Narraganset *naiaganset*, lit., people of the small point, fr. *naiagans* small point of land (dim. of *naiag* point) + *-et*, locative suffix] **1 a :** an Indian people of Rhode Island west of Narragansett Bay **b :** a member of such people **2 :** an Algonquian language of the Narraganset people **3 :** NARRAGANSETT

nar·ra·gan·sett \ˈ"\ *n, usu cap* [fr. *Narragansett*, Rhode Island] **1** *also* **narranganset pacer** **a** *usu cap N&P* **:** an extinct breed of American pacing saddle horses **b** -S *usu cap N* **:** an animal of this breed **2** -S **:** a domestic turkey of a variety developed in Rhode Island that is characterized by medium size and black plumage marked with white giving a grayish cast to the feathers

nar·ran·te \nəˈräntā\ *adv* (*or adj*) [It, narrating, pres. part. of *narrare* to narrate, fr. L — more at NARRATE] **:** in a declamatory style — used as a direction in music

nar·rat·able \(ˈ)naˈrād·əbəl\ *adj* **:** capable of being narrated

nar·ra·tage \ˈnarəd·ij\ *n* -S [*narrate* + *-age*] **:** a technique sometimes used in plays and films and on television whereby the voice of a narrator usu. begins and often supplements the actual story and gives thereby the illusion that the story itself is merely an expansion of his own words

nar·rate \ˈnaˌrāt, naˈr- *also* ˈneˌr- *or* neˈr- *sometimes* nəˈr-, *usu* -ād-+V\ *vb* -ED/-ING/-S [L *narratus*, past part. of *narrare* to make known, narrate, fr. L *gnarus* knowing, known; akin to L *gnoscere*, *noscere* to know — more at KNOW] *vt* **:** to tell or recite the happenings of (a story) ~ *vi* **:** to act or function as a storyteller **syn** see RELATE

nar·ra·tion \naˈrāshən *also* ne- *sometimes* nəˈ-\ *n* -S [ME *narracion*, fr. L *narration-*, *narratio*, fr. *narratus* + *-ion-*, *-io* -ion] **1 :** the act or process of telling the particulars of an act, occurrence, or course of events ⟨the ~ of the course of battle⟩ ⟨the ~ of a fairy story⟩ **2 :** something that is narrated **:** STORY, NARRATIVE **3 :** the recitation of a succession of events usu. in chronological order and usu. with description of the persons involved — **nar·ra·tion·al** \-shənᵊl, -shnəl\ *adj*

¹nar·ra·tive \ˈnarəd·|iv, -at| *also* ˈner-\ *n* -S [MF, fr. fem. of *narratif*, adj.] **1** *Scots law* **:** the part of a document containing the recitals; *specif* **:** the part of a deed immediately following the name and designation of the grantor reciting the inducement for making it **2 :** something that is narrated (as the account of a series of events) **:** STORY, NARRATION **3 :** the art or study of narrating **4 :** the representation in painting of an event or story or an example of such a representation ⟨the ~ of St. Francis of Assisi⟩

²narrative \ˈ"\ *adj* [F or LL; F *narratif*, fr. LL *narrativus*, fr. L *narratus* (past part. of *narrare* to make known, narrate) + *-ivus* -ive — more at NARRATE] **1 a :** of or relating to narration ⟨a good ~ technique⟩ **b :** having the form of a story ⟨a ~ treatment of an historical event⟩ **2** *of a painting* **:** showing or having the quality of a narrative

nar·ra·tive·ly \|əvlē\ *adv* **1 :** in the style or manner of narration **2 :** in respect to narrative character ⟨a book amusing ~ but shallow⟩

narrative past *or* **narrative preterit** *n* **:** PAST TENSE

nar·ra·tor \ˈnaˌrād·ə(r), ˈnarə- -ātə- *also* ˈneˌ- *or* neˈr- *sometimes* naˈr- *or* ˈnarəd·- *or* ˈnerəd·-\ *n* -S [L, fr. *narratus* + *-or*] **:** one that narrates

narrawood *var of* NARRA

nar·rin·yeri \ˌnarənˈyerē\ *n, pl* **narrinyeri** *or* **narrinyeris** *usu cap* **1 a :** a people native to the Lake Alexandria region of So. Australia **b :** a member of such people **2 :** the language of the Narrinyeri people

¹nar·row \ˈna(ˌ)rō, -rə *also* ˈne(-, *often* -rəw+V\ *adj* -ER/-EST [ME *narwe*, *naru*, *narowe*, fr. OE *nearu*; akin to OHG *narwa* scar, narrow mark of a scar, *snuor* cord, ON *snœri* twisted rope, Goth *snorjo* basket, net, Gk *narnax* box, chest, Lith *nerti* to dive, thread; basic meaning: twisting] **1 a :** of little breadth esp. in comparison with length ⟨a ~ bay⟩ ⟨a ~ table⟩ **b :** not possessing usual or expected width ⟨a ~ sidewalk⟩ **c** *of a textile* **:** woven narrow (as in widths less than 18 inches) and suitable for ribbon, tape, webbing, or braid — compare BROAD **2 a :** limited in size or scope **:** RESTRICTED, CIRCUMSCRIBED ⟨~ resources⟩ ⟨~ nations⟩ ⟨in a ~*er* sense, history is the record of human events —A.L.Guérard⟩ **b :** close around **:** CONFINING ⟨~ bounds⟩ **3 a** (1) **:** possessed of insufficient means **:** MEAGER ⟨a ~ income⟩ ⟨~circumstances⟩ (2) **:** MEAGER, BIGOTED, SMALL ⟨a ~ individual⟩ ⟨a ~ mind⟩ **b** *chiefly dial* **:** STINGY, NIGGARDLY **4 a :** having only a little margin **:** having barely sufficient space, time, or number **:** CLOSE ⟨winner in the election by a ~ margin⟩ **b :** uncomfortably close to failure **:** barely successful ⟨a ~ escape⟩ **5 a :** concentrating on minute particulars **:** CLOSE ⟨a ~ inspection⟩ **b :** extremely precise ⟨a machine with ~ tolerances⟩ **6** *of an animal ration* **:** relatively rich in protein as compared with carbohydrate and fat — compare WIDE **7 a :** TENSE 3 **b** *of pronunciation transcription* **:** representing by diacritical symbols many differences in and varieties of sounds including nonphonemic differences — compare BROAD **8 :** of limited activity (as with little or no demand or supply for particular issues) ⟨a ~ market⟩; *also* **:** characterized by very small price changes ⟨a ~ price range⟩

syn STRAIT: NARROW is the ordinary term signifying not broad or wide ⟨a *narrow* tape⟩ ⟨a *narrow* street⟩ ⟨a *narrow* entrance⟩ It commonly extends to signify cramped, restricted, or circumscribed ⟨a *narrow* squeeze through a passage⟩ ⟨a *narrow* interpretation of a law⟩ and often suggests the provincial, sectional, or partisan ⟨a *narrow* sectarian opinion on a national problem⟩ ⟨a *narrow* mind⟩ STRAIT, now archaic or dialect except in the phrase *the strait and narrow path*, more strongly than *narrow* implies tightness and closeness, commonly extending in meaning to include the idea of the strictness or rigorousness of great and distressing restraints ⟨narrow is the gate and *strait* is the way, which leadeth unto life —Mt 7:14 (DV)⟩ ⟨a *strait* prison⟩ ⟨to reform . . . some *strait* decrees that lie too heavy on the commonwealth —Shak.⟩

²narrow \ˈ"\ *n* -S [ME *narwe*, fr. *narwe*, adj.] **:** the narrow part of something: as **a :** a narrow passage (as in a mountain pass or street) **b :** a contracted part of a stream, lake, or sea; *specif* **:** a strait connecting two bodies of water ⟨the *Narrows* of New York harbor⟩ — usu. used in pl. but sometimes sing. in constr. **c :** a narrow gallery in a mine

³narrow \ˈ"\ *vb* -ED/-ING/-S [¹*narrow*] *vt* **1 :** to decrease the breadth or extent of **:** CONTRACT; *specif* **:** DECREASE 2 **2 :** to contract the reach or sphere of ⟨~ the powers of executive authority⟩ **:** make less liberal or broad **:** LIMIT ⟨~ one's views on education⟩ ~ *vi* **:** to become less broad **:** CONTRACT, LESSEN ⟨the river ~*s* above the town⟩

narrow dock *n* **:** CURLED DOCK

nar·row·er \ˈnarōə(r), -rəwə(r) *also* ˈner-\ *n* -S **:** one that narrows

narrow-fisted \ˌ=(ˌ)=ˈ==\ *adj* **:** CLOSEFISTED

¹narrow-gage *also* **narrow-gaged** \ˌ=(ˌ)=ˈ=\ *adj* **1 :** using track of less than standard gage ⟨a *narrow-gage* railway⟩; *also* **:** of a gage less than standard ⟨*narrow-gage* track⟩ **2** *usu* **narrow-gauge :** RESTRICTED, PROVINCIAL, PETTY ⟨*narrow-gauge* views⟩ the stereotypes of *narrow-gauge* business standards —Lewis Mumford⟩

²narrow-gage \ˈ=(ˌ)=ˌ=\ *n* [¹*narrow-gage*] **:** a narrow-gage railway, track, locomotive, or car

narrowhearted \ˌ=(ˌ)=ˈ==\ *adj* **:** MEAN, PARSIMONIOUS, UNGENEROUS — **nar·row·heart·ed·ness** *n* -ES

narrowing *n* -S [fr. gerund of ³*narrow*] **1 :** the act or process of becoming or making narrow **2 :** an instance of narrowing; *specif* **:** DECREASE 3

nar·row·ing·ness *n* -ES **:** the quality of becoming narrow or a tendency to become narrow

narrow-leaved plantain \ˈ=(ˌ)=ˌ=-\ *n* **:** a ribgrass (*Plantago lanceolata*)

narrow-leaved vetch *n* **:** an annual or winter annual vetch (*Vicia angustifolia*) with linear upper leaves

nar·row·ly *adv* [ME *narowly*, fr. OE *nearulice*, fr. *nearu* narrow + *-lice* -ly — more at NARROW] **:** in a narrow manner: as **a :** with little width or extent ⟨a ~ constructed causeway⟩ **b :** by a slight margin **:** BARELY ⟨~ escaped⟩ ⟨the Indian onslaught . . . ~ missed extinguishing the colony —*Amer. Guide Series: Va.*⟩ **c** (1) **:** with strict adherence to details, rules, or norms ⟨a ~ interpreted constitution⟩ (2) **:** with minute scrutiny **:** CAREFULLY ⟨search an area ~⟩ **d :** with utmost vigor **:** INTENSELY ⟨a ~ pursued course of action⟩ **e :** in a particularly petty, illiberal, or narrow-minded way ⟨not ~ moral —F.R.Leavis⟩

narrow-minded \ˌ=(ˌ)=ˈ==\ *adj* **1 a :** of limited mental or spiritual capabilities **:** SHALLOW ⟨*narrow-minded* public officials⟩ **b :** PETTY, PROVINCIAL ⟨*narrow-minded* blue laws⟩ **2 :** restricted or hampered by bigotry ⟨a *narrow-minded* interpretation⟩ ⟨brilliant, but *narrow-minded* judges⟩ — **nar·row-mind·ed·ly** *adv* — **nar·row-mind·ed·ness** *n* -ES

narrow-mouthed toad \ˈ=(ˌ)=ˌ=-\ *n* **:** a toad of the family Brevicipitidae

nar·row·ness *n* -ES **:** the quality or state of being narrow ⟨the ~ of a point of view⟩ ⟨the ~ of a road⟩

narrow pennant *n* **:** LONG PENNANT

narrows *pl of* NARROW, *pres 3d sing of* NARROW

nar·sar·suk·ite \ˌnärsə(r)ˈsəˌkīt\ *n* -S [*Narsarssuak*, near Ivigtut, So. Greenland + E *-ite*] **:** a mineral $Na_2(Ti,Fe)Si_4(O,F)$ consisting of a silicate and fluoride of sodium, iron, and titanium

nar·sin·ga \nərˈsiŋgə\ *n* -S [Hindi *narsīgā*, perh. fr. Skt *nala* reed, tube + *śṛṅga* horn — more at HORN] **:** a curved metal trumpet used throughout India

nar·the·cal \(ˈ)närˈthēkəl\ *adj* [LGk *narthēk-*, *narthēx* + E *-al*] **:** of the nature of or relating to a narthex of a church

nar·the·ci·um \närˈthēs(h)ēəm\ *n, cap* [NL, fr. Gk *narthēkion* asphodel, dim. of *narthēk-*, *narthēx* giant fennel] **:** a genus of bog herbs (family Liliaceae) having linear leaves and greenish yellow flowers in racemes and with conspicuously bearded filaments — see BOG ASPHODEL

nar·thex \ˈnärˌtheks\ *n* -ES [LGk *narthēx*, fr. Gk, giant fennel, prob. of Sem origin like Gk *nardos* nard; fr. the resemblance in shape of the thin porch to a stalk of giant fennel — more at NARD] **1 :** a western porch (as in early Christian churches) used orig. by persons (as women, penitents, or catechumens) not entering the church itself and being usu. one side or member of the atrium or outer court surrounded by ambulatories; *also* **:** a vestibule (as within an early Christian church) used for similar purposes **2 :** a vestibule leading to the nave of a church — see BASILICA illustration

nartje *or* **nartjie** *var of* NAARTJE

nar·whal *or* **nar·wal** \ˈnärˌ(h)wäl, -rwəl, -ˌ(h)wȯl\ *or* **nar·whale** \-ˌ(h)wāl\ *n* -S [*narwhal*, *narwal* modif. (influenced by E *whale*) of Norw & Dan *narhval* & Sw *narval*, prob. modif. of Icel *náhvalur*, fr. ON *nāhvalr*, fr. *nār* corpse + *hvalr* whale; *narwhale* part trans. of Dan & Norw *narhval* & Sw *narval*; fr. the resemblance of its color to that of a human corpse; akin to OE *nēo-*, *-nē* corpse, Goth *naus*, ORuss *navĭ* corpse, Goth *nauths* need — more at NEED, WHALE] **:** an arctic cetacean (*Monodon monoceros*) that has no dorsal fin, is marbled gray or white in color, becomes when mature about 20 feet long, and possesses in the male one or infrequently two long twisted pointed tusks projecting like a horn and furnishing ivory of commercial value — **nar·whal·ian** \(ˈ)närˈ(h)wälēən, -wȯl-, -wāl-\ *adj*

narwhal

nary \ˈnarē, ˈner-, ˈnaar-, -ri, *South also* ˈnar *or* ˈnaə\ *adj* [alter of *ne'er a*, fr. *ne'er* + ²*a*] *dial* : not one — **nary a** *or* **nary an** : not a single : never a ⟨sold merchandise to a friend, with *nary an* entry on the books —J.K.Lasser⟩

nas- *or* **naso-** *also* **nasi-** *comb form* [L *nasus* nose — more at NOSE] **1** : nose : nasal ⟨*nasicorn*⟩ ⟨*nasitis*⟩ ⟨*nasology*⟩ ⟨*nasoscope*⟩ ⟨*nasosinusitis*⟩ **2** : nasal and ⟨*nasethmoid*⟩ ⟨*nasopalatine*⟩ ⟨*nasolabial*⟩

NAS *abbr* naval air station

¹**na·sal** \ˈnāzəl\ *n* -s [MF *nasal*, *nasel*, fr. OF, fr. *nes* nose, fr. L *nasus* — more at NOSE] **1** : a part of a helmet serving as a guard for the nose — called also *nosepiece* **2** : a part near or entering into the structure of the nose (as a nasal bone or scale) **3** : a nasal consonant or vowel

²**nasal** \"\ *adj* [F, fr. L *nasus* nose + F *-al* (adj. suffix)] **1 a** : of or relating to the nose ⟨~ inflammation⟩ **b** : of or relating to a plate or scale through or by which the nostril opens (as in various reptiles) **2 a** : uttered with the nose passage open by reason of a lowered velum and with the mouth passage occluded at some point (as at the lips in \m\, the tongue tip in \n\, or the tongue back in \ŋ\ **b** (1) : uttered with the mouth open, with the velum lowered, and with the nose passage producing a phonemically essential resonance — used of a vowel as in French and Portuguese (2) : uttered by some speakers with purely oral resonance (as in English) : uttered with the mouth open, with the velum at least partly open, and with the nose passage producing a phonemically nonessential resonance objectionable to some listeners — used of a vowel or a continuant **c** : containing or using sounds that are nasal or that are made through the nose — used of speech or a speaker **3** *of a musical tone* : having a quality characteristically sharp and penetrating and lacking in resonance; *esp* : having a predominance of upper partials

nasal bone *n* : either of two bones of the skull of vertebrates above the fishes lying in front of the frontal bones and being in man oblong in shape forming by their junction the bridge of the nose and partly covering in the nasal cavity

nasal breadth *n* **1** *on the skull* : the distance between the two most lateral points on the rim of the nasal opening **2** *on the living* : the distance between the two most lateral points on the wings of the nostrils

nasal capsule *n* : the structures enclosing the nasal fossae or olfactory organ of a vertebrate

nasal cartilage *n* : any of the cartilages forming the anterior part of the nose

nasal cavity *n* : the vaulted chamber that lies between the floor of the cranium and the roof of the mouth of higher vertebrates extending from the external nares to the pharynx, being enclosed by bone or cartilage and usu. incompletely divided into lateral halves by the septum of the nose, and having its walls lined with mucous membrane that is rich in venous plexuses and ciliated in the lower part which forms the beginning of the respiratory passage and warms and filters the inhaled air and that is modified as sensory epithelium in the upper olfactory part — see NOSE 1

nasal concha *n* : TURBINATE BONE

nasal duct *n* : a nasolacrimal duct

nasal eminence *n* : GLABELLA

nasal fly *n* : any of several botflies that develop in nasal passages and frontal sinuses of various mammals

nasal fossa *n* **1** : either lateral half of the nasal cavity **2** : one of the depressions or grooves on the bill in which the nostrils of most birds are situated

nasal gamma *n* : GAMMA NASAL

nasal height *n* : the height of the nose from the nasion to the middle of the lower margin of the anterior nares

nasal index *n* : the ratio of nasal breadth to nasal height multiplied by 100

na·sa·lis \nāˈz|aləs, -ˈs|, |äl-, |āl-\ *n* [NL, fr. L *nasus* nose + *-alis* -al — more at NOSE] **1** -ES : a small muscle on each side of the nose that constricts the nasal aperture by the action of (1) a triangular transverse portion which draws the lateral part of the aperture upward and (2) a quadrangular alar portion which draws it downward **2** *cap* : a genus of monkeys (family Cercopithecidae) that comprises the proboscis monkey

na·sal·ism \ˈnāzə,lizəm\ *n* -s : nasality of utterance

na·sal·i·ty \nāˈzaləd·ē, -ətē, -i\ *n* -ES [prob. fr. F *nasalité*, fr. *nasal* + *-ité* -ity — more at NASAL] : the quality or an instance of being nasal esp. in utterance

na·sal·iza·tion \,nāzələ'zāshən, -,lī'-\ *n* -s : the act or process of making, being, or becoming nasal

na·sal·ize \ˈnāzə,līz\ *vb* -ED/-ING/-S *vt* : to make nasal; *specif* : to change to a sound that is nasal ~ *vi* : to speak in a nasal manner

na·sal·ly \-lē, -li\ *adv* **1** : in a nasal manner ⟨~ pronounced⟩ **2** : in the direction of nasalization ⟨a ~ altered consonant⟩

nasal mite *n* : any of several mites of the family Rhinonyssidae and order Acarina that are parasitic in the nasal passages of birds

nasal nerve *n* : NASOCILIARY NERVE

nasal notch *n* : the rough surface on the anterior lower border of the frontal bone between the orbits which articulates with the nasal bones and superior maxillaries

nasal process *n* : the upwardly extending part of the maxillary bone that forms part of the sides of the nose

nasal sac *n* : OLFACTORY PIT 2

nasal scale *n* : NARICORN

nasal septum *n* : the bony and cartilaginous partition between the nasal passages

nasal sill *n* : the floor of the nasal opening

nasal spine *n* : any of three median bony processes adjacent to the nasal passages — see ANTERIOR NASAL SPINE, FRONTAL NASAL SPINE, POSTERIOR NASAL SPINE

nasal twang *n* : TWANG 2a

nasard *var of* NAZARD

na·sat \ˈnä,zät\ *n* -s [G, modif. of F *nazard* — more at NAZARD] : NAZARD

na·saump \nəˈsȯmp\ *n* -s [Narraganset] : HOMINY

nasca *usu cap, var of* NAZCA

nas·cence \ˈnasᵊn(t)s, ˈnās-, ˈnaas-, ˈnais-\ *n* -s [L *nascentia*] : NASCENCY

nas·cen·cy \-ᵊnsē, -si\ *n* -ES [L *nascentia*, fr. *nascent-*, *nascens* (pres. part. of *nasci* to be born) + *-ia* -y — more at NATION] : condition of being nascent : BIRTH, ORIGIN

nas·cent \-ᵊnt\ *adj* [L *nascent-*, *nascens*, pres. part. of *nasci* to be born] **1** : undergoing the process of being born : beginning to exist ⟨~ revolutionary tendencies⟩ **2** : of, relating to, or being an atom or substance at the moment of its formation usu. with the implication of greater reactivity than otherwise ⟨~ hydrogen⟩ ⟨~ state⟩

nase *var of* NAZE

nase·ber·ry \ˈnāz- — *see* BERRY\ *n* [by folk etymology (influence of E *berry*) fr. Sp *néspera*, *níespera*, fr. L *mespila* — more at MEDLAR] : SAPODILLA 2

na·seth·moid \(ˈ)nā¦zeth,mȯid\ *adj* [*nas-* + *ethmoid*] : of or relating to the nasal and ethmoid bones

nash \ˈnash\ *var of* NESH

nash·gab \ˈnash,gab\ *also* **nash·gob** \-gäb\ *n* [Sc *nash* impertinence + *gab* or *gob* alter. of *gab*] **1** *archaic Scot* : rude gossip **2** *archaic Scot* : an impertinent oaf

nashi *usu cap, var of* NA-KHI

nash·ville \ˈnash,vil, ˈnaash-, ˈnaish-, *esp in southern US* -,vəl\ *adj, usu cap* [fr. *Nashville*, Tennessee] : of or from Nashville, the capital of Tennessee ⟨an old *Nashville* mansion⟩ : of the kind or style prevalent in Nashville

nashville warbler *n, usu cap N* : a common greenish-backed yellow-breasted swamp warbler (*Vermivora ruficapilla*) of eastern No. America — see CALAVERAS WARBLER

nash·vil·lian \nash'vilyən\ *n* -s *cap* [*Nashville*, Tennessee + E *-ian*] : a native or resident of Nashville, Tenn.

¹**nasi** *pl of* NASUS

²**na·si** \ˈnä(,)sē\ *n* -s [Heb *nāsī'* exalted one] **1** *often cap* : the chief presiding officer of the Sanhedrin according to the rabbinical tradition **2** : PATRIARCH

nasi- — see NAS-

na·si·al \ˈnāzēəl\ *adj* [NL *nasion* + E *-al*] : of or relating to the nasion

¹**na·si·corn** \ˈnāzə,kȯrn\ *adj* [*nas-* + L *cornu* horn] **1** : bearing a horn or horns on the nose **2** [NL *Nasicornia*, division of mammals containing the rhinoceroses in former classifications, fr. *nas-* + *-cornia* (fr. L *cornu* horn + NL *-ia*) — more at HORN] : of or relating to a former taxonomic group consisting of the rhinoceroses

²**nasicorn** \"\ *n* -s [(assumed) NL *nasicornus*] : RHINOCEROS

na·si·on \ˈnāzē,än\ *n* -s [NL, fr. *nas-* + Gk *-ion*, dim. suffix] : the middle point of the nasofrontal suture — see CRANIOMETRY illustration

nas·ka·pi \ˈnaskəpē\ *n, pl* **naskapi** *or* **naskapis** *usu cap* **1 a** : an Indian people of northern Quebec and interior Labrador, Canada **b** : a member of such people **2** : a dialect of Cree

naskhi *usu cap, var of* NESKHI

nas·myth's membrane \ˈnā|z,miths-, ˈna|, |,smiths-\ *n, usu cap N* [after Alexander *Nasmyth* †1848 Scottish anatomist and dentist] : the thin cuticular remains of the enamel organ which surrounds the enamel of a tooth during its fetal development and for a brief period after birth

naso- — see NAS-

na·so·basilar \¦nāzō+\ *adj* [*nas-* + *basilar*] : of or relating to the nasion and the basion ⟨~ diameter⟩

na·so·ciliary \"+\ *adj* [*nas-* + *ciliary*] : nasal and ciliary

nasociliary nerve *n* : a branch of the ophthalmic division of the trigeminal nerve distributed in part to the ciliary ganglion and in part to the mucous membrane and skin of the nose

na·so·labial fold \"+ . . . -\ *n* [ISV *nas-* + *labial*] : the crease that runs from the ala of the nose to the corner of the mouth of the same side

na·so·lacrimal *also* **na·so·lachrymal** \"+\ *adj* [*nas-* + *lacrimal*, *lachrymal*] : of or relating to the lacrimal apparatus and nose ⟨the ~ duct transmits tears from the lacrimal sac to the inferior meatus of the nose⟩

na·sol·o·gy \nāˈzäləjē\ *n* -ES [*nas-* + *-logy*] : a scientific study of noses

na·son flute \ˈnāzᵊn-\ *n* [*nason* perh. irreg. fr. L *nasus* nose — more at NOSE] : a 4-foot or 8-foot gedeckt with a prominent second harmonic

na·son·ite \ˈnāsᵊn,īt\ *n* -s [Frank L. *Nason* †1928 Am. geologist + E *-ite*] : a mineral $Ca_4Pb_6Si_6O_{21}Cl_2$ consisting of lead calcium silicate with chloride and occurring as granular white masses

na·so·palatine *also* **na·so·palatal** \¦nāzō+\ *adj* [*nas-* + *palatine* or *palatal*] : of, relating to, or connecting the nose and the palate

na·so·pharyngeal \"+\ *adj* [*nas-* + *pharyngeal*] : of or relating to the nose and pharynx or the nasopharynx

na·so·phar·yn·gi·tis \,nāzō,farənˈjīd·əs\ *n* [NL, fr. *nas-* + *pharyngitis*] : inflammation of the nose and pharynx

na·so·pha·ryn·go·scope \,nāzōfəˈriŋgə,skōp\ *n* [NL *nasopharyng-*, *nasopharynx* + E *-o-* + *-scope*] : an instrument equipped with an optical system and used in examining the nasal passages and pharynx — **na·so·pha·ryn·go·scop·ic** \¦==¦==¦skäpik\ *adj*

na·so·pharynx \¦nāzō+\ *n* [NL, fr. *nas-* + *pharynx*] : the upper part of the pharynx continuous with the nasal passages

na·so·scope \ˈnāzə,skōp\ *n* [*nas-* + *-scope*] : an instrument for inspecting the nasal passages

na·so·sinusitis *also* **na·so·sinuitis** \¦nāzō+\ *n* [NL, fr. *nas-* + *sinusitis*, *sinuitis*] : inflammation of the nasal sinuses

na·so·spi·na·le \,nāzō,spīˈnalē, -nälē, -nälē\ *n* -s [NL, fr. *nas-* + LL *spinale*, neut. of *spinalis* spinal — more at SPINAL] *anthropol* : the point of intersection of a line uniting the lowest points on the margin of each nasal opening with the midsagittal plane

na·so·turbinal \¦nāzō+\ *n* [ISV *nas-* + *turbinal*] : the middle turbinate bone

nas·sa \ˈnasə\ [NL, fr. L, fish basket — more at NET] *syn of* NASSARIUS

nas·sa·ri·idae \,nasəˈrīə,dē\ *n pl, cap* [NL, fr. *Nassarius*, type genus + *-idae*] : a large family of widely distributed marine snails (suborder Stenoglossa) having a long broad foot, long siphon, and a heavy usu. sculptured shell and including numerous basket shells

nas·sar·i·us \nəˈsa(a)rēəs\ *n, cap* [NL, fr. *Nassa* + L *-arius* -ary] : the type genus of Nassariidae comprising various typical basket shells

nas·sau \ˈna(,)sȯ\ *n* -s *usu cap* [fr. *Nassau*, capital city of the Bahama islands] : a golf match in which winning the first nine holes counts one point, winning the second nine one point, and winning eighteen one point

nassau grouper *n, usu cap N* [fr. *Nassau*, Bahama islands] : ²HAMLET

nas·sel·la \nəˈselə\ *n, cap* [NL, dim. of L *nassa* fish basket — more at NET] : a small genus of So. American and chiefly Chilean tufted perennial grasses that resemble sedges and have narrow few-branched panicles — see NASSELLA TUSSOCK

nassella tussock *n* : an aggressive Chilean grass (*Nassella trichotoma*) that has been introduced accidentally in various regions and is a serious weed in New Zealand rangeland

nast \ˈnast\ *n* -s [back-formation fr. ¹*nasty*] *dial Eng* : FILTH, DIRT

nas·ta·liq \ˈnastə,lēk\ *n* -s [Per *nasta'līq*, fr. Ar *naskhī ta'līq*, fr. *naskhī* neskhi + *ta'līq*, a script — more at NESKHI] : an Arabic script developed about the 15th century, characterized by a tendency to slope downward from right to left, and used mainly for Persian poetical writings and in Urdu and Malay manuscript

nas·tic \ˈnastik\ *adj* [Gk *nastos* close-pressed, firm, solid (fr. *nassein* to press, stamp down) + E *-ic*] : of, relating to, or constituting a nastic movement

nastic movement *n* : movement of a flat plant part (as a leaf or bud scale) that is oriented in respect to the plant rather than an external source of stimulation, is brought about by disproportionate growth or increase of turgor in the tissues of one surface of the part, and typically involves a curling or bending outward or inward of the whole part in a direction away from the more active surface ⟨the opening and closing of four-o'clocks involves *nastic movements*⟩ — compare TROPISM

nas·ti·ly \ˈnastəlē, -aas-, -li\ *adv* : in a nasty manner or condition

nas·ti·ness \-tēnəs, -tin-\ *n* -ES **1** : the quality or state of being nasty ⟨the ~ of crooked politics⟩ ⟨the ~ of weather in the north Atlantic⟩ **2** : something that is nasty ⟨the vermin, rags, disease, and other ~*es* of slum areas⟩

nas·tur·tium \nəˈstərshəm, na'-, naa'-, -stəsh-\ *n* [NL, fr. L *nasturtium*, *nasturcium*, a cress, perh. fr. *nasus* nose + *-turtium*, *-turcium* (fr. *torquēre* to twist); fr. its strong smell — more at NOSE, TORTURE] **1** *cap* : a genus of aquatic herbs (family Cruciferae) with succulent smooth stems, often pinnate leaves, and flowers with white petals twice as long as the sepals — see WATERCRESS 1 **2** -s : any plant of the genus *Tropaeolum* (as *T. majus* and *T. minus*) **3** -s **a** : NASTURTIUM RED **b** : CADMIUM YELLOW

nasturtium

nasturtium family *n* : TROPAEOLACEAE

nasturtium red *n* **1** *or* **nasturtium** : a strong reddish orange **2** : a dark reddish orange

nasturtium yellow *n* **1** : CADMIUM YELLOW **2** : a strong orange yellow that is redder and paler than average marigold (sense 3b) and slightly stronger and very slightly lighter than Spanish yellow

¹**nasty** \ˈnastē, -aas-, -ais-, -äs-, -ti\ *adj* -ER/-EST [ME] **1 a** : filthy to the point of exciting disgust ⟨~ living conditions⟩ **b** : exciting physical repugnance : VILE ⟨a ~ taste⟩ ⟨~ food⟩ ⟨~ medicine⟩ **2 a** : morally reprehensible : INDECENT, OBSCENE ⟨~ language⟩ **b** : lacking the decencies of good taste : grossly indelicate ⟨~ literature⟩; *specif* : crudely or immaturely preoccupied with matters of sex ⟨a ~ book⟩ **c** : devoid of real value : TAWDRY, CHEAP ⟨using cheap and ~ articles and living a cheap and ~ life —G.B.Shaw⟩ **3 a** : extremely difficult, hazardous, or threatening ⟨~ storms⟩ ⟨a ~ tide rip⟩ ⟨a ~ crossfire⟩ **b** : excessively unpleasant, uncomfortable, or awkward ⟨would not go again in that ~ little clipper ship . . . where the passengers were cooped up —George Santayana⟩ **4 a** : difficult to understand, handle, or solve : VEXATIOUS ⟨a ~ question⟩ **b** : psychologically unsettling : DISTURBING ⟨the ~ realization that money has run out⟩ **5 a** : characterized by a sharp lack of sportsmanship, generosity, or good nature : MEAN ⟨a ~ trick⟩ ⟨a ~ disposition⟩ **b** : prone to display petty maliciousness : SNIDE ⟨~ underpaid clerks⟩ **c** : socially offensive : ILL-BRED, OAFISH ⟨~ little urchins⟩ **syn** see DIRTY

²**nasty** \"\ *vt, chiefly dial* : to get dirty : SOIL ⟨don't ~ your new dress⟩

-nas·ty \,nastē, -aas-, -ti\ *n comb form* -ES [G *-nastie*, fr. Gk *nastos* close-pressed, firm + G *-ie* -y] : nastic movement of a plant part in a (specified) direction, of a (specified) kind, or resulting from a (specified) class of stimulus ⟨*epinasty*⟩ ⟨*nyctinasty*⟩ ⟨*thermonasty*⟩

na·sua \ˈnāshəwə\ *n* [NL, fr. L *nasus* nose] **1** *cap* : a genus of mammals (family Procyonidae) consisting of the coatis **2** -s : COATI

na·sus \ˈnāsəs\ *n, pl* **na·si** \-ā,sī\ [NL, fr. L, nose — more at NOSE] : a prolongation on the front of the head of a crane fly or of various termites

¹**na·sute** \(ˈ)nā¦süt\ *adj* [L *nasutus* having a large nose, fr. *nasus* nose] **1** : having a well-developed proboscis ⟨a lean, ~ leprechaun, given to tricks —*Newsweek*⟩ **2** : having a nasus — **na·sute·ness** *n* -ES

²**nasute** \"\ *n* -s : a member of a caste of highly modified soldier termites in which the jaws are reduced and the top of the head is drawn out into a snoutlike process from which a sticky fluid can be ejected

na·su·ti·form \(ˈ)nā¦süd·ə,fȯrm\ *adj* [¹*nasute* + *-iform*] : having a nasus projection of the front of the head

na·su·ti·ter·mes \nā,süd·əˈtər(,)mēz\ *n, cap* [NL, fr. *nasuti-* (fr. L *nasutus*) + L *termes* woodworm — more at TERMITE] : a large genus of termites of the family Termitidae whose soldiers are mainly nasutes

na·su·tus \nāˈsüd·əs\ *n, pl* **na·su·ti** \-ü,tī\ [NL, fr. L, having a large nose] : NASUTE

¹**nat** \ˈnat\ *dial Brit var of* NOT

²**nat** \ˈnät\ *n* -s [Burmese *nāt*, fr. Skt *nātha* protector, lord] : one of a general class of spirits in the folklore and aboriginal religion of Burma ⟨house ~*s* and river ~*s* — all of whom have to be propitiated —*N. Y. Times*⟩

nat *abbr* **1** national; nationalist **2** native **3** natural; naturalist; naturalized

na·ta·ka \ˈnäd·əkə\ *n* -s [Skt *nāṭaka*] : the drama in India; *specif* : the heroic comedy that is the chief of the ten main types of the drama in India

¹**na·tal** \ˈnād·ᵊl, -ātᵊl\ *adj* [ME, fr. L *natalis*, fr. *natus* (past part. of *nasci* to be born) + *-alis* -al — more at NATION] **1** : NATIVE — used of places ⟨princes' children took names from their ~ places —William Camden⟩ ⟨most weeds have ~ countries whence they have sortied —D.C.Peattie⟩ **2 a** : of or relating to birth ⟨on the nation's ~ day —C.G.Bowers⟩ ⟨lowering the ~ death rate —*Jour. Amer. Med. Assoc.*⟩ **b** : connected with or dating from one's birth ⟨~ star⟩ **c** : present at birth ⟨the ~ down of the young ducklings is soon dry —*Canadian Geog. Jour.*⟩ ⟨their ~ and acquired faculties —H.O.Taylor⟩

²**natal** \"\ *adj* [L *natis* buttock + E *-al* — more at NATES] : of or relating to the buttocks : GLUTEAL

na·tal aloes \nəˈtal-, -täl-\ *n pl, usu cap N* [fr. *Natal*, province of Union of So. Africa] : a commercial variety of aloes — compare ALOIN

natal brown *n, usu cap N* : NEW COCOA

natal grass *also* **natal redtop** *n, usu cap N* : a showy grass (*Rhynchelytrum roseum* syn. *Tricholaena rosea* or *T. repens*) of southern Africa grown for forage and hay esp. in Australia

natal hemp *n, usu cap N* : SISAL

na·tal·ian \nəˈtalēən, -täl-, -lyən\ *n* -s *cap* [*Natal*, province of Union of So. Africa + E *-ian*] : a native or resident of Natal, Union of So. Africa

natalitial *adj* [L *natalitius*, *natalicius* (fr. *natalis* natal) + E *-al* — more at NATAL] *obs* : NATAL

na·tal·i·ty \nəˈtaləd·ē, naˈ-, -ətē, -i\ *n* -ES [F *natalité*, fr. *natal* (fr. L *natalis*) + *-ité* -ity] : BIRTHRATE ⟨looked on the decreasing ~ of France as a source of economic . . . weakness —*Century Mag.*⟩ ⟨the effect of crowding upon the ~ of grain-infesting insects —*Experiment Station Record*⟩

natal mahogany *n, usu cap N* [fr. *Natal*, province of Union of So. Africa] : MAFURA

natal orange *n, usu cap N* : a spiny shrub (*Strychnos spinosa*) of tropical and southern Africa having greenish yellow edible berries and ovate to orbicular leaves with veins hairy beneath and cultivated as an ornamental

natal plum *n, usu cap N* **1** : either of two shrubs of southern Africa (*Carissa bispinosa* and *C. grandiflora*) having forked spines and edible scarlet fruits resembling plums **2** : the fruit of the Natal plum

na·tant \ˈnātᵊnt\ *adj* [L *natant-*, *natans*, pres. part. of *natare* to swim, float; akin to L *nare* to swim, float — more at NOURISH] : swimming or floating in water

na·tan·tia \nəˈtanchə\ *n pl, cap* [NL, fr. L, neut. pl. of *natant-*, *natans*, pres. part. of *natare*] : a suborder of Decapoda comprising crustaceans (as the shrimps, prawns, and related forms) that have the rostrum usu. long, the first antenna with a stylocerite, the second antennal scale larger, and the abdomen well-developed, somewhat compressed laterally, and frequently flexed ventrally — compare REPTANTIA

na·ta·tion \nəˈtāshən, nāˈ-\ *n* -s [L *natation-*, *natatio*, fr. *natatus* (past part. of *natare*) + *-ion-*, *-io* -ion] : the action or art of swimming ⟨their dexterity at ~ —George Borrow⟩

na·ta·tor \ˈnād·əd·ə(r)\ *n* -s [L, fr. *natatus* + *-or*] : SWIMMER ⟨the first woman ~ to negotiate the . . . passage —*Emporia (Kans.) Gazette*⟩

na·ta·to·ri·al \¦nād·ə¦tōrēəl, -ātə¦-, -tȯr-\ *adj* [LL *natatorius* + E *-al*] **1** : of or relating to swimming ⟨~ skill⟩ **2** : adapted to or characterized by swimming ⟨~ birds⟩

na·ta·to·ri·um \,==ˈtōrēəm, -tȯr-\ *n* -s [LL, fr. L *natatus* + *-orium*] : a place for swimming; *esp* : an indoor swimming pool

na·ta·to·ry \ˈ==,tōrē, -tȯr-, -ri\ *adj* [LL *natatorius*, fr. L *natatus* + *-orius* -ory] **1** : adapted for or used in swimming ⟨~ organs⟩ **2** : of, relating to, or characterized by swimming ⟨~ feats⟩

¹**natch** \ˈnach\ *dial Brit var of* NOTCH

²**natch** \"\ *n* -ES [prob. fr. ¹*natch*] : a knob and a corresponding notch on respective halves of a plaster mold used in ceramics to keep the halves in proper position

³**natch** \"\ *adv* [by shortening and alter.] *slang* : NATURALLY ⟨the witch doctor charged for his services, ~ —Jeff Daniels⟩

natch·bone \ˈnach,bōn\ *n* [fr. (assumed) ME *nachebon* — more at AITCHBONE] : AITCHBONE

natch·e·san \ˈnachəsən\ *n* -s *usu cap* [*Natchez* (of AmerInd origin) + E *-an*] **1** : a linguistic family of the Natchez-Muskogean stock comprising the Natchez language **2 a** : the peoples speaking Natchesan languages (as the Natchez, Taensa, and Avoyel) **b** : a member of any of the Natchesan peoples

natch·ez \ˈnachəz\ *n, pl* **natchez** *usu cap* [F, of AmerInd origin] **1 a** : a Natchesan people of southwestern Mississippi **b** : a member of such people **2** : the language of the Natchez people

natchez-muskogean \¦==¦==¦===\ *n, usu cap N&M* : a language stock comprising the Natchesan and Muskogean language families

natch·i·toches \ˈnakə,täsh\ *n, pl* **natchitoches** *usu cap* **1 a** : a Caddo confederacy of northwestern Louisiana **b** : a member of any of the peoples of such confederacy **2 a** : an Indian people of the Natchitoches confederacy **b** : a member of such people

na·tes \ˈnā,tēz\ *n pl* [NL, fr. L, pl. of *natis* buttock, rump; akin to Gk *nōtos*, *nōton* back] **1** : something suggesting the buttocks: as **a** : the anterior pair of elevations of the corpora quadrigemina **b** : the umbones of a bivalve shell **2** [L] : BUTTOCKS

nathe *n* -s [ME, by alter.] *obs* : ¹NAVE

nathe·less \ˈnāthləs\ *or* **nath·less** \ˈnath-\ *adv* [ME *natheles*, *nathles*, fr. OE *nā thē lǣs*, fr. *nā* not + *thē*, *thȳ* (instrumental of *sē* the, that) + *lǣs* less — more at NO, THE, LESS] *archaic* : NEVERTHELESS : NOTWITHSTANDING ⟨somewhat they doubted, ~ forth they passed —William Morris⟩

nathemore *adv* [ME *nathemore*, fr. *na* not + *the* (adv.) + *more*

— more at MORE] *obs* : never the more ⟨but ~ would that courageous swain to her yield passage —Edmund Spenser⟩

nathless *prep* [*natheless, nathless,* adv.] : in spite of : NOTWITHSTANDING ⟨~ the dread which I had of these creatures —Edmund O'Donovan⟩

nat·i·ca \'nad·əkə\ *n, cap* [NL, perh. fr. LL, buttock, fr. L *natis* — more at NATES] : a large genus (the type of the family Naticidae) of active marine snails having a thick nearly smooth shell and a large foot with a fold reflected over the head and characterized by burrowing beneath sand or mud along the seashore and drilling other shells

na·tic·i·dae \nə'tisə,dē\ *n pl, cap* [NL, fr. *Natica*, type genus + *-idae*] : a family of carnivorous marine gastropod mollusks (suborder Taenioglossa) that have strong globose umbilicate shells, a long retractile proboscis, and a firm dark-colored operculum and that deposit their eggs in firm sandy ribbons — see MOON SHELL, NATICA, SAND COLLAR

na·tick \'nād·ik\ *n* -s *usu cap* : a dialect of Massachuset

[1]**nat·i·coid** \'nad·ə,kȯid\ *adj* [ISV *natic-* (fr. NL *Natica*) + *-oid*] : resembling or related to the Naticidae

[2]**naticoid** \"\ *n* -s : a naticoid snail

na·ti·form \'nād·ə,fȯrm\ *adj* [L *natis* buttock + E *-form* — more at NATES] : resembling the buttocks

[1]**na·tion** \'nāshən\ *n* -s [ME *nacioun*, fr. MF *nation*, fr. L *nation-, natio* birth, race, people, nation, fr. *gnatus, natus* (past part. of *nasci* to be born) + *-ion-, -io* -ion; akin to L *gignere* to beget — more at KIN] **1 a** (1) : NATIONALITY 5a ⟨after the division of Poland . . . the ~ existed without a state —F.A.Magruder⟩ ⟨three Slav peoples . . . forged into a Yugoslavia without really fusing into a Yugoslav ~ —Hans Kohn⟩ (2) : a politically organized nationality; *esp* : one having independent existence in a nation-state **b** : a community of people composed of one or more nationalities and possessing a more or less defined territory and government ⟨India is . . . a member ~ of the British Commonwealth —*N. Y. Times Mag.*⟩ ⟨Canada is a ~ with a written constitution —B.K.Sandwell⟩ — compare STATE **c** : a territorial division containing a body of people of one or more nationalities and usu. characterized by relatively large size and independent status ⟨a Roman province was far above a satrapy though far below a ~ —Goldwin Smith⟩ ⟨a ~ of vast size with a small population —Mary K. Hammond⟩ **2** *archaic* : a particular group or aggregation (as of men or animals) ⟨the scaly ~*s* of the sea profound —John Dryden⟩ ⟨you are a subtle ~, you physicians —Ben Jonson⟩ **3 a** : a division of the student body forming a relatively independent community within a medieval university and comprising students from a particular locality (as a country or region) **b** : a similar division of students at Glasgow and Aberdeen universities in Scotland for the purpose of electing a rector ⟨the ~*s* into which the body of matriculated students is divided —*Glasgow Univ. Cal.*⟩ **4 a** : TRIBE : a federation of tribes (as of American Indians); *specif* : one having a measure of political cohesion ⟨that part of the Shawnee ~ inhabiting the upper Savannah river —Geraldine De Courcy⟩ ⟨the five ~*s* of Iroquois⟩ **b** : the territory occupied by such a tribe or federation of American Indians **syn** see RACE

[2]**nation** \"\ *adj* [short for *damnation*, fr. *damnation*, n.] *chiefly dial* : GREAT, LARGE ⟨there was a ~ sight of folks there —T.C.Haliburton⟩

[3]**nation** \"\ *adv* [short for *damnation*, fr. *damnation*, n.] *chiefly dial* : EXTREMELY, VERY ⟨I'm ~ sorry for you —Mark Twain⟩

[4]**nation** \"\ *n* -s [short for *damnation*] *chiefly dial* : DAMNATION ⟨~ seize such husbands as you seem to get —Thomas Hardy⟩ ⟨what in the ~ are we doing down here —MacKinlay Kantor⟩ ⟨how in the ~ are these fellows going to be ransomed —Mark Twain⟩

[1]**na·tion·al** \'nashənᵊl, -shnəl, -'naash-, 'naish-\ *adj* [MF, fr. *nation* + *-al*] **1** : of or relating to a nation: as **a** : of, affecting, or involving a nation as a whole esp. as distinguished from subordinate areas ⟨the ~ desire to win a war —E.L.Bernays⟩ ⟨the Republican party is not ~ in scope —Arthur Krock⟩ ⟨~ newspapers⟩ ⟨~ advertising⟩ — compare LOCAL **b** : of, relating to, or affecting one nation as distinguished from several nations or a supranational group ⟨protected only by ~ action in concert with that of another power —O.W.Holmes †1935⟩ ⟨the basis . . . is neither ~ nor continental but planetary —Lewis Mumford⟩ ⟨a ~ king⟩ — compare INTERNATIONAL **c** : identified with or symbolic of a specific nation ⟨regards wine and brandy as ~ beverages —G.G.Weigend⟩ ⟨the ~ poet of the empire —James Bryce⟩ ⟨~ game⟩ ⟨~ flower⟩ ⟨~ costume⟩ **d** : having a size or importance of significance for a nation as a whole ⟨his performances . . . brought him ~ distinction —*Providence (R. I.) Evening Bull.*⟩ ⟨a vice-president . . . is not a ~ figure in the fullest sense —R.H.Rovere⟩ **2** : NATIONALIST ⟨intensely ~⟩ **3** : of, having the characteristics of, or being a nationality ⟨his ~ accent was plainly audible —Elinor Wylie⟩ ⟨the doctrine of ~ self-determination acquired greater prominence —Oscar Handlin⟩ ⟨the various ~ groups that settled in the state —*Amer. Guide Series: Pa.*⟩ **4** : of, maintained, or sponsored by the government of a nation ⟨one mile from a ~ tarred road —*advt*⟩ ⟨one of four ~ cemeteries in Louisiana —*Amer. Guide Series: La.*⟩ ⟨a ~ park⟩ **5** : of, relating to, or being a government formed in a parliamentary system by representatives of most or all major political parties usu. in a period of crisis **6** *usu cap* : of, relating to, or constituting a minor political party composed of the Greenbackers **7** *usu cap* : of, relating to, or being a major political party in New Zealand generally favoring private enterprise and tending to represent agricultural and business as contrasted with labor interests ⟨the anti-Labour forces represented in the *National* party are miscellaneous —Alexander Brady⟩

[2]**national** \"\ *n* -s **1** : one that owes permanent allegiance to a nation without regard to place of residence or to possession of a more formal status (as that of citizen or subject) ⟨citizens of Guam and ~*s* but not citizens of the United States —D.L. Oliver⟩ ⟨under that act a person might be a Canadian ~ without being a British subject —T.N.M.Buesst⟩ ⟨American ~*s* in China⟩ **2** : NATIONAL BLUE **3** : the national or major competition held in various sports — usu. used in pl. ⟨runner-up to the champion in the ~*s* —*Springfield (Mass.) Union*⟩ **4** : an organization (as a fraternity or labor union) having local units on a nationwide basis **syn** see CITIZEN

national anthem *or* **national air** *or* **national hymn** *n* : a patriotic song or hymn; *esp* : one adopted officially and played or sung on formal occasions as a mark of loyalty to the nation

national assembly *n* : an assembly composed of the representatives of a nation and usu. constituting a legislative body or a constituent assembly

national bank *n* **1** : a bank having association with the finances of a nation ⟨a *national bank* of Libya was established —*Statesman's Yr. Bk.*⟩ **2** : a commercial bank that is organized under the provisions of congressional legislation and that is chartered by and operates under the supervision of the federal government

national bank note *n* : a bank note issued by a national bank on the security of government bonds deposited with the U. S. Treasury and circulating as full legal tender

national blue *n* : a moderate to deep blue — called also *bleu de Lyon, opal blue*

national chairman *n* : the chairman of the national committee of a political party who usu. acts as the head of the party's permanent organization and has general direction of party strategy esp. during election campaigns

national church *n* **1** : an autonomous church organized and administered on a national scale ⟨the churches of Norway and Denmark are both *national churches*⟩ **2** : a church established by law in a particular nation as a national institution

national committee *n* : the chief executive agency of a political party usu. consisting of members chosen by the national convention to represent geographical areas or constituent elements in the party and having general supervisory powers over the organization of national conventions and the planning of campaigns ⟨the *national committee* . . . was brought into being for the purpose of directing the presidential campaign —H.R. Penniman⟩

national convention *n* : a convention of a political party usu. composed of delegates chosen by state primaries or conventions and meeting primarily to nominate candidates for president and vice-president and to adopt a platform ⟨the supreme organ of the national party is still the *national convention* —F. A.Ogg & P.O.Ray⟩

national day *n* : a day having significance for and usu. celebrated throughout a nation ⟨the 26th is a *national day* of mourning and all activities cease —*Stamps*⟩; *specif* : NATIONAL HOLIDAY ⟨each colony tended to celebrate its own foundation day to the exclusion of the *national day* —Ira Raymond⟩

national debt *n* : the total financial obligations of the central government of a nation usu. in the form of interest-bearing government bonds — called also *public debt*

national democratic *adj, usu cap N&D* : of, relating to, or being a political party composed of Gold Democrats running a separate ticket in the presidential election of 1896 in opposition to the stand of the regular Democrats in favor of the free coinage of silver

national economy *n* : the economy of a nation; *specif* : the economy of a nation as a whole that is an economic unit and is usu. held to have a unique existence greater than the sum of the individual units within it

national emergency *n* : a state of emergency resulting from a danger or threat of danger to a nation from foreign or domestic sources and usu. declared to be in existence by governmental authority ⟨therefore I . . . do proclaim the existence of a *national emergency* —H.S.Truman⟩

national ensign *n* : ENSIGN 1

national flag *n* : a flag serving as a distinctive emblem of a particular nation; *esp* : one so designated (as by custom, decree, or law) in distinction from other flags of the nation serving other purposes — compare ENSIGN 1, MERCHANT FLAG

national flag blue *n* : a dark purplish blue that is slightly darker than Scotch blue and slightly stronger and very slightly darker than homage blue

national forest *n* : a usu. forested area of considerable extent that is preserved by government decree from private exploitation and harvested only under supervision and that is often used for the practice and demonstration of proper silvicultural methods

national guard *n, usu cap N&G* : a militia force that is recruited and partly maintained by each state and equipped and partly maintained by the federal government and that may be employed by the state (as in law enforcement or the suppression of insurrection) or called into federal service as part of the U. S. Army — compare HOME GUARD

national holiday *n* **1** : a holiday celebrated throughout a nation; *esp* : one commemorating the birth or independence of a nation ⟨the Bolivian *national holiday*⟩ **2** : a legal holiday established by the central government of a nation rather than by state or local authorities ⟨there are no annual legal *national holidays* in the United States —*Literary Digest*⟩

national income *n* : the aggregate of all earnings arising from the current production of goods and services in a nation's economy and comprising the compensation of employees, the profits of business after taxes, interest, and rental income ⟨net national product . . . less indirect business taxes equals *national income* —H.H.Maynard & T.N.Beckman⟩ — compare GROSS NATIONAL PRODUCT, NET NATIONAL PRODUCT

national interest *n* : the interest of a nation as a whole held to be an independent entity separate from the interests of subordinate areas or groups and also of other nations or supranational groups ⟨any foreign policy which operates under the standard of the *national interest* —H.J.Morgenthau⟩

na·tion·al·ism \'nashənᵊl,izəm, -shnə,li-, 'naash-, 'naish-\ *n* -s [[1]*national* + *-ism*] : loyalty and devotion to a nation; *esp* : an attitude, feeling, or belief characterized by a sense of national consciousness, an exaltation of one nation above all others, and an emphasis on loyalty to and the promotion of the culture and interests (as political independence) of one nation as opposed to subordinate areas or other nations and supranational groups ⟨~ is a relatively recent phenomenon —F.H.Heller⟩ — compare INTERNATIONALISM, LOCALISM, PARTICULARISM, PATRIOTISM

[1]**na·tion·al·ist** \-shənᵊləst, -shnəl-\ *n* -s [[1]*national* + *-ist*] **1** : an advocate of or believer in nationalism ⟨a true ~ places his country above everything —C.J.H.Hayes⟩ ⟨has gone through evolution as a cultural ~ and today is a cultural chauvinist —J.T.Farrell⟩ **2** *usu cap* : a member of a political group usu. associated with advocacy of national independence or the creation and development of a strong national government: as **a** : a member of a British political party advocating the independence of Ireland and constituting an important element in the House of Commons until the establishment of Irish independence **b** : a member of a political party in the Union of So. Africa characterized chiefly by strong Afrikaner nationalism **c** : a member of an Australian political party evolving from groups opposed to the Labour party and later becoming part of the Liberal party

[2]**nationalist** \"\ *adj* **1** : of, relating to, or advocating nationalism ⟨the ~ aspirations of the Korean people —Homer Bigart⟩ ⟨an alleged ~ orthodoxy . . . seeking to control the schools —*Living Church*⟩ **2** *usu cap* : of, relating to, or being a political group advocating or associated with nationalism ⟨the Turkish *Nationalist* forces attack the sultan's troops —*Literary Digest*⟩

na·tion·al·is·tic \¦nashənᵊl¦istik, -shnə,li-, ¦naash-, ¦naish-, -tēk\ *adj* **1** : of, favoring, or having the characteristics of nationalism ⟨the highly ~ tone of the election speeches —*Listener*⟩ ⟨the ~ demand that America rise to meet her destiny —R.A.McConnell⟩ **2** : of, relating to, or favoring a nation : NATIONAL 1 ⟨examined from a world rather than a strictly ~ standpoint —W.A.Noyes b.1898⟩ ⟨minor ~ differences —A.E.Wier⟩ — **na·tion·al·is·ti·cal·ly** \-tək(ə)lē, -tēk-, -li\ *adv*

na·tion·al·i·ty \,nashə'naləd·ē, ,naash-, ,naish-, -ətē, -i\ *n* -ES [[1]*national* + *-ity*] **1 a** : national quality or character ⟨those peculiar institutions which colored all their ~ —J.T.Graves⟩ **b** : the quality of being distinctively national ⟨the question of the value of ~ in art —Edward Hopper b.1882⟩ **2** : NATIONALISM ⟨the anglicizing policy . . . robbed Irish ~ of a great deal of its native force —Aidan Mulloy⟩ **3 a** : the fact or state of belonging to a nation : the status of being a national; *specif* : a legal relationship between an individual and a nation involving allegiance on the part of the individual and usu. protection on the part of the state ⟨until . . . recently voluntary resignation of ~ was not generally recognized —Edward Jenks⟩ **b** : the quality or state of being a national of a particular nation ⟨a local citizenship in addition to their British ~ —*News from New Zealand*⟩ ⟨before a national can acquire the ~ of another state —D.V.Sandifer⟩ **4** : the quality or state of being a nation; *specif* : political independence or existence as a separate nation ⟨product of Canada's own evolving ~ —H.W.Baehr⟩ ⟨if the ~ of any of the smaller German states were extinguished —*Examiner*⟩ **5 a** : a usu. large and closely associated aggregation of people having a common and distinguishing origin, tradition, and language and potentially capable of or actually being organized in a nation-state ⟨the diverse *nationalities* of the Austro-Hungarian Empire desired independence⟩ **b** : a group of people having a common and distinguishing racial, linguistic, and cultural background and forming one constituent element of a larger group (as a nation) : an ethnic group ⟨in China . . . some fifty *nationalities* have been noted —John De Francis⟩ ⟨Russia's population consists of some 140 *nationalities* —*Pulaski Foundation Bull.*⟩ **6** : national or ethnic background ⟨immigrants . . . of the same language and ~ seek one another —Edith T. Bremer⟩

na·tion·al·iza·tion \,nashənᵊlə'zāshən, -shnələ'-, ,naash-, ,naish-, -ᵊl,ī'-, -nə,lī'-\ *n* -s : the action or process of nationalizing : the state of being nationalized ⟨the ~ of culture, taste, mind —P.W.Kurtz⟩ ⟨a bill proposing the ~ of mines —C.W.A. Veditz⟩ ⟨the Bolsheviks . . . decreed immediate ~ and distribution of all the land —M.W.Straight⟩

na·tion·al·ize \'nashənᵊl,īz, -shnə,līz, 'naash-, 'naish-\ *vt* -ED/-ING/-S *see -ize in Explan Notes* [prob. fr. F *nationaliser*, fr. *national* + *-iser* -ize] **1** : to give a national character to : make distinctively national ⟨factors tending to ~ American politics⟩ **2** : to invest in the central government of a nation the control or ownership of ⟨it . . . *nationalized* ownership of all agricultural estates, factories, . . . and all means of production —A.J.Osgniach⟩ ⟨the movement to ~ industry —P.H. Douglas⟩ — compare COLLECTIVIZE, SOCIALIZE

na·tion·al·iz·er \-zə(r)\ *n* -s : one that advocates nationalization ⟨the English railway ~*s* proposed that the state should own the lines —*Contemporary Rev.*⟩

na·tion·al·ly \-nᵊlē, -nəlē, -i\ *adv* **1** : by, with regard to, or in terms of a nation as a whole ⟨farm purchasing power has declined ~ —A.G.Mezerik⟩ ⟨the people . . . might be represented as ~ Christianized —Rufus Anderson⟩ **2** : on a national scale : throughout a nation ⟨it costs a lot of money to advertise ~ —Sherwood Anderson⟩ ⟨made available ~ at prices . . . everyone could afford —Gordon Russell⟩

national meridian *n* : a meridian chosen in a particular nation as the zero point in measuring longitude for that nation — compare PRIME MERIDIAN

national mission *n* : HOME MISSION

national monument *n* : a monument reserved by the federal government as public property ⟨permits presidents to make *national monuments* of historically . . . interesting places —C.L.Wirth⟩

national park *n* : an area of special scenic, historical, or scientific importance set aside and maintained by a national government esp. for recreation or study ⟨the fourth of Britain's *national parks* —*Brit. Book News*⟩ ⟨Canada's western *national parks* —L.S.Marceau⟩ ⟨*national parks* in the U.S. are managed by the Department of the Interior⟩

national product *n* **1** : GROSS NATIONAL PRODUCT **2** : NET NATIONAL PRODUCT

national republican *n, usu cap N&R* : a member of a political party formed in opposition to the Jacksonian Democrats and after being decisively defeated in the presidential election of 1832 fused with other elements to form the Whig party

nationals *pl of* NATIONAL

national salute *n* **1** : a salute of 21 guns in honor of the president of the U.S. or of the head or flag of an independent foreign nation **2** : SALUTE TO THE UNION

national school *n* : a voluntary school in Great Britain established or aided by a national society (as the National Society for Promoting the Education of the Poor in the Principles of the Established Church)

national school–bus chrome *n* : a variable color averaging a vivid orange yellow that is redder, lighter, and stronger than bright marigold

national service *n, Brit* : SELECTIVE SERVICE

national service life insurance : life insurance made available by the federal government to members of the armed forces during and after World War II

national silver *adj, usu cap N&S* : of, relating to, or being a political party composed of dissident Republicans favoring the free coinage of silver and endorsing the Democratic ticket in the election of 1896 — compare GOLD DEMOCRAT, NATIONAL DEMOCRATIC

national socialism *n* [trans. of G *nationalsozialismus*] : NAZISM 1 ⟨the anti-Jewish policy of *national socialism* —G.H. Sabine⟩

national socialist *adj* [trans. of G *nationalsozialistisch*] : of, relating to, or having the characteristics of nazism ⟨theories . . . advanced to explain the *national socialist* movement in Germany —J.H.Hallowell⟩ ⟨the *national socialist* notion of the racial folk —G.H.Sabine⟩

national state *n* : NATION-STATE ⟨in the nineteenth century the *national state* became the basis of all political systems —W.J. Ehrenpreis⟩

na·tion·hood \'nāshən,hu̇d\ *n* : the quality or state of being a nation ⟨colonies emerging into ~ —R.S.Sayers⟩ ⟨claim the full status of ~ for the Dominions —*Nineteenth Century*⟩ ⟨animated by a . . . strong sense of ~ —Isaac Deutscher⟩

na·tion·less \-nləs\ *adj* : belonging to no nation

nations *pl of* NATION

nation–state \'=='=\ *n* : a form of international political organization developing in the 16th century from earlier feudal units and characterized chiefly by a relatively homogeneous group of people with a feeling of common nationality living within the defined boundaries of an independent and sovereign state : a state containing one as opposed to several nationalities

nationwide \'==¦=\ *adj* : extended or existing throughout an entire nation ⟨political oratory . . . in this day of the ~ broadcast —Max Eastman⟩ ⟨a ~ coal strike⟩ ⟨attracted ~ attention⟩

[1]**na·tive** \'nād·|iv, -āt|, |ēv *also* |əv\ *adj* [ME *natif*, fr. MF, fr. L *nativus*, fr. *natus* (past part. of *nasci* to be born) + *-ivus* -ive — more at NATION] **1** : belonging to one by nature : conferred by birth : derived from origin : born with one : not acquired : INHERENT, INBORN ⟨a ~ shrewdness and an ability to make the right decision by instinct —A.J.P.Taylor⟩ ⟨ambition and ~ aptitude —Bertrand Russell⟩ ⟨a certain ~ capacity is needed to meet academic requirements —W.K.Hicks⟩ **2** : belonging to or associated with a particular place (as a region or country) by birth ⟨~ artists left the state and studied . . . abroad — *Amer. Guide Series: Mich.*⟩ ⟨a ~ Englishman⟩ **3** *archaic* : closely related (as by birth or race) ⟨the head is not more ~ to the heart . . . than is the throne of Denmark to thy father —Shak.⟩ **4 a** : of, relating to, or connected with one as a result of birth in a given place or circumstances ⟨hailed in his ~ Sweden as an influential dramatist —William Peden⟩ ⟨returned to his ~ countryside —I.M.Price⟩ ⟨my foot is on my ~ heath —Sir Walter Scott⟩ **b** : belonging to or associated with one by birth into a particular region or people ⟨~ language⟩ ⟨~ costume⟩ **5 a** : according to nature : NATURAL, NORMAL ⟨think France and England . . . the ~ leaders of Europe —Janet Flanner⟩ ⟨if fiction chooses to abandon its ~ approach —Bernard DeVoto⟩ — often used with following *to* ⟨sitting there, as ~ to the stool as a cat —Jean Stafford⟩ **b** : naturally implied or involved (as in a text or term) : not forced in interpretation or construction ⟨the ~ sense of a word⟩ **6 a** : grown, produced, or originating in a particular place (as a region or country) : not foreign or exotic ⟨whose paintings retained a ~ quality despite his close familiarity with the styles of European art —*Amer. Guide Series: Pa.*⟩ ⟨the Edinburgh groat . . . was the first ~ coin of Scotland —*advt*⟩ ⟨the first ~ use of the harp in Ireland —Richard Hayward⟩ **b** : grown, produced, or originating in the vicinity : not transported from a distant region : LOCAL ⟨your requirements are either ~ or nearby —*Delaware*⟩ ⟨a one-story structure of ~ stone —Seth King⟩ **c** : living or growing naturally in a given region : INDIGENOUS ⟨tobacco is ~ to the American continent —C.H.Thienes⟩ ⟨where tropical . . . plants will grow ~ —Marjory S. Douglas⟩ ⟨a ~ species⟩ **d** : of, relating to, or being livestock found typically in a particular region; *often* : inferior and not of a recognized breed **7** : left or remaining in a natural state : being without embellishment or artificial change : SIMPLE, UNADORNED, UNAFFECTED ⟨our feelings still ~ and entire, unsophisticated by pedantry —Edmund Burke⟩ **8** *archaic* : belonging to or associated with one by birth ⟨that man should thus . . . abridge him of his just and ~ rights —William Cowper⟩ **9** *obs* : having a right or title by birth : RIGHTFUL **10** : constituting the original substance or source of something ⟨the way I must return to ~ dust —John Milton⟩ **11 a** : occurring in nature esp. uncombined with other elements ⟨~ gold⟩ ⟨~ sulfur⟩ **b** : as found in nature : not artificially prepared ⟨~ gypsum⟩ ⟨salt in the ~ state⟩ ⟨conversion of a ~ protein to a denatured protein⟩ **12** [[2]*native*] **a** : of, relating to, or composed of a people inhabiting a territorial area at the time of its discovery or its becoming familiar to a foreigner ⟨~ societies⟩ ⟨a ~ worker⟩ **b** : of, relating to, or having the characteristics of such a people having a less complex civilization ⟨the ~ Indian tribes of the American prairie⟩ ⟨~ reserve⟩ **c** *usu cap, Africa* : of, relating to, or being a Negro of unmixed descent ⟨the vast *Native* labor resources of the country —A.J.Bruwer⟩ ⟨the third *Native* woman to qualify as a doctor —*Johannesburg Sunday Express*⟩ **13** *chiefly Austral* : having a usu. superficial resemblance to a specified English plant or animal ⟨~ cat⟩ ⟨~ robin⟩ ⟨~ cherry⟩ **14** : free from branding marks : UNBRANDED — used of cattle and hides

syn INDIGENOUS, ENDEMIC, ABORIGINAL, AUTOCHTHONOUS: NATIVE applies to one having birth or origin in a locality indicated; it may imply concord or compatibility with that locality ⟨except for highly technical work, the company employs only *native* whites —*Amer. Guide Series: La.*⟩ ⟨2,479 European and 37,032 *native* teachers —*Americana Annual*⟩ ⟨interest centers on our *native* roots, the American past that here is many strata deep —Bernard DeVoto⟩ INDIGENOUS may apply to that which is not only native but which, insofar as can be known, has never been introduced, transported, or brought from another area into the locality in question ⟨southern Rhodesia at present employs about half a million Africans, of whom half are *indigenous* and half are migrants from neighboring territories —Peter Scott⟩ ⟨the sugarcane, a plant *indigenous* to the island —Herman Melville⟩ ⟨no rich heritage of *indigenous* folk song —C.A. & Mary Beard⟩ ENDEMIC may but does not necessarily add to INDIGENOUS the notion of being peculiar to a specific locality or sphere ⟨the Russia of the czars was backward, poor, threatened by an *endemic* revolutionary crisis, tyrannical and inefficient in practically all aspects of its life —D.W.Brogan⟩ ⟨keen competition among universities in educational affairs and the pursuit of knowledge is necessary as a corrective to that complacency which is an *endemic* disease of academic groups —J.B.Conant⟩ ⟨malaria is *endemic* in 17 states of our own South and Southwest —*Harper's*⟩ ABORIGINAL is likely to apply to the primitive native belonging to the earliest extant race inhabiting an area ⟨a primitive *aboriginal* race in the southeast of Sumatra —J.G. Frazer⟩ ⟨the squatters who staked off so-called government lands pushed the *aboriginal* inhabitants back into the mountains and deserts —*Amer. Guide Series: Calif.*⟩ AUTOCHTHONOUS (along with its variants) applies to that which either definitely or presumably had its eventual origin or emergence at the locality in question ⟨*autochthonous* cases of malaria have never been reported from these islands —*Biol. Abstracts*⟩ ⟨born in the West of Britain, a Welshman, into that tribe of *autochthonous* types who were living in the Island before the Danes, Romans, Angles, Saxons, Vikings, and other aggressors arrived —Henry Williamson⟩

[2]**native** \"\ *n* -S [in sense 1, fr. ME *natif*, fr. ML *nativus*, fr. L *nativus*, adj., belonging by birth, native; in other senses fr. [1]*native*] **1 :** one born in a state of bondage or serfdom **:** a born thrall ⟨these lairds had also their ~*s* and husbandmen for labor in feudal services —James Colville⟩ **2** *archaic* **a :** one born under a particular sign or planet **b :** the subject of a nativity or other horoscope **3 a :** one born in a particular place **:** one connected with a place (as by parental domicile or childhood residence) even though actually born or later resident elsewhere ⟨the total numbers of ~*s* and foreign-born persons —*Population Census Methods*⟩ — often used with following *of* ⟨a ~ of Hoboken, where he was born on March 26 —*Current Biog.*⟩ **b** *Austral* **:** a white person born in the country as distinguished from one born abroad **4** *obs* **:** a fellow countryman **:** COMPATRIOT — used in pl. ⟨the king (distrusting his ~*s*) ... many French foreigners —Thomas Fuller⟩ **5 a :** one of a people inhabiting a territorial area at the time of its discovery or becoming familiar to a foreigner; *esp* **:** one belonging to a people having a less complex civilization ⟨a protest against the attitude of the white population toward the ~*s* —*Irish Digest*⟩ **b :** one held to resemble such a person **:** an inhabitant of a region spoken of as if strange or newly discovered **c** *usu cap, Africa* **:** a Negro of unmixed descent; *specif* **:** BANTU ⟨*Natives* and Coloreds who live along this public road —*Farmer's Weekly So. Africa*⟩ — compare [2]AFRICAN 1, AFRIKANER, [2]ASIATIC 2, CAPE COLORED, [2]EUROPEAN 2b **6** *dial Brit* **:** one's native country or locality ⟨when he came back to his ~ ... he knew no one —*Cornhill Mag.*⟩ **7 a :** a local resident; *esp* **:** a person who has lived all his life in a place as distinguished from a visitor or a temporary resident ⟨give visitors — and the mere ... ~ — a new aspect of a city —*Irish Digest*⟩ ⟨~*s* and old-time summer residents —*N.Y.Times*⟩ ⟨the split between ~*s* and refugees —Dolf Sternberger⟩ **b :** such a person inhabiting a small town or village **8 a :** something (as an animal, vegetable, or mineral) indigenous to a particular locality **:** one produced in a given area and not normally produced or found elsewhere ⟨improbable that corn could have been a ~ of the region —P.C.Mangelsdorf⟩ ⟨the Mexican bean beetle, a ~ of Central America —*Amer. Guide Series: N.J.*⟩ **b** *Brit* **:** an oyster grown in local waters ⟨eating ~*s* until the man who opened them grew pale —Charles Dickens⟩ **9 :** a very old and large snapper — called also *rock native*

[1]**native american** *adj, usu cap N&A* [[1]*native*] **:** of, relating to, or characterized by Native Americanism ⟨in 1835 a *Native American* party was formed —D.D.McKean⟩

[2]**native american** *n, usu cap N&A* **:** a member of a minor American political group having a brief existence in the early 19th century before evolving into the Know-Nothing party ⟨the *Native Americans* ... were pledged not to vote for any foreigner for office —C.H.Haswell⟩

native american church *n, usu cap N&A&C* **:** an intertribal American Indian religious organization adapting Christianity to native beliefs and practices and including esp. the sacramental use of peyote

native americanism *n, usu cap N&A* **:** the principles and policies of the Native Americans; *esp* **:** hostility toward all but native-born Protestant Americans

native bear *n, Austral* **:** KOALA

native beech *n* **1 :** either of two Australian trees: **a :** FLINDOSA **b :** a shrubby tree (*Callicoma serratifolia*) of the family Cunoniaceae having wood that contains saponin and being often cultivated for its heads of petalless bright yellow flowers with showy elongated stamens and anthers **2** *or* **native birch** *NewZeal* **:** NEW ZEALAND BEECH

native-born \ˌ==ˈ=\ *adj* **:** belonging to or associated with a particular place (as a country) by birth therein ⟨a *native-born* American⟩ ⟨*native-born* stock —*Survey Graphic*⟩ ⟨supply of *native-born* labor in the South is equal to the demand —*Textile World*⟩ — compare NATURAL-BORN

native box *n* **:** an Australian prickly shrub or small tree (*Bursaria spinosa*) useful as a browse plant — called also *boxthorn*

native bread *n* **:** BLACKFELLOWS' BREAD

native broom *n* **:** DOGWOOD 2d(1)

native cabbage *n* **:** a succulent Australian shrub (*Scaevola koenigii*)

native cat *n* **:** any of several Australian predaceous carnivorous marsupials of the genus *Dasyurus* (esp. *D. viverrinus*)

native cherry *n* **1 :** a low shrubby Australian tree (*Exocarpus cupressiformis*) of the family Santalaceae with a fruit that is a drupe and rests on an enlarged succulent bright red edible pedicel **2 :** the fruit or pedicel of the native cherry

native cod *n* **:** SHORE COD

native companion *n, Austral* **:** BROLGA

native cranberry *n* **:** either of two Australian shrubs of the genus *Styphelia* (*S. sapida, S. humifusa*) having thin-fleshed fruits resembling cranberries

native currant *n* **:** any of several Australian trees bearing small edible acid berries resembling currants: as **a :** a tree (*Coprosma billardieri*) **b :** any of several shrubs or trees of the genus *Leptomeria* (family Santalaceae) **c :** BLUEBERRY 2a(1) **d :** BLACK NIGHTSHADE

native daphne *n* **:** NATIVE LAUREL

native dog *n, Austral* **:** DINGO

native flax *n* **1 :** an Australian flax (*Linum marginale*) **2 :** NEW ZEALAND FLAX

native fuchsia *n* **1** *NewZeal* **:** KONINI **2 :** any of several plants of the genera *Correa* or *Epacris* having showy flowers

native guava *n* **1 :** an Australian shrub or small tree (*Rhodomyrtus psidioides*) of the family Myrtaceae resembling the true guava **2 a :** an Australian timber tree (*Eupomatia laurina*) **b :** the edible fruit of the native guava **3 :** IVORYWOOD

native hen *n* **:** an Australian rail (*Tribonyx mortierii*)

native hop *n, Austral* **:** HOPBUSH

native juniper *n* **:** BLUEBERRY 2a(2)

native laurel *n* **1 :** a medium-sized Australian tree (*Pittosporum undulatum*) with shining evergreen leaves and fragrant creamy white flowers in terminal clusters **2 :** an Australian timber tree (*Polyscias elegans*) of the family Araliaceae having whitish wood

native lime *n* **1 :** either of two Australian citrus trees (*Citrus australis* and *Microcitrus australasica*) having very acid fruit **2 :** the fruit of a native lime tree

na·tive·ly \ˈnād·əvlē, -ātə-, -li\ *adv* **:** in a native manner; *specif* **:** by birth, origin, or inherent qualities **:** INNATELY, NATURALLY ⟨a ~ gifted ... individual —A.L.Kroeber⟩ ⟨they were ~ courteous —Ernie Pyle⟩

native millet *n* **:** AUSTRALIAN MILLET

native mistletoe *n* **:** an Australian plant of the genus *Loranthus*

native mulberry *n* **:** any of several Australian trees that are felt to resemble the mulberry: as **a :** a tree (*Pipturus argenteus*) of the family Urticaceae having edible white berries **b :** a tree (*Hedycarya angustifolia*) of the family Monimiaceae **c :** an evergreen tree (*Litsea dealbata*) of the family Lauraceae **d :** a thorny bush (*Cudrania javanensis*) of the family Moraceae

native myrtle *n* **:** any of several Australian shrubs or trees that are felt to resemble the true myrtles: as **a :** BRUSH CHERRY 1 **b :** AUSTRALIAN MYRTLE **c :** BLUEBERRY 2a(2)

na·tive·ness *n* -ES **:** the quality or state of being native **:** NATURALNESS

native olive *n* **1 a :** an indigenous Australian olive (*Olea paniculata*) **b :** the fruit of this plant **2 :** an Australian ironwood (*Notelaea ligustrina*)

native orange *n* **1** *Austral* **:** NATIVE LIME 1 **2** *Austral* **:** NATIVE POMEGRANATE

native peach *n* **1** *Austral* **a :** QUANDONG **b :** the fruit of the quandong **2** *Austral* **:** EMU APPLE 1

native pear *n* **:** an Australian tree (*Xylomelum pyriforme*) of the family Proteaceae having a pear-shaped fruit with a thick woody epicarp

native pheasant *n* **:** LEIPOA

native plum *n* **1 :** any of several Australian trees that are felt to resemble the plums: as **a :** BLACK APPLE **b :** a Tasmanian tree (*Cenarrhenes nitida*) of the family Proteaceae **c :** a plant of the genus *Owenia* **2 :** the fruit of a native plum

native pomegranate *n* **1 :** any of several Australian plants of the genus *Capparis* **2 :** the edible fruit of a native pomegranate resembling the pomegranate

native porcupine *n, Austral* **:** ECHIDNA

native potato *n* **1 :** an Australian orchid (*Gastrodia sesamoides*) having tubers resembling potatoes **2 :** an Australian plant of the genus *Marsdenia*

native quince *n* **:** a small shrubby Australian tree (*Petalostigma quadriloculare*) that is related to the eucalypts and has a very bitter bark

native rabbit *n, Austral* **:** a bandicoot (*Thylacomys lagotis*)

native rat *n, NewZeal* **:** KIORE

natives *pl of* NATIVE

native sarsaparilla *n* **:** an Australian purple-flowered twining plant (*Kennedya monophylla*) of the family Leguminosae having roots sometimes used as a substitute for sarsaparilla

native sloth *n* **:** KOALA

native son *n* **:** NATIVE 3a

native sparrow *n* **:** either of two Australian weaverbirds (*Zonaeginthus oculatus* and *Z. bellus*)

native state *n* **:** a former territorial division of India not constituting an integral part of British India but ruled by its own prince with British advice and supervision

native teak *n* **:** either of two Australian trees: **a :** a flindersia (*Flindersia bennettiana*) that is native to New So. Wales and has been introduced into southern Africa as a shelter and timber tree **b :** FLINDOSA

native thrush *n* **:** an Australian whistler (*Pachycephala olivaceus*)

native trout *n* **1 a :** BROOK TROUT **b :** CUTTHROAT TROUT **2 :** a small pale green Australian salmonoid fish (*Galaxias attenuatus*)

native turkey *n* **:** PLAIN TURKEY

native willow *n* **:** any of several Australian trees having foliage resembling that of a willow: as **a :** BOOBYALLA **b :** COOBA **c :** POISONBERRY TREE **d :** WILGA

native yam *n* **:** an Australian yam (*Dioscorea transversa*)

na·tiv·ism \ˈnād·ə̇ˌvizəm, -ātə̇-\ *n* -S **1 :** the attitude or policy of favoring the native inhabitants of a country as against immigrants ⟨forces of racism and ~ —D.S.Myer⟩ ⟨a persistent ~ in American politics —D.D.McKean⟩; *specif* **:** such an attitude or policy held by the 19th century Native Americans ⟨the rise of ~ and eventually Know-Nothingism —Wallace Stegner⟩ **2 a :** the doctrine that the mind possesses elements of knowledge not derived from sensation **b :** a theory emphasizing heredity or bodily constitution in determining man's perceptions, attitudes, and behavior — compare EMPIRICISM, GENETICISM **3 :** a nativistic reaction of a usu. primitive people against acculturation

[1]**na·tiv·ist** \-ˌvə̇st\ *n* -S [[1]*native* + *-ist*] **:** one that believes in or advocates nativism ⟨a bigoted ~ who published feverish anti-immigration and anti-Catholic tracts —Marshall Davidson⟩

[2]**nativist** \"\ *adj* **1 :** of, having the characteristics of, or supporting political nativism ⟨the die-hard Know-Nothings ... were both ~ and proslavery —M.M.Hunt⟩ ⟨old ~ prejudice against the ... foreign businessman —*Springfield (Mass.) Republican*⟩ **2 :** of, relating to, or composed of nativists ⟨~ rural audiences in the south —W.G.Carleton⟩

na·tiv·is·tic \ˌ==ˈvistik, -tēk\ *adj* **1 :** NATIVIST ⟨the ~ tendencies of the Whig party —*Nation*⟩ **2 :** of, advocating, or having the characteristics of psychological nativism ⟨the traditional controversy between the ~ and empiristic theories of space perception —H.H.Price⟩ **3 :** of, being, or having the characteristics of a movement (as among a primitive people) advocating or advancing the perpetuation or reestablishment of native culture traits and a concomitant restriction or removal of foreign culture elements often accompanied by a strong messianic or ceremonial cult ⟨the ~ faith preaches the old values —C.K.Kluckhohn⟩

na·tiv·i·ty \nə'tivəd·ē, nā'-, -ətē, -i\ *n* -ES [ME *nativite*, fr. MF *nativité*, fr. ML *nativitat-, nativitas* birth, birth of Christ, fr. LL, birth, fr. L *nativus* native + *-itat-, -itas* -ity — more at NATIVE] **1** *usu cap* **:** the birth or coming into the world of Christ — usu. used with *the* ⟨his sermons on the *Nativity* —R.H.Bainton⟩ **2** *usu cap* **a :** an annual church festival commemorating the birth of Christ **:** CHRISTMAS 1 **b :** an annual festival held in some churches to commemorate the birth of other religious figures (as the Virgin Mary and St. John the Baptist) **3 :** the process, fact, or circumstances (as time, place, or manner) of being born **:** BIRTH ⟨the country of one's ~⟩ ⟨I have served him from the hour of my ~ —*Shak.*⟩ **4 :** a horoscope at or of the time of one's birth **5 :** the fact or status of being born a native of a particular place ⟨the Yankee ~ of many Florida editors —*Amer. Guide Series: Fla.*⟩ ⟨percentage distribution of the population by ~ for Connecticut —*Amer. Guide Series: Conn.*⟩ **6** *usu cap* **:** a work of art (as a picture or relief sculpture) representing or symbolizing the earliest infancy of Christ

nativity play *n* **:** a play dealing with the nativity of Christ — compare PASSION PLAY

na·tiv·ize \ˈnād·ə̇ˌvīz\ *vt* -ED/-ING/-S [[1]*native* + *-ize*] **:** to modify in conformity with local customs or usages

natl *abbr* national

natr- *or* **natro-** *comb form* [G, fr. *natron*, fr. F — more at NATRON] **1 :** natron **2 :** sodium ⟨*natr*ium⟩ ⟨*natro*lite⟩ ⟨*natro*philite⟩

nat·ri·cine \ˈna·trəˌsīn, -sə̇n\ *n* -S [NL *Natric-, Natrix* + E *-ine*] **:** any of various predominantly aquatic snakes belonging to *Natrix* and closely related genera

na·tri·um \ˈnā·trēəm\ *n* -S [NL, fr. *natr-* + *-ium*] **:** SODIUM — symbol *Na*

na·trix \ˈnā·triks\ *n, cap* [NL, fr. L, water snake — more at ADDER] **:** a large widely distributed genus of colubrid aquatic snakes that includes all the true water snakes of No. America

na·tro·alunite \ˌnā·trō, ˌna·trō+\ *n* [*natr-* + *alunite*] **:** a mineral $NaAl_3(SO_4)_2(OH)_6$ consisting of a basic sulfate of aluminum and sodium isomorphous with alunite — called also *almerite*

na·tro·chal·cite \ˌnā·trōˈkalˌsīt, ˌna-\ *n* -S [G *natrochalzit*, fr. *natro-* natr- + *chalz-* chalc- + *-it* -ite] **:** a mineral $NaCu_2(SO_4)_2(OH).H_2O$ consisting of a hydrous basic sodium copper sulfate

na·tro·jarosite \ˌnā·trō, ˌna·trō+\ *n* [*natr-* + *jarosite*] **:** a mineral $NaFe_3(SO_4)_2(OH)_6$ in which sodium takes the place of potassium in jarosite

na·tro·lite \ˈna·trəˌlīt, ˈna-\ *n* -S [G *natrolith*, fr. *natro-* natr- + *-lith* -lite] **:** a hydrous sodium aluminum silicate $Na_2Al_2Si_3O_{10}.2H_2O$ belonging to the zeolite family

na·tro·montebrasite \ˌnā·trō, ˌna·trō+\ *n* [F, fr. *natr-* + *montebrasite*] **:** a mineral (Na, Li)Al(PO_4)(OH, F) consisting of a basic phosphate of sodium, lithium, and aluminum isomorphous with amblygonite and montebrasite

na·tron \ˈnāˌträn, ˈna-, -ˌtrən\ *n* -S [F, fr. Sp *natrón*, fr. Ar *natrūn*, fr. Gk *nitron* — more at NITER] **:** a hydrous sodium carbonate $Na_2CO_3.10H_2O$ occurring mainly in solution or solid and with other salts

na·troph·i·lite \nəˈträfəˌlīt\ *n* -S [*natr-* + *-phil* + *-ite*] **:** a mineral $NaMn(PO_4)$ consisting of phosphate of sodium and manganese almost isostructural with varulite but having sodium and manganese disordered

nats *pl of* NAT

nat·te \nəˈtā\ *n* -S [F *natté*, fr. past part. of *natter* to plait, braid, fr. *natte* mat, fr. LL *natta*, alter. of *matta* — more at MAT] **:** a basket weave made with contrasting colors in the warp and weft; *also* **:** a fabric with such a weave woven usu. from silk, rayon, and cotton

[1]**nat·ter** \ˈnad·ə(r), -atə-\ *vi* -ED/-ING/-S [alter. of *gnatter*] **1** *dial Eng* **:** to find fault **:** GRIPE **2** *chiefly Brit* **:** to talk a great deal but say little **:** CHATTER ⟨willing to sit for hours and ~ away about nothing —*Vancouver (Canada) Sun*⟩ ⟨~ to the neighbors' women, exchanging gossip —Peter Mayne⟩

[2]**natter** \"\ *n* -S *chiefly Brit* **:** a conversation usu. of a trivial nature **:** CHAT

nat·ter·jack \ˈnad·ə(r)ˌjak\ *n* [origin unknown] **:** a common brownish yellow toad (*Bufo calamita*) of western Europe having short hind legs and progressing by running rather than by hopping

nat·tier blue \naˈtyā-\ *n* [after Jean Marc *Nattier* †1766 Fr. portrait painter] **:** a moderate azure

nat·ti·ly \ˈnad·ᵊlē\ *adv* **:** in a natty manner **:** SMARTLY ⟨everything seemed to be arranged so carefully and ~ —Hall Caine⟩

nat·ti·ness \-d·ēnə̇s\ *n* -ES **:** the quality or state of being natty **:** SMARTNESS ⟨his familiar ~ of attire —John Buchan⟩

nat·tle \ˈnatᵊl\ *vi* -ED/-ING/-S [imit.] *dial Eng* **:** to make a usu. slight rattling or tapping noise

nat·tock \ˈnad·ək\ *n* -S [origin unknown] **:** WEASEL LEMUR

nat·ty \ˈnad·ē, -at, ǀi\ *adj* -ER/-EST [perh. alter. of earlier *netty*, fr. [3]*net* + *-y*] **:** trimly neat and tidy **:** SMART, SPRUCE ⟨a glamorous air hostess in gray uniform and a ~ cap —*Blackwood's*⟩ ⟨a ~ marine captain —E.L.Beach⟩

[1]**na·tu·fi·an** \nəˈtüfēən\ *adj, usu cap* [Wadi en-*Natuf*, valley in Palestine + E *-ian*] **:** of, relating to, or having the characteristics of a food-gathering, cave-dwelling Mesolithic culture of Palestine characterized by microliths, composite tools of microliths, small bare zoomorphic carvings in bone or stone, and the use of sickles suggesting some agriculture

[2]**natufian** \"\ *n* -S *usu cap* **:** a Mesolithic cave dweller of Mount Carmel and other localities in Palestine

[1]**nat·u·ral** \ˈnach(ə)rəl + V *also* -chərl\ *adj* [ME, fr. MF *natural, naturel*, fr. L *naturalis*, fr. *natura* nature + *-alis* -al — more at NATURE] **1 :** based upon the innate moral feeling or inherent sense of right and wrong held to characterize mankind ⟨principles of equity and ~ justice —J.D.Johnson⟩ — see NATURAL LAW **2 a :** in accordance with or determined by nature **:** based upon the operations of the physical world ⟨~ year⟩ — see NATURAL LOGARITHM, NATURAL NUMBER; compare DAY 1, 2 **b :** having or constituting a classification or other method of arrangement based on features existing in nature **3 a** *chiefly dial* (1) **:** begotten as distinguished from adopted; *esp* **:** begotten in wedlock **:** LEGITIMATE ⟨all the children, whether male or female, ~ or adopted —Thomas Robinson⟩ (2) **:** being a relation by actual consanguinity or kinship by descent as distinguished from adoption ⟨any child ... found guilty of cursing or striking his ~ parents —*Amer. Guide Series: Conn.*⟩ **b** (1) **:** born out of wedlock; *specif* **:** ILLEGITIMATE — see NATURAL CHILD (2) **:** being a relation by consanguinity as opposed to a legally recognized relationship **4 :** having an essential relationship with someone or something **:** possessing a normal connection with someone or something **:** consonant with the nature or character of someone or something ⟨his guilt is a ~ deduction from the facts⟩ **5 :** implanted or held to be implanted by nature **:** existing or present from birth **:** being part of the constitution of a person **:** not acquired **:** INBORN, INNATE ⟨some ~ inability to observe —Ellen Glasgow⟩ ⟨our ~ abhorrence of war —F.D.Roosevelt⟩ — see NATURAL PARTS 2 **6 :** of, relating to, or concerned with nature as an object of study and research ⟨some ~ observations made —*Philosophical Transactions*⟩ — see NATURAL HISTORY, NATURAL PHILOSOPHY, NATURAL SCIENCE **7 :** having a specified character by nature ⟨~ fool⟩ ⟨~ idiot⟩ ⟨~ pacer⟩ ⟨a ~ leader⟩ **8 :** WHITE 3c ⟨~ magic⟩ **9 a :** occurring in conformity with the ordinary course of nature **:** not supernatural, marvelous, or miraculous ⟨the ~ process of growth —H.W.H.King⟩ ⟨a world where ~ forces overwhelmed him —R.B.West⟩ ⟨the rate of ~ increase of the ... population was quite high —Kingsley Davis⟩ ⟨~ causes⟩ **b :** having a normal or usual character **:** not exceptional ⟨digressions ... ~ in a work taken down from oral dictation —G.F.Hudson⟩ **10 :** having a relationship with something by reason of the conditions, events, or circumstances of the case or in line with normal experience ⟨theory and practice are a kind of ~ opposites —C.E.Montague⟩ ⟨the ~ enemies of originality —Clive Bell⟩ **11 :** characterized by qualities (as warm and genuine feelings, affection, or gratitude) held to be part of the nature of man ⟨a wicked old screw ... why wasn't he ~ in his lifetime —Charles Dickens⟩ **12** *obs* **:** NATURAL-BORN ⟨~ subjects⟩ **13 a :** planted or growing by itself **:** not cultivated or introduced artificially ⟨~ grass⟩ **b :** existing in or produced by nature **:** consisting of objects so existing or produced **:** not artificial (as in form or construction) ⟨agricultural commodities in their raw and ~ state —*U.S. Code*⟩ ⟨these ~ deposits of potassium salts —A.C.Morrison⟩ ⟨the vast ~ wealth of the country —William Tate⟩ **14 a :** being in a state of nature without spiritual enlightenment **:** UNREGENERATE ⟨the ~ man receiveth not the things of the Spirit of God —1 Cor 2:14 (AV)⟩ **b :** living in or as if in a state of nature untouched by the influences of civilization and society ⟨an apotheosis of ~ man, with consequent exaltation of appetite —W.L.Grossman⟩ **15 a :** having a physical or real existence as contrasted with one that is spiritual, intellectual, or psychical ⟨the ~ world⟩ **b :** of, relating to, or operating in the physical as opposed to the spiritual world ⟨~ laws ... merely describe what actually happens —Maurice Cranston & J.W.N.Watkins⟩ **16** *obs* **:** NATIVE-BORN **17 a :** closely resembling the object imitated **:** true to nature **:** according to life ⟨the Israeli flag ... illustrated in ~ colors —K.B.Stiles⟩ ⟨doves ~ do not have little crests —F.M. Ford⟩ ⟨drawn to ~ scale⟩ **b :** having the ease or simplicity of nature **:** free from artificiality, affectation, or constraint **:** springing from true sentiment **:** EASY, SIMPLE ⟨successful people are genuine and ~ rather than synthetic and imitative —Gilbert Seldes⟩ ⟨at ease with us ..., always spontaneous and ~ —Dorothy Bussy⟩ **c :** having a form or appearance found in nature ⟨~ hair⟩ **18 a :** having neither flats nor sharps — used of a key or scale in music ⟨the ~ scale of C major⟩ **b :** being neither sharped nor flatted — used of a musical note or tone **c :** having the pitch as indicated in musical notation modified by the natural (sense 7a) **d :** produced without aid of stops, valves, slides, or other supplementary devices — used of a harmonic or tone from a wind and stringed instrument **e :** not falsetto — used of a man's singing voice **19 a :** not being the joker or a wild card — used of a playing card **b :** containing no wild card — used of a combination of cards **20 :** of the color natural

syn SIMPLE, UNAFFECTED, ARTLESS, UNSOPHISTICATED, INGENUOUS, NAÏVE: NATURAL stresses easy freedom from the artificial, stiff, constrained, or formal ⟨the fact is that a poetic language which appears *natural* to one age will appear unnatural or artificial to another —C.D.Lewis⟩ ⟨the poor man had no *natural*, spontaneous human speech ... he habitually expressed himself in a book-learned language —Willa Cather⟩ SIMPLE indicates lack of duplicity and artifice in one's character or thought along with suggestion of lack of complexity and artificiality ⟨the straight and *simple*, the homespun, *simple*, valiant English Truth —H.G.Wells⟩ ⟨*simple* and earnest people, however, being accustomed to speak from their genuine impulses, cannot easily, as craftier men do, avoid the subject which they have at heart —Nathaniel Hawthorne⟩ UNAFFECTED stresses lack of affectation and indicates a simple naturalness without connoting much else ⟨his simple manners and *unaffected* friendliness were attractive —A.W.Long⟩ ⟨she's the best-natured and most *unaffected* young creature —W.M. Thackeray⟩ ARTLESS indicates freedom from calculation about the effects of what one says or does and a consequent ease ⟨her simple, *artless* behaviour, and modest kindness of demeanour, won all their unsophisticated hearts —W.M.Thackeray⟩ ⟨almost every turn in the *artless* little maid's prattle touched a new mood in him —George Meredith⟩ UNSOPHISTICATED stresses lack of knowledge of and experience with worldly matters bringing discretion, reserve, adroitness, smoothness ⟨not elegant or artificial, too much the *unsophisticated* child of nature —Rose Macaulay⟩ ⟨a race almost wholly *unsophisticated* by intercourse with strangers —Herman Melville⟩ INGENUOUS indicates lack of any subtlety, dissimulation, calculation; it indicates unrestrained and unmasked frankness ⟨Father had set a dog on him. A less *ingenuous* character would be silent about such passages —H.G.Wells⟩ ⟨"yet I've done very well this year. Oh yes," he went on with *ingenuous* enthusiasm —Thomas Hardy⟩ NAÏVE stresses lack of worldly wisdom and sophistication with resulting freshness, candor, or innocence untutored and unchecked by convention ⟨the future arch master of love proved to be a *naïve* and candid swain at the beginning of his career —P.H.Lang⟩ ⟨that *naïve* patriotism which leads every race to regard itself as evidently superior to every other —J.W.Krutch⟩ **syn** see in addition REGULAR

²natural \" \ *n* -s [partly fr. MF *naturel, natural,* fr. *naturel, natural,* adj.; partly fr. E ¹*natural*] **1** *obs* **:** a native inhabitant of a place (as a region or country) **2 naturals** *pl, obs* **:** the gifts, powers, and abilities with which a person is endowed by nature ⟨a person of excellent ~s —Theophilus Gale⟩ **3 :** one born without the usual powers of reason and understanding **:** a half-witted person **:** IDIOT ⟨with the vacant grin of a ~ —Charles Gibbon⟩ **4 naturals** *pl, obs* **:** the objects of the natural world **:** natural as distinguished from unnatural or supernatural things **5** *obs* **:** the natural character or disposition of a person **:** the natural form or condition of an animate object (as a flower) **6 naturals** *pl, obs* **a :** a natural state or condition ⟨in their pure ~s, they were wonderfully abstemious —Thomas Fuller⟩ **b :** a state of nakedness — usu. used in the phrase *in one's pure naturals* **7 a :** the character or sign ♮ placed on any degree of the musical staff to nullify the effect of a preceding sharp or flat **b :** a note or tone affected by the natural sign **8 :** a result or combination that immediately wins the stake in a game: as **a :** a throw of 7 or 11 on the first cast in craps **b :** BLACKJACK 6c **c :** a count of 8 or 9 in the first two cards at baccarat **d :** RANCHE **9 :** something that is natural as distinguished from artificial or supernatural ⟨all culture is thus . . . a negation of the ~ —Leon Livingstone⟩ ⟨this social philosophy, based like contemporary science on the ~ —*New Republic*⟩ ⟨study the supernatural as the philosopher studies the ~ —Frederic Myers⟩ **10 :** a shot in billiards held to be easy because the ball can be pocketed directly or in carom billiards by a simple angle shot **11 :** a variable color averaging a yellowish gray that is lighter and slightly redder than average sand and redder and deeper than ivory tint **12 a :** one having natural skills, talents, or abilities often to an unusual degree and usu. requiring no special training or development for success in a specific line of endeavor ⟨as an actor, he was a ~⟩ **b :** something that by its very nature is or is likely to become an immediate and genuine success ⟨as much a ~ as rubber on the end of a pencil —Irving Kolodin⟩ ⟨fight fans discussed the . . . rematch as a ~ —*Newsweek*⟩ ⟨the idea of this book is a ~ —Carl Bridenbaugh⟩ **c :** one constituting an easy, appropriate, and usu. successful selection for a specific purpose by possession of various natural qualities ⟨the review characterizing some new novel as a ~ for pictures —P.S. Nathan⟩ ⟨the legal process . . . is a ~ for delaying tactics —Titus Lord⟩ ⟨fearless and cool in the face of disaster, he was a ~ for the job —*Newsweek*⟩ **13 :** a close pase in bullfighting done with the muleta in the left hand—compare DERECHAZO **syn** see FOOL

natural allegiance *n* **:** the allegiance owed to his country by a native-born subject or citizen — compare ALLEGIANCE 1 b (2), LOCAL ALLEGIANCE

natural area *n* **:** a geographical area (as in a city) having a physical and cultural individuality developed through natural growth rather than design or planning

natural astrology *n* **:** a branch of astrology formerly concerned with the prediction of events in inanimate nature and being in part legitimate astronomical science

natural bark *n* **:** virgin cinchona bark; *specif* **:** the bark first removed from the tree in alternate longitudinal strips — compare MOSSED BARK, RENEWED BARK

natural–born \¦=(=)=¦=\ *adj* **:** having a specified status or character by birth ⟨a *natural-born* describer with a memory for details —Ernestine Evans⟩ ⟨she's a *natural-born* nurse —Winston Churchill⟩; *esp* **:** having the legal status of citizen or subject ⟨no person except a *natural-born* citizen . . . shall be eligible to the office of president —*U. S. Constitution*⟩ — compare NATIVE-BORN

natural bridge *n* **:** a usu. arch formation created by nature and resembling a bridge

natural cement *n* **:** a hydraulic cement made from a naturally occurring limestone containing up to 25 percent argillaceous material — compare PORTLAND CEMENT

natural bridge

natural child *n* **1 :** a child born out of lawful wedlock **:** an illegitimate child **:** BASTARD 1 **2 :** a child under Louisiana law that is born out of lawful wedlock but to parents capable of entering into lawful marriage at the time of the birth and that unlike a bastard may be legitimized

natural childbirth *n* **:** a system of management of parturition in which prenatal reeducation and psychologic conditioning largely replace the use of anesthesia, sedation, or surgical intervention in the course of normal childbirth

natural day *n* **1 :** DAY 1 **2 :** DAY 2

natural death *n* **:** death occurring in the course of nature and from natural causes (as age or disease) as opposed to accident or violence ⟨Hindu orthodoxy opposes any cattle slaughter . . . on the grounds sacred beasts should be allowed *natural deaths* —*Associated Press*⟩ ⟨the industry died a *natural death* —Ada Darling⟩ — compare CIVIL DEATH, NATURAL LIFE

natural dualism *n* **:** NATURAL REALISM

natural dye *n* **:** a dye (as logwood or cochineal) from a plant or animal source — see DYE table I

na·tu·ra·le \¦nätü¦rälā\ *adv (or adj)* [It, natural, fr. L *naturalis* — more at NATURAL] **:** in a natural manner — used as a direction in music to cancel a previous direction

natural english *n, usu cap E* **:** RUNNING ENGLISH

nat·u·ral·esque \¦nach(ə)rə¦lesk *also* -chər¦-\ *adj* **:** faithfully imitating nature **:** conforming closely to natural details (as of objects represented) ⟨~ designs of birds⟩

natural frequency *n* **1 :** the frequency or wavelength with which a circuit or part of a circuit is in tune **2 :** the lowest frequency or highest wavelength with which an antenna without added capacity or inductance is in tune — called also NATURAL WAVELENGTH

natural function *n* **:** a trigonometric function as distinguished from its logarithm

natural gas *n* **:** gas issuing from the earth's crust through natural openings or bored wells; *esp* **:** any of various combustible gaseous mixtures that when in the dry state contain largely methane and in the wet state in association with petroleum contain also higher hydrocarbons (as ethane, propane, butanes, and pentanes) and that are used chiefly as fuels directly or by recovery of gasoline or conversion to other liquid fuels and as raw materials for the manufacture of carbon black and many other products (as nitroparaffins and synthesis gas) — see CASINGHEAD GAS

natural gasoline *n* **:** a very volatile gasoline recovered from natural gas and used in blending with gasoline from petroleum and other sources to increase the volatility — called also *casinghead gasoline*

natural gender *n* **:** the phenomena in a language that resemble grammatical gender but are not ⟨the use of the pronoun *she* in the sentence *the girl may do as she likes* is an instance of *natural gender,* since the choice of the pronoun *she* is not determined by the noun *girl* but by the actual sex of the person to whom the noun *girl* refers⟩

natural glass *n* **:** a silica-rich noncrystalline solid of either volcanic or cosmic origin — compare OBSIDIAN, TEKTITE

natural guardian *n* **1 :** a guardian by natural relationship having custody of the person but not the property of a minor and under common law being constituted by the father if fit and upon his death or incapacity the mother and in the absence of lawful parents the grandparents or other close relatives **2 :** the person who is in fact exercising parental authority over a minor as distinguished from a guardian appointed by a court to have custody of the person or property of the minor — called also *guardian by nature;* compare GUARDIAN FOR NURTURE, GUARDIAN IN SOCAGE

natural harmonic *n* **1 :** a harmonic produced on an open string of a stringed musical instrument — compare ARTIFICIAL HARMONIC **2 :** one of the overtones produced without the use of a slide or valves on a wind instrument

natural hexachord *n* **:** the hexachord beginning on C

natural historian *n* **:** a student of or writer on natural history

natural history *n* **1 :** a treatise on any aspect of natural history but esp. on ecology ⟨edited a *natural history* of spiders⟩ **2 a :** the natural development of something (as of an organism or disease) over a period of time ⟨increasing knowledge of the *natural histories* of tumors —H.S.N.Greene⟩ **b :** a chronicle of the natural development of something over a period of time usu. presenting an assemblage of principal facts and characteristics ⟨the plays are a shrewd *natural history* of . . . Bohemian New York —Francis Fergusson⟩ **3 a :** a former branch of knowledge embracing the study, description, and classification of natural objects (as animals, plants, and minerals) and thus including the modern sciences of zoology, botany, and mineralogy in so far as they existed at that time **b :** a modern branch of inquiry usu. restricted to a consideration of these subjects from an amateur or popular rather than a technical and professional point of view

natural horn *n* **:** the simplest form of the horn consisting of a tapering brass tube with mouthpiece and bell curved upon itself and without keys or valves and producing only those tones appearing in the harmonic series

natural horn

natural immunity *n* **:** immunity possessed by a group (as a race, strain, or species) and occurring in an individual as part of its natural biologic makeup — compare ACQUIRED IMMUNITY

nat·u·ral·ism \ˈnach(ə)rə,lizəm *also* -chər,-\ *n* -s **1 :** action, inclination, or thought based on natural desires and instincts alone **2 :** a theory that expands conceptions drawn from the natural sciences into a world view and that denies that anything in reality has a supernatural or more than natural significance; *specif* **:** the doctrine that cause-and-effect laws (as of physics and chemistry) are adequate to account for all phenomena and that teleological conceptions of nature are invalid **3 a :** a theory that art or literature should conform exactly to nature or depict every appearance of the subject that comes to the artist's attention; *specif* **:** a theory in literature emphasizing the role of heredity and environment upon human life and character development **b :** the quality, rendering, or expression of art or literature executed according to this theory **:** close adherence to nature — compare REALISM **4 :** a doctrine that religious truth is derived from nature and not from miraculous or supernatural revelation **:** a denial of the miraculous and supernatural in religion **5 :** a view in ethics that distinctions between good and bad and right and wrong can be made on the basis of natural phenomena or that ethical terms and statements can be expressed in terms of or be reduced to nonnormative factual terms and statements

¹nat·u·ral·ist \-ləst\ *n* -s [MF *naturaliste,* fr. *natural, naturel* natural + *-iste* -ist — more at NATURAL] **1 a :** an adherent of naturalism (as in theology or philosophy) **b :** one that believes in, practices, or teaches naturalism (as in art or literature) **2 a** *archaic* **:** one versed in natural science **:** NATURAL PHILOSOPHER **b :** a student of natural history; *esp* **:** a field biologist in contrast to a laboratory worker

²naturalist \" \ *adj* **:** NATURALISTIC ⟨belong to the ~ school, an offshoot of realism —Marjorie Wheeler⟩ ⟨the ~ imprint upon a work of fiction —Philip Rahv⟩

nat·u·ral·is·tic \¦nach(ə)rə¦listik, -tēk *also* -chər¦-\ *adj* **:** of, characterized by, or in accordance with naturalism ⟨more ~ behavior⟩ ⟨in ~ colors⟩ ⟨the school of ~ writers⟩ ⟨a ~ interpretation of the deity —Helmut Kuhn⟩

nat·u·ral·is·ti·cal·ly \-tək(ə)lē, -tēk-, -li\ *adv* **:** in a naturalistic style or manner ⟨animals shown ~ and humans fantastically —*African Abstracts*⟩ ⟨a ~ constructed novel⟩

naturalistic fallacy *n* **:** the process of defining ethical terms (as the good) in nonethical descriptive terms (as happiness, pleasure, and utility)

nat·u·ral·i·ty \,nachəˈraləd·ē\ *n* -ES [MF *naturalité,* fr. LL *naturalitat-, naturalitas,* fr. L *naturalis* natural + *-itat-, -itas* -ity — more at NATURAL] **1** *obs* **:** natural quality or character **2 :** natural feeling or behavior ⟨to rouse lethargic friends into ~ —Jane W. Carlyle⟩

nat·u·ral·iza·tion \,nach(ə)rə¦ləˈzāshən |,līˈ- *also* -chər|\ *n* -s [MF *naturalisation,* fr. *naturaliser* to naturalize + *-ation*] **:** the act or process of naturalizing **:** the state of being naturalized ⟨Australian citizenship may also be acquired by . . . ~ —T.N.M.Buesst⟩ ⟨the ~ of . . . these new terms in English —A.E.Bestor⟩

nat·u·ral·ize \ˈnach(ə)rə,līz *also* -chər,-\ *vb* -ED/-ING/-S [MF *naturaliser,* fr. *natural, naturel* natural + *-iser* -ize — more at NATURAL] *vt* **1 a :** to establish in new surroundings **:** introduce into a new area or into common use ⟨he *naturalized* among us the Renaissance manner which he had learned —F.J.Mather⟩ ⟨these tales . . . had become *naturalized,* developed, adapted to American settings —DeLancey Ferguson⟩ **b :** to receive or adopt into the vernacular language ⟨some Latin phrases . . . have become completely *naturalized* —A.H. Weston⟩ **c :** to cause to adapt and grow or multiply as if native ⟨several Old World weeds have become *naturalized* here⟩ ⟨the steelhead and rainbow trout have become *naturalized* . . . in the Lake Superior region —*Amer. Guide Series: Minn.*⟩ **d :** to plant (as a flowering bulb) in sod so as to give an effect of wild growth ⟨*naturalized* daffodils in open shade⟩ **2 :** to make less artificial or conventional **:** to bring into accord or conformity with nature **3 :** to confer the rights and privileges of a native subject or citizen on **:** admit (an alien) to the rights and status of citizenship ⟨all persons born or *naturalized* in the United States . . . are citizens —*U. S. Constitution*⟩ **4** *obs* **:** to render familiar by custom and habit ⟨custom has *naturalized* his labor to him —Robert South⟩ **5 a :** to treat as natural as opposed to supernatural **:** place on a natural basis ⟨willing to contradict the falsity and thus ~ the miracle —Jeremy Bentham⟩ **b :** to express in natural terms esp. in a manner not conflicting with scientific theories ⟨find a way to ~ the idealistic traditions —J.H.Randall⟩ **~** *vi* **1 :** to become naturalized **:** become as if native **2 :** to carry on investigations in natural history

natural key *n* **:** a key used to determine the name of a plant or animal and based on genetic relationships esp. as shown by chromosome counts — compare ARTIFICIAL KEY

natural language *n* **:** a language that is the native speech of a people (as English, Tamil, Samoan) — compare ARTIFICIAL LANGUAGE

natural law *n* **1 :** a body of law derived from nature and binding upon human society in the absence of or in addition to institutional law: as **a :** the principles of justice discernible (as by the Stoics) by right reason **b :** JUS GENTIUM **c :** the part of divine law discernible (as by the Scholastics) to reason but not directly revealed **d :** a set of principles derived from an analysis of human societies and based (as by 18th century rationalists) principally upon certain natural rights having prior validity to institutional law **e :** the body of rules or customs derived from the general development of mankind and essential to the maintenance of human society **2 :** a specific principle belonging to the total body of natural law **3 :** LAW OF NATURE

natural life *n* [ME] **:** the period of a person's earthly existence terminated by natural as opposed to civil death

natural logarithm *n* **:** a logarithm with *e* as a base

nat·u·ral·ly \ˈnach(ə)rəlē, -li *also* -chərl-\ *adv* [ME, fr. *natural* + *-ly*] **1 :** by nature **:** by natural or inherent character **:** by native endowment **:** by innate tendency or feeling ⟨one child . . . was ~ good —Margaret Deland⟩ ⟨poetry or music . . . may be said to be ~ pleasing —Joshua Reynolds⟩ ⟨her face, ~ pale as marble —Charlotte Brontë⟩ **2 a :** according to or by the operation of the laws of nature ⟨the snow loads will begin to slide off the ~ drooping branches —G.R.Stewart⟩ ⟨the changes which are ~ wrought by time —H.F.Tozer⟩ **b :** as a natural result or consequence **:** as might be expected from the circumstances ⟨the doomed retainers . . . ~ bewailed their sad fate —A.M.Young⟩ ⟨its insular situation . . . led ~ to the seafaring activities —Kemp Malone⟩ ⟨money flows ~ to those who can produce something of value —W.J.Reilly⟩ **3 :** in a natural manner ⟨she did not seem to die ~ —Ann Radcliffe⟩ ⟨you will feel your body weight shift ~ to the left leg —Bob Nichols⟩ **4 a :** by natural growth **:** without cultivation **:** without the use of art or effort **:** SPONTANEOUSLY ⟨her hair curls ~⟩ ⟨an older and more ~ wooded area —*Amer. Guide Series: Minn.*⟩ **b :** INDIGENOUSLY ⟨the cypress grows ~ in the southeastern U. S.⟩ **5 :** with truth to nature or life **:** in a lifelike manner **:** REALISTICALLY ⟨the artist who represents objects ~⟩ **6 :** with ease and simplicity **:** without affectation ⟨write ~ and spontaneously, just as you'd thank your friend in person —Barbara Peterson⟩

natural magnet *n* **:** MAGNET 1a

natural minor scale *n* **:** a minor scale with the diatonic intervals being whole steps except those half-steps between 2–3 and 5–6 and corresponding in pattern to the Aeolian church mode — compare HARMONIC MINOR SCALE, MELODIC MINOR SCALE

nat·u·ral·ness *n* -ES **1** *obs* **:** natural feeling, conduct, or sympathy **2 :** the quality or state of being natural ⟨the spontaneous ~ . . . of his manner —Frank Budgen⟩

natural number *n* **:** any one of the numbers 1, 2, 3, 4, etc. **:** a positive integer

natural order *n* **1 :** the orderly system comprising the physical universe and functioning according to natural as distinguished from human or supernatural laws **2 :** FAMILY 6 a — not now used technically

natural parts *n pl* **1** *obs* **:** GENITALIA **2** *archaic* **:** native ability ⟨a rough man, with good *natural parts* —Horace Walpole⟩

natural period *n* **:** the period of one complete oscillation of a body or system

natural person *n* **:** a human being as distinguished in law from an artificial or juristic person ⟨extended to corporations the rights and immunities guaranteed to *natural persons* —G.W. Johnson⟩ — compare CORPORATION 3

natural philosopher *n* **:** one that studies or is skilled in natural philosophy

natural philosophy *n* [ME] **:** the study of nature in general; *specif* **:** NATURAL SCIENCE — compare MENTAL PHILOSOPHY, MORAL PHILOSOPHY

natural porcelain *n* **:** a porcelain (as Chinese porcelain) made from a single raw material

natural premium *n* **:** the amount required to meet the mortality cost of life insurance for each particular year and increasing from year to year for any given unit of protection

natural price *n* **:** a price which is determined by the costs of production and about which the market price can oscillate

natural pruning *n* **:** a natural falling or dropping off of branches and twigs of trees and shrubs esp. as caused by suppression or death of branches and twigs — compare ABSCISSION 2

natural rate of interest : the rate of interest at which the demand for funds and the supply of savings exactly agree

natural realism *n* **:** a doctrine (as elaborated by the philosophers of the Scottish school) that perception gives direct and indubitable evidence of the independent existence of both mind and matter — called also *commonsense realism*

natural religion *n* **:** a religion validated on the basis of human reason and experience apart from miraculous or supernatural revelation; *specif* **:** a religion that is universally discernible by all men through the use of human reason apart from any special revelation — compare REVEALED RELIGION

natural resin *n* **:** an unmodified resin (as a copal or a dammar) from a natural source (as a tree) **:** RESIN 1 a — distinguished from *synthetic resin*

natural resources *n pl* **:** capacities (as native wit) or materials (as mineral deposits and waterpower) supplied by nature

natural right *n* **:** a right conferred upon man by natural law ⟨a *natural right* . . . would hold in the absence of organized government —Lucius Garvin⟩ — compare LEGAL RIGHT

natural rubber *n* **:** rubber or rubber latex from a plant (esp. *Hevea brasiliensis*) **:** RUBBER 2a — distinguished from *synthetic rubber*

naturals *pl of* NATURAL

natural science *n* **:** branches of science (as physics, chemistry, biology) that deal with matter, energy, and their interrelations and transformations or with objectively measurable phenomena

natural selection *n* **:** a natural process tending to cause the survival of those individuals or groups best adjusted to the conditions under which they live, resulting from the interaction of the organism in its entirety with all the factors of the environmental complex although any one factor may appear to be decisive for survival or extinction in particular circumstances, and recognized today as a mechanism equally important for the perpetuation of desirable genetic qualities and for the elimination of undesirable as these are brought forward by recombination or mutation of genes — compare DARWINISM, MACROEVOLUTION, MENDEL'S LAWS, MICROEVOLUTION

natural slope *n* **:** the slope assumed by a mass of earth thrown up into a heap

natural spirits *n pl, obs* **:** a vaporous principle formerly supposed to arise from the blood and exert control over the functions of nutrition, growth, and reproduction

natural steel *n* **:** steel made by the direct refining of cast iron in a refinery or (as wootz) by a direct process from the ore

natural system *n* **:** a biological classification based upon morphological and anatomical relationships and affinities considered in the light of phylogeny and embryology; *specif* **:** a system in botany other than the artificial or sexual system established by Linnaeus

natural theologian *n* **:** a theologian who uses the methodology of natural theology

natural theology *n* **:** theology deriving its knowledge of God from the study of nature independent of special revelation

natural virtue *n* **:** one of the four cardinal virtues prudence, justice, temperance, or fortitude distinguished in scholasticism from the three theological virtues

natural wavelength *n* **:** NATURAL FREQUENCY

natural wine *n* **:** TABLE WINE

¹na·ture \ˈnāchə(r)\ *n* -s [ME, fr. MF, fr. L *natura,* fr. *natus,* (past part. of *nasci* to be born) + *-ura* -ure — more at NATION] **1** *dial Eng* **:** normal and characteristic quality, strength, vigor, or resiliency ⟨she cooked the meat till it lost all its ~⟩ **2 a :** the essential character or constitution of something ⟨the ~ of the controversy⟩ ⟨inquire into the ~ of heredity —Theodosius Dobzhansky⟩; *esp* **:** the essence or ultimate form of something **b :** the distinguishing qualities or properties of something ⟨the ~ of mathematics⟩ ⟨the ~ of a literary movement⟩ **3 a :** the fundamental character, disposition, or temperament of a living being usu. innate and unchangeable ⟨it was in his ~ to look after others —F.A.Swinnerton⟩ ⟨devotion that it was not in her ~ to return —Naomi Lewis⟩ **b :** the fundamental character, disposition, or temperament of mankind as a whole **:** HUMAN NATURE b ⟨not interested in any particular man . . . but in the ~ of man —Peter Dunne⟩ **c (1) :** a specified kind of individual character, disposition, or temperament ⟨his kindly ~⟩ **(2) :** a being possessing or characterized by such a specified character, disposition, or temperament ⟨who, like so many buoyant ~*s*, had a talent for worrying —S.H.Adams⟩ **4 :** a creative and controlling agent, force, or principle operating in something and determining wholly or chiefly its constitution, development, and well-being: **a :** such a force or agency in the universe acting as a creative guiding intelligence **:** a set of principles held to be established for the regulation of the universe or observed in its operation **b :** an inner driving or prompting force (as instinct, appetite, desire) or the sum of such forces in an individual **5 :** a life-giving or health-giving force in an animate being **6 :** kind, order, or general character ⟨most of his public acts are of a ceremonial ~ —*London Calling*⟩ ⟨island songs of a Hawaiian ~ —Eve Langley⟩ **7 :** the qualities, characteristics, properties, organs, and functions that together make up the vital being of a human being or other organism: **a :** such organs or functions requiring nourishment **b :** an excretory organ or function — usu. used in the phrase *call of nature* **8 :** normality esp. as prescribed by law for sexual relations — usu. used in the phrase *against nature* ⟨their women did change the natural use into that which is against ~ —Rom. 1:26 (AV)⟩; compare CRIME AGAINST NATURE **9 :** feeling (as kindliness or affection) that is genuine, spontaneous, or unstudied in expression **:** NATURALNESS 2 ⟨that no compunctious visitings of ~ shake my fell purpose —Shak.⟩ **10 a** (1) **:** the created world in its entirety (2) **:** the totality of physical reality exclusive of things mental **b :** the total system of spatiotemporal phenomena and events that can be explained by other occurrences in the same system **11 :** the state of an unregenerate soul ⟨the difference between a state of ~ and a state of grace —Robert South⟩ ⟨the congenital ~ of men is evil, the goodness in them acquired —E.R.Hughes⟩ **12 a :** a theoretical condition or stage of existence usu. held to reveal man in his original or proper state: as (1) **:** the normal and ideal character both of particular things and of the universe as a whole sometimes equated with reason and the rational ⟨the full meaning of the Stoic injunction that we live according to ~ —Frank Thilly⟩ (2) **:** a simple, undomesticated, uncivilized mode of life among primitive men having few wants and obligations **:** a state of existence preceding the foundation of organized society **b :** a simplified mode of life esp. as lived out of doors apart from communities and other civilizing and restraining influences ⟨escape from civilization and get back to ~⟩ **13 :** substance or essence that is the principle of specific proper acts or operations ⟨the union of two ~*s* in Christ⟩ ⟨in the Trinity, three persons in one divine ~⟩ **14 :** the genetically controlled qualities of an organism ⟨~ . . . modified by nurture —E.G.Conklin⟩ — compare NURTURE **15 :** a particular order of existence or of existing things that is the subject matter of art: as **a :** one having an unchanged as contrasted with a developed, ordered, perfected, or man-made character **b :** real and objective existence **:** the world of mind and matter external to an observer **:** reality as observed **c :** the aspect of out-of-doors (as a landscape) **:** natural scenery **syn** see TYPE

²nature \"\ *vi* -ED/-ING/-S [ML *naturare*, fr. L *natura*] **:** to give to each thing its specific nature

³nature \", *in sense 2* nə'tü(ə)r\ *adj* [¹*nature*] **1 :** of or relating to nature **2** [F, plain, unadulterated (used of food or drink), fr. *nature*, n.] **:** BRUT

na·tured \'nāchə(r)d\ *adj* [¹*nature* + *-ed*] **:** having a specified nature, temper, or disposition ⟨others, similarly ~, will not permit him . . . to do this —Herbert Spencer⟩ — usu. used in combination ⟨good-*natured*⟩ ⟨ill-*natured*⟩

nature faker *n* **:** one (as a writer) that misrepresents facts about nature usu. attributing to animals traits or habits which they are not known to possess

nature philosophy *n* **:** NATURAL PHILOSOPHY; *esp* **:** an ancient Grecian and Renaissance philosophy undertaking to explain phenomena by natural causes and without recourse to mythical beings

nature print *n* **:** a print made by nature printing

nature printing *n* **:** a process in which an object (as a leaf or piece of lace) is pressed into a plane surface (as of soft metal) to make either a direct printing surface or a matrix

nature study *n* **:** a study of the objects and phenomena of nature (as birds, flowers, minerals, and weather) usu. on an amateur or superficial basis ⟨botany is taught in every high school and *nature study* in the grades —*Amer. Botanist*⟩

na·tur·ism \'nāchə,rizəm\ *n* -S **1 :** NATURALISM **2 :** a form of religious belief and practice characterized by a worship of usu. personified powers of nature — compare ANIMISM **3 :** NUDISM

na·tur·ist \-,rəst\ *n* -S **:** a follower of naturism; *specif* **:** a believer in or adherent of naturism

na·tur·is·tic \¦==¦ristik\ *adj* **:** of, relating to, or resembling naturism

na·tur·o·path \'nāchərə,path, 'nach-\ *n* -S [*nature* + *-o-* + *-path*] **:** a practitioner of naturopathy

na·tur·o·path·ic \¦===¦pathik\ *adj* **:** of, relating to, or by means of naturopathy

na·tur·op·a·thy *also* **na·ture·op·a·thy** \,nāchə'räpəthē, ,nach-\ *n* -ES [*nature* + *-o-* + *-pathy*] **:** a system of treatment of disease emphasizing assistance to nature and sometimes including the use of various medicinal substances (as herbs, vitamins, and salts) and certain physical means (as manipulation and electrical treatment)

na·tya \'nätyə\ *n* -S [Skt *nātya*; prob. akin to Skt *nṛtyati* he dances] **:** the theatrical dance art of India originating in the temple and still devoted largely to the enactment of divine epics and embracing an elaborate system of body postures, hand gestures, and foot movements

¹nau·co·rid \'nȯkərəd, -,rid\ *adj* [NL *Naucoridae*] **:** of or relating to the Naucoridae

²naucorid \"\ *n* -S **:** a bug of the family Naucoridae

nau·cor·i·dae \nȯ'kȯrə,dē, -kär-\ *n pl, cap* [NL, fr. *Naucoris*, type genus + *-idae*] **:** a widely distributed family of aquatic predaceous hemipterous insects comprising the water creepers and having the body broad, oval, and flat and the front femora greatly enlarged

nau·co·ris \'nȯkərəs\ *n, cap* [NL, fr. Gk *naus* ship + *koris* bedbug — more at NAVE, COREIDAE] **:** the type genus of the family Naucoridae comprising water creepers of Europe and Asia

nau·cra·tes \'nȯkrə,tēz\ *n, cap* [NL, fr. LGk *naukratēs* pilot fish, fr. Gk *naus* ship + *-kratēs* ruler (fr. *kratos* strength, power) — more at HARD] **:** a genus of amberfishes including the pilot fish (*N. ductor*)

naufrage *n* -S [MF, fr. L *naufragium*, *navifragium*, fr. *navis* ship + *-fragium* (fr. *frangere* to break) — more at NAVE, BREAK] *obs* **:** SHIPWRECK

nau·ger \'nōgə(r)\ *n* -S [ME — more at AUGER] *chiefly dial* **:** AUGER

¹naught *or* **nought** \'nȯt, 'nät, *usu* -d·+V\ *pron* [ME, fr. OE *nāwiht*, *nōwiht* (akin to OHG *neowiht*), fr. *nā*, *nō* no + *wiht* creature, thing — more at NO, WIGHT] **1 a :** NOTHING ⟨can do ~ but give ourselves wholly to it —L.A.White⟩ ⟨has heard ~ but good of me —J.H.Wheelwright⟩ **b :** a state of utter ineffectualness **:** an insignificant result ⟨these promising beginnings . . . were brought to ~ —Stephen Ullmann⟩ ⟨his efforts to purge his own party came to ~ —Norman Thomas⟩ **2** *obs* **:** what is wrong in morals or method **:** EVIL, ERROR

²naught *or* **nought** \"\ *n* -S [ME, fr. OE *nāwiht*, *nōwiht*, fr. *nāwiht*, *nōwiht*, pron.] **1 a :** NOTHING **b** (1) **:** NOTHINGNESS, NONEXISTENCE ⟨a shift of emphasis from existential analysis to ontology . . . from the ~ to what the ~ manifests concerning the real —James Collins⟩ (2) *usu cap, cabalism* **:** the depths of the Godhead ⟨communion with the *Naught*, . . . a much higher rank than communion with the Shekhinah —G.G. Scholem⟩ **2 :** the arithmetical symbol 0 **:** ZERO, CIPHER — see NUMBER table

³naught *or* **nought** \"\ *adj* [ME, fr. OE *nāwiht*, fr. *nāwiht*, pron.] **1** *archaic* **:** of no worth **:** BAD, UNFIT ⟨the water is ~ and the ground barren —2 Kings 2:19 (AV)⟩ **2 :** of no existence, importance, or effect **:** INSIGNIFICANT ⟨why give him publicity and importance when our critics are convinced that he is ~ —*United India & Indian States*⟩ **:** NONEXISTENT ⟨a whole city made ~ by the bomb⟩ **:** RUINED

naugh·ti·ly \'nȯd|ᵊlē, |t|, |ᵊli, |əl- *also* 'näl\ *adv* **:** in a naughty manner **:** MISCHIEVOUSLY ⟨behaved ~ before guests⟩

naugh·ti·ness \|ēnəs, |in-\ *n* -ES **1 :** the quality or state of being naughty **2 :** a naughty act or impulse

naughts–and–crosses *var of* NOUGHTS-AND-CROSSES

naugh·ty \'nȯd|ē, |t|, |i *also* 'näl\ *adj* -ER/-EST [²*naught* + *-y*] **1 a** *archaic* **:** of inferior quality **:** POOR ⟨very ~ figs, which could not be eaten —Jer 24:2 (AV)⟩ **b** *chiefly Scot* **:** INSIGNIFICANT, GOOD-FOR-NOTHING **2 a** *archaic* **:** vicious in moral character **:** WICKED ⟨~ persons . . . have practiced dangerously against your state —Shak.⟩ **b :** guilty of disobedience or misbehavior ⟨treated like a grown-up gangster, whereas he ought to be treated as a ~ boy —*Times Lit. Supp.*⟩ **3 :** violating accepted standards of morality, good taste, or polite behavior ⟨books . . . with ~ illustrations —Thomas Wolfe⟩ ⟨will be ~ for the young generation to question anything —Sinclair Lewis⟩ **syn** see BAD

naughty pack *n, archaic* **:** a person of bad character; *esp* **:** a loose woman ⟨she was a *naughty pack* —Jonathan Swift⟩

nau·ja·ite \'naùyə,īt\ *n* -S [*Naujakasik*, Greenland + E *-ite*] **:** a nephelite-sodalite-syenite rock having a poikilitic texture

nau·ja·ka·site \,==='kä,sīt\ *n* -S [*Naujakasik*, Greenland + E *-ite*] **:** a mineral $Na_4FeAl_4Si_8O_{25}.2H_2O$ (?) consisting of a hydrous aluminosilicate of sodium or of sodium and iron

nau·ma·chia \nȯ'mākēə\ *n, pl* **naumachi·ae** \-kē,ē\ *or* **naumachias** [L, fr. Gk, naval battle, fr. *naus* ship + *-machia* -machy — more at NAVE] **1 :** an ancient Roman spectacle representing a naval battle **2 :** a place for naumachiae; *esp* **:** an artificial body of water surrounded by seats

nau·mann·ite \'nȯmə,nīt, 'naùm-\ *n* -S [G *naumannit*, fr. Karl F. *Naumann* †1873 Ger. mineralogist + G *-it* -ite] **:** a mineral (Ag_2Se) consisting of a silver selenide in iron-black cubic crystals or massive (sp. gr. 8)

¹naum·keag \'nȯm,keg\ *or* **naumkeag machine** *or* **naumkeag scourer** *n* -S *often cap N* [prob. fr. *Naumkeag*, old name for Salem, Mass., shoe manufacturing city] **:** a machine having a rubber buffing disk for smoothing the surface of shoe soles or heels before finishing

²naumkeag \"\ *vb* -ED/-ING/-S *vi* **:** to buff a shoe bottom (as on a naumkeag machine) prior to the finishing process ~ *vt* **:** to buff (a shoe bottom) prior to finishing

naum·keag·er \-gə(r)\ *n* -S **:** an operator of a naumkeag machine

naunt \'nänt, -ā-,-ä-\ *n* -S [alter. (resulting fr. incorrect division of *mine aunt*) of *aunt*] *dial chiefly Eng* **:** AUNT

nau·pa·ka \naù'päkə\ *n* -S [Hawaiian] **:** a Hawaiian shrub (*Scaevola frutescens*) of the family Goodeniaceae found in mountains and near the coast and conspicuous for their white flowers that look like half flowers

nau·path·ia \nȯ'pathēə\ *n* -S [NL, fr. Gk *naus* ship + NL *-pathia* — more at NAVE] **:** SEASICKNESS

nau·pli·ar \'nȯplēə(r)\ *adj* [NL *nauplius* + E *-ar*] **:** of, relating to, or being a nauplius

nau·pli·iform \'nȯplēᵊ,fȯrm\ *adj* [NL *nauplius* + E *-iform*] **1 :** resembling the nauplius of a crustacean **2** *of a hymenopterous larva* **:** having large sickle-shaped mandibles and a pair of bifurcate caudal processes

nau·pli·o·so·ma \,==='sōmə\ *n* -S [NL, fr. *nauplius* + *-o-* + *-soma*] **:** a pelagic larva that precedes the phyllosoma of various marine decapod crustaceans (as some spiny lobsters)

nau·pli·us \'nȯplēəs\ *n, pl* **nau·plii** \-ē,ī\ [NL, fr. L, a shellfish, fr. Gk *nauplios*] **:** a crustacean larva in usu. the first stage after leaving the egg and with three pairs of appendages corresponding to antennules, antennae, and mandibles, a median eye, and little or no segmentation of the body

na·u·ru \nä'ü(,)rü\ *adj*, [fr. *Nauru*, island in the western Pacific] **:** of or from the island of Nauru **:** of the kind or style prevalent in Nauru

na·u·ru·an \nä'ürəwən\ *n* -S *usu cap* [*Nauru* + E *-an*] **:** a Micronesian native or inhabitant of Nauru

nau·ruz \(')naù'rüz\ *n* -ES *usu cap* [Per *naurūz*, *nau·rōz*, lit., new day, fr. *nau* new + *rūz*, *rōz* day, fr. OPer *raucha-*; akin to Skt *nava* new & to Skt *rocate* he shines — more at NEW, LIGHT] **:** the Persian New Year's Day celebrated at the vernal equinox as a day of great festivity

nau·sea \'nȯ|shə, |zēə, |sēə, |zhə *sometimes* |zyə, |syə, |shēə, |zhēə\ *n* -S [L, lit., seasickness, fr. Gk *nausia*, *nautia* nausea, seasickness, fr. *naus* ship — more at NAVE] **1 a :** a sensation of discomfort in the region of the stomach usu. associated with an urge to retch or vomit **b :** a feeling of distress associated with loathing of food and sometimes aroused by the sight of food **2 :** extreme disgust **:** LOATHING ⟨the victory of his party . . . is considerably more the product of ~ with the present situation —P.B.Rice⟩ **3 :** a state of revulsion accompanying the frightening awareness of one's inescapable freedom as an individual human self

¹nau·se·ant \|shēənt, |zē-, |sē-, |zhē-\ *n* -S [*nausea* + *-ant*, n. suffix] **:** an agent that induces nausea; *esp* **:** an expectorant that liquefies and increases the secretion of mucus

²nauseant \"\ *adj* [*nausea* + *-ant*, adj. suffix] **:** inducing nausea **:** NAUSEATING

nau·se·ate \-ē,āt, *usu* -äd·+V\ *vb* -ED/-ING/-S [L *nauseatus*, past part. of *nauseare*, fr. *nausea*] *vi* **1 :** to become affected with nausea **2 :** to feel disgust ~ *vt* **1 a** *archaic* **:** to reject with nausea or loathing **:** sicken at **b :** to feel disgust or aversion to **:** ABHOR, LOATHE ⟨the mind ~*s* the thought of processions of learned dunces —Holbrook Jackson⟩ **2 a :** to cause to sicken **:** affect with nausea ⟨was something in the dinner that *nauseated* him⟩ **b :** to create an aversion in **:** affect with loathing ⟨the antics of Party discipline soon *nauseated* him —Eugene Gressman⟩ **syn** see DISGUST

nau·se·at·ing·ly *adv* **:** in a nauseating manner or to a nauseating degree ⟨of America . . . he expressed the view that it was ~ materialist —H.J.Laski⟩

nau·se·at·ing·ness *n* -ES **:** the quality or state of being nauseating

nau·seous \'nȯ|shəs, |zēəs, |sēəs, |zhəs\ *adj* [L *nauseosus* causing nausea, fr. *nausea* + *-osus* -ous] **1 :** affected with or inclined to nausea **:** NAUSEATED ⟨began to feel ~⟩ **2 :** causing or such as might be expected to cause nausea **:** SICKENING, LOATHSOME, DISGUSTING ⟨a ~ odor⟩ ⟨~ hypocrisy⟩ — **nau·seous·ly** *adv* — **nau·seous·ness** *n* -ES

nau·set \'nȯsət\ *n, pl* **nauset** *also* **nausetts** *usu cap* **1 :** an Indian people of Cape Cod **2 :** a member of the Nauset people

naut *abbr* nautical

nautch \'nȯch\ *n* -ES [Hindi *nāc*, fr. Prakrit *nacca*, fr. Skt *nṛtya*, fr. *nṛtyati* he dances, acts] **1 :** an entertainment in India consisting chiefly of dancing by professional dancing girls **2** *or* **nautch dance :** a suggestive Eastern dance performed by a dancing girl

nau·ther \'nȯthə(r)\ *conj* [ME — more at NEITHER] *dial chiefly Eng* **:** NEITHER

nau·ti·cal \'nȯd·|əkəl, 'nä|, |t|, |ēk-\ *adj* [L *nauticus* (fr. Gk *nautikos*, fr. *nautēs* sailor — fr. *naus* ship — + *-ikos* -ic) + E *-al* — more at NAVE] **:** of, relating to, or associated with seamen, navigation, or ships ⟨a glossary of ~ terms⟩

nautical astronomy *n* **:** practical astronomy by which the position of a ship or airplane is found by astronomical observations

nautical distance *n* **:** the length in nautical miles of the rhumb line joining any two places on the earth's surface

nau·ti·cal·i·ty \,nȯd·ə'kaləd·ē\ *n* -ES **:** the quality of being nautical ⟨a seaman of overpowering ~ —John Lardner⟩

nau·ti·cal·ly \'nȯd|·ək(ə)lē, 'nä|, |t|, |ēk-, -li\ *adv* **:** in a nautical manner **:** with reference to nautical affairs ⟨a ~ powerful nation⟩

nautical mile *n* **:** any of various units of distance used for sea and air navigation based on the length of a minute of arc of a great circle of the earth and differing because the earth is not a perfect sphere: as **a :** a British unit equ[al] to 6080 ft. or 1853.2 meters — called also *Admiralty mile* **b** a [U.S.] unit no longer in official use equal to 6080.20 ft. or 1853.248 meters **c :** an international unit equal to 6076.11549 ft. or 1852 meters used officially in the U.S. since July 1, 1959

nautical planisphere *n* **:** the projection of the terrestrial globe on a plane for navigators' use

nautical star *n* **:** a star selected with special reference to its fitness for navigators' use in ascertaining longitude and latitude

nautical tables *n pl* **:** arithmetical tables esp. adapted to facilitate a navigator's work in solving problems particularly in nautical astronomy

nautical twilight *n* **:** the period before sunrise or after sunset during which the sun is not more than 12 degrees below the horizon

nau·ti·la·cea \,nȯd·ᵊl'āshēə\ [NL, fr. *Nautilus* + *-acea*] *syn of* NAUTILOIDEA

¹nau·ti·la·cean \¦==¦āshən\ *adj* [NL *Nautilacea* + E *-an*] **:** NAUTILOID

²nautilacean \"\ *n* -S **:** NAUTILOID

nau·til·i·cone \nȯ'tilə,kōn\ *n* [NL *Nautilus* + E *-i-* + *cone*] **:** a nautiloid cephalopod shell coiled in a plane spiral with the outer whorls embracing the inner

nau·til·i·dae \-,dē\ *n pl, cap* [NL, fr. *Nautilus*, type genus + *-idae*] **:** a family of cephalopod mollusks that comprises nautiloids with closely coiled shells and includes all recent members of the order Nautiloidea — see NAUTILUS 1 b

nau·til·i·form \-,fȯrm\ *adj* [NL *Nautilus* + E *-iform*] **:** having the form of a nautilus shell

nau·ti·lite \'nȯd·ᵊl,īt\ *n* -S [NL *Nautilus* + E *-ite*] **:** a fossil nautilus

¹nau·ti·loid \-,ȯid\ *adj* [NL *Nautiloidea*] **1** *also* **nau·ti·loi·de·an** \¦==¦ȯidēən\ [*nautiloidean* fr. NL *Nautiloidea* + E *-an*] **:** of or relating to the Nautiloidea **2** [*nautili*cone + *-oid*] *of a shell* **:** having the form of a nautilicone

²nautiloid \"\ *also* **nautiloidean** \"\ *n* -S **:** a mollusk of the group Nautiloidea

nau·ti·loi·dea \,=='ȯidēə\ *n pl, cap* [NL, fr. *Nautilus* + *-oidea*] **1 :** an order or other subdivision of Tetrabranchia comprising cephalopods having an external chambered shell that is either straight (as in *Orthoceras*) or variously curved or coiled and being important in the Ordovician and esp. the Silurian but now represented only by the genus *Nautilus* **2** *in some classifications* **:** a subclass or other subdivision of Cephalopoda that is coextensive with Tetrabranchia

nau·ti·lus \'nȯd·ᵊləs, 'näl, |tᵊl-\ *n* [NL, fr. L, paper nautilus, fr. Gk *nautilos*, lit., sailor, fr. *naus* ship — more at NAVE] **1 a** *pl* **nautilus·es** \-ᵊləsəz\ *or* **nauti·li** \-ᵊl,ī\ **:** any of several cephalopod mollusks of the southern Pacific and Indian oceans that constitute a genus (*Nautilus*), that are contained in the outermost chamber of a spiral chambered shell with an outer porcelaneous layer and an inner pearly layer, and that have numerous small tentacles arranged in groups and without suckers or hooks, no ink sac, four gills, four auricles, four nephridia, and a siphon consisting of two lobes not fused to form a tube — called also *chambered nautilus, pearly nautilus* **b** *cap* **:** the type genus and sole recent representative of the family Nautilidae comprising nautiluses and extinct related forms of which some date back to the Tertiary **2** [L] **:** PAPER NAUTILUS

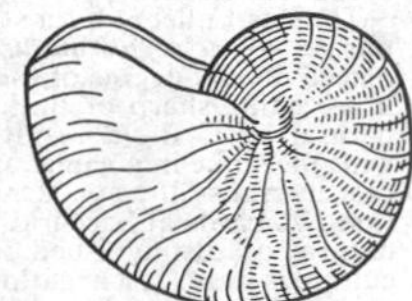
shell of pearly nautilus

nav *abbr* **1** naval **2** navigable **3** navigate; navigation; navigator **4** navy

nava·ho *or* **nava·jo** \'navə,hō, 'näv-\ *n, pl* **navaho** *or* **navahos** *or* **navahoes** *or* **navajo** *or* **navajos** *or* **navajoes** [Sp (*Apache de*) *Navajó*, lit., Apache of Navajó, fr. *Navajó*, a pueblo, fr. Tewa *Navahú*, lit., great planted-fields] **1** *usu cap* **a :** an Athapaskan people of northern New Mexico and Arizona ranging also into Colorado and Utah — called also *Diné* **b :** a member of such people **2** *usu cap* **:** the language of the Navaho people **3** *usu navaho, pl navahos, often cap* **:** a strong to vivid orange that is redder than orpiment orange and slightly redder and darker than Big Four yellow

navaho blanket *also* **navaho rug** *n, usu cap N* **:** a blanket woven by the Navaho in symbolic designs of symbolic meaning

navajo stitch *n, usu cap N* **:** a coiled basketry stitch in which the binding strand encloses the working coil and the previous coil in a figure eight

¹na·val \'nāvəl\ *adj* [L *navalis*, fr. *navis* ship + *-alis* -al — more at NAVE] **1** *obs* **:** of or relating to ships or shipping **2 a :** of, relating to, or belonging to, connected with, or used in a navy ⟨~ vessels⟩ ⟨U. S. ~ history⟩ ⟨~ personnel⟩ ⟨a ~ academy⟩ ⟨~ supplies⟩ **b :** engaged in by ships of war ⟨a ~ battle⟩ ⟨a ~ bombardment⟩ **c :** consisting of or based on a navy ⟨a ~ force⟩ ⟨~ power⟩

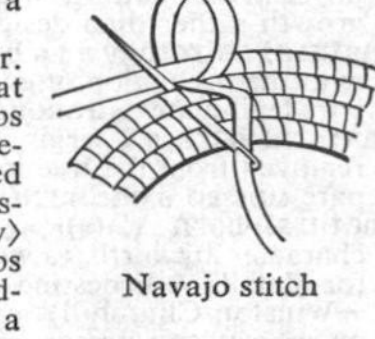
Navajo stitch

²naval *or* **naval orange** *var of* NAVEL ORANGE

naval architect *n* **:** MARINE ARCHITECT

naval attaché *n* **:** a naval officer detailed on duty with the diplomatic representative of his country at a foreign capital

naval auxiliary *n* **:** a naval vessel (as a tanker or supply ship) auxiliary to the fighting ships

naval aviator *n* **:** an officer or petty officer in the U. S. Navy who has completed the requisite course of training as a pilot of heavier-than-air craft

naval base *n* **:** an area command normally including a seaport that includes and integrates the shore activities (as a shipyard, ammunition depot, hospital) which provide local logistic services to the fleet

naval brass *also* **naval bronze** *n* **:** brass composed usu. of 60 percent copper, 39 percent zinc, 1 percent tin and used for bolts or other parts usu. under water

naval brigade *n* **:** NAVAL MILITIA

naval cadet *n* **:** a young man in training for service as a naval officer; *specif* **:** a midshipman in the U. S. Naval Academy between 1882 and 1902

naval crown *n* [trans. of L *corona navalis*] **1 :** a golden crown given as a reward for sea service in ancient Rome that consists of galley prows arranged in a circle to form the rim **2** *or* **naval coronet :** a heraldic representation of a crown of gold with ship sterns and square sails arranged alternately on the fillet

naval crown 2

naval district *n* **:** a geographical area in which all naval activities except those of the fleet come under the command of its commandant

naval establishment *n* **:** all the activities under the secretary of the navy including the operating forces, the navy department, and the shore establishment

na·val·ism \'nāvə,lizəm\ *n* -S **:** the policy of maintaining naval interests; *also* **:** dominance of the naval class or of naval policies ⟨radio propaganda for ~ —*N. Y. Herald Tribune*⟩

na·val·ist \-ləst\ *n* -S **:** an advocate of navalism — **na·val·is·tic** \¦==¦listik\ *adj* — **na·val·is·ti·cal·ly** \-tək(ə)lē\ *adv*

na·val·ly \'nāvəlē, -li\ *adv* [*naval* + *-ly*] **1 :** with a naval crown ⟨an eagle . . . and on the sinister a stork proper, each ~ gorged —*Burke's Peerage*⟩ **2 :** in a naval manner or from a naval standpoint ⟨~, the U. S. controls the Pacific —F.H. Cramer⟩

naval militia *n* **:** a naval force maintained by some states in a similar manner to the National Guard

naval officer *n* **1 :** an officer in a navy **2 :** a customs official of the U. S. who handles manifests and entries, permits, clearances, and other documents

naval pipe *n* **:** CHAIN PIPE

naval reserve *n* **:** an organization of trained officers and men that can be called upon to strengthen the regular navy in war

naval shipyard *n* **:** a naval activity manned by civilian engineers and workers and administered by engineer duty officers that builds, repairs, alters, docks, converts, and fits out all types of warship — called also *navy yard*

naval station *n* **:** a command ashore whose mission is to provide local logistic support to units of the operating forces (as in ship repair, personnel administration, pilotage, aerology, flight control, medical care)

naval stores *n pl* **1 :** permanent or consumable supplies for warships excluding armament stores **2 :** products (as tar, pitch, turpentine, pine oil, rosin, terpenes) obtained from the oleoresin of pine and other coniferous trees

nav·ar \'na,vär, -vȧ(r\ *n* -s [*nav*igational and traffic control *radar*] **:** a system of radar navigation in which the position and identity of all aircraft in the area about an airport are determined by ground radar and retransmitted so that a pilot has a detailed picture of all aerial activity on his radarscope

na·va·ra·tra \,nəvə'rä·trə\ *n* -s [Skt *navarātra* period of nine nights, fr. *nava* nine + *rātri* night; perh. akin to Skt *rāma* black — more at NINE] **:** a nine-day Hindu festival in honor of Durga held in the month Asin

na·varch \'nā,värk\ *n* -s [L *navarchus, nauarchus,* fr. Gk *nauarchos,* fr. *naus* ship + *-archos* -arch — more at NAVE] **:** the commander of a fleet in ancient Greece

nav·a·rho \'navə,rō\ *n* -s [*nav*igation + *aid* + *rho* (ρ), a symbol for distance in navigation] **:** a long-range omnidirectional radio navigation system presenting position information in the simplified form of an azimuth reading and a distance reading on two dials in the cockpit

na·va·rin \nȧvärаⁿ\ *n, pl* **navarins** \"\ [F] **:** a mutton stew prepared with vegetables

[1]**navar·rese** \¦navə¦rēz, ¦näv-, -rēs\ *adj, usu cap* [*Navarre* ancient kingdom now divided between Spain and France + E *-ese*] **:** of, relating to, or characteristic of Navarre

[2]**navarrese** \"\ *n, pl* **navarrese** \"\ *cap* **1 :** a native or inhabitant of Navarre **2 :** a dialect of Basque spoken on both sides of the French-Spanish border in the western Pyrenees

[1]**nave** \'nāv\ *n* -s [ME, fr. OE *nafu;* akin to OHG *naba* nave, ON *nöf* nave, OE *nafela* navel — more at NAVEL] **:** a block in the center of a wheel from which the spokes radiate and in which the axle is fixed **:** HUB

[2]**nave** \"\ *n* -s [ML *navis,* fr. L, ship; akin to OE *nōwend* skipper, sailor, OHG *nuosc* trough, ON *nōr* ship, Gk *naus,* Skt *nau*] **1 :** the main part of the interior of a church: as **a :** the long narrow central hall in a cruciform church that rises higher than the aisles flanking it to form a clerestory and is usu. not considered to include the central part of the transept and choir — see BASILICA illustration **b :** the part of a church between the rear wall and the chancel **2 :** a large open central space in a building (as a railway station)

nave arcade *n* **:** an arcade marking the separation between a nave and its side aisles

na·vel \'nāvəl\ *n* -s [ME *navel, navele,* fr. OE *nafela;* akin to OHG *nabalo* navel, ON *nafli,* L *umbilicus* navel, *umbo* boss of a shield, Gk *omphalos* navel, Skt *nabhya* nave of a wheel, *nābhi* navel, nave of a wheel] **1 :** a mark or depression in the middle of the abdomen, marking the point of attachment of the umbilical cord or yolk stalk **:** UMBILICUS **2 :** the central point or part of something **:** MIDDLE ⟨the blessed Mediterranean . . . the ~ of the earth —Harold Nicolson⟩ ⟨the hero as the incarnation of God is himself the ~ of the world, the umbilical point through which the energies of eternity break into time —Joseph Campbell⟩ **3** *or* **navel point :** NOMBRIL

navel ill *n* **:** a serious septicemia of newborn animals caused by pus-producing bacteria entering the body through the umbilical cord or opening and typically marked by joint inflammation or arthritis accompanied by generalized pyemia, rapid debilitation, and commonly death — called also *joint evil;* compare MUSHY CHICK

navel orange *also* **navel** \"\ *or* **na·val** \"\ *or* **naval orange** *n* -s [*naval* by folk etymology fr. *navel*] **:** a seedless or nearly seedless orange originated in Brazil and much grown in California with fruit that encloses a small secondary fruit and has a pit at the apex of the rind

navel orangeworm *n* **:** a caterpillar that is the larva of a phycitid moth (*Paramyelois transitella*) and that is a serious pest of almonds and walnuts esp. in California

navel string *n* **:** UMBILICAL CORD

navelwort \'≈,≈\ *n* [ME, fr. *navel* + *wort*] **1 :** a European succulent herb (*Cotyledon umbilicus*) having round peltate leaves with a central depression **2 :** an herb of the genus *Omphalodes* of the family Boraginaceae **3 :** MARSH PENNYWORT

na·vet \nȧvā\ *or* **na·vette** \nȧvet\ *n* -s [MF *navet* turnip, rape (fr. OF *naviet,* dim. of *nef* turnip, rape, fr. L *napus*) & *navette* rape, alter. of *navet*] **:** RAPE 2

na·ve·ta \nə'vād·ə, -ved·ə\ *n* -s [Catal, navicula, naveta, dim. of *nau* ship, fr. L *navis*] **:** a megalithic long barrow of the Balearic islands resembling an inverted boat

na·vette \nȧvet\ *n* -s [F, shuttle, navicula, marquise, fr. OF, shuttle, dim. of *nef* ship, fr. L *navis* — more at NAVE] **:** MARQUISE 3

nav·i·cel·la \,navə'selə\ *n* -s [ML, fr. LL, small ship, dim. of L *navis* ship — more at NAVE] **:** an ornamental object shaped like a ship

nav·i·cert \'navə,sərt\ *n* -s [*navi*gation *cert*ificate] **:** a certificate issued by authorized British officials (as consular officers) exempting a noncontraband consignment from seizure or search by British blockade patrols

na·vic·u·la \nə'vikyələ\ *n* [in sense 1, fr. ML, fr. L, small ship, dim. of L *navis* ship; in sense 2, NL, fr. L] **1** -s **:** an incense boat **2 a** *cap* **:** a very large genus (the type of the family Naviculaceae) of diatoms having a lanceolate or boat-shaped usu. free-floating frustule covered with minute striae **b** -s **:** a plant of the genus *Navicula*

[1]**na·vic·u·lar** \-lə(r)\ *adj* [in sense 1, fr. L *navicula* small ship + E *-ar;* in sense 2, fr. NL *Navicula* + E *-ar;* in sense 3, irreg. fr. MF *naviculaire,* fr. L *navicula* + MF *-aire* -ary] **1 :** resembling or having the shape of a boat ⟨a ~ bone⟩ **:** CYMBIFORM, SCAPHOID **2 :** resembling a diatom of the genus *Navicula* **3 :** of, relating to, or involving a navicular bone ⟨~ fractures⟩

[2]**navicular** \"\ *also* **na·vic·u·lare** \≈,≈≈'la(a)rē, -lärē\ *n* -s [partly fr. [1]*navicular;* partly fr. NL (*os*) *naviculare* navicular bone] **:** a navicular bone; *esp* **:** the lateral bone on the radial side of the proximal row of the carpus

navicular disease *also* **navicular** *n* -s **:** inflammation of the navicular bone and forefoot of the horse resulting in a shortened stride and persistent lameness and regarded as due to repeated bruising or strain esp. in individuals exhibiting a hereditary predisposition

navies *pl of* NAVY

nav·i·ga·bil·i·ty \,navəgə'biləd·ē, -ətē, -i\ *n* **:** the quality or state of being navigable

nav·i·ga·ble \'≈≈gəbəl\ *adj* [MF or L; MF *navigable,* fr. L *navigabilis,* fr. *navigare* to navigate + *-abilis* -able] **1 :** capable of being navigated **:** deep enough and wide enough to afford passage to ships ⟨a ~ river⟩ ⟨canals ~ at a length of about 2,700 miles and floatable at a length of about 26,500 miles —*Statesman's Yr. Bk.*⟩ **2 :** capable of being navigated or steered ⟨a ~ balloon⟩ — **nav·i·ga·ble·ness** *n* -ES

navigable airspace *n* **:** airspace above the minimum safe altitudes of flight as legally prescribed

navigable waters *n pl, law* **:** waters which form in their ordinary condition by themselves or by uniting with other waters a continuous highway over which commerce in the customary mode in which it is conducted by water is or may be carried on with other states or foreign countries, their status as such waters being established by evidence of actual commercial or private use or of the feasibility of removing the obstructions to their use for such interstate or foreign commerce

nav·i·ga·bly \-blē, -li\ *adv* **:** in a navigable manner or to a navigable degree

nav·i·gate \'navə,gāt, *usu* -ād·+V\ *vb* -ED/-ING/-S [L *navigatus,* past part. of *navigare,* fr. *navis* ship + *-igare* (fr. *agere* to lead, drive) — more at NAVE, AGENT] *vi* **1 a :** to go from one place to another by ship **:** SAIL **b :** to sail or manage a boat **2 :** to direct one's course through any medium; *specif* **:** to operate an airplane or airship ⟨~ by instrument⟩ **3 :** to get about **:** WALK ⟨well enough to ~ under his own power⟩ **:** MOVE ⟨as to the state of the roads . . . it might be another week or two before wheels could ~ in any comfort —Esther Forbes⟩ ~ *vt* **1 a :** to sail over, on, or through ⟨the first ships to ~ the Atlantic⟩ ⟨cargo ships that can ~ inland waters⟩ ⟨having successfully *navigated* the pack ice off the . . . coast —Rene Cutforth⟩ **b :** to make one's way on, about, or through ⟨had trouble *navigating* the stairs⟩ ⟨managed to ~ the house on his knees —Alice Lake⟩ ⟨~ the dangerous age range from 50 to 70 —Flanders Dunbar⟩ **2 a :** to steer, direct, or manage in sailing **:** conduct (a boat) upon the water by the art or skill of seamen **b :** to operate, steer, or control the course of (an aircraft)

navigating officer *n* **:** a navigator of a ship or aircraft

nav·i·ga·tion \,navə'gāshən\ *n* -s [MF or L; MF *navigation* fr. L *navigation-, navigatio,* fr. *navigatus* + *-ion-, -io* -ion] **1 :** the act or practice of navigating ⟨feats of ~ among migratory animals —W.H.Dowdeswell⟩ **2 a :** the science or art of conducting ships or aircraft from one place to another; *esp* **:** the method of determining position, course, and distance traveled over the surface of the earth by the principles of geometry and astronomy and by reference to devices (as radar beacons or instruments) designed as aids **b :** skill in this art or science **3 :** an instance of navigating **:** VOYAGE ⟨pigeons and shearwaters can exhibit . . . a successful ~ homeward —R.M.Lockley⟩ **4 :** ship traffic or commerce **:** SHIPPING ⟨open to ~ as soon as the ice is out⟩ **5 :** a navigable waterway formed artificially **:** PASSAGE ⟨the lake itself being some six miles long, tolerable ~ was thus established for a distance of eleven miles —John Burroughs⟩

nav·i·ga·tion·al \¦≈≈¦gāshənᵊl, -shnəl\ *adj* **:** of, relating to, or used in navigation ⟨~ difficulties⟩ ⟨~ astronomy⟩ ⟨the ~ planets Venus, Mars, Jupiter, and Saturn⟩ — **nav·i·ga·tion·al·ly** \-ᵊlē, -əl|, |i\ *adv*

navigation light *n* **:** one of a set of lights on an airplane indicating its position and direction of motion and consisting of a red light and a green light on the port and starboard wing tips respectively and a white light at the tail

nav·i·ga·tor \'navə,gād·ə(r), -gāt-\ *n* -s [L, fr. *navigatus* + *-or*] **1 :** one that navigates or is qualified to navigate: as **a :** an officer on a ship or aircraft responsible for its navigation **b :** one who explores by ship **c :** an automatic device that registers or directs the course of an aircraft or missile **2 a** *Brit* **:** a laborer employed in constructing a canal **b :** NAVVY

na·vite \'nā,vīt\ *n* -s [G *navit,* fr. L *Nava* Nahe river, Germany + G *-it* -ite] **:** a mineral consisting of a coarse-grained olivine-basalt with phenocrysts of altered olivine and a little augite and basic plagioclase in a holocrystalline groundmass of labradorite and augite

navr *abbr* navigator

[1]**nav·vy** \'navē, -vi\ *n* -ES [by shortening & alter. fr. *navigator*] **1** *Brit* **:** an unskilled laborer; *esp* **:** one doing excavation or construction **2** *Brit* **:** a machine for excavating **:** STEAM SHOVEL

[2]**navvy** \"\ *vb* -ED/-ING/-ES *Brit, vi* **:** to work as a navvy ~ *vt* **:** EXCAVATE

na·vy \'nāvē, -vi\ *n, pl* **navies** *see sense 4, often attrib* [ME *navie,* fr. MF, fr. L *navigia,* pl. of *navigium* ship, fr. *navigare* to navigate] **1 :** the ships of one nation or owner or gathering **:** FLEET ⟨the country's merchant ~⟩ **2 :** the war vessels belonging to a nation composed formerly chiefly of ships of the line, frigates, and gun vessels and in modern times of warships (as aircraft carriers, battleships, cruisers, command ships, destroyers and submarines), amphibious ships (as attack transports and attack cargo ships), patrol vessels (as escort vessels and gunboats), mine warfare vessels (as minelayers and minesweepers), and logistic support vessels (as tenders, tankers, repair ships and ammunition ships) **3** *often cap* **:** the complete military organization of a nation for sea warfare including yards, shops, stations, men, ships, offices, and officers **:** the naval establishment **4** *pl* **navys :** NAVY BLUE **5** *or* **navy plug :** a strong dark plug tobacco

navy agent *n* **:** a British attorney who acts for naval officers in financial matters connected with the service (as distribution of prize money)

navy bean *n* **:** a white-seeded kidney bean that is grown esp. for its nutritious seeds

navy blue *n* **:** a variable color averaging a grayish purplish blue that is duller and bluer than average delft, bluer and duller than Windsor blue or Turkish blue, bluer and darker than regimental, and duller than Wedgwood blue (sense 2)

navy exchange *n* **:** SHIP'S SERVICE

navy green *n* **:** LIGHT CHROME GREEN

navy yard *n* **:** NAVAL SHIPYARD

na·wab \nə'wäb, -wȯb\ *n* -s [Hindi *nawāb* — more at NABOB] **1 a :** a deputy ruler or viceroy under the Mogul government **b :** a Muslim prince inferior only to a Nizam — sometimes used as a courtesy title **2 :** NABOB

[1]**nay** \'nā\ *adv* [ME *nay, nei,* fr. ON *nei,* fr. *ne* not + *ei* ever — more at NE, AYE] **1 :** NO — used formerly as a negative answer to a question asked or a request made and now superseded by *no* except in oral voting **2 :** not this merely but also **:** not only so but — used to mark addition or substitution of a more explicit or emphatic phrase and thus interchangeable with *yea* ⟨each of us is peculiar, ~, in a sense, unique —S.J. Brown⟩

[2]**nay** \"\ *n* -s **1 :** DENIAL, REFUSAL, PROHIBITION **2 a :** a negative reply or vote ⟨the ~*s* outnumbering the ayes⟩ **b :** one who votes no ⟨voted among the ~*s*⟩

[3]**nay** \"\ *n* -s [Ar *nāy,* fr. Per] **:** a vertical end-blown flute of ancient origin used in Muslim lands

na·ya·di \'nīədē\ *n, pl* **nayadi** *or* **nayadis** *usu cap* [Malayalam *nāyāti* hunter, fr. *nay* dog + *āti* one who moves] **:** a member of one of the lowest of the untouchable Hindu castes of the Malabar coast of India

nayak *var of* NAIK

na·ya pai·sa \nə,yä,pī'sä\ *n, pl* **na·ye pai·se** \nə,yā,pī'sā\ [Hindi *nayā paisā,* lit., new pice] **:** a subsidiary unit of value of the Republic of India equal to ¹⁄₁₀₀ rupee established April 1957 **:** PAISA

nayar *or* **nair** \'nī(ə)r\ *n, pl* **nayar** *or* **nayars** *or* **nair** *or* **nairs** *usu cap* [Malayalam *nāyar,* fr. Skt *nāyaka* — more at NAIK] **1 :** a people of the Malabar coast of India that are probably Dravidians with Aryan admixture and are noted for polyandry in which women are free to contract alliances as they please outside their own clan with men of equal or better rank, children belong to the mother's clan, and property descends through the female line **2 :** a member of the Nayar people

na·ya·rit \,näyə'rēt\ *or* **na·ya·ri·ta** \-rēd·ə\ *n* -s *usu cap* [Sp *nayarita,* of AmerInd origin] **:** CORA 2

na·yaur \nə'yaȯr\ *n* -s [perh. modif. of Nepali *nahūr* nahoor] **:** a Tibetan wild sheep (*Ovis ammon hodgsoni*) that is a variety of the argali

[1]**nay·say** \'nā,sā\ *n* [[1]*nay* + *say,* n.; after the phrase *to say one nay*] **:** REFUSAL, DENIAL

[2]**naysay** \(')≈¦≈\ *vt* [[1]*nay* + *say,* vb.] **:** DENY, REFUSE, OPPOSE ⟨there might have been . . . for anything he could ~ —W.F. DeMorgan⟩ — **naysayer** \(')≈¦≈≈\ *n* -s

nay·word \'nā,≈\ *n* [*nay-* (of unknown origin) + *word*] **1 :** a word used as a signal **:** WATCHWORD 1b **2** *obs* **:** a proverb of reproach **:** BYWORD

na·zard *or* **na·sard** \nə'zär(d)\ *n* -s [F, fr. *nazard, nasard,* having a nasal sound, fr. L *nasus* nose — more at NOSE] **:** a mutation organ stop of 2⅔-foot pitch with metal pipes

naz·a·re·an \¦nazə¦rēən\ *n* -s *cap* [LL *Nazaraeus* (fr. Gk *Nazēraios,* fr. *Nazareth, Nazeret* Nazareth) + E *-an*] **:** NAZARENE 1

[1]**naz·a·rene** \¦nazə¦rēn\ *n* -s [ME *Nazaren,* fr. LL *Nazarenus,* fr. Gk *Nazarēnos,* fr. *Nazareth, Nazeret* Nazareth, town in ancient Palestine] **1** *cap* **:** a native or resident of Nazareth in Galilee, Palestine ⟨Jesus Christ, the *Nazarene*⟩ **2** *usu cap* **a :** a follower of Jesus of Nazareth **:** CHRISTIAN **b :** a member of an early sect of Jewish-Christians holding that Christians of Jewish descent should observe the Jewish law **c :** a member of a sect of pietistic, pacifistic Christians in Hungary **d :** a member of the Church of the Nazarene, a Protestant Christian denomination deriving from the merging in 1907–8 of three independent holiness groups and adhering closely to the original teachings of Methodism (as the doctrines of holiness and sanctification) **3** *usu cap* **:** one of a group of 19th century German painters in Rome seeking to restore Christian art to its medieval purity

[2]**nazarene** \"\ *adj, usu cap* **:** of or relating to Nazareth or the Nazarenes

naz·ca *also* **nas·ca** \'näskə\ *adj, usu cap* [fr. *Nazca* (*Nasca*), town in southwestern Peru] **:** of or relating to a culture of the coast of southern Peru dating from about 2000 B.C. and characterized by a thin hard coiled pottery painted in many brilliant colors and conventionalized symbolic design, by expert weaving, and by irrigated agriculture in an area now desert

naze *or* **nase** \'nāz\ *n* -s [perh. from the *Naze,* promontory in Essex, England] **:** PROMONTORY, HEADLAND

[1]**na·zi** \'nä|ts|ē, 'na|, 'nȧ|, |i *sometimes* |z|\ *n* -s [G, by shortening and alter. fr. *nationalsozialist* National Socialist, fr. *national* + *sozialist* socialist] **1** *usu cap* **:** a member of the former National Socialist German Workers' party founded on fascist principles in 1919 and headed by Adolf Hitler from 1921 **2** *often cap* **:** an adherent of a party or movement similar to that of the Nazis

[2]**nazi** \"\ *adj, often cap* **1 :** of or relating to Nazism or a Nazi ⟨~ ideology⟩ ⟨~ officials⟩ ⟨the ~ party⟩ **2 :** controlled or carried out by Nazis ⟨a ~ government⟩ ⟨~ persecution⟩

na·zi·dom \-dəm\ *n* -s *often cap* **:** NAZISM 2

na·zi·fi·ca·tion \,≈≈fə'kāshən\ *n* -s *often cap* [fr. *nazify,* after such pairs as E *amplify: amplification*] **:** the act or process of nazifying

na·zi·fy \'≈≈,fī\ *vt* -ED/-ING/-ES *often cap* [[1]*Nazi* + *-fy*] **:** to subject to Nazi control or imbue with Nazism

na·zim \'näzəm\ *n* -s [Hindi *nāzim,* fr. Ar *nāzim* arranger, organizer] **:** a military governor in India

na·zi·phile *pronunc at* NAZI + ,fīl\ *n* -s *often cap* [[1]*Nazi* + *-phile*] **:** a person favorable toward Nazism

na·zir \'nä,zi(ə)r\ *n* -s [Hindi *nāzir,* fr. Ar *nāzir*] **1 :** a native court official in India who serves processes, acts as treasurer, and performs other similar duties **2 :** any of various officials in Muslim countries

naz·i·rite *or* **naz·a·rite** \'nazə,rīt, *usu* -īd·+V\ *n* -s *usu cap* [LL *nazaræus* Nazarite (fr. Gk *nazaraios, naziraios,* fr. Heb *nāzīr,* fr. *nāzar* to consecrate) + E *-ite*] **:** a man of ancient Israel or Judah consecrated to God for a given time by an ascetic vow esp. to avoid drinking wine, cutting the hair, and being defiled by a corpse

naz·i·rit·ism \-,rīd·,izəm\ *n* -s *usu cap* **:** the practice of a Nazirite

na·zism \'nät,sizəm *sometimes* 'nä,zizəm *or* 'na- *or* 'nȧ-\ *or* **na·zi·ism** *pronunc at* NAZI +,izəm\ *n* -s *usu cap* [[1]*Nazi* + *-ism*] **1 :** the body of political and economic doctrines held and put into effect by the National Socialist German Workers' party in the Third German Reich including the totalitarian principle of government, state control of all industry, predominance of groups assumed to be racially superior, and supremacy of the führer **:** German fascism **2 :** a Nazi movement or regime

na·zist \'nä|ts|əst, 'na|, 'nȧ| *sometimes* |z|\ *or* **na·zis·tic** \(')nät¦sistik *sometimes* (')nä¦zi- *or* (')na- *or* (')nȧ-\ *adj, usu cap* **:** adhering to or resembling Nazism

naz·o·re·an \¦nazə¦rēən\ *n* -s *cap* [Gk *nazōraios,* fr. *Nazareth* Nazareth] **:** NAZARENE 1

NB *abbr* **1** naval base **2** no ball **3** no bid **4** northbound **5** [L *nota bene*] note well; take notice

Nb *symbol* niobium

n balance *n, usu cap N* **:** NITROGEN BALANCE

NBP *abbr* normal boiling point

NC *abbr* **1** new charter **2** new crop **3** nitrocellulose **4** no change **5** no charge **6** no connection **7** noncollectible **8** nurse corps

NCA *abbr* neurocirculatory asthenia

NCO \¦en,sē¦ō\ *abbr or n* -s noncommissioned officer

NCS *abbr* net control station

NCUP *abbr* no commission until paid

NCV *abbr, often not cap* no commercial value

-nd *symbol* — used after the figure 2 to form the ordinal *second* or an ordinal that ends in *second* ⟨a 32*nd* note⟩ — compare -D

ND *abbr* **1** national debt **2** navy department **3** *often not cap* no date; not dated

Nd *symbol* neodymium

NDB *abbr* nondirectional beacon

nde·be·le \,endə'bē(,)lē\ *n, pl* **ndebele** *or* **ndebeles** *usu cap* **1 a :** a Bantu people of the northern Transvaal and Southern Rhodesia — called also *Matabele* **b :** a member of such people **2 :** a dialect of Zulu spoken by the Ndebele people

NDGA *abbr* nordihydroguaiaretic acid

ndon·ga *n, pl* **ndonga** \ən'dȯŋgə\ *or* **ndongas** *usu cap* **1 a :** a people of South-West Africa near the Angola border **b :** a member of such people **2 :** a Bantu language spoken by the Ndonga people

ndo·ro·bo \,endə'rō(,)bō\ *n, pl* **ndorobo** *or* **ndorobos** *usu cap* **1 :** a hunting people of small stature living in the Kikuyu-Masai region and northward in Kenya and possibly related to the Pygmies **2 :** a member of the Ndorobo people

[1]**ne** \'nē, ˌnə\ *adv* [ME, fr. OE *ne, ni* — more at NO] *chiefly dial* **:** NOT

[2]**ne** \"\ *conj* [ME, fr. OE *ne, ni,* fr. [1]*ne*] *chiefly dial* **:** NOR

[3]**né** \'nā\ *adj* [F, lit., born (past part. of *naître* to be born, fr L *nascere,* fr. *nasci*), fr. L *natus,* past part. of *nasci* to be born — more at NATION] **:** originally or formerly called or named — used (1) to indicate and introduce the former name of a man or boy usu. after mention of the name actually being used ⟨John Doe ~ Smith⟩ or (2) sometimes to indicate and introduce the former name of a group ⟨the Los Angeles Dodgers ~ the Brooklyn Dodgers⟩ or thing ⟨Kernville ~ Whiskey Flat⟩ usu. after mention of the name actually being used; compare NÉE

ne- *or* **neo-** *comb form* [Gk, fr. *neos* new — more at NEW] **1 a :** new **:** recent ⟨*neo*logism⟩ ⟨*neo*phyte⟩ **b :** a new and different period or form of something (as a faith, school, or language) — often joined to the second element with a hyphen ⟨*neo*-Chippendale⟩ ⟨*Neo*-Darwinism⟩ ⟨*Neo*-Latin⟩ ⟨*Neo*platonism⟩ **c :** of recent forms — opposed to *pale-* ⟨*neo*botanist⟩ ⟨*neo*botany⟩ ⟨*neo*ntology⟩ **d :** neozoic — opposed to *pale-* ⟨*Neo*crinoidea⟩ ⟨*Neo*lithic⟩ **e :** imitation **:** pseudo **f :** the New World ⟨*Ne*arctic⟩ ⟨*Neo*tropical⟩ **g :** an immature form ⟨*neo*fetus⟩ **h :** a more recently developed part (as of a plant or animal) ⟨*neo*morph⟩ **i :** an abnormal new formation ⟨*neo*plasm⟩ **2 a :** the one among several isomeric hydrocarbons that has been recently classified and contains at least one carbon atom connected directly with four other carbon atoms ⟨*neo*hexane⟩ — compare IS-, NORMAL 10e **b :** a new chemical compound isomeric with or otherwise related to the one to whose name it is prefixed ⟨*neo*arsphenamine⟩ **3 :** the latest subdivision of a division of geologic time ⟨*Neo*paleozoic⟩ — distinguished from *mes-* and *eo-*

NE *abbr* **1** national emergency **2** new edition **3** no effects **4** nonessential **5** northeast; northeastern **6** not exceeding; not to exceed

Ne *symbol* neon

neaf \'nēf\ *chiefly dial var of* [1]NIEVE

neal \'nēl, -ēəl\ *vb* [by shortening] *chiefly dial* **:** ANNEAL

ne·allotype \(')nē+\ *n* [*ne-* + *allotype*] **:** a type specimen of the opposite sex to the holotype and collected and described later than the holotype — compare ALLOTYPE

[1]**ne·an·der·thal** *also* **ne·an·der·tal** \nē'andə(r),t(h)ȯl, -'aan-; nā'ändə(r),täl, nā'ändə(r),tȧl\ *adj, usu cap* [*Neanderthal* (*man*) *or Neandertal* (*man*)] **1 :** belonging or relating to or resembling Neanderthal man ⟨*Neanderthal* cave⟩ ⟨*Neanderthal* jaw⟩ **2 a :** suggesting primitive man in appearance or behavior ⟨*Neanderthal* ferocity⟩ **b :** extremely old-fashioned or out-of-date ⟨*Neanderthal* conservatism⟩

[2]**neanderthal** \"\ *n* -s *usu cap* **1 :** a member of the Neanderthal race **2 :** a rugged or uncouth person **:** CAVEMAN

ne·an·der·thal·er \-lə(r)\ *n* -s *usu cap* [G, lit., inhabitant of the Neanderthal, fr. *Neanderthal,* valley in western Germany] **:** NEANDERTHAL

[1]**ne·an·der·thal·ian** \≈¦≈¦≈lēən, -lyən\ *adj, usu cap* [*Neanderthal* (*man*) + *-ian*] **:** belonging or relating to Neanderthal man

[2]**neanderthalian** \"\ *n* -s *usu cap* **:** NEANDERTHAL

neanderthal man *also* **neandertal man** *n, usu cap N* [fr. *Neanderthal* (*Neandertal*), valley in western Germany where the remains were first discovered] **:** a type or race or species of Middle Paleolithic man (*Homo neanderthalensis* or *Palaeoanthropus neanderthalensis*) known from skeletal remains found at many sites in Europe, northern Africa, and western Asia usu. in association with Mousterian artifacts and distinguished by a stocky, heavily muscled build, proportionally short forearm and lower leg, and an extremely dolichocephalic skull with projecting occiput, heavy supraorbital torus, receding forehead, and undeveloped chin

[1]**ne·an·der·thal·oid** \≈¦≈¦≈,lȯid\ *adj, usu cap* [*Neanderthal* (*man*) + *-oid*] **:** like or relating to Neanderthal man or to the Neanderthal type of skull

²neanderthaloid \"\ *n* -s *often cap* **:** a specimen or a fossil type resembling Neanderthal man

ne·an·ic \nē'anik\ *adj* [Gk *neanikos* youthful, vigorous, fr. *neanias* young man + -*ikos* -ic; akin to Gk *neos* new — more at NEW] **:** YOUTHFUL; *specif* **:** constituting the pupal stage of insect development

ne·anthropic \¦nē+\ *also* **neo·anthropic** \¦nēō+\ *adj* [*ne-* + *anthrop-* + *-ic*] **:** of, like, or belonging to man of the surviving species (*Homo sapiens*) as distinguished from primitive hominids (as Neanderthal man or Pithecanthropus) that are known only through fossil remains ⟨~ man⟩

ne·an·thro·pi·nae \nē,an(t)thrə'pī,nē\ *n pl, usu cap* [NL, fr. *ne-* + *anthrop-* + *-inae*] **:** recent man (*Homo sapiens*) when treated by anthropologists as though distinct from more primitive species of the same genus at the subfamily level

¹neap \'nēp\ *adj* [ME *neep*, fr. OE *nēp* being at the stage of neap tide] **:** of, relating to, or constituting a neap tide

²neap \"\ *vi* -ED/-ING/-S [¹*neap*] *of a tide* **:** to tend toward the neap stage

³neap \"\ *n* -s [prob. fr. E dial. *nape*, *neap* piece of wood used to hold up the front or the tongue of a wagon, of Scand origin; akin to Norw dial. *neip* forked stick, hayfork, Icel *neip* space between two fingers, ON *hnippa* to prod — more at NIP] *NewEng* **:** the tongue of a cart

neaped *adj* [fr. past part. of ²*neap*] **:** left aground by the high water of a spring tide **:** STRANDED, GROUNDED

¹ne·a·pol·i·tan \¦nēə¦pälət°n *also* -ətən *or* -əd·ən\ *adj, usu cap* [L *neapolitanus*, fr. Gk *neapolitēs* citizen of Naples (fr. *Neapolis* Naples + *-itēs* -ite) + L *-anus* -an] **:** of, relating to, or characteristic of Naples, Italy, or its residents

²neapolitan \"\ *n* -s **1** *cap* **:** a native or resident of Naples, Italy **2** *usu cap* **:** NEAPOLITAN ICE CREAM

neapolitan ice cream *n, usu cap N* **:** a brick of from two to four layers of ice cream of different flavors usu. including lemon ice or orange ice

neapolitan mandolin *n, usu cap N* **:** a mandolin having four pairs of strings — compare MILANESE MANDOLIN

neapolitan ointment *n, usu cap N* **:** MERCURIAL OINTMENT

neapolitan sixth *n, usu cap N* **:** the first inversion of the major triad formed on the lowered second degree of the musical scale

neapolitan yellow *n, often cap N* **:** NAPLES YELLOW

neap rise *n* **:** the difference in level between low water at spring tide and high water at neap tide

neap tide *also* **neap** *n* -s **:** a tide of minimum range occurring at the first and the third quarters of the moon — compare SPRING TIDE

¹near *adv* [ME *ner*, *nere*, fr. OE *nēar* — more at ²NEAR] *obs* **:** NEARER

²near \'ni(ə)r, -iə\ *adv* -ER/-EST [ME *ner*, *nere*, partly fr. *ner*, *nere* nearer, fr. OE *nēar*, comparative of *nēah* nigh; partly fr. ON *nær* nearer, near, comp. of *nā-* near — more at NIGH] **1 :** at, within, or to a short distance ⟨don't shoot until they come ~⟩ or a short time ⟨sunset was drawing ~⟩ ⟨getting ~*er* to the true explanation⟩ **2 :** within little **:** ALMOST, NEARLY ⟨~ exhausted by the heat⟩ ⟨dark brown coming ~ to black⟩ ⟨not ~ so many⟩ ⟨came ~ to being the best speller in the class⟩ **3 a :** CLOSELY ⟨copy it as ~ as you can⟩ ⟨*near*-related terms⟩ ⟨*near*-actual mock battle⟩ **b :** INTIMATELY ⟨~ allied unto the duke —Shak.⟩ **4 :** THRIFTILY, STINGILY

³near \"\ *prep* [ME *ner*, *nere*, fr. *ner*, *nere* adv.] **:** not far distant from esp. in place, time, or degree **:** close to ⟨bombs fell ~ the building⟩ ⟨several beaches ~ the city⟩ ⟨came home ~ midnight⟩ ⟨seemed to be ~ death⟩ ⟨was in a state ~ collapse⟩

⁴near \"\ *adj* -ER/-EST [ME *ner*, *nere*, fr. *ner*, *nere*, adv.] **1 a :** closely akin ⟨~ relative⟩ **b :** closely or intimately related or associated ⟨~ relations⟩ ⟨~ affairs⟩ ⟨his ~*est* and dearest friend⟩ **2 a :** not far distant in time, place, or degree ⟨in the ~ future⟩ ⟨his ~*est* approach to success⟩ **:** ADJACENT, NIGH ⟨saw only his ~*est* neighbors⟩ ⟨hunting rabbits in the ~ fields⟩ **b :** that barely avoids, passes, or misses ⟨~ disaster⟩ ⟨~ miracle⟩ **:** CLOSE, NARROW ⟨he won the match but it was a very ~ thing⟩ **3 a :** being the closer of two ⟨~ side of the mountain⟩ — opposed to *far* **b :** being the left-hand one of a pair ⟨~ horse⟩ ⟨~ hind foot⟩ ⟨~ wheel of a cart⟩ — opposed to *off* **4 :** DIRECT, SHORT — used chiefly in the comparative or superlative ⟨four miles by the ~*est* road⟩ **5 :** CLOSEFISTED, PARSIMONIOUS, STINGY **6 a :** closely resembling or following ⟨a version very ~ the original⟩ **b :** approaching closely in extent or degree ⟨~ equivalent⟩ ⟨the ~*est* thing to perfect happiness⟩ **c :** approximating the genuine ⟨~ silk⟩ — often used in combination ⟨*near*-antique⟩

⁵near \"\ *vb* -ED/-ING/-S [²*near*] *vi* **:** to come closer in space or time ⟨every year when the baseball season ~*s*⟩ ~ *vt* **:** to draw near to **:** APPROACH ⟨ship was ~*ing* the dock⟩

⁶near *var of* NEER

nearabout \¦≠≠¦≠\ *also* **nearabouts** \¦≠≠¦≠\ *adv* [*nearabout* fr. ²*near* + *about*; *nearabouts* fr. ²*near* + *about* + *-s*] *chiefly South & Midland* **:** NEARLY, ALMOST

near-at-hand \¦≠≠¦≠\ *adj* [fr. *near at hand*, adv. phrase, fr. ME *nere at hand*] **:** NEARBY ⟨lumber from *near-at-hand* sources⟩ **:** IMMEDIATE ⟨concerned mostly with *near-at-hand* problems⟩

near beer *n* **:** any of various malt liquors resembling beer but considered nonalcoholic because containing less than ½ percent alcohol

¹nearby \¦≠¦≠\ *adv* [ME *nerby*, *nere by*, fr. *ner*, *nere* near + *by*, adv.] **1 :** near at hand **:** close by ⟨~ flows a river⟩ ⟨plane lands ~⟩ **2** *Scot* **:** NEARLY, THEREABOUTS ⟨sixty miles or ~⟩

²nearby \"\ *prep* [ME *nerby*, *nereby*, fr. *nerby*, *nere by*, adv.] **:** close to **:** hard by **:** NEAR ⟨put up attractive churches ~ a university —W.L.Sperry⟩

³nearby \"\ *adj* [¹*nearby*] **:** being or set close at hand **:** ADJACENT, NEIGHBORING ⟨water from a ~ river⟩

⁴nearby \'≠,≠\ *n* -s **:** something produced in the neighborhood — usu. used in pl. ⟨steady market on . . . colored eggs . . . but ~*s* were weaker —*Jour. of Commerce*⟩

ne·arctic \(')nē+\ *adj, usu cap* [*ne-* + *arctic*] **:** of, relating to, or being the biogeographic subregion that includes Greenland, arctic America, and the northern and mountainous parts of No. America and that is now usu. considered a subdivision of the Holarctic region

near eastern *adj, usu cap N&E* **:** of, relating to, or concerned with the countries of the Near East — used orig. of the Balkan States, later of the region included in the Ottoman Empire, and now often of all the countries of southeastern Europe, No. Africa, and southwestern Asia, sometimes including the entire area extending from Libya or Morocco, Ethiopia, and Somalia to Greece, Turkey, Iran, Afghanistan, and sometimes India; compare FAR EASTERN, MIDDLE EASTERN

near-fall \'≠¦≠\ *n* **:** a wrestling fall scoring usu. two points and achieved by pinning both shoulders to the mat for more than one but less than two seconds or by holding both shoulders to within two inches of the mat for at least two seconds

¹near hand *adv* [ME *nerhand*, *nerehand*, fr. *ner*, *nere* near + *hand*] *chiefly Scot* **1 :** close by **2 :** ALMOST, NEARLY

²near hand *prep* [ME *nerhand*, *nerehand*, fr. *nerhand*, *nerehand*, adv.] *chiefly Scot* **:** close to **:** next to **:** NEAR

³near hand *adj* [¹*near hand*] *chiefly Scot* **:** ADJACENT, NEAR

near·ish \'ni(ə)rish, -rēsh\ *adj* [⁴*near* + *-ish*] **:** rather near ⟨not really miserly, but ~⟩ ⟨a ~ escape from serious injury⟩

near-legged *U S usu* '≠¦legəd, *Brit usu* -gd\ *adj, of a horse* **:** having the two fore or two hind legs set close together; *esp* **:** having them so near that the feet interfere

near·ly \'ni(ə)rlē, -iəlē, -li\ *adv, sometimes* -ER/-EST [⁴*near* + *-ly*] **1 :** at close range **:** with careful scrutiny **2 a :** closely as to relationship, personal connection, or interest ⟨~ related⟩ **:** PARTICULARLY ⟨other things that concerned me more ~ to think of —W.H.Hudson †1922⟩ ⟨~ acquainted⟩ **b :** closely as to similarity ⟨~ identical⟩ ⟨two cities . . . grown to a status so ~ equal —*Amer. Guide Series: Minn.*⟩ **c :** with an approach to completeness or exactness **:** APPROXIMATELY ⟨such words are ~ meaningless⟩ ⟨lying ~ at right angles⟩ **d** *archaic* **:** closely as to location ⟨some danger does approach you ~ —Shak.⟩ **3 :** within a little **:** all but **:** ALMOST ⟨~ a year later⟩ ⟨~ a hundred dollars⟩ ⟨~ missed the train⟩

near-miss \'≠¦≠\ *n* **:** a miss (as with a bomb) close enough to the target to cause damage; *broadly* **:** something that falls just short of complete success

near-money \'≠¦≠≠\ *n* **:** demand or short-term obligations easily converted into cash or bank deposits **:** liquid assets

near·most \'≠,mōst *also chiefly Brit* -,məst\ *adj* [⁴*near* + *-most*] **:** NEAREST

near·ness *n* -ES [ME *nernes*, fr. *ner* near + *-nes* -ness] **:** the quality or state of being near: as **a :** close relationship or resemblance ⟨confused by the ~ of their names⟩ **b :** INTIMACY ⟨lost the ~ of the first months of their marriage⟩ **c :** proximity in space or time ⟨shyly aware of her ~ to the cowboy —Zane Grey⟩ **d :** FRUGALITY, STINGINESS

near point *n* **:** the point nearest the eye at which an object is accurately focused on the retina when the maximum degree of accommodation is employed, having an approximate value of 4 inches in infancy, 10 inches in the normal adult eye, and 13 inches in extreme old age — compare FAR POINT; see RANGE OF ACCOMMODATION

near-print \'≠¦≠\ *n* **:** a duplicating process (as typewriting and offset) that resembles typographical printing but does not involve the setting of metal type — called also *nomic*

nears *pres 3d sing of* NEAR

near seal *n* **:** a fur (as rabbit) dressed to simulate true seal

nearshore \'≠¦≠\ *adj* **:** extending seaward or lakeward an indefinite but generally short distance from a shore ⟨~ deposits⟩ ⟨~ current⟩

nearside \'≠¦≠\ *adj* [so called fr. the custom of approaching, mounting, or leading horses and cattle from the left side] *chiefly Brit* **:** being on the left-hand side ⟨never quite knows where his ~ wheels are —*New Statesman & Nation*⟩

nearsighted \'≠¦≠≠\ *adj* **:** seeing distinctly at short distances only **:** affected with myopia **:** SHORTSIGHTED, MYOPIC

near·sight·ed·ly *adv* **:** in a nearsighted manner ⟨peered ~ at the visitor —Josephine Pinckney⟩

near·sight·ed·ness *n* -ES **1 :** the quality or state of being nearsighted **2 :** MYOPIA

ne·ar·thro·sis \¦nē+\ *n* [NL, fr. *ne-* + *arthrosis*] **:** a false joint **:** PSEUDARTHROSIS

near wilt *n* **:** a disease of peas caused by a fungus (*Fusarium oxysporum pisi*) and differing from true wilt in that it is found only on scattered plants, develops more slowly, and causes brick red rather than orange coloration

ne·as·cus \nē'askəs\ *n* -ES [NL, fr. *ne-* + Gk *askos* sack, bladder — more at ASCUS] **:** BLACK GRUB

¹neat \'nēt, *usu* -ēd·+V\ *n, pl* **neat** [ME *net*, *neet*, fr. OE *nēat*; akin to OHG *nōz* head of cattle, ON *naut*; all fr. a prehistoric NGmc-WGmc noun akin to OE *nēotan* to make use of, enjoy, OHG *niozzan*, ON *njōta*, Goth *niutan*] **:** the common domestic bovine (*Bos taurus*); *also* **:** cattle of this or sometimes of other species of the genus *Bos* ⟨~ cattle⟩ ⟨~ stall⟩ ⟨~ leather⟩ ⟨a lion in a herd of ~ —Shak.⟩

²neat \"\ *adj* -ER/-EST [MF *net*, fr. L *nitidus* bright, lustrous, neat, fr. *nitēre* to shine; akin to MIr *niam* luster, beauty, OIr *nōib* holy, OPer *naiba-* beautiful] **1 :** BRIGHT, SHINING — used chiefly in the phrase *neat as a new pin* **2 a :** free from admixture or adulteration **:** UNDILUTED ⟨~ brandy⟩ ⟨a remark is not to be taken ~, but watered with the ideas of common sense —O.W.Holmes †1894⟩ **b :** made without sand ⟨~ cement⟩ ⟨~ plaster⟩ **c** *of raw silk* **:** free from loops, lumps, breaks, or hairiness **3** *obs* **:** finely or smartly dressed ⟨still to be ~, still to be dressed as if going to a feast —Ben Jonson⟩ **4 a :** free from whatever clutters, blurs, or confuses **:** having sharp outlines on even, smooth surfaces ⟨~ patch⟩ ⟨~ joint⟩ ⟨~ handwriting⟩ **b :** free from complication or irregularity or contradiction **:** simply or symmetrically arranged or constituted ⟨~ set of rules⟩ ⟨hated to have her ~ plans upset⟩ ⟨not all human problems have ~ solutions⟩ **c :** achieved or performed with precision and economy of effort **:** DEFT, ADROIT ⟨~ theft⟩ ⟨a ~ way of carving up a chicken⟩ ⟨mathematics . . . retains the ~ exactness of the surgeon's knife —Bertrand Russell⟩ **d :** CLEVER, INGENIOUS ⟨saw through his ~ little plan⟩ ⟨~ device for shelling peas⟩ **e :** capable of quick and accurate performance ⟨small ~ hands⟩ ⟨a *neat*-fingered worker⟩ **5 :** ORDERLY, TIDY ⟨~ housewife⟩ ⟨the cat is ~ in its habits⟩ **6 a :** CLEAR, NET ⟨~ profit⟩ **b :** GRATIFYING ⟨a ~ little fortune⟩ **7** *slang* **:** WONDERFUL, FINE, ADMIRABLE — used to express general enthusiastic approval ⟨~ bicycle⟩ ⟨we had a ~ time at the circus⟩

syn TIDY, TRIM, TRIG, SNUG, SHIPSHAPE, SPICK-AND-SPAN: NEAT may call forth suggestions of blended clearness and order, particularly the latter, freedom from clutter, jumble, disorder, confusion, complication, or adventitious addition ⟨she could be to the last degree slatternly. Or she could be as *neat* as a pin —Arnold Bennett⟩ ⟨as a rule he was *neat* in his person, but now his clothes were in disorder —W.S.Maugham⟩ ⟨*neat* minds, who prefer things in their proper places, ticketed and pigeon-holed —W.M.Dixon⟩ TIDY now commonly suggests a pleasing neatness and order diligently maintained ⟨he's always *tidy* without being smart; his coat is old and his trousers are uncreased, but they're both clean, and nothing's loose or torn —Richard Harrison⟩ ⟨he told me of his childhood in the *tidy* brick house, and of his mother's passionate orderliness —W.S. Maugham⟩ TRIM suggests neat smartness like that given by clean lines, good proportion, and compact, orderly arrangement ⟨a *trim* clipper ship⟩ ⟨spotless and *trim*, with shining spectacles and a white apron —Eden Phillpotts⟩ ⟨the sward was *trim* as any garden lawn —Alfred Tennyson⟩ TRIG may suggest jaunty neatness ⟨so *trig* in fashionable clothes that he made me feel awkward and uncomfortable —Irving Bacheller⟩ SNUG may suggest trim neatness with compact order in stowage and fine firmness of line and construction ⟨a *snug* little ship⟩ ⟨Farmer Matson reached the *snug* little cabin which was his headquarters —F.V.W.Mason⟩ SHIPSHAPE implies a tidiness and order befitting a ship likely to undergo sudden peril or difficulty ⟨in *shipshape* order⟩ ⟨leaving the account in *shipshape* condition⟩ SPICK-AND-SPAN suggests the brightness and freshness of the completely clean ⟨no spots came on his clothes. No slovenly habits crept upon him. He was always *spick-and-span* —W.A.White⟩ ⟨the automobile owner who likes to keep his car *spick-and-span* between washings —*New Yorker*⟩

³neat *vt* -ED/-ING/-S **1** *obs* **:** to make neat **:** TRIM, GROOM **2** *obs* **:** ⁴NET

⁴neat \'nēt, *usu* -ēd·+V\ *adv* **:** NEATLY

neat·en \'nēt°n\ *vt* **neatened; neatened; neatening** \-t-(°)niŋ\ **neatens** [²*neat* + *-en*] **1 :** to set in order **:** make neat ⟨~*ing* the books in a low bookcase —E.B.White⟩ **2 :** to finish (as a piece of sewing) carefully ⟨oversewing edges to ~ them⟩

neater *comparative of* NEAT

neatest *superlative of* NEAT

neath \'nēth, -ēth\ *prep* [by shortening fr. *aneath* & *beneath*] *dial* **:** BENEATH

neat-handed \'≠¦≠≠\ *adj* **:** neat and deft in handling things **:** DEXTEROUS — **neat-hand·ed·ly** *adv* — **neat-hand·ed·ness** *n* -ES

neat·herd \'nēt,hərd, -həd, -əid\ *n* [ME *netherde*, fr. *net* head of cattle + *herde* herdsman — more at NEAT, HERD] **:** HERDSMAN, COWHERD

neath·most \'≠,mōst *also chiefly Brit* -,məst\ *adj* [*neath* + *-most*] *Scot* **:** LOWEST

neat line *n* [²*neat*] **1 :** the line to which the face of a masonry wall is supposed to conform disregarding minor irregularities **2 :** the innermost of a series of lines that frame a map or mechanical drawing

neat·ly *adv* [²*neat* + *-ly*] **:** in a neat manner ⟨hair ~ combed⟩ **:** TIDILY ⟨~ kept room⟩ **:** DEFTLY, CLEVERLY ⟨~ removed the bones from the fish⟩

neat·ness *n* -ES **:** the quality or state of being neat

neat's-foot oil \'≠,≠-\ *n* [¹*neat*] **:** a pale yellow fatty oil made by boiling the feet and shinbones esp. of cattle and used chiefly as a leather dressing and fine lubricant

neat soap *n* [²*neat*] **:** molten soap formed during manufacture esp. after fitting and settling out of nigre and lye and used for making bars, chips, or powders

neb \'neb\ *n* -s [ME *neb*, *nebb*, fr. OE; akin to ON *nef* beak, nose, MLG *nebbe*, and prob. to OHG *snabul* beak] **1 :** the beak of a bird or tortoise **:** BILL; *also* **:** a person's mouth **2 :** something suggestive of a bill esp. in being jutting or pointed; *specif* **:** NOSE 1 **3 :** the pointed or narrowed end of a thing **:** TIP; *specif* **:** the point of a pen or pencil **4 :** ¹EAR 4h

ne·ba·lia \nə'bālēə\ *n, cap* [NL] **:** a genus of small marine crustaceans (order Nebaliacea) having the body enclosed in a bivalved carapace, the thoracic feet leaflike, the abdominal feet biramous, and the abdomen composed of eight segments — **ne·ba·li·an** \-ēən\ *adj or n* — **ne·ba·li·oid** \-ē,ȯid\ *adj or n*

ne·ba·li·a·cea \≠,≠≠'āsh(ē)ə\ *n pl, cap* [NL, fr. *Nebalia* + *-acea*] **:** a small order of marine crustaceans (division Phyllocarida) comprising *Nebalia* and a few other genera of recent or extinct forms

nebbed \'nebd\ *adj* **:** having a neb

neb·by \'nebē, -bi\ *adj* -ER/-EST [*neb* + *-y*] **1** *dial* **:** rudely inquisitive **:** MEDDLESOME **2** *dial Brit* **:** sharp-natured **:** SPITEFUL

ne·bel \'nā¦bəl, 'nē¦\ *or* **ne·vel** \¦vəl\ *n* -s [Heb *nēbhel*] **:** NABLA

ne·ben·kern \'nābən,kərn\ *n* -s [G, fr. *neben-* secondary, accessory (fr. *neben* beside, next to) + *kern* kernel, nucleus] **:** an extranuclear organized body of the spermatid possibly derived from the chondriosomes — compare ACROSOME

neb-neb \'neb,neb\ *n* -s [Senegalese] **:** BABUL 2

ne·bras·ka \nə'braskə, -raas-\ *adj, usu cap* [*Nebraska*, state in the central U. S., fr. *Nebraska*, former name for the Platte river] **:** of or from the state of Nebraska ⟨*Nebraska* farmers⟩ **:** of the kind or style prevalent in Nebraska **:** NEBRASKAN

¹ne·bras·kan \-kən\ *also* **ne·bras·ki·an** \-kēən\ *adj, usu cap* [*Nebraska* state + E *-an*, *-ian*] **1 :** of, relating to, or characteristic of Nebraska or Nebraskans **2 :** belonging to the first glacial stage during the glacial epoch in No. America

²nebraskan \"\ *also* **nebraskian** \"\ *n* -s *cap* **:** a native or resident of the state of Nebraska

neb·ris \'nebrəs\ *n* -ES [L, fr. Gk, fr. *nebros* fawn] **:** a fawn skin shown in classic art as worn by Dionysus, Silenus, satyrs, and bacchanals

neb·u·chad·nez·zar \,neb(y)əkəd'nezə(r)\ *n* -s *usu cap* [after *Nebuchadnezzar* II †562 B.C. king of Babylon] **:** an oversize wine bottle holding about 20 quarts ⟨a ~ of champagne⟩

neb·u·la \'nebyələ\ *n, pl* **nebu·las** \-ləz\ *or* **nebu·lae** \-,lē, -,lī\ [NL, fr. L, mist, cloud; akin to OE *nifol* cloudy, dark, OS *nebal* fog, OHG *nebul* fog, ON *njōl* darkness, night, Gk *nephelē*, *nephos* cloud, Skt *nabhas* mist] **1 a :** any of many immense bodies of highly rarefied gas or dust in the interstellar space of our own Milky Way and other galaxies that when located in our own Milky Way are observed by absorption of light from objects farther away be observed as a dark cloud or may by reflection or reemission of light from associated nearby stars be observed as a bright cloud **b :** GALAXY; *specif* **:** a galaxy outside the Milky Way galaxy — see PLANETARY NEBULA, SPIRAL NEBULA **2 a :** a white spot or a slight opacity of the cornea **3 :** a liquid preparation intended for medicinal spraying

neb·u·lar \-lə(r)\ *adj* [NL *nebula* + E *-ar*] **:** of or relating to a nebula **:** of the nature of or resembling a nebula **:** CLOUDY

nebular hypothesis *n* **:** a hypothesis in astronomy: the solar system has evolved from a hot gaseous nebula

neb·u·lat·ed \'nebyə,lād·əd\ *adj* [LL *nebulatus* (past part. of *nebulare* to cloud, obscure, fr. L *nebula* mist, cloud) + E *-ed*] **:** indistinctly marked **:** CLOUDED, CLOUDY

neb·u·lé \¦nebyə¦lā, -¦lē\ *also* **neb·u·ly** \'nebyəlē\ *adj* [MF *nebulé*, fr. L *nebula* + F *-é* -ate, adj. suffix (fr. L *-atus* -ate)] **1 :** composed of successive short curves made to resemble a cloud — used of a heraldic line by which an ordinary or subordinary may be bounded **2** *of a molding* **:** consisting of an overhanging band the lower projecting edge of which conforms in shape to a continuous undulating curve

ne·bu·li·um \nə'byülēəm, ne'-\ *n* -s [NL, fr. *nebula* + *-ium*] **:** a hypothetical chemical element formerly inferred from certain lines in the spectra of nebulae now believed to arise from transitions in oxygen and nitrogen that are forbidden under ordinary laboratory conditions

neb·u·li·za·tion \,nebyələ'zāshən, -,lī'z-\ *n* -s **:** reduction (as of a medicinal solution) to a mist, spray, or vapor

neb·u·lize \'≠≠,līz\ *vt* -ED/-ING/-S [NL *nebula* + E *-ize*] **:** to reduce (as a medicinal solution) to a fine spray **:** AEROSOLIZE — **neb·u·liz·er** \-zə(r)\ *n* -s

neb·u·lose \-,lōs\ *adj* [L *nebulosus* — more at NEBULOUS] **:** NEBULOUS

neb·u·los·i·ty \,≠≠'läsəd·ē, -ətē, -i\ *n* -ES [F or LL; F *nébulosité*, fr. LL *nebulositat-*, *nebulositas*, fr. L *nebulosus* + *-itat*, *-itas* -ity] **1 :** the quality or state of being nebulous **:** CLOUDINESS **2 :** nebulous matter **:** NEBULA ⟨faintly luminous ~ is abundant in the vicinity of Orion —R.H.Baker⟩

neb·u·lous \'≠≠ləs\ *adj* [L *nebulosus*, fr. *nebula* mist, cloud + *-osus* -ous, -ose — more at NEBULA] **1** *archaic* **:** full of clouds **:** CLOUDY, FOGGY **2 a :** lacking clarity of feature or sharpness of outline **:** HAZY, INDISTINCT ⟨~ memory⟩ ⟨~ line between confidence and overconfidence —*Wall Street Jour.*⟩ **b :** vaguely defined **:** poorly grasped **:** dimly realized ⟨~ hopes and fears⟩ ⟨~ social values —A.H.MacCormick⟩ **3 :** not transparent **:** TURBID, CLOUDED **4 :** of, relating to, or resembling a nebula **:** NEBULAR — **neb·u·lous·ly** *adv* — **neb·u·lous·ness** *n* -ES

nebulous cluster *n* **:** a cluster of stars containing or enveloped in nebulosity

ne·ca·tor \nə'kād·ə(r)\ *n* [NL, fr. LL, killer, fr. L *necatus* (past part. of *necare* to kill, fr. *nec-*, *nex* violent death) + *-or* — more at NOXIOUS] **1** *cap* **:** a common genus of hookworms that have buccal teeth resembling flat plates, that include internal parasites of man and various other mammals, and that are prob. of African origin though first identified in No. America — compare ANCYLOSTOMA **2** -s **:** any hookworm of the genus *Necator*

nec·es·sar \'nesəsər\ *Scot var of* NECESSARY

nec·es·sar·i·an \¦nesə¦serēən -sa(a)r-, -sär-\ *n or adj* [²*necessary* + *-an*] **:** NECESSITARIAN

nec·es·sar·i·an·ism \,≠≠'≠≠ə,nizəm\ *n* -s [¹*necessarian* + *-ism*] **:** NECESSITARIANISM

nec·es·sar·i·ly \¦≠≠¦serəlē, -li\ *adv* [ME, fr. *necessary* + *-ly*] **1 :** in such a way that it cannot be otherwise **:** of necessity **:** INEVITABLY, UNAVOIDABLY ⟨the audience was ~ small⟩ ⟨political philosophy ~ implies the attitude of the philosopher toward politics —Hannah Arendt⟩ ⟨occupying precious space with a ~ lengthy chapter —Peter Heaton⟩ **2 :** as a necessary result or consequence ⟨their whole political outlook was ~ determined by this condition —G.L.Dickinson⟩ ⟨inconsistency, flat contradiction, and irrelevance ~ prevent an armed doctrine from achieving great success —D.W.Brogan⟩

nec·es·sar·i·ness \-rēnəs, -rin-\ *n* -ES *archaic* **:** the quality or state of being necessary **:** NECESSITY

¹nec·es·sary \'nesə,serē, -ri, *in rapid speech* 'nes,se-\ *n* -ES [ME *necessaries* (pl.), fr. L *necessaria*, fr. neut. pl. of *necessarius* necessary (adj.)] **1 a** (1) **necessaries** *pl* **:** items (as of food, clothing, shelter, medical care, equipment or furnishing) that cannot be done without **:** things that must be had (as for the preservation and reasonable enjoyment of life) **:** ESSENTIALS ⟨was provided with at least the *necessaries* of life⟩ ⟨gave away so much that he could only have kept just enough to keep himself in bare *necessaries* —Flora Thompson⟩ ⟨household *necessaries*⟩; *specif* **:** such items as are essential to the proper maintenance and support of those (as married women) who are legally dependent or those (as infants, children, the mentally ill) who are legally incompetent (2) **:** one such essential item ⟨salt is a ~⟩ **b :** whatever is essential for some purpose ⟨supplies of the ~ were hard to come by —Brian James⟩; *esp* **:** MONEY — used with *the* **2** *chiefly NewEng* **:** PRIVY 2

²necessary \"\ *adj* [ME *necessarie*, fr. L *necessarius*, fr. *necesse* unavoidable, inevitable, necessary (fr. *ne* not + *-cesse*, fr. *cedere* to withdraw) + *-arius* -ary — more at NO, CEDE] **1 a :** that must be by reason of the nature of things **:** that cannot be otherwise by reason of inherent qualities **:** that is or exists or comes to be by reason of the nature of being and that cannot be or exist or come to be in any other way **:** that is determined and fixed and inevitable ⟨death is a ~ feature of the human condition⟩ ⟨it is ~ that a whole be greater than any of its parts⟩ ⟨patience . . . is a ~ mark of the liberal mind —John Dewey⟩ **b :** of, relating to, or having the character of something that is logically required or logically inevitable or that cannot be denied without involving contradiction ⟨a ~ judgment⟩ ⟨a ~ relation between two things⟩ ⟨a ~ truth⟩ ⟨a ~ conclusion⟩ — opposed to *contingent* **c :** that is inevitably fixed or determined or produced by a previous condition of things ⟨a ~ result⟩ ⟨the ~ outcome of the affair⟩ **d** (1) **:** that is produced in a mechanical way through conditioning (as by previous actions, experiences) so as to be devoid of freedom of the will ⟨a ~ submission to evil⟩ (2) **:** that is driven by circumstances or other outside forces so as to have little or no independence of volition : not exercising free choice : acting under compulsion ⟨the ~ agent of some crimes⟩ **2** : that cannot be done without : that must be done or had : absolutely required : ESSENTIAL, INDISPENSABLE ⟨food is ~ for all⟩ ⟨was ~ to her peace of mind⟩ ⟨the ~ secrecy of my trip —F.D. Roosevelt⟩ ⟨the ~ conditions of freedom —F.C.Neff⟩ ⟨a ~ tool⟩ ⟨a ~ law⟩ ⟨took all ~ steps⟩ ⟨a ~ act⟩ **syn** see NEEDFUL

necessary condition *n* : CONDITION 2a(3)

necessary deposit *n* : a deposit arising where the owner of property entrusts it to another in a sudden emergency or overwhelming calamity (as in case of fire or earthquake)

necessary house *n, chiefly dial* : PRIVY

necessary improvement *n* : an improvement to property that is made to prevent its deterioration

necessary woman *n, archaic* : a personal maid

¹**ne·ces·si·tar·i·an** \nə¦sesə¦terēən, -ta(a)r-, -tār-\ *n* -s [*necessity* + *-arian*] : one that accepts or advocates necessitarianism — contrasted with *libertarian*

²**necessitarian** \"\ *adj* : of or relating to a necessitarian or necessitarianism

ne·ces·si·tar·i·an·ism \-ə,nizəm\ *n* -s : the theory or doctrine that results follow by invariable sequence from causes : the doctrine of philosophical necessity : DETERMINISM

¹**ne·ces·si·tate** \-ˈ==,tāt, *usu* -ād.+V\ *vt* -ED/-ING/-S [ML *necessitatus*, past part. of *necessitare* to compel, constrain, fr. L *necessitas* necessity — more at NECESSITY] **1** : to make necessary: as **a** (1) : to make inevitable : make unavoidable ⟨difficult circumstances seemed to ~ a certain gloominess on his part⟩ (2) : to involve as an essential element or inevitable outcome or unavoidable consequence ⟨goodness ~*s* a sharing of itself⟩ ⟨his private practice grew to large proportions, *necessitating* the employment of assistants —G.M.Lewis b.1899⟩ **b** : to cause to be required as an indispensable preparation, condition, or accompaniment ⟨the complexity of the problem ~*s* careful thought and good judgment⟩ ⟨world changes which *necessitated* a new approach —Bruce Bliven b.1889⟩ **2** : to put under the obligation of : force into : CONSTRAIN, COMPEL ⟨was *necessitated* to choose some other route⟩ **3** *archaic* : to reduce to a state of necessity : cause to be hard up

²**necessitate** *adj* [ML *necessitatus*] *obs* : forced by necessity ⟨being ~ to leave London —Anne Halkett⟩

ne·ces·si·ta·tion \=,==ˈtāshən\ *n* -s : the act of necessitating or condition of being necessitated ⟨the absence of ~ by the past —A.C.Ewing⟩ ⟨is good by free choice, not ~ —Nicholas Rescher⟩

ne·ces·si·tous \=ˈsesəd·əs, -ətəs\ *adj* [F *nécessiteux*, fr. *nécessité* necessity (fr. L *necessitat-, necessitas*) + *-eux* -ous] **1 a** : hard up : reduced to a state of marked want : NEEDY ⟨was a ~ widower with a marriageable daughter —Norman Douglas⟩ ⟨the most ~ members of the community —T.B. Macaulay⟩ **b** : STRAITENED ⟨~ circumstances⟩ **2** : URGENT, PRESSING ⟨except for the most ~ reasons —Walter Goodman⟩ **3** : that is essential by reason of circumstances : that is unavoidable ⟨will be unable to do its ~ financing —Allan Sproul⟩ **syn** see POOR

ne·ces·si·tude \-ə,tüd, -ə·,tyüd\ *n* -s [L *necessitudo*, fr. *necesse* necessary + *-i-* + *-tudo* -tude] *archaic* : NECESSITY

¹**ne·ces·si·ty** \nəˈsesəd·ē, -ətē, -ˈsestē, -i\ *n* -ES [ME *necessite*, fr. MF *necessité*, fr. L *necessitat-, necessitas*, fr. *necesse* necessary + *-itat-, -itas* -ity — more at NECESSARY] **1** : the quality or state or fact of being necessary: as **a** : a condition arising out of circumstances that compels to a certain course of action ⟨as if there were some ~ for being together that only the two of them understood —C.B.Flood⟩ **b** : INEVITABLENESS, UNAVOIDABILITY ⟨the ~ of death⟩ **c** : great or absolute need : INDISPENSABILITY ⟨the ~ of full and fair news service —F.L. Mott⟩ ⟨the ~ of civil, academic, and scientific liberty —George Soule⟩ **d** (1) : absence of physical or moral liberty : physical or moral compulsion ⟨did it, not because he wanted to, but by ~⟩ ⟨making a virtue of ~⟩ (2) : constraint or compulsion arising out of the natural constitution of things : impossibility of a contrary order or condition of things ⟨submitting to the ~ imposed by the physical laws of the universe⟩ ⟨logical ~⟩ ⟨physical ~⟩ **2** : the quality or state or fact of being in difficulties or in need ⟨came to help them in their ~⟩; *esp* : POVERTY ⟨was reduced to the most abject ~⟩ **3** : something that is necessary : REQUIREMENT, REQUISITE ⟨daily *necessities*⟩ ⟨is a ~ for happy living⟩ ⟨the *necessities* of life⟩ — **of necessity** *adv* : NECESSARILY ⟨something that *of necessity* must be so⟩

²**necessity** \"\ *adj* [*necessity (money)*] : consisting of, used as, or designed for necessity money ⟨a ~ coin⟩

necessity money *n* : money (as a coin, token, note) issued for a period of emergency (as a war, siege, financial crisis) and typically consisting of substitute materials

¹**neck** \ˈnek\ *n* -s [ME *necke, nekke*, fr. OE *hnecca*; akin to OHG *hnac* nape of the neck, ON *hnakki* nape of the neck, OE *hnutu* nut—more at NUT] **1 a** (1) : the usu. constricted part of an animal that connects the head with the body; *specif* : the cervical region of a vertebrate (2) : the part of a tapeworm immediately behind the scolex from which new proglottides are produced — see ECHINOCOCCUS illustration (3) : the siphon of a bivalve mollusk (as a clam) — not used technically **b** : the part of a garment that covers or is next to the neck; *esp* : NECKLINE **2** : a relatively narrow or constricted part joining two other parts or located at an end and suggestive of a neck: as **a** (1) : the narrowed part of a bottle running from the body of the bottle to the mouth (2) : the slender end of a gourd or of some other fruits **b** : the narrow part of the uterus : CERVIX **c** (1) : COLLET 3 (2) : the tapering distal part of an archegonium (3) : the terminal usu. elongated part of a perithecium or pycnidium in some fungi (4) : the part of the trunk of a tree or of the stem of a shrub that is at the surface of the soil (5) : the restricted part of the leaf cluster just above the bulb of an onion **d** (1) : GORGERIN (2) : the narrow part of a column or baluster shaft just below the capital **e** : a part reduced in circumference (as the part forming the journal of a shaft) formed by a groove around and usu. near the end of an object **f** (1) : the slender part of a cascabel between the knob and the fillet (2) : the part of a cannon immediately behind the swell of the muzzle (3) : the cylindrical part of a cartridge case that has an inside diameter about equal to the projectile diameter **g** : the part of a stringed musical instrument which extends from the body and to which are attached the fingerboard and the strings **h** : BEARD 4d **i** : a thread shank for a button **3 a** : a narrow stretch of land (as an isthmus, cape, promontory, or mountain pass) **b** (1) : a narrow body of water between two larger bodies : STRAIT (2) : a narrow current flowing seaward through incoming surf **c** : a mass of solidified massive or fragmental lava or igneous rock that fills or formerly filled a conduit leading upward to a volcanic vent or a laccolith **d** : a narrow vertically elongated ore body **4** : a brick wall that is usu. 60 bricks long, 24 to 30 high, and 3 thick placed on each side of an upright or double battering wall to form a clamp **5 a** : the approximate length of the neck of a horse plus that of the head ⟨won by a ~⟩ **b** : a narrow margin of victory ⟨won the election campaign by a ~⟩ **6** : WAKE, TRAIL — used with *in, on, upon* ⟨this bad news followed on the ~ of the letter⟩ — **in the neck** *adv* : to a severe or painful extent : without sparing ⟨really got it *in the neck* for his impudence⟩

²**neck** \"\ *vb* -ED/-ING/-S *vt* **1 a** : to strike sharply (as with the side of the hand) on the neck **b** : BEHEAD **c** : to twist or pull the neck of (as of a fowl) so as to kill **2** : to reduce the diameter of esp. by making a groove around — often used with *down* or *in* ⟨~ down a cylinder⟩ ⟨~*ing* down a cartridge case⟩ **3** *chiefly West* : to tie (animals) loosely together by means of something (as a rope, thong) fastened about the neck **4** : to hold tightly and fondle and kiss amorously ⟨~*ing* the co-eds on the steps of the lecture hall —*Time*⟩ ~ *vi* **1** : to engage in fondling and kissing ⟨a young couple ~*ing* on the park bench⟩ **2** : to undergo a constriction or reduction of cross section — used esp. of a solid rod subjected to tension beyond the yield value

³**neck** \"\ *n* -s [origin unknown] *dial Eng* : the last sheaf of grain cut often with traditional ceremonies at harvest time and sometimes decorated and preserved

neck ail *n, chiefly NewEng* : a cobalt deficiency disease of sheep and cattle

neck and crop *adv* : with brisk dispatch and completeness : SUMMARILY ⟨turned her out into the street *neck and crop* —W.S.Maugham⟩

neck and heels *adv* **1** : neck and crop **2** : SECURELY ⟨tied him up *neck and heels*⟩

neck and neck *adj* (*or adv*) : very close together (as in a race, contest, campaign, game) so that the winner is not yet certain ⟨were *neck and neck* in the polls through most of the election campaign⟩

neckatee *n* -s [¹*neck* + *-atee* (origin unknown)] *obs* : NECKERCHIEF

neckband \ˈ=,=\ *n* [ME *nekbande*, fr. *nek, nekke* neck + *bande* strip — more at BAND] **1** : a usu. ornamental band worn about the neck **2 a** : the part of a garment that encircles the neck and finishes the neckline ⟨the ~ of a sweater⟩ **b** : the band of a shirt to which a collar is sewed or buttoned

neckbreaking \ˈ=¦==\ *adj* : BREAKNECK

neck canal cell *n* [trans. of G *halskanalzelle*] : one of the cells in the neck of an archegonium

neck cell *n* : one of the sterile cells constituting the jacket that surrounds the canal cells in an archegonium

neckcloth \ˈ=,=\ *n* **1 a** : a large folded ornamental cloth formerly worn loosely about the neck by men **b** : NECKERCHIEF **2** *archaic* : NECKTIE

neck-deep \ˈ=¦=\ *adj* (*or adv*) : sunk or absorbed or involved in something almost to the point of total submersion ⟨was *neck-deep* in trouble —*Time*⟩ : up to the limit of involvement ⟨fell *neck-deep* into difficulties⟩

necked \ˈnekt\ *adj* [¹*neck* + *-ed*] **1** : having a neck or necks of a specified kind or number ⟨red-*necked*⟩ ⟨short-*necked*⟩ ⟨two-*necked*⟩ **2** : having a neck ⟨~ barnacles⟩

neck·er \ˈnekə(r)\ *n* -s [¹*neck* + *-er*] : one that stitches around the neckline of neckties

neck·er·cher \ˈnekə(r)chə(r)\ *n* -s [¹*neck* + *kercher*] *chiefly dial* : NECKERCHIEF

neck·er·chief \-chəf, -(,)chif, -,chēf\ *n, pl* **neckerchiefs** *also* **neckerchieves** \-fs, -vz; *see pl at* HANDKERCHIEF\ [ME *nekkerchef*, fr. *nekke* neck + *kerchef* kerchief — more at NECK, KERCHIEF] : a folded ornamental square of cloth worn about the neck like a scarf or worn esp. by sailors as part of a uniform

neck handkerchief *n, archaic* : NECKCLOTH

neckhole \ˈ=,=\ *n* : an opening in a garment for the head and neck to pass through

neck·ing \ˈnekiŋ, -ēŋ\ *n* -s [¹*neck* + *-ing*] **1** : a small molding near the top of a column or pilaster **2** : GORGERIN

¹**neck·lace** \ˈnekləs\ *n* [¹*neck* + *lace*] **1 a** (1) : a string of beads or of other small objects (as precious stones) that is worn about the neck as an ornament (2) : a chain or band usu. of metal often specially decorated (as with enamel work, precious stones) and worn about the neck as an ornament **b** (1) : a trimming or decoration that resembles or is suggestive of a necklace (2) : a stripe of different color about the neck of an animal **c** : a series of identical or similar things arranged or lying in a circular or semicircular pattern or otherwise linked together like a necklace ⟨with a ~ of barbed wire gun pits ringing it about —T.H.White b.1915⟩ ⟨a ~ of islands⟩ **2** : a rope or chain fitted around a mast near the top to hold hanging blocks

²**necklace** \"\ *vt* : to provide with or as if with a necklace ⟨*necklaced* the statue with a wreath of flowers⟩ ~ *vi* : to become formed into or as if into a necklace ⟨boats *necklacing* about the pier⟩

necklace poplar *n* [so called fr. the arrangement of its pods] : BALSAM POPLAR

necklace tree *n* [so called fr. the use of its seeds as beads] : a tree of the genus *Ormosia*; *esp* : JUMBY BEAN 1a

necklaceweed \ˈ==,=\ *n* [so called fr. its pearly white berries] **1** : WHITE BANEBERRY **2** : FALSE GROMWELL

neck·less \ˈnekləs\ *adj* : having no neck

neck·let \-lət\ *n* -s [¹*neck* + *-let*] **1** : an ornamental piece (as of fur) worn about the neck **2** : a close-fitting necklace

necklike \ˈ=,=\ *adj* : resembling a neck

neckline \ˈ=,=\ *n* **1** : the line formed by the neck opening of a garment ⟨the little pleated frill that finished the ~ of her gown —Edna Ferber⟩ **2** : the line formed by the edge of the hair across the back of the neck

neckmold \ˈ=,=\ *or* **neck molding** *n* : NECKING

neck of the woods 1 : a settlement in a wooded country **2** : NEIGHBORHOOD, REGION ⟨haven't been in that *neck of the woods* for a long time⟩

neck or nothing *also* **neck or nought** *adv* : with complete abandon and recklessness ⟨launched my scheme *neck or nought* —W.C.Hazlitt⟩

neckpiece \ˈ=,=\ *n* **1** : an article of apparel (as a fur) worn about the neck **2** : MIDDLE PIECE

neck-rein \ˈ=,=\ *vi, of a saddle horse* : to respond to the pressure of a rein on one side of the neck by turning in the opposite direction ~ *vt* : to guide or direct (a horse) by pressures of the rein on the neck

neck rot *n* : a disease of onions caused by a fungus of the genus *Botrytis* and marked by rotting of the leaf cluster just above the bulb

necks *pl of* NECK, *pres 3d sing of* NECK

necktie \ˈ=,=\ *n* : a rather long narrow length of soft material (as silk or wool) worn about the neck usu. under a collar with a knot, loop, or bow tied in front and with the two ends usu. falling free vertically; *esp* : FOUR-IN-HAND — compare BOW TIE

necktie party *n, slang* : LYNCHING, HANGING ⟨were threatened with mob violence, with tar and feathering and a *necktie party* —Mari Sandoz⟩

neck-verse \ˈ=,=\ *n* [ME *neke verse*; fr. the possibility of its saving the accused person's neck] : a verse usu. consisting of the first lines of a Latin version of the 51st psalm formerly set before an accused person claiming benefit of clergy so that the person might vindicate his claim by an intelligent reading aloud of the verse before examiners

neckwear \ˈ=,=\ *n* : articles of clothing worn about the neck (as ties, collars, scarfs)

neckweed \ˈ=,=\ *n* [so called fr. its use for treating scrofula] : an American speedwell (*Veronica peregrina*)

necr- *or* **necro-** *comb form* [LL, fr. Gk *nekr-, nekro-*, fr. *nekros* dead body, dead person — more at NOXIOUS] **1 a** : those that are dead : the dead : corpses ⟨*necrophilism*⟩ **b** : one that is dead : corpse ⟨*necropsy*⟩ **2** : death ⟨*necrobiosis*⟩ : conversion to dead tissue : atrophy ⟨*necrosis*⟩ **3** : extinct : fossil ⟨*necrotype*⟩

nec·ro \ˈne(,)krō\ *n* -s [by shortening] : NECROTIC ENTERITIS

nec·ro·bacillary \¦nekrō+\ *adj* [NL *necrobacillosis* + E *-ary*] : of, relating to, or marked by necrobacillosis

nec·ro·bacillosis \"+\ *n* [NL *necrophorus* & *necrophorum* (specific epithets of *Sphaerophorus necrophorus* & *Necrobacterium necrophorum* respectively; fr. *necr-* + *-phorus* or *-phorum*, neut. of *-phorus*) + *bacillosis*] : infection with or disease caused by a bacterium (*Sphaerophorus necrophorus* or *Necrobacterium necrophorum*) that is either localized (as in foot rot) or disseminated through the body of an affected mammal and that is characterized by inflammation and ulcerative or necrotic lesions — compare BULLNOSE, CALF DIPHTHERIA, QUITTOR

ne·cro·bia \nəˈkrōbēə, neˈ-\ *n, cap* [NL, fr. *necr-* + *-bia*] : a genus of widely distributed beetles that include the copra beetle, are related to the family Cleridae, and feed on animal and cereal products

nec·ro·bi·o·sis \¦nekrō,bīˈōsəs\ *n, pl* **necrobioses** \-,sēz\ [NL, fr. *necr-* + *-biosis*] : death of a cell or group of cells within a tissue whether normal (as in various epithelial tissues) or part of a pathologic process — compare NECROSIS

nec·ro·biotic \"+\ *adj* [fr. NL *necrobiosis*, after such pairs as NL *neurosis*: E *neurotic*] : of, relating to, or being in a state of necrobiosis

nec·ro·gen·ic \¦==ˈjenik\ *or* **ne·crog·e·nous** \nəˈkräjənəs, neˈ-\ *adj* [*necr-* + *-genic, -genous*] : relating to, living in, or coming from carrion

ne·crog·ra·pher \nəˈkrägrəfə(r), neˈ-\ *n* -s [*necr-* + *-grapher*] : NECROLOGIST

ne·crol·a·try \-ˈkrälə·trē, -ri\ *n* -ES [LGk *nekrolatreia*, fr. Gk *nekr-* necr- + *-latreia* -latry] : superstitious worship or veneration of the dead

nec·ro·log·i·cal \¦nekrə¦läjəkəl\ *also* **nec·ro·log·ic** \-jik\ *adj* : of, relating to, or having the nature of a necrology ⟨a ~ notice in a newspaper⟩ — **nec·ro·log·i·cal·ly** \-jək(ə)lē\ *adv*

ne·crol·o·gist \nəˈkräləjəst, neˈ-\ *n* -s : one that writes or compiles a necrology

nec·ro·logue \ˈnekrə,lȯg *also* -läg\ *n* -s [alter. (influenced by *catalogue*) of *necrology*] : NECROLOGY

ne·crol·o·gy \nəˈkräləjē, neˈ-, -ji\ *n* -ES [NL *necrologium*, fr. *necr-* + *-logium* (as in *eulogium* eulogy, epitaph) — more at EULOGY] **1 a** : an ecclesiastical or monastic register in which are recorded the dates of death of persons (as benefactors) closely associated with the church or monastery where the register is kept **b** : a list of persons that have died at or within a certain time ⟨the publication carried a ~ of contributors who had died during the year⟩ **2** [F *nécrologie*, fr. NL *necrologium*] : a death notice : OBITUARY

nec·ro·man·cer \ˈnekrə,man(t)sə(r)\ *n* -s [alter. (influenced by LL *necromantia* necromancy) of *nigromancer*, fr. ME, fr. MF, fr. *nigromance* necromancy + *-er*] : one that practices necromancy

¹**nec·ro·manc·ing** \-,man(t)siŋ, -sēŋ\ *adj* [*necromancer* + *-ing*] : practicing necromancy

²**necromancing** \"\ *n* -s : the practice of necromancy

nec·ro·man·cy \-n(t)sē, -si\ *n* -ES [alter. (influenced by LL *necromantia*) of ME *nigromancie*, fr. MF *nigromance, nigromancie*, fr. ML *nigromantia*, by folk etymology (influence of L *nigr-, niger* black) fr. LL *necromantia*, fr. LGk *nekromanteia*, fr. Gk *nekr-* necr- + *-manteia* -mancy — more at NEGRO] **1 a** (1) : the art or practice of magically revealing the future, of magically influencing the course of natural events, or of magically attaining other purposes esp. through communication with and the intervention of the dead (2) : the art or practice of magically conjuring up the souls of the dead **b** : magic in general esp. when directed toward the attainment of evil purposes : WITCHCRAFT, SORCERY **2** : an instance of the practice of necromancy

nec·ro·mant \-,mant\ *n* -s [Gk *nekromantis*, fr. *nekr-* necr- + *mantis* seer, prophet — more at MANTIS] : NECROMANCER

nec·ro·man·tic \¦==ˈmantik\ *adj* [LL *necromanticus*, fr. *necromantia* + L *-icus* -ic] **1** : given to the practice of necromancy ⟨a ~ sorcerer⟩ **2 a** : of, relating to, or associated with necromancy ⟨mysterious ~ rites⟩ **b** : accomplished or produced by necromancy ⟨~ delusions⟩ **3** : used in necromancy ⟨strange ~ powders and other weird objects⟩ — **nec·ro·man·ti·cal·ly** \-tək(ə)lē\ *adv*

nec·ro·man·ti·cal *obs var of* NECROMANTIC

ne·croph·a·ga \nəˈkräfəgə, neˈ-\ *n pl, cap* [NL, fr. *necr-* + *-phaga*] : a group composed of the burying beetles

nec·ro·pha·gia \,nekrəˈfājēə\ *n* -s [NL, fr. *necr-* + *-phagia*] : the act or practice of eating corpses or carrion

ne·croph·a·gous \nəˈkräfəgəs, neˈ-\ *adj* [Gk *nekrophagos*, fr. *nekr-* necr- + *-phagos* -phagous] : feeding on corpses or carrion ⟨~ savages⟩ ⟨~ insects⟩

ne·croph·a·gy \-jē\ *n* -ES [*necr-* + *-phagy*] : NECROPHAGIA

nec·ro·phile \ˈnekrə,fīl\ *also* **nec·ro·phil** \-,fil\ *n* -s [*necr-* + *-phile, -phil*] : one that is affected with necrophilia

nec·ro·phil·ia \,==ˈfilēə\ *n* -s [NL, fr. *necr-* + *-philia*] : fascination with the dead; *specif* : obsession with and usu. erotic attraction toward and stimulation by corpses typically evidenced by overt acts (as copulation with a corpse)

¹**nec·ro·phil·i·ac** \¦==¦filē,ak\ *adj* [NL *necrophilia* + E *-ac* (fr. Gk *-akos*, adj. suffix)] : NECROPHILIC

²**necrophiliac** \"\ *n* -s : NECROPHILE

¹**necrophil·ic** \-lik\ *adj* [*necr-* + *-philic*] : of, relating to, or marked by necrophilia

²**necrophilic** \"\ *n* -s : NECROPHILE

ne·croph·i·lism \nəˈkräfə,lizəm, neˈ-\ *n* -s **1** : NECROPHILIA **2** : an act prompted by necrophilia

ne·croph·i·list \-ləst\ *n* -s : NECROPHILE

ne·croph·i·lous \-ləs\ *adj* [*necr-* + *-philous*] **1** : NECROPHAGOUS **2** : NECROPHILIC

ne·croph·i·ly \-lē\ *n* -ES [*necr-* + *-phily*] : NECROPHILIA

nec·ro·phobe \ˈnekrə,fōb\ *n* -s [*necr-* + *-phobe*] : one that exhibits necrophobia

nec·ro·pho·bia \,==ˈfōbēə\ *n* [NL, fr. *necr-* + *-phobia*] : an exaggerated fear of death or horror of dead bodies — **nec·ro·pho·bic** \¦==¦fōbik *also* -fäb-\ *adj*

ne·croph·o·rus \nəˈkräf(ə)rəs, (ˈ)neˈk-\ *n, cap* [NL, fr. Gk *nekrophoros* burying the dead, fr. *nekr-* necr- + *-phoros* bearing, burying (fr. *pherein* to bear, carry to burial) — more at BEAR] : a genus of large burying beetles

nec·ro·pole \ˈnekrə,pōl\ *n* -s [back-formation fr. NL *necropoles*, pl. of *necropolis*] : NECROPOLIS

ne·crop·o·lis \nəˈkräpələs, neˈ-\ *n, pl* **necropolis·es** \-ləsəz\ *or* **necropo·les** \-,lēz\ *also* **necropo·leis** \-,līs\ *or* **necropo·li** \-,lī\ [LL, city of the dead, fr. Gk *nekropolis*, fr. *nekr-* necr- + *-polis*] **1 a** : CEMETERY; *esp* : a large elaborate cemetery of an ancient city **b** : an ancient or prehistoric burying place **2** : a place (as an abandoned city or town) devoid of life and inhabited by or as if by only the dead

¹**ne·crop·sy** \ˈne,kräpsē, -nəˈk-, neˈk-\ *n* -ES [*necr-* + *-opsy*] : POSTMORTEM EXAMINATION

²**necropsy** \"\ *vt* -ED/-ING/-ES : to perform a postmortem examination upon

necrose \nəˈkrōs, neˈ-, -ōz, ˈne,k-\ *vb* -ED/-ING/-S [back-formation fr. *necrosis*] *vi* : to undergo necrosis ⟨tissues subjected to prolonged pressure may ~ to form bedsores⟩ ~ *vt* : to affect with or cause to undergo necrosis ⟨infarction commonly ~*s* tissues deprived of blood⟩

nec·ro·sin \ˈnekrəsən\ *n* -s [ISV *necros-* (fr. *necrosis*) + *-in*] : a toxic substance associated with euglobulin in injured tissue and inflammatory exudates that induces leukopenia and hastens blood coagulation and is regarded by some as a proteolytic enzyme

ne·cro·sis \nəˈkrōsəs, neˈ-\ *n, pl* **necro·ses** \-,sēz\ [LL, fr. Gk *nekrōsis*, fr. *nekroun* to make dead, mortify, fr. *nekros* dead body — more at NOXIOUS] **1** : death of living tissue: as **a** : death of a portion of animal tissue differentially affected by loss of blood supply, corrosion, burning, the local lesion of a disease (as tuberculosis), or other local injury — compare NECROBIOSIS **b** : localized or general death of plant tissue caused by low temperatures, fungi, or other factors and often characterized by a brownish or black discoloration **2** : DEADARM

nec·ro·sper·mia \,nekrəˈspərmēə\ *n* -s [NL, fr. *necr-* + *-spermia*] : a condition in which the spermatozoa in seminal fluid are dead or motionless

ne·crot·ic \nəˈkräd·ik, neˈ-,-ätik\ *adj* [Gk *nekrōtikos*, fr. (assumed) *nekrōtos* (verbal of *nekroun*) + *-ikos* -ic] : affected with, characterized by, or producing necrosis

necrotic enteritis *n* : a serious infectious disease of young swine caused by a bacterium (*Salmonella suipestifer* or *S. choleraesuis*) and marked by fever and by necrotic and ulcerative inflammation of the intestinal wall — called also *necro, swine typhoid, paratyphoid*; see HOG CHOLERA

necrotic ring spot *n* : a virus leaf spot of cherries characterized by small dark water-soaked sometimes incomplete rings which may alternate with the normal green tissue and later often drop out and give the leaf a shredded or tattered appearance

necrotic stomatitis *n* : CALF DIPHTHERIA

nec·ro·tize \ˈnekrə,tīz\ *vb* -ED/-ING/-S *see -ize in Explan Notes* [*necrotic* + *-ize*] *vi* : to undergo necrosis ⟨a *necrotizing* lesion⟩ ~ *vt* : to cause or affect with necrosis

ne·crot·o·my \nəˈkräd·əmē, neˈ-, -mi\ *n* -ES [*necr-* + *-tomy*] **1** : dissection of dead bodies **2** : surgical removal of necrosed bone

nec·ro·type \ˈnekrə,tīp\ *n* [*necr-* + *type*] : an extinct organism or group of organisms

nect- *or* **necto-** *comb form* [NL, fr. Gk *nēktos*, fr. *nēchein* to swim — more at NESO-] : swimming : for swimming ⟨*nectocalyx*⟩

-nec·tae \ˈnek(,)tē\ *n pl comb form* [NL, fr. Gk *nēktai*, pl. of *nēktēs* swimmer, fr. *nēchein* to swim] : ones that swim in a (specified) way — in taxonomic names in zoology ⟨*Cystonectae*⟩

nec·tan·dra \nekˈtandrə\ *n, cap* [NL, fr. L *nectar* + NL *-andra*; fr. the nectar glands of the anthers] : a large genus of tropical American trees of the family Lauraceae having pinnately veined leaves and small paniculate flowers — see BEBEERU, GREENHEART

¹**nec·tar** \ˈnektə(r)\ *n* [L, fr. Gk *nektar*, prob. lit., overcoming death, fr. *nek-* (prob. akin to L *nec-, nex* death) + *-tar* (prob. akin to Skt *tarati* he crosses over, overcomes) — more at NOXIOUS, TERM] **1 a** : the drink of the Greek and Roman gods

b : any delicious drink; *often* **:** one of blended fruit juices **c :** a sweet liquid that is secreted by the nectaries of a plant and that is the chief material used by bees in the production of honey **2 :** a grayish red that is yellower and paler than apple-blossom, bluer and paler than bois de rose, and bluer, less strong, and slightly lighter than Pompeian red

²nectar \"\ *usu cap* — a communications code word for the letter *n*

nectar bird *n* **1 :** HONEY EATER **2 :** SUNBIRD

nec·tar·e·al \(ˈ)nek¦ta(a)rēəl\ *adj* [L *nectareus* of or like nectar (fr. Gk *nektareos*, fr. *nektar*) + E *-al*] *archaic* **:** NECTAROUS

nec·tar·e·an \-ēən\ *adj* [L *nectareus* + E *-an*] *archaic* **:** NECTAROUS

nec·tared \ˈnektə(r)d\ *adj* [*nectar* + *-ed*] **1** *archaic* **:** filled or imbued or mingled with nectar ⟨each to his lips applied the ~ urn —Alexander Pope⟩ **2** *archaic* **:** deliciously sweet or fragrant **:** NECTAROUS ⟨the blue ~ air —Julian Hawthorne⟩

nec·tar·e·ous \(ˈ)nek¦ta(a)rēəs\ *adj* [L *nectareus*] **:** NECTAROUS

nec·tar·i·al \-rēəl\ *adj* [*nectary* + *-al*] **:** relating to or consisting of a nectary

nec·tar·i·an \-ən\ *adj* [alter. of *nectarean*] *archaic* **:** NECTAROUS

nec·ta·ried \ˈnektərēd\ *adj* [*nectary* + *-ed*] **:** having nectaries

nec·tar·if·er·ous \¦nektə¦rif(ə)rəs\ *adj* [*nectar* + *-i-* + *-ferous*] **:** producing nectar ⟨the ~ organs of flowers⟩

¹nec·tar·ine \ˈnektərən\ *adj* [*nectar* + *-ine*] *archaic* **:** NECTAROUS

²nec·tar·ine \¦==¦rēn\ *n* -s [¹*nectarine*] **1 :** a peach (*Prunus persica nectarina*) that has a smooth-skinned fruit and is a frequent somatic mutation of the normal peach; *also* **:** its fruit **2 :** a light to moderate yellowish pink that is redder and stronger than seashell pink

nec·ta·rin·ia \ˌ==ˈrinēə\ *n, cap* [NL, fr. L *nectar* + *-inus* -ine + NL *-ia*] **:** a genus (the type of the family Nectariniidae) of Old World oscine birds

nec·ta·ri·ni·idae \ˌ==rəˈnīəˌdē\ *n pl, cap* [NL, fr. *Nectarinia*, type genus + *-idae*] **:** a family of Old World oscine birds consisting of the sunbirds

nec·tar·i·ous \(ˈ)nek¦ta(a)rēəs\ *adj* [alter. of *nectareous*] *archaic* **:** NECTAROUS

nec·tar·i·um \=ˈta(a)rēəm, -terē-, -tār-\ *n, pl* **nectar·ia** \-rēə\ *or* **nectariums** [NL, irreg. fr. L *nectar* + *-arium*] **:** NECTARY

nec·tar·iv·o·rous \¦nektə¦riv(ə)rəs\ *adj* [*nectar* + *-i-* + *-vorous*] **:** feeding on nectar ⟨~ insects⟩

nec·tar·ous \ˈnektərəs\ *adj* [*nectar* + *-ous*] **:** having the nature of or consisting of nectar **:** resembling nectar (as in deliciousness, sweetness, fragrance) ⟨~ drinks —Andrew Young⟩

nec·ta·ry \-rē\ *n* -ES [NL *nectarium*] **1 :** a plant gland that secretes nectar and that in flowers is usu. at the base of the corolla or petals or (as in the larkspur or violet) in the spur **2 :** an organ or part that contains a nectary

-nec·tes \ˈnek,tēz\ *n comb form* [NL, fr. Gk *nēktēs* swimmer, fr. *nēchein* to swim — more at NESO-] **:** one that swims in a (specified) way — in generic names in zoology ⟨*Chironectes*⟩

necto- — see NECT-

nec·to·calycine \¦nektō+\ *adj* [NL *nectocalyc-, nectocalyx* + E *-ine*] **:** of, relating to, or resembling a nectocalyx

nec·to·calyx \"+\ *n* [NL, fr. *nect-* + *calyx*] **:** a swimming bell of a siphonophore

necton *var of* NEKTON

nec·to·nematoidea *n pl, cap* \¦nektō+\ [NL, fr. *Nectonemat-, Nectonema* (fr. *nect-* + *-nema*) + *-oidea*] **:** a cosmopolitan order (coextensive with a family Nectonematidae and genus *Nectonema*) of Nematomorpha comprising marine hairworms with a parasitic stage in various crustaceans, a double row of natatory bristles, and an expansive pseudocoel — compare GORDIOIDEA

nec·to·phore \ˈnektə,fō(ə)r\ *n* -s [*nect-* + *-phore*] **:** NECTOCALYX

nec·to·pod \-,päd\ *n* -s [*nect-* + *-pod*] **:** a limb (as of a mollusk) adapted for swimming

nec·to·some \-,sōm\ *n* -s [*nect-* + *-some*] **:** the part of the colony of some complex siphonophores that bears swimming bells

nec·tria \ˈnektrēə\ *n* [NL, irreg. fr. Gk *nēktris* female swimmer, fr. *nēchein* to swim — more at NESO-] **1** *cap* **:** a genus (the type of the family Nectriaceae) of ascomycetous fungi that have bright-colored superficial perithecia — see CORAL SPOT, EUROPEAN CANKER **2** -s **:** any fungus of the genus *Nectria*

nec·tri·a·ce·ae \ˌ==ˈāsē,ē\ *n pl, cap* [NL, fr. *Nectria*, type genus + *-aceae*] **:** a family of ascomycetous fungi (order Hypocreales) that have superficial perithecia with or without a stroma

nec·tri·a·ceous \¦==¦āshəs\ *adj* [NL *Nectriaceae* + E *-ous*] **:** of or relating to the Nectriaceae

nec·trid·ia \nekˈtridēə\ *n pl, cap* [NL, fr. Gk *nēktrid-, nēktris* female swimmer + NL *-ia*] **:** an order of Lepospondyli comprising extinct amphibians of the Pennsylvanian and Lower Permian characterized by markedly aquatic forms with the limbs weak or reduced and the body elongated like that of an eel or broadly flattened like that of a skate — **nec·trid·i·an** \(ˈ)=¦tridēən\ *adj or n*

nec·tri·oid·a·ce·ae \ˌnektrē,ōiˈdāsē,ē\ [NL, fr. *Nectria* + L *-oides* -oid + NL *-aceae*] *syn of* ZYTHIACEAE

nec·tu·rus \nekˈtu̇rəs\ *n* [NL, fr. *nect-* + *-urus*] **1** *cap* **:** a genus of large No. American gilled aquatic salamanders of the family Proteidae — see MUD PUPPY **2** *pl* **nectu·ri** \-,rī\ *or* **necturuses :** a salamander of the genus *Necturus*

ned·der \ˈnedə(r)\ *n* -s [ME *neddre, naddre* — more at ADDER] *dial chiefly Brit* **:** ADDER

ned·dy \ˈnedē, -di\ *n* -ES [fr. *Neddy*, nickname for *Edward*] **1** *dial chiefly Brit* **:** DONKEY **2** *dial chiefly Brit* **:** HORSE

ne·der·lands \ˈnādə(r),länts\ *n* -ES *cap* [D, fr. *Nederland* Netherlands] **:** DUTCH 1b

née *or* **nee** \ˈnā *sometimes* ˈnē\ *adj* [F *née*, fem. of *né*] **1 :** born into a family surnamed ⟨Rebecca Crawley, ~ Sharp —W.M. Thackeray⟩ ⟨Mrs. Jane Doe ~ Roe⟩ ⟨Mrs. John Doe ~ Roe⟩ ⟨Aunt Margaret, ~ Sheridan —Mary McCarthy⟩ — used to identify a woman by her maiden family name usu. after mention of her name by marriage; sometimes used of a male ⟨Don Lockwood ~ Kosinski —J.S.Redding⟩ **2 :** originally or formerly called or named — used to identify (1) a girl or woman usu. after mention of an assumed or acquired name ⟨John Doe, whose widow ~ Jane Roe⟩ ⟨with his charming bride, ~ Miss Carol Milford —Sinclair Lewis⟩ ⟨the actress Madam X ~ Jane Roe⟩ ⟨requiem high mass for Sister AB ~ Jane Roe⟩; (2) sometimes a man or boy usu. after mention of another name being used ⟨Lord Byron, ~ George Pappas —Joseph Auslander & Audrey Wurdemann⟩; and (3) sometimes similarly a group ⟨the Atlanta Braves ~ the Boston Braves⟩, place ⟨Kernville, ~ Whiskey Flat —Ray Millholland⟩, or thing ⟨sonata for flute, oboe, and basso continuo ~ sonata for violin and harpsichord —P.H.Lang⟩; compare NÉ

¹need \ˈnēd\ *n* -s [ME *ned, nede*, fr. OE *nēd, nīed, nēad, nēod* distress, force, necessity, need; akin to OHG *nōt* distress, force, necessity, need, ON *nauth*, Goth *nauths*, and prob. to OE *nēo* corpse, ON *nār*, Goth *naus;* basic meaning: to be exhausted] **1 :** necessary duty **:** OBLIGATION ⟨if ~ be⟩ ⟨no ~ to apologize —B.K.Thorne⟩ ⟨the ~ to pay taxes —Peter Scott⟩ ⟨the ~ to evade in order to survive —S.D.Cutter⟩ **2 a :** a want of something requisite, desirable, or useful ⟨our daily ~s⟩ ⟨meet every ~⟩ ⟨a building adequate for the company's ~s⟩ ⟨eliminates all ~ for stitches and glue —*Book Production*⟩ ⟨the urgent ~ for discussion —*Manchester Guardian Weekly*⟩ ⟨order and discipline were the crying ~s —Kemp Malone⟩ ⟨the classless society in which each would receive according to his ~s —C.I.Glicksberg⟩ **b :** a physiological or psychological requirement for the maintenance of the homeostasis of an organism ⟨tissue ~s⟩ ⟨the ~ of a better education⟩ ⟨fundamental ~s (besides sex and organic satisfaction) are for prestige, security, and some form of generalized activity —Frederick Creedy⟩ ⟨she experienced the ~ of being petted and made much of by a man —Robert Grant †1940⟩ ⟨an equilibrium in which society's ~s and the ~s of the individual are one —W.H.Whyte⟩ **3 :** a condition requiring supply or relief **:** EXIGENCY ⟨in his ~⟩ ⟨at a time of ~⟩ ⟨whenever the ~ arises⟩ ⟨a friend in ~ is a friend indeed⟩ **4 :** want of the means of subsistence **:** DESTITUTION, POVERTY ⟨the community provides for those in ~⟩ — **at need** *adv* **:** in time of need ⟨a supply to draw on *at need*⟩

²need *adv* [ME *nede*, fr. OE *nēde, nīede, nēade, nēode*, instrumental of *nēd, nīed, nēad, nēod* necessity] *obs* **:** NEEDS

³need \ˈnēd\ *vb* **needed; needed; needing; needs** *or* **need** [ME *needen, neden*, fr. OE *nēodian* to be necessary, fr. *nēod* necessity] *vi* **1 :** to be in want ⟨give to them who ~⟩ **2 :** to be needful **:** be necessary ⟨playing as quietly as ~*ed* —Warwick Braithwaite⟩ ⟨is less effective than ~*s* be —Leo Wiener⟩ **~** *vt* **:** to be in need of **:** have cause or occasion for **:** REQUIRE ⟨children ~ milk⟩ ⟨he ~*s* advice⟩ ⟨great art does not ~ a theory —Herbert Read⟩ ⟨he does not ~ to be told when he is failing⟩ ⟨we ~ to guard against the private seizure of power —T.W.Arnold⟩ ⟨really ~ to ask ourselves —Frank Fremont-Smith⟩ ⟨something urgently ~*s* doing —Joaquin Noval⟩ ⟨it ~*s* little more than wise words —Barbara Ward⟩ — sometimes used before an infinitive without *to* ⟨I did not ~ appear —Herbert Hoover⟩ ⟨one ~*s* point out —J.B.Cabell⟩ ~ *verbal auxiliary* **:** be under necessity or obligation to ⟨the last group . . . we ~ deal with —W.E.Swinton⟩ ⟨one ~ only look at the management . . . to realize —Wayne Morse⟩ ⟨no necessitarian ~ ever abandon his hypothesis —L.S.Feuer⟩ ⟨talks more than he ~⟩ ⟨he ~ not answer⟩ ⟨~ she explain⟩ ⟨all the poet ~ do is to remind the reader —Joseph Jones⟩ **syn** see LACK

need–be \ˈ=,=\ *n* -s [fr. the phrase *need be*, fr. ³*need* + *be*, vb.] *archaic* **:** a necessary reason **:** NECESSITY

need·ces·si·ty \nēdˈsesəd·ē\ *n* -ES [alter. (influenced by *need*) of *necessity*] *dial* **:** NECESSITY

needfire \ˈ=,=\ *n* [¹*need* + *fire*] **:** a purificatory fire traditionally kindled usu. by friction of dry wood in time of distress (as during a cattle plague) in the belief that it would ward off evil spirits; *specif* **:** the fire lighted on the night of St. John the Baptist's Day (June 24) to ward off sickness and ill luck — compare SAINT JOHN'S FIRE

¹need·ful \ˈnēdfəl\ *adj* [ME *nedefull, nedfull*, fr. *nede, ned* need + *-full* -ful] **1 :** having need **:** NEEDY ⟨~ families⟩ **2 :** necessary for supply or relief **:** REQUISITE, INDISPENSABLE ⟨the one thing ~⟩ ⟨provided with everything ~ and remain aboard —Herman Melville⟩ ⟨power to . . . make all ~ rules and regulations —*U. S. Constitution*⟩ ⟨buying only what was strictly ~ —W.S. Maugham⟩

syn NEEDFUL, NECESSARY, REQUISITE, INDISPENSABLE, and ESSENTIAL can mean, in common, required, usu. urgently. NEEDFUL is the weakest, applying to anything required to fill a want or need ⟨the town fathers found it *needful* to seek a new place to the west for grazing —*Amer. Guide Series: Mass.*⟩ ⟨pots and pans, kettles and cranes, axes and nails, and other *needful* things which could not be made by men hewing homes from a wilderness —Harriot B. Barbour⟩ NECESSARY implies more pressing need ⟨until we know how much of this damage can be repaired and how quickly the *necessary* repairs can be made —F.D.Roosevelt⟩ ⟨we are making them independent of the knowledge *necessary* to make their work satisfactory —M. R.Cohen⟩ ⟨amino acids *necessary* for protein synthesis —*Americana Annual*⟩ REQUISITE suggests an imposed requirement, applying usu. to what is necessary by the nature of the end or the larger purpose to be served ⟨attack their other studies with the vigor *requisite* to success —C.H.Grandgent⟩ ⟨the skill *requisite* to direct these immense machines is proportionate to their magnitude and complicated mechanism —T.L.Peacock⟩ INDISPENSABLE applies to something that cannot be done without if the end is to be attained ⟨eliminate irrelevancies and retain what is *indispensable* —John Dewey⟩ ⟨reading quite *indispensable* to a wise man —R.W.Emerson⟩ ⟨stability of cost is *indispensable* to sound business planning —H.S.Truman⟩ ESSENTIAL is often interchangeable with *indispensable* though less dramatic in implication, implying simply inherent necessity ⟨food is *essential* to life⟩ ⟨the award of fellowships and research grants is *essential* to the accomplishment of this high purpose —Dexter Perkins⟩ ⟨unrestrained competition, which is generally regarded as *essential* to modern capitalism —M.R.Cohen⟩

²needful \"\ *n* -s **:** something needed or requisite: **a :** the thing that must be done — used with *the* ⟨do the ~⟩ **b :** a personal necessary (as a piece of apparel or a toilet article) ⟨summer ~s⟩ ⟨small ~s⟩ **c :** MONEY — used with *the* ⟨had the ~ to buy what he wanted⟩

need·ful·ly \ˈnēdfəlē\ *adv* [ME *nedfully*, fr. *nedfull* + *-ly*] *archaic* **:** NECESSARILY

need·ful·ness *n* -ES [ME *nedefulnes*, fr. *nedefull* + *-nes* -ness] **:** the quality or state of being needful

needier *comparative of* NEEDY

neediest *superlative of* NEEDY

need·i·ness \ˈnēdēnəs\ *n* -ES [ME *nedynes*, fr. *nedy* needy + *-nes* -ness] **:** the quality or state of being needy

¹nee·dle \ˈnēdᵊl\ *n* -s *often attrib* [ME *nedle*, fr. OE *nǣdl;* akin to OHG *nādala* needle, ON *nāl*, Goth *nēthla;* all fr. a prehistoric Gmc noun akin to OHG *nājan* to sew, L *nēre* to spin, Gk *nēn* to spin, *nēma* thread, Skt *snāyu* sinew] **1 a** (1) **:** a small slender rodlike instrument for hand sewing that has a round or elongated eye for thread at one end and a blunt or sharp point at the other and that is made usu. of steel or bone in straight or curved form (2) **:** a similar steel instrument for machine sewing that has an eye in the pointed end and is shaped at the other end for attachment to the machine **b :** any of various devices for carrying thread and making stitches in crocheting, knitting, netting, or hooking — see KNITTING NEEDLE **c** (1) **:** a pointed slender instrument used for sewing or puncturing tissues **:** SURGICAL NEEDLE (2) **:** a slender hollow instrument that has one end pointed and beveled and the other enlarged and modified for attachment to various devices and that is used chiefly for introducing material into or removing material from the body parenterally ⟨intravenous ~⟩ (3) **:** a hollow device designed to contain radioactive material (4) **:** ELECTRIC KNIFE **2 :** a slender usu. sharp-pointed indicator on a dial instrument (as a magnetic compass or an ammeter); *specif* **:** MAGNETIC NEEDLE **3 a :** a slender pointed object resembling a needle: as (1) **:** a pointed crystal (2) **:** a sharp rock (3) **:** OBELISK ⟨Cleopatra's ~⟩ **b :** a needle-shaped leaf (as of the pine, spruce, larch) **4 :** a short stout timber, steel, or iron beam passing through a hole in a wall esp. to support the end of a shore **5 a :** ETCHING NEEDLE **b :** a slender piece of a jewel or of steel, wood, or fiber with a rounded tip used in a phonograph to transmit vibrations from the record — called also *stylus* **6** [by shortening] *archaic* **:** NEEDLEWOMAN **7 a :** one of a set of parallel wires found in knitting machines and jacquard looms **b :** a usu. platinum wire used for transferring microorganisms into culture mediums **8 a :** part of the knotting mechanism of a grain binder **b :** a slender tapering rod set in a bore during charging and then withdrawn leaving an opening for the priming, fuse, or squib — called also *pricker* **c :** a slender pointed rod controlling a fine inlet or outlet (as in a valve) **d :** a slender pointed rod mounted on a handle and used to sort or to arrange hand-sorted punch cards — **needle in a haystack :** an object hard to find or attain

1 2 3 4

needles 1 a (1) and 1b: *1* dressmaker's needle, *2* crochet needle, *3* knitting needle, *4* netting needle

²needle \"\ *vb* **needled; needled; needling** \-d(ᵊ)liŋ\ **needles** *vt* **1 :** to sew with a needle ⟨fabrics which are woven, *needled* and printed —W.C.Smith⟩ **2 a :** to pierce or treat with or as if with a needle ⟨*needling* a blister until it bursts —James Baldwin⟩ ⟨the pangs of terror now *needled* his soul —James Hogg⟩ **b :** to puncture, operate on, or inject (as a person) with a needle ⟨*needling* a cataract⟩ ⟨~*s* the population against polio⟩ **3 a :** to push (something) through like a needle ⟨words . . . *needled* into one's self —Christopher Morley⟩ ⟨have to talk fast to ~ it in between . . . speeches —*Nat'l Home Monthly*⟩ ⟨*needling* their way through a crowd⟩ **b :** to put a needle beam under a wall for support **4 :** to vex by repeated sharp prods or gibes **:** goad or incite often to a specified action ⟨thoroughly enjoys *needling* his stuffy relatives —James Gray⟩ ⟨*needled* him into it —James Jones⟩ **5 :** to increase the interest and attractiveness of **:** add strength or pungency to ⟨~ a speech with humor⟩ ⟨*needled* with irony⟩; *specif* **:** to strengthen (a beverage) by adding raw alcohol ⟨~ beer⟩ **~** *vi* **:** to sew or embroider with a needle ⟨groups of women . . . *needling* away —W.M.Thackeray⟩

³needle \"\ *adj* [¹*needle*] *chiefly Brit, of a game or athletic contest* **:** highly important **:** CRUCIAL ⟨the most heated moments of a ~ match —*Rugger*⟩

needle and thread *n* **:** a needlegrass (*Stipa comata*)

needlebar \ˈ==,=\ *n* **:** a bar on a sewing or knitting machine for holding the needle or needles

needle bath *n* **:** a bath in which water is forcibly projected on the body in fine jets

needle beam *n* **1 :** NEEDLE 4 **2 :** a transverse floor beam in a bridge

needle bearing *n* **:** a roller bearing with very slender rollers varying typically from 0.08 to 0.16 inch in diameter

needle beer *n* [²*needle*] **:** beer made with ether alcohol often illicitly and under makeshift conditions ⟨for a big depression buck, you could get ten glasses of *needle beer* —*Crime Detective*⟩

needlebill \ˈ==,=\ *also* **needle–billed snipe** \ˈ==,=-\ *n* **:** WILSON'S PHALAROPE

needle biopsy *n* **:** a biopsy esp. of deep tissues done with a hollow needle

needle blight *or* **needle cast** *n* **:** LEAF CAST

needle board *n* **1 :** a board covered with very short fine wires that is used for pressing pile fabrics **2 a :** the perforated board in a jacquard mechanism through which the ends of the actuating needles project **b :** a board carrying the needles in a punch loom or needle loom

needle bug *n* [so called fr. its long slender body] **:** a bug of the genus *Ranatra*

needlebush \ˈ==,=\ *n* **1 :** any of several Australian shrubs or trees with rigid needle-shaped leaves; *esp* **:** a plant of the genus *Hakea* **2 :** CHAPARRAL PEA

needle chatter *n* **:** NEEDLETALK

needlecraft \ˈ==,=\ *n* [ME *nedle craft*, fr. *nedle* needle + *craft*] **:** NEEDLEWORK

needled *adj* [fr. past part. of ²*needle*] **1 :** done with a needle ⟨~ embroidery⟩ **2** [¹*needle* + *-ed*] **:** resembling a needle ⟨~ crystals⟩

needle dam *n* **:** a barrier consisting of horizontal bars dropped into grooves in the abutments of a pass through a dam or of planks set on end and removable in case of flood

needle file *n* **:** a very small file having any of the usual shapes of cross section and having the tang end extended to a long rodlike handle

needle fir *n* **:** a Chinese evergreen tree (*Abies holophylla*) with pectinate leaves and erect cones

needlefish \ˈ==,=\ *n, pl* **needlefish** *or* **needlefishes 1 :** any of numerous voracious elongate teleost fishes of *Belone* and related genera that resemble superficially but are not related to the freshwater ganoids, that are green and silvery in color with even the bones often bright green, and that include a common European fish (*Belone belone*) and well-known American forms belonging to the genus *Tylosurus* — called also *billfish, gar* **2 :** any of various other slender elongated fishes (as a halfbeak or a pipefish) with projecting jaws

needle furze *n* **:** a prickly shrub (*Genista anglica*) of western Europe having bluish green foliage and racemose yellow flowers

needle grama *n* **:** an annual grama (*Bouteloua aristidoides*) with three awns longer than the spikelet

needlegrass \ˈ==,=\ *n* **1 :** any of several grasses of the genus *Stipa* (esp. *S. comata*) of the western U. S. with filiform leaves and slender awns on the spikelet **2 :** any of several grasses of the genus *Aristida* (esp. *A. longiseta*) of the western U. S. furnishing poor forage — called also *triple-awned grass*

needle gun *n* **:** a rifle of the later 19th century having a needle-shaped firing pin which upon penetrating a paper, oiled linen, or oiled silk cartridge passes through the powder charge to detonate the cap loaded at the base of the bullet

needle ice *n* **:** FRAZIL

needle ironstone *or* **needle iron ore** *n* **:** goethite in acicular crystals

needle juniper *n* **:** an Asiatic evergreen shrubby tree (*Juniperus rigida*) with needle-shaped rigid leaves that is sometimes used as an ornamental

needle lace *n* **:** NEEDLEPOINT 1

needlelike \ˈ==,=\ *adj* **:** resembling a needle in slenderness, pointedness, or sharpness ⟨~ crystals⟩ ⟨~ leaves⟩ ⟨~ pick⟩ ⟨~ spire⟩

needle loom *n* **1 :** a loom in which the filling is carried through the shed by a long eye-pointed needle **2 :** PUNCH LOOM

nee·dle·man \ˈnēdᵊlmən\ *n, pl* **needlemen** *archaic* **:** TAILOR

needle–miner \ˈ==,==\ *n* **:** an insect larva that forms minute mines within the needles of various coniferous trees; *esp* **:** a lepidopterous larva of such habits

needle ore *n* **:** AIKINITE

needle palm *n* **:** BLUE PALMETTO

¹needlepoint \ˈ==,=\ *n* **1 :** lace worked entirely with a needle over a paper pattern in buttonhole stitch — compare BOBBIN LACE **2 :** embroidery worked over or on canvas usu. in simple even stitches across counted threads; *esp* **:** GROS POINT

²needlepoint \"\ *adj* **1 :** of, relating to, or resembling needlepoint ⟨~ lace⟩ ⟨~ embroidery⟩ ⟨~ silk⟩ ⟨~ holder⟩ **2 :** of or relating to a fabric with a fine pebbled or nubby surface formed by uneven yarns or fancy weaves

³needlepoint \"\ *n* **:** something resembling the point of a needle (as in sharpness or minuteness) ⟨admits the ~ of that argument —*Times Lit. Supp.*⟩ ⟨the towerman has to balance on a thin beam . . . virtually on a ~ —Beatrice Schapper⟩

needle–pointed \¦==¦==\ *adj* **:** resembling a needle in sharpness of point ⟨*needle-pointed* cleaners used to clean clogged burner holes —K.A.Henderson⟩

nee·dler \ˈnēd(ᵊ)lə(r)\ *n* -s [in sense 1, fr. ¹*needle* + *-er;* in other senses fr. ²*needle* + *-er*] **1 :** one that makes, uses, or deals in needles **2** *Brit* **:** one that sews up packages **3 :** one that goads or prods; *esp* **:** one that indulges in sharp and often captious criticism of others ⟨the moderator was an able discussion leader rather than just a plain ~ —John Withall⟩

needlerun \ˈ==,=\ *adj* [¹*needle* + *run*, past part. of *run* to sew] **:** ornamented or joined by needlework — used esp. of pillow lace or machine-made net with hand-sewn designs

needlerush \ˈ==,=\ *n* **1 :** a rush (*Juncus roemerianus*) chiefly of the southeastern U. S. with terete rigid leaves and sharp-pointed sepals **2 :** NEEDLE SPIKE RUSH

needles *pl of* NEEDLE, *pres 3d sing of* NEEDLE

needle scale *n* **:** a homopterous insect of the family Coccidae that feeds on conifers

needle scratch *n* **:** SURFACE NOISE

needle spike rush *n* **:** a common perennial sedge (*Eleocharis acicularis*) with needlelike leaves — called also *needlerush*

need·less \ˈnēdləs\ *adj* [ME *nedeles*, fr. *nede* need + *-les* -less] **:** not needed **:** UNNECESSARY, GRATUITOUS ⟨~ movement⟩ ⟨~ controversy⟩ ⟨~ to say⟩ ⟨outraged by . . . ~ wickedness —F.L.Paxson⟩ — **need·less·ly** *adv* — **need·less·ness** *n* -ES

needletalk \ˈ==,=\ *n* **:** noise radiated directly by the needle of a phonograph pickup or by a record as distinguished from the sound produced by the complete phonograph — called also *needle chatter*

needle telegraph *n* **:** a telegraph signaling by the deflections of a magnetic needle (as when the receiver is a galvanometer with vertical needle)

needle tooth *n* **:** a small dark sharp tooth of a newborn pig — called also *black tooth*

needle trade *n* **:** any of the various businesses involved in the manufacture of clothing — usu. used in pl. with *the* ⟨immigrants worked as peddlers or entered the expanding *needle trades* —*Amer. Guide Series: N.Y. City*⟩

needle valve *n* **:** a valve consisting essentially of a slender pointed rod or needle fitting into a conoidal seat and capable of fine adjustment

needle whin *n* **:** NEEDLE FURZE

needlewoman \ˈ==,==\ *n, pl* **needlewomen :** a woman who does needlework

needle wood *n* **1** *usu* **needlewood** \ˈ==,=\ **:** a needlebush of the genus *Hakea; esp* **:** a white-flowered shrub or small shrubby tree (*H. leucoptera*) with a hard tough heavy reddish brown wood that is used locally for small cabinetwork **2 :** an Indian-Burmese tree (*Schima wallichii*) of the family Theaceae with light red or reddish brown wood **3 :** the wood of a needle wood

needlework \'=,=\ *n* [ME *nedle werk*, fr. *nedle* needle + *werk* work] **1 :** work done with a needle; *specif* **:** work (as embroidery, knitting, needlepoint) other than plain sewing **2 :** the occupation of one who does needlework

needleworker \'=,=,=\ *n* **:** one that does needlework

needle zeolite *n* [so called fr. the shape of its crystals] **:** NATROLITE

needling *n* -s [fr. gerund of ²*needle*] **1 :** the action or process of using a needle ⟨from their authentic styling to their fine ~ —*N.Y. Times*⟩; *specif* **:** the action or process of using an etching needle **2 :** a temporary support of needle beams **3 :** irritatingly persistent goading or prodding ⟨the give-and-take, the ~ . . . and sometimes the downright abuse involved in dealing with newsmen —F.L.Mott⟩

nee·dly \'nēd(ᵊ)lē\ *adj* -ER/-EST [¹*needle* + -*y*] **:** resembling a needle ⟨ragged and ~ ice —Rudyard Kipling⟩

need·ment \'nēdmənt\ *n* -s **:** a thing needed or wanted; *esp* **:** a necessary item of personal luggage — usu. used in pl. ⟨the old canvas bag in which all his poor ~*s* for a long journey were packed —Jack Kerouac⟩

need-not \'=,=\ *n* -s [fr. the phrase *need not*, fr. ³*need* + *not*] **:** something not needed **:** SUPERFLUITY ⟨purchasing *need-nots*⟩

needs \'nēdz\ *adv* [ME *nedes*, fr. OE *nēdes*, fr. gen. of *nēde* necessity — more at NEED] **:** of necessity **:** NECESSARILY, INDISPENSABLY ⟨would ~ be left open —*U.S. Daily*⟩ — usu. used with *must* ⟨must ~ be objective —W.B.Yeats⟩ ⟨must ~ examine her bracelet —Henry Lapham⟩

¹**needy** \'nēdē, -di\ *adj* -ER/-EST [ME *nedy*, fr. *ned* need + -*y*] **:** marked by want of the means of living **:** POVERTY-STRICKEN ⟨~ families⟩ ⟨the ~ blind⟩ ⟨the *neediest* cases⟩ **syn** see POOR

²**needy** \"\ *n*, *sing or pl in constr* **:** one that is unable to maintain economic self-sufficiency or that must receive public or private assistance of some kind ⟨take care of the ~⟩

neeld \'nēld\ *dial chiefly Eng var of* NEEDLE

neem \'nēm\ *or* **neem tree** *also* **neemba** \'nēmbə\ *n* -s [Hindi & Skt; Hindi *nīm*, fr. Skt *nimba*] **:** MARGOSA

neem-oil \'=,=\ *n*, *sometimes cap* **:** a medicinal aromatic oil yielded by the fruit and seeds of the neem tree

ne·encephalon \¦nē+\ *n* [NL, fr. *ne-* + *encephalon*] **:** the part of the brain having the most recent phylogenetic origin; *specif* **:** the cerebral cortex and parts developed in relation to it — compare PALEENCEPHALON

neep \'nēp\ *n* -s [ME *nepe*, fr. OE *nǣp*, fr. L *napus*] *chiefly Scot* **:** TURNIP

neep·er \'nēpə(r)\ *Scot var of* NEIGHBOR

neer \'nēr\ *n* -s [ME *nere* — more at NEPHRITIS] *chiefly Scot* **:** KIDNEY

ne'er \(ˈ)ne\|(ə)r, (ˈ)na(ə)\|, \|ə\ *adv* [ME *ner*, *nere*, contr. of *never*, *nevere*] **:** NEVER

ne'er-do-weel \'ner(,)dü,wēl\ *chiefly Scot var of* NE'ER-DO-WELL

¹**ne'er-do-well** \'ner(,)dü,wel, 'neə(-\ *n* -s [fr. the phrase *ne'er do well*] **:** a person who never does well **:** GOOD-FOR-NOTHING ⟨the backwash of society . . . tramps, prostitutes and *ne'er-do-wells* —F.J.Jirka⟩ ⟨charming, desirable, yet essentially a *ne'er-do-well* —John Nerber⟩

²**ne'er-do-well** \"\ *adj* **:** never doing well **:** SHIFTLESS, INCOMPETENT ⟨a *ne'er-do-well* couple that has neglected farm, home, and church —H.H.Reichard⟩

neet \'nēt\ *dial Eng var of* NIGHT

ne ex·e·at \nē'eksē,at\ *n* [L, let him not leave] **1 :** a high prerogative writ formerly used in England in matters of state to restrain a person from leaving the country **2 :** a writ issued out of chancery or equity to restrain a person from leaving the jurisdiction of the court pending an action

ne exeat re·pub·li·ca \-rē'pəbləkə\ *n* [L, let him not leave the state] **:** a writ issued to restrain a person from leaving the jurisdiction of the court pending an action — compare NE EXEAT

¹**neeze** *also* **neese** \'nēz\ *vi* -ED/-ING/-S [ME *nesen*, of Scand origin; akin to ON *hnjōsa* to sneeze; akin to OHG *niosan* to sneeze] *chiefly Scot* **:** SNEEZE

²**neeze** *also* **neese** \"\ *n* -s *chiefly Scot* **:** SNEEZE

nef \'nef\ *n* -s [F, nave, boat-shaped vessel, fr. ML *navis* — more at NAVE] **1** *obs* **:** NAVE **2 :** a 16th century clock in the form of a ship having mechanical devices to illustrate astronomical movements **3 :** an ornamental table utensil (as for holding a napkin, knife, and spoon) shaped like a ship

ne·fan·dous \nə'fandəs\ *adj* [L *nefandus*, fr. *ne-* not + *fandus*, gerundive of *fari* to speak — more at NO, BAN] *archaic* **:** unfit to be spoken of **:** IMPIOUS, EXECRABLE ⟨~ wickedness —Increase Mather⟩

ne·far·i·ous \nə'fa(a)rēəs, nē'-, -fer-, -fār-\ *adj* [L *nefarius*, fr. *nefas* crime, wrong, fr. *ne-* not + *fas* right, divine law; akin to L *fari* to speak] **:** heinously or impiously wicked **:** DETESTABLE, INIQUITOUS ⟨~ schemes⟩ ⟨~ practice⟩ ⟨race prejudice is most ~ on its politer levels —H.E.Clurman⟩ **syn** see VICIOUS

ne·far·i·ous·ly *adv* **:** in a nefarious manner ⟨~ involved in a conspiracy⟩

ne·far·i·ous·ness *n* -ES **:** the quality or state of being nefarious ⟨the ~ of the deed⟩

ne·fast \nə'fast\ *adj* [L *nefastus*, fr. *nefas* crime, wrong] **:** WICKED

nef·fy \'nefē\ *dial var of* NEPHEW

neft·gil \'neft,gil\ *n* -s [G, fr. Per *naftdagil* naphtha clay] **:** OZOKERITE

neg *abbr* **1** negative **2** negotiable

ne·ga·ra \nə'gärə\ *n* -s [Indonesian, fr. Skt *nagara* city] **:** an autonomous or federative state in the republic of Indonesia

¹**ne·gate** \nə'gāt, nē'-, *usu* -ād·+V *sometimes* 'ne,g *or* 'nē,g-\ *vb* -ED/-ING/-S [L *negatus*, past part. of *negare*] *vt* **1 :** to deny the existence or truth or fact of **:** refuse to admit ⟨*negated* and denied her own honest reactions —Sara H. Hay⟩ **2 :** to cause to be ineffective or invalid **:** NEGATIVE ⟨the conception of limitless growth is even more obviously *negated* by the death of the individual —Reinhold Niebuhr⟩ ~ *vi* **:** to deny something **:** negative something ⟨the . . . dictator is the force that always ~*s* —F.H.Cramer⟩ **syn** see NULLIFY

²**negate** \"\ *n* -s [L *negatus*, past part. of *negare*] **:** the contradictory of something ⟨either this statement or its ~ is verifiable —R.J.Richman⟩

ne·ga·tion \nə'gāshən, nē'-, ne'-\ *n* -s [MF or L; MF *negation*, fr. L *negation-*, *negatio*, fr. *negatus* (past part. of *negare* to say no, deny, fr. *neg-* no, not, akin to *ne-* not) + *-ion-*, *-io* -ion — more at NO] **1 a :** the action of negating **:** DENIAL, CONTRADICTION ⟨conformity is the very ~ of the liberties enjoyed by a free society —*New Republic*⟩; *specif* **:** the operation of forming a negation **b :** an instance of negating **:** a negative doctrine or statement or proposition or judgment; *specif* **:** a statement that is true provided the unqualified original statement is false **c :** a negating particle (as *not*) **:** NEGATIVE **2 a :** something that is merely the absence of something actual **:** something without real existence of its own **:** NONENTITY ⟨anarchy is not law but its ~ —B.N.Cardozo⟩ **b :** something considered the opposite of something regarded as positive ⟨black is the ~ of all color⟩ — **ne·ga·tion·al** \-shənᵊl, -shnəl\ *adj*

ne·ga·tion·ist \-sh(ə)nəst\ *also* **ne·ga·tion·al·ist** \-shənᵊl-əst, -shnel-\ *n* -s **:** an adherent of a doctrine or theory of mere negation

neg·a·tiv·ate \'negəd·ə,vāt\ *vt* -ED/-ING/-S [¹*negative* + -*ate*] **:** NEGATE ⟨is directly *negativated* by plain facts —A.N.Whitehead⟩

¹**neg·a·tive** \'negəd·iv, -ətiv\ *adj* [MF or L; MF *negatif*, fr. L *negativus*, fr. *negatus* + *-ivus* -ive] **1 a :** that expresses or implies or contains negation **:** that denies or contradicts or prohibits or refuses ⟨a ~ answer⟩ ⟨a ~ opinion⟩ **b** (1) **:** denying a predicate of a subject or of a part of a subject or asserting the falsity of something ("no A is B", "some A is not B", and "it is false that A is B" are ~ propositions)— contrasted with *affirmative* (2) **:** denoting the absence of something or the contradictory of something ⟨*not-white* is a ~ term⟩ **2 a :** that is marked by the absence of positive features ⟨a colorless ~ personality⟩ **b :** that is marked by features (as hostility, perversity, withdrawal) that oppose constructive treatment or development ⟨delinquents retarded by their ~ outlook on life⟩ **3 a :** less than zero and of such nature that when added to a like number of positive sign zero is produced ⟨the ~ number −2 added to +2 yields zero⟩ **b :** that is opposite in direction or position to an arbitrarily chosen regular direction or position **4 a :** relating to, charged with, or composed of negative electricity **b :** gaining electrons **:** ELECTRONEGATIVE 2a, ACID 2a **5 a :** not affirming the presence of the organism or condition in question ⟨a ~ diagnosis⟩ ⟨a ~ reaction⟩ **b :** directed or moving away from a source of stimulation ⟨a ~ tropism⟩ **c :** less than the pressure of the atmosphere ⟨the role of intrathoracic ~ pressure in respiration⟩ **6 a :** being or exhibiting rotation to the left **:** LEVOROTATORY **b :** having or characterized by a smaller index of refraction for the extraordinary ray than for the ordinary ray — used of doubly refracting crystals **7 :** having or reproducing the bright parts of the original subject as dark areas and the dark parts as light areas — used of a photographic image or of the material on which it is reproduced **8** *geol* **a :** frequently submerged **b :** subjected to downward movement or extensive erosion **c :** displaying less than normal gravitational or magnetic properties **9 a :** that is a no-trump response made on a weak hand in bridge for the purpose of keeping the bidding open **b** *of a double in bridge* **:** INFORMATORY

²**negative** \"\ *n* -s **1 a :** a proposition by which something is denied or contradicted **:** an opposite or contradictory term or conception or sense; *specif* **:** a statement or judgment expressing or implying or containing denial or contradiction **b** (1) **:** a reply by which is indicated the withholding of assent about something **:** REFUSAL (2) *archaic* **:** a right of veto (3) *obs* **:** a vote expressing opposition **:** adverse vote **2 :** something that is the opposite or negation of something else **3 a :** a word or particle or term or phrase (as *not*, *no*) that expresses negation or denial — often used adverbially esp. in radiotelephone communication ⟨is he there? —~⟩ **b :** a mathematical quantity or symbol that has a minus value **4 a :** the side that upholds the contradictory proposition in a debate — opposed to *affirmative* **b :** a speaker on the contradictory side in a debate **5 :** the plate of a voltaic or electrolytic cell that is at the lower potential **6 a :** a photographic image that reproduces the bright parts of the photographed subject as dark areas and the dark parts as light areas, that is usu. on transparent material, and that is used for printing positive pictures **b :** the material on which this image is reproduced **7 :** a reverse impression or mold taken from a piece of sculpture or ceramics — **in the negative** *adv (or adj)* **1 :** in favor of or with the effect of rejection or refusal ⟨the vote was wholly *in the negative*⟩ **2 :** with a negative answer ⟨invited her to go but she answered *in the negative*⟩

³**negative** \"\ *vb* -ED/-ING/-S *vt* **1 a :** to refuse assent to (as a candidate, proposal, program) **:** refuse to accept **b** (1) **:** to reject by or as if by a vote (2) **:** VETO **2 :** to demonstrate the falsity of **:** DISPROVE **3 :** CONTRADICT **4 :** COUNTERACT ~ *vi* **:** to deny or reject or refuse something **syn** see DENY, NEUTRALIZE

negative acceleration *n* **1 :** RETARDATION **2 :** acceleration in a negative direction

negative afterimage *n* **1 :** COMPLEMENTARY AFTERIMAGE **2 :** a visual afterimage in which light portions of the original sensation are replaced by dark portions and dark portions are replaced by light portions — opposed to *positive afterimage*

negative angle *n* **:** an angle generated in a direction opposite to an arbitrarily chosen usu. clockwise direction

negative catalysis *n* **:** catalysis in which the catalyst has an inhibiting effect on the reaction (as the retardation of the aging of rubber and oils by antioxidants)

negative catalyst *n* **:** a substance that brings about negative catalysis

negative crystal *n* **1 :** a cavity that has the form of a crystal and occurs in a mineral mass **2 :** a crystal showing negative double refraction

negative curvature *n* **:** curvature of a graph in such a way that it is concave downward

negative easement *or* **negative servitude** *n* **:** an easement enabling its holder to prevent the possessor of the land subject to the easement from doing certain acts or exercising certain rights of ownership he would otherwise have a legal right to ⟨a *negative easement* to receive air and light without interference by an adjoining owner⟩

negative electricity *n* **:** electricity of which the elementary unit is the electron

negative electron *n* **:** ELECTRON

negative eugenics *n pl but usu sing in constr* **:** improvement of the genetic makeup of a population by preventing the reproduction of the obviously unfit

negative feedback *n* **:** the returning of a fraction of the output of an electric oscillator to the input in such a way as to decrease the oscillation amplitude **:** DEGENERATION — called also *inverse feedback*

negative form *n* **:** one of a pair of congruent crystal forms that together correspond to a single form in a crystal class of higher symmetry

negative glow *n* **:** a narrow luminous region that occurs in an electrical discharge in a gas at low pressure (as in a Crookes tube) and that is often the second such region from the cathode

negative lens *n* **:** DIVERGING LENS

negative logarithm *n* **:** COLOGARITHM

neg·a·tive·ly \'negəd·əvlē, -ətə-, -li\ *adv* **:** in a negative manner: as **a** (1) **:** by way of denial or contradiction **:** in the negative **:** on the negative side ⟨answered ~⟩ ⟨with a sphere of action defined more ~ than positively —*Times Lit. Supp.*⟩ (2) **:** in a negative direction ⟨a disk rotating ~⟩ (3) **:** in such a way as to indicate refusal or lack of agreement or of sympathy ⟨viewed all their efforts ~⟩ **b :** with negative electricity ⟨~ charged⟩

negative misprision *n* **:** concealment of something known by one that has the duty of revealing it to proper authority — distinguished from *positive misprision*

negative modulation *or* **negative transmission** *n* **:** amplitude-modulated signals in television in which the maximum carrier corresponds to the dark part of the picture

neg·a·tive·ness *n* -ES [¹*negative* + -*ness*] **:** NEGATIVITY

negative-painted \¦=,=,=\ *adj* **:** painted by negative painting

negative painting *n* **:** an ancient process of decorative painting (as of Peruvian Indian pottery) marked by application of wax or gum to parts of a surface and by application of color to the entire surface and by subsequent removal of the wax or gum so as to leave a pattern created by the parts of the surface thus left unpainted

negative phase *n* **:** a phase of lowered resistance that may follow the injection of foreign antigen in active immunization

negative plate *n* **:** the electrode of a voltaic cell or storage cell that is at the lower potential when the circuit is open

negative pole *n* **:** the terminal of a voltaic cell or storage cell that is connected to the negative plate

negative potential *n* **:** an electric potential lower than that of the earth or other conductor taken as an arbitrary zero of potential

negative pregnant *n*, *pl* **negatives pregnant** [²*negative* + *pregnant*, adj.] **:** a legal denial that admits or involves an affirmative implication which is favorable to the pleader's adversary

negative pressure *n* [¹*negative*] **:** pressure that is less than existing atmospheric pressure taken as a zero of reference

negative proton *n* **:** ANTIPROTON

negative resistance *n* **:** a resistance phenomenon (as exhibited by an electric arc or vacuum tube) in which the voltage drop across the circuit decreases as the current increases

negative sign *n* **:** MINUS SIGN 1

negative skewness *n* **:** skewness in which the mean is less than the mode

negative staining *n* **:** a method of demonstrating the form of small objects (as bacteria) by surrounding them with a stain that they do not take up so that they appear as sharply outlined unstained bright bodies on a colored ground

negative theology *n* **:** theology that conceives of ultimate reality as so transcending human thought that it can be described only negatively — distinguished from *positive theology*

negative valence *n* **1 :** the valence of a negatively charged ion **2 :** the number of electrons an atom can take up ⟨oxygen has a *negative valence* of 2⟩

neg·a·tiv·ism \'negəd·ə,vizəm, -gətə,-\ *n* -s [¹*negative* + -*ism*] **1 :** an attitude of mind marked by regular denial of or skepticism about nearly everything affirmed by others **:** habitual skepticism **2 :** a tendency to refuse to do what is asked, to do the opposite of what is asked, or to do something capriciously at variance with what is asked

neg·a·tiv·ist \-vəst\ *n* -s **:** one who adheres to or practices negativism

neg·a·tiv·is·tic \¦=,=,=¦vistik, -tēk\ *also* **negativist** *adj* **:** of, relating to, or marked by negativism

neg·a·tiv·i·ty \,negə'tivəd·ē\ *n* -ES **:** the quality or state of being negative **:** NEGATIVISM

ne·ga·tor *or* **ne·gat·er** \nə'gād·ə(r)\ *n* -s [*negator* fr. LL, fr. L *negatus*, past part. of *negare* to deny + -*or* -or; *negater* fr. ¹*negate* + -*er* — more at NEGATION] **:** one that negates

neg·a·to·ry \'negə,tōrē\ *adj* [MF and LL; MF *negatoire*, fr. LL *negatorius*, fr. L *negatus* + *-orius* -ory] **:** marked by or having the nature of negation **:** NEGATIVE ⟨~ criticism⟩

neg·a·tron \'negə,trän\ *also* **neg·a·ton** \-gə,tän\ *n* -s [*negatron* fr. ¹*negative* + *electron*; *negaton* fr. ¹*negative* + -*on*] **:** ELECTRON

ne·ger \'nēgə(r)\ *n* -s [MF *negre*, fr. Sp or Pg *negro* black, Negro] *dial chiefly Eng* **:** NEGRO

negidim *pl of* NAGID

¹**ne·glect** \nə'glekt, nē'-\ *vt* -ED/-ING/-S [L *neglectus*, past part. of *neglegere*, *negligere*, *neclegere*, fr. *nec-* not (akin to *ne-* not) + *legere* to choose, gather — more at NO, LEGEND] **1 a :** to give little or no attention or respect to **:** consider or deal with as if of little or no importance **:** DISREGARD, SLIGHT ⟨some of the most significant issues have been ~*ed* —Bruce Payne⟩ ⟨~*ed* the real needs of the students⟩ **b :** to fail to attend to sufficiently or properly **:** not give proper attention or care to ⟨a great deal of its important work must either be ~*ed* or only inadequately done —J.E.Smith⟩ ⟨~*ed* her clothes and hair⟩ ⟨~*ed* his correspondence⟩ **2 :** to carelessly omit doing (something that should be done) either altogether or almost altogether **:** leave undone or unattended to through carelessness or by intention **:** pass lightly over ⟨~*ing* their obvious duty⟩ ⟨~*ed* to mention that he was a convict —Bernard Smith⟩ **3** *obs* **:** to cause to be neglected ⟨my absence doth ~ no great design —Shak.⟩

syn NEGLECT, OMIT, DISREGARD, IGNORE, OVERLOOK, SLIGHT, and FORGET can mean in common to pass over something without giving it due or sufficient attention. NEGLECT implies failure to give full or proper attention to someone or something that has a claim on one's attention ⟨*neglect* the duties of a citizen⟩ ⟨*neglect* one's friends⟩ OMIT implies to neglect entirely, as by oversight or inattention, an important detail or aspect of a whole or of a series of related things ⟨wished his parents had *omitted* to have him baptized —Bruce Marshall⟩ ⟨small possessions of her own which she had *omitted* to remove from the . . . room —Arnold Bennett⟩ DISREGARD usu. implies a voluntary inattention ⟨efface and injure something in ourselves, when we hurry by and *disregard* what does not seem to profit our own existence —Laurence Binyon⟩ ⟨wished to affirm her right to *disregard* the feelings of all the world —Joseph Conrad⟩ IGNORE implies an intention to disregard or a failure to regard something more or less obvious ⟨he who *ignores* outsiders is naturally ignored himself —G.G.Coulton⟩ ⟨get a reputation for clarity by avoiding or *ignoring* all the tangled jungles, by detouring round the blind alleys and dead ends of thought —Irwin Edman⟩ ⟨*ignore* trivial irritations⟩ OVERLOOK implies a disregarding typically through haste or lack of care ⟨some of the most significant issues have been neglected, and many revealing lessons of past experience have been *overlooked* —Bruce Payne⟩ ⟨promised to give him some background work, a promise he later *overlooked* —*Amer. Guide Series: La.*⟩ SLIGHT usu. implies cursory treatment, often contemptuous, or a disdainful disregarding ⟨nothing in the service was *slighted*, every phrase and gesture had its full value —Willa Cather⟩ ⟨these systems sometimes do not receive their full share of attention and may be *slighted* in the design —H.J. Petersen⟩ ⟨felt as if he had been *slighted* by a close friend⟩ FORGET in this comparison can imply a willful ignoring but more often suggests an absentminded neglecting ⟨the matter seemed important but I was told by my superiors, who were afraid of trouble, to *forget* it⟩ ⟨*forgot* to turn off the gas before leaving the house⟩

²**neglect** \"\ *n* -s [L *neglectus*, fr. *neglectus*, past part. of *neglegere*] **1 a :** the action of neglecting something ⟨could not understand his ~ of her⟩ ⟨one other element which may have contributed to the ~ of this problem —H.G.Armstrong⟩ **b :** the condition of being neglected ⟨would sink back into relative ~ and stagnation —Harold Griffin⟩ **2 a :** the fact of neglecting or of being neglected ⟨cannot deny the total ~ of the house⟩ **b** *archaic* **:** an instance of neglecting or of being neglected ⟨recovering from . . . ravages and ~*s* —J.H.Stocqueler⟩ **syn** see FAILURE

ne·glect·able \-təbəl\ *adj* [¹*neglect* + -*able*] *archaic* **:** NEGLIGIBLE

neglected *adj* [fr. past part. of ¹*neglect*] **1 :** not properly or sufficiently attended to or cared for ⟨a very ~ child⟩ **2 :** that evidences improper or insufficient attention or care ⟨had a ~ appearance⟩ — **ne·glect·ed·ly** *adv* — **ne·glect·ed·ness** *n* -ES

ne·glect·er *also* **ne·glec·tor** \-tə(r)\ *n* -s [*neglecter* fr. ¹*neglect* + -*er*; *neglector* fr. LL, fr. L *neglectus* (past part. of *neglegere*) + -*or* -or] **:** one that neglects

ne·glect·ful \-tfəl\ *adj* [²*neglect* + -*ful*] **1 :** that neglects or is given to neglecting **:** CARELESS, HEEDLESS ⟨~ of what people might think⟩ ⟨telling the nurse she was as ~ as the rest of us —W.H.Wright⟩ **2 :** NEGLECTED 2 ⟨the ~ condition of the cemetery⟩ **syn** see NEGLIGENT

ne·glect·ful·ly \-fəlē, -li\ *adv* **:** in a neglectful manner

ne·glect·ful·ness *n* -ES **:** the quality or state of being neglectful

ne·glec·tion \nə'glekshən\ *n* -s [L *neglection-*, *neglectio* neglect, fr. *neglectus* (past part. of *neglegere* to neglect) + *-ion-*, *-io* -ion — more at NEGLECT] *chiefly dial* **:** NEGLECT

ne·glec·tive \-ktiv\ *adj* [¹*neglect* + -*ive*] *archaic* **:** NEGLECTFUL

neg·li·gee *or* **nég·li·gé** *or* **neg·li·gé** *also* **neg·li·ge** \,neglə'zhā, '=,=,=\ *n* -s [F *négligé*, fr. past part. of *négliger* to neglect, fr. L *negligere*, *neglegere*] **1 a :** a loose gown worn by women in the 18th century **b :** a woman's long flowing dressing gown usu. dressy in style and trimmed (as with lace, ruffles, fur) **2 :** carelessly informal or incomplete attire ⟨was lounging about at home in ~⟩

neg·li·gence \'negləjən(t)s\ *n* -s [ME *negligence*, *necgligence*, fr. MF & L; MF *negligence*, fr. L *neglegentia*, *neclegentia*, fr. *neglegent-*, *neglegens* + *-ia* -y] **1 a :** the quality or state of being negligent **b :** a failure to exercise the care that a prudent person usu. exercises — opposed to *diligence*; see GROSS NEGLIGENCE, ORDINARY NEGLIGENCE, SLIGHT NEGLIGENCE **2 :** an instance of negligence ⟨remembered his past ~*s*⟩

neg·li·gen·cy \-nsē\ *n* -ES [L *neglegentia*] *archaic* **:** NEGLIGENCE

¹**neg·li·gent** \-nt\ *adj* [ME *negligent*, *necgligent*, fr. MF & L; MF *negligent*, fr. L *neglegent-*, *neglegens*, pres. part. of *neglegere* to neglect — more at NEGLECT] **1 :** that is marked by or given to neglect **:** that is neglectful esp. habitually or culpably ⟨was a careless workman, ~ of detail —Edith Hamilton⟩ ⟨~ in his correspondence⟩; *specif* **:** not exercising the care usu. exercised by a prudent person ⟨~ about traffic regulations⟩ **2 :** that is marked by or given to a carelessly easy manner in such a way as to produce a usu. agreeable effect ⟨~ speech⟩ ⟨~ action⟩ **:** marked by a nonchalant indifference **:** free from stiffness or restraint **:** not labored or artificial **:** UNSTUDIED, OFFHAND ⟨converse with ~ ease upon indifferent topics —Arnold Bennett⟩ ⟨wore clothes with a ~ grace⟩

syn NEGLECTFUL, LAX, SLACK, REMISS: NEGLIGENT suggests culpable inattentiveness resulting in imperfection, incompleteness, slovenliness, or danger or damage to others ⟨so *negligent* in his poetical style . . . so slovenly, slipshod, and infelicitous —Matthew Arnold⟩ ⟨would come from the kitchen and pass slowly about the table, vaguely *negligent* unless she was directed by . . . brief orders —Elizabeth M. Roberts⟩ ⟨*negligent* about not maintaining a steady watch on the fire⟩ NEGLECTFUL may be more censorious in centering attention without palliation on the fact of neglect ⟨was not *neglectful* and would write as soon as he found anything good —Upton Sinclair⟩ ⟨peoples who when they dress themselves are utterly *neglectful* of what we consider the first requirements of decency —Edward Westermarck) LAX implies a want of strictness, stringency, precision, severity, or careful attention, usu. a blameworthy want ⟨scandalously *lax* in restraining drunkards from annoying the sober —G.M.Trevelyan⟩ ⟨their rather *lax* mental processes allow sweeping generalizations about the riddle of the universe and the mystery that is man —W.L.Sperry⟩ SLACK suggests want of necessary due care, diligence, attention, or application ⟨if they were *slack* in performing these arduous duties —G.M.Trevelyan⟩ ⟨one of the oars slipped from her *slack* grasp and floated beside the drifting skiff —B.A.Williams⟩ REMISS strongly implies the fact of blameworthiness or culpability without implication about the degree ⟨so *remiss* did they become in their attentions that we could no longer rely upon their bringing us the daily supply of food —Herman Melville⟩ ⟨shamefully *remiss* about paying them —H.E.Scudder⟩

²**negligent** \"\ *n* -s *archaic* **:** a negligent person

negligent escape *n* **:** the escape of a prisoner without prison breach and without the custodian's consent and arising through the custodian's negligence — contrasted with *voluntary escape*

neg·li·gent·ly *adv* [ME, fr. ¹*negligent* + *-ly*] **:** in a negligent manner ⟨did their work ~⟩ ⟨was strolling ~ toward them, smoking a cigarette —Dorothy Sayers⟩

neg·li·gi·bil·i·ty \ˌnegləjə'biləd·ē, -lēj-, -ətē, -i\ *n* -ES **:** the quality or state of being negligible ⟨differences between the two positions dwindle to ~ —Lucius Garvin⟩

neg·li·gi·ble *also* **neg·lige·able** \'negləjəbəl, -lēj-\ *adj* [*negligible* fr. *neglig-* (fr. L *negligere*) + *-ible*; *negligeable* fr. F *négligeable*, fr. *négliger* to neglect (fr. L *negligere*) + *-able*] **:** that can or should easily be disregarded: **a :** that is so tiny or unimportant or otherwise of so little consequence as to require or deserve little or no attention **:** TRIFLING ⟨the error involved is ~ —W.H.Dowdeswell⟩ **b :** that is of so little substance or extent or worth as to be practically nonexistent and so requiring or deserving little or no attention or respect ⟨trade or industry is practically ~ —S.J.Roche⟩ ⟨made ~ progress⟩ ⟨poisonous plants in Arizona are so rare as to be ~ —*Amer. Guide Series: Ariz.*⟩ ⟨a pious and good man, but an utterly ~ personality —Compton Mackenzie⟩

neg·li·gi·bly \-blē\ *adv* [*negligible* + *-ly*] **:** to a negligible extent ⟨are small, but not ~ small —Fred Hoyle⟩

negociate *archaic var of* NEGOTIATE

ne·go·tia·bil·i·ty \nəˌgōsh(ē)ə'biləd·ē, nē,-, -ətē, -i\ *n* **:** the quality or state of being negotiable

ne·go·tia·ble \nə'gōsh(ē)əbəl, nē'-\ *adj* [*negotiate* + *-able*] **:** that can be negotiated: as **a :** that can be transferred or assigned from one person to another in return for equivalent value by being delivered either with endorsement (as of an instrument payable to order) or without endorsement (as of an instrument payable to bearer) so that the title passes to the transferee who is not prejudiced in his rights by any defect or flaw in the title of prior parties nor by personal defenses available to prior parties among themselves provided in both cases that the transferee is a bona fide holder without notice ⟨bills of exchange, promissory notes, and checks that are payable to bearer or order are ~ instruments, as are also, in some jurisdictions, some other instruments (as bonds, some forms of stock)⟩ ⟨~ paper⟩ ⟨~ securities⟩ **b** (1) **:** that can be successfully traversed ⟨the road, normally ~ by jeep —Herbert Passin⟩ ⟨a difficult but ~ path through the forest⟩ ⟨going up or down ⟨a ~ hill⟩ or otherwise successfully managed ⟨a sharp curve in the road that is ~ if one goes slowly⟩ (2) **:** that can be met and successfully dealt with **:** that does not pose insurmountable problems ⟨familiar and ~ situations —Anthony West⟩ (3) **:** that can be arrived at **:** that can be done or accomplished or realized **:** ATTAINABLE ⟨thought that some kind of treaty was ~⟩ ⟨not readily ~ by empirical method —V.C. Aldrich⟩ (4) **:** that can be readily understood ⟨disclose its fundamental motives in widely ~ language —H.E.Clurman⟩ **c** (1) **:** that is utilizable in a practical way ⟨the old rhetoric ... is no longer ~ —E.R.Bentley⟩ (2) **:** that has characteristics favoring wide acceptance ⟨have found a home where their ideas are ~ —R.M.Weaver⟩ ⟨is ~ to the widest possible public —W.L.Miller⟩ **:** that has high commercial value ⟨seems to be highly ~ at the box office —Barbara B. Jamison⟩ **d :** that is open to discussion or question or dispute ⟨criticism, which is public and ~ —J.C.Ransom⟩ ⟨have declared that their claim ... is not ~ —*New Republic*⟩

ne·go·ti·ant \-sh(ē)ənt\ *n* -s [L *negotiant-, negotians* trader, fr. pres. part. of *negotiari*] **:** NEGOTIATOR

ne·go·ti·ate \-s(h)ēˌāt, *usu* -ād·+V\ *vb* -ED/-ING/-S [L *negotiatus*, past part. of *negotiari* to carry on business, fr. *negotium* business, fr. *neg-* not (akin to *ne-* not) + *otium* leisure — more at NO] *vi* **1 :** to communicate or confer with another so as to arrive at the settlement of some matter **:** meet with another so as to arrive through discussion at some kind of agreement or compromise about something **:** come to terms esp. in state matters by meetings and discussions ⟨*negotiated* with him on the political and economic program to be carried out —*Current Biog.*⟩ ⟨wanted to ~ before naming a final price⟩ ⟨*negotiating* with the foreign ministers⟩ **2** *obs* **:** to carry on business or trade **:** TRAFFIC ~ *vt* **1 a :** to deal with (some matter or affair that requires ability for its successful handling) **:** MANAGE, HANDLE, CONDUCT ⟨*negotiated* his business deals with remarkable skill⟩ **b** (1) **:** to arrange for or bring about through conference and discussion **:** work out or arrive at or settle upon by meetings and agreements or compromises ⟨*negotiating* a peace treaty⟩ ⟨one of his first actions was to ~ a monetary understanding with the British government —*Current Biog.*⟩ (2) **:** to influence successfully in a desired way by discussions and agreements or compromises ⟨*negotiated* them into doing exactly what he wanted⟩ **2 a :** to transfer or assign (as a check, bill of exchange, promissory note) to another by delivery or endorsement or both in return for equivalent value **b :** to convert (as a check) into cash or the equivalent value ⟨*negotiating* securities⟩ **c :** to give equivalent value for (as a check) ⟨offered to ~ any checks properly drawn up⟩ **3 a :** to successfully get over or across (as a road) or up or down (as a hill) or through (as an obstacle) ⟨carefully *negotiated* the winding road⟩ ⟨took me almost an hour to ~ the almost perpendicular trail —V.W. Von Hagen⟩ **b :** to encounter and dispose of (as a problem, challenge) with completeness and satisfaction **:** tackle successfully ⟨*negotiated* the difficult arpeggios of the song cleanly and confidently —*Current Biog.*⟩ **c :** COMPLETE, ACCOMPLISH ⟨~*s* the trip in 4 hours⟩

ne·go·ti·a·tion \=ˌ==ˈāshən\ *n* -s [L *negotiation-, negotiatio*, fr. *negotiatus* + *-ion-, -io* -ion] **1** *obs* **a :** a business transaction **b :** TRADING, TRAFFICKING **2 :** the action or process of negotiating or of being negotiated ⟨the dispute is now under ~⟩ — often used in pl. ⟨proposed resumption of ~*s* on the long treaty draft —*Americana Annual*⟩

ne·go·ti·a·tor \=ˈ==ˌād·ə(r), -ātə-\ *n* -s [L, trader, fr. *negotiatus* + *-or* -or] **:** one that negotiates

ne·go·ti·a·to·ry \nə'gōshēəˌtōrē\ *adj* [*negotiate* + *-ory*] **:** of or relating to negotiation ⟨a ~ association that was formed for carrying on discussions with trade unions⟩ ⟨have been restricted to ~ functions —Dale Yoder⟩

ne·go·ti·a·tress \nə'gōshēəˌtrəs\ *n* -ES [*negotiator* + *-ess*] **:** a female negotiator

ne·go·ti·a·trix \-riks\ *n* -ES [NL, fem. of *negotiator*] **:** NEGOTIATRESS

ne·go·ti·o·rum ges·tio \nəˌgōd·ē'ōˌrüm'gestēˌō\ *n* [LL, fr. L, management of business] **:** GESTION 2

neg·re \'negrā\ *n* -s [origin unknown] **:** RED GROUPER

ne·gress \'nēgrəs\ *n* -ES *usu cap* [F *négresse*, fr. *nègre* Negro (fr. Sp or Pg *negro*, black, Negro) + *-esse* -ess] **:** a female Negro — usu. taken to be offensive

ne·gri body \'nāgrē-\ *n, usu cap N* [after Adelchi *Negri* †1912 Ital. physician] **:** an inclusion body found in the nerve cells in rabies

ne·grid \'nēgrəd\ *n* -s *often cap* [ISV *negr-* Negro (fr. ¹*negro*) + *-id*] **1 :** NEGRITO **2 :** NEGRILLO

ne·gril·lo \nə'griˌ(l)lō\ *n, pl* **negrillos** *or* **negrilloes** *usu cap* [Sp, dim. of *negro* black, Negro] **:** a member of a people (as Bushmen, Pygmies) belonging to a group of negroid peoples of small stature found in Africa — usu. distinguished from *Negrito*

ne·grit·ic \nə'grid·ik\ *adj, often cap* [partly fr. *negro* + *-itic*; partly fr. *negrito* + *-ic*] **:** of, relating to, or resembling Negroes or Negritos

ne·gri·to \nə'grē(ˌ)tō\ *n, pl* **negritos** *or* **negritoes** [Sp, dim. of *negro*] **1** *usu cap* **:** a member of a people (as the Andamanese) belonging to a group of negroid peoples of small stature found in Oceania and the southeastern part of Asia — usu. distinguished from *Negrillo* **2 :** PARADISE TREE 1a

ne·grit·oid \-riˌtȯid\ *adj, often cap* [*negrito* + *-oid*] **:** of, relating to, or having the characteristics of Negritos

¹**ne·gro** \'nē(ˌ)grō, *esp South* 'ni(ˌ)- *or* -grə\ *n* -ES [Sp or Pg *negro*, black, Negro, fr. L *nigr-, niger* black] **1** *usu cap* **a :** a member of the black race of mankind as opposed by classification according to physical features (as skin color, hair form, or body or skeletal characteristics) but without regard to language or culture to members of the Caucasian, Mongoloid, or other races of mankind; *esp* **:** a member of a people belonging to the African branch of the black race and marked typically by dark pigmentation and woolly hair and everted lips and broad flat noses and prognathism **b :** a person of Negro ancestry; *esp* **:** a person whose pigmentation is dark like that of typical African Negroes and who often (as with mulattoes) has other physical characteristics of typical African Negroes **2 :** a black to dark grayish yellowish brown — called also *Saint Benoit*; see MINERAL BROWN

²**negro** \"\ *adj, usu cap* **:** of, relating to, or having the characteristics of Negroes

negro-african \ˌ=(ˌ)=ˈ===\ *n, cap N&A* **1** *in former classifications* **:** a family of African languages **2 :** the indigenous languages of Africa south of the Sahara

negro ant *n* **:** a common widely distributed black ant (*Formica fusca*)

negro bug *n, sometimes cap N* **:** any of numerous minute convex black bugs that constitute the genus *Corimelaena* and that feed on plant juices and impart a foul taste to fruits (as raspberries) over which they crawl; *esp* **:** a common pest (*C. pulicaria*) of the U.S. east of the Rocky mountains that is sometimes very destructive to celery, corn, and wheat

negro cloth *or* **negro cotton** *n, often cap N* **:** a strong coarse cloth formerly used in making clothes for Negro slaves

negro coffee *n, often cap N* **:** COFFEE SENNA

negrohead \'=(ˌ)=ˌ=\ *n* [fr. its color] **1 :** a dark lump or mass of tobacco or inferior rubber **2 :** NIGGERHEAD 3

negrohead beech *n* **:** an Australian timber tree (*Nothofagus moorei*) having dark green foliage

¹**ne·groid** \'nēˌgrȯid\ *adj, often cap* [ISV *negr-* Negro (fr. ¹*negro*) + *-oid*] **:** of, resembling, or related to the Negro race

²**negroid** \"\ *n* -s *usu cap* **:** a negroid individual

ne·gro·ism \'nēgrōˌizəm\ *n* -s *often cap* **1 :** advancement of Negro interests; *specif* **:** advocacy of the cause of equal rights for Negroes **2 :** a quality or trait distinctive or taken to be distinctive of Negroes; *esp* **:** a word, phrase, or manner of expression distinctive or taken to be distinctive of the speech of Negroes

ne·gro·ize \-ˌīz\ *vt* -ED/-ING/-S *sometimes cap* **1 :** to cause to be Negro (as in qualities, personnel) ⟨*negroized* speech⟩ ⟨a new *negroized* stage production⟩ ⟨a *negroized* unit⟩ **2 :** to imbue with negroism ⟨a *negroized* philanthropic group⟩

negro monkey *n* **1 :** MOOR MACAQUE **2 :** a black langur (*Presbytis maurus*) **3** *or* **negro tamarin :** a black Brazilian tamarin (*Leontocebus ursulus*)

negro peach *n* **1 :** a stout spreading or semiclimbing shrub (*Sarcocephalus esculentus*) of tropical Africa and Ceylon with round brownish warty fruit having a reddish watery pulp **2 :** the fruit of the negro peach

¹**ne·gro·phile** \'nēgrōˌfīl\ *also* **ne·gro·phil** \-fil\ *n* -s *often cap* [¹*negro* + *-phile*] **:** one that is esp. friendly to Negroes and their interests; *esp* **:** one that favors negroism

²**negrophile** \"\ *adj, often cap* **:** having the qualities of a negrophile

ne·groph·i·lism \nə'gräfəˌlizəm\ *n* -s *often cap* **:** NEGROISM

ne·groph·i·list \nə'gräfələst\ *n* -s *often cap* **:** NEGROPHILE

¹**ne·gro·phobe** \'nēgrōˌfōb\ *n* -s *often cap* **:** one that strongly dislikes or fears Negroes

²**negrophobe** \"\ *adj, often cap* **:** having the qualities of a negrophobe

ne·gro·pho·bia \ˌ==ˈfōbēə\ *n, often cap* [NL, fr. E *negro* + NL *-phobia*] **:** strong dislike or fear of Negroes — **ne·gro·pho·bic** \ˌ==ˈfōbik, -bēk *also* -fäb-\ *adj, often cap*

negro vine *n* **:** an herbaceous vine (*Vincetoxicum hirsutum*) with hairy foliage and dark purple flowers

ne·gun·do \nə'gən(ˌ)dō\ *n* [NL, fr. a native name in India for plants of the genus *Vitex*, fr. Skt *nirgundī*] **1** *cap, in some classifications* **:** a genus of trees set off from *Acer* on the basis of the pinnate leaves **2** -s **:** BOX ELDER

¹**ne·gus** \'nēgəs\ *n* -ES [Amharic *negūs*, fr. Eth *nĕgūša, nagašt* king of kings] **:** KING — used as a title of the sovereign of Ethiopia

²**negus** \"\ *n* -ES [after Francis *Negus* †1732 Eng. colonel, its originator] **:** a beverage of claret, port, or other wine heated with hot water, sweetened, and often flavored with lemon juice and nutmeg

ne·hu \'neˌ(ˌ)hü\ *n, pl* **nehu** *or* **nehus** [Hawaiian] **:** a small Hawaiian anchovy (*Anchoviella purpureus*) much used for bait

NEI *abbr, often not cap* **1** [L *non est inventus*] he was not found **2** not elsewhere included; not elsewhere indicated

nei·bour \'nēbə(r)\ *Scot var of* NEIGHBOR

neid \'nēd\ *Scot var of* NEED

ne·id·i·dae \nē'idəˌdē\ *n pl, cap* [NL, fr. *Neides*, type genus, + *-idae*] **:** a family of long-legged slender-bodied bugs with elbowed antennae of which the first joint is long and clubbed and the last is spindle-shaped — see STILT BUG

¹**neif** \'nēf\ *n* -s [fr. (assumed) AF *neif, naif*, fr. OF *naif* native, fr. L *nativus* — more at NATIVE] **:** one born a serf

²**neif** \'nēf\ *chiefly dial var of* ¹NIEVE

¹**neigh** \'nā\ *vb* -ED/-ING/-S [ME *neyen*, fr. OE *hnǣgan*; akin to MHG *nēgen* to neigh, ON *gneggja*; all fr. a prehistoric Gmc vb. of imit. origin] *vi* **:** to make the loud prolonged calling cry typical of a horse ~ *vt* **:** to utter by or as if by neighing

²**neigh** \"\ *n* -s **:** the loud prolonged calling cry typical of a horse

¹**neigh·bor** \'nābə(r)\ *n* -s *see -or in Explan Notes* [ME *neighbor, neighebor*, fr. OE *nēahgebūr*; akin to MD *nāgebuur*, OHG *nāhgibūr*; all fr. a prehistoric WGmc compound whose first element is represented by OE *nēah* near and whose second element is represented by OE *gebūr* dweller — more at NIGH, BOOR] **1 a :** one whose house or other place of residence immediately adjoins or is relatively near that of another **:** one that lives next to or near another **b :** one whose town or district or country immediately adjoins or is relatively near that of another **c** (1) **:** one whose position (as in sitting, standing) immediately adjoins or is relatively near that of another ⟨each of the students in the classroom passed his paper to his ~⟩ (2) **:** CORNER 7 **d :** something located in a position immediately adjoining or relatively near that of another ⟨Canada is the northern ~ of the U.S.⟩ ⟨Venus is one of Earth's nearest ~*s*⟩ **2 a :** a fellow creature; *esp* **:** a fellow human being ⟨thou shalt love thy ~ as thyself —Mt 19:19 (AV)⟩ ⟨closing their eyes and their hearts to the misfortune of a ~ who is unknown and far away —Pius XII⟩ **b :** one that evidences true kindness and charity toward his fellowman ⟨proved ~ to the man who fell among the robbers —Lk 10:36 (RSV)⟩ **3** — used as a term of familiar direct address esp. to one whose name is not known ⟨say, ~, give me a hand⟩ and often with an implication of stiff reserve or condescension or mild hostility ⟨better not say things you oughtn't, ~⟩ **4** *chiefly Scot* **:** one of a pair

²**neighbor** \"\ *adj* **:** that immediately adjoins or is relatively near another **:** that is a neighbor **:** NEIGHBORING ⟨promised our ~ American republics —Blair Bolles⟩

³**neighbor** \"\ *vb* **neighbored; neighbored; neighboring** \-b(ə)riŋ\ **neighbors** *vt* **1 a :** to adjoin immediately or lie relatively near to **:** border upon ⟨the U.S. ~*s* the northern border of Mexico⟩ **b** *archaic* **:** to come close to **:** APPROACH ⟨can pretty nigh ~ it with a guess —George Meredith⟩ **2 :** to put into the position or relationship of having (something indicated) immediately adjoining or closely situated ⟨a building of admirable proportions is this, ~*ed* by other public structures of vast size —Aubrey Drury⟩ ~ *vi* **1 a :** to have one's house or other place of residence immediately adjoining or relatively near that of another ⟨she ~*ed* close upon the street where her former friend lived⟩ **b :** to have an immediately adjoining or relatively near position or location ⟨the earth ~*s* near to the sun⟩ **2 :** to associate in a friendly way (as by exchanging visits, having informal chats, offering other help and advice) with another that is a neighbor **:** make the agreeable easy social contacts usual among congenial neighbors ⟨it was a quiet farmplace, standing among fields . . . yet it was near enough the town for ~*ing* —Maristan Chapman⟩ ⟨had no mind to ~ with them —V.L.Parrington⟩

neigh·bor·hood \-(r)ˌhu̇d\ *n* [ME *neighborhode*, fr. ¹*neighbor* + *-hode*, -hood] **1 :** friendly association with another that is a neighbor **:** the agreeable easy relationship usual among congenial neighbors ⟨if there are remoter nations that wish us not good but ill, they know that we are strong; they know that we can and will defend our ~ —F.D.Roosevelt⟩ **2 :** the quality or state of being immediately adjacent or relatively near to something **:** PROXIMITY ⟨the ~ of the earth to the sun⟩ ⟨refugees from the country, driven by fear or the ~ of armies —F.L.Paxson⟩ **3 a :** the approximate area or point of the location or position of something ⟨traveled to a region somewhere in the ~ of that city⟩ **b :** the approximate amount or extent or degree — usu. used with *in* and a qualifying phrase ⟨has in the ~ of $10,000,000⟩ ⟨a highway in the ~ of 100 miles long⟩ **4 a :** a number of people forming a loosely cohesive community within a larger unit (as a city, town) and living close or fairly close together in more or less familiar association with each other within a relatively small section or district of usu. somewhat indefinite boundaries and usu. having some common or fairly common identifying feature (as approximate equality of economic condition, similar social status, similar national origins or religion, similar interests) and usu. some degree of self-sufficiency as a group (as through local schools, churches, libraries, business establishments, cultural and recreational facilities) ⟨thought the whole ~ would hear about it⟩ **b :** the particular section or district that is lived in by these people and that is marked by individual features (as type of homes and public establishments) that together establish a distinctive appearance and atmosphere ⟨now lives in a beautiful ~⟩ **c :** an area or region of usu. vague limits that is usu. marked by some fairly distinctive feature of the inhabitants or terrain ⟨would never want to live in that ~ of the country⟩ **5 :** the assemblage of all points whose distances from a given point are not greater than a given positive number

neighborhood house *n* **:** SETTLEMENT 6g

neighboring *adj* [fr. pres. part. of ³*neighbor*] **1 :** that is immediately adjacent or relatively near ⟨where the men from the ~ towns gathered —Phyllis Duganne⟩ ⟨~ countries⟩ ⟨~ planets⟩ **2** *of atoms or groups in a molecule* **:** attached to atoms united to each other; *esp* **:** attached to carbon atoms united to each other in aliphatic or alicyclic compounds — compare VICINAL 3

neighboring tone *n* **:** AUXILIARY TONE

neigh·bor·less \'nābə(r)ləs\ *adj* **:** having no neighbor

neighborlike \'==ˌ=\ *adj* **:** NEIGHBORLY

neigh·bor·li·ness \'nābə(r)lēnəs, -lin-\ *n* -ES **:** the quality or state of being neighborly

¹**neigh·bor·ly** \-lē, -li\ *adv* [*neighbor* + *-ly*, adv. suffix] *archaic* **:** in a neighborly manner ⟨you called in here ~ —John Drinkwater⟩

²**neighborly** \"\ *adj* [*neighbor* + *-ly*, adj. suffix] **1 :** of, relating to, or typical of neighbors, esp. congenial neighbors **:** suited to neighbors ⟨a ~ conversation⟩ ⟨has ~ chores —Mary Welsh⟩ ⟨~ helpfulness⟩ **2 :** that readily associates in a friendly way (as by exchanging visits, having informal chats, offering ordinary help and advice) with a neighbor **:** that has the agreeable easy sociability typical of a congenial neighbor ⟨a pleasant ~ person⟩ **syn** see AMICABLE

neigh·bor·ship \-(r)ˌship\ *n* [ME *nychtbourschip*, fr. *nychtbour, neighbor* + *-schip, -ship* -ship] **1** *archaic* **:** PROXIMITY **2** *archaic* **:** the relationship and activity of a neighbor ⟨its true interest is a good ~ —Jedediah Morse⟩

neigh·er \'nikə(r)\ *vi* -ED/-ING/-S [imit.] *Scot* **:** ⁴NICKER

ne·i·lah \ˌneē'lä, neˈēlə\ *n* -s [Heb *nĕ'īlāh* closing of gates; fr. the closing of the gates of the Temple at Jerusalem at the end of the service] **:** the concluding portion of the liturgy on Yom Kippur

nei·per \'nēpə(r)\ *Scot var of* NEIGHBOR

neis·se·ria \nī'sirēə\ *n, cap* [NL, fr. Albert L. S. *Neisser* †1916 Ger. physician + NL *-ia*] **:** a genus of parasitic bacteria (the type of the family Neisseriaceae) growing in pairs and occas. tetrads and thriving best at 98.6°F in the animal body or serum media — see GONOCOCCUS, MENINGOCOCCUS

neis·ser·i·a·ce·ae \nīˌsirē'āsēˌē\ *n pl, cap* [NL, fr. *Neisseria*, type genus + *-aceae*] **:** a small family of spherical nonmotile gram-negative bacteria (order Eubacteriales) that are obligate parasites of warm-blooded vertebrates — see NEISSERIA

neis·se·ri·an \(')nīˌsirēən\ *adj* [NL *Neisseria* + E *-an*] **:** of, relating to, or caused by the gonococcus

neist \'nēst\ *chiefly Scot var of* NEXT

¹**nei·ther** \'nēthə(r), 'nīth-; *see* EITHER\ *pron* [ME *neither, naither* not either of two, pron., conj. & adj., alter. (influenced by *either, aither* either) of *nauther*, pron. & conj., *nouther, nowther*, pron., conj. & adj., *nother*, pron. & adj., fr. OE *nāhwæther, nawther*, pron. & conj., *nōhwæther, nowther*, pron., *nōther*, pron., fr. *nā, nō* not + *hwæther* which of two, whether — more at NO, WHETHER] **:** not one of two or more **:** not either: **a :** not the one and not the other of two ⟨made two suggestions and ~ was accepted⟩ **b :** not any one of more than two ⟨~ of the three men stood up —Luke Short⟩ — usu. sing. in constr. except when a periphrastic genitive intervenes between *neither* and the verb form in which circumstance the verb is often plural in form ⟨~ of them were in —John Galsworthy⟩; often qualified by a periphrastic genitive and used in apposition with a plural pronominal subject to emphasize the exclusion of each of the individuals included in the subject from the thing predicated ⟨we ~ of us moved —Wendy Wood⟩ ⟨two English painters who are ~ of them abstract or surrealist —Geoffrey Grigson⟩

²**neither** \"\ *conj* [ME *neither, naither*] **1** — used as a function word before two or more coordinate words, phrases, or clauses now joined usu. by *nor* or sometimes by *or* or archaically by *neither* to indicate that what immediately follows is the first of two or more alternatives both or all of which are rejected ⟨~ my father nor I were by nature inclined to faith in the unintelligible —George Santayana⟩ **2 :** nor yet **:** also not **:** no more ⟨just as the serf was not permitted to leave the land, so ~ was his offspring —G.G.Coulton⟩ ⟨an illiterate author cannot get very far, and ~ can a musical composer who has not learned musical notation —Thomas Munro⟩ ⟨justice is ~ new nor old —Mark Van Doren⟩ ⟨sat at bare tables and ~ ate, drank, nor smoked —Mary Cable⟩ ⟨~ by day nor by night⟩ ⟨we believe ~ in prescribing or proscribing books —*Publisher's Weekly*⟩ ⟨this court ~ approves or condemns any legislative policy —O.J.Roberts⟩

³**neither** \"\ *adj* [ME *neither, naither*] **:** not either ⟨on ~ side of the street are there any trees⟩

⁴**neither** \"\ *adv, chiefly dial* **:** EITHER — used esp. to emphasize a negative in a foregoing clause ⟨others speak so fast and sputter that they are not to be understood ~ —Earl of Chesterfield⟩

neive \'nēv\ *chiefly dial var of* ¹NIEVE

nejd \'nejd\ *also* **nej·di** \-dē\ *adj, usu cap* [*nejd* fr. *Nejd*, state of Saudi Arabia; *nejdi* fr. Ar *najdīy*, fr. *Najd* Nejd] **:** of or relating to the inland state of Nejd in Saudi Arabia

nejdi *n* -s *cap* [Ar *najdīy*] **:** a native or inhabitant of Nejd

nek·ton *also* **nec·ton** \'nektən\ *n* -s [G *nekton*, fr. Gk *nēkton*, neut. of *nēktos* swimming — more at NECT-] **:** free swimming aquatic animals essentially independent of wave and current action — compare PLANKTON — **nek·ton·ic** \(')nek'tänik\ *adj*

nell \'nel\ *n* -s [by shortening & alter.] **:** MENEL

nel·lore \nə'lō(ə)r\ *n, usu cap* [fr. *Nellore*, town in southeast Indian Union] **:** an Indian breed of large steel-gray to almost white cattle used chiefly for heavy draft and introduced in many warm regions for crossbreeding with European cattle

nel·ly \'nelē\ *n* -ES [perh. fr. *Nelly*, nickname for *Helen*] **1 :** GIANT PETREL **2 :** SOOTY ALBATROSS

nel·ma \'nelmə\ *n* -s [Russ *nel'ma*] **:** INCONNU

¹**nel·son** \'nelsən\ *adj, usu cap* [fr. *Nelson*, provincial district of New Zealand] **:** of or from the provincial district of Nelson, New Zealand **:** of the kind or style prevalent in the Nelson provincial district

2nelson \"\ *n* -s [prob. fr. the name *Nelson*] : a wrestling hold marked by a distinctive application of leverage against an opponent's arm and neck and head — see FULL NELSON, HALF NELSON, QUARTER NELSON, THREE-QUARTER NELSON

nelson bighorn sheep *n, usu cap N* [prob. fr. the name *Nelson*] : a large dark-coated wild sheep that is a variety (*Ovis canadensis nelsoni*) of the bighorn distinguished by its very large horns and now rare over much of its range in the mountainous regions of western No. America

nelson's oriole *n, usu cap N* [after Edward W. *Nelson* †1934 Am. naturalist] : HOODED ORIOLE

ne·lum·bi·um \nəˈləmbēəm\ [NL, fr. Sinhalese *nelumbu* + NL *-ium*] *syn of* NELUMBO

ne·lum·bo \-ləm(ˌ)bō\ *n* [NL, fr. Sinhalese *nelumbu*, Indian lotus] **1** *cap* : a genus that includes large water lilies having flowers with 4 to 5 sepals, numerous petals, and the discrete carpels embedded in a fleshy receptacle and that is usu. considered to constitute a subfamily of Nymphaeaceae but is sometimes isolated in a separate family **2** *or* **nelumbium** -s : any plant of the genus *Nelumbo* — compare LOTUS 3

nem- *or* **nema-** *or* **nemo-** *comb form* [Gk & NL; NL *nem-*, *nemo-*, fr. Gk *nēma*] **1** : thread ⟨*nema*thecium⟩ ⟨*Nem*ichthys⟩ ⟨*Nemo*cera⟩ **2** : nematode ⟨*nema*cide⟩ ⟨*nem*ic⟩

NEM *abbr, often not cap* not elsewhere mentioned

ne·ma \ˈnēmə\ *n* -s [NL, fr. Gk *nēma* thread — more at NEEDLE] **1** : a tubular filament that connects the disk of attachment of a graptolite with the primary theca **2** : NEMATODE, ROUNDWORM, EELWORM

-ne·ma \ˈnēmə\ *n comb form, pl* **-nema·ta** \ˈnēməd·ə, ˈnem-, -mətə\ *or* **-nemas** [NL, fr. Gk *nēma* thread] : one having, being, or resembling (such) a thread ⟨chromo*nema*⟩ — esp. in generic names in botany and zoology ⟨Hyalo*nema*⟩ ⟨Scyto*nema*⟩

nemacide *var of* NEMATOCIDE

nem·a·line \ˈneməˌlīn, -ˌlən\ *adj* [*nem-* + connective *-l-* + *-ine*] *of a mineral* : having the form of threads : FIBROUS

ne·ma·li·on \nəˈmālēən\ *n, cap* [NL, irreg. fr. Gk *nēma* thread] : a genus of reddish brown gelatinous wormlike branching algae (family Helminthocladiaceae) found clinging to rocks in the intertidal zone in the north Atlantic

ne·ma·li·o·na·ce·ae \nəˌmālēōˈnāsēˌē\ [NL, fr. *Nemalion* + *-aceae*] *syn of* HELMINTHOCLADIACEAE

ne·ma·li·o·na·les \-ˈnā(ˌ)lēz\ *n pl, cap* [NL, fr. *Nemalion* + *-ales*] : an order of red algae (class Rhodophyceae) that have only a gametophytic generation and carpospores which develop from end cells of short filaments sprouting from a carpogonium

nem·a·lite \ˈneməˌlīt\ *n* -s [Gk *nēma* thread + E *-lite*] : a fibrous brucite

nem·a·sto·ma·ce·ae \ˌneməstōˈmāsēˌē, nəˌmas-\ *n pl, cap* [NL, fr. *Nemastoma*, type genus (fr. *nem-* + *stoma*) + *-aceae*] : a family of red algae (order Cryptonemiales) with cylindrical, flat, or leaflike thalli and sunken cystocarps

nema·sty·lis \ˌneməˈstīləs\ *n, cap* [NL, fr. *nem-* + Gk *stylis* small pillar, dim. of *stylos* pillar — more at STOW] : a genus of bulbous perennial herbs (family Iridaceae) that are characterized by terete stems, few plicate leaves, few-flowered spathes, and threadlike style branches

nemat- *or* **nemato-** *comb form* [NL, fr. Gk *nēmat-*, *nēma* thread] **1** : thread ⟨*nemat*ic⟩ ⟨*Nemato*spora⟩ **2** : nematode ⟨*nemato*cide⟩

nem·a·tel·mia \ˌneməˈtelmēə\ *or* **nem·a·tel·min·thes** \-ˌtelˈmin(t)(ˌ)thēz\ [*Nematelmia* fr. NL, fr. *nemat-* + *-elmia* (fr. Gk *helminth-*, *helmis* intestinal worm, parasitic worm); *Nematelminthes* fr. NL, fr. *nemat-* + *-elminthes* (fr. Gk *helminth-*, *helmis*) — more at HELMINTH-] *syn of* NEMATHELMINTHES

nem·a·the·cial \ˌneməˈthēsh(ē)əl, -thēsēəl\ *adj* [*nemathecium* + *-al*] : of or relating to a nemathecium

nem·a·the·ci·um \ˌneməˈthēs(h)ēəm\ *n, pl* **nemathe·cia** \-ēə\ [NL, fr. *nem-* + *-thecium*] : a wartlike prominence on the thallus of a red alga containing tetraspores, antheridia, or cystocarps

nem·a·thel·mia \ˌneməˈthelmēə\ [NL, fr. *nemat-* + *-helmia* (fr. Gk *helminth-*, *helmis*)] *syn of* NEMATHELMINTHES

nem·a·thel·minth \-lˌmin(t)th\ *n* -s [NL *Nemathelminthes*] : a worm of the phylum Nemathelminthes

nem·a·thel·min·thes \-ˌthelˈmin(t)(ˌ)thēz\ *n pl, cap* [NL, fr. *nemat-* + *Helminthes*] *in some classifications* : a phylum including the Nematoda and Nematomorpha and sometimes the Acanthocephala, the Rotifera, the Gastrotricha, and the Kinorhyncha, all being more or less wormlike animals with a cylindrical unsegmented body covered by an unciliated ectoderm that secretes an external cuticle

ne·mat·ic \nəˈmad·ik\ *adj* [ISV *nemat-* + *-ic*] : of, relating to, or being the phase of a liquid crystal characterized by arrangement of the long axes of the molecules in parallel lines but not layers — compare CHOLESTERIC 2, SMECTIC

nem·a·to·blas·tic \ˌneməd·əˈblastik, nəˌmad-\ *adj* [ISV *nemat-* + *blastic*] *of metamorphic rock* : having a texture corresponding to the fibrous texture in igneous rock

nem·a·toc·era \ˌneməˈtäsərə\ *n pl, cap* [NL, fr. *nemat-* + *-cera*] : a suborder of Diptera including the mosquitoes, fungus gnats, and crane flies — **nem·a·toc·er·an** \ˌ==ˈ==rən\ *adj or n* — **nem·a·toc·er·ous** \-rəs\ *adj*

nem·a·to·ci·dal *also* **nem·a·ti·ci·dal** \ˌneməd·əˈsīdᵊl, nəˌmad-\ *or* **nema·ci·dal** \ˌneməˈs-\ *adj* [*nematocide*, *nematicide*, *nemacide* + *-al*] : capable of destroying nematodes

nem·a·to·cide *also* **nem·a·ti·cide** \ˈneməd·əˌsīd, nəˈmad-\ *or* **nem·a·cide** \ˈneməˌs-\ *n* -s [*nematocide* fr. *nemat-* + *-cide*; *nematicide* fr. *nemat-* + *-i-* + *-cide*; *nemacide* fr. *nem-* + *-cide*] : a substance or preparation used to destroy nematodes, esp. those that attack crop plants — compare ANTHELMINTIC

nem·a·to·cyst \ˈneməd·əˌsist, nəˈmad-\ *n* [ISV *nemat-* + *cyst*] : one of the minute stinging organs of hydrozoans, scyphozoans, and actinozoans — compare TRICHOCYST — **nem·a·to·cys·tic** \ˌ===ˈsistik, =ˌ==-\ *adj*

nem·a·to·cyte \ˈ===ˌsīt, =ˈ==-\ *n* -s [*nemat-* + *-cyte*] : CNIDOBLAST

nem·a·to·da \ˌneməˈtōdə\ *n pl, cap* [NL, fr. *nemat-* + *-oda* (irreg. fr. *-oidea*)] : a class of Aschelminthes or a separate phylum comprising elongated cylindrical worms without an epithelial coelomic lining, with dorsal and ventral nerve cords, and with lateral excretory ducts, that are parasites of man, animals, or plants or free-living dwellers in soil or water and are known as roundworms, eelworms, or nematodes

1nem·a·tode \ˈneməˌtōd\ *adj* [NL *Nematoda*] : of or relating to the Nematoda

2nematode \"\ *n* -s [NL *Nematoda*] : a worm of the class or phylum Nematoda

nem·a·to·di·a·sis \ˌnemə(ˌ)tōˈdīəsəs\ *n, pl* **nematodia·ses** \-əˌsēz\ [NL, fr. *Nematoda* + *-iasis*] : infestation with or disease caused by nematode worms

nem·a·to·di·rus \ˌneməd·əˈdīrəs, nəˌmad-\ *n, cap* [NL, fr. *nemat-* + *-dirus* (prob. fr. Gk *deirē* neck, throat) — more at DER-] : a genus of reddish nematode worms (family Strongylidae) having slender elongated necks and being parasitic in the small intestine of ruminants and sometimes other mammals

ne·mat·o·gen \nəˈmad·əjən, ˈneməd-, -ˌjen\ *also* **ne·mat·o·gene** \-ˌjēn\ *n* -s [*nemat-* + *-gen*] : the form of a mesozoan of the order Dicyemida that occurs in the immature host and that consists of an outer layer of cells enclosing one or more large elongated axial cells which give rise to other nematogens by means of agametes — compare RHOMBOGEN

nem·a·tog·nath \ˌneməˈtägˌnath\ *n* -s [NL *Nematognathi*] : a siluroid fish : CATFISH

nem·a·tog·na·thi \ˌneməˈtägnəˌthī\ *n pl, cap* [NL, fr. *nemat-* + *-gnathi* (fr. *-gnathi*, pl. of *-gnathus* -gnathous)] *in some classifications* : an order of scaleless fishes that comprises the catfishes and is equivalent to the suborder Siluroidea of the order Ostariophysi — **nem·a·tog·na·thous** \ˌ==ˈ==ˌthəs\ *adj*

ne·mat·o·gone \nəˈmad·əˌgōn, ˈneməd-\ *n* -s [ISV *nemat-* + *-gone* (fr. Gk *gonē* seed, offspring) — more at GONE] : one of the thin-walled propagative cells in the gemmae of various mosses

nem·a·tog·o·nous \ˌneməˈtägənəs\ *adj* : of or relating to a nematogone

1nem·a·toid \ˈneməˌtȯid\ *or* **nem·a·toi·de·an** \ˌ==ˈtȯidēən\ *adj* [*nematoid* fr. NL *Nematoidea*; *nematoidean* fr. NL *Nematoidea* + E *-an*, adj. suffix] **1** : resembling or related to the Nematoda **2** : NEMATODE

2nematoid \"\ *or* **nematoidean** \"\ *n* -s [*nematoid* fr. NL *Nematoidea*; *nematoidean* fr. NL *Nematoidea* + E *-an*, n. suffix] **1** : a nematoid worm : NEMATHELMINTH **2** : NEMATODE

nem·a·toi·dea \ˌ==ˈtȯidēə\ [NL, fr. *nemat-* + *-oidea*] *syn of* NEMATODA

nem·a·to·log·i·cal \ˌneməd·əˈläjəkəl, nəˌmad-\ *adj* : of or relating to nematology

nem·a·tol·o·gist \ˌneməˈtäləjəst\ *n* -s : a specialist in nematology

nem·a·tol·o·gy \-jē\ *n* -ES [*nemat-* + *-logy*] : a branch of zoology that deals with nematodes

nem·a·to·mor·pha \ˌneməd·əˈmȯrfə, nəˌmad-\ *n pl, cap* [NL, fr. *nemat-* + *-morpha*] : a class of Aschelminthes or a separate phylum comprising the horsehair worms formerly often grouped with the nematodes but distinguished from these by possession of a true body cavity, gonads discontinuous with their ducts, and an atrophied digestive tract in the adult — see GORDIOIDEA, NECTONEMATOIDEA — **nem·a·to·mor·phan** \ˌ===ˈmȯrfən, =ˌ==-\ *adj or n*

nem·a·toph·o·ra \ˌneməˈtäfərə\ *n pl, cap* [NL, fr. *nemat-* + *-phora*] *in former classifications* : a phylum or other division of invertebrates comprising the true nematocyst-bearing coelenterates as distinguished from the Ctenophores

nem·a·toph·y·ton \ˌneməˈtäfəˌtän\ *n* -s [NL, fr. *nemat-* + Gk *phyton* plant — more at PHYT-] : a large branching fossil plant found in Devonian rocks, believed to be a thallophyte, and often considered to offer evidence of a relationship between brown algae and vascular plants

nem·a·tos·po·ra \ˌneməˈtäspərə; ˌneməd·əˈspōrə, nəˌmad-\ *n, cap* [NL, fr. *nemat-* + *-spora*] : a genus of yeasts (family Saccharomycetaceae) having ascospores with needle-shaped, fusiform, or threadlike nonvibratile extensions

nem·a·to·zooid \ˌneməd·ə, nəˌmad·ə+\ *n* [*nemat-* + *zooid*] : a defensive zooid in a hydroid or siphonophore

Nem·bu·tal \ˈnembyəˌtȯl *sometimes* -tal\ *trademark* — used for the sodium salt of pentobarbital

nem·bu·tsu \nemˈbu̇t(ˌ)sü\ *n* -s *often cap* [Jap, fr. *nen* thought, feeling + *Butsu* Buddha] : repetition of an Amidist devotional formula as a means of salvation

nem con *abbr* [NL *nemine contradicente*] no one contradicting

nem diss *abbr* [NL *nemine dissentiente*] no one dissenting

-neme \ˌnēm\ *n comb form* -s [NL *-nema*] : thread ⟨axo*neme*⟩ ⟨desmo*neme*⟩

ne·me·an \nəˈmēən, nəˈm-\ *adj, usu cap* [L *nemeus* Nemean (fr. Gk *nemeos*, *nemeois*, fr. *Nemea*, valley in northern Argolis in ancient Greece) + E *-an*] : of, relating to, or held in Nemea in ancient Greece ⟨*Nemean* festivals included athletic and musical competitions⟩

ne·mer·tea \nəˈmərd·ēə\ *n pl, cap* [NL, fr. *Nemertes*, included genus (fr. Gk *Nēmertēs* Nemertes, one of the Nereids) + *-ea* (fr. L, neut. pl. of *-eus* -eous)] : a class or other category of Platyhelminthes comprising soft-bodied often brightly colored unsegmented acoelomate worms that have an anterior mouth and posterior anus, a long eversible proboscis, and a definite circulatory system, are typically elongate and contractile, and are usu. marine and littoral and burrow in sand or mud though a few live in fresh water or on land — see ANOPLA, ENOPLA — **ne·mer·te·an** \-ēən\ *adj or n*

1nem·er·tine \ˈnemə(r)ˌtīn, -tēn\ *or* **nem·er·tin·e·an** \ˌ==ˈtinēən\ *adj* [*nemertinean* fr. NL *Nemertinea* + E *-an*, adj. suffix; *nemertine* fr. NL *Nemertinea*, *Nemertina*, *Nemertini*] : of or relating to the Nemertea

2nemertine \"\ *or* **nemertinean** \"\ *n* -s [*nemertinean* fr. NL *Nemertinea* + E *-an*, n. suffix; *nemertine* fr. NL *Nemertinea*, *Nemertina*, *Nemertini*] : a worm of the group Nemertea

nem·er·tin·ea \ˌneməˈtinēə\ *also* **nem·er·ti·na** \-tīnə,-tēnə\ *or* **nem·er·ti·ni** \-tīˌnī, -tē(ˌ)nē\ [*Nemertinea* fr. NL, fr. *Nemertes* + *-inea* (fr. L, neut. pl. of *-ineus* — as in *gramineus* gramineous); *Nemertina*, *Nemertini* fr. NL, fr. *Nemertes* + *-ina* or *-ini*] *syn of* NEMERTEA

1nem·er·toid \ˈneməˌtȯid, nəˈmər-\ *adj* [NL *Nemertea* + E *-oid*] : resembling or related to the Nemertea : NEMERTEAN

2nemertoid \"\ *n* -s : one of the Nemertea : a nemertoid worm

ne·me·sia \nəˈmēzh(ē)ə\ *n* [NL, fr. Gk, pl. of *nemesion* catchfly] **1** *cap* : a genus of African herbs or subshrubs (family Scrophulariaceae) having variously colored, irregular, slightly spurred, mostly racemose flowers **2** -s : a plant of the genus *Nemesia*

nem·e·sis \ˈneməsəs\ *n, pl* **neme·ses** \-əˌsēz\ *or* **neme·sis·es** [L *Nemesis*, goddess of divine retribution, fr. Gk, fr. *nemesis* retribution, righteous anger, fr. *nemein* to distribute — more at NIMBLE] **1 a** : one that inflicts retribution ⟨many a pursued man fell before his ~ in the streets —Agnes M. Cleaveland⟩ **b** : one that avenges relentlessly or destroys inevitably **c** : a formidable and usu. victorious rival or opponent ⟨the baseball team was defeated by the first-rate pitching of its old ~⟩ **2 a** : an act or effect of retributive justice ⟨whether in the individual or in the community, overweening self-assertion . . . was regarded as justly provoking ~ —Walter Moberly⟩ ⟨if they jumped their duty, not one survivor would there be to pursue them with the ~ of outraged humanity —D.C. Peattie⟩ **b** : an inevitable result ⟨this propensity to self-destruction is the ~ of irrationality —Lewis Mumford⟩ ⟨the crisis is the recurrent ~ of democracy —Harvey Wheeler⟩

1neme·stri·nid \ˌneməˈstrīnəd\ *adj* [NL *Nemestrinidae*] : of or relating to the Nemestrinidae

2nemestrinid \"\ *n* -s [NL *Nemestrinidae*] : an insect of the family Nemestrinidae

nem·e·strin·i·dae \-ˈrinəˌdē\ *n pl, cap* [NL, fr. *Nemestrinus*, type genus (perh. fr. LL *Nemestrinus*, god of groves) + *-idae*] : a family of dipterous insects occurring mostly in hot and arid regions and having larvae that are parasitic on other insects

nem·ic \ˈnemik\ *adj* [*nem-* + *-ic*] : of or relating to nematodes

nem·ich·thy·i·dae \ˌnemikˈthīəˌdē\ *n pl, cap* [NL, fr. *Nemichthys*, type genus + *-idae*] : a family of eels (order Apoda) comprising the snipe eels and related deep-sea forms — see NEMICHTHYS

nem·ich·thys \nəˈmikthəs\ *n, cap* [NL, fr. *nem-* + *-ichthys*] : a genus (the type of the family Nemichthyidae) of fragile slender-bodied deep-sea eels

ne·mi·ne con·tra·di·cen·te \ˌneməˌnēˌkänˌträdəˈsentē\ *adv (or adj)* [NL, lit., no one contradicting] : without a dissenting vote ⟨the votes of thanks were endorsed by . . . all parties and were passed *nemine contradicente* —*Times Hist. of the War*⟩

ne·mi·ne dis·sen·ti·en·te \-ˌdəˌsentēˈentē\ *adv (or adj)* [NL, lit., no one dissenting] : without dissent ⟨resolutions are sometimes . . . agreed to *nemine dissentiente* in the House of Lords —T.E.May⟩

ne·mo \ˈnē(ˌ)mō\ *n* -s [perh. alter. of *remote*] : a radio or television broadcast that originates outside the studio (as at a football game or a banquet)

nemo- — see NEM-

ne·mo·bi·us \nəˈmōbēəs\ *n, cap* [NL, fr. Gk *nemos* wooded pasture, glade + NL *-bius*] : a widely distributed genus of crickets most of which inhabit open fields

ne·moc·era \nəˈmäsərə\ [NL, fr. *nem-* + *-cera*] *syn of* NEMATOCERA

ne·moph·i·la \nəˈmäfələ\ *n* [NL, fr. Gk *nemos* wooded pasture, glade + NL *-phila*] **1** *cap* : a genus of ornamental chiefly Californian annual herbs (family Hydrophyllaceae) having flowers with a reflexed or spreading appendage in each sinus of the calyx — see BABY BLUE-EYES **2** -s : a plant of the genus *Nemophila*

1ne·mop·ter·id \nəˈmäptərəd\ *adj* [NL *Nemopteridae*] : of or relating to the Nemopteridae

2nemopterid \"\ *n* -s [NL *Nemopteridae*] : an insect of the family Nemopteridae

nemop·ter·i·dae \ˌnēˌmäpˈterəˌdē, ˌneˌ-\ *n pl, cap* [NL, fr. *Nemoptera*, type genus (fr. *nem-* + *-ptera*) + *-idae*] : a family of neuropterous insects whose hind wings are elongate and ribbonlike and whose larvae inhabit dusty or sandy regions and prey on small insects

nem·o·ral \ˈnem(ə)rəl\ *adj* [L *nemoralis*, fr. *nemor-*, *nemus* wood, grove + *-alis* -al; akin to Gk *nemos* wooded pasture, glade, Skt *namas* obeisance, *namati* he bends, bows] : of, relating to, or inhabiting a wood or grove

nemorhaedus *syn of* NAEMORHEDUS

ne·mori·cole \nəˈmȯrəˌkōl, ˈnemər-\ *or* **nem·o·ric·o·line** \ˌneməˈrikəˌlīn, -ˌlən\ *or* **nem·o·ric·o·lous** \-ˌləs\ *adj* [L *nemor-*, *nemus* grove + E *-i-* + *-cole* or *-coline* or *-colous*] : inhabiting groves

1ne·mou·rid \nəˈmu̇rəd\ *adj* [NL *Nemouridae*] : of or relating to the Nemouridae

2nemourid \"\ *n* -s [NL *Nemouridae*] : a stone fly of the family Nemouridae

ne·mou·ri·dae \-rəˌdē\ *n pl, cap* [NL, fr. *Nemoura*, type genus (fr. *nem-* + Gk *oura* tail) + *-idae* — more at -URA] : a widely distributed family of stone flies (order Plecoptera) having small or vestigial cerci

ne·ne \ˈnāˌ(ˌ)nā\ *n, pl* **nene** [Hawaiian *nēnē*] : a nearly extinct goose (*Nesochen sandvicensis*) of the Hawaiian islands that inhabits waterless uplands and feeds on berries and vegetation

nen·tsi *or* **nen·tsy** \ˈnentsē\ *or* **nien·tsi** \nēˈe-\ *n, pl* **nentsi** *or* **nentsy** *or* **nientsi** *cap* [Russ *Nentsy*, pl. of *Nenets*, fr. Yurak *ńenetś* man] : SAMOYED

nenu·phar \ˈnenyəˌfär, nəˈn(y)üfər\ *n* -s [ML *nenufar*, fr. Ar *naynūfar*, *naylūfar*, fr. Per *nīlūfar*, fr. Skt *nīlotpala*, fr. *nīla* dark blue + *utpala* nenuphar blossom] : WATER LILY; *esp* : EGYPTIAN LOTUS 1

neo- — see NE-

neo·abietic acid \ˌnē(ˌ)ō+ . . .\ *n* [*neoabietic* fr. *ne-* + *abietic* (in *abietic acid*)] : a crystalline resin acid $C_{19}H_{29}COOH$ that is isomeric with abietic acid and is found esp. in oleoresins from pine trees

Neo-Ant·er·gan \ˌnē(ˌ)ōˌantˈərgən\ *trademark* — used for pyrilamine

neo·anthropic \ˌnē(ˌ)ō+\ *adj* [*ne-* + *anthrop-* + *-ic*] : belonging to the same species (*Homo sapiens*) as recent man : modern in anatomy or type — used of fossil hominids; compare PALEOANTHROPIC

neo·an·thro·pi·nae \ˌnē(ˌ)ōˌanthrəˈpī(ˌ)nē\ *n pl, cap* [NL, fr. *ne-* + *anthrop-* + *-inae*] : an anthropological subdivision of Hominidae coextensive with a species (*Homo sapiens*) but regarded as comparable to a subfamily — compare ARCHANTHROPINAE, PALEOANTHROPINAE — **neo·an·thro·pine** \ˌnē(ˌ)ōˈanthrəˌpīn\ *adj or n*

neo·aplec·ta·na \ˌnē(ˌ)ō(ˌ)āˈplektənə\ *n, cap* [NL, fr. *ne-* + *Aplectana*, genus of nematode worms, fr. *a-* + *-plectana* (fr. Gk *plektanē* coil, fr. *plekein* to plait, twine) — more at PLY] : a genus of nematode worms (order Rhabditida) that are parasitic in insects and that include one form (*N. glaseri*) which has been used in attempts to establish biological control of the Japanese beetle

neo·arsphenamine \ˌnē(ˌ)ō+\ *n* [*ne-* + *arsphenamine*] : a yellow powder $C_{12}H_{11}As_2N_2O_2CH_2SO_2Na$ similar to arsphenamine in structure and uses

neo-assyrian \"+\ *n, often cap N & usu cap A* [*ne-* + *assyrian*] : a dialect of Akkadian used in Assyria after 1000 B.C.

1neo-babylonian \"+\ *adj, often cap N & usu cap B* [*ne-* + *babylonian*] : of or relating to the later Babylonian empire

2neo-babylonian \"+\ *n, often cap N & usu cap B* : CHALDEAN 1 b

neo·balaena \ˌnē(ˌ)ō+\ *n, cap* [NL, fr. *ne-* + *Balaena*] : a genus of relatively small whalebone whales of the waters about Australia and New Zealand

neo·baroque \"+\ *adj* [*ne-* + *baroque*] : of, relating to, or having the characteristics of art or architecture based on study of 17th century baroque ⟨the free-form flights of fancy of the ~ experimenters —Ada Louise Huxtable⟩

ne·o·blast \ˈnēəˌblast\ *n* [ISV *ne-* + *-blast*] : any of various large undifferentiated cells of annelid worms that participate in regeneration of lost parts

ne·o·blas·tic \ˌnēəˈblastik\ *adj* [*ne-* + *-blastic*] : relating to or constituting new growth

neo·calamites \ˌnē(ˌ)ō+\ *n, cap* [NL, fr. *ne-* + *Calamites*] : a genus of Mesozoic fossil plants (order Equisetales) having large strap-shaped leaves

ne·o·cene \ˈnēəˌsēn\ *adj or n, usu cap* [*ne-* + *-cene*] : NEOGENE

neo·ceratodus \ˌnē(ˌ)ō+\ *n, cap* [NL, fr. *ne-* + *Ceratodus*] : a genus of dipnoan fishes comprising the recent lungfishes of Australia — see BARRAMUNDA; compare CERATODUS

neo·cerebellar \"+\ *adj* [*neocerebellum* + *-ar*] : of or relating to the neocerebellum

neo·cerebellum \"+\ *n* [NL, fr. *ne-* + ML *cerebellum*] : the phylogenetically youngest part of the cerebellum associated with the cerebral cortex in the integration of voluntary limb movements and comprising most of the cerebellar hemispheres and the superior vermis — compare ARCHICEREBELLUM, PALEOCEREBELLUM

neo-christianity \"+\ *n, often cap N & usu cap C* [*ne-* + *christianity*] : a reinterpretation of Christianity in terms of a current philosophy (as rationalism in the 19th century)

neo·classic *or* **neo·classical** \"+\ *adj* [*ne-* + *classic* or *classical*] **1** : of, relating to, or having the characteristics of a style of artistic expression that is based on or felt to be based on the classical style: as **a** : of or relating to a revival or contemporary adaptation of classical taste or style in art or architecture ⟨not all buildings erected in Rome during the Fascist era were in the severe *neoclassical style* —*Architectural Rev.*⟩ ⟨in France meanwhile the classic grandeur of Versailles had given way to the *neoclassical* delicacy of the Place de la Concorde and the Petit Trianon —Nikolaus Pevsner⟩ **b** : of or relating to a revival or adaptation of classical style in literature; *esp* : of, relating to, or being the dominant style of English literature of the 18th century ⟨*neoclassical* poetry, for example, is characterized by the simile, periphrasis, the ornamental epithet, epigram, balance, antithesis —René Wellek & Austin Warren⟩ ⟨the most accomplished poet of the ~ school itself, however, was Alexander Pope; other members of the school included Addison, Swift, and Dr. Samuel Johnson —D.S.Norton & Peters Rushton⟩ — compare ROMANTIC **c** : of or relating to a style of musical composition of the 20th century characterized by the incorporation of the impersonal features and formal restrictions of the classic and earlier periods into a contemporary style **2** : of, relating to, or being the theories or teachings of the postclassical economists esp. Alfred Marshall and his followers whose most distinguishing feature is their substitution of marginal utility for the labor theory of value of the classical school

neoclassical arabic *n, cap A* : literary Arabic that follows the grammatical conventions of classical Arabic, has a modernized vocabulary, and is commonly the written language of Arab countries

neo·classicism \"+\ *n* [*ne-* + *classicism*] **1** : the principles or the style of neoclassical literature, art, architecture, music, or economics ⟨in drama, ~ was marked by devotion to the "Rules": the three unities, the use of a chorus, the avoidance of violence on the stage, the use of only royal or noble characters in tragedy —Cleanth Brooks & R.B.Heilman⟩ **2** : CLASSICISM 3

neo·classicist \"+\ *n* [*ne-* + *classicist*] : an advocate or follower of neoclassical style, models, or theory — compare ROMANTICIST

ne·o·co·mi·an \ˌnēəˈkōmēən\ *adj, usu cap* [F *néocomien*, fr. *Neocomium* (latinized form of *Neuchâtel*, canton in western Switzerland) + F *-en* -an (fr. L *-anus*)] : of or relating to a division of the European Cretaceous — see GEOLOGIC TIME table

neo-confucian *or* **neo-confucianist** \ˌnē(ˌ)ō+\ *adj, often cap N & usu cap C* [*ne-* + *confucian* or *confucianist*] : of or relating to neo-Confucianism or the neo-Confucianists

neo-confucianism \"+\ *n, often cap N & usu cap C* [*ne-* + *confucianism*] : a rationalistic revival of Confucian philosophy in the 11th century A.D. that exercised a pronounced influence on Chinese thought for over 800 years ⟨*neo-Confucianism*, in which many traits of both Buddhism and Taoism were blended with the more naturalistic tenets of Confucius —L.J.Walker⟩

neo-confucianist \"+\ *n* -s *often cap N & usu cap C* [*ne-* + *confucian* + *-ist*] : an adherent or advocate of neo-Confucianism

neo·cortex \"+\ *n* [NL, fr. *ne-* + L *cortex* bark — more at CORTEX] : the cortical part of the neencephalon

neo·cosmic \"+\ *adj* [*ne-* + *cosmic*] : of or relating to the universe in its present state or to races of men known to history

neo·crinoidea \"+\ *n pl, cap* [NL, fr. *ne-* + *Crinoidea*] *in some classifications* : an order of crinoids comprising forms in which the actinal surface is not closed — compare PALAEOCRINOIDEA

neo·criticism \"+\ *n* [ISV *ne-* + *criticism*] : a form of neo-Kantianism developed principally by C. B. Renouvier and his followers rejecting the noumena of Kant and restricting knowledge to phenomena as constituted by a priori categories

neo·cyanine \"+\ *n* [*ne-* + *cyanine*] : a cyanine dye derived from lepidine and used for sensitizing photographic emulsions to infrared rays

neo–darwinian \"+\ *adj, often cap N & usu cap D* [*ne-* + *darwinian*] : of or relating to neo-Darwinism

neo–darwinism \"+\ *n, often cap N & usu cap D* [*ne-* + *darwinism*] : a theory that holds natural selection to be the chief factor in the evolution of plants and animals and specif. denies the possibility of inheriting acquired characters — compare NEO-LAMARCKISM, WEISMANNISM

neo–darwinist \"+\ *n, often cap N & usu cap D* [*ne-* + *darwinist*] : an advocate or follower of neo-Darwinism

neo·di·pri·on \ˌnē(ˌ)ōˌdīˈprīˌän\ *n, cap* [NL, fr. *ne-* + *Diprion*, genus of sawflies, fr. *di-* + *-prion*] : a genus of sawflies including forms that in the larval stage feed on and often cause serious defoliation of pines and other conifers

neo·dym·i·um \ˌnēōˈdimēəm\ *n* -s [NL, fr. *ne-* + *-dymium* (fr. *didymium*)] : a faintly yellow trivalent metallic element of the rare-earth group that occurs in monazite sand associated esp. with cerium, lanthanum, and praseodymium, that forms pink salts, and that is used chiefly in the form of the oxide to impart a violet color to glass and porcelain — symbol *Nd;* see DIDYMIUM, ELEMENT table

neo–egyptian \ˌnē(ˌ)ō+\ *n, often cap N & cap E* [*ne-* + *egyptian*] : NEW EGYPTIAN

neo·fabraea \"+\ *n, cap* [NL, fr. *ne-* + *Fabraea*] : a genus of plant-parasitic fungi (family Mollisiaceae) that form brightly colored apothecia in conidial stromata — see APPLE ANTHRACNOSE

neo·fascism \"+\ *n* [ISV *ne-* + *fascism*] : a political movement arising in Europe after World War II and characterized by policies designed to incorporate the basic principles of fascism (as nationalism and opposition to democracy) into existing political systems

¹neo·fascist \"+\ *n* [ISV *ne-* + *fascist*] : one who advocates or supports neofascism

²neofascist \"\ *adj* : of, relating to, or favoring neofascism

neo·fetus \ˌnē(ˌ)ō+\ *n* [NL, fr. *ne-* + L *fetus*] : the embryo during the eighth and ninth weeks of gestation

neo·fiber \"+\ *n, cap* [NL, fr. *ne-* + *Fiber*] : a genus of rodents (family Cricetidae) comprising solely the round-tailed muskrat

neo·formation \"+\ *n* [ISV *ne-* + *formation*] : a new growth: as **a** : TUMOR **b** : an anatomical anomaly peculiar to a small racial group and regarded as recent in appearance — **neo·formative** \"+\ *adj*

neo–freudian \"+\ *n, often cap N & usu cap F* [*ne-* + *freudian*] : any of a group of psychoanalysts who differ from orthodox Freudians in emphasizing the importance of socio-cultural factors in the development of an individual's personality

neo·gae·an *or* **neo·ge·an** \ˌnēōˈjēən\ *adj, usu cap* [NL *Neogaea, Neogea*, biogeographic region that is coextensive with the neotropical biogeographic region and is regarded as one of three primary biogeographic realms (fr. *ne-* + *-gaea*) + E *-an*] : NEOTROPICAL

ne·og·a·mous \(ˈ)nēˈägəməs\ *adj* [*ne-* + *-gamous*] : of or relating to neogamy

ne·og·a·my \nēˈägəmē\ *n* -ES [*ne-* + *-gamy*] : association in gregarines occurring prior to the adult stage of the life cycle

¹ne·o·gene \ˈnēəˌjēn\ *adj, usu cap* [ISV *ne-* + *-gene* (fr. Gk *-genēs* born) — more at -GEN] : relating to or being the later part of the Tertiary including the Miocene and Pliocene

²neogene \"\ *n* -s *usu cap* : the Neogene period or system

neo·genesis \ˌnēō+\ *n* [NL, fr. *ne-* + L *genesis*] : new formation : REGENERATION ⟨~ of tissue⟩

neo·ge·net·ic \ˌnēōjəˈnedˌik\ *or* **neo·gen·ic** \-ˈjenik\ *adj* [*neogenetic* ISV, fr. *neogenesis*, after such pairs as E *antithesis: antithetic; neogenic* alter. (influenced by *-genic*) of *neogenetic*] : of, relating to, or characterized by neogenesis

ne·og·na·thae \nēˈägnəˌthē\ *n pl, cap* [NL, fr. *ne-* + *-gnathae*] : a superorder of Neornithes that includes most existing birds and that is characterized by reduction of the median bones of the palate — see PALAEOGNATHAE — **ne·og·nath·ic** \ˌnēˌägˈnathik\ *adj* — **ne·og·na·thous** \(ˈ)nēˈägnəthəs\ *adj*

neo–gothic \ˌnē(ˌ)ō+\ *adj, often cap N & usu cap G* [*ne-* + *gothic*] : of, relating to, or having the characteristics of art or architecture based on study of medieval Gothic models (as in the Gothic revival of 1840 in England and similar movements in Germany, France, and the U.S.) ⟨the *neo-Gothic* treatment of railway signal towers —R.D.Altick⟩

neo·grammarian \"+\ *n* [*ne-* + *grammarian;* trans. of G *junggrammatiker*] : one of a school of philologists arising in Germany about 1875, advocating the more exact formulation of phonetic law and its more rigid application to linguistic phenomena, maintaining that phonetic laws admit no real exceptions, and recognizing analogy as a normal factor in linguistic change

neo–greek \"+\ *n, often cap N & cap G* [ISV *ne-* + *greek*] : the modern Greek language

neo–hawaiian \"+\ *n, often cap N & cap H* [*ne-* + *hawaiian*] : an individual born in Hawaii of Hawaiian and other (usu. Caucasian, Chinese, or Japanese) ancestry

neo–hebraic \"+\ *n, often cap N & cap H* [*ne-* + *hebraic*] : NEO-HEBREW

neo–hebrew \"+\ *n, often cap N & cap H* [*ne-* + *hebrew*] : Hebrew as used by learned Jews of the Christian era

¹neo–hegelian \"+\ *n, often cap N & usu cap H* [*ne-* + *hegelian*] : an advocate of neo-Hegelianism

²neo–hegelian \"\ *adj, often cap N & usu cap H* : of or relating to neo-Hegelianism

neo–hegelianism \"+\ *n, often cap N & usu cap H* [*ne-* + *hegelianism*] **1** : the philosophy of a school of chiefly British and American idealists following Hegel in his logical method and emphasizing organismic rather than atomistic conceptions **2** : one of a group of philosophical theories based on Hegelian principles advanced esp. by German and Italian philosophers

neo–hellenism \"+\ *n, often cap N & usu cap H* [*ne-* + *hellenism*] : Hellenism as surviving or revived in modern times : the practice of ancient Greek ideals in modern life or art

neo·hexane \ˌnē(ˌ)ō+\ *n* [*ne-* + *hexane*] : a volatile flammable liquid hydrocarbon $(CH_3)_3CC_2H_5$ that is usu. made from isobutane and ethylene and is used in aviation fuel and other special fuels for increasing power; 2,2-dimethyl-butane

neo·hipparion \"+\ *n, cap* [NL, fr. *ne-* + *Hipparion*] : a genus of extinct American Pliocene horses with one large and two small toes on each foot

neo–humanism \"+\ *n* [*ne-* + *humanism*] : NEW HUMANISM

neo–humanist \"+\ *n* [*ne-* + *humanist*] : NEW HUMANIST

neo–impressionism \"+\ *n, often cap N&I* [F *néo-impressionisme*, fr. *né-* ne- + *impressionisme* impressionism] : art whose exponents are critical of impressionism and seek a carefully integrated pictorial structure involving simplified and solidified forms and a pointillist rendering of light; *specif* : a French art theory and practice of the last decade of the 19th century characterized by an attempt to make impressionism more precise in form and the use of a pointillist painting technique — compare DIVISIONISM

¹neo–impressionist \"+\ *n, often cap N&I* [F *néo-impressioniste*, fr. *né-* ne- + *impressioniste* impressionist] : a practitioner or advocate of neo-impressionism

²neo–impressionist \"\ *adj, often cap N&I* : of, relating to, or having the characteristics of neo-impressionism or the neo-impressionists

¹neo–kantian \ˌnē(ˌ)ō+\ *n, often cap N & usu cap K* [*ne-* + *kantian;* prob. trans. of G *neukantianer*] : an adherent of neo-Kantianism

²neo–kantian \"\ *adj, often cap N & usu cap K* : derived from Kant or based on his theories or his philosophy ⟨a *neo-Kantian* movement⟩ ⟨a *neo-Kantian* hypothesis⟩

neo–kantianism \ˌnē(ˌ)ō+\ *n, often cap N & usu cap K* [*ne-* + *kantianism;* prob. trans. of G *neukantianismus*] : a philosophical movement opposing mid-19th century materialism and idealism, developing from Kant's epistemology, considering the thing-in-itself as a borderline concept and emphasizing normative considerations in ethics and jurisprudence

neol *abbr* neologism

ne·o·la·lia \ˌnēōˈlālēə\ *n* -s [NL, fr. *ne-* + *-lalia*] : speech esp. of a psychotic that includes words that are new and meaningless to the hearer

¹neo–lamarckian \ˌnē(ˌ)ō+\ *adj, often cap N & usu cap L* [*ne-* + *lamarckian*] : of or relating to neo-Lamarckism

²neo–lamarckian \"+\ *n, often cap N & usu cap L* : an advocate or follower of neo-Lamarckism

neo–lamarckism \ˌnē(ˌ)ō+\ *n, often cap N & usu cap L* [*ne-* + *lamarckism*] : a modern theory of evolution based on Lamarckism and retaining the fundamental concept that acquired characters are inherited: as **a** : the theory that evolution results from the action of natural selection upon acquired characters **b** : the theory that evolutionary change is the direct product of the interaction of organism and environment — compare NEO-DARWINISM

neo·la·si·op·tera \ˌnē(ˌ)ōˌlāzēˈäptərə, -āsē-\ *n, cap* [NL, fr. *ne-* + *Lasioptera*, genus of Diptera, fr. *lasio-* (fr. Gk *lasios* shaggy) + *-ptera*; akin to Gk *lēnos* wool — more at WOOL] : a genus of gall midges (family Cecidomyiidae) whose larvae cause the formation of galls chiefly on the stems of asters, viburnums, dogwoods, and various other plants

neo–latin \ˌnē(ˌ)ō+\ *n, often cap N & cap L* [ISV *ne-* + *latin*] **1** : NEW LATIN **2** : ROMANCE 5

neo·liberal \"+\ *n* [ISV *ne-* + *liberal*] : an advocate or adherent of neoliberalism

neo·liberalism \"+\ *n* [ISV *ne-* + *liberalism*] **1** : a movement or doctrine that attempts to modify the principles of classical liberalism in the light of 20th century conditions **2** : a modern movement in Protestant Christian theology that is critical of earlier 20th century liberalism while affirming many of its fundamental assumptions and that is held to have arisen as a reaction against the new supernaturalism and the conservative doctrines of neoorthodoxy

ne·oligochaeta \(ˌ)nē+\ *n pl, cap* [NL, fr. *ne-* + *Oligochaeta*] *in some classifications* : a division of Oligochaeta comprising relatively large complex chiefly terrestrial worms that ordinarily reproduce only by sexual means (as those of the genera *Lumbricus, Allolobophora*, and *Megascolex*) — compare EARTHWORM, MEGADRILI, TERRICOLAE — **ne·oligochaete** \"+\ *adj or n*

neo·linguist \ˌnē(ˌ)ō+\ *n* [*ne-* + *linguist;* trans. of It *neolinguista*] : an adherent of areal linguistics

neo·linguistic \"+\ *adj* [*ne-* + *linguistic;* trans. of It *neolinguistico*] : of or relating to areal linguistics

neo·linguistics \"+\ *n pl but usu sing in constr* [*ne-* + *linguistics;* trans. of It *neolinguistica*] : AREAL LINGUISTICS

ne·o·lith \ˈnēəˌlith\ *n* -s [back-formation fr. *neolithic*] : a neolithic stone implement

ne·o·lith·ic \ˌnēəˈlithik\ *adj* [*ne-* + *-lithic*] **1** *usu cap* : of, being, or relating to the latest period of the Stone Age following the Mesolithic and Aeneolithic and characterized by the use of polished stone implements, the art of grinding stone, horn, bone, and ivory tools with sandstone, pottery making, the use of bow and arrow, domestication of animals, the cultivation of grain and fruit trees, the invention of the wheel, linen weaving, and the beginning of settled village life **2** : belonging to an earlier age and now outmoded ⟨defense of the ~ liberals who once inhabited these lands —W.A.White⟩

neo·local \ˌnēō+\ *adj* [*ne-* + *local*] : having a new location; *specif* : located apart from the families of either spouse ⟨a ~ residence⟩ — compare AVUNCULOCAL, MATRILOCAL, PATRILOCAL — **neo·locality** \ˌnē(ˌ)ō+\ *n*

ne·o·lo·gian \ˌnēəˈlōj(ē)ən\ *n* -s [*neology* + *-an*] : NEOLOGIST

ne·o·log·i·cal \ˌnēəˈläjəkəl\ *also* **ne·o·log·ic** \-jik\ *adj* [*neological* fr. F *néologique* neological (fr. *né-* ne- + *-logique*, fr. *-logie* -logy + *-ique* -ic) + E *-al; neologic* fr. F *néologique*] : of, relating to, or characterized by neology

ne·ol·o·gism \nēˈäləˌjizəm *sometimes* ˈnēəl-\ *n* -s [F *néologisme*, fr. *né-* ne- + *log-* + *-isme* -ism] **1 a** : a new word, usage, or expression ⟨all ~s begin as slang, except in those branches of terminology where . . . there is an established tradition of word coinage or redefinition —R.A.Hall b.1911⟩ **b** : a usu. compound word coined by a psychotic and meaningless to the hearer **2** : NEOLOGY 2

ne·ol·o·gist \nēˈäləjəst\ *n* -s [prob. fr. F *néologiste*, fr. *neologisme*, after such pairs as F *purisme* purism: *puriste* purist] : a proponent of a new doctrine : an advocate of neology

ne·ol·o·gis·tic \(ˌ)nēˌäləˈjistik, ˌnēəl-\ *adj* [*neologist* + *-ic*] : of or relating to neology

ne·ol·o·gize \nēˈäləˌjīz *sometimes* ˈnēəl-\ *vi* -ED/-ING/-S [*neology* + *-ize*] : to practice neology

ne·ol·o·gy \nēˈäləjē\ *n* -ES [F *néologie*, fr. *né-* ne- + *-logie* -logy] **1 a** : the use of a new word or expression or of an established word in a new or different sense : the use of new expressions that are not sanctioned by conventional standard usage : the introduction of such expressions into a language **b** : NEOLOGISM 1a **2** : a new doctrine; *esp* : a new method of theological interpretation

neo–malthusian \ˌnē(ˌ)ō+\ *adj, often cap N & usu cap M* [*ne-* + *malthusian*] : being or relating to the doctrine that only through the limitation of births by the use of artificial contraceptives can the numbers of the population be sufficiently controlled to make possible the elimination of vice and misery and a general elevation of the standard of living

neo–malthusianism \ˌnē(ˌ)ō+\ *n, often cap N & usu cap M* : neo-Malthusian views or beliefs

neo–melanesian \ˌnē(ˌ)ō+\ *n, often cap N & cap M* [*ne-* + *melanesian*] : an English-based pidgin language used in New Guinea and the Solomon islands

neo–mendelian \"+\ *adj, often cap N & usu cap M* [*ne-* + *mendelian*] : of or relating to neo-Mendelism

neo–mendelism \"+\ *n, often cap N & usu cap M* [*ne-* + *mendelism*] : Mendelism as modified and extended by recent biologists; *esp* : such principles including the concepts of linkage and multiple factors

ne·o·me·nia \ˌnēəˈmēnēə\ *n* -s [ME, fr. LL, fr. Gk *neomēnia*, fr. *ne-* + *-mēnia* (fr. *mēnē* moon) — more at MOON] : the time of the new moon; *also* : the festival of the new moon

neo–mercantilism \ˌnē(ˌ)ō+\ *n* [*ne-* + *mercantilism*] : a revived theory of mercantilism emphasizing trade restrictions and commercial policies as means of increasing domestic income and employment

neo·modal \ˌnēō+\ *adj* [*ne-* + *modal*] : characterized by the modification of major-minor tonality by the use of ecclesiastical modes or of new modes (as whole-tone scale, pentatonic scale)

neo·morph \ˈnēəˌmȯrf\ *n* [*ne-* + *-morph*] **1** : a structure that is not derived from a similar structure in an ancestor **2** : a mutant gene having a function distinct from that of any nonmutant gene of the same locus — **neo·mor·phic** \ˌnēəˈmȯrfik\ *adj* — **neo·mor·phism** \ˈnēəˌmȯrˌfizəm, ˌ=ˈ=ˌ==\ *n* -s

neo·mor·pha \ˌnēəˈmȯrfə\ *n, cap* [NL, fr. *ne-* + *-morpha*] : a genus of New Zealand passerine birds including solely the huia

neo·mor·pho·sis \ˌnēəˈmȯrfəsəs, -ˌmȯrˈfōs-\ *n* [NL, fr. *ne-* + *-morphosis*] : regeneration in which one part is replaced by an unlike part (as production of a leg in place of an antenna)

ne·o·my·cin \ˌnēəˈmīsᵊn\ *n* -s [*ne-* + *-mycin*] : an antibiotic or mixture of antibiotics that is produced by a soil actinomycete (*Streptomyces fradiae*) and that is active against a wide variety of bacteria — compare FRADICIN

¹ne·on \ˈnēˌän *sometimes* ˈnēən\ *n* -s [Gk, neut. of *neos* new — more at NEW] **1** : a colorless odorless inert gaseous element that occurs in air to the extent of about two thousandths of a percent by volume, is obtained by separating from liquid air, gives a reddish glow in a vacuum tube, and is used in electric lamps — symbol *Ne;* see ELEMENT table **2 a** : NEON LAMP **b** : a sign composed of neon lamps; *esp* : one used for advertising **c** : the illumination provided by such lamps or signs ⟨a street of narrow shops and faulty ~ —Martin Dibner⟩

²neon \"\ *adj* **1** : of, relating to, or resembling the light of neon lamps **2** : lighted by or composed of neon lamps ⟨a ~ roadside stand⟩ ⟨a ~ sign⟩

neo·natal \ˌnēə+\ *adj* [*ne-* + *natal*] : of, relating to, or affecting the newborn and esp. the human infant during the first month after birth ⟨~ period⟩ ⟨~ death⟩ ⟨~ serum⟩ — compare ANTENATAL, INTRANATAL, POSTNATAL — **neo·natally** \"+\ *adv*

ne·o·nate \ˈnēəˌnāt\ *n* -s [NL *neonatus*, fr. *ne-* + L *natus*, past part. of *nasci* to be born — more at NATIVE] : a newborn child; *specif* : a child less than one month old

neo·naturalism \ˌnē(ˌ)ō+\ *n* [*ne-* + *naturalism*] : a Protestant theology that seeks to reinterpret the Christian faith with new relevance on the basis of the biblical gospel and within the philosophical framework of process philosophy

neo·naturalist \"+\ *adj* [*ne-* + *naturalist*] : of, relating to, or adhering to neonaturalism

ne·oned \ˈnēˌänd *sometimes* ˈnēənd\ *adj* [¹*neon* + *-ed*] : of, equipped with, or lighted by neon lamps

neon lamp *also* **neon light** *or* **neon tube** *n* : a gas-discharge lamp in which the electrical discharge takes place through a mixture of gases containing a large proportion of neon

ne·o·no·mi·an \ˌnēəˈnōmēən\ *n* -s [*ne-* + *-nomian* (as in *antinomian*)] : one who advocates or adheres to new laws; *esp* : one who holds that the Christian gospel is a new law supplanting the Mosaic

ne·o·no·mi·an·ism \-mēəˌnizəm\ *n* -s : the doctrine of the neonomians

neon tetra *n* : a brightly colored So. American characin fish (*Hyphessobrycon innesi*) often kept in a tropical aquarium

ne·on·to·log·ic \(ˌ)nēˌäntəˈläjik\ *or* **ne·on·to·log·i·cal** \-jəkəl\ *adj* [*neontology* + *-ic* or *-ical*] : of or relating to neontology

ne·on·tol·o·gist \ˌnēˌänˈtäləjəst, ˌnēən-\ *n* -s [*neontology* + *-ist*] : a specialist in neontology

ne·on·tol·o·gy \-jē\ *n* -ES [*ne-* + *ont-* + *-logy*] : the study of recent organisms — distinguished from *paleontology*

neo·onych·i·um \ˌnēəˈnikēəm\ *n, pl* **neonych·ia** \-kēə\ *or* **neonychi·ums** [NL, fr. *ne-* + *-onychium*] : a protective pad enclosing a fetal claw

neo·orthodox \ˌnē(ˌ)ō+\ *adj* [*ne-* + *orthodox*] : of, relating to, or adhering to neoorthodoxy

neo·orthodoxy \"+\ *n* [*ne-* + *orthodoxy*] : a 20th century movement in Protestant theology characterized by a reaction against liberalism, reemphasis on some orthodox Reformation doctrines (as God's transcendence, the fallen state of man, the inevitability of man's sin and his responsibility for it, discontinuity between time and eternity), and renewed stress on classic Protestant formularies interpreted through biblical language and symbolism — compare CRISIS THEOLOGY, DIALECTICAL THEOLOGY

neo·pagan \"+\ *adj* [*ne-* + *pagan*] : of, relating to, or characterized by neopaganism

neo·paganism \"+\ *n* [*ne-* + *paganism*] : revived or new paganism

¹neo·paleozoic \"+\ *adj, usu cap* [*ne-* + *paleozoic*] : late Paleozoic — used of the entire period including the Devonian and the Permian

²neopaleozoic \"\ *n, usu cap* : the Neopaleozoic period

neo·pal·li·al \ˌnēōˈpalēəl\ *adj* [*neopallium* + *-al*] : of, relating to, or mediated by the neopallium

neo·pal·li·um \-lēəm\ *n* [NL, fr. *ne-* + *pallium*] : the phylogenetically new part of the cerebral cortex that develops from the area between the pyriform lobe and the hippocampus, comprises the nonolfactory region of the cortex, and attains its maximum development in man where it makes up the greater part of the cerebral hemisphere on each side — compare ARCHIPALLIUM

neo·pentane \ˌnē(ˌ)ō+\ *n* [*ne-* + *pentane*] : a gaseous or very volatile liquid hydrocarbon $(CH_3)_4C$ found in small amounts in petroleum and natural gas; dimethyl-propane or tetramethylmethane

neo·pentyl \"+\ *n* -s [*neopentane* + *-yl*] : the pentyl radical $(CH_3)_3CCH_2$— derived from neopentane; 2,2-dimethyl-propyl

neo·phobia \ˌnēə+\ *n* [NL, fr. *ne-* + *-phobia*] : dread of or aversion to novelty — **neophobic** *adj*

ne·o·phron \ˈnēəˌfrän\ *n, cap* [NL, fr. Gk *Neophrōn*, man transformed into a vulture in the *Metamorphoses* of Antoninus Liberalis, 2d cent. A.D. Greek writer of narrative prose] : a genus of Old World vultures characterized by horizontal nostrils and containing the Egyptian vulture

neo·phy·o·sis \ˌnēəˌfīˈōsəs\ *n* -ES [NL, fr. *ne-* + Gk *phyein* to grow + *-osis* -osis] : rejuvenation of a citrus strain long vegetatively reproduced by seedlings developing from nucellar buds and reproducing the original characters of the strain

ne·o·phyte \ˈnēəˌfīt, *usu* -īd·+V\ *n* -s [LL *neophytus* recently converted, recently planted, fr. Gk *neophytos*, fr. *ne-* + *phytos*, verbal of *phyein* to grow, bring forth — more at BE] **1** : a new convert : PROSELYTE; *esp* : a convert to the Christian faith in the early church **2** *Roman Catholicism* **a** : a newly ordained priest **b** : a novice in a convent **3** : a young or inexperienced practitioner or student : TYRO, BEGINNER ⟨to the ~, the desert may be only a barren waste —Gladwin Hill⟩ ⟨psychic code-deciphering that makes Freud look like a ~ and Jung like an amateur —Joseph Frank⟩ **syn** see NOVICE

ne·o·phyt·ic \ˌnēəˈfid·|ik, -it|, |ēk\ *adj* : of or relating to a neophyte

ne·o·phyt·ism \ˈnēəˌfīd·ˌizəm, -īˌti-\ *n* -s : the state of being a neophyte

neo·pilina \ˌnē(ˌ)ō+\ *n, cap* [NL, fr. *ne-* + *Pilina*, genus of mollusks] : a genus of primitive segmented mollusks that have conical shells, are believed to have existed from the Cambrian on, and are of uncertain systematic position often being isolated in a distinct class

ne·o·pine \ˈnēəˌpēn, -ˌpən\ *n* -s [ISV *ne-* + *-opine* (as in *atropine*)] : an opium alkaloid $C_{18}H_{21}NO_3$ isomeric with codeine

ne·o·pla·sia \ˌnēəˈplāzh(ē)ə\ *n* -s [NL, fr. *ne-* + *-plasia*] **1** : the abnormal state characterized by the growth and development of tumors **2** : the bodily alterations involved in the formation of tumors and esp. of malignant tumors

ne·o·plasm \ˈnēəˌplazəm\ *n* [ISV *ne-* + *-plasm*] : a new growth of animal or plant tissue resembling more or less the tissue from which it arises but serving no physiologic function and being benign, potentially malignant, or malignant in character — compare CARCINOMA, NEOPLASIA, SARCOMA

ne·o·plas·tic \ˌnēəˈplastik\ *adj* [ISV *ne-* + *-plastic*] **1** : of, relating to, or having the characteristics of a neoplasm or neoplasia **2** : of or relating to neoplasticism

neo·plasticism \ˌnē(ˌ)ō+\ *n* [*ne-* + *plasticism;* intended as trans. of D *nieuwe beelding* new form-construction] : the de Stijl art principle of reducing form to horizontal and vertical lines and planes and excluding all colors except white, black, and the primaries

neo·plas·ti·cist \-səst\ *n* -s [*neoplasticism* + *-ist*] : an advocate or a practitioner of neoplasticism

neo·platonic \ˌnē(ˌ)ō+\ *adj, usu cap* [*ne-* + *platonic*] : of, relating to, or resembling Neoplatonism or Neoplatonists

neo·platonism \"+\ *n, usu cap* [ISV *ne-* + *platonism*] **1** : a philosophical school originating in Alexandria about A.D. 200, modifying the teachings of Plato to accord with Aristotelian, post-Aristotelian, and oriental conceptions and conceiving of the world as an emanation from the One with whom the soul is capable of being reunited in trance or ecstasy — compare EMANATION, NOUS **2** : teachings and doctrines similar to those of the ancient Neoplatonists (as those promulgated in medieval times by mystics and in the Renaissance by Italian humanists) — compare CAMBRIDGE PLATONISTS

neo·platonist \"+\ *n, usu cap* [*ne-* + *platonist*] : an advocate of Neoplatonism

neo·positivism \"+\ *n* [ISV *ne-* + *positivism*] : LOGICAL POSITIVISM

neo·positivist \"+\ *n* : an advocate or adherent of neopositivism — **neo·positivistic** \"+\ *adj*

ne·o·prene \ˈnēəˌprēn\ *n* -s [*ne-* + *-prene* (as in *chloroprene*)] : a synthetic rubber made by the polymerization of chloroprene and characterized by superior resistance to oils, gasoline, sunlight, ozone, and heat and by lower permeability to gases than rubber — compare POLYCHLOROPRENE

ne·op·tera \nēˈäptərə\ *n pl, cap* [NL, fr. *ne-* + *-ptera*] : a major division of the subclass Pterygota comprising winged insects that are able to flex the wings over the abdomen when not in use and including all orders of winged insects except Odonata and Plectoptera — **ne·op·ter·ous** \(ˈ)nēˈäptərəs\ *adj*

¹ne·opte·ryg·ian \(ˌ)nēˌäptəˈrij(ē)ən, ˌnē(ˌ)ōtə-\ *adj* [NL *Neopterygii* + E *-an*] : of or relating to the Neopterygii

²neopterygian \"\ *n* -s : a fish of the subclass Neopterygii

ne·opte·ryg·ii \(ˌ)nēˌäptəˈrijēˌī, ˌnē(ˌ)ōtə-\ *n pl, cap* [NL, fr. *ne-* + *-pterygii*] *in some classifications* : a subclass of Osteichthyes including all the higher bony fishes — compare PALAEOPTERYGII

neo·pterygota \ˌnē(ˌ)ō+\ [NL, fr. *ne-* + *Pterygota*] *syn of* NEOPTERA

neo-punic \"+\ *n, often cap N & cap P* [*neo-* + *punic*] : the later Punic language

neo-pythagorean \"+\ *n, often cap N & usu cap P* [*ne-* + *pythagorean*] : an advocate of neo-Pythagoreanism

neo-pythagoreanism \"+\ *n, often cap N & usu cap P* [*ne-* + *pythagoreanism*] : the doctrines of a school of philosophy originating in Alexandria about the beginning of the first century A.D. and reviving with mystical interpretations many Pythagorean ideas

neo·realism \"+\ *n* [*ne-* + *realism*] **1** : NEW REALISM **2** : a revived realism ⟨like the postwar Italian movies of consequence, the novels have turned to ~, with truth taking the place of a happier ending —*New Yorker*⟩

neo·realist \"+\ *n* [*ne-* + *realist*] : an advocate or follower of neorealism — **neo·realistic** \"+\ *adj*

ne·or·ni·thes \nē'ȯrnə,thēz, ˌnē,ȯr'nī(ˌ)thēz\ *n pl, cap* [NL, fr. *ne-* + *-ornithes*] : a subclass of birds comprising all recent and fossil birds except the Archaeornithes — **ne·or·nith·ic** \ˌnē,ȯrˈnithik\ *adj*

¹neo·romantic \ˌnē(ˌ)ō+\ *adj* [*ne-* + *romantic*] : of or relating to a new or revived romanticism esp. in art or literature ⟨~ is a term that may most accurately be applied to those writers of recent years who have shown marked allegiance to the principles of Wordsworth, Coleridge, and Shelley or who have in a distinctive way exemplified romantic modes of mind and practice —C.D.Thorpe & N.E.Nelson⟩ ⟨the unhampered imaginative and emotional conception of the art of painting that distinguishes what is best in British art at this moment and may be qualified, for reasons of convenience, as ~ —Robin Ironside⟩

²neoromantic \"\ *n* : an advocate or follower of neoromanticism

neo·romanticism \ˌnē(ˌ)ō+\ *n* [*ne-* + *romanticism*] : neoromantic principles or characteristics

Neo·sal·var·san \ˌnē(ˌ)ōˈsalvə(r)ˌsan\ *trademark* — used for neoarsphenamine

neo-sanskrit \ˌnē(ˌ)ō+\ *n, often cap N & cap S* [*ne-* + *sanskrit*] : the modern Indic languages — **neo-sanskritic** \"+\ *adj, often cap N & usu cap S*

neo-scholastic \"+\ *adj, sometimes cap S* [ISV *ne-* + *scholastic*] : of or relating to neo-scholasticism

neo-scholasticism \"+\ *n, sometimes cap S* [*ne-* + *scholasticism*] **1** : a movement begun in the middle of the 19th century among Catholic scholars and having for its aims the restatement and exposition of the methods and teachings of the medieval Schoolmen in a manner suited to the intellectual needs of the present and further speculation that makes use of the findings of modern research and is grounded on principles derived from the Greeks and the Schoolmen **2** : SCHOLASTICISM 2

neo·schon·gas·tia \ˌnē(ˌ)ō,shänˈgastēə\ *n, cap* [NL, fr. *ne-* + *Schongastia*, genus of Arachnida, prob. fr. the name *Schöngast* + NL *-ia*] : a genus of trombiculid mites parasitic in their larval stage on poultry

neo·sisten \ˌnē(ˌ)ō+\ *or* **neosistens** *n, pl* **neosistens** *or* **neosistentes** [NL *neosistens*, fr. *ne-* + *sistens* sisten] : a first-stage nymph of an adelgid bug that hibernates, reaches maturity in the spring, and lays eggs which develop parthenogenetically

neo-sogdian \"+\ *n, often cap N & usu cap S* [*ne-* + *sogdian*] : UIGHUR 2b

neo·spo·rid·ia \ˌnē(ˌ)ōspəˈridēə\ *n pl, cap* [NL, fr. *ne-* + *-sporidia*] *in some classifications* : a division of Sporozoa including Cnidosporidia and Acnidosporidia — **neo·spo·rid·i·an** \-ēən\ *adj or n*

ne·os·sol·o·gy \ˌnē,äˈsäləjē, ˌnēəˈs-\ *n* -ES [Gk *neossos* young bird (fr. *neos* young, new) + E *-logy*] : the study of young birds

ne·os·sop·tile \ˌnēəˈsäptəl, -ˌtīl\ *n* -S [Gk *neossos* young bird + E *-ptile*] : one of the downy feathers of a newly hatched bird

neo·stig·mine \ˌnē(ˌ)ōˈstig,mēn, -,mən\ *n* -S [*ne-* + *-stigmine* (as in *physostigmine*)] : a cholinergic drug used in the form of the bromide [$(CH_3)_2NCOOC_6H_4N(CH_3)_3$]Br or the methyl sulfate derivative in the diagnosis and treatment of myasthenia gravis and the relief of postoperative atony of the intestines and urinary bladder

neo·striatum \ˌnē(ˌ)ō+\ *n, pl* **neostriatums** *or* **neostriata** [NL, fr. *ne-* + *striatum*] : the phylogenetically new part of the corpus striatum consisting of the caudate nucleus and putamen

neo-sumerian \"+\ *n, often cap N & cap S* [*ne-* + *sumerian*] : the later form of the Sumerian language

neo·supernaturalism \"+\ *n* [*ne-* + *supernaturalism*] : a revival of supernaturalism esp. in religious thought; *specif* : NEOORTHODOXY

Neo–Sy·neph·rine \ˌnē(ˌ)ōsəˈnefrən, -,rēn\ *trademark* — used for phenylephrine

neo-syriac \ˌnē(ˌ)ō+\ *n, often cap N & cap S* [*ne-* + *syriac*] : a modern form of Syriac that is spoken by Christians in northwestern Iran and that is akin to the ancient literary Syriac though not directly from it

neo·technic \ˈnēō+\ *adj* [*ne-* + *technic*] : of, relating to, or constituting the most recent period of industrial development marked by the use of electricity and alloys — compare PALEOTECHNIC

ne·o·tenic \ˌnēəˈtēnik, -ten-\ *also* **ne·o·te·nous** \-tēnəs\ *or* **ne·o·tei·nic** \-tēnik, -tīn-,-tān-\ *adj* [*neotenic, neoteinic* ISV *neoten-, neotein-* (fr. NL *neotenia, neoteinia* neoteny) + *-ic*; *neotenous* fr. *neoteny* + *-ous*] **1** : of, relating to, or exhibiting neoteny **2** *usu neoteinic* : being a newly developed king or queen of a termite colony following the loss of the previous royalties

ne·o·te·ny \nēˈätᵊnē\ *also* **ne·o·tei·nia** \ˌnēəˈtēnēə, -tīn-, -tān-\ *n, pl* **neotenies** *also* **neoteinias** [NL *neotenia, neoteinia*, fr. *ne-* + *-tenia, -teinia* (fr. Gk *teinein* to stretch) — more at THIN] **1** : the attainment of sexual maturity during the larval stage (as in the axolotl) **2** : the retention of some larval or immature characters in adulthood (as in complemental reproductives of termites) — compare FETALIZATION

¹ne·o·ter·ic \ˌnēəˈterik\ *adj* [LL *neotericus*, fr. LGk *neōterikos*, fr. Gk, youthful, fr. *neōteros* more recent, newer (compar. of *neos* young, new) + *-ikos* -ic — more at NEW] : recent in origin : MODERN **syn** see NEW

²neoteric \"\ *n* -S : MODERN 1; *esp* : a modern writer

ne·o·ter·i·cal·ly \-rək(ə)lē\ *adv* : in a neoteric manner

ne·ot·er·ism \nēˈäd·ə,rizəm\ *n* -S [Gk *neōterismos* innovation, fr. *neōteros* + *-ismos* -ism] : a newly invented word or phrase : the introduction of new expressions — compare NEOLOGISM

neo·thalamus \ˌnē(ˌ)ō+\ *n* [NL, fr. *ne-* + *thalamus*] : the phylogenetically more recent part of the thalamus including the lateral nucleus and the pulvinar together with the geniculate bodies

neo-thomism \ˌnē(ˌ)ō+\ *n, often cap N & usu cap T* [ISV *ne-* + *thomism*] : neo-scholastic philosophy or theory concerned with the teachings of Thomas Aquinas

¹neo-thomist \"+\ *n, often cap N & usu cap T* [ISV *ne-* + *thomist*] : an adherent of neo-Thomism

²neo-thomist \"\ *or* **neo-thomistic** *adj, often cap N & usu cap T* : of or relating to neo-Thomism or neo-Thomists

neo·thunnus \ˌnē(ˌ)ō+\ *n, cap* [NL, fr. *ne-* + *Thunnus*] : a genus of fishes (family Scombridae) containing the yellowfin tuna

ne·ot·o·cite \nēˈäd·ə,sīt\ *n* -S [Sw *neotokit*, fr. Gk *neotokos* newborn (fr. *ne-* + *tokos* childbirth, offspring, fr. *tiktein* to give birth to, beget) + Sw *-it* -ite — more at THANE] : a mineral consisting of a hydrous silicate of manganese and iron but having an uncertain formula

ne·ot·o·ma \nēˈäd·əmə\ *n, cap* [NL, fr. *ne-* + *-toma* (fr. Gk *temnein* to cut) — more at TOME] : a genus of rodents (family Cricetidae) comprising the wood rats or pack rats of western No. America

ne·ot·ra·gus \nēˈä·trəgəs\ *n, cap* [NL, fr. *ne-* + Gk *tragos* he-goat — more at TRAGEDY] : a genus of western African antelopes including only the royal antelope

ne·o·trema·ta \ˌnēə·ˈtremәd·ə, -rēm-\ *n pl, cap* [NL, fr. *ne-* + *-tremata*] : an order of inarticulate brachiopods that have the peduncle restricted throughout life to the ventral valve or atrophied in the adults and are known from the Cambrian to the present — **ne·o·tremate** \ˌ==ˌmāt\ *n* -S — **ne·o·trema·tous** \ˌ==ˈ=məd·əs\ *adj*

ne·o·treme \ˈnēə,trēm\ *adj* [NL *Neotremata*] : of or relating to the Neotremata

neo·tropical *also* **neo·tropic** \ˌnē(ˌ)ō+\ *adj, usu cap* [ISV *ne-* + *tropical* or *tropic*] : of, relating to, or constituting the biogeographic region that includes So. America, the West Indies, and tropical No. America

neo·tropics \"+\ *n pl* [*ne-* + *tropics*] : the Neotropical region

neo·type \ˈnēə,tīp\ *n* [*ne-* + *type*] : a type specimen selected subsequent to the description of a species to replace a preexisting type that has been lost or destroyed

neo·vitalism \ˌnē(ˌ)ō+\ *n* [ISV *ne-* + *vitalism*] : modern vitalism

neo·vitalist \"+\ *n* [*ne-* + *vitalist*] : an advocate of neovitalism

neo·washingtonia \ˌnē(ˌ)ō+\ [NL, fr. *ne-* + *Washingtonia*] *syn of* WASHINGTONIA

ne·o·za pine \nēˈōzə-\ *n* [Bhutanese *neoza*] : a tall Himalayan pine (*Pinus gerardiana*) with silvery bark and edible nuts

neo·zo·ic \ˌnēəˈzōik\ *adj, usu cap* [*ne-* + *-zoic*] : of, relating to, or constituting the entire period from the end of the Mesozoic to the present time

¹nep \ˈnep\ *n* -S [ME *nep, nepte*, fr. OE *nepte*, fr. L *nepeta*] *dial chiefly Brit* : CATNIP

²nep \"\ *vt* **nepped; nepped; nepping; neps** [origin unknown] : to form neps in (cotton) during processing

³nep \"\ *n* -S **1** : any of the little knots formed by irregular growth of cotton fibers or by the rubbing together of the fibers esp. in ginning **2** : a cluster of fibers occurring in wool staple

NEP *abbr* new economic policy

ne·pa \ˈnēpə\ *n, cap* [NL, fr. L, scorpion] : the type genus of the family Nepidae containing various typical elongate-oval water scorpions — compare RANATRA

NEPA *abbr* nuclear energy for propulsion of aircraft

ne·pal \nəˈpȯl, -päl,-pal,-päl\ *adj, usu cap* [fr. *Nepal*, country on northeast frontier of India] : of or from Nepal : of the kind or style prevalent in Nepal : NEPALESE

¹nep·a·lese \ˌnepəˈlēz, -ēs\ *adj, usu cap* [*Nepal* + E *-ese*] **1** : of, relating to, or characteristic of Nepal **2** : of, relating to, or characteristic of the people of Nepal

²nepalese \"\ *n, pl* **nepalese** *cap* : NEPALI

¹ne·pali \nəˈpȯlē, -pä-,-pa-,-pá-\ *adj, usu cap* [Hindi *naipālī*, fr. Skt *naipāliya*, fr. *Nepāla* Nepal] **1 a** : of, relating to, or characteristic of Nepal **b** : of, relating to, or characteristic of the people of Nepal **2** : of, relating to, or characteristic of the Nepali language

²nepali \"\ *n, pl* **nepali** *also* **nepalis** *cap* **1** : the Indic language of Nepal **2** : a native or inhabitant of Nepal

nepen·tha·ce·ae \ˌnepənˈthāsē,ē, ˌnē,pen-\ *n pl, cap* [NL, fr. *Nepenthes*, type genus + *-aceae*] : a family of plants coextensive with the genus *Nepenthes*

ne·pen·the \nəˈpen(t)thē\ *n* -S [L *nepenthes*, fr. Gk *nēpenthes*, neut. of *nēpenthēs* banishing pain and sorrow, fr. *nē-* not + *penthos* grief, sorrow — more at NO, PATHOS] **1 a** : a potion or drug used by the ancients to give forgetfulness of pain and sorrow and held by some to have been opium or hashish **b** : something capable of causing oblivion of grief or suffering ⟨only in occasional visits to the movies and lending libraries, in idle chatter and consoling gossip and scandal, and in the more unendurable cases in drink, can they find ~ —G.J. Nathan⟩ **2** : a plant yielding nepenthe — **ne·pen·the·an** \-ēən\ *adj*

ne·pen·thes \-n(t)(ˌ)thēz\ *n* [L] **1** *pl* **nepenthes** : NEPENTHE **2** *cap* [NL, fr. L, nepenthe] : a genus of Malaysian climbing insectivorous plants constituting a distinct family of the order Sarraceniales and having leaves with the midrib prolonged to a tendril and the apex expanded to a pitcher-shaped appendage — see PITCHER PLANT

ne·per \ˈnēpə(r), ˈnāp-\ *n* -S [after John *Neper* (Napier) †1617 Scot. mathematician who invented logarithms] : a unit on a natural logarithmic scale for expressing the relationship between two amounts of power (as electric power or acoustic power) equal to one half the natural logarithm of the ratio of the two powers compared : 8.686 decibels

nep·e·ta \ˈnepəd·ə\ *n, cap* [NL, fr. L, catnip] : a large genus of Eurasian mints having dentate leaves and verticillate clusters of white or blue flowers with a tubular 15-nerved calyx and a 2-lipped corolla — see CATNIP, GROUND IVY

neph·a·lism \ˈnefə,lizəm\ *n* -S [MGk *nēphalismos* soberness, fr. Gk *nēphalios* sober (fr. *nēphein* to be sober, drink no wine) + *-ismos* -ism; akin to Arm *nautʻi* sober] : total abstinence from alcoholic beverages

neph·a·list \-ləst\ *n* -S : an advocate or practitioner of nephalism — **neph·a·lis·tic** \ˌnefəˈlistik\ *adj*

nephel- *or* **nephelo-** *comb form* [F *néphél-*, fr. Gk *nephel-*, *nephelo-*, fr. *nephelē* — more at NEBULA] **1** : cloud ⟨*nephelognosy*⟩ **2** : cloudiness ⟨*nephelometer*⟩

neph·e·line \ˈnefə,lēn, -lən\ *or* **neph·e·lite** \-,līt\ *n* -S [*nepheline* fr. F *néphéline*, fr. Gk *nephelē* cloud + F *-ine*; *nephelite* fr. *nepheline* + *-ite*] : a hexagonal mineral $KNa_3Al_4Si_4O_{16}$ consisting of a silicate of sodium, potassium, and aluminum, occurring as glassy crystals or grains or as coarse crystals or masses of greasy luster without cleavage in various igneous rocks, and constituting an essential constituent of some rocks — **neph·e·lin·ic** \ˌnefəˈlinik\ *adj*

neph·e·lin·ite \ˈnefələ,nīt\ *n* -S [ISV *nepheline* + *-ite*; prob. orig. formed as G *nephelinit*] : a silica-deficient igneous rock having nepheline as the predominant mineral

neph·e·lin·iza·tion \ˌnefələnəˈzāshən, -ˌlēn-, -ˌnīˈz-\ *n* -S [*nepheline* + *-ization*] : the transformation of a rock into one having nepheline as an essential mineral

ne·phe·li·um \nəˈfēlēəm, neˈ-\ *n, cap* [NL, fr. LL *nephelion*, a plant, prob. burdock, fr. Gk *nephelion* small cloud, dim. of *nephelē* cloud] : a genus of Asiatic and Australian trees (family Sapindaceae) having terminal panicles of small flowers succeeded by fruits with a sweet edible pulp and a warty crust — see RAMBUTAN

neph·e·log·no·sy \ˌnefəˈlägnəsē\ *n* -ES [*nephel-* + *-gnosy*] : scientific observation of clouds

neph·e·lom·e·ter \ˌnefəˈlämәd·ə(r)\ *n* [ISV *nephel-* + *-meter*] : an instrument for measuring cloudiness: as **a** : a set of barium chloride or barium sulfate standards used for estimating the turbidity of a fluid and thereby the number of bacteria in suspension **b** : an instrument for determining the concentration or particle size of suspensions by means of transmitted or reflected light **c** : TURBIDIMETER — **neph·e·lo·met·ric** \ˌnefələˈme·trik\ *also* **neph·e·lo·met·ri·cal** \-rəkəl\ *adj* — **neph·e·lo·met·ri·cal·ly** \-k(ə)lē\ *adv* — **neph·e·lom·e·try** \ˌnefəˈlämə·trē\ *n* -ES

neph·e·lo·scope *also* **neph·e·le·scope** \ˈnefələ,skōp\ *n* [*nepheloscope* fr. *nephel-* + *-scope*; *nephelescope* fr. Gk *nephelē* cloud + E *-scope*] : an instrument for demonstrating cloud formation in the laboratory by expansion of moist air

neph·ew \ˈne(ˌ)fyü, *chiefly Brit* -)vyü\ *n* -S [ME *nevew* nephew, grandson, fr. OF *neveu*, fr. L *nepot-, nepos* grandson, nephew, descendant; akin to OE *nefa* grandson, nephew, OHG *nevo* grandson, kinsman, ON *nefi* nephew, kinsman, Gk *nepodes* children, Skt *napāt* grandson, descendant] **1 a** (1) : the son of a brother or sister (2) : the son of a brother-in-law or sister-in-law **b** : an illegitimate son of an ecclesiastic **2** *obs* **a** : a lineal descendant ⟨on that day Adam shall see all his ~s together —John Trapp⟩; *esp* : GRANDSON ⟨among the ancient Greeks the name of the grandfather was commonly given to the ~ —Richard Bentley †1742⟩ **b** : GRANDNEPHEW **c** : COUSIN ⟨Henry the Fourth, grandfather to this King, depos'd his ~ Richard, Edward's son —Shak.⟩

neph·ew·ship \-,ship\ *n* : the relationship of a nephew

neph·i·la \ˈnefələ\ *n, cap* [NL, fr. Gk *nēn* to spin + NL *-phila* — more at NEEDLE] : a genus of large elongate brightly marked mainly tropical spiders of the family Argiopidae — see SILK SPIDER

neph·i·lim \ˈnefə,lim, -ləm\ *n, pl in constr, usu cap* [Heb *Nĕphīlīm*] : a biblical race of giants or demigods ⟨the *Nephilim* were on the earth in those days —Gen 6:4 (RSV)⟩

nephite \ˈnē,fīt, ˈneˌ-\ *n* -S *usu cap* [*Nephi*, son of the Jewish prophet Lehi in the *Book of Mormon* (1 Nephi 1) + E *-ite*] *Mormonism* : a member of a people descended from Nephi, a son of the Jewish prophet Lehi who led a colony from Jerusalem to America about 600 B.C., organized as a church by the risen Christ, and exterminated by the Lamanites leaving the scriptures recorded in the Book of Mormon

nepho- *comb form* [ISV, fr. Gk, fr. *nephos* — more at NEBULA] : cloud ⟨*nephology*⟩

nepho·gram \ˈnefə,gram\ *n* [*nepho-* + *-gram*] : a photograph of clouds

nepho·graph \-,raf, -räf\ *n* [ISV *nepho-* + *-graph*] : an instrument for photographing clouds

ne·phol·o·gy \neˈfäləjē\ *n* -ES [*nepho-* + *-logy*] : a branch of meteorology dealing with clouds

neph·o·scope \ˈnefə,skōp\ *n* [ISV *nepho-* + *-scope*] : an instrument for observing the direction of motion and velocity of clouds

nepho·tet·tix \ˌnefəˈted·iks\ *n, cap* [NL, fr. *nepho-* + Gk *tettix* cicada] : a genus of leafhoppers including one (*N. apicalis*) that transmits a virus causing dwarf disease of rice

nephr- *or* **nephro-** *comb form* [LL *nephr-* & NL *nephro-*, fr. Gk *nephr-, nephro-*, fr. *nephros* — more at NEPHRITIS] **1** : kidney ⟨*nephric*⟩ ⟨*nephrology*⟩ **2** : nephric and ⟨*nephroabdominal*⟩ ⟨*nephrogastric*⟩

-nephra *pl of* -NEPHROS

ne·phrec·to·mize \nəˈfrektə,mīz, neˈ-\ *vb* -ED/-ING/-S *vt* : to perform nephrectomy upon ~ *vi* : to remove a kidney

ne·phrec·to·my \-mē\ *n* -ES [ISV *nephr-* + *-ectomy*] : the surgical removal of a kidney

neph·ric \ˈnefrik\ *adj* [*nephr-* + *-ic*] : of or relating to the kidneys : RENAL

ne·phrid·i·al \nəˈfridēəl\ *adj* [*nephridium* + *-al*] : of or relating to a nephridium

nephridial gland *n* : NEPHRIDIUM

ne·phrid·io·blast \-ēə,blast\ *n* [*nephridio-* (fr. *nephridium*) + *-blast*] : a single large coelomic cell that is the precursor of a nephridium in some worms

ne·phrid·io·duct \-,dəkt\ *n* [*nephridio-* (fr. *nephridium*) + *duct*] : the duct of a nephridium connecting nephrostome and nephridiopore and often serving as a common excretory and genital outlet

ne·phrid·io·pore \-,pō(ə)r\ *n* [*nephridio-* (fr. *nephridium*) + *-pore*] : the excretory orifice of a nephridium

ne·phrid·io·stome \-,stōm\ *n* -S [*nephridio-* (fr. *nephridium*) + *-stome*] : NEPHROSTOME

ne·phrid·i·um \nəˈfridēəm\ *n, pl* **nephrid·ia** \-ēə\ [NL, fr. *nephr-* + *-idium*] **1** : an excretory organ that is characteristic of various coelomate invertebrates (as annelid worms, mollusks, brachiopods, and some arthropods), occurs paired in each body segment or as a single pair serving the whole body, typically consists of a tube opening at one end into the coelom by a nephrostome and discharging at the other end by a nephridiopore on the exterior of the body, is often lengthened and convoluted, and has glandular walls **2** : any of various primarily excretory structures; *esp* : NEPHRON

neph·rite \ˈne,frīt\ *n* -S [G *nephrit*, fr. *nephr-* + *-it* -ite] : a compact tremolite or actinolite constituting the less valuable kind of jade and formerly worn as a remedy for kidney diseases

¹ne·phrit·ic \nəˈfrid·ik, (ˈ)neˈf-\ *adj* [LL *nephriticus*, fr. Gk *nephritikos*, fr. *nephritis* + *-ikos* -ic] **1** : arising from, originating in, or affecting the kidneys **2** : of, relating to, or affected with nephritis

²nephritic \"\ *n* -S : a person affected with nephritis

nephritic wood *n* **1** : the wood of the rosilla tree formerly used in an infusion for kidney diseases **2** : the wood of the East Indian horseradish tree formerly used in an infusion for kidney diseases

ne·phri·tis \nəˈfrīd·əs, neˈf-\ *n, pl* **nephrit·i·des** \-ˈrid·ə,dēz\ *also* **nephri·tis·es** [LL, fr. Gk, fr. *nephr-* (fr. *nephros* kidney) + *-itis*; akin to ME *nere* kidney, OHG *nioro* kidney, testicle, ON *nȳra* kidney, Lanuvian *nebrundines* testicles] : inflammation of the kidney affecting the structure (as of the glomerulus or parenchyma), being acute or chronic, and caused by infection, degenerative process, or vascular disease ⟨parenchymatous ~⟩ ⟨glomerular ~⟩ — distinguished from *nephrosclerosis* and *nephrosis*; compare BRIGHT'S DISEASE

nephro- — see NEPHR-

neph·ro·blast \ˈnefrə,blast\ *n* [*nephr-* + *-blast*] : NEPHRIDIOBLAST

neph·ro·calcinosis \ˌne(ˌ)frō+\ *n* [NL, fr. *nephr-* + *calcinosis*] : a condition marked by calcification of the tubules of the kidney

neph·ro·coel *or* **neph·ro·coele** \ˈnefrə,sēl\ *n* -S [*nephr-* + *-coele*] : the cavity of a nephrotome

neph·ro·cy·ta·ry \ˌnefrəˈsīd·ərē\ *adj* [*nephrocyte* + *-ary*] : of or relating to a nephrocyte

neph·ro·cyte \ˈnefrə,sīt\ *n* -S [ISV *nephr-* + *-cyte*] : an excretory cell; *specif* : a cell that has the ability to store up substances of an excretory nature

neph·ro·gen·ic \ˌnefrəˈjenik\ *also* **ne·phrog·e·nous** \nəˈfräjənəs, (ˈ)neˈf-\ *adj* [*nephr-* + *-genic* or *-genous*] **1** : originating in the kidney : caused by factors originating in the kidney ⟨~ hypertension⟩ **2** : developing into or producing kidney tissue ⟨strands of ~ cells⟩

neph·ro·gonaduct \ˌne(ˌ)frō+\ *n* [*nephr-* + *gonoduct*] : a nephridium that serves as a gonoduct

neph·roid \ˈne,frȯid\ *adj* [Gk *nephroeidēs* like a kidney, fr. *nephr-* + *-oeidēs* -oid] : RENIFORM

neph·rol·e·pis \nəˈfräləpəs, neˈ-\ *n, cap* [NL, fr. *nephr-* + *-lepis*] : a small genus of mainly tropical ferns (family Polypodiaceae) having large pinnate fronds, the pinnae articulated at the rachis, and the sori on the upper branches of the free veins — see SWORD FERN

neph·ro·lith \ˈnefrə,lith\ *n* -S [ISV *nephr-* + *-lith*] : RENAL CALCULUS

neph·ro·li·thi·a·sis \ˌnefrō+\ *n, pl* **nephrolithiases** [NL, fr. *nephr-* + *lithiasis*] : a condition marked by the presence of renal calculi

neph·ro·lith·ic \ˌnefrəˈlithik\ *adj* [ISV *nephrolith* + *-ic*] : of or relating to renal calculi

neph·ro·li·thot·o·my \ˌnefrələˈthäd·əmē\ *n* -ES [ISV *nephrolith* + *-o-* + *-tomy*] : the surgical operation of removing a calculus from the kidney

ne·phrol·o·gist \nəˈfräləjəst, neˈ-\ *n* -S [ISV *nephrology* + *-ist*] : a specialist in nephrology

ne·phrol·o·gy \-jē\ *n* -ES [ISV *nephr-* + *-logy*] : the science that deals with the kidneys, esp. their structure, functions, or diseases

ne·phro·ma \nəˈfrōmə, neˈ-\ *n, pl* **nephromas** \-məz\ *also* **nephroma·ta** \-məd·ə\ [NL, fr. *nephr-* + *-oma*] : a malignant tumor of the renal cortex

neph·ro·mere \ˈnefrə,mi(ə)r\ *n* -S [*nephr-* + *-mere*] : a segment of the mesoblast giving rise to a part of the kidney

neph·ro·mix·i·um \ˌnefrəˈmiksēəm\ *n, pl* **nephromix·ia** \-ēə\ [NL, fr. *nephr-* + *-mixium* (perh. fr. Gk *mixis* act of mixing, fr. *mignynai* to mix) — more at MIX] : a nephridium that functions as an excretory organ and a genital duct

neph·ron \ˈne,frän\ *also* **neph·rone** \-rōn\ *n* -S [G *nephron*, fr. Gk *nephros* kidney — more at NEPHRITIS] : a single excretory unit; *esp* : such a unit in the vertebrate kidney typically consisting of a Malpighian corpuscle, proximal convoluted tubule, loop of Henle, distal convoluted tubule, collecting tubule, and vascular and supporting tissues and discharging by way of a renal papilla into the renal pelvis

ne·phrop·a·thy \neˈfräpəthē\ *n* -ES [ISV *nephr-* + *-pathy*] : an abnormal state of the kidney; *esp* : one associated with or secondary to some other pathologic process ⟨diabetic ~⟩

neph·ro·pexy \ˈnefrə,peksē\ *n* -ES [ISV *nephr-* + *-pexy*] : surgical fixation of a floating kidney

neph·ro·pore \-,pō(ə)r\ *n* -S [*nephr-* + *-pore*] : NEPHRIDIOPORE

neph·rops \ˈne,fräps\ *n, cap* [NL, fr. *nephr-* + *-ops*] : a genus of lobsters including the Norway lobster

ne·phrop·si·dae \neˈfräpsə,dē\ *n pl, cap* [NL, fr. *Nephrops* + *-idae*] *in some classifications* : a family of crustaceans coextensive with Homaridae

neph·rop·to·sis \ˌne,fräpˈtōsəs, ˌnefrəˈtō-\ *n, pl* **nephroptoses** \-ō,sēz\ [NL, fr. *nephr-* + *-ptosis*] : abnormal mobility of the kidney : floating kidney

ne·phror·rha·phy \ne'frȯrəfē\ *n* -ES [ISV *nephr-* + *-rrhaphy*] **:** the fixation of a floating kidney by suturing it to the posterior abdominal wall

-neph·ros \ˌnefrəs, -ˌfräs\ *also* **-neph·ron** \-ən,-ˌän\ *n comb form, pl* **-nephroi** *also* **-nephra** [NL, fr. Gk *nephros*] **:** kidney ⟨*pronephros*⟩

neph·ro·sclerosis \ˌne(ˌ)frō+\ *n* [NL, fr. *nephr-* + *sclerosis*] **:** hardening of the kidney; *specif* **:** a condition that is characterized by sclerosis of the renal arterioles with reduced blood flow and contraction of the kidney, that is associated usu. with hypertension, and that terminates in renal failure and uremia

ne·phro·sis \nə'frōsə̇s, ne'-\ *n, pl* **nephro·ses** \-ō,sēz\ [NL, fr. *nephr-* + *-osis*] **:** noninflammatory degeneration of the kidneys chiefly affecting the renal tubules — distinguished from *nephritis, nephrosclerosis*

neph·ro·stome \'nefrəˌstōm\ *also* **neph·ro·stom** \-täm\ *or* **ne·phros·to·ma** \nə'frästəmə, ne'-\ *n, pl* **nephrostomes** \-tōmz\ *also* **nephrostoms** \-tämz\ *or* **neph·ro·sto·ma·ta** \ˌnefrə'stōmədə\ [NL *nephrostoma*, fr. *nephr-* + *-stoma*] **:** the ciliated funnel-shaped coelomic opening of a typical nephridium — **neph·ro·stomic** \ˌnefrə¦stōmik, -täm-\ *adj*

¹ne·phrot·ic \nə'frädik, ne'-\ *adj* [fr. *nephrosis*, after such pairs as E *narcosis: narcotic*] **:** of, relating to, or affected by nephrosis

²nephrotic \"\ *n* -S **:** one that is affected with nephrosis

neph·ro·tome \'nefrəˌtōm\ *n* -S [*nephr-* + *-tome*] **:** the modified part of a somite of a vertebrate embryo that develops into a segmental excretory tubule of the primitive kidney

ne·phrot·o·my \nə'frädəmē, ne'-\ *n* -ES [NL *nephrotomia*, fr. *nephr-* + *-tomia* -tomy] **:** surgical incision of a kidney (as for the extraction of a stone)

neph·ro·toxic \ˌnefrō+\ *adj* [ISV *nephr-* + *toxic*] **:** poisonous to the kidney ⟨a ~ serum⟩ **:** sufficient to poison the kidney ⟨a ~ dose⟩ **:** resulting from or marked by poisoning of the kidney ⟨~ nephritis⟩ — **neph·ro·toxicity** \ˌne(ˌ)frō+\ *n* -ES

neph·thy·tis \nef'thīdə̇s, 'nefthəd-\ *n* [NL, fr. Gk *Nephthys*, Egyptian goddess] **1** *cap* **:** a small genus of tropical western African creeping or twining rhizomatous herbs (family Araceae) that usu. have long-petioled sagittate leaves and include some (as *N. afzelii*) that are cultivated as ornamental foliage plants **2** *pl* **nephthytis a :** any plant of the genus *Nephthytis* **b :** any of several plants that are confused with or have formerly been included among members of the genus *Nephthytis*

¹nepid \'nepə̇d, 'nēp-\ *adj* [NL *Nepidae*] **:** of or relating to the Nepidae

²nepid \"\ *n* -S [NL *Nepidae*] **:** an insect of the family Nepidae

nep·i·dae \'nepəˌdē\ *n pl, cap* [NL, fr. *Nepa*, type genus + *-idae*] **:** a family of true bugs comprising the water scorpions — see NEPA, RANATRA

nepi·on·ic \ˌnepē¦änik, ¦nēp-\ *adj* [Gk *nēpios* infant + E *-onic* (as in *embryonic*)] **:** IMMATURE, LARVAL ⟨~ forms of many of the common larger fossils —*Jour. of Geol.*⟩

ne plus ul·tra \ˌnēˌplə'səl-trə; ˌnāˌplü'sül-trə, -ˌträ\ *n, pl* **ne plus ultras** [NL, no further] **1 a :** the highest point capable of being reached or attained **:** the summit of achievement **:** ACME ⟨the *ne plus ultra* of original philosophy —O.W.Holmes †1935⟩ ⟨the most sophisticated people in the *ne plus ultra* of civilized society —Edith Hamilton⟩ **b :** the highest degree of a quality or state ⟨found a small clerical job in the town — the *ne plus ultra* of humiliation —Van Wyck Brooks⟩ **2** *archaic* **:** a prohibition against or obstacle to further advance or achievement ⟨her fancy of no limit dreams, no *ne plus ultra* bounds her schemes —Hannah More⟩

nep·man \'nepmən, -ˌman\ *n, pl* **nepmen** [Russ, fr. *nep* New Economic Policy (fr. *Novaya Ekonomicheskaya Politika* New Economic Policy) + *-man* (prob. fr. G *mann* man, fr. OHG *man*) — more at MAN] **:** one of a group of small private traders and merchants appearing briefly in Russia during the third decade of the 20th century as a result of a temporary relaxation by the Communist government of its ban on private enterprise

nepo·tal \'nepəd·ᵊl, ne'pōd·-\ *adj* [L *nepot-, nepos* + E *-al*] **:** of, relating to, or resembling a nephew

nepote \'neˌpōt, 'nē,-\ *n* -S [L *nepot-, nepos*] *Scot* **:** NEPHEW

ne·pot·ic \(')ne¦pädik, nə'-\ *adj* [fr. *nepotism*, after such pairs as E *despotism: despotic*] **1 :** of or relating to nepotism **:** disposed to nepotism **2 :** NEPOTAL

nep·o·tism \'nepəˌtizəm\ *n* -S [F *népotisme*, fr. It *nepotismo*, fr. *nipote, nepote* nephew (fr. L *nepot-, nepos* grandson, nephew) + *-ismo* -ism — more at NEPHEW] **:** favoritism shown to nephews and other relatives (as by giving them positions because of their relationship rather than on their merits) ⟨continued some of the earlier traditions . . . of ~, creating the duchy of Parma for his vicious illegitimate son —R.A.Hall b.1911⟩ ⟨British administration at the beginning of the 19th century was honeycombed with ~ —C.J.Friedrich⟩

nep·o·tist \-pəd·ə̇st, -pətə-\ *n* -S [*nepotism* + *-ist*] **:** one who practices nepotism

nep·o·tis·tic \¦nepə¦tistik\ *or* **nep·o·tis·ti·cal** \-stə̇kəl\ *adj* **:** of or relating to nepotism or nepotists

ne·pou·ite \nə'püˌīt\ *n* -S [ISV *nepou-* (fr. *Népoui*, New Caledonia, its locality) + *-ite*] **:** a mineral $(Ni,Mg)_3Si_2O_5(OH)_4$ consisting of a hydrous nickel magnesium silicate

nepped *past of* NEP

nep·pi·ness \'nepēnə̇s\ *n* -ES **:** the quality or state of being neppy

nepping *pres part of* NEP

nep·py \'nepē\ *adj* -ER/-EST [¹*nep* + *-y*] **:** having neps **:** containing many neps ⟨~ cotton⟩ ⟨~ yarns⟩

neps *pl of* NEP, *pres 3d sing of* NEP

¹nep·tic·u·lid \(')nep¦tikyələd, ¦neptə¦kyül-\ *adj* [NL *Nepticulidae*] **:** of or relating to the Nepticulidae

²nepticulid \"\ *n* -S [NL *Nepticulidae*] **:** a moth of the family Nepticulidae

nep·ti·cu·li·dae \ˌneptə'kyüləˌdē\ *n pl, cap* [NL, fr. *Nepticula*, type genus (fr. LL *nepticula* little granddaughter, dim. of L *neptis* granddaughter) + *-idae* — more at NIECE] **:** a family of minute and widely distributed moths whose larvae occur as leaf miners on many deciduous trees

nep·tune \'nep,t(y)ün *sometimes* -p,chün\ *n* -S [after *Neptune*, Roman god of waters, fr. L *Neptunus*] **1** *usu cap* **:** OCEAN, SEA ⟨full often hath she . . . sat with me on *Neptune's* yellow sands —Shak.⟩ **2 :** a copper or brass plate or pan used in trade with the natives of Africa **3** *or* **neptune green** *often cap N* **:** a light to moderate green that is bluer and stronger than surf green

neptune's cup *also* **neptune's goblet** *n, usu cap N* **:** either of two very large cup-shaped sponges (*Poterion neptuni* and *P. amphitritae*) sometimes four feet high

neptune shell *n* **:** a large whelk (*Neptunea decemcostata*) of the eastern coast of northern No. America distinguished by 10 raised reddish bands surrounding the body whorl of the drab-colored shell

¹nep·tu·ni·an \(')nep¦t(y)ünēən *sometimes* -¦chü-\ *adj* [L *neptunius* Neptunian (fr. *Neptunus*) + E *-an*] **1** *usu cap* **:** of or relating to the god Neptune, the planet Neptune, or the ocean **2 a :** formed by the agency of water **b :** of or relating to neptunism or the neptunists

²neptunian \"\ *n* -S **:** NEPTUNIST

nep·tun·ism \'=ˌ=ˌnizəm\ *n* -S [ISV *neptun-* (fr. L *Neptunus*) + *-ism*] **:** the theory of the neptunists

nep·tun·ist \-nə̇st\ *n* -S [ISV *neptun-* (fr. L *Neptunus*) + *-ist*] **:** one holding the now obsolete theory that all of the rocks of the earth's crust were formed by the agency of water — compare PLUTONIST

nep·tun·ite \-ˌnīt\ *n* -S [Sw *neptunit*, fr. L *Neptunus* Neptune + Sw *-it* -ite] **:** a mineral $(Na,K)_2(Fe,Mn)TiSi_4O_{12}$ consisting of a silicate of iron, manganese, potassium, sodium, and titanium

nep·tu·ni·um \nep't(y)ünēəm *sometimes* -p'chü-\ *n* -S [NL, fr. ISV *Neptune*, the planet Neptune (fr. L *Neptunus*, the god Neptune) + NL *-ium*] **:** a radioactive metallic element of the actinide series that is similar chemically to uranium, that was discovered as a short-lived isotope by spontaneous emission of an electron from uranium 239 produced in turn by neutron bombardment of uranium 238, and that is obtained as the longest-lived isotope in nuclear reactors as a by-product in the production of plutonium — symbol *Np*; see ELEMENT table

neptunium series *n* **:** a radioactive series that does not now occur in nature and that begins with plutonium of mass number 241 and continues to americium, to the longest-lived member of the series neptunium of mass number 237, and eventually to the stable end product bismuth

ne·ral \'niˌral, 'nē,-\ *n* -S [ISV *nerol* + *-al*] **:** the cis form of citral

¹ne·re·id \'nirēə̇d\ *n* -S *usu cap* [L *Nereid-, Nereis*, fr. Gk *Nēreid-, Nēreis, Nēreid-, Nēreis*, fr. *Nēreus* Nereus, god of the sea + Gk *-id-, -is* fem. patronymic suffix] **1 :** any of the 50 or 100 sea nymphs held in Greek mythology to be the daughters of Nereus and Doris and attendants on Poseidon and represented as riding sea horses and other sea monsters and usu. as having the human form **2 :** an often malevolent nymph of Greek folklore dwelling in springs or trees as well as in the sea

²nereid \"\ *adj* [NL *Nereidae*] **:** of or relating to the Nereidae

³nereid \"\ *n* -S [NL *Nereidae*] **:** a worm of the family Nereidae

ne·re·idae \nə'rēəˌdē\ *n pl, cap* [NL, fr. *Nereis*, type genus + *-idae*] **:** a large family of predaceous marine polychaete worms that have an elongated many-segmented body with large complex parapodia on most segments and a well-defined head with paired tentacles and palps, four prostomial eyes, eight peristomial cirri, and large jaws which bite transversely and that include burrowing and free-swimming forms — see NEREIS

ne·re·idi·for·mia \ˌnirēˌidə'fȯrmēə, nəˌrēəd-\ *n pl, cap* [NL, fr. *Nereid-, Nereis*, genus of polychaete worms + *-iformia* (fr. L, neut. pl. of *-iformis* -iform)] *in some classifications* **:** a division of polychaete worms nearly equivalent to Errantia

ne·re·is \'nirēə̇s\ *n* [NL *Nereid-, Nereis*, fr. L, Nereid] **1** *cap* **:** the type genus of Nereidae comprising usu. large, often dimorphic, and frequently greenish polychaete worms — see CLAM WORM **2** *pl* **nereides :** any marine worm of the genus *Nereis*

ne·reo·cys·tis \ˌnirēō'sistə̇s\ *n, cap* [NL, fr. *nereo-* (fr. Gk *Nēreus* Nereus) + *-cystis*] **:** a monotypic genus of probably annual brown algae (family Laminariaceae) of the northern Pacific that have a stipe which sometimes exceeds 100 feet in length, is hollow in its upper part, and terminates in a large spherical float supporting dependent long thin dichotomously branched laminae and that have been used as a source of potash — see SEA-OTTER'S-CABBAGE

ne·ri \'nā(ˌ)rē\ *n pl, usu cap* [It, lit., blacks, pl. of *nero* black, fr. L *nigr-, niger*] **:** a political faction of the Guelphs in Tuscany, Italy, about 1300 opposed to the Bianchi

ne·ri·ne \nə'rī(ˌ)nē\ *n* [NL, fr. L *Nerine* Nereid, fr. Gk *Nēreus* Nereus] **1** *cap* **:** a genus of southern African bulbous herbs (family Amaryllidaceae) with strap-shaped leaves and showy red flowers resembling lilies — see GUERNSEY LILY **2** -S **:** any plant of the genus *Nerine*

ne·ri·ta \nə'rīd·ə\ *n* [NL, fr. L, sea snail, fr. Gk *nēreitēs, nēritēs*, fr. *Nēreus* Nereus] **1** *cap* **:** the type genus of Neritidae comprising marine snails with the shell short and smooth or spirally ridged and with a thick usu. toothed outer lip and a toothed operculum **2** -S **:** any mollusk of the genus *Nerita* — see BLEEDING TOOTH — **neri·toid** \nə'rīˌtȯid, 'nerə,-\ *adj*

ner·ite \'neˌrīt\ *n* -S [NL *Nerita*] **:** NERITID

ne·rit·ic \nə'rid·ik\ *adj* [ISV *nerit-* (perh. fr. NL *Nerita*) + *-ic*] **:** of, relating to, or constituting the belt or region of shallow water adjoining the seacoast and usu. considered to extend from low-tide mark to a depth of 100 fathoms ⟨the ~ zone⟩ ⟨a characteristic ~ fauna⟩ — compare OCEANIC, PELAGIC

¹ne·ritid \nə'rīd·ə̇d, -rid·ə̇d\ *adj* [NL *Neritidae*] **:** of or relating to the Neritidae

²neritid \"\ *n* -S [NL *Neritidae*] **:** a snail of the family Neritidae

ne·rit·i·dae \nə'rid·əˌdē\ *n pl, cap* [NL, fr. *Nerita*, type genus + *-idae*] **:** a family of operculate snails (suborder Rhipidoglossa) with turbinate shells having the aperture shaped like a half-moon and a columella resembling a shelf — see NERITA, NERITINA

ner·i·ti·na \ˌnerə'tīnə, -tēnə\ *n* [NL, fr. L *nerita* sea snail + NL *-ina*] **1** *cap* **:** a genus of ornately marked and brightly colored snails (family Neritidae) chiefly inhabiting fresh and brackish waters **2** -S **:** any snail of the genus *Neritina*

ne·ri·um \'nirēəm\ *n, cap* [NL, fr. L, oleander, fr. Gk *nērion*] **:** a small genus of tropical Old World shrubs (family Apocynaceae) having coriaceous verticillate leaves and large red or white fragrant flowers — see OLEANDER

nernst effect \'ne(ə)rn|zt-, 'nərn|, |(t)st-\ *n, usu cap N* [after Walther H. *Nernst* †1941 Ger. physicist & chemist] **:** a transverse electromotive force produced when a metal through which a flow of heat occurs is placed in a magnetic field and observed when the magnetic lines of force are perpendicular to the thermal flux

nernst heat theorem *n, usu cap N* **:** a theorem in thermodynamics: no change in entropy is involved in a physical or chemical process taking place in the vicinity of the absolute zero of temperature

nernst lamp *n, usu cap N* **:** an electric incandescent lamp whose filament or rod consists of a mixture of magnesia with oxides of the rare earth metals that on being raised to a high temperature (as by a glowing platinum spiral) becomes luminous and conducting and may be kept thus by the passage of a comparatively weak current and without a vacuum

ne·ro an·ti·co \¦nā(ˌ)rōˌan'tē(ˌ)kō, rō,än-\ *n* [It, lit., ancient black] **:** an ornamental black marble found in fragments among Roman ruins and believed to have come from ancient Laconia

nerol \'neˌrōl, 'ni,-, -rōl\ *n* -S [ISV *ner-* (fr. *neroli oil*) + *-ol*] **:** a liquid unsaturated alcohol $C_{10}H_{17}OH$ that has a rose scent, that occurs in many essential oils (as neroli, petitgrain, and rose oils), that is prepared from its stereoisomer geraniol, and that is used in perfumery esp. in rose and orange blossom scents — compare CITRAL

Nerol \"\ *trademark* — used for a dye; see DYE table I (under *Acid Black 26B*)

ne·ro·li·dol \ne'rōləˌdōl, -rȯl-, -dōl\ *n* -S [ISV *nerol* + *-ide* + *-ol*] **:** a liquid acyclic sesquiterpenoid tertiary alcohol $C_{15}H_{25}OH$ that has a floral odor, that is isomeric with farnesol, and that occurs in many essential oils (as neroli oil and the oil from Peru balsam)

ner·o·li oil \'nerəlē-\ *n* [F *néroli*, fr. It *neroli*, fr. Anna Maria de la Tremoille, princess of *Nerole fl* 1670] **:** a fragrant pale yellow essential oil that darkens on standing, that is obtained from the flowers esp. of the sour orange, and that is used chiefly in cologne and other perfumes and as a flavoring material — called also *orange-flower oil*

ne·ro·ni·an \nə'rōnēən, nē'-\ *or* **ne·ron·ic** \-ränik\ *adj, usu cap* [*neronian* fr. L *neronianus*, fr. *Neron-, Nero* Nero †A.D.68 Rom. emperor + L *-anus, -ianus* -an; *neronic* fr. L *Neron-, Nero* + E *-ic*] **1 :** resembling Nero in some characteristic (as moral depravity) **2 :** of or relating to Nero or his times

ne·ro·nize \'nērəˌnīz, 'nir-\ *vt* -ED/-ING/-S *often cap* [L *Neron-, Nero* + E *-ize*] **:** to tyrannize over in the manner of Nero

ner ta·mid \ˌnā(ə)rtä'mēd\ *n, usu cap N&T* [Heb *nēr tāmīdh*, lit., eternal light] **:** a light that hangs in front of and above the ark in the synagogue and is symbolic of the light of truth and the presence of God

ner·thri·dae \'nərthrəˌdē\ [NL, fr. *Nerthra*, genus of toad bugs + *-idae*] *syn of* GELASTOCORIDAE

nerts \'nərts, -əts,-əits\ *n pl* [by alter.] *slang* **:** NUT 6b

nerv- *or* **nervi-** *or* **nervo-** *comb form* [ME *nerv-*, fr. L, fr. *nervus* sinew, nerve] **1 :** nerve ⟨*nervate*⟩ ⟨*nerviduct*⟩ **2 :** nervous and ⟨*nervomuscular*⟩

ner·val \'nərvəl\ *adj* [L *nervalis*, fr. *nervus* nerve + *-alis* -al] **:** of or relating to nerves or nervous tissue **:** NEURAL

¹ner·vate \'nərˌvāt\ *vt* -ED/-ING/-S [*nerv-* + *-ate*, v. suffix] *archaic* **:** NERVE, INSPIRIT, SUPPORT

²nervate \"\ *also* **ner·vat·ed** \-ād·ə̇d\ *adj* [*nervate* prob. fr. (assumed) NL *nervatus*, fr. L *nervus* sinew, nerve + *-atus* -ate (adj. suffix); *nervated* prob. fr. (assumed) NL *nervatus* + E *-ed*] **:** NERVED

ner·va·tion \ˌnər'vāshən\ *n* -S [prob. fr. (assumed) NL *nervation-, nervatio*, fr. (assumed) NL *nervatus* nervate + L *-ion-, -io* -ion] **:** an arrangement or system of nerves; *often* **:** VENATION

ner·va·ture \'nərvəˌchü(ə)r, -ˌchər\ *n* -S [prob. fr. (assumed) NL *nervatura*, fr. (assumed) NL *nervatus* nervate + L *-ura* -ure] **:** NERVATION

¹nerve \'nərv, -əv,-əiv\ *n* -S [L *nervus* sinew, nerve; akin to Gk *neuron* sinew, nerve, string, Skt *snāvan* sinew, Gk *nēn* to spin — more at NEEDLE] **1 a :** SINEW, TENDON — used in the phrase *to strain every nerve* **b :** a sinew or tendon taken (as for a bowstring or for thread) from an animal **2 :** one of the filamentous bands of nervous tissue that connect parts of the nervous system with the other organs of the body and conduct nervous impulses to or away from these organs and that are made up of nerve fibers together with protective and supportive structure with the fibers of larger nerves being gathered into funiculi surrounded by a perineurium and the funiculi being enclosed in a common epineurium **3 a :** the mainspring of action, drive, force, or vitality **:** the center or source of energy or direction ⟨develops and finds the ~ of its own style —Milton Klonsky⟩ ⟨proved again and again that he himself was the heart and ~ of the whole undertaking⟩ **b :** power of endurance, self-command, equilibrium, or control **:** FORTITUDE, HEART, STAMINA, STRENGTH ⟨knew that now he was to face some trial of mind and ~ —Gilbert Parker⟩ **c :** BOLDNESS, DARING ⟨true leadership begins when a statesman . . . has the ~ to dwell on distasteful facts —Fremont Rider⟩; *often* **:** presumptuous audacity or hardihood **:** BRASS, EFFRONTERY, ¹GALL 3 ⟨the ~ of her⟩ **4 a :** a sore or sensitive point **:** a touchy subject or aspect ⟨touched the pocketbook ~⟩ **b nerves** *pl* **:** nervous disorganization or collapse **:** HYSTERIA ⟨went all to pieces with ~*s*⟩ **5 :** VEIN 3a ⟨magnesium deficiency causes a light yellow discoloration of the old leaves except for the parenchyma along the ~*s* —Charles Coster⟩ **6 :** the sensitive pulp of a tooth **7 :** VEIN 3c **8 :** the aggregate of the physical properties (as firmness, strength, and elasticity) characteristic of crude rubber **:** rubbery quality ⟨low-grade soft rubbers lack ~⟩ **syn** see TEMERITY

²nerve \"\ *vt* -ED/-ING/-S **:** to give strength, vigor, or courage to **:** supply with physical or moral force ⟨this feeling . . . *nerved* him to break through the awe-inspiring aloofness of his captain —Joseph Conrad⟩ **syn** see ENCOURAGE

nerve block *n* **:** an interruption of the passage of impulses through a nerve (as with pressure or narcotization); *sometimes* **:** BLOCK ANESTHESIA

nerve canal *n* **:** PULP CANAL

nerve cavity *n* **:** PULP CAVITY

nerve cell *n* **:** one of the cells that constitute nervous tissue, that have the property of transmitting and receiving nervous impulses, and that are typically composed in higher animals and man of somewhat reddish or grayish protoplasm with a large nucleus containing a conspicuous nucleolus, irregular cytoplasmic granules, and cytoplasmic processes which are highly differentiated as frequently multiple dendrites or usu. solitary axons and which conduct impulses toward and away from the nerve cell body **:** NEURON; *sometimes* **:** a nerve cell body exclusive of its processes **:** the major structural element of the gray matter of the brain and spinal cord, the ganglia, and the retina

nerve center *n* **1 :** CENTER 2e **2 :** the essential part of a body or system **:** the place or source of leadership, control, or influence ⟨the political and economic *nerve center* of the archipelago —R.S.Kain⟩

nerve cord *n* **:** a cord of nervous tissue; *specif* **:** the pair of closely united ventral longitudinal nerves with their segmental ganglia that is characteristic of many elongate invertebrates (as earthworms)

nerved \-vd\ *adj* [¹*nerve* + *-ed*] **1 :** having nerves; *esp* **:** having nerves of a specified character — often used in combination ⟨fan-*nerved*⟩ **2 :** showing courage or strength **:** BOLD, POISED ⟨broad hand ~ and vital in bronze as if in actual flesh —Dymphna Cusack & Florence James⟩

nerve ending *also* **nerve end** *n* **:** the structure in which the distal end of the axon of a nerve fiber terminates

nerve fiber *n* **:** an axon or dendrite covered with both a medullary sheath and a neurilemma (as in the peripheral nervous system), with a medullary sheath only (as in the central nervous system), or with a neurilemma only (as in the sympathetic system), or not covered at all (as in the gray matter)

nerve gas *n* **:** a war gas that is absorbed into the body through the skin, ingested, or inhaled and that has a paralyzing or other harmful effect esp. on the nervous and respiratory systems

nerve impulse *also* **nervous impulse** *n* **:** the progressive alteration in the protoplasm of a nerve fiber that follows stimulation of the fiber, is accompanied by a wave of alteration of electrical potential, and serves to transmit a record of sensation from a receptor or an instruction to act to an effector

nerve·less \'=lə̇s\ *adj* **1 :** destitute of strength or courage **:** FEEBLE, POWERLESS ⟨a weak, ~ fool, devoid of energy and promptitude —Nathaniel Hawthorne⟩ **2 :** lacking nerves or nervures **3 :** exhibiting control or balance **:** COOL, POISED ⟨surely one of the most ~ champions in the history of the tournament —*New Yorker*⟩ — **nerve·less·ly** *adv* — **nerve·less·ness** *n* -ES

nerve·let \'=lə̇t\ *n* -S [¹*nerve* + *-let*] **:** a little nerve

nerve net *n* **:** a network (as in various lower invertebrates and possibly the wall of the vertebrate intestine) that consists of primitive nerve cells each of which appears continuous with adjacent cells without intervening synapses and that conducts stimulation in all directions with a decrement

nerve of lan·ci·si \-län'chēzē\ *usu cap L* [after Giovanni M. *Lancisi* †1720 Ital. anatomist] **:** STRIA LONGITUDINALIS

nerve of wris·berg \-'rizˌbərg, *Ger* -'vris,berk\ *usu cap W* [after Heinrick A. *Wrisberg* †1808 Ger. anatomist] **:** GLOSSOPALATINE NERVE

nerve-racking *or* **nerve-wracking** \'=ˌ==\ *adj* **:** extremely trying on the nerves

nerve ring *n* **:** a ring of nervous tissue; *esp* **:** a ring of concentrated nervous tissue about the pharynx of various invertebrate animals

nerveroot \'=ˌ=\ *n* **:** MOCCASIN FLOWER

nerves *pl of* NERVE, *pres 3d sing of* NERVE

nerve sheath *n* **:** NEURILEMMA

nerve trunk *n* **:** a bundle of nerve fibers enclosed in a connective tissue sheath

nervi *pl of* NERVUS

nervi- — see NERV-

ner·vi·duct \'nərvəˌdəkt\ *n* [*nerv-* + *duct*] **:** a bony or cartilaginous passage for a nerve

nervier *comparative of* NERVY

nerviest *superlative of* NERVY

ner·vii \'nərvēˌī, 'nervēˌē\ *n pl, usu cap* [L] **:** a Celtic-German people of Belgium almost exterminated by Julius Caesar

ner·vi·ly \'nərvəlē, -əv-,-əiv-, -lī\ *adv* **:** in a nervy manner

ner·vi·muscular \¦nərvə̇, -vē+\ *or* **ner·vo·muscular** \-(ˌ)vō+\ *adj* [*nerv-* + *muscular*] **:** NEUROMUSCULAR

¹ner·vine \'nərˌvēn *sometimes* -vīn\ *adj* [*nerv-* + *-ine*] **:** affecting the nerves **:** tending to soothe nervous excitement

²ner·vine \'nərˌvēn, ˌ='=\ *n* -S **:** a nerve tonic

ner·vi ner·vo·rum \ˌnərˌvīˌnər'vōrəm, ¦nerˌvēˌner-\ *n pl* [NL, lit., nerves of nerves] **:** small nerve filaments innervating the sheath of a larger nerve

nerv·i·ness \'nərvēnə̇s, -əv-,-əiv-, -vin-\ *n* -ES **:** the quality or state of being nervy ⟨the scramble and ~ of competitive living —George Farwell⟩

nerv·ing \-viŋ,-vēŋ\ *n* -S [¹*nerve* + *-ing*] **:** the removal of part of a nerve trunk in chronic inflammation to destroy sensation in the parts supplied and thus cure lameness (as in a horse)

nerv·ish \-vish,-vēsh\ *adj, dial* **:** NERVOUS

nervo- — see NERV-

ner·von \'nərˌvän\ *also* **ner·vone** \-vōn\ *n* -S [ISV *nerv-* + *-on* or *-one*] **:** a crystalline cerebroside $C_{48}H_{91}NO_8$ found together with a hydroxy derivative in the brain

ner·von·ic acid \(')nər¦vänik-\ *n* [*nervonic* ISV *nervon* + *-ic*] **:** a crystalline unsaturated fatty acid $C_{23}H_{45}COOH$ obtained from nervon by hydrolysis and also found in some fish-liver oils — called also *selacholeic acid*

ner·vose \'nərˌvōs, ˌ='=\ *adj* [L *nervosus* sinewy, vigorous, energetic] **1** *obs* **:** of, relating to, affecting, or consisting of nerves **2** *of a leaf* **:** having nerves **:** NERVED

ner·vos·i·ty \ˌnər'värsəd·ē\ *n* -ES [L *nervositat-, nervositas* strength, thickness, fr. *nervosus* + *-itat-, -itas* -ity] **:** NERVOUSNESS

ner·vous \ˈnərvəs, -ə̄v-,-əiv-\ *adj* [ME, fr. L *nervosus* sinewy, vigorous, energetic, fr. *nervus* sinew, nerve + *-osus* -ose — more at NERVE] **1 a** *archaic* : having strong sinews : VIGOROUS **b** *obs* : having abundant tendons — used of animals and meat **2** : manifesting vigor of mind : marked by strength of thought, feeling, or style : highly organized : FORCIBLE, SPIRITED ⟨the texture of her writing is compact and ~ —G.F.Whicher⟩ ⟨vivid pages in simple, ~, racy language —Carl Van Doren⟩ **3** : of, relating to, or made up of nervous tissues ⟨the ~ layer of the eye⟩ **4 a** : of or relating to the nerves : originating in or affected by the nerves ⟨~ energy⟩ ⟨~ excitement⟩ **b** : exhibiting, suggesting, or originating in undue irritability : JERKY, JUMPY, UNSTEADY ⟨a hurried and ~ conclave —G.G. Coulton⟩ ⟨in the ~ atmosphere thus created, a tragic event occurred —*Amer. Guide Series: Wash.*⟩ **c** : TIMID, APPREHENSIVE ⟨permitted a ~ smile to flit across her face —Louis Bromfield⟩ — often used with *of* in British speech ⟨we were ~ of broaching it —Harry Lauder⟩ **d** *archaic* : affecting or used as medication for the nerves ⟨a ~ draught⟩ **5 a** : tending to produce nervousness or agitation : CRITICAL, DIFFICULT ⟨the moment was ~ — as far as the private secretary knew, quite the most critical moment in the records of American diplomacy —Henry Adams⟩ **b** : appearing or acting unsteady, irregular, or erratic — used of inanimate things ⟨climbed carefully into his ~ kayak —Farley Mowat⟩ **syn** see VIGOROUS

nervous breakdown *also* **nervous prostration** *n* **1** : NEURASTHENIA **2** : a case of neurasthenia ⟨she had a *nervous breakdown* last year⟩

nervous fluid *n* : a fluid formerly supposed to circulate through nerves and function as the essential agent in transmitting nerve impulses

ner·vous·ly *adv* : in a nervous manner

nervous nel·lie \-ˈnelē, -li\ *n, usu cap 2d N* [*nervous* + *Nellie*, dim. of *Ellen, Eleanor*, or *Helen*] : a timid or ineffectual person ⟨the *nervous Nellies*, who always come into a bull market too late, pushed prices too high —Burton Crane⟩

ner·vous·ness *n* -ES : the quality or state of being nervous

nervous system *n* : the bodily system that in vertebrates is made up of brain and spinal cord, nerves, ganglia, and parts of the receptor organs and that receives and interprets stimuli and transmits impulses to the effector organs — see AUTONOMIC NERVOUS SYSTEM, CENTRAL NERVOUS SYSTEM

ner·vule \ˈnər(ˌ)vyül\ *n* -S [prob. fr. (assumed) NL *nervulus*, fr. L *nervus* sinew, nerve + *-ulus*] **1** : a small nerve **2** : NERVURE

ner·vu·lose \ˈnərvyəˌlōs\ *adj* [*nervule* + *-ose*] : minutely nerved

ner·vu·ra·tion \ˌnərvyəˈrāshən\ *n* -S [*nervure* + *-ation*] : the neuration of an insect's wing

ner·vure \ˈnərvyər, -ˌvyü(ə)r\ *n* -S [F, fr. MF *nerveure* leather strap used to strengthen a shield, fr. *nerf* sinew, fr. L *nervus* sinew] : VEIN 3c

ner·vus \ˈnərvəs, ˈnerv-\ *n, pl* **ner·vi** \ˈnərˌvī, ˈne(ə)rˌvē\ [L] : NERVE

nervus ter·mi·nalis \-ˌtərməˈnaləs, -nāl-; -ˌterməˈnäl-\ *n* [NL, lit., terminal nerve] : a slender ganglionated nerve associated with the olfactory nerves in most vertebrates from fishes to man

nervy \ˈnərvē, -ə̄v-,-əiv-, -vi\ *adj* -ER/-EST [¹*nerve* + *-y*] **1** *archaic* : SINEWY, STRONG ⟨his ~ knees —John Keats⟩ **2 a** : showing calm courage : BOLD, INTREPID ⟨all good tacklers, and ~, no matter how much they may be outclassed —Paul Withington⟩ **b** : marked by effrontery or presumption : BRASH, IMPUDENT ⟨unwelcome, and knowing he was unwelcome, he was ~ enough to come anyway⟩ **3** : marked by nervousness : EXCITABLE, JERKY ⟨smoked one cigarette after another; he was very ~ and couldn't sit still —Christopher Isherwood⟩ **4** *of rubber* : having nerve

NES *abbr, often not cap* not elsewhere specified

ne·science \ˈne|sh(ē)ən(t)s, |sēən- *also* ˈnē|\ *n* -S [LL *nescientia*, fr. L *nescient-, nesciens* (pres. part. of *nescire* not to know, fr. *ne-*, negative prefix + *scire* to know) + *-ia* -y — more at NO, SCIENCE] **1** : lack of knowledge or awareness : IGNORANCE ⟨his apparent ~ of contemporary literature was not a pose —A.T.Quiller-Couch⟩ **2** : a conviction or doctrine that ultimate or immaterial realities cannot be known through the rational processes of the mind : AGNOSTICISM

¹ne·scient \-ənt\ *adj* [L *nescient-, nesciens*] : exhibiting or characterized by nescience : IGNORANT, AGNOSTIC **syn** see IGNORANT

²nescient \ˈ"\ *n* -S : AGNOSTIC

nese \ˈnēz\ *n* -S [ME *nese, neose;* akin to MD *nēse, neuse* nose, MLG *nese* and prob. to OE *nasu* nose — more at NOSE] *now chiefly Scot* : NOSE

¹nesh \ˈnesh\ *adj* [ME *nesshe, nesche*, fr. OE *hnesce;* akin to OHG *nascōn* to nibble, eat dainties, Goth *knasqus* soft, fine, tender, Gk *kneōron, kneōros* spurge flax, Skt *kiknasa* particles of ground grain, groats, L *ciner-, cinis* ashes — more at INCINERATE] **1** *chiefly dial* : SOFT, JUICY, TENDER ⟨~ grass in the spring⟩ **2** *chiefly dial* **a** : DELICATE, RETIRING **b** : GENTLE, KINDLY **c** : extremely fastidious or dainty **d** : TIMID

²nesh \ˈ"\ *vi* -ED/-ING/-ES [ME *nesshen, neschen* to make soft, become soft, fr. OE *hnescian*, fr. *hnesce*, adj.] *dial Eng* : to act timidly

nes·khi *or* **nes·ki** \ˈneskē\ *or* **nas·khi** \ˈnas-\ *n* -S *usu cap* [Ar *naskhīy*, fr. *nasakha* to copy] : the ordinary cursive Arabic script used in writing scientific and religious books — compare KUFIC

neso- *comb form* [NL, fr. Gk *nēso-*, fr. *nēsos;* akin to Gk *nēchein, nēchesthai* to swim, L *nare* — more at NOURISH] : island ⟨*Neso*gaean⟩

neso·gae·an *or* **neso·ge·an** \ˌnēsəˈjēən, ˌnes-\ *adj, usu cap* [NL *Nesogaea* Polynesia (fr. *neso-* + *-gaea*) + E *-an*] : POLYNESIAN 3

ne·so·kia \nəˈsōkēə\ *n, cap* [NL] : a genus of burrowing Indian scaly-tailed murine rats including important vectors of plague

neso·silicate \ˈnē(ˌ)sō, ˈne(- + \ *n* [prob. fr. *neso-* + *silicate*] : a mineral silicate (as olivine) that contains independent tetrahedral silicon-oxygen anionic groups SiO_4 : ORTHOSILICATE — compare INOSILICATE

ne·sot·ra·gus \nəˈsä·trəgəs\ *n, cap* [NL, fr. *neso-* + Gk *tragos* goat — more at TRAGEDY] : a genus of very small antelopes of southeastern Africa comprising the Sunis and closely related to the royal antelopes

nes·pe·lem \ˈnespəˌlem, -ˌləm\ *or* **nes·pe·lim** \-ˌlim, -ˌləm\ *n, pl* **nespelem** *or* **nespelems** *or* **nespelim** *or* **nespelims** *usu cap* **1 a** : a Salishan people of northeastern Washington **b** : a member of such people **2** : a dialect of Okanagon

nes·que·ho·nite \ˌneskwəˈhōˌnīt\ *n* -S [*Nesquehoning*, Pa. + E *-ite*] : a mineral $MgCO_3.3H_2O$ consisting of a colorless hydrous magnesium carbonate in prismatic crystals

ness \ˈnes\ *n* -ES [ME *naisse, nasse*, fr. OE *naess, naessa, ness;* akin to ON *nes* ness, MD *nesse, nes*, MLG *nes* ness, OE *nasu* nose — more at NOSE] : CAPE, HEADLAND, PROMONTORY

-ness \nəs *sometimes esp when an unstressed syllable precedes & esp in the pl* ,nes; *see* BUSINESS\ *n suffix* -ES [ME *-nes, -ness, -nesse*, fr. OE *-nes, -ness, -nyss, -nys;* akin to OS *-nissi, -nussi* -ness, MD *-nisse, -nesse*, OHG *-nissa, -nassi, -nussi*, Goth *-inassus* (*-n-, -in-* being orig. part of the stem)] : state : condition : quality : degree ⟨good*ness*⟩ ⟨great*ness*⟩ ⟨sick*ness*⟩

ness·ber·ry \ˈnes- — *see* BERRY\ *n, sometimes cap* [Helge *Ness* †1928 Am. horticulturist born in Norway + E *berry*] : a hybrid bramble with fruit of superior flavor but inferior picking and shipping qualities produced by interbreeding dewberries and red raspberries and grown to a limited extent in the southern U.S.

nes·sel·rode pie \ˈnesəlˌrōd-\ *n, usu cap N* [after Count Karl R. *Nesselrode* †1862 Russ. statesman] : cream pie filled with mixed preserved fruits and topped with shaved chocolate

nesselrode pudding *n, usu cap N* : a frozen pudding containing chestnuts and maraschino

ness·ler·iza·tion \ˌneslərəˈzāshən, -ˌrīˈz-\ *n* -S *sometimes cap* : the process of nesslerizing

ness·ler·ize \ˈnesləˌrīz\ *vt* -ED/-ING/-S *sometimes cap* [Julius *Nessler* †1905 Ger. agricultural chemist + E *-ize*] : to treat or test with Nessler's reagent

ness·ler's reagent *or* **nessler's solution** \ˈneslə(r)z-\ *n, usu cap N* [after Julius *Nessler*] : an alkaline solution of potassium mercuric iodide used in chemical analysis esp. in a delicate test for ammonia in aqueous solution (as when obtained from water, blood, urine) with which it forms a yellowish brown color or precipitate

nessler tube *n, usu cap N* [after Julius *Nessler*] : a narrow glass cylinder with a flat bottom used in colorimetry (as in nesslerization) for comparing the colors of liquids

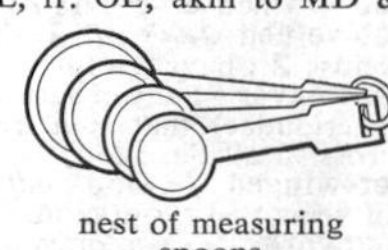

nest of measuring spoons

¹nest \ˈnest\ *n* -S *often attrib* [ME, fr. OE; akin to MD & OHG *nest*, L *nidus*, OIr *net* nest, Skt *nīḍa* resting place, nest; all from a prehistoric IE compound whose first constituent is represented by Skt *ni* down and whose second constituent is akin to the root of E *sit* — more at NETHER] **1 a** : the bed, receptacle, or location prepared by a bird for holding its eggs and for hatching and rearing its young **b** : the settled and often concealed place in which the eggs of animals (as insects, fishes, or turtles) are laid and hatched and the young are reared **2 a** : a place of rest, retreat, or lodging : HOME, SHELTER ⟨a cozy little blanketed ~ which she had arranged and furnished herself —Zane Grey⟩ **b** : the place of resort of persons of like character or purpose esp. regarded as bad or hostile : DEN, HANGOUT ⟨the ~ of Saracen marauders . . . in the Alpine passes —R.W.Southern⟩ **3 a** : the family, group, or swarm of animals occupying a nest **b** : the persons frequenting a place of resort **4 a** : a group of similar things : AGGREGATION ⟨it had become a ~ of empty paint jars —John Updike⟩ ⟨rammed into a ~ of sampans —Chesley Wilson⟩ ⟨right up into a ~ of giant mountains —Helen MacInnes⟩ **b** : a center or home of practices or habits of thought of a particular kind ⟨felt most strongly that, in practice, the Court of Rome was a ~ of abuses —G.G.Coulton⟩ **5** : a group of objects made to fit close together or graduated in size to fit one within another ⟨a ~ of picnic plates⟩ — compare NEST OF TABLES **6** : a receptacle or locating device shaped to hold something ⟨a ~ to receive the Continental-type spare tire mounting —Jeff Taylor⟩ ⟨there is a sudden rush of air into the bilges under the tube ~ —E.L.Beach⟩ **7** : a small isolated mass of ore or mineral within another formation **8 a** : a compact group of devices (as pulleys, gears, springs) working together **b** : a group of things (as boilers or tubes in a water-tube boiler) **c** : a group of holes or pins for locating work in a jig or die **9** : an isolated collection or clump of cells in tissue of a different structure ⟨a ~ of sarcomatous cells in the liver⟩ **10** : an emplaced group of weapons ⟨a ~ of machine guns⟩

²nest \ˈ"\ *vb* -ED/-ING/-S [ME *nesten*, fr. *nest*, n.] *vi* **1** : to build or occupy a nest : settle down in or as if in a nest ⟨birds ~ in many places⟩ **2** : to fit compactly together or within one another ⟨to solve the schools' storage problem, the chairs stack easily, the tables ~ —*Time*⟩ ~ *vt* **1** : to fit or settle into a bed or suitable receptacle : adjust into a protective place ⟨~ their jelly bottles in green tissue paper —John Haverstick⟩ ⟨the old method of ~*ing* a fragile product in a great mass of loose cushioning material —*Modern Packaging*⟩ **2** : to pack or fit compactly together (as in a stack or a close or graduated series) ⟨cooking pans and racks ~*ed* under an aluminum dome —*New Yorker*⟩ **3** : to assemble (as boiler tubes or piles) in a group **4** : to arrange (tobacco) so that the better bundles are exposed to view in a warehouse

nest·able \-təbəl\ *adj* : capable of being nested

nest·age \-tij\ *n* -S : a place or group of nests or a nest

nest box *n* : a box provided for the nesting of domesticated animals (as hens or rabbits)

nest egg *n* **1** : a natural or artificial egg left in the nest of a domestic fowl to induce her to continue to lay there **2** *archaic* : something used as an inducement, lure, or decoy **3 a** : a fund of money accumulated as a reserve or as a basis for further acquisition ⟨a retirement-fund *nest egg*, built up over a 15-year period —E.R.Leibert⟩ **b** : a nucleus or accumulation intended to promote further growth or development ⟨will have a *nest egg* of 128 — only five less than half the 266 needed to win —H.H.Martin⟩

nest·er \-tə(r)\ *n* -S **1** : one that nests (as a bird) ⟨enough fish to make the kingfishers constant ~*s* in their banks —John Masefield⟩ **2** *West* : a homesteader or squatter who takes up rangeland for a farm ⟨not all of the ~*s* stayed to prove up, but enough did to settle the West —Seth Agnew⟩

nest fungus *n* : a fungus of the family Nidulariaceae

nes·tle \ˈnesəl\ *vb* **nestled; nestled; nestling** \-s(ə)liŋ\ **nestles** [ME *nestlen*, fr. OE *nestlian*, fr. *nest* + *-lian* -le] *vi* **1** *archaic* **a** : to make or occupy a nest : settle in a nest **b** : to make one's home : take up abode **2 a** : to settle snugly or comfortably : take up a cozy, warm, or affectionate position ⟨*nestled* quietly into the cushions⟩ ⟨the infant *nestled* at his mother's breast⟩ **b** : to press or lie close : CUDDLE ⟨she had *nestled* down with him, that his head might lie upon her arm —Charles Dickens⟩ **3** : to lie embosomed, embedded, or sheltered : seem at home or naturally located ⟨settlements *nestled* in narrow valleys and ravines —J.F.Embree & W.L. Thomas⟩ **4** *dial chiefly Eng* : to be restless : FIDGET ~ *vt* **1** : to settle, shelter, or house in or as if in a nest ⟨*nestled* himself into the warm bed⟩ ⟨*nestled* the monkey's body in the crook of his arm —Joseph Whitehill⟩ **2** : to press or snuggle close or affectionately ⟨*nestled* her shoulder close against him⟩

nes·tler \-s(ə)lə(r)\ *n* -S : one that nestles : NESTLING

nest·ling \ˈnes(t)liŋ\ *n* -S [ME, fr. *nest* + *-ling*] **1** : a young bird that has not abandoned the nest **2 a** : a young animal still living in the parental nest **b** : a young child

nest of tables : a set of small tables graduated in size so that they fit one beneath another

nest of tables

nes·tor \ˈnestə(r); -ˌstȯ(ə)r, -ȯ(ə)\ *n* [after *Nestor*, legendary Greek hero known for long life and wisdom (fr. L & Gk; L, fr. Gk *Nestōr*)] **1** -S *often cap* : a wise elder counselor : a grand old man : one regarded as patriarch or leader in his field ⟨the *Nestor* of that great-statured generation —J.R. Chamberlain⟩ ⟨the ~ of American philosophy —D.D.Runes⟩ **2** *cap* [NL, fr. L] : a genus of large parrots of New Zealand and the Papuan subregion that include the kaka and the kea and with related forms constitute a subfamily of Psittacidae or in some classifications a separate family **3** -S [by alter.] : NESTER 2 ⟨horse-and-cow-men, when they got to timbered country, found ~*s* and sodbusters, who were their natural enemies —W.F.Harris⟩

¹nes·to·ri·an \neˈstōrēən\ *n* -S *usu cap* [ME, fr. LL *Nestorianus*, fr. *Nestorius* †ab451 patriarch of Constantinople + L *-anus* -an] **1** : a member of the Church of the East that originated in the ancient Persian Empire, rejected the condemnation of Nestorius by the Council of Ephesus in 431, and survives among Assyrians in Iraq, Iran, Syria, and the U.S. **2** : an adherent of Nestorianism **3** : ASSYRIAN 3

²nestorian \(ˈ)ˈ≤≤≤\ *adj, usu cap* : of or relating to the Nestorians, to Nestorius, or to Nestorianism

nestorian alphabet *n, usu cap N* : a Syriac alphabet widely spread by Nestorian missionaries

nes·to·ri·an·ism \≤ˈ≤≤≤ˌnizəm\ *n* -S *usu cap* **1** : Nestorian Christianity **2** : the doctrines imputed to Nestorius or the Nestorians; *esp* : the doctrine that a divine and a human personality were joined in Jesus Christ in perfect harmony of action but remained distinct with the corollary that Mary should not be called the Mother of God

nestorian syriac *n, cap N & S* **1** : an eastern dialect of Syriac **2** : NEO-SYRIAC

nes·to·rine \ˈnestəˌrīn, -rēn\ *adj* [NL *Nestor* + E *-ine*] : of or relating to the genus *Nestor* or the parrots belonging to it

nests *pl of* NEST, *pres 3d sing of* NEST

nes·ty \ˈnesti\ *Scot var of* NASTY

¹net \ˈnet, *usu* -ed·+V\ *n* -S *often attrib* [ME *net, nett, nette*, fr. OE *net, nett;* akin to OS *net, netti* net, MD *net, nette*, OHG *nezzi*, ON *net, nēt*, Goth *nati* net, L *nodus* knot, OIr *nascim* I bind, and prob. to L *nassa* fish basket and perh. to Skt *nahyati* he binds; basic meaning: to knot, weave] **1 a** : a meshed arrangement of threads, cords, or ropes that have been twisted, knotted, or woven together at regular intervals **b** : any of various devices made of net and used esp. for catching fish, birds, or insects **c** : something made of net and used esp. for protecting, confining, carrying, or dividing (as a cargo net or tennis net) **2** : something designed to entrap or ensnare ⟨a man that flatters his neighbor spreads a ~ for his feet —Prov 29:5 (RSV)⟩ ⟨the engineer cannot escape the ~ of circumstances in which he is caught —W.P.Webb⟩ **3 a** : a machine-twisted fabric in fine to coarse geometric meshes made usu. of silk, rayon, nylon, or cotton and used for dresses, curtains, veils, or trimmings **b** : a handmade or machine-made background fabric for lace usu. in fine geometric meshes **4** : something resembling a net in reticulation : a network of lines, fibers, or figures ⟨a perfect ~ of steamer, bus and air service —Frederick Arnold⟩ **5 a** : a three-sided structure that consists of poles and netting enclosing a wicket and that is used in cricket for batting and bowling practice **b** : a three-sided structure enclosed in netting and used as a goal in hockey or lacrosse — often used in pl. **c** : a return of the ball in a racket game that goes into the net **6 a** : a rigging of ropes and twine on a free balloon that supports the weight of the basket and distributes the load over the entire upper surface of the envelope **b** : a rectangular net of cordage used to restrain the envelope of a kite, balloon, or airship during inflation and before the car is attached **7 a** : a group of communications stations operating under unified control on assigned frequencies and in accordance with a plan for the systematic handling and relay of radio traffic ⟨Army radio ~⟩ **b** : NETWORK 5 **8** : a device made usu. of canvas stretched in a frame and used for catching persons leaping from a building or other structure

²net \ˈ"\ *vb* **netted; netted; netting; nets** *vt* **1** : to cover or enclose with or as if with a net ⟨to leave his favorite tree . . . after . . . *netting* it to keep off the birds —Maria Edgeworth⟩ ⟨how dense a fold of danger ~*s* him round —Alfred Tennyson⟩ **2** : to make in the style of or by means of network ⟨is *netting* herself the sweetest cloak you can conceive —Jane Austen⟩ **3** : to catch as if in a net : capture by stratagem or wile ⟨and now I am here, *netted* and in the toils —Sir Walter Scott⟩ **4 a** : to use nets in for catching fish ⟨*netted* the wallow and brought out scores of small fish —Francis Birtles⟩ **b** : to catch by means of a net ⟨*netted* 15 tons of smelt in 10 minutes —*Amer. Guide Series: Mich.*⟩ **5** : to cover with or as if with a network ⟨her high plump cheeks were *netted* with little purple veins —Marguerite Steen⟩ **6** : to hit (a ball) into the net for the loss of a point in a racket game ~ *vi* **1** : to make nets or netting ⟨was *netting* away as if nothing unusual had occurred —Elizabeth C. Gaskell⟩ **2** : to hit a ball into the net for the loss of a point in a racket game **3** : to combine into a communications net or network

³net \ˈ"\ *adj* [ME, fr. MF — more at NEAT (bright)] **1** *archaic* : NEAT, TRIM **2** *obs* : CLEAN, BRIGHT **3** : free from all charges or deductions: as **a** : remaining after the deduction of all charges, outlay, or loss ⟨~ earnings⟩ ⟨~ proceeds⟩ — opposed to *gross* **b** : excluding all tare or tret ⟨~ weight⟩ **4 a** : free from adulteration : PURE ⟨~ wine⟩ **b** : excluding all nonessential or extraneous considerations : BASIC, FUNDAMENTAL ⟨the ~ effect is one that disturbs many scholars —C.V.Newsom⟩ ⟨the ~ result is a huge canvas of small-town life —C.J. Rolo⟩

⁴net \ˈ"\ *vt* **netted; netted; netting; nets 1 a** : to make by way of profit : CLEAR ⟨*netted* $8000 a year from the restaurant⟩ **b** : to produce by way of profit : YIELD ⟨the restaurant *netted* $8000 a year⟩ **2** : to get possession, control, use, or benefit of : GAIN ⟨war experiences which *netted* him just about all the decorations there are —Clarence Woodbury⟩ ⟨*netting* us less security than we would otherwise enjoy —Sidney Hook⟩

⁵net \ˈ"\ *n* -S **1** : a net amount, profit, weight, or price ⟨reduced taxes . . . partly accounted for the high ~ —*Time*⟩ **2** : the score of a golfer in a handicap match after deducting his handicap from his gross **3** : the fundamental point : ESSENCE, GIST ⟨the ~ of all these articles is that competition is dying —Raymond Moley⟩

⁶net \ˈ"\ *vt* **netted; netted; netting; nets** [MF *netir*, fr. OF, fr. *net* clean, pure, bright — more at NEAT] *dial chiefly Eng* : WASH, RINSE

NET *abbr, often not cap* not earlier than

net area *n* [³*net*] : the part of the cross-sectional area of a masonry unit effective in carrying load

net assets *n pl* **1** : the excess of value of resources over liabilities to creditors — called also *net worth* **2** : ADMITTED ASSETS

net ball \ˈ≤ˌ≤\ *n* **1** : a ball that on the service (as in tennis and volleyball) strikes the top of the net and lands in the service court but must be served over — compare ²LET 2 **2** : a ball that during play in tennis is hit into the net for loss of point

netball \ˈ≤ˌ≤\ *n* [¹*net* + *ball*] : a game that resembles basketball and that is played with a soccer ball between 2 teams of 7 players each on a hard court 100 feet long and 50 feet wide

net blotch *n* [¹*net*] : a disease of barley characterized by spots on the leaves and caused by a fungus (*Helminthosporium teres*)

net earnings *n pl* [³*net*] : NET INCOME

net·ful \ˈnetˌfu̇l\ *n* -S : as much or as many as will fill a net ⟨a ~ of fish⟩

neth·er \ˈnet͟hə(r)\ *adj* [ME *nether, nethere, nithere*, fr. OE *nithera*, fr. *nither, nithor*, adv., down, downward; akin to OS *nithiri*, adj., nether, *nithar*, adv., down, OHG *nidari, nidaro*, adj., nether, *nidar*, adv., down, ON *nethri, netharri*, adj., nether, *nithr*, adv., down; all fr. a Gmc word that is a compar. of a word akin to Skt *ni* down; akin to OE *in* — more at IN] **1** : situated down or below : lying beneath or in the lower part : LOWER, UNDER ⟨wandered onward till they reached the ~ margin of the heath —Thomas Hardy⟩ ⟨her ~ lip crept up between her upper and lower teeth —F.V.W.Mason⟩ ⟨caught between the ~ millstone of higher labor costs and the upper millstone of . . . rigidly set price ceilings —Clark Kerr⟩ ⟨her first contact with the ~ side of the smooth social surface —Edith Wharton⟩ **2** : situated or believed to be situated beneath the surface of the earth ⟨captured her and carried her off to the ~ world to be his wife —S.V.McCasland⟩

neth·er·land \-lənd\ *adj, usu cap* : NETHERLANDS

neth·er·land·er \ˈnet͟hə(r)ˌlandə(r), -lən-, -ˌlaan-, ˌ≤≤ˈla(a)n-\ *n* -S *cap* [*Netherlands*, country in Europe (trans. of D *Nederlanden*, pl. of *Nederland*) + E *-er*] : a native or inhabitant of the Netherlands

¹neth·er·land·ish \-dish,-dēsh\ *adj, usu cap* [*Netherlands* + E *-ish*] **1 a** : of, relating to, or characteristic of the Netherlands **b** : of, relating to, or characteristic of the people of the Netherlands **2** : of, relating to, or characteristic of the language of the Netherlands

²netherlandish \ˈ"\ *n* -ES *cap* : the Germanic language of the Netherlanders

neth·er·lands \ˈnet͟hə(r)lən(d)z\ *adj, usu cap* [fr. the *Netherlands*, country of Europe] : of or from the Netherlands : of the kind or style prevalent in the Netherlands : DUTCH, NETHERLANDISH

nethermore \ˈ≤≤ˌ≤\ *adj* [ME, fr. *nether* + *more*] : LOWER ⟨the heavens expelled them; nor them the ~ abyss receives —H.W. Longfellow⟩

nethermost \ˈ≤≤ˌmōst, *esp Brit also* -ˌməst\ *adj* [ME *nethermast*, fr. *nether* + *-mast*, *-most* -most] : LOWEST ⟨a grin of malice which would have held its own in the ~ hell —Bram Stoker⟩

neth·er·stock \ˈ≤≤ˌstäk\ *n* [*nether* + *stock* (stocking)] : STOCKING; *specif* : a 16th century stocking reaching above the knee and worn with upperstocks

netherstock: *1* trunk hose, *2* upperstock, *3* netherstock

neth·er·ward \-ˌwə(r)d\ *adj* [*nether* + *-ward*] : DOWNWARD ⟨in the ~ black of the night —Walt Whitman⟩

neth·er·wards \-dz\ *adv* [alter. (influenced by such words as *afterwards, downwards*) of earlier *netherward*, fr. ME *netherward, nitherward*, fr. OE *nitherward, nitherweardes;* OE *nitherweard*, fr. *nither* down + *-werd, -weard* -ward; OE *nitherweardes*, fr. *nither* down + *-weardes* -wards — more at NETHER] : DOWNWARD

netherworld \ˈ≤≤ˌ≤\ *n* [*nether* + *world*] **1** : the world of the dead ⟨journeys to the ~ to plead for his wife's return —*Time*⟩ **2** : UNDERWORLD

⟨sheds a withering light on the ~ of deceit, subversion, and espionage —R.M.Nixon⟩

ne·thi·nim \ˌnetēˈnēm\ *n pl, usu cap* [Heb *nĕthīnīm*, lit., those given] **:** servants performing the lowest menial services about an ancient Jewish tabernacle and temple

net income *n* **:** the balance of gross income remaining after deducting related costs and expenses usu. for a given period and losses allocable to the period

net interest *n* **:** PURE INTEREST

net–knot \ˈ≈,≈\ *n* [¹*net*] **:** KARYOSOME

netlayer \ˈ≈,≈≈\ *n* **:** a small naval vessel equipped to lay and repair harbor defense nets

netleaf \ˈ≈,≈\ *or* **netleaf plantain** *n, pl* **netleafs** *or* **netleaf plantains** **:** a common rattlesnake plantain (*Goodyera pubescens*)

net lease *n* [³*net*] **:** a lease requiring the lessee to assume all operating expenses (as maintenance, insurance, taxes) in addition to the payment of rent

netlike \ˈ≈,≈\ *adj* **:** resembling a net

N et M \ˌeˌnedˈ¦em\ *abbr, often not cap N & M* [L *nocte et mane*] night and morning

netmaker \ˈ≈,≈≈\ *n* [ME, fr. *net* + *maker*] **:** a maker of nets

net·man \ˈnet,man, -ˌmən\ *n, pl* **netmen** **1 :** a worker who takes care of fishing nets **2 :** a tennis player; *esp* **:** the partner in a doubles match who stays near the net when his teammate serves

net national product *n* **:** the net value of the goods and services produced in a nation during a specific period (as a year) computed by subtracting from the gross national product charges for depreciation of capital assets — compare NATIONAL INCOME

net necrosis *n* **:** a necrosis of the phloem of the potato tuber caused by frost or the leaf roll virus in which the pith and cortex contain a broken netlike pattern of necrotic cells

ne·top \ˈnē,täp\ *n* -S [of Algonquian origin; akin to Narraganset *netoup* my friend, companion, Abnaki *nidanbé*] *chiefly NewEng* **:** FRIEND — often used in salutation to an Indian by the American colonists

net plankton *n* **:** plankton consisting of small and usu. microscopic organisms that are large enough to be retained by a net of number 25 mesh silk bolting cloth — compare NANNOPLANKTON

net premium *n* [³*net*] **:** an insurance premium consisting of the amount required to pay the insurance liability on its becoming due without paying any expenses or contingent charges

net quick assets *n pl* [³*net* + *quick assets*] **:** the excess of quick assets over current liabilities

Ne·trop·sin \nəˈträpsən\ *trademark* — used for an antibiotic obtained from bacteria of the genus *Streptomyces*

nets *pl of* NET, *pres 3d sing of* NET

net sales *n pl* **:** the balance of gross sales remaining after deducting trade discounts, returned sales, and sales allowances

net silk *n* [¹*net*] *Brit* **:** THROWN SILK

nets·man \ˈnetsmən\ *n, pl* **netsmen** **:** one who uses a net (as in fishing)

ne·tsu·ke \ˈnetskē, -ˌskā, -ˌsəˌkā\ *n* -S [Jap] **:** a small object carved in wood or ivory or wrought in metal, pierced with holes, and used by the Japanese as a toggle to fasten a small pouch or purse to the kimono sash

nett *Brit var of* NET

net·ta·ble \ˈned·əbəl, -etə-\ *adj* **:** capable of being netted

net·ta·pus \ˈned·əpəs\ *n, cap* [NL, fr. Gk *nētta, nēssa* duck + NL *-pus* — more at ANAS] **:** a genus of small chiefly tropical Old World geese with the legs so short as to be nearly useless on land — see PYGMY GOOSE

net tare *n* [³*net*] **:** CLEAR TARE

net·ta·stom·i·dae \ˌned·əˈstäməˌdē\ *n pl, cap* [NL, fr. *Nettastoma*, type genus (fr. Gk *nētta* duck + NL *-stoma*) + *-idae*] **:** a family of slender fragile-bodied deep-sea eels (order Apodes) that have an elongated upper jaw and thin black≈pigmented skin

netted *past of* NET

netted melon *or* **net melon** *n* **:** a melon (*Cucumis melo reticulatus*) that is a variety of the muskmelon and has a thin rind with reticulated surface and deep green sweet flesh — called also *nutmeg melon*

net tender *n* **:** a small naval vessel that tends the openings in a harbor defense net

net·ter \ˈned·ə(r), -etə-\ *n* -S [ME, netmaker, fr. *net* + *-er*] **:** one that makes or uses nets (as for fishing)

¹net·ting \ˈnetiŋ\ *n* -S [ME, prob. fr. MD or MLG *netten* to wet + ME *-ing*; akin to OHG *nezzen* to wet, Goth *natjan*, denominative causatives fr. a root represented by OHG *naz, nazz* wet, MD *nat*; perh. akin to Gk *noteros* wet, damp — more at NOURISH] *dial Eng* **:** URINE

²net·ting \ˈned·iŋ, -et|, |ēŋ\ *n* -S [¹*net* + *-ing*] **1 :** NETWORK: as **a :** a network of ropes used on a ship (as for stowing away sails or hammocks) **b :** a material of crossed, twisted, or knotted cords, threads, ropes, or wires with open spaces between **c :** the reticulation on the surface of a melon **2** [fr. gerund of ²*net*] **:** the act or process of making a net or network **3** [fr. gerund of ²*net*] **:** the act, process, or right of fishing with a net

netting knot *n* **:** SHEET BEND

net·ti·on \ˈned·ē,än\ *n, cap* [NL, fr. Gk *nēttion* duckling, dim. of *nētta* duck] *in some classifications* **:** a genus of ducks comprising the common European teal, the American green≈winged teal, and several related birds that are now usu. included in *Anas*

¹net·tle \ˈned·ᵊl, -etᵊl\ *n* -S *often attrib* [ME *nettle, netle*, fr. OE *netle, netel, netele*; akin to MD *netel* nettle, OHG *nazza, nezzila*, ON *nötr*, MIr *nenaid*, Gk *adikē* nettle, and perh. to OE *net, nett* net — more at NET] **1 :** a plant of the genus *Urtica* or the family Urticaceae **2 :** any of numerous prickly or stinging plants not of the family Urticaceae — usu. used with preceding modifier

²nettle \"\ *vb* **nettled; nettled; nettling** \-d·ᵊliŋ, -t(ᵊ)liŋ\ **nettles** [ME *netlen, nettyllen*, fr. *netle, nettle*, n.] *vt* **1 a :** to whip or sting with nettles **b :** to cause to be stung by nettles **2 :** to arouse displeasure, impatience, or anger in **:** PROVOKE, VEX ⟨ashamed at having been *nettled* by so minor a cause —Edwin O'Connor⟩ **3 :** to stir up **:** INCITE ~ *vi* **:** to become irritated, vexed, or provoked **syn** see IRRITATE

³nettle \"\ *or* **knet·tle** \"\ *or* **knit·tle** \ˈnid·ᵊl, -itᵊl\ *n* -S [alter. of earlier *knettel*, fr. ME *knittel*, fr. OE *cnyttels* string, sinew, fr. *cnyttan* to knit, bind, tie — more at KNIT] **1 :** a small line made of rope yarn and used esp. for hammock clews or seizings **2 nettles** *pl* **:** halves of yarns in the end of a rope twisted up for pointing

nettle butterfly *n* **:** any of several butterflies (as the red admiral) whose larvae feed on nettles

nettle cell *n* **:** NEMATOCYST

nettle family *n* **:** URTICACEAE

nettlefish \ˈ≈≈,≈\ *n* **:** JELLYFISH

nettlehead \ˈ≈≈,≈\ *n* **:** a virus disease of the hop characterized by leaves that curl and cluster so as to resemble those of a nettle (*Urtica dioica*)

nettle–leaved goosefoot *or* **nettleleaf goosefoot** \ˈ≈≈,≈-\ *n* **:** an annual European goosefoot (*Chenopodium murale*) with coarsely dentate leaves that is widespread in the U. S. and southern Canada

net·tler \ˈned·lə(r), -et(ᵊ)lə-\ *n* -S **:** one that nettles

nettle rash *n* **:** an eruption on the skin caused by or resembling the condition produced by stinging with nettles **:** URTICARIA

net·tle·some \ˈned·ᵊlsəm, -etᵊl-\ *adj* [²*nettle* + *-some*] **1 :** readily nettled **:** IRRITABLE ⟨was not the least ~ of his countrymen —*Life of Quin*⟩ **2 :** causing vexation **:** IRRITATING ⟨will anticipate such ~ problems as traffic rules for orbiting spacecraft —*Newsweek*⟩

nettle tree *n* **1 :** a tree of the genus *Celtis* (esp. *C. australis*) **2 :** a tree of the genus *Laportea*; *esp* **:** AUSTRALIAN NETTLE TREE **3 :** a tree of the genus *Trema*

net·tling \ˈned·ᵊliŋ, -et(ᵊ)liŋ\ *n* -S [³*nettle* + *-ing*] **1 :** a process resembling splicing by which two ropes are joined end to end so as to form one rope **2 :** a process of tying together the ends of yarns in pairs so as to prevent tangling

nettling cell *n* [fr. pres. part. of ²*nettle*] **:** NEMATOCYST

net·ty \ˈned·ᵊlē, -etᵊlē, -ᵊli\ *adj* -ER/-EST **1 :** having a profusion of nettles **2 :** NETTLESOME

net ton *n* **:** TON 1b

net tonnage *n* **:** the gross tonnage of a ship less deductions for space occupied by crew's quarters, machinery for navigation, engine room, and fuel

net tracery *n* **:** window tracery (as in 14th-century Gothic work) in which the openings are of nearly the same size and of approximately the same form

net·ty \ˈned·|ē, -et|, |i\ *adj* -ER/-EST **:** NETLIKE

net–veined \ˈ≈,≈\ *adj* **1** *of a leaf* **:** having netted or reticulated veins **2 :** having a fine network of veins ⟨a *net-veined* wing⟩

net weaver *n* **:** any of various sedentary spiders (as of the family Theridiidae) that spin irregular webs in which the threads cross in all directions

net–winged \ˈ≈,wiŋd\ *adj* **:** having wings with a fine network of veins **:** NEUROPTEROID

¹network \ˈ≈,≈\ *n, often attrib* [¹*net* + *work*] **1 :** a fabric or structure of threads, cords, or wires that cross each other at regular intervals and are knotted or secured at the crossings ⟨ribbons, lace and embroidery wrought together in a most curious piece of ~ —Joseph Addison⟩ **2 :** a system of lines or channels that interlace or cross like the fabric of a net ⟨a ~ of highways⟩ ⟨a ~ of rivers⟩ ⟨a ~ of veins⟩ ⟨a ~ of roots⟩ ⟨a ~ of nerves⟩ **3 :** an interconnected or interrelated chain, group, or system ⟨a ~ of secret agents⟩ ⟨a ~ of alliances⟩ ⟨a ~ of beliefs⟩ **4 :** a system of electrical conductors in which conduction takes place between certain points by more than one path **5 a :** a group of local radio or television stations linked by wire or radio relay for the usu. simultaneous broadcasting or televising of the same program **b :** a radio or television company that produces programs to be relayed to local stations for broadcast by radio or television ⟨sold the show to a big ~⟩ **syn** see SYSTEM

²network \"\ *vt* **:** to cover with or as if with a network ⟨a continent . . . so ~*ed* with navigable rivers and canals —*Lamp*⟩

net worth *n* **:** NET ASSETS

neuf·châ·tel \ˌn(y)üshəˈtel, ¦nə(r)sh-, ¦nəsh-\ *or* **neufchâtel cheese** *n* -S *usu cap N* [F *neufchâtel*, fr. *Neufchâtel*, France] **:** a small soft unripened cheese made from whole or skim milk with or without cream and often with condiments added — compare CREAM CHEESE 1

neuk \ˈnyük\ *chiefly Scot var of* NOOK

neu·ma \ˈn(y)ümə\ *n* -S [ML] **:** NEUME

neu·mat·ic \n(y)üˈmad·ik\ *adj* [F *neumatique*, fr. ML *neumaticus*, fr. *neumat-, neuma* + L *-icus* -ic] **:** consisting of or characterized by neumes

neume *also* **neum** *or* **pneume** \ˈn(y)üm\ *n* -S [*neume, neum*, fr. F, fr. MF, fr. ML *neuma, pneuma* (also, group of notes sung to a final syllable as long as the breath lasts), fr. Gk *pneuma* breath; *pneume* fr. ML *pneuma* — more at PNEUMATIC] **1 :** a symbol in the musical notation of the middle ages derived from the Greek system of accents, indicating from one to usu. four notes, and showing only relative pitch **2 :** one of the square symbols in the plainsong notation of the Roman Catholic Church **3 :** PNEUMA 2a — **neu·mic** \-mik\ *adj*

neur- *or* **neuro-** *comb form* [NL, fr. Gk *neur-*, nerve, sinew, fr. *neuron*; *neuro-* fr. NL, fr. Gk, nerve, sinew, fr. *neuron* — more at NERVE] **1 :** neural tissue **:** nerve ⟨*neuro*anatomy⟩ ⟨*neuro*sarcoma⟩ ⟨*neuro*trophy⟩ **2 :** neural ⟨*neur*ectoderm⟩ ⟨*neuro*cyte⟩ ⟨*neuro*malacia⟩ ⟨*Neuro*ptera⟩ **3 :** neural and ⟨*neuro*cardiac⟩ ⟨*neuro*psychic⟩ ⟨*neuro*vascular⟩

-neu·ra \ˈn(y)ürə, -ürə\ *n comb form, pl* **-neura** [NL, fr. Gk *neuron* nerve] **:** one or ones having (such) nerves or veins — in taxonomic names ⟨Dasy*neura*⟩ ⟨Strepto*neura*⟩

neu·rad \ˈn(y)ü(ˌ)rad\ *adv* [*neur-* + *-ad*] **:** toward the neural side — opposed to *hemad*; compare HEMAL 2

neu·ral \ˈn(y)ürəl, -ür-\ *adj* [*neur-* + *-al*] **1 :** of, relating to, or affecting a nerve or the nervous system **2 :** situated in the region of or on the same side of the body as the neural axis — used of vertebrate anatomical relations as an equivalent to *dorsal*; opposed to *hemal* — **neu·ral·ly** \-rəlē\ *adv*

neural arch *n* **:** the cartilaginous or bony arch on the dorsal side of a vertebra **:** the series of neural arches forming the canal in which the spinal cord is situated

neural axis *n* **:** CEREBROSPINAL AXIS

neural canal *n* **1 :** the canal formed by the series of vertebral neural arches **2 :** the neurocoele of the vertebrate embryo

neural cavity *n* **:** the cavity comprising the spinal canal and the interior of the cranium

neural crest *n* **:** the ridge of a neural fold giving rise to the spinal ganglia and various autonomic structures

neural fold *n* **:** the lateral longitudinal fold on each side of the neural plate that by folding over and fusing with the opposite fold gives rise to the neural tube

neu·ral·gia \n(y)üˈraljə, n(y)ə'-\ *n* -S [NL, fr. *neur-* + *-algia*] **:** an acute paroxysmal pain radiating along the course of one or more nerves usu. without demonstrable changes in the nerve structure — compare NEURITIS — **neu·ral·gic** \-jik\ *adj*

neu·ral·gi·form \-jə,fȯrm\ *adj* [NL *neuralgia* + E *-form*] **:** resembling neuralgia or that of neuralgia ⟨~ pains⟩

neural gland *n* **:** a glandular mass in ascidians that lies in close relation to the nerve ganglion and is possibly homologous with the pituitary body of vertebrates

neural groove *n* **1 :** the longitudinal hollow that separates the neural crest from the main body of the neural plate **2 :** MEDULLARY GROOVE

neu·ral·gy \n(y)əˈraljē, -ji\ *n* -ES [NL *neuralgia*] *dial* **:** NEURALGIA

neural lamina *n* **:** one of the medullary folds

neural plate *n* **1 :** a thickened plate of ectoderm along the dorsal midline of the early vertebrate embryo that gives rise to the neural tube and crests **2 :** one of the bony plates in the middorsal part of the carapace of most turtles

neural process *n* **:** the lateral half of the neural arch of a vertebra equivalent to the pedicle and lamina together

neural ridge *n* **:** NEURAL CREST — compare NEURAL PLATE

neural shield *n* **:** any of a number of horny shields above the neural plates on the carapace of turtles

neural spine *n* **:** the median dorsal spine of a vertebra **:** SPINOUS PROCESS

neural tube *n* **:** the hollow longitudinal tube formed by infolding and subsequent fusion of the opposite neural folds in the vertebrate embryo

neur·aminic acid \¦n(y)ür+-\ *n* [ISV *neur-* + *aminic*] **:** an amino acid $C_9H_{17}NO_8$ of carbohydrate character occurring in the form of acyl derivatives — see SIALIC ACID

neur·apophysis \"+\ *n, pl* **neurapophyses** [NL, fr. *neur-* + *apophysis*] **1 :** NEURAL PROCESS **2 :** NEURAL SPINE

neur·asthenia \"+\ *n* [NL, fr. *neur-* + *asthenia*] **:** a syndrome marked by ready fatigability of body and mind, usu. by worrying and depression, and often by headache and by gastrointestinal and circulatory disturbances

¹neur·asthenic \"+\ *adj* [NL *neurasthenia* + E *-ic*] **:** of, relating to, or having neurasthenia ⟨before the ~ tendencies of the patient are developed —*Jour. Amer. Med. Assoc.*⟩ — **neu·ras·then·i·cal·ly** \-nək(ə)lē, -nēk-, -li\ *adv*

²neurasthenic \"\ *n* -S **:** one affected with neurasthenia

neu·ra·tion \n(y)üˈrāshən, n(y)ə-\ *n* -S [*neur-* + *-ation*] **:** VENATION — used esp. of the veins of an insect's wing

neur·axial \(ˈ)n(y)ür+\ *adj* [*neur-* + *axial*] **:** of or relating to a neuraxis

neur·axis \"+\ *n* [NL, fr. *neur-* + *axis*] **1 :** AXON **2 :** CEREBROSPINAL AXIS

neur·axon \"+\ *also* **neur·axone** \"+\ *n* [NL *neuraxon*, fr. *neur-* + *axon*] **:** NEURAXIS

neur·ectoblast \"+\ *n* [*neur-* + *ectoblast*] **:** embryonic ectoderm destined to produce neural tissue

neur·ectoderm \"+\ *n* [*neur-* + *ectoderm*] **:** ectoderm destined to give rise to neural tissues

neu·rec·to·my \n(y)üˈrektəmē\ *n* -ES [*neur-* + *-ectomy*] **:** the excision of part of a nerve

neur·enteric \¦n(y)ür+\ *adj* [*neur-* + *enteric*] **:** being or relating to a canal that in embryos of many vertebrates and tunicates temporarily connects the neural tube and the primitive intestine

neu·rer·gic \(ˈ)n(y)üˈrərjik\ *adj* [*neur-* + *erg-* + *-ic*] **:** of or relating to the action of a nerve

neu·ri·lem·ma *also* **neu·ri·lema** *or* **neu·ro·lemma** \ˌn(y)ürəˈlemə\ *n* -S [NL, fr. *neur-* + Gk *eilēma* covering, coil, fr. *eilein* to wind (akin to Gk *eilyein* to enfold, wrap); influenced by Gk *lemma* peel, rind, fr. *lepein* to peel, husk — more at VOLUBLE, LEPER] **1 :** the delicate nucleated outer sheath of a nerve fiber **2 :** PERINEURIUM — **neu·ri·lem·mal** \¦≈≈ˈleməl\ *or* **neu·ri·lem·mat·ic** \-ləˈmad·ik\ *or* **neu·ri·lem·ma·tous** \-ˈlemədəs\ *adj*

neu·ri·lem·mo·ma *or* **neu·ri·le·mo·ma** \ˌ≈≈ləˈmōmə\ *n, pl* **neu·ri·lem·mo·mas** \-məz\ *or* **neu·ri·lem·mo·ma·ta** \-məd·ə\ *or* **neurilemomas** *or* **neurilemomata** [NL, fr. *neurilemma* or *neurilema* + *-oma*] **:** a tumor of the sheath of a peripheral nerve

neu·ril·i·ty \n(y)üˈriləd·ē, -ətē, -i\ *n* -ES [*neur-* + ¹*-ile* + *-ity*] **:** the special properties and functions of the nerves

neu·rine \ˈn(y)ü,rēn, ˈn(y)ürən\ *also* **neu·rin** \ˈn(y)ürən\ *n* -S [ISV *neur-* + *-ine* or *-in*] **:** a syrupy poisonous quaternary ammonium hydroxide $CH_2{=}CHN(CH_3)_3OH$ that has a fishy odor, that is obtained esp. from animal sources (as brain, bile, egg yolk), and that is formed by dehydration of choline (as by boiling with barium hydroxide solution and in the putrefaction of flesh)

neu·ri·no·ma \ˌn(y)ürəˈnōmə\ *n, pl* **neurino·mas** \-məz\ *or* **neurinoma·ta** \-məd·ə\ [NL, fr. *neur-* + *-inoma* (as in L *carcinoma*)] **:** a nerve tumor supposed to be derived from the neurilemma

neu·rite \ˈn(y)ü,rīt\ *n* -S [ISV *neur-* + *-ite*] **:** AXON

¹neu·rit·ic \(ˈ)n(y)üˈrid·ik, n(y)ə'-, -itik, -ēk\ *adj* [NL *neuritis* + E *-ic*] **:** of, relating to, or affected by neuritis

²neuritic \"\ *n* -S **:** an individual affected with neuritis

neu·ri·tis \n(y)üˈrīd·əs, n(y)ə'-, -ītəs\ *n, pl* **neuritides** *or* **neuritises** [NL, fr. *neur-* + *-itis*] **:** an inflammatory or degenerative lesion of a nerve characterized by pain, sensory disturbances, paralysis, muscle atrophy, and impaired or lost reflexes in the part innervated — compare NEURALGIA

neu·ro- *in pronunciations below*, ¦≈≈≈ˈn(y)ü(ˌ)rō *or* ¦n(y)ürō *or* ˈn(y)ürə\ — see NEUR-

neu·ro·anatomic \¦≈≈+\ *also* **neu·ro·anatomical** \"+\ *adj* [*neuroanatomy* + *-ic* or *-ical*] **:** of or relating to the structure of nervous tissue or the nervous system

neu·ro·anatomist \"+\ *n* **:** a specialist in neuroanatomy

neu·ro·anatomy \"+\ *n* [*neur-* + *anatomy*] **1 :** the study of the structure of nervous tissue and the nervous system **2 :** the structural makeup of nervous tissue and the nervous system

neu·ro·bio·tac·tic \"+¦bīəˈtaktik\ *or* **neu·ro·bio·tac·ti·cal** \-təkəl\ *adj* [*neurobiotaxis*, after such pairs as NL *chemotaxis*: E *chemotactic*; *neurobiotactical* fr. *neurobiotactic* + *-al*] **:** of, relating to, or involving neurobiotaxis — **neu·ro·bio·tac·ti·cal·ly** \-tək(ə)lē\ *adv*

neu·ro·bio·taxis \"+¦bīōˈtaksəs\ *n* [NL, fr. *neur-* + *bi-* + *-taxis*] **:** a hypothetical directed and oriented shift of nerve cells in the course of phylogeny toward a region of maximum stimulation that has been held to explain cephalization and brain evolution

neu·ro·blast \ˈn(y)ürə,blast\ *n* [ISV *neur-* + *-blast*] **:** a cellular precursor of a nerve cell; *esp* **:** an undifferentiated embryonic nerve cell — **neu·ro·blas·tic** \¦≈≈ˈblastik\ *adj*

neu·ro·blas·to·ma *pronunc at* NEURO- +,blaˈstōmə\ *n, pl* **neuroblasto·mas** \-məz\ *or* **neuroblastoma·ta** \-məd·ə\ [NL, fr. ISV *neuroblast* + NL *-oma*] **:** a malignant tumor formed of embryonic ganglion cells

neu·ro·canal \"+\ *n* [*neur-* + *canal*] **:** the central canal of the spinal cord

neurocele *var of* NEUROCOELE

neu·ro·central \¦≈≈ *at* NEURO- +\ *adj* **1** [*neur-* + *central*] **:** of, relating to, or situated between the neural arch and the centrum of a vertebra **2** [NL *neurocentrum* + E *-al*] **:** of, relating to, or being a neurocentrum

neu·ro·centrum \"+\ *n* [NL, fr. *neur-* + *centrum*] **:** the dorsal element of a vertebra that unites with its fellow of the opposite side to form a neural arch from which the vertebral spine is developed

neu·ro·chondrite \"+\ *n* [*neur-* + *chondr-* + *-ite*] **:** NEUROCENTRUM

neu·ro·chord \ˈn(y)ürə+,-\ *n* [*neur-* + *chord*] **:** a prominent strand of nervous tissue **:** a nerve cord: as **a :** the primitive chordate central nervous system (as in a lancelet) **b :** one of the very large longitudinal nerve fibers of various segmented worms

neu·ro·circulatory \¦≈≈ *at* NEURO- +\ *adj* [*neur-* + *circulatory*] **:** of or relating to both the nervous and circulatory systems

neurocirculatory asthenia *n* **:** CARDIAC NEUROSIS

neu·ro·coele *or* **neu·ro·coel** *also* **neu·ro·cele** \ˈn(y)ürə,sēl\ *n* -S [*neur-* + *-coele*] **:** the cavity or system of cavities in the interior of the vertebrate central nervous system comprising the central canal of the spinal cord and the ventricles of the brain — **neu·ro·coe·li·an** \¦≈≈ˈsēlēən\ *adj*

neu·ro·cranium \¦≈≈ *at* NEURO- +\ *n* [NL, fr. *neur-* + *cranium*] **:** the portion of the skull that encloses and protects the brain — compare BRANCHIOCRANIUM, SPLANCHNOCRANIUM

neu·ro·crine \ˈn(y)ürəkrən; -,krin, -rīn, -rēn\ *adj* [*neur-* + *endocrine*] **:** of, relating to, or being a hormonal substance that influences the activity of the nerves ⟨~ synaptic transmission⟩ — **neu·ro·crin·ism** \-ˌkrəˌnizəm, -ˌkrī,-, -ˌkrē,-\ *n* -S

neu·ro·cutaneous \¦≈≈ *at* NEURO- +\ *adj* [*neur-* + *cutaneous*] **:** of, relating to, or affecting the skin and nerves ⟨~ syndrome⟩

neu·ro·cyte \ˈn(y)ürə,sīt\ *n* [*neur-* + *-cyte*] **:** the cell body of a neuron; *broadly* **:** NEURON

neu·ro·cy·to·ma \¦≈≈ *at* NEURO- +,sīˈtōmə\ *n, pl* **neurocytomas** \-məz\ *or* **neurocytoma·ta** \-məd·ə\ [NL, fr. *neur-* + *cyt-* + *-oma*] **:** any of various tumors of nerve tissue arising in the central or sympathetic nervous system

neu·ro·dendrite \¦≈≈ *at* NEURO- +\ *or* **neu·ro·dendron** \"+\ *n* [*neurodendrite* fr. *neur-* + *dendrite*; *neurodendron*, NL, fr. *neur-* + *-dendron*] **:** DENDRITE 3

neu·ro·dermatitic \"+\ *adj* [NL *neurodermatitis* + E *-ic*] **:** of, relating to, or exhibiting neurodermatitis

neu·ro·dermatitis \"+\ *n* [NL, fr. *neur-* + *dermatitis*] **:** a chronic allergic disorder of the skin characterized by patches of an itching lichenoid eruption and occurring esp. in persons of nervous and emotional instability

neu·ro·ectoderm \"+\ *n* [*neur-* + *ectoderm*] **:** embryonic ectoderm destined to give rise to nervous tissue — **neu·ro·ectodermal** \"+\ *adj*

neu·ro·effector \"+\ *adj* [*neur-* + *effector*] **:** of, relating to, or involving both neural and effector components

neu·ro·endocrine \"+\ *adj* [*neur-* + *endocrine*] **:** NEUROCRINE

neu·ro·epidermal \"+\ *adj* [*neur-* + *epidermal*] **:** relating or giving rise to the central nervous system and epidermis

neu·ro·epithelial \"+\ *adj* **1** [NL *neuroepithelium* + E *-al*] **:** of or relating to neuroepithelium **2** [*neur-* + *epithelial*] *of a cell* **:** having qualities of both neural and epithelial cells

neu·ro·epithelium \"+\ *n* [NL, fr. *neur-* + *epithelium*] **1 :** the part of the embryonic ectoderm that gives rise to the nervous system **2 :** the modified epithelium of an organ of special sense

neu·ro·fibril \"+\ *n* [NL *neurofibrilla*] **:** one of a system of many minute fibrils in a neuron believed by some to be conducting elements

neu·ro·fibrilla \"+\ *n* [NL, fr. *neur-* + *fibrilla*] **:** NEUROFIBRIL

neu·ro·fibrillary \"+\ *adj* [NL *neurofibrilla* + E *-ary*] **:** of or relating to neurofibrils ⟨~ network⟩

neu·ro·fibroma \"+\ *n* [NL, fr. *neur-* + *fibroma*] **:** a fibroma originating in the fibrous tissue of a nerve sheath

neu·ro·fibromatosis \"+\ *n* [NL, fr. *neurofibromat-*, *neurofibroma* + *-osis*] **:** a condition marked by the presence of many neurofibromas chiefly in the subcutaneous tissues

neu·ro·formative system \"+-\ *n* [*neur-* + *formative*] **:** NEUROMOTOR SYSTEM

neu·ro·gen \ˈn(y)ürəjən, -,jen\ *n* -S [*neur-* + *-gen*] **:** a hypothetical specific primary organizer that induces formation of neural structures in an embryo

neu·ro·gen·ic \¦≈≈ˈjenik\ *adj* [*neur-* + *-genic*] **1 a :** originating in nervous tissue ⟨a ~ tumor⟩ **b :** induced, controlled, or modified by nervous factors ⟨~ intestinal lesions⟩ ⟨a ~ suckling reflex⟩; *esp* **:** disordered because of abnormally altered neural relations ⟨the ~ kidney⟩ **2 a :** constituting the neural component of a bodily process ⟨~ factors in disease⟩ **b** *of cardiac muscular contraction* **:** taking place or viewed as taking place in ordered rhythmic fashion under the control of a net of nerve cells scattered in the cardiac muscle — compare MYOGENIC 2 — **neu·ro·gen·i·cal·ly** \-nə̇k(ə)lē\ *adv*

neu·rog·e·nous \(ˈ)n(y)u̇ˈräjənəs\ *adj* [*neur-* + *-genous*] : NEUROGENIC

neu·ro·glandular \¦==at NEURO- +\ *adj* [*neur-* + *glandular*] **1** : of or relating to a gland with its nerves and their nerve centers **2** : having the properties of both nervous and glandular tissue ⟨the pituitary body is ~⟩

neu·ro·glia \n(y)u̇ˈrōglēə, -ˈräg-; ˌn(y)u̇rəˈglīə, -lēə\ *n* -s [NL, fr. *neur-* + MGk *glia* glue — more at CLAY] : sustentacular tissue that fills the interstices and supports the essential elements of nervous tissue esp. in the brain, spinal cord, and ganglia, is of ectodermal origin, and is composed of a network of fine fibrils and of flattened stellate cells with numerous radiating fibrillar processes — compare MICROGLIA — **neu·ro·gli·al** \-əl\ *or* **neu·ro·gli·ar** \-ə(r)\ *adj*

neu·ro·gli·o·ma \n(y)u̇ˌrōglīˈōmə, -ˌräg-, -lēˈ-\ *n* [NL, fr. *neuroglia* + *-oma*] : a tumor developed from neuroglia cells : GLIOMA

neu·ro·gli·o·sis \-ˈōsə̇s\ *n, pl* **neuroglio·ses** \-ˌsēz\ [NL, fr. *neuroglia* + *-osis*] : a condition marked by the development of multiple neurogliomas throughout the nervous system

neu·ro·gram \ˈn(y)u̇rəˌgram\ *n* [*neur-* + *-gram*] : the postulated modified neural structure resulting from activity and serving to retain whatever has been learned : a neural engram — **neu·ro·gram·mic** \¦==¦gramik\ *adj*

neu·ro·graphic \¦==+\ *adj* : of or relating to neurography

neu·rog·ra·phy \n(y)u̇ˈrägrəfē\ *n* -ES **1** [NL *neurographia*, fr. *neur-* + *-graphia* -graphy] : a description of the nervous system **2** [*neur-* + *-graphy*] **a** : the postulated formation of neurograms **b** : the postulated system of engrams present in an individual's brain

neu·ro·hormonal \¦== at NEURO- +\ *adj* [*neur-* + *hormonal*] : involving both neural and hormonal mechanisms ⟨~ factors in certain forms of heart disease⟩

neu·ro·hormone \"+\ *n* [ISV *neur-* + *hormone*] : a hormone produced by or acting on nervous tissue

neu·ro·humor \"+\ *n* [*neur-* + *humor*] : a substance liberated at a nerve ending that participates in the transmission of a nerve impulse

neu·ro·humoral \"+\ *adj* : of or relating to neurohumors

neurohumoral theory *n* : a theory in physiology: transmission of nerve impulses are due to chemical mechanisms — compare CHEMICAL MEDIATION THEORY

neu·ro·hypnotic \"+\ *adj* : HYPNOTIC 2

neu·ro·hypnotism \"+\ *n* [*neur-* + [1]*hypnotic* (soporific) + *-ism*] : HYPNOTISM

neu·ro·hypophysis \"+\ *n* [NL, fr. *neur-* + *hypophysis*] : the portion of the pituitary gland derived from the embryonic brain and made up of the infundibulum and of the posterior lobe which is associated with the secretion of various hormones (as one regulating the renal mechanism that controls the salt and water balance of the body) — compare ADENOHYPOPHYSIS

neu·roid \ˈn(y)u̇ˌrȯid, ˈn(y)ü,-\ *adj* [*neur-* + *-oid*] **1** : resembling a nerve or nerve tissue **2** : of or relating to the transmission of excitation through tissues without nerve fibers

neu·ro·keratin \¦== at NEURO- +\ *n* [ISV *neur-* + *keratin*] : a pseudokeratin present in nerve tissue (as in the sheath of the axis cylinder of medullated nerve fibers)

neu·ro·kyme \ˈn(y)u̇rəˌkīm\ *n* -s [*neur-* + Gk *kyma* wave — more at CYME] : the kinetic energy of neural activity

neurolemma *var of* NEURILEMMA

neu·ro·log·i·cal \ˌn(y)u̇rəˈläjə̇kəl, -jēk-\ *or* **neu·ro·log·ic** \-jik, -jēk\ *adj* [*neurology* + *-ical* or *-ic*] : of or relating to neurology ⟨combined with the study of brain ~ sciences —*Jour. Amer. Med. Assoc.*⟩ — **neu·ro·log·i·cal·ly** \-k(ə)lē\ *adv*

neu·rol·o·gist \n(y)u̇ˈräləjə̇st, n(y)əˈ-\ *n* -s : one specializing in neurology; *esp* : a physician skilled in the diagnosis and treatment of disease of the nervous system — distinguished from *psychiatrist*

neu·rol·o·gize \-ˌjīz\ *vt* -ED/-ING/-S [*neurology* + *-ize*] : to explain behavioral phenomena in neural terms

neu·rol·o·gy \-jē, -ji\ *n* -ES [NL *neurologia*, fr. Gk *neuro-* nerve, sinew (fr. *neuron*) + NL *-logia* -logy — more at NERVE] : the scientific study of the nervous system esp. in respect to its structure, functions, and abnormalities

neu·ro·lymphomatosis \¦== at NEURO- +\ *n* [NL, fr. *neur-* + *lymphomatosis*] : a disease of the avian leukosis complex that is marked by mononuclear cell infiltration of peripheral nerves esp. of the legs and wings of chickens approaching maturity, that results in flaccid paralysis, and that is sometimes held due to a specific virus infection — called also *fowl paralysis, range paralysis*

neu·rol·y·sis \=ˈräləsə̇s\ *n* [NL, fr. *neur-* + *-lysis*] **1** : the breaking down of nerve substance (as from disease or exhaustion) **2** : the operation of freeing a nerve from adhesions

neu·ro·lyt·ic \ˌn(y)u̇rə¦lidik\ *adj* [fr. NL *neurolysis*, after such pairs as NL *histolysis*: E *histolytic*] : of, relating to, or causing neurolysis

neu·ro·ma \n(y)u̇ˈrōmə\ *n, pl* **neuro·mas** \-məz\ *or* **neuro·ma·ta** \-mədə\ [NL, fr. *neur-* + *-oma*] **1** : a tumor or mass growing from a nerve and usu. consisting of nerve fibers **2** : a mass of nerve tissue in an amputation stump resulting from abnormal regrowth of the stumps of severed nerves — called also *amputation neuroma, pseudoneuroma*

neu·ro·mast \ˈn(y)u̇rəˌmast\ *n* -s [*neur-* + Gk *mastos* hillock, breast — more at MEAT] : one of the characteristic sensory organs of the lateral lines of fishes and various other lower vertebrates consisting of a cluster of sensory cells connected with nerve fibers — **neu·ro·mas·tic** \¦==¦mastik\ *adj*

neu·ro·mere \ˈn(y)u̇rəˌmi(ə)r\ *n* -s [*neur-* + *-mere*] **1** : a metameric segment of the vertebrate nervous system ⟨the ~s of the spinal cord are identified by the exits of the spinal nerves⟩ **2** : a primitive nerve ganglion of an invertebrate

neu·rom·er·ism \n(y)u̇ˈräməˌrizəm\ *n* -s : metamerism of the nervous system

neu·ro·motor \¦== at NEURO- +\ *adj* [*neur-* + *motor*] : relating to efferent nervous impulses

neu·ro·motorium \"+\ *n* [NL, fr. *neur-* + *motorium*] : NEUROMOTOR SYSTEM

neuromotor system *also* **neuromotor apparatus** *n* : a system of noncontractile cytoplasmic fibrils that is often associated with a motorium in various protozoans and may be analogous to the nervous system of higher forms

neu·ro·muscular \¦== at NEURO- +\ *adj* [ISV *neur-* + *muscular*] : of, relating to, or involving both nerves and muscles or nervous and muscular tissue

neuromuscular spindle *n* : MUSCLE SPINDLE

neu·ro·my·al \¦== at NEURO- + ¦mīəl\ *also* **neu·ro·my·ic** \-īik\ *adj* [*neur-* + *my-* + *-al* or *-ic*] : NEUROMUSCULAR

neu·ro·myelitis \"+\ *n* [NL, fr. *neur-* + *myelitis*] **1** : inflammation of the medullary substance of the nerves **2** : inflammation of both spinal cord and nerves

neu·ron \ˈn(y)üˌrän, ˈn(y)u̇rˌ-\ *also* **neu·rone** \-ˌrōn\ *n* -s [NL *neuron*, fr. Gk, nerve, sinew — more at NERVE] **1** *archaic* : the brain and spinal cord **2** : a nerve cell esp. with all its processes — **neu·ro·nal** \ˈn(y)u̇rənəl, (ˈ)n(y)u̇¦rōnᵊl\ *or* **neu·ron·ic** \(ˈ)n(y)u̇¦ränik\ *adj*

neuron doctrine *or* **neuron theory** *n* : a theory in anatomy and physiology: the nervous system is composed of nerve cells each of which is a structural unit in contact with other units but not in continuity, a genetic unit derived from a single embryonic neuroblast, a functional unit or unit of conduction with the nervous pathways being chains of such units, and a trophic unit with the nerve processes degenerating when severed from the cell body and being replaced by outgrowths from the cell body

neu·ro·neuronal \¦== at NEURO- +\ *adj* [*neur-* + *neuronal*] : between nerve cells or nerve fibers ⟨~ synapses⟩

neu·ron·ism \ˈn(y)u̇rəˌnizəm\ *n* -s [NL *neuron* + E *-ism*] : a theory in psychology that stresses the brain neurons as the vehicles of mental processes

neu·ron·ist \-nə̇st\ *n* -s : one who accepts neuronism

neu·ron·i·tis \ˌn(y)u̇rəˈnīdə̇s, -ītə̇s\ *n* -ES [NL, fr. *neuron* + *-itis*] : inflammation of neurons; *esp* : neuritis involving nerve roots and nerve cells within the spinal cord

neu·ro·no·pha·gia \n(y)u̇ˌrōnōˈfājēə\ *also* **neu·ro·noph·a·gy** \ˌn(y)u̇rəˈnäfəjē\ *n, pl* **neuronophagias** *also* **neuronophagies** [*neuronophagia*, NL, fr. *neuron* + *-o-* + *-phagia*; *neuronophagy*, ISV, fr. NL *neuron* + *-o-* + ISV *-phagy*] : destruction of neurons by phagocytic cells

neu·ro·path \ˈn(y)u̇rəˌpath\ *n* -s [*neur-* + *-path*] : a person subject to nervous disorders or to neuroses

neu·ro·path·ic \¦==¦pathik -thēk\ *adj* [*neur-* + *-pathic*] : of or relating to neuropathy : being or having nervous disease — **neu·ro·path·i·cal·ly** \-thə̇k(ə)lē -thēk, -li\ *adv*

neu·ro·pathologic \¦== at NEURO- +\ *or* **neu·ro·pathological** \"—\ *adj* [*neuropathology* + *-ic* or *-ical*] : of, relating to, or involving neuropathology

neu·ro·pathologist \"+\ *n* : a specialist in neuropathology

neu·ro·pathology \"+\ *n* [ISV *neur-* + *pathology*] : pathology of the nervous system

neu·rop·a·thy \n(y)u̇ˈräpəthē, n(y)əˈ-\ *n* -ES [ISV *neur-* + *-pathy*] : any of various abnormal states of the nervous system or nerves esp. when involving degenerative changes; *also* : a systemic condition (as muscular atrophy) that stems from a primary degeneration of nervous tissue

neu·ro·phile \ˈn(y)u̇rəˌfīl\ *or* **neu·ro·phil·ic** \¦==¦filik\ *adj* [*neurophile*, ISV *neur-* + *-phile*; *neurophilic* fr. *neur-* + *-philic*] : NEUROTROPIC

neu·ro·physiological \¦== at NEURO- +\ *also* **neu·ro·physiologic** \"+\ *adj* [*neur-* + *physiological* or *physiologic*] : of or relating to neurophysiology — **neu·ro·physiologically** \"+\ *adv*

neu·ro·physiologist \"+\ *n* : a specialist in neurophysiology

neu·ro·physiology \"+\ *n* [*neur-* + *physiology*] : physiology of the nervous system

neu·ro·pil \ˈn(y)u̇rəˌpil\ *also* **neu·ro·pile** \-ˌpīl\ *n* -s [ISV *neur-* + *-pil*, *-pile* (fr. Gk *pilos* felt) — more at PILE (hair)] **1** : a feltwork of delicate unmyelinated nerve fibers interrupted by numerous synapses and found in concentrations of nervous tissue esp. throughout the vertebrate central nervous system and esp. in parts of the brain where it is highly developed and constitutes with interspersion of myelinated fibers the reticular formations **2** : a delicate terminal branch of a nerve fiber — **neu·ro·pi·lar** \¦==¦pīlə(r)\ *adj*

neu·ro·plasm \ˈ==ˌplazəm\ *n* [*neur-* + *-plasm*] : the ground cytoplasm of a nerve cell — contrasted with *neurofibril* — **neu·ro·plasmatic** \¦==+\ *or* **neu·ro·plasmic** \"+\ *adj*

neu·ro·po·di·al \ˌn(y)u̇rə¦pōdēəl\ *adj* [NL *neuropodium* + E *-al*] : of or relating to a neuropodium

neu·ro·po·di·um \ˌ==ˈ=dēəm\ *n, pl* **neuropo·dia** \-ēə\ [NL, fr. *neur-* + *-podium*] **1** : one of the delicate terminal branches of an axon **2** *also* **neu·ro·pod** \ˈ==ˌpäd\ : the ventral lobe of a parapodium

neu·rop·o·dous \n(y)u̇ˈräpədəs\ *adj* [*neur-* + *-podous*] : having ventrally directed limbs or limbs with neuropodia — used of certain annelid worms

neu·ro·pore \ˈn(y)u̇rəˌpō(ə)r\ *n* [*neur-* + *pore*] : either of the openings to the exterior at the anterior and posterior ends of the neural tube of a vertebrate embryo

neu·ro·psychiatric \¦== at NEURO- +\ *adj* [*neur* + *psychiatric*] : of or relating to neuropsychiatry — **neu·ro·psychiatrically** \"+\ *adv*

neu·ro·psychiatrist \"+\ *n* : a specialist in neuropsychiatry

neu·ro·psychiatry \"+\ *n* [*neur-* + *psychiatry*] : a branch of medicine concerned with both the psychic and organic aspects of mental disorder

neu·ro·psychological \"+\ *adj* [*neur-* + *psychological*] : of or relating to neuropsychology

neu·ro·psychologist \"+\ *n* [*neur-* + *psychologist*] : a specialist in neuropsychology

neu·ro·psychology \"+\ *n* [*neur-* + *psychology*] : a science that attempts to correlate psychological and neurological facts

neu·rop·ter \n(y)u̇ˈräptə(r)\ *n* -s [NL *Neuroptera*] : NEUROPTERON

neu·rop·tera \-tərə\ *n pl, cap* [NL, fr. *neur-* + *-ptera*] : an order of usu. net-winged insects that have holometabolous development and that include the lacewings, ant lions, and related insects — see MEGALOPTERA — **neu·rop·ter·an** \(ˈ)=-¦=tərən\ *adj or n* — **neu·rop·ter·ous** \-rəs\ *adj*

neu·rop·ter·is \=ˈ=tərə̇s\ *n, cap* [NL, fr. *neur-* + *-pteris*] : a genus of fossil seed ferns represented by abundant fronds and stems from the Devonian to the Triassic

neu·rop·ter·ist \-rə̇st\ *n* -s [NL *Neuroptera* + E *-ist*] : a student of the neuropterous insects

[1]**neu·rop·ter·oid** \(ˈ)=¦==ˌrȯid\ *adj* [NL *Neuroptera* + E *-oid*] : resembling or related to the Neuroptera

[2]**neuropteroid** \"\ *n* -s [NL *Neuropteroidea*] : an insect of the superorder Neuropteroidea

neu·rop·ter·oi·dea \=ˌ==ˈrȯidēə\ *n pl, cap* [NL, fr. *Neuroptera*, order of insects + *-oidea*] : a superorder of insects including the orders Neuroptera, Mecoptera, Trichoptera, Lepidoptera, Diptera, and Siphonaptera

neu·rop·ter·ol·o·gy \-ˈräləjē\ *n* -ES [NL *Neuroptera* + E *-o-* + *-logy*] : a branch of entomology that is concerned with the Neuroptera

neu·rop·ter·on \=ˈ=ˌrän\ *n* -s [NL, sing. of *Neuroptera*] : an insect of the order Neuroptera

neu·ro·retinitis \¦== at NEURO- +\ *n* [NL, fr. *neur-* + *retinitis*] : inflammation of the optic nerve and the retina

neu·ro·secretion \"+\ *n* [ISV *neur-* + *secretion*] **1** : a secretion produced by nerve cells **2** : the act or process of producing a neurosecretion

neu·ro·secretory \"+\ *adj* : relating to or promoting neurosecretion

neu·ro·sis \n(y)u̇ˈrōsə̇s, n(y)əˈ-\ *n, pl* **neuro·ses** \-ˌsēz\ [NL, fr. *neur-* + *-osis*] **1** : a functional disorder of the central nervous system usu. manifested by anxiety, phobias, obsessions, or compulsions but frequently displaying signs of somatic disorder involving any of the bodily systems with or without other subjective or behavioral manifestations and having its most probable etiology in intrapsychic or interpersonal conflict ⟨somatic changes such as induced by drugs or by fatigue may act as precipitating, and constitutional factors as predisposing, influences in ~⟩ ⟨it is the feeling of isolation, of being shut out, which is the painful sting of every ~ —Erich Fromm⟩ ⟨a ~ or a neurotic fantasy always relates to a reality, and a neurotic expression of a reality is likely to have more force than a "normal" one —Lionel Trilling⟩ **2** : individual or group behavior that is characterized by rigid adherence to an idealized concept of the personal or social organism esp. when that concept is significantly at variance with reality and that results in interpersonal, cultural, or political conflict and in the development of discomforting intraorganismal tensions ⟨the atmosphere of conformity, induced by our present ~⟩

neu·ro·some \ˈn(y)u̇rəˌsōm\ *n* -s [ISV *neur-* + *-some* (body)] **1** : the cell body of a neuron **2** : one of various small particles in the cytoplasm of a neuron

neu·ro·spon·gi·um \ˌn(y)u̇rəˈspənjēəm, -pän-\ *n, pl* **neu·rospon·gia** \-ēə\ [NL, fr. *neur-* + *-spongium*] **1** : a network of fibrils in the cytoplasm of a nerve cell **2** : the inner reticular stratum of the retina

neu·ros·po·ra \n(y)u̇ˈräspərə\ *n, cap* [NL, fr. *neur-* + *-spora*] : a genus of ascomycetous fungi (family Sphaeriaceae) used extensively in genetic research, having black perithecia and persistent asci, and including some forms that have salmon pink or orange spore masses and cause severe damage in bakeries

neu·ro·surgeon \¦== at NEURO- +\ *n* [*neur-* + *surgeon*] : a surgeon specializing in neurosurgery

neu·ro·surgery \"+\ *n* [*neur-* + *surgery*] : surgery of the brain, spinal cord, nerves, or other nervous structures

neu·ro·surgical \"+\ *adj* [*neur-* + *surgical*] : of, relating to, or performed by means of neurosurgery

neu·ro·syphilis \"+\ *n* [NL, fr. *neur-* + *syphilis*] : syphilis of the central nervous system

neu·ro·tendinous \"+\ *adj* [*neur-* + *tendinous*] : of or relating to a nerve and tendon; *esp* : being any of various nerve endings in tendons

[1]**neu·rot·ic** \(ˈ)n(y)u̇¦räd·ik, n(y)əˈr-, -ätik, -ēk\ *n* -s [Gk *neur-* nerve, sinew (fr. *neuron*) + E *-otic* (as in *narcotic*, n.) — more at NERVE] **1** *archaic* : a drug acting esp. noxiously on the nervous system **2** [[2]*neurotic*] : an emotionally unstable individual or one affected with a neurosis

[2]**neurotic** \"\ *adj* [fr. NL *neurosis*, after such pairs as NL *narcosis*: E *narcotic*] **1 a** : of, relating to, or involving the nerves : seated in the nerves ⟨a ~ disorder⟩ **b** : being a neurosis : NERVOUS ⟨a ~ disease⟩ **2** : affected with, relating to, or characterized by neurosis ⟨a ~ person has become estranged from himself —Karen Horney⟩

neu·rot·i·cal·ly \-ə̇k(ə)lē, -ēk-, -li\ *adv* : in a neurotic manner : as a result of or as though affected by neurosis ⟨an embittered pedant, ~ conscious of his personal dignity —*Contemporary Rev.*⟩

neu·rot·i·cism \=ˈräd·əˌsizəm, -ätə-\ *n* -s [[2]*neurotic* + *-ism*] : a neurotic condition, character, or trait ⟨imputation of ~ to the intelligentsia as a group —Philip Rahv⟩ ⟨the apparently *normal* world of men and women whose ~s are concealed, even from themselves, by their adherence to fixed behavior patterns —*Tomorrow*⟩

neu·roto·gen·ic \n(y)u̇¦räd·ə¦jenik\ *adj* [[1]*neurotic* + *-o-* + *-genic*] : tending to produce neurosis ⟨~ effects⟩

neu·rot·oid \=ˈräd·ˌȯid\ *adj* [[1]*neurotic* + *-oid*] : resembling or simulating neurosis ⟨~ behavior⟩

neu·ro·tome \ˈn(y)u̇rəˌtōm\ *n* -s [*neur-* + *-tome*] : NEUROMERE

neu·rot·o·my \n(y)u̇ˈräd·əmē\ *n* -ES [*neur-* + *-tomy*] **1** : the dissection or cutting of nerves **2** : the division of a nerve (as to relieve neuralgia)

neu·ro·toxic \¦== at NEURO- +\ *adj* [*neur-* + *toxic*] : toxic to the nerves or nervous tissue ⟨~ snake venom⟩ — **neu·ro·toxicity** \"+\ *n*

neu·ro·toxicologist \"+\ *n* [*neur-* + *toxicologist*] : a specialist in the study of neurotoxins and their effects

neu·ro·toxicology \"+\ *n* [*neur-* + *toxicology*] : the study of neurotoxins and their effects

neu·ro·toxin \"+\ *n* [ISV *neur-* + *toxin*] : a poisonous protein complex that is present in various snake venoms and that exerts its principal effect as a nervous system depressant

neu·ro·trope \ˈn(y)u̇rəˌtrōp\ *n* -s [prob. fr. F or G; F, adj., neurotropic, fr. G *neurotrop*, fr. *neuro-* neur- + *-trop* -trope] : a neurotropic agent

neu·ro·troph·ic \¦== at NEURO- + ¦träfik, -rōf-\ *adj* [ISV *neur-* + *-trophic*] **1** : relating to or dependent on the influence of nerves on the nutrition of tissue **2** [prob. by alter.] : NEUROTROPIC

neu·ro·trop·ic \¦==¦träpik, -rōp-\ *adj* [ISV *neur-* + *-tropic*] **1** : having an affinity for nerve tissue ⟨~ drugs⟩ ⟨~ poisons⟩ ⟨~ stains⟩ **2** : localizing selectively in nerve tissue ⟨tested for ~ viruses⟩ ⟨~ infectious agents⟩ — compare ORGANOTROPIC, PANTROPIC

neu·rot·ro·pism \n(y)u̇ˈrä·trəˌpizəm\ *n* [ISV *neur-* + *tropism*] : the quality or state of being neurotropic

neu·ro·tubule \¦== at NEURO- +\ *n* [*neur-* + *tubule*] : one of the tubular elements sometimes considered to be a fundamental part of the nerve-cell axon

neu·ro·vascular \"+\ *adj* [*neur-* + *vascular*] : of, relating to, or involving both nerves and blood vessels

neu·ro·vegetative \"+\ *adj* [*neur-* + *vegetative*] : AUTONOMIC 2b

neu·ru·la \ˈn(y)u̇r(y)ələ\ *n, pl* **neuru·lae** \-ˌlē, -ˌlī\ *or* **neuru·las** \-ləz\ [NL, fr. *neur-* + *-ula*] : an early vertebrate embryo which follows the gastrula and in which the basic vertebrate pattern begins to emerge esp. by the formation of the neural tube and the beginning of differentiation of nervous tissue — **neu·ru·lar** \-lə(r)\ *adj* — **neu·ru·la·tion** \ˌ==ˈlāshən\ *n* -s

neu·si·ok \ˈn(y)üsēˌäk\ *n, pl* **neusiok** *or* **neusioks** *usu cap* **1** : an Indian people of uncertain linguistic affiliation south of the lower Neuse river in No. Carolina **2** : a member of the Neusiok people

neus·tic \ˈn(y)üstik\ *or* **neus·ton·ic** \(ˈ)=¦stänik\ *adj* [*neustic*, ISV *neuston* + *-ic*; prob. orig. formed as G *neustisch*; *neustonic* fr. *neuston* + *-ic*] : of, relating to, or being neuston

neus·ton \ˈn(y)üˌstän\ *n* -s [G, fr. Gk, neut. of *neustos* swimming, verbal of *nein* to swim; akin to L *nutrire* to nourish — more at NOURISH] : minute organisms that float in the surface film of water

[1]**neus·tri·an** \ˈn(y)üstrēən\ *adj, usu cap* [ML *Neustria*, northwestern portion of the Frankish empire + E *-an*] **1** : of, relating to, or characteristic of Neustria, the northwestern portion of the Frankish empire including most of the territory between the Loire and the Scheldt **2** : of, relating to, or characteristic of the people of Neustria

[2]**neustrian** \"\ *n* -s *cap* : a native or inhabitant of Neustria

neut *abbr* **1** neuter **2** neutral

[1]**neu·ter** \ˈn(y)üd·ə(r), -ütə-\ *adj* [ME *neutre*, fr. MF & L; MF *neutre*, fr. L *neuter*, lit., neither, fr. *ne-* (negative prefix) + *uter* which of two — more at NO, WHETHER] **1 a** : belonging to, connected with, or constituting the gender that ordinarily includes most words or grammatical forms referring characteristically to things that are neither masculine nor feminine ⟨a ~ noun⟩ ⟨the ~ gender⟩ ⟨a ~ ending⟩ **b** : neither active nor passive : INTRANSITIVE; *also* : restricted to mere existence or state — used of verbs and verb forms **2** : taking no side : free from marked bias or partiality : NEUTRAL **3** : belonging to neither of two usu. opposed classes **4 a** : having no generative organs : SEXLESS **b** : having imperfectly developed or nonfunctional generative organs either permanently or seasonally ⟨the worker bee is ~⟩ — **neu·ter·ly** *adv* — **neu·ter·ness** *n* -ES

[2]**neuter** \"\ *n* -s **1 a** : a noun, pronoun, adjective, or inflectional form or class of the neuter gender **b** : the neuter gender **2 a** : one that is neutral **b** *usu cap* : NEUTRAL 1b **3 a** : an imperfectly developed female of various social insects (as ants and honeybees) that performs labors of the community : WORKER **b** : a spayed or castrated animal (as a cat)

[3]**neuter** \"\ *vt* -ED/-ING/-S : CASTRATE, ALTER

[1]**neu·tral** \ˈn(y)ü·trəl\ *adj* [MF, fr. (assumed) ML *neutralis*, fr. L, of neuter gender, fr. *neutr-*, *neuter* neuter + *-alis* -al] **1 a** : not engaged on either side : not siding with or assisting either of two or more contending parties **b** *of a state or power* : lending no active assistance to either or any belligerent **2** : of or belonging to a neutral state or power : not involved in hostilities ⟨~ territory⟩ **3 a** : being neither one thing nor the other : belonging to neither of two usu. opposed or contrasted classes : not decided or pronounced as to characteristics : MIDDLING, INDIFFERENT ⟨a ~ character without marked virtues or vices⟩ **b** (1) : totally lacking in saturation : ACHROMATIC, HUELESS (2) : not decided in color : nearly achromatic : of low saturation **c** (1) : NEUTER 4 (2) : lacking stamens or pistils **d** (1) : neither acid nor basic : neither acid nor alkaline; *specif* : having a pH value of 7.0 ⟨a ~ solution contains both hydrogen ions and hydroxide ions at the same concentration, 1.00x10^{-7} —Linus Pauling⟩ (2) : NORMAL 10c ⟨a ~ salt⟩ (3) : neither degressive nor progressive ⟨~ burning of propellants in which the total surface remains nearly constant⟩ **e** (1) : not electrically charged ⟨a ~ particle⟩ (2) : being at an arbitrary zero of electrical potential (3) : being at a potential midway between extremes **f** : being the position in which a propelling mechanism although itself revolving freely transmits no motion to the parts to be driven **g** (1) : neither distinctively physical nor distinctively mental ⟨~ stuff⟩ ⟨~ entities⟩ (2) : common to the knowing mind and the object known **h** : being neither milk nor meat nor prepared with dairy products or meat derivatives : PAREVE **i** *usu cap* : TRANSITION **4 a** (1) *of the tongue or lips* : being in a rest position intermediate between extreme positions to which movable (2) *of the tongue* : lying low in the mouth and having no effort-produced arching ⟨the ~ articulation of either vowel of \əˈbəv\ *above*⟩ (3) *of the lips* : open and with the corners of the mouth neither closely approximated nor widely separated ⟨the ~ articulation of the vowel of *hut* or *art*⟩ **b** *of a vowel* : produced with the tongue in a position of rest : having brief duration : not of strongly defined or readily perceptible quality : UNSTRESSED ⟨either ~ vowel of \əˈbəv\ *above*⟩ ⟨the ~ vowel schwa⟩ — **neu·tral·ly** \-rəlē, -li\ *adv* — **neu·tral·ness** \-lnə̇s\ *n* -ES

[2]**neutral** \"\ *n* -s **1 a** : a person, party, ship, or nation that takes or belongs to one who takes no part in a contest between others : one that exhibits neutrality **b** *usu cap* (1) **neutrals** *pl* : an Iroquoian people of the region about Lake Erie in Canada and the U.S. (2) a member of such people **2** : a neutral color **3** : a neutral substance: as **a** : NEUTRAL LARD **b** : NEUTRAL OIL 2 **4 a** : an electrically neutral point, wire, conductor, bus bar, or other element **b** : a neutral position of driving and driven parts of a machine : a position of disengagement (as of gears from the motive power) ⟨when the transmission is in ~, it means simply that the flow of power is

cut off in the transmission so that rotation of the clutch shaft is not transmitted to the main shaft —Joseph Heitner⟩

neutral axis *n* **:** the line in a beam or other member subjected to a bending action in which the fibers are neither stretched nor compressed or where the longitudinal stress is zero

neutral brandy *n* **:** brandy of 170 proof or over but of less than 190 proof used chiefly for fortifying wines or as a base for various fruit-flavored brandies — compare NEUTRAL SPIRITS

neutral conductor *n* **:** the intermediate conductor in a three-wire electrical system usu. grounded or maintained at zero potential

neutral corner *n* **:** either of the two diagonally opposite corners of a boxing ring that are not appropriated to one or the other of the contestants

neutral dye *n* **1 :** a dye capable of dyeing fibers (as cotton) directly in a neutral or faintly alkaline bath **2 :** a salt formed by interaction of an acid dye (as eosin) and a basic dye (as methylene blue) — called also *neutral stain*

neutral flame *n* **:** a flame resulting from the burning of gases supplied in the proper proportions for perfect combustion (as approximately equal volumes of acetylene and oxygen)

neutral gray *n* **:** GRAY 3a

neutral gray G *n* **:** a direct dye — see DYE table I (under *Direct Black 3*)

neu·tral·ism \'n(y)ü-trə,lizəm\ *n* -s [¹*neutral* + *-ism*] **1 a :** NEUTRALITY **b :** a policy or the advocacy of neutrality esp. in international affairs (as with respect to a conflict between world powers) **c :** the practice or an attitude of neutrality; *also* **:** the expression of neutral sentiments **2 :** NEUTRAL MONISM

neu·tral·ist \-ləst\ *n* -s **1 :** a professor or practicer of neutrality **2 :** one that favors the neutralization of a state or region — **neu·tral·is·tic** \¦==¦listik\ *adj*

neu·tral·i·ty \n(y)ü'tralәd·ē, -әtē, -i\ *n* -ES [MF or ML; MF *neutralité* state or condition of being neutral, fr. ML *neutralitat-, neutralitas*, fr. (assumed) ML *neutralis* neutral + L *-itat-, -itas* -ity — more at NEUTRAL] **1** *archaic* **:** a party that is neutral **:** a combination of neutral powers or states — used with *the;* see ARMED NEUTRALITY **2 a :** the quality or state of being neutral **:** a condition of being uninvolved in contests or controversies between others or of refraining from taking part on either side of such contest or controversy **b :** the condition of a state or government that refrains from taking part directly or indirectly in a war between other powers **c :** a condition of immunity from invasion or use by belligerents in the course of operations against each other that is sometimes guaranteed by treaty (as to a nation or of a waterway) **3 :** the particular character conveyed to something belonging to a state (as a citizen or place) by the maintenance of neutrality by that state during hostilities ⟨insisted on recognition of the ~ of the port⟩ **4 :** the quality or state of being intermediate, falling between extremes, or belonging to neither one nor the other of two well-defined categories or classes ⟨a solution of perfect ~ is neither acid nor basic⟩ **5 :** the quality or state of being neuter

neu·tral·i·za·tion \,n(y)ü·trələ'zāshən, -,lī'-\ *n* -s [*neutralize* + *-ation*] **1 :** an act or process of neutralizing **2 :** the quality or state of being neutralized **3 :** the absence in some contexts of a phonetic or grammatical contrast found elsewhere or formerly in a language (as the contrast between final \s\ and \z\ after \t\ in English or between the nominative and accusative neuter case in Latin)

neutralization number *also* **neutralization value** *n* **:** a number indicating the degree of acidity or alkalinity of a substance determined by finding the amount of alkali or acid required for neutralization; *specif* **:** the weight in milligrams of potassium hydroxide required to neutralize the acid in one gram of an oil (as a hydrocarbon oil)

neu·tral·ize \'n(y)ü-trə,līz\ *vb* -ED/-ING/-S *see -ize in Explan Notes* [¹*neutral* + *-ize*] *vt* **1 :** to make chemically neutral ⟨~ an acid with a base⟩ **:** destroy the peculiar properties or effect of ⟨stimulated the adrenals to secrete a hormone that *neutralized* rheumatism —G.W.Gray b.1886⟩ **2 :** to destroy the peculiar properties or opposite dispositions of **:** reduce to inefficiency **:** counteract the activity or effect of ⟨*neutralized* his effort by a show of force⟩ ⟨*neutralizing* these arguments with consummate skill⟩ **3 :** to make void of electricity or electrically inert by combining equal positive and negative quantities **4 :** to invest (as a country) with conventional or obligatory neutrality conferring inviolability under international law by belligerents **5 :** to reduce or destroy the combat effectiveness of (as an enemy force or an artillery installation) **6 :** to make (a color) neutral by blending with the complement **7 :** to make inoperative (a phonetic or grammatical contrast found elsewhere or formerly) ⟨with many speakers the \t\-\d\ opposition in *latter: ladder* is *neutralized*⟩ ~ *vi* **1 :** to prevent regeneration by inserting a device to balance signal feedback from the output to the input of an electronic device **2 :** to undergo neutralization

syn COUNTERACT, NEGATIVE: NEUTRALIZE indicates an equalizing, making ineffectual or inoperative, or nullifying by an opposing force, power, agency, or effect ⟨a quinine that can *neutralize* his venom; it is called courage —Elmer Davis⟩ ⟨*neutralize* the effects of propaganda with counterpropaganda so as to render the international environment favorable —Earl Latham⟩ ⟨our esteem for facts has not *neutralized* in us all religiousness —William James⟩ COUNTERACT may indicate merely neutralizing or counterbalancing; it is often used in situations in which the good and bad or the beneficial and deleterious are opposed ⟨these two principles have often sufficed, even when *counteracted* by great public calamities and by bad institutions, to carry civilization rapidly forward —T.B. Macaulay⟩ ⟨frequently visited the Choctaws, in an effort to *counteract* the influence of the French and to win them to an alliance with the English —W.J.Ghent⟩ NEGATIVE indicates an annulling, contradicting, making futile, useless, or ineffective, or vitiating by an opposing force, effect, or trend ⟨as if the wind might blow it over, thus *negativing* the idea of solidity —Arnold Bennett⟩ ⟨it is only in literature that the paradoxical and even mutually *negativing* anecdotes in the history of a human heart can be juxtaposed and annealed by art into verisimilitude and credibility —William Faulkner⟩

neu·tral·iz·er \-zə(r)\ *n* -s **:** one that neutralizes: as **a :** any of various devices that neutralize or eliminate some unwanted or side effect (as static from radio, excess acidity from a solution) **b :** a worker who neutralizes something (as a product of acid hydrolysis by suitable treatment with a base) as his regular work **c :** a worker who cleans metal objects in an acid bath **d :** a chemical solution used to terminate the action of a permanent waving solution **e :** ¹CLOCKER 3

neutral lard *n* **:** lard of high quality that is rendered at temperatures not exceeding 131° F from leaf fat or back fat of a hog and is used esp. in the manufacture of oleomargarine

neutral money *n* **:** money that functions in such a manner as to leave economic results unchanged from those of a barter economy

neutral monism *n* **:** a philosophical monism that takes primordial reality to be neither mind nor matter but something more fundamental than either of these

neutral oil *n* **1 :** an oil that is neither acid nor alkaline **2 :** a lubricating oil of low or medium viscosity (as prepared from paraffin-base petroleum without chemical treatment)

neutral orange *n* **:** BITTERSWEET ORANGE

neutral point *n* **:** the temperature at which the thermoelectric power of two metals is zero and which is midway between the temperature of the cold junction and the corresponding temperature of inversion

neutral position *n* **1** *or* **neutral line :** the position of the brushes of a dynamoelectric machine for least sparking **2 :** a position in amateur wrestling in which neither contestant has advantage over his opponent — compare ADVANTAGE POSITION

neutral red *n* **1** *sometimes cap N&R* **:** a basic phenazine dye used chiefly as a biological stain and acid-base indicator **2 :** a dark red to purplish red that is lighter and stronger than plum violet or sultana and paler than wild cherry

neutrals *pl of* NEUTRAL

neutral shoreline *n* **:** a shoreline the major features of which are not a result of either submergence or emergence of the adjacent land

neutral spirits *n pl but sing or pl in constr* **:** ethyl alcohol of 190 or higher proof used esp. for blending other alcoholic liquors — compare NEUTRAL BRANDY

neutral spore *n* **:** MONOSPORE

neutral stain *n* **:** NEUTRAL DYE 2

neutral tint *n* **1 :** a gray pigment of various shades used by artists **2 :** a color approximating to gray; *specif* **:** a nearly neutral slightly purplish black that is very slightly bluer and lighter than slate black or sooty black

neutral wire *n* **:** the wire in a three-wire distribution system usu. required to be grounded for safety of both linemen and householders

neutral zone *n* **1 :** the position on the armature of a direct-current machine where the magnetic flux from the field poles is zero, being midway between the poles at no load **2 a :** a space between the two lines of scrimmage in American football equivalent to the length of the ball that may not be encroached upon by either team until the ball is put in play **b :** the portion of an ice hockey rink between the attacking and defensive zones — see ICE HOCKEY illustration

neu·tret·to \n(y)ü·'tred·(,)ō\ *n* -s [*neutron* + It *-etto* (dim. suffix)] **:** a neutral meson

neu·tri·no \n(y)ü·'trē(,)nō\ *n* -s [It, fr. *neutrone* neutron (prob. fr. E *neutron*) + *-ino* (dim. suffix)] **:** an uncharged elementary particle that comes in two forms associated respectively with the electron and the muon, that is a lepton with one-half quantum unit of spin and is believed to be massless, and that interacts very weakly with matter after its creation in the process of particle decay

neutro- *comb form* [LL, fr. L *neutr-, neuter* of neuter gender — more at NEUTER] **1 :** neutral ⟨*neutro*phile⟩ ⟨*neutro*ceptor⟩ **2 :** neutrophil ⟨*neutro*penia⟩

neu·tro·cep·tor \¦n(y)ü·trō¦septə(r)\ *n* -s [*neutro-* + *receptor*] **:** a receptor for stimuli that are not necessarily either harmful or beneficial — compare NOCICEPTOR

neu·tro·clu·sion \¦==¦klüzhən\ *n* -s [*neutro-* + *occlusion*] **:** the condition in which the anteroposterior occlusal relations of the teeth are normal

neu·tro·cyte \'n(y)ü·trə,sīt\ *n* -s [*neutro-* + *-cyte*] **:** NEUTROPHIL — **neu·tro·cyt·ic** \¦==¦sid·ik\ *adj*

neu·tron \'n(y)ü,trän\ *n* -s [prob. fr. ¹*neutral* + *-on*] **:** an uncharged elementary particle that has a mass nearly equal to that of the proton, that by itself is unstable with an average lifetime of 1013 seconds, that can be stabilized when joined to a proton, and that is present in all known atomic nuclei except the lightest hydrogen nucleus

neu·tro·pe·nia \,n(y)ü·trə'pēnēə\ *n* -s [NL, fr. *neutro-* + *-penia*] **:** leukopenia in which the decrease in white blood cells is chiefly in neutrophils — **neu·tro·pe·nic** \¦==¦=nik\ *adj*

¹**neu·tro·phil** \'n(y)ü·trə,fil\ *or* **neu·tro·phil·ic** \¦==¦filik\ *also* **neu·tro·phile** \'==,fīl\ *adj* [*neutrophil, neutrophile*, ISV *neutro-* + *-phil* or *-phile* (adj. comb. forms); *neutrophilic*, ISV *neutrophil* + E *-ic*] **:** staining to the same degree with acid or basic dyes ⟨~ granulocytes⟩

²**neu·tro·phil** \-,fil\ *also* **neu·tro·phile** \-,fīl\ *n* -s [*neutrophil* or *neutrophile*, adj.] **:** a finely granular cell that is the chief phagocytic leukocyte of the blood

neu·tro·phil·ia \,==·'filēə\ *n* -s [NL, fr. ISV *neutrophil* + NL *-ia*] **:** leukocytosis in which the increase in white blood cells is chiefly in neutrophils

neu·tro·phil·ine \-'fi,lēn, -,lən\ *also* **neu·tro·phil·in** \-,lən\ *n* -s [*neutrophil* + *-ine* or *-in*] **:** a substance produced by the liver that is believed to stimulate the release of leukocytes from the bone marrow into the circulation

neu·troph·i·lous \n(y)ü·'träfələs\ *adj* [ISV *neutrophil* (adj.) + E *-ous*] **1 :** NEUTROPHIL **2 :** preferring or thriving in an environment without excess of either acid or base

neu·wi·der green \(')nȯi¦vēdə(r)-\ *n, often cap N* [part trans. of G *neuwieder grün*, fr. *neuwieder* of Neuwied (fr. *Neuwied*, Germany) + G *grün* green] **:** a light yellowish green to green

neu·wied blue \(')nȯi¦vēd-\ *n, often cap N* [fr. *Neuwied*, Germany; prob. trans. of G *neuwieder blau*] **:** BREMEN BLUE

ne·va·da \nə'vadə, -ädə, -ādə\ *adj, usu cap* [fr. *Nevada*, state in the western U.S., fr. Sierra *Nevada*, mountain range in Calif., fr. Sp, lit., snow-covered mountain range, fr. *sierra* mountain range + *nevada*, fem. of *nevado* snow-covered, prob. fr. L *nivatus* cooled with snow, fr. *niv-, nix* snow + *-atus* -ate — more at SNOW] **:** of or from the state of Nevada ⟨a *Nevada* mine⟩ **:** of the kind or style prevalent in Nevada **:** NEVADAN

nevada bluegrass *n, usu cap N* [*nevada* + *blue grass*] **:** a tall bluegrass (*Poa nevadensis*) of the Mohave desert and adjacent mountain slopes having a large panicle with appressed branches

¹**ne·va·dan** \nə'vadᵊn, -äd-, -ad-\ *also* **ne·va·di·an** \-dēən\ *adj, usu cap* [*Nevada* state + E *-an*] **1 :** of, relating to, or characteristic of Nevada or Nevadans **2 :** of or relating to a mountain-making movements of the American Mesozoic era — see GEOLOGIC TIME table

²**nevadan** \"\ *also* **nevadian** \"\ *n* -s *cap* **:** a native or resident of the state of Nevada

ne·va green \'nēvə-\ *n* [*neva* (origin unknown) + *green*] **:** a strong yellow green to brilliant yellowish green

ne·val \'nēvəl\ *adj* [NL *nevus* + E *-al*] **:** of or relating to a nevus ⟨~ cells⟩

nevar *var of* NEWAR

né·vé \(')nā¦vā\ *n* -s [F (Swiss dial.), fr. L *niv-, nix* snow] **:** the partially compacted granular snow that forms the surface part of the upper end of a glacier; *broadly* **:** a field of granular snow — called also *firn*

¹**nev·el** *also* **nev·ell** \'nevəl\ *vt* **nevelled; nevelled; nevelling; nevels** *also* **nevells** [perh. fr. obs. E *neve* fist (fr. ME) + E *-el* (as in *pommel*) — more at NIEVE] *chiefly Scot* **:** to beat with the fists

²**nevel** *var of* NEBEL

névé line *n* **:** a line or zone marking the lower limit of the névé on a glacier

nev·er \'nevə(r)\ *adv* [ME *never, nevere*, fr. OE *nǣfre*, fr. *ne* not, no + *ǣfre* ever — more at NO, EVER] **1 :** not ever **:** not at any time **:** at no time ⟨~ saw his equal⟩ — often used to form emphatic double negatives ⟨I ~ had no trouble with him before⟩ **2 :** not in any degree **:** not in the least **:** not in any way **:** not under any condition — used in emphatic negation ⟨~ fear⟩ ⟨he had ~ a cent⟩ ⟨~ the wiser for his experience⟩ ⟨answered him to ~ a word —Mt 27:14 (AV)⟩

neverland \'==,=\ *n* [short for *never-never land*] **:** NEVER-NEVER 1

nevermind \¦==¦=\ *n* [fr. the phrase *never mind*] **:** a serious affair **:** matter of concern **:** strict attention — used in negative constructions ⟨that's no ~ of theirs⟩ ⟨not paying nobody no ~ —Stetson Kennedy⟩

nevermore \¦==¦=\ *adv* [ME *nevermore, nevermor, nevermar*, fr. *never* + *more, mor, mar* more] **:** never again **:** at no time hereafter ⟨quoth the raven, "*Nevermore*" —E.A.Poe⟩

never-never \¦==¦==\ *n* -s [short for *never-never land*, prob. fr. redupl. of *never* + *land*] **1** *or* **never-never land** *also* **never-never country** *a Austral* **:** sparsely settled country in the northern and western part of Queensland **b :** a remote or sparsely settled region **:** a barren or frontier area **c :** an ideal or imaginary place or region ⟨that *never-never land* of true romance and pure love —Rollene W. Saal⟩ **2 :** an illusory existence **3** [redupl. of *never*] *Brit* **:** a system of installment purchase

never-say-die \¦==,=¦=\ *adj* [fr. the phrase *never say die*] **:** INDOMITABLE ⟨a *never-say-die* spirit⟩

never so *adv* [ME, fr. OE *nǣfre swā*, fr. *nǣfre* never + *swā* so — more at NEVER, SO] **:** to an exceptional or unheard-of degree or extent **:** ESPECIALLY, PARTICULARLY ⟨though he offered *never so* much money for our help⟩

nevertheless \¦===¦=\ *adv* [ME *never the lesse*, fr. *never* + *the* (adv.) + *lesse, less* less (adv.)] **:** in spite of that **:** NOTWITHSTANDING **:** YET

never-was \¦==¦=\ *n, pl* **never-weres** [fr. the phrase *never was*] **:** one that has attained no rank, success, or eminence

nev·ey *or* **nev·vy** \'nevē, -vi\ *dial var of* NEPHEW

ne·vile and win·ther's acid \'nävəl, 'vintə(r)z-\ *n, usu cap N&W* [after R.H.C. *Nevile*, 19th cent. chemist and Adolph *Winther*, 20th cent. Ger. chemist] **:** a crystalline phenolic sulfonic acid $HOC_{10}H_6SO_3H$ made by sulfonation of alpha-naphthol and used as a dye intermediate; 1-naphthol-4-sulfonic acid

ne·vo·carcinoma \¦nēvō+\ *n* [NL, fr. *nevo-* (fr. *nevus*) + *carcinoma*] **:** a carcinoma developing from a nevus

ne·void *also* **nae·void** \'nē,vȯid\ *adj* [NL *nevus* or L *naevus* + E *-oid*] **:** resembling a nevus ⟨a ~ tumor⟩ **:** accompanied by nevi or similar superficial lesions ⟨idiocy with ~ lesions⟩

nev·oy \'nevi\ *Scot var of* NEPHEW

ne·vus *also* **nae·vus** \'nēvəs\ *n, pl* **ne·vi** *also* **nae·vi** \-,vī\ [NL *nevus*, fr. L *naevus*] **:** a congenital pigmented area on the skin **:** BIRTHMARK, MOLE; *esp* **:** a tumor made up chiefly of blood vessels (as dilated arteries, veins, or capillaries) — see BLUE NEVUS

nev·yansk·ite \nev'yan(t),skīt\ *n* -s [G *newjanskit*, fr. *Newjansk* Nevyansk, U.S.S.R. + G *-it* -ite] **:** iridosmine containing over 40 percent of iridium and occurring in tin-white scales

¹**new** \'n(y)ü; *in geographical names, before a stressed syllable often* n(y)ə *(as in* n(y)ə'yȯ(ə)rk *for "New York") or* + *V* n(y)əw *(as in* nyə'wiŋglənd *for "New England")*\ *adj* **newer** \'n(y)üə(r); -ü(ə)r, -üə\ **newest** \-üəst\ [ME *new, newe*, fr. OE *nīwe, nēowe, niewe;* akin to MD *nieuwe, niewe, nūe* new, OS & OHG *niuwi*, ON *nȳr*, Goth *niujis*, OIr *nūe*, W *newydd*, L *novus*, Gk *neos*, Skt *nava, navya*, Lith *naujas*, OSlav *novŭ* and prob. to the root of E *now*] **1 :** having existed or having been made but a short time **:** having originated or occurred lately **:** not early or long in being **:** RECENT, FRESH, MODERN — opposed to *old* ⟨a ~ coat⟩ ⟨a ~ regime⟩ ⟨~ fashions⟩ **2 a :** having been seen or known but a short time although perhaps existing before **:** recently manifested, recognized, or experienced **:** NOVEL ⟨a ~ crop for this region⟩; *broadly* **:** STRANGE, UNFAMILIAR ⟨~ doctrines⟩ ⟨~ concepts⟩ ⟨liked to visit ~ places⟩ **b :** being other than the former or old **:** having freshly come into a relation (as use, connection, or function) ⟨turn a ~ leaf⟩ ⟨the ~ teacher⟩ ⟨a ~ product⟩ **c** *of land* **:** undergoing or about to undergo cultivation for the first time ⟨broke 10 acres of ~ ground that winter⟩ **d :** being the first or earliest available of the current season's crop ⟨~ potatoes⟩ ⟨~ peas are sometimes ready by July 4⟩ **3 :** having been in a relationship, position, or condition but a short time and usu. lacking full adaptation thereto ⟨a ~ member⟩ ⟨~ from school⟩ ⟨~ to the plow⟩ **4 a :** beginning or appearing as the recurrence, resumption, or repetition of a previous act or thing ⟨a ~ year⟩ ⟨a ~ start⟩ ⟨a ~ edition⟩ **b :** RENOVATED, RECREATED, REGENERATED ⟨rest had made him a ~ man⟩ **5 :** different or distinguished from a person, place, or thing of the same kind or name that has longer or previously existed ⟨the ~ reservoir⟩ ⟨the ~ theology⟩ **6 a :** not of ancient lineage **:** of a family previously unknown or undistinguished **:** having recently acquired an improved status (as of rank or wealth) ⟨a ~ family⟩ ⟨the ~ rich⟩ **b :** of dissimilar origin and usu. of superior quality to or capable of causing improvement in what preexists ⟨introducing ~ blood into an ancient but outworn line⟩ ⟨try a ~ strain of hybrid corn⟩ **7** *usu cap, of a language* **:** MODERN; *esp* **:** having been in use after medieval times

syn NEW, NOVEL, NEW-FASHIONED, NEWFANGLED, NEOTERIC, MODERN, MODERNISTIC, ORIGINAL, and FRESH can apply to something very recently come into existence, employment, or recognition. NEW implies that the thing was not known, thought of, manufactured, or experienced before its advent or has only recently been acquired, employed, put to use, and so on ⟨a *new* invention⟩ ⟨a *new* type of adding machine⟩ ⟨a *new* movie star⟩ ⟨a *new* experience⟩ ⟨a *new* pan⟩ ⟨a *new* baby⟩ ⟨a *new* president⟩ NOVEL applies to something that is not only new but also markedly out of the ordinary in its type of newness often to the point of seeming strange or startling ⟨built a *novel* fort of parallel log walls filled with earth —*Amer. Guide Series: Minn.*⟩ ⟨vacationists who like *novel* activities can sail to a remote part of the islands . . . for buried treasure —L.A. Werden⟩ ⟨the book was *novel* to the point of seeming bizarre —W.L.Sperry⟩ ⟨in a *novel* and highly photogenic setting —Rome's new, deluxe depot —Arthur Knight⟩ ⟨the experiment of appointing as a teacher of law one who had never practiced the profession was *novel* —Samuel Williston b.1861⟩ NEW-FASHIONED suggests a newness of form, style, or character that challenges curiosity or that has been only recently popularly accepted ⟨the type of old-fashioned scholarship . . . the type of *new-fashioned* criticism —S.E.Hyman⟩ ⟨the *new-fashioned* girl in light, comfortable clothes⟩ NEWFANGLED is disparaging in suggesting unnecessary or objectionable and usu. ingenious novelty ⟨its villages have avoided any incongruous *newfangled* type of building —S.P.B.Mais⟩ ⟨quite a modern hostelry for its time. It had such *newfangled* doodads as mechanical dishwashers and potato peelers —Green Peyton⟩ ⟨the empress Tzu Hsi, who again seized the reins of government and revoked all the *newfangled* regulations —Olga Lang⟩ MODERN and the now rare or literary NEOTERIC imply a belonging to the present time in a broad sense or to the present era, often suggesting up-to-dateness and sometimes novelty ⟨Pineville is even more *modern* in appearance, most of its residences having been rebuilt after a destructive cyclone in 1923 —*Amer. Guide Series: La.*⟩ ⟨telephone line, house, and highway, although giving the *modern* touch, are far from being truly up-to-date —G.R.Stewart⟩ ⟨pianoforte compositions. In these, Bach is more *modern* than Haydn, Mozart or even Beethoven —*Encyc. Americana*⟩ ⟨*modern* English dates from the 16th century⟩ ⟨the *modern* era in geology covers many thousands of years⟩ ⟨a girl anxious to be considered *modern*, not oldfashioned⟩ ⟨*neoteric* brass playing by a group of young men who are obviously fond of J. S. Bach —Wilder Hobson⟩ MODERNISTIC, sometimes interchangeable with MODERN, usually adds to MODERN a contemptuous suggestion of the ephemerally novel ⟨his adoption of many *modernistic* harmonic procedures makes his works tantalizing by the very incongruity of their essence and their idiom —Nicolas Slonimsky⟩ ⟨the jury . . . felt called upon to point out that Conway's work was "in no way *modernistic*, though distinctly modern" —*Time*⟩ ⟨when I refer to modern music, I do not mean necessarily "*modernistic*" music, much of which is a pale afterglow of the great and original modernism of yesteryear —Virgil Thomson⟩ ORIGINAL applies to what is or produces something new, novel, and the first of its kind ⟨the Aztec character was perfectly *original* and unique —W.H. Prescott⟩ ⟨the would-be *original* veers perilously towards the extravagant and the eccentric —J.L.Lowes⟩ ⟨an interesting and *original* mind that despised imitation⟩ FRESH in this connection applies to what is new and still retaining a first liveliness, energy, virginal quality, and so on ⟨a *fresh* and vital painting⟩ ⟨a lively and *fresh* active mind⟩ ⟨a *fresh* point of view upon an old problem⟩

²**new** \"\ *n* -s [ME *new, newe*, fr. OE *nīwe*, fr. *nīwe, nēowe, niewe*, adj.] **1 :** a new thing **:** something new ⟨the ~ ever supplants the old⟩; *esp* **:** the first phase ⟨in the ~ of the moon⟩ **2 :** FRESHNESS, NEWNESS ⟨wear the ~ off these shoes⟩

³**new** \"\ *adv* [ME *new, newe*, fr. OE *nīwe*, fr. *nīwe, nēowe, niewe*, adj.] **:** NEWLY, RECENTLY, ANEW, AFRESH ⟨grass ~ washed by rain⟩ — often used in combination ⟨*new*-mown⟩

ne·war *also* **ne·var** *or* **ni·war** \nə'wär\ *n, pl* **newar** *or* **newars** *usu cap* **:** one of the Mongoloid Nepalese

ne·wa·ri \nə'wärē\ *n* -s *usu cap* **:** the Tibeto-Burman language of the Newars

new·ark \'n(y)üə(r)k\ *adj, usu cap* [fr. *Newark*, N.J.] **:** of or from the city of Newark, N.J. ⟨the *Newark* parks⟩ **:** of the kind or style prevalent in Newark

newark charging system *n, usu cap N* **:** a system of charging library books in which when a book is lent the date of issue or the date due is stamped on the book card, on a plate in the book, and on the borrower's card and the borrower's name or number also is recorded on the book card which is filed until the book is returned and the return is recorded on the borrower's card

new·ark·er \-kə(r)\ *n* -s *cap* [*Newark*, N.J. + E *-er*] **:** a native or resident of Newark, N.J.

new art *n, usu cap N&A* [trans. of F *art nouveau*] **:** ART NOUVEAU

new bedford *adj, usu cap N&B* [fr. *New Bedford*, Mass.] **:** of or from the city of New Bedford, Mass. ⟨the *New Bedford* harbor⟩ **:** of the kind or style prevalent in New Bedford

new·bery·ite \'n(y)üb(ə)rē,īt, -,ber-\ *n* -s [G *newberyit*, fr. J. Cosmo *Newbery*, 19th cent. Australian mineralogist + G *-it* -ite] **:** a mineral $MgHPO_4.3H_2O$ consisting of an acid magnesium phosphate occurring as white orthorhombic crystals in guano

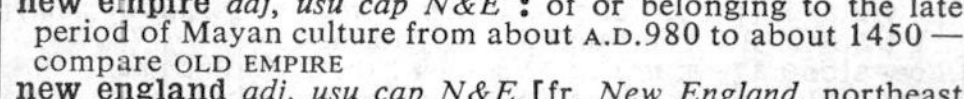

new birth *n* : REGENERATION 2

new blood *n* : an agent that is expected to convey vitality or superior qualities to or renew them in something (as a natural strain or an organization) ⟨as retirements provide openings for *new blood* in the directorate⟩

new blue *n* [prob. trans. of G *neublau*] **1** : any of several blue pigments: as **a** : cobalt blue containing chromium **b** : ULTRAMARINE 1b **c** : any of various iron blue pigments **2** : any of several blue dyes — see DYE table I (under *Basic Blue 6*) **3** : FRENCH BLUE

[1]**newborn** \ˈ=ˌ=\ *adj* [ME *new born*] **1 a** : recently born ⟨a ~ kitten⟩ **b** : affecting or relating to the newborn ⟨the ~ period⟩ ⟨~ disorders⟩ **2** : born anew ⟨~ and whole in spirit⟩

[2]**newborn** \"\ *n, pl* **newborn** *or* **newborns** : a newborn individual : NEONATE

new bronze *n* : a moderate brown that is yellower, lighter, and less strong than bay, yellower and slightly lighter than auburn, and lighter and slightly yellower and stronger than chestnut brown — called also *Brussels brown, cowboy*

new broom *n* [fr. the proverb "a *new broom* sweeps clean"] : a person recently established in a position of authority and vigorous in exercise of his duties

new bruns·wick \-ˈbrənz(ˌ)wik\ *adj, usu cap N&B* [fr. *New Brunswick*, province of Canada] : of or from the province of New Brunswick : of the kind or style prevalent in New Brunswick

new bruns·wick·er \-kə(r)\ *n* -s *cap N&B* [*New Brunswick*, province of Canada + E *-er*] **1** : a native or resident of New Brunswick province, Canada **2** [*New Brunswick*, N.J. + E *-er*] : a native or resident of New Brunswick, N.J.

new brunswick green *n, often cap B* : CHROME GREEN 1b

new·burg *or* **new·burgh** \ˈn(y)üˌbərg, -ōg, -əig\ *adj, usu cap* [prob. fr. (*lobster*) *newburg*] : made of cream, butter, sherry or Madeira, and yolks of eggs or dressed with a rich sauce ⟨a *Newburg* sauce⟩ — usu. used postpositively with the names of seafoods ⟨shrimp *Newburg*⟩

new·cal \ˈn(y)ükəl\ *or* **new·ca'd** \-kəd\ *adj* [[3]*new* + *cal* (short for *calved*) *or ca'd* (contr. of *calved*)] *chiefly Scot, of a cow* : newly calved

[1]**new caledonian** *adj, usu cap N&C* [*New Caledonia*, Fr. island and territory in the southwest Pacific + E *-an*] : of or from New Caledonia : of the kind or style prevalent in New Caledonia

[2]**new caledonian** *n, cap N&C* : a native or inhabitant of New Caledonia

new caledonian pine *n, usu cap N&C* : a very tall columnar araucaria (*Araucaria columnaris*) of New Caledonia and the New Hebrides that is often confused with Norfolk Island pine

new candle *n* : CANDLE 4b

[1]**new·cas·tle** \ˈ=ˌkasəl, -aas-,-ais-,-äs-; *the Brit places are locally often* =ˈ==\ *adj* **1** *or* **newcastle-upon-tyne** \-ˌ=ˌ=ˈtīn\ *usu cap N&T* [fr. *Newcastle* upon Tyne, England] : of or from Newcastle upon Tyne, England : of the kind or style prevalent in Newcastle upon Tyne **2** *or* **newcastle-under-lyme** \-ˌ==ˈlīm\ *usu cap N&L* : of or from Newcastle under Lyme, England : of the kind or style prevalent in Newcastle under Lyme **3** *usu cap* [fr. *Newcastle*, New So. Wales] : of or from Newcastle, New So. Wales : of the kind or style prevalent in Newcastle

[2]**newcastle** \"\ *n* -s *usu cap* [prob. fr. *Newcastle* upon Tyne, England] **1** : an old English round dance for eight participants **2** [by shortening] : NEWCASTLE DISEASE

newcastle disease *n, usu cap N* [fr. *Newcastle* upon Tyne] : a virus disease of domestic fowl and other birds resembling bronchitis or coryza but in later stages distinguished by nervous invasion leading to incoordination, tremors, and twitching of the head and being esp. destructive of young birds although all ages may be attacked — called also *avian pneumoencephalitis*; compare INFECTIOUS LARYNGOTRACHEITIS

newcastle thorn *n, usu cap N* [prob. fr. *Newcastle*, a name or place name] : COCKSPUR THORN

new christian *n, sometimes cap N & usu cap C* [prob. trans. of Sp *cristiano nuevo*] : MARRANO

new chum *n, chiefly Austral* : a recent immigrant esp. from the British Isles : NEWCOMER

new cocoa *n* : a grayish brown that is yellower and slightly lighter than chestnut and slightly yellower and lighter than coconut — called also *mahal, Natal brown*

new·comb \ˈn(y)ükəm\ *also* **newcomb ball** *n* -s *usu cap N* [prob. fr. the name *Newcomb*] : a game resembling volleyball in which a ball is thrown back and forth across a net by the opposing players by whom it has been caught

newcome \ˈ=ˌ=\ *adj* [ME *newcum, new-cumen*, fr. OE *nīwcumen*, fr. *nīwe*, adv., new + *cumen*, past part. of *cuman* to come — more at NEW, COME] : recently come

new·com·er \-mə(r)\ *n* : one that has recently arrived: as **a** : IMMIGRANT **b** : NOVICE 2 **c** : something that is advancing toward a position of greater prominence or eminence

new connexion *usu cap N&C* **1** : a former division of the General Baptists of England founded in 1770 **2** : a former division of British Methodists formed in 1797

new covenant *n* : a new promise of redemption by God to men as individuals rather than as a nation and on the basis of grace rather than law ⟨Christ is . . . the mediator of a *new covenant* —*Interpreter's Bible*⟩

new critic *n, usu cap N&C* : a practitioner of the New Criticism

new criticism *n, usu cap N&C* : an analytic literary criticism focusing intensively upon the language, imagery, and emotional or intellectual tensions in particular literary works (as poems) in an attempt to explain their total formal aesthetic organization — usu. used with *the*

new–cut \ˈ=ˌ=\ *n* [[1]*new* + *cut*, n.] : a card game played in England in the 16th and 17th centuries

new–day \ˈ=ˌ=\ *adj* [[1]*new* + *day*, n.] : current, modern, or stylish at the time in question : UP-TO-DATE ⟨*new-day* society⟩ ⟨various *new-day* conveyances⟩

new deal *n* [so called fr. the supposed resemblance to the situation of freshness and equality of opportunity provided by a fresh deal in a card game] : a fundamental reevaluation and reorganization (as of a government's duties and responsibilities) designed to have far-reaching and usu. liberalizing effects ⟨it would require a complete *new deal* to solve the problem⟩

new dealer *n* [*new deal* + *-er*] : a political liberal in government service : a proponent or supporter of a governmental new deal

new–deal·ish \ˈ=ˈ=lish\ *adj* [*new deal* + *-ish*] : suited to a new deal esp. in liberal or radical tendencies

new deal·ism \-ˌlizəm\ *n, pl* **new dealisms** [*new deal* + *-ism*] : political orientation based on the use of new deal techniques in government : advocacy of a governmental new deal

new delhi *adj, usu cap N&D* [fr. *New Delhi*, India] : of or from New Delhi, the capital of India : of the kind or style prevalent in New Delhi

new duck disease *n* : ANATIPESTIFER INFECTION

new dunker *n, usu cap N&D* : a member of the Church of God organized in 1848 and distinguished from other Dunker churches chiefly by insistence on a biblical name for the church

new egyptian *n, cap N&E* : the language of Egypt under the 18th to 21st dynasties

new·el \ˈn(y)üəl\ *n* -s [ME *nowell*, fr. MF *nouel, noiel* stone of a fruit, newel, fr. OF, stone of a fruit, fr. LL *nucalis* like a nut, fr. L *nuc-, nux* nut + *-alis* -al — more at NUT] **1** *or* **newel–post** \ˈ==ˌ=\ **a** : an upright post or the upright made of the inner or smaller ends of the steps about which the steps of a circular staircase wind **b** : the principal post at the foot of a stairway with straight flight or a secondary one at a landing — see HOLLOW NEWEL **2** : a cylindrical pillar terminating a wing wall of a bridge or viaduct

newel stair *n* : a stair with newels at the angles to receive the ends of the strings; *also* : a spiral stair in which the inner or smaller ends of the steps are engaged in a solid vertical core

new·el·ty \ˈn(y)üəltē, -ti\ *n* -ES [ME *newelte*, alter. (influenced by *new, newl* new) of *novelte* novelty — more at NEW, NOVELTY] *chiefly dial* : NOVELTY

newel 1b

new empire *adj, usu cap N&E* : of or belonging to the late period of Mayan culture from about A.D.980 to about 1450 — compare OLD EMPIRE

new england *adj, usu cap N&E* [fr. *New England*, northeast section of U.S.] : of or from New England : of the kind or style prevalent in New England

new england aster *n, usu cap N & E* : a common perennial aster (*Aster novae-angliae*) of eastern No. America having showy purplish flowers and being one of the parents of the Michaelmas daisies

new england boiled dinner *n, usu cap N&E* : BOILED DINNER

new england boxwood *n, usu cap N&E* : FLOWERING DOGWOOD

new england clam chowder *n, usu cap N&E* : clam chowder made of minced clams, salt pork, onions, potatoes, and milk — compare MANHATTAN CLAM CHOWDER

new england colonial *n, usu cap N&E* [*New England* + *colonial*, adj.] : architecture of or based on the style typical of colonial New England characterized by the saltbox house and the Cape Cod cottage

new englander *n, cap N&E* [*New England* + E *-er*] : a native or resident of New England

new england hemlock *n, usu cap N&E* : EASTERN HEMLOCK

new en·gland·ish \-dish — *see* [1]NEW\ *adj, usu cap N&E* [*New England* + E *-ish*] : like or like that of New England : typical or suggestive of New England

new en·gland·ism \-ˌdizəm\ *n, pl* **new englandisms** *usu cap N&E* [*New England* + E *-ism*] **1** : the traits, ideas, or attitudes distinctive of native New Englanders **2** : a locution or pronunciation characteristic of New England

new en·gland·ly *adv, usu cap N&E* [*New England* + E *-ly*] : in the manner of a New Englander ⟨thinks and acts *New Englandly*⟩

new england pine *n, usu cap N&E* : WHITE PINE 1a

new england short o *n, usu cap N&E* : a vowel short in duration, of a quality that varies from \ō\-like to \ȯ\-like to \ˈə\= like, and less and less used in New England in some or all of approximately 50 consonant-final monosyllables and their compounds and derivatives that in other dialects have the vowel of *no* (as in *coat, road, stone, whole, wholly*)

new england theology *n, usu cap N&E* : the modified Calvinism originated by Jonathan Edwards (1703–58)

[1]**new english** *adj, usu cap N&E* : of or relating to New England ⟨puritanism of *New English* life —Mervyn Jones-Evans⟩

[2]**new english** *n, cap N&E* : Modern English

newer *comparative of* NEW

newest *superlative of* NEW

[1]**new·fan·gle** \ˈn(y)üˈfaŋgəl, -aiŋ-\ *adj* [ME *newefangel*, fr. *newe* new + *-fangel* (fr. OE *fangen*, past part. of *fōn* to take, seize) — more at NEW, PACT] : NEWFANGLED

[2]**newfangle** \"\ *n* -s *archaic* : a newfangled thing

[3]**newfangle** \"\ *vt* -ED/-ING/-S *archaic* : to make newfangled ⟨not . . . to the scripture —John Milton⟩

new·fan·gled \-ld\ *adj* [ME *newe fangled*, fr. *newefangel* + *-ed*] **1** : attracted to new or novel things or modes ⟨not ~ enough to please the crowd⟩ **2** : newly made or of the newest fashion ⟨swore he'd never wear those ~ pajamas⟩ **syn** see NEW

new·fan·gled·ly *adv* : in a newfangled style or manner

new·fan·gled·ness *n* -ES : the quality or state of being newfangled

new·fan·gle·ment \=ˈ=gəlmənt\ *n* -s : a novelty or a newfangled thing ⟨tired of all these changes and ~*s*⟩

new–fashioned \ˈ=ˈ==\ *adj* [[3]*new* + *fashioned*, past part. of [2]*fashion*] **1** : made in a new fashion or form : lately come into fashion **2** : following the newest fashions : UP-TO-DATE **syn** see NEW

new·fie \ˈn(y)üfē, -fi\ *n* -s *usu cap* [by shortening and alter.] **1** : NEWFOUNDLANDER **2** : NEWFOUNDLAND 2

new fire ceremony *also* **new fire** *n* [*new fire ceremony* fr. *new fire* (fr. [1]*new* + *fire*) + *ceremony*] : a ceremony that recurs in many cultures, is symbolic of new life, the new year, or rebirth, and involves the extinguishing of all household fires and their rekindling on the hearths from a newly kindled ceremonial fire

newfish \ˈ=ˌ=\ *n, New South Wales* : AUSTRALIAN SALMON

new forest pony *n, usu cap N&F&P* [fr. *New Forest*, region of southern England] **1** : a British breed of hardy largeheaded ponies of the New Forest region of southern England 12 to 14 hands high with short neck, sturdy shoulders, and deep body that make excellent surefooted saddle ponies when trained **2** : a pony of the New Forest breed

newfound \ˈ=ˌ=\ *adj* [ME *newe founde*, fr. *newe*, new, adv., new + *founde*, past part. of *finden* to find — more at NEW, FIND] : newly found, uncovered, or made evident ⟨his ~ aggressiveness⟩

new foundation *n, usu cap N&F, Church of England* : the status of having been founded at the Reformation with a new organization — compare OLD FOUNDATION

[1]**new·found·land** \ˈn(y)üfən(d)lənd; ˈ==ˌland, -laa(ə)nd, ˌ==ˈ=; nyüˈfaun(d)land, n(y)əˈ-\ *adj, usu cap* [fr. *Newfoundland*, province of Canada] : of or from the province of Newfoundland : of the kind or style prevalent in Newfoundland

[2]**newfoundland** \"\ *n, usu cap* **1** : a breed of very large vigorous highly intelligent dogs that are believed to have been developed in Newfoundland during the 17th century by crossing dogs of European fishermen and possibly introducing some native blood, are vigorous swimmers, stand 26 to 28 inches high, weigh from 110 to 150 pounds, have a strong massive build with large broad head, decided stop, and squarish muzzle, and develop a coarse flat dense coat that is usu. black though black and white or bronze sometimes appear **2** *also* **newfoundland dog** -s : a dog of the Newfoundland breed

newfoundland caribou *n, usu cap N* : a large caribou (*Rangifer caribou terraenovae*) that is a variety of the woodland caribou confined to Newfoundland

new·found·land·er \-də(r)\ *n* -s *cap N* [*Newfoundland* + E *-er*] **1** : a native or resident of Newfoundland, Canada **2** : a Newfoundland boat

new franc *n* : the franc established as the French legal unit of value effective Jan. 1, 1960 — see MONEY table

new fuchsine *n, often cap N&F* : a dye closely related to fuchsine — see DYE table I (under *Basic Violet 2*)

new greek *n, cap N&G* : Greek as used by the Greeks for literature and for speech since the end of the medieval period — compare GREEK, LATE GREEK, MIDDLE GREEK

newground \ˈ=ˌ=\ *n, chiefly South & Midland* : a piece of land recently cleared and put under cultivation

newgrowth \ˈ=ˌ=\ *n* : NEOPLASM

new guinea *adj, usu cap N&G* [fr. *New Guinea*, island of eastern Malay Archipelago] : of or from the island of New Guinea : of the kind or style prevalent in New Guinea

new guinea butter bean *n, usu cap N&G* : SNAKE GOURD

[1]**new guinean** *adj, usu cap N&G* [*New Guinea*, island + E *-an*] **1** : of, relating to, or characteristic of the island of New Guinea **2** : of, relating to, or characteristic of the people of New Guinea

[2]**new guinean** *n, cap N&G* : a native or inhabitant of New Guinea

new guinea wood *or* **new guinea walnut** *n, usu cap N&G* : the light gray to brown wood of a tree (*Dracontomelum mangiferum*) of the family Anacardiaceae that is native to the southern Pacific islands, has black markings and a high figure, and is used esp. in veneers

[1]**new hampshire** *adj, usu cap N&H* [fr. *New Hampshire*, state in the northeastern U.S.] : of or from the state of New Hampshire ⟨a *New Hampshire* road⟩ : of the kind or style prevalent in New Hampshire

[2]**new hampshire** *also* **new hampshire red** *n, usu cap N&H&R* [*new hampshire* fr. *New Hampshire* state; *new hampshire red* fr. *new hampshire* + (*rhode island*) *red*] **1** : a breed of general purpose domestic fowls that were developed chiefly in New Hampshire by selection from Rhode Island Red, resemble members of the parent breed but are always single-combed, and are noted for rapid maturing and for heavy winter egg production **2** : a bird of the New Hampshire breed

new hamp·shire·man \-*pronunc at* HAMPSHIRE +mən\ *n, pl* **new hampshiremen** *cap* [*New Hampshire* + E *man*] : NEW HAMPSHIRITE

new hamp·shir·ite \-ˌīt\ *n, cap N&H* [*New Hampshire* + E *-ite*] : a native or resident of the state of New Hampshire

new ha·ven \-ˈhāvən\ *adj, usu cap N&H* [fr. *New Haven*, Conn.] : of or from the city of New Haven, Conn. ⟨*New Haven* schools⟩ : of the kind or style prevalent in New Haven

new ha·ven·er \-v(ə)nə(r)\ *n* -s *cap N&H* [*New Haven*, Conn. + E *-er*] : a native or resident of New Haven, Conn.

new haven theology *n, usu cap N&H* : TAYLORISM

new hebrew *n, cap N & H* : ISRAELI HEBREW

new humanism *n* [[1]*new* + *humanism*] : a 20th century doctrine marked by a belief in moderation, the dignity of the human will, a sense of permanent values, and a dualistic order of existence

new humanist *n* : one who advocates or accepts new humanism

new·ing \ˈnyüən, -üiŋ\ *n* -s [ME *neweinge* novelty, something new, fr. *newing*, gerund of *newen* to renew, fr. OE *nīwian*, fr. *nīwe, niewe*, adj., new — more at NEW] *dial chiefly Brit* : NEWS — usu. used in pl.

new·ish \ˈn(y)üish, -ēsh\ *adj* [[1]*new* + *-ish*] : rather new : not yet showing signs of use or wear

new israel *n, usu cap N&I* : the Christian fellowship of believers : the Christian Church

new jersey *adj, usu cap N&J* [fr. *New Jersey*, state in the eastern U.S.] : of or from the state of New Jersey ⟨*New Jersey* truck farms⟩ : of the kind or style prevalent in New Jersey

new jerseyite *n, cap N&J* [*New Jersey* + E *-ite*] : a native or resident of the state of New Jersey

new jersey pine *n, usu cap N&J* : JERSEY PINE

new jersey tea *n, usu cap N&J* [so called fr. its leaves having been used as a substitute for tea during the Am. Revolution] : a low deciduous shrub (*Ceanothus americanus*) of the eastern U.S. with ovate to ovate-oblong dull green leaves and with small white flowers borne in large terminal panicles in summer

new jerusalem *n, usu cap N&J* [fr. the phrase "the holy city, *New Jerusalem*" (Rev 21: 2); trans. of LL *Jerusalem nova*, trans. of Gk *Hierousalēm kainē*] : the abode of the redeemed

new je·ru·sa·lem·ite \-*pronunc at* JERUSALEM +ˌīt\ *n, pl* **new jerusalemites** *usu cap N&J* [*New Jerusalem* (*Church*) church holding the doctrines taught by Emanuel Swedenborg †1772 Swed. philosopher and religious writer (fr. *New Jerusalem* + *church*) + E *-ite*] : SWEDENBORGIAN

new latin *n, cap N&L* : Latin as used since the end of the medieval period; *esp* : Latin as used in scientific description and classification — compare LATE LATIN, LATIN, MEDIEVAL LATIN

new learning *n, usu cap N&L* **1** : learning of the 15th and 16th centuries based on the study of the Bible and the classics (as Greek) in the original **2** : the learning and doctrines of the English Reformation

new licht \ˈnyü,likt\ *n, usu cap N&L* [Sc, lit., new light] : a member of one of the parties in the Scottish Secession Churches both Burgher and Antiburgher that supported the principle of voluntarism in opposition to the Auld Lichts

new light *n, usu cap N&L* : a person who accepts new usu. more modern or more liberal religious views, doctrines, or methods: as **a** : a member of a group favoring revivalism and emotionalism in religion (as in Congregational, Presbyterian, and Baptist Churches) during and following the American revival movement of 1740–42 — compare OLD LIGHT **b** : NEW LICHT **c** : DISCIPLE 2

newlight \ˈ=ˌ=\ *n* [*new light*; fr. its association with [1]*campbellite*] : CRAPPIE

new·lins \ˈnyülənz\ *adv* [alter. of earlier *newlingis*, fr. ME, fr. *new* (adj.) + *-lingis, -linges* -lings] *archaic Scot* : NEWLY

new look *n* : the changed appearance or makeup of something into which radical innovations have been recently introduced ⟨this year's car has a *new look*⟩ ⟨the *new look* of current Broadway plays⟩ ⟨a military *new look* to suit world conditions⟩

new·ly \ˈn(y)ülē, -li\ *adv* [ME *newly, newliche*, fr. OE *nīwlīce*, fr. *nīwe*, adj., new + *-līce* -ly — more at NEW] **1** : LATELY, RECENTLY ⟨~ blossomed trees⟩ **2** : ANEW, AFRESH ⟨a ~ floored stable⟩ **3** : in a new way ⟨a house ~ furnished⟩ ⟨a thought ~ expressed⟩

newlywed \ˈ==ˌ=\ *n* -s [*newly* + *wed* (past part.)] : one recently married

new man *n* [fr. the phrase "put on the *new man*" (Eph 4: 24 —AV); trans. of LL *novus homo*, trans. of Gk *kainos anthrōpos*] : man as regenerated by religious conversion or experience

new·man·ism \ˈn(y)ümə,nizəm\ *n* -s *usu cap* [John Henry *Newman* †1890 Eng. theologian + E *-ism*] : the theological and ecclesiastical views taught by John Henry Newman while a member of the Church of England in which he argued that the language of the Thirty-nine Articles admits of a Catholic interpretation by distinguishing between the corruptions against which they were directed and the doctrines they did not oppose

new·man·ite \-ˌnīt\ *n* -s *usu cap* [John Henry *Newman* + E *-ite*] : a follower of John Henry Newman : an adherent of Newmanism

new·mar·ket \ˈn(y)ü,märkət, -mȧk-, *usu* -ȯd·+V\ *n* [fr. *Newmarket*, England] **1** *sometimes cap* : a long close-fitting coat worn in the 19th century **2** *usu cap* : a card game of English origin equivalent to the U.S. game of Michigan

[1]**new mexican** *adj, usu cap N&M* [*New Mexico* state + E *-an*] : of, relating to, or characteristic of New Mexico or New Mexicans

[2]**new mexican** *n, cap N&M* : a native or resident of the state of New Mexico

new mexican locust *n, usu cap N&M* : a thorny shrub or small tree (*Robinia mexicana*) of dry rocky uplands of the southwestern U.S. and adjacent Mexico that is an important browse plant

new mexican piñon *n, usu cap N&M* : a nut pine (*Pinus edulis*)

new mexico *adj, usu cap N&M* [fr. *New Mexico*, state in the southwestern U.S.] : of or from the state of New Mexico ⟨a *New Mexico* pueblo⟩ : of the kind or style prevalent in New Mexico : NEW MEXICAN

new–mint \ˈ=ˈ=\ *vt* [[3]*new*] : to coin anew; *specif* : to give a fresh meaning to (as a word or phrase)

new–model \ˈ=ˈ==\ *vt* [prob. fr. *New Model*, the English parliamentary army as reorganized in 1645] : REORGANIZE, REMODEL

new moon *n* [ME *newe mone, newe moone*, fr. OE *nīwe mōna*] **1 a** : the moon's phase when it is in conjunction with the sun so that its dark side is turned toward the earth — see MOON illustration **b** : the moon's dark appearance when at the new moon phase **c** : the position in the orbit when the moon is new **d** : the thin crescent moon seen in the western evening sky shortly after sunset for a few days after the actual occurrence of the new moon phase **2 a** : the day when the new moon is first seen **b** : ROSH HODESH

new negro *n, usu cap 2d N* : a Negro brought from Africa to the New World as a slave

new·ness *n* -ES [ME *newnes*, fr. OE *nīwnes*, fr. *nīwe*, adj., new + *-nes* -ness — more at NEW] : the quality or state of being new ⟨the ~ of this system⟩

new norse *n, cap both Ns* : LANDSMÅL

new order *n* : a reorganized and usu. fundamentally reoriented basis of action

new orleanian *n* -s *cap N&O* [*New Orleans*, La. + E *-an*] : ORLEANIAN

new or·leans \-ˈȯrlēənz, -lənz, -lyənz, -ˈō(ə)l-, *chiefly by outsiders* ˌ=ˈ=ˈlēnz\ *adj, usu cap N&O* [fr. *New Orleans*, La.] : of or from New Orleans ⟨the *New Orleans* Mardi Gras⟩ : of the kind or style prevalent in New Orleans

new orleans molasses *n* : a molasses that is comparatively light in color and rich in sugar

new philharmonic pitch *n* : a tuning standard of 435 to 439 vibrations per second for A above middle C adopted in Britain at the end of the 19th century to replace the old philharmonic pitch

new platonism *n, usu cap N&P* : NEOPLATONISM

new·port \ˈn(y)ü,pō(ə)rt, -ō(ə)r|, |, -ōə|, -ō(ə)|, *usu* |d·+V\ *adj, usu cap* **1** [*Newport*, Monmouthshire, England] : of or from the county borough of Newport, Monmouthshire, England : of the kind or style prevalent in Newport, Monmouthshire **2** [*Newport*, Isle of Wight, England] : of or from Newport, county seat of the Isle of Wight, England : of the kind or style prevalent in Newport, Isle of Wight **3** [*Newport*, R.I.] : of or from the city of Newport, Rhode Island : of the kind or style prevalent in Newport, Rhode Island

new realism *n* : a form of realism that was developed at the beginning of the 20th century in opposition to idealism, that emphasizes the distinction between the object and the act of sensation, and that holds the objective world to exist independently of the knowing mind and to be directly knowable — compare CRITICAL REALISM, MONISM

new realist *n* **:** an advocate of new realism

¹new–rich \ˈ≈,≈\ *n* [trans. of F *nouveau riche*] **:** NOUVEAU RICHE

²new–rich \"\ *adj* **1 :** recently become rich **2 :** typical of a new-rich person ⟨*new-rich* snobbery⟩

¹news \ˈn(y)üz\ *n pl but sing or pl in constr, often attrib* [ME *newes*, fr. pl. of *new, newe*, adj., new; prob. trans. of MF *nouvelles*] **1 :** a report of a recent event **:** new information **:** fresh tidings ⟨gave the bad ~⟩ ⟨wanted to tell her as quickly as he could his evil ~ —Pearl Buck⟩ **2 a :** what is reported in a newspaper, news periodical, or news broadcast **b :** matter that is interesting to newspaper readers or news broadcast audiences **:** matter that is suitable for news copy **3** [by shortening] **a :** NEWSBOARD **b :** NEWSPRINT **c :** NEWSPAPER **d :** NEWSCAST

²news \"\ *vb* -ED/-ING/-ES *vt* **:** to tell or repeat as news ⟨it is being ~*ed* about that the report is inaccurate⟩ ~ *vi* **:** to tell or repeat news **:** GOSSIP ⟨were ~*ing* over the teacups⟩

news agency *n* **1 :** the place of business of a newsagent **2 :** a commercial organization that collects and supplies news to subscribing newspapers, periodicals, and news broadcasters — compare PRESS ASSOCIATION

newsagent \ˈ≈,≈≈\ *n* [¹*news* + *agent*] **:** a dealer in newspapers and magazines

news analyst *n* **:** COMMENTATOR b

newsbeat \ˈ≈,≈\ *n* **:** BEAT 7 e

news bell *n, now dial Eng* **:** a singing in the ears supposed to portend news

newsboard \ˈ≈,≈\ *n* **1** *chiefly Brit* **:** a bulletin board for posting news **2 :** paperboard made chiefly from repulped newspapers

newsboat \ˈ≈,≈\ *n* **:** a boat that puts out to passing ships to supply and receive news

newsbook \ˈ≈,≈\ *n* **:** a publication popular in 17th century England consisting of one or two sheets folded octavo to make 8 or 16 pages and containing domestic news

newsboy \ˈ≈,≈\ *n* **:** a person that delivers or sells newspapers at retail **:** CARRIER 2e

newsbreak \ˈ≈,≈\ *n* **:** a newsworthy event

news case *n* **:** either of a pair of type cases one containing lowercase letters and the other uppercase letters

newscast \ˈ≈,≈\ *n* [¹*news* + *broadcast*] **:** a radio or television broadcast of news

news·cast·er \-tə(r)\ *n* -s [¹*news* + *broadcaster*] **:** a person engaged to broadcast news **:** COMMENTATOR

¹newscasting \ˈ≈,≈≈\ *n* [¹*news* + *broadcasting*] **:** the broadcasting of news

²newscasting \"\ *adj* **:** of or relating to the broadcasting of news

new school *n, usu cap N&S* **:** the more liberal of two parties into which the Presbyterian Church in the U.S. was divided about 1825, later organized as a separate church from 1838 to 1869 when a reunion was effected with the more conservative party

newsclip \ˈ≈,≈\ *n* **:** ⁴CLIP 2a

news conference *n* **:** PRESS CONFERENCE

news dealer *n* **:** a seller of newspapers and periodicals

news feature *n* **:** FEATURE 4b(1)

newsgirl \ˈ≈,≈\ *n* **:** a girl that sells or delivers newspapers to individual customers

newshawk \ˈ≈,≈\ *n* **:** NEWSHOUND

newshound \ˈ≈,≈\ *n* **:** a reporter for a newspaper, news periodical, or news agency

new side *adj, usu cap N&S* **:** of, relating to, or constituting a more liberal division among American Presbyterians resulting from a great religious awakening in the colonies beginning about 1734, favoring revivalism and employing its methods, and separating from Old Side Presbyterians in 1741 but reuniting with them in 1758

newsie *var of* NEWSY

newsier *comparative of* NEWSY

newsies *pl of* NEWSY

newsiest *superlative of* NEWSY

new silver *n* **:** a yellowish gray that is greener and less strong than sand and greener and duller than natural — compare OLD SILVER

news·i·ness \ˈn(y)üzēnəs, -zin-\ *n* -ES **:** the quality or state of being newsy

newsing *pres part of* NEWS

news·less \ˈn(y)üzləs\ *adj* **:** lacking news **:** not receiving or producing news — **news·less·ness** *n* -ES

newsletter \ˈ≈,≈≈\ *n* **1 :** a circular letter formerly written or printed for the dissemination of news **2 :** a printed sheet, pamphlet, or small newspaper containing news or information of current interest to or bearing upon the interests of a special group ⟨the Commerce Department is planning to begin publication in January of a semimonthly, four-page ~ containing all information stemming from the department which might be useful to small businessmen —*Newsweek*⟩

newsmagazine *n* **:** a periodical typically published weekly and devoted chiefly to summarizing and analyzing current news

news·man \ˈn(y)üzmən, -,man,-,maa(ə)n\ *n, pl* **newsmen 1** *archaic* **:** a bearer of news **2 :** one who gathers, reports, or comments on the news **:** REPORTER, CORRESPONDENT

newsmonger \ˈ≈,≈≈\ *n* **:** a gossipy person **:** one active in gathering and repeating news

new south wales *adj, usu cap N&S&W* [fr. *New South Wales*, Australia] **:** of or from the state of New South Wales, Australia **:** of the kind or style prevalent in New South Wales

¹news·pa·per \ˈn(y)üz,pāpə(r), -üs,pā-\ *n, often attrib* [¹*news* + *paper*] **1 :** a paper that is printed and distributed daily, weekly, or at some other regular and usu. short interval and that contains news, articles of opinion (as editorials), features, advertising, or other matter regarded as of current interest **2 :** an organization engaged in composing and issuing a newspaper **3 :** newsprint or the paper making up newspapers ⟨wrap the dirty shoes in ~⟩ ⟨sketching on unprinted ~⟩

²newspaper \"\ *vi* **:** to do newspaper work (as running a newspaper or reporting or editing news)

newspaperboy \ˈ≈,≈≈,≈\ *n* **:** NEWSBOY

news·pa·per·ish \-p(ə)rish\ *adj* **:** like or like that of a newspaper ⟨a brisk ~ style⟩

news·pa·per·man \-,man, -,aa(ə)n\ *n, pl* **newspapermen 1 a :** a person regularly employed as writer or editor on the editorial staff of a newspaper or news agency **b :** one who writes professionally for newspapers, news periodicals, or news agencies **2 :** one who owns or runs a newspaper or news agency

newspaper post *n* **:** the postal service of the British Post Office providing for special rates on newspapers that are registered as such with the General Post Office and that thus constitute a classification of mail corresponding to second class in the U.S.

newspaperwoman \ˈ≈,≈≈,≈≈\ *n, pl* **newspaperwomen :** a woman engaged in newspaper work

news·pa·po·ri·al \,n(y)üz,pā,pōrēəl, -üspə¦-, -¦pȯr-\ *adj* [irreg. (influenced by *-or*) fr. ¹*newspaper* + *-ial*] **:** of or relating to newspapers **:** suitable to a newspaper ⟨~ items⟩ ⟨~ labors⟩

newsprint \ˈ≈,≈\ *n* **:** cheap machine-finished paper made chiefly from groundwood with a little chemical pulp to give strength and used mostly for newspapers

new–sprung \ˈ≈¦≈\ *adj* [³*new* + *sprung*, past. part. of *spring*] **:** recently come into being

newsreader \ˈ≈,≈≈\ *n, Brit* **:** NEWSCASTER

newsreel \ˈ≈,≈\ *n* **:** a short motion-picture film portraying or dealing with current events

newsroom \ˈ≈,≈\ *n* **1 :** a room or place where newspapers or periodicals are sold **2 :** a reading room primarily devoted to newspapers and periodical literature **3 :** the office, offices, or portion of an office in which news is processed by a newspaper, news agency, or radio or television station

news service *n* **:** NEWS AGENCY 2

news·sheet \ˈn(y)üz(h),shēt, *usu* -ēd·+V\ *n* **:** NEWSPAPER, NEWSLETTER

news·stand \ˈ≈,≈\ *n* **:** a place (as a counter or an outdoor stall) where newspapers and periodicals are sold

news stick *n* **:** a composing stick permanently set to a fixed measure

new star *n* [prob. trans. of It *nuova stella* or NL *nova stella*] **1 :** NOVA **2 :** a star that is newly formed

new stone age *n, usu cap N&S&A* **:** the Neolithic age

new style *adj, usu cap N&S* **:** using or according to the Gregorian calendar — abbr. *N.S.*

new suit *n* **:** a suit when bid for the first time in the current auction of a bridge game

news vendor *n* **:** a seller of newspapers

newsweekly \ˈ≈,≈≈\ *n* **:** a periodical issued weekly and devoted primarily to current events of general interest or of interest to a special group ⟨the leading theatrical ~⟩

newsworthiness \ˈ≈,≈≈≈\ *n* **:** the quality or state of being newsworthy

newsworthy \ˈ≈,≈≈\ *adj* **:** sufficiently interesting to a general public to warrant reporting in the news

¹newsy \ˈn(y)üzē, -zi\ *adj* -ER/-EST [¹*news* + *-y* (adj. suffix)] **1 a :** filled with news ⟨a ~ letter⟩ **b :** given to gossip ⟨a ~ old aunt⟩ **2 :** likely to give rise to news **:** designed to attract attention — often used of styles in women's dress ⟨a ~ new cut about the shoulder⟩

²newsy *or* **news·ie** \"\ *n, pl* **newsies** [*news*boy + *-y* or *-ie* (dim. n. suffix)] **:** NEWSBOY

newt \ˈn(y)üt, *usu* -üd·+V\ *n* -s [ME *newte*, alter. (resulting from incorrect division of *an ewte*) of *ewte, evete* — more at EFT] **:** any of various small semiaquatic salamanders esp. of the genus *Triturus* **:** EFT, TRITON

newt

new·take \ˈnyü,tāk\ *n, Brit* **:** a field of moorland newly placed under cultivation

new testament *n, cap N&T* [ME *newe testament*, trans. of LL *novum testamentum* new testament, new covenant, trans. of Gk *kainē diathēkē* new covenant (2 Cor 3: 6)] **:** the covenant of God with man embodied in the coming of Christ and the teaching of Christ and his followers as set forth in the Bible — abbr. *N. T.*

new thought *n, cap N&T* **:** a mental healing movement embracing a number of small groups and organizations devoted generally to such ideas as spiritual healing, the creative power of constructive thinking, and personal guidance from an inner presence

new·ton \ˈn(y)üt³n\ *n* -s [after Sir Isaac *Newton* †1727 Eng. natural philosopher and mathematician] **:** the unit of force in the mks system of physical units that is of such size that under its influence a body whose mass is one kilogram would experience an acceleration of one meter per second per second ⟨one ~ equals 10^5 dynes⟩

¹new·to·ni·an \(ˈ)n(y)ü¦tōnēən\ *adj, usu cap* [Sir Isaac *Newton* + E *-an*] **:** of, relating to, or following Sir Isaac Newton, his discoveries, or doctrines

²newtonian \"\ *n* -s *usu cap* **1** *also* **new·ton·ist** \ˈn(y)üt³nəst\ **:** a follower of Sir Isaac Newton **2** [by shortening] **:** NEWTONIAN TELESCOPE

newtonian fluid *or* **newtonian liquid** *n, usu cap N* **:** a fluid whose viscosity does not change with rate of flow

newtonian force *n, usu cap N* **:** any of the forces that like gravitation are subject to the inverse-square law

new·to·ni·an·ism \n(y)üˈtōnēə,nizəm\ *n* -s *usu cap* [¹*newtonian* + *-ism*] **:** the doctrine of the universe as expounded in Newton's *Principia; esp* **:** Newton's mathematical theory of universal gravitation

newtonian mechanics *n pl but sing or pl in constr, usu cap N* **:** classical mechanics

newtonian physics *n pl but sing or pl in constr, usu cap N* **:** classical physics

newtonian potential *n, usu cap N* **:** a potential in a field of force obeying the inverse-square law; *esp* **:** GRAVITATIONAL POTENTIAL

newtonian telescope *n, usu cap N* **:** a reflecting telescope including a spherical or paraboloidal primary mirror and a flat reflecting surface (as of a mirror or prism) set at 45 degrees to the optical axis to reflect the light to a focus at the side of the telescope tube

newton's disk *n, usu cap N* [after Sir Isaac *Newton*] **:** a disk divided into sectors of proper relative dimensions bearing the different colors of the spectrum so that fusion of the colors by rotation gives a white or gray

newton's first law of motion *usu cap N* **:** LAW OF MOTION 1

newton's law of cooling *usu cap N* **:** a statement in physics: the rate at which an exposed body changes temperature through radiation is approximately proportional to the difference between its temperature and that of its surroundings

newton's rings *n pl, usu cap N* **:** colored rings due to light interference that are seen about the contact of a convex lens with a plane surface or of two lenses differing in curvature

newton's second law of motion *usu cap N* **:** LAW OF MOTION 2

newton's third law of motion *usu cap N* **:** LAW OF MOTION 3

new town *n, usu cap N&T* **:** any of several recent British urban developments that constitute small and essentially self-sufficient cities with accommodations for about 20,000 persons each and a planned ordering of residential, industrial, and commercial development

new wheat disease *or* **new wheat poisoning** *n* **:** BLUE COMB

new woman *n* **:** a woman esp. of the late 19th century actively resisting traditional controls and seeking to fill a complete role in the world

new world *n, usu cap N&W* **:** the western hemisphere; *esp* **:** the continental landmass of No. and So. America

new–world monkey *n* [*New World*] **:** a platyrrhine monkey

new world porcupine *n, usu cap N&W* **:** any of numerous more-or-less arboreal porcupines constituting a family (Erethizontidae) restricted to No. and So. America

new world vulture *n, usu cap N&W* **:** a bird of the family Cathartidae

new year *n* [ME *newe yere*] **1 a** *often cap N&Y* (1) **:** the calendar year following the current Gregorian year; *also* **:** the Gregorian calendar year just begun (2) **:** the year following the current year in any calendar **b** *usu cap N&Y* **:** NEW YEAR'S DAY; *also* **:** New Year's Day and succeeding days at the beginning of the new year **2** *usu cap N&Y* **:** the first day and traditionally also the second day of Tishri, the first month of the Jewish civil year — called also *Rosh Hashanah*

new–year \ˈ≈,≈\ *also* **new year's** *adj, often cap N&Y* [ME *newyere, new yeer, new yeres, newe yeers*, fr. *newe yere*, n.] **:** of, relating to, or suitable for the commencement of the year ⟨*new-year* resolutions⟩ ⟨a *new year's* party⟩

new year's day *or* **new year's** *n, usu cap N&Y&D* [*new year's day* fr. ME *new yeres day, newe yeersday; new year's*, short for *new year's day*] **:** the first day of the calendar year observed as a legal holiday in many countries (as the U.S., Canada, Scotland)

new year's eve *n, usu cap N&Y&E* [ME *newe yeres even*] **:** the eve of New Year's Day

new york \(ˈ)n(y)ü¦yȯ(ə)rk, -ȯ(ə)k *sometimes* nə'y-\ *adj* **1** *or* **new york city** *usu cap N&Y&C* [fr. *New York* or *New York City*, N. Y.] **:** of or from New York, N.Y. ⟨a *New York* skyscraper⟩ ⟨*New York City* police⟩ **:** of the kind or style prevalent in New York **2** *or* **new york state** *usu cap N&Y & often cap S* [fr. *New York, New York State*, middle Atlantic state of the U.S.] **:** of or from the state of New York ⟨*New York* freeways⟩ **:** of the kind or style prevalent in New York

new york aster *n, usu cap N&Y* **:** an erect perennial herb (*Aster novibelgii*) of northeastern No. America with slender lanceolate leaves and showy violet-rayed heads

new york cut *adj, usu cap N&Y, of beef sirloin* **:** cut with the hipbone included

new york dressed *adj, usu cap N&Y, of poultry* **:** killed, bled, and picked for marketing but with head, feet, and viscera intact — compare FULL-DRESSED

new york·er \n(y)ü¦yȯrkər, -ȯ(ə)kə(r *sometimes* nə'-\ *n, cap N&Y* [*New York* (city or state) + E *-er*] **:** a native or resident of the city or state of New York

new york·ese \,n(y)ü,yȯrˈkēz, -ēs\ *n, usu cap N&Y* [*New York City* + E *-ese*] **:** the speech or an item of the speech (as of vocabulary or pronunciation) characteristic of New York City

new york fern *n, usu cap N&Y* **:** a slender shield fern (*Dryopteris noveboracensis*) of moist woods in eastern No. America

new york point *n, usu cap N&Y* **:** an embossed system of writing for the blind that is now largely disused, is similar to braille but employs a cell two dots high and variable up to four dots in width arranged in accommodation to the frequency of letter occurrence, and provides for mathematical expression and a full musical notation

new york weasel *n, usu cap N&Y* **:** a common weasel (*Mustela frenata noveboracensis*) widely distributed in the eastern U.S. that is a variety of the No. American long-tailed weasel

new york weevil *n, usu cap N&Y* **:** PEACH WEEVIL

new–yorky \n(y)üˈyȯrkē\ *adj, usu cap N&Y* [*New York* (city or state) + E *-y* (adj. suffix)] **:** suggestive of or like that of New York ⟨*New-Yorky* sophistication⟩

¹new zea·land \(ˈ)n(y)ü¦zēlənd\ *adj, usu cap N&Z* [fr. *New Zealand*, Brit. dominion in the south Pacific ocean] **1 :** of or from New Zealand **:** of the kind or style prevalent in New Zealand **2 :** of, relating to, or being the biogeographic region or subregion of the Australian region that includes New Zealand and a few adjacent islands

²new zealand \"\ *n, usu cap N&Z* **1 :** an American breed of medium-sized white or reddish tan domestic rabbits **2** *pl* **new zealands :** an animal of the New Zealand breed

new zealand beech *n, usu cap N&Z* **:** any of several tall New Zealand trees of the genus *Nothofagus* some of which yield useful timber

new zealand birch *n, usu cap N&Z* **:** NEW ZEALAND BEECH

new zealand blue cod *n, usu cap N&Z* **:** smoked Australian freshwater catfish

new zealand bramble *n, usu cap N&Z* **:** a leafless prickly bramble (*Rubus australis*) of New Zealand that forms impenetrable thickets — called also *bush lawyer, wait-a-bit*

new zealand broom *n, usu cap N&Z* **:** a leguminous plant of the genus *Carmichaelia* (esp. *C. australis*)

new zealand bur *n, usu cap N&Z* **:** a creeping mat-forming New Zealand plant (*Acaena microphylla*) that is sometimes cultivated for its grayish to rosy bronze foliage and showy crimson spines

new zealand cotton *n, usu cap N&Z* **:** a fiber from the bast of the ribbon tree

new zea·land·er \-də(r)\ *n, cap N&Z* [*New Zealand* + E *-er*] **:** a native or inhabitant of New Zealand

new zealand flax *or* **new zealand hemp** *n, usu cap N&Z* **1 :** a tall New Zealand herb (*Phormium tenax*) having erect, sword-shaped leaves and scarlet or yellow flowers **2 :** the strong fiber from the leaves of New Zealand flax used chiefly for cordage, twine, and mattings

new zealand frog *n, usu cap N&Z* **:** a rare frog (*Liopelma hochstetteri*) peculiar to New Zealand and the only amphibian known from that region

new zealand honeysuckle *n, usu cap N&Z* **:** REWA-REWA

new zealand pepper tree *n, usu cap N&Z* **:** an aromatic and pungent evergreen tree (*Drimys axillaris*) with pinnate leaves and greenish flowers succeeded by red berrylike drupes

new zealand spinach *n, usu cap N&Z* **:** a coarse annual chiefly Australasian herb (*Tetragonia expansa*) of the family Aizoaceae used as a potherb

new zealand tea tree *n, usu cap N&Z* **:** a tea tree (*Leptospermum scoparium*) of New Zealand and Australia

new zealand white pine *n, usu cap N&Z* **:** KAHIKATEA

nex·al \ˈneksəl\ *adj* [L *nexum* + E *-al*] **:** of, relating to, or constituting the contract of nexum

¹next \ˈnekst, *before a consonant* " *or* ˈneks\ *adj* [ME *next, nexte*, fr. OE *nēhst, nīehst, nȳhst*, superl. of *nēah, nēh* nigh — more at NIGH] **1 :** being the nearest **:** having nothing similar intervening: as **a :** adjoining in a series **:** immediately preceding or following in order (as of place, rank, relation, or time) ⟨the ~ verse⟩ ⟨the ~ house⟩ ⟨is ~ in line⟩ ⟨the ~ day⟩ ⟨~ Monday⟩ **b :** following that approaching or in progress ⟨cannot go this Christmas, but I hope to go ~⟩ ⟨our ~ job will be clearing the land⟩ **c :** first in nearness without implication of succession or contiguity **:** first located, appearing, happening, or otherwise made relevant ⟨his ~ neighbor was five miles away⟩ **2** *archaic* **:** most pressing, convenient, ready, direct, or available **3** *slang* **a :** aware of what is happening or planned ⟨~ to their schemes⟩ **b :** INTIMATE, CLOSE ⟨planned to be ~ to her to learn the scandal when it broke⟩ **4** *of a suit in euchre* **:** of the same color as the exposed or otherwise indicated suit — **next·ness** *n* -ES

²next \"\ *adv* [ME *next, nest*, fr. OE *nīehst, nēhst, nȳhst* next, last, nearly, superl. of *nēah, nēh* near, nigh — more at NIGH] **1 :** in the time, place, or order nearest or immediately succeeding ⟨~ we drove home⟩ **:** in next order (as of place, rank, relation, or time) ⟨the ~ widest horizon he knew —C.S.Forester⟩ ⟨my ~ newest dress⟩ — compare NEAR **2 :** on the first occasion to come ⟨when ~ we meet⟩

³next \"\ *prep* [ME *nexte, nest*, fr. OE *nēahst, nēhst, nȳhst*, fr. *nīehst, nēhst, nȳhst*, adv.] **:** nearest or adjacent to (as in place or order) ⟨a mad dog . . . will fly upon and bite anyone that comes ~ him —Daniel Defoe⟩ ⟨one ~ himself in power —John Milton⟩

next best *n* **:** SECOND BEST

next friend *n* [trans. of AF *prochein ami*] **:** a person that is admitted to or appointed by a court as a special guardian to act for the benefit of an infant, a married woman, or any person not sui juris (as in a suit at law) **:** PROCHEIN AMI, GUARDIAN AD LITEM

next·ly *adv* **:** in the next place **:** so as to be or come next

next of kin *n, pl* **next of kin 1 :** a person in the nearest degree of relationship by blood to another person ⟨divided among children and other *next of kin* —G.B.Shaw⟩ **2 :** STATUTORY NEXT OF KIN **3 :** a person closely related to another person by blood, marriage, or court decision ⟨*next of kin* are being notified of his death⟩

¹next to *prep* [ME, fr. *next* (adj.) + *to*] **:** immediately following or adjacent to (as in space, time, or importance) ⟨*next to* the best flavor of all⟩ ⟨the top news *next to* the war⟩

²next to *adv* **:** very nearly **:** ALMOST, PRACTICALLY ⟨*next to* impossible to win⟩ ⟨had *next to* no food left⟩

next ways *adv* [irreg. (influenced by the *ways* in *a good ways, a great ways*) fr. the phrase obs. E *next way* nearest way] **:** by the shortest way or route **:** DIRECTLY

nex·um \ˈneksəm\ *n* -s [L, fr. neut. of *nexus*, past part. of *nectere* to bind] *Roman law* **:** a formal contract of loan with coin and balance in the presence of five witnesses under which the obligor could be seized and held in bondage for failure to perform

nex·us \ˈneksəs\ *n, pl* **nexuses** *or* **nexus** *see sense 4* [L, fr. *nexus*, past part. of *nectere* to bind — more at ANNEX] **1 :** CONNECTION, INTERCONNECTION, TIE, LINK **2 :** a connected group or series **3 :** a predicative relation or a construction consisting of grammatical elements either actually or felt as so related — compare JUNCTION, RANK **4** *pl* **nexi** \-k,sī\ [L, fr. *nexus* (past part.)] *Roman law* **:** a person bound by a contract of nexum

nez percé *or* **nez perce** \ˈnezˈpərs\ *n, pl* **nez percé** *or* **nez percés** *or* **nez perce** *or* **nez perces** *usu cap N&P* [F, lit., pierced nose] **1 a :** a Shahaptian people of central Idaho and adjacent parts of Washington and Oregon **b :** a member of such people **2 :** a language of the Nez Percé people

NF *abbr* **1** near face **2** no funds **3** nonferrous **4** nonfundable **5** not fordable

NFD *abbr, often not cap* no fixed date

NFS *abbr* not for sale

NG *abbr* **1** national guard **2** nitroglycerin **3** \(ˈ)en¦jē\ no good; not good

nga·dju \əŋˈgä(,)jü\ *also* **ngadju dayak** *n, pl* **ngadju** *or* **ngadjus** *also* **ngadju dayak** *or* **ngadju dayaks** *usu cap N&D* **1 a :** a Dayak people inhabiting the interior of Borneo **b :** a member of such people **2 :** the Austronesian language of the Ngadju people

ngai camphor \əŋˈgī-\ *n* [*ngai*, prob. native name in Borneo] **:** a camphor found in various essential oils (as the oil of the Asiatic woody shrub *Blumea balsamifera*); levorotatory borneol

ngaio \ˈnī(,)ō\ *n* -s [Maori] **:** a small tree (*Myoporum laetum*) of the New Zealand coast with edible fruit and light tough wood

nga·la \əŋˈgälə\ *n, pl* **ngala** *or* **ngalas** *usu cap* **1 a :** a Bantu people of French Equatorial Africa **b :** a member of such people **2 :** a Bantu language of the Ngala people **3 :** a trade language based on Ngala (sense 2) and widely used in the Belgian Congo

n'gana *var of* NAGANA

nga·na·sa·ni *also* **nga·na·sa·ne** \ŋ,gänə'sänē\ *n, pl* **nganasani** *or* **nganasanis** *also* **nganasane** *or* **nganasanes** *cap* **1 :** a Samoyed people inhabiting the Taimyr peninsula of Siberia **2 :** a member of the Nganasani people

ngan·dong man \əŋ'gän,dóŋ\ *n, usu cap N* [fr. *Ngandong*, fossil site near Trinil, south central Java] **:** SOLO MAN

ngba·ka \əŋ'bäkə\ *n, pl* **ngbaka** *or* **ngbakas** *usu cap* **1 a :** a people of the northwest Congo **b :** a member of such people **2 :** an Adamawa-Eastern language of the Ngbaka people

nge·ge \əŋ'gāgē\ *n, pl* **ngege** *or* **ngeges** [native name in East Africa] **:** an important African cichlid food fish (*Tilapia esculenta*) — compare TILAPIA

NGF *abbr* naval gunfire

ngo·ko \əŋ'gō(,)kō\ *n* -S *usu cap* **:** a dialect of Javanese used in speaking to inferiors

ngo·lok \əŋ'gō,läk\ *n, pl* **ngolok** *or* **ngoloks** *usu cap* **1 :** a nomadic Tibetan people **2 :** a member of the Ngolok people

ngo·ni \əŋ'gōnē\ *or* **ngu·ni** \-günē\ *n, pl* **ngoni** *or* **ngonis** *or* **nguni** *or* **ngunis** *usu cap* **1 a :** a prominent people of the region of Lake Nyasa in south central Africa **b :** a member of such people **2 a :** a group of closely related Bantu languages consisting of Zulu, Xhosa, and Swazi **b :** a dialect of Zulu more or less mixed with adjoining languages spoken in Nyasaland and Tanganyika

ngt *abbr* night

ngwa·na \əŋ'gwänə\ *n, pl* **ngwana** *or* **ngwanas** *usu cap* **:** KINGWANA

ngwa·to \əŋ'gwä(,)tō\ *n, pl* **ngwato** *or* **ngwatos** *usu cap* **:** a Bantu-speaking people of Bechuanaland in south central Africa

NH *abbr* **1** never hinged **2** nonhygroscopic

nham·bi·qua·ra *or* **nham·bi·cua·ra** \,nyambə'kwärə, nē,am-\ *usu cap, var of* NAMBICUARA

nhang \'nyaŋ, nē'aŋ\ *n, pl* **nhang** *or* **nhangs** *usu cap* **:** GIAI

NHP *abbr, often not cap* nominal horsepower

ni *abbr* night

NI *abbr* naval intelligence

Ni *symbol* nickel

ni·a·cin \'nīəsən\ *n* -S [*ni*cotinic *a*cid + *-in*] **:** NICOTINIC ACID

ni·a·cin·a·mide \,nīə'sinə,mīd\ *n* [*niacin* + *amide*] **:** NICOTINAMIDE

ni·ag·a·ra \nī'ag(ə)rə, -aig-, *attributively* (')=¦=(=)=\ *n* -S *often cap* [fr. *Niagara* Falls waterfall of the Niagara river between Ontario, Canada and New York State] **:** an overwhelming flood **:** TORRENT ⟨a ~ of curses⟩ ⟨a ~ of cheap fiction⟩

niagara green *n, often cap N* [fr. *Niagara* Falls *or Niagara* river] **:** a light bluish green that is greener and duller than average aqua green (sense 1), greener and paler than average turquoise green, and greener and stronger than robin's-egg blue (sense 2)

ni·ag·a·ran \-rən\ *adj, usu cap* [*Niagara* River + E *-an*] **:** of or relating to a division of the American Silurian — see GEOLOGIC TIME table

nia·mey \nē'ä(,)mā, ¦nē(,)ä¦mā\ *adj, usu cap* [fr. *Niamey*, Niger Republic] **:** of or relating to Niamey, capital of the Niger Republic **:** of the kind or style prevalent in Niamey

ni·aou·li \nē'aùlē\ *n* -S [native name in New Caledonia] **:** a small irregular evergreen tree (*Melaleuca viridiflora*) of the southwestern Pacific islands that is closely related to the Indian cajeput and similarly used

ni·as \'nē,äs\ *n* -ES *usu cap* **:** the Austronesian language of the Niasese people

ni·a·sese \¦nēə¦sēz, -ēs\ *n, pl* **niasese** *usu cap* [*Nias*, island in the Indian ocean + E *-ese*] **1 :** a people inhabiting the island of Nias west of Sumatra **2 :** a member of the Niasese people

ni·as·san \'nēəsən\ *n* -S *cap* [*Nias*, island in the Indian ocean, west of Sumatra + E *-an*] **:** an Indonesian native or inhabitant of Nias and adjacent islands

¹nib \'nib\ *n* -S [prob. alter. of *neb*] **1 :** BILL, BEAK, NEB **2 a :** the sharpened point of a quill pen **b :** each of the two divisions of a pen point **c :** a pen point (as of gold or steel) intended for insertion into a holder **3 :** a small pointed or projecting part: as **a :** the scorer of an auger bit **b :** the tip of a caliper or a scriber **c :** a sharp tip (as a diamond) on a cutting tool **d :** a small lug (as on a roofing tile) **e :** the tongue of a buckle **f :** TOOTH 3e **4** *dial Eng* **a :** one of the handles which project from a scythe snath **b :** one of the shafts on the pole of a wagon **5 a :** a cacao seed with germ removed **b :** COFFEE BEAN **6 a :** a tiny knot or lump (as in raw silk or wool or in a woven or knitted fabric) **b :** a small lump or particle in a film (as of paint or varnish) **c :** irregularly twisted or lumpy leaves of oolong tea

²nib \"\ *vt* **nibbed; nibbed; nibbing; nibs :** to furnish with a nib; *esp* **:** to mend the point of (a pen)

³nib \"\ *vb* [prob. by shortening] *dial chiefly Eng* **:** NIBBLE

nibbana *usu cap, var of* NIRVANA

nib·ber \'nibə(r)\ *n* -S [¹*nib* & ²*nib* + *-er*] **1 :** one that nibs; *esp* **:** one who puts nibs on buckles **2 :** a worker who cuts nibs from hosiery **3 :** a machine for crushing cacao beans; *also* **:** its operator

¹nib·ble \'nibəl\ *vb* **nibbled; nibbled; nibbling** \-b(ə)liŋ\ **nibbles** [origin unknown] *vt* **1 :** to bite lightly or gently **:** eat in small bits ⟨leaves had been *nibbled* away by deer⟩ **2 :** to take away or conserve bit by bit **3 a :** to trim or shape (glass) by breaking off small bits **b :** to cut (as metal) with a nibbling machine ~ *vi* **1 a :** to take gentle or cautious bites ⟨a cracker to ~ on⟩ ⟨fish *nibbled* at the bait⟩ **b :** to make small attempts **:** deal with or attack something cautiously or timidly — used with *at* ⟨legislation was *nibbling* away at the worst abominations of . . . housing —F.L.Allen⟩ **2 :** to make petty criticisms **:** CARP — used with *at*

²nibble \"\ *n* -S **1 :** an act of nibbling **:** a small or cautious bite or an attempt to take such a bite **2 :** a bit (as of food) such as might be taken in a small bite **:** a trifling quantity

³nibble \"\ *chiefly dial var of* NIPPLE

nib·bler \-b(ə)lə(r)\ *n* -S **:** one that nibbles: as **a :** CUNNER **b** *also* **nibbling machine :** a machine for cutting sheets or plates of metal by punching a succession of overlapping holes along the desired contour

¹nib·by \'nibē, -bi\ *n* -ES [¹*nib* + *-y*] *chiefly Scot* **:** a hooked staff such as is used by a shepherd

²nibby \"\ *adj* -ER/-EST [¹*nib* + *-y*] *dial* **:** INQUISITIVE, NOSY

nib·lick *also* **nib·lic** \'niblik, -lēk\ *n* -S [origin unknown] **:** an iron golf club with a wide deeply slanted face used for short shots out of sand or long grass or for shots where quick loft and little roll is desired — called also *number nine iron;* see IRON illustration

ni·bong \'nē,bóŋ\ *or* **ni·bung** \-bəŋ\ *n* -S [Malay] **:** a Malay feather palm (*Oncosperma fasciculata*)

nibs \'nibz\ *n pl but sing or pl in constr* [perh. alter. of *nabs*] **:** a person of importance or authority **:** CHIEF, BOSS — used chiefly in *his nibs* as if a title of honor

¹ni·cae·an \(')nī¦sēən\ *adj, usu cap* [*Nicaea*, ancient city, Asia Minor (fr. L) + E *-an* — more at NICENE] **:** NICENE

²nicaean \"\ *n* -S **1** *cap* **:** a native or inhabitant of Nicaea **2** *usu cap* **:** a 4th or 5th century adherent of the Nicene Creed

nic·a·ra·gua \¦nikə¦rägwə, -rág- *sometimes* -gyəwə, *chiefly Brit* -rag-\ *adj, usu cap* [fr. *Nicaragua*, republic, Central America] **:** of or from Nicaragua **:** of the kind or style prevalent in Nicaragua **:** NICARAGUAN ⟨Nicaragua coffee⟩

¹nic·a·ra·guan \-gwən, -gyəw-\ *adj, usu cap* [*Nicaragua*, republic, Central America + E *-an*] **:** of or relating to Nicaragua or its inhabitants

²nicaraguan \"\ *n* -S *cap* **:** a native or resident of Nicaragua

nicaragua wood *n, usu cap N* **:** BRAZILETTE

nic·a·rao \¦nikə¦raù\ *n, pl* **nicarao** *or* **nicaraos** *usu cap* [prob. fr. AmerSp] **1 :** a Uto-Aztecan people of southwestern Nicaragua **2 :** a member of the Nicarao people

nic·colic \'nikə(,)lik; ni'kälik, -kōl-\ *or* **nic·co·lous** \'nikələs\ *adj* [NL *niccolum* nickel + E *-ic, -ous*] **:** composed of or containing nickel

nic·co·lite \'nikə,līt\ *n* -S [NL *niccolum* nickel (prob. fr. Sw *nickel*) + E *-ite* — more at NICKEL] **:** a mineral NiAs of a pale copper red color and metallic luster usu. occurring massive and composed essentially of a nickel arsenide (hardness 5–5.5, sp. gr. 7.33–7.67)

niccolo *var of* NICOLO

¹nice \'nīs\ *adj* -ER/-EST [ME, foolish, wanton, fr. OF, simpleminded, stupid, fr. L *nescius* ignorant, not knowing, fr. *nescire* not to know — more at NESCIENCE] **1** *obs* **a :** LEWD, WANTON, DISSOLUTE **b :** COY, MODEST, DIFFIDENT, RETICENT **2 a :** showing fastidious, particular, or finical tastes ⟨too ~ about his food to like camp cooking⟩ ⟨an animal ~ about its diet⟩ **b :** satisfying a dainty palate **:** pleasing delicate tastes ⟨the ~ dishes at the banquet⟩ **3 :** marked by refinement and culture, refined tastes, or wise discrimination ⟨the popular ear, none too ~ to distinguish between sense and fustian —V.L.Parrington⟩ **4 :** showing, marked by, or requiring meticulous choice, tactful handling, careful consideration, or precise and scrupulous conduct ⟨a diplomatic mission requiring ~ judgment⟩ ⟨the highest standards which a man of . . . the *nicest* sense of honor might impose —B.N.Cardozo⟩ **5 :** requiring, marked by, or capable of delicate discrimination, precision, closely accurate measurement, subtle analysis, or minute treatment ⟨the balance was ~ enough . . . to make both parties appeal for popular support —G.G.Coulton⟩ ⟨a ~ question of ethics⟩ ⟨~ measurements with a micrometer⟩ **6** *obs* **a :** lacking vigor, strength, or endurance **b :** lacking significance **:** TRIVIAL ⟨the letter was not ~ but full of charge —Shak.⟩ **7 :** pleasant and satisfying: as **a :** COMPLAISANT, AFFABLE, AGREEABLE, CONSIDERATE ⟨the duty of being ~ to one's mother-in-law —F.D.Roosevelt⟩ ⟨what a ~ fellow you are, and we all thought you so nasty —George Meredith⟩ **b :** ENJOYABLE, ATTRACTIVE, PLEASING, DELIGHTFUL ⟨a ~ time at the party⟩ ⟨~ and warm by the fire⟩ ⟨we have four ~ bedrooms upstairs to make them comfortable —Willa Cather⟩ **c :** very good **:** well-executed **:** well-conducted **:** OUTSTANDING ⟨a ~ bit of satire⟩ ⟨a ~ shot bringing down the bird⟩ **d :** well-intentioned **:** BENIGN ⟨~ people support charities⟩ **e :** MILD, CLEMENT, PLEASING ⟨the ~ weather of late spring⟩ ⟨the ~ old days of the the past⟩ **f :** well or appropriately dressed **:** NEAT, PERSONABLE, COMELY ⟨always a ~ dresser⟩ ⟨a *nice*-looking American businessman with a quiet calm manner and a friendly face —Dorothy C. Fisher⟩ **g :** FITTING, APPROPRIATE, SUITABLE ⟨the ~ clothes she wears⟩ ⟨not a ~ word for use in church⟩ **h —** used with *and* as an intensive ⟨blankets are ~ and dry⟩ ⟨this soup is ~ and hot⟩ **8 :** most inappropriate **:** UNPLEASANT, UNATTRACTIVE **:** MEAN, TREACHEROUS — used ironically ⟨a chronic alcoholic is certainly a ~ one to talk about temperance⟩ ⟨a ~ friend, who would have me . . . cover myself with eternal infamy —J.A.Froude⟩ ⟨got himself in a ~ fix⟩ **9 :** marked by conformity to convention: as **a :** given to accustomed practices **:** established in conventional normal ways of life **:** not unusual, bizarre, wild, morbid, wayward ⟨unpopular with the *nicer* people of the town⟩ **b :** not marked by sexual license **:** VIRTUOUS, CHASTE **c :** not profane, indecent, or obscene **:** PROPER

syn DAINTY, FASTIDIOUS, FINICAL, PARTICULAR, FUSSY, SQUEAMISH, PERNICKETY: NICE implies fine discrimination in perception and evaluation ⟨a *nice* taste in literature —Compton Mackenzie⟩ NICE may indicate a tender or squeamish disinclination to countenance the questionable or raw ⟨boycotted by the respectables, who were too *nice* to accept socially those whose business they tolerated —W.A.White⟩ DAINTY may describe a tendency to pick and choose with delicate sensibility and, sometimes, to reject disdainfully ⟨*dainty* feeders who expect perfection —A.W.Long⟩ ⟨the tough jargon of the East Side no less than the *dainty* discourse of the Four Hundred —C.H.Grandgent⟩ FASTIDIOUS implies a meticulously careful judgment, often with disdainful rejection of what does not meet with very high standards occas. set capriciously ⟨a *fastidious* critic both of the written and the spoken word, hating anything which savored of the fantastic or the turgid —John Buchan⟩ ⟨the *fastidious* author could never satisfy himself, and the result is a production more remarkable for high polish than warmth of poetic feeling —Richard Garnett †1906⟩ ⟨the *fastidious* lady whom it was most difficult to please —L.P.Smith⟩ FINICAL describes an affected, capricious fastidiousness that sometimes seems composed partly of a determination to be displeased or dissatisfied ⟨I am possibly a trifle overscrupulous about the conventions, but you must contrive to forgive a *finical* old friend —Elinor Wylie⟩ PARTICULAR may indicate a demand that all details satisfy an exacting standard ⟨every year it used to get a nice coat of paint —Papa was very *particular* about the paint —Lillian Hellman⟩ ⟨they wear gloves, hats and stockings, and are usually *particular* about grooming because they were brought up in the stricter times —Agnes M. Miall⟩ FUSSY may blend the suggestions of FINICAL and PARTICULAR with a hint of querulousness ⟨a busy, *fussy* sort of man, much concerned with regulating everything —A.M.Young⟩ ⟨so *fussy* about the punctilious observance of orders that almost any brakeman would take a chance once in a while, from natural perversity —Willa Cather⟩ SQUEAMISH describes a sensitive or prudish readiness to be nauseated, disgusted, or antagonized by whatever does not satisfy one's delicate standards or preferences ⟨his conditioning had made him not so much pitiful as profoundly *squeamish*. The mere suggestion of illness or wounds was to him not only horrifying, but even repulsive and rather disgusting —Aldous Huxley⟩ ⟨not *squeamish* about the soft fleshy mud creeping round his ankles, or about the things which slid from under his feet —Audrey Barker⟩ PERNICKETY is deprecatory in indicating exasperating crusty fussiness ⟨the grammarian, the purist, the *pernickety* stickler for trifles —Brander Matthews⟩ **syn** see in addition CORRECT, DECOROUS

²nice \"\ *adv* **:** NICELY

³nice \'nēs\ *adj, usu cap* [fr. *Nice*, seaport of France] **:** of or from the city of Nice, France **:** of the kind or style prevalent in Nice

nice·ish \'nīsish\ *adj* [¹*nice* + *-ish*] **:** fairly nice **:** rather pleasant or agreeable ⟨seemed to be ~ people⟩ ⟨~ income⟩

nice·ling \'nīsliŋ\ *n* -S [¹*nice* + *-ling*] **1 :** an overfastidious person **2 :** one who makes fine distinctions

¹nice·ly \'nīslē, -li\ *adv* [ME, foolishly, fr. *nice* (adj.) + *-ly*] **1 :** PRECISELY ⟨~ calculated stroke⟩ **2 :** SCRUPULOUSLY **3 :** SATISFACTORILY, AGREEABLY, PLEASANTLY

²nicely \"\ *adj, chiefly dial* **:** being in good health **:** WELL

ni·cene \'nī,sēn, =¦=\ *adj, usu cap* [ME, fr. LL *Nicenus*, *Nicaenus*, fr. L *Nicea*, *Nicaea* Nicaea, fr. Gk *Nikaia*] **1 :** of or relating to Nicaea or Nice, an ancient city of Asia Minor **2 :** of or relating to a confession of Christian faith formulated and decreed by the First Council of Nicaea in A.D. 325 in opposition to Arianism and reaffirmed by the First Council of Constantinople in A.D. 381 or to one of the later forms of this confession

nice nelly *or* **nice nellie** \'=¦nelē\ *n, usu cap 2d N* [prob. fr. ¹*nice* + *Nelly, Nellie*, the name] **1 :** PRUDE ⟨I'm no *nice Nelly* —Ethel Merman⟩ **2 :** a euphemistic term or expression

nice-nelly *or* **nice-nellie** \'=¦==\ *adj, often cap 2d N* [*nice Nelly* or *nice Nellie*] **:** overly delicate **:** PRUDISH, EUPHEMISTIC ⟨*nice-nelly* . . . terms for the sexual and excretory functions —George Devereux⟩

nice-nel·ly·ism \(')nī¦snelē,izəm\ *n* -S *often cap 2d N* **1 :** PRUDERY, PRUDISHNESS **2 :** EUPHEMISM

nice·ness \'nīsnəs\ *n* -ES **:** the quality or state of being nice ⟨scrutinize his conduct with a ~ —J.A.Froude⟩ ⟨revolt against formal and philistine ~ —Max Eastman⟩

ni·ce·ni·an \nī'sēnēən\ *also* **ni·cen·ist** \'nī,sēnəst, =¦==\ *n* -S *usu cap* [*Nicene* + *-ian* or *-ist*] **:** NICAEAN 2

niceno- *comb form, usu cap* [*Nicene*] **:** Nicene and ⟨*Niceno*-Constantinopolitan⟩

nicer *comparative of* NICE

nicest *superlative of* NICE

ni·ce·ty \'nīsəd·ē, -ətē, -i\ *n* -ES [ME *nicete* (also, foolishness), fr. MF *niceté* foolishness, fr. *nice* (adj.) + *-té* -ty] **1 :** the quality or state of being nice **:** NICENESS **2 :** a dainty, delicate, or elegant thing or feature ⟨enjoy the *niceties* of civilized life⟩ **3 :** an expression, act, mode of treatment, distinction involving delicacy or subtlety **:** a minute distinction, point, or detail ⟨*niceties* of workmanship⟩ ⟨~ of a problem⟩ **4 :** delicacy or exactness of perception or discrimination **:** PRECISION, ACCURACY ⟨depicted the scene with the greatest ~⟩ ⟨the ~ of a trained eye and hand⟩ **5 :** the quality of demanding delicacy and accuracy of treatment ⟨a question of great ~⟩ **6 a :** delicacy of taste or feeling **:** FASTIDIOUSNESS **b :** excessive fastidiousness **:** SQUEAMISHNESS, PRUDISHNESS **— to a nicety** *adv* **:** PRECISELY, ACCURATELY

¹niche \'nich *sometimes* 'nish *or* 'nēsh\ *n* -S [F, fr. MF, fr. *nicher* to nest, fr. OF *nichier*, fr. (assumed) VL *nidicare*, fr. L *nidus* nest — more at NEST] **1 :** a recess in a wall: as **a :** a hollowed space in a wall made esp. for a statue, bust, or other ornament **b :** a vaulted passage or alcove made usu. within the thickness of a wall **c :** a space provided at the side of a roadway (as of a tunnel, bridge, highway) for emergency use **2 :** a covert or retreat resembling a niche in its formation or privacy **3 :** a place, condition of life or employment, or position suitable for the capabilities or merits of a person or qualities of a thing ⟨his poetry fills a ~ of its own⟩ **4 :** CRATER 1d **5 a :** the sum of the physical and biotic life-controlling factors (as climate, food sources, water supply, enemies); *also* **:** a site or habitat supplying these factors characteristically necessary for the successful existence of an organism or species in a given habitat **b :** the role of an organism in an ecological community involving esp. its way of life and its effect on the environment (as through its relations to other biotic factors and to abiotic factors) **c :** MICROHABITAT — not used technically

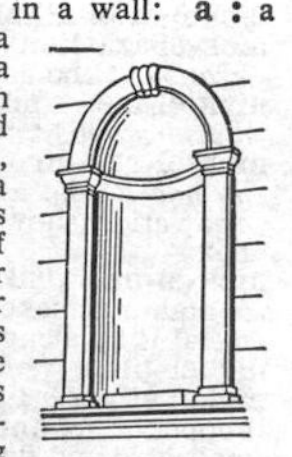
niche 1a

²niche \"\ *vb* -ED/-ING/-S [partly fr. ¹*niche* and partly fr. F *nicher* to nest] *vt* **1 :** to place in or as if in a niche: as **a :** to put into a position to attract attention or veneration ⟨safely *niched* as classics⟩ **b :** to settle snugly or cozily **c :** SECRETE **2 :** to construct as or furnish with a niche ~ *vi* **:** to settle or grow in a niche **:** NESTLE

ni·chi·ren \¦nichə¦ren\ *n* -S *cap* [after *Nichiren* †1282 Jap. religious teacher and founder of the sect] **:** a Japanese Buddhist sect based doctrinally on the Saddharma-pundarika Sutra and noted historically for its militant nationalism

nich·ol·son's hydrometer \'nikəlsənz-\ *n, usu cap N* [after Wm. *Nicholson* †1815 Eng. scientist] **:** a hydrometer with a submerged pan for determining the specific gravities of solids by weighing them in water and in air

nich·ols terrace \'nikəlz-\ *n, usu cap N* [after Mark L. *Nichols* b1888 Am. agricultural engineer] **:** a broad-channel terrace with a wide bank constructed along a contour usu. on gently sloping land

nicht \'nikt\ *Scot var of* NIGHT

¹nick *vt* -ED/-ING/-S [ME *nicken*, fr. OE *niccan*, fr. *nic*, *nicc*, adv., not I, no, contr. of *ne* not + *ic* I — more at NO, I] **:** to say nay to **:** DENY

²nick \'nik\ *n* -S [ME *nyke*, prob. alter. of *nocke* nock — more at NOCK] **1 a :** a cut made or occurring in a surface or edge **:** NOTCH; *usu* **:** a small sharp-edged cut made typically with one blow or stroke and without intention ⟨the razor had bad ~*s*⟩ ⟨~*s* in the table⟩ **b** *chiefly Scot* **:** a gap or slight opening in a range of hills **c :** a notch on the belly of a piece of type — compare GROOVE; — see TYPE illustration **2 a** *archaic* **:** a cut (as in a stick) serving as a tally **b** *obs* **:** RECKONING, ACCOUNT **c :** a particular point or place considered as marked by a cut **:** a precise or critical moment ⟨help came in the ~ of time⟩ **d** [fr. the obs. phrase *nick and froth*] *obs* **:** a false bottom in a beer mug **3 a :** the exact mark aimed at ⟨just what he needed, mum; it was in the ~ —Joyce Cary⟩ ⟨his rejoinder hit the ~⟩ **b :** the junction line of wall and floor in court tennis, squash, handball **c** [³*nick* (to breed)] **:** an individual superior to either parent; *also* **:** a mating that produces such offspring **4 :** the sound produced by a slight or brief impact **:** TICK **5** *Austral* **:** physical condition **:** SHAPE ⟨in great ~⟩ **6 a** *also* **nick point :** a place of abrupt change in a stream gradient **b :** a sharp angle cut at the base of a cliff (as by waves and currents or by shore ice) — compare NIP 5

³nick \"\ *vb* -ED/-ING/-S *vt* **1 a :** to make a nick in **:** NOTCH ⟨~ a tree⟩ ⟨~ a steel bar before sawing⟩ **b :** to injure by denting or chipping the surface or edge of ⟨~ a knife blade⟩ ⟨~ a china cup⟩ ⟨~ a table leg⟩ **2 a :** to score by making a nick on a tally **b :** to jot down **:** RECORD, SCORE **3** *obs* **:** to tally with **:** correspond to **:** copy closely **4** [partly short for ²*nickname*] *obs* **:** to fix a fitting name upon **:** NICKNAME **5** *obs* **a :** to provide (a beer mug) with a false bottom **b :** CHEAT, DEFRAUD **6 a :** to cut off or cut out **:** cut short ⟨cold weather ~*ed* steel and automobile output —*Time*⟩ **b :** to cut into slightly **:** wound lightly ⟨bullet ~*ed* his leg⟩ ⟨~*ed* himself while shaving⟩ **c :** to make a crosscut on the underside of (the tail of a horse) to effect a higher carrying position **:** cut beneath the tail of (a horse) **7 :** to hit, grasp, or catch precisely at the right point or time ⟨~ an opportunity⟩ ⟨~ a secret⟩ ⟨~ a train⟩ **8 a** *slang Brit* **:** to catch off guard **:** ARREST **b** *slang Brit* **:** STEAL **c :** to take from as payment or loan **:** CHARGE ⟨complained they were being ~*ed* as high as $30 a ton more for special steels —*Time*⟩ ~ *vi* **1 :** to make petty attacks **:** SNIPE, HACK ⟨people who ~ at the American system —*Saturday Rev.*⟩ **2** *of a ball in court games* **:** to strike the wall and floor simultaneously **3 :** to outrun and take the inner course from another (as in racing) **:** cut in **4 :** to complement one another genetically **:** breed together and produce offspring of good quality

nickar nut *var of* NICKER NUT

nick-eared \'=¦=\ *adj* [²*nick*] **:** CROP-EARED 1

¹nick·el \'nikəl\ *n* -S *often attrib* [prob. fr. Sw, short for *kopparnickel* niccolite, part trans. of G *kupfernickel*, prob. fr. *kupfer* copper (fr. OHG *kupfar*) + *nickel* goblin, demon, fr. *Nickel*, nickname for *Nikolaus* Nicholas — more at COPPER] **1 :** a nearly silver-white hard malleable ductile ferromagnetic metallic element capable of a high polish and resistant to corrosion that occurs native esp. in meteorites and combined in minerals (as garnierite and pentlandite associated with pyrrhotite and chalcopyrite), that is usu. obtained by roasting, smelting, sintering to the oxide, reducing to the metal, and refining by electrolysis or by formation and decomposition of nickel carbonyl, that is closely related chemically to cobalt and iron forming a monoxide and characteristic green bivalent salts, and that is used chiefly in alloys (as nickel steel and nickel silver) and as a catalyst (as Raney nickel) esp. in hydrogenation — symbol *Ni;* see ELEMENT table **2 a** *also* **nick·le** \"\ **:** the U.S. 5-cent piece regularly containing 25 percent nickel and 75 percent copper **b :** the Canadian 5-cent piece **3 a :** five cents **b :** a trifling sum of money ⟨not worth a ~⟩ **4 :** a nearly neutral, slightly reddish, medium gray

²nickel *vt* **nickeled** *or* **nickelled; nickeled** *or* **nickelled; nickeling** *or* **nickelling** \-k(ə)liŋ\ **nickels :** to plate with nickel

nick·el·age \-kəlij\ *n* -S [ISV ¹*nickel* + *-age*] **:** the art, act, or process of nickel plating

nickel bloom *or* **nickel ocher** *n* [*nickel bloom* trans. of G *nickelblüte; nickel ocher* trans. of NL *ochra niccoli*] **:** ANNABERGITE

nickel carbonyl *or* **nickel tetracarbonyl** *n* **:** a volatile flammable poisonous liquid compound $Ni(CO)_4$ obtained by passing carbon monoxide over finely divided nickel and readily decomposed by heating

nickel-chromium stainless steel *n* **:** a stainless steel containing 8 percent of nickel and 18 percent of chromium that is strong and ductile and suitable for chemical processing equipment

nickeled *or* **nickelled** *adj* **:** NICKEL-PLATED, SHINY

nickel glance *n* [G *nickelglanz*, fr. *nickel* + *glanz* glance (mineral sulfide)] **:** GERSDORFFITE

nickel green *n* **:** a dark grayish green that is bluer, lighter, and stronger than average ivy, yellower than persian green, and yellower and lighter than hemlock green — called also *frosty green*

nickel gymnite *n* **:** GENTHITE

nick·el·ic \ni'kelik, 'nikəl-\ *adj* [¹*nickel* + *-ic*] **:** of, relating to, or containing nickel — used esp. of compounds in which this element is regarded as having a higher valence than two

nick·el·if·er·ous \¦nikə¦lif(ə)rəs\ *adj* [¹*nickel* + *-iferous*] **:** containing nickel ⟨~ pyrrhotite⟩

¹nick·el·ine \'nikə,līn, -lēn\ *adj* [¹*nickel* + *-ine*] **:** NICKELIC

²nick·el·ine \¦nikə¦lēn\ *n* -S [F, fr. *nickel* (fr. Sw) + *-ine*] **:** any of several varieties of nickel silver

nickel-iron \'=¦=¦=\ *n* [prob. part trans. of G *nickeleisen*, fr. *nickel* + *eisen* iron] **:** an alloy of nickel and iron (Ni,Fe) occurring native terrestrially in pebbles, grains, and fine scales and in meteorites as fine borders about and intimate intergrowths with kamacite

nickel–iron alkaline battery *n* : EDISON BATTERY
nick·el·iza·tion \ˌnikələ'zāshən, -ˌlī'z-\ *n* -s [¹*nickel* + *-ization*] : the act or process of plating with nickel
nick·el·ize \'nikəˌlīz\ *vt* -ED/-ING/-S [back-formation fr. *nickelization*] : NICKEL
nick·el·ode·on \ˌnikə'lōdēən\ *n* -s [prob. blend of ¹*nickel* + *melodeon*] **1** : a theater affording a motion-picture exhibition or a variety show for an admission price of five cents **2** : JUKEBOX
nick·el·ous \'nikələs\ *adj* [¹*nickel* + *-ous*] : of, relating to, or containing nickel — used esp. of compounds in which this metal is bivalent ⟨light green ~ hydroxide⟩
nickel–plate \'≈≈'≈\ *vt* : to electroplate with nickel
nickel silver *n* : a silver-white alloy that consists essentially of copper, zinc, and nickel usu. in the proportion 3:1:1, that is malleable and ductile and not affected by exposure to the air, and that is used for tableware, keys, and restaurant and hospital equipment — called also *German silver*
nickel–skutterudite \'nikəl+\ *n* : a mineral $(Ni,Co)As_3$ consisting of a tri-arsenide of nickel and cobalt having more nickel than cobalt and isomorphous with skutterudite, smaltite, and chloanthite
nickel steel *n* : steel containing nickel
nickel sulfate *n* : a salt $NiSO_4$ obtained usu. as the green or blue crystalline hexahydrate and used chiefly in nickel-plating baths — called also *single nickel salt*
¹**nick·el·type** \'nikəlˌtīp\ *n* [¹*nickel* + electro*type*] : a nickel-faced electrotype made usu. by first electrodepositing nickel and then thinly coating on the back with copper prior to backing with lead — called also *steelfaced electrotype*
²**nickeltype** \"\ *vt* : to make a nickeltype from (a printing surface) ~ *vi* : to be reproducible by nickeltyping
¹**nick·er** \'nikə(r)\ *n* -s [ME *niker*, fr. OE *nicor*; akin to MD *nicker* water sprite, OHG *nihhus* water monster, water sprite, *nicchessa* mermaid, ON *nykr* water monster, L *noegeum* white upper garment, OIr *nigim* I wash, Gk *nizein*, *niptein* to wash, Skt *nejana* act of washing, *nenekti* he washes] : a fabulous water monster : WATER SPRITE, NIX
²**nicker** \"\ *n* -s [³*nick* + *-er*] : one that nicks: as **a** : one of the 18th century night brawlers of London noted for breaking windows with halfpence **b** : an operator of a machine for making cuts on the curved edges of shoe vamps, uppers, tongues, tips, and piping so that the edges may be folded under smoothly — called also *snipper*
³**nicker** \"\ *vi* **nickered; nickered; nickering** \-k(ə)riŋ\ **nickers** [perh. alter. of ¹*neigh*] **1** : to neigh gently : WHICKER **2** : SNICKER
⁴**nicker** \"\ *n* -s **1** : NEIGH **2** : SNICKER
⁵**nicker** \"\ *n, pl* **nicker** *or* **nickers** [perh. fr. ²*nicker*] *slang Brit* : one pound sterling
nick·er nut *also* **nicker** *or* **nicker–seed** *or* **nick·ar nut** \'nikə(r)(-)\ *n* -s [*nicker*, prob. fr. obs. *nicker* marble, modif. of D *knikker*, fr. *knikken* to crack, snap, fr. MD *cnicken*, prob. of imit. origin like MLG *knicken* to crack, snap, MHG *knacken* to make a cracking noise — more at KNACK] : the very hard shiny gray seed of bonduc (sense 2)
nicker tree *n* **1** : BONDUC 2 **2** *dial* : KENTUCKY COFFEE TREE
nick·ey \'nikē\ *n* -s [perh. fr. *Nicholas*, name of frequent occurrence among Cornishmen who first brought it to the Isle of Man] : a lug-sailed fishing boat common on the Manx fishing grounds

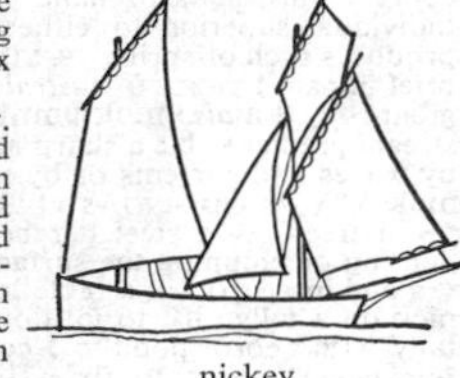

nickey

nick·ing \'nikiŋ\ *n* -s [fr. gerund of ³*nick*] **1** : gouged or notched carving frequent on cabinetwork of the 17th and early 18th centuries — called also *gouge carving*, *notch carving* **2** : localized constriction of a retinal vein by the pressure from an artery crossing it seen esp. in arterial hypertension
nickle *var of* NICKEL
nicknack *or* **nicnac** *var of* KNICKKNACK
¹**nick·name** \'nikˌnām\ *n* [ME *nekename*, an additional name, alter. (resulting from incorrect division of *an ekename*) of *ekename*, fr. *eke* (n.) + *name*] **1** : a usu. descriptive name (as Shorty, Tex) given instead of or in addition to the one belonging to a person, place, or thing **2** : a familiar form of a proper name (as Bill, Tommy)
²**nickname** \"\ *vt* **1** : to misapply the name of (one person or thing) to another : MISNAME, MISCALL ⟨psychical research is so often *nicknamed* ghost hunting —A.G.N.Flew⟩ **2** : to give a nickname to : call by a nickname
nick·name·less \-ləs\ *adj* : having no nickname
nick·nam·er \-mə(r)\ *n* [²*nickname* + *-er*] : one who invents or applies a nickname ⟨the ~ of genius called this brand of genius "pig philosophy" —T.H.Huxley⟩
nick off *vi* [prob. fr. ³*nick*] *Austral* : to go away : DEPART
nick point *n* : NICK 6a
nicks *pres 3d sing of* NICK, *pl of* NICK
nickstick \'≈,≈\ *n* [²*nick* or ³*nick* + *stick*] : a stick on which a reckoning is kept by notches : TALLY
nick·um \'nikəm\ *n* -s [perh. alter. & contr. of the phrase *nick them* or *nick him*, fr. ³*nick* (cheat) + *them* or *him*] **1** *slang* : SHARPER **2** *Scot* : SCAMP, WAG
nicky \'nikē\ *n* -ES [perh. fr. ²*nick* + *-y*] *dial chiefly Eng* : a bundle of wood
nic·o·bar·ese \ˌnikə,bä'rēz, -ēs\ *n, pl* **nicobarese** *usu cap* [*Nicobar* islands, Bay of Bengal + E *-ese*] **1 a** : the people of the Nicobar islands in the Bay of Bengal **b** : a member of such people **2** : the Mon-Khmer language of the Nicobarese people
nicobar pigeon *n, usu cap N* [fr. *Nicobar* islands] : a green pigeon (*Caloenas nicobarica*) of the Malayan and Polynesian islands
nic·o·de·mite \ˌnikə'dēˌmīt\ *n* -s *usu cap* [*Nicodemus*, the Jewish ruler who came to Jesus by night (fr. L, fr. Gk *Nikodēmos*) (John 3:1–21) + E *-ite*] : a secret follower or adherent; *specif* : a 16th century Protestant Christian who to escape persecution concealed his Protestantism while living in a Roman Catholic country
nic·o·la·i·tan \ˌnikə'lāət°n\ *n* -s *usu cap* [ME *Nicholaite* Nicolaitan (fr. Gk *Nikolaïtēs* follower of Nicolaus, fr. *Nikolaos* Nicolaus, a reputed heretic + *-itēs* -ite) + E *-an*] **1** : one of a group reproved in Rev 2:6, 14–15 and generally associated with those who were rebuked for eating things offered to idols and for fornication **2** : one of a group of 3d century antinomian Gnostics **3** [ML *Nicolaitae*, pl., Nicolaitans, heretics (fr. Gk *Nikolaitai*, pl. of *Nikolaïtēs*) + E *-an*] : one of the married or concubinary clergy in the medieval period; *also* : an opponent of clerical celibacy
¹**nic·o·lo** \'nikəˌlō\ *n* -s [It] : a large 17th century reed bombardon
²**nicolo** \"\ *also* **nic·co·lo** \"\ *n* -s [obs. It *niccolo*, prob. dim. of OIt *onice* onyx, fr. L *onych-*, *onyx* onyx] : a variety of onyx having a faint bluish layer over black
nic·ol prism \'nikəl-\ *also* **nicol** *n* -s *usu cap N* [after William *Nicol* †1851 Brit. physicist who invented it] : a device used for the production or analysis of polarized light consisting of the two parts of a rhombohedron of clear calcite bisected obliquely at a particular angle and subsequently cemented together with a transparent cement of which the refractive index lies between that of calcite for the ordinary ray which is totally reflected at the cement interface and the maximum refractive index of calcite for the extraordinary ray which is alone transmitted, both rays being plane-polarized at right angles to each other
nic·o·sia \ˌnikə'sēə\ *adj, usu cap* [fr. *Nicosia*, Cyprus] : of or from Nicosia, the capital of Cyprus : of the kind or style prevalent in Nicosia
nicotia *n* -s [NL, fr. Jean *Nicot* †1600 Fr. diplomat and scholar who introduced tobacco into France + NL *-ia*] *obs* : NICOTINE, TOBACCO
ni·co·tian \ni'kōshən\ *n* -s [MF *nicotiane*, prob. fr. NL *nicotiana* (in *herba nicotiana* Nicot's herb, tobacco), fem. of *nicotianus*, adj., of Nicot fr. Jean *Nicot* †1600 + L *-ianus* -an] **1** *obs* : TOBACCO **2** *archaic* : a user of tobacco
ni·co·ti·ana \ni,kōshē'anə, -'ä-,-'ā-\ *n* [NL, prob. fr. *nicotiana* (in *herba nicotiana*)] **1** *cap* : a genus of American and Asiatic herbs or shrubs (family Solanaceae) having viscid foliage and tubular flowers with a cleft or divided calyx and a many-seeded capsule — see TOBACCO **2** -s : FLOWERING TOBACCO
nicotin– *or* **nicotino–** *comb form* [*nicotin-* fr. *nicotine; nicotino-* fr. *nicotine* + *-o-*] **1** : nicotine : tobacco ⟨*nicotinism*⟩ ⟨*nicotinophobe*⟩ **2** [*nicotin-* ISV, fr. *nicotinic; nicotino-* ISV *nicotinic* + *-o-*] : nicotinic acid ⟨*nicotinamide*⟩ ⟨*nicotinonitrile*⟩
nic·o·ti·na \ˌnikə'tēnə\ *n* -s [NL, fr. Jean *Nicot* †1600 + L *-ina* (fem. of *-inus* -ine, adj. suffix)] *archaic* : NICOTINE
nic·o·tin·amide \ˌnikə'tēnəˌmīd, -məd\ *n* [ISV *nicotin-* + *amide*] : a bitter crystalline basic amide $C_5H_4NCONH_2$ that is a member of the vitamin B complex and is interconvertible with nicotinic acid in the living organism, that occurs naturally usu. as a constituent of coenzymes, and that is used similarly to nicotinic acid; the amide of nicotinic acid — called also *niacin*; see PYRIDINE NUCLEOTIDE
nic·o·tin·ate \-ēˌnāt\ *n* -s [*nicotinic* + *-ate*] : a salt or ester of nicotinic acid
nic·o·tine \'nikəˌtēn, ˌ≈≈'≈\ *n* -s [F, fr. NL *Nicotiana* + F *-ine*] **1** : a very poisonous volatile weakly basic liquid alkaloid $C_{10}H_{14}N_2$ that constitutes the chief active principle of tobacco, that darkens on exposure, that causes an acrid burning sensation in the mouth, that is obtained usu. as a by-product of the tobacco industry, and that is used as an insecticide in various forms (as the free alkaloid or as a solution of the sulfate) **2** : FLOWERING TOBACCO
nic·o·tined \-ēnd\ *adj* **1** : full of, stained with, or saturated with tobacco smoke ⟨~ fingers⟩ **2** : drugged with nicotine
nic·o·tine·less \-ēnləs\ *adj* : lacking nicotine
nic·o·tin·ian *also* **nic·o·tin·ean** \ˌnikə'tēnēən, -tin-\ *adj* [*nicotine* + *-an*] : relating to or caused by use of tobacco
nic·o·tin·ic \-ēnik, -tin-\ *adj* [ISV *nicotin-* + *-ic*] **1** : of or relating to nicotine or nicotinic acid **2** : producing a transitory stimulation followed by paralysis in autonomic ganglion cells ⟨~ effect⟩ ⟨a ~ drug⟩ — compare MUSCARINIC
nicotinic acid *n* : a crystalline acid C_5H_4NCOOH that is a member of the vitamin B complex occurring usu. in the form of a complex of nicotinamide in various animal and plant parts (as blood, liver, yeast, bran, legumes), is made by oxidation of nicotine, quinoline, or methylethy pyridine, and is effective in preventing and treating human pellagra and blacktongue of dogs; 3-pyridine-carboxylic acid — called also *niacin*
nic·o·tin·ism \'nikəˌtēˌnizəm, ˌ≈≈'≈ˌ≈≈\ *n* -s [ISV *nicotin-* + *-ism*] : the effect of the excessive use of tobacco
nic·o·tin·ize \-tēˌnīz\ *vt* -ED/-ING/-S [*nicotin-* (fr. *nicotine*) + *-ize*] : to drug with nicotine
nic·o·ti·no·yl \ˌnikə'tēnəwəl, -tin-\ *or* **nic·o·ti·nyl** \-tēn°l\ *n* -s [*nicotin-* + *-yl*] : the radical $NC_5H_4CO–$ of nicotinic acid
nic·o·tin·uric acid \ˌnikəˌtē'nyůrik-\ *n* [ISV *nicotinuric*, fr. *nicotin-* + *-uric*] : a crystalline acid $NC_5H_4CONHCH_2COOH$ found in the urine of some animals as a product of the metabolism of nicotinic acid; *N*-nicotinoyl-glycine
nic·tate \'nikˌtāt\ *vi* -ED/-ING/-S [L *nictatus*, past part. of *nictare* — more at CONNIVE] : WINK — **nictation** *n* -s
nic·ti·tant \'niktətənt\ *adj* [*nictitate* + *-ant*] : adapted for winking ⟨~ membrane of a snake⟩
nic·ti·tate \'niktəˌtāt *sometimes probably by* t-*dissimilation* ÷-kə-\ *vi* -ED/-ING/-S [alter. (influenced by L freq. verbs in *-itare*) of *nictate*] : WINK — **nic·ti·ta·tion** \ˌ≈≈'tāshən\ *n* -s
nictitating membrane *n* [*nictitating* fr. pres. part. of *nictitate*] : a thin membrane found in many animals at the inner angle or beneath the lower lid of the eye and capable of extending across the eyeball
nictitating spasm *n* : clonic spasm of the eyelid
nic·u·ri \ˌnikə'rē\ *n* -s [prob. fr. Pg, modif. of Tupi *aricuri*] : OURICURY
NID *abbr* naval intelligence department; naval intelligence division
ni·dal \'nīd°l\ *adj* [L *nidus* nest + E *-al*] : of or relating to a nidus
nida·men·tal \ˌnīdə'ment°l\ *adj* [L *nidamentum* materials for a nest (fr. *nidus* nest) + E *-al* — more at NEST] : relating to or producing a capsule or covering for an egg or mass of eggs
ni·da·tion \nī'dāshən\ *n* -s [L *nidus* nest + E *-ation*] **1** : the development of the epithelial membrane lining the inner surface of the uterus following menstruation **2** : IMPLANTATION 1b
nida·to·ry \'nīdəˌtōrē, 'nid-\ *adj* [L *nidus* nest + E *-atory*] : of or relating to a nest
nid·der·ing *or* **nid·er·ing** \'nid(ə)riŋ\ *n* -s [*niddering*, alter. of *nidering*, alter. of ME *nithing*] *archaic* : COWARD
nid·dick \'nidik\ *n* -s [origin unknown] *dial Eng* : the nape of the neck
nid·dle \'nid°l\ *vi* -ED/-ING/-S [origin unknown] *chiefly Scot* : to move quickly
niddle–noddle \'nid°l'näd°l\ *adj* [redupl. & alter. of ²*noddle*] : having an unstably nodding head
nid·dy nod·dy \ˌnidē'nädē\ *n* [perh. fr. obs. *niddy-noddy* to nod to and fro unsteadily, by redupl. & alter. of ¹*nod*] : a hand reel for yarn
nide \'nīd\ *n* -s [L *nidus* nest] *chiefly Brit* : a family or group of pheasants
¹**nidge** \'nij\ *vi* -ED/-ING/-S [origin unknown] : SHAKE, QUIVER
²**nidge** *var of* NIG
nid·get \'nijət\ *n* -s [alter. of earlier *nidiot*, alter. (from incorrect division of *an idiot*) of ¹*idiot*] *archaic* : IDIOT, FOOL
nidi *pl of* NIDUS
ni·dic·o·lous \(')nī'dikələs\ *adj* [L *nidi-* (fr. *nidus* nest) + E *-colous*] **1** : reared for a time in a nest : ALTRICIAL — compare NIDIFUGOUS **2** : living in a nest; *esp* : sharing the nest of another kind of animal ⟨some beetles are ~ with ants⟩
nid·i·fi·cant \'nidəfəkənt, (')nī'dif-\ *adj* [L *nidificant-*, *nidificans*, pres. part. of *nidificare*] : building a nest
nid·i·fi·cate \'nidəfəˌkāt, nī'dif-\ *vi* -ED/-ING/-S [L *nidificatus*, past part. of *nidificare*] : to build a nest
nid·i·fi·ca·tion \ˌnidəfə'kāshən, (ˌ)nīˌdif-\ *n* -s [ML *nidification-*, *nidificatio*, fr. L *nidificatus* (past part.) + *-ion-*, *-io* -ion] : the act or process of nidificating : the construction of a nest — **nid·i·fi·ca·tion·al** \-shən°l, -shnəl\ *adj*
ni·dif·u·gous \(')nī'difyəgəs\ *adj* [L *nidi-* (fr. *nidus* nest) + E *-fugous* (as in *lucifugous*)] : leaving the nest soon after hatching : PRECOCIAL — compare NIDICOLOUS
nid·i·fy \'nidəˌfī\ *vi* -ED/-ING/-ES [L *nidificare*, fr. *nidi-* (fr. *nidus* nest) + *-ficare* -fy — more at NEST] : to build a nest
nid–nod \'nid,näd\ *vi* [redupl. & alter. of ¹*nod*] : to nod repeatedly from drowsiness
ni·dol·o·gist \nī'däləjəst\ *n* -s [L *nidus* nest + E *-ologist*] : one who specializes in the study of birds' nests
ni·dol·o·gy \-jē\ *n* -ES [L *nidus* nest + E *-ology*] : the study of birds' nests
ni·dor \'nīˌdȯ(ə)r, -dər\ *n* -s [L; akin to OE *hnītan* to thrust, gore, knock, encounter, *gehnǣst* collision, battle, ON *hnīta* to strike, *hnita* to weld, *hnissa* smell from cooking, unpleasant taste, MIr *cned* wound, Gk *knizein* to scratch, tickle, tease, *knisma* scratch, *knismos* irritation, itching, *knisa*, *knisē* smell of burnt sacrifice, nidor, Latvian *kniest* to itch and to L *ciner-*, *cinis* ashes — more at INCINERATE] : a strong smell : REEK; *esp* : the smell of cooking or burning meat or fat
ni·dor·ous \'nīdərəs\ *adj* [LL *nidorosus* steaming, reeking, fr. L *nidor* + *-osus* -ous] : rankly odorous : smelling of or like burning or decaying animal matter
nid·u·lant \'nijələnt\ *adj* [L *nidulant-*, *nidulans*, pres. part. of *nidulari*] : EMBEDDED, NESTLING; *specif* : lying free in a cavity
nid·u·lar·ia \ˌnijə'la(a)rēə\ *n*, *cap* [NL, fr. L *nidulus* small nest + NL *-aria*] : a genus of fungi (the type of the family Nidulariaceae) having a sessile globose peridium opening by a lacerate mouth
nid·u·lar·i·a·ce·ae \-ˌla(a)rē'āsēˌē\ *n pl, cap* [NL, fr. *Nidularia*, type genus + *-aceae*] : a family of small fungi (order Nidulariales) comprising the bird's-nest fungi and having the spores formed in peridioles borne in the peridium like eggs in a nest — compare SPHAEROBOLACEAE — **nid·u·lar·i·a·ceous** \ˌ≈≈ˌ≈≈'āshəs\ *adj*
nid·u·lar·i·a·les \ˌ≈≈ˌ≈≈'ā(ˌ)lēz\ *n pl, cap* [NL, fr. *Nidularia* + *-ales*] : a small order of basidiomycetous fungi (subclass Homobasidiomycetes) usu. including the families Nidulariaceae and Sphaerobolaceae
nid·u·late \'nijəˌlāt\ *adj* [L *nidulatus*, past part. of *nidulari* to make a nest, fr. *nidulus* small nest, dim. of *nidus* nest — more at NEST] : NIDULANT
nid·u·la·tion \ˌnijə'lāshən\ *n* -s [obs. E *nidulate* to make a nest (fr. L *nidulatus*, past part.) + E *-ion*] : nest building : NESTING
nid·u·li·tes \-'līd·(ˌ)ēz\ *n*, *cap* [NL, fr. L *nidulus* small nest + NL *-ites*] : a genus of hollow ovoidal calcareous fossils that have walls with a honeycomb structure and are often considered to belong among or to be related to the Porifera but are sometimes treated as calcareous algae
nid·u·lus \'nijələs\ *n*, *pl* **niduli** [NL, fr. L, small nest] : CENTER 2e
ni·dus \'nīdəs\ *n*, *pl* **ni·di** \-ˌdī\ *or* **ni·dus·es** [NL, fr. L, nest] **1** : a nest for the eggs of insects, spiders, small animals **2 a** : a breeding place; *esp* : a place or substance in an animal or plant where the germs of a disease or other organisms lodge and multiply **b** : a place of development for spores or seeds **c** : a group of regenerative epithelial cells of the insect ventriculus **3 a** : a place where something originates or is fostered or develops ⟨hysterical symptoms often grow from an organic ~, congenital or acquired —D.N.Parfitt⟩ **b** : a place where something is settled, lodged, or located
niece \'nēs\ *n* -s [ME *nece*, fr. AF *nece* niece & OF *niece* granddaughter, niece, fr. LL *neptia*, fr. L *neptis* granddaughter; akin to L *nepos*, grandson, nephew — more at NEPHEW] **1** *obs* : a female descendant or relative: as **a** : GRANDDAUGHTER **b** : GRANDNIECE **2 a** : a daughter of one's brother or sister **b** : a daughter of one's brother-in-law or sister-in-law
niece·less \-sləs\ *adj* : having no niece
nief *var of* NEIF
ni·el·lat·ed \nē'eˌlād·əd\ *or* **ni·elled** \-eld\ *adj* [*niellated* fr. It *niellato* (past part. of *niellare* to inlay with niello, fr. *niello*) + E *-ed*; *nielled*, perh. fr. F *nieller* to inlay with niello (fr. *nielle* niello, fr. It *niello*) + E *-ed*] : NIELLOED
ni·el·list \-eləst\ *n* -s : a maker of or worker in niello
¹**ni·el·lo** \-e(ˌ)lō\ *n*, *pl* **ni·el·li** \-ˌlē\ *or* **niellos** [It, fr. ML *nigellum*, fr. neut. of L *nigellus* blackish, dark, dim. of *niger* black] **1** : any of several metallic alloys of sulfur with silver, copper or lead having a deep black color **2** : the art, process, or method of decorating metal with incised designs filled with niello; *also* : work of this kind **3** : an object decorated with niello **4** : an impression on paper taken from the engraved or incised surface before niello has been inlaid
²**niello** \"\ *vt* -ED/-ING/-S : to inlay or ornament with niello
niel·sen method \'nēlsən-\ *n*, *usu cap N* [after Holger *Nielsen* †1955 Dan. army officer who originated it] : BACK PRESSURE–ARM LIFT METHOD
nie·mann–pick disease \'nēˌmän'pik-\ *n*, *usu cap N&P* [after Albert *Niemann* †1921 Ger. surgeon and Ludwig *Pick* †1944 Ger physician] : a familial disease of infants characterized by gastrointestinal disturbances, malnutrition, and enlargement of the spleen, liver, and lymph nodes, and marked by abnormalities of the blood-forming organs
nie·nock \'nēnək\ *n* -s *often cap* [origin unknown] : AMERICAN LOTUS
nientsi *usu cap, var of* NENTSI
nie·pa \'nēpə\ *n* -s [prob. fr. the native name in East India] **1** : an East Indian tree (*Samadera indica*) whose bark contains a bitter principle similar to quassia **2** *also* **niepa bark** : the bark of the niepa tree
nie·rem·ber·gia \ˌnirəm'bərjēə, -rgēə\ *n* [NL, fr. Juan E. *Nieremberg* †1658 Span. Jesuit naturalist and author + NL *-ia*] **1** *cap* : a genus of tropical American creeping herbs (family Solanaceae) having solitary white or purple flowers and a slender corolla tube bearing five exserted stamens at its apex **2** -s : any plant of the genus *Nierembergia* — called also *cupflower*
nies·hout \'nēsˌhaůt\ *n* -s [Afrik, fr. *nies* to sneeze (fr. D *niezen*) + *hout* wood (fr. D)] : SNEEZEWOOD
¹**nietz·sche·an** \'nēchēən\ *adj*, *usu cap* [Friedrich W. *Nietzsche* †1900 Ger. philosopher and poet + E *-an*] : of or relating to the philosopher Nietzsche or to Nietzscheanism
²**nietzschean** \"\ *n* -s *usu cap* : an adherent to Nietzscheanism : an advocate of the ideas of Nietzsche
nietz·sche·an·ism \-əˌnizəm\ *or* **nietz·sche·ism** \-chēˌizəm\ *n* -s *usu cap* [*nietzscheanism* fr. ¹*nietzschean* + *-ism*; *nietzscheism* fr. F. W. *Nietzsche* + E *-ism*] : the philosophical theories of Nietzsche advocating the overcoming of both a threatening nihilism and a slave morality as exemplified for him in historical Christianity through a reevaluation of all values on the basis of a will to power epitomized in his doctrine of the superman and the idea of the eternal recurrence of all things
¹**nieve** \'nēv\ *also* **nief** \'nēf\ *n* -s [ME *neve*, *nefe*, fr. ON *hnefi*] **1** *chiefly dial* : a person's hand **2** *chiefly dial* : FIST
²**nieve** \"\ *n* -s [AF *neife*, *nieje*, *niej*, fem. of (assumed) *neij*, *naif* neif — more at NEIF] : a female neif
nie·ve pen·i·ten·te \nē'āvāˌpenə'tentā, 'nyāv-\ *n*, *pl* **nie·ves peniten·tes** \-vās . . . tās\ [Sp, lit., penitent snow; fr. the illusion of kneeling human figures] : a jagged sometimes curved pinnacle of ice or névé produced by uneven melting of a snowbank or of the surface of a glacier; *also* : an assemblage of such pinnacles — compare SERAC
nie·ve·ta \ˌnēə'vēd·ə, nyə'-\ *n* -s [AmerSp, fr. *nieve* snow, fr. L *niv-*, *nix* — more at SNOW] : a low Californian herb of the genus *Cryptantha* (family Boraginaceae) with small white flowers like forget-me-nots
niev·ie–niev·ie–nick–nack \'nēvē'nēvē'nikˌnak\ *n* -s [prob. fr. redupl. of *nievie* (dim. of ¹*nieve*) + *nick-nack*, alter. of *knickknack*] : a child's guessing game
¹**nif·fer** \'nifə(r)\ *vb* -ED/-ING/-S [perh. alter. of ¹*nieve*] *chiefly Scot* : EXCHANGE, TRADE
²**niffer** \"\ *n* -s *chiefly Scot* : BARGAIN, DICKER, EXCHANGE
niff–naff \'nifˌnaf\ *vi* -ED/-ING/-S [origin unknown] *dial Brit* : TRIFLE
niff–naf·fy \-ˌnafi\ *adj*, *Scot* : TRIFLING
ni·fle \'nīfəl, 'nif-\ *or* **nif·fle** \'nif-\ *n* -s [ME *nifle*] *chiefly dial* : a trivial or worthless person or thing
¹**nif·ty** \'niftē, -ti\ *adj* -ER/-EST [origin unknown] : very good : very attractive : SMART, STYLISH ⟨~ clothes⟩ ⟨a ~ blond⟩ : well-executed ⟨a ~ right to the jaw⟩ : SPLENDID ⟨a ~ show⟩ : HANDY ⟨a ~ little machine⟩ : CLEVER, ADEPT ⟨~ hands of a third baseman —John McNulty⟩
²**nifty** \"\ *n* -ES : something that is nifty; *esp* : a clever or neatly turned phrase or joke ⟨hurled a few fistfuls of crackling *nifties* at them —Bob Hope⟩
¹**nig** \'nig\ *n* -s [by shortening] : NIGGER
²**nig** \"\ *vi* **nigged; nigged; nigging; nigs** [short for *renig*] : RENEGE, REVOKE
³**nig** \"\ *or* **nidge** *vt* **nigged** *or* **nidged; nigged** *or* **nidged; nigging** *or* **nidging; nigs** *or* **nidges** [origin unknown] : to dress (stone) with a sharp-pointed hammer
ni·gel·la \nī'jelə\ *n* [NL, fr. LL, black caraway, fr. fem. of L *nigellus* blackish, dark — more at NIELLO] **1** *cap* : a genus of erect annual European herbs (family Ranunculaceae) having dissected leaves and blue or white flowers — see LOVE-IN-A-MIST **2** -s : any plant of the genus *Nigella*
¹**niger** *n* -s [prob. modif. (influenced by L *niger*, adj., black, dark) of Sp *negro*] *obs* : NEGRO
²**ni·ger** \'nījə(r)\ *also* **niger morocco** *n* -s [fr. *Niger* river, West African river flowing through Nigeria] : leather from Nigerian goats used chiefly for fine bookbinding
³**niger** \"\ *adj*, *usu cap* [fr. *Niger* Republic, western Africa] : of or relating to the Niger Republic : of the kind or style prevalent in the Niger Republic
niger–congo \ˌ≈≈'≈(ˌ)≈\ *n*, *usu cap N&C* [fr. *Niger*, river of West Africa + *Congo*, river of central Africa] : a language family that consists of the West-Atlantic, Mande, Gur, Kwa. Ijo, Central, and Adamawa-Eastern branches and that is spoken by most of the indigenous peoples of west, central, and south Africa
ni·ge·ria \(')nī'jirēə\ *adj*, *usu cap* [fr. *Nigeria*, state in West Africa] : of or from Nigeria : of the kind or style prevalent in Nigeria : NIGERIAN
¹**ni·ge·ri·an** \≈'≈≈≈\ *n* -s *cap* [*Nigeria*, West Africa + E *-an*] : a native or inhabitant of Nigeria
²**nigerian** \(')≈'≈≈≈\ *adj*, *usu cap* : of or relating to Nigeria
ni·ger·ite \'nījəˌrīt\ *n* -s [*Nigeria*, its locality + E *-ite*] : a mineral $(Zn,Fe,Mg)(Sn,Zn)_2(Al,Fe)_{12}O_{22}(OH)_2$ consisting of an oxide and hydroxide of aluminum, iron, tin, zinc, and magnesium

ni·ge·rois \ˈnēzhər¦wä, -ˌzher-\ *n, pl* **nigerois** \-wä(z)\ *cap* [(assumed) F, fr. *Niger*, country in western Africa + F *-ois* -ese, fr. L *-ensis*] **:** a native or inhabitant of the Republic of Niger

niger seed *n* [prob. fr. *Niger* river, West Africa, where it originated] **:** the seed of ramtil that yields a valuable oil

niger-seed oil *n* [*niger seed*] **:** a drying oil obtained from the seeds of ramtil and used in food, soap, and paints

1nig·gard \ˈnigə(r)d\ *n* -s [ME *nigart, nigard, niggard*, prob. fr. earlier *nig* niggard (of Scand origin) + *-art, -ard;* akin to ON *hnøggr* niggardly, stingy, *hnøggva, hnyggja* to humble, bring down; akin to OE *hnēaw* niggardly, stingy, OHG *hniuwan* to crush, Gk *knyein* to scratch, *knoos, knous* grating noise of an axle, sound of footsteps, *knuos* itch, Latvian *knūt, knūst* to itch and to L *ciner-, cinis* ashes — more at INCINERATE] **:** a person meanly close and covetous **:** MISER

2niggard \"\ *adj* [ME *nigart*, adj. & n.] **1 :** NIGGARDLY, STINGY ⟨~ storekeepers who refused to pay . . . his modest monthly honorarium —Ben Riker⟩ ⟨cold, unappreciative, very ~ in even modified praise —Arnold Bennett⟩ **2 :** resulting from or displaying niggardliness **:** SCANTY ⟨the shop-windows' show is ~ and shabby —W.C.Brownell⟩

3niggard *vb* -ED/-ING/-S *vi, obs* **:** to act niggardly ~ *vt, obs* **:** to treat in a niggardly manner

nig·gard·li·ness \-dlēnəs\ *n* -ES **:** the quality or state of being niggardly

1nig·gard·ly \-lē, -li\ *adj* [1*niggard* + *-ly*] **1 :** grudgingly loath to part with money or possessions or to grant favors ⟨they were not ~, these tramps, and he who had money did not hesitate to share it —W.S.Maugham⟩ ⟨so ~ about entry to their country —Bernard Pares⟩ **2 :** provided in meanly limited supply **:** SCANTY ⟨the country has been handicapped by ~ transport resources —V.H.Whitney⟩ **syn** see STINGY

2niggardly \"\ *adv* [2*niggard* + *-ly*] **:** in the manner of a niggard ⟨the people of our respective states . . . cannot afford to deal ~ with their universities —L.M.Chamberlain⟩

nig·gard·ness *n* -ES [2*niggard* + *-ness*] **:** NIGGARDLINESS

1nig·ger \ˈnigə(r)\ *n* -s *often attrib* [alter. of *neger* or 1*niger*] **1 a :** NEGRO — usu. taken to be offensive **b :** a member (as an East Indian, a Filipino, an Egyptian) of any very dark-skinned race — usu. taken to be offensive **2 :** any of several dark-colored insect larvae (as of some ladybugs and of the turnip sawfly) **3 :** COTTON SPINNER **4 :** a steam-operated capstan for warping river steamboats over snags and shallows **5 :** a long-toothed power-propelled lever arm used to position logs on a carriage (as in a sawmill)

2nigger \"\ *vt* -ED/-ING/-S **:** to divide (a log) by burning — usu. used with *off* ⟨~*ed* off into lengths —Conrad Richter⟩

nigger baby *n, Southwest* **:** either of two herbs: **a :** a sanicle (*Sanicula bipinnatifida*) with purple flowers **b :** a blue-eyed grass (*Sisyrinchium bellum*) with purplish blue flowers — usu. used in pl.

nigger bug *n* **:** NEGRO BUG

nigger chaser *n* **:** a small firework that shoots about on the ground

nigger daisy *n* **:** BLACK-EYED SUSAN 1

niggerfish \ˈ==,=\ *n* **:** CONEY 5a

niggergoose \ˈ==,=\ *n, pl* **niggergeese :** CORMORANT

niggerhead \ˈ==,=\ *n* **1 :** a dark-colored mound or clump of vegetation (as a hummock of tundra or a tussock of sedge in a permafrost bog) found in far northern regions (as Alaska) **2 :** a strong black chewing tobacco **:** NEGROHEAD **3 a :** a hard dark-colored nodule or boulder **b :** a coral boulder broken off and thrown to the surface by wind and wave action (as on the Great Barrier reef) **4 :** a large blackish smooth-shelled freshwater mussel (*Quadrula ebena*) used in button making and sometimes producing valuable pearls **5 a** (1) **:** any of various plants of the genus *Rudbeckia* (2) **:** a ribgrass (*Plantago lanceolata*) (3) **:** a wild peony (*Paeonia brownii*) of the western U. S. (4) **:** the common greenbrier (*Smilax rotundifolia*) of eastern No. America (5) **:** PURPLE CONEFLOWER **b** *Austral* (1) **:** the spiny head of a saltwort (2) **:** NEGROHEAD BEECH **6 a :** a drum on a windlass **b :** BOLLARD **7** *Canad* **:** SCOTER **8 a :** a small wire nail driven into the furniture of a form on a cylinder press to produce a black mark on the feed-gauge edge of the printed sheet as a guide for trimming and folding **b** (1) **:** a mark made by a niggerhead (2) **:** a similar mark used as a collating mark

niggerhead cactus *n* **:** BISNAGA

nigger heaven *n, slang* **:** the highest balcony or row of seats in a theater

nigger in the woodpile : something (as a concealed motive or obscure factor) contrary to appearances in a situation

nigger pine *n* **:** JERSEY PINE

nigger-shooter \ˈ==,==\ *n* **:** SLINGSHOT

niggertoe \ˈ==,=\ *n* **1** *South* **:** any of various herbs (as of the genera *Gaillardia, Coreopsis*, and *Rudbeckia*) having flower heads with black or dark-colored disks **2 :** BRAZIL NUT

niggerweed \ˈ==,=\ *n* **:** JOE-PYE WEED

niggerwool \ˈ==,=\ *n* **:** a sedge (*Carex filifolia*) of the western Great Plains of No. America that is used for mulch in erosion control

nig·gery \ˈnigərē\ *adj* [1*nigger* + *-y*] **:** characteristic of a Negro

niggling *pres part of* NIG

nig·gle \ˈnigəl\ *vb* **niggled; niggled; niggling** \-g(ə)liŋ\ **niggles** [origin unknown] *vi* **1 a :** TRIFLE ⟨didn't ~ with . . . prepositions but printed the lecture title as it was received —*Newsweek*⟩ **b :** to work meticulously; *esp* **:** to spend too much effort on minor details **2 :** to find fault constantly in a petty way **:** CARP ⟨she haggles, she ~*s*, she wears out our patience —Virginia Woolf⟩ **3 :** GNAW ⟨a tiny *niggling* noise like a mouse —Ruth Park⟩ ⟨the question which had *niggled* insistently at his brain —J.E.Macdonnell⟩ ~ *vt* **:** to give stingily or in tiny portions ⟨it seems greedier to me to . . . ~ it out in tiny bits —Florence Bullock⟩

nig·gler \-g(ə)lə(r)\ *n* -s **:** one that niggles ⟨the ~*s* . . . take great pride in their discovery of a trifling error and go to immense lengths to point it out —Philip Wylie⟩

nig·gli·ite \ˈniglē,īt\ *n* -s [Paul *Niggli* †1953 Swiss mineralogist + E *-ite*] **:** a mineral $PtTe_3(?)$ consisting of a telluride of platinum found in Griqualand East

niggling *adj* [fr. pres. part. of *niggle*] **1 :** PETTY ⟨impatient with small patterns and regular meters, which they find ~ and hampering —Louise Bogan⟩ **2 a :** METICULOUS ⟨begin some ~ task, usually the preparation of a very careful drawing —*Lancet*⟩ **b :** overelaborate or feeble in execution ⟨the brushwork trailed off in ~ strokes —*Atlantic*⟩ — **nig·gling·ly** *adv*

nig·gly \ˈnig(ə)lē\ *adj* -ER/-EST [*niggle* + *-y*] **:** NIGGLING

niggun *var of* NIGUN

1nigh \ˈnī\ *adv* -ER/-EST [ME *nigh, neigh, neih, neh*, adv. & adj., fr. OE *nēah, nēh;* akin to OS *nāh*, adv. & adj., nigh, MD *nā*, prep. & adv., OHG *nāh*, adv. & adj., nigh, prep., nigh, after, ON *nā-* (in composition) nigh, Goth *nehw, nehwa*, adv., nigh, and perh. to Skt *naśati* he attains, reaches — more at ENOUGH] **1 :** near in place, time, or relationship — often used with *on, onto*, or *unto* ⟨served . . . for ~ on forty years —M.S.Tisdale⟩ ⟨my end draws ~; 'tis time that I were gone —Alfred Tennyson⟩ **2 :** NEARLY, ALMOST ⟨the already ~ obliterated records of childhood —Osbert Sitwell⟩

2nigh \"\ *adj* -ER/-EST [ME *nigh, neigh, neih, neh*, fr. OE *nēah, nēh*, adj. & adv.] **1 :** CLOSE ⟨man in . . . friend, brother, ~*est* neighbor —Walt Whitman⟩ — often used predicatively ⟨vow that my heart, when death is ~ —Sidney Lanier⟩; often used with a preposition ⟨some so silent, dark, and ~ to death —Walt Whitman⟩ **2** *chiefly dial* **:** DIRECT, SHORT ⟨took a ~ cut through the hill paths home —J.H. Stuart⟩ **3 :** 4NEAR 3b **4** *chiefly dial* **:** STINGY

3nigh \"\ *prep* [ME *nigh, neigh, neih, neh*, fr. OE *nēah, nēh*, prob. fr. *nēah, nēh*, adv.] **:** NEAR ⟨everyone wanted to be next and ~ me —Padraic Colum⟩

4nigh \"\ *vb* -ED/-ING/-S [ME *nighen, neighen, neihen, neghen*, fr. *nigh, neigh, neih*, adv.] *vt* **:** to draw or come near to **:** APPROACH ⟨strapped, noosed, ~*ing* his hour —A.E.Housman⟩ ~ *vi* **:** to draw near

nigh-hand \ˈ=¦=\ *adv* [ME *nigh hand, neih hond*, fr. OE *nēh hand*, fr. *nēh*, adv., nigh + *hand*] **1 :** near at hand **:** close by ⟨living *nigh-hand* to where the new house was to be built —A.H.Bullen⟩ **2 :** NEARLY, ALMOST ⟨wasn't it enough for you to *nigh-hand* kill one o' my horses —Samuel Lover⟩

nigh·ly *adv* [ME *neli*, fr. OE *nēalice*, fr. *nēah*, adv. & adj., nigh + *-lice* -ly] **:** NEARLY, ALMOST

nigh·ness *n* -ES [ME, fr. *nigh* (adj.) + *-ness*] **:** the quality or state of being nigh

1night \ˈnīt, *usu* -īd·+V\ *n* -s [ME *night, niht*, fr. OE *niht, næht, neaht;* akin to MD *nacht* night, OS & OHG *naht*, ON *nōtt, nātt*, Goth *nahts* night, OIr in-*nocht* tonight, W *nos* night, L *noct-, nox*, Gk *nykt-, nyx*, Skt *nakt, nakti*, Lith *naktis*, OSlav *noštĭ*] **1 :** the part of the solar day when the sun is beneath the horizon; *esp* **:** the time from dusk to dawn when no light of the sun is visible ⟨had an exhausting ~ alone in the woods⟩ ⟨extra pay for working at ~⟩ ⟨dine, drink, dance, or gamble by ~ —T.H.Fielding⟩ — compare DAY **2 a :** an evening or night taken as an occasion or point of time ⟨saw the opera on the opening ~⟩ ⟨saw the satellite on the third ~⟩ **b** (1) **:** an evening set aside for a particular purpose ⟨it was bingo ~ and everybody was at the movies —Theodora Keogh⟩ (2) **:** an evening program ⟨hold an amateur ~⟩ ⟨plan a ladies' ~ for the men's next club meeting⟩ **c :** the evening following a particular day ⟨Christmas ~⟩ ⟨their wedding ~⟩ ⟨election ~⟩ — compare EVE **3 a :** DARKNESS ⟨under cover of ~ swooped in among the cumbersome ships of the line —Frank Yerby⟩ **b :** a condition or period felt to resemble the darkness of night; *specif* **:** a period of dreary inactivity or affliction **:** mental or moral darkness ⟨the glories of Roman civilization were lost in a gloomy ~ of ignorance, superstition, and barbarism —R.A.Hall b.1911⟩ **c :** the beginning of darkness **:** NIGHTFALL ⟨rainbow at ~, sailors' delight⟩ ⟨waited until it was ~⟩ **4 a :** the period between sunset or the evening meal and bedtime ⟨went bowling every ~⟩ ⟨Thursday evening is their maid's ~ out⟩ **b :** the period between nightfall or 6 p.m. and midnight ⟨the ~ of May 1⟩ **c :** the period between bedtime and morning usu. spent in bed ⟨slept quietly all ~⟩ **d :** a time for sexual intercourse **e :** a period of gainful employment coming during or chiefly during the night ⟨began his ~ at eleven and got off at seven⟩ ⟨paid the lecturer $500 a ~⟩ **5** *archaic* **:** TONIGHT — used with *the* **6 :** a night's rest ⟨the patient had a good ~⟩

2night \"\ *vi* -ED/-ING/-S [ME *nighten*, fr. *night*, n.] **:** to remain during the night **:** to spend the night

3night \"\ *adj* [1*night*] **1 :** of, relating to, or associated characteristically with the night ⟨~ poetry⟩ ⟨~ air⟩ **2 :** intended for use at night ⟨a ~ lamp⟩ ⟨the ~ bell⟩ **3 :** existing, occurring, or carried out during the night ⟨the ~ view of the city⟩ ⟨~ noises⟩ ⟨~ baseball⟩ **4 a** (1) **:** working at night ⟨a ~ nurse⟩ ⟨the ~ clerk⟩ (2) **:** of or relating to work done at night ⟨posted the ~ hours⟩ **b :** operating at night ⟨the ~ train⟩ **5 :** active or effective at night ⟨a ~ fly⟩

night adder *n* **:** any of several nocturnal African vipers (genus *Causus*) with greatly enlarged venom glands extending along the neck

night and day *adv* [ME, fr. OE *næht & dæg*] **:** CONTINUALLY

night ape *n* **1 :** any of several small nocturnal Central and So. American monkeys of the genus *Aotes* with whitish ruff, long nonprehensile tail, short ears, and very large yellow eyes — called also *owl monkey* **2 :** BUSH BABY

night ark *n, Brit* **:** a small chicken house with a slatted floor often measuring six by three feet

night bird *n* **1 :** a bird associated with night: as **a :** OWL **b :** NIGHTINGALE **c :** MOORHEN **d :** MANX SHEARWATER **2 :** NIGHTHAWK 2

night-blind \ˈ=,=\ *adj* [back-formation fr. *night blindness*] **:** afflicted with night blindness

night blindness *n* **:** NYCTALOPIA

night-blooming cereus \ˈ=,==-\ *n, pl* **night-blooming cereuses :** any of several night-blooming cacti: as **a :** a slender sprawling or climbing cactus (*Selenicereus grandiflorus*) that has ribbed stems and yellow spines and is often cultivated for its very large showy white strongly-scented flowers which are followed by yellow red-streaked fruits **b :** any of several cacti of the genera *Cereus* and *Hyalocereus* with flexuous climbing angled branches and large fragrant white flowers

night blue *n* **:** a dark grayish blue that is greener and paler than indigo

night bolt *n* **1 :** the bolt of a night latch **2 :** an auxiliary bolt on the inside of a door to prevent opening from the outside except by a key

nightcap \ˈ=,=\ *n* [ME *night cappe*, fr. 1*night* + *cappe* cap] **1 a :** a cloth cap worn with nightclothes **b** *or* **nightcap wig** *archaic* **:** a close-fitting wig **2 :** a cloud resting about the summit of a mountain or hill **3 :** something usu. soporific (as hot cocoa or toddy) taken at bedtime **4 :** the final race or contest of a day's sports; *esp* **:** the final game of a baseball doubleheader

nightcap 1a

nightcaps *n pl but sing or pl in constr* [pl. of *nightcap*] **:** WOOD ANEMONE a

night cart *n* **:** a cart for removing night soil

night chair *n* **:** CLOSESTOOL

nightchurr \ˈ=,=\ *n* -s **:** the European goatsucker

nightclothes \ˈ=,=\ *n pl* **1 :** garments worn in bed ⟨left me in total darkness, to scramble into my ~ as I could —Jane W. Carlyle⟩ **2** *obs* **:** informal evening wear

night cloud *n* **:** STRATUS

1nightclub \ˈ=,=\ *n* **:** a restaurant open at night usu. serving liquor, having a floor show, and providing music and space for dancing

2nightclub \"\ *vi* **:** to patronize nightclubs ⟨*nightclubbed* until the early hours . . . with a long-haired blond —*Associated Press*⟩ — **nightclubber** \"+ə(r)\ *n*

night court *n* **:** a criminal court in a large city that sits at night (as for summary disposition of criminal charges and the granting of bail)

night crawler *n* **:** EARTHWORM; *esp* **:** a large earthworm found on the surface of the soil usu. at night and used for fish bait

night crow *n* [ME *nihtcrowe, night crowe*, fr. *niht, night* night + *crowe* crow] **:** a bird that cries in the night; *esp* **:** NIGHT HERON

night dial *n* **1 :** a dial showing time by the moon's shadow — called also *moondial* **2 :** a clockface made luminous at night by a light from behind or by radioluminescent paint

nightdress \ˈ=,=\ *n* **1 :** NIGHTGOWN **2 :** NIGHTCLOTHES

night·ed \ˈnīd·əd\ *adj* [fr. past part. of obs. *night* to become night, grow dark, benight, fr. ME *nighten* (also, to spend the night) — more at NIGHT (v.)] **1 :** DARKENED, CLOUDED **2 :** BENIGHTED

night editor *n* **:** an editor in charge of the final makeup of a morning paper

night effect *n* **:** a shifting of the apparent direction of arrival of radio waves received with a direction finder that is sometimes accompanied by other irregularities of wave behavior and is most commonly observed at night

night emerald *n* **:** chrysolite or olivine having by artificial light a color resembling emerald and being used as a gem

night·ery \ˈnīd·ərē\ *n* -ES **:** NIGHTCLUB

nightfall \ˈ=,=\ *n* **:** the close of the day **:** DUSK

night fighter *n* **:** a fighter plane equipped with searchlights or radar and used at night as an interceptor

nightflit \ˈ=,=\ *n* [prob. fr. 1*night* + *flit* (v.)] **:** WOODCOCK

night-flowering catchfly \ˈ=,==-\ *n* **:** a European herb (*Silene noctiflora*) naturalized in No. America and having fragrant white or pink night-blooming flowers

nightfowl \ˈ=,=\ *n* **:** NIGHT BIRD

nightgear \ˈ=,=\ *n* **:** NIGHTCLOTHES 1

night glass *n* **:** a telescope having a low f-number to increase the light-gathering power for use at night

night glasses *n pl* **:** binoculars of similar design to the night glass

nightgown \ˈ=,=\ *n* [ME *nightgoun*, fr. 1*night* + *goun* gown] **1** *archaic* **:** a loose gown suitable for wear on evenings at home **:** DRESSING GOWN ⟨found him . . . wrapped in a tartan ~ —Sir Walter Scott⟩ **2 :** a garment resembling a dress or shirt designed for wear in bed ⟨she rose in her pale ~ —W.B. Yeats⟩ ⟨stockinet ~*s* are comfortable . . . for the baby —Benjamin Spock⟩

night green *n* [so called because it retains its greenness at night even under a dim gaslight] **:** a strong yellowish green that is paler than shamrock green and greener and less strong than Cyprus green

nighthawk \ˈ=,=\ *n* **1 a :** any of several No. American goatsuckers of the genus *Chordeiles* related to the whippoorwill; *specif* **:** a goatsucker (*C. minor*) common in the eastern U.S. that is marbled black, brown, and ocherous with white on the wings, throat, and in the male also on the tail and that feeds on insects which it secures on the wing principally at twilight flying at a considerable height and often diving almost vertically **b :** the European nightjar **c :** any of several large petrels of the genera *Pterodroma* and *Priofinus* inhabiting southern seas **d** *Austral* **:** MOREPORK 1 **2 :** a person who habitually stays up or goes about late at night **3 :** an independent taxicab operated chiefly at night **4 :** a ranch hand who works at night on the range; *specif* **:** a hand who herds the saddle horses at night

night heron *n* **:** any of various nocturnal or crepuscular herons of *Nycticorax* and related genera found in most temperate and tropical regions; *esp* **:** a heron (*N. nycticorax*) that ranges from southern Europe to India and northern Africa — see BLACK-CROWNED NIGHT HERON, YELLOW-CROWNED NIGHT HERON

night hitch *n* [1*night* + *hitch* (v.); fr. its use on night duty] **:** BUNKER SUIT

night horn *n* [prob. trans. of G *nachthorn*] **:** COR-DE-NUIT

night·ie *also* **nighty** \ˈnīd·ē\ *n, pl* **nighties** [*night*gown + *-ie* or *-y*] **:** NIGHTGOWN 2; *esp* **:** one for a woman or child

nighting *pres part of* NIGHT

night·in·gale \ˈnīˌtᵊnˌgāl, |d·ən,-, |tən,- *sometimes* |d·iŋ,g- *or* |d·eŋ,g- *or* |ti- *or* |tē-\ *n* -s [ME *nihtegale, nightingale*, fr. OE *nihtegale*, fr. *niht* night + *-gale* (fr. *galan* to sing); akin to OS *nahtigala* nightingale, MD *nachtegale*, OHG *nahtagala* — more at NIGHT, YELL] **1 :** any of several Old World thrushes of the genus *Luscinia:* as **a :** a thrush (*L. megarhyncha*) common in Great Britain that is about six inches long and russet brown above with the rump and tail lighter and the under parts whitish and that is noted for the sweet song of the male often heard at night during the breeding season **b :** a similar but larger thrush (*L. luscinia*) of eastern Europe **2 :** any of various birds that sing at night

night intruder *n* **:** an airplane equipped with navigation and radar equipment for flying into enemy territory at night

night intrusion *n* **:** the air tactic of interdicting enemy supply lines at night

nightjar \ˈ=,=\ *n* [1*night* + *jar* (pound); fr. its harsh sound] **:** a common grayish brown European nocturnal bird (*Caprimulgus europaeus*) that is speckled and barred with dark brown and buff and in the male has white markings on wing tips and outer tail feathers; *broadly* **:** GOATSUCKER — used esp. of Old World forms

night jasmine *n* **1 :** HURSINGHAR **2 :** a tropical shrub (*Cestrum nocturnum*) with tubular yellow flowers

night kaka *n* **:** KAKAPO

night key *n* **:** a key for operating a night latch

night latch *or* **night lock** *n* **:** a door lock having a spring bolt operated from the outside by a key and from the inside by a knob

night·less \ˈnītləs\ *adj* **:** having no night — **night·less·ness** *n* -ES

night letter *also* **night lettergram** *n* **:** a telegram sent at night at a reduced rate per word

night life *n* **:** the activity of pleasure-seekers at night (as in nightclubs)

night lifer *n* [*night life* + *-er*] **:** a person taking part in night life **:** NIGHTCLUBBER ⟨the *night lifers* . . . listen to the best Negro bands and pay feverish prices for liquor —Earl Brown⟩

night-light \ˈ=,=\ *n* **:** a light kept burning at night

night line *n* **:** a fishline set overnight

1nightlong \ˈ=,=\ *adj* [1*night* + *long*] **:** lasting the whole night ⟨a ~ festivity⟩

2nightlong \"\ *adv* **:** through the whole night ⟨working ~ to save whom they could —*Newsweek*⟩

1night·ly \ˈnītlē, -li\ *adj* [ME *nightly, nihtlich*, fr. OE *nihtlīc*, fr. *niht*, n., night + *-lic* -ly] **1 :** of or relating to the night or every night ⟨peering into the ~ murk —*Springfield (Mass.) Union*⟩ **2 :** happening, done, or used by night or every night ⟨giving five-minute ~ analyses of the news —*Current Biog.*⟩

2nightly \"\ *adv* [ME, fr. *nightly*, adj.] **:** every night ⟨gathered ~ to listen to the band concerts⟩; *also* **:** at or by night

night·man \ˈnītmən, *in sense 2* -ˌman *or* -ˌmaa(ə)n\ *n, pl* **nightmen 1 :** a man who empties privies by night **2** *usu* **night man :** a man whose work is at night; *specif* **:** NIGHT WATCHMAN 1

1night·mare \ˈnītˌma(a)(ə)r, -me|, |ə\ *n* [ME, fr. 1*night* + *mare* (spirit)] **1 :** an evil spirit formerly thought to oppress people during sleep: as **a :** INCUBUS **b :** SUCCUBUS **c :** a hag sometimes believed to be accompanied by nine attendant spirits ⟨the ~, with her whole ninefold, seems to make it the scene of her gambols —Washington Irving⟩ **2 :** a frightening dream accompanied by a sense of oppression or suffocation that usu. awakens the sleeper **3 a :** something producing a feeling of burden, agitation, anxiety, or terror **:** a source of trouble or worry ⟨the worst ~*s* were the bridges high above rushing torrents —Dillon Ripley⟩ ⟨the ~ of the surgeon dealing with battle wounds is infection —C.L.Boltz⟩ **b :** APPREHENSION, WORRY ⟨the life of a hotel man here is precarious and full of ~*s* —Sam Schneider⟩ **4 :** an experience, situation, or work of imagination having the monstrous character of a nightmare ⟨their existence would be one living ~ of hideous watchfulness and dread —*Blue Bk.*⟩ ⟨signs that we dwellers in the modern ~ love one another —F.A.Swinnerton⟩ ⟨an enormous imitation palace . . . a ~ of pretentiousness —John Hersey⟩ **syn** see FANCY

2nightmare \"\ *adj* **1 :** of or relating to a nightmare ⟨a ~ obsession in some current poetry⟩ **2 :** NIGHTMARISH ⟨began a ~ existence in an iron lung —*N.Y. Times Book. Rev.*⟩ ⟨years that seemed to pass with ~ speed —William DuBois⟩

night·mar·ish \-ma(a)rish, -mer-, -rēsh\ *adj* **:** resembling or suggestive of a nightmare ⟨had a ~ memory of certain doorknobs . . . horrible in color and in shape —Royal Cortissoz⟩ ⟨paints a ~ picture —Henry Hazlitt⟩ — **night·mar·ish·ly** *adv* — **night·mar·ish·ness** *n* -ES

night monkey *n* **:** NIGHT APE

night owl *n* **:** a person who keeps late hours at night **:** NIGHTHAWK

night parrot *n* **1 :** KAKAPO **2 :** a nearly extinct nocturnal terrestrial parrot (*Geopsittacus occidentalis*) of western Australia

night partridge *or* **night peck** *n* [*night partridge* fr. 1*night* + *partridge; night peck* fr. 1*night* + *peck* (v.)] **:** WOODCOCK

night piece *n* **:** a work (as a picture, composition, or writing) dealing with night

night rail *n* **:** a woman's loose robe or gown formerly worn as a nightgown or dressing gown

night raven *n* [ME, fr. OE *niht-hræfn*, fr. *niht* night + *hræfn* raven] **:** a bird that cries at night; *esp* **:** NIGHT HERON

night rider *n* **:** one that rides at night; *esp* **:** a member of a secret band who ride masked at night doing acts of violence for the purpose of punishing or terrorizing

night-riding \ˈ=,==\ *n* **:** activity of or resembling that of night riders

night-robe \ˈ=,=\ *n* **:** NIGHTGOWN ⟨in her *night-robe* loose she lay reclined —Sir Walter Scott⟩

night rocket *n* **:** DAME'S VIOLET

nights \ˈnīts\ *adv* [ME *nightes*, fr. OE *nihtes*, adverbial gen. of *niht* night — more at NIGHT] **:** in the nighttime repeatedly ⟨he had written it ~ and over weekends —*Current Biog.*⟩ **:** on any night ⟨gets little sleep ~⟩

night-scented stock \ˈ=,==-\ *n* **:** an annual or biennial stock (*Matthiola bicornis*) having very fragrant lilac or purplish flowers followed by forked elongated seed pods

night school *n* **:** school held in the evening; *specif* **:** a course offered (as by a university or high school) for people in working life and often stressing vocational training and recreational activities as well as general education — compare ADULT EDUCATION

nightshade \ˈ=,=\ *n* [ME *nighteschede, nightschode*, fr. OE *nihtscada*, prob. fr. *niht* night + *sceadu* shade; akin to MD *nachtschade* nightshade, OHG *nahtscato* — more at SHADE] **1 :** any plant of the genus *Solanum:* as **a :** BLACK NIGHTSHADE **b :** BITTERSWEET 2a **2 :** BELLADONNA 1 **3 :** HENBANE 1a

nightshade family *n* **:** SOLANACEAE
night shift *n* **1 :** a shift worked chiefly at night (as between 10 p.m. and 8 a.m.) **2 :** the workers on a night shift
nightshirt \ˈ=,=\ *n* **:** a nightgown resembling a shirt
nightside \ˈ=,=\ *n* **:** the staff that works on a morning edition of a newspaper — contrasted with *dayside*
night singer *n* **:** a bird that sings at night; *specif* **:** SEDGE WARBLER
night soil *n* **:** human excrement collected for fertilizing the soil
night song *n* **:** COMPLINE
night sparrow *n* **:** CHIPPING SPARROW
night spot *n* **:** NIGHTCLUB
nightstand \ˈ=,=\ *n* **:** NIGHT TABLE
nightstick \ˈ=,=\ *n* [so called fr. its being originally carried by night] **:** a policeman's club
nightstock \ˈ=,=\ *n* **:** DAME'S VIOLET
nightstool \ˈ=,=\ *n* **:** CLOSESTOOL

nightshirt

night sweat *n* **:** profuse sweating during sleep that is sometimes a symptom of febrile disease
night table *n* **:** a small bedside table or stand — called also *nightstand*
night terror *n* **:** a sudden awakening in dazed terror occurring in children and often preceded by a sudden shrill cry uttered in sleep
nighttide \ˈ=,=\ *n* **1 :** NIGHTTIME **2 :** a flood tide occurring during the night
nighttime \ˈ=,=\ *n* [ME, fr. ¹*night* + *time*] **:** the time from dusk to dawn
night vision *n* **:** ability to see in dim light (as provided by moon and stars)
nightwalker \ˈ=,==\ *n* [ME, fr. ¹*night* + *walker*] **1 a :** a person who roves about at night esp. with criminal intent **b :** a prostitute who walks the street at night **2 a :** an animal active at night **b** *chiefly North* **:** NIGHT CRAWLER

night table

night warbler *n* **:** SEDGE WARBLER
night watchman *n* **1 :** a watchman on duty by night **2 :** a member of a night watch
nightwear \ˈ=,=\ *n* **:** NIGHTCLOTHES 1
night willow herb *n* **:** an evening primrose (*Oenothera biennis*)
nightworks \ˈ=,=\ *n pl* **:** the parts of a lock mechanism which make the lock inoperable from the outside except by a key
nighty *var of* NIGHTIE
nig·nay \ˈnig,nā\ *also* **nig·nye** \-nī\ *n* -s [origin unknown] *chiefly Scot* **:** TRIVIALITY, TRIFLE
nig·ra \ˈnigrə\ *n* -s [by alter.] **:** NEGRO — often taken to be offensive
ni·gran·i·line \nīˈgranᵊlən\ *n* [ISV *nigr-* (fr. L *nigr-*, *niger* black) + *aniline*] **:** a dark blue basic compound yielding blue salts with acids that is formed from emeraldine as an intermediate in the production of aniline black
nig·ra scale \ˈnigrə-\ *n* [NL *nigra* (specific epithet of *Saissetia nigra*, species of coccid), fr. L, fem. of *niger* black, dark] **:** a coccid (*Saissetia nigra*) that is a serious pest on cotton, coffee, and other plants of warm temperate regions
ni·gre \ˈnīgə(r), ˈnig-\ *n* -s [prob. alter. of obs. E *nigger*, fr. E ¹*nigger*] **:** a dark-colored water solution of soap and impurities formed during manufacture of soap by settling from the neat soap
ni·gres·cence \nīˈgresᵊn(t)s\ *n* -s [*nigrescent* + *-ence*] **1 :** a process of becoming black or dark **2 :** BLACKNESS, DARKNESS; *specif* **:** darkness of complexion
ni·gres·cent \(ˈ)nī;gresᵊnt\ *adj* [L *nigrescent-*, *nigrescens*, pres. part. of *nigrescere* to become black, fr. *nigr-*, *niger* black] **:** BLACKISH
nig·ri·cant \ˈnigrə̇kənt\ *adj* [L *nigricant-*, *nigricans*, pres. part. of *nigricare* to be blackish, fr. *nigr-*, *niger* black] **:** BLACKISH
nig·ri·fy \ˈnigrəfī\ *vt* -ED/-ING/-ES [LL *nigrificare* to blacken, fr. L *nigr-*, *niger* black + *-ficare* -fy] **:** BLACKEN
ni·grine \ˈnīgrən\ *n* -s [G *nigrin*, fr. L *nigr-*, *niger* black + G *-in* -ine] **:** a mineral consisting of black ferruginous rutile
ni·gri·tian \nə̇ˈgrishən\ *adj, usu cap* [*Nigritia*, former name of the Sudan (fr. L *nigr-*, *niger* black) + E *-an*] **:** SUDANESE
nig·ri·tude \ˈnigrə,tüd, -ə,tyüd\ *n* -s [L *nigritudo*, fr. *nigr-*, *niger* black + *-tudo* -tude] **:** intense darkness **:** BLACKNESS
ni·gro·man·cer \ˈnīgrə,man(t)sə(r)\ *archaic var of* NECROMANCER
ni·grom·e·ter \nīˈgrämədə(r)\ *n* [*nigro-* (fr. L *nigr-*, *niger* black) + *-meter*] **:** an instrument for measuring degree of blackness (as of paints or dyes)
ni·gro·sine \ˈnīgrə,sēn, -,sən\ *also* **ni·gro·sin** \-,sən\ *n* -s *often cap* [L *nigr-*, *niger* black + E *-ose* + *-ine* or *-in*] **:** any of several azine dyes closely related to the indulines: as **a** *or* **nigrosine base B** *usu cap N & both Bs* **:** an oil-soluble bluish black dye obtained as the free base by heating aniline and aniline hydrochloride with nitrobenzene or nitrophenol in the presence of iron and used chiefly in coloring waxes, shoe polish, plastics, and lacquers and as wood stains — see DYE table I (under *Solvent Black 7*) **b** *or* **nigrosine spirit soluble** *usu cap N & both Ss* **:** a chloride of the free base that is soluble in alcohol and is used similarly — see DYE table I (under *Solvent Black 5*) **c** *or* **nigrosine water soluble** *usu cap N&W&S* **:** a water-soluble sulfonation product of the free base or of its chloride used chiefly in dyeing leather and paper and as a biological stain — see DYE table I (under *Acid Black 2*)
ni·grous \ˈnīgrəs\ *adj* [L *nigr-*, *niger* black + E *-ous*] **:** BLACK
nigs *pl of* NIG, *pres 3d sing of* NIG
ni·gua \ˈnēgwə\ *n* -s [Sp, fr. Taino] **:** CHIGOE
ni·gun *or* **nig·gun** \nēˈgün\ *n, pl* **ni·gu·nim** *or* **nig·gu·nim** \,nēgüˈnēm\ [LHeb *niggūn*, fr. Heb *naggēn* to play an instrument] **:** MELODY; *specif* **:** a traditional synagogal or folk melody
ni·hil de·bet \ˈnī,hilˈdē,bet\ *n* [L, he owes nothing] **:** a legal plea of the general issue in an action of debt on a simple contract or on a specialty when the deed is the only inducement to the action
nihil di·cit \-ˈdī,sit\ *n* [L, he says nothing] **1 :** a refusal or neglect by the defendant to plead or answer **2 :** a judgment rendered against a defendant charged with nihil dicit
nihil ha·bet \-ˈhā,bet\ *n* [L, he has nothing] **:** a return by a sheriff or other officer made on a scire facias or other writ indicating that the defendant has no property within reach of the process, and the defendant has not been served
ni·hil·ian·ism \nīˈhilyə,nizəm\ *n* -s [L *nihil* nothing + E *-ianism* (as in *pelagianism*) — more at NIL] **:** a doctrine that the human nature of Christ was nothing having true subsistence
ni·hi·lism \ˈnīə,lizəm, ˈnihə̇,-, ˈnēə,- *sometimes* ˈnīhə̇,- *or* ˈnēhə̇,-\ *n* -s [G *nihilismus*, fr. L *nihil* nothing + G *-ismus* -ism] **1 a :** a viewpoint that all traditional values and beliefs are unfounded and that all existence is consequently senseless and useless **:** a denial of intrinsic meaning and value in life **b :** a doctrine that denies or is taken as denying any objective or real ground of truth; *specif* **:** an ethical doctrine that denies any objective ground of moral principles — called also *ethical nihilism, moral nihilism* **2 a :** a doctrine that no reality exists **b :** a profession of nihilistic delusions **3 :** an annihilation (as by mystical contemplation) of desires and self-consciousness **4 a** [Russ *nigilizm*, fr. F *nihilisme*, fr. G *nihilismus*] (1) **:** a doctrine or belief that conditions in the social organization are so bad as to make destruction desirable for its own sake independent of any constructive program or possibility (2) *usu cap* **:** the program or doctrine of a Russian party or succession of parties of the 19th and 20th centuries who proposed various schemes of revolutionary reform and resorted to terrorism and assassination **b :** revolutionary propaganda **:** TERRORISM **5 :** scepticism as to the therapeutic value of a drug or method ⟨therapeutic ~⟩ **6 :** the advocacy or practice of nihilism **7 :** a nihilistic belief, act, or utterance
¹**ni·hi·list** \-ˌlə̇st\ *n* -s *sometimes cap* [F *nihiliste*, fr. L *nihil* nothing + F *-iste* -ist] **1 :** an advocate of nihilism **2** [Russ *nigilist*, fr. F *nihiliste*] **:** a member of a Russian nihilistic party resorting to terrorism
²**nihilist** \ˈ" *or* **ni·hi·lis·tic** \;==ˈlistik\ *adj* **:** of, relating to, or characterized by nihilism — **ni·hi·lis·ti·cal·ly** \-tə̇k(ə)lē\ *adv*
nihilist cipher *n, usu cap N* [¹*nihilist*; fr. its use by the Russian nihilists] **:** a substitution method replacing each letter by its row and column numbers in an alphabet square
nihilistic delusion *n* **:** the belief that oneself, a part of one's body, or the real world does not exist or has been destroyed
ni·hil·i·ty \nīˈhiləd·ē\ *n* -ES [F *nihilité*, fr. MF, fr. ML *nihilitat-*, *nihilitas*, fr. L *nihil* nothing + *-itat-*, *-itas* -ity] **1 :** NOTHINGNESS **2 :** a thing amounting to nothing **:** NULLITY, TRIFLE
nihil ob·stat \-ˈäbz,tat, -b,st-\ *n* [L, nothing hinders] **1 :** the certification by an official censor of the Roman Catholic Church that a book has been examined and found to contain nothing opposed to faith and morals **2 :** authoritative or official approval ⟨the surest road to fame was . . . through the imprimatur and *nihil obstat* of a foreign critic —P.H.Odegard⟩
ni·i·ga·ta \,nēˈēgäd·ə\ *adj, usu cap* [fr. *Niigata*, Japan] **:** of or from the city of Niigata, Japan **:** of the kind or style prevalent in Niigata
nij·me·gen \ˈnī,māgən\ *adj, usu cap* [fr. *Nijmegen*, Netherlands] **:** of or from the city of Nijmegen, Netherlands **:** of the kind or style prevalent in Nijmegen
ni·kau \ˈnē,kaů\ *or* **nikau palm** *n* -s [Maori *nikau*] **:** a graceful pinnate-leaved New Zealand palm (*Kentia sapida*)
nik·eth·amide \nə̇ˈkethə,mīd, -məd\ *n* [*nik-* (alter. of *nicotinic acid*) + *diethyl* + *amide*] **:** a bitter viscous liquid or crystalline compound $C_5H_4NCON(C_2H_5)_2$ used chiefly in aqueous solution as a respiratory stimulant; *N,N*-diethyl-nicotinamide
nik·ko \ˈni(,)kō\ *n* -s *often cap* [prob. fr. *Nikko*, Japan] **:** CHINA BLUE
nikko fir *n, usu cap N* [fr. *Nikko*, village in central Japan] **:** a Japanese evergreen tree (*Abies homolepis*) widely cultivated for ornament and having deeply grooved branchlets, cones that are purple when young, and leaves slightly bifid at the apex
ni·ko·la·ev \,nikəˈlīəf\ *adj, usu cap* [fr. *Nikolaev*, U.S.S.R.] **:** of or from the city of Nikolaev, U.S.S.R. **:** of the kind or style prevalent in Nikolaev
¹**nil** \ˈnil\ *n* -s [L, nothing, contr. of *nihil*, *nihilum*, prob. fr. *ne-* (negative prefix) + *hilum* small thing, trifle — more at NO] **1 :** NOTHING, ZERO ⟨reducing to almost ~ the relevant collection work —John Fiddler⟩ **2** *chiefly Brit* **:** a score of nothing ⟨a game won by a goal to ~⟩ ⟨a *nil*-all draw⟩
²**nil** \ˈ"\ *adj* **:** NONEXISTENT — usu. used predicatively ⟨tuition fees are ~ or nominal —B.K.Sandwell⟩
³**nil** \ˈ"\ *n* -s [short for *nilgai*] **:** a male nilgai
nil di·cit \-ˈdī,sit\ *n* [L, he says nothing] **:** NIHIL DICIT
nile \ˈnīl *esp before pause or consonant* -īəl\ *or* **nile green** *n* -s *often cap N* [fr. *Nile* river, Africa] **:** a variable color averaging a pale yellow green that is greener and stronger than smoke gray and greener and deeper than oyster gray — called also *boa, eau de Nile*
nile bird *n, usu cap N* [fr. *Nile*, river in Africa] **1** *dial Eng* **:** WRYNECK **2 :** CROCODILE BIRD
nile blue *n* [fr. *Nile*, river in Africa] **1** *often cap N* **:** a light bluish green, greener and deeper than average aqua green (sense 1), bluer and paler than average turquoise green, and bluer and stronger than robin's-egg blue (sense 2) **2** *or* **nile blue A** *usu cap N & sometimes cap B* **:** an oxazine dye used chiefly in the form of the sulfate as a biological stain (as for staining neutral fat red in the presence of dilute sulfuric acid)
nile crocodile *n, usu cap N* **:** a widely distributed and dangerous African crocodile (*Crocodylus niloticus*)
nile goose *n, usu cap N* **:** EGYPTIAN GOOSE
nile perch *n, usu cap N* **:** a large predacious food fish (*Lates nilotica*) of the rivers and lakes of northern and central Africa that may exceed 200 pounds in weight — called also *capitaine*
nil·gai *also* **nil·ghai** \ˈnil,gī\ *n, pl* **nilgais** *or* **nilgai** *also* **nilghais** *or* **nilghai** [Hindi *nīlgāw* blue bull (fem. *nīlgāī*), fr. Skt *nīla* dark blue + *go* bull, cow — more at ANILINE, COW (animal)] **:** a large bluish gray antelope (*Boselaphus tragocamelus*) of India, the male of which has short horns, a black mane, and a bunch of long hair on the throat — called also *blue bull*
nil·gi·ri nettle *or* **nil·ghi·ri nettle** \ˈnilgərē-\ *n, usu cap 1st N* [fr. *Nilgiri* Hills, India] **:** any of several plants (genus *Girardinia*) of the family Urticaceae; *esp* **:** an East Indian fiber plant (*G. palmata*) with stinging foliage and stems that yield a strong fiber useful for cordage
nil grade *n* **:** ZERO GRADE
¹**nill** \ˈnil\ *vb* -ED/-ING/-S [ME *nilen*, *nellen*, fr. OE *nyllan*, *nellan*, fr. *ne* not + *wyllan* to wish — more at NO, WILL] *vi*, *archaic* **:** to be unwilling ⟨will you ~ you, I will marry you —Shak.⟩ ~ *vt, archaic* **:** not to will **:** REFUSE, REJECT, PREVENT
²**nill** \ˈ"\ *dial Eng var of* NEEDLE
nil·ly-wil·ly \;nilē;wilē\ *adv* [by alter.] **:** WILLY-NILLY
ni·lo-hamite \;nī(,)lō+\ *n, usu cap N&H* [¹*nilotic* + *hamite*] **:** a member of a group of East African pastoral peoples including esp. the Masai and others linguistically, traditionally, and otherwise culturally affiliated with these
ni·lo-hamitic \ˈ"+\ *n, usu cap N&H* [¹*nilotic* + *hamitic*] **:** the eastern branch of the Nilotic languages
ni·lom·e·ter \nīˈlämədə(r)\ *n, often cap* [modif. (influenced by E *-meter*) of NL *nilometrion*, fr. Gk *neilometrion*, fr. *Neilos* Nile, river in Africa + *-metrion* (fr. *metron* measure) — more at MEASURE] **:** a gauge for measuring the height of water in the Nile esp. during its flood; *specif* **:** a graduated scale cut on a natural rock or in the stone wall of a pit communicating with the river — **ni·lo·met·ric** \,nīləˈme·trik\ *adj, often cap*
ni·lot \ˈnī,lät, -,lət\ *n, pl* **ni·lo·tes** \nīˈlōd·(,)ēz, -ō,tēz\ *usu cap* [modif. (influenced by E *-ot* as in *cypriot*) of Gk *Neilōtēs* in the Nile, on the Nile, fr. *Neilos* Nile] **:** a native of the region of the Upper Nile
¹**ni·lot·ic** \(ˈ)nī;läd·|ik, -ät|, |ēk\ *adj, usu cap* [L *niloticus* of the Nile, fr. *nilotis*, fem. adj. (fr. Gk *neilōtis*, fr. *Neilos* Nile) + *-icus* -ic] **1 :** of or relating to the Nile or the peoples dwelling in the territory directly drained by it ⟨the *Nilotic* year⟩; *specif* **:** of or relating to the Dinka, Luo, Nuer, Shilluk and linguistically related peoples who constitute a distinctive negroid race or subrace characterized particularly by extreme height **2 :** of, relating to, or constituting the Nilotic group of Sudanic languages
²**nilotic** \ˈ"\ *n* -s *usu cap* **1 :** a member of a Nilotic people **2 :** a group of languages spoken in the Nile valley above Khartoum and southeastward into Kenya and Tanganyika, divided into western containing Acholi, Alur, Dinka, Lango, Luo, Nuer, and Shilluk and eastern containing Bari, Karamojong, Masai, Nandi, and Teso, and variously considered as a family or as a branch of the Chari-Nile family **3 :** the western division only of the Nilotic languages in distinction to the eastern branch called Nilo-Hamitic
nils *pl of* NIL
¹**nim** \ˈnim\ *vb* **nimmed; nimmed; nimming; nims** [fr. earlier *nim* to take, fr. ME *nimen*, fr. OE *niman* — more at NIMBLE] *vt* **:** STEAL, FILCH ⟨this snuff-box . . . *nimm'd* two nights ago in the park —John Gay⟩ ⟨a kirtle that I would not have *nimmed* from a hedge —E.G.Bulwer-Lytton⟩ ~ *vi, archaic* **:** THIEVE
²**nim** \ˈ"\ *n* -s [prob. fr. ¹*nim*] **:** any of various games in which counters are laid out in one or more piles of agreed numbers, each of two players in turn draws one or more counters, and the object is to take the last counter, force the opponent to take it, or take the most or the fewest counters
³**nim** *var of* NEEM
nimb \ˈnim *also* -mb\ *n, pl* **nimbs** \-mz\ [L *nimbus*] **:** NIMBUS, HALO ⟨with an aureate ~ —Thomas Hardy⟩
nimbed \-md\ *also* **nim·bat·ed** \-m,bād·ə̇d\ *adj* [*nimb* + *-ed* or *-ated* (fr. *-ate* + *-ed*)] **:** having a nimbus esp. around the head ⟨apostles, martyrs, and saints all ~ with glory —Daniel Rock⟩
¹**nim·ble** \ˈnimbəl\ *adj* **nim·bler** \-b(ə)lə(r)\ **nim·blest** \-b(ə)lə̇st\ [ME *nymel*, *nemel*, fr. OE *numol* holding much, quick at grasping, *nǣmel* receptive, both from *niman* to take; akin to OHG *neman* to take, ON *nema*, Goth *niman*, L *numerus* number, Gk *nemein* to distribute, pasture, manage, *nomos* pasture, district, *nomos* usage, custom, law, Av *nəmah* loan; basic meaning: to assign] **1 a :** marked by quick light movement **:** moving easily or dexterously **:** AGILE, LIVELY ⟨~ fingers⟩ ⟨a ~ rabbit⟩ ⟨a ~ leap⟩ ⟨a ~ climber⟩ ⟨a ~ well-schooled colt with a smooth, powerful, effortless stride —G.F. T.Ryall⟩ ⟨a ~, fast-moving shovel —*Steel*⟩ **b** *of money* **:** circulating rapidly ⟨~ shilling⟩ ⟨a ~ sixpence is better than a slow shilling —*North Carolina Folklore*⟩ **2 a :** marked by quick, alert, clever conception, comprehension, or resourcefulness ⟨~ mind⟩ ⟨~ tongue⟩ ⟨her lines combine the closest observation and the *nimblest* imagination —Louis Untermeyer⟩ ⟨the amiability of these Italians, aided by their sharp and ~ wits, caused them to overflow with plausible suggestions —Nathaniel Hawthorne⟩ ⟨writes ~ dialogue —Bernard Hollowood⟩ **b :** marked by ready sensitive responsiveness ⟨a ~ listener⟩ ⟨nothing like playacting to make you ~ in your feelings —Mary Austin⟩ ⟨disinclination of every ~ spirit to bruise itself against walls —*Nation*⟩ **syn** see AGILE
²**nimble** \ˈ"\ *vi* **nimbled; nimbled; nimbling;** \-b(ə)liŋ\ **nimbles** *archaic* **:** to move or act nimbly
nimble kate \ˈ==,kāt\ *n, usu cap K* [so called fr. its climbing habits] **:** BUR CUCUMBER 1
nimbleness *n* -ES **:** the quality or state of being nimble
nimble will \ˈ==,wil\ *n, often cap W* [so called fr. its rapid spreading] **:** a slender branching American grass (*Muhlenbergia schreberi*) of some value for grazing in the central U.S.
nim·bly \-blē, -bli\ *adv* [ME *nemely*, fr. *nemel* nimble + *-ly*] **:** in a nimble manner ⟨~ scaling an iron gate —Charles Dickens⟩ ⟨speaks crisply, ~, and neatly —Francis Fergusson⟩
nimbo- *comb form* [NL *nimbus*] **:** nimbus and ⟨*nimbo*stratus⟩
nim·bo·ran \ˈnimbə,ran\ *n, pl* **nimboran** *or* **nimborans** *usu cap* **1 :** a Papuan people of Netherlands New Guinea **2 :** a member of the Nimboran people
nim·bose \ˈnim,bōs\ *adj* [L *nimbosus*, fr. *nimbus* + *-osus* -ose] **:** CLOUDY, STORMY
nim·bo·stratus \;nim(,)bō+\ *n* [NL, fr. *nimbo-* + *stratus*] **:** a low dark gray rainy cloud layer
nim·bus \ˈnimbəs\ *n, pl* **nim·bi** \-(,)bī\ *or* **nimbus·es** [L, rainstorm, cloud; akin to Pahlavi *namb* dew, mist and perh. to L *imber* rain, *nebula* mist — more at IMBRICATE] **1 a :** a luminous vapor, cloud, or atmosphere about a god or goddess when on earth **b :** a cloud or atmosphere (as of romance) about a person or thing ⟨before the ~ of idolatry enveloped him —*N.Y.Herald Tribune Bk. Rev.*⟩ **2 :** an indication in an art work (as a painting) of radiant light or glory around or above the head of a sacred or venerated personage; *specif* **:** a circle, disk, rectangle, triangle, or rayed structure about the head of a drawn or sculptured divinity, saint, or sovereign — see AUREOLE 2 **3 a :** the rain cloud characterized by its uniform grayness and extending over the entire sky in seasons of continued rain **b :** a cloud from which rain is falling
nim·bused \-bəst\ *adj* **:** furnished with or surrounded by a nimbus ⟨they were ~ . . . by the last light of a sun that had set —Hugh MacLennan⟩
ni·mi·e·ty \nə̇ˈmīəd·ē\ *n* -ES [LL *nimietas*, fr. *nimie-* (fr. L *nimius* too much, adj., fr. *nimis*, adv.) + *-tas* -ty; perh. akin to L *ne-* not and to L *minor* — more at NO, MINOR] **:** EXCESS, REDUNDANCY ⟨Edwardian ~ made poems drowsier, pictures bigger . . . meals heavier than ever before —*Times Lit. Supp.*⟩
niminy *adj* [by shortening] **:** NIMINY-PIMINY
nim·i·ny-pim·i·ny \;nimənē;pimənē\ *adj* [prob. alter. of *namby-pamby*] **:** MIMINY-PIMINY ⟨the . . . press is already too *niminy-piminy*, too nice altogether, too refined —*Persuasion*⟩
nim·i·ous \ˈnimēəs\ *adj* [ME *nymyos*, fr. L *nimius*] **:** EXCESSIVE, EXTRAVAGANT ⟨the author . . . is never ~; there is nothing in excess —Sydney Smith⟩
nimmed *past of* NIM
nim·mer \ˈnimə(r)\ *n* -s [¹*nim* + *-er*] **:** THIEF, PILFERER
nimming *pres part of* NIM
nim·ra·vus \nimˈrāvəs\ *n, cap* [NL] **:** a genus of Oligocene and Miocene No. American saber-toothed tigers that is usu. made type of a distinct subfamily
nim·rod \ˈnim,räd\ *n* -s [fr. *Nimrod*, son of Cush, described as a mighty man and hunter (Gen 10:8–9)] **1** *usu cap, obs* **:** TYRANT **2** *sometimes cap* **:** HUNTER ⟨more squirrel hunters than any other kind of ~s in Alabama —*Ala. Dept. of Conservation*⟩ — **nim·rod·ian** \(ˈ)nim;rädēən, -rōd-\ *adj, sometimes cap*
nims *pres 3d sing of* NIM, *pl of* NIM
nim·shi \ˈnim(p)shē\ *n* [prob. alter. of E dial. *nimshie* flighty girl] *North* **:** a silly person **:** FOOL
nim tree *n* [Hindi *nīm* — more at NEEM] **:** MARGOSA
nin·com *or* **nin·cum** \ˈninkəm, -iŋk-\ *n* -s [by shortening] **:** NINCOMPOOP
nin·com·poop \ˈninkəm,püp *also* -iŋk-\ *n* -s [origin unknown] **:** FOOL, SIMPLETON ⟨compelled to vote for dummies and ~s —G.B.Shaw⟩ — **nin·com·poop·ery** \-üpərē, -ri, ,==ˈ===\ *n* -ES
¹**nine** \ˈnīn *sometimes for emphasis, as by telephone operators*, -īən\ *adj* [ME *nyne*, *nigen*, fr. OE *nigon*; akin to OHG & Goth *niun* nine, ON *nīu*, L *novem*, Gk *ennea*, Skt *nava*] **:** being one more than eight in number ⟨~ years⟩ — see NUMBER table
²**nine** \ˈ"\ *pron, pl in constr* [ME *nyne*, fr. OE *nigone*, fr. *nigon*, adj.] **:** nine countable persons or things not specified but under consideration and being enumerated ⟨~ are here⟩ ⟨~ were found⟩
³**nine** \ˈ"\ *n* -s [ME, fr. *nyne*, adj. & pron.] **1 :** one more than eight **:** three threes **:** the square of three **2 a :** nine units or objects ⟨a total of ~⟩ **b :** a group or set of nine ⟨arranged by ~s⟩ **3 a :** the numerable quantity symbolized by the arabic numeral 9 **b :** the figure 9 **4 :** nine o'clock — compare BELL table, TIME illustration **5 :** the ninth in a set or series: as **a :** a playing card marked to show that it is ninth in a suit **b :** an article of clothing of the ninth size ⟨wears a ~⟩ **6 :** something having as an essential feature nine units or members: as **a :** a playing team of nine members; *esp* **:** a baseball team **b :** the first or last 9 holes of an 18-hole golf course ⟨fired a two-under-par 33 on the front ~ and held his advantage in the back ~ —*Vancouver (Canada) Sun*⟩ — **to the nines** *also* **up to the nines :** to the highest point, degree, or mark ⟨dressed *to the nines* —*Harper's Bazaar*⟩ ⟨the paper . . . is done *to the nines* with a sensitiveness worthy of its subject —Leonard Bacon⟩ ⟨garnished *up to the nines* —C.E.Montague⟩
nine-banded armadillo \ˈ=,==-\ *n* **:** PEBA
ninebark \ˈ=,=\ *n* **:** an American white-flowered shrub of the genus *Physocarpus* having bark which separates into many thin layers
nine days' wonder *n* **:** an object or event that creates a short-lived sensation ⟨those political explosions . . . that make a *nine days' wonder* till something fresh comes along —Mary Deasy⟩ ⟨a *nine days' wonder*, fated to sink swiftly into obscurity —*Times Lit. Supp.*⟩
nine-eyes \ˈ=,=\ *n pl but sing or pl in constr, also* **nine-eyed eel** \ˈ=,=-\ [fr. its numerous spiracles] **:** LAMPREY
¹**ninefold** \ˈ=;=\ *adj* **1 :** having nine parts or aspects **2 :** being nine times as large, as great, or as many as some understood size, degree, or amount ⟨a ~ increase⟩
²**ninefold** \ˈ"\ *adv* **:** to nine times as much or as many **:** by nine times ⟨increased ~⟩
nineholes \ˈ=,=\ *n pl but sing in constr* **1 :** a game in which balls or marbles are rolled into nine holes in the ground or through arches in a board **2 :** a difficult situation — usu. used in the phrase *in the nineholes*
nine-killer \ˈ=,==\ *n* [trans. of D *negendoder* or G *neuntöter*; fr. the belief that it kills nine birds a day] **:** SHRIKE
nine-men's morris *n* **:** morris played with nine counters
nine mile fever *n, usu cap N&M* [fr. *Nine Mile* Creek, Mont., where it was first recognized] **:** a rickettsial disease identical with or closely related to Q fever that affects man and various mammals in parts of the northwestern U.S.
nine·pence *Brit* ˈnīnpən(t)s *sometimes* -īmp-, *US* " *or* -īn,pen-\ *n, pl* **ninepence** *or* **ninepences 1 :** the sum of nine usu. British pennies **2 :** an old Irish shilling worth in England about nine British pennies **3 :** the old Spanish real formerly worth in New England about 12½ cents
nine·pen·ny \-pənē, -ni; -,penē\ *adj* **:** costing or having the value of ninepence
ninepenny morris *n* **:** NINE-MEN'S MORRIS
ninepin \ˈ=,=\ *n* **1 :** a pin used in ninepins **2 ninepins** *pl but sing in constr* **:** a bowling game played with nine wooden pins **:** tenpins played without the headpin
ninepin block *n* **:** a fairlead shaped like a ninepin
nine-spined stickleback \ˈ=,=-\ *n* **:** a stickleback (*Pungitius pungitius*) of both Europe and America

ninepins set up ready for play

¹**nine·teen** \(ˈ)nīn-ˈtēn, -īntˈtēn\ *adj* [ME *nynetene*, *nigentene*, fr. OE *nigontīene*, *nigontȳne*, *nigontēne* (akin to OHG *niunzehan*, ON *nītjān*), fr.

nigon nine + *-tiene, -tȳne, -tēne* (fr. *tien, tȳn, tēn* ten) — more at NINE, TEN] **:** being one more than 18 in number ⟨~ years⟩ — see NUMBER table; used prepositively to designate various years of the 20th century ⟨the *nineteen*-eighties⟩ ⟨the early *nineteen*-hundreds⟩

2nineteen \"\ *pron, pl in constr* [ME *nynetene, nigentene,* fr. *nynetene, nigentene* nineteen, adj.] **:** nineteen countable persons or things not specified but under consideration and being enumerated ⟨~ are here⟩ ⟨~ were found⟩

3nineteen \"\ *n* -s **1 :** 10 and nine **2 a :** 19 units or objects ⟨a total of ~⟩ **b :** a group or set of 19 **3 :** the numerable quantity symbolized by the arabic numerals 19 **4 :** the nineteenth in a set or series; *esp* **:** an article of clothing of the nineteenth size ⟨wears a ~⟩ **5 :** something having as an essential feature nineteen units or members **6** [so called from the fact that no hand can score exactly 19] **:** a score of zero in cribbage

nineteen order *n* **:** a train order for which the engineer or other member of a train crew does not have to sign — compare THIRTY-ONE ORDER

1nine·teenth \-ēn(t)th\ *adj* [ME *nyntenthe,* adj. & n., alter. (influenced by *nynetene* nineteen) of *nyentethe,* fr. OE *nigontēotha,* fr. *nigontiene, nigontȳne, nigontēne* nineteen + *-otha, -tha* -th] **1 :** being number 19 in a countable series ⟨the ~ day⟩ — see NUMBER table **2 :** being one of 19 equal parts into which something is divisible ⟨a ~ share of the money⟩

2nineteenth \"\ *n, pl* **nineteenths** \-ēn(t)s,-ēn(t)ths\ **1 :** number 19 in a countable series ⟨the ~ of the month⟩ **2 :** the quotient of a unit divided by 19 **:** one of 19 equal parts of something ⟨one ~ of the total⟩ **3 a :** a musical interval of two octaves and a fifth **b :** an organ stop sounding pitches two octaves and a fifth above the keys used

nineteenth hole *n* **:** the locker room or other convivial gathering place of golfers after play on the course

1nine·ti·eth \ˈnīntēə̇th, -ti\ *adj* [ME *nyntithe,* fr. OE *nigontigotha,* fr. *nigontig* ninety + *-otha, -tha* -th] **1 :** being number 90 in a countable series ⟨the ~ day⟩ — see NUMBER table **2 :** being one of 90 equal parts into which something is divisible ⟨a ~ share of the money⟩

2ninetieth \"\ *n* -s **1 :** number 90 in a countable series **2 :** the quotient of a unit divided by 90 **:** one of 90 equal parts of something ⟨one ~ of the total⟩

1nine·ty \ˈnīntē, -ti\ *adj* [ME *nynety, nigenti,* fr. OE *nigontig,* short for *hundnigontig,* fr. *hundnigontig,* n., group of 90, fr. *hund* hundred + *nigon* nine + *-tig* group of ten — more at EIGHTY] **:** being one more than 89 in number ⟨~ years⟩ — see NUMBER table

2ninety \"\ *pron, pl in constr* **:** ninety countable persons or things not specified but under consideration and being enumerated ⟨~ are here⟩ ⟨~ were found⟩

3ninety \"\ *n* -ES **1 :** nine tens **:** twice 45 **:** three times 30 **:** five times 18 **:** six fifteens **:** fourscore and 10 **2 a :** 90 units or objects ⟨a total of ~⟩ **b :** a group or set of 90 **3 :** the numerable quantity symbolized by the arabic numerals 90 **4 :** the 90th in a set or series **5 :** something having as an essential feature 90 units or numbers **6 nineties** *pl* **a :** the numbers 90 to 99 inclusive ⟨a golf score in the *nineties*⟩ ⟨all his grades in that subject are in the *nineties*⟩ **b (1) :** the members of a series or set of successive numbers that end in 90 to 99 inclusive ⟨the *nineties* of the preceding century⟩ ⟨lives in the *nineties* in the next block⟩ **(2)** *usu cap* **:** the years of the last decade of the 19th century ⟨the Gay *Nineties*⟩ ⟨the so-called decadent romantics of the *Nineties* —*Publ's Mod. Lang. Assoc. of Amer.*⟩ **c :** the portion of a continuum lying between 90 and 100 on a scale of measurement or segmentation ⟨temperatures in the high *nineties* tomorrow⟩ ⟨a man in his *nineties*⟩ ⟨overcoats selling in the *nineties*⟩

ninety-day wonder *n* **:** a person commissioned as an officer in one of the armed services after 90 days or a relatively short length of training

1ninety-eight \¦==¦=\ *adj* **:** being one more than 97 in number ⟨*ninety-eight* years⟩ — see NUMBER table

2ninety-eight \"\ *pron, pl in constr* **:** ninety-eight countable persons or things not specified but under consideration and being enumerated ⟨*ninety-eight* are here⟩ ⟨*ninety-eight* were found⟩

3ninety-eight \"\ *n* **1 :** eight and 90 **:** two times 49 **:** seven times 14 **2 a :** 98 units or objects ⟨a total of *ninety-eight*⟩ **b :** a group or set of 98 **3 :** the numerable quantity symbolized by the arabic numerals 98

1ninety-eighth \¦==¦=\ *adj* **1 :** being number 98 in a countable series ⟨the *ninety-eighth* day⟩ — see NUMBER table **2 :** being one of 98 equal parts into which something is divisible ⟨a *ninety-eighth* share of the money⟩

2ninety-eighth \"\ *n* **1 :** number 98 in a countable series **2 :** the quotient of a unit divided by 98 **:** one of 98 equal parts of something

1ninety-fifth \¦==¦=\ *adj* **1 :** being number 95 in a countable series ⟨the *ninety-fifth* day⟩ — see NUMBER table **2 :** being one of 95 equal parts into which something is divisible ⟨a *ninety-fifth* share of the money⟩

2ninety-fifth \"\ *n* **1 :** number 95 in a countable series **2 :** the quotient of a unit divided by 95 **:** one of 95 equal parts of something

1ninety-first \¦==¦=\ *adj* **1 :** being number 91 in a countable series ⟨the *ninety-first* day⟩ — see NUMBER table **2 :** being one of 91 equal parts into which something is divisible ⟨a *ninety-first* share of the money⟩

2ninety-first \"\ *n* **1 :** number 91 in a countable series **2 :** the quotient of a unit divided by 91 **:** one of 91 equal parts of something

1ninety-five \¦==¦=\ *adj* **:** being one more than 94 in number ⟨*ninety-five* years⟩ — see NUMBER table

2ninety-five \"\ *pron, pl in constr* **:** ninety-five countable persons or things not specified but under consideration and being enumerated ⟨*ninety-five* are here⟩ ⟨*ninety-five* were found⟩

3ninety-five \"\ *n* **1 :** five and 90 **:** five times 19 **2 a :** 95 units or objects ⟨a total of *ninety-five*⟩ **b :** a group or set of 95 **3 :** the numerable quantity symbolized by the arabic numerals 95

1ninety-four \¦==¦=\ *adj* **:** being one more than 93 in number ⟨*ninety-four* years⟩ — see NUMBER table

2ninety-four \"\ *pron, pl in constr* **:** ninety-four countable persons or things not specified but under consideration and being enumerated ⟨*ninety-four* are here⟩ ⟨*ninety-four* were found⟩

3ninety-four \"\ *n* **1 :** four and 90 **:** two times 47 **2 a :** 94 units or objects ⟨a total of *ninety-four*⟩ **b :** a group or set of 94 **3 :** the numerable quantity symbolized by the arabic numerals 94

1ninety-fourth \¦==¦=\ *adj* **1 :** being number 94 in a countable series ⟨the *ninety-fourth* day⟩ — see NUMBER table **2 :** being one of 94 equal parts into which something is divisible ⟨a *ninety-fourth* share of the money⟩

2ninety-fourth \"\ *n* **1 :** number 94 in a countable series **2 :** the quotient of a unit divided by 94 **:** one of 94 equal parts of something

nine·ty·ish \ˈnīntēish, -ti·ish\ *adj* **:** resembling what was current in the 1890s ⟨the tale of macabre horror is definitely ~ —F.B.Millett⟩

1ninety-nine \¦==¦=\ *adj* **:** being one more than 98 in number ⟨*ninety-nine* years⟩ — see NUMBER table

2ninety-nine \"\ *pron, pl in constr* **:** ninety-nine countable persons or things not specified but under consideration and being enumerated ⟨*ninety-nine* are here⟩ ⟨*ninety-nine* were found⟩

3ninety-nine \"\ *n* **1 :** nine and 90 **:** three times 33 **:** nine times 11 **2 a :** 99 units or objects ⟨a total of *ninety-nine*⟩ **b :** a group or set of 99 **3 :** the numerable quantity symbolized by the arabic numerals 99 — often used with *and* instead of a hyphen

1ninety-ninth \¦==¦=\ *adj* **1 :** being number 99 in a countable series ⟨the *ninety-ninth* day⟩ — see NUMBER table **2 :** being one of 99 equal parts into which something is divisible ⟨a *ninety-ninth* share of the money⟩

2ninety-ninth \"\ *n* **1 :** number 99 in a countable series **2 :** the quotient of a unit divided by 99 **:** one of 99 equal parts of something

1ninety-one \¦==¦=\ *adj* **:** being one more than 90 in number ⟨*ninety-one* years⟩ — see NUMBER table

2ninety-one \"\ *pron, pl in constr* **:** ninety-one countable persons or things not specified but under consideration and being enumerated ⟨*ninety-one* are here⟩ ⟨*ninety-one* were found⟩

3ninety-one \"\ *n* **1 :** one and 90 **2 a :** seven times 13 **:** 91 units or objects ⟨a total of *ninety-one*⟩ **b :** a group or set of 91 **3 :** the numerable quantity symbolized by the arabic numerals 91

1ninety-second \¦==¦=\ *adj* **1 :** being number 92 in a countable series ⟨the *ninety-second* day⟩ — see NUMBER table **2 :** being one of 92 equal parts into which something is divisible ⟨a *ninety-second* share of the money⟩

2ninety-second \"\ *n* **1 :** number 92 in a countable series **2 :** the quotient of a unit divided by 92 **:** one of 92 equal parts of something

1ninety-seven \¦==¦=\ *adj* **:** being one more than 96 in number ⟨*ninety-seven* years⟩ — see NUMBER table

2ninety-seven \"\ *pron, pl in constr* **:** ninety-seven countable persons or things not specified but under consideration and being enumerated ⟨*ninety-seven* are here⟩ ⟨*ninety-seven* were found⟩

3ninety-seven \"\ *n* **1 :** seven and 90 **2 a :** 97 units or objects ⟨a total of *ninety-seven*⟩ **b :** a group or set of 97 **3 :** the numerable quantity symbolized by the arabic numerals 97

1ninety-seventh \¦==¦=\ *adj* **1 :** being number 97 in a countable series ⟨the *ninety-seventh* day⟩ — see NUMBER table **2 :** being one of 97 equal parts into which something is divisible ⟨a *ninety-seventh* share of the money⟩

2ninety-seventh \"\ *n* **1 :** number 97 in a countable series **2 :** the quotient of a unit divided by 97 **:** one of 97 equal parts of something

1ninety-six \¦==¦=\ *adj* **:** being one more than 95 in number ⟨*ninety-six* years⟩ — see NUMBER table

2ninety-six \"\ *pron, pl in constr* **:** ninety-six countable persons or things not specified but under consideration and being enumerated ⟨*ninety-six* are here⟩ ⟨*ninety-six* were found⟩

3ninety-six \"\ *n* **1 :** six and 90 **:** two times 48 **:** three times 32 **:** four times 24 **:** six times 16 **:** eight times 12 **:** eight dozen **2 a :** 96 units or objects ⟨a total of *ninety-six*⟩ **b :** a group or set of 96 **3 :** the numerable quantity symbolized by the arabic numerals 96

1ninety-sixth \¦==¦=\ *adj* **1 :** being number 96 in a countable series ⟨the *ninety-sixth* day⟩ — see NUMBER table **2 :** being one of 96 equal parts into which something is divisible ⟨a *ninety-sixth* share of the money⟩

2ninety-sixth \"\ *n* **1 :** number 96 in a countable series **2 :** the quotient of a unit divided by 96 **:** one of 96 equal parts of something

1ninety-third \¦==¦=\ *adj* **1 :** being number 93 in a countable series ⟨the *ninety-third* day⟩ — see NUMBER table **2 :** being one of 93 equal parts into which something is divisible ⟨a *ninety-third* share of the money⟩

2ninety-third \"\ *n* **1 :** number 93 in a countable series **2 :** the quotient of a unit divided by 93 **:** one of 93 equal parts of something

1ninety-three \¦==¦=\ *adj* **:** being one more than 92 in number ⟨*ninety-three* years⟩ — see NUMBER table

2ninety-three \"\ *pron, pl in constr* **:** ninety-three countable persons or things not specified but under consideration and being enumerated ⟨*ninety-three* are here⟩ ⟨*ninety-three* were found⟩

3ninety-three \"\ *n* **1 :** three and 90 **:** three times 31 **2 a :** 93 units or objects ⟨a total of *ninety-three*⟩ **b :** a group or set of 93 **3 :** the numerable quantity symbolized by the arabic numerals 93

1ninety-two \¦==¦=\ *adj* **:** being one more than 91 in number ⟨*ninety-two* years⟩ — see NUMBER table

2ninety-two \"\ *pron, pl in constr* **:** ninety-two countable persons or things not specified but under consideration and being enumerated ⟨*ninety-two* are here⟩ ⟨*ninety-two* were found⟩

3ninety-two \"\ *n* **1 :** two and 90 **:** two times 46 **:** four times 23 **2 a :** 92 units or objects ⟨a total of *ninety-two*⟩ **b :** a group or set of 92 **3 :** the numerable quantity symbolized by the arabic numerals 92

nin·e·vite *or* **nin·i·vite** \ˈninə,vīt\ *n* -s *usu cap* [*Nineveh, Ninive,* ancient capital of Assyria + E *-ite*] **:** an inhabitant of the ancient Assyrian city of Nineveh

ningle *n* -s [alter. (resulting fr. incorrect division of *an ingle*) of *ingle*] *obs* **:** CATAMITE

ning·po \ˈniŋ¦pō\ *adj, usu cap* [fr. Ningpo, China] **:** of or from the city of Ningpo, China **:** of the kind or style prevalent in Ningpo

nin·gre·ton·go \,niŋgrā¦täŋ(,)gō\ *n* -s *usu cap N&T* [prob. fr. Taki-Taki, fr. E *nigger* + *tongue*] **:** TAKI-TAKI

nin·hy·drin \ninˈhīdrən\ *n* -s [fr. *Ninhydrin,* a trademark] **:** a poisonous crystalline mild oxidizing agent $C_9H_4O_2(OH)_2$ used chiefly as an analytical reagent; 1,2,3-indan-trione hydrate or triketo-hydrindene hydrate

ninhydrin reaction *n* **:** a reaction of ninhydrin with amino acids or related amino compounds used for the colorimetric determination of amino acids, peptides, or proteins by measuring the intensity of the blue to violet to red color formed or for the quantitative determination of alpha-amino acids by measuring the amount of carbon dioxide produced

nin·ny \ˈninē, -ni\ *n* -ES [perh. by shortening and alter. fr. *an innocent*] **:** FOOL, SIMPLETON ⟨don't stand there fiddling like a ~ —Paul Gallico⟩ — **nin·ny·ish** \-ish\ *adj*

nin·ny·ham·mer \-,hamə(r)\ *n* **:** NINNY

nin·ny·watch \-,wäch\ *n* [origin unknown] *dial Brit* **:** DISTURBANCE, COMMOTION

ni·non \ˈnē,nōⁿ, ≈ˈ≈\ *n* -s [prob. fr. F *Ninon,* nickname for *Anne*] **:** a smooth sheer fabric made in a plain close weave and novelty open weaves usu. of silk, rayon, or nylon and used esp. for women's clothing and curtains

ni·nox \ˈnī,näks\ *n, cap* [NL] **:** a large genus of owls having bristly feet and long wings and ranging from Madagascar to Australian and Indo-Malayan regions

1ninth \ˈnīn(t)th\ *adj* [ME *nynthe,* adj. & n., alter. (influenced by *nyne, nigen* nine) of *nithe,* fr. OE *nigotha* (akin to OS *nigutho,* MLG *negede*), fr. *nigon* nine + *-otha, -tha* -th — more at NINE] **1 :** being number nine in a countable series ⟨the ~ day⟩ — see NUMBER table **2 :** being one of nine equal parts into which something is divisible ⟨a ~ share of the money⟩

2ninth \"\ *n, pl* **ninths** \-īn(t)s,-īn(t)ths\ **1 :** number nine in a countable series ⟨the ~ of the month⟩ **2 :** the quotient of a unit divided by nine **:** one of nine equal parts of something ⟨one ~ of the total⟩ **3 a :** a musical interval embracing an octave and a second **b :** a tone at this interval **c :** NINTH CHORD

ninth 3a

3ninth \"\ *adv* **1 :** in the ninth place **2 :** with eight exceptions ⟨the nation's ~ largest city⟩

ninth chord *n* **:** a dominant seventh chord with the ninth added **:** a chord composed of four superposed thirds

ninth cranial nerve *or* **ninth nerve** *n* **:** GLOSSOPHARYNGEAL NERVE

ninth·ly \-īn(t)thlē, -li\ *adv* **:** in the ninth place ⟨~ and lastly, they were wholly unintelligible —Rudyard Kipling⟩

ninth of ab *usu cap N&A* [1ab] **:** TISHAH B'AB

nin·ut \ˈninət\ *n* -s [origin unknown] *Brit* **:** MAGPIE 1a

ni·o·bate \ˈnīə,bāt\ *n* -s [NL *niobium* + E *-ate*] **:** a salt of niobic acid — called also *columbate*

ni·o·bic \(ˈ)nī¦ōbik\ *adj* [NL *niobium* + E *-ic*] **:** of, relating to, or containing niobium — used esp. of compounds in which this element is pentavalent

niobic acid *n* **:** a gelatinous hydrated form $Nb_2O_5.nH_2O$ of niobium pentoxide that reacts with alkalies to yield salts (as sodium niobate $NaNbO_3$) — called also *columbic acid*

ni·o·bite \ˈnīə,bīt\ *n* -s [G *niobit,* fr. NL *niobium* + G *-it* -ite] **:** COLUMBITE

ni·o·bi·um \nīˈōbēəm\ *n* -s [NL, fr. *Niobe,* daughter of Tantalus + NL *-ium* — so called fr. its occurrence in tantalite] **:** a platinum-gray ductile chiefly pentavalent metallic element of brilliant luster that occurs combined in columbite and various other rare minerals but almost always associated with tantalum which it closely resembles chemically and from which it is separated as a by-product and that is used esp. in alloys (as in small amounts in stainless steels to inhibit intergranular corrosion) — called also *columbium;* symbol *Nb;* see ELEMENT table

niobium pentoxide *n* **:** a compound Nb_2O_5 obtained as a white infusible powder

ni·o·bous \(ˈ)nī¦ōbəs\ *adj* [NL *niobium* + *-ous*] **:** of, relating to, or containing niobium — used esp. of compounds in which this element has a lower valence than in niobic compounds

ni·o·ta \nēˈōd·ə\ *or* **niota bark** *n* -s [Malayalam *ñoṭṭa*] **:** NIEPA 2

1nip \ˈnip\ *vb* **nipped** *or archaic* **nipt; nipped** *or archaic* **nipt; nipping; nips** [ME *nippen;* akin to MD *nīpen* to nip, ON *hnippa* to prod, Gk *knips,* an insect, *skniptein* to nip, *konis* dust — more at INCINERATE] *vt* **1 a :** to catch hold of and squeeze tightly between two surfaces, edges, or points **:** compress esp. by pinching or biting **:** CLAMP ⟨the dog *nipped* him on the leg⟩ ⟨*nipped* his grandson between his knees —Ethel Anderson⟩ ⟨a little gold ring . . . *nipped* to the top of an ear —Christopher Rand⟩ **b :** to secure or stop (a cable or rope) with seizing **c** *obs* **:** to close up (a glass vessel or tube) by pressing together the heated mouth or neck **2 a :** to sever by or as if by pinching sharply or biting ⟨choosing a slender cigar . . . he *nipped* it carefully and lit it —Ann Bridge⟩ ⟨*nipped* out pieces from the ends of the bar —L.A.Werden⟩ ⟨salient, in danger of being *nipped* off anytime —Earle Birney⟩; *specif* **:** to pinch or clip off (as a bud or shoot) in horticulture ⟨in the spring the blooms are *nipped,* allowing the bulb to retain the full nourishment of the plant juices —*Amer. Guide Series: La.*⟩ **b :** to destroy the growth, progress, maturing, or fulfillment of ⟨his designs were . . . *nipped* in their infancy —T.L.Peacock⟩ — often with *in the bud* ⟨the political leaders would . . . ~ the conspiracy in the bud —William Clark⟩ **:** check sharply ⟨government fiscal policy was used to ~ a downswing —J.R. Chamberlain⟩ **c :** to diminish by cutting off bits ⟨the Atlantic . . . nibbling away at the rocks, *nipping* off a bit here and swallowing a valley there —Alastair Borthwick⟩ **3 :** to censure sharply or bitingly ⟨when her brother whom she despised grew sentimental . . . she *nipped* him —Rose Feld⟩ **4 a :** to make numb with cold **:** CHILL ⟨the wind . . . *nipped* him to the bone —Rudyard Kipling⟩ **b :** to cause injury to (vegetation) **:** BLIGHT ⟨see if this frost has not *nipped* my fruit trees —James Boswell⟩ **c :** to affect painfully and closely ⟨these tidings ~ me and I hang the head —Shak.⟩ **5 :** to seize suddenly and forcibly **:** SNATCH; *esp* **:** STEAL ⟨whoever *nipped* the whiskey, *nipped* the money, too —Mark Twain⟩ **6 a :** to apply momentary mechanical pressure to (as a book or something mounted) so as to compact the leaves or promote adhesion — compare SMASH 4 **b :** to shape up (the raised bands on the backbone of a leather-covered book) with band nippers **7 :** to beat (an opponent) by a very small margin of score, distance, or time ⟨*nipped* him by 6 in. at the tape —*Time*⟩ **~** *vi, chiefly Brit* **:** to move briskly, nimbly, or quickly ⟨~ up there and fetch me down a book —James Ronald⟩: as **a :** JUMP, HOP ⟨*nipping* in and out of buses and taxis —Alan Moorehead⟩ ⟨*nipping* on a tram —Richard Llewellyn⟩ **b (1) :** HURRY ⟨~ back here with the key —Dodie Smith⟩ **(2) :** hurry away — used with *off* ⟨we *nipped off* while they was milking —Audrey Barker⟩ **(3) :** DART ⟨*nipping* in under his host's arm —Elizabeth Bowen⟩ **c :** to make a quick trip **:** HOP 2b ⟨shall I ~ out and buy one —Alan Paton⟩ **d :** INTERRUPT, INTRUDE — used with *in* or *into* ⟨*nipped* in with a neat query —*Punch*⟩

2nip \"\ *n* -s **1 :** something (as a quality or element of a thing) that nips: as **a :** a sharp, biting comment **:** 2DIG 1b ⟨many a privy ~ has he given him —Andrew Marvell⟩ **b :** a sharp, stinging cold ⟨the ~ of the air had startled her —Willa Cather⟩; *esp* **:** a frost that checks or destroys the growth of vegetation ⟨some tender slip saved with care from Winter's ~ —John Milton⟩ **c :** a biting or pungent flavor: **(1)** *Scot* **:** TANG ⟨cheese with a ~⟩ **(2) :** PIQUANCY ⟨a scholar with a ~ in his words —H.J.Laski⟩ **2 :** a compression between two surfaces, edges, or points: as **a :** a sharp bite **:** PINCH ⟨the . . . ~s of the timid black widow spider —Donald Carlisle⟩ **b :** a pinch of a coal seam **c (1) :** the pressure of a rope when it is bent around or held by something **(2) :** a sharp bend or turn in a rope where chafing occurs ⟨in calm weather the ~ of a cable is usually freshened every 24 hours —*Manual of Seamanship*⟩ **d :** the crushing pressure on a ship caught in the ice **e (1) :** the region of a calender or other squeezing or crushing device where the rolls or jaws are closest together **(2) :** the line of contact of any pair of the rolls used in papermaking (as press and calender rolls) between which the paper passes **(3) :** the distance between the corrugations of a pair of rollers (as those used in flour milling) in the course of rotation **3 :** a sly thief **:** CUTPURSE, PICKPOCKET ⟨punishment of foists and ~s caught in the act was prompt —*Times Lit. Supp.*⟩ **4 :** a small portion **:** 3BIT ⟨wrapped a loaf of bread and a ~ of cheese in the blanket —A.B.Mayse⟩ **5 :** a low cliff often with a narrow platform at its base cut by waves and currents in an initial stage of their activity

3nip \"\ *n* -s [alter. of 1*nep*] *dial chiefly Eng* **:** CATNIP

4nip \"\ *n* -s [prob. short for *nipperkin*] **:** a small quantity of liquor **:** SIP ⟨might take a little ~ now and then —Hamilton Basso⟩ ⟨gin at threepence a ~ —Fred Majdalany⟩

5nip \"\ *vi* **nipped; nipped; nipping; nips :** to take liquor in nips **:** TIPPLE ⟨getting higher all the time by *nipping* at . . . bottles filled with martinis —Daniel Curley⟩

6nip \"\ *n or adj, usu cap* [by shortening] **:** NIPPONESE — usu. used disparagingly

ni·pa \ˈnēpə\ *n* [prob. fr. It, fr. Malay *nipah* an East Indian palm] **1** -s **:** an alcoholic beverage made from the fermented sap of an Australasian palm **2** *cap* [NL, fr. Malay *nipah*] **:** a monotypic genus of creeping semiaquatic palms whose sap is a source of nipa and of sugar, whose seeds are edible, and whose long strong pinnate leaves are extensively used in thatching and basketry **3** -s **a** *or* **nipa palm :** any palm of the genus *Nipa* **b :** thatch made of nipa leaves ⟨a row of ~ huts⟩

nip and tuck \¦nipən¦tək\ *adj (or adv)* **:** so close that the lead or advantage shifts rapidly from one contestant to another **:** neck and neck ⟨the race was *nip and tuck* for a time —*Our Dumb Animals*⟩ ⟨until about the 25th lap, it was a *nip and tuck* go —*Illustrated Speedway News*⟩

nipcheese \ˈ=,=\ *n* **1** *slang* **:** a ship's purser ⟨that's our ~ —Frederick Marryat⟩ **2** *slang* **:** MISER ⟨the old ~ . . . has been wasting his time —T.B.Costain⟩

nip draw *n* **:** a short draw shot used in billiards when the cue ball and first object ball are in close proximity

nip·e·cot·ic acid \¦nipə¦käd·ik-\ *n* [ISV, prob. blend of *nicotinic* and *piperidine*] **:** a crystalline heterocyclic amino acid HNC_5H_9COOH obtained by hydrogenation of nicotinic acid; 3-piperidine-carboxylic acid

nip·is·sing \ˈnipəsiŋ\ *n, pl* **nipissing** *or* **nipissings** *usu cap* **1 a :** an Algonkian people of southeastern Ontario **b :** a member of such people **2 :** the Algonquian language of the Nipissing people

nip·kow disc \ˈnip(,)kō-\ *n, usu cap N* [after Paul G. *Nipkow* †1940 Ger. television pioneer] **:** a mechanical television scanner consisting of a rotating disk with small holes upon its periphery through which narrow beams of light pass

1nip·per \ˈnipə(r)\ *n* -s [1*nip* + *-er*] **1 :** any of various devices for nipping: as **a :** small pincers that are used for gripping, breaking, or cutting — usu. used in pl. **b :** long slender-nosed pliers or pincers used for seizing the end of a key in a lock to turn it — usu. used in pl. **c :** a device for squeezing tar from rope yarn **d nippers** *pl* **:** handcuffs or leg irons **e :** a grab for seizing heavy objects (as large stones) for hauling or hoisting **f nippers** *pl* **:** EYEGLASSES; *specif* **:** PINCE-NEZ **g nippers** *pl* **:** a nail or cuticle cutter with short curved blades **h :** a short selvagee or sennit for securing a nautical hemp cable temporarily to a messenger to assist in the raising of an anchor **i (1) :** a power press that compresses the leaves of books during the binding process by means of momentary pressure **(2) :** a small hand press used to compress single books or mounted material **2 a :** an incisor of a horse; *esp* **:** one of the middle four incisors **b :** one of the large claws or pincers of a crab or lobster **3** *chiefly Brit* **a :** a boy employed as a helper (as of a carter or hawker) **b :** CHILD, KID ⟨from fat, solemn babies . . . to ~s of nine or ten —Gavin Casey⟩ **4 a :** CUNNER b **b** *or*

nipper crab : a European crab (*Polybius henslowii*) **c** *Austral* (1) : PRAWN (2) : SNAPPING SHRIMP **5 a** (1) : a workman who assists miners (as by distributing drill steel or carrying blasting powder) (2) : one that tends ventilation doors in a mine (3) : BRAKEMAN 1a(2) **b** : a workman who holds up railroad ties to the rails with a bar or other tool while the rails are being spiked in place **6** : a thick band or mitten worn by deep-sea fishermen to protect the hand from the lines

²nip·per \"\ *vt* -ED/-ING/-S : to secure (a ship's cable) with nippers : RACK 7

nip·per·kin \ˈnipə(r)kən\ *n* -S [origin unknown] **1** : a liquor container or vessel with a capacity of a half pint or less **2** : a quantity of liquor contained in or able to be contained in a nipperkin

nip·pi·ly \ˈnipəlē\ *adv* : in a nippy manner : BRISKLY, NIMBLY ⟨a panther could not have moved more ~ —P.G.Wodehouse⟩

nip·pi·ness \-pēnəs\ *n* -ES : the quality or state of being nippy : AGILITY

¹nipping *adj* [fr. pres. part. of ¹*nip*] : that nips : SHARP, CAUSTIC, CHILLING ⟨in her most ~ tones —Harriet B. Stowe⟩ ⟨there was a ~ wind on deck —Robert Grant †1940⟩

²nipping *n* -S [fr. gerund of ¹*nip*] : the act or process of holding ties up to the rails in track laying

nippingly *adv* : in a nipping manner

nippitate *adj* [fr. *nippitaty*, *nippitate*, n.] *obs, of liquor* : strong and good : EXCELLENT

nippitaty *also* **nippitate** *or* **nippitato** *or* **nippitatum** *n* [origin unknown] *obs* : particularly good and strong liquor; *esp* : good ale

¹nip·ple \ˈnipəl\ *n* -S [earlier *neble*, *nible*, prob. dim. of *neb*, *nib*] **1 a** : a more or less conical eminence surmounting the mammary gland in all higher mammals that contains the terminal and usu. fused parts of the lactiferous ducts of the gland and is the part of the breast or udder from which the young animal draws milk in suckling : TEAT — called also *mammilla*, *pap* **b** : any papilla marking the outlet of a gland **2** : any of various devices resembling a nipple in appearance or function: as **a** : an artificial teat through which an infant sucks milk from a nursing bottle **b** : a device (as a stopcock) with an orifice through which the discharge of a liquid can be regulated **c** : a hollow conical projection on the percussion lock of a firearm on which the cap is placed and through which fire from the exploding cap is conveyed to the charge **3 a** : any eminence or protuberance (as the crest of a mountain) resembling or suggesting the nipple of a breast **b** : a small projection through which oil or grease is injected into machinery **4** : a pipe coupling consisting of a short piece of tubing usu. with an external screw thread at each end

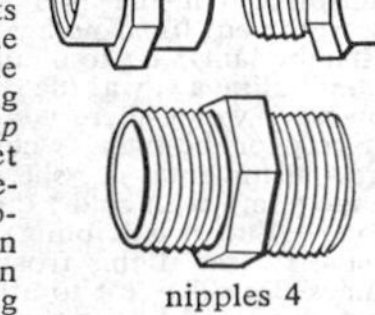

nipples 4

²nipple \"\ *vt* **nippled**; **nippled**; **nip·pling** \-p(ə)liŋ\ **nipples** : to provide with a nipple : cover with or as if with nipples ⟨a rain of fire *nippling* the water —H.D.Skidmore⟩

nipplewort \ˈ==,=\ *n* [so called fr. its use as a medication for nipples] : a slender branching annual herb (*Lapsana communis*) with loose-panicled small heads of yellow flowers

¹nip·pon·ese \ˌnipəˈnēz, -ēs\ *adj, usu cap* [*Nippon* (Japan) + E *-ese*] : JAPANESE

²nipponese \"\ *n, pl* **nipponese** *cap* : JAPANESE

nip·pon·ism \ˈ==,nizəm\ *n* -S *usu cap* : JAPANISM

nip·pon·ize \-,nīz\ *vt* -ED/-ING/-S *often cap* : JAPANIZE

nip·po·strongylus \ˌni(,)pō+\ *n, cap* [NL, fr. *nippo-* (fr. *Nippon*) + *Strongylus*] : a genus of strongyloid nematode worms that comprise intestinal parasites of rodents and are much used in biological research

nip·py \ˈnipē, -pi\ *adj* -ER/-EST **1** : marked by a tendency to nip : NIPPING, SNAPPISH, MORDANT ⟨a narrower and *nippier* breed —G.D.Brown⟩ ⟨the dialogue got much *nippier* —J.P. O'Donnell⟩ **2** : brisk, quick, or nimble in movement : SNAPPY ⟨~ little chaps —Rudyard Kipling⟩ ⟨in good physical trim and exceptionally . . . ~ on his feet —Tyrone Guthrie⟩ ⟨an excellent pony . . . ~, fast, and intelligent —*Farmer's Weekly* (*So. Africa*)⟩ ⟨a . . . ~ little car —A.J.Liebling⟩ **3** : PUNGENT, SHARP ⟨~ cheese⟩ ⟨~ cider⟩ **4** : CHILLY, CHILLING ⟨a canter on a ~ fall day —Henry Cavendish⟩

ni pri *abbr* nisi prius

nip roll *n* : one of a pair or set of rolls for squeezing materials (as in a wringer)

nips *pres 3d sing of* NIP, *pl of* NIP

nipt \ˈnipt\ *archaic past of* NIP

nip·ter \ˈniptə(r)\ *n* -S [MGk *niptēr*, fr. Gk, washbasin, fr. *niptein*, *nizein* to wash — more at NICKER] : the ceremony of foot washing on Maundy Thursday in the Eastern Orthodox Church — compare MAUNDY 1

nip-up \ˈni,pəp\ *n, pl* **nip-ups** **1** : KIP-UP ⟨doing *nip-ups* and handsprings during meetings with his top military aides —R.L. Taylor⟩ **2** : STUNT, CAPER ⟨vaudeville came back with a *nip-up* that made news —*Newsweek*⟩

nir·gran·tha \nirˈgrantə, -iəˈ-, -ran-\ *n, pl* **nirgrantha** *or* **nirgranthas** *usu cap* [Skt, free from ties, fr. *nir-*, *nis-* out, without + *grantha* tying, fr. *grathnāti* he ties] : JAIN

nirles \ˈnirlz\ *n pl* [origin unknown] *chiefly Scot* : an eruption resembling measles or chicken pox — usu. used with *the* ⟨suffering from the ~⟩

nir·ma·na·ka·ya \nirˈmänəˈkäyə, -iəˈ-\ *n* -S [Skt *nirmāṇakāya* body of magic transformation, fr. *nirmāṇa* measuring, creating, magical creation (fr. *nir-* *nis-* out + *māti* he measures) + *kāya* body, fr. *cinoti* he piles in order — more at MEASURE, POET] : the historically manifested body of Buddha in the doctrine of trikaya

nir·va·na \nirˈvänə, niəˈ-, nə(r)ˈ-, -anə\ *n* -S [Skt *nirvāṇa*, lit., blowing out, fr. *nir-*, *nis-* out + *vāti* it blows — more at WIND] **1** *usu cap* **a** *Hinduism, Jainism, Buddhism* : the state of freedom from karma, extinction of desire, passion, illusion, and the empirical self, and attainment of rest, truth, and unchanging being : SALVATION — contrasted with *samsara* **b** *also* **nib·ba·na** \niˈbänə\ [*nibbana* fr. Pali *nibbāna*, fr. Skt *nirvāṇa*] *Buddhism* : the state of enlightenment in which karma is transcended, desire, hatred, delusion, and the empirical self are extinguished, and rest, harmony, and unchanging being are attained **c** *Jainism* : the state of omniscient passive peace attained by a soul liberated from matter, the effects of karma, and the course of samsara **2** *often cap* **a** : a place or state of rest, harmony, or pleasure : OBLIVION, PARADISE ⟨his old roommate of the clipping shack was in an alcoholic ~ —Herman Wouk⟩ **b** : a goal hoped for but apparently unattainable : DREAM ⟨that ~ of the . . . weatherman: a foolproof system of forecasting —*Newsweek*⟩

nirvana principle *n* : the psyche's characteristic tendency to reduce inner tensions and approach an inorganic state as if responding to the death instinct

nir·va·nic \(ˈ)=ˈvänik, -an-\ *adj* : of, relating to, or resembling nirvana ⟨~ calm⟩

nis·an *or* **nis·san** \ˈnisən, (ˈ)nēˈsän\ *n* -S *usu cap* [Heb *Nīsān*, fr. Assyr-Bab] : the 7th month of the civil year or the 1st month of the ecclesiastical year in the Jewish calendar — see MONTH table

ni·sei \(ˈ)nēˈsā\ *n, pl* **nisei** *also* **niseis** *often cap* [Jap, lit., second generation, fr. *ni* second + *sei* generation] : a son or daughter of issei parents who is born and educated in America and esp. in the U.S. — distinguished from *kibei*; compare SANSEI

ni·sha·da \niˈshädə\ *n* -S *usu cap* [Skt *niṣāda*, fr. *Niṣāda*, name of a wild non-Aryan tribe] : a member of a low caste in India : the offspring of a Brahman and a Sudra

ni·shi·no·mi·ya \ˌnē,shē(,)nōˈmēyə\ *adj, usu cap* [fr. *Nishinomiya*, city in western Japan] : of or from the city of Nishinomiya, Japan : of the kind or style prevalent in Nishinomiya

ni·si \ˈnī,sī, ˈnē(,)sē\ *adj* [L, unless, fr. *ne-* not + *si* if — more at NO] : not final or absolute — used in law to denote that a rule, decree, or order shall take effect at a given time unless before that time it is modified or avoided by cause shown or further proceedings or by the fulfillment of some condition therein named ⟨the decree is ~ and not absolute —*Economist*⟩ ⟨a rule ~⟩ — compare DECREE NISI

ni·sin \ˈnīsən\ *n* -S [origin unknown] : a crystalline polypeptide antibiotic that is produced by a bacterium of the genus *Streptomyces* (*S. lactis*) and inhibits many gram-positive organisms

nisi pri·us \-ˈprīəs\ *n* [ME, fr. ML, lit., unless before (words introducing a clause in the writ)] **1 a** : a cause involving issues of fact that being begun in the courts of Westminster was appointed to be tried there in an Easter or Michaelmas term by a jury from the county wherein the cause of action arose unless before the day appointed the judges of assize came into the county in question and there tried the cause **b** : an issue of fact triable at the assizes **2 a** (1) : a writ commanding the sheriff to provide a jury at the Court of Westminster on a day certain unless the judges of assize previously come to the county from which the jury is to be returned (2) : the clause in this writ introduced by the words *nisi prius* (3) : the authority or commission conferred by this clause on the judges of assize **b** : an action tried or to be tried in an English court under such a writ **c** (1) : the trial of civil causes by the judges of assize (2) : the trial of issues of fact in civil causes or other such court business (as the trial of causes before the judges of the King's Bench Division in London) **3 a** : a court of record in the U.S., Great Britain, and other English-speaking countries that tries an issue of fact before a jury and a single judge **b** : the proceedings in such a court — compare *in banc* at BANC

nis·ka \ˈniskə\ *n, pl* **niska** *or* **niskas** *usu cap* **1 a** : a Tsimshian people or group of peoples of the Nass river valley and contiguous Pacific coast, British Columbia, Canada **b** : a member of any of such peoples **2** : the language of the Niska people

nis·nas \ˈnisnəs\ *n, pl* **nisnas** [Ar *nisnās*] : a guenon (*Cercopithecus griseoviridis*) of northeastern Africa or a monkey of a related species

ni·spe·ro \ˈnēspə,rō\ *n* -S [AmerSp *níspero*, fr. Sp, medlar, fr. (assumed) VL *nespilus*, fr. L *mespilus*, *mespilum*, fr. Gk *mespilon*] **1** : any of various plants of the genus *Achras* found in Spanish America; *esp* : SAPODILLA **2** : LOQUAT

nis·qual·li *also* **nis·qual·ly** \niˈskwälē, ˈniz,kw-\ *n, pl* **nisqualli** \"\ *or* **nisquallis** *usu cap* **1 a** : a Salishan people of Puget Sound, Wash. **b** : a member of such people **2** : the language of the Nisqualli people

nis·se \ˈnisə\ *n, pl* **nisser** *or* **nisses** [Sw or Dan or Norw, alter. of *Nils* (Saint) Nicholas] : a friendly goblin or brownie of Scandinavian folklore that frequents farm buildings : KOBOLD ⟨~ . . . a harmless creature, dressed in red blouse and pantaloons and wearing a red cap —*Nat'l Geographic*⟩

nis·sen hut \ˈnisᵊn-\ *n, usu cap N* [after Lieut. Col. Peter N. *Nissen* †1930 Brit. mining engineer and inventor] : a barrel-shaped prefabricated shelter of corrugated iron with cement floor

nissl bodies \ˈnisəl-\ *or* **nissl corpuscles** *or* **nissl granules** *or* **nissl's bodies** *or* **nissl's corpuscles** *or* **nissl's granules** *n pl, usu cap N* [after Franz *Nissl* †1919 Ger. neurologist] : discrete bodies of variable size that are found in the cytoplasm of nerve cells and that stain deeply with methylene blue

nissl substance \"-\ *n, usu cap N* : the material of Nissl bodies

ni·sus \ˈnīsəs\ *n, pl* **nisus** [L, fr. *nisus*, past part. of *niti* to bear down, strive; akin to L *conivēre*, *connivēre* to close the eyes — more at CONNIVE] **1** : a conative state or condition : STRIVING, INCLINATION ⟨a ~ or energizing towards a presented object —L.P.Hickok⟩ ⟨this ~ towards individuality —R.H. Gault & D.T.Howard⟩ ⟨a ~ towards large generalizing —George Saintsbury⟩ **2** : a tendency or principle in reality according to some philosophers exhibited in the emergence of higher levels of existence (as life, mind, deity) ⟨there is a ~ in space-time which, as it has borne its creatures forward through matter and life to mind, will bear them forward to some higher level of existence —Samuel Alexander⟩

¹nit \ˈnit, *usu* -id·+V\ *n* -S [ME *nite*, *nitte*, fr. OE *hnitu*; akin to OHG *hniz* nit, Gk *konid-*, *konis*] : the egg of a louse or other parasitic insect; *also* : the insect itself when young

²nit \"\ *n* -S [alter. of *nut*] *chiefly Scot* : NUT; *esp* : HAZELNUT

³nit \"\ *adv* [perh. fr. Yiddish, not, no, fr. MHG *niht*, *nit* nothing, not, fr. OHG *niwiht*, *neowiht* — more at NAUGHT] *slang* : NO — used as a negative response

⁴nit \"\ *n* -S [origin unknown] *Austral* : GUARD, WATCH — usu. used with *keep* ⟨with galahs and cockatoos keeping ~ —*Sporting Life*⟩

ni·tel·la \nīˈtelə\ *n, cap* [NL, fr. L *nitēre* to shine + NL *-ella* — more at NEAT] : a genus of delicate branching stoneworts (family Characeae) differing from *Chara* in lacking a cortical layer of cells and in having the leaves all branched

ni·ter *also* **ni·tre** \ˈnīd·ə(r), -ītə-\ *n* -S [ME *nitre* natron, fr. MF, fr. L *nitrum*, fr. Gk *nitron*, fr. Egypt *ntry*] **1** *usu nitre, obs* : NATRON **2 a** : potassium nitrate esp. occurring naturally (as in desert deposits in northern Chile) **b** : SODIUM NITRATE; *esp* : CHILE SALTPETER **c** *archaic* : NITRATE 1 **3** *usu nitre, obs* : a supposed nitrous substance or element occurring esp. diffused through the air **4** *usu nitre* : ETHYL NITRITE ⟨spirit of ~⟩ — compare ETHYL NITRITE SPIRIT **5** : SUGAR SAND

niter-blue \ˈ==ˈ=\ *vt* : to make (steel) blue by immersing in a molten niter mixture

niter cake *n* : SODIUM BISULFATE; *esp* : a caked form obtained as a by-product in the original manufacture of nitric acid from sodium nitrate and sulfuric acid or in the manufacture of hydrochloric acid from common salt and sulfuric acid

ni·te·rói *or* **ni·te·roi** \ˌnēd·əˈrȯi\ *adj, usu cap* [fr. *Niterói*, city in southeast Brazil] : of or from the city of Niterói, Brazil : of the kind or style prevalent in Niterói

nit·ery \ˈnīd·ərē, -ītə-, -ri\ *n* -ES [*nite* (alter. of *night*) + *-ery*] : NIGHTCLUB

nit fly *n* : a horse botfly (*Gasterophilus intestinalis*)

nit grass *n* : an annual grass (*Gastridium ventricosum*) of the family Gramineae that is native to the Mediterranean region but adventive in some parts of the southern U.S. and has small shining spikelets

¹nith·er \ˈnith̲ə(r)\ *vt* -ED/-ING/-S [ME *nitheren*, fr. OE *nitherian*; akin to OHG *nideren* to lower, debase, ON *nithra* to lower; all fr. a prehistoric NGmc-WGmc verb derivative fr. the root of OE *nither* down — more at NETHER] *chiefly Scot* **1** : DEBASE, HUMILIATE **2** : BLAST, BLIGHT ⟨~*ed* plants⟩

²nither \"\ *vi* -ED/-ING/-S [prob. of Scand origin] *chiefly Scot* : to shiver or tremble esp. with cold

³nither \"\ *dial var of* NEITHER

nithing *n* -S [ME, fr. OE *nīthing*, fr. ON *nīthingr*, fr. *nīth* scorn, contumely + *-ingr* -ing; ON *nīth* akin to OE *nīth* envy, hatred, strife, OHG *nīd* envy, hatred, Goth *neith* envy and perh. to L *nitēre* to shine — more at NEAT] **1** *obs* : COWARD, POLTROON **2** *obs* : NIGGARD

nit·id \ˈnid·əd\ *also* **nit·i·dous** \-ədəs\ *adj* [L *nitidus* — more at NEAT] : BRIGHT, GLOSSY, LUSTROUS ⟨Nereids beneath the ~ moon —P.B.Rice⟩ ⟨apex with a depressed, glabrous, *nitidous* flange — *Pan-Pacific Entomologist*⟩

ni·tid·i·ty \nīˈtidəd·ē\ *n* -ES : the quality or state of being nitid : BRILLIANCY, SHEEN

¹ni·tid·u·lid \nəˈtijələd\ *adj* [NL *Nitidulidae*] : of or relating to the Nitidulidae

²nitidulid \"\ *n* -S : a beetle of the family Nitidulidae

nit·i·du·li·dae \ˌnid·əˈd(y)üləˌdē\ *n pl, cap* [NL, fr. *Nitidula*, type genus (fr. LL, fem. of *nitidulus* natty, dim. of L *nitidus* bright, neat) + *-idae*] : a family of small beetles having 5-jointed tarsi and antennae ending in a 3-jointed clavate expansion, including some that are believed to be vectors of the oak wilt fungus, and having larvae that develop usu. in decaying vegetation but sometimes attack healthy plants

nit·i·nat \ˈnid·ə,nat\ *n, pl* **nitinat** *or* **nitinats** *usu cap* **1 a** : a subdivision of the Nootka **b** : a member of such subdivision **2** : the dialect of the Nitinat people

ni·to \ˈnē(,)tō\ *n* -S [Tag *nitó*] : any of several climbing ferns (genus *Lygodium*) whose stems are used in the Philippines for making hats and baskets

ni·ton \ˈnīd·,än, ˈnē-\ *n* -S [L *nitēre* to shine + ISV *-on*; fr. its phosphorescent properties — more at NEAT] : RADON 1

nitr- *or* **nitro-** *comb form* [L & Gk; L *nitrum* natron, fr. Gk *nitron* — more at NITER] **1** : nitrate ⟨*nitro*bacteria⟩ ⟨*nitro*gen⟩ **2 a** : containing nitrogen in combined form esp. when derived from an acid (as nitric acid) ⟨*nitr*amide⟩ ⟨*nitro*hydrochloric acid⟩ **b** *usu nitro-* : containing the univalent group $-NO_2$ composed of one nitrogen and two oxygen atoms united through nitrogen to (1) carbon or nitrogen; (2) oxygen; or (3) a central atom — in names respectively of (1) organic compounds ⟨*nitro*benzene⟩ ⟨*nitro*methane⟩ ⟨*nitr*amines⟩; (2) organic nitrates ⟨*nitro*glycerin⟩ ⟨*nitro*cellulose⟩; (3) coordination complexes ⟨*nitro*-pentammine-cobalt ion $[Co(NO_2)(NH_3)_5]^{++}$⟩ — compare ISONITRO-, NITRITO-, NITRYL

ni·tra·mide \nīˈtra,mīd, ˈnī·trə,m-, -,məd\ *n* [ISV *nitr-* + *amide*] : a crystalline weakly acid compound NH_2NO_2 that is made from a nitro-carbamate (as nitro-urethane) or from nitro-urea and that decomposes on heating into nitrous oxide; the amide of nitric acid

ni·tra·mine \ˌnī·trəˈmēn, nīˈtramən\ *n* [ISV *nitr-* + *amine*] **1** : any of a class of compounds characterized by the grouping $>NNO_2$ consisting of a nitro group attached to nitrogen and regarded either as *N*-nitro derivatives of amines or as organic derivatives of nitramide; *esp* : TETRYL **2** : NITRAMIDE

nitraniline *var of* NITROANILINE

¹ni·trate \ˈnī,trāt, -,trət, *usu* -d·+V\ *n* -S [F, fr. *nitr-* + *-ate*] **1** : a salt or ester of nitric acid, most of the salts being soluble in water and some of them (as the sodium, potassium, and calcium salts) constituting the principal source of nitrogen for higher plants **2** : sodium nitrate or potassium nitrate used as a fertilizer **3** : cellulose nitrate or its products (as a plastic)

²ni·trate \-,trāt, *usu* -ād·+V\ *vt* -ED/-ING/-S : to treat or combine with nitric acid or a nitrate; *esp* : to convert (an organic compound) into a nitro compound or a nitrate (as by treating with a mixture of nitric acid and sulfuric acid)

nitrate bacterium *n* : a bacterium that converts nitrites into nitrates in the nitrogen cycle

nitrate group *or* **nitrate ion** *n* : the univalent group or anion NO_3 or $-ONO_2$ characteristic of nitric acid and nitrates

nitrate of iron : a dark red chiefly ferric sulfate liquid made usu. by oxidizing a solution of ferrous sulfate with nitric acid and used as a mordant in dyeing

nitrate of lime : calcium nitrate esp. for use as a fertilizer

nitrate of potash : potassium nitrate esp. for use as a fertilizer

nitrate of soda : SODIUM NITRATE

ni·tra·tine \ˈnī·trə,tēn, -,tən\ *n* -S : native sodium nitrate : CALICHE 1

ni·tra·tion \nīˈtrāshən\ *n* -S : the process of nitrating

nitrato- *comb form* [ISV *nitrate*] : containing the nitrate group — esp. in names of coordination complexes ⟨ammonium hexa-*nitrato*-cerate $(NH_4)_2[Ce(NO_3)_6]$⟩

ni·tra·tor \ˈnī,trād·ə(r)\ *n* -S : one that nitrates: as **a** : an acid-resistant vessel with cooling equipment used for the nitration of organic substances **b** : one who tends a nitrator

nitre *var of* NITER

ni·tri·ary \ˈnī·trē,erē\ *n* -ES [F *nitrière*, fr. L *nitraria* natron bed, fr. *nitrum* natron + *-aria* -ary — more at NITER] : an artificial bed of refuse animal matter for the manufacture of niter by nitrification

ni·tric \ˈnī·trik, -ēk\ *adj* [F *nitrique*, fr. *nitr-* + *-ique* -ic] : derived from nitrogen — used esp. of compounds in which this element has a higher valence than in corresponding nitrous compounds ⟨~ oxide⟩

nitric acid *n* [trans. of F *acide nitrique*] : a corrosive liquid inorganic acid HNO_3 made usu. by the catalytic oxidation of ammonia or by the action of sulfuric acid on nitrates and used chiefly as an oxidizing agent (as in rocket propellants), in nitrations, and in the manufacture of fertilizers, explosives, dyes, nitroparaffins, and a variety of other organic compounds : AQUAFORTIS — see AQUA REGIA, FUMING NITRIC ACID

nitric anhydride *n* : NITROGEN PENTOXIDE

nitric oxide *n* : a colorless poisonous gas NO that is obtained by oxidation of nitrogen or ammonia in making nitric acid or by reduction of nitrous acid and that turns brown in air by oxidation to nitrogen dioxide; nitrogen monoxide — called also *nitrogen(II) oxide*

ni·trid·a·tion \ˌnī·trəˈdāshən\ *n* -S : conversion into a nitride : NITRIDING

¹ni·tride \ˈnī,trīd, -,trəd\ *n* -S [ISV *nitr-* + *-ide*] : a binary compound of nitrogen with a more electropositive element (as boron, silicon, and most metals)

²ni·tride \-,trīd\ *vt* -ED/-ING/-S : to convert into a nitride; *esp* : to treat (steel) by the process of nitriding

nitriding *n* -S [fr. gerund of ²*nitride*] : a process of case hardening steel by impregnating with nitrogen usu. by being heated in ammonia gas between 900 and 1000°F

ni·trid·ize \-,dīz\ *vt* -ED/-ING/-S [¹*nitride* + *-ize*] : to combine with nitrogen; *also* : to change (a compound) by increasing the proportion of the electronegative part or to deprive (an atom or ion) of electrons by means of nitrogen — compare OXIDIZE

nitrido- *comb form* [¹*nitride*] : NITRILO- — esp. in names of inorganic compounds ⟨*nitrido*-tri-sulfuric acid $N(SO_3H)_3$⟩

ni·tri·fac·tion \ˌnī·trəˈfakshən\ *n* -S [*nitr-* + *-i-* + *-faction*] : formation of niter

ni·trif·er·ous \(ˈ)nīˈtrif(ə)rəs\ *adj* [*nitr-* + *-iferous*] : containing or yielding niter

ni·tri·fi·able \ˌnī·trəˈfīəbəl\ *adj* [*nitrify* + *-able*] : capable of nitrification

ni·tri·fi·ca·tion \ˌ==,fəˈkāshən\ *n* -S [F, fr. *nitrifier* to nitrify, after such pairs as F *amplifier* to amplify: *amplification*] : the process of nitrifying; *specif* : the oxidation by bacteria of ammonium salts to nitrites and the further oxidation of nitrites to nitrates wherever the proper conditions of temperature, air, moisture, and alkalinity allow the nitrobacteria to act (as in all productive soils and in the heaps of waste organic matter formerly used in manufacturing potassium nitrate) — see NITROGEN CYCLE, NITROGEN FIXATION 2; compare DENITRIFICATION

ni·tri·fier \ˈ==,fī(ə)r, -iə\ *n* -S : one that nitrifies

ni·tri·fy \-,fī\ *vt* -ED/-ING/-ES [F *nitrifier*, fr. *nitre* niter + *-ifier* -ify] **1** : to combine or impregnate with nitrogen or a nitrogen compound **2** : to convert by oxidation into nitric acid or nitrous acid or their salts : subject to or produce by nitrification — compare NITROSIFY

ni·trile \ˈnī·trəl; -,trēl, -īl\ *n* -S [ISV *nitr-* + *-ile*] : any of a class of compounds characterized by the presence of the trivalent nitrogen radical N≡ and derivable from oxygen-containing acids by complete removal of the elements of water from their ammonium salts; *usu* : a compound (as acetonitrile, benzonitrile) that is characterized by the presence of the cyanogen group, is derivable from a carboxylic acid or its amide, and yields the acid on complete hydrolysis : an organic cyanide

nitrile rubber *n* : any of a class of synthetic rubbers that are made by copolymerizing butadiene and acrylonitrile, are characterized by good resistance to swelling caused by oils, solvents, and greases, and are used esp. in hose for carrying oils and gasoline, in tank linings, and in gaskets

nitrilo- *comb form* [ISV *nitrile*] : containing the trivalent radical N≡ characteristic of nitriles — esp. in names of organic compounds ⟨*nitrilo*-tri-acetic acid $N(CH_2COOH)_3$⟩

ni·trite \ˈnī,trīt, *usu* -īd·+V\ *n* -S [*nitr-* + *-ite*] : a salt or ester of nitrous acid

nitrite group *or* **nitrite ion** *n* : the univalent group or anion NO_2 or ONO characteristic of nitrous acid and nitrites in which it is united through oxygen and hence is isomeric with the nitro group

nitrito- *comb form* [*nitrite*] : containing the nitrite group — esp. in names of coordination complexes ⟨*nitrito*-pentammine-cobalt ion $[Co(ONO)(NH_3)_5]^{++}$⟩ — compare NITR- 2b

ni·tri·toid \ˈnī·trə,tȯid\ *adj* [ISV *nitrite* + *-oid*] : resembling a nitrite or being something (as poisoning) caused by a nitrite ⟨a severe ~ crisis may follow arsphenamine injection⟩

¹ni·tro \ˈnī·(,)trō\ *adj* [*nitr-*] : containing or being the univalent group $-NO_2$ united through nitrogen — used esp. of organic compounds in which the group is united to carbon or nitrogen; compare NITR- 2b, NITRITE GROUP, NITRYL

²nitro \"\ *n* -S : any of various nitrated products: as **a** [by shortening] : NITROGLYCERIN **b** [short for *nitrocellulose*] : CELLULOSE NITRATE **c** : NITRO POWDER

ni·tro- *in pronunciations below*, ˈ==ˈnī·(,)trō *or* -,trə\ — see NITR-

ni·tro·amine \ˈ==+\ *n* [*nitro-* + *amine*] : a nitro derivative of an amine; *esp* : NITRAMINE 1

ni·tro·aniline \"+\ *also* **ni·tran·i·line** \(ˈ)nīˈtranᵊlən *sometimes* -,īn *or* -,ēn\ *n* [ISV *nitr-* + *aniline*] : a nitro derivative of aniline: as **a** : the bright yellow crystalline para mono derivative $H_2NC_6H_4NO_2$ made usu. from *para*-nitro-chlorobenzene by reaction with ammonia or from acetanilide by nitration and hydrolysis and used chiefly as an intermediate for azo and azoic dyes **b** : the orange-yellow crystalline ortho isomer made similarly to the para derivative **c** : the yellow crystalline meta isomer made usu. from *meta*-dinitrobenzene by partial reduction and used chiefly as a dye intermediate

ni·tro·bac·ter \ˈ⸗⸗,baktə(r)\ *n* [NL, fr. *nitr-* + *-bacter*] **1** *cap* **:** a genus of rod-shaped nonmotile bacteria (family Nitrobacteriaceae) occurring in soil, securing energy for growth by oxidizing nitrites to nitrates, and growing poorly on organic media **2** -s **:** any bacterium of the genus *Nitrobacter* **:** NITRIC BACTERIUM

ni·tro·bacteria \ˈ⸗⸗+\ *n pl* [NL, fr. *nitr-* + *bacteria*] **1 :** the soil bacteria concerned in nitrification **2 :** NITRIC BACTERIA — compare NITROSOBACTERIA

ni·tro·bacteriaceae \"+\ *n pl, cap* [NL, irreg. fr. *Nitrobacter*, type genus + *-aceae*] **:** a family of Eubacteriales (order Pseudomonadales) comprising rod-shaped or rarely spherical bacteria capable of using carbon dioxide as a source of carbon and obtaining energy by oxidation of ammonia or nitrites — compare THIOBACTERIACEAE

ni·tro·bar·ite \"+\ *n* [*nitr-* + *baryta* + *ite*] **:** native barium nitrate

ni·tro·benzene \"+\ *n* [ISV *nitr-* + *benzene*] **:** a poisonous insoluble oil $C_6H_5NO_2$ of slightly yellow color and sweetish odor that is made by nitration of benzene and that is used chiefly as a solvent, mild oxidizing agent, and starting material in making aniline and other dye intermediates

ni·tro·calcite \"+\ *n* [*nitr-* + *calc-* + *-ite*] **:** native calcium nitrate $Ca(NO_3)_2.4H_2O$ occurring as an efflorescence (as on old walls and in limestone caves)

ni·tro·cellulose \"+\ *n* [ISV *nitr-* + *cellulose*] **:** nitrated cellulose **:** CELLULOSE NITRATE ⟨~ lacquers⟩ — **ni·tro·cel·lulosic** \"+\ *adj*

ni·tro·chloroform \"+\ *n* [*nitr-* + *chloroform*] **:** CHLOROPICRIN

ni·tro·cotton \"+\ *n* **:** cellulose nitrate made from cotton; *esp* **:** GUNCOTTON

ni·tro·ethane \"+\ *n* [ISV *nitr-* + *ethane*] **:** a volatile liquid nitroparaffin $C_2H_5NO_2$ obtained usu. along with the nitropropanes and used as an industrial solvent and in chemical synthesis

ni·tro·form \ˈnī·trə,fȯrm\ *n* [ISV *nitr-* + *-form* (as in *chloroform*)] **:** a crystalline explosive compound $CH(NO_2)_3$ analogous to chloroform; trinitro-methane

ni·tro·furan \¦⸗⸗ *at* NITRO- +\ *n* [*nitr-* + *furan*] **:** any of several derivatives of furan containing a nitro group in the alpha or 2- or 5-position and used as antibacterial agents

ni·tro·fu·ra·zone \,⸗⸗ˈfyu̇rə,zōn\ *n* -s [*nitr-* + *fur-* + semi*carbazone*] **:** a pale yellow crystalline compound $O_2NC_4H_2$-$OCH{=}NNHCONH_2$ used chiefly externally as a bacteriostatic or bactericidal dressing (as for wounds and infections); 5-nitro-2-furfural semicarbazone

ni·tro·ga·tion \,nī·trəˈgāshən\ *n* -s [*nitr-* + *irrigation*] **:** fertilization of the soil with nitrogen by the addition of anhydrous ammonia from pressure tanks to the irrigation water

ni·tro·gelatin *or* **ni·tro·gelatine** \¦⸗⸗ *at* NITRO- +\ *n* [ISV *nitr-* + *gelatin*] **:** BLASTING GELATIN

ni·tro·gen \ˈnī·trəjən, -rēj-\ *n* -s [F *nitrogène*, fr. *nitr-* + *-gène* -gen] **:** a common nonmetallic element that in the free form is normally a colorless odorless tasteless insoluble inert diatomic gas comprising 78 percent of the atmosphere by volume, obtained industrially by fractional distillation of liquid air, and used chiefly as an inert atmosphere (as in industrial processes) and that in the combined form has a wide range of valences (as from −3 in ammonia to +5 in nitric acid and nitrates) and is a constituent of biologically important compounds (as proteins, nucleic acids, alkaloids) and hence of all living cells as well as of industrially important substances (as cyanides, fertilizers, dyes, antibiotics) — symbol *N;* see ELEMENT table, NITROGEN CYCLE, NITROGEN FIXATION

ni·tro·gen·ate \-jə,nāt, nīˈträjə-, *usu* -ād.+V\ *vt* -ED/-ING/-S **:** to combine with nitrogen **:** NITROGENIZE — **ni·tro·gen·a·tion** \,nī·trəjəˈnāshən, nī·,träjə'-\ *n* -s

nitrogen balance *n* **1 :** the difference between nitrogen intake and nitrogen excretion in the animal body, a greater intake resulting in a positive balance and an increased excretion causing a negative balance — see NITROGEN EQUILIBRIUM **2 :** the net loss or gain of soil nitrogen resulting from the removal of nitrogen (as by cropping, leaching, denitrification, and soil erosion) and the addition of nitrogen (as through fertilizers and nitrogen fixation by organisms)

nitrogen base *or* **nitrogenous base** *n* **:** a basic derivative of ammonia (as hydroxylamine); *esp* **:** an organic derivative (as methylamine, pyridine)

nitrogen chloride *n* **:** NITROGEN TRICHLORIDE

nitrogen cycle *n* **:** a continuous series of natural processes by which nitrogen passes through successive stations in air, soil, and organisms involving principally decay, nitrogen fixation, nitrification, and denitrification

nitrogen dioxide *n* **:** a suffocating poisonous strongly oxidizing gas that is reddish brown and has the formula NO_2 at 150°C but becomes paler on being cooled because it dimerizes to nitrogen tetroxide, that is usu. obtained in an equilibrium mixture with nitrogen tetroxide by oxidation (as of nitric oxide or ammonia), by reduction of nitric acid, or by decomposition of lead nitrate, and that is used in either gaseous or liquefied form chiefly in making concentrated nitric acid, in nitration processes, and as an oxidizing agent (as in rocket propellants) — called also *nitrogen(IV) oxide*

nitrogen equilibrium *n* **:** nitrogen balance when intake and excretion of nitrogen are equal

nitrogen family *n* **:** the related elements nitrogen, phosphorus, arsenic, antimony, and bismuth forming a subdivision of group V of the periodic table

nitrogen fixation *n* **1 :** the conversion of free nitrogen into combined forms useful as such or as starting materials for fertilizers, explosives, and a variety of chemicals by any of several industrial processes (as the synthesis of ammonia, the synthesis of calcium cyanamide, the synthesis of nitric oxide and nitrogen dioxide from nitrogen and oxygen of the air at very high temperatures produced in an electric arc or by combustion of natural gas) — compare CYANAMIDE PROCESS, SYNTHETIC AMMONIA PROCESS **2 :** the metabolic assimilation of atmospheric nitrogen by heterotrophic bacteria (as free-living members of the genera *Azotobacter* and *Clostridium* in soil or symbiotic rhizobia in root nodules of leguminous plants) the nitrogen being utilized in the presence of carbohydrate to build bacterial protein and released for plant use by nitrification in the soil on the death of the bacteria that initially fix it

nitrogen fixer *n* **:** any of various soil organisms involved in the process of nitrogen fixation

nitrogen-fixing \¦⸗⸗⸗¦⸗⸗\ *adj* [*nitrogen* + *fixing*, fr. pres. part. of [1]*fix*] **:** having the power of nitrogen fixation ⟨*nitrogen-fixing* bacteria⟩; *broadly* **:** contributing to the process of nitrogen fixation ⟨*nitrogen-fixing* plants⟩

ni·tro·gen·iza·tion \nī-,träjənəˈzāshən, ,nī·trəjə-, -,nīˈz-\ *n* -s **:** the process of nitrogenizing

ni·tro·gen·ize \nīˈträjə,nīz, ˈnī·trəjə-,-\ *vt* -ED/-ING/-S **:** to combine or impregnate with nitrogen or its compounds

nitrogen monoxide *n* **1 :** NITROUS OXIDE **2 :** NITRIC OXIDE

nitrogen mustard *n* **:** any of a group of toxic blistering compounds that are analogous in composition to mustard gas but with nitrogen replacing sulfur and that typically are chlorinated tertiary alkylamines; *esp* **:** an amine $CH_3N(CH_2CH_2Cl)_2$ used in the form of its crystalline hydrochloride in treating neoplastic diseases (as Hodgkin's disease and leukemia); methyl-bis-(2-chloroethyl)-amine

ni·trog·e·nous \(ˈ)nī-¦träjənəs\ *adj* [*nitrogen* + *-ous*] **:** of, relating to, or containing nitrogen in combined form (as in nitrates or proteins) ⟨~ fertilizers such as ammonium nitrate and tankage⟩ ⟨~ feeds⟩

nitrogenous equilibrium *n* **:** NITROGEN EQUILIBRIUM

nitrogen oxide *n* **:** any of several oxides of nitrogen some of which are formed in a mixture as toxic fumes by the action of nitric acid on oxidizable material (as organic substances or metals) or by the decomposition of nitrates or nitro compounds and are used as catalysts in the chamber process of making sulfuric acid: as **a :** NITROUS OXIDE **b :** NITRIC OXIDE **c :** NITROGEN TRIOXIDE **d :** NITROGEN DIOXIDE **e :** NITROGEN PENTOXIDE

nitrogen pentoxide *n* **:** a white crystalline unstable compound N_2O_5 obtainable by oxidation of nitrogen dioxide with ozone or by dehydration of nitric acid and yielding nitric acid on combination with water with evolution of much heat; di-nitrogen pentoxide — called also *nitric anhydride, nitrogen(V) oxide*

nitrogen peroxide *n* **:** the oxide nitrogen dioxide as such, as its dimer nitrogen tetroxide, or as a mixture of these two

nitrogen tetroxide *n* **1 :** a colorless poisonous gas N_2O_4 that is obtained by cooling nitrogen dioxide, that condenses to a colorless or pale yellow liquid at 21°C, and that freezes to colorless crystals at −11°C **2 :** a brown liquid produced commercially and containing both nitrogen tetroxide and nitrogen dioxide

nitrogen trichloride *n* **:** a pungent volatile explosive yellow oil NCl_3 formerly used in bleaching and aging flour

nitrogen trioxide *n* **:** a compound N_2O_3 obtained at a low temperature as a deep blue unstable liquid that readily decomposes into nitric oxide and nitrogen dioxide; di-nitrogen trioxide — called also *nitrogen(III) oxide, nitrous anhydride*

ni·tro·glycerin *or* **ni·tro·glycerine** \¦⸗⸗ *at* NITRO- +\ *n* [ISV *nitr-* + *glycerin*; prob. orig. formed as F *nitroglycérine*] **:** a heavy oily explosive poisonous liquid compound $C_3H_5(ONO_2)_3$ that is almost colorless when pure and has a sweet taste, that is obtained by nitrating glycerol, that burns quietly in the open air but explodes on heating in a closed vessel or esp. on percussion with the formation of about 10,000 times its own volume of gas, and that is used chiefly in making dynamites and propellant explosives (as blasting gelatin) and in medicine as a vasodilator (as in angina pectoris) — called also *glyceryl trinitrate*

ni·tro·guanidine \"+\ *n* [ISV *nitr-* + *guanidine*] **:** a crystalline smokeless flashless propellant $HN{=}C(NH_2)NHNO_2$ obtained usu. by treating guanidine nitrate with concentrated sulfuric acid and used as a component in military smokeless powder (as in guns requiring rapid firing without overheating the barrel of the gun)

ni·tro·hydrochloric acid \"+-\ *n* [*nitr-* + *hydrochloric*] **:** AQUA REGIA

ni·trol·amine \¦nī·,trōl, -ōl+\ *n* [G *nitrolamin*, fr. *nitro-* (fr. *nitros-*) + *-lamin* (fr. *hydroxylamin* hydroxylamine)] **:** any of a class of compounds obtained by the action of amines or ammonia on nitrosates, nitrosites, or nitrosochlorides

ni·tro·lic acid \(ˈ)nī-¦trōlik, -rälik-\ *n* [*nitr-* + *-ol* + *-ic*] **:** any of a class of weak acids of the general formula $RC({=}NOH)NO_2$, that are formed by the action of nitrous acid on primary nitroparaffins RCH_2NO_2 and that react with alkalies to give intensely red-colored solutions of their salts ⟨aceto-*nitrolic acid* $CH_3C({=}NOH)NO_2$⟩ — compare PSEUDONITROLE

ni·tro·lim \ˈnī·trə,lim\ *or* **ni·tro·lime** \-,līm\ *n* -s [*nitrolim* alter. of *nitrolime*, fr. *nitr-* + *-lime*] **:** CALCIUM CYANAMIDE — used chiefly commercially

ni·tro·magnesite \¦⸗⸗ *at* NITRO- +\ *n* [*nitr-* + *magnesium* + *-ite*] **:** native magnesium nitrate $Mg(NO_3)_2.6H_2O$ occurring as an efflorescence in limestone caverns

ni·tro·mersol \,⸗⸗ˈmər,sȯl, -ōl\ *n* -s [*nitr-* + *mercury* + *cresol*] **:** a brownish yellow to yellow solid organic mercurial $C_7H_5HgNO_3$ that is a derivative of *ortho*-cresol used chiefly in the form of a solution of its sodium salt as an antiseptic and disinfectant

ni·trom·e·ter \nīˈträməd·ə(r)\ *n* [*nitr-* + *-meter*] **:** an apparatus for collecting and measuring the volume of gaseous nitrogen or other gas that is liberated from a substance during analysis — **ni·tro·met·ric** \¦⸗⸗ *at* NITRO- +¦me·trik\ *adj*

ni·tro·methane \¦⸗⸗ *at* NITRO- +\ *n* [ISV *nitr-* + *methane*] **:** a liquid nitroparaffin CH_3NO_2 that boils at 101°C, that is obtained usu. along with the nitropropanes, and that is used chiefly as an industrial solvent, as a rocket monopropellant, and in chemical synthesis

ni·tro·muriatic acid \"+-\ *n* [*nitr-* + *muriatic*] **:** AQUA REGIA

nitro musk *n* **:** any of several synthetic musks (as musk ambrette, musk ketone, musk xylene) that are nitro derivatives of substituted benzenes

ni·tro·naphthalene \¦⸗⸗ *at* NITRO- +\ *n* [ISV *nitr-* + *naphthalene*] **:** either of two yellow crystalline compounds $C_{10}H_7NO_2$: **a :** the alpha or 1-isomer made by direct nitration of naphthalene and used in making alpha⸗ naphthylamine **b :** the beta or 2-isomer made indirectly (as by nitration of tetrahydronaphthalene followed by dehydrogenation)

nitrometer

ni·trone \ˈnī·,trōn\ *n* -s [*nitr-* + *-one*] **:** any of a class of compounds that contain the grouping $>C{=}N(O)-$ consisting of carbon and oxygen attached to nitrogen and that are made from alkyl or aryl derivatives of hydroxylamine by interaction with aldehydes or ketones or from nitroso compounds and derivatives of diazomethane ⟨phenyl-*N*-methyl-nitrone C_6H_5-$CH{=}N(O)-CH_3$ ⟨oxime-*nitrone* tautomerism⟩

ni·tron·ic acid \(ˈ)nī-¦tränik-\ *n* [*nitronium* + *-ic*] **:** a tautomeric form of a nitroparaffin characterized by the isonitro group $=NO(OH)$

ni·tro·ni·um \nīˈtrōnēəm\ *n* -s [NL, fr. *nitr-* + *-onium*] **:** NITRYL; *esp* **:** the nitryl cation NO_2^+ ⟨~ perchlorate NO_2ClO_4⟩

ni·tro·paraffin \¦⸗⸗ *at* NITRO- +\ *n* [ISV *nitr-* + *paraffin*] **:** a nitro derivative (as nitromethane, nitropropane) of any member of the methane series, the mononitro derivatives of the lower members of the series being dense liquids of pleasant odor that form crystalline salts with alkalies

ni·tro·phenol \"+\ *n* [ISV *nitr-* + *phenol*] **1 :** a nitro derivative of phenol: as **a :** a yellow crystalline compound O_2N-C_6H_4OH used chiefly in organic synthesis — called also *ortho⸗ nitrophenol* **b :** a colorless to yellowish isomeric compound $O_2NC_6H_4OH$ used chiefly as an acid-base indicator, as a fungicide, and in organic synthesis — called also *para-nitrophenol* **2** *usu* **nitro phenol :** a nitro derivative of any of the class of phenols

ni·troph·i·lous \(ˈ)nī-¦träfələs\ *adj* [ISV *nitr-* + *-philous*] **:** preferring or thriving in a soil rich in nitrogen

ni·tro·phyte \ˈnī·trə,fīt\ *n* -s [ISV *nitr-* + *-phyte*] **:** a plant requiring a soil rich in nitrogen — **ni·tro·phyt·ic** \¦⸗⸗¦fid·ik\ *adj*

nitro powder *n* **:** an explosive powder made from nitrated organic materials (as guncotton, smokeless powder)

ni·tro·propane \¦⸗⸗ *at* NITRO- +\ *n* **:** either of two liquid nitroparaffins $C_3H_7NO_2$ made usu. by hot vapor-phase nitration of propane and used chiefly as industrial solvents and in chemical synthesis: **a :** the primary derivative $CH_3CH_2CH_2NO_2$ — called also *1-nitropropane* **b :** the secondary derivative $CH_3CH(NO_2)CH_3$ — called also *2-nitropropane*

ni·tro·prussiate \"+\ *n* [ISV *nitr-* + NL *prussia* Prussian blue + ISV *-ate*] **:** NITROPRUSSIDE

ni·tro·prusside \"+\ *n* -s [ISV *nitr-* + NL *prussia* Prussian blue + ISV *-ide*] **:** a salt containing the anion $[Fe(CN)_5NO]^{--}$ composed of five cyanogen groups and one nitrosyl group coordinated with iron; penta-cyano-nitrosyl-ferrate — see SODIUM NITROPRUSSIDE

nitros- *or* **nitroso-** *comb form* [NL *nitrosus* nitrous] **:** containing the univalent group —NO composed of one nitrogen and one oxygen atom — esp. in names of organic compounds ⟨*nitroso*benzene C_6H_5NO⟩ ⟨*nitros*amines⟩; compare ISONITROSO-, NITROSYL 1, NITR- 2b

ni·tros·amine \,nī·trōsəˈmēn, -ōˈsamən\ *n* -s [*nitros-* + *amine*] **:** any of a class of neutral compounds formed from secondary amines by action of nitrous acid and characterized by the grouping $>NNO$ consisting of a nitroso group attached to nitrogen; an *N*-nitroso-amine

[1]**ni·tro·sate** \ˈnī·trə,sāt, -,sət\ *n* -s [G *nitrosat*, contr. of *nitrosonitrat*, fr. *nitros-* + *nitrat* nitrate] **:** any of a class of compounds obtained by the action of nitrogen dioxide on unsaturated hydrocarbons (as terpenes)

[2]**nitrosate** \-,sāt\ *vt* -ED/-ING/-S [*nitros-* + *-ate* (vb. suffix)] **:** to introduce the nitroso group into (a compound) **:** convert into a nitroso compound

ni·tro·sa·tion \,⸗⸗ˈsāshən\ *n* -s [ISV *nitros-* + *-ation*] **:** the process of converting into a nitroso compound

ni·tros·i·fy \nīˈtrōsə,fī\ *vt* -ED/-ING/-ES [NL *nitrosus* nitrous + E *-ify*] **:** to convert by oxidation into nitrous acid or nitrites — compare NITRIFY

ni·tro·site \ˈnī·trə,sīt\ *n* -s [G *nitrosit*, contr. of *nitrosonitrit*, fr. *nitros-* + *nitrit* nitrite] **:** any of a class of compounds obtained by the action of nitrous acid or nitrogen trioxide on unsaturated hydrocarbons (as terpenes)

ni·tro·so \nīˈtrō(,)sō\ *adj* [*nitros-*] **:** containing or being the univalent group —NO — used esp. of organic compounds; compare NITRO, NITROS-, NITROSYL 1

ni·tro·so·bacteria \⸗¦⸗⸗+\ *n pl* [NL, fr. *nitrosus* nitrous + *-o-* + *bacteria*] **:** the nitrobacteria that oxidize ammonia to nitrites **:** NITROUS BACTERIA

ni·tro·so·chloride \"+\ *n* [*nitros-* + *chloride*] **:** any of a class of crystalline compounds obtained by the action of nitrosyl chloride or of alkyl nitrites and hydrochloric acid on unsaturated hydrocarbons (as terpenes) and characterized by the grouping $>CCl-C(NO)<$ or $>CCl-C({=}NOH)<$

ni·tro·so·coc·cus \⸗,⸗⸗ˈkäkəs\ *n, cap* [NL, fr. *nitros*us nitrous + *-o-* + *-coccus*] **:** a genus of large nonmotile spherical bacteria (family Nitrobacteriaceae) comprising a single species (*N. nitrosus*) that oxidizes ammonia compounds to nitrites in the soil or on suitable media

ni·tro·som·o·nas \,nī·(,)trōˈsämənəs, -,nas\ *n, cap* [NL, fr. *nitrosus* + *-o-* + *-monas*] **:** a genus of ellipsoidal autotrophic soil bacteria (family Nitrobacteriaceae) that obtain energy for growth by oxidizing ammonia to nitrites and grow poorly on organic matter

ni·tro·so·phenol \nī-¦trō(,)sō+\ *n* [ISV *nitros-* + *phenol*] **:** a nitroso derivative of phenol; *esp* **:** the unstable pale yellow to light brown crystalline para derivative ONC_6H_4OH that is tautomeric with quinone oxime, is made from phenol by reaction with nitrous acid, and is used as a dye intermediate

ni·tro·so·sulfuric acid \"+-\ *n* [*nitros-* + *sulfuric*] **:** NITROSYLSULFURIC ACID

ni·tro·starch \ˈnī·trə+,-\ *n* [ISV *nitr-* + *starch*] **:** a high explosive that is similar to cellulose nitrate, that is obtained as a white powder by nitrating starch, and that is used chiefly in blasting and demolition explosives — called also *starch nitrate*

ni·tro·syl \-,sil, -ēl\ *n* -s [ISV *nitros-* + *-yl*] **1 :** the nitroso group, radical, or cation — used esp. in names of inorganic compounds ⟨~ chloride⟩ and coordination complexes; compare NITROPRUSSIDE **2 :** a compound of the nitrosyl radical with a metal analogous to a carbonyl ⟨cobalt tricarbonyl ~ $Co(CO)_3NO$⟩

nitrosyl chloride *n* **:** an orange-red corrosive gaseous compound NOCl that has an odor like chlorine, that is present in aqua regia but is made usu. by reaction of nitric oxide with chlorine or of nitric acid with common salt, and that is used chiefly in bleaching flour and in chemical synthesis

nitrosylsulfuric acid \¦⸗⸗,⸗+-\ *n* [ISV *nitrosyl* + *sulfuric*] **:** a crystalline acid $NOHSO_4$ that is formed by the reaction of nitrogen oxides or fuming nitric acid with sulfuric acid or sulfur dioxide (as in the manufacture of sulfuric acid by the chamber process) and that is used chiefly in the form of a straw-colored corrosive oily liquid containing over half sulfuric acid in making dyes and dye intermediates (as by diazotization); nitrosyl hydrogen sulfate

ni·tro·toluene \¦⸗⸗ *at* NITRO-+\ *n* [ISV *nitr-* + *toluene*] **:** a nitro derivative of toluene or a mixture of such derivatives: as **a :** the yellow liquid ortho mono derivative $CH_3C_6H_4NO_2$ made by nitration of toluene and used chiefly as an intermediate for azo dyes **b :** the colorless crystalline solid para isomer obtained along with the ortho derivative and used similarly

ni·trous \ˈnī·trəs\ *adj* [NL *nitrosus*, fr. L, full of natron, fr. *nitrum* natron + *-osus* -ous — more at NITER] **1 :** of, relating to, containing, or impregnated with niter **:** of the nature of or like niter ⟨~ powder⟩ ⟨Priestley's name for nitric oxide was ~ air⟩ **2 :** of, relating to, or containing nitrogen — used esp. of compounds in which this element has a lower valence than in corresponding nitric compounds ⟨~ oxide⟩ ⟨~ acid⟩

nitrous acid *n* **:** an unstable acid HNO_2 known only in pale blue solutions and esp. in the form of its salts and used chiefly in diazotization processes

nitrous anhydride *n* **:** NITROGEN TRIOXIDE

nitrous bacterium *n* **:** a bacterium that oxidizes ammonia to nitrites **:** one of the nitrosobacteria

nitrous ether *n* **:** ETHYL NITRITE

nitrous oxide *n* **:** a colorless gas N_2O that is obtained usu. by heating ammonium nitrate, that when inhaled produces incoordination of movement and loss of sensibility to pain preceded by exhilaration and sometimes laughter, and that is used chiefly as an anesthetic (as in dentistry) and in preparing whipped cream and other food aerosols; di-nitrogen monoxide — called also *laughing gas, nitrogen(I) oxide*

nitrous vitriol *n* **:** strong sulfuric acid in which nitrogen oxides have been absorbed in the Gay-Lussac tower in the chamber process of making sulfuric acid — see GLOVER TOWER

ni·trox·yl \nīˈträksəl\ *n* [ISV *nitr-* + *oxy-* + *-yl*] **:** NITRYL

ni·tryl \ˈnī·,tril, -rēl\ *n* -s [ISV *nitr-* + *-yl*] **:** the nitro group, radical, or cation — esp. in names of inorganic compounds ⟨~ chloride NO_2Cl⟩

nits *pl of* NIT

nit·ta·ny turkey \ˈnit(ᵊ)nē, -ni-\ *n, usu cap N* [fr. *Nittany* valley, Pennsylvania] **:** a domesticated strain of the native wild turkey developed in Pennsylvania and being smaller and darker than the domestic Bronze turkey which it considerably resembles

nit·ta tree \ˈnid·ə-\ *n* [perh. fr. Mandingo *nete* leguminous mimosa] **:** any of several Old World tropical trees of the genus *Parkia* (as *P. biglobosa* and *P. filicoidea*)

nit·ter \ˈnid·ə(r)\ *n* -s [[1]*nit* + *-er*] **:** an insect (as a botfly) that deposits nits on horses

nit·ty \ˈnid·ē, -i\ *adj* -ER/-EST [[1]*nit* + *-y*] **:** full of or infested with nits

nitweed \ˈ⸗,⸗\ *n* [[1]*nit* + *weed;* fr. its minute leaves] **:** ORANGE GRASS

nit·wit \ˈnit·,⸗\ *n* [prob. fr. G dial. *nit* not (fr. OHG *niwiht*, *neowiht* nothing) + E *wit* — more at NAUGHT] **:** an empty⸗ headed or stupid person ⟨convention that the characters of farce should be ~s devoid of feeling —Eric Keown⟩

nit·witted \(ˈ)⸗·¦⸗⸗\ *adj* **:** EMPTY-HEADED, STUPID, SILLY

nitzsch·ia \ˈnichēə\ *n, cap* [NL, fr. Christian L. *Nitzsch* †1837 Ger. naturalist + NL *-ia*] **:** a genus (the type of the family Nitzschiaceae) of mostly solitary and free-floating diatoms that are elongate with rhomboidal cross section

nitzsch·i·a·ce·ae \,⸗⸗ˈāsē,ē\ *n pl, cap* [NL, fr. *Nitzschia*, type genus + *-aceae*] **:** a family of diatoms (order Pennales) having the features of the genus *Nitzschia*

[1]**niu·e·an** \(ˈ)n(y)ü¦(w)āən\ *adj, usu cap* [*Niue* Island, south central Pacific ocean + E *-an*] **1 a :** of, relating to, or characteristic of the island of Niue **b :** of, relating to, or characteristic of the people of Niue **2 :** of, relating to, or characteristic of the Polynesian language of the Niuean people

[2]**niuean** \"\ *n* -s *usu cap* **1 :** a Polynesian of Niue Island **2 :** the Polynesian language of the Niuean people

ni·val \ˈnīvəl\ *adj* [L *nivalis*, fr. *niv-*, *nix* snow + *-alis* -al — more at SNOW] **:** characterized by, abounding with, or living in or under snow **:** of or relating to a region of perennial snow ⟨~ flora⟩ ⟨~ climate⟩

ni·va·tion \nīˈvāshən\ *n* -s [L *niv-*, *nix* snow + E *-ation*] **:** erosion of rock or soil caused by the alternate thawing and freezing of meltwater beneath and at the margins of snowbanks

ni·veau \(ˈ)nē¦vō\ *n, pl* **ni·veaux** \"\ [F, fr. MF *niveau*, *nivel*, alter. of *livel* — more at LEVEL] **:** a level or plateau (as of existence or achievement) esp. in a progression ⟨cultural ~ and religious level —Joachim Wach⟩ ⟨the life history and achievement of ~ of the patient-to-be —*Scientific Monthly*⟩

niv·en·ite \ˈnivə,nīt\ *n* -s [William *Niven* †1937 Am. mineralogist + E *-ite*] **:** a velvet-black variety of uraninite containing cerium and yttrium

niv·e·ous \ˈnivēəs\ *adj* [L *niveus*, fr. *niv-*, *nix* snow] **:** of or relating to snow **:** resembling snow (as in whiteness) **:** SNOWY ⟨~ rock⟩ ⟨a ~ landscape⟩

niv·er \ˈnivə(r)\ *dial var of* NEVER

niwar *usu cap, var of* NEWAR

[1]**nix** \ˈniks\ *n* -ES [G, fr. OHG *nihhus* — more at NICKER] **:** a supernatural creature orig. in Germanic folklore and conceived of in many forms but usu. as having the form of a woman or as half human and half fish, dwelling in fresh water usu. in a beautiful palace, and usu. unfriendly to man ⟨haunting, penetrating, pining as voice of ~ or siren —Walter de la Mare⟩ — called also *nixie*

[2]**nix** \"\ *n* -ES [G *nichts* nothing, fr. MHG *nihtes*, gen. of *niht*

nothing, fr. OHG *niwiht, neowiht* — more at NAUGHT] **1** *slang* : NOTHING : NO ONE ⟨what a man means to say signifies ~ in politics —*Emporia (Kans.) Gazette*⟩ **2** : ²NIXIE

³nix \"\ *adv, slang* : NO — used to express disagreement or the withholding of permission ⟨if I were to say ~ on the books he'd be miserable —*Everybody's Mag.*⟩

⁴nix \"\ *vt* -ED/-ING/-ES *slang* : VETO, FORBID, PROHIBIT, BAN, REJECT, CANCEL ⟨~*ed* a request for a $2500 business loan —Carl Sifakis⟩ ⟨tried to ~ the idea of a lie-detector test —Barbara Graham⟩

¹nix·ie \'niksē, -si\ *n* -s [G, female nix, fr. OHG *nicchessa*, fem. of *nihhus* nix] : ¹NIX

²nixie *also* **nixy** \"\ *n, pl* **nixies** [²*nix* + *-ie, -y*] : a piece of mail that is undeliverable because illegibly or incorrectly addressed

³nixie *also* **nixy** \"\ *vt* **nixied; nixied; nixying; nixies** : to stamp (a piece of mail) as a nixie and dispatch to sender or to dead-letter office

nix·ta·mal \ˌnēshtə'mäl\ *n, pl* **nixtamal** \"\ *or* **nixtama·les** \-(ˌ)läs\ [MexSp, fr. Nahuatl, fr. *nextli* ashes + *tamalli* tamale] : limed kernels of corn that is ready to be ground into masa

ni·yo·ga \nē'yōgə\ *n* -s [Skt, order, duty, fr. *niyunakti* he orders, enjoins, fr. *ni-* down, into + *yunakti* he yokes, joins — more at NETHER, YOKE] *Hindu law* : an appointed task; *specif* : the appointment of a brother or any near kinsman to raise up issue to a deceased childless husband by marrying his widow

ni·zam \nə'zäm, (')nī¦-, -zam\ *n* [Hindi *nizām* order, arrangement, governor, fr. Ar *nizām*] **1** *pl* **nizams** : one of the sovereigns of Hyderabad, India reigning from 1713 to 1950 **2** *pl* **nizam** [Turk, fr. Ar *nizām*] : a Turkish soldier

ni·zam·ate \-ˌmāt\ *n* -s [*nizam* + *-ate*] : the territory or office of the nizam

nizh·ni ta·gil \'nizhnētə'gil\ *adj, usu cap N&T* [fr. *Nizhni Tagil*, U.S.S.R.] : of or from the city of Nizhni Tagil, U.S.S.R. : of the kind or style prevalent in Nizhni Tagil

nizy \'nizē, -zi\ *n* -ES [perh. fr. ¹*nice* + *-y*] *dial chiefly Brit* : FOOL, LUNKHEAD

nja·ve \'nyävə\ *or* **dja·ve** \'jä-\ *n* -s [native name in Africa] : a very large tropical African tree (*Mimusops njave*) that has a termite-resistant wood somewhat resembling mahogany, a slightly acid edible fruit, and a seed rich in a fat that resembles shea butter

njo·ro·an \nyə'rōən\ *adj, usu cap* [fr. *Njoro*, Bantu stock in Kenya + E *-an*] : of or relating to a Neolithic culture of Kenya characterized by polished stone axes and extended burial in cemeteries

nk *abbr* neck

NK *abbr* not known

nko·le \ən'kōlə\ *n, pl* **nkole** *or* **nkoles** *usu cap* : NYANKOLE

NL *abbr* **1** *often not cap* new line **2** night letter **3** *often not cap* [L *non licet*] it is not permitted **4** *often not cap* [L *non liquet*] it is not clear **5** *often not cap* [L *non longe*] not far **6** north latitude

NLO *abbr* naval liaison officer

NLT *abbr* **1** net long ton **2** night letter **3** *often not cap* not later than **4** *often not cap* not less than

NM *abbr, often not cap* **1** nautical mile **2** night message **3** no mark; not marked **4** [L *nocte et mane*] night and morning

NME *abbr* national military establishment

NMT *abbr, often not cap* not more than

NN *abbr, often not cap* **1** names **2** nomen novum **3** nomen nudum **4** notes **5** not to be noted **6** nouns

NN *symbol* place for the insertion of two or more usu. given names of a person (as in a ceremonial statement)

NNE *abbr* north-northeast

NNW *abbr* north-northwest

¹no \'nō\ ; *when expressing disgust, impatience, or strong disagreement* 'nō, 'nä, 'nā, (*esp. when reduplicated*) 'nə, 'ˀm'ˀm, 'ˀəˀə, *or* 'ˀäⁿ,'ˀäⁿ\ *adv* [ME *no, na*, fr. OE *nō, nā*, fr. *ne* not, no + *ā, ō* ever, always; akin to OS & OHG *ni, ne* not, ON *ne, nē*, Goth *ni*, OIr *ni, nī*, L *ne-* not (negative prefix), *nē* not, Gk *nē-*, Skt *na, nā*, OSlav *ne* — more at AYE (ever)] **1 a** *chiefly Scot* : NOT ⟨have walked forty miles and yet am ~ wearied —Hugh Mitchell⟩ ⟨and he's ~ rightly young either —John Buchan⟩ **b** — used as a function word to express the negative of an alternative choice or possibility ⟨whether he was satisfied or ~ —H.J.Laski⟩ ⟨shall we write a letter or ~ —J.H.Robinson †1936⟩ **2** : in no respect or degree : not at all — used in comparisons ⟨regard criticism . . . as ~ better than blasphemy —Elmer Davis⟩ ⟨is ~ more serious than the rest of them⟩ ⟨your experience was ~ different from mine⟩ **3** : not so — used to express negation, dissent, denial, or refusal in answer to a question or request ⟨are you going? *No*, I am not going⟩ ⟨~, you can't have any more candy⟩ or to introduce a statement correcting or contradicting a preceding statement ⟨~, that's not the way the accident happened⟩ **4** — used with a following adjective to imply a meaning expressed by the opposite positive statement ⟨express his opinions in ~ uncertain terms —B.W.Bond⟩ ⟨a teacher of ~ mean ability —L.W.Fox⟩ ⟨an item of ~ small importance —B.H. Hibbard⟩ **5** — used as a function word to emphasize a following negative or to introduce a more emphatic, explicit, or comprehensive statement ⟨none is righteous, ~, not one —Rom 3:10 (RSV)⟩ ⟨had the ambition, ~, the conviction, that he would . . . be a great singer —Hans Herbert⟩ **6** — used as an interjection to express surprise, doubt, or incredulity ⟨~, that's impossible⟩ ⟨~, you couldn't have been the one responsible⟩

²no \'nō\ *adj* [ME *no, non, na, nan*, fr. OE *nān* — more at NONE] **1 a** : not any ⟨let there be ~ strife between you and me —Gen 13:8 (RSV)⟩ ⟨and ~ birds sing —John Keats⟩ ⟨with ~ dancing in the streets or ritual bonfires —Mollie Panter-Downes⟩ ⟨wanted ~ part of army routine —Georg Meyers⟩ ⟨show little or ~ concern for the . . . rest of the population —Vera M. Dean⟩ ⟨~ two of the rugged, scarecrow figures were dressed alike —F.V.W.Mason⟩ **b** : hardly any : very little ⟨in ~ time other families followed —John Mason Brown⟩ ⟨it's ~ distance from the house to the store⟩ **2** : not a : quite other than a : far from being a — usu. used to modify a predicate noun ⟨whether this is true . . . I don't know; I'm ~ anatomist —Deems Taylor⟩ ⟨that goodness is ~ name and happiness ~ dream —Lord Byron⟩ ⟨this was ~ Bohemia, but a workshop in the woods —*Amer. Guide Series: N.H.*⟩ ⟨it was ~ job to pull the elk cows out of the water —F.B.Gipson⟩ **3** : not any possible — used to modify a gerund that follows a finite form of the verb *to be* ⟨there's ~ speaking a word but you fly into a passion —Fanny Burney⟩ ⟨there's ~ accounting for tastes⟩ **4** : that is absent, lacking, or nonexistent ⟨frankly confide to yourself these opinions or rather ~ opinions of mine —Thomas Jefferson⟩ — usu. used in combination ⟨thoroughly frightened with certain *no*-persons called ghosts —Henry Fielding⟩ ⟨a dog such as I have described, whatever be this breed or his *no*-breed —William Carnegie⟩ — **no dice 1** *of a cast of dice* : not valid : VOID **2** *slang* — used chiefly in the predicate to emphasize a negative attitude, result, or expectation ⟨tried for a scholarship but it was *no dice*⟩ ⟨to such a proposition I can only say *no dice*⟩

³no \"\ *n, pl* **noes** *or* **nos 1** : an act or instance of refusing or denying by the use of the word *no* : DENIAL ⟨my wooing mind shall be expressed in russet yeas and honest kersey ~*es* —Shak.⟩ ⟨the Everlasting *No* —Thomas Carlyle⟩ **2 a** : a negative vote or decision ⟨110 ayes were cast and only 16 ~*es*⟩ **b** *noes or nos pl* : persons voting in the negative ⟨the chairman asked the ~*es* to raise their right hands⟩

⁴no *or* **noh** \"\ *n, pl* **no** *or* **noh** *often cap* [Jap *nō*, lit., talent, ability] : classic Japanese dance-drama that is heroic in subject and in the use of measured chants and movements — called also *nogaku*

no *abbr* **1** north **2** nose **3** [L *numero*, abl. of *numerus*] number

NO *abbr* **1** name of **2** natural order **3** naval officer **4** nonofficial **5** no orders **6** not out

No *symbol* nobelium

noa \'nōə\ *adj* [Hawaiian, Tahitian, & Maori] : charged with little or no supernatural power : free or freed from taboo : COMMON, PROFANE

¹no–account \'≈ˌ≈\ *or* **no–count** \'≈ˌ≈\ *adj* [fr. the phrase *of no account*] *chiefly dial* : worthless and lazy : of no account : TRIFLING ⟨those *no-account* relatives of his⟩

²no–account \"\ *or* **no–count** \"\ *n* -s : a worthless or shiftless person

no·a·chi·an \(')nō¦ākēən\ *also* **no·a·chic** \-kik\ *adj, usu cap* [Heb *Nōaḥ* Noah, patriarch who built an ark to save his family and representative living creatures from the Flood (Gen 5:28–10:32) + E *-an* or *-ic*] **1** : of or relating to the patriarch Noah or his time **2** : ANCIENT, ANTIQUATED

no·a·chite \'nōəˌkīt\ *n* -s [perh. fr. F, fr. Heb *Nōaḥ* Noah + F *-ite*] **1** : a Freemason who has taken the 21st degree of the Scottish rite — called also *Prussian Knight* **2** : FREEMASON

no·ah's ark \'nōəz-\ *n, usu cap N* [so called fr. the supposed similarity to Noah's ark (Gen 6:14–20)] **1** *also* **noah's ark shell** : ARK SHELL; *esp* : a common ark shell (*Arca noae*) **2** : a series of straight parallel narrow bands of cloud that by perspective appear to spring from common points on opposite sides of the horizon and to arch and spread apart as they approach the zenith **3** : a set of toys representing Noah's ark and the animals in it **4 a** : LADY'S SLIPPER 1 **b** : a monkshood (*Aconitum napellus*)

noap *dial Brit var of* ¹NOPE

¹nob \'näb\ *n* -s [prob. alter. of ¹*knob*] **1** *slang* : HEAD 1 **2** *slang* : a blow on the head **3** : a jack of the same suit as the starter scoring in cribbage one point for the holder

²nob \"\ *vb* **nobbed; nobbed; nobbing; nobs** *vt* : to strike (as a person) in the head ~ *vi* : to strike blows at or on the head ⟨*nobbed* away without connecting once⟩

³nob \"\ *n* -s [perh. fr. ¹*nob*] *chiefly Brit* : one in a superior position in life or of superior attainments (as in a field of specialization) : SWELL, TOFF

⁴nob \"\ *var of* KNOB

NOB *abbr* naval operating base

no ball *n* [fr. the umpire's call "no ball"] : a bowled ball in a cricket game that because ruled unfair by the umpire cannot take a wicket, does not count as a ball in the over, and counts one run if not otherwise scored from — compare EXTRA

no–ball \'≈ˌ≈\ *vt* [*no ball*] : to declare a delivery by (a cricket bowler) to be a no ball

nob·bily \'näbəlē\ *adv* : in a nobby manner

¹nob·ble \'näbəl\ *vt* **nobbled; nobbled; nobbling** \-b(ə)liŋ\ **nobbles** [perh. alter. of ²*nab* + *-le*] **1** *Brit* : to incapacitate (a racehorse) esp. by drugging **2** *slang Brit* **a** : to win over to one's side (as by bribery or flattery) **b** : STEAL, TAKE **c** : SWINDLE, CHEAT

²nobble \"\ *vt* -ED/-ING/-S [²*nob* + *-le*] *dial chiefly Eng* : to strike on the head

¹nob·bler \-b(ə)lə(r)\ *n* -s [¹*nobble* + *-er*] **1** *Brit* : one that nobbles horses **2** *Brit* : SWINDLER

²nobbler \"\ *n* -s [origin unknown] *Austral* : a drink of liquor or beer

³nobbler \"\ *n* -s [²*nobble* + *-er*] **1** *slang Brit* : a blow on the head : KNOCKOUT **2** *slang Brit* : ²NOBBY 1

nobbly *var of* KNOBBLY

nob·but \'näbət\ *adv* [ME *no but*, fr. *no* (adv.) + *but*] **1** *dial Brit* : ONLY, JUST ⟨tha's ~ had one marriage —Eric Knight⟩ **2** *dial Brit* : nothing but ⟨~ warts o' trees —Marjorie Whitaker⟩

¹nob·by *also* **knob·by** \'näbē, -bi\ *adj* -ER/-EST [³*nob* + *-y*] : of the first quality or style : of the finest design or finish : EXCELLENT, SMART, STYLISH

²nobby \"\ *n* -ES [perh. fr. ²*nob* + *-y*] **1** : a stick sometimes used by anglers for killing fish **2** : a small fishing boat used off the Isle of Man

no–being \'≈ˌ≈≈\ *n* [²*no* + *being*] : the negation of being : NONEXISTENCE

no·bel·ist \nō'beləst\ *n* -s *often cap* [*Nobel* (*Prize*), a prize usu. awarded annually for the encouragement of men and women who work for the interests of humanity (after Alfred B. *Nobel* †1896 Swed. manufacturer, inventor, and philanthropist, who left his entire estate for the establishment of such prizes) + E *-ist*] : a winner of a Nobel Prize

no·bel·i·um \nō'belēəm\ *n* -s [NL, fr. Alfred B. *Nobel* + NL *-ium*] : a radioactive element produced artificially (as by bombardment of curium with ions of carbon) — symbol *No*; see ELEMENT table

nob·i·le of·fi·ci·um \'näbəlēə'fishēəm\ *n* [L, noble office] *Scots law* : the equitable discretion of the Court of Sessions to afford relief in cases where none is possible at law

no·bil·i·ary \nō'bilēˌerē, -lyarē\ *adj* [*nobility* + *-ary*] : of or relating to the nobility

no·bi·li's ring \'nōbəlēz-, 'nōb-\ *n, usu cap N* [after Leopoldo *Nobili* †1835 It. physicist] : one of the colored rings formed upon a metal plate by electrolytic deposition (as of copper or lead peroxide) — usu. used in pl.

no·bil·i·tate \nō'biləˌtāt\ *vt* -ED/-ING/-S [L *nobilitatus*, past part. of *nobilitare*, fr. *nobilis* famous, noble] : ENNOBLE — **no·bil·i·ta·tion** \ˌ≈≈'tāshən\ *n* -s *archaic*

no·bil·i·ty \nō'bilədē, -ətē, -i\ *n* -ES [ME *nobilite*, fr. MF *nobilité*, fr. L *nobilitat-, nobilitas*, fr. *nobilis* famous, noble + *-itat-, -itas* -ity] **1** : the quality or state of being noble: as **a** : the condition of possessing characteristics or properties of a very high kind or order : superiority in excellence, value, or importance ⟨the ~ of gold⟩ ⟨the ~ of his prose⟩ **b** : superiority of mind or of character : commanding moral worth or excellence : EMINENCE ⟨a man of true ~⟩ **c** : the quality or state of being of noble or high birth or of exalted rank or station either inherited or acquired : preeminence or distinction by rank or title ⟨in many Continental countries . . . ~, once conferred, extends to every member of the family in all generations —Valentina Heywood⟩ **2 a** : the body of persons forming the noble class in a country or state : ARISTOCRACY; *specif* : the British peerage — usu. used with *the* ⟨a street where many of the ~ reside —Samuel Johnson⟩ **b** : a noble class or a body of nobles — used with *a* ⟨the Venetians were a ~ of merchants —C.C.Clarke⟩ **3** : a manifestation of noble spirit

nobill \'≈ˌ≈\ *vt* [fr. the phrase *no bill* (of indictment)] : to release from charges by failing to find a true bill ⟨the grand jury ~*ed* her after the murder⟩

no–bill \'≈ˌ≈\ *n* -s [prob. fr. ²*no* + waybill] *slang* : a nonunion railroad employee

¹no·ble \'nōbəl\ *adj* **nobler** \-b(ə)lə(r)\ **noblest** \-b(ə)ləst\ [ME, fr. OF, fr. L *nobilis* knowable, known, well known, famous, noble, fr. OL *gnobilis*; akin to L *noscere* (OL *gnoscere*) to come to know — more at KNOW] **1 a** *of a person* : possessing outstanding qualities (as of eminence, dignity) : ILLUSTRIOUS **b** *of a deed* : FAMOUS, NOTABLE **2** : having the power of transmitting by inheritance some recognized preeminence founded on hereditary succession : of high birth or exalted rank : of, belonging to, or constituting the nobility : HIGHBORN, ARISTOCRATIC ⟨my sire is of a ~ line —S.T.Coleridge⟩ **3 a** : possessing very high or excellent qualities or properties : belonging to a kind that is considered exceptionally fine ⟨~ wines⟩ **b** : very good or excellent : superior of its kind ⟨inherited a ~ estate⟩ **4** : outstanding or impressive esp. by reason of grandeur, largeness, magnificence ⟨a ~ cathedral⟩ ⟨these ~ edifices⟩ **5** : possessing, characterized by, arising from, or indicating superiority or commanding excellence of mind or character, or high ideals or morals : LOFTY ⟨a man of ~ nature⟩ **6** : resisting chemical action : chemically inert or inactive esp. toward oxygen : relatively stable ⟨a ~ metal⟩ ⟨a ~ gas⟩ ⟨~ patina⟩ **syn** see GRAND, MORAL

²noble \"\ *n* -s [ME, partly fr. *noble*, adj., and partly fr. MF *noble*, fr. *noble*, adj.] **1** : a person of noble rank or birth : a member of the nobility : NOBLEMAN, PEER **2 a** (1) : an old English gold coin first issued by Edward III as equivalent to 6s 8d and orig. weighing a little over 138 grains but reduced to 128, then to 120 grains, and then debased by Henry IV to 108 grains — see RYAL (2) : a corresponding unit of value ⟨half-*noble* and quarter-*noble* coins were issued⟩ **b** (1) : a Scottish gold coin similar to the English noble (as one issued by David II another by James VI) (2) : a silver coin, the half-mark piece of James VI, worth 6s 8d **3** *slang* : a captain of strikebreakers or an overseer in charge of strikebreaking operations

noble art *or* **noble science** *n* [*noble art* short for *noble art of boxing*; *noble science* short for *noble science of defense*] : BOXING

noble cane *n* : any of various sugarcanes that are considered to represent the highest development of the species and are characterized by thick barrel-shaped internodes, large soft-rinded juicy stalks, and high sugar content

noble fir *n* : a valuable evergreen timber tree (*Abies procera*) attaining a height of 250 feet in the Cascade mountains being distinguished by cones with taper pointed bracts that project beyond and are reflexed over the scales, and yielding a useful timber resembling that of spruce — called also *Oregon larch*

noble gas *n* : INERT GAS 2

noble hawk *n* : FALCON 1b — used in the technical language of falconry

noble liverwort *n* : a hepatica (*Hepatica triloba*)

no·ble·man \'nōbəlmən\ *n, pl* **noblemen** [¹*noble* + *man*] **1** : a man of noble rank : one belonging to the nobility : NOBLE, PEER **2 noblemen** *pl* : the pieces as distinguished from the pawns in chess

no·ble·man·ly \-nlē\ *adj* : of, relating to, or befitting a nobleman

noble metal *n* [ME *noble metall*] : a metal (as gold, silver, or platinum) or alloy relatively superior in resistance to corrosion or oxidation — opposed to *base metal*; compare PRECIOUS METAL

noble–minded \¦≈≈¦≈≈\ *adj* : having or characteristic of an honorable, upright, and superior mind ⟨a *noble-minded* reply⟩ — **no·ble–mind·ed·ly** *adv* — **no·ble–mind·ed·ness** *n* -ES

no·ble·ness *n* -ES [ME *nobilnes*, fr. *nobil, noble noble* + *-nes* -ness] **1** : the quality or state of being noble: as **a** : elevation of mind, character, or station **b** *obs* : SPLENDOR, GRANDEUR **2** *obs* **a** : ²NOBLE 1 **b** : NOBILITY 2a

noble pine *n* : PIPSISSEWA

nobler *comparative of* NOBLE

noble rot *n* [trans. of F *pourriture noble*] **1** : an alteration of various wine grapes that is caused by the action of a fungus on the grapes when allowed to hang on the vine until overripe and that is responsible for the characteristic flavor of sauternes and related wines **2** *also* **noble mold** : the imperfect fungus (*Botrytis cinerea*) that causes noble rot

no·blesse \nō'bles\ *n* -s [ME *noblesse, noblesce*, fr. OF *noblesce*, fr. *noble*] **1** : noble birth or condition : NOBILITY 1c **2** : NOBILITY 2b; *esp* : the members of the French nobility

noblesse oblige \-ō'blēzh\ *n* [F, lit., nobility obligates] : the obligation of honorable, generous, and responsible behavior that is a concomitant of high rank or birth

noblest *superlative of* NOBLE

noblewoman \'≈≈ˌ≈\ *n, pl* **noblewomen** : a woman of noble rank : PEERESS

no·bly \'nōb(ə)lē, -li\ *adv* [ME *nobly, nobliche*, fr. *noble* (adj.) + *-ly, -liche* -ly] **1** : with greatness of soul : GALLANTLY ⟨a deed ~ done⟩ **2** : SPLENDIDLY, MAGNIFICENTLY ⟨a ~ planned work⟩ ⟨~ clad attendants⟩ **3** : of noble extraction ⟨~ born⟩

¹no·body \'nōˌbädē, -(ˌ)bədē, -di\ *pron* [ME *no body*] : no person : not anybody

²nobody \"\ *n* : a person of no influence, importance, social standing, or other outstanding quality

no–bond resonance *n* [²*no* + *bond*, n.] : HYPERCONJUGATION

nob·ut \'näbət\ *var of* NOBBUT

no·cake \'nōˌkāk\ *n* [of Algonquian origin; akin to Narraganset *nokehick* parched corn meal, lit., it is soft, Natick *nookhic*] : Indian corn parched and pounded into a powder

no·car·dia \nō'kärdēə\ *n* [NL, fr. Edmond I. E. *Nocard* †1903 Fr. veterinarian and biologist + NL *-ia*] **1** *cap* : a genus of aerobic actinomycetes (family Actinomycetaceae) that form limited mycelia which tends to break up into rod-shaped cells, develop neither conidia nor endospores but occas. form spores by fragmentation of the parent cell, and include various pathogens as well as some soil-dwelling saprophytes **2** -s : any organism of the genus *Nocardia*

no·car·di·o·sis \nōˌkärdē'ōsəs\ *n, pl* **nocardio·ses** \-ˈō,sēz\ [NL, fr. *Nocardia* + *-osis*] : actinomycosis caused by actinomycetes of the genus *Nocardia* and characterized by production of spreading granulomatous lesions — compare MADUROMYCOSIS

nocence *also* **nocency** *n, pl* **nocences** *also* **nocencies** [LL *nocentia*, fr. L *nocent-, nocens* (pres. part.) + *-ia* -y] *obs* : GUILT

no·cent \'nōsᵊnt\ *adj* [ME, fr. L *nocent-, nocens* harmful, criminal, fr. pres. part. of *nocēre* to harm, hurt — more at NOXIOUS] **1** : doing harm or having a tendency to harm : HURTFUL, HARMFUL ⟨a ~ dose⟩ **2** *archaic* : GUILTY, CRIMINAL — opposed to *innocent*

no·cer·ite \'nōsəˌrīt, nō'chä,-\ *n* -s [*Nocera*, Italy, its locality + E *-ite*] : a mineral $Ca_3Mg_3F_8O_2$ that is a calcium magnesium oxyfluoride

nocht \'näkt\ *chiefly Scot var of* NAUGHT

noci- *comb form* [L *nocēre* to hurt, harm + E *-i-*] : pain ⟨*noci*perception⟩

no·ci·cep·tive \¦nōsē¦septiv\ *adj* [*noci-* (fr. L *nocēre* to hurt) + *receptive*] **1** *of a stimulus* : PAINFUL, INJURIOUS **2** : of, induced by, or responding to a nociceptive stimulus — used esp. of receptors or protective reflexes

no·ci·cep·tor \-tə(r)\ *n* -s [*noci-* + *receptor*] : a receptor for injurious or painful stimuli : a pain sense organ — compare NEUTROCEPTOR

no·ci·fen·sor \-¦fen(t)sə(r)\ *adj* [*noci-* + *-fensor* (prob. fr. *defense* + *-or*)] : of, relating to, or constituting a system of cutaneous nerve fibers believed to mediate diffuse pain sensations

no·ci·perception \¦nōsē+\ *n* [*noci-* + *perception*] : perception of injurious stimuli

no·ci·perceptive \"+\ *adj* : of or relating to nociperception

no·cive \'nōsiv\ *adj* [MF or L; MF *nocif*, fr. L *nocivus*, fr. *nocēre* to hurt + *-ivus* -ive — more at NOXIOUS] : HARMFUL, INJURIOUS ⟨~ effects of insecticides⟩

¹nock \'näk\ *n* -s [ME *nocke, nokke*; akin to OE *hnocc* penis, MD *nocke* tip, summit, end of a yardarm, ON *hnúka* to sit cowering, *hnykill* clew of yarn, tumor, Sw *nock, nocke* pin, peg, end of a yardarm, OIr *cnocc* lump, hill, L *nux* nut — more at NUT] **1 a** (1) : either of two tips of horn fastened on the ends of a bow and having notches for holding the string (2) : one of the notches cut in these or in the bow itself **b** (1) : the part of an arrow having a notch for the bowstring whether as formerly a thick bulbous wooden end containing the notch or as now usu. an attached fixture (as of horn or plastic) : the butt end of any arrow (2) : the notch itself — see ARROW illustration **2** *obs* : the cleft between the buttocks **3** [prob. fr. D *nok*, fr. MD *nocke* tip, summit] : the upper fore corner of a boom sail or a staysail when cut with a square tack

²nock \"\ *vt* -ED/-ING/-S : to make a notch in or fit into or by means of a notch: as **a** : to slip (the eye of a bowstring) into a bow nock in bracing a bow **b** : to fit (an arrow) on the string of a bow **c** : to furnish (an arrow or bow) with a nock

nock·erl \'näkər(ə)l\ *n, pl* **nock·erln** \-ln\ [G dial. (Austria), dim. of *nock*, a kind of mountain, dumpling; akin to MD *nocke* tip, summit] : a rich light dumpling

nock·et \'näkət\ *var of* NACKET

nocking point *n* [*nocking*, gerund of ²*nock*] : the commonly reinforced point on a bowstring where an arrow is nocked

no–count *var of* NO-ACCOUNT

noct- *or* **nocti-** *or* **nocto-** *comb form* [*noct-* fr. NL, fr. L *noct-, nox*; *nocti-* fr. L, fr. *noct-, nox*; *nocto-* fr. *noct-* + *-o-* — more at NIGHT] : night : during the night ⟨*nocti*florous⟩ ⟨*nocto*vision⟩

noc·tam·bu·lant \(')näk¦tambyələnt\ *adj* [*noctambulation* + *-ant*] **1** : NOCTAMBULOUS **2** : walking by night ⟨a ~ rogue⟩

noc·tam·bu·la·tion \ˌnäkˌtambyə'lāshən\ *or* **noc·tam·bu·lism** \'≈'≈≈ˌlizəm\ *n* -s [*noctambulation* fr. *noct-* + *ambulation*; *noctambulism*, prob. fr. F *noctambulisme*, fr. *noctambule* + *-isme* -ism] **1** : SOMNAMBULISM **2** : a stroll by night

noc·tam·bule \näk'tamˌbyül\ *n* -s [F, fr. NL *noctambulo*] : SOMNAMBULIST

noc·tam·bu·lic \(')näk¦tambyəlik\ *also* **noc·tam·bu·lis·tic** \(ˌ)näk¦tambyə¦listik\ *adj* [*noctambule* fr. *noctambule* + *-ic*; *noctambulistic* fr. *noctambulist* + *-ic*] : of or relating to noctambulation

noc·tam·bu·list \-'≈≈ləst\ *n* -s [*noctambulation* + *-ist*] : one who walks at night esp. in his sleep

noctambulo *n, pl* **noctambulones** *or* **noctambuloes** *or* **noctambulos** [NL, fr. *noct-* + *-ambulo* (fr. L *ambulare* to walk) — more at AMBLE] *obs* : SOMNAMBULIST

noc·tam·bu·lous \(ˈ)näkˈtambyələs\ *adj* [*noctambulation* + *-ous*] **:** of, relating to, or given to walking by night ⟨given way to ~ habits —*Times Lit. Supp.*⟩

noc·ti·diurnal \ˌnäktə+\ *adj* [*noct-* + *diurnal*] **:** comprising a sequence of day and night

noc·til·io \näkˈtilē,ō\ *n, cap* [NL, fr. *noct-* + *-ilio* (as in *Vespertilio*)] **:** a genus (the type of the family Noctilionidae) of tropical American fish-eating mastiff bats

noc·ti·lu·ca \ˌnäktəˈlükə\ *n* [NL, fr. L, moon, lantern, fr. *nocti-* noct- + *-luca*, fr. *lucēre* to shine — more at LIGHT (n.)] **1** *-s obs* **:** PHOSPHOR 2 **2** *cap* [NL, fr. L, moon] **:** a genus of marine plantlike flagellates (order Dinoflagellata) that are unusually large, complex in structure, and bioluminescent and that when present in numbers are responsible for much of the phosphorescence of the sea **3** *pl* **noctilucas** \-kəz\ *or* **noctilu·cae** \-ü,sē\ **:** any organism of the genus *Noctiluca*

noc·ti·lu·cence \ˌ==ˈlüsᵊn(t)s\ *n* -s [NL *noctiluca* + E *-ence*] **:** BIOLUMINESCENCE

noc·ti·lu·cent \-ᵊnt\ *adj* **1** [fr. *noctilucence*, after such pairs as E *translucence: translucent*] **:** BIOLUMINESCENT **2** [*noct-* + *lucent*] **:** visible or glowing at night — see NOCTILUCENT CLOUD

noctilucent cloud *n* **:** a luminous cloud seen at night at a height of about 275,000 feet

noc·ti·lu·cine \ˌ==ˈlü,sēn, -,sən\ *n* -s [F, fr. NL *Noctiluca*, genus of flagellates + F *-ine*] **:** an extract from luminous organisms to which their luminescence has been attributed — compare LUCIFERIN

noc·ti·lu·cous \ˌ==ˈlükəs\ *adj* [NL *noctiluca* (phosphor) + E *-ous*] **:** shining at night **:** PHOSPHORESCENT

noc·tiv·a·gant \(ˈ)näkˈtivəgənt\ *adj* [L *noctivagus* night-wandering (fr. *noct-*, *nox* night + *vagus* wandering) + E *-ant* — more at NIGHT, VAGARY] **:** going about in the night **:** night-wandering

noc·tiv·a·ga·tion \ˌnäk,tivəˈgāshən\ *n* -s [*noctivagant* + *-ation*] **:** a roving or going about in the night

noctivagator *n* -s [*noctivagation* + *-or*] *obs* **:** NIGHTWALKER

noc·tiv·a·gous \(ˈ)näkˈtivəgəs\ *adj* [L *noctivagus*] **:** NOCTIVAGANT

noc·to·graph \ˈnäktə,graf, -rȧf\ *n* [*noct-* + *-graph*] **:** a writing frame for the blind

noc·to·vis·ion \ˈnäktə,vizhən\ *n* [*nocto-* + *television*] **:** television in which the use of infrared rays makes it possible to transmit the image of a subject not visible to the eye (as because of darkness or fog)

noc·tua \ˈnäkchəwə\ *n, cap* [NL, fr. L, night owl, owl; akin to L *nox* night] **:** a large and widely distributed genus (the type of the family Noctuidae) of moths having larvae that are cutworms

noc·tu·ary \ˈnäkchə,werē\ *n* -ES [L *noctu*, adv., by night + E *-ary*; akin to L *nox* night] *archaic* **:** a journal of nocturnal incidents

¹noc·tu·id \ˈnäkchəwəd\ *adj* [NL *Noctuidae*] **:** of or relating to the Noctuidae

²noctuid \"\ *n* -s **:** a moth of the family Noctuidae

noc·tu·i·dae \näkˈtüə,dē\ *n pl, cap* [NL, fr. *Noctua*, type genus + *-idae*] **:** a large nearly cosmopolitan family of medium-sized stout-bodied dull-colored night-flying moths with usu. naked larvae that include many destructive agricultural pests (as the cutworms and armyworms) — see NOCTUA, OWLET MOTH; compare BOLLWORM, COTTON LEAFWORM, DAGGER MOTH, UNDERWING

noc·tule \ˈnäk,chül\ *n* -s [prob. fr. NL *noctula* (used as specific epithet), fr. LL *noctula* small owl, dim. of L *noctua* owl] **:** PIPISTRELLE

noc·tu·ria \näkˈtùrēə\ *n* -s [NL, fr. *noct-* + *-uria*] **:** urination at night esp. when excessive — called also *nycturia*

¹noc·turn \ˈnäk,tərn\ *n* -s [ME *nocturne*, fr. MF, fr. ML *nocturna*, fr. fem. of L *nocturnus* nocturnal] *Roman Catholicism* **:** one of the three principal divisions of the office of matins, formerly sung or recited between midnight and 4 o'clock in the morning, but now often on the preceding afternoon or evening

²nocturn \(ˈ)=ˈ=\ *adj* [MF or L; MF *nocturne*, fr. L *nocturnus*] *archaic* **:** NOCTURNAL

¹noc·tur·nal \(ˈ)näkˈtərnᵊl, -tən-\ *adj* [MF or LL; MF *nocturnal*, *nocturnel*, fr. LL *nocturnalis*, fr. L *nocturnus* of night, nocturnal + *-alis* -al; akin to L *nox* night — more at NIGHT] **1 :** of or relating to night **:** done, held, or occurring in the night ⟨~ darkness⟩ ⟨a ~ journey⟩ **2 a :** active at night — used of animals and sometimes plants that perform most of their functions (as feeding, breeding, or blooming) at night; compare DIURNAL **b :** characterized by nocturnal activity ⟨a ~ form of filariasis⟩ ⟨a ~ flower⟩ **3 :** suggestive of or having the character of a nocturne **4** *of a sign of the zodiac* **:** EVEN 5a — **noc·tur·nal·ly** \-ᵊlē, -ᵊli\ *adv*

²nocturnal \"\ *n* -s **1 :** NIGHT PIECE; *specif* **:** a play in which the action takes place to a considerable extent on a darkened stage **2 :** one that is abroad or active at night **:** NIGHTWALKER **3 :** an astrolabe formerly used for finding the time at night or determining latitude

nocturnal emission *n* **:** an involuntary discharge of semen during sleep often accompanied by an erotic dream — see WET DREAM

noc·tur·nal·ity \ˌnak,tərˈnaləd·ē\ *also* **noc·tur·nal·ism** \näkˈtərnᵊl,izəm\ *n, pl* **nocturnalities** *also* **nocturnalisms** **:** the condition of being nocturnal ⟨many rodents exhibit strict ~⟩

noc·turne \ˈnäk,tərn, -tōn\ *n* -s [F, adj., nocturnal, fr. L *nocturnus*] **1 :** a musical night piece; *esp* **:** a dreamy pensive composition for the piano **2 :** a painting of a scene at night **:** NIGHT PIECE

noc·u·ous \ˈnäkyəwəs\ *adj* [L *nocuus*, fr. *nocēre* to harm, hurt — more at NOXIOUS] **:** likely to cause injury **:** HARMFUL, DAMAGING ⟨~ grubs in the soil⟩ ⟨a ~ stimulus⟩ — **noc·u·ous·ly** *adv*

¹nod \ˈnäd\ *vb* **nodded; nodded; nodding; nods** [ME *nodden*; akin to OHG *hnotōn* to shake, ON *hnjótha* to rivet, clinch, L *cinis* ashes — more at INCINERATE] *vi* **1 :** to incline the head with a quick motion **:** make a quick downward motion of the head whether as a sign (as of assent, salutation, or command) or involuntarily (as from drowsiness) ⟨her cousin *nodded* in agreement⟩ ⟨sat *nodding* by the fire⟩ **2 :** to incline or sway from the vertical as though ready to fall ⟨the *nodding* debris that once was a city⟩ **3 :** to bend or sway the upper part downward or forward with a quick motion **:** bob gently ⟨the plumes that ~ on his helmet⟩ **4 :** to be for the moment inattentive, inaccurate, or careless **:** make a slip or error in a moment of abstraction **~** *vt* **1 :** to incline (as the head) or bend downward or forward; *specif* **:** to make a quick downward motion of (the head) as a sign or involuntarily ⟨*nodded* his head in approval⟩ **2 :** to bring, invite, or send by a nod ⟨~ one back⟩ **3 :** to signify by a nod ⟨~ approbation⟩ **4 :** to cause to bend **:** SWAY

²nod \"\ *n* -s **:** the act of one that nods or an instance of nodding: as **a :** NAP **b :** a signal of approval or victory **c :** a careless or inattentive fault **:** SLIP, LAPSE

³nod \"\ *n* -s [prob. back-formation fr. ¹*noddle*] *dial Eng* **:** the nape of the neck

nod·al \ˈnōdᵊl\ *adj* [¹*node* + *-al*] **:** being, relating to, or located at or near a node or nodes — **nod·al·ly** \-ᵊlē\ *adv*

no·dal·i·ty \nōˈdaləd·ē\ *n* -ES **:** the quality or state of being nodal

nodal point *n* **:** NODE; *esp* **:** either of two points so located on the axis of a lens or optical system that any incident ray directed through one will produce a parallel emergent ray directed through the other

nodal slide *n* **:** a device for locating the nodal points of a lens or lens system

no·dat·ed \ˈnō,dād·əd\ *adj* [L *nodatus* (past part. of *nodare* to make knotty, knot, fr. *nodus* knot) + E *-ed* — more at NODE] **:** having or forming a node ⟨a ~ hyperbola⟩

nod·der \ˈnädə(r)\ *n* -s **:** one that nods

nodding *adj* [fr. pres. part. of ¹*nod*] **1 :** bending downward or forward **:** PENDULOUS, DROOPING ⟨a plant with ~ flowers⟩ **2 :** DROWSY ⟨the ~ bees⟩ — **nod·ding·ly** *adv*

nodding acquaintance *n* **1 :** a very slight or superficial knowledge or understanding of something ⟨had no more than a *nodding acquaintance* with economic theory⟩ **2 :** a person with whom one is on terms of casual and distant civility

nodding cap *or* **nodding pogonia** *n* **:** a slender tuberous woodland orchid (*Triphora trianthophora*) of eastern No. America having a pale pink or whitish nodding flower with three-lobed lip

nodding catchfly *n* **:** a perennial European sticky herb (*Silene nutans*)

nodding ladies' tresses *n pl but sing or pl in constr* **:** SCREW AUGER

nodding lily *n* **1 :** MEADOW LILY **2 :** TURK'S-CAP LILY b

nodding mandarin *n* **:** a No. American disporum (*Disporum maculatum*) with yellow purple-spotted flowers

nodding onion *n* **:** a widely distributed No. American bulbous herb (*Allium cernuum*) with white to deep rose flowers — called also *wild onion*

nodding thistle *n* **:** MUSK THISTLE

nodding trillium *n* **:** a No. American trillium (*Trillium cernuum*) with whitish or creamy to pinkish or roseate nodding flowers nearly hidden under the leaves

¹nod·dle \ˈnädᵊl\ *n* -s [ME *nodel*, *nodle*] **1 a** *obs* **:** the back of the head **b** *chiefly dial* **:** the nape of the neck **2 :** HEAD, PATE, BRAIN

²noddle \"\ *vb* **noddled; noddled; noddling** \-d(ᵊ)liŋ\ **noddles** [¹*nod* + *-le*] **:** NOD

nod·dy \ˈnädē, -di\ *n* -ES [prob. short for obs. *noddypoll*, alter. (influenced by ¹*nod*) of *hoddypoll*] **1 :** a stupid person **:** DUNCE, SIMPLETON, FOOL **2 a** *also* **noddy tern :** any of several stout-bodied terns of the genera *Anoüs* and *Micranous* chiefly of tropical and subtropical seas; *esp* **:** a dark sooty brown tern (*A. stolidus*) common on the southern Atlantic and Gulf coasts of the U.S. **b** *Midland* **:** RUDDY DUCK **c :** FULMAR **d :** RAZORBILL **3 a :** an old card game resembling cribbage **b :** JACK 1c(1) **4** [prob. fr. ¹*nod* + *-y*] **a :** a small usu. 2-wheeled one-horse hackney vehicle formerly used in Ireland and Scotland **b :** an inverted pendulum consisting of a short vertical flat spring that supports a rod having a bob at the top and used for measuring slight horizontal vibrations

node \ˈnōd\ *n* -s [L *nodus* knot, node — more at NET] **1 :** a complication or difficulty (as in a drama) **:** PREDICAMENT, ENTANGLEMENT **2 :** a thickened or swollen enlargement (as on the trunk of a tree) **:** KNOB, PROTUBERANCE **a :** a pathological swelling or enlargement (as one in the neighborhood of a joint affected by rheumatism or gout or a firm tumor) **b :** a body part resembling a knot; *esp* **:** a discrete mass of one kind of tissue enclosed in tissue of a different kind ⟨the lymph ~s of the intestinal wall⟩ **3 :** either of the two points where the orbit of one celestial body intersects a specific reference plane (as the ecliptic in the solar system or the plane of the sky for a double star system) — see ASCENDING NODE, DESCENDING NODE **4 :** a point at which subsidiary parts originate or center: **a :** the often swollen or otherwise modified point on a stem or similar structure at which a leaf or leaves are inserted **b :** a point at which a curve intersects itself in such a manner that the branches have different tangents **c :** a point in an electrical network at which several branches come together **5 :** a point, line, or surface of a vibrating system that is constantly free or relatively free from vibratory motion (as the middle point of a stretched vibrating string constrained to vibrate in two equal segments or a point in a conductor at which the current or voltage remains zero or at a minimum)

nod·ed \-dəd\ *adj* **:** having or divided into nodes

node of ran·vier \-rän'vyā\ *usu cap R* [after Louis A. *Ranvier* †1922 Fr. histologist] **:** a constriction in the medullary sheath of a medullated nerve fiber

nodi *pl of* NODUS

no·di·ak \ˈnōdē,ak\ *n* -s [prob. native name in New Guinea] **:** the 3-toed echidna (*Zaglossus bruijnii*) of New Guinea

nod·i·cal \ˈnädəkəl, ˈnōd-\ *adj* [*node* + *-ical*] **:** of or relating to astronomical nodes **:** measured from node to node ⟨the ~ revolution of the moon⟩

nodical month *n* **:** the mean time of the moon's revolution in its orbit from ascending node to ascending node equal to 27 days, 5 hours, 5 minutes, 35.8 seconds of mean solar time — called also *draconic period*

no·di·corn \ˈnōdə,kȯrn\ *adj* [prob. fr. F *nodicorne*, fr. *nodi-* (fr. L *nodus* knot) + *-corne*, fr. L *-cornis* -corn] **:** having nodose antennae

no·dif·er·ous \(ˈ)nōˈdif(ə)rəs\ *adj* [ISV *nod-* (fr. L *nodus* knot, node) + *-iferous*] **:** producing or having nodes

no·di·form \ˈnōdə,fȯrm\ *adj* [*node* + *-iform*] **:** resembling a node

no·do·sa·ria \ˌnōdəˈsa(a)rēə\ *n, cap* [NL, fr. L *nodosus* knotty + NL *-aria*] **:** a genus of foraminiferans having the shell composed of chambers arranged in a straight or gently curved line — **no·do·sa·ri·an** \ˌ==ˈsa(a)rēən\ *adj or n* — **no·do·sar·oid** \-(a),rȯid\ *adj*

no·do·saur \ˈnōdə,sȯ(ə)r\ *n* -s [NL *Nodosaurus*] **:** a dinosaur of the genus *Nodosaurus*

no·do·sau·rus \ˌ==ˈsȯrəs\ *n, cap* [NL, fr. L *nodus* node, knot + NL *-saurus*] **:** a genus of heavily armored No. American Upper Cretaceous dinosaurs somewhat resembling gigantic horned toads

no·dose \(ˈ)nō,dōs\ *also* **no·dous** \ˈnōdəs\ *adj* [L *nodosus*, fr. *nodus* knot, node + *-osus* -ose, -ous — more at NET] **:** having numerous or conspicuous protuberances **:** KNOTTY, KNOBBED ⟨~ antennae⟩ ⟨~ leaf petioles⟩

no·dos·i·ty \nōˈdäsəd·ē\ *n* -ES [F or It or LL; F *nodosité* & It *nodosita*, fr. LL *nodositat-*, *nodositas* knottiness, fr. L *nodosus* knotty + *-itat-*, *-itas* -ity] **1 :** the quality or state of being nodose **2 :** PROTUBERANCE, SWELLING, NODE ⟨a surface dotted with *nodosities*⟩

nods *pres 3d sing of* NOD, *pl of* NOD

nod·u·lar \ˈnäjələ(r)\ *adj* [*nodule* + *-ar*] **1 :** of, relating to, characterized by, or having nodules ⟨~ vaginitis⟩ **2 :** occurring in the form of nodules ⟨a ~ ore⟩ ⟨~ graphites⟩ **3 :** infested with nodular worms ⟨a section of ~ intestine⟩

nodular disease *also* **nodule disease** *n* **:** infestation with or disease caused by nodular worms of the genus *Oesophagostomum* esp. in sheep

nodular iron *n* **:** cast iron in which the graphite is present as tiny nodules of characteristic structure

nodular worm *also* **nodule worm** *n* **1 :** any of several nematode worms (genus *Oesophagostomum*) that are parasitic in the large intestine of ruminants and swine where they cause swellings of the intestinal wall resembling abscesses **2 :** a filarial worm (*Onchocerca gibsoni*) causing nodular swellings in the skin and subcutaneous tissues of Australian cattle

nod·u·late \-jə,lāt\ *vb* -ED/-ING/-S [prob. back-formation fr. *nodulated*, adj.] *vt* **1 :** NODULIZE **2 :** to cause the formation of nodules on or in ⟨some rhizobia are capable of *nodulating* several different legumes⟩ **~** *vi* **:** to form or multiply in nodules — used of symbiotic nitrogen-fixing bacteria

nod·u·lat·ed \-lād·əd\ *adj* [*nodule* + *-ated*] **1 a :** having nodules; **b** *cf a leguminous plant* **:** having nodules containing symbiotic bacteria on the roots **2 :** NODULAR 2

nod·u·la·tion \ˌ==ˈlāshən\ *n* -s [*nodulated* (adj.) + *-ion*] **1 :** the process of becoming or condition of being nodular or nodulated **2 :** NODULE

nod·ule \ˈnä,jül\ *n* -s [L *nodulus* small knot, dim. of *nodus* knot, node — more at NET] **1** *obs* **:** a small quantity of medicinal material tied up in a bag or bit of cloth **2 :** a small rounded mass of irregular shape **:** a little lump: as **a :** a small rounded lump of a mineral or mineral aggregate ⟨a ~ of ironstone⟩ **b** (1) **:** a plant bud or gemma (2) **:** a thickening on the valve of a diatom (3) **:** one of the swellings on the roots of a leguminous plant that contains symbiotic bacteria **c :** the nodulus of the cerebellum **d :** a small abnormal knobby protuberance (as of tumorous growth or of calcification near an arthritic joint)

nod·uled \-ld\ *adj* **:** having or occurring in the form of nodules

nod·u·lize \ˈnäjə,līz\ *vt* -ED/-ING/-S **:** to convert (as finely divided ores) into nodules

nod·u·lose \ˌ==ˈlōs\ *also* **nod·u·lous** \ˈ==ləs\ *adj* [*nodule* + *-ose* or *-ous*] **:** having minute nodules **:** finely knobby — see ROOT illustration

nod·u·lus \ˈnäjələs\ *n, pl* **nodu·li** \-jə,lī\ [L, small knot] **:** NODULE; *esp* **:** a prominence on the inferior surface of the cerebellum forming the anterior end of the vermis

no·dus \ˈnōdəs\ *n, pl* **no·di** \ˈnō,dī\ [L, knot, node] **:** NODE: as **a :** COMPLICATION, DIFFICULTY **b :** a center or central point **c :** a hinge on the front margin of the wings of insects of the order Odonata

NOE *abbr* not otherwise enumerated

noe·genesis \ˌnōē+\ *n* [NL, fr. Gk *noē-* (as in *noēma*, understanding, thought, *noēsis* intelligence, understanding) + *genesis*] **:** a schema for the production of knowledge including three processes: (1) observation; (2) discovery of relations; and (3) the bringing to mind or the creation of ideas that stand in a given relation to given ideas

no·e·ge·ne·tic \ˌnōējəˈned·ik\ *adj* [fr. NL *neogenesis*, after E *genesis: genetic*] **:** of, relating to, or involving noegenesis

noek·kel·ost \ˈnōkə,lōst\ *or* **nok·kel·ost** \ˈnäkə,lōst\ *n* -s [Norw *nøkkelost*, fr. *nøkkel* key + *ost* cheese; fr. its being modeled after cheese from Leiden, Holland, that was marked with the crossed keys of Leiden's escutcheon] **:** a dark cheese made from whole or partly skimmed milk and spiced with cumin, caraway, or cloves, or all three

no·el \nōˈel\ *n* -s [F *noël*, fr. L *natalis* birthday, fr. *natalis*, adj., natal — more at NATAL] **1 :** a Christmas carol **2 :** the Christmas season

no·e·ma \nōˈēmə\ *n, pl* **noema·ta** \-məd·ə\ [NL, fr. Gk *noēma* perception, thought understanding, mind, fr. *noein* to perceive, think] *in Husserlian philos* **:** the objective aspect of or the content within an intentional experience — distinguished from *noesis*

no·e·ma·tach·o·graph \nō,ēməˈtakə,graf, -rȧf\ *n* [Gk *noēma* thought, understanding + E *tacho-* + *-graph*] **:** an instrument for measuring complex reaction time

no·e·ma·ta·chom·e·ter \nō,ēməd·əˈkäməd·ə(r)\ *n* [ISV *noema-* (fr. Gk *noēma* thought, understanding) + *tacho-* + *-meter*] **:** an instrument for measuring simple reaction time

no·e·mat·ic \ˌnōēˈmad·ik\ *adj* [prob. fr. G *noematisch*, fr. LGk *noēmatikos* rational, fr. Gk *noēmat-*, *noēma* thought, understanding + *-ikos* -ic] **:** of, relating to, or involved in noema

noes *pl of* NO

no·e·sis \nōˈēsəs\ *n* -ES [Gk *noēsis*, fr. *noein* to perceive, think] **1 :** purely intellectual apprehension: **a** *Platonism* **:** the highest kind of knowledge or knowledge of the eternal forms or ideas — contrasted with *dianoia* **b** *in Husserl* **:** the subjective aspect of or the act in an intentional experience — distinguished from *noema* **2 :** cognition esp. when occurring through direct knowledge

¹no·et·ic \(ˈ)nōˈed·ik\ *adj* [Gk *noētikos*, fr. *noētos* (verbal of *noein* to perceive, fr. *noos*, *nous* mind) + *-ikos* -ic] **:** of, relating to, or characterized by noesis ⟨~ experiences⟩: as **a :** apprehended only by the intellect ⟨~ truths⟩ **b :** given to purely intellectual or abstract reasoning ⟨a ~ thinker⟩

²noetic \"\ *n* -s **1 :** one that is noetic **2 :** the logical doctrine of axioms or of the laws of thought — often used in pl.

no-fines concrete *n* [*no-fines*, fr. ²*no* + *fines*] **:** porous concrete made without the use of fine aggregate

¹nog \ˈnäg *sometimes* ˈnȯg\ *n* -s [origin unknown] **:** a wooden peg, pin, or block of the size of a brick; *esp* **:** a small block built into a wall as a hold for nails

²nog \"\ *vt* **nogged; nogged; nogging; nogs :** to fill in (as between scantling) with brickwork ⟨~ partitions⟩

³nog *also* **nogg** \"\ *n* -s [origin unknown] **1 :** a strong ale formerly brewed in Norfolk, England **2** [by shortening] **:** EGGNOG **3 :** any of various mixed drinks usu. containing beaten egg, milk, or both and often spirits ⟨a brandy ~⟩ ⟨a prune ~⟩

⁴nog \ˈnäg\ *n* -s [by shortening] *dial Brit* **:** NOGGIN

no·gai \ˈnō,gī\ *n, pl* **nogai** *or* **nogais** *usu cap* [of Altaic origin; akin to Tatar & Kirghiz *Nogai*] **1 a :** a nomad Tatar people of the northeastern Caucasus **b :** a member of such people **2 :** a Turkic language of the Nogai people

no·ga·ku \ˈnō,gäkü\ *n, pl* **nogaku** [Jap *nōgaku*, fr. *nō* no (drama) + *gaku* music] **:** ⁴NO

no·gal \nōˈgäl\ *n* -ES [Sp, walnut tree, fr. LL *nucalis* like a nut — more at NEWEL] *chiefly Southwest* **:** a walnut, pecan, or hickory tree

nog·gin \ˈnägən\ *also* **nag·gin** \ˈnag-\ *n* -s [origin unknown] **1 a :** a small mug or cup **b :** a small usu. wooden pail **2 :** a small quantity of drink usu. equivalent to a gill ⟨a ~ of milk⟩ **3 :** a person's head

nogging *n* -s [fr. gerund of ²*nog*] **1 :** rough brick masonry used to fill in the open spaces of a wooden frame **2** *also* **nogging piece :** a horizontal reinforcement or furring strip between vertical studs

no-go gage \ˈ=,=-\ *n* [*no-go*, fr. the phrase *no go*] **:** a limit gage that will not go in or on the part being tested or will not screw on more than a given number of turns — compare GO GAGE

¹no-good \ˈ=ˈ=\ *adj* [fr. the phrase *no good*] **:** having no virtue, value, or chance of success **:** WORTHLESS, HOPELESS, USELESS ⟨he was *no-good* at anything tedious⟩ ⟨it's *no-good* to argue⟩ ⟨see what that *no-good* dog has done⟩

²no-good \ˈ=ˈ=\ *n* **:** a no-good person or thing

noh *var of* NO

no-hit \ˈ=ˈ=\ *adj* [fr. the phrase *no hit*] **:** of, relating to, or being a baseball game in which the pitcher allows the opposition no base hits

no-hit·ter \ˈnōˈhid·ə(r)\ *n* **:** a no-hit game in baseball

no-holds-barred \ˈ=ˈ=ˈ=\ *adj* [fr. the phrase *no holds barred*] **:** free from hampering rules or conventions ⟨the discussion on a *no-holds-barred* basis⟩

no-hoper \ˈnōˈhōpə(r)\ *n* [fr. the phrase *no hope* + *-er*] *Austral* **:** a shiftless individual without ideals or ambitions

nohow \ˈnō,hau̇\ *adv* [²*no* + *how*] **1 :** in no manner or way **:** not at all ⟨could ~ make out the writing⟩ ⟨was ~ equal to the task⟩ — often used dial. following another negative ⟨couldn't see him ~⟩ **2** *chiefly Midland* **:** ANYWAY ⟨where are you going ~⟩ **3** *chiefly dial* **:** in a state of confused disorder **:** out of sorts — usu. used with *all* ⟨was all ~ at the thought of going⟩

NOHP *abbr* not otherwise herein provided

NOIBN *abbr* not otherwise indexed by name

no·ib·wood \ˈnōib,wu̇d\ *also* **noib** *n* -s [*noib* (of unknown origin)] **:** BETHABARA

NOIC *abbr* naval officer in charge

noil \ˈnȯi(ə)l\ *n* -s [origin unknown] **:** short fiber removed during the combing of a textile fiber (as wool, silk, camel's hair) and spun into yarn for cloth ⟨whereas silk ~ is often waste, that of camel's hair is the best part of the fleece⟩

noint \ˈnȯint\ *vb* -ED/-ING/-S [ME *nointen*, prob. alter. of *anointen* — more at ANOINT] *archaic* **:** ANOINT

noir \ˈnwär\ *n* -s [F, fr. *noir*, adj., black, fr. L *niger*] **:** the black numbers in roulette when a bet is made on them

¹noise \ˈnȯiz\ *n* -s [ME, fr. OF, noise, noisy strife, quarrel, fr. L *nausea* seasickness, nausea — more at NAUSEA] **1 :** loud, confused, or senseless shouting or outcry **:** din or uproar of persons **2 a** (1) **:** sound or a sound that lacks agreeable musical quality or is noticeably loud, harsh, or discordant ⟨~ results from irregular vibrations and produces an unpleasant sound —Henry Melnik⟩ ⟨~ represents sounds in which the energy is more or less uniformly distributed over a considerable frequency range without a definite pitch being present —F.E.Terman⟩ (2) **:** the din or loud persistent incoherent sound that is a feature of most communities or activities ⟨the ~ of a rookery⟩ ⟨far away from city ~ and disorder⟩ **b :** any sound that is undesired or that interferes with something to which one is listening (as a hum or the scratching of a needle produced by a sound recording or reproducing system) **c :** an unwanted signal that enters an electronic communication system (as telephone, radio, television) or that is created in it and that tends to interfere with the desired signals ⟨a hissing sound in a telephone receiver, static in a radio receiver, and snow in a television receiver are forms of ~⟩ **3** *obs* **:** general or common talk or discussion **:** RUMOR; *esp* **:** evil or slanderous report **4 a :** sound or a sound that is not regarded as unpleasing or that has a pleasing melodious quality ⟨the tinkling ~s of the brook⟩ ⟨the ~ of heavenly choirs⟩ **b** *obs* **:** a company of musicians

²noise \"\ *vb* -ED/-ING/-S [ME *noisen*, fr. *noise*, n.] *vt* **:** to spread by rumor or report — usu. used with *abroad* or *about* ⟨it was *noised* about that the troops were to be returned home⟩ ⟨a rumor is being *noised* abroad⟩ **~** *vi* **1 :** to talk much or loudly **2 :** to make a noise or outcry

noise factor *or* **noise figure** *n* **:** the ratio of the noise output of an electronic device to that of a similar ideal device

noise field intensity *n* **:** the electromagnetic field intensity produced by waves of an interfering character in radio reception

noise·ful \ˈnȯizfəl\ *adj* [ME, fr. *noise* + *-ful*] **:** full of noise: as **a :** full of, abounding in, or making sounds **:** NOISY **b** *obs* **:** full of evil report—**noise·ful·ly** \-fəlē\ *adv*

noise·less \-zləs\ *adj* [¹*noise* + *-less*] **1 :** making or causing no noise or stir **:** free from noise **:** SILENT, QUIET ⟨kittens on ~ feet⟩ **2 a :** making less noise than is typical of its kind **b** *of a typewriter* **:** having a type-bar action that is quieter than that of a standard typewriter — **noise·less·ly** *adv* — **noise·less·ness** *n* -ES

noiseless recording *n* **:** a method of film recording in which the average density of the unmodulated track of the negative is decreased during silent and soft passages in order to reduce background noise

noise limiter *n* **:** an electronic device that eliminates some types of noise (as one due to strong pulses of interference) in radio receivers

noisemaker \ˈ=,==\ *n* **:** one that makes noise; *specif* **:** any of several devices (as a horn, clapper, rattle) used to make noise at a celebration or merrymaking — **noisemaking** \ˈ=,==\ *n or adj*

noiseproof \ˈ=;=\ *adj* **:** SOUNDPROOF

noise spectrum *n* **:** the array of frequencies involved in noise

¹noi·sette \nwäˈzet\ *n* -S [F, hazel nut, fr. MF, fr. OF, dim. of *nois, noix* nut, fr. L *nuc-, nux* — more at NUT] **1 :** a small rounded morsel of food: as **a :** a small piece of lean meat (as the eye of a chop or a small slice of tenderloin) **b :** a small potato ball browned in butter **2** *or* **noisette brown** [*noisette*, fr. F, adj., hazel, light brown, fr. *noisette* hazel nut] **:** HAZEL 4

²noisette \"\ *adj* [F] **:** prepared with, consisting principally of, or dressed with browned butter ⟨a ~ sauce⟩ ⟨cutlets ~⟩

noi·sette rose \nwäˈzet\ *also* **noisette** *n* -S *usu cap N* [after Philippe *Noisette*, brother of Louis Claude *Noisette* †1849 Fr. horticulturist] **:** any of various hardy garden roses supposedly descended from a hybrid between the China rose (*Rosa chinensis*) and the moss rose (*R. centifolia muscosa*)

nois·i·ly \ˈnȯizəlē, -li\ *adv* **:** in a noisy manner **:** so as to produce usu. disturbing noise

nois·i·ness \-zēnəs\ *n* -ES **:** the quality or state of being noisy

noi·some \ˈnȯisəm\ *adj* [ME *noysome*, fr. *noy* annoy (alter. of *anuy, anoi*) + *-some* — more at ANNOY (n.)] **1 :** NOXIOUS, HARMFUL, UNWHOLESOME, DESTRUCTIVE ⟨a ~ environment⟩ **2 :** offensive to the smell or other senses **:** DISGUSTING, DISTASTEFUL ⟨foul breath is ~ —Shak.⟩ **3** *obs* **:** ANNOYING — **noi·some·ly** *adv* — **noi·some·ness** *n* -ES

noisy \ˈnȯizē, -zi\ *adj* -ER/-EST [¹*noise* + *-y*] **1 :** making or given to making noise **:** CLAMOROUS, VOCIFEROUS ⟨the ~ crowd⟩ ⟨never rode in a *noisier* car⟩ **2 :** full of or characterized by the presence of noise ⟨that ~ night⟩ ⟨such a ~ office⟩ **3 :** tending to attract attention usu. by reason of showiness, gaudiness, or brightness of color **:** LOUD ⟨a ~ sweater⟩

noisy friarbird *n* **:** FRIARBIRD 1

noisy pitta *n* **:** DRAGOON BIRD

no·ki \ˈnōkē\ *n* -S [prob. the native name in So. Africa] **:** a rock rat (*Petromys typicus*)

nokkelost *var of* NOEKKELOST

no·ko \ˈnō(,)kō\ *n* -S *usu cap* **:** NGOKO

no·li me tan·ge·re \ˈnōlē;māˈtäŋgə,rā\ *n, pl* **noli me tangeres** [L, do not touch me] **1 :** a warning against touching or interference **2 a :** a person or thing not to be touched or meddled with **b** [so called fr. Christ's warning to Mary Magdalene in the Vulgate (John 20:17)] **:** a painting representing Christ's appearance to Mary Magdalene after the Resurrection

no·li·na \nōˈlīnə\ *n* [NL, after P. C. *Nolin* 18th cent. Fr. botanist and cleric] **1** *cap* **:** a genus of perennial plants (family Liliaceae) of the southern U.S. and Mexico that resemble yuccas and have a thick woody trunk often much dilated at its base and narrow rigid finely serrate leaves which have been used as a source of a hard cordage fiber **2** -S **:** any plant of the genus *Nolina* **:** BEAR GRASS

no·li·tion \nōˈlishən\ *n* -S [prob. fr. F, fr. MF, fr. L *nolle* not to will, to be unwilling (fr. *ne-* not + *velle* to will, wish, be willing) + MF *-ition* (as in *volition*) — more at NO, WILL] **:** adverse action of will **:** UNWILLINGNESS — opposed to *volition*

noll \ˈnōl\ *n* -S [ME *noll, nolle*, fr. OE *knoll, knol* top, crown of the head; akin to MD *nolle, nol* top, crown or back of the head, OHG *knol, nol* top, *knel* top, crown of the head and to OE *hneeca* neck — more at NECK] *dial Eng* **:** HEAD

nol·le \ˈnälē\ *vt* -ED/-ING/-S [short for *nolle pros*] **:** NOL-PROS

nolle pros \-ˈpräs\ *vt* **nolle prossed; nolle prossed; nolle prossing; nolle prosses** [*nolle prosequi*] **:** NOL-PROS

nolle pros·e·qui \-ˈpräsə,kwī\ *n, pl* **nolle prosequis** [L, to be unwilling to pursue] **:** an entry on the record of a legal action denoting that the prosecutor or plaintiff will proceed no further in his action or suit either as a whole or as to some count or as to one or more of several defendants — abbr. *nol pros;* compare NON PROSEQUITUR

noll-kholl \ˈnōl,kōl\ *n* -S [D *knolkool*, fr. *knol* turnip + *kool* cabbage] *India* **:** KOHLRABI

no·lo \ˈnō(,)lō\ *n* -S [by shortening] **:** NOLO CONTENDERE

nolo con·ten·de·re \-kənˈtendərē\ *n, pl* **nolo contenderes** [L, I do not wish to contend] **:** a plea by the defendant in a criminal prosecution that without admitting guilt subjects him to a judgment of conviction as in case of a plea of guilty but does not preclude him from denying the truth of the charges in a collateral proceeding

nol-pros \ˈnälˈpräs\ *vt* **nol-prossed; nol-prossed; nol-prossing; nol-prosses** [*nolle prosequi*] **:** to discontinue by entering a nolle prosequi

nom *abbr* **1** nomenclature **2** nominal **3** nominative

no·ma \ˈnōmə\ *n* -S [NL, fr. L *nome* spreading ulcer, fr. Gk *nomē* pasturage, food from pasturing, spreading ulcer; akin to Gk *nemein* to distribute, pasture — more at NIMBLE] **:** a spreading invasive gangrene chiefly of the lining of cheek and lips most often occurring in persons severely debilitated by disease or profound nutritional deficiency

¹no·mad *also* **no·made** \ˈnō,mad\ *n* -S [L *nomad-, nomas*, fr. Gk; akin to Gk *nemein* to pasture, distribute] **1 :** a member of a people that has no fixed residence but wanders from place to place usu. seasonally and within a well-defined territory for the purpose of securing its supply of food either by gathering of plants and hunting of animals, by using suitable grounds for quick crops, or esp. by finding grazing lands and water for its herds — compare MIGRANT **2 :** an individual that roams about aimlessly or without a fixed pattern of movement

²nomad \"\ *adj* **:** being a nomad **:** ROVING, NOMADIC ⟨~ herdsmen⟩

no·mad·ic \(ˈ)nōˈmadik, -dēk\ *adj* [Gk *nomadikos* pastoral, wandering, fr. *nomad-, nomas* nomad + *-ikos* -ic] **1 :** of, relating to, or characteristic or suggestive of a people of nomads or their way of life ⟨a ~ tribe⟩ ⟨the ~ habits of the Bedouins⟩ **2 :** roaming about from place to place aimlessly or without a fixed pattern of movement **:** VAGRANT ⟨many ownerless dogs are ~ —E.M.Pullar⟩ ⟨girls . . . make up from one eighth to one third of the ~ group —W.C.Naw⟩

no·mad·i·dae \nōˈmadə,dē\ *n pl, cap* [NL, fr. *Nomada*, type genus (fr. Gk *nomad-, nomas* nomad) + *-idae*] **:** a family of small bees resembling wasps — see CUCKOO BEE

no·mad·ism \ˈnō,ma,dizəm\ *n* -S **1 :** the mode of life of a nomadic people ⟨pastoral ~⟩ **2 :** the mode of life or behavior of an individual that roams about aimlessly or without any fixed pattern of movement; *specif* **:** VAGRANCY ⟨sometimes a roaming instinct — the trait of ~ —appears —J.A.O'Brien⟩ ⟨incidence of ~ — about twice as frequent in the broken home group —Nathan Blackman⟩

no·mad·ize \-dīz\ *vb* -ED/-ING/-S [¹*nomad* + *-ize*] *vi* **:** to live the life of a nomad **:** roam about **~** *vt* **:** to make nomadic ⟨*nomadized* by evacuation from the bombed cities —*Foreign Affairs*⟩

no man *n* [ME *no man, naman, non man, nan man*, fr. OE *nān man*, fr. *nān* no, none + *man* — more at NONE] **1 :** no person **:** NOBODY **2** *usu* **no-man** \ˈ=,=\ [²*no* + *man*] **:** a man who is accustomed or inclined to disagree in an independent manner or to decline requests in a firm resolute way ⟨surrounded by a number of *no-men* to resist me at every point —Sir Winston Churchill⟩ — compare YES-MAN

no·man·cy \ˈnōmən(t)sē\ *n* -ES [obs. F *nomancie*, alter. of *onomancie* — more at ONOMANCY] **:** divination by letters

no-man's-land \ˈ=,=,=\ *n* [*no man's* (gen. of *no man*) + *land*] **1 a :** an area of unowned, unclaimed, or uninhabited land ⟨a *no-man's-land* of bottomlands and islands aggregating up to forty square miles —*N.Y.Times*⟩ ⟨many metropolitan areas will become a kind of *no-man's-land* should they become heavily contaminated —R.E.Lapp⟩ ⟨starting down into a *no-man's-land* where once had stood busy streets —S.P.B.Mais⟩ **b :** a belt of ground between the most advanced elements of opposing armies **:** an area in a theater of operations not controlled by either side **2 :** an area of anomalous, ambiguous, or indefinite character ⟨lived in a *no-man's-land* between slavery and freedom —*World*⟩ ⟨the *no-man's-land* between political theory, theology, and political history —Richard Mayne⟩ ⟨the *no-man's-land* that was neither wholly good nor wholly evil —Nigel Dennis⟩

nom·arch \ˈnä,märk\ *n* -S [Gk *nomarchēs, nomarchos* (also, governor of a region or province), fr. Gk *nomos* district + *-archēs, -archos* -arch — more at NIMBLE] **1 :** the chief magistrate of a nome in ancient Egypt **2** [NGk *nomarchēs*, fr. Gk] **:** the chief administrator of a nomarchy in modern Greece

nom·archy \-,mə(r)kē\ *n* -ES [NGk *nomarchia*, fr. Gk *nomarchia* province or district of a nomarch, fr. *nomos* district + *-archia* -archy] **:** a province or department of modern Greece **:** NOME

no·mar·thra \nōˈmärthrə\ [NL, fr. Gk *nomos* law + *arthron* joint — more at NIMBLE, ARTHR-] *syn of* PHOLIDOTA

nombles *var of* NUMBLES

nom·bril \ˈnämbrəl\ *or* **nombril point** *n* -S [MF *nombril*, lit., navel, fr. OF, prob. alter. of *lombril*, fr. *le* the + *ombril* navel, fr. (assumed) VL *umbiliculus*, dim. of L *umbilicus* navel — more at LA, NAVEL] **:** the center point of the lower half of an armorial escutcheon — called also *navel;* see POINT illustration

nom de guerre \,nämdəˈga(ə)r, -ger\ *n, pl* **noms de guerre** \-m(z)d-\ [F, lit., war name] **:** a fictitious name **:** PSEUDONYM ⟨drawings . . . shall be signed with a device or *nom de guerre* —*Pencil Points*⟩

nom de plume \,nämdəˈplüm\ *n, pl* **noms de plume** \-m(z)d-\ *also* **nom de plumes** \-m(z)\ [F, pen name; prob. coined in E] **:** a pseudonym assumed by a writer **:** PEN NAME ⟨the author hid under a *nom de plume*⟩

¹nome \ˈnōm\ *n* -S [Gk *nomos* place of pasturage, district, province — more at NIMBLE] **1 :** a province of ancient Egypt **2** [NGk *nomos*, fr. Gk] **:** a province or department of modern Greece **:** NOMARCHY

²nome \"\ *n* -S [Gk *nomos* (also, usage, custom, melody) — more at NIMBLE] **:** a musical composition of ancient Greece intended either for instrumental performance alone or to be accompanied by a recitation of epics

no·me·i·dae \nōˈmēə,dē\ *n pl, cap* [NL, fr. *Nomeus*, type genus + *-idae*] **:** a family of usu. small fishes most of which are found in the open sea

no·men \ˈnōmən\ *n, pl* **nom·i·na** \ˈnämənə, ˈnōm-\ [L — more at NAME] **1 :** NAME ⟨no longer a ~ of bitter sarcasm —Gertrude Atherton⟩ **2 :** the name of the gens being the second of the three usual names of a person among the ancient Romans — compare AGNOMEN, COGNOMEN, PRAENOMEN **3 :** a grammatical form with the functions of a noun **:** NOUN, SUBSTANTIVE

no·men·cla·tive \ˈnōmən,klād·iv\ *adj* [¹*nomenclature* + *-ive*] **:** of or relating to name or the act of naming ⟨the family connection might seem a little remote . . . for such ~ prominence —M.D.Geismar⟩

no·men·cla·tor \-d·ə(r)\ *n* -S [L, slave in ancient Rome who attended a candidate for office to tell him the names of influential persons whom they met, slave who told his master the names of the other slaves, fr. *nomen* name + *-clat-* (fr. *calare* to call) + *-or* — more at CLAIM] **1 :** a book containing collections or lists of words **:** VOCABULARY **2 a :** a person who calls persons or things by their names **b** *archaic* **:** one who announces the names of guests or of persons generally **3 :** one who gives names to or invents names for things **:** a classifier of objects under appropriate names ⟨the ~ of the English Gothic styles —Tudor Edwards⟩

no·men·cla·to·ri·al \nō;menkləˈtōrēəl\ *adj* **:** NOMENCLATURAL — **no·men·cla·to·ri·al·ly** \-ēəlē\ *adv*

no·men·cla·tur·al \;nōmən;klāch(ə)rəl\ *adj* **:** relating to or connected with nomenclature — **no·men·cla·tur·al·ly** \-rəlē\ *adv*

¹no·men·cla·ture \ˈnōmən,klāchə(r) *sometimes* nōˈmenklәch-\ *n* -S [L *nomenclatura* act of calling by name, list of names, fr. *nomenclator* + *-ura* -ure] **1 a :** NAME, APPELLATION, DESIGNATION ⟨the patricians — mainly of Etruscan origin and ~ —R.A.Hall b.1911⟩ ⟨the generally accepted ~ of *Theileria* was proposed —John Legg⟩ ⟨whose main obsession was his ~ —*Sydney (Australia) Bull.*⟩ ⟨an example of the odd ~ of coal patches —*Amer. Guide Series: Pa.*⟩ ⟨has a magnitude of ~ second to none —St. Clair McKelway⟩ ⟨the changing ~ of her streets is even more baffling —Cornelia O. Skinner⟩ **b :** the collective names given to or borne by places in a particular area or region ⟨whose names are preserved in the village ~ of the Danelaw —F.M.Stenton⟩ **2 :** the act or process or an instance of naming ⟨by an odd quirk of ~ —Green Peyton⟩ ⟨problems of ~⟩ ⟨~ . . . is at its simplest the task of assigning a name to each distinct species —R.I.Smith⟩ **3 a :** LIST, CATALOG ⟨no more than an annotated ~ of the rich and varied writings —R.L.Bruckberger⟩ **b** *obs* **:** VOCABULARY, DICTIONARY, GLOSSARY **4 a :** a system or set of names, designations, or symbols used by a person or group ⟨the following ~ is used in the paper —A.W.Cochardt⟩ ⟨employs a very strange ~⟩ ⟨most textual critics have refused to adopt this ~ —B.M. Metzger⟩ **b :** a system or set of names or designations used in a particular science, discipline, or art and formally adopted or sanctioned by the usage of its practitioners **:** TERMINOLOGY ⟨the course includes a survey of the nature of law; its subject matter . . . and ~ —*College of William & Mary Catalog*⟩ ⟨the standard ~ of diseases and operations —*Jour. Amer. Med. Assoc.*⟩ ⟨reflects changes in the aircraft ~ —William Wallrich⟩ ⟨the ~s of politics and law —E.J.Kimble⟩ **c :** an international vocabulary of New Latin names of kinds and groups of kinds of animals and plants standardized under rules set up by international commissions sponsored by the basic biological taxonomic disciplines — see BINARY NOMENCLATURE, BINOMIAL NOMENCLATURE; compare FAMILY, GENUS, ORDER, SPECIES; -ACEAE, -ALES, -IDAE, -INAE; TAXONOMY **d :** a set of chemical names that may be systematic (as according to decisions of the International Union of Pure and Applied Chemistry) or not and that aims to tell the composition and often the structure of a given compound by naming the elements, groups, radicals, or ions present and employing suffixes denoting function (as *-ic* and *-ate* for acids and salts, *-ane, -ol, -one* for hydrocarbons and some of their derivatives, *-ine* for organic bases), prefixes denoting composition (as *hypo-, per-, chloro-*, Greek numerical prefixes), configuration prefixes (as *cis-, syn-, xylo-, meso-*), operational prefixes (as *cyclo-, dehydro-, deoxy-, homo-*), arabic numbers or Greek letters for indicating structure (as positions of substituents), or Roman numerals for indicating oxidation state — see GENEVA SYSTEM, STOCK SYSTEM; compare STRUCTURAL FORMULA

²nomenclature \"\ *vt* -ED/-ING/-S **:** NAME, DESIGNATE

no·men·cla·tur·ist \;nōmən;klāch(ə)rəst\ *n* -S **:** NOMENCLATOR 3

no·men con·ser·van·dum \ˈnōmən,kän(t)sə(r)ˈvandəm\ *n, pl* **nom·i·na con·ser·van·da** \ˈnämənə, . . . də\ [L, name to be preserved] **:** a name that should not be changed; *specif* **:** a biological generic name or other taxon to be preserved by special sanction in exception to the usual rules (as of priority)

nomen no·vum \-ˈnōvəm\ *n, pl* **nomina no·va** \-və\ [L, new name] **:** a taxonomic name for a plant or animal substituted for an untenable one

nomen nu·dum \-ˈnüdəm\ *n, pl* **nomina nu·da** \-də\ [L, naked name, mere name] **:** a proposed taxonomic name invalid because the group designated is not described or illustrated sufficiently for recognition, having no nomenclatural status, and consequently capable of being used as though never previously proposed

nomes *pl of* NOME

no·me·us \nōˈmēəs\ *n, cap* [NL, fr. Gk, herdsman; akin to G *nemein* to distribute, pasture — more at NIMBLE] **:** a genus (the type of the family Nomeidae) of fishes including the man-of-war fish

no·mia \ˈnōmēə\ *n, cap* [NL, fr. Gk *nomios* of shepherds, pastoral; akin to Gk *nomeus* shepherd, herdsman] **:** a genus of bees (family Halictidae) some of which are important pollinators of legumes

¹nom·ic \ˈnämik, ˈnōm-\ *adj* [Gk *nomos* nome, melody, custom + E *-ic* — more at NIMBLE] **:** relating to a musical nome

²nomic \"\ *adj* [Gk *nomikos*, fr. *nomos* usage, custom, law + *-ikos* -ic — more at NIMBLE] **1 :** having the general force of natural law **:** generally valid ⟨a ~ statement⟩ **2 a :** CUSTOMARY, ORDINARY, CONVENTIONAL **b** *of spelling* **:** ORTHOGRAPHIC, NONPHONETIC

³no·mic \ˈnōmik\ *n* -S [*no metal in composition*] **:** NEAR-PRINT

nomina *pl of* NOMEN

nomina conservanda *pl of* NOMEN CONSERVANDUM

¹nom·i·nal \ˈnämənᵊl *sometimes* -mnəl\ *adj* [ME *nominalle*, fr. ML *nominalis*, fr. L, of or relating to a name, fr. *nomin-, nomen* name + *-alis* -al — more at NAME] **1 a :** of, relating to, or being a noun **:** SUBSTANTIVAL **b :** of, relating to, or being a word that is otherwise characteristically an adjective or adverb but that takes a noun construction in a given context (as *good* in "the good die young" **2** [²*nominal*] **:** of or relating to the nominalists **3 a :** of, relating to, being, or consisting in a name ⟨the Russian system of ~ brevity —Irwin Ross⟩ **b :** bearing or mentioning the name of a specific person ⟨~ shares⟩ **c :** containing or being a set of names ⟨~ lists of priests —Robert Graves⟩ ⟨taxable males as revealed by the ~ rolls —M.D.W.Jeffreys⟩ **4 a** (1) **:** existing or being something in name or form but usu. not in reality **:** FORMAL, OSTENSIBLE — distinguished from *actual* ⟨a large majority of indifferent and lukewarm ~ Christians —Emil Brunner⟩ ⟨was both the ~ and the real head of his party⟩ ⟨that sign of the ~ virgin —J.H. Wheelwright⟩ ⟨we'll consider that the jewelry had only a ~ value —Erle Stanley Gardner⟩ ⟨the budget continued in ~ balance —*Collier's Yr. Bk.*⟩ ⟨the plaintiff is only a ~ party and not the real party in interest —D.C.Cook & Myer Feldman⟩ ⟨the ~ spokesman for a continent in travail —*Time*⟩ ⟨the pleasure derived from them . . . is practically ~ —Herbert Spencer⟩ (2) **:** measured in money as distinct from actual purchasing power ⟨~ wages⟩ — compare REAL **b :** being so small, slight, or negligible as scarcely to be entitled to the name **:** TRIFLING, INSIGNIFICANT ⟨parts are supplied at a ~ cost —R.S.Casey & J.W.Perry⟩ ⟨will pay a ~ price when it suits him —Walter Lippmann⟩ **c :** not known to exist except as a name ⟨a ~ species⟩ — compare NOMINATE **5 a :** APPROXIMATE, RATED ⟨although described as 4 inch by 4 inch, which is the ~ size, a piece which has been dried and dressed on four sides is actually 3⅝ by 3⅝ inch —*Amer. Builder Catalog Directory*⟩ ⟨the ~ voltage of a circuit, or system, is a value assigned to a circuit, or system of a given voltage class, for the purpose of convenient designation —*Electrical Engineering*⟩ **b** *of a price* **:** based on opinions of value expressed by buyers and sellers rather than on actual transactions when there is little or no trading in a particular commodity — **nom·i·nal·ly** \-ᵊlē, -mnəl-, -i\ *adv*

²nominal \"\ *n* -S **1 :** an individual that exists or is something in name or form but not in reality ⟨the Republican side . . . includes a lot of ~s —R.H.Rovere⟩ **2 :** a note from which a scale or other series of musical tones is named

nominal account *n* **:** any one of the income or expense accounts — compare MIXED ACCOUNT, REAL ACCOUNT

nominal damages *n pl* **:** a small or token sum awarded to a person who has been wronged but who has not shown such an injury as to be entitled to compensatory damages

nominal definition *n* **:** a statement giving the meaning of a name, word, or expression ⟨a purely *nominal definition*, completely lacking in operational utility —Morris Watnick⟩ — contrasted with *real definition*

nominal essence *n, Lockeanism* **:** an abstract complex idea that has been given a distinct general name ⟨the *nominal essences* of things, expressed by their common name, rest upon the experienced resemblances that cause objects to fall into different groups and to receive different appellations —B.A.G. Fuller⟩ — contrasted with *real essence*

nom·i·nal·ism \-ᵊl,izəm, -mnə,li-\ *n* -S **1 a :** a theory that there are no universal essences in reality and that the mind can frame no single concept or image corresponding to any universal or general term; *specif* **:** a theory advanced by the medieval thinker Roscellinus that universal terms such as indicate genus or species and all general collective words or terms such as *animal, man, tree, air, city, nation, wagon* have no objective real existence corresponding to them but are mere words, names, or terms or mere vocal utterances and that only particular individual things and events exist — compare CONCEPTUALISM, REALISM **b :** a logical or mathematical theory excluding from its language any names or variables for such abstract or higher level entities as classes — contrasted with *platonism* **2 :** a sociological doctrine or theory that holds that society is merely an aggregate of discrete individuals and that it has no superorganic reality — contrasted with *realism*

no·mi·nal·ist \-ᵊləst, -ləst\ *n* -S [prob. fr. F *nominaliste*, fr. MF, fr. *nominal* nominalist (fr. ML *nominalis*, fr. L *nominalis*, adj., of or relating to a name) + *-iste* -ist — more at NOMINAL] **:** an advocate of nominalism

nom·i·nal·is·tic \;==nᵊl;istik, ;==;listik, -tēk\ *adj* **:** of, relating to, or advocating nominalism — **nom·i·nal·is·ti·cal·ly** \-tək(ə)lē\ *adv*

nom·i·nal·ize \ˈnämənᵊl,īz, -mnə,līz\ *vt* -ED/-ING/-S [¹*nominal* + *-ize*] **:** to convert into or use as a noun ⟨*nominalized able* into *ability*⟩ ⟨~s the adjective *poor* into *the poor*⟩

nominal partner *n* **:** a person who holds himself out as a partner or permits a partner to hold him out as a copartner though in fact he is not a partner

nominal rate *n* **:** a rate of interest used in adding compound interest to a principal sum when interest is compounded other than annually — compare EFFECTIVE RATE

nominal sentence *n* **:** an equational sentence

nominal value *n* **:** PAR VALUE

nomina nova *pl of* NOMEN NOVUM

nomina nuda *pl of* NOMEN NUDUM

¹nom·i·nate \ˈnämənət, -mə,nāt, *usu* -d·+V\ *adj* [L *nominatus* (past part.)] **1** *Roman & civil law* **:** having a special or certain name **:** being a contract involving the delivery of property for which the actual property or similar property was to be returned (as in the case of a loan, deposit, or pledge) — distinguished from *innominate* **2 :** appointed to an office — chiefly used in Scots law of a tutor appointed by a father or since 1886 by a mother in a will or some other sufficient writing **3 :** being the first named and by rule a tautonymic subdivision of a species ⟨*Icterus cucullatus cucullatus* is a ~ race⟩ ⟨the ~ race of this oriole —*Condor*⟩

²nom·i·nate \ˈnämə,nāt, *usu* -ād·+V\ *vt* -ED/-ING/-S [L *nominatus*, past part. of *nominare*, fr. *nomin-, nomen* name — more at NAME] **1 a :** to call by some name or title **:** DESIGNATE, NAME, DENOMINATE ⟨the first of the commonly so *nominated* explorers of the American Arctic —Vilhjalmur Stefansson⟩ **b :** to mention by name **:** give the name of **:** call or name off ⟨~ . . . all the islets of the sound would entail a couple of hours' work —A.A.MacGregor⟩ ⟨becomes more and more difficult to ~ the real criminals —R.H.S.Crossman⟩ **2 a** (1) **:** to appoint to an office or place ⟨the person *nominated* by the deceased's will as his executor —Edward Jenks⟩ (2) **:** to propose by name for office as a preliminary to appointment upon approval or confirmation by some person or body ⟨the President . . . shall ~, and, by and with the advice and consent of the Senate, shall appoint ambassadors —*U.S.Constitution*⟩ **b** (1) **:** to propose, select, or formally enter by any of various methods (as the caucus, the convention, the primary, or petition) as a candidate for public office (2) **:** to propose or enter as a candidate for a nonpublic office ⟨*nominated* for club chairman but lost by a few votes⟩ **3** *obs* **:** FIX, SPECIFY ⟨let the forfeit be *nominated* —Shak.⟩ **4 :** to put forward or propose formally or informally for some honor, eminence, or status ⟨do not share the taste that ~s these poems for greatness —A.S.Stein⟩ ⟨~ him as the best model football player of 1952 —Eddie Beachler⟩ **5 a** (1) **:** to select (as a bull) for the serving of a particular female (2) **:** to request service for (as a mare) from a particular male **:** offer to book service for — used with *to* ⟨the mare should be *nominated* to a stallion whose qualities complement her own⟩ **6 :** to enter (a horse) in a race **syn** see DESIGNATE

nom·i·nate·ly *adv* **:** by name

no·mi·na·tim \,näməˈnād·əm\ *adv* [L, fr. *nomin-, nomen* name] **:** by name **:** EXPRESSLY

nom·i·na·tion \,näməˈnāshən\ *n* -S [ME *nominacioun*, fr. MF *nomination*, fr. L *nomination-, nominatio*, fr. *nominatus* (past part.) + *-ion-, -io* -ion] **1 :** an act, process, or an instance of nominating: as **a** (1) **:** an act or right of designating by name for an office or duty : APPOINTMENT 〈won for the crown the right of ~ to all benefices〉 (2) : the act or an instance of proposing by name for offices as a preliminary to appointment upon approval or confirmation by some person or body 〈the senate approved all the president's ~*s*〉 (3) : the act, process, or an instance of proposing, selecting, or formally entering by any of various methods as a candidate for a public or non-public office 〈the process whereby party members select the person they wish to bear the party emblem in the race . . . is called ~ —O.P.Field, P.S.Sikes, & J.E.Stoner〉 **b** *Church of England* : the naming of a clergyman by a patron to the rightful authority for presentation in cases where patronage does not include the legal rights of a presenter **2** : the state of being nominated 〈competition for the ~ was very keen〉 — often used in the phrase *in nomination* 〈kind enough to put my name in ~ for this job —Rolfe Humphries〉 **3** *archaic* **a** : NAME, DENOMINATION **b** : assignment of a name **4** : the part of the Roman legal formula that designates by name the judex or the recuperatores **5** : the preliminary entry in a race of a horse by name

1nom·i·na·tive *in sense 1 usu* 'näm(ə)nəd·iv *or* -nətiv; *in other senses* " *or* 'nämə,nād·¦iv *or* -āt¦ *or* ¦ēv *also* ¦əv\\ *adj* [ME *nominatif*, fr. L *nominativus*, fr. *nominatus* (past part.) + *-ivus* -ive] **1 a** : marking typically the subject of a verb 〈Latin *filius* in *filius amat matrem suam*, "the son loves his mother", is in the ~ case〉 — used esp. in the grammar of languages that have relatively full inflection **b** *of a word or word group* : being the subject of a verb even when the relation is not marked by any inflective element (as *John* in *John sees Henry*) **c** : of or relating to the nominative case 〈a ~ ending〉 **2** : nominated or appointed by nomination **3** : bearing a person's name : NOMINAL 〈~ shares〉

2nom·i·na·tive \\'näm(ə)nəd·iv\\ *n* -s : the nominative case of a language or a form in the nominative case

nominative absolute *also* **nominative independent** *n* : a construction in English consisting of a noun in the common case or a pronoun in the nominative case joined with a predicate that does not include a finite verb and functioning usu. as a sentence modifier but also sometimes capable of being construed as the modifier of a particular word in the sentence (as *her head erect* in "she walked along, her head erect" or *he being absent* in "he being absent, no business was transacted")

nom·i·na·tive·ly \\-d·əvlē\\ *adv* : in the manner of a nominative

nom·i·na·tor \\'nämə,nād·ə(r), -ātə-\\ *n* -s [LL, fr. L *nominatus* (past part.) + *-or*] **1** : one that nominates **2** : a person in whose name a horse is entered for a race

no·mi·na·tum \\,nämə'nād·əm\\ *n, pl* **nomina·ta** \\-d·ə\\ [L, neut. of *nominatus*, past part of *nominare* to name — more at NOMINATE] : the thing that is named by a sign, word, or linguistic expression 〈the ~ of a proper name is the object itself which is designated thereby —Herbert Feigl & W.S. Sellars〉 — compare DESIGNATUM

nom·i·nee \\¦nämə¦nē\\ *n* -s [2*nominate* + *-ee*] **1** : a person named as the recipient in an annuity or grant **2** : a person named or proposed for an office, duty, or position; *esp* : a candidate selected to represent a party in an election **3** : a person in whose name a stock or registered bond certificate is registered but who is not the actual owner

nom·i·ny \\'näməni\\ *n* -ES [prob. fr. L *in nomine* in the name] **1** *dial Eng* : a formulaic or conventional piece of rhyming doggerel; *also* : RIGMAROLE **2** *dial Eng* : a long-winded speech

no·mism \\'nō,mizəm\\ *n* -s [Gk *nomos* custom, usage, law + E *-ism* — more at NIMBLE] : ethical or religious basing of conduct on the observance of moral law : LEGALISM

no·mis·ma \\nō'mizmə\\ *n, pl* **nomisma·ta** \\-əd·ə\\ [Gk, something established by usage, current coin, money, fr. *nomizein* to use customarily, fr. *nomos* usage, custom] : the Byzantine solidus

no·mis·tic \\(')nō¦mistik\\ *adj* : based on or conforming to moral law

no·mi·us \\'nōmēəs\\ *n, cap* [NL] : a genus of ground beetles (family Carabidae) one of which (*N. pygmaeus*) occurs in parts of Europe and No. America and produces a strong offensive odor

nom·la·ki \\näm'läkē\\ *n, pl* **nomlaki** *or* **nomlakis** *usu cap* **1** : a Wintun people of the lower Sacramento river valley, Calif. **2** : a member of the Nomlaki people

nom nov *abbr* nomen novum

nom nud *abbr* nomen nudum

nomo- *comb form* [Gk, fr. *nomos* — more at NIMBLE] : usage : law 〈*nomo*logy〉

no·mo·ca·non \\,nōmə'kä,nōn\\ *n* -s *often cap* [MGk *nomokanōn*, fr. *nomo-* + LGk *kanōn* canon, rule, fr. Gk, measuring rod, rule, standard — more at CANON] : a collection of the ecclesiastical laws of the ancient Eastern Orthodox Church and the Byzantine imperial laws that pertained to the administration of the church

no·moc·ra·cy \\nō'mäkrəsē\\ *n* -ES [*nomo-* + *-cracy*] : government in accordance with a system of law

no·mo·genesis \\¦nōmə+\\ *n* [NL, fr. *nomo-* (fr. Gk) + L *genesis*] : a theory of evolution that regards evolutionary change as due to inherent orderly processes fundamental to organic nature and independent of environmental influences

nom·o·gram \\'nämə,gram, 'nōm-\\ *or* **nom·o·graph** \\-raf\\ *n* [ISV *nomo-* + *-gram* or *-graph*] : a graphic representation of numerical relations by any of various systems; *specif* : a graph that enables one by the aid of a straightedge to read off the value of a dependent variable when the values of two or more independent variables are given 〈if the viscosity of a slag is known at one temperature, the entire viscosity-temperature relationship for the liquid slag can be ascertained from the ~ . . . which readily gives the viscosity of a liquid slag at any desired temperature if the viscosity is known at a particular temperature —*Kent's Mech. Engineers' Handbook*〉

no·mog·ra·pher \\nō'mägrəfə(r)\\ *n* -s [Gk *nomographos* one who drafts laws (fr. *nomo-* + *-graphos* -grapher) + E *-er*] : a writer of laws : one who is expert in nomography

nom·o·graph·ic \\¦nämə¦grafik, ¦nōm-\\ *adj* **1** : of or relating to nomography **2** : of, being, or relating to a nomogram 〈~ chart〉 — **nom·o·graph·i·cal·ly** \\-fək(ə)lē\\ *adv*

no·mog·ra·phy \\nō'mägrəfē\\ *n* -ES [Gk *nomographia*, fr. *nomo-* + *-graphia* -graphy] **1** : the art of or a treatise on drafting laws **2** : the theory, making, and use of nomograms

nom·o·log·i·cal \\¦nämə¦läjəkəl, ¦nōm-\\ *adj* **1** : of or relating to nomology **2** : of, relating to, or in accordance with laws

no·mol·o·gy \\nō'mäləjē\\ *n* -ES [*nomo-* + *-logy*] : the science of the laws of the mind

nom·o·pel·mous \\¦nämə¦pelməs, ¦nōm-\\ *adj* [*nomo-* + *-pelmous*] : having a separate and simple tendon to flex the hallux 〈~ birds〉

1no more *n* [ME *nomare*, *nomore*, *namare*, *namore*, fr. OE *nā māre*, fr. *nā* no + *māre* more — more at NO, MORE] : nothing more : nothing further 〈it is a fantasy and *no more* —D.W. Brogan〉 〈will hear *no more* of this nonsense〉

2no more *adv* [ME *namare*, *namore* (adv. & n.)] **1 a** : no longer 〈those stately homes stand *no more*〉 **b** : no longer in existence : DEAD, DEPARTED 〈the glory of his house is *no more*〉 〈the great leader is *no more*〉 **2** : to no greater extent : in no greater degree 〈can *no more* attempt to do intricate law-business than to play the piano —W.M.Thackeray〉 **3** : NEVERMORE 〈these fields and hills shall see thee *no more*〉 **4** : NEITHER 〈he won't hear of it. *No more* will I —W.C.Williams〉 〈*no more* you'll have to, if you don't want —William Faulkner〉

3no more *adj* [ME *namore*, *nomore* (adj. & n.)] : not any more 〈there's *no more* milk or bread in the house〉

no·mos \\'nō,mäs\\ *n, pl* **no·moi** \\-mȯi\\ [Gk — more at NIMBLE] : LAW 〈natural slavery and slavery according to ~ —C.J.O'Neil〉

nom·o·thet·ic \\¦nämə¦thed·ik\\ *adj* [Gk *nomothetikos* of or relating to legislation, legislative, fr. *nomothetēs* lawgiver (fr. *nomo-* + *-thetēs* one who establishes, fr. *tithenai* to establish, place, set) + *-ikos* -ic — more at DO] : relating to, involving, or dealing with the abstract, recurrent, universal : formulating general statements or scientific laws — contrasted with *idiographic*

noms de guerre *pl of* NOM DE GUERRE

noms de plume *pl of* NOM DE PLUME

-no·my \\nəmē, -mi\\ *n comb form* -ES [ME *-nomie*, fr. OF, fr. L *-nomia*, fr. Gk, fr. *-nomos* distributing, arranging + *-ia* -y; akin to Gk *nemein* to distribute, manage — more at NIMBLE] : system of laws governing or sum of knowledge regarding a (specified) field 〈astro*nomy*〉 〈agro*nomy*〉

1non- \\(¦)nän *sometimes* ¦nən\\ *prefix* [ME, fr. MF, fr. L *non* not, fr. OL *noenum*, fr. *ne-* not + *oinom*, neut. of *oinos* one — more at NO, ONE] : not : reverse of : absence of 〈*non*academic〉 〈*non*conformity〉 〈*non*breakable〉 〈*non*productive〉 〈*non*intervention〉 〈*non*-Arabic〉 〈*non*-Mormon〉 〈*non*rush hours〉

2non- *or* **nona-** *comb form* [L *non-*, fr. *nonus* ninth — more at NOON] : ninth : nine 〈*nona*gon〉 〈*non*ane〉

non·ability \\¦⸗ *at* NON- +\\ *n* **1** : lack of ability or capacity; *specif* : lack of legal capacity (as in bringing suit) **2** : a plea or exception raising a lack of legal capacity

non·abrasive \\"+\\ *adj* : not abrasive

non·absorbable \\"+\\ *adj* : not capable of being absorbed 〈~ silk sutures〉

non·academic \\(¦)⸗+\\ *adj* : not academic: as **a** : other than academic : TECHNICAL, PROFESSIONAL, PRACTICAL 〈children in need of ~ training〉 **b** (1) : not conforming to the rules of a literary or artistic school (as one characterized by conservatism or strict adherence to tradition) (2) *of art* : NONREPRESENTATIONAL **c** : not connected with or foreign to academic life, atmosphere, or activity 〈prefers to move in ~ circles〉 〈the ~ world of competitive industry〉

non·acceptance \\¦⸗+\\ *n* : failure or refusal to accept

non·access \\(')⸗ *at* NON- +\\ *n* : the nonexistence of opportunity for sexual intercourse esp. between husband and wife or the absence of such intercourse

non·achromatic \\(¦)⸗+\\ *adj* [1*non-* + *achromatic*] : CHROMATIC

non·acid \\(')⸗+\\ *adj* : not acid : destitute of acid properties 〈a ~ radical〉

non·a·co·sane \\,nänə'kō,sān\\ *n* -s [ISV *nonacos-* (fr. 2*non-* + *-cos-* — fr. *eicosa-*) + *-ane*] : a paraffin hydrocarbon $C_{29}H_{60}$; *esp* : the crystalline normal hydrocarbon $CH_3(CH_2)_{27}CH_3$

non·activistic \\(¦) *at* NON- + \\ *adj* : not activist

non·adaptive \\¦⸗ *at* NON-+\\ *adj* : not serving to adapt the individual to his environment 〈~ traits〉

non·a·dec·ane \\,nänə'de,kān\\ *n* -s [ISV *nonadec-* (fr. 2*non-* + *deca-*) + *-ane*] : a paraffin hydrocarbon $C_{19}H_{40}$; *esp* : the crystalline normal hydrocarbon $CH_3(CH_2)_{17}CH_3$

non·adherence \\¦⸗ *at* NON-+\\ *n* : a lack of adherence

non·adhesive \\"+\\ *adj* : not adhesive

non·adjacent \\"+\\ *adj* : not adjacent

non·adjustable \\"+\\ *adj* : not adjustable

non·adjustive \\"+\\ *adj* [1*non-* + *adjustive*] : tending to produce maladjustment 〈~ behavior〉

nonadministrative \\"+\\ *adj* : not administrative

non·admitted asset \\"+-\\ *n* : an asset (as past due accounts, furniture, and fixtures) of an insurer not permitted by state regulations to be reckoned in determining its financial condition — compare ADMITTED ASSET

non·aesthetic \\"+\\ *adj* : not aesthetic

1non·age \\'nänij, 'nōn-, *sometimes* 'nən- *or* -nēj\\ *n* [ME, fr. MF, fr. *non-* 1non- + *age*, fr. OF *aage*, *eage* — more at AGE] **1** : the condition of being under 21 and consequently not of age to manage one's property and affairs : the condition of not being of the required legal age to enter into some particular transaction (as marriage) — compare FULL AGE, MINOR 2 **2 a** : a period of youth, childhood, or infancy 〈the brook we leaped so nimbly in our ~ —R.S.Hillyer〉 〈these slight novels of his ~ —*Time*〉 **b** : IMMATURITY 〈bored with the ~ of her contemporaries —*Newsweek*〉

2no·nage \\'nōnij, 'nän-, -nēj\\ *n* -s [ML *nonagium*, fr. L *nonus* ninth + ML *-agium* -age (fr. OF *-age*)] : the ninth part of movable goods of a decedent sometimes payable to the clergy

nonaged *adj* [1*nonage* + *-ed*] *obs* : belonging to the period of nonage : YOUTHFUL, MINOR

1nona·ge·nar·i·an \\,nänəjə'nerēən, ,nōn-, -na(a)r-, -nār-\\ *n* -s [L *nonagenarius* containing or consisting of ninety (fr. *nonageni* ninety each — fr. *nonaginta* ninety — + *-arius* -ary) + E *-an*, n. suffix] : a person who is 90 or more and less than 100 years old

2nonagenarian \\¦⸗⸗⸗¦⸗⸗⸗\\ *adj* : 90 or more and less than 100 years old

nona·ges·i·mal \\¦⸗⸗¦jesəməl\\ *adj* [L *nonagesimus* ninetieth (fr. *nonaginta* ninety, fr. *nona-* — akin to L *novem* nine — + *-ginta* — akin to L *-ginti* in *viginti* twenty) + E *-al* — more at NINE, VICENARY] : NINETIETH

non·aggression \\¦⸗ *at* NON-+\\ *n* : forbearance or refrainment from aggression 〈proposed an all-European ~ treaty —*N. Y. Times*〉 〈~ and arbitration of all disputes —*Rev. of Reviews*〉

non·a·gon \\'nänə,gän, *sometimes* -ōgən\\ *n* -s [2*non-* + *-gon*] : a plane polygon of nine angles and therefore nine sides

nonagon

non·agreement \\¦⸗ *at* NON-+\\ *n* : a lack of agreement

non·agricultural \\(¦)⸗+\\ *adj* : not agricultural: as **a** : being other than agricultural : not being a product of agriculture **b** : not devoted to or engaged in agriculture 〈the primitive ~ people of Cuba —*Amer. Antiquity*〉

nona·hydrate \\¦nänə+\\ *n* [2*non-* + *hydrate*] : a chemical compound with nine molecules of water

non·alcoholic \\(¦)⸗ *at* NON-+\\ *adj* : not containing alcohol

non·allelic \\¦⸗+\\ *adj* [1*non-* + *allelic*] *of genes* : not behaving as alleles toward one another

non·alphabetic \\(¦)⸗+\\ *adj* : not alphabetic

non·amino \\¦⸗+, (')⸗+\\ *adj* [1*non-* + *amino*] : not in the form of the amino group 〈~ nitrogen〉

non·analytic \\(¦)⸗+\\ *adj* : not analytic

no·nane \\'nō,nān, 'nä,-\\ *n* -s [ISV 2*non-* + *-ane*] : any of several liquid isomeric paraffin hydrocarbons C_9H_{20}; *esp* : the normal hydrocarbon $CH_3(CH_2)_7CH_3$ obtained esp. from petroleum

non·a·no·ic acid \\¦nänə¦nōik-\\ *n* [*nonanoic* ISV *nonane* + *-oic*] : PELARGONIC ACID — used in the system of the International Union of Pure and Applied Chemistry

no·na·nol \\'nōnə,nōl, 'nän-, -nōl\\ *n* -s [*nonane* + *-ol*] : any of five isomeric liquid water-insoluble alcohols $C_9H_{19}OH$ derived from normal nonane; *esp* : the fragrant primary or 1-isomer $CH_3(CH_2)_7CH_2OH$ that occurs as an ester in sweet orange oil — compare NONYL ALCOHOL

non·antigenic \\(¦)⸗ *at* NON-+\\ *adj* : not antigenic

non·apparent easement \\¦⸗+-\\ *n* : an easement not involving any permanent visible sign of its existence (as an easement of a way or of drawing a net upon a shore) — distinguished from *apparent easement*

non·appearance \\"+\\ *n* [ME *noun apperaunce*, fr. *noun-*, *non-* 1non- + *apperaunce* appearance — more at APPEARANCE] : default of appearance (as in court) to prosecute or defend : failure to appear

non·aquatic \\"+\\ *adj* : not aquatic : not restricted to living in water or at the waterside

non·aqueous \\(')⸗+\\ *adj* : not aqueous : of, relating to, or having the characteristics of a liquid other than water 〈a ~ solvent such as benzene〉 : made from, with, or by means of a liquid other than water 〈~ solutions〉

non·arcing *or* **non·arcking** \\"+\\ *adj* [1*non-* + *arcing*, pres. part. of *arc*, v.] : not capable of readily maintaining an electric arc 〈~ metals of the zinc group〉

non·aromatic \\(¦)⸗+\\ *adj* : not aromatic

non·assessable \\¦⸗+\\ *adj* [1*non-* + *assessable*] : exempting the owner from further contributions to the capital or business of an issuing corporation and when fully paid for entailing no further liability on the part of the owner either to the corporation or its creditors 〈~ stock〉

nonassessable mutual *n* : a mutual company issuing policies not subject to assessment

non as·sump·sit \\¦nänə'səm(p)sət, ¦nōn-\\ *n* [NL, he did not undertake] : a general plea or denial in an action of assumpsit

non·athletic \\¦⸗ *at* NON-+\\ *adj* : not athletic

non·attendance \\"+\\ *n* : neglect or failure to attend 〈school authorities complained of the child's ~〉

non·attributive \\"+\\ *adj* : not attributive — **non·attribu·tively** \\"+\\ *adv*

non·automotive \\(¦)⸗+\\ *adj* : not automotive

non·bank \\(')⸗+\\ *adj* [1*non-* + *bank*, n.] : being or done by someone other than a bank : not being or done by a bank 〈~ borrowing〉 〈~ lenders〉 〈~ investors〉

non·bearing partition \\"+-\\ *or* **nonbearing wall** *n* [*nonbearing* fr. 1*non-* + *bearing*, pres. part. of *bear*, v.] : a dividing wall that supports no vertical weight other than its own weight

non·being \\"+\\ *n* : absence or lack of being : NONEXISTENCE, VOID

non·believer \\¦⸗ *at* NON-+\\ *n* **1** : a person who does not believe or have faith in something 〈a ~ in ghosts〉 **2** : a person without religious beliefs : ATHEIST

non·belligerency \\"+\\ *n* [1*non-* + *belligerency*] **1** : the status of not being at war : the status of not being a belligerent **2** : the status or attitude of a country that refrains from direct participation in a war but openly favors and usu. gives unneutral aid in varying degree and kind to one of the belligerents 〈after the fall of France the United States shifted to ~ and intervention —A.P.Whitaker〉

1non·belligerent \\"+\\ *adj* [1*non-* + *belligerent*, adj.] : being a nonbelligerent

2nonbelligerent \\"\\ *n* : a country whose status or attitude is one of nonbelligerency

non·beverage \\(')⸗ *at* NON-+\\ *adj* [1*non-* + *beverage*] : not used as a beverage : not suitable for use as a beverage 〈~ products〉

non·biting \\"+\\ *adj* : not given to or characterized by biting

non·board \\"+\\ *adj* [1*non-* + *board*, n.] : not being a member of a rate-making association or bureau 〈a ~ insurance firm〉

non·book \\"+\\ *adj* [1*non-* + *book*, n.] : being something other than a book : being a manuscript, microfilm, map, or other library holding that is not a book 〈housing and arrangement of ~ materials —W.H.Jesse〉

non·brachiating \\"+\\ *adj* : not brachiating

non·breeding \\"+\\ *adj* : not breeding 〈~ mice〉 : gone beyond the time for breeding

non·broody \\"+\\ *adj* : not broody 〈~ hens〉

non·business \\"+\\ *adj* : not related to business

non·calcarea \\¦⸗+\\ *n pl, cap* [NL, fr. 1*non-* + *Calcarea*] *in some classifications* : a class of Porifera including all sponges not placed in Calcarea

non·calcareous \\"+\\ *adj* : lacking or deficient in lime

non·callable \\(')⸗+\\ *adj* : not capable of or susceptible to being called

non·cancelable \\"+\\ *adj* [1*non-* + *cancelable*] : not subject to cancellation; *esp* : guaranteed renewable from year to year 〈a ~ accident policy〉

non·canonical \\¦⸗+\\ *adj* : not forming part of or being a canon 〈~ writings〉

non·carbohydrate \\(¦)⸗+\\ *n* : a substance that is not a carbohydrate; *esp* : one (as an aglycon) combined with a carbohydrate (as a sugar) — compare GLYCOSIDE

non·carnivorous \\¦⸗+\\ *adj* : not carnivorous

non·carrying \\(')⸗+\\ *adj* [1*non-* + *carrying*, pres. part. of *carry*, v.] : keeping within the range 0 to 9 by adding or dropping tens 〈in ~ addition and subtraction $3+9=2$ and $3-9=4$〉 — see 2ADDITIVE 3

non·cash \\"+\\ *adj* [1*non-* + *cash*, n.] : other than cash 〈~ income〉

non·caste \\"+\\ *adj* [1*non-* + *caste*] : being of no caste or rank

1nonce \\'nän(t)s, *sometimes* 'nən-\\ *n* -s [ME *nones*, fr. *nanes*, alter. (resulting from incorrect division of *then anes* in such phrases as *to then anes* for the one purpose, fr. *to* + *then* — dat. sing. neut. of *the*, def. art. — + *anes* one purpose) of *anes* one purpose, alter. (prob. influenced by *anes* once) of *ane*, dat. sing. neut. of *an* one, fr. OE *ān* — more at ONE, ONCE] : the one, particular, or present occasion, purpose, or use — **for the nonce** *adv* **1** *dial chiefly Eng* : for the particular or express purpose 〈had an anger fit *for the nonce* —*Ballad Book*〉 **2 a** *archaic* : for the one, single, or particular occasion **b** : for the time being 〈we had changed characters *for the nonce* —W.H.Hudson †1922〉 〈*for the nonce*, conditions were reasonably normal —P.G.Wodehouse〉

2nonce \\"\\ *adj* : occurring, used, or made only once or for a special occasion 〈the words which he cites . . . represent mainly ~ loans —C.E.Reed〉 〈even factitious and ~ names have been listed —F.G.Cassidy〉 〈chose one of four societies as a ~ police —*Jour. of the Royal Anthrop. Inst. of G. Brit. & Ire.*〉 〈~ uses〉

non·cellular \\(')⸗ *at* NON- +\\ *adj* : not made up of or divided into cells : ACELLULAR

non·centric \\"+\\ *adj* : not centric

nonce word *n* : a word (as *ringday* in "four girls I know have become engaged today: this must be ringday") coined and used apparently to suit one particular occasion sometimes independently by different writers or speakers but not adopted into use generally 〈Coleridge coined *mammonolatry* in 1820 as a *nonce word*〉 〈I still think I heard it, though so seldom that it had more or less the air of a *nonce word* —S.T.Byington〉

non·cha·lance \\¦nänshə¦län(t)s, -ȧn(t)s; '⸗⸗,lən(t)s\\ *n* -s [F, fr. OF, fr. *nonchalant* (pres. part. of *nonchaloir* to disregard, make light of), after such pairs as OF *abundant: abundance*] : an attitude marked by or reflecting lack of concern, anxiety, or excitement esp. under circumstances that might be expected to provoke such feelings : a display or air of jaunty unconcern or indifference : IMPERTURBABILITY, POISE, SANGFROID 〈just takes a little practice, ~, and stability —T.H.Fielding〉 〈the ~ of boys who are sure of a dinner —R.W.Emerson〉

non·cha·lant \\-nt\\ *adj* [F, fr. OF, fr. pres. part. of *nonchaloir* to disregard, make light of, fr. *non-* 1non- + *chaloir* to be of interest to, concern, fr. L *calēre* to be warm — more at LEE] : marked by or reflecting an attitude of nonchalance : having a manner or air of jaunty unconcern or indifference : UNRUFFLED, IMPERTURBABLE 〈a hastily assumed air of ~ confidence —J.B.Priestley〉 〈drove the car with ~ abandon〉 〈~ amid the booming of guns〉 **syn** see COOL

non·cha·lant·ly *adv* : in a nonchalant manner

non·cha·lant·ness *n* -ES : the quality or state of being nonchalant

non·charitable \\(')⸗ *at* NON- +\\ *adj* : not charitable

non·chemical \\"+\\ *adj* : not chemical

non·chitinous \\"+\\ *adj* : not chitinous

non·circular \\"+\\ *adj* : not circular : ECCENTRIC

non·citizen \\"+\\ *n* : a person who is not a citizen; *esp* : a person residing in a country but not a citizen thereof 〈the legal right to employ a ~ —*Veteran's Guide*〉

non·claim \\"+\\ *n* [ME *noun cleime*, fr. *noun-*, *non-* 1non- + *cleime*, *claim*, *claime* claim] : neglect or failure to make a demand within the time limited by law

non·classical \\"+\\ *adj* : not classical

non·clerical \\"+\\ *adj* : not clerical 〈a ~ democracy〉

non·climax \\"+\\ *adj* [1*non-* + *climax*, n.] : not having a climax : not being in a climactic environment

non·clotting \\"+\\ *adj* : not clotting

non·cognitive \\"+\\ *adj* [1*non-* + *cognitive*] : not based on or incapable of being reduced to empirical factual knowledge

non·cognitivism \\"+\\ *n* [*noncognitive* + *-ism*] : a theory holding that ethical statements cannot be reduced without remainder to empirical cognitive statements by reason of the emotive or imperative elements in their content; *specif* : EMOTIVISM

non·cognitivist \\"+\\ *n* [*noncognitive* + *-ist*] : an advocate of noncognitivism in ethics

non·coital \\"+\\ *adj* : not involving heterosexual copulation

non·collectible \\¦⸗+\\ *adj* : not collectible

non·colloid \\(')⸗+\\ *n* [1*non-* + *colloid*, n.] : CRYSTALLOID

non·com \\(')⸗ *at* NON- + ¦käm\\ *n* -s *often attrib* [by shortening] : NONCOMMISSIONED OFFICER 〈most of the ~*s* were killed and wounded —Marjory S. Douglas〉 〈with the ~ marks still on him —William Chamberlain〉

non·combat \\(')⸗+\\ *adj* [1*non-* + *combat*, n.] : not involving combat 〈~ service〉 : not combatant

1non·combatant \\¦⸗+, (')⸗+\\ *n* [1*non-* + *combatant*] : a person (as a chaplain or a member of the medical services) whose military or naval duties do not include fighting; *also* : CIVILIAN

2noncombatant \\"\\ *adj* **1** : not usu. engaged in or assigned to combat or combat duties 〈~ personnel〉 **2** : not designed for or normally used in combat 〈~ stores〉 **3** : not constituting or directly forwarding combat 〈~ operations〉

1non·combustible \\¦⸗+\\ *adj* : not combustible : incapable of catching fire and burning when subjected to fire 〈asbestos and carbon dioxide are ~〉 — compare INCOMBUSTIBLE

2noncombustible \\"\\ *n* : a noncombustible substance

non·commensurable \"+\ *adj* **:** not commensurable **:** INCOMMENSURABLE

non·commercial \"+\ *adj* **:** not commercial: as **a :** not used in commerce **:** having no commercial importance ⟨a ~ species of fish —H.P.Clemens⟩ **b :** not commercially motivated ⟨their friendly ~ attitude —*Atlantic*⟩ ⟨the ~ theater⟩

non·commissioned \"+\ *adj* **:** not having a commission

noncommissioned officer *n* **:** a subordinate officer in a branch of the armed services appointed usu. on the basis of examination from enlisted personnel and holding one of various grades (as corporal, sergeant, petty officer)

1non·committal \"+\ *n* [*1non-* + *committal*] **:** the state of being noncommittal to a particular position or point of view **:** refusal to commit oneself

2noncommittal \"\ *adj* **1 :** taking no clear position or giving no clear indication of attitude, feeling, or point of view **:** RESERVED ⟨finally consent to sign the brief and ~ communiqué —A.L.Funk⟩ ⟨her tone was friendly but ~ —Helen Howe⟩ ⟨did not greet him with flowery excitement but with a ~ "hello" —Sinclair Lewis⟩ ⟨elicited a ~ grunt —C.G.D. Roberts⟩ **2 :** having no clear, sharply defined, or distinctive character, meaning, or significance ⟨a ~ word that might be used of anything from babies to furnaces —J.C.Swaim⟩ ⟨pitched in the null, ~ surroundings of a rehearsal room —Osbert Sitwell⟩ — **non·com·mit·tal·ly** \-ᵊlē, -i\ *adv*

non·com·mit·tal·ism \-ᵊlˌizəm\ *n* -s **:** a noncommittal position or policy

non·communicable \ˈ; *at* NON-+\ *adj* **:** not capable of being communicated; *specif* **:** not transmissible by direct contact ⟨a ~ disease⟩

non·communicant \"+\ *n* **:** a person who is not a communicant **:** one who does not receive Communion; *specif* **:** one who does not attend church

non·communion \"+\ *n* **:** neglect or refusal to receive Communion

non–communist \(ˈ)= *at* NON-+\ *adj, usu cap C* **1 :** not Communist **:** being other than Communist ⟨~ labor leaders⟩ **2 :** affirming or certifying to nonmembership in the Communist party ⟨*non-Communist* oaths⟩

non·conquer \(ˈ)=+\ *n* [MexSp, fr. Sp *non-* 1non- + MexSp *comoquer*] **:** an ace or king that can be combined in panguingue and other Mexican forms of rummy with other cards of the same rank (as the ace of spades and two aces of hearts) — compare COMOQUER

non·compearance \ˈ=+\ *n, Scots law* **:** default in appearing in court

non·competent \(ˈ)=+\ *adj* **:** not competent; *specif* **:** not legally qualified or capable ⟨declared ~ by the government —F.B.Gipson⟩

non·competing \ˈ=+\ *adj* **:** not competing

non·competitive \"+\ *adj* **:** not competitive: as **a :** not subject to competition **:** not filled by competitive examinations ⟨~ positions⟩ **b :** lacking competitive spirit or not motivated by a spirit of competition ⟨stimulate ~ interest in games —*Atlantic*⟩

non·complementary \(ˈ)=+\ *adj* **:** not complementary

non·compliance \ˈ=+\ *n* **:** failure or refusal to comply

non·com·pos \(ˈ)nänˈkämpəs\ *n, pl* **noncompos·es** *or* **non·compos·ses** \-səz\ [L *non compos* (in the phrase *non compos mentis*)] **:** a person who is non compos mentis

non compos \"\ *adj* [L *non compos* (in the phrase *non compos mentis*)] **:** non compos mentis ⟨they'll say you're *non compos* —Kenneth Roberts⟩

non compos men·tis \-pəˈsmentəs\ *adj* [L, lit., not having mastery of one's mind] **:** not of sound mind **:** wholly lacking mental capacity to understand the nature, consequences, and effect of a situation or transaction

non·compound \(ˈ)= *at* NON-+\ *adj* **:** not compound

non·compounder \ˈ=+\ *n* **:** **1** one that does not compound **2** *usu cap* **:** one of the Jacobites who desired the unconditional restoration of James II of England after his abdication

noncon *abbr* nonconformist

non·concentric \ˈ= *at* NON- +\ *adj* **:** not concentric

non·concur \ˈ= *at* NON-+\ *vb* [*1non-* + *concur*] *vt, archaic* **:** to refuse to concur in **:** dissent from ~ *vi* **:** to refuse to concur ⟨moved to ~ with the lower board —*Springfield* (*Mass.*) *Union*⟩ ⟨*nonconcurred* in the Senate's adjournment resolution —H.W.Sparrow⟩

non·concurrence \"+\ *n* [*1non-* + *concurrence*] **:** the act or an instance of nonconcurring

non·concurrency \"+\ *n* [*1non-* + *concurrency*] **:** the state of being nonconcurrent

non·concurrent \"+\ *adj* [*1non-* + *concurrent*] **:** having unlike provisions or application to a loss ⟨a ~ insurance policy⟩

non·condensing engine \"+-\ *or* **noncondensing turbine** *n* **:** a steam engine or turbine not provided with a condenser

non·conducting \"+\ *adj* **:** not conducting ⟨~ material⟩

non·conductor \"+\ *n* [*1non-* + *conductor*] **:** a substance that conducts heat, electricity, or sound only in very small degree

non·confidence \(ˈ)=+\ *n* **:** lack of confidence; *esp* **:** lack of confidence in a government by a parliamentary body ⟨the cabinet fell as a result of a formal vote of ~⟩

1nonconform *adj* [*1non-* + *conform*, adj.] *obs* **:** NONCONFORMING

2non·conform \ˈ= *at* NON-+\ *vi* [*1non-* + *conform*, v.] **:** to fail to conform

nonconformable *adj* [*1non-* + *conformable*] *obs* **:** NONCONFORMING — **non·conformably** \"+\ *adv*

non·conformance \"+\ *n* [*1non-* + *conformance*] **:** failure to conform ⟨~ to the established traditions —Bernard Taper⟩

non·conformer \"+\ *n* [*1non-* + *conformer*] **:** one that does not conform ⟨a natural-born ~ —*Newsweek*⟩

non·conforming \"+\ *adj* [*1non-* + *conforming*, pres. part. of *conform*] **:** not conforming **:** declining conformity ⟨pressures on ~ individuals —*New Yorker*⟩; *esp* **:** not conforming to the established church ⟨~ ministers⟩ ⟨~ sects⟩

non·conformism \"+\ *n* [*nonconformist* + *-ism*] **:** the principles or practices of nonconformity ⟨their individualism . . . constantly drives them to ~ —Janet Flanner⟩ ⟨their vociferous ~ —Norman Lewis⟩ ⟨deeply averse to excitement and ~ —Robert Pick⟩

1non·conformist \"+\ *n* [*1non-* + *conform*, v. + *-ist*] **1 a :** a person who does not conform to an established church or its doctrine, discipline, or polity ⟨Lutheran churchmen and Swedish ~*s* cooperate —N.G.Sahlin⟩ **b** *often cap* (1) **:** one of the clergymen numbering about 2000 who left the Church of England in 1662 rather than submit to the Act of Uniformity (2) **:** a member of a religious body separated from the Church of England **:** DISSENTER ⟨a desire to bring *Nonconformists* within the established church —*Brit. Book News*⟩ **2 a :** a person who fails or refuses to conform to some norm **:** one who deviates from a generally accepted or socially approved way or pattern of thought or action ⟨the Bureau of Naval Personnel soon returned these ~*s* to a civilian status —A.A.Ageton⟩ **b :** a person who dissents on principled grounds from an established or conventional creed, rule, or practice **:** one who displays a courageous independence of thought in refusing to conform blindly or timidly to a prevailing dogma or orthodoxy ⟨whoso would be a man must be a ~ —R.W.Emerson⟩ ⟨those who have done most for the world . . . have been the dissenters and ~*s* —R.J.McCracken⟩ **3 :** a natural object that does not function or behave according to rule or in a manner typical of its kind ⟨gallium is a ~ among metals —L.J.Briggs⟩ ⟨type of variable star had been recognized as a ~ since 1946 —J.M.Chamberlain⟩

2nonconformist \"\ *adj* **1 a :** nonconforming to an established church **b** *often cap* **:** relating to a member of or being a religious body separated from the Church of England ⟨~ ministers gathered⟩ ⟨a poor, *Nonconformist* family —*Time*⟩ **2 :** nonconforming to some norm or socially approved pattern of thought or behavior or to an established creed, rule, or practice ⟨whose rabidly ~ deportment has made them legendary figures —*New Yorker*⟩ ⟨also ~, also biased by abnormality —Edmund Wilson⟩ ⟨the old, stubborn, ~ spirit of the earliest settlers —R.M.Coates⟩

non·conformity \ˈ= *at* NON-+\ *n* [*1non-* + *conformity*] **1 a** (1) **:** failure or refusal to conform to an established church **:** the principles or practices of religious nonconformists ⟨the early church was hostile to all ~⟩ (2) *often cap* **:** neglect or refusal esp. by Protestant dissenters to conform to the Church of England or its doctrine, discipline, or polity **:** the movement, doctrines, or principles of English Protestant dissent ⟨*Nonconformity* reached its height of political power . . . round the beginning of the century —D.W.Brogan⟩ (3) *often cap* **:** the body of English nonconformists ⟨efforts on behalf of persecuted *Nonconformity* —Douglas Bush⟩ ⟨made many friends in the circles of prosperous ~ —John Buchan⟩ **b :** refusal to conform to an established or conventional creed, rule, or practice ⟨totalitarian orthodoxy hates defiant ~ —A.E.Stevenson †1965⟩ ⟨the world . . . with its tenor of ~ —Mary Webb⟩ **2 :** absence of agreement or correspondence ⟨the striking ~ of his ideas and his practice⟩ **3 :** a surface of contact between sedimentary rocks and underlying eroded igneous or metamorphic rocks upon which they were deposited **:** a depositional contact; *also* **:** an unconformity occurring between two nonparallel sequences of strata

non·conscious \(ˈ)=+\ *adj* **:** not conscious ⟨~ psychic processes —A.A.Brill⟩

non·consumable \ˈ=+\ *adj* **:** not consumable

non·contagious \"+\ *adj* **:** not contagious ⟨a ~ disease⟩

non·content \"+\ *n* [*1non-* + *content*, n.] **:** a member of the British House of Lords who gives a negative vote

non·contentious \"+\ *adj* **:** not contentious

non·continuous \"+\ *adj* **:** not continuous **:** DISCONTINUOUS

noncontinuous easement *n* **:** DISCONTINUOUS EASEMENT

non·contraband \(ˈ)=+\ *adj* **:** not being contraband

non·contractile \ˈ=+\ *adj* **:** not contractile

non·contradiction \(ˈ)=+\ *n* **:** absence of logical contradiction

non·contradictory \"+\ *adj* **:** not contradictory

non·contributory \ˈ=+\ *adj* **:** making or involving no contribution: as **a :** involving, related to, or constituting a pension plan whereby the employer pays the total cost **b :** making no contribution to a medical diagnosis ⟨the past history was ~ —*Seminar*⟩

non·convertible \"+\ *adj* **:** not convertible ⟨~ bonds⟩

non·convulsive \"+\ *adj* **:** not convulsive

non·cooperation \"+\ *n* **:** failure or refusal to cooperate; *specif* **:** refusal through civil disobedience (as by nonpayment of taxes or by boycott of courts, legislative councils, schools) of a people to cooperate with the government of a country — used esp. of the policy of Gandhi and his followers in India — **non·cooperationist** \"+\ *n*

non·cooperative \"+\ *adj* **:** of, relating to, or characterized by noncooperation

non·cooperator \"+\ *n* **:** one who practices noncooperation

non·corroding \" +\ *adj* **:** not corrodible

non·crystalline \(ˈ)=+\ *adj* **:** not crystalline

noncum *abbr* noncumulative

non·cumulative \(ˈ)= *at* NON-+\ *adj* [*1non-* + *cumulative*] **:** not entitled to future payments of dividends or interest passed when normally due ⟨~ stock⟩ ⟨~ income bonds⟩

non·current \"+\ *adj* **:** not current

non·cyclic *or* **non·cyclical** \"+\ *adj* **:** not cyclic

non·da \ˈnändə\ *also* **nonda plum** *n* -s [*nonda* native name in southeast Queensland, Australia] **1 :** an edible fruit of an Australian tree that resembles a plum **2 :** the tree (*Parinarium nonda*) that bears nondas

non·deciduata \ˌnän+\ *n pl, cap* [NL, fr. *1non-* + *Deciduata*] **:** mammals having a nondeciduate placenta — used as if it were a taxon

non·deciduate \ˈ= *at* NON-+\ *adj* [*1non-* + *deciduate*] *of a placenta* **:** having the fetal and maternal tissues but superficially associated so that no maternal tissue is lost at parturition (as in ungulates and whales)

non·deductibility \"+\ *n* [*1non-* + *deductibility*] **:** the condition of being nondeductible

non·deductible \"+\ *adj* [*1non-* + *deductible*] **:** not deductible; *esp* **:** not deductible for income tax purposes ⟨~ losses⟩

non·degradable \"+\ *adj* **:** not degradable ⟨~ bottles⟩

non·delegable \(ˈ)=+\ *adj* **:** not capable of being delegated

non·delinquent \ˈ= +\ *n* **:** one that is not a delinquent

non·delivery \ˈ=+\ *n* **:** neglect or failure to deliver

non·democratic \(ˈ)=+\ *adj* **:** not democratic **:** not believing in or practicing democratic ideals and principles

non·denominational \ˈ=+\ *adj* **:** not restricted to a denomination ⟨a ~ church⟩

non·denominationalism \"+\ *n* **:** the principle of being nondenominational or of not emphasizing denominationalism

non·deposition \"+\ *n* **:** DIASTEM 3

1non·de·script \ˌnändəˈskript\ *adj* [*1non-* + L *descriptus*, past part. of *describere* to describe — more at DESCRIBE] **1** *archaic* **:** not hitherto described **2 :** lacking distinguishing characteristics or a distinctive character **:** belonging or appearing to belong to no particular class or kind **:** not easily described **:** UNCLASSIFIABLE, INDETERMINATE, INDESCRIBABLE ⟨clad in ~ gray clothes and battered black hat —Rex Ingamells⟩ ⟨a section of ~ row houses —*Amer. Guide Series: Va.*⟩ ⟨a ~ mixture of styles in the worst possible taste —G.B.Shaw⟩

2nondescript \"\ *n* -s **1** *archaic* **:** something (as a species of plant or mineral) not hitherto described **2 :** someone or something lacking distinguishing characteristics or a distinctive character **:** an individual not easily classified or of no particular class or kind ⟨the famous turquoise eyes had washed out to a milky ~ —Budd Schulberg⟩ ⟨a wizened old ~ —Norman Douglas⟩ ⟨the rush of prospectors, middlemen, gamblers, outlaws, and ~*s* —*Amer. Guide Series: Nev.*⟩ ⟨ranging from the landlord to the lowest stable ~ —Charles Dickens⟩ ⟨cattle in the region, 80 percent of which were crossbred ~*s* —*Farmer's Weekly* (*So. Africa*)⟩ **3 :** the bottom or near the bottom grade of marketable tobacco

non·deteriorative \ˈ= *at* NON- +\ *adj* **:** not deteriorative

non de·ti·net \(ˈ)nänˈdetᵊnˌet\ *n, pl* **non detinets** [L, he does not detain] **:** the general issue in an action of detinue putting in issue only the question of detainer

non·detonating \(ˈ)= *at* NON- +\ *adj* **:** not detonating **:** reacting by deflagration

non·development \ˈ=+\ *n* **:** a failure or lack of development

non·diffusible \"+\ *adj* **:** not diffusible

non·diffusing \"+\ *adj* **:** not diffusing

non·digestible \"+\ *adj* **:** not digestible

non·directional \"+\ *adj* **:** not directional **:** OMNIDIRECTIONAL ⟨a ~ beacon⟩

non·directive \"+\ *adj* [*1non-* + *directive*] **1 :** of or relating to psychotherapy or counseling in which the counselor refrains from interpretive or associative comment but usu. by repeating phrases used by the client encourages him to express, clarify, and restructure his problems — contrasted with *directive* **2 :** of or relating to interviewing (as by an anthropologist of a native informant) which avoids direct questioning and prompts the person being interviewed to talk freely, informally, or spontaneously ⟨prolonged . . . ~ interviews —B.J.Siegel⟩

non·disclosure \"+\ *n* **:** a failure to reveal facts bearing upon a transaction

non·disjunction \"+\ *n* [ISV *1non-* + *disjunction*] *n* **:** the failure of two homologous chromosomes to separate during reduction division — **non·disjunctional** \"+\ *adj*

non·distinctive \"+\ *adj* [*1non-* + *distinctive*] *of a speech sound* **:** having no signaling value **:** NONFUNCTIONAL

non·distribution \(ˈ)=+\ *n* **:** a lack or absence of distribution

non·divided \ˈ=+\ *adj* **:** not divided

non·do \ˈnän(ˌ)dō\ *n* -s [origin unknown] **:** a perennial herb (*Levisticum canadense*) of the eastern U.S. having an aromatic root

non·dollar \(ˈ)= *at* NON- +\ *adj* [*1non-* + *dollar*] **1 :** being an area where the U.S. dollar is not used as a basis for exchange and currencies usu. cannot be converted freely into dollars ⟨~ countries⟩ **2 :** not consisting in or composed of dollars ⟨a ~ loan⟩ ⟨~ currencies⟩

non·dormant \"+\ *adj* [*1non-* + *dormant*] **1 :** being in such a condition that germination is possible ⟨~ seeds⟩ **2 :** being in active vegetative growth ⟨~ plants⟩

non·dramatic \ˈ=+\ *adj* **:** not dramatic

non·drying \(ˈ)=+\ *adj* **:** not drying

nondrying oil *n* **:** a natural or synthetic oil (as olive oil) characterized by low unsaturation and consequent inability to solidify readily when exposed in a thin film to the air

non·dualism \"+\ *n* [*1non-* + *dualism*] **1 :** a doctrine of classic Brahmanism holding that the essential unity of all is real whereas duality and plurality are phenomenal illusion and that matter is materialized energy which in turn is the temporal manifestation of an incorporeal spiritual eternal essence constituting the innermost self of all things **2 :** any of various monistic or pluralistic theories of the universe

non·durables \"+\ *or* **nondurable goods** *n pl* **:** consumer goods or producer goods (as textiles, food, clothing, petroleum, chemical products) that are serviceable for a comparatively short period of time or that are consumed or destroyed in a single usage

1none \ˈnən\ *pron, sing or pl in constr* [ME *noon, none*, pron. & adj., fr. OE *nān*, fr. *ne* not + *ān* one — more at NO, ONE] **1 a :** not any ⟨~ of them were intellectually absorbing enough —Winthrop Sargeant⟩ ⟨~ of our scholars has written a monograph on him —Norman Douglas⟩ ⟨~ of our creeds are entirely free from guesswork —M.R.Cohen⟩ **b :** NEITHER ⟨of which ~ of the two can wholly be responsible —*Science & Culture*⟩ **2 a :** one that is not or lacks the requisite qualities of the thing or person mentioned ⟨how to make a brave or wise man of one that is ~⟩ **b** *archaic* **:** one that is not at all the thing or person mentioned — used in the phrase *none of* ⟨thou art ~ of my brother —*Ballad Book*⟩ **3 :** not one **:** NO ONE, NOBODY ⟨~ is said to be left now —Stark Young⟩ ⟨~ is immune from the feeling and need for individuality —John Sirjamaki⟩ ⟨in the morning ~ was visible —*Time*⟩ ⟨~ were deeper in that labyrinthine ambition —G.K.Chesterton⟩ **4 :** not any such thing or person ⟨half a loaf is better than ~⟩ **5 :** no part **:** NOTHING ⟨had ~ of the condescension of the foreigner —Walter Lippmann⟩ ⟨seemed to want ~ of it —*Time*⟩ ⟨will have ~ of this theory —R.S.Bourne⟩ ⟨a sluttish sort and I want ~ of her —Marcia Davenport⟩

2none \"\ *adj* [ME *noon, none*, pron. & adj., fr. OE *nān*] *archaic* **:** not any **:** NO ⟨thou shalt have ~ other gods before me —Deut 5:7 (AV)⟩

3none \"\ *adv* [ME *noon, none* not, fr. *noon, none*, pron. & adj.] **1 :** by no means **:** not at all ⟨the authenticity of many . . . is ~ too clear —A.L.Kroeber⟩ ⟨~ too prosperous, it sought to save itself —*Amer. Guide Series: Pa.*⟩ **2 :** in no way **:** to no extent — often used in substandard speech with another negative ⟨ain't heard her ~ this morning —Burl Ives⟩

4none \ˈnōn\ *n* -s *often cap* [LL *nona*, fr. L. ninth hour of the day counting from sunrise — more at NOON] **1 :** a canonical hour that according to ancient Roman and Eastern reckoning is the ninth hour **2 :** a religious office formerly recited at 3 p.m. but now in the Roman Catholic Church often somewhat earlier

non·economic \(ˈ)= *at* NON-+\ *adj* **:** not economic: as **a :** being other than economic ⟨~ kinds of motivation —Harold Koontz & Cyril O'Donnell⟩ ⟨over any ~ issue such as the union shop —*U.S. Code*⟩ **b :** having no economic importance or implication ⟨a number of . . . ~ plants —*Encyc. Americana*⟩

non·economist \ˈ=+\ *n* **:** one that is not an economist

non·eczematous \ˈ=+\ *adj* **:** not eczematous

1non·effective \"+\ *adj* **1 :** not effective **2 :** not fit or available for military or naval duty

2noneffective \"\ *n* **:** a soldier or sailor unavailable for regular duty because of unfitness (as from sickness or wounds)

non·effervescent \(ˈ)=+\ *adj* **:** not effervescent

non·ego \(ˈ)=+\ *n* [*1non-* + *ego*; trans. of G *nicht-ich*] **:** the external world or object of knowledge as contrasted with the subject or ego — used esp. in the idealistic doctrines of Fichte and Schelling

nonelastic \ˈ=+\ *adj* **:** not elastic

non·electrolyte \ˈ=+\ *n* [*1non-* + *electrolyte*] **:** a substance (as sugar or benzene) that is not appreciably ionized (as in aqueous solution) and therefore is a poor conductor of electricity **:** a nonpolar substance

non·empirical \"+\ *adj* **:** not empirical ⟨~ intuition⟩

no·nene \ˈnōˌnēn, ˈnä,-\ *n* -s [ISV *2non-* + *-ene*] **:** any of four liquid straight-chain hydrocarbons C_9H_{18} of the ethylene series

non·ent \(ˈ)näˈnent\ *n* -s [ML *nonent-*, *nonens*, fr. L *non* not + ML *ent-*, *ens* ens — more at NON-, ENS] **:** something that does not exist

non·entanglement \ˈ= *at* NON- +\ *n* **1 :** abstention from becoming entangled ⟨policy of ~ —*Amer. Scholar*⟩ **2 :** the condition of not being entangled ⟨his ~ in that scandal⟩

non·entitative \(ˈ)=+\ *or* **non·en·ti·tive** \"+ˈentəd·iv\ *adj* [*nonentitative* fr. *1non-* + *entitative*; *nonentitive* fr. *nonentity* + *-ive*] **:** NONEXISTENT

non·entity \(ˈ)= *at* NON-+\ *n* **1 :** something that does not exist or exists only in the imagination ⟨the whole realm of *nonentities*, such as "the round square" . . . "Apollo", "Hamlet" —Herbert Feigl & W.S.Sellars⟩ ⟨in one day . . . high-heaped money-wages became fairy-money and ~ —Thomas Carlyle⟩ **2 :** the quality or state of not existing **:** NONEXISTENCE **3 a :** a person who is totally undistinguished or unimpressive in mind, character, or achievement **:** one of small or mediocre talents ⟨manifested by hacks and *nonentities* put in nomination —*New Republic*⟩ ⟨there can be no leaders if all the followers are *nonentities* —W.L.Sullivan⟩ ⟨becoming a moral ~ —Lionel Trilling⟩ **b :** something of no consequence or significance **:** something totally lacking in distinction ⟨this building therefore sinks . . . a ~, into the dismal swamp of buildings around it —Lewis Mumford⟩ **c :** the condition of being a nonentity ⟨his shrunken figure relapsed into drab ~ —Gerald Beaumont⟩ ⟨emerging from the unfathomable abyss of ~ —H.L. Mencken⟩ ⟨after five and a half months of political ~ —*Time*⟩

non·en·tres *or* **non·en·tresse** \(ˈ)näˈnen·trəs\ *n, pl* **nonentreses** *or* **nonentresses** [ME (Sc) *none entress*, fr. *none-*, *non-* 1non- + *entress*, *entres* entrance, entry, fr. ME *entren* to enter + *-ess*, *-es*, *-esse* (as in *duresse* duress, restraint) — more at ENTER] *Scots feudal law* **:** failure of an heir to land to make an entry thereon and to obtain investiture of the feu from the superior; *also* **:** the feudal casualty arising from such failure

non·entry \(ˈ)= *at* NON-+\ *n* [ME (Sc) *nonentree*, fr. ME *1non-* + *entree*, *entre* entry — more at ENTRY] **1 :** the fact of not entering **2** *Scots feudal law* **:** NONENTRES

non·episcopal \ˈ=+\ *adj* **:** not episcopal

non·eruptive \ˈ=+\ *adj* **:** not eruptive

nones \ˈnōnz\ *n pl but sing or pl in constr* [ME *nonys*, fr. L *nonae*, fr. fem. pl. of *nonus* ninth — more at NOON] **1 :** the ninth day before the ides according to ancient Roman reckoning that is not found in his jurisdiction **2** *often cap* [pl. of *4none*] **:** 4NONE

none–so–pretty \ˈ=(ˌ)=ˈ=\ *n, pl* **none–so–pretties** **1 :** a decorative braid or tape used in the late 18th century **2 a :** LONDON PRIDE 1 **b :** LOBEL'S CATCHFLY

1non·essential \ˈ= *at* NON-+\ *adj* **:** not essential **:** not of prime or central importance ⟨~ to the integral meanings of poetry —*Publ's Mod. Lang. Assoc. of Amer.*⟩ ⟨guard carefully against unnecessary uniformity in ~ matters —E.P.Cubberley⟩

2nonessential \"\ *n* **:** something that is not essential

nonessential clause *n* **:** NONRESTRICTIVE CLAUSE

non est fac·tum \ˌnäˌnestˈfaktəm, ˈnō,-\ *n, pl* **non est factums** [NL, it was not done] **:** the plea of the general issue in an action of debt on bond or other specialty and on any written instrument in some states

non est in·ven·tus \-inˈventəs\ *n, pl* **non est inventuses** [ME, fr. ML, he has not been found] **:** the return of a sheriff on a writ when the defendant or person to be served or arrested is not found in his jurisdiction

1none·such \ˈnənˌsəch\ *or* **non·such** \"*sometimes* ˈnän-\ *n* -ES [*1none* + *such*] **1 :** a person or thing without an equal in some respect or category **:** one that has no match or rival **:** PARAGON, NONPAREIL ⟨the team's ~ . . . began throwing his famous passes —*New Yorker*⟩ ⟨only a ~ could go through a schedule like that —G.F.T.Ryall⟩ ⟨made him a ~ in New York politics —*Atlantic*⟩ **2** *also* **nonesuch clover :** BLACK MEDIC

2nonesuch \"\ *or* **nonsuch** \"\ *adj* **:** UNEQUALED, UNRIVALED, MATCHLESS ⟨a ~ hero of space opera —J.F.McComas⟩

nonesuch chest *var of* NONSUCH CHEST

no·net \nōˈnet\ *n* -s [It *nonetto*, fr. *nono* ninth (fr. L *nonus*) + *-etto* (as in *duetto* duet) — more at NOON] **:** a combination of nine instruments or voices; *also* **:** a musical composition for such a combination

nonetheless \ˈ=ˈ=\ *adv* [fr. the phrase *none the less*] **:** NEVERTHELESS ⟨there is ~ that risk —Henry Wynmalen⟩ ⟨~, the presentation . . . is so reasonable one cannot resist being convinced despite the method of reasoning —A.D.Kossoff⟩

non·ethical \(ˈ)⸗ *at* NON- +\ *adj* **:** not ethical

non·etymological \(ˌ)⸗+\ *adj* **:** not etymological

non-euclidean *also* **non-euclidian** \ˌ⸗ *at* NON- +\ *adj, often cap E* [prob. trans. of G *nichteuklidisch*] **:** not euclidean; *specif* **:** not assuming all the axioms and postulates assumed in the *Elements* of Euclid

non·exempt \"+\ *adj* **:** not exempt ⟨~ property⟩

non·existence \"+\ *n* **1 :** absence of existence **:** the negation of being **2 :** something that has no existence

¹non·existent \"+\ *adj* **:** not having existence

²nonexistent \"\ *n* **:** one that does not exist

non·expendable \ˌ⸗+\ *adj* [ˈ*non-* + *expendable*] **:** not consumed in use and not losing identity in use ⟨~ tooling such as dies, jigs, and templates —P.T.Sherwood⟩

non·explosive \"+\ *adj* **:** not explosive ⟨a ~ gas⟩

non·extant \(ˈ)⸗+, ˌ⸗+\ *adj* **:** not extant; *esp* **:** no longer existing or accessible through loss or destruction ⟨its ~ original was written on vellum —G.B.Saul⟩

non·fabricated \(ˈ)⸗+\ *adj* **:** not fabricated

non·farm \(ˈ)⸗+\ *adj* [ˈ*non-* + *farm*, n.] **:** not of or related to a farm: as **a :** not engaged in, devoted to, or derived from farming ⟨~ jobs⟩ ⟨approximately one half of the rural population . . . was classed as ~ —Alexander Heard⟩ **b :** not composed of or belonging to farm families ⟨farmers have failed to make clear beyond all doubt to ~ America —*Country Gentleman*⟩ ⟨~ homes⟩ **c :** of or relating to commodities other than agricultural ⟨~ prices⟩

non·fat \"+\ *adj* **:** lacking fat **:** having fat removed

non·fea·sance \nänˈfēzᵊn(t)s\ *n* -s [ˈ*non-* + obs. E *feasance* performance, doing, fr. AF *fesance*, fr. MF, *faisance*, act, fr. OF, fr. *fais-* (stem of *faire* to do, fr. L *facere*) + *-ance* — more at DO] **:** omission to do esp. what ought to be done

non·febrile \(ˈ)⸗ *at* NON- +\ *adj* **:** not febrile

non·feeding \"+\ *adj* **:** not feeding

non·ferrous \"+\ *adj* **:** not containing, including, or relating to iron ⟨~ metal⟩ **:** relating to metals other than iron

non·fibrous \"+\ *adj* **:** not fibrous

non·fiction \"+\ *n* **:** literary works other than novels or stories ⟨the best-selling ~ of that spring —*Current Biog.*⟩

non·fictional \"+\ *adj* **:** not fictional

non·figurative \"+\ *adj* **:** NONOBJECTIVE ⟨~ art⟩

non·filamentous \(ˌ)⸗+\ *adj* **1 :** not having the form of a thread **2 :** not made up of filamentous parts

non·filterable \(ˈ)⸗+\ *adj* **:** not filterable

non·financial \ˌ⸗+\ *adj* **:** being or relating to an enterprise or economic activity (as manufacturing, trade, or public utilities) other than financial **:** not engaged in the banking or insurance business ⟨~ corporations⟩ ⟨controlled 49 percent of all the ~ corporate wealth of the country —P.H.Douglas⟩

non·fissionable \(ˈ)⸗+\ *adj* **:** not fissionable

non·flagellated \"+\ *adj* **:** not flagellated

non·flam \(ˈ)⸗+ˌflam\ *adj* [by shortening] **:** not flammable

non·flammable \"+\ *adj* [ˈ*non-* + *flammable*] **:** not flammable **:** incapable of being easily ignited and of burning with extreme rapidity

non·flowering \"+\ *adj* **:** producing no flowers; *specif* **:** lacking a flowering stage in the life cycle — used esp. of liverworts, mosses, ferns, and fern allies

non·forfeiture \"+\ *n* **:** no forfeiture

non·forfeiture benefit \"+-\ *or* **nonforfeiture value** *n* **:** a benefit (as in cash or insurance) received by a policyholder who after making premium payments for at least the minimum period as provided wishes to discontinue further premium payments

nonforfeiture law *n* **:** a law requiring life insurance companies within certain limitations to grant surrender values on policies for which premium payments have been discontinued

non·fossiliferous \(ˌ)⸗+\ *adj* **:** not fossiliferous

non·fraternal \ˌ⸗+\ *adj* **:** not fraternal **:** not connected with a fraternal order or association

non·freezing \"+\ *adj* **:** not subject to freezing **:** resistant to freezing

non·fulfillment \ˌ⸗+\ *n* **:** a lack of fulfillment

non·functional \(ˈ)⸗+\ *adj* **:** not functional: as **a :** having no function **:** serving or performing no useful purpose ⟨there is no merit in ~ footnotes —G.W.Sherburn⟩ ⟨spending an extra hundred thousand dollars for ~ . . . decorations —Paul Woodring⟩ **b :** not performing or able to perform its regular function

non·fundable \"+\ *adj* **:** not capable of being funded

non·game \"+\ *adj* [ˈ*non-* + *game*, n.] **:** not hunted for food, sport, or fur ⟨~ birds⟩

non·generic \ˌ⸗+\ *adj* **:** not generic

non·genetic \ˌ⸗+\ *adj* **:** not genetic

non·genic \(ˈ)⸗+\ *adj* **:** not genic

non·glandular \"+\ *adj* **:** not glandular

non·government \(ˈ)⸗+\ *adj* **:** not belonging to or affiliated with the government

non·governmental \(ˌ)⸗+\ *adj* **:** not governmental

non gra·ta *see* PERSONA NON GRATA\ *adj* [L (in *persona non grata*)] **:** not approved **:** UNWELCOME ⟨a sign informed us that the public was *non grata* at the gathering —*New Yorker*⟩

non·gregarious \ˌ⸗ *at* NON- +\ *adj* **:** not gregarious

non·halation \"+\ *adj* **:** ANTIHALATION

non·hardening \"+\ *adj* **:** not hardening

non·hardy \(ˈ)⸗+\ *adj* **:** not capable of enduring low winter temperatures — compare TENDER

non·harmonic \ˌ⸗+\ *adj* **:** not harmonic; *specif* **:** not belonging to the essential musical harmony ⟨a ~ note⟩

non·heritable \(ˈ)⸗+\ *adj* **:** not heritable

non·historical \ˌ⸗+\ *adj* **:** not historical

non·homogeneous \(ˌ)⸗+\ *adj* **:** not homogeneous

non·homologous \ˌ⸗+\ *adj* **:** being of unlike genic constitution — used of chromosomes of one set containing nonallelic genes

non·human \(ˈ)⸗+\ *adj* **1 :** being other than a human being ⟨~ animals⟩ ⟨the great world of ~ spirits —*Amer. Mercury*⟩ **2 :** not belonging or appropriate to or produced by human beings ⟨a babel of ~ noises —*N.Y. Times*⟩

non·hygroscopic \"+\ *adj* **:** not hygroscopic

no·ni \ˈnō(ˌ)nē\ *n* -s [Hawaiian & Marquesan] *central Polynesia & Hawaii* **:** INDIAN MULBERRY 1

no·nil·lion \nōˈnilyən\ *n* -s *often attrib* [F, fr. MF, fr. L *nonus* ninth + MF *-illion* (as in *million*) — more at NOON] — see NUMBER table

non·immigrant \(ˈ)⸗ *at* NON- +\ *n* **:** an alien (as a foreign tourist, government official, or student) who enters the U.S. for a temporary period or a resident alien returning from a temporary stay abroad

¹non·immune \ˌ⸗+\ *adj* **:** not immune **:** being a nonimmune

²nonimmune \"\ *n* **:** one that lacks immunity to a particular disease **:** SUSCEPTIBLE

non·importation \(ˌ)⸗+\ *n, often attrib* **:** cessation or prohibition of the import of goods from another country esp. as employed against Great Britain by the American colonies in the Revolutionary era in retaliation for the Townshend Acts and by the U.S. in the Napoleonic era as a measure of reprisal for British violations of American neutral rights ⟨~ associations made effective use of an economic boycott —*Amer. Guide Series: N.C.*⟩ ⟨the device of ~ was tried, in resistance to British political and economic aggression —J.C.Fitzpatrick⟩

non·inbred \(ˈ)⸗+\ *adj* **:** free from or not produced by inbreeding

non·inductive \ˌ⸗+\ *adj* **:** having negligible inductance ⟨a ~ electrical resistor⟩ — **non·inductively** \"\ *adv* — **non·in·duc·tiv·i·ty** \(ˌ)⸗+ˌin,dəkˈtivəd·ē, -ətē, -i\ *n*

non·industrial \ˌ⸗+\ *adj* **:** not industrial

non·infectious \ˌ⸗+\ *adj* **:** not infectious

non·inflammable \"+\ *adj* **:** not inflammable **:** NONFLAMMABLE

non·inflammatory \"+\ *adj* **:** not inflammatory

non·inflationary \"+\ *adj* **:** not inflationary

non·inflectional \"+\ *adj* **:** not inflectional

non·inherent \"+\ *adj* **:** not inherent

non·inheritable \"+\ *adj* **:** not inheritable

non·institutional \(ˌ)⸗+\ *adj* **:** not institutional

non·intercourse \(ˈ)⸗+\ *n* **:** suspension or absence of dealings or relations ⟨diplomatic ~ between the two states continued 25 years⟩; *esp* **:** suspension by one country of commercial relations with another esp. as employed during the Napoleonic era by the U.S. against Great Britain and France in retaliation for their violations of American neutral rights

non·interference \(ˌ)⸗+\ *n* **:** the fact or an instance of refraining from interference

non·intersecting \"+\ *adj* **:** not intersecting

non·intervention \"+\ *n, often attrib* [ˈ*non-* + *intervention*] **1 :** the state or habit of not intervening **:** refusal or failure to intervene; *esp* **:** a systematic policy or practice of refraining from interference in the affairs of other states ⟨had to preserve the legal fiction of ~ —*Collier's Yr. Bk.*⟩ ⟨the outworn doctrine of ~ —*New Republic*⟩ ⟨a ~ pact⟩ ⟨~ is overwhelmingly supported by our people⟩ **2 :** an instance of nonintervention ⟨advocated ~ in the civil war across the border⟩

¹non·interventionist \"+\ *n* [ISV *nonintervention* + *-ist*] **:** one who does not intervene or favors nonintervention ⟨the God of the Deists was . . . a ~ —W.L.Sperry⟩; *esp* **:** one who favors nonintervention in the affairs of another country ⟨the trend of his votes revealed him as a ~ —*Current Biog.*⟩

²noninterventionist \"\ *adj* **:** implementing or favorable to nonintervention ⟨~ policies⟩ ⟨turned from a ~ stand to one of internationalism —*Current Biog.*⟩

non·intoxicant \ˌ⸗+\ *n* **:** a beverage that does not intoxicate

non·intoxicating \"+\ *adj* **:** not conducive to intoxication

non·intrusion \"+\ *n* **:** absence of intrusion **:** refusal to intrude; *specif* **:** the principle historically upheld by the Church of Scotland that a minister may not be settled in a parish against the will of the people — **non·in·tru·sion·ism** \-ˌnizəm\ *n* — **non·in·tru·sion·ist** \-ˌnəst\ *n*

non in·ven·tus \ˌnäˌninˈventəs, ˌnō,-\ *n, pl* **non inventuses** [L, not found] **:** NON EST INVENTUS

non·involvement \ˌ⸗ *at* NON- +\ *n* **:** refusal to become involved or committed **:** the condition of not being involved or committed ⟨much to be said . . . for ~ in the affairs of the Orient —*Saturday Rev.*⟩

¹non·ionic \"+\ *adj* **:** not ionic **:** NONPOLAR

²nonionic \"\ *n* -s **:** a nonionic substance; *esp* **:** NONIONIC DETERGENT

nonionic detergent *n* **:** any of a class of synthetic detergents (as long-chain ether derivatives or esters of alcohols or phenols) that are neither anionic nor cationic but produce electrically neutral colloidal particles in solution

non·irrigated \(ˈ)⸗+\ *adj* **:** not irrigated

nonis *pl of* NONI

non·isobaric \(ˌ)⸗ *at* NON- +\ *adj* **:** not directly associated with any definite form of isobars or isobaric gradients

non·issuable \(ˈ)⸗+\ *adj* **:** not being of such a nature as to raise a fact in issue determinative of the merits of a case ⟨a ~ plea⟩

non·joinder \"+\ *n* **:** the omission of a necessary party, plaintiff, or defendant to a suit at law or in equity

non·ju·ran·cy \(ˈ)nänˈju̇rənsē\ *n* -ES [*nonjurant* + *-cy*] **:** the state of being a nonjuror **:** nonjuring principles

¹non·ju·rant \(ˈ)⸗ˈju̇rənt\ *adj* [ˈ*non-* + L *jurant-, jurans*, pres. part. of *jurare* to swear — more at JURY] **:** NONJURING **:** relating to or characteristic of nonjurors

²nonjurant \"\ *n* -s **:** NONJUROR

non·juridical \ˌ⸗ *at* NON- +\ *adj* **:** not juridical

non·ju·ring \(ˈ)nänˈju̇riŋ, -rēŋ\ *adj* [ˈ*non-* + L *jurare* to swear + E *-ing*] **:** not swearing allegiance — used esp. of a member of a party in Great Britain that would not swear allegiance to William and Mary or to their successors

non·juror \(ˈ)⸗ *at* NON- +\ *n* [ˈ*non-* + *juror*] **:** a person refusing to take an oath (esp. of allegiance, supremacy, or abjuration): **a :** one of the beneficed clergy in England and Scotland refusing to take an oath of allegiance to William and Mary or to their successors after the revolution of 1688 **b :** one of the Scotch Presbyterians refusing to take an oath of abjuration as involving recognition of episcopacy

non·laminated \"+\ *adj* **:** not laminated

non·lateral \"+\ *adj* **:** not lateral ⟨~ oral sound⟩

non·laying \"+\ *adj* **:** not laying ⟨~ hens⟩

non·ledger assets \"+-\ *n pl* [*nonledger* fr. ˈ*non-* + *ledger*, n.] **1 :** assets (as interest, rent, premiums), receivable in the current year but not received as of a given date **2 :** excess of market values of investments over book values

non·legal \"+\ *adj* **:** not legal; *specif* **:** not being within the province of the law so as to be either required as legal or forbidden as illegal

non·legato \ˌ⸗+\ *adv (or adj)* [ˈ*non-* + *legato*] **:** with breaks between successive tones **:** with a bow stroke for each tone — used as a direction in music esp. for a bowed instrument

non·legislative \(ˈ)⸗+\ *adj* **:** not legislative

non·lethal \"+\ *adj* **:** not lethal

non·letterpress \"+\ *adj* **:** not consisting of or printed by letterpress

non·lexical \"+\ *adj* **:** not lexical

non·life \"+\ *n* **:** absence of life ⟨somewhere along the road . . . life and ~ seem to merge —*Treasury of Science*⟩

non·linear \"+\ *adj* **:** not linear

non·linearity \(ˌ)⸗+\ *n* [ˈ*non-* + *linearity*] **:** the failure of an output signal in an electronic reproducing system to reproduce an input signal faithfully

non·linguist \(ˈ)⸗+\ *n* [ˈ*non-* + *linguist*] **:** one not versed or accomplished in language

non·linguistic \ˌ⸗+\ *adj* **1 :** not consisting of or related to language **2 :** lacking ability to learn or use foreign languages ⟨we are a ~ people, and most of our professors are unable to deliver lectures in a foreign tongue —*Survey Graphic*⟩

non li·quet \(ˈ)nänˈlīkwət, (ˈ)nōn-, -lik-\ *n, pl* **non liquets** [L, it is not clear] **:** an expression or condition of doubt or uncertainty as to the facts or where the truth lies ⟨questions which can be answered only with a *non liquet* —Louis Infield⟩ — used by Roman judges in rendering a decision in a doubtful case or in asking leave to be excused

non·liquid \(ˈ)⸗ *at* NON- +\ *adj* **:** not liquid

non·literary \"+\ *adj* **:** not literary

¹non·literate \"+\ *adj* **1 :** having no written language ⟨primitive people are above all ~ people —A.L.Kroeber⟩ **2 :** characterized by a lack of written language, simple technology, and relatively simple social organization **:** PRELITERATE, PRIMITIVE ⟨~ cultures⟩

²nonliterate \"\ *n* **:** a person having no written language ⟨ethnological fieldwork with ~s⟩

non·liturgical \ˌ⸗+\ *adj* **:** not liturgical

non·living \(ˈ)⸗+\ *adj* **:** not having or characterized by life ⟨~ matter⟩

non·load-bearing tile \(ˈ)⸗+-\ *n* **:** tile (as partition tile or furring tile) not capable of carrying superimposed loads for use in masonry construction

non·local \(ˈ)⸗+\ *adj* **:** not local

non·localized vector \(ˈ)⸗+-\ *n* **:** a vector that requires for its description only its magnitude and direction

non·logical \(ˈ)⸗+\ *adj* **:** not based on or derived from a process of reasoning or logic **:** based on or proceeding from insight, intuition, or the unconscious ⟨~ actions⟩ ⟨his cardinal doctrine is that most human behavior is ~ —H.J.Muller⟩ — compare ILLOGICAL

non·luminescent \(ˌ)⸗+\ *adj* **:** not luminescent

non·luminous \(ˈ)⸗+\ *adj* **:** lacking luminosity **:** not luminous

non·lustrous \"+\ *adj* **:** not lustrous

non·magnetic \ˌ⸗+\ *adj* **:** lacking magnetic qualities

non·mailable \(ˈ)⸗+\ *adj* **1 :** being in an unfit condition for mailing ⟨a hole in the paper as the result of poor erasing should render a paper ~ —Virginia Reva⟩ **2 :** not lawful to mail ⟨had the right to declare particular issues of the paper ~ —O.K.Fraenkel⟩

non·malignant \ˌ⸗+\ *adj* **:** not malignant

non·mammalian \"+\ *adj* **:** not mammalian

non·man \(ˈ)⸗+\ *n, pl* **nonmen :** a being that is not a man ⟨a man who is completely dehumanized by snobbery, a ~, a monster —E.R.Bentley⟩

non·mandatory \"+\ *adj* **:** not mandatory

non·marine \ˌ⸗+\ *adj* **:** not marine ⟨~ sandstone⟩

non·market \(ˈ)⸗+\ *adj* [ˈ*non-* + *market*, n.] **:** not relating to or characteristic of a market

non·marketable \"+\ *adj* [ˈ*non-* + *marketable*] **:** capable of being cashed at or before maturity only by the registered holder or one authorized to act for him ⟨~ securities⟩

non·master \"+\ *n* **:** a player in a U. S. contract-bridge tournament having too few master points to qualify for masters' tournaments

non·matching \"+\ *adj* **:** not matching

non·material \ˌ⸗+\ *adj* **:** not material: as **a :** being spirit or soul **:** IMMATERIAL, SPIRITUAL ⟨finds no evidence in man of a ~ faculty which . . . can be filled up with knowledge like a tank —Albert Lynd⟩ **b :** CULTURAL, INTELLECTUAL, AESTHETIC ⟨there are few ~ compensations for these material hardships —*Report: (Canadian) Royal Commission on Nat'l Development*⟩ **c :** of or relating to those aspects of a culture that constitute its ideological superstructure **:** not directly serving the sustenance and maintenance of life ⟨the ~ elements of a culture⟩ ⟨the beliefs and theories of the hated infidel, his ~ culture —H.E.Barnes & H.P.Becker⟩

non·mechanical \"+\ *adj* **:** not mechanical

non·medical \"+\ *adj* **:** not medical

nonmedical insurance *n* **:** life, accident, or health insurance issued without medical examination of the applicant

non·medullated \(ˈ)⸗+, ˌ⸗+\ *adj* **:** not medullated

non·member \(ˈ)⸗+\ *n* **:** an individual that is not a member

nonmember bank *n* **1 :** a bank that is not a member of the Federal Reserve system **2 :** a bank that is not a member of a clearinghouse association

non·membership \(ˈ)⸗+\ *n* **:** the state or status of a non-member

non·mental \"+\ *adj* **:** not mental

non·metal \"+\ *n* [ˈ*non-* + *metal*] **:** a chemical element (as boron, carbon, phosphorus, nitrogen, oxygen, sulfur, chlorine, argon) that is not classed as a metal because it does not exhibit most of the typical metallic properties **:** an element that in general is characterized chemically by the ability to form anions, acidic oxides and acids, and stable compounds with hydrogen — compare METALLOID

¹non·metallic \ˌ⸗+\ *adj* [ˈ*non-* + *metallic*] **1 :** not metallic (as in luster or other physical properties) **2 :** of, relating to, or being a nonmetal ⟨~ elements⟩

²nonmetallic \"\ *n* -s **:** a mineral or other naturally occurring substance (as rock or clay) that is not used for extraction of its metal content

non·metameric \(ˌ)⸗+\ *adj* **:** not divided into or originating from metameric segments ⟨a ~ nervous system⟩

non·metered \(ˈ)⸗+\ *adj* [ˈ*non-* + *metered*, past part. of *meter*] **:** used for nonmetered mail ⟨~ permit⟩ ⟨~ postage⟩

nonmetered mail *n* **:** mail for which postage is paid by the batch at the time of mailing according to special permits for batches of identical pieces of any one class of mail and which bears indicia printed by some device other than a postage meter

non·metrical \"+\ *adj* **:** not metrical

non·migratory \"+\ *adj* **:** not migratory

non·military \(ˈ)⸗+\ *adj* **:** not military

non·miscible \"+\ *adj* **:** not miscible

non·modifying \"+\ *adj* **:** not modifying

non·moral \"+\ *adj* **1 :** neither moral nor immoral **:** not in the sphere of morals or ethics **:** AMORAL ⟨make religion ~, a matter of inner experience and personal attitude —J.H.Randall⟩ **2 :** not moralistic **:** having no moral ⟨a ~ story⟩

non·motile \"+\ *adj* **:** not motile

non·muscular \"+\ *adj* **:** not muscular

non·mutant \"+\ *adj* **:** not mutant

non·nasal \(ˈ)⸗+\ *adj* **:** not nasal

¹non·native \"+\ *adj* **:** not native: as **a :** not being an aborigine; *esp* **:** being a member of the colonizing or dominant race or nation ⟨the ~ population of South Africa⟩ **b :** not born in the place or region to which reference is had ⟨relatively large proportions of ~ population —W.C.Bagley⟩

²nonnative \"\ *n* **:** an individual who is not a native ⟨to ~s of his state —Vance Packard⟩

non·natural \"+\ *adj* [ˈ*non-* + *natural*] **1 :** not natural: as **a** *or* **non·naturalistic** \(ˌ)⸗+\ **:** not dependent on, explainable in terms of, or reducible to natural or empirical observable characteristics but existing objectively as a spiritual or metaphysical reality apprehended by a priori intuition ⟨~ properties⟩ **:** INTUITIONIST ⟨nonnaturalistic ethics⟩ **b :** not conforming to the natural interpretation **:** FORCED ⟨a ~ way of viewing things⟩ **2** *or* **nonnaturalistic :** of, relating to, or having the characteristics of nonnaturalism or nonnaturalists

non·naturalism \(ˈ)⸗+\ *n* [ˈ*non-* + *naturalism*] **1 :** an art style that avoids representation of the objects and appearances of the natural world **:** an abstract or nonobjective art style **2 :** an ethical theory opposed to naturalism; *esp* **:** INTUITIONISM

non·naturalist \"+\ *n* [ˈ*non-* + *naturalist*] **:** an advocate or supporter of nonnaturalism

non·naturals \"+\ *n pl* [*nonnatural*] **:** the six things held in old medicine to be necessary to health

non·necessity \ˌ⸗+\ *n* **1 :** the condition of being unnecessary ⟨a certificate of ~⟩ **2 :** something that is unnecessary

non·negotiable \"+\ *adj* **:** not negotiable

non·nitrogenous \"+\ *adj* **:** not containing nitrogen

non·normative \(ˈ)⸗+\ *adj* **:** not based upon or employing a norm **:** OBJECTIVE ⟨analyzing political data in ~ empirical statements of verifiable relationships about the political behavior of men —Avery Leiserson⟩

non·notification \(ˌ)⸗+\ *n* [ˈ*non-* + *notification*] **:** a sale to a finance company or factor of an account receivable without informing the debtor who continues to remit to the vendor

non·novelist \(ˈ)⸗+\ *n* **:** one that is not a novelist

non·nucleated \(ˈ)⸗+\ *adj* **:** not nucleated

non·ny-non·ny \ˌnänēˈnänē, -äni\ [origin unknown] *archaic* — used as a refrain esp. in songs of the Elizabethan era

non·objective \ˌ⸗ *at* NON- +\ *adj* [ˈ*non-* + *objective*] **:** representing or intended to represent no concrete object of nature or natural appearance **:** NONREPRESENTATIONAL, ABSTRACT ⟨~ art⟩ ⟨~ paintings⟩ — **non·objectivity** \(ˌ)⸗+\ *n*

non·objectivism \ˌ⸗+\ *n* **:** the theory or practice of nonobjective painting

non·objectivist \"+\ *n* **:** an adherent or supporter of nonobjectivism

non·obligatory \ˌ⸗+, (ˈ)⸗+\ *adj* **:** not obligatory

non·observance \ˌ⸗+\ *n* **:** a lack of observance **:** failure to observe

non·ob·stan·te \ˌnänəbˈstantē, ˌnōn-\ *n* -s [ME *non obstante*, fr. L, notwithstanding, being no hindrance; fr. the medieval English use in statutes and letters patent of the L words *non obstante aliquo statuto in contrarium* notwithstanding any statute to the contrary] **1 :** a license from the crown to do a thing notwithstanding any statute to the contrary **2** *obs* **a :** a dispensation from or relaxation of a law or rule **b :** an exception to a rule

non obstante \"\ *prep* [L] **:** NOTWITHSTANDING — abbr. *non obst.*

non obstante ve·re·dic·to \-ˌverəˈdik(ˌ)tō\ [ML] **:** notwithstanding a verdict — used of a judgment entered by order of the court on motion of one party for that party notwithstanding a verdict for the other party (as when the record shows that the party for whom the verdict was rendered is not entitled to judgment as a matter of law) ⟨refer to judgment *non obstante veredicto* —Richard Hartshorne b.1888⟩

non·occurrence \ˌ⸗ *at* NON- +\ *n* **:** an absence or lack of occurrence

non·official \"+\ *adj* **:** not official: as **a :** not relating to, proceeding from, or approved by officials **:** having no official status ⟨~ points of view —*Atlantic*⟩ ⟨the panel of ~ advisers —*Manchester Guardian Weekly*⟩ **b :** UNOFFICIAL — **non·officially** \"+\ *adv*

no·no·ic acid \nōˈnōik-\ *n* [*nonoic* fr. *nonane* + *-oic*] **:** any of the numerous monocarboxylic acids $C_8H_{17}COOH$ (as pelargonic acid) derived from the nonanes

non·olfactory \ˌ⸗ *at* NON- +\ *adj* **:** not olfactory

no-nonsense \ˈ⸗ˌ⸗⸗\ *adj* [fr. the phrase *no nonsense*] **:** tolerating no nonsense **:** not frivolous **:** SERIOUS, BUSINESSLIKE ⟨the somber *no-nonsense* manner of a prosecuting attorney —Russell Baker⟩ ⟨a warmhearted, *no-nonsense* patrolman —*Lamp*⟩

¹non·op \(ˈ)näˈnäp\ *n, pl* **nonops** [short for *nonoperator*] **1 :** NONOPERATOR **2 :** a union composed of nonoperators ⟨the 17 ~s previously reached such an agreement with the Eastern railroads —*Progressive Labor World*⟩

²nonop \"\ *adj* [by shortening] **:** NONOPERATING ⟨agreed to the union shop for their ~ unions —*Americana Annual*⟩

non·opaque \(ˌ)⸗ *at* NON- +\ *adj* **:** not opaque

non·operating \(ˈ)⸗ *at* NON- +\ *adj* [ˈ*non-* + *operating*] **:** not operating: as **a :** of or relating to railroad employees (as telegraph operators, train dispatchers, signalmen) not directly engaged in train operation ⟨~ unions⟩ ⟨~ railroad workers⟩

b : arising from the minor operations of a business **:** AUXILIARY, SUPPLEMENTARY ⟨~ profits⟩

non·operator \"+\ *n* [¹*non-* + *operator*] **:** a nonoperating railroad employee

non·operculate \¦≠+\ *adj* **:** not operculate

non·optical \(')≠+\ *adj* **:** not optical

non·organic \¦≠+\ *adj* **:** not organic

non·palatal \(')≠+\ *adj* **:** not palatal

non·par \(')≠+\ *adj* [¹*non-* + *par*, n.] **:** being a bank that has not agreed to pay all checks drawn on it at par and so cannot join the par clearance system of the Federal Reserve system

non·parallel \"+\ *adj* **:** not parallel

non·parametric \(¦)≠+\ *adj* **:** not involving the estimation of parameter values of a distribution function ⟨~ methods⟩

non·parasitic \"+\ *adj* **:** not parasitic; *esp* **:** not caused by parasites — **non·parasitically** \"+\ *adv*

¹**non·pa·reil** \¦nänpə¦rel *sometimes* ¦nən- *or* -rī(ə)l *or* -rā(ə)l *or* -rē(ə)l *or, by British printers* 'nänprəl *or* 'nämp-\ *adj* [MF, fr. *non-* ¹non- + *pareil* equal, fr. (assumed) VL *pariculus*, fr. L *par* equal — more at PAIR] **:** having no equal **:** PEERLESS ⟨a lover's triumph in the ~ beauty of his mistress —Robert Lynd⟩

²**nonpareil** \"\ *n* -s **1 :** an individual of unequaled excellence **:** PARAGON ⟨the very ~ of tidiness and cleanliness —Eric Linklater⟩ ⟨~*s* whose conduct was a model for all time —Maurice Collis⟩ ⟨a virtuoso, a master, a ~ —S.H.Adams⟩ **2** [F *nonpareille*, fr. fem. of *nonpareil*, adj.] **a :** an old size of type (approximately 6 point) between agate and minion **b :** 6-point interlinear space or spacing material **3** [F *nonpareille*, fr. fem. of *nonpareil*, adj.] **a :** a small flat disk of chocolate covered with very small white pellets of sugar **b :** sugar in the form of small pellets of various colors used in covering candy or decorating cakes or cookies **4 :** PAINTED BUNTING

non·participant \¦≠ *at* NON-+\ *n* [¹*non-* + *participant*, n.] **:** one who does not participate

non·participating \"+\ *adj* **:** not participating; *specif* **:** not participating or not giving the right to participate in surplus or profit

non·participation \"+\ *n* **:** an absence or lack of participation

¹**non·partisan** \(')≠+\ *adj* **:** not partisan: as **a :** not affiliated with or committed to the support of a particular political party **:** politically independent ⟨labor will continue playing its ~ role of helping friends, opposing enemies —Sam Stavisky⟩ **b :** viewing matters or policies without party bias **:** OBJECTIVE, IMPARTIAL ⟨expected to be ~ in foreign affairs —Norman Hill & Eugene Haugse⟩ **c :** held or organized with all party designations or emblems absent from the ballot ⟨legislation to substitute ~ for partisan election of judges —G.R.Winters⟩ **d :** composed, appointed, or elected without regard to the political party affiliations of members ⟨a ~ ticket⟩ ⟨a ~ board⟩ ⟨a ~ commission⟩ — **non·partisanship** \"+\ *n*

²**nonpartisan** \"\ *n* **:** a person who is nonpartisan

nonpartisan ballot *n* **:** a ballot bearing no party designations

nonpartisan primary *n* **:** a direct primary in which all qualified voters may participate without regard to political affiliations and may vote usu. for two nominees for each office who are the two receiving the highest vote and whose names are placed on the ballot without any party designation

non·party \(')≠ *at* NON-+\ *adj* **:** not party: **a :** not affiliated with any political party ⟨~ delegates to a congress⟩ **b :** not based upon or representing political parties ⟨a ~ regime —*Atlantic*⟩ **c :** not actuated by party spirit **:** NONPARTISAN ⟨the ~ report by British members of Parliament —*Manchester Guardian Weekly*⟩

non·passerine \"+\ *adj* **:** not passerine — used esp. of birds of the order Coraciiformes

¹**non·past** \'≠¦≠\ *adj* [¹*non-* + *past*] *of a verb* **:** lacking inflection for a past tense **:** PRESENT **:** present and future

²**nonpast** \"\ *n* **:** a verb form or set of verb forms lacking inflection for a past tense

non·paternity \¦≠+\ *n* **:** the condition of not being the father of a particular child ⟨comparative blood tests established his ~ beyond question⟩

non·pathogenic \(¦)≠+\ *adj* **:** not capable of inducing disease — compare AVIRULENT

non·payment \(')≠+\ *n* [ME *nonpayement*, fr. ¹*non-* + *payement* payment] **:** neglect or failure to pay ⟨imprisonment for ~ of ordinary debts —Edward Jenks⟩

non·pecuniary \¦≠+\ *adj* **:** not consisting of money ⟨~ compensation allowable under law —*U. S. Code*⟩

non·performance \"+\ *n* **:** neglect or failure to perform

non·periodic \(¦)≠+\ *adj* **:** not periodic

non·peripteral \¦≠+\ *adj* **:** being without a row of columns ⟨a ~ temple⟩

non·perishable \(')≠+\ *adj* [¹*non-* + *perishable*] **:** processed or packaged to withstand prolonged storage — used esp. of foods; distinguished from *fresh* ⟨~ staples⟩

non·permanent \"+\ *adj* **:** not permanent; *specif* **:** being any one of six member states of the United Nations elected by the General Assembly for two-year terms as members of the Security Council who are not eligible for immediate reelection

non·personal \"+\ *adj* **:** not personal

non·petaloid \"+\ *adj* **:** not petaloid

non·philatelic \(')≠+\ *adj* **:** not philatelic

non·philosophic \"+\ *adj* **:** not philosophic

non·phonemic \(¦)≠+\ *adj* **:** not phonemic

non·phonetic \"+\ *adj* **:** not phonetic

non·physical \(')≠+\ *adj* **:** not physical **:** INTANGIBLE

non·physiological \(¦)≠+\ *adj* **:** not physiological

non·pictorial \¦≠+\ *adj* **:** not pictorial

non·pigmented \(')≠+\ *adj* **:** not pigmented

non·placental \¦≠+\ *adj* **:** lacking a placenta ⟨~ mammals⟩ **:** not involving a placenta ⟨~ gaseous exchange⟩

non pla·cet \(')nän'plāsət, (')nōn-\ *n, pl* **non placets** [L, it does not please] **:** a negative vote or expression of disapproval — used in ecclesiastical assemblies and in the legislative assemblies of some universities

non–placet \"\ *vt* -ED/-ING/-S [*non placet*] **:** to vote negatively on **:** REJECT, VETO ⟨the *non-placeted* ambassador to the Vatican —E.A.Peers⟩

non·plastic \(')≠ *at* NON- +\ *adj* **:** not plastic

¹**non·plus** \(')nän¦pləs\ *n, pl* **nonpluses** *or* **nonplusses** [L *non plus* no more] **:** a state of bafflement or perplexity **:** inability to proceed or decide **:** QUANDARY, DILEMMA ⟨reducing the young man to a ~ —Leigh Hunt⟩ ⟨appear to be at a ~ —George Borrow⟩

²**non·plus** *adj, obs* **:** NONPLUSSED, PERPLEXED

³**non·plus** \(')nän¦pləs\ *vt* **nonplussed** *also* **nonplused; nonplussed** *also* **nonplused; nonplussing** *also* **nonplusing; nonplusses** *also* **nonpluses :** to cause to be at a loss as to what to say, think, or do **:** reduce to a state of total incapacity to act or decide **:** PERPLEX, BAFFLE, STUMP ⟨this turn of events *nonplusses* me —J.R.Perkins⟩ ⟨*nonplussed* by the disclosure —*Newsweek*⟩ ⟨for a moment the girl was *nonplussed* —A.R. Williams⟩ **syn** see PUZZLE

non·poisonous \(')≠ *at* NON-+\ *adj* **:** not poisonous

non·polar \"+\ *adj* **:** not polar: **a :** relating to or being a combination in which two or more atoms with incomplete electron shells make up for their instability by sharing electrons and thus achieve completed outer shells which neither could attain individually **:** COVALENT **b :** lacking a dipole **:** having a low dielectric constant **:** NONIONIC

non·political \¦≠+\ *adj* **:** not political: as **a :** not influenced by or concerned with political considerations or issues ⟨our foundations are clearly ~ —L.U.Hauke⟩ ⟨~ experts appointed by Congress to serve as counselors —*Tomorrow*⟩ ⟨on a ~ tour inspecting the drought devastation —*Atlantic*⟩ **b :** NONPARTISAN ⟨appoint a ~ commission to cooperate with similar bodies in the states —*Rev. of Reviews*⟩ **c :** not interested in or concerned with politics **:** APOLITICAL ⟨the large ~ element in the population⟩

non·porous \(')≠+\ *adj* [¹*non-* + *porous*] **:** not porous; *specif* **:** not possessing vessels extending along the grain that appear as pores ⟨~ wood⟩

non·positive \"+\ *adj* **:** not positive **:** NEGATIVE, PRIVATIVE

non·possession \¦≠+\ *n* **:** an absence or lack of possession

non·possessor \"+\ *n, usu cap* [¹*non-* + *possessor*] **:** a member of a 16th century monastic movement within the Russian Orthodox Church, dedicated to prayer and meditation, to simplicity of life and dissociation from worldly affairs esp. as achieved through a life of solitude, and to the ideal of poverty to the extent of preferring to own no property either singly or collectively and particularly opposing the established custom of monasteries' owning farms worked by secular laborers

non pos·su·mus \(')nän'päs(y)əməs, (')nōn-\ *n, pl* **non possumus** [L, we cannot] **:** a statement expressing inability to do something ⟨had been compelled to express a *non possumus* —*Canadian Mining Jour.*⟩

non·precipitation \¦≠ *at* NON-+\ *n* **:** an absence or lack of precipitation

non·pregnant \(')≠+\ *adj* **:** not pregnant

non·prehensile \¦≠+\ *adj* **:** not prehensile

non·prescription drug \¦≠+-\ *or* **nonprescription medicine** *n* **:** a drug or medicine that can be bought without a doctor's prescription — see PROPRIETARY 6c

non·pressure \(')≠+\ *adj* **:** not having pressure

non·principled \(')≠+\ *adj* **:** having no concern with or awareness of principles **:** AMORAL ⟨not exactly unprincipled, but ~ —Joseph Furphy⟩

non·printing \"+\ *adj* **:** not printing

non·producer \¦≠+\ *n* **:** one that is not productive ⟨they carry the load, while the ~*s* ride —*Atlantic*⟩

non·productive \"+\ *adj* **1 :** failing to produce or yield **:** UNPRODUCTIVE ⟨consisted of four vines, all ~ —*Current Biog.*⟩ ⟨a ~ oil well⟩ **2 :** not directly productive **:** not creating exchangeable values ⟨~ labor⟩ **3** *of a cough* **:** not effective in raising mucus or exudate from the respiratory tract **:** DRY — **non·productively** \"+\ *adv* — **non·productiveness** \"+\ *n*

¹**non·professional** \"+\ *adj* **:** not professional: as **a :** having no profession ⟨the ~ . . . wives of their male colleagues —H.M.Parshley⟩ **b :** not belonging to or trained in a particular profession ⟨will not be read by very many ~ citizens —B.F. Wright⟩ **c :** engaging in or practicing some craft or art without previous training or professional status **:** AMATEUR ⟨~ actors⟩ — **non·professionally** \"+\ *adv*

²**nonprofessional** \"\ *n* **:** a person who is not a professional: as **a :** a person who does not belong to or possess training in a particular profession ⟨a book is of great value if it can give the ~ a clear, intelligible answer —Lise Meitner⟩ **b :** a person who engages in or practices some craft or art without previous training or professional status ⟨build a cast of ~*s* around an established cast —*Current Biog.*⟩

non·professionalism \"+\ *n* **:** an absence or lack of professionalism

non·profit \(')≠+\ *adj* [¹*non-* + *profit*, n.] **1 :** not conducted or maintained for the purpose of making a profit ⟨a ~ agency supported by endowments and private contributions —*Current Biog.*⟩ **2 :** not based on the profit motive **:** not organized on capitalistic principles **:** SOCIALIST ⟨decreed the creation of a ~ society —*Time*⟩

non·profitable \"+\ *adj* **:** not profitable

non·progressive \¦≠+\ *adj* **:** not progressive

non·proportional \"+\ *adj* **:** not proportional

non·propositional \(¦)≠+\ *adj* **:** not propositional

non·proprietary \¦≠+\ *adj* **:** not proprietary

non·pros \(')≠+¦präs\ *vt* **nonprossed; nonprossed; nonprossing; nonprosses** [fr. *non pros*, abbr. of *non prosequitur*] **:** to enter a non prosequitur against

non pro·se·qui·tur \¦nän(,)prō'sekwəd·ə(r), ¦nōn-\ *n, pl* **non prosequiturs** [LL, he does not prosecute] **:** a judgment entered against the plaintiff in a suit in which he does not appear to prosecute — abbr. *non pros.*; compare NOLLE PROSEQUI

non·protein \(')≠ *at* NON-+\ *n, often attrib* **1 :** a substance that is not a protein — compare PROSTHETIC **2 :** any or the sum of all of the plant or animal nitrogenous constituents (as asparagine of plants or urea and uric acid of urine or various extractives of muscle) that are less complex in structure than proteins ⟨~ nitrogen⟩

non·proven \"+\ *adj* **:** not established by proof **:** not proved ⟨what is ~ is its value —Anne Fremantle⟩

non·psychiatric \(¦)≠+\ *adj* **:** not psychiatric

non·public \(')≠+\ *adj* **:** not public

non·pungent \"+\ *adj* [¹*non-* + *pungent*] **:** UNPOINTED, BLUNT ⟨flexible ~ fin rays⟩

non·quota \"+\ *adj* [¹*non-* + *quota*, n.] **1 :** not included in or subject to a quota **:** of or relating to a nonquota immigrant ⟨~ visas⟩ **2 :** exceeding a quota ⟨a penalty tax on his ~ cotton —*Time*⟩

nonquota immigrant *n* **:** an immigrant not subject to the quota restrictions imposed by various U. S. immigration laws

non·radially \(')≠+\ *adv* **:** not radially

non·radioactive \(¦)≠+\ *adj* **:** not radioactive

non·random \"+\ *adj* **:** not random — **non·randomness** \"+\ *n*

non·rational \"+\ *adj* **:** not based on, guided by, or employing reason **:** not rational **:** IRRATIONAL ⟨they fight from ~ causes of a lower kind —Norman Angell⟩ ⟨there is a great deal that is ~ in modern cultures —*American Anthropologist*⟩

non·reactive \¦≠+\ *adj* [¹*non-* + *reactive*] **:** having no inductance or capacitance — used of a circuit offering only ohmic resistance to a current

nonreactive load *n* **:** a load consisting of ohmic resistance only

non·reader \(')≠ *at* NON-+\ *n* **:** a person who lacks the ability or desire to read; *specif* **:** a child in school whose progress in learning to read is exceedingly slow

non·realistic \(¦)≠+\ *adj* **:** not realistic: as **a :** not viewing matters in their true light **:** not practical **:** IMPRACTICAL, VISIONARY ⟨a ~ point of view⟩ **b :** not characterized by realism in conception and portrayal ⟨a ~ style⟩

non·reciprocal \¦≠+\ *adj* **:** not reciprocal or reciprocating

non·reciprocity \(¦)≠+\ *n* **:** the absence of reciprocity

non·recognition \"+\ *n* **:** absence of recognition **:** failure or refusal to recognize ⟨the doctrine of ~ of governments established by revolutionary means⟩

non·recourse \(¦)≠+\ *adj* [¹*non-* + *recourse*, n.] **:** not giving a holder the right to sue the borrower or endorser for a deficiency or loss — used esp. of price-support loans to farmers made by the Commodity Credit Corporation

nonrecourse loan *n* **:** a loan by which a lender agrees to accept the collateral security in lieu of repayment from the borrower if he is unable to pay or if the value of the security falls below the amount of the loan **:** a loan in which a lender under an endorsement without recourse discounts commercial paper for an endorser and agrees to accept the security and to hold the party primarily liable responsible and not the immediate endorser

non·rectilinear \"+\ *adj* **:** not rectilinear

non·recurrent \¦≠+\ *adj* **:** not recurrent

non·recurring \"+\ *adj* **:** not recurring

non·reducing \"+\ *adj* **:** not reducing; *specif* **:** not readily reducing Fehling solution or a similar reagent

non·reflexive \"+\ *adj, of a pronoun* **:** not reflexive

non·regent \(')≠+\ *n* **:** a Master of Arts at an English university whose regency has expired

non·regulation \(¦)≠+\ *adj* **:** not being in accordance with regulations ⟨a ~ uniform⟩

non·reimbursable \"+\ *adj* **:** not reimbursable

non·religious \¦≠+\ *adj* **1 :** not religious **:** not having a religious character **:** SECULAR ⟨the ~ nature of the art —*Nat'l Geographic*⟩ ⟨the state is not irreligious; it is simply ~ —W.L.Sperry⟩ **2 :** having no religion **:** IRRELIGIOUS ⟨a ~ individual may see little but show and outward circumstance in all this business —*Amer. Mercury*⟩

non·removable \"+\ *adj* **:** not removable

non rep *abbr* [L *non repetatur*] not to be repeated

¹**non·repatriable** \¦≠ *at* NON-+\ *adj* **:** being not repatriable; *specif* **:** displaced and stateless or not capable of being repatriated for any of a variety of reasons (as unwillingness to return to one's former country) ⟨a plan to rehabilitate and resettle these ~ victims of German action —Eli Ginzberg⟩

²**nonrepatriable** \"\ *n* -s **:** a person who is nonrepatriable

non·representational \(¦)≠+\ *adj* **:** not representing or imitating external reality or the objects of nature **:** ABSTRACT, NONFIGURATIVE, NONOBJECTIVE ⟨~ art⟩ — **non·representationalism** \"+\ *n*

non·representative \"+\ *adj* **:** not representative: as **a :** not typical or characteristic ⟨rendered them ~ of the great majority —*Popular Science Monthly*⟩ **b :** NONREPRESENTATIONAL ⟨stressing ~ design —Thomas Munro⟩

non·residence \(')≠+\ *also* **non·residency** \"+\ *n* [*nonresidence* fr. ME *noun residense*, fr. *noun-*, *non* ¹non- + *residense*, *residence* residence; *nonresidency* fr. ¹*non-* + *residency*] **:** the state or fact of being nonresident

¹**non·resident** \"+\ *adj* [¹*non-* + *resident*] **1 :** not residing in a particular place or a place referred to by implication ⟨a ~ student⟩; *specif* **:** having one's permanent residence away from one's benefice, charge, or estate ⟨a ~ clergyman⟩ **2 :** of or relating to a nonresident ⟨nearly four hundred ~ licenses were sold —*Alaska Sportsman*⟩

²**nonresident** \"\ *n* **:** a nonresident person ⟨most of the land is owned by ~*s* —J.L.Christian⟩

non·residenter \"+\ *n* [*nonresident* + *-er*] **:** NONRESIDENT

non·residential \(¦)≠+\ *adj* **:** not residential

non·resistance \¦≠+\ *n* [¹*non-* + *resistance*] **:** the principles or practice of a nonresistant **:** passive obedience or submission

¹**non·resistant** \"+\ *adj* [¹*non-* + *resistant*] **:** not resistant: as **a :** practicing or adhering to nonresistance ⟨pacifist and ~ in attitude and program —G.F.Hershberger⟩ **b :** not capable of resisting **:** incapable of offering opposition (as to a disease) **:** SUSCEPTIBLE ⟨~ strains of mice⟩

²**nonresistant** \"\ *n* **:** a person who maintains or acts on the theory that no resistance should be made to constituted authority even when unjust or oppressive; *also* **:** one who holds that violence should never be resisted by force

non·resister \¦≠+\ *n* **:** NONRESISTANT

non·resisting \"+\ *adj* **:** not resisting **:** NONRESISTANT

non·restraint \"+\ *n* **:** an absence or lack of restraint

non·restricted \"+\ *adj* **:** not restricted **:** not subject to restrictions

non·restrictive \"+\ *adj* **:** not restrictive; *specif* **:** not limiting the reference of a modified word or phrase

nonrestrictive clause *n* **:** a descriptive clause that adds information but is so loosely attached to the main clause as to be not essential to the definiteness of its meaning and to be marked off from it by commas (as in "the aldermen, *who were present*, assented")

non·retractable \"+\ *adj* **:** not retractable

non·retractile \"+\ *adj* **:** not retractile

non·returnable \"+\ *adj* **:** not returnable; *specif* **:** not returnable to the vendor or dealer ⟨the ~ beer bottle⟩

non·return valve \"+-\ *n* **:** CHECK VALVE

non·revenue \(')≠+\ *adj* [¹*non-* + *revenue*] **1 :** not productive of revenue ⟨~ equipment⟩ **2 :** not arising from current revenue

nonreversible \¦≠+\ *adj* **:** not reversible

non·rhythmic \(')≠+\ *adj* **:** not rhythmic

¹**non·rigid** \"+\ *adj* [¹*non-* + *rigid*] **:** maintaining form by pressure of contained gas ⟨a ~ airship⟩

²**nonrigid** \"\ *n* -s **:** an airship of nonrigid type

non·rotatable \(¦)≠+\ *adj* **:** that does not rotate

non·ruminant \"+\ *adj* **:** not ruminant

non·ruminantia \¦≠+\ *n pl, cap* [NL, fr. ¹*non-* + *Ruminantia*] *in some classifications* **:** the Artiodactyla exclusive of the Ruminantia

non·sacred \(')≠ *at* NON- +\ *adj* **:** not sacred

non·sapi·ens \(')nän¦sapēənz, -sāp- *also* -ē,enz *or* -ē,en(t)s\ *adj* [¹*non-* + NL *sapiens* (specific epithet of *Homo sapiens*) fr. L *sapient-*, *sapiens* wise — more at SAPIENT] **:** of, relating to, or being any of the extinct men that are usu. treated as distinct from recent man at a species or higher level

non·scheduled \(')≠ *at* NON- +\ *adj* [¹*non-* + *scheduled*, past part. of *schedule*] **:** licensed to carry passengers or freight by air between authorized points as frequently as demand requires and not on a regular schedule ⟨a ~ airline⟩ ⟨~ service⟩

non·school \'≠¦-\ *adj* **1 :** not being in school **2 :** not connected with school

non·scientific \(¦)≠+\ *adj* **:** not scientific: as **a :** not based on fact or empirical methods of inquiry **:** not being in conformity with the methods or principles of science ⟨~ theories⟩ **b :** not having the professional status of a scientist **:** not trained in science ⟨the ~ reader⟩

non·scientist \(')≠+\ *n* **:** a person who is not a scientist or who lacks training in the sciences

non·seasonal \"+\ *adj* **:** not seasonal

non·secretor \¦≠+\ *n* [¹*non-* + *secretor*] **:** an individual who lacks water-soluble group-specific substances

non·secretory \"+\ *adj* **:** not secretory

non·sectarian \"+\ *adj* **:** not having a sectarian character **:** not restricted to or dominated by a particular religious group ⟨~ colleges⟩ ⟨religious training in a ~ atmosphere⟩

non·segregated \(')≠+\ *adj* **:** UNSEGREGATED ⟨not one of us ever spent a day in a ~ school —F.A.Perry⟩

non·segregation \(¦)≠+\ *n* **:** the absence of segregation esp. of individuals or groups from a larger group or from society ⟨a defiant enclave of ~ in segregated Virginia —*Time*⟩ — compare DESEGREGATION, INTEGRATION

non·selective \¦≠+\ *adj* **:** not selective

non–self–governing \(¦)≠+\ *adj* **:** not self-governing **:** not independent ⟨*non-self-governing* territories⟩

¹**non·sense** \'nän,sen(t)s, -sən-\ *n* **1 a :** something that is not sense or has no sense **:** words or language having no meaning or conveying no intelligible ideas ⟨apples harvest — the words are now ~; they have lost their grammar —Charlton Laird⟩ **b :** something written or said that is absurd or contrary to good sense **:** TWADDLE, DRIVEL ⟨a lot of ~ has been uttered —R.A. Lester⟩ ⟨no throaty oratorical ~ was there —W.A.White⟩ **c** (1) **:** conduct or a course of action that is absurd or contrary to good sense **:** a piece of absurdity ⟨this, of course, makes ~ of the liberation policy —*New Statesman & Nation*⟩ ⟨this attitude is, manifestly, ~ —Allan Sangster⟩ ⟨the ~ that the ragged rebels spoke of as their War for Independence —F.V. W.Mason⟩ (2) **:** an instance of nonsensical action ⟨if this did happen to be just a ~ —Nigel Balchin⟩ ⟨dispelling his many ~*s* —*Amer. Anthropologist*⟩ **d :** a concrete object whose acceptance or use is contrary to good sense ⟨an Eskimo cloak makes perfect sense in the Arctic regions, though it . . . is ~ in Guayaquil —Gustave Weigel⟩ ⟨never pay any attention to the ~ of omens —George Meredith⟩ **2 a :** things of no importance or value **:** TRIFLES, FOLDEROL, FRILLS ⟨the raincoats are classic, without any ~ —*New Yorker*⟩ **b :** foolish, affected, impudent or frivolous conduct or manner **:** FOOLING, HUMBUG ⟨the Indians of those regions would stand no ~ —S.E.Morison & H.S.Commager⟩ ⟨were taught to recite poetry when asked and no ~ —Katherine A. Porter⟩ ⟨a brisk old lady with no ~ about her —Jean Stafford⟩

²**nonsense** \"\ *adj* **1** *archaic* **:** NONSENSICAL **2 a :** being a verse (as *ibbety, bibbety, sibbety, sab*) consisting of words or syllables arranged primarily with regard to meter and not to sense **b :** being a poem or other literary composition of humorous or whimsical character typically with odd, grotesque, or anomalous themes, characters, and actions and often marked by the use of words coined for the purpose that sometimes have an evocative character but no precise or generally accepted meaning ⟨limericks and other types of ~ poetry⟩ **3 :** being a simulated unit of speech (as a word or syllable) fabricated by arbitrary grouping of speech sounds or symbols and pronounced to provide a test as of ability to apprehend speech sounds or word or syllable boundaries ⟨'shkrög,thyəmpth is a ~ word⟩ ⟨a linguistic response like the ~ syllable provides . . . a highly differentiable but easily recognizable response —J.B.Carroll⟩

non·sen·si·cal \(')nän¦sen(t)səkəl, -sēk-\ *adj* **1 a :** being nonsense or full of nonsense **:** UNMEANING, ABSURD, FOOLISH, PREPOSTEROUS ⟨asked a ~ question —W.F.de Morgan⟩ ⟨refused to modify his opinions, even when the plain facts made them ~ —Douglas Stewart⟩ **b :** characterized by or revealing absurd or foolish speech, thoughts, or acts ⟨subjected to strains and stresses by their ~ wives —*Irish Digest*⟩ **2 a :** NONSENSE 3 ⟨if ~ syllables are used as test material —G.A.Miller⟩ **b :** NONSENSE 2 ⟨represented by a few light ~ sketches —Marc Slonim⟩ — **non·sen·si·cal·i·ty** \,≠(,)≠≠'kaləd·ē, -ətē, -i\ *n* -ES — **non·sen·si·cal·ly** \-sək(ə)lē, -ēk-, -li\ *adv* — **non·sen·si·cal·ness** \(')≠¦sen(t)səkəlnəs, -sēk-\ *n* -ES

non·sensitive \(ˈ)≡ *at* NON- +\ *adj* **:** not sensitive; *specif* **:** not involving or related to the national security ⟨employees in ~ jobs may not be dismissed as security risks —*Time*⟩
non·septate \"+\ *adj* **:** not septate
non se·qui·tur \(ˈ)nän'sekwəd·ə(r), ˈnōn-, -sākwə̇,tü(ə)r\ *n, pl* **non sequiturs** [L, it does not follow] **:** an inference that does not follow from the premises; *specif* **:** a fallacy resulting from a simple conversion of a universal affirmative proposition or from the transposition of a condition and its consequent
non·settler \(ˈ)≡ *at* NON- +\ *n* [¹*non-* + *settler*] **:** a domestic animal (as a cow) persistently failing to conceive or settle to service or insemination
non·sexual \"+\ *adj* **:** not sexual
¹**non·significant** \¦≡+\ *n* [¹*non-* + *significant*, n.] **:** ²NULL 2
²**nonsignificant** \"\ *adj* [¹*non-* + *significant*, adj.] **:** not significant: as **a :** having slight or no importance **:** INSIGNIFICANT ⟨cluttered up with ~ features —R.A.Hall b.1911⟩ **b :** having or conveying no meaning ⟨inserted ~ symbols —W.W.R.Ball⟩
non·silicate \(ˈ)≡+\ *n* **:** a substance that is not a silicate
non·sked \"+¦sked\ *n* -s [by shortening & alter. fr. *nonscheduled*] **:** an air transport carrier that offers service at irregular times, at less frequent intervals, and often at lower fares than certificated scheduled service; *also* **:** a nonscheduled transport plane
¹**non·skid** \(ˈ)≡+\ *adj* [¹*non-* + *skid*, n. or *skid*, v.] **1 :** designed to reduce or prevent skidding **2** *of an automobile tire* **:** having the tread corrugated or otherwise specially constructed to resist skidding
²**nonskid** \"\ *n* **:** a nonskid tire
non·slaveholding \"+\ *adj* **:** not allowing slavery or not inhabited by slaveholders ⟨the ~ North⟩ ⟨~ states⟩
non·slip \"+\ *adj* [¹*non-* + *slip*, n. or *slip*, v.] **:** designed to reduce or prevent slipping ⟨~ concrete⟩
non·smoker \"+\ *n* **:** a person who does not smoke
non·social \"+\ *adj* **:** having no social character; *specif* **:** not directed toward others ⟨~ behavior⟩
non·solid \"+\ *adj* **:** not solid
non·spatial \"+\ *adj* **:** not spatial
non·speaking \"+\ *adj* **:** involving no spoken lines ⟨~ part in a play⟩
non·specialist \"+\ *n* **:** a person who is not a specialist in a particular subject
non·specialized \"+\ *adj* **:** not specialized ⟨~ duties⟩
non·specific \¦≡+\ *adj* **:** not specific; *esp* **:** not caused by a specific agent ⟨~ adenitis⟩ ⟨~ enteritis⟩
non·spectral \(ˈ)≡+\ *adj* [¹*non-* + *spectral*] **:** not being in the spectrum; *esp* **:** purple in the range from red to violet
non·speculative \"+\ *adj* **:** not speculative
non·spillable \"+\ *adj* **:** not spillable
non·spore–forming \"+\ *adj* **:** not producing spores
non·sporting \"+\ *adj* **1 :** lacking the qualities characteristic of a gundog or hunting dog ⟨the Newfoundland is a ~ breed that has contributed valuable characteristics to various of the retrievers⟩ **2** *of a plant or animal variety* **:** not giving rise to sports **:** not subject to frequent mutation
non·staining \"+\ *adj* **:** not staining ⟨a ~ medicine⟩ **:** incapable of being stained ⟨~ elements in cells⟩
non·standard \"+\ *adj* **1 :** not standard **2** *of language* **:** not conforming in pronunciation, grammatical construction, idiom, or choice of word to the usage generally characteristic of educated native speakers of the language ⟨the common core of ~ words and phrases in folk speech —A.R.Dunlap⟩ — compare SUBSTANDARD
non·stellar \"+\ *adj* **:** not stellar; *specif* **:** being a celestial object (as an asteroid) that resembles a star but is not a star
non·stock \"+\ *adj* [¹*non-* + *stock*, n.] **:** not organized for profit and so having no stock outstanding ⟨~ corporations⟩
non·stoichiometric \(¦)≡+\ *adj* **:** not stoichiometric
¹**non·stop** \(ˈ)≡+\ *adj* [¹*non-* + *stop*, n.] **1 :** made without a stop ⟨a ~ journey⟩; *specif* **:** made without intermediate landings between takeoff and destination ⟨a ~ flight⟩ **2 :** made or held without a pause or interruption ⟨a ~ dive-bombing attack⟩ ⟨a ~ performance⟩ ⟨a 25-hour ~ conference —*Time*⟩
²**nonstop** \"\ *adv* **:** without a stop ⟨rushed ~ through his Latin —Bruce Marshall⟩
non·striated \(ˈ)≡+\ *adj* **:** being without striations
nonstriated muscle *n* **:** SMOOTH MUSCLE
nonstriker \"+\ *n* [¹*non-* + *striker*] **1 :** a batsman in cricket who is in but is not receiving the bowling — compare STRIKER **2 :** a worker who is not on strike
non·structural \"+\ *adj* **:** not structural
non·subjective \¦≡+\ *adj* **:** not subjective
non·subscriber \"+\ *n* **:** a person who does not subscribe; *specif* **:** one who refuses to subscribe to a confession of faith or covenant (as the National Covenant of 1638 in the Church of Scotland)
nonsuch *var of* NONESUCH
non·such chest *also* **none·such chest** \ˈnən,səch-\ *n* [perh. fr. *Nonsuch* palace, Cheam, Surrey] **:** a chest popular in the later 16th and early 17th centuries with front panels decorated in inlay of architectural design
non·sugar \ˈ≡ *at* NON- +\ *n* **:** a substance that is not a sugar; *esp* **:** AGLYCON
¹**non·suit** \(ˈ)≡ *at* NON- +\ *n* [ME, fr. AF *nounsuyte*, fr. *noun-* ¹*non-* + OF *suite, sieute* following, pursuit — more at SUIT] **:** a judgment given against a plaintiff because of his failure to prosecute his case or his inability to establish a prima facie case at the trial
²**nonsuit** \"\ *adj* [ME *non suit*, fr. *nonsuit*, n.] *archaic* **:** NONSUITED
³**nonsuit** \"\ *vt* [¹*nonsuit*] **1 :** to determine, adjudge, or record (a plaintiff) as having terminated a suit by default or failure to establish a good cause of action **:** subject to a nonsuit — used in strict common-law practice only of the termination of the suit on motion of the defendant against a defaulting plaintiff but in modern practice of other terminations of a case not on the merits (as by a nolle prosequi); compare DISCONTINUANCE **2** *obs* **:** to deny the suit of
non·superconducting \(¦)≡+\ *adj* **:** not superconducting
non·superimposable \"+\ *adj* **:** not capable of being superimposed
non·support \¦≡+\ *n* **1 :** lack of support **:** failure to support ⟨use the threat of ~ . . . to bring recalcitrants in his party to heel —R.H.Rovere⟩ **2 :** failure on the part of one under obligation either by contract or by statutory liability to provide maintenance or means of sustenance
non·surgical \(ˈ)≡+\ *adj* **:** not surgical
non·syllabic \¦≡+\ *adj* **:** not constituting a syllable or the nucleus of a syllable: **a** *of a consonant* **:** accompanied in the same syllable by a vowel ⟨\n\ is syllabic in \ˈbätᵊnē\ *botany*, — in \ˈbätnē\⟩ **b** *of a vowel* **:** having vowel quality less prominent than that of another vowel in the syllable ⟨the second vowel of a falling diphthong, as \i\ in \ȯi\, is ~⟩
non·symbiotic \(¦)≡+\ *adj* **:** not living or occurring in a state of mutualism or symbiosis — **non·symbiotically** \"+\ *adv*
non·symmetrical \¦≡+\ *adj* **:** UNSYMMETRICAL
non·sync \(ˈ)≡+¦siŋk\ *n* -s [short for *nonsynchronous turntable*, fr. *nonsynchronous* not synchronous (fr. ¹*non-* + *synchronous*) + *turntable*] **:** an accessory pair of ordinary phonograph turntables and pickups in a sound-on-film reproducing system used to provide musical interludes and background music for silent films
non tan·to \(ˈ)nän·ˈtän·(,)tō, (ˈ)nōn-, -tȧn-\ *adv (or adj)* [It, lit., not so much] **:** NON TROPPO
nontaster \ˈ≡ *at* NON- +\ *n* **:** a person unable to taste the chemical phenylthiourea
non·tax \(ˈ)≡+\ *adj* **1 :** not related to taxation ⟨~ matters⟩ **2 :** not derived directly from taxation ⟨~ funds⟩
non–tax–paid \(ˈ)≡+\ *adj* **:** not having had the tax paid ⟨contained eighty gallons of *non-tax-paid* liquor —*Beam v. Georgia*⟩
non·technical \(ˈ)≡*at* NON- +\ *adj* **:** not technical: as **a :** not related to technique or to technical skills or subjects ⟨~ training⟩ ⟨the ~ aspects of a performance⟩ **b :** not employing the words, expressions, or meanings peculiar or largely confined to a particular occupation or science ⟨~ language⟩ **:** written or phrased in a plain manner easily comprehended by laymen ⟨an excellent ~ guide —D.H.Kupfer⟩ — **nontechnically** *adv*
non·temporal \"+\ *adj* **:** not temporal
non·tenure \"+\ *n* [AF *nountenure*, fr. *noun-* ¹*non-* + MF *tenure*] **:** a former plea in bar made by a defendant in a real action setting up that he did not hold the land **:** a plea denying a demise or letting
non·term \"+\ *n* **:** the vacation between two terms of a law-court
non·terminal \"+\ *adj* **:** not terminal
non·theatrical \¦≡+\ *adj* **:** not theatrical: as **a :** not designed for or presented in a theater ⟨tended to be more dramatic in his ~ works —Irving Kolodin⟩ **b :** of or relating to a moving picture esp. on film of substandard size that is designed primarily for showing in the home, classroom, or assembly hall ⟨the wholly ~ film tends to be of two- to three-reel length —Raymond Spottiswoode⟩
non·theistic \"+\ *adj* **:** not theistic
non·tidal \(ˈ)≡+\ *adj* **:** not tidal
non·tournament \"+\ *adj* **:** not involving tournament play
non·toxic \"+\ *adj* **:** not toxic; *often* **:** free from toxicity for an indicated organism or a warm-blooded vertebrate at concentrations normally employed ⟨~ insecticides⟩
non·traditional \¦≡+\ *adj* **:** not traditional; *specif* **:** not conforming to tradition ⟨~ practices⟩ ⟨~ designs⟩
nontransferable \(¦)≡+\ *adj* **:** not transferable
non·transparency \¦≡+\ *n* **:** the quality or state of being not transparent
non·transparent \(¦)≡+\ *adj* **:** not transparent
non·tron·ite \ˈnän·trə,nīt\ *n* -s [F *nontronite*, fr. *Nontron*, town in southwest France + F *-ite*] **:** a pale yellow or greenish clay mineral that consists chiefly of hydrous iron silicate and is classed as montmorillonite in which iron has replaced more or less of the aluminum
non·tropical \(ˈ)≡ *at* NON- +\ *adj* **:** not tropical
nontropical sprue *n* **:** CELIAC DISEASE
non trop·po \(ˈ)nän'trä(,)pō, (ˈ)nōn-, -trȯ-, -trō-\ *adv (or adj)* [It, lit., not too much] **:** without excess — used to qualify a direction in music ⟨*non troppo* presto⟩
non·trump \(ˈ)≡ *at* NON- +\ *adj* [¹*non-* + *trump*, n.] **:** not having a trump ⟨a ~ hand⟩ **:** not being trumps ⟨a ~ suit⟩
non·umbilicate \(¦)≡+\ *adj* **:** characterized by lack or closure of the umbilicus ⟨~ shells⟩
non·uniform \(ˈ)≡+\ *adj* [¹*non-* + *uniform*] **:** not uniform — **non·uniformly** \"+\ *adv*
non·uniformist \"+\ *n* [*nonuniform* + *-ist*] **:** a person who believes that past changes in the structure of the earth have proceeded from cataclysms or processes more violent than are now operating — called also *nonuniformitarian*
non·uniformitarian \(¦)≡+\ *n* [*nonuniformity* + *-arian*] **:** NONUNIFORMIST
non·uniformity \"+\ *n* [¹*non-* + *uniformity*] **:** the fact, condition, or an instance of being nonuniform **:** absence of uniformity ⟨such *nonuniformities* are greater with the faster heating process —F.O.Hess⟩ ⟨~ of composition⟩
¹**non·union** \(ˈ)≡+\ *adj* [¹*non-* + *union*, adj.] **1 :** not belonging to or affiliated with a trade union ⟨~ carpenters⟩ **2 :** not recognizing or favoring trade unions or trade unionists ⟨a ~ contractor⟩
²**nonunion** \"\ *n* [¹*non-* + *union*, n.] **:** lack of union **:** failure to unite; *specif* **:** failure of the fragments of a broken bone to knit together
non·unionism \"+\ *n* [*nonunion* + *-ism*] **:** the theories, opinions, or practices of those who do not support trade unions
non·unionist \"+\ *n* [¹*non-* + *unionist*] **:** a person who does not belong to a trade union
nonunion shop *n* **1 :** an establishment in which the employer recognizes no labor union and excludes from employment anyone affiliated with a labor union **2 :** a shop in which a labor union forbids its members to accept employment
non·uple \ˈnä,n(y)üpəl, ≡ˈ≡≡; ˈnänəp-\ *adj* [F, fr. MF, fr. L *nonus* ninth + MF *-ple* (as in *quadruple*) — more at NOON] **1 :** consisting of nine **:** being nine times as great or as many **:** NINEFOLD **2 :** taken by nines or in groups of nine
non·u·plet \-plə̇t\ *n* -s [L *nonus* ninth + E *-plet* (as in *triplet*)] **1 :** a combination of nine of a kind **2 :** a group of nine musical notes to be performed in the time of eight or six
non·use \(ˈ)≡ *at* NON- +\ *n* **1 :** failure to use ⟨influence consumers in their use or ~ of citrus products —*Consumers' Use of & Opinions About Citrus Products*⟩ **2 :** the fact or condition of not being used ⟨difficult to explain its ~ by scholars⟩
¹**non·user** \"+\ *n* [¹*non-* + *-user* (as in ²*misuser*)] **:** neglect or omission to use **:** failure to exercise a legal right or privilege
²**nonuser** \"\ *n* [¹*non-* + *user*] **:** one who is not a user
non·vascular \"+\ *adj* **:** not vascular
non·venomous \"+\ *adj* **:** not venomous
non·verbal \"+\ *adj* **:** not verbal: as **a :** being other than verbal ⟨the various ~ elements which are background to conversation —David Abercrombie⟩ **b :** involving, using, or requiring minimal or no use of language ⟨~ tests⟩ ⟨animal communication is always ~ —Stuart Chase⟩ **c :** ranking low in verbal skill **:** lacking facility in the use and comprehension of words ⟨simplified spelling for ~ types —W.H.Auden⟩ ⟨rural students . . . often come from ~ background —Julia F. Sherbourne⟩
non·vernalized \"+\ *adj* **:** not vernalized; *specif* **:** not subjected to low temperatures in early stages of germination to hasten flowering and fruiting ⟨~ seeds⟩
non·viable \"+\ *adj* **:** not viable **:** not capable of living, growing, or developing and functioning successfully ⟨a ~ theory⟩ ⟨~ embryos⟩
non·vibratile \"+\ *adj* **:** not vibratile
non·vibratory \"+\ *adj* **:** not vibratory
non·vintage \"+\ *adj* [¹*non-* + *vintage*, n.] **:** undated and usu. blended to approximate a standard ⟨a ~ wine⟩
non·violence \"+\ *n* **:** abstention on principled grounds from all use of violence; *also* **:** the ideal, doctrine, or principle of such abstention from all use of violence ⟨complete ~ is complete absence of ill will against all —D.M.Brown⟩ ⟨exalt ~, which . . . they consider the sublime ethics —Albert Schweitzer⟩
non·violent \"+\ *adj* **:** abstaining on principled grounds from all use of violence **:** not carried on or done with the use of violence **:** PEACEFUL ⟨by methods of . . . passive resistance and ~ sabotage —Edmond Taylor⟩ — **non·violently** \"+\ *adv*
non·viscous \"+\ *adj* **:** not viscous
non·vocal \"+\ *adj* **:** not vocal
non·vocalic \"+\ *adj* **:** not vocalic ⟨~ phonemes⟩
non·volatile \"+\ *adj* **:** not volatile; *esp* **:** not volatilizing readily ⟨a ~ acid⟩
nonvolatile vehicle *n* **:** the liquid portion of a paint aside from its volatile thinner and water
non·voting \(ˈ)≡*at* NON- +\ *adj* **1 :** not voting **:** not exercising the right to vote ⟨the ~ element in the population⟩ **2 :** not entitling the holder to vote ⟨~ preferred stock⟩
non vult con·ten·de·re \¦nän,vəltkən'tendə,rē, ¦nōn-\ *or* **non vult** *n, pl* **non vult contenderes** *or* **non vults** [L *non vult contendere* he does not wish to contend] **:** NOLO CONTENDERE
non·war \(ˈ)≡ *at* NON- +\ *adj* **:** not serving or used for military purposes ⟨~ industries⟩ ⟨~ products⟩
non·white \"+\ *n* **:** a person who is not of the white race ⟨thousands of ~s —D.T.Bogue⟩
²**nonwhite** \"\ *adj* **:** of or relating to a race that is not white ⟨47 percent of the ~ population . . . were under 20 years of age —H.W.Odum⟩
non·worker \(ˈ)≡+\ *n* **1 :** a person who does not work ⟨the rule is that ~s shall not eat⟩ **2 :** a person (as a self-employed man) who is not an employee
non·woven \"+\ *adj* **:** made without weaving; *esp* **:** having textile fibers bonded together by adhesive resins, rubber, or plastic or felted together under pressure ⟨~ fabrics⟩
non·yl \ˈnä,nil, ˈnō,-, -ēl\ *n* -s [ISV *nonane* + *-yl*] **:** an alkyl radical C_9H_{19} derived from a nonane; *esp* **:** the normal radical $CH_3(CH_2)_7CH_2$—
nonyl alcohol *n* **:** any of several alcohols $C_9H_{19}OH$ derived from the nonanes; *esp* **:** primary or 1-nonanol
non·yl·ene \ˈnänᵊl,ēn, ˈnō-\ *n* -s [ISV *nonyl* + *-ene*] **:** any of several liquid isomeric hydrocarbons C_9H_{18} of the ethylene series
no·nyl·ic acid \nō'nilik-\ *n* [*nonylic* ISV *nonyl* + *-ic*] **:** NONOIC ACID
non·zero \(ˈ)≡ *at* NON- +\ *adj* **:** not being or involving zero
noo \ˈnü\ *dial var of* NOW
noo- *comb form* [LGk *noo-*, fr. Gk *noos, nous*] **:** mind ⟨*noo*scopic⟩
¹**noo·dle** \ˈnüdᵊl\ *n* -s [perh. alter. of ¹*noddle*] **1 :** a stupid person **:** SIMPLETON, BLOCKHEAD, NINNY **2 :** NODDLE, HEAD ⟨try to get this into your ~⟩
²**noodle** \"\ *n* -s [G *nudel*] **:** a food paste made with egg and shaped typically in ribbon form
³**noodle** \"\ *vt* **noodled; noodled; noodling** \-d(ə)liŋ\ **noodles** [prob. fr. G *nudeln*, fr. *nudel*, n.] **:** to feed (geese) forcibly with a fattening mixture in the form of an elongated roll
⁴**noodle** \"\ *vb* -ED/-ING/-S [origin unknown] *vt, chiefly Midland* **:** to catch (fish) with the bare hands or with a crude hook held in the hand **:** GUDDLE **~** *vi, chiefly Midland* **:** to fish with the bare hands
⁵**noodle** \"\ *vb* -ED/-ING/-S [imit.] *vi* **1 :** to prelude or improvise on an instrument in an informal or desultory manner ⟨background of soft *noodling* by a clarinet⟩ ⟨went to the piano and *noodled* around until the tune came back to him⟩ **2 :** to work over or elaborate the lines (as of a drawing) so as to impair the spontaneity and freedom **~** *vt* **:** to work over (a drawing)
noo·dle·dom \-ᵊldəm\ *n* -s **1 :** the world of fools **2 :** FOOLISHNESS, STUPIDITY
noodlehead \ˈ≡,≡\ *n* **:** NOODLE, BLOCKHEAD
noo·goo·ra burr \nü'gürə\ *n, usu cap N* [*noogoora* (of unknown origin) + *burr*] **:** a European cocklebur (*Xanthium pungens*) that is a noxious weed in Australia
nook \ˈnu̇k\ *n* -s [ME *noke, nok*, perh. of Scand origin; akin to Norw dial. *nok* hook] **1** *chiefly Scot* **:** a corner of a rectangular piece (as of paper or cloth) or surface (as a field) **2** *obs* **:** a projecting piece of land **:** PROMONTORY **3** *chiefly Scot* **:** a projecting corner of a building or of an obstruction (as a hedge) **4 a :** an interior angle formed by two meeting walls **:** RECESS ⟨chimney ~⟩ **b :** a remote, secluded, sheltered, or out-of-the-way place or part ⟨odd ~s and corners of knowledge⟩ ⟨searched every ~ and cranny⟩ ⟨resting in a shady ~⟩
nooked \ˈnu̇kt\ *adj, chiefly Scot* **:** having corners or angles ⟨a four-*nooked* bit of paper —Sir Walter Scott⟩
nook·ery \ˈnu̇k(ə)rē\ *n* -ES **:** a snug or cozy place or room
nook·let \-klə̇t\ *n* -s **:** a little nook
nook·sack *or* **nook·sak** \ˈnu̇k,sak\ *also* **noot·sack** *or* **noot·sak** \ˈnüt,-, ˈnu̇t,-\ *n, pl* **nooksack** *or* **nooksacks** *or* **nooksak** *or* **nooksaks** *usu cap* **1 a :** a Salishan people of the Nooksack river valley, Washington **b :** a member of such people **2 :** the language of the Nooksack people
nook shaft *n* **:** a column set in a reentering angle (as that made by the parts of a compound pier) differing from an angle shaft in standing free and being therefore usu. larger
nook·shot·ten \ˈnu̇k,shätᵊn\ *adj* [*nook* + obs. E *shotten*, past part. of E *shoot*] *chiefly dial* **:** jutting out at numerous angles
¹**nooky** \ˈnu̇kē, -ki\ *adj* -ER/-EST [*nook* + *-y*, adj. suffix] **1 :** full of nooks **2 :** like a nook
²**nooky** \"\ *n* -ES [prob. fr. *nook* + *-y*, n. suffix forming diminutives] **:** ⁴PUSSY — usu. considered vulgar
no·olog·i·cal \¦nōə¦läjə̇kəl\ *adj* [*noology* + *-ical*] **:** relating to mind or to mental character ⟨~ anthropology⟩
no·ol·o·gy \nō'äləjē\ *n* -ES [LGk *noo-* (fr. Gk *noos, nous* mind) + E *-logy*] **:** the study of mind **:** the science of phenomena regarded as purely mental in origin
¹**noon** \ˈnün\ *n* -s *often attrib* [ME, ninth hour of the day counting from sunrise, noon, midday, fr. OE *nōn* ninth hour of the day counting from sunrise, fr. L *nona*, fr. fem. of *nonus* ninth; akin to Skt *navama* ninth, L *novem* nine — more at NINE] **1** *obs* **:** ⁴NONE **2 :** the middle of the day **:** the time when the sun is on the meridian **:** twelve o'clock in the daytime **:** MIDDAY ⟨several hours before ~⟩ ⟨~ meal⟩ ⟨the ~ line on a sundial⟩ **3 :** MIDNIGHT — used chiefly in the phrase *noon of night* **4 :** the highest point **:** CULMINATION ⟨~ of life⟩
²**noon** \"\ *vi* -ED/-ING/-S **1** *chiefly dial* **:** to take a rest or stop for a meal at noon **2 :** to reach the culmination
noonday \ˈ≡,≡\ *n* **:** MIDDAY ⟨seek for it . . at broad ~ —Virginia Woolf⟩ ⟨~ heat⟩
no one *pron* **:** no person **:** NOBODY, NONE ⟨we saw *no one*⟩
no. 1 *adj, usu cap N* **:** NUMBER ONE
noonflower \ˈ≡,≡\ *n* **:** GOATSBEARD 1
noon·ing \ˈnüniŋ\ *n* -s [¹*noon* + *-ing*] **1** *chiefly dial* **:** NOONTIME **2** *chiefly dial* **:** a meal eaten at noon **3** *chiefly dial* **:** a period at noon for eating or resting
noonlight \ˈ≡,≡\ *n* **:** the light of noon **:** the brightest daylight
noon·stead \ˈnün,sted\ *n, chiefly dial* **:** the position of the sun at noon
noon·tide \-,tīd\ *n* [ME *none-tyde*, fr. OE *nōntīd* ninth hour of the day counting from sunrise, fr. *nōn* + *tīd* time — more at NOON, TIDE] **1 :** the time of noon **:** MIDDAY **2 :** the highest or culminating point ⟨the bright ~ of southern gastronomy was somewhere in the past —Lucius Beebe⟩
noon·time \-,tīm\ *n, often attrib* [ME *none tyme*, fr. *none*, noon noon + *tyme*, *time* time] **:** MIDDAY, NOONTIDE
no·oscop·ic \¦nōə¦skäpik\ *adj* [*noo-* + *-scopic*] **:** of or relating to the examination of the mind
¹**noose** \ˈnüs\ *n* -s [prob. fr. Prov *nous* knot, fr. L *nodus* — more at NET] **1 :** a loop with a running knot (as in a hangman's halter or a lariat) that binds closer the more it is drawn **2 :** TIE, BOND, SNARE ⟨matrimonial ~⟩ **3 :** the free end of a bowstring fastened to the bow nock by a timber hitch — compare EYE 2d(5)
²**noose** \"\ *vt* -ED/-ING/-S **1 :** to secure by or as if by a noose **:** catch or capture in a noose **:** put a noose round **:** ENTRAP ⟨~ a snake⟩ **2 :** to execute by hanging **:** HANG **3 :** to furnish with a noose **:** make a noose in or of **:** pass (as a rope) around something so as to make a noose
noot·ka \ˈnu̇tkə, ˈnüt-\ *n, pl* **nootka** *or* **nootkas** *usu cap* **1 a :** a Wakashan people of Vancouver Island and the Cape Flattery region in northwestern Washington **b :** a member of such people **2 :** the Wakashan language of the Nootka people
nootka cypress *or* **nootka sound cypress** *n, usu cap N&S* [*Nootka Sound*, Vancouver Island, British Columbia] **:** YELLOW CEDAR 1a
noot·kan \-kən\ *adj, usu cap* [*Nootka* + E *-an*] **:** belonging or relating to the Nootka people
nootsack *or* **nootsak** *usu cap, var of* NOOKSACK
NOP *abbr* **1** not otherwise provided for **2** not our publication
no·pal \ˈnōpəl\ *n* -s [Sp, fr. Nahuatl *nopalli*] **:** a cactus of the genus *Nopalea* (as the cochineal fig); *broadly* **:** PRICKLY PEAR
no·pa·lea \nō'pālēə\ *n, cap* [NL, fr. Sp *nopal*] **:** a genus of cacti differing from *Opuntia* with which it is sometimes combined by the erect petals and scarlet flowers with stamens that are much longer than the petals
no·pal·ry \ˈnōpəlrē\ *n* -ES **:** a plantation of nopal for raising the cochineal insect
no–par \ˈ≡¦≡\ *or* **no–par–value** *adj* [fr. the phrase *no par* or *no par value*] **:** having no nominal value ⟨*no-par* share⟩ ⟨*no-par* common stock⟩
¹**nope** \ˈnōp\ *n* -s [earlier *nowpe*, prob. alter. (resulting from incorrect division of *an owpe*) of obs. E *owpe*, prob. alter. of E dial. ¹*alp*] *dial Brit* **:** BULLFINCH
²**nope** \ˈnōp\ *adv* [alter. of ¹*no*] **:** definitely not **:** NO — not often in formal use; compare YEP
no·pi·nene \ˈnōpə,nēn\ *n* -s [ISV *nopin-* (as in *nopinic acid* $C_{10}H_{16}O_3$) (prob. anagram of *pinon-* — in *pinonic acid*) + *-ene* — more at PINONIC ACID] **:** a terpene $C_{10}H_{16}$ associated with alpha-pinene in turpentine oils and hyssop oil **:** a liquid bicyclic terpene that is usu. levorotatory in its natural oils and that isomerizes to alpha-pinene (as on heating) — called also *beta-pinene, 2(10)-pinene*
no place *adv* [fr. the phrase *no place*] **:** NOWHERE
¹**nor** \nə(r), (¦)nȯ(ə)r, (¦)nȯ(ə), *in R speech in the southern US also* (¦)när\ *conj* [ME, contr. of *nother* nor, neither, fr. *nother*, pron. & adj., not either of two, neither — more at NEITHER] **1 :** or not — used to introduce the second member ⟨neither here ~ there⟩ or last member ⟨does not drink, smoke, ~ gamble⟩ or second and each following member ⟨not to be done by you ~ by me ~ by anyone⟩ of a series of two or more items of which each is negated **2 a —** used with *neither* as a negative correlative ⟨neither good ~ bad⟩; also used archaically to imply a negative in a preceding member ⟨thou ~ I have made the world —Alfred Tennyson⟩ **b —** used archaically to introduce both alternatives in a negative statement ⟨~ bits ~ bridles can his rage sustain —John Dryden⟩ **3 :** and not — often used with inversion of subject and predicate after an affirmative that is equivalent to or implies a negative ⟨the crisis . . . was simple; ~ was it really serious —Ernest Barker⟩ ⟨forbear, ~ carry out the scheme you've planned —W.S.

Gilbert⟩ **4** *chiefly dial* **:** AND, OR — used with a negative (as *not, never, no*) ⟨it cannot ~ it will not come to good —Shak.⟩

[2]nor \"\ *conj* [ME, perh. fr. [1]*nor*] *dial* **:** THAN ⟨did you ever . . . see a poorer place ~ this place —Donn Byrne⟩

nor- *comb form* [ISV, fr. [1]*normal*] **1 :** parent compound from which (a specified compound) may be regarded as derived (as by removal of side chains from a ring system) — esp. in names of terpenes ⟨*nor*bornane⟩ **2 :** compound of normal structure isomeric with the one to the name of which it is prefixed ⟨*nor*leucine⟩ **3 :** homologue lower by one methylene group — esp. in names of steroids and alkaloids ⟨*nor*cholane⟩ ⟨*nor*nicotine⟩

nor *abbr* **1** normal **2** north; northern

nor·adrenaline \ˌnȯr+\ *n* [ISV *nor-* + *adrenaline*] **:** NOREPINEPHRINE

no·rate \nōˈrāt, ˈ=,=\ *vb* -ED/-ING/-S [alter. of *narrate*] *vt* **1** *chiefly South & Midland* **:** to spread (news) by word of mouth **2** *chiefly South & Midland* **:** to make deprecating statements about (a person) ~ *vi, chiefly South & Midland* **:** GOSSIP

no·ra·tion \nōˈrāshən\ *n* -S [alter. of *narration*] *Midland* **:** RUMOR

nor·berg·ite \ˈnȯrˌbərˌgīt\ *n* -S [Sw *norbergit*, fr. Norberg, Västmanland, Sweden, its locality + Sw *-it* -ite] **:** a mineral $Mg_3SiO_4(F,OH)_2$ of the humite group composed of a magnesium silicate with fluorine and hydroxyl

nor·bert·ine \ˈnȯ(r)bə(r)d·ən\ *adj or n, usu cap* [St. *Norbert* †1134 Ger. ecclesiastic + E *-ine*, adj. suffix] **:** PREMONSTRATENSIAN

nor·bornane \(ˈ)nȯr+\ *n* [*nor-* + *bornane*] **:** a bicyclic crystalline hydrocarbon C_7H_{12} that is the parent compound of various terpenoids (as camphor and fenchone) and that is obtained by adding ethylene to cyclopentadiene under heat and pressure and then hydrogenating; 1,4-methano-cyclohexane; bicyclo[2.2.1]heptane — called also *norcamphane*

nor·camphane \"+\ *n* [*nor-* + *camphane*] **:** NORBORNANE

nord·cap·er \ˈnȯ(r)dˌkāpə(r)\ *n* -S [D *noordkaper*, fr. *Noordkaap* North Cape, northern Norway + D *-er*] **:** RIGHT WHALE

nor·den·skiol·dine \ˈnȯ(r)dᵊnˌshōldən\ *n* -S [Norw *nordenskiöldin*, fr. Baron Nils A.E. *Nordenskjöld* †1901 Swed. geologist + Norw *-in* -ine] **:** a mineral $CaSn(BO_3)_2$ consisting of a calcium tin borate

nord·hau·sen acid \ˈnȯ(r)dˌhau̇zᵊn-\ *n, usu cap N* [fr. *Nordhausen*, city in central Germany where it was orig. manufactured] **:** OLEUM 2

[1]nor·dic \ˈnȯrdik, ˈnȯ(ə)d-, -dēk\ *adj, usu cap* [F *nordique*, fr. *nord* north (fr. OF, fr. OE *north*) + *-ique* -ic — more at NORTH] **1 :** of or relating to the Germanic peoples of northern Europe **2 :** of or relating to a physical type characterized by tall stature, long head, light skin and hair, and blue eyes, occurring most frequently in northern Europe, and regarded by some as a racial division of the Caucasian **:** TEUTONIC — compare ALPINE, MEDITERRANEAN **3 :** ARYAN 3a **4 :** of or relating to Norway, Sweden, Denmark, Iceland, and Finland

[2]nordic \"\ *n* -S *cap* **1 :** a native of northern Europe **2 a :** a person representative of the Nordic physical type **b :** a member of the hypothetical Nordic division of the Caucasian race **3 :** a member of the Norwegian, Swedish, Danish, Icelandic, or Finnish peoples **:** SCANDINAVIAN

nordic combined *n, pl* **nordic combineds** *usu cap N* **:** a competitive ski event consisting of both ski jumping and cross-country racing — compare ALPINE COMBINED

nor·di·cism \ˈnȯ(r)dəˌsizəm\ *n* -S *usu cap* **1 :** the belief in or the doctrine of the superiority of the hypothetical Nordic racial type and its cultural capacities — compare ARYANISM **2 :** qualities or traits regarded as distinctive of the hypothetical Nordic race

nor·di·cist \-ˌsəst\ *n* -S **:** a believer in the doctrine of Nordic preeminence and supremacy

nor·di·hy·dro·guai·a·ret·ic acid \ˌnȯ(r)ˌdīˌhīdrōˌg(w)īəˌred·-ik-\ *n* [*nordihydroguaiaretic* fr. *nor-* + *dihydr-* + *guaiaretic* (in *guaiaretic acid* $C_{20}H_{24}O_4$) (ISV *guaia-* — fr. NL *Guaiacum* — + *ret-* — fr. Gk *rhētinē* resin — + *-ic*)] **:** a crystalline derivative $[(HO)_2C_6H_3CH_2CH(CH_3)-]_2$ of pyrocatechol obtained esp. from the creosote bush or made synthetically and used in trace amounts as an antioxidant to prevent rancidity of lard and other fats or oils — abbr. *NDGA*

nord·mann's fir \ˈnȯrdmənz-\ *n, usu cap N* [after A. von *Nordmann* †1866 Russ. naturalist] **:** an ornamental evergreen tree (*Abies nordmanniana*) native to the Caucasus region having rigid horizontal branches

nord·mark·ite \ˈnȯrdˌmärˌkīt\ *n* -S [*Nordmark*, Sweden, its locality + E *-ite*] **:** a variety of staurolite containing manganese

nor·ephedrine \ˌnȯr, (ˈ)nȯr+\ *n* [*nor-* + *ephedrine*] **:** a crystalline compound $C_6H_5CHOHCH(CH_3)NH_2$ known in three optically isomeric forms of which the levoratatory form occurs naturally with ephedrine; 1-phenyl-2-amino-1-propanol — called also *phenylpropanolamine*

nor·epinephrine \ˌnȯr+\ *n* [*nor-* + *epinephrine*] **:** a crystalline compound $(HO)_2C_6H_3CH(OH)CH_2NH_2$ that occurs in the levoratatory form as a hormone with epinephrine and that has a strong vasoconstrictor action and mediates transmission of sympathetic nerve impulses but lacks or exhibits weakly most other epinephrine effects (as on cardiac output or blood-sugar concentration) — called also *arterenol, noradrenaline;* compare SYMPATHIN

[1]nor·folk \ˈnȯr\|fək, ˈnȯ(ə)\|; *in sense 2 also* \|ˌfȯk *sometimes* \|ˌfōk\ *adj, usu cap* [fr. *Norfolk*, county in eastern England] **1 :** of or from the county of Norfolk, England **:** of the kind or style prevalent in Norfolk **2** [fr. *Norfolk*, city in southeast Virginia] **:** of or from the city of Norfolk, Virginia ⟨*Norfolk* shipyards⟩ **:** of the kind or style prevalent in Norfolk

[2]nor·folk \ˈnȯrfək, ˈnȯ(ə)f-\ *n* -S *often cap* [fr. *Norfolk*, county in eastern England] **:** NORFOLK JACKET

norfolk island pine *n, usu cap N&I* [fr. *Norfolk Island*, island in the southern Pacific ocean administratively attached to Australia] **:** an evergreen tree (*Araucaria excelsa*) of Australia and Norfolk Island with whorls of horizontal branches densely set with deep green awl-shaped leaves that in its native home grows to 200 feet but is often grown in pots and there seldom exceeds a few feet in height

norfolk jacket *n, often cap N* [fr. Norfolk, county in eastern England] **:** a single-breasted usu. loose-fitting jacket with four box pleats, one at each side of the front and back, and a belt that typically runs through them

Norfolk jacket

norfolk plover *n, usu cap N* [fr. *Norfolk*, county in eastern England] **:** STONE CURLEW

norfolk spot *n, usu cap N* [fr. *Norfolk*, city in southeast Virginia] **:** SPOT 7

norfolk trotter *n, usu cap N&T* [fr. *Norfolk*, county in eastern England] **:** HACKNEY 2a

norfolk turkey *n, usu cap N* [fr. *Norfolk*, county in eastern England] **:** a medium-sized greenish black turkey that has pink feet which turn slaty black with age and that is sometimes considered to constitute a distinct breed

norfolk wherry *n, usu cap N* [fr. *Norfolk*, county in eastern England] **:** WHERRY 2

no·ri \ˈnōrē\ *n* -S [Jap] **:** AMANORI

no·ria \ˈnōrēə\ *n* -S [Sp, fr. Ar *nāʿūrah*] **:** a Persian wheel of the bucket type

nor·ie \ˈnäri\ *n* -S [origin unknown] *chiefly Scot* **:** a cormorant (*Phalacrocorax carbo*)

nor·i·mon \ˈnärəˌmän\ *n* -S [Jap *norimono*, fr. *nori* riding + *mono* thing] **:** a Japanese covered litter carried by men

nor·it \ˈnȯrət\ *n* -S [fr. *Norit*, a trademark] **:** a commercially produced activated carbon that is used as an adsorbent (as for decolorizing sugar solutions or isolating vitamins or antibiotics)

nor·ite \ˈnȯˌrīt\ *n* -S [Norw *norit*, fr. *Norge* Norway + Norw *-it* -ite] **:** a variety of gabbro consisting of a granular aggregate of basic plagioclase, orthorhombic pyroxene, and usu. some magnetite — **nor·it·ic** \(ˈ)nȯˌrid·ik\ *adj*

no·ri·to \ˈnōrəˌtō\ *n pl* [Jap] **:** Shinto ritualistic prayers

nor·land \ˈnȯrlənd\ *n* [contr. of *northland*] **1** *chiefly dial* **:** the land in the north **:** north country **2** *chiefly Scot* **:** NORLANDER

nor·land·er \-də(r)\ *n* -S *chiefly dial* **:** a person from the north country **:** NORTHERNER

nor·leucine \(ˈ)nȯ(r)+\ *n* [ISV *nor-* + *leucine*] **:** a crystalline amino acid $CH_3(CH_2)_3CH(NH_2)COOH$ isomeric with leucine and usu. made synthetically; alpha-amino-caproic acid

norm \ˈnȯ(ə)rm, ˈnȯ(ə)m\ *n* -S [L *norma* carpenter's square, pattern, rule] **1 :** an authoritative rule or standard **:** MODEL, TYPE, PATTERN; *specif* **:** a hypothetical mineral composition of a rock calculated according to certain definite rules and usu. differing widely from the actual mineral composition or mode **2 :** a standard of conduct or ethical value **:** a principle of right action **:** MAXIM; *esp* **:** an imperative statement asserting or denying that something ought to be done or has value ⟨~*s* or ideals or values that are not held, that don't become peoples' interests, will be peculiarly valueless, no matter what inherent validity they may possess —Lucius Garvin⟩ **3 :** an ideal standard binding upon the members of a group and serving to guide, control, or regulate proper and acceptable behavior ⟨no society lacks ~*s* governing conduct —R.K.Merton⟩ **4 :** AVERAGE ⟨$10,000 per annum is the ~ in this community⟩: as **a :** a set standard of development or achievement usu. derived from the average or median achievement of a large group ⟨these students . . . scored above the national ~*s* for teachers college graduates —*Education Digest*⟩; *specif* **:** a production quota set for a worker **b :** the average score of a specified class of persons on a specified test ⟨grade ~⟩ ⟨age ~⟩ **c :** a pattern or trait taken or estimated to be typical in the behavior of a social group because most frequently observed ⟨studies aimed at establishing the ~*s* of sexual behavior among the middle classes⟩ **syn** see AVERAGE

norm- *or* **normo-** *comb form* [ISV, fr. [1]*normal*] **:** normal ⟨*norm*ergy⟩ ⟨*normo*blast⟩ ⟨*normo*tension⟩

nor·ma \ˈnȯrmə\ *n, pl* **nor·mae** \-rˌmē\ [L, carpenter's square, pattern, rule] **1 :** RULE, MODEL, STANDARD, NORM **2** *anthrop* **a :** a standard position for viewing a part (as the skull); *also* **:** an aspect of a bodily part (as the cranium) **b :** a line or pattern indicating the contour of the cranium

[1]nor·mal \ˈnȯrməl, ˈnȯ(ə)m-\ *adj* [in sense 1, fr. L *normalis* according to a square, forming a right angle, fr. *norma* carpenter's square, pattern, rule (prob. fr. Gk *gnōmona*, accus. of *gnōmōn* interpreter, discerner, pointer on a sundial, carpenter's square) + *-alis* -al; in senses 2–7 and 9–10, fr. LL *normalis* according to rule, fr. L, according to a square; in sense 8, trans. of F *normale* (in *école normale* normal school) — more at GNOMON] **1 :** forming a right angle **:** PERPENDICULAR **2 :** according to, constituting, or not deviating from an established norm, rule, or principle **:** conformed to a type, standard, or regular pattern **:** not abnormal **:** REGULAR ⟨~ word order of subject and verb⟩ ⟨~ working hours⟩ ⟨~ pronunciation⟩ **3 a :** unaffected by or not exposed to any particular infection or experimental treatment ⟨a ~ control animal⟩ **b :** occurring naturally and not because of disease, inoculation, or any experimental treatment ⟨~ immunity⟩ **4 a :** of, relating to, or characterized by average intelligence or development **:** free from intellectual defect **b :** free from mental disorder **:** having neither neurosis, personality disorder, nor psychosis **:** SANE **c :** characterized by balanced, well-integrated functioning of the organism as a whole within the limits imposed by the environment and in accord with the pattern of one's biological endowment **5 :** relating to or conforming with long-run expectations or to a permanent standard deviations from which on the part of individual economic phenomena are to be regarded as self-corrective ⟨a ~ price corresponds to long-run costs of production⟩ **6 a :** approximating the statistical norm or average ⟨a ~ infant mortality rate⟩ ⟨~ rainfall of the region⟩ **b :** consistent with the social norm ⟨~ married life⟩ **7 :** average over many years at a particular place and for a definite time, a certain day, or some other specified period — used of a meteorological element **8 :** of or relating to the training of teachers ⟨~ college⟩ ⟨~ department⟩ **9 :** of, relating to, or characterized by full ablaut grade **10 a** *of a solution* **:** having a concentration of one gram equivalent of solute per liter ⟨~ hydrochloric acid⟩ — abbr. *N* **b :** being an assumed fundamental compound (as an acid from which the known acids are obtained by dehydration) ⟨~ sulfuric acid $S(OH)_6$⟩ — compare ORTH- 3a **c :** containing neither basic hydroxyl nor acid hydrogen ⟨~ silver phosphate Ag_3PO_4⟩ — used of a compound (as a salt, ester, or amide) **d :** not associated ⟨~ liquids⟩ ⟨~ molecules⟩ **e :** having a straight-chain structure ⟨~ pentane⟩ ⟨~ butyl alcohol⟩ — abbr. *n;* used of an aliphatic hydrocarbon, one of its derivatives, or an alkyl radical; compare IS- 2b **f :** CIS — used esp. of stereoisomeric compounds containing two fused saturated rings; contrasted with *allo* ⟨the allo and ~ forms of steroids⟩ **syn** see REGULAR

[2]normal \"\ *n* -S **1** *math* **a :** PERPENDICULAR: (1) **:** a line perpendicular to the tangent line to a curve at a point of the curve (2) **:** a plane perpendicular to the tangent plane to a surface at a point on the surface **b :** the intercept on the normal line between a curve and the x-axis **2 :** one that is normal: as **a :** a normal person or organism **b :** a normal level (as of temperature, pressure, rainfall, price) **:** MEAN, AVERAGE **c :** NORMAL SCHOOL **3 :** a form or state regarded as the norm **:** STANDARD

normal barrage *n* **:** a standing barrage which is to be fired in an attack and for which batteries are habitually laid on a target line with the barrage being fired on call from the appropriate area

normal curve *n* **:** a bell-shaped curve representing a Gaussian distribution (as of random error)

nor·mal·cy \ˈnȯ(r)məlsē, -si\ *n* -ES **:** the state, condition, or fact of being normal **:** NORMALITY ⟨a return to ~ after war⟩

normal dispersion *n* **:** dispersion (as of light by an optical grating) in which the separation of components in any one spectrum increases continuously and almost uniformly with the wavelength, the separation being a monotonic function of the dispersion variable

normal distribution *n* **:** GAUSSIAN DISTRIBUTION

normal dropper *n* **:** DROPPER 4b

normal equation *n* **:** any of a set of simultaneous equations involving experimental unknowns and derived from a larger number of observation equations in the course of least-squares adjustment of observations

normal fault *n* **:** an inclined fault in which the hanging wall has slipped down relative to the footwall

normal form *n, logic* **:** a canonical or standard fundamental form of a statement to which others can be reduced; *esp* **:** a compound statement in the propositional calculus consisting of nothing but a conjunction of disjunctions whose disjuncts are either elementary statements or negations thereof

normal honey *n* **:** honey produced from floral nectars as distinguished from that produced from honeydew

normal horizontal separation *n* **:** the horizontal separation measured in a direction at right angles to the strike of a faulted stratum

nor·mal·i·ty \nȯ(r)ˈmaləd·ē, -ətē, -i\ *n* -ES [prob. fr. F *normalité*, fr. *normal* according to or constituting an established norm, normal (fr. LL *normalis* according to rule) + *-ité* -ity — more at NORMAL] **1 :** the quality or state of being normal **:** conformity with the norm ⟨~ of human behavior⟩ ⟨~ of structure in an organism⟩ **2** *of a solution* **:** concentration expressed in gram equivalents of solute per liter **3 :** conformity (as of statistical data) to the Gaussian distribution law

nor·mal·iza·tion \ˌnȯ(r)mələˈzāshən, -ˌlī-\ *n* -S [*normalize* + *-ation*] **:** the act or process of making normal ⟨~ of diplomatic relations⟩

nor·mal·ize \ˈnȯ(r)məˌlīz\ *vt* -ED/-ING/-S *see -ize in Explan Notes* [[1]*normal* + *-ize*] **:** to make normal **:** make conform to or reduce to a norm or standard: **a :** to secure uniformity and destroy coarse structure and strains in (metal) esp. by heating to a temperature at which recrystallization takes place or (in steel) by heating above the upper transformation temperature and then cooling in still air — compare HEAT-TREAT **b :** to make (a text, dialect, or language) regular as to spelling and inflection by using consistently only one symbol or group of symbols for each phoneme and only one of several variants for each grammatical form

nor·mal·iz·er \-zə(r)\ *n* -S **:** one that normalizes; *specif* **:** one that heat-treats metal to relieve internal strains and strengthen it during or after the annealing process

nor·mal·ly \-ˌlē, -li\ *adv* **1 :** in a normal manner ⟨acting ~ in spite of his anxiety⟩ **:** to a normal degree ⟨~ educated person⟩ **2 :** COMMONLY, USUALLY ⟨the ~ stabilizing middle class —E.B. George⟩ **:** in normal circumstances **:** under normal conditions ⟨contract ~ would have expired in January⟩

normal minor scale *n* **:** NATURAL MINOR SCALE

normal moisture capacity *n* **:** FIELD CAPACITY

normalness *n* -ES **:** NORMALITY

normal overlap *n* **:** an individual normal in phenotype although possessing a genotype that should cause deviation from normal — compare PENETRANCE

normal pitch *n* **:** the distance between points of intersection of the line of action of gear teeth with the working faces of two adjacent teeth

normal place *n* **:** the apparent position of a planet or comet at a specified time as determined from a considerable number of observations

normal pressure *n* **:** standard pressure usu. taken to be equal to that of a column of mercury 760 millimeters in height, the mercury being 0° C and gravity being that at 45 degrees latitude **:** one atmosphere

normal saline solution *also* **normal salt solution** *n* **:** PHYSIOLOGICAL SALINE

normal school *n* [trans. of F *école normale;* fr. the fact that the first school so named in France was intended to serve as a model for other teacher training schools] **:** a school for the training chiefly of elementary schoolteachers commonly state-supported and usu. offering a two-year course to high school graduates — compare TEACHERS COLLEGE

normal state *n* **:** GROUND STATE

normal tax *n* **:** a basic rate of taxation (as on income) applied to large groups of taxpayers to which varying surtaxes may be added for smaller subgroups

normal valence *n* **:** the usually accepted valence of a chemical element or of an atom or radical ⟨the *normal valence* of oxygen is −27⟩

normal volume *n* **:** the volume of a gas at 0° C and 760 millimeters pressure as ascertained either by direct observation or by calculations in accordance with the laws of Boyle and Charles

[1]nor·man \ˈnȯrmən, ˈnȯ(ə)m-\ *n* -S *cap* [ME, fr. OF *normant*, fr. ON *Northmann-*, *Northmathr* Norwegian, Scandinavian, fr. *northr* north + *mann-*, *mathr* man — more at NORTH, MAN] **1 :** a native or inhabitant of Normandy: **a :** one of the Scandinavians who conquered Normandy in the 10th century **b :** a member of the Norman-French people who conquered England in 1066 under William the Conqueror **2 :** NORMAN-FRENCH

[2]norman \"\ *adj, usu cap* **:** of, relating to, or characteristic of Normandy or the Normans ⟨*Norman* castle⟩

[3]norman \"\ *n* -S [origin unknown] **1 :** a heavy wooden or iron bar to insert into a hole in a bitt or stanchion in order to guide or secure a cable or rope **2 :** a pin used in a hole for any of various purposes (as a fid through a rudderhead)

norman architecture *n, usu cap N* **1 :** a Romanesque style first appearing in and near Normandy about A.D. 950 **2 :** architecture resembling or imitating this style

norman crimson *or* **norman red** *n, often cap N* **:** vermilion or a color resembling it

nor·mand \ˈnȯrmənd\ *n* -S *cap* [ME *Normand*, *Normant*, fr. MF, Norman] **:** a modern descendant of the Normans or Norman-French **:** a native of Normandy

nor·mande sauce \(ˈ)nȯrˌmänd-\ *or* **nor·man·dy sauce** \ˈnȯ(r)məndē-\ *n, often cap N* [*normande sauce* fr. F *normande* (in *sauce normande* normande sauce) (fem. of *normand*, adj., Norman, fr. *Normand*, n., Norman, fr. OF *Normant*) + E *sauce; normandy sauce* fr. *Normandy*, region of northwest France + E *sauce*] **:** a white sauce made of fish stock, flavored with wine, and enriched with cream and yolks of eggs

norman–french \ˌ==ˌ=\ *n* -ES *cap N&F* **1 a :** the French language used by the medieval Normans **b :** the modern dialect of Normandy **2 :** LAW FRENCH

nor·man·ism \ˈnȯ(r)məˌnizəm\ *n* -S *usu cap* **1 :** the quality or traits distinctive of the Normans; *also* **:** partiality for Norman culture or civilization **2 :** a Norman idiom or expression

nor·man·iza·tion \ˌnȯ(r)mənəˈzāshən\ *n* -S *often cap* [*normanize* + *-ation*] **:** the act or process of making Norman ⟨~ of England after the Conquest⟩

nor·man·ize \ˈnȯ(r)məˌnīz\ *vt* -ED/-ING/-S *see -ize in Explan Notes, often cap* [[1]*Norman* + *-ize*] **:** to make Norman in quality, traits, or culture; *also* **:** to bring under the military or civil control of Normans

nor·man·nic \(ˈ)nȯ(r)ˌmanik\ *adj, usu cap* **:** relating to or characteristic of the Normans

nor·ma·tive \ˈnȯ(r)məd·\|iv, -ət\|\ *adj* [F *normatif*, fr. *norme* norm (fr. L *norma* carpenter's square, pattern, rule) + *-atif* -ative — more at NORMAL] **1 :** of, relating to, or dealing with norms, their nature, or mode of discovery and existence ⟨~ discipline⟩ **2 :** explicating, inferring, or discovering a norm ⟨a ~ judgment⟩ ⟨~ statements⟩ **3 :** creating, prescribing, or imposing a norm ⟨a ~ law⟩ **4 a :** REGULATIVE, HEURISTIC ⟨guiding ~ principles⟩ **b :** PRESCRIPTIVE, DIDACTIC ⟨governing, ~ rules⟩ ⟨~ grammar⟩ **5 :** relating to norms of mineral composition — **nor·ma·tive·ly** \\|əvlē, -li\ *adv* — **nor·ma·tive·ness** \\|ivnəs\ *n* -ES

normative currency *n* **:** a currency system in which the unit is based upon a metallic standard — compare FREE CURRENCY

normative science *n* **:** a science that tests or evaluates and not merely describes or generalizes facts; *specif* **:** the group comprising logic, ethics, and aesthetics

normative truth *n* **:** the truth about values that is presumably not determinable simply by the existence or nonexistence of things or by logic alone without reference to something further (as the human will or objective ideals) — called also *aesthetic truth, ethical truth, ideal truth*

nor·mer·gic \(ˈ)nȯrˌmərjik\ *adj* **:** having the degree of sensitivity toward an allergen typical of age group and community — distinguished from *hyperergic* and *hypoergic*

nor·mer·gy \ˈnȯ(r)mə(r)jē\ *n* -ES [ISV *norm-* + all*ergy*] **:** the quality or state of being normergic

normo- — see NORM-

nor·mo·blast \ˈnȯ(r)məˌblast\ *n* [ISV *norm-* + *-blast*] **:** an immature red blood cell containing hemoglobin and a pycnotic nucleus and normally present in bone marrow but appearing in the blood in many anemias — compare ERYTHROBLAST — **nor·mo·blas·tic** \ˌ==ˌblastik\ *adj*

nor·mo·chro·mia \ˌnȯ(r)məˈkrōmēə\ *n* -S [NL, fr. *norm-* + *-chromia*] **:** the condition of red blood cells that contain a normal amount of hemoglobin whatever their other deficiencies

nor·mo·chro·mic \ˌ==ˌkrōmik\ *adj* [*normochrom*ia + *-ic*] **1** *of blood* **:** having a normal color **2** *of anemia* **:** accompanied by normal color of the red blood cells **:** not marked by decrease in the hemoglobin content of the individual red blood cells

nor·mo·cyte \ˈnȯ(r)məˌsīt\ *n* -S [ISV *norm-* + *-cyte*] **:** a red blood cell normal in size and in hemoglobin content

nor·mo·cyt·ic \ˌ==ˌsid·ik\ *adj* **1** *of blood* **:** containing red blood cells that are normal in size and usu. also in hemoglobin content **2** *of anemia* **:** marked by the presence of diminished numbers of normal red blood cells in the circulating blood

nor·mo·splanchnic \ˌnȯ(r)mō+\ *adj* [ISV *norm-* + *splanchnic;* orig. formed as It *normosplàncnico*] **:** having average or intermediate body-build — distinguished from *macrosplanchnic* and *microsplanchnic*

nor·mo·tension \"+\ *n* [*norm-* + *tension*] **:** normal blood pressure

[1]nor·mo·ten·sive \ˌnȯ(r)mōˌten(t)siv\ *adj* [*normotens*ion + *-ive*] **:** having a blood pressure typical of the age group and community to which one belongs — compare HYPERTENSIVE

[2]normotensive \"\ *n* -S **:** a person with normal blood pressure

norms *pl of* NORM

norn \ˈnȯ(ə)rn\ *n* -S *often cap* [ON] **:** a goddess presiding over personal destiny **:** a fate of Norse mythology ⟨blinks and croaks like a toad or a *Norn* —R.P.Warren⟩ — usu. used in pl. ⟨buy something you cannot afford as a gesture of defiance at the *Norns* —Frank Sullivan⟩

nor·nicotine \(ˈ)nȯ(r)+\ *n* [*nor-* + *nicotine*] **:** a liquid alkaloid $C_9H_{12}N_2$ found in tobacco and obtained from nicotine by demethylation; 3-α-pyrrolidyl-pyridine

nor·roy \ˈnäˌrȯi\ *n* -S *usu cap* [ME *norrey*, prob. fr. MF *nord* north (fr. OF, fr. OE *north*) + *rey, roy* king, fr. L *reg-*, *rex* — more at NORTH, ROYAL] **1 :** NORROY KING OF ARMS **2 :** NORROY AND ULSTER KING OF ARMS

norroy and ulster king of arms *also* **norroy and ulster** *usu cap N&U&K&Arms* [*Ulster*, former province in northern Ireland] **:** a king of arms having jurisdiction in England north of the river Trent and in Northern Ireland — compare COLLEGE OF ARMS, CLARENCEUX KING OF ARMS, GARTER KING OF ARMS; see NORROY KING OF ARMS, ULSTER KING OF ARMS

norroy king of arms *usu cap N&K&A* **:** one of the English kings of arms, having jurisdiction north of the river Trent and since 1943 given an expanded jurisdiction and called *Norroy and Ulster King of Arms;* compare COLLEGE OF ARMS, CLARENCEUX KING OF ARMS, GARTER KING OF ARMS, ULSTER KING OF ARMS

1**norse** \\'nȯ(ə)rs, 'nȯ(ə)s\\ *n, pl* **norse** *cap* [prob. fr. obs. D *noorsch*, adj., Norwegian, Scandinavian (now *noors* Norwegian), alter. of obs. D *noordsch*, adj., northern (now *noords*), fr. D *noord* north + *-sch* -ish; akin to OE *north* and to OE *-isc* -ish — more at NORTH, -ISH] **1** *norse pl* **a :** SCANDINAVIANS **b :** NORWEGIANS **2 a :** NORWEGIAN 2 **b :** any of the western Scandinavian dialects or languages **c :** the Scandinavian group of Germanic languages

2**norse** \\"\\ *adj, usu cap* **1 :** of or relating to ancient Scandinavia or the language of its inhabitants ⟨*Norse* mythology⟩ **2 :** of or relating to Norway or the Norwegians **:** NORWEGIAN

1**norse-american** \\¦==¦===\\ *adj, usu cap N&A* **:** Norwegian and American; *specif* **:** of, relating to, or being an American of Norwegian origin or descent

2**norse-american** \\"\\ *n, cap N&A* **:** an American of Norwegian origin or descent

nor·sel \\'nȯrsəl\\ *n* -s [alter. of ME *nostul, nostylle*, fr. OE *nostle* fillet, band; akin to OHG *nestila, nestilo* bow, band, shoelace — more at LANYARD] **:** a short line for fastening fishnets or fishhooks

nor·sel·ler \\-lər\\ *n* -s **:** one that attaches norsels to fishnets

norse·man \\'nȯrsmən, 'nȯ(ə)s-\\ *n, pl* **norsemen** *cap* **1 :** one of the ancient Scandinavians — called also *Northman* **2 :** SCANDINAVIAN; *specif* **:** NORWEGIAN

nor·ski *or* **nor·skie** *or* **nor·sky** \\'nȯrskē\\ *n, pl* **norskis** *or* **norskies** *usu cap* [*norskie, norsky* fr. Norw *norsk*, adj., Norwegian (fr. ONorw, prob. contr. of — assumed — ONorw *norrænsk*, fr. ONorw *norrænn*, adj., Norwegian — akin to OE *northerne* northern — + *-sk* -ish, akin to OE *-isc* -ish) + E *-ie* or *-y; norski* alter. of *norskie, norsky* — more at NORTHERN, -ISH] **:** a Norwegian or Norwegian-American — used as a nickname

nor·te \\'nȯrtā\\ *n* -s [Sp, north wind, north, fr. MF *nord* north, fr. OF, fr. OE *north*] **:** a strong northerly wind esp. in Mexico or Central America **:** NORTHER

nor·te·amer·i·ca·no \\¦nȯ(r)tāə͵merə¦kä(͵)nō\\ *n* -s [Sp, adj. & n., fr. *norte* north + *americano* American] **:** NORTH AMERICAN 2

1**north** \\'nȯ(ə)rth, 'nȯ(ə)th\\ *adv* [ME, fr. OE; akin to OHG *nord* north, ON *northr* north, Umbrian *nertru* left, Gk *nerteros* lower, infernal; basic meaning: left] **:** to, toward, or in the north **:** NORTHWARD

2**north** \\"\\ *adj* [ME, fr. OE *north-*, fr. *north*, adv.] **1 a :** situated toward or at the north ⟨the ~ entrance⟩ ⟨the ~ country⟩ **b** [ME, fr. OE *northan-*, fr. *northan*, adv.; akin to ON *northan* from the north; derivative fr. the root of E 1*north*] **:** coming from the north ⟨the ~ wind⟩ **2 :** in the direction of the left side of a church looking from the nave toward the altar or chancel

3**north** \\"\\ *n* -s [ME, fr. *north*, adv.] **1 a :** the direction of the north terrestrial pole **:** the direction to the left of one facing east **:** the direction to the left of one facing the sunrise when the sun is near one of the equinoxes **b :** the part of the sky lying to the left of an observer facing east **c :** the cardinal point directly opposite to south — abbr. *N;* see COMPASS CARD **d :** the direction along any meridian toward that pole of the earth viewed from which the earth's rotation is counterclockwise — compare MAGNETIC NORTH **e :** the direction on the celestial sphere to the left when one faces the direction of its apparent rotation **:** the direction to the left when one faces the direction of revolution around the sun of the earth and the principal planets **2** *usu cap* **a :** regions or countries lying to the north of a specified or implied point of orientation (as in the U. S. the states lying in general north of Mason and Dixon's Line and the Ohio river) **b :** something (as people, culture, or institutions) characteristic of the North ⟨the *North* favored certain legislative proposals⟩ **3 :** the north wind **4** *often cap* **a :** the one of four positions at 90-degree intervals that lies toward the north **b :** a person (as a bridge player) occupying such a position in the course of a specific activity

4**north** \\"\\ *vb* -ED/-ING/-S [1*north*] **:** to move or veer toward the north

northabout \\'==͵=\\ *adv (or adj)* **:** about in tacking so as to head north; *broadly* **:** toward the north **:** NORTHWARD

1**north african** *adj, usu cap N&A* [*North Africa*, the countries of northern Africa + E *-an*] **1 :** of, relating to, or characteristic of North Africa — often used specif. of the region including Morocco, Algeria, Tunisia, Libya, and Egypt **2 :** of, relating to, or characteristic of the North Africans

2**north african** *n, cap N&A* **:** a native or inhabitant of North Africa — usu. used specif. of the natives and inhabitants of Morocco, Algeria, Tunisia, Libya, and Egypt

north america *adj, usu cap N&A* [fr. *North America*, continent in the western hemisphere] **:** of or from the continent of North America **:** of the kind or style prevalent in North America **:** NORTH AMERICAN

1**north american** *n, cap N&A* [*North America* + E *-an*, n. suffix] **1 :** a native or inhabitant of North America **2** [trans. of Sp *norteamericano*] **:** a native or inhabitant of the U. S. as distinguished esp. from the Latin natives or inhabitants of Mexico, Central America, the West Indies, and So. America — compare ANGLO-AMERICAN

2**north american** *adj, usu cap N&A* [*North America* + E *-an*, adj. suffix] **1 :** of, relating to, or characteristic of North America **2 :** of, relating to, or characteristic of the people of North America **3** [trans. of Sp *norteamericano*] **:** of, relating to, or characteristic of the people of the U. S. as distinguished esp. from the Latin peoples of Mexico, Central America, the West Indies, and So. America ⟨a strong sensitive face, too quick and mobile to be *North American* —Thurston Scott⟩

north american blastomycosis *n, usu cap N&A* **:** blastomycosis that involves esp. the skin, lymph nodes, and lungs and that is caused by infection with a fungus (*Blastomyces dermatitidis*)

north american indian *n, usu cap N&A&I* **:** an Indian of the North American continent; *esp* **:** an Indian of the U. S. and Canada

north·amp·ton \\(')nȯ(r)¦tham(p)tən, -(r)th¦ha-\\ *adj, usu cap* [fr. *Northampton*, city and county in central England] **:** of or from the city of Northampton, England **:** of the kind or style prevalent in Northampton

north·amp·ton·shire \\-n͵shi(ə)r, -͵shiə, -͵shə(r)\\ *or* **northampton** *adj, usu cap* [fr. *Northamptonshire, Northampton*, county in central England] **:** of or from the county of Northampton, England **:** of the kind or style prevalent in Northampton

north arabic *n, usu cap N&A* **:** a group of Semitic dialects spoken in northern and central Arabia from the 4th century onward, one of which forms the basis of classical and modern Arabic

northbound \\'=͵=\\ *adj* **:** traveling or headed in a northerly direction ⟨~ traffic⟩ — compare EASTBOUND

north briton *n, cap N&B* **:** SCOT

1**north by east :** a compass point that is one point east of due north **:** N 11° 15′ E — abbr. *N b E, N by E;* see COMPASS CARD

2**north by east** *adv (or adj)* **1 :** toward north by east **2 :** from north by east

1**north by west :** a compass point that is one point west of due north **:** N 11° 15′ W — abbr. *N b W, N by W;* see COMPASS CARD

2**north by west** *adv (or adj)* **1 :** toward north by west **2 :** from north by west

north carolina *adj, usu cap N&C* [fr. *North Carolina*, south Atlantic state of the U. S., fr. 2*north* + *Carolina*, English colony from which No. and So. Carolina were formed — more at CAROLINIAN] **:** of or from the state of North Carolina ⟨the *North Carolina* coast⟩ **:** of the kind or style prevalent in North Carolina **:** NORTH CAROLINIAN

north carolina bay *n, usu cap N&C* **:** a mountain magnolia (*Magnolia fraseri*)

north carolina pine *n, usu cap N&C* **1 a :** SHORTLEAF PINE **b :** the wood of shortleaf pine **2 a :** LOBLOLLY PINE **b :** the wood of loblolly pine **3 :** JERSEY PINE

1**north carolinian** *n, cap N&C* [*North Carolina* (state) + E *-an*, n. suffix] **:** a native or resident of North Carolina

2**north carolinian** *adj, usu cap N&C* [*North Carolina* (state) + E *-an*, adj. suffix] **1 :** of, relating to, or characteristic of the state of North Carolina **2 :** of, relating to, or characteristic of the people of North Carolina

north celestial pole *n* **:** NORTH POLE 1a

north central *adj, usu cap N&C* **:** of, relating to, or characteristic of the states of the Mississippi valley and the Great Lakes region lying north of the Ohio river and the southern boundaries of Kansas and Missouri and between the eastern boundaries of Montana, Wyoming, and Colorado and the western boundary of Pennsylvania

north-countryman \\'='===\\ *n, pl* **north-countrymen** *cap N* [*north country* (fr. ME *north cuntree*, fr. 2*north* + *cuntree* country) + *man*] *Brit* **:** a native or inhabitant of the northern counties of England

north dakota *adj, usu cap N&D* [fr. *North Dakota*, northwestern state of the U. S., fr. 2*north* + *Dakota* (*territory*), former region of the U. S. including No. & So. Dakota — more at DAKOTA] **:** of or from the state of North Dakota ⟨the *North Dakota* plains⟩ **:** of the kind or style prevalent in North Dakota **:** NORTH DAKOTAN

1**north dakotan** *adj, usu cap N&D* [*North Dakota* (state) + E *-an*] **1 :** of, relating to, or characteristic of the state of North Dakota **2 :** of, relating to, or characteristic of the people of North Dakota

2**north dakotan** *n, cap N&D* **:** a native or resident of the state of North Dakota

1**north·east** \\(')nȯr¦thēst, -ȯ(ə)¦-, *usual nautical pronunciation* (')nȯ¦rēst\\ *adv* [ME *northest*, fr. OE *northēast*, fr. 1*north* + *ēast* adv., east] **:** to, toward, or in the northeast **:** NORTHEASTWARD

2**northeast** \\"\\ *n* [ME *northest*, fr. *northest*, adv.] **1 a :** the general direction between north and east **b :** the part of the northern sky lying east of the observer's meridian **c :** the point of the compass midway between the cardinal points north and east **:** the point directly opposite to southwest — abbr. *NE;* see COMPASS CARD **2** *usu cap* **a :** regions or countries lying to the northeast of a specified or implied point of orientation **b :** something (as people or institutions) characteristic of the Northeast ⟨the *Northeast* was solidly against the bill⟩ **3 :** the northeast wind

3**northeast** \\"\\ *adj* [ME *northest*, fr. *northest*, adv.] **1 :** coming from the northeast ⟨the ~ wind⟩ **2 :** situated toward or at the northeast ⟨the ~ section of land⟩

1**northeast by east :** a compass point that is one point east of due northeast **:** N 56° 15′ E — abbr. *NE b E, NE by E;* see COMPASS CARD

2**northeast by east** *adv (or adj)* **1 :** toward northeast by east **2 :** from northeast by east

1**northeast by north :** a compass point that is one point north of due northeast **:** N 33° 45′ E — abbr. *NE b N, NE by N;* see COMPASS CARD

2**northeast by north** *adv (or adj)* **1 :** toward northeast by north **2 :** from northeast by north

north·east·er \\-tə(r)\\ *n* [3*northeast* + *-er*] **1 :** a strong northeast wind **2 :** a storm with northeast winds ⟨a good ~, which usually means three days of wind and rain —J.P. Marquand⟩

1**north·east·er·ly** \\-tərlē, -li, *-R* -təl- *sometimes* -tᵊl-\\ *adv (or adj)* [fr. 3*northeast*, after E 2*east:* 2*easterly*] **1 :** from the northeast ⟨the wind blew ~⟩ ⟨~ gales⟩ **2 :** toward the northeast ⟨voyaging ~ for several days⟩ ⟨a ~ voyage⟩

2**northeasterly** \\"\\ *n* **:** a wind from the northeast

north·east·ern \\-tə(r)n, *-R also* -tᵊn\\ *adj* [2*northeast* + *-ern* (as in *eastern*)] **1** *often cap* **:** of, relating to, originating or dwelling in, or characteristic of a region (as of the U. S.) conventionally designated Northeast ⟨~ seaports⟩ ⟨~ schools⟩ **2 :** situated toward or coming from the northeast ⟨the ~ suburbs of a city⟩

north·east·ern·er *R* -tə(r)nər, *-R* -tənə(r *also* -tᵊnə(r\\ *n, usu cap* **:** a native or inhabitant of a northeastern region (as of the U. S.)

north·east·ern·most \\-n͵mōst, *esp Brit also* -͵məst\\ *adj* **:** farthest to the northeast **:** most northeastern

1**north·east·ward** \\-twə(r)d\\ *adv (or adj)* **:** toward the northeast **:** in a northeast direction

2**northeastward** \\"\\ *n* **:** NORTHEAST ⟨to the ~⟩

north·east·ward·ly \\-dlē\\ *adv (or adj)* **:** toward or from the northeastward **:** NORTHEASTERLY

north·east·wards \\-dz\\ *adv* **:** NORTHEASTWARD

northed *past of* NORTH

1**north·er** \\'nȯrt͟hər, 'nȯ(ə)t͟hə(r\\ *vi* -ED/-ING/-S [1*north* + *-er* (as in 1*batter*)] **:** to turn, veer, or shift to the north — used chiefly of the wind

2**norther** \\"\\ *n* -S [2*north* + *-er*, n. suffix] **:** a northerly wind; *esp* **:** a sudden strong north wind over the Plains or such a wind in Texas and on the Gulf of Mexico and western Caribbean sea — compare BLUE NORTHER, NORTE

north·er·li·ness \\-t͟hə(r)lēnə̇s\\ *n* -ES **:** the situation of being northerly

1**north·er·ly** \\-lē, -li\\ *adj* [fr. 2*north*, after E 2*east:* 1*easterly*] **1 :** situated or directed toward the north **:** NORTHERN ⟨~ slopes of hills⟩ ⟨~ flight of birds⟩ ⟨the color characterizes the peculiar ~ atmosphere —Dorothy Adlow⟩ **2 :** blowing from the north ⟨the wind's much more ~ —David Beaty⟩

2**northerly** \\"\\ *adv* **1 :** from the north ⟨the wind blew ~⟩ **2 :** toward the north ⟨streets running ~⟩

3**northerly** \\"\\ *n* -ES **:** a wind from the north ⟨the morning ~ was making up —G.W.Brace⟩

north·er·most \\-t͟hə(r)͵mōst, *esp Brit also* -͵məst\\ *adj* [fr. 2*north*, after such pairs as E 2*east*: *eastermost*] **:** NORTHERNMOST

1**north·ern** *R* 'nȯrt͟hərn *sometimes* -t͟hən, *-R* 'nȯ(ə)t͟hən\\ *adj* [ME *northerne*, fr. OE; akin to OHG *nordrōni* northern, ON *norrænn* Norwegian; derivative fr. the root of E 1*north*] **1** *often cap* **a :** of, relating to, originating or dwelling in, or characteristic of a region (as of the U. S. or England) conventionally designated North ⟨~ factories⟩ ⟨the ~ autumn⟩ **b :** of, relating to, or typical of northern dialect **2 a :** lying toward the north ⟨the ~ lakes⟩ ⟨~ suburbs⟩ **b :** coming from the north ⟨a ~ snowstorm⟩ **3** *of a sign of the zodiac* **:** situated north of the equator

2**northern** \\"\\ *n* -S **1** *usu cap* **:** an inhabitant of the North **:** NORTHERNER **2** *or* **northern dialect** *usu cap N* **:** the dialect of English spoken in the part of the U. S. that lies north of a line running northwest from central New Jersey across the northern tier of counties in Pennsylvania and through northern Ohio, Indiana, and Illinois **3 :** 4PIKE 1a

northern anchovy *n* **:** a large-mouthed anchovy (*Engraulis mordax*) of the Pacific coast of No. America much used for bait and sometimes as food

northern anthracnose *n* **:** a disease of clovers (as red and crimson clovers) in No. America, Asia, and Europe caused by a fungus (*Kabatulla caulivora*) of the family Tuberculariaceae causing sunken linear brown lesions on the stems and petioles

northern athapaskan *n, usu cap N&A* **:** DÉNÉ

northern baptist *n, cap N&B* **:** AMERICAN BAPTIST

northern barracuda *n* **:** a small barracuda (*Sphyraena borealis*) of the Atlantic coast of the U. S. from Cape Fear to Cape Cod

northern bedstraw *n* **:** a stoloniferous perennial No. American bedstraw (*Galium boreale*) sometimes used as an ornamental and having several-veined leaves in fours and white flowers

northern black currant *n* **1 :** an erect unarmed shrub (*Ribes hudsonianum*) of northern No. America **2 :** the edible black fruit of the northern black currant — called also *quinsyberry*

northern catfish *n* **:** a catfish that constitutes a northern subspecies (*Ictailurus lacustris lacustris*) of the channel catfish

northern cattle grub *n* **:** the larva of a warble fly (*Hypoderma bovis*) — see BOMB FLY

northern dusky wing *n* **:** a common No. American butterfly (*Thorybes pylades*) of the family Hesperidae

northern eider *n* **:** a No. American duck that constitutes a subspecies (*Somateria mollissima borealis*) of the European eider

north·ern·er *R* 'nȯrt͟hə(r)nər, *-R* 'nȯt͟hənə(r)\\ *n* -S *usu cap* **:** a native or inhabitant of the North; *esp* **:** a native or inhabitant of the northern states of the U. S.

northern fowl mite *n* **:** a parasitic mite (*Ornithonyssus silviarum*) of the family Laelaptidae that is a serious pest of poultry, pigeons, and other birds in both Europe and No. America — called also *fowl mite*

northern fox grape *n* **:** FOX GRAPE c

northern hartebeest *n* **:** an African hartebeest (*Alcelaphus buselaphus*) also found in Arabia

northern hemisphere *n* **:** the half of the earth that lies north of the equator

northern ireland *adj, usu cap N&I* [fr. *Northern Ireland*, division of the United Kingdom of Great Britain and Northern Ireland occupying the northeast section of the island of Ireland] **:** of or from Northern Ireland, a division of the United Kingdom of Great Britain and Northern Ireland **:** of the kind or style prevalent in Northern Ireland

north·ern·ize \\-t͟hə(r)͵nīz\\ *vt* -ED/-ING/-S *sometimes cap* **:** to imbue with qualities native to or associated with residents of northern U. S.

northern lights *n pl* **:** AURORA BOREALIS

north·ern·ly \\-t͟hə(r)nlē, -li\\ *adv (or adj)* **:** NORTHERLY

northern mammoth *n* **:** WOOLLY MAMMOTH

northern masked chafer *n* **:** a beetle (*Cyclocephala borealis*) of the family Lucanidae the grubs of which feed on turf roots

north·ern·most \\-n͵mōst, *esp Brit also* -͵məst\\ *adj* **:** farthest to the north **:** most northern

northern muskellunge *n* **:** CHAUTAUQUA MUSKELLUNGE

northern paiute *n, usu cap N&P* **1 a :** a group of Shoshonean peoples in western Nevada, southeastern Oregon, and northeastern California **b :** a member of any such peoples **2 :** any of the dialects of the Shoshonean language family spoken by the Northern Paiute peoples

northern phalarope *n* **:** a phalarope (*Lobipes lobatus*) breeding in the arctic regions of the Old and New Worlds and often occurring in large flocks far out at sea

northern pike *also* **northern pickerel** *n* **:** 4PIKE 1a

northern pine *n* **1 :** SCOTCH PINE **2 :** WHITE PINE 1a **3 :** the wood of northern pine

northern porgy *n* **:** SCUP a

northern rat flea *n* **:** a common and widely distributed flea (*Nosopsyllus fasciatus*) parasitic on rats

northern red oak *n* **:** RED OAK 1a

northern shrike *n* **:** a shrike (*Lanius borealis*) occurring in northern No. America — called also *butcher-bird*

northern sucker *n* **:** a sucker (*Catostomus catostomus*) of northern No. America reaching a length of two and a half feet and being from the Great Lakes northward a valuable food fish

northern tehuelche *n, usu cap N&T* **:** PUELCHE

northern union football *n, usu cap N&U* [*Northern Union*, unofficial name of *The Northern Rugby Football Union*, football league that was formed in the North of England in 1895 and changed its name to The Rugby Football League in 1922] **:** RUGBY LEAGUE FOOTBALL

northern water thrush *n* **:** a No. American water thrush (*Seiurus noveboracensis*)

northern white cedar *n* **:** AMERICAN ARBORVITAE

northern white pine *n* **:** WHITE PINE 1 a

northern whiting *n* **:** a whiting (*Menticirrhus saxatilis*) of the east coast of the U. S. closely resembling the king whiting but having a filament extending from the first spine of the dorsal fin

northers *pres 3d sing of* NORTHER, *pl of* NORTHER

north geographical pole *n* **:** NORTH POLE 1b

north germanic *n, cap N&G* **:** a subdivision of the Germanic languages that includes Icelandic, Faeroese, Norwegian, Swedish, Danish — see INDO-EUROPEAN LANGUAGES table

north·ing \\'nȯr|th|iŋ, 'nȯ(ə)|, |t͟h|, |ēŋ\\ *n* -S [1*north* + *-ing*] **1 :** difference in latitude to the north from the last preceding point of reckoning ⟨the problem is to determine differences of ~ between distant points by means of angular observations at each end of the base line —L.G.Trorey⟩ **2 :** northerly progress **:** a going northward ⟨our progress was slow, but we made steady ~ —Deneys Reitz⟩ ⟨the captains decided to make as much ~ as they could —Bernard DeVoto⟩

north·land \\'nȯrth͵land, 'nȯ(ə)th-, -aa(ə)nd, -͵lənd\\ *n, often cap* [ME, fr. OE, fr. 1*north* + *land*] **:** land in the north **:** the north of a country ⟨my stay in the *Northland* was ended —W.E. Ekblaw⟩ ⟨when winter closes in over the ~ —Melvin Beck⟩

north light *n* **1 :** light admitted to a room (as a studio) that comes solely from the north and in the northern hemisphere is preferred by artists because it is there more neutral in color and less productive of variation than light from any other direction **2 :** a window or skylight furnishing a north light

north·man \\-thmən\\ *n, pl* **northmen** **1** *cap* **:** NORSEMAN **2** *often cap* **:** a native or inhabitant of a northern region (as of northern Europe or northern Canada)

north·most \\-th͵mōst, *esp Brit also* -͵məst\\ *adj* **:** NORTHERNMOST

north·ness *n* -ES **:** the quality or state of being north

1**north-northeast** \\(¦)=¦=¦=\\ *adv (or adj)* [ME *north northest*, fr. 1*north* + *northest* northeast] **1 :** toward north-northeast **2 :** from north-northeast

2**north-northeast** \\"\\ *n* **:** a compass point that is two points east of due north **:** N 22° 30′ E — abbr. *NNE;* see COMPASS CARD

1**north-northwest** \\(¦)=¦=¦=\\ *adv (or adj)* [ME *north northwest*, fr. 1*north* + *northwest*, adv.] **1 :** toward north-northwest **2 :** from north-northwest

2**north-northwest** \\"\\ *n* [ME *north northwest*, fr. *north northwest*, adv.] **:** a compass point that is two points west of due north **:** N 22° 30′ W — abbr. *NNW;* see COMPASS CARD

north oscan *adj, usu cap N&O* **:** of or being a group of Italic languages comprising Paelignian, Marrucinian, and Vestinian

north polar distance *n* **:** the angular distance of a celestial body measured along its hour circle from the north celestial pole

north pole *n* [ME] **1 a :** the zenith of the heavens as viewed from the north terrestrial pole **b** *often cap N&P* **:** the northernmost point of the earth **:** the northern extremity of the earth's axis — see ZONE illustration **2** *of a magnet* **:** the pole that points toward the north when the magnet is freely suspended

norths *pl of* NORTH, *pres 3d sing of* NORTH

north-seeking pole *n* **:** NORTH POLE 2

north semitic *n, cap N&S* **:** NORTHWEST SEMITIC

north star *n, usu cap N&S* [ME *north sterre*] **:** POLESTAR

north temperate *adj, often cap N&T* **:** of or relating to the north temperate zone of the earth lying between the tropic of Cancer and the arctic circle — see ZONE illustration

north terrestrial pole *n* **:** NORTH POLE 1b

north·um·ber \\nȯ(r)'thəmbə(r)\\ *n* -S *cap* [ME *Northhumbre*, fr. OE *Northhymbre* (pl.), fr. 1*north* + *-hymbre* (fr. *Humbre* Humber, river in eastern England] **:** an inhabitant of ancient Northumbria

north·um·ber·land \\nȯ(r)'thəmbə(r)lənd\\ *adj, usu cap* [fr. *Northumberland*, county in northeast England] **:** of or from the county of Northumberland, England **:** of the kind or style prevalent in Northumberland **:** NORTHUMBRIAN

1**north·um·bri·an** \\(')nȯ(r)¦thəmbrēən\\ *adj, usu cap* [*northumber* + *-an*] **1 a :** of, relating to, or characteristic of ancient Northumbria **b :** of, relating to, or characteristic of the people of Northumbria **c :** of, relating to, or characteristic of the Old English dialect of Northumbria **2 a :** of, relating to, or characteristic of Northumberland **b :** of, relating to, or characteristic of the people of Northumberland **c :** of, relating to, or characteristic of the modern English dialect of Northumberland

2**northumbrian** \\"\\ *n* -S *cap* **1 :** a native or inhabitant of ancient Northumbria **2 :** a native or inhabitant of Northumberland **3 a :** the Old English dialect of Northumbria **b :** the modern English dialect of Northumberland

northumbrian burr *n, usu cap N* **:** a uvularly trilled *r* said to be characteristic of some Northumbrian speech

nor·thup·ite \\'nȯ(r)thə͵pīt\\ *n* -S [C. H. *Northup*, 19th cent. Am. mineral collector who first obtained it + E *-ite*] **:** a mineral $Na_3MgCl(CO_3)_2$ composed of a magnesium sodium carbonate with chloride and occurring in colorless octahedral crystals

1north·ward \'nȯrthwərd, 'nȯ(ə)thwəd\ *adv (or adj)* [ME, fr. OE *northweard*, fr. 1*north* + *-weard* -ward] **:** toward the north ⟨sailing ~⟩ ⟨a journey ~⟩ ⟨the ~ flight of birds⟩

2northward \"\ *n* -s **:** northward direction or part ⟨sailing to the ~⟩

north·ward·ly \-dlē, -li\ *adv (or adj)* **:** in a northern direction ⟨the seabed extending ~ approximately 250 feet —*Bahamas Acts*⟩ ⟨a ~ wind⟩

north·wards \-dz\ *adv* [ME *northwardis*, fr. OE *northweardes*, fr. *northweard* northward + *-es* -s (adv. suffix)] **:** NORTHWARD

1north·west \(')nȯr¦thwest, -ō(ə)¦-, *usual nautical pronunciation* (')nȯr¦w- *or* -ō(ə)¦w-\ *adv* [ME, fr. OE, fr. 1*north* + *west*, adv.] **:** to, toward, or in the northwest **:** NORTHWESTWARD

2northwest \"\ *n* [ME, fr. *northwest*, adv.] **1 a :** the general direction between north and west **b :** the part of the northern sky lying west of the observer's meridian **c :** the point of the compass midway between the cardinal points north and west **:** the point directly opposite to southeast — abbr. *NW;* see COMPASS CARD **2** *usu cap* **a :** regions or countries lying to the northwest of a specified or implied point of orientation **b :** something (as people or institutions) characteristic of the Northwest **3 :** the northwest wind

3northwest \"\ *adj* [ME, fr. *northwest*, adv.] **1 :** coming from the northwest ⟨a ~ storm⟩ **2 :** situated toward or at the northwest ⟨the ~ passage⟩

1northwest by north : a compass point that is one point north of due northwest **:** N 33° 45′ W — abbr. *NW b N, NW by N;* see COMPASS CARD

2northwest by north *adv (or adj)* **1 :** toward northwest by north **2 :** from northwest by north

1northwest by west : a compass point that is one point west of due northwest **:** N 56° 15′ W — abbr. *NW b W, NW by W;* see COMPASS CARD

2northwest by west *adv (or adj)* **1 :** toward northwest by west **2 :** from northwest by west

northwest coast indian *n, usu cap N&C&I* **:** a member of any of the peoples living along the Pacific coast from northern California to Alaska and comprising the Haida, Tlingit, Tsimshian, Bellabella, Kwakiutl, Nootka, Chinook, and Makah

north·west·er \-tə(r)\ *n* [3*northwest* + *-er*] **1 :** a strong northwest wind **2** *usu cap* **:** an employee of a fur-trading company formerly operating in western Canada

1north·west·er·ly \-tərlē, -li, *-R* -təl- *sometimes* -tᵊl-\ *adv (or adj)* [fr. 3*northwest*, after E *west: westerly*] **1 :** from the northwest ⟨winds blowing ~⟩ ⟨~ frosts —*Spectator*⟩ **2 :** toward the northwest ⟨steered the ship ~⟩ ⟨journeyed ~ all day⟩

2northwesterly \"\ *n* **:** a wind from the northwest

north·west·ern \-tə(r)n, *-R also* -tᵊn\ *adj* [2*northwest* + *-ern* (as in *western*)] **1** *often cap* **:** of, relating to, originating or dwelling in, or characteristic of a region (as of the U. S.) conventionally designated Northwest ⟨~ forests⟩ ⟨~ folklore⟩ **2 :** situated toward or coming from the northwest ⟨the ~ counties⟩

northwestern anthracnose *n* **:** APPLE ANTHRACNOSE

northwestern apple box *n* **:** a nailed paper-lined wooden fruit box designed to produce little or no compression of contents

north·west·ern·er *R* -tə(r)nər, *-R* -tənə(r *also* -tᵊnə(r)\ *n, usu cap* **:** a native or inhabitant of a northwestern region (as of the U.S.)

northwest semitic *n, cap N&S* **:** a division of the Semitic languages consisting of Aramaic and Canaanitic languages

northwest shipworm *n, often cap N* **:** a large destructive shipworm (*Bankia setacea*) of the Pacific coast of No. America

1north·west·ward \-twə(r)d\ *adv (or adj)* [ME, fr. 1*northwest* + *-ward*] **:** toward the northwest **:** in a northwest direction

northwestern apple box

2northwestward \"\ *n* -s **:** NORTHWEST ⟨to the ~⟩

north·west·ward·ly \-dlē\ *adv (or adj)* **:** toward or from the northwest **:** NORTHWESTERLY

north·west·wards \-dz\ *adv* **:** NORTHWESTWARD

nor·valine \(')nȯ(r)+\ *n* [ISV *nor-* + *valine*] **:** a crystalline amino acid $C_2H_5CH_2CH(NH_2)COOH$ isomeric with valine and usu. made synthetically; alpha-aminovaleric acid

1nor·ward \'nȯrwərd\ *adv (or adj)* [by contr.] **:** NORTHWARD

2norward \"\ *n* -s **:** NORTHWARD

nor·way \'nȯr,wā, 'nō(ə),-\ *adj, usu cap* [fr. *Norway*, country in northwest Europe] **:** of or from Norway **:** of the kind or style prevalent in Norway **:** NORWEGIAN

norway haddock *n, usu cap N* **:** ROSEFISH

norway iron *n, usu cap N* **:** a high grade of wrought iron produced in Sweden but usu. finished in and exported from Norway

norway lobster *n, usu cap N* **:** a lobster (*Nephrops norvegicus*) of European seas resembling the American lobster but much slenderer

norway maple *n, usu cap N* **:** a European maple (*Acer platanoides*) with dark green or often reddish or red-veined leaves that is much planted for shade in the U.S.

norway pine *n, usu cap N* **1 :** RED PINE 1a **2 :** the wood of Norway pine

norway rat *n, usu cap N* **:** BROWN RAT

norway spruce *n, usu cap N* **:** a widely cultivated spruce (*Picea abies*) native to northern Europe and having pyramidal shape, spreading branches and pendulous branchlets, dark foliage, and long pendulous cones

1nor·we·gian \(')nȯ(r)¦wējən\ *adj, usu cap* [ML *Norvegia, Norwegia* Norway + E *-an*, adj. suffix] **1 a :** of, relating to, or characteristic of Norway **b :** of, relating to, or characteristic of the Norwegians **2 :** of, relating to, or characteristic of the Norwegian language

2norwegian \"\ *n* -s *cap* [ML *Norvegia, Norwegia* Norway + E *-an*, n. suffix] **1 a :** a native or inhabitant of Norway **b :** a person of Norwegian descent **2 :** the Germanic language of the Norwegian people — see LANDSMÅL, RIKSMÅL; INDO-EUROPEAN LANGUAGES table

norwegian elkhound *n* **1** *usu cap N&E* **:** a Norwegian breed of medium-sized compact short-bodied dogs having a very heavy gray coat tipped with black and developed for herding sheep, guarding farms, hunting, and for draft purposes **2** *usu cap N & often cap E* **:** a dog of the Norwegian Elkhound breed

norwegian saltpeter *n, usu cap N* **:** CALCIUM NITRATE

norwegian whist *n, usu cap N* **:** whist in which each player in turn offers to win or lose tricks, bidding grand or nullo, there being no trumps

nor·wich \'nȯr,wich, 'närij\ *adj, usu cap* [fr. *Norwich*, county borough in eastern England] **:** of or from the county borough of Norwich, England **:** of the kind or style prevalent in Norwich

norwich terrier *n, usu cap N* **:** a terrier of a small active low-set English breed with rather long straight wiry coat of red, black and tan, or grizzle

nos *pl of* NO

nos- *or* **noso-** *comb form* [prob. fr. LL *noso-*, fr. Gk *nos-, noso-*, fr. *nosos*] **:** disease ⟨*nos*etiology⟩ ⟨*noso*geography⟩

NOS *abbr* not otherwise specified

1nose \'nōz\ *n* -s [ME, fr. OE *nosu;* akin to OE *nasu* nose, OHG *nasa*, ON *nǫs*, L *nasus*, Skt *nāsā*] **1 a :** the prominent part of the face of man or other mammals that bears the nostrils and covers the anterior part of the nasal cavity; *broadly* **:** this part together with the nasal cavity ⟨his ~ is stopped up with a cold⟩ ⟨people who speak through their ~s⟩ **b :** the anterior part of the head above or projecting beyond the mouth **:** SNOUT, PROBOSCIS, MUZZLE ⟨hit the shark over the ~ with an oar⟩ **2 a :** the sense of smell **:** OLFACTION; *also* **:** ability to track by scent ⟨this dog has a good ~⟩ **b :** SCENT; *esp* **:** AROMA ⟨the ~ of well-cured leafy hay⟩ **c :** the bouquet of an alcoholic beverage **3 :** the vertebrate olfactory organ consisting essentially of a moist layer of sensory epithelium derived from invaginated embryonic ectoderm and in intimate contact with terminations of the olfactory nerve, lying in higher vertebrates in the upper part of the nasal cavity and in fishes in small sacs on each side of the head, and communicating with the external environment through the nares **4 a :** the front or forward end or projection of something ⟨I pushed on, the ~ of my car headed for the tropics —Francis Birtles⟩ **b :** the projecting or working end of a tool or a machine part (as a spindle) ⟨a quarter-inch radius is specified for the ~ of this lathe tool⟩ ⟨pliers with a long ~⟩ **c :** the end of a projectile that is forward in flight ⟨could blow half a dozen men to pieces by dropping a cartridge on the point of that ~ —Wirt Williams⟩ **d :** the forward end of an airplane; *specif* **:** the part of a fuselage or nacelle projecting in front **e :** the distal end of a gooseberry, currant, apple, or other fruit **f :** the projecting edge of a molding or stair tread **5 a :** the stem of a boat **b :** the protective metal covering a boat's stem **6 a :** an anticlinal flexure plunging downward at one end and opening broadly at the other **b :** a buttress of usu. overhanging rock **7 :** the nose regarded as a symbol of officious or prying concern, interest, or intervention ⟨a clever fellow . . . with his ~ in all sorts of dark corners —H.J.Laski⟩ ⟨why can't he keep his big ~ out of things —James Jones⟩ **8 :** the knack for discovering or the instinct for recognizing or discerning **:** FLAIR ⟨anyone with a ~ for it might scent out a drama even in the meager information just provided —E.R.Bentley⟩ ⟨has an unerring ~ for humbug of any sort —Frank O'Connor⟩ ⟨a ~ for news⟩ ⟨one of the keener ~s for hit tunes —R.G.Hubler⟩ **9 a :** the approximate length of the nose (as of a horse) ⟨won the race by a ~⟩ **b :** an extremely narrow margin of victory ⟨won the election by a ~⟩ — compare HEAD, NECK — **nose to the grindstone :** in a state of hard, monotonous, servile, or unremitting work ⟨his demanding wife and large growing family are keeping his *nose to the grindstone*⟩ — **on the nose** *adv (or adj)* **1 :** to a prescribed or specified measure or limit of size or time **:** on the button **:** EXACTLY, PRECISELY ⟨ended the broadcast at 12 *on the nose*⟩ ⟨the 1.5314 inches dimension checked out *on the nose*⟩ **2 :** to win — used of horse or dog racing bets ⟨bet $10 on the favorite *on the nose*⟩ — **through the nose** *adv* **:** with the resonance characteristic of a stopped-up or defective nose ⟨*m* pronounced *through the nose* sounds like *b*⟩ — **under the nose of :** in plain sight of; *esp* **:** in bold and successful defiance of ⟨carried off the floating vote *under the* very *nose of* the conservative candidate⟩

2nose \"\ *vb* -ED/-ING/-S *vt* **1 :** to perceive the odor of **:** detect by or as if by smell **:** SCENT **:** smell out **2** *archaic* **:** to treat insolently **:** deal irreverently or disrespectfully with **:** BEARD **3 a :** to push or move with the nose ⟨the dog *nosed* the door open⟩ ⟨wolves or foxes had *nosed* aside some of the rocks —Farley Mowat⟩ **b :** to push or make (one's way) with the nose ⟨the plane . . . ~s its way into the whirling mass of clouds —Nona B. Brown⟩ **c :** to advance the nose, prow, or forward end into **:** push ahead in ⟨our craft . . . *nosed* the first strong swell —J.R.Perkins⟩ **4 :** to touch or rub with the nose **:** thrust the nose against or into in affection or curiosity **:** NUZZLE ⟨as he sat despairing his dog came up and *nosed* him⟩ **5 :** to round off or bevel the end of (as a log for skidding) **6 a :** to defeat by the length of a nose in a horse race **b :** to defeat by a narrow margin in a sport or contest ~ *vi* **1 :** to use the nose in examining, smelling, or showing affection **:** SCENT, SNIFF, NUZZLE **2 :** to pry or search impertinently **3 :** to move ahead esp. slowly or cautiously ⟨the cars had begun to move again, *nosing* out into the main road —Maurice Duggan⟩ ⟨had been *nosing* along the shores in pinnace, yacht, or bark —*Amer. Guide Series: Md.*⟩ **4 :** to dip or run in the form of a geological nose — **nose around :** to sniff around **:** EXPLORE ⟨plant auditors may also be found *nosing around* scrap heaps to see whether material is being wasted —Hugh Morrow⟩ — **nose into :** to poke or pry into with or as if with the nose ⟨she was *nosing into* everything around here —Edwin Lanham⟩

no·se·an \'nōzēən\ *n* -s [obs. G *nosian* (now *nosean*), fr. Karl W. *Nose* †1835 Ger. geologist + G *-ian*] **:** NOSELITE

nose ape *n* **:** PROBOSCIS MONKEY

nose bag *n* **:** a usu. canvas bag that is used for feeding an animal (as a horse) and that is fastened on top of the head and covers the muzzle — called also *feed bag*

noseband \'⸗,⸗\ *n* **:** the part of a headstall that passes over a horse's nose — see BRIDLE illustration

nose bit *n* **:** a wood bit similar to a gouge or pod bit but having a cutting edge on one side of its boring end

nose bag

nosebleed \'⸗,⸗\ *n* [1*nose* + *bleed*, v.] **1 a :** bleeding from the nose — called also *epistaxis* **b :** an attack of nosebleed ⟨had a severe ~⟩ **2** [ME *noseblede* yarrow, fr. 1*nose* + *blede, bleden* to bleed] **a :** either of two red-flowered plants: (1) **:** a trillium (*Trillium erectum*) (2) **:** INDIAN PAINTBRUSH **b** [so called fr. its use in folk medicine to check epistaxis] **:** YARROW

nose bot *or* **nose fly** *n* **:** a widely distributed botfly (*Gasterophilus haemorrhoidalis*) parasitic in the larval stage on horses and mules

noseclip \'⸗,⸗\ *n* **:** a small clamp usu. of rubber or plastic worn to keep water out of a swimmer's nose

nose cone *n* **:** a protective cone constituting the forward end of a rocket or missile and capable of withstanding the heat caused by reentry into the earth's atmosphere

nosed \'nōzd\ *adj* [1*nose* + *-ed*] **1 :** having a nose esp. of a specified kind — usu. used in combination ⟨thick, snub-*nosed*, ankle-high shoes —Robert Shaplen⟩ **2** *obs* **:** keen of scent

nose dive *n* **1 :** the downward nose-first plunge of an airplane or other flying object (as a kite) ⟨a pilot must have altitude in order to get out of a *nose dive* —E.J.David⟩ **2 :** a sudden extreme drop (as of prices) ⟨the blue chips were seriously off, and speculative favorites had gone into a *nose dive* —J.K. Galbraith⟩

nose-dive \'⸗,⸗\ *vi* [*nose dive*] **:** to plunge headlong

nose down *vi* **:** to head down **:** depress the nose ⟨the airplane *nosed down* out of the overcast⟩ ~ *vt* **:** to turn, point, or direct (an airplane's nose) down **:** head (an airplane) down ⟨she *nosed* the airplane *down* —Robert Craig⟩

nose drops *n pl* **:** a medicated liquid instilled into the nostrils with a medicine dropper

no-see-um \nō'sēəm\ *n* -s [fr. the group of words (as supposedly spoken by American Indians) *no see um* you don't see them] **:** BITING MIDGE

nose flute *n* **:** a flute played by blowing through the nostrils

nosegay \'⸗,⸗\ *n* [ME, fr. 1*nose* + *gay*, n.] **1 a :** a small bunch of flowers suitable to be worn on the person **:** POSY **b :** something likened to a bouquet: as (1) **:** an expression of compliment or praise (2) **:** a collection of lovely things ⟨this ~ of 18 sprightly short stories —James Kelly⟩ **2** *archaic* **:** an odorous object or its scent

nose glasses *n pl* **:** PINCE-NEZ

nose-heavy \'⸗,⸗⸗\ *adj* **:** having the center of gravity located forward of the center of lift so that the nose tends to drop when the longitudinal control is released in level flight ⟨a *nose-heavy* airplane⟩ — compare TAIL-HEAVY

nosehole \'⸗,⸗\ *n, dial chiefly Eng* **1 :** NOSTRIL **2 :** BYE HOLE

nose iron *n* **:** an adjustable pivot assembly in a weighing scale for changing the multiplication of a lever

nose leaf *n* **:** an expansion of skin resembling a leaf on the nose of various bats that is believed to have a delicate tactile function

nose·less \'nōzləs\ *adj* [ME *noseles*, fr. 1*nose* + *-les* -less] **:** having no nose — **nose·less·ly** *adv* — **nose·less·ness** *n* -ES

nose line *n* **:** a line drawn on the profile of a stairway following the outer edges of the treads and marking the slope of the stairway — compare NOSING

no·se·lite \'nōzə,līt\ *n* -s [G *noselith*, fr. Karl W. *Nose* †1835 Ger. geologist who described it + G *-lith* -lite] **:** a grayish, bluish, or brownish mineral $Na_5Al_3Si_3O_{12}(SO_4)$ that is a sodium aluminosilicate and sulfate related to hauynite

no·se·ma \nō'sēmə\ *n, cap* [NL, fr. Gk *nosēma* disease, fr. *nosein* to be sick, fr. *nosos* disease] **:** a genus (the type of the family Nosematidae) of microsporidian protozoans that includes various parasites of insects and other invertebrates — see NOSEMA DISEASE; compare GLUGEA

nosema disease *n* **:** a disease of bees caused by a microsporidian (*Nosema apis*) that invades the stomach and midgut causing dysentery and varying degrees of paralysis in the affected host

nose-nippers \'⸗,⸗⸗\ *n pl* **:** PINCE-NEZ

nose of wax : a pliant person or thing **:** one readily influenced or turned in any direction ⟨am neither an untrue man . . . nor a mere *nose of wax* to be twisted this way and that —Sir Walter Scott⟩

nose out *vt* **1 :** to discover by prying **:** ferret out **:** smell out ⟨found that detectives were *nosing out* divorce evidence⟩ ⟨our horses were able to *nose out* the trail despite the darkness⟩ **2 :** to defeat by a narrow margin ⟨he was *nosed out* in the primary⟩

nose over *vi* **:** to turn over by pivoting on the nose (as in a faulty airplane landing)

nosepiece \'⸗,⸗\ *n* **1 :** a piece of armor for protecting the nose **:** NASAL **2 :** NOSEBAND **3 a :** the endpiece of a microscope body to which an objective is attached **b :** a revolving holder for two or more microscope objectives **4 :** the bridge of a pair of eyeglasses

noseprint \'⸗,⸗\ *n* **:** an impression of the bare surface of an animal's nose used to identify a particular individual by means of the unique pattern of pores and lines — compare FINGERPRINT

nose putty *n* **:** a material used in plastic alteration of the nose (as in theatrical makeup)

nos·er \'nōzə(r)\ *n* -s **1** *archaic* **:** a blow or fall on the nose **2** *archaic* **:** a wind full in one's face

nose ring *n* **1 :** a ring worn in the nose for ornament **2 :** a ring fixed in the nose of an animal in order to control it (as to prevent a pig from rooting or to lead a bull)

noses *pl of* NOSE, *pres 3d sing of* NOSE

nose stiffener *n* **:** BOW STIFFENER

nose·thirl \'nōz,thərl\ *n* -s [ME — more at NOSTRIL] *chiefly dial* **:** NOSTRIL

nose-thumbing \'⸗,⸗⸗\ *n* **:** the placing of thumb to nose in derision or contempt

nose up *vi* **:** to head up **:** elevate the nose ⟨the airplane *nosed up* into the sky⟩ ~ *vt* **:** to turn, point, or direct (an airplane's nose) up **:** head (an airplane) up

nosewheel \'⸗,⸗\ *n* **:** a landing-gear wheel located under the nose of an airplane

nosewing \'⸗,⸗\ *n* **:** a nasal ala ⟨laughed . . . slyly, rubbing her ~ with a finger —Thomas Wolfe⟩

nose·wise \'nōz,wīz\ *adj* **1** *archaic* **:** CONCEITED **2** *obs* **:** keen-scented

1nosey \'nōzē\ *n* -s [1*nose* + *-y*, adj. suffix] *archaic* **:** a person having a conspicuous nose

2nosey *var of* NOSY

nosey par·ker \-'pärkər\ *n, often cap P* [prob. fr. a name *Nosey Parker*, fr. *nosy* (used as a nickname) + *Parker* (the surname)] **:** a meddlesome prying busybody

no-show \'⸗'⸗\ *n* [1*no* + *show*, v. (as in *show up*)] **:** a person who reserves space on a train, a ship, or esp. an airplane but neither uses nor cancels the reservation

no side *n* [2*no* + *side*, n. (one of the contesting parties in a game)] **:** the end of a Rugby game

nos·i·ly \'nōzəlē\ *adv* **:** in a nosy manner

nos·i·ness \-zēnəs\ *n* -ES **:** the quality or state of being nosy

nos·ing \'nōziŋ\ *n* -s [1*nose* + *-ing*] **1 a :** the usu. rounded edge of a stair tread that projects over the riser **b :** any of various similar rounded projections (as of molding) **2 a :** the end of a bridge pier **b :** the transverse horizontal motion of a locomotive that exerts a lateral force on the track

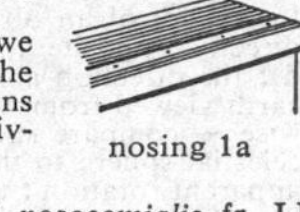

nosing 1a

nos·ism \'nō,sizəm, 'nä,-\ *n* -s [L *nos* we + E *-ism* — more at US] **1** *archaic* **:** the conceit or pride of a group of persons **2** *archaic* **:** the practice of using *we* in giving one's opinions

noso- — see NOS-

noso·co·mi·al \¦näsə¦kōmēəl\ *adj* [NL *nosocomialis*, fr. LL *nosocomium* hospital (fr. LGk *nosokomeion*, fr. Gk *nosokomos* one that tends the sick, fr. *nos-* + *-komos*, akin to Gk *kamnein* to work) + L *-alis* -al — more at COMA] **:** originating or taking place in a hospital ⟨~ infection⟩

noso·geographic \¦näsō+\ *or* **noso·geographical** \"+\ *adj* **:** of or relating to nosogeography

noso·geography \"+\ *n* [ISV *nos-* + *geography*] **:** the geography of disease **:** GEOMEDICINE

nos·o·graph·ic \¦näsə¦grafik\ *adj* [prob. fr. (assumed) NL *nosographicus*, fr. NL *nosographia* nosography + L *-icus* -ic] **:** of or relating to nosography

no·sog·ra·phy \nō'sägrəfē\ *n* -ES [prob. fr. NL *nosographia*, fr. *nos-* + L *-graphia* -graphy] **:** a description or classification of diseases

nos·o·log·ic \¦näsə¦läjik\ *or* **nos·o·log·i·cal** \-jəkəl\ *adj* [*nosologic* prob. fr. (assumed) NL *nosologicus*, fr. NL *nosologia* nosology + L *-icus* -ic; *nosological* prob. fr. (assumed) NL *nosologicus* + E *-al*] **:** relating to a classification of diseases — **nos·o·log·i·cal·ly** \-jək(ə)lē\ *adv*

no·sol·o·gist \nō'säləjəst *sometimes* nō'zä-\ *n* -s [prob. fr. (assumed) NL *nosologistes*, fr. NL *nosologia* nosology + L *-istes* -ist] **:** a specialist in nosology

no·sol·o·gy \-jē, -ji\ *n* -ES [prob. fr. NL *nosologia*, fr. *nos-* + L *-logia* -logy] **:** a branch of medical science that deals with orderly relating or classification of diseases; *sometimes* **:** a classification or list of diseases or a treatise comprising such a classification

nos·o·psyl·lus \,näsə'siləs\ *n, cap* [NL, fr. *nos-* + *-psyllus* (fr. Gk *psylla* flea) — more at PSYLLA] **:** a genus of fleas that includes the northern rat flea (*N. fasciatus*)

nos·tal·gia \nə'stalj(ē)ə, nä'- *sometimes* nō'- *or* nȯ'- *or* -täl-\ *n* -s [NL (trans. of G *heimweh*), fr. Gk *nostos* return home + NL *-algia;* akin to OE *genesan* to survive, OHG *ginesan* to survive, Goth *ganisan* to get well, be saved, Skt *nasate* he approaches, joins] **1 a** *archaic* **:** a severe melancholia caused by protracted absence from home or native place **b :** HOMESICKNESS **2 :** a wistful or excessively sentimental sometimes abnormal yearning for return to or return of some real or romanticized period or irrecoverable condition or setting in the past ⟨~ for his more impressionable youth⟩ ⟨felt a sudden pang of ~ for German music⟩ — **nos·tal·gic** \nə'staljik, (')nä¦s-, -jēk *sometimes* (')nō¦s- *or* (')nȯ¦s- *or* -täl-\ *adj or n* — **nos·tal·gi·cal·ly** \-jək(ə)lē, -jēk-, -li\ *adv*

nos·tal·gy \nə'staljē, nä'-\ *n* -ES [NL *nostalgia*] *archaic* **:** NOSTALGIA

nos·toc \'nä,stäk\ *n* [NL] **1** *cap* **:** a widely distributed genus (the type of the family Nostocaceae) of blue-green algae having filaments enveloped and united by a gelatinous substance into a generally spherical colony living on damp ground or in the water — see STAR JELLY, WITCHES'-BUTTER **2** -s **:** any plant of the genus *Nostoc*

nos·to·ca·ce·ae \,nästə'kāsē,ē\ *n pl, cap* [NL, fr. *Nostoc*, type genus + *-aceae*] **:** a family of minute freshwater blue-green algae (order Hormogonales) consisting of moniliform filaments and reproducing by hormogonia — see ANABAENA — **nos·to·ca·ceous** \¦⸗⸗¦kāshəs\ *adj*

nos·to·ca·les \,nästə'kā(,)lēz\ *n pl, cap* [NL, fr. *Nostoc* + *-ales*] *in some classifications* **:** an order equivalent to Hormogonales

nos·tra·da·mus \,nästrə'dāməs, ,nōstrə'dä̈məs\ *n* -ES *usu cap* [after *Nostradamus* †1566 Fr. physician and astrologer] **:** one professing to foretell future events ⟨one does not have to be a *Nostradamus* to predict tomorrow's weather —*Domestic Commerce*⟩

nos·tril \'nä|strəl *sometimes* 'nō| *or* |(,)stril\ *n* -s [ME *nostrill, nosethirl*, fr. OE *nosterl, nosthyrl, nosthyrel*, fr. *nosu* nose + *thyrel* hole — more at NOSE, THIRL] **1 a :** an external naris; *broadly* **:** a naris with the adjoining passage on the same side of the nasal septum **:** the anterior part of a nasal fossa with its naris **b :** the fleshy lateral wall of the nose **:** a nasal ala **2 :** a small hole for passage of combustion air or waste gas in any of various industrial furnaces

nos·triled *or* **nos·trilled** \-ld\ *adj* **:** having nostrils

nostril fly *n* **:** a fly of the family Oestridae; *esp* **:** SHEEP BOTFLY

nos·tril·i·ty \nä'strilədē\ *n* -ES **:** prominence of nostril

nos·trum \'nästrəm *sometimes* 'nōs-\ *n* -s [L, neut. of *noster* our, ours, fr. *nos* we — more at US] **1 :** a remedy or medicine of secret composition recommended by its preparer but usu. lacking general repute or acceptance **:** a dubious specific ⟨remedies which can have no possible value as medicine, as in the case of a ~ offered for the treatment of diabetes at $12 a pint —*Encyc. Americana*⟩ **2 :** a questionable remedy or scheme **:** CURE-ALL, PANACEA ⟨have never been able to believe wholeheartedly in any simple ~ by which all ills are to be cured —Bertrand Russell⟩ ⟨identify this spiritually impotent but socially powerful ~ with Christianity —H.N.Fairchild⟩

no·su \'nō(,)sü\ *n, pl* **nosu** *or* **nosus** *usu cap* **1 :** a Tibeto-Burman people of the high plateaus and mountains of southwest Szechwan, former eastern Sikang and northern Yunnan — called also *Lolo* **2 :** a member of the Nosu people

nosy *or* **nosey** \'nōzē, -zi\ *adj* **nosier; nosiest** [¹*nose* + -*y*] **1** *archaic* **a :** bad-smelling **b :** FRAGRANT **2 :** of prying or inquisitive disposition or quality **:** INTRUSIVE ⟨~ neighbors⟩ ⟨~ questions⟩ **syn** *see* CURIOUS

¹not \'nät, *usu* -äd·+V\ *or* **-nt** *or* **-n't** \(ə)n(t), (ᵊ)n(t)\ *also* **-not** \(')nät *sometimes* -,nət, *usu* -d·+V\ *adv* [ME, alter. of *nought*, fr. *nought*, pron. — more at NAUGHT] **1 a** — used as a function word to turn an expression consisting of a word or group of words into an implicitly opposite expression ⟨~ pregnant⟩ ⟨~ in sight⟩ ⟨the team did ~ win⟩ ⟨if he will ~ go⟩ ⟨the telephone is ~ ringing⟩ ⟨will ~ pay the bill⟩ ⟨there has ~ been time —Lois M. Miller⟩ ⟨a faint smell of disinfectant, but it did ~ reek of the stuff —Phil Stong⟩ ⟨we could ~ defend the Philippines —James Forrestal⟩ ⟨recommend that we ~ offend against charity —G.H.Dunne⟩ ⟨may insist that prefabricated products be ~ used in the buildings they work in —T.W.Arnold⟩ ⟨can*not* read or write —Vicki Baum⟩ ⟨yield ~ to temptation⟩ **b :** NO ⟨my cold is ~ worse than yesterday⟩ ⟨was ~ less fortunate in marriage —T.B.Macaulay⟩ ⟨there were ~ cleaner windows . . . in the whole street —Charles Dickens⟩ ⟨should like to know how language evolved from what was ~ language —C.F.Hockett⟩ **c :** in no manner or degree **:** in no way **:** NOWISE ⟨~ at all satisfactory⟩ ⟨~ near so expensive⟩ ⟨it is certainly ~ the viewpoint of the minister —C.F.Hunter⟩ ⟨thou shalt ~ kill⟩ **d** — used as a function word to stand for the opposite of a preceding group of words ⟨changes in the environment are sometimes beneficial to the animals and sometimes ~ —W.H.Dowdeswell⟩ ⟨the little girl used to sit very quiet and be good and the little boy used ~ —James Stephens⟩ ⟨if ~, you'll be sorry⟩ and often correlatively ⟨will he be here or ~⟩ ⟨whether you need to make decisions or ~ —W.J. Reilly⟩ **e** — used esp. with *think* to negate a following noun clause ⟨I do*n't* think it will rain⟩ ⟨do*n't* think I'll go⟩ or without a verb to introduce a clause ⟨~ that it matters⟩ ⟨~ that it doesn't matter⟩ ⟨~ that my congratulations to her would not have been tempered with misgivings —Walter de la Mare⟩ ⟨the poem is bad, ~ because it is didactic —S.E.Hyman⟩ ⟨~ to go is a mistake⟩ **f** — used without modifying the meaning of an expression containing another negative ⟨could*n't* stand it no longer —Mark Twain⟩; compare DOUBLE NEGATIVE **2** — used as a generalized negative function word to express an unspecified degree of comparative difference varying from almost identical to almost opposite ⟨today is ~ Wednesday⟩ ⟨in better light you can see the cloth is ~ black⟩ ⟨~ a full cup, please⟩ ⟨five dollars does*n't* count in that place⟩ ⟨the question is ~ as simple as it seems —A.G.Hays⟩ ⟨will be found that it is ~ so easy as it seems —J.A.Powell⟩ ⟨in the auditorium there were many ~ idolaters who found their admiration mixed with apprehension —John Mason Brown⟩ ⟨the holdups he took part in were ~ carefully planned —Croswell Bowen⟩ ⟨was ~ merely a man of words —*Quarterly Jour. of Speech*⟩ ⟨he's ~ all there⟩ ⟨try ~ to hurt me so much⟩ ⟨~ paying careful attention to the warnings⟩ ⟨charged with ~ assuming full responsibility⟩ ⟨after your ~ heavy body shrunken in death —Amy Lowell⟩ **3 :** not even **:** not so much as ⟨~ a red cent⟩ ⟨~ a dog would bark at him —Washington Irving⟩ ⟨five wounded and ~ a man killed —S.C.Williams⟩ **4 :** NEVER ⟨ten years old and ~ been to a circus⟩ **5 :** OTHERWISE ⟨whalers were more often than ~ three or four years away from port —Sacheverell Sitwell⟩ **6 :** slightly less than **:** somewhat less than **:** HARDLY ⟨while ~ as interesting as similar works —E.C.Carter⟩ — usu. used with an intensive (as *very, quite, always, wholly*) and sometimes with *half* ⟨the clergy and elders . . . by and large, are ~ very helpful —John Cogley⟩ ⟨for the armed forces, life is ~ quite as trying as it is for the civilian —Emily Hahn⟩ ⟨the canvasses by other writers have ~ been as revealing —Harold Fields⟩ ⟨the irony of this ~ altogether heartening disclosure —*Sat. Eve. Post*⟩ ⟨the conditions today are ~ half bad⟩ **7** — used as a function word before a negative word to express an intentionally unemphatic affirmation ⟨~ dishonest⟩ ⟨~ implausibly⟩ ⟨~ atypical⟩ ⟨~ inconsistent with law —*U.S.Code*⟩ ⟨~ unreasonable or unexpected —*Atlantic*⟩ **8** — used as the first element of the correlatives *not only . . . but* ⟨will have brought about ~ only the defect of evil, but some permanent good —Julian Huxley⟩ ⟨effective ~ only in terminating an unlawful conspiracy, but in limiting price increases —T.W.Arnold⟩; of the correlatives *not only . . . but also* ⟨~ only the spelling of the words, but also the grammatical forms become conventionalized —William Chomsky⟩; of the correlatives *not . . . but* ⟨~ a country town but a metropolis —Leslie Stephen⟩ ⟨our most significant contribution to general culture, however, was made ~ in modern times but in Saxon times —Kemp Malone⟩; of the correlatives *not . . . nor* ⟨~ for wealth nor for fame did he strive —J.A.Powell⟩ ⟨did ~ speak nor stir —B.A.Williams⟩; or of the correlatives *not . . . or* ⟨such quotations do ~ discredit or impair the sincerity —William Hard⟩ ⟨~ folded bud, or wave that laps a shore —Phyllis McGinley⟩ — **not a little :** to a considerable extent or degree ⟨*not a little* embarrassed by the lack of adequate references —R.W.Chapman⟩

²not \'nät, *usu* -äd·+V\ *n* -S **:** NEGATION, NEGATIVE

³not \"\ *prep* **:** other than **:** EXCEPT ⟨nobody ~ a professor has the remotest idea —W.L.Sullivan⟩

⁴not *or* **nott** \"\ *adj* [ME, close-cropped, fr. OE *knot*] *dial Eng* **:** POLLED

⁵not *or* **nott** \"\ *n* -S *dial Eng* **:** a hornless sheep, cow, or steer

¹not- *or* **noto-** *comb form* [NL, fr. Gk *nōt-, nōto-*, fr. *nōtos, nōton* back — more at NATES] **:** back **:** back part ⟨*noto*chord⟩ ⟨*not*algia⟩

²not- *or* **noto-** *comb form* [NL, fr. Gk *notos* south wind, south, southwest; akin to Gk *noteros* damp — more at NOURISH] **:** south **:** southern ⟨*Noto*therium⟩

-not \(,)nät, 'nät, ,nət, *usu* -d·+V\ *adv comb form* [¹*not*] **:** not ⟨*can*not⟩

nota *pl of* NOTUM

no·ta be·ne \,nōd·ə'benē, -ōtə-, -ni *sometimes* -bēn-; ,nō,tä-'be(,)nā, -tä'-\ [L, mark well] — used to call attention to something important ⟨whom, *nota bene*, I had never seen —Joseph Conrad⟩

no·ta·bilia \,nōd·ə'bilēə, -bēl-, -lyə\ *n pl* [L, neut. pl. of *notabilis*] **:** things worthy of note ⟨collected ~ into groups —G.U.Yule⟩

no·ta·bil·i·ty \,nō|d·ə'bilod·ē, |tə-, -ləté, -i, *in sense 1* " *or* ,nä|\ *n* -ES [¹*notable* + -*ity*] **1** *archaic* **:** the industry or management appropriate to a housewife **2 :** a notable or prominent person ⟨all the *notabilities* gave balls —Lady Hanson⟩

¹no·ta·ble \'nō|d·əbəl, |tə-, *in sense 3* " *or* 'nä|\ *adj* [ME, fr. MF, fr. L *notabilis*, fr. *notare* to note + -*abilis* -able — more at NOTE] **1 a (1) :** worthy of note **:** STRIKING, CONSPICUOUS, REMARKABLE ⟨~ chiefly for its sublime unreality —G.B. Hurff⟩ ⟨wins the ~ distinction of being feared by all —H.A. Overstreet⟩ ⟨the ~ increase in joint production of films —*College English*⟩ ⟨the clock kept time with ~ accuracy —*New Yorker*⟩ ⟨the most ~ exception to this statement —Alfred Cobban⟩ ⟨~ for their endurance . . . and resignation —W.C. Huntington⟩ **(2) :** being of much weight, scope, or significance **:** IMPORTANT, MEMORABLE ⟨a ~ intrigue was set in motion —Claudia Cassidy⟩ ⟨appeared as chief counsel in many ~ cases⟩ ⟨~ deposits were found in other parts of the area⟩ **b (1) :** noteworthy for excellence, quality, merit, or high rank or standing **:** DISTINGUISHED, PROMINENT ⟨had aid and comfort from that ~ scholar —Leonard Bacon⟩ ⟨attended by the most ~ persons of the community⟩ ⟨his conduct toward the one that survived was very ~ —Nancy Mitford⟩ ⟨based on the journal of that ~ trader —*Amer. Guide Series: Ore.*⟩ ⟨a ~ technique wedded to an austere and searching subject —Hollis Alpert⟩ ⟨married into a ~ family⟩ **(2) :** NOTORIOUS ⟨a ~ criminal⟩ ⟨cleaned out a crew of ~ horse thieves —S.H.Holbrook⟩ **2 :** capable of being noted **:** OBSERVABLE ⟨other important events . . . were ~ throughout 1948 —*Collier's Yr. Bk.*⟩ **3** *archaic* **a :** efficient or capable in performance of housewifely duties ⟨~ mothers, who knew what it was to keep children whole and sweet —George Eliot⟩ **b :** of or relating to household management — **no·ta·ble·ness** *n* -ES

²notable \"\ *n* -S **1 :** a prominent or conspicuous figure **:** a person of note **:** NOTABILITY ⟨~*s* from princes to publishers have been involved —Al Brannon⟩ ⟨has been a ~ in the cafeterias, diners, barrooms —Joseph Mitchell⟩ **2 a :** a person of high social rank **:** a member of the wealthy or upper class ⟨employed as domestic servants in the homes of ~*s* —J.F. Embree & W.L.Thomas⟩ **b notables** *pl, often cap* **:** a group of prominent persons usu. of the aristocracy summoned esp. in monarchical France or regions under its political influence to act as a deliberative body ⟨an assembly of *Notables* decided in favor of the establishment in Mexico of a monarchy —W.S. Robertson⟩

no·ta·bly \-blē, -bli\ *adv* [ME, fr. ¹*notable*] **1 :** in a notable manner **:** to an extreme or considerable degree **:** REMARKABLY, STRIKINGLY ⟨club operators are ~ close-mouthed on sales figures —Mitchell Gordon⟩ ⟨became apparent that the seasons vary ~ in length —Benjamin Farrington⟩ ⟨American English has tended to be ~ euphemistic —Thomas Pyles⟩ ⟨beef consumption was ~ higher —*Dun's Rev.*⟩ ⟨were both ~ stubborn —Hugh MacLennan⟩ **2 :** ESPECIALLY, PARTICULARLY ⟨neither comfortable nor ~ uncomfortable —Andy Logan⟩ ⟨other powers, ~ Britain and the United States —C.A.Fisher⟩ ⟨continued to be produced, ~ in recent years —I.M.Price⟩ **3 :** in a manner likely to attract attention **:** NOTICEABLY, CONSPICUOUSLY ⟨could not really be called united, with so many countries ~ absent —Mollie Panter-Downes⟩

no·ta·canth \'nōd·ə,kan(t)th\ *n* -S [NL *Notacanthus*, type genus of Notacanthidae, fr. ¹*not-* + Gk *akantha* thorn, spine — more at ACANTH-] **:** a fish of the family Notacanthidae

no·ta·can·thid \,==¦kan(t)thəd\ *n* -S [NL *Notacanthidae*] **:** NOTACANTH

no·ta·can·thi·dae \-n(t)thə,dē\ *n pl, cap* [NL, fr. *Notacanthus*, type genus + -*idae* — more at NOTACANTH] **:** a small family of deep-sea fishes (order Heteromi) resembling eels and having long dorsal and anal fins with both spines and soft rays

no·ta·can·thous \,==¦kan(t)thəs\ *adj* [¹*not-* + Gk *akantha* + E -*ous*] **:** having spines on the back

no·tae·al \(')nō¦tēəl\ *adj* [NL *notaeum* + E -*al*] **:** of or relating to a notaeum

no·tae ti·ro·ni·a·nae \'nōd·,ētə,rōnē'ā,nē, -ōd·,ī-, -ā,nī\ *n pl, cap T* [NL, characters of Tiro, after M. Tullius *Tiro*, secretary of Cicero] **:** a system of shorthand employed in ancient Rome

no·tae·um *or* **no·te·um** \nō'tēəm\ *n, pl* **no·taea** *or* **no·tea** \-ēə\ [NL, fr. Gk *nōtaios* of the back, fr. *nōton, nōtos* back — more at NATES] **:** the upper surface of a bird's body

no·tal \'nōd·ᵊl, -ōtᵊl\ *adj* [¹*not-* + -*al*] **1 :** of or belonging to the back **:** DORSAL **2** [NL *not*um + E -*al*] **:** of or belonging to a notum

no·ta·lian \(')nō¦tālēən, -lyən\ *adj, usu cap* [NL *Notalia* south temperate marine biogeographic realm (fr. ²*not-* + -*alia*) + E -*an*] **:** of, relating to, or being the south temperate marine biogeographic realm that is bounded by the southern isocrymes of 68° and 44° F

no·tam \'nō,tam\ *n* -S [*notice to airmen*] **:** a notice providing pilots with general information essential for the safe and efficient operation of airplanes (as the establishment or condition of or change in any aeronautical facility, service, procedure, or hazard)

no·tan \'nō'tän\ *n* -S [Jap *nōtan*] **:** the combination of lights and darks esp. as used in Japanese art **:** the design or pattern of a work of art as seen in flat areas of dark and light values only — compare CHIAROSCURO

no·tan·dum \nō'tandəm\ *n, pl* **notan·da** \-də\ *also* **notan·dums** [L, neut. of *notandus*, gerundive of *notare* to note — more at NOTE] **:** something to be noted or an entry of it **:** NOTE, MEMORANDUM

no·tar \'nōd·ə(r)\ *n* [ME, alter. of *notary*] *archaic Scot* **:** NOTARY

no·tar·i·al \(')nō¦ta(a)rēəl\ *adj* [*notary* + -*al*] **:** of, relating to, or characteristic of a notary **:** done, executed, framed, or taken by a notary ⟨~ documents⟩ — **no·tar·i·al·ly** \-əlē\ *adv*

no·ta·ri·za·tion \,nōd·ərə'zāshən, -ōtə-, -,rī'-\ *n* -S [*notarize* + -*ation*] **1 :** the act of a notary in authenticating a document or verifying it under oath **2 :** the act or an instance of causing a document to be authenticated by a notary or to be verified under oath before him **3 :** the notarial certificate appended to a document

no·ta·rize \'==,rīz\ *vt* -ED/-ING/-S [*notary* + -*ize*] **1 :** to acknowledge or attest as a notary public ⟨~ a legal paper⟩ **2 :** to cause (a document) to be acknowledged or attested before or authenticated by a notary public

no·ta·ry \-rē, -ri\ *n* -ES [ME, fr. L *notarius* stenographer, secretary, fr. *notarius* of shorthand, fr. *nota* mark, shorthand character + -*arius* -ary] **1** *obs* **a :** CLERK, SECRETARY **b :** NOTER, OBSERVER **2 a** *or* **notary public** *pl* **notaries public** *or* **notary publics** [ME, fr. *notary* + *public*, adj.] **:** a public officer appointed in the U. S. usu. by the governors of the states and in England where he is still nominally an ecclesiastical official by the Archbishop of Canterbury to take acknowledgment of or otherwise attest or certify deeds and other writings or copies of them usu. under official seal to make them authentic and to take affidavits, depositions, and protests of negotiable paper **b :** a French official who draws up and records documents and instruments of legal importance and certifies to copies of judgments and records and to protests of commercial paper, who is appointed by the president of the Republic, and who cannot serve as advocate or engage in any other business **c :** an official in Quebec who draws up and records instruments, makes titles, and does noncontentious legal business

no·ta·ry·ship \'===,ship\ *n* **:** the office, tenure, or dignity of a notary

¹no·tate \'nō,tāt, *usu* -ād·+V\ *adj* [L *nota* mark + E -*ate*] **:** marked with spots or lines

²notate \"\ *vt* -ED/-ING/-S [back formation fr. *notation*] **:** to put into notation

no·ta·tion \nō'tāshən\ *n* -S [L *notation-, notatio*, fr. *notatus* (past part. of *notare* to note, denote) + -*ion-, -io* -ion — more at NOTE] **1** *obs* **:** etymological explanation or denotation **2 a :** ANNOTATION, NOTE ⟨damage, according to the constable's ~*s*, consisted of broken front bumper —Richard Joseph⟩ ⟨if a letter refers to an enclosure, add the appropriate ~ to the closing lines —D.D.Lessenberry & T.J.Crawford⟩ **b :** an act of noting **:** OBSERVATION **3 a :** the act, process, method, or an instance of representing by a system or set of marks, signs, figures, or characters **b :** a system of characters, symbols, or abbreviated expressions used in an art or science to express technical facts, quantities, or other data **4 a (1) :** the act, process, or system of recording music or musical details by means of written notes or symbols to indicate pitch, rhythm, tempo, harmonic combinations, style, and specific directions for performance **(2) :** musical notes and symbols **b :** the representation of dance movements by means of written symbols **c :** the recording of chess moves **d :** the system of signs and symbols used in symbolic logic — compare TRUTH table **5 :** the act or an instance of recording (as natural appearances or states of mind) through artistic or literary means ⟨swift ~*s* of a light quite different from that of the Caribbean —Virgil Barker⟩ ⟨exact ~ of qualities, tones, rapports of colors and forms —Meyer Schapiro⟩ ⟨the whole purport of literature . . . is the ~ of the heart —Thornton Wilder⟩

no·ta·tion·al \(')=¦tāshənᵊl, -shnəl\ *adj* **:** of or relating to notation

no·ta·tive \'nōd·əd·iv, -ōtətiv\ *adj* [L *notatus* + E -*ive*] **:** suggesting the characteristics or things denoted

no·ta·tor \(')nō¦tād·ə(r), -ātə-\ *n* -S [L *notatus* (past part. of *notare* to note) + E -*or* — more at NOTE] **:** a specialist in musical or dance notation

no·tau·lix \nō'tȯ(,)liks\ *n, pl* **notauli·ces** \-,lə,sēz\ [NL, fr. ¹*not-* + LL *aulic-, aulix* furrow, MS error for *aulac-, aulax*, fr. Gk *aulak-, aulax*] **:** a longitudinal furrow in the anterior part of the mesonotum of various insects

not–being \'=¦==\ *n* **:** the state of not being

¹notch \'näch\ *n* -ES [perh. alter. (resulting from incorrect division of *an otch*) of (assumed) *otch*, fr. MF *oche*] **1 a :** a V-shaped indentation or hollow (as in a surface or edge) **b (1) :** a slit or cut made in something esp. to serve as a mark or record **:** NICK ⟨supposed to be three ~*es* on the butt of his business six-shooter —Green Peyton⟩ **(2) :** a run in cricket **c :** UNDERCUT **d :** a half-moon (as in a thumb index) cut in book leaves at the fore edge to provide space for an identification guide **e :** a space cut out in the safety roller of lever escapements and in the staff of duplex escapements of watches to permit passage of a safety finger piece during impulse to the balance **f (1) :** a small V-shaped cut or one of several cuts along the edge of clothing patterns to be used as an aid in assembling a garment **(2) :** a V-shaped angle at the joining of lapel and collar on a garment **2 :** a narrow passage between two mountains or other elevations **:** a deep close pass **:** DEFILE, GAP ⟨the most historic of nine ~*es* . . . which are scattered through these mountains —*Ford Times*⟩ — often used in place names ⟨Crawford *Notch*⟩ **3 :** a degree, step, or peg ⟨his voice rose another ~ —Earle Birney⟩ ⟨this book . . . is ~*es* above the usual product —Louise D. Rich⟩

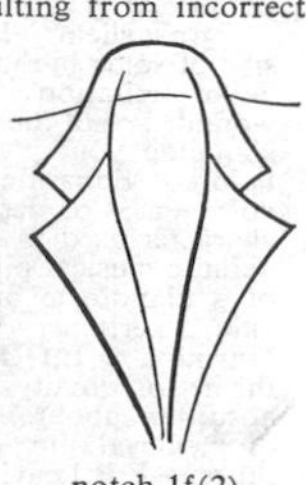

notch 1f(2)

²notch \"\ *vb* -ED/-ING/-ES *vt* **1 a** *obs* **:** to cut (the hair) unevenly or poorly **b (1) :** to cut or make a notch in **:** INDENT ⟨fitted together by ~*ing* the ends —*Amer. Guide Series: Minn.*⟩ ⟨the much steeper continental slope, ~*ed* by the mouths of the gorges —R.E.Coker⟩ **(2) :** to score, mark, or record by or as if by means of a notch ⟨~*ed* another kill on the butt of his gun⟩ **(3) :** to score, gain, or achieve successfully ⟨~*ed* his second victory against three losses —*N.Y.Times*⟩ ⟨wrote the thesis which ~*ed* him his M.D. —Sydney (*Australia*) *Bulletin*⟩ ⟨~*ed* his thirteenth consecutive perfect performance —*Postal Service News*⟩ ⟨~*ed* himself a place in Spanish history —Hamilton Basso⟩ **c :** to make an undercut in ⟨~ a tree⟩ **2 :** to fit (the arrow) to the string **:** NOCK **3 a :** to fasten or insert by means of a notch ⟨logs being ~*ed* into each other at the corners —*Amer. Guide Series: Texas*⟩ **b :** to give a particular shape or form to by making notches — used with *into* **4 :** to change the position of (a control device) step by step ~ *vi* **:** to make or form a notch ⟨the path ~*ed* into the jungle wall —William Faulkner⟩

notch block *n* **:** SNATCH BLOCK

notchboard \'=,=\ *n* **:** a board that receives the ends of the steps in a staircase

notch carving *n* **:** NICKING

notched \'nächt\ *adj* [partly fr. past part. of ²*notch*, partly fr. ¹*notch* + -*ed*] **1 :** having a notch **:** INDENTED, SERRATED ⟨a ~ collar⟩ ⟨a ~ log⟩ ⟨a medicinal tablet . . . which is ~ down the middle —Richard Joseph⟩ ⟨brow . . . already ~ with care —Julian Maclaren-Ross⟩ ⟨a leaf with ~ edges⟩ **2** *archaic* **:** having the hair cut unevenly

notched binding *n* **:** the fastening of sets of single leaves (as of books or magazines) with a series of glue-filled grooves at the backbone edge rather than by sewing

notched falcon *n* **:** any of several So. American kites (genus *Harpagus*) having the maxilla doubly toothed

notched wrack *n* **:** a common rockweed (*Fucus serratus*) of the northern Atlantic

notch·er \'nächə(r)\ *n* -S **:** one who cuts notches: as **a :** UNDERCUTTER **b :** an operator of a machine for notching tin plate to facilitate the flanging and seaming operations in the making of tin cans **c :** an instrument for making notches

notch graft *n* **:** a graft similar to a cleft graft except that a slit in the stock is made with a saw and the scion is inserted in the slit

notch grafting *or* **notch graftage** *n* **:** the process of making a notch graft

notching *n* -S [fr. gerund of ²*notch*] **1 a :** the act or an instance of making notches **:** an act of cutting into small hollows **b :** a method of joining (as timbers or scantling) by notching (as at the ends) and overlapping or interlocking the notched portions; *also* **:** a joint so formed **c :** the removal of a wedge of bark above a bud (as on a branch of an apple tree) to induce the formation of a branch from the bud **2 :** a small hollow formed by notching **:** NOTCH

notchweed \'=,=\ *also* **notchwort** \'=,=\ *n* **:** STINKING GOOSEFOOT

notchwing \'=,=\ *n* **:** a European moth (*Peronia caudana*) of the family Tortricidae

not content *n, pl* **not contents** [¹*not* + *content*, adj.] **:** NON-CONTENT

¹note \'nōt, *usu* -ōd·+V\ *n* -S [ME, use, profit, benefit, fr. OE *nutu;* akin to OE *nēotan* to use, enjoy — more at NEAT] *dial Eng* **:** a cow's lactation period

²note \"\ *vt* -ED/-ING/-S [ME *noten*, fr. OF *noter*, fr. L *notare*, fr. *nota* note, mark] **1 a (1) :** to record or fix in the mind or memory **:** take due or special notice of **:** notice or observe with care ⟨must be *noted* that some southern Negroes were able to rise —Mercer Cook⟩ ⟨please ~ that payment in full is enclosed⟩ ⟨*noted* the fine stature of the Indian males —*Amer. Guide Series: Oreg.*⟩ ⟨pleased to ~ that I will be summoned to appear in court —Oris Turner⟩ **(2) :** to record or preserve in writing **:** make a note of ⟨*noted* on the margin his disagreement with the writer⟩ — often used with *down* ⟨*noted* down his impressions of the city⟩ **(3)** *archaic* **:** to set down in or provide with notes esp. musical notes **(4) :** to make a notarial memorandum of nonpayment of (a negotiable bill) on presentation **(5) :** to make notes in; *also* **:** ANNOTATE ⟨*noted* cases for the attorney general —John Buchan⟩ **b :** to recognize the existence or presence of **:** PERCEIVE, OBSERVE ⟨in these brilliant and gifted inhabitants . . . one may ~ a number of characteristics —W.K.Ferguson⟩ ⟨edema is likely to be *noted* first in the legs —Morris Fishbein⟩ ⟨too good and simple himself to ~ what was implied —Mary Austin⟩ ⟨one ~*s* the scars pocking the buildings —H.L.Matthews⟩ ⟨quick to ~ a shadow of pain across his pale features —W.J.Locke⟩ **2** *obs* **:** DENOTE, SIGNIFY **3 a :** to call attention to in speech or writing **:** make separate or special mention of **:** REMARK ⟨the odds, someone *noted*, were stacked . . . in favor of the house —T.H.White b. 1915⟩ ⟨~*s* with gallant approval the civilizing influences of British administrators —Hal Lehrman⟩ ⟨the magazine *noted* his understanding of international problems —*Current Biog.*⟩ **b :** to indicate or show ⟨records fail to ~ what became of him⟩ ⟨on this occasion she was merely *noted* as a member of the company —F.C.Schang⟩ ⟨scales that can ~ the absence of a dime in a batch of thousands —*Buick Mag.*⟩ **4** *obs* **:** CHARGE, ACCUSE, BRAND — usu. used with *of, for*, or *with* **syn** see SEE

³note \"\ *n* -S [L *nota* note, mark, character, brand] **1 a (1) :** a

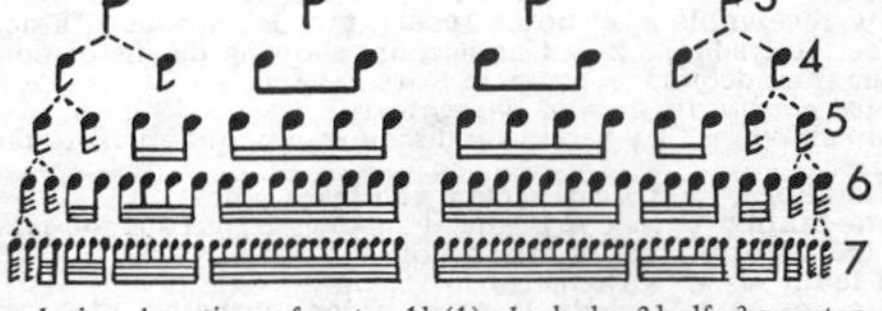

relative duration of notes 1b(1): *1* whole, *2* half, *3* quarter, *4* eighth, *5* sixteenth, *6* thirty-second, *7* sixty-fourth notes

melody or song ⟨mine ear is much enamored of thy ~ —Shak.⟩ **(2) :** a tone of definite pitch (as of a musical instrument or the voice) **(3) :** CRY, CALL, SOUND ⟨heard the iron on the roof give an uneasy warning ~ —Eve Langley⟩ ⟨not even the loon, in whose voice there is a human ~ —Charlton Laird⟩ **(4) :** the musical call or song of a bird ⟨you know its ~: the liquid clarity is so perfect that when it sings the other birds . . . grow silent —Harold Laski⟩ (5) **:** a tone of voice expressive of some mood, attitude, or emotion ⟨her voice carried a ~ of irritation —Louis Bromfield⟩ ⟨would cry with the wounded ~ of the utterly betrayed —Mary Austin⟩ ⟨her deep-sounding young voice with a ~ in it he had never heard before —Edna Ferber⟩ ⟨a wild anxiety had come into her voice—a ~ of desperate pleading —O.E.Rölvaag⟩ **b** (1) **:** a character used to indicate relative duration by its shape and definite musical pitch by its position on the staff (2) **:** a key of a pianoforte or similar instrument **c :** ODOR, SMELL ⟨a valued perfumery synthetic with a lily-of-the-valley ~ —J.E. Hawkins & E.G.Rietz⟩ **2 a** (1) **:** a characteristic feature, theme, or quality **:** ELEMENT, MOTIF ⟨there was such a ~ of absurdity about it —T.B.Costain⟩ ⟨those are the main ~s of medieval life —G.G.Coulton⟩ ⟨the essential ~s of his satire —F.R.Leavis⟩ ⟨a fixed ~ of my father's life —Van Wyck Brooks⟩ ⟨two ~s of gentility our family maintained —R.M.Lovett⟩ ⟨a strong ~ of realism —Ellen L. Buell⟩ ⟨there isn't a ~ in you which I don't know —Thomas Hardy⟩ (2) **:** an identifying or dominant theme, characteristic, or motif ⟨the hard, varnished, cosmopolitan cleverness which is the ~ of the hour —Sinclair Lewis⟩ ⟨strikes at once the ~ of his career —H.E.Scudder⟩ (3) **:** a concrete object that sets the tone or constitutes an identifying or characteristic feature ⟨vast ranches whose one modern ~ is an occasional oil derrick —*Amer. Guide Series: Texas*⟩ (4) **:** MOOD, TONE, TENOR ⟨hadn't intended to end on this ~ —F.R.Leavis⟩ ⟨answered on the same detached ~ —Francis King⟩ ⟨began . . . on a ~ of urgency —Christine Weston⟩ ⟨inject a ~ of intimacy into their contacts —T.B.Costain⟩ **b** *archaic* **:** STIGMA, REPROACH **3 a** (1) **:** an abstract of particulars recorded in the conveyance by fine (2) *Scots law* **:** a short and concise statement used as a pleading of an action or defense and setting forth without argument the statutes or cases relied upon **b** (1) **:** a brief writing intended to assist the memory or to serve as the basis for a fuller statement **:** MEMORANDUM, MINUTE ⟨made a ~ on a piece of paper —Barnaby Conrad⟩ (2) **:** a condensed record of a speech, lecture, lesson, or discussion made at the time of listening ⟨takes extensive ~s in all his classes⟩ (3) **:** an artist's rough sketch esp. of a detail **c** (1) **:** a brief remark by way of explanation or information **:** a comment or explanation (as penciled in the margin of a page) **:** a critical explanation or illustrative observation (2) **:** a printed comment or reference that is set apart from the main text and usu. in smaller type — see FOOTNOTE, SHOULDER NOTE, SIDENOTE; compare REFERENCE MARK (3) **:** explanatory printed comment on a work of art ⟨program ~s for a concert⟩ ⟨~s on a record album⟩ **d** (1) *archaic* **:** ACCOUNT, BILL (2) **:** a written or printed paper acknowledging a debt and promising payment **:** a written promise to pay ⟨has my ~ for $1000⟩ (3) **:** a bank note or other form of paper that is current money ⟨deposited the sum in ~s and coin⟩ (4) *obs* **:** a signed receipt **:** VOUCHER **e** (1) **:** a short informal letter (2) **:** a formal diplomatic communication regularly bearing the signature of the person who sends it, addressed personally to the minister or other official to whom it is sent, usually written in the first person although sometimes in the third, and typically used for the most important correspondence — compare AIDE-MÉMOIRE, MEMORANDUM, NOTE VERBALE (3) **:** any of a number of diplomatic communications of varying character or formality **f** (1) **:** a short account, essay, or sketch ⟨not attempting in this brief ~ to recount again the public battles of that far-off time —Bruce Bliven b.1889⟩; *specif* **:** a communication (as to a scholarly or technical journal) usu. considerably shorter in length than an article and severely restricted in scope or subject matter ⟨a brief ~ . . . reported the find of an association of human burials and artifacts —G.W.Hewes⟩ (2) **:** an often informal record of impressions or incidents — usu. used in pl. ⟨~s on a journey to the headwaters of the Amazon⟩ (3) **:** a brief item in a newspaper or magazine **:** JOTTING ⟨financial ~s⟩ ⟨household ~s⟩ ⟨social ~s⟩ **4 a :** DISTINCTION, REPUTATION, EMINENCE ⟨other animal stories of ~ —Ellen L. Buell⟩ ⟨a figure of almost international ~ —John Buchan⟩ **b :** OBSERVATION, NOTICE, HEED — usu. used with *take* ⟨took full ~ of all that had happened⟩ **c :** KNOWLEDGE, INFORMATION ⟨his popularity has long been a matter of ~ —*Current Biog.*⟩ **5 :** an incident or situation of an unexpected, startling, or disagreeable character ⟨wasn't that a ~ for a chief officer to swallow —Sam Ross⟩ ⟨that's a hell of a ~ —Ernest Hemingway⟩ **syn** see CHARACTER, SIGN

notebook \ˈ⸗,⸗\ *n* **1 :** a book in which notes or memoranda are recorded **2 :** a book with blank leaves used by students for taking notes during a class or lecture

note broker *n* **:** a broker who deals in short-term negotiable instruments (as acceptances, bills, or notes)

notecase \ˈ⸗,⸗\ *n*, *Brit* **:** a pocketbook for banknotes **:** WALLET

note col·lec·tive \ˈnōt,kȯ,lekˈtēv\ *n*, *pl* **notes collectives** \-ōts,kȯ,lekˈtēv\ [F] **:** a formal diplomatic communication addressed by two or more states to one or more states that is usu. signed and not merely initialed by the representatives of the states presenting it

not·ed \ˈnōd·əd, -ōtəd\ *adj* [ME, fr. past part. of *noten* to note] **1 :** well-known by reputation **:** EMINENT, CELEBRATED ⟨a ~ educator⟩ ⟨a ~ landmark⟩ ⟨a ~ beauty⟩ ⟨a ~ racehorse⟩ **2 :** provided with musical notes or score — **not·ed·ly** *adv* — **not·ed·ness** *n* -ES

note di·plo·ma·tique \ˈnōt,dipləˌmaˈtēk\ *n*, *pl* **notes diplomatiques** \-ōts,dipləˌmaˈtēk\ [F] **:** a formal diplomatic communication signed and not merely initialed and understood to speak for and under the direction of the government presenting it

notehead \ˈ⸗,⸗\ *or* **noteheading** \ˈ⸗,⸗⸗\ *n* **:** a sheet of writing paper that has a printed or engraved heading and is usu. somewhat smaller than a letterhead; *also* **:** the heading itself

noteholder \ˈ⸗,⸗⸗\ *n* **:** a person who holds a note

not·e·laea \ˌnäd·əˈlēə\ *n*, *cap* [NL, fr. ²*not-* + Gk *elaia* olive tree — more at OLIVE] **:** a small genus of chiefly Australian trees or shrubs (family Oleaceae) most of which have very hard wood

note·less \ˈnōtləs\ *adj* **1 :** not noted or not noticed **:** UNDISTINGUISHED ⟨some ~ Gaelic poet —W.B.Yeats⟩ **2 :** devoid of musical notes or tones **:** UNMUSICAL — **note·less·ly** *adv* — **note·less·ness** *n* -ES

note·let \-lət\ *n* -S **:** a little or short note

note·man \-mən, -ˌman\ *n*, *pl* **notemen :** a member of a surveying party who keeps the records of the data secured

note of exclamation *also* **note of admiration :** EXCLAMATION POINT

note of hand : PROMISSORY NOTE

note of interrogation : QUESTION MARK

notepaper \ˈ⸗,⸗⸗\ *n* **:** writing paper of a quality, size, or fold suitable for notes, letters, memoranda

note payable *n*, *pl* **notes payable 1 :** a note of indebtedness of the maker **2** *pl* **:** an account showing details of notes owed to creditors — compare NOTE RECEIVABLE

note-perfect \ˈ⸗ˈ⸗⸗\ *adj* **:** perfect in every note ⟨it is not quite *note-perfect* —Edward Sackville-West & Desmond Shawe-Taylor⟩

not·er \ˈnōd·ə(r), -ōtə-\ *n* -S **:** one that notes

note receivable *n*, *pl* **notes receivable 1 :** a note of a debt due the creditor **2** *pl* **:** an account showing details of notes due from debtors — compare NOTE PAYABLE

notes *pl of* NOTE, *pres 3d sing of* NOTE

note shaver *n* **:** a person who discounts notes at an exorbitant rate

notetaker \ˈ⸗,⸗⸗\ *n* **:** a person who takes notes

note-taking \ˈ⸗,⸗⸗\ *n* [³*note* + *taking*, fr. gerund of *take*] **:** the act or process of taking notes

no·teum *var of* NOTAEUM

note ver·bale \ˌ⸗verˈbäl\ *n*, *pl* **notes verbales** \ˌnōt(s),⸗ˈbäl(z)\ [F, lit., verbal note] **:** a diplomatic note that is more formal than an aide-mémoire and less formal than a note, is drafted in the third person, and is never signed

noteworthily \ˈ⸗,⸗⸗⸗\ *adv* **:** in a noteworthy manner

noteworthiness \ˈ⸗,⸗⸗⸗\ *n* -ES **:** the quality or state of being noteworthy

noteworthy \ˈ⸗,⸗⸗\ *adj* **:** worthy of note **:** REMARKABLE, NOTABLE ⟨made ~ contributions in diverse fields —M.R. Cohen⟩ ⟨the damage to the promenade . . . was ~ —J.A. Steers⟩

not-go gage \ˈ⸗ˈ⸗-\ *n* **:** NO-GO GAGE

not guilty *adj* — used as the term of general issue to deny the whole indictment in legal actions

noth- *or* **notho-** *comb form* [NL, fr. Gk *noth-*, *notho-*, fr. *nothos* bastard, spurious, born of unequal parents] **:** bastard **:** spurious **:** hybrid ⟨*Noth*arctus⟩ ⟨*Notho*saurus⟩

¹**no·tharc·tid** \nəˈthärktəd\ *adj* [NL *Notharctidae*, family including *Notharctus*] **:** of or relating to *Notharctus* or a closely related genus

²**notharctid** \"\ *or* **no·tharc·tine** \-tīn, -tən\ *n* -S **:** a lemur of *Notharctus* or a closely related genus

no·tharc·tus \-təs\ *n*, *cap* [NL, fr. *noth-* + Gk *arktos* bear — more at ARCTIC] **:** a genus of primitive No. American Eocene lemurs with large orbits and 40 teeth of which the incisors are not procumbent, that is related to *Adapis*, and known from the No. American Eocene

¹**noth·er** \ˈnəthə(r)\ *pron* [ME, alter. (resulting fr. incorrect division of *an other, none other*) of *other*, pron.] *chiefly dial* **:** OTHER

²**nother** \"\ *adj* [ME, alter. (resulting fr. incorrect division of *an other, none other*) of *other*, adj.] *chiefly dial* **:** OTHER

¹**noth·ing** \ˈnəthiŋ, -thēŋ\ *pron* [ME *nothing, nathing, non thing*, fr. OE *nāthing, nān thing*, fr. *nān* no + *thing* — more at NONE] **1 :** not any thing **:** no thing ⟨~ in the . . . document precludes the existence of regional arrangements —Vera M. Dean⟩ ⟨leaving ~ to chance—Fred Majdalany⟩ ⟨the dead feel ~, hear ~ —Carson McCullers⟩ ⟨had done little or ~ toward solving the really fundamental problem —*Collier's Yr. Bk.*⟩ ⟨just say ~ —Lilian Balch⟩ **2 :** no share, element, or part ⟨wrote ~ of an acceptance message in advance —J.A.Huston⟩ ⟨~ of him that doth fade —Shak.⟩ **3 a :** one that is of no interest, value, or consequence to a person ⟨she's ~ to me, and I am ~ to her —Thomas Hardy⟩ ⟨the work he does . . . is ~ to him —T.P.Whitney⟩ **b :** no gain or advantage — often used in the phrase *nothing in it* ⟨there was ~ in it for him —L.C.Douglas⟩ **c :** no point or element of advantage **:** no superiority of condition — usu. used in the phrase *have nothing on* ⟨palaces had . . . ~ on her lovely thatched cottage —*No. Amer. Rev.*⟩ **d :** no substance or reality ⟨there's ~ to that story⟩ **e :** no complexity or difficulty ⟨the inexperienced hunter, who, after having killed a dozen or so of the animals . . . begins to think there is ~ in it —James Stevenson-Hamilton⟩ ⟨there's ~ to it if you know how⟩ **f :** no money or resources ⟨lived . . . on next to ~ —Ellen Glasgow⟩ ⟨left with ~⟩ **g :** no incriminating or damning evidence — usu. used in the phrase *have nothing on* ⟨the police had ~ on him⟩ — **for nothing** *adv* **1 :** to no purpose **:** in vain ⟨not born in the hills of Tennessee *for nothing* —W.C.Fridley⟩ **2 :** for no reason ⟨crying *for nothing* at all⟩ **3 :** without cost or payment ⟨delight of impressions given by nature *for nothing* —Henry Adams⟩ — **in nothing flat** *adv* **:** in the shortest possible time ⟨the rain swallowed up the tail light *in nothing flat* —E.S. Gardner⟩ ⟨put away her sandwiches *in nothing flat* —*New Yorker*⟩ — **nothing but :** nothing other than **:** ONLY ⟨has *nothing but* the clothes on his back⟩ — **nothing doing 1 :** by no means **:** definitely no ⟨*nothing doing* was the substance of his reply⟩ **2 :** no result or accomplishment ⟨there was *nothing doing* —W.R.Frye⟩ — **nothing for it :** no alternative ⟨*nothing for it* but to ride away . . . for the doctor —D.M. Davin⟩ ⟨there is *nothing for it*, but to keep her under close watch —Henry Wynmalen⟩ — **nothing if not :** above all **:** EXTREMELY ⟨*nothing if not* persistent —J.D.Carr⟩

²**nothing** \"\ *adv* [ME *nothing, nathing*, fr. OE *nāthing, nān thing*, fr. *nāthing, nān thing*, pron.] **:** not at all **:** in no degree ⟨that he should become a deity is ~ surprising —A.M. Young⟩ ⟨~ daunted, they dive into the icy water —G.W. Long⟩ — **nothing like** *adv* **:** NOWHERE NEAR **:** not nearly ⟨is *nothing like* as big as it looks on the map —Harry Gilroy⟩

³**nothing** \"\ *n* -S [¹*nothing*] **1 a :** no thing at all **:** something that does not exist ⟨an emissary of the primeval ~ —Thomas Carlyle⟩ ⟨~ cannot become an object of consciousness —Herbert Spencer⟩ **b** (1) **:** the absence of all magnitude or quantity **:** ZERO (2) **:** the symbol naught **:** CIPHER **c :** something that is characterized by utter absence of determination **:** perfect indistinguishableness ⟨pure ~⟩ **d** *obs* **:** utter insignificance **:** NOTHINGNESS ⟨find the emptiness of all things and the ~ of what is past —Sir Thomas Browne⟩ **2 a** (1) **:** something of no or slight value or significance **:** TRIFLE, BAGATELLE ⟨a little ~ of a dress —Lois Long⟩ ⟨love at first sight is a romantic ~ —Walter Le Beau⟩ ⟨so badly damaged that they looked like ~ —J.P.Blank⟩ (2) **:** a trifling or inane remark ⟨the glories of silent appreciation were shattered by garrulous ~s —William Beebe⟩ ⟨having drinks and saying sweet ~s —Hugh Gaitskell⟩ **b :** a person or other living individual who is supremely insignificant or inconsequential **:** one with no claim to note **:** NULLITY ⟨his wife . . . is strictly a ~ —*New Yorker*⟩ ⟨the bull . . . had temporarily become a ~ —Jean Stafford⟩ — **no nothing :** nothing at all ⟨no drama, no astonishing shots—*no nothing* —*New Yorker*⟩

noth·ing·ar·i·an \ˌ⸗⸗ˈerēən\ *n* -S [¹*nothing* + *-arian*] **:** a person of no belief, creed, or particular sect

¹**noth·ing·ly** *adj* [³*nothing* + *-ly*] **:** VALUELESS, INEFFECTUAL

²**nothingly** \"\ *n* -ES **:** CIPHER

noth·ing·ness *n* -ES **1 :** the quality or state of being nothing: as **a :** absence of being **:** NONEXISTENCE ⟨the smoke . . . was snatched and scattered into ~ —Gordon Webber⟩ **b :** utter insignificance, worthlessness, or futility ⟨would be intimidated into meek ~ —Sinclair Lewis⟩ **c :** DEATH ⟨human reason cannot conceive of ~, yet men fear it —*Time*⟩ ⟨cannot believe in ~ being the destined end of all —T.B.Cabell⟩ **d :** the state or quality of utter indistinguishableness **:** total absence of determination or particularity **2 :** something that is utterly insignificant or valueless **3 :** EMPTINESS, VOID ⟨beyond the window was only a gray ~ —Hugh MacLennan⟩ ⟨ran behind a great green wall into ~ —Ira Wolfert⟩ **4 :** the conceptualization or reification of the affective content in an emotional experience (as of anxiety) that is negatively colored ⟨~ is . . . a distinctive metaphysical entity —J.A.Franquiz⟩; *also* **:** MEANINGLESSNESS ⟨the utter ~ of not being —Jean Wahl⟩

nothing off [²*nothing*] — used as an order to a steersman to keep the ship close to the wind

notho- — see NOTH-

notho·cli·nal \ˌnäthəˈklīnᵊl\ *adj* **:** of, relating to, or constituting a nothocline

notho·cline \ˈ⸗⸗,klīn\ *n* -S [*noth-* + *cline*] **:** a gradation of forms resulting from interspecific hybridization **:** a hybrid cline

noth·o·fa·gus \ˌ⸗⸗ˈfāgəs\ *n*, *cap* [NL, fr. *noth-* + *Fagus*] **:** a genus of timber trees of the cooler parts of the southern hemisphere differing from the genus *Fagus* in the chiefly evergreen smaller leaves and in the flowers of both sexes being solitary or in threes — see EVERGREEN BEECH, NEW ZEALAND BEECH

noth·o·lae·na \-ˈlēnə\ *n*, *cap* [NL, fr. *noth-* + L *laena* cloak, fr. Gk *chlaina*] **:** a genus of rock-inhabiting ferns (family Polypodiaceae) of very diverse habit and with pinnate, bipinnate, or tripinnate fronds that are silky, hairy, tomentose, or farinose

noth·o·saur \ˈ⸗⸗,sȯ(ə)r\ *n* -S [NL *Nothosaurus*] **:** a reptile or fossil of the suborder Nothosauria

noth·o·sau·ria \ˌ⸗⸗ˈsȯrēə\ *n pl*, *cap* [NL *Nothosaurus* + *-ia*] **:** a suborder of primitive chiefly marine European Triassic reptiles (order Sauropterygia) —see NOTHOSAURUS — **noth·o·sau·ri·an** \ˌ⸗⸗ˈsȯrēən\ *adj or n*

noth·o·sau·rus \ˌ⸗⸗ˈsȯrəs\ *n*, *cap* [NL, fr. *noth-* + *-saurus*] **:** a genus of extinct reptiles (suborder Nothosauria) resembling the plesiosaurs but having longer and more slender limbs less completely modified for swimming

noth·o·scor·dum \-ˈskȯrdəm\ *n*, *cap* [NL, fr. *noth-* + Gk *skordon* garlic] **:** a genus of bulbous plants (family Liliaceae) that resemble the related onions and are sometimes cultivated for their terminal umbels of showy flowers — see CROW POISON

¹**no·tice** \ˈnōd·əs, -ōtəs\ *n* -S [ME *notice*, fr. MF *notice* acquaintance, fr. L *notitia*, fr. *notus* (past part. of *noscere* to become acquainted with) + *-itia* -ice — more at KNOW] **1 a** (1) **:** formal or informal warning or intimation of something **:** ANNOUNCEMENT ⟨subject to change without ~ —*Dun's Rev.*⟩ ⟨was ~ that Britain meant to crack down on violence —*Time*⟩ ⟨give ~ of the fat and wrinkles coming to the young bride —H.M.Parshley⟩ (2) **:** a warning, announcement, or intimation given a specified time before the event to take place ⟨evacuating a school building . . . in a minute's ~ —Rose Bernadette⟩ ⟨upon reasonable ~, these charges are subject to adjustment —*Bull. of Bates Coll.*⟩ ⟨ready to leave at short ~⟩ ⟨allow me ten minutes' ~⟩ (3) **:** notification by one of the parties to an agreement or relation (as by an employer to a laborer) of intention of terminating it at a specified time ⟨tenants' right freely to give ~ —Store Bolin⟩ (4) **:** a communication of intelligence or of a claim or demand often required by statute or contract and prescribing the manner or form of giving it ⟨a ~ to quit leased premises⟩ (5) **:** the condition of being warned or notified — usu. used in the phrase *on notice* ⟨are on ~ that their military supply centers . . . would no longer be a privileged sanctuary —*N.Y.Times*⟩ ⟨putting all . . . court personnel on ~ that fundamental rights had to be observed —E.E.Nobleman⟩ **b :** INFORMATION, INTELLIGENCE ⟨~ of any errors . . . should be addressed —*Federal Guide (Australia)*⟩ ⟨give ~ of a poet —H.A.Larrabee⟩ **c** (1) *archaic* **:** KNOWLEDGE (2) **:** actual knowledge of a pertinent legal fact — called also *actual notice, express notice* (3) **:** knowledge of a particular fact (as the terms of a lease when one knows a tenant is in possession) capable of being acquired by the exercise of reasonable care on the part of the person legally chargeable with it — called also *implied notice* (4) **:** knowledge of a particular fact (as from deeds recorded in a public registry office) imputed by a positive rule of law to a person regardless of his actual knowledge — called also *constructive notice* **d** *obs* **:** NOTION, IDEA **2 a** (1) **:** ATTENTION, HEED, OBSERVATION ⟨first attracted ~ with his short novel⟩ ⟨will be brought under the ~ of the police —Priscilla Hughes⟩ ⟨the first . . . to receive ~ from history —W.J.Entwistle & W.A.Morison⟩ — often used in the phrase *take notice* ⟨doubted whether she would take much ~ —Gerard Bourke⟩ ⟨you sit up and take ~⟩ (2) **:** the condition of being noticed ⟨brought him into public ~ —Gearoid O'Sullivan⟩ **b :** polite or favorable attention **:** FAVOR, RESPECT, CIVILITY ⟨she had very little ~ from any but him —Jane Austen⟩ **3 :** a written or printed announcement or bulletin ⟨one sees crude ~s of patent medicines —*Amer. Guide Series: Fla.*⟩ ⟨inserted a ~ in the newspaper⟩ ⟨all the societies put up printed ~s of their activities —S.P.B.Mais⟩ **4 a :** a critical account or commentary on a play or other public performance ⟨the stage play received . . . glowing ~s —C.J.Rolo⟩ ⟨opened to enthusiastic ~s —*Current Biog.*⟩ **b :** BOOK REVIEW ⟨presume that your book . . . is not out yet though I have heard rumors of ~s —O.W.Holmes †1935⟩ ⟨a collection of book ~s —*Brit. Book News*⟩ **c :** critical examination **:** REVIEW, EVALUATION ⟨the books under ~ . . . are a valuable addition —*Times Lit. Supp.*⟩ ⟨considered 2,179 publications and selected 887 for ~ —L.H.Evans⟩

²**notice** \"\ *vb* -ED/-ING/-S [in sense 1a, fr. ME *notysen* to notify, fr. *notyce*; in other senses fr. ¹*notice*] *vt* **1 a** *archaic* **:** NOTIFY, INTIMATE **b :** to give notice of the scheduling of (a legal proceeding) by placing on a court calendar ⟨hearing on the motion was *noticed* for February 14 —Caryl Chessman⟩ **2 a :** to comment or remark upon **:** make mention of **:** refer to ⟨the city merchant's house . . . that is *noticed* in another chapter —Elizabeth Montizambert⟩ ⟨three of the four men *noticed* by name —H.M.Reichard⟩ **b :** to write a notice of **:** REVIEW ⟨asked me to ~ the volume —O.W.Holmes †1935⟩ ⟨*noticed* in these pages when it came out last year —*Times Lit. Supp.*⟩ **3 a :** to pay polite or favorable attention to **:** treat with attention or civility **:** GREET, RECOGNIZE ⟨were *noticed* only by a curtsey —Jane Austen⟩ **b** (1) **:** to take notice of with the senses **:** pay attention to **:** SEE, SENSE, NOTE ⟨*noticed* a strange odor in the room⟩ ⟨some attractive feature that can be *noticed* —Agnes M. Miall⟩ ⟨doesn't ~ a word —Charles Dickens⟩ ⟨began to ~ other men —*Time*⟩ ⟨barely *noticed* the clock strike midnight —Erle Stanley Gardner⟩ (2) **:** to take notice of with the mind **:** MARK ⟨the first thing that we ~ is that our thought moves with . . . incredible rapidity —J.H.Robinson †1936⟩ ⟨worth while to ~ that belief in the supernatural presupposes a belief in natural law —W.R.Inge⟩ **4 :** to give a formal notice or notification to **:** serve a notice on ⟨~ a tenant⟩ ~ *vi* **:** to take notice **syn** see SEE

no·tice·abil·i·ty \ˌnōd·əsəˈbiləd·ē, -ōtə-, -lətē, -i\ *n* -ES **:** the quality or state of being noticeable

no·tice·able \ˈ⸗⸗⸗bəl\ *adj* **1 :** worthy of notice **:** likely to attract attention **:** CONSPICUOUS ⟨~ for the variety and harmony of its coloring —O. Elfrida Saunders⟩ **2 :** capable of being observed ⟨gives the water a ~, but not unpleasant taste —*Amer. Guide Series: Mich.*⟩

syn REMARKABLE, PROMINENT, OUTSTANDING, CONSPICUOUS, SALIENT, SIGNAL, STRIKING, ARRESTING: NOTICEABLE applies to whatever is worthy of notice or unlikely to escape notice ⟨the influence of northern architecture and farming methods is still *noticeable* —*Amer. Guide Series: La.*⟩ REMARKABLE applies to that which commands attention or comment as extraordinary or exceptional ⟨a sudden and *remarkable* transformation of feeling —W.A.Swanberg⟩ ⟨the *remarkable* belief of some primitive peoples which associates twins with water and especially with rain —J.G.Frazer⟩ PROMINENT describes that which stands out from its setting or environment and demands notice as superior or more important ⟨the 25-foot cylindrical marble shaft, surmounted with draped flags and an eagle, occupies a *prominent* position in a traffic island on the main street —*Amer. Guide Series: Pa.*⟩ ⟨his inflammatory speeches against the Hitler regime won him a *prominent* place on the Nazi blacklist —*Americana Annual*⟩ OUTSTANDING, close to PROMINENT in meaning and connotation, heightens the notion of rising above or excelling others ⟨fortunate, too, in the men of *outstanding* ability who planned our resources and our campaigns —Clement Attlee⟩ ⟨trout appeared at several points along the main stream and have steadily increased in number, until the Au Sable is known as the *outstanding* trout stream in the state —*Amer. Guide Series: Mich.*⟩ CONSPICUOUS describes that which thrusts itself into notice and is unlikely to be overlooked or ignored ⟨*conspicuous* natural features like mountain ranges, waterfalls, and high cliffs overlooking rivers and lakes —*Amer. Guide Series: N.Y.*⟩ ⟨did not loom up in a room as such formidable and *conspicuous* pieces of furniture as the older pianos —A.E.Wier⟩ SALIENT may suggest a demanding attention as esp. significant ⟨days rich in *salient* news —C.E. Montague⟩ ⟨whoever called Africa the dark continent was guilty of a half truth. The *salient* point about South Africa is its brightness —N.F.Busch⟩ SIGNAL describes what is entitled to notice and remark as extraordinarily indicative or significant ⟨this work is not intelligible unless we appreciate a few *signal* facts in the history of psychoanalytic theory —Abram Kardiner⟩ ⟨even to do the very trifling thing will be of *signal* value, provided he catches hold of the underlying idea —H.A. Overstreet⟩ STRIKING suggests that which forcefully, powerfully, and suddenly calls attention ⟨everyone agreed that the most *striking* feature of the Plains was the absence of trees —R.H.Brown⟩ ⟨a *striking* figure. Handsome, graceful, cool, he personally led his soldiers to battle —F.P.Gaines⟩ ARRESTING indicates a being able to bring about a focusing of absorbed interest ⟨her magnificent agate-green eyes must at any age have been *arresting*; they seemed to concentrate the light of the intellect as a powerful lens does the sun —Edmund Wilson⟩ ⟨it is an *arresting* thought that murderers' skulls so often show quite normal shaped heads while the skulls of poets, scientists, lawyers and the rest are often abnormal in shape —S.P.B.Mais⟩

no·tice·ably \-blē, -li\ *adv* **:** in a noticeable manner

notice board \ˈ⸗⸗,⸗\ *n*, *chiefly Brit* **:** a board displaying a notice or warning; *specif* **:** BULLETIN BOARD

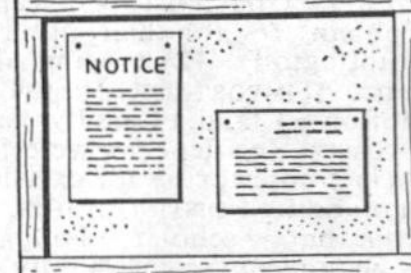

notice board

noticed *past of* NOTICE

notice of dishonor : a notice by the holder to the drawer and each endorser of a negotiable bill or note that has been dishonored with failure to give such notice to any person liable generally discharging the obligation of that person

notices *pl of* NOTICE, *pres 3d sing of* NOTICE

noticing *pres part of* NOTICE

no·tid·a·ni \nōˈtidəˌnī\ *n pl*, *cap* [NL, fr. pl. of *Notidanus*] *in some classifications* **:** an order of sharks that comprises forms with embolomerous vertebrae and 6 or 7 pairs of gill slits, includes Hexanchidae and sometimes Chlamydoselachidae — see NOTIDANOIDEA

no·tid·a·noi·dea \¦=·=ˈnòidēə\ *n pl, cap* [NL, fr. *Notidanus* + *-oidea*] **:** a suborder of Pleurotremata equivalent to the order Notidani

no·tid·a·nus \-ˌnəs\ [NL, fr. Gk *nōtidanos* small shark, fr. *nōt-* not- + *idanos* comely, fr. *idein* to see — more at WIT] *syn of* HEXANCHUS

no·ti·fi·a·ble \¦nōd·ə¦fīəbəl, -ōtə-\ *adj* [*notify* + *-able*] **:** requiring notice to be given; *specif* **:** required by law to be reported to official health authorities ⟨~ diseases⟩

no·ti·fi·ca·tion \ˌ==fəˈkāshən\ *n* -s [ME *notificacioun*, fr. MF *notification*, fr. ML *notification-, notificatio*, fr. LL *notificatus* (past. part. of *notificare* to make known) + L *-ion-* *-io* -ion — more at NOTIFY] **1 :** the act or an instance of notifying **:** INTIMATION, NOTICE; *esp* **:** the act of giving official notice or information **2 a :** a written or printed matter that gives notice **3 :** the notifying of a borrower's debtors that their accounts have been sold or assigned and that they are requested to make payment to the finance company or bank making the loan ⟨a loan on the ~ basis⟩

notified *adj* [fr. past part. of *notify*] *archaic* **:** CELEBRATED, NOTORIOUS

no·ti·fier \ˈnōd·ə,fī(ə)r, -ōtə-, -īə\ *n* -s **:** one that notifies

no·ti·fy \-ˌfī\ *vb* -ED/-ING/-ES [ME *notifien*, fr. MF *notifier* to make known, fr. LL *notificare*, fr. L *notus* (past. part. of *noscere* to come to know) + *-ificare* -ify — more at KNOW] *vt* **1** *obs* **a :** to take notice of **:** OBSERVE **b :** to point out **:** INDICATE, DENOTE **2 a :** to give notice of **:** make known **:** DECLARE, PUBLISH ⟨Her Majesty's pleasure not to disallow this act is *notified* in the *Gazette* —*Bahamas Acts*⟩ **b :** to report the occurrence of (a communicable disease or an individual suffering from such disease) in a community to public-health or other authority ⟨~ any cow which . . . appears to be affected with tuberculosis —*Control of Certain Diseases of Dairy Cows*⟩ **3 :** to give notice to **:** inform by notice ⟨*notified* the citizens to meet at the city hall⟩ **~** *vi* **:** to give notice **syn** see INFORM

noting *pres part of* NOTE

no·tion \ˈnōshən\ *n* -s [L *notion-, notio* idea, conception, act of coming to know, fr. *notus* + *-ion-, -io* -ion] **1 a** (1) **:** a mental apprehension or picture of whatever may be known or imagined **:** the meaning or content assigned by the mind to a term **:** CONCEPTION, IDEA ⟨my ~ of the country gentleman of the 17th century —T.B.Macaulay⟩ ⟨have no adequate ~ of what we mean by causation —Edward Sapir⟩ ⟨outraged her mother's ~*s* of economic and amorous propriety —*N.Y.Times*⟩ ⟨her ~ of a delta was a lot of channels and islands —C.S. Forester⟩ (2) *obs* **:** a form, character, or sense in which a thing is taken or exists (3) *obs* **:** CONNOTATION, MEANING (4) **:** PHRASE, TERM ⟨the meaning of the ~ *law*⟩ **b :** a general or universal concept ⟨introduced the ~ of organism into the world of minute beings —A.N.Whitehead⟩ ⟨the ~ of an established body of alphabetical symbols —Charlton Laird⟩ ⟨arriving at the ~ of law —Irving Babbitt⟩ **c** (1) *Lockeanism* **:** a complex idea that has its original and constant existence in the thoughts of men rather than in the reality of things (2) *Berkeleianism* **:** a conception that in distinction from an idea has no corresponding sense impression but nevertheless has something real corresponding to it (as minds and their operations, including God) ⟨it must be owned at the same time that we have some ~ of soul, spirit, and the operations of the mind, such as willing, loving, hating, inasmuch as we know or understand the meaning of those words —George Berkeley⟩ (3) [trans. of G *begriff*] *Hegelianism* **:** the organized unity of a differentiated whole corresponding to some universal; *specif* **:** the dialectical synthesis of Being and Essence approaching the Absolute Idea (4) *Kantianism* **:** a pure concept of reason — compare NOUMENON **2 a :** an idea, theory, or belief held by someone ⟨had a vague ~ that some supervision should be exercised —Robertson Davies⟩ ⟨disliked this ~ of begging of strange people —Pearl Buck⟩ ⟨this ~ of a basically honest mankind —L.A.Fiedler⟩ ⟨man's ~*s* about his history have altered tremendously —L.C.Eiseley⟩ **b** (1) **:** an inclination, whim, or fancy ⟨it's a queer ~ of the old gentleman —George Meredith⟩ — often used in the phrase *take a notion* ⟨took the ~ of having a ball in costume —Winston Churchill⟩ ⟨rocks their ancestors had taken a ~ to —Willa Cather⟩ (2) **:** a perverse, crotchety, or flighty idea or fancy ⟨don't go getting any ~*s* into your head —Maeve Brennan⟩ ⟨get ~*s* before he was fifty —Jean Stafford⟩ ⟨some of it was just ~*s* that the poor woman had got into her head —B.A.Williams⟩ **c** *dial chiefly Brit* **:** a fondness for one of the opposite sex **3 a** *obs* **:** MIND, INTELLECT **b :** UNDERSTANDING, KNOWLEDGE, INKLING ⟨has not the least ~ of what it's all about⟩ ⟨has no more ~ of how to run a business than a child⟩ ⟨had no ~ . . . that you analysed people like that —Walter de la Mare⟩ **4 a :** an ingenious device **:** any of various small articles or wares **:** KNICKKNACK **b notions** *pl* **:** small articles usu. sold in one department of a store (as findings for sewing, ribbons, buttons, small personal and clothing items) **syn** see IDEA

no·tion·al \-shənᵊl, -shnəl\ *adj* [*notion* + *-al*] **1 a :** having an abstract or speculative character **:** not based on fact or empirical investigation **:** THEORETICAL ⟨distinguishes between . . . ~ assent and apprehension and real assent and apprehension —*Times Lit. Supp.*⟩ ⟨a ~ figure of cost is given to them so that they may determine their production costs —*Packet Foods*⟩ ⟨more ~ than empirical⟩ **b** *archaic* **:** given to speculation or holding speculative views **2 :** existing in the mind only **:** VISIONARY, IMAGINARY, UNREAL ⟨is fictional only, as furnishing . . . a repository and ~ vehicle for the later transfer of title —*McLean v. Keith*⟩ **3 a :** given to, marked by, or reflecting foolish or fanciful moods or ideas **:** WHIMSICAL, CROTCHETY ⟨subject to all the ~ vagaries of childhood —Gerald Beaumont⟩ ⟨ships weren't ~ —Richard Hallet⟩ ⟨both reactionary and ~ to reject so much of modern history —L.P.Curtis⟩ **b** *dial* **:** being of the opinion ⟨I'm ~ that there is something queer afoot —S.H.Adams⟩ **4 a :** of, relating to, or being a notion or idea ⟨can improve ~ comprehension —J.T.Clark⟩ **b** (1) **:** carrying a full meaning of its own **:** having descriptive value in presenting an idea of a thing or quality ⟨*has* is ~ in *he has luck*, relational in *he has gone*⟩ (2) **:** of or representing what exists or occurs in the world of things as distinguished from syntactic categories ⟨sex is a ~, gender a syntactic category⟩ — **no·tion·al·i·ty** \ˌnōshəˈnaləd·ē\ *n* -ES — **no·tion·al·ly** \ˈnōshənᵊlē, -shnəl-, -i\ *adv*

no·tion·al·ist \ˈnōshənᵊləst, -shnəl-\ *n* -s *archaic* **:** THEORIST

no·tion·ary \ˈnōshəˌnerē\ *adj, archaic* **:** NOTIONAL

no·tion·ate \-ˌnət, *usu* -əd·+V\ *adj* [*notion* + *-ate*] **1** *chiefly dial* **:** FANCIFUL, NOTIONAL **2** *chiefly dial* **:** HEADSTRONG, STUBBORN

no·tion·ist \-nəst\ *n* -s *archaic* **:** a person whose religious opinions are characterized by extravagance

no·tion·less \ˈnōshənləs\ *adj* **:** devoid of any notion or idea

no·tiony \-nē\ *adj, chiefly dial* **:** given to notions **:** WHIMSICAL, FANCIFUL, CROTCHETY ⟨it'll keep time . . . it's just ~ —*Chapel Hill (N.C.) News Leader*⟩ ⟨wildflowers . . . are shy, ~ little things —H.H.Martin⟩

no·tio·sorex \ˌnōshēō+\ *n, cap* [NL, fr. *notio-* southern (fr. L *notius*, fr. Gk *notios*, fr. *notos* south wind, south) + *Sorex* — more at NOT-] **:** a genus of shrews of the southern U.S. and Mexico having only 28 teeth

notio·thau·mi·dae \-ˈthómə,dē\ *n pl, cap* [NL, fr. *Notiothauma*, type genus (fr. *notio-* + Gk *thauma* wonder) + *-idae* — more at THEATER] **:** a family of primitive insects (order Mecoptera) containing a single Chilean species (*Notiothauma reedi*)

no·ti·tia \nōˈtish(ē)ə\ *n, pl* **notiti·ae** \-shē,ē\ [LL, fr. L, acquaintance, knowledge — more at NOTICE] **:** a list or register esp. of ecclesiastical sees or districts

noto- — see NOT-

no·to·cen·tral \¦nōd·ō¦sen·trəl\ *or* **no·to·cen·trous** \-rəs\ *adj* [NL *notocentrum* + E *-al* or *-ous*] **:** of, relating to, or being a notocentrum

no·to·cen·trum \ˌ==ˈ=trəm\ *n* [NL, fr. 1*not-* + *centrum*] **:** the centrum of a vertebra when formed by the dorsal arches (as in a toad or frog)

no·to·chord \ˈnōd·ə,kȯrd, -ōtə-, -ō(ə)d\ *n* [1*not-* + L *chorda* cord — more at CORD] **:** a longitudinal flexible rod of cells that acts as a specific inductor of neural plate formation, that in the lowest chordates (as amphioxus and the lampreys) and in the embryos of the higher vertebrates forms the supporting axis of the body, being almost obliterated in the adult of the higher vertebrates as the bodies of the vertebrae develop, and that arises as an outgrowth from dorsal lip of the blastopore extending forward between epiblast and hypoblast in the middorsal line — **no·to·chord·al** \¦==¦kȯrdᵊl, -ō(ə)d-\ *adj*

1**no·to·don·tid** \¦nōd·ə¦dän·təd\ *adj* [NL *Notodontidae*] **:** of or relating to the Notodontidae

2**notodontid** \"\ *n* -s **:** a moth of the family Notodontidae

no·to·don·ti·dae \ˌ==ˈdäntə,dē\ *n pl, cap* [NL, fr. *Notodonta*, type genus (fr. 1*not-* + *-odonta*) + *-idae*] **:** an extensive family of moths which resemble the Noctuidae but are distinguished from them chiefly by the venation of the forewings and whose larvae are usu. naked and often of grotesque form with humps, spines, or fleshy processes — compare LOBSTER MOTH, PUSS MOTH

1**no·to·don·toid** \¦==¦=,tȯid\ *adj* [NL *Notodontidae* + E *-oid*] **:** resembling or related to the Notodontidae

2**notodontoid** \"\ *n* -s **:** a notodontoid moth

no·to·ed·res \ˌ==ˈe,drēz\ *n, cap* [NL, fr. 1*not-* + Gk *hedra* seat, abode — more at SIT] **:** a genus of mites (family Sarcoptidae) containing mange mites that attack various mammals

no·to·ed·ric \¦==¦edrik\ *adj* [NL *Notoedres* + E *-ic*] **1 :** of or relating to the genus *Notoedres* **2 :** caused by mites of the genus Notoedres

no·to·gae·an *or* **no·to·ge·an** \¦==¦jēən\ *also* **no·to·gae·al** *or* **no·to·ge·al** \-ēəl\ *or* **no·to·gae·ic** *or* **no·to·ge·ic** \-ēik\ *adj, usu cap* [NL *Notogaea, Notogea* south temperate terrestrial biogeographic realm (fr. 2*not-* + *-gaea, -gea*) + E *-an, -al, -ic*] **:** of, relating to, or being a biogeographic realm that includes the Australian and New Zealand regions and the islands of the southwestern Pacific

1**no·tom·ma·tid** \nəˈtäməd·əd\ *adj* [NL *Notommatidae*] **:** of or relating to the Notommatidae

2**notommatid** \"\ *n* -s **:** a rotifer of the family Notommatidae

no·tom·mat·i·dae \ˌnōd·əˈmad·ə,dē\ *n pl, cap* [NL, fr. *Notommata*, type genus (fr. 1*not-* + Gk *ommat-, omma* eye) + *-idae* — more at OPTIC] **:** a large family of rotifers (order Monogononta) including many typical and common forms that usu. have a nearly cylindrical body with a slender posterior foot ending in two toes

no·to·mys \ˈnōd·ə,mis\ *n, cap* [NL, fr. 2*not-* + *-mys*] **:** a genus of jerboa rats

no·to·nec·tal \¦nōd·ə¦nektəl\ *adj* [NL *Notonectidae* + E *-al*] **:** of or relating to the Notonectidae

no·to·nec·tid \ˌ==ˈ=təd\ *n* -s [NL *Notonectidae*] **:** a bug of the family Notonectidae

no·to·nec·ti·dae \-tə,dē\ *n pl, cap* [NL, fr. *Notonecta*, type genus (fr. 1*not-* + *-necta* swimmer, fr. Gk *nēktēs*, fr. *nēchein* to swim) + *-idae* — more at NESO-] **:** a family of aquatic carnivorous insects (order Hemiptera) having the back strongly convex and the hind legs long and resembling oars and habitually swimming back downward

no·to·po·di·al \¦==¦pōdēəl\ *adj* [NL *notopodium* + E *-al*] **:** of or relating to a notopodium

no·to·po·di·um \ˌ==ˈpōdēəm\ *also* **no·to·pod** \ˈ==,päd\ *n, pl* **notopo·dia** \ˌ==ˈpōdēə\ *also* **notopods** [NL *notopodium*, fr. 1*not-* + *-podium*] **:** the dorsal lobe or branch of a parapodium

1**no·top·ter·id** \nəˈtäptərəd, -ˌrid\ *adj* [NL *Notopteridae*] **:** of or relating to the Notopteridae

2**notopterid** \"\ *n* -s **:** a fish of the family Notopteridae

no·top·ter·i·dae \ˌnō,täpˈterə,dē\ *n pl, cap* [NL, fr. *Notopterus*, type genus (fr. 1*not-* + *-pterus*) + *-idae*] **:** a small family of freshwater fishes (order Isospondyli) of West Africa and southeastern Asia having the dorsal fin when present short and high, the anal fin long and confluent with the caudal, and the air bladder complex

1**no·top·ter·oid** \nəˈtäptə,rȯid\ *adj* [NL *Notopteridae* + E *-oid*] **:** resembling or related to the Notopteridae

2**notopteroid** \"\ *n* -s **:** a notopteroid fish

notorhynchus *syn of* NOTORYNCHUS

no·to·ri·e·ty \ˌnōd·əˈrīəd·ē, ˌnōtəˈrīətē, -i\ *n* -ES [MF or ML; MF *notorieté*, fr. ML *notorietat-, notorietas*, fr. *notorie-* (fr. *notorius*) + L *-tat-, -tas* -ty] **1 :** the quality or state of being notorious: as **a :** the condition of being publicly or generally known ⟨a fact of such ~ hardly requires documentation⟩ **b :** the condition of being an object of wide or general attention, interest, and comment ⟨the ~ surrounding the awards dates back only to 1949 —*Advertising Age*⟩ ⟨won favorable ~ as counsel —C.B.Swisher⟩ **c :** the condition of being an object of wide or general attention, interest, and comment but for something reprehensible or scandalous ⟨enjoys a most unenviable ~ —J.C.Snaith⟩ ⟨reputation is to ~ what real turtle is to mock —Douglas Jerrold⟩ ⟨certain personalities . . . whose fame would better be described by another word . . . ~ —*Phoenix Flame*⟩ ⟨the city's ~ for corrupt and incompetent government —R.E.Merriam⟩ **2 :** a notorious person; *esp* **:** one notorious for something sensational or scandalous ⟨love to have notabilities and *notorieties* under one roof —*Times Lit. Supp.*⟩ **syn** see FAME

no·to·ri·ous \(ˈ)nō¦tōrēəs, nə¦-, -ȯr-\ *adj* [ML *notorius*, irreg. fr. LL *notorium* information, indictment, fr. neut. of (assumed) LL *notorius*, adj., making known, fr. L *notus* (past part. of *noscere* to come to know) + *-orius* -ory — more at KNOW] **1 a** (1) **:** being or constituting something commonly known **:** well known ⟨iron is a ~ conductor of heat—Lewis Mumford⟩ ⟨the ~ mass-energy relation —P.W.Bridgman⟩ ⟨the possession must be open and ~ —C.S.Lobingier⟩ ⟨contradicted by multiple and ~ documentation —G.G.Coulton⟩ ⟨in mathematics it is ~ that we start from absurdities to reach a realm of law —Havelock Ellis⟩ (2) **:** well known or celebrated for a particular quality or trait ⟨the tapeworms are ~ in this respect —W.H.Dowdeswell⟩ ⟨it is ~ for its ability to dive instantly —Ralph Hoffmann⟩ ⟨novelists are ~ for their howlers —V.S. Pritchett⟩ ⟨~ as a sane level-headed man —Arnold Bennett⟩ **b** (1) **:** widely and unfavorably known as an individual of a specified kind or class ⟨a ~ chiseler⟩ ⟨a ~ gangster⟩ ⟨a ~ gambler⟩ ⟨this bird is a ~ destroyer of poultry⟩ (2) **:** widely and unfavorably known or discussed for something reprehensible or scandalous or for some negative quality or trait ⟨an area ~ for soot, smog, and dust —*Pliotron*⟩ ⟨this scandal made the little town ~ —*Amer. Guide Series: Mich.*⟩ ⟨his front was a ~ law firm —George Carter⟩ ⟨the most ~ of Confederate prisons —W.B.Hesseltine⟩ **2** *obs* **:** CONSPICUOUS, EVIDENT, MANIFEST — **no·to·ri·ous·ly** *adv* — **no·to·ri·ous·ness** *n* -ES

no·tor·nis \nəˈtȯrnəs\ *n* [NL, fr. 2*not-* + NL *-ornis*] **1** *cap* **:** a genus of flightless birds of New Zealand related to the gallinules **2** *pl* **notornis :** any bird of the genus *Notornis*

no·to·ryc·tes \ˌnōd·əˈrik,tēz\ *n, cap* [NL, fr. 2*not-* + Gk *oryktēs* digger, fr. *oryssein* to dig — more at ROUGH] **:** a genus of small burrowing Australian marsupials comprising solely the marsupial mole

1**no·to·ryc·tid** \¦==¦=təd\ *adj* [NL *Notoryctidae* (family including *Notoryctes*), fr. *Notoryctes* + *-idae*] **:** of or relating to the genus *Notoryctes*

2**notoryctid** \"\ *n* -s **:** MARSUPIAL MOLE

no·to·ryn·chus \ˌ==ˈriŋkəs\ *n, cap* [NL, irreg. fr. 1*not-* + *-rhynchus*] **:** a genus of cow sharks with seven pairs of external gill openings

no·to·stig·ma \-ˈstigmə\ *n pl, cap* [NL, fr. 1*not-* + *-stigma* (neut. pl. of *-stigmus*, fr. Gk *stigma* mark, brand) — more at STIGMA] *in some classifications* **:** a subclass of centipedes distinguished by seven dorsal unpaired tracheal spiracles — compare ANAMORPHA

no·tos·tra·ca \nōˈtästrəkə\ *n pl, cap* [NL, fr. 1*not-* + *-ostraca*] **:** an order of small freshwater crustaceans (subclass Branchiopoda) having a shield-shaped carapace, sessile paired eyes, vestigial antennae, and 40 to 63 pairs of trunk appendages — see TRIOPS — **no·tos·tra·can** \-kən\ *adj or n*

no·to·the·ri·um \ˌnōd·əˈthirēəm\ *n, cap* [NL, fr. 2*not-* + NL *-therium*] **:** a genus of gigantic herbivorous diprotodont marsupials of the Pleistocene of Australia

no·to·tre·ma \ˌnōd·əˈtrēmə\ *n, cap* [NL, fr. 1*not-* + *-trema*] **:** a genus consisting of the marsupial frogs

no·to·ungulata \ˌnōd·ˌō+\ *n pl, cap* [NL, fr. 2*not-* + *Ungulata*] **:** an order of extinct New World herbivorous mammals widely distributed in So. America from the Paleocene to the Pleistocene

1**no·to·un·gu·late** \¦=·=¦əŋgyələt, -ˌlāt, *usu* -d·+V\ *or* **no·tun·gu·late** \(ˈ)nō¦təŋ-\ *adj* [NL *Notoungulata*] **:** of or relating to the Notoungulata

2**notoungulate** \"\ *or* **notungulate** \"\ *n* **:** a mammal or fossil of the order Notoungulata

no·tour \ˈnōd·ər\ *adj* [ME, fr. MF *notoire*, fr. ML *notorius* — more at NOTORIOUS] *chiefly Scot* **:** NOTORIOUS, INFAMOUS

notour bankrupt *n* **1** *Scots law* **:** a debtor who has fled to a sanctuary to escape imprisonment for debt **2** *Scots law* **:** a debtor who is declared bankrupt

not out *adj, of a batsman in cricket* **:** not dismissed (as after an opponent's unsuccessful appeal to an umpire) ⟨with innings uncompleted (as at the end of a day's play)

not-out \ˈ=¦=\ *n* -s **:** a batsman in cricket who is not out

not proved *or* **not proven** *adj, Scots law* — used as a verdict of acquittal brought in by a jury who find the evidence insufficient for conviction of guilt

no·tro·pis \ˈnōtrəpəs\ *n, cap* [NL, irreg. fr. 1*not-* + Gk *tropis* keel of a ship, fr. *trepein* to turn — more at TROPE] **:** a genus of No. American fishes (family Cyprinidae) comprising typical shiners

1**no-trump** \ˈ=¦=\ *adj* [2*no* + *trump*] **:** being without trumps; *specif* **:** being a bid or contract to play or a hand suitable to play without any suit being trumps

2**no-trump** \"\ *also* **no-trumps** *n, pl* **no-trump** *or* **no-trumps** **1 :** a bridge bid, declaration, or contract that names no suit as trumps and that outranks the suit bids **2 :** a hand played without any suit named as trumps

no-trump·er \-pə(r)\ *n* [*no-trump* + *-er*] **:** a no-trump bridge hand or contract or a hand considered strong enough for a no-trump bid or declaration

nots *pl of* NOT

not-self \ˈ=¦=\ *n* **:** something that is other than or objective to the self **:** NONEGO ⟨the world is in some manner a *not-self*, whose nature is both like and unlike my own —Weston La Barre⟩

nott \ˈnät, *usu* -äd·+V\ *dial var of* NOT

not·ta·way \ˈnäd·ə,wā\ *n, pl* **nottaway** *or* **nottaways** *usu cap* [Algonquian *nadowa*, perh. fr. *natowe* rattlesnake] **1 a :** an extinct Iroquoian people of southeastern Virginia **b :** a member of such people **2 :** a language of the Nottaway people

not·ting·ham \ˈnäd·iŋəm, ˈnätiŋ- *sometimes* -ŋ,ham\ *adj, usu cap* [fr. *Nottingham*, city and county of north central England] **1 :** of or from the city of Nottingham, England **:** of the kind or style prevalent in Nottingham **2 :** NOTTINGHAMSHIRE

nottingham lace *n, usu cap N* **:** any of the various flat laces and nets machine-made orig. at Nottingham, England and used for curtains, dresses, tablecloths

not·ting·ham·shire \-ˌshi(ə)r, -ˌshiə, -ˌshə(r)\ *or* **not·ting·ham** *adj, usu cap* [fr. *Nottinghamshire, Nottingham* county in north central England] **:** of or from the county of Nottingham, England **:** of the kind or style prevalent in Nottingham

not·tur·no \nəˈtu̇r(ˌ)nō, nōˈ-\ *n, pl* **nottur·ni** \-(ˌ)nē\ [It, adj., of night, fr. L *nocturnus* — more at NOCTURNAL] **1 :** an 18th century piece for an instrumental group composed in several movements and resembling the serenade or divertimento **2 :** NOCTURNE

no·tum \ˈnōd·əm\ *n, pl* **no·ta** \-ōd·ə\ [NL, fr. Gk *nōton* back — more at NATES] **:** a back part or surface of an animal; *specif* **:** the dorsal surface of a thoracic segment of an insect

no·tun·gu·la·ta \nō,təŋgyəˈläd·ə, -ˈlād·ə\ [NL, fr. 2*not-* + *Ungulata*] *syn of* NOTOUNGULATA

notungulate *var of* NOTOUNGULATE

-no·tus \ˈnōd·əs, -ōtəs\ *n comb form* [NL, fr. Gk *nōtos, nōton* back — more at NATES] **:** one having a (specified) kind of back — in generic names of animals ⟨Campo*notus*⟩ ⟨Pycno*notus*⟩

1**notwithstanding** \¦==¦==\ *prep* [ME *notwithstonding*, fr. 1*not* + *withstanding*, pres. part. of *withstonden* to withstand] **:** without prevention or obstruction from or by **:** in spite of ⟨~ its wide distribution, it is an animal seldom encountered —James Stevenson-Hamilton⟩ — often used after its substantive and in this position still sometimes taken as a negative present participle joined with the substantive in a nominative absolute construction ⟨anything in the Constitution or laws of any state to the contrary ~ —*U.S. Constitution*⟩

2**notwithstanding** \"\ *adv* [ME *notwithstanding*, fr. *notwithstanding*, prep.] **:** NEVERTHELESS, HOWEVER, YET ⟨you are welcome ~ —Shak.⟩

3**notwithstanding** \"\ *conj* [ME *notwithstanding*, fr. *notwithstanding*, prep.] **:** ALTHOUGH ⟨unknown to most, ~ he had lived here many years⟩

nouak·chott \ˈnwäk,shät, nəˈwä-, -shōt, (ˌ)=¦=\ *adj, usu cap* [fr. *Nouakchott*, Mauritania] **:** of or relating to Nouakchott, the capital of Mauritania **:** of the kind or style prevalent in Nouakchott

nou·gat \ˈnügət, *usu* -əd·+V; -ˌgä\ *n* -s [F, fr. Prov, fr. OProv *nogat*, fr. *noga* nut (fr. L *nuc-, nux*) + *-at* -ate; akin to OE *hnutu* nut — more at NUT] **:** a confection made by mixing nuts or sometimes fruit pieces in a sugar paste whose composition is varied to give either a chewy or a brittle consistency

nou·ga·tine \¦nügə¦tēn\ *n* -s [*nougat* + *-ine*] **:** a chocolate with a nougat center

nought *var of* NAUGHT

noughts-and-crosses \ˈ==ˈ==\ *n pl but sing in constr, chiefly Brit* **:** TICKTACKTOE

noughty \ˈnȯd·ē, -i\ *adj* [ME, fr. *nought* naught + *-y*] *chiefly Scot* **:** WORTHLESS

nould \ˌnəd, (ˈ)nu̇d\ *vb* [ME *nolde*, fr. OE, 1st & 3d sing. past indic. of *nillan* to be unwilling — more at NILL] *archaic* **:** would not

nou·me·ite \ˈnümē,īt, =ˈmā,īt\ *also* **nou·me·a·ite** \nüˈmāə,īt\ *n* -s [*Nouméa*, New Caledonia + E *-ite*] **:** GARNIERITE; *esp* **:** a dark green unctuous variety of garnierite

nou·me·nal \ˈnümənəl, ˈnaüm-\ *adj* **:** of or relating to the noumenon or noumena — contrasted with *phenomenal* ⟨these elemental, unconscious and ~ needs —A.L.Rowse⟩ — **nou·me·nal·ly** \-nəlē\ *adv*

nou·me·nal·ism \-ˌlizəm\ *n* -s **:** the doctrine of the existence of things-in-themselves

nou·me·nal·ist \-ˌləst\ *n* -s **:** an adherent of noumenalism

nou·me·non \ˈnümə,nän, ˈnaüm-\ *n, pl* **noume·na** \-ˌnə\ [G, fr. Gk *nooumenon* that which is conceived, thought, fr. neut. of pres. pass. part. of *noein* to conceive, think, fr. *nous* mind] **1** *Kantianism* **a :** an object that is conceived by reason and consequently thinkable but is not knowable by the senses **:** THING-IN-ITSELF **b :** an unknowable object (as God or the soul) whose existence is theoretically problematic **2 :** an object of purely rational apprehension as opposed to an object of perception

noun \ˈnaün\ *n* -s *often attrib* [ME *nowne*, fr. AF *noun* name, noun, fr. OF *nun, non, nom*, fr. L *nomen* — more at NAME] **1 :** a word that is the name of a subject of discourse (as a person, animal, plant, place, thing, substance, quality, idea, action, or state) and that in languages with grammatical number, case, and gender is inflected for number and case but has inherent gender **2 :** a word except a pronoun used in a sentence as subject or object of a verb, as object of a preposition, as the predicate after a copula, or as a name in an absolute construction — see COMMON NOUN, COUNT NOUN, MASS NOUN, PROPER NOUN

noun·al \-nᵊl\ *adj* **:** of, relating to, or of the nature, function, or quality of a noun — **noun·al·ly** \-ᵊlē\ *adv*

noun equivalent *n* **:** a word group (as *to err* in "to err is human") or a word (as *they* in "they are hungry") not otherwise a noun in a syntactic function that is ordinarily performed by a noun

noun of multitude : a noun that is collective

nouns \ˈnaünz\ *interj* [alter. of *wounds*, fr. pl. of *wound*, n.] *archaic* — a mild oath

noup \ˈnüp\ *n* -s [ON *nūpr, gnūpr* peak; perh. akin to OE *hnutu* nut — more at NUT] *Scot* **:** a high steep promontory

nou·rice \ˈnürəs\ *chiefly Scot var of* NURSE

nour·ish \ˈnər·ish, ˈnə·r|, |ēsh, *chiefly in pres part* |əsh\ *vb* -ED/-ING/-ES [ME *nurishen, norishen, norissen*, fr. OF *norriss-*, stem of *norrir*, fr. L *nutrire*; akin to L *nare*, *natare* to swim, Gk *nan* to flow, *nein* to swim, *noteros* damp, Skt *snauti* it drips, *snāti* he bathes] *vt* **1 a :** to bring up **:** RAISE, NUR-

TURE, REAR ⟨to save my boy, to ~ and bring him up —Shak.⟩ ⟨it was for Chaucer, ~*ed* in other literatures . . . to make rapid advances on the road of English poetry —H.S.Bennett⟩ ⟨~*ed* in the old bootlegger days . . . demanded his cut from every pie —George Carter⟩ **b** *archaic* **:** to bring up (an animal) **:** RAISE ⟨episcopal visitors were recording . . . that it was scandalous to ~ hunting dogs in monasteries —G.G. Coulton⟩ **2 :** to promote or stimulate the growth or development of **:** BUILD UP, STRENGTHEN ⟨has ~*ed* in us the dream of liberty —Liston Pope⟩ ⟨no occasions to exercise the feelings nor ~ passion —L.O.Coxe⟩ **3 :** BREAST-FEED, SUCKLE ⟨wish she would not see fit to sit down and ~ her baby in my poor old bachelor drawing room —H.G.Wells⟩ **4 a :** to furnish or sustain with food or nutriment ⟨the human body can be ~*ed* on any food —R.W.Emerson⟩ ⟨the rain which ~*ed* the bushes —Laura Krey⟩ ⟨the heart speeds up and the blood pressure rises to better ~ the tissues —H.G.Armstrong⟩ **b :** to provide with sustenance ⟨the glow of a fire ~*ed* by partially dried logs —P.A.Talbot⟩ ⟨this great work ~*ed* American lawyers —Howard M. Jones⟩ **c :** to provide for **:** MAINTAIN, SUPPORT ⟨thou shalt dwell in the land of Goshen . . . and there will I ~ thee —Gen. 45:10–11 (AV)⟩ ⟨welfare committees whose task it is to ~ the social life of old people —M.A.Abrams⟩ ⟨their profits flow into the underworld and ~ other criminal activities —Beverly Smith⟩ **5 a** *archaic* **:** to grow or let grow (one's hair) ⟨~*ed* two locks, which graceful hung behind in equal curls —Alexander Pope⟩ **b** *archaic* **:** to cultivate (as plants or trees) ⟨it's a' for the apple he'll ~ the tree —Robert Burns⟩ **6 :** to cherish or keep alive (as a feeling or plan) ⟨~*ed* the hope that something might come of it later —L.C.Douglas⟩ ⟨~ a shrewd distrust of anybody who looked like a big tycoon —F.L.Allen⟩ ⟨for many years had ~*ed* the project of a trip abroad⟩ ~ *vi* **1** *obs* **:** to furnish nourishment ⟨grains and roots ~ more than the leaves —Francis Bacon⟩ **2 :** to receive nourishment **:** be fed ⟨thrives and ~*es* where poverty prevails —M.O.Purcell⟩ **syn** see FEED

nour·ish·able \-shəbəl\ *adj* [ME, fr. *nurishen* + *-able*] **1** *obs* **:** capable of giving nourishment **2 :** capable of receiving nourishment

nour·ish·er \-shə(r)\ *n* -S [ME *norysshere*, fr. *norishen* + *-er*] **:** one that nourishes

nourishing *adj* [ME *norisshing*, fr. pres. part. of *norishen*] **:** giving nourishment **:** NUTRITIOUS — **nour·ish·ing·ly** *adv*

nour·ish·ment \-mənt\ *n* -S [ME *norysshement*, fr. MF *norrissement*, fr. *norriss-* (stem of *norrir*) + *-ment*] **1 :** something that nourishes **:** FOOD, NUTRIMENT, SUSTENANCE ⟨takes little ~ between breakfast and dinner⟩ ⟨the soil was poor and gave almost no ~ to the plants⟩ ⟨a few books provided his only intellectual ~⟩ **2 :** the act of nourishing or the state of being nourished ⟨devoted himself to the ~ of education⟩

nour·i·ture \-əchə(r), -ēch-, -‚chu̇(ə)r, -ūə\ *n* -S [ME *noriture*, fr. MF *nourreture*, partly fr. *norrir* to nourish, partly fr. ML *nutritura* upbringing, fr. LL, nursing, suckling, fr. L *nutritus* (past part. of *nutrire* to nourish) + *-ura* -ure] **1 :** NOURISHMENT **2** *obs* **:** NURTURE

nous \'nüs, 'nau̇s\ *n* -ES [Gk *noos*, *nous* mind] **1 a :** an intelligent purposive principle controlling and ordering the world of matter **:** the highest intellect **:** MIND, REASON **b** *Platonism* (1) **:** a purely teleological and completely immaterial principle (2) **:** the capacity for the highest intuitive and immediate insight **c** *Aristotelianism* **:** reason regarded either as passive (as in sense perception) or as active and creative **d** *Neoplatonism* **:** the divine reason as the first emanation or creation of God **2** *Brit* **:** mental quickness **:** ALERTNESS, COMMON SENSE ⟨may be full of erudite theories but is liable to go astray from lack of practical sense and ordinary ~ —Jacquetta & Christopher Hawkes⟩

nout \'nōt, 'nōt\ *dial Eng var of* NAUGHT

nou·ther \'nōthə(r)\ *dial var of* NEITHER

nou·veau \(')nü¦vō\ *adj* [F, new, fr. OF *novel* — more at NOVEL] **:** newly arrived or developed **:** IMMATURE, RAW ⟨the Hollywood rich were flamboyantly ~ in the 1920's —Budd Schulberg⟩ ⟨the ~ society of his adopted home —John Farrelly⟩

nouveau riche \¦nü‚vō'rēsh\ *n, pl* **nou·veaux riches** \"\ [F, fr. *nouveau* + *riche* rich (of Gmc origin; akin to OE *rīce* rich)] **:** a person of newly acquired wealth but limited education or culture **:** PARVENU ⟨had made his money quickly, and the curse of the *nouveau riche* had fallen upon him —Leslie Charteris⟩ ⟨the typical inferiority complex of the *nouveaux riches*: the desire to possess foreign culture through wealth —J.D.Hart⟩

nou·velle \(')nü'vel\ *n* -S [F, trans. of It *novella*] **:** NOVELLA 2

nov- *or* **novo-** *comb form* [L *novus* new — more at NEW] **:** new ⟨*Nov*anglian⟩

no·va \'nōvə\ *n, pl* **no·vas** \-vəz\ *or* **no·vae** \-‚vē, -‚vī\ [NL, fem. of L *novus* new] **:** a star that suddenly increases its light output tremendously (as 10,000 times or more within a few days) and then fades away less rapidly and reaches its former obscurity in a few months or years — see RECURRENT NOVA, SUPERNOVA

no·va·chord \'nōvə‚kȯrd, -ō(ə)d\ *n* [fr. *Novachord*, a trademark] **:** a musical instrument resembling a piano and electrically producing and controlling by means of vacuum tubes musical tones ranging in quality from those of the piano and organ to those of stringed and woodwind instruments

no·vac·u·lite \nō'vakyə‚līt\ *n* -S [L *novacula* razor (fr. — assumed — L *novare* to shave, whet + L *-cula*, suffix denoting an instrument) + E *-ite*; akin to Skt *kṣṇauti* he whets, ON *snøggr* shorn, bald, OE *besnyth̄ian* to deprive, MHG *snœde* contemptible, ON *snauthr* bereft, poor, OE *-heord* hair of a woman's head — more at HURDS] **:** a very hard fine-grained siliceous rock used for whetstones and thought to be of sedimentary origin

no·va·lia \nō'vālēə\ *n pl* [L, pl. of *novale* fallow land, land ploughed for the first time, fr. *novus* new — more at NEW] *Scots law* **:** lands newly reclaimed for improvement or agriculture; *specif* **:** lands not liable for teinds

¹no·van·gli·an \nō'vaŋglēən, -aiŋ-\ *also* **no·van·gli·can** \-lәkən, -ēk-\ *adj, usu cap* [*novanglian* fr. NL *Nova Anglia* New England + E *-an*; *novanglican* fr. NL *novanglicus* of New England (fr. *Nova Anglia* + L *-icus* -ic) + E *-an*] **1 :** of, relating to, or characteristic of New England **2 :** of, relating to, or characteristic of the people of New England ⟨rather admire this stolid self-reliance and Novanglian assumption —Bayard Taylor⟩

²novanglian \"\ *also* **novanglican** \"\ *n* -S *cap* **:** a native or inhabitant of New England

nov·arsenobenzene \(¦)nōv+\ *or* **nov·ar·se·no·ben·zol** \-‚zȯl, -ōl\ *n* [*novarsenobenzene* fr. *nov-* + *arsenobenzene*; *novarsenobenzol* fr. *nov-* + *arsen-* + *benzol*] **:** NEOARSPHENAMINE

no·va sco·tia \¦nōvə¦skōshə\ *adj, usu cap N&S* [fr. *Nova Scotia*, province of southeastern Canada] **:** of or from the province of Nova Scotia **:** of the kind or style prevalent in Nova Scotia **:** NOVA SCOTIAN

¹nova sco·tian \¦==¦skōshən\ *adj, usu cap N&S* [*Nova Scotia*, province of Canada + E *-an*] **1 :** of, relating to, or characteristic of Nova Scotia **2 :** of, relating to, or characteristic of the people of Nova Scotia

²nova scotian \"\ *n* -S *cap* **:** a native or inhabitant of the province of Nova Scotia, Canada

no·vate \nō'vāt, '==, *usu* -ād·+V\ *vt* -ED/-ING/-S [L *novatus*, past part. of *novare* to make new, fr. *novus* new — more at NEW] **:** to replace (an old obligation) by a new obligation

no·va·tian \nō'vāshən\ *n* -S *usu cap* [ME, fr. LL *novatianus*, fr. *Novatianus*, 3d cent. antipope and founder of the sect] **:** one of an early Christian schismatic sect existing from A.D. 251 to the 6th or 7th century that denied that the church should restore lapsed Christians to membership and advocated a rigidly purist conception of church membership

no·va·tian·ism \-‚nizəm\ *n* -S *usu cap* [*Novatian*, *Novatianus*, 3d cent. sectarian + E *-ism*] **:** the denial of the church's right to restore lapsed Christians to membership

no·va·tian·ist \-nəst\ *n* -S *usu cap* **:** NOVATIAN

no·va·tion \nō'vāshən\ *n* -S [LL *novation-*, *novatio*, fr. L *novatus* + *-ion-*, *-io* -ion] **1 :** INNOVATION **2 :** the substitution of a new legal obligation for an old one (as by a substitution of a new contract, a new debtor, or a new creditor for an old one) — see DELEGATION

no·va·tor \-ād·ə(r)\ *n* -S [L, renewer, fr. *novatus* + *-or*] **:** INNOVATOR

¹nov·el \'nävəl\ *n* -S [ME *novele*, fr. MF *novele*, fr. fem. of *novel* new, fr. L *novellus*, fr. *novus* new] **1 a** *chiefly dial* **:** NEWNESS, NOVELTY **b** *obs* **:** a piece of news **2** [It *novella*] **a** *archaic* **:** NOVELLA 1 — usu. used in pl. **b :** an invented prose narrative of considerable length and a certain complexity that deals imaginatively with human experience through a connected sequence of events involving a group of persons in a specific setting **c :** the literary type constituted by such narratives ⟨the ~ is the chief literary form of the present day⟩ **3** *usu cap* [NL *novella*, fr. LL *novellae constitutiones*, lit., new statutes] **:** a Roman imperial enactment issued supplementary to a code; *esp* **:** one of a collection of statutes of Justinian and his immediate successors promulgated subsequent to the Justinian Code ⟨the nine collations, the legal standard of modern tribunals, consist of ninety-eight *Novels* —Edward Gibbon⟩

²novel \"\ *adj* [ME, fr. MF] **1 :** not resembling something formerly known **:** having no precedent **:** NEW ⟨the great geographical discoveries posed ~ practical problems in navigation —S.F.Mason⟩ ⟨the opportunity to experiment in providing four-year courses on ~ lines —James Britton⟩ **2 :** original or striking in conception or style **:** STRANGE, UNUSUAL ⟨if a man cannot write what is new, at least he can write what is ~ —Richard Hallet⟩ ⟨the feverish search for the ~ and the disquieting, the odd, and the macabre —Bernard Smith⟩ **syn** see NEW

novel assignment *n* [²*novel*] *law* **:** a new assignment or specification of the cause of action set forth in a previous assignment (as where more certainty or particularity is required)

novel disseizin *n* [ME, fr. AF *novele disseisine*] **:** an ancient remedy in English law, abolished in 1833, for the recovery of land from which the owner had been recently disseized

nov·el·ese \¦nävə'lēz, -ēs\ *n* -S **:** a style characteristic of bad novels; *esp* **:** a style marked by the use of trite expressions ⟨the revolting ~ that the English translator spreads upon the page —J.M.Barzun⟩

nov·el·esque \-esk\ *adj* **:** suitable for or resembling a novel

nov·el·ette *also* **nov·el·et** \¦nävə¦let\ *n* -S **1 a :** a brief novel or long short story ⟨is also buying ~s of around 15,000 words —Iris Litt⟩ ⟨all of it is short; nothing exceeding ~ length —Richard Sullivan⟩ **b** *Brit* **:** a light usu. sentimental romantic novel ⟨was a great reader of ~*s* and had romantic ideas —Flora Thompson⟩ ⟨weeping over a sentimental ~ —F.M. Ford⟩ **2** [G *novellette*, fr. *novelle* novel (fr. It *novella*) + *-ette* — more at NOVELLA] **:** a romantic piano piece of free form characteristically containing a number of contrasting sections

nov·el·et·tish \-ed·ish\ *adj* **1 :** of, relating to, or characteristic of a novelette **2 :** CHEAP, SENTIMENTAL ⟨its situations and dialogue are at times ~, its humour stilted and elementary —T.R.Fyvel⟩ ⟨a mawkish schoolgirl with a crude, ~ mind —*Times Lit. Supp.*⟩

nov·el·et·tist \-d·əst\ *n* -S **:** one who writes novelettes

nov·el·ish \'nävəlish\ *adj* [¹*novel* + *-ish*] **:** NOVELISTIC

nov·el·ism \-‚lizəm\ *n* -S [¹*novel* + *-ism*] **1** *obs* **:** INNOVATION **2 :** the writing of novels ⟨the text itself . . . is rarely much beyond talented facility and expert ~ —*New Republic*⟩

nov·el·ist \-ləst\ *n* -S [¹*novel* + *-ist*] **1** *obs* **:** one who likes novelty **:** INNOVATOR **2** *archaic* **:** a bearer of news **:** NEWSMONGER **3 :** a writer of novels ⟨the ~ is concerned with the nature of man's constant experience as it can be illustrated in character —Douglas Grant⟩

nov·el·is·tic \¦==¦listik\ *adj* **:** of, relating to, or characteristic of a novel ⟨slowness . . . is an element essential to the ~ form — as opposed to the dramatic or short-story form —R.C. Hutchinson⟩ ⟨the ~ fashions he parodied and superseded —William Irvine⟩ — **nov·el·is·ti·cal·ly** \-tə̇k(ə)lē\ *adv*

nov·el·i·za·tion \‚nävələ'zāshən, -‚lī'-\ *n* -S **:** the act or process of novelizing ⟨~*s* of successful films which were not originally based on novels —J.T.Farrell⟩ ⟨the mere skillful ~ of a chapter in a psychiatry casebook —Clifton Fadiman⟩

nov·el·ize \'==‚līz\ *vt* -ED/-ING/-S **1 :** to convert into the form of a novel ⟨that queer, clumsy mongrel species . . . the *novelized* play —*Nation*⟩ ⟨comb Hollywood for its outstanding scenarios and ~ them —*Newsweek*⟩ **2 :** to treat as fiction **:** FICTIONALIZE ⟨what he sees he ~*s* into a string of anecdotes —*Saturday Rev.*⟩ ⟨*novelized* biography and history⟩

no·vel·la \nō'velə\ *n, pl* **novel·las** \-ləz\ *or* **novel·le** \-(‚)lā\ *see numbered senses* [It, fr. fem. of *novello* new, fr. L *novellus*, fr. *novus* new — more at NEW] **1** *pl* **novelle :** a story with a compact and pointed plot ⟨found the plots of several of his plays in Italian *novelle*⟩ **2** *pl usu* **novellas :** a short novel **:** a work of fiction intermediate in length and complexity between a short story and a novel ⟨is not a major work of fiction, but as a ~ it is a gem —*Newsweek*⟩ — called also *nouvelle*

nov·el·ly \'näv(ə)lē, -li\ *adv* [²*novel* + *-ly*] **:** in a novel manner

novel news *or* **novel paper** *n* [¹*novel*] **:** a paper similar to newsprint but often somewhat more bulky that is used in pulp magazines

nov·el·ty \'nävəltē, -ti\ *n* -ES *often attrib* [ME *novelte*, fr. MF *noveleté*, fr. *novel* + *-té* -ty] **1 :** something novel **:** a new or unusual thing or event ⟨men in uniform are no ~ to a city which considers itself the army's home town —Green Peyton⟩ ⟨found it a ~ and a satisfaction to work on the soil —Martha Sharp⟩ ⟨~ seekers⟩ ⟨the ballet season produced only two *novelties*⟩ ⟨a ~ song⟩ **2 :** the quality or state of being novel **:** recentness of origin or introduction **:** NEWNESS ⟨a general uncritical acceptance of ~ as advance —Howard M. Jones⟩ ⟨the ~ of space travel⟩ ⟨the charm of ~⟩ ⟨~ appeal⟩ **3 a :** a small manufactured article intended mainly for decoration or adornment and marked by unusual or novel design ⟨a ~ shop⟩ ⟨~ goods⟩ ⟨factories that manufacture paper, wooden *novelties*, and snowplows —*Amer. Guide Series: Mich.*⟩ — usu. used in pl. **b :** a short-lived fashion **:** an article (as a fabric or garment) of unusual or fancy design created for a special season or occasion ⟨~ sweaters⟩

novelty siding *n* **:** DROP SIDING

¹no·vem·ber \nə'vembə(r), (')nō¦v-\ *n* -S *usu cap* [ME *novembre*, fr. OF, fr. L *november* (ninth month), fr. *novem* nine — more at NINE] **:** the eleventh month of the Gregorian calendar — abbr. *Nov.*; see MONTH table

²november \"\ *usu cap* — a communications code word for the letter *n*

no·vem·decillion \¦nō‚vem+\ *n, often attrib* [L *novemdecim* nineteen (fr. *novem* nine + *-decim*, fr. *decem* ten) + E *-illion* (as in *million*) — more at TEN] — see NUMBER table

no·ve·na \nō'vēnə\ *n* -S [ML, fr. L, fem. of *novenus* nine each, ninefold, fr. *novem*] *Roman Catholicism* **:** a nine days' devotion for a religious intention

¹nov·e·nary \'nävə‚nerē, nō'vēnərē, -ri\ *adj* [L *novenarius*, fr. *novenus* + *-arius* -ary] **:** of or relating to the number nine **:** based on the number nine

²novenary \"\ *n* -ES [*novena* + *-ary*] **:** NOVENA

no·ver·cal \nə'vərkəl\ *adj* [L *novercalis*, fr. *noverca* stepmother + *-alis* -al — more at ANEROID] **:** of, relating to, or characteristic of a stepmother ⟨of true ~ type, dragon and devil —Robert Browning⟩

¹nov·go·rod·i·an \¦nävgə¦rädēən, -rōd-\ *adj, usu cap* [*Novgorod*, city of northwest U. S. S. R. + E *-ian*] **1 :** of, relating to, or characteristic of Novgorod, U. S. S. R. **2 :** of, relating to, or characteristic of the people of Novgorod

²novgorodian \"\ *n* -S *cap* **:** a native or resident of Novgorod, U. S. S. R.

nov·ice \'nävəs\ *n* -S [ME *novice*, *novis*, fr. MF *novice*, fr. ML *novicius*, fr. L, new, inexperienced, fr. *novus*] **1 a :** one who has entered a religious house and is on probation **:** a postulant who has received the habit in a religious house and is under training **b :** one newly received into the church or one newly converted to the Christian faith **2 :** one who has no previous training or experience in a specific field or activity **:** BEGINNER, TYRO ⟨a ~ in cooking who had never prepared a meal⟩ ⟨a ~ who was teaching his first class⟩ ⟨a ~ at bridge⟩ **3 :** an animal that has never won a first prize in show competition

syn NOVITIATE, APPRENTICE, PROBATIONER, POSTULANT, NEOPHYTE: NOVICE and the less common NOVITIATE may designate any inexperienced beginner in a trade, career, or way of life, especially in a religious order ⟨superiors instructing *novices*⟩ ⟨her book shows the uneven hand of a *novice* at writing —Rose Feld⟩ ⟨to show the Communist *novitiate* as a human being with idealistic impulses —Daniel Bell⟩ APPRENTICE may apply to a beginner placed, sometimes formally, under a master or supervisor for training or instruction ⟨while still an *apprentice*, he had made his first attempt at engraving —R.C.Smith⟩ ⟨the breathless, the fructifying adoration of a young *apprentice* in the atelier of some great master of the Renaissance —Van Wyck Brooks⟩ PROBATIONER indicates a beginner on trial in which he must demonstrate aptitude ⟨the *probationer* is not allowed to take part in assemblies or to sit as a judge —*Current Biog.*⟩ POSTULANT designates a candidate on probation, especially for admission to a religious order ⟨a master in the field of diplomacy but a *postulant* in democratic politics —M. W.Straight⟩ NEOPHYTE is applicable to one, often eager and unsophisticated, newly connected with or entered into a group, society, faith, or pursuit ⟨the old philosopher of Monticello was more than pleased with this ardent *neophyte*, who offered to purchase books for him in Europe —Van Wyck Brooks⟩ ⟨in many states it is almost impossible to differentiate between the *neophyte* and the confirmed criminal —C.R.Cooper⟩

nov·ice·ship \-və(sh)‚ship *also* -vəs‚sh-\ *n* **:** NOVITIATE

no·vi·lla·da \‚nōvē'yädə\ *n* -S [Sp, fr. *novillo*] **:** a bullfight in which novilleros fight immature, overage, or defective bulls ⟨the best bullfight to see first would be a ~ —Ernest Hemingway⟩

no·vi·lle·ro \-'ye(ə)(‚)rō\ *n* -S [Sp, fr. *novillo*] **:** an aspiring bullfighter who has not yet attained the rank of matador

no·vi·llo \nō'vē(‚)(y)ō\ *n* -S [Sp, young bull, fr. L *novellus* new — more at NOVEL] **:** a bull used in a novillada ⟨sell me like a ~ to the butcher —Budd Schulberg⟩

no·vi·tiate *also* **no·vi·ciate** \nō'vish(ē)ət, nə'-, -shē‚āt, *usu* -d·+V\ *n* -S [F *noviciat*, fr. ML *noviciatus*, *novitiatus*, fr. *novicius*, *novitius* novice + L *-atus* -ate] **1 a :** the probationary period or state of a novice in a religious order ⟨monks were to be admitted first for a ~ of one year —K.S.Latourette⟩ **b :** a period or state of initiation or apprenticeship in an activity or occupation ⟨some of these early works were hung in the Paris Salon during his ~ —W.H.Downes⟩ **2 a :** a novice in a religious order or priesthood ⟨entered the Sisters of Charity Convent . . . as a ~ —*Newsweek*⟩ ⟨must pass some time as a ~ in a Buddhist monastery —John Gunther⟩ **b :** APPRENTICE, BEGINNER ⟨the ~ at this business of motoring south —Jack Westeyn⟩ ⟨has little to offer a person already knowledgeable about India, but it provides a pleasant sojourn for the ~ —Marguerite A. Brown⟩ **3 :** a place where novices are trained and housed ⟨all their German, Czech and Austrian ~*s* were closed, the buildings confiscated —Anne Fremantle⟩ **syn** see NOVICE

nov·i·ty \'nävəd·ē, -ətē, -i\ *n* -ES [ME *novitee*, fr. MF *novité*, fr. L *novitat-*, *novitas*, fr. *novus* new + *-tat-*, *-tas* -ty — more at NEW] **:** NOVELTY

novo- — see NOV-

no·vo·bi·o·cin \‚nō(‚)vō'bīəsən\ *n* -S [prob. fr. *nov-* + anti*biotic* + streptomy*cin*] **:** an acid antibiotic $C_{31}H_{36}N_2O_{11}$ that is produced by actinomycetes of the genus *Streptomyces* (as *S. niveus* or *S. spheroides*) and is active esp. against gram-positive bacteria (as staphylococci)

No·vo·cain \'nōvə‚kān\ *trademark* — used for a preparation containing procaine hydrochloride

no·vo·caine \'nōvə‚kān\ *n* -S [ISV *nov-* + *cocaine*; orig. formed as G *novokain*] **:** procaine or its hydrochloride

no·vo·da·mus \‚nō(‚)vō'dāməs, ‚və'-\ *n* -ES [L (*de*) *novo damus* we grant anew] *Scots law* **:** a clause sometimes added to a grant, charter, or deed granting anew certain rights, privileges, or estates and thereby confirming or validating them; *also* **:** the written instrument containing such a grant

no·vo·kuz·netsk \‚nō(‚)vōku̇z'netsk\ *adj, usu cap* [fr. *Novokuznetsk*, U.S.S.R.] **:** of or from the city of Novokuznetsk, U.S.S.R. **:** of the kind or style prevalent in Novokuznetsk

no·vo·si·birsk \¦nō(‚)vōsə¦birsk\ *adj, usu cap* [fr. *Novosibirsk*, U.S.S.R.] **:** of or from the city of Novosibirsk, U.S.S.R. **:** of the kind or style prevalent in Novosibirsk

¹now \(¦)nau̇\ *adv* [ME, fr. OE *nū*; akin to OHG *nū*, *nu* now, ON *nū*, Goth *nu*, L *nunc*, Gk *ny*, *nyn*, Skt *nū*, *nu*] **1 a :** at the present time **:** at this moment ⟨he is busy ~⟩ ⟨is ~ abroad⟩ ⟨is ~ writing a new play⟩ ⟨he teaches ~⟩ **b :** in the time immediately before the present **:** very lately **:** a moment ago ⟨was here just ~⟩ ⟨we were thinking of you just ~⟩ **c :** in the time immediately to follow **:** without delay **:** FORTHWITH ⟨steps to correct this weakness must be taken ~⟩ ⟨must write ~ or it will be too late⟩ **2 —** used with the sense of present time weakened or lost to express command, request, or admonition ⟨~ hear this⟩ ⟨~ be a good boy and do as I tell you⟩ ⟨~ don't get me angry⟩ **3 —** used with the sense of present time weakened or lost to introduce an important point or indicate a transition from one idea to another ⟨~, this central cord is present in all the vertebrate animals we have so far mentioned —W.E.Swinton⟩ ⟨~ this point of view . . . seems to me absolutely unhistorical —Edmund Wilson⟩ **4 :** SOMETIMES ⟨full of pathos and humor, ~ gay, ~ sad —H.H.Reichard⟩ ⟨the foothills roll along on either side, ~ bare and ~ wooded —*Amer. Guide Series: Vt.*⟩ **5 :** under the present conditions **:** in view of the existing circumstances ⟨after his quick victory over his last opponent, he is ~ favored to defeat the champion⟩ ⟨since my plan has failed, we must ~ try his⟩ **6 :** at the time under consideration **:** at the time referred to ⟨the people ~ proceeded to give him almost every important honor within their gift —E.M.Coulter⟩ ⟨~ the ore is loaded in chutes from towering trestled docks —Meridel Le Sueur⟩ **7 :** reckoning to the present time **:** by this time ⟨spurned as the lowest form of wit for several centuries ~ —Esther K. Sheldon⟩ ⟨a good many years ago ~, when I was a soldier —John Connell⟩

²now \"\ *conj* [ME, fr. OE *nū*, fr. *nū*, adv.] **:** seeing that at or by this time **:** in view of the fact that **:** SINCE ⟨~ he is better, he can return to school⟩ — often followed by *that* ⟨~ that I have seen her, I can understand your feeling for her⟩

³now \'nau̇\ *n* -S [ME, fr. ¹*now*] **:** the present time or moment **:** PRESENT ⟨the ~ is that which limits and determines the before and after of time —W.A.Gerhard⟩ ⟨about three times as large as any dining alcove of ~ —Sylvia T. Warner⟩

⁴now \"\ *adj* [ME, fr. ¹*now*] **1 :** of or relating to the present time **:** EXISTING ⟨was working for the ~ judge —*Time*⟩ **2 :** currently fashionable **:** UP-TO-DATE ⟨the ~ point of view⟩

¹now·a·days \'nau̇(ə)‚dāz\ *also* **now·a·day** \-‚dā\ *adv* [*nowadays* fr. ME *now a dayes*, fr. ¹*now* + *a dayes* adays; *nowaday* fr. ME, fr. ¹*now* + *aday*, fr. ¹*a-* + *day*] **:** in these days **:** at the present time ⟨it is solely by their language that the upper classes ~ are distinguished —Nancy Mitford⟩

²nowadays \"\ *also* **nowaday** \"\ *adj* **:** of or relating to the present time ⟨the tendency of the *nowaday* producer —Johnston Forbes-Robertson⟩

³nowadays \"\ *n* **:** the present time ⟨the land of ~ that we never discover —Booth Tarkington⟩

now and again *or* **now and then** *adv* **:** from time to time **:** OCCASIONALLY ⟨*now and again* . . . our grandmother would put the good book back on the shelf —Rumer Godden⟩ ⟨as they drove along, the beautiful scenery *now and then* attracted his attention⟩

now·a·nights \-‚nīts\ *adv* [¹*now* + *anights*] **:** on present nights ⟨outspread ~ down the high dark coast road —Max Beerbohm⟩

no·way \'nō‚wā\ *adv* [ME *na wai*, fr. *na* no + *wai* way] **1 :** in no way whatever **:** not at all ⟨is ~ to blame⟩ **2** *dial* **:** ANYHOW ⟨me and my wife ain't got much longer to live, ~ —Erskine Caldwell⟩ ⟨you ain't goin' to git in ~, so you've got all the time there is —T.S.Stribling⟩

no·ways \-āz\ *adv* [ME *nanes weies*, *nanwais*, *naways*, fr. gen. of *nan wei*, *nan wai* no way, fr. *nan* no, none + *wai* way] **:** NOWAY

nowed \'nüəd, 'nau̇d\ *adj* [modif. (influenced by E *-ed*) of MF *noué*, past. part. of *nouer* to knot, fr. L *nodare*, fr. *nodus* knot — more at NET] *heraldry* **:** twisted into a knot **:** KNOTTED

¹now·el *or* **now·ell** \nō'el, 'nōəl\ *n* -S [ME, fr. MF *noel*] **:** NOEL

²now·el \'nōəl, 'nau̇əl\ *n* -S [ME *nowell* newel — more at NEWEL] **1 :** the core of a mold for casting a large hollow object **2 :** the bottom part of a mold or of a flask, in distinction from the cope **:** DRAG

¹no·where \'nō‚(h)we(ə)r, -wa(ə)‚ ‚ə; *when a stressed syllable, as "else," follows, sometimes* -ōwə(r)\ *adv* [ME *nowher*, fr.

OE *nāhwær*, fr. *nā* no + *hwær* where, anywhere — more at WHERE] **1 a :** not anywhere **:** not in or at any place ⟨the book is ~ to be found⟩ ⟨he discovered gold ~⟩ ⟨has property everywhere and a home ~⟩ **b :** to no place ⟨has gone ~ for months⟩ **2 :** not in any part of a book **:** in no written work or writer ⟨this word is ~ used by Shakespeare⟩ ⟨these facts are ~ stated⟩ **3 a :** far behind **:** out of the running ⟨is ~ when it comes to the race for class president⟩ ⟨a dazzling exhibition of grace and beauty that left her rivals ~ —*Current Biog.*⟩ **b :** to no position or state of advancement ⟨a project going ~⟩ ⟨the team will get ~ this year⟩

²nowhere \"\ *n* **1 :** a place that does not exist ⟨as if all truth was gone out, and night and ~ had the world —Horace Bushnell⟩ **2 :** an unknown or undeveloped place **:** WILDERNESS ⟨lost forever in the ~ of South America —Marcia Davenport⟩ ⟨the lumbermen, construction workers and miners who are carving towns out of ~ in Canada —Bill Wolf⟩ **3 :** a state of not existing or of not being known to exist ⟨out of the ~ into the here came trouble —W.A.White⟩ ⟨an officer appeared from ~ to strike the soldier sharply —Kenneth Roberts⟩ ⟨a gossipy, clucking crowd materialized from ~ —Anne S. Mehdevi⟩ **4 :** a state of being unknown **:** OBSCURITY ⟨starting from ~, he became a leading politician in a few years⟩ ⟨came out of ~ to become a big-league star⟩ **5 :** an inhabited place ⟨found a cattleman with a broken leg miles from ~ —Ellen Buell⟩

nowhere near *adv* **:** not nearly **:** not by a great deal ⟨purposes *nowhere near* as good —J.R.Wiggins⟩ ⟨operates at *nowhere near* its theoretical efficiency —*Collier's Yr. Bk.*⟩

no·wheres \|(ə)rz, |əz\ *adv* [*nowhere* + *-s*] *chiefly dial* **:** NOWHERE

no whit *adv* [²*no* + *whit*] **:** not at all **:** not in the least

nowhither \ˈ≈,≈≈, ≈ˈ≈≈\ *adv* [ME *nowhider*, fr. OE *nāhwider*, fr. *nā* no + *hwider* whither, anywhither — more at WHITHER] **:** to or toward no place **:** NOWHERE ⟨allures us into byways leading ~ —J.B.Cabell⟩

nowise \ˈ≈,≈\ *adv* [ME *nawise, no wise*, fr. *na, no* no + *wise*, n.] **:** in no manner or degree **:** not at all ⟨the human values that we have taken for granted are ~ different from those of the past —Norman Foerster⟩

nown \ˈnōn\ *archaic var of* OWN

now·ness \ˈnau̇nə̇s\ *n* -ES [¹*now* + *-ness*] **:** the quality or state of existing at or belonging to the present time ⟨concerned with the present moment, the ~ of life —Alwyn Berland⟩

nows *pl of* NOW

nows and nans \ˈnüzᵊnˈnanz\ *adv* [alter. of *nows and thens*] *Scot* **:** OCCASIONALLY ⟨Tam drank *nows and nans* —J.M.Barrie⟩

¹nowt \ˈnōt\ *dial Eng var of* NAUGHT

²nowt \ˈnau̇t, ˈnōt\ *n, pl* **nowt** *often attrib* [ME, fr. ON *naut* — more at NEAT] **1** *chiefly Scot* **:** OX, BULLOCK — usu. used in pl. **2** *chiefly Scot* **:** BLOCKHEAD, LOUT

now·ther \ˈnōthə(r)\ *dial var of* NEITHER

nowy \ˈnaüē, ˈnōē\ *adj* [F *noué*, fr. L *nodatus* having a knot, fr. *nodus* knot + *-atus* -ate — more at NET] *of a cross* **:** expanded into a circle at the junction of the arms

noxa \ˈnäksə\ *n, pl* **nox·ae** \-,sē, -sī\ [NL, fr. LL, that which has caused damage, fr. L, damage, offense — more at NOXIOUS] **:** something that exerts a harmful effect on the body

nox·ae de·di·tio \ˈnäk,sēdəˈdishē,ō, -,sīd-, -did-ē,ō\ *n* [LL, lit., surrender of that which has caused damage] **:** NOXAL SURRENDER

nox·al \ˈnäksəl\ *adj* [LL *noxalis*, fr. *noxa* + L *-alis* -al] **:** of or relating to damage or an injury caused by another's chattel

noxal action *n* [LL *noxalis actio*] **:** an action brought against someone for damage or injury done by a person or animal belonging to him

noxal surrender *n* [trans. of LL *noxae deditio*] **:** the surrender of a person or thing that has done damage to the damaged person in satisfaction of his damage or injury; *also* **:** the right (as among the Romans and in medieval Europe) to make this surrender in full satisfaction of damages

nox·ious \ˈnäkshəs\ *adj* [L *noxius*, fr. *noxa* damage, offense, harm; akin to L *nocēre* to harm, *nec-*, *nex* violent death, Gk *nekros* dead body, Skt *naśyati* he disappears, perishes] **1 :** harmful or destructive to man or to other organisms ⟨dust, fumes, effluvia, sometimes ~ for human organisms —Lewis Mumford⟩ ⟨the ~ wastes in the stream killed the fish⟩ ⟨~ weeds that prevent the growth of food plants⟩ **2 :** having or regarded as capable of having a harmful influence on thought or behavior **:** INJURIOUS, PERNICIOUS ⟨a ~ book⟩ ⟨a ~ doctrine⟩ ⟨a ~ system of education⟩ **3 :** DISTASTEFUL, OBNOXIOUS ⟨this ~ political scandal —H.L.Ickes⟩ ⟨the Transcendentalists and their ~ crew —Van Wyck Brooks⟩ **syn** see PERNICIOUS

nox·ious·ly *adv* **:** in a noxious manner

nox·ious·ness *n* -ES **:** the quality or state of being noxious

no·yade \(ˈ)nwäˈyäd, (ˈ)nwīˈäd\ *n* -S [F, fr. *noyer* to drown, fr. LL *necare*, fr. L, to kill, fr. *nec-*, *nex* violent death] **:** an execution by drowning **:** a mass drowning

noyance *n* -S [ME *noiaunce*, short for *anoiaunce* annoyance] *obs* **:** ANNOYANCE

no·yau \(ˈ)nwäˈyō, (ˈ)nwīˈō\ *n, pl* **no·yaux** \-ō(z)\ [by shortening] **:** CRÈME DE NOYAU

no·zi \ˈnōzē\ *n, pl* **nozi** *or* **nozis** *usu cap* **:** YANA

¹noz·zle \ˈnäzəl\ *n* -S [dim. of *nose*] **1 :** a socket on a candlestick or sconce into which the lower end of a candle fits **2 a :** a projecting vent of something **:** a small spout or other projecting part with an opening ⟨the ~ of a bellows⟩ ⟨the ~ of a gun⟩ **b :** a short tube or duct that usu. tapers or has a constriction, often forms the vent of a hose or pipe, and is used to direct the flow of fluid or to increase the velocity of flow ⟨delivery of fuel to an injection ~ at each engine cylinder —William Landon⟩ **c :** any of several channels through which steam or gas is conveyed to the rotor vanes of a turbine **d :** a part in a rocket engine that accelerates the exhaust gases from the combustion chamber to a high velocity **3** *slang* **:** NOSE ⟨longed to clout him in the ~ —J.H.Wheelwright⟩

²nozzle \"\ *vb* **nozzled; nozzled; nozzling** \-z(ə)liŋ\ **nozzles** *vt* **1 :** to furnish with a nozzle or something resembling a nozzle **2 :** to press the nose against ⟨pawing and *nozzling* some remnants of fodder —J.L.Allen⟩ **3 :** to spray or eject through or as if through a nozzle ⟨seemed as though every gun . . . *nozzled* a cone of fire at it —H.M.Forgy⟩ ~ *vi* **:** to nose about ⟨hungry birds will force their way into broken reeds . . . to spatter and ~ for food —*Pall Mall Mag.*⟩

noz·zle·man \-mən\ *n, pl* **nozzlemen :** one who works with a stream of water or sand projected through a nozzle (as in firefighting, hydraulic mining, sandblasting)

np *abbr* neap

NP *abbr* **1** net proceeds **2** neuropsychiatric; neuropsychiatry **3** *often not cap* new paragraph **4** nickel-plated **5** nisi prius **6** *often not cap* nonparticipating **7** *often not cap* no paging **8** *often not cap* no place **9** no protest **10** notary public **11** noun phrase

Np *symbol* neptunium

n paper *n, usu cap N* **:** paper containing significant imperfections and graded below M paper — compare P PAPER

NPD *abbr* north polar distance

NPF *abbr, often not cap* not provided for

NPL *abbr* nonpersonal liability

NPN *abbr* nonprotein nitrogen

NPNA *abbr* no protest nonacceptance

NP *or* **D** *abbr, often not cap* no place or date

NPT *abbr* normal pressure and temperature

NPV *abbr* no par value

nr *abbr* **1** near **2** number

NR *abbr, often not cap* **1** net register **2** [L *non repetatur*] not to be repeated **3** no risk

NRAD *abbr, often not cap* no risk after discharge

n-radiation \ˈ≈,≈≈ˈ≈≈\ *n, usu cap N* **:** X rays emitted when an electron becomes an N electron in an atom

nrit·ta \enˈrid·ə\ *n* -S [Skt *nritta* dance] **:** a purely abstract type of bharata natya dance in southern India

nrit·ya \enˈrityə\ *n* -S [Skt *nritya* dance, play] **:** a narrative type of bharata natya dance in southern India

nrml *abbr* normal

NRT *abbr, often not cap* net register ton

n's *or* **ns** *pl of* N

NS *abbr* **1** national society **2** near side **3** new school **4** new series **5** new side **6** new style **7** nickel steel **8** [F *Notre Seigneur*] Our Lord **9** not specified **10** not sufficient **11** nuclear ship **12** numismatic society

nsam·bya \enˈsämbyə\ *n* -S [native name in Uganda, eastern Africa] **1 :** an African timber tree (*Markhamia platycalyx*) of the family Bignoniaceae having yellow flowers and tough durable wood **2 :** the wood of the nsambya tree used chiefly for poles and construction work

NSF *abbr* not sufficient funds

NSIC *or* **NSJC** *abbr* [L *Noster Salvator Iesus* (*Jesus*) *Christus*] Our Savior Jesus Christ

NSO *abbr* naval staff officer

NSP *abbr* navy standard part

NSPF *abbr* not specifically provided for

n star *n, usu cap N* **:** a star of spectral type N — see SPECTRAL TYPE table

nstd *abbr* nested

nt *abbr* **1** net **2** neuter **3** night

NT *abbr* **1** net ton **2** new terms **3** new translation

-n't *or* **-nt** \ᵊnt, n(t), ᵊn(t)\ *adv comb form* [by contr.] **:** not ⟨*isn't*⟩ ⟨*needn't*⟩ ⟨*can't*⟩

NTC *abbr, often not cap* negative temperature coefficient

ntfy *abbr* notify

nth \ˈen(t)th\ *adj* [*n* + *-th*] **1 :** numbered with some unspecified or indefinitely large ordinal number ⟨a polynomial of the ~ degree⟩ ⟨hunting up the ~ decimal of pi —Lucius Garvin⟩ ⟨fascinated . . . by the consideration of space to the ~ dimension —Peter Watson⟩ **2 :** EXTREME, UTMOST ⟨all the components of dullness and boringness to the ~ degree —S.H.Adams⟩ ⟨never quite attains the ~ power of enthusiasm —William Beebe⟩ ⟨the art of photography raised to its ~ power —Margaret A. Barnes⟩

nthn *abbr* northern

ntla·kya·pa·muk \,entləˈkyäpə,mək\ *n, pl* **ntlakyapamuk** *or* **ntlakyapamuks** *usu cap* **:** THOMPSON

NTM *abbr, often not cap* net ton mile

NTO *abbr* not taken out

NTP *abbr* **1** normal temperature and pressure **2** no title page

NTS *abbr* not to scale

n-tu·ple \ˈen,t(y)üpəl, ≈ˈ≈≈; ˈentəp-\ *adj* [*n* + *-tuple* (as in *quintuple*)] **:** multiple in the degree denoted by *n* — **n-tu·ply** *adv*

¹nu \ˈn(y)ü\ *n* -S [Gk *ny*, of Sem origin; akin to Heb *nūn* nun] **:** the 13th letter of the Greek alphabet — symbol N or ν; see ALPHABET table

²nu \ˈnü\ *or* **nu–tzu** \-ˈdzü\ *n, pl* **nu** *or* **nus** *or* **nu–tzu** *or* **nu–tzus** *usu cap* [Chin (Pek) *Nu⁴ Tzu³*] **1 :** the Tibeto-Burman inhabitants of the upper Salween river region in Yunnan **2 :** a member of any of various Tibeto-Burman groups of the upper Salween region related to the Nu and including the Chingpaw and Lisu

NU *abbr* **1** name unknown **2** national union **3** number unobtainable

¹nu·ance \ˈn(y)ü,än(t)s, ≈ˈ≈ *also* -ᵊⁿs *sometimes* ˈn(y)üən-\ *n* -S [F, fr. MF, shade of color, fr. *nuer* to make shades of color (fr. *nue* cloud, fr. L *nubes*) + *-ance*; akin to Gk *nythos* dark, W *nudd* mist, Av *snaotha* clouds and perh. to Gk *nan* to flow — more at NOURISH] **1 a :** a shade of difference **:** minute variation **:** delicate gradation **:** subtle distinction ⟨the play of surfaces, the dance of subtle lights and shadows, the ~s of color, tones, atmosphere —Lewis Mumford⟩ ⟨~s of flavor and fragrance cannot be described accurately —Scott Seegers⟩ ⟨a quick ear for ~s in mood —Irwin Edman⟩ **b :** a subtle expressive variation in a musical performance (as in tempo, dynamic intensity, or timbre) that is not indicated in the score ⟨the jazz world's increasing preoccupation with melodic and harmonic ~s —Wilder Hobson⟩ **2 :** a subtle or implicit quality, aspect, or device **:** NICETY ⟨a sense of the ~s of plain words —E.F.Goldman⟩ ⟨its vernacular shape may have given it a ~ of humor —R.A.Hall⟩ ⟨captures both the essence and the ~s of different theological positions —*Rev. of Religion*⟩ ⟨a very singular ~ of a boy's character — the one which decides what he will or will not consider to be sneaking —W.F. De Morgan⟩ **3 :** sensibility to, awareness of, or ability to express delicate shadings (as of meaning, feeling, or value) **:** extreme finesse ⟨form of acting, which has no ~ or restraint —*Current Biog.*⟩ ⟨a performance of remarkable pliability and ~ —Irving Kolodin⟩

²nuance \"\ *vt* -ED/-ING/-S **:** to give nuances to **:** express or perform with nicety or precision **:** depict in delicate gradations (as of colors or tones) ⟨it is not color as such that lends enchantment to a painting, it is the manner in which it is *nuanced* —Frederic Taubes⟩ ⟨an individually *nuanced* pronunciation —Edward Sapir⟩ ⟨the treatment of the first movement is excessively *nuanced* —B.A.Haggin⟩

¹nub \ˈnəb\ *n* -S [alter. of *knub*] **1 :** KNOB, LUMP, PROTUBERANCE **2** [by shortening] **:** NUBBIN ⟨a ~ of corn⟩ ⟨a ~ of pencil⟩ ⟨a ~ of land⟩ ⟨puffed at the ~ of his cigarette —Lionel Shapiro⟩ ⟨saw a fawn standing at a ~ of grass —Jack Kerouac⟩ **3 :** CORE, CRUX, GIST, KERNEL, POINT ⟨the ~ of an argument⟩ ⟨the ~ of a problem⟩ ⟨if this is the ~ of the book —W.W.Howells⟩ **4 :** a small bunch of fibers usu. made on the card, dyed, and interspersed in yarn during spinning ⟨jacket of tobacco-colored wool dotted with fat black ~s —Lois Long⟩ — **to the nub** *or* **to a nub** *adv* **:** to a state of fatigue or exhaustion **:** to the condition of being worn out ⟨worn *to a nub* doing the extra work the baby entails —Alma K. Reck⟩ ⟨danced me clean down *to the nub* last time —Ross Santee⟩

²nub \"\ *vt* **nubbed; nubbed; nubbing; nubs** [perh. fr. ¹*nub*] **1** *dial Eng* **:** NUDGE **2** *obs* **:** to execute by hanging

³nub \"\ *vt* **nubbed; nubbed; nubbing; nubs** [¹*nub*] **:** to provide with nubs ⟨*nubbed* silk⟩ ⟨*nubbed* weaves⟩ ⟨*nubbed* pottery⟩

nu·ba \ˈnübə\ *n, pl* **nuba** *or* **nubas** *usu cap* [LL *Nuba*, sing. of L *Nubae* Nubians] **1 a :** any of numerous diverse peoples constituting a loose community in the Nuba hills of So. Kordofan believed by some to be related to the Nubians **b :** a member of any such people **2 :** any of several languages spoken by the Nuba people — compare NUBIAN

nub·bin \ˈnəbə̇n\ *n* -S [¹*nub*] **1 :** something (as a fruit) that is small of its kind, stunted, undeveloped, or imperfect ⟨made cider of the ~s⟩ ⟨blackberry ~s⟩ ⟨found some potato ~s about the size of small marbles —Ross Santee⟩; *esp* **:** a small or imperfect ear of Indian corn **2 :** something that remains after a large part has been removed or worn away **:** a small piece or chunk **:** STUB, STUMP ⟨drew spider webs with a ~ of pink chalk —Jean Stafford⟩ ⟨a ~ of coal⟩ **3 :** NUB 3 ⟨further questions before you get to the ~ and ask your victim how he or she actually intends to vote —Stewart Alsop⟩ ⟨the ~ of hard intelligence in their opponents' argument —John Chamberlain⟩

nubbin disease *n* **:** CUCUMBER MOSAIC

nubbing cheat *n* [*nubbing* fr. gerund of ²*nub*] *obs* **:** GALLOWS

nub·ble \ˈnəbəl\ *n* -S [dim. of ¹*nub*] **1 :** a small knob or lump ⟨ **:** NUB ⟨a ~ of sod —W.D.Edmonds⟩ **2 :** a small hill **3 :** ISLET

nub·bly *also* **knub·bly** \ˈnəb(ə)lē, -li\ *adj* -ER/-EST [*nubble* or *knubble* + *-ly*] **1 :** having or like nubbles **:** KNOBBY, LUMPY ⟨~ steel walls —R.M.Hodesh⟩ ⟨sharp, ~ grains provide more cutting points —*advt*⟩ ⟨little ~ reefs —D.C.Peattie⟩ ⟨a ~ magenta carpet —Alexander Laing⟩ **2 :** NUBBY 2

nub·by *also* **knub·by** \ˈnəbē, -bi\ *adj* -ER/-EST [¹*nub* or *knub* + *-y*] **1 :** NUBBLY 1 ⟨thin ~ shoulders —Shirley A. Grau⟩ ⟨~ branches sprouting fan-sized leaves —D.W.Dresden⟩ **2** *of a textile* **:** having nubs ⟨enabling the fabric stylist to create all sorts of ~ and slubby effects —J.B.Goldberg⟩

nu·bec·u·la \n(y)üˈbekyələ\ *n, pl* **nubecu·lae** \-yə,lē\ [NL, fr. L, little cloud, dim. of *nubes* cloud] *med, archaic* **:** a cloudy formation (as in urine) or speck (as in the eye)

nu·bia \ˈn(y)übēə\ *n* -S [alter. (influenced by NL *-ia*) of earlier *nube*, fr. Sp, cloud, nubia, fr. L *nubes* cloud] **:** a woman's knitted or crocheted scarf for the head and shoulders

¹nu·bi·an \ˈn(y)übēən\ *adj, usu cap* [*Nubia*, region in Nile valley, northeastern Africa + E *-an*, adj. suffix] **1 a :** of, relating to, or characteristic of Nubia **b :** of, relating to, or characteristic of the Nubians **2 :** of, relating to, or characteristic of a Nubian language

²nubian \"\ *n* -S *usu cap* [*Nubia*, region in Nile valley + E *-an*, n. suffix] **1 :** one of the people of Nubia; *esp* **:** a member of one of the group of negroid tribes who were early Christianized and formed a powerful empire between Egypt and Ethiopia from the 6th to the 14th centuries when they were conquered by the Arabs and converted to the Muslim religion **2 a :** any of several languages spoken in central and northern Sudan esp. by the Nuba people and including some dialects that are extremely distantly related if at all **b :** a branch of the Chari-Nile language family containing the Nubian language of the Nuba people **c :** CUSHITIC **3 a** *also* **nubian horse :** an Arabian horse from Nubia **b** *also* **nubian goat :** a breed of long-legged roman-nosed brown or black goats of northern Africa the does of which are relatively heavy milkers; *also* **:** a goat of this breed — compare ANGLO-NUBIAN

nu·bile \ˈn(y)übəl\ *adj* [F, fr. L *nubilis*, fr. *nubere* to marry — more at NUPTIAL] **:** of marriageable condition or age **:** physically suited for or desirous of sexual relationship — used esp. of girls or young women ⟨~ provincial schoolgirls —Janet Flanner⟩ ⟨an excessively ~ young woman —Anthony West⟩

nu·bil·i·ty \n(y)üˈbiləd·ē\ *n* -ES [F *nubilité*, fr. *nubile* + *-ité* -ity] **:** the quality or state of being nubile

nu·bi·lous \ˈn(y)übələs\ *adj* [L *nubilus*, fr. *nubes* cloud — more at NUANCE] **1 :** CLOUDY, FOGGY, MISTY ⟨trade-wind clouds which are constantly piling up in ~ traffic jams —S.E.Morison⟩ **2 :** OBSCURE, VAGUE ⟨some ~ notions about an ideal society⟩

nubs *pl of* NUB, *pres 3d sing of* NUB

nub yarn *n* [¹*nub*] **:** a yarn with nubs; *specif* **:** KNOP YARN

nu·ca·ment \ˈn(y)ükəmənt\ *n* -S [L *nucamenta* fir cones, lit., things shaped like nuts, fr. *nuca-* (fr. *nuc-*, *nux* nut) + *-menta*, pl. of *-mentum* -ment — more at NUT] **:** AMENT

nu·cel·lar \(ˈ)n(y)üˈselə(r)\ *adj* [NL *nucellus* + E *-ar*] **:** of or relating to a nucellus ⟨~ seedling⟩

nu·cel·lus \n(y)üˈseləs\ *n, pl* **nucel·li** \-e,lī\ [NL, fr. L *nucella* small nut, fr. *nuc-*, *nux* nut + *-ella* -el] **:** a mass of thin-walled parenchymatous cells that composes the central and chief part of the body of an ovule and that contains the embryo sac and is surrounded by one or more integuments

nu·cha \ˈn(y)ükə\ *n, pl* **nu·chae** \-ü,kē\ [ML, nape, fr. Ar *nukhā'* spinal marrow] **1 a** *obs* **:** SPINAL CORD **b :** ¹NAPE **2** [NL, fr. ML, nape] **:** the hind part of the thorax of an insect bearing the petiole of the abdomen

¹nu·chal \-ükəl\ *adj* [in sense 1, fr. *nucha* + *-al*; in other senses, fr. (assumed) NL *nuchalis*, fr. NL *nucha* + L *-alis* -al] **1 :** of, relating to, or lying in the region of the nape **2 :** situated on the back of the prothorax of an insect immediately behind the head **3 :** of or relating to a nucha

²nuchal \"\ *n* -S **:** a nuchal element (as a scale or bone)

nu·che fly \ˈnüchā-\ *n* [*nuche* fr. AmerSp] **:** HUMAN BOT-FLY

nu·ci·form \ˈn(y)üsə,fȯrm\ *adj* [F *nuciforme*, fr. *nuc-* (fr. L *nuc-*, *nux* nut) + *-iforme* -iform] **:** like a nut in shape

nucle- *or* **nucleo-** *also* **nuclei-** *comb form* [F *nuclé-*, *nucléo-*, *nucléi-*, fr. NL *nucleus*] **1 :** nucleus **:** nuclear ⟨*nucleo*fugal⟩ ⟨*nucle*on⟩ ⟨*nucle*iform⟩ ⟨*nucleo*geny⟩ **2 :** nucleic acid ⟨*nucleo*protein⟩

nu·cle·al \ˈn(y)üklēəl\ *adj* [ISV *nucle-* + *-al*; orig. formed as F *nucléal*] **:** NUCLEAR

nucleal reaction *or* **nucleal stain :** FEULGEN REACTION

nu·cle·ar \ˈn(y)üklēə(r), ≈ˈ≈ -kyələ(r)\ *adj* [ISV *nucle-* + *-ar*; orig. formed as F *nucléaire*] **1 :** of or relating to a nucleus **:** constituting or like a nucleus ⟨annexation of the suburban fringe by the ~ metropolis —W.H.Wickwar⟩ ⟨the oldest or ~ parts of the continents —O. D. von Engeln⟩ ⟨~ budding⟩ **2 a** *of an atom or group of atoms* **:** attached directly to a nucleus or ring in a molecule **b :** ¹CENTRAL 1 — used of an atom or ion in a coordination complex **3 a :** of or relating to the atomic nucleus ⟨~ particle⟩ ⟨~ forces⟩ ⟨~ physics⟩ ⟨~ scientist⟩ ⟨~ structure⟩ **b :** of or relating to atomic energy ⟨~ inventions⟩ ⟨~ studies⟩: as (1) **:** being, involving, or relating to a weapon or missile that utilizes atomic energy (as in the atom bomb) ⟨~ attack⟩ ⟨~ device⟩ ⟨~ war⟩ (2) **:** being, propelled by, produced by, or relating to atomic power (as that produced by a reactor) ⟨~ airplane⟩ ⟨~ engineering⟩ ⟨~ propulsion⟩ ⟨~ ship⟩ ⟨~ submarine⟩

nuclear bomb *n* **:** ATOM BOMB 2

nuclear chemistry *n* **:** RADIOCHEMISTRY 1

nuclear cycle *n* **:** the cyclic nuclear changes (as between haplophase and diplophase) characteristic of the life cycles of various fungi and algae and occurring in many without accompanying marked changes in form and mode of life

nuclear emulsion *n* **:** a photographic emulsion for recording the track of a nucleon or other ionizing particle as a definite arrangement of developed silver grains

nuclear energy *n* **:** ATOMIC ENERGY

nuclear exclusion clause *or* **nuclear clause** *n* **:** a clause in a fire or similar insurance policy excluding loss from nuclear reaction or from nuclear radiation or radioactive contamination

nuclear family *n* **:** a family group consisting of father, mother, and children — opposed to *extended family*

nuclear fission *n* **:** FISSION 4

nuclear fuel *n* **:** FUEL 1c

nuclear fusion *n* **:** FUSION 2g

nuclear isomer *n* **:** ISOMER 2

nuclear magneton *n* **:** a unit of magnetic moment of a nuclear particle involving the mass of the proton instead of the electron and equaling ¹⁄₁₈₃₇ Bohr magneton

nuclear membrane *n* **:** the boundary of a nucleus variously interpreted as an organized physical structure or a visible interface or colloidal phase boundary — see CELL illustration

nuclear plate *n* **:** METAPHASE PLATE

nuclear-powered \ˌ≈≈≈ˈ≈\ *adj* **:** utilizing atomic power (as for propulsion) ⟨*nuclear-powered* submarine⟩

nuclear reaction *n* **:** REACTION 4b

nuclear reactor *n* **:** REACTOR 4b

nuclear reticulum *or* **nuclear network** *n* **:** the diffuse intermeshed granular threads that represent the chromosomes in the resting or metabolic nucleus

nuclear sap *n* **:** KARYOLYMPH

nuclear spindle *n* **:** the spindle-shaped figure that is formed in mitosis

nu·cle·ase \ˈn(y)üklē,ās\ *n* -S [ISV *nucleic* (in *nucleic acid*) + *-ase*; orig. formed as G *nuklease*] **:** any of the enzymes found in plants and animals that promote hydrolysis of nucleic acids (as into nucleotides) — see DEOXYRIBONUCLEASE, RIBONUCLEASE

¹nu·cle·ate \ˈn(y)üklē,āt\ *vb* -ED/-ING/-S [LL *nucleatus*, past part. of *nucleare* to become kernelly, hard, fr. L *nucleus* kernel, dim. of *nuc-*, *nux* nut — more at NUT] *vt* **1 :** to form into a nucleus **:** CLUSTER ⟨almost no community life or social solidarity, the *nucleating* factors being rooming houses, bars, pool rooms —J.H.Burma⟩ ⟨business establishments are compactly *nucleated* —H.W.H.King⟩ ⟨vague but tremendous expectations were gradually *nucleated* in certain symbolic demands —*Yale Rev.*⟩ **2 :** to act as a nucleus for (as crystallization or precipitation) ⟨light-diffusing crystals whose precipitation is *nucleated* by submicroscopic silver particles formed photographically within the glass —S.D.Stookey⟩ ⟨an oasis *nucleated* by a hamlet —P.K.Hitti⟩; *also* **:** to cause (as particles) to nucleate ~ *vi* **:** to form a nucleus **:** CLUSTER ⟨new communities *nucleating* as the boundaries of older ones⟩

²nu·cle·ate \-ēət, -ē,āt\ *adj* [L *nucleatus*, fr. *nucleus* kernel + *-atus* -ate] **:** having a nucleus or nuclei ⟨~ cells⟩

³nucleate \"\ *n* -S [ISV *nucleic* (in *nucleic acid*) + *-ate*] **:** a salt or ester of a nucleic acid

nu·cle·a·tion \,n(y)üklēˈāshən\ *n* -S **:** the process of nucleating or clustering ⟨the ~ of communities in villages and cities —A.J.Bruwer⟩: as **a :** the formation of nuclei (as in a supersaturated vapor or the free air) ⟨kept a continuous record of atmospheric ~ for several years —*Science*⟩ **b :** the action of a nucleus in starting a process (as condensation, crystallization, or precipitation) ⟨pearlitic structure . . . is formed by a process of ~ and growth —Frederick Seitz⟩ **c :** the process of seeding a cloud for the production of rain

nu·cle·a·tor \ˈ≈≈,ād·ə(r)\ *n* -S **:** one that nucleates

nuclei *pl of* NUCLEUS

nuclei- — see NUCLE-

nu·cle·ic acid \n(y)üˈklēik-, -lā|, |ēk-\ *n* [*nucleic* ISV *nucle-* + *-ic*; orig. formed in G] **:** any of two groups of complex acids that are found in all living cells esp. in combination as nucleoproteins, that are polynucleotides yielding on partial hydrolysis less highly polymerized nucleotides, nucleosides, and finally purine bases, pyrimidine bases, a pentose sugar, and phosphoric acid — see DEOXYRIBONUCLEIC ACID, RIBONUCLEIC ACID

nu·cle·in \ˈn(y)üklēən\ *n* -S [ISV *nucle-* + *-in*; orig. formed as G *nuklein*] **1 :** NUCLEOPROTEIN **2 :** NUCLEIC ACID

nu·cle·in·ation \ˌn(y)üklēə'nāshən\ *n* -s [*nuclein* + *-ation*] : the deposition of nucleic acids on the chromosomes during the stage of prophase coiling
nucleo- — see NUCLE-
nu·cleo·centrosome \ˌn(y)üklē,ō+\ *n* [*nucle-* + *centrosome*] : an intranuclear division center (as in some protozoans)
nu·cleo·cytoplasmic \"+\ *adj* [*nucle-* + *cytoplasmic*] : of or relating to nucleus and cytoplasm
nucleocytoplasmic ratio *n* : the more or less constant proportionality between the volume of nucleus and cytoplasm characteristic of any given type of cell
nu·cle·og·o·ny \ˌn(y)üklē'ägənē\ *n* -ES [*nucle-* + *-gony*] : nuclear division accompanied by chromatin growth but not by cell division
nu·cleo·histone \ˌn(y)üklē,ō+\ *n* [ISV *nucle-* + *histone*] : a nucleoprotein derived from a histone
[1]**nu·cle·oid** \'n(y)üklē,ȯid\ *adj* [*nucle-* + *-oid*] : resembling a nucleus
[2]**nucleoid** \"\ *n* -s [ISV *nucle-* + *-oid*] : a body (as in some bacteria) resembling a nucleus in composition and behavior but not proved to be such
nucleol- *or* **nucleolo-** *comb form* [ISV, fr. NL *nucleolus*] : nucleolus ⟨*nucleolo*centrosome⟩ ⟨*nucleol*oid⟩
nu·cle·o·lar \n(y)ü'klēələ(r) *also* ˌn(y)üklē'ōlə(r)\ *adj* [ISV *nucleol-* + *-ar*; prob. orig. formed as F *nucléolaire*] : of, relating to, or constituting a nucleolus ⟨~ proteins⟩
nucleolar organizer *also* **nucleolar zone** *n* : NUCLEOLUS ORGANIZER
nu·cle·o·lat·ed \n(y)ü'klēə,lād·əd, 'n(y)üklēə,-\ *also* **nu·cle·o·late** \-,lāt, -lət\ *adj* [*nucleolated* fr. NL *nucleolus* + E *-ate* + *-ed*; *nucleolate* ISV *nucleol-* + *-ate*] : having a nucleolus or nucleoli
nu·cle·ole \'n(y)üklē,ōl\ *n* -s [NL *nucleolus*] : NUCLEOLUS
nu·cle·o·li·nus \ˌn(y)üklēō'līnəs\ *n*, *pl* **nucleoli·ni** \-ī,nī\ [NL, dim. of *nucleolus*] : a differentiated body within a nucleolus
nu·cle·o·lo·centrosome \n(y)ü'klēə,lō+\ *n* [ISV *nucleol-* + *centrosome*; prob. orig. formed as G *nucleolozentrosom*] : NUCLEOCENTROSOME
nu·cle·o·loid \n(y)ü'klēə,lȯid\ *adj* [*nucleol-* + *-oid*] : resembling a nucleolus
nu·cle·o·lus \n(y)ü'klēələs\ *n*, *pl* **nucleo·li** \-ə,lī\ [NL, fr. L, small kernel, dim. of *nucleus* kernel — more at NUCLEUS] **1** : an organized body of predominantly protein structure that is typical of the metabolic nucleus, is variously regarded as a center of synthetic activity or as a storage organelle, and is usu. absent during mitosis being formed anew after each division in contact with the nucleolus organizer of the SAT-chromosome : PLASMOSOME — see CELL illustration **2** : any differentiated nuclear body other than a chromosome (as an endosome, karyosome, or nucleocentrosome)
nucleolus organizer *n* : the part of a SAT-chromosome that is associated with and possibly responsible for nucleolus reorganization following nuclear division
nu·cle·ol·y·sis \ˌn(y)üklē'äləsəs\ *n* [NL, fr. *nucle-* + *-lysis*] : KARYOLYSIS
nu·cle·ome \'n(y)üklē,ōm\ *n* -s [ISV *nucle-* + *-ome*; orig. formed as F *nucléome*] : the entire nuclear content of a protoplast
nu·cle·om·e·ter \ˌn(y)üklē'ämәd·ə(r)\ *n* [*nucle-* + *-meter*] : a sensitive counting device for nuclear particles
nu·cle·on \'n(y)üklē,än\ *n* -s [ISV *nucle-* + *-on*] : a proton or neutron esp. in the atomic nucleus — **nu·cle·on·ic** \ˌ==ˈänik\ *adj*
nu·cle·on·ics \ˌ=='äniks\ *n pl but sing or pl in constr* [*nucleon* + *-ics*] : a branch of physical science that deals with nucleons or with all phenomena of the atomic nucleus esp. in their practical applications
nu·cle·o·phil·ic \ˌn(y)üklēəˈfilik\ *adj* [*nucle-* + *-philic*] : having an affinity for atomic nuclei : donating electrons to atomic nuclei : ANIONOID — contrasted with *electrophilic* ⟨~ reagents⟩ ⟨~ displacement reactions⟩
nu·cle·o·plasm \'n(y)üklēə,plazəm\ *n* -s [ISV *nucle-* + *-plasm*; prob. orig. formed as G *nucleoplasma*] **1** : the protoplasm of a nucleus — distinguished from *cytoplasm* **2** : KARYOLYMPH — **nu·cle·o·plas·mat·ic** \ˌ===ˌplazˈmad·ik\ *or* **nu·cle·o·plas·mic** \ˌ==='plazmik\ *adj*
nu·cleo·protamine \ˌn(y)üklē,ō+\ *n* [*nucle-* + *protamine*] : a nucleoprotein derived from a protamine
nu·cleo·protein \"+\ *n* [ISV *nucle-* + *protein*] : any of a class of conjugated proteins that are combinations of a protein and a nucleic acid, that occur in all living cells in the nuclei or the cytoplasm, and that constitute either the whole or the essential portion of genes and viruses (as tobacco mosaic virus)
nu·cle·o·sid·ase \'n(y)üklēə,sī,dās\ *n* -s [ISV *nucleoside* + *-ase*] **1** : an enzyme that promotes the hydrolysis of a nucleoside **2** : a phosphorylase that promotes reversibly the reaction of a nucleoside with phosphate forming a base and a phosphate of ribose or deoxyribose — called also *nucleoside phosphorylase*
nu·cle·o·side \-,sīd\ *n* -s [ISV *nucle-* + *-ose* + *-ide*] : a crystalline compound formed by partial hydrolysis of a nucleic acid or a nucleotide and consisting typically of a glycosyl-amine derived from ribose or deoxyribose and one of the purine bases adenine or guanine or one of the pyrimidine bases cytosine, uracil, or thymine — see ADENOSINE, CYTIDINE, GUANOSINE, THYMIDINE, URIDINE
nucleoside phosphorylase *n* : NUCLEOSIDASE 2
nu·cle·o·tid·ase \'n(y)üklēə,tī,dās\ *n* -s [*nucleotide* + *-ase*] : a phosphatase that promotes hydrolysis of a nucleotide (as into a nucleoside and phosphoric acid)
nu·cle·o·tide \-,tīd\ *n* -s [ISV *nucle-* + *-t-* + *-ide*] **1** : a compound that is formed by partial hydrolysis of a nucleic acid or occurs free in tissues, that is an ester of a nucleoside and a phosphoric acid, and that may consist of one or more units of phosphate-pentose-nitrogen base — see ADENYLIC ACID, CYTIDYLIC ACID, GUANYLIC ACID, THYMIDYLIC ACID, URIDYLIC ACID **2** : any of various compounds chemically related to those obtained from nucleic acids and including some coenzymes (as coenzyme A, the pyridine nucleotides, riboflavin phosphate)
nu·cleo·toxic \ˌn(y)üklēō+\ *adj* [*nucle-* + *toxic*] : toxic to the nuclei of cells ⟨c-mitotic agents are basically ~⟩
nu·cle·us \'n(y)üklēəs\ *n*, *pl* **nu·clei** \-ē,ī\ *also* **nucleuses** [NL, fr. L, kernel, dim. of *nuc-*, *nux* nut — more at NUT] **1 a** : the relatively small, brighter, and denser portion of a galaxy, of the head of a comet, or of another celestial body **b** : the hot faint central star of a planetary nebula **2 a** : central point, part, group, or mass about which gathering, concentration, or accretion takes place : a center for subsequent increase or growth ⟨the ~ of masters and students that should grow into a university —H.O.Taylor⟩ ⟨a ~ of fact beneath the incrustation of fable over famous names —Edward Clodd⟩ ⟨enough patients . . . to form the ~ of a new practice —O.S.J.Gogarty⟩ ⟨not primarily boarding schools but rather day schools with a ~ of boarders —J.B.Conant⟩ ⟨frontiers of pioneer settlement have appeared around the margins of the original ~*es* —P.E.James⟩: as **a** : an element of the protoplasm of most plant and animal cells that is regarded as an essential agent in their metabolism, growth, and reproduction and in the transmission of hereditary characters and that typically consists of a more or less rounded mass of nucleoplasm made up of a hyaline ground substance in which is suspended a network rich in nucleoproteins from which the mitotic chromosomes and one or more nucleoli condense, the whole being enclosed by a nuclear membrane — see MACRONUCLEUS, MICRONUCLEUS; compare COENOCYTE, ENERGID, PROTOPLAST; KARYOLYMPH, LININ; MEIOSIS, MITOSIS; see CELL illustration **b** : the earliest formed part of a shell, operculum, or other similar structure **c** : a visceral mass containing the stomach and other organs of some tunicates **d** : MADREPORITE **e** : FOCUS 8 **f** : the hilum of a starch granule **g** : CORE 1 k **h** : a mass of gray matter or group of nerve cells in the central nervous system **i** : a small mass of bees and combs of brood used in forming a new colony or in rearing queens **j** : a characteristic and stable complex of atoms or groups in a molecule; *esp* : a ring system : RING ⟨the naphthalene ~⟩ — compare BENZENE RING **k** : a particle on which metal forms and grows (as in solidification, condensation, recrystallization, or transformation from one solid crystalline form to another) **l** : a particle upon which water vapor condenses in free air — called also *kern* **m** : the positively charged central portion of an atom that comprises nearly all of the atomic mass and that consists of protons and neutrons except in hydrogen in which it consists of one proton only — see ATOMIC NUMBER, MASS NUMBER **n** (1) : the peak of energy in the utterance of a syllable (2) : the syllable that is the seat of maximum stress in a stress group **o** : HEAD 25 **syn** see CENTER
nucleus dor·sa·lis \-dór'saləs, -sal-, -säl-\ *n*, *pl* **nuclei dorsa·les** \-a(,)lēz, -ā(,)lēz, -ä(,)lās\ [NL, lit., dorsal nucleus] : an elongated longitudinal strand of neurons in the spinal cord with its axons passing into the direct cerebellar tract
nucleus of pan·der \-'pändə(r)\ *usu cap P* [after Christian H. *Pander* †1865 Russ. zoologist] : the expanded upper end of the flask-shaped mass of white yolk in a bird's egg
nucleus pul·po·sus \-,pəl'pōsəs\ *n*, *pl* **nuclei pulpo·si** \-ō,sī\ [NL, lit., pulpy nucleus] : an elastic pulpy mass lying in the center of each intervertebral fibrocartilage and regarded as a remnant of the notochord
nu·clide \'n(y)ü,klīd\ *n* -s [*nucleus* + *-ide* (irreg. fr. Gk *eidos* species, form) — more at IDOL] : a species of atom characterized by the constitution of its nucleus and hence by the number of protons, the number of neutrons, and the energy content : an atom of specified atomic number and mass number — compare ISOBAR, ISOTONE, ISOTOPE, RADIOISOTOPE ⟨the different isotopes of an element are composed of ~*s* having the same atomic number but different mass numbers⟩ — **nu·clid·ic** \(')n(y)ü'klidik\ *adj*
nucquedah *var of* NAKHODA
nu·cu·la \'n(y)ükyələ\ *n* [NL, fr. L, nutlet, fr. *nuc-*, *nux* nut + *-ula* -ule] **1** *cap* : the type genus of Nuculidae **2** -s **a** : a mollusk of the genus *Nucula* **b** : a nut shell or beaked cockle
nu·cu·la·na \-yə,lanə, -länə, -lānə\ *n*, *cap* [NL, fr. *Nucula* + *-ana* (fr. L, neut. pl. of *-anus* -an)] : the type genus of Nuculanidae comprising various beaked cockles
nu·cu·lan·i·dae \ˌ=='lanə,dē\ *n pl*, *cap* [NL, fr. *Nuculana*, type genus + *-idae*] : a family of marine bivalve mollusks (order Protobranchia) related to and formerly included in Nuculidae but distinguished by a shell that is produced posteriorly and considerably elongated — see BEAKED COCKLE
nu·cu·la·ni·um \ˌn(y)ükyə'lānēəm\ *also* **nu·cu·lane** \'==,lān\ *n*, *pl* **nucula·nia** \-ēə\ *also* **nuculanes** [*nuculanium* fr. NL, fr. L *nucula* nutlet + connective *-n-* + NL *-ium*; *nuculane* fr. NL *nuculanium*] : an indehiscent fleshy fruit (as the grape) resembling a berry except in being superior
nu·cule \'n(y)ü,kyül\ *n* -s [F, nutlet, fr. L *nucula*] **1** : NUTLET **2** : the female reproductive organ in plants of the family Characeae
[1]**nu·cu·lid** \'n(y)ükyələd\ *adj* [NL *Nuculidae*] : of or relating to the Nuculidae
[2]**nuculid** \"\ *n* -s [NL *Nuculidae*] : a mollusk of the family Nuculidae
nu·cu·li·dae \n(y)ü'kyüləd·ē\ *n pl*, *cap* [NL, fr. *Nucula*, type genus + *-idae*] : a large widely distributed family of marine bivalve mollusks (order Protobranchia) having a small nutlike equivalve shell and very large labial palps and including the typical nut shells — see NUCULANIDAE
[1]**nu·cu·loid** \'n(y)ükyə,lȯid\ *adj* [NL *Nucula* + E *-oid*] : resembling or related to the Nuculidae
[2]**nuculoid** \"\ *n* -s : a nuculoid mollusk
nu·da \'n(y)üdə\ *n pl*, *cap* [NL, fr. L, neut. pl. of *nudus* naked] : a class of ctenophores without tentacles including but one genus (*Beroë*)
nuda pacta *pl of* NUDUM PACTUM
[1]**nude** \'n(y)üd\ *adj* -ER/-EST [L *nudus* naked — more at NAKED] **1 a** : lacking some essential particular : being without consideration : NAKED, UNSUPPORTED **b** *Roman & civil law* : having no cause — compare NUDUM PACTUM **2** : devoid of some natural, conventional, or customary covering, furnishing, or adornment ⟨a ~ hillside⟩ ⟨a broad ~ valley —R.L.Stevenson⟩ **3 a** : devoid of clothing : UNCLOTHED **b** : UNDRAPED — used of an artistic representation of a human figure esp. in sculpture and painting **4** : of the color nude **syn** see BARE
[2]**nude** \"\ *n* -s **1 a** : a picture or other representation of an unclothed undraped human figure **b** : an unclothed person **2** : the condition of being unclothed or undraped — usu. used with *the* **3** : a brownish pink that is slightly yellower, lighter, and stronger than atmosphere
nude·ly *adv* : in a nude manner
nude matter *n* : MATTER IN PAIS 1
nude·ness *n* -ES : the quality or state of being nude
nude pact *n* [trans. of ML *nudum pactum*] : NUDUM PACTUM
nude tan *n* : a moderate yellowish pink that is duller and much yellower than coral pink and yellower and duller than peach pink
[1]**nudge** \'nəj\ *vb* -ED/-ING/-S [perh. of Scand origin; akin to Icel *nugga* to push, rub, ON *gnaga* to gnaw — more at GNAW] *vt* **1** : to touch or push gently (as with the elbow) usu. to call attention or convey an intimation **2** : to prod lightly : urge into action ⟨needled and *nudged* and worried him till finally he consented —Ellery Sedgwick⟩ **3** : to ease along : assist in maneuvering ⟨impudent little tugboats . . . *nudged* our ship out of its slip —June W. Brown⟩ **4** : to get close to : NEAR ⟨its circulation is *nudging* the four million mark —Bennett Cerf⟩ ⟨defense in the old protective sense is *nudging* the impossible —*Sydney (Australia) Bull.*⟩ ~ *vi* : to give a nudge ⟨well-polished automobiles . . . ~ into a parking space —*Amer. Guide Series: N. Y. City*⟩ ⟨the annual supply vessel should ~ through the bay ice —*Nat'l Geographic*⟩
[2]**nudge** \"\ *n* -s : a slight push, poke, or jog (as with the elbow) ⟨he felt a sharp ~ in his side —Scott Fitzgerald⟩ ⟨some further ~*s* toward integrity —R.W.McEwen⟩
nudg·er \-jə(r)\ *n* -s : one that nudges
nudi- *comb form* [LL, fr. L *nudus* naked] : naked : bare ⟨*Nudi*branchia⟩ ⟨*nudi*ped⟩
[1]**nu·di·branch** \'n(y)üdə,braŋk\ *adj* [back-formation fr. obs. *nudibranchial*, fr. NL *Nudibranchia* + E *-al*] : of or relating to the Nudibranchia
[2]**nudibranch** \"\ *n* -s [NL *Nudibranchia*] : a mollusk of the suborder Nudibranchia
nu·di·bran·chia \ˌ=='braŋkēə\ *n pl*, *cap* [NL, fr. *nudi-* + *-branchia*] : a suborder of Opisthobranchia comprising numerous highly varied marine gastropod mollusks lacking a shell in the adult state and without true ctenidia and typically having a body suggesting that of a slug usu. with brightly colored often branching respiratory cerata on the back — **nu·di·bran·chi·an** \ˌ=='braŋkēən\ *adj* — **nu·di·bran·chi·ate** \-ēət, -ē,āt\ *adj or n*
nu·di·bran·chi·a·ta \ˌ==,braŋkē'äd·ə, -'ād·ə\ *syn of* NUDIBRANCHIA
nu·di·caudate \ˌn(y)üdə+\ *adj* [ISV *nudi-* + *caudate*] : having a hairless tail
nu·di·caul \'n(y)üdə,kȯl\ *or* **nu·di·cau·lous** \ˌ=='kȯləs\ *adj* [*nudicaul* fr. (assumed) NL *nudicaulis*, fr. *nudi-* + L *caulis* stem; *nudicaulous* fr. *nudi-* + *caul-* + *-ous* — more at COLE] : having leafless stems
nu·di·flo·rous \ˌn(y)üdə'flōrəs\ *adj* [fr. (assumed) NL *nudiflorus*, fr. *nudi-* + LL *-florus* -florous] : having flowers naked and esp. without hairs or glands
[1]**nu·di·ped** \'n(y)üdə,ped\ *adj* [F *nudipède*, fr. LL *nudiped-*, *nudipes*, fr. *nudi-* + L *ped-*, *pes* foot — more at FOOT] : having feet without a natural covering (as of hair or feathers)
[2]**nudiped** \"\ *n* -s [*nudi-* + *-ped*] : a nudiped animal
nud·ish \'n(y)üdish\ *adj* : nearly nude : approaching nudity
nud·ism \-ü,dizəm\ *n* -s [[1]*nude* + *-ism*] : the cult or custom of going unclothed as a social practice
[1]**nud·ist** \-dəst\ *n* -s [[1]*nude* + *-ist*] : an advocate or practitioner of nudism
[2]**nudist** \"\ *adj* : of or relating to nudists or nudism
nu·di·ty \'n(y)üdəd·ē, -ətē, -i\ *n* -ES [F or LL; F *nudité*, fr. LL *nuditat-*, *nuditas*, fr. L *nudus* + *-itat-*, *-itas* -ity] **1** : the quality or state of being nude **2** : a nude figure esp. as depicted in art
nud·nick *or* **nud·nik** \'nüdnik\ *n* -s [Yiddish *nudnik*, fr. Russ *nudnyĭ* tiresome, boring (fr. *nuda* need, boredom) + Yiddish *-nik* (n. suffix denoting a person engaged in or connected with something specified), fr. Pol & Russ; akin to OSlav *nužda* need, OE *nēd* — more at NEED] : a person who is a bore : NUISANCE, PEST
nu·dum pac·tum \ˌnü,düm'päk,tüm\ *n*, *pl* **nu·da pac·ta** \-üdə'päktə\ [ML, naked pact] : a pact or agreement not enforceable by action because lacking in or bare of certain legal essentials or formalities: as **a** *Roman law* : a pact or agreement not in the form required for a binding stipulation **b** *common law* : a promise unenforceable for lack of the required consideration **c** *civil law* : a promise unenforceable for lack of a lawful motive
nu·er \'nüə(r)\ *n*, *pl* **nuer** *or* **nuers** *usu cap* **1 a** : a numerous and widespread Nilotic people in the Sudan and on the Ethiopian border **b** : a member of such people **2** : a Nilotic language of the Nuer people
nuernberg *usu cap, var of* NUREMBERG
nu·ga·cious \(')n(y)ü'gāshəs\ *adj* [L *nugac-*, *nugax* trifling + E *-ous*] : TRIFLING, TRIVIAL — **nu·ga·cious·ness** *n* -ES
nu·gac·i·ty \n(y)ü'gasəd·ē\ *n* -ES [LL *nugacitas*, fr. L *nugac-*, *nugax* trifling (fr. *nugae* trifles, jokes) + *-itas* -ity] **1** : TRIVIALITY **2** : something frivolous or trivial ⟨hummed the scrambled fragments of two or three *nugacities* —Robertson Davies⟩
nugation *n* -s [ML *nugation-*, *nugatio*, fr. L *nugatus* (past part. of *nugari* to trifle, joke, fr. *nugae* trifles, jokes) + *-ion*, *-io* -ion] *obs* : the act or an instance of trifling
nu·ga·to·ry \'n(y)ügə,tōrē, -tȯr-, -ri\ *adj* [L *nugatorius*, fr. *nugatus* + *-orius* -ory] **1** : having little or no consequence : WORTHLESS **2** : having no force : INVALID **syn** see VAIN
nug·gar \nə'gär\ *n* -s [Ar *nuqqār*] : a cargo boat used on the Nile
nug·get \'nəgət, *usu* -əd·+V\ *n* -s [origin unknown] **1 a** : a solid lump; *esp* : a native lump of precious metal ⟨a ~ of gold⟩ ⟨a few ~*s* of uranium —Harrison Smith⟩ **b** : something resembling a nugget of precious metal ⟨~*s* of wisdom —C.J.Rolo⟩ ⟨odd ~*s* of information —*Newsweek*⟩ **2** *Austral* : a sturdy and thickset person or animal **3** : BRONZE YELLOW

nuggar

nugget gold *n* : a strong yellow that is redder and deeper than yolk yellow, gamboge, or light chrome yellow
nug·gety \-gəd·ē\ *adj* **1** : having or resembling a nugget : occurring in nuggets; *also* : covered with small rocks **2** *Austral* : short and thickset : COMPACT ⟨a sardonic ~ old prospector —George Farwell⟩
nuik \'nyük\ *chiefly Scot var of* NOOK
[1]**nui·sance** \'n(y)üsᵊn(t)s\ *n* -s [ME *nusaunce*, fr. AF *nusaunce*, *nuisance*, fr. OF *nuisir* to hurt, harm (fr. L *nocēre*) + *-aunce*, *-ance* -ance — more at NOXIOUS] **1** : HARM, INJURY ⟨relieving the ~ of poisonous fumes from rural factories —*Collier's Yr. Bk.*⟩ **2** *law* : an offensive, annoying, unpleasant, or obnoxious thing or practice : a cause or source of annoyance that although often a single act is usu. a continuing or repeated invasion or disturbance of another's right — see PRIVATE NUISANCE, PUBLIC NUISANCE **3** : a person that annoys usu. by obtrusion : PEST ⟨he was a perfect ~, running through the house slamming doors⟩ **4 a** : a vexing, difficult, or distressing practice or state of things ⟨the ~ of litter in the countryside —*Manchester Guardian Weekly*⟩ **b** : something that is disagreeable or troublesome : ANNOYANCE ⟨timber was cheap, in fact, a ~ to those who wanted farms —S.H.Holbrook⟩ ⟨motels . . . accessible without the ~ of city traffic —*Look*⟩
[2]**nuisance** \"\ *adj* **1** : possessing the ability to annoy, distress, or hamper ⟨burn off the ~ scrub growth —Frank Cameron⟩ ⟨the ~ strikes in public services that seriously injured the tourist season —W.H.Chamberlin⟩ **2** : constituting a nuisance — used esp. of wild animals ⟨transfer of ~ beavers⟩
nuisance tax *n* : an excise tax levied on a wide range of miscellaneous commodities and borne mostly by the consumer (as the American excises on telephone services and firearms)
nuisance value *n* : value, importance, or usefulness arising from a capacity to annoy, frustrate, harass, or injure ⟨atolls and islands having a high *nuisance value* —W.V.Pratt⟩ ⟨the business of the minor parties is to develop so great a *nuisance value* that one of the major parties will take over their programs —H.S.Commager⟩ ⟨alert to opportunities to institute representative suits solely for their *nuisance value* —G.B.Hurff⟩
nu·ku·hi·van \ˌnükə'hēvən\ *n* -s *usu cap* [*Nuku Hiva* Island, Marquesas islands + E *-an*] : the Polynesian language of Nukuhiva : MARQUESAN
nul \'nəl\ *adj*, *sometimes* -ER/-EST [F, fr. MF] *law* : not any : NO
[1]**null** \'nəl\ *adj* [MF *nul*, lit., none, not any, fr. L *nullus*, fr. *ne-* not + *ullus* any (akin to *unus* one) — more at NO, ONE] **1 a** : having no legal or binding force or validity : of no efficacy : INVALID, VOID — often used in the phrase *null and void* **b** : capable of being regarded as void : voidable at the option of an injured party **2** : amounting to nothing : NIL, NONEXISTENT ⟨the ~ uselessness of the wireless transmitter that lacks a receiving station —Fred Majdalany⟩ **3 a** : having no value : of no consequence : INSIGNIFICANT ⟨news as ~ as nothing —Emily Dickinson⟩ **b** : lacking distinction, character, or personality ⟨the scene . . . was pitched in the ~, noncommittal surroundings of a rehearsal room —Osbert Sitwell⟩ **4 a** : having no members : EMPTY ⟨the ~ class⟩ **b** (1) : having the character or value of zero ⟨the ~ element⟩ (2) : having a zero radius ⟨a ~ sphere⟩ **5** : indicating usu. by a zero reading on a scale when current or voltage is zero — used of an instrument **6** : of, being, or relating to zero ⟨the photoelectric current through a load resistor produces a voltage drop that is balanced by a potentiometer, thus giving a ~ reading for each condition of balance —*Jour. of Research*⟩ **7** : relating to the null of a radio receiver
[2]**null** \"\ *n* -s **1 a** : ZERO 2a(1) ⟨a *null*-reading instrument⟩ ⟨the various signals can combine so that a substantial ~ in transmission exists at certain frequencies —B.D.Loughlin⟩ **b** : a condition of a radio receiver existing when minimum or zero signal is received and resulting from adjustment of parts (as rotation of the directional antenna or tuning of the circuit) **2** : a meaningless letter or code group introduced to impede cryptanalysis
[3]**null** \"\ *vt* -ED/-ING/-S [ML *nullare*, fr. L *nullus* null, adj.] **1** : to reduce to nothing : DESTROY, EXPUNGE, OBLITERATE **2** : to make void : ANNUL, NULLIFY ⟨the first election he ~*ed* because its irregularity was glaring —Edmund Burke⟩ ⟨election ~*ed* by the courts⟩
[4]**null** \"\ *n* -s [by alter.] : KNUR
[5]**null** \"\ *n* -s [by alter.] : KNURL 1; *esp* : a raised convex boss or ornament on a flat surface on a piece of furniture
[6]**null** \"\ *vt* -ED/-ING/-S [back-formation fr. *nulling*] : KNURL
[7]**null** \"\ *n* -s [[3]*null*] **1** : NULLO **2** : a game of skat played without a trump suit in which the bidder undertakes to lose every trick
nul·la \'nələ\ *n* -s [by shortening] : NULLA-NULLA
nul·la bo·na \ˌnələ'bōnə\ *n* [NL, no goods] : the return made upon a writ of fieri facias or execution by a sheriff or other officer when he has found no leviable goods
nul·lah *also* **nul·la** \'nələ\ *or* **nal·lah** *or* **na·la** *n* -s [Hindi *nālā*, prob. of Dravidian origin; akin to Tamil *ñeḷḷal* hollow, pit, Kanarese *naḷḷu* nullah] : a watercourse that is often dry : GULLY, RAVINE
null and void *adj* : having no force, binding power, or validity : utterly invalid
nul·la-nul·la \'nələ'nələ\ *n* [native name in Australia] : a hardwood club of a type used by the Australian aborigines
nulled \'nəld\ *adj* [by alter.] : KNURLED
null hypothesis *n* [[1]*null*] : a statistical hypothesis to be tested and accepted or rejected in favor of an alternative; *specif* : the hypothesis that an observed difference (as between the means of two samples) is due to chance alone and not due to a systematic cause
nulli- *comb form* [LL, fr. L *nullus*] : no : none : null ⟨*nulli*fidian⟩ ⟨*nulli*form⟩ ⟨*nulli*parous⟩
nul·li·bic·i·ty \ˌnələ'bisəd·ē\ *also* **nul·li·bi·e·ty** \-bīəd·ē\ *n* -ES [L *nullibi* nowhere (fr. *nullus* null + *ibi* here, there) + E *-icity* (as in *simplicity*) or *-ety* (as in *society*); akin to Gk *itha-* here, Skt *iha* here, L *ita* thus — more at NULL, ITERATE] : the quality or state of being nowhere

nul·li·bist \ˈnələbəst\ *n* -s [L *nullibi* nowhere + E *-ist*] **:** one who denies that the soul exists in space

nul·li·fi·ca·tion \ˌnələfəˈkāshən\ *n* -s [LL *nullification-*, *nullificatio*, fr. *nullificatus* (past part. of *nullificare* to nullify) + L *-ion-*, *-io* -ion] **1 :** the act of nullifying or the state of being nullified **2 :** the action of a state of impeding or attempting to prevent the operation and enforcement within its territory of a law of the U. S. — **nul·li·fi·ca·tion·ist** \-sh(ə)nəst\ *n* -s

nul·li·fi·ca·tor \ˈ===ˌkād·ə(r)\ *n* -s **:** NULLIFIER

[1]**nul·li·fid·i·an** \ˌnələˈfidēən\ *n* -s [LL *nulli-* + L *fides* faith + E *-an* — more at FAITH] **1 :** a person of no faith or religion **:** SKEPTIC, UNBELIEVER **2 :** one lacking in faith **:** DISBELIEVER

[2]**nullifidian** \ˌ==ˌ===\ *adj* **:** having no faith or religion **:** SKEPTICAL

nul·li·fi·er \ˈnələˌfī(ə)r, -īə\ *n* -s **:** one that nullifies; *specif* **:** one maintaining the right of nullification against the U. S. government

nul·li·fy \-fī\ *vt* -ED/-ING/-ES [LL *nullificare*, fr. *nulli-* + L *-ficare* -fy] **1 :** to make null; *specif* **:** to make legally null and void ⟨we are asked to ~ legislation as an undue encroachment upon the sphere of individual liberty —B.N.Cardozo⟩ **2 :** to make of no value or consequence **:** reduce to nothing **:** EFFACE ⟨the lightning *nullified* the meager table lamp —R.A.W. Hughes⟩ ⟨the small gains made in the Colony were *nullified* by the Revolution —*Amer. Guide Series: N. C.*⟩

syn INVALIDATE, NEGATE, ANNUL, ABROGATE: although these five verbs are almost interchangeable, NULLIFY and INVALIDATE carry the most general and inclusive meanings. NULLIFY means to counteract completely the force, effectiveness, or value of something ⟨the earlier devices for *nullifying* the effects of the Fifteenth Amendment were becoming outworn —Helen Sullivan⟩ ⟨at least 19 international cartels which threaten to *nullify* efforts to reduce trade barriers —*Current Biog.*⟩ ⟨a lack of . . . confidence tends to *nullify* and destroy the results of enormous effort in technical and interpretative development —A.E.Wier⟩ INVALIDATE carries this general sense but adds the idea of rendering unacceptable by reason of legal or official requirements or condition not adequately met ⟨a priest of wisdom with a flaw in his ordination and an *invalidating* clause in his commission —W.L.Sullivan⟩ ⟨so many reservations, explicit and implicit, as to *invalidate* that pact from the outset —Vera M. Dean⟩ ⟨we do not say that we have met with an instance which *invalidates* the mathematical proposition that the sum of the three angles of a Euclidean triangle is 180 degrees —A.J. Ayer⟩ NEGATE suggests a canceling out or a nullification of one thing by another of two mutually exclusive things ⟨excellent clauses regarding the employment of children, they are *negated* not only by the negligence and venality of some local officials but also by the sheer facts of existence among the poor —George Woodcock⟩ ⟨he discovers he has appended his signature to contracts which *negate* each other —Richard Maney⟩ ⟨shock may temporarily *negate* the effects of drinking —Theodore Loveless⟩ ANNUL suggests a rendering ineffective by depriving of the power to function or rendering nonexistent, often officially or legally ⟨the two opposing electricities, so proportioned and so disposed that each of them *annuls* the actions which the other would produce outside the block if it were by itself —K.K.Darrow⟩ ⟨mystery does not *annul* meaning but enriches it —Reinhold Niebuhr⟩ ⟨war, as it becomes more and more total, practically *annuls* the difference as to injury and exposure to danger which formerly existed between armed forces and noncombatants —H.M.Huber⟩ ⟨the Emancipation Proclamation *annulled* all prior laws regarding slaves⟩ ABROGATE is much like *annul* but has a stronger association with a legal or official purposeful act ⟨the military clique *abrogated* the existing constitution —*Americana Annual*⟩ ⟨the Council of Ministers . . . has the power to *abrogate* actions of the constituent republics which contravene laws or decrees of the central government —F.A.Ogg & Harold Zink⟩ ⟨his audience had reached the point where it had *abrogated* all desire to think about anything —Nigel Dennis⟩

nul·li·gravida \ˌnələ+\ *n* [NL, fr. *nulli-* + L *gravida* pregnant woman — more at GRAVIDA] **:** a woman who has never been pregnant — compare NULLIPARA

nul·ling \ˈnəliŋ\ *n* -s [alter. of *knurling*] **:** KNURLING; *esp* **:** a quadrant-shaped decorative detail carved on moldings (as in Jacobean architecture)

nul·lip·a·ra \(ˌ)nəˈlipərə\ *n*, *pl* **nulliparas** \-rəz\ *also* **nul·lipa·rae** \-pəˌrē\ [NL, fr. *nulli-* + *-para*] **:** a woman who has never borne a child — compare NULLIGRAVIDA — **nul·lip·a·rous** \(ˌ)nəˌlipərəs\ *adj*

nul·li·pennate \ˌnələ+\ *adj* [*nulli-* + *pennate*] **:** having no flight feathers

nul·li·pen·nes \ˌnələˈpeˌnēz\ [NL, fr. *nulli-* + *-pennes* (fr. L *penna* feather, wing); akin to Gk *pteron* wing, feather — more at FEATHER] *syn of* APTERYGIFORMES

nul·li·plex \ˈnələˌ pleks\ *adj* [*nulli-* + *-plex* -fold — more at SIMPLE] **:** homozygously recessive at a specified locus or for a specified factor — used of a polyploid ⟨~ for color intensifiers⟩

nul·li·pore \ˈnələˌpō(ə)r\ *n* -s [ISV *nulli-* + *-pore*] **:** any of several lime-secreting coralline algae formerly thought to be animals — **nul·lip·o·rous** \(ˌ)nəˌlipərəs, ˌnələˌpōrəs\ *adj*

nul·li·some \ˈnələˌsōm\ *n* -s [*nulli-* + *-some*] **:** NULLISOMIC

[1]**nul·li·so·mic** \ˌnələˌsōmik\ *adj* [ISV *nulli-* + *-somic*] **:** having two less than the diploid number of chromosomes due to loss of one chromosome pair

[2]**nullisomic** \"\ *n* -s **:** a nullisomic individual

nul·li·ty \ˈnələd·ē, -ətē, -i\ *n* -ES [MF *nullité*, fr. ML *nullitat-*, *nullitas*, fr. LL *nulli-* + L *-itat-*, *-itas* -ity] **1 a** (1) **:** the state or fact of being legally null or void **:** INVALIDITY (2) **:** a case of nullity (3) **:** a nullifying or invalidating fact or circumstance **b** (1) *Eng law* **:** the total absence of legal effect or existence (2) **:** a judicial declaration of the invalidity of a marriage ab initio **:** ANNULMENT **c :** any act or proceeding void of legal effect either absolutely (as in English law) or relatively (as sometimes in the civil law) **2 a :** the state of being null or nothing **:** want of efficacy or force **:** NOTHINGNESS ⟨a haunting and growing sense of the ~ of human life —Edmund Wilson⟩ **b :** a mere nothing **:** NONENTITY ⟨a diplomacy that results in pure *nullities* —R.H.Rovere⟩ ⟨taken a nice ~ as his central character —Sidney Alexander⟩

nul·li·us fi·li·us \ˌnəˌlēəsˈfēlēəs, ˌnülēəs-\ *n* [NL] **:** an illegitimate child **:** a bastard having no heritable rights in common law

nullius ju·ris \-ˈjürəs\ *adj* [ML] **:** having no standing in law **:** without legal effect or validity

null method *n* **:** a method of measurement in which an unknown quantity (as of electric current) is compared (as in a Wheatstone bridge) with a known quantity of the same kind and found equal by zero response of the detector

nul·lo \ˈnə(ˌ)lō\ *n* -s [alter. of [3]*null*] **1 a :** a bid in a card game by which a player undertakes to win no tricks **b :** a condition of play in which each trick counts against instead of for the player winning it **2 :** [7]NULL 2

nulls *pl of* NULL, *pres 3d sing of* NULL

nul tiel record \-ˈtēl-\ *n* [AF, lit., no such record] **:** a plea alleging the record on which the action is founded does not exist

nul tort *n* [AF, lit., no wrong] **:** a former plea of the general issue in the real action of novel disseizin whereby the defendant denies he did anything wrong

num *abbr* **1** number **2** numeral

[1]**numb** \ˈnəm\ *adj* -ER/-EST [ME *nomen*, fr. *nome*, *nomen* (past part. of *nimen* to take), fr. OE *numen*, past part. of *niman* to take — more at NIMBLE] **1 a :** devoid of sensation esp. due to cold **:** BENUMBED ⟨my right cheek has been ~ all day —Jack London⟩ ⟨had to lay him down again and rest her ~ arms —Elsie Singmaster⟩ **b :** devoid of emotion **:** DESENSITIZED, INDIFFERENT ⟨prisoners . . . ~ from suffering and anguish —E.M.Lustgarten⟩ ⟨personally, I am ~, and can't rouse . . . interest in anybody —Anthony Boucher⟩ **c :** devoid of skill or sensitivity ⟨he is tough, ~, and simple-minded —J.W.Aldridge⟩ **2 :** NUMBING ⟨it was a listless and ~ gray day —Edith Sitwell⟩ **3 :** characterized by numbness ⟨a deep sensation of cold . . . a ~ feeling —R.S.Woodworth⟩

[2]**numb** \"\ *vb* -ED/-ING/-S *vt* **:** to make numb **:** DEADEN ⟨fatigue ~*ed* his legs —William Chamberlain⟩ ⟨his body was ~*ed* with fear —Liam O'Flaherty⟩ ⟨the ~*ing* hand of officialdom —*Britain Today*⟩ ~ *vi* **:** to become numb ⟨tried to shield his face . . . but his jaw ~*ed* and his teeth ached —Andrew Hamilton⟩

numb *abbr* numbered

num·bat \ˈnəmˌbat\ *n* -s [native name in Australia] **:** BANDED ANTEATER

numbed \ˈnəmd\ *adj* [short for *benumbed*] **:** made inert or insensitive — **numbed·ly** \-mədlē, -md-\ *adv*

[1]**num·ber** \ˈnəmbə(r)\ *n* -s [ME *noumbre*, *nombre*, fr. OF *nombre*, fr. L *numerus* — more at NIMBLE] **1 a :** an arithmetical total **:** sum of the units involved **:** AGGREGATE ⟨~ of desks in the room⟩ ⟨~ of people in the hall⟩ ⟨owing to the ~ of prior

CARDINAL NUMBERS[1]

NAME[2]	SYMBOL arabic[3]	SYMBOL roman[4]
naught *or* zero *or* cipher	0	
one	1	I *or* i *also* j[5]
two	2	II *or* ii
three	3	III *or* iii
four	4	IV *or* iv *also* IIII
five	5	V *or* v
six	6	VI *or* vi
seven	7	VII *or* vii
eight	8	VIII *or* viii
nine	9	IX *or* ix
ten	10	X *or* x
eleven	11	XI *or* xi
twelve	12	XII *or* xii
thirteen	13	XIII *or* xiii
fourteen	14	XIV *or* xiv
fifteen	15	XV *or* xv
sixteen	16	XVI *or* xvi
seventeen	17	XVII *or* xvii
eighteen	18	XVIII *or* xviii
nineteen	19	XIX *or* xix
twenty	20	XX *or* xx
twenty-one	21	XXI *or* xxi
twenty-two	22	XXII *or* xxii
twenty-three	23	XXIII *or* xxiii
twenty-four	24	XXIV *or* xxiv
twenty-five	25	XXV *or* xxv
twenty-six	26	XXVI *or* xxvi
twenty-seven	27	XXVII *or* xxvii
twenty-eight	28	XXVIII *or* xxviii
twenty-nine	29	XXIX *or* xxix
thirty	30	XXX *or* xxx
thirty-one	31	XXXI *or* xxxi
thirty-two *etc*	32	XXXII *or* xxxii
forty	40	XL *or* xl *also* XXXX
forty-one	41	XLI *or* xli
forty-two *etc*	42	XLII *or* xlii
fifty	50	L *or* l
sixty	60	LX *or* lx
seventy	70	LXX *or* lxx
eighty	80	LXXX *or* lxxx *also* XXC
ninety	90	XC *or* xc *also* LXXXX
one hundred	100	C *or* c
one hundred and one *or* one hundred one *etc*	101	CI *or* ci
one hundred and two	102	CII *or* cii
one hundred and fifty	150	CL *or* cl
two hundred	200	CC *or* cc
three hundred	300	CCC *or* ccc
four hundred	400	CD *or* cd *also* CCCC
five hundred	500	D *or* d *also* IↃ[6]
six hundred	600	DC *or* dc *also* IↃC
seven hundred	700	DCC *or* dcc *also* IↃCC
eight hundred	800	DCCC *or* dccc
nine hundred	900	CM *or* cm
one thousand *or* ten hundred *etc*	1,000[7]	M *or* m *also* CIↃ
two thousand *etc*	2,000	MM *or* mm
five thousand	5,000	$\overline{V}$[6]
ten thousand	10,000	$\overline{X}$
one hundred thousand	100,000	$\overline{C}$
one million	1,000,000	$\overline{M}$

[1]The cardinal numbers are used in simple counting or in answer to "how many?" The words for these numbers may be used as nouns (he counted to *twelve*), as pronouns (*twelve* were found), or as adjectives (*twelve* boys)

[2]In formal contexts the numbers one to one hundred and in less formal contexts the numbers one to nine are commonly written out, while larger numbers are given in numerals. In nearly all contexts a number occurring at the beginning of a sentence is usually written out. Numerals are invariably used for dates except in very formal contexts

[3]The arabic numerals were first used in India and were introduced to the West by the Arabs. They are sometimes called *Hindu numerals* or *Hindu-Arabic numerals*. In an early form arabic numerals are called *gobar numerals*

[4]The roman numerals are built up on seven basic symbols: I, V, X, L, C, D, and M according to the following rules:

1. A symbol following one of equal or greater value adds its value (II=2)
2. A symbol preceding one of greater value subtracts its value (IV=4; XL=40)
3. When a symbol stands between two of greater value, its value is subtracted from the second and the remainder is added to the first (XIV=14; LIX=59)

ORDINAL NUMBERS[8]

NAME[9]	SYMBOL[10]
first	1st
second	2d *or* 2nd
third	3d *or* 3rd
fourth	4th
fifth	5th
sixth	6th
seventh	7th
eighth	8th
ninth	9th
tenth	10th
eleventh	11th
twelfth	12th
thirteenth	13th
fourteenth	14th
fifteenth	15th
sixteenth	16th
seventeenth	17th
eighteenth	18th
nineteenth	19th
twentieth	20th
twenty-first	21st
twenty-second	22d *or* 22nd
twenty-third	23d *or* 23rd
twenty-fourth	24th
twenty-fifth	25th
twenty-sixth	26th
twenty-seventh	27th
twenty-eighth	28th
twenty-ninth	29th
thirtieth	30th
thirty-first	31st
thirty-second *etc*	32d *or* 32nd
fortieth	40th
forty-first	41st
forty-second *etc*	42d *or* 42nd
fiftieth	50th
sixtieth	60th
seventieth	70th
eightieth	80th
ninetieth	90th
hundredth *or* one hundredth	100th
hundred and first *or* one hundred and first *etc*	101st
hundred and second	102d *or* 102nd
two hundredth	200th
three hundredth	300th
four hundredth	400th
five hundredth	500th
six hundredth	600th
seven hundredth	700th
eight hundredth	800th
nine hundredth	900th
thousandth *or* one thousandth	1,000th
two thousandth *etc*	2,000th
ten thousandth	10,000th
hundred thousandth *or* one hundred thousandth	100,000th
millionth *or* one millionth	1,000,000th

4. Of two equivalent ways of representing a number, that in which the symbol of larger denomination precedes is preferred (XIV, not VIX, for 14; XLV, not VL, for 45); in modern usage a short form by subtraction is preferred to a long form by addition (IV rather than IIII for 4, although IIII is seen on some clock faces; IX for 9 rather than VIIII; MCM for 1900 rather than MDCCCC)

[5]In medieval roman numerals the symbol for 1 was J and in modern times the lowercase j for a final i may be found, as in medical prescriptions (ij=2; vj=6)

[6]Several methods were employed in expressing the larger numbers in roman numerals, but none of them frequently since there was little use for the larger numbers themselves. The apostrophus Ↄ was used in ancient and medieval times following I to express 500 and repeated after the IↃ to express larger numbers, as IↃↃ for 5,000 and IↃↃↃ for 50,000. To represent numbers twice as great as these, C was repeated as many times before the stroke I as the Ↄ was after it as CCIↃↃ for 10,000 and CCCIↃↃↃ for 100,000. A straight line over a letter was sometimes used, esp. in medieval times, to indicate multiples of a thousand

[7]Arabic numerals from 1,000 to 9,999 are often written without commas (1000, 9999). Year numbers are always written without commas (1783)

[8]The ordinal numbers are used to show the order or succession in which such items as names, objects, and periods of time are considered (the *twelfth* month; the *fourth* row of seats; the *18th* century)

[9]Each of the terms for the ordinal numbers excepting *first* and *second* is used in designating one of a number of parts into which a whole may be divided (a *fourth;* a *sixth;* a *tenth*) and as the denominator in fractions designating the number of such parts constituting a certain portion of a whole (one *fourth;* three *fifths;* five *sixths;* seven *tenths*). The fractions when used as nouns are usually written as two words, although they are often hyphenated as nouns and regularly hyphenated as adjectives (a *two-thirds* majority; a *three-fourths* vote). When fractions are written in numerals, the cardinal symbols are used (¼, ⅗, ⅚)

DENOMINATIONS ABOVE ONE MILLION

American system[11]

NAME[12]	VALUE IN POWERS OF TEN	NUMBER OF ZEROS[13]	NUMBER OF PERIODS OF 0's AFTER 1,000[12]
billion[14]	10^{9}	9	2
trillion[14]	10^{12}	12	3
quadrillion	10^{15}	15	4
quintillion	10^{18}	18	5
sextillion	10^{21}	21	6
septillion	10^{24}	24	7
octillion	10^{27}	27	8
nonillion	10^{30}	30	9
decillion	10^{33}	33	10
undecillion	10^{36}	36	11
duodecillion	10^{39}	39	12
tredecillion	10^{42}	42	13
quattuordecillion	10^{45}	45	14
quindecillion	10^{48}	48	15
sexdecillion	10^{51}	51	16
septendecillion	10^{54}	54	17
octodecillion	10^{57}	57	18
novemdecillion	10^{60}	60	19
vigintillion	10^{63}	63	20
centillion	10^{303}	303	100

British system[11]

NAME	VALUE IN POWERS OF TEN	NUMBER OF ZEROS[13]	POWERS OF 1,000,000[12]
milliard	10^{9}	9	—
billion	10^{12}	12	2
trillion	10^{18}	18	3
quadrillion	10^{24}	24	4
quintillion	10^{30}	30	5
sextillion	10^{36}	36	6
septillion	10^{42}	42	7
octillion	10^{48}	48	8
nonillion	10^{54}	54	9
decillion	10^{60}	60	10
undecillion	10^{66}	66	11
duodecillion	10^{72}	72	12
tredecillion	10^{78}	78	13
quattuordecillion	10^{84}	84	14
quindecillion	10^{90}	90	15
sexdecillion	10^{96}	96	16
septendecillion	10^{102}	102	17
octodecillion	10^{108}	108	18
novemdecillion	10^{114}	114	19
vigintillion	10^{120}	120	20
centillion	10^{600}	600	100

[10]The arabic symbols for the cardinal numbers may be read as ordinals in certain contexts (January 1=January first; August 15=August fifteenth; 1 Chronicles=First Chronicles; 2 Samuel =Second Samuel). The roman numerals are sometimes read as ordinals (Henry IV=Henry the Fourth; the *Argonaut II*= the *Argonaut the Second*); sometimes they are written with the ordinal suffixes (XIXth Dynasty, XXth Dynasty)

[11]The American system of numeration for denominations above one million was modeled on the French system but more recently the French system has been changed to correspond to the German and British systems. In the American system each of the denominations above 1,000 millions (the American *billion*) is 1,000 times the one preceding (one trillion=1,000 billions; one quadrillion=1,000 trillions). In the British system the first denomination above 1,000 millions (the British *milliard*) is 1,000 times the preceding one, but each of the denominations above 1,000 milliards (the British *billion*) is 1,000,000 times the preceding one (one trillion=1,000,000 billions; one quadrillion=1,000,000 trillions)

[12]The names of the denominations in the American system correspond to the number of periods of zeros (groups of three zeros) that come after 1,000 (the numeral for one billion [1,000,000,000] contains two [bi-]; and the numeral for one trillion [1,000,000,000,000] contains three [tri-]. The names of the British denominations correspond to the values expressed in powers of one million (one billion=a million to the 2d power; one trillion=a million to the 3d power)

[13]For convenience in reading large numerals the thousands, millions, etc., are usually separated by commas (21,530; 1,155,465) or by half spaces (1 155 465). Serial numbers (as a social security number or the engine number of a car) are often written with hyphens (583-695-20), spaces, or other devices.

[14]The usual French term for the American billion is *milliard*, the British term is *milliard*, and the German is *Milliarde*. The British billion (1,000 milliards or 1,000,000 millions) is equivalent to the American trillion.

applications, he shortly withdrew —J.C.Archer⟩ **b :** an ascertainable total **:** the possibility of numbering ⟨the sands of the seashore are beyond ~⟩ ⟨times without ~⟩ **c :** an allotted total **:** COMPLEMENT ⟨the whole ~ of Senators —*U.S.Constitution*⟩ **d :** a total of units of a particular kind ⟨an enormous ~ of languages —J.B.Carroll⟩ ⟨there is a limited ~ of such laboratories —P.D.Close⟩ ⟨the city is . . . continuing to draw increasing ~*s* of visitors —H.W.H.King⟩ ⟨archery clubs have been established . . . and their ~ is growing rapidly —*Amer. Guide Series: Minn.*⟩ **e :** an unspecified total **:** SEVERAL ⟨a ~ of solutions have been proposed —S.H.Hofstadter⟩ ⟨the . . . concern occupies a ~ of brick buildings —*Amer. Guide Series: N.H.*⟩ ⟨collection which he has exhibited a ~ of times —Mary Zimmer⟩; *esp* **:** quite a few ⟨a ~ of instances⟩ **2 a :** a select company ⟨I want to be in that ~ when the saints go marching in —*When the Saints Go Marching In*⟩ **b** *obs* (1) **:** a designated class **:** CATEGORY ⟨a mineral . . . of the ~ of bitumens —A. Cooper⟩ (2) **:** a specified group of people ⟨this happy ~ that have endured shrewd days and nights with us —Shak.⟩ (3) **:** a numerous group **:** MULTITUDE; *specif* **:** PROLETARIAT ⟨the ~ may be hanged, but not be crowned —Alexander Pope⟩ **3 :** the enumerative aspect of things existing in countable units ⟨a weak sense of time and ~ —G.T.Trewartha & Wilbur Zelinsky⟩ **4 a :** an abstract unit in a numerical series ⟨seven is his lucky ~⟩ ⟨a ~ divisible by two⟩ **b numbers** *pl* **:** the art of computation **:** ARITHMETIC ⟨teach children their ~*s*⟩ ⟨from simple ~*s* to the calculus —*Brit. Book News*⟩ **5 a :** distinction of word form to denote reference to one or to more than one or in some languages also to two usu. expressed by an inflectional change; *also* **:** the distinctive form itself (as of noun, adjective, or verb) or one of the groups of forms so distinguished — compare PLURAL, SINGULAR **b** (1) *obs* **:** tuneful cadence **:** RHYTHM ⟨in full harmonic ~ joined —John Milton⟩ (2) **numbers** *pl, archaic* **:** musical sounds **:** NOTES ⟨holy ~*s* which thou warblest —W.M.Praed⟩ **c numbers** *pl* (1) **:** symmetry of cadence **:** PERIOD ⟨melodic ~*s* of the classic orators⟩ (2) **:** metrical structure **:** METER ⟨most by ~*s* judge a poet's song —Alexander Pope⟩ (3) **:** metrical lines **:** VERSES ⟨these ~*s* will I tear, and write in prose —Shak.⟩ **6 a :** a written word, symbol, or group of symbols representing a number ⟨spell out ~*s* under three digits —Kate L. Turabian⟩; *specif* **:** NUMERAL ⟨the code employs letters as well as ~*s*⟩ **b :** a numerical label or designation: as (1) **:** a digit or group of digits used as a means of identification ⟨house ~⟩ ⟨catalog ~⟩ ⟨stamped a ~ on each ball —Millen Brand⟩; *specif* **:** LICENSE PLATE ⟨the victim remembered the ~ of the getaway car⟩ — symbol # ⟨apartment #32⟩ (2) **:** an allotted position in a numerical sequence ⟨take ~ two position in column —Wirt Williams⟩; *specif* **:** relative position on a promotion roster ⟨for the grounding of his ship . . . he was reduced ten ~*s* —Allan Westcott⟩ (3) **:** an individual identified by position in a sequence or by a numerical label ⟨opened fire on ~ three —*Oxford Bk. of English Talk*⟩ ⟨tackled on the line of scrimmage by ~ 22⟩ ⟨to the keeper I was just a new ~, another dirty blanket to issue —Gilbert Millstein⟩ — compare OPPOSITE NUMBER (4) **:** the specified position of an article in a series with respect to established criteria (as of size or quality) ⟨~ nine shoe⟩ ⟨~ one manila⟩ ⟨a ~ two can of tomatoes⟩ — compare ²COUNT 8a (5) **:** a telephone number ⟨dialed a ~ on the interoffice telephone —Hamilton Basso⟩ (6) **:** a numerical value obtained as the result of a chemical test and used in characterizing the substance tested ⟨the iodine ~ of a fatty oil⟩ **7 :** a large supply **:** QUANTITY, SWARM ⟨squaretails in ~ —Stewart Holbrook⟩ — usu. used in pl. ⟨~*s* of this shark sometimes attack shoals of sardines —J.L.B.Smith⟩ ⟨individuals of great wealth will certainly not exist in any ~*s* in another decade or so —*Persuasion*⟩ ⟨~*s* of beauties major and minor —F.R.Leavis⟩ **8 numbers** *pl* **a :** a numerous group **:** MANY ⟨~*s* died on the way —Marjory S. Douglas⟩ **b :** a numerical preponderance ⟨there is safety in ~*s*⟩ **c :** units of population ⟨their ~*s* outstrip their resources —Barbara Ward⟩ ⟨the graduate school doubled its ~*s* —C.F.Smith⟩ **9 a :** a single issue of a periodical ⟨a year's subscription brings you 12 ~*s*⟩ ⟨this article will appear in the February ~⟩ **b :** one that is singled out from a group: as (1) **:** one of a company of people **:** PERSON ⟨two . . . stokers as ammunition ~*s* —*The Crowsnest*⟩; *esp* **:** GIRL ⟨a cute ~ in a yellow dress —R.L. Strout⟩ ⟨a blondined ~ . . . draped in silver fox —Margaret Long⟩ (2) **:** a musical, theatrical, or literary selection or production ⟨a catchy little ~ in waltz time —A.E.Stevenson †1965⟩ ⟨contains perhaps half a dozen ~*s* that are among the best things he ever wrote —Robert Collet⟩ ⟨novel . . . was going to turn out to be one of those amnesia ~*s* —E.J.Fitzgerald⟩ ⟨supported this cheery little ~ for just fifteen performances —Deems Taylor⟩ ⟨the tango ~ late in Act I —*Theatre Arts*⟩ (3) **:** an item of merchandise offered for sale ⟨put that black velvet ~ with the sequins on the blonde dummy —Bennett Cerf⟩ ⟨the new nylon ~ which he calls an armored vest —*New Yorker*⟩ ⟨costs a lot of money to bring out any new toy ~ —*Marketing Toys*⟩ ⟨a more modestly priced blanket is an all-wool ~ —Hamilton Basso⟩ **10 :** information about or insight into a person's ability or character ⟨the other side had his ~ and was riding him —Mary Deasy⟩ ⟨she was incapable of subterfuge and it didn't take him long to get her ~⟩ **11 numbers** *pl but sing or pl in constr* **a :** a form of lottery played in the U.S. in which one may select any three digits from 001 to 999 and bet on them to appear in a specified order or in any combination and in which the winning numbers and order are determined by figures regularly published in newspapers (as clearinghouse or stock market receipts, pari-mutuel payoffs, or the cards in an article on contract bridge) — called also *number pool, numbers game* **b :** POLICY 2a

syn NUMBER, NUMERAL, FIGURE, DIGIT, and INTEGER can mean in common a character by which an arithmetical value is designated. NUMBER may refer to a character or to a word ⟨the *number* forty-five⟩ ⟨the *number* 45⟩ or to a character with an affix ⟨the ordinal *numbers* 2d, 3d, and 4th⟩ NUMERAL applies to the characters as numbers as distinguished from the words standing for the same numbers ⟨a license plate with both letters and the *numerals* 13249⟩ ⟨the Roman numerals V, VI, and XLII⟩ FIGURE stresses the characters as characters, usu. arabic ⟨write the numbers in *figures* wherever possible to save space⟩ ⟨his salary went into five *figures*⟩ DIGIT refers expressly to one of the characters in Arabic notation ⟨if you include 0, Arabic numerals consist of 10 *digits*, though some authorities exclude 0 as a digit⟩ INTEGER, in this connection, is an arithmetical term for a whole number, one that is not or does not contain a fraction ⟨11½ is not an *integer*⟩ **syn** see in addition SUM

— **any number :** quite a few ⟨laid out with *any number* of trees of different species —B.C.Cronwright⟩ — **by the numbers** *adv* **1 :** in unison to a specific count or cadence **2 :** in a systematic, routine, or mechanical manner ⟨a program run not *by the numbers* but with concern for the participants⟩ — **have one's number on it :** to be destined by fate to cause the death of one — usu. used of a projectile (as a bullet)

²**number** \"\ *vb* **numbered; numbered; numbering** \-b(ə)riŋ\ **numbers** [ME *noumbren, nombren*, fr. OF *nombrer*, fr. L *numerare*, fr. *numerus* number] *vt* **1 a :** to ascertain the number of **:** COUNT ⟨~*s* his friends by the hundreds⟩ **b** *archaic* **:** to determine by mathematical processes **:** COMPUTE ⟨was desirous of accurately ~*ing* the interval of time from one . . . festival to another —Thomas Taylor⟩ **c** *obs* **:** to gauge the amount of **:** ESTIMATE ⟨poets cannot think, speak, cast, write, sing, ~ . . . his love —Shak.⟩ **2 :** to claim as part of a total **:** INCLUDE ⟨it is only by accident that I am ~*ed* among American philosophers —George Santayana⟩ ⟨writers resident in Texas ~*ed* none of note whose literary work was not incidental —*Amer. Guide Series: Texas*⟩ ⟨prudence . . . is ~*ed* with the cardinal virtues —H.O.Taylor⟩ **3 :** to restrict to a limited or definite number ⟨doctors told him his days were ~*ed* —H.E.Starr⟩ **4 :** to assign a number to esp. as a means of identification ⟨~ the pages of a book⟩ ⟨stay on ~*ed* highways⟩ ⟨we use letters to ~ the rows of seats in an assembly room —D.E.Smith⟩ ⟨five thousand dollars of the stolen money was in ~*ed* bills —E.S. Gardner⟩ **5** *archaic* **a :** to report the number of **:** ENUMERATE ⟨the quantities of . . . furnitures following so royal an army, what pen can ~ —Robert Johnson⟩ — often used with *up* ⟨you ~*ed* up the acts of trust —R.H.Hutton⟩ **b :** to check over one by one **:** TELL ⟨let my brother ~ his beads devoutly —Philip Massinger⟩ **c :** APPORTION, DIVIDE ⟨days of this life's pilgrimage . . . to ~ wisely —J.W.Warter⟩ ⟨my . . . fellows I ~*ed* into two companies —William Morris⟩ **6** *archaic* **:** to experience the passage of (an interval of time) ⟨I since then have ~*ed* o'er some thrice three years —Alfred Tennyson⟩; *esp* **:** to reach or have (a specified age) in years ⟨of as able body as when he ~*ed* thirty —Shak.⟩ **7 :** to comprise in number **:** TOTAL ⟨they were a miscellaneous lot . . . ~*ing* in all some 20 or 30 —R.W.Southern⟩ ⟨his extensive collection . . . ~*ing* many thousand specimens —Witmer Stone⟩ ~ *vi* **1 :** to reach a total **:** COUNT ⟨controls . . . literally ~ in the thousands —Harold Koontz & Cyril O'Donnell⟩ **2 :** to call off numbers in sequence ⟨*neng, song, sam*, she ~*ed* in Siamese —Kathryn Grondahl⟩; *esp* **:** to call off one's number as a member of a squad or group ⟨men fall in in single rank and ~ from the right in fours —*Fire Service Drill Bk.*⟩ — often used with *off* ⟨lined up and ~*ed* off⟩ **syn** see COUNT

³**numb·er** \ˈnəmə(r)\ *comparative of* NUMB

num·ber·able \ˈnəmb(ə)rəbəl\ *adj* **:** capable of being numbered

number agreement *n* **:** grammatical concord in form (as singular, dual, or plural) of adjective with noun, finite verb with subject, or pronoun with antecedent

number-board \ˈ==,=\ *n* **:** SLATE 3b

number eight iron *n* **:** PITCHING NIBLICK

num·ber·er \-bərə(r)\ *n* -s **:** one that numbers

number field *or* **number system** *n* **:** the aggregate of all numbers of a given type (as integers, irrationals, complex numbers, vectors) which can be combined by addition or multiplication to obtain a result of the same type

number five iron *n* **:** MASHIE

number four iron *n* **:** MASHIE IRON

numbering machine *n* **:** a device for the rapid stamping or printing of usu. consecutive numbers on successive pages, sheets, or discrete items

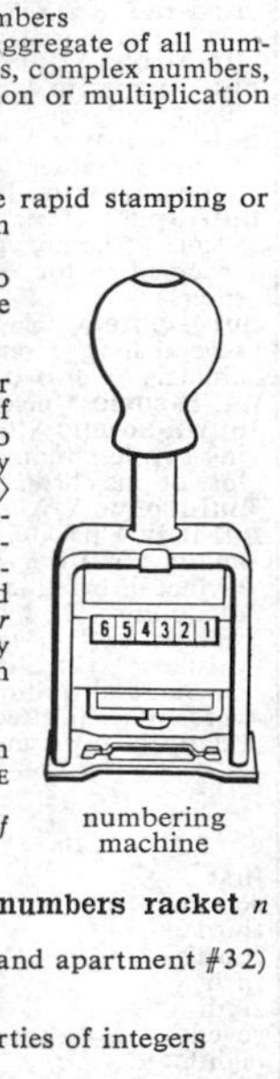

numbering machine

num·ber·less \-bə(r)ləs\ *adj* **:** too many to be counted **:** INNUMERABLE ⟨the possible combinations are ~ —Alfred Marshall⟩

number nine iron *n* **:** NIBLICK

¹**number one** *n* **:** one's own interests or welfare **:** ONESELF ⟨he's very careful of *number one*⟩ ⟨never neglects a chance to exploit a personal advantage on the theory that you've got to look out for *number one*⟩

²**number one** *adj* **1 :** first in rank, importance, or influence **:** FOREMOST ⟨America's *number one* woman golfer —*Providence (R.I.) Evening Bull.*⟩ ⟨declared stamp collecting to be "the nation's *number one* hobby" —H.M.Ellis⟩ ⟨public enemy *number one*⟩ **2 :** of highest or of high quality **:** A1 2 ⟨a real *number one* dinner⟩

number one iron *n* **:** DRIVING IRON 2

number plate *n* **:** a plate or tab bearing an identifying number; *specif* **:** LICENSE PLATE

number pool *n* **:** NUMBER 11

numbers *pl of* NUMBER, *pres 3d sing of* NUMBER

number seven iron *n* **:** PITCHER 4

numbers game *also* **numbers pool** *or* **numbers racket** *n* **:** NUMBER 11

number sign *n* **:** a sign # (as in #2 pencil and apartment #32) used before a numeral to denote number

number six iron *n* **:** MASHIE NIBLICK

number theory *n* **:** the study of the properties of integers

number three iron *n* **:** MID-MASHIE

number two iron *n* **:** MIDIRON

numbest *superlative of* NUMB

numbfish \ˈ=,=\ *n* [¹*numb* + *fish*; fr. the numbing effect of its shocks] **:** ELECTRIC RAY

numbing *adj* [fr. pres. part. of ²*numb*] **:** causing numbness **:** DEADENING, STUPEFYING ⟨a deep ~ hurt way down inside me —Billie Hamlet⟩ ⟨the significance of the title . . . is explained at ~ length —Wolcott Gibbs⟩ — **numb·ing·ly** *adv*

num·bles *also* **nom·bles** \ˈnəmbəlz\ *n pl* [ME *noumbles, nombles*, fr. MF *nombles*, pl. of *nomble* muscle from the thigh of a deer, fillet of beef, pork loin, modif. of L *lumbulus* small loin, fr. *lumbus* loin + *-ulus* -ule — more at LOIN] **:** certain edible viscera (as the heart, lights, liver) of an animal (as a deer) **:** UMBLES — compare GIBLET 1

numb·ly *adv* **:** in a numb manner **:** INSENSIBLY, DULLY ⟨his . . . arms hung down ~ —Peter Schmid⟩ ⟨the men . . . stared up at him ~ —Irwin Shaw⟩

numb·ness *n* -ES [¹*numb* + *-ness*] **1 :** reduced sensibility to touch ⟨patients subsequently experienced a feeling of ~ . . . in the thighs —*Jour. Amer. Med. Assoc.*⟩ **2 :** reduced sensitivity to perception or emotion **:** STUPOR ⟨a drowsy ~ pains my sense, as though of hemlock I had drunk —John Keats⟩ ⟨slipped from her waking ~ into complete oblivion —Mary Webb⟩

numbrous *adj* [MF *nombreux*, fr. *nombre* number + *-eux* -ous — more at NUMBER] *obs* **:** NUMEROUS

numbs *pres 3d sing of* NUMB

numbskull *var of* NUMSKULL

num·dah \ˈnəmdə\ *or* **nam·mad** *or* **na·mad** \ˈnəməd\ *n* -s [Hindi *namdā*, fr. Per *namad*, fr. MPer *namat*; akin to Av *nəmata-* brushwood] **:** a thick felted rug of India and Persia usu. made of pounded goat's hair and embroidered with bird or floral designs in colored wool yarn — compare DRUGGET

nu·men \ˈn(y)ümən\ *n, pl* **nu·mi·na** \-mənə\ [L, nod, divine will, numen; akin to MHG *nucken* to nod off, MLG *nucke* sudden push, L *nuere* to nod, Gk *neuein* to nod, *nyssein, nyttein* to prick, sting, Skt *navate, nauti* he moves, turns] **1 a :** a spirit believed by animists to inhabit a natural object or phenomenon ⟨said to have set up one of the stones . . . and to have poured oil on the top of it as an offering to the indwelling ~ —E.O.James⟩ **b :** a presiding spirit **:** a local deity ⟨the ~ that exercised watch and ward over the whole household —J.B. Noss⟩ **2 :** a dynamic or creative force **:** GENIUS ⟨the strange and powerful ~ which, he felt, used him as its tabernacle —Aldous Huxley⟩

nu·me·ni·us \n(y)üˈmēnēəs\ *n, cap* [NL, fr. LGk *noumēnios*, a bird, perh. the curlew, fr. Gk *noumēnia, neomēnia* new moon, first of the month, fr. *ne-* + *mēn* month + *-ia* — more at MOON] **:** a genus of birds (family Scolopacidae) consisting of the curlews

nu·mer·a·ble \ˈn(y)üm(ə)rəbəl\ *adj* [L *numerabilis*, fr. *numerare* to count + *-abilis* -able — more at NUMBER] **:** capable of being counted ⟨the small ~ band of runaway planets —A.N.Whitehead⟩

¹**nu·mer·al** \ˈn(y)üm(ə)rəl\ *adj* [MF, fr. LL *numeralis*, fr. L *numerus* number + *-alis* -al — more at NIMBLE] **1 :** of, relating to, or expressing numbers ⟨~ adjective⟩ ⟨used the letters of their alphabet for ~ symbols —D.E.Smith⟩ **2 :** consisting of numbers or numerals ⟨~ cipher⟩ — **nu·mer·al·ly** \-rəlē, -li\ *adv*

²**numeral** \"\ *n* -s **1 :** NUMBER 6 **2 numerals** *pl* **:** the numbers designating by year a school or college class ⟨carried a banner with the class ~*s* on it in the reunion parade⟩ ⟨won ~*s* in basketball, baseball, and track⟩ — compare LETTER 6 **syn** see NUMBER

nu·mer·ate \ˈn(y)üməˌrāt\ *vt* -ED/-ING/-S [L *numeratus*, past part. of *numerare* to count] **:** to give a detailed list of **:** ENUMERATE ⟨might have been illuminating had he *numerated* the mistakes made by each side —Mary K. Hammond⟩

nu·mer·a·tion \ˌ==ˈrāshən\ *n* -s [ME *numeracion*, fr. L *numeration-, numeratio*, fr. *numeratus* (past part. of *numerare* to count) + *-ion-, -io* -ion] **1 a :** a system or process of enumeration ⟨the positional system which came at length by way of the Arabs to supersede the clumsy ~ of the Romans —*Times Lit. Supp.*⟩ **b :** the application of enumerative processes **:** COMPUTATION ⟨study of African or American Indian languages shows systems of ~, often on a decimal scale —D.J. Struik⟩ **c :** an act or instance of counting or of applying numbers to something **:** CENSUS, NUMBERING ⟨make an exact ~ of the inhabitants of Ireland —Edmund Burke⟩ ⟨a fourteenth century Arabic ~ is written in the lower outer corner of the verso of the leaves —Jack Finegan⟩ **2 :** arithmetical skill; *esp* **:** the art of reading off in words numbers set down in figures

¹**nu·mer·a·tive** \ˈn(y)ümərəd·iv, -məˌrād·-\ *adj* [*numerate* + *-ive*] *archaic* **:** of or relating to number or numeration ⟨a ~ noun interposed between it and the substantive —R.K.Douglas⟩

²**numerative** \"\ *n* **:** CLASSIFIER 2

nu·mer·a·tor \ˈn(y)üməˌrād·ə(r), -ātə-\ *n* -s [F *numérateur*, fr. LL *numerator* one that counts, fr. L *numeratus* (past part. of *numerare* to count) + *-or*] **1 :** the part of a fraction that is above the line and signifies the number of parts of the denominator taken **:** DIVIDEND **2** [LL] **:** one that numbers

nu·mer·ic \(ˈ)n(y)ü¦merik\ *adj* [L *numerus* number + E *-ic*] **:** NUMERICAL 1; *esp* **:** denoting a number or a system of numbers ⟨~ code⟩ ⟨a ~ sign⟩

nu·mer·i·cal \-rəkəl, -rēk-\ *adj* [L *numerus* number + E *-ical*] **1 a :** of or relating to numbers ⟨~ analyst⟩ ⟨~ superiority of the enemy⟩ **b :** denoting a number ⟨letters of the alphabet were employed as ~ signs —William Chomsky⟩ **c :** expressed in figures rather than letters ⟨spies . . . used a very simple ~ cipher, which changed every day —Alexander d'Agapeyeff⟩ ⟨the ~ proportions of hybrid crosses —Lancelot Hogben⟩ ⟨~ equation⟩ **d :** designated by number ⟨conscious of his ~ standing in every class —Harry Levin⟩ **e :** of or relating to ability to think in or work with numbers ⟨~ skill⟩ ⟨the ~ factor of a test⟩ — compare VERBAL **2 a** *archaic* **:** of a corresponding type **:** INDISTINGUISHABLE, SAME ⟨many of these ~ postures . . . are found in statues of the ancients —John Bulwer⟩ **b** *obs* **:** IDENTICAL ⟨in a river we swim in the same place, though not in the same ~ water —Robert Burton⟩ ⟨probably that very ~ book . . . kept in the temple —Thomas Fuller⟩

numerical aperture *n* **:** a quantity that indicates the resolving power of a microscope objective and that is numerically equal to the product of the index of refraction of the medium in front of the objective and the sine of the angle which the most oblique ray entering it makes with the optical axis

nu·mer·i·cal·ly \-rək(ə)lē, -rēk-, -li\ *adv* **1 a :** in respect to number **:** in numbers ⟨a ~ inferior but intellectually potent group —K.S.Davis⟩ **b :** according to number ⟨copy . . . is filed ~ —E.M.Robinson⟩ **c :** in figures ⟨if a date is written ~ —Marjorie E. Skillin & R.M.Gay⟩ **2 :** in a precisely similar way **:** INDISTINGUISHABLY ⟨the emotion . . . is not ~ identical —John Dewey⟩

numerical rating system *n* **:** a system of establishing insurance premium rates for substandard lives on the basis of numerical weights for various impairments

numerical value *n* **1 a :** a quantitative value assigned to a letter of the alphabet ⟨exegetical rule . . . according to which every Hebrew letter has a *numerical value* —S.A.Binion⟩ **b :** a sum obtained by adding together the numerical equivalents of the letters in a word or phrase ⟨if two names had the same *numerical value*, this fact showed some relation between the individuals —D.E.Smith⟩ — compare GEMATRIA **2 :** ABSOLUTE VALUE

nu·mer·ist \ˈn(y)ümərəst\ *n* -s [L *numerus* number + E *-ist*] *archaic* **:** NUMEROLOGIST

nu·mer·o·log·i·cal \¦n(y)ümərə¦läjəkəl\ *adj* **:** of or relating to numerology

nu·mer·ol·o·gist \ˌn(y)üməˈräləjəst\ *n* -s **:** a specialist in numerology ⟨bets $2000 on a horse, after consulting his private ~ —Malcolm Cowley⟩

nu·mer·ol·o·gy \-jē, -ji\ *n* -ES [L *numerus* number + E *-o-* + *-logy*] **:** the study of the occult significance of numbers — compare GEMATRIA

nu·mer·os·i·ty \ˌn(y)üməˈräsəd·ē\ *n* -ES [MF *numerosité* numerousness, fr. LL *numerositat-, numerositas*, fr. L *numerosus* numerous + *-itat-, -itas* -ity] **1 :** NUMEROUSNESS ⟨the earliest scales of measurement were scales of ~ — scales for the counting of pebbles or cattle or warriors —S.S.Stevens⟩ **2** *archaic* **:** melodic flow

nu·mer·ous \ˈn(y)üm(ə)rəs\ *adj* [MF *numereux*, fr. L *numerosus*, fr. *numerus* number + *-osus* -ous — more at NIMBLE] **1 a :** consisting of great numbers of units **:** existing in abundance **:** MANY, PLENTIFUL ⟨decked out with . . . ~ ribbons and a thousand other joyous trifles —Osbert Sitwell⟩ ⟨mutation . . . has occurred ~ times under natural conditions —Theodosius Dobzhansky⟩ ⟨legends regarding buried treasure . . . are as ~ as they are improbable —Thomas Barbour⟩ **b :** consisting of a great number of individuals **:** LARGE, MULTITUDINOUS ⟨it was too bad that the family was ~: each man got only one share . . . instead of two —Ernest Beaglehole⟩ ⟨this species has become infinitely more ~ during the past five or six years —Thomas Heinitz⟩ **c** *archaic* **:** of or relating to a great number of individuals ⟨the birds begun at four o'clock . . . a music ~ —Emily Dickinson⟩ **2** *archaic* **:** musically cadenced **:** RHYTHMICAL ⟨blank verse . . . falling occasionally almost into ~ prose —Henry Hallam⟩

nu·mer·ous·ly *adv* **:** in large numbers **:** ABUNDANTLY ⟨letters have been arriving ~ of late —Virgil Thomson⟩

nu·mer·ous·ness *n* -ES **:** the quality or state of being numerous

nu·me·rus clau·sus \¦nüməˌrüˈsklau̇ˌsu̇s\ *n* [NL, lit., closed or restricted number] **:** a quantity fixed as the maximal number or percentage (as of applicants of a particular race or class) admissible to an academic institution

nu·mi·da \ˈn(y)ümədə\ *n, cap* [NL, fr. L *Numida* Numidian, fr. Gk *Nomada*] **:** the type genus of Numididae comprising the domesticated guinea fowls and closely related African wild guinea fowls

¹**nu·mid·i·an** \(ˈ)n(y)ü¦midēən\ *adj, usu cap* [L *Numidianus*, fr. *Numidia* + *-ianus* -ian] **:** of or relating to Numidia, an ancient country of No. Africa nearly coextensive with modern Algeria

²**numidian** \"\ *n* -s *cap* **1 :** a native or inhabitant of ancient Numidia **2 :** the Berber language of the Numidian people

numidian alphabet *n, usu cap N* **:** LIBYAN ALPHABET

numidian crane *n, usu cap N* **:** DEMOISELLE 2a

nu·mid·i·dae \n(y)üˈmidəˌdē\ *n pl, cap* [NL, fr. *Numida*, type genus + *-idae*] **:** a family of African and Madagascan birds that are closely related to the pheasants and peacocks and often included with them in the family Phasianidae and that comprise the guinea fowls — see NUMIDA

numina *pl of* NUMEN

¹**nu·mi·nous** \ˈn(y)ümənəs\ *adj* [L *numin-, numen* numen + E *-ous* — more at NUMEN] **1 a :** of, relating to, or characteristic of a numen **:** SUPERNATURAL ⟨a single dark and ~ power ruling the world —Aldous Huxley⟩ **b :** dedicated to or hallowed by association with a deity **:** SACRED ⟨a ~ wood⟩ **c :** having talismanic properties **:** MAGICAL ⟨all quests are concerned with some ~ object, the waters of life, the Grail, buried treasure —W.H.Auden⟩ **2 a :** filled with a sense of the presence of divinity **:** HOLY ⟨the holiest, most ~ moment in the Mass — the moment of transubstantiation —V.C.Aldrich⟩ **b :** inspiring reverence ⟨as beautiful and as ~ as a cathedral —C.E.Raven⟩ **3 a :** appealing to the higher emotions or to the aesthetic sense **:** SPIRITUAL ⟨when tradition has lost its . . . ~ authority —George Santayana⟩ ⟨the candle was a graceful . . . and ~ method of illumination —*New Yorker*⟩ **b :** beyond understanding or description **:** MYSTERIOUS, INCOMPREHENSIBLE ⟨emphasizes the ~ aspect of writing —*Times Lit. Supp.*⟩

²**numinous** \"\ *n* -ES [G *numinos*, fr. L *numin-, numen* numen] **:** an unseen but majestic presence that inspires both dread and fascination and constitutes the nonrational element characteristic of vital religion **:** a psychic revelation of deity producing religious awe and ecstasy — usu. used with *the* ⟨African Bushmen, awed by the presence of the ~ at a given place . . . throwing a few grains into a hole in the hallowed ground —Joachim Wach⟩ ⟨the unanimity of prophets and seers regarding their experiences of the ~ —William Telfer⟩

nu·mis·mat·ic \¦n(y)üməz¦mad·ik, -məs¦-, -at|, |ēk\ *also* **nu·mis·mat·i·cal** \|əkəl, |ēk-\ *adj* [*numismatic* fr. F *numismatique*, fr. L *numismat-, numisma, nomismat-, nomisma* money, coin (fr. Gk *nomismat-, nomisma* custom, usage, currency, coin) + F *-ique*; *numismatical* fr. L *numismat-, numisma* + E *-ical*; akin to Gk *nomos* custom, usage, law — more at NIMBLE] **1 :** of or relating to numismatics ⟨will accept any dime but would prefer it to be of some ~ value —J.M.Hageman⟩ **2 :** of or relating to currency **:** MONETARY ⟨cowrie shells because of their ~ . . . significance were given the technical name of *Cypraea moneta* —*Numismatist*⟩

nu·mis·mat·i·cal·ly \|ək(ə)lē, |ēk-, -li\ *adv* **:** from a numismatic point of view **:** with regard to numismatics ⟨coins in this ~ and historically interesting series —*Numismatist*⟩

nu·mis·mat·ics \ˌ==ˈmad·iks\ *n pl but sing in constr* [F *numismatique*, fr. *numismatique*, adj.] **1 :** the study of coins, tokens, medals, paper money, and objects closely resembling them in form or purpose **2 :** the collecting of numismatic objects

nu·mis·ma·tist \n(y)üˈmizməd·əst, -ism-, -ətəst\ *n* -s [L *numismat-, numisma* + E *-ist*] **1 :** a specialist in numismatics **2 :** a collector of numismatic objects **:** a coin collector

nu·mis·ma·tol·o·gist \n(y)üˌmizməˈtäləjəst, -ism-\ *n* -s [*numismatology* + *-ist*] **:** NUMISMATIST

nu·mis·ma·tol·o·gy \-jē\ *n* -ES [*numismatic* + *-ology*] **:** NUMISMATICS

num·ma·ry \ˈnəmərē\ *adj* [L *nummarius*, fr. *nummus* coin, money (fr. Gk *nomimos* customary, lawful) + *-arius* -ary; akin to Gk *nomos* custom, usage, law — more at NIMBLE] **:** of, relating to, or dealing with money or coins

num·mi·form \ˈnəməˌfȯrm\ *adj* [F *nummiforme*, fr. L *nummus* coin + F *-forme* -form] **:** NUMMULAR

num·mu·lar \ˈnəmyələ(r)\ *adj* [F *nummulaire*, fr. L *nummulus* (dim. of *nummus* coin) + F *-aire* -ar] **1 :** circular or oval in shape ⟨~ lesions⟩ **2 a :** marked by circular or oval lesions ⟨~ dermatitis⟩ **b :** forming circular or oval drops ⟨~ sputum⟩

num·mu·la·ria \ˌnəmyəˈla(a)rēə\ *n, cap* [NL, fr. L *nummulus*, dim. of *nummus* coin + NL *-aria*] **:** a genus of mostly saprophytic fungi (family Xylariaceae) forming generally amorphous crustose round or discoid black stromata — see BLISTER CANKER

num·mu·lary \ˈnəmyəˌlerē\ *adj* [L *nummularius* of or relating to money changing, fr. *nummulus* some money, money (dim. of *nummus* coin) + *-arius* -ary] *archaic* **:** NUMMARY

num·mu·line \ˈnəmyəˌlīn, -ˌlən\ *adj* [*nummulite* + *-ine*] **:** NUMMULITIC

num·mu·lite \ˈnəmyəˌlīt\ *n* -s [NL *Nummulites*] **:** a foraminifer or fossil of the family Nummulitidae — **num·mu·lit·ic** \ˌ==ˈlid·ik\ *adj*

num·mu·li·tes \ˌnəmyəˈlīd·(ˌ)ēz\ *n, cap* [NL, fr. L *nummulus* (dim. of *nummus* coin) + NL *-ites* -ite] **:** the type genus of the family Nummulitidae

nummulitic limestone *n* **:** the most widely distributed and distinctive formation of the Eocene in Europe, Asia, and northern Africa attaining a thickness of thousands of feet and being composed chiefly of the remains of foraminifers (esp. of the genus *Nummulites*)

num·mu·lit·i·dae \ˌnəmyəˈlid·əˌdē\ *n pl, cap* [NL, fr. *Nummulites*, type genus + *-idae*] **:** a family of foraminifers that are mostly extinct, have a calcareous symmetrical usu. lenticular or discoidal shell composed of numerous chambers spirally or concentrically arranged, and form whole strata in some Eocene and Oligocene deposits of eastern and southern Asia and the Mediterranean region from their shelly remains

num·mu·li·toid \ˌ==ˈlīˌtȯid\ *adj* [NL *Nummulites* + E *-oid*] **:** resembling or related to the genus *Nummulites*

num·mu·loi·dal \ˌ==ˈlȯidᵊl\ *adj* [*nummulite* + *-oidal*] **:** shaped like a nummulite

num·nah \ˈnəmnə\ *n* -s [Hindi *namdā* — more at NUMDAH] **:** a felt or sheepskin pad placed between a horse's back and the saddle to prevent chafing ⟨a soft . . . ~ under the saddle has been known to cure some buckjumpers —W.A.Kerr⟩

nu movable *n* [*nu* fr. Gk *ny*] **:** a nu inserted in ancient and modern Greek at the end of vowel-final words of certain classes when followed by a vowel-initial word or by a pause or inserted in poetry even before an immediately following word with a single initial consonant to provide two consonants to make a preceding short vowel long by position — compare MOVABLE 5

num·skull *or* **numb·skull** \ˈnəmˌskəl\ *n* [¹*numb* + *skull*] **1 :** a dull or stupid person **:** BONEHEAD, DUNCE ⟨the moment he sits down at the piano only a ~ wouldn't know he was a genius —Robert Rice⟩ **2 :** a thick or muddled head ⟨the wooden sound of ~s being soundly hit—Edith Sitwell⟩ — **num·skulled** \-ld\ *adj*

¹**nun** \ˈnən\ *n* -s *except sense 2c(1)* [ME, fr. OE *nunne*, fr. LL *nonna* nun, child's nurse; of baby-talk origin like Gk *nanna*, *nenna* female relative, aunt, W *nain* grandmother, Alb *nanë* mother, child's nurse, Russ *nyanya* child's attendant, Skt *nanā* mother, little mother] **1 a** *obs* **:** a priestess of a pagan deity ⟨prohibited all but the emperor and vestal ~s to be buried within the city —John Houghton⟩ **b :** a woman belonging to a religious order ⟨in primitive Buddhism there were four ecclesiastical orders: monks, ~s, devout laymen, and devout laywomen —*Religions in Japan*⟩; *esp* **:** a woman living in a convent under vows of poverty, chastity, and obedience ⟨a convent of ~s vowed to contemplation who . . . never went outside the convent walls —L.P.Smith⟩ **2 a** *dial Eng* **:** BLUE TIT **b** *chiefly Brit* **:** SMEW **c (1)** *usu cap* **:** a German breed of domestic pigeons **(2) :** a bird of this breed that is white with a colored head, tail, and wing tips and has a semicircular crest of white feathers curving forward from the back of the head **d :** a weaverbird of the genus *Lonchura* **3 :** NUN MOTH **4** [by shortening] **:** NUN BUOY

²**nun** \"\ *vt* **nunned; nunned; nunning; nuns :** to confine in or as if in a nunnery

³**nun** \ˈnün, ˈnůn\ *n* -s [Heb *nūn*] **1 :** the 14th letter of the Hebrew alphabet — symbol נ; see ALPHABET table **2 :** the letter of the Phoenician alphabet or of any of various other Semitic alphabets corresponding to the Hebrew nun

nun·a·tak \ˈnənəˌtak\ *n* -s [Esk] **:** a hill or mountain completely surrounded by glacial ice

nun bird *n* **:** any of several dark-colored So. American puffbirds of the genus *Monasa* having white around the face and throat

nun buoy *n* **:** a red metal buoy made of two cones joined at the base and usu. marking the starboard side of a channel approached from the sea — see BUOY illustration

nun·cheon *also* **nun·chion** \ˈnənshən, ˈnən-, -nch-\ *or* **nunch** \ˈnənsh, ˈnən-, -nch\ *n, pl* **nuncheons** *also* **nunchions** *or* **nunches** [*nuncheon, nunchion* fr. ME *nonechench, noneschench*, lit., noon drink, fr. *none* noon + *schench* drink, cup, fr. OE *scenc*; akin to OE *scencan* to pour out drink, give to drink, OHG *skenken* to pour out, ON *skakkr* crooked, askew; *nunch* short for *nuncheon, nunchion* — more at NOON, SHANK] *dial chiefly Eng* **:** a light midmorning or midafternoon snack consisting typically of bread, cheese, and beer

nun·ci·ate \ˈnən(t)sēˌāt\ *n* -s [L *nuncius, nuntius* messenger, message + E *-ate*] *archaic* **:** one that proclaims **:** NUNCIO

nun·ci·a·ture \ˈnən(t)sēəˌchů(ə)r\ *n* -s [It *nunciatura, nunziatura*, fr. *nunciato, nunziato* (past part. of *nunciare, nunziare* to announce, proclaim) (fr. L *nunciatus, nuntiatus*, past part. of *nunciare, nuntiare* to announce, relate, inform, fr. *nuncius, nuntius* messenger, message) + *-ura* -ure (fr. L)] **1 :** the office or period of office of a papal nuncio **2 :** an official delegation from the pope to a foreign power ⟨negotiations . . . for establishing an apostolic ~ in Washington and an American embassy accredited to the Vatican —*N.Y.Times*⟩

nun·cio \ˈnən(t)sēˌō, ˈnůn|, |shēˌō, |chēˌō\ *n* -s [It *nuncio, nunzio*, fr. L *nuncius, nuntius* messenger, message] **1 a :** a top-ranking diplomatic envoy of the pope accredited to a civil government — distinguished from *legate a latere*; compare APOSTOLIC DELEGATE, INTERNUNCIO **b** *obs* **:** MESSENGER ⟨she will attend it better in thy youth, than in a ~'s of more grave aspect —Shak.⟩ **2 :** a member of the former Polish diet

nun·cle \ˈnəŋkəl\ *n* -s [alter. (resulting fr. incorrect division of *an uncle*) of *uncle*] *chiefly dial* **:** UNCLE

nunc pro tunc \ˈnůŋkˌprōˈtůŋk\ [NL] **:** now for then — used of a legal entry, judgment, or decree made currently to have effect as of an earlier date when it ought to have been made, done, or recorded

nun·cu·pate \ˈnəŋkyəˌpāt\ *vt* -ED/-ING/-S [L *nuncupatus*, past part. of *nuncupare* to name, declare, dedicate, contr. of *nomen capere*, fr. *nomen* name + *capere* to take — more at NAME, HEAVE] **1** *obs* **a :** to inscribe to by way of compliment **:** DEDICATE ⟨*nuncupating* my litany to your ladyship —John Bastwick⟩ **b :** to utter solemnly **:** PRONOUNCE ⟨they do here . . . ~ this deliberate vow —Edmund Burke⟩ **2 :** to declare (a will) publicly **:** PROCLAIM ⟨how doth that will appear . . . in whose presence did he ~ it —Isaac Barrow⟩

nun·cu·pa·tion \ˌ==ˈpāshən\ *n* -s [L *nuncupation-, nuncupatio*, fr. *nuncupatus* (past part. of *nuncupare* to name, declare) + *-ion-, -io* -ion] **:** an oral will ⟨the dying seaman made a ~ in favor of his mother⟩

nun·cu·pa·tive \ˈ==ˌpād·iv, (ˈ)nəŋˈkyüpəd·iv, (ˈ)nən|-\ *adj* [ML *nuncupativus*, fr. LL, so-called, fr. L *nuncupatus* (past part. of *nuncupare* to name, declare) + *-ivus* -ive] **1 :** stated verbally **:** ORAL — used chiefly of a will **2** *archaic* **:** DESIGNATIVE ⟨participles substantive or ~ —T.F.Middleton⟩ — **nun·cu·pa·tive·ly** \-d·əvlē\ *adv*

nuncupative will *n* [trans. of ML *testamentum nuncupativum*] **1** *Roman law* **:** a will consisting orig. in the simple oral declaration of the testator's testamentary dispositions in the presence of seven witnesses and later in such a declaration made before a magistrate **2 a :** a will primarily evidenced by the testator's oral declaration to a witness of his testamentary dispositions as distinguished from one primarily evidenced by a written disposition **b :** *English law* **:** an oral will made by a person in extremis

nuncupatory *adj* [prob. fr. (assumed) NL *nuncupatorius*, fr. ML, naming, fr. L *nuncupatus* (past part. of *nuncupare* to name, declare) + *-orius*, -ory] **1** *obs* **:** ORAL **2** *obs* **:** DEDICATORY

nun·di·nal \ˈnəndənᵊl\ *adj* [L *nundinalis*, fr. *nundinae* nundine + *-alis* -al] **:** of or relating to a nundine

nundinal letter *n* **:** one of the first eight letters of the alphabet used by the ancient Romans in the Sabine calendar after adoption of the seven-day week, the first seven letters being repeated consecutively in one column to designate days of the week and all eight in a parallel column to mark the recurrence of market days under an older eight-day cycle

nun·di·na·tion \ˌnəndəˈnāshən\ *n* -s [F, fr. L *nundination-, nundinatio*, fr. *nundinatus* (past part. of *nundinari* to trade, market, fr. *nundinae* nundine) + *-ion-, -io* -ion] *archaic* **:** an act or instance of bartering **:** SALE ⟨the ~ of indulgences —Isaac Taylor⟩

nun·dine \ˈnənˌdīn, -ˌdən\ *n* -s [L *nundinae*, pl., market time, lit., nine days, fr. *nundinus* of nine days, alter. of *novem dies* nine days, fr. *novem* nine + *dies* day; fr. its being held every ninth day of the Roman calendar — more at NINE, DEITY] **:** a market day held every ninth day according to ancient Roman reckoning

nung \ˈnůŋ\ *n, pl* **nung** *or* **nungs** *usu cap* **1 :** a Thai-speaking group of peoples known by a variety of names with slight phonetic variations and mainly found in Kwangsi province of China but also in northern Vietnam — compare GIAI **2 a :** a Tibeto-Burman people related to the Chingpaw in north Burma but having a more archaic language **b :** a member of such people

nun·hood \ˈnənˌhůd\ *n* -s [¹*nun* + *-hood*] **:** the status or calling of a nun

nun·let \ˈnənlət\ *n* -s [¹*nun* + *-let*] **:** any of several small So. American puffbirds of the genus *Nonnula*

nunlike \ˈ=ˌ=\ *adj* **:** resembling or characteristic of a nun or her habit ⟨~ serenity⟩ ⟨~ coif⟩

nun moth *n* **:** a European tussock moth (*Lymantria monacha*) that often damages coniferous forest trees

nun·na·ri \ˈnənərē\ *or* **nunnari root** *n* -s [*nunnari* prob. native name in India] **:** INDIAN SARSAPARILLA

nun·na·tion \ˌnəˈnāshən\ *n* -s [NL *nunnation-, nunnatio*, fr. Ar *nūn*, letter n of the Arabic alphabet + L *-ation-, -atio* -ation] **:** the addition of a final *n* in declension of nouns (as in Arabic)

nunned *past of* NUN

nun·nery \ˈnən(ə)rē, -ri\ *n* -ES [ME *nunnerie*, fr. ¹*nun* + *-erie* -ery] **1 :** an establishment housing a community of nuns **:** CONVENT **2 :** an order of nuns **:** SISTERHOOD

nun·ni \ˈnənē\ *n, pl* **nunni** *or* **nunnis** [Sechuana *nōnē*] **:** BLESBOK

nunning *pres part of* NUN

nun·nish \ˈnənish\ *adj* **:** of, relating to, or characteristic of a nun

nun·ny·watch \ˈnənē-\ *var of* NINNYWATCH

nun of the visitation *usu cap N & V, Roman Catholicism* **:** a member of a religious order founded by St. Jane Frances de Chantal under the direction of St. Francis de Sales in 1610 at Annecy, Savoy, and now chiefly devoted to teaching

nuns *pl of* NUN, *pres 3d sing of* NUN

nun·ship \ˈnənˌship\ *n* [¹*nun* + *-ship*] **:** NUNHOOD

nun's veiling *n* **:** a fine sheer clothing fabric in plain weave usu. made of worsted, silk, or cotton

nun·ti·us \ˈnənshēəs\ *n, pl* **nun·tii** \-ēˌī\ [L — more at NUNCIO] **:** NUNCIO 1a

nu·pe \ˈnüpā\ *n, pl* **nupe** *or* **nupes** *usu cap* **1 a :** a Negro people of west central Nigeria **b :** a member of such people **2 :** a Kwa language of the Nupe people

Nu·per·caine \ˈn(y)üpə(r)ˌkān\ *trademark* — used for dibucaine

nu·phar \ˈn(y)üfə(r)\ *n, cap* [NL, fr. Ar *nūfar*, short for *naynūfar* — more at NENUPHAR] **:** a genus of water lilies (family Nymphaeaceae) having flowers with showy usu. yellow sepals and minute petals that resemble stamens or scales, leaves with a deep sinus, and a cylindrical creeping rootstock — see SPATTERDOCK

nupson *n* [*nup* of unknown origin + *son*] *obs* **:** FOOL, SIMPLETON

¹**nup·tial** \ˈnəpsh|əl, -pch|, *chiefly in substandard speech* |əwəl\ *adj* [L *nuptialis*, fr. *nuptiae* wedding (fr. *nuptus*, past part. of *nubere* to marry a man) + *-alis* -al; akin to Gk *nymphē* bride, nymph, OSlav *snibiti* to couple] **1 :** of or relating to marriage or the marriage ceremony ⟨the ~ day⟩ ⟨a ~ hymn⟩ **2 a :** capable of breeding ⟨several large ~ males⟩ **b :** characteristic of the breeding season ⟨~ coloration⟩ **c :** concerned with or preliminary to copulation ⟨~ behavior⟩

²**nuptial** \"\ *n* -s **:** MARRIAGE, WEDDING ⟨must employ you in some business against our ~ —Shak.⟩ — usu. used in pl. ⟨preparations . . . for the approaching ~s —W.H.Prescott⟩

nuptial father *n, archaic* **:** one who represents the bride's father at a wedding

nuptial flight *n* **:** a flight of sexually mature social insects (as bees) in which mating takes place and which is usu. a prelude to the forming of a new colony; *esp* **:** the mass flight and mating of winged sexual forms of ants after leaving the parent nest

nup·ti·al·i·ty \ˌnəpshēˈaləd·ē, ˌnəpˈshal-\ *n* -ES [F *nuptialité*, fr. *nuptial* of marriage (fr. L *nuptialis*) + *-ité* -ity] **:** the marriage rate ⟨~ . . . being very high in the general rural population —B.W.Gussman⟩

nuptial plumage *also* **nuptial dress** *n* **:** the specialized plumage assumed by the males of many birds while the gonads are enlarging prior to the start of the annual breeding period and characterized by greater brilliance of color and form than that of the nonbreeding males — called also *breeding plumage*; compare ECLIPSE PLUMAGE

nuque \ˈn(y)ük\ *n* -s [MF, fr. ML *nucha* — more at NUCHA] **:** the back of the neck

nu·ra·ghe \nüˈrägā\ *n, pl* **nura·ghi** \-gē\ *or* **nuraghes** [It (Sardinian dial.), perh. fr. *Nura, Nurra*, locality in Nuoro province, central Sardinia, Italy] **:** a large stone structure of Sardinia built in the shape of a truncated cone and held to date from the bronze age ⟨the *nuraghi* . . . are easily the equal of the sphinx in mystery and grandeur —P.E.Deutschman⟩ — **nuraghic** *adj*

nur·em·berg \ˈn(y)ůrəmˌbərg\ *or* **nürn·berg** *or* **nurn·berg** *or* **nuern·berg** \ˈnᵺrnˌberk\ *adj, usu cap* [fr. *Nuremberg*, city in southern Germany] **:** of or from the city of Nuremberg, Germany **:** of the kind or style prevalent in Nuremberg

nuremberg violet *n, often cap N* **:** MANGANESE VIOLET

¹**nurse** \ˈnərs, ˈnɘs, ˈnəis\ *n* -s *often attrib* [ME *nurse, norse, nurice*, fr. OF *norrice, nurice*, fr. LL *nutricia*, fr. L, fem. of *nutricius*, *nutritius* nourishing — more at NUTRITIOUS] **1 a :** a woman who suckles and takes care of an infant that is not her own **:** WET NURSE **b :** a woman who takes care of a young child **:** DRY NURSE **2 a :** a person who looks after or gives advice to another **b :** something that serves as a fostering agency or influence ⟨time is a ~ and breeder of all good —Shak.⟩ **3 a :** a person skilled in caring for and waiting on the infirm, the injured, or the sick; *specif* **:** one esp. trained to carry out such duties under the supervision of a physician **b :** a person esp. trained to assist a physician or dentist (as in an operating room) **4 :** NURSE TREE **5 a :** a worker form of a social insect (as an ant or bee) that cares for the young **b :** an asexual oozooid that produces and carries the blastozooids in some ascidians (as of the genus *Doliolum*) **c :** a female mammal used to suckle the young of another female usu. of her own kind — usu. used with following noun ⟨~ doe⟩ ⟨~ cow⟩ ⟨~ mare⟩ **6 :** the act of nursing the balls in billiards — **to nurse** *adv* **1** *or* **at nurse :** under the care of a nurse ⟨would send for the baby, though I entreated him . . . to put it out *to nurse* —Charlotte Brontë⟩ **2 :** under the control of trustees ⟨put his estate *to nurse* —Tobias Smollett⟩

²**nurse** \"\ *vb* -ED/-ING/-S [alter. (influenced by ¹*nurse*) of ME *nurshen* to nourish, contr. of *nurishen* — more at NOURISH] *vt* **1 a :** to nourish at the breast **:** SUCKLE ⟨four women were unable to ~ their infants —J.P.Greenhill⟩ ⟨keep the kittens alive till the mother can ~ them —Eleanor B. Simmons⟩ **b :** to take nourishment from the breast of **:** suck milk from ⟨possible for a baby to contract tuberculosis from *nursing* its mother —L.H.Brevard⟩ ⟨the foal should not be permitted to ~ the mare when she is hot and sweating —James Law & M.S. Shahan⟩ **2 :** to bring up **:** REAR, EDUCATE ⟨for we were *nursed* upon the selfsame hill —John Milton⟩ **3 a :** to promote the growth, development, or progress of ⟨anything to ~ the arts and bring them into the homes of the . . . people —M.R. Cohen⟩ ⟨the policy of attracting original work and *nursing* authors of promise —*Times Lit. Supp.*⟩ **b :** to cultivate (a plant) with care ⟨*nursed* the long rows of vines that were their livelihood —Margaret Evans⟩ **c :** to manage (as a business) with care or economy ⟨on his hundreds of thousands of dollars — *nursed* into millions — a substantial Boston family had been built —J.A.Michener⟩ **d :** to take charge of and watch over in the manner of a nurse ⟨to ensure that performers arrive on time he ~s them from show to show —Don Everitt⟩ ⟨trout are hatched and *nursed* to planting age —*Amer. Guide Series: Wash.*⟩ **e :** to cause to develop ⟨fancied it to be their interest . . . to ~ the embers of the old enmity into a flame —Edward Edwards⟩ **4 a :** to care for and wait on (as an injured or infirm person) **:** ATTEND ⟨great-grandfather was bedridden . . . and my mother *nursed* him —Ellen Glasgow⟩ **b :** to attempt a cure of (as an ailment) by care and treatment ⟨would stay in her room and ~ a sick headache —Louis Auchincloss⟩ ⟨had been pitched against a bridge . . . and was *nursing* a painfully bruised arm —Llewellyn Howland⟩ **5 :** to hold in one's heart or mind **:** keep in memory or consideration ⟨had spent the night watches in *nursing* his wrath —John Buchan⟩ ⟨did not ~ the idea that her life was at an end —Arnold Bennett⟩ ⟨*nursed* a plan to invade the South and forcibly liberate the slaves —B.B.Stutler⟩ **6 :** to hold or grasp carefully or firmly ⟨~ my fat briefcase on my knees and go through my papers —Christopher Morley⟩ ⟨took her hands again and *nursed* them against my cheek —Mary Austin⟩ **7 a :** to use, handle, or drive carefully so as to conserve energy or avoid injury ⟨trying to ~ a gigantic crippled plane back over many hundreds of miles of open ocean —J.A.Michener⟩ **b :** to use with forethought and care so as to conserve or stretch out ⟨~s his time so that he may keep his brain in rested condition for decisions —*Atlantic*⟩ **c :** to consume slowly so as to conserve or stretch out ⟨like to ~ a drink . . . and watch the people around us —Dwight Taylor⟩ ⟨~s a cup of coffee and a doughnut until it is morning —Norman Mailer⟩ **8** *chiefly Brit* **:** to attract or sustain the favorable attention of usu. by personal contacts and the dispensing of favors in order to sustain electoral support ⟨is busy *nursing* his constituency and calculating how he can be reelected —W.E.Binkley⟩ **9 :** to keep (billiard balls) close together and in good position for a series of caroms ~ *vi* **1 a :** to give suck **b :** to feed at the breast **:** SUCK **2 :** to act or serve as a nurse

syn CULTIVATE, NURTURE, FOSTER, CHERISH: NURSE implies careful sustaining of an infant, person, thing, or notion. CULTIVATE is likely to differ from NURSE in suggesting methods of sustaining and protecting the useful in the plant world; it implies sedulous and steady care but lacks the human warmth suggested in many of the other words in this group ⟨spinning theories of fiction is my favorite amusement . . . a good habit to *cultivate* —Ellen Glasgow⟩ ⟨whatever physical gifts she may have are carefully *cultivated* —Lafcadio Hearn⟩ ⟨the morbid curiosity *cultivated* in Browning by his father's tasks and inclinations —Ruth R. Chapman⟩ NURTURE places stress on giving that which sustains and affording a safe environment pointing toward a certain development or course ⟨men who have not been *nurtured* in dissecting rooms and other laboratories —C.S.Peirce⟩ ⟨had been *nurtured* in sentiments opposed to the institution of human servitude —R.P.Warren⟩ FOSTER may suggest the relationship of foster parent to child in implying caring for, encouraging, sustaining, and maintaining growth ⟨such a sentiment is *fostered* by all those agencies of the mind and spirit which may serve to gather up the traditions of the people —Felix Frankfurter⟩ ⟨the pope . . . used his powers to *foster* abuses that brought wealth to the Roman court —G.M.Trevelyan⟩ ⟨we must *foster* on every campus the principle of individualism as contrasted with docile receptivity —C.M. Fuess⟩ CHERISH implies fondness or love for something with incidental nurturing of it ⟨a cause which is embraced and *cherished* by so vast a portion of American society —Kenneth Roberts⟩

³**nurse** \"\ *n* -s [earlier *nuse*, fr. ME *nusse*] **:** NURSE SHARK

nurse cell *n* **:** a cell of a type present in the ovary of many animals that supplies nourishment to the developing egg cell and is commonly believed to be a rudimentary egg cell

nurse-child \ˈ=ˌ=\ *n* **:** a child under the care or supervision of a nurse

nurse crop *n* **:** a crop planted with another presumably to shelter it from competition with weeds or other undesirable plants — compare COMPANION CROP, NURSE GRASS

nursed *past of* NURSE

nurse-father *n* [prob. trans. of MF *pere nourricier*] *obs* **:** a foster father

nurse frog *n* **:** OBSTETRICAL TOAD

nurse-garden *n, obs* **:** NURSERY 4

nurse graft *n* **:** a plant graft in which the stock is intended to remain united with the scion only temporarily usu. until the latter establishes roots of its own

nurse grass *n* **:** a quick-growing grass planted to shade and protect other grass and to help suppress weeds — compare NURSE CROP

nursehound \ˈ=ˌ=\ *n* [³*nurse* + *hound*] **:** a European dogfish (*Scyliorhinus canicula*)

nursekeeper \ˈ=ˌ==\ *n, archaic* **:** a nurse for the sick

nurseling *var of* NURSLING

¹**nursemaid** \ˈ=ˌ=\ *n* [¹*nurse* + *maid*] **1 :** one who is regularly employed to look after children **2 :** one who guards or takes care ⟨became to his people a combination oracle and ~ —M.R. Werner⟩ ⟨was the ~ to . . . polo ponies —James Jones⟩

²**nursemaid** \"\ *vt* -ED/-ING/-S **:** to watch over or take care of in a solicitous manner ⟨grateful to a conductor who ~s six soloists —Virgil Thomson⟩ ⟨that engine . . . was greased and cleaned and ~*ed* —C.S.Forester⟩ ⟨in the midst of the school crossing . . . ~*ing* moppets —R.M.Stern⟩

nurs·er \ˈnərsər\ *n* -s **1 :** one that nurses ⟨known as a ~ of nickels⟩ **2 :** NURSING BOTTLE

nur·sery \ˈnərs(ə)rē, ˈnɘs-, ˈnəis-, -ri\ *n* -ES *often attrib* [ME *norserie*, fr. *norse* nurse + *-erie* -ery] **1** *obs* **:** attentive care **:** FOSTERAGE ⟨thought to set my rest on her kind ~ —Shak.⟩ **2 :** a place designed for the care or training of children: **a :** a child's bedroom **b :** a room or apartment in a house set aside for the use of children **c :** a room or place in a public building (as a church) where children are temporarily cared for in their parents' absence by trained attendants **d :** DAY NURSERY **e :** NURSERY SCHOOL **3 a :** something that fosters, develops, or promotes ⟨the inland seas became the first *nurseries* of seamanship and commerce —W.G.East⟩ ⟨an equal claim to be noticed as a ~ of the arts —*Times Lit. Supp.*⟩ **b :** a place in which persons are trained or educated ⟨the chancery became a ~ of clever and unscrupulous churchmen —E.A.Freeman⟩ ⟨France at this time . . . was a ~ for good surgeons —Harvey Graham⟩ **4 :** an area where trees, shrubs, or plants are grown for transplanting, for use as stocks for budding and grafting, or for sale **5 :** a place where young animals are cared for: as **a :** a pond, trough, or box in which young fish are kept until the yolk sac is absorbed **b :** BROODER 2a **6 :** a handicap horse race for 2-year-olds

nurserymaid \ˈ=(=)ˌ=\ *n* **:** NURSEMAID

nur·sery·man \ˈ=(=)=mən\ *n, pl* **nurserymen :** one whose occupation is the scientific cultivation of trees, shrubs, and plants

nursery rhyme *n* **:** a tale in rhymed verse for children

nursery school *n* **:** a school for children usu. under five years of age — compare KINDERGARTEN

nursery stock *n* **:** young plants grown in a nursery
nurses *pl of* NURSE, *pres 3d sing of* NURSE
nurse's aide *n* **:** a worker who assists trained nurses in a hospital by performing nonspecialized services (as making beds or giving baths)
nurse shark *n* [2*nurse*] **1 :** GREENLAND SHARK **2 :** any of various sharks of a widely distributed family (Orectolobidae); *esp* **:** GATA **3 :** a large pale Australian sand shark (*Carcharias arenarius*)
nurse-tender \ˈ=,==\ *n, chiefly Irish* **:** a nurse who cares for the sick
nurse tree *n* **:** a tree that protects or fosters the growth of other young trees
nursing *n* -s [fr. gerund of 2*nurse*] **1 :** the profession of a nurse ⟨modern schools of ~⟩ **2 :** the varied activities that constitute the duties of a nurse ⟨proper ~ is no easy job⟩
nursing anemia *or* **nursing sickness** *n* **:** an abnormality of ranch-reared nursing mink that is marked by extreme emaciation, loss of appetite, and death and is apparently due to dietary deficiencies superimposed on the strain of milk production
nursing bottle *n* **:** a bottle to which a rubber nipple is attached and which is used in supplying food to infants — called also *feeding bottle*
nursing chair *n* **:** an armless chair with a low seat
nursing home *n* **1** *chiefly Brit* **:** a private hospital **2 :** a private home or other place where maintenance and personal or nursing care are provided for three or more persons who are unable to care for themselves properly
nursing sister *n, Brit* **:** GRADUATE NURSE
nur·sle \ˈnərsəl\ *vt* -ED/-ING/-S [prob. alter. (influenced by 2*nurse*) of 2*nuzzle*] **:** to bring up **:** NURTURE ⟨*nursled* . . . under a regime of religious liberty —S.R.Gardiner⟩
nurs·ling *also* **nurse·ling** \ˈnərsliŋ, ˈnə̄s-, ˈnəis-, -lēŋ\ *n* -s [1*nurse* + *-ling*] **1 :** one that is solicitously cared for and fostered ⟨was the child and ~ of that Burgundian court —Sarah Austin⟩ **2 :** a nursing child or other young nursing mammal; *esp* **:** one that is suckled by another than its mother

nursing bottle

nur·tur·al \ˈnərchərəl\ *adj* **:** of, relating to, or resulting from nurture
1**nur·ture** \ˈnərchər, ˈnə̄chə(r, ˈnəichə(r\ *n* -s [ME *nurture, norture*, fr. MF *norriture, norreture*, fr. LL *nutritura* act of nursing or suckling, fr. L *nutritus* (past part. of *nutrire* to suckle, nourish) + *-ura* -ure — more at NOURISH] **1 a :** the breeding, education, or training that one receives or possesses **:** UPBRINGING ⟨the poverty she lived in was utterly unbefitting her gentle ~ —George Meredith⟩ **b** *obs* **:** moral training **2 :** something that nourishes **:** FOOD ⟨fed him well and nourished himself and took ~ for the road —R.D.Blackmore⟩ **3 :** the process of bringing up **:** TUTELAGE ⟨the best moral atmosphere for the ~ of creative scientists —Weston La Barre⟩ **4 :** the sum of the influences modifying the expression of the genetic potentialities of an organism — compare NATURE
2**nurture** \"\ *vt* **nurtured; nurtured; nurturing** \-ch(ə)riŋ\ **nurtures** [ME *nurturen, norturen*, fr. *nurture, norture*, n.] **1 :** to supply with food, nourishment, and protection ⟨was not *nurtured* by the best of mothers —O.W.Holmes †1894⟩ **2 a :** to train by or as if by instruction **:** EDUCATE ⟨will ask for the financial support of the alumni whom they have *nurtured* —C.M.Fuess⟩ **b** *obs* **:** to give moral training to **:** DISCIPLINE **3 :** to further the development of **:** promote the growth of **:** FOSTER ⟨~ your mind with great thoughts —Benjamin Disraeli⟩ **syn** see NURSE
nur·ture·less \-chə(r)ləs\ *adj* **:** lacking nurture or nourishment
nur·tur·er \-ch(ə)rə(r)\ *n* -s **:** one that nurtures
nus *pl of* NU
nu·sai·ri \nüˈsīrē\ *n* -s *usu cap* [Ar *Nuṣayrīyah* Nusairis] **:** a member of a syncretistic religious sect of northern Syria that lives in comparative isolation and mingles religious beliefs from Islamic, Christian, and native sources — called also *Ansarie*
1**nut** \ˈnət, *usu* -əd·+V\ *n* -s [ME *nute, note*, fr. OE *hnutu*; akin to OHG *nuz*, *hnuz* nut, ON *hnot*, MIr *cnū*, L *nuc-, nux*] **1 a** (1) **:** a hard-shelled dry fruit or seed having a more or less distinct separable rind or shell and interior kernel or meat — used to include various forms (as peanuts and Brazil nuts) not botanically true nuts (2) **:** the kernel of a nut **b :** a dry indehiscent one-seeded fruit (as an acorn, hazelnut, or chestnut) with a woody pericarp developing from an inferior syncarpous ovary — see FRUIT illustration **2 :** something resembling a nut in the difficulty it represents: as **a :** a problem to be solved — often used with *to crack* ⟨communications were a tough ~ —John Dos Passos⟩ ⟨many hard ~*s* to crack in developing satisfactory processes —J.P.Baxter b.1893⟩ **b :** an undertaking to be shouldered — usu. used with *to crack* ⟨climbed the lower slopes but the summit proved too hard a ~ to crack⟩ **c :** a person to be conciliated ⟨tried to convince him but he was a tough old ~⟩ **3 :** a perforated block that is usu. a small piece of metal of square or hexagonal section, that has an internal screw thread, and that is used on a bolt or screw for tightening or holding something or for transmitting motion **4 :** a projection on the shank of an anchor to secure the stock in place **5 a :** the ridge in a stringed musical instrument over which the strings pass on the upper end of the fingerboard nearest the head and pegbox **b :** the movable piece at the lower end of a bow (as a violin bow) by which the hairs may be tightened **6 nuts** *pl* **a** *slang* **:** a source of joy and pleasure **:** DELIGHT — usu. used with *the* ⟨they thought this one was the ~*s* when they built it —Calder Willingham⟩ ⟨it's the ~*s* — you can splash around all you want to —*Better Homes & Gardens*⟩ **b :** NONSENSE — often used interjectionally to express disapproval or annoyance; sometimes considered vulgar ⟨~*s* to you and your friends⟩ **c :** TESTES — usu. considered vulgar **7** *slang* **:** a person's head ⟨you get this in your ~ —Richard Llewellyn⟩ ⟨should think there was something wrong in his ~ —H.J.Laski⟩ **8 a** *slang Austral* **:** LARRIKIN **b** (1) **:** one whose thinking or conduct is eccentric ⟨his contemporaries sometimes considered him just a prodigiously talented ~ —*Time*⟩ (2) **:** one who is or seems to be mentally unbalanced ⟨a ~ got into the . . . reception and started screaming obscenities —Toni Howard⟩ (3) **:** one who is overenthusiastic about a particular matter (as a hobby) ⟨some golf ~ who had ranged the world collecting out-of-the-way golf courses —E.J.Kahn⟩ **c** *slang Brit* **:** a smartly or sprucely dressed person **9 :** a rounded cake or biscuit (as a doughnut or spice nut) **10 :** the complete expense involved — usu. used of the costs of a stage or television production **11 :** EN ⟨indent one ~⟩ — **for nuts** *adv, slang chiefly Brit* **:** at all ⟨may be good at lessons, but she can't sew *for nuts* —Flora Thompson⟩ ⟨they can't write *for nuts* either —S.M.Lipset⟩ — **off one's nut :** CRAZY ⟨we're all rude to each other and if we weren't we'd go *off our nuts* —H.E.Bates⟩

nuts 3

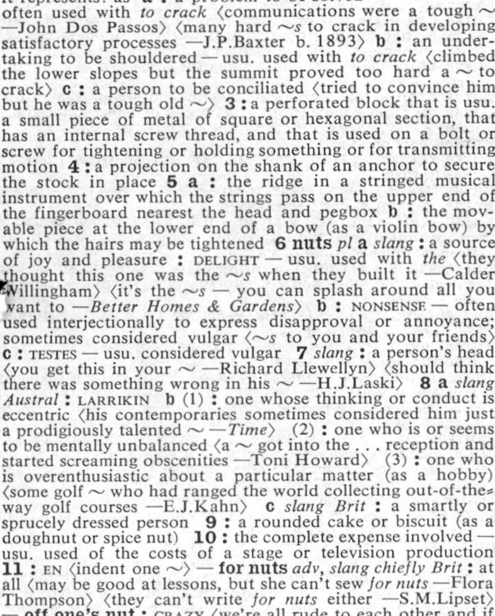

2**nut** \"\ *adj* [ME *nute, note*, fr. OE *hnut-*, fr. *hnutu* nut, n.] **1 :** of, relating to, or characteristic of a nut **:** having nuts ⟨my little ~ tree⟩ **2 :** serving as a receptacle for nuts ⟨~ dish⟩
3**nut** \"\ *vi* **nutted; nutted; nutting; nuts** [1*nut*] **:** to gather or seek nuts — usu. used in the form *nutting*
nu·tant \ˈn(y)üt³nt\ *adj* [L *nutant-, nutans*, pres. part. of *nutare* to nod, sway] **:** DROOPING, NODDING ⟨the equestrian statue . . . rode under the ~ trees —Malcolm Lowry⟩
nu·tate \ˈn(y)ü,tāt\ *vi* -ED/-ING/-S [L *nutatus*, past part. of *nutare* to nod, sway] **:** to exhibit nutation
nu·ta·tion \n(y)üˈtāshən\ *n* -s [L *nutation-, nutatio*, fr. *nutatus* (past part. of *nutare* to nod, sway, rock, freq. of *nuere* to nod) + *-ion-, -io* -ion — more at NUMEN] **1 :** the act of nodding; *esp* **:** an involuntary nodding of the head **2 a :** a small inequality in the motion of precession **:** a libratory motion of the earth's axis like the nodding of a top due to joint action of the sun and moon by which its inclination to the plane of the ecliptic varies with a period of about 19 years and with a range of only a few seconds of arc so that the celestial poles describe wavy rather than circular parallels round the poles of the ecliptic **3 :** a more or less rhythmical change in the position of growing plant organs due to variation in growth rates on different sides of the growing apex **:** an autonomic movement — compare CIRCUMNUTATION **4 :** the vibratory displacement of the axis of a precessing top or gyroscope from the cone-shaped figure traced by the axis during precession
nu·ta·tion·al \-shən³l, -shnəl\ *adj* **:** of or relating to nutation
nut bone *n* **:** a large transversely extended sesamoid bone behind the joint between the coronary bone and coffin bone in the foot of a horse
nutbreaker \ˈ=,==\ *n* [trans. of G *nussbrecher*] **:** NUTCRACKER 2
nut-brown \ˈ=ˈ=\ *adj* **:** brown as a nut
nut brown *n* **:** a color of brown nuts (as hazel, chestnut, or walnut)
nut·burg·er \ˈnət,bərgər\ *n* [1*nut* + *-burger*] **:** a patty containing ground nuts
nutcake \ˈ=,=\ *n* [1*nut* + *cake*] **1** *NewEng* **:** DOUGHNUT **2 :** a cake containing nuts
nut coal *n* [by shortening] **1 :** CHESTNUT COAL **2 :** bituminous coal of medium size having varying top and bottom limits in different localities and ranging between top sizes of 1½ to 2 inches and bottom sizes of ¾ to 1½ inches
1**nutcracker** \ˈ=,==\ *n* [1*nut* + *cracker*] **1 a :** an implement for cracking nuts **b :** something resembling a nutcracker ⟨squeezed in the ~ of taxes and inflation —*Jour. of Accountancy*⟩ **2 a** [trans. of G *nussbrecher*] **:** a European bird (*Nucifraga caryocatactes*) of the family Corvidae that is dark brown spotted with white **b :** CLARK NUTCRACKER

nutcracker 1a

2**nutcracker** \"\ *adj* **:** suggestive of or resembling the jaws of a nutcracker esp. from lack of teeth ⟨a thin young man with a ~ nose and jaw —David Garnett⟩
nutfall \ˈ=,=\ *n* **:** the normal or precocious dropping of nuts from a tree
nutgall \ˈ=,=\ *n* **:** a nutlike gall; *esp* **:** a gall produced on oak
nut grass *n* **1 :** any of several aggressively weedy sedges of the genus *Cyperus*; *esp* **:** a perennial sedge (*C. rotundus*) of wide distribution having slender rootstocks that bear small edible nutlike tubers **2 :** any of several American sedges of the genus *Scleria*
nut·hatch \ˈnət,hach\ *n* [alter. (influenced by 1*hatch*) of ME *nuthak*, alter. (influenced by *hak* hack) of *notehache*, fr. *note* nut + *hache* ax, hatchet (fr. OF, battle-ax); fr. its way of breaking nuts for food — more at NUT, HACK, HASH] **:** any of various birds of the family Sittidae that are chiefly small with long wings and a short tail, creep over the trunk and branches of trees, and have character and habits intermediate between the titmice and the creepers — see RED-BREASTED NUTHATCH, WHITE-BREASTED NUTHATCH
nuth·er \ˈnəthə(r)\ *dial var of* NEITHER
nuthook *n* [1*nut* + *hook*] **1** *obs* **:** a hook at the end of a pole to pull down boughs for gathering nuts **2** *obs Brit* **:** CONSTABLE
nuthouse \ˈ=,=\ *n* [1*nut* + 1*house*] *slang* **:** an insane asylum
nut·job·ber \ˈnət,jäbə(r)\ *n* [1*nut* + *jobber* (fr. 4*job* + *-er*)] *dial Brit* **:** NUTHATCH
nut·let \ˈnətlət\ *n* -s [1*nut* + *-let*] **1 :** a small nut **2 :** a small nutlike fruit (as of many plants of the family Boraginaceae) **3 :** the stone of a drupelet
nutlike \ˈ=,=\ *adj* **1 :** resembling a nut; *often* **:** being or having the characteristics of a nut **2 :** suggesting or like that of a nut **:** NUTTY ⟨a ~ flavor⟩
nut margarine *n* **:** margarine made principally from coconut and peanut oils churned with soured whole or skimmed milk and salt
nutmeat \ˈ=,=\ *n* [1*nut* + *meat*] **:** the kernel of a nut
1**nut·meg** \ˈnət,meg, -mäg\ *n* -s *often attrib* [ME *notemuge*, part trans., part modif. of OF *nois muguete, nois muguede* nutmeg, alter. of *nois muscade*, fr. OProv *noz muscada*, fr. *noz* nut (fr. L *nuc-, nux*) + *muscada*, fem. of *muscat* musky — more at NUT, MUSCAT] **1 a :** a hard aromatic spheroidal seed that is widely used as a spice — see 3MACE **b** *or* **nutmeg tree :** a small evergreen tropical tree (*Myristica fragrans*) native to the Molucca islands but widely cultivated for its spherical yellow drupaceous fruits which yield mace and nutmeg **2 :** any of various trees related to or in some respect resembling the nutmeg: as **a :** any of several trees of the genus *Myristica* having seeds that resemble but are generally inferior to the true nutmegs **b :** a Central and So. American banak (*Virola koschnii*) yielding a timber used for veneer and plywood **c :** CALIFORNIA NUTMEG **d :** NUTMEG HICKORY **e :** a western African tree (*Pycnanthus kombo*) of the family Myristicaceae with a somewhat aromatic arillode and seed which is of importance primarily as a source of oil **3 :** DARK BEAVER
2**nutmeg** \"\ *or* **nut·meg·ger** \-gə(r)\ *n* -s *cap* [*nutmeg* short for *wooden nutmeg*; fr. the notion that wooden or imitation nutmegs came from Connecticut and were examples of Yankee inventiveness; *nutmegger* fr. *Nutmeg* State, nickname of the state of Connecticut (fr. the phrase *wooden nutmeg state*) + E *-er*] **:** a native or resident of Connecticut — used as a nickname
nutmeg apple *n* **:** the fruit of the nutmeg tree
nutmeg butter *n* **:** a soft yellowish or orange fat of nutmeg odor obtained from nutmegs and used chiefly in ointments
nutmeg family *n* **:** MYRISTICACEAE
nutmeg flower *n* **:** a European annual herb (*Nigella sativa*) with small black aromatic seeds sometimes used as a flavoring agent and insect repellent
nutmeg geranium *n* **:** a cultivated pelargonium (*Pelargonium odoratissimum*) with round fragrant leaves and small white flowers
nutmeg hickory *n* **:** a hickory (*Carya myristicaeformis*) of the southern U. S. and Mexico having a nutmeg-shaped fruit
nutmeg liver *n* **:** a liver appearing mottled like a nutmeg when cut because of congestion and associated with impaired circulation esp. from heart or lung disease
nutmeg melon *n* **:** NETTED MELON
nutmeg oil *n* **:** either an oil or a fat obtained from nutmegs: **a :** a colorless or pale yellow essential oil of nutmeg odor distilled from nutmegs and used chiefly in flavoring and in medicine as a local stimulant — called also *myristica oil* **b :** NUTMEG BUTTER
nutmeg pigeon *n* **:** any of several pigeons of the genus *Ducula* (syn. *Myristicivora*) of the East Indies and Australia that feed on wild nutmegs
nutmeg shell *n* [so called fr. its rough, warty surface] **:** a marine snail of the genus *Cancellaria*
nut of bahera : a myrobalan that is the fruit of a tall East Indian tree (*Terminalia belerica*) and that is used in tanning and dyeing and in folk medicine
nut oil *n* [prob. trans. of D *noot olie*] **:** an oil obtained from nuts: as **a :** WALNUT OIL **b :** TUNG OIL **c :** PEANUT OIL
nut palm *n* **:** an Australian cycad (*Cycas media*) having edible seeds
nutpecker \ˈ=,==\ *n* [1*nut* + *pecker*] **:** NUTHATCH
nutpick \ˈ=,=\ *n* [1*nut* + *pick*] **:** a small sharp-pointed table implement for extracting the kernels from nuts
nut pine *n* **:** a pine with edible seeds: as **a :** any of several piñons (as *Pinus edulis* or *P. cembroides*) **b :** STONE PINE 2 **c :** SWISS PINE
nut plate *n* **:** a nut with an extended flat base so that it may be secured to a surface and made captive
nu·tria \ˈn(y)ütrēə\ *n* -s [Sp *nutria, nutra* coypu, otter, modif. of L *lutra* otter; akin to Gk *hydros* water snake — more at OTTER] **1 a :** COYPU 1 **b :** the fur of the coypu that is usu. light brown but occas. black, is durable, and is plucked and blended to imitate beaver **2 :** an olive gray that is paler than the color rat and redder and darker than stone gray — called also *beaverpelt, grège*
nu·tri·cial \(ˈ)n(y)üˈtrishəl\ *adj* [L *nutricius, nutritius* nourishing, nursing + E *-al* — more at NUTRITIOUS] **:** of or relating to nursing or rearing ⟨~ castration in worker bees⟩
nu·tri·cism \ˈn(y)ü·trə,sizəm\ *n* -s [prob. fr. (assumed) NL *nutricismus*, fr. L *nutric-, nutrix* nurse + *-ismus* -ism — more at NUTRITIOUS] **:** symbiosis in which one organism is nourished or protected by the other without apparently being of reciprocal benefit **:** COMMENSALISM
nu·tri·culture \ˈn(y)ü·trə+,-\ *n* [*nutrient* solution + *culture*] **:** HYDROPONICS
1**nu·tri·ent** \ˈn(y)ü·trēənt\ *adj* [L *nutrient-, nutriens*, pres. part. of *nutrire* to nourish — more at NOURISH] **:** furnishing nourishment **:** promoting growth **:** NUTRITIOUS ⟨feed avidly on water hyacinths, but they do not make good fodder and are not ~ —Thomas Barbour⟩ ⟨magnesium is the ~ element in plant growth —*Market Growers Jour.*⟩
2**nutrient** \"\ *n* -s **:** a nutritious substance or component; *esp* **:** a chemical element or inorganic compound (as a nitrate) taken in by a green plant and used in organic synthesis
nu·tri·fy \-rə,fī\ *vb* -ED/-ING/-ES [LL *nutrificare*, fr. L *nutrire* to nourish + *-ficare* -fy] *vt, archaic* **:** NOURISH ~ *vi, archaic* **:** to supply nourishment
nu·tri·lite \ˈn(y)ü·trə,līt\ *n* -s [*nutrition* + *-lite* (as in *metabolite*)] **:** a substance (as a vitamin or growth factor) required in small quantities for normal metabolism and growth and obtained by an organism in its food
nu·tri·ment \ˈn(y)ü·trəmənt\ *n* -s [L *nutrimentum*, fr. *nutrire* to nourish + *-mentum* -ment] **:** something that nourishes **:** something that promotes growth and repairs the natural waste of animal or vegetable life **:** ALIMENT, FOOD, NOURISHMENT
nu·tri·men·tal \ˌ==ˈment³l\ *adj* [ME, fr. LL *nutrimentalis*, fr. L *nutrimentum* nourishment + *-alis* -al] **:** NUTRITIOUS
nu·tri·tial \(ˈ)n(y)üˈtrishəl\ *adj* [L *nutritius, nutricius* nourishing + E *-al* — more at NUTRITIOUS] **:** NUTRICIAL
nu·tri·tion \n(y)üˈtrishən\ *n* -s [MF, fr. LL *nutrition-, nutritio*, fr. L *nutritus* (past part. of *nutrire* to nourish) + *-ion-, -io* -ion] **:** the act or process of nourishing or being nourished; *specif* **:** the sum of the processes by which an animal or plant takes in and utilizes food substances in animals typically involving ingestion, digestion, absorption, and assimilation
nu·tri·tion·al \(ˈ)=ˈ=shən³l, -shnəl\ *adj* **:** of, relating to, or functioning in nutrition — **nu·tri·tion·al·ly** \-³lē, -əlē, -i\ *adv*
nutritional anemia *n* **:** anemia which results from inadequate intake or assimilation of nutrients or other elements essential to the production of red blood cells and hemoglobin (as hypochromic anemia)
nutritional deficiency *n* **:** an inadequate supply of essential nutrients (as vitamins and minerals) in the diet resulting in malnutrition or disease
nutritional encephalomalacia *n* **:** CRAZY CHICK DISEASE
nutritional roup *n* **:** avitaminosis of poultry
nu·tri·tion·ist \=ˈ=sh(ə)nəst\ *n* -s **:** a specialist in the study of nutrition
nu·tri·tious \(ˈ)n(y)üˈtrishəs\ *adj* [L *nutritius, nutricius*, fr. *nutric-, nutrix* nurse + *-ius* -ious; akin to L *nutrire* to nourish — more at NOURISH] **:** promoting growth and repairing the natural waste **:** NOURISHING, NUTRITIVE — **nu·tri·tious·ly** *adv*
nu·tri·tious·ness *n* -ES **:** the quality or state of being nutritious
1**nu·tri·tive** \ˈn(y)ü·trəd·|iv, -ət|\ *adj* [ME *nutritif*, fr. MF & LL; MF *nutritif*, fr. LL *nutritivus*, fr. L *nutritus* (past part. of *nutrire* to nourish) + *-ivus* -ive — more at NOURISH] **1 :** of, relating to, or concerned in nutrition ⟨the ~ functions⟩ **2 :** affording nourishment **:** NUTRITIOUS ⟨~ food⟩ — **nu·tri·tive·ly** \|əvlē, -li\ *adv*
2**nutritive** \"\ *n* -s [ME, fr. *nutritif* nutritive, adj.] **:** a nutritive substance **:** a nourishing food
nu·tri·tive·ness \|ivnəs\ *n* -ES **:** the quality or state of being nutritive
nutritive plasma *n* **:** TROPHOPLASM
nutritive polyp *n* **:** GASTROZOOID
nutritive ratio *n* **:** the ratio of digestible protein to other digestible nutrients in a foodstuff or ration ⟨*the nutritive ratio* of shelled corn is about 1 to 10⟩
nu·tri·to·ry \ˈn(y)ü·trə,tōrē\ *adj* [LL *nutritorius*, fr. L *nutritus* (past part. of *nutrire* to nourish) + *-orius* -ory] **:** NUTRITIVE
nu·tri·ture \ˈn(y)ü·trə,chù(ə)r, -,chər\ *n* -s [It *nutritura*, fr. LL, fr. L *nutritus* + *-ura* -ure] **:** NOURISHMENT
nut rush *n* **1 :** a sedge of the genus *Scleria* having hard bony achenes **2 :** NUT GRASS 1
nuts \ˈnəts\ *adj* [fr. pl. of 1*nut*] **1 :** eagerly enthusiastic **:** fervently ardent **:** KEEN, WILD ⟨everyone seems ~ about it —Lois Long⟩ ⟨she was ~ about the boy next door⟩ **2 :** CRAZY, DEMENTED ⟨thought I would go ~ waiting around —Polly Adler⟩ ⟨she thought I was ~ but she liked me —Agnes de Mille⟩
nutsch filter \ˈnüch-\ *or* **nutsch** *n* -ES *sometimes cap N* [G *nutsch, nutsche*, lit., sucking bottle, fr. *nutschen* to suck, of imit. origin] **:** a filter of a simple type adapted to batch operation; *esp* **:** such a filter operated by suction
nut sedge *n* **:** NUT GRASS
1**nutshell** \ˈ=,=\ *n* [ME *nut schell*, fr. 1*nut* + *schell* shell — more at SHELL] **1 :** the shell or hard external covering in which the kernel of a nut is enclosed **2 a** *obs* **:** something of little or no value ⟨don't stake your life against a ~ —Jeremy Collier⟩ **b :** something of little or small compass, size, amount, or length ⟨a little ~ of people here —Owen Wister⟩ ⟨wisdom in these ~*s* of poems —*Times Lit. Supp.*⟩ — **in a nutshell** *adv* **:** in or within a small compass or limit **:** in a very brief statement **:** in a few words ⟨explained the situation *in a nutshell*⟩
2**nutshell** \"\ *vt* **:** to state or sum up in a few words ⟨he ~*ed* the whole plan for them⟩
nut shell *n* **:** a marine bivalve mollusk of the family Nuculidae or sometimes of the related Nuculanidae — see NUCULA
nutsy \ˈnətsē\ *adj* -ER/-EST [*nuts* + *-y*, adj. suffix] **:** LUNATIC
nut·tall blister beetle \ˈnəd-,ȯl-\ *n, usu cap N* [after Thomas *Nuttall* †1859 Am. botanist and ornithologist born in England] **:** a metallic green and copper-colored blister beetle (*Lytta nuttallii*) that feeds on bean and pea plants
1**nut·tal·lia** \nəˈtalēə\ [NL, fr. Thomas *Nuttall* †1859 Am. botanist and ornithologist + NL *-ia*] *syn of* MENTZELIA
2**nuttallia** \"\ *n, cap* [NL, fr. George H. F. *Nuttall* †1937 Am. biologist + NL *-ia*] **:** a genus sometimes treated as a subgenus of *Babesia* and comprising tick-borne protozoan parasites of mammals — compare BABESIIDAE
nut·tal·li·a·sis \,nəd·³lˈīəsəs\ *or* **nut·tal·li·o·sis** \nə,talēˈōsəs\ *n, pl* **nuttallia·ses** \-ī,sēz\ *or* **nuttallio·ses** \-ō,sēz\ [NL, fr. 2*Nuttallia* + *-iasis* or *-osis*] **:** infection with or disease caused by protozoans of the genus *Nuttallia* — compare PIROPLASMOSIS
nuttall oak *or* **nuttall's oak** *n, usu cap N* [after Thomas *Nuttall* †1859 Am. botanist and ornithologist] **:** a large tree (*Quercus nuttallii*) of Missouri, Mississippi, and Texas having dark brownish gray bark and a nut with a thin-walled cup that has cinereous-puberulent scales
nut·ted \ˈnəd·əd\ *adj* [1*nut* + *-ed*] **:** furnished with or secured by a nut
nut·ter \ˈnəd·ə(r)\ *n* -s [3*nut* + *-er*] **:** a gatherer of nuts
nut·tery \ˈnəd·ərē\ *n* -ES [1*nut* + *-ery*] **:** a place where nut trees grow; *also* **:** a place for storing nuts
nut·ti·ly \ˈnəd·|³lē, -ət|, |³li, |əl-\ *adv* **:** in a nutty manner
nut·ti·ness \|ēnəs, |in-\ *n* -ES **:** the quality or state of being nutty
nutting *pres part of* NUT
nut·ty \|ē, |i\ *adj* -ER/-EST [1*nut* + *-y*, adj. suffix] **1 :** having or producing nuts ⟨the pine . . . letting fall its ripe ~ cones —Cyril Connolly⟩ **2 a :** NUTS 1 ⟨most sixteen-year-olds are ~ about cars⟩ **b :** CRACKBRAINED, ECCENTRIC; *also* **:** mentally unbalanced ⟨the projects in progress that summer seemed fairly ~ —Bruce Bliven b.1916⟩ ⟨the cranks who send ~ letters to editors —C.W.Morton⟩ ⟨all as ~ as fruitcakes —Nancy Hale⟩ **3 :** full of a pleasant zest **:** STIMULATING ⟨the fine ~ flavor of American politics —D.C.Coyle⟩ ⟨his thoughts, many of them thin, diffuse, abstract, others ~ . . . phrased in a rare flowing antique style —V.W.Brooks⟩ **4** *Brit* **:** spruce in appearance **5 :** having a flavor like that of nuts ⟨poured a fine old ~ sherry⟩ ⟨a strip of rich ~ blubber —Rudyard Kipling⟩
nut weevil *n* **:** a weevil (as of the genus *Balaninus*) whose larva lives in nuts
nux vom·i·ca \ˌnəksˈvämәkə\ *n, pl* **nux vomica** [NL, lit., emetic nut] **1 :** the poisonous seed of an Asiatic tree (*Strychnos nux-vomica*) that contains several alkaloids but chiefly strychnine and brucine **2 :** the tree that yields nux vomica — see FALSE ANGOSTURA BARK
nu·zi \ˈnüzē\ *n* -s *usu cap* [fr. *Nuzi*, ancient city south of Kirkuk, northeastern Iraq, where cuneiform tablets in this dialect were discovered] **:** a dialect of Akkadian in use at Nuzi
nuz·zer \ˈnəzə(r)\ *n* -s [Hindi *nazr*, fr. Ar] **:** a ceremonial offering to a superior in India

¹nuz·zle \'nəzəl\ *vb* **nuzzled; nuzzled; nuzzling** \-z(ə)liŋ\ **nuzzles** [earlier *nosill, nousle,* fr. ME *noselen* to bring the nose towards the ground, fr. ¹*nose* + *-elen, -len* -le] *vi* **1 :** to work with or as if with the nose **:** root, rub, or snuff with the nose ⟨feedboxes where once horses had *nuzzled* —H.P.Kishbaugh⟩ ⟨carp in the shadows . . . *nuzzling* for crumbs under lily pads —Amy Lowell⟩ ⟨felt a nose *nuzzling* at his shoulder —George Orwell⟩ **2 :** to poke, press, or rub against something ⟨two tugs *nuzzled* up gently to the bow . . . and began to push —Vernon Pizer⟩ **3 :** to lie close or snug **:** associate intimately **:** NESTLE ~ *vt* **:** to root, rub, or touch with or as if with the nose **:** NUDGE, PUSH, THRUST ⟨horses stopped by the fence and began *nuzzling* the snow —Ellen Glasgow⟩ ⟨*nuzzled* her face into her pillow —Maritta Wolff⟩ ⟨*nuzzling* his lips against her hair —Adria Langley⟩ ⟨*nuzzled* his shoulder blades more comfortably into the pillows —Olive H. Prouty⟩

²nuzzle \"\ *vt* -ED/-ING/-S [origin unknown] **1** *obs* **:** to bring up or train in a practice **:** NURTURE ⟨possessed with blind zeal, and *nuzzled* with superstition —Robert Burton⟩ **2** *chiefly Brit* **:** to make snug **:** nestle with **:** NURSE

NV *abbr* **1** new version **2** nonvoting

NVM *abbr* **1** Nativity of the Virgin Mary **2** nonvolatile matter

NVR *abbr* no voltage release

NW *abbr* **1** naked weight **2** net weight **3** northwest; northwestern

NWG *abbr* national wire gauge

NY *abbr* **1** navy yard **2** new year **3** no year

nya·la \'nyälə\ *n, pl* **nyalas** *or* **nyala** [Tsonga & Venda] **1 :** a harnessed antelope (*Tragelaphus angasi*) of southeastern Africa with a shaggy black mane on the male underside — called also *inyala* **2 :** a grayish chestnut rather shaggy antelope (*Tragelaphus buxtoni*) of some central eastern mountains of Africa

nyam·we·zi \nyäm'wāzē\ *n, pl* **nyamwezi** *or* **nyamwezis** *usu cap* **1 :** a Bantu-speaking people of the Unyamwezi region of western Tanganyika comprising one of the two largest communities of the territory **2 :** a Bantu language of the Nyamwezi people

nyan·ja \'nyanjə\ *n, pl* **nyanja** *or* **nyanjas** *usu cap* **1 a :** a people of Nyasaland who live chiefly around Lake Nyasa, the lower shores of the Shire river, and Lake Shirwa **b :** a member of such people **2 :** a Bantu language of the Nyanja people

nyan·ko·le \nyäŋ'kōlā\ *n, pl* **nyankole** *or* **nyankoles** *usu cap* **1 :** the Bantu-speaking peoples of the kingdom of Ankole in Uganda presumed to be cognate with the Nyoro and other neighboring peoples **2 :** a Bantu language of the Nyankole peoples

¹ny·asa \(')nī¦asə, nē'a-, 'nya-\ *adj, usu cap* [fr. *Nyasa*land, southeastern Africa] **1 :** of, relating to, or characteristic of Nyasaland ⟨*Nyasa* Africans⟩ ⟨*Nyasa* Europeans⟩ **2 :** of, relating to, or characteristic of the people of Nyasaland

²nyasa \"\ *n* -S *cap* [fr. *Nyasa*land, southeastern Africa] **:** a native or inhabitant of Nyasaland

ny·asa·land·er \-ə,landə(r)\ *n* -S *usu cap* [*Nyasaland,* southeastern Africa + E *-er*] **:** NYASA

nyaya \'nyäyə\ *n* -S *usu cap* [Skt *nyāya* rule, model, maxim, logic, fr. *ni* down, back (i.e., to an original model) + *eti* he goes — more at NETHER, ISSUE] **:** an orthodox philosophical system in Hinduism dealing primarily with logic and epistemological analysis

nych·them·er·al *also* **nyc·them·er·al** \(')nik¦them(ə)rəl\ *adj* [*nychthemeron, nycthemeron* + *-al*] **:** of or relating to a nychthemeron

nych·them·er·on *also* **nyc·them·er·on** \=ˈ=mə,rän\ *n, pl* **nychthem·era** \-m(ə)rə\ *or* **nychthemerons** [Gk *nychthēmeron,* fr. *nykt-, nyx* night + *-hēmeron* (fr. *hēmera* day) — more at NIGHT, HEMERA] **:** a full period of a night and a day

nyct- *or* **nycti-** *or* **nycto-** *comb form* [NL, fr. L, fr. Gk *nykt-, nykti-, nykto-,* fr. *nykt-, nyx* night — more at NIGHT] **:** night ⟨*Nyct*anthes⟩ ⟨*nycti*tropic⟩ ⟨*nycto*phobia⟩

nyc·ta·gi·na·ce·ae \,niktəjə'nāsē,ē\ *n pl, cap* [NL, fr. *Nyctagin-, Nyctago,* type genus (obs. syn. of *Mirabilis*) (fr. *nyct-* + *-agin-, -ago* — as in *Plantagin-, Plantago* —) + *-aceae*] **:** a family of chiefly American herbs and rarely shrubs or trees (order Caryophyllales) having apetalous flowers with an involucre simulating a calyx and fruit enclosed by the persistent base of the perianth — **nyc·ta·gi·na·ceous** \¦===¦nāshəs\ *adj*

nyc·ta·lope \'niktə,lōp\ *n* -S [MF, fr. Gk *nyktalōp-, nyktalōps*] **:** one affected with nyctalopia

nyc·ta·lo·pia \,==ˈlōpēə\ *n* -S [NL, fr. ML, fr. L *nyctalops* unable to see at twilight (fr. Gk *nyktalōp-, nyktalōps,* fr. *nykt-* nyct- + *alaos* blind + *-ōp-, ōps* eye) + *-ia* -y — more at EYE] **1 :** a defect of vision characterized by reduced visual capacity in faint light or at night — called also *night blindness* **2 :** HEMERALOPIA — **nyc·ta·lop·ic** \¦==¦läpik\ *adj*

nyc·tea \'niktēə\ *n, cap* [NL, fr. *nyct-* + L *-ea* (neut. pl. suffix)] **:** a genus of birds (family Strigidae) consisting of the snowy owl

nyc·tem·era \nik'tem(ə)rə\ *n, cap* [NL, fr. Gk *nyktēmeron, nychthēmeron* night and day; prob. fr. the black-and-white color of the moths] **:** a genus of Australian and New Zealand black-and-white moths — see MAGPIE MOTH b

nyc·te·reu·tes \,niktə'rüd·ēz\ *n, cap* [NL, fr. Gk *nyktereutēs* one who hunts or fishes by night, fr. *nykt-* nyct- + *ereutēs* collector, exactor, fr. *ereuein* to search, investigate, ask; akin to ON *raun* attempt, examination, *reyna* to test, experience] **:** a genus of mammals (family Canidae) consisting of the raccoon dogs

¹nyc·te·ribi·id \¦niktə¦ribēəd\ *adj* [NL *Nycteribiidae*] **:** of or relating to the Nycteribiidae

²nycteribiid \"\ *n* -S [NL *Nycteribiidae*] **:** an insect of the family Nycteribiidae

nyc·te·ri·bi·i·dae \,niktərə'bīə,dē\ *n pl, cap* [NL, fr. *Nycteribia,* type genus (fr. Gk *nykteris* bat + NL *-bia*) + *-idae*] **:** a family consisting of the bat flies

¹nyc·ter·is \'niktərəs\ *n, cap* [NL, fr. Gk *nykteris* bat, fr. *nykt-, nyx* night — more at NIGHT] **:** a genus (the type of the family Nycteridae) of African and Asiatic bats comprising the hollow-faced bats

²nycteris \"\ [NL, fr. Gk *nykteris* bat] *syn of* LASIURUS

-nycteris \"\ *n comb form* [NL, fr. *Nycteris*] **:** bat — in generic names

nycthemeral *var of* NYCHTHEMERAL

nycthemeron *var of* NYCHTHEMERON

nycti- — see NYCT-

nyc·tic·o·rax \nik'tikə,raks\ *n, cap* [NL, fr. Gk *nyktikorax* long-eared owl, fr. *nykt-* nyct- + *korax* raven — more at RAVEN] **:** a genus of herons consisting of the typical night herons

nyc·tim·e·ne \nik'timənē\ *n, cap* [NL, fr. L *Nyctimene,* Lesbian king's daughter who was transformed into an owl, fr. Gk *Nyktimenē*] **:** a genus of East Indian fruit bats — see HARPY BAT 1

nyc·ti·nas·tic \¦niktə¦nastik\ *adj* **:** of, relating to, or caused by nyctinasty — **nyctinastically** *adv*

nyc·ti·nas·ty \'==,nastē\ *n* -ES [ISV *nyct-* + *-nasty;* prob. orig. formed as G *nyktinastie*] **:** a nastic movement (as the opening and closing of some flowers) that is associated with diurnal changes of temperature or light intensity

nyc·ti·pelagic \¦niktə+\ *adj* [ISV *nyct-* + *pelagic*] **:** bathypelagic and appearing at the surface only at night ⟨~ fauna⟩

nyc·ti·pi·the·cus \,niktəpə'thēkəs, -tə'pithəkəs\ [NL, fr. *nyct-* + *-pithecus*] *syn of* AOTES

nyc·ti·trop·ic \¦niktə¦träpik\ *adj* [ISV *nyct-* + *-tropic*] **:** exhibiting nyctitropism

nyc·tit·ro·pism \nik'ti·trə,pizəm\ *n* -S [ISV *nyct-* + *-tropism*] **:** a sleep movement in plants characterized by response to a stimulus that is greatest or exclusively from one direction — compare NYCTINASTY

nycto- — see NYCT-

nyc·turia \nik'türēə, -k·'tyü-\ *n* -S [NL, fr. *nyct-* + *-uria*] **:** NOCTURIA

NYD *abbr, often not cap* not yet diagnosed

nye \'nī\ *n* -S [ME *neye, nye,* fr. MF *nyee, niee* brood, flock, fr. OF, fr. *ni* nest, fr. L *nidus* — more at NEST] *chiefly Brit* **:** a brood or flock of pheasants

ny·lon \'nī,län\ *n* -S *often attrib* [coined word] **1 :** any of numerous synthetic materials consisting of polyamides that are made from a dicarboxylic acid (as adipic acid or sebacic acid) and a diamine (as hexamethylenediamine) or from an omega-amino acid or its lactam (as caprolactam), that can be formed from a melt or solution into fibers, filaments, bristles, or sheets (as by extrusion through spinnerets and drawing or by casting), that are characterized when cold-drawn by toughness, elasticity, and strength, and that are used chiefly in making yarn, fabrics, cordage, resins, and plastics (as for molded products requiring high resistance to wear, heat, or chemicals) ⟨gears made of ~⟩ ⟨~ rope⟩ ⟨~ cord tires⟩ **2 a :** a quick-drying fiber made from nylon in filament and staple form and often blended with other fibers in fabrics ⟨~ velvet⟩ **b :** yarn or fabric made from nylon ⟨~ hosiery⟩ ⟨~ tricot⟩ **3 a :** an article made of nylon fibers **b nylons** *pl* **:** stockings made of nylon

ny·loned \-nd\ *adj* **:** wearing nylon stockings ⟨crossing her ~ legs —William Sansom⟩

nylon salt *n* **:** a white crystalline salt made by mixing dicarboxylic acid and the diamine in the first step of nylon manufacture

nymph \'nim(p)f\ *n, pl* **nymphs** \-m(p)fs, -mps\ [ME *nimphe,* fr. MF, nymph, fr. L *nympha* bride, nymph, fr. Gk *nymphē* — more at NUPTIAL] **1** *Greek & Roman mythol* **:** one of the minor divinities of nature that are represented as beautiful maidens dwelling in the mountains, forests, meadows, and waters — compare NAIAD, NEREID, OCEANID, OREAD, WOOD NYMPH 1 ⟨she fled as if she were a startled ~ —E.A.Peeples⟩ **2 a :** GIRL **b :** a woman of loose morals **3 a :** any of various hemimetabolic insects in an immature stage: as (1) **:** a late larva (as of a true bug) in which wing pads and rudiments of the genitalia are present; *broadly* **:** any insect larva that differs chiefly in size and degree of differentiation from the imago (2) **:** NAIAD 2 **b :** a mite or tick in the first 8-legged form that immediately follows the last larval molt **c :** a nymphal stage in the life cycle of an insect or acarid **4 :** NYMPH PINK **5 :** an artificial fly of a type made in imitation of the larval stage of the Ephemeridae

nymph- *or* **nympho-** *also* **nymphi-** *comb form* [F *nymph-,* fr. L, fr. Gk, fr. *nymphē*] **1 :** nymph ⟨*nympho*lepsy⟩ **2 :** nymphae ⟨*nympho*tomy⟩ ⟨*nymph*itis⟩ **3 :** nymphaea ⟨*nympho*ides⟩ **4 :** nympha ⟨*nympho*sis⟩

nym·pha \'nim(p)fə\ *n, pl* **nym·phae** \-,fē\ [L — more at NYMPH] **1 :** NYMPH 3 **2** *nymphae pl* [NL, fr. L, pl. of *nympha* nymph] **:** LABIA MINORA **3** [NL, fr. L *nymphae* labia minora] **:** one of the thickened marginal processes behind the beak of many bivalves where the ligament is attached

¹nym·phaea \nim'fēə\ *n* [NL, fr. L, water lily, fr. Gk *nymphaia;* akin to Gk *nymphē* bride, nymph] **1** *cap* **:** the type genus of the family Nymphaeaceae including numerous typical water lilies with sometimes fragrant flowers that have four green sepals and numerous petals which are as large as the sepals in the outer whorls and diminish centrally to the size and appearance of stamens and occur in white, pink to red, blue, and yellow in various members of the genus **2** -S **:** any plant of the genus *Nymphaea*

²nymphaea \"\ [NL, fr. L, water lily] *syn of* NUPHAR

nym·phae·a·ceae \,nim(p)fē'āsē,ē\ *n pl, cap* [NL, fr. *Nymphaea,* type genus + *-aceae*] **:** a family of aquatic plants (order Ranales) having long-stalked often peltate leaves, large flowers with 3 to 5 sepals and numerous petals and stamens, and polycarpellary indehiscent fruit and comprising the water lilies — see NELUMBO, NUPHAR, NYMPHAEA, VICTORIA — **nym·phae·a·ceous** \¦==¦āshəs\ *adj*

nym·phae·um *also* **nym·phe·um** \nim'fēəm\ *n, pl* **nym·phaea** \-ēə\ [F *nymphaeum,* fr. L, lit., shrine of nymphs, fr. Gk *nymphaion,* fr. *nymphē* nymph] **:** a Roman building or room containing a fountain, adorned with plants and sculpture, and serving as a place of rest

nymph·al \'nim(p)fəl\ *adj* [F, fr. MF, fr. *nymphe* nymph + *-al*] **:** of, relating to, or being a nymph **:** consisting of nymphs ⟨during the ~ period the mite may molt one or more times —Nathan Banks⟩ ⟨the first ephemerids . . . crack their ~ shucks —Richard Salmon⟩ ⟨will result in lower ~ populations —*Biol. Abstracts*⟩

¹nym·pha·lid \nim'faləd, -fāl-, -fäl-\ *adj* [NL *Nymphalidae*] **:** of or relating to the Nymphalidae

²nymphalid \"\ *n* -S **:** a butterfly of the family Nymphalidae

nym·phal·i·dae \nim'falə,dē\ *n pl, cap* [NL, fr. *Nymphalis,* type genus + *-idae*] **:** a widely distributed family of butterflies mostly of medium or large size and distinguished by having the forelegs much reduced in size in both sexes so that they are useless in walking and are carried folded on the breast, usu. absent tarsal claws, larvae that are usu. spiny or provided with fleshy processes, and pupae that are usu. of angular outline and hang suspended by the tip of the tail — see FOUR-FOOTED BUTTERFLY

nym·pha·lis \nim'faləs, -fāl-, -fäl-\ *n, cap* [NL, fr. L, nymphal, fr. *nympha* nymph + *-alis* -al — more at NYMPH] **:** a widely distributed genus of nymphalid butterflies

nym·phe·an \'nim(p)fēən, nim'f-\ *adj* [*nymph* + *-an*] **:** of or appropriate to nymphs **:** inhabited by nymphs ⟨~ grace and beauty —G.W.Cable⟩

nymph·et \(')nim¦fet, 'nim(p)fət\ *n* -S [MF *nymphette,* fr. *nymphe* nymph + *-ette* -et — more at NYMPH] **1 :** a young nymph ⟨the ~s sporting there —Michael Drayton⟩ **2 :** a sexually precocious girl **:** a loose young woman

nymph·id \-fəd\ *n* -S [*nymph* + *-id,* n. suffix] **:** NYMPH 3

nym·phi·dae \'nim(p)fə,dē\ *n pl, cap* [NL, fr. *Nymphes,* type genus (fr. L *nympha* nymph) + *-idae*] **:** a small family of primitive neuropterous insects related to the ant lions and confined to the Australian region

nym·phip·a·ra \nim'fipərə\ [NL, fr. *nymph-* + *-para* (fr. L, neut. pl. of *-parus* -parous)] *syn of* PUPIPARA

nymph·ish \'nim(p)fish\ *adj* **:** of, relating to, or resembling a nymph

nymphlike \'=,=\ *adj* **:** resembling a nymph (as in grace or beauty)

nym·pho \'nim(p)(,)fō\ *n* -S [by shortening] **:** NYMPHOMANIAC

nympho- — see NYMPH-

nym·phoi·des \nim'fȯidēz\ *n, cap* [NL, fr. *nymph-* + L *-oides* -oid] **:** a genus of aquatic herbs (family Menyanthaceae) mostly of tropical regions and having floating round or cordate leaves and small yellow or white umbellate flowers — see FLOATING HEART

nym·pho·lep·sy \'nim(p)fə,lepsē\ *n* -ES [*nymph-* + *-lepsy*] **1 :** a species of demoniac enthusiasm supposed by the ancients to seize one possessed or bewitched by a nymph **2 :** a frenzy of emotion (as for some unattainable ideal)

¹nym·pho·lept \-pt\ *n* -S [Gk *nympholēptos* caught by nymphs, raptured, frenzied, fr. *nymphē* nymph + *lēptos,* verbal of *lambanein* to take, seize — more at NUPTIAL, LATCH] **:** one seized with nympholepsy ⟨the ~s of old —Augustine Birrell⟩

²nympholept \"\ *adj* **:** NYMPHOLEPTIC

nym·pho·lep·tic \¦==¦leptik\ *adj* [Gk *nympholēptos* + E *-ic*] **:** of, relating to, or affected with nympholepsy

nym·pho·ma·nia \,nim(p)fə'mānēə\ *n* [NL, fr. *nymph-* + LL *mania*] **:** excessive desire by a female for sexual activity usu. based on feelings of personal inadequacy — called also *uteromania;* compare SATYRIASIS

¹nym·pho·ma·ni·ac \-ē,ak\ *n* **:** one affected by nymphomania

²nymphomaniac \¦==¦==,=\ *also* **nym·pho·ma·ni·a·cal** \¦nim(p)fōmə¦nīəkəl\ *or* **nym·pho·man·ic** \¦nim(p)fə¦manik\ *adj* [*nymphomaniac* fr. *nymphomaniac,* n.; *nymphomaniacal* fr. ¹*nymphomaniac* + *-al; nymphomanic* fr. *nymphomania* + *-ic*] **:** of, affected with, or characterized by nymphomania

nym·pho·sis \nim'fōsəs\ *n, pl* **nym·pho·ses** \-ō,sēz\ [NL, fr. *nymph-* + *-osis*] **:** the change of an insect into a nymph

nymph pink *n* **:** a moderate to strong pink that is bluer and darker than hermosa pink or peachblossom (sense 1)

nymphs *pl of* NYMPH

nymss \'nim(p)s\ *n* -ES [native name in Egypt] **:** an ichneumon (*Herpestes ichneumon*)

ny·o·ro \'nyō(,)rō\ *n, pl* **nyoro** *or* **nyoros** *usu cap* **1 :** a Bantu-speaking people of Uganda constituting a socially and economically complex society organized as a kingdom and presumed to be cognate with the Nyankole and other neighboring peoples **2 :** a Bantu language of the Nyoro people

NYP *abbr* not yet published

NYR *abbr* not yet returned

ny·ro·ca \nə'rōkə\ [NL, fr. Russ *nyrok* diver (duck), fr. *nyryat* to dive; akin to Lith *nerti* to dive, thread — more at NARROW] *syn of* AYTHYA

nys·i·us \'nisēəs\ *n, cap* [NL] **:** a large and widely distributed genus of bugs (family Lygaeidae) that includes the false chinch bugs

nys·sa \'nisə\ *n, cap* [NL, perh. fr. Gk, meta, post] **:** a small genus of American and Asiatic trees (family Nyssaceae) having flowers with imbricate petals and a single or 2-cleft style — see BLACK GUM, TUPELO

nys·sa·ce·ae \nə'sāsē,ē\ *n pl, cap* [NL, fr. *Nyssa* + *-aceae*] **:** a family of dicotyledonous trees (order Myrtales) containing the sour gums and having alternate leaves without stipules, inconspicuous greenish flowers in small heads, a 1- or 2-locular ovary, and the fruit a drupe

nys·tag·mic \nə'stagmik\ *adj* [ISV *nystagm-* (fr. NL *nystagmus*) + *-ic*] **:** of, relating to, characterized by, or constituting nystagmus

nys·tag·moid \-g,mȯid\ *adj* [NL *nystagmus* + E *-oid*] **:** resembling that which is characteristic of nystagmus ⟨the eyes may show rapid lateral ~ movements —W.S.Weidorn⟩

nys·tag·mus \-gməs\ *n* -ES [NL, fr. Gk *nystagmos* drowsiness; akin to Gk *nystazein* to doze, Lith *snusti* to doze off and perh. to Gk *nythos* dark — more at NUANCE] **:** a rapid involuntary oscillation of the eyeballs occurring normally with dizziness during and after bodily rotation or abnormally after injuries (as to the cerebellum or the vestibule of the ear)

nys·ta·tin \'nistəd·ən\ *n* -S [*New York State,* where it was developed + E *-in*] **:** a pale yellow crystalline antibiotic isolated from cultures of a soil actinomycete (*Streptomyces noursei*) that is active against fungi and is useful esp. in the treatment of moniliasis (as of the mouth, skin, or intestines)

ny·tril \'nī·trəl\ *n* -S [*vinylidene dinitrile*] **:** a synthetic fiber composed chiefly of a long-chain polymer of vinylidene dinitrile

-nyx·is \'niksəs\ *n comb form, pl* **-nyx·es** \-k,sēz\ [NL, fr. Gk *nyxis* act of pricking, of stabbing; akin to Gk *nyssein, nyttein* to prick, sting — more at NUMEN] **:** puncture ⟨pyro*nyxis*⟩ ⟨sclero*nyxis*⟩

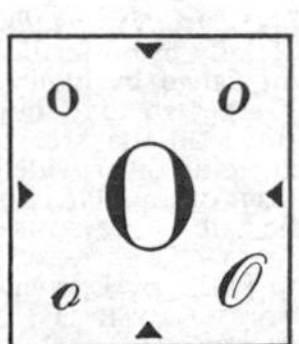

¹o \'ō\ *n, pl* **o's** *or* **os** \'ōz\ *often cap, often attrib* **1 a :** the 15th letter of the English alphabet **b :** an instance of this letter printed, written, or otherwise represented **c :** a speech counterpart of orthographic *o* (as long *o* in *code,* short *o* in *cod,* or *o* in *cord*) **2 :** a printer's type, a stamp, or some other instrument for reproducing the letter *o* **3 :** someone or something arbitrarily or conveniently designated *o* esp. as the 14th or when j is used for the 10th the 15th in order or class **4 :** something having the shape of the capital letter O ⟨made an enthusiastic *O* with his thumb and forefinger —John Dos Passos⟩ ⟨the Roman girl's eyes widened, her mouth formed an *O* —F.V.W.Mason⟩; *esp* **:** ZERO ⟨wrote a couple of *O's*⟩

²o *usu cap, var of* OH

³o *abbr, often cap* **1** object **2** oblast **3** observation; observer **4** occident; occidental **5** ocean **6** [L *octarius*] pint **7** October **8** [L *oculus*] eye **9** off **10** office; officer **11** official **12** ohm **13** oil **14** old **15** only **16** opening **17** operation **18** [L *optimus*] best **19** order **20** [L *ordinis*] of the order of **21** [L *ordo*] order **22** ordnance **23** oriental **24** original **25** [L *os*] bone **26** out **27** outfield **28** outlet **29** over **30** overcast **31** owner

⁴o *symbol, cap* **1** octavo **2** oxygen

¹o- *or* **oo-** *comb form* [Gk *ōi-, ōio-*, fr. *ōion* egg — more at EGG] **:** egg ⟨*o*idium⟩ ⟨*oo*logy⟩; *specif* **:** ovum ⟨*oo*genesis⟩ ⟨*oo*gonium⟩

²o- *abbr* ortho-

¹-o \(,)ō\ *n suffix* -s [perh. fr. ¹*oh*] **:** one that is or that constitutes or that has the qualities of or that is in some way associated with ⟨boy*o*⟩ ⟨buck*o*⟩ — chiefly in informal or nonstandard speech; often in place of the missing element in a shortened word ⟨comp*o*⟩ ⟨comb*o*⟩; in writing sometimes attached to its base by a hyphen ⟨daddy-*o*⟩ or sometimes attached to the reduplicated final consonant of its base ⟨kidd*o*⟩

²-o \"\ *interj suffix* [prob. fr. ¹*oh*] — in interjections formed from other parts of speech ⟨cheeri*o*⟩ ⟨right*o*⟩, esp. imitative words ⟨smack*o*⟩ ⟨bang*o*⟩

-o- [ME, fr. OF, fr. L, fr. Gk, thematic vowel of many nouns and adjectives in combination] — used as a connective vowel orig. to join two elements of Greek origin and now also to join two elements of Latin or other origin and being either identical with ⟨chrys*o*prase⟩ or analogous to ⟨Angl*o*-Saxon⟩ an original Greek stem vowel or simply inserted ⟨jazz*o*phile⟩ ⟨dramatic*o*-musical⟩; compare -I-

o' *also* **o** \ə\ *prep* [in sense 1 fr. ME *o, o-*, alter. of *on;* in sense 2 fr. ME *o, o-*, alter. of *of*] **1** *chiefly dial* **:** ON **2 :** OF — now chiefly in dial. use except in a few set phrases (as *o'clock*)

OA *abbr* **1** on account **2** open account **3** overall

OAA *abbr* old-age assistance

oaf \'ōf\ *n* -s [of Scand origin; akin to ON *alfr* elf — more at ELF] **1** *obs* **a :** CHANGELING 2b(2) **b :** a deformed or mentally defective child **2 :** a stupid person **:** SIMPLETON, DUMBBELL, BOOB ⟨numerous readers who may not be such ~*s* as they suppose —F.L.Allen⟩ **3 :** a big clumsy slow-witted fellow **:** LOUT, LUMMOX

oaf·ish \-fish, -ēsh\ *adj* **:** having the qualities typical of an oaf **:** STUPID, LOUTISH ⟨~ remarks⟩ — **oaf·ish·ly** *adv* — **oaf·ish·ness** *n* -ES

¹oa·hu·an \ō'ähüən,-hwən\ *n* -s *cap* [*Oahu*, Hawaii + E *-an* n. suffix] **:** a native or resident of Oahu, the chief island of the state of Hawaii

²oahuan \"\ *adj, usu cap* [*Oahu*, Hawaii + E *-an*, adj. suffix] **:** of, relating to, or characteristic of Oahu or Oahuans

oak \'ōk\ *n, pl* **oaks** *or* **oak** *often attrib* [ME *ok, oke,* fr. OE *āc;* akin to OHG *eih* oak, ON *eik,* Gk *aigilōps* havergrass, Turkey oak and perh. to L *aesculus,* an oak] **1 a :** a tree or shrub of *Quercus* or the related genus *Lithocarpus* **b** (1) **:** the tough hard durable wood of an oak tree; *esp* **:** such wood (as of the white oak, red oak, bur oak, cork oak, English oak) having a distinct pattern produced by prominent medullary rays (2) **:** furniture made of this wood ⟨bought ~ for the living room⟩ **c :** the leaves of an oak used as a decoration ⟨a wreath of ~⟩ ⟨hung with ~⟩ **2 a :** any of various plants resembling oaks (as in foliage) — usu. used with a qualifying adjective or other attributive word; see POISON OAK, SILK OAK **b** *Austral* **:** CASUARINA 2 **3 :** a moderate to strong brown that is yellower and slightly darker than Vassar tan and yellower and slightly lighter than Arabian brown — called also *briar*

oak apple *n* [ME *oke appil,* fr. *oke* oak + *appil* apple; fr. its shape — more at APPLE] **:** an oak gall resulting from the presence of a larva of one of the cynipid wasps (esp. *Amphibolips concluentus* or *Andricus californicus*)

oak beauty *n* **:** a British moth (*Amphidasis prodomaria*) of the family Geometridae whose larva feeds on the oak

oak blight *n* **:** a black plant louse (*Anoecia guerci*) that lives on the small branches of oak trees and on the dogwood

oak borer *n* **:** any of several cerambycid beetles with larvae that excavate galleries in the heartwood of oak and hickory

oak brown *n* **:** a moderate brown that is yellower, stronger, and slightly lighter than bay, yellower and stronger than auburn, and stronger and slightly yellower than chestnut brown

oak chestnut *n* **:** a tree of the genus *Castanopsis*

oak·en \'ōkən\ *adj* [ME *oken,* fr. *ok* oak + *-en*] **1 a :** made of oak wood ⟨an ~ door⟩ ⟨~ paneling⟩ **b** *archaic* **:** made of oak leaves or oak twigs ⟨around her head an ~ wreath was seen —William Falconer⟩ **2** *archaic* **:** belonging to or coming from an oak tree ⟨a fall of ~ leaves —Richmond Lattimore⟩ **3** *archaic* **:** consisting of oak trees ⟨with breezes from our ~ glades —Alfred Tennyson⟩

oakenshaw \'ˌ=ˌ=\ *n* [*oaken* + *shaw*] **:** an oak grove ⟨when winds were in the ~*s* —A.E.Housman⟩

oak family *n* **:** FAGACEAE

oak fern *n* [trans. of L *dryopteris*] **:** a widely distributed fern (*Thelypteris dryopteris*) of the family Polypodiaceae chiefly of damp acid woodlands of boreal and alpine parts of the northern hemisphere that has a slender subterraneous rhizome and delicate solitary triangular fronds

oak fungus *n* **:** SHOESTRING FUNGUS

oak gall *n* **:** a gall on oak caused by the presence of insect larvae esp. of the family Cynipidae

oak green *n* **:** AUCUBA GREEN

oakie *usu cap, var of* OKIE

oak lace bug *n* **:** a bug (*Corythucha arcuata*) of the family Tingidae that feeds on No. American oaks

oak·land \'ōklənd\ *adj, usu cap* [fr. *Oakland,* Calif.] **:** of or from the city of Oakland, Calif. ⟨*Oakland* canneries⟩ **:** of the kind or style prevalent in Oakland

oak·land·er \-də(r)\ *n* -s *cap* [*Oakland* + E *-er*] **:** a native or resident of Oakland, Calif.

oakleaf brown \'ˌ=ˌ=-\ *n* **:** FEUILLE MORTE

oak leaf miner *n* **:** a larva of any of several insects that tunnels in oak leaves

oak leather *n* **1 :** a mycelial mat formed in decaying oak wood **2** *or* **oak-tanned leather** \'ˌ=ˌ=-\ **:** leather tanned with tannin derived from oak bark alone or from oak bark and other materials

oak-leaved goosefoot *also* **oak leaf goosefoot** *n* **:** an annual European goosefoot (*Chenopodium glaucum*) that has leaves farinose beneath with inflated white hairs and greenish flowers in axillary or terminal spikes and that is common as a weed in the northern part of the U.S. and Canada

oak·ling \'ōkliŋ, -lēŋ\ *n* -s [*oak* + *-ling*] **:** a young or small oak tree

oak looper *n* **:** a larva of a geometrid moth (*Lambdina somniaria*)

oakmoss \'ˌ=ˌ=\ *n* **:** any of several lichens that grow on oak trees and yield a resin used in perfumery

oak of cap·pa·do·cia \-ˌkapə'dōsh(ē)ə\ *usu cap C* [*cappadocia* fr. *Cappadocia,* ancient country in extreme eastern Asia Minor] **:** SEA RAGWEED

oak of jerusalem *or* **oak of paradise** *usu cap J&P* **:** JERUSALEM OAK

oak opening *n* **:** an open usu. even-aged stand of white oak or bur oak in a turf of native grasses forming a characteristic natural plant community adjoining or interspersed by prairie in much of Illinois and southern Wisconsin prior to the establishment of settlements and agriculture

oak pruner *or* **oak twig pruner** *n* **:** a twig pruner (*Hypermallus villosus*) that is sometimes abundant on oak

oak root fungus *n* **:** SHOESTRING FUNGUS

oak scale *n* **:** any of several scales attacking oaks

oaktag \'ˌ=ˌ=\ *n* **:** TAGBOARD

oak toad *n* **:** a small toad (*Bufo quercicus*) of Georgia and neighboring coastal states

oa·kum \'ōkəm\ *n* -s [ME *okum,* fr. OE *ācumba* hurds, tow, lit., off-combings, fr. *ā-* (separative and perfective prefix) + *-cumba* (akin to OE *camb* comb) — more at ABEAR, COMB] **:** loosely twisted fiber usu. of hemp or jute impregnated with tar or with a tar derivative (as creosote or asphalt) and used in caulking seams (as of the wood hulls and decks of ships) and in packing joints (as of pipes, caissons)

oak wilt *n* **:** a destructive disease of oak trees caused by a fungus (*Chalara quercina*) characterized by wilting and by yellow and red discoloration of the foliage that begins at the top or at the branch extremities and usu. progresses downward and inward and that is often accompanied or followed by defoliation

oakwood \'ˌ=ˌ=\ *n* **:** a moderate brown that is lighter, stronger, and slightly yellower than auburn, lighter, stronger, and slightly redder than chestnut brown, and yellower and slightly stronger than toast brown

oak worm *n* **:** any of several lepidopterous insect larvae that feed on oak leaves — usu. used with a qualifying term ⟨red-humped *oak worm*⟩

oaky \'ōkē\ *adj* -ER/-EST [*oak* + *-y,* adj. suffix] **:** of, relating to, or having the characteristics of oak trees

oam \'ōm\ *n* -s [perh. fr. (assumed) ME *oom;* akin to ON *eimr* steam, vapor — more at EMBER] *Scot* **:** warm vaporous air

O and R *abbr* ocean and rail

o antigen \'ō-\ *n, usu cap O* [G, fr. *ohne hauch antigen,* fr. *ohne hauch* without breath + *antigen*] **:** SOMATIC ANTIGEN

o antiphon *n, usu cap O&A* [²*o;* fr. the fact that it opens with O (as O Adonai)] **:** GREAT ANTIPHON

OAP *abbr* old-age pension

¹oar \'ō(ə)r, 'ȯ(ə)r, 'ōə, 'ȯə\ *n* -s [ME *oor, or,* fr. OE *ār;* akin to ON *ār* oar] **1 a :** a long rather heavy wooden pole with a broad fairly flat blade at one end that is used for propelling and steering or stopping a boat and that is usu. held in place in an oarlock at the side of a boat or sometimes at the stern (as of a gondola) so that the shorter usu. narrower end can be readily grasped and manipulated by a rower in the boat in such a way that the blade can be dipped into and pulled against and raised from the water or otherwise manipulated so as to propel or steer or stop the boat **b** *archaic* **:** something (as an arm, the wing of a bird) used for propulsion through water or air and suggestive in its action of an oar **2 a** *archaic* **:** ROWBOAT — usu. used in pl. and often with *pair* ⟨went into a pair of ~*s* that was ready —Edward Hyde⟩ **b** *or* **oars** *pl but sing in constr* **:** OARSMAN **c oars** *pl but sing or pl in constr* **:** the position of holding a boat's oars horizontal and at right angles with the boat's sides and with the blade ends parallel with the water — often used as a command to prepare to row or to rest from rowing **3 :** a stick or pole or paddle used for stirring something (as mash) — **lay on one's oars** *or* **lay on the oars :** to lie on one's oars — **lie on one's oars** *or* **lie on the oars** *or* **rest on one's oars** *or* **rest on the oars 1 :** to take the position of oars **2 :** to cease effort **:** take it easy **:** REST, RELAX ⟨had not been content entirely to *rest on his oars* during that ten days —F.W.Crofts⟩ — **put one's oar in** *also* **shove one's oar in** *or* **stick one's oar in :** to offer usu. unwanted advice or assistance **:** take part in another's affairs usu. without being asked or wanted **:** be meddlesome **:** INTERFERE ⟨had to *put their oar in* all the time —Robert Westerby⟩ ⟨was trying to *stick his oar in* —J.G.Cozzens⟩ ⟨wasn't afraid to *shove in his oar* now and again —Elizabeth Goudge⟩

²oar \"\ *vb* -ED/-ING/-S *vt* **1 :** to propel with or as if with oars **:** ROW ⟨~*ed* the boat forward⟩ **2** *archaic* **:** to manipulate (as one's arm) like an oar ~ *vi* **:** to go along by or as if by using oars ⟨~*ing* slowly over the water⟩ ⟨a lazy troupe of rooks flapped over the sky, cawing as they ~*ed* along —Richard Church⟩

oar·age \-rij, -rēj\ *n* -s [¹*oar* + *-age*] **1** *archaic* **:** the action of oaring **2** *archaic* **a :** rowing equipment **:** oars and oar fittings **b :** something resembling oars in appearance or movement ⟨the ~ of the wings of a single great bird —C.E.Montague⟩

oared shrew *n* [so called fr. its fringed feet] **:** the European water shrew

oar feather *n* **:** REMEX

oarfish \'ˌ=ˌ=\ *n* **1 :** any of several fishes of the genus *Regalecus* that have narrow soft delicate bodies ranging from 20 to 30 feet in length, a dorsal fin running the entire length of the body with red-tipped anterior rays rising above the head, and ventral fins reduced to long filaments, that lack a caudal fin, and that are found off the coasts of Europe and Asia and the Pacific coast of America **2 :** a fish of the family Lophotidae that resembles the oarfish

oar-footed \'ˌ=ˌ=ˌ=\ *adj* **:** having feet adapted for swimming

oarlock \'ˌ=ˌ=\ *n* [ME *orlok,* fr. OE *ārloc,* fr. *ār* oar + *loc* lock — more at LOCK] **:** a usu. U-shaped device or arrangement for supporting and holding an oar in place **:** ROWLOCK: as **a :** a metal fork or stirrup pivoted in the gunwale or on an outrigger **b :** a single pin swiveling in the gunwale or on an outrigger and passing through a hole in the oar or having the oar attached (as by a grommet) to it **c :** a pair of pins set vertically in the gunwale or on an outrigger **d :** a U-shaped notch in the gunwale

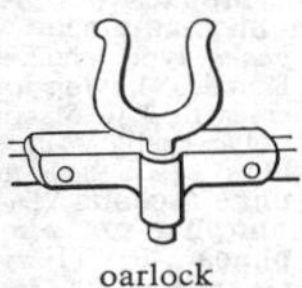

oarlock

oars·man \'ō(ə)rzmən, 'ȯ(ə)rz-, 'ōəz-,'ȯəz-\ *also* **oar·man** \'=mən\ *n, pl* **oarsmen** *also* **oarmen** [*oarsman* fr. *oar's* (gen. of ¹*oar*) + *man*] **:** one that rows **:** ROWER; *esp* **:** one that is skilled in rowing

oars·man·ship \-ˌship\ *n* **:** skill in rowing

oarweed \'ˌ=ˌ=\ *n* [E dial. *oare, ore* seaweed (fr. ME *ware,* fr. OE *wār*) + E *weed;* akin to OE *wīr* myrtle, MD *wier* seaweed, and prob. to ON *visk* wisp — more at WHISK] **:** any of several large brown algae esp. of the genus *Laminaria* including some used as a source of iodine and other chemicals, as fertilizer, and sometimes as food

oary \'ōrē, 'ȯrē, -ri\ *adj* [¹*oar* + *-y*] **1** *archaic* **a :** resembling or having the qualities or function of oars **b :** widely outspread ⟨~ wings⟩ **2** *archaic* **:** equipped with oars

OAS *abbr* on active service

oa·sal \(')ō¦āsəl\ *or* **oa·se·an** \-sēən\ *adj* [*oasis* + *-al* or *-an*] **:** OASITIC

OASI *abbr* old-age and survivors insurance

oa·sis \ō'āsəs, 'ōəsəs\ *n, pl* **oa·ses** \-ˌsēz\ [LL, fertile land in the Libyan desert, fr. Gk, prob. of Hamitic origin; akin to Coptic *wahe*] **1 :** a small isolated fertile area (as in the midst of a sandy desert) that is surrounded by general aridity or barrenness and that is typically marked by trees or other greenery and that has a water supply furnished by local springs or wells or by local seepage or by water flowing from a distant source either naturally or through artificial irrigation **2 :** something (as a place of refuge or a time of relaxation) existing or occurring in an isolated way (as in the midst of surrounding dreariness or monotony or tiresomeness) and affording welcome refreshment or relief or contrast ⟨an ~ of calm in a troubled and turbulent universe —Douglas MacArthur⟩ ⟨an ~ of prosperity in an increasingly impoverished world —P.G.Worsthorne⟩ ⟨a lovely intellectual ~ —Green Peyton⟩ **3 :** any of numerous small dark roundish spots on the planet Mars at the intersection of its canals

oa·sit·ic \¦ōə¦sid·ik\ *adj* [*oasis* + *-itic*] **:** of, relating to, or resembling an oasis ⟨the conditions observed in ~ areas⟩

oast \'ōst\ *or* **oasthouse** \'ˌ=ˌ=\ *n* -s [*oast* fr. ME *ost,* fr. OE *āst;* akin to MD *eest, est* kiln, L *aestus* heat, *aestas* summer — more at EDIFY] **:** a kiln or group of kilns often of a distinctive conical shape and used for drying hops, malt, or tobacco

¹oat \'ōt, *usu* ōd.+V\ *n* -s *often attrib* [ME *ote,* fr. OE *āte*] **1 a** (1) **:** a plant of the genus *Avena; esp* **:** a cereal grass (*Avena sativa*) that is an important grain crop in temperate regions through its wide cultivation as a source of food for both human beings and animals (2) *usu* **oats** *pl but sing or pl in constr* **:** a crop of oats ⟨~*s* can be grown further north than wheat⟩; *also* **:** a field or plot of growing oats ⟨the ~*s* are doing well⟩ **b** *usu* **oats** *pl but sing or pl in constr* **:** oat seed; *esp* **:** the seed of the cultivated oat plant **2** *archaic* **:** a crude reed instrument made of an oat straw **:** an oaten pipe

²oat \"\ *vt* -ED/-ING/-S *archaic* **:** to feed (a horse) with oats

oatcake \'ˌ=ˌ=\ *n* **:** a thin flat cake made of oatmeal mixed with water, milk, or buttermilk and cooked on a griddle or in an oven

-o·ate \ə,wāt, *usu* -ād.+V\ *n suffix* -s [-*oic* + *-ate*] **:** salt or ester of a carboxylic acid with a name ending in *-oic* ⟨capro*ate*⟩ ⟨octan*oate*⟩

oat·en \'ōtᵊn\ *adj* [ME *oten,* fr. *ote* + *-en*] **1 :** made of oat grain or of oatmeal ⟨~ bread⟩ **2 :** made of oat straw or of an oat stem ⟨a shepherd playing on an ~ pipe⟩ ⟨~ thatch⟩ **3 :** of or relating to oat plants ⟨~ hay⟩ ⟨~ chaff⟩

oat 1a (1)

oat·er \'ōd·ə(r)\ *n* -s **:** HORSE OPERA

oat grass *n* **1 :** WILD OAT 1a **2 :** one of several grasses of the genera *Danthonia* and *Trisetum* **3 a** *Austral* **:** ULLA GRASS **b :** an Australian forage grass (*Anisopogon avenaceus*)

¹oath \'ōth\ *n, pl* **oaths** \-ths,-t͟hz\ [ME *ooth, oth,* fr. OE *āth;* akin to OHG *eid* oath, ON *eithr,* Goth *aiths;* all prob. fr. a prehistoric Gmc word of Celt origin; akin to MIr *ōeth* oath] **1 a** (1) **:** a solemn usu. formal calling upon God or a god to witness to the truth of what one says or to witness to the fact that one sincerely intends to do what one says (2) **:** a usu. formal affirmation made solemn by being coupled with the invocation of something viewed as sacred or of something highly revered (3) **:** a usu. formal affirmation that is in some way made solemn without such an appeal or without such an invocation **b :** something (as the truth of what one says, a promise that one makes) that is corroborated by an oath **c :** a form of expression used in taking an oath **2 a :** an irreverent or thoughtless or otherwise profane use (as in giving vent to anger, expressing ill will or annoyance, expressing surprise, corroborating a trivial statement) of the name of something viewed as sacred (as the name of God, Christ) **b :** a word or phrase identical with or derived from or in some other way involving the name of something viewed as sacred that is used in such an irreverent or thoughtless or otherwise profane way — **under oath** *or* **on oath** *also* **upon oath :** under the solemn obligation of an oath ⟨was *under oath* to tell all he knew⟩

²oath \"\ *vb* -ED/-ING/-S *archaic* **:** SWEAR

oathay \'ˌ=ˌ=\ *n, Brit* **:** unthreshed oats used as hay

oath helper *n, Old Eng law* **:** one brought into court to swear to the truth of his principal's oath in a wager of law

oath of calumny [trans. of LL *juramentum calumniae*] **:** an oath taken by a plaintiff or defendant that attests to the plaintiff's or defendant's good faith and to his conviction that there exists a good ground of action

oatmeal \'ˌ=ˌ=\ *n* [ME *ote-mele,* fr. *ote* oat + *mele* meal — more at OAT, MEAL] **1 a** (1) **:** meal made by grinding oats from which the husks have been removed (2) **:** ROLLED OATS **b :** porridge made from ground or rolled oats **2 :** a grayish yellow that is greener and paler than chamois, paler and very slightly greener than old ivory, and paler and slightly redder than crash **3 :** a fabric (as of wool, cotton) with a rough pebbled surface made with fine warp yarns and coarse filling yarns

oatmeal paper *or* **oatmeal wallpaper** *n* **:** a wallpaper that is given a coarse surface by the addition of sawdust to the fiber finish

oat nematode *n* **:** an Old World plant-parasitic nematode (*Heterodera major* or *Heterodera avenae*) that is destructive to the roots of oats, barley, and several other cereals and that has become established in parts of Canada

oat opera *n* **:** HORSE OPERA

oats *pl of* OAT, *pres 3d sing of* OAT

¹oaves \'ōvz, -vəs\ *dial Eng var of* EAVES

²oaves \'ōvz\ *archaic pl of* OAF

ob- *prefix* [ME, fr. OF, fr. L, to, toward, against, over, completely, fr. *ob* to, before, against, on account of — more at EPI-] **1 :** inward ⟨*ob*imbricate⟩ **2 :** incompletely ⟨*ob*rotund⟩ ⟨*ob*round⟩ **3 :** in reverse order ⟨*ob*diplostemonous⟩ **4 :** inverse ⟨*ob*ovate⟩ ⟨*ob*conic⟩ ⟨*ob*cordate⟩

ob *abbr* **1** [L *obiit*] he died **2** obiter **3** oblong **4** oboe **5** [L *obolus*] halfpenny **6** observation **7** obstetrical; obstetrician; obstetrics

OB *abbr* **1** opening of books **2** ordered back **3** order of battle **4** outboard **5** outward bound

oba *also* **ob·ba** \'ōbə\ *n* -s [native name in western Nigeria] **:** a ruler of any of several African peoples of western Nigeria — used as a form of address

ob·am·bu·late \ä'bambyə,lāt, ə'-\ *vi* [L *obambulatus,* past part. of *obambulare* to walk to or before, fr. *ob-* to, against, over + *ambulare* to walk — more at OB-, AMBLE] *archaic* **:** to walk about **:** WANDER

oban \'ō,ban\ *or* **obang** \-aŋ\ *n* -s [Jap *ōban,* fr. *ō-* large + *ban* size] **:** a large oval Japanese gold coin of the 16th to 19th centuries that varied in size and weight

obb *abbr* obbligato

ob·ben·ite \'äbə,nīt\ *n* -s *usu cap* [*Obbe* Philipszoon †1568 Du. religious leader + connective *-n-* + E *-ite*] **:** a member of an Anabaptist group arising in the 16th century

¹ob·bli·ga·to *also* **ob·li·ga·to** \ˌäblə'gäd.(ˌ)ō, -lē-, -ä(ˌ)tō\ *adj* [It *obbligato* (past part. of *obbligare* to obligate), fr. L *obligatus,* past part. of *obligare* to obligate — more at OBLIGATE] **:** obligatory and not to be omitted — used as a musical direction ⟨accompaniment ~⟩; distinguished from *ad libitum*

²obbligato *also* **obligato** \"\ *n, pl* **obbliga·tos** \-ōz\ *also* **obbliga·ti** \-d.(ˌ)ē, -(ˌ)tē\ **1 :** a prominent part of semi-independent melodic character accompanying a solo voice or principal melody and usu. played by a single instrument ⟨a song with violin ~⟩ **2 :** an accompaniment to something; *esp* **:** an attendant sound ⟨arrived with a flourish accompanied by an ~ of honking geese and barking dogs⟩

obcaecation *n* -s [obs. F *obcecation,* fr. MF, fr. LL *obcaecation-, obcaecatio, occaecation-, occaecatio* act of hiding, fr. L *obcaecatus, occaecatus* (past part. of *obcaecare, occaecare* to blind, fr. *ob-, oc-* toward, against, over + *caecare* to blind, fr. *caecus* blind) + *-ion-, -io* -ion — more at OB-, CECUM] *obs* **:** BLINDNESS

ob·clavate \(')äb+\ *adj* [ISV *ob-* + *clavate*] **:** inversely clavate

ob·clude \äb'klüd\ *vt* -ED/-ING/-S [alter. (influenced by *ob-*) of *occlude*] **:** to hide from view **:** OCCLUDE

ob·compressed \¦äb+\ *adj* [*ob-* + *compressed*] **:** flattened vertically or anteriorly rather than laterally

ob·conic \(')äb+\ *also* **ob·conical** \"+\ *adj* [*ob-* + *conic* or *conical*] **:** conical with the apex below or forming the point of attachment ⟨an ~ capsule⟩

ob·cordate \"+\ *adj* [*ob-* + *cordate*] *of a leaf* **:** heart-shaped with the notch apical **:** inversely cordate — compare RETUSE

ob·cuneate \"+\ *adj* [*ob-* + *cuneate*] **:** inversely cuneate

ob·deltoid \"+\ *adj* [*ob-* + *deltoid*] **:** inversely deltoid **:** triangular with downward pointing apex

ob·diplostemonous \(¦)äb+\ *adj* [prob. fr. (assumed) NL *obdiplostemonus,* fr. NL *ob-* + (assumed) NL *diplostemonus* diplostemonous — more at DIPLOSTEMONOUS] **:** having the stamens in two whorls with those of the outer whorl opposite the petals — compare DIPLOSTEMONOUS — **ob·diplostemony** \"+\ *n* -ES

obdt *abbr* obedient

ob·duce \äb'd(y)üs\ *vt* -ED/-ING/-S [L *obducere,* fr. *ob-* toward, over + *ducere* to draw, lead — more at OB-, TOW] **:** to cover with **:** draw over **:** envelop in

obduction *n* -s [L *obduction-, obductio,* fr. *obductus* (past part. of *obducere* to obduce) + *-ion-, -io* -ion] **:** an act or instance of drawing or laying something (as a covering) over

ob·du·ra·cy \'äbd(y)ərəsē, äb'd(y)ürə-, əb'-, -si\ *n* -ES [¹*obdurate* + *-cy*] **:** the quality or state or an instance of being obdurate

¹ob·du·rate \-rət, *usu* -əd.+V\ *adj* [ME *obdurat,* fr. L *obduratus,* past part. of *obdurare* to harden, fr. *ob-* toward, over + *durare* to harden — more at OB-, DURE] **1 a :** hardened in feelings esp. against moral or mollifying influences **:** stubbornly persistent in wrongdoing ⟨that ~ old sinner⟩ **b :** resistant to persuasion or softening influences **:** INFLEXIBLE, UNYIELDING ⟨~ in his determination⟩ ⟨remaining ~ to her husband's advances —Edith Wharton⟩ **2 :** hard and resistant **:** HARSH, RUGGED, ROUGH ⟨wringing a livelihood from that ~ soil⟩ — **ob·du·rate·ly** *adv* — **ob·du·rate·ness** *n* -ES

²obdurate \-ˌrāt, *usu* -ād·+V\ *vt* -ED/-ING/-S [L *obduratus*, past part. of *obdurare* to harden] **:** to make obdurate; *esp* **:** to make stubbornly persistent in ill-doing — **ob·du·ra·tion** \ˌäbd(y)əˈrāshən\ *n* -S

¹ob·dure \äbˈd(y)u̇(ə)r, -u̇ə\ *vb* -ED/-ING/-S [L *obdurare* to harden] *archaic* **:** HARDEN

²obdure \"\ *adj* [*ob-* + *dure*, adj.] *archaic* **:** OBDURATE

obe \ˈōb\ *n* -S [Gk (Laconian dial.) *ōba*; akin to Gk *oiē* village] **:** a subdivision of a phyle or clan in ancient Laconia

obe·ah \ˈōbēə\ *also* **obi** \ˈōbē\ *n* -S [of African origin; akin to Edo *o³bi¹* poison, Twi *a¹bi¹a³*, a creeper used in making medicine and charms] **1** *often cap* **:** a system of belief that is probably of Ashanti origin, has long been practiced but is of increasingly declining influence among Negroes chiefly of the British West Indies, the Guianas, and the southeastern U.S., and is characterized by the use of sorcery and magic ritual — compare VOODOOISM **2 a :** a charm or fetish used in obeah **b :** the influence of obeah ⟨put ~ on a person⟩

obeah man *also* **obeah doctor** *n* **:** an adept or leader in the practice of obeah **:** WITCH DOCTOR

obe·che *also* **obe·chi** \ōˈbēchē\ *n* -S [native name in Nigeria] **1 :** a large West African tree (*Triplochiton scleroxylon*) with soft white to pale yellow wood — called also *arere, samba* **2 :** the wood of the obeche used esp. for veneering

obe·di·ence \ōˈbēdēən(t)s, əˈ-\ *n* -S [ME, fr. OF, fr. L *oboedientia*, fr. *oboedient-, oboediens* (pres. part. of *oboedire* to obey) + *-ia* -y — more at OBEY] **1 :** the act or fact of obeying or the quality or state of being obedient **:** compliance with that which is required by authority **:** subjection to rightful restraint **2 a :** JURISDICTION, CONTROL, RULE — now used chiefly of the spiritual authority of the Roman Catholic Church over its members **b :** a sphere of jurisdiction **:** an ecclesiastical or sometimes a secular dominion **3** *dial chiefly Eng* **:** BOW, CURTSY **4** [ML *obedientia*, fr. L *oboedientia* obedience] **a :** an official position or specific assigned task or responsibility within a monastic establishment; *also* **:** the part of such an establishment devoted to the activities of a particular function **b :** conformity to the rule of a monastic order and to the will of its superior **c :** a specific and usu. written precept or injunction from a superior in a religious order to one of the congregation ⟨hoping that his abbot will place him under ~ to use his singular talents —J.A.O'Brien⟩ **5 :** a system of dog training designed to develop the intelligent response of the animal to the demands of his handler by means of a graded series of specific problem situations of increasing difficulty ⟨goes big for ~ . . . running all five classes off in the first day —*All-Pets Mag.*⟩

obe·di·en·cer \-nsə(r)\ *n* -S [ME, fr. *obedience* + *-er*] *archaic* **:** OBEDIENTIARY

obe·di·en·cy \-nsē, -si\ *n* -ES [L *oboedientia* (fr. *oboedient-, oboediens*) + *-ia* -y] **:** OBEDIENCE 1

¹obe·di·ent \-nt\ *adj* [ME, fr. OF, fr. L *oboedient-, oboediens*, pres. part. of *oboedire* to obey] **1 a :** submissive to the restraint, control, or command of authority **:** willing to obey ⟨an ~ child⟩ ⟨the most modest . . . of little men, and as ~ to his wife —W.M.Thackeray⟩ **b :** SUBJECT, SUBSERVIENT ⟨that Germany would become an ~ sovietized state under the tight grip of the Soviet Union —*Collier's Yr. Bk.*⟩ **2 a :** conformable or conforming to the control of an indicated agent ⟨drifting ~ to winds and tides⟩ ⟨~ instruments of his will —Max Lerner & Edwin Mims⟩ **b :** acting in conformance to an indicated situation ⟨~ to his nature he pried into everything⟩

syn DOCILE, TRACTABLE, AMENABLE, BIDDABLE: OBEDIENT suggests due and accustomed recognition of and compliance with the commands of recognized authority ⟨as second in command, Abercromby proved himself an *obedient* and trustworthy officer —Stanley Pargellis⟩ ⟨he seemed to have lost all power of will; he was like an *obedient* child —W.S.Maugham⟩ DOCILE may stress a disposition to submit, either to due guidance and control or to imposition and oppression ⟨that is a question which you must excuse my child from answering. Not, sir, from want of will, for she is *docile* and obedient —W.H.Hudson †1922⟩ ⟨a state which dwarfs its men in order that they may be more *docile* instruments in its hands —Howard M. Jones⟩ TRACTABLE suggests characteristics that make for easy guiding, leading, ordering, or managing ⟨they are the tamest, the most abject creatures that we can possibly imagine: mild, peaceable, and *tractable*, they seem to have no will or power to act but as directed by their masters —William Bartram⟩ ⟨a wave of rebelliousness ran through the countryside. Bulls which had always been *tractable* suddenly turned savage —George Orwell⟩ AMENABLE indicates a disposition to be agreeable or complaisant and a lack of assertive independent or stubborn truculence ⟨strikingly individual, never *amenable* to group coercion, expressing their convictions freely and ready to uphold their views by the code of the duel —V.L.Parrington⟩ ⟨she therefore tackled her brother, anticipating a curt refusal, but determined nevertheless to stick to her point. Hermann, however, proved quite *amenable*, and admitted his liability without discussion —J.D.Beresford⟩ BIDDABLE, often applied to children, indicates a ready, constant inclination to follow orders, requests, and suggestions ⟨well-behaved children, *biddable*, meek, neat about their clothes, and always mindful of the proprieties —Willa Cather⟩ ⟨so used to being *biddable* that words and wishes said and shown by older folks were still like orders to her —A.B.Guthrie⟩

²obedient \"\ *n* -S **:** an obedient person

obe·di·en·tial \≈ˌ≈≈ˈenchəl\ *adj* [ML *obedientialis*, fr. *obedientia* rule of obedience, obedience (fr. L *oboedientia* obedience) + L *-alis* -al] **:** according to a rule of obedience — **obe·di·en·tial·ly** \-ch(ə)lē\ *adv*

obe·di·en·tia·ry \-ch(ə)rē, -ri\ *n* -ES [ML *obedientiarius*, fr. *obedientia* obedience + *-arius* -ary — more at OBEDIENCE] **1** *obs* **:** one owing or yielding obedience **:** SUBJECT **2 :** one of the minor officials in a medieval monastery appointed by the abbot

obe·di·ent·ly *adv* [ME, fr. ¹*obedient* + *-ly*] **:** in an obedient manner ⟨procured fire, which ~ to human purpose cooks and gives warmth —A.N.Whitehead⟩

obedient plant *n* [so called fr. the fact that its blossoms will remain for some time in the direction in which they are moved] **:** FALSE DRAGONHEAD 1

obei·sance \ōˈbās³n(t)s, əˈ-, -bēs-\ *n* -S [ME *obeisaunce*, fr. MF *obeissance*, fr. *obeissant* (fr. OF) + *-ance*] **1** *obs* **:** OBEDIENCE 1, 2 **2 a :** a movement of the body (as a bending or prostration) or other gesture made in token of respect or submission **:** BOW, CURTSY ⟨after making his ~*s* he approached the altar⟩ **b :** an attitude of respect **:** DEFERENCE, HOMAGE ⟨an author could hardly ask for more than this cultivated ~ —Wolcott Gibbs⟩ **syn** see HONOR

obei·sant \-s³nt\ *adj* [ME *obeisaunt, obeisant*, fr. OF *obeissant*, pres. part. of *obeir* to obey — more at OBEY] **1** *obs* **:** OBEDIENT **2 a :** DEFERENTIAL **b :** SERVILE, OBSEQUIOUS **c :** bowing in homage — **obei·sant·ly** *adv*

o-be-joyful \ˈ≈(ˌ)≈ˈ≈≈\ *n* -S *slang* **:** intoxicating drink

obe·lia \ōˈbēlyə, -lēə\ *n* [NL, prob. fr. Gk *obelias*, a cake, fr. *obelos* spit (rod used in baking)] **1** *cap* **:** a genus of small delicate colonial hydroids having a medusa that lacks a velum and being widely distributed in temperate seas and a common colonial hydrozoan about wharves and pilings **2** -S **:** a member of the genus *Obelia; broadly* **:** any colonial hydroid of similar form

obe·li·al \-lēəl\ *also* **obe·li·ac** \-ēˌak\ *adj* [*obelion* fr. NL *obelion* + E *-al*; *obeliac* fr. NL *obelion* + E *-ac* (fr. L *-acus*, adj. suffix, fr. Gk *-akos*)] **:** of or relating to the obelion

obe·li·on \-lēˌän, -ēən\ *n, pl* **obe·lia** \-ēə\ [NL, fr. Gk *obelos* spit, pointed pillar + *-ion*, n. suffix] **:** a point on the sagittal suture that lies between two small openings through the superior dorsal aspect of the parietal bones and is used in craniometric determinations — see CRANIOMETRY illustration

ob·e·lis·cal \ˌäbəˈliskəl\ *adj* [L *obeliscus* obelisk + E *-al*] **:** of, relating to, or being an obelisk

ob·e·lis·coid *or* **ob·e·lis·koid** \-ˌskȯid\ *adj* **:** shaped like an obelisk

¹ob·e·lisk \ˈ≈≈ˌlisk\ *n* -S [MF *obelisque*, fr. L *obeliscus*, fr. Gk *obeliskos* small spit, obelisk, dim. of *obelos* spit, pointed pillar, obelus] **1 :** an upright, 4-sided, and usu. monolithic pillar that gradually tapers as it rises and terminates in a pyramid ⟨Cleopatra's Needle and the Washington Monument are ~*s*⟩ **2 a :** OBELUS **b :** DAGGER 1b(1) **3 :** a decorative feature (as on a lamp base or on a chandelier) having a tall slender tapering form

obelisk

²obelisk \"\ *vt* -ED/-ING/-S **:** to mark or designate with an obelisk

ob·e·lism \-ˌlizəm\ *n* -S [MGk *obelismos*, fr. Gk *obelizein* to obelize + *-ismos* -ism] **:** the act of obelizing

ob·e·lize *also* **ob·e·lise** \-ˌlīz\ *vt* -ED/-ING/-S [Gk *obelizein*, fr. *obelos* obelus + *-izein* -ize] **:** to designate or annotate with an obelus; *esp* **:** so to mark as doubtful or spurious

ob·e·lus \-ləs\ *n, pl* **obe·li** \-ˌlī\ [LL, fr. Gk *obelos* obelus, lit., spit, pointed pillar] **:** a symbol — or ÷ used in ancient manuscripts (as of the Septuagint) to mark the beginning of a suspected passage — compare METOBELUS

obe·rea \ōˈbirēə\ *n, cap* [NL] **:** a widely distributed genus of beetles (family Lamiidae) having larvae that are stem borers in various woody plants — see RASPBERRY CANE BORER

obe·rek \ōˈberək\ *n* -S [Pol] **:** a Polish folk dance characterized by acrobatics for the man and marching steps for both partners

ober·hau·sen \ˈōbə(r)ˌhau̇z³n\ *adj, usu cap* [fr. *Oberhausen*, Germany] **:** of or from the city of Oberhausen, Germany **:** of the kind or style prevalent in Oberhausen

ober·re·al·schu·le \-(r)rāˈälˌshülə\ *n, pl* **oberrealschu·les** \-ləz\ *or* **oberrealschu·len** \-lən\ [G, fr. *ober* upper (fr. OHG *obaro*) + *realschule*; akin to OHG *ubar* over — more at OVER, REALSCHULE] **:** a German secondary school preparing students for the university and emphasizing modern languages and natural sciences rather than Latin or Greek — compare GYMNASIUM

obese \ōˈbēs\ *adj* [L *obesus*, fr. past part. of *obedere* to eat away, devour, fr. *ob-* toward, over + *edere* to eat — more at OB-, EAT] **1 :** excessively fat **:** CORPULENT ⟨~ adults compulsively stuffing themselves —Warren Boroson⟩ **2 :** unusually large in size or extent ⟨occupied two ~ divans —Philip Wylie⟩ ⟨a document quite ~ with self-congratulation —*Times Lit. Supp.*⟩

obe·si·ty \ōˈbēsəd·ē, -bes-, -ətē, -i\ *n* -ES [L *obesitas*, fr. *obesus* obese + *-itas* -ity] **:** a bodily condition marked by excessive generalized deposition and storage of fat **:** CORPULENCE

obex \ˈōˌbeks\ *n* -ES [L *obic-, obex*, fr. *obicere, objicere* to throw in the way, to hinder — more at OBJECT] **1 :** OBSTACLE **2** [NL, fr. L, obstacle] **:** a thin triangular lamina of gray matter in the roof of the fourth ventricle of the brain

obey \ōˈbā, əˈ-\ *vb* -ED/-ING/-S [ME *obeien*, fr. OF *obeir*, fr. L *oboedire* to listen to, obey, fr. *ob-* to, toward, over + *-oedire* (fr. *audire* to hear) — more at OB-, AUDIBLE] *vt* **1 :** to fit one's conduct to and perform as directed or requested by ⟨~ one's parents⟩ ⟨~*ing* a superior's order⟩ **2 :** to submit to or accord with **a :** to rule one's conduct in accordance with ⟨the fiercest rebel against society . . . ~*s* most of its conventions —H.J. Muller⟩ ⟨~*ed* his sense of justice even when it ran counter to his own interests —E.M.Violette⟩ **b :** to act or react in conformity with ⟨the ship ~*ed* the helm⟩ ⟨concluded that by analogy electrical force also ~*ed* the inverse square law —S.F. Mason⟩ ~ *vi* **1** *obs* **:** to accord with orders or requests and do as told or asked — used with *to* ⟨~*ed to* the king's command⟩ **2 :** to perform or behave as directed often without question or attempt at independent decision **:** be obedient ⟨a people gentle, submissive, prompt to ~ —Agnes Repplier⟩

syn MIND, COMPLY: OBEY is the general term indicating to accord with another's commands or wishes ⟨*obey* one's father⟩ ⟨*obey* orders⟩ It may suggest lack of questioning or attempting independent judgment ⟨hear and *obey*⟩ ⟨the submissive way of one long accustomed to *obey* under coercion —Charles Dickens⟩ OBEY is wider in application than MIND or COMPLY since it may be used in reference to laws, principles, moral forces, abstractions ⟨what *obeys* reason, is free —John Milton⟩ ⟨*obey* at all costs the call of what was felt as truth —Havelock Ellis⟩ As a synonym for *obey* MIND is likely to be used in connection with children or juniors; it often suggests admonition to an inferior, ward, or charge ⟨*mind* your mother⟩ ⟨children refusing to *mind* their teachers⟩ COMPLY may suggest a yielding or giving in to another's wishes or orders or to rules or requirements, perhaps through complaisance or lack of strong opinion ⟨should you think ill of that person for *complying* . . . without waiting to be argued into it —Jane Austen⟩ ⟨on being invited by the brute to go outside, what could he do but *comply* —Arnold Bennett⟩

obey·able \-əbəl\ *adj* **:** capable of being obeyed ⟨~ laws⟩

obey·ance \-ən(t)s\ *n* -ES **:** an act or the custom of obeying **:** OBEDIENCE ⟨~ of laws⟩

obey·er \-ə(r)\ *n* -S **:** one that obeys

obfirm *also* **obfirmate** *vt* -ED/-ING/-S [*obfirm* fr. L *obfirmare, offirmare*, fr. *ob-, of-* to, against, over + *firmare* to make firm; *obfirmate* fr. L *obfirmatus, offirmatus*, past part. of *obfirmare, offirmare* to make firm — more at OB-, FIRM] *obs* **:** to make obdurate

obfirmation *n* -S [ML *obfirmation-, obfirmatio*, fr. L *obfirmatus, offirmatus* + *-ion-, -io* -ion] *obs* **:** confirmation in ill-doing **:** OBDURACY

ob·fusc \(ˈ)äbˈfəsk, əbˈf-\ *adj* [by shortening] **:** OBFUSCATED

ob·fus·ca·ble \äbˈfəskəbəl, əbˈ-\ *adj* **:** capable of being obfuscated

¹ob·fus·cate \(ˈ)äbˈfəˌskāt, əbˈf-, -ˌskət, *usu* -d·+V\ *adj* [LL *obfuscatus, offuscatus*, past part. of *obfuscare, offuscare* to darken] **:** OBFUSCATED

²obfuscate \äbˈfəˌskāt, əbˈf; ˈäb(ˌ)fə,-; *usu* -ād·+V\ *vt* -ED/-ING/-S [LL *obfuscatus, offuscatus*, past part. of *obfuscare, offuscare* to darken, fr. L *ob-, of-* over, completely + *fuscare* to darken, fr. *fuscus* dark brown, blackish — more at OB-, DUSK] **1 :** CONFUSE, BECLOUD; *esp* **:** to cause confusion in the mind of ⟨to give the reader all the facts and yet ~ him as to meaning⟩ **2 :** to make obscure: **a :** to make difficult of comprehension or interpretation ⟨the small facts could not be ignored without *obfuscating* the main dramatic purpose⟩ **b :** to make unnecessarily complex usu. to the point of confusion ⟨his use of symbolism became a mere mechanical device for *obfuscating* the commonplace and intelligible⟩ **3 :** to throw into shadow **:** make difficult to see **:** DARKEN **syn** see OBSCURE

obfuscated *adj* **:** confused and baffled

ob·fus·ca·tion \ˌäb(ˌ)fəˈskāshən\ *n* -S [LL *obfuscation-, obfuscatio, offuscation-, offuscatio*, fr. *obfuscatus, offuscatus* + L *-ion-, -io* -ion] **1 :** the quality or state of being obfuscated **2 :** an act or instance of obfuscating something

ob·fus·ca·tor \äbˈfəˌskād·ə(r), əbˈ-; ˈäb(ˌ)fə,-\ *n* -S **:** one that obfuscates

ob·fus·ca·to·ry \äbˈfəskəˌtōrē, əbˈ-; ˈäb(ˌ)fəˌskād·ərē, -ri\ *adj* [²*obfuscate* + *-ory*] **:** tending to obfuscate **:** CONFUSING, OBSCURING

ob·fusque \äbˈfəsk, əbˈ-\ *vt* -ED/-ING/-S [MF *obfusquer*, fr. LL *obfuscare, offuscare*] **:** OBFUSCATE

ob·fus·ti·cat·ed \äbˈfəstəˌkād·əd, əbˈ-\ *adj* [alter. of *obfuscated*] *dial* **:** OBFUSCATED, CONFUSED, BEWILDERED

¹obi *var of* OBEAH

²obi \ˈōbē\ *n* -S [Jap] **:** a broad Japanese sash wound around the waist over the main kimono and tied at the back

obis·po \ōˈbi(ˌ)spō, əˈ-\ *n* -ES [Sp, lit., bishop, fr. LL *episcopus*; fr. the resemblance of its head to a bishop's mitre — more at BISHOP] **:** SPOTTED EAGLE RAY

obispo pine *n* **:** BISHOP PINE

obit \ˈōbət, ˈäb- *also chiefly in sense 3* ōˈbit\ *n* -S [ME, fr. MF, fr. L *obitus*, fr. *obitus*, past part. of *obire* to die, fr. *ob-* to, over, completely + *ire* to go — more at OB-, ISSUE] **1** *obs* **a :** a person's death **:** DECEASE **b :** a funeral solemnity **:** OBSEQUIES; *specif* **:** a requiem mass and office of the dead **2** *archaic* **:** a service for the soul of a deceased person (as by an institution in memory of its founder) on his deathday **:** a regularly recurrent memorial service **3 :** a notice or record of a person's death and the date thereof; *esp* **:** OBITUARY 1

obital *adj* [*obit* + *-al*] *obs* **:** OBITUARY

¹obi·ter \ˈōbəd·ə(r) *sometimes* ˈäb-\ *adv* [L, fr. *ob* to, before, against + *iter* way, journey, fr. *ire* to go — more at EPI-] **:** in passing **:** INCIDENTALLY

²obiter \"\ *n* -S [by shortening] **:** OBITER DICTUM

obiter dic·tum \ˌ≈≈≈ˈdiktəm\ *n, pl* **obiter dic·ta** \-tə\ [LL] **1 :** an incidental and collateral opinion uttered by a judge and therefore not material to his decision or judgment and not binding — compare RESPONSA PRUDENTIUM **2 :** an incidental and casually interjected remark, reflection, comment, or opinion

obit·u·al \ōˈbichəwəl, əˈ-\ *adj* [L *obitus* death + E *-al*] **:** OBITUARY

obit·u·ar·ist \-chəˌwerəst, -chər-\ *n* -S **:** a writer of obituaries or the writer of an obituary

obit·u·a·rize \-chəwəˌrīz, -chəˌr-\ *vi* -ED/-ING/-S [*obituar*ist + *-ize*] **:** to write an obituary

¹obit·u·ary \-chəˌwerē, -chər-, -ri\ *n* -ES [ML *obituarium*, fr. L *obitus* death + *-arium*] **1 a :** a record or notice of a person's death **b :** a usu. short account of the significant aspects and accomplishments of a person's life published (as in a newspaper) upon the person's death **2 :** something suggesting an obituary in signaling or seeming to signal the end or death of an enterprise or plan

²obituary \"\ *adj* **:** of, relating to, or recording the death of a person or persons

obj *abbr* object; objection; objective

¹ob·ject \ˈäbjikt, -jēkt *sometimes* -ˌjekt\ *n* -S [ME, fr. ML *objectus*, fr. L *objectus*, past part. of *objicere, obicere* to throw in the way, hinder, object, fr. *ob-* to, toward, against + *-jicere, -icere* (fr. *jacere* to throw) — more at OB-, JET] **1 :** something that is put or may be regarded as put in the way of some of the senses **:** a discrete visible or tangible thing ⟨saw an ~ in the distance⟩ **2 :** something that arouses feelings (as of pity, amusement, disgust) in an observer **:** SIGHT, SPECTACLE **3 a :** something (as an end, aim, or motive) by which the mind or any of its activities is directed **:** something on which the purposes are fixed as the end of action or effort **:** something that is sought for **:** final cause ⟨let our ~ be, our country, our whole country, and nothing but our country —Daniel Webster⟩ ⟨the attainment of wealth was the ~ of his every effort⟩ **b** (1) **:** something that is set or may be regarded as set before the mind so as to be apprehended or known ⟨an ~ of fear⟩ ⟨such ~*s* of study⟩ (2) **:** something of which the mind by any of its activities takes cognizance, whether a thing external in space and time or a conception formed by the mind itself ⟨the opinion that the four main kinds of ~*s* are cultural objects, other minds, physical objects, and data of our minds —Jørgen Jørgensen⟩ — sometimes distinguished from *ego, self-consciousness*, and *subject* **3 :** the totality of external phenomena constituting the not-self — compare INTENTION **4** *obs* **:** REPRESENTATION, APPEARANCE, SHOW **5 a :** a noun or noun equivalent denoting in verb constructions that on or toward which the action of a verb is directed either actually or as conceived (as *ball* in *I struck the ball* and *what had happened* in *I saw what had happened*) and either immediately (as *thanks* in *I give thanks*) or less immediately (as *you* in *I give you thanks*) **b :** a noun or noun equivalent having with an adjective or adverb a relation analogous to that of object with verb (as *trouble* in *worth the trouble* and *brother* in *like his brother*) **c :** a noun or noun equivalent in a prepositional phrase (as *table* in *on the table* and *city* in *from the city*) **syn** see INTENTION

²ob·ject \əbˈjekt\ *vb* -ED/-ING/-S [ME *objecten*, fr. L *objectus*, past part. of *objicere, obicere* to object] *vt* **1** *archaic* **a :** to set before or against **:** bring into opposition **:** OPPOSE, INTERPOSE **b :** to bring or place in view **:** EXPOSE **c :** to offer as supportive evidence **:** bring forward as an argument or reason **2 :** to offer in opposition (as by way of accusation or reproach) **:** adduce as an objection or adverse reason ⟨~*ed* that the statement was misleading⟩ **3** *obs* **a :** to expose to danger or other hazard **b :** IMPUTE ~ *vi* **1 :** to oppose something with words or arguments — usu. followed by *to* ⟨~*ed* vigorously to their statements⟩ **2 :** to feel aversion or distaste for something ⟨any honest man will ~ to such a policy⟩

syn PROTEST, REMONSTRATE, EXPOSTULATE, KICK: OBJECT focuses attention on the fact of voiced dislike, aversion, or dissent without implication about its manner or content ⟨*objecting* as a matter of principle⟩ ⟨*objecting* because the evidence was unclear⟩ PROTEST may suggest uttered objection delivered either with orderly formality or with emotion ⟨the bill was passed despite the arguments of the *protesting* senators⟩ ⟨he went here and there swearing and *protesting* against every delay in the work —Sherwood Anderson⟩ REMONSTRATE may apply to utterance blending objection and desire to persuade, influence, or convince ⟨now and then a well-meaning friend of Sir Austin's ventured to *remonstrate* on a dangerous trial he was making in modeling any new plan of Education for a youth —George Meredith⟩ EXPOSTULATE may suggest earnest explanation of something objected to coupled with urgent insistence on change ⟨I resolved, for Johnny's sake, to protest, and that very evening drew Gibbings aside and *expostulated* with him —A.T.Quiller-Couch⟩ KICK, often considered colloquial, suggests strenuous or recalcitrant objecting ⟨employees *kicking* about the new regulations⟩ ⟨the crew *kicking* about their food⟩ ⟨newspaper editorials *kicking* about the delay⟩

ob·ject·able \-təbəl\ *adj* [²*object* + *-able*] *archaic* **:** OBJECTIONABLE

ob·ject·ant \-tənt\ *n* -S **:** one that objects (as to military service or some matter in a legal proceeding)

object ball *n* **:** the ball that is first struck by the cue ball in pool or billiards; *also* **:** any ball that may be hit by the cue ball

object color *n* **:** color that is perceived as belonging to an object and is classifiable as bulky color for interiors of non-opaque objects or as surface color

ob·jec·tee \ˌäbˌjekˈtē, əbˌjekˈtē\ *n* -S [²*object* + *-ee*] **:** one that is objected to

object glass *n* **:** OBJECTIVE 5

ob·jec·ti·fi·able \əbˌjektəˈfīəbəl\ *adj* [*objectify* + *-able*] **:** capable of being made objective

ob·jec·ti·fi·ca·tion \≈ˌ≈≈fəˈkāshən\ *n* -S [fr. *objectify*, after such pairs as E *identify: identification*] **1 :** an act or instance or the process of making objective ⟨Schopenhauer declared . . . that, in contemplating works of art, we contemplate the ~ of will —John Dewey⟩ **2 a :** the state of being objectified **b :** something that is objectified

ob·jec·ti·fy \≈ˈ≈≈ˌfī\ *vt* -ED/-ING/-ES [¹*object* + *-ify*] **1 a :** to cause to become or to assume the character of an object **b :** to render objective; *specif* **:** to give the status of external or independent reality to (something in the mind) **2 :** to externalize visually (as in hallucinatory vision)

ob·jec·tion \əbˈjekshən\ *n* -S [ME *objeccioun*, fr. MF *objection*, fr. LL *objection-, objectio*, fr. L *objectus* (past part. of *objicere, obicere* to object) + *-ion-, -io* -ion — more at OBJECT] **1 :** an act of objecting ⟨prevent action by ~⟩ **2 a :** something that is or may be presented in opposition **:** adverse reason or argument **:** reason for objecting or opposing ⟨presented his ~*s* in a formal report⟩ **b :** a feeling of disapproval ⟨I have no ~ to going⟩ **3** *obs* **:** presentation or representation to the view or to the mind

ob·jec·tion·abil·i·ty \≈ˌ≈sh(ə)nəˈbiləd·ē, -ətē, -i\ *n* **:** the quality or state of being objectionable

¹ob·jec·tion·able \≈ˈ≈sh(ə)nəbəl\ *adj* **:** arousing objection **:** OFFENSIVE — **ob·jec·tion·able·ness** \-bəlnəs\ *n* -ES — **ob·jec·tion·ably** \-blē, -li\ *adv*

²objectionable \"\ *n* -S **:** an objectionable individual

ob·jec·tion·al \-shən³l, -shnəl\ *adj* **1 :** of or relating to objection **2 :** OBJECTIONABLE

ob·jec·ti·val \ˌäbjekˈtīvəl, -jek-\ *adj* [¹*objective* + *-al*] **:** of, relating to, or constituting an object esp. in grammar

ob·jec·ti·vate \əbˈjektəˌvāt, äb-\ *vt* -ED/-ING/-S [¹*objective* + *-ate*] **:** OBJECTIFY — **ob·jec·ti·va·tion** \-ˌ≈≈ˈvāshən\ *n* -S

¹ob·jec·tive \əbˈjektiv, äb-, -tēv *also* -əv\ *adj* [It *obiettivo*, fr. ML *objectivus*, fr. L *objectus* object + *-ivus* -ive — more at OBJECT] **1 a :** of or relating to an object of action or feeling **:** forming an object of attraction or a final cause **b :** contained in, constituting, or having the status of an object: as (1) **:** existing only in relation to mind **:** relating to the thing known considered merely in its relation to the knowing subject or to the thing willed or desired in its relation to the agent willing or desiring (2) **:** existing independent of mind **:** relating to an object as it is in itself or as distinguished from consciousness or the subject (3) **:** belonging to nature or the sensible world **:** publicly or intersubjectively observable or verifiable esp. by scientific methods **:** independent of what is personal or private in our apprehension and feelings **:** of such nature that rational minds agree in holding it real or true or valid ⟨his first impression was disproved by ~ reality⟩ (4) *of a symptom of disease* **:** perceptible to persons other than an affected individual **c :** emphasizing or expressing the nature of reality as it is apart from self-consciousness **:** treating events or phenomena as external rather than as affected by personal reflections or feelings **d :** expressing or involving the use of facts without distortion by personal feelings or prejudices ⟨an ~ analysis⟩ ⟨~ tests⟩ **2 :** perceptible to the senses or derived from sense perception ⟨~ data⟩ **3 :** belonging or relating to an object to be delineated ⟨an ~ line⟩ ⟨~ planes⟩ **4** *of a lens* **:** nearest the object — see PRISM BINOCULAR illustration **5 a :** relating to, characteristic of, or being the case which follows a verb used transitively or a preposition **:** being the case that denotes the relation of object; *also* **:** relating to the relation itself **b :** expressing a relation that resembles that of an object to its verb ⟨the ~ genitive *member's* in *a member's expulsion from the club*⟩ **c :** taking an object or noun complement — used of an adjective or adverb (as *worth* in *worth his salt* and *like* in *like his mother*) and of a transitive verb in contrast to an intransitive verb **syn** see FAIR, MATERIAL

²**objective** \"\ *n* -s **1 :** something toward which effort is directed **:** an aim or end of action **:** GOAL, OBJECT **2 :** something that is objective; *specif* **:** something external to the mind **3 a :** the objective case that in modern English replaces the Old English accusative and dative **b :** a word in the objective case **4 :** a strategic position to be attained, the purpose to be satisfied (as the destruction of the effectiveness of an enemy's force), or the designated terrain feature to be reached by a military or naval operation **5 :** a lens or system of lenses that forms an image of the object on a screen (as in a camera or projector) or in the focal plane of an eyepiece (as in a telescope or microscope) **syn** see INTENTION

objective complement *or* **objective predicate** *n* **:** a noun, adjective, or pronoun used in the predicate as complement to a factitive verb or a verb of choosing, naming, thinking and as qualifier of its direct object (as *chairman* in *make John chairman, angry* in *make him angry*, and *red* in *paint his nose red*)

objective correlative *n* **:** something (as a situation or chain of events) that symbolizes or renders objective an emotion and may be employed in creative writing to evoke a desired emotional response in the reader

objective idealism *n* **:** the acceptance of nature as ultimately ideal or spiritual and existing independently of any subjects; *specif* **:** the philosophy of F.W.J. von Schelling according to which nature is visible intelligence and intelligence invisible nature — contrasted with *subjective idealism*

objective line *n* **:** a line drawn on the geometrical plane to be represented

ob·jec·tive·ly \əbˈjektəvlē, äb-, -li\ *adv* **:** in an objective manner **:** with objectivity

ob·jec·tive·ness \-tivnəs, -tēv- *also* -əv-\ *n* -ES **:** OBJECTIVITY

objective plane *n* **:** the plane tangent to the ground at a military objective

objective prism *n* **:** a transparent prism of small apex angle but large size that is placed in front of the objective of a telescope to cause all stars and other objects to appear as short spectra in the focal plane where they may be photographed together on a single plate of the field

objective test *n* **:** a test designed to exclude as far as possible the subjective element on the part of both those taking and grading it by presenting a number of factual questions to be answered by one word or a check mark instead of verbal expression and organization of material — compare ESSAY EXAMINATION

objective time *n* **:** time that is an objectively determinable order in which durations are measured and an absolute present is indifferent — contrasted with *subjective time;* called also *public time*

ob·jec·tiv·ism \əbˈjektəˌvizəm, äb-\ *n* -s **1 a** (1) **:** any of various philosophical theories that stress the external elements of reality to the relative neglect of the mental (2) **:** a theory that asserts human knowledge to have objective validity **b :** any theory or system of analysis that stresses objectivity through the rigid exclusion of data that do not admit of quantitative treatment — compare BEHAVIORISM **2 :** an ethical theory considering the moral good to be objective and independent of personal or merely human feelings: **a :** such a theory considering the moral good to be something natural and observable without a special faculty or insight **b :** such a theory (as in intuitionism) considering the moral good to be something nonnatural **3 :** the theory or practice of objective art or literature

ob·jec·tiv·ist \-ˌvəst\ *n* -s **:** an adherent or advocate of objectivism

ob·jec·tiv·is·tic \=ˌ==ˈvistik, -ēk\ *adj* **:** of or relating to objectivism

ob·jec·tiv·i·ty \ˌäb(ˌ)jekˈtivəd·ē, -jək-, -vətē, -i\ *n* -ES **1 :** the quality, state, or relation of being objective ⟨his completely unimpassioned ~⟩ **2 :** objective reality

ob·jec·ti·vi·za·tion \əbˌjektəvəˈzāshən, äb-, -ˌvīˈz-\ *n* -s **:** the act or process of making or becoming objective

ob·jec·tiv·ize \əbˈjektəˌvīz, äb-\ *vt* -ED/-ING/-s [²*objective* + -*ize*] **:** OBJECTIFY

ob·ject·ize \ˈäb(ˌ)jekˌtīz, -jək-\ *vt* -ED/-ING/-s [¹*object* + -*ize*] **:** OBJECTIFY

object language *n* **1 :** a language dealing with objects or entities outside itself or referring to things, events, and their properties **2 :** a language that is being talked about or is an object of investigation by another language — compare METALANGUAGE

ob·ject·less \ˈäbjəktləs, -jek-\ *adj* **:** lacking an object **:** having no clear-cut purpose or intent ⟨~ rambles⟩ — **ob·ject·less·ly** *adv* — **ob·ject·less·ness** *n* -ES

object lesson *n* **1 :** a lesson in which a material object is made the basis of instruction **2 :** something that teaches by exemplifying a principle in concrete form

object libido *n* [part trans. of G *objekt libido*] **:** erotic desire directed toward another individual than the self — compare EGO-LIBIDO

object matter *n* **:** SUBJECT MATTER

object of art [by trans.] **:** OBJET D'ART

ob·jec·tor \əbˈjektə(r)\ *n* -s [²*object* + -*or*] **:** one that objects (as to a proposition or measure)

objects *pl of* OBJECT, *pres 3d sing of* OBJECT

object space *n* **:** the space in relation to an optical system in which are located the objects to be imaged by the system — compare IMAGE SPACE

ob·jet d'art \ˌȯbˌzhäˈdär, -dȧ(r\ *n, pl* **ob·jets d'art** \"\ [F, lit., art object] **1 :** an article of artistic worth **2 :** BIBELOT, CURIO, TRINKET

ob·ji·cient \əbˈjishənt\ *n* -s [L *objicient-, objiciens, obicient-, obiciens*, pres. part. of *objicere, obicere* to object — more at OBJECT] **:** OBJECTOR

ob·ju·ra·tion \ˌäbjəˈrāshən\ *n* -s [L *objurare* to bind by oath (fr. *ob-* + *jurare* to swear) + E *-ation* — more at JURY] **:** a binding or charging by or as if by oath

ob·jur·gate \ˈäbjə(r)ˌgāt\ *vt* -ED/-ING/-s [L *objurgatus*, past part. of *objurgare* to scold, blame, fr. *ob-* against, over + *jurgare* to quarrel, blame, bring a lawsuit, fr. *jur-, jus* law + *-gare* (fr. *agere* to drive, lead, act, do) — more at OB-, JUST, AGENT] **:** to decry vehemently ⟨*objurgated* the custom of garnishing poems with archaisms —T.R.Weiss⟩ **:** to castigate with harsh or violent language **:** VITUPERATE **syn** see EXECRATE

ob·jur·ga·tion \ˌäbjə(r)ˈgāshən\ *n* -s [MF or L; MF, fr. L *objurgation-, objurgatio*, fr. *objurgatus* + *-ion-, -io* -ion] **:** an act or instance of objurgating **:** a harsh or violent reproof

ob·jur·ga·tive \əbˈjərgəd·iv\ *adj* **:** OBJURGATORY — **ob·jur·ga·tive·ly** \-d·ə̇vlē\ *adv*

ob·jur·ga·tor \ˈäbjə(r)ˌgād·ə(r)\ *n* -s **:** one that objurgates

ob·jur·ga·to·ri·ly \əbˌjərgəˈtōrəlē, (ˌ)äb-\ *adv* **:** in an objurgatory manner

ob·jur·ga·to·ry \əbˈjərgəˌtōrē\ *adj* [L *objurgatorius*, fr. *objurgatus* (past part. of *objurgare* to objurgate) + *-orius* -ory] **:** constituting objurgation ⟨~ speeches⟩ **:** expressing rebuke ⟨relapse from her official ~ tone —George Eliot⟩

ob·jur·ga·trix \ˌäbjərˈgāˌtriks\ *n, pl* **objurgatri·ces** \ˌ==ˈgā·trəˌsēz; əbˌjərgəˈtrī(ˌ)sēz, ˌäb-\ [ML, fem. of L *objurgator* scolder, fr. *objurgatus* + *-or*] *archaic* **:** COMMON SCOLD

obl *abbr* **1** obligation **2** oblique **3** oblong

OBL *abbr* order bill of lading

ob·lanceolate \(ˈ)äb+\ *adj* [*ob-* + *lanceolate*] **:** inversely lanceolate ⟨an ~ leaf⟩ — see LEAF illustration

ob·last \ˈäˌblast, ˈȯ,-\ *n, pl* **oblasts** \-sts\ *also* **oblasti** \-stē\ [Russ *oblast'* province, oblast, fr. OSlav, fr. *ob-* (fr. *ob* to, on) + *vlast'* dominion, government; akin to L *ob* to, before, against and to Lith *veldėti* to rule — more at EPI-, WIELD] **:** a governmental subdivision of the U. S. S. R. corresponding to an autonomous province or state

oblat \ōblȧ\ *n* -s [F, fr. ML *oblatus* oblate, n., fr. L *oblatus*, suppletive past part. of *offerre* to carry to, offer] **:** OBLATE

ob·la·ta \äˈblād·ə, -ād·ə\ *n pl* [ML, oblates, neut. pl. of *oblatus* oblate, n.] *archaic* **:** old debts or gifts to the crown remaining unpaid to the English Exchequer; *also* **:** the entries for them in the rolls of the Exchequer

¹**ob·late** \äˈblāt, əˈ-, *usu* -ād.+V\ *vt* -ED/-ING/-s [L *oblatus* (suppletive past part. of *offerre* to carry to, offer) fr. *ob-* to, towards + *latus* carried (suppletive past part. of *ferre* to carry) — more at OB-, BEAR, TOLERATE] **:** OFFER; *esp* **:** to make an oblation of

²**ob·late** \(ˈ)äˈblāt, (ˈ)ō;-, əˈblāt, *usu* -ād- + V\ *adj* [prob. fr. (assumed) NL *oblatus*, lit., carried forward, stretched, fr. L, suppletive past part. of *offerre*] **:** flattened or depressed at the poles ⟨an ~ leaf⟩ ⟨~ teapot⟩ ⟨~ spheroid⟩ — opposed to *prolate* — **ob·late·ly** *adv*

³**oblate** \"\ *n* -s [ML *oblatus*, fr. L, suppletive past part. of *offerre*] **1** *Roman Catholicism* **:** one offered or devoted to the monastic life or to some special religious service or work: **a :** a child dedicated in his or her early years by the parents to the monastic life **b :** one of a class of persons who have offered themselves and their property to a monastery in which they live **2** *usu cap, Roman Catholicism* **:** a member of one of the religious orders devoted to a particular work

oblate ellipsoid of revolution [²*oblate*] **:** the ellipsoid of revolution obtained by revolving an ellipse about its minor axis

ob·late·ness *n* -ES [²*oblate* + *-ness*] **:** oblate state or character; *specif* **:** ELLIPTICITY 1 ⟨~ of a planet⟩

ob·la·tio \äˈblāshēˌō, -(ˌ)shō\ *n* -s [LL, oblation] *Roman civil law* **:** a tender of something (as a payment) due

ob·la·tion \əˈblāshən, ōˈb-, äˈb-\ *n* -s [ME *oblacioun*, fr. MF *oblation*, fr. LL *oblation-, oblatio*, fr. L *oblatus* (suppletive past part. of *offerre* to carry to, offer) + *-ion-, -io* -ion] **1 a :** a religious or ritualistic offering usu. of something without life in contrast to a sacrifice of living things **b** *usu cap* **:** the act of offering the eucharistic elements to God in a Christian communion service **2 :** something offered or presented in worship or sacred service **:** OFFERING, SACRIFICE **3 :** an offering made to a church ⟨tithing her ~s for aid to the poor⟩ **4** *usu cap* **:** one of several loaves of leavened bread offered by members of an Eastern Orthodox church for use in the Eucharist

ob·la·tion·al \-shənᵊl, -shnəl\ *adj* **:** OBLATORY

ob·la·tion·ary \-shəˌnerē, -ri\ *n* -ES [ML *oblationarius*, fr. LL *oblation-, oblatio* oblation + L *-arius* -ary] **:** an ecclesiastic who receives the oblations offered in the celebration of the Eucharist

ob·la·to·ry \ˈäbləˌtōrē, -tȯr-, -ri\ *adj* [ML *oblatorius*, fr. L *oblatus* + *-orius* -ory] **:** of or relating to oblation

ob·lec·ta·tion \ˌäˌblekˈtāshən\ *n* -s [MF or L; MF, fr. L *oblectation-, oblectatio*, fr. *oblectatus* (past part. of *oblectare* to delight, fr. *ob-* to, over, completely + *lactare*, freq. of *lacere* to allure) + *-ion-, -io* -ion — more at OB-, DELIGHT] **:** PLEASURE, SATISFACTION, DELIGHT ⟨~ of the senses⟩

obleege \əˈblēj\ *chiefly dial var of* OBLIGE

ob·ley \ˈäblē, -li\ *n* -s [ME, fr. MF *oublee*, fr. ML *oblata*, fem. of *oblatus* offering, oblate — more at OBLATE] **:** a small flat cake or wafer; *esp* **:** a wafer of altar bread

ob·li·ga·bil·i·ty \ˌäbləgəˈbiləd·ē, -lēg-\ *n* **:** the quality or state of being obligable

ob·li·ga·ble \ˈ==gəbəl\ *adj* [*obligation* + *-able*] **:** subject to or involving obligation

ob·li·gant \-gənt\ *n* -s [L *obligant-, obligans*, pres. part. of *obligare* to oblige — more at OBLIGE] **:** OBLIGOR

¹**ob·li·gate** \-gət, -lə,gāt\ *adj* [ME *obligat*, fr. L *obligatus*, past part. of *obligare*] **1 a** *obs* **:** placed under obligation **:** BOUND **b :** restricted to a particular condition of life ⟨an ~ parasite⟩ ⟨~ anaerobes⟩ **2 :** completely unavoidable **:** ESSENTIAL, NECESSARY ⟨the presence of mycorrhiza appears ~ to the healthy growth of many plants⟩ ⟨following an ~ course of development⟩ — **ob·li·gate·ly** *adv*

²**obligate** \ˈäbləˌgāt, *usu* -ād.+V\ *vt* -ED/-ING/-s [L *obligatus*, past part. of *obligare* to oblige — more at OBLIGE] **1** *obs* **:** BIND, FASTEN **2 a :** to pledge as security **b :** to assign or commit (as funds) to meet a particular obligation ⟨the treasury had *obligated* anticipated receipts from the new tax⟩ **3 a :** to constrain or bind to some course of action (as by legal measures, moral or social considerations, or force of circumstances) ⟨*obligated* to pay alimony⟩ ⟨community life ~s each of us to certain restraints and conformities⟩ **b :** OBLIGE 3a ⟨hoping to ~ enough of his colleagues to put over the measure⟩ ⟨I don't like to be *obligated* to anybody⟩ **4 :** to put under a promise, vow, or oath esp. as part of a ceremony of initiation into an organization

ob·li·ga·tion \ˌ==ˈgāshən\ *n* -s [ME *obligacioun*, fr. OF *obligation*, fr. L *obligation-, obligatio*, fr. *obligatus* + *-ion-, -io* -ion] **1 :** an act of obligating oneself to a course of action **:** a putting under a promise, vow, or oath (as in initiation into an organization) **2 a :** an obligating factor or instrument **:** something (as a promise, vow, or demand of ideals or conscience) that binds or constrains to a course of action **:** the obligating power inherent in such a factor or instrument ⟨the ~s of conscience⟩ **b :** a bond with a condition annexed and a penalty for nonfulfillment; *broadly* **:** a formal and binding agreement or acknowledgment of a liability to pay a specified sum or do a specified thing **c :** an investment security ⟨corporate bonds and other ~s⟩ **3 a :** something that one is bound to do or forbear **:** an imperative duty (as imposed by promise, religion, conscience, ideals, or social standards) **b :** a duty arising by contract **:** a legal liability **4 a :** a condition or feeling of being bound legally or ethically **b :** a condition or feeling of social indebtedness (as for kindnesses and favors granted) ⟨their repeated assistance left him with an intolerable sense of ~⟩ **5 :** money committed to a particular purpose **:** LIABILITY, ENCUMBRANCE **6** *Roman & civil law* **:** a legal relationship or tie in accordance with which one party is able to compel another in a personal action and under the existing circumstances to do or not to do a specified act (as to pay money or transfer property) or to refrain from specified conduct and which arises out of a contract, quasi contract, delict, or quasi delict

syn DUTY and OBLIGATION are often interchangeable but OBLIGATION can apply to what one must do or refrain from doing usu. by an immediate constraint inherent in position, occupation, relationship, or belief ⟨the *obligation* of the courts to refuse to enforce any legislation which violates freedom of speech —Zechariah Chafee⟩ ⟨Christians differ in their understanding of religious *obligation* —J.C.Swaim⟩ ⟨one of the most compelling *obligations* of the good citizen —John Lodge⟩ ⟨one's *obligation* to provide for one's family⟩ whereas DUTY can suggest less immediate compulsion but a greater general compulsion on moral or ethical grounds ⟨one's *duty* to one's family⟩ ⟨considered that every one owed a certain *duty* to society —A.C.Benson⟩ ⟨the *duty* of self-preservation —W.R. Inge⟩ ⟨still has his *duty* to his mother —Mary Austin⟩ **syn** see in addition DEBT

ob·li·ga·tion·al \ˌ==ˈgāshənᵊl, -shnəl\ *adj* **:** of, relating to, or constituting an obligation; *specif* **:** qualified to create a legal or financial obligation ⟨an ~ authority⟩

ob·li·ga·tive \ˈ==ˌgād·iv\ *adj* [L *obligatus* (past part. of *obligare* to oblige) + E *-ive*] **1 :** entailing an obligation **:** OBLIGATORY ⟨an ~ contract⟩ **2 :** OBLIGATE 1b **3 a :** characterized by or relating to the obligative mood **b :** containing a form in the obligative mood

obligative mood *n* **:** modal expression of obligation or propriety (as in "the door *should* be closed")

obli·gato *var of* OBBLIGATO

ob·li·ga·tor \ˈäbləˌgād·ə(r)\ *n* -s [ML, fr. L *obligatus* + *-or*] **1 :** OBLIGOR **2 :** OBLIGER

oblig·a·to·ri·ly \əˌbligəˈtōrəlē, ˌäbləg-, -lēg-, -tȯr-, -li, *chiefly Brit* ˈäbləˌgāt(ə)rəli\ *adv* **:** in an obligatory manner **:** so as to be obligatory ⟨they are infinitesimally small, living things, ~ parasitic —W.A.Hagan⟩

ob·li·ga·to·ri·ness \-rēnəs, -rin-\ *n* -ES **:** the quality or state of being obligatory

oblig·a·to·ry \əˈbligəˌtōrē, ˈäbləg-, -lēg-, -tȯr-, -ri, *chiefly Brit* ˈäbləˌgātəri *or* -ā·tri\ *adj* [ME, fr. MF *obligatoire*, fr. LL *obligatorius*, fr. L *obligatus* + *-orius* -ory] **1 a :** demanded or required by existing obligations esp. of a moral or legal nature; *specif* **:** binding in law or conscience **b :** imposing or constituting duty or obligation — often used with *on* or *upon* ⟨obedience is ~ on a soldier⟩ **2 :** relating to or used to create or enforce an obligation ⟨a writ ~⟩ **3 :** having to be coped with (as by studying, acting, paying) **:** REQUIRED ⟨physical education is ~⟩ ⟨an ~ contribution⟩ **4 :** OBLIGATE 1b

ob·li·ga·tum \ˌäbləˈgād·əm, -ād·əm\ *n, pl* **obliga·ta** \-ād·ə, -ād·ə\ [NL, lit., obligation, fr. L, neut. of *obligatus*, past part. of *obligare*] **:** a proposition that is not self-contradictory and that is assumed for argument in scholastic disputation

oblige \əˈblīj\ *vb* -ED/-ING/-s [ME *obligen*, fr. OF *obliger*, fr. L *obligare*, fr. *ob-* to, against, over + *ligare* to bind, tie — more at OB-, LIGATURE] *vt* **1 :** to constrain (as another or oneself) by physical, moral, or legal force **:** put under obligation to do or to forbear from doing something ⟨necessity *obliged* him to this crime⟩ ⟨we *obliged* ourselves to settle our father's bills⟩ ⟨the soldiers were *obliged* to retreat⟩ ⟨the law ~s everyone to pay his taxes⟩ **2 a** *obs* **:** to pledge as security **:** PAWN, MORTGAGE **b** *obs* **:** to bind as subject to a penalty (as by a bond) **c :** to make (oneself) liable to punishment under the law **3 a :** to bind by a favor or service performed **:** place under obligation by helping or favoring **:** make indebted by such treatment ⟨you will ~ me greatly if you get there early⟩ **b :** to do a favor or minor service for ⟨always seeking to ~ his friends⟩ **c** *obs* **:** PLEASE, ACCOMMODATE, GRATIFY **d** *dial* **:** to work for esp. in a domestic capacity ⟨used to ~ a few favored neighbors on festive occasions⟩ **e :** to make a loan to ⟨can you ~ me with a few dollars⟩ **~** *vi* **:** to do something as or as if a favor ⟨the sun *obliged* somewhat fitfully —Mollie Panter-Downes⟩: as **a :** to perform by way of entertainment ⟨the quartet will ~ with a song⟩ **b** *dial* **:** to work for someone esp. in a domestic capacity ⟨she *obliged* for the cottagers in summer⟩

syn OBLIGE, ACCOMMODATE, FAVOR all signify to do a service or perform a courtesy. OBLIGE suggests the doing of something that is so pleasing or so esp. convenient for someone else that it could be thought to, though does not necessarily, create an obligation ⟨*oblige* a friend by lending him money⟩ ⟨the hotel *obliged* by serving them meals at odd hours with no extra charge⟩ ⟨*oblige* me by retiring for the night —George Meredith⟩ ACCOMMODATE, often interchangeable with *oblige*, usu. suggests the putting of oneself to some inconvenience or sacrifice to oblige; in its very common use in business it frequently suggests a practical or commercial motive above that of goodwill ⟨*accommodate* a friend with the loan of a car⟩ ⟨keep exotic foods in stock to *accommodate* special customers⟩ FAVOR usu. confines the service or courtesy to one of goodwill ⟨*favor* one's friends with many small kindnesses⟩ ⟨*favor* an audience with an encore⟩ although it has come, in this sense, to suggest often a supercilious or patronizing quality in the action ⟨*favor* common people around him with a cold smile⟩ ⟨*favor* his admirers with a glance⟩ ⟨*favor* his parents with a yearly letter⟩ **syn** see in addition FORCE

obliged \-jd\ *adj* **1 :** full of appreciation **:** OBLIGATED **2 a :** FATED, SURE ⟨it's ~ to rain soon⟩ **b :** FORCED ⟨~ to continue on foot⟩ — **oblig·ed·ly** \-jədlē, -li\ *adv* — **oblig·ed·ness** \-jədnəs\ *n* -ES

ob·li·gee \ˌäbləˈjē\ *n* -s [*oblige* + *-ee*] **1 a :** one to whom another is obligated **:** one toward whom another has undertaken an obligation **:** one in a position to enforce a legal duty owed by another — opposed to *obligor* **b :** a person whose interests are protected under a surety bond **2 :** one who is obliged — opposed to *obliger*

oblige·ment \əˈblījmənt\ *n* -s [F, fr. *obliger* to oblige + *-ment*] **:** an obligation or accommodation esp. resulting from a service or favor

oblig·er \-jə(r)\ *n* -s **:** one that obligates or obliges

obliging *adj* [fr. pres. part. of *oblige*] **1** *archaic* **:** OBLIGATING, OBLIGATORY **2 :** willing to do services or favors **:** accommodating to others **:** HELPFUL, COOPERATIVE ⟨was very ~ and offered to do anything in his power —Bram Stoker⟩ **syn** see AMIABLE

oblig·ing·ly *adv* **:** in an obliging manner **:** PLEASANTLY, COOPERATIVELY

oblig·ing·ness *n* -ES **:** the quality or state of being obliging

ob·li·gis·tic \ˌäbləˈjistik\ *adj* [NL *obligatum* + E *-istic*] **:** of or relating to the obligata of scholastic disputation ⟨an ~ proposition⟩

ob·li·gor \ˌäbləˈgȯ(ə)r, -ō(ə)\ *n* -s [*oblige* + *-or*] **1 :** one that binds himself or gives his bond to another **:** one that places himself under a legal obligation — opposed to *obligee* **2 a :** a surety or surety company that writes a bond **b :** the person bonded under a surety bond

obliquate *vt* -ED/-ING/-s [L *obliquatus*, past part. of *obliquare* to bend aside, turn aside, fr. *obliquus* oblique] *obs* **:** to turn or bend aside or to one side — **obliquation** *n* -s *obs*

¹**oblique** \əˈblēk, ōˈ-, -līk\ *adj* [ME *oblike*, fr. L *obliquus*, fr. *ob-* to, towards, over + *-liquus* (akin to L *liquis* oblique); akin to L *ulna* elbow — more at OB-, ELL] **1 a :** neither perpendicular nor parallel **:** having a slanting direction or position **:** INCLINED **b** *of a solid* **:** having the axis not perpendicular to the base **2 a :** not straightforward **:** INDIRECT, OBSCURE ⟨~ glances⟩ ⟨~ accusations⟩ ⟨~ perspective⟩ **b :** DEVIOUS, UNDERHAND, PERVERSE, SINISTER ⟨behaving in a curiously ~ manner⟩ **c** (1) **:** SKEW ⟨an ~ arch⟩ ⟨~ bridges⟩ (2) *of a leaf* **:** having the two sides of the blade unequal esp. at the base **3 :** not direct in descent **:** COLLATERAL **4** *of a muscle* **:** situated obliquely and having one end that is not inserted on bone ⟨the ~ muscles of the eye or abdomen⟩ **5 :** taken from an airplane with the camera axis intentionally directed horizontally or downward but not vertically — used of a photograph of the surface of the earth — **oblique·ly** *adv* — **oblique·ness** *n* -ES

²**oblique** \"\ *n* -s **1 :** an oblique thing (as a line or photograph) **2 :** any of several oblique muscles: as **a :** one of the thin flat muscles forming the middle and outer layers of the lateral walls of the abdomen and having aponeuroses that extend medially to ensheathe the rectus muscles and fuse in the midventral line in the linear alba **b** (1) **:** a long thin muscle that is inserted on the upper part of the eyeball and that moves the eye downward and laterally — called also *superior oblique* (2) **:** a short muscle that is inserted slightly in front of and below the superior oblique and that moves the eye upward and laterally — called also *inferior oblique* **3 :** DIAGONAL 4 **4 :** a printed letter characterized by essentially the same form and degree of inclination as italic **5 a :** OBLIQUE CASE **b :** an inflection of an oblique case

³**oblique** \əˈblīk, ōˈ-\ *vi* -ED/-ING/-s [F *obliquer*, fr. L *obliquare* to bend aside, turn aside, fr. *obliquus* oblique] *of a military formation* **:** to march or advance obliquely at an angle of about 45 degrees to the original front formerly by oblique steps but now by direct steps with the participants half-faced to right or left and marching forward

oblique angle *n* **:** an acute or obtuse angle — distinguished from *right angle*

oblique case *n* **:** a grammatical case other than the nominative and vocative

oblique coordinates *n pl* **:** Cartesian coordinates that are not rectangular

oblique drawing *n* **:** a projective drawing of which the frontal lines are given in true proportions and relations and all others at suitable angles other than 90 degrees without regard to the rules of linear perspective

oblique fault *n* **:** a geological fault whose trend is oblique to the strike

oblique helicoid *n* **:** a helicoid whose generating half line maintains a constant oblique angle with the helix axis

oblique lamination *n* **:** CROSS-BEDDING

oblique·ly *adv* **:** in an oblique way or direction

oblique·ness *n* -ES **:** the quality or state of being oblique

oblique projection *n* **1 :** a representation in a mechanical drawing of an object usu. placed with its front face or with two of its principal axes parallel to a plane of projection by means of lines of projection that make angles of other than 90 degrees with the plane **2 :** a map projection not centered upon one of the poles or on the equator and not using the equator or a meridian as a center line of orientation

oblique sailing *n* **:** the movement of a vessel when it sails upon a course making an oblique angle with the meridian

oblique section *n* **:** a section in a mechanical drawing that is neither a cross section nor a longitudinal section

oblique sphere *n* **:** the celestial sphere and its analogous terrestrial sphere when oriented so the heavenly bodies rise and set at angles other than a right angle (as for an observer at any point on the earth except the poles and the equator)

oblique triangle *n* **:** a triangle that is not a right triangle

ob·liq·ui·tous \ə'blikwəd·əs, ō'-, -ətəs\ *adj* **:** exhibiting or characterized by obliquity

ob·liq·ui·ty \-wəd·ē, -ətē, -i\ *n* -ES [ME *obliquitee*, fr. MF *obliquité*, fr. L *obliquitat-, obliquitas*, fr. *obliquus* oblique + *-itat-, -itas* -ity — more at OBLIQUE] **1 a :** deviation from moral rectitude or sound thinking **b** *obs* **:** deviation from ordinary rules **2 a** (1) **:** the quality or state of being oblique **:** deviation from parallelism or perpendicularity (2) **:** the amount of such deviation **:** DIVERGENCE **b** *or* **obliquity of the ecliptic :** the angle between the planes of the earth's equator and orbit having a mean value of 23°26′40″.16 in 1960 and diminishing 0″.47 per year **3 a :** indirectness or deliberate obscurity of speech or conduct **b :** an obscure or confusing statement ⟨hiding their thoughts behind such *obliquities*⟩

ob·lit·er·a·ble \ə'blid·ərəbəl, ō'-, ä'-, -itər-\ *adj* **:** capable of being obliterated

1ob·lit·er·ate \-rət\ *adj* [L *obliteratus, oblitteratus*, past part. of *obliterare, oblitterare* to obliterate] **1 :** blotted out **:** OBLITERATED **2 :** FAINT, INDISTINCT, OBSCURE — used esp. of markings on an insect

2obliterate \-,rāt, *usu* -ād.+V\ *vb* -ED/-ING/-S [L *obliteratus, oblitteratus*, past part. of *obliterare, oblitterare*, prob. fr. *ob-* to, against, over + *litera, littera* letter — more at OB-, LETTER] *vt* **1 :** to remove from significance and bring to nothingness: as **a :** to make undecipherable or imperceptible by obscuring, covering, or wearing or chipping away ⟨a dimness . . . envelops consciousness as mist ~*s* a crag —Emily Dickinson⟩ ⟨only copper so worn that even the stamp is *obliterated* —Amy Lowell⟩ **b :** to remove utterly from recognition, cognizance, consideration, or memory ⟨a successful love crowned all other successes and *obliterated* all other failures —J.W.Krutch⟩ **c** (1) **:** to remove from existence **:** make nonexistent **:** destroy utterly all traces, indications, significance of ⟨many of our monuments . . . seem to shout for a friendly zeppelin to ~ them —W.R.Inge⟩ (2) **:** to cause to disappear (as a body part, scar, or the lumen of a duct) **:** REMOVE ⟨possible to ~ the gall bladder by electrosurgical methods⟩ **2 :** to withdraw utterly from attention and make as inconspicuous as if nonexistent ⟨those hero-worshipers who ~ themselves —Robert Lynd⟩ **3 :** CANCEL ~ *vi* **:** to become obliterated **syn** see ERASE

ob·lit·er·at·ing·ly *adv* **:** in an obliterating manner **:** so as to obliterate

ob·lit·er·a·tion \ə,blid·ə'rāshən, ō,-, ä,-, -litə-\ *n* -S [L *obliteratio, oblitteratio*, fr. *obliteratus, oblitteratus* + *-ion-, -io* -ion] **1 :** an act or instance of obliterating **2 :** the state of being obliterated **:** EXTINCTION

ob·lit·er·a·tive \ə'=·=,rād·iv, ,rə|, |t|, |ēv *also* |əv\ *adj* **:** inducing or characterized by obliteration: as **a :** causing or accompanied by collapse or closure of a lumen (as of a blood vessel) ⟨~ endarteritis⟩ **b :** tending to make inconspicuous ⟨the characteristic ~ shading of fishes⟩ ⟨~ behavior⟩ — **ob·lit·er·a·tive·ly** \|əvlē, -li\ *adv*

ob·lit·er·a·tor \-,rād·ə(r), -ātə-\ *n* -S [LL *obliterator, oblitterator*, fr. L *obliteratus, oblitteratus* + *-or*] **:** one that obliterates; *esp* **:** a device for canceling postage stamps

ob·li·ves·cence \,äblə'ves°n(t)s\ *n* -S [alter. (influenced by *-escence*) of *obliviscence*] **:** an act or the process of forgetting

ob·liv·i·al \ə'blivēəl\ *adj* [L *oblivialis*, fr. *oblivion-, oblivio* oblivion + *-alis* -al] **:** OBLIVIOUS **:** causing oblivion — **ob·liv·i·al·i·ty** \=,==ʼaləd·ē\ *n* -ES

ob·liv·i·ate \ə'===,āt\ *vt* -ED/-ING/-S [L *oblivion-, oblivio* oblivion + E *-ate*] **:** FORGET

ob·liv·i·on \ə'blivēən, ō'-, ä'-\ *n* -S [ME, fr. MF, fr. L *oblivion-, oblivio*, fr. *oblivisci* to forget (perh. fr. *ob-* to, over, completely + *levis* smooth) + *-ion-, -io* -ion — more at OB-, LIME] **1 :** an act of forgetting or the fact of having forgotten **:** FORGETFULNESS, OBLIVIOUSNESS ⟨seeking ease and the ~ of sleep⟩ **2 :** the quality or state of being forgotten ⟨contentedly accepted his political ~⟩ **3 :** official ignoring of offenses **:** general pardon **:** AMNESTY ⟨an act of ~⟩

ob·liv·i·on·ize \-,nīz\ *vt* -ED/-ING/-S **:** to relegate to oblivion

ob·liv·i·ous \ə'blivēəs, ō'-, ä'-\ *adj* [ME, fr. L *obliviosus*, fr. *oblivion-, oblivio* oblivion + *-osus* -ous] **1 :** lacking remembrance, memory, or mindful attention **:** characterized by forgetfulness ⟨~ old age⟩ — usu. used with *of* ⟨~ of past slights⟩ **2** *archaic* **:** relating to or associated with forgetfulness **3 :** lacking active conscious knowledge or awareness **:** UNNOTICING, UNAWARE — usu. used with *of* or *to* ⟨~ to the risk she ran⟩ ⟨~ of the surrounding crowds⟩ **syn** see FORGETFUL

ob·liv·i·ous·ly *adv* **:** without remembrance or awareness **:** in an oblivious manner

ob·liv·i·ous·ness *n* -ES **:** the quality or state of being oblivious

ob·li·vis·cence \,äblə'vis°n(t)s\ *n* -S [L *oblivisci* to forget + E *-ence*] **:** FORGETFULNESS

ob·lo·cu·tor \ä'blo'kyüd·ə(r)\ *n* -S [L, fr. *oblocutus* (past part. of *obloqui* to speak against) + *-or* — more at OBLOQUY] **:** DISPUTER, GAINSAYER, DETRACTOR — used chiefly in law

ob·long \'ä,blȯŋ *also* -läŋ\ *adj* [ME *oblonge*, fr. L *oblongus* elongated, somewhat long, fr. *ob-* toward, over, completely + *longus* long — more at OB-, LONG] **:** deviating from a square or circular form through elongation: **a :** rectangular with adjacent sides unequal **b :** rectangular with the normally horizontal dimension the greater — used of a plane surface or of an object with a principal plane surface ⟨an ~ sheet of paper⟩ ⟨~ tables⟩ — **ob·long·ly** *adv* — **ob·long·ness** *n* -ES

2oblong \"\ *n* -S **:** an oblong figure ⟨a border of silver ~*s*⟩

ob·lon·ga·ta \,ä,blȯŋ'gäd·ə\ *n, pl* **oblonga·tas** \-äd·əz\ *or* **ob·lon·ga·tae** \-äd·,ē\ [NL, lit., oblong, fem. of *oblongatus*, past part. of *oblongare* to elongate, fr. L *oblongus* oblong] **:** MEDULLA OBLONGATA

ob·long·atal \'ä,blȯŋ'gäd·°l *also* -läŋ-\ *adj* [NL *oblongata* + E *-al*] **:** of, relating to, occurring or originating in, or affecting the medulla oblongata

ob·long·at·ed \(')ä¦blȯŋ,gād·əd *also* -läŋ-\ *adj* [NL *oblongatus* (past part. of *oblongare* to prolong, elongate) + E *-ed*] **:** PROLONGED, ELONGATED

ob·long·ish \'ä,blȯŋish, -ŋēsh *also* -läŋ-\ *adj* **:** somewhat oblong

ob·lo·qui·al \ä'blōkwēəl,ə'-\ *adj* **:** relating to or constituting obloquy

obloquious *adj, obs* **:** characterized by obloquy

ob·lo·quy \'äbləkwē, -kwi\ *n* -ES [LL *obloquium*, fr. L *obloqui* to speak against, fr. *ob-* toward, against + *loqui* to speak — more at OB-] **1 a :** a strongly and often intemperately condemnatory utterance **:** defamatory or calumnious language **:** abusive or slanderous reprehension **:** CALUMNY ⟨names . . . mentioned with ~ and detraction —Joseph Addison⟩ **b** *obs* **:** a calumnious utterance **2 a :** the condition of one that is subjected to or deserving of obloquy **:** a blending of ill fame, hatred, and contempt on the one hand with distress and shame on the other ⟨living out his days in the ~ of one who had betrayed a solemn trust⟩ **b** *obs* **:** a cause or source of reproach **:** DISGRACE **syn** see ABUSE, DISHONOR

ob·mu·tes·cence \,äbmyə'tes°n(t)s\ *n* [L *obmutescere* to become mute (fr. *ob-* to, toward + *mutescere* to become mute, fr. *mutus* mute) + E *-ence* — more at OB-, MUTE] **:** a becoming or keeping silent or mute

ob·neb·u·late \äb'nebyə,lāt, əb-\ *vt* -ED/-ING/-S [*ob-* + L *nebula* mist, cloud + E *-ate* — more at NEBULA] **:** BECLOUD, BEFOG

ob·nounce \=ʼnaùn(t)s\ *vi* -ED/-ING/-S [L *obnunciare, obnuntiare*, lit., to announce, fr. *ob-* to, toward + *nunciare, nuntiare* to report, relate — more at NUNCIATURE] **:** to tell of an ill omen

ob·nox·i·e·ty \,äb,näk'sīəd·ē\ *n* -ES [ML *obnoxietas*, fr. L *obnoxius* obnoxious + *-tas* -ty] **:** LIABILITY

ob·nox·ious \əb'näkshəs, äb'-\ *adj* [L *obnoxiosus* subjected, submissive, fr. *obnoxius* subject to harm (fr. *ob-* to, toward + *noxius* harmful, noxious) + *-osus* -ous — more at OB-, NOXIOUS] **1 a** *archaic* **:** subject to the authority or power of another **:** exposed or open to a particular action or influence **b** *obs* **:** SUBMISSIVE, OBSEQUIOUS **2 :** subject, liable, exposed, or open (as to a hurtful influence) — used with *to* ⟨actions ~ to censure⟩ **3 :** deserving of censure **:** REPREHENSIBLE **4** [influenced in meaning by L *noxius*] *obs* **:** HARMFUL, NOXIOUS **5 :** forming an object of dislike or disgust **:** OFFENSIVE, ODIOUS, OBJECTIONABLE ⟨thoroughly ~ views⟩ ⟨~ to his associates⟩ **syn** see HATEFUL

ob·nox·ious·ly *adv* **:** in an obnoxious manner **:** so as to be obnoxious

ob·nox·ious·ness *n* -ES **:** the quality or state of being obnoxious

ob·nu·bi·late \äb'n(y)übə,lāt, əb'-\ *vt* -ED/-ING/-S [L *obnubilatus*, past part. of *obnubilare* to cover with clouds, fr. *ob-* to, over + *nubilus* cloudy, fr. *nubes* cloud — more at OB-, NUANCE] **1 :** to cover or obscure by or as if by clouds **:** BECLOUD ⟨vision *obnubilated* by fatigue⟩ **2 a :** to make cloudy of mind ⟨*obnubilated* by scholastic philosophy⟩ **b :** to induce torpor in ⟨~ with drugs⟩ **syn** see OBSCURE

ob·nu·bi·la·tion \=,==ʼlāshən\ *n* -S [LL *obnubilation-, obnubilatio*, fr. L *obnubilatus* (past part. of *obnubilare*) + *-ion-, -io* -ion] **:** the quality or state of being or making something be cloudy or obscure ⟨~ of the intellect⟩

1oboe \'ō(,)bō\ *n* -S [It, fr. F *hautbois*, fr. MF — more at

oboe

HAUTBOIS] **1 :** a nontransposing orchestral woodwind instrument having a conical body with a slightly flaring end, a double reed mouthpiece, a range from B-flat below to third G above middle C, and a nasal and penetrating tone quality and forming the highest and chief member of a family of double-reed instruments — compare BASSOON, ENGLISH HORN **2 :** an organ reed stop that gives a tone resembling that of an oboe **3 :** a chanter in a bagpipe

2oboe \"\ *usu cap* — a communications code word for the letter *o*

3oboe \"\ *n* -S *usu cap* [prob. so called fr. its being a key word for the letter O] **:** a radar blind-bombing and navigation system in which one airplane flies a circular course while two ground stations measure the distance to a radar beacon in the plane

oboe da cac·cia \¦ō(,)bōdə'kächə, ,ōbə,wäd-\ *n, pl* **oboi da caccia** \,ōbə,wēd-\ *or* **oboe da caccias** \-chəz\ [It, lit., oboe of the hunt] **:** an alto oboe that is the forerunner of the modern English horn

oboe d'a·mo·re \¦ō(,)bōdə'mōrē, ,ōbə,wäd-\ *n, pl* **oboi d'amore** \,ōbə,wēd-\ *or* **oboe d'amores** \-r,ēz\ [It, lit., oboe of love, prob. trans. of F *hautbois d'amour*] **1 :** a mezzo-soprano oboe having a pear-shaped bell and a rich somber tone **2** *or* **oboe d'a·mour** \¦ō(,)bōdə'mü(ə)r\ *pl* **oboe d'a·mours** \-rz\ [modif. (influenced by ¹*oboe*) of F *hautbois d'amour*] **:** a pipe-organ oboe stop having a veiled and pathetic tone

obo·ist *or* **oboe·ist** \'ō(,)bōəst, -,bəwəst\ *n* -S [*oboist* prob. fr. It *oboista*, fr. *oboe* + *-ista* -ist (fr. L); *oboeist* fr. *oboe* + *-ist*] **:** an oboe player

obol \'äbəl, 'ōb-\ *n* -S [L *obolus*, fr. Gk *obolos*, lit., nail; akin to Gk *obelos* spit, pointed pillar, obelus] **1 :** a unit of weight of ancient Greece equivalent in the Attic standard to ⅙ drachma or 11¼ grains or 0.71 grams **2 :** an ancient Greek coin equal to ⅙ drachma **3 a :** OBOLE **b :** any of several old small coins of the European continent

ob·ole \'ä,bōl\ *n* -S [F, fr. L *obulus*] **:** the medieval half denier of France

ob·o·lus \'äbələs\ *n, pl* **obo·li** \-,lī\ [L] **:** OBOL 2, 3

ob·omegoid \¦äb+\ *adj* [*ob-* + *omegoid*] **:** obversely omegoid

obon·go \ō'bäŋ(,)gō\ *n, pl* **obongo** *or* **obongos** *usu cap* **:** ABONGO

ob·ovate \(')äb+\ *adj* [*ob-* + *ovate*] **:** inversely ovate **:** ovate with the narrower end basal ⟨an ~ leaf⟩ — see LEAF illustration

ob·ovoid \"+\ *adj* [*ob-* + *ovoid*] **:** ovoid with the broad end toward the apex ⟨an ~ fruit⟩

ob·pyramidal \¦äb+\ *adj* [ISV *ob-* + *pyramidal*] **:** inversely pyramidal — compare CUNEATE

ob·pyriform \(')äb+\ *adj* [*ob-* + *pyriform*] **:** inversely pyriform

ob·rep·tion \ä'brepshən\ *n* -S [L *obreption-, obreptio* act of creeping upon, stealing upon, deceiving, fr. *obreptus* (past part. of *obrepere* to steal upon, surprise, deceive, fr. *ob-* to, toward, over + *repere* to creep) + *-ion-, -io* -ion — more at OB-, REPTILE] *canon & Scots law* **:** the obtaining of or attempting to obtain a dispensation from ecclesiastical authority or a gift from the sovereign by fraud — distinguished from *subreption*

ob·rep·ti·tious \¦ä,brep¦tishəs\ *adj* [LL *obrepticius, obreptitius*, fr. L *obreptus* (past part. of *obrepere*) + *-icius, -itius* -itious] **:** marked by obreption **:** done or obtained by trickery or by concealing the truth — **ob·rep·ti·tious·ly** *adv*

o'bri·en potatoes \ō'brīən-\ *n pl, usu cap O&B* [prob. fr. the name *O'Brien*] **:** diced potatoes sautéed in butter and dressed with chopped sweet pepper

ob·ro·gate \'äbrə,gāt, *usu* -ād.+V\ *vt* -ED/-ING/-S [L *obrogatus*, past part. of *obrogare* to obrogate, fr. *ob-* toward, against + *rogare* to ask, propose, propose a law — more at OB-, RIGHT] **:** to modify or repeal (a law) in whole or in part by passing a new law — compare ABROGATE 1 — **ob·ro·ga·tion** \,==ʼgāshən\ *n*

ob·rok \ä'bräk, ə'brȯk\ *n* -S [Russ, fr. *ob-* (fr. *ob* to, on) + *rok* regulation, term, fate, lot; akin to L *ob* to, before, against and to OE *regn-* might, ON *rögn*, pl., the decreeing powers, gods, Goth *ragin* counsel, decision, Skt *racayati* he completes, builds — more at EPI-] **:** a yearly tax formerly paid by a Russian peasant engaged in trade

ob·ro·tund \'äbrə¦tənd\ *adj* [LL *obrotundus*, fr. L *ob-* to, over, completely + *rotundus* round — more at OB-, ROUND] **:** nearly spherical but with one diameter slightly exceeding the others **:** OBROUND

ob·round \(')äb+\ *adj* [*ob-* + *round*] **:** having the form of a flattened cylinder with the sides parallel and the ends hemispherical

obs *abbr* **1** obscure **2** observation; observatory; observed **3** obsolete **4** obstacle **5** obstruction

ob·scene \əb'sēn, (')äb¦s-\ *adj* -ER/-EST [MF, fr. L *obscenus, obscaenus*; prob. fr. a prehistoric Latin compound whose first constituent is akin to L *ob* to, before, and whose second constituent is akin to L *caenum* filth, Sw dial. *hven* swamp, Latvian *svīns* dirtied — more at EPI-] **1 a :** disgusting to the senses usu. because of some filthy, grotesque, or unnatural quality ⟨~ fungi clothed the wall of that dank cavern⟩ ⟨dressed in ~ rags⟩ **b :** grossly repugnant to the generally accepted notions of what is appropriate **:** SHOCKING ⟨death under the stars is ~ somehow —*Infantry Jour.*⟩ **2 :** offensive or revolting as countering or violating some ideal or principle: as **a :** abhorrent to morality or virtue **:** stressing or reveling in the lewd or lustful; *specif* **:** inciting or designed to incite to lust, depravity, indecency ⟨the dance often becomes flagrantly ~ and definitely provocative —Margaret Mead⟩ ⟨a sly and ~ humor, the whispering and important lecheries of an old worn-out rake —Thomas Wolfe⟩ **b :** marked by violation of accepted language inhibitions and by the use of words regarded as taboo in polite usage ⟨~ chantey —Sinclair Lewis⟩ **c :** repulsive by reason of malignance, hypocrisy, cynicism, irresponsibility, crass disregard of moral or ethical principles ⟨the ~ little counterdemonstration lewdly exulting in the forthcoming deaths —T.R.Ybarra⟩ ⟨the debate . . . was almost ~ in its irresponsibility —*New Republic*⟩ **syn** see COARSE

ob·scene·ly *adv* **:** to an obscene degree **:** in an obscene manner

ob·scene·ness \-nnəs\ *n* -ES **:** OBSCENITY 1a

ob·scen·i·ty \əb'senəd·ē, äb'-, -sēn-, -əti, -i\ *n* -ES [F *obscenité*, fr. L *obscenitat-, obscenitas, obscaenitat-, obscaenitas*, fr. *obscenus, obscaenus* obscene + *-itat-, itas* -ity] **1 a :** the quality or state of being obscene ⟨the ~ of a writing may lie as much in intent as in wording⟩ **b** *archaic* **:** FILTHINESS, FOULNESS **2 :** something (as an utterance or act) that is obscene — usu. used in pl. ⟨*obscenities* in the public press⟩

1ob·scu·rant \əbz'kyùrənt, äb-, -b'sk-\ *n* -S [F, fr. L *obscurant-, obscurans*, pres. part. of *obscurare* to obscure] **:** one who obscures esp. by striving to prevent enlightenment or to hinder the progress of knowledge and wisdom — compare OBSCURANTIST

2obscurant \"\ *or* **ob·scu·ran·tic** \¦äbzkyə¦rantik, -bsk-\ *adj* **1 :** tending to make obscure **2 :** of or relating to obscurants or obscurantism

ob·scu·ran·tism \əbz'kyùrən·,tizəm, äb-, -b'sk-; ,äbzkyə'ran-, -bsk-\ *also* **ob·scu·ran·ti·cism** \,äbzkyə'rantə,sizəm, -bsk-\ *n* -S [*obscurantism* fr. F *obscurantisme*, fr. *obscurant* + *-isme* -ism; *obscuranticism* fr. *obscurantic* + *-ism*] **1 :** deprecation of or positive opposition to enlightenment or the spread of knowledge; *esp* **:** a policy (as in art or social science) of deliberately making something obscure or withholding knowledge from the general public **2 a :** a style (as in literature or art) characterized by haziness and lack of sharp definition **b :** an act or instance of obscurantism **:** an obscure utterance or one intended to confuse ⟨legal ~*s*⟩

1ob·scu·ran·tist \əbz'kyùrəntəst, äb-, -b'sk-; ,äbzkyə'ran-, -bsk-\ *n* -S [¹*obscurant* + *-ist*] **:** a practitioner of or believer in obscurantism

2obscurantist \=ʼ===, ¦==¦==\ *adj* **1 :** of, relating to, or constituting obscurantism ⟨~ doctrines⟩ **:** affected by obscurantism ⟨an American society made sterile and ~ by big business —H.N.Smith⟩ **2 :** being or characteristic of an obscurantist ⟨a notably ~ leader⟩

ob·scu·ra·tion \,äbzkyə'rāshən, -bsk-\ *n* -S [ME, fr. L *obscuration-, obscuratio*, fr. *obscuratus* (past part. of *obscurare* to obscure) + *-ion-, -io* -ion] **:** an act of obscuring or the quality or state of being obscured

ob·scu·ra·tive \əbz'kyùrəd·iv, äb-, -b'sk-\ *adj* [L *obscuratus* (past part. of *obscurare*) + E *-ive*] **:** tending to obscure

1ob·scure \əbz'kyù(ə)r, (')äbz¦k-, -b'sk-, -b¦sk-, -ùə\ *adj, sometimes* -ER/-EST [ME, fr. MF *obscur*, fr. L *obscurus*, fr. *ob-* to, against, over + *-scurus* (akin to OHG *scūr* covered place, shelter, OFris *skūre* barn, shed, Icel *skūrr* sheltering roof, Gk *keuthein* to conceal, *skytos* skin, leather — more at OB-, HIDE] **1 :** lacking or inadequately supplied with light **:** DARK, DIM, GLOOMY ⟨the ~ dusk of the shuttered room⟩ **2 :** not readily perceived: as **a** *of a place* **:** withdrawn from the centers of human activity **:** REMOTE, RETIRED, SECRET ⟨these ~ regions⟩ ⟨settled in an ~ country village⟩ **b :** not readily understood **:** lacking clarity or legibility **:** not clearly expressed **:** ABSTRUSE ⟨an ~ reference⟩ ⟨an ~ writing⟩ **c :** lacking showiness, worth, or prominence by which the attention might be attracted **:** INCONSPICUOUS, HUMBLE ⟨such ~ everyday people⟩ ⟨an ~ Roman poet⟩ ⟨this ~ cottage housed an unnoticed genius⟩ **d :** lacking clarity or distinctness of form or outline **:** FAINT, INDISTINCT ⟨~ markings on the wing of a butterfly⟩ ⟨a delicate pattern of ~ lines⟩ **e :** indistinctly or imperfectly felt or apprehended ⟨an ~ pulse⟩ ⟨sounds ~ in the distance⟩ **3 :** of or relating to darkness **:** frequenting or enveloped in darkness **:** UNSEEN ⟨the ~ powers of evil⟩ ⟨standing ~ in the deepest shade⟩ **4 :** constituting the unstressed vowel \ə\ or having unstressed \ə\ as its value

syn DARK, VAGUE, ENIGMATIC, CRYPTIC, AMBIGUOUS, EQUIVOCAL: OBSCURE may apply to communication the meaning of which is hidden or veiled, often through some defect of expression, sometimes through abstruse or arcane nature ⟨there are more *obscure* poems written and printed every year than clear ones —R.B.West⟩ ⟨the communiqué was apt to be *obscure* as to its sense, so that the priests might have to clarify it —W.W. Howells⟩ DARK may refer to what is imperfectly revealed and hence somewhat mysterious, often possibly with ominous or sinister suggestion ⟨they hunt for clues to our present duty and future destiny among the *dark* sayings of Daniel, Micah, and the Book of Revelations —Brand Blanshard⟩ VAGUE may describe that which lacks clear distinctness as not susceptible to definitive formulation or as imperfectly conceived or not definitively thought out ⟨much *vaguer* and indeed obscure allegory —Rex Warner⟩ ⟨only a *vague*, genial theory as a policy with inadequate preparation, and lacking a clear-cut, definitive, and detailed plan —R.E.Danielson⟩ ⟨a *vague* sense of obligation was replaced by an exacting set of rules —R.W.Southern⟩ ENIGMATIC refers to what puzzles by suggestive unclarity of allusion or ramification ⟨this *enigmatic* utterance —Jack London⟩ ⟨fell to conjecturing the meaning of Farfrae's *enigmatic* words about not daring to ask her what he fain would —Thomas Hardy⟩ CRYPTIC may describe that which is purposefully darkly enigmatic or esoteric ⟨a very *cryptic* text —S.F.Mason⟩ ⟨that *cryptic* unintelligibility, the sibylline phrase, which, if it has a meaning, sometimes guards it all too well from the bewildered reader —*Amer. Guide Series: Mass.*⟩ AMBIGUOUS applies to communication admitting of more than one interpretation ⟨most words are *ambiguous* as regards their plain sense, especially in poetry —I.A.Richards⟩ ⟨the title of this chapter is *ambiguous* —A.S.Eddington⟩ EQUIVOCAL may describe whatever admits of false interpretation, often purposefully phrased or delivered as an expedient to deceive or evade ⟨to veil the matter, with utterances capable of more *equivocal* meaning —H.O.Taylor⟩ ⟨the Moral Law speaks in *equivocal* tones to those who listen most scrupulously for its dictates —L.P.Smith⟩ **syn** see in addition DARK

2obscure \"\ *vt* -ED/-ING/-S [L *obscurare*, fr. *obscurus* obscure] **1 :** to make obscure: as **a :** to make dim **:** DARKEN ⟨the soot on the lampshade *obscured* the light⟩ **b :** to conceal or hide from view as by or as if by covering wholly or in part **:** make difficult to discern ⟨the fine sunburn somewhat *obscured* the inherent transparency of his complexion —Elinor Wylie⟩; *also* **:** DISGUISE ⟨no dukedom even, however high-sounding and traditional, could ~ for him native idiocy —Osbert Sitwell⟩ **c :** to dim in glory or significance **:** OVERSHADOW ⟨in the shadow of Emerson and Thoreau, the wit of Back Bay is in danger of being *obscured* —V.L.Parrington⟩ **d :** to make unintelligible or vague **:** make difficult to understand ⟨too much use of symbolism *obscured* his poetic thought⟩ **e :** to make (as a sound or line) indistinct or undefined ⟨writing *obscured* by age and mildew⟩; *also* **:** to make indistinct in logical or rational order ⟨reasoning *obscured* by emotion⟩ **f :** to make (as the judgment) weak **:** IMPAIR ⟨her blood being stirred . . . her judgment was slightly *obscured* —Arnold Bennett⟩ **2 :** to use unstressed \ə\ for (an item of spelling) or instead of (another vowel in a variant spelling or gradational form)

syn OBSCURE, DIM, BEDIM, DARKEN, ECLIPSE, CLOUD, BECLOUD, FOG, BEFOG, OBFUSCATE, OBNUBILATE: of these terms OBSCURE, DIM, BEDIM, and DARKEN all suggest the effect obtained by the lessening or the removal of illumination — the making of an object difficult to see clearly or the weakening or impairing of the ability to see with the eye or the mind. OBSCURE stresses the indistinctness, often concealment, of the object or idea or the unclearness of the vision or the comprehension ⟨there are readers of papers who . . . like the ordinary, average day, with its good human humdrum; they do not want to have its nature denied or *obscured* —C.E.Montague⟩ ⟨the faded yellow building, its original austerity of line somewhat *obscured* by a comfortable porch —*Amer. Guide Series: Vt.*⟩ DIM and BEDIM stress the diminishing of light or of clarity, intensity, or luster or the consequent diminishing of capacity to see, distinguish, or comprehend; BEDIM is usually found in a more literary context than DIM ⟨celestial tears *bedimm'd* her large blue eyes —Lord Byron⟩ ⟨the old patriotic glow began to *dim* its ineffectual fires —Howard M. Jones⟩ DARKEN, although like

DIM and BEDIM suggesting a diminishing of illumination, is much richer metaphorically in suggesting strongly the alteration of an object or the impairment of clear or normal vision or mental comprehension by reason of confusion, ignorance, or evil ⟨the yearly migrations of passenger pigeons . . . literally *darkening* the sky —*Amer. Guide Series: Mich.*⟩ ⟨his intellect was indeed *darkened* by many superstitions and prejudices —T.B.Macaulay⟩ ⟨evils enough to *darken* all his goodness —Shak.⟩ ECLIPSE may stand alone in suggesting the effect of an actual astronomical eclipse, the partial or total darkening or concealment of one object by another and, hence, the overshadowing or supplanting of one object by another ⟨in the English field, Anglo-Saxon never *eclipsed* the study of Shakespeare or Milton —A.L.Guérard⟩ CLOUD, BECLOUD, FOG, BEFOG, OBFUSCATE, and OBNUBILATE all suggest the obstruction or impairment of vision by clouds, fog, or other vapor or, in figurative extension, the making of the mental perception or object of that perception murky or confused. CLOUD and BECLOUD stress the obscuring of the object, or the murky view of the object; BECLOUD is somewhat more literary than CLOUD ⟨the beginnings of our physical universe are necessarily *beclouded* in the swirling mists of countless ages past —F.L. Whipple⟩ ⟨smoke *clouding* the prospect before us⟩ ⟨the actual issues *clouded* by prejudice and politics⟩ ⟨reasoning *clouded* by hysteria⟩ FOG and BEFOG are applied possibly more frequently than CLOUD and BECLOUD to matters of the understanding or mental comprehension and usu. suggest a greater obstruction or impairment of clear vision of eye and mind and, so, a greater and more unnecessary indistinctness, illogicality, or confusion; BEFOG is somewhat more literary than FOG ⟨the willfully created misunderstandings that so often *befog* the American political scene —Carl Sandburg⟩ ⟨the landscape *fogged* by the smoke from the forest fire⟩ ⟨eyes *fogged* by sleep⟩ ⟨a mind *befogged* by fatigue⟩ ⟨truth *fogged* by the imperfections of human sight⟩ ⟨a text *fogged* by careless scholarship⟩ OBFUSCATE found usu. in a literary context suggests strongly an avoidable, often willful, obscuring of an object or confusing of the mind by darkening or illogicality ⟨the process, not of enlightening but of *obfuscating* the mind —H.D.Thoreau⟩ OBNUBILATE confines itself in modern usage chiefly to a nontechnical medical use to designate the radical impairing of the mental faculties to the point of torpor ⟨*obnubilate* the patient with thiopentone and then wake him up with some cerebral stimulant —*Lancet*⟩

[3]**obscure** \"\ *n* -s [[1]*obscure*] **:** something (as an unknown place, the darkness of night, or a part in a picture) that is obscure **:** OBSCURITY

obscured *past of* OBSCURE

ob·scur·ed·ly \əbz'kyu̇rədlē, äb-, -b'sk-\ *adv* **:** so as to be obscure **:** in an obscure manner

obscure glass *n* **:** sheet glass made translucent or opaque (as by roughening one side) ⟨used *obscure glass* panels to enclose the patio⟩

ob·scure·ly *adv* **:** in an obscure manner **:** INDISTINCTLY, VAGUELY

ob·scure·ment \əbz'kyu̇(ə)rmənt, äb-, -b'sk-, -u̇əm-\ *n* -s [F, fr. *obscurer* to obscure (fr. L *obscurare*) + *-ment*] **:** OBSCURATION

ob·scure·ness *n* -ES **:** the quality or state of being obscure

ob·scur·er \-rə(r)\ *n* -s **:** one that obscures

ob·scu·ri·fy \-rə,fī\ *vt* -ED/-ING/-ES [[1]*obscure* + *-ify*] **:** to make obscure

obscuring *pres part of* OBSCURE

ob·scur·ing·ly *adv* **:** so as to obscure **:** to an obscuring degree ⟨fog drifted ~ into the valley⟩

ob·scu·ri·ty \əbz'kyu̇rəd·ē, äb-, -b'sk-, -ətē, -i\ *n* -ES [MF & L; MF *obscurité*, fr. L *obscuritat-*, *obscuritas*, fr. *obscurus* obscure + *-itat-*, *-itas* -ity] **1 :** the quality or state of being obscure, inconspicuous, unknown, uncomprehended, or imperspicuous **2 :** someone or something obscure ⟨these silly *obscurities* mar his writing⟩

obsd *abbr* observed

ob·se·crate \'äbsə,krāt\ *vt* -ED/-ING/-S [L *obsecratus*, past part. of *obsecrare* to beseech, pray, fr. *ob-* toward, over + *sacrare* to consecrate, fr. *sacr-*, *sacer* sacred — more at OB-, SACRED] *archaic* **:** BESEECH, SUPPLICATE, BEG

ob·se·cra·tion \,==ˈkrāshən\ *n* -s [ME *obsecracioun*, fr. L *obsecration-*, *obsecratio*, fr. *obsecratus* (past part. of *obsecrare* to beseech) + *-ion-*, *-io* -ion] **1 :** SUPPLICATION; *specif* **:** a supplicatory prayer mentioning in its appeal things or events held to be sacred ⟨"through thy victory over death, O Lord, deliver us" is an ~⟩ **2 :** DEESIS

ob·sede \əb'sēd\ *vt* -ED/-ING/-S [F *obséder*, fr. L *obsidēre* to sit at, possess — more at OBSESS] **:** OBSESS

ob·se·quence \'äbsəkwən(t)s\ *n* -s [L *obsequentia*, fr. *obsequent-*, *obsequens*, (pres. part. of *obsequi* to yield) + *-ia*] **:** OBSEQUIOUSNESS, COMPLIANCE

[1]**ob·se·quent** \'äbsəkwənt\ *adj* [L *obsequent-*, *obsequens*, pres. part.] **1** *obs* **:** YIELDING, SUBMISSIVE, OBSEQUIOUS **2 a** *of a stream* **:** flowing in a direction opposite to that of the dip of the local strata and joining a subsequent valley developed along the strike of poorly resistant beds **b :** produced by differential erosion of fault blocks and facing in a direction opposite to that of a previous fault scarp — used of fault-line scarps and cliffs

[2]**obsequent** \"\ *n* -s **:** an obsequent stream

ob·se·qui·al \əb'sēkwēəl, äb-\ *adj* **:** of or relating to obsequies **:** FUNEREAL

ob·se·qui·ence \-ēən(t)s\ *n* -s [by alter. (influence of *obsequious*)] **:** OBSEQUENCE

ob·se·qui·ous \-ēəs\ *adj* [ME, fr. L *obsequiosus*, fr. *obsequium* compliance (fr. *obsequi* to yield, fr. *ob-* to, toward, over + *sequi* to follow) + *-osus* -ose — more at OB-, SUE] **1 a :** exhibiting ready and proper compliance to the will of another **:** prompt and dutiful in attendance on the wishes of one in authority **b** *obs* **:** dutiful in regard to the dead and in the proper and appropriate performance of obsequies **2 :** meanly or servilely attentive **:** compliant to excess **:** exhibiting a servile and sycophantic complaisance ⟨an ~ toady⟩ ⟨fawning ~ behavior⟩ **syn** see SUBSERVIENT

ob·se·qui·ous·ly *adv* **:** in an obsequious manner

ob·se·qui·ous·ness *n* -ES [ME *obsequiousnesse*, fr. *obsequious* + *-nesse* -ness] **:** the quality or state of being obsequious

ob·seq·ui·ty \əb'sekwəd·ē, äb-, -sēk-\ *n* -ES [*obsequious* + *-ity*] **:** OBSEQUIOUSNESS

ob·se·qui·um \äb'sēkwēəm\ *n*, *pl* **obsequ·ia** \-ēə\ [L, lit., compliance] **:** the customary respectful behavior due from a freedman to his patron or former master under ancient Roman law including freedom from lawsuit by the freedman except with the consent of the praetor and the duty to support the patron when needy

ob·se·quy \'äbsəkwē, -wi\ *n* -ES [ME *obsequie*, *obseque*, fr. MF, fr. ML *obsequiae*, alter. (influenced by L *exsequiae* funeral rites) of L *obsequia* obsequies, pl. of *obsequium* compliance — more at EXEQUY] **1 :** the last duty or service to a person rendered after his death; *esp* **:** a rite or ceremony relating to burial — usu. used in pl. **2** [ME, fr. L *obsequium*] *obs* **:** COMPLIANCE, OBSEQUIOUSNESS; *also* **:** RITUAL

ob·serv·abil·i·ty \əb,zərvə'biləd·ē, -zə̄v-, -zəiv-, -lətē, -i\ *n* **:** capacity for or possibility of being observed

[1]**ob·serv·able** \əb'zərvəbəl, -zə̄v-, -zəiv-\ *adj* [F, fr. L *observabilis*, fr. *observare* to observe + *-abilis* -able — more at OBSERVE] **1 :** requiring or suitable to be observed, regarded, or kept ⟨a very ~ old custom⟩ ⟨forms ~ in social intercourse⟩ **2 a :** deserving of observation **:** NOTEWORTHY **b** *obs* **:** REMARKABLE, NOTABLE **3 :** capable of being observed **:** DISCERNIBLE, DETECTABLE, NOTICEABLE ⟨an ~ decline in health⟩ ⟨an ~ phenomenon⟩ — **ob·serv·able·ness** \-bəlnəs\ *n* -ES — **ob·serv·ably** \-blē, -li\ *adv*

[2]**observable** \"\ *n* -s **1** *archaic* **:** something noteworthy or unusual **2 :** an event that is perceptible directly or indirectly (as by the medium of instruments) through the senses **:** PHENOMENON ⟨such ~*s* as size, energy, momentum, or viscosity⟩

ob·serv·ance \-vən(t)s\ *n* -s [ME *observaunce*, fr. OF *observance*, fr. LL *observantia*, fr. L, regard, respect, fr. *observant-*, *observans* (pres. part. of *observare*) + *-ia*] **1 a :** something (as an act of religious or ceremonial nature) that is carried out in accord with prescribed forms **:** a customary practice, rite, or ceremony **b :** a rule or set of regulations governing members of a religious order **c** *usu cap*, *Roman Catholicism* **:** the ordinances governing the strict Franciscans **2 a :** the performance of a customary rite (as of ceremony or religion) ⟨do the ~ due to sprightly May —John Dryden⟩ ⟨our customary Sabbath ~*s*⟩ **b :** an act or the practice of paying due heed to something established (as a rule, law, custom) **:** an attending, participating in, or following with care ⟨~ of the speed laws⟩ **3** *archaic* **:** respectful and dutiful service or attention (as to a person) **:** deferential courtesy **4 :** an act or instance of observing **:** ATTENTION, OBSERVATION ⟨~ of life⟩

ob·serv·an·cy \-nsē\ *n* -ES [LL *observantia*] **:** OBSERVANCE

observandum *n*, *pl* **observanda** [L, neut. of *observandus*, gerundive of *observare*] *obs* **:** a thing to be observed

[1]**observant** *n* -s [ME, fr. L *observant-*, *observans*, pres. part. of *observare* to observe] **1** *obs* **:** OBSERVER **2** *obs* **:** an assiduous or obsequious servant or attendant

[2]**ob·serv·ant** \əb'zərvənt, -zə̄v-, -zəiv-\ *adj* [F, fr. pres. part. of *observer* to observe, fr. L *observare*] **1 :** taking notice **:** viewing or noticing attentively **:** ATTENTIVE ⟨~ spectators⟩ ⟨an ~ habit of mind⟩ **2** *archaic* **:** RESPECTFUL, DEFERENTIAL **3 :** attentive in observing **:** REGARDFUL, MINDFUL — used with *of* ⟨~ of rules⟩ ⟨carefully ~ of the niceties of life⟩ **4** *obs* **:** OBSERVABLE **5 :** CAREFUL, HEEDFUL ⟨~ to avoid offense⟩ — **ob·serv·ant·ly** *adv* — **ob·serv·ant·ness** *n* -ES

[1]**ob·ser·va·tion** \,äbsə(r)'vāshən, -bzə-\ *n* -s [MF, fr. L *observation-*, *observatio*, fr. *observatus* (past part. of *observare* to observe) + *-ion-*, *-io* -ion — more at OBSERVE] **1** *obs* **:** something (as an ordinance, rite, or custom) that must be observed **:** OBSERVANCE 1a **2 :** OBSERVANCE 2a **3 :** an act or the faculty of observing or taking notice **:** an act of seeing or fixing the mind upon something **4 a :** an act of recognizing and noting some fact or occurrence (as in nature) often involving the measurement of some magnitude with suitable instruments ⟨made an ~ of the sun's altitude⟩ ⟨temperature ~*s*⟩ **b :** a record so obtained **5 :** an expression of a judgment upon what one has observed; *broadly* **:** REMARK, STATEMENT, UTTERANCE ⟨a very childish ~⟩ **6 :** a conclusion drawn from observing **:** VIEW, REFLECTION **7** *obs* **:** deferential courtesy **:** HEED **8 :** the condition of one that is seen, examined, or noticed ⟨stooping to avoid the risk of ~⟩ ⟨under ~ at the hospital⟩ **9 :** a game in which players examine an assortment of articles for a short time and then write down the names of as many of the objects as they can remember

[2]**observation** \"\ *adj* **:** used or for use in viewing (as scenery) or in making observations ⟨an ~ tower⟩ ⟨the ~ car⟩

ob·ser·va·tion·al \-shənᵊl, -shnəl\ *adj* **:** of, relating to, or based on observation — sometimes distinguished from *experimental* — **ob·ser·va·tion·al·ly** \-ᵊl|ē, -əl|, |i\ *adv*

ob·ser·va·tion·al·ism \-ᵊl,izəm, -əl-\ *n* -s **:** a theory that knowledge is based on observation

observation battalion *n* **:** a military artillery unit that performs sound, flash, and radar ranging and furnishes topographic and meteorological data

observation equation *n* **:** an equation expressing a measured value of some function of one or more unknown quantities

observation kite *n* **:** WAR KITE

ob·serv·a·tive \əb'zərvəd·iv, -zə̄v-, -zəiv-\ *adj* [L *observatus* (past part. of *observare* to observe) + E *-ive*] **:** OBSERVANT

ob·ser·va·tor \'äbzər,vād·ər, -bsə-, -zə(r),vād·ə(r), -ātə-\ *n* -s [MF *observateur*, fr. L *observator*, fr. *observatus* (past part. of *observare*) + *-or*] **:** OBSERVER

ob·serv·a·to·ri·al \əb¦zərvə¦tōrēəl, -zə̄v-, -zəiv-, -tȯr-\ *adj* **:** of or relating to an observer or an observatory

[1]**ob·serv·a·to·ry** \='==,tōrē, -tȯr-, -ri\ *n* -ES [prob. fr. (assumed) NL *observatorium*, fr. L *observatus* (past part. of *observare* to observe) + *-orium*] **1 :** a building or place given over to or equipped for observation of natural phenomena (as in astronomy, magnetism, meteorology, ornithology); *also* **:** an institution whose primary purpose is making such observations **2 :** a situation, position, or place (as a building or elevated chamber) affording or commanding a wide view **:** LOOKOUT

[2]**observatory** \"\ *adj* [L *observatus*, past part. + E *-ory*] **:** relating to observation esp. when scientific

[1]**ob·serve** \əb'zərv, -zə̄v, -zəiv\ *vb* -ED/-ING/-S [ME *observen*, fr. MF *observer*, fr. L *observare* to watch, guard, observe, fr. *ob-* to, over, completely + *servare* to keep, guard, observe — more at OB-, CONSERVE] *vt* **1 :** to take notice of by appropriate conduct **:** conform one's action or practice to **:** HEED, OBEY ⟨~ rules⟩ ⟨*observing* common decencies⟩ **2** *obs* **:** to give heed to (as in deference) **:** WORSHIP, HONOR **3 :** to inspect or take note of as an augury, omen, or presage ⟨*observed* the sacred geese⟩ ⟨*observed* the stumble of his horse and turned back⟩ **4 :** to celebrate or solemnize (as a ceremony, rite, or festival) after a customary or accepted form ⟨we always *observed* birthdays at home⟩ ⟨~ the Sabbath⟩ **5 :** to see or sense esp. through directed, careful, analytic attention ⟨in order to get fresh light on this subject, I have *observed* my own children carefully —Bertrand Russell⟩ ⟨keeping an ear pricked to ~ the movements of the viceroy —Victoria Sackville-West⟩ **6 :** to come to realize or know esp. through consideration of noted facts ⟨have *observed* that profane men living in ships . . . develop traits of profound resemblance —Joseph Conrad⟩ ⟨as we trace . . . the development of the Greek mind, we can ~ their intellect and their moral sense expanding —G.L.Dickinson⟩ **7 :** to express as a result of observation **:** utter as a remark **:** say in a casual or incidental way **:** REMARK **8 :** to make an observation on or of **:** ascertain by scientific observation ⟨~ phenomena⟩ ⟨*observed* the height of the sun⟩ ~ *vi* **1 a :** to take notice **:** be attentive **b :** to make observations **:** WATCH **2 :** REMARK, COMMENT — usu. used with *on* or *upon* **syn** see KEEP, SEE

[2]**observe** \"\ *n* -s *Scot* **:** REMARK, OBSERVATION ⟨a clever ~⟩

ob·serv·ed·ly \-vədlē, -li\ *adv* **:** to a significant degree **:** NOTABLY

ob·serv·er \-və(r)\ *n* -s **:** one that observes: as **a :** a keeper of or adherent to something established (as a law, custom, regulation, rite, or vow) **:** one that conforms to an accepted, usual, or traditional practice **b :** one that pays attention to something; *esp* **:** one engaged in or trained in the methods of close and exact observation ⟨an astronomical ~⟩ **c :** one that makes a remark **d** *obs* **:** a dutiful attendant or sycophantic follower **e :** a representative sent to observe and listen but not to participate officially in a gathering **f** (1) **:** one that accompanies the pilot of an airplane in order to make observations during flight (2) **:** an officer or other person that ascends in a captive balloon (as to reconnoiter or observe) (3) **:** an aeronautical rating for a member of an air crew with a special duty (as navigator, radar operator, bombardier) other than piloting — called also *aircraft observer* **g :** a subject in introspective analysis who describes his experiences under physical conditions arranged by an experimenter

observing *adj* **1 :** attentive to what passes **:** OBSERVANT **2 :** engaged in making observations — **ob·serv·ing·ly** *adv*

ob·sess \əb'ses, äb-\ *vt* -ED/-ING/-ES [L *obsessus*, past part. of *obsidēre* to sit at, possess, besiege, fr. *ob-* toward, against, over + *sedēre* to sit — more at OB-, SIT] **1** *obs* **:** BESIEGE, INVEST **2 a** *archaic* **:** HAUNT, POSSESS, BESET **b :** to occupy an undue or disproportionate place in the mind of **:** trouble continuously in mind ⟨he was ~*ed* by details⟩

ob·sess·ed·ly \-sədlē, -stlē, -li\ *adv* **:** in an obsessed manner

ob·sess·ing·ly *adv* **:** to an obsessing degree **:** so as to obsess

ob·ses·sion \əb'seshən, äb-\ *n* -s [L *obsession-*, *obsessio*, fr. *obsessus* (past part. of *obsidēre* to besiege) + *-ion-*, *-io* -ion] **1** *obs* **:** SIEGE **2 :** the act of a devil or a spirit in besetting a person or impelling him to action from without **:** the fact of being so beset or impelled — distinguished from *possession* **3 a :** a persistent and disturbing intrusion of or anxious and inescapable preoccupation with an idea or feeling esp. if known to be unreasonable — compare COMPULSION **b :** an emotion or idea causing such intrusion

ob·ses·sion·al \-shənᵊl, -shnəl\ *adj* **:** relating to, characterized by, or constituting an obsession **:** OBSESSIVE ⟨the ~ character of his response⟩ — **ob·ses·sion·al·ly** \-ᵊlē, -əlē, -li\ *adv*

obsessional neurosis *n* **:** an obsessive-compulsive neurosis in which obsessive thinking predominates with little need to perform compulsive acts

ob·ses·sion·ist \-sh(ə)nəst\ *n* -s **:** one that is obsessed

[1]**ob·ses·sive** \-'sesiv, -sēv *also* -səv\ *adj* [*obsession* + *-ive*] **1 a :** tending to provoke obsession **b :** excessive in some quality (as interest, concern, urgency) to or nearly to the point of abnormality ⟨an ~ nurse⟩ ⟨our ~ need for quick solutions —A.E.Stevenson b.1900⟩ **2 :** relating to, characterized by, or constituting obsession — **ob·ses·sive·ly** \-səvlē, -li\ *adv* — **ob·ses·sive·ness** \-sivnəs, -sēv- *also* -səv-\ *n* -ES

[2]**obsessive** \"\ *n* -s **:** a person that is obsessed **:** an obsessional neurotic

[1]**obsessive-compulsive** \=¦===¦==\ *adj* **:** relating to or characterized by obsessions and compulsions esp. as symptoms of a neurotic state — compare ANANKASTIC

[2]**obsessive-compulsive** \"\ *n* -s **:** a person affected with an obsessive-compulsive neurosis

obsessive-compulsive neurosis *or* **obsessive-compulsive reaction** *n* **:** a psychoneurotic disorder in which the patient is beset with obsessions or compulsions or both and suffers extreme anxiety or depression through failure to think the obsessive thoughts or perform the compelling acts

ob·ses·sus \əb'sesəs\ *n* -ES [ML, fr. L, past part. of *obsidēre* to possess, besiege — more at OBSESS] *archaic* **:** a person believed to be possessed by an evil spirit

ob·sid·i·an \əb'sidēən, äb-\ *n* -s [NL *obsidianus*, fr. L *Obsidianus* lapis (MS var. of *Obsianus* lapis), lit., stone of Obsidian, fr. *Obsidius* (MS var. of *Obsius*), Roman traveler named by Pliny as its discoverer + *-ianus* -ian] **:** volcanic glass that is generally black, banded, or spherulitic and has a marked conchoidal fracture, a bright luster, and a composition similar to rhyolite but usu. with more water

ob·sid·i·an·ite \-ə,nīt\ *n* -s [ISV *obsidian* + *-ite*] **:** a material composed of small approximately spherical balls of natural glass that are usu. black, green, or brown

ob·sid·i·o·nal \əb'sidē·ənəl\ *adj* [L *obsidionalis*, fr. *obsidion-*, *obsidio* siege (fr. *obsidēre* to besiege + *-ion-*, *-io* -ion) + *-alis* -al — more at OBSESS] **1 :** of or relating to a siege **2** *of a piece of money* **:** issued for use during a siege

obsidional crown *n* [trans. of L *corona obsidionalis*] **:** a crown bestowed in ancient Rome upon a general who raised the siege of a beleaguered place or upon one who held out against a siege

ob·sid·i·o·nary \='===,nerē\ *adj* [L *obsidion-*, *obsidio* + E *-ary*] **:** OBSIDIONAL 2

ob·sid·i·ous \='==əs\ *adj* [L *obsidium* siege (fr. *obsidēre* to besiege + *-ium*, n. suffix) + E *-ious*] **:** BESETTING

ob·sig·na·tion \,äb(,)sig'nāshən\ *n* -s [LL *obsignation-*, *obsignatio*, fr. L, action of sealing, fr. *obsignatus* (past part. of *obsignare* to mark upon, fr. *ob-* + *signare* to mark) + *-ion-*, *-io* -ion — more at SIGN] **:** a formal ratification (as by an official seal)

obsn *abbr* observation

ob·so·lesce \¦äbsə¦les\ *vi* -ED/-ING/-S [L *obsolescere*] **:** to be or become obsolescent

ob·so·les·cence \,=='lesᵊn(t)s\ *n* -s [*obsolescent* + *-ence*] **1 a :** the process of becoming obsolete or the condition of being nearly obsolete ⟨the gradual ~ of machinery⟩ ⟨reduced to ~⟩ **b :** the process of becoming or condition of being vestigial or nonfunctional ⟨the ~ of the wings of some strictly terrestrial birds⟩ **2 :** a factor included in depreciation to cover decline in value of fixed assets due to invention of new and better processes or machines, changes in demand, in design, or in the art, and other technical or legal changes but not to cover physical deterioration

ob·so·les·cent \¦==¦lesᵊnt\ *adj* [L *obsolescent-*, *obsolescens*, pres. part. of *obsolescere*] **1 :** going out of use **:** falling into disuse esp. as unable to compete with something more recent ⟨animal transport is largely ~⟩ **2 :** becoming obsolete; *esp* **:** VESTIGIAL — **ob·so·les·cent·ly** *adv*

[1]**ob·so·lete** \¦äbsə¦lēt, *usu* -ēd·+V\ *adj* [L *obsoletus*, past part. of *obsolescere* to grow old, fall into disuse, perh. fr. *ob-* to, toward + *-solescere* (fr. *solēre* to be accustomed) — more at OB, INSOLENT] **1 :** no longer active or in use **:** DISUSED, NEGLECTED: as **a :** formerly but no longer current ⟨an ~ word⟩ ⟨an ~ construction⟩ **b :** of a kind or style no longer current **:** OUTMODED ⟨~ equipment⟩ ⟨an ~ theory⟩ **c** (1) *of a postage or revenue stamp* **:** no longer issued by a post office **:** no longer on sale as a postal or revenue item (2) *of a piece of currency* **:** no longer legal tender because demonetized or issued by an authority that is no longer in existence **d** *of a business firm* **:** gone out of existence **:** having ceased to conduct business **2 :** worn out **:** reduced to a trace **:** EFFACED: as **a** *of a plant or animal part* **:** indistinct or imperfect as compared with a corresponding part in related organisms **:** REDUCED, RUDIMENTARY, VESTIGIAL ⟨spotting and ridges ~⟩ **b** *of a lesion or an infective process* **:** DIMINISHED, INDISTINCT, EFFACED **3 :** regarded as out of date whether currently in use or not ⟨this model makes all other cars ~⟩ ⟨the colonial system is ~⟩ **syn** see OLD

[2]**obsolete** \"\ *vt* -ED/-ING/-S [L *obsoletus*, past part. of *obsolescere*] **:** to make obsolete

[3]**obsolete** \"\ *n* -s [[1]*obsolete*] **:** something that is obsolete (as a word or phrase)

ob·so·lete·ly *adv* **:** in an obsolete manner **:** so as to be out of date or fashion

ob·so·lete·ness *n* -ES **:** the quality or state of being obsolete

ob·so·le·tion \,äbsə'lēshən\ *n* -s [[1]*obsolete* + *-ion*] **:** the act of becoming or condition of being obsolete

ob·so·let·ism \'==,lēd·,izəm\ *n* -s **1 :** something (as a custom or a word) that is obsolete **2 :** OBSOLETENESS

obsr *abbr* observer

[1]**ob·sta·cle** \'äbz(,)tikəl, -,tək-, -tēk-; 'äb(,)stik-, -,stək-, -stēk-\ *n* -s *often attrib* [ME, fr. MF, fr. L *obstaculum*, fr. *obstare* to stand before, hinder, fr. *ob-* to, against + *stare* to stand — more at OB-, STAND] **1 :** something that stands in the way or opposes **:** something that hinders progress **:** a physical or moral impediment or obstruction **:** HINDRANCE **2** *obs* **:** OPPOSITION, RESISTANCE

syn OBSTACLE, OBSTRUCTION, IMPEDIMENT, BAR, and SNAG can signify, in common, something which hampers or stops action or progress. OBSTACLE applies to anything which stands in one's way or stops passage ⟨the removal of an *obstacle* in the throat —F.D.Smith & Barbara Wilcox⟩ ⟨the poverty of some of the . . . districts is an *obstacle* to good education —B.K.Sandwell⟩ ⟨those *obstacles*, placed in the path of westward-marching pioneers by nature, must be surmounted before the continent was settled —R.A.Billington⟩ OBSTRUCTION stresses a blocking of the way or passage ⟨can only be used in straight stretches of water where there are no *obstructions* —W.H.Dowdeswell⟩ ⟨science deals with a psychological complex much as it deals with an *obstruction* in the bowels —Albert Dasnoy⟩ ⟨circumvent the *obstructions* placed in the way of emigration —*Amer. Guide Series: N.Y.*⟩ IMPEDIMENT, often interchangeable with OBSTACLE, usu. suggests something that hinders or delays as by entangling ⟨the rugged hills of the peninsula were no *impediment* to the discharge of his clerical duties —*Amer. Guide Series: Maine*⟩ ⟨the most important *impediment* . . . to reform, perhaps, is the number and diversity of the plans which have been submitted as possible cures —R.M.Dawson⟩ ⟨the increasing *impediments* to international trade —D.W.Brogan⟩ BAR implies something interposed as between a person and his goal ⟨there were, of course, no *bars* against immigration in those days —Paul Blanshard⟩ ⟨difference in language should be no *bar* to friendship⟩ SNAG applies to an obstacle or a delay encountered suddenly and unexpectedly ⟨his plan to build hit its first *snag* in the building code⟩ ⟨the operations were constantly running into legal *snags* which delayed progress considerably⟩

[2]**obstacle** *adj*, *obs* **:** OBSTINATE

[3]**obstacle** *pronunc at n*\ *vt* -ED/-ING/-S [obs. F *obstacler*, fr. F *obstacle*, n., fr. MF] **:** to resist or harass with obstacles

obstacle course *n* **:** a military training area filled with obstacles (as hurdles, fences, walls, ditches) that must be surmounted

obstacle sense *n* **:** the enhanced sensitivity that some blind persons exhibit to the presence of a large mass being approached

ob·stet·ric \əbz'te·trik, əb'st-, (')äbz¦t-, (')äb¦st-, -rēk\ *or* **ob·stet·ri·cal** \-rəkəl, -rēk-\ *adj* [*obstetric* prob. fr. (assumed) NL *obstetricus*, fr. L *obstetric-*, *obstetrix* midwife, lit., one who stands before (i.e., to receive the child), fr. *obstare* to stand before; *obstetrical* fr. L *obstetric-*, *obstetrix* + E *-al* — more at OBSTACLE] **:** of or relating to obstetrics **:** belonging to or associated with pregnancy and childbirth ⟨~ shock⟩ ⟨the ~ canal⟩ — **ob·stet·ri·cal·ly** \-rək(ə)lē, -rēk-, -li\ *adv*

obstetrical toad *n* **:** either of two rather small toads (*Alytes obstetricans* and *A. cisternasi*) of central and southwestern Europe the male of which takes up and fastens about his

hind legs the strings of eggs laid by the female and carries them about until they hatch
ob·stet·ri·cate \ə'ste·trə,kāt\ *vb* -ED/-ING/-S [LL *obstetricatus*, past part. of *obstetricare* to act as midwife, fr. L *obstetric-, obstetrix* midwife] *vi, archaic* : to function as a midwife ~ *vt, obs* : to attend (a woman) as a midwife at childbirth
obstetric forceps *n* : a forceps for grasping the fetal head or other part to facilitate delivery in difficult labor

obstetric forceps

ob·ste·tri·cian \,äbz,te·'trishən, ,äb,st-, -bztə-, -bstə-\ *n* -S [*obstetrics* + *-an*] : a physician or veterinary specializing in obstetrics
ob·stet·rics \əbz'te·triks, -b'st-; äbz't-, -b'st-\ *n pl but sing or pl in constr* [*obstetric* + *-s*, pl. suffix] : a branch of medical science that deals with birth and with its antecedents and sequels
ob·stet·rist \-rəst\ *n* -S [*obstetrics* + *-ist*] : OBSTETRICIAN
ob·sti·na·cy \'äbztənəsē, -bst-, -si\ *n* -ES [ME, fr. ML *obstinatia*, fr. L *obstinatus* (past part. of *obstinare* to be set upon, be obstinate) + *-ia* -y] **1 a** : the quality or state of being obstinate : fixedness in will, opinion, or resolution : firm and usu. unreasonable adherence to an opinion, purpose, or system : STUBBORNNESS, PERTINACITY, PERSISTENCY **b** : the quality or state of being difficult to remedy, relieve, or subdue ⟨the ~ of tuberculosis⟩ ⟨the ~ of this evil⟩ **2** : an instance of being obstinate : an obstinate action or stand ⟨irritated by his neighbor's petty *obstinacies*⟩
ob·sti·nance \-nən(t)s\ *or* **ob·sti·nan·cy** \-nənsē\ *n, pl* **obstinances** *or* **obstinancies** [ML *obstinantia*, fr. *obstinant-, obstinans* (pres. part. of *obstinare*) + *-ia* -y] : OBSTINACY
[1]**ob·sti·nate** \-nət, *usu* -əd+V\ *adj* [ME *obstinat*, fr. L *obstinatus*, past part. of *obstinare* to be set upon, be obstinate, fr. *ob-* to, over + *-stinare* (akin to *stare* to stand) — more at OB-, STAND] **1** : pertinaciously adhering to an opinion, purpose, or course : not yielding to reason, arguments, or other means **2** : not yielding readily : not easily subdued or removed ⟨~ fever⟩ ⟨these ~ obstructions⟩
syn OBSTINATE, DOGGED, STUBBORN, PERTINACIOUS, MULISH, STIFF-NECKED, PIGHEADED, and BULLHEADED can mean, in common, fixed or unyielding in one's course, purpose, opinion, and so on. OBSTINATE implies persistent adherence to an opinion, purpose, or course, suggesting unreasonableness or perversity rather than steadfastness ⟨a man so *obstinate* as to resist the strongest arguments can never be brought to repentance, for he can never be persuaded of his errors —Leslie Stephen⟩ ⟨so stupid and so *obstinate* that it was impossible to get him to do or understand anything —Anthony Trollope⟩ ⟨not courageous, only quarrelsome; not determined, only *obstinate*; not masterful, only domineering —G.B. Shaw⟩ DOGGED adds the idea of downright or tenacious persistence, usu. connoting stolid determination or unwavering purpose ⟨the immense amount of planning, of *dogged* study; the tireless, constant activity, the ability to get what he was after —Adria Langley⟩ ⟨the dull, *dogged*, unspectacular heroism which was needed for fighting filth and ignorance and disease —Louis Bromfield⟩ ⟨*dogged* hope and resolution for a peaceful union of nations —Laurence Stapleton⟩ STUBBORN implies the unyielding adherence of OBSTINATE and the stolid determination of DOGGED, carrying strongly the idea of fixedness of character, in a person, that resists attempts to change his purpose, course, or opinion, or, in a thing, that makes it hard to work with or manipulate ⟨the *stubborn* resistance which he met showed that the temper of the people was not easily broken —J.R.Green⟩ ⟨his *stubborn* refusal to accept the consequences of his own discoveries —J.B.Conant⟩ ⟨she was so *stubborn* that she wouldn't adjust her opinions —Sinclair Lewis⟩ ⟨man and beast joined against *stubborn* nature and her grudging soil —Ann F. Wolfe⟩ PERTINACIOUS stresses a sticking to a chosen pursuit, purpose, and so on, with an unusual, often annoying, persistence ⟨a *pertinacious* newsman⟩ ⟨a *pertinacious* mosquito⟩ MULISH suggests the unreasonable obstinacy of a mule ⟨in refusing to accept ardent suitors who were urged upon her, she was obstinately *mulish* —*Fashion Digest*⟩ ⟨a *mulish* determination to make the worst of everything —T.S.Eliot⟩ ⟨there is a *mulish* quality about vellum that renders it difficult to cope with —Edith Diehl⟩ STIFF-NECKED, even more than OBSTINATE or STUBBORN, stresses inflexibility, suggesting a haughtiness or arrogance that will not be directed ⟨*stiff-necked* in his determination to wage a national campaign rather than a series of local campaigns —*Newsweek*⟩ ⟨the *stiff-necked* secretaries of Cromwell's army who had been glad to stand in pillories and suffer their ears to be cropped rather than put bread in the mouths of priests —V.W.Brooks⟩ PIGHEADED and BULLHEADED, terms of severe reproach, suggest a particularly perverse or stupid kind of obstinacy, PIGHEADED stressing rather imperviousness to reason, BULLHEADED stressing rather headstrong determination ⟨too . . . *pigheaded* to listen to reason —Dashiell Hammett⟩ ⟨a *pigheaded* refusal to budge from an untenable political position⟩ ⟨a *bullheaded* driving at a private goal no matter who else is hurt along the way⟩
[2]**ob·sti·nate** \-,nāt\ *vt* -ED/-ING/-S [ME *obstinaten*, fr. L *obstinatus*, past part. of *obstinare* to be obstinate] : to make obstinate
ob·sti·nate·ly *adv* [ME *obstinatly*, fr. [1]*obstinat* + *-ly*] : in an obstinate manner : with obstinacy
ob·sti·nate·ness *n* -ES : the quality or state of being obstinate
ob·sti·na·tion \,äbztə'nāshən, -bat-\ *n* -S [ME *obstinacioun*, fr. MF *obstination*, fr. L *obstination-, obstinatio*, fr. *obstinatus* (past part. of *obstinare*) + *-ion-, -io* -ion] : OBSTINACY
ob·sti·pate \'äbztə,pāt, -bst-\ *vt* -ED/-ING/-S [back-formation fr. *obstipation*] : to bind up : constipate severely
ob·sti·pa·tion \,==ˈpāshən\ *n* -S [LL *obstipation-, obstipatio* close pressure, fr. L *ob-* + *stipare* to press together + *-ion-, -io* -ion — more at STIFF] : BLOCKAGE ⟨~ of a body passage⟩; *specif* : severe and obstinate constipation
ob·strep·er·ate \əbz'trepə,rāt, äb-, -b'st-\ *vi* -ED/-ING/-S [*obstreperous* + *-ate*] *archaic* : to make a noise
ob·strep·er·ous \-p(ə)rəs\ *adj* [L *obstreperus*, fr. *obstrepere* to make noise against, fr. *ob-* to, against + *strepere* make noise; akin to OE *thræft* quarrel, discord, MLG *drevelinge* vain chatter, ON *thrapt* chatter; all of imit. origin — more at OB-] **1** : marked by or engaging in aggressive noisiness : LOUD, CLAMOROUS ⟨~ roaring⟩ **2** : stubbornly defiant : resisting control or restraint often with a show of noisy disorder : TURBULENT, UNMANAGEABLE ⟨an ~ crew⟩ ⟨~ elephants —Faubion Bowers⟩ **syn** see VOCIFEROUS
ob·strep·er·ous·ly *adv* : in a loud, clamorous, or disorderly manner : REBELLIOUSLY
ob·strep·er·ous·ness *n* -ES : the quality or state of being obstreperous
obstriction *n* -S [LL *obstriction-, obstrictio*, fr. L *obstrictus* (past part. of *obstringere* to bind, obligate, fr. *ob-* to, over + *stringere* to draw tight, bind) + *-ion-, -io* -ion — more at OB-, STRAIN] *obs* : the condition of being obligated : OBLIGATION
ob·strop·o·lous \əbz'träpələs, äb-, -b'st-\ *dial var of* OBSTREPEROUS
ob·struct \əbz'trəkt, äb-, -b'st-\ *vb* -ED/-ING/-S [L *obstructus*, past part. of *obstruere* to build against, block up, fr. *ob-* to, against + *struere* to pile up, build — more at OB-, STRUCTURE] *vt* **1** : to block up : stop up or close up : place an obstacle in or fill with obstacles or impediments to passing ⟨traffic ~*ing* the street⟩ ⟨veins ~*ed* by clots⟩ **2** : to be or come in the way of : hinder from passing, action, or operation : IMPEDE, RETARD ⟨unwise rules ~ legislation⟩ ⟨constant interruptions ~ our progress⟩ **3** : to cut off from sight : shut out ⟨the high wall ~*ed* the view⟩ ~ *vi* : to place obstacles in the way : IMPEDE **syn** see HINDER
ob·struc·tion \-kshən\ *n* -S [L *obstruction-, obstructio* fr. *obstructus* (past part. of *obstruere* to obstruct) + *-ion-, -io* -ion] **1** : an act of obstructing or the condition of being obstructed: as **a** : a condition of being clogged or blocked ⟨intestinal ~⟩ ⟨respiratory ~ due to thyroid disease⟩ **b** *obs* : arrest of vital functions : DEATH **c** : a delay or attempted delay of business by dilatory parliamentary tactics in a deliberative body (as a legislature) — compare FILIBUSTER 2 **d** : the illegal hindrance of the progress of an opponent in a game (as soccer) by remaining in the path he wants to follow **2** : something that obstructs or impedes : IMPEDIMENT, HINDRANCE ⟨removing ~*s* from the path⟩ ⟨this was the major ~ to the success of our plan⟩ **syn** see OBSTACLE
ob·struc·tion·ism \-,nizəm\ *n* -S [*obstructionist* + *-ism*] : the practice of an obstructionist : deliberate interference with progress or business
ob·struc·tion·ist \-,nəst\ *n* -S *often attrib* : one that hinders progress : one that deliberately and often by indirect or delaying tactics obstructs business (as in a legislative body) — **ob·struc·tion·is·tic** \=;==;nistik\ *adj*
[1]**ob·struc·tive** \əbz'trəktiv, äb-, -b'st-, -ēv *also* -əv\ *adj* [L *obstructus* + E *-ive*] **1** : tending to obstruct : presenting obstacles : HINDERING **2** : of, relating to, or characterized by obstruction — **ob·struc·tive·ly** \-təvlē\ *adv* — **ob·struc·tive·ness** \-tivnəs, -tēv- *also* -təv-\ *n* -ES
[2]**obstructive** \"\ *n* -S : an obstructive person or thing
obstructive jaundice *n* : jaundice due to obstruction of the biliary passages (as by gallstones or tumor)
ob·struc·tor \əbz'trəktə(r), äb-, -b'st-\ *n* -S : one that obstructs
[1]**ob·stru·ent** \'äbztrəwənt -bst-\ *adj* [L *obstruent-, obstruens*, pres. part. of *obstruere* to obstruct — more at OBSTRUCT] **1** *archaic* : causing obstruction : blocking up **2** *phonetics* : characterized by stoppage or friction
[2]**obstruent** \"\ *n* -S : a speech sound in the articulation of which the breath passage is obstructed completely or to the point of producing friction : STOP, FRICATIVE — compare RESONANT
obstruse *adj* [L *obstrusus*, MS var. of *abstrusus* concealed — more at ABSTRUSE] *obs* : ABSTRUSE
ob·stu·pe·fy \äbz't(y)üpə,fī, -b'st-\ *vt* [L *obstupefacere*, fr. *ob-* to, against, over + *stupefacere* to stupefy — more at OB-, STUPEFY] : STUPEFY
obt *abbr* **1** obedient **2** [L *obiit*] he died
ob·tain \əb'tān, äb-\ *vb* -ED/-ING/-S [ME *obteinen*, fr. MF & L; MF *obtenir*, fr. L *obtinēre* to take hold of, fr. *ob-* to, completely + *-tinēre* (fr. *tenēre* to hold) — more at OB-, THIN] *vt* **1 a** : to gain or attain possession or disposal of usu. by some planned action or method ⟨ability to doubt until evidence is ~*ed* —John Dewey⟩ ⟨~*ing* the information easily⟩ **b** : to bring about or call into being : EFFECT ⟨~ quiet for their annual meetings —*Amer. Guide Series: N.Y.City*⟩ **2** *obs* : HOLD, KEEP, POSSESS, OCCUPY ⟨he who ~*s* the monarchy of heaven —John Milton⟩ **3** *obs* : to arrive at : ATTAIN, REACH ~ *vi* **1** *archaic* : SUCCEED **2** *obs* : ATTAIN, ARRIVE — used with *to* or *unto* **3** : to have a firm footing : become recognized or established : be prevalent or general ⟨the custom ~*s* of going to the seashore in summer⟩ ⟨a greater degree of free expression than usually ~*s* in film production —Roger Manvell⟩ **syn** see GET
ob·tain·able \-nəbəl\ *adj* : capable of being obtained : AVAILABLE
ob·tain·al \-nᵊl\ *n* -S [*obtain* + *-al*] : OBTAINMENT
ob·tain·er \-nə(r)\ *n* -S : one that obtains
ob·tain·ment \-mənt\ *n* -S **1** : the act or process of obtaining **2** : something that is obtained
obtd *abbr* obtained
ob·tect \əb'tekt\ *also* **ob·tect·ed** \-təd\ *adj* [*obtect* fr. L *obtectus*, past part. of *obtegere* to cover up, fr. *ob-* to, over + *tegere* to cover; *obtected* fr. L *obtectus* + E *-ed* — more at OB-, THATCH] : enclosed in or characterized by enclosure in a firm chitinous case or covering ⟨an ~ pupa⟩ ⟨~ metamorphosis⟩ — compare EXARATE
ob·tem·per \əb'tempər\ *vt* [MF *obtemperer*, fr. L *obtemperare*, fr. *ob-* to, over + *temperare* to temper, mingle properly — more at OB-, TEMPER] *Scots law* : SUBMIT, COMPLY, OBEY
ob·tem·per·ate \-,rāt\ *vt* [ME *obtemperat*, fr. L *obtemperatus*, past part. of *obtemperare* to comply, obey] *archaic* : OBEY
obtend *vt* [L *obtendere* to stretch before, draw out, pretend, fr. *ob-* to, toward + *tendere* to stretch — more at OB-, TEND] **1** *obs* : to offer as a reason : PRETEND **2** *obs* : OPPOSE
ob·ten·e·brate \äb'tenə,brāt\ *vt* -ED/-ING/-S [LL *obtenebratus*, past part. of *obtenebrare* to darken, fr. L *ob-* to, toward, over + *tenebrare* to darken, fr. *tenebrae* darkness — more at OB-, TEMERITY] : to darken by or as if by shadowing
ob·ten·tion \əb'tenchən, äb-\ *n* -S [F, fr. L *obtentus* (past part. of *obtinēre* to take hold of) + F *-ion* — more at OBTAIN] : an act or instance of obtaining : OBTAINMENT
ob·test \äb'test\ *vb* [MF *obtester*, fr. L *obtestari*, fr. *ob-* to, toward + *testari* to be a witness — more at OB-, TESTAMENT] *vt* **1** : BESEECH, SUPPLICATE **2** : to call to witness : invoke as a witness ~ *vi* **1** : SUPPLICATE **2** : PROTEST
ob·tes·ta·tion \,=,te'stāshən\ *n* -S [L *obtestation-, obtestatio*, fr. *obtestatus* (past part. of *obtestari*) + *-ion-, -io* -ion] : an act of obtesting : solemn supplication or adjuration
obtrect *vt* -ED/-ING/-S [L *obtrectare* to detract from, fr. *ob-* + *-trectare* (fr. *tractare* to draw, handle, manage, treat) — more at TREAT] *obs* : SLANDER — **obtrectation** *n* -S *obs* — **obtrectator** *or* **obtrector** *n* -S *obs*
ob·trude \əb'trüd, äb-\ *vb* -ED/-ING/-S [L *obtrudere*, fr. *ob-* to, toward, against + *trudere* to thrust — more at OB-, THREAT] *vt* **1** : to thrust out : push or extend into sight : EXTRUDE ⟨the snail slowly *obtruded* his tentacle⟩ **2** : to thrust forward, present, or call to notice without warrant or request ⟨not a man to ~ his beliefs casually⟩ ⟨forced to ~ ourselves into their party⟩ ~ *vi* : to thrust oneself or some other matter upon attention : INTRUDE ⟨do what we may our childhood background will ~⟩
ob·trud·er \-də(r)\ *n* -S : one that obtrudes
ob·truncate \(')äb+\ *vt* [L *obtruncatus*, past part. of *obtruncare* to cut off, fr. *ob-* toward, against, over + *truncare* to cut off, fr. *truncus* trunk — more at OB-, TRUNCATE] : to cut the head or top from
ob·tru·sion \əb'trüzhən, äb-\ *n* -S [LL *obtrusion-, obtrusio* fr. L *obtrusus* (past part. of *obtrudere* to obtrude) + *-ion-, -io* -ion] **1** : an act of obtruding : a thrusting upon others by force or unsolicited **2** : something that is obtruded
ob·tru·sive \əb'trüs|iv, (')äb|t-, -ēz|, |ēv *also* |əv\ *adj* [L *obtrusus* + E *-ive*] **1** : thrust out : PROTRUDING ⟨a sharp ~ edge⟩ **2 a** : disposed to obtrude : FORWARD, PUSHING, INTRUSIVE ⟨~ behavior⟩ **b** : undesirably or unattractively noticeable or showy ⟨hats will be less ~ this season⟩ ⟨the propaganda was occasionally ~⟩ **syn** see IMPERTINENT
ob·tru·sive·ly \|əvlē, -li\ *adv* : in an obtrusive manner : so as to be obtrusive
ob·tru·sive·ness \ ivnəs, |ēv *also* |əv- *n* -ES : the quality or state of being obtrusive
ob·tund \äb'tənd\ *vt* -ED/-ING/-S [ME *obtunden*, fr. L *obtundere* to beat against, to dull — more at OBTUSE] : to reduce the edge or violence of : DULL, BLUNT ⟨~*ed* reflexes⟩ ⟨agents that ~ pain⟩
[1]**ob·tund·ent** \(')=;təndənt\ *adj* [L *obtundent-, obtundens*, pres. part. of *obtundere*] : blunting irritation or lessening pain
[2]**obtundent** \"\ *n* -S : an agent that blunts pain or dulls sensibility
ob·tu·rate \'äbt(y)ə,rāt\ *vt* -ED/-ING/-S [L *obturatus*, past part. of *obturare* to stop up, fr. *ob-* toward, over + *-turare* (akin to *tumēre* to swell) — more at OB-, THUMB] : OBSTRUCT, CLOSE; *esp* : to stop (a gun breech) so as to prevent the escape of gas in firing — **ob·tu·ra·tion** \,==ˈrāshən\ *n* -S
ob·tu·ra·tor \'==,rād·ə(r)\ *n* -S *often attrib* [NL, fr. L *obturatus* + *-or*] : one that closes or stops up an opening: **a** : either of two muscles arising from the obturator membrane and adjacent bony surfaces: (1) *or* **obturator ex·ter·nus** \-ek'stərnəs\ : a muscle arising from the outer surface of the membrane and being inserted into the trochanteric fossa of the femur (2) *or* **obturator in·ter·nus** \-in'tərnəs\ : a muscle arising from the inner surface of the membrane and being inserted into the greater trochanter of the femur **b** : a prosthetic device that usu. has the form of a plate and is designed to bridge an unnatural opening (as a fissure of the palate) **c** : a device for preventing the escape of gas through the breech mechanism of a breech-loading gun **d** : a hooded swelling of the placenta that fits over the nucellus in some plants
obturator artery *n* : an artery that passes out through the obturator canal and dividing into two branches is distributed to the muscles and fasciae of the hip and thigh
obturator canal *n* : the small patent opening of the obturator foramen through which nerves and vessels pass
obturator foramen *n* : an opening that is situated between the pubic and ischial parts of the innominate bone and that is largely closed by the obturator membrane — see OBTURATOR CANAL
obturator membrane *n* : a firm fibrous membrane covering most of the obturator foramen and serving as origin of the obturator muscles
obturator nerve *n* : a branch of the lumbar plexus arising from the second, third, and fourth lumbar nerves and supplying the hip and knee joints, adductor muscles of the thigh, and skin
obturator vein *n* : a tributary of the internal iliac vein that accompanies the obturator artery
ob·turbinate \(')äb+\ *adj* [ISV *ob-* + *turbinate*] : inversely turbinate
ob·tuse \əb't(y)üs, (')äb|-\ *adj, sometimes* -ER/-EST [L *obtusus*, past part. of *obtundere* to beat against, to dull, fr. *ob-* to, against + *tundere* to beat — more at OB-, STUTTER] **1** : lacking acuity of sensibility or perceptions : having neither delicate feelings nor alert awareness : DENSE ⟨too ~ to take a hint⟩ ⟨a dull ~ person⟩ **2 a** *of an angle* : exceeding 90 degrees but being less than 180 degrees — see ANGLE illustration **b** : not pointed or acute : BLUNT ⟨an ~ contour⟩ **c** *of a leaf* : blunt or rounded at the free end of : OBTUSE-ANGLED **3** : not causing an acute impression : MILD ⟨an ~ pain⟩ **syn** see DULL
obtuse-angled \-;==\ *also* **obtuse-angular** \-;===\ *adj* : having one or more angles that are obtuse
obtuse bisectrix *n* : the bisectrix of the obtuse angle formed by the axes of a biaxial crystal — called also *second mean line*
ob·tuse·ly *adv* : in an obtuse manner : so as to be obtuse
ob·tuse·ness *n* -ES : the quality or state of being obtuse
obtusi- *comb form* [NL, fr. L *obtusus*, past part.] : obtusely ⟨*obtusi*rostrate⟩ ⟨*obtusi*folious⟩
ob·tu·sion \äb't(y)üzhən\ *n* -S [LL *obtusion-, obtusio*, fr. L *obtusus* (past part. of *obtundere*) + *-ion-, -io* -ion] : a blunting or a condition of being blunted
ob·tu·si·ty \-üsəd·ē\ *n* -ES [ML *obtusitas*, fr. L *obtusus* + *-itas* -ity] : OBTUSENESS; *esp* : human density and insensitivity
ob-ugrian \(')äb+\ *n* -S *usu cap O&U* [*Ob*, river in Siberia + *Ugrian*] : a member of an Ostyak and Vogul people of Siberia that is of Finno-Ugrian ethnic classification, has a primitive hunting and fishing economy, and is closest linguistic ally to the Magyar peoples
ob·um·brant \(')ä;bəmbrənt\ *adj* [L *obumbrant-, obumbrans*, pres. part. of *obumbrare* to overshadow] : OVERHANGING ⟨~ hackle feathers⟩
[1]**obumbrate** *adj* [L *obumbratus*, past part. of *obumbrare* to overshadow, fr. *ob-* to, over + *umbrare* to shade, fr. *umbra* shadow — more at OB-, UMBRAGE] *obs* : darkened by or as if by shadow
[2]**ob·um·brate** \ä'bəm,brāt\ *vt* -ED/-ING/-S [L *obumbratus*, past part. of *obumbrare*] **1** : SHADE, DARKEN, CLOUD **2** *archaic* : ADUMBRATE — **ob·um·bra·tion** \,ä,bəm'brāshən\ *n* -S
obus \ōbēs, -ʊz; 'ōbəs\ *n, pl* **obus** \"\ *or* **obus·es** \'ōbəsəz\ [F, fr. G *haubitze* howitzer — more at HOWITZER] : an artillery shell
obv *abbr* obverse
ob·vallate \(')äb+\ *adj* [L *obvallatus*, past part. of *obvallare* to surround with a wall, fr. *ob-* toward, over + *vallare* to surround with a wall, fr. *vallum* wall, rampart — more at OB-, WALL] : surrounded by or as if by a wall ⟨~ papillae⟩
ob·ve·la·tion \,äbvə'lāshən\ *n* -S [LL *obvelare* to cover over, hide (fr. *ob-* toward, over + *velare* to cover, fr. *velum* covering, veil) + E *-ation* — more at OB-] : VEILING, CONCEALING — compare REVELATION
ob·ven·tion \äb'venchən\ *n* -S [ME *obvencioun*, fr. MF *obvention*, fr. L *obvention-, obventio* income, revenue, fr. L *obventus* (past part. of *obvenire* to come about, fr. *ob-* to, toward + *venire* to come) + *-ion-, -io* -ion — more at OB-, COME] : something that comes casually (as an incidental advantage or an occasional religious offering)
[1]**ob·verse** \əb'vərs, (')äb|v-, -vəs,-vəis\ *adj* [L *obversus*, past part. of *obvertere* to turn towards] **1** : facing the observer or opponent — opposed to *reverse* **2** : having the base or end next the attachment narrower than the top or free end ⟨an ~ tool⟩ ⟨an ~ leaf⟩ **3** : constituting a counterpart or complement — **ob·verse·ly** *adv*
[2]**ob·verse** \'äb,vərs, äb'vərs, -vəs,-vəis\ *n* -S [L *obversus*, past part. of *obvertere*] **1 a** : the side of a coin, token, medal, or currency note that is considered the front and that bears the principal device and lettering; *broadly* : a front or principal surface **b** : the more conspicuous of two possible sides, things, or cases ⟨the ~ of this situation⟩ **2 a** : a counterpart necessarily involved in or answering to a fact or truth **b** *logic* : a proposition which may be inferred immediately from another and in which the quality of the given proposition is changed, the subject term remains unaltered, and the predicate is the negative of that which is given ⟨the ~ of "all *A* is *B*" is "no *A* is not *B*"⟩ **syn** see CONVERSE
ob·ver·sion \äb'vərzhən, -vəzh-, -vəizh- *also* -shən\ *n* -S [LL *obversion-, obversio*, fr. *obversus* (past part. of *obvertere*) + *-ion-, -io* -ion] *logic* : the operation of immediate inference that gives the obverse
ob·vert \='vərt, -vət, -vəit\ *vt* -ED/-ING/-S [L *obvertere* to turn towards, fr. *ob-* to, toward + *vertere* to turn — more at OB-, WORTH] **1** : to turn so as to present a different surface to view : to change the appearance or seeming of **2** : to subject (a proposition in logic) to obversion
ob·ver·tend \'äbvə(r),tend\ *n* -S [L *obvertendus*, gerundive of *obvertere* to obvert] : a proposition upon which the operation of obversion is performed
ob·vi·a·ble \'äbvēəbəl\ *adj* [*obviate* + *-able*] : capable of being obviated
ob·vi·ate \'äbvē,āt, *usu* -ād+V\ *vt* -ED/-ING/-S [LL *obviatus*, past part. of *obviare* to meet, withstand, oppose, fr. L *obviam* in the way] **1** : to meet or anticipate and dispose of : make unnecessary ⟨~ the necessity of going⟩ **2** *obs* : OPPOSE **syn** see PREVENT
ob·vi·a·tion \,==ˈāshən\ *n* -S [ME *obviacioun*, fr. LL *obviation-, obviatio*, fr. *obviatus* + *-ion-, -io* -ion] : an act or instance of obviating or being obviated
[1]**ob·vi·a·tive** \'äbvē,ād·iv\ *adj* [*obviate* + *-ive*] *of a grammatical form* : denoting the second of two third persons referred to in a context (as in the construction in some languages corresponding to "he held *his* [another's] horse") — compare PROXIMATE
[2]**obviative** \"\ *n* -S : an obviative grammatical form
ob·vi·ous \'äbvēəs *in rapid speech often* 'ävē-\ *adj* [L *obvius*, fr. *obviam* in the way, towards, about to, fr. *ob* to, before, against + *viam*, accus. of *via* way, road — more at EPI-, VIA] **1 a** *obs* : presenting itself in the way : occurring often **b** *archaic* : being in the way or to the front : OPPOSITE, FRONTING **c** : so placed as to be easily or inevitably perceived or noticed ⟨an ~ light switch⟩ **2** *archaic* : liable or exposed to some effect (as injury or mockery) : OPEN, SUBJECT **3** : capable of easy perception: **a** : readily perceived by the senses : hard not to perceive, sense, or grasp ⟨the invisible as opposed to the ~ —M.R.Cohen⟩ **b** : readily and easily perceived by the sensibilities or mind : requiring very little insight or reflection to perceive, recognize, or comprehend ⟨all was taken in at a glance; the fell purpose . . . was ~ —Herman Melville⟩ **c** : easily understood : requiring no thought or consideration to understand or analyze : so simple and clear as to be unmistakable ⟨poetry, in fact, whatever else it may or may not be, must be poetry—a sound, if ~, conclusion —C.D.Lewis⟩ **d** : disappointingly simple and easy to discover or interpret : wanting in any challenging or interesting complexity or ingenuity ⟨the devices . . . are rather too ~ —Henry Adams⟩ **syn** see EVIDENT
ob·vi·ous·ly *adv* : in an obvious manner : CERTAINLY
ob·vi·ous·ness *n* -ES : the quality or state of being obvious
ob·vo·lute \'äbvə,lüt *also* -əl,yüt, *usu* -üd+V\ *adj* [L *obvolutus*, past part. of *obvolvere*] : OVERLAPPING, CONTORTED, CONVOLUTE
ob·volve \äb'välv\ *vt* -ED/-ING/-S [L *obvolvere* to roll around, wrap around, fr. *ob-* to, over + *volvere* to roll — more at OB-, VOLUBLE] *archaic* : ENWRAP
oc *abbr* ocean
OC *abbr* **1** of course **2** office copy **3** officer candidate

4 officer commanding **5** officer in charge **6** officer's cook **7** official classification **8** old charter **9** old crop **10** on center **11** *often not cap* only child **12** open charter **13** open cover **14** *often not cap* [L *opere citato*] in the work cited **15** order canceled **16** original cover **17** outing club **18** overcharge **19** oxygen consumed

oca *or* **oka** \'ōkə\ *n* -s [Sp *oca*, fr. Quechua *ókka*] **:** either of two So. American wood sorrels (*Oxalis crenata* and *O. tuberosa*) cultivated for their edible tubers

oc·a·ri·na \ˌäkə'rēnə\ *n* -s [It, dim of *oca* goose, fr. LL *auca*, fr. (assumed) VL *avica*, back-formation fr. L *avicula* small bird, dim. of *avis* bird — more at AVIARY] **:** a simple wind instrument or toy of the flute class having a mouthpiece and finger holes and usu. made of terracotta in various sizes — called also *sweet potato*

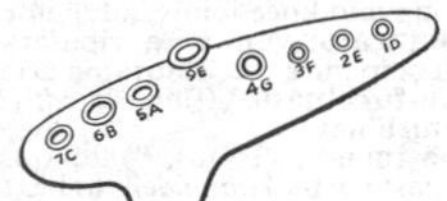

ocarina

occ *abbr* **1** occasional; occasionally **2** occulting

oc·ca·mism *usu cap, var of* OCKHAMISM

occam's razor *usu cap O, var of* OCKHAM'S RAZOR

oc·ca·nee·chi \ˌäkə'nēchē\ *n, pl* **occaneechi** *or* **occaneechis** *usu cap* **1 :** an extinct Siouan people formerly found on the middle island in the Roanoke river, Virginia **2 :** a member of the Occaneechi people

¹oc·ca·sion \ə'kāzhən\ *n* -s [ME *occasioun*, fr. MF or L; MF *occasion*, fr. L *occasion-, occasio*, fr. *occasus* (past part. of *occidere* to fall down, fr. *ob-* + *cadere* to fall) + *-ion-, -io* -ion — more at CHANCE] **1 :** a situation or set of circumstances favorable to a particular purpose or development **:** a timely chance **:** OPPORTUNITY ⟨rose to the ~⟩ ⟨was equal to the ~⟩ ⟨took ~ by the forelock⟩ ⟨only those living in exceptionally fortunate localities had ~ to grow surplus products —Samuel Van Valkenburg & Ellsworth Huntington⟩ ⟨while the new science has achieved wonders in medicine and surgery, it has also produced and spread ~*s* for diseases and weaknesses — John Dewey⟩ **2 a :** something that produces an effect or brings about an event ⟨a formula that has been the ~ for a considerable amount of misunderstanding —I.A.Richards⟩ ⟨any ~ which prompts a mind to ask some fundamental question —Hunter Mead⟩ ⟨an ~ of sin⟩ **b :** something that helps to bring about an event or produce an effect without directly causing it **:** a contributing or incidental cause ⟨the birthday . . . was merely the ~, not the cause, of the guests' effusions —Lillian Ross⟩ ⟨the specific ~ of the poem is not known —C.S.Kilby⟩ ⟨a casual mention of the house by a friend was the ~ of their buying it⟩ ⟨an inspiring teacher was the ~ of his great achievements in science⟩ **3 :** a circumstance, occurrence, or state of affairs that provides ground or reason for something ⟨there is no ~ for alarm: it is a very mild illness⟩ ⟨his graduation with honors is ~ for celebration⟩ **4 a :** a particular occurrence **:** HAPPENING, INCIDENT ⟨well adapted for treatment as a row of detached episodes or ~*s* —Percy Lubbock⟩ ⟨everybody has been terribly kind since my recent sad ~ —Thomas Kelly⟩ **b :** a particular time at which something takes place **:** a time marked by some happening ⟨on the ~ of his daughter's wedding⟩ ⟨on the ~ of the signing of the peace treaty⟩ **5 a :** a need arising from a particular circumstance **:** EXIGENCY, REQUIREMENT ⟨there had been no ~ for being so definite —Sherwood Anderson⟩ ⟨knowledge for which he will never have any ~ —C.H. Grandgent⟩ **b** *archaic* **:** a personal want or need — usu. used in pl. ⟨my purse, my person, my extremest means lie all unlock'd to your ~*s* —Shak.⟩ **6 occasions** *pl* **:** something that one has to do **:** necessary affairs **:** BUSINESS ⟨minded his own ~*s* and was content to let other folk mind theirs —S.H. Adams⟩ ⟨going about their lawful or unlawful ~*s* all over the seven seas —Douglas Bush⟩ **7 a :** a religious ceremonial; *specif* **:** a Scottish communion service **b :** a special event or ceremony **:** CELEBRATION ⟨he liked the ~ —the Changing of the Guard at St. James's Palace, parties, and balls, and such things as that —Basil Taylor⟩ ⟨sat in the big parlor as though this was an ~ —Agnes S. Turnbull⟩ **syn** see CAUSE, OPPORTUNITY — **on occasion** *adv* **:** now and then **:** OCCASIONALLY ⟨he lives in the country, though he visits the city *on occasion*⟩

²occasion \"\ *vt* -ED/-ING/-S **1 :** to give occasion to **:** bring about **:** give rise to **:** CAUSE ⟨a violent storm ~*ed* a new delay of two weeks —Oscar Handlin⟩ ⟨social and commercial intercourse will ~ movement of language —Charlton Laird⟩ **2 :** to cause to do something ⟨was almost at the end of his financial resources, which fact ~*ed* him to turn away from a pretentious hotel —Zane Grey⟩

¹oc·ca·sion·al \-zhən°l, -zhnəl\ *adj* **1 :** occurring or operating on a particular occasion **:** proceeding from the occasion ⟨the cabinet has ~ special meetings to deal with urgent matters⟩ ⟨a budget must be able to meet ~ demands as well as regular ones⟩ **2 :** acting as the occasion or contributing cause of something ⟨nothing else ~ of my long silence —D.G. Rossetti⟩ **3 :** written for a particular occasion or to celebrate a particular event or anniversary ⟨an ~ essay⟩ ⟨an ~ poem⟩ ⟨~ verse⟩ **4 :** met with, appearing, or occurring irregularly and according to no fixed or certain scheme **:** INFREQUENT ⟨takes an ~ vacation⟩ ⟨sees an ~ visitor⟩ ⟨runs into an ~ storm⟩ **5 :** acting in a specified capacity on a particular occasion or from time to time ⟨an ~ speaker⟩ ⟨an ~ chauffeur⟩ ⟨an ~ fisherman⟩ **6 :** designed or constructed to be used as the occasion demands ⟨an ~ chair⟩ ⟨an ~ table⟩

²occasional \"\ *n* -s **:** something occasional —usu. used in pl. ⟨the furniture department has a good selection of ~*s*⟩

occasional cause *n* **1 a :** a mental state (as desire or decision) considered as the occasion but not the real cause of a physical phenomenon (as bodily behavior) **b :** a physical phenomenon considered similarly as the occasion of a mental state — compare OCCASIONALISM **2 :** a circumstance that precedes an effect and that without being the real cause is the occasion of its action

oc·ca·sion·al·ism \-zhən°l,izəm, -zhnə,li-\ *n* -s [ISV ¹*occasional* + *-ism*] **:** a doctrine held by the Cartesian philosophers Geulincx and Malebranche that mind and matter are inherently incapable of affecting each other and that their apparent reciprocal action must therefore be due to the intervention of God who on the occasion of a change in one produces a corresponding change in the other — compare OCCASIONAL CAUSE

oc·ca·sion·al·ist \-ləst\ *n* -s [ISV ¹*occasional* + *-ist*] **:** an adherent of occasionalism

oc·ca·sion·al·is·tic \ə¦kāzhən°l¦istik, -zhnə¦li-\ *adj* **:** of or relating to occasionalism or occasionalists

oc·ca·sion·al·i·ty \əˌkāzhə'naləd·ē\ *n* -ES **:** the quality or state of being occasional

oc·ca·sion·al·ly \ə'kāzhən°lē, -zhnəlē, -i *sometimes* -zhənl-\ *adv* **1 :** now and then **:** here and there **:** SOMETIMES ⟨open areas are only ~ interrupted by clumps of aspen —*Amer. Guide Series: Nev.*⟩ **2** *dial chiefly Eng* **:** on a particular occasion **:** for the occasion

oc·ca·sion·er \-nə(r)\ *n* -s **:** one that occasions

occasions *pl of* OCCASION, *pres 3d sing of* OCCASION

oc·ci·dent \'äksədənt *also* -d°nt *or* -ˌdent\ *n* -s [ME, west, fr. MF, fr. L *occident-, occidens*, fr. pres. part. of *occidere* to fall down, go down, set — more at OCCASION] **1** *obs* **:** the part of the firmament or of the world where the sun sets — compare ORIENT **2** *usu cap* **:** WEST 2 ⟨sailed for the *Occident*⟩

¹oc·ci·den·tal \¦==¦dent°l\ *adj* [ME, fr. L *occidentalis*, fr. *occident-, occidens* + *-alis* -al] **1** *often cap* **:** of, relating to, or situated in the Occident **:** WESTERN — compare ORIENTAL **2 a** *often cap* **:** of, relating to, or having the characteristics of Occidentals ⟨~ culture⟩ ⟨~ art⟩ **b :** of, relating to, or characteristic of the western U.S. ⟨the ~ plane tree⟩ **3 :** of inferior grade, luster, or value ⟨~ agate⟩ — compare ORIENTAL 2a — **oc·ci·den·tal·ly** \-°lē, -i\ *adv*

²occidental \"\ *n* -s *usu cap* **:** a member of one of the indigenous peoples of the Occident ⟨the *Occidental* regards much oriental and primitive music as mere noise —Thomas Munro⟩

oc·ci·den·tal·ism \ˌ==ˈdent°l,izəm\ *n* -s *usu cap* **:** the characteristic features of occidental peoples or culture

oc·ci·den·tal·ist \-ləst\ *n* -s *often cap* **:** one who favors occidental culture

oc·ci·den·tal·iza·tion \ˌ==ˌdent°lə'zāshən\ *n* -s *often cap* **:** the process of occidentalizing or the state of being occidentalized

oc·ci·den·tal·ize \ˌ==ˈdent°lˌīz\ *vt* -ED/-ING/-S *sometimes cap* **:** to make occidental **:** cause to conform to western standards or culture ⟨served to widen the gulf between the small *occidentalized* intelligentsia and the great mass of the people —Virginia Thompson & Richard Adloff⟩

occipit- *or* **occipito-** *comb form* [ML *occipit-* & NL *occipito-*, fr. L *occipit-, occiput*] **1 :** occiput ⟨*occipit*ad⟩ **2 :** occipital and ⟨*occipito*nasal⟩

oc·cip·i·tad \(')äk¦sipə,tad\ *adv* [*occipit-* + *-ad*] **:** toward the occiput

¹oc·cip·i·tal \(')äk¦sipəd·°l, -ət°l\ *adj* [MF, fr. ML *occipitalis*, fr. L *occipit-, occiput* occiput + *-alis* -al — more at OCCIPUT] **1 :** of or relating to the occiput or an occipital part **2 :** lying near or oriented toward the occiput — **oc·cip·i·tal·ly** \-°lē, -i\ *adv*

²occipital \"\ *n* -s **1 :** OCCIPITAL BONE **2 :** a part or structure lying near or on the occiput (as certain scales on reptiles)

occipital arch *n* **:** a part of the insect cranium between the occipital and postoccipital sutures

occipital artery *n* **:** a branch of the external carotid supplying the muscles and other structures of the back of the neck and head

occipital bone *n* **:** a compound bone that forms the posterior part of the skull and surrounds the foramen magnum, bearing the condyle or condyles for articulation with the atlas, in higher vertebrates being usu. composed of four more or less completely united elements and in man much curved and of trapezoid outline, ending in front of the foramen magnum in the basilar process, and bearing on its outer surface behind the foramen magnum the two curved transverse superior and inferior nuchal lines besides a median crest and protuberance

occipital condyle *n* **1 :** an articular surface on the occipital bone by which the skull articulates with the atlas **2 :** a projection of the border of the postocciput of the insect head to which the lateral neck plates articulate

occipital crest *n* **1 :** either of the two ridges connecting the occipital protuberances and foramen magnum **2 :** a transverse ridge at the upper posterior border of the skull of many animals between the occipital and parietal segments **3 :** a crest of feathers on the back of the head of certain birds

occipital foramen *n* **1 :** FORAMEN MAGNUM **2 :** an opening at the back of an insect's head through which the alimentary canal and other organs pass to the thorax

occipital ganglion *n* **:** one of the paired ganglia of the stomodaeal nervous system of an insect that are located just behind the brain

oc·cip·i·ta·lis \äk,sipə'taləs, -tāl-, -täl-\ *n* -ES [NL, fr. ML, occipital] **:** the posterior muscular part of the occipitofrontalis

occipital lobe *n* **:** the posterior lobe of the cerebral hemisphere that is indistinctly separated from the parietal lobe in front and the temporal lobe below and has the form of a 3-sided pyramid

occipital plate *n* **:** a scute on the back of the head of certain reptiles

occipital point *n* **:** the point on the occiput farthest removed from the glabella

occipital protuberance *n* **:** either of two prominences on the occipital bone: **a :** a prominence on the outer surface of the occipital bone midway between the upper border and the foramen magnum that gives attachment to the ligamentum nuchae — called also *external occipital protuberance* **b :** a prominence similarly situated on the inner surface of the occipital bone — called also *internal occipital protuberance*

occipital sinus *n* **:** a venous sinus lodged in a groove on the internal occipital crest

oc·cip·i·to·frontalis \äk¦sipəd·ō+\ *n* [NL, fr. *occipit-* + *frontalis* frontal] **:** a fibrous layer covering each side of the vertex of the skull from the eyebrow to the occiput and continuous anteriorly and posteriorly with the frontalis and occipitalis muscles respectively — called also *epicranius*

oc·cip·i·to·mastoid \"+\ *adj* [*occipit-* + *mastoid*] **:** of, relating to, lying between, or distributed to the occipital and mastoid bones ⟨~ suture⟩

oc·cip·i·to·parietal index \"+ . . -\ *n* [*occipitoparietal* ISV *occipit-* + *parietal*] **:** the ratio of the breadth of the skull between the asterions to its greatest breadth multiplied by 100

oc·ci·put \'äksə(,)pət, *usu* -d·+V\ *n, pl* **occiputs** \-ts\ *or* **oc·cip·i·ta** \äk'sipəd·ə\ [L *occipit-, occiput*, back-formation (influenced by L *capit-, caput* head) fr. *occipitium* back part of the head, occiput, fr. *ob-* + *-cipitium* (fr. *capit-, caput* head) — more at HEAD] **1 :** the back part of the head of a vertebrate or insect — see DOG illustration **2 :** the back part of the skull

oc·ci·sion \äk'sizhən\ *n* -s [ME *occisioun*, fr. MF *occision*, fr. L *occision-, occisio*, fr. *occisus* (past part. of *occidere* to kill, fr. *ob-* + *caedere* to cut, strike, kill) + *-ion-, -io* -ion — more at CONCISE] **:** SLAUGHTER ⟨applauded their pitiless ~ —R.S.Ellery⟩

oc·clude \ə'klüd\ *vb* -ED/-ING/-S [L *occludere*, fr. *ob-* + *claudere* to shut, close — more at CLOSE] *vt* **1 :** to shut or stop up so as to prevent the passage of something **:** CLOSE, OBSTRUCT ⟨a thrombus *occluding* a coronary artery⟩ ⟨an *occluded* bronchus⟩ ⟨sank ships to ~ the harbor⟩ **2 :** to bar the passage of **:** shut in or out ⟨concern with the mechanics of pronunciation ~*s* comprehension of the author's ideas —A.S.Artley⟩ ⟨the dandy's world is friendly, formal, and heartless, *occluding* the imagination —Cyril Connolly⟩ **3 :** to bring (upper and lower teeth) into occlusal relations **4 :** to take in and retain (a substance) in the interior rather than on an external surface **:** SORB ⟨proteins in precipitating may ~ alcohol⟩ — used esp. of metals sorbing gases ⟨palladium ~*s* large volumes of hydrogen⟩ **5 :** to cut off from contact with the surface of the earth and force aloft by the convergence of a cold front upon a warm front ⟨an *occluded* cyclone⟩ ⟨*occluded* warm air⟩ ⟨an *occluded* low⟩ ~ *vi* **1 :** to close with the cusps fitting together ⟨his teeth do not ~ properly⟩ **2 :** to become cut off from contact with the earth's surface ⟨the cyclone ~*s* and is left behind by the storm below —T.M.Longstreet⟩

occluded front *n* **:** OCCLUSION 1 c (2) — see FRONT illustration

oc·clud·ent \-d°nt\ *adj* [L *occludent-, occludens*, pres. part. of *occludere*] **:** serving to occlude

occlus- *or* **occluso-** *comb form* [prob. fr. (assumed) NL *occlus-*, fr. L *occlusus*, past part. of *occludere* to occlude] **1 :** occlusion ⟨*occlusal*⟩ ⟨*occluso*meter⟩ **2 :** occlusal and ⟨*occluso*gingival⟩

oc·clu·sal \ə'klüs°l\ *adj* [*occlus-* + *-al*] **:** of or relating to the grinding or biting surface of a tooth or occlusion of the teeth ⟨~ surface⟩ ⟨~ relationship⟩ ⟨an ~ neurosis⟩

oc·clu·sion \-üzhən\ *n* -s [prob. fr. (assumed) NL *occlusion-, occlusio*, fr. L *occlusus* (past part. of *occludere* to occlude) + *-ion-, -io* -ion] **1 :** the act of occluding or the state of being occluded **:** a shutting off or obstruction of something ⟨a coronary ~⟩ ⟨the silting up and ~ of the mouth of the river⟩ ⟨the ~ of sources of information⟩: as **a :** a blocking of the central passage of one reflex by preoccupation of nerve relays with passage of another **b (1) :** the complete obstruction of the breath passage in the articulation of a stop (2) **:** the complete obstruction of the mouth passage in the articulation of a nasal consonant **c (1) :** the meteorological process of occluding (2) **:** something that has been occluded; *specif* **:** the front formed by a cold front overtaking a warm front and lifting the warm air above the earth's surface **2 a :** the bringing of the opposing surfaces of the teeth of the two jaws into contact; *also* **:** the relation between the surfaces when in contact **b :** the transient approximation of the edges of a natural opening ⟨~ of the eyelids⟩ **3 :** SORPTION; *esp* **:** sorption of gases

¹oc·clu·sive \-üsiv, -sēv *also* -sev\ *adj* [ISV *occlus-* + *-ive*] **1 :** serving to occlude ⟨an ~ dressing for a wound⟩ ⟨~ arterial disease⟩ **2 :** characterized by occlusion

²occlusive \"\ *n* -s **1 :** STOP 9 **2 :** a nasal consonant

oc·clu·sor \-üsə(r)\ *n* -s [NL, fr. L *occlusus* (past part. of *occludere*) + NL *-or*] **:** a body part that closes or blocks another ⟨~ muscles⟩ ⟨the operculum forms an effective ~ of the snail's shell⟩

occn *abbr* occasion

¹oc·cult \ə'kəlt, 'ä,kəlt\ *vb* -ED/-ING/-S [L *occultare*, fr. *occultus*, past part. of *occulere* to cover up] *vt* **1 :** to hide from sight **:** CONCEAL ⟨the lids lowered again, ~*ing* the old eyes' softened gleam —*MacLean's Mag.*⟩ ⟨if his ~*ed* guilt do not itself unkennel in one speech —Shak.⟩ **2 :** to conceal or extinguish the light of by intervention **:** ECLIPSE ⟨planets, like stars, may be ~*ed*; but as a planet shows a disk, and does not appear as a mere point, the disappearance is gradual —Patrick Moore⟩ ~ *vi* **:** to become concealed or to have its light extinguished ⟨the beam of the lighthouse ~*s* at regular intervals⟩

²occult \"\ *adj* [L *occultus*, past part. of *occulere* to cover up, fr. *ob-* + *-culere* (akin to L *celare* to conceal) — more at HELL] **1 :** deliberately kept hidden **:** not revealed to others **:** SECRET, UNDISCLOSED ⟨too ~ to be shown to uninitiate eyes —Elinor Wylie⟩ ⟨deep subterranean ~ jealousy —J.C.Powys⟩ **2 :** not to be apprehended or understood **:** demanding more than ordinary perception or knowledge **:** ABSTRUSE, MYSTERIOUS, RECONDITE ⟨as far as the general public was concerned, the museum was an esoteric, ~ place —Aline B. Saarinen⟩ ⟨~ matters like nuclear physics, radiation effects and the designing of rockets —Robert Bendiner⟩ ⟨the ~ properties of the ductless glands —W.R.Inge⟩ **3 a :** hidden from view **:** not able to be seen **:** CONCEALED ⟨the silica may appear in crystalline form . . . or it may remain ~ in the groundmass —G.W. Tyrrell⟩ **b** *archaic* **:** of or relating to lines drawn in dots or meant to be erased **4 :** of, relating to, or dealing in matters regarded as involving the action or influence of supernatural agencies or some secret knowledge of them ⟨deals in the ~ arts⟩ ⟨an ~ fortune-teller⟩ **5 :** not manifest or detectable by clinical methods alone ⟨~ carcinoma⟩ ⟨~ infection⟩; *esp* **:** not present in macroscopic amounts ⟨~ blood in the feces⟩ — compare GROSS — **oc·cult·ly** *adv*

³occult \"\ *n* -s **:** something mysterious or supernatural — usu. used with *the* ⟨he is a student of the ~⟩

oc·cul·ta·tion \ˌä(ˌ)kəl'tāshən\ *n* -s [ME *occultacion* concealment, fr. L *occultation-, occultatio*, fr. *occultatus* (past part. of *occultare* to conceal) + *-ion-, -io* -ion] **1 :** the state of being hidden from view or lost to notice **:** disappearance from the public eye ⟨his fame was already emerging from the ~ of changing fashion —*Times Lit. Supp.*⟩ **2 :** the shutting off of the light of a celestial body by the intervention of some other celestial body; *esp* **:** an eclipse of a star or planet by the moon

occult balance *n* **:** an asymmetrical mode of composition (as in flower arrangement or Chinese and Japanese painting)

oc·cult·er \ə'kəltə(r), 'ä,k-\ *n* -s [¹*occult* + *-er*] **:** an occulting opaque object

occulting *adj* [fr. pres. part. of ¹*occult*] **:** of or relating to any of various devices for cutting off from view a light or light-giving body ⟨an ~ disk located in the optical system of the coronagraph blacks out . . . the face of the sun to establish a perpetual, artificial, total eclipse —*Christian Science Monitor*⟩

occulting light *n* **:** a navigational light whose beam is interrupted at regular intervals by a brief period of darkness

oc·cult·ism \ə'kəl,tizəm, 'ä(,)kə-\ *n* -s [ISV ²*occult* + *-ism*] **:** occult theory or practice **:** a belief in hidden or mysterious powers and the possibility of subjecting them to human control ⟨~*s*, incantations, glimpses of the beyond, intimations of another world —L.P.Smith⟩ ⟨a kind of experimental ~ which relied on psychic phenomena for its proofs —*Times Lit. Supp.*⟩

oc·cult·ist \-təst\ *n* -s [ISV ²*occult* + *-ist*] **:** an adherent of occultism **:** one thought to be proficient in occult practices

occult mineral *n* **:** a mineral molecule shown by calculation of chemical analyses to be present in a rock (as plagioclase in orthoclase) but not actually seen under the microscope

oc·cult·ness *n* -ES **:** the quality or state of being occult

occult spavin *n* **:** spavin in which there is pronounced lameness without apparent enlargement on the hock joint

oc·cu·pance \'äkyəpən(t)s\ *n* -s [fr. *occupant*, after such pairs as E *assistant: assistance*] **:** OCCUPANCY ⟨the sequent ~ of the valleys and their adjacent benchlands —*Geog. Rev.*⟩

oc·cu·pan·cy \-nsē, -si\ *n* -ES [*occupant* + *-cy*] **1 a :** the taking and holding possession of real property under a lease or tenancy at will **b :** the act of taking possession of something that has no owner (as a waif or derelict) and thus acquiring title to it **2 a :** the act of becoming an occupant or the condition of being an occupant ⟨between successive human *occupancies*, the caves were often used by wild animals —R.W. Murray⟩ ⟨the essential quality of his existence consists in his ~ of this world of symbols and ideas —L.A.White⟩ ⟨ten years of uninterrupted ~ of this position⟩ **b :** the condition of being occupied ⟨though the village site showed two levels of ~, the temple mound showed three —*Amer. Guide Series: Tenn.*⟩ ⟨ghetto-slums which were both substandard and homogeneous in their ~ —Charles Abrams⟩ **3 :** the particular use or type of use to which property (as a building or part of a building) is put ⟨residential ~⟩ ⟨industrial ~⟩ ⟨storage ~⟩ **4 :** an occupied building or part of a building (as an apartment or office)

oc·cu·pant \-nt\ *n* -s [MF, fr. pres. part. of *occuper* to take possession of — more at OCCUPY] **1 a :** one who takes the first possession of something that has no owner and thereby acquires title by occupancy **b :** one who takes possession under title, lease, or tenancy at will **2 a :** one who occupies a particular place or premises **:** TENANT, RESIDENT ⟨the influence of sudden variations in temperature . . . on the ~*s* of a small pond —W.H.Dowdeswell⟩ ⟨the only year-around ~*s* of snowcapped Mount Washington —R.S.Monahan⟩ ⟨the human body has fascinated, pleased and frightened its ~*s* for many an age —R.M.Yoder⟩ **b :** one who holds a particular post ⟨a study of the ~*s* of the supreme court bench⟩ ⟨the first ~ of the post of assistant to the president⟩ **3 :** one who has the actual use or possession of something ⟨limped hurriedly to grab a table whose ~*s* had scarcely risen fully to their feet —William Sansom⟩

oc·cu·pa·tion \ˌäkyə'pāshən\ *n* -s [ME *occupacioun*, fr. MF *occupation*, fr. L *occupation-, occupatio*, fr. *occupatus* (past part. of *occupare* to take possession of, occupy, employ) + *-ion-, -io* -ion — more at OCCUPY] **1 a :** an activity in which one engages **:** a way of passing the time ⟨declared she had always plenty of ~ for herself while he was away —William Black⟩ ⟨bathing or loafing on the beaches are obviously a major ~ hereabouts —Ann Panners⟩ **b :** the principal business of one's life **:** a craft, trade, profession or other means of earning a living **:** EMPLOYMENT, VOCATION ⟨his ~ is farming⟩ ⟨has gone from one ~ to another without settling down to any⟩ ⟨writing has been his ~ for many years⟩ **2 :** the function or use of something ⟨if the ~ of steamboats be a matter of such general notoriety —John Marshall⟩ ⟨it is . . . the great ~ of the graphic arts to give us first of all order and variety in the sensuous plane —Roger Fry⟩ **3 a :** the actual possession and use of real estate (as by lease) **:** OCCUPANCY, TENANCY ⟨this fairly old house . . . was otherwise in doctors' and dentists' ~ —Elizabeth Bowen⟩ ⟨the last of the historic private houses in the metropolis . . . still in the ~ of its hereditary owner —*Sydney (Australia) Bull.*⟩ **b :** the possession or settlement of a place or area **:** TENURE ⟨many relics of this early Indian ~ have been found —*Amer. Guide Series: N. H.*⟩ ⟨from this section westward evidences of ancient human ~ are many —*Amer. Guide Series: Texas*⟩ **c :** the holding of an office or position ⟨it is only . . . the ~ . . . of two offices at the same time that offends public policy —W.D.Miller⟩ **d** *Brit* **:** land held by a tenant **:** HOLDING **4 :** the act or process of occupying or taking possession of a place or area **:** SEIZURE ⟨the fate of New Spain depended on forestalling England's ~ of that waterway —R.A.Billington⟩ **5 a :** the usu. temporary holding and control of a country or a part of a country by a foreign military force ⟨their ~ of the divided capital city —*Current Biog.*⟩ **b** *often cap* **:** the military force occupying a country or the policies carried out by such a force ⟨the broad program of the ~ was being carried out without disturbance —*Collier's Yr. Bk.*⟩ ⟨the *Occupation* removed this requirement in order to decrease the sense of regimentation —Hugh & Mabel Smythe⟩ **syn** see WORK

¹oc·cu·pa·tion·al \¦==¦pāshən°l, -shnəl\ *adj* **:** of or relating to occupation or an occupation ⟨~ troops⟩ ⟨~ choice⟩ — **oc·cu·pa·tion·al·ly** \-°lē, -əlē, -i\ *adv*

²occupational \"\ *n* -s **:** OCCUPATION STAMP

occupational disease *n* **1 :** an illness caused by factors arising from one's occupation ⟨dermatitis is often an *occupational disease*⟩ **2 :** an exaggerated or harmful attitude, tendency, or type of behavior associated with a particular occupation ⟨to diagnose the ills of our liberal arts colleges has become almost an *occupational disease* among college presidents —J.B. Conant⟩

occupational neurosis *n* **:** a condition that is caused by overuse of a muscle or set of muscles in repetitive performance of an operation (as in milking or dancing) and that is marked by loss of ability to constrain the muscles to perform the particular operation involved

occupational therapist *n* **:** one trained in or engaged in the practice of occupational therapy

occupational therapy *n* **:** therapy by means of mental or physical activity; *specif* **:** prescribed creative activity carried out under supervision for its effect in promoting recovery or rehabilitation following disease or injury

occupation bridge *n* **:** a bridge connecting the parts of an estate separated by a railroad, highway, or canal

occupation currency *n* **:** currency issued by the occupying power of a conquered country

occupation day *n, usu cap O&D* **:** July 25 observed in Puerto Rico as a holiday commemorating the anniversary of the landing of American troops at Guanica in 1898

occupation stamp *n* **:** a postage stamp issued for use in a country occupied by forces of a foreign country

oc·cu·pa·tive \ˈäkyə,pād·iv\ *adj* [L *occupatus* (past part. of *occupare* to take possession of, occupy, employ) + E *-ive*] **1 :** held by occupation ⟨an ~ field⟩ **2 :** of or relating to an occupation ⟨Smith is an ~ name⟩

oc·cu·pi·able \ˈäkyə,pīəbəl, ˌ≈≈ˈ≈≈\ *adj* **:** capable of being occupied or fit for occupancy ⟨an ~ room⟩

oc·cu·pied \ˈäkyə,pīd\ *adj* [ME *occupyed,* fr. past part. of *occupien* to occupy] **1 :** held by occupation ⟨an ~ country⟩ ⟨an ~ area⟩ ⟨an ~ house⟩ **2 :** engaged in activity **:** BUSY, EMPLOYED ⟨a constantly ~ person⟩ **3 :** taken up **:** FILLED ⟨has few ~ days⟩ **4 :** technically published whether valid or not

oc·cu·pi·er \-ī(ə)r, -īə\ *n* -s [ME, fr. *occupien* to occupy + *-er*] **:** one that occupies a place ⟨the region is not burdened with unpalatable space ~s —W.S.Hopkins⟩: as **a** *Brit* **:** one who holds possession of property as owner or tenant ⟨the hovels which still exist under the name of cottages almost always belong to the ~s themselves —G.E.Fussell⟩ ⟨the present ~s of the . . . mansion do not follow the generous custom of the owners in admitting the public —Elizabeth Montizambert⟩ **b :** a member of a foreign military force occupying a country or part of a country

oc·cu·py \ˈäkyə,pī\ *vt* -ED/-ING/-ES [ME *occupien* to take possession of, occupy, employ, modif. of MF *occuper,* fr. L *occupare,* fr. *ob-* + *-cupare* (akin to L *capere* to seize) — more at HEAVE] **1 :** to engage the attention or energies of **:** BUSY, EMPLOY ⟨the deeper issues which have *occupied* modern thinkers —A.N.Whitehead⟩ ⟨had to be given extra work to ~ her —Jean Stafford⟩ ⟨was *occupied* in national service throughout that period —*Current Biog.*⟩ **2 a :** to fill up (a place or extent) ⟨*occupies* an attractive site along the bay shore —*Amer. Guide Series: Mich.*⟩ ⟨the center of the house was *occupied* by a magnificent mahogany staircase —R.M.Lovett⟩ **b :** to take up (a specified time) ⟨they must have *occupied* tens of thousands of years —W.H.Dowdeswell⟩ ⟨a ten-day race meet *occupies* the last week of July and the first week of August —*Amer. Guide Series: Md.*⟩ **3 a :** to take possession of by conquest **:** SEIZE ⟨the enemy troops, in a massive attack, quickly *occupied* the eastern half of the country⟩ **b :** to take up residence in **:** settle in ⟨the area was discovered in 1820 and was *occupied* soon after by pastoralists —H.W.H.King⟩ **c :** to maintain possession or control of by military occupation ⟨second-grade troops, useful mainly to ~ parts of the country that have already been pacified —Brian Crozier⟩ **4 a :** to hold possession of ⟨*occupied* a ridge from which they dominated the crossroads⟩ **b :** to fill and perform the functions of ⟨ ~ the newly created office of chancellor —*Current Biog.*⟩ ⟨the woman *occupied* . . . a position very like that of the father in our society —Abram Kardiner⟩ **5 :** to reside in as an owner or tenant ⟨*occupies* the house that his grandfather built fifty years ago⟩ ⟨*occupies* the apartment on a two-year lease⟩ **6** *archaic* **:** USE ⟨bind me fast with new ropes that never were *occupied* —Judg 16:11 (AV)⟩ **7** *obs* **:** to have sexual intercourse with **8** *archaic* **:** to use in commerce **:** trade with **:** INVEST ⟨~ thy merchandise —Ezek 27:9 (AV)⟩

oc·cur *R* əˈkər, +V -kər·; *-R* əˈkə, + *suffixal vowel* əˈkər· *also* əˈkər, + *vowel in a word following without pause* əˈkər· *or* əˈkə *also* əˈkər\ *vi* **occurred; occurred; occurring; occurs** [L *occurrere,* fr. *ob-* + *currere* to run — more at CURRENT] **1 :** to be present or met with **:** EXIST ⟨this bird ~s in the Middle Atlantic states throughout the year —F.C.Lincoln⟩ **2 :** to present itself **:** come to pass **:** take place **:** HAPPEN ⟨successful marriages do not ~, but are created —Katharine F. Gerould⟩ **3 :** to come to mind **:** suggest itself ⟨something *occurred* to him which he had never thought of before —Louis Bromfield⟩ **4 :** to fall on the same day as another festival — used esp. of Christian festivals; compare CONCUR **syn** see HAPPEN

oc·cur·rence \əˈkər·ən(t)s *also* əˈkərə-\ *n* -s [prob. fr. ¹*occurrent,* after such pairs as E *abstinent: abstinence*] **1 :** something that takes place; *esp* **:** something that happens unexpectedly and without design **:** HAPPENING ⟨a happy ~⟩ ⟨a disastrous ~⟩ ⟨an unusual ~⟩ **2 a :** the action or process of happening or taking place ⟨the ~ of a genuine dispute —R.M.Dawson⟩ **b :** the action or process of being met with or coming into view **:** APPEARANCE ⟨the ~ of mammal remains falls sharply throughout the summer —*Ecology*⟩ ⟨a fish of regular ~ along the southern coast of California⟩ **:** the fact of being met with or of taking place **3 :** the presence of a natural form or material at a particular place; *also* **:** the mineral, rock, or deposit thus occurring ⟨evidence of oil ~⟩ ⟨the ~ of shallow coal beds in this region⟩ **4 :** the occurring of Christian festivals

syn INCIDENT, EPISODE, EVENT, CIRCUMSTANCE: OCCURRENCE is a general term for taking place or happening and lacks much connotational range; it may suggest a happening without plan, intent, or volition ⟨*occurrences* which we not only do not, but cannot perceive —Bertrand Russell⟩ INCIDENT may suggest either a trivial happening unworthy of attention or a more consequential or unusual happening having some effect ⟨his unexpected appearances and disappearances were *incidents* in the house —Willa Cather⟩ ⟨the faculty for myth . . . seizes with avidity upon any *incidents,* surprising or mysterious —W.S. Maugham⟩ EPISODE stresses the notion that the occurrence in question has an apartness or unity by itself, with no implication about the significance, or lack of it, of the occurrence ⟨the dumb creation lives a life made up of discrete and mutually irrelevant *episodes* —Aldous Huxley⟩ EVENT is more likely than others in this set to suggest a happening or occurrence of moment or significance or a happening logically ensuing from or giving rise to another happening ⟨assassination was an *event* of daily occurrence —T.B.Macaulay⟩ ⟨it is, in fact, almost a routine incident in a distinguished career. In the case of Mark Twain it became a historic *event* —Van Wyck Brooks⟩ ⟨*events* acting upon us in unexpected, abrupt, and violent ways —John Dewey⟩ CIRCUMSTANCE in the general sense here involved indicates specific or detailed incident ⟨stood reflecting on the *circumstances* of the preceding hours —Thomas Hardy⟩

¹**oc·cur·rent** \-nt\ *adj* [MF, fr. L *occurrent-, occurrens,* pres. part. of *occurrere* to occur] **1 a :** presently occurring **:** CURRENT **b :** happening by the way **:** INCIDENTAL **2 :** of or relating to an occurrent (sense 2)

²**occurrent** \"\ *n* -s **1** *archaic* **:** OCCURRENCE **2 :** something that occurs as distinguished from that which continues to exist **:** an alterable state — contrasted with *continuant*

ocean \ˈōshən\ *n* -s *often attrib* [ME *occean,* fr. OF, fr. L *oceanus* fr. Gk *ōkeanos* ocean, great river believed to encompass the earth] **1 :** the whole body of salt water that covers nearly three fourths of the surface of the globe, that has an average depth of about 13,000 feet and a maximum reported depth of 35,040 feet, that contains on the average 3½ percent of dissolved salts comprising mainly common salt with smaller amounts of magnesium and calcium salts, that has a density of 1.026, and that has a floor sometimes level or gently undulating and sometimes quite irregular with narrow elongated depressions called trenches and with elevations of various shapes and sizes (as ridges, rises, seamounts and swells) — called also *sea* **2 :** one of the large bodies of water into which the great ocean is regarded as divided (as the Atlantic, Pacific, Indian, Arctic, and Antarctic) **3 :** an immense expanse **:** an apparently unlimited space or quantity ⟨that mighty tropical ~ of foliage —William Beebe⟩ ⟨first began navigating the ~ of air —H.L.Smith b.1906⟩

ocea·nar·i·um \,ōshəˈna(a)rēəm, -ner-, -när-\ *n, pl* **oceanariums** \-mz\ *or* **oceanar·ia** \-ēə\ [*ocean* + *-arium*] **:** a large marine aquarium

ocean basin *n* **:** BASIN 3e — compare CONTINENTAL PLATEAU

ocean bug *n* **:** an insect of *Halobates* or related genera (order Hemiptera) found on the surface of the sea far from land

ocean deep *n* **:** a part of an ocean basin in which the depth greatly exceeds the average for the basin as a whole

oceanfront \ˈ≈≈,≈\ *n, often attrib* **:** the waterfront of a resort town or area situated along the ocean

oceangoing \ˈ≈≈,≈≈\ *adj* **:** of, relating to, or suitable for travel on the ocean ⟨~ commerce⟩ ⟨an ~ ship⟩

ocean green *n* **:** a light yellowish green that is yellower and paler than apple green (sense 2) or crayon green and paler than pistachio

¹**oce·an·i·an** \,ōshēˈanēən, -ˈän-\ *adj, usu cap* [F *océanien,* fr. *Oceania,* region of the central and south Pacific + F *-en, -ien* -an] **1 :** of, relating to, or characteristic of the region of Oceania comprising the islands and archipelagoes of the central and south Pacific **2 :** of, relating to, or characteristic of the people of Oceania

²**oceanian** \"\ *n* -s *cap* **:** a native or inhabitant of Oceania

oce·an·ic \-ˈanik, -nēk\ *adj* [F *océanique,* fr. MF *oceanique,* fr. *ocean, occean* ocean + *-ique* -ic] **1 a :** of, relating to, occurring in, living in, or frequenting the ocean ⟨~ currents⟩ ⟨~ depths⟩ ⟨~ rock⟩ ⟨~ birds⟩ **b :** affected by or produced by the ocean ⟨a wet, windy, ~ climate —C.D.Forde⟩ **c :** resembling the ocean esp. in immensity of size or extent ⟨October gives the grain belt an ~ vastness of gold —W.W.Haines⟩ ⟨the ~ violence of his rage against the miseries of man's life —Walter McElroy⟩ **2** *usu cap* **:** OCEANIAN **3 :** of, relating to, constituting, or living in the open sea as distinguished from littoral or neritic regions ⟨~ waters⟩ ⟨~ life⟩ — compare ABYSSAL, PHOTIC **4** *usu cap* **:** relating to, belonging to, or characterizing the Austronesian family of languages or the Melanesian and Polynesian divisions of that family

oceanic area *n* **:** the ocean as contrasted with the neritic zone consisting of a photic zone which extends down as far as light penetrates with a twilight zone as its lower limit and an abyssal zone which extends thence to the bottom

oceanic bonito *n* **:** any of several bonitos (as of the genus *Katsuwonus*); *esp* **:** SKIPJACK 2a(2)

oceanic island *n* **:** an island in the ocean far from any continent — compare CONTINENTAL ISLAND

oce·a·nid \ōˈsēənəd\ *n, pl* **oceanids** *also* **oce·an·i·des** \(,)ōsēˈanəˌdēz\ *usu cap* [Gk *ōkeanid-, ōkeanis,* fr. *Okeanos* Oceanus, deity identified as a great river believed to encompass the earth + Gk *-id-, -is,* fem. patronymic suffix] **:** an ocean nymph

oce·an·i·ty \,ōshēˈanəd·ē\ *n* -ES [ISV *ocean* + *-ity*] **1 :** the quality or state of being oceanic **2 :** the degree to which a climate has oceanic qualities — compare CONTINENTALITY

ocean lane *n* **:** LANE 3a

ocean liner *n* **:** a liner for navigating the ocean

ocean marine insurance *n* **:** insurance against risks incident to transportation by sea — compare INLAND MARINE INSURANCE, MARINE INSURANCE

ocea·nod·ro·mous \,ōshəˈnädrəməs\ *adj* [*ocean* + *-o-* + *-dromous*] *of a fish* **:** migratory in salt water

ocean·og·ra·pher \,ōshəˈnägrəfə(r)\ *n* -s [*oceanography* + *-er*] **:** a specialist in oceanography

ocean·o·graph·ic \,ōshənəˈgrafik\ *or* **ocean·o·graph·i·cal** \-fəkəl\ *adj* [*oceanographic* ISV *oceanography* + *-ic; oceanographical* fr. *oceanography* + *-ical*] **:** of or relating to oceanography — **ocean·o·graph·i·cal·ly** \-fək(ə)lē\ *adv*

ocean·og·ra·phy \,ōshəˈnägrəfē\ *n* -ES [ISV *ocean* + *-o-* + *-graphy*] **:** a science that deals with the ocean and its phenomena — see BIOLOGICAL OCEANOGRAPHY, DYNAMIC OCEANOGRAPHY, PHYSICAL OCEANOGRAPHY

ocean·ol·o·gist \-ˈäləjəst\ *n* -s [*oceanology* + *-ist*] **:** OCEANOGRAPHER

ocean·ol·o·gy \-äləjē\ *n* -ES [*ocean* + *-o-* + *-logy*] **:** OCEANOGRAPHY

ocean perch *n* **:** ROSEFISH

ocean pout *n* **:** EELPOUT

oceans *pl of* OCEAN

ocean sea *n, often cap O&S* **:** OCEAN 1

ocean spray *n* **:** a white-flowered shrub (*Holodiscus discolor*) of western U. S. — called also *arrowwood, creambush*

ocean station vessel *n* **:** a ship assigned to a specific station at sea to take weather observations, assist aircraft in determining position, and help in rescue operations

ocean sunfish *n* **:** a large usu. gray or brown marine fish (*Mola mola*) that has a deep compressed body truncated behind, no pelvic fins, and very long dorsal and anal fins nearly adjoining the short caudal fin and that is widely distributed in warm and temperate seas; *also* **:** a closely related fish (*Masturus lanceolatus*)

ocean tramp *n* **:** TRAMP 6

ocean whitefish *n* **:** a large showy brownish food and sport fish (*Caulolatilus princeps*) found along the warmer parts of the Pacific coast from Peru to central California — see BLANQUILLO

oc·el·lana \,äsəˈlanə\ *n, pl* **ocel·lanae** \-a,nē\ [NL, fr. *ocellus* + *-ana* (fr. L, fem. of *-anus* -an)] **:** STEMMA

ocel·lar \ōˈselə(r)\ *adj* [prob. fr. (assumed) NL *ocellaris,* fr. NL *ocellus* + L *-aris* -ar] **1 :** of, relating to, or connecting with an ocellus **2 :** of or relating to a type of rock structure characterized by radiated aggregates resembling eyes

ocellar center *n* **:** an aggregation of ganglia in the ocellar pedicel of an insect

ocellar pedicel *n* **:** a slender stalk consisting of nerve fibers that connect the ocellus in an insect with the forebrain

ocel·lat·ed \ōˈse,lād·əd, ˈäsə,- *also* **ocel·late** \-,lāt, -ˌlət\ *adj* [*ocellated* prob. fr. (assumed) NL *ocellatus* ocellated (fr. NL *ocellus* + L *-atus* -ate) + E *-ed; ocellate* prob. fr. (assumed) NL *ocellatus*] **1 :** having ocelli **2 :** resembling an ocellus **:** EYELIKE ⟨an ~ spot⟩

ocellated argus *n* **:** ARGUS 2; *esp* **:** an argus (*Rheinartia ocellata*) of southeastern Asia that is predominantly brown with in the male elaborate spotting in black, white, and buff, a long pointed tail patterned with nonmetallic ocelli, and a large occipital crest

ocellated blenny *n* **:** a dusky brown blenny (*Blennius ocellaris*) of the Mediterranean and western European coastal waters that has the body barred with dark crossbars and a round black white-bordered spot on the dorsal fin

ocellated lizard *n* **:** a moderately large lizard (*Lacerta ocellata*) found in parts of southern Europe and No. Africa and having black-edged blue spots on the sides

ocellated turkey *n* **:** a wild turkey (*Agriocharis ocellata*) of Yucatan, Honduras, and Guatemala that is slightly smaller than the common turkey and has the tail feathers margined with rich coppery color and ornamented with greenish blue

oc·el·la·tion \,äsəˈlāshən\ *n* -s [prob. fr. (assumed) NL *ocellation-, ocellatio,* fr. (assumed) NL *ocellatus* + L *-ion-, -io* -ion] **1 :** the state of being ocellated **2 :** OCELLUS

oc·el·loc·u·lar \,äsəˈläkyələ(r)\ *adj* [*ocellus* + *ocular*] **:** lying or extending between the compound eye and the median simple eye of an insect ⟨~ distance⟩

ocel·lus \ōˈseləs\ *n, pl* **ocel·li** \-e,lī, -e(,)lē\ [NL, fr. L, small eye, dim. of *oculus* eye — more at EYE] **1 a :** a minute simple eye or eyespot found in many organisms; *specif* **:** one of usu. three simple eyes in an insect located in a triangle between the compound eyes **b :** one of the elements of a compound eye **2 :** a spot of color encircled by a band of another color **:** an eyelike spot ⟨a butterfly with a striking ~ on its wing⟩

oce·lot \ˈōsə,lät, ˈäs- *sometimes* -lət, *usu* -d·+V\ *n* -s [F, fr. Nahuatl *ocelotl* jaguar] **1 :** a medium-sized American wildcat (*Felis pardalis*) ranging from Texas to Patagonia and having a tawny yellow or grayish coat that is dotted and striped with black **2 :** the fur or pelt of the ocelot

ocelot

och \ˈäk\ *interj* [ScGael & IrGael] *Irish & Scot* — used to express regret or surprise

¹**ocher** *or* **ochre** \ˈōkə(r)\ *n* -s [ME *oker,* fr. MF *ocre,* fr. L *ochra,* fr. Gk *ōchra,* fr. *ōchros* yellow, pale] **1 a :** an earthy usu. red or yellow and often impure iron ore that is extensively used as a pigment; *also* **:** any of various ferruginous clays — compare HEMATITE, LIMONITE **b :** an earthy metallic oxide ⟨tungstic ~⟩ **2 :** the color of ocher, esp. of yellow ocher **:** OCHER YELLOW **3 :** any of various chiefly yellow to orange pigments prepared from the natural ochers (as by washing, grinding, and sometimes calcining) — see BURNT OCHER; compare SIENNA, UMBER

²**ocher** *or* **ochre** \"\ *vt* **ochered** *or* **ochred; ochered** *or* **ochred; ochering** *or* **ochring** \-k(ə)riŋ\ **ochers** *or* **ochres** **:** to color with ocher

ocher brown *n* **:** a moderate orange that is yellower and deeper than honeydew, yellower and darker than Persian orange, and duller than mikado orange — called also *brown ocher, doubloon, golden ocher, Roman ocher*

ocher·ish *or* **ochre·ish** \ˈōk(ə)rish\ *adj* **:** resembling or suggesting ocher (as in color) **:** somewhat like ocher

ocher orange *n* **:** a strong orange that is yellower and stronger than pumpkin, deeper and slightly redder than cadmium orange, and redder and deeper than cadmium yellow — called also *burnt Roman ocher, orange ocher, Spanish ocher, Tangier*

ocher·ous \ˈōk(ə)rəs\ *or* **ochre·ous** \", ˈōkrēəs\ *also* **ochrous** \ˈōkrəs\ *adj* [¹*ocher* + *-ous* or *-eous*] **1 :** of or relating to ocher **:** containing or resembling ocher **2 :** of the color ocher yellow

ocher red *n* **:** a dark reddish orange that is yellower, less strong, and slightly darker than average lacquer and redder and slightly darker than burnt sienna — called also *faded rose*

ochery \ˈōk(ə)rē\ *or* **ochry** \ˈōkrē\ *or* **ochrey** \ˈōk(ə)rē\ *adj* [¹*ocher* + *-y*] **:** OCHEROUS

ocher yellow *n* **:** YELLOW OCHER

och·i·dore \ˈäkə,dō(ə)r\ *n* -s [origin unknown] **:** SHORE CRAB

och·loc·ra·cy \äkˈläkrəsē\ *n* -ES [Gk & MF; MF *ochlocratie,* fr. Gk *ochlokratia,* fr. *ochlos* crowd, mob + *-kratia* -cracy] **:** government by the mob **:** mob rule

och·lo·crat \ˈäklə,krat\ *n* -s [F *ochlocrate,* back-formation fr. *ochlocratie* & *ochlocratique*] **:** a partisan of ochlocracy

och·lo·crat·ic \ˌ≈≈ˈkrad·ik\ *or* **och·lo·crat·i·cal** \-d·əkəl\ *adj* [*ochlocratic* fr. F *ochlocratique,* fr. MF, fr. *ochlocratie* + *-ique* -ic; *ochlocratical* fr. F *ochlocratique* + E *-al*] **:** of or relating to ochlocracy — **och·lo·crat·i·cal·ly** \-d·ək(ə)lē\ *adv*

och·lo·pho·bia \,äkləˈfōbēə\ *n* [NL, fr. Gk *ochlos* crowd + NL *-phobia*] **:** morbid fear of crowds

och·lo·pho·bist \-bəst\ *n* -s [NL *ochlophobia* + E *-ist*] **:** one who is afflicted with ochlophobia

och·na \ˈäknə\ *n, cap* [NL, fr. Gk *ochnē, onchnē* pear tree; prob. akin to Gk *achras,* a wild pear tree (prob. *Pyrus amygdaliformis*) — more at ACHRAS] **:** a genus (the type of the family Ochnaceae) of African and Asiatic trees and shrubs having yellow flowers with coriaceous petaloid sepals and numerous stamens

och·na·ce·ae \äkˈnāsē,ē\ *n pl, cap* [NL, fr. *Ochna,* type genus + *-aceae*] **:** a family of tropical trees, shrubs, or rarely herbs (order Parietales) having thick shining parallel-veined leaves and paniculate flowers with elongated anthers — **och·na·ceous** \(ˈ)äkˈnāshəs\ *adj*

ocho·an \ōˈchōən\ *adj, usu cap* [*Ochoa,* locality in southeastern New Mexico + E *-an*] **:** of or relating to a subdivision of the American Permian — see GEOLOGIC TIME table

och·one \äˈkōn\ *interj* [ScGael & IrGael *ochōn*] *Irish & Scot* — used as an exclamation of regret or grief

och·o·to·na \,äkəˈtōnə\ *n, cap* [NL, fr. Mongolian *ochodona* pika] **:** the type genus of Ochotonidae comprising the pikas

och·o·ton·i·dae \-ˈtänə,dē\ *n pl, cap* [NL, fr. *Ochotona,* type genus + *-idae*] **:** a family of short-eared lagomorph mammals that comprises the pikas and various extinct related forms

ochra·ceous \ōˈkrāshəs\ *adj* [prob. fr. (assumed) NL *ochraceus,* fr. L *ochra* ocher + *-aceus* -aceous] **:** OCHEROUS

ochre *var of* OCHER

ochrea *var of* OCREA

ochroid \ˈō,krȯid\ *adj* [Gk *ōchroeidēs* pallid, fr. *ōchros* yellow, pale + *-eidēs* -oid] **:** resembling ocher or yellow ocher in color

och·ro·ma \äˈkrōmə\ *n, cap* [NL, fr. Gk *ōchrōma* pallor, fr. *ōchros* yellow, pale] **:** a genus of tropical American trees (family Bombacaceae) having very light wood and seeds enveloped in silky floss — see BALSA

ochro·no·sis \,ōkrəˈnōsəs\ *n, pl* **ochrono·ses** \-nō,sēz\ [NL, fr. Gk *ōchros* yellow, pale + NL *-nosis* (irreg. — influenced by NL *-osis* — fr. Gk *nosos* disease)] **:** a rare familial condition often associated with alkaptonuria and marked by pigment deposits in cartilages, ligaments, and tendons

ochro·not·ic \ˌ≈≈ˈnäd·ik\ *adj* [fr. *ochronosis,* after such pairs as E *narcosis: narcotic*] **:** of, relating to, or marked by ochronosis ⟨~ arthritis⟩

ochrous *var of* OCHEROUS

ochry *var of* OCHERY

¹**ocht** \ˈäkt\ *chiefly Scot var of* AUGHT

²**ocht** \"\ *Scot & Irish var of* OUGHT

oc·i·mene \ˈäsə,mēn\ *n* -s [ISV *ocim-* (fr. NL *Ocimum*) + *-ene*] **:** an acyclic terpene hydrocarbon $C_{10}H_{16}$ that occurs in several essential oils (as basil oil) and that resinifies readily in air and isomerizes on heating

oc·i·mum \ˈäsəməm\ *n, cap* [NL, fr. L, basil, fr. Gk *ōkimon*] **:** a large genus of mints (family Labiatae) found chiefly in warm climates and having flowers with a reflexed calyx and a very short corolla tube — see BASIL 1, HOLY BASIL, SWEET BASIL

-ock \ək *or, in many words,* ik *or* ēk\ *n suffix* -s [ME *-oc, -ok,* fr. OE *-uc, -oc*] **:** small one ⟨bittock⟩ ⟨lassock⟩

ock·ham·ism *or* **oc·cam·ism** \ˈäkə,mizəm\ *n* -s *usu cap* [William of *Ockham* (or *Occam*) †1349? Eng. scholastic philosopher + E *-ism*] **:** the philosophy developed by Ockham and consisting essentially of a revival of nominalism

ock·ham·ist *or* **oc·cam·ist** \-,məst\ *also* **ock·ham·ite** \-,mīt\ *or* **oc·cam·ite** *n* -s *usu cap* [William of *Ockham* (or *Occam*) + E *-ist* or *-ite*] **:** an adherent of Ockhamism

ock·ham·is·tic *or* **oc·cam·is·tic** \ˌ≈≈ˈmistik\ *adj, usu cap* **:** of or relating to Ockham or his philosophy

ock·ham's razor *or* **oc·cam's razor** \ˈäkəmz-\ *n, usu cap O* **:** the philosophic rule that entities should not be multiplied unnecessarily

o'·clock \əˈkläk\ *adv* [contr. of *of the clock*] **1 :** according to the clock **:** by the clock ⟨the time is three ~⟩ **2 :** on a clock dial imagined in a horizontal position with the observer at the center facing the numeral 12 or in a vertical position in front of and facing the observer with the numeral 12 at the top — used for indicating position or direction ⟨the pilot saw a plane approaching at eleven ~⟩ ⟨a bullet hit the target at three ~⟩

oco·nee bells \əˈkōnē-\ *n pl but sing or pl in constr* [prob. fr. *Oconee* river, central Georgia] **:** a stemless perennial herb (*Shortia galacifolia*) that has crenate-dentate glossy leaves

oco·te \əˈkōtā\ *or* **ocote pine** *n* -s [MexSp, fr. Nahuatl *ocotl* torch] **:** a resinous Mexican pine (*Pinus montezumae*) with prominently ridged young shoots

oco·tea \əˈkōd·ēə\ *n, cap* [NL, fr. a native name in Guiana] **:** a genus of tropical trees and shrubs (family Lauraceae) having alternate coriaceous leaves and small panicled flowers — see STINKWOOD

ocotea cymbarum oil *n, usu cap 1st O* [NL *Ocotea cymbarum* (species name of a Brazilian tree) + E *oil*] **:** an essential oil obtained by steam distillation from the wood of Brazilian trees (*Ocotea cymbarum*) and used chiefly as a source of safrole and as a substitute for sassafras oil in technical but not medicinal preparations

oco·ti·llo \,ōkəˈtē(,)(y)ō\ *also* **oco·ti·lla** \-ē(y)ə\ *n* -s [MexSp, dim. of *ocote*] **1 :** a desert shrub (*Fouquieria splendens*) of southwestern U.S. and Mexico characterized by naked thorny branches that after the rainy season put forth fo[illegible] and clusters of scarlet flowers **2 :** an ashy gray M[illegible]

shrub (*Gochnatia hypoleuca*) of the family Compositae that is used for making charcoal
-oc·ra·cy \'äkrəsē, -si\ — see -CRACY
-ocrat — see -CRAT
oc·rea *or* **och·rea** \'äkrēə, 'ōk-\ *n, pl* **ocre·ae** *or* **ochre·ae** \-ē,ē\ [NL, fr. L *ocrea* greave, legging; perh. akin to L *ocris* stony mountain — more at MEDIOCRE] **:** a tubular sheath around the base of the petiole consisting of a single stipule in the red clover or of a pair of coherent stipules in the buckwheat family (Polygonaceae)
oc·re·ate \-ēət, -ē,āt\ *adj* [NL *ocreatus*, fr. L, wearing greaves or leggings, fr. *ocrea* + *-atus* -ate] **:** provided with ocreae
OCS *abbr or n* -S **:** officer candidate school
OCS *abbr* Old Church Slavonic
oct *abbr* octavo
octa- *or* **octo-** *also* **oct-** *comb form* [Gk *okta-*, *oktō-*, *okt-* (fr. *oktō*) & L *octo-*, *oct-* (fr. *octo*) — more at EIGHT] **1 :** eight ⟨*Octa*cnemus⟩ ⟨*octa*merous⟩ ⟨*octo*ploid⟩ ⟨*oct*ose⟩ **2 :** containing eight atoms, groups, or equivalents ⟨*octa*cetate⟩
oc·ta·acetate \¦äktə+\ *n* [*octa-* + *acetate*] **:** an acetate containing eight acetate groups ⟨sucrose ~⟩
oc·ta·chord \'äktə,kȯrd\ *n* [L *octachordos* with eight strings, fr. Gk *oktachordos*, fr. *okta-* octa- + *-chordos* stringed — more at -CHORD] **1 :** a musical instrument having eight strings **2 :** a system of eight tones (as the diatonic octave)
oc·tac·ne·mus \,äk,tak'nēməs\ *n, cap* [NL, fr. *octa-* + *-cnemus*] **:** a genus of deep-sea tunicates of the order Ascidiacea found in the south Pacific ocean
oc·ta·co·sane \,äktə'kō,sān\ *n* -S [ISV *octacos-* (fr. *octa-* + *-cos-* — fr. *eicosa-*) + *-ane*] **:** a solid paraffin hydrocarbon $C_{28}H_{58}$; *esp* **:** the normal hydrocarbon $CH_3(CH_2)_{26}CH_3$
oc·tad \'äk,tad\ *n* -S [Gk *oktad-*, *oktas* number eight, body of eight men, fr. *okta-* octa- + *-ad-*, *-as* -ad] **:** a group or arrangement of eight; *esp* **:** a group of eight figures representing consecutive powers of ten in ancient mathematical notation
oc·ta·dec·a·di·e·no·ic acid \¦äktə¦dekə¦dīə¦nōik-\ *n* [*octadecadienoic* ISV *octadecadiene* $C_{18}H_{34}$ (ISV *octadeca-* — fr. *octa-* + *deca-* — + *-diene*) + *-oic*] **:** any of several unsaturated fatty acids $C_{17}H_{31}COOH$ some of which (as linoleic acid) occur in fats and oils
oc·ta·dec·ane \,äktə'de,kān\ *n* [ISV *octadec-* (fr. *octa-* + *deca-*) + *-ane*] **:** any of numerous isomeric hydrocarbons $C_{18}H_{38}$ of the paraffin series; *esp* **:** the crystalline normal hydrocarbon $CH_3(CH_2)_{16}CH_3$
oc·ta·dec·a·no·ic acid \¦==¦dekə¦nōik-\ *n* [*octadecanoic* ISV *octadecane* + *-oic*] **:** STEARIC ACID
oc·ta·dec·a·nol \,==='dekə,nōl, -nōl\ *n* [*octadecane* + *-ol*] **:** any of several alcohols $C_{18}H_{37}OH$ derived from normal octadecane; *esp* **:** STEARYL ALCOHOL
oc·ta·dec·e·no·ic acid \¦äktə¦desə¦nōik-\ *n* [*octadecenoic* ISV *octadecene* $C_{18}H_{36}$ (ISV *octadec-* — fr. *octa-* + *deca-* — + *-ene*) + *-oic*] **:** any of several unsaturated fatty acids $C_{17}H_{33}COOH$ some of which (as oleic acid, vaccenic acid) occur in fats and oils
oc·ta·dec·yl \,äktə'desəl\ *n* [ISV *octadecane* + *-yl*] **:** an alkyl radical $C_{18}H_{37}$ derived from an octadecane by removal of one hydrogen atom; *esp* **:** the normal radical $CH_3(CH_2)_{16}CH_2$–
oc·ta·drachm *or* **oc·to·drachm** \'äktə,dram\ *n* [Gk *oktadrachmos* worth eight drachmas, fr. *okta-* octa- + *drachmē* drachma — more at DRAM] **:** an ancient Greek coin weighing or worth eight drachmas
oc·ta·gon \'äktə,gän *sometimes* -tägən\ *n* -S [L *octagonum*, *octogonum*, fr. Gk *oktagōnon*, fr. neut. of *oktagōnos* octagonal, fr. *okta-* octa- + *-gōnos* (fr. *gōnia* angle); akin to Gk *gony* knee — more at KNEE] **1 :** a plane polygon of eight angles and therefore eight sides — see AREA table **2 :** an octagonal object ⟨the central ~ was covered by a dome —E.H. Short⟩

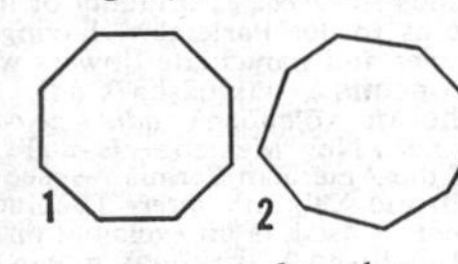

octagons: *1* regular, *2* irregular

oc·tag·o·nal \(')äk¦tagənᵊl, -taig-\ *adj* [alter. (influenced by *octagon*) of earlier *octogonal*, fr. MF, fr. *octogone* octagon (fr. L *octagonum*, *octogonum*) + *-al*] **:** having eight sides ⟨built a mansion in the shape of an octagon, which started quite a fashion for ~ houses —*Time*⟩ — **oc·tag·o·nal·ly** \-ᵊlē, -ᵊli\ *adv*
oc·ta·he·dral \¦äktə¦hēdrəl\ *adj* [*octahedron* + *-al*] **1 :** having eight plane faces **2 :** of, relating to, or formed in octahedrons ⟨~ crystals⟩ — **oc·ta·he·dral·ly** \-lē\ *adv*
octahedral cleavage *n* **:** cleavage of minerals parallel to the octahedral faces
octahedral iron ore *n* **:** MAGNETITE
oc·ta·he·drite \,äktə'hē,drīt\ *n* -S [F *octaédrite*, fr. *octaèdre* octahedron (fr. Gk *oktaedron*) + *-ite*] **1 :** ANATASE **2 :** an iron meteorite having plates of kamacite with narrow selvages of taenite and interstitial plessite constituting a very intimate mixture of kamacite and taenite — compare WIDMANNSTAETTEN FIGURES
oc·ta·he·dron \,äktə'hēdrən\ *n, pl* **octahedrons** \-nz\ *also* **octahe·dra** \-rə\ [Gk *oktaedron*, fr. neut. of *oktaedros* octahedral, fr. *okta-* octa- + *hedra* seat — more at SIT] **:** a solid bounded by eight plane faces
oc·tal \'äktᵊl\ *adj* [*octa-* + *-al*] **1 :** of, relating to, or based on the number eight ⟨~ notation⟩ ⟨~ coding⟩ **2** *of an electronic tube* **:** having eight connecting pins arranged symmetrically on the base
oc·ta·mer \'äktəmə(r)\ *n* -S [*octa-* + *-mer*] **:** a polymer formed from eight molecules of a monomer

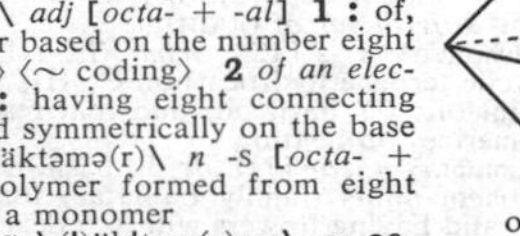
octahedron

oc·tam·er·ous \(')äk¦tam(ə)rəs\ *or* **oc·tom·er·ous** \-täm-\ *adj* [*octa-* + *-merous*] **:** having eight parts or having organs arranged in eights ⟨an ~ flower⟩
¹oc·tam·e·ter \(')äk¦tamәd·ә(r), -mәtә-\ *adj* [LL, fr. LGk *oktametros*, fr. Gk *okta-* octa- + *metron* measure — more at MEASURE] **:** having eight metrical feet
²octameter \"\ *or* **oc·tom·e·ter** \-¦täm-\ *n* **:** a line consisting of eight metrical feet (as in Poe's "Deep into the darkness peering, long I stood there wond'ring, fearing")
oc·ta·meth·yl·py·ro·phos·phor·a·mide \,äktə,methəl,pīrō-,fäs'fȯrə,mīd\ *n* [*octamethyl-* (fr. *octa-* + *methyl*) + *-pyrophosphoramide* (fr. *pyrophosphor-* — in *pyrophosphoric acid* — + *amide*)] **:** SCHRADAN
oc·ta·nal \'äktə,nal\ *n* -S [ISV *octane* + *-al*] **:** a liquid aldehyde $CH_3(CH_2)_6CHO$ of powerful characteristic odor found in the essential oils of many plants — called also *caprylaldehyde*
oc·tan·dria \äk'tandrēə\ *n pl, cap* [NL, fr. *octa-* + *-andria*] *in some classifications* **:** a class of plants comprising all those having flowers with eight stamens — **oc·tan·dri·an** \(')=¦==ən\ *adj* — **oc·tan·dri·ous** \-əs\ *adj*
oc·tane \'äk,tān *sometimes* =¦=\ *n* -S [ISV *octa-* + *-ane*] **1 :** any of several isomeric liquid paraffin hydrocarbons C_8H_{18}: as **a :** the normal hydrocarbon $CH_3(CH_2)_6CH_3$ found in petroleum **b :** ISOOCTANE b **2 :** OCTANE NUMBER ⟨100-octane gasoline⟩ **3 :** motor fuel as rated by octane number ⟨octane-propelled vehicles⟩ ⟨100-octane cracking plants⟩
octane number *or* **octane rating** *n* **:** a number that is used to measure the antiknock properties of a liquid motor fuel and that represents the percentage by volume of isooctane (sense b) in a reference fuel consisting of a mixture of isooctane and normal heptane and matching in knocking properties the fuel being tested, the higher the number the less likely being the fuel to detonate
oc·tan·gu·lar \(')äk¦taŋgyələ(r)\ *adj* [L *octangulus* octagonal (fr. *oct* — fr. *octo* eight — + *angulus* angle) + E *-ar* — more at EIGHT, ANGLE] **:** OCTAGONAL
oc·ta·no·ate \,äktə'nōət, -ō,āt\ *n* -S [ISV *octanoic* (in *octanoic acid*) + *-oate*] **:** CAPRYLATE
oc·ta·no·ic acid \¦äktə¦nōik-\ *n* [*octanoic* ISV *octane* + *-oic*] **:** CAPRYLIC ACID — used in the nomenclature adopted by the International Union of Pure and Applied Chemistry
oc·ta·nol \'äktə,nōl, -nōl\ *n* -S [*octane* + *-ol*] **:** any of four liquid alcohols $C_8H_{17}OH$ derived from normal octane: as **a :** the primary alcohol $CH_3(CH_2)_6CH_2OH$ having a penetrating odor, occurring free or in the form of esters in oils from plant seeds and fruits, and used chiefly in organic synthesis and in perfumes — called also *1-octanol*, *n-octyl alcohol* **b :** a viscous oily secondary alcohol $CH_3(CH_2)_5CH(OH)CH_3$ having an aromatic odor, made by heating the sodium soap of castor oil, and used chiefly as a solvent, in organic synthesis, and in perfumes — called also *2-octanol*
oc·ta·no·yl \¦äktə¦nōəl; äk'tanə,wil, -,wēl\ *n* -S [ISV *octanoic* (in *octanoic acid*) + *-yl*] **:** CAPRYLYL
oc·tant \'äktənt\ *n* -S [L *octant-*, *octans* half quadrant, fr. *octo* eight] **1 a :** the position or aspect of a celestial body (as the moon or a planet) when halfway between conjunction or opposition and quadrature **b :** an instrument used for observing altitudes of a celestial body from a moving ship or aircraft and having a maximum angle of 45 degrees between its reflecting mirrors — compare SEXTANT **2 a :** one of the eight regions into which three usu. orthogonal planes meeting in a point divide all three-dimensioned space around it **b :** any of the eight parts into which a space is divided by three coordinate planes
oc·ta·phyllite \¦äktə+\ *n* [*octa-* + *phyllite*] **:** any of various micas (as biotite) in which there are eight cations for every ten oxygen and two hydroxyl ions — compare HEPTAPHYLLITE
oc·ta·pla \'äktəplə\ *n* -S *often cap* [LGk *oktapla*, fr. Gk, neut. pl. of *oktaplous*, *oktaploos* eightfold, fr. *okta-* octa- + *-plous*, *-ploos* -fold (as in *diploos* double) — more at DOUBLE] **:** an edition or work in eight texts or versions in parallel columns; *esp* **:** an edition of a portion of the Old Testament compiled by Origen in the 3d century A.D. and consisting of the Hebrew text and seven Greek versions of it — compare HEXAPLA
octaploid *var of* OCTOPLOID
oc·ta·pod·ic \¦äktə¦pädik\ *adj* [*octapody* + *-ic*] **:** having eight metrical feet
oc·tap·o·dy \äk'tapədē\ *n* -ES [*octa-* + *-pody* (as in *dipody*)] **:** OCTAMETER
oc·tarch \'äk,tärk\ *adj* [*octa-* + *-arch*] **:** having eight xylem groups ⟨~ roots⟩
oc·tar·chy \'äk,tärkē\ *n* -ES [*octa-* + *-archy*] **1 :** a government by eight persons **2 :** a confederacy of Anglo-Saxon kingdoms considered as having eight rulers — compare HEPTARCHY
oc·ta·stich \'äktə,stik\ *also* **oc·tas·ti·chon** \äk'tastə,kän\ *n, pl* **octastichs** \-ks\ *also* **octasti·cha** \-stəkə\ [LGk *oktastichon*, neut. of *oktastichos* consisting of eight lines, fr. Gk *okta-* octa- + *stichos* line; akin to Gk *steichein* to go — more at STAIR] **:** a verse unit of eight lines
oc·ta·stroph·ic \¦äktə¦sträfik\ *adj* [*octa-* + *strophic*] **:** having eight strophes
oc·ta·style *also* **oc·to·style** \'äktə,stīl\ *adj* [L *octastylos*, fr. Gk *oktastylos*, fr. *okta-* octa- + *-stylos* -style] **:** marked by columniation with eight columns across the front — compare DISTYLE
oc·ta·sty·los \,==='stī,läs\ *n* -ES [L *octastylos*, adj.] **:** an octastyle building
oc·ta·teuch \'äktə,tük, -ə-,tyük\ *n* -S *often cap* [LL *octateuchus*, fr. Gk *oktateuchos*, fr. *okta-* octa- + *teuchos* vessel, case for holding a roll of papyrus; akin to Gk *teuchein* to make, build — more at DOUGHTY] **:** a collection of eight books; *esp* **:** the first eight books of the Old Testament
oc·ta·val \(')äk¦tāvəl, 'äktəv-\ *adj* **:** of or relating to an octave
oc·ta·valent \¦äktə+\ *adj* [*octa-* + *valent*] **:** having a valence of eight
oc·ta·vary \'äktə,verē\ *n* -ES [NL *octavarium*, fr. ML *octava* octave + NL *-arium*] **:** a Roman Catholic service book containing collects and lections for use within festival octaves
¹oc·tave \'äktəv, -tēv, -,tāv\ *n* -S [ME, fr. ML *octava*, fr. L,

octave 3a

fem. of *octavus* eighth, fr. *octo* eight — more at EIGHT] **1 a :** the eighth day counting the festival day after a church festival **b :** the eight day period beginning with the festival day **2 a :** a stanza of eight lines **:** OTTAVA RIMA **b :** the first two quatrains or first eight verses of a sonnet — called also *octet*; compare SESTET **3 a :** a musical interval embracing eight diatonic degrees **b :** a tone or note at this interval **c :** the harmonic combination of two tones an octave apart **d :** the whole series of notes, tones, or digitals comprised within this interval and forming the unit of the modern scale **e :** an organ stop giving tones an octave above those corresponding to the digitals **4 :** a parry or guard position in fencing defending the lower outside target in which the hand is to the right in a position of supination with the tip of the blade directed at the opponent's knee — compare SECONDE **5 :** a group of eight ⟨an ~ of oarsmen⟩ **6** *in a spectrum of vibrations* **:** an interval analogous to the musical octave and being such that the frequencies at its beginning and end are to each other as 1 : 2 ⟨the visible or photic portion of the 60 or more ~s of the electromagnetic spectrum of radiant energy, extending from wireless waves to cosmic rays, constitutes about 1 ~ and has wavelengths ranging from the red end of the spectrum (7700A) to the extreme violet end (about 4000A) —Charles Sheard⟩ **7 a :** a cask for wine holding ⅛ pipe **b :** a unit of liquid capacity equal to ⅛ pipe or 13½ gallons **8** *archaic* **:** a series of eight chemical elements in order of increasing atomic weights
²octave \"\ *adj* **1 :** consisting of eight units **2 :** sounding or producing sounds at the octave ⟨an ~ organ stop⟩
octave flute *n* **1 :** PICCOLO **2 :** a 4-foot flute stop in a pipe organ
octave species *n* **:** a specific arrangement of the whole-step and half-step intervals comprising the diatonic scale of the octave **:** MODE, SCALE
oc·ta·vo \äk'tā(,)vō, -tä(-\ *n* -S [L, abl. of *octavus* eighth — more at OCTAVE] **:** the size of a piece of paper cut eight from a sheet; *also* **:** paper or a page of this size — abbr. *8vo*; symbol *8°*; see BOOK tables
oc·tene \'äk,tēn\ *n* -S [ISV *octa-* + *-ene*] **:** any of the four oily liquid straight-chain octylenes
oc·ten·ni·al \(')äk¦tenēəl\ *adj* [LL *octennium* period of eight years (fr. L *oct-* — fr. *octo* eight — + *-ennium*, fr. *annus* year) + E *-al* — more at EIGHT, ANNUAL] **1 :** happening every eighth year **2 :** lasting for a period of eight years
oc·tet *also* **oc·tette** \(')äk¦tet, *usu* -ed·+V\ *n* -S [*octa-* + *-et* or *-ette*; trans. of It *ottetto*] **1 a :** a musical composition for eight parts (as eight instruments or voices) **b :** a group of eight singers or players in joint performance **2 :** OCTAVE 2b **3 :** a group of eight electrons in the outer valence shell of an atom that are considered to constitute a stable arrangement and to be present in pairs which may or may not be shared with another atom — compare COVALENCE, LEWIS-LANGMUIR THEORY
oc·til·lion \äk'tilyən\ *n* -S *often attrib* [F, fr. MF, fr. *octa-* + *-illion* (as in *million*)] — see NUMBER table
octine *var of* OCTYNE
octo- — see OCTA-
oc·to·ate \'äktə,wāt\ *n* -S [*octoic* (in *octoic acid*) + *-ate*] **:** a salt or ester of an octoic acid: as **a :** CAPRYLATE **b :** ETHYLHEXOATE
oc·to·bass \'äktə,bās\ *n* [F *octobasse*, *octabasse*, fr. *octa-* + *basse* bass, contrabass, fr. fem. of *bas* low, of little height — more at BASE] **:** a huge contrabass having three strings stopped by finger keys and pedals
oc·to·ber \äk'tōbə(r)\ *n* -S *usu cap* [ME *octobre*, fr. OF, fr. L *october* (eighth month), fr. *octo* eight] **1 :** the tenth month of the Gregorian calendar — abbr. *Oct.*; see MONTH table **2** *Brit* **:** ale made in October ⟨sent down to the storehouse for a bottle of rum and a bottle of *October* —B.M.Carew⟩
oc·to·brist \-brəst\ *n* -S *usu cap* [*octobr-* (fr. *october*) + *-ist*; trans. of Russ *oktyabrist*] **1 :** a member of a moderately liberal political party in czarist Russia whose principles of constitutional government and measures of reform were expressed in an imperial manifesto of October, 1905 **2** [trans. of Russ *oktyabrenok*; fr. the Russian Communist revolution that began on October 25, 1917, Old Style (November 7, New Style)] **:** a member of a Russian Communist youth organization with members between the ages of 8 and 10 — compare PIONEER
oc·to·co·ral·lia \,äktōkə'ralēə\ [NL, fr. *octa-* + L *corallia*, pl. of *corallium* coral] *syn of* ALCYONARIA
oc·tode \'äk,tōd\ *n* -S [ISV *octa-* + *-ode*] **:** a vacuum tube with eight electrodes comprising a cathode, an anode, a control grid, and five additional electrodes that are usu. grids
oc·to·de·cil·lion \¦äktōdə'silyən\ *n, often attrib* [L *octodecim* eighteen + E *-illion* (as in *million*)] — see NUMBER table
oc·to·dec·i·mo \¦äktō'desə,mō\ *n* -S [L, abl. of *octodecimus* eighteenth, fr. *octodecim* eighteen, fr. *octo* eight + *-decim* (fr. *decem* ten) — more at TEN] **:** EIGHTEENMO — symbol *T;* see BOOK tables
oc·to·don \'äktə,dän\ *n* [NL *Octodont-*, *Octodon*, fr. *octa-* + *-odont-*, *-odon* -odon] **1** *cap* **:** a genus (the type of the family Octodontidae) of small long-eared social rodents of western So. America having combs of long stiff hairs at the base of the claws **2** -S **:** any rodent of the genus *Octodon* **:** DEGU
¹oc·to·dont \'äktə,dänt\ *adj* [NL *Octodont-*, *Octodon*] **1 :** having eight teeth **2 :** of or relating to the genus *Octodon* or the family Octodontidae
²octodont \"\ *n* -S [NL *Octodont-*, *Octodon*] **:** an octodont rodent
octodrachm *var of* OCTADRACHM
oc·to·echos \,äktō'ē,käs\ *n* -ES [NGk *oktōēchos*, *oktaēchos*, fr. Gk *okta-* octa- + *ēchos* sound — more at ECHO] **:** a liturgical book of the Eastern Orthodox Church attributed to St. John of Damascus and containing all hymns to be used at offices throughout the whole week
¹oc·to·foil \'äktə,fȯil\ *adj* [*octo-* + *foil*, n.] **:** having eight leaves ⟨a temple column of ~ plan⟩
²octofoil \"\ *n* **1 :** an octofoil figure ⟨the chancel . . . window has an ~ above three cusped lights —Nikolaus Pevsner⟩ **2 :** DOUBLE QUATREFOIL
¹oc·to·ge·nar·i·an \,äktəjə'na(a)rēən, -tōj-, -ner-, -nār-\ *n* -S [L *octogenarius* containing or consisting of eighty + E *-an*, n. suffix] **:** a person who is 80 or more but less than 90 years old
²octogenarian \¦===¦===\ *adj* **:** 80 or between 80 and 90 years old
oc·to·ge·nar·i·an·ism \,==='=rēə,nizəm\ *n* -S **:** the state of being an octogenarian
oc·tog·e·nary \(')äk¦täjə,nerē\ *adj* [L *octogenarius* containing or consisting of eighty, fr. *octogeni* eighty each (fr. *octoginta* eighty, fr. *octo* eight + *-ginta* — akin to *-ginti* in *viginti* twenty) + *-arius* -ary — more at VICENARY] **1 :** OCTOGENARIAN **2 :** based on the number 80
oc·to·gyn·ia \,äktə'jinēə\ *n pl, cap* [NL, fr. *octa-* + *-gynia*] *in some classifications* **:** an order of plants having flowers with eight pistils
oc·to·ic acid \äk'tōik-\ *n* [*octoic* fr. *octane* + *-oic*] **:** any of the monocarboxylic acids $C_7H_{15}COOH$ derived from the octanes: as **a :** CAPRYLIC ACID **b :** ETHYLHEXOIC ACID
oc·toid \'äk,tȯid\ *adj* [*octa-* + *-oid*] **:** being a gear tooth form that is commonly used for generated bevel gear teeth and that closely approximates the involute
octomerous *var of* OCTAMEROUS
octometer *var of* OCTAMETER
oc·to·nar·ius \,äktə'na(a)rēəs\ *n, pl* **octonar·ii** \-ē,ī\ [L *octonarius*, adj.] **:** an eight-foot verse (as of four iambic or trochaic dipodies)
¹oc·to·nary \'äktə,nerē\ *n* -ES [L *octonarius*, adj., containing or consisting of eight, fr. *octoni* eight each (fr. *octo* eight) + *-arius* -ary] **:** a stanza or group of eight verses; *esp* **:** one of the stanzas of the 119th Psalm
²octonary \"\ *adj* [L *octonarius*, adj.] **:** of or relating to the number eight **:** consisting of eight **:** in sets of eight
oc·to·noc·u·lar \¦äktə¦näkyələ(r)\ *adj* [L *octoni* eight each + E *ocular*] **:** having eight eyes
oc·to·pal \'äktəpəl\ *adj* [*octopus* + *-al*] **:** resembling or having the characteristics of an octopus ⟨all the slow ~ movements of her temper —Thomas Wolfe⟩
oc·to·pe·an \¦äktə¦pēən, (')äk¦tōp-\ *or* **oc·to·pine** \'äktə-,pīn, -,pən\ *adj* [*octopus* + *-an* or *-ine*] **:** of, relating to, or like an octopus
oc·toph·thal·mous \¦äk,täf¦thalməs\ *adj* [*octa-* + *-ophthalmous* (fr. Gk *ophthalmos* eye) — more at OPHTHALMIA] **:** having eight eyes
¹oc·to·ploid *also* **oc·ta·ploid** \'äktə,plȯid\ *adj* [ISV *octa-* + *-ploid*] **:** eightfold in appearance or arrangement; *specif* **:** having a chromosome number eight times the basic chromosome number — **oc·to·ploi·dy** \'==,plȯidē\ *n* -ES
²octoploid \"\ *n* -S **:** an octoploid individual
¹oc·to·pod \'äktə,päd\ *adj* [Gk *oktōpod-*, *oktapod-*, *oktōpous*, *oktapous*, fr. *okta-* octa- + *pod-*, *pous* foot — more at FOOT] **1 :** having eight feet, limbs, or arms **2** [NL *Octopoda*] **:** of or relating to the Octopoda
²octopod \"\ *n* [partly fr. ¹*octopod*, partly fr. NL *Octopoda*] **:** an individual having eight limbs; *specif* **:** OCTOPUS
oc·top·o·da \äk'täpədə\ *n pl, cap* [NL, fr. Gk *oktōpoda*, *oktapoda*, neut. pl. of *oktōpod-*, *oktapod-*, *oktōpous*, *oktapous* octopod] **:** an order of cephalopod mollusks (subclass Dibranchia) comprising the octopuses, argonauts, and related mollusks that have eight arms with sessile suckers devoid of horny rims and that often have vestiges of an internal shell but have an external shell only in the argonaut — **oc·top·o·dan** \(')=¦==dᵊn\ *adj or n*
oc·to·pod·i·dae \,äktə'pädə,dē\ *n pl, cap* [NL, fr. *Octopod-*, *Octopus*, type genus + *-idae*] **:** a family of mollusks comprising the typical octopuses that are comparatively large eight-armed cephalopods with a small saclike body, a large head armed with a strong beak, highly developed eyes, and the arms united at the base by a membrane and usu. provided with two rows of suckers by which they cling to the sea bottom or hold their prey
oc·top·o·dous \(')äk¦täpədəs\ *adj* [Gk *oktōpod-*, *oktapod-*, *oktōpous*, *oktapous* octopod + E *-ous*] **:** OCTOPOD
oc·to·pole *also* **oc·tu·pole** \'äktə,pōl\ *n* [*octopole* fr. *octa-* + *pole*; *octupole* alter. (influenced by *quadrupole*) of *octopole*] **:** a system composed of eight electric charges arranged as four dipoles or two quadrupoles
oc·to·pus \'äktəpəs *sometimes* -tə,pu̇s\ *n* [NL *Octopod-*, *Octopus*, fr. Gk *oktōpod-*, *oktapod-*, *oktōpous*, *oktapous* octopod] **1 a** *cap* **:** a genus formerly including all of the common octopuses but now restricted to a few typical forms and being the type of the family Octopodidae **b** *pl* **octopuses** \-səz\ *or* **octo·pi** \-tə,pī\ *also* **oc·top·o·des** \äk'täpə,dēz, -tōp-\ **:** any mollusk of this genus; *broadly* **:** any member of the order Octopoda usu. excepting the paper nautilus **2** *pl* **octopuses** *or* **octopi :** something that resembles or is thought to resemble an octopus esp. in having many branches centrally directed or in exerting control over others by many means ⟨an ~ of a corporation which lends, buys, produces, and sells —*Atlantic*⟩
oc·to·roon \¦äktə¦rün\ *n* -S [*octa-* + *-roon* (as in *quadroon*)] **:** a person of one-eighth Negro ancestry
oc·tose \'äk,tōs\ *n* -S [*octa-* + *-ose*] **:** any of a class of synthetic monosaccharides $C_8H_{16}O_8$ containing eight carbon atoms in the molecule
oc·to·spore \'äktə,spō(ə)r\ *n* [ISV *octa-* + *spore*] **:** one of eight carpospores commonly produced by red algae of the family Bangiaceae — **oc·tos·po·rous** \(')äk¦täspərəs, ¦äktə-¦spōrəs\ *adj*
oc·tos·ti·ate \(')äk¦tästēət, -ē,āt\ *adj* [NL *Octostiatae*, fr. *octa-* + *-ostiatae* (fr. fem. pl. of *-ostiatus* having a specified number of ostia, fr. *ostium* + L *-atus* -ate] **1 :** having eight ostia **2 :** belonging to a group of spiders having eight cardiac ostia
octostyle *var of* OCTASTYLE
¹oc·to·syllabic \¦äktə, ¦äktō+\ *adj* [LL *octosyllabus*, *octasyllabus* octosyllabic (fr. Gk *oktasyllabos*, fr. *okta-* octa- + *-syllabos*, fr. *syllabē* syllable) + E *-ic* — more at SYLLABLE] **:** having eight syllables or composed of verses having eight syllables ⟨an ~ line⟩ ⟨an ~ poem⟩
²octosyllabic \"\ *n* -S **:** a verse of eight syllables
oc·to·syllable \"+\ *adj* [part trans. of LL *octosyllabus*, *octasyllabus*] **:** OCTOSYLLABIC
²octosyllable \"\ *n* **:** a word or line of eight syllables
oc·troi \'äk,trōi, (')äk¦trwä\ *n* -S [F, fr. MF, fr. *octroyer*] **1 :** a concession or privilege granted by an absolute sovereign and serving as a limitation on his authority **2 a :** a tax on commodities brought into a town or city esp. in certain Euro-

pean countries : a municipal customs **b** : the agency for collecting such a tax or the city entrance at which it is collected

oc·troy \'äk,trȯi\ *vt* -ED/-ING/-S [MF *octroyer*, fr. OF *otreier*, fr. ML *auctorizare* to authorize, warrant, consent — more at AUTHORIZE] : to grant or concede as a privilege ⟨such charters, or constitutions, are said to be ~*ed*, or issued by royal fiat —R.G.Gettell⟩

oc·tuor \'äktüˌȯr\ *n* -S [F, fr. *octa-* + *-uor* (as in *quatuor*)] : OCTET

¹oc·tu·ple \'äk,t(y)üpəl, ≐'≐≐; 'äktəp-\ *adj* [L *octuplus*, fr. *oct-* (fr. *octo* eight) + *-uplus* (as in *quadruplus* quadruple) — more at EIGHT] **1** : consisting of eight : being eight times as great or as many : EIGHTFOLD **2** : taken by eights or in groups of eight

²octuple \"\ *n* -S : a sum eight times as great as another : an eightfold amount : the eighth multiple

³octuple \"\ *vb* **octupled; octupled; octupling** \-p(ə)liŋ\ **octuples** *vt* : to make eight times as much or as many ~ *vi* : to increase or grow to eight times as much or as many

octuple press *n* : a rotary newspaper press that prints 64 pages per revolution

oc·tup·let \(')äk¦təplət, -¦t(y)üp-, 'äktəp-, *usu* -əd.+V\ *n* -S [¹*octuple* + *-et*] **1** : a combination of eight of a kind **2** : a group of eight musical notes or tones to be performed in the time of six of the same value

¹oc·tu·pli·cate \(')äk¦t(y)üpləkət, -lə,kāt\ *adj* [L *octuplicatus* eightfold, fr. *octuplus*, after L *quadruplus* quadruple: *quadruplicatus* (past part. of *quadruplicare* to quadruple, quadruplicate)] : made in eight identical copies : EIGHTFOLD

²octuplicate \"\ *n* -S **1** : an eighth thing like seven others of the same kind **2** : eight copies all alike — used with *in* ⟨typed in ~⟩

³oc·tu·pli·cate \≐'≐plə,kāt\ *vt* -ED/-ING/-S : to multiply by eight : OCTUPLE : reproduce seven times; *specif* : to make at one time an original and seven carbon copies of

octupole *var of* OCTOPOLE

oc·tyl \'äktᵊl\ *n* -S [ISV *octane* + *-yl*] : an alkyl radical C_8H_{17} derived from an octane: as **a** : the normal radical $CH_3(CH_2)_6CH_2$— **b** : the radical $CH_3(CH_2)_3CH(C_2H_5)CH_2$— having a branched chain; 2-ethyl-hexyl

octyl alcohol *n* : any of several alcohols $C_8H_{17}OH$ derived from the octanes; *esp* : OCTANOL **a** — compare ISOOCTYL ALCOHOL

oc·tyl·ene \'äktə,lēn\ *n* -S [ISV *octyl* + *-ene*] : any of numerous isomeric hydrocarbons C_8H_{16} belonging to the ethylene series and including the octenes — compare DIISOBUTYLENE

oc·tyne *also* **oc·tine** \'äk,tīn\ *n* -S [ISV *octa-* + *-yne* or *-ine*] : any of four straight-chain hydrocarbons C_8H_{14} of the acetylene series

ocul- *or* **oculo-** *comb form* [L *ocul-*, fr. *oculus* — more at EYE] **1** : eye ⟨*oculomotor*⟩ **2** : ocular and ⟨*oculauditory*⟩ ⟨*oculofacial*⟩

¹oc·u·lar \'äkyələ(r)\ *adj* [LL *ocularis* of the eyes, fr. L *oculus* eye + *-aris* -ar] **1 a** : done or carried out by means of the sight ⟨~ measurement⟩ ⟨~ inspection⟩ ⟨the density of the vegetation as determined by ~ estimate —*Ecology*⟩ **b** (1) : addressed to or perceived by the eye : received by actual sight : VISIBLE ⟨be sure of it; give me the ~ proof —Shak.⟩ ⟨~ evidence for my belief that those books were written and were published —Max Beerbohm⟩ (2) : based on what has been seen ⟨~ testimony⟩ **c** : of or relating to the sense of sight : VISUAL ⟨of wondrous ~ excitement to any art-minded provincial youth —Janet Flanner⟩ ⟨this correction of ~ illusions was a practice of Greek architects —Benjamin Farrington⟩ **2 a** : of, relating to, or connected with the eye ⟨~ diseases⟩ ⟨~ muscles⟩ **b** : used by or expressed by the eye ⟨the ~ dialect needs no dictionary —R.W.Emerson⟩ ⟨~ approval⟩ **c** : resembling or suggesting an eye in form or function ⟨spindly balusters, ~ windows —Frederic Beck⟩

²ocular \"\ *n* -S **1** : EYE ⟨stick an eyeglass in his ~ —W.S. Gilbert⟩ **2** : EYEPIECE **1** ⟨the perfect ~ exists only in the astronomer's wistful imagination —*Times Lit. Supp.*⟩ **3** : an ocular scale or shield (as in certain reptiles)

oc·u·lar·i·um \,äkyə'la(a)rēəm\ *n, pl* **ocular·ia** \-ēə\ [ML, fr. L *oculus* eye + *-arium*] : a slit for vision in a barrel helm

oc·u·lar·ly *adv* **1** : by means of the eyes or the sight ⟨expressed her feelings ~⟩ **2** : to the sight ⟨demonstrated ~⟩

ocular micrometer *n* **1** : MICROMETER EYEPIECE **2** : EYEPIECE MICROMETER

ocular sclerite *n* : a narrow circular strip of the insect cranium surrounding the compound eye

ocular spectrum *n* : AFTERIMAGE

ocular spot *n* : a pigmented organ or part believed to be sensitive to light

oc·u·late \'äkyələt, -yə,lāt\ *adj* [LL *oculatus* having ornaments resembling eyes, fr. L, having eyes, fr. *oculus* eye + *-atus* -ate] : having spots or holes resembling eyes : OCELLATED

oc·u·lau·di·to·ry \,äkyə'lȯdə,tōrē\ *adj* [*ocul-* + *auditory*] : combining the sense of sight and that of hearing

oc·u·li·na \,äkyə'līnə\ *n, cap* [NL, fr. L *oculus* eye + NL *-ina*] : a genus (the type of the family Oculinidae) of tropical aporose corals comprising the typical ivory corals — **oc·u·lin·id** \-linəd\ *n* -S — **oc·u·lin·oid** \,≐≐'li,nȯid\ *adj*

oc·u·list \'äkyələst\ *n* -S [F *oculiste*, fr. MF, fr. L *oculus* eye + MF *-iste* -ist] **1** : OPHTHALMOLOGIST **2** : OPTOMETRIST

oc·u·li sunday \'äkyə,lī-\ *n, cap O&S* [L *oculi*, pl. of *oculus* eye; from the fact that the introit for the day, Ps 24: 15 (Vulgate), begins with the word *oculi*] : the third Sunday in Lent

oculo- — see OCUL-

oc·u·lo·gy·ric \¦äkyəlō¦jīrik\ *also* **oc·u·lo·gy·ral** \-rəl\ *adj* [*oculogyric* fr. *ocul-* + *gyr-* (fr. Gk *gyros* circle) + *-ic*; *oculogyral* fr. *ocul* + *gyral* — more at GYRE] : relating to or involving circular movements of the eyeballs

oculogyric crisis *n* : a spasmodic attack that occurs in some nervous diseases and is marked by fixation of the eyeballs in one position usu. upward

¹oc·u·lo·motor \¦äkyəlō+\ *adj* [*ocul-* + *motor*] **1** : moving or tending to move the eyeball **2** : involving movement of the eyeball ⟨~ palsies⟩

²oculomotor \"\ *n* : an oculomotor part; *esp* : OCULOMOTOR NERVE

oculomotor nerve *n* : either nerve of the 3d pair of cranial nerves that are motor nerves with some associated autonomic fibers, arise from the midbrain, and supply muscles of the eye except the superior oblique and the lateral rectus with motor fibers and the ciliary body and iris with autonomic fibers by way of the ciliary ganglion

oc·u·lus \'äkyələs\ *n, pl* **ocu·li** \-yə,lī\ [L, lit., eye — more at EYE] **1** : an architectural member resembling or suggesting an eye: as **a** : the central boss of a volute **b** : a round opening in a dome **c** : OEIL-DE-BOEUF **2** : EYE **3** : a painted or metal image of a human eye placed on the bow or other part of a boat (as in ancient Egypt)

oculus mun·di \-'mən,dī\ *n, pl* **oculi mundi** [L, eye of the world] : OPAL

ocyp·o·da \ō'sipədə\ *syn of* OCYPODE

ocyp·o·de \-dē\ *n* [NL, irreg. fr. Gk *ōkypod-*, *ōkypous* swift-footed, fr. *ōkys* swift + *pod-*, *pous* foot; akin to L *ocior* swifter, Skt *āśu* swift, and perh. to L *acer* sharp — more at EDGE, FOOT] **1** *cap* : a genus (the type of the family Ocypodidae) of square-bodied, long-legged, and swift-running crabs that are related to the fiddler crabs and live in holes in the sand along the seashore **2** -S : any crab of the genus *Ocypode* — **oc·y·po·di·an** \¦äsə¦pōdēən\ *adj or n* — **ocyp·o·doid** \ō'sipə,dȯid\ *adj*

ocyr·oe \ō'sirəwē\ *n, cap* [NL, fr. Gk *ōkyroēs* swift-flowing, fr. *ōkys* swift + *-roēs* (akin to *rhein* to flow) — more at STREAM] : a genus (coextensive with the family Ocyroidae) of ctenophores of the Gulf of Mexico and the Caribbean sea that swim by means of a large winglike process on each side of the body

¹od *also* **odd** \'äd\ *interj, often cap* [euphemism for *God*] — a mild oath

²od \'äd, 'ōd\ *n* -S [G, coined 1850 by Baron Carl-Ludwig von Reichenbach †1869 Ger. chemist and natural philosopher] : a force or natural power formerly held by some to reside in certain individuals and things and to underlie hypnotism and magnetism and some other phenomena

OD \(')ō'dē\ *abbr or n* -S **1** : OFFICER OF THE DAY **2** : OLIVE DRAB : an olive drab uniform **3** : a doctor of optometry

OD *abbr* **1** [L *oculus dexter*] right eye **2** on demand **3** on duty **4** ordinary seaman **5** ordnance datum **6** outside diameter; outside dimensions **7** overdraft; overdrawn

oda *or* **odah** \'ōdə, ō'dä\ *n, pl* **odas** *or* **oda** *or* **odahs** *or* **odah** [Turk *oda* room, chamber] **1** : a room in a harem **2** : ODALISQUE

odac·i·dae \ō'dasə,dē\ *n pl, cap* [NL, fr. *Odac-*, *Odax*, type genus + *-idae*] : a family of labroid fishes that is usu. made coextensive with the genus *Odax*

¹odal *or* **odel** *also* **odhal** *or* **odhall** \'ōdᵊl\ *n* -S [ON *ōthal* — more at ATHELING] : alodium owned by individuals or families belonging to Teutonic and esp. Scandinavian peoples in the premedieval or medieval period

²odal \'ōdᵊl\ *adj* : of, relating to, or constituting odal ⟨~ soil⟩

oda·lisque *also* **oda·lisk** *or* **oda·lisc** \'ōdᵊl,isk\ *n* -S [F *odalisque*, alter. of *odalique*, fr. Turk *odalık*, fr. *oda* room + *-lık*, n. suffix] : a female slave or concubine in a harem

odal·ler \'ōdᵊlə(r)\ *n* -S : an owner of odal

odax \'ō,daks\ *n, cap* [NL, fr. Gk, adv., by biting, irreg. (influence of *odous* tooth), fr. the stem of *daknein* to bite — more at TOOTH, TONGS] : a genus of marine fishes of Australian and New Zealand seas that resemble sparid fishes but have a jaw with the front margin modified into a sharp cutting edge that replaces teeth — see ODACIDAE

¹odd \'äd\ *adj, usu* -ER/-EST [ME *odde*, fr. ON *oddi* point of land, triangle, odd number (as in such compounds as *odda-mathr* odd man, *oddatala* odd number); akin to OE *ord* point of a weapon, OHG *ort*, ON *oddr*, and prob. to Lith *usnis* thistle, hawthorn, Alb *usht* ear of grain] **1 a** : that is without its corresponding mate : that lacks its complementary match : that is unpaired ⟨found two pairs of shoes and an ~ shoe in the closet⟩ ⟨lost a glove somewhere and was unable to match the ~ one⟩ **b** (1) : that exists alone or is present alone in contrast with others that are paired or coupled or grouped : that is left over ⟨four of them began playing bridge, and the ~ player drew up a chair and watched⟩ ⟨came without his wife and so turned out to be the ~ guest at the party⟩ (2) : that exists alone or is present alone as something that forms or that is designed to form part of a complete set or series : that is separated from an actual or contemplated complete set or series ⟨had in his possession only two or three ~ volumes of the original 12-volume set⟩ **c** *chiefly dial* : that is the only one : SINGLE ⟨just for this ~ night —Margery Sharp⟩ **d** *obs* : excelling in a unique way : CHOICE **2 a** (1) : being somewhat though insignificantly more than the indicated round number or than the indicated approximate quantity or extent or degree — used formerly with a preceding *and* ⟨the eighty and ~ pigeons —Matthew Arnold⟩ but now usu. used immediately following the numerical adjective and usu. connected with it by a hyphen ⟨a book of 300-*odd* pages⟩ ⟨was 40-*odd* years old⟩ (2) : increased by the addition of a fraction of one of the indicated units — now usu. used following the substantive qualified by a numerical adjective ⟨will cost 23 dollars ~⟩ **b** (1) : that constitutes a remainder in comparison with an expressed or implied unitary amount (as of money) : that is left over as a remainder ⟨used most of the check for necessary expenses and spent the ~ dollars on his hobby⟩ (2) : that does not total up to any very considerable amount : that does not constitute any very considerable unitary amount ⟨had some ~ change in his pocket⟩ ⟨some ~ nickels and dimes⟩ **c** *archaic* : SOME, SEVERAL — used to indicate an indefinite usu. small number of unitary amounts of lesser extent than an immediately preceding unitary amount ⟨two thousand ~ hundred cavalry —R.T.Wilson⟩ ⟨three thousand and ~ hundred clouds —Henry Petowe⟩ **3 a** : being any member of a sequence of positive integers beginning with one and counting by twos : not divisible exactly by two — opposed to EVEN **b** : having an odd number as one of a series ⟨read every other ~ page of the book⟩ **c** : marked by an odd number of units (as of measurement) ⟨needed two *odd*-length boards, one of 3 feet and one of 5 feet⟩ **4** : that exists or occurs or is produced in addition to or apart from what is regular or planned in advance or taken into account: as **a** (1) : that is a scrap or fragment ⟨swept up the ~ bits of metal left on the floor⟩ (2) : that is one of several or many mixed or varied usu. unrelated things : MISCELLANEOUS ⟨rummaged around and picked up a few ~ things we needed⟩ (3) : HAPHAZARD, RANDOM, SCATTERED ⟨collected ~ bits of information⟩ ⟨found a few ~ references to the book⟩ **b** (1) : that occurs at an irregular or indefinitely determined time ⟨the matter was brought up at one of the club's ~ sessions⟩ (2) : that occurs largely by chance : that occurs unpredictably : ACCIDENTAL, FORTUITOUS ⟨an ~ stroke of luck⟩ (3) : that occurs at some indefinitely indicated time : that comes along at some time or other ⟨told her he would see her again some ~ day⟩ (4) : that occurs sporadically or in an isolated way : that crops up or materializes from time to time : happening or becoming available now and then : OCCASIONAL, STRAY ⟨manages to get in some reading at ~ moments⟩ ⟨at ~ moments as a boy he was set to hoeing the family garden —*Current Biog.*⟩ **c** (1) : that does not form part of a regular schedule (as of work) : that is done or engaged in or attended to over and above a regular program or routine : INCIDENTAL ⟨does ~ chores around the house, potters ineffectually round the garden —Geoffrey Gorer⟩ ⟨try to supplement their pensions by taking on ~ jobs —M.A.Abrams⟩ (2) : that is engaged to do miscellaneous work esp. requiring little training or skill ⟨hired a couple of ~ hands for the farm⟩ ⟨had begun life as an ~ boy in various steelworks —R.W.Pickford⟩ **d** : that is produced over and above what comes from a regular source : EXTRA ⟨hoped to make a few ~ dollars during his summer vacation⟩ **e** : CASUAL 4 b (2) ⟨wear ~ jackets and slacks —Richard Joseph⟩ **5** : that has an out-of-the-way location : SECLUDED, REMOTE ⟨found it in some ~ corner of the house⟩ **6** : that differs markedly from what is usual or ordinary or accepted : that is hardly or not at all the expected or normal thing : PECULIAR: as **a** (1) : strange in behavior or action ⟨a very ~ way to show gratitude⟩ ⟨has ~ little habits⟩ (2) : eccentric or mentally unbalanced ⟨there must have been something ~ about the man, or he wouldn't have buried himself alive —G.K.Chesterton⟩ **b** (1) : strange in appearance ⟨had an ~ look in her eyes⟩ (2) : grotesque or freakish in appearance ⟨was one of the ~*est* creatures I had ever seen⟩ **c** (1) : altogether unusual : most uncommon : quite extraordinary : SINGULAR, CURIOUS, QUEER ⟨it's ~ you didn't know⟩ ⟨an ~ collection of books⟩ (2) : BAFFLING, MYSTERIOUS, INEXPLICABLE ⟨suffered an ~ impulse to get up and kick his chair over —Mary Austin⟩ ⟨the young man had an ~ effect on her, making her almost giddily loquacious —Harriet La Barre⟩ **syn** see STRANGE

²odd \"\ *adv* [ME *odde*, fr. *odde*, adj.] *archaic* : ODDLY

³odd \"\ *n* -S [¹*odd*] **1 a** : a stroke in golf that when played will be one more than the number of strokes played for a hole by one's opponent **b** : a stroke deducted from a weaker opponent's golf score for a hole **2** : ODD TRICK 1

¹oddball \'≐,≐\ *n* [¹*odd* + *ball*] : one whose behavior is eccentric or otherwise peculiar ⟨talked like an ~, and he had a funny look in his eyes —Everett Wilson⟩

²oddball \'≐,≐\ *adj* : ECCENTRIC, PECULIAR, ODD ⟨~ humor⟩

odd-come-short \¦≐(,)≐¦≐\ *n, pl* **odd-come-shorts** **1** *archaic* **a** : a cast-off garment or piece of cloth **b** *odd-come-shorts pl* : ODDS AND ENDS **2** *archaic* : some day or other

odd-come-shortly \¦≐(,)≐¦≐≐\ *n, pl* **odd-come-shortlys** *or* **odd-come-shortlies** *archaic* : an undetermined day in the future ⟨one of these *odd-come-shortlies* —W.F.De Morgan⟩

odd court *n* : the left half court in a singles racket game — compare EVEN COURT

odder *comparative of* ODD

oddest *superlative of* ODD

odd-eyed \'≐¦≐\ *adj* : having the two eyes of different colors ⟨an *odd-eyed* cat⟩

odd fellow *n, usu cap O & F* : a member of one of the major benevolent and fraternal orders

odd fish *n, pl* **odd fish** : ODDBALL

odd function *n* : a function such that $f(-x) = -f(x)$ where the sign is reversed but the absolute value remains the same if the sign of the independent variable is reversed

odd·ish \'ädish, -dēsh\ *adj* : somewhat odd

odd·i·ty \'ädəd·ē, -ətē, -i\ *n* -ES **1** : something odd: as **a** : a peculiar quality or trait or feature : PECULIARITY, ECCENTRICITY ⟨an ~ of character⟩ ⟨the *oddities* of this particular pilot —J.A.Michener⟩ ⟨any *oddities* in his behavior will be commented upon —Robert Graves⟩ **b** (1) : an eccentric or otherwise peculiar individual ⟨had all sorts of *oddities* visiting me —H.J.Laski⟩ (2) : something strange or grotesque or freakish (as in appearance) ⟨among *oddities* of the sea are the opalescent squid and the sea squirt —*Amer. Guide Series: Wash.*⟩ (3) : something unique or curiously unusual or anomalous : CURIOSITY ⟨a good piece of steak is an ~ —Green Peyton⟩ **c** : a strange event : peculiar occurrence ⟨the *oddities* of history⟩ ⟨meeting her there was a real ~⟩ **2** : the quality or state of being odd ⟨the ~ of the situation⟩ ⟨saw for myself one example of his ~ —S.P.B.Mais⟩ ⟨the ~ of our own temperaments —Virginia Woolf⟩

odd-job \'≐¦≐\ *vi* [fr. the n. phrase *odd job*] : to work at odd jobs esp. those requiring little training or skill ⟨gone in to work in town, *odd-jobbing* —Paul Annixter⟩

odd-job·ber \(')≐¦jäbə(r)\ *n* [*odd job* + *-er*] : ODD-JOBMAN

odd-job·man \-mən\ *n, pl* **odd-jobmen** [*odd job* + *man*] : one that works at odd jobs

odd-leg caliper \'≐,≐-\ *n* **1** : a caliper having the points of its legs bent in the same direction for measurements on stepped surfaces or similar surfaces **2** : HERMAPHRODITE CALIPER

odd-leg caliper

odd legs *n pl but sing in constr* : ODD-LEG CALIPER

odd·ling \'ädliŋ, -lēŋ\ *n* -S **1** *chiefly dial* : a mildly eccentric individual **2 oddlings** *pl, Brit* : ODDS AND ENDS

odd lot *n* : a number or quantity other than the usual unit in transactions; *specif* : a quantity of less than 100 shares of stock — compare ROUND LOT

odd·ly \'ädlē, -li\ *adv* [ME *oddely*, fr. *odde* odd + *-ly* — more at ODD] : in an odd manner ⟨seem to have acted ~ —Nigel Balchin⟩ ⟨was quite happy, ~ enough⟩ or to an odd extent ⟨sensed that he was ~ disturbed —Wilson Collison⟩

odd man *n* **1** : one that casts or may cast a decisive vote when a vote is otherwise tied **2 a** : a player (as in the game of odd man wins) whose coin shows a face different from two other coins tossed or matched **b** : ODD MAN OUT 2 **3** [*odd* (*job*)] **a** *chiefly Brit* (1) : one that does odd jobs (2) : DAY LABORER **b** : FLOATER 4 b, 4 d

odd man out *n* **1** : a method or game of choosing or eliminating one of a number of persons (as by matching coins) **2 a** : an individual singled out from others (as by matching coins) **b** : one that by choice or circumstances does not share in the ordinary affairs of others

odd man wins *n* : a gambling game in which three players match coins and declare the winner the one whose coin does not match the others

odd mark *n, dial Eng* : a portion of arable land lying fallow in preparation for seeding

odd·ment \'ädmənt\ *n* -S [¹*odd* + *-ment*] **1 oddments** *pl* : ODDS AND ENDS ⟨clawing the ~*s* out of his pockets —Verne Athanas⟩ **2 a** : something left over or remaining or isolated (as a garment or piece of goods from a larger stock, a book from a complete set) ⟨an ~ sale⟩ — usu. used in pl. ⟨a display of ~*s*⟩ **b** : a garment designed for casual or otherwise informal wear ⟨frivolous ~*s* for summer —*New Yorker*⟩ — usu. used in pl. **3** *chiefly Brit* **a** : a page (as the title page) of a book that does not carry the actual text or other central material — usu. used in pl. **b oddments** *pl* : pages of a book remaining over after complete sections are made up **4** : something odd : ODDITY — usu. used in pl. ⟨a museum where were gathered those ~*s* that rich men seem disposed to accumulate —Agnes M. Cleaveland⟩ ⟨various ~*s* of humanity —G.F. Whicher⟩ ⟨explains some nice ~*s* of behavior —Russell Lynes⟩

odd·ness *n* -ES [ME *oddenesse*, fr. *odde* odd + *-nesse* -ness] **1** : the quality or state of being odd ⟨comical in their ~ —George Meredith⟩ **2** : an instance of oddness ⟨were warned off by his ~*es* —Thomas Hughes⟩

odd or even *or* **odd and even** *or* **odds or evens** *n* : one of several games of chance or skill in which there is guessing or betting as to whether a certain number will be odd or even: as **a** : a game in which one player selects and holds an odd or even number of counters (as beans) and the other guesses which it is **b** : a game of betting on casts of dice or turns of a wheel **c** : a simplified form of fan-tan (sense 1) **d** : a mathematical game similar to nim in which the object is to take or leave an odd number of counters

odd-pinnate \'≐¦≐,≐\ *adj, of a compound leaf* : having leaflets on each side of the petiole and having a single leaflet at the tip of the petiole — see LEAF illustration — **odd-pinnately** *adv*

¹odds \'ädz\ *n pl but sometimes sing in constr* [¹*odd* + *-s*] **1 a** *archaic* : INEQUALITIES, DISPARITIES ⟨death looks down with nods and smiles and makes the ~ all even —W.M.Praed⟩ **b** *obs* : degree of unlikeness ⟨a manifest ~ between the bigness of the diameter —John Locke⟩ **2 a** : amount of difference by which one thing exceeds or falls short of another : amount in excess or defect ⟨won the election by considerable ~⟩ **b** (1) : difference favoring one of two opposed things : balance of advantage or weight of opposition ⟨the overwhelming ~ it affords the sportsman over bird and animal —Richard Jefferies⟩ ⟨one man's determination to win through despite heavy ~ —Robert Nicholas⟩ ⟨has managed to beat the ~ against him —Frank O'Leary⟩ ⟨would assume that the ~ were against him —Gilbert Highet⟩ (2) *archaic* : the state or fact of being in an advantageous position (3) : difference in the way of advantage or disadvantage or of benefit or detriment : significant difference : IMPORTANCE : advantage to be gained : PROFIT, BENEFIT, USE, PERCENTAGE ⟨it makes no ~ what you do⟩ ⟨she'll do it anyway, so what's the ~ of telling her not to⟩ ⟨it was little ~ what they sang, for they were all singing out of tune —Michael McLaverty⟩ ⟨what's the ~, if thinking so makes them happy —Flora Thompson⟩ **c** (1) : the probability that one thing is so rather than another or that one thing will happen rather than another : balance of probability : greater likelihood : CHANCES ⟨the night is clear and the ~ are that it'll stay that way until morning —H.D.Cooper⟩ ⟨the ~ are against it⟩ (2) : the ratio of probability that one thing is so rather than another or that one thing will happen rather than another ⟨it is even ~ which makes the more noise —Claudia Cassidy⟩ **3** : DISAGREEMENT, DISSENSION, VARIANCE — now usu. used with *at* ⟨was at ~ with everything she represented —Cliff Farrell⟩ ⟨were at moral ~ among themselves —*Time*⟩ **4 a** (1) : an advantage (as a head start in a footrace) given to a less skilled or otherwise weaker competitor ⟨allowed ~ to the other team⟩ (2) : special favor : special treatment or consideration : PARTIALITY ⟨I ask no ~ of them, no more than I do of the dirt I walk on —H.C.Kimball⟩ **b** (1) : the advantage of an unequal wager that is granted by one making a bet to one accepting the bet and that is made proportionate to and is designed to equalize the assumed chances favoring the one or the other of the bettors ⟨offered him ~ of 3 to 1 but he refused to take the bet⟩ (2) : the ratio assumed to exist or actually arrived at (as by preliminary placement of bets) with regard to the probabilities of winning or losing and used as a basis for placing bets; *specif* : the ratio existing between the amount to be paid off for a winning bet and the amount of the bet placed ⟨the horse was running at ~ of 6 to 1⟩ — **by all odds** *also* **by long odds** *or* **by odds** *adv* : from every viewpoint : in every way : without question : far and away ⟨was *by all odds* the outstanding public question in the United States —*New Republic*⟩ ⟨is *by long odds* the most rigidly intellectual —G.W.Johnson⟩ ⟨social life centered in the palace of the governor, *by odds* the most pretentious and stately house in town —C.G.Bowers⟩

²odds \"\ *vt, past or past part* **oddsed**; *pres 3d sing* **odds** *dial Eng* : to make some adjustment in (as by altering)

odds and ends *n pl* **1 a** : small often trifling items that are usu. varied and often unrelated : miscellaneous things : miscellaneous articles ⟨*odds and ends* found lying around the attic⟩ ⟨threw some *odds and ends* into a suitcase⟩ **b** : miscellaneous small matters (as of business) to be attended to ⟨have some *odds and ends* to do tomorrow morning⟩ **2** : miscellaneous bits or fragments or scraps or remnants or leftovers ⟨*odds and ends* of information⟩ ⟨*odds and ends* of food⟩

odds bobs or **odds bob** *often cap O, var of* ODS-BOBS

odds fish *also* **odsfish** \'ˌ=ˌ=\ *interj, often cap O* [gen. of 1*od,* *odd* + *fish*] — a mild oath

1**odds-on** \'=ˌ=\ *adj* [*odds* + *on,* adv.] **1 a :** that is more likely to win or that is viewed as being more likely to win than not ⟨an *odds-on* favorite at the racetrack⟩ **:** having or viewed as having a better than even chance to win ⟨an *odds-on* political candidate⟩ **b :** that is viewed as being more likely to be so or more likely to turn out so than not ⟨the book is an *odds-on* best seller⟩ ⟨an *odds-on* candidate for reform school —*Newsweek*⟩ fairly sure **:** quite probable ⟨it's *odds-on* she did it —Ngaio Marsh⟩ **2 :** that does not involve much risk **:** fairly good ⟨an *odds-on* chance of getting out⟩ **:** fairly safe **:** pretty sure ⟨if you were given the opportunity to make a fresh start, it is an *odds-on* bet you'd wind up in much the same sort of job —Stanley Frank⟩

2**odds-on** \"\ *n* -s **:** favorable odds — usu. used with *at* ⟨won the chief event and at *odds-on*⟩

odd trick *n* **1 :** the first trick in excess of six won by the same side in whist **2 :** each trick in excess of six won by declarer's side at bridge or by either side at whist or bridge-whist

ode \'ōd\ *n* -s [MF or LL; MF, fr. LL *ode, oda,* fr. Gk *aoidē* (Attic *ōidē*), fr. *aeidein* (Attic *aidein*) to sing; akin to OHG *farwāzan* to deny, Gk *audē* voice, sound, speech, Toch A & Toch B *wätk-* to command, Skt *vadati* he says, sings, plays music] **1 :** a lyric poem usu. marked by particular exaltation of feeling and style and typically marked by varying length of line and by complexity of stanza forms **2 a :** one of nine scriptural canticles used in the morning office of the Eastern Church on certain days **b :** one of nine hymns of a canon (sense 10)

1**-ode** \ˌōd\ *n comb form* -s [F, fr. Gk *-ōdēs,* prob. fr. the stem of *ozein* to smell — more at ODOR] **:** thing that resembles ⟨placode⟩

2**-ode** \"\ *n comb form* -s [Gk *-odos,* fr. *hodos* — more at CEDE] **1 :** way **:** path **:** road ⟨electrode⟩ **2 :** electrode ⟨diode⟩

-o·dea \'ōdēə\ *n pl comb form* [NL, fr. Gk *-ōdēs* -ode] **:** animals belonging to or resembling — in names of higher taxa (as orders, suborders) ⟨Blattodea⟩ ⟨Embiodea⟩

odel *var of* ODAL

oden·se \'ōthənsə\ *adj, usu cap* [fr. *Odense,* Denmark] **:** of or from the city of Odense, Denmark **:** of the kind or style prevalent in Odense

-o·des \'ō(ˌ)dēz\ *n comb form* [NL, fr. Gk *-ōdēs* -ode] **:** animal or plant resembling — in generic names ⟨Goniodes⟩

odes·sa \ō'desə\ *adj, usu cap* [fr. *Odessa,* U.S.S.R.] **:** of or from the city of Odessa, U.S.S.R. **:** of the kind or style prevalent in Odessa

odes·san \-sᵊn\ *n* -s *cap* [*Odessa* + E *-an*] **:** a native or resident of Odessa, U.S.S.R.

ode·um \ō'dēəm, 'ōdēəm\ *also* **ode·on** \'ōdēˌän, -ən\ *n, pl* **ode·ums** \-mz\ *also* **odeons** \-nz\ *or* **odea** \-ēə\ [L & Gk; L *odeum,* fr. Gk *ōideion,* fr. *ōidē* song, ode — more at ODE] **1 :** a relatively small typically circular roofed theater of ancient Greece and Rome used chiefly for competitions in music and poetry that were attended by the public **2 :** a contemporary theater or concert hall

odhal *or* **odhall** *var of* ODAL

1**od·ic** \'ädik, 'ōd-\ *adj* [ISV 2*od* + *-ic*] **:** of or relating to od

2**od·ic** \'ōdik\ *adj* [*ode* + *-ic*] **:** of, relating to, or forming an ode ⟨~ stanzas⟩

-odies *pl of* -ODY

odif·er·ous \(')ō¦dif(ə)rəs\ *adj* [ME *odeferus,* contr. of *odoriferous* — more at ODORIFEROUS] **1 :** ODORIFEROUS ⟨the ~ principles of natural musk —*Swiss Industry & Trade*⟩ **2 :** having a strong gamy often acrid odor ⟨the long ~ line of baggage camels —A.R.Griffin⟩

odin·ic \(')ō¦dinik\ *adj, usu cap* [*Odin,* the chief god of the ancient Scandinavians (fr. ON *Óthinn*) + E *-ic*] **:** of or relating to the god Odin

odin·ism \'ōdᵊnˌizəm\ *n* -s *usu cap* [*Odin* + E *-ism*] **:** worship of Odin **:** the Odinic cult

odin·ist \-ᵊnəst\ *n* -s *usu cap* [*Odin* + E *-ist*] **:** a worshiper of Odin

odi·om·e·ter \ˌōdē'ämədə(r)\ *n* [*odio-* (irreg. fr. *odor*) + *-meter*] **:** an olfactometer measuring the greatest dilution of an odorous vapor detectable by smell

odi·ous \'ōdēəs\ *adj* [ME, fr. MF *odieus,* fr. L *odiosus,* fr. *odium* + *-osus* -ous] **:** exciting or deserving odium **:** HATEFUL ⟨was in some mysterious way ~ and unlovable —Joseph Conrad⟩ ⟨the ~ feelings he must have —John Galsworthy⟩ ⟨his cruelty to such a charming woman made him ~ to her —Jane Austen⟩ — **odi·ous·ly** *adv* — **odi·ous·ness** *n* -ES

od·ist \'ōdəst\ *n* -s [*ode* + *-ist*] **:** a writer of odes

odi·um \'ōdēəm\ *n* -s [L; akin to L *odi* I hate, OE *atol* terrible, horrible, ON *atall* fierce, loathsome, Gk *odyssasthai* to be angry, Arm *ateam* I hate, and perh. to L *odor* — more at ODOR] **1 a :** the state or fact of being subjected to widespread or deep hatred and severe condemnation and often loathing or contempt usu. as a result of a despicable act or blameworthy situation ⟨these three artists had finally started losing their ~ —Janet Flanner⟩ **b :** hatred and condemnation often marked by loathing or contempt and usu. directed toward one guilty of or held responsible for some despicable act or situation **:** DETESTATION ⟨was compelled to ... face the ~ —John Buchan⟩ ⟨heaps ~ on those responsible for the defeat —*Americas*⟩ ⟨would risk the ~ that would come from overthrowing him —*N.Y.Times*⟩ **2 a** (1) **:** the qualities of something (as a despicable act or situation) that excite hatred and condemnation and often loathing or contempt **:** HATEFULNESS ⟨has endeavored to remove that ~ —Elmer Davis⟩ (2) **:** a mark of disgrace or reproach **:** STIGMA ⟨the whole ~ fell on the girl —Margaret Mead⟩ ⟨shift the burden and the ~ of decision —G.B.Sansom⟩ **b :** great disrepute or infamy attached to something **:** OPPROBRIUM ⟨prizefighting had not yet escaped the ~ which clung to it throughout the bareknuckle days —F.R.Dulles⟩ ⟨no ~ attached to those who didn't go to football games —John Reed⟩ ⟨eliminate the ~ attaching to the word —William James⟩ **3 :** an object of widespread or deep hatred and condemnation ⟨other ~*s* were abolished —Mark Harris⟩ **syn** see DISHONOR

odium the·o·lo·gi·cum \ˌ=ˌ==ˌthēə'läjəkəm\ *n* [NL, lit., theological hatred] **:** bitterness developed during or typical of controversy about religion and giving rise to an unyielding refusal to continue a discussion ⟨the *odium theologicum* which prevented any real understanding —*Times Lit. Supp.*⟩

odly *abbr* orderly

odo·ben·i·dae \ˌōdō'benəˌdē\ *n pl, cap* [NL, fr. *Odobenus,* type genus + *-idae*] **:** a small family of marine mammals (suborder Pinnipedia) that are related to the seals, have a thick tough nearly hairless skin underlaid by a thick layer of blubber and the upper canines enlarged into tusks, and include the walruses and extinct related forms

odo·be·nus \-'bēnəs\ *n, cap* [NL, fr. Gk *odōn* tooth + *bainein* to walk; fr. the belief that walruses use their tusks in sequence — more at TOOTH, COME] **:** the type genus of Odobenidae comprising the walruses

odo·coi·le·us \-'kōilēəs\ *n, cap* [NL, fr. Gk *odōn* tooth + *koilos* hollow — more at CAVE] **:** a genus including the Virginia deer, mule deer, black-tailed deer, and related American species

odo·graph \'ōdəˌgraf\ *n* [*odo-* (as in *odometer*) + *-graph*] **1 :** an instrument for automatically plotting the course and distance traveled by a vehicle **2 :** a device for recording the length and rapidity of stride and the number of steps taken by a walker

odom·e·ter \ō'dämədə(r)\ *n* [F *odomètre,* modif. of Gk *hodometron, hodometros* instrument for measuring distance, fr. *hodos* way, road + *metron* measure — more at CEDE, METER] **1 :** an instrument attached to a vehicle to measure the distance traversed ⟨some speedometers are equipped with a trip ~ which registers distance traveled up to 999.9 miles —Ernest Venk & William Landon⟩ **2 :** a wheel used by surveyors that registers the miles and rods traversed

-o·don \əˌdän, ōˌ-, -ˌdən\ *n comb form* -s [NL, fr. Gk *odōn* tooth — more at TOOTH] **:** animal having teeth of a (specified) kind — chiefly in the names of genera in zoology ⟨Iguanodon⟩ ⟨mastodon⟩

odo·na·ta \ˌōdᵊn'ädə, -'ādə; ō'dänədə\ *n pl, cap* [NL, irreg. fr. Gk *odōn* tooth + NL *-ata*] **:** an order of insects containing the dragonflies and damselflies and characterized by aquatic larvae that are nymphs or naiads and by predaciousness in both adult and larval forms

1**odo·nate** \'ōdᵊnˌāt, -ət\ *n* -s *sometimes cap* [NL *Odonata*] **:** an insect of the order Odonata ⟨nymphs of certain of the larger ~*s* ... capture and eat small fish —*Biol. Abstracts*⟩

2**odonate** \"\ *adj* **:** of or relating to the Odonata ⟨~ larvae⟩ ⟨~ nymphs⟩ ⟨~ life⟩

odo·na·tol·o·gist \ˌōdᵊnə'täləjəst\ *n* -s **:** a specialist in odonatology

odo·na·tol·o·gy \-jē\ *n* -ES [NL *Odonata* + E *-o-* + *-logy*] **:** the study of the Odonata

odont- *or* **odonto-** *comb form* [F, fr. Gk, fr. *odont-, odōn* — more at TOOTH] **:** tooth ⟨odontitis⟩ ⟨odontocete⟩ ⟨odontogeny⟩ ⟨odontology⟩ ⟨odontorrhagia⟩

-o·dont \əˌdänt, ōˌd-\ *adj comb form* [Gk *odont-, odōn* tooth] **:** having or being teeth of a (specified) nature ⟨heterodont⟩ ⟨lophodont⟩

-o·don·ta \əˌdäntə, ōˌd-\ *n comb form, pl* **-odonta** [NL, fr. Gk *odont-, odōn* tooth] **:** animal or animals having teeth of a (specified) nature — in names of zoological taxa ⟨Bunodonta⟩ ⟨Creodonta⟩ ⟨Heterodonta⟩ ⟨Labyrinthodonta⟩

odon·tal·gia \ˌōˌdän'talj(ē)ə\ *n* -s [NL, fr. Gk *odontalgeia,* fr. *odont-* + *-algeia* -algia] **:** TOOTHACHE

odon·tal·gic \ˌōˌdän¦taljik\ *adj* [F *odontalgique,* fr. *odontalgie* odontalgia (fr. Gk *odontalgeia*) + *-ique* -ic] **:** of or relating to toothache

odon·tas·pid·i·dae \(ˌ)ōˌdänˌta'spidəˌdē\ *also* **odon·tas·pi·dae** \ˌōˌdän'taspəˌdē\ [NL, fr. *Odontaspid-, Odontaspis* + *-idae*] *syn of* CARCHARIIDAE

odon·tas·pis \ˌōˌdän'taspəs\ [NL, fr. *odont-* + Gk *aspis* shield — more at ASPID-] *syn of* CARCHARIAS

-o·don·tes \ə'dänˌtēz, ō'd-\ *n comb form, pl* **-odontes** [NL, fr. Gk *odontes,* pl. of *odōn* tooth — more at TOOTH] **:** animal or animals having teeth of a (specified) nature — in names of zoological taxa ⟨Gymnodontes⟩ ⟨Priodontes⟩

odon·tia \ō'dänch(ē)ə\ *n, cap* [NL, fr. *odont-* + *-ia;* fr. its conical spines] **:** a widely distributed genus of fungi (family Hydnaceae) including some that are pathogens of economic plants — see STELLATE-CRYSTAL FUNGUS

1**-o·don·tia** \ə'dänch(ē)ə, ō'd-\ *n comb form, pl* **-odontia** [NL, fr. Gk *odont-, odōn* tooth] **:** animal or animals having teeth of a (specified) nature — in taxonomic names in zoology ⟨Anomodontia⟩ ⟨Aplodontia⟩ ⟨Dicynodontia⟩

2**-odontia** \"\ *n comb form* -s [NL, fr. *odont-* + *-ia*] **:** form, condition, or mode of treatment of the teeth ⟨macrodontia⟩ ⟨saprodontia⟩ ⟨orthodontia⟩ — compare -ODONT

odon·ti·a·sis \ˌōˌdän'tīəsəs\ *n, pl* **odontia·ses** \-ˌsēz\ [NL, fr. Gk *odontian* to cut teeth (fr. *odont-, odōn* tooth) + NL *-sis*] **:** cutting of the teeth **:** TEETHING

-odonties *pl of* -ODONTY

odon·ti·tis \ˌōˌdän'tīdəs\ *n, pl* **odon·tit·i·des** \-'tidəˌdēz\ [NL, fr. *odont-* + *-itis*] **:** inflammation of a tooth

odon·to·blast \ō'däntəˌblast\ *n* [ISV *odont-* + *-blast*] **:** one of the elongated radially arranged outer cells of the dental pulp that secrete the dentin of a tooth — **odon·to·blas·tic** \=ˌ==¦blastik\ *adj*

odon·to·cer·i·dae \=ˌ=='serəˌdē\ *n pl, cap* [NL, fr. *Odontocera,* type genus (fr. *odont-* + Gk *keras* horn) + NL *-idae* — more at HORN] **:** a small family of widely distributed caddis flies

1**odon·to·ce·te** \ˌōˌdäntə'sēˌtē\ [NL, fr. *odont-* + L *cete,* pl. of *cetus* whale] *syn of* ODONTOCETI

2**odon·to·cete** \=ˈ==ˌsēt\ *also* **odon·to·ce·tous** \=¦==¦sēdəs\ *adj* **:** of or relating to the Odontoceti

odon·to·ce·ti \=ˌ=='sēˌtī\ *n pl, cap* [NL, fr. *odont-* + L *ceti,* pl. of *cetus* whale — more at CETE] **:** a suborder of Cetacea comprising the toothed whales — compare MYSTICETI

odon·to·clast \=ˈ==ˌklast\ *n* -s [*odont-* + *-clast*] **:** one of the large multinucleate cells that are active during the absorption of the roots of the milk teeth

odon·to·gen·ic \=¦==¦jenik\ *adj* [*odont-* + *-genic*] **1 :** forming or capable of forming teeth ⟨~ tissues⟩ **2 :** containing or arising from odontogenic tissues ⟨an ~ tumor⟩

odon·to·glos·sum \=ˌ=='gläsəm, -lȯs-\ *n* [NL, fr. *odont-* + *-glossum* (fr. Gk *glōssa* tongue) — more at GLOSS] **1** *cap* **:** a large genus of showy tropical American epiphytic orchids having flowers with the tip not spurred and distinct from the column and including many that are cultivated and of great diversity in form and color **2** -s **:** any plant of the genus *Odontoglossum*

odon·tog·na·thae \ˌ=ˌdän'tägnəˌthē\ *n pl, cap* [NL, fr. *odont-* + *-gnathae*] **:** a superorder of extinct toothed birds (subclass Neornithes) — **odon·tog·na·thous** \¦=¦=¦==thəs\ *also* **odon·to·gnath·ic** \ˌōˌdänˌtō¦nathik\ *adj*

odon·to·graph \ō'däntəˌgraf\ *n* [ISV *odont-* + *-graph*] **:** an instrument for marking or laying off the outlines of gear teeth

odon·tog·ra·phy \ˌōˌdän'tägrəfē\ *n* -ES [*odont-* + *-graphy*] **:** scientific description of the teeth (as of their gross structure); *also* **:** a treatise on this subject

1**odon·toid** \ō'dänˌtȯid\ *adj* [Gk *odontoeidēs,* fr. *odont-* + *-oeidēs* -oid] **1 :** having the form of a tooth **:** TOOTHLIKE **2 :** of or relating to the odontoid process

2**odontoid** \"\ *n* -s **:** ODONTOID PROCESS

odontoid ligament *n* **:** any of the three ligaments that pass from the odontoid process to the margins of the foramen magnum

odontoid process *n* **:** a toothlike process that projects from the anterior end of the centrum of the axis vertebra, serves as a pivot on which the atlas vertebra rotates, and is morphologically the centrum of the atlas though detached from that vertebra and more or less perfectly united with the next one behind

odon·tol·cae \ˌōˌdän'tälˌsē\ *n pl, cap* [NL, fr. *odont-* + *-olcae* (fr. Gk *holkos, holkē* furrow) — more at SULCUS] *in some classifications* **:** a superorder of Aves including *Hesperornis* and related genera of extinct aquatic birds with teeth set in a groove

odon·to·lite \ō'däntᵊlˌīt\ *n* -s [F, fr. *odont-* + *-lite*] **:** a mineral consisting of fossil bone or tooth made bright blue by phosphate of iron — called also *bone turquoise, fossil turquoise*

odon·tol·o·gist \ˌōˌdän'täləjəst, ˌäˌd-\ *n* -s **:** a specialist in odontology

odon·tol·o·gy \-jē, -ji\ *n* -ES [F *odontologie,* fr. *odont-* + *-logie* -logy] **:** a science that treats of the teeth, their structure and development, and their diseases

odon·to·lox·ia \ˌōˌdäntə'läksēə\ *n* -s [NL, fr. *odont-* + Gk *loxos* slanting, crosswise + NL *-ia*] **:** irregularity of the teeth

odon·to·ma \ˌōˌdän'tōmə, ˌäˌd-\ *n, pl* **odonto·mas** \-məz\ *also* **odontoma·ta** \-mədə\ [NL, fr. *odont-* + *-oma*] **:** a tumor originating from a tooth and containing dental tissue (as enamel, dentin, cementum)

odon·tom·e·ter \-'tämədə(r)\ *n* [*odont-* + *-meter*] **:** ODONTOGRAPH

odon·toph·o·ral \¦=ˌdän¦täf(ə)rəl\ *also* **odon·toph·o·rine** \-fəˌrīn, -ˌrən\ *adj* **:** of or relating to an odontophore

odon·to·phore \ō'däntəˌfō(ə)r\ *n* -s [ISV *odont-* + *-phore*] **1 :** a usu. more or less protrusible structure in the mouths of most mollusks except the bivalves that supports the radula **2 :** RADULA

odon·toph·o·rous \¦=ˌdän¦täf(ə)rəs\ *adj* **:** having an odontophore

odon·toph·o·rus \ˌōˌdän'täf(ə)rəs\ *n, cap* [NL, fr. *odont-* + *-phorus*] **:** a genus of Central and South American crested partridges that resemble quails and are placed in a distinct subfamily of Phasianidae or sometimes isolated in a distinct family

odon·top·te·ris \ˌōˌdän'täptərəs\ *n, cap* [NL, fr. *odont-* + Gk *pteris* fern; akin to Gk *pteron* wing, feather — more at FEATHER] **:** a genus of fossil seed ferns found in the coal measures of the Carboniferous that have pinnatifid fronds with indistinct midribs and veins not forming a network

odon·top·ter·yx \-tə(ˌ)riks\ *n, cap* [NL, fr. *odont-* + *-pteryx*] **:** a genus of serrate-jawed totipalmate birds from the Lower Eocene of England

odon·to·rhyn·chous \ō¦däntə¦riŋkəs\ *adj* [*odont-* + *rhynch-* + *-ous*] **:** LAMELLIROSTRAL

odon·tor·mae \ˌōˌdän'tȯr(ˌ)mē\ *n pl, cap* [NL, alter. of *Odontotormae*] *in some classifications* **:** a higher group coextensive with the family Ichthyornithidae

odon·tor·ni·thes \ˌōˌdän·'tȯrnəˌthēz, -ˌtȯr'nī(ˌ)thēz\ *n pl, cap* [NL, fr. *odont-* + Gk *ornithes,* pl. of *ornis* bird — more at ERNE] *in some classifications* **:** a group of Mesozoic toothed birds comprising the Odontolcae and the Odontormae — **odon·tor·nith·ic** \¦=ˌdänˌtȯr¦nithik\ *adj*

odon·to·sis \ˌōˌdän'tōsəs, ˌäˌd-\ *n, pl* **odonto·ses** \-ˌsēz\ [NL, fr. *odont-* + *-sis*] **:** DENTITION

odon·to·syl·lis \ˌōˌdänˌtō+\ *n, cap* [NL, fr. *odont-* + *Syllis*] **:** a genus of polychaete worms (family Syllidae) that are bioluminescent during the breeding period

odon·tot·o·my \ˌōˌdän'tädəmē\ *n* -ES [*odont-* + *-tomy*] **:** the operation of cutting into a tooth

odon·to·tor·mae \ˌōˌdänˌtō'tȯr(ˌ)mē\ [NL, fr. *odont-* + *-tormae* (fr. Gk *tormos* socket) — more at TERM] *syn of* ODONTORMAE

-o·don·ty \əˌdäntē, ōˌd-, -ti\ *n comb form* -ES [*odont-* + *-y*] **:** condition of having a (specified) type of tooth formation — chiefly in terms employed in anthropometry ⟨selenodonty⟩

odor \'ōdə(r)\ *n* -s *see -or in Explan Notes* [ME *odour,* fr. OF, fr. L *odor;* akin to L *olēre* to smell, Gk *ozein* to smell, *odmē, osmē* smell, odor, Lith *uosti* to smell, and perh. to Sw *os* odor, ill-smelling gas] **1 a :** a quality of something that affects the sense of smell **:** SCENT, FRAGRANCE, AROMA ⟨one ... system classifies all ~*s* according to six fundamental sensations or combinations of sensations: namely, spicy, flowery, fruity, resinous, foul and burnt —F.J.Gruber⟩ **b :** one of a class of sensations resulting from adequate chemical stimulation of the receptors for the sense of smell **:** SMELL ⟨emit an ~⟩ ⟨a sweet ~⟩ ⟨a disagreeable ~⟩ ⟨the ~ of a bakery —William Black⟩ ⟨the penetrating, acid ~ of hardwood smoke —Rufus Jarman⟩ ⟨a new ~ ... the sweet, intense smell of overripe fruit —William Beebe⟩ **2 a :** a characteristic or predominant quality **:** FLAVOR ⟨the ~ of earnestness is not good for melodrama —E.R.Bentley⟩ ⟨an ~ of ... unsavory politics —G.F. Cronkhite⟩ ⟨a faint ~ of romance —*Nation*⟩ **b :** REPUTE, ESTIMATION ⟨another ... committee in equally bad ~ as regards the propriety of its procedures —R.D.Leigh⟩ **3** *archaic* **:** something (as incense, spice, a flower) that emits a sweet or pleasing scent **:** PERFUME ⟨throw in ... all sorts of spices and sweet ~*s* —James Maxwell⟩ **syn** see SMELL

1**odor·ant** \'ōdərənt\ *adj* [ME *odoraunt,* fr. MF *odorant,* fr. L *odorant-, odorans,* pres. part. of *odorare* to perfume, fr. *odor,* n.] **:** ODOROUS, ODORIFEROUS

2**odorant** \"\ *n* -s **:** an odorous substance ⟨~*s* used as warning agents in natural gas⟩

odor·ate \-rət\ *adj* [L *odoratus,* past part. of *odorare*] *archaic* **:** SCENTED

odored \'ōdə(r)d\ *adj* **:** having an odor **:** SCENTED — used chiefly in combination ⟨ill-odored⟩

odo·ri \ō'dȯrˌē\ *n* -s [Jap, dancing, dance] **:** any lively Japanese folk or theater dance characterized by rapid footwork — distinguished from *mai*

odor·if·er·ous \ˌōdə¦rif(ə)rəs\ *adj* [L *odorifer* odoriferous (fr. *odor* + *-i-* + *-fer* -ferous) + E *-ous* — more at ODOR] **1 :** bearing or yielding an odor **:** ODOROUS ⟨the constituents of perfumes ... the vehicle or solvent, the fixative, and the ~ elements —R.N.Shreve⟩: **a :** sweet-smelling **:** FRAGRANT, BALMY ⟨~ flowers⟩ ⟨~ spices⟩ **b :** ill-smelling **:** MALODOROUS ⟨~ stockyards⟩ ⟨~ fumes⟩ **2 :** morally offensive ⟨~ legislation⟩ — **odor·if·er·ous·ly** *adv* — **odor·if·er·ous·ness** *n* -ES

odor·im·e·ter \ˌōdə'rimədə(r)\ *n* [*odor* + *-i-* + *-meter*] **:** ODOROMETER

odor·im·e·try \-mətrē\ *n* -ES [ISV *odor* + *-i-* + *-metry*] **:** the measurement of the intensity of odors

odor·i·phore \ō'dȯrəˌfō(ə)r\ *n* -s [*odor* + *-i-* + *-phore*] **:** OSMOPHORE

odor·i·vec·tor \-ˌvektə(r)\ *n* [*odor* + *-i-* + L *vector* bearer — more at VECTOR] **:** a substance that gives rise to an odor

odor·iza·tion \ˌōdərə'zāshən, -ˌrī'z-\ *n* -s **:** the act or process of odorizing ⟨*reodorization* of rubber and leather articles —A.C.Morrison⟩; *esp* **:** the act or process of odorizing gas ⟨odor tests should be made on the gas at the point of ~ —*Chem. Abstracts*⟩

odor·ize \'ōdəˌrīz\ *vt* -ED/-ING/-s [*odor* + *-ize*] **:** to make odorous **:** SCENT, PERFUME ⟨~ a room⟩ ⟨~ industrial products to mask bad smells⟩; *specif* **:** to add a characteristic detectable odor to (a relatively odorless domestic fuel gas) as a safety measure ⟨some city and state utility regulatory bodies have made it mandatory to ~ natural, propane, and butane gases supplied in their territories —H.A.Gollamer⟩

odor·less \'ōdə(r)ləs\ *adj* **:** lacking an odor **:** INODOROUS, SCENTLESS ⟨~ gas⟩ ⟨~ flowers⟩

odorless phosphate *n* **:** BASIC SLAG

odor of sanctity [trans. of ML *odor sanctitatis*] **1 :** a fragrance held to proceed from the person, clothing, or domicile of a saint during life or after death ⟨died in the *odor of sanctity* and ... was canonized —Charles Speroni⟩ **2 a :** an appearance of or reputation for goodness and righteousness ⟨the *odor of sanctity* that seemed to cling about his every utterance —Kenneth Roberts⟩ **b :** SANCTIMONIOUSNESS

odor·om·e·ter \ˌōdə'rämədə(r)\ *n* [*odor* + *-o-* + *-meter*] **:** an instrument for measuring the intensity of odors of substances in varying concentrations in air — compare OSMOSCOPE

odor·o·phore \ō'dȯrəˌfō(ə)r\ *n* -s [*odor* + *-o-* + *-phore*] **:** a substance that produces an odor **:** ODORANT

odor·ous \'ōdərəs\ *adj* [L *odorus,* fr. *odor,* n.] **:** having or emitting an odor **:** SCENTED ⟨~ materials ... captured by the mucous lining of the nostrils —F.A.Geldard⟩: as **a :** FRAGRANT ⟨the ~ air of the orchard —H.W.Longfellow⟩ ⟨~ gums from the East —Oscar Wilde⟩ ⟨fresh, moist, ~ bread —Della Lutes⟩ **b :** MALODOROUS ⟨grievances of the men ... salt junk and weevily hardtack —H.A.Chippendale⟩ — **odor·ous·ly** *adv*

odorous house ant *or* **odorous ant** *n* **:** a common No. American ant (*Tapinoma sessile*) that emits a characteristic odor and that frequently invades buildings

odors *pl of* ODOR

odour \'ōdə(r)\ *chiefly Brit var of* ODOR

ods *pl of* OD

ODs *pl of* OD

ods–bobs \(')ädz'bäbz\ *interj, often cap* [prob. euphemism for *God's body*] *archaic* — a mild oath

ods·bod·i·kins \(')ädz'bädəkənz, -dēk-\ *also* **ods bodkins** \-'bädkənz\ *interj, often cap* [prob. euphemism for *God's bodykins*] *archaic* — a mild oath

ods·bud \-'bəd\ *also* **od's–buds** *interj, often cap* [euphemism for *God's blood*] *archaic* — a mild oath

odsfish *often cap, var of* ODDS FISH

od·so \'äd¦sō\ *interj, sometimes cap* [euphemism for obs. *Godso,* by folk etymology fr. It *cazzo,* lit., penis — more at CATSO] — used typically as a mild oath or as an expression of surprise

odum \ō'düm\ *n* -s [native name in western Africa] **:** IROKO

-o·dus \ədəs\ *n comb form* [NL *-odont-, -odus,* fr. Gk *odont-, odous* tooth — more at TOOTH] **:** animal having teeth of a (specified) kind — in generic names in zoology ⟨Gyrodus⟩

-o·dy \ˌōdē, -di\ *n comb form* -ES [Gk *-ōdia,* fr. *-ōdēs* -ode + *-ia* -y] **:** process of becoming like **:** metamorphosis into (something specified) — chiefly in botanical terms ⟨sepalody⟩

od·yl *or* **od·yle** \'ädᵊl, 'ōd-\ *n* -s [ISV 2*od* + Gk *hylē* forest, wood, material — more at -YL] **:** OD

odyl·ic \(')ō¦dilik\ *adj* **:** of or relating to odyl

odylic force *n* **:** OD

od·yl·ism \'ädᵊlˌizəm, 'ōd-\ *n* -s **:** the theory of od

od·y·ne·rus \ˌädə'nīrəs\ *n, cap* [NL, fr. Gk *odynēros* painful, fr. *odynē* pain; akin to Gk (Homeric) *edmenai* to eat — more at EAT] **:** a genus of solitary wasps having a very short abdominal peduncle and often resembling yellow jackets in coloration

-o·dyn·ia \ə'dinēə, ō'd-\ *n comb form* -s [NL, fr. Gk, state of pain, fr. *odynē* pain + *-ia* -y] **:** pain ⟨crymodynia⟩ ⟨neurodynia⟩ ⟨omodynia⟩ — **-odyn·ic** \(')ō¦dinik, ə'd-\ *adj comb form*

od·ys·se·an \¦ädə¦sēən\ *adj, usu cap* [*Odyssey* + E *-an*] **:** of, relating to, or having the characteristics of Homer's *Odyssey*

od·ys·sey \'ädəsē, -si\ *n* -s [fr. the *Odyssey,* long epic poem recounting the adventures of Odysseus on his way home from the siege of Troy and attributed to Homer, Greek poet who prob. lived *ab* 8th cent. B.C., fr. L *Odyssea,* fr. Gk *Odysseia,* fr. *Odysseus,* its hero + Gk *-ia* -y] **1 a :** a long wandering **:** a series of adventurous journeys usu. marked by many changes of fortune ⟨the journey of these unwilling adventurers . . . is certainly one of the strangest ~s in modern fiction —James Stern⟩ ⟨his ~ up and down the land as a journeyman printer —W.A.White⟩ ⟨the ~ of man through time —*Think*⟩ **2 :** an extensive intellectual or spiritual wandering or quest ⟨everyone's philosophic ~ —Anthony Nemetz⟩ ⟨the course of his political ~ —Sidney Hook⟩ ⟨the random and voracious reading ~s of your childhood —J.H.Burns⟩ ⟨the emotional ~ of an intelligent and romantic young girl —*Times Lit. Supp.*⟩ ⟨less a historical novel than the story of a spiritual ~ —Ann F. Wolfe⟩

od·zooks \äd'zu̇ks, -üks\ *also* **od·zook·ers** \-kə(r)z\ *interj, sometimes cap* [*od* (euphemism for *God*) + *-zooks* or *-zookers* (origin unknown)] — a mild oath

oe \'ō\ *n* -s [Faroese *óthi*, fr. *óthur* mad, furious, fr. ON *ōthr* — more at WOOD] **:** a violent whirlwind off the Faroe islands

OE *abbr* **1** Old English **2** *often not cap* omissions excepted

oe- or **oeco-** — see EC-

oe·can·thus \ē'kan(t)thəs\ *n, cap* [NL, fr. ²*ec-* + *-anthus*] **:** a genus of Orthoptera that includes the tree crickets

-oe·cia \'ēs(h)ēə\ *n pl comb form* [NL, fr. Gk *oikia* building, house, dwelling, fr. *oikos* house + *-ia* -y — more at VICINITY] **:** plants of a (specified) type — in names of botanical taxa ⟨*Monoecia*⟩ ⟨*Dioecia*⟩

oe·ci·a·cus \ē'sīəkəs\ *n, cap* [NL, fr. Gk *oikiakos* member of a household, fr. *oikiakos* of a house, fr. *oikia* house] **:** a genus of bugs related to the bedbugs and including a parasite (*O. vicarius*) of swallows

oe·cist \'ēsəst\ or **oe·kist** \-kəst\ *n* -s [Gk *oikistēs*, fr. *oikos* house + *-istēs* -ist] **:** COLONIZER

oe·ci·um \'ēs(h)ēəm\ *n, pl* **oe·cia** \-s(h)ēə\ [NL, fr. ²*ec-* + *-ium*] **:** OVICELL

oecoid *var of* ECOID

oecology *var of* ECOLOGY

oe·con·o·mus \ē'känəməs\ *n, pl* **oecono·mi** \-,mī\ [LL, fr. Gk *oikonomos* steward — more at ECONOMY] **:** a steward or manager of the temporalities of a diocese, college, or religious society

¹oe·coph·o·rid \ē'käfərəd\ *adj* [NL *Oecophoridae*] **:** of or relating to the Oecophoridae

²oecophorid \"\ *n* -s **:** a moth of the family Oecophoridae

oe·co·phor·i·dae \,ēkə'fȯrə,dē, fär-\ *n pl, cap* [NL, fr. *Oecophora*, type genus (fr. ²*ec-* + *-phora*) + *-idae*] **:** a large family of small mostly inconspicuous moths whose larvae feed on leaves and flowers

oecumenical *var of* ECUMENICAL

oe·cus \'ēkəs\ *n, pl* **oe·ci** \'ē,sī\ [L, fr. Gk *oikos* house — more at VICINITY] **:** an apartment, room, or hall in an ancient Roman dwelling house

oedema *var of* EDEMA

¹oe·de·me·rid \,ēdə'mirəd\ *adj* [NL *Oedemeridae*] **:** of or relating to the Oedemeridae

²oedemerid \"\ *n* -s [NL *Oedemeridae*] **:** a beetle of the family Oedemeridae

oe·de·mer·i·dae \,==='merə,dē\ *n pl, cap* [NL, fr. *Oedemera*, type genus (fr. Gk *oidein* to swell + *mēros* thigh) + NL *-idae* — more at EDEMA, MEMBER] **:** a family of soft-bodied elongate beetles that have heteromerous tarsi, usu. strikingly colored adults which frequent flowers, and larvae which feed on decaying wood and sometimes are injurious to damp timbers of wharves, bridges, and mines

oe·dic·ne·mus \,ē(,)dik'nēməs\ [NL, *oidi-* (fr. Gk *oidein* to swell) + *-cnemus* (fr. Gk *knēmē* shinbone) — more at HAM] *syn of* BURHINUS

oed·i·pal \'edəpəl, 'ēd-\ *adj, often cap* [*Oedipus (complex)* + *-al*] **:** of, relating to, characterized by, or resulting from the Oedipus complex — **oed·i·pal·ly** \-p(ə)lē, -li\ *adv, often cap*

oed·i·pe·an \,=='pēən\ *adj, usu cap* [*Oedipus*, Theban hero + E *-ean*] **:** of or relating to Oedipus or the Oedipus complex

oed·i·pus \'==pəs\ *adj, usu cap* [*Oedipus (complex)*] **:** OEDIPAL

oedipus complex *also* **oedipus** \"\ *n, pl* **oedipus complexes** *also* **oedipuses** *usu cap O* [G *Ödipuskomplex*, after *Ödipus* (Oedipus), Theban hero of ancient Greek legend who slew his father and married his mother, fr. L *Oedipus*, fr. Gk *Oidipous*] **1 :** the positive esp. libidinal feelings that a child develops usu. between the ages of three and six toward the parent of the opposite sex and that are largely repressed because of the fear of retaliation by the parent of the same sex who is viewed as a rival and toward whom unconscious hostility is generated — used esp. of the male child; see ELECTRA COMPLEX **2 :** the unresolved oedipal feelings persisting into adult life that are conceived as a source of personality disorder

oe·do·go·ni·a·ce·ae \,ēdə,gōnē'āsē,ē\ *n pl, cap* [NL *Oedogonium*, type genus + *-aceae*] **:** a family (usu. coextensive with the order Oedogoniales but sometimes placed in Chaetophorales) of filamentous green algae having a characteristic method of growth that gives rise to series of narrow cells at various intervals in the filaments and developing large zoospores with a crown of cilia and also oogonia and antheridia that are sometimes on the same plant but frequently on separate plants with the male plants being often of only a few cells and attached to the female filaments — **oe·do·go·ni·a·ceous** \==,==;āshəs\ *adj*

oe·do·go·ni·a·les \-'ā(,)lēz\ *n pl, cap* [NL, fr. *Oedogonium* + *-ales*] **:** an order of simple or branched filamentous freshwater green algae (class Chlorophyceae) with zoospores having many flagella and oogamous reproduction

oe·do·go·ni·um \,=='gōnēəm\ *n, cap* [NL, fr. Gk *oidos* swelling, tumor + *gonos* offspring, seed + NL *-ium* — more at ATTER, GON-] **:** a genus (the type of the family Oedogoniaceae) of freshwater green algae that have long unbranched filaments usu. free-floating when mature but attached by special basal cells when young

oeil-de-boeuf \,ərdə'bə(r)f, ¦əd-, ¦əid-, ¦ād-, -bōf, œydəbœf\ *n, pl* **oeils-de-boeuf** \"\ [F, lit., eye of an ox] **:** a circular or oval window

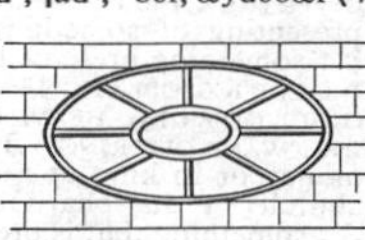

oeil-de-boeuf

oeil·lade \,ə(r)'yäd, ə'y-,əi'y-,ā'y-, œ'yäd\ *n, pl* **oeillades** \-d(z)\ [F, fr. MF, fr. *oeil* eye (fr. L *oculus* eye) + *-ade* — more at EYE] **:** a glance of the eye; *esp* **:** OGLE

oekist *var of* OECIST

oen- or **oeno-** *also* **en-** or **eno-** *comb form* [L *oen-*, *oeno-*, fr. Gk *oin-*, *oino-*, fr. *oinos* — more at WINE] **:** wine ⟨*oenin*⟩ ⟨*oenology*⟩ ⟨*oenopoetic*⟩

oenanthaldehyde *var of* ENANTHALDEHYDE

oenanthate *var of* ENANTHATE

¹oe·nan·the \ē'nan(,)thē\ *n, cap* [NL, fr. L, a kind of dropwort, a bird (perh. the wheatear), fr. Gk *oinanthē*, fr. *oin-* oen- + *anthē* bloom, blossom, fr. *anthos* flower — more at ANTHOLOGY] **:** a genus of Old World herbs (family Umbelliferae) having compound umbels of white flowers without carpophores — see WATER DROPWORT

²oenanthe \"\ *n, cap* [NL, fr. L, a bird (perh. the wheatear)] **:** a small genus of Old World passerine birds comprising the wheatears

¹oe·nan·thic acid \(')ē¦nan(t)thik-\ *n* [ISV *oenanth-* (fr. L *oenanthe* wild grape) + *-ic* — more at ENANTHIC ACID] **:** an acid or mixture of acids obtained by hydrolysis of an oenanthic ester

²oenanthic acid *var of* ENANTHIC ACID

oenanthic ester *also* **oenanthic ether** *n* **1 :** an oily liquid that is obtained in the distillation of wine and that is held to be responsible for the flavor characteristic of wines in general and to consist of a mixture of esters **2 :** the ethyl ester of enanthic acid

oe·ne·is \ē'nēəs\ *n, cap* [NL] **:** a genus of alpine and arctic butterflies belonging to the family Satyridae

oe·nin *also* **enin** \'ēnən\ *n* -s [ISV *oen-* + *-in*; prob. orig. formed as G *önin*] **:** an anthocyanin pigment occurring in the skin of the blue grape and forming a dark red or reddish brown crystalline chloride $C_{23}H_{25}ClO_{12}$

oe·no·car·pus \,ēnə'kärpəs\ *n, cap* [NL, fr. *oen-* + *-carpus*] **:** a genus of So. American pinnate-leaved palms that have a slender spadix which resembles a broom, a woody double caducous spathe, and edible black or purplish oily fruit — see BACABA

oe·noch·oe \ē'näkə(,)wē\ *also* **oi·noch·oe** \ȯi'n-\ *n, pl* **oenocho·es** \-ə,wēz\ or **oenocho·ae** \-ə,wē\ [Gk *oinochoē*, fr. *oino-* oen- + *choē* action of pouring out, drink offering, fr. *cheín* to pour — more at FOUND] **:** an ancient Greek wine pitcher or jug usu. with a trefoil-shaped mouth

oenochoe

oe·no·cyte \'ēnə,sīt\ *n* -s [ISV *oen-* + *-cyte*] **:** one of the large straw-colored cells that are segmentally arranged in connection with the fat bodies and tracheae of most insects and that may have important secretory functions — **oe·no·cyt·ic** \¦==¦sid·ik\ *adj*

oe·no·cy·toid \,=='sī,tȯid\ *n* -s [*oenocyte* + *-oid*] **:** a large blood cell resembling an oenocyte and occurring in insects

oe·nol·o·gist \ē'näləjəst\ *n* -s **1 :** FERMENTOLOGIST **2 :** one versed in enology

oenology *var of* ENOLOGY

oe·no·mel \'ēnə,mel\ *n* -s [LL *oenomeli*, fr. Gk *oinomeli*, fr. *oino-* oen- + *meli* honey — more at MELLIFLUOUS] **1 :** an ancient Greek beverage of wine and honey **2 :** something resembling oenomel ⟨memories to my thinking make a better ~ —Elizabeth B. Browning⟩

oe·no·phile \-,fīl\ or **oe·noph·i·list** \ē'näfələst\ *n* -s [*oen-* + *-phile*, *-philist*] **:** a lover or connoisseur of wine

oe·no·thera \,ēnə'thirə, ē'näthərə\ *n, cap* [NL, fr. L *oenothera*, *onothera*, a plant of the genus *Epilobium*, fr. Gk *oinothēras*, *onothēras*] **:** a genus of mostly No. American annual or biennial herbs (family Onagraceae) having usu. nocturnal yellow flowers with erect buds and terete seeds in two rows in a capsule — see EVENING PRIMROSE, KNEIFFIA

oe·no·therapy \¦ēnə+\ *n* [*oen-* + *therapy*] **:** a use of wine for therapeutic purposes

¹o'er \'ō(ə)r, 'ōə, 'ȯ(ə)r, 'ȯ(ə)\ *adv* [by contr.] **:** OVER

²o'er \"\ *prep* [by contr.] **:** OVER

oer·li·kon \'ərlə,kän\ *n* -s *usu cap* [fr. *Oerlikon*, suburb of Zurich, Switzerland, noted for its gun manufacturing] **:** any of several automatic aircraft or antiaircraft cannon shooting 20 millimeter greased ammunition

oer·sted \'ər,sted\ *n* -s [after Hans Christian *Oersted* †1851 Dan. physicist] **:** the cgs electromagnetic unit of magnetic intensity equal to the intensity of a magnetic field in a vacuum in which a unit magnetic pole experiences a mechanical force of one dyne in the direction of the field — used instead of *gauss* after official adoption in 1932

oes *pl of* O *or of* OE

oesophag- — see ESOPHAG-

oesophageal *var of* ESOPHAGEAL

oesophageal ganglion *n* **:** OCCIPITAL GANGLION

oe·soph·a·go·stome \ə'säfəgə,stōm, ē's-\ *n* -s [NL *Oesophagostomum*] **:** a nematode worm of the genus *Oesophagostomum*

oe·soph·a·go·sto·mi·a·sis \=,==(,)gōstə'mīəsəs\ *n, pl* **oesophagostomiases** [NL, fr. *Oesophagostomum* + *-iasis*] **:** infestation with or disease caused by nematode worms of the genus *Oesophagostomum* **:** NODULAR DISEASE

oe·soph·a·gos·to·mum \=,=='gästəməm\ *n, cap* [NL, fr. *esophag-* + *-stomum*] **:** a genus of nematode worms (family Strongylidae) comprising the nodular worms of ruminants and swine and other worms affecting primates including man, esp. in Africa

oesophagus *var of* ESOPHAGUS

oestradiol *var of* ESTRADIOL

oes·trel·a·ta \e'streləd·ə, ē's-\ [NL, fr. Gk *oistrēlatos* driven by a gadfly, fr. *oistros* gadfly + *-elatos* (fr. *elan* to drive) — more at IRE, ELASTIC] *syn of* PTERODROMA

oes·tri·a·sis \e'strīəsəs, ē's-\ *n, pl* **oestria·ses** \-,sēz\ [NL, fr. ¹*Oestrus* + *-iasis*] **:** infestation with or disease caused by botflies of the genus *Oestrus*

¹oes·trid \'estrəd, 'ēs-\ *adj* [NL *Oestridae*] **:** of or relating to the Oestridae

²oestrid \"\ *n* -s **:** a fly of the family Oestridae

oes·tri·dae \-trə,dē\ *n pl, cap* [NL, fr. ²*Oestrus*, type genus + *-idae*] **:** a family of two-winged flies consisting of the botflies and formerly including also the warble flies

oestrin *var of* ESTRIN

oestriol *var of* ESTRIOL

oestrogen *var of* ESTROGEN

oestrone *var of* ESTRONE

oes·tro·scope \'estrə,skōp, 'ēs-\ *n* [²*oestrus* + *-o-* + *-scope*] **:** a device for determining the existence of estrus in cattle by measuring the viscosity of the cervical mucus

oestrous or **oestral** or **oestrual** *var of* ESTROUS

oestruation *var of* ESTRUATION

¹oes·trus \'estrəs, 'ēs-\ *n* [L, gadfly, fr. Gk *oistros* gadfly, desire, frenzy — more at IRE] **1** -ES *archaic* **:** a biting or tormenting fly **2** *cap* [NL, fr. L] **:** the type genus of *Oestridae* comprising the sheep botfly

²oestrus or **oestrum** *var of* ESTRUS

oeu·vre \'ə(r)v(rᵊ), 'əv-, -vrə, F œvr(ᵊ) or -v(rə)\ *n, pl* **oeuvres** \"\ [F *œuvre* work (something produced by labor), fr. L *opera*, fr. pl. of *opus* work — more at OPERATE] **:** a substantial body of work constituting the lifework of a writer, an artist, or a composer ⟨even without an ~, some dramatists can effect a satisfying unity and significance of pattern in single plays —T.S.Eliot⟩ ⟨the ~ of one and the same painter sometimes is divided into two strata —Wolfgang Born⟩ ⟨the most popular of all the music in the Wagnerian ~ —P.H.Lang⟩

¹of \,əv; *esp before a consonant* -,ə; *after an unstressed or lightly stressed vowel sometimes* v (*as in* t͟həsīdēəvābz *for "this idea of Abe's"*) *or, before a voiceless consonant,* f (*as in* t͟həsīdēəftämz *for "this idea of Tom's"*) *or, before* f, *without pronunciation* (*as in* t͟həsīdēəfredz *for "this idea of Fred's"*); *when emphatic, as when it is the last or the first word in a sentence,* ¦əv *or* ¦äv\ *prep* [ME, of, off, fr. OE (also adv.), away, off]; akin to OHG *aba*, prep., off, away from, & adv., off, away, down, ON *af*, prep., off, from, Goth *af* from, away from, since, L *ab* from, Gk *apo* away from, off, Skt *apa* away, off] **1** *obs* — used as a function word to indicate the place or thing from which anything moves, comes, goes, or is directed or impelled ⟨with the least drawing blood ~ another —Samuel Purchas⟩ **2** *archaic* — used as a function word to indicate an anterior condition from which a transition has been made ⟨I, ~ brute, human; ye, ~ human, gods —John Milton⟩ **3 :** at an interval or in a direction with respect to — used to indicate something from which position or reckoning is defined ⟨north ~ the lake⟩ ⟨the arrow went wide ~ the mark⟩ ⟨passed within a foot ~ the rock⟩ ⟨waited upwards ~ an hour⟩ ⟨within a few hours ~ birth⟩ ⟨I know you ~ old, you don't fool me⟩ **4** — used as a function word to indicate something from which a person or thing is delivered ⟨cured him ~ being late⟩ ⟨eased ~ her pain⟩ ⟨rid the barn ~ rats⟩ or with respect to which someone or something is made destitute ⟨robbed ~ his sleep⟩ ⟨stripped ~ all his titles⟩ ⟨relieved ~ his command⟩ **5 a :** from by birth or descent ⟨born ~ a royal house⟩ ⟨he is ~ a well-to-do family⟩ **b :** from as the place of birth, production, or distribution **:** having as its base of operation, point of initiation, or source of issuance or derivation ⟨~ or relating to Italy, its language, or its people⟩ **c :** from as cause or occasion **:** in regard to ⟨I wish him joy ~ her —Shak.⟩ ⟨vote yes . . . because they are frightened ~ their skins —John Gunther⟩ **d :** from as possessor, seller, loser, giver ⟨buy our eggs ~ a farmer⟩ ⟨held his lands ~ the duke⟩ **e :** from as one that is looked to for something ⟨asked a favor ~ me⟩ ⟨too much to expect ~ a child⟩ **f :** from undergoing or coping with — used with *it* ⟨had a hard time ~ it at school⟩ ⟨make a good job ~ it⟩ **6** — used as a function word to indicate the cause, motive, or reason by which a person or thing is actuated or impelled ⟨die ~ shame⟩ ⟨this milk tastes ~ garlic⟩ ⟨dead ~ violence⟩ ⟨afraid ~ his own shadow⟩ ⟨went ~ their own free will⟩ ⟨did it ~ necessity⟩ **7** — used as a function word to indicate the agent or doer of an act or action (1) archaically after such participles as *loved*, *ordained*, *forgotten* ⟨despised and rejected ~ men —Isa 53:3 (AV)⟩, (2) after an adjective or adjective phrase characterizing the act or conduct ⟨it was kind ~ him to offer it⟩, and (3) after a noun indicating the maker or doer often with the force of a subjective genitive ⟨plays ~ Shakespeare⟩ ⟨the mercy ~ the Lord⟩ ⟨the ruins ~ time⟩ **8** *archaic* — used as a function word to indicate the means or instrument by which an action is carried out ⟨it is pouring ~ rain⟩ ⟨pave it ~ gold⟩ **9** — used as a function word to indicate the material, parts, or elements composing something or the contents held by something ⟨throne ~ gold⟩ ⟨company ~ 20 men⟩ ⟨distance ~ five miles⟩ ⟨genus ~ mammals⟩ ⟨cup ~ water⟩ **10 a** — used as a function word to indicate a particular example belonging to the class denoted by the preceding noun ⟨the city ~ Rome⟩ ⟨month ~ August⟩ ⟨goes under the name ~ charity⟩ ⟨the crime ~ murder⟩ **b** — used as a function word to indicate simple or definitional apposition ⟨great barn ~ a house⟩ ⟨that fool ~ a husband⟩ ⟨jewel ~ a woman⟩ **11 :** relating to **:** with reference to **:** as regards **:** ABOUT ⟨stories ~ his travels⟩ ⟨the truth ~ the matter⟩ ⟨judge ~ the case⟩ ⟨dreaming ~ home⟩ ⟨think ~ a way out⟩ ⟨complaining ~ the heat⟩ ⟨test ~ skill⟩ **12** — used as a function word indicating the object of an action denoted or implied by the preceding noun ⟨love ~ nature⟩ ⟨care ~ children⟩ ⟨creation ~ the world⟩ ⟨the polishing ~ a diamond⟩ ⟨pursuit ~ happiness⟩ ⟨knowledge ~ the past⟩ **13** — used as a function word (1) idiomatically after some adjectives implying action or process or perception ⟨fruitful ~ results⟩ ⟨sparing ~ words⟩ ⟨greedy ~ gain⟩ ⟨neglectful ~ his duties⟩ or (2) chiefly dial. after verbs and participles ⟨felt ~ his head⟩ ⟨ever trying ~ something new —Adrian Bell⟩ ⟨stop pestering ~ your father⟩ **14 :** in respect to ⟨slow ~ speech⟩ ⟨light ~ step⟩ ⟨forty years ~ age⟩ ⟨problems difficult ~ solution⟩ **15** — used as a function word to indicate a quality or possession characterizing or distinguishing a subject ⟨a fellow ~ infinite jest —Shak.⟩ ⟨men ~ goodwill⟩ ⟨persons ~ refinement⟩ ⟨boy ~ ten years⟩; used with *all* to indicate a temporary quality or condition ⟨all ~ a tremble⟩ ⟨all ~ a sweat⟩; used with a following noun denoting or implying action usu. with a possessive ⟨wine ~ choice⟩ ⟨rulers ~ their own choosing⟩ ⟨girl ~ his dreams⟩ ⟨boat ~ his own design⟩ **16 a** — used as a function word indicating the aggregate or whole that includes the part or quantity denoted by the preceding word ⟨most ~ the army⟩ ⟨many ~ those present⟩ ⟨ton ~ coal⟩ ⟨three glasses ~ beer⟩ ⟨first years ~ life⟩ **b** — used as a function word to indicate a whole or quantity from which some is removed or expended by the action of the preceding verb ⟨gave generously ~ his time⟩ ⟨partook ~ the morning meal⟩ **17 a** — used as a function word indicating a possessive relationship ⟨gates ~ heaven⟩ ⟨courage ~ the pioneers⟩ ⟨lateness ~ the hour⟩ ⟨cube ~ six⟩ ⟨member ~ parliament⟩ or close association in time ⟨in the days ~ the Roman emperors⟩ ⟨knights ~ yore⟩; used often with a following possessive ⟨a friend ~ mine⟩ ⟨an acquaintance ~ the colonel's⟩ ⟨through no fault ~ his⟩ **b** — used as a function word to indicate such relationships as ruler and subject, owner and property ⟨king ~ England⟩ ⟨Mary ~ Scotland⟩ ⟨chiefs ~ state⟩ ⟨captain ~ Company A⟩ ⟨head ~ the household⟩ **18** — used as a function word to indicate a point or space in time relating either to a single or to a usual action or occurrence ⟨he died ~ a Monday⟩ ⟨likes to visit a bar ~ an evening⟩ ⟨plays golf ~ a Sunday⟩ **19** — used as a function word indicating position before the clock hour ⟨ten minutes ~ eight⟩ ⟨twenty-five ~ five⟩ ⟨quarter ~ ten⟩ **20 a** *now dial* **:** ON ⟨a plague ~ all cowards —Shak.⟩ ⟨fell flat ~ his back in the grass —F.B.Gipson⟩ **b** *chiefly Brit* **:** IN ⟨continue her full membership ~ the Commonwealth —*Brit. Information Services*⟩ **c** *chiefly dial* **:** WITH ⟨what's the matter ~ her⟩

²of \,ə(v)\ *verbal auxiliary* [by alter.] **:** HAVE — used esp. in written dialogue to represent a supposed dial. or substand. speech ⟨meant to ~ written you —Christopher La Farge⟩ ⟨hadn't ought to ~ fooled with figures —Delos Avery⟩ ⟨told you we should ~ quit —William English⟩

OF *abbr* **1** Old French **2** oxidizing flame

ofay \'(')ō¦fā\ *n* -s [origin unknown] **:** a white person ⟨stays in Harlem and learns to hate ~s —*New Republic*⟩

ofc *abbr* office

ofcl *abbr* official

ofcr *abbr* officer

¹off \'ȯf *also* 'äf\ *adv* [ME *of*, fr. OE — more at OF] **1 a :** from a place or position ⟨march ~⟩ ⟨fly ~⟩ ⟨send a letter ~⟩; *specif* **:** in a direction away from land ⟨ship stood ~ to sea⟩ **b :** so as to prevent close approach ⟨drove the dogs ~⟩ ⟨fighting ~ drowsiness⟩ ⟨buy ~ an enemy⟩ **c :** from a course **:** in a slanting or oblique direction **:** ASIDE ⟨turned ~ into a bypath⟩ ⟨veered ~ to avoid collision⟩ ⟨his drive fell ~ to the left of the green⟩; *specif* **:** away from the wind ⟨ship eased ~ a point or two⟩ **d :** into an unconscious state **:** into sleep ⟨dozed ~ for a while⟩ ⟨must have dropped ~⟩ **2 :** to a state or condition of separateness **:** so as not to be supported ⟨rolled to the edge of the table and ~⟩ or covering or enclosing ⟨blew the lid ~⟩ ⟨took his coat ~⟩ or attached ⟨the handle came ~⟩ ⟨peeled ~ the skin⟩ ⟨married ~ two daughters⟩ or united ⟨surface marked ~ into squares⟩ **3 a :** to a state of discontinuance ⟨shut ~ an engine⟩ ⟨turn ~ the water⟩ ⟨break ~ a conversation⟩ or exhaustion ⟨drain ~ excess fluid⟩ ⟨drink ~ a glass at one draft⟩ or completion ⟨the weather has cleared ~⟩ ⟨coat of paint to finish it ~⟩ ⟨smooth ~ the corners⟩ ⟨sweep ~ the porch steps⟩ ⟨rattle ~ a string of clichés⟩ ⟨run ~ a series of racing heats⟩ ⟨play ~ a tie⟩ **b :** into a state of relief resulting from an orgasm ⟨go ~⟩ ⟨dream ~⟩ — not often in formal use **4 :** in absence from or suspension of regular work or service ⟨take time ~ for lunch⟩ ⟨ask for a day ~⟩ **5 :** at a distance in space or time ⟨stood ten paces ~⟩ ⟨Christmas is only two weeks ~⟩ ⟨lives ~ in the hills⟩ **6 :** OFFSTAGE ⟨turns and goes ~ left⟩ ⟨knocking is heard ~⟩ **7** *substand* — used as a function word with *and* to express abruptness or unexpectedness or directness of an action ⟨he ~ and bought a whole new outfit⟩ ⟨~ and busted him in the jaw⟩; compare HAUL OFF — **off with** — used interjectionally to express a command or exhortation that something be taken off or away or cast aside ⟨*off with* the old, on with the new⟩ ⟨*off with* his head⟩

²off \"\ *prep* [ME *of* — more at OF] **1 a** — used as a function word to indicate a supporting surface or a position of rest, attachment, or union from which separation is made ⟨take it ~ the table⟩ ⟨eat ~ a plate⟩ ⟨bullet glanced ~ the wall⟩ ⟨took the property ~ his hands⟩ ⟨cut two yards ~ the roll of cloth⟩ **b :** down from ⟨stepped ~ the train⟩ **2 a :** from the charge or possession of ⟨bought it ~ a wandering peddler⟩ ⟨had his wallet stolen ~ him⟩ **b :** from as a source of supply **:** at the expense of ⟨lived ~ the county⟩ ⟨lived ~ his sister⟩ ⟨got two runs ~ the first pitcher⟩ ⟨made his living ~ the tourists⟩ ⟨liked the money he made ~ it —Will Rogers b.1911⟩ **c :** so as to consume ⟨dined ~ oysters and champagne⟩ **3 :** to seaward of ⟨two miles ~ shore⟩ **4** — used as a function word to indicate something that one has been but is not now partaking of, occupied with, or engaged upon ⟨~ duty⟩ ⟨recently gone ~ smoking⟩ **5 a** — used as a function word to indicate a standard or level from which there is a reduction or falling away ⟨~ his usual tennis form⟩ ⟨fifteen percent ~ the list price⟩ ⟨two seconds ~ the track record⟩ **b :** diverging from (a main course) ⟨two points ~ the wind⟩ ⟨~ center⟩ ⟨~ balance⟩ ⟨kept getting ~ the subject⟩ ⟨got ~ the route at the park⟩ ⟨a street opening ~ the avenue⟩ **:** situated or occurring apart from (a principal place or proceeding) ⟨little shop just ~ Main Street⟩ ⟨speaking ~ the record⟩ — used often in combination ⟨*off*-Broadway play⟩ ⟨talks . . . to imaginary people that are carefully *off*-camera —*Newsweek*⟩ — **off the mark** *adv (or adj)* **:** away from the main point or focal center

³off \"\ *adj* [¹*off*] **1 a :** more removed or distant **:** opposite to the main part or side ⟨went round to the ~ side of the building⟩ ⟨the ~ side of the medal was blank⟩ **b :** situated to one side **:** not main or principal ⟨~ street⟩ ⟨~ branch of the river⟩ **c :** being on the side away from the shore **:** SEAWARD ⟨keeping the buoy on her ~ side⟩ **d :** being or relating to the side of an animal, team, or vehicle that is farther from the driver as he walks or rides at his mounts **:** RIGHT ⟨~ horse in a team⟩ ⟨~ leg⟩ ⟨~ wheel⟩ — opposed to *near* **e :** of or relating to the side of the cricket field opposite to that on which the batsman stands ⟨an ~ hit⟩ ⟨an ~ play⟩ ⟨an ~ stroke⟩ **2 a :** set in motion **:** started on the way ⟨~ on one of his tirades⟩ ⟨~ on a spree⟩ **b :** not taking place or staying in effect ⟨the picnic is ~⟩ ⟨in case of a tie all bets are ~⟩ **c** *bridge* **:** having lost or destined to lose ⟨the spade finesse was ~⟩ **d :** off side (sense 3) **e :** not flowing **:** checked from flowing by a closed valve or opened switch ⟨repairs made while the current is ~⟩ ⟨the lever is in the ~ position⟩ ⟨hot water is ~⟩ **f** *of a braking device* **:** not applied **:** RELEASED,

INOPERATIVE **3 a :** not corresponding to fact **:** divergent or erring from a true line or exact figure ⟨~ in his reckoning⟩ ⟨your guesses are way ~⟩ **b :** not being up to normal condition or usual efficiency **:** not being at one's best ⟨every performer has his ~ days⟩ **c :** not entirely sane **:** mentally unstable **:** ODD, ECCENTRIC ⟨the poor fellow is a little ~⟩ ⟨psychiatrists . . . understand that a person can be ~ on one topic and fully normal in others —Ruth P. Randall⟩ **d :** REMOTE, SLIGHT ⟨only an ~ chance of his being right⟩ **e :** not familiar or well-known **:** not well advertised ⟨suspicious of ~ brands⟩ **4 a :** taken or spent off duty or in relaxation ⟨reading on his ~ days⟩ **b :** marked by a falling off or by less than ordinary activity or productiveness or amount of business **:** SLACK ⟨~ season in European travel⟩ **5 a :** slightly tinged with some or another hue or with gray ⟨~ shades⟩ ⟨an ~ kind of blue —C. B.Kelland⟩ **b :** being of inferior quality ⟨~ grade of oil⟩ **:** detracting from quality ⟨trying to keep butter free from any ~ odors⟩; *also* **:** TAINTED ⟨this cream is ~⟩ **c :** being at a lower level ⟨industrial stocks were 1.12 points ~ for the day⟩ ⟨railroad traffic was ~ 5 percent⟩ — opposed to *up* **d** *of a racetrack* **:** not being in good condition **:** not fast ⟨ran his best races on ~ tracks⟩ **e** *of a bridge hand* **:** short of the ideal or normal requirement ⟨~ by two aces⟩ **6 :** having completed a pressrun whether or not removed from the press ⟨form is ~⟩ **7 :** conditioned or circumstanced esp. as to material welfare ⟨not rich but comfortably ~⟩ ⟨thought he was just as well ~ without a wife⟩ ⟨the house was badly ~ for paint⟩ **8** *of an animal's age* **:** more than a specified number of years ⟨a mare four ~ but not yet rising five⟩ **9 :** relating to the sale of liquor that is to be consumed away from the premises ⟨an ~ license⟩

⁴off \"\ *vb* -ED/-ING/-S [¹*off*] *vt* **:** to take off **:** DOFF **~** *vi* **1** *of a ship* **:** to move away from shore **:** start out to sea **2 a :** to go away **:** DEPART — used chiefly as an imperative ⟨~, or I shoot⟩ **b :** to get or be off — used chiefly as an imperative ⟨~, ye lendings —Shak.⟩

⁵off \"\ *n* -S [³*off*] **1 :** the condition or state of being off ⟨their engagement had its ~*s* and ons⟩ **2 :** the side of a cricket field bisected by a straight line passing through both middle stumps from boundary to boundary opposite to that on which the batsman stands — compare LEG, ON; see CRICKET illustration

off *abbr* **1** offered **2** office; officer; official **3** officinal

of·fal \ˈȯfəl, ˈäf-\ *n* -S [ME, fr. *of* off + *fal, fall* fall — more at OFF, FALL] **1 :** material that is left as waste or by-product of a process of preparation or manufacture: as **a :** the stalks and dust from tobacco leaves **b :** less valuable portions (as the belly, head, and shoulders) of a hide **c :** the by-products of milling (as of wheat or barley) used esp. for stock feed **d :** the parts of a butchered animal that are removed in dressing, that consist largely of the viscera (as brain, heart, sweetbreads, liver) and the trimmings (as tail, hooves, blood, skin, head meat), and that are used as edible products or as raw material in the manufacture of by-products **e :** small or inferior or unmarketable fish **2 a :** a dead or slaughtered animal or parts of it considered inedible by nature or through tainting **:** CARRION **b :** something thrown away as worthless **:** RUBBISH, GARBAGE **c :** worthless, vicious, or outcast persons ⟨~ of the jails and brothels —T.B.Macaulay⟩ **syn** see REFUSE

of·fa·ly \ˈäfəlē, -li\ *adj, usu cap* [fr. County *Offaly*, Ireland] **:** of or from County Offaly, Ireland **:** of the kind or style prevalent in County Offaly

off and on *adv* **1 :** with interruptions or intermissions **:** INTERMITTENTLY ⟨the war lasted *off and on* for thirty years⟩ ⟨rained *off and on* all evening⟩ **2 :** on different tacks alternately toward and away from the land ⟨the ship stood *off and on* until morning⟩

off–axis reflector \(ˈ)ˌ=ˌ==-\ *n* **:** HERSCHELIAN TELESCOPE

off–balance \ˈ=ˌ==\ *adj (or adv)* **1 :** not well proportioned **:** out of balance ⟨the plans are *off-balance*⟩ ⟨their military is *off-balance*⟩ **2 :** not standing, sitting, or resting in normal physical equilibrium ⟨caught *off-balance* and knocked down —Jack Dempsey⟩ **3 a :** upset from or in a state of being upset by confusion **:** UPSETTING ⟨the *off-balance* presentation of alternatives —S.L.Payne⟩ ⟨keep us *off-balance*⟩ **b :** into a state of surprise from the unexpected ⟨may turn us momentarily *off-balance* by saying one thing when he means another —R.B.West⟩

off–bar \ˈ=ˌ=\ *vb* **:** to bar off

off–bear \ˈ=ˌ=\ *vt* **:** to take away (as bricks from a molding bench or boards or slabs from a saw)

off–bearer \ˈ=ˌ==\ *n* **:** a worker who removes partly processed or completed products from a machine, conveyor belt, power saw, or other equipment and piles them, packs them, or trucks them away

¹offbeat \ˈ=ˌ=\ *n* [³*off* + *beat*] **:** the part of a musical measure other than the principally accented one — compare DOWNBEAT

²offbeat \ˈ=ˌ=\ *adj* [fr. the phrase *off beat*] **:** diverging from the main stream of current fashion **:** UNCONVENTIONAL, UNORTHODOX ⟨~ advertising⟩ ⟨~ style of comedy⟩

off–board \ˈ=ˌ=\ *adj* **:** OVER-THE-COUNTER ⟨*off-board* market for securities⟩

offbreak \ˈ=ˌ=\ *n* **:** a bowled ball in cricket that breaks from the off side to the leg side

¹offcast \ˈ=ˌ=\ *adj* [¹*off* + *cast*, past part. of *cast* (after *cast off*)] **:** cast off **:** DISCARDED, REJECTED

²offcast \"\ *n* **:** CASTOFF

off–center \ˈ=ˈ==\ *or* **off–centered** \ˈ=ˈ==\ *adj* **1 :** having an axis (as of rotation or equilibrium) deviating from the geometrical center ⟨*off-center* revolving disk⟩ ⟨*off-center* placing of a letterhead⟩ ⟨an *off-centered* postage stamp⟩ **2 :** not entirely normal or sound **:** not perfectly balanced **:** ECCENTRIC ⟨suspicion that existentialism is *off-center*, that it has elevated experiences that all of us have occasionally into permanent and decisive qualities of life —Charles Frankel⟩

off–color \ˈ=ˈ==\ *or* **off–colored** \ˈ=ˈ==\ *adj* **1 a :** not having the right or standard color **:** not colorless ⟨*off-color* diamond⟩ ⟨*off-color* paper⟩ ⟨*off-color* show dog⟩ ⟨*off-colored* racial mixtures⟩ **b :** not being up to a required standard **:** not being in sound condition or good health ⟨feeling *off-color* and out of sorts⟩ **2 :** being of doubtful propriety **:** not socially acceptable **:** DUBIOUS ⟨*off-color* reputation⟩ **:** RISQUÉ ⟨*off-color* anecdotes⟩

offcome \ˈ=ˌ=\ *n* -S [³*off* + *come*] *chiefly Scot* **1 :** OUTCOME **2 :** EXCUSE

¹offcut \ˈ=ˌ=\ *n* [³*off* + *cut* (after *cut off*)] **:** something that is cut off: as **a :** a portion cut from a sheet of paper to reduce it to the press size **b :** a part of a printed sheet cut off and folded separately **c :** an odd or waste piece of lumber ⟨plywood ~*s*⟩

²offcut \ˈ=ˌ=\ *adj* [¹*off* + *cut*, past part. of *cut* (after *cut off*)] **:** not being of the usual or standard sizes ⟨~ lumber⟩

offed *past of* OFF

off·en \ˈȯfən\ *prep* [alter. of *off from*] *substand* **:** OFF

of·fen·bach \ˈäfən,bäk, ˈȯf-, -ä\underline{k}\ *adj, usu cap* [fr. *Offenbach*, Germany] **:** of or from the city of Offenbach, Germany **:** of the kind or style prevalent in Offenbach

of·fend \əˈfend\ *vb* -ED/-ING/-S [ME *offenden*, fr. MF *offendre*, fr. L *offendere*, fr. *of-* (fr. *ob-* to, toward, against) + *-fendere* to strike — more at OB-, DEFEND] *vi* **1** *obs* **:** TRIP, STUMBLE **2 a :** to transgress the moral or divine law **:** SIN ⟨if it be a sin to covet honor, I am the most ~*ing* soul alive —Shak.⟩ **b :** to act in violation of a law, rule, or code **:** do wrong — used often with *against* ⟨that only those . . . who will never again ~ against the law should be paroled —Fred Finsley⟩ **3 a :** to cause difficulty or discomfort or injury ⟨took off his shoe and removed the ~*ing* pebble⟩ **b :** to cause dislike, anger, or vexation ⟨take care that your dog does not . . . ~ on the common staircase —Agnes M. Miall⟩ ⟨a fabric of brick and asbestos that would not ~ in that landscape —Bryan Morgan⟩ **~** *vt* **1 a :** VIOLATE, TRANSGRESS ⟨a contract not ~*ing* a statute . . . might still be in restraint of trade —C.A. Cooke⟩ ⟨at the risk of ~*ing* the canons of reviewing —J.N.L. Baker⟩ **b** *obs* **:** to strike against **:** ATTACK, ASSAIL **c :** to cause pain to **:** HURT, INJURE ⟨tasteless billboards that ~ the eye⟩ ⟨the horse . . . develops . . . bony growths around the joints that have been ~*ed* —R.R.Dykstra⟩ **2** *obs* **:** to oppose or obstruct in duty **:** cause to sin ⟨if thy right eye ~ thee, pluck it out —Mt 5:29 (AV)⟩ **3 :** to cause to feel vexed or resentful **:** hurt the feelings of ⟨some people might be ~*ed* at mentioning a novelist in church —Compton Mackenzie⟩ ⟨friend of my youth may remember something in a different shape and be ~*ed* with my book —W.B.Yeats⟩

syn AFFRONT, INSULT, OUTRAGE: OFFEND indicates causing vexation, resentment, or hurt feelings or occas. violating notions of what is proper or right ⟨begged pardon for having displeased her. In a softened tone she declared herself not at all *offended* —Jane Austen⟩ ⟨hurt and *offended* by Ivy's rudeness —Willa Cather⟩ ⟨an old man asks her to become his mistress: she is not much *offended* morally, nor is she horrified —E.K. Brown⟩ AFFRONT indicates treating with incivility, lack of consideration, rudeness, or contempt, either with willful intent or deliberate indifference to courtesy ⟨a vigor, resolution, and at times an arrogance, which *affronted* his contemporaries —*New Republic*⟩ ⟨further *affronted* every soldier by saying that as things stood, England's only defense was the navy —Anthony West⟩ INSULT indicates a deliberate, insolent, wanton causing of another's shame, hurt pride, or humiliation ⟨he would *insult* them flagrantly; he would fling his hands in the air and thunder at their ignorance —Louis Auchincloss⟩ OUTRAGE applies to flagrant, egregious offense calling forth extreme feelings ⟨*outraged* at the aspersions upon the character of his old friend —S.H.Adams⟩ ⟨deputies, *outraged* because they thought Mendès was appealing over their heads to the people, broke into an angry roar —*Time*⟩

of·fend·ed·ly *adv* **:** in an offended manner

of·fend·er \əˈfendə(r)\ *n* -S **1 :** one that offends **:** one that violates a law, rule, or code of conduct **:** one that commits an offense **:** WRONGDOER, TRANSGRESSOR ⟨the ruler should have a power . . . to pardon some ~*s* —John Locke⟩ **2 :** something that causes injury or annoyance

of·fense *or* **of·fence** \əˈfen(t)s, ˈȯ,f-, ˈä,f-\ *n* -S [ME, fr. MF, fr. L *offensa*, fr. fem. of *offensus*, past part. of *offendere* to offend — more at OFFEND] **1 a** *obs* **:** act of stumbling ⟨for a rock of ~ to both the houses of Israel —Isa 8:14 (AV)⟩ **b** *archaic* **:** a cause or occasion of sin **:** STUMBLING BLOCK ⟨woe unto the world because of ~*s* —Mt 18:7 (AV)⟩ **2** *obs* **:** DISFAVOR, DISGRACE **3** *archaic* **:** INJURY, DAMAGE **4 :** something that outrages the moral or physical senses **:** NUISANCE ⟨~ to the public conscience⟩ ⟨such chord successions are an ~ to the ear⟩ **5 a :** the act of attacking **:** ATTACK, ASSAULT ⟨weapons of ~⟩ **b :** the means or method of attacking or of attempting to score **c :** the offensive team or members of a team playing offensive positions **d :** scoring ability **6 a :** the act of displeasing, affronting, or angering ⟨no ~ intended and none taken, I hope⟩ ⟨his words have given great ~ at court⟩ **b :** the state of being displeased, insulted, or morally outraged ⟨likly to take ~ at the least word of criticism⟩ **7 a :** a breach of moral or social conduct **:** SIN, TRANSGRESSION, MISDEED ⟨tolerant of his youthful ~*s*⟩ **b :** an infraction of law **:** CRIME, MISDEMEANOR ⟨nor shall any person be subject for the same ~ to be twice put in jeopardy —*U. S. Constitution*⟩; *sometimes* **:** a misdemeanor not indictable but subject to summary punishment ⟨a record of petty ~*s*⟩

syn RESENTMENT, UMBRAGE, PIQUE, DUDGEON, HUFF: OFFENSE (or OFFENCE), commonly as the object of *give* or *take*, refers to the hurt displeasure one feels at a slight, insult, or indignity ⟨some demon of contradiction impelled her to find a point of *offense* everywhere —Ellen Glasgow⟩ ⟨could say things that from anyone else would sound outrageous, but he phrased them so amusingly, and was so lacking in malice, that he never gave *offense* —V.G.Heiser⟩ ⟨this tiny breath of genuine criticism had given deep *offense* —E.M.Forster⟩ RESENTMENT may apply to a feeling longer lasting, deeper, and marked by more indignation and smoldering ill will than OFFENSE ⟨actuated in great measure by *resentment* at not having received leave of absence to visit his dying wife, he made very serious charges against the personal character of his commandant —Edward Breck⟩ ⟨requited their hospitality by robbing them of much of their supplies. So fierce was their *resentment* that Hudson was forced to put from shore —*Amer. Guide Series: Maine*⟩ UMBRAGE, chiefly in the phrase *to take umbrage*, may suggest blended hurt pride, jealousy, suspicion of another's motives, and ill will ⟨a man took *umbrage* at being called a certain kind of fool —W.F.Hambly⟩ ⟨although the rector was not inclined to take *umbrage* at the treatment they had received, he showed . . . that he was quite aware that it was not what might have been considered due to them —Archibald Marshall⟩ PIQUE applies to the roiled displeasure of one taking offense or irritation at a petty cause that wounds vanity or shakes composure ⟨a ridiculous sense of *pique* at being left out, like a child shut out from a room in which a vitally interesting game is being played —H.G.Wells⟩ ⟨fits of jealous *pique* when one or the other rated special questioning —*Newsweek*⟩ DUDGEON, usu. used with *in*, suggests an irate fit of indignation ⟨this offended Mr. Barrow, who retired in *dudgeon* to the remotest part of the field —Dorothy Sayers⟩ ⟨sometimes the employer, flanked by his lawyer, will in a *dudgeon* refuse to sit in the same room with the union representatives —Dorothy Bromley⟩ HUFF, also usu. used with *in*, suggests a peevish or petulant fit of anger, often short-lived, at some petty cause ⟨at the first hint that we were tired of waiting and that we should like the show to begin, he was off in a *huff* —Henry James †1916⟩ ⟨read the letter, flew into a rage, and left the country in a *huff* —Virginia Woolf⟩

of·fense·less \-ləs\ *adj* **:** incapable of offending or attacking **:** INOFFENSIVE — **of·fense·less·ly** *adv*

of·fen·sible \əˈfen(t)səbəl\ *adj* [MF, fr. LL *offensibilis* liable to stumble, fr. L *offensus* (past part. of *offendere* to stumble, offend) + *-ibilis* -ible — more at OFFEND] **1** *obs* **:** OFFENSIVE, HARMFUL, INJURIOUS **2 :** liable to be offended

¹of·fen·sive \əˈfen(t)siv, ˈȯ,f-, ˈä,f-, -sēv *also* -səv\ *adj* [MF or ML; MF *offensif*, fr. ML *offensivus*, fr. L *offensus* (past part. of *offendere*) + *-ivus* -ive] **1 :** making attack **:** relating to or characterized by attack **:** AGGRESSIVE **:** fitted for or used in attacking ⟨~ weapons⟩ ⟨~ maneuver⟩ ⟨~ strength⟩ — opposed to *defensive* **2 a** *obs* **:** causing injury or damage **:** HARMFUL **b :** giving painful or unpleasant sensations **:** NAUSEOUS, OBNOXIOUS, REVOLTING ⟨~ odor of garbage⟩ **3 :** causing displeasure or resentment **:** giving offense **:** INSULTING, AFFRONTING ⟨loud, ~ behavior⟩ ⟨~ advertising⟩ ⟨it's ~ to a gentleman's feelings when his word isn't believed —Dorothy Sayers⟩ **4** *obs* **:** OFFENDING, TRANSGRESSIVE, SINFUL

syn LOATHSOME, REPULSIVE, REPUGNANT, REVOLTING: OFFENSIVE describes what is disagreeable or nauseating or painful because of outrage to taste and sensibilities or affronting insultingness ⟨her head thrown back, her face discolored, her eyes bulging, her mouth wet and yawning: a sight horribly *offensive* —Arnold Bennett⟩ ⟨bad manners and a blatancy that, for some reason, seemed much more *offensive* than any mere peasant crudeness of their parents —Edmund Wilson⟩ ⟨his jeering voice had an *offensive*, deliberately insulting tone —O.E.Rölvaag⟩ LOATHSOME applies to what is foul or corrupt to the point of being quite disgusting or abhorrent ⟨upon the bed, before that whole company, there lay a nearly liquid mass of *loathsome* — of detestable putrescence —E.A.Poe⟩ ⟨picturing on many pages of his immortal comedy of hell, purgatory, and paradise the most horrible monsters and tortures, and the most *loathsome* and noisome abominations —C.W.Eliot⟩ REPULSIVE describes whatever produces strong physical disgust or aversion ⟨there was something *repulsive* about his touch. I shrank from his hand; my flesh revolted —Jack London⟩ ⟨rats, mice, dogs, cats, and such *repulsive* substitutes for food —J.L.Motley⟩ REPUGNANT describes what is highly offensive as in conflict with one's nature, principles, or tastes ⟨intensely *repugnant* to human nature, being a condition of chronic terror that at last became unbearable —G.B.Shaw⟩ ⟨if violence was incompatible with the character of a Virginia gentleman, how much more *repugnant* must it appear to the ideal of pure womanhood —Ellen Glasgow⟩ REVOLTING applies to what is offensive or repulsive and calls forth a determination to resist, rebel, or escape, esp. on the part of a person of delicate sensibilities ⟨his whole body shivered and started into awe-inspiring movement, monstrous and inhuman, *revolting* . . . yet pitiful —Liam O'Flaherty⟩ ⟨the maneuvers of selfishness and duplicity must ever be *revolting* —Jane Austen⟩

²offensive \"\ *n* -S **1 :** the state or posture of one that is attacking **:** aggressive attitude **:** act of the attacking party ⟨took the ~⟩ — opposed to *defensive* **2 :** a sustained or large-scale attack ⟨~ aimed at the enemy's capital⟩ **:** an aggressive action or movement ⟨an economic ~ can often prevent the necessity for a . . . military defense —W.H. Draper⟩

of·fen·sive·ly \-sȯvlē, -li\ **:** in an offensive manner ⟨~ conceited⟩ ⟨smelling ~ of cheap perfume⟩

of·fen·sive·ness \-sivnəs, -sēv- *also* -səv-\ *n* -ES **:** the quality or state of being offensive ⟨the ~ of his continual bragging⟩

¹of·fer \ˈȯfə(r), ˈäf-\ *vb* **offered; offered; offering** \-f(ə)riŋ\ **offers** [ME *offren, offeren*, in sense 1, fr. OE *offrian*, fr. LL *offerre*, fr. L, to present, tender, proffer, offer, fr. *of-* (fr. *ob-* to, toward, against) + *ferre* to carry; in other senses, fr. OF *offrir*, fr. L *offerre* — more at OB-, BEAR] *vt* **1 a :** to present as an act of worship or devotion **:** SACRIFICE ⟨to the Catholic church where she would ~ a candle or so to his recovery —F.M.Ford⟩ **b :** to utter (as a prayer) in devotion — often used with *up* ⟨~*ed* up prayers of thanksgiving⟩ **2 a :** to present for acceptance or rejection **:** hold out **:** TENDER, PROFFER ⟨~ a bribe⟩ ⟨~ a bill to the legislature⟩ ⟨~*ed* his hand in marriage⟩ ⟨was ~*ed* a job⟩ **b :** to present in order to meet a requirement ⟨candidates for the degree may ~ English as one of their foreign languages⟩ **3 a :** to bring or put forward for action or consideration **:** PROPOSE, SUGGEST ⟨~ an opinion⟩ ⟨~ a proposition⟩ ⟨~*ed* himself as a candidate for governor⟩ **b :** to declare one's readiness or willingness — used with an infinitive object ⟨~*ed* to help me⟩ ⟨~*ed* to join in the search⟩ **4 a :** to try or begin to exert ⟨~*ed* stubborn resistance⟩ ⟨don't shoot unless they ~ violence⟩ **b :** UNDERTAKE, ATTEMPT — used with an infinitive object ⟨~*ed* to strike him with his cane⟩ ⟨~*ed* to kiss her⟩ ⟨a young bruiser . . . can hardly ~ to beat up on an old man —W.L.Gresham⟩ **5 :** to make available or accessible **:** SUPPLY, AFFORD ⟨summit ~*s* a magnificent panorama⟩ ⟨stream ~*ing* excellent fishing⟩ ⟨the college ~*s* courses in Russian⟩; *esp* **:** to place (merchandise) on sale ⟨~*s* a range of cameras at reasonable prices⟩ **6 :** to present in performance or exhibition ⟨~ a new comedy⟩ **7 :** to propose as payment **:** BID ⟨~*ed* me $10 for it⟩ **~** *vi* **1 :** to present something as an act of worship or devotion **:** make an offering or sacrifice **:** SACRIFICE ⟨in no other country . . . do people pray and ~ as much as they do in Tibet —Heinrich Harrer⟩ **2** *archaic* **:** to make an attempt — used with *at* **3 :** to come to hand **:** present itself ⟨buying land whenever opportunity ~*ed*⟩ **4 :** to make a proposal; *esp* **:** to propose marriage **5** *Brit* **:** to be or to become available ⟨free choice to get work where work is ~*ing* —*Sydney (Australia) Bull.*⟩ ⟨corn that is ~*ing* is quite suitable —*Farmer's Weekly* (*So. Africa*)⟩

syn OFFER, PROFFER, TENDER, PRESENT, and PREFER can mean, in common, to put something before another for acceptance. OFFER in itself usu. implies no more than the common meaning ⟨*offer* a cigarette⟩ ⟨*offer* a helping hand⟩ ⟨*offer* a solution to a problem⟩ ⟨*offer* to help out in a crisis⟩ ⟨*offer* a good evening's entertainment⟩ PROFFER, more literary than OFFER, adds, or throws stress on, the idea of voluntariness, spontaneity, or courtesy on the part of the doer or subject of the verb ⟨*proffer* one's hand to a lady⟩ ⟨*proffer* hospitality to strangers in trouble⟩ ⟨sympathy should be *proffered* to the bereaved —Alexander MacDonald⟩ TENDER, a term with a legal currency implying an offering of something according to the terms of the law for approval or acceptance, in general use adds to OFFER the idea of the modesty, humility, or gentleness of the doer or subject of the verb ⟨*tender* your resignation⟩ ⟨*tender* your services⟩ ⟨*tender* your friendship⟩ PRESENT can carry a strong suggestion of formalness or a ceremoniousness or outward show in the act of offering or can suggest the character of a gift in the thing offered ⟨*present* a prize to a winning team⟩ ⟨*presented* the Davy-Faraday Laboratory to the Royal Institution —S.F.Mason⟩ ⟨the analysis of experimental science *presented* in this foreword —J.B.Conant⟩ ⟨words by which one scholar can *present* clearly to another the results of an investigation on this complex subject —E.S. McCartney⟩ PREFER in the sense of PROFFER or PRESENT is current only in legal use, though it is common in literary works up to the late nineteenth century ⟨the government of which the victim is a subject may justly *prefer* a claim —*Encyc. Americana*⟩ ⟨has *preferred* some serious charges —Reginald Bretnor⟩ ⟨I don't *prefer* any claim to being the soul of romance —Charles Dickens⟩

²offer \"\ *n* -S [ME *offre*, fr. MF, fr. OF, fr. *offrir*] **1 :** an act of offering: as **a :** a presenting for acceptance **:** PROFFER ⟨refused all ~*s* of assistance⟩ ⟨considering job ~*s* from several firms⟩; *specif* **:** a proposal of marriage ⟨if she was still single it was not for lack of ~*s*⟩ **b :** an undertaking upon terms that embodies a promise given in consideration and in exchange for another's stipulated act or forbearance or designated reciprocal promise and that calls for acceptance or rejection by that other — compare CONTRACT **2** *obs* **:** OFFERING **3 :** a price named by one proposing to buy **:** BID ⟨had several good ~*s* for his house⟩ **4 a :** ATTEMPT, TRY ⟨made an ~ to catch the ball⟩ **b :** an action or movement indicating a purpose or intention of doing something ⟨halfhearted ~ of resistance⟩ ⟨made an ~ of jumping out of the car⟩ **5 :** a small knob on a deer's antler **:** a rudimentary tine — **on offer** *adv (or adj)* **:** on sale **:** for sale

of·fer·able \-f(ə)rəbəl\ *adj* **:** capable of being offered

of·fer·ee \ˌȯfəˈrē, ˌäf-\ *n* -S **:** one to whom an offer is made ⟨a contract is formed when there is mutual assent between an offeror and an ~ —*College & Univ. Business*⟩

of·fer·er *or* **of·fer·or** \ˈȯf(ə)rə(r), ˈäf-\ *n* -S [ME *offerer*, fr. *offeren* to offer + *-er* — more at OFFER] **1 :** one that offers **:** one that makes an offer or an offering ⟨~ of a bribe⟩ ⟨~ of a sacrifice⟩ **2** *now usu* **offeror :** one that communicates an offer (as of purchase) to another ⟨*offeror* and offeree have agreed on terms of the contract⟩

of·fer·ing \-f(ə)riŋ, -rēŋ\ *n* -S [ME *offring, offering*, fr. OE *offrung*, fr. *offrian* to offer, sacrifice + *-ung* -ing — more at OFFER] **1 :** the act of one who offers **:** PROFFERING: as **a :** a presenting of something as an act of worship or devotion **b :** something presented as an expiation or atonement for sin **:** SACRIFICE, OBLATION — see BURNT OFFERING, DRINK OFFERING, GUILT OFFERING, HEAVE OFFERING, PEACE OFFERING, SIN OFFERING, WAVE OFFERING **2 :** GIFT, PRESENT; *esp* **:** a gift made in money or in kind at a church service for the support of the church or its charitable, missionary, or other activities **3 :** something that is presented or made available for purchase ⟨large ~ of long-term securities⟩ ⟨~*s* for last month on the wool market⟩ or patronage ⟨~*s* of an opera company⟩ ⟨latest ~*s* of the leading novelists⟩ ⟨~*s* of a television network⟩ **4 :** an opportunity for instruction or study in a specific subject provided by an educational institution ⟨several new ~*s* in the history department⟩

offering plate *n* **:** a plate for collecting offerings from the members of a church congregation

offering price *n* [*offering* fr. pres. part. of ¹*offer*] **:** the price quoted for a commodity or service in a schedule of prices or price list

offering plate

of·fer·to·ry \ˈȯfə(r),tōrē, ˈäf-, -tȯr-, -ri\ *n* -ES [ML *offertorium*, fr. *offertus* (past part. of LL *offerre* to offer) + L *-orium* -ory — more at OFFER] **1** *often cap* **a :** a part of a eucharistic service in which bread and wine are offered to God before they are consecrated **b :** prayers said by the priest when making the offerings **2** *often cap* **:** an antiphon, anthem, or other musical selection sung or played during a liturgy or during a religious service in which an offering is received from the congregation **3 a :** an offering received from the congregation in a Christian worship service during the playing or singing of the offertory **b :** a collection of money taken at a religious service

offerture *n* -S [MF, fr. ML *offertura*, fr. *offertus* + L *-ura* -ure] **1** *obs* **:** act of offering (as in worship) **2** *obs* **:** PROPOSAL, OVERTURE

off–face \ˈ=ˈ=\ *adj* **:** OFF-THE-FACE

off–flavor \ˈ=ˌ==\ *n* **:** a flavor that is not natural or up to standard owing to deterioration or contamination ⟨*off-flavors* of cream⟩

off–glide \ˈ=ˌ=\ *n* **:** a glide produced by the movement of the vocal organs from the articulatory position of a speech sound to a position of inactivity or to the articulatory position of an immediately following speech sound — compare ON-GLIDE

off-go \'=,=\ *n* [³*off* + *go* (after *go off*)] **:** a going or starting off **:** START

offgoing \'=,==, ='==\ *n* [³*off* + *going*] **:** a going off **:** DEPARTURE, REMOVAL

¹**offgrade** \'=¦=\ *adj* [fr. the phrase *off grade*] **:** varying from and inferior to a standard grade ⟨~ fruit⟩ ⟨~ ore⟩

²**offgrade** \"\ *n* **:** a product (as lumber) that is below standard

¹**offhand** \'=¦=\ *adv* [²*off* + *hand*] **1 :** without previous study or preparation **:** EXTEMPORE ⟨couldn't give the figures ~⟩ ⟨reasons she would give ~ if you asked her why she read novels —Bernard DeVoto⟩ **2 :** from a standing position **:** without a support or rest ⟨fire ~ with . . . accuracy in . . . deer shooting —Claude Parmalee⟩

²**offhand** \"\ *adj* **1 a :** done or made offhand **:** EXTEMPORANEOUS; IMPROMPTU ⟨~ excuses⟩ **b :** showing no premeditation or preparation **:** CASUAL, INFORMAL ⟨bored, ~ manner⟩ ⟨grumbled about the ~, grudging service —*Time*⟩ ⟨her clothes usually gave an ~ effect⟩ **2 a :** shaped by hand without the use of molds ⟨~ glassworking⟩ **b :** done with a workpiece held in the hand ⟨~ grinding⟩ ⟨~ polishing⟩ **3 :** fired from a standing position ⟨rifle too heavy for ~ shooting⟩

offhanded \'=¦==\ *adj* **:** OFFHAND ⟨trying to sound ~ and reassuring —H.L.Davis⟩ — **off·hand·ed·ly** *adv* — **off·hand·ed·ness** *n*

off-hour \'=¦=\ *n* **1 :** a period of time spent off duty or away from work **2 a :** a period of time other than rush hour ⟨cut-rate tickets for *off-hour* travelers —William White⟩ or regular business hours ⟨a small store depends on customers during *off-hours*⟩ **b :** a time when one is not up to one's usual standard

¹**of·fice** \'ȯfəs, 'äf-\ *n* -S [ME, fr. OF, fr. L *officium* service, kindness, activity, duty, office, alter. of (assumed) *opifacium*, fr. *opus* work + *-i-* + *-facium* (fr. *facere* to do, make) — more at OPERATE, DO] **1 a :** a special duty, charge, or position conferred by an exercise of governmental authority and for a public purpose **:** a position of authority to exercise a public function and to receive whatever emoluments may belong to it ⟨qualified to hold public ~⟩ **b :** a position of responsibility or some degree of executive authority **c :** the fact or state of holding a public position of authority ⟨permitting . . . Socialism to be corrupted by ~ —*Times Lit. Supp.*⟩ **2** [ME, fr. OF, fr. LL *officium*, fr. L] **:** a set form of prayer or other religious service drawn up by church authority and sanctioned as the approved usu. obligatory form to be used by particular individuals (as clerics) or on particular occasions: as **a** *often cap* **:** the service of the breviary **:** DIVINE OFFICE ⟨a priest reciting his ~⟩ **b :** the rites or one of the rites of the missal ⟨the ~ of the mass⟩ **c :** a prayer service (as evensong) used in churches of the Anglican communion **3 a :** a religious or social ceremonial observance **:** RITE **b offices** *pl* **:** rites for the dead **4 a :** something that one ought to do or must do **:** an assigned or assumed duty, task, or role ⟨his ~ was merely to . . . point the way to new achievements —Frank Thilly⟩ ⟨to suppose she would shrink . . . from the ~ of a friend —Jane Austen⟩ **b :** something that is done or performed by a particular thing **:** the proper or customary action of something **:** FUNCTION ⟨the sentence through its ~ of assertion —R.M.Weaver⟩ ⟨numbed ears refused their proper ~ of conveying meanings to the mind —Kenneth Roberts⟩ **c :** something that a person does for another **:** SERVICE ⟨light the lights for them, the last ~ of welcome that she would ever be able to do here —*New Yorker*⟩ **d** INQUEST OF OFFICE **5 :** a place where a particular kind of business is transacted or a service is supplied: as **a :** a place in which the functions (as consulting, record-keeping, clerical work) of a public officer are performed **b :** the directing headquarters of an enterprise or organization ⟨continuing point of contact of the new student with the college ~ —*Official Register of Harvard Univ.*⟩ ⟨directives to branch factories were sent out from the New York ~⟩ **c :** the place in which a professional man (as a physician or lawyer) conducts his professional business **6 offices** *pl, chiefly Brit* **:** the apartments, attached buildings, or outhouses (as kitchens, pantries, laundries, stables) in which the activities attached to the service of a house are carried on ⟨3 bedrooms, bathroom and compact ~*s* —*Country Life*⟩ **7 :** the company whose place of business is in an office; *specif, Brit* **:** an insurance company **8 a** *Brit* **:** a principal branch or division of governmental administration **:** DEPARTMENT ⟨War *Office*⟩ ⟨Colonial *Office*⟩ **b :** a branch or subdivision of governmental administration that ranks (in the national government) below the department ⟨Patent *Office*⟩ ⟨*Office* of Education⟩ **9** *slang* **:** PRIVY **10** *slang* **:** a private usu. covert signal, warning, or cue ⟨in case the boss gives you the ~ that the cops . . . are going to investigate —John Scarne & Clayton Rawson⟩ **syn** see FUNCTION

²**office** \"\ *vb* -ED/-ING/-S *vt, obs* **:** to appoint to or place in office ~ *vi* **:** to maintain or occupy a professional or business office ⟨the old Vienna doctors have always had the habit of *officing* in their homes —Ernst Waldinger⟩

office-bearer \'==,==\ *n, Brit* **:** OFFICEHOLDER, OFFICER

office-block ballot \'==,=- *or* **office-group ballot** \'==,=-\ *n* **:** an Australian ballot on which the names of candidates with or without party labels are grouped under the titles of the offices to be filled — compare INDIANA BALLOT, MASSACHUSETTS BALLOT

office boy *n* **:** a boy employed for errands and odd jobs in a business office

office copy *n* **1 :** an authenticated or certified copy of an official or legal record **2 :** a copy made or kept to be used in an office

office found *n* **:** the return of a verdict by an inquest of office

officeholder \'==,==\ *n* **:** one holding a public office esp. in the civil service

office hours *n pl* **:** the hours set for business, work, or professional service in an office

office lawyer *n* **:** a lawyer whose practice is largely work carried on in his office rather than litigated cases requiring trials or hearings in the courts

of·fice·less \'ȯfəsləs, 'äf-\ *adj* [ME *officeles*, fr. *office* + *-les* -less] **:** lacking an office **:** not holding an office

office lock *n* **:** a door lock having the keyhole above the knob

office machine *n* **:** BUSINESS MACHINE

office of arms 1 : a body of officers of arms of a nation organized as a corporate body or as a division of the government **2** *usu cap 1st O&A* **:** the office in Dublin, terminated March 31, 1943, of which Ulster king of arms was head, having charge of heraldic matters in the island of Ireland

office lock

office premium *n* **:** GROSS PREMIUM

¹**of·fi·cer** \'ȯfəsə(r), 'äf- *sometimes* -fs-\ *n* -S [ME, fr. MF *officier*, fr. ML *officiarius*, fr. L *officium* office + -arius -ary — more at OFFICE] **1 a** *obs* **:** one charged with a duty **:** AGENT **b :** one charged with administering and maintaining the law (as a constable, bailiff, sheriff) ⟨~*s* of the peace⟩ ⟨the ~ on duty at a traffic corner⟩ **c :** a chief official engaged in domestic management or service in a large household or a college ⟨~*s* of the royal household⟩ **2 :** one who holds an office **:** one who is appointed or elected to serve in a position of trust, authority, or command esp. as specif. provided for by law ⟨~*s* of state⟩ ⟨~ in the foreign service⟩ ⟨~*s* of a bank⟩ ⟨the club held a meeting to elect its ~*s* for the year⟩ — distinguished from *employee* and sometimes from *official* **3 a :** one who holds a position of authority or command in the armed forces; *specif* **:** one who holds a commission ⟨separate clubs for ~*s* and enlisted men⟩ — see NONCOMMISSIONED OFFICER, PETTY OFFICER, WARRANT OFFICER **b :** the master or any of the mates of a merchant or passenger ship ⟨the ~*s'* rooms opened off the dining room —H.A.Chippendale⟩ **4 a :** a member of an honorary order in a grade above the lowest ⟨~ of the Legion of Honor⟩ **b** *in the Salvation Army* **:** a person trained and commissioned to engage in paid full-time service — see SALVATIONIST; compare LOCAL OFFICER

²**officer** \"\ *vt* -ED/-ING/-S **1 :** to furnish with officers **:** appoint officers over ⟨supply and ~ a militia⟩ **2 :** to command or direct as an officer ⟨veterans ~*ed* the recruits⟩ ⟨the troops were well ~*ed*⟩

officer at arms *obs* **:** OFFICER OF ARMS

of·fi·cer·less \'ȯfəsə(r)ləs, 'äf-\ *adj* **:** lacking officers

officer of arms [ME *officers of armes*] **:** any officer of whatever specific rank (as king of arms, herald, or pursuivant) having the duties of a herald or having supervision over officers who have such duties

officer of the day : the officer who acting directly under the commanding officer of a military organization or installation is responsible on an assigned day for overseeing the guard, preserving order, protecting property, enforcing inspection regulations, and guarding prisoners

officer of the deck : the officer in charge of a naval vessel for an assigned period (as a 4-hour watch) who is stationed on the bridge while at sea or on the quarterdeck while in port, who represents the commanding officer, and who for the duration of such duty is superior to all other officers except the executive officer

officer of the watch : the officer representing the engineering officer for an assigned period and serving in the engine room

of·fi·cer·ship \'===,ship\ *n* **:** the post or rank of an officer

offices *pl of* OFFICE, *pres 3d sing of* OFFICE

office seeker *n* **:** one who tries to gain public office ⟨after a few weeks of heading off *office seekers* he will move into the White House —*Nation*⟩

¹**of·fi·cial** \ə'fishəl, ō'f-\ *n* -S [ME, fr. MF, fr. ML *officialis*, fr. LL, adj.] **1** *or* **official principal :** a person appointed (as by an archbishop, bishop, dean, chapter, archdeacon) to exercise jurisdiction in an ecclesiastical court **2 a :** one who holds or is invested with an office **:** OFFICER ⟨government ~*s*⟩ **b :** a person authorized to act for a government, corporation, organization, or for another person esp. in administering or directing in a subordinate capacity ⟨~*s* of a sports contest⟩ ⟨railroad ~*s*⟩ **3 :** OFFICIAL STAMP

²**official** \"\ *adj* [LL *officialis*, fr. L *officium* duty, office + *-alis* -al — more at OFFICE] **1** *obs* **:** performing a function or service **2 :** belonging or relating to an office, position, or trust **:** connected with holding an office ⟨~ duties⟩ ⟨~ routine⟩ **3 :** holding an office or serving in a public position **:** authorized to perform a service ⟨~ messenger⟩ ⟨president's ~ representative⟩ **4 a :** derived from the proper office or officer or authority **:** made or communicated by virtue of authority **:** AUTHORIZED, AUTHORITATIVE ⟨~ statement⟩ ⟨~ biography⟩ **b :** prescribed or recognized as authorized ⟨~ ballot⟩ ⟨~ language of a region⟩ ⟨~ architecture⟩ ⟨~ record for the mile⟩; *specif* **:** described by the U. S. Pharmacopeia or the National Formulary ⟨~ species of a plant genus⟩ **5 :** befitting or characteristic of a person in office or acting in his capacity of an officer **:** FORMAL ⟨was extended an ~ greeting⟩ ⟨~ condolences⟩ ⟨faults to which ~ writing is especially prone —Ernest Gowers⟩ **6 :** serving in a legislature of a British dependency by virtue of nomination by the governor from the public service of the colony — compare UNOFFICIAL 1c

official at bat *or* **official time at bat :** AT BAT 2

of·fi·cial·dom \-dəm\ *n* -S **:** officials as a class or as a body ⟨the kind of ~ which characterized the Roman Empire —K.S. Latourette⟩ ⟨referring to all ~ — executives, legislators and judges —D.R.Richberg⟩ ⟨people are informed of only so much as ~ decides they need to be told —Arthur Krock⟩

of·fi·cial·ese \=,fishə¦lēz, -lēs\ *n* -S **:** the characteristic language of official statements **:** wordy, pompous, or obscure language ⟨handbooks which would fortify civil servants against the reduction of ~ —C.J.Rolo⟩

of·fi·cial·ism \='==,lizəm\ *n* -S **:** action characteristic of an official **:** official system or routine **:** BUREAUCRACY, RED-TAPEISM ⟨where there is ~ every human relation suffers —E.M. Forster⟩

of·fi·ci·al·i·ty \ə,fishē'alәd·ē, ,ō,f-\ *n* -ES [F *officialité*, fr. LL *officialitat-, officialitas*, fr. *officialis* + L *-itat-, -itas* -ity] **1 :** the ecclesiastical charge, office, court, or jurisdiction of an official principal **2 :** the state or fact of being official **:** OFFICIALISM **3 :** OFFICIALS

of·fi·cial·iza·tion \ə,fishələ'zāshən, ō,f-, -,lī'z-\ *n* -S **:** the process of becoming or being made official **:** act of placing under the control of officials

of·fi·cial·ize \='fishə,līz\ *vt, see -ize in Explan Notes* [²*official* + *-ize*] **:** to make official **:** subject to official routine **:** bring under public control

of·fi·cial·ly \-sh(ə)lē, -li\ *adv* **1 :** with official authorization **:** FORMALLY ⟨the bridge will be ~ opened next week⟩ **2 :** in an official capacity ⟨~ responsible for the disaster, as the man charged . . . with the security of all frontiers —Robert Graves⟩ **3 :** PROFESSEDLY, PUBLICLY, OSTENSIBLY ⟨this is the dry season; ~, no rain should fall —Marjory J. Douglas⟩ — often contrasted with *actually*

official oath *n* **:** the promissory oath required by law of an officer upon qualifying for his office in which he promises faithfully to perform the duties of the office and makes all other declarations or promises required by law — compare JUDICIAL OATH

official principal *n* **:** OFFICIAL 1

official receiver *n* **:** RECEIVER 2b(4)

official stamp *n* **:** a postage stamp for use by government officials on government mail

of·fi·ci·ant \ə'fishēənt\ *n* -S [ML *officiant-, officians*, pres. part. of *officiare* to officiate] **:** an officiating priest or minister

¹**of·fi·ci·ary** \-shē,erē, -ri\ *n* -ES [ML *officiarius* — more at OFFICER] **1 :** OFFICER, OFFICIAL **2 :** a body of officers or officials

²**officiary** \"\ *adj* [L *officium* office + E *-ary* — more at OFFICE] **:** connected with, derived from, or having a title or rank in virtue of holding an office ⟨~ earl⟩

¹**of·fi·ci·ate** \ə'fishē,āt, ō'f-, *usu* -ād·+V\ *vb* -ED/-ING/-S [ML *officiatus*, past part. of *officiare*, fr. LL *officium* (ecclesiastical) office — more at OFFICE] *vi* **1 a :** to perform a prescribed religious service or ceremony ⟨~ at a Communion service⟩ ⟨~ at a coronation⟩ ⟨~ at a wedding⟩ **b :** to carry through a prescribed or traditional ceremony **:** perform a social duty ⟨~ as toastmaster at a banquet⟩ ⟨~ as hostess at a formal dinner⟩ **2 a :** to act in an official capacity **:** fill a position ⟨asked her to ~ temporarily as his personal secretary⟩ **b :** to act as an official at a sports contest ~ *vt* **1 :** to carry out (an official duty or function) **2 :** to serve as a leader or celebrant of (a ceremony) **3 :** to administer the rules of (a game or sport) esp. as a referee or umpire

²**officiate** \-ēət\ *n* -S [L *officium* + E *-ate*] **:** a body of officials

of·fi·ci·a·tion \=,=='āshən\ *n* -S **:** the act or term of officiating **:** performance of a ceremony ⟨no provisions for a civil marriage, hence some kind of religious ~ is obligatory —Alfred Werner⟩

of·fi·ci·a·tor \='==,ād·ə(r)\ *n* -S [ML, fr. *officiatus* + L *-or*] **:** one that officiates

¹**of·fi·ci·nal** \ə'fisᵊnəl, ¦ȯfə'sīnᵊl, ¦äf-\ *adj* [ML *officinalis* of a storeroom, fr. *officina* storeroom (fr. L, workshop, alter. of *opificina*, fr. *opific-, opifex* artisan — fr. *opus* work + *-i-* + *-fic-, fex*, fr. *facere* to do, make — + *-ina*, fr. fem. of *-inus* -ine) + L *-alis* -al — more at OPERATE, DO] **1 a :** kept in stock by druggists **:** available without special preparation or compounding **:** not magistral ⟨~ drugs⟩ ⟨~ medicines⟩ **b :** OFFICIAL 4b **2** *of a plant* **:** MEDICINAL ⟨~ herbs⟩ ⟨~ rhubarb⟩ — **of·fic·i·nal·ly** \-əlē, -ᵊlē, -li\ *adv*

²**officinal** \"\ *n* -S **:** an official drug, medicine, or plant

officing *pres part of* OFFICE

of·fi·cious \ə'fishəs\ *adj* [L *officiosus*, fr. *officium* service, kindness, duty, office + *-osus* -ous — more at OFFICE] **1 a** *obs* **:** eager to serve or help **:** KIND, OBLIGING ⟨~ humility of a heart devoted to the assistance merely of the inquisitive —Laurence Sterne⟩ **b** *obs* **:** DUTIFUL **c** *obs* **:** OFFICIAL, FORMAL **2 :** volunteering one's services where they are neither asked nor needed **:** MEDDLESOME ⟨a college . . . should excise ~ administration . . . in order to let learning happen —F.N. Davis⟩ ⟨shouting orders and generally making an ~ nuisance of himself⟩ **3 :** having a connection with official matters or duties merely through the position of the speaker or doer or the nature of the matters or duties **:** of an informal or unauthorized nature **:** UNOFFICIAL ⟨~ conversation between foreign ministers⟩ — opposed to *official* **syn** see IMPERTINENT

of·fi·cious·ly *adv* **:** in an officious manner ⟨nothing so fatal as to strive too directly or too ~ for an abstract quality like beauty —Herbert Read⟩

of·fi·cious·ness *n* -ES **:** officious quality or behavior

off·ing \'ȯfiŋ, 'äf-, -fēŋ\ *n* -S [¹*off* + *-ing*] **1 a :** the part of the open sea that is in sight of but a safe distance from the shore ⟨ships lay in the ~ waiting for a favorable wind⟩ **b :** a position or course near to but safely clear of the land ⟨steered southwest to get a good ~ . . . when he was sufficiently offshore . . . set course for the Canaries —S.E.Morison⟩ **c :** the act of anchoring offshore ⟨decided to make an ~ at the African village . . . to do some trading —H.A.Chippendale⟩ **2 :** the near or foreseeable future ⟨a wedding was in the ~ —D.R. Morris⟩ or the near distance ⟨a waiter hovered in the ~⟩

off·ish \'ȯfish *also* 'äf- *or* -fēsh\ *adj* [¹*off* + *-ish*] **1 :** inclined to stand off **:** stiffly or rudely unapproachable in manner **2 :** somewhat off in health or quality — **off·ish·ly** \-fəshlē, -fēsh-\ *adv* — **off·ish·ness** \-fishnəs, -fēsh-\ *n* -ES

off-key \'=¦=\ *adj* **1 :** varying in pitch from the proper notes of a melody ⟨his *off-key*, squeaky voice . . . as he hummed his favorite hymn —Lynn Montross⟩ ⟨band . . . caterwauling away . . . more stridently *off-key* than ever —*Time*⟩ **2 :** INCONGRUOUS, UNACCOUNTABLE, ANOMALOUS ⟨symbols are sometimes *off-key*; his details of plot are occasionally eccentric —Gene Baro⟩ ⟨sensed something *off-key* about the disastrous fire —Denis Daly⟩

offlap \'=,=\ *n* [³*off* + *lap*] **:** the progressive withdrawal of a sea from the land; *also* **:** the arrangement of the strata deposited on the floor of such a sea during its regression — compare ONLAP, OVERLAP

off·let \'=,=\ *n* -S [³*off* + *let* (after *let off*)] **:** a pipe or channel for letting off water or other fluid

off-license \'=,==\ *n, Brit* **:** a license to sell liquor to be consumed off the premises; *also* **:** an establishment so licensed

off limits *adj* **:** not to be entered or patronized by a designated class (as military personnel, students, athletes in training) ⟨*off limits* section of town⟩ ⟨the casino was declared *off limits* to the airmen at the base⟩

off-line \'=¦=\ *adj* [²*off* + *line*] **:** located at a point not in the immediate area served by a particular railroad ⟨*off-line* ticket agent⟩ ⟨*off-line* destination⟩

off-list \'=¦=\ *adj* [²*off* + *list*] *of merchandise* **:** bought and sold below the list price

off-load \'=¦=\ *vb* [trans. of Afrik *aflaai*] **:** UNLOAD

off-lying \'=¦==\ *adj* [¹*off* + *lying* (after *lie off*)] **1 :** situated off the shore ⟨*off-lying* islands⟩ or off the main part ⟨*off-lying* apartment for servants⟩ **2 :** OUTLYING, REMOTE ⟨*off-lying* provinces⟩

off-mike \'=¦=\ *adj* [²*off* + *mike*] **:** recorded or transmitted at less than normal volume **:** distant from or turned away from the microphone ⟨background of *off-mike* voices⟩

off'n \'ȯfən\ *prep* [alter. of *off from*] *dial* **:** off from **:** OFF

off-odor \'=,==\ *n* **:** an odor that is not natural or up to standard owing to deterioration or contamination ⟨the butter smelled of fish and other *off-odors*⟩

off of *prep* **:** OFF

off-peak \'=¦=\ *adj* [²*off* + *peak*] **:** not at the maximum ⟨the *off-peak* load of a power plant⟩

off-presser \'=,==\ *n* [³*off* + *presser* (after *press off*, v.)] **:** an operator of a machine designed for pressing a particular part (as collar, sleeves, top of trousers) of a garment

¹**offprint** \'=,=\ *n* [trans. of G *abdruck*] **:** an excerpt (as a magazine article) separately printed

²**offprint** \"\ *vt* **:** to reprint as an offprint

offr *abbr* officer

offs *pres 3d sing of* OFF, *pl of* OFF

offsaddle \'=,==\ *vb* [trans. of Afrik *afsaal*] *chiefly Brit* **:** UNSADDLE

off-sale \'=¦=\ *adj, of a license* **:** permitting sale of alcoholic beverages only in sealed containers for off-premises consumption

off·scape \'ȯf,skāp *also* 'äf-\ *n* [³*off* + *-scape*] **:** the distant part of a landscape; *specif* **:** the visible surroundings of a tract to be landscaped ⟨plantings . . . will be used along the roadside to screen objectionable ~*s* —B.D.Tallamy⟩

offscour \'=¦=\ *vt* [¹*off* + *scour*] **:** to scour off **:** CLEANSE

offscouring \'=¦==\ *n* -S [³*off* + *scouring* (after *scour off*, v.)] **1 :** something that is scoured off **:** cast-off filth **:** REFUSE **2 :** someone driven off from society **:** SCUM, OUTCAST — usu. used in pl. ⟨~*s* of the nation, but they were hardy men —C.B. Kelland⟩

offscreen \'=¦=\ *adj* [²*off* + *screen*] **:** taking place or produced out of the viewer's sight ⟨~ voice⟩ ⟨~ violence⟩

off-season \'=¦==\ *n* **:** a time of suspended or reduced activity ⟨springtime, once considered an *off-season*, has become a thriving vacation period —Bert Pierce⟩

¹**offset** \'=,=\ *n, pl* **offsets** [³*off* + *set*, n. (after *set off*, v.)] **1 a** *archaic* **:** OUTSET, START **b :** CESSATION — opposed to *onset* ⟨rapid regular beating of the heart . . . characterized by sudden onset and sudden ~ —H.J.Stewart⟩ **2 a (1) :** a short prostrate lateral shoot arising from the base of the parent plant (as a houseleek) **(2) :** a small bulb arising from the base of a mother bulb **b :** a lateral or collateral branch of a family or race **:** OFFSHOOT **c :** a spur from a range of hills or mountains **d :** a short drift or crosscut driven from a main level or gangway of a mine **3 a :** a horizontal ledge on the face of a wall, pier, or buttress formed by a diminution of its thickness above **b :** a level terrace on a bank or hillside **c :** horizontal displacement in faulting of strata from previous alignment **:** STRIKE SLIP **d :** an abrupt change in the dimension or profile of an object (as a bowl) or the part set off by such change **4 :** something that sets off to advantage or embellishes something else **:** FOIL **5 a :** an abrupt bend in an object (as a pipe or rod) by which one part is turned aside out of line but nearly parallel with the rest; *also* **:** the part thus bent aside **b :** a short distance measured usu. at right angles from a line (as to a boundary in computing the area of an irregular-shaped piece of land or to a continuation of a line parallel to itself at some distance away to avoid an obstruction) **c :** the distance of any point in a ship's structure from one of the three reference planes measured normal to that plane **6 :** something that serves to counterbalance or to compensate for something else ⟨the ~ of a century of industry was the universal ugliness —Sacheverell Sitwell⟩; *specif* **:** either of two equivalent items on the two sides of an account ⟨these agencies . . . borrow money in order to relend it, and have ~*s* consisting of debts owed them —*New Republic*⟩ **7 :** OFFSET WELL **8** [fr. past part. of ²*offset*] **a :** unintentional transfer of ink (as from the surface of a freshly printed sheet to the back of the sheet placed on top of it); *also* **:** the ink or image so transferred — called also *setoff* **b** *or* **offset lithography :** a printing process in which an inked impression (usu. from a dampened planographic surface) is first made on a rubber-blanketed cylinder and then transferred to the paper being printed — compare DRY OFFSET, LITHOGRAPHY, PHOTO-OFFSET, PLANOGRAPHY **9 :** a rip current running out from or along a beach **:** SEA PUSS **10 :** difference in value or direction **:** DEVIATION, DISCREPANCY ⟨modern man cannot divest himself of his desire to act in the old way . . . the result is an ~ between his desires and his possibilities —W.P.Webb⟩

²**offset** \'=¦=\ *vb* [¹*off* + *set*, v.] *vt* **1 a :** to place over against **:** BALANCE ⟨~ items of deposit and withdrawal⟩ **b :** COUNTERBALANCE, COMPENSATE ⟨had speed enough to ~ his opponents' greater weight⟩ **2 :** to form an offset in (as a wall, rod, pipe) **3** *geol* **:** to move horizontally to one side out of alignment by faulting **4 :** to transfer (an inked impression) from one surface to another by contact ~ *vi* **:** to receive an unintentionally transferred impression **:** set off ⟨interleaving to prevent *offsetting*⟩

³**offset** \"\ *adj* [fr. past part. of ²*offset*] **1 :** placed or moved out of line or out of the center ⟨fishing rod with ~ handle⟩ ⟨~ wheels⟩ **2 :** neither parallel nor intersecting — used esp. of the axes of gears or pulleys **3 :** printed by the offset method ⟨an ~ postage stamp⟩

offset arch *n* **:** CORBEL ARCH

offset screwdriver *n* **:** a screwdriver with the blade at right angles to the shaft for use where a straight screwdriver cannot reach the screwhead

offset screwdriver

offset sheet *n* **:** SLIP SHEET
offset tool *n* **:** a cutting tool whose cutting edge is not in line with the shank
offset well *n* **:** an oil well drilled opposite another oil well on an adjoining property
off-shade \'⸗ˌ⸗\ *adj* **:** imperfectly matching an original or desired color ⟨least mistake in the quantities of dyed wool means *off-shade* yarn —*Dyestuffs*⟩
off-shears \'⸗ˌ⸗\ *adj* [²*off* + *shears*] *Austral* **:** of or relating to sheep that have been shorn ⟨*off-shears* sale⟩ ⟨*off-shears* dipping⟩
offshoot \'⸗ˌ⸗\ *n* [³*off* + *shoot*] **1 :** a branch of a main stem **2 a :** a lateral branch (as of a mountain range) **b :** a collateral or derived branch, descendant, or member **:** OUTGROWTH ⟨the Roman law and its ~*s*⟩ ⟨American culture began as an ~ of Europe —Peter Viereck⟩ **c :** a minor or secondary activity or product ⟨devoted to fiction, and these nonfictional pieces are . . . ~*s* of this activity —J.T.Farrell⟩
¹**offshore** \'⸗ˌ⸗\ *adv* [²*off* + *shore*] **1 :** from the shore ⟨a breeze blowing ~⟩ **:** at a distance from the shore ⟨a boat sailing along ~⟩ **2 :** outside the country **:** ABROAD ⟨purchasing weapons ~⟩
²**offshore** \"\ *adj* **1 :** coming or moving away from the shore ⟨an ~ breeze⟩ ⟨an ~ current⟩ **2 a :** situated off the shore or within a zone generally considered to extend to three miles from low-water line ⟨~ bar⟩ ⟨~ islands⟩ ⟨~ oil reserves⟩ **b :** distant from the shore ⟨~ navigation⟩ ⟨~ fishing⟩ **c :** placed or made abroad ⟨~ procurement⟩
offshore bar *n* **:** BARRIER 2b(1)
off side *adv (or adj)* **1 :** illegally in advance of the ball or puck: as **a :** beyond or across the line of scrimmage in football before the ball is snapped **b :** in the opponent's territory in field hockey or soccer in advance of a teammate having the ball when less than two opponents are between ball and goal line **2 :** in poor taste **:** OFF-COLOR ⟨comedy line cut out as being *off side*⟩ **3 :** in such position as to cause a finesse to lose ⟨the queen is *off side*⟩
offside \'⸗ˌ⸗\ *n* [³*off* + *side*] **1 a** *chiefly Brit* **:** the right side (as of a horse or a vehicle) **b :** the far or inferior side ⟨into the rough surroundings of Chicago's ~ —*Science*⟩ **2** [*off side*] **:** an instance of being off side in a game ⟨five-yard penalty for ~⟩
off·sid·er \'⸗ˌsīdə(r)\ *n, Austral* **:** HELPER, ASSISTANT, ASSOCIATE, FOLLOWER ⟨wanted him as ~ on the boat —Vance Palmer⟩ ⟨an ~ of the governor, too —Thomas Wood †1950⟩
off-sorts \'⸗ˌ⸗\ *n pl* [²*off* + *sorts*] **:** the less desirable parts of the fleece separated during wool-sorting
off soundings *adv* **:** offshore beyond the 100 fathom line
offspin \'⸗ˌ⸗\ *n* [³*off* + *spin*] **:** spin imparted to a bowled ball in cricket that tends to cause it to break from the off side to the leg side
off·spring \'ȯfˌspriŋ *also* 'äf-\ *n, pl* **offspring** *also* **offsprings** [ME *ofspring*, fr. OE, fr. *of* off + *springan* to spring — more at OF, SPRING] **1 :** something that springs from an animal or plant reproducing its kind **:** YOUNG, PROGENY, CHILD, ISSUE ⟨a mother of numerous ~⟩ **2 :** something that comes into being as a result **:** PRODUCT ⟨atomic bomb is the ~ of 20th century physics —I.I.Rabi⟩ **3** *obs* **a :** GENERATION **b :** ancestral stock **:** RACE **c :** LINEAGE, DESCENT **d :** SOURCE, ORIGIN
offstage \'⸗ˌ⸗\ *adv (or adj)* [²*off* + *stage*] **1 :** off or away from the stage **:** out of sight of the audience ⟨the actual murder is carried out ~⟩ ⟨voices heard ~⟩ **2 :** in private life ⟨known ~ as a kindly man⟩ **3 :** behind the scenes **:** out of the public view **:** UNOFFICIALLY ⟨much of the important work of the conference was done ~⟩
off-street \'⸗ˌ⸗\ *adj* [²*off* + *street*] **:** located outside the boundary lines of any street ⟨an *off-street* parking facility⟩
off stump *n* **:** the outside stump farther from the batsman in cricket — compare LEG STUMP
offtake \'⸗ˌ⸗\ *n* [³*off* + *take* (after *take off*, v.)] **1 :** the act of taking off: as **a :** the taking off or purchase of goods **b :** the amount of goods purchased during a given period **2 :** a channel or passage for taking or leading off (as a liquid or gas) ⟨~ of a distilling flask⟩
off-taste \'⸗ˌ⸗\ *n* **:** an unwanted taste imparted by spoilage or contamination
off-the-face \ˌ⸗⸗'⸗\ *adj, of a woman's hat* **:** brimless or having a brim that does not shade the face
off theory *n* **:** a cricket strategy in which a concentration of fielders is placed on the off side esp. in the slips and the bowling aimed generally at or outside of the off stump — compare LEG THEORY
off-trail \'⸗ˌ⸗\ *adj (or adv)* [²*off* + *trail*] **:** UNUSUAL, UNCONVENTIONAL, UNHACKNEYED ⟨the plot, which is an odd and *off-trail* one —Anthony Boucher⟩ ⟨interesting *off-trail* body designs —Roger Huntington⟩
offtype \'⸗ˌ⸗\ *adj* [²*off* + *type*] **:** not true to type **:** markedly deviating from the normal or standard ⟨~ individuals cropping out within a breed of rabbits⟩
off·ward \'ȯfwə(r)d *also* 'äf-\ *also* **off·wards** \-dz\ *adv* [¹*off* + *-ward*, *-wards*] **:** off or away from something as to direction or position; *specif* **:** off or away from the shore ⟨the deck was canting ~⟩
off-wheeler \'⸗ˌ⸗⸗\ *n* [*off wheel* right wheel + *-er*] **:** a wheelhorse on the right side
off-white \'⸗ˌ⸗\ *n* **:** a color (as cream, oyster, beige) closely resembling white but having a slight tinge of gray or of a pale hue **:** a yellowish or grayish white ⟨cloths handwoven in *off-white* with wide borders —*New Yorker*⟩
off year *n* **:** a year characterized by or noted for diminished activity or inferior production: as **a :** a year in which there are no national elections; *esp* **:** a year in which no president is elected — compare MIDTERM **b :** the year of light bearing in biennial-bearing fruit trees
of·lag \'ȯˌfläg\ *n* -S [G, short for *offizierslager* officers' camp] **:** a German prison camp for officers
ofo \'ō(ˌ)fō\ *n, pl* **ofo** *or* **ofos** *usu cap* **1 a :** a Siouan people of the Yazoo river valley, Mississippi **b :** a member of such people **2 :** the language of the Ofo people
OFr *abbr* Old French
oft \'ȯft\ *adv, sometimes* -ER/-EST [ME, fr. OE *oft*; akin to OHG *ofto* often, ON *opt*, Goth *ufta*] **:** OFTEN — now used chiefly in compound adjectives ⟨an ~ neglected factor⟩ ⟨~ repeated question⟩ ⟨~ quoted statement⟩
¹**of·ten** \'ȯfən, -ftən\ *adv, usu* -ER/-EST [ME, alter. of *oft*] **:** on many occasions **:** in many instances or places ⟨numerous plates ~ in color⟩ **:** not seldom **:** FREQUENTLY ⟨are ~ puzzled and sometimes annoyed by the ways of other peoples —W.A. Parker⟩ ⟨in the sense in which the Dialect Society ~*est* employs the word *dialect* —Louise Pound⟩ ⟨now and then he finds adventure by imagining it, ~*er* he transforms his own experience —Walter Lippmann⟩
²**often** \"\ *adj* [ME, fr. *often*, adv.] *archaic* **:** frequently occurring **:** FREQUENT ⟨use a little wine for . . . thine ~ infirmities —1 Tim 5:23 (AV)⟩
of·ten·ness \-n(n)əs\ *n* -ES **:** FREQUENCY
of·tens \-nz\ *adv* [¹*often* + *-s*] *dial chiefly Eng* **:** OFTEN
oftentimes \'⸗⸗ˌ⸗\ *also* **oftentime** \'⸗⸗ˌ⸗\ *adv* [ME, alter. of *ofttime*, *ofttimes*] **:** OFTEN
oft·time \'ȯf(t)ˌtīm\ *adv* [ME, fr. *oft* + *time*] *archaic* **:** OFTEN
oft·times \-mz\ *adv* [ME, fr. *oft* + *times*] **:** OFTEN
OG *abbr* **1** officer of the guard **2** original gum **3** outside guard
o gage *n, usu cap O* [²*oh*, *o*] **:** a gage of track in model railroading in which the rails are approximately 1¼ inches apart
ogalala *usu cap, var of* OGLALA
og·co·ce·phal·i·dae \ˌägkōsə'faləˌdē\ *n pl, cap* [NL, fr. *Ogcocephalus*, type genus + *-idae*] **:** a small family of sluggish spiny bottom-dwelling marine fishes (order Pediculati) with broad flat head and body, slender tapering tail, small mouth and feeble teeth, a short illicium, and jugular pelvic fins resembling limbs by means of which they crawl about — see BATFISH
og·co·ceph·a·lus \ˌägkō'sefələs\ *n, cap* [NL, irreg. fr. Gk *onkos* bulk + NL *-cephalus*; akin to Gk *enenkein* to carry — more at ENOUGH] **:** the type genus of the family Ogcocephalidae comprising various typical batfishes
og·do·ad \'ägdōˌad\ *n* -S *usu cap* [Gk *ogdoad-*, *ogdoas*, fr. *ogdoos* eighth (fr. *oktō* eight) + *-ad-*, *-as*, fem. suffix denoting descent from or connection with — more at EIGHT] **1** *Gnosticism* **:** a group of eight divine beings or of eight aeons **2** *Gnosticism* **:** the seat of rule of the higher archon and his son
¹**ogee** *also* **OG** \(')ō¦jē\ *n* -S [fr. obs. E *ogee* ogive, modif. of F *ogive*; fr. the use of such moldings in ogives — more at OGIVE] **1 a :** a molding with a profile in the form of a letter S **:** CYMA RECTA, CYMA REVERSA **b :** a reverse curve like the profile of an ogee molding **2 :** an ogee arch
²**ogee** *also* **OG** \"\ *adj* **1 :** having the outline of an ogee molding ⟨an ~ bracket foot⟩ — see FOOT illustration **2 :** having an outline composed of two contrasted ogee curves meeting in a point at the apex ⟨an ~ arch⟩ ⟨an ~ doorhead⟩ — see ARCH illustration

ogee 1a

ogee·chee lime \ō'gēchē-\ *n, usu cap O* [fr. *Ogeechee* river, Ga.] **1 :** the acid olive-shaped drupe of a tupelo (*Nyssa ogeche*) of the southern U.S. **2 :** a tree whose fruits are Ogeechee limes
ogee clock *or* **OG clock** *n* **:** a 19th century U. S. shelf clock with S-curve molding
ogeed \(')ō¦jēd\ *adj* [¹*ogee* + *-ed*] **:** shaped like an ogee or like two meeting contrasted ogees
og·ham *or* **og·am** *also* **og·um** \'ägəm, 'ȯg-\ *n* -S [IrGael & MIr; IrGael *ogham*, fr. MIr *ogom*, *ogum*] **1** *sometimes cap* **:** a system of alphabetic writing which is known principally from inscriptions in Old Irish running vertically up rough standing memorial stones that date from at least as early as the 5th century and are found in the British Isles esp. in southern Ireland and which in its typical form had 15 consonant symbols consisting of lines touching or crossing an edge of the stone and five vowel symbols consisting of notches on the edge **2 :** a letter of the ogham alphabet **3 :** an inscription in ogham characters **4 :** the form of Old Irish appearing in ogham inscriptions

ogham

ogham·ic *or* **ogam·ic** \ō'gamik\ *adj* **1 :** of, relating to, characteristic of, or constituting ogham ⟨~ characters⟩ ⟨the ~ alphabet⟩ **2 :** inscribed or written in ogham
og·ham·ist \'ägəməst, 'ȯg-\ *n* -S **:** one that practices inscribing or writing in ogham ⟨embellishments by an ~ no longer bound by practical tradition —Howard Meroney⟩
ogham stone *n* **:** a usu. roughly worked upright stone placed over a grave in ancient Ireland and having at least one sharp edge on which a memorial inscription in ogham is cut
oghuz \ō'güz\ *n, pl* **oghuz** *usu cap* **:** GHUZ
ogi·val \(')ō¦jīvəl\ *adj* [F, fr. *ogive* + *-al*] **1 :** of, relating to, or having the form of an ogive **2 :** characterized by the use of pointed arches and ribbed vaulting **:** GOTHIC **3 :** shaped like an ogee or like two meeting contrasted ogees ⟨an ~ chair arm⟩
ogive \(')ō¦jīv\ *n* -S [F, fr. MF *ogive*, *augive*, perh. fr. *auge* trough (fr. L *alveus* tub, trough) + *-ive* — more at ALVEOLUS] **1 a :** a diagonal arch or rib across a Gothic vault **b :** a pointed arch **c :** a contour like that of a pointed arch **2 a :** the curve determining the shape of the head of modern pointed projectiles that is struck on a line perpendicular to the axis of the projectile on a radius expressed in calibers **b :** the ogival head of a projectile **3 :** a graph each of whose ordinates represents the sum of all the frequencies up to and including a corresponding frequency in a frequency distribution **4 :** OGEE 1a
ogived \-vd\ *adj* **:** shaped like an ogive
og·la·la \äg'lälə\ *or* **og·a·la·la** \ˌägə'-\ *n, pl* **oglala** *or* **oglalas** *or* **ogalala** *or* **ogalalas** *usu cap* **1 a :** a Teton Dakota people **b :** a member of such people **2 :** the language of the Oglala people
¹**ogle** \'ōgəl *sometimes* 'äg-\ *vb* **ogled; ogled; ogling** \-g(ə)liŋ\ **ogles** [prob. fr. LG *oegeln*, freq. of *oegen* to look at, fr. *oog* eye; akin to OHG *ouga* eye — more at EYE] *vi* **:** to glance coquettishly or provocatively **:** look with amorous invitation or challenge ⟨subject to temptation to ~ at young ladies —Lucius Garvin⟩ ~ *vt* **1 :** to eye amorously **:** glance at admiringly, provocatively, or enticingly ⟨lounged in front of a sidewalk cafe, *ogling* the women who passed —Steve Nelson⟩ **2 :** to look at esp. with greedy or interested attention ⟨was still *ogling* the drinks on the next table —William DuBois⟩
²**ogle** \"\ *n* -S **1** *slang* **:** EYE ⟨y'll 'ave to clap a beefsteak on that ~ of yours —G.B.Shaw⟩ **2 :** an amorous or coquettish glance ⟨gave him two or three ~*s* accompanied by . . . a captivating smile —T.L.Peacock⟩
ogler \-g(ə)lə(r)\ *n* -S **:** one that ogles
oglio *archaic var of* OLIO
og·mic \'ägmik\ *adj* [irreg. fr. *ogham* + *-ic*] **:** OGHAMIC
ogre \'ōgə(r)\ *n* -S [F, prob. fr. L *Orcus*, god of the underworld] **1 :** a hideous giant represented in fairy tales and folklore as feeding on human beings **:** MONSTER ⟨he was going to strike her in terror, thinking her an ~ from his dreams, when she spoke —Liam O'Flaherty⟩ **2 :** a dreaded person or object **:** someone or something very difficult to cope with ⟨the ~ of nonuniformity of laws comes up again and again —*Motor Transportation in the West*⟩
ogre·ish *also* **ogrish** \'ōg(ə)rish, -rēsh\ *adj* **:** resembling or befitting an ogre — **ogre·ish·ly** *adv*
ogress \'ōgrəs\ *n* -ES [F *ogresse*, fr. *ogre* + *-esse* -ess] **1** *heraldry* **:** a roundel sable **:** GUNSTONE, PELLET **2 :** a female ogre
ogyg·i·an \ō'jijēən\ *adj, usu cap* [L *ogygius* Ogygian (fr. Gk *ōgygios*, fr. *Ōgygos*, *Ōgygēs*, ancient legendary king of Boeotia) + E *-an*] **1 :** of or relating to the legendary Greek King Ogyges or to a deluge said to have taken place in his reign **2 :** ANCIENT, PRIMEVAL
¹**oh** *or* **o** \'ō(ˌ)\ *interj, usu cap when spelled o* [ME *o*] **1** — used to express various emotions (as astonishment, pain, or desire) **2** — used in direct address ⟨*Oh*, porter! Come here, please⟩
²**oh** \'ō\ *or* **o** *n* -S *usu cap when spelled o* [¹*o*; fr. the similarity of the symbol for zero (0) to the letter O] **:** ZERO ⟨the number is three six ~ seven (3607)⟩
OH *abbr* **1** open hearth **2** overhead
ohe·lo \ō'hā(ˌ)lō\ *n* -S [Hawaiian *'ohelo*] **:** an endemic Hawaiian blueberry (*Vaccinium reticulatum*) with a shining fleshy rather astringent red or yellow berry
OHG *abbr* Old High German
oh hell *or* **oh pshaw** *n* **:** a card game for three to six players in which a player scores only if he has correctly predicted the exact number of tricks he will win
ohia \ō'hēə\ *n* -S [Hawaiian *'ōhi'a*] **1** *or* **ohia-lehua** \⸗'⸗⸗⸗-'⸗⸗\ [*ohia-lehua* fr. Hawaiian *'ōhi'a-lehua*, fr. *'ōhi'a* + *lehua* fruit of the lehua tree] *Hawaii* **:** LEHUA **2** *also* **ohia-ai** \⸗'⸗⸗'ī\ [*ohia-ai* fr. Hawaiian *'ōhi'a-'ai*, fr. *'ōhi'a* + *'ai* food, food plant] *Hawaii* **:** MALAY APPLE
ohi·an \ō'hīən\ *n* -S *cap* [*Ohio* state + *-an*] **:** OHIOAN
ohio \ō'hī(ˌ)ō\ *adj, usu cap* [fr. *Ohio*, north central state of the U. S., fr. the *Ohio* river, perh. fr. Iroquois *oheo* beautiful] **:** of or from the state of Ohio ⟨*Ohio* clay products⟩ **:** of the kind or style prevalent in Ohio **:** OHIOAN
¹**ohio·an** \ō'hīəwən\ *adj, usu cap* [*Ohio* state + E *-an*] **1 :** of, relating to, or characteristic of the state of Ohio **2 :** of, relating to, or characteristic of the people of Ohio
²**ohioan** \"\ *n* -S *cap* **:** a native or resident of the state of Ohio
ohio buckeye *n, usu cap O* **:** a buckeye (*Aesculus glabra*) that occurs chiefly in the central U. S. and has gray bark which is much-furrowed and broken into scaly plates and leaves which have usu. five finely toothed leaflets more or less glabrous beneath
ohio curcuma *n, usu cap O* **:** GOLDENSEAL
ohio horsemint *n, usu cap O* **:** a stiff hairy perennial mint (*Blephilia ciliata*) having showy purple irregular flowers
ohm \'ōm\ *n* -S [after Georg Simon *Ohm* †1854 Ger. physicist] **1 :** the practical mks unit of electric resistance that is equal to the resistance of a circuit in which a potential difference of one volt produces a current of one ampere or to the resistance in which one watt of power is dissipated when one ampere flows through it and that is taken as standard in the U. S. **2 :** a unit of electrical resistance equal to 1.00049 ohms that was formerly taken as the standard in the U. S. — called also *international ohm* **3 :** the cgs unit of acoustic resistance, reactance, and impedance corresponding to a pressure amplitude of one dyne per square centimeter per cubic centimeter per second of flux (volume-velocity) amplitude — called also *acoustic ohm*
ohm·age \-mij\ *n* -S **:** the resistance of a conductor expressed in ohms
ohm-ammeter \'⸗'⸗ˌ⸗⸗\ *n* **:** a combined ohmmeter and ammeter
ohm·ic \'ōmik\ *adj* [ISV *ohm* + *-ic*] **1 :** of or relating to an ohm **:** measured in ohms **2 :** relating to a material or an electrical contact for which the electrical resistance is not dependent on the applied voltage
ohmic resistance *n* **:** electrical resistance as distinguished from inductive or capacitive reactance
ohm·me·ter \'ō(m)ˌmēd·ə(r), -ētə-\ *n* [ISV *ohm* + *-meter*] **:** an instrument for indicating directly resistance in ohms
OHMS *abbr* On Her Majesty's Service; On His Majesty's Service
ohm's law *n, usu cap O* [after G. S. *Ohm*] **1 :** a law in electricity: the strength or intensity of an unvarying electrical current is directly proportional to the electromotive force and inversely proportional to the resistance of the circuit **2 :** a statement in acoustics: the human ear in perceiving a complex sound receives not a sensation of a single sound but sensations of the separate components of the complex wave causing the sound
oho \ō'hō\ *interj* [ME] — used to express various emotions (as taunting or amused surprise)
ohone \ä'kōn\ *var of* OCHONE
OHV *abbr, often not cap* overhead valve
OIC \ˌōˌī'sē, 'ȯik\ *n* [*Ohio Improved Chester White*] **1 :** a breed of low set white lard-type swine developed in Ohio by selection from a strain of the Chester White breed **2** -S **:** any hog of the OIC breed
-o·ic \'ōik, ¦ēk\ *adj suffix* [*-o-* + *-ic*] **:** containing carboxyl or a derivative of it — in names of acids and related compounds ⟨capr*oic*⟩ ⟨hex*oic*⟩ ⟨naphth*oic*⟩; *esp* **:** containing carboxyl in place of methyl ⟨hexan*oic* acid⟩
¹**-oid** \ˌȯid\ *n suffix* -S [L *-oides*, fr. *-oīdes*, adj. suffix] **:** something resembling a (specified) object or having a (specified) quality ⟨cylindr*oid*⟩ ⟨glob*oid*⟩ ⟨hyperbol*oid*⟩
²**-oid** \"\ *adj suffix* [MF *-oïde* & L *-oides*, fr. Gk *-oeidēs*, fr. *-o-* + *-eidēs*, fr. *eidos* form, shape, kind — more at WISE] **:** resembling **:** having the form or appearance of ⟨asbest*oid*⟩ ⟨Caucas*oid*⟩ ⟨crystall*oid*⟩ ⟨granit*oid*⟩ ⟨intellectual*oid*⟩
-oi·dal \ˌȯidᵊl\ *adj suffix* [¹*-oid* + *-al*] **:** -OID ⟨asbest*oidal*⟩
-oi·dea \ˌȯidēə\ *or* **-oi·da** \-də\ *or* **-oi·dei** \-dēˌī\ *n pl suffix* [*-oidea*, NL, fr. L *-oides* -oid + *-ea*, neut. pl. of *-eus* -eous; *-oida*, NL, fr. L *-oides*; *-oidei*, NL, fr. L *-oides* + *-ei*, masc. pl. of *-eus* -eous] **:** animals characterized by or of the nature of — in names of higher taxa in zoology ⟨Echin*oidea*⟩ ⟨Hydr*oida*⟩ ⟨Gan*oidei*⟩
oid·i·oid \ō'idēˌȯid\ *adj* [NL *Oidium* + E *-oid*] **1 :** of, relating to, or resembling fungi of the genus *Oidium* **2 :** producing oidia
oid·i·o·my·co·sis \ōˌidēōˌmī'kōsəs\ *n* [NL, fr. *Oidium* + *-o-* + NL *-mycosis*] **:** infection with or disease caused by fungi of the genus *Oidium*
oid·i·um \ō'idēəm\ *n* [NL, fr. *o-* + *-idium*] **1 a** *cap* **:** a genus of imperfect fungi (family Moniliaceae) including many now considered to represent conidial stages of various powdery mildews — compare BLASTOMYCETES, THRUSH **b** *pl* **oid·ia** \-ēə\ **:** a fungus of this genus **c** *pl* **oidia :** one of the small conidia borne in chains by various fungi (as members of the genus *Oidium*) — called also *arthrospore* **2** *pl* **oidia :** a powdery mildew caused by a fungus of the genus *Oidium* esp. in the grape — compare OIDIOMYCOSIS
oiko- — see ²EC-
¹**oi·ko·mo·nad** \ˌȯikə¦mōˌnad\ *adj* [NL *Oikomonad-*, *Oikomonas*] **:** of or relating to the genus *Oikomonas* or to the family Oikomonadidae
²**oikomonad** \"\ *n* -S **:** a protozoan of the genus *Oikomonas* or the family Oikomonadidae
oi·kom·o·nas \ȯi'kämənəs\ *n, cap* [NL, fr. ²*ec-* + *-monas*] **:** a cosmopolitan genus (the type of the family Oikomonadidae) of minute uniflagellate protozoans common in stagnant water, soil, and sewage
oi·ko·plast \'ȯikəˌplast\ *n* -S [²*ec-* + *-plast*] **:** one of the ectodermal cells that secrete the gelatinous layer in the Appendicularia
oi·ko·pleu·ra \ˌȯikə'plùrə\ *n, cap* [NL, fr. ²*ec-* + *-pleura*] **:** a cosmopolitan genus of small tunicates (order Larvacea) with egg-shaped body and long tail
¹**oil** \'ȯil\ *dial* 'īl, *esp before pause or consonant* |əl\ *n* -S *often attrib* [ME *olie*, *oile*, fr. OF, fr. L *oleum* olive oil, oil, fr. Gk *elaion*, fr. *elaia* olive — more at OLIVE] **1 a :** any of various substances that typically are unctuous viscous combustible liquids or solids easily liquefiable on warming and are not miscible with water but are soluble in ether, naphtha, and often alcohol and other organic solvents, that leave a greasy not necessarily permanent stain (as on paper or cloth), that may be of animal, vegetable, mineral, or synthetic origin, and that are used according to their types chiefly as lubricants, fuels and illuminants, as food, in soap and candles, and in perfumes and flavoring materials — compare ESSENTIAL OIL, FAT, FATTY OIL, MINERAL OIL **b :** PETROLEUM **2 :** a substance of an oily consistency: as **a :** a cosmetic preparation containing oil ⟨bath ~⟩ ⟨hair ~⟩ ⟨sunburn ~⟩ **b :** NITROGLYCERIN **3 a :** an oil color used by an artist ⟨paints in ~*s*⟩ **b :** a painting done in oil colors ⟨suggests that his best ~*s* retain the sharp conviction of his sketches —J.T.Soby⟩ **4 :** unctuous or flattering speech **:** smooth or persuasive utterance ⟨it's just the old ~ —Harris Downey⟩ **5** *slang Austral* **:** INFORMATION **6 oils** *pl* **:** stocks or bonds of oil companies
²**oil** \"\ *vb* -ED/-ING/-S [ME *oilen*, fr. *oile*, n.] *vt* **1** *obs* **:** to anoint ceremonially with oil (as a king at coronation) **2 a :** to smear or rub over with oil **:** furnish or feed with oil **:** LUBRICATE ⟨carefully ~*ed* the bearings of the machine⟩ ⟨liberal contributions ~*ed* the campaign machinery⟩ **b :** to spray oil on (a dirt road) **3 :** to make bland or smooth ⟨I learned to use a soft voice to ~ my words —Lillian Smith⟩ **4 :** to turn into or make of the consistency of oil (as grease by melting) ~ *vi* **1 a :** to become like oil in consistency **b :** to separate with the formation of an oily portion (as butter fat) — used with *off* ⟨cream poured into hot coffee ~*s* off⟩ **2 :** to take on fuel oil — used chiefly of ships and locomotives — **oil the hand** *or* **oil the palm :** BRIBE, TIP ⟨a cop whose *palm* I'd *oiled* —Polly Adler⟩
oil and gas lease *n* **:** a deed by which a landowner authorizes exploration for and production of oil and gas on his land usu. in consideration of a royalty
oil bag *n* **:** a canvas bag containing cotton, oakum, or other absorbent material soaked with oil that is sometimes dropped with a sea anchor to create an oil slick tending to reduce surface wave violence
oil bath *n* **:** a bath of oil: as **a :** a volume of oil in which a solid is submerged (as for lubrication, preservation, or tempering) **b :** the container for oil so used **c :** a stream of oil flowing upon a cutting tool to cool it
oil beetle *n* **:** a beetle of *Meloe* or a related genus having a swollen body and short elytra that overlap instead of meeting in a straight line, passing through more than the usual number of larval instars, and emitting a yellowish liquid from the leg joints when disturbed
oilbird \'⸗ˌ⸗\ *n* **:** a nocturnal bird (*Steatornis guácharo*) of northern So. America and Trinidad that is related to the goatsuckers and in some characters to the owls, nests in caverns, feeds chiefly on oily fruits of various nut palms, is believed to employ a form of echo-location comparable to that of bats, and has fatty young from which an oil is extracted for use instead of butter — called also *guacharo*
oil-break switch *n* **:** a switch in which the contacts are immersed in oil — compare AIR-BREAK SWITCH
oil burner *n* **1 :** a burner equipped to vaporize or atomize fuel oil, mix it with air and ignite the mixture, and direct the flame upon the surface to be heated **2 :** a ship whose boilers are oil-fired **3 :** a gasoline engine that consumes an excessive amount of oil
oil cake *n* **:** the solid residue that remains after expressing or

extracting most of the oil from various seeds (as of cotton, hemp, flax, and soybeans) and that is then often ground to make oil meal

oilcan \ˈ≈,≈\ *n* **:** a can for oil; *esp* **:** a can equipped with a slender spout for lubricating machinery

oilcloth \ˈ≈,≈\ *n* **1 a :** cotton cloth coated with a dull or glossy finish that usu. contains oil, clay, and colored pigment and used for waterproof coverings **b :** an article (as a tablecloth) made of this material **2 :** a floor covering made of a strong open canvas treated with linseed-oil paint, smoothed with pumice, and printed from blocks as in calico printing — compare LINOLEUM

oilcan

oil color *n* **1 :** a pigment used for oil paint **2 :** OIL PAINT **3 :** a concentrated dispersion of a colored pigment in linseed oil or other drying oil

oil column *or* **oil crane** *n* **:** a vertical pipe with control valve and spout for supplying oil to the tenders of oil-burning locomotives

oil cup *n* **:** a cup connected with a bearing as a lubricator and usu. having a wick, valve, or other means for regulating the delivery of oil

oil·dom \ˈȯi(ə)ldəm\ *n* -S [¹*oil* + *-dom*] **1 :** a petroleum region **2 :** the petroleum industry

oiled *adj* **1 a :** lubricated with oil **b :** polished, dressed, or impregnated with oil **c :** coated or treated with oil or an oil compound ⟨~ silk⟩ ⟨~ paper⟩ **2** *slang* **:** DRUNK ⟨thoroughly ~ and very talkative —*Amer. Mercury*⟩

oil–electric \¦≈¦≈\ *adj* **:** DIESEL-ELECTRIC

oil·er \ˈȯilə(r)\ *n* -S **1 a :** one who is employed to do routine oiling and greasing of mechanical equipment (as in a mill, factory, power plant, railroad yard, or on a vessel) **b :** one who works oil or grease into hides or skins to soften and protect the leather **2 :** an oilcan, oil cup, or other receptacle or device for applying oil to mechanical bearing surfaces **:** LUBRICATOR **3 :** a producing oil well **4 a :** a ship using oil as fuel **b :** an oil cargo ship **:** TANKER **5 oilers** *pl* **:** OILSKINS **6 a :** a device that automatically applies an oil or insecticide to the hide of a domestic animal that rubs against it

oilfeeder \ˈ≈,≈≈\ *n, Brit* **:** a force-feed oilcan

oil field *n* **:** a region rich in petroleum deposits; *esp* **:** a region containing numbers of producing oil wells

oil·field·er \ˈȯil,fēldə(r)\ *n* **:** a worker in an oil field

oilfish \ˈ≈,≈\ *n* **:** ESCOLAR

oil gas *n* **:** gas (as blau gas or Pintsch gas) made usu. by vaporizing and cracking a petroleum distillate (as a heavy oil) — compare CARBURETED WATER GAS, GAS OIL

oil geologist *n* **:** PETROLEUM GEOLOGIST

oil gilding *or* **oil gold** *n* **:** gilding on a surface coated with oil paint and size

oil gland *n* **:** a gland that secretes oil; *specif* **:** UROPYGIAL GLAND

oil groove *n* **:** a groove in the bearing surface of a machine part that distributes lubricating oil injected through an oilhole

oil–harden \ˈ≈¦≈≈\ *vt* **:** to quench (steel) in oil for the purpose of hardening

oil heater *n* **:** a heater that burns fuel oil

oilhole \ˈ≈,≈\ *n* **:** a small hole through which oil is injected to lubricate a mechanical bearing surface

oilhole drill *also* **oil drill** *n* **:** a twist drill having oilholes through which a lubricant is fed to its cutting edge while drilling

oilier *comparative of* OILY

oiliest *superlative of* OILY

oil·i·ly \ˈȯiləlē\ *adv* **:** in an oily manner **:** UNCTUOUSLY ⟨waddled forward, smiling ~ —John Buchan⟩

oil–immersion lens *n* **:** IMMERSION LENS

oil·i·ness \ˈȯilēnəs, -lin-\ *n* -ES **:** the quality or state of being oily

oiling *pres part of* OIL

oil–in–water \¦≈≈¦≈≈\ *adj* **:** consisting of oil dispersed in water ⟨*oil-in-water* emulsions⟩

oil length *n* **:** the ratio of drying oil to resin in a varnish or similar coating expressed usu. as the number of gallons of oil per 100 pounds of resin ⟨varnishes are usually classified as to *oil length* as well as to the major types of oil and resin used —S.B.Levinson⟩ — compare LONG-OIL, SHORT-OIL

oil·less \ˈȯilləs\ *adj* **:** lacking oil **:** not lubricated with oil **:** not requiring oil — **oil·less·ness** *n* -ES

oilless bearing *n* **:** a bearing that does not require oil; *esp* **:** one in which a lubricant (as powdered graphite) is incorporated in the material of which the bearing is made

oil·let \ˈȯilət\ *n* -S [ME *oilet* — more at EYELET] *archaic* **:** ¹EYELET 2

oil·man \ˈ≈,man, -,maa(ə)n, -mən\ *n, pl* **oilmen 1 :** an entrepreneur or leader in the petroleum industry **2 :** one who sells or delivers oil

oil meal *n* **:** a meal made by grinding oil cake and fed to livestock or used as fertilizer

oil mill *n* [ME, fr. *oile* + *mill*] **1 :** a machine that crushes seeds (as cottonseed or soybeans) to extract their oil **2 :** a factory using oil mills

oil nut *n* **1 :** BUFFALO NUT **2 :** any of several nuts and seeds yielding oil: as **a :** COCONUT **b :** the fruit of the oil palm **c :** BUTTERNUT; *esp* **:** this nut with its husks used while still soft and immature for pickling whole

oil of catechumens : holy oil used in baptism, ordination, consecration of churches, and coronation of rulers

oil of hartshorn : BONE OIL 1

oil of philosophers : PHILOSOPHERS' OIL

oil of the sick : holy oil used in extreme unction

oil of vitriol : concentrated sulfuric acid

oil·om·e·ter \ȯiˈläməd·ə(r)\ *n* [¹*oil* + *-o-* + *-meter*] **1 :** OLEOMETER **2 :** a reservoir for oil **:** an oil tank

oil paint *n* **:** paint in which a drying oil is the vehicle

oil painting *n* **1 a :** the act or art of painting in oil colors **b :** a picture painted in oils **2 :** painting that uses pigments orig. ground in oil

oil palm *n* **:** a palm of the genus *Elaeis*; *esp* **:** AFRICAN OIL PALM

oil pan *n* **:** the lower section of the crankcase used as a lubricating-oil reservoir on an internal-combustion engine

oilpaper \ˈ≈,≈≈\ *n* **:** paper made translucent and waterproof by soaking in oil ⟨dim light . . . streamed in through ~ windows —J.H.Cutler⟩

oil plant *n* **:** a plant that yields oil: as **a :** SESAME **b :** CASTOR-OIL PLANT

oil pool *n* **:** ¹POOL 3

oil press *n* **:** a press for expressing oil (as from nuts, olives, seeds)

oil process *n* **:** a photographic printing process in which a layer of gelatin is sensitized with a bichromate solution, exposed under a negative, soaked in water, and inked with an oily printing ink by a brush, the unexposed portions of the gelatin swelling in the water and repelling the oily ink while the exposed portions tanned by the light action remain unswollen and accept the ink

¹oilproof \¦≈¦≈\ *adj* [¹*oil* + *proof*] **:** impervious to oil

²oilproof \"\ *vt* **:** to make oilproof

oil red *n, often cap O&R* **:** any of several oil-soluble red dyes — see DYE table I (under *Solvent Red 26 and 27*)

oil ring *n* **1 :** a seal engravers' finger ring having a small receptacle containing a mixture of oil and diamond dust used in replenishing the engraving tool **2 :** RING OILER **3 :** a piston ring designed to secure proper distribution of lubricating oil over the length of cylinder wall traversed by the piston

oil rock *n* **:** the stratum usu. of sandstone, limestone, or shale from which petroleum is produced

oils *pl of* OIL, *pres 3d sing of* OIL

oil sand *n* **:** a porous sandstone from which petroleum is obtained by drilled wells

oil seal *n* **:** a device (as a gland with packing) for preventing the escape or entrance of oil

oilseed \ˈ≈,≈\ *n* **1 :** any of various seeds grown largely for oil: as **a :** CASTOR BEAN **b :** SESAME **c :** COTTONSEED **d :** LINSEED **e :** RAPESEED **2 a :** GOLD OF PLEASURE **b :** the seed of gold of pleasure yielding cameline oil

oil shale *n* **:** shale from which oil may be produced by distillation

oil shark *n* **:** any of several sharks from whose livers oil is obtained: as **a :** BASKING SHARK **b :** SOUPFIN SHARK

oilskin \ˈ≈,≈\ *n* **1 :** an oiled cloth (as of cotton) used for waterproof coverings and garments **2 :** an oilskin raincoat **3 oilskins** *pl* **:** an oilskin suit usu. consisting of coat and trousers

oil–skinned \"+d\ *adj* **:** dressed in or protected with oilskin

oil slick *n* **:** a film of oil floating on water

oil–soluble \ˈ≈¦≈≈≈\ *adj* **:** soluble or dispersible in oils **:** FAT-SOLUBLE ⟨*oil-soluble* dyes⟩ ⟨*oil-soluble* resins⟩

oil spot *n* **1 :** one of the pale transparent areas on the upper leaf surface in the early stages of downy mildew of the grape **2 :** OLEOCELLOSIS

oilstock \ˈ≈,≈\ *n* **:** a vessel for holding holy oil

¹oilstone \ˈ≈,≈\ *n* [¹*oil* + *stone*] **1 :** a whetstone for use with oil **2 :** stone from which oilstones may be made

²oilstone \"\ *vt* **:** to sharpen with an oilstone **:** polish with oilstone powder or oilstone slips

oilstove \ˈ≈,≈\ *n* **:** a stove that burns oil (as kerosene)

oil switch *n* **:** a switch in which the contacts are immersed in oil

oil tanning *n* **:** the conversion of hides into leather by impregnation with oil — see CHAMOIS 2b

oil–temper \ˈ≈¦≈≈\ *vt* **:** to harden (steel) by quenching in oil after heating

oiltight \ˈ≈¦≈\ *adj* **:** so tight as to prevent the passage of oil ⟨~ joints⟩ — **oil·tight·ness** *n*

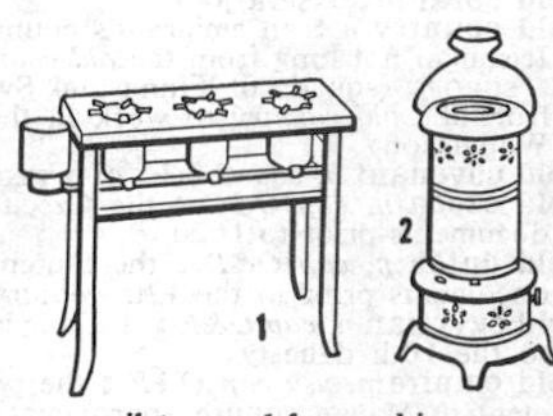

oilstoves: *1* for cooking, *2* for heating

oil transfer process *n* **:** a photographic printing process in which an image in oily ink produced in the oil process is transferred to another support (as paper) by contact and pressure

oil tube *n* **:** VITTA 1

oil varnish *n* **:** a varnish consisting of a solution of natural or synthetic resins in a drying oil (as linseed oil or tung oil)

oilway \ˈ≈,≈\ *n* **:** a channel by which oil may reach a part to be lubricated

oil well *n* **:** a well from which petroleum is obtained

¹oily \ˈȯilē, -li\ *adj* -ER/-EST [¹*oil* + *-y*] **1 :** of, relating to, or consisting of oil **:** containing oil **:** having the nature or qualities of oil **2 :** covered or impregnated with oil **:** GREASY ⟨rid of rubbish and ~ rags —*My Weekly Reader*⟩ **3 :** unctuously ingratiating or insinuating **:** PLAUSIBLE, SMOOTH, SUAVE ⟨an ~, sycophantic press agent —Lee Rogow⟩

²oily \"\ *adv* **:** OILILY ⟨of ~ smooth texture⟩

oily bean *or* **oily grain** *n* **:** SESAME

oil yellow *n* **1** *often cap O&Y* **3 a :** any of several oil-soluble yellow dyes — see DYE table I (under *Solvent Yellow*) **b** *or* **oil yellow II :** a carcinogenic azo dye $C_6H_5N_2C_6H_4N(CH_3)_2$ formerly used in coloring butter and oils; *para*-dimethyl-aminoazobenzene — called also *butter yellow, methyl yellow;* see DYE table I (under *Solvent Yellow 2*) **2 :** a moderate greenish yellow that is greener and duller than citron yellow and deeper than linden green

oily–tongued \¦≈≈¦≈\ *adj* **:** excessively smooth-spoken **:** UNCTUOUS

oi·me *also* **oi·mee** \ȯiˈmā\ *interj* [It *oimè, ohimè,* fr. *ohi* alas + *me* me] *archaic* — used to express grief or lamentation

-oin \əwən, ōwən, ,ōin, ˈōən\ *n suffix* -S [ISV *-o-* + *-in*] **:** acyloin ⟨acetoin⟩

¹oink \ˈȯiŋk\ *n* -S [imit.] **:** the natural grunt of a hog

²oink \"\ *vi* -ED/-ING/-S **:** to utter the natural grunt of a hog

oinochoe *var of* OENOCHOE

oint \ˈȯint\ *vt* -ED/-ING/-S [ME *ointen,* fr. MF *oint,* past part. of *oindre,* fr. L *ungere, unguere*] *chiefly dial* **:** ANOINT

oint·ment \ˈȯintmənt\ *n* -S [ME, alter. (influenced by *ointen* to anoint) of *oignement, oinement,* fr. OF *oignement,* fr. (assumed) VL *unguimentum,* alter. of L *unguentum,* fr. *unguent-, unguens,* pres. part. of *unguere* to anoint, smear; akin to OHG *ancho, anko* butter, OIr *imb,* W *ymenyn* butter, Skt *añjati, anakti* he salves] **:** a salve or unguent for application to the skin; *specif* **:** a semisolid medicinal preparation usu. having a base of fatty or greasy material (as petrolatum, lard, wool fat) — see SIMPLE OINTMENT

o'io \ˈōē,ō\ *n* -S [Hawaiian *ʻōʻio*] *Hawaii* **:** BONEFISH

oi·ti·ci·ca \,ȯid·əˈsēkə\ *n* -S [Pg, fr. Tupi] **:** any of several So. American trees; *esp* **:** a tall tree (*Licania rigida*) of northeastern Brazil having a fruit like the pecan with a kernel that yields oiticica oil

oiticica oil *n* **:** a drying oil obtained from the kernels of the fruit of the oiticica tree, similar to tung oil in many properties, and used chiefly in varnishes, paints, and printing inks

ojib·wa *or* **ojib·way** \ōˈjib,wā\ *n, pl* **ojibwa** *or* **ojibwas** *or* **ojibway** *or* **ojibways** *usu cap* [Ojibwa *ojib-ubway* moccasin with a puckered seam (such as the Ojibwa traditionally wore), lit., to roast till puckered up] **1 a :** an Indian people of the region around Lake Superior and westward **b :** a member of such people **2 :** an Algonquian language of the Ojibwa, Salteaux, Ottawa, and Algonkian peoples — called also *Chippewa*

¹OK *or* **okay** *also* **okey** *or* **okeh** \(ˈ)ō¦kā\ *adj* [abbr. of *oll korrect,* facetious alter. of *all correct*] **:** all right ⟨an *OK* battery commander —John Phillips⟩ ⟨will print anything however bad which is politically *OK* —George Orwell⟩ ⟨there are people, nice people, *okay* people, who do their own housework, cooking, and serving —Laura Hobson⟩

²OK *or* **okay** *also* **okey** *or* **okeh** \"\ *adv* **:** all right **:** YES ⟨*OK,* Doctor, I'll let you know —John Hersey⟩ ⟨*okay, okay,* but be good to him —C.O.Gorham⟩

³OK *or* **okay** *also* **okey** *or* **okeh** \"\ *vt* **OK'd** *or* **okayed; OK'd** *or* **okayed; OK'ing** *or* **okaying; OK's** *or* **okays :** APPROVE, AUTHORIZE, SANCTION ⟨read and *OK'd* every script —Sam Balter⟩ ⟨all right, I'll *okay* that —James Hilton⟩ ⟨*okehs* easing small business tax —*Sacramento (Calif.) Bee*⟩

⁴OK *or* **okay** *also* **okey** *or* **okeh** \"\ *n* -S **:** APPROVAL, ENDORSEMENT, SANCTION, AUTHORIZATION ⟨he gets the *OK* of the Production Code censors —Joseph Wechsberg⟩ ⟨an ad presented to the publisher for *okey* —*Publishers' Weekly*⟩

¹oka *var of* OCA

²oka \ˈōkə\ *n* -S *usu cap* [CanF, fr. *Oka,* village in Quebec, Canada, where it is made] **:** a Trappist cheese made by Trappist monks in Quebec

OKA *abbr, often not cap* otherwise known as

oka·na·gon \,ōkəˈnägən\ *n, pl* **okanagon** *or* **okanagons** *usu cap* **1 a :** a Salishan people of the Okanagon river valley of Washington and British Columbia **b :** a member of such people **2 :** a language of the Okanagon, Colville, Nespelem, Sanpoil, and Senijextee people

oka·pi \ōˈkäpē\ *n* -S [native name in Africa] **:** a mammal (*Okapia johnstoni*) discovered in the deep forests of the Belgian Congo in 1900 and closely related to and in many respects resembling the giraffe but being somewhat smaller than an ox, having a relatively short neck, a coat of solid reddish chestnut on the body, the cheeks yellowish white, and the upper parts of the legs ringed with cream and purplish black

okapi

oka·ya·ma \,ōkəˈyämə\ *adj, usu cap* [fr. *Okayama,* Japan] **:** of or from the city of Okayama, Japan **:** of the kind or style prevalent in Okayama

¹oke \ˈōk\ *or* **oka** \ˈōkə\ *n* -S [F, NGk & Turk; F *oque,* fr. NGk & Turk; NGk *oka,* fr. Turk *okka,* fr. Ar *ūqīyah,* prob. fr. Gk *oungia, ounkia* ounce, fr. L *uncia* — more at OUNCE] **:** any of three units of weight varying around 2.8 pounds and used respectively in Greece, Turkey, and Egypt

²oke \ˈōkē\ *n* -S [by shortening & alter.] **:** OKOLEHAO

oken·ite \ˈōkə,nīt\ *n* -S [G *okenit,* fr. Lorenz *Oken* †1851 Ger. naturalist + G *-it* -ite] **:** a compact or fibrous mineral $CaSi_2O_4(OH)_2.H_2O$ consisting of a whitish hydrous calcium silicate

okey·doke \,ōkēˈdōk\ *or* **okey·dokey** \-dōkē\ *adv* (*or adj*) [redupl. of ²*OK*] *slang* **:** all right

okie *also* **oakie** \ˈōkē\ *n* -S *usu cap* [*Ok*lahoma + *-ie*] **:** a migrant agricultural worker; *esp* **:** such a worker from Oklahoma — compare ARKIE

¹oki·na·wan \¦ōkə¦näwən, -naùən\ *adj, usu cap* [*Okinawa,* island and island group of the Ryukyu islands, between the East China sea and the Pacific ocean + E *-an*] **1 :** of, relating to, or characteristic of the island of Okinawa **2 :** of, relating to, or characteristic of the people of Okinawa

²okinawan \"\ *n* -S *cap* **:** a native or inhabitant of Okinawa

okla·bar \ˈōklə,bär\ *n* -S *usu cap* [fr. ¹*okla*homa + *bar*] **1 :** a breed of autosexing gold or silvery barred domestic fowls developed in Oklahoma and notable for fast feathering and good meat conformation **2** *often cap* **:** a bird of the Oklabar breed

¹okla·ho·ma \¦ōklə¦hōmə\ *adj, usu cap* [fr. *Oklahoma,* state in the southwestern U. S., fr. Choctaw *okla humma, okla homma* red people] **:** of or from the state of Oklahoma **:** of the kind or style prevalent in Oklahoma **:** OKLAHOMAN

²oklahoma \"\ *n* -S *usu cap* **1 :** a form of rummy related to canasta **2** *or* **oklahoma gin :** a form of gin rummy in which the rank of the first upcard determines the minimum count on which one may knock

oklahoma city *adj, usu cap O&C* [fr. *Oklahoma City,* Okla.] **:** of or from Oklahoma City, the capital of Oklahoma **:** of the kind or style prevalent in Oklahoma City

¹okla·ho·man \-mən\ *adj, usu cap* [*Oklahoma* + E *-an*] **1 :** of, relating to, or characteristic of the state of Oklahoma **2 :** of, relating to, or characteristic of the people of Oklahoma

²oklahoman \"\ *n* -S *cap* **:** a native or resident of Oklahoma

oklahoma plum *n, usu cap O* **:** a low shrub (*Prunus gracilis*) with white flowers and globose red fruit

oko·le·hao *also* **oko·le·hau** \,ōkəlāˈhaù\ *or* **okulehau** *n* -S [Hawaiian *ʻōkolehao* iron try-pot still, okolehao, lit., iron buttocks] *Hawaii* **:** an alcoholic liquor distilled from ti or taro roots

okou·me *or* **oku·me** \,ōkəˈmā\ *n* -S [F *okoumé,* fr. native name in Africa] **:** GABOON 2a

okra *also* **okro** \ˈōkrə, *chiefly in southern U. S.* -rē *or* -ri\ *n* -S [of African origin; akin to Twi *ŋkuˈrūmā* okra] **1 :** a tall annual (*Hibiscus esculentus*) widely cultivated in the southern U. S. and the West Indies for its mucilaginous green pods that are pickled or used as the basis of soups and stews **2 :** the pods of the okra **3 :** ¹GUMBO 2 a

okra

ok·vik \ˈäkvik\ *adj, usu cap* [fr. *Okvik,* site on Punuk Island, S.E. of St. Lawrence Island in the Bering sea] **:** of or belonging to an early phase of the Old Bering Sea culture in northern Alaska and northeastern Siberia that produced an art style in which patterns suggesting scrolls are noticeable

ol *abbr* oleum

OL *abbr* **1** occupational level **2** [L *oculus laevus*] left eye **3** overflow level **4** overhead line **5** overload **6** Old Latin

¹-ol \,ȯl, ,ōl, ,ōl\ *n suffix* -S [ISV, fr. *alcohol*] **:** chemical compound containing hydroxyl ⟨hydrol⟩ — esp. in names of alcohols and phenols ⟨glycerol⟩ ⟨methanol⟩ ⟨cresol⟩

²-ol — see -OLE; not used systematically

³-ol *also* **-ole** \,ȯl, ,ōl, ,ōl\ *n comb form* -S [ISV, fr. L *oleum* oil — more at OIL] **:** hydrocarbon of the benzene series esp. in a commercial mixture containing homologous hydrocarbons ⟨xylol⟩ — not used systematically; compare -ENE

ola *also* **ol·la** \ˈälə\ *n* -S [Pg *ola,* fr. Malayalam *ōla*] **1 :** a leaf or strip from the leaf of the talipot palm used in India for writing paper **2 :** a document written on olla

ol·a·ca·ce·ae \,äləˈkāsē,ē\ *n pl, cap* [NL, fr. *Olac-, Olax,* type genus + *-aceae*] **:** a family of tropical trees or shrubs (order Santalales) having simple leaves and small flowers with a one-celled ovary followed by a one-seeded fruit — **ol·a·ca·ceous** \¦≈≈¦kāshəs\ *adj*

OL and T *abbr* owners, landlords, and tenants

ola·tion \ōˈlāshən\ *n* -S [¹*-ol* + *-ation*] **:** the formation of polynuclear coordination complexes by means of hydroxyl groups as bridges

olax \ˈō,laks\ *n, cap* [NL, fr. LL *olax* odorous, fr. L *olēre* to smell; fr. the unpleasant odor of the wood — more at ODOR] **:** a genus (the type of the family Olacaceae) of evergreen trees and shrubs distributed through the tropics of Asia, Africa, and Australia and having distichous leaves and small racemose flowers with three stamens

ol·cha \ˈōlchə\ *n, pl* **olcha** *or* **olchas** *usu cap* **1 :** a Tungusic people living near the mouth of the Amur river in Asia — compare TUNGUS **2 :** a member of the Olcha people

¹old \ˈōld, *before a consonant often* ˈōl\ *adj* -ER/-EST [ME *ald, old,* fr. OE *eald, ald;* akin to OS *ald* old, OHG *alt* old, ON *aldr* age, *ala* to bring up, nourish, Goth *alds* period of time, age (of a person), *altheis* old, *alan* grown up, L *alere* to feed, nourish, *alescere* to grow, *altus* high, Gk *aldēskein* to grow, *analtos* insatiable, Skt *anala* fire (lit., the insatiable one), *ṛdhnoti* he flourishes, succeeds; basic meaning: to grow, nourish] **1 a :** dating from the remote past **:** ANCIENT ⟨beautiful ~ Japanese traditions —Lafcadio Hearn⟩ **b :** persisting from an earlier time **:** CHRONIC ⟨~ pains keep . . . gnawing at your heart —Joseph Conrad⟩ **c :** of long standing **:** having a status strengthened by the passage of time ⟨an ~ friend⟩ ⟨~ residents of the vicinity —John De Meyer⟩ ⟨comes from an ~ family⟩ **2 a :** distinguished from an object of the same kind by being of an earlier date ⟨new . . . standards for ~ jobs —Bruce Payne⟩ ⟨the ~ name was readopted at the time of incorporation —*Amer. Guide Series: Pa.*⟩ ⟨how slow this ~ moon wanes —Shak.⟩; *specif, usu cap* **:** belonging to an early period in the development of a language or literature and preceding a middle period **b :** constituting an earlier geographic entity ⟨the ~ Roman Empire⟩ ⟨repeatedly toured the ~ Northwest —E.S.Bates⟩ **c** *of a holiday* **:** celebrated on the Old Style date ⟨*Old* Christmas⟩ ⟨*Old* Midsummer Day⟩ **3 a :** having existed for a specified period of time ⟨a little girl three years ~⟩ ⟨a gambrel roofed house over 200 years ~⟩ ⟨the campaign was scarcely two days ~ —P.W.Thompson⟩ **b :** exceeding a specified age ⟨~ geese retailed at 47¢ lb.⟩ **4 a :** performed in or descriptive of the distant past ⟨~ sacrifices to the Cretan bulls⟩ ⟨mentioned in ~ histories⟩ **b :** of, relating to, or characteristic of antiquity or of a past era **:** ANTIQUE, BYGONE ⟨interpreting ~ writers in their own tongue —Benjamin Farrington⟩ ⟨~ Hitchcock chairs⟩ ⟨rural simplicity and innocence because in ~ days, as now, this region lay apart from the active life . . . near the sea —Samuel Van Valkenburg & Ellsworth Huntington⟩ **c :** stemming from or reminiscent of a past era ⟨tenacity of ~ opinion —H.T. Buckle⟩ ⟨giving new meanings to ~ words —M.R.Cohen⟩ ⟨chandeliers, which are merely ~, as opposed to antique —*New Yorker*⟩ **d :** famed through the ages ⟨the ~ historical lands of Europe —Mark Pattison⟩ **5 a :** advanced in years **:** nearing the end of the normal life span ⟨an ~ man with a long white beard⟩ ⟨a tall ~ virgin pine . . . spared by fire and woodcutter —*Amer. Guide Series: Minn.*⟩ **b :** exhibiting the physical or mental characteristics of age ⟨looked ~ at 20 because of prolonged suffering⟩ ⟨wake up . . . in a world where no one was conventional or stuffy or ~ —Margery Sharp⟩ **6 :** having a knowledge or ability gained through long practice **:** EXPERIENCED ⟨~ in the ways of conspirators —Max Peacock⟩ **7 a :** identified with an earlier period ⟨the ~ democratic objection to despotism —G.K.Chesterton⟩ ⟨ministers . . . who spoke the ~ tongue —Oscar Handlin⟩ ⟨the grandfather's clock still stands in the same ~ place⟩ ⟨retained all of his ~ alertness and charm —F.J.Mather⟩ **b :** during an earlier period **:** FORMER ⟨hundreds of his ~ students were present —L.M.Crosbie⟩ ⟨the badge . . . is treasured among ~ members of our squadron —L.G.Pine⟩ **8 a :** deteriorated or mellowed by or as if by time or use : AGED, WORN ⟨~ books⟩ ⟨~ wine⟩ ⟨~ pasture⟩ ⟨marks the northern end of an ~ sea wall —H.Lovegrove⟩ — often used to express disparagement ⟨give mamma that dirty ~ stick⟩, generalized affection ⟨good ~ Santa Claus⟩ ⟨our little ~ wobbledy calf —Eugene Field⟩ ⟨a great ~ establishment —Sinclair Lewis⟩, familiarity ⟨fifty years ago, there was only one kind of pneumonia — just plain ~ pneumonia —R.J.Huebner⟩ ⟨back to the same ~ grind⟩, personalization ⟨the ~ stomach did a buck and wing —P.G.Wodehouse⟩, or as an intensive ⟨having a high ~ time⟩ esp. of *any* ⟨come any ~ time, I'll be home all day⟩ ⟨not any ~ ink will print well —Séan Jennett⟩ **b :** well advanced toward reduction to baselevel — used of topography and topographic features or their age ⟨a wide, nearly level floor . . . characterizes an ~ valley —W.J.Miller⟩ **c** *obs* **:** dressed in old clothes : SHABBY ⟨the rest were ragged, ~, and beggarly —Shak.⟩ **d :** no longer in use : DISCARDED ⟨the profitable . . . reworking of ~ tailings —*Amer. Guide Series: Nev.*⟩ **e :** of a grayish or dusty tone — used of a color

syn ANCIENT, VENERABLE, ANTIQUE, ANTIQUATED, ANTEDILUVIAN, ARCHAIC, OBSOLETE: OLD is a general term opposed to *young* or *new*, describing whatever has had a long life or existence. ANCIENT, often opposed to *modern*, applies to what has been in existence from the remote past; it may suggest possession of valuable characteristics (as rarity or wisdom) accruing from age, describe an aspect of the distant now dead past, or be used to indicate hoary antiquity ⟨some illustrious line so *ancient* that it has no beginning —Edward Gibbon⟩ ⟨the civilization of China is *ancient* —Havelock Ellis⟩ ⟨poets of *ancient* Greece⟩ ⟨*ancient* pre-Inca Peruvians —Current Biog.⟩ ⟨the decrepit manager who was too *ancient* and incompetent for more serious employment —Ellen Glasgow⟩ VENERABLE usu. implies respect or veneration ⟨*venerable* men, you have come down to us from a former generation —Daniel Webster⟩ ⟨the ruins, Etruscan, Roman, Christian, *venerable* with a threefold antiquity —Nathaniel Hawthorne⟩ but sometimes emphasizes decrepitude ⟨a *venerable* Hudson whose driver makes periodic stops to wield a screwdriver and siphon gasoline —Claudia Cassidy⟩ ANTIQUE is a close synonym of ANCIENT; it is likely to apply to something old-fashioned that has acquired value through rarity or nostalgic charm ⟨a savor of the *antique*, primeval world and the earliest hopes and victories of mankind —Laurence Binyon⟩ ⟨*antique* monsters, older than Italy and Greece, than Babylon and Carthage —Llewelyn Powys⟩ ⟨such prosperous cities had already in Leland's day outgrown their *antique* suits of stone armor —G.M.Trevelyan⟩ ⟨an *antique* clock⟩ ANTIQUATED usu. applies to what is discredited or deprecated as outmoded ⟨we are apt to scorn our neighbor because his rate of motion is faster or more sluggish than our own. He is *antiquated* if he clings to the values of yesterday —A.L.Guérard⟩ ⟨as *antiquated* as the powdered periwig of an eighteenth century courtier —Waldemar Kaempffert⟩ ANTEDILUVIAN carries an even stronger sense of deprecation ⟨up-to-date models of scientific inquiry have steadily replaced the *antediluvian* constructions of an earlier generation —Ethel Albert⟩ ARCHAIC applies to what belongs to or has the characteristics of an earlier period ⟨when new opinions have overthrown the *archaic* institutions, they will create new institutions in harmony with themselves —S.M.Crothers⟩ ⟨Portugal at this time, *archaic* in its chivalry, had the most resplendent court in Europe —Francis Hackett⟩ ⟨*methinks* is an *archaic* construction⟩ OBSOLETE applies to what has been entirely displaced or superseded ⟨*obsolete* as the feudal baron —J.C.Snaith⟩ ⟨the relationship between the English king and the English people is a relationship far more modern and far better fitted to the needs of the times than the *obsolete* language and the *obsolete* trappings of the court suggest —D.W.Brogan⟩ ⟨instructing his civil officers in California to regard General Kearny's orders as *obsolete* —Irving Stone⟩

[2]old \"\ *n* -s [ME *ald, old,* fr. *ald, old,* adj.] **1** *obs* **:** an advanced stage : OLD AGE ⟨they must not be gelded . . . in the ~ of the moon —Richard Surflet & Gervase Markham⟩ **2 :** an earlier time or period ⟨in days of ~ when knights were bold —Edward Thomas⟩ **3 :** one that is of a specified age — usu. used in combination ⟨had come to the park when she was a five-year-*old* —W.A.White⟩ ⟨for 14 and 15 year ~*s* the reduction has been about 38 percent —*Amer. Child*⟩ ⟨entered a promising two-year-*old* in the Derby⟩ — **of old** *adv* **:** in times past : FORMERLY ⟨more . . . committees than *of old* were appointed —Allan Nevins⟩ ⟨still must the poet as *of old* . . . starve, freeze, and fashion verses —Edna S. V. Millay⟩

[3]old \ˌōl(d)\ *adv* [[1]old] **:** of old : ANCIENTLY — used chiefly in combination ⟨*old*-established⟩

old adam *n, usu cap A* [after the Biblical *Adam*, the first man and first sinner] **:** unregenerate man ⟨grant that the *old Adam* in this child may be so buried —*Bk. of Com. Prayer*⟩ ⟨the *old Adam* in me . . . rises and asserts himself —R.W. Jackson⟩ — called also *old man*

old age *n* [ME] **1 :** the final stage of the normal life span : SENESCENCE ⟨for purposes of the conference *old age* was considered to be 65 years or over —*Progressive Labor World*⟩ **2 :** the final stage in a cycle of erosion — compare ADOLESCENCE, INFANCY, MATURITY ⟨plains that illustrate the extreme of erosional *old age* —V.C.Finch & G.T.Trewartha⟩

old–age \ˈ=ˈ=\ *adj* [*old age*] **1 :** of or relating to senescence ⟨*old-age* pension⟩ **2 :** of or relating to the final stage in an erosion cycle ⟨there is abundant evidence of an *old-age* topography in the summit area —*Jour. of Geol.*⟩

old–age and survivors insurance *n* **:** national insurance under the U. S. government providing retirement benefits at age 65 and payments to survivors upon death of the insured — compare SOCIAL SECURITY

old akkadian *n, cap O&A* **:** the Akkadian language exemplified in texts before 1900 B.C.

old american *n, usu cap O&A* **:** an American descended from white ancestors who for three or more generations have been born in the U. S.

old armenian *n, cap O&A* **:** the Armenian language exemplified in documents from the 5th century through the medieval period

old army game *n* **1 :** a game or device whereby an inexperienced or unwary person is fleeced or victimized — used esp. from time to time of various gambling games (as craps, poker, blackjack) **2 :** the practice of shifting responsibility to another esp. when faced with an unpleasant situation

old assyrian *n, cap O&A* **:** the dialect of Akkadian used in Assyria from 2000 B.C. to 1500 B.C.

old babylonian *n, cap O&B* **:** the dialect of Akkadian used in Babylonia from 2000 B.C. to 1500 B.C.

old believer *n, usu cap O&B* [trans. of Russ *Starover*] : RASKOLNIK

old belt *n* [fr. the *Old Belt*, the piedmont area of Virginia and North Carolina] **:** a flue-cured tobacco produced mostly in north-central No. Carolina

old ber·ing sea \-ˈberiŋ-, -ˈbiriŋ-\ *adj, usu cap O&B&S* [fr. the *Bering sea*, part of the northern Pacific ocean] **:** of or belonging to an Eskimo culture of northern Alaska and northeastern Siberia about A.D. 100–500 characterized esp. by fossil-ivory implements

old blue *n* **:** a pale blue that is redder and duller than average powder blue, greener and less strong than Sistine, and greener and paler than average cadet gray — called also *bleu passé*

old boy *n* **1** *usu cap O&B* : OLD NICK **2 a :** an often sprightly or waggish old man ⟨that incorrigible broth of an *old boy* —Peter Forster⟩ **b :** a man of a past era or of established prestige ⟨not in the nature of these tough *old boys* to give way —O.S.Nock⟩ ⟨I find the *old boys* . . . too long-winded —O.W. Holmes†1935⟩ **3** *chiefly Brit* **:** a graduate of a boys' school : ALUMNUS ⟨heard a headmaster say that the test of a school was the quality of the *old boys* —*Manchester Guardian Weekly*⟩

old brain *n* : ARCHIPALLIUM

old bulgarian *n, cap O&B* : OLD CHURCH SLAVONIC

old catholic *n, usu cap O&C* **1 :** a member of a separate religious communion formed by members of the Roman Catholic Church who rejected the dogma of papal infallibility as adopted by the Vatican Council of 1870 **2 :** a member of an American communion that retains most of the doctrines and customs of the Roman Catholic Church but has rejected the ecclesiastical authority of the Roman Catholic hierarchy

old cedar *n* : CASTILIAN BROWN

old china *n* **1 :** a moderate blue that is greener and duller than average copen or Dresden blue and redder and less strong than azurite blue **2 :** a grayish blue that is redder and paler than electric, less strong and slightly redder than copenhagen, and redder and stronger than Gobelin

old christmas *n, usu cap C, chiefly Midland* **:** January 6 : TWELFTHNIGHT

old church slavonic *or* **old church slavic** *n, cap O&C&S* **:** the Slavic language used in the Bible translation of Cyril and Methodius and later continued as the liturgical language of many of the Eastern churches

old–clothes·man \ˈōl(d)ˈklō(th)z,man, -,maa(ə)n, -,mən\ *n, pl* **old–clothesmen :** a dealer in secondhand clothing

old coral *n* : JASPER RED

old country *n* **:** an emigrant's country of origin ⟨big-talking Irishman not long from the *old country* —Mari Sandoy⟩; *esp* : EUROPE ⟨squads of Finns and Swedes were brought over from the *old country* to work in the granite quarries —S.T. Williamson⟩

old covenant *n, cap O&C* : OLD TESTAMENT

old czech *n, cap O&C* **:** the Czech language exemplified in documents prior to 1620

old dutch *n, cap O&D* **:** the Dutch language exemplified in documents prior to the 12th century

old egyptian *n, cap O&E* **:** the language of Egypt from the 1st to the 10th dynasty

old empire *n, usu cap O&E* **:** the period of highest development in Mayan culture approximately A.D. 200–600 — compare NEW EMPIRE

[1]old·en \ˈōldən\ *adj* [ME, fr. [2]*old* + *-en* (adj. suffix)] **1 :** of or relating to a bygone era : ANCIENT, QUAINT ⟨Denmark in very ~ times was a wooded country —Erik Schacke⟩ ⟨in the ~ days, water wheels were used to drive some of the machinery —L.D.Stamp⟩ ⟨a style which resembles that of the ~ chronicles —P.J.Searles⟩ **2 :** advanced in years : OLD ⟨assented to the judgment of an ~ rabbinic teacher —Leonard Bernstein⟩

[2]olden \"\ *vb* -ED/-ING/-S [[1]*old* + *-en* (v. suffix)] *vi* **:** to grow old : AGE ⟨saw an ~*ing* flaccid face —Maurice Walsh⟩ ~ *vt archaic* **:** to make older ⟨experience . . . had ~*ed* him —W.M. Thackeray⟩

ol·den·burg \ˈōldən,bərg\ *adj, usu cap* [fr. *Oldenburg*, Germany] **:** of or from the city of Oldenburg, Germany : of the kind or style prevalent in Oldenburg

old english *n, cap O&E* **1 a :** the language of the English people from the time of the earliest documents in the 7th century to about 1100; *specif* : WEST SAXON — distinguished from *Middle English;* called also *Anglo-Saxon;* see INDO-EUROPEAN LANGUAGES table **b :** English of any period prior to Modern English **2 :** BLACK LETTER **3 a :** a style of architecture popular esp. for residences in 16th century England and featuring heavy half-timbering **b :** a contemporary adaptation of 16th century English architecture

old english alphabet *n, cap O&E* : ANGLO-SAXON ALPHABET

old english brown *n, often cap E* **:** a dark grayish to dark yellowish brown — called also *broncho, Indian brown*

old english game *n, usu cap O&E&G* **:** a class of game fowls characterized by conventional form and now bred almost wholly for show — compare MODERN GAME

old english sheepdog *n* **1** *usu cap O&E&S* **:** an English breed of medium-sized sheep and cattle dogs believed to trace back to the Roman occupation of the British Isles, having no tail or a very short one, a square large skull, nose tapered but blunt-ended, body short and compact with deep brisket and well-sprung ribs, forelegs straight, and hind legs well-muscled, being in length and height from about 21 to 26 inches each, and having a profuse, shaggy, blue-gray and white coat that often obscures the eyes and hangs from the body almost to the ground **2** *usu cap O&E, sometimes cap S* **:** a dog of the Old English Sheepdog breed — called also *bobtail*

ol·den·lan·dia \ˌōldənˈlandēə\ *n, cap* [NL, fr. H.B.*Oldenland* †*ab*1697 Dan. physician and botanist + NL *-ia*] **:** a large genus of chiefly tropical herbs (family Rubiaceae) with usu. elongated leaves and crowded axillary or terminal cymes of small flowers — see CLUSTERED BLUET

older *comparative of* OLD

oldest *superlative of* OLD

oldest profession *n* : PROSTITUTION

old ewe disease *n* : PREGNANCY DISEASE

old face *n, chiefly Brit* : OLD STYLE 2

old–fan·gled \ˈōl(d)ˈfaŋgəld\ *adj* : OLD-FASHIONED

old–farrand \ˈ(ˌ)=ˈ=\ *adj* : AULD-FARRANT

old–fashion \ˈ=ˈ=\ *adj, archaic* : OLD-FASHIONED

[1]old–fashioned \ˈ=ˈ==\ *adj* **1 a :** of, relating to, or characteristic of a past era : ANCIENT, ANTIQUATED ⟨wears an *old-fashioned* black bow tie —Green Peyton⟩ ⟨*old-fashioned* houses, with their ornamental cornices and high gables —*Amer. Guide Series: Mich.*⟩ ⟨men with the *old-fashioned* hellfire in their sermons —*Atlantic*⟩ ⟨suggested reviving *old-fashioned* home and classroom discipline with physical punishment —*N.Y. Times*⟩ **b :** adhering to traditions or standards of a past era : CONSERVATIVE ⟨my mother's family . . . more *old-fashioned*, more pious, and in a word more Victorian even than the English county families of the time —Harold Nicolson⟩ **c :** reminiscent of the past : NOSTALGIC, QUAINT ⟨two editions, one of them bound in *old-fashioned* blue gingham —H.H.Reichard⟩ ⟨attendants carried *old-fashioned* bouquets —*Springfield (Mass.) Union*⟩ **2 :** out of date : supplanted by something more modern : OBSOLETE ⟨thirty *old-fashioned* propeller planes —J.A.Michener⟩ ⟨*old-fashioned* methods for making maple sugar —Murray Schumach⟩ ⟨propaganda — the *old-fashioned* name for psychological warfare —George Fischer⟩ **3** *dial chiefly Eng* **:** of a mature or intelligent nature : KNOWING ⟨the collie . . . had turned on him an *old-fashioned* eye —John Buchan⟩ **4 :** growing wild : of early hybrid origin — used esp. of a rose — **old–fash·ioned·ly** *adv*

[2]old–fashioned \"\ *adv* [[1]*old-fashioned*] **1** *dial chiefly Eng* **:** in a knowing way : QUIZZICALLY **2 :** in an outmoded way : QUAINTLY ⟨a dress . . . cut kind of *old-fashioned* —J.B. Benefield⟩

[3]old–fashioned \"\ *n* -s [*old-fashioned (cocktail)*] **1 :** a cocktail usu. made of whiskey, bitters, sugar, a twist of lemon peel, and a small amount of water or soda, served with ice, and often garnished with fruit (as orange, pineapple, maraschino cherry) **2 :** a short broad glass usu. with a flared top, a sham bottom, and a capacity of seven or eight ounces

old-fashioned 2

old–fash·ioned·ness *n* -ES **:** the quality or state of being old-fashioned

old field *n* **1 :** land exhausted by cultivation and no longer tilled **2 :** a field that has produced a particular crop (as alfalfa) for many years

old–field birch *n* : AMERICAN GRAY BIRCH

old–field clover *n* : RABBIT-FOOT CLOVER

old–field colt \ˈ=ˌ=-\ *or* **old–fields colt** \ˈōl(d),fēldz-\ *n* : WOODS COLT

old–field lark *n, chiefly South & Midland* : MEADOWLARK 1

old–field pine *n* **1 :** LOBLOLLY PINE 1 **2 :** SAND PINE **3 :** SHORTLEAF PINE **4 :** JERSEY PINE

old–field school *n* **:** a rural elementary school often built in an exhausted corn or tobacco field and common in the South before the Civil War

old flemish *n, cap O&F* **:** the Flemish language exemplified in documents prior to the 12th century

old foundation *n, usu cap O&F, Church of England* **:** the status of having been founded prior to the Reformation — compare NEW FOUNDATION

old franconian *n, cap O&F* **:** the Franconian dialects in use before 1100

old frankish *n, cap O&F* : OLD FRANCONIAN

old french *n, cap O&F* **:** the French language from the time of the earliest documents preserved until the time of Modern French or approximately from the 9th to the 16th century; *esp* **:** French from the 9th to the 13th century as distinguished from Middle French of the 14th to the 16th century

old frisian *n, cap O&F* **:** the Frisian language exemplified in documents prior to the 16th century

old fustic *n* **1 :** any of several trees of the family Moraceae; *esp* : FUSTIC 1a — see MACLURIN, MORIN **2 :** [6]LIME 3

old german baptist brethren *n pl, usu cap O&G&B&B* **:** Dunkers withdrawing from the Church of the Brethren in 1881 in protest over Sunday schools, higher education, missions, and church societies — called also *Old Order Dunkers*

old girl *n, chiefly Brit* **:** a graduate of or former student at a girls' school : ALUMNA

old glory blue *n* [fr. *Old Glory*, nickname for the flag of the U.S.] **:** a moderate purplish blue that is redder and stronger than marine blue, duller than average cornflower, and redder and darker than gentian blue

old glory red *n* **:** a vivid red that is yellower and duller than apple red or carmine and duller and very slightly bluer than scarlet

old gold *n* **1 :** a variable color averaging a dark yellow that is redder and slightly darker than average antique gold (sense 1) and redder, stronger, and slightly lighter than mustard (sense 3 a) **2 :** a light olive that is less strong than citrine

old gooseberry *n, usu cap O&G* : OLD NICK

old growth *n* **1 :** a mature or overmature forest growth more or less uninfluenced by human activity — called also *virgin forest* **2 :** a stand consisting mainly of mature trees

old guard *n, often cap O&G* [fr. the *Old Guard*, the imperial French guard created by Napoleon I in 1804; trans. of F *Vieille Garde*] **:** a group of established prestige and influence ⟨the *old guard* of the socially elect —F.L.Allen⟩ ⟨among physicists . . . he had become the leader of the *Old Guard* —Bertrand Russell⟩; *esp* **:** a dominant usu. conservative element of a political party ⟨proceeded to undermine . . . the caucus, which the *Old Guard* of that day dominated —H.R. Penniman⟩

old guard·ism \-ˈgär,dizəm\ *n, often cap O&G* **:** conservatism esp. in politics

old guardist *n, often cap O&G* **:** a member or supporter of a conservative group : DIEHARD

old·ham \ˈōldəm\ *adj, usu cap* [fr. *Oldham*, England] **:** of or from the county borough of Oldham, England : of the kind or style prevalent in Oldham

old·ham·ite \ˈōldə,mīt\ *n* -s [Thomas *Oldham* †1878 Irish geologist + E *-ite*] **:** a mineral CaS consisting of sulfide of calcium and found in meteorites

old·ham's coupling \ˈōldəmz-\ *n, usu cap O* [fr. the name *Oldham*] **:** a coupling for parallel shafts slightly out of line consisting of a disk on the end of each shaft and an intermediate disk having two mutually perpendicular feathers on opposite sides that engage slots in the respective shaft disks

old hand *n* **1 :** one having knowledge or ability gained through long experience : VETERAN ⟨viewed it with the lenient, slightly bored cynicism of an *old hand* —Francis Hackett⟩ ⟨even *old hands* had to gear up anew for these new jobs —J.A.Conway⟩; *esp* **:** one having detailed knowledge of a geographical area due to extended residence or activity there ⟨an *old* China *hand*⟩ **2** *Austral* **:** an ex-convict; *esp* **:** one of the early immigrants to Australia

old harry *n, usu cap O&H* : OLD NICK

old hat *adj* **1 a :** that is behind the times : OLD-FASHIONED, REACTIONARY ⟨in today's climate suffragism seems *old hat* —Helen B. Woodward⟩ ⟨the very young still regarded the rather young as *old hat* —R.L.Duffus⟩ **b :** lacking in freshness : HACKNEYED, TRITE ⟨a buyer's main problem is . . . dropping the trend before it becomes *old hat* —*Fashion Accessories*⟩ ⟨accustomed to dismiss Dutch 17th century painting as *old hat* —Emily Genauer⟩ **2 :** inferior to present methods or practices : DATED, OBSOLETE ⟨the company's microwave loop . . . (coaxial cable is *old hat* now) —*New Yorker*⟩ ⟨such crude methods are *old hat* —R.G.Spivack⟩

old helio *n* : MADDER VIOLET

old high german *n, cap O&H&G* **:** High German exemplified in documents prior to the 12th century — see INDO-EUROPEAN LANGUAGES table

old home week *n* **1** *often cap O&H&W* **:** a week of special festivities during which a community invites former residents to return for a reunion ⟨the social activities of an *Old Home Week* —Agnes Repplier⟩ **2 :** a reunion of former associates marked by special warmth or cordiality ⟨a little knot of alumni having an *old home week* in the stadium parking lot⟩

old house borer *n* **:** a cerambycid beetle (*Hylotrupes bajulus*) orig. European but now established in the U. S. whose larvae feed on dry coniferous wood and frequently do serious damage to old rafters and flooring

old hunker *n, usu cap O&H* : [2]HUNKER 1

old icelandic *n, cap O&I* **:** Icelandic spoken or written from the 9th century to the 16th century — compare OLD NORSE; see INDO-EUROPEAN LANGUAGES table

old identity *n, Austral* **:** an old and well-known inhabitant of a locality

old·ie *also* **oldy** \ˈōldē, -di\ *n, pl* **oldies** [[1]*old* + *-ie, -y*] **:** something trite : an old chestnut ⟨take the ~, "Never use a preposition to end a sentence with" —C.E.Borklund⟩; *esp* **:** a popular song of an earlier day ⟨students favor ~*s*, such as "When Irish Eyes Are Smiling" —Kathryn Murray⟩

old indo–aryan *or* **old indic** *n, cap O&I&A* : SANSKRIT

old injun *n* : OLD-SQUAW

old ionic *n, cap O&I* **:** the Greek dialect of the Homeric epics

old iranian *n, cap O&I* **:** any Iranian language in use in the period B.C.

old irish *n, cap O&I* **:** the Irish in use between the 7th and 11th centuries — compare IRISH GAELIC; see INDO-EUROPEAN LANGUAGES table

old·ish \ˈōldish, -dēsh\ *adj* **:** somewhat elderly

old italian book hand *n, usu cap I* : SEMICURSIVE

old ivory *n* **:** a grayish yellow that is duller and slightly greener than chamois, slightly redder and stronger than crash, and darker and very slightly greener than flax

old lady *n* **1 a :** WIFE ⟨my *old lady* . . . said when we were first hooked up it was usually the bills —Adela R. St. Johns⟩ — not often in formal use **b :** MOTHER ⟨used to fight with my *old lady* about taking a bath once a week —L.M.Uris⟩ — not often in formal use **2 :** OLD MAID 2

old lag *n* [[5]*lag*] *chiefly Brit* : HABITUAL CRIMINAL

old·land \ˈōld,land, -lənd\ *n* **:** an extensive area of ancient crystalline rocks reduced to low relief by long erosion

old lang syne *n* : AULD LANG SYNE

old latin *n, cap O&L* **:** the Latin used in the early inscriptions and in the literature prior to the classical period

old lavender *n* **1 :** a pale violet that is paler than dusty lavender and redder and duller than dusty periwinkle blue **2 :** a dark grayish purple that is bluer and less strong than raisin black, redder and less strong than average purple wine, and redder and duller than average orchid taupe

old light *n, usu cap O&L* **1 :** AULD LICHT **2 :** a member of a conservative group in colonial America (as in a Baptist, Congregationalist, or Presbyterian church) opposed to revivalism and emotionalism in religion — compare NEW LIGHT

old–line \ˈ=ˌ=\ *adj* [fr. the phrase *old line*] **1 a :** having a reputation or authority based on seniority : ESTABLISHED, EXPERIENCED ⟨*old-line* bankers, remembering 1929, shuddered at the shaky loans their young executives . . . were willing to make —H.H.Martin⟩ ⟨there is not a single *old-line* movie company that doesn't now have some business connection with television —T.M.Pryor⟩ ⟨he is an *old-line* Yankee⟩ **b :** out of date : OLD-FASHIONED ⟨endorsement of the *old-line* and supposedly discredited control —S.H.Adams⟩ **2 :** adhering to old policies or practices : CONSERVATIVE, TRADITIONAL ⟨the *old-line* purchasing agent who . . . defies improvements —G.W.H.Ahl⟩ ⟨*old-line* political parties . . . had lost the confidence of the public —A.P.Whitaker⟩ ⟨earned . . . the displeasure of the *old-line* Humanists —G.C.Sellery⟩ **3 :** of or relating to a legal-reserve insurance company established prior to the rise of fraternal benefit societies ⟨most *old-line* policies cannot be turned in for cash till after the third year —*Time*⟩

old–line company *n* **:** a nonfraternal insurance company that writes an absolute contract, collects a fixed level premium, and accumulates the legal reserve

old liner *n* [*old line* + *-er*] : [2]CONSERVATIVE 2, 3

old low franconian *or* **old low frankish** *n, cap O&L&F* **:** the Germanic dialects of the lower Rhine valley used prior to about 1100

old low german *n, cap O&L&G* **:** Low German exemplified in documents prior to the 12th century

old maid *n* **1 :** SPINSTER 3 **2 :** a prim nervous person of either sex who frets over inconsequential details **:** FUSSBUDGET **3 :** a simple game of matching cards which is played with a pack with one queen removed and in which the player holding the odd queen at the end of the game is an "old maid" **4 a** *West Indies* **:** ¹PERIWINKLE 1c **b :** a common garden zinnia (*Zinnia elegans*)

old maidhood *n* **:** the status or condition of being an old maid

old–maidish \ˈ⸗⸗⸗\ *adj* [*old maid* + *-ish*] **:** characteristic of an old maid **:** FUSSY, OLD-WOMANISH — **old–maid·ish·ly** *adv*

old–maid·ish·ness *n* -ES **:** the prim conservatism of an old maid

old–maid's–bonnet \ˈ⸗,⸗ˈ⸗⸗\ *n* **:** WILD LUPINE

old–maid's–nightcap \ˈ⸗,⸗ˈ⸗,⸗\ *n* **:** SPOTTED CRANESBILL

old–maid's–pink \ˈ⸗,⸗ˈ⸗\ *n* **1 :** CORN COCKLE **2 :** SOAPWORT 1

old man *n* **1 a :** HUSBAND ⟨a married woman steppin out on her *old man* —James Jones⟩ — not often in formal use **b :** FATHER ⟨my *old man* was not any great shakes as a parent —Damon Runyon⟩ — not often in formal use **c** *usu cap O&M* **:** BOSS ⟨was not wholly satisfied with the way the *Old Man* was running the department —H.S.Commager⟩; *esp* **:** COMMANDING OFFICER ⟨the *Old Man* pointed her head for Nantucket Sound —H.A. Chippendale⟩ — not often in formal use **2 a :** one having the skill or status acquired through long experience **:** recognized authority ⟨the great *old man* of Eurasian archaeology —O.J. Maenchen-Helfen⟩ **b :** a senior member or former member of an organization (as a military unit) ⟨the *old men* who had fought in the regiment's first two battles —Dan Levin⟩ **c** (1) **:** a tribal elder or sage ⟨the *old man* . . . presides at ceremonials —C.D.Forde⟩ (2) *usu cap O&M* **:** CULTURE HERO ⟨marks on the birch tree . . . inflicted in a moment of anger by *Old Man* —W.D.Wallis⟩ **d** (1) **:** OLD ADAM ⟨put off . . . the *old man*, which is corrupt according to the deceitful lusts —Eph 4: 22 (AV)⟩ (2) **:** GOD **3** *Austral* **:** a full-grown male kangaroo **4 a :** SOUTHERNWOOD **b :** ROSEMARY **5** *dial Eng* **:** the last sheaf of the harvest sometimes shaped into a human effigy and buried **6 :** a drilling post for use with a ratchet, electric, or pneumatic drill

old–man–and–woman \ˈ⸗ˈ⸗⸗ˈ⸗⸗\ *n* -S **:** HOUSELEEK

old–man cactus *n* **:** a Mexican cactus (*Cephalocereus senilis*) having its joints crowned by drooping white hairs

old–man fern *n* **:** an Australasian tree fern (*Dicksonia antarctica*) with very large tripinnate fronds

old man saltbush *n* **:** a tall Australian shrub (*Atriplex nummularia*)

old–man's–beard \ˈ⸗,⸗ˈ⸗\ *n* **1 :** any of several clematises: as **a :** an American virgin's bower (*Clematis virginiana*) **b :** a European traveler's-joy (*C. vitalba*) **2 a :** SPANISH MOSS **b :** BEARD LICHEN **3 :** FRINGE TREE **4** *dial Eng* **:** any of several plants of the genus *Equisetum*

old–man's–flannel \ˈ⸗,⸗ˈ⸗⸗\ *n* **:** MULLEIN

old–man's–pepper \ˈ⸗,⸗ˈ⸗⸗\ *n* **:** YARROW

old–man's–root \ˈ⸗,⸗ˈ⸗\ *n* **:** the American spikenard (*Aralia racemosa*)

old master *n* **1 :** a superior artist or craftsman of established reputation; *esp* **:** a distinguished painter of the 16th, 17th, or early 18th century **2 :** a work by an old master — **old masterly** *adv*

old–mine \ˈ⸗ˈ⸗\ *adj* **:** having a deep crown and cut in an obsolete style that gives it less sparkle than the modern brilliant — used of a diamond ⟨a Victorian diamond necklace with thirty-eight *old-mine* diamonds —*N. Y. Herald Tribune*⟩

old moss *or* **old moss green** *n* **:** a light olive color that is greener, stronger, and slightly darker than citrine, deeper than grape green, and redder and duller than average willow green — called also *lizard bronze, moss*

old ned \-ˈned\ *n, usu cap N* [prob. fr. *Old Ned*, nickname for the devil] *Midland* **:** home-cured hog meat and esp. salt pork or bacon

old·ness *n* -ES [ME *oldnes*, fr. OE *ealdnes*, fr. *eald* old + *-nes* -ness — more at OLD] **:** AGE, ANTIQUITY

old nick *n, usu cap O&N* **:** the personification of evil **:** DEVIL, SATAN — called also *Old Boy, Old Gooseberry, Old Harry, Old One, Old Scratch, Old Serpent*

old norse *n, cap O&N* **:** the North Germanic language of the Scandinavian peoples prior to about A.D. 1350; *specif* **:** the western branch of Old Norse including Old Norwegian and Old Icelandic — see INDO-EUROPEAN LANGUAGES table

old north french *n, cap O&N&F* **:** the northern dialects of Old French including esp. those of Normandy and Picardy

old norwegian *n, cap O&N* **:** the Norwegian language before the Reformation

old olive *n* **:** OLIVE BROWN

old one *n, usu cap both Os* **1 :** OLD NICK **2 :** the creator or chief deity in many primitive religions

old order amish *n, usu cap both Os&A* **:** a member of the Old Order Amish Mennonite Church adhering strictly to the older forms of worship and attire

old order brethren *n pl, usu cap both Os&B* **:** YORKER BRETHREN

old order dunkers *n pl, usu cap both Os&D* **:** OLD GERMAN BAPTIST BRETHREN

ol·do·wan \ˈäldəwən\ *adj, usu cap* [*Oldoway* gorge, Tanganyika + E *-an*] **:** of or belonging to a Lower and Middle Pleistocene culture of East Africa characterized by crude pebble choppers, scrapers, and hand axes

old persian *n, cap O&P* **:** one of the two ancient languages composing Old Iranian and known from cuneiform inscriptions of the 6th and 5th centuries B.C. — compare AVESTAN

old pink *n* **:** a light brown that is yellower, stronger, and slightly darker than blush and redder, stronger, and slightly lighter than cork

old provençal *n, cap O&P* **:** the Provençal language exemplified in documents from the 11th to the 16th centuries

old prussian *n, cap O&P* **1 :** a member of an early people related to the Lithuanians and inhabiting the shores of the Baltic sea east of the Vistula **:** BORUSSIAN **2 :** the Baltic language of the Old Prussian people

old rail *n, slang* **:** a veteran or retired railroad employee

old red *n* **:** BURNT CARMINE

old red sandstone *n, usu cap O&R&S* **:** a thick series of fragmental chiefly sandstone rocks of nonmarine origin, predominantly red in color, and representing the Devonian system in some parts of Great Britain and elsewhere in northwestern Europe

old regime *n* **:** ANCIEN REGIME

old ritualism *n, usu cap O&R* **:** the doctrines and practices of the Raskolniks

old ritualist *n, usu cap O&R* **:** RASKOLNIK

old rose *n* **:** a variable color averaging a grayish red that is bluer and paler than bois de rose, bluer and lighter than blush rose, and bluer and paler than appleblossom or Pompeian red

old roseleaf *n* **:** a dark red that is yellower and less strong than cranberry and yellower and paler than average garnet or average wine — called also *chocolate maroon, Cuyahoga red*

old russian *n, cap O&R* **:** the Russian language exemplified in documents of the 12th to 15th centuries

olds *pl of* OLD

old salt *n* **:** an experienced sailor **:** a seafaring man ⟨nothing pleases the *old salts* more than a yarn with the boys on the dock —Anthony Anable⟩

old saxon *n, cap O&S* **:** the language of the Saxons of northwest Germany between the Rhine and Elbe rivers until about the 12th century — compare LOW GERMAN; see INDO-EUROPEAN LANGUAGES table

old scandinavian *n, cap O&S* **:** OLD NORSE

old school *n* **1 :** adherents to the conservative policies and practices of the past ⟨the charming self-portrait of a gentleman of the *old school* —Frank Meyer⟩ ⟨of the *old school* that believed the only way to make money was by hard work⟩ **2** *usu cap O&S* **:** adherents to conservative theology or practice and opponents of innovation; *specif* **:** OLD LIGHT 2

old school baptist *n, usu cap O&S&B* **:** PRIMITIVE BAPTIST

old school tie *n, sometimes cap O&S&T* **1 a :** a necktie displaying the colors of an English public school ⟨entitled to wear the very best of *old school ties*, the Etonian pale blue and black —*Fortune*⟩ **b :** an attitude of conservatism, aplomb, and upper-class solidarity associated with English public school graduates ⟨the traditional prejudice against the British, their aristocratic society and their *old school ties* —*Atlantic*⟩ **c :** a graduate of an English public school ⟨to the *old school ties* the dictators seem ignorant uneducated rebels —G.B.Shaw⟩ **2 :** CLANNISHNESS, CLIQUISM ⟨the War and Navy departments each accumulated growing prestige which fostered the spirit of the *old school tie* —Beirne Lay⟩

old scratch *n, usu cap O&S* **:** OLD NICK

old serpent *n, usu cap O&S* [ME] **:** OLD NICK

old–shoe \ˈ⸗ˈ⸗\ *adj* **:** characterized by familiarity or freedom from restraint **:** COMFORTABLE, UNPRETENTIOUS ⟨*old-shoe* and easy to talk with —Ernie Pyle⟩

old side *adj, usu cap O&S* **:** of or relating to a conservative element among Presbyterians in colonial America favoring stricter adherence to a confession of faith and opposing the more revivalistic methods — compare NEW SIDE

old silver *n* **:** a nearly neutral slightly yellowish medium gray that is darker than gull (sense 2a) or agate gray and very slightly redder than flint gray — compare NEW SILVER, SILVER

old slavic *or* **old slavonic** *n, cap O&S* **:** OLD CHURCH SLAVONIC

old sledge *n* **:** SEVEN-UP

old soldier *n, slang* **:** an emptied liquor bottle

old–squaw \ˈ⸗ˈ⸗\ *n* **:** a common sea duck (*Clangula hyemalis*) of the more northern parts of the northern hemisphere of which the adult male is marked with sharply contrasted black and white and has the middle tail feathers very long and slender and the female is plainer and lacks the long tail feathers — called also *old injun, oldwife*

old stager *n, chiefly Brit* **:** OLD HAND 1

old·ster \ˈōl(d)stə(r), -(d)st-\ *n* -S **1 :** an experienced hand ⟨∼s pass it down faithfully to each newcomer —Elmont Waite⟩; *specif* **:** a midshipman of four years' standing in the British navy — distinguished from *youngster* **2 :** an aging or elderly person ⟨gray-bearded ∼s go swaggering down the boulevards —Hubert Herring⟩ ⟨the accumulated wisdom and lore of the ∼s —E.A.Hoebel⟩

old stone age *n, usu cap O&S&A* **:** the Paleolithic period

old story *n* **:** something well established **:** an idea or object no longer a novelty ⟨by the time Virginia was first settled secular schools were an *old story* in England —G.W.Johnson⟩

¹**old style** *n* **1 :** something belonging to or characteristic of an earlier period **2 :** a style of type resembling an 18th century design of William Caslon and distinguished by graceful irregularity among individual letters, slanted ascender serifs, and but slight contrast between light and heavy strokes

(as in this example of Old Style)

— contrasted with *modern*

²**old style** *adj, usu cap O&S* **:** using or according to the Julian calendar — abbr. *O.S.*

old testament *n, cap O&T* [ME, trans. of LL *Vetus Testamentum*, trans. of Gk *Palaia Diathēkē*] **:** the covenant of God with the Hebrews as set forth in the Bible — abbr. *O.T.*; called also *Old Covenant*

old–time \ˈ⸗ˈ⸗\ *adj* **1 :** of, relating to, or characteristic of an earlier period ⟨an *old-time* community sing⟩ ⟨loved the conservative *old-time* ways —Van Wyck Brooks⟩ ⟨using the *old-time* . . . mule-power grinding mills —*Amer. Guide Series: N. C.*⟩ **2 :** of long standing **:** EXPERIENCED, VETERAN ⟨many *old-time* bowlers are back bowling this year —*Deerfield (Wisc.) Independent*⟩ ⟨*old-time* summer residents —*N. Y. Times*⟩

old–tim·er \ˈ⸗ˈtīmə(r)\ *n* -S **1 a :** OLD HAND, VETERAN ⟨the stranger must compete with the *old-timers* already established —Justina Hill⟩ ⟨the eternal friction between *old-timer* and rookie —Dixon Wecter⟩ **b :** OLDSTER 2 ⟨service for . . . *old-timers* beyond retirement age —W.R.Wood⟩ **2 :** something that is old-fashioned **:** ANTIQUE ⟨a collar . . . one of those hard-boiled *old-timers* which calls for gold collar buttons front and rear —F.C.Othman⟩

old–timey *also* **old–timy** \ˈ⸗ˈtīmē\ *adj* **:** of a kind or style prevalent in or reminiscent of an earlier period **:** OLD-TIME ⟨hollyhocks and *old-timey* roses —C.F.Saunders⟩ ⟨our *old-timey*, crotchety operative . . . from London —*New Yorker*⟩

old tuberculin *n* **:** tuberculin prepared by boiling, filtering, and concentrating a broth culture of tubercle bacilli and orig. introduced as a proposed curative agent for tuberculosis

old welsh *n, cap O&W* **:** the Welsh language exemplified in documents prior to about 1150 — see INDO-EUROPEAN LANGUAGES table

oldwench \ˈ⸗,⸗\ *n* **:** QUEEN TRIGGERFISH

old wife *n, pl* **old wives** [ME] **:** a prattling old woman **:** GOSSIP ⟨a mishmash of *old wives'* tales —J.N.Leonard⟩

oldwife \ˈ⸗,⸗\ *n, pl* **oldwives 1** [perh. so called fr. the large belly] **:** any of several fishes: as **a :** the European black sea bream (*Cantharus lineatus*) **b :** any of several triggerfishes; *esp* **:** QUEEN TRIGGERFISH **c :** LONGFIN POMPANO **d :** ¹SPOT 7 **e :** ²ALEWIFE 1a **f :** MENHADEN **g :** an Australian fish (*Enoplosus armatus*) resembling a perch **2 :** OLD-SQUAW

old wine *n* **:** a variable color averaging a dark red that is yellower and paler than average wine or average garnet and yellower, less strong, and slightly darker than cranberry

old witchgrass *n* **:** WITCHGRASS 2

old woman *n* **1 a :** WIFE — not often in formal use **b :** MOTHER — not often in formal use **2** *chiefly dial* **:** BEACH WORMWOOD

old–wom·an·ish \ˈ⸗ˈwu̇mənish\ *adj* **:** OLD-MAIDISH

old–woman's–bitter \ˈ⸗,⸗ˈ⸗⸗\ *n* **:** a tropical American fiddlewood (*Citharexylum fruticosum*)

old wood *n* **:** a grayish red that is bluer and darker than bois de rose and yellower and deeper than appleblossom

old world *n, usu cap O&W* **:** EASTERN HEMISPHERE; *specif* **:** the continent of Europe ⟨renaissance . . . in the countries of the *Old World* —Hellmut Lehmann-Haupt⟩

old–world \ˈ⸗ˈ⸗\ *adj* [*Old World*] **:** OLD-FASHIONED, PICTURESQUE ⟨the *old-world*, vacillating, pathetically likable headmaster of the school —Leslie Rees⟩ ⟨as quaint . . . as any *old-world* continental city —Arnold Bennett⟩

old–world monkey *n* **:** a catarrhine monkey; *esp* **:** a monkey of the family Cercopithecidae widely distributed in the warmer parts of the Old World

old world porcupine *n, usu cap O&W* **:** a porcupine of the family Hystricidae; *esp* **:** a rather bulky short-tailed terrestrial porcupine of the common widely distributed genus *Hystrix*

olé \ōˈlā\ *n* -S [Sp *ole, olé*, fr. Ar *wa-llāh*, fr. *wa-* and + *allāh* God] **:** ²BRAVO ⟨the generous approbation and shouted ∼s of these warm Mexican people —George Sklar⟩ — often used interjectionally in applauding a superior performance

ole– *or* **oleo–** *also* **olei–** *comb form* [F *olé-, oléo-*, fr. L *ole-*, fr. *oleum* — more at OIL] **1 :** oil ⟨*olei*ferous⟩ ⟨*ole*in⟩ ⟨*oleo*graph⟩ ⟨*oleo*cyst⟩ **2 a :** olein ⟨*oleo*-di-stearin⟩ **b :** oleic acid ⟨*ole*oyl⟩

¹**–ole** *also* **–ol** \,ōl, ˈōl, ,ȯl, ˈōl\ *n comb form* -S [ISV, fr. L *oleum* oil — more at OIL] **1 :** chemical compound containing a five-membered ring usu. heterocyclic ⟨imidaz*ole*⟩ ⟨pyrr*ole*⟩ **2** *usu -ole* **:** chemical compound not containing hydroxyl — esp. in names of several ethers ⟨anis*ole*⟩ ⟨phenet*ole*⟩

²**–ole** — see -OL

³**–ole** \,ōl\ *n suffix* -S [F, fr. L *-olus, -olum, -ola*, dim. suffix] **:** little one ⟨veni*ole*⟩

¹**olea** \ˈōlēə\ *n, cap* [NL, fr. L, olive tree, olive, fr. Gk *elaia* — more at OLIVE] **:** a genus (the type of the family Oleaceae) of trees or shrubs having simple entire leaves, axillary flowers with induplicate calyx lobes, and oily drupaceous fruit — see MAIRE, OLIVE

²**olea** *pl of* OLEUM

ole·a·ce·ae \,ōlēˈāsē,ē\ *n pl, cap* [NL, fr. *Olea*, type genus + *-aceae*] **:** a family of shrubs and trees (order Oleales) having opposite or rarely alternate exstipulate leaves, tetramerous flowers, and the fruits a berry, drupe, or capsule

ole·a·ceous \ˌ⸗⸗ˈāshəs\ *adj* [NL *Oleaceae* + E *-ous*] **:** of or relating to the Oleaceae

ole·a·ci·na \,ōlēəˈsīnə\ *n, cap* [NL, prob. fr. L *oleaceus* oily (fr. *ole-* + *-aceus* -aceous) + NL *-ina*] **:** a genus of West Indian carnivorous land snails (suborder Stylommatophora) having elongate usu. smooth glassy brownish shells and feeding generally on other snails

ole·a·cin·i·dae \-sinə,dē\ *n pl, cap* [NL, fr. *Oleacina*, type genus + *-idae*] **:** a family of carnivorous land snails (suborder Stylommatophora) that feed chiefly on other snails — see EUGLANDINA

ole·ag·i·nous \,ōlēˈajənəs\ *adj* [MF *oleagineux*, fr. L *oleaginus, oleagineus* of an olive tree, of an olive, fr. *olea* olive tree, olive, fr. Gk *elaia* — more at OLIVE] **1 :** resembling or having the properties of oil ⟨∼ liquid⟩ ⟨an ∼ smear⟩ **:** containing or producing oil **:** OILY ⟨∼ matter keeps his wavy black hair slick —Darrell Berrigan⟩ ⟨the crop of winter ∼ seeds —Kay Boyle⟩ **2 :** characterized by suave urbanity or sickly sentimentality ⟨∼ disc-plugging crooners —Bernard Hollowood⟩

ole·ag·i·nous·ly *adv* **:** in an oily manner **:** UNCTUOUSLY

ole·ag·i·nous·ness *n* -ES *archaic* **:** the quality or state of being oily ⟨the ∼ of urinous spirits —Robert Boyle⟩

ole·a·les \,ōlēˈā(,)lēz\ *n pl, cap* [NL, fr. *Olea* + *-ales*] **:** an order of dicotyledonous woody plants including the single family Oleaceae and being often included in the order Gentianales

ole·an·der \ˈōlēˌandə(r)\ *n* -S [ML *oleander*, alter. of *arodandrum, lorandrum*, prob. alter. of L *rhododendron* — more at RHODODENDRON] **:** a plant of the genus *Nerium*; *specif* **:** an ornamental evergreen shrub (*Nerium oleander*) that is native to the East Indies but widely cultivated and naturalized in warm regions and that has narrow entire leaves and clusters of fragrant white to red flowers

oleander aphid *n* **:** an aphid (*Aphis nerii*) that infests foliage and flower buds of oleander

oleander fern *n* **:** a tropical fern (*Oleandra neriiformis*) of the family Polypodiaceae having coriaceous fronds that resemble oleander leaves

oleander scale *n* **:** any of several scales injurious to the oleander, orange, and lemon; *esp* **:** a common greenhouse scale (*Aspidiotus hederae*)

ole·an·drin \,ōlēˈandrən\ *n* -S [ISV *oleander* + *-in*] **:** a poisonous crystalline glycoside $C_{32}H_{48}O_9$ found in oleander leaves and resembling digitalis in its action

ole·a·no·lic acid \,ōlēəˈnōlik-\ *n* [ISV *olea-* (fr. L *olea* olive tree, olive) + connective *-n-* + *-olic* — more at OLEA] **:** a crystalline triterpenoid acid $C_{29}H_{47}COOH$ derived from beta-amyrin and occurring free or in the form of saponins or other glycosides (as in olive leaves, clove buds, sugar beets)

ole·ar·ia \,ōlēˈa(a)rēə\ *n, cap* [NL, fr. Adam Ölschläger (Latinized *Olearius*) †1671 Ger. traveler + NL *-ia*] **:** a large genus of Australasian shrubs or low trees (family Compositae) with alternate leaves and rather large heads of flowers having white or purple rays, the pappus capillary, and the receptacle without chaff

o'lea·ry \ōˈlirē, -ler-\ *n* -ES *usu cap O&L* [prob. alter. of ME *a-lery, aliri* crossed (used of the legs)] **:** a game in which a child bounces a ball and executes prescribed movements (as crossing one leg over the ball) at certain words of an accompanying verse

ole·as·ter \,ōlēˈastə(r)\ *n* -S [L, fr. *olea* olive tree, olive — more at OLEA] **1 :** any of several plants of the genus *Elaeagnus*; *esp* **:** RUSSIAN OLIVE **2 :** a wild tree of the commonly cultivated olive

oleaster family *n* **:** ELAEAGNACEAE

ole·ate \ˈōlē,āt, -ēət\ *n* -S [F *oléate*, fr. *olé-* ole- + *-ate*] **1 :** a salt or ester of oleic acid **2 :** a liquid or semisolid preparation of a medicinal dissolved in an excess of oleic acid ⟨mercury ∼⟩ ⟨∼ of quinine⟩

olec·ra·nal \ōˈlekrənᵊl, ,ōlēˈkrānᵊl\ *adj* [NL *olecranon* + E *-al*] **:** of, belonging to, or relating to the olecranon

olec·ra·non \-rə,nän, -rā,-\ *n* -S [NL, fr. Gk *ōlekranon*, fr. *ōlenē* elbow + *kranion* head, skull — more at ELL, CRANIUM] **:** the large process of the ulna that projects behind the elbow joint, forms the bony prominence of the elbow, and receives the insertion of the triceps muscle — see FUNNY BONE 1

ole·fi·ant gas \,ōləˈfīənt-; ōˈlēfēənt-, ōˈlef\ *n* [part trans. of F *gaz oléfiant*, fr. *gaz* gas + *oléfiant*, fr. *olé-* ole- + *-fiant*, pres. part. of *-fier* -fy] *archaic* **:** ETHYLENE

ole·fin *also* **olefine** \ˈōləfən, -ə,fēn\ *n* -S [ISV *olef*iant (*gas*) + *-in, -ine*] **:** an unsaturated open-chain hydrocarbon containing at least one double bond; *esp* **:** a member of the ethylene series **:** ALKENE — compare CYCLOOLEFIN, DIOLEFIN, TRIOLEFIN

ole·fin·ic \ˌ⸗⸗ˈfinik\ *adj* **:** of, relating to, or being an olefin **:** ETHYLENIC ⟨∼ bonds⟩ ⟨∼ terpenes⟩

olei– — see OLE-

ole·ic \(ˈ)ōˈlēik\ *adj* [*ole-* + *-ic*] **1 :** relating to, derived from, or contained in oil **2 :** of or relating to oleic acid or its derivatives ⟨∼ esters⟩

oleic acid *n* **:** a liquid unsaturated fatty acid $CH_3(CH_2)_7CH{=}CH(CH_2)_7COOH$ that occurs in the form of glycerides in vegetable oils (as olive oil) and animal fats and oils (as depot fats), that is usu. obtained commercially from inedible tallow or grease as a colorless to red or brown oil, that yields stearic acid on hydrogenation and azelaic acid and pelargonic acid on cleavage by oxidation, and that is used chiefly in making textile soaps, synthetic detergents, lubricants (as for textile fibers), sulfonated oils and cosmetics, and in compounding rubber; *cis*-9-octadecenoic acid — see ELAIDIC ACID, RED OIL

olei·cul·ture \ˈōlēə+,-\ *n* [F *oléiculture*, fr. L *olea* olive + F *-i-* + *culture* — more at OLEA, CULTURE] **:** the production, processing, and marketing of olives

ole·if·er·ous \,ōlēˈif(ə)rəs\ *adj* [*ole-* + *-ferous*] **:** producing oil ⟨∼ seeds⟩

ole·in \ˈōlēən\ *n* -S [F *oléine*, fr. *olé-* ole- + *-ine*] **1 :** an ester of glycerol and oleic acid; *esp* **:** TRIOLEIN **2** *also* **ole·ine** \ˈ", -ē,ēn\ **a :** the liquid portion of any fat — distinguished from *stearin* **b :** SULFONATED OIL **c :** commercial oleic acid ⟨white ∼⟩ — compare RED OIL 1a

ole·nel·lid \,ōləˈneləd\ *n* -S [NL *Olenellidae* family of trilobites, fr. NL *Olenellus*, type genus + *-idae*] **:** a trilobite of the genus *Olenellus*

ole·nel·lus \-ləs\ *n, cap* [NL, dim. of *Olenus*] **:** a genus of Lower Cambrian trilobites having a large spine on the fifteenth thoracic segment

olent \ˈōlənt\ *adj* [L *olent-, olens*, pres. part. of *olēre* to smell — more at ODOR] *archaic* **:** having a scent **:** ODOROUS

ole·nus \ˈōlēnəs\ *n, cap* [NL, after *Olenus*, character in Greco-Roman mythology who was changed into a stone pillar, fr. L, fr. Gk *Ōlenos*] **:** a genus of trilobites from the Upper Cambrian of Europe having 12–15 thoracic segments, pleurae with sharp back-bent extremities, and a small pygidium

oleo \ˈōlē,ō\ *n* -S [in sense 1, short for *oleomargarine*; in sense 2, fr. *ole-*; in sense 3, short for *oleograph*] **1 a :** OLEOMARGARINE **b :** OLEO OIL **2** *or* **oleo gear :** a shock-absorbing device that utilizes the damping action produced by the flow of a column of liquid through an orifice of variable area **3 a :** OLEOGRAPH **b :** a backdrop for a television scene

oleo– — see OLE-

oleo·calcareous \,ōlēō+\ *adj* [ISV *ole-* + *calcareous*] **:** consisting of or containing a mixture of oil and lime

ole·o·cel·lo·sis \,ōlēō,seˈlōsəs\ *n, pl* **oleocello·ses** \-ˈlō,sēz\ [NL, fr. *ole-* + ISV *cell* + NL *-osis*] **:** a spotting of citrus fruits by oil liberated from the oil glands of the rind — called also *green spot*

ole·o·cyst \ˈōlēō,sist\ *n* [*ole-* + *-cyst*] **:** a diverticulum of the nectocalyx in various Calycophora that contains oil

ole·o·graph \ˈōlēə,graf, -rȧf\ *n* [ISV *ole-* + *-graph*] **1 :** a chromolithograph printed on canvas or other cloth to imitate an oil painting **2 :** the peculiar form or figure assumed by a drop of oil when placed on water or some other immiscible lubrication — **oleographic** *adj*

ole·og·ra·phy \,ōlēˈägrəfē\ *n* -ES [ISV *ole-* + *-graphy*] **1 :** the art or process of producing oleographic pictures **2 :** a process of identifying oils by their oleographs

oleo–gum–resin \ˈ⸗⸗,⸗ˈ⸗ˈ⸗⸗\ *n* [*ole-* + *gum* + *resin*] **:** a solid plant exudation (as asafetida or myrrh) consisting of a mixture of volatile oil, gum, and resin

oleo·margaric \,ōlēō+\ *adj* **:** of, relating to, or containing oleomargarine

oleo·margarine *also* **oleo·margarin** \"+\ *n* [F *oléomargarine*, fr. *oléo-* ole- + *margarine* — more at MARGARINE] **1 :** OLEO OIL **2 :** MARGARINE

ole·om·e·ter \,ōlēˈämədə(r)\ *n* [ISV *ole-* + *-meter*; prob. orig. formed as F *oléomètre*] **1 :** a hydrometer for determining the specific gravity of oils **2 :** an apparatus (as a Soxhlet extractor) for determining the percentage of oil in a material

oleo oil *n* **1 :** a yellow oil of buttery consistency expressed usu. from edible tallow and used in making margarine and soap and in lubrication — compare OLEOSTEARIN **2 :** any of various oils (as a hydrogenated vegetable oil) used in making margarine

ole·o·phil·ic \¦ōlēō¦filik\ *adj* [*ole-* + *-philic*] **:** having or relating to strong affinity for oils **:** HYDROPHOBIC — compare LIPOPHILIC

ole·o·pho·bic \-fōbik\ *adj* [*ole-* + *-phobic*] **:** having or relating to a lack of strong affinity for oils **:** HYDROPHILIC

ole·o·plast \'ōlēō,plast\ *n* -s [ISV *ole-* + *-plast*] **:** ELAIOPLAST

ole·op·tene \,ōlē'äp,tēn\ *n* -s [ISV *ole-* + Gk *ptēnos* winged — more at ELEOPTENE] **:** ELEOPTENE

oleo·refractometer \¦ōlēō+\ *n* [ISV *ole-* + *refractometer;* prob. orig. formed as F *oléoréfractomètre*] **:** a refractometer for use with oils

oleo·resin \"+\ *n* [ISV *ole-* + *resin*] **1 :** a natural plant product (as copaiba, elemi) consisting essentially of essential oil and resin; *esp* **:** TURPENTINE 1 b — compare BALSAM **2 :** a solid, liquid, or semiliquid preparation extracted (as from capsicum, cubebs, ginger) usu. by means of ether or acetone and consisting essentially of fatty or essential oil holding resin in solution

oleo·resinous \"+\ *adj* [ISV *oleoresin* + *-ous*] **1 :** of, relating to, or containing oleoresin ‹the ~ exudation of the balsam fir› **2 :** made of drying oils and resins usu. cooked — used esp. of a varnish or a paint vehicle

ole·o·sac·cha·rum \,ōlēō'sakərəm\ *n, pl* **oleosaccha·ra** \-rə\ [NL, fr. *ole-* + L *saccharum* sugar — more at SACCHARINE] **:** a homogeneous mixture used in pharmacy that is made by triturating sugar with a small amount of essential oil

ole·o·some \'ōlēə,sōm\ *n* -s [ISV *ole-* + *-some*] **:** a fat or fatty inclusion in cytoplasm

oleo·stearin *also* **oleo·stearine** \¦ōlēō+\ *n* [ISV *ole-* + *stearin, stearine*] **:** a solid residue of tallow remaining after removal of oleo oil or tallow oil and used chiefly in lard substitutes

oleo strut \'ōlē,ō-\ *n* [*ole-* + *strut*] **:** a cylindrical strut with a built-in telescopic shock absorber that damps or absorbs rectilinear shock (as in an aircraft landing gear) by forcing oil up through an orifice in the bottom of a hollow piston into an air-compression chamber

oleo strut: *1* inner cylinder, *2* orifice, *3* oil, *4* outer cylinder

oleo·thorax \¦ōlēō+\ *n* [NL, fr. *ole-* + *thorax*] **:** a state in which oil is present in the pleural cavity usu. as a result of injection — compare PNEUMOTHORAX

ole·ous \'ōlēəs\ *also* **ole·ose** \-ē,ōs\ *adj* [L *oleosus*, fr. *ole-* + *-osus* -ous, -ose] *archaic* **:** OILY

oleo·vitamin \¦ōlēō+\ *n* [*ole-* + *vitamin*] **:** a preparation containing one or more fat-soluble vitamins or derivatives in oil (as a fish-liver oil or an edible vegetable oil) ‹~ A› ‹synthetic ~ D›

ole·o·yl \ō'lēə,wil\ *n* -s [*ole-* + *-oyl*] **:** the radical $C_{17}H_{33}CO$– of oleic acid

ol·er·a·ceous \,älə'rāshəs\ *adj* [L *oleraceus, holeraceus*, fr. *oler-, olus, holer-, holus* potherb + *-aceus* -aceous; akin to L *helvus* light-bay-colored — more at YELLOW] **:** having the qualities of a potherb ‹~ plants›

ol·eri·culture \'älərə, ō'lerə+,-\ *n* [L *oler-, olus, holer-, holus* + E *-i-* + *culture*] **:** a branch of horticulture that deals with the production, storage, processing, and marketing of vegetables

ol·eri·culturist \,==+\ *n* -s **:** a specialist in olericulture

olés *pl of* OLÉ

-oles *pl of* -OLE

¹ole·threu·tid \¦ōlə¦thrüd·əd\ *adj* [NL *Olethreutidae*] **:** of or relating to the Olethreutidae

²olethreutid *n* -s **:** a moth of the family Olethreutidae

ole·threu·ti·dae \,==thrüd·ə,dē\ *n pl, cap* [NL, fr. *Olethreutes*, type genus (fr. Gk *olethreuein* to slay, destroy, fr. *olethros* destruction) + *-idae*] **:** a large family of small moths including the codling moth and the oriental peach moth

ole·um \'ōlēəm\ *n, pl* **olea** \-ēə\ *or* **oleums** [L — more at OIL] **1** *pl* **olea :** OIL — used chiefly in phrases that are the Latin names of oils ‹~ thae piperitae› **2** *pl* **oleums :** a heavy oily strongly corrosive liquid that consists of a solution of sulfur trioxide in anhydrous sulfuric acid, that fumes in moist air and reacts violently with water with the evolution of heat, and that is used chiefly in sulfonation and sulfation processes, in mixed acid for nitration, and in petroleum refining — called also *fuming sulfuric acid* ‹the strength of ~ is designated as percent by weight of free sulfur trioxide: thus 20% ~ contains 20% SO_3 and 80% H_2SO_4 by weight —B.M.Carter›

ole·yl \ō'lēəl\ *n* -s [*ole-* + *-yl*] **1 :** OLEOYL **2 :** the univalent radical $C_{17}H_{33}CH_2$– derived from oleyl alcohol

oleyl alcohol *n* **:** an oily liquid unsaturated compound $C_{17}H_{33}CH_2OH$ found in fish oils and other marine-animal oils that is made by reduction or hydrogenation of esters of oleic acid and is used chiefly in making surface-active agents and plasticizers; *cis*-9-octadecen-1-ol

ol·fac·tion \äl'fakshən\ *n* -s [L *olfactus, olefactus* (past part. of *olfacere, olefacere* to smell) + E *-ion* — more at OLFACTORY] **1 :** the sense of smell **2 :** the act or process of smelling

ol·fact·ive \(')äl¦faktiv\ *adj* [L *olfactus, olefactus* + E *-ive*] **:** OLFACTORY

ol·fac·tol·o·gy \,äl,fak'täləjē\ *n* -ES [L *olfactus* smell (fr. *olfactus, olefactus*, past part. of *olfacere, olefacere*) + E *-o-* + *-logy*] **:** the scientific study of smells or of the sense of smell

ol·fac·tom·e·ter \-tämәd·ə(r)\ *n* [ISV *olfacto-* (fr. L *olfactus* smell) + *-meter*] **:** an instrument for measuring the sensitivity of the sense of smell

ol·fac·to·met·ric \äl¦faktə¦me·trik\ *adj* **:** of, relating to, or marked by the use of olfactometry — **ol·fac·to·met·ri·cal·ly** \-rək(ə)lē\ *adv*

ol·fac·tom·e·try \,äl,fak'tämə·trē\ *n* -ES [ISV *olfacto-* + *-metry*] **:** the testing and measurement of the sensitivity of the sense of smell

ol·fac·to·ri·ly \(')äl¦fakt(ə)rəlē, (')ōl¦-\ *adv* **:** in respect to the sense of smell

ol·fac·to·ry \-rē, -ri\ *adj* [L *olfactorius*, fr. *olfactus, olefactus* (past part. of *olfacere, olefacere*, fr. *olēre* to smell + *facere* to make, do) + *-orius* -ory — more at ODOR, DO] **:** of, relating to, or connected with the sense of smell ‹~ receptors›

olfactory area *n* **1 :** the sensory area for olfaction lying in the hippocampal convolution **2 :** the area of nasal mucosa in which the olfactory organ is situated

olfactory bulb *n* **:** a bulbous anterior projection of the olfactory lobe in which the olfactory nerves terminate, being esp. well developed in lower vertebrates (as many fishes)

olfactory capsule *n* **:** NASAL CAPSULE

olfactory cell *n* **:** a sensory cell specialized for the reception of sensory stimuli caused by odors; *specif* **:** one of the spindle-shaped nerve cells buried in the nasal mucous membrane of vertebrates, each having a round nucleus and two slender processes of which the inner constitutes an olfactory nerve fiber and the short outer one is modified peripherally to form the actual sensory receptor — see OLFACTORY ORGAN

olfactory gyrus *n* **:** either a lateral or a medial gyrus by which the olfactory tract on either side communicates with the olfactory area of the brain

olfactory lobe *n* **:** a lobe of the brain that projects forward from the anterior lower part of each cerebral hemisphere, is continuous anteriorly with the olfactory nerve and well developed in most vertebrates, but is reduced to a narrow elongated body in man — see OLFACTORY BULB; BRAIN illustration

olfactory nerve *also* **olfactory** *n* -ES **:** either of the first pair of cranial nerves, being a sensory nerve, arising from the olfactory cells as discrete bundles of nonmedullated fibers that pass in small groups (in man, about 20) through the cribriform plate of the ethmoid and terminate in the olfactory bulb, and serving to conduct sensory stimuli from the olfactory organ to the brain

olfactory organ *n* **:** an organ of chemical sense that receives stimuli interpreted as odors from volatile and soluble substances in low dilution, that lies in the walls of the upper part of the nasal cavity, and that forms a mucous membrane continuous with the rest of the lining of the nasal cavity and made up of tall columnar supporting cells containing golden brown pigment interspersed with olfactory cells the outer processes of which project between the supporting cells as small vesicles surmounted by delicate sensory filaments and the inner ends of which are continuous with fibers of the olfactory nerves

olfactory pit *n* **1 :** an olfactory organ having the form of a small depression (as in amphioxi and various invertebrates) **2 :** a depression on the head of an embryo that becomes converted into a nasal passage — called also *nasal sac*

ol·fac·ty \äl'faktē\ *n* -ES [L *olfactus* smell + E *-y* — more at OLFACTOLOGY] **:** an arbitrary unit used in olfactometry for measuring the strength of an odorous stimulus

olib·a·num \ō'libənəm\ *n* -s [ME, fr. ML, fr. Ar *al-lubān* the frankincense] **:** FRANKINCENSE 1

-o·lic \'ōlik, ¦äl-, -lēk\ *adj suffix* [ISV *-ol* + *-ic*] **1 :** containing a triple bond — in names of acids ‹propi*olic* acid› **2 :** containing hydroxyl and carboxyl — in names of hydroxy acids ‹oleano*lic* acid›

ol·id \'äləd\ *adj* [L *olidus*, fr. *olēre* to smell — more at ODOR] **:** having a strong disagreeable smell **:** FETID

olifant *var of* OLIPHANT

olig- *or* **oligo-** *comb form* [ML, fr. Gk, fr. *oligos;* akin to Gk *loigos* ruin, havoc, OIr *líach* miserable, unhappy, Lith *liga* sickness, Arm *ałkat* poor, scant, and perh. to Gk *liazesthai* to bend, recoil, sink — more at LESS] **1 :** few ‹*Oligo*chaeta› ‹*oligo*gene› ‹*oligo*myodian› **:** few things ‹*oligo*phagous› **2** *med* **:** deficiency **:** insufficiency ‹*oligo*chromemia› ‹*olig*uria› **3 :** little **:** small ‹*oligo*lecithal›

ol·i·garch \'älə,gärk, -gäk\ *n* -s [Gk *oligarchēs*, fr. *olig-* + *-archēs* -arch] **:** a member or supporter of an autocratic clique ‹bureaucratic ~s in striped pants or khaki —Edmond Taylor›; *esp* **:** a member of a political oligarchy ‹the factional violence between democrats and ~s with which the Greek cities of the late fifth and early fourth centuries were sadly familiar —G.R.Morrow›

ol·i·gar·chal \¦==¦gärkəl\ *adj* **:** OLIGARCHIC

ol·i·gar·chic \¦älə¦gärkik, -gák-, -kēk\ *or* **ol·i·gar·chi·cal** \-kəkəl, -kēk-\ *adj* [Gk *oligarchikos*, fr. *oligarchia* + *-ikos* -ic, -ical] **:** of, relating to, characteristic of, or supporting oligarchy — **ol·i·gar·chi·cal·ly** \-kək(ə)lē\ *adv*

ol·i·gar·chy \'==,gärkē, -gák-, -ki\ *n* -ES [Gk *oligarchia*, fr. *olig-* + *-archia* -archy] **1 a** (1) **:** despotic power exercised by a privileged clique ‹a plutocratic ~ exercising all the old kingly powers —G.B.Shaw› — compare ARISTOCRACY (2) **:** government by the few ‹democracy and ~ shade into each other and are chiefly distinguished by the degree of the citizens' participation in government —D.D.McKean› **b :** autocratic control of any group or organization by a small faction ‹the alarming growth of economic ~ resulting from corporate concentration —C.C.Rodee› **2 a :** a group or organization that is controlled by a privileged few ‹high schools are *oligarchies* . . . or whatever you like, but not democracies —*Saturday Rev.*› **b :** the faction in control of such a group or organization ‹rival *oligarchies* supporting similar programs within the same party —H.R.Penniman› ‹the Millennium — old domination of the landowning and merchant ~ —D.M.Friedenberg›

ol·i·ge·mia \,älə'gēmēə, -'jē-\ *n* -s [NL, fr. Gk *oligaimia*, fr. *olig-* + *-aimia* -emia] **:** a condition in which the total volume of the blood is reduced — **ol·i·ge·mic** \¦==¦=mik\ *adj*

ol·i·gist \'äləjəst\ *or* **oligist iron** *n* -s [F *oligiste*, fr. Gk *oligistos* least, superl. of *oligos* small, few — more at OLIG-] **:** HEMATITE — **ol·i·gis·tic** \¦==¦jistik\ *or* **ol·i·gis·ti·cal** \-təkəl\ *adj*

ol·i·go·cene \'äləgō,sēn, ə'ligə,-\ *adj, usu cap* [ISV *olig-* + *-cene;* orig. formed as G *oligozän*] **:** of or relating to a subdivision of the Tertiary — see GEOLOGIC TIME table

ol·i·go·chae·ta \,äləgō'kēd·ə, ə,ligə'-\ *n pl, cap* [NL, fr. *olig-* + Gk *chaitē* long hair — more at CHAETA] **:** a class or in former classifications an order of Chaetopoda comprising hermaphroditic terrestrial and aquatic annelids distinguished from the polychaetes by possession of compact localized gonads and simple direct life histories without formation of a trochophore and by lack of parapodia and head specialization — see ARCHIOLIGOCHAETA, NEOLIGOCHAETA

¹ol·i·go·chaete *also* **ol·i·go·chaet** *or* **ol·i·go·chete** \'äləgō,kēt, ə'ligə,-\ *adj* [NL *Oligochaeta*] **:** of or relating to the Oligochaeta

²oligochaete *also* **oligochaet** *or* **oligochete** \"\ *n* -s **:** an annelid worm of the class Oligochaeta

ol·i·go·chae·to·log·i·cal \¦äləgō¦kēd·ə¦läjəkəl, ə¦ligə¦kē-\ *adj* **:** of or relating to oligochaetology

ol·i·go·chae·tol·o·gy \,äləgōkē'täləjē, ə,ligəkē'-\ *n* -ES [NL *Oligochaeta* + E *-o-* + *-logy*] **:** a branch of zoology that deals with the oligochaete worms

ol·i·go·chro·me·mia \,äləgōkrō'mēmēə, ə,ligək-\ *n* -s [NL, fr. *olig-* + *chrom-* + *-emia*] **:** deficiency of hemoglobin in the blood

ol·i·go·chronometer \¦äləgō, ə¦ligə+\ *n* [ISV *olig-* + *chronometer*] **:** an instrument for measuring very small time intervals

ol·i·go·clase \'äləgō,klās, ə'ligə,-\ *n* -s [G *oligoklas*, fr. *oligo-* olig- + *-klas* -clase] **:** a mineral of the plagioclase series — compare FELDSPAR

ol·i·go·cy·the·mia \,äləgō,sī'thēmēə, ə,ligə,s-\ *n* -s [NL, fr. *olig-* + *cyt-* + *-hemia*] **:** absolute deficiency in the number of red blood cells present in the body — compare ANEMIA — **ol·i·go·cy·the·mic** \¦äləgə,sī¦thēmik, ə,ligə,s-\ *adj*

ol·i·go·dac·tyl·ism \,äləgō'daktə,lizəm, ə,ligə'-\ *also* **ol·i·go·dac·tyly** \-'daktᵊlē\ *n, pl* **oligodactylisms** *also* **oligodactylies** [*olig-* + *-dactylism, -dactyly*] **:** a deficiency of fingers or toes

ol·i·go·den·dro·cyte \,äləgō'dendrə,sīt, ə,ligə'-\ *n* -s [ISV *olig-* + *dendr-* + *-cyte*] **:** a neuroglial cell resembling an astrocyte but small with few and slender processes having few branches

ol·i·go·den·drog·lia \,äləgō,den'dräglēə, ə,ligə,de-\ *n* -s [NL, fr. *olig-* + *dendr-* + *-glia*] **:** neuroglia made up of oligodendrocytes that is often prominent in pathologic states

ol·i·go·den·dro·gli·o·ma \,äləgō,dendrō,glī'ōmə, ə,ligə,de-\ *n, pl* **oligodendrogliomas** *or* **oligodendrogliomata** [NL, fr. *oligodendroglia* + *-oma*] **:** a tumor of the nervous system composed of oligodendroglia

ol·i·go·dynamic \¦äləgō, ə¦ligə+(,)¦==\ *adj* [ISV *olig-* + *dynamic;* orig. formed as G *oligodynamisch*] **1 :** active in very small quantities ‹an ~ germicide› **2 a :** produced by very small quantities ‹~ action of finely divided silver in disinfecting water› **b :** of or relating to the action of such quantities **3 :** of, relating to, or being produced by the specific activity of an oligodynamic substance ‹the ~ action of some pyridine derivatives on pathogenic microorganisms›

ol·i·go·gene \'äləgō,jēn, ə'ligə,-\ *n* [*olig-* + *gene*] **:** a gene that alone or with a few other genes controls the inheritance of a qualitative character or one showing typical Mendelian distribution — see POLYGENE; compare PARTICULATE INHERITANCE — **ol·i·go·gen·ic** \¦äləgō¦jenik, ə¦ligə¦-\ *adj*

ol·i·go·hydramnios \¦äləgō, ə¦ligə+,=¦==\ *n* [NL, fr. *olig-* + *hydramnios*] **:** deficiency of amniotic fluid sometimes resulting in embryonic defect through adherence between embryo and amnion

ol·i·go·lecithal \"+\ *adj* [ISV *olig-* + *lecithal*] **:** MICROLECITHAL

ol·i·go·menorrhea \"+\ *n* [NL, fr. *olig-* + *menorrhea*] **:** abnormally infrequent or scanty menstrual flow

ol·i·gom·era \,älə'gämərə\ *n pl, cap* [NL, fr. *olig-* + *-mera* (fr. Gk *meros* part) — more at MERIT] *in some classifications* **:** a division of invertebrate animals having the body divided into few or obscure segments

ol·i·go·my·o·di·an \¦äləgō,mī¦ōdēən, ə¦ligə,-\ *adj* [*olig-* + Gk *myōdēs* muscular (fr. *mys* mouse, muscle + *-ōdēs* -ode) + E *-ian* — more at MOUSE] **:** having few syringeal muscles

ol·i·go·nephric \¦äləgō, ə¦ligə+\ *adj* [*olig-* + *nephric*] *of an insect* **:** having few Malpighian tubules

ol·i·go·neu·ri·el·li·dae \,äləgō,n(y)ùrē'elə,dē, ə,ligə,n-\ *n pl, cap* [NL, fr. *Oligoneuriella*, type genus (dim. of *Oligoneuria*, genus of mayflies, fr. *olig-* + *neur-* + *-ia*) + *-idae*] **:** a large and widely distributed family of mayflies

ol·i·go·nite \'äləgō,nīt, ə'ligə,-\ *n* -s [G *oligonit*, fr. Gk *oligon* (neut. sing. of *oligos* little) + G *-it* -ite — more at OLIG-] **:** a mineral consisting of a manganiferous variety of siderite

ol·i·goph·a·gous \¦älə¦gäfəgəs\ *adj* [*olig-* + *-phagous*] **:** eating only a few specific kinds of food — used esp. of an insect subsisting on a few usu. related plants — compare MONOPHAGOUS — **ol·i·goph·a·gy** \,==¦gäfəjē\ *n* -ES

ol·i·go·phre·nia \,äləgō'frēnēə, ə,ligə'-\ *n* -s [NL, fr. *olig-* + *-phrenia*] **:** mental deficiency **:** FEEBLEMINDEDNESS

¹ol·i·go·phren·ic \¦äləgō¦frenik, ə¦ligə¦-\ *adj* **:** of, relating to, or exhibiting mental deficiency

²oligophrenic *n* -s **:** a mentally deficient person

ol·i·go·pod \'äləgō,päd, ə'ligə,-\ *adj* [*olig-* + *-pod*] *of an insect larva* **:** having thoracic legs fully developed and the abdomen completely segmented ‹carabid beetles have ~ larvae›

ol·i·gop·o·list \,älə'gäpələst\ *n* -s **:** a member of an oligopolistic industry or market

ol·i·gop·o·lis·tic \¦==¦gäpə¦listik\ *adj* **:** of or relating to an oligopoly

ol·i·gop·o·ly \,==¦gäpəlē\ *n* -ES [*olig-* + *monopoly*] **:** a market situation in which each of a limited number of producers is strong enough to influence the market but not strong enough to disregard the reaction of his competitors — compare DUOPOLY, MONOPOLY

ol·i·gop·so·nist \,älə'gäpsənəst\ *n* -s **:** a member of an oligopsonistic industry or market

ol·i·gop·so·nis·tic \¦==¦gäpsə¦nistik\ *adj* **:** of or relating to an oligopsony

ol·i·gop·so·ny \,==¦gäpsənē\ *n* -ES [*olig-* + Gk *opsōnia* purchase of victuals, catering — more at DUOPSONY] **:** a market situation in which each of a limited number of buyers is strong enough to influence the market but not strong enough to disregard the reaction to such influence by his competitors — compare DUOPSONY, MONOPSONY

ol·i·go·pyrene \¦äləgō, ə¦ligə+\ *adj* [ISV *olig-* + *pyrene;* prob. orig. formed as G *oligopyren*] **:** containing less than the normal amount of chromatin — used of a sperm cell; compare APYRENE, EUPYRENE

ol·i·go·saccharide \"+\ *n* [ISV *olig-* + *saccharide;* orig. formed as G *oligosaccharid*] **:** any of the saccharides that contain a known small number of constituent monosaccharide units and include esp. the disaccharides, trisaccharides, and tetrasaccharides — compare POLYSACCHARIDE

ol·i·go·saprobic \"+\ *adj* [ISV *olig-* + *saprobic;* orig. formed as G *oligosaprobisch*] **:** living in or being a highly oxygenated aquatic environment in which little organic material and a minimum of fermentation is present — compare MESOSAPROBIC, POLYSAPROBIC

ol·i·go·siderite \"+\ *n* [F, fr. *olig-* + *siderite*] **:** a meteorite characterized by the presence of only a small amount of metallic iron

ol·i·go·spermatic \"+\ *adj* [*olig-* + *spermatic*] **:** affected with or exhibiting oligospermia

ol·i·go·sper·mia \,äləgō'spərmēə, ə,ligə'-\ *n* -s [NL, fr. *olig-* + *-spermia*] **:** scantiness of semen or of living spermatozoa in the semen

ol·i·got·ri·cha \,älə'gä·trəkə\ *n pl, cap* [NL, fr. *olig-* + *-tricha*] **:** a suborder of Spirotricha comprising ciliated protozoans having the body ciliation reduced to a few large bristles or entirely absent and including numerous free-living aquatic forms (as the tintinnids) as well as the cellulose-digesting ciliates of the ruminant stomach — compare OPHRYOSCOLECIDAE, TINTINNIDAE — **ol·i·got·ri·chous** \¦==¦==kəs\ *adj*

ol·i·go·trich·i·da \,äləgō'trikədə, ə,ligə-'-\ [NL, fr. *olig-* + *trich-* + *-ida*] *syn of* OLIGOTRICHA

ol·i·go·troph·ic \¦äləgō¦träfik, ə¦ligə¦-\ *adj* [ISV *olig-* + *-trophic;* orig. formed as G *oligotrophisch*] *of a lake* **:** deficient in plant nutrients and usu. having abundant dissolved oxygen with no marked stratification — compare DYSTROPHIC, EUTROPHIC

ol·i·go·trop·ic \-räpik\ *adj* [ISV *olig-* + *-tropic*] **:** visiting only a few kinds of flowers for nectar — used of a bee; compare MONOTROPIC, POLYTROPIC

ol·i·go·zo·ic \-¦zōik\ *adj* [ISV *olig-* + *-zoic*] **:** containing few kinds or small numbers of animals — used of a habitat

ol·i·go·zo·o·sper·mia \,äləgō,zōə'spərmēə, ə,ligə,z-\ *n* -s [NL, fr. *olig-* + *zo-* + *-spermia*] **:** OLIGOSPERMIA

ol·i·gu·ria \,älə'g(y)ùrēə\ *n* -s [NL, fr. *olig-* + *-uria*] **:** reduced excretion of urine

olin·ia \ō'linēə\ *n, cap* [NL, fr. Johan Henrik *Olin*, 18th cent. Swed. botanist + NL *-ia*] **:** a small genus (coextensive with the family Oliniaceae of the order Myrtales) of African shrubs with opposite coriaceous leaves, small flowers in bracted cymes, and drupaceous fruits — see HARD PEAR 1

olio \'ōlē,ō\ *n* -s [modif. of Sp *olla* — more at OLLA] **1 :** OLLA PODRIDA 1 **2 a :** a miscellaneous mixture **:** HODGEPODGE ‹an incredibly bourgeois ~ of fancy stonework, stained glass, and light-opera staircases —R.H.Rovere› **b :** a miscellaneous collection (as of literary or musical selections) ‹a rich ~ of literary fare —Ray Corsini› **3 :** vaudeville numbers performed usu. in front of the curtain between acts or as a variety bill at the end of a burlesque or minstrel show ‹the ~ consisted of clog dancing, acrobatic acts —C.F.Wittke›

ol·i·phant *or* **ol·i·fant** \'äləfənt\ *n* -s [F *olifant*, fr. OF *olifant, oliphant* elephant, ivory, horn made of ivory — more at ELEPHANT] **:** a hunter's horn made from an elephant tusk

ol·i·prance \'äləprən(t)s\ *n* [ME *olipraunce*] *archaic* **:** boisterous merrymaking **:** FROLIC

olis·thops \'äləs,thäps, ə'lis-\ *n, cap* [NL, fr. Gk *olisthos* slippery (akin to *olisthanein* to slip) + NL *-ops* — more at SLIDE] **:** a genus of Pacific scarid fishes including the Australian herring-cale

¹ol·i·to·ry \'älə,tōrē\ *adj* [L *olitorius, holitorius*, fr. *olitor, holitor* vegetable gardener, fr. *olus, holus* potherb — more at OLERACEOUS] *archaic* **:** of, relating to, or produced in a kitchen garden

²olitory \"\ *n* -ES *archaic* **:** KITCHEN GARDEN

oli·va \ō'līvə\ *n, cap* [NL, fr. L, olive — more at OLIVE] **:** a genus of carnivorous marine snails (the type of the family Olividae) — see OLIVE SHELL

ol·i·va·ceous \¦älə¦vāshəs\ *adj* [*olive* + *-aceous*] **1 :** resembling an olive **2 :** of the color olive or olive green ‹~ markings on a bird›

ol·i·vary \'älə,verē, -ri\ *adj* [L *olivarius*, fr. *oliva* olive + *-arius* -ary] **1 :** shaped like an olive **2 :** of or relating to an olivary body

olivary body *n* **1 :** INFERIOR OLIVE **2 :** SUPERIOR OLIVE

¹ol·ive \'äləv, -lēv\ *n* -s [ME, fr. OF, fr. L *oliva*, fr. (assumed) OGk *elaiwa* (whence Gk *elaia*), prob. of non-IE origin; akin to the source of Arm *eul* oil] **1 a :** a plant of the genus *Olea; specif* **:** a tree (*Olea europaea*) cultivated for its fruit from antiquity in Asia Minor and southern Europe and more recently elsewhere and having a trunk that is often gnarled, leaves resembling the willow, and yellow flowers **b :** any of various shrubs and trees resembling the olive — compare WILD OLIVE **2 :** the oblong or ovoid drupaceous fruit of the olive tree that is eaten as a pickle or relish either when unripe and green or when bluish black and ripe and that yields a valuable oil **3 :** the hard yellow often attractively variegated wood of the olive tree used esp. in turnery **4 :** OLIVE BRANCH **5 :** something that is shaped like an olive: as **a :** a small slice of meat seasoned, rolled up, and cooked — usu. used in pl. ‹~s of veal› **b :** OLIVARY BODY **6 :** any of several colors resembling that of the unripe fruit of the olive tree that are yellow to yellow green in hue, of medium to low lightness, and of moderate to low saturation **7 a :** OLIVE SHELL **b :** OLIVE FLY

olive: *1* flowering branch, *2* fruit

²olive \"\ *adj* **1 :** of the color olive or olive green **2** *of a complexion* **:** approaching closer in color to olive than the average complexion

³oli·ve \ō'lēvā\ *n, pl* **olive** *or* **olives** *usu cap* [Sp, of AmerInd origin] **1 a :** an Indian people of northeastern Mexico **b :** a member of such people **2 :** a language of the Olive people that is of unknown relationship

olive acanthus *n, archit* **:** an acanthus with lobes resembling olive leaves

olive-backed thrush \'==,=-\ *or* **olive back** *n* **:** a common thrush (*Hylocichla ustulata*) of northern No. America migrating to the tropics that is brownish olive above and whitish beneath and has a ring about the eye and the sides of the head buff and the chest buff marked with black — compare GRAY-CHEEKED THRUSH

olive branch *n* [ME] **1 a :** a branch of the olive tree esp. when used as an emblem of peace ⟨making their submission through a boy clad in ash-color and bearing an *olive branch* —E.K.Chambers⟩ **b :** an offer or gesture of conciliation or goodwill ⟨his belief that the *olive branch* should be extended by loyal Democrats to . . . dissident party members —J.N. Popham⟩ **2 :** CHILD ⟨the rest of his letter is only about . . . his expectation of a young *olive branch* —Jane Austen⟩

olive brown *n* **:** any of a group of colors intermediate in hue between yellowish browns and olives; *typically* **:** a moderate olive that is lighter and very slightly redder than the color autumn — called also *bronze nude, old olive*

olive drab *n* **1 :** a variable color averaging a grayish olive that is greener, lighter, and slightly stronger than average covert brown and redder, lighter, and slightly stronger than bronzesheen **2 a :** a wool or cotton fabric of an olive drab color used esp. for making uniforms **b :** a uniform of this fabric

olive family *n* **:** OLEACEAE

olive fruit fly *n* **:** a small acalyptrate trypetid fly of the genus *Dacus* (*D. oleae*) having a larva that is a pest of the olive in Europe

olive G *n, usu cap O* **:** a sulfur dye — see DYE table I (under *Sulfur Green 11*)

olive gray *n* **:** a variable color averaging a grayish yellow green that is yellower and paler than average sage green or palmetto and yellower and duller than mermaid or celadon

olive green *n* **:** a variable color that is greener, lighter, and stronger than average olive color

olive gum *n* **:** a gummy exudation from the olive tree used as a drug by the ancients and now used as a perfume

olive hole *n* **:** a hole in a jeweled watch bearing whose sharp corners have been ground off to reduce the friction between the sides of the hole and the pivot that turns in it

olive knot *n* **:** a bacterial disease of the olive caused by a bacterium (*Pseudomonas savastonoi*) and characterized by small or large excrescences on leaves, branches, or even the main trunk — called also *olive tubercle*

olive lace bug *n* **:** a lace bug (*Froggattia olivina*) injurious to olives in Australia

ol·i·vel·la \\ˌäləˈvelə\\ *n* [NL, dim. of L *oliva* olive — more at OLIVE] **1** *cap* **:** a genus of small marine snails (family Olividae) having an operculum and a smooth shining shell formerly used by some Indians of the Pacific coast of No. America as money and for ornament — compare OLIVE SHELL **2** -s **:** any shell or animal of the genus *Olivella*

olive mangrove *n* **:** BLACK MANGROVE

olive moth *n* **:** a moth (*Prays oleellus*) of the family Yponomeutidae with a larva that feeds on the buds, leaves, and fruits of olives

oliv·en·ite \\ōˈlivəˌnīt, ˈäləvə-\\ *n* -s [G *olivenit*, fr. *olive* (fr. L *oliva*) + *-it* -ite] **:** a mineral $Cu_2(AsO_4)(OH)$ consisting of a basic arsenate of copper that is olive green, dull brown, or yellowish in color

olive oil *n* **:** a pale yellow to yellowish green nondrying oil obtained from the pulp of olives usu. by expression and used chiefly as a salad oil and in cooking, in toilet soaps, as an emollient, and as a wool oil — compare SULFUR OIL

olive-oil castile soap *n* **:** CASTILE 1

olive plum *n* **1 :** the fruit of a shrub or tree of the genus *Elaeodendron* (family Celastraceae) having simple leathery leaves, small greenish or white flowers in axillary clusters, and a drupaceous fruit **2 :** a tree of the genus *Elaeodendron*

ol·i·ver \\ˈäləvə(r)\\ *n* -s [prob. fr. the name *Oliver*] **1 :** an old form of smith's hammer worked by means of a treadle and normally held off the work by a spring pole **2 :** a device consisting of a pair of swages held together by a spring handle

¹ol·i·ve·ri·an \\ˌäləˈvirēən\\ *n* -s *usu cap* [*Oliver* Cromwell †1658 Eng. general and statesman + E *-ian*] **:** an adherent or partisan of Oliver Cromwell

²oliverian \\ˈ"\\ *adj, usu cap* **:** CROMWELLIAN 1

oliver's bark *n, usu cap O* [fr. the name *Oliver*] **:** the dried bark of a tree of the genus *Cinnamomum* (*C. oliveri*) of New So. Wales and Queensland that is used as a substitute for cinnamon

olives *pl of* OLIVE

olive scab *n* **:** a disease of the olive caused by a fungus (*Cycloconium oleaginum*) and characterized by blotches on the leaves and peduncles

olive scale *n* **:** any of several scales that attack olives: as **a :** an armored scale (*Parlatoria oleae*) that is a serious pest in California **b :** BLACK SCALE 1

ol·i·ves·cent \\ˌäləˈvesᵊnt\\ *adj* [²*olive* + *-escent*] **:** verging on olive in color

olivesheen \\ˈ==ˌ=\\ *n* **:** a dark grayish yellow that is greener and stronger than California green and greener, less strong, and slightly darker than honey or yellowstone

olive shell *n* **:** any of numerous chiefly tropical marine gastropod mollusks of the genus *Oliva* or the family Olividae having an elongate smooth highly polished shell with a very short spire, a narrow mouth notched in front, a plicate columella, a large foot, and a mantle that envelops the shell — compare OLIVELLA

olive-sided flycatcher \\ˈ=ˌ==-\\ *n* **:** a medium-sized flycatcher (*Nuttallornis borealis*) of eastern No. America

ol·i·vet \\ˌäləˈvet\\ *n* -s [*olivette* dim. of *olive* — more at OLIVE] **:** an imitation pearl esp. of a kind made for trading with primitive peoples in Africa

olive terra verte *n* **:** AUCUBA GREEN

olive tree *n* [ME] **1 :** OLIVE 1 **2 :** TUPELO 1

olive-tree agaric *n* **:** a red luminescent mushroom (*Pleurotus phosphoreus*) of Europe

ol·i·vette *also* **ol·i·vet** \\ˌäləˈvet\\ *n* -s [F *olivette*, dim. of *olive*] **:** a theatrical floodlight consisting of a 1000-watt bulb in an open-front metal box usu. mounted on a telescopic pipe stand or hung from a batten

olive tubercle *n* **:** OLIVE KNOT

olive wood *n* **1 :** the wood of the olive tree **2 a :** OLIVE PLUM 2 **b :** the wood of the olive plum **3 :** American-grown black ash esp. when quartersawed for veneer **4 :** a grayish yellowish brown that is darker and slightly redder than deer and slightly redder and darker than acorn — called also *brun doré, collie*

olive yellow *n* **:** a variable color averaging a dark greenish yellow that is greener, stronger, and very slightly darker than chartreuse green

oliv·i·dae \\ōˈlivəˌdē\\ *n pl, cap* [NL, fr. L *Oliva*, type genus + NL *-idae*] **:** a family of burrowing snails (suborder Stenoglossa) with cylindrical, glossy, and often brightly colored shells

ol·i·vif·er·ous \\ˌäləˈvif(ə)rəs\\ *adj* [L *olivifer* oliviferous (fr. *oliva* olive + *-fer* -ferous) + E *-ous* — more at OLIVE] **:** producing olives

oliv·i·form \\ōˈlivəˌfȯrm\\ *adj* [ISV ¹*olive* + *-iform*] **:** shaped like an olive or an olive shell

ol·i·vine \\ˈäləˌvēn, -vən\\ *n* -s [G *olivin*, fr. *olive* + *-in* -ine — more at OLIVENITE] **1 a :** a mineral $(Mg,Fe)_2SiO_4$ consisting of a silicate of magnesium and iron and comprising the isomorphous series forsterite-fayalite that is used in making refractories; *broadly* **:** a member of the isomorphous system $(Mg,Fe,Mn,Ca)_2SiO_4$ including forsterite, fayalite, tephroite, and a hypothetical calcium orthosilicate — see PERIDOT **b :** DEMANTOID **2 :** a light yellowish green that is yellower and paler than apple green (sense 2), lighter and stronger than pistachio, and deeper than ocean green

ol·i·vin·ic \\ˌ==ˈvinik\\ *or* **ol·i·vi·nit·ic** \\ˌäləvəˈnid·ik\\ *adj* [ISV *olivine* + *-ic* or *-itic*] **:** relating to, resembling, or containing olivine

¹ol·la \\ˈälə, ˈō(l)yə, ˈȯ(l)yə\\ *n* -s [Sp, fr. L *aulla, aula, olla* pot — more at OVEN] **1** *chiefly Southwest* **:** a large earthenware jar with a globular body often having a wide mouth and looped handles and used esp. as a stewpot or as a container for water **2** *chiefly Southwest* **:** OLLA PODRIDA 1

²olla *var of* OLA

ol·la po·dri·da \\ˌäləpəˈdrēdə, ˌō(l)yə-, ˌȯ(l)yə-\\ *n, pl* **olla podridas** \\-ēdəz\\ *also* **ollas podridas** \\-yəzp-\\ [Sp, lit., rotten pot] **1 :** a highly seasoned soup or stew made of one or more meats and several vegetables usu. including chick-peas cooked in an olla **2 :** OLIO 2

ol·lav *or* **ol·lave** *or* **ol·lamh** \\ˈäləv\\ *n* -s [IrGael *ollamh*, fr. MIr *ollam*] **:** a learned man in ancient Ireland

olluco *var of* ULLUCO

olm \\ˈōlm\\ *n* -s [G, fr. OHG] **:** an elongated European cave-dwelling aquatic salamander (*Proteus anguinus*) with permanent external gills and small eyes covered by the skin

¹ol·mec \\ˈälˌmek\\ *also* **ol·me·ca** \\älˈmākə\\ *n, pl* **olmec** *or* **olmecs** *also* **olmeca** *or* **olmecas** *usu cap* [Sp *olmeca*, of AmerInd origin] **:** an ancient people of the Isthmus of Tehuantepec in southern Mexico antedating or being contemporary with the Mayas

²olmec \\ˈ"\\ *adj, usu cap* **:** of or relating to an early culture of southeastern Mexico characterized by stone and jade carvings **:** LA VENTA

ol·o·gist \\ˈäləjəst\\ *n* -s [fr. *-ologist* (as in *geologist, psychologist*)] **:** SPECIALIST

ol·o·graph \\ˈäləˌgraf, -räf\\ *n* [by alter.] **:** HOLOGRAPH

ol·o·gy \\ˈäləjē\\ *n* -ES [fr. *-ology* (as in *geology, psychology*)] **:** a branch of knowledge **:** SCIENCE ⟨at least a dozen *ologies* will be represented on any one expedition nowadays —S.A. Korff⟩

olo·liu·qui \\ˌōləˈl(y)ükē\\ *n* -s [Sp *ololiuque*, fr. Nahuatl *ololiuhqui*, lit., one that covers, fr. *ololoa* to cover] **:** a woody stemmed Mexican vine (*Rivea corymbosa*) of the family Convolvulaceae having small fleshy fruits with single seeds resembling lentils that are used by the Indians for medicinal, narcotic, and religious purposes

olo·na \\ˌōləˈnä\\ *n* -s [Hawaiian *olonā*] **1 :** a Hawaiian shrub (*Touchardia latifolia*) of the family Urticaceae with erect stems, large thick leaves, and small flowers in globose clusters **2 a :** the strong bark fiber of the olona used for making fishnets and ropes resistant to sea water **b :** a cord made from this fiber

olo·nets \\əˈlōnəts\\ *also* **ol·nets** \\ˈälˌnets\\ *n, usu cap* [fr. *Olonets*, town on Lake Ladoga in northwestern Russia] **:** a dialect of Karelian spoken east of Lake Ladoga

olor \\ˈōˌlō(ə)r\\ *n, cap* [NL, fr. L, swan — more at AUK] **:** a genus of swans with no frontal knob including the whistling and trumpeter swans

olo·ro·so \\ˌōləˈrō(ˌ)sō\\ *n* -s [Sp, fr. *oloroso*, adj., fragrant, fr. *olor* odor (fr. L, fr. *olēre* to smell) + *-oso* -ous (fr. L *-osus*) — more at ODOR] **:** a sherry of golden color and medium sweetness

ölöt \\ˈüˈlüt\\ *n, pl* **ölöt** *or* **ölöts** *usu cap* **1 :** a Mongol people of Chinese Turkestan and Mongolia **2 :** a member of the Ölöt people

olp \\ˈälp\\ *also* **olph** \\ˈälf\\ *dial Eng var of* ¹ALP

ol·pe \\ˈälpē\\ *n, pl* **olpes** \\-ēz\\ *or* **ol·pae** \\-ē\\ [Gk *olpē*; akin to Gk *elpos* oil — more at SALVE] **:** either of two ancient Greek containers: **a :** a leather flask for oils or other liquids **b :** a wine pitcher resembling the oenochoe but more cylindrical in body

ol·pid·i·a·ce·ae \\älˌpidēˈāsēˌē\\ *n pl, cap* [NL, fr. *Olpidium*, type genus + *-aceae*] **:** a family of fungi (order Chytridiales) in which each thallus develops into a single sporangium

ol·pid·i·as·ter \\ˌ=ˌ==ˈastə(r)\\ *n, cap* [NL, fr. *Olpidium* + *-aster*] **:** a genus of fungi (family Olpidiaceae) resembling *Olpidium* but having a sporangium without a neck

ol·pid·i·um \\älˈpidēəm\\ *n, cap* [NL, fr. Gk *olpid-*, *olpis* leather flask; akin to Gk *elpis* oil — more at SALVE] **:** a genus of fungi (family Olpidiaceae) having a sporangium with a neck and retaining the spores in a sac until fully matured

-ols *pl of* -OL

ol·y·koek *also* **ol·y·cook** \\ˈäləˌku̇k\\ *n* -s [D *oliekoek*, fr. *olie* oil (fr. MD, fr. L *oleum*) + *koek* cake — more at OIL, COOKIE] *North* **:** DOUGHNUT

olym·pia \\ōˈlimpēə\\ *adj, usu cap* [fr. *Olympia*, Wash.] **:** of or from Olympia, capital of the state of Washington ⟨*Olympia* residents⟩ **:** of the kind or style prevalent in Olympia

olym·pi·ad \\ōˈlimpēˌad\\ *n* -s *often cap* [MF *Olympiade*, fr. L *Olympiad-*, *Olympias*, fr. Gk, fr. *Olympia*, plain in Elis in the northwestern Peloponnesus where the ancient Olympian games took place (fr. *Olympos*, a mountain in Elis + Gk *-ia* -y) + Gk *-ad-*, *-as*, fem. suffix denoting descent from or connection with] **1 :** one of the four-year intervals between Olympian games by which time was reckoned in ancient Greece ⟨the city was taken on the third month, on the day of the fast, upon the hundred and seventy-ninth ~ —R.L.Odom⟩ **2 a :** a quadrennial celebration of the modern Olympic Games ⟨India, in the past five ~*s*, has won 20 contests without defeat —*Amateur Athlete*⟩ **b :** OLYMPIC GAMES ⟨national ~*s*⟩

¹olym·pi·an \\-ēən\\ *adj, usu cap* [L *Olympius* Olympian (fr. Gk *Olympios*, fr. *Olympia*) + E *-an*] **1 :** of or relating to the ancient Greek region of Olympia **2 a :** of, relating to, or constituting the Olympian games **b :** ²OLYMPIC 2

²olympian \\ˈ"\\ *n* -s **1** *cap* **:** a native or inhabitant of ancient Olympia **2** *usu cap* **:** a participant in Olympic Games ⟨two American *Olympians* and other red-capped, blue-jacketed competitors —*Newsweek*⟩

³olympian \\ˈ"\\ *adj, usu cap* [L *Olympius* Olympian (fr. Gk *Olympios*, fr. *Olympos* Olympus, mountain in Thessaly that was considered the abode of the chief gods of ancient Greece) + E *-an*] **1 :** of or relating to Mount Olympus in Thessaly ⟨*Olympian* deities⟩ **2 :** befitting or characteristic of the gods conceived as inhabiting Mount Olympus **:** displaying majestic omniscience or detachment **:** LOFTY, SUPERLATIVE ⟨verdicts based on *Olympian* detachment and austere standards —Richard Watts⟩ ⟨lies in *Olympian* beauty gazing upon it all with . . . serene composure —C.B.Tinker⟩

⁴olympian \\ˈ"\\ *n* -s *usu cap* **1 :** one of the gods conceived as inhabiting Mount Olympus ⟨something lofty and sinister like an *Olympian's* caprice —Joseph Conrad⟩ **2 :** a being of lofty detachment or superior attainments ⟨side by side with these *Olympians* are the less conspicuous who are glad for modest honors —C.M.Fuess⟩

olympian blue *n, often cap O* [³*Olympian*] **:** MATELOT 2

olympian games *n pl, usu cap O* [¹*Olympian*] **:** a Panhellenic festival dedicated to Zeus, originating in 776 B.C. and held every fourth year in the first month after the summer solstice, and consisting of contests in sports, music, and literature with the victor's prize a crown of wild olive, a palm branch, and the right to erect a statue in the central enclosure of the sacred precincts — compare AGON a

olympian green *n, often cap O* [³*Olympian*] **:** MALACHITE GREEN 3

olym·pi·an·ism \\-ēəˌnizəm\\ *n* -s *usu cap* [³*Olympian* + *-ism*] **:** worship of the Olympian gods

olym·pi·an·ly *adv, usu cap* [³*Olympian* + *-ly*] **:** in an Olympian manner ⟨the accident was *Olympianly* disregarded except by the butler —Jean Stafford⟩

olympia oyster *n, usu cap 1st O* **:** a small flavorful native oyster (*Ostrea lurida*) of the Puget Sound area of the Pacific coast of No. America

¹olym·pic \\ōˈlimpik, -pēk\\ *adj, often cap* [L *Olympicus*, fr. Gk *Olympikos*, fr. *Olympos* Mt. Olympus + Gk *-ikos* -ic] **:** ³OLYMPIAN

²olympic \\ˈ"\\ *adj, often cap* [L *Olympicus*, fr. Gk *Olympikos*, fr. *Olympia*, region in Elis + Gk *-ikos* -ic] **1 :** ¹OLYMPIAN 1 **2 :** of or relating to the Olympic Games

olympic blue *n, often cap O* [¹*Olympic*] **:** COBALT BLUE 2

olympic games *n pl, usu cap O&G* [²*Olympic*] **1 :** OLYMPIAN GAMES **2 :** a modified revival of the Olympian games originating in Athens in 1896, held once every four years, and consisting of international athletic contests — called also *Olympics*

olym·pics \\-ks\\ *n pl, usu cap* [²*olympic* + *-s*] **:** OLYMPIC GAMES

olyn·thi·an \\ōˈlin(t)thēən\\ *n* -s *cap* [*Olynthus*, town in ancient Macedonia + E *-an*] **:** a native or inhabitant of Olynthus in ancient Macedonia

olyn·thus \\ōˈlin(t)thəs\\ *n* -ES [NL, fr. Gk *olynthos* fig] **:** a young calcareous sponge immediately after fixation of the free larva where it resembles a vase in form and has a simple and asconoid body wall — compare ASCON

om *also* **aum** \\ˈōm\\ *interj* [Skt *om*] — used in Hinduism, Sikhism, and Lamaism as a mantra in mystical contemplation of ultimate reality

om *also* **aum** \\ˈōm, ˈōm\\ *n* [Skt *om*] **:** a mantra consisting of the sound \\ˈōm\\ or \\ˈōm\\ and used in Hinduism, Sikhism, and Lamaism in mystical contemplation of ultimate reality

OM *abbr* **1** old measurement **2** outer marker

-o·ma \\ˈōmə\\ *n suffix, pl* **-omas** \\-məz\\ *or* **-oma·ta** \\-məd·ə, -ətə\\ [L *-omat-*, *-oma*, fr. Gk *-ōmat-*, *-ōma*] **1 :** tumor of a (specified) kind ⟨aden*oma*⟩ ⟨melan*oma*⟩ ⟨hygr*oma*⟩ or consisting predominantly of a (specified) kind of cell or tissue ⟨fibr*oma*⟩ ⟨my*oma*⟩ ⟨myelocyt*oma*⟩ or occurring in a (specified) organ ⟨nephr*oma*⟩ **2 :** -OME

oma·dhaun \\ˈäməˌthȯn\\ *n* -s [IrGael *amadān*] *chiefly Irish* **:** FOOL, IDIOT, SIMPLETON

oma·gua \\ōˈmä(g)wə\\ *n, pl* **omagua** *or* **omaguas** *usu cap* **1 a :** a Tupian people of western Brazil and Peru **b :** a member of such people **2 :** the language of the Omagua people

¹oma·ha \\ˈōməˌhȯ, -hä\\ *also* **ma·ha** \\məˈ=\\ *n, pl* **omaha** *or* **omahas** *also* **maha** *or* **mahas** *usu cap* [Omaha, lit., those going upstream or against the wind] **1 a :** a Siouan people in the Missouri river valley in northeastern Nebraska **b :** a member of such people **2 :** a dialect of Dhegiha

²omaha \\ˈ"\\ *adj, usu cap* [fr. *Omaha*, city in eastern Nebraska, fr. *Omaha* (Siouan people)] **:** of or from the city of Omaha, Nebr. **:** of the kind or style prevalent in Omaha

oma·han \\-ˌhȯn, -hän\\ *n* -s *cap* [*Omaha*, Nebraska + E *-an*] **:** a native or resident of Omaha, Nebr.

oman \\(ˈ)ōˈmän\\ *adj, usu cap* **:** Muscat and Oman

¹oma·ni \\ōˈmänē\\ *n* -s *cap* [Ar *ʽumānī*, fr. *ʽumān* Oman] **:** a native or inhabitant of Muscat and Oman

²omani *adj, usu cap* **:** of, relating to, or characteristic of Muscat and Oman or its people

omao \\ōˈmau̇\\ *n* -s [Hawaiian] **:** a thrush (*Phaeornis obscurus*) of Hawaii

omar·ian \\ōˈmärēən\\ *n* -s *usu cap* [*Omar* Khayyám †*ab*1123 Pers. poet and astronomer + E *-an*] **:** a student or admirer of the poetry of Omar Khayyám

omar stanza \\ˈōˌmär-\\ *n, usu cap O* [after *Omar* Khayyám] **:** RUBAIYAT STANZA

oma·sal \\(ˈ)ōˈmāsəl\\ *adj* [*omasum* + *-al*] **:** of or relating to the omasum

oma·si·tis \\ˌōməˈsīd·əs\\ *n* -ES [NL, fr. *omasum* + *-itis*] **:** inflammation of the omasum

oma·sum \\ōˈmāsəm\\ *n, pl* **oma·sa** \\-sə\\ [NL, fr. L, tripe of a bullock] **:** the third chamber of the ruminant stomach that is situated between the reticulum and the abomasum — called also *manyplies, psalterium*

o·mayyad *usu cap, var of* UMAYYAD

¹om·bre *also* **om·ber** \\ˈämbə(r)\\ *n, pl* **ombres** *also* **ombers** [alter. of *umber*] **:** a European grayling (*Thymallus thymallus*)

²om·bre *also* **om·ber** *or* **hom·bre** \\ˈämbə(r)\\ *n* -s [F or Sp; F *hombre*, fr. Sp, lit., man — more at HOMBRE] **:** a 3-handed card game played throughout Europe in the 17th and 18th centuries and still played in Spain; *also* **:** the player in this game who elects to name the trump and oppose the other 2 players

³om·bré *or* **om·bre** \\(ˈ)ōmˈbrā, (ˈ)ämˈb-\\ *adj* [F *ombré*, past part. of *ombrer* to shade, fr. It *ombrare*, fr. *ombra* shade, shadow, fr. L *umbra* — more at UMBRAGE] **:** SHADED — used esp. of fabrics with a dyed or woven design in which the color is graduated from light to dark and often into stripes of varying shades of one or more colors ⟨some hats are of ~ blues and lavenders —Lois Long⟩

⁴ombré *or* **ombre** \\ˈ"\\ *n* -s **1 :** an ombré design **2 :** a fabric with an ombré design ⟨a gray leaf-and-fern pattern printed on a pink-to-red ~ —Lois Long⟩

om·bres chi·noises \\ˌämbrəˌshēnˈwäz\\ *n pl, sometimes cap* [F, lit., Chinese shadows] **:** shadows of puppets or persons thrown upon a transparent screen and used as characters in a dramatic presentation

ombrette *var of* UMBRETTE

ombro- *comb form* [Gk, fr. *ombros* — more at IMBRICATE] **:** rain ⟨*ombro*logy⟩

om·bro·graph \\ˈämbrəˌgraf\\ *n* [ISV *ombro-* + *-graph*] **:** a self-registering rain gage

om·brol·o·gy \\ämˈbräləjē\\ *n* -ES [*ombro-* + *-logy*] **:** a branch of meteorology that deals with rain

om·brom·e·ter \\ämˈbräməd·ə(r)\\ *n* [Gk *ombros* rain + E *-meter*] **:** RAIN GAGE

om·bro·phile \\ˈämbrəˌfīl\\ *n* -s [ISV *ombro-* + *-phile*] **:** an ombrophilous plant

om·broph·i·lous \\(ˈ)ämˈbräfələs\\ *also* **om·bro·phil·ic** \\ˌämbrəˈfilik\\ *adj* [*ombrophilous* ISV *ombro-* + *-philous*; *ombrophilic* fr. *ombrophilous* + *-ic*] *of a plant* **:** capable of withstanding or thriving in the presence of much rain — **om·broph·i·ly** \\ämˈbräfəlē\\ *n* -ES

om·bro·phobe \\ˈämbrəˌfōb\\ *n* -s [ISV *ombro-* + *-phobe*] **:** an ombrophobous plant

om·broph·o·bous \\(ˈ)ämˈbräfəbəs\\ *adj* [ISV *ombro-* + *-phobous*] *of a plant* **:** incapable of withstanding long-continued rain — **om·broph·o·by** \\=ˈ==bē\\ *n* -ES

om·bu \\ämˈbü\\ *n* -s [Sp *ombú*, fr. Guarani *umbú*] **:** a large herbaceous So. American tree (*Phytolacca dioica*) having an immensely broad trunk, soft spongy wood, and dark green oval leaves

om·deh *also* **om·da** \\ˈämdə\\ *n* -s *sometimes cap* [Ar *ʽumdah* column, authority] **:** the leader of an Egyptian village ⟨the tendency of village ~*s* . . . to back the winning horse —*Economist*⟩

om·dur·man \\ˌämdə(r)ˈman\\ *adj, usu cap* [fr. *Omdurman*, city in Sudan] **:** of or from the city of Omdurman, Sudan **:** of the kind or style prevalent in Omdurman

-ome \\ˌōm\\ *n suffix* -s [NL *-omat-*, *-oma*, fr. L *-omat-*, *-oma*] **:** abstract entity **:** group **:** mass **:** stem ⟨caul*ome*⟩ ⟨mest*ome*⟩

¹omega \\ōˈmegə, -ˈmēgə, -ˈmāgə *sometimes* ˈōmigə *or* ˈōmēgə *or* ˈōˌmegə *or* ˈōˌmāgə\\ *n* -s [Gk *ō mega*, lit., large o] **1 :** the 24th and last letter of the Greek alphabet — symbol Ω or ω; see ALPHABET table **2 :** the last (as in sequence, order, classification) **:** ENDING ⟨between her alpha and ~, a span of fifty years —Jean Stafford⟩ — compare ALPHA

²omega \\ˈ"\\ *or* ω *adj* **:** of, relating to, or being an end group or position ⟨~ oxidation of fatty acids⟩ ⟨ω-chloro-styrene $C_6H_5CH{=}CHCl$⟩

omega·tron \\=ˈ==ˌträn\\ *n* -s [*omega* + *-tron*] **:** a small instrument utilizing the principle of the cyclotron for the measurement of the masses of atomic particles

omegoid \\ōˈmeˌgȯid, -ˈmē-, -ˈmā-\\ *adj* [*omega* + *-oid*] **:** having the form of the Greek capital letter omega

om·e·let *also* **om·e·lette** \\ˈäm(ə)lət, *usu* -əd.+V\\ *n* -s [F *omelette*, fr. MF, alter. of *amelette*, alter. of *alumette*, alter. (influenced by *-ette*) of *alumelle*, lit., blade (of a sword or knife), fr. OF *alemelle*, *alemele*, alter. of *lemelle*, *lemele*, fr. L *lamella* small metal plate, dim. of *lamina* thin plate] **:** eggs beaten to a froth, cooked without stirring until set, and served in a half-round form by folding one half over the other ⟨cheese ~⟩ ⟨jelly ~⟩

¹omen \\ˈōmən\\ *n* -s [L *omin-*, *omen*] **:** an occurrence or phenomenon believed to portend or show the character of a future event **:** AUGURY, FORETOKEN, PRESAGE ⟨priests took ~*s* before the warriors went into battle —Ralph Linton⟩ ⟨the ghostly bidding of the cloud, the ~ of thunder —C.P.Aiken⟩

²omen \\ˈ"\\ *vt* -ED/-ING/-S **:** to divine or to foreshow by signs or portents **:** have omens or premonitions regarding **:** AUGUR, PRESAGE ⟨the blazing red of the setting sun ~*ed* fine weather⟩

oment- *or* **omento-** *comb form* [*omentum*] **:** omentum ⟨*oment*itis⟩ ⟨*omento*pexy⟩

omen·tal \\(ˈ)ōˈmentəl\\ *adj* [*omentum* + *-al*] **:** of, relating to, or formed from an omentum

omen·to·pexy \\ōˈmentəˌpeksē\\ *n* -ES [ISV *oment-* + *-pexy*] **:** the operation of suturing the omentum esp. to another organ ⟨nephro-*omentopexy*⟩

omen·tu·lum \\ōˈmenchələm\\ *n, pl* **omentu·la** \\-lə\\ [NL, fr. L *omentum* + *-ulum*] **:** LESSER OMENTUM

omen·tum \\ōˈmentəm\\ *n, pl* **omen·ta** \\-tə\\ *or* **omentums** [L, fr. *o-* (akin to L *-uere* to put on) + *-mentum* — more at EXUVIAE] **:** a free fold of peritoneum or one connecting or supporting viscera or other abdominal structures — see GREATER OMENTUM, LESSER OMENTUM; compare MESENTERY

omer \\ˈōmə(r)\\ *n* -s [Heb *ʽōmer*] **1 :** an ancient Hebrew unit of dry capacity equal to 1/10 ephah or about ½ peck **2** *often cap* **a :** a wave offering of a sheaf or omer measure of barley representing the first reaping of the grain harvest and presented to the priest in a temple ceremony on the second day of the Passover **b :** a period of seven weeks between the second day of the Passover and Shabuoth during which in traditional Judaism various restrictive laws (as the prohibition of festivities except on Rosh Hodesh and Lag b'Omer) are in force and each day is formally counted in the evening service ⟨hast commanded us concerning the counting of the ~ —*Jewish Daily Prayer Book*⟩

om·i·cron *also* **om·i·kron** \ˈämə,krän, *chiefly Brit* ōˈmīkrən\ *n* -s [Gk *o mikron*, lit., small o] **:** the 15th letter of the Greek alphabet — symbol O or o; see ALPHABET table

om·i·nate \ˈämə,nāt\ *vb* -ED/-ING/-s [L *ominatus*, past part. of *ominari*, fr. *omin-*, *omen* omen] *vt* **1** *archaic* **:** to prophesy from signs and omens **:** AUGUR **2** *archaic* **:** to be a portent or omen of ~ *vi* **1** *obs* **:** to utter prophecies or forebodings **2** *obs* **:** to serve as a prophecy

omination *n* -s [L *omination-*, *ominatio*, fr. *ominatus* + *-ion-*, *-io* -ion] *obs* **:** the act of prophesying

om·i·nous \ˈämənəs\ *adj* [L *ominosus*, fr. *omin-*, *omen* + *-osus* -ose] **1 :** of or relating to an omen **:** being or exhibiting an omen ⟨the continual wars and revolutions so ~ of the future —Margaret Parton⟩ **2 :** indicative of future misfortune or calamity **:** causing anxiety and fear **:** potentially disastrous ⟨the ~ waves of cloud seemed to advance with terrific speed —O.E.Rölvaag⟩ ⟨a dead and ~ silence prevailed everywhere —J.A.Froude⟩ ⟨the ~ sounds the motor was making —Herbert Passin⟩

syn PORTENTOUS, FATEFUL, INAUSPICIOUS, UNPROPITIOUS: OMINOUS applies to that which shows a menacing, threatening, and frightful character foreshadowing evil or tragic developments, sometimes rather vague ⟨there was something *ominous* about it, and in intangible ways one was made to feel that the worst was about to come —Jack London⟩ ⟨they formed together an *ominous* cloud charged with forces of uncertain magnitude, but of the reality of which Italy had already terrible experience —J.A.Froude⟩ PORTENTOUS is now likely to indicate the prodigious, huge, impressive, marvelous, or monstrous, and only secondarily to suggest the character of a portent, a forewarning of calamity to come ⟨in the midst of a *portentous* silence, the consul unrolled his papers, evidently intending to produce an effect by the exceeding bigness of his looks —Herman Melville⟩ ⟨something quivered in every fiber of his being, like moonlit ripples on the sea. He felt at the same time a *portentous* stillness and an immense enterprise —H.G.Wells⟩ FATEFUL may imply an especial importance, often solemn, decreed by fate; it is often simply a synonym for *momentous* ⟨the moving, *fateful* story of his death —H.O.Taylor⟩ ⟨the hour seemed awful to them, and the hearts within them burned as though of *fateful* matters their souls were newly learned —William Morris⟩ ⟨six thousand years ago, the Nile, the begetter of water and grain, was as *fateful* to the fellah as it is today —Mary Lindsay⟩ INAUSPICIOUS and UNPROPITIOUS may suggest the presence of distinctly unfavorable signs or may be simply synonyms for *unlucky* or *unfavorable* ⟨while my words with *inauspicious* thunderings shook Heaven —P.B.Shelley⟩ ⟨*unpropitious* weather⟩ ⟨an *unpropitious* attitude for a politician seeking reelection to take⟩

om·i·nous·ly *adv* **:** in an ominous manner ⟨the steps to the veranda sagged ~ under his weight —Harold Sinclair⟩ ⟨the night sky glowed ~ red —O.S.Nock⟩

om·i·nous·ness *n* -ES **:** the quality or state of being ominous

omis·si·bil·i·ty \ō,misəˈbilədē\ *n* -ES **:** the quality or state of being omissible

omis·si·ble \ōˈmisəbəl\ *adj* [L *omissus* (past part. of *omittere*) + E *-able*] **:** that may be omitted **:** subject to or suitable for omission

omis·sion \ōˈmishən,əˈm-\ *n* -s [ME *omissioun*, fr. LL *omission-*, *omissio*, fr. L *omissus* (past part. of *omittere*) + *-ion-*, *-io* -ion] **1 a :** apathy toward or neglect of duty **:** lack of action ⟨allowed themselves to be engulfed . . . through ~ or commission —*N. Y. Times Mag.*⟩ — compare COMMISSION 5 **b :** something neglected or left undone ⟨pondered many ~*s* that night in the rectory's best bedroom —J.D.Beresford⟩ **2 :** the act of omitting whether by leaving out or by abstention from inserting or by failure to include or perform; *also* **:** the state of being omitted ⟨the ~ of clues essential to understanding —J.H. Wheelock⟩ ⟨when the ~ was discovered, they would send somebody —Margaret Kennedy⟩

omis·sive \ōˈmisiv\ *adj* [L *omissus* (past part. of *omittere*) + E *-ive*] **:** leaving out **:** failing or neglecting to do **:** OMITTING — **omis·sive·ly** *adv*

omit \ōˈmit, əˈm-, *usu* -id·+V\ *vt* **omitted; omitted; omitting; omits** [ME *omitten*, fr. L *omittere*, fr. *ob-* to, against, over + *mittere* to send — more at OB-, SMITE] **1 :** to leave out or leave unmentioned **:** fail to insert, include, or name ⟨if you ~ the industrial areas . . . this way of life is pastoral, parochial, picturesque —W.G.Hardy⟩ ⟨will not wish to ~ this valuable book from his reading —Harry Schwartz⟩ **2 :** to fail to perform or make use of **:** leave alone or undone **:** FORBEAR ⟨nor could I think well of the man who should ~ an occasion of testifying his respect —Jane Austen⟩ ⟨most visitors ~ to walk round the walls in their hurry —S.P.B.Mais⟩ **3** *obs* **:** to leave unnoticed or unregarded ⟨~ him not; blunt not his love nor lose the good advantage of his grace —Shak.⟩ **4** *obs* **:** to refrain or cease from keeping **:** let go ⟨traitors . . . having sense of beauty do ~ their mortal natures —Shak.⟩ **syn** see NEGLECT

omittance *n* -s [*omit* + *-ance*] *obs* **:** OMISSION

-om·ma \ˈämə\ *n comb form* [NL *-ommat-*, *-omma*, fr. Gk *ommat-*, *omma* eye; akin to Gk *ōps* eye — more at EYE] **:** one having (such) an eye or (such or so many) eyes — in generic names in zoology ⟨*Loxomma*⟩

om·mas·tre·phes \əˈmastrə,fēz\ *n, cap* [NL, fr. Gk *omma* eye + *strephein* to turn — more at STROPHE] **:** a widely distributed genus (type of the family Ommastrephidae) of extremely active cephalopods (order Decapoda) having a cylindrical body, large rhombic terminal fins, and short strong arms

om·ma·te·al \ˈäməˈtēəl\ *adj* [*ommateum* + *-al*] **:** of, relating to, or having compound eyes

om·ma·te·um \,==ˈtēəm\ *n, pl* **omma·tea** \-ēə\ [NL, fr. Gk *ommat-*, *omma* eye] **:** COMPOUND EYE

om·ma·tid·i·al \ˈäməˈtidēəl\ *adj* [*ommatidium* + *-al*] **:** of, relating to, or having ommatidia

om·ma·tid·i·um \,==ˈ==ēəm\ *n, pl* **ommatid·ia** \-ēə\ [NL, fr. Gk *ommat-*, *omma* eye + NL *-idium*] **:** one of the elements corresponding to a small simple eye or ocellus that make up the compound eye of an arthropod and that typically consist of an external corneal lens beneath which is a crystalline cone and below it a rhabdom which is enclosed in a sensitive retinula protected by pigment

om·ma·tin \ˈämədən\ *n* -s [Gk *ommat-*, *omma* eye + E *-in*] **:** an ommochrome (as a brown pigment in the eye of the fruit fly) of low molecular weight

om·mat·o·phore \əˈmadə,fō(ə)r\ *n* -s [prob. fr. (assumed) NL *ommatophorus*, fr. Gk *ommat-*, *omma* eye + NL *-o-* + *-phorus* -phore] **:** a movable peduncle bearing an eye ⟨a snail probing with his eyes at the end of their ~*s*⟩ — **om·ma·toph·o·rous** \,äməˈtäf(ə)rəs\ *adj*

ommiad *usu cap, var of* UMAYYAD

om·mo·chrome \ˈämə,krōm\ *n* [*ommo-* (fr. Gk *omma* eye) + *-chrome*] **:** any of various pigments derived from tryptophan and found esp. in the eyes of insects

omn- *or* **omni-** *comb form* [ME *omni-*, fr. MF, fr. L, fr. *omnis* all] **:** all **:** universal **:** universally **:** without restriction ⟨*omni*meter⟩ ⟨*omni*present⟩ ⟨*omn*ist⟩

om·ne·i·ty \ämˈnēədē\ *n* -ES [L *omne* (neut. of *omnis* all) + E *-ity*] **:** the state of being all-comprehensive **:** ALLNESS

om·ni·bearing \ˈämnə,-nē+,-\ *n* [*omn-* + *bearing*] **:** the bearing of an omnidirectional radio range station from an airplane usu. expressed in terms of magnetic rather than true north

¹om·ni·bus \ˈämnə,bəs,-nē-, -bəs\ *n* -ES [F, fr. L, for all, dat. pl. of *omnis* all; perh. akin to L *ops* wealth — more at OPULENT] **1 :** a public vehicle usu. automotive and 4-wheeled and designed to carry a comparatively large number of passengers **:** BUS **2 :** OMNIBUS BILL ⟨this bill is an ~ and is being reviewed at length by the author —E.H.Wilson⟩ **3 :** BUSBOY ⟨little ~*es* in white suits moved about gathering up papers or napkins dropped by careless diners —H.S.Harrison⟩ **4 :** a book containing reprints of a number of works (as of a single author or on a single subject or related subjects)

²omnibus \ˈ"\ *adj* **:** of, relating to, or providing for many things or classes at once **:** containing or including many items ⟨meager appropriation in view of the ~ nature of its assignment —*Nation's Business*⟩ ⟨a sort of ~ tribute, touching on the natives, the huts, the palm trees, . . . hookworm, dysentery —R.L.Taylor⟩

omnibus bill *n* **:** a legislative bill that includes a number of miscellaneous provisions or appropriations ⟨a tough *omnibus bill* he could dump as a single package —*Time*⟩

omnibus box *n* **:** a large box in a theater or opera house adapted to contain many persons

omnibus clause *n* **:** a clause or section (as of a contract or statute) intended to cover various items not otherwise specifically covered; *esp* **:** a clause in an automobile insurance policy that extends protection to others than the named insured

om·ni·competence \ˈämnə,-nē+\ *n* [fr. *omnicompetent*, after E *competent: competence*] **:** the quality or state of being omnicompetent ⟨they act on an identical assumption of ~ —Hannah Arendt⟩

om·ni·competent \"+\ *adj* [*omn-* + *competent*] **:** having jurisdiction or legal capacity to act in all matters ⟨too little aware of the peril in a monopoly of political and economic power in the hands of the ~ state —Reinhold Niebuhr⟩

om·ni·directional \"+\ *adj* [ISV *omn-* + *directional*] **1 :** receiving or sending radiations equally well in all directions ⟨~ radio transmitter⟩ ⟨~ antenna⟩ **2** *of a microphone* **:** not directional

omnidirectional radio range *or* **omnidirectional range** *n* **:** OMNIRANGE

om·ni·far·i·ous \ˈämnəˈfa(a)rēəs, -fer-, -fār-\ *adj* [LL *omnifarius*, fr. L *omni-* omn- + *-farius* (as in *bifarius* twofold) — more at BIFARIOUS] **:** of all varieties, forms, or kinds ⟨his ~ reading . . . craved books of poetry and chivalry —E.A.Weeks⟩ — **om·ni·far·i·ous·ly** *adv* — **om·ni·far·i·ous·ness** *n* -ES

om·nif·ic \(ˈ)ämˈnifik\ *adj* [ML *omnificus*, fr. L *omni-* omn- + *-ficus* -fic] **:** being all-creating **:** OMNIFICENT

om·nif·i·cence \ämˈnifəsən(t)s\ *n* -s [fr. *omnificent*, after such pairs as E *benevolent: benevolence*] **:** the quality or state of being omnificent

om·nif·i·cent \-nt\ *adj* [*omn-* + *-ficent* (as in *magnificent*)] **:** creating all that comes into existence **:** unlimited in creative power

om·ni·fy \ˈämnə,fī\ *vt* -ED/-ING/-ES [*omn-* + *-fy*] **:** to make universal **:** ENLARGE

om·nig·e·nous \(ˈ)ämˈnijənəs\ *adj* [L *omnigenus*, fr. *omni-* omn- + *genus* kind — more at KIN] **:** composed of or containing all varieties

om·ni·graph \ˈämnə,graf, -räf\ *n* [*omn-* + *-graph*] **:** a device for automatically producing dot-and-dash sounds of the telegraph code used in instructing radiotelegraph operators

om·nil·e·gent \(ˈ)ämˈniləjənt\ *adj* [*omn-* + L *legent-*, *legens*, pres. part. of *legere* to read — more at LEGEND] **:** reading or having read everything **:** characterized by encyclopedic reading ⟨no historians have been more ~, more careful of the document —George Saintsbury⟩

om·nim·e·ter \ämˈnimədə(r)\ *n* [*omn-* + *-meter*] **:** a theodolite having a microscope rigidly attached to the telescope so that the vertical angular movement of the telescope can be observed through the microscope

om·ni·phib·i·ous \ˈämnəˈfibēəs\ *adj* [*omn-* + *-phibious* (as in *amphibious*)] *of an airplane* **:** able to land on any surface (as water, snow, ice, or land)

om·nip·o·tence \ämˈnipəd·ən(t)s, əmˈ-, -ətən- *also* -ət°n-\ *n* [LL *omnipotentia*, fr. L *omnipotent-*, *omnipotens* + *-ia* -y] **1 a :** the quality or state of being omnipotent **:** almighty or unlimited power **b :** an agency or force of unlimited power and influence ⟨I could not share the popular faith in the ~ of education —M.R.Cohen⟩ **2** *cap* **:** DEITY 1b

om·nip·o·ten·cy \-nsē, -si\ *n* -ES [ME *omnipotencie*, fr. LL *omnipotentia*] **:** OMNIPOTENCE

¹om·nip·o·tent \-nt\ *adj* [ME, fr. MF, fr. L *omnipotent-*, *omnipotens*, fr. *omni-* omn- + *potent-*, *potens* potent — more at POTENT] **1** *often cap* **:** ALMIGHTY 1a ⟨lift up our mind in contemplation of the aid of the *Omnipotent* Deity —P.N.Ure⟩ **2 a** *obs* **:** ARRANT ⟨this is the most ~ villain that ever cried "Stand!" to a true man —Shak.⟩ **b :** having virtually unlimited authority or influence **:** ALL-POWERFUL **:** possessing infinite capacity ⟨for five years this man was the ~ leader of the Roman mob —J.A.Froude⟩ ⟨enjoy smoothly functioning and ~ libraries —H.N.Southern⟩

²omnipotent \"\ *n* -s **1 :** one who is omnipotent **2** *cap* **:** ²ALMIGHTY

om·nip·o·tent·ly *adv* **:** in an omnipotent manner **:** with unlimited power

om·ni·pres·ence \,ämnəˈprez°n(t)s\ *n* [ML *omnipraesentia*, fr. *omnipraesent-*, *omnipraesens* omnipresent + L *-ia* -y] **:** the quality or state of being omnipresent **:** UBIQUITY ⟨find some positive value in life to pose against the ~ of death —Joseph Frank⟩ ⟨the ~ of scholarship as a background —R.P.Blackmur⟩

om·ni·pres·ent \ˈ==ˈprez°nt\ *adj* [ML *omnipraesent-*, *omnipraesens*, fr. L *omni-* omn- + *praesent-*, *praesens* present — more at PRESENT] **:** present in all places at all times **:** UBIQUITOUS ⟨an ~ Deity⟩ ⟨had always been conscious of poverty as . . . an ~ reality which ate its way into the marrow of life —Christine Weston⟩ ⟨the most ~ sign without words . . . is the red and green traffic light —Stuart Chase⟩ — **om·ni·pres·ent·ly** *adv*

om·ni·range \ˈämnə, -nē+,-\ *n* [*omnirange* fr. *omn-* + *range*] **:** a system of radio navigation in which any bearing relative to a special radio transmitter on the ground may be chosen and flown by an airplane pilot

om·ni·science \ämˈnishən(t)s\ *also* **om·ni·scien·cy** \-nsē, -si\ *n, pl* **omnisciences** *also* **omnisciencies** [ML *omniscientia*, fr. L *omni-* omn- + *scientia* knowledge — more at SCIENCE] **:** the quality or state of being omniscient: **a :** infinite knowledge ⟨in ~ . . . there is only an unmediated timeless knowledge —J.R.Everett⟩ **b :** universal or complete learning or knowledge ⟨a company should possess enough humility to deny ~ and to invite help and advice —L.H.Bristol⟩

¹om·ni·scient \(ˈ)=ˈnishənt\ *adj* [NL *omniscient-*, *omnisciens*, back-formation fr. ML *omniscientia*] **1 :** having infinite awareness, understanding, and insight **:** knowing all things **:** infinitely wise ⟨would take an ~ Deity to know what you're talking about —Edith Wharton⟩ **2 :** possessed of universal or complete knowledge **:** exhaustively learned ⟨was as ~ as the scholarship and science of his day permitted —O.S.J. Gogarty⟩ — **om·ni·scient·ly** *adv*

²omniscient \"\ *n* -s **1 :** a being or person that is omniscient **2** *cap* **:** ²GOD

om·ni·scope \ˈämnə,skōp\ *n* [*omn-* + *-scope*] **:** PERISCOPE

om·nist \ˈämnəst\ *n* -s [*omn-* + *-ist*] **:** one that believes in all religions

om·ni·tude \ˈämnə,tüd, -ə,tyüd\ *n* -s [*omn-* + *-tude*] **:** TOTALITY, UNIVERSALITY ⟨no other metropolitan area so reflects American civilization's ~ —D.W.Lantis⟩

om·ni·um \ˈämnēəm\ *n* -s [L, of all, gen. pl. of *omnis* all — more at OMNIBUS] **1 :** the total of the different stocks and other items formerly offered by the British government for the capital subscribed in funding a loan or for a unit of subscribed capital **2** *Brit* **:** the total of the items in any fund or stock made up by combination of various independent constituents **3 :** WHATNOT

omnium–gath·er·um \-ˈgathərəm\ *n* -s [L *omnium* + E *gather* + L *-um* (inflectional ending of many neuter nouns and of the neuter of many adjectives)] **:** a miscellaneous collection of a variety of things or persons **:** a confused mixture **:** HODGEPODGE ⟨at least part of the *omnium-gatherum* of my research —G.T.Hellman⟩; *also* **:** a place for holding such a collection ⟨an *omnium-gatherum*, stocked to meet all common family wants —*Atlantic*⟩

om·ni·verse \ˈämnə,vərs, -vəs, -vəis\ *n* -s [*omn-* + *-verse* (as in *universe*)] **:** a universe that is spatiotemporally four-dimensional

om·niv·o·ra \ämˈnivərə\ *n pl* [NL, fr. L, neut. pl. of *omnivorus* omnivorous] **1** *cap, in some esp former classifications* **:** a group comprising the pigs and the hippopotamuses **2** *often cap* **a :** omnivorous animals **b :** man and swine — used when it is desired to stress fundamental similarities of habits and physiology

om·ni·vore *also* **om·ni·vor** \ˈämnə,vō(ə)r\ *n* -s [NL *Omnivora*] **:** one that is omnivorous

om·niv·o·rous \(ˈ)ämˈniv(ə)rəs\ *adj* [L *omnivorus*, fr. *omni-* omn- + *-vorus* -vorous] **1 :** eating everything; *esp* **:** feeding on both animal and vegetable substances ⟨only a very few insects appear to be normally . . . ~ —C.T.Brues⟩ — compare CARNIVOROUS **2 :** avidly taking in everything as if devouring or consuming ⟨became an ~ reader of the classics —T.S. Lovering⟩ ⟨an expression of ~ but benevolent curiosity —A.J. Liebling⟩ ⟨an ~ collector of antiques⟩ — **om·niv·o·rous·ly** *adv* — **om·niv·o·rous·ness** *n* -ES

omnivorous leaf tier *n* **:** a tortricid moth (*Cnephasia longana*) whose larva is a pest on many plants (as strawberry, flax, and cultivated flowers) in Europe and parts of the western U. S.

omo- — see OM-

om·odyn·ia \,ōmōˈdinēə, ,ämə-\ *n* -s [NL, fr. *om-* + *-odynia*] **:** pain in the shoulder

¹omo·hyoid \,ōmō, ˈämō+\ *adj* [*om-* + *hyoid*] **:** of or relating to the shoulder and the hyoid bone; *specif* **:** being a muscle that arises from the upper border of the scapula and is inserted in the body of the hyoid bone

²omohyoid \"+\ *n* **:** an omohyoid muscle

omo·hy·oi·de·us \,==,hīˈȯidēəs\ *n, pl* **omohyoi·dei** \-ē,ī\ [NL, fr. *om-* + *hyoides* hyoid bone + L *-eus* -eous — more at HYOID BONE] **:** OMOHYOID

omoi·de·um \ōˈmȯidēəm\ *n* -s [NL, fr. *om-* + *-oideum* (fr. L *-oides* -oid + *-eum*, neut. of *-eus* -eous)] **:** the pterygoid bone of a bird

omo·pho·ri·on \,ōməˈfōrēən, ,äm-\ *n, pl* **omopho·ria** \-ēə\ [LGk *ōmophorion*, fr. Gk *ōm-* om- + LGk *-phorion* (fr. Gk *pherein* to bear, carry) — more at BEAR] **:** the distinctive vestment of bishops of the Eastern Church corresponding to the pallium of the Western Church but made in two forms and worn in one form or the other by all bishops during the celebration of liturgical offices

omo·plate \ˈōmə,plāt, ˈäm-; ōˈmäplə,tē\ *n* [MF, fr. Gk *ōmoplatē*, fr. *ōm-* om- + *platē* blade of an oar; akin to Gk *platys* flat, broad — more at PLACE] **:** SCAPULA

omo·pla·tos·co·py \,ōmōpləˈtäskəpē, ,äm-; ō,mäp-\ *n* -ES [MGk *ōmoplatoskopia*, fr. Gk *ōmoplatē* + *-o-* + *-skopia* -scopy] **:** SCAPULIMANCY

omos·te·gite \ōˈmästə,jīt\ *n* -s [*om-* + *-stegite*] **:** the part of a crustacean's carapace covering the thorax

omo·sternum \ˈōmō, ˈämō+\ *n* [NL, fr. *om-* + *sternum*] **1 :** a median bony element of the sternum of amphibians extending forward from the ventral ends of the precoracoids and bearing the episternum at its anterior end **2 :** an interarticular cartilage or bone between the sternum and each clavicle in many mammals

OMPA \ˈō,empēˈā\ *n* -s [*oc*tamethyl*py*rophosphor*a*mide] **:** SCHRADAN

om·pha·cite \ˈäm(p)fə,sīt\ *n* -s [G *omphazit*, fr. Gk *omphakitēs* green stone, fr. *omphak-*, *omphax* unripe grape + *-itēs* -ite] **:** a mineral consisting of a grass-green granular or foliated pyroxene found in the rock eclogite

omphal- *or* **omphalo-** *comb form* [Gk, fr. *omphalos* — more at NAVEL] **1 :** umbilicus ⟨*omphalo*id⟩ ⟨*omphalo*skepsis⟩ **2 :** umbilical and ⟨*omphalo*mesenteric⟩

om·pha·lia \ämˈfālēə\ *n, cap* [NL, fr. *omphal-* + *-ia*] **:** a genus of fungi (family Agaricaceae) having white spores, small caps usu. with a central indentation, and a very narrow fragile stipe

om·phal·ic \(ˈ)ämˈfalik\ *adj* [*omphal-* + *-ic*] **:** of or relating to the umbilicus

om·pha·li·on \ämˈfālēən\ *n* -s [NL, fr. Gk, small navel, dim. of *omphalos* navel] **:** the center of the umbilicus

om·pha·li·tis \,äm(p)fəˈlīd·əs\ *n, pl* **ompha·lit·i·des** \-lid·ə,dēz\ [NL, fr. *omphal-* + *-itis*] **1 :** inflammation of the umbilicus **2 :** avian navel ill **:** MUSHY CHICK

om·pha·lo·di·um \,==ˈlōdēəm\ *or* **omphalode** \ˈ==,lōd\ *n, pl* **omphalo·dia** \-ˈlōdēə\ *or* **ompha·lodes** \-,lōdz\ [NL *omphalodium*, fr. Gk *omphalōdēs* like a navel (fr. *omphal-* + *-ōdēs* -ode) + NL *-ium*] **:** the scar at the hilum of a seed; *also* **:** HILUM

om·pha·loid \ˈ==,lȯid\ *adj* [*omphal-* + *-oid*] **:** resembling an umbilicus **:** UMBILICATE

om·pha·lo·mesenteric \ˈäm(p)fə(,)lō+\ *adj* [*omphal-* + *mesenteric*] **:** of or relating to the umbilicus and mesentery ⟨the ~ arteries of an embryo⟩

omphalomesenteric duct *n* **:** VITELLINE DUCT

om·pha·lo·phlebitis \ˈäm(p)fə(,)lō+\ *n* [NL, fr. *omphal-* + *phlebitis*] **:** NAVEL ILL

om·pha·lo·pleure \ˈäm(p)fəlō,plü(ə)r\ *n* -s [*omphal-* + *-pleure* (fr. *-pleura*)] **:** an embryonic membrane constituted in part of the yolk sac wall

om·pha·lopsy·chite \,äm(p)fəlōˈsī,kīt, -ˈläpsə,k-\ *n* -s [*omphal-* + *psyche* + *-ite*] **:** one who stares fixedly at his navel to induce a mystical trance — often used of the hesychasts

om·pha·los \ˈäm(p)fə,läs, -ləs\ *n, pl* **ompha·li** \-,lī, -,lē\ [Gk, lit., navel] **1 :** a central part **:** FOCAL POINT ⟨come to a sort of ~ of the whole projected history —George Saintsbury⟩ **2** *also* **om·pha·lus** \-ləs\ [NL, fr. Gk *omphalos*] **:** UMBILICUS

om·pha·lo·skep·sis \,äm(p)fəlōˈskepsəs\ *n* -ES [*omphal-* + Gk *skepsis* act of viewing, examination; akin to Gk *skeptesthai* to view — more at SPY] **:** meditation while staring fixedly at one's navel practiced by Eastern mystics as an aid toward inducing a mystical trance

om·rah \ˈämˈrä\ *n* -s [Hindi *umrā*, fr. Ar *umarā'*, pl. of *amīr* ruler, commander] **:** a lord or grandee of a Muslim court in India

OMS *abbr* output per man shift

omsk \ˈȯmzk, ˈäm-, -m(p)sk\ *adj, usu cap* [fr. *Omsk*, city in the western part of Asiatic Russia, U.S.S.R.] **:** of or from the city of Omsk, U.S.S.R. **:** of the kind or style prevalent in Omsk

omu·ta \ˈōmə,tä\ *adj, usu cap* [fr. *Omuta*, city in northwest Kyushu, Japan] **:** of or from the city of Omuta, Japan **:** of the kind or style prevalent in Omuta

¹on \(ˈ)ȯn, (ˈ)än, *in the southeastern US sometimes* (ˈ)ōn\ *prep* [ME, prep. & adv., fr. OE *an*, *on*, prep. & adv.; akin to OHG *ana*, prep. & adv., on, at, ON *ā*, prep. & adv., Goth *ana*, prep. & adv., on, at, L *an-* (in *anhelare* to pant) Gk *ana*, prep. & adv., up, on, Skt *ana*, prep. & adv., after] **1 a** — used as a function word to indicate position over and in contact with that which supports from beneath ⟨the book is ~ the table⟩ ⟨was built ~ an island⟩ ⟨kept his hands ~ the desk⟩ **b** — used as a function word to indicate presence within ⟨rode there ~ a train⟩ ⟨booked passage ~ an ocean liner⟩ **c** — used as a function word to indicate situation along a whole surface ⟨a streak ~ the wall running from top to bottom⟩ or at any particular point on a surface ⟨there wasn't a mark ~ it⟩ or to indicate situation at the projecting usu. supporting edge or point or end of something ⟨their clothes hung ~ a couple of nails in the wall⟩ or situation inside of something (as clothing) worn by or covering the principal object of attention ⟨found a knife ~ him⟩ **2** — used as a function word to indicate contiguity or dependence; esp. (1) contact and support from elsewhere than beneath ⟨a fly ~ the ceiling⟩ ⟨hanging ~ the wall⟩; (2) location closely adjoining something ⟨a town situated ~ the river⟩ or location very near some point of a narrowly extended area (as a street) ⟨lives ~ the principal street of the town⟩; (3) imminence or beginning (as of some action or activity) ⟨the storm is ~ us⟩; (4) connection or employment or activity with or in or with regard to something ⟨works ~ the committee⟩ ⟨is now ~ the third problem⟩ ⟨will be ~ duty⟩ ⟨has long been successful ~ the stage⟩; (5) engagement in doing something ⟨are now ~ a tour around the country⟩; (5) source or support or basis on which something (as an action, opinion) turns or rests ⟨learned it ~ good authority⟩ ⟨his reliance ~ her⟩ ⟨will do it ~ one condition⟩ **3 a** — used as a function word to indicate position with regard to place, direction, or time; esp. (1) position with regard to a point of the compass ⟨~ the west are rolling plains⟩; (2) position near a specified part of something ⟨~ the side of the house is a garden⟩; (3) occurrence during the course of a specified day ⟨will see them ~ Monday⟩ or of some other divisions of time ⟨said he would write ~ the morrow⟩ or at a set time ⟨trains leave here every hour ~ the hour⟩; (4) occurrence at the same time as or following or as a result of something ⟨will send a check ~ receipt of the book⟩ ⟨will do it ~ your arrival⟩ ⟨was uneasy ~ arriving home and finding no one there⟩ **b** — used as a function word to indicate location in or progress along something taken as a standard ⟨~ the right road⟩ ⟨a boat keeping ~ course⟩ **4 a** — used as a function word to indicate involvement in a specified condition ⟨the house is ~ fire⟩ ⟨beer ~ tap⟩ ⟨merchandise ~ sale⟩ or process ⟨business is ~ an upturn⟩ **b** — used as a function word to indicate participation in a condition of privilege ⟨has been ~ sick leave⟩ or subjection to a condition of restriction ⟨is ~ probation⟩ **5** — used as a function word to indicate manner ⟨did it ~ the sly⟩ ⟨cut it ~ the bias⟩ **6** — used as a function word to indicate the object of action or motion; esp. (1) the object of action or motion coming esp. down from above so as to touch or strike the surface or cover the upper part ⟨watched the rain fall ~ the earth⟩ ⟨put a lid ~ the jar⟩; (2) the object of action or motion directed up to or against the object ⟨crept up ~ him⟩ ⟨marched ~ the ancient fortress⟩; (3) the object of action or motion directed toward the object without actual physical contact ⟨smiled ~ her⟩ ⟨blamed it ~ them⟩ ⟨was always bent ~ fighting⟩; (4) the object of some emotion ⟨had pity ~ them⟩ or formality ⟨served an injunction ~ him⟩ or obligation ⟨a charge ~ an overdue book⟩; (5) the object in connection with which payment, computation of interest, reduction, or similar settlement is made ⟨paid off a substantial sum ~ the mortgage⟩ ⟨creditors received about 75 cents ~ the dollar⟩ ⟨a rebate of 15 cents ~ a ton⟩ ⟨an inroad ~ supplies⟩ **7 a :** with regard to : with reference or relation to : ABOUT ⟨agreed ~ a price⟩ ⟨a monopoly ~ wheat⟩ ⟨a satire ~ society⟩ ⟨at variance ~ what to do⟩ **b** *chiefly dial* : OF ⟨be not jealous ~ me —Shak.⟩ **8** — used as a function word to indicate means or agency ⟨cut her finger ~ a knife⟩ ⟨playing the latest hits ~ the piano⟩ ⟨heard it ~ the radio⟩ **9** — used as a function word to indicate reduplication or succession in a series ⟨trouble ~ trouble followed his involvement with her⟩ ⟨loss ~ loss⟩ **10** — used as a function word to indicate an object of reference; esp. (1) an object having some advantage or disadvantage ⟨is very talented but has nothing ~ her brother who is a real genius⟩ ⟨his brother has two inches ~ him in reach⟩; (2) an object subjected to expense or cost ⟨drinks are ~ the house⟩ ⟨the joke was ~ me⟩; (3) an object that bears some stress or strain ⟨long hours began to tell ~ him⟩; (4) an object subjected to indicated annoyance ⟨the fire went out ~ him⟩ ⟨don't try to pull that ~ me⟩ or discomfiture or some other unwanted or detrimental thing

²**on** \"\ *adv* [ME, prep. & adv., fr. OE *an, on*, prep. & adv.] **1 :** in or into the position of being in contact with the upper surface of something or of being supported from beneath by the upper surface ⟨the plates are ~⟩ ⟨put a jazz recording ~⟩ **2 :** in or into the position of being attached to or covering a surface ⟨has suspenders ~⟩ ⟨put a clean shirt ~⟩ ⟨keep your hat ~⟩ **3 a** (1) **:** toward a point that lies ahead in space or time : FORWARD, ONWARD ⟨spent a day there and then went ~ to the next town⟩ ⟨from here ~ you'll need help⟩ (2) **:** at a more advanced point in space or time ⟨will do it later ~⟩ ⟨did not see her until well ~ in the evening⟩ ⟨was well ~ in years⟩ **b :** with forward movement or action : in constant progression : without break : CONTINUOUSLY ⟨read ~ late into the night⟩ ⟨spoke ~ without hesitation⟩ ⟨slept peacefully ~⟩ **c :** in succession : from one to another : in continuance ⟨a tradition handed ~ through the centuries⟩ ⟨pass the note ~⟩ **4 a :** in or into action or operation ⟨the radio was ~⟩ ⟨turn the lights ~⟩ : in or into a functioning state : in or into a state of activity ⟨the water is ~⟩ ⟨the electricity finally came ~⟩ **b :** in or into a position designed to set something into action or otherwise produce some activity ⟨the light switch is ~⟩ ⟨had a large fish ~⟩ : in or into an operative position ⟨the brake is ~⟩ **5 :** in or into the process of doing something : in or into engagement in some function or activity ⟨two speeches had already been given and he was told he would be ~ next⟩ ⟨has worked two nights and will also be ~ tomorrow night⟩ ⟨a well-known star will be ~ in the role when the show opens⟩ **6 a :** with an indicated part turned toward a point of contact, approach, or observation ⟨the two cars smashed together head ~⟩ ⟨the boats collided bows ~⟩ **b :** with direction toward something ⟨didn't want to play but preferred simply to look ~⟩ **7 :** in a condition of being decided upon or planned for or regarded as something that must be done ⟨has nothing particular ~ for tonight⟩ **8 :** in or into a state of being aware of something ⟨wasn't ~ to what had happened⟩ : in or into a knowledgeable state about something ⟨quickly got ~ to what they were trying to do⟩ — usu. used with *to* **9 :** in a state of being willing to participate in something ⟨told them about the plan and asked if they were ~⟩ **10** *printing* : UP ⟨printed eight ~⟩ **11 :** on base in baseball

³**on** \"\ *adj* **1** *cricket* : that sends the ball to the on ⟨an ~ hit⟩ ⟨an ~ drive⟩ **2** *cricket* : that is on the on side of the wicket ⟨an ~ stroke⟩ **3 :** permitted to flow by means of an opened valve or closed switch : FLOWING ⟨the water was ~⟩

⁴**on** \"\ *n* -s : the side of the wicket on which a batsman stands in the game of cricket or the corresponding side of the field — compare OFF; see CRICKET illustration

¹**-on** \ˌän\ *n suffix* -s [ISV, alter. of *-one*] **:** chemical compound not a ketone or other oxo compound ⟨nerv*on*⟩ — sometimes distinguished from *-one*

²**-on** \"\ *n suffix* -s [fr. *-on* (in *anion, cation, & ion*)] **1 :** elementary particle ⟨nucle*on*⟩ **2 a :** unit : quantum ⟨magnet*on*⟩ ⟨phot*on*⟩ **b :** basic hereditary component ⟨cistr*on*⟩ ⟨oper*on*⟩

³**-on** \"\ *n suffix* -s [NL, fr. Gk, neut. of *-os* (nom. sing. masc. ending of many adjectives)] **:** inert gas ⟨rad*on*⟩

ON *abbr* **1** octane number **2** order notify

ona \ˈōnə\ *n, pl* **ona** *or* **onas** *usu cap* **1 a :** a Chonan people of Tierra del Fuego off the southern tip of So. America — compare FUEGIAN **b :** a member of such people **2 :** the language of the Ona people

on-again-off-again \ˈ⸗,⸗ˈ⸗,⸗\ *adj* [fr. the phrase *on again, off again*] **:** occurring suddenly and irregularly and vanishing quickly : becoming briefly existent and then disappearing in an intermittent unpredictable way : FITFUL, SPASMODIC ⟨*on-again-off-again* fads⟩ ⟨troubled with *on-again-off-again* headaches⟩ ⟨months of *on-again-off-again* negotiations —Kennett Love⟩

on·a·ger \ˈänəjə(r)\ *n* -s [ME, wild ass, fr. L *onager, onagrus*, fr. Gk *onagros*, fr. *onos* ass + *agros* (fr. *agros* field) — more at ASS, ACRE] **1 :** a small pale-colored kiang having a broad dorsal stripe and being usu. treated as a natural variety but sometimes considered to constitute a distinct species (*Equus onager*) **2** [LL, fr. L] **:** an ancient and medieval heavy catapult used for hurling heavy stones and made up basically of a strong lever with a receptacle at one end for the stones and of ropes twisted so as to pull the lever back under great strain until suddenly released

onager 2

onagra \ōˈnagrə, ˈänəg-\ [NL, fr. Gk, oleander] *syn of* OENOTHERA

on·a·gra·ce·ae \ˌänəˈgrāsē,ē\ *n pl, cap* [NL, fr. *Onagra* + *-aceae*] **:** a large widely distributed family of plants of the order Myrtales having an inferior ovary, 2 or 4 petals, 1 to 8 stamens, and a simple style — **on·a·gra·ceous** \ˌänəˈgrāshəs\ *adj*

on and off *adv (or adj)* **:** off and on ⟨we've been living together *on and off* —Paul Scott⟩

on and on *adv (or adj)* **:** at great often tedious length ⟨talked *on and on*⟩

onan·ism \ˈōnə,nizəm\ *n* -s [prob. fr. (assumed) NL *onanismus*, fr. *Onan*, son of Judah described in Gen 38: 9 as practicing coitus interruptus + L *-ismus* -ism] **1 :** COITUS INTERRUPTUS **2 :** MASTURBATION **3 :** SELF-GRATIFICATION ⟨the kind of intellectual ~ to which he was dedicated —Esther P. Shiverick⟩ — **onan·is·tic** \ˌōnəˈnistik\ *adj*

onan·ist \ˈōnənəst\ *n* -s [ISV *onanism* + *-ist*] **:** one that practices onanism

onc- *or* **onco-** *also* **onch-** *or* **oncho-** *or* **onci-** *comb form* [NL, fr. Gk *onkos* barbed hook — more at ANGLE] **1 :** barb : hook ⟨*Onco*rhynchus⟩ ⟨*Onci*dium⟩ ⟨*onch*ium⟩ ⟨*Oncho*cerca⟩ **2 :** barbed ⟨*Onci*cola⟩

¹**once** \ˈwən(t)s\ *adv* [ME *ones, anes*, fr. gen. of *on, an* one — more at ONE] **1 :** one time and no more : just one time : one time only ⟨visited her father ~ a month⟩ ⟨spoke to her ~ and didn't see her again⟩ ⟨have read it only ~⟩ **2 a :** at any one time : in any possible contingency : under any circumstances whatsoever ⟨don't ~ let them know⟩ ⟨couldn't ~ succeed in doing what was asked⟩ **b :** at all : ONLY, MERELY, JUST ⟨if you thought about it ~, you'd see I'm right⟩ **c :** EVER ⟨if they ~ lose hope, their failure is certain⟩ ⟨didn't ~ guess the truth⟩ — usu. used in negative or conditional clauses **3 a :** at some indefinite time in the past : at one time : FORMERLY ⟨~ knew her well, but had now forgotten her name⟩ ⟨was ~ very happy⟩ **b** *archaic* : at some indefinite time in the future : at some future time : SOMEDAY **4** *obs* **a :** one time for all times : once and finally : once and for all ⟨if I have him not, I am resolved to die a maid, that's ~ —John Dryden⟩ **b :** in short : in a word : by way of summing up **5 :** by one degree of relationship ⟨is a cousin ~ removed⟩ ⟨lives a life only ~ removed from that of animals⟩ **6** *dial* — used as a vague sentence expletive esp. in imperative constructions ⟨come here ~⟩ ⟨hand me that hammer ~⟩ — **once and a while** [by alter.] **:** once in a while ⟨*once and a while* to think of my first love —R.D.Blackmore⟩ — **once and for all** *or* **once for all 1 :** once and finally : once and decisively : once and be done with it ⟨make up your mind *once and for all*⟩ : DEFINITIVELY : with such finality as to preclude reservation or modification ⟨deciding to settle the matter *once for all*⟩ **2 :** for the last time : one time to end all times ⟨I'm telling you *once and for all*⟩ — **once in a way** *also* **once and a way** *chiefly Brit* : once in a while : one time by way of exception ⟨were permitted to hear, for *once in a way*, the pizzicato accompaniment —*Manchester Guardian Weekly*⟩ — **once in a while :** now and then : occasionally but not often : from time to time : at infrequent intervals : SOMETIMES ⟨spend most of their time at home and go out *once in a while*⟩ — **once upon a time :** once at some indefinite time in the past usu. long ago ⟨had *once upon a time* known them well⟩ ⟨*once upon a time* there was a beautiful princess⟩

²**once** \"\ *adj* **:** that once was : FORMER ⟨the ~ province of Britain —J.N.Pomeroy⟩

³**once** \"\ *n* -s **:** one single time : one sole time ⟨thought it was only the ~ —Anne D. Sedgwick⟩ ⟨please listen to me just this ~⟩ : one time at least : one time by way of exception ⟨for ~ you seem to know what I'm talking about⟩ — **all at once** *adv* **1 :** all at the same time ⟨seemed happy and sad *all at once*⟩ **2 :** with great suddenness : suddenly and unexpectedly ⟨*all at once* there was a clatter of dishes⟩ — **to once** *adv, dial* : at once

⁴**once** \"\ *also* **once that** *conj* **:** when once : if once : at the moment when : as soon as ⟨~ the job is finished, we'll have nothing to worry about⟩ ⟨*once that* he finds out, you'll have to be careful⟩

once-accented octave *n* : ONE-LINE OCTAVE

once and again *adv* **1 a :** once and once more ⟨spoke to her *once and again*⟩ **b :** two or more times ⟨have heard it said *once and again*⟩ **2 :** now and again : from time to time : OCCASIONALLY, SOMETIMES ⟨*once and again* this sort of thing will happen⟩

once-born \ˈ⸗,⸗\ *adj* **:** not having been or not needing to be regenerated spiritually

once more *or* **once again** *adv* [*once more* fr. ME *ones more*, fr. *ones* once + *more*; *once again* fr. ¹*once* + *again*] **:** one more time ⟨decided to try *once more*⟩

once or twice *adv* [ME *ones or twies*, fr. *ones* once + *or* + *twies* twice] **:** a couple of times : a few times : OCCASIONALLY ⟨have seen her *once or twice* during the past month⟩

once-over \ˈ⸗,⸗⸗\ *n* -s [fr. the phrase *once over*] **:** a single swift examination or consideration or treatment of something : rapid survey; *esp* : a swift comprehensive appraising glance ⟨gave every new applicant the *once-over*⟩ ⟨as she walked in she got the *once-over*⟩

¹**once-over-lightly** \ˈ⸗,⸗⸗ˈ⸗⸗\ *n* -ES [fr. the phrase *once over lightly*] : ONCE-OVER; *esp* : an esp. casual or cursory or gingerly once-over ⟨had given political problems the *once-over-lightly* —Sigrid Arne⟩

²**once-over-lightly** \ˈ⸗,⸗⸗ˈ⸗⸗\ *adj* **:** swift and usu. casual or cursory or gingerly ⟨gets the *once-over-lightly* treatment —Sidney Hyman⟩

onc·er \ˈwən(t)sə(r)\ *n* -s [¹*once* + *-er*] **:** one that does or has done something only once

oncet \ˈwənzt, -n(t)st\ *substand var of* ONCE

onch- *or* **oncho-** *or* **onci-** — see ONC-

on·chi·di·idae \ˌäŋkəˈdīə,dē\ *n pl, cap* [NL, fr. *Onchidium*, type genus + *-idae*] **:** a family of slugs (suborder Stylommatophora) — see ONCHIDIUM

on·chid·i·um \äŋˈkidēəm, änˈ-\ *n, cap* [NL, fr. *onc-* + *-idium*] **:** a genus (the type of the family Onchidiidae) of chiefly Indo-Pacific marine air-breathing slugs that live chiefly on rocky shores between tide levels or in mangrove swamps

on·chi·um \ˈäŋkēəm\ *n, pl* **on·chia** \-ēə\ [NL, fr. *onc-* + *-ium*] **:** one of the hooks or rasps located in the buccal cavity of various nematode worms and serving to grasp and break up prey

on·cho·cer·ca \ˌäŋkəˈsərkə\ *n, cap* [NL, fr. *onc-* + *-cerca* (fr. Gk *kerkos* tail)] **:** a genus of long slender filarial worms (family Dipetalonematidae) that are parasites of subcutaneous and connective tissues of mammals with their adults enclosed in fibrous nodules and their larvae free in the tissues — see ONCHOCERCIASIS — **on·cho·cer·cal** \ˌ⸗⸗ˈ⸗kəl\ *adj*

on·cho·cer·ci·a·sis *also* **on·co·cer·ci·a·sis** \ˌäŋkō,sərˈkīəsəs\ *n, pl* **onchocerciases** \-ə,sēz\ [NL, fr. *Onchocerca* + *-iasis*] **:** infestation with or disease caused by filarial worms of the genus *Onchocerca*; *esp* : a disease of man caused by a worm (*O. volvulus*) native to Africa but now present in parts of tropical America, transmitted by several biting flies, and marked by subcutaneous nodules containing adult worms and migration of larvae through the tissues causing local irritation and itching and when the eyes are involved sometimes blindness — compare CRAW-CRAW

on·cho·cer·co·ma \-ˈkōmə\ *n* -s [NL, fr. *Onchocerca* + *-oma*] **:** the subcutaneous nodule of onchocerciasis that contains encysted parasites

on·cho·cer·co·sis \-ˈkōsəs\ *n, pl* **onchocerco·ses** \-ō,sēz\ [NL, fr. *Onchocerca* + *-osis*] : ONCHOCERCIASIS

on·cho·sphere *also* **on·co·sphere** \ˈäŋkə,sfi(ə)r\ *n* [ISV ¹*onco-* + *sphere*] **:** the hexacanth embryo that is the earliest differentiated stage of a cyclophyllidean tapeworm

on·cic·o·la \änˈsikələ\ *n, cap* [NL, fr. *onc-* + *-cola*] **:** a genus of small acanthocephalan worms having the adults parasitic in the intestines of dogs and coyotes and the infective larvae encysted in turkeys and armadillos

on·cid·i·um \änˈsidēəm\ *n* [NL, fr. *onc-* + *-idium*; fr. the shape of the labellum] **1** *cap* **:** a genus of showy tropical American epiphytic or terrestrial orchids with the column short and winged and the labellum usu. at right angles to it **2** -s **:** any plant of the genus *Oncidium* — called also *butterfly plant*

¹**onco-** *or* **oncho-** *comb form* [NL, fr. Gk *onkos* bulk, mass; akin to Gk *enenkein* to carry — more at ENOUGH] **1 :** tumor ⟨*onco*logy⟩ **2 :** bulk : mass ⟨*oncho*sphere⟩ ⟨*onco*meter⟩

²**onco-** — see ONC-

on·co·chaeta \ˌäŋkō+\ *n, pl* **oncochaetae** *or* **oncochaetas** [NL, fr. *onc-* + *-chaeta*] **:** a hair or bristle with a hooked tip ⟨*onchochaetae* on the thorax of a fly⟩

on·co·cyte \ˈäŋkō,sīt\ *n* -s [¹*onco-* + *-cyte*] **1 :** an acidophilic granular cell esp. of the parotid gland **2 :** a tumor cell

on·co·gen·ic \ˌäŋkōˈjenik\ *also* **on·cog·e·nous** \(ˈ)äŋˈkäjənəs, (ˈ)än-\ *adj* [¹*onco-* + *-genic* or *-genous*] **:** relating to tumor formation : tending to cause tumors ⟨~ tars⟩

on·cog·e·ny \äŋˈkäjənē, änˈ-\ *n* -ES [¹*onco-* + *-geny*] **:** the process of tumor formation

on·co·graph \ˈäŋkō,graf, -räf\ *n* [ISV ¹*onco-* + *-graph*] **:** a recording device attached to an oncometer — **on·cog·ra·phy** \äŋˈkägrəfē, änˈ-\ *n* -ES

on·co·log·i·cal \ˌäŋkəˈläjikəl\ *also* **on·co·log·ic** \-jik\ *adj* **:** of or relating to oncology

on·col·o·gist \äŋˈkäləjəst, änˈ-\ *n* -s **:** a specialist in oncology

on·col·o·gy \-jē\ *n* -ES [ISV ¹*onco-* + *-logy*] **:** the study of tumors

on·col·y·sis \-ləsəs\ *n* [NL, fr. ¹*onco-* + *-lysis*] **:** the destruction of tumor cells — **on·co·lyt·ic** \ˌäŋkōˈlid·ik\ *adj*

oncome \ˈ⸗,⸗\ *n* [ME, fr. *on* + *come, cume* action of coming, fr. *comen, cumen* to come (after *comen on* to come on)] — more at COME] **1** *chiefly Scot* : ONSET, BEGINNING **2** *chiefly Scot* : an attack of disease

on·co·melania \ˌäŋkō+\ *n, cap* [NL, perh. fr. ¹*onco-* + *Melania*] **:** a genus of amphibious operculate snails (family Bulimidae) of Asiatic and Pacific island freshwaters that is sometimes extended to include *Katayama, Schistosomophora*, and possibly other genera and that comprises forms which are intermediate hosts of the blood fluke (*Schistosoma japonicum*)

oncomer \ˈ⸗,⸗⸗\ *n* [*on* + *comer* (after *come on*, v.)] : COMER 2 ⟨~s being developed for our international teams —*Lawn Tennis & Badminton*⟩

on·com·e·ter \äŋˈkämәd·ə(r), änˈ-\ *n* [ISV ¹*onco-* + *-meter*] **:** an instrument for measuring variations in size or volume of the internal organs of the body

¹**oncoming** \ˈ⸗,⸗⸗\ *adj* [²*on* + *coming*, adj. (after *come on*, v.)] **1 a :** coming nearer in space or time : moving forward upon one : APPROACHING ⟨blinded by the lights of an ~ car⟩ ⟨during the ~ year⟩ **b :** that is to be : FUTURE ⟨not for just a few of our ~ citizens, but also for all present citizens —L.L. Medsker⟩ ⟨discussed the ~ visit⟩ **2 :** RISING, EMERGENT ⟨~ generations began to seek new goals —Hunter Mead⟩

²**oncoming** \ˈ⸗,⸗⸗, ⸗ˈ⸗⸗\ *n* -s [*on* + *coming*, n. (after *come on*, v.)] *archaic* : APPROACH

on·co·pel·tus \ˌäŋkōˈpeltəs\ *n, cap* [NL, fr. *onc-* + *-peltus* (fr. Gk *peltē* small shield) — more at PELTA] **:** a genus of lygaeid bugs including the common milkweed bug (*O. fasciatus*)

on·cop·era \äŋˈkäpərə, änˈ-\ *n, cap* [NL, fr. *onc-* + Gk *pēra* pouch] **:** a genus of moths (family Hepialidae) whose caterpillars are serious pests on grass in Australia and Tasmania

on·co·rhyn·chus \ˌäŋkōˈriŋkəs\ *n, cap* [NL, fr. *onc-* + *-rhynchus*] **:** a genus of salmons that are related to those of the genus *Salmo* but have a greater number of anal rays, branchiostegals, pyloric caeca, and gill rakers and that include commercially important fishes of the north Pacific and of the coastal streams of both America and Asia

oncosphere *var of* ONCHOSPHERE

oncost \ˈ⸗,⸗\ *n* -s [ME *oncost, uncost*, fr. MD *oncost* extra charge, fr. *on-* un- (akin to OE *un-*) + *cost* expense, charge, prob. fr. OF — more at UN-, COST] *Brit* : indirect expense : OVERHEAD

on·cot·ic pressure \(ˈ)äŋ¦käd·ik-, (ˈ)äŋ|\ *n* [*oncotic* prob. ISV ¹*onco-* + *-tic* (as in *osmotic*)] **:** the pressure exerted by plasma proteins on the capillary wall and made up of the osmotic and imbibition pressures of the hydrophilic colloid systems in which these proteins exist

on·cot·o·my \äŋˈkädəmē, änˈ-\ *n* -ES [NL *oncotomia*, fr. ¹*onco-* + *-tomia* -tomy] **:** surgical incision of a swelling (as an abscess or tumor)

onct *like* ONCET\ *substand var of* ONCE

on·dat·ra \änˈdatrə\ *n, cap* [NL, fr. F, muskrat, fr. Huron] **:** a genus of rodents (family Cricetidae) comprising the muskrats

ondé *var of* UNDÉ

ondes mu·si·cales \ōⁿdmüzēkäl\ *or* **ondes martenot** \ōⁿdmártənō\ *n, pl* **ondes musicales** *like sing*\ *or* **ondes martenot** *like sing*\ *often cap O&M* [*ondes musicales* fr. F, lit., musical waves; *ondes martenot* fr. F, lit., Martenot waves, after Maurice *Martenot* b1898 Fr. musician, its inventor] **:** a melodic electrophone capable of producing quarter tones and eighth tones

on·dine \(ˈ)änˈdēn, (ˈ)ȯnˈ-, (ˈ)ōⁿˈ-\ *n* -s [F, fr. NL *undina* — more at UNDINE] **1 :** UNDINE **2 :** a pale green that is bluer, lighter, and slightly less strong than celadon gray and duller than spray green

on·ding \ˈän,diŋ\ *n* -s [²*on* + *ding*, v. (to beat) (after the verb phrase *ding on*)] *chiefly Scot* : a heavy fall of rain or snow ⟨the rain was such an ~ by now —Maristan Chapman⟩

on-dit \(ˈ)ōⁿˈdē\ *n, pl* **on-dits** \-ē(z)\ [F, fr. *on dit* they say, it is said] **:** a piece of gossip : vague rumor : REPORT ⟨the *on-dits* and surreptitious tales that float about —*Saturday Rev.*⟩ ⟨there were incredible *on-dits* —Clare Sheridan⟩

on·di·um mar·te·not \ˈändēəm,märtəˈnō\ *n, often cap O&M* [*ondium* fr. *ond-* (fr. *ondes musicales*) + *-ium* (as in *harmonium*)] : ONDES MUSICALES

on·do·graph \ˈändə,graf, -räf\ *n* [F *ondographe*, fr. *onde* wave (fr. L *unda*) + *-o-* + *-graphe* -graph — more at WATER] **:** an instrument for autographically recording the wave forms of varying electrical currents and esp. rapidly varying alternating currents

on·du·le \ˌändəˈlā, -njə-\ *n* -s [F *ondulé* wavy, fr. past part. of *onduler* to wave, ripple, back-formation fr. *ondulation* wave, concentric wave-motion in a liquid or gas, prob. fr. (assumed) NL *undulation-, undulatio* concentric wave motion in a liquid or gas — more at UNDULATION] **:** a wavy weaving pattern produced by a special reed that alternately spreads and converges a small group of warp threads

ondy *var of* UNDÉ

¹**one** \ˈwən\ *adj* [ME *oon, on*, fr. OE *ān*; akin to OHG *ein* one, ON *einn*, Goth *ains*, L *unus* one, Gk *oinē* ace on dice, Skt *eka* one, and perh. to L *is* he, that — more at ITERATE] **1 a :** being a single unit or entire being or thing and no more — see NUMBER table **b :** existing alone in a specified sphere ⟨there is ~ apple in the basket⟩ **2 a** (1) **:** being a particular unit or entire being or thing singled out (as by way of contrast, difference) from two or more identical or similar units or beings or things ⟨spent ~ day of our vacation exploring the forest⟩ ⟨have mentioned ~ important point out of the several that will have to be considered⟩ ⟨went from ~ side to the other⟩ (2) **:** being an individual that is preeminently what is indicated ⟨is really ~ fine person⟩ **b :** existing as at least a single unit or being or thing : that is at least something : one at any rate : one in any case ⟨well, that's ~ thing you can be proud of⟩ ⟨that's ~ consolation, anyway⟩ **3 a** (1) **:** existing as something actually or virtually the same as something else : that is identical with or substantially the same as something else ⟨the writer and his principal character are ~⟩ ⟨~ and the same substance⟩ (2) **:** single in kind : quite the same : EQUAL ⟨are of ~ age⟩ (3) **:** that is not marked by any notable differences from something else : that amounts to the same thing ⟨it's all ~ to me what you do⟩ (4) **:** that is commonly shared by two or more individuals ⟨~ plague was on you all —I Sam 6:4 (AV)⟩ **b** (1) **:** constituting a unified entity made up of or formed from or produced by two or more components or sources ⟨combined the elements in such a way as to form ~ substance⟩ ⟨cried out with ~ voice⟩ (2) **:** that is so united to or merged with something else as to form a single harmonious whole with it : that is at one : that is in agreement : UNITED ⟨is ~ with you in all you do⟩ **4 :** existing or occurring as something not definitely fixed or placed (as in time) ⟨will see you again ~ day⟩ or as something merely mentioned with little or no specifying description : a certain ⟨~ John Doe got up and made a speech⟩ — compare ²A 4 d **5 :** that is the only individual of an indicated or implied kind ⟨was the ~ person she wanted to marry⟩

²**one** \"\ *pron* [ME *oon, on*, fr. OE *ān*, adj.] **1 a :** a certain indefinitely indicated person or thing usu. of a kind mentioned or under consideration ⟨saw ~ of his classmates⟩ ⟨had several current novels and let her borrow ~⟩ **b** (1) **:** an individual of a vaguely indicated group : anyone at all : anyone in a general way ⟨~ wouldn't like to see that happen⟩ (2) — sometimes used as a 3d-person substitute for a pronoun of the first person (as *I, we*) ⟨~ supposes you will come⟩ **2 :** something of an indicated or implied kind: as **a :** JOKE, LAUGH ⟨that's ~ on you⟩ **b :** BLOW, SOCK ⟨got ~ on the jaw which he remembered for a long time —John Masefield⟩ **3** *chiefly Midland* : one or the other — used after the second of two alternatives to indicate the necessity of a choice between the two ⟨stay in bed or go to school, ~⟩ — **by one and one** *archaic* : one by one — **in one** *adv* : in or into a single whole : TOGETHER ⟨is a source of information and pleasure, all *in one*⟩ — **one by one** *also* **one after one** *adv* : with one following the other : one after another : one at a time : SINGLY, SUCCESSIVELY ⟨came into the room *one by one*⟩

³**one** \", *in sense 1c(2)* ˌwən\ *n* -s [ME *oon, on*, fr. OE *ān*, adj. & pron.] **1 a :** the first whole number above zero and below two : the number denoting unity **b :** a single unit or entire being or thing and no more ⟨has the ~ but will need another⟩ **c** (1) **:** a particular unit or entire being or thing singled out (as by way of contrast, difference) from two or more identical or similar units or beings or things ⟨this is the ~ that is best⟩ (2) **:** an individual of a particular kind ⟨that's really a splendid ~⟩ **2 a :** the numerable quantity symbolized by the arabic numeral 1 **b :** the figure 1 **c :** the letter I **3 :** one o'clock — compare BELL table, TIME illustration **4 a :** a domino with one spot on one of its halves **b :** a die with one spot on the uppermost side **c :** an article of clothing of the first size; *esp* : a baby's shoe of the first size ⟨wears a ~⟩ **5 a :** a pound note **b :** a one-dollar bill **6** *cap* : the ulti-

mate being : the first principle of all things : the Absolute : GOD **7 a** : DEVOTEE, FAN ⟨was a ~ for football —Naomi G. Royde-Smith⟩ **b** : an extraordinary or unique or eccentric individual ⟨you're quite the ~⟩ ⟨you are a ~, aren't you⟩

⁴one \ˈwən\ *vt* **oned; oned; oneing; ones** [ME *onen*, fr. *oon*, *on*, adj. — more at ¹ONE] : UNITE ⟨prayer . . . ~*s* the soul to God —Walter Lippmann⟩

-one \ˌōn\ *n suffix* -s [ISV, fr. Gk *-ōnē* (fem. patronymic suffix)] **1** : ketone or oxo compound not a true ketone — in names of specific organic compounds ⟨acet*one*⟩ ⟨pentan*one*⟩ ⟨5-pyrazol*one*⟩ **2** : chemical compound containing oxygen esp. in a carbonyl or analogous group (as sulfonyl) — in names of classes of compounds ⟨ket*one*⟩ ⟨lact*one*⟩ ⟨sulf*one*⟩ **3** : ¹-ON

one–a–cat *var of* ONE OLD CAT

one and all *pron* [ME *oon and al*] : each one individually and jointly ⟨I greet you, *one and all*⟩

one–and–thirty \ˌ=ˌ==\ *n, archaic* : THIRTY-ONE

one another *pron* [ME *oon . . . another*] : EACH OTHER ⟨were madly in love with *one another* —C.G.Norris⟩ ⟨they all knew *one another*⟩

one–arm \ˈ=ˌ=\ *adj* : marked by the use of chairs having one arm extended and broadened in such a way as to support a tray of food ⟨ate in . . . *one-arm* joints —Saul Bellow⟩

one–armed bandit *also* **one–arm bandit** \ˈ=ˌ=-\ *n* [so called fr. the handle that is pulled to make the wheels spin] : SLOT MACHINE 2

one–base hit \ˈ=,=-\ *or* **one–bagger** \ˈ=ˈbagə(r), -ˈbaag-, -ˈbaig-\ *n* : a base hit that enables a batter to reach first base safely — called also *single*

one–berry \ˈwən— *see* BERRY\ *n* **1** : HACKBERRY **2** : PARTRIDGEBERRY 1 **3** : JACK-IN-THE-PULPIT

one–crop \ˈ=ˌ=\ *adj* : marked by the raising of only one kind of crop on the same land over a long time ⟨*one-crop* farming⟩

one–dimensional \ˌ=(ˌ)=ˈ=(=)=\ *adj* : lacking depth : SUPERFICIAL ⟨seems rather *one-dimensional* and unimportant —Merle Miller⟩ ⟨the characters are *one-dimensional* stereotypes —Anthony Boucher⟩ ⟨too often give us only *one-dimensional* news —Elmer Davis⟩

one–egg \ˈ=ˌ=\ *adj* : MONOZYGOTIC ⟨*one-egg* twins⟩

one–eighty \ˌ=ˈ==\ *n* -s : a complete turn of 180 degrees ⟨did a *one-eighty* and crashed —*Infantry Jour.*⟩

one–eye \ˈ=,=\ *also* **one–eyed card** \ˈ=,=-\ *n* : one of three face cards (as the jack of hearts or jack of spades or king of diamonds) that in a standard pack of playing cards carry a profile view

one–eyed \ˈ=ˌ=\ *adj* [ME *oon-eyed*, fr. *oon* one + *eyed*] **1** : having one eye : having the sight of only one eye **2** : lacking breadth of vision : narrow in outlook ⟨our naive submission to the *one-eyed* methodology of the physical sciences —Lewis Mumford⟩ — **one–eyed·ness** \ˌ=ˈ=(ə)dnəs\ *n* -ES

one–eyed cat \ˌwənəˌkat, ˌwəˌnīdˌk-\ *n* : ONE OLD CAT

one–flowered wintergreen *or* **one–flowered pyrola** \ˈ=,=-\ *n* : a delicate perennial herb (*Moneses uniflora*) of the family Ericaceae that resembles the wintergreen and has a solitary white terminal flower

one·fold \ˈwənˌfōld\ *adj* : constituting a single undivided whole ⟨simple counterpoint in which the many sounds are ~ —*Encyc. Britannica*⟩

one–foot pitch *n* : the pitch of a one-foot stop on a pipe organ

one–foot stop *n* : a pipe-organ stop sounding pitches three octaves higher than the notes indicate — compare EIGHT-FOOT STOP

one–for–one \ˌ==ˈ=\ *adj* : ONE-TO-ONE ⟨a *one-for-one* correspondence between symbols and syllables —Kenneth Croft⟩

one–gallus *or* **one–gallused** \ˈ=ˌ==\ *adj, Midland* : low-class and often ignorant and backward

one·gite \ōˈneˌgīt, ˈäni,g-\ *n* -s [G *onegit*, fr. Lake *Onega*, northwest U.S.S.R., its locality + G *-it* -ite] : a pale amethyst gemstone penetrated by needles of goethite

oneg shab·bat \ˌō,neg(ˌ)shäˈbät\ *n, pl* **oneg shabbat** *often cap O&S* [NHeb *ʿōneg shabbath*, lit., Sabbath delight] : a Jewish social gathering held on Saturday afternoon or Friday evening and typically marked by talks and community singing

one–handed \ˈ=ˌ==\ *adj* [ME *oon handyd*, fr. *oon* one + *-handyd*, *-handed* having (such or so many) hands (fr. *hand* + *-ed*)] **1** : having or using only one hand ⟨said he could beat him up *one-handed*⟩ **2** *or* **one–hand a** : designed for or requiring the use of only one hand ⟨a *one-hand* alphabet for the use of deaf-mutes⟩ **b** : effected by the use of only one hand ⟨made an amazing *one-handed* catch of the ball⟩

one–horse \ˈ=,=\ *adj* **1 a** : designed to be drawn by only one horse ⟨a *one-horse* wagon⟩ **b** : using or owning only one horse ⟨a *one-horse* farm⟩ **2 a (1)** : that falls woefully below usual or expected standards : most inferior or inadequate : distinctly below par : SECOND-RATE ⟨put on an art exhibition that was pretty much a *one-horse* affair⟩ ⟨elected a *one-horse* committee⟩ ⟨a *one-horse* newspaper⟩ ⟨*one-horse* lawyer struggling to get along —Hamilton Basso⟩ **(2)** : that lacks substance and force : that is of little real importance or consequence : TRIVIAL ⟨advanced some kind of *one-horse* theory⟩ ⟨a *one-horse* argument⟩ **b** : that is small in size and limited in resources and narrowly provincial in outlook, atmosphere, and development : JERKWATER, INSULAR ⟨stop overnight in a *one-horse* town⟩

one–hundred–percent \ˌ=ˌ===ˈ=\ *adv (or adj)* : HUNDRED-PERCENT

one–hundred–percenter \ˌ=ˌ==pə(r)ˈsentə(r)\ *n* -s : HUNDRED-PERCENTER

one–hundred–percentism \-pə(r)ˈsent-ˌizəm\ *n* -s : HUNDRED-PERCENTISM

onei·da \ōˈnīdə\ *n, pl* **oneida** *or* **oneidas** *usu cap* [Iroquois *Oneyóde'*, lit., standing rock] **1 a** : an Iroquoian people orig. living near Oneida Lake in the state of New York **b** : a member of such people **2** : the language of the Oneida people

one–ideaed *or* **one–idea'd** \ˌwə,nīˈdēəd\ *adj* : having or possessed by only one idea ⟨her *one-ideaed* peasant mind was as inaccessible as a closed iron safe —Joseph Conrad⟩ ⟨sneered at him as a *one-ideaed* abolitionist —David Donald⟩

oneing *pres part of* ONE

oneir- *or* **oneiro-** *also* **onir-** *or* **oniro-** *comb form* [Gk *oneir-*, *oneiro-*, fr. *oneiros*, *oneiron*; akin to Arm *anurǰ* dream] : dream ⟨*oneiro*logy⟩

onei·ric \ōˈnīrik\ *adj* [*oneir-* + *-ic*] **1** : of or relating to dreams ⟨those ~ images which have had so profound an effect on certain kinds of twentieth-century art —J.T.Soby⟩ **2** : DREAMY **2** : ANAGOGIC 2

onei·ro·crit·ic \ōˌnīrōˈkrid·ik\ *n* -s [Gk *oneirokritikos*, adj.] : an interpreter of dreams

onei·ro·crit·i·cal \-d·əkəl\ *adj* [Gk *oneirokritikos* oneirocritical (fr. *oneir-* + *kritikos* able to discern or judge) + E *-al* — more at CRITIC] : of, relating to, or specializing in the interpretation of dreams — **onei·ro·crit·i·cal·ly** \-k(ə)lē\ *adv*

onei·ro·crit·i·cism \-d·əˌsizəm\ *n* [fr. *oneirocritical*, after E *critical*: *criticism*] : the interpreting of dreams

onei·ro·crit·ics \-d·iks\ *n pl but usu sing in constr* [modif. (influenced by E *-ics*) of Gk *oneirokritika*, fr. neut. pl. of *oneirokritikos*, adj.] : ONEIROCRITICISM

onei·ro·man·cy \ōˈnīrōˌman(t)sē\ *n* -ES [*oneir-* + *-mancy*] : divination by means of dreams

one–legged \ˈ=ˌ=(=)\ *adj* **1** : having only one leg ⟨a *one-legged* veteran⟩ **2** : lacking some important part or element so as to be faulty or altogether ineffective ⟨a *one-legged* law⟩

one–line octave *n* [so called fr. the one accent mark of the symbol C′ representing middle C] : the musical octave that begins on middle C — see PITCH illustration

one–lung \ˈ=ˌ=\ *adj* **1** *or* **one–lunged** \ˈ=ˌləŋd\ : having only one lung **2** *slang* : having only one cylinder ⟨a *one-lung* jalopy⟩ ⟨a *one-lung* motorboat⟩

one–lung·er \ˈ=ˈləŋə(r)\ *n* -s **1** *slang* : a one-cylinder engine **2** *slang* : a vehicle or craft powered by a one-cylinder engine

one–man \ˈ=ˌ=\ *adj* : of or relating to just one individual (as a man): as **a** : consisting of only one individual ⟨a *one-man* government⟩ ⟨a *one-man* staff⟩ ⟨a *one-man* committee⟩ ⟨a *one-man* band⟩ **b (1)** : done, presented, or produced by only one individual ⟨a *one-man* stage play⟩ **(2)** : that features the work of a single artist (as a painter) and that is usu. exhibited by the artist ⟨a *one-man* show of oils⟩ **c (1)** : designed for or limited to one individual ⟨a *one-man* job⟩ ⟨a small *one-man* boat⟩ or operation by one individual ⟨a *one-man* typesetting machine⟩ **(2)** : managed or controlled by only one individual ⟨a *one-man* business⟩ **(3)** : originating with or supported by or dependent upon only one individual ⟨started a *one-man* revolution⟩ ⟨a *one-man* political movement⟩ **d** : that obeys or is friendly toward only one individual ⟨a *one-man* dog⟩ ⟨a *one-man* horse that no one else could ride⟩

one–many \ˈ=ˌ==\ *adj, of a relation in logic* : constituted so that if the first term is given any of many things can be the second term whereas if the second term is given only one thing can be the first term ⟨the relation "father-child" is *one-many*⟩ — compare MANY-ONE, ONE-ONE

one·ness \ˈwənnəs\ *n* -ES **1** : the quality or state or fact of being one: as **a (1)** : SINGLENESS ⟨a ~ of purpose⟩ **(2)** : UNIQUENESS ⟨the ~ of man⟩ **b** : WHOLENESS, INTEGRITY ⟨achieving a ~ of personality⟩ **c** : HARMONY, CONCORD ⟨a ~ of thoughts and desires⟩ **d** : SAMENESS, IDENTITY ⟨numerical ~⟩ **e** : UNITY, UNION ⟨physical and spiritual ~ with each other⟩ **2** *archaic* : SOLITARINESS

one–night stand \ˈ=,=-\ *also* **one–night·er** \ˈwənˈnīd·ə(r)\ *n, pl* **one–night stands** *also* **one–nighters** **1** : a performance (as of a play, concert) given and designed to be given (as by a traveling group of actors, musicians) only once in separate localities : a single night's performance ⟨the television show was considerably more wearing for him than *one-night stands* —Harold Brown⟩ **2 a** : a locality (as a city, town) used for one-night stands ⟨these cities became *one-night stands* for road companies —*Amer. Guide Series: N.Y.*⟩ **b** : a stopover for a one-night stand ⟨making *one-night stands* all over the Midwest —R.J.Donovan⟩

one–o'clock \ˈ==,=\ *n* : DANDELION 1

one old cat \ˌwənəˌkat, ˌwəˌnōlˌk-\ *or* **one o' cat** *also* **one–a–cat** \ˌwənəˌk-\ *n* : a ball game in which a batter hits a ball and then tries to run from home base to the single other base and back home again without being put out by the other players

one–one \ˈ=ˌ=\ *adj* **1** *of a relation in logic* : constituted so that if one term is given only one thing can be the other term ⟨in a monogamous society the relation "husband-wife" is *one-one*⟩ — compare MANY-ONE, ONE-MANY **2** : ONE-TO-ONE ⟨a *one-one* correlation between the names of things and the things named —W.E.Johnson⟩

one·o·ta \ˌōnēˈōd·ə\ *adj, usu cap* [*Oneota*, village in eastern Minnesota] : of, relating to, or constituting a culture of the Upper Mississippi phase of the Mississippi culture pattern that in some areas has been definitely related to the Siouan peoples

one–over–one \ˌ=,==ˈ=\ *n* **1** : a forcing bid in contract bridge of one in a suit made in response to a partner's opening bid of one in a suit **2** : a system of bidding in contract bridge in which the one-over-one bid is an essential

one over the eight *Brit* : one drink too many

one–part code *n* : a code having code groups assigned in alphabetical or numerical order to an alphabetically and logically arranged list of plaintext segments — compare TWO-PART CODE

one–piece \ˈ=ˌ=\ *adj* : that consists of or is made in a single undivided piece ⟨a *one-piece* bathing suit⟩ — **one–piec·er** \ˈ=ˈpēsə(r)\ *n* -s

one–point perspective *n* : PARALLEL PERSPECTIVE

one–pound·er \ˈ=ˈpaundə(r)\ *n* : a gun firing a one-pound shot or shell

on·er \ˈwənə(r)\ *n* -s [*one* + *-er*] *Brit* : something unique or extraordinary

oner·ous \ˈänərəs, ˈōn-\ *adj* [ME, fr. MF *onereus*, fr. L *onerosus*, fr. *oner-*, *onus* burden + *-osus* -ose; akin to Skt *anas* cart and perh. to Gk *ania* grief] **1 a** : that involves, imposes, or constitutes much oppressive or irksome work, effort, difficulty, or responsibility : heavily demanding : TROUBLESOME, BURDENSOME ⟨~ duties⟩ ⟨an ~ political system⟩ ⟨an ~ task⟩ **b** : that involves, imposes, or constitutes a legal burden ⟨~ property⟩ ⟨an ~ option⟩ **2** : of or relating to something done or given for an equivalent ⟨an ~ grant⟩

syn ONEROUS, BURDENSOME, OPPRESSIVE, and EXACTING can mean, in common, imposing great trouble, labor, or hardship. ONEROUS implies laboriousness or heaviness and usu. connotes irksomeness ⟨an unending, tiring, *onerous* job⟩ ⟨the tyranny of a majority might be more *onerous* than that of a despot —A.N. Whitehead⟩ ⟨a permanent agreement which should remove *onerous* taxes —*Encyc. Americana*⟩ BURDENSOME usu. implies both mental and physical strain ⟨a *burdensome* responsibility⟩ ⟨the *burdensome* customs regulations and the unfair tax laws —Allan Nevins & H.S.Commager⟩ ⟨a *burdensome* bureaucratic structure —*Current Biog.*⟩ OPPRESSIVE adds to BURDENSOME the idea of distress to spirit or body, usu. implying extreme harshness or severity and suggesting excessive impositions, cruelty, or tyranny ⟨the utter solitude and silence were *oppressive* —Herman Melville⟩ ⟨*oppressive* taxes⟩ ⟨others who have lived under *oppressive* governments get into the fixed habit of not telling the truth to government officials —M.R.Cohen⟩ ⟨one distant universal enemy is less *oppressive* than a thousand unchecked pilferers and plotters at home —George Santayana⟩ EXACTING implies great demands, suggesting rigor, sternness, or extreme fastidiousness rather than oppression ⟨aristocrats subjected themselves as proudly and willingly to the *exacting* discipline of the warrior —Edith Hamilton⟩ ⟨the pity of it was that even the least *exacting* husband should so often desire something more piquant than goodness —Ellen Glasgow⟩ ⟨an *exacting* standard for the economic system —J.M.Clark⟩ ⟨*exacting* specifications⟩

oner·ous·ly *adv* : in an onerous manner

oner·ous·ness *n* -ES : the quality or state of being onerous

onery *var of* ORNERY

ones *pl of* ONE, *pres 3d sing of* ONE

-ones *pl of* -ONE

one–seat·er \ˈwənˈsēd·ə(r)\ *n* : SINGLE-SEATER

one–seed juniper *n* : a small hardy drought-resistant tree (*Juniperus monosperma*) used for hedges and windbreaks esp. in the southern U.S.

one·self *also* **one's self** \(ˌ)wən *sometimes* (ˌ)wənz + *pronunc at* SELF\ *pron* **1** : a person's self : the self of one : one's own self — compare HIMSELF, HERSELF; used (1) reflexively as object of a preposition or direct or indirect object of a verb ⟨one is a long time finding out how different others are from ~ —Van Wyck Brooks⟩ ⟨one can easily fool ~⟩ ⟨willingness to sacrifice ~ —E.P.Cubberley⟩ ⟨one must buy ~ whatever is necessary⟩; (2) for emphasis in apposition with *one* or sometimes *who, that*, or a noun ⟨if one does not have the information ~, one can ask others⟩; (3) for emphasis instead of *one* or instead of *one oneself* as subject of a verb ⟨an undertaking which is so much bigger than anything ~ would even try to engage in —H.J. Morgenthau⟩ or as predicate nominative ⟨one can trust only one person and that is ~⟩ or in comparisons after *than* or *as* ⟨one usually associates with people of the same age as ~⟩ **2** : one's normal, healthy, or sane condition : one's normal, healthy, or sane self ⟨in such a place one could not be ~⟩ ⟨after a short interval one will come to ~⟩

¹one–shot \ˈ=,=\ *adj* **1 a** : that is complete or effective through being done or used or applied only once and that does not require repetition ⟨a *one-shot* cure⟩ ⟨a *one-shot* riveting machine⟩ **b** : that is successful in only one try ⟨those *one-shot* Johnnies who make a lucky strike and then spend the rest of their lives trying to repeat —Hamilton Basso⟩ **2 a (1)** : that is not followed and is not designed to be followed by something else of the same kind : that is not open to repetition or subsequent modification ⟨a *one-shot* sale⟩ ⟨a *one-shot* business deal⟩ **(2)** : that is limited to just one time, occasion, or instance ⟨a *one-shot* criminal⟩ ⟨a *one-shot* bank robbery⟩ ⟨a *one-shot* job in a nightclub⟩ **(3)** : existing or occurring only once ⟨a *one-shot* affair⟩ **b (1)** : that is not followed and is not designed to be followed by a second issue : that does not appear as one of a series ⟨books and pamphlets are usually produced as *one-shot* publications⟩ **(2)** : that is not one of a series of productions of the same kind : performed or produced or put on just once ⟨a *one-shot* television program⟩

²one–shot \"\ *also* **one–shot·ter** \ˈ=ˈshäd·ə(r)\ *n* -s **1** : something that is not followed and is not designed to be followed by something else of the same kind: as **a** : a book or other publication that is not to be published in successive issues **b** : a program (as a theater production) that is put on and designed to be put on only once **2** *usu* **one–shotter** : one that performs an act or that functions only once

one–shot camera *n* : a color camera in which three color-separation negatives are made with a single exposure by using semitransparent reflectors to divide the beam that has passed through the lens so as to form three geometrically identical images on three plates or films through three different color filters

one–sided \ˈ=ˈ==\ *adj* **1 a** : having or existing or occurring on one side only : having one side prominent or more developed ⟨a *one-sided* leaf⟩ **b** : limited to one side : PARTIAL, UNJUST, UNFAIR ⟨a *one-sided* interpretation⟩ **2** : UNILATERAL ⟨a *one-sided* decision⟩ — **one–sid·ed·ly** *adv* — **one–sid·ed·ness** *n* -ES

¹one–step \ˈ=,=\ *n* **1** : a ballroom dance popular in the early 20th century and marked by quick walking steps backward and forward in ¾ time **2** : a piece of music for the one-step

²one–step \"\ *vi* : to dance the one-step

one–sucker *n* : a tobacco produced in western Kentucky and north central Tennessee and suckered only once or topped only just before cutting and used in the manufacture of chewing tobacco

one–suiter \ˈ=ˈsüd·ə(r)\ *n* -s : a man's wardrobe case designed to hold one suit and accessories

¹onetime \ˈ=,=\ *adj* : FORMER, SOMETIME, QUONDAM ⟨a ~ professor of history⟩

²onetime \"\ *adv* : FORMERLY ⟨said they ~ knew him very well⟩

one–to–one \ˌ=təˈ=, -dəˈ-\ *adj* **1** : pairing each element of a set uniquely with an element of another set ⟨a *one-to-one* correspondence between the sounds of a language and the symbols used to represent the sounds⟩ **2** : ONE-ONE 1

one–track \ˈ=ˌ=\ *adj* **1 a** : that lacks flexibility and nimbleness and can handle only one thing at a time ⟨is an unimaginative person and has a *one-track* mind⟩ **b** : marked by often narrowly constricted attention to or absorption in just one thing ⟨a *one-track* party member⟩ **2** : that lacks variety or breadth : limited in scope : UNDIVERSIFIED ⟨areas where *one-track* farming has been the rule —A.J.Bruwer⟩

one–two \ˈ=ˈ=\ *n* **1** : a fencing attack made by simulating a disengagement and followed by delivery of a thrust in the original line if the adversary's parry is drawn **2** *or* **one–two punch** \ˈ=ˈ=-\ : delivery of two short blows in rapid succession in boxing; *esp* : delivery of a jab with the left hand followed at once by a hard straight blow with the right

one–upmanship *n* : the art or practice of going a friend or competitor one better or keeping one jump ahead of him (as by appearing to have better information, connections, possessions, or experience) ⟨a branch of *one-upmanship* that involves playing one milieu off against another —Edmund Wilson⟩

¹one–way \ˈ=ˈ=\ *adj* **1 a (1)** : that moves in only one direction ⟨*one-way* traffic⟩ ⟨a *one-way* stream of time —A.J.Toynbee⟩ **(2)** : that exists on one side only : ONE-SIDED ⟨was pretty much a *one-way* conversation —G.K.Wynne⟩ : UNILATERAL ⟨a *one-way* agreement⟩ **b** : that allows or provides for or is limited to movement in only one direction ⟨a *one-way* path along which there can be no retreat —S.A.Coblentz⟩ ⟨a *one-way* plane ticket⟩; *esp* : that is limited to vehicles moving in only one direction ⟨a *one-way* street⟩ **2** : that functions in only one of two or more possible ways ⟨a *one-way* radio for receiving but not transmitting broadcast signals⟩

²one–way \"\ *or* **one–way disc plow** *n* : a disc plow that has relatively small discs set at a sharp angle in the same direction and that is designed to turn soil only partially

onfall \ˈ=,=\ *n* [*on* + *fall*, n.; prob. trans. of G *anfall*] : ATTACK, ASSAULT ⟨intend to make an ~ —J.H.Wheelwright⟩

onflow \ˈ=,=\ *n* [*on* + *flow*, n. (after the verb phrase *flow on*)] : the action or fact of flowing on : onward flow

onga–onga \ˈäŋgəˈäŋgə\ *n* -s [Maori] : a New Zealand shrubby nettle (*Urtica ferox*) with copious stinging hairs

on·ge *or* **on·gi** \ˈäŋjē\ *n, pl* **onge** *or* **onges** *or* **ongi** *or* **ongis** *usu cap* **1** : a people of the Andaman islands in the Bay of Bengal **2** : a member of the Onge people

on–glaze \ˈ=,=\ *adj* [prob. fr. the phrase *on glaze*, fr. ¹*on* + *glaze*, n.] : OVERGLAZE

on–glide \ˈ=,=\ *n* [*on* + *glide*, n.] : a glide produced by the movement of the vocal organs to the articulatory position of a speech sound from a position of inactivity or from the articulatory position of an immediately preceding speech sound — compare OFF-GLIDE

¹ongoing \ˈ=,==\ *n* [*on* + *going*, n. (after *go on*, v.)] **1 ongoings** *pl* : GOINGS-ON ⟨the ~*s* in the Orient —*Forbes*⟩ **2** : the action of going on : the action of continued forward movement : PROGRESS, DEVELOPMENT ⟨throughout this entire period of the world's ~ —P.W.Sinks⟩

²ongoing \"\ *adj* [²*on* + *going*, adj. (after *go on*, v.)] : that is going on: **a** : that is actually in process ⟨~ and contemplated research on language —*Amer. Anthrop. Assoc. Bull.*⟩ ⟨~ activities of the world —S.H.Horton⟩ **b** : that is continuously moving forward : making progress : GROWING, DEVELOPING ⟨the long ~ history of Christian thought —W.L.Sperry⟩ ⟨~ human society exacts a high degree of conformity —Bernard Rosenberg⟩ — **on·go·ing·ness** *n* -ES

on·gole \ˈän,gōl, ˈäŋ,-\ *n, usu cap* [fr. *Ongole*, town in southeast India] : NELLORE

onhanger \ˈ=,==\ *n* [*on* + *hanger* (after *hang on*, v.)] : HANGER-ON

-on·ic \ˈänik, -nēk\ *adj suffix* [ISV, fr. *-onic* (in *gluconic acid*)] : containing carboxyl esp. when formed by oxidizing the aldehyde group of an aldose sugar ⟨ald*onic* acid⟩ ⟨hex*onic* acid⟩ ⟨lact*onic*⟩

onio·ma·nia \ˌōnēōˈmānēə\ *n* [NL, fr. Gk *ōnios* to be bought, for sale (fr. *ōnos* price) + LL *mania* — more at VENAL] : a mania for buying things — **onio·ma·ni·ac** \-ē,ak\ *n*

¹on·ion \ˈənyən, *dial* ˈiŋə(r)n\ *n* -s *often attrib* [ME *onion*, *union*, fr. MF *oignon*, fr. L *union-*, *unio*, perh. fr. *unus* one — more at ONE] **1 a (1)** : a widely cultivated orig. Asiatic plant (*Allium cepa*) that has slender hollow tubular leaves and an edible rounded bulb made up of close concentric easily separable layers, that has a notably strong sharp smell and taste, and that is widely used as a vegetable **(2)** : the bulb of this plant **b** : any plant of the genus *Allium* including several that are cultivated for their showy heads of flowers **2** *obs* : a rounded knob or similar projection; *esp* : BUNION — **off one's onion** *also* **off one's onions** *chiefly Brit* : FOOLISH, CRAZY ⟨thought he was a trifle *off his onion* —Walter Murdoch⟩

onion 1a(2)

²onion \"\ *vt* -ED/-ING/-s : to apply an onion to

onion couch *or* **onion twitch** *n* : TALL OAT GRASS

onion flute *n* : KAZOO

onion fly *n* **1** : a dipterous insect of the family Anthomyiidae whose larva feeds on onion bulbs; *esp* : an orig. European insect (*Hylemya antiqua*) now widely distributed in America **2** : an insect (*Tritoxa flexa*) of the family Otitidae with habits like those of the onion fly — called also *black onion fly*

onion foot *n, pl* **onion foots** : BUN FOOT

oniongrass \ˈ==,=\ *n* : MELIC GRASS

onion maggot *n* : the larva of the onion fly

onion mildew *n* **1** : a downy mildew of the onion **2** : a fungus (*Peronospora destructor*) that causes onion mildew

onion red \ˈ==ˈ=\ *or* **onionpeel** \ˈ==,=\ *n* : a grayish red that is bluer and deeper than Pompeian red, bluer and darker than bois de rose, and deeper than livid brown

onion set *n* : a small onion bulb planted in the spring to produce an early crop esp. of green onions

onionskin \ˈ==,=\ *n* : a thin strong translucent paper of very light weight

onionskin pink *n* : a light brown that is stronger and slightly redder and darker than alesan, stronger and slightly yellower and darker than blush, lighter, stronger, and slightly redder than French beige, and redder, stronger, and slightly lighter than cork

onion smudge *or* **onion scab** *n* **1** : a common fungus disease of the onion characterized by black concentric internal rings or smutty spots on the surface of the bulb scales **2** : the fungus (*Colletotrichum circinans*) that causes onion smudge

onion smut *n* **1** : a fungus disease of the onion that is esp. destructive to seedlings and is characterized by elongate blackish blisters on the scales and leaves **2 :** the fungus (*Urocystis cepulae*) that causes onion smut

onion thrips *also* **onion louse** *n* **:** a minute widely distributed thrips (*Thrips tabaci*) that is often very injurious to the foliage of onions and in some regions to tobacco

on·iony \ˈənyənē\ *adj* **:** flavored with or tasting or smelling of onions ⟨~ soup⟩ ⟨an ~ breath⟩

onir- *or* **oniro-** — see ONEIR-

onis·coi·dea \ˌänəˈskȯidēə, ˌōn-\ *n pl, cap* [NL, fr. *Oniscus* + *-oidea*] **:** a suborder of Isopoda that includes all terrestrial isopods and a few that are to some extent aquatic — **onis·coi·de·an** \ˌ≈≈ˈ≈dēən\ *adj or n*

onis·cus \ōˈniskəs\ *n, cap* [NL, fr. L, wood louse, fr. Gk *oniskos*, fr. *onos* wood louse, ass + *-iskos*, dim. n. suffix — more at ASS, -ISH] **:** a genus (the type of the family Oniscidae) comprising isopods that cannot roll into a ball and formerly including most of the known isopods but now restricted to a few chiefly Old World terrestrial forms with flattened body, large eyes, and 3-jointed antennal flagella

oni·um \ˈōnēəm, ˈōnyəm\ *adj* [*-onium*] **:** characterized by a cation that is usu. complex (as oxonium, pyridinium, or a substituted ammonium) — compare QUATERNARY AMMONIUM COMPOUND

-o·ni·um \"\ *n suffix* -s [ISV, fr. NL *ammonium*] **:** an ion having a positive charge — in names of complex cations containing hydrogen or one or more organic radicals coordinated to a central atom ⟨*oxonium*⟩ ⟨*phosphonium*⟩ ⟨*sulfonium*⟩; compare -IUM 1b

on·kos \ˈäŋkəs\ *n, pl* **on·koi** \-ˌkȯi\ *or* **onkos·es** \-ˌkəsəz\ [Gk, lit., bulk, mass — more at ONCO-] **:** a topknot worn on the mask in ancient Greek tragedy

onlap \ˈ≈ˌ≈\ *n* [*on* + *lap*, n.] **1 :** progressive submergence of land by an advancing sea **2 :** the arrangement of strata deposited on the floor of an advancing sea during its advance — compare OFFLAP, OVERLAP

¹onlay \(ˈ)≈ˈ≈\ *vt* [²*on* + *lay*] **:** to lay on; *specif* **:** to mount (an onlay) on a surface

²onlay \ˈ≈ˌ≈\ *n* **1 :** material mounted on a surface usu. so as to be in relief and usu. for decorative effect; *esp* **:** a thin ornamental piece of leather mounted on the surface of a leather bookbinding **2 :** INLAY 2b

on–license \ˈ≈ˌ≈≈\ *n* **:** a license to sell liquor for consumption on the premises

on·li·est \ˈōnlēəst\ *adj* [¹*only* + *-est*] *dial* **:** ONLY ⟨couldn't see anything to cause a loving father to let go his ~ daughter —Miriam Michelson⟩

on limits *adj* **:** available or approved for military personnel

on·li·ness \ˈōnlēnəs\ *n* -ES **:** the quality or state of being the only one of an indicated or implied kind or category ⟨was an only child and was lonely in his ~⟩

onload \ˈ≈ˌ≈\ *vb* [²*on* + *load*] **:** LOAD ⟨~*ing* cargo⟩

onlooker \ˈ≈ˌ≈≈\ *n* [*on* + *looker* (after *look on*, v.)] **:** one that looks on ⟨curious ~*s*⟩; *esp* **:** a passive spectator ⟨a crowd of indifferent ~*s*⟩

onlooking \ˈ≈ˌ≈≈\ *adj* [²*on* + *looking*, pres. part. of *look* (after *look on*, v.)] **:** that looks on ⟨walked by the ~ crowd⟩

¹on·ly \ˈōnlē, -li\ *adj* [ME *only, oonly*, fr. OE *ānlīc*, fr. *ān* one + *-līc* -ly — more at ONE] **1 :** that is unequaled (as in quality, rank) **:** unquestionably the best or the most outstanding **:** PEERLESS ⟨was convinced that the team was the ~ one⟩ **:** that alone is worth serious consideration ⟨the ~ actor on Broadway⟩ **2** *dial chiefly Eng* **:** that is without companions or associates **:** LONE, ISOLATED **3 :** being one or more of which there exist no others of the same class or kind **:** alone in an indicated or implied category ⟨is the ~ authority you can really rely on⟩ ⟨said she was the ~ one for him⟩ ⟨was the ~ book deserving to be read⟩ **:** SOLE, SINGLE ⟨was an ~ child⟩ ⟨had an ~ brother⟩ ⟨is the ~ known species⟩ ⟨the ~ begotten son⟩

²only \"\ *adv* [ME *only, oonly*, fr. *only, oonly*, adj.] **1 a :** as a single solitary fact or instance or occurrence **:** as just the one simple thing and nothing more or different **:** SIMPLY, MERELY, JUST ⟨has ~ lost one election —George Orwell⟩ ⟨if ~ she had yellow hair —Jean Stafford⟩ ⟨saw my father three times ~ —T.B.Costain⟩ ⟨has ~ two dollars⟩ **b :** EXCLUSIVELY, SOLELY ⟨will tell it ~ to you⟩ ⟨is ~ known to scholars —Stephen Spender⟩ **2 a :** at the very least **:** without going any further than necessary ⟨it was ~ too true⟩ ⟨it was ~ too probable that my inquiries would be reported —Allen Upward⟩ **b :** by that much indeed **:** all the more as a matter of fact ⟨such significance ~ adds to the value of such literature —Herbert Read⟩ ⟨the risk ~ makes the whole thing more interesting⟩ **3 a :** in the final outcome **:** at last **:** as a final result ⟨it will ~ make you sick⟩ ⟨a period of personal rule which ~ ended with revolution —R.A.Billington⟩ **b :** with nevertheless the final outcome or result ⟨won a great deal, ~ to lose it all later on⟩ **4 :** as recently as ⟨saw her ~ last week⟩ **:** in the immediate past ⟨I ~ just talked to her⟩

³only \"\ *conj* [ME *only, oonly*, fr. *only, oonly*, adv.] **1 a :** with the qualification or restriction that **:** BUT ⟨you may go, ~ come back early⟩ **b :** and yet **:** HOWEVER ⟨they look very nice, ~ we can't use them⟩ **2 :** were it not that **:** if it weren't for the fact that **:** EXCEPT ⟨he would have come over, ~ we never expected you as early as this —J.G.Cozzens⟩

⁴only \"\ *prep* [²*only*] *chiefly dial* **:** EXCEPT

onmarch \ˈ≈ˌ≈\ *n* [*on* + *march*, n. (after the verb phrase *march on*)] **:** a march onward ⟨the ~ of history —*Science*⟩

on·mun \ˈȯnmən\ *or* **en·mun** \ˈenm-\ *n* -s *often cap* [Korean] **:** HANKUL

ono \ˈō(ˌ)nō\ *n, pl* **ono** *or* **onos** [Hawaiian, Marquesan, & Tahitian] **:** WAHOO

on·o·bry·chis \ˌänəˈbrīkəs\ *n, cap* [NL, fr. Gk *onobrychis*, a leguminous plant, fr. *onos* ass + *-brychis* (fr. *brykein*, *brychein* to eat greedily, gnash the teeth) — more at ASS, BRUXISM] **:** a genus of Old World herbs of the family Leguminosae having pinnate leaves, pink or white racemose flowers, and flat unjointed pods

ono·centaur \ˈ¦änə+\ *n* [LL *onocentaurus*, a wild animal inhabiting waste places, fr. Gk *onokentauros*, fr. *onos* ass + *kentauros* centaur] **:** a mythological creature having the head and arms and upper torso of a human being and the body and legs of an ass

on·o·clea \ˌänəˈklēə\ *n, cap* [NL, fr. Gk *onokleia* anchusa] **:** a genus of ferns (family Polypodiaceae) of cold temperate regions having fronds that are broad and pinnatifid or that consist of segments rolled up into berrylike structures enclosing the sori — **on·o·cle·oid** \ˌ¦änə¦klēˌȯid\ *n or adj*

on·o·man·cy \ˈ¦änəˌman(t)sē, ōˈnäm ənsē\ *n* -ES [obs. F *onomancie*, fr. MF, irreg. fr. Gk *onoma* name + MF *-mancie* -mancy] **:** divination from the letters of a name

on·o·ma·si·o·log·ic \ˌ¦änə¦māsēə¦läjik, -āzē-\ *or* **on·o·ma·si·o·log·i·cal** \-jəkəl\ *adj* **:** relating to the gathering or comparison of lists of words that designate similar or associated concepts

on·o·ma·si·ol·o·gy \ˌ≈≈ˌ≈≈ˈäləjē\ *n* -ES [Gk *onomasia* name, expression (fr. *onomazein* to call, name) + E *-o-* + *-logy*] **:** the study of words and expressions having similar or associated concepts and a basis (as social, regional, occupational) for being grouped

on·o·mas·tic \ˌ¦änəˈmastik\ *adj* [Gk *onomastikos*, fr. *onomazein* to name, fr. *onoma* name — more at NAME] **1 :** of, relating to, or consisting of a name or names ⟨published an ~ study⟩ **2** *of a signature* **:** written in the handwriting of the author of a letter or document or in the handwriting of one subscribing to a letter or document the body of which is in the handwriting of another person

on·o·mas·ti·con \ˌänəˈmastəˌkän, -ˌkən\ *n* -s [NL, fr. Gk *onomastikon*, fr. neut. of *onomastikos* onomastic] **1 a :** a collection or listing of words esp. in a specialized field (as science or commerce) **b :** a work containing such a collection or listing **:** WORDBOOK, LEXICON **2 a :** a collection or listing of proper names of persons or places usu. with etymologies **b :** a work containing such a collection or listing

on·o·mas·tics \-stiks\ *n pl but usu sing in constr* [modif. (influenced by E *-ics*) of F *onomastique*, fr. *onomastique* onomastic, fr. Gk *onomastikos*] **1 a :** the science or study of the origins and forms of words esp. as used in a specialized field (as science or commerce) ⟨a course in ~⟩ **b :** the science or study of the origin and forms of proper names of persons or places ⟨any student of ~ and of surnames in particular —Otto Springer⟩ **2 :** the system underlying the formation and use of words esp. for proper names or of words used in a specialized field ⟨according to rules of Indo-European ~ —E.E.Herzfeld⟩

onomato- *comb form* [LL, fr. Gk, fr. *onomat-, onoma*] **:** name **:** word ⟨*onomato*mania⟩

on·o·ma·tol·o·gy \ˌänəməˈtäləjē *sometimes* ōˌnäm-\ *n* -ES [F *onomatologie*, fr. *onomato-* + *-logie* -logy] **:** ONOMASTICS

on·o·mato·mania \ˌänəˌmad·əˈmānēə *sometimes* ōˌnäməd- *or* ˌänəˌmäd-\ *n* [NL, fr. *onomato-* + LL *mania*] **:** uncontrollable obsession with words or names or their meanings or sounds; *esp* **:** a mania for repeating certain words or sounds

onoma·tope \ˈänəməˌtōp, ōˈnäm-\ *n* -s [irreg. fr. *onomatopoeia*] **:** an onomatopoeic word ⟨fondness of comic-strip artists for ~s —H.L.Mencken⟩

on·o·mat·o·poe·ia \ˌänəˌmad·əˈpēə, ¦tə'- *sometimes* ōˌnäm- *or* ˌänəˌmä¦ *or* -pēyə\ *n* -s [LL, fr. Gk *onomatopoiia*, fr. *onomato-* + *-poiia* (fr. *poiein* to make + *-ia* -y) — more at POET] **1 a :** formation of words in imitation of natural sounds **:** the naming of a thing or action by a more or less exact reproduction of the sound associated with it (as *buzz, hiss, bobwhite*) **:** the imitative or echoic principle in language — compare BOWWOW THEORY **b :** a word so formed ⟨the international stock of ~s —Leo Spitzer⟩ **2 :** the use of words whose sound suggests the sense ⟨a study of the poet's ~⟩ — **on·o·mat·o·poe·ian** \-¦pē(y)ən\ *adj*

on·o·mat·o·poe·ic \-ēik\ *also* **on·o·mat·o·poe·i·cal** \-ēəkəl\ *adj* [*onomatopoeic* fr. F *onomatopéique*, fr. *onomatopée* onomatopoeia (fr. LL *onomatopoeia*) + *-ique* -ic; *onomatopoeical* fr. *onomatopoeic* + *-al*] **:** of, relating to, or characterized by onomatopoeia **:** imitative in origin **:** ECHOIC ⟨~ words⟩ ⟨~ imitation of noises —Cecil Sprigge⟩ — **on·o·mat·o·poe·i·cal·ly** \-k(ə)lē\ *adv*

on·o·mat·o·po·et·ic \ˌ≈≈ˌ≈≈pōˌed·ik, ≈¦≈≈≈-\ *adj* [fr. MGk *onomatopoiētis*, after L *poesis* poetry, poem: *poeticus* poetic — more at POESY] **:** ONOMATOPOEIC ⟨independently developed in more than one place as an ~ term —Harry Hoijer⟩ — **on·o·mat·o·po·et·i·cal·ly** \-k(ə)lē\ *adv*

on·o·mat·o·py \ˌänəˈmad·əpē\ *n* -ES [LL *onomatopoeia*] **:** ONOMATOPOEIA ⟨the possibility that ~ has produced in different languages similar but genetically unrelated words —George Herzog⟩

on·on·da·ga \ˌänənˈdȯgə, -dägə *or, prob by* n-*dissimilation*, ˌänəˈd-\ *n, pl* **onondaga** *or* **onondagas** *usu cap* [Iroquois *Onōtāge'*, principal village of the Onondaga people, lit., on top of the hill] **1 a :** an Iroquoian people in and about Onondaga county in the central part of the state of New York **b :** a member of such people **2 :** the language of the Onondaga people — **on·on·da·gan** \ˌ≈≈ˈ≈gən\ *adj, usu cap*

ono·nis \ōˈnōnəs\ *n, cap* [NL, fr. Gk *onōnis* restharrow] **:** a genus of European herbs (family Leguminosae) that resemble clovers and have red or yellow solitary or clustered flowers — see RESTHARROW

on·o·por·don \ˌänəˈpȯrdᵊn, -ˌdän\ *n, cap* [NL, fr. Gk *onopordon* pellitory, fr. *onos* ass + *-pordon* (fr. *pordē* expulsion of intestinal gas); akin to Gk *perdesthai* to break wind — more at ASS, FART] **:** a genus of Eurasian herbs (family Compositae) with tomentose prickly foliage and large heads of purplish flowers — see COTTON THISTLE

on·os·mo·di·um \ˌänəzˈmōdēəm, -nəˈsm-\ *n, cap* [NL, irreg. fr. Gk *onosma*, a boraginaceous plant, fr. *onos* ass + *-osma* (fr. *osmē* odor) — more at ODOR] **:** a genus of No. American perennial herbs (family Boraginaceae) with hispid foliage and small yellowish or greenish flowers — see FALSE GROMWELL

on-plant \ˈ≈ˌ≈\ *adj* [¹*on* + *plant*, n.] **:** IN-PLANT

onroll \ˈ≈ˌ≈\ *n* [*on* + *roll*, n. (after the verb phrase *roll on*)] **:** a rolling forward or onward

onrush \ˈ≈ˌ≈\ *n* [*on* + *rush*, n. (after the verb phrase *rush on*)] **1 :** a rushing forward or onward ⟨the ~ of industrialization created a serious housing shortage —Nels Anderson⟩ **2 :** ONSET, ONSLAUGHT ⟨the first ~ of some sudden grief —Laura Krey⟩

onrushing \ˈ≈ˌ≈≈\ *adj* **:** rushing forward rapidly or impetuously

-ons *pl of* -ON

on–sale \ˈ≈ˌ≈\ *adj* **1** *of a license* **:** that permits sale and consumption of alcoholic beverages on the premises ⟨secured an *on-sale* license for his restaurant⟩ **2 a :** authorized to sell ⟨an *on-sale* retailer⟩ or buy ⟨*on-sale* patrons⟩ alcoholic beverages under the conditions of an on-sale license **b :** sold ⟨*on-sale* liquor⟩ or licensed ⟨an *on-sale* restaurant⟩ under the conditions of an on-sale license

¹onset \ˈ≈ˌ≈\ *n* [*on* + *set*, n. (after *set on*, v.)] **1 :** ATTACK, ASSAULT ⟨unable to withstand the ~ of the army⟩ **2 a :** BEGINNING, COMMENCEMENT, START ⟨the ~ of winter⟩ **b :** the initial existence or symptoms of a disease ⟨the ~ of scarlet fever⟩ **c :** the initial formation of a speech sound ⟨the ~ of a voiceless consonant⟩ **3 :** ELECTRONOGRAPHY

²on·set \ˈänˌset, -ˌsət\ *n* [*on* + *set*, n.] *chiefly Scot* **:** a farmhouse with its outbuildings

onsetter \ˈ≈ˌ≈≈\ *n* [*on* + *setter* (after *set on*, v.)] **:** CAGER 1a

¹onshore \(ˈ)≈ˈ≈\ *adv* [¹*on* + *shore*, n.] **1 :** toward or onto the shore ⟨a breeze blowing ~⟩ **:** near the shore ⟨a boat sailing along ~⟩ **2 :** within the country **:** DOMESTICALLY ⟨did all his business ~⟩

²onshore \"\ *adj* **1 :** coming or moving toward or onto the shore ⟨an ~ breeze⟩ ⟨an ~ current⟩ **2 a :** situated on or near the shore ⟨~ oil reserves⟩ ⟨~ fishing⟩ **b :** placed or made within the country **:** DOMESTIC ⟨~ purchases⟩

on side *adv (or adj)* **1 :** not off side **:** in a position legally to play the ball or puck or to receive it from a teammate **2 :** in a position to make a finesse in a card game successful ⟨the king is *on side*⟩

onside kick \ˈ≈ˌ≈-\ *n* **:** a free kick (as a kickoff) in football that a kicker deliberately aims only slightly beyond the defensive restraining line in the hope of recovering the ball which becomes free after crossing the restraining line

on·slaught \ˈȯnˌslȯt, ˈän-, *usu* -ȯd·+V\ *n* -s [alter. (influenced by E *on* and obs. E *slaught* slaughter, fr. ME, fr. OE *sleaht*) of earlier *anslaight*, modif. of D *aanslag* act of striking, fr. MD *aenslach* act of striking, attack, fr. *aen* on, at + *slach* blow, stroke; akin to OE *an, on* on and to OE *slēan* to strike, beat — more at ON, SLAY, SLAUGHTER] **:** an esp. fierce attack ⟨the tremendous ~ across the Rhine —Sir Winston Churchill⟩ ⟨an ~ of disease⟩ ⟨less resilient under his wife's verbal ~s —D.G.Gerhaty⟩

onst *like* ONCE\ *dial var of* ONCE

onstage \(ˈ)≈ˈ≈\ *adv (or adj)* [¹*on* + *stage*, n.] **:** on a part of the stage visible to the audience **:** toward the central part of the stage ⟨is ~ almost continuously —Philip Hamburger⟩ ⟨began to walk ~⟩ ⟨has good ~ diction⟩

on·stead \ˈänzˌted, -nˌst-, -ˌtəd, -ˌstəd\ *n* [*on* + *stead*, n.] *Scot* **:** a farmhouse with its outbuildings

on–stream *adj* [fr. the phrase *on stream*] **:** moving through or flowing (as in a pipe or filter) in the desired operational direction ⟨*on-stream* chemical reactions⟩ ⟨the *on-stream* time for a filter varies widely —D.P.Thornton⟩

on stream *adv* **:** in operation **:** into operation ⟨a new polypropylene plant will go *on stream*⟩

ont- *or* **onto-** *comb form* [NL, fr. LGk *onto-*, fr. Gk *ont-*, *ōn*, pres. part. of *einai* to be — more at IS] **1 :** being **:** existence ⟨*ontic*⟩ **2 :** individual living thing **:** living organism ⟨*ontogeny*⟩

-ont \ˌänt\ *n comb form* -s [Gk *ont-, ōn*, pres. part. of *einai* to be] **:** cell **:** organism ⟨*gamont*⟩

¹on·tar·i·an \(ˈ)änˈterēən, -ta(a)r-, -tär-\ *adj, usu cap* [*Ontario*, province of southern and central Canada + E *-an*, adj. suffix] **1 :** of, relating to, or characteristic of the province of Ontario in south central Canada **2** [Lake *Ontario*, lake lying between the state of New York and the Canadian province of Ontario + E *-an*, adj. suffix] **:** of, relating to, or characteristic of Lake Ontario lying between the state of New York and Canada

²ontarian \"\ *also* **on·tar·io·an** \≈ˈ≈≈ˌōən\ *n* -s *cap* [*Ontario* (province) + E *-an*, n. suffix] **:** a native or inhabitant of the province of Ontario

on·tar·io \≈ˈ≈≈ˌō\ *adj, usu cap* **:** of or from the province of Ontario **:** of the kind or style prevalent in Ontario **:** ONTARIAN

ontario violet *n, often cap O* **:** a pale purplish blue that is redder and paler than hydrangea blue and redder and deeper than starlight blue — called also *blue lavender*

on·thoph·a·gus \änˈthäfəgəs\ *n, cap* [NL, fr. Gk *onthos* dung + NL *-phagus* (fr. Gk *-phagos* -phagous)] **:** a widely distributed genus of scarabaeid beetles

on·tic \ˈäntik\ *also* **on·tal** \-tᵊl\ *adj* [*ont-* + *-ic* or *-al*] **:** of, relating to, or having real being or existence **:** NOUMENAL ⟨~ aspects of experience —Fritz Kaufmann⟩ ⟨the alleged ~ status of moral values —Ernest Nagel⟩ — distinguished from *phenomenal* — **on·ti·cal·ly** \-tək(ə)lē\ *adv*

on·to \ˈȯntə, ˈän-, -ntü, -n·(ˌ)tü, +V *often* -ntəw\ *prep* [²*on* + *to*] **1 a :** to a position or point on or upon ⟨slipped away from the table ~ the floor —C.D.Lewis⟩ ⟨water splashed down from the roof ~ my hat —Joseph Wechsberg⟩ ⟨jumped off the boat and ~ the dock⟩ ⟨climbed out ~ the roof⟩ **b** *chiefly dial* **:** in position on ⟨the coat has big buttons ~ it —Delia H. Pugh⟩ **2 :** in or into a state of awareness or knowledgeability about ⟨he's a shrewd bird and he's ~ me —Mark Schorer⟩ ⟨was ~ something that should have been pursued further —Bosley Crowther⟩ — compare ²ON 8

onto·genesis \ˌäntə+\ *n* [NL, fr. *ont-* + L *genesis*] **:** ONTOGENY

on·to·ge·net·ic \ˌ¦äntəjə¦ned·ik\ *adj* [ISV, fr. NL *ontogenesis*, after such pairs as LL *antithesis: antitheticus* antithetical] **1 :** of or relating to ontogeny **2 :** based on visible morphological characters and not necessarily indicative of natural evolutionary relationships ⟨an ~ key to the Lygaeidae⟩ **3 :** appearing in the course of ontogenetic development **:** INDIVIDUAL ⟨~ traits⟩ ⟨an ~ modification⟩ — **on·to·ge·net·i·cal·ly** \-d·ək(ə)lē\ *adv*

on·to·gen·ic \ˌ¦äntə¦jenik\ *adj* [ISV *ontogeny* + *-ic*] **:** ONTOGENETIC — **on·to·gen·i·cal·ly** \-enək(ə)lē\ *adv*

on·tog·e·nist \änˈtäjənəst\ *n* -s **:** a student of ontogeny

on·tog·e·ny \-jənē\ *n* -ES [ISV *ont-* + *-geny*] **:** the biological development or course of development of an individual organism — distinguished from *phylogeny*

on·to·log·i·cal \ˌ¦äntᵊl¦äjəkəl, ¦äntə¦lä-\ *also* **on·to·log·ic** \-jik\ *adj* [*ontological* fr. *ontologic* + *-al*; *ontologic* prob. fr. (assumed) NL *ontologicus*, fr. NL *ontologia* ontology + L *-icus* -ic] **1 :** of or relating to ontology **2 :** of or relating to being or existence; *esp* **:** based upon or drawn from analysis of the nature of being ⟨the ~ argument for the existence of God⟩ — **on·to·log·i·cal·ly** \-jək(ə)lē\ *adv*

on·tol·o·gism \änˈtäləˌjizəm\ *n* -s [ISV *ontology* + *-ism*] **1 :** a philosophical method that analyzes reality on ontological principles (as from a consideration of the categories) **2 :** a theory in philosophy: the order of intellectual apprehension follows the order of real being and knowledge of God is immediate and intuitive

on·tol·o·gist \-jəst\ *n* -s [*ontology* + *-ist*] **1 :** a specialist in ontology **2 :** an advocate or adherent of ontologism — **on·tol·o·gis·tic** \(ˌ)än¦tälə¦jistik\ *adj*

on·tol·o·gize \änˈtäləˌjīz\ *vt* -ED/-ING/-S [ISV *ontology* + *-ize*] **:** to convert into ontological entities or express ontologically

on·tol·o·gy \-jē\ *n* -ES [NL *ontologia*, fr. *ont-* + *-logia* -logy] **1 a** (1) **:** a science or study of being; *specif* **:** a branch of metaphysics relating to the nature and relations of being (2) **:** a particular system according to which problems of the nature of being are investigated **b :** FIRST PHILOSOPHY **2 :** a theory concerning the kinds of entities and specif. the kinds of abstract entities that are to be admitted to a language system

onus \ˈōnəs\ *n* -ES [L — more at ONEROUS] **1 a :** something (as a task, duty, responsibility) that involves considerable difficulty or annoyance or necessitates rather strenuous effort or results in notable strain or fatigue **:** BURDEN ⟨the job of caring for his dependents was a real ~⟩ ⟨believe it to be the ~ on every man to add . . . to the sum total of human knowledge —Douglas Carruthers⟩ **b :** something distasteful or objectionable and difficult to bear: as (1) **:** a disagreeable necessity of doing something ⟨free of all ~ of retort or comment —Richard Blaker⟩ (2) **:** BLAME ⟨tried to shift the ~ for causing the war onto the other country⟩ ⟨adroitly transfer the ~ from the accused to the accusers —Eugene Lyons⟩ (3) **:** STIGMA ⟨excusing himself ahead of time so that the ~ would be less if his failure was realized —Norman Mailer⟩ **2** *or* **onus pro·ban·di** \-prōˈbanˌdī, -ndē\ **:** BURDEN OF PROOF ⟨put forth a theory that left the ~ squarely on him⟩

onwaiting \ˈ≈ˌ≈≈\ *n* [*on* + *waiting*, gerund of *wait* (after the verb phrase *wait on*)] *Scot* **:** the act of awaiting

¹on·ward \ˈȯnwə(r)d, ˈän-\ *also* **on·wards** \-dz\ *adv* [ME *onward*, fr. ²*on* + *-ward*] **:** toward or at a point lying ahead in space or time **:** FORWARD, AHEAD ⟨moved ~ into the forest⟩ ⟨the bridge was farther ~ along that road⟩ ⟨from the 6th century ~⟩

²onward \"\ *adj* **:** directed or moving onward **:** FORWARD ⟨the difficult and dangerous ~ path which we must tread —Sir Winston Churchill⟩ ⟨the ~ course of events⟩ ⟨the ~ march of agricultural settlement —B.K.Sandwell⟩

on·ward·ness *n* -ES **:** the quality or state of being directed forward or of moving forward ⟨~ that he found among these youthful liberals —Francis Biddle⟩

ony \ˈānē\ *dial var of* ANY

onych- *or* **onycho-** *comb form* [L *onych-*, fr. Gk *onych-*, *onycho-*, fr. *onych-*, *onyx* — more at ONYX] **:** nail of the finger or toe ⟨*onych*auxis⟩ **:** claw ⟨*Onycho*phora⟩

on·y·cha \ˈänəkə\ *n* -s [ME, fr. LL, fr. Gk, acc. of *onych-*, *onyx* aromatic substance, onyx, nail of the finger or toe] **:** an ingredient of the incense anciently used in some religious ceremonies of the Jews

on·ych·aux·is \ˌänəˈkȯksəs\ *n, pl* **onychauxes** [NL, fr. *onych-* + *-auxis* (fr. Gk *auxein* to increase) — more at EKE] **:** overgrowth of the nails

onych·ia \ōˈnikēə\ *n* -s [NL, fr. *onych-* + *-ia*] **:** inflammation of the matrix of the nail leading to suppuration and loss of the nail

-onychia \"\ *n comb form* -s [NL, fr. *onych-* + *-ia*] **:** condition of the nails of the fingers or toes ⟨leuk*onychia*⟩

on·y·chi·tis \ˌänəˈkīd·əs\ *n, pl* **ony·chit·i·des** \-kid·əˌdēz\ [NL, fr. *onych-* + *-itis*] **:** ONYCHIA

onych·i·um \ōˈnikēəm\ *n, pl* **onych·ia** \-ēə\ [NL, fr. Gk *onychion* little claw, dim. of *onych-, onyx* nail of the finger or toe, claw] **:** EMPODIUM

-onychium \"\ *n comb form* -s [NL, fr. Gk *onychion* little claw] **:** fingernail **:** toenail **:** region of the fingernail or toenail ⟨ep*onychium*⟩ ⟨hyp*onychium*⟩

on·y·chog·a·le \ˌanəˈkägə(ˌ)lē\ *syn of* ONYCHOGALEA

on·y·cho·ga·lea \ˌänəkōˈgālēə\ *n, cap* [NL, fr. *onych-* + Gk *galē, galeē* weasel, ferret — more at GALEA] **:** a genus of marsupials comprising the nail-tailed wallaby

on·y·cho·gryposis \ˌ¦änəkō+\ *n* [NL, fr. *onych-* + *gryposis*] **:** an abnormal state of the nails (as in acromegaly) characterized by marked hypertrophy and increased curvature

on·y·choid \ˈänəˌkȯid\ *adj* [*onych-* + *-oid*] **:** resembling a fingernail in shape or texture

on·y·chol·y·sis \ˌänəˈkäləsəs\ *n* [NL, fr. *onych-* + *-lysis*] **:** a loosening of a nail from the nail bed beginning at the free edge and proceeding to the root

on·y·cho·ma·de·sis \ˌänəkōməˈdēsəs\ *n* -ES [NL, fr. *onych-* + Gk *madēsis* loss of hair, fr. *madan* to be bald, be moist; akin to L *madēre* to be wet — more at MEAT] **:** loosening and shedding of the nails

on·y·cho·mycosis \ˌänəkō+\ *n* [NL, fr. *onych-* + *mycosis*] **:** a fungous disease of the nails

onych·o·mys \ōˈnikəməs\ *n, cap* [NL, fr. *onych-* + *-mys*] **:** a genus of rodents (family Cricetidae) comprising the No. American grasshopper mice

on·y·cho·pha·gia \ˌänəkōˈfāj(ē)ə\ *n* -s [NL, fr. *onych-* + *-phagia*] **:** NAIL-BITING

on·y·choph·a·gy \ˌänəˈkäfəjē\ *n* -ES [NL *onychophagia*, fr. *onych-* + *-phagia* -phagy] **:** NAIL-BITING

on·y·choph·o·ra \ˌänəˈkäfərə\ *n pl, cap* [NL, fr. *onych-* + *-phora*] **:** a class of Arthropoda or an independent phylum comprising small elongated velvety-skinned terrestrial invertebrate animals of damp dark habitats in warm regions that are in some respects intermediate between annelid worms and typical arthropods, that have an unsegmented vermiform body, numerous pairs of short unsegmented legs with terminal bifid claws, and a head bearing a pair of segmented antennae, a pair of oral papillae on which slime glands open, a pair of simple eyes, and a pair of jaws resembling blades, that possess a hemocoel as a body cavity, and that breathe by means of tracheae and excrete by means of nephridia — **on·y·choph·oran**

\ˌ⸗⸗ˈ⸗⸗rən\ *adj or n* — **onycho·phore** \ōˈnikəˌfō(ə)r, ˈänəkō,-\ *n* -s — **on·y·choph·o·rous** \ˌänəˈkäfərəs\ *adj*

on·y·chor·rhex·is \ˌänəkəˈreksəs\ *n, pl* **onychorrhexes** [NL, fr. *onych-* + *-rrhexis*] : longitudinal ridging and splitting of the finger and toe nails

on·y·cho·schiz·ia \ˌänəkōˈskitsēə, -izēə\ *n* -s [NL, fr. *onych-* + *-schizia* (fr. Gk *schizein* to split) — more at SCHISM] : a condition of the nails marked by lamination in two or more layers and by scaling away in thin flakes

on·y·cho·sis \ˌänəˈkōsəs\ *n, pl* **onycho·ses** \-ōˌsēz\ [NL, fr. *onych-* + *-osis*] : a disease of the nails

on–year \ˈ⸗ˌ⸗\ *n* : a year marked by the regular or expected or full occurrence of something ⟨looked forward to a good yield from his biennial fruit trees during their *on-year*⟩

onyg·e·na \ōˈnijənə\ *n, cap* [NL, irreg. fr. Gk *onyx* nail of the finger or toe, claw, hoof + NL *-gena* (fr. Gk *-genēs* born) — more at -GEN] : a genus (the type of the family Onygenaceae) of ascomycetous fungi that have stalked capitate ascocarps and occur typically on decaying animal materials (as hooves or feathers)

-o·nym \əˌnim\ *n comb form* -s [ME *-onyme*, fr. L *-onymum*, fr. Gk *-ōnymon*, fr. neut. of *-ōnymos*, adj. comb. form (as in *homōnymos* having the same name) — more at HOMONYMOUS] : name : word ⟨allo*nym*⟩ ⟨hypo*nym*⟩

on·y·mous \ˈänəməs\ *adj* [back-formation fr. *anonymous*] : bearing a name; *esp* : giving or bearing the author's name ⟨an ~ article in a magazine⟩ — opposed to *anonymous* — **on·y·mous·ly** *adv*

-on·y·my \ˈänəmē, -mi\ *n comb form* -ES [L *-onymia*, fr. Gk *-ōnymia*, fr. *-ōnymos* (as in *homōnymos*) + *-ia* -y] **1** : kind of name or word : kind or set of names or words ⟨hydr*onymy*⟩ **2** : study of a (specified) kind of names or words ⟨anthrop*onymy*⟩

¹onyx \ˈäniks, -nēks *sometimes* ˈōn-\ *n* -ES [ME *onix, oniche*, fr. OF & L; OF *onix, oniche*, fr. L *onych-, onyx*, fr. Gk, nail of the finger or toe, claw, onyx — more at NAIL] **1 a** : a chalcedony that has straight parallel alternating bands of color (as white and black or white and brown) and that is used esp. in making cameos — compare SARDONYX **b** : BLACK ONYX **2** *or* **onyx marble** : ALABASTER 1b

²onyx \ˈ"\ *adj* : of the color jet black ⟨the ~ night sky —Flora Lewis⟩ ⟨~ days of the depression —Maurice Zolotow⟩

-onyx \ˈäniks, ˌəniks, ³niks, -nēks\ *n comb form* [NL, fr. Gk *onych-, onyx* nail of the finger or toe, claw] : one having (such) nails or claws — chiefly in generic names of animals ⟨Coleo*nyx*⟩

onyx·is \ōˈniksəs\ *n* -ES [NL, irreg. fr. Gk *onych-, onyx*] : an ingrowing of the nail

on·za \ˈōnzə, -n(ˌ)sä, -n(ˌ)thä\ *n* -s [Sp, lit., ounce, fr. L *uncia* ounce, twelfth part — more at OUNCE] : an old Spanish gold doubloon

oo \ˈōˌō\ *n* -s [Hawaiian *ʻōʻō*] : an Hawaiian honey eater of the genus *Moho*; *esp* : a bird (*M. nobilis*) having yellow axillary tufts used in native featherwork after the extinction of the mamo until it too became extinct

OO *abbr* **1** order of **2** ordnance office; ordnance officer **3** or order

oo- — see O-

o–o–a–a \ˈōˌōˈäˌä, ˌōəˈ-\ *n* -s [Hawaiian *ʻōʻō-ʻāʻā*, fr. *ʻōʻō* oo + *ʻaʻa* dwarf] : a bird of the family Meliphagidae (*Moho braccatus*) confined to the island of Kauai

oo·blast \ˈōəˌblast\ *n* [*o-* + *-blast*] **1** : a cellular precursor of an ovum **2** : a tube by which the diploid nucleus resulting from fertilization in red algae is carried to an auxiliary cell — called also *connecting filament*

oo·blas·te·ma filament \ˌōəˌblaˈstēmə-\ *n* [NL *ooblastema* fertilized ovum, fr. *o-* + *blastema*] : OOBLAST 2

oo·capt \ˈōəˌkapt\ *n* -s [*o-* + *-capt*, fr. Gk *kaptein* to gulp down — more at HEAVE] : a muscular enlargement of the beginning of the oviduct of various worms that serves to draw the egg into the oviduct

oo·cyesis \ˌōə +\ *n, pl* **oocyeses** [NL, fr. *o-* + *cyesis*] : extrauterine pregnancy in an ovary

oo·cyst \ˈōəˌsist\ *n* [ISV *o-* + *-cyst*] : ZYGOTE; *specif* : a sporozoan zygote undergoing sporogenous development

oo·cys·ta·ce·ae \ˌōəsəˈstāsēˌē\ *n pl, cap* [NL, fr. *Oöcystis*, type genus (fr. *o-* + *-cystis*) + *-aceae*] : a family of free-floating green algae (order Chlorococcales) which are unicellular or colonial with an indefinite number of cells and in which the cells are often retained within the distended gelatinized wall of the old mother cell — **oo·cys·ta·ceous** \ˌ⸗⸗⸗ˈstāshəs\ *adj*

oo·cyte \ˈōəˌsīt\ *n* -s [ISV *o-* + *-cyte*] : an egg before maturation : a female gametocyte or macrogametocyte

OOD *abbr* officer of the deck

oo·din·i·um \ˌōəˈdinēəm\ *n, cap* [NL, fr. *o-* + *Dinoflagellata* + *-ium*] : a genus of parasitic dinoflagellates occurring esp. on marine and freshwater fish

oo·dles \ˈüdᵊlz\ *also* **oo·dlins** \ˈüdlənz\ *n pl but sometimes sing in constr* [*oodles* perh. alter. of *huddles*, pl. of ²*huddle*; *oodlins* perh. alter. of *huddlings*, pl. of *huddling*, fr. gerund of ¹*huddle*] : a great quantity : ABUNDANCE, HEAP, LOT ⟨~ of money⟩ ⟨jolly picnics and ~ of good food —E.J.Fitzgerald⟩ ⟨~ of eyelet cottons are blossoming out all over the place this spring —*Christian Science Monitor*⟩

ooe·cial \(ˈ)ōˈēsh(ē)əl\ *adj* : of or relating to an ooecium

ooe·ci·um \(ˈ)ōˈēs(h)ēəm\ *n, pl* **ooe·cia** \-ēə\ [NL, fr. *o-* + *oecium*] : an ovicell of a bryozoan

oof *var of* OUF

oof·tish \ˈüftish\ *or* **oof** *n, pl* **ooftishes** *or* **oofs** [*ooftish* fr. Yiddish *uf tish* on (the) table; *oof* short for *ooftish*] *slang* : MONEY

oofy \ˈüfi\ *adj* -ER/-EST [*oof* + *-y*] *slang* : RICH, WEALTHY

oo gage \ˈ⸗ˌdəbəlˈō-\ *n, usu cap both Os* [so called fr. its being smaller than O gage] : a gage of track in model railroading in which the rails are approximately ¾ inch apart

oo·gamete \ˌōə+\ *n* [*o-* + *gamete*] : a female gamete; *specif* : a relatively large nonmotile gamete containing reserve material for use by the developing zygote that results when a sperm fuses with such a gamete

oog·a·mous \(ˈ)ōˈägəməs\ *adj* [*o-* + *-gamous*] **1** *of sexual reproduction* : characterized by fusion of a small actively motile male gamete and a large immobile female gamete — compare ANISOGAMOUS, HETEROGAMOUS, ISOGAMOUS **2** : having oogamous reproduction — **oog·a·my** \ōˈägəmē\ *n* -ES

oo·genesis \ˌōə+\ *n* [NL, fr. *o-* + *genesis*] : formation and maturation of the egg

oo·genetic \ˌ"+\ *adj* [*o-* + *genetic*] : of or relating to oogenesis

oog·e·ny \ōˈäjənē\ *n* -ES [*o-* + *-geny*] : OOGENESIS

oo·glea *or* **oo·gloea** \ˌōəˈglēə\ *n* -s [NL *o-* + *gloea*] : EGG CEMENT

oo·go·ni·al \ˌōəˈgōnēəl\ *adj* : of or relating to an oogonium

oo·go·ni·um \ˌōəˈgōnēəm\ *n* [NL, fr. *o-* + *gonium*] **1** : the female sexual organ in oogamous algae and fungi that corresponds to the archegonium of ferns and mosses but is unicellular in structure and lacks differentiation into neck and venter and that contains one or more eggs which after fertilization develop into oospores — compare ANTHERIDIUM **2** : one of the descendants of a primordial germ cell that give rise to oocytes

¹ooid \ˈōˌȯid\ *or* **ooi·dal** \(ˈ)ōˈȯidᵊl\ *adj* [Gk *ōioeidēs*, fr. *ōi-* o- + *-eidēs* -oid] : shaped like an egg

²ooid \ˈ"\ *n* -s [¹*ooid*] : one of the individual spherical concretionary bodies that characterize an oolite

ook *var of* OUK

oo·kinesis \ˌōə+\ *n, pl* **ookineses** [NL, fr. *o-* + *-kinesis*] : the nuclear phenomenon incidental to maturation and fertilization of an egg

oo·ki·nete \ˌōəˈkīˌnēt, -kəˈnēt, -kīˈnēt\ *n* -s [*o-* + Gk *kinētos* moving — more at KINETIC] : a motile zygote in various protozoans (as the malaria parasite)

oo·kinetic \ˌ"+\ *adj* : of or relating to ookinesis

oolachan *var of* EULACHON

oo·lem·ma \ˌōəˈlemə\ *n* -s [NL, fr. *o-* + Gk *lemma* rind, husk — more at LEMMA] : a membrane surrounding an egg: **a** : ZONA PELLUCIDA **b** : VITELLINE MEMBRANE

oo·lite \ˈōəˌlīt\ *n* -s [prob. fr. F *oolithe* (fr. *o-* + *-lithe* -lite), trans. of G *rogenstein*, lit., roe stone] : a rock consisting of small round grains that resemble the roe of fish, are cemented together, and consist of small concretions which usu. are of calcium carbonate forming a variety of limestone but sometimes are of silica or iron oxide — **oo·lit·ic** \ˌōəˈlid·ik\ *adj*

oolitic limestone *n* : calcareous oolite quarried chiefly for building purposes

oo·log·i·cal \ˌōəˈläjəkəl\ *also* **oo·log·ic** \-jik\ *adj* : of or relating to oology — **oo·log·i·cal·ly** \-jək(ə)lē\ *adv*

ool·o·gist \ōˈäləjəst\ *n* -s **1** : one specializing in oology **2** : a collector of birds' eggs

ool·o·gize \-ˌjīz\ *vi* -ED/-ING/-S **1** : to study oology **2** : to hunt for birds' nests and eggs

ool·o·gy \-jē\ *n* -ES [*o-* + *-logy*] : a branch of zoology that treats of eggs and esp. of the collection of birds' eggs and the study of their shape and coloration

oo·long \ˈüˌlȯŋ *also* -ˌläŋ\ *n* -s [Chin *wu¹ lung²*, lit., black dragon, fr. *wu¹* black + *lung²* dragon] : a tea that is partially fermented before drying and combines the characteristics of black and green teas

oom·an \ˈümən\ *dial var of* WOMAN

oo·man·cy \ˈōəˌman(t)sē\ *also* **oo·man·tia** \ˌōəˈmantēə\ *n, pl* **oomancies** *also* **oomantias** [*oomancy* fr. *o-* + *-mancy*; *oomantia*, NL, fr. *o-* + *-mantia* -mancy] : divination by means of eggs

oom·e·ter \ōˈämədˑə(r)\ *n* [*o-* + *-meter*] : an instrument for measuring eggs — **oo·met·ric** \ˌōəˈme·trik\ *adj* — **oom·e·try** \ōˈämə·trē\ *n* -ES

oomiak *also* **oomiack** *var of* UMIAK

oom·pah \ˈüm(ˌ)pä, ˈüm-\ *n* -s [imit.] : an insistent or monotonous bass accompaniment in a band or orchestra

oomph \ˈüm(p)f\ *n* -s [prob. imit. of an appreciative *mm* uttered by a man at the sight of an attractive woman] **1** : personal charm or magnetism : ATTRACTIVENESS, GLAMOUR ⟨a magician lends all his own ~ to the spell he is making —W.W.Howells⟩ ⟨the singer with the extra special and highly individual ~ in his voice —Margaret Hinxman⟩ ⟨had a lot of friends, but very little political ~ —Volta Torrey⟩ ⟨type of book . . . may not possess that curious ~ which spells "Sales Appeal" —R.E.Danielson⟩ **2** : SEX APPEAL ⟨a girl liberally endowed with ~ —P.G.Wodehouse⟩ **3** : SPIRIT, VITALITY, ENTHUSIASM, ANIMATION ⟨sings with her accustomed ~ two arias —Roland Gelatt⟩ ⟨lack of meat is sapping British ~ needed to keep the export drive in high gear —*Wall Street Jour.*⟩

oo·mycete \ˌōə+\ *n* -s [NL *Oomycetes*] : a fungus of the subclass Oomycetes

oo·my·ce·tes \ˌōəˌmīˈsēd·ēz\ *n pl, cap* [NL, fr. *o-* + *-mycetes*] : a subclass of parasitic or saprophytic fungi (class Phycomycetes) that includes water molds, white rusts, and downy mildews and that is distinguished from the Zygomycetes by having the gametangia usu. differentiated into antheridia and oogonia and by producing oospores as a result of the sexual process — **oo·my·ce·tous** \-d·əs\ *adj*

oo·my·ceti·dae \ˌōəˌmīˈsēd·əˌdē, -sed-\ [NL, fr. *Oomycetes* + *-idae*] *syn of* OOMYCETES

¹oon \ˈün\ *dial Brit var of* OVEN

²oon \ˈ"\ *dial Brit var of* ONE

oo·nop·i·dae \ˌōəˈnäpəˌdē\ *n pl, cap* [NL, fr. *Oonops*, type genus (irreg. fr. Gk *ōion* egg + NL *-ops*) + *-idae* — more at EGG] : a family of small hunting spiders (suborder Dipneumonomorphae) having six eyes or none and six spinnerets

oons \ˈünz\ *interj* [alter. of *wounds*, fr. pl. of *wound*, n.] — used as a mild oath

¹oont \ˈünt\ *dial Eng var of* WANT

²oont \ˈ"\ *n* -s [Hindi *ūt*, fr. Skt *uṣṭra*] *India* : CAMEL

¹oop \ˈüp\ *dial var of* UP

²oop \ˈüp\ *vt* -ED/-ING/-S [origin unknown] *Scot* : BIND, UNITE

oo·pak *also* **oo·pack** \ˈüˌpak\ *n* -s [fr. *Hupeh*, province in east central China] : any of several black teas grown in the Hupeh province of China

ooph·a·gous \(ˈ)ōˈäfəgəs\ *adj* [*o-* + *-phagous*] : living or feeding on eggs — used of insects or reptiles

oophor- *or* **oophoro-** *comb form* [NL *oophoron*] : ovary : ovarian ⟨*oophor*ectomy⟩ ⟨*oophoro*tomy⟩

oo·phore \ˈōəˌfō(ə)r\ *n* -s [*o-* + *-phore*] : OOPHYTE — **oo·pho·ric** \ˌōəˈfȯrik\ *adj*

oo·pho·rec·to·mize \ˌōəfəˈrektəˌmīz\ *vt* -ED/-ING/-S [*oophorectomy* + *-ize*] : OVARIECTOMIZE

oo·pho·rec·to·my \-ˌmē\ *n* -ES [ISV *oophor-* + *-ectomy*] : OVARIECTOMY

oo·pho·ri·tis \ˌōəfəˈrīd·əs\ *n* -ES [NL, fr. *oophor-* + *-itis*] : inflammation of one or both ovaries : OVARITIS

ooph·o·ron \ōˈäfəˌrän\ *n* -s [NL, fr. *o-* + Gk *-phoron* -phore] : OVARY

oo·phyte \ˈōəˌfīt\ *n* -s [*o-* + *-phyte*] : the sexual generation in the life cycle of an archegoniate plant (as a moss, fern, liverwort) : the stage in which sexual organs are developed — compare GAMETOPHYTE, SPOROPHYTE — **oo·phyt·ic** \ˌōəˈfid·ik\ *adj*

oo·plasm \ˈōəˌplazəm\ *n* -s [*o-* + *-plasm*] : the cytoplasm of an egg — **oo·plas·mic** \ˌōəˈplazmik\ *adj*

oo·plast \ˈōəˌplast\ *n* -s [*o-* + *-plast*] : OOSPHERE

oo·pod \ˈōəˌpäd\ *n, pl* **oop·o·da** \ōˈäpədə\ [*o-* + *pod-*] : any of the pieces composing the ovipositor or sting of an insect — **oop·o·dal** \(ˈ)ōˈäpədᵊl\ *adj*

oo·porphyrin \ˌōə+\ *n* [ISV *o-* + *porphyrin*] : a pale brown pigment in eggshells (as of the domestic hen)

oops \ˈ(w)ü(ə)p(s) *also* ˈwə(-ə)p(s) *or* ˈ(w)üp(s) *or* ˈ(w)ōp\ *interj* [origin unknown] — used typically to express mild apology, surprise, or dismay (as when one drops an object or makes a faux pas)

oo·pu·hue \ˌōˌōpəˈhüē\ *n* -s [Hawaiian *ʻoʻopu-hue*, fr. *ʻoʻopu* gobioid fish + *hue* gourd] *Hawaii* : GLOBEFISH

oor \(ˈ)ür\ *chiefly Scot var of* OUR

oo·ra·li *or* **u·ra·li** \üˈrälē\ *n* -s [Carib *urali, urari, kurari*] : CURARE

oorial *var of* URIAL

oorie *var of* OURIE

oo·scope \ˈōəˌskōp\ *n* [*o-* + *-scope*] : an instrument for viewing the interior of an egg

oos·co·py \ōˈäskəpē\ *n* -ES [*o-* + *-scopy*] : use of an ooscope; *also* : OOMANCY

oo·some \ˈōəˌsōm\ *n* -s [ISV *o-* + *-some*; orig. formed as It *oosoma*] : a disk-shaped mass of protoplasm near the posterior pole of an insect egg

oo·sorp·tion \ˌōəˈsȯrpshən\ *n* -s [*o-* + *resorption*] : resorption of ripe or developing eggs that constitutes a physiological response of a parasitic hymenopteran to the absence of the appropriate host — **oo·sorp·tive** \-ptiv\ *adj*

oo·sperm \ˈōəˌspərm\ *n* [*o-* + *sperm*] : a fertilized egg : ZYGOTE, OOSPORE

oo·sphere \-ˌsfi(ə)r\ *n* [ISV *o-* + *sphere*] : an unfertilized egg : a female gamete that is fully mature and ready for fertilization : OVUM 1 a — used esp. of lower plants

oos·po·ra \ōˈäspərə\ *n, cap* [NL, fr. *o-* + *-spora*] : a genus of imperfect fungi (order Moniliales) comprising parasitic and saprophytic forms with short hyphae, sparse mycelium, and usu. globose conidia — see ACHORION; compare OIDIUM

oo·spore \ˈōəˌspō(ə)r\ *n* [ISV *o-* + *spore*] : ZYGOTE; *esp* : a resting spore produced by heterogamous fertilization that ultimately produces the sporophytic generation of a plant — compare ZYGOSPORE — **oo·spo·ric** \ˌōəˈspōrik\ *adj* — **oospo·rous** \ˌōəˈspōrəs, (ˈ)ōˈäspərəs\ *adj*

oo·spor·if·er·ous \ˌōəˌspōrˈif(ə)rəs\ *adj* [*oospore* + *-iferous*] : bearing or producing oospores

oos·te·gite \ōˈästəˌjīt\ *n* -s [*o-* + *-stegite*] : a platelike expansion of the basal segment of a thoracic appendage in many crustaceans that helps to form a receptacle for the eggs — **oos·te·git·ic** \(ˌ)ōˌästəˈjid·ik\ *adj*

oos·te·go·pod \ōˈästəgəˌpäd\ *n* -s [*oostegite* + *-o-* + *-pod*] : a modified thoracic leg bearing an oostegite in a crustacean

oot \ˈüt\ *chiefly Scot var of* OUT

oo·the·ca \ˌōəˈthēkə\ *n, pl* **oothe·cae** \-ēˌ(ˌ)sē\ [NL, fr. *o-* + *-theca*] : a firm-walled and distinctive egg case (as of many mollusks or of a cockroach) — **oo·the·cal** \ˌōəˈthēkəl\ *adj*

oo·tid \ˈōəˌtid\ *n* -s [irreg. (influenced by *spermatid*) fr. *o-* + *-id*] : an egg cell after meiosis — compare SPERMATID

oo·type \ˈōəˌtīp\ *n* -s [*o-* + *-type*] : the part of the oviduct of most flatworms in which the eggs are furnished with a shell

¹ooze \ˈüz\ *n* -s [ME *wose*, fr. OE *wāse* mud, mire; akin to ON *veisa* slime, stagnant water, L *virus* slimy liquid, poison — more at VIRUS] **1** : a soft deposit on the bottom of a body of water ⟨to tread the ~ of the salt deep —Shak.⟩: as **a** : soft mud or slime typically in the bed of a river or estuary : earth so wet as to flow gently or easily yield to pressure **b** : a soft deposit that resembles mud, covers large areas of the ocean bottom, and is composed largely or mainly of the shells or other hard parts of minute organisms (as foraminiferans, radiolarians, and diatoms) **2** : a stretch or piece of muddy ground : a marsh or bog that results from the flow of a spring, stream, or brooklet **3** *archaic* : SEAWEED

²ooze \ˈ"\ *n* -s [ME *wose*, fr. OE *wōs*] **1** : JUICE, SAP ⟨dyed . . . threads in the ~ she wrung from herbs —George McMillan⟩ **2 a** : a decoction of vegetable material used for tanning leather : tanning liquor **b** : OOZE LEATHER **3** : the action of oozing : gentle flow ⟨bleeding in the form of a profuse ~ from surgical wounds —*Anesthesia Digest*⟩ **4** : something that oozes : a slow stream

³ooze \ˈ"\ *vb* -ED/-ING/-S [ME *wosen*, fr. *wose* ooze (juice)] *vi* **1** : to pass slowly or in small amounts through the pores or small openings of a body : flow slowly through interstices ⟨blood appears to have *oozed* from a varicose vein —Morris Fishbein⟩ ⟨water *oozed* from the ground —Harry Gilroy⟩ ⟨sweet potatoes baked in the peeling until the juice ~s out —*Amer. Guide Series: N.C.*⟩ ⟨a weak tear *oozed* from each eye —Agnes S. Turnbull⟩ **2 a** : to pass through or as if through small openings or crevices ⟨we could hear the wind . . . ~ through the briar thickets —J.H.Stuart⟩ ⟨a voice ~s from a slit of a door —Francis Aldor⟩ ⟨the clatter of typewriters *oozed* from every transom —Herbert Hoover⟩ **b** : to move slowly or imperceptibly ⟨what they skim off ~s across the floor —R.A.W.Hughes⟩ ⟨the crowd began to ~ forward —Bruce Marshall⟩ **3 a** : to exude moisture; *specif* : to exude blood **b** : to exude something in a way suggestive of the emitting of moisture — usu. used with *with* ⟨a writing that ~s with hostility⟩ ⟨a person *oozing* with good cheer⟩ **4** : to escape slowly and quietly — often used with *out* or *away* ⟨courage *oozing* out at his finger tips —A.T.Weaver⟩ ⟨satisfaction would ~ away —*Times Lit. Supp.*⟩ ⟨failure *oozed* out of the very pores of his skin —Ellen Glasgow⟩ ~ *vt* **1** : to emit or give out slowly (as air or liquid) ⟨thick steaks *oozing* blood —Marcia Davenport⟩ **2** : to exude or give off in a way suggestive of the emitting of moisture ⟨popular songs which ~ optimism —J.T.Farrell⟩ ⟨his voice *oozing* sarcasm —Walter Goodman⟩ ⟨*oozing* charm from every pore —*Irish Digest*⟩ **syn** see EMIT

ooze leather *n* [²*ooze*] : leather usu. made from calfskins by the vegetable tanning process and having a soft sueded finish on the flesh side

oo·zooid \ˌōə+\ *n* -s [*o-* + *zooid*] : a sexually produced compound tunicate larva that by budding gives rise to blastozooids

oozy \ˈüzē, -zi\ *adj* -ER/-EST [ME *wosie*, fr. *wose* ooze, mud + *-ie* -y] **1** : containing or composed of ooze : resembling ooze : MUDDY, MIRY **2** [³*ooze* + *-y*] : exuding moisture : damp with exuded or deposited moisture : SLIMY

op *abbr* **1** opera **2** operation; operative; operator **3** opposite **4** opus

OP *abbr* **1** observation plane **2** observation post **3** old prices **4** open policy **5** opposite prompt; opposite prompter **6** out of print **7** outpost **8** overprint **9** overproof

opa·cate \ōˈpāˌkāt, ˈōpəˌk-\ *vt* -ED/-ING/-S [L *opacatus*, past part. of *opacare* to shade, darken, fr. *opacus* shaded, dark — more at OPAQUE] : to make opaque : DARKEN, DIM

opaci·fi·ca·tion \ōˌpasəfəˈkāshən, ōˌpakə-\ *n* -s [fr. *opacify*, after such pairs as E *amplify*: *amplification*] : an act or the process of becoming or rendering opaque ⟨~ of the cornea following ulceration⟩ ⟨~ of the bile passages for roentgenographic examination⟩

opaci·fi·er \⸗ˈ⸗⸗ˌfī(ə)r\ *n* -s : a constituent or additive (as of an enamel, a paint, a glass) that tends to opacify the system of which it is a part

opaci·fy \-ˌfī\ *vb* -ED/-ING/-ES [ISV *opaci-* (fr. L *opacus*) + *-fy*] *vt* : to cause (as glass or enamel) to become opaque ~ *vi* : to become opaque ⟨~*ing* gradually in the heat of the furnace⟩

opa·cim·e·ter \ˌōpəˈsimədˑə(r)\ *n* [ISV *opaci-* + *-meter*] : an instrument (as a turbidimeter or a nephelometer) for measuring opacity

opac·i·ty \ōˈpasəd·ē, -sətē, -i\ *n* -ES [F *opacité*, fr. L *opacitat-, opacitas*, fr. *opacus* shaded, dark + *-itat-, -itas* -ity] **1** : the quality or state or an instance of being shaded or obscure : DARKNESS, OBSCURITY **2 a** : the quality or state of a body that renders it impervious to the rays of light : lack of transparency or translucency **b** : degree of nontransparency ⟨titanium dioxide has the greatest ~ and tinctorial strength of all white pigments —Andries Voet⟩ **c** : the property of a photographic image that causes partial absorption of rays of light **d** : the capacity of matter to obstruct by absorption or reflection the transmission of forms of radiant energy in addition to light (as radio waves, infrared radiation, sound) ⟨the ~ to ultrasound of porous media —A.B.Wood⟩; *also* : a measure of this capacity : the reciprocal of the transmissivity **3 a** : obscurity of sense : lack of clearness : UNINTELLIGIBLENESS **b** : mental dimness or obtuseness : DULLNESS **4** : an opaque spot on a normally transparent structure (as the cornea or lens of the eye)

opa·cous \ōˈpākəs\ *adj* [L *opacus*] *archaic* : OPAQUE

opah \ˈōpə\ *n* -s [Ibo *úbà*] : a large marine elliptical fish (*Lampris regius* syn. *L. luna*) that is nearly cosmopolitan in warm and temperate seas and that has brilliant colors and rich oily red flesh

opa·ka·pa·ka \ˌōpəkəˈpäkə\ *n* -s [Hawaiian *ʻōpakapaka*] : any of several brightly colored chiefly Hawaiian snappers of the genus *Pristipomoides* including some that are important food fishes

opal \ˈōpəl\ *n* -s *often attrib* [L *opalus*, fr. Skt *upala* stone, jewel, upper millstone; perh. akin to Skt *upari* over — more at OVER] **1** : a mineral $SiO_2.nH_2O$ that is a hydrated amorphous silica softer and less dense than quartz and typically with definite and often marked iridescent play of colors — see BLACK OPAL, HARLEQUIN OPAL **2 a** : OPAL GLASS **b** : OPALINE

opal blue *n* **1** : a grayish blue that is redder and paler than electric, greener and paler than copenhagen, and redder and lighter than Gobelin **2** : NATIONAL BLUE

opal·esce \ˌōpəˈles\ *vi* -ED/-ING/-S [back-formation fr. *opalescence* & *opalescent*] : to emit or exhibit a play of colors like those of an opal

opal·es·cence \ˌōpəˈlesᵊn(t)s\ *n* -s [*opal* + *-escence*] : the quality or state of being opalescent ⟨that mother-of-pearl ~ which shimmers in the hollowness of certain seashells —J.C. Powys⟩

opal·es·cent \ˌōpəˈlesᵊnt\ *adj* [*opal* + *-escent*] **1** : reflecting an iridescent light : having a milky iridescence **2** : having a colored smooth surface that gives the effect of cloudiness and diffusion due to the intentional presence of fissures, striae, and bubbles ⟨~ glass⟩

opal·es·cent·ly *adv* : as if opalescent : so as to appear opalescent

opal·esque \ˌōpəˈlesk\ *adj* [*opal* + *-esque*] : suggesting opal : OPALESCENT

opaleye \ˈ⸗⸗ˌ⸗\ *n* [*opal* + *eye*] : any of several fishes of the family Girellidae; *esp* : a small green shorefish (*Girella nigricans*) of the California coast that feeds chiefly on seaweeds and is a minor food fish — called also *greenfish*

opal glass *n* : a translucent or opaque glass; *esp* : a milky white glass that is prepared by adding impurities (as fluorine compounds) which disperse as crystallites within the matrix of glass and that is used esp. for ornamental pressed glass and for diffusing light without serious loss of lighting efficiency — compare MILK GLASS

opal gray *n* : a reddish gray that is duller and slightly yellower than evenglow and yellower and duller than mist gray

opa·li·na \ˌōpəˈlīnə, -lēnə\ *n, cap* [NL, fr. L *opalus* opal + NL *-ina*] : a genus (the type of the family Opalinidae) of large flattened multinucleate protociliates that are endozoic in the rectum of amphibians

¹opal·ine \ˈōpəˌlīn, -lēn\ *adj* [*opal* + *-ine*] : resembling opal esp. in appearance : OPALESCENT

²opal·ine \ˈōpəˌlēn\ *n* -s **1** : any of several minerals related to or resembling opal **2 a** : A French decorative opalescent glassware developed in the late 18th century **b** : MILK GLASS **3** : an opaline color or surface

opaline green *n* : a very light green

¹opa·linid \ˌōpəˈlinəd, -lēn-,-lin-\ *adj* [NL *Opalinidae*, family of protociliates, fr. *Opalina*, type genus + *-idae*] : of or relating to the genus *Opalina* or the family Opalinidae

²opalinid \ˈ"\ *n* -s [NL *Opalinidae*] : PROTOCILIATE

opal·iza·tion \ˌōpələ'zāshən, -ˌlī'z-\ *n* -s **:** the process of opalizing

opal·ize \'ōpəˌlīz\ *vt* -ED/-ING/-S **1 :** to replace with or convert into opal ⟨*opalized* trunks of trees, most of them of prehistoric species —*Nat'l Geographic*⟩ **2 :** to make opalescent ⟨~ glass⟩

opal lamp *n* **:** an incandescent electric lamp with a bulb of opal glass

opal matrix *n* **:** a matrix of opal

opal·oid \'ōpəˌlȯid\ *adj* [*opal* + *-oid*] **:** milky and translucent **:** OPALINE

¹opaque \(')ō¦pāk\ *adj, sometimes* -ER/-EST [alter. (influenced by F *opaque*) of earlier *opake*, fr. L *opacus* shaded, dark, perh. fr. *op-*, *ob* to, before — more at EPI-] **1** *archaic* **:** lacking illumination **2 :** neither reflecting nor emitting light — not in current technical use **3 a :** impervious to the rays of visible light **:** not transparent or translucent ⟨his eyes were light, large, and bright, but it was that kind of brightness which belongs to an ~, and not to a transparent body —Anthony Trollope⟩ **b :** impervious to forms of radiant energy other than visible light (as infrared radiation or radio waves) ⟨organic compounds containing iodine or bromine are also ~ to roentgen rays —C.H.Thienes⟩ **4 a :** hard to understand, solve, or explain **:** not simple, clear, or lucid ⟨how ~ and incredible the past seems to us —L.P.Smith⟩ **b :** impervious to reason **:** STUPID, DULL, DENSE ⟨too ~ to recognize the insult⟩ **syn** see DARK

²opaque \"\ *n* -s **:** something that is opaque **:** an opaque medium or space: as **a :** an opaque paint or other preparation for blocking out portions of a photographic negative or print **b :** an opaque photographic print — contrasted with *transparency*

³opaque \"\ *vt* -ED/-ING/-S **1 :** to make opaque **2 :** to apply opaque to (as parts of a photographic negative or positive)

opaque·ly *adv* **:** in an opaque manner

opaque·ness \ō'pāknəs\ *n* -ES **:** the quality or state of being opaque

opaque projector *n* **:** a projector for projection by reflected light of an image of an opaque object or of a picture or other graphic matter on an opaque support

opaqu·er \ō'pākə(r)\ *n* -s **:** a worker who applies photographic opaque

opa·ta \ō'pād·ə\ *n, pl* **opata** *or* **opatas** *usu cap* [Pima, lit., hostile people] **1 a :** a Taracahitian people or group of peoples of the northeastern part of the state of Sonora, Mexico **b :** a member of such people or group of peoples **2 :** the language of the Opata people

op cit *abbr* opere citato; opus citatum

¹ope \'ōp\ *adj* [ME, alter. of ¹*open*] **:** OPEN

²ope \"\ *vb* -ED/-ING/-S [ME *open*, alter. of *openen* to open] **:** OPEN

³ope \"\ *n* -s [¹*ope*] **1** *archaic* **a :** APERTURE, OPENING **b :** OPPORTUNITY **2** *dial chiefly Eng* **:** a narrow covered passage between houses

-ope \ˌōp\ *n comb form* -s [F, fr. LL *-op-*, *-ops* having (such) eyes, fr. Gk *ōp-*, *ōps* eye, face — more at EYE] **:** one having eyes with a (specified) defect ⟨hypermetr*ope*⟩

opeg·ra·pha \ō'pegrəfə\ *n, cap* [NL, fr. Gk *opē* hole, opening (akin to Gk *ōp-*, *ōps*) + *graphē* writing, fr. *graphein* to write — more at CARVE] **:** a genus of crustaceous lichens occurring chiefly on bark and forming markings like writing or hieroglyphics

opei·do·scope \ō'pīdəˌskōp\ *n* [Gk *opa* (acc.) voice + *eidos* form + E *-scope* — more at VOICE, IDOL] **:** an instrument consisting essentially of a tube across one end of which is stretched a thin flexible membrane bearing a small mirror and used for exhibiting upon a screen by rays reflected from the mirror vibratory motions caused by sounds

ope·let \'ōplət\ *n* -s [¹*ope* + *-let*] **:** a bright-colored European actinian (*Anemonia sulcata*) with permanently expanded tentacles

ope·lu \'ōpəˌlü\ *n* -s [Hawaiian *'ōpelu*] **1** *Hawaii* **:** JAPANESE MACKEREL **2** *Hawaii* **:** a common Pacific mackerel scad (*Decapterus sanctae-helenae*) much used as bait

¹open \'ōpən, *esp before consonants* -pᵊm\ *adj* **opener** \-p(ə)nə(r)\ **openest** \-p(ə)nəst\ [ME, fr. OE; akin to OHG *offan* open, ON *opinn*; all fr. a prehistoric NGmc-WGmc past part. of a verb derived from the root of OE *ūp* up] **1 :** so arranged or governed as to permit ingress, egress, or passage: as **a :** having no enclosing or confining barrier **:** free from fences, boundaries, or other restrictive margins ⟨an ~ village⟩ ⟨the ~ moor⟩ **b** (1) **:** adjusted in a position that permits passage **:** not shut or fast ⟨an ~ door⟩ ⟨these ~ gates⟩ (2) **:** having a movable barrier so adjusted ⟨the house is ~⟩ **c** (1) **:** not stopped by a finger ⟨the four ~ strings of a violin⟩ (2) **:** unstopped by the hand or by a mute ⟨~ horn⟩ (3) **:** produced by an open string or on a wind instrument by the lip without the use of slides, valves, or keys ⟨~ tone or note⟩ (4) **:** having clarity and resonance unimpaired by undue tension or constriction of the throat ⟨an ~ vocal tone⟩ **2 a :** completely free from concealment **:** exposed to general or particular perception or knowledge ⟨now lay ~ all your plans⟩ ⟨an ~ ballot⟩ ⟨~ total war⟩ **b :** free from reserve or pretense **:** natural, forthright, and free **:** not concealing or intended to conceal one's thoughts or actions ⟨very ~ about his plans⟩ ⟨~ and uninhibited in speech⟩ ⟨a very ~ manner⟩ **3 a :** having no roof, lid, or other covering ⟨an ~ boat⟩ **b :** having no protective or concealing cover **:** BARE, NAKED ⟨~ wiring⟩ ⟨laying the arm ~ to the bone⟩ **c** (1) *obs, of the face* **:** UNCOVERED, UNABASHED (2) **:** not covered with wool or enshrouding hair ⟨a ewe with an ~ face⟩ **d :** lacking some immaterial protection **:** LIABLE, SUBJECT ⟨~ to infection⟩ ⟨~ to challenge⟩ **e** (1) **:** not covered, enclosed, or scabbed over ⟨an ~ lesion⟩ ⟨an ~ running ulcer⟩ (2) **:** not involving or encouraging a covering (as by bandages or overgrowth of tissue) or enclosure ⟨~ treatment of burns⟩ (3) **:** shedding the infective agent to the exterior ⟨~ tuberculosis⟩ **f** (1) **:** not completely enclosed by defining lines ⟨an ~ drawing⟩ (2) **:** not defined by a figure or outline — used in the phrase *open color* **g** (1) **:** lacking covers or parts that restrict ventilation **:** not enclosed ⟨an ~ motor⟩ (2) **:** FREE 13e **h :** using a plain language text in conjunction with code or cipher: as (1) **:** using a concealment cipher (2) **:** using a jargon code **4 a :** requiring no special status, identification, or permit for entry or participation **:** generally available or known ⟨this house is ~ to all that need help⟩ ⟨an ~ Communion service⟩ ⟨an ~ secret⟩ **b :** not restricted to a particular group or category of participants ⟨~ to the public⟩ ⟨~ bowling⟩ **c :** enterable by both amateur and professional contestants ⟨an ~ golf tournament⟩ **d :** enterable by competitors of different classes ⟨~ to dogs of all breeds⟩ **5 :** fit to be traveled over or through **:** presenting no serious obstacle to passage or view: as **a :** free from hampering obstructions ⟨an ~ stretch of road⟩ **b :** free from woods, buildings, or large rocks ⟨an ~ field⟩ ⟨~ country⟩ **c :** presenting no surface impediment (as ice) or underwater hazard (as shoals) to the passage of a boat **d** (1) **:** unobstructed by congestion ⟨~ sinuses⟩ (2) **:** not constipated ⟨~ bowels⟩ **e** (1) **:** relatively free from snow and cold ⟨~ winter⟩ (2) **:** not foggy or misty ⟨as the sun warmed the air patches of ~ water began to appear⟩ (3) **:** not frozen solid ⟨an ~ harbor⟩ **6 a** *obs* **:** lying or sailing in full view **b :** having a visible opening between ⟨steer so as to keep the two spires ~⟩ **7 a :** spread out **:** UNFOLDED **:** having the parts or surfaces laid back in an expanded position **:** not drawn together, folded, or contracted ⟨an ~ letter⟩ ⟨left the book ~⟩ ⟨an ~ rose⟩ **b :** removed from a carcass by splitting down the mid-ventral line and along the inner surfaces of each limb and cured and dressed flat ⟨an ~ hide⟩ **8 a** *obs* **:** uttered with the mouth open **b** (1) *of a vowel* **:** LOW 1a (5) (2) *of one of two vowels constituting a pair because similar in articulation or orthography or in both* **:** formed with the tongue in a lower position ⟨Italian has an ~ *e*⟩ (3) **:** characterized by moderate lip-rounding (4) *of a consonant* **:** formed with the articulating organs narrowed without contact or with loose contact (as \s\ or \k̟\) **:** CONTINUANT, SPIRANT, FRICATIVE — contrasted with *stopped* **9 a** (1) **:** available to use **:** ACCESSIBLE, SUITABLE, USABLE **:** free and unoccupied ⟨keep an hour ~ on Friday⟩ ⟨the invitation is still ~⟩ ⟨there are only two courses ~ to us⟩ (2) **:** not now pregnant ⟨an ~ heifer⟩ **b :** available for consideration or decision **:** adjustable according to the requirements of circumstances **:** not finally closed or determined ⟨considered it an ~ question⟩ **c :** kept available for future custom ⟨an ~ pattern⟩ ⟨~ stocks⟩ **d :** remaining available for use or filling until canceled ⟨an ~ order for four more⟩ **:** OPERATIVE **:** not terminated or liquidated **e :** legally available for hunting, fishing, and similar sports ⟨an ~ season on deer⟩ ⟨an ~ brook⟩ **f :** unoccupied and undefended by military forces and divested of any military installation and when so proclaimed and acknowledged immune under international law from enemy bombardment ⟨an ~ city⟩ **10 :** characterized by ready accessibility and usu. cooperative attitude: as **a :** generous in giving **b :** willing to hear and consider or to accept and deal with **:** RESPONSIVE ⟨~ to suggestion⟩ ⟨~ to an offer⟩ **c :** permitting the registration of a high-grade animal conforming to breed type as well as of an animal having both sire and dam registered ⟨an ~ studbook⟩ **d :** accessible to the influx of new factors (as new members and ideas or foreign goods) ⟨an ~ class system⟩ ⟨an ~ market⟩ **e :** tolerant of internal change (as by social mobility, reforms, and the development of new ideas, values, and customs) and permissive of diversity in social, religious, and political institutions ⟨an ~ society⟩ **11 :** having openings, interruptions, interstices, or spaces ⟨~ banks⟩ ⟨*open*-grained lumber⟩: as **a :** light, porous, and friable so as to be easily tilled and receptive to water infiltration ⟨~ soil⟩ **b :** sparsely distributed **:** SCATTERED ⟨~ population⟩ **c** (1) **:** having relatively wide spacing between words or lines ⟨~ type⟩ ⟨~ printed matter⟩ (2) **:** having each leaf separate and distinct from the others after the bolts are opened or trimmed off ⟨the ~ signatures of a book⟩ **d :** having the warp threads of a shed always divided into two sections and never coming together as one section **e :** having cambium between the xylem and phloem portions — used of a vascular bundle **f** (1) **:** widely apart — used of dancers or the position of their feet (2) **:** having the participants well separated — used of a dance or dance figure **g :** characterized by open-chain structure **h :** GRANULAR, HARD ⟨soap in an ~ condition⟩ — used in soap manufacturing **12 :** ready to operate **:** actively functioning **:** ACTIVE ⟨the store is ~ from 9 to 5⟩ ⟨an ~ microphone⟩ **13 a** (1) **:** characterized by lack of effective control or regulation of various commercial enterprises (as amusements) ⟨notorious as an ~ town⟩ (2) **:** not repressed by legal controls ⟨~ gambling⟩ **b :** using a minimum of physical restrictions and custodial restraints upon the freedom of movement of inmates ⟨an ~ prison⟩ **c :** not yielding to usu. controlling factors **:** free from checking or hampering restraints ⟨an ~ economy⟩ ⟨faced with ~ inflation⟩ **d :** relatively unguarded by opponents in a sports competition ⟨~ ice⟩ ⟨~ court⟩ **14** *of an expression in logic* **:** containing one or more free variables **15 :** not crossed ⟨an ~ pulley belt⟩ ⟨~ eccentric rods⟩ **16 :** characterized by a free development of chess pieces in front of the pawns **17 a :** having been opened by a first ante, bet, or bid ⟨an ~ pot in poker⟩ ⟨the bidding is ~⟩ **b** (1) **:** having cards properly exposed ⟨the dummy is the ~ hand⟩ (2) **:** played or to be played with cards exposed **c :** interrupted or incomplete by a break in card sequence ⟨an ~ straight⟩ **18 a** *of punctuation* **:** characterized by omission of commas where possible without ambiguity **b** *of the punctuation of a letter* **:** characterized by the omission of punctuation marks at the end of the lines of the heading and after the complimentary close — opposed to *close* **syn** see FRANK, LIABLE

²open \"\ *vb* **opened** \-pənd,-pᵊmd\ **opened** \"\ **opening** \-p(ə)niŋ, -pniŋ\ **opens** \-pənz,-pᵊmz\ [ME *openen*, fr. OE *openian*; akin to OHG *offanōn* to open, ON *opna*; all fr. a prehistoric NGmc-WGmc denominative fr. the root of OE ¹*open*] *vt* **1 a :** to move (as a door or lid) from its shut position ⟨~ the windows⟩ ⟨slowly ~*ed* her eyelids⟩ ⟨~ a switch⟩ **b :** to make available for entry or passage by turning back (as a barrier), removing (as a cover), or clearing away (as an obstruction) ⟨the janitor ~*s* the building at 7 o'clock⟩ ⟨~*ing* the road after the flood⟩ ⟨~ your heart to mercy⟩: as (1) **:** to free (a body passage) of an occluding agent ⟨used cathartics to ~ the bowels⟩ ⟨an inhalator for ~*ing* congested nasal passages⟩ (2) **:** to make available for or active in a regular function ⟨plan to ~ a new store soon⟩ ⟨at what time do you ~ your office⟩; *also* **:** to make accessible for a particular purpose ⟨~*ed* new land for settlement⟩ (3) **:** to declare (as a public building or park) to be open to the public usu. by a formal ceremony **2 a :** to expose to view **:** DISCLOSE, REVEAL, UNBOSOM **b** *archaic* **:** INTERPRET, EXPOUND **c :** to make more discerning or responsive **:** ENLIGHTEN **d :** to bring into view or come in sight of by changing position so as to remove an intervening object from the line of sight ⟨sailed on until we ~*ed* a bay⟩ **3 a :** to make one or more openings in **:** cut or break into ⟨~*ed* the boil⟩ ⟨planned to ~ the tombs of the ancient kings⟩ **b :** to loosen and make less compact usu. by separating the constituent parts ⟨~ the soil by cultivating⟩ ⟨~*ed* the matted wool by shaking vigorously⟩ **c :** to salt out — used in soap manufacturing **4 :** to spread out **:** UNFOLD, UNROLL, EXTEND ⟨the rose ~*s* its dewy petals⟩ ⟨~*ed* the book near the middle⟩ **5 a :** to enter upon **:** BEGIN ⟨~*ed* the meeting⟩ ⟨will ~ his campaign soon⟩ **b** (1) **:** to make the statement by which the trial of (a case) is begun and put before the court (2) **:** to be the first to speak in summing up or arguing (a case) **c :** to commence action in a card game by making (a first bid), putting a first bet in (the pot), or playing (a specified card or suit) as first lead **6 :** to restore or recall (as an order, rule, judgment) from a finally determined state to a state in which the parties are free to prosecute or oppose by further legal proceedings **7 :** to shift the feet so as to assume (an open stance) in golf or batting ~ *vi* **1 a :** to become open **:** UNCLOSE ⟨the door ~*ed* slowly⟩ **b :** to open a door or other barrier or make open a closed place usu. so as to give admittance ⟨~ in the name of the law⟩ **c :** to have the doors opened for admittance of the public ⟨the store ~*s* at 9⟩ **2 a :** to spread out **:** EXPAND ⟨the buds are beginning to ~⟩ **b :** to separate or come apart usu. with an effect of spreading out ⟨the wound ~*ed* under the strain⟩ ⟨the book ~*ed* to my place⟩ **c :** to expand into view **:** become disclosed **:** spread out in the sight esp. so that elements come to be seen as distinct ⟨a lovely vista ~*ed* before us⟩ **3 :** to become enlightened or responsive ⟨my heart ~*s* to your words⟩ **4 a :** to give access ⟨an arch ~*s* into the dining room⟩ **b :** to have an opening, passage, or outlet ⟨all the rooms ~ onto a long hall⟩ **c :** to open in an indicated direction ⟨the door ~*s* toward the hall⟩ **5 :** to bark on first finding scent **:** give tongue to a scent trail ⟨the dog ~*ed* almost at once⟩ **6 :** to bare or make plain one's mind, feelings, or knowledge by speaking **:** speak out **:** be open in speech ⟨finally ~*ed* freely on the subject⟩ **7 a :** to begin action **:** commence in some course or activity ⟨the artillery ~*ed* on the enemy⟩ ⟨the stock ~*ed* at par⟩ **b :** to commence by a first incident (as a performance of a drama, a concert, or a day's hunting) ⟨the opera season ~*s* Friday⟩ **c :** to make a bet, bid, or lead in commencing a round or hand of a card game — **open one's eyes 1 :** to cause one to stare with wonder or amazement **2 :** to awaken one to a knowledge or realization of something usu. unpleasant — **open one's heart 1 :** to disclose one's intimate thoughts or feelings **2 :** to behave with generosity — **open one's mouth 1 :** to begin speaking **2 :** to give power of speech **:** induce to speak (as by bribery) **3 :** to speak indiscreetly or disclose confidential matters in speech — **open one's shoulders** *cricket* **:** to use the long handle in batting — **open ranks :** to execute a movement in infantry drill in which the third rank stands fast and the others take a varying number of steps forward or back from it — **open the books :** to resume use of corporation or other record books after temporary closing: as **a :** to reopen stock transfer books after they have been closed because of a forthcoming stockholders' meeting or other purpose **b :** to begin to accept subscriptions to a new offering ⟨*the books will be opened* for the new Treasury issue⟩

³open \"\ *adv* [ME, fr. ¹*open*] **:** in an open manner

⁴open \"\ *n* -s [ME, in sense 1 fr. *openen* to open; in other senses fr. ¹*open*] **1 :** OPENING **2 :** open and unobstructed space: as **a :** land without trees, buildings, or obstructions ⟨finally broke out of the forest into the ~⟩ **b :** countryside free from hedges or fences **c** (1) **:** cultivated land as distinguished from some protected place (as a greenhouse) ⟨grapes grown in the ~ have a distinctive tang⟩ (2) **:** outdoors as distinguished from inside ⟨spent the day in the ~⟩ **d :** open water esp. of the ocean or a lake **3 :** a public or unconcealed state or position ⟨bring the facts into the ~⟩ **4 :** a style of type characterized by letters in outline

LIKE THIS

5 : a break in an electric circuit **6 :** an open contest, competition, or tournament (as in a sport)

open·able \'ōp(ə)nəbəl\ *adj* **:** capable of being opened

open-access \¦==¦=\ *adj, Brit* **:** OPEN-SHELF

open account *n* **1 :** CURRENT ACCOUNT 1a **2 :** an account with a debtor or creditor having a balance due or payable

open air *n* **:** the space where air is unconfined; *esp* **:** out of doors ⟨exercise in the *open air*⟩

open-air \¦==¦=\ *adj* [*open air*] **1 :** taking place, done, existing in, or characteristic of the open air **:** OUTDOOR ⟨an *open-air* meeting⟩ **2 :** plein air

open-and-shut \ˌōp(ə)nən¦shət\ *adj* **1 :** perfectly simple **:** OBVIOUS **2** *chiefly dial* **:** partly cloudy **:** alternately overcast and clear

open-and-shut block *n* **:** a football block preceded by a side step to gain position and used by a lineman or a wingback to block inwardly a tackler who is on his outside shoulder

open-and-shut case \¦===¦-\ *n* [so called fr. the fact that it may be closed as soon as opened] **:** a case open to no doubts as to the legal principles to be applied and the necessary result

open arc lamp *n* **:** an arc lamp operated in the open air — compare ENCLOSED ARC LAMP

open arms *n pl* **:** an eager or warm welcome ⟨greeted them with *open arms*⟩

open-arse \'==ˌ=\ *n* [ME *openers*, fr. OE *openærs*, fr. *open* + *ærs*, *ears* ass; fr. the large open disk between the lobes of the calyx — more at ASS] *dial Brit* **:** ¹MEDLAR 1

open back *n* **:** HOLLOW BACK

openband \'==ˌ=\ *adj, of a twist in textile manufacture* **:** right-hand or Z-shaped — compare CROSSBAND

openbeak \'==ˌ=\ *n* **:** OPENBILL

openbill \'==ˌ=\ *n* **:** a stork of the genus *Anastomus* characterized by a grooved bill with the upper and lower parts touching only at the base and tip

open book *n* **:** something that is widely or fully known **:** a thing completely free from mystery or concealment ⟨her life is an *open book*⟩

open-book examination *n* **:** a written examination during which an examinee is permitted to consult references to answer questions calling for organization, analysis, or judgment, rather than memorization

open bridle *n* **:** a bridle having no blinders

open caisson *n* **:** a small cofferdam that is set in place, pumped dry, and filled with concrete to form a foundation (as for a pier)

¹opencast \'==ˌ=\ *n, chiefly Brit* **:** ¹OPENCUT 1

²opencast \"\ *adv (or adj), chiefly Brit* **:** ²OPENCUT ⟨~ mining⟩

open chain *n* **:** an arrangement of atoms represented in a structural formula by a chain whose ends are not joined so as to form a ring — opposed to *closed chain*

open charge *n* **:** a charge placed against a defendant usu. to enable the police to gain time for the discovery of further evidence so that another more serious charge may be made

open check *n, Brit* **:** an unindorsed check payable to the order of the bearer

open circuit *n* **:** an electrical circuit in which the continuity is broken so that current does not flow

open cluster *n* **:** a cluster of stars in which all the individual members may be discerned with an optical aid and which is much less compact and has fewer members than a globular cluster; *often* **:** a galactic cluster

open commission *n* **:** a commission to take testimony in which the witnesses to be examined are not named or in which the scope of the inquiry is not limited to specific questions

open communion *n* **:** Communion open to all Christians and not restricted to those of a particular denomination or those meeting a specific qualification (as baptism by immersion) — opposed to *close communion*

open compound *n* **:** a compound whose word components are separated by a space in printing or writing — compare SOLID COMPOUND

open couplet *n* **:** a couplet the sense of which requires completion by what follows

open court *n* **1 :** a court that is in session and lawfully organized and engaged in the transaction of official business as distinguished from a court taking evidence in camera or from a judge in chambers or elsewhere exercising his powers as a magistrate rather than as a court **2 :** a session of court at the transactions of which the public are free to be present

open craps *n* **:** craps in which a house or banker undertakes to cover all bets at its established odds but also permits players to bet among themselves

open cure *n* **:** hot vulcanization of rubber in the presence of steam

¹opencut \¦==¦=\ *n* **1 :** a mine working in which excavation is performed from the surface — compare STRIP MINE **2 :** a trench for the passage of a roadway or railway through an obstruction (as a hill) — distinguished from *tunnel*

²opencut \"\ *adv (or adj)* **:** with the surface exposed to the air or worked from the exposed surface ⟨an ~ iron mine⟩ ⟨a copper mine worked ~⟩

open-delta connection *n* **:** a usu. temporary or emergency connection of a three-phase electrical circuit in which one of the three transformers is omitted and its load carried by the two transformers — called also *V-connection*

open diapason *n* **:** a pipe organ foundation stop having a full sonorous tone and consisting usu. of metal pipes of 8-foot pitch open at the top

open door *n* **1 a :** a recognized right of admittance (as to the presence or attention of a superior) **:** freedom of access **b :** free and unhampered opportunity or a source of such ⟨education is an *open door* to advancement⟩ **2 :** a policy giving all nations equal opportunity for commercial and other intercourse with a country controlled by more powerful states and abolishing special concessions to a favored nation

open-door \¦==¦=\ *adj* [*open door*] **1 :** done or carried on with or as if with the doors open **:** PUBLIC **2 :** of, relating to, or sustaining the open door in foreign relations ⟨trade was on an *open-door* basis⟩ ⟨an *open-door* policy was initiated⟩

open-eared \¦==¦=\ *adj* **1 :** attentive to what is heard **2 :** responsive to appeal, suggestion, or other utterance

opened *past of* OPEN

open-end \¦==¦=\ *adj* **:** organized, formulated, or constituted to contain possibilities for various contingencies whether unspecified, merely inferable, or definitely stated: as **a :** permitting additional debt to be incurred under the original indenture subject to specified conditions ⟨an *open-end* bond issue⟩ — compare OPEN-END MORTGAGE **b :** offering for sale or having issued outstanding capital shares redeemable on demand usu. at liquidating value or at a slight discount ⟨an *open-end* investment company⟩ — opposed to *closed-end* **c :** calling for the filling by a particular contractor of all government needs for a specific product during a specified period ⟨an *open-end* contract⟩ **d :** having blank spaces for the insertion of commercials ⟨*open-end* transcription for a new TV program⟩ **e** *usu* **open-ended** \¦==¦==\ **:** having no fixed set of alternative replies and permitting spontaneous and unguided responses for expression (as of attitudes, opinions, and intent) ⟨an *open-ended* question⟩ ⟨*open-ended* interview⟩

open-end mortgage *n* **:** a mortgage under which additional funds may be borrowed without making a new mortgage — contrasted with *closed mortgage*

open-end straight *n* **:** four cards in poker sequence (as 4, 5, 6, 7) that can be filled at either end

open end wrench *n* **:** a wrench with jaws having a fixed width of opening at one or both ends of the handle

open end wrench

¹open·er \'ōp(ə)nə(r)\ *n* -s [²*open*] **:** one that opens ⟨a can ~⟩: as **a** *obs* **:** APERIENT **b :** a machine in which textile fiber (as cotton) is loosened and partially cleaned **c open-**

ers *pl* **:** cards of sufficient value for a player to open the betting in a poker game **d :** the first item on a multiple bill (as of vaudeville acts) or of a series (as of professional baseball games)
²opener *comparative of* OPEN
openest *superlative of* OPEN
open-eyed \ˈ≈≈ˈ≈\ *adj* **1 :** having the eyes open (as in surprise or amazement) ⟨watching in *open-eyed* wonder⟩ **2** *also* **open-eye :** characterized by alert vigilance and attention **:** WATCHFUL, DISCERNING ⟨a policy of *open-eyed* awareness⟩
open-faced *or* **open-face** \ˈ≈≈ˈ≈\ *adj* **:** having an open face: as **a** *of a watch* **:** having the face or dial covered only with a glass — compare HUNTING CASE **b :** having a frank, ingenuous, or undisguised face **c :** lacking a top covering — used of a made dish (as a pie or sandwich) **d :** BAREFACED
open-field \ˈ≈≈ˈ≈\ *adj* **1 :** of, relating to, or constituting a system of agriculture widely practised in medieval Europe and based upon dividing the arable land into unenclosed strips usu. subject to a 3-year rotation and upon distributing it among different cultivators **2** *of a football player* **:** notably capable of gaining yardage in a broken field ⟨an *open-field* runner⟩
open field *n* **1 :** BROKEN FIELD **2 :** an unhampered chance ⟨given an *open field* to experiment⟩
open file *n* **:** a chess file void of pawns; *also* **:** a file with neither pieces nor pawns on it
open-file \ˈ≈≈ˈ≈\ *adj* **:** not restricted as to circulation or possession ⟨*open-file* reports⟩
open fire *n* **1 :** a fire (as in a fireplace) that is not wholly enclosed by a stove or furnace **2 :** a fire in a forge in which combustion takes place on the top of the fuel
open-fire \ˈ≈≈ˈ≈\ *adj, ceramics* **:** exposed to direct contact with the fire as opposed to muffled firing
open flash *n* **:** a method of taking flashlight pictures by leaving the camera shutter open while the lamp is flashed and then closing it
open flow *n* **:** the total flow produced by an oil or gas well in a given time with the main valve wide open
open form *n* **:** a crystal form (as a prism) whose faces do not completely enclose a space
open frame *n* **:** a frame in which a bowler scores neither a strike nor a spare
open furrow *n* **:** a furrow not filled by a furrow slice
open fuse *n* **:** a fuse not enclosed in a cartridge
open gait *n* **:** the gait of a trotting horse that places his hind feet outside the forward ones in action
open gate *n* **:** a slalom obstacle placed at right angles to the vertical descent of a ski slope — compare CLOSED GATE
open-grained *or* **open grain** \ˈ≈≈ˈ≈\ *adj* **:** having a coarse texture; *esp* **:** having large pores ⟨*open-grained* woods⟩
openhanded \ˈ≈≈ˈ≈≈\ *adj* **1 :** generous in giving **:** MUNIFICENT **2** *obs* **:** ready to accept bounty **3 :** OBVIOUS, BRAZEN ⟨~ extortion⟩ **syn** see LIBERAL
open·hand·ed·ly *adv* **:** in an openhanded manner **:** GENEROUSLY
open·hand·ed·ness *n* **:** GENEROSITY, MUNIFICENCE
open-handled \ˈ≈≈ˈ≈≈\ *adj* **:** OPEN 7b
open harmony *n* **:** an arrangement of the note or tones of a musical chord in which the three upper parts encompass an octave or more — called also *open position;* compare CLOSE HARMONY
open hawse *n* **:** an arrangement of starboard and port anchor cables in which the cables run directly to the anchors — compare FOUL HAWSE
open-headed \ˈ≈≈ˈ≈≈\ *adj* **:** trained and pruned without a central leader and with the center open in order to facilitate spraying and other operations and provide superior exposure to sunlight ⟨*open-headed* apple trees⟩
openhearted \ˈ≈≈ˈ≈≈\ *adj* **1 :** candidly straightforward **:** freely communicative **:** FRANK **2 :** responsive to emotional appeal **:** generously kind — **open·heart·ed·ly** *adv* — **open·heart·ed·ness** *n* -ES
open hearth *n* **1 :** the shallow hearth of a reverberatory

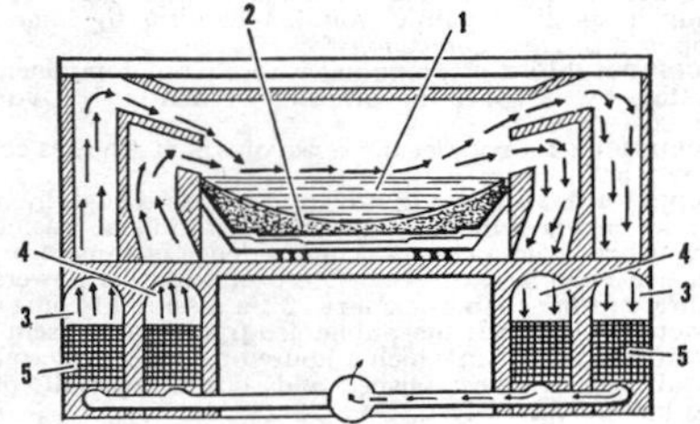

cross section of an open hearth 2: *1* molten steel, *2* lining, *3* air, *4* gas, *5* checker

melting furnace heated by hot gases above it **2 :** an open-hearth furnace
open-hearth \ˈ≈≈ˈ≈\ *adj* [*open hearth*] **:** of, relating to, involving, or produced by an open hearth ⟨*open-hearth* steel⟩ ⟨an *open-hearth* ladle⟩
open-hearth process *n* **:** a process of making steel in a furnace of the regenerative reverberatory type from pig iron usu. charged molten by adding to it with lime and other slag-forming constituents either steel scrap or iron ore or both
open hole *n* **:** an oil well or portion of an oil well that has not been cased
open house *n* **1 :** ready and usu. informal hospitality or entertainment ⟨kept *open house* for the young people of the neighborhood⟩ **2 a :** an occasion when a person or institution (as a club) entertains a large number of guests often by general rather than specific invitation **b :** an occasion or period during which an organization puts its special features (as products) on public display
open ice *n* **:** ice on navigable waters sufficiently broken up to permit passage of a ship
open·ing \ˈōp(ə)niŋ, -pn̄iŋ\ *n* -S [ME, fr. gerund of *openen* to open] **1 a :** an act or instance of making or becoming open ⟨the slow ~ of the door⟩ ⟨the ~ of distant markets⟩ **b :** an act or instance of beginning **:** a first step toward starting or activating (as of an enterprise) ⟨the ~ of two new stores helped the neighborhood⟩; *esp* **:** a formal and usu. public event by which something new is put officially into operation ⟨the mayor spoke at the ~ of the new bridge⟩ **2 :** something that is open: as **a** (1) **:** BREACH, APERTURE ⟨planned the ~*s* for the doors and windows⟩ (2) **:** an open width **:** SPREAD, SPAN **b :** an indentation of water into land **:** STRAIT, BAY, GULF **c :** an area without trees or with scattered usu. mature trees that occurs as a break in a forest — compare OAK OPENING **d :** two pages that face one another in a book **e :** the daily beginning of trading on an exchange; *also* **:** the prices of the initial transaction in a particular stock or commodity futures contract on an exchange **3 :** something that constitutes a beginning **:** an initial stage, instance, part, or event ⟨the ~ of his speech⟩: as **a :** a lawyer's statement of his case prior to adducing evidence **b :** the first phase of a game (as of chess or cards); *specif* **:** a planned series of moves made at the beginning of a game of chess or checkers — compare END GAME, MIDDLE GAME **c :** the introductory and often burlesque part of a pantomime — compare HARLEQUINADE **d :** a first performance (as of a play or an artist) **4 a :** something (as a circumstance) that constitutes an opportunity or occasion ⟨waiting for an ~ to tell his story⟩ **b :** a professional or business vacancy **:** an opportunity for employment ⟨there are always ~*s* for qualified engineers⟩ **c :** a scoring opportunity in a sports competition esp. as a result of a mistake or lapse by the opponent
opening bid *n* **:** ORIGINAL BID
opening bit *n* **:** BROACH, REAMER
opening day *n* **:** the first of a sequence of days related by some common factor ⟨the *opening day* of deer season⟩ ⟨a baseball park filled on *opening day*⟩
opening die *n* **:** a screw-cutting die head that automatically opens to clear the cut thread at the end of each run
opening gun *n* **:** the initial event of a sequence of related events ⟨the *opening gun* of the campaign⟩
opening material *n, ceramics* **:** material (as grog or sand) not affected by water that is added to plastic clay to increase the rate of drying and reduce shrinkage
open interest *n* **:** the total in physical units of outstanding long and short futures contracts on a commodity exchange
open-jaw \ˈ≈≈ˈ≈\ *or* **open-jaw ticket** *n* **:** a round trip ticket having a terminal point that is not the originating point — used esp. in respect to air transportation
open joint *n* **:** the depression in a case-bound book between the shoulder of the backbone and the edge of the cover board that forms the joint — compare TIGHT JOINT
open juncture *or* **open internal juncture** *n* **:** a juncture between two consecutive sounds in speech having less mutual assimilation than a close juncture and less hiatus than a terminal juncture
open-kettle \ˈ≈≈ˈ≈≈\ *adj* **1 :** consisting of or made by evaporation of sap or the juice of sugarcane in open pans ⟨*open-kettle* molasses⟩ **2 :** canned by the hot-pack method
open letter *n* **:** a letter of protest or appeal intended for the general public and printed in a newspaper or periodical
open-letter proof *n* **:** a proof (as of an engraving) with title or other inscription in outline letters
open listing *n* **:** a system whereby two or more real-estate brokers are given the right to sell property for a commission to be paid to the broker making the sale but permitting the owner to sell it himself if possible with no obligation to pay the broker — compare MULTIPLE LISTING
open·ly \ˈōpənlē, -pᵊnl-, -lī\ *adv* [ME, fr. OE *openlīce*, fr. ¹*open* + *-līce* -ly] **:** in an open manner **:** freely and without concealment
open market *n* **:** a freely competitive market in which any buyer or seller may trade and in which prices are determined by competition
open-market \ˈ≈≈ˈ≈≈\ *adj* [*open market*] **1 :** of, relating to, or occurring in an open market ⟨*open-market* operations⟩ **2 :** arrived at through or resulting from freely competitive bidding ⟨an *open-market* price⟩ ⟨*open-market* exchange rates⟩
open-minded \ˈ≈≈ˈ≈≈\ *adj* **:** receptive of arguments or ideas **:** free from rigidly fixed preconceptions **:** UNPREJUDICED ⟨an *open-minded* curiosity that made him receptive to new ideas —V.L.Parrington⟩ — **open-mind·ed·ly** *adv* — **open-mind·ed·ness** *n* -ES
openmouthed \ˈ≈≈ˈ≈\ *adj* **1 :** having the mouth widely open (as for gasping, seizing, or crying out) **2 :** struck with amazement or wonder **3 :** urgent or determined in speech or protest **:** CLAMOROUS, VOCIFEROUS — **open·mouth·ed·ly** \-ˈmaůthədlē, -thədlē,-thtlē,-thdlē\ *adv* — **open·mouth·ed·ness** \-thədnəs, -thədn-, -th(t)n-, -th(d)n-\ *n* -ES
openmouthed grunt *n* **:** FRENCH GRUNT
open·ness \ˈōpənnəs, ˈ-pmnəs\ *n* -ES **:** the quality or state of being open ⟨the unusual ~ of that winter⟩ ⟨behaved with perfect ~⟩
open newel *n* **:** HOLLOW NEWEL
open-newel stair *n* **:** a stair having successive flights or a continuous spiral surrounding a space left open between the strings
open note *n* **1 :** a musical note with an outline head instead of with a solid one (as a half note) **2 :** a natural harmonic of the fundamental tone of the instrument occurring in the playing of a brass wind instrument — called also *open tone*
open order *n* **1 :** a military formation in which the units are separated by considerable intervals **:** EXTENDED ORDER **2 :** an order to buy securities or commodity futures that remains effective until filled or canceled — compare DAY ORDER **3 :** an order for merchandise expressed in very general terms so that the seller has considerable latitude in selecting the articles actually provided ⟨sent an *open order* for 60 better-class suits⟩
open-pit \ˈ≈≈ˈ≈\ *n or adj or adv* **:** OPENCUT
open plan *n* **:** the disposition of interior space in a building (as a dwelling) without distinct or conventional barriers between areas designed for different uses
open policy *n* **:** a continuous policy of marine insurance that is terminable by either party after notice, covers specific shipments automatically, and has the premiums determined by the values reported
open-pollinated \ˈ≈≈ˈ≈≈,≈≈\ *adj* **:** pollinated by natural agencies (as wind or insects) without direct human control or intervention ⟨*open-pollinated* and hybrid sweet corns⟩
open port *n* **1 :** a port open to foreign commerce **2 :** a port free from ice the year round
open position *n* **:** OPEN HARMONY
open price *n* **:** a price at which goods or commodities are sold or are to be sold and which is filed by businesses at a central point of registration and open to all businesses concerned
open primary *n* **:** a primary in which the voter is not required to indicate party affiliation — compare CLOSED PRIMARY
open question *n* **1 a :** a matter that is undecided or unsettled ⟨it's an *open question* whether the landlord is responsible⟩ **b :** a matter on which a political party has not taken a positive stand **2 :** a question that is so phrased as to encourage an expression of opinion as distinguished from a simple negative or affirmative
open rate *n* **1 :** a railroad rate included in a published tariff **2 :** a rate charged by publishers for advertising space that is subject to discounts for volume purchased or frequency of use
open reduction *n* **:** realignment of a fractured bone after incision into the fracture site — compare ¹REDUCE 7
open rein *n* **:** DIRECT REIN
open riser *n* **:** the space between two adjacent stairs when not closed by a solid riser
opens *pres 3d sing of* OPEN, *pl of* OPEN
open-sand \ˈ≈≈ˈ≈\ *adj, of a foundry mold or casting* **:** made entirely of sand or in sand without a flask or cover
open sandwich *n* **:** a sandwich lacking a top covering of bread
open score *n* **:** a musical choral or orchestral score in which each part has a staff to itself — compare CLOSE SCORE
open sea *n* **1 :** the part of the sea not enclosed between headlands or included in narrow straits **:** the main sea **2 :** the part of the sea outside the territorial jurisdiction or maritime belt of any country — compare MARE CLAUSUM
open secret *n* **:** a matter that is ostensibly secret but generally known
open section *n* **:** a railway Pullman accommodation providing seats that are not enclosed for day use and upper and lower berths closed off with curtains for night use
open ses·a·me \,≈≈ˈsesəmē, -mi\ *n, sometimes cap O* [fr. *open sesame*, the magical command used to open the door of the robbers' den by Ali Baba in the *Arabian Nights* tale of *Ali Baba and the Forty Thieves*] **:** something that unfailingly brings about a desired end ⟨believe that education is for them . . . an *open sesame* to a good life —E.O.Melby⟩
open setting *n* **:** arrangement of ceramic ware in a kiln so that it is exposed to the fire and is not in a muffle
open-shelf \ˈ≈≈ˈ≈\ *adj* **:** of, used in, or constituting a system of library organization in which books are so shelved as to permit direct examination and selection by patrons ⟨an *open-shelf* room⟩ ⟨the *open-shelf* idea⟩
open shop *n* **:** an establishment in which eligibility for employment and retention on the payroll are not determined by membership or nonmembership in a labor union though there may be an agreement by which a union is recognized as sole bargaining agent — compare CLOSED SHOP
open-shop·per \ˈ≈≈ˈshäpə(r)\ *n* **:** an operator of an open shop or an advocate of open shops
openside \ˈ≈≈ˈ≈\ *adj* **:** having one side left unobstructed for the accommodation of large work ⟨an ~ punchpress⟩
openside planer *n* **:** a planer having the crossrail supported by a housing on one side only
open sight *n* **:** a firearm rear sight having an open notch instead of a peephole or a telescope
open-stack \ˈ≈≈ˈ≈\ *adj* **:** OPEN-SHELF
open stance *n* **:** a preparatory position (as in baseball batting or golf) in which the left foot of a right-handed person is drawn back farther from the line of play than the right — contrasted with *closed stance*
open station *n* **:** a railway station to which freight can be shipped COD — contrasted with *prepaid station*
open string *n* **:** a string in stairs having its upper edge cut to fit underneath the steps, and its ends overlapping the edge
open syllable *n* **:** a syllable ended by a vowel or diphthong
open-tank \ˈ≈≈ˈ≈\ *adj* **:** of, relating to, or constituting a nonpressure process of treating wood with chemicals (as creosote and oil) to guard against decay
open-timbered *or* **open-timber** \ˈ≈≈ˈ≈≈\ *adj* **:** having the timbers exposed ⟨an *open-timbered* gable⟩
open-timbered roof *n* **:** a timber roof of which the constructional parts together with the under side of the covering or its lining are treated ornamentally and left to form the ceiling of an apartment below
open-to-buy \ˈ≈≈ˈ≈\ *n* [fr. the phrase *open to buy*] **:** the portion of a budget allotment remaining available for additional purchases at any given moment of a budgetary period ⟨an *open-to-buy* is an amount which is budgeted for the placement of purchase orders —H.D.Broehm⟩
open tone *n* **:** OPEN NOTE 2
open traverse *n* **:** a surveying traverse that fails to terminate where it began and therefore does not completely enclose a polygon — compare ERROR OF CLOSURE 2
open tunnel *n* **:** a square dance figure with a space between the outstretched arms of joined couples for the passage of other couples
open turn *n* **:** a turn in dancing made with the partners in open position
open up *vi* **1 :** to commence firing **2 a :** to become communicative **b** *of a hound* **:** to give tongue **3 :** to spread out or come into view ⟨the road *opens up* ahead⟩ **4 :** to turn toward an audience or camera **5 :** to launch an offensive esp. in competitive sport ⟨*open up* with forward passes⟩ ⟨*open up* with a series of quick punches⟩ ~ *vt* **1 :** to cut into; *esp* **:** to open surgically **2 a :** to make plain or visible **:** DISCLOSE ⟨her account *opened up* a whole new line of investigation⟩ **b :** to bring into view ⟨means to place his drive so as to *open up* the green for his approach —Paul Gallico⟩ **3 :** to make available ⟨new opportunities were *opened up* as the population grew⟩ **4 :** to force (a defense) to spread itself thin ⟨split the line to *open up* this defense —Jim Tatum⟩
open valley *n* **:** a roofing valley laid with a broad open gutter with the slates, tiles, or shingles lapping over the edges of the metal
open verdict *n* **:** a verdict on a preliminary investigation finding the fact of a crime but not stating the criminal or finding the fact of a violent death without disclosing the cause
open water *n* **:** water less than one tenth of which is covered with floating ice
open-well stair *n* **:** OPEN-NEWEL STAIR
openwork \ˈ≈≈,≈\ *n, often attrib* **:** work so constructed or manufactured as to show openings through its substance **:** work that is perforated or pierced ⟨an ~ sweater⟩ ⟨balconies decked with wrought-iron ~⟩ — **open-worked** \ˈ≈≈,≈\ *adj*
ope·pe \ˈōpəpē\ *n* -S [Yoruba *òpepe*] **:** a large African forest tree (*Sarcocephalus diderrichii*) that yields a strong hard durable yellow to golden brown lumber
¹ope·ra \ˈōpərə, ˈäp-\ *pl of* OPUS
²op·era \ˈäp(ə)rə\ *n* -S [It, work, opera, fr. L, work, pains; akin to L *oper-, opus* work — more at OPERATE] **1 :** a drama in which music is the essential factor comprising songs with orchestral accompaniment (as *recitative, aria, chorus*) and orchestral preludes and interludes — compare MUSIC DRAMA **2 :** the score of a musical drama **3 a :** the performance of an opera or a house where operas are performed ⟨a season of ~⟩ ⟨heard it at the ~⟩ **b :** an organization that produces and performs operas **4 :** musical drama as a form of art ⟨the origin of ~⟩ ⟨French ~⟩ **5** [by shortening] **a :** OPERA PUMP **b :** OPERA SLIPPER **6 :** a showy unrealistic literary or theatrical production — see HORSE OPERA, SOAP OPERA, SPACE OPERA
³opera \ˈ"\ *adj* **:** used or suitable for use at or in an opera ⟨~ chairs⟩; *esp* **:** of a formal style suitable for wear at the opera ⟨an ~ cloak⟩
opé·ra bal·let \ˈäp(ə)rə+*pronunc at* ²BALLET; *or* ōpārābȧlā\ *n* [F] **:** an opera in which ballet dancing constitutes a principal feature
op·er·a·bil·i·ty \,äp(ə)rəˈbilǝd-ē\ *n* **:** the quality or state of being operable — compare RESECTABILITY
op·er·a·ble \ˈäp(ə)rəbəl\ *adj* [LL *operabilis* working, efficacious, fr. L *operari* to work + *-abilis* -able] **1 :** fit, possible, or desirable to use **:** PRACTICABLE ⟨a highly ~ machine⟩ **2 :** suitable for surgical treatment ⟨an ~ cancer⟩ — compare RESECTABLE — **op·er·a·bly** \-blē\ *adv*
opéra bouffe \,äp(ə)rəˈbüf, ōpārābüf\ *n* [F, fr. It *opera buffa*] **:** a light comic opera having a light or sentimental subject and characterized by parody or burlesque
opéra-bouffe \ˈ"\ *adj* [*opéra bouffe*] **:** fit for opéra bouffe **:** being a parody of the thing specified ⟨*opéra-bouffe* revolutions⟩
ope·ra buf·fa \,äp(ə)rəˈbüfə, ,ōpärä'büffä\ *n* [It]**:** an Italian comic opera particularly of the 18th century of farcical character with dialogue in recitative
opé·ra co·mique \,äp(ə)rə,käˈmēk, ōpārȧkōmēk\ *n* [F] **:** an opera characterized by spoken dialogue interspersed between the set arias and ensemble numbers — compare GRAND OPERA
opera glass \ˈ≈(≈)≈,≈\ *n* **:** a small binocular optical instrument similar to the field glass and adapted for use at the opera or theater — often used in pl.

opera glasses

opera hat *n* **:** a man's hat worn with evening dress having a narrow brim and a high cylindrical crown with slightly concave sides and consisting usu. of a dull silky fabric stretched over a steel frame that may be collapsed by a spring device
opera house *n* **:** a theater devoted principally to the performance of operas; *broadly* **:** THEATER
op·er·ance \ˈäpərən(t)s\ *n* -S [fr. ¹*operant*, after such pairs as E *expectant: expectance*] **:** the act of operating or working something **:** OPERATION
op·er·an·cy \-nsē\ *n* -ES [¹*operant* + *-cy*] **:** the quality or state of being operative **:** OPERATION
op·er·and \ˈäpə,rand\ *n* -S [L *operandum*, neut. of gerundive of *operari* to work, operate — more at OPERATE] **1 :** a quantity upon which a mathematical operation is performed or which arises from an operation **2** *logic* **a :** something that is operated on by an operator **b :** the scope of an operator
¹op·er·ant \ˈäpərənt\ *adj* [L *operant-, operans*, pres. part. of *operari*] **1 :** functioning or tending to produce effects **:** EFFECTIVE ⟨an ~ conscience⟩ **2 :** of, relating to, or being a behavioral operant ⟨~ conditioning⟩
²operant \ˈ"\ *n* -S **1 :** one that operates **:** OPERATIVE, OPERATOR **2 :** behavior or responses that operate on the environment to produce rewarding and reinforcing effects
ope·ra om·nia \,ōpərəˈämnēə, ˈäp-\ *n pl* [L, lit., all works] **:** the complete works of a writer
opera pink *n* **:** a light yellowish pink that is redder and less strong than light apricot and darker than petal pink
opera pump *n* **:** a woman's low-cut, high-heeled shoe usu. cut from a single piece of leather or fabric and untrimmed
operas *pl of* OPERA
ope·ra se·ria \,äp(ə)rəˈsirēə\ *n* [It] **:** an 18th century opera with a heroic or legendary subject chiefly characterized musically by the highly stylized treatment and preponderant use of the aria and recitative
opera slipper *n* **1 :** OPERA PUMP **2 :** a man's house slipper cut low on both sides at the shank
op·er·at·able \ˈäpə,rād-əbəl, ,≈≈ˈ≈≈≈\ *adj* **:** possible to operate or to operate on **:** OPERABLE
op·er·ate \ˈäpə,rāt *sometimes* ˈä,prāt; *usu* -ād·+V\ *vb* -ED/-ING/-S [L *operatus*, past part. of *operari* to work, fr. *oper-, opus* work, labor; akin to Skt *apas* work, OHG *uoben* to put to work, be active, OE *efnan* to perform, ON *efna*] *vi* **1 :** to perform a work or labor **:** exert power or influence **:** produce an effect ⟨a plain reason ~*s* on the mind of a learned hearer⟩ ⟨factors *operating* against our success⟩ ⟨this remark

opera slipper 2

operated to close the meeting in disorder⟩ **2 :** to produce or take an appropriate effect **:** issue in the result designed ⟨the drug *operated* quickly⟩ **3 a :** to perform an operation or series of operations ⟨a mill for *operating* on the crude ore⟩ **b :** to perform surgery ⟨the doctor ~*s* from 8 to 10⟩ **c :** to carry on a military or naval action or mission **d :** to function through the use of a specified agent ⟨the tractor ~*s* on diesel oil⟩ **4 :** to trade or speculate in securities or commodities **:** act as a dealer or broker in the markets ⟨*operated* largely in cotton futures⟩ **5 :** to follow a course of conduct or way of life, esp. one that is irregular or antisocial ⟨*operated* as a salesman⟩ ⟨crooked gamblers *operating* on the Atlantic liners⟩ ~ *vt* **1 :** to cause to occur **:** bring about by or as if by the exertion of positive effort or influence **:** INITIATE ⟨such influences may ~ remarkable changes⟩ **2 a :** to cause to function usu. by direct personal effort **:** WORK ⟨~ a car⟩ ⟨*operating* a drill press⟩ **b :** to manage and put or keep in operation whether with personal effort or not ⟨*operated* a grocery store⟩ **3 :** to perform surgery on ⟨not all surgeons will ~ malignant growths⟩ ⟨the *operated* limb regained strength slowly⟩ **syn** see ACT

[1]**op·er·at·ic** \ˌäpəˈrad·ik, -rat|, |ēk\ *adj* [fr. *opera*, after such pairs as E *drama: dramatic*] **:** of, relating to, resembling, or suitable to opera — **op·er·at·i·cal·ly** \|ək(ə)lē, |ēk-, -li\ *adv*

[2]**operatic** \"\ *n* -s **1 operatics** *pl but sing or pl in constr* **a :** the performance or production of opera **b :** noisily histrionic behavior ⟨no excuse for such ~*s*⟩ **2 :** an operatic recording

operating *adj* [fr. pres. part. of *operate*] **1 :** engaged in some form of operation **:** FUNCTIONAL ⟨an ~ motor⟩; *esp* **:** engaged in active business (as manufacture, transportation, merchandising) **2 a :** arising out of or concerned with the current operations of a concern engaged in transportation or manufacturing as distinct from its financial transactions and its permanent improvements ⟨~ expense⟩ ⟨~ personnel⟩ **b :** of or dealing with profit and loss or income and expenses ⟨an ~ statement⟩ **3 :** used for or in operations ⟨the ~ room in a hospital⟩

op·er·a·tion \ˌäpəˈrāshən\ *n* -s [ME *operacioun*, fr. MF *operation*, fr. L *operation-, operatio*, fr. *operatus* (past part. of *operari* to work) + *-ion, -io* -ion — more at OPERATE] **1 a** *obs* **:** a doing or performing esp. of action **:** WORK, DEED **b :** a doing or performing of a practical work or of something involving practical application of principles or processes often experimentally or as part of a series of actions ⟨the mechanical ~*s* involved in sculpture⟩ ⟨practice until you can go through the whole ~ without hesitation or thinking⟩ **2 a :** an exertion of power or influence **:** FUNCTIONING, WORKING ⟨depending on the ~*s* of the intelligence⟩ ⟨the ~ of a drug⟩ **b :** the quality or state of being functional or operative — usu. used with *in* or *into* ⟨the plant has been in ~ for several weeks⟩ ⟨the new line will be put into ~ soon⟩ **c :** method or manner of functioning ⟨a machine of very simple ~⟩ ⟨the ~ of the circulation⟩ **3 a :** capacity for action or functioning **:** EFFICACY, POTENCY — archaic except in legal usage **b** *archaic* **:** result of the action or existence (as of a disease, an activity) **:** INFLUENCE **4** *obs* **a :** PRODUCTION, CREATION **b :** a product of creative activity **5 :** actual energy or activity viewed as expressing the agent's nature or natures ⟨the ~ of the Holy Spirit⟩ **6 :** a procedure carried out on a living body for the purpose of altering an existing esp. abnormal state or condition by means of instruments (as in surgery) or the hands of a surgeon (as by manipulation of joints) — compare BLOODLESS SURGERY, ELECTROSURGERY **7 a :** a process whereby one quantity or expression is derived from another or others **b** *logic* (1) **:** TRANSFORMATION (2) **:** a function or correlation when conceived as a process of proceeding from one or more entities to another according to a definite rule **c :** the checking of the applicability of a given term or concept to a concrete situation by means of observation and usu. manipulation ⟨determining the acidity of a liquid by indicators constitutes an ~⟩ **8 a :** a military or naval action, mission, or maneuver, including its planning and execution — often used in combination with a designating code word **b operations** *pl* **:** the office on the flight line of an airfield where pilots file clearances for flights and which controls flying from the field **c operations** *pl* **:** the staff agency (as in a U.S. air headquarters) for transacting the principal planning and operating functions of a headquarters and its subordinate units **9 a :** a business transaction esp. when speculative ⟨continued his ~*s* in cotton futures⟩ **b :** the whole process of planning for and operating a business or other organized unit ⟨the ~ of a large household⟩ ⟨the ~ of a steel mill⟩ **c :** a phase of a business or of business activity ⟨the new forge shop has proved a valuable addition to our ~*s*⟩ **10 :** the operating of or putting and maintaining in action of something (as a machine or an industry) ⟨careful ~ of a motor car⟩ ⟨problems in the ~ of a railroad⟩

op·er·a·tion·al \ˌäpəˈrāshənᵊl, -shnəl\ *adj* **1 :** of or relating to operation or an operation **2 :** concerned with, involving, or based on operations ⟨~ symbols⟩ ⟨an ~ definition⟩ — see OPERATIONAL CALCULUS **3 a :** of, engaged in, or connected with execution of military or naval operations in campaign and battle as distinguished from training, testing, observation ⟨an ~ leave⟩ ⟨~ patrols⟩ **b :** ready for or in condition to undertake a destined function ⟨the new pool should be ~ in a few weeks⟩; *esp* **:** serviced in readiness for action ⟨the fleet is fully manned and ~⟩

operational calculus *n* **:** a branch of mathematics that subjects to algebraic operations symbols of operation as well as of magnitude

operational fatigue *n* **:** COMBAT FATIGUE

op·er·a·tion·al·ism \ˌäpəˈrāshənᵊlˌizəm, -shnəˌli-\ *n* -s **:** the view that the concepts or terms used in nonanalytic scientific statements must be definable in terms of identifiable and repeatable operations

op·er·a·tion·al·ist \-ᵊləst, -əl-\ *n* -s **:** an advocate or adherent of operationalism

op·er·a·tion·al·ly \ˌäpəˈrāshənᵊlē, -shnəl|, |li\ *adv* **1 :** in an operational condition or manner **:** so as to be operational **2 :** in respect to operation **:** as observed in actual use or function ⟨reported the machine ~ satisfactory⟩ ⟨a well-trained staff that is ~ adequate⟩

operational research *n, chiefly Brit* **:** OPERATIONS RESEARCH

op·er·a·tion·ism \-shəˌnizəm\ *n* -s **:** OPERATIONALISM

op·er·a·tion·is·tic \ˌäpəˌrāshəˈnistik\ *adj* **:** of or relating to operationalism **:** OPERATIONAL

operations analysis *n* **:** the systematic examination of a tactic or other military procedure usu. by mathematical and statistical methods to determine its efficiency and to devise or indicate possible improvements

operations research *n* **:** the application of scientific and esp. mathematical methods to the study and analysis of complex problems (as of industrial, governmental, or military activity) that are not traditionally considered to fall within the field of profitable scientific inquiry

[1]**op·er·a·tive** \ˈäp(ə)rə|d·iv, ˈäpəˌrā|, |t|, |ēv *also* |əv\ *adj* [MF *operatif*, fr. L *operatus* (past part. of *operari* to work) + MF *-if* -ive — more at OPERATE] **1 :** producing an appropriate or designed effect **:** EFFICACIOUS ⟨an ~ dose⟩ ⟨an ~ word⟩ **2 :** having the power of acting **:** exerting force or influence **:** OPERATING ⟨an ~ motive⟩ ⟨an ~ force⟩ **3 a :** involving or having to do with physical operations (as of the hands or of machines) ⟨~ arts⟩ ⟨~ skills⟩ **b :** engaged in or doing work **:** occupied in productive labor **:** WORKING ⟨an ~ craftsman⟩ ⟨~ freemasons working at their craft⟩ **4 :** based upon or consisting of an operation or operations ⟨~ surgery⟩ ⟨~ dentistry⟩ — **op·er·a·tive·ly** \|əvlē, -li\ *adv* — **op·er·a·tive·ness** \|ivnəs, |ēv- *also* |əv-\ *n* -ES

[2]**operative** \"\ *n* -s **:** one that operates **:** OPERATOR: as **a :** a person engaged in an occupation or profession; *esp* **:** a skilled or semiskilled employee in industry (as in a mill or factory) **:** ARTISAN, MECHANIC ⟨machine ~*s*⟩ ⟨wool ~*s*⟩ **b :** a secret agent **:** PRIVATE DETECTIVE

op·er·a·tize \ˈäp(ə)rəˌtīz\ *vt* -ED/-ING/-S [fr. *opera*, after such pairs as E *drama: dramatize*] **:** to convert (as a drama) into opera

op·er·a·tor \ˈäpəˌrād·ə(r), -ātə- *sometimes* ˈäˌprā-\ *n* -s [LL, worker, fr. L *operatus* + *-or*] **1 :** one that produces a physical effect or engages himself in the mechanical aspect of any process or activity: as **a :** one (as an operative surgeon or dentist) that performs surgical operations **b** (1) **:** a worker who operates a usu. specified machine or device as his regular trade ⟨loom ~*s*⟩; *broadly* **:** one that uses or operates a machine or device professionally or otherwise — sometimes used to distinguish the user of fixed devices from the driver of automotive devices (2) **:** DRIVER 1b ⟨~*s* of motor vehicles⟩ **c :** a person in charge of a telephone switchboard, connecting and disconnecting the lines and routing calls; *also* **:** a supervisor of such persons **d :** a person who transmits or receives telegraphic or radio messages or who operates electronic communications equipment (as radar or computer installation) **2 a** *obs* **:** MAKER, CREATOR **b** (1) *obs* **:** a maker of quack medicines or of shoddy or fraudulent articles; *broadly* **:** MOUNTEBANK, FRAUD (2) **:** a shrewd and skillful person who knows how to evade or circumvent restrictions, controls, or difficulty **:** one that is smooth and highly expert in some line **3 a** (1) **:** a dealer or speculator in stocks or commodities (2) **:** a person who regularly or professionally engages in some usu. financial activity esp. on a large scale ⟨an important ~ around the gambling houses⟩ **b :** a person that actively operates a business (as a mine, a farm, or a store) whether as owner, lessor, or employee **4 a :** a mathematical symbol denoting an operation to be performed ⟨$\frac{d}{dx}$ is the differentiating ~⟩ **b :** something that performs a logical operation or forms a symbol denoting such an operation (as a quantifier or a sentential connective) **c :** FUNCTION WORD ⟨a preposition, auxiliary, or conjunction is an ~⟩ **5 :** HYPNOTIST

[1]**op·er·a·to·ry** \ˈäp(ə)rəˌtōrē\ *adj* [*operate* + *-ory*] **:** OPERATIVE

[2]**operatory** \"\ *n* -ES [ML *operatorium*, fr. L *operatus* + *-orium* -ory] **:** a working space (as of a dentist or engineer) **:** LABORATORY, SURGERY

oper·cle \ōˈpərkəl, ˈōpər-\ *n* -s [L *operculum* cover — more at *operculum*] **:** OPERCULUM; *specif* **:** the upper posterior and usu. the largest bone of the operculum of a fish

oper·cled \-kəld\ *adj* [*opercle* + *-ed*] **:** OPERCULATE

[1]**oper·cu·lar** \(ˈ)ōˌpərkyələr\ *adj* [*operculum* + *-ar*] **:** of, relating to, or resembling an operculum

[2]**opercular** \"\ *n* -s **:** an opercular part; *esp* **:** the opercle of a fish

opercular bones *n pl* **:** the bony plates developed in and supporting the gill cover in most fishes and being usu. the opercle, preopercle, subopercle, and interopercle

[1]**oper·cu·late** \-lət, -ˌlāt\ *also* **oper·cu·lat·ed** \-ˌlād·əd\ *adj* [*operculum* + *-ate*] **:** having an operculum

[2]**operculate** \"\ *n* -s **:** an operculate gastropod

operculi- *comb form* [NL *operculum*] **:** operculum ⟨*operculi*ferous⟩ ⟨*operculi*form⟩

oper·cu·lum \ōˈpərkyələm\ *n, pl* **opercu·la** \-lə\ *also* **oper·culums** [NL, fr. L, cover, lid, fr. *operire* to cover, shut (fr. *op-, ob* to, before + — assumed — *verire* to shut) + *-culum*, suffix denoting instrument — more at EPI-, WEIR] **1 :** a lid or covering flap (as of a moss capsule, of an ascus, of a pyxidium in a seed plant, or of the pitcher in some pitcher plants) **2 :** a part of the cerebrum bordering the lateral fissure and concealing the island of Reil **3 :** a body process or part that suggests a lid: as **a :** the horny or shelly plate that develops on the posterior dorsal surface of the foot in many gastropod mollusks (as in Streptoneura) and serves to close the shell when the animal is retracted **b :** the two or more movable plates of the shell of a barnacle **c :** the first pair of abdominal appendages of a king crab which are united and cover the other pairs **d :** one of the small plates covering the orifice of a trachea or lung sac in a spider **e :** the fold of integument usu. supported by bony plates that protects the gills in most fishes and some amphibians **:** GILL COVER — see FISH illustration **f :** the principal bony plate of the gill cover **:** OPERCLE **g :** a flap that covers the mouth of some bryozoans **h :** a circular lid at one end of the egg of various invertebrates

ope·re ci·ta·to \ˌōpəˌrākəˈtäd·(ˌ)ō, -ˌsīˈtäd-\ *adv* [L] **:** in the work quoted — abbr. *op. cit.* or *o.c.*

op·er·et·ta \ˌäpəˈred·ə, -etə *sometimes* äˈpre-\ *also* **op·er·ette** \ˌäpəˈret, *usu* -ed·+V\ *n* -s [It., fr. *opera* + *-etta* ette] **1** *archaic* **:** LIGHT OPERA **2 :** a light musical-dramatic production having usu. a romantic plot and containing spoken dialogue and dancing scenes; *also* **:** the musical score of such a work

op·er·et·tist \ˌäpəˈred·əst, äˈpre-\ *n* -s **:** one that composes operettas

op·er·ose \ˈäpəˌrōs\ *adj* [L *operosus*, fr. *oper-, opus* work + *-osus* -ose — more at OPERATE] **1 :** wrought with labor **:** requiring or involving effort ⟨an ~ affair⟩ **2 :** DILIGENT, BUSY, INDUSTRIOUS — **op·er·ose·ly** *adv* — **op·er·ose·ness** *n* -ES

op·er·os·i·ty \ˌäpəˈräsəd·ē\ *n* -ES [L *operositas*, fr. *operosus* + *-itas* -ity] **:** OPEROSENESS

operous *adj* [L *operosus*] *obs* **:** OPEROSE

opes *pres 3d sing of* OPE, *pl of* OPE

-opes *pl of* -OPE

opg *abbr* opening

[1]**ophe·lia** \ōˈfēlyə, əˈf-, -lēə\ *n, cap* [NL, prob. fr. Gk *ophis* serpent + *helos* marsh + NL *-ia* — more at HELODES] **:** a genus of small littoral burrowing polychaete worms with rudimentary parapodia of which the dorsal cirri are modified into gills

[2]**ophelia** \"\ *n* -s *often cap* [prob. fr. *Ophelia*, feminine proper name] **:** a grayish reddish purple to purplish red

ophe·lim·i·ty \ˌäfəˈliməd·ē, ˌōf-\ *n* -ES [It *ofelimità*, fr. Gk *ōphelimos* useful, helpful (fr. *ōphelein* to help, fr. *ophelos* advantage, help) + It. *-ità* -ity; akin to Skt *ā* toward and to Skt *phalam* fruit, profit — more at ACHARYA] **:** economic satisfaction ⟨the seller's net ~ varies with the price⟩

ophi- *or* **ophio-** *comb form* [Gk, fr. *ophis* snake — more at ANGUIS] **1 :** snake **:** serpent ⟨*ophio*phagous⟩ ⟨*ophio*latrous⟩ **2 a :** thing suggesting a snake ⟨*ophi*calcite⟩ **b :** being or resembling a snake in respect to a (specified) structure or quality ⟨*ophio*cephalus⟩

ophi·an \ˈäfēən, ˈōf-\ *n* -s *usu cap* [LGk *ophianoi*, pl., fr. Gk *ophis* + *-anoi*, pl. of *-anos* -an] **:** [2]OPHITE

ophic \ˈäfik, ˈōf-\ *adj* [irreg. fr. *ophi-* + *ic*] **:** of or relating to snakes ⟨~ worship⟩

ophi·cal·cite \ˌäfə, ˌōfə+\ *n* [*ophi-* + *calcite*] **:** crystalline limestone or marble spotted with greenish serpentine **:** VERD ANTIQUE — called also *ophite*

ophi·ce·phal·i·dae \ˌäfəsəˈfaləˌdē, ˌōf-\ *n pl, cap* [NL, fr. *Ophicephalus*, type genus (fr. *ophi-* + *-cephalus*) + *-idae* — more at -CEPHALIC] **:** a family of elongated cylindrical carnivorous labyrinth fishes comprising the snakehead mullets of eastern Asia and Africa and usu. made coextensive with a suborder of Percomorphi

oph·ich·thy·i·dae \ˌäˌfikˈthīəˌdē, ˌōˌf-\ *n pl, cap* [NL, fr. *Ophichthys, Ophicthys*, type genus (irreg. fr. *ophi-* + *-ichthys*) + *-idae*] **:** a family of slender tropical eels comprising the snake eels

ophi·cleide \ˈäfəˌklīd, ˈōf-\ *n* -s [F *ophicléide*, fr. *ophi-* + Gk *kleid-, kleis* key — more at CLEID-] **1 :** a deep-toned brass wind musical instrument of the key bugle class, consisting of a large tapering tube bent double and provided with finger keys **2 :** a powerful organ reed stop of 8-foot or 16-foot pitch — **ophi·clei·de·an** \ˌ==ˈklīdēən\ *adj*

ophi·cleid·ist \ˈ==ˌklīdəst\ *n* -s **:** one who plays the ophicleide

ophicleide

ophid·ia \ōˈfidēə\ *n pl* [NL, irreg. fr. Gk *ophis* snake + NL *-ia* — more at ANGUIS] *syn of* SERPENTES

[1]**ophid·i·an** \ōˈfidēən\ *adj* [NL *Ophidia* + E *-an*] **:** of, relating to, or resembling that of snakes **:** SNAKELIKE — **ophid·i·an·ly** *adv*

[2]**ophidian** \"\ *n* -s **:** SNAKE 1

[1]**ophid·i·id** \ōˈfidēəd; ˈäfəˌdīəd, ˈōf-\ *adj* [NL *Ophidiidae*] **:** of or relating to the Ophidiidae

[2]**ophidiid** \"\ *n* -s **:** a fish of the family Ophidiidae

ophi·di·idae \ˌäfəˈdīəˌdē, ˌōf-\ *n pl, cap* [NL, fr. *Ophidion*, type genus (fr. L *ophidion*, fish resembling the conger, fr. Gk, dim. of *ophis*) + *-idae*] **:** a family of elongate compressed somewhat eel-shaped fishes comprising the cusk eels and with related forms constituting a suborder of Percomorphi

ophid·io·batrachia \ōˌfidē(ˌ)ō+\ *or* **ophio·batrachia** \ˌäfē(ˌ)ō, ˌōf- +\ [*Ophidiobatrachia*, NL, fr. Gk *ophidion* + NL *Batrachia*; *Ophiobatrachia*, NL, fr. *ophi-* + *Batrachia*] *syn of* GYMNOPHIONA

[1]**ophid·i·oid** \ōˈfidēˌȯid; ˈäfəˈdīˌȯid, ˈōf-\ *adj* [NL *Ophidiidae* + E *-oid*] **:** like or related to the family Ophidiidae

[2]**ophidioid** \"\ *n* -s **:** an ophidioid fish

ophi·ob·o·lus \ˌäfēˈäbələs, ˌōf-\ *n, cap* [NL, fr. *ophi-* + Gk *-bolos* throwing, casting, fr. *ballein* to throw — more at DEVIL] **:** a genus of fungi (family Pleosporaceae) characterized by spindle-shaped several-septate ascospores — see TAKE-ALL

ophio·ce·phal·i·dae \ˌäfē(ˌ)ōsəˈfaləˌdē, ˌōfē-\ *syn of* OPHICEPHALIDAE

ophio·glos·sa·ce·ae \ˌäfē(ˌ)ō(ˌ)gläˈsāsēˌē, ˌōf-\ *n pl, cap* [NL, fr. *Ophioglossum*, type genus + *-aceae*] **:** a family of eusporangiate ferns (order Ophioglossales) that are more or less succulent and have a stem and usu. a single frond with thin sheathing stipules and sporophylls forming a spike or panicle, the sporangia opening by transverse slits — see OPHIOGLOSSUM — **ophio·glos·sa·ceous** \ˌ==(ˌ)=(ˌ)=ˈsāshəs\ *adj*

ophio·glos·sa·les \ˌ==(ˌ)=(ˌ)gläˈsāˌlēz\ *n pl, cap* [NL, fr. *Ophioglossum* + *-ales*] **:** an order of Filicineae coextensive with the family Ophioglossaceae

ophio·glos·sum \ˌ===ˈgläsəm\ *n, cap* [NL, fr. *ophi-* + *-glossum*, fr. Gk *glōssa* tongue — more at GLOSS (explanation)] **:** the type genus of the family Ophioglossaceae comprising the adder's-tongues and having a solitary simple frond with netted venation and a terminal spike formed of two rows of coalescent sporangia

ophi·ol·a·try \ˌäfēˈäləˌtrē, ˌōf-\ *n* -ES [*ophi-* + *-latry*] **:** the worship of or attribution of divine or sacred nature to snakes

ophi·o·lite \ˈäfēəˌlīt, ˈōf-\ *n* -s [F *ophiolithe*, fr. *ophi-* + *lithe* -lite] **1** *obs* **:** SERPENTINE **2 :** OPHICALCITE — **ophi·o·lit·ic** \ˌ===ˈlid·ik\ *adj*

ophi·o·log·i·cal \ˌäfēəˈläjəkəl, ˌōf-\ *adj* [*ophiology* + *-ical*] **:** of or relating to ophiology

ophi·ol·o·gy \ˌ==ˈäləjē\ *also* **ophi·dol·o·gy** \ˌäfəˈdä-, ˌōf-\ *n* -ES [*ophiology* fr. *ophi-* + *-logy*; *ophidology* fr. NL *ophidion* (irreg. fr. Gk *ophis* serpent) + E *-logy*] **:** a branch of herpetology concerned with the study of snakes

ophio·mor·pha \ˌ==əˈmȯrfə\ [NL, fr. *ophi-* + *-morpha*] *syn of* GYMNOPHIONA

ophio·mor·phic \ˌ===ˈfik\ *adj* [*ophi-* + *-morphic*] **1 :** snakelike in form **2** [NL *Ophiomorpha* + E *-ic*] **:** of or relating to the Gymnophiona

ophi·on \ōˈfīˌän; ˈäfēˌän, ˈōf-\ *n* [NL, fr. Gk *ophiōn*, a fabulous animal of Sardinia] **1** *cap* **:** a widely distributed genus of ichneumon flies that have a compressed abdomen and are parasitoid on the caterpillars of various moths in which they lay a single egg **2** -s **:** any insect of the genus *Ophion* — **ophi·o·nine** \ōˈfīəˌnīn; ˈäfēə-, ˈōfēə-\ *adj or n*

ophi·oph·a·gous \ˌäfēˈäfəgəs, ˌōfē-\ *adj* [Gk *ophiophagos*, fr. *ophi-* + *-phagos* -phagous] **:** feeding on snakes

ophio·pluteus \ˌäfē(ˌ)ō, ˌōf- +\ *n* [NL, fr. *ophi-* + *pluteus*] **:** the pluteus of a brittle star

ophio·po·gon \ˌ===ˈpōˌgän\ *n, cap* [NL, fr. *ophi-* + *-pogon*] **:** a genus of stoloniferous scapose grass-leaved herbs (family Liliaceae) having racemes or spikes of white, blue, violet, or lilac flowers with the ovary inferior — see LILYTURF

ophio·sau·rus \-ˈsȯrəs\ *syn of* OPHISAURUS

ophi·os·to·ma \ˌ==ˈästəmə\ [NL, fr. *ophi-* + *-stoma*] *syn of* CERATOSTOMELLA

-o·phis \əfəs\ *n comb form* [Gk *ophis* snake — more at *anguis*] **:** snake **:** serpent — in generic names esp. in herpetology ⟨Hydr*ophis*⟩

ophi·sau·rus \ˌäfəˈsȯrəs, ˌōf-\ *n, cap* [NL, fr. *ophi-* + *-saurus*] **:** a genus of lizards comprising the glass snakes

ophism \ˈäˌfizəm, ˈōˌf-\ *n* -s **1** *usu cap* **:** the doctrines and rites of the Ophites **2 :** serpent worship or the use of serpents as magical agents **:** OPHIOLATRY — compare SNAKE DANCE

[1]**ophite** \-ˌfīt\ *n* -s [L, fr. Gk *ophitēs* (*lithos*), lit., serpentine stone, fr. *ophitēs* like a snake, fr. *ophis*] **:** any of various usu. green and often mottled or blotched rocks (as a serpentine or serpentine marble)

[2]**ophite** \"\ *n* -s *usu cap* [LL *Ophitae*, pl., fr. LGk *Ophitai*, pl., fr. Gk *ophis* snake + *-itae*, pl. of *-ites* -ite — more at ANGUIS] **:** a member of a Gnostic sect or group of sects including the Naassenes and Perates that revered the serpent as the symbol of the hidden divine wisdom and as having befriended Adam and Eve by persuading them to eat of the tree of knowledge

ophit·ic \(ˈ)äˌfid·ik, (ˈ)ō;-\ *adj* [[1]*ophite* + *-ic*] **:** having a rock fabric in which lath-shaped plagioclase crystals are enclosed wholly or in part in later formed augite ⟨diabase has an ~ structure⟩

ophi·ura \ˌäfēˈ(y)u̇rə, ˌōf-\ *n, cap* [NL, fr. *ophi-* + *-ura*] **:** a very large and widely distributed genus of brittle stars

ophi·urae \-u̇ˌrē\ [NL, pl. of *Ophiura*] *syn of* OPHIUROIDEA

ophi·uran \ˌ==ˈrən\ *adj or n* [NL *Ophiura* + E *-an*] **:** OPHIUROID

[1]**ophi·urid** \ˌ==ˈrəd\ *adj* [NL *Ophiurida*] **:** of or relating to the Ophiurida; *broadly* **:** OPHIUROID

[2]**ophiurid** \"\ *n* -s **:** a member of the order Ophiurida **:** a typical brittle star; *broadly* **:** OPHIUROID

ophi·uri·da \ˌ==ˈrədə\ *n pl, cap* [NL, fr. *Ophiura* + *-ida*] **:** an order or other division of Ophiuroidea comprising brittle stars with simple unbranched arms

[1]**ophi·uroid** \ˌ==ˌrȯid\ *adj* [NL *Ophiuroidea*] **:** of or relating to the Ophiuroidea

[2]**ophiuroid** \"\ *n* -s **:** an echinoderm of the subclass Ophiuroidea **:** BRITTLE STAR, BASKET STAR

ophi·uroi·dea \ˌ==ˌ(y)əˈrȯidēə\ *n pl, cap* [NL, fr. *Ophiura* + *-oidea*] **:** a subclass or class of Echinodermata comprising the brittle stars and basket stars and being distinguished from Asteroidea by the slender flexible arms that are sharply marked off from the central disc, contain neither intestinal ceca nor prolongations of the gonads, and lack ambulacral grooves and by the location of the madreporite on the ventral surface adjacent to the mouth — see EURYALIDA, OPHIURIDA

ophry·on \ˈäfrēˌän, ˈōf-\ *n* -s [NL, fr. Gk *ophrys*, brow, eyebrow — more at BROW] **:** a craniometric point in the median line of the forehead and immediately above the orbits — see CRANIOMETRY illustration

ophryo·scolec·i·dae \ˌäfrē(ˌ)ōskōˈlesəˌdē, ˌōf-\ *n pl, cap* [NL, fr. *Ophryoscolec-, Ophryoscolex*, type genus (fr. Gk *ophrys* + NL *-o-* + *-scolec-, -scolex*) + *-idae*] **:** a large family of oligotrichous ciliates that are endocommensals in the stomach of ruminants where they break down starches and probably cellulose and presumably contribute protein to their hosts

ophrys \ˈäfrəs, ˈōf-\ [NL, fr. Gk, brow, eyebrow, a plant with two leaves] *syn of* LISTERA

ophthalm- *or* **ophthalmo-** *comb form* [Gk, fr. *ophthalmos* eye — more at OPHTHALMIA] **1 :** eye **:** eyeball ⟨*ophthalmo*tomy⟩ ⟨*ophthalm*ectomy⟩ **2 :** of or affecting the eyes ⟨*ophthalmo*carcinoma⟩ ⟨*ophthalm*algia⟩

-oph·thal·ma \ˌäfˈthalmə, ÷äp|th-\ *or* **-oph·thal·mia** \-mēə\ *n pl comb form* [-*ophthalma*, NL, fr. Gk, neut. pl. of adj. comb. form *-ophthalmos* having a (specified) eye, fr. *ophthalmos*; *-ophthalmia*, NL, fr. Gk *ophthalmos* + NL *-ia*] **:** ones having a (specified) eye — used in higher taxa esp. of arthropods ⟨Edri*ophthalma*⟩ ⟨Pod*ophthalmia*⟩

oph·thalm·encephalon \(ˌ)äfˌthalm, ÷(ˌ)äpˈth- +\ *n* [NL, fr. *ophthalm-* + *encephalon*] **:** the neural visual apparatus including the retinas, the optic nerves, and the parts of the brain functioning in vision

oph·thal·mia \äfˈthalmēə, ÷ äpˈth-\ *n* -s [ME *obtalmia*, fr. LL *ophthalmia*, fr. Gk, fr. *ophthalmos* eye, prob. fr. *op-* (root of *opsesthai* to be going to see) + *-thalmos*, alter. of *thalamos* chamber, room — more at OPTIC, THALAMUS] **:** an inflammation of the conjunctiva or of the eyeball

-oph·thal·mia \ˌäfˈthalmēə, ÷ˌäpˈth-\ *n comb form* -s [NL, fr. Gk, fr. *ophthalmos* eye + *-ia* -y] **:** condition of having (such) eyes ⟨micr*ophthalmia*⟩

ophthalmia neo·na·to·rum \-ˌnēənəˈtōrəm\ *n* [NL] **:** acute inflammation of the eyes in the newborn from infection during passage through the birth canal

oph·thal·mi·a·ter \äfˈthalmēˌad·ə(r), ÷äpˈth-\ *n* -s [*ophthalm-* + Gk *iatēr* healer, fr. *iasthai* to heal — more at IATRIC] **:** OCULIST

oph·thal·mic \(ˈ)äfˈthalmik, -mēk, ÷ äpˈth-\ *adj* [Gk *ophthalmikos* fr. *ophthalm-* + *-ikos* -ic] **1 :** of, relating to, or near the eye : OCULAR **2** : for use on or in the eye ⟨an ~ ointment⟩

ophthalmic artery *n* : a branch of the internal carotid following the optic nerve through the optic foramen into the orbit and supplying the eye and adjacent structures

ophthalmic ganglion *n* : CILIARY GANGLION

ophthalmic glass *n* : glass similar to optical glass but annealed in rolled sheets and used primarily for spectacle lens blanks

ophthalmic nerve *n* : the first division of the trigeminal nerve, arising from the gasserian ganglion and by its branches supplying sensory fibers to the lachrymal gland, eyelids, ciliary muscle, nose, forehead, and adjoining parts

ophthalmic optician *n, Brit* : OPTOMETRIST

ophthalmic vein *n* : either of two veins, a superior and an inferior, that pass from the orbit through the superior orbital fissure to the cavernous sinus

oph·thal·mite \ə'⸗,mīt\ *n* -s [*ophthalm-* + *-ite*] : an eyestalk of a crustacean

oph·thal·mi·tis \,⸗,⸗'mīd·əs, - thəl-\ *n* -ES [NL, fr. *ophthalm-* + *-itis*] : OPHTHALMIA

oph·thal·mo·diastimeter \äf¦thal(,)mō, ÷äp¦th-\ *n* [*ophthalm-* + *diastimeter*] : an instrument for adjusting the distance between the eyes and lenses (as of spectacles)

ophthalmodynamometer \"+\ *n* [ISV *ophthalm-* + *dynamometer*; prob. orig. formed as F *ophtalmodynamomètre*] : an instrument used to determine the nearest point to which the two eyes can be made to converge

oph·thal·mo·graph \äf'thalmə,graf, -rȧf, ÷äp'th-\ *n* [*ophthalm-* + *-graph*] : an instrument that photographs the movements of the eyes during reading

oph·thal·mo·leu·ko·scope *also* **oph·thal·mo·leu·co·scope** \(,)äf,thalmə'lükə,skōp, ÷ (,)äp,th-\ *n* [*ophthalm-* + *leuc-* + *-scope*] : an apparatus for testing the color sense by means of colors produced by polarized light

oph·thal·mo·log·ic \(¦)äf¦thalmə¦läjik, ÷(¦)äp¦th-, ¦⸗ thəl-, -jēk, *by* l-*dissimilation* ÷_thəmə-\ *also* **oph·thal·mo·log·i·cal** \-jəkəl, -jēk-\ *adj* : of or relating to ophthalmology — **oph·thal·mo·log·i·cal·ly** \-jək(ə)lē, -jēk-, -li\ *adv*

oph·thal·mol·o·gist \,äf,thal'mäləjəst, ÷,äp,th-, -_thəl-, *by* l-*dissimilation* ÷-_thə'm-\ *n* -s : a physician that specializes in the study and treatment of defects and diseases of the eye — compare OPTICIAN, OPTOMETRIST

oph·thal·mol·o·gy \-jē,-ji\ *n* -ES [*ophthalm-* + *-logy*] : a branch of medical science concerned with the structure, functions, and diseases of the eye — compare OPTOMETRY

oph·thal·mom·e·ter \,⸗,thal'mämәd·ə(r), -_thəl-\ *n* [ISV *ophthalm-* + *-meter*] : an instrument for measuring the eye; *specif* : an instrument for measuring the size of a reflected image on the convex surface of the cornea of the eye by which its principal meridians and the presence and amount of astigmatism may be determined

oph·thal·mo·met·ric \(¦)äf¦thalmə¦me·trik, ÷(¦)äp,th-\ *or* **oph·thal·mo·met·ri·cal** \-rəkəl\ *adj* : of, relating to, or by means of an ophthalmometer or ophthalmometry

oph·thal·mom·e·try \,⸗,⸗'mäm·ə·trē, -_thəl-\ *n* -ES [ISV *ophthalm-* + *-metry*] : the measuring of the corneal curvatures of the eye and of their deviations from normal (as in astigmatism) usu. by means of an ophthalmometer

oph·thal·mo·phore \⸗'thalmə,fō(ə)r\ *also* **oph·thal·mo·pho·ri·um** \(,)⸗,⸗mə'fōrēəm\ *n, pl* **ophthalmophores** \-,fō(ə)rz\ *also* **ophthalmopho·ria** \-'fōrēə\ [*ophthalmophore* fr. *ophthalm-* + *-phore*; *ophthalmophorium* fr. NL, fr. E *ophthalmophore*] : OMMATOPHORE — **oph·thal·moph·o·rous** \¦⸗,⸗¦mäfərəs, -_thəl-\ *adj*

oph·thal·mo·ple·gia \(,)⸗,thalmə'plēj(ē)ə\ *n* -s [NL, fr. *ophthalm-* + *-plegia*] : paralysis of the muscles of the eye — **oph·thal·mo·ple·gic** \(¦)⸗¦⸗¦plējik\ *adj*

oph·thal·mo·pod \ə'⸗⸗,päd\ *n* -s [*ophthalm-* + *-pod*] : EYESTALK

ophthalmo-reaction \⸗'⸗(,)mō+\ *n* [ISV *ophthalm-* + *reaction*] : a serological diagnostic reaction involving the use of a test antigen (as tuberculin) on the mucous membrane of the eye, a positive response indicative of infection being signalized by hyperemia, swelling, and lacrimation

oph·thal·mo·sau·rus \(,)⸗,⸗mə'sȯrəs\ *n, cap* [NL, fr. *ophthalm-* + *-saurus*] : a genus of Jurassic and Lower Cretaceous ichthyosaurs of England having no or only a few small teeth

oph·thal·mo·scope \⸗'⸗mə,skōp\ *n* [ISV *ophthalm-* + *-scope*; prob. orig. formed as G *ophthalmoskop*] : an instrument for viewing the interior of the eye consisting of a concave mirror with a hole in the center through which the observer examines the eye, a source of light that is reflected into the eye by the mirror, and lenses in the mirror which can be rotated into the opening in the mirror to neutralize the refracting power of the eye being examined and thus make the image of the fundus clear — **oph·thal·mo·scop·ic** \(¦)⸗¦⸗¦skäpik\ *adj* — **oph·thal·mo·scop·i·cal·ly** \-pək(ə)lē\ *adv*

oph·thal·mos·co·py \,äf,thal'mäskəpē, -_thəl-, ÷,äp(,)th-\ *n* -ES [ISV *ophthalm-* + *-scopy*] : examination of the eye with an ophthalmoscope

oph·thal·mo·trope \⸗'thalmə·,trōp\ *n* -s [*ophthalm-* + *-trope*] : a mechanical eye for demonstrating the movement of the eye muscles

oph·thal·mo·tropometer \(¦)⸗¦thalmō +\ *n* [*ophthalm-* + *tropometer*] : an instrument for measuring ocular movements

-oph·thal·mus \,äf'thalməs, ÷,äp'th-\ *n comb form* [NL, fr. Gk *-ophthalmos*, fr. *ophthalmos* eye — more at OPHTHALMIA] **1** : one having a (specified) kind of eye — in generic names usu. of arthropods ⟨Megophthalmus⟩ **2** -ES : eyes of a (specified) form or in a (specified) state ⟨megalophthalmus⟩

-o·pia \'ōpēə\ *n comb form* [NL, fr. Gk *-ōpia*, fr. *ōps* eye, face + *-ia* -y — more at EYE] **1** *also* **-o·py** \,ōpē, -pi\ *pl* **-opias** *also* **-opies** [NL *-opia*] **a** : vision : condition of having (such) vision ⟨diplopia⟩ ⟨amblyopy⟩ **b** : possession of an eye or eyes with a (specified) defect ⟨anopia⟩ **2** : one having a (specified) kind of eye — in generic names in zoology ⟨Heteropia⟩

opi·an·ic acid \¦ōpē¦anik-\ *n* [*opiane*, obs. syn. of *narcotine* (fr. *opium* + *-ane*) + *-ic*] : a bitter crystalline aldehyde acid $C_6H_2(OCH_3)_2(CHO)COOH$ obtained by the oxidation of narcotine and hydrastine

¹**opi·ate** \'ōpēət, -ē,āt, *usu* -d·+V\ *adj* [ML *opiatus*, fr. L *opium* + *-atus* -ate] **1** : containing or mixed or impregnated with opium **2 a** : inducing sleep : SOMNIFEROUS, NARCOTIC **b** : causing rest, dullness, or inaction

²**opiate** \"\ *n* -s **1** : a medicine containing or derived from opium and tending to induce sleep and to alleviate pain **2** : a synthetic drug capable of producing or sustaining addiction similar to that characteristic of morphine and cocaine : NARCOTIC — used esp. in modern law **3** : something that induces rest or inaction or quiets uneasiness ⟨price fixing is a most dangerous ~ —T.W.Arnold⟩

³**opiate** \-ē,āt, *usu* -ād·+V\ *vt* -ED/-ING/-S [*opium* + *-ate*, vb. suffix] **1 a** : to subject to the influence of an opiate : put to sleep **b** : to diminish the force, intensity, or sensitiveness of : DEADEN **2** : to impregnate or mix with opium

opi·at·ic \¦ōpē¦ad·ik\ *adj* : of, relating to, or like opiates

-opies *pl of* -OPY

opifice *n* -s [L *opificium*, fr. *opific-* *opifex* workman, irreg. fr. *opus* work + *-fic*, *-fex* (fr. *facere* to do, make) — more at OPERATE, DO] *obs* : LABOR, WORKMANSHIP; *also* : a piece of work

opif·i·cer \ō'pifəsə(r)\ *n* -s [L *opific-* *opifex* + E *-er*] : ARTIFICER, WORKMAN, MAKER

opi·hi \ō'pē(,)hē\ *n* -s [Hawaiian *'opihi*] *Hawaii* : any of several edible limpets (genus *Helcioniscus*)

opil·ia \ō'pilēə\ *n, cap* [NL, perh. fr. *Opilio*, genus of arachnids — more at OPILIONEA] : a small genus (the type of the family Opiliaceae) of Old World tropical climbing shrubs

opil·i·a·ce·ae \,⸗,⸗⸗'āsē,ē\ *n pl, cap* [NL, fr. *Opilia*, type genus + *-aceae*] : a family of tropical shrubs or trees (order Santalales) having coriaceous leaves, small flowers, and drupaceous fruit — **opil·i·a·ceous** \⸗¦⸗⸗¦āshəs\ *adj*

opil·i·o·nea \ō,pilē'ōnēə\ *or* **opil·i·o·nes** \-,nēz\ *or* **opil·i·o·ni·na** \-ə'nīnə\ [NL, fr. *Opilion-*, *Opilio*, genus of arachnids, fr. L *opilion-*, *opilio* shepherd, fr. *ovis* sheep + *-pilion-*, *-pilio* driver (fr. *pellere* to drive) — more at EWE, FELT] *syn of* PHALANGIDA

opil·i·o·nine \⸗'⸗⸗ə,nīn, -_nən\ *adj or n* [NL *Opilionina*] : PHALANGID

opinable *adj* [L *opinabilis*, fr. *opinari*, to have an opinion, think + *-abilis* -able — more at OPINE] **1** *obs* : being a matter of opinion **2** *obs* : capable of being opined : constituting an object of opinion

op·i·nant \'äpənənt, ō'pīn-\ *n* -s [F, fr. pres. part. of *opiner* to opine, fr. L *opinari*] : OPINER

¹**opin·a·tive** \ō'pīnəd·iv\ *adj* [LL *opinativus* expressing a conjecture, fr. L *opinatus* (past part. of *opinari*) + *-ivus* -ive] **1** *obs* : OBSTINATE, OPINIONATED **2** : of, relating to, or constituting opinion : UNCERTAIN — **opinatively** *adv, obs*

²**opinative** \"\ *n* -s : an opinionated person

opinator *n* -s [L, fr. *opinatus* + *-or*] *obs* : OPINER, THEORIST

opine \ō'pīn, ə'p-\ *vb* -ED/-ING/-S [MF *opiner*, fr. L *opinari* to have an opinion, think; perh. akin to L *optare* to choose, desire, *option-*, *optio* free choice, Gk *epiopsesthai* to be going to choose] *vt* **1** : to express in form as one's opinion : give a formal opinion about : STATE ⟨*opined* that the weather would improve⟩ **2** : to have, hold, or form an opinion about ⟨some things we know, some we only ~⟩ ~ *vi* : to form or express opinions ⟨you may ~ about anything under the sun⟩

opin·er \-nə(r)\ *n* -s : one that opines

oping *pres part of* OPE

opin·i·ate \ō'pinē,āt, ə'p-\ *vt* -ED/-ING/-S [irreg. fr. *opinion* + *-ate*] **1** *archaic* : OPINE, SUPPOSE **2** *archaic* : to establish in an opinion **3** *archaic* : to declare an opinion on

opin·i·a·tive \ō'pinē,ād·iv, ə'p-\ *adj* [MF *opiniatif*, irreg. fr. *opinion* + *-atif* -ative] : OPINIONATIVE — **opin·i·a·tive·ness** *n* -ES

¹**opiniatre** *also* **opiniastre** *or* **opiniaster** *adj* [MF *opinionastre*, *opiniatre*, fr. *opinion*] *obs* : OPINIONATED

²**opiniatre** *also* **opiniastre** *or* **opiniaster** *n* -s *obs* : an opinionated person

³**opiniatre** *vb* -ED/-ING/-S [F *opiniâtrer*, fr. *opiniâtre* opiniated, fr. MF *opiniatre*] *vt*, *obs* : to obstinately maintain (an opinion) or persist in (a course of action) ~ *vi*, *obs* : to obstinately maintain an opinion or persist in a course of action

opiniatrety *also* **opiniatry** *n* -ES [*opiniatrety* fr. F *opiniâtreté*, fr. *opiniâtre* + *-té* -ty; *opiniatry* fr. F *opiniastrie*, fr. MF *opiniastre* + *-ie* -y] *obs* : the quality or state of being opinionated : mental obstinacy or inflexibility

opin·i·cus \ō'pinəkəs\ *n* -ES [origin unknown] **1** : a fabulous beast represented esp. in heraldry much like a griffon but with a short tail **2** : an insignia bearing or consisting of an opinicus

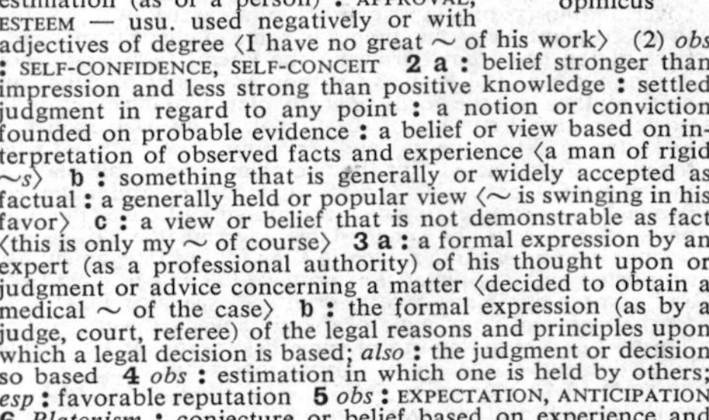

opinicus

¹**opin·ion** \ə'pinyən *sometimes* ō'p-\ *n* -s [ME, fr. MF, fr. L *opinion-*, *opinio*; akin to L *opinari*] **1 a** : a view, judgment, or appraisal formed in the mind about a particular matter or particular matters ⟨why ask my ~ if you have already decided⟩ **b** (1) : favorable impression or estimation (as of a person) : APPROVAL, ESTEEM — usu. used negatively or with adjectives of degree ⟨I have no great ~ of his work⟩ (2) *obs* : SELF-CONFIDENCE, SELF-CONCEIT **2 a** : belief stronger than impression and less strong than positive knowledge : settled judgment in regard to any point : a notion or conviction founded on probable evidence : a belief or view based on interpretation of observed facts and experience ⟨a man of rigid ~s⟩ **b** : something that is generally or widely accepted as factual : a generally held or popular view ⟨~ is swinging in his favor⟩ **c** : a view or belief that is not demonstrable as fact ⟨this is only my ~ of course⟩ **3 a** : a formal expression by an expert (as a professional authority) of his thought upon or judgment or advice concerning a matter ⟨decided to obtain a medical ~ of the case⟩ **b** : the formal expression (as by a judge, court, referee) of the legal reasons and principles upon which a legal decision is based; *also* : the judgment or decision so based **4** *obs* : estimation in which one is held by others; *esp* : favorable reputation **5** *obs* : EXPECTATION, ANTICIPATION **6** *Platonism* : conjecture or belief based on experience and perception

syn VIEW, BELIEF, CONVICTION, PERSUASION, SENTIMENT: these nouns have in common the sense of a more or less clearly formulated idea or judgment which one holds as true. OPINION implies a conclusion concerning something on which ideas may differ, not, however, excluding a careful consideration or weighing of evidence or pros and cons, but usu. stressing the subjectivity and disputability of the conclusion ⟨opposing political *opinions*⟩ ⟨a man of strong likes and dislikes but few *opinions*⟩ ⟨a dissenting *opinion* handed down by a Supreme Court judge⟩ ⟨to prefer to deal in facts rather than *opinions*⟩ VIEW is an opinion or set of opinions usu. more or less colored by individual feeling, sentiment, or bias ⟨the political *views* of the opposing party⟩ ⟨expressed her *views* on the role of education in the integration of home and community life —*Current Biog.*⟩ ⟨to air one's *views*⟩ BELIEF differs from *view* or *opinion* in implying a conclusion or set of interrelated conclusions not necessarily formulated by the individual but often constituting a dogma, doctrine, or proposition already formulated prior to the individual's acceptance or adoption of it; it emphasizes the individual's assent to the conclusion or his assurance of its truth ⟨religious *beliefs*⟩ ⟨old customs and old *beliefs* —Wilfrid Goatman⟩ ⟨to hold the *belief* that man has certain inalienable rights⟩ CONVICTION is a belief held strongly because one has no doubts about its truth ⟨the *conviction* that where one was born and lives is the best place in the world —E.L.Ullman⟩ ⟨along with that faith have lost the old . . . *conviction* that most people are good and that evil is merely an accident —Malcolm Cowley⟩ ⟨a man of many positive *convictions*⟩ PERSUASION suggests a belief or set of beliefs held strongly, often predominantly though by no means exclusively on nonlogical or nonrational grounds ⟨Christians of all *persuasions* —*Current Biog.*⟩ ⟨the childish *persuasion* that we have the only rational way of doing things —Gustave Weigel⟩ ⟨an artist who is not of the contemporary *persuasion* —*Sydney (Australia) Bull.*⟩ SENTIMENT, rather infrequent today in this sense, suggests a more or less settled opinion, often involving feelings or emotions ⟨a speech in which he expressed an apparent reversal of his known conservative *sentiments* —A.L. Funk⟩ ⟨to express strong *sentiments* on a political issue⟩ — **be of the opinion** : to hold as an opinion : THINK

²**opinion** \"\ *vb* -ED/-ING/-S *chiefly dial* : OPINE

opin·ion·able \-nəbəl\ *adj* [²*opinion* + *-able*] : admitting of opinion : having no single provable solution

opin·ion·al \-nəl\ *adj* : of, relating to, or constituting opinion

¹**opin·ion·ate** \-nə́t, -,nāt\ *adj* [¹*opinion* + *-ate*, adj. suffix] **1** *obs* : grounded on opinion : lacking firm factual bases **2** *obs* : OPINIONATED — **opin·ion·ate·ly** *adv*

²**opin·ion·ate** \-,nāt, *usu* -ād·+V\ *vt* -ED/-ING/-S [¹*opinion* + *-ate*, vb. suffix] : OPINE

opin·ion·at·ed \-,nād·əd, -ātəd\ *adj* [¹*opinionate* + *-ed*] **1** *obs* : having or holding a specified opinion : OPINIONED; *specif* : CONCEITED **2** : stiff in opinion : firmly or unduly adhering to one's own opinion or to preconceived notions : OBSTINATE — **opin·ion·at·ed·ly** *adv* — **opin·ion·at·ed·ness** *n* -ES

opin·ion·a·tive \-,nād·iv\ *adj* [*opinion* + *-ative*] **1** *obs* **a** : based on opinion : CONJECTURAL, IMAGINARY **b** : PROUD, CONCEITED **2** : of, relating to, or consisting of opinion or belief : DOCTRINAL **3** : unduly attached to one's own opinions : tending to be opinionated — **opin·ion·a·tive·ly** \-d·əvlē\ *adv* — **opin·ion·a·tive·ness** \-d·ivnəs\ *n* -ES

opin·ion·a·tor \-,nād·ə(r)\ *n* -s [²*opinionate* + *-or*] : an expresser, holder, or creator of opinion

opin·ioned \ə'pinyənd *sometimes* ō'p-\ *adj* [¹*opinion* + *-ed*] **1** : having or holding an opinion : possessed of a usu. specified opinion ⟨are we so hardly ~ as to hear no arguments⟩ **2** : having a usu. favorable opinion with respect to a particular thing ⟨arrogant fellows very well ~ of themselves⟩ **3** : OPINIONATED ⟨a biased and ~ editorial⟩

opin·ion·ist \-nəst\ *n* -s **1** : one who holds an unusual or heretical belief or opinion : SECTARY **2** : a person holding a specified opinion

opin·ion·naire *also* **opin·ion·aire** \ə¦pinyə¦na(a)|(ə)r, -ne|, |ə\ *n* -s [*opinion* + *questionnaire*] : a questionnaire designed to elicit views on matters of opinion from which generalizations may be abstracted

opinion poll *n* : a recording of the replies to a question or set of questions of opinion given by a small percentage of the members of a group or of the general public and used as a basis for gauging group opinion or public opinion on a particular issue

opinions *pl of* OPINION, *pres 3d sing of* OPINION

opio- *comb form* [Gk *opion* opium — more at *opium*] : opium ⟨*opiomania*⟩ ⟨*opiophagous*⟩

opio·phile \'ōpēə,fīl\ *n* -s [*opio-* + *-phile*] : a user of opium

opip·a·rous \ō'pipərəs\ *adj* [L *opiparus*, fr. *ops* riches + *parare* to provide, prepare — more at OPULENT, PARE] *archaic* : SUMPTUOUS — **opip·a·rous·ly** *adv, archaic*

op·i·som·e·ter \,äpə'sämәd·ə(r)\ *n* [fr. Gk *opisō* backwards + E *-meter*; akin to Gk *opisthen*] : an instrument used for measuring curved lines (as on a map) and consisting essentially of a screw with a wheel-shaped nut that is made to rotate forward along the curved lines and then backward to its original position on the screw along a straight scale

opisth- *or* **opistho-** *comb form* [Gk, fr. *opisthen*, *opithen* behind, in the rear; akin to Gk *epi* on, upon — more at EPI-] **1** : having something (specified) located dorsally or posteriorly ⟨*opisthotic*⟩ ⟨*opisthandric*⟩ **2** : dorsal or posterior ⟨*opisthaptor*⟩ ⟨*opisthodome*⟩

op·is·thap·tor \¦äpəs¦thaptə(r)\ *n* [NL, fr. *opisth-* + *haptor*] : the posterior and usu. complex adhesive organ of a monogenetic trematode

opis·the·nar \ə'pisthə,när, -ȧ(r\ *n* [NL, fr. Gk, fr. *opisth-* + *thenar*] : the back of the hand

opis·thi·on \ə'pisthē,än\ *n, pl* **opis·thia** \-ēə\ *or* **opisthions** [NL, fr. Gk, neut. of *opisthios* hinder, fr. *opisthen*] : the median point of the posterior border of the foramen magnum

opisometer

¹**opis·tho·branch** \ə'pisthə,braŋk\ *adj* [NL *Opisthobranchia*] : of or relating to the Opisthobranchia

²**opisthobranch** \"\ *n* -s : a mollusk of the order Opisthobranchia

opis·tho·bran·chia \⸗,⸗⸗'braŋkēə\ *n pl, cap* [NL, fr. *opisth-* + *-branchia*] *zool* : a large order of Euthyneura comprising marine gastropod mollusks having the gills when present posterior to the heart and having no operculum — compare STREPTONEURA; see NUDIBRANCHIA, TECTIBRANCHIA — **opis·tho·bran·chi·ate** \⸗¦⸗⸗¦braŋkēət, -ē,āt\ *adj or n*

opis·tho·bran·chi·a·ta \⸗,⸗⸗,⸗⸗'ād·ə, -ād·ə\ *syn of* OPISTHOBRANCHIA

opis·tho·coe·la \⸗,⸗⸗'sēlə\ *n pl, cap* [NL, fr. neut. pl. of *opisthocoelus* hollow behind — more at OPISTHOCOELOUS] : a suborder of Salientia comprising frogs and toads having short free ribs and vertebrae that are concave behind but not in front and including the families Discoglossidae and Pipidae — **opis·tho·coe·lan** \-lən\ *n* -s — **opis·tho·coe·lid** \⸗¦⸗⸗¦lə̇d\ *adj or n*

opis·tho·coe·lia \⸗,⸗⸗'sēlēə\ [NL, fr. *opisthocoelus* + *-ia*] *syn of* SAUROPODA

opis·tho·coe·li·an \⸗¦⸗⸗¦lēən\ *adj* [NL *opisthocoelus* + E *-ian*] : OPISTHOCOELOUS

opis·tho·coe·lous \-ləs\ *adj* [NL *opisthocoelus*, fr. *opisth-* + Gk *koilos* hollow — more at CAVE] : of, relating to, or being a vertebra that is concave behind with the anterior end of the centrum flat or convex and the posterior concave

opis·tho·come \ə'pisthə,kōm\ *n* -s [NL *Opisthocomus*, fr. LGk *opisthokomos* wearing the hair long behind, from Gk *opisth-* + *komē* hair] : HOATZIN

op·is·thoc·o·mi \,äpəs'thäkə,mī\ *n pl, cap* [NL, pl. of *Opisthocomus*] : a suborder of Galliformes constituted by the hoatzin

opis·tho·com·i·dae \ə,pisthə'kämə,dē\ *n pl, cap* [NL, fr. *Opisthocomus*, type genus + *-idae*] : a family of birds coextensive with the suborder Opisthocomi

opis·tho·cra·ni·on \-'krānē,än\ *n* -s [NL, fr. LGk *opisthokranion*, fr. Gk *opisth-* + *kranion* skull — more at CRANIUM] : the posteriormost point in the midsagittal plane of the occiput

opis·tho·det·ic \⸗¦⸗⸗¦ded·ik\ *adj* [Gk *opisthodetos* tied behind (fr. *opisth-* + *detos*, verbal of *dein* to tie, bind) + E *-ic* — more at DIADEM] : situated behind the beak — used of the ligament of a bivalve mollusk — compare PROSODETIC

opis·tho·dome \ə'pisthə,dōm\ *n* [Gk *opisthodomos*, fr. *opisth-* + *domos* house — more at TIMBER] : a back chamber; *esp* : the part of the naos of a classical temple farthest from the main entrance

op·is·thod·o·mos \,äpəs'thädəməs, -,mäs\ *or* **op·is·thod·o·mus** \-_məs\ *n* -ES [*opisthodomos*, Gk; *opisthodomus*, L, fr. Gk *opisthodomos*] : OPISTHODOME

opis·tho·dont \ə'pisthə,dänt\ *adj* [*opisth-* + *-odont*] : having back teeth only ⟨~ snakes⟩

opis·tho·gastric \ə¦pisthə+\ *adj* [F *opisthogastrique*, fr. *opisth-* + *gastrique* gastric] : situated behind the stomach

opis·tho·glos·sa \⸗,⸗⸗'gläsə, -lȯsə\ *n pl, cap* [NL, fr. *opisth-* + *-glossa*] : a division of Salientia comprising amphibians with the tongue attached in front and free behind — **opis·tho·glos·sal** \⸗¦⸗⸗¦gläsəl, -lȯs-\ *or* **opis·tho·glos·sate** \-sə̇t, -,sāt\ *adj*

¹**opis·tho·glyph** \⸗'⸗⸗,glif\ *or* **opis·tho·glyph·ous** \⸗¦⸗⸗¦glifəs\ *also* **opis·tho·glyph·ic** \-fik\ *adj* [*opisthoglyph* fr. NL *Opisthoglypha*; *opisthoglyphous* fr. NL *Opisthoglypha* + E *-ous*; *opisthoglyphic* fr. NL *Opisthoglypha* + E *-ic*] : of or relating to the Opisthoglypha : having teeth of the type characteristic of this group

²**opisthoglyph** \"\ *n* -s : an opisthoglyph snake

op·is·thog·ly·pha \,äpəs'thägləfə, ə,pisthə'glifə\ *n pl, cap* [NL, neut. pl. of *opisthoglyphus*, carved behind, fr. *opisth-* + Gk *-glyphos*, fr. *glyphein* to carve — more at CLEAVE] : a group of snakes having one or a few posterior maxillary teeth grooved to conduct venom from the enlarged upper labial glands and comprising the families Homalopsidae, Elachistodontidae and Boigidae — compare PROTEROGLYPHA

opis·tho·gnath·i·dae \ə,pisthə'nathə,dē, -,thäg'n-\ *n pl, cap* [NL, fr. *Opisthognathus*, type genus, (fr. *opisth-* + *-gnathus*) + *-idae*] : a family of large-mouthed percoid fishes with a large naked head and the body covered with small cycloid scales — see JAWFISH

op·is·thog·na·thism \,äpəs'thägnə,thizəm\ *n* -s [ISV *opisth-* + *gnathism*] : the condition of being markedly opisthognathous

op·is·thog·na·thous \¦⸗¦⸗¦⸗⸗ thəs\ *adj* [*opisth-* + *-gnathous*] **1** : having retreating jaws — opposed to *prognathous* **2** : having the mouthparts ventral and posterior to the cranium — used esp. of hemipterons

opis·tho·go·ne·a·ta \ə,pisthə,gōnē'ād·ə, -ād·ə\ *n pl, cap* [NL, fr. *opisth-* + Gk *gonē* genitalia (fr. Gk *gignesthai* to be born) + NL *-ata* — more at KIN] : a primary division of Arthropoda comprising forms with single posterior genital aperture and including the insects and centipedes or sometimes only the latter

opis·tho·go·ne·ate \⸗¦⸗⸗¦⸗⸗ə̇t, -,āt\ *adj* [*opisth-* + Gk *gonē* + E *-ate*] **1** : having the genital opening near the hind end of the body — distinguished from *progoneate* **2** [NL *Opisthogoneata*] : of or relating to the Opisthogoneata

opis·tho·graph \ə'pisthə,graf\ *n* [L *opisthographus* written on the back, fr. Gk *opisthographos*, fr. *opisth-* + *-graphos* -graph] : an ancient manuscript or tablet written or inscribed upon both the back and the front — **opis·tho·graph·ic** \⸗¦⸗⸗¦grafik\ *or* **opis·tho·graph·i·cal** \-fəkəl\ *adj* — **op·is·thog·ra·phy** \,äpəs'thägrəfē\ *n* -ES

opis·tho·gyrate \ə¦pisthə+\ *adj* [*opisth-* + *gyrate*] : curving toward the posterior ⟨a bivalve shell with ~ umbones⟩ — compare PROSOGYRATE

opis·tho·mere \⸗'⸗⸗,mi(ə)r\ *n* -s [*opisth-* + *-mere*] : any of several terminal plates of the abdomen of the female earwig that unite to form a horny sclerite

opis·tho·mi \-,mī\ *n pl, cap* [NL, pl. of *opisthomus* with the shoulder behind fr. *opisth-* + Gk *ōmos* shoulder — more at HUMERUS] : a small order of freshwater carnivorous fishes of Africa and southern Asia that resemble eels and have modified tubular nostrils and highly developed olfactory organs — **opis·tho·mous** \-_məs\ *adj*

opis·tho·neph·ros \⸗,⸗⸗'ne,fräs\ *n, pl* **opis·tho·neph·roi** \-,frȯi\ [NL, fr. *opisth-* + Gk *nephros* kidney — more at

NEPHRITIS] : the adult kidney of animals (as some amphibians) that are commonly considered mesonephric as adults, resembling but not identical to the embryonic mesonephros

opis·tho·par·ia \ə,pisthə'pa(a)rēə\ *n pl, cap* [NL, fr. *opisth-* + *-paria* (fr. Gk *pareia* cheek)] : an order of trilobites including those in which the genal angles or spines are borne by the free cheeks — **opis·tho·par·i·an** \ ;==;pa(a)rēən\ *n or adj*

opis·thor·chi·a·sis \ə,pis,thò(r)'kīəsəs\ *n* -ES [NL, fr. *Opisthorchis* + *-iasis*] : infestation with or disease caused by liver flukes of the genus *Opisthorchis*

¹**op·is·thor·chi·id** \,äpəs¦thò(r)kēəd\ *adj* [NL *Opisthorchiidae*] : of or relating to the Opisthorchiidae

²**opisthorchiid** \"\ *n* -S : a trematode of the family Opisthorchiidae

opis·thor·chi·idae \ə,pis,thò(r)'kīə,dē\ *n pl, cap* [NL, fr. *Opisthorchis*, type genus + *-idae*] : a family of digenetic trematodes that are parasitic as adults in the bile ducts of various birds and mammals including man, that are ingested with fish as encysted metacercaria and freed in the digestive tract to make their way into the liver, and that are distinguished by the absence of a cirrus pouch and the presence of the ovary anterior to the testes — see CLONORCHIS, OPISTHORCHIS

op·is·thor·chis \,äpəs'thò(r)kəs\ *n, cap* [NL, fr. *opisth-* + Gk *orchis* testicle — more at ORCHIS] : the type genus of Opisthorchiidae including several trematodes that are casual or incidental parasites of the human liver

opis·tho·so·ma \ə,pisthə'sōmə\ *n, pl* **opisthosomata** [NL, fr. *opisth-* + *-soma*] : the posterior portion of the body of an arthropod esp. when unsegmented or when the segmentation is obscured

opis·tho·somal \ə¦pisthə+\ *also* **opis·tho·somatic** \"+\ *adj* **1** : of, relating to, or lying in the posterior region of the body **2** : forming an opisthosoma ⟨an ~ mass⟩

opis·tho·the·lae \ə;==;'thē(,)lē\ *n pl, cap* [NL, fr. *opisth-* + *-thelae* (fr. Gk *-thēlai*, fr. *thēlē* nipple)] *in some classifications* : a large suborder of Araneida containing spiders that have nonsegmented abdomens and the first pair of spinnerets unbranched — compare LIPHISTIOMORPHAE

¹**op·is·thot·ic** \,äpəs'thäd·ik\ *adj* [*opisth-* + *-otic*] : of, relating to, or constituting the posterior and inferior of the bony elements of the capsule of the internal ear

²**opisthotic** \"\ *n* -S : an opisthotic bone or cartilage

opis·tho·ton·ic \ə¦pisthə¦tänik\ *adj* [Gk *opisthotonikos*, fr. *opisthotonos* + *-ikos* -ic] : characteristic of or affected with opisthotonos ⟨an ~ posture⟩

op·is·thot·o·nos \,äpəs'thät'nəs, -ᵊn,äs\ *n* -ES [Gk, drawn backwards, fr. *opisth-* + *tonos* stretching — more at TONE] : a condition of tetanic spasm of the muscles of the back, causing the head and lower limbs to bend backward and the trunk to arch forward

op·is·thot·o·nus \-ᵊnəs\ *n* -ES [NL, fr. Gk *opisthotonos*] : OPISTHOTONOS

opi·um \'ōpēəm\ *n* -S *often attrib* [ME, fr. L, fr. Gk *opion* poppy juice, opium, dim. of *opos* vegetable juice, sap; perh. akin to L *sucus, succus* juice, sap — more at SUCCULENT] **1** : a drug that consists of the dried milky juice of the opium poppy obtained from incisions made in the unripe capsules of the plant, that has a brownish yellow color, a faint smell, and a bitter and acrid taste, that is a stimulant narcotic poison usu. producing a feeling of well-being, hallucinations, and drowsiness terminating in coma or death if the dose is excessive, that was formerly much used in medicine to soothe pain but is now often replaced by derivative alkaloids (as morphine or codeine) or synthetic substitutes, that is smoked as an intoxicant with baneful effects, and that on continued use in any form causes an addiction which is difficult to break and eventually results in physical and mental deterioration **2** : something having an effect like that of opium : STUPEFIER

opi·um·ism \-,mizəm\ *n* -S **1** : the habitual use of opium **2** : the state resulting from habitual use of opium

opium poppy *n* : a variable erect annual Eurasian poppy (*Papaver somniferum*) that has cordate leaves with wavy toothed margins and large usu. white or lavender and sometimes double flowers on long stiff peduncles and that has been cultivated since antiquity as the source of opium, for its edible oily seeds, or for ornament — see ⁶MAW, POPPY SEED OIL

op·leg·nath·i·dae \,ä(,)pleg'nathə,dē\ *n pl, cap* [NL, fr. *Oplegnathus*, type genus (fr. Gk *hoplē* hoof + NL *-gnathus*) + *-idae*] : a small family of short deep-bodied marine percoid fishes with small mouths and the teeth fused into a plate or beak — see PARROT FISH

opn *abbr* **1** operation **2** opinion

opng *abbr* opening

opo- *comb form* [Gk, fr. *opos* — more at OPIUM] : juice : sap ⟨*opo*therapy⟩

op·o·bal·sam \,äpə'bòlsəm\ *or* **op·o·bal·sa·mum** \-'balsəməm\ *n* [L *opobalsamum*, fr. Gk *opobalsamon*, fr. *opo-* + *balsamon* balsam — more at BALM] : BALM OF GILEAD 2 a

op·o·del·doc \-'del,däk\ *n* -S [NL *oppodeltoch*, prob. fr. *opo-* + *-deltoch* (origin unknown)] **1** *obs* : a medical plaster for external use **2** : any of various soap liniments; *esp* : an unofficial camphorated soap liniment of a soft semisolid consistency

opop·a·nax \ə'päpə,naks\ *n* [L, fr. Gk, fr. *opo-* + *panax*] **1** *also* **opop·o·nax** \"\ -ES **a** : an odorous gum resin formerly used in medicine and believed to be obtained from Hercules' allheal **b** : BISABOL **2 a** *cap* : a genus of southern European herbs (family Umbelliferae) having compound umbels of yellow flowers and fruit with numerous oil tubes **b** -ES : a plant of the genus *Opopanax; specif* : HERCULES' ALLHEAL **3** -ES : HUISACHE

¹**opor·to** \ō'pōrd·(,)ō\ *adj, usu cap* [fr. *Oporto*, Portugal] : of or from the city of Oporto, Portugal : of the kind or style prevalent in Oporto

²**oporto** \"\ *n* -S *often cap* [¹*oporto*] *archaic* : ⁹PORT 1

opos·sum \ə'päsəm, ō'p-\ *n, pl* **opossums** *also* **opossum** *often attrib* [fr. *āpäsûm* (in some Algonquian language of Virginia), lit., white animal] **1 a** : any of various American marsupials of the family Didelphidae; *esp* : a common omnivorous largely nocturnal and arboreal mammal (*Didelphis virginiana*) of the eastern U. S. that is naturalized on the Pacific coast, is about 2½ feet long including the scaly prehensile tail, has coarse grayish fur mingled with whitish hairs and an abdominal pouch to which the young are transferred at birth, reputedly feigns death when startled or alarmed, and is esteemed as food in some sections **b** : the pelt or fur of an opossum ⟨an ~ coat⟩ **2** *Austral* : any of several phalangers that somewhat resemble the true opossums

opossum

opossum mouse *n* : any of several small Australian phalangers (genus *Cercaërtus* syn. *Dromicia*) that resemble mice

opossum rat *n* : any of several small So. American marsupials of the genus *Caenolestes*

opossum shrimp *n* : a small crustacean of the order Mysidacea with females that carry their eggs in a pouch between the legs

opossum tree *n* **1** : OPOSSUM WOOD 2 **2** : LIQUIDAMBAR

opossum wood *n* **1 a** : SILVER BELL **b** : the close-grained hard pinkish wood of the silver bell **2** : an Australian timber tree (*Quintinia sieberi*)

op·o·therapy \¦äpə+\ *n* [ISV *opo-* + *therapy*] : ORGANOTHERAPY

opp *abbr* **1** opportunity **2** opposed; opposite

OPP *abbr* out of print at present

op·pen·auer oxidation \'äpə,naù(ə)r, -aùə-\ *n, usu cap 1st O* [after Rupert V. *Oppenauer* 20th cent. Austrian chemist] : the oxidation of a saturated or unsaturated secondary alcohol (as cholesterol) to the corresponding ketone by reaction with acetone or other ketone in the presence of aluminum *tert*-butoxide or aluminum isopropoxide — compare MEERWEIN-PONNDORF REACTION

op·pen·heim·er \'äpən,hīmə(r)\ *n* -S [G, of *Oppenheim*, fr. *Oppenheim*, town in Hesse, Germany] : a white table wine of the Rhine wine group from Rheinhessen, Germany

¹**op·pi·dan** \'äpədən, -dᵊn\ *n* -S [L *oppidanus*, fr. *oppidanus*, adj.] **1** : a resident of a town : TOWNSMAN **2** *obs* **a** : an inhabitant of a university town not a member of the university **b** : a university student living in the town rather than at a college **3** : a student at Eton College living in a residence owned by the school but situated in the town outside the limits of the original foundation — compare COLLEGER

²**oppidan** \"\ *adj* [L *oppidanus*, fr. *oppidum* + *-anus* -an] : of or relating to a town or to town as opposed to country

op·pi·dum \-dəm\ *n, pl* **oppi·da** \-də\ [L, fortified town, barriers of a circus; prob. fr. *ob* to, before, in the way of + *ped-, pes* foot — more at EPI-, FOOT] : an ancient Roman provincial town lacking self-government; *esp* : one having walls and fortifications and serving as a provincial strong point

op·pig·no·rate *or* **op·pig·ne·rate** \ə'pignə,rāt\ *vt* -ED/-ING/-S [L *oppignoratus, oppigneratus*, past. part. of *oppignorare, oppignerare* to pawn, fr. *ob-* + *pignorare, pignerare* to pledge — more at PIGNORATION] *archaic* : PLEDGE, PAWN

op·pi·late \'äpə,lāt\ *vt* -ED/-ING/-S [L *oppilatus*, past part. of *oppilare* to stop up, fr. *ob-* + *pilare* to ram down, thrust, fr. *pila* mortar; akin to L *pinsere* to pound, crush — more at PESTLE] *archaic* : to stop up : fill with obstructions : block up : OBSTRUCT

op·pi·la·tion \,==;'lāshən\ *n* -S [L *oppilation-, oppilatio*, fr. *oppilatus* + *-ion-, -io* -ion] *archaic* : an act of oppilating or the state of being oppilated : OBSTRUCTION

op·pi·la·tive \'==,lād·iv\ *adj* [L *oppilatus* + E *-ive*] *archaic* : tending to oppilate : OBSTRUCTIVE, CONSTIPATING

op·po \'ä(,)pō\ *n* -S [prob. fr. opposite (in *opposite number*) + *-o*] *Brit* : FRIEND, COMPANION; *esp* : SWEETHEART

oppone *vb* -ED/-ING/-S [L *opponere* — more at OPPONENT] *obs* : OPPOSE

op·po·nen·cy \ə'pōnənsē\ *n* -ES [²*opponent* + *-cy*] **1** : OPPOSITION, ANTAGONISM **2** *archaic* : the action of maintaining an opposing argument in or opening an academic disputation (as in trying for a degree) by proposing objections to a tenet

op·po·nens \ə'pō,nenz\ *n, pl* **op·po·nen·tes** \,äpə'nen·(,)tēz\ *or* **opponens** [NL, fr. L, pres. part. of *opponere* to oppose] : any of several muscles of the hand or foot that tend to draw one of the lateral digits across the palm or sole toward the others

¹**op·po·nent** \ə'pōnənt\ *n* -S [L *opponent-, opponens*, pres. part. of *opponere* to place against, oppose, fr. *ob-* + *ponere* put, place — more at POSITION] **1 a** : one that opposes a tenet or thesis in a disputation, argument, or other verbal controversy **b** *archaic* : one that opens an academic disputation by attacking a thesis or proposition — distinguished from *respondent, defendant* **2** : one that opposes : ADVERSARY, FOE **3** : a muscle that opposes or serves to counteract and limit the action of another : ANTAGONIST

²**opponent** \"\ *adj* [L *opponent-, opponens*] **1** : OPPOSING, ADVERSE, ANTAGONISTIC **2** : situated in front : OPPOSITE

op·por·tune \¦äpə(r)¦tün, -(r)·¦tyün\ *adj* [ME, fr. MF *opportun*, fr. L *opportunus*, fr. the phrase *ob portum* (*veniens*) coming to harbor, fr. *ob* to, towards + *portum*, accus. of *portus* harbor, port — more at PORT] **1 a** : fit, suitable, or convenient for a particular occurrence ⟨made his bid for power at an ~ moment⟩ ⟨couldn't have chosen a more ~ spot⟩ **b** : occurring at a suitable time : TIMELY ⟨this most ~ assistance⟩ ⟨~ words of reassurance⟩ **2** *obs* : ADVANTAGEOUS, HELPFUL, USEFUL **3** *obs* : open or liable to : EXPOSED **syn** see SEASONABLE

op·por·tune·ly *adv* : at a suitable time or place : so as to be opportune

op·por·tune·ness \-n(n)əs\ *n* -ES : the quality or state of being opportune

op·por·tun·ism \-ü,nizəm\ *n* -S [It *opportunismo*, fr. *opportuno* opportune (fr. L *opportunus*) + *-ismo* -ism] : the art, policy, or practice of taking advantage of opportunities or circumstances, esp. with little regard for principles or ultimate consequences

¹**op·por·tun·ist** \-ˌnəst\ *n* -S [F *opportuniste*, fr. *opportunisme* opportunism, fr. It *opportunismo*] : one who practices opportunism ⟨an aristocracy of ~s who sought power for no end except their own —Victor Canning⟩

²**opportunist** \"\ *or* **op·por·tun·is·tic** \¦==;=¦nistik, -tēk\ *adj* : of, relating to, or having the characteristics of an opportunist : marked by opportunism ⟨the rare kind of honesty that refuses to be ~ —E.B.Barrett⟩ ⟨is superbly *opportunistic*, taking advantage of every break —Alfred Bester⟩ — **op·por·tun·is·ti·cal·ly** \-tək(ə)lē, -tēk-, -li\ *adv*

op·por·tu·ni·ty \,äpə(r)'tünəd·ē, -(r)·'tyü-, -nətē, -i\ *n* -ES [ME *opportunite*, fr. MF *opportunité*, fr. L *opportunitat-, opportunitas*, fr. *opportunus* + *-itat-, -itas* -ity] **1 a** : a combination of circumstances, time, and place suitable or favorable for a particular activity or action ⟨the many small rivers . . . offered unlimited *opportunities* for water transport —*Amer. Guide Series: R. I.*⟩ ⟨artists are given ~ to do creative work —*Amer. Guide Series: N. H.*⟩ **b** : an advantageous circumstance or combination of circumstances esp. when affecting security, wealth, or freedom (as from constraint) : a time, place, or condition favoring advancement or progress ⟨to strike out in search of new *opportunities* in new surroundings —H.S.Truman⟩ ⟨sons of poor and ignorant farmers, blacksmiths, tanners and backwoodsmen, with few *opportunities* —E.G.Conklin⟩ **2** *obs* : FITNESS, COMPETENCY **3** : the quality or state of being opportune : TIMELINESS **4** *archaic* : convenience or advantage of situation **5** [by confusion] *obs* : IMPORTUNITY

syn OCCASION, CHANCE, BREAK, TIME: OPPORTUNITY indicates a combination of circumstances facilitating a certain action or inviting a certain decision ⟨it was deemed advisable to continue the case . . . in order that we might have an *opportunity* of giving to the whole subject a more deliberate consideration —R.B.Taney⟩ OCCASION is likely to convey the notion of the period or time at which an opportunity is offered; since this may be fleeting, OCCASION may suggest a combination of circumstances that are urgent and quite likely to evoke action or that have evolved it ⟨afterward she can explain . . . as *occasion* shall require —F.W.Maitland⟩ ⟨so long as a child is with adults, it has no *occasion* for the exercise of a number of important virtues —Bertrand Russell⟩ CHANCE is close to OPPORTUNITY in this sense ⟨the most challenging *opportunity* of all history — the *chance* to help create a new society —Wendell Willkie⟩ It may suggest a situation arising accidentally ⟨in war lay the greatest *chance* of his life —H.L.Mencken⟩ or a fair situation arising in an equitable allotment of things ⟨only those who have a special cause to plead will hold that . . . children of the poor [have] the same *chances* as those of the well-to-do —John Dewey⟩ BREAK, formerly a slang term and more common in the U. S. than in England, suggests a turn of luck or an opportunity offered by luck or by an act of kindliness from one with power or influence ⟨not a single day of storm, not one day of flat calm, only a few days of variables did he experience. He had all the *breaks* —S.E. Morison⟩ ⟨Communist promises of a better *break* for the common people —A.E.Stevenson b. 1900⟩ TIME may be used as a synonym for opportune time or occasion ⟨an adversary of no common prowess was watching his *time* —T.B.Macaulay⟩

opportunity cost *n* : the monetary or other advantage surrendered for something in order to acquire it in competition with other potential users ⟨the *opportunity cost* method is clearly applicable in determining the value of a property that can be shifted to another use —M.S.Kendrick⟩ ⟨by putting such things as leisure, safety, and agreeableness of work into the utility scales of the individuals, the disutility of any occupation can be represented as an *opportunity cost* —B.E.Lippincott⟩

opportunity school *n* : a school designed to meet the special needs of particular groups (as adult illiterates, foreigners seeking competency in a language, or persons requiring vocational retraining)

oppos *pl of* OPPO

op·pos·abil·i·ty \ə,pōzə'biləd·ē, -lətē, -i\ *n* : the quality or state of being opposable

op·pos·able \ə'pōzəbəl\ *adj* **1** : capable of being opposed or resisted **2** : capable of being placed opposite something else ⟨the thumb is ~ to the forefinger⟩

opposal *n* -S [ME *opposaille*, fr. *opposen* to oppose + *-aille* -al] **1** *obs* **a** : a putting of questions : EXAMINATION **b** : something that poses or puzzles **2** *obs* : OPPOSITION

op·pose \ə'pōz\ *vb* -ED/-ING/-S [in sense 1, fr. ME *opposen*, fr. MF *opposer*; in other senses, fr. F *opposer*, fr. MF, modif. (influenced by *poser* to put, place) of ML *opponere*, fr. L, to place against or opposite, to adduce in contradiction (perfect stem *oppos-*), fr. *ob-* + *ponere* to put, place — more at POSITION, POSE] *vt* **1** *obs* : to confront with hard or searching questions or objections **2 a** : to place opposite ⟨uncertain which of two *opposed* doors he should enter⟩ **b** (1) : to place the ball of (a first digit) against the corresponding part of a second digit of the same hand or foot ⟨some monkeys ~ the great toe as freely as the thumb⟩ (2) : to bring the palmar surfaces of (the forepaws) into contact ⟨various rodents ~ the paws in handling food⟩ **3** : to place over against something so as to provide resistance, counterbalance, or contrast ⟨principles that may be *opposed* to this modern confusion —Irving Babbitt⟩ ⟨to ~ one military force to another⟩ ⟨diametrically *opposed* political beliefs⟩ ⟨concreteness as *opposed* to abstraction —L. E.Lynch⟩ **4** : to offer resistance to, contend against, or forcefully withstand ⟨~ the enemy⟩ ⟨~ a congressional bill⟩ ⟨*opposed* every tendency toward nationalism —E.R.Dobson⟩ **5** *obs* : to lay (as oneself) open : EXPOSE ~ *vi* : to offer opposition to something **syn** see CONTEST

opposed *adj* [fr. past part. of *oppose*] **1** : set or placed in opposition : OPPOSITE, CONTRARY, ADVERSE **2 a** *of two engine cylinders* : opposite to each other : placed on opposite sides of a common crankshaft **b** *of an engine* : having cylinders so placed

op·pose·less \ə'pōzləs\ *adj* [*oppose* + *-less*] : IRRESISTIBLE

op·pos·er \-zə(r)\ *n* -S : one that opposes; *specif* : one that formally seeks to prevent registration of a trademark

opposing *adj* [fr. pres. part. of *oppose*] **1** : opposite in position **2** : active in or offering opposition — **op·pos·ing·ly** *adv*

opposing train *n* : a train that is moving in a direction opposite to and toward another train on the same track

¹**op·po·site** \'äpəzət, -psət, *usu* -əd·+V\ *n* -S [ME, fr. MF, fr. *opposite*, adj.] **1** *obs* **a** : the opposed point of the heavens **b** : OPPOSITION 1 **2** : one that opposes: as **a** : one taking an opposite position (as on a public question) or exhibiting opposite qualities or characteristics ⟨though twins they were complete ~s in temperament⟩ **b** *archaic* : ANTAGONIST, OPPONENT **c** : the person occupying the position opposite to one's own in square dancing **3 a** : something that is opposed to some other usu. specified thing ⟨vice and virtue are ~s⟩ **b** : ANTONYM ⟨what is the ~ of good⟩ **4 a** : a proposition in logic that is characterized by opposition (sense 2a(2)) **b** **opposites** *pl* : CONTRARY TERMS

²**opposite** \"\ *adj* [ME, fr. MF, fr. L *oppositus*, past part. of *opponere* to place against — more at OPPOSE] **1 a** : set over against something that is at the other end or side of an intervening line or space : FACING: as (1) *of two sides of a quadrilateral* : not adjacent : sharing no point at which the intervening space is zero (2) *of two angles formed by the intersection of a pair of lines* : having contact only at the apex, sharing no common side, and usu. having a combined magnitude of other than 180 degrees (3) *of two points on the circumference of a circle* : terminating the same diameter **b** (1) : situated in pairs on an axis each being separated from the other by half the circumference of the axis — used esp. of leaves; compare PHYLLOTAXY (2) *of floral parts* : SUPERPOSED (3) : situated side by side ⟨bordered pits ~⟩ — distinguished from *alternate* **2 a** : OPPOSED, HOSTILE ⟨belonged to the ~ faction⟩ ⟨~ sides of the question⟩ **b** : diametrically different : CONTRARY, ANTAGONISTIC, ANTONYMIC ⟨~ meanings⟩ **3** : being the other of a matching or contrasting pair : corresponding or complementary in position, function, or nature ⟨his courtesy toward all members of the ~ sex⟩ ⟨the chess king is set up on a square of the ~ color⟩

syn CONTRADICTORY, CONTRARY, ANTITHETICAL or ANTITHETIC, ANTIPODAL or ANTIPODEAN, ANTONYMOUS: OPPOSITE may apply to ideas, statements, conditions, or forces marked by sharp, unmistakable contrast, conflict, or antagonism ⟨the reaction against the follies of the old rationalism has led them to the *opposite* extreme of irrationalism —M.R.Cohen⟩ ⟨self-interest and sympathy, *opposite* in quality —John Dewey⟩ CONTRADICTORY applies to statements or tendencies that completely negate each other; it may imply that if one is true or valid, the other must be untrue or invalid ⟨the reconciliation of the seemingly *contradictory* facts, that the power of the many over production is at once paramount and small —W.H. Mallock⟩ ⟨*contradictory* predictions are being made, some gloomy, some optimistic —J.T.Farrell⟩ CONTRARY suggests extreme, perhaps diametrical, divergence or opposition ⟨foolishly began to teach matters *contrary* to the faith, and in the end was condemned as a heretic —H.O.Taylor⟩ ⟨*contrary* to general opinion young pilots are not the safest —H.G. Armstrong⟩ ⟨this hypothesis is not only unfounded but *contrary* to all reasonable assumptions —Edward Westermarck⟩ ANTITHETICAL or ANTITHETIC may stress diametrical opposition, the contrast involved being useful to highlight a certain significance or nature ⟨a combination of *antithetical* elements which are at eternal war with one another —W.S.Gilbert⟩ ⟨the *antithetic* consciousness of alienation from, and of communion with, the unseen power which surrounds us —W.R.Inge⟩ ANTIPODAL and ANTIPODEAN indicate a diametrical opposition and also a remoteness, as though located at opposite poles of the earth ⟨hunters, like pipe smokers, are recruited from two *antipodal* types of men — gentlemen and worthless loafers —D.C.Peattie⟩ ⟨two men *antipodean* in all their tastes⟩ ANTONYMOUS refers to words expressing opposite meanings ⟨*hot* and *cold* are *antonymous*⟩

³**opposite** \"\ *adv* : on opposite sides : in an opposed position

⁴**opposite** \"\ *prep* [²*opposite* & ³*opposite*] **1** : across an intervening space from and usu. facing or on the same level with ⟨make a check ~ a name⟩ ⟨live ~ the post office⟩ **2** : in a role complementary to ⟨played ~ the leading man⟩

opposite lady *n* : the woman of the couple opposite a man in a square dance set — compare CORNER LADY, PARTNER

opposite-leaved \¦=(=)¦=\ *adj* : having opposite leaves

op·po·site·ly *adv* : in an opposite position : so as to be opposite

op·po·site·ness *n* -ES : the quality or state of being opposite

opposite number *n* **1** : a member of a system or class who holds relatively the same position as a particular member in a corresponding system or class ⟨the Secretary of State and his *opposite number*, the Minister of Foreign Affairs⟩ ⟨union executives met their *opposite numbers* in industry⟩ **2** : a corresponding or comparable establishment, area, implement, publication, word, esp. in a different country or language

opposite tide *n* : high tide at a corresponding place on the opposite side of the earth accompanying a high tide at any given place — compare DIRECT TIDE

oppositi- *comb form* [L *oppositus*] : situated opposite : having the corresponding parts opposite ⟨*oppositi*folious⟩ ⟨*oppositi*sepalous⟩

op·po·si·tion \,äpə'zishən\ *n* -S [ME *opposicioun*, fr. ML *opposition-, oppositio*, fr. L, act of opposing, fr. *oppositus* (past part. of *opponere* to place against) + *-ion-, -io* -ion — more at OPPOSE] **1** : a configuration in which one celestial body is opposite another in the sky or in which the elongation is near or equal to 180 degrees — see CONFIGURATION **2 a** (1) *obs* : a setting of one rhetorical proposition against another : a counter proposition (2) : the relation that occurs between two propositions in logic having the same subject and predicate but differing in quantity, in quality, or in both and that is usu. considered to occur in the four forms of contrariety, subcontrariety, subalternation, and contradiction **b** *obs* : OPPOSITE, CONTRARY, CONTRAST **3** : an act of setting opposite or over against or the condition of being so set **4 a** : hostile or contrary action or condition : action designed to constitute a barrier or check ⟨offered strong ~ to the advance of the enemy⟩ ⟨a child's automatic ~ to maturity⟩ ⟨held up a hand in ~ to oncoming traffic⟩ **b** : a position of the king in chess preventing the advance of the enemy king either directly or obliquely **c** : a position of one's blade when crossed with that of one's opponent such that the latter cannot hit in the line of engagement **d** (1) : refusal of a creditor to assent to the debtor's discharge in a bankruptcy proceeding (2) : a formal action for preventing the registration of a trademark **5 a** : something that opposes; *specif* : the aggregate of those in opposition to a particular thing (as a political policy or party) **b** *often cap* : a political party that actively opposes the party in power and is prepared to replace it if opportunity offers ⟨Her Majesty's Loyal *Opposition*⟩ ⟨last election saw considerable strengthening of the ~⟩ **6** : movement of diagonally opposite limbs (as in various complex reflexes and some dance patterns) **7 :** the relationship of partial difference between two partially similar elements of a language (as oral versus nasal with *b* and *m* or singular versus plural with *man's* and *men's*)

op·po·si·tion·al \¦==¦zishən³l, -shnəl\ *adj* **1 :** relating to or constituting opposition ⟨~ activities⟩ **2 :** acting in opposition to one another ⟨~ alleles⟩

op·po·si·tion·ary \-shə,nerē\ *adj* **:** OPPOSITIONAL 1

op·po·si·tion·ism \-,nizəm\ *n* -S **:** a policy of opposition (as in politics)

op·po·si·tion·ist \-_nəst\ *n* -S **:** a member of an opposition or one who advocates or practices oppositionism

op·po·si·tion·less \-nləs\ *adj* **:** lacking opposition

op·po·si·tious \¦==¦zishəs\ *adj* [*opposition* + *-ous*] **:** inclined to oppose **:** determined in opposition

op·pos·i·tive \ə'päzəd·iv, -ətiv\ *adj* [L *oppositus* (past part. of *opponere* to set against) + E *-ive* — more at OPPOSE] **:** tending to oppose **:** functioning in the expression of contrariety — **op·pos·i·tive·ly** \-əvlē, -li\ *adv*

op·po·sure \ə'pōzhə(r)\ *n* -S [*oppose* + *-ure*] **:** OPPOSITION

op·press \ə'pres\ *vt* -ED/-ING/-ES [ME *oppressen*, fr. MF *oppresser*, fr. ML *oppressare*, fr. L *oppressus*, past part. of *opprimere* to press down, fr. *ob-* + *-primere* (fr. *premere* to press) — more at PRESS] **1 a** *archaic* **:** to put down **:** SUPPRESS, QUELL **b :** to crush, burden, or trample down by or as if by abuse of power or authority **:** treat with unjust vigor or with cruelty ⟨rulers that ~ the people⟩ **2 a :** to burden spiritually or mentally as if by pressure **:** weigh heavily upon **:** weigh down ⟨~*ed* by a sense of failure⟩ ⟨~*ed* by prolonged sultry weather⟩ **b** *obs* **:** HARASS, DISTRESS **3** *archaic* **a :** to press upon with physical violence **:** injure by physical pressure **:** CRUSH, TRAMPLE **b :** to overpower in or as if in battle **:** overwhelm by numbers **c :** OVERCOME — used of sleep, death, or other vital phenomena **4** *obs* **a :** to take unawares **b :** RAPE, RAVISH **syn** see DEPRESS, WRONG

oppressed *adj* [fr. past part. of *oppress*] **:** subjected to debruising

op·press·ible \ə'presəbəl\ *adj* **:** subject to oppression **:** unable to resist oppression

op·pres·sion \ə'preshən\ *n* -S [MF, fr. L *oppression-*, *oppressio*, fr. *oppressus* + *-ion-*, *-io* -ion] **1 a :** unjust or cruel exercise of authority or power esp. by the imposition of burdens; *esp* **:** the unlawful, excessive, or corrupt exercise of power other than by extortion by any public officer so as to harm anyone in his rights, person, or property while purporting to act under color of governmental authority **b :** something that so oppresses **:** EXACTION ⟨unfair taxes and other ~*s*⟩ **2 a :** the act of weighing down (as a person, his mind or spirits) ⟨the continued ~ of the heat⟩ **b :** the condition of being weighed down (as by misfortune) **3 :** an act of pressing down **:** PRESSURE, WEIGHT **4 :** a sense of heaviness or obstruction in the body or mind **:** DEPRESSION, DULLNESS, LASSITUDE ⟨an ~ of spirits⟩ ⟨an ~ of the lungs⟩

op·pres·sive \ə'presiv, -sēv *also* -səv\ *adj* [ML *oppressivus*, fr. L *oppressus* + *-ivus* -ive] **1 :** unreasonably burdensome **:** unjustly severe, rigorous, or harsh **:** constituting oppression ⟨~ legislation⟩ ⟨~ taxes⟩ ⟨~ exactions⟩ **2 :** using or depending upon oppression **:** TYRANNICAL ⟨an ~ ruler⟩ **3 :** overpowering or depressing to the spirit or senses **:** hard to be borne ⟨~ grief⟩ ⟨an ~ climate⟩ ⟨to ease the soul of one ~ weight —Alexander Pope⟩ **syn** see ONEROUS

op·pres·sive·ly \-əvlē, -li\ *adv* **:** in an oppressive manner **:** so as to oppress

op·pres·sive·ness \-sivnəs,-sēv-\ *n* -ES **:** the quality or state of being oppressive

op·pres·sor \-sə(r)\ *n* -S [ME, fr. AF *oppressour*, fr. L *oppressor* crusher, destroyer, fr. *oppressus* + *-or*] **:** one that oppresses esp. when in a position of public authority ⟨the orphan pines while the ~ feeds —Shak.⟩

op·pro·bri·ate \ə'prōbrē,āt\ *vt* -ED/-ING/-S [ML *opprobriatus*, past part. of *opprobriare*, fr. L *opprobrium*] **:** to regard or speak of as opprobrious

op·pro·bri·ous \-ēəs\ *adj* [ME, fr. MF or LL; MF *opprobrieux*, fr. LL *opprobriosus*, fr. L *opprobrium* + *-osus* -ous] **1 :** expressive of opprobrium **:** conveying or intended to convey disgrace **:** SCURRILOUS, CONTUMELIOUS — used chiefly of utterances ⟨~ language⟩ **2 :** deserving of opprobrium **:** INFAMOUS, DESPICABLE ⟨this ~ monument to human greed⟩ ⟨this dark, ~ den of shame —John Milton⟩ — **op·pro·bri·ous·ly** *adv* — **op·pro·bri·ous·ness** *n* -ES

op·pro·bri·um \-ēəm\ *n* -S [L, fr. *opprobrare* to reproach, fr. *ob-* + *probrum* disgraceful act, infamy, reproach, fr. *prober* guilty, subject to reproach; akin to Gk *propherein* to bring forward, reproach — more at FOR, BEAR] **1 :** something that gives occasion for disgrace or reprobation **:** opprobrious behavior **2** *obs* **:** opprobrious utterance **3 a :** public or known disgrace or ill fame that ordinarily follows from or is attached to conduct considered grossly wrong or vicious **:** INFAMY ⟨I can name four from thereabouts who have been in the pen. To only one . . . who . . . turned out to be truly criminal, does ~ attach —Oliver La Farge⟩ **b :** contempt or distaste usu. mingled with reproach and an implication of inferiority ⟨*cold storage* was once a term of ~⟩ ⟨there has always been ~ attached to ignorance of grammar —Charlton Laird⟩ **syn** see DISHONOR

op·pro·bry \ə'prōbrē\ *n* -ES [ME, fr. L *opprobrium*] *archaic* **:** OPPROBRIUM

op·pugn \ə'pyün\ *vb* -ED/-ING/-S [ME *oppugnen*, fr. L *oppugnare*, fr. *ob-* + *pugnare* to fight — more at PUGNACIOUS] *vt* **1 a :** to fight against **b** *obs* **:** WITHSTAND **2 :** to call in question **:** challenge the accuracy, propriety, probity, or other quality of **:** CONTROVERT ~ *vi* **:** stand in opposition **:** CONTEND

op·pug·nan·cy \ə'pəgnənsē, -si\ *n* -ES [LL *oppugnantia*, fr. L *oppugnant-* *oppugnans* + *-ia* -y] **:** OPPOSITION, HOSTILITY, RESISTANCE

¹op·pug·nant \-nənt\ *adj* [L *oppugnant-*, *oppugnans*, pres. part. of *oppugnare*] **:** HOSTILE, OPPOSING, ANTAGONISTIC

²oppugnant \"\ *n* -S **:** OPPONENT, ANTAGONIST

op·pug·nate \-,nāt\ *vt* -ED/-ING/-S [L *oppugnatus*, past part. of *oppugnare*] *archaic* **:** OPPUGN

op·pug·na·tion \,ä(,)pəg'nāshən\ *n* -S [L *oppugnation-*, *oppugnatio*, fr. *oppugnatus* + *-ion-*, *-io*, -ion] **:** ATTACK, OPPOSITION

op·pugn·er \ə'pyünə(r)\ *n* -S **:** one that oppugns

oppy *abbr* opportunity

opr *abbr* operate; operator

oprich·nik \ä'prichnik\ *n*, *pl* **oprich·ni·ki** \-nəkē\ *or* **oprichniks** [Russ., fr. *oprichina* corps of life-guards of Ivan IV] **:** a member of an imperial Russian police force

op·ry \'äprē, -ri\ *dial var of* OPERA

-ops \,äps\ *n comb form* [Gk *-ōp-*, *-ōps*, fr. *ōp-*, *ōps* eye, face — more at EYE] **1** *pl* **-ops** *or* **-opses :** organism with a (specified) kind of eye or face — chiefly in generic names ⟨*megalops*⟩ ⟨*Stylops*⟩ ⟨*Selenops*⟩ **2 :** organism resembling a (specified) thing — in generic names usu. combined with the names of other genera ⟨*Echinops*⟩ ⟨*Dryobalanops*⟩

-op·sia \'äpsēə\ *or* **-op·sy** \,äpsē, -si\ *n comb form*, *pl* **-opsias** *or* **-opsies** [*-opsia* fr. NL, fr. Gk, fr. *opsis* appearance, vision + *-ia* -y; *-opsy* fr. Gk *-opsia* — more at *-opsis*] **:** vision of a (specified) kind or condition ⟨*anopsia*⟩ ⟨*hemiopsia*⟩

op·si·math \'äpsə,math\ *n* -S [Gk *opsimathēs* late in learning, fr. *opse*, *opsi* late (akin to Gk *epi* on, to) + *-mathēs*, fr. *manthanein* to learn — more at EPI-, MATHEMATICAL] **:** a person who begins to learn late in life

op·sin \'äpsən\ *n* -S [prob. back-formation fr. *rhodopsin*] **:** any of various colorless proteins formed together with retinene by the action of light on a visual pigment (as rhodopsin or porphyropsin)

-op·sis \'äpsəs\ *n comb form* [NL, fr. Gk, fr. *opsis* appearance, vision — more at OPTIC] **1 a :** organism resembling or having a part that resembles a (specified) thing — in generic names ⟨*Chilopsis*⟩ ⟨*Ampelopsis*⟩ **b** *pl* **-opses :** structure resembling a (specified) thing ⟨*caryopsis*⟩ **2** *pl* **-opses :** -OPSIA

op·sis·form \'äpsəs,fȯrm\ *also* **op·sis·type** \-,tīp\ *n* [Gk *opsis* + E *form*, *type*] **:** a rust fungus that lacks uredinia — compare EU-FORM

opson- *or* **opsono-** *comb form* [*opsonin*] **:** opsonin ⟨*opsonic*⟩ ⟨*opsonotherapy*⟩ ⟨*opsonophilic*⟩

op·son·ic \(')äp¦sänik, -nēk\ *adj* [*opson-* + *-ic*] **:** of, relating to, or involving opsonin ⟨an ~ test⟩

opsonic index *n* **:** the ratio of the phagocytic index of a tested serum to that of normal serum taken as the unit

op·son·i·fi·ca·tion \(,)äp,sänəfə'kāshən\ *n* -S [*opson-* + *-i-* + *-fication*] **:** the action or the effect of opsonins in making bacteria more readily phagocytized

op·so·nin \'äpsənən\ *n* -S [L *opsonium* relish (fr. Gk *opsōnion* victuals, money for victuals, fr. *opsōnein* to purchase victuals + E *-in* — more at DUOPSONY] **:** a constituent of blood serum that makes foreign cells (as invading pathogenic bacteria) more susceptible to the action of the phagocytes

op·so·nize \-,nīz\ *vt* -ED/-ING/-S **:** to modify (as a bacterium) by the action of opsonins

op·so·no·cytophagic test \¦äpsə,nō+-\ *n* [*opson-* + *cytophagic*] **:** a test for immunity to or infection by a pathogenic organism (as of brucellosis or whooping cough) based on the assumption that the serum of an immune or infected individual contains specific opsonins capable of facilitating phagocytosis of the organism in question

-opsy \,äpsē, ,əp-, -si\ *n comb form* -ES [Gk *-opsia*] **1 :** -OPSIA **2 :** examination ⟨*biopsy*⟩

opt \'äpt\ *vi* -ED/-ING/-S [F *opter* to choose, desire, fr. L *optare* — more at OPINE] **1 :** to make a choice of citizenship; *esp* **:** to choose between a former citizenship and that of a new sovereign state made of a territory transferred by treaty ⟨~*ed* to retain his nationality⟩ **2 a :** to decide to do one of two or more alternatively possible things ⟨~*ed* to go to Europe⟩ **b :** to decide in favor of one or more alternatively available things or courses ⟨give the people an opportunity to ~ for statehood —Rupert Emerson⟩ ⟨would still ~ for a good jazz band⟩

opt *abbr* **1** operate **2** optative **3** optical; optician; optics **4** option; optional

optable *adj* [L *optabilis* desirable, fr. *optare* + *-abilis*, -able] *obs* **:** worthy to be chosen **:** DESIRABLE

op·tant \'äptənt\ *n* -S [G & Dan, fr. L *optant-*, *optans*, pres. part. of *optare* to choose] **:** one who opts

op·tate \'äp,tāt\ *vi* -ED/-ING/-S [L *optatus*, past part. of *optare*] **:** OPT 2 — **op·ta·tion** \äp'tāshən\ *n* -S

¹op·ta·tive \'äptəd·iv, -ətiv; (')äp¦tād·iv, -ātiv\ *adj* [MF *optatif*, fr. LL *optativus*, fr. L *optatus* + *-ivus* -ive] **1 a :** of, relating to, characterizing, or being a mood of verbs in Greek and other languages that is expressive of wish or desire and various related distinctions **b :** characterizing or being a sentence that is expressive of wish or hope and marked as optative by the subjunctive mood and by word order (as in *Heaven help him*) **2 :** expressing desire or wish — **op·ta·tive·ly** \-d·əvlē, -təv-, -li\ *adv*

²optative \"\ *n* -S **1 a :** the optative mood **b :** a verb or verbal form denoting the optative mood **2 :** something to be desired

¹op·tic \'äptik, -tēk\ *adj* [MF *optique*, fr. ML *opticus*, fr. Gk *optikos*, fr. *optos* (verbal of *opsesthai* to be going to see) + *-ikos* -ic; akin to Gk *opsis* sight, appearance, vision, *ōps* eye, face, *ommat-*, *omma* eye — more at EYE] **1 a :** of or relating to vision ⟨~ phenomenon⟩ **b :** dependent chiefly on vision for orientation ⟨man is basically an ~ animal⟩ — compare OSMATIC **2 a :** of or relating to the eye **:** OCULAR ⟨the ~ axis⟩ **b :** affecting the eye or an optic structure **3** *archaic* **:** relating to optics **:** OPTICAL

²optic \"\ *n* -S [in sense 1, prob. trans. of It *ottica*, fr. L *optice*, fr. Gk *optikē*, fr. fem. of *optikos*; in other senses, fr. ¹*optic*] **1** *obs* **:** OPTICS **2 :** an organ of sight **:** EYE — not used technically **3 :** any of the lenses, prisms, or mirrors of an optical instrument ⟨the ~*s* of this instrument⟩ ⟨interchangeable ~*s* of quartz, glass, rock salt —R.A.Sawyer⟩

op·ti·cal \-təkəl, -tēk-\ *adj* [in sense 1, fr. ²*optic* + *-al*; in other senses, fr. ¹*optic* + *-al*] **1 a :** relating to the science of optics **b :** dealing with or expert in optics **2 :** relating to vision **:** OCULAR, VISUAL ⟨an ~ illusion⟩ **3 a :** designed or constructed to aid the vision ⟨an ~ magnifier⟩ **b :** acting by means of light or in accord with the principles of optics

optical activity *n* **:** ability to rotate the plane of polarization of light — compare OPTICAL ROTATION

optical anomaly *n* **:** an apparent lack of harmony between the crystal form of a mineral and its optical properties

optical antipode *n* **:** ENANTIOMORPH 2

optical axis *n* **1 a :** a straight line perpendicular to the front of the cornea of the eye and extending through the center of the pupil **b :** the axis of symmetry of a radially symmetrical optical system **2 :** OPTIC AXIS 1

optical bench *n* **:** a horizontal rod or movable track that is fitted with movable clamps, is usu. provided with a linear scale, and is used for the convenient location and adjustment of light sources, optical devices, and screens employed in the observation and measurement of optical phenomena

optical bleach *n* **:** FLUORESCENT BRIGHTENER

optical calcite *n* **:** calcite suitable for use in optical instruments

optical center *n* **1 :** a point on the axis of a lens that is so located that any ray of light passing through it in passing through the lens suffers no net deviation and that may be within, without, or on either surface of the lens **2 :** the part of a flat surface (as a printed page or sheet) that appears to the eye to be in the center esp. when not coincident with the geometric center

optical constant *n* **:** any of several quantities characteristic of the optical behavior of a substance (as the refractive index, absorption coefficient, or reflectivity for a specified wavelength)

optical contact *n* **:** juxtaposition of two surfaces (as of glass) with a separation small compared to the wavelength of light so that interference fringes are not observable

optical correction *n* **:** a slight modification of geometrically correct lines (as of a building) for the purpose of making them appear correct to the eye

optical density *n* **:** DENSITY 5

optical double star *also* **optical double** *or* **optical pair** *n* **:** DOUBLE STAR 2 — compare PHYSICAL DOUBLE STAR

optical electron *n* **:** VALENCE ELECTRON

optical flat *n* **:** FLAT 6 a

optical gage *n* **:** a gage (as a micrometer comparator) that makes no direct contact with the object measured but measures an optical image of it

optical glass *n* **:** flint or crown glass of extreme purity and well-defined optical characteristics that is used chiefly for making lenses, prisms, and other optical forms

optical haze *n* **:** a condition of impaired atmospheric transparency resulting when the juxtaposition of air masses of different densities over a heated surface induces irregular refraction

optical inversion *n* **:** INVERSION 5 a

optical isomer *n* **:** one of two or more forms of a compound exhibiting optical isomerism

optical isomerism *n* **:** stereoisomerism in which the isomers have different effects on polarized light and in which asymmetry of the molecule as a whole or the presence of one or more asymmetric atoms is held to be responsible for such effects — compare ASYMMETRIC CARBON ATOM, DIASTEREOISOMERISM, ENANTIOMORPHISM, GEOMETRIC ISOMERISM

optical lever *n* **:** an arm or lever the displacement of which is measured by an attached mirror and a fixed telescope and scale commonly used for measuring small lengths

op·ti·cal·ly \'äptək(ə)lē, -tēk-, -li\ *adv* [*optical* + *-ly*] **1 :** by means of sight **:** with or to the eye ⟨as viewed ~⟩ ⟨an ~ accurate measurement⟩ **2 :** with reference to or by means of optics or to optical properties ⟨vitamins measured ~⟩ ⟨~ ground surfaces⟩ — compare OPTICALLY ACTIVE

optically active *adj* **:** capable of rotating the plane of polarization of light to the right or left **:** either dextrorotatory or levorotatory ⟨*optically active* substances may be divided into two classes depending upon whether activity is due to crystal structure —R.L.Shriner & Roger Adams⟩ — see ASYMMETRIC CARBON ATOM

optically inactive *adj* **:** INACTIVE c (2)

optical maser *n* **:** LASER

optical microscope *n* **:** a microscope in which light rays are seen directly by the observer as distinguished from one (as an electron microscope) in which some transformation or system of indirect viewing is used

optical path *n* **:** the path followed by a ray of light through an optical system

optical printer *n* **:** an apparatus for transferring a photographic picture or sound image from one film to another by means of various optical elements and devices that permit changing the size of the image and the production of special effects (as fades, dissolves, wipes) not usu. possible with contact printing

optical pyrometer *n* **:** a pyrometer that measures temperature by means of determining the intensity of the light of a particular wavelength emitted by a hot body

optical rotation *n* **:** the angle through which the plane of polarization of polarized light that traverses an optically active substance is rotated depending on the nature of the substance, on the length of the layer of the substance traversed, and on the wavelength of the light

optical section *n* **:** a plane in a translucent object (as a slip of tissue or a cell) brought into view by adjustment of the focus of a microscope

optical square *n* **:** a small hand instrument used by surveyors for laying off a right angle by means of two mirrors set at an angle of 45 degrees

optical system *n* **:** a combination of lenses, mirrors, and prisms that constitutes the optical part of an optical instrument (as a microscope or telescope)

optical train *n* **:** OPTICAL SYSTEM

optical wedge *n* **:** a graded sheet or block (as of glass or film on which is coated a layer of neutral or colored substance varying progressively in transmittance with distance along the sheet) for reducing the intensity of light or radiation gradually or in steps

optic angle *n* **1 a :** the angle formed by the optical axes of the two eyes when directed to the same point **b :** VISUAL ANGLE **2 :** the angle between the optic axes of a biaxial crystal

optic atrophy *n* **:** degeneration of the optic nerve

optic axis *n* **1 :** a line in a doubly refracting medium that is parallel to the direction in which all components of plane-polarized light travel with the same speed **2 :** OPTICAL AXIS 1

optic capsule *n* **:** either of a pair of cartilaginous capsules that develop around the eyes of elasmobranch fishes and of embryos of higher vertebrates

optic chiasma *also* **optic chiasm** *n* **:** the X-shaped partial decussation on the undersurface of the hypothalamus through which the optic nerves are continuous with the brain

optic cup *n* **:** the optic vesicle after invaginating to form a two-layered cup from which the retina and pigmented layer of the eye will develop

optic disk *n* **:** the nearly circular light-colored area at the back of the retina where the optic nerve enters the eyeball

optic foramen *n* **:** the passage in the sphenoid bone traversed by the optic nerve and ophthalmic artery — see OPTIC GROOVE

optic groove *n* **:** a narrow transverse groove that lies near the front of the superior surface of the body of the sphenoid bone, is continuous with the optic foramen, and houses the optic chiasma

op·ti·cian \äp'tishən\ *n* -S [F *opticien*, fr. ML *optica* optics + F *-ien* -ian] **1** *archaic* **:** one skilled in optics **2 a :** a maker of or dealer in optical items and instruments **b :** one that grinds spectacle lenses to prescription and dispenses spectacles — compare OCULIST, OPTOMETRIST

op·ti·cist \'äptəsəst\ *n* -S **:** a specialist in optics

optic lobe *n* **1 :** either of the anterior pair of corpora quadrigemina of a mammal **2 :** either of the corpora bigemina of a lower vertebrate **3 :** a lateral lobe of the forebrain of some arthropods containing the visual centers of the compound eyes

optic nerve *also* **op·tic** \'äptik, -tēk\ *n* -S [*optic nerve* trans. of MF *nerf optique*, trans. of ML *nervus opticus*; *optic* fr. ¹*optic*] **:** either of the second pair of cranial nerves being a sensory nerve, arising from the ventral part of the diencephalon, forming in higher vertebrates an optic chiasma before passing to the eye and spreading over the anterior surface of the retina, and serving to conduct visual stimuli from the retina to the brain; *sometimes* **:** the portion of this nerve lying between the retina and the optic chiasma — see EYE illustration; OPTIC TRACT

optic neuritis *n* **:** inflammation of the optic nerve

optico- *comb form* [F, fr. Gk *optikos* — more at OPTIC] **1 :** optical and ⟨*optico*chemical⟩ **2 :** relating or belonging to the eye **:** ocular ⟨*optico*pupillary⟩ **3 :** optic and ⟨supra*optico*hypophyseal⟩ ⟨*optico*chiasmatic⟩

op·ti·coel \'äptə,sēl\ *n* -S [blend of *optic* and *-coel* (fr. Gk *koilos* hollow) — more at CAVE] **:** the cavity of the optic vesicle

op·ti·con \'-,kän\ *n* -S [NL, fr. Gk *optikon*, neut. of *optikos* optic] **:** an external enlargement of the optic lobe of the insect brain that is the innermost of the ganglionic masses connected with the compound eye

-op·ti·con \'-_kən, -,kän\ *n comb form* -S [*stereopticon*] **:** stereopticon ⟨*pan*opticon⟩ ⟨*sci*opticon⟩

optic orientation *also* **optical orientation** *n* **:** the relation between the principal vibration directions of a crystal and the crystallographic axes

optic papilla *n* **:** a slight elevation that is nearly coextensive with the optic disk and is produced by the thick bundles of the fibers of the optic nerve in entering the eyeball

optic placode *n* **:** LENS PLACODE

optic radiation *n* **:** any of several neural radiations concerned with the visual function; *esp* **:** one made up of fibers from the pulvinar and lateral geniculate body to the cuneus and other parts of the occipital lobe

optic rod *n* **:** RHABDOM

¹op·tics \'äptiks, -tēks\ *n pl but usu sing in constr* [ML *optica*, fr. Gk *optika*, fr. neut. pl. of *optikos* optic] **:** a science that deals with light, its genesis and propagation, the effects that it undergoes and produces, and other phenomena closely associated with it — see GEOMETRICAL OPTICS, PHYSICAL OPTICS

²optics *pl of* OPTIC

optic sign *n* **:** the distinctive character of the double refraction of a crystal

optic stalk *n* **:** the constricted part of the optic vesicle by which it remains continuous with the embryonic forebrain

optic thalamus *n* **:** either of two masses of nerve tissue in the floor of the diencephalon from which the optic nerves take their origin

optic tract *n* **:** the portion of each optic nerve between the chiasma and the diencephalon proper

optic vesicle *n* **:** an outpouching of each lateral wall of the forebrain of a vertebrate embryo from which the essential nervous structures of the eye develop

optima *pl of* OPTIMUM

op·ti·ma·cy \'äptəməsē\ *n* -ES [NL *optimatia*, fr. L *optimat-*, *optimas* optimate + *-ia* -y] *archaic* **:** the best people **:** ARISTOCRACY

op·ti·mal \-məl\ *adj* [*optimum* + *-al*] **:** most desirable or satisfactory **:** OPTIMUM ⟨~ concentration of a drug⟩ — **op·ti·mal·i·ty** \,==¦maləd·ē\ *n* -ES — **op·ti·mal·ly** \'==məlē\ *adv*

op·ti·mal·ize \'==mə,līz\ *vt* -ED/-ING/-S **:** to make optimal; *specif* **:** to bring (as an industrial plant) to a peak of economic efficiency esp. by the use of precise analytical methods

op·ti·me \'äptə,mē\ *n* -S [fr. the L phrase *optime disputasti* you have argued very well] **:** a student at Cambridge University, England, prior to the 20th century obtaining honors but failing to get placed among the wranglers in the mathematical tripos

op·tim·e·ter \äp'timəd·ə(r)\ *n* [*optic* + *-meter*] **:** an instrument for measuring the accuracy of gage blocks or similar devices by means of an optical lever

op·ti·mism \'äptə,mizəm\ *n* -S [F *optimisme*, fr. L *optimum* that which is best, (fr. neut. of *optimus* best) + F *-isme* -ism; akin to L *ops* power, wealth, help — more at OPULENT] **1 a :** a doctrine that this world is the best possible world based on the argument that God being all-wise must know all possible worlds, being all-powerful must be able to create whichsoever he might choose, and being all-good must choose the best — used orig. in reference to this doctrine as formulated by Leibniz **b :** a doctrine or opinion that reality is essentially good, completely good, or as good as it conceivably could be **c :** a doctrine that the goods of life overbalance the pain and evil of it and that life is preponderantly good — compare PESSIMISM **2 a :** the quality of being the best or for the best **b :** the best possible or conceivable condition **3 :** an inclination to put the most favorable construction upon actions and happenings, to minimize adverse aspects, conditions, and possibilities, or to anticipate the best possible outcome **:** a cheerful and hopeful temperament

op·ti·mist \-ˌməst\ *n* -s [F *optimiste*, fr. L *optimum* + F *-iste* -ist] **:** one given to optimism; *esp* **:** an adherent of philosophical optimism — opposed to *pessimist*

op·ti·mis·tic \ˌ══ˈmistik, -tēk\ *also* **op·ti·mis·ti·cal** \-tə̇kəl, -tēk-\ *or* **op·ti·mist** \ˈ══ˌməst\ *adj* [*optimist* + *-ic* or *-ical*] **1 :** of or relating to optimism **:** tending or conforming to the opinion that all events are ordered for the best **2 :** anticipating the best often to an unwise extent or on scanty evidence **:** notably hopeful **:** SANGUINE ⟨an ~ view⟩ — **op·ti·mis·ti·cal·ly** \ˌ══ˈmistə̇k(ə)lē, -tēk-, -li\ *adv*

op·tim·i·ty \äpˈtimədˑē\ *n* -ES [LL *optimitat-*, *optimitas* fr. *optimus* + *-itat-*, *-itas* -ity] **:** the condition or fact of being best or for the best

op·ti·mi·za·tion \ˌäptəmə̇ˈzāshən, -ˌmīˈz-\ *n* -s **:** an act of optimizing or the fact of being optimized

[1]**op·ti·mize** \ˈ══ˌmīz\ *vb* -ED/-ING/-s [back-formation fr. *optimist*] *vi* **:** to be optimistic ⟨*optimizing* about the future⟩ ~ *vt* **:** to make the best of **:** treat optimistically

[2]**optimize** \"\ *vt* [*optimum* + *-ize*] **:** OPTIMALIZE **:** to make as perfect, effective, or functional as possible ⟨~ the distribution of raw materials⟩

[1]**op·ti·mum** \-ˌməm\ *n, pl* **opti·ma** \-mə\ *also* **optimums** [L, neut. of *optimus* best — more at OPTIMISM] **1 :** the amount or degree of something that is most favorable to some end; *esp* **:** the most favorable condition (as of temperature, light, moisture, food) for the growth and reproduction of an organism **2 a :** greatest degree (as of growth, activity, or effectiveness) attained under implied or specified conditions ⟨this pest reaches its ~ further south⟩ **b :** a period of warmer and drier climate than that of the present ⟨the post-Wisconsin ~ of the northern hemisphere is considered to have occurred between 6000 B.C. and 3000 B.C.⟩

[2]**optimum** \"\ *adj* **1 :** most favorable or most conducive to a given end esp. under fixed conditions ⟨~ temperature for incubation⟩ ⟨question is one of combining these various techniques to ~ advantage —H.V.R.Iengar⟩ **2 :** greatest or best possible under a restriction expressed or implied ⟨~ safe speed⟩ ⟨an ~ return on capital⟩

opting *pres part of* OPT

[1]**op·tion** \ˈäpshən\ *n* -s [F, fr. L *option-*, *optio* free choice — more at OPINE] **1 :** an act of choosing **:** exercise of the power of choice ⟨at the student's ~ and with the professor's permission —*Loyola Univ. Bull.*⟩ ⟨hard to make one's ~ between such alternatives⟩ **2** *obs* **:** expression of a desire **:** WISH **3 a :** the power or right to choose (as between alternatives) **:** freedom of choice ⟨have an ~ . . . between accepting its findings or sticking to what we call traditional grammar —W.N. Francis⟩ **b :** a right formerly belonging to an archbishop of the Church of England to select any one dignity or benefice in the gift of a suffragan bishop consecrated or confirmed by him for bestowal by himself when next vacant **c** (1) **:** a privilege of demanding fulfillment of a contract on any day within a specified limit (2) **:** a right (as a put or call) to buy or sell designated securities or commodities at a specified price during the period of the contract **d :** a right of an insured person to choose the form in which various payments due him on a policy shall be made or applied **4 :** something that is offered for choice or that is chosen; *esp, chiefly Brit* **:** ELECTIVE **syn** see CHOICE

[2]**option** \"\ *vt* -ED/-ING/-s **:** to grant or take an option (as to purchase or rent) on ⟨~*ed* a building site to an out-of-state company⟩ ⟨ready to ~ the film rights from the author⟩

[1]**op·tion·al** \-shənᵊl, -shnəl\ *adj* **:** involving or depending on the exercise of an option **:** left to the discretion of the one concerned **:** not compulsory or obligate ⟨an ~ activity⟩ ⟨formal dress is ~⟩ — **op·tion·al·i·ty** \ˌäpshəˈnaləd·ē\ *n* -ES — **op·tion·al·ly** \ˈäpshənᵊlē, -shnəlē, -li\ *adv*

[2]**optional** \"\ *n* -s **1 :** something that is optional **2** *chiefly Brit* **:** ELECTIVE

op·tion·al·ize \ˈäpshənᵊlˌīz, -shnəˌlīz\ *vt* -ED/-ING/-s **:** to make optional

optional pass *n* **:** an offensive maneuver in football in which the quarterback may select the receiver for a pass or may himself run with the ball

optional referendum *n* **:** a referendum held in an area and on a subject (as a piece of legislation) that the legislature may deem advisable

optional writ *n* **:** an original legal writ that gives a defendant a choice either of doing some act that immediately provides a remedy to the plaintiff or of defending his own action **:** PRAECIPE

op·tion·ary \ˈäpshəˌnerē\ *adj* **:** OPTIONAL

op·tion·ee \ˌäpshəˈnē\ *n* -s [[1]*option* + *-ee*] **:** the grantee in an option contract

op·tion·or \ˈäpshənə(r); ˌ══ˈnȯ(ə)r, -ȯ(ə)\ *n* -s [[1]*option* + *-or*] **:** the grantor in an option contract

option play *n* **:** a football play (as an optional pass) in which an offensive player reacts to the situation rather than according to a predetermined pattern

op·tive \ˈäptiv\ *adj* [L *optivus* chosen; akin to L *option-*, *optio* free choice — more at OPINE] *Roman law* **:** chosen or appointed to an office or trust by an interested person — compare DATIVE, NOMINATIVE, TESTAMENTARY

opto- *comb form* [Gk *optos*, verbal of *opsesthai* to be going to see — more at OPTIC] **1 :** vision ⟨*optometer*⟩ **2 :** eye ⟨*optoblast*⟩ ⟨*optotype*⟩ **3 :** optic **:** optic and ⟨*optokinetic*⟩ ⟨*optocoele*⟩

op·to·gram \ˈäptəˌgram\ *n* [ISV *opto-* + *-gram*, orig. formed as G *optogramm*] **:** an image of an external object fixed on the retina by the photochemical action of light on the visual purple

op·to·kinetic \ˌäp,tō+\ *adj* [*opto-* + *kinetic*] **:** of, relating to, or involving movements of the eyes

op·tom·e·ter \äpˈtäməd·ə(r)\ *n* [*opto-* + *-meter*] **:** an instrument for measuring the power and range of vision

op·to·met·ric \ˌäptəˈme·trik, -rēk\ *also* **op·to·met·ri·cal** \-rə̇kəl, -rēk-\ *adj* **:** of or relating to optometry

op·tom·e·trist \äpˈtämə·trə̇st\ *n* -s **:** a specialist in optometry **:** REFRACTIONIST — compare OPTICIAN

op·tom·e·try \-rē, -ri\ *n* -ES [ISV *opto-* + *-metry*] **1 :** measurement of visual powers (as by use of an optometer) **2 :** an art or occupation consisting of the examination of the eye for defects and faults of refraction and the prescription of correctional lenses and exercises but not including the use of drugs or surgery — compare OPHTHALMOLOGY

op·to·mo·tor reaction \ˌäptəˈmōd·ə(r)-\ *n* [*opto-* + *-motor* (as in loco*motor*, vaso*motor*)] **:** a reflex involving turning of head or body in response to moving stripes of differing luminosity

op·to·phone \ˈäptəˌfōn\ *n* [*opto-* + *-phone*] **:** an instrument by which light variations are converted into sound variations so that a blind person is enabled by its use to locate and estimate varying degrees of light through the ear and thus even to read printed matter

op·to·type \-ˌtīp\ *n* [NL *optotypus*, fr. *opto-* + *typus* type, fr. L, character — more at TYPE] **:** type of different size used in testing the acuity of vision — usu. used in pl.

opts *pres 3d sing of* OPT

op·u·lence \ˈäpyələn(t)s\ *also* **op·u·len·cy** \-nsē, -si\ *n, pl* **opulences** *also* **opulencies** [L *opulentia*, fr. *opulentus* + *-ia* -y] **1 :** WEALTH, RICHES, AFFLUENCE **2 a :** PLENTY, PROFUSION, AMPLITUDE **b :** showy florid fullness (as of utterance or musical style)

op·u·lent \-nt\ *adj* [L *opulentus*, fr. *ops* power, wealth, help; akin to Skt *apnas* possession, property, Gk *ompnē* food, prosperity, L *oper-*, *opus* work — more at OPERATE] **:** exhibiting or characterized by opulence: as **a :** having a large estate or property **:** WEALTHY, AFFLUENT **b :** amply or plentifully provided or fashioned **:** LUXURIANT, PROFUSE, LAVISH ⟨~ blossoms⟩ ⟨an ~ bosom⟩ **syn** see LUXURIOUS, RICH

op·u·lent·ly *adv* **:** with opulence **:** in an opulent manner

opun·tia \ōˈpənch(ē)ə, -ntēə\ *n* [NL, fr. L, a plant, fr. fem. of *opuntius* of Opus, fr. *Opunt-*, *Opus* Opus, ancient city of Locris, Greece, fr. Gk *Opount-*, *Opous*] **1** *cap* **:** a very large genus of cacti comprising the prickly pears, being native to America but naturalized in most warm regions, having flat or terete joints usu. studded with tubercles that bear sharp spines, prickly hairs, or both, and producing mostly yellow flowers followed by pulpy edible fruits **2** -s **:** any cactus of the genus *Opuntia*

opun·ti·a·les \ˌ══chēˈā(ˌ)lēz, -tēˈā-\ *n pl, cap* [NL, fr. *Opuntia* + *-ales*] **:** an order of succulent dicotyledonous plants coextensive with the family Cactaceae

opun·ti·oid \ˌ══ˈchēˌȯid, -tē-\ *adj* [NL *Opuntia* + E *-oid*] **:** resembling a prickly pear

opus \ˈōpəs, *chiefly Brit* ˈäp-\ *n, pl* **opera** \ˈōpərə, ˈäp-\ *also* **opuses** [L *oper-* *opus* — more at OPERATE] **:** WORK: as **a :** a musical composition or set of compositions usu. numbered in the order of its issue — abbr. *op* **b :** EMBROIDERY — used in combination; see OPUS ANGLICANUM

opus an·gli·ca·num \-ˌaŋgləˈkānəm, -ka-, -kā-\ *n, pl* **opera anglica·na** \-nə\ [ML, lit., English work] **:** fine English medieval embroidery having pictorial designs following early paintings and being used esp. for ecclesiastical vestments

opus ci·ta·tum \-kə̇ˈtäd·əm, -ˌsīˈtäd-\ *n, pl* **opera cita·ta** \-d·ə\ [NL] **:** the work quoted from — abbr. *op cit*

opus·cu·lar \(ˈ)ōˈpəskyələ(r)\ *adj* **:** of or relating to an opuscule

opus·cule \ōˈpə(ˌ)skyül\ *also* **opus·cle** \ōˈpəsəl\ *n* -s [*opuscule* fr. F, fr. L *opusculum*; *opuscle* fr. L *opusculum*] **:** a small or petty work **:** OPUSCULUM

opus·cu·lum \ōˈpəskyələm\ *n, pl* **opuscu·la** \-lə\ [L, dim. of *opus*] **:** a minor work (as of literature) — usu. used in pl.

opus la·te·ri·ci·um \-ˌlad·əˈrikēəm, -ishē-\ *or* **opus la·te·ri·ti·um** \-ˌlad·əˈrid·ēəm, -ishē-\ *n, pl* **opera lateri·cia** *or* **opera lateri·tia** \-ēə\ [L *opus latericium*, lit., work of brick] **:** masonry of bricks or tiles of baked clay laid in mortar and much used in Greco-Roman building for the facing of walls in stone masonry

opus li·tho·stra·tum \-ˌlithəˈsträd·əm, -rā-\ *n, pl* **opera lithostra·ta** \-d·ə\ [NL, lit., work paved with stone] **:** a facing or covering of stone

opus mu·si·vum \-müˈsēvəm; -myüˈsīvəm, -ˈzī-\ *n, pl* **opera musi·va** \-və\ [LL, lit., mosaic work] **:** mosaic decoration of walls often employing glass or enamel

opus ope·ran·tis \-ˌäpəˈrantə̇s\ *n, pl* **opera operan·tes** \-n·ˌtēz\ [ML, lit., work of the worker] **:** the efficacy of the agent — compare EX OPERE OPERANTIS

opus ope·ra·tum \-ˌäpəˈräd·əm, -rā-\ *n, pl* **opera opera·ta** \-d·ə\ [ML, lit., work done] **:** the efficacy of the action — compare EX OPERE OPERATO

opus qua·dra·tum \-kwäˈdräd·əm, -rā-\ *n, pl* **opera quadra·ta** \-d·ə\ [NL, lit., squared work] **:** Roman masonry of squared blocks

opus sec·ti·le \-ˈsektəlē\ *n, pl* **opera sec·til·ia** \-ˌsekˈtilēə\ [NL, lit., cut work] **:** stone inlay or tiling using pieces cut to follow the outline of the design

opus tes·se·la·tum \-ˌtesəˈläd·əm,-lā-\ *n, pl* **opera tessela·ta** \-d·ə\ [NL, lit., checkered work] **:** mosaic work employing cubes in simple geometric arrangements

opus ver·mi·cu·la·tum \-və(r)ˌmikyəˈläd·əm, -lā-\ *n, pl* **opera vermicula·ta** \-d·ə\ [NL, lit., work in the form of worms] **:** mosaic work employing small stones arranged in patterns of curving lines or in pictorial designs

-opy — see -OPIA

oquas·sa \ōˈkwäsə\ *n, pl* **oquassa** *or* **oquassas** [fr. *Oquassa* (Rangeley lake), lake in western Maine] **:** a small rather slender trout (*Salvelinus oquassa*) found in the Rangeley lakes of Maine

[1]**or** \ə(r), (ˌ)ȯ(ə)r, (ˌ)ȯ(ə), *in southern US also* (ˌ)ä(r)\ *conj* [ME *other, or*, fr. OE *oththe, otūtha, eththa*; akin to OHG *eddo, odo, oaar* or, ON *etha*, Goth *aiththau*] **1** — used as a function word to indicate (1) an alternative between different or unlike things, states, or actions ⟨wolves ~ bears are never seen in that part of the country⟩ ⟨sick ~ well, he should not be here⟩ ⟨eat ~ go hungry is all the same to him⟩; (2) choice between alternative things, states, or courses ⟨will you have tea ~ coffee⟩ ⟨decide to study medicine ~ law⟩ ⟨to be, ~ not to be: that is the question —Shak.⟩; (3) the synonymous, equivalent, or substitutive character of two words or phrases ⟨fell over a precipice ~ cliff⟩ ⟨the off ~ far side⟩ ⟨lessen ~ abate⟩; (4) correction or greater exactness of phrasing or meaning ⟨these essays, ~ rather rough sketches⟩ ⟨the present king had no children — ~ no legitimate children —Max Peacock⟩; (5) approximation, doubt, or uncertainty ⟨will be Tuesday ~ Wednesday before he arrives⟩ ⟨in five ~ six days⟩ ⟨it's scarlet fever ~ diphtheria⟩; (6) succession by turns ⟨one ~ the other will watch over him all night⟩; (7) the operation or logical connective symbolized by v or by +; compare TRUTH TABLE **2** *archaic* **:** EITHER — used with a second paired *or* ⟨no man can ~ foretoken or forefend —Walter de la Mare⟩ **3 :** or else **:** OTHERWISE ⟨do what I say, ~ you'll suffer the consequences⟩ ⟨pay ~ I'll sue⟩ **4** *archaic* **:** WHETHER — used with a second paired *or* ⟨~ rich or poor —*Baltimore (Md.) Sun*⟩ **5 :** on another occasion **:** as another instance **:** AGAIN ⟨~, an electron may serve merely to measure —L.A.White⟩

[2]**or** \"\ *prep* [ME *ar, or*, prep. & conj., fr. *ar, or*, adv., early, earlier, before, fr. ON *ār* early — more at ERE] *chiefly dial* **:** BEFORE

[3]**or** \"\ *conj* [ME *ar, or*] **1** *chiefly dial* **:** sooner than **:** UNTIL, BEFORE, ERE ⟨~ the porter was at the gate, the boy was in the hall —*Ballad Book*⟩ **2** *chiefly dial* **:** THAN

[4]**or** \ˈȯ(ə)r, ˈȯ(ə)\ *n* -s [MF, gold, fr. L *aurum* — more at ORIOLE] **1 :** a heraldic metal conventionally supposed to be the color of gold but in practice also represented as any of various shades of yellow **2 :** the color gold or the color yellow represented in drawing or engraving by small dots — compare TINCTURE

[5]**or** \"\ *adj* **:** being of the heraldic metal or **:** GOLDEN, YELLOW

[1]**-or** \ə(r)\ *sometimes* ˌȯ(ə)r *or* ˌȯ(ə)\ *n suffix* -s [ME *-or, -our*, fr. OF *-eor, -eur* & L *-or;* OF *-eor, -eur*, partly fr. L *-or;* partly fr. L *-ator*, fr. *-atus* -ate + *-or*] **:** one that does a (specified) thing ⟨grantor⟩ ⟨alternator⟩ ⟨occlusor⟩ ⟨elevator⟩

[2]**-or** \"\ *n suffix* -s [ME *-or, -our*, fr. OF *-eur*, fr. L *-or*] **:** condition **:** activity ⟨demeanor⟩

or *abbr* **1** oriental **2** original

OR *abbr* **1** official receiver **2** on request **3** operating room **4** operations room **5** ordered recorded **6** other ranks **7** owner's risk

[1]**ora** \ˈōrə\ *n, pl* **oras** \-rəz\ *also* **orae** \ˈōrˌē, ˈōrˌī\ [OE *ōra*, of Scand origin; akin to ON *aur-*, *eyrir* ounce (usu. of silver), money (in pl.) — more at EYRIR] **:** a money of account introduced into England by the Danish invaders and valued in A.D. 920 at 2½ shillings and in the Domesday Book of 1086 at 20*d* sterling

[2]**ora** *pl of* OS

ora *abbr* oratorio

ora·bas·su \ˌōrəˈbäˌsü\ *n* -s [Tupi *oyapussá*] **:** any of several So. American titi monkeys of the genus *Callicebus*

or·ache *or* **or·ach** \ˈärach\ *n, pl* **oraches** [ME *arage, orage*, fr. MF *arache*, modif. of L *atriplic-*, *atriplex*, fr. Gk *atraphaxys*] **:** a plant of the genus *Atriplex; esp* **:** GARDEN ORACHE

[1]**or·a·cle** \ˈȯrəkəl, ˈär-, -rēk-\ *n* -s [ME, fr. MF, fr. L *oraculum*, fr. *orare* to speak + *-culum*, suffix denoting means, place, or instrument — more at ORATION] **1 a** (1) **:** a revelation received from the God of Judaism and Christianity **:** a divine revelation (2) **:** a typically ambiguous or enigmatic revelation or utterance believed to issue from a divinity through a medium (as a priest or priestess) thought to be inspired **b :** an authoritative or wise expression **:** an answer delivered with an aspect of oracular certainty ⟨could utter ~*s* of Delphian ambiguity —Thomas Hardy⟩ **2 a** (1) **:** a medium by which a pagan god reveals hidden knowledge or makes known the divine purpose (2) **:** a medium of communication from the Hebraic or Christian God **:** an expounder or interpreter of God's will **b :** a place where a divine revelation or an utterance believed to issue from a divinity is given **3 a :** a person of great authority or wisdom whose opinions or judgments are regarded with great respect **:** one who is considered or professes to be infallible ⟨a systematic philosopher, not a dabbler or ~ —W.W.Austin⟩ **b :** something (as a scientific instrument) on which one can rely for guidance or direction **:** an infallible guide ⟨electronic computers are rapidly becoming the ~*s* of industry —*Time*⟩

[2]**oracle** \"\ *vb* **oracled; oracled; oracling** \-kliŋ\ **oracles** *archaic* **:** to proclaim or speak as an oracle

oracle bone *n* **:** a bone used in early China esp. during the Shang dynasty 1765–1123 B.C. in divination by writing a question upon it, heating it, and divining the answer from the resultant cracks

orac·u·lar \ōˈrakyələ(r), äˈr-, əˈr-\ *adj* [L *oraculum* oracle + E *-ar* — more at ORACLE] **1 :** of, relating to, or being an oracle **:** used to forecast or divine **:** FORECASTING, DIVINING ⟨~ bone inscriptions —Chung-Yuan Chang⟩ ⟨~ instruments —Nathaniel Micklem⟩ ⟨able by ~ means to expose a witch —*Notes & Queries on Anthropology*⟩ **2 :** resembling an oracle esp. in solemnity of delivery or obscurity of thought ⟨the ~ sayings of Victorian poets —René Wellek & Austin Warren⟩ — **orac·u·lar·ly** *adv* — **orac·u·lar·ness** *n* -ES

orac·u·lar·i·ty \ˌ══ˈlarəd·ē\ *n* -ES **:** the quality, state, or an instance of being oracular

orac·u·late \ˌ══ˌlāt\ *vb* -ED/-ING/-s [L *oraculum* + E *-ate*] **:** ORACLE

orac·u·lous \-ˌləs\ *adj* [L *oraculum* + E *-ous*] *archaic* **:** ORACULAR — **orac·u·lous·ly** *adv, archaic*

orad \ˈōrˌad, ˈȯˌr-\ *adv* [L *or-*, *os* mouth + E *-ad*] **:** toward the mouth or oral region

orae serratae *pl of* ORA SERRATA

[1]**oral** \ˈōrəl, ˈōr-, ˈär-\ *adj* [L *or-*, *os* mouth + E *-al;* akin to OE *ōr* beginning, origin, *ōra* border, bank, shore, ON *ōss* mouth of a river, L *ora* edge, border, MIr *ā* (gen. sing.) mouth, Skt *ās*] **1 a :** uttered by the mouth or in words **:** not written **:** SPOKEN ⟨~ traditions⟩ ⟨~ delivery⟩ ⟨~ testimony⟩ **b :** using lip movement and voice articulation **:** conducted or delivered by the spoken word ⟨~ reading⟩; *specif* **:** emphasizing lip reading and the development of vocal expression rather than the use of manual signs in teaching the deaf ⟨~ teacher⟩ ⟨~ method⟩ ⟨~ system⟩ **2 a** (1) **:** of, relating to, or belonging to the mouth **:** BUCCAL ⟨the ~ mucous membrane⟩ (2) **:** given or taken through or by way of the mouth ⟨doses for ~ administration⟩ (3) **:** acting on the mouth ⟨~ diseases⟩ ⟨a skillful ~ surgeon⟩ **b :** articulated between lips and uvula and with the velum raised so that there is no nasal resonance ⟨~ speech sounds⟩ ⟨an ~ consonant⟩ **c** (1) **:** being the surface on which the mouth is situated ⟨the ~ surface of a starfish⟩ (2) **:** relating to or located on an oral surface ⟨the water-vascular system is chiefly ~⟩ — opposed to *aboral* **3 a :** of, relating to, or characterized by the first stage of psychosexual development in which libidinal gratification is derived from intake (as of food), by sucking, and later by biting **b :** of, relating to, or characterized by personality traits of passive dependency and aggressiveness — compare ANAL, GENITAL — **oral·ly** \-rəlē, -li\ *adv*

[2]**oral** \"\ *n* -s **1 :** an oral part (as a plate or valve) **2 :** an oral examination — usu. used in pl. ⟨had to clear this hurdle before reaching your ~*s* —Francis Biddle⟩

oral arm *n* **:** one of the prolongations of the distal end of the manubrium of a jellyfish

oral disc *n* **1 :** LOPHOPHORE **2 :** the more or less flattened upper or free end of the body bearing the mouth in its center and tentacles near or at its border in most polyps **3 :** the sucker-bordered mouth of some trematode worms

ora·le \ōˈrā(ˌ)lē\ *n* -s [ML, fr. L *or-*, *os* mouth + *-ale*, neut. of *-alis* -al] **:** FANON d

oral·er \ˈōrələ(r), ˈōr-, ˈär-\ *n* -s [[1]*oral* + *-er*] **:** one who bets (as on a race) by word of mouth without giving or receiving any ticket or slip

oral groove *n* **:** a depressed peristome resembling a groove

oral hood *n* **:** a prolongation of the metapleural folds surrounding the mouth in an amphioxus and bearing the oral cirri

oral·ism \ˈōrəˌlizəm, ˈōr-, ˈär-\ *n* -s **:** advocacy or use of the oral method of teaching the deaf

oral·ist \-ˌləst\ *n* -s **:** a practicer of oralism

oral·i·ty \ōˈraləd·ē, ōˈr-, äˈr-\ *n* -ES **:** the quality or state of being oral

oral law *n* **1 :** law handed down and perpetuated by word of mouth rather than by writing **2** *usu cap O&L* **:** MISHNAH

oral lobe *n* **:** a labial palp of a bivalve mollusk

oral method *n* **:** a method of instructing the deaf by which they are taught to speak and to understand the speech of others by lipreading

oral·o·gy \ōˈraləjē, ōˈr-, äˈr-\ *n* -ES [irreg. fr. [1]*oral* + *-logy*] **:** STOMATOLOGY

oral plate *also* **oral membrane** *n* **:** STOMODAEUM

oral surgeon *n* **:** one that specializes in oral surgery

oral surgery *n* **1 :** a branch of dentistry that deals with the diagnosis and treatment of oral conditions requiring surgical intervention **2 :** a branch of surgery that deals with conditions of the jaws and mouth structures requiring surgery

oran \ōˈrän\ *adj, usu cap* [*Oran*, Algeria] **:** of or from the city of Oran, Algeria **:** of the kind or style prevalent in Oran

or/and \ˈȯ(ə)ˈr(ə)nd\ *conj* **:** AND/OR

orang *also* **ourang** *n* -s [by shortening] **:** ORANGUTAN

[1]**or·ange** \ˈȯrənj, ˈär-, -rēnj, *in rapid speech esp in pl or in compounds* -rnj\ *n* -s [ME *orenge, orange*, fr. MF, fr. OProv *auranja*, fr. Ar *nāranj*, fr. Per *nārang*, fr. Skt *nāraṅga*, of Dravidian origin; akin to Tamil *naru* fragrant] **1 a :** any of various globose to subglobose tropical or subtropical fruits that are technically berries with a reddish yellow leathery aromatic rind containing many oil glands and used extensively in confectionery, preserves, and cookery and with a usu. sweet but acid juicy edible pulp rich in minerals and vitamin C — see MANDARIN ORANGE, NAVEL ORANGE, SOUR ORANGE, SWEET ORANGE **b :** any of various rather small evergreen and often spiny trees of the genus *Citrus* (as *C. aurantium*, *C. sinensis*, or *C. reticulata*) that have pointed ovate unifoliate leaves, hard yellow wood, and usu. fragrant white flowers and that produce fruits which are oranges — see TRIFOLIATE ORANGE **2 a :** the evergreen orange tree usu. not over 30 feet in height with oval unifoliate leaves, hard yellow wood, and a fragrant white blossom **b :** any of several trees or fruits resembling the orange **3** [[2]*orange*] **a :** any of a group of colors about midway between red and yellow in hue, of medium lightness, and of moderate to high saturation **b :** a hue midway between red and yellow that is evoked in the normal observer under normal conditions by radiant energy of the wavelength 610 millimicrons **c :** a pigment or dye producing an orange color — see DYE table I (under *Acid Orange*), ORANGE G, ORANGE II **4 :** a roundel tenné

orange 2 (flowering branch)

[2]**orange** \"\ *adj* **1 :** of or relating to an orange **2 :** being of the color orange ⟨an ~ ribbon⟩

[3]**orange** \"\ *adj, usu cap* [fr. *Orange*, princely family of Europe to which belong William III of England and the present reigning family of the Netherlands] **1 :** of or relating to the Orange family or house in the Netherlands **2 :** of or relating to the Orangemen **:** being or relating to those belonging to or in sympathy with them

or·ange·ade \ˌȯrənˈjād, ˌär-, -rēn-, *in rapid speech* (ˈ)ȯrn- *or* (ˈ)ärn-\ *n* [F, fr. *orange* + *-ade*] **:** a beverage of orange juice sweetened and mixed with plain or carbonated water

or·ange·a·do \ˌȯrənˈjä(ˌ)dō, ˌär-, -rēn-\ *n* -s [prob. modif. (influenced by [1]*orange*) of Sp *naranjado, naranjada*, fr. *naranja* orange (fr. Ar *nāranj*) + *-ado* -ate (fr. L *-atus*) or *-ada*, fem. of *-ado* — more at ORANGE] *archaic* **:** candied orange peel

orange aphid *n* **:** COTTON APHID

orange aurora *n* **:** AURORA 3

orange basketworm *n* **:** a grub that is the larva of a small moth (*Platoeceticus gloveri*), lives on the orange tree, and forms an oval larval case

orange bat *or* **orange horseshoe bat** *n* **:** a common bat (*Rhinonicteris aurantius*) of northwest Australia with soft fur that is bright orange on the male and pale yellow on the female

orange berry *n* **1 :** LIMEBERRY **2 :** EUROPEAN CRANBERRY

orangebird \ˈ═(ˌ)═ˌ═\ *n* **:** a Jamaican tanager (*Spindalis zena nigricephala*) with a bright orange breast

orange bitters *n pl but usu sing in constr* **:** an orange-flavored bitters; *esp* : one made in England from the bitter Seville orange and used chiefly as a cocktail ingredient

orange blossom *n* **1** : a white fragrant blossom that is the flower of the orange and is a favorite flower at weddings and a source of a fragrant oil used as an ingredient of eau de cologne **2** : BIRTHROOT **3** : MEXICAN ORANGE **4** : a cocktail consisting of gin, orange juice, and sugar or sometimes honey shaken with ice and strained before serving

orange-blossom orchid *n* : an orchid (*Sarcochilus falcatus*) of Australia having white flowers with purple and orange markings on the lip

orange chrome *n* : CHROME ORANGE

orange chrome yellow *n* : CHROME ORANGE

orange chromide *n* : CHROMIDE

orange creeper *n* : a very showy Brazilian woody vine (*Pyrostegia venusta*) of the family Bignoniaceae commonly cultivated for its showy crimson-orange flowers in hanging panicles

orange-crowned warbler \'⸗(⸗),⸗-\ *n* : a small grayish green and yellowish American warbler (*Vermivora celata*) having a concealed orange crown patch

orangecup lily \'⸗(⸗),⸗-\ *n* : WOOD LILY 1b

orange daisy *or* **orange fleabane** *n* : a perennial herb (*Erigeron aurantiacus*) of Turkestan with nearly double orange-yellow flower heads

orange dog *n* : the larva of the orange-tree butterfly (*Papilio cresphontes*)

orange drink *n* : a still beverage consisting of orange oils, citric acid, sugar, and water

orange fin *n*, *Brit* : a young sea trout : a sea trout smolt

orange flower *n* **1** : ORANGE BLOSSOM **2** : MEXICAN ORANGE **3** : MOCK ORANGE

orange-flower oil *n* : NEROLI OIL

orange-flower water *n* : a saturated solution of neroli oil used in pharmaceutical preparations and toilet water

orange fly *n* : any of several small flies whose larvae burrow in oranges; *esp* : MEXICAN FRUITFLY

orange fruit moth *n* : any of several moths able to pierce oranges and other fruits

orange G *n*, *usu cap O* : an acid azo dye made by coupling diazotized aniline and G acid and used chiefly in dyeing wool and leather and as a biological stain — see DYE table I (under *Acid Orange 10*)

orange grass *n* : a No. American weed (*Hypericum gentianoides*) with wiry stems, minute leaves resembling scales, and small bright yellow flowers

orange hawkweed *n* : a European hawkweed (*Hieracium aurantiacum*) that has flower heads with bright orange-red rays and is troublesome as a weed esp. in northeastern No. America

or·ange·ism \'ȯrən,jizəm, 'är-, -rēn-\ *n* -s *usu cap* [[3]*orange* + *-ism*] : attachment to the principles of the society of Orangemen : the tenets or practices of the Orangemen

orange jessamine *or* **orange jasmine** *n* : an East Indian shrub or small tree (*Murraya paniculata*) with evergreen pinnate leaves and fragrant white bell-shaped flowers

orange lead *n* : ORANGE MINERAL

orange leaf rust *n* : a rust of wheat and other grasses caused by a fungus (*Puccinia triticina*), characterized by orange-colored pustules on the leaves, resulting in decreased yield and quality of grain, and involving as alternate host of the parasite a meadow rue or related plant

orange lily *n* : either of the two European lilies (*Lilium croceum* and *L. bulbiferum*) having erect bright orange or orange-red flowers

oran·ge·lo \ə'ranjə,lō\ *n* -s [blend of *orange* and *pomelo*] : a hybrid citrus fruit produced by crossing an orange and a pomelo

orange madder *n* : MADDER ORANGE

orange maggot *n* : the larva of an orange fly

or·ange·man \'⸗(⸗)mən, -,man, -,maa(ə)n\ *n*, *pl* **orangemen** *usu cap* [William III †1702 king of England and prince of *Orange* + E *man*] **1** : a member of a secret society organized in the north of Ireland in 1795 to defend the reigning sovereign of Great Britain, to support the Protestant religion, and to maintain the laws of the kingdom **2** : a Protestant Irishman esp. of Ulster

orange margined blue \'⸗(⸗),⸗⸗-\ *n* : any of several lycaenid butterflies of the genus *Lycaeides*

orange melon *n* : MANGO MELON

orangemen's day *n*, *usu cap O&D* : July 12 observed in northern Ireland as a holiday commemorating the Battle of Aughrim in 1691 and the Battle of the Boyne in 1690

orange milkweed *n* : BUTTERFLY WEED

orange milkwort *n* : an annual bog herb (*Polygala lutea*) of the pine barrens of the southeastern U. S. with yellow-orange spikes of irregular flowers

orange mineral *n* : a pigment that is similar in composition to red lead but lighter in color and is usu. obtained by roasting white lead

orange ocher *n* : OCHER ORANGE

orange oil *n* : an essential oil from orange peel or orange flowers: as **a** : a yellow to deep orange oil obtained from the peel of the sweet orange and used chiefly as a flavor and perfume — called also *sweet orange oil* **b** : a similar but bitter pale yellow or yellowish brown oil from the peel of the sour orange — called also *bitter orange oil*

orange I *n* : an acid dye — see DYE table I (under *Acid Orange 20*)

orange peel *n* **1** : the peel of an orange **2** : a rough surface resembling that of an orange that may occur with a fast-drying coating (as shellac or lacquer) or with some ceramic glazes **3** : a strong orange color that is yellower, lighter, and stronger than pumpkin and slightly redder and darker than cadmium orange

orange-peel bucket *n* : a bucket having three or more crescent-shaped jaws resembling segments of orange peel hinged to a single support at the top

orange pekoe *n* **1 a** : a tea formerly made from the tiny leaf and end bud of the spray **b** : a similar small-leaved tea of India and Ceylon obtained by screening fired tea **2** : a good grade of India or Ceylon tea; *esp* : one made from the first and second leaves of the shoot

orange plume *n* : YELLOW FRINGED ORCHID

orange puppy *n* : ORANGE DOG

orange quit *n* : a Jamaican honey-creeper (*Glossiptila ruficollis*)

orange R *n*, *usu cap O* : an acid dye — see DYE table I under *Acid Orange 8*

or·ange·rie *like* ORANGERY\ *n* -s [F — more at ORANGERY] : ORANGERY

orange-peel bucket

orange rockfish *n* : a rockfish (*Sebastodes pinniger*) found from Puget Sound to southern California that becomes two feet long, is olive gray blotched with orange shading to grayish white below, and is a common market fish

orangeroot \'⸗(⸗),⸗\ *n* [[2]*orange* + *root*] **1** : GOLDENSEAL **2** : BUTTERFLY WEED 1

orange-rufous \¦⸗(⸗)¦⸗⸗\ *adj* : of any of several colors averaging a strong orange that is deeper than pumpkin and redder and darker than cadmium orange

orange rust *n* **1** : either of two diseases of raspberries and blackberries caused by two rusts (*Gymnoconia peckiana* and *Kunkelia niteus*) and characterized by retarded growth and curled and stunted usu. small leaves lacking in green color and with bright red or orange powder on the under surfaces; *also* : the fungus causing either disease **2** : a strong yellowish brown that is redder, stronger, and slightly darker than buckthorn brown and redder and deeper than centennial brown

or·ange·ry \'ȯrənjrē, 'är-, -rēnj-, -ri, -rnj-\ *n* -ES [F *orangerie*, fr. *orange* + *-erie* -ery — more at ORANGE] **1** : a greenhouse or other protected place for raising oranges in cool climates **2** *obs* **a** : orange perfume **b** : orange-scented snuff

oranges *pl of* ORANGE

oranges and lemons *n pl but sing or pl in constr* : an old singing game played like London Bridge

orange scab *n* : citrus scab of the orange

orange scale *n* : any of several scales that infest orange trees: as **a** : PURPLE SCALE **b** : GLOVER SCALE **c** : RED SCALE **d** : BROWN SCALE

orange shellac *n* : SHELLAC 1

orange sneezeweed *n* : WESTERN SNEEZEWEED

orange spoon *n* : a teaspoon that tapers to a sharp point or teeth and that is used for citrus fruits and melons

orange spoon

orangespotted sunfish \'⸗(⸗),⸗⸗-\ *or* **orangespot sunfish** \'⸗(⸗),⸗-\ *n* : a very small orange-marked sunfish (*Lepomis humilis*) widely distributed in silty waters of the central U. S.

orange star *n* : a star of spectral type K

orange stick *n* : a thin stick like a pencil usu. of orangewood with pointed and rounded ends for manicuring

orange-sucker \'⸗(⸗),⸗⸗\ *n* : ORANGE FRUIT MOTH

orange swallowwort *n* : BUTTERFLY WEED 1

orange-tawny \¦⸗(⸗)¦⸗⸗\ *adj* : of any of several colors averaging the color Mars orange

orange tip *n* : any of several small pierid butterflies in which the males or both males and females usu. have a conspicuous orange blotch at the tip of the forewing

orange tortrix *n* : a tortricid moth (*Argyrotaenia citrana*) whose larva infests oranges and also feeds on several fruit trees and various other cultivated and wild plants esp. in California

orange-tree butterfly *n* : a large black and yellow butterfly (*Papilio cresphontes*) — see ORANGE DOG

orange II *n* : an acid azo dye made by coupling diazotized sulfanilic acid with beta-naphthol and used chiefly in dyeing wool and leather, in making pigments (as for wallpaper), and as a biological stain — see DYE table I (under *Acid Orange 7*)

orange vermilion *n* : a strong reddish orange that is yellower and paler than poppy or paprika and slightly yellower and lighter than scarlet vermilion

orange wine *n* : a wine variously made by fermenting orange juice or orange peel

orangewood \'⸗(⸗),⸗\ *n* : the wood of the orange tree used esp. in turnery and carving

orange worm *n* : the larva of any of several moths that are pests on oranges; *esp* : ORANGE TORTRIX

orang laut \'ōraŋ,lau̇t\ *n*, *pl* **orang laut** *or* **orang lauts** *usu cap O&L* [Malay, fr. *orang* person, man + *laut* sea] : BAJAU

orangs *pl of* ORANG

orang·utan *or* **orang·ou·tan** *or* **orang·ou·tang** *also* **oran·utan** *or* **ou·rang·ou·tang** \ə'raŋə,taŋ, ō'r-, ȯ'r-, -raiŋə,taiŋ *sometimes* ⸗'⸗yü,- *or* ⸗'⸗⸗,tan *or* -,taa(ə)n *or* ¦ō,⸗-'(y)ü,⸗ *or* ¦ō,⸗'⸗,⸗ *or* ,ōraŋ'(y)üt'n *or with* n *instead of* ŋ *after the vowel of the second syllable*\ *n* -s [Malay *orang hutan*, fr. *orang* man, person + *hutan* forest] : a largely herbivorous arboreal anthropoid ape (*Pongo pygmaeus*) of low swampy forests of Borneo and Sumatra that is about two thirds as large as the gorilla with the adult male standing four feet high and weighing up to 250 pounds, is distinguished by its small ears, brown skin, long sparse reddish brown hair, and very long arms, and has the face, hands, and feet naked and the cheeks in old males flattened and expanded

orangutan

or·angy *or* **or·ang·ey** \'ȯrənjē, 'är-, -rēn-, -ji, *in rapid speech* -rnj-\ *adj*, *sometimes* **orang·i·er**; **orang·i·est** [[1]*orange* + *-y*] **1** : resembling or suggestive of an orange (as in flavor or color) ⟨an ~ pink —Tamara T. Rice⟩ **2** *of a color of gems* : having the orange component strong ⟨~ yellow is midway between orange yellow and yellow⟩

oran·ian \ō'rānēən\ *adj*, *usu cap* [*Oran*, seaport and department in northwestern Algeria + E *-ian*] : of or relating to an Upper Paleolithic culture of western Algeria and Morocco typified by tiny crescent-backed blades

orans \'ō,ranz\ *n*, *pl* **oran·tes** \ō'ran·(,)tēz\ [ML or NL] : ORANT

orant \'ōrənt\ *or* **oran·te** \ō'ran·(,)tē\ *n* -s [*orant* fr. ML or NL *orant-, orans*, fr. L, pres. part. of *orare* to pray; *orante* fr. It, fr. ML or NL *orant-, orans* — more at ORATION] **1** : a female figure in the posture of prayer in ancient Greek art **2** : a usu. female figure standing with outstretched arms as if in prayer used in early Christian art as a symbol of the faithful dead

ora·on \ō'rä,ōn\ *n*, *pl* **oraon** *or* **oraons** *usu cap* **1** : KURUKH **2** : the Kurukh language

ora·ri·on \ō'rärē,ōn\ *or* **orar·i·um** \ō'ra(a)rēəm, -rer-, -rar-\ *n*, *pl* **oraria** \-rēə\ [MGk & LL; MGk *ōrarion*, fr. LL *orarium*, fr. L *or-, os* mouth + *-arium* -ary — more at ORAL] : a stole worn hanging over the left shoulder by a deacon in the Eastern Church

oras *pl of* ORA

ora ser·ra·ta \¦ōrəsə'rād·ə, -rād·ə\ *n*, *pl* **orae serra·tae** \¦ō,rī,sə'rād·,ī, ¦ōr,ēsə'rād·,ē\ [NL, lit., serrated margin] : the dentate border of the retina

orate \ō'rāt, ȯ'r-, '⸗,⸗, *usu* -ād·+V\ *vb* -ED/-ING/-S [back-formation fr. [1]*oration*] *vi* **1** : to deliver an oration ⟨~ in the sonorous periods of a rhetoric long forgotten —Patrick Balfour⟩ **2** : to talk in a declamatory, grandiloquent, or impassioned manner : HARANGUE ⟨love to hear him ~ with waving hands about the racial sins of his native land —Ben Burns⟩ ⟨go around *orating* about pure Southern womanhood —James Street⟩ ~ *vt* : to talk to in a declamatory, grandiloquent, or impassioned manner : HARANGUE ⟨*orated* the Italian people into that tragic aggression —Herbert Hoover⟩

[1]**ora·tion** \ə'rāshən, ə'r-\ *n* -s [in sense 1, fr. ME *oracione*, fr. LL *oration-, oratio*, fr. L, speech, language, style, harangue, oration, fr. *oratus* (past part. of *orare* to recite a ritual, plead, pray, speak) + *-ion-, -io* -ion; in other senses, fr. L *oration-, oratio*; akin to Gk *ara, arē* prayer, Russ *orat'* to yell, cry, and perh. to Skt *āryati* he acknowledges, praises; basic meaning: to speak, call] **1** *archaic* : PETITION, PRAYER ⟨the bells tolled the hour of ~ —Washington Irving⟩ **2** : an elaborate discourse delivered in public and treating an important subject in a formal and dignified manner; *esp* : a formal discourse on some special occasion (as a funeral or an anniversary) **3** *dial Eng* : CLAMOR, UPROAR

[2]**oration** \"\ *vi* -ED/-ING/-S : to deliver an oration

ora·tio obli·qua \ō¦räd·ē,ōə'blēkwə\ *n* [L, indirect speech] : discourse that is indirect : a paraphrase rather than an exact quotation

or·a·tor \'ȯrəd·ə(r), 'är-, -ətə- *also* -,tō(ə)r *or* -ō(ə)\ *n* -s [ME *oratour*, fr. MF *orateur*, fr. L *orator*, fr. *oratus* (past part. of *orare*) + *-or*] **1 a** *obs* : ADVOCATE, PLEADER **b** : PETITIONER, SUPPLIANT **c** : the petitioner or plaintiff in a bill of information or petition in a court of justice esp. in chancery **2 a** : a public speaker : one who delivers an oration; *esp* : one distinguished for his skill and power as a public speaker ⟨might have been a spouter who thought he was an ~ —W.A.White⟩ **b** (1) : an officer of an English university who represents the university on public occasions, writes addresses and letters of a public nature, and presents candidates for honorary degrees (2) : a college or high school student selected to deliver an oration at commencement or other public occasion **c** : one of the officers of the Masonic order and some other secret societies

or·a·to·ri·al \,ȯrə¦tōrēəl, ¦är-, -tȯr-\ *adj* [L *oratorius* oratorial (fr. *orator*) + E *-al*] : ORATORICAL

[1]**or·a·to·ri·an** \-rēən\ *n* -s *usu cap* [*Oratory* of St. Philip Neri + E *-an*] : a member of the Oratory of St. Philip Neri established in Rome in 1564 as a religious society of diocesan priests that live a community life but do not make special vows

[2]**oratorian** \"\ *adj*, *usu cap* : of or relating to the Oratorians

or·a·tor·i·cal \¦⸗⸗¦tȯrəkəl, -tär-, -rēk-\ *also* **or·a·tor·ic** \-rik, -rēk\ *adj* [*orator* & *oratory* + *-ical, -ic*] **1** : of, relating to, or suggestive of an orator or oratory : RHETORICAL ⟨the pomp and glitter of ~ prose —Pedro Salinas⟩ ⟨the letters grow more ~ —T.L.Robertson⟩ ⟨harangued his men in an ~ way —Robert Graves⟩ **2** : given to oratory — **or·a·tor·i·cal·ly** \-rək(ə)lē, -rēk-, -li\ *adv*

or·a·to·rio \,ȯrə'tōrē,ō, ,ärə-, -tȯr-\ *n* -s [It, fr. the *Oratorio* di San Filippo Neri (Oratory of St. Philip Neri) in Rome, where musical religious services similar to mystery plays were held in the 16th century] **1** : a musical composition having a libretto based usu. on a religious or scriptural subject and consisting typically of recitatives, arias, choruses, orchestral interludes and accompaniment, and sometimes spoken dialogue or narration but having no action, scenery, or costume **2** : a performance of such a composition

[1]**or·a·to·ry** \'⸗⸗,tōrē, -tȯr-, -ri\ *n* -ES [ME *oratorie*, fr. LL *oratorium*, fr. L *oratus* (past part. of *orare* to pray) + *-orium* -ory — more at ORATION] **1** : a place of orisons or prayer; *esp* : a chapel or small room set apart for private devotions **2** *often cap* : an establishment or house of the Oratorians

[2]**oratory** \"\ *n* -ES [L *oratoria*, fr. fem. of *oratorius* oratorial — more at ORATORIAL] **1** : the art of an orator : the art of speaking in public eloquently or effectively : the exercise of rhetorical skill in discourse : ELOQUENCE ⟨a student of ~⟩ **2** : an example or instance of rhetorical speech or art : the substance of such speech ⟨his ~ was pure bombast⟩ ⟨campaign ~⟩ ⟨your general's speeches . . . are admirable as ~ but damnably unhistorical —Robert Graves⟩

or·a·trix \'ȯrə,triks, 'är-\ *n*, *pl* **or·atrices** \,⸗⸗'trī(,)sēz\ [L, fem. of *orator* — more at -TRIX] : a female orator

[1]**orb** \'ō(ə)rb, 'ȯ(ə)b\ *n* -s [AF *orbe*, fr. OF *orbe* blind, without light, fr. L *orbus* orphaned, bereft, blind — more at ORPHAN] : a detail in medieval architecture of uncertain character but prob. a recessed panel surrounded by moldings (as one member of a blind arcade or one of the spaces between the ribs of a Gothic vault)

[2]**orb** \"\ *n* -s [MF *orbe*, fr. L *orbis* circle, disk, orb; akin to L *orbita* track, rut] **1 a** : any of the azure transparent spheres in old astronomy surrounding the earth one within the other and carrying the heavenly bodies in their revolutions **b** (1) : a globular celestial object (as the sun or moon, a planet or star) ⟨the celestial ~s revolve with uniform circular movements—G.C.Sellery⟩ (2) : EARTH ⟨solid, ironical, rolling ~—Walt Whitman⟩ **c** (1) : a spherical body : something of globular shape : GLOBE ⟨skewering the smaller ~s where they cowered amid their leaves —A.B.Mayse⟩ (2) : EYE ⟨her sightless ~s —Arnold Bennett⟩ (3) : a sphere surmounted by a cross symbolizing kingly power and justice and forming part of the English regalia (4) : a similar sphere on top of a scepter or crown **d** *archaic* (1) : a collective whole : WORLD (2) : a sphere of action : STATION ⟨in our ~s we'll live so round and safe —Shak.⟩ **2 a** : something circular (as a disk, wheel, ring) : CIRCLE ⟨the wheeling ~ of change —Alfred Tennyson⟩ **b** (1) *obs* : a period of time marked off by the revolution of a heavenly body (2) *archaic* : the orbit or the plane of the orbit of a planet or other heavenly body

orb 1c (3)

[3]**orb** \"\ *vb* -ED/-ING/-S *vt* **1** : to form into a disk or circle : round out **2** *archaic* : ENCIRCLE, SURROUND, ENCLOSE ~ *vi* : to move in an orbit

ORB *abbr* **1** omnidirectional radio beacon **2** owner's risk of breakage

orbed \'ō(ə)rbd, 'ō(ə)bd, *in poetry often* -bəd\ *adj* [[1]*orb* + *-ed*] : having the form of an orb : ROUND

or·bic \'ȯrbik, 'ō(ə)b-, -bēk\ *or* **or·bi·cal** \-bəkəl, -bēk-\ *adj* [*orbic* fr. L *orbicus*, fr. *orbis* + *-icus* -ic; *orbical* fr. L *orbicus* + E *-al*] : ORBICULAR

or·bi·cel·la \,ȯ(r)bə'selə\ *n*, *cap* [NL, fr. L *orbis* orb, circle + L *cella* cell — more at ORB, CELL] : a genus of usu. massive star corals with the zooids widely separated

or·bic·u·lar \ȯ(r)'bikyələ(r)\ *adj* [ME *orbiculer*, fr. MF or LL; MF *orbiculaire*, fr. LL *orbicularis* circular, fr. L *orbiculus* small disk + *-aris* -ar — more at ORBICULE] **1 a** : resembling or having the form of an orb : SPHERICAL, CIRCULAR ⟨nearly ~ in shape —P.S.Barnhart⟩ **b** : containing rounded bodies consisting of minerals in generally radial or tangential groupings usu. in successive concentric zones ⟨~ rocks⟩ **c** : encircling a part or opening ⟨an ~ ligament⟩ **2** : COMPLETE, ROUNDED, INTEGRAL ⟨an ~ system of political thought⟩ — **or·bic·u·lar·i·ty** \,⸗,⸗⸗'larəd·ē\ *n* -ES — **or·bic·u·lar·ly** *adv*

or·bi·cu·lar·is \ȯ(r),bikyə'la(a)rəs, -lär-\ *n*, *pl* **orbicula·res** \-(,)rēz\ [NL, fr. LL *orbicularis*, adj.] : a muscle encircling an orifice ⟨the ~ that encircles the opening of the orbit⟩

orbicularis oris \-'ōrəs\ *n*, *pl* **orbiculares oris** [NL, lit., orbicularis of the mouth] : a muscle made up of several layers of fibers passing in different directions that encircles the mouth and controls most movements of the lips (as compressing, closing, or pursing movements)

orbicular ligament *n* : ANNULAR LIGAMENT b

or·bic·u·late \ȯ(r)'bikyələ¦t, -,lā|, *usu* |d·+V\ *adj* [L *orbiculatus*, fr. *orbiculus* + *-atus* -ate] : having the form of an orb : circular or nearly circular in outline : ORBICULAR ⟨an ~ leaf⟩ — see LEAF illustration — **or·bic·u·late·ly** *adv*

or·bi·cule \'ō(r)bə,kyül\ *n* -s [L *orbiculus* small disk, dim. of *orbis* disk, circle — more at ORB] : a more or less spherical body found in some granites and other rocks, varying in size from a pellet visible only under the microscope to a sphere 10 feet or more in diameter, and having its constituents arranged in concentric shells

orbier *comparative of* ORBY

orbiest *superlative of* ORBY

[1]**or·bit** \'ȯrbət, 'ō(ə)b-, *usu* -əd·+V\ *n* -s [L *orbita* track, rut, orbit] **1** [ML *orbita*, fr. L] **a** : the bony cavity perforated for the passage of nerves and blood vessels that occupies the lateral front of the skull immediately beneath the frontal bone on each side and encloses and protects the eye and its appendages — called also *eye socket* **b** : the skin around the eye of a bird **2 a** : a path described by a celestial body, an artificial satellite, or a spacecraft in its revolution around another body ⟨the ~ of the earth around the sun⟩ ⟨the ~ of a spacecraft around the moon⟩; *also* : one complete revolution of an orbiting body ⟨a spacecraft making two ~s of the moon⟩ **b** : the course of an orbiting airplane **c** (1) : the usu. curved path of a body in a field of force (as the path of an electron in the presence of a nucleus, or of a charged particle in electric and magnetic fields, or of the earth in the sun's gravitational field) (2) : a state of a particle as determined by its energy, angular momentum, and other factors as it moves in a force field — used esp. of an electron in the presence of a nucleus **3** : range or sphere of activity, experience, influence, or interest ⟨Roman political power swept the Mediterranean world into its ~ —Benjamin Farrington⟩ ⟨within the ~ of my curiosity —Alec Waugh⟩ **4** : BALL, ORB **syn** see RANGE

[2]**orbit** \"\ *vb* -ED/-ING/-S *vt* **1** : to revolve in an orbit around ⟨a satellite ~*ing* the earth⟩ **2** : to send up and make revolve in an orbit ⟨~ a satellite⟩ ~ *vi* : to travel in circles : CIRCLE ⟨a plane ~*ing* over a landing field⟩

[1]**or·bit·al** \'ȯ(r)bəd·ᵊl, -bət[ə]l\ *adj* [[1]*orbit* + *-al*] **1** : of or relating to an orbit ⟨~ revolution⟩ **2** : OCULAR ⟨an ~ scale⟩

[2]**orbital** \"\ *n* -s **1** : a solution of the Schrödinger wave equation describing a possible mode of motion of a single electron in an atom or molecule **2** : the state that is described by the orbital

orbital arch *n* : the curved upper edge of the orbit of the eye

or·bi·tale \,ȯ(r)bə'ta(,)lē, -ā(,)lē, -ä(,)lē\ *n* -s [NL, fr. ML *orbita* orbit + L *-ale*, neut. of *-alis* -al — more at ORBIT] : the lowest point on the lower edge of the cranial orbit

orbital electron *n* **:** one of the electrons that according to the theory of Rutherford and Bohr revolve in an orbit about the nucleus of an atom

orbital fissure *n* **:** either of two openings transmitting nerves and blood vessels to or from the orbit with a superior lying between the greater and the lesser wing of the sphenoid bone and an inferior between the greater wing of the sphenoid and the maxilla

orbital fossa *n* **:** a depression in the front of the carapace of a crustacean from which the eyestalk arises

orbital index *n* **:** the ratio of the greatest height of the orbital cavity to its greatest width multiplied by 100 where the width is measured from the dacryon to the farthest point on the opposite border and the height is measured along a line perpendicular to the width — see CHAMAECONCH, HYPSICONCH, MESOCONCH

orbital lobe *n* **:** the part of the lower surface of the frontal lobe of the brain that overlies the orbits

orbital moment *n* **:** the angular momentum of an atomic electron corresponding to its supposed motion in an orbit

orbital nerve *n* **:** ZYGOMATIC NERVE

orbital point *n* **:** ORBITALE — see CRANIOMETRY illustration

orbital process *n* **:** a process of the palatine bone that forms part of the floor of the orbit

orbital quantum number *n* **:** AZIMUTHAL QUANTUM NUMBER

or·bi·te·lous spider \ˌȯ(r)bə¦tēləs-\ *n* [*orbitelous* fr. NL *Orbitelae*, tribe of Argiopidae (fr. L *orbis* circle, disk, orb + *tela* web) + E *-ous* — more at ORB, TOIL] **:** ORB WEAVER

or·bit·er \ˈȯ(r)bəd·ə(r), -ətə-\ *n* -s **:** one that orbits; *esp* **:** a man-made satellite ⟨the successful achievement of space ~*s* —J.B.Medaris⟩

¹**or·bi·toid** \ˈȯ(r)bəˌtȯid\ *adj* [NL *Orbitoides*] **:** of or relating to the genus *Orbitoides*

²**orbitoid** \"\ *n* -s **:** a member of the genus *Orbitoides*

or·bi·toi·des \ˌ==ˈtȯi(ˌ)dēz\ *n, cap* [NL, fr. L *orbita* orbit + *-oides* -oid — more at ORB] **:** a genus of Upper Cretaceous to Miocene foraminiferans similar to *Nummulites* but characterized by radially arranged chambers and several layers of small chambers superimposed on both surfaces of the layer of large chambers

or·bi·to·li·na \ˌ=bəd·əˈlīnə, -lēnə\ *n, cap* [NL, fr. *Orbitolites* + *-ina*] **:** a genus of foraminiferans very abundant in the Cretaceous having a bowl-shaped or depressed conic siliceous test with agglutinated sandy particles

or·bit·o·lite \ȯ(r)ˈbid·ᵊlˌīt\ *n* -s [NL *Orbitolites*] **:** a fossil of the genus *Orbitolites*

or·bi·to·li·tes \ˌȯ(r)bəd·əˈlīd·(ˌ)ēz\ *n, cap* [NL, fr. L *orbita* track, rut, orbit + NL *-o-* + *-lites* -lite — more at ORB] **:** a genus of foraminiferans of the Eocene that form thin, broad, circular disks containing numerous small chambers disposed concentrically about a few spirally wound primordial chambers

¹**or·bi·to·sphenoid** \ˌȯ(r)bəd·(ˌ)ō+\ *also* **or·bi·to·sphenoi·dal** \"+\ *adj* [¹*orbit* + *-o-* + *sphenoid, sphenoidal*] **:** being or relating to a paired element of the skull between the presphenoid and frontal that in man forms the lesser wing of the sphenoid

²**orbitosphenoid** \"\ *n* -s **:** an orbitosphenoid bone or process

or·bi·to·stat \ˈȯ(r)bəd·əˌstat, =ˈbid·ə,-\ *n* -s [ISV ¹*orbit* + *-o-* + *-stat*] **:** a device used for measuring the axis of the cranial orbit

orbits *pl of* ORBIT, *pres 3d sing of* ORBIT

or·bi·ty \ˈȯ(r)bəd·ē\ *n* -ES [MF *orbité*, fr. L *orbitat-, orbitas*, fr. *orbus* orphaned, childless, bereft + *-itat-, -itas* -ity — more at ORPHAN] *archaic* **:** CHILDLESSNESS

orb·less \ˈȯrbləs, ˈȯ(ə)b-\ *adj* [²*orb* + *-less*] **:** lacking an orb

orbs *pl of* ORB, *pres 3d sing of* ORB

orb-spider \ˈ=ˌ==\ *n* **:** ORB WEAVER

or·bu·li·na \ˌȯ(r)byəˈlīnə, -lēnə\ *n, cap* [NL, fr. L *orbis* circle, disk + *-ulus* -ule + NL *-ina*] **:** a genus of minute foraminiferans having a globular unilocular shell

orb weaver *n* [²*orb*] **:** a spider of the family Argiopidae — compare GEOMETRIC SPIDER

orb web *n* **:** a web made by an orb weaver

orby \ˈȯrbē, ˈȯ(ə)bē, -bi\ *adj* -ER/-EST [²*orb* + *-y*] *archaic* **:** having the course of an orb **:** like an orb **:** REVOLVING

orc \ˈȯ(ə)rk, ˈȯ(ə)k\ *n* -s [MF *orque*, fr. L *orca*, a whale, prob. fr. Gk *oryga*, acc. of *oryx*, a whale] **1 :** GRAMPUS; *also* **:** a sea animal held to resemble it **2 :** a horrid creature (as a sea monster, giant, or ogre) of horrid form or aspect

ORC *abbr* owner's risk of chafing

¹**or·ca** \ˈȯrkə\ [NL, fr. L, a whale] *syn of* ORCINUS

²**orca** \"\ *n* -s [NL *Orca*] **:** KILLER WHALE

¹**or·ca·di·an** \(ˈ)ȯ(r)¦kādēən\ *n* -s *cap* [L *Orcades* Orkney islands + E *-ian*] **:** a native or inhabitant of the Orkney islands

²**orcadian** \"\ *adj, usu cap* **1 :** of or relating to the Orkney islands **2 :** of or relating to the people of the Orkneys

or·ca·nette *also* **or·ca·net** *or* **or·cha·net** \ˈȯ(r)kəˌnet\ *n* -s [MF *orcanette*, alter. of OF *arquenet*, dim. of *arcanne, alcanne* henna, fr. ML *alchanna* — more at ALKANNA] **:** ALKANET 1b, 2

or·ce·in \ˈȯ(r)sēən\ *n* -s [F *orcéine*, fr. *orcine* orcin + *-éine* -ein] **:** a purple nitrogenous dye that is the essential coloring matter of cudbear and archil and is obtained from orcinol by action of aqueous ammonia and atmospheric oxygen

orch *abbr* orchestra

or·chard \ˈȯrchərd, ˈȯ(ə)chəd\ *n* -s [ME, fr. OE *ortgeard, orceard*, fr. L *hortus* garden + OE *geard* enclosure, yard — more at YARD] **1 :** a plantation or enclosure containing fruit trees, nut-bearing trees, or sugar maples; *also* **:** the trees of such a plantation **2** *archaic* **:** a grove of wild fruit-bearing trees

orchard bush *n, chiefly Brit* **:** open woodland of tropical uplands in which the individual trees are more or less uniformly distributed

orchard fruit *n* **:** TREE FRUIT

orchard grass *n* **:** a widely grown tall stout hay and pasture grass (*Dactylis glomerata*) growing in tufts with loose open panicles — called also *cocksfoot, cockspur*

orchard heating *n* **:** the protection of fruit trees in bloom or fruit from frost injury by means of numerous small heaters utilizing as fuel crude oil, coke, coal, or wood or by large heaters burning oil and supplying radiant heat — compare SMUDGE

orchard house *n* **:** a greenhouse for raising fruit trees

or·chard·ing \ˈȯ(r)chə(r)diŋ\ *n* -s **1 :** the cultivation of orchards **2 :** orchard land **:** ORCHARDS

or·chard·ist \-dəst\ *n* -s **:** a person who is engaged in orcharding

or·chard·man \dmən\ *n, pl* **orchardmen :** ORCHARDIST

orchard oriole *n* **:** an oriole (*Icterus spurius*) of eastern No. America smaller than the Baltimore oriole with the adult male a rich chestnut with a black head, neck, and upper back

orchectomy *var of* ORCHIECTOMY

or·chel·la weed \ȯrˈchelə\ *n* **:** ARCHIL 2

or·che·sis \ȯ(r)ˈkēsəs\ *n* -ES [Gk *orchēsis* action or art of dancing, fr. *orcheisthai* to dance + *-sis*] **:** the art of dancing in the Greek chorus

or·che·sog·ra·phy \ˌȯ(r)kəˈsägrəfē\ *n* -ES [F *orchésographie*, fr. MF *orchesographie*, fr. Gk *orchēsis* dancing + MF *-o-* + *-graphie* -graphy] **:** CHOREOGRAPHY

or·ches·tia \ȯ(r)ˈkestēə\ *n, cap* [NL, fr. Gk *orchēstēs* dancer (fr. *orcheisthai* to dance, leap) + NL *-ia*] **:** a genus (the type of the family Orchestiidae) of semiterrestrial amphipod crustaceans comprising the widely distributed beach fleas of sandy seacoasts

¹**or·ches·ti·id** \(ˈ)=¦kestēəd\ *adj* [NL *Orchestiidae*, family of crustaceans, fr. *Orchestia*, type genus + *-idae*] **:** of or relating to the genus *Orchestia* or the family Orchestiidae

²**orchestiid** *n* -s **:** an orchestiid crustacean

or·ches·tra \ˈȯ(r)kəstrə *also* -ˌkes-\ *n* -s [L, fr. Gk *orchēstra*, fr. *orcheisthai* to dance; akin to Skt *ṛghāyati* he raves, rages, trembles and perh. akin to Gk *ornynai* to urge on, incite, call forth — more at RISE] **1 a :** a circular space used by the chorus in front of the proscenium in an ancient Greek theater — see THEATER illustration **b :** a corresponding semicircular space in a Roman theater used for the seats of persons of distinction **2 a :** a large group of players of musical instruments including typically strings, woodwinds, brasses, and percussion organized esp. for performing one of the larger forms of concert music (as a symphony) or for accompanying an oratorio or other dramatic work (as a ballet or opera) or for playing light or popular music ⟨symphony ~⟩ ⟨pops ~⟩ **b :** a

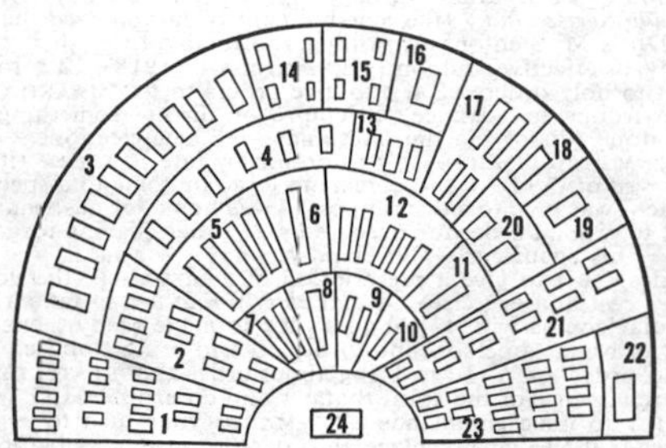

orchestra: typical arrangement: *1* first violins, *2* cellos, *3* basses, *4* French horns, *5* bassoons, *6* contrabassoons, *7* oboes, *8* English horn, *9* flutes, *10* piccolo, *11* bass clarinet, *12* clarinets, *13* trumpets, *14* percussion, *15* timpani, *16* chimes, *17* trombones, *18* tuba, *19* piano, *20* saxophones, *21* violas, *22* harp, *23* second violins, *24* podium

small group of musicians organized specif. to play for dining and dancing ⟨a small 4-piece ~⟩ **c** (1) **:** a space in a modern theater or other public hall that is used by a band of instrumental performers and that is commonly just in front of the stage and at or below the level of the auditorium floor (2) **:** the forward section of seats on the main floor of a theater (3) **:** the main floor of a theater

orchestra bells *n pl* **:** GLOCKENSPIEL 2

orchestra circle *n* **:** PARQUET CIRCLE

or·ches·tral \(ˈ)ȯ(r)¦kestrəl *sometimes* ˈ=ˌkəs-\ *adj* [*orchestra* + *-al*] **1 a :** of, relating to, or designed for an orchestra ⟨seek new ~ works in Paris —*Current Biog.*⟩ ⟨~ concerts⟩ ⟨~ programs⟩ **b :** imitating a specified orchestral instrument — used in the names of organ stops ⟨~ oboe⟩ **2 :** suggestive of an orchestra or its characteristic musical qualities or effects ⟨a poem of ~ sweep and grandeur⟩ — **or·ches·tral·ly** \-trəlē, -li\ *adv*

or·ches·tra·less *pronunc at* ORCHESTRA + ləs\ *adj* **:** having no orchestra

orchestral organ *n* **:** SOLO ORGAN

orchestra pit *n* **:** a pit underneath the forestage from which an orchestra plays

or·ches·trate \ˈȯ(r)kəˌstrāt, *usually* -ād·+V\ *vb* -ED/-ING/-s [F *orchestrer* to orchestrate (fr. *orchestre* orchestra, fr. L *orchestra*) + E *-ate*] *vt* **1 :** to compose or arrange (music) for an orchestra **:** provide with orchestration ⟨~ a ballet⟩ ⟨~ a waltz⟩ **2 :** to arrange, develop, organize, or combine so as to achieve a desired or maximum effect ⟨must ~ the best thoughts of mankind —K.F.Leidecker⟩ ⟨the teller of tall tales . . . who would always ~ his facts —H.A.L. Craig⟩ ⟨separate periods of time are *orchestrated* according to the novel's needs —Bernard DeVoto⟩ **~** *vi* **:** to arrange or compose music for an orchestra ⟨~*s* very well⟩

or·ches·tra·tion \ˌ==ˈstrāshən\ *n* -s [F, fr. *orchestrer* + *-ation*] **1 :** the arranging of music for an orchestra; *specif* **:** the treatment of a composition with regard to the structure, manipulation, compass, and timbre of the orchestral instruments and their effective combination, the proper distribution of the harmony, and the writing of orchestral scores — compare INSTRUMENTATION **2 :** harmonious organization, integration, or combination ⟨an exquisite ~ of activity —G.W.Gray b. 1886⟩ ⟨develop a world community through ~ of cultural diversities —L.K.Frank⟩

or·ches·tra·tor *also* **or·ches·trat·er** \ˈ==ˌstrād·ə(r), -ātə-\ *n* -s **:** a person that arranges music for orchestral use or provides with orchestration

or·ches·trelle \¦ȯ(r)kə¦strel\ *n* -s [*orchestra* + F *-elle*, dim. suffix] **:** a reed organ of the late 19th and early 20th centuries constructed on the principle of the mechanical player piano and designed to imitate the effect of an orchestra

or·ches·tric \(ˈ)ȯ(r)¦kestrik\ *adj* [*orchestra* + *-ic*] **:** ORCHESTRAL

or·ches·tri·na \ˌȯ(r)kəˈstrēnə\ *n* -s [*orchestra* + *-ina*] **:** ORCHESTRION

or·ches·tri·on \ȯ(r)ˈkestrēən\ *n* -s [*orchestra* + *-ion* (as in *melodion*)] **:** a mechanical device provided with different stops capable of imitating a variety of musical instruments

or·chid \ˈȯrkəd, ˈȯ(ə)k-\ *n* -s [NL *Orchidaceae*] **1 :** a plant of the family Orchidaceae **2 :** a variable color averaging a light purple **3 :** PRAISE, COMMENDATION, COMPLIMENT — usu. used in pl. ⟨an unsung editor deserves some of the ~*s* —S.L.A. Marshall⟩ ⟨extended ~*s* to industry for its encouragement of such students —*Ethyl News*⟩

or·chi·da·ce·ae \ˌ=kəˈdāsēˌē\ *n pl, cap* [NL, fr. *Orchid-, Orchis*, type genus + *-aceae*] **:** a very large family of highly specialized perennial herbaceous monocotyledonous plants (order Orchidales) that have entire sheathing or scalelike leaves, tuberous or bulbous or thickened roots, and extremely complex usu. showy flowers with a calyx of three often petaloid sepals, a corolla of three petals of which one forms a distinctive and often spurred labellum, a column consisting of the variously fused style, stigma, and stamen, the pollen usu. aggregated into pollinia which adhere to visiting insects, and an inferior ovary and that reproduce by minute seeds lacking endosperm and containing chlorophyll — see ORCHID, ORCHIS

or·chi·da·cean \ˌ==ˈdāshən\ *n* -s [NL *Orchidaceae* + E *-an*] **:** a plant of the family Orchidaceae

or·chi·da·ceous \¦==¦shəs\ *adj* [NL *Orchidaceae* + E *-ous*] **1 :** of, relating to, or resembling the Orchidaceae or an orchid **2 a :** SHOWY, OSTENTATIOUS ⟨from the modern standpoint she was a very ~ writer —*N.Y. Herald Tribune*⟩ **b :** marked by or displaying a showy or luxurious beauty ⟨an ~ lady of no definite profession —William Du Bois⟩ — **or·chi·da·ceous·ly** *adv*

or·chi·da·les \ˌ==ˈ=(ˌ)lēz\ *n pl, cap* [NL, fr. *Orchid-, Orchis* + *-ales*] **:** an order of monocotyledonous plants with irregular flowers, an inferior compound ovary, and minute seeds that lack endosperm — see BURMANNIACEAE, ORCHIDACEAE

orchid cactus *n* **:** a cactus of the genus *Epiphyllum*

or·chi·dec·to·my \ˌȯ(r)kəˈdektəmē\ *n* -ES [irreg. fr. Gk *orchis* testicle + E *-ectomy*] **:** ORCHIECTOMY

orchid family *n* **:** ORCHIDACEAE

orchid fly *n* **:** CATTLEYA FLY

orchid gray *n* **:** a variable color averaging a grayish purple that is redder, lighter, and stronger than telegraph blue, bluer and stronger than mauve gray, and bluer and paler than average rose mauve

orchid haze *n* **:** a light purplish gray that is stronger and very slightly bluer than lilac gray

-or·chi·dism \ˈȯ(r)kəˌdizəm\ *n comb form* -s [NL *-orchidismus*, irreg. fr. Gk *orchis* testicle + L *-ismus* -ism] **:** -ORCHISM ⟨crypt*orchidism*⟩

or·chid·ist \ˈȯ(r)kədəst\ *n* -s **:** a cultivator of orchids

orchid mist *n* **:** a variable color averaging a grayish purplish pink that is bluer and paler than cameo pink and bluer, stronger, and slightly lighter than dawn pink

or·chid·ol·o·gist \ˌȯ(r)kəˈdäləjəst\ *n* -s **:** a specialist in orchidology

or·chid·ol·o·gy \-jē, -ji\ *n* -ES [*orchid* + *-o-* + *-logy*] **:** a branch of botany or horticulture dealing with orchids

or·chi·do·pexy \ˈȯ(r)kədōˌpeksē\ *n* -ES [irreg. fr. Gk *orchis* testicle + E *-pexy*] **:** surgical fixation of a testis

orchid peat *n* **:** the stipes, roots, and other parts of ferns chopped up and used for potting ferns, orchids, and epiphytes

orchid pink *n* **:** a variable color averaging a light purplish pink

orchid rose *n* **:** a variable color averaging a deep purplish pink that is redder and less strong than amaranth pink

orchid taupe *n* **:** a variable color averaging a dark grayish purple that is redder and paler than average purple wine, bluer and paler than raisin black, and bluer, lighter, and stronger than old lavender (sense 2)

orchid tint *n* **:** a pale purplish pink that is bluer and paler than mauve pink

orchid tree *n* **:** MOUNTAIN EBONY

or·chi·ec·to·my \ˌȯ(r)kēˈektəmē\ *also* **or·chec·to·my** \ȯ(r)ˈkektəmē\ *n* -ES [Gk *orchis* testicle + E *-ectomy* — more at ORCHIS] **:** excision of a testis

or·chil *var of* ARCHIL

or·chil·la weed *n* \ȯrˈchilə\ **:** ARCHIL 2

or·chi·o·pexy \ˈȯ(r)kēōˌpeksē\ *n* -ES [Gk *orchis* testicle + E *-o-* + *-pexy*] **:** ORCHIDOPEXY

or·chis \ˈȯrkəs\ *n* [NL *Orchid-, Orchis*, fr. L *orchis* orchid, fr. Gk, testicle, orchid; fr. the shape of the roots; akin to MIr *uirgge* testicle, Alb *herdhe* testicle, Av *ərəzi-* scrotum] **1** *cap* **:** a genus (the type of the family Orchidaceae) of terrestrial or epiphytic herbs having fleshy tubers or rootstocks and spicate flowers with a spurred lip and having the pollinia borne in a common pouch — see MALE ORCHIS, SALEP **2** -ES **:** ORCHID; *specif* **:** any plant of the genus *Orchis*

-or·chism \ˈȯ(r)ˌkizəm\ *n comb form* -s [NL *-orchismus*, fr. Gk *orchis* testicle + L *-ismus* -ism] **:** a (specified) form or condition of the testes ⟨crypt*orchism*⟩

or·chit·ic \(ˈ)ȯ(r)¦kid·ik\ *adj* [NL *orchitis* + E *-ic*] **:** of, producing, or affected with orchitis

or·chi·tis \ȯ(r)ˈkīd·əs\ *n* -ES [NL, fr. Gk *orchis* testicle + NL *-itis*] **:** inflammation of a testis

or·cin \ˈȯrsən\ *n* -s [ISV *orchil* + *-in*] **:** ORCINOL

or·cin·ol \-ˌnōl, -nȯl\ *n* -s [ISV *orcin* + *-ol*] **:** a crystalline dihydroxy phenol $CH_3C_6H_3(OH)_2$ obtained from various lichens (as of the genera *Roccella* and *Lecanora*), from extract of aloes, and synthetically from some derivatives of toluene; 5-methyl-resorcinol

or·ci·nus \ȯ(r)ˈsīnəs\ *n, cap* [NL, fr. L *orca*, a whale + *-inus* -ine — more at ORC] **:** the genus consisting of the killer whale

orcs *pl of* ORC

ord *abbr* **1** ordained **2** order **3** orderly **4** ordinal **5** ordinance **6** ordinary **7** ordnance

ORD *abbr* owner's risk of damage

or·dain \ȯrˈdān, ȯ(ə)ˈ-\ *vb* -ED/-ING/-s [ME *ordeinen*, fr. OF *ordener* (3d sing. pres. *ordeine*), fr. LL & L; LL *ordinare* to ordain (a clergyman), fr. L, to put in order, arrange, appoint, fr. *ordin-, ordo* order — more at ORDER] *vt* **1 :** ARRANGE, ORDER, REGULATE, MANAGE, CONDUCT ⟨a boy not yet fit to ~ his life —Oliver La Farge⟩ **2 a** (1) **:** to invest with ministerial or sacerdotal functions **:** introduce into the office of the Christian ministry by the laying on of hands or by other forms **:** set apart by the ceremony of ordination — compare CONSECRATE (2) **:** to invest with regal functions by a religious ceremony ⟨~*ed* king in Westminster Abbey —F.M.Stenton⟩ **b :** to establish by appointment, decree, or law **:** CONSTITUTE, INSTITUTE, ENACT ⟨the plan was ~*ed* by the governor and judges —*Amer. Guide Series: Mich.*⟩ ⟨~*ed* a form of government closely resembling an absolute monarchy —E.O.Hauser⟩ **c :** to predestine or destine as part of a divine plan, by the force of circumstances, or as necessary in the nature of things **:** FATE ⟨truly ~*ed* to be one of the world's great crossroads —H.F. Bain⟩ ⟨~*ed* to be hewers of wood and drawers of water —*Newsweek*⟩ ⟨the end is ~*ed* by fate —C.H.Rickword⟩ **d :** to order by fiat or by virtue of great or supreme authority **:** COMMAND, DECREE ⟨~*ed* that the best gumtrees were to be left standing —Rex Ingamells⟩ ⟨cannot ~ that so many tons of steel be produced when the ore and steel plants are not in existence —F.A.Ogg & Harold Zink⟩ **~** *vi* **:** to issue an order **:** DECREE, COMMAND ⟨so great Jove ~*s*⟩ **syn** see DICTATE

or·dain·er \-nə(r)\ *n* -s [ME *ordeinour*, fr. OF *ordeneor*, fr. *ordener* + *-eor* -or] **1 :** one that ordains **2 :** *often cap* **:** one of a commission of 21 nobles and prelates appointed under Edward II in 1310 to frame ordinances esp. for regulating the king's household

or·dain·ment \-nmənt\ *n* -s **:** appointment or ordinance esp. by divine power or fate **:** ORDINATION

¹**or·deal** \(ˈ)ȯr¦dēl, (ˈ)ȯ(ə)¦-, *esp before pause or consonant* -ēəl\ *n* -s [ME *ordal*, fr. OE *ordāl, ordēl*; akin to OFris *ordēl, urdēl* judgment, verdict, ordeal, OS *urdēli* judgment, verdict, OHG *urteili, urteil*; all fr. a prehistoric WGmc compound derived fr. a compound verb represented by OHG *irteilen* to render a verdict, judge, bestow, distribute, fr. *ir-*, perfective prefix + *teilen* to divide, render a verdict — more at ABEAR, DEAL] **1 :** a primitive means used to determine guilt or innocence by submitting the accused to dangerous or painful tests believed to be under divine or superhuman control with escape from injury ordinarily taken as a vindication of innocence ⟨~ by battle⟩ ⟨~ by fire⟩ ⟨~ by water⟩ **2 :** something that tests or is used to test character or endurance **:** a severe trial **:** a trying experience ⟨recover from the ~ of that climb —John Hunt & Edmund Hillary⟩ ⟨the ~ of watching the last dollars disappear —Irving Stone⟩ ⟨an encounter with the headmaster could be something of an ~ —A.F.Fforde⟩

²**ordeal** \"\ *adj* **:** of or relating to trial by ordeal

ordeal bark *n* [so called fr. its use as an ordeal poison] **:** the poisonous bark of a West African tree (*Erythrophloeum guineense*) of the family Leguminosae **:** SASSY BARK

ordeal bean *n* **:** CALABAR BEAN

ordeal tree *n* **1 :** a poisonous Madagascan tree (*Tanghinia venenifera*) having fruit resembling plums and poisonous seeds **2 :** ORDEAL BARK **3 :** a southern African tree (*Acocanthera venenata*) **4 :** a poisonous central African shrub (*Strychnos densiflora*)

¹**or·der** \ˈȯrdər, ˈȯ(ə)də(r\ *n* -s [MF *ordre, order*, fr. OF *ordene, ordne, ordre*, fr. ML & L; ML *ordin-, ordo* order (in ecclesiastical senses), fr. L (in other senses); akin to L *ordiri* to lay the warp, begin to weave, begin, and perh. to Gk *arariskein* to fit together, fasten, suit — more at ARM] **1 a** (1) **:** one of the nine grades of angels in medieval theology; *also* **:** an analogous class of supernatural beings ⟨an ~ of spirits who abuse and persecute those they possess —Ralph Linton⟩ (2) *sometimes cap* **:** any of the several grades of the Christian ministry — see MAJOR ORDER, MINOR ORDER (3) **orders** *pl* **:** the office and dignity of a person in the Christian ministry ⟨in deacon's ~*s*⟩ (4) **:** ORDINATION — usu. used in pl. ⟨received ~*s*⟩ (5) *often cap* **:** a ritually prescribed form of service (as for the administration of a sacrament) ⟨the ~ of baptism⟩ **b** (1) **:** a religious body typically an aggregate of separate communities living under a distinctive rule, discipline, or constitution **:** a monastic brotherhood or society (2) **:** any of several knightly fraternities bound by a discipline both religious and military and typically originating in the era of the crusades (3) **:** a society patterned on the knightly fraternities of the middle ages but typically founded by a sovereign, a prince, or a national legislature for the conferring of honorary distinction (4) **:** the badge, medal, or other insignia of such a society; *also* **:** a military decoration for bravery or distinguished service (5) **:** a fraternal society or other association of private character ⟨the Masonic *Order*⟩ ⟨the *Order* of Gregg Artists is the largest and best-known shorthand organization in the world —Florence E. Ulrich⟩ ⟨a secret ~ of conspirators⟩ **c** (1) **:** one of the classes comprising a hierarchical or stratified society **:** a social class or grouping ⟨there are two main ~*s*, the natural aristocracy and the common people —C.J.Friedrich⟩ — often used in the phrases *higher orders, lower orders* ⟨the lower ~*s* of whites were all but beyond the reach of democracy —Van Wyck Brooks⟩ (2) **:** a narrowly delimited group of persons having a common interest and forming a distinct class by profession, special privileges, or other common interests ⟨the first two ~*s*, the clergy and the nobility —D.W.S.Lidderdale⟩ ⟨the ~ of baronets⟩ (3) **:** the totality of social, political, and cultural arrangements prevailing in a particular place and time **:** a particular sociopolitical

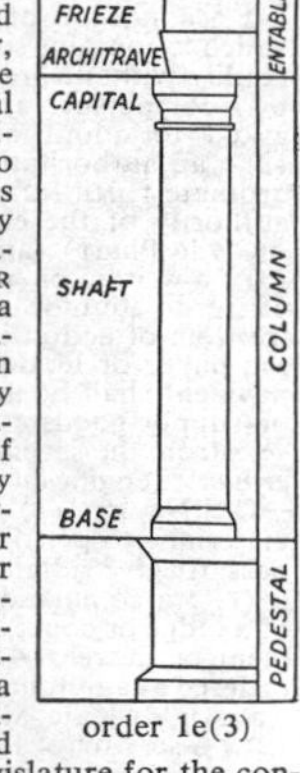

order 1e(3)

system ⟨inclined to oppose radical changes in the established ~ —*Amer. Guide Series: Maine*⟩ ⟨symbols of the decaying ~*s* they headed —Claude Pepper⟩ ⟨the ceremonies are part of the traditional ~ —*Brit. Book News*⟩ **d** (1) *archaic* **:** a rank, row, or series of objects (2) **:** level or degree of importance, quality, or value **:** RANK ⟨a world power of the first ~ —S.L.Sharp⟩ ⟨the productions booked for these communities were of a low ~ —*Amer. Guide Series: Mich.*⟩ ⟨realism of the highest ~ —A.L.Guérard⟩ (3) **:** a category, type, class, or kind of thing of distinctive character or rank ⟨there is an ~ of mind which is perpetually modern —Edith Hamilton⟩ ⟨cultivated after his fashion the ~ of verse —*Times Lit. Supp.*⟩ ⟨in the same ~ of ideas —O.G.Frazer⟩ ⟨in emergencies of this ~ —R.B.Westerfield⟩ ⟨revolutions are a different ~ of events —John Strachey⟩ ⟨presents a problem of the severest ~ —J.B.Gallagher⟩ **e** (1) **:** a style of building (2) **:** a type of column and entablature that with its forms, proportions, and mode of decoration is the unit of a style ⟨Corinthian ~⟩ ⟨Doric ~⟩ (3) **:** a columnar treatment based on the classic orders **f** (1) **:** arrangement of objects in position or of events in time (2) **:** the number of times differentiation is applied successively ⟨derivatives of higher ~⟩ (3) **:** the order of the highest order derivative in a differential equation (4) **:** DEGREE 11a, 11b (5) **:** the number of rows and columns in a matrix ⟨the ~ of a matrix with 2 rows and 3 columns is 2 by 3⟩ (6) **:** ORDER OF MAGNITUDE 2 **g** (1) **:** degree or grade in a series based on size or quantity ⟨lines, of the ~ of one third of an inch in diameter —R.E.Coker⟩ (2) **:** general or approximate size, quantity, or level of magnitude or a figure indicative thereof ⟨a population of the ~ of 40,000 —W.G.East⟩ ⟨all explosions were divided into two general types — low ~ and high ~ —H.A.Holsinger⟩ ⟨at a date of the ~ of 50,000 years ago —R.C.Murphy⟩ ⟨the time period is of the ~ of a thousand years —A.N.Whitehead⟩ **h :** a category of taxonomic classification ranking above the family and below the class and in botany characteristically having a name ending in *-ales* (as Rosales) and often being made up of several families — see NATURAL ORDER **i :** position in a sequence of interference or diffraction phenomena ⟨a grating spectrum of the third ~⟩ **j** (1) **:** a sequential arrangement of mathematical elements (2) **:** a degree, type, level, or rank within an order ⟨a predicate of a higher ~⟩ **k :** the broadest category in soil classification ⟨zonal ~⟩ ⟨intrazonal ~⟩ **l :** a class of consonants whose common characteristic is that they have the same place of articulation ⟨the bilabials \p\, \b\, \m\ belong to the same ~⟩ **2 a** (1) **:** the manner in which one thing succeeds another **:** sequence or succession in space or time ⟨let me tell of these events in their ~⟩ ⟨were issued in a strange ~ —Edward Sackville-West & Desmond Shawe-Taylor⟩ (2) **:** sequence in respect of value, importance, or some other criterion ⟨good to know the goods in their ~ —R.M.Hutchins⟩ ⟨osmium, iridium and platinum in that ~ are the three heaviest metals known —W.R.Jones⟩ ⟨necessary to establish some ~ of importance —G.P.Wibberley⟩ ⟨the children came in proper ~, first the oldest, then their juniors⟩ (3) **:** the sequence of constituents as a device for conveying meaning (as in *Cain* [subject] *killed* [predicate] *Abel* [object]) **b** (1) **:** the totality of arrangements composing some sphere of action or being **:** a system functioning according to some definite laws or rules ⟨the contemporary economic ~⟩ ⟨our political ~⟩ ⟨should take the lead in reconstructing the social ~ —Paul Woodring⟩ ⟨whose loyalty to the English ~ of things was suspect —*Amer. Guide Series: Mich.*⟩; *also* **:** a prevailing mode, style, or trend ⟨the new ~ in literary criticism⟩ (2) *obs* **:** customary mode of procedure **:** established usage (3) **:** the customary, established, or prescribed mode of procedure in debate or other business (as of a deliberative or legislative body or a public meeting) ⟨rose to a point of ~⟩ ⟨a book on the rules of ~⟩ (4) **:** the condition of being in conformity with such a mode of procedure — usu. used in the phrases *in order, out of order* ⟨your motion is out of ~⟩ ⟨the amendment was inconsistent with the resolution and hence out of ~ —Walter Goodman⟩ (5) **:** the attentive, orderly, or decorous behavior or state appropriate to the conduct of deliberative or legislative business ⟨will the meeting please come to ~⟩ — compare CALL TO ORDER **c** (1) **:** the manner in which something is ordered **:** ARRANGEMENT, FORMATION, ARRAY ⟨the troops retired in good ~⟩ ⟨in his ~ of battle his center . . . was pushed forward —Tom Wintringham⟩ (2) **:** regular or harmonious arrangement or disposition **:** SYSTEM, PATTERN, METHOD ⟨there was a feminine ~ in the arrangement —Jean Stafford⟩ ⟨a world whose lack of ~ . . . must inspire them with a certain fear —Herbert Read⟩ ⟨the stuff of our lives is . . . a tangled web, yet in the end there is ~ —Havelock Ellis⟩ (3) **:** a condition in which everything is so arranged as to play its proper part ⟨a lover of ~⟩ ⟨values rank and station and ~ above other things in politics —R.G.F.Robinson⟩ ⟨the sense of ~ we associate with the medieval world —Wallace Fowlie⟩ (4) **:** the rule of law or proper authority **:** freedom from disturbance **:** public quiet ⟨restore ~ in a lawless community⟩ ⟨the victory of ~ . . . must be assured at all costs —*Times Lit. Supp.*⟩ (5) *archaic* **:** provision or disposition to achieve some end — usu. used in the phrase *take order* (6) **:** state or condition with regard to quality, functioning, or repair ⟨a square grand piano in good ~ —D.D.Martin⟩ ⟨found the equipment in the worst possible ~⟩ ⟨erect and maintain in good ~ a gate —*Farmer's Weekly* (*So. Africa*)⟩ (7) **:** a sound, proper, orderly, or functioning condition ⟨the finances and plans of the . . . institute have been set in ~ —W.G.Penfield⟩ ⟨the telephone is out of ~⟩ ⟨had his place put in ~ —Everett Lloyd⟩ ⟨his passport is not in ~⟩ (8) **:** the condition of being proper, appropriate, or required by the circumstances — used in the phrases *in order, out of order* ⟨this retraction is in ~ —Alexander MacDonald⟩ ⟨your suggestion is completely out of ~⟩ ⟨technically, his conviction was in ~ —S.H.Adams⟩ ⟨nominations for president are now in ~⟩ (9) **:** ORDER ARMS **d :** a condition of the tobacco leaf in the curing process in which it contains sufficient moisture to be pliable and handled readily without breaking **3 a** (1) **:** a rule or regulation made by a competent authority ⟨the Board of Aldermen will also be asked to adopt an ~ —*Springfield* (*Mass.*) *Daily News*⟩ (2) **:** an authoritative mandate usu. from a superior to a subordinate **:** INJUNCTION, INSTRUCTION ⟨refusal to recognize the authority of the emperor amounted to a refusal to take ~*s* —Clyde Pharr⟩ ⟨an executive ~⟩ ⟨under ~ to sail for home⟩ (3) **:** a written or oral directive from a senior military or naval officer to a junior telling him what to do but giving him certain freedom of action in complying **b** (1) **:** a direction by which the payee or holder of negotiable paper prescribes to whom payment shall be made (2) **:** a commission to purchase, sell, or supply goods **:** a direction in writing to furnish supplies ⟨~*s* from the seven canners had been too small —*Pacific Fisherman*⟩ ⟨engines built to the ~ of the Ministry of Supply —O.S.Nock⟩ (3) **:** a formal written authorization to deliver materials, to perform work, or to do both **c :** a direction or pass to give admittance (as to a building or entertainment) **d** (1) **:** a command or direction of a court (2) **:** a direction of a judge or court entered in writing and not entered in a judgment or decree **4 a** (1) **:** the merchandise, goods, or items ordered as a purchase ⟨should receive your ~ promptly —Sarah Taintor & Kate Monro⟩ ⟨the ~ arrived in good condition⟩ (2) **:** a serving of food ordered in a public eating place ⟨bring me my ~ right away⟩ ⟨one ~ of mashed potatoes⟩; *also* **:** an oral or written direction to serve such food ⟨the waitress will take your ~ now⟩ **b :** an assigned or requested undertaking ⟨this is a large ~, which would seem to require a much longer book —K.E.Poole⟩ ⟨trying to move loose horses through snow was almost as tall an ~ —H.L.Davis⟩ — **in order that** *conj* **:** THAT ⟨invite you *in order that* you may see for yourself⟩ — **in order to 1** *obs* **:** in regard or reference to **2 :** for the purpose of **:** as a means to ⟨ran *in order to* get home in time⟩ — **on the order of :** after the fashion of **:** LIKE ⟨something *on the order of* a state park —W.D.Hartley⟩ ⟨much *on the order of* Great Lakes bulk carriers —*Ships and the Sea*⟩ — **to order** *adv* **:** in fulfillment of an order given ⟨shoes made *to order*⟩

2**order** \"\ *vb* **ordered; ordered; ordering** \-d(ə)riŋ\ **orders** [ME *ordren*, fr. *ordre*, n.] *vt* **1 a** (1) **:** to arrange or dispose according to some plan or with reference to some end **:** put in a particular order **:** arrange in a series or sequence ⟨~*s* the arts and sciences according to their value in his Christian system —H.O.Taylor⟩ (2) *archaic* **:** to draw up in battle array **:** ARRAY, MARSHAL (3) **:** to put in order **:** make neat or orderly ⟨~*ed* her dress —D.C.Peattie⟩ **b :** to manage by rule or regulation ⟨~*ed* his affairs to the tempo of an earlier day —*Amer. Guide Series: Ind.*⟩ ⟨the marshal controlled and ~*ed* the hall —Doris M. Stenton⟩ ⟨unwilling and unable to ~ their economy in effective fashion —E.S.Furniss b. 1918⟩ **2 :** to admit to holy orders **3 a :** to give orders to **:** COMMAND ⟨~*ed* the troops to advance⟩ **:** require or direct (something) to be done ⟨dissolving the Diet and ~*ing* new elections —F.A. Ogg & Harold Zink⟩ **b :** to ordain by fate **:** DESTINE ⟨it was so ~*ed* of God⟩ **c :** to command to go or come to a specified place ⟨was ~*ed* to a distant post⟩ ⟨~*ed* home for misbehavior⟩ **d :** to give an order for **:** secure by an order ⟨having forgotten to ~ his chauffeur —Cleveland Amory⟩ ⟨~ a meal⟩ ⟨~ groceries⟩ **e :** to give a prescription of **:** PRESCRIBE ⟨the doctor ~*ed* rest and exercise⟩ **4** *dial chiefly Eng* **a :** to take a particular course with **:** deal with **b :** to make ready **:** PREPARE **c :** to bring (a person) into order **5 :** to bring (tobacco leaf) into order ~ *vi* **1 :** to bring about order **:** REGULATE, DIRECT ⟨a renascence of the spirit that ~*s* and controls —H.G.Wells⟩ **2 a :** to issue commands **:** COMMAND ⟨your turn to ~ next week⟩ **b :** to give or place an order ⟨be sure to ~ before it's too late⟩ **3 :** to become the object of an order ⟨slacks are ~*ing* with renewed strength —*Women's Wear Daily*⟩

syn ORDER, ARRANGE, MARSHAL, ORGANIZE, SYSTEMATIZE, METHODIZE can mean to put (a number of things) in their proper places or into a fit place, esp. in an interrelation or organization. ORDER in the sense of to put in a given sequence is somewhat archaic; in more general current use it means to put into an interrelationship thought of as reasoned or effective or to dispose so that system is achieved or confusion or friction is eliminated ⟨the ceremony is not well *ordered;* in fact there is here no single ceremony but a group of separate little rituals —C.L.Jones⟩ ⟨life as it came to him without conscious *ordering* —Virginia Woolf⟩ ⟨free to *order* their affairs as they choose —W.L.Sperry⟩ ⟨trees, lawns, terraces, rock gardens, paved walks, and many benches, all cleverly *ordered* in harmonious composition —*Amer. Guide Series: N. Y. City*⟩ ARRANGE is usu. used to apply to a putting of things in a proper, fit, or pleasing sequence or relationship, often by straightening up or adjusting to fixed circumstantial things, sometimes, however, suggesting contrivance or manipulation of things to a given end ⟨*arrange* the articles on a desk⟩ ⟨each of us *arranges* the world according to his own notion of the fitness of things —Joseph Conrad⟩ ⟨made his bed and *arranged* his room —Willa Cather⟩ ⟨the distressingly difficult task of *arranging* a peaceful world —K.F.Mather⟩ ⟨*arrange* things so that Father could go to Santa Fe —Mary Austin⟩ MARSHAL implies an assembling and arranging (of things, or sometimes diverse elements of a thing) esp. in preparation for or to facilitate a particular move or operation ⟨resources of the government have been *marshaled* in support of science —A.T.Waterman⟩ ⟨*marshals* his facts and arguments with lucidity and detachment —*Times Lit. Supp.*⟩ ⟨*marshaled* the evidence in his client's behalf —H.D.Hazeltine⟩ ⟨*marshal* a case before going into court⟩ ORGANIZE implies an arrangement in which several or many parts function in smooth interrelation ⟨our most successful historians . . . can *organize* their materials clearly and cogently —W.G.Carleton⟩ ⟨man, as a highly *organized* whole —H.J.Muller⟩ ⟨*organized* the hospital work of the Crimean war —G.B.Shaw⟩ ⟨the daily routine was gradually *organized* after a fashion —André Maurois⟩ SYSTEMATIZE implies arrangement according to a predetermined scheme ⟨if grammar was to become a rational science, it had to *systematize* itself through principles of logic —H.O.Taylor⟩ ⟨everything was *systematized* to an extraordinary extent. There was a way for doing everything, or rather sixteen, or thirty-six, or some other consecrated number of ways, each distinct and defined and each with a name —Laurence Binyon⟩ METHODIZE differs from SYSTEMATIZE in suggesting more the imposition of orderly procedure than a fixed scheme ⟨modern criticism has developed a number of specialized procedures of its own and *methodized* them, sometimes on the analogy of scientific procedure —S.E. Hyman⟩ **syn** see in addition COMMAND

order arms *n* [fr. the imper. phrase *order, arms*] **:** a position in the manual of arms in which the rifle is held vertically at the right side with the butt on the ground — often used as a command

order bill of lading : a negotiable receipt and contract between carrier and shipper by which legal possession of the shipment may be ordered by endorsement from person to person — compare STRAIGHT BILL OF LADING

orderboard \'==,=\ *n* **:** a manual signal used at railroad stations, a vertical position of the signal indicating that there are no orders, a horizontal position indicating to the crew of an approaching train that train orders must be picked up

order book *n* **1 :** a book in which orders from customers are entered **:** a specially printed book for making multiple copies of orders including one for the customer **2** *often cap O&B* **:** a calendar of future business of a session of the English House of Commons or other legislative body of the British Commonwealth — called also *order paper*

order buyer *n* **:** a buyer who purchases (as produce or livestock) for another's account

ordered *adj* **:** characterized by order: as **a :** marked by system, regularity, or discipline **:** carefully regulated or managed ⟨theirs was an ~ life —C.B.Flood⟩ ⟨my quiet, ~ house —L.P. Smith⟩ **b :** marked by a regular or harmonious arrangement or disposition **:** arranged or disposed so as to form a pattern ⟨the trim and ~ landscape —Oscar Handlin⟩ ⟨society before the industrial revolution . . . was ~ and relatively stable —R.C.Beatty⟩ ⟨the ~ structure of crystals —J.L.Hoard & Seymour Galler⟩ **c** *of a solid solution* **:** characterized by a regular arrangement of solvent and solute atoms

ordered lattice *n* **:** the crystal lattice of a substitutional alloy in which the substituted atoms occur in a regular order of spacing

or·der·er \'ó(r)dərə(r)\ *n* -s [alter. of ME *orderour*, fr. *ordren* to order + *-our* -or — more at ORDER] **:** one that orders

order–in–council \'===' ==\ *n, pl* **orders–in–council :** an order having the full force of law that is issued by the British monarch acting by and with the advice of the Privy Council or by a governor-general acting by and with the advice of the privy council or similar body of a member nation of the British Commonwealth usu. as a means of giving legal effect to a decision of the cabinet in areas not involving parliamentary action ⟨the promulgation of *orders-in-council* both in pursuance of royal prerogative and under authority of statute —F.A.Ogg & Harold Zink⟩

ordering *n* -s [ME, fr. gerund of *ordren* to order] **:** the act, an instance, or the result of ordering: as **a :** MANAGEMENT, REGULATION ⟨determined to have the ~ of things in its hands —John Buchan⟩ **b :** mode or product of ordering **:** ARRANGEMENT ⟨the polity is a certain ~ of the inhabitants of the polis —C.H.McIlwain⟩ ⟨the distinction between the two ~*s* of knowledge —C.W.Berenda⟩ **c :** the process of applying water to tobacco either as steam, moist air, or spray to make it soft and pliable for handling

or·der·less \'ó(r)də(r)ləs\ *adj* **:** lacking order, regularity, or system **:** DISORDERLY

or·der·li·ness \-lēnəs, -lin-\ *n* -ES **:** the quality or state of being orderly

1**or·der·ly** \-lē, -li\ *adv* [ME, fr. *ordre, order* + *-ly* (adv. suffix)] **:** in or according to due order **:** REGULARLY, METHODICALLY, DULY ⟨will find the following lessons ~ arranged —Whitcomb Crichton⟩

2**orderly** \"\ *adj* [1*order* + *-ly* (adj. suffix)] **1 a** (1) **:** arranged, disposed, or organized in some order, pattern, or sequence **:** conforming to a plan **:** well ordered **:** REGULAR ⟨the city plan is ~ —*Amer. Guide Series: Mich.*⟩ ⟨~ rows of shacks —*Amer. Guide Series: Fla.*⟩ (2) **:** not disordered **:** NEAT, TIDY ⟨found the room and its belongings in ~ condition⟩ **b :** governed by law or system **:** not haphazard **:** REGULATED, SYSTEMATIC ⟨gives rise to ~ involuntary motor responses —H.G.Armstrong⟩ ⟨a series of ~ actions at regular hours —Ellen Glasgow⟩ **c :** characterized by methodical ways or procedures **:** systematic in action or thought ⟨an ~ mind⟩ ⟨an ~ person⟩ **d :** reflecting or exhibiting a methodical mind or temper ⟨admired his ~ ways⟩ **2 :** having regard for good order, authority, or rule **:** not unruly **:** PEACEFUL, QUIET ⟨thrifty, ~ New England —Allan Nevins & H.S.Commager⟩ ⟨the parts of provincial Africa which lay near the desert were less ~ —James Bryce⟩ **3 :** relating to or charged with the transmission of military orders

syn ORDERLY, METHODICAL, SYSTEMATIC can apply to what follows closely a set arrangement, design, or pattern. ORDERLY implies an observance of due sequence or proper arrangement as in the disposition of things, in the observance of rules, in keeping a place free from litter, or in the making of a plan or the following of a scheme ⟨an *orderly* setting of a table⟩ ⟨an *orderly* election⟩ ⟨an *orderly* household⟩ ⟨an *orderly* housekeeper⟩ ⟨an *orderly* mind⟩ METHODICAL implies the careful observance of an order of things or actions that is worked out, usu. carefully, in advance or that is logical or inevitable ⟨a *methodical* search for the facts⟩ ⟨a *methodical* course of instruction⟩ ⟨a *methodical* cleaning up of a yard⟩ ⟨a *methodical* housekeeper following a more or less fixed routine⟩ SYSTEMATIC comes close to METHODICAL but puts stress upon the integrity and completeness of the order adopted or followed ⟨a *systematic* course in astronomy⟩ ⟨a cold-blooded and *systematic* destruction of one's enemies⟩ ⟨a *systematic* devotee of physical exercise⟩ ⟨a *systematic* workman⟩

3**orderly** \"\ *n* -ES **1 :** a soldier who attends a superior officer to carry his orders or to give other service; *also* **:** a soldier detailed to look after a room or otherwise assist in a hospital ward **2 :** a hospital attendant who does routine or heavy work (as cleaning, carrying supplies, or moving patients to surgery)

orderly book *n, Brit* **:** a book kept at a military headquarters in which orders and instructions received from higher authority are recorded

orderly officer *n* **1** *Brit* **:** OFFICER OF THE DAY **2** *Brit* **:** ORDERLY

orderly room *n* **:** a room in barracks sometimes occupied by the first sergeant that contains the company, troop, or battery records and is used for company business

orderly sergeant *n, archaic* **:** FIRST SERGEANT

order of a reaction : a number that relates the rate of a chemical reaction with the concentrations of the reacting substances **:** the sum of all the exponents of the terms expressing concentrations of the molecules or atoms determining the rate of the reaction — compare FIRST-ORDER REACTION, SECOND-ORDER REACTION, THIRD-ORDER REACTION, ZERO-ORDER REACTION; MOLECULARITY

order of battle 1 : a particular disposition of troops or ships made in preparation for combat **2 :** a tabular compilation by unit showing organization, commanders, movements, and other details over an extended time

order of business 1 : the precedence or priority under the rules or practice of a deliberative or legislative body in which different proceedings, reports, motions, and general business will be considered or will take place **2 :** a program or sequence of different matters or classes of business arranged in the order in which they are to be taken up by an assembly **3 :** a matter or problem calling for attention or solution **:** TASK ⟨the problem of congestion is the first *order of business* with the commission —S.H.Hofstadter⟩

order of contact : a numerical measure of contact equal to or less than the number of points that coincide

order of magnitude 1 : ORDER 1g(2) ⟨two explosions of the same low *order of magnitude*⟩ **2 :** a range of magnitude extending from some value to ten times that value ⟨two quantities are of the same *order of magnitude* if one is no larger than ten times the other, but if one is one hundred times the other it is larger by two *orders of magnitude*⟩

order of service : the arrangement of the various parts of a religious service in Protestant Christianity

order of the day 1 a : the order of business appointed for an assembly for a given day **:** AGENDA ⟨*order of the day* will include three conferences, rosary in common, confessions —*Springfield* (*Mass.*) *Union*⟩; *esp* **:** the order of business appointed for a legislative body for a given day ⟨the House . . . proceeded to the *order of the day* —Christopher Morley⟩ **b :** a stage of a bill or other matter that the House of Commons or other legislative body of the British Commonwealth has ordered to be taken under consideration on a particular day **2 :** a statement issued by a commander to his troops usu. in commemoration of some achievement **3 :** the salient, characteristic, or dominant custom, theme, feature, or activity of a particular time **:** HALLMARK, KEYNOTE ⟨lavishness is the *order of the day* —Betty Pepis⟩ ⟨minuets, cancan, and ballet were the *order of the day* —*N.Y. Times*⟩ ⟨expansionism was the *order of the* new *day* —R.H.Brown⟩

order of worship : the arrangement of the various parts of a worship service within Protestant Christianity

order paper *n, often cap O&P* **:** ORDER BOOK 2

order pro confesso *n* **:** an order in U.S. equity practice that takes a bill as confessed for want of appearance or want of answer

orders *pl of* ORDER, *pres 3d sing of* ORDER

order up *vt* **1 :** to summon up for active military duty **:** call up ⟨*ordered up* all the militia regiments⟩ **2 :** to direct an opposing dealer to take (the trump) into his hand and discard in euchre — compare ASSIST 3a

or·di·na·ble \'ó(r)d(ə)nəbəl\ *adj* [ML *ordinabilis*, fr. L *ordinare* to put in order, arrange, appoint + *-abilis* -able — more at ORDAIN] **:** capable of being ordered or arranged

1**or·di·nal** \'órd(ə)nəl, 'ó(ə)d-\ *n* -s [ME, fr. ML *ordinale*, fr. LL, neut. of *ordinalis*, adj.] **1** *usu cap* **a :** a book containing directions for Roman Catholic services every day in the year **b :** a collection of forms to be used in the Anglican Communion in the consecration of bishops and the ordination of priests and deacons **2** [LL *ordinalis*, fr. *ordinalis*, adj.] **:** ORDINAL NUMBER **3 :** the divisor in a fraction as spoken or written out (as *hundredth* in *one hundredth* or *hundredths* in *three hundredths*

2**ordinal** \"\ *adj* [LL *ordinalis*, fr. *ordin-*, *ordo* order + *-alis* -al — more at ORDER] **1 :** being of a specified order or rank (as sixth) in a numberable series **2 :** of or relating to an order ⟨family and ~ names . . . of fishes are badly jumbled in the text —*N. Y. Herald Tribune Bk. Rev.*⟩

ordinal number *n* **:** a number designating the place (as first, second, third) occupied by any item in an ordered sequence — distinguished from *cardinal number;* see NUMBER table

or·di·nance \'órd(ə)nən(t)s, 'ó(ə)d-\ *n* -s [ME *ordinaunce*, fr. MF & ML; MF *ordenance*, lit., art of ordering, arranging, fr. ML *ordinantia*, fr. L *ordinant-*, *ordinans* (pres. part. of *ordinare* to put in order, arrange, appoint + *-ia* -y — more at ORDAIN] **1 a :** an authoritative decree or direction **:** ORDER ⟨our swift ~*s* on their way over the whole earth —Walt Whitman⟩ **b :** a public enactment, rule, or law promulgated by governmental authority: as (1) **:** one of a number of laws or regulations issued at various periods of English history without the assent of one of the three powers (Crown, House of Lords, and House of Commons) necessary to an act of Parliament (2) **:** a regulation or decree promulgated in Great Britain by any authority less than the sovereign enacting power (3) **:** any of several acts of the U. S. Congress under the Articles of Confederation (4) **:** a local law or regulation enacted by a city council or other similar body under powers delegated to it by the state **2 a :** the act or an instance of ordering or arranging **:** DIRECTION, DISPENSATION, CONTROL ⟨insistence upon a higher and rational ~ throughout the world —G.G.Coulton⟩ **b :** something ordained or decreed by fate or a deity **:** a decree or disposition of divine or providential origin ⟨an ~ of the Christian God —G.F.Hudson⟩ **c** *obs* **:** ordained or appointed place or condition **3 a :** established rule, policy, or practice ⟨a positive ~ . . . that there should be no sketching until lessons were done —Arnold Bennett⟩ **b :** an established and fully authoritative religious ceremony, rite, or usage that is not considered a sacrament **syn** see LAW

or·di·nand \'órdə,nand\ *n* -s [LL *ordinandus*, gerundive of *ordinare* to ordain — more at ORDAIN] **:** a person about to be ordained

1**or·di·nant** \-d(ə)nənt\ *adj* [L *ordinant-*, *ordinans*, pres. part.] **:** that ordains, decrees, or regulates

2**ordinant** \"\ *n* -s [LL *ordinant-*, *ordinans*, pres. part.] **:** a person who ordains

or·di·nar·i·ate \,ó(r)d(ə)n'erēət, -ē,āt\ *n* -s [1*ordinary* + *-ate*] **1 :** the administrative division of a particular Roman Catholic diocese or archdiocese **2 :** a group of members of an Eastern rite in communion with the Pope who are subject to the personal jurisdiction of an appointed prelate (as a titular bishop) of the same rite — see MILITARY ORDINARIATE

or·di·nar·i·ly \ˌȯ(r)dᵊnˈerəlē, -li *sometimes* -dəˌne- *or* -dˌne-\ *adv* **:** in an ordinary manner: as **a :** in the ordinary course of events **:** USUALLY ⟨~ took notice of such things —Ross Annett⟩ ⟨were ~ sung in the court by the minstrel —R.A. Hall b. 1911⟩ **b :** to the usual extent **:** MODERATELY ⟨could afford, if he was ~ conscientious, to keep an assistant priest —G.G.Coulton⟩ **c :** in a commonplace or inferior way **:** without distinction ⟨two apartments . . . very ~ furnished —Walt Whitman⟩

or·di·nar·i·ness \ˈȯ(r)dᵊnˌerēnəs, -rin- *sometimes* -dəˌne- *or* -dˌne-\ *n* -ES **:** the quality or state of being ordinary: as **a :** routine or commonplace character ⟨the ~ of our sun which has accomplished the creation of life —*Think*⟩ **b :** everyday or typical quality or character ⟨either too pretty or too brutal; it lacks ~ —Virginia Woolf⟩

1**or·di·nary** \-rē, -ri\ *n* -ES [ME *ordinarie*, fr. AF & ML; AF, fr.

ordinary 2d

ML *ordinarius*, fr. L *ordinarius*, adj.] **1 a** (1) *often cap* **:** a prelate exercising actual ecclesiastical jurisdiction over a specified territory ⟨the local ~ of a province is an archbishop⟩ (2) **:** a clergyman appointed formerly in England to give spiritual assistance to condemned criminals and to prepare them for the ordeal of the death penalty **b** (1) *civil & Scots law* **:** a judge having jurisdiction in his own right; *specif* **:** a lord ordinary in Scotland (2) **:** a judge of probate in some states of the U. S. **c** *obs* **:** the persons formerly employed to care for warships when laid up **d** *obs* **:** a courier in regular service; *also* **:** MAIL **e :** the second rank in the sea exploring program of the Boy Scouts of America **2 a** (1) *obs* **:** regular provision or allowance (as of food) (2) *Brit* **:** a meal served to all comers at a fixed price in distinction from one where each dish is separately charged for ⟨lunching . . . on the very excellent ~ —Elizabeth Montizambert⟩ (3) *chiefly Brit* **:** a tavern or eating house where regular meals are served; *also* **:** the dining room in such a house **b** (1) **:** regular, customary, or ordinary condition or course of things **:** such as is ordinarily met with or experienced — usu. used in the phrase *out of the ordinary* ⟨nothing out of the ~ —Glenway Wescott⟩ (2) **:** someone or something of ordinary or routine character ⟨the little *ordinaries* of life⟩ **c** (1) **:** a heraldic charge or bearing (as the bend, chevron, chief, cross, fess, pale, or saltire) of simple form and in constant use — see SUBORDINARY (2) **:** a book containing a collection of coats of arms arranged by design — compare ARMORY **d :** an early bicycle with a very large and a very small wheel as distinguished from a safety bicycle **e** *Brit* **:** common stock or a share of it **3** *often cap* **a :** an ecclesiastical order of service; *specif* **:** the parts of the mass that do not vary from day to day **b :** the part of a missal containing the ordinary of the mass — **by ordinary** *adv* **:** in the ordinary course of events **:** ORDINARILY ⟨*by ordinary* retained the elaborately cordial manner he had brought —Shelby Foote⟩ — **in ordinary 1 :** regularly attending or serving — used in titles ⟨the royal sculptor *in ordinary* —*Springfield (Mass.) Union*⟩ ⟨physician *in ordinary* —*Notes & Queries*⟩ **2** *of a ship* **:** laid up (as for repairs)

2**ordinary** \"\ *adj, sometimes* -ER/-EST [ME *ordinarie*, fr. L *ordinarius*, fr. *ordin-, ordo* order + *-arius* -ary — more at ORDER] **1 a** (1) **:** occurring or encountered in the usual course of events **:** not uncommon or exceptional **:** not remarkable **:** ROUTINE, NORMAL ⟨the ~ experience common to everyone —W.V. Houston⟩ ⟨a spring van, ~ in shape but singular in color —Thomas Hardy⟩ ⟨the ~ traffic had been stopped . . . to allow of the passage of troops and guns —H.G.Wells⟩ (2) *obs* **:** being of frequent occurrence **:** COMMON, ABUNDANT (3) *archaic* **:** commonly experienced or practiced **b :** characterized by common quality, merit, rank, or ability **:** lacking in excellence, superior merit, uncommon appeal, or distinctive characteristics ⟨just ~ people, with no more authority or judgment than they had themselves —Rose Macaulay⟩ ⟨not the ~ rice, but rice which has been specially planted and tended —J.G.Frazer⟩ **c :** being of a poor or mediocre quality **:** SECOND-RATE, INFERIOR ⟨a very ~ wine⟩ **d :** not advanced or honorary ⟨an ~ examination⟩ ⟨an ~ degree⟩ **e :** of or relating to life insurance sold in amounts of $1000 or more with premiums payable annually, semiannually, or quarterly — compare INDUSTRIAL LIFE INSURANCE **2 a :** having or constituting immediate or original jurisdiction as opposed to that which is delegated **:** having jurisdiction of his own right or by virtue of office; *also* **:** belonging to such jurisdiction **b** *Brit* **:** constituting the common-law branch of the Chancery Court

syn see COMMON

ordinary care *or* **ordinary diligence** *or* **ordinary prudence** *n* **:** the care that an average reasonable man exercises to prevent harm to the person or property of others and failure to exercise which when under a duty to do so constitutes actionable negligence on the part of one causing such harm

ordinary differential equation *n* **:** DIFFERENTIAL EQUATION

ordinary lay *n* **:** a lay of a wire rope in which the twist of the strands is the reverse of that of the wires

ordinary life insurance *n* **:** life insurance for which premiums are payable as long as the insured lives

ordinary negligence *n* **:** a failure to exercise or an absence of such care and diligence as a person of ordinary care, precaution, and diligence would exercise under the same or similar circumstances that is one of the three degrees of negligence recognized both at common law and in the civil law in many jurisdictions and in some jurisdictions is the only degree of negligence recognized — compare GROSS NEGLIGENCE, SLIGHT NEGLIGENCE

ordinary of the season : an established Christian service or any part of it appointed for any ordinary Sunday or weekday from the octave of Epiphany to the first Sunday in Lent and from Trinity to Advent

ordinary point *n* **:** any point on a curve that is not a singular point

ordinary ray *n* **:** the part of a ray divided in two by double refraction that follows the ordinary laws of refraction because its speed is the same in all directions through the doubly refracting medium

ordinary's court *n* **:** ORDINARY 1b(2)

ordinary seaman *n* **:** a seaman of some experience but not as skilled as an able-bodied seaman

1**or·di·nate** \ˈȯrd(ᵊ)nət, ˈȯ(r)d-, -dᵊnˌāt, *usu* -d·+V\ *adj* [ME *ordinat*, fr. L *ordinatus*, past part. of *ordinare* to put in order, arrange — more at ORDAIN] **:** ORDERLY, REGULAR ⟨~ markings⟩

2**or·di·nate** \-dᵊnˌāt\ *vt* -ED/-ING/-S [L *ordinatus*, past part. of *ordinare*] *archaic* **:** ORDER, ORDAIN

3**or·di·nate** \-d(ᵊ)nət, -dᵊnˌāt, *usu* -d·+V\ *n* -S [NL (*linea*) *ordinate* (*applicata*) & (*linea*) *ordinatim* (*applicata*), lit., line applied in an orderly manner; NL *ordinate, ordinatim*, adv., fr. L *ordinatus*, past part.] **:** the vertical coordinate of a point in a plane Cartesian coordinate system obtained by measuring parallel to the y-axis — compare ABSCISSA

or·di·na·tion \ˌȯ(r)dᵊnˈāshən\ *n* -S [in sense 1, fr. ME *ordinacioun*, fr. LL *ordination-, ordinatio*, fr. L *ordinatus* (past part. of *ordinare* to ordain) + L *-ion-, -io* -ion; in sense 2, fr. L *ordination-, ordinatio*, fr. *ordinatus* (past part. of *ordinare* to put in order, arrange) + *-ion-, -io* -ion — more at ORDAIN] **1 :** the act or an instance of ordaining or state of being ordained **:** APPOINTMENT; *specif* **:** the admission into the Christian ministry **2 :** DISPOSITION, ARRANGEMENT, ORDERING ⟨a sign . . . of God's ~ of the world —Isaac Rosenfeld⟩

or·di·na·tor \ˈ===ˌād·ə(r)\ *n* -S [in sense 1, fr. LL, fr. *ordinatus* + L *-or*; in sense 2, fr. L, fr. *ordinatus* + *-or*] **1 :** one that ordains into the Christian ministry **2 :** one that orders ⟨an ~ of states and a guide to destinies —H.B.Alexander⟩

or·di·nee \ˌȯ(r)dᵊnˈē\ *n* -S [LL *ordinare* to ordain + E *-ee* — more at ORDAIN] **:** one who has been or is being ordained

ordines *pl of* ORDO

ord·nance \ˈȯrdnən(t)s, ˈȯ(ə)d-\ *n* -S *often attrib* [ME *ordinaunce*, fr. MF *ordenance*, lit., act of ordering, arranging — more at ORDINANCE] **1 a :** military supplies including weapons, ammunition, combat vehicles, and the necessary maintenance tools and equipment **b :** a service of the army charged with the duty of procuring by purchase or manufacture and distributing the necessary ordnance for the army and organized militia and of establishing and maintaining arsenals and depots for their manufacture and safekeeping ⟨*Ordnance* had to start pretty close from scratch —*Time*⟩ ⟨*Ordnance* Corps⟩ **2 :** heavy firearms discharged from mounts **:** CANNON, ARTILLERY

ord·nance·man \ˈ==ˌ=\ *n, pl* **ordnancemen :** a person who is engaged in the testing, assembling, storing, maintenance, or transportation of ordnance equipment

ordnance officer *n* **1 :** an officer of an ordnance corps or department; *also* **:** a staff officer who advises and assists the commander in ordnance matters **2 :** GUNNERY OFFICER

ordnance stores *n pl* **:** ORDNANCE

or·do \ˈȯr(ˌ)dō\ *n, pl* **ordos** \-ōz\ *or* **or·di·nes** \-rdəˌnēz\ *usu cap* [ML, fr. L, order — more at ORDER] **:** an annual publication containing the list of offices and feasts of the Roman Catholic Church for each day of the year

or·don·nance \ˈȯ(r)dənən(t)s\ *n* -S [F, alter. of MF *ordenance*, lit., act of ordering, arrangement — more at ORDINANCE] **1 :** disposition of the parts of a composition with regard to one another and the whole **:** ARRANGEMENT, STRUCTURE ⟨there are design and ~ in it —C.D.Lewis⟩ **2** [F (*compagnie d'*) *ordonnance*, lit., ordinance company; fr. the *Ordonnance Royale* (Royal Ordinance) of 1437 which created the first standing army of France] **:** a company of French men-at-arms **3 a :** DECREE, LAW, ORDER ⟨the ~s of France are so unfavorable to strangers —Tobias Smollett⟩ **b :** an orderly compilation of a body of law on a particular subject (as of prizes and captures at sea)

1**or·do·vi·cian** \ˌȯ(r)dəˈvishən\ *adj, usu cap* [*Ordovices*, ancient people in northern Wales (fr. L) + E *-ian*] **:** of or relating to the period between the Cambrian and the Silurian — called also *Lower Silurian*; see GEOLOGIC TIME table

2**ordovician** \"\ *n* -S *usu cap* **:** the Ordovician period or system of rocks

or·dure \ˈȯrjər, ˈȯ(ə)jə(r\ *n* -S [ME, filth, excrement, fr. MF, fr. *ord* filthy, foul (fr. L *horridus* horrid) + *-ure* — more at HORRID] **1 :** EXCREMENT **2 :** something (as pornographic material) that is morally degrading ⟨these ~s are rapidly depraving the public taste —Thomas Jefferson⟩

1**ore** \ˈō(ə)r, ˈȯ(ə)r, ˈōə, ˈȯ(ə)\ *n* -S *often attrib* [ME *oor, or*, fr. OE *ār* brass, copper, ore; akin to OHG *ēr* bronze, ON *eir* bronze, copper, Goth *aiz* bronze, L *aes* bronze, copper, money, Skt *ayas* metal, iron] **1 a :** a natural or native mineral that can usu. be profitably mined and treated for the extraction of any of its constituents ⟨iron ~⟩ ⟨copper ~⟩ **b :** a source from which valuable matter is extracted **c :** an unrefined condition or material **2 :** PRECIOUS METAL

2**ore** \"\ *n* -S [OE *ōra* — more at ORA] **:** ORA

3**öre** \ˈœrə, ˈərə\ *n, pl* **öre** [Dan & Norw *øre* & Sw *öre*, fr. L *aureus*, a gold coin — more at AUREUS] **1 :** a Danish and Norwegian unit of value equal to 1/100 krone; *also* **:** a coin representing this unit — see MONEY table **2 :** a Swedish unit of value equal to 1/100 krona; *also* **:** a coin representing this unit — see MONEY table

ore- *or* **oreo-** *comb form* [L, fr. Gk, fr. *ore-, oros* mountain, hill — more at RISE] **:** mountain ⟨*Oreophasis*⟩ ⟨*Oreortyx*⟩ ⟨*Oreamnos*⟩ — compare 1ORO-

ore·ad \ˈōrēˌad, -ēəd\ *n* -S *often cap* [L *Oread-, Oreas*, fr. Gk *Oreiad-, Oreias*, fr. *oreios* of a mountain (fr. *oros* mountain) + *-ad-, -as*, fem. suffix denoting descent from or connection with] **:** one of the nymphs of mountains and hills

ore·am·nos \ˌōrēˈamnəs\ *n, cap* [NL, fr. *ore-* + Gk *amnos* lamb — more at YEAN] **:** a genus of ruminant mammals consisting of the mountain goat

ore body *n* **:** a more or less solid mass of ore that may consist of low-grade as well as high-grade ore and that is of different character from the adjoining rock

ore bridge *n* **:** a large gantry crane for loading or unloading ore at stockpiles

orec·tic \ōˈrektik\ *adj* [Gk *orektikos* appetitive, fr. *orektos* stretched out, longed for (fr. *oregein* to stretch, reach for, desire) + *-ikos* -ic — more at RIGHT] **:** of or relating to the desires; *specif* **:** impelling to gratification **:** APPETITIVE ⟨the ~ mechanism . . . does not consist simply of a number of instincts —C.E. Spearman⟩

orec·to·lob·i·dae \ōˌrektəˈläbəˌdē\ *n pl, cap* [NL, fr. *Orectolobus*, type genus + *-idae*] **:** a large family of chiefly Pacific and tropical sharks including the carpet shark, having two dorsal fins, a well-developed fleshy barbel at the anterior margin of the nostril, and small teeth with several cusps, and being mostly small often brilliantly marked bottom dwellers of shallow waters

orec·tol·o·bus \ōˌrekˈtäləbəs, ˌōrˌe-\ *n, cap* [NL, fr. Gk *orektos* stretched out + NL *-lobus*] **:** the type genus of the family Orectolobidae

ore dressing *n* **:** mechanical treatment (as of low-grade ore) to separate a metallic or other valuable mineral from gangue rock and sometimes from other minerals that includes preparation (as by crushing or grinding) and concentration (as by gravity separation, flotation, magnetic separation) — compare METALLURGY

oregano [AmerSp *orégano*, fr. Sp, wild marjoram, fr. L *origanum* — more at ORIGANUM] *var of* ORIGANUM

or·e·gon \ˈȯrēgən, ˈär-, -rəg-, *chiefly by outsiders* -ēˌgän\ *adj, usu cap* [*Oregon*, state in the northwestern U. S., fr. the *Oregon* river, former name for the Columbia river in southwestern Canada and northwestern U. S.] **:** of or from the state of Oregon **:** of the kind or style prevalent in Oregon **:** OREGONIAN

oregon alder *n, usu cap O* **:** RED ALDER

oregon ash *n, usu cap O* **1 :** a timber tree (*Fraxinus oregona*) of western No. America **2 :** the hard light wood of the Oregon ash tree

oregon balsam *n, usu cap O* **1 :** a liquid oleoresin obtained from the Douglas fir **2 :** a mixture of rosin and turpentine **3** *also* **oregon balsam fir :** DOUGLAS FIR

oregon boot *n, usu cap O* **:** a heavy iron shackle attached to the ankle and foot of a prisoner to prevent escape (as while being transported)

oregon box *n, usu cap O* **:** a low evergreen shrub (*Pachistima myrsinites*) of western No. America with tiny reddish brown flowers — called also *goatbrush, mountain lover*

oregon cedar *n, usu cap O* **:** PORT ORFORD CEDAR

oregon char *n, usu cap O* **:** DOLLY VARDEN 2

oregon cliff brake *n, usu cap O* **:** a No. American fern (*Pellaea densa*) with wiry light brown stipes that is cultivated for ornament — called also *pod fern*

oregon crab apple *n, usu cap O* **:** a small tree (*Malus fusca*) of western No. America having white flowers

oregon fir *or* **oregon douglas fir** *n, usu cap O&D* **:** DOUGLAS FIR

oregon grape *also* **oregon holly grape** *n, usu cap O* **:** either of two small evergreen shrubs (*Mahonia aquifolium* or *M. nervosa*) that have stiff pinnate dark green leaves tending to turn bronzy in winter, fascicled racemes of usu. yellow flowers, and globose blue berries, are native to the Pacific coast from northern California to British Columbia, and are cultivated in many temperate areas as shade-tolerant ornamentals — called also *hollygrape, holly-leaved barberry, mountain grape*

oregon graperoot *n, usu cap O* **:** BERBERIS 2

1**or·e·go·nian** \ˌȯrəˈgōnēən, ˌär-, -rēˈg-, -nyən\ *n* -S *cap* [*Oregon* state + E *-ian*] **:** a native or resident of the state of Oregon

2**oregonian** \ˈ==ˈ=(=)=\ *adj, usu cap* **:** of, relating to, or characteristic of Oregon or Oregonians

oregon jargon *n, usu cap O & J* **:** CHINOOK JARGON

oregon jay *n, usu cap O* **:** a crestless jay (*Perisoreus canadensis obscurus*) of northwestern No. America resembling the typical Canada jay but brownish

oregon larch *n, usu cap O* **1 :** WESTERN LARCH **2 :** NOBLE FIR

oregon lily *n, usu cap O* **:** a slender bulbous herb (*Lilium columbianum*) of western No. America with scattered leaves and showy orange-red purple-spotted flowers

oregon maple *n, usu cap O* **:** a large-leaved maple (*Acer macrophyllum*) of the Pacific coast of No. America

oregon myrtle *n, usu cap O* **:** CALIFORNIA LAUREL

oregon oak *or* **oregon white oak** *n, usu cap 1st O* **:** an oak (*Quercus garryana*) of western No. America with light-gray bark and obovate pinnatifid leaves — called also *Garry oak*

oregon pine *n, usu cap O* **:** DOUGLAS FIR

oregon robin *n, usu cap O* **:** VARIED THRUSH

oregon triton *n, usu cap O* **:** a large whelk (*Argobuccinum oregonensis*) of the Pacific coast of No. America with a heavy hairy epidermis covering the shell

oreide *var of* OROIDE

ore·jón \ˌōrəˈhōn\ *n, pl* **orejón** \"\ *or* **ore·jo·nes** \-ō(ˌ)nās\ *usu cap* [Sp, lit., big ear, aug. of *oreja* ear, fr. L *auricula* external ear — more at AURICLE] **1 :** any of various No. American or So. American Indian peoples known to distend the earlobes with metal or wooden disks or ornaments: as **a :** 2COTO **b :** CHANÉ **c :** a Witotoan people of southern Colombia and eastern Ecuador **d :** a Coahuiltec people of Texas **e :** any of several peoples of the northwest coast of the U. S. **2 :** a member of any of the Orejón peoples

orel \ȯrˈyȯl, ōˈrel\ *adj, usu cap* [fr. *Orel*, U.S.S.R.] **:** of or from the city of Orel, U.S.S.R. **:** of the kind or style prevalent in Orel

ore·less \ˈō(ə)rləs, ˈȯ-\ *adj* **:** having no ore

or else *conj* **:** if not — see 1ELSE 2a

oren·da \ōˈrendə\ *n* -S [Wyandot] **:** extraordinary invisible power believed by the Iroquois Indians to pervade in varying degrees all animate and inanimate natural objects as a transmissible spiritual energy capable of being exerted according to the will of its possessor ⟨a successful hunter's ~ overcomes that of his quarry⟩

oreo- — see ORE-

oreo·car·ya \ˌōrē(ˌ)ōˈka(a)rēə\ *n, cap* [NL, fr. *ore-* + *-carya* (fr. Gk *karyon* nut) — more at CAREEN] **:** a genus of perennial herbs (family Boraginaceae) that resemble forget-me-nots, have leafy stems and small white or yellow flowers in one-sided spikes or racemes, and are found in the western U. S. and adjacent Mexico

1**ore·odon** \ˈōrēəˌdän, ōˈr-\ [NL, fr. *ore-* + *-odon*] *syn of* MERYCOIDODON

2**oreodon** \"\ *n* -S [NL *Oreodon*] **:** an ungulate mammal of the genus *Merycoidodon*

1**ore·odont** \-nt\ *adj* [NL *Oreodontidae*] **:** of or relating to the Merycoidodontidae

2**oreodont** \"\ *n* -S **:** an ungulate mammal of the family Merycoidodontidae

ore·odon·ti·dae \ˌōrēōˈdäntəˌdē, ōˌr-\ [NL, fr. *Oreodont-, Oreodon*, type genus + *-idae*] *syn of* MERYCOIDODONTIDAE; see MERYCOIDODON

oreo·doxa \ˌōrēōˈdäksə\ *n, cap* [NL, fr. *ore-* + Gk *doxa* glory, splendor — more at DOXOLOGY] **:** a small genus of tropical So. American palms that is closely related to *Roystonea* and in some classifications includes the royal palm

oreography *var of* OROGRAPHY

oreo·pha·sine \ˌōrēōˈfāˌsīn\ *adj* [NL *Oreophasinae*, subfamily of Cracidae, fr. *Oreophasis*, type genus + *-inae*] **:** of or relating to the genus *Oreophasis*

oreo·pha·sis \ˌ===ˈ=səs\ *n, cap* [NL, fr. *ore-* + Gk *Phasis*, a river (now Rion) in Colchis (now western Georgia, U.S.S.R.), the etymon of Gk *phasianos* pheasant] **:** a genus of curassows including the mountain curassow

ore·or·tyx \ˌōrēˈȯrdˌiks\ *n, cap* [NL, fr. *ore-* + Gk *ortyx* quail; akin to Skt *vartaka, vartika* quail] **:** a genus of birds (family Perdicidae) comprising the mountain quail of the western U. S.

oreo·tra·gus \ˌōrēˈä·trəgəs\ *n, cap* [NL, fr. *ore-* + Gk *tragos* male goat — more at TRAGEDY] **:** a genus of antelopes comprising the klipspringer

oreo·troch·i·lus \ˌōrēōˈträkələs\ *n, cap* [NL, fr. *ore-* + L *trochilus* wren — more at TROCHILUS] **:** a genus of hummingbirds found near the snow line in the So. American Andes

ore pocket *n* **:** a bin for temporary storage of ore in a mine

ores *pl of* ORE

ore shoot *n* **:** a usu. large and more or less vertical rich body of ore

ore te·nus \ˌōrēˈtenəs\ *adv* [L, by mouth] **:** by spoken word **:** ORALLY ⟨pleading done *ore tenus*⟩

-o·rex·ia \ōˈreksēə, ȯ'-\ *n comb form* -S [NL, fr. Gk *orexis* desire, appetite, longing + L *-ia* -y] **:** desire **:** appetite ⟨*cynorexia*⟩ ⟨*parorexia*⟩

orex·is \-səs\ *n* -ES [L, fr. Gk, fr. *oregein* to stretch, reach for, desire + *-sis* — more at RIGHT] **:** the feeling and striving aspect of mind as contrasted with the intellectual **:** DESIRE, APPETITE

orey-eyed \ˌōrēˈīd\ *adj* [*orey* of unknown origin] **:** very angry **:** WILD-EYED ⟨this bad steer . . . was an *orey-eyed* old devil —F.B.Gipson⟩ ⟨sure can make me *orey-eyed* —Helen Rich⟩

orf \ˈȯ(ə)f\ *n* -S [alter. of E dial. *hurf*, prob. of Scand origin; akin to ON *hrūfa* crust on a wound, scab — more at DANDRUFF] *Brit* **:** SORE MOUTH 1

ORF *abbr* **1** owner's risk of fire **2** owner's risk of freezing

orfe \ˈȯ(ə)rf\ *n* -S [G *orf, orfe*, fr. OHG *orvo*, fr. L *orphus*, a sea fish, fr. Gk *orphos, orphōs*; perh. akin to OE *eorp, earp* dark, dusky, OHG *erpf* brown, ON *jarpr* brown, Gk *orphnos* dark] **:** an ide of a golden variety that is often stocked in ornamental pools; *broadly* **:** 2IDE

or·fe·vre·rie \ȯrfevrərē\ *n* -S [F *orfèvrerie*, fr. *orfèvre* goldsmith (fr. OF *orfevre*, fr. *or* gold + *fevre* smith, fr. L *fabr-, faber*) + *-erie* -ery — more at OR, DAFT] **:** goldsmith's or jeweler's work **:** gold or silver plate **:** JEWELRY

orf·gild \ˈȯrfˌgild\ *n* -S [OE *orf* cattle + *gield, geld, gild* tax, tribute; akin to OE *ierfe* inheritance — more at ORPHAN, GELD] **:** a fine imposed for taking away cattle and payable under old English law by the hundred to which the wrongdoer belonged

orfray *or* **orfrey** *var of* ORPHREY

org *abbr* **1** organic **2** organization; organized

1**or·gan** \ˈȯrgən, ˈȯ(ə)g- *sometimes* -gᵊŋ\ *n* -S [ME, partly fr. OE *organa*, fr. L *organum*, fr. Gk *organon*, lit., tool, instrument; partly fr. OF *organe*, fr. L *organum*; akin to Gk *ergon* work — more at WORK] **1 a** *archaic* **:** a musical instrument ⟨the harp . . . the solemn pipe, and dulcimer, all ~s of sweet stop —John Milton⟩; *esp* **:** WIND INSTRUMENT ⟨praise him with stringed instruments and ~s —Ps 150: 4 (AV)⟩ **b :** any of several large musical instruments producing sustained tones and played by means of a keyboard: (1) **:** a wind instrument consisting of sets of pipes sounded by compressed air, controlled by manual and pedal keyboards, and capable of producing a variety of musical timbres and orchestral effects — called also *pipe organ* (2) **:** REED ORGAN (3) **:** an instrument in which the sound and resources of the pipe organ are approximated by means of electronic devices **c :** one of various similar cruder instruments (as the barrel organ) **d :** a division of a pipe organ consisting of a group of stops with their actions and usu. an independent keyboard set on a single wind-chest — see CHOIR ORGAN, ECHO ORGAN, GREAT ORGAN, SOLO ORGAN, SWELL ORGAN **2 a :** a differentiated structure (as a heart, kidney, leaf, or stem) in an animal or plant made up of various cells and tissues and adapted for the performance of some specific function and grouped with other structures sharing a common function into systems — see HOLLOW ORGAN **b :** bodily parts performing a function or cooperating in an activity ⟨the eyes and related structures that make up the visual ~⟩ **c :** PENIS **3 :** an instrumentality exercising some function or accomplishing some end ⟨the political cartoon is one of the greatest ~s of propaganda —A.C.W.Harmsworth⟩; *specif* **:** a governmental instrumentality operating as a part of a larger organization ⟨the cabinet's function as a general ~ of government without special regard to the king's wishes —*Times Lit. Supp.*⟩ **4 :** a publication (as a newspaper or magazine) expressing the view of a single person or a special group or specif. serving a special group ⟨a newspaper that is the official ~ of the government⟩; *broadly* : PERIODICAL ⟨newspaper and magazine clippings should be accompanied by the name of the ~ from which they are taken —*Western Folklore*⟩ **syn** see MEAN

2**organ** \"\ *vt* **organed** \-nd,-ŋd\ **organed** \"\ **organing** \-gəniŋ\ **organs** \-gənz,-gᵊŋz\ : to play on an organ

3**organ** \"\ *n* -s [by alter.] *dial chiefly Eng* : ORIGAN

organ- *or* **organo-** *comb form* [ME, fr. ML, fr. L *organum* — more at 1ORGAN] **1 a** : organ ⟨*organ*elle⟩ ⟨*organo*genesis⟩ ⟨*organ*onymy⟩ **b** : organic substance or life ⟨*organo*genic⟩ **2 a** : organic : organic and ⟨*organo*chemical⟩ ⟨*organo*mineral⟩ **b** : organometallic ⟨*organo*tin⟩ ⟨*organo*arsenic⟩ ⟨*organo*phosphorus⟩

or·ga·nal \'ȯ(r)gənᵊl\ *adj* [*organ*um + *-al*] : of or being an organum ⟨an ~ voice⟩ ⟨the ~ parts⟩

organ beater *n* : a medieval organist

organbird \'==,=\ *n* **1** : a Tasmanian magpie (*Gymnorhina hyperleuca*) whose discordant notes suggest an organ out of tune **2** : a wren (*Leucolepis arada*) of northern So. America

organ cactus *var of* ORGAN-PIPE CACTUS

organ coral *n* : ORGAN-PIPE CORAL

or·gan·dy *also* **or·gan·die** \'ȯ(r)gəndē, -di, *chiefly Brit sometimes* ='gan-\ *n, pl* **organdies** [F *organdi*] : a very fine transparent plain-woven muslin with a temporary or permanent finish for crispness made orig. of cotton and now imitated in other fibers and used esp. for clothing, curtains, and trimmings

or·gan·elle \¦ȯ(r)gə¦nel\ *also* **or·gan·el·la** \,=='nelə\ *n* -s [NL *organella*, fr. *organ-* + *-ella*] : a specialized part of a cell (as a cilium or a cytopharynx) performing functions analogous to those of the organs of many-celled animals — compare ORGANOID 1

or·gan·ette \¦ȯ(r)gə¦net\ *n* -s [1*organ* + *-ette*] **1** : a small portable organ sometimes mechanically played **2** : a large accordion

organ genus *n* : a genus of fossil plants diagnosed on the basis of single organs or restricted groups of connected organs — compare FORM GENUS

organ-grinder \'==,==\ *n* : one that cranks a hand organ; *esp* : an itinerant street musician who grinds a barrel organ

organ gun *n* : a piece of ordnance with several chambers or barrels arranged side by side

1**or·gan·ic** \(')ȯ(r)¦ganik, -nēk\ *adj* [L *organicus*, fr. Gk *organikos*, fr. *organon* tool, instrument, organ + *-ikos* -ic — more at ORGAN] **1** *archaic* : serving as an instrument or means : INSTRUMENTAL **2** [F *organique*, fr. MF, fr. LL *organicus*, fr. Gk *organikos*] **a** : of or relating to an organ or a system of organs; *specif* : relating to or affecting the internal organs of the body ⟨~ changes in emotion⟩ **b** : consisting of or containing organs ⟨the ~ structure of animals and plants⟩ **c** : produced by an organ ⟨~ pleasure⟩; *specif* : having origin in demonstrable somatic pathology ⟨~ psychoses⟩ — compare FUNCTIONAL **d** : affecting the structure of the organism ⟨an ~ disease⟩ — compare FUNCTIONAL **3 a** (1) : of, relating to, or derived from living organisms ⟨~ evolution⟩ ⟨~ matter⟩ : being, composed of, or containing matter of plant or animal origin ⟨~ remains in the Silurian rocks⟩ ⟨a highly ~ soil⟩ (2) : relating to, produced with, or based on the use of organics as fertilizers without employment of chemically formulated fertilizers or pesticides ⟨~ farming⟩ ⟨~ vegetables⟩ **b** : exhibiting characters or qualities peculiar to living organisms ⟨~ growth⟩ ⟨~ nature⟩; *broadly* : forming or belonging to the animate world ⟨the powers of the atom bomb to effect strict ~ and inorganic destruction —W.D.Pardridge⟩ ⟨~ life⟩ **4 a** : being, containing, or relating to carbon compounds esp. in which hydrogen is attached to carbon whether derived from living organisms or not — usu. distinguished from *inorganic* or *mineral* ⟨~ solvents⟩ ⟨~ pigments⟩ **b** : being in the form of such a carbon compound ⟨~ nitrogen in proteins⟩ **5 a** (1) : forming an integral element of a whole : FUNDAMENTAL, INHERENT, VITAL ⟨incidental music rather than ~ parts of the action —Francis Fergusson⟩ (2) : involving or inherent in the basic character or structure (as of a nation or church) : CONSTITUTIONAL, ORGANIZATIONAL ⟨the ~ union of what had been two denominations⟩ (3) : belonging etymologically to the structure of a word ⟨~ *t* in *dental*⟩ ⟨~ *d* in *hound* contrasted with *d* in *sound* [L *sonus*]⟩ (4) : assigned to and constituting a permanent part of a military organization (as a regiment) under its table of organization and equipment **b** (1) : constituting a whole whose parts are mutually dependent or intrinsically related : having systematic coordination : ORGANIZED ⟨an overall perceivable pattern into which the parts can be fitted to make an ~ whole —Irving Stone⟩ (2) : forming a complex entity in which the whole is more than the sum of the individual parts and the parts have a life and character deriving from their participation in the whole : having the character of an organism ⟨form and content . . . wrought into a unique ~ whole outside of which neither element has any relevant meaning —Carlos Lynes⟩ ⟨in such an ~ society the concept of individual liberty was virtually unknown —H.J.Laski⟩ **6 a** : arising and developing in a manner resembling the growth of a living plant or animal ⟨~ form in poetry⟩ ⟨the romantic principle asserts that form is an ~ event, proceeding from the intuitive experience of the artist —Kathleen Raine⟩ ⟨many new coinages in modern Hebrew stem from the normal ~ structure of the language —William Chomsky⟩ : having the character of a natural outgrowth ⟨an ~ connection between the Koran and the Old and New Testaments —Norman Cousins⟩ **b** (1) : having a form suggesting natural growth as opposed to one that is calculated and contrived ⟨~ crystal formations⟩ (2) : having a form growing out of inherent factors (as function, site) rather than convention ⟨a clear ~ architecture . . . whose function is clearly recognizable in the relation of its forms —Walter Gropius⟩ **7** : being or relating to the law by virtue of which a government or organization exists as such : incorporated or involved in the organization of a state, political organism, or other organized association ⟨their nation has written the separation of church and state into its ~ law —Paul Blanshard⟩ ⟨the purpose of the weather bureau as defined in its ~ act is to provide meteorological information —F.W.Reichelderfer⟩ **8** : interpreting something (as human society) as having the characteristics of a living plant or animal : ORGANISMIC ⟨an ~ concept of the novel⟩ ⟨the ~ theory of the state⟩

2**organic** \"\ *n* -s : an organic substance : as **a** : a fertilizer consisting only of matter or products of plant or animal origin **b** : a pesticide whose active component is an organic compound or mixture of organic compounds

or·gan·i·cal \-nəkəl, -nēk-\ *adj* [L *organic*us + E *-al*] *archaic* : ORGANIC

or·gan·i·cal·ly \-k(ə)lē, -li\ *adv* : in an organic manner ⟨~ diseased⟩ ⟨smaller combines consisting of ~ linked plants —*Economist*⟩

organic base *n* : a basic compound containing carbon; *esp* : an organic nitrogen base (as an amine)

organic chemistry *n* : a branch of chemistry that deals chiefly with hydrocarbons and their derivatives — compare INORGANIC CHEMISTRY

or·gan·i·cism \ȯ(r)'ganə,sizəm\ *n* -s [ISV 1*organic* + *-ism*] : a theory interpreting something as organic in character: as **a** : a theory that disease is always associated with a structural lesion of an organ **b** : a theory holding in contrast to vitalism on the one hand and mechanism on the other that life and living processes are the manifestation of an activity possible only in virtue of the state of autonomous organization of the system rather than because of its individual components — compare HOLISM, OBJECTIVE IDEALISM, PHILOSOPHY OF ORGANISM **c** : a conception of society as a superindividual organism constituted of ideas, beliefs, and volitions or as an entity analogous to a biological organism and subject to the same stages of birth, maturity, and death

or·gan·i·cist \-‚səst\ *n* -s [ISV 1*organic* + *-ist*] : an advocate of organicism ⟨the ~ believes that every actual event in the world is a more or less concealed organic process —S.C. Pepper⟩ — **or·gan·i·cis·tic** \(¦)ȯ(r)¦ganə¦sistik\ *adj*

or·ga·nic·i·ty \,ȯ(r)gə'nisəd·ē\ *n* -ES [1*organic* + *-ity*] : the quality or state of being organic

organic mechanism *n* : PHILOSOPHY OF ORGANISM

organic memory *n* : the permanent modification of an organism by stimulation and activity; *also* : MNEME

organic pigment *n* : an insoluble coloring matter consisting essentially of a dye that is itself insoluble or has been converted into an insoluble product ⟨the expression "lakes and toners" has come to be used synonymously with *organic pigments* —E.R.Allen⟩ — distinguished from *mineral pigment;* see DYE table I, 4LAKE 1b, TONER a

organic selection *n* : a process by which acquired individual characters are sometimes considered to protect heritable variations while these are still insufficiently developed to be perpetuated by natural selection

organic sensation *n* : a sensation (as hunger, nausea) arising from internal organs

organic soil *n* : soil composed mostly of plant material

organic synthesis *n* : the synthesis of organic compounds including pharmaceuticals and dyes

organing *pres part of* ORGAN

organise *Brit var of* ORGANIZE

or·ga·nism \'ȯ(r)gə,nizəm\ *n* -s [*organ-* + *-ism*] **1** : organic structure : ORGANIZATION ⟨the man of large and imperious physical ~ —Havelock Ellis⟩ **2** : something felt to resemble a living plant or animal: as **a** (1) : an entity having an existence independent of or more fundamental than its elements and having distinct members or parts whose relations and powers or properties are determined by their function in the whole ⟨the nation is not merely the sum of individual citizens at any given time, but it is a living ~, a mystical body . . . of which the individual is an ephemeral part —Joseph Rossi⟩ (2) : a being in which every part is at once a means and an end to every other **b** : something arising and developing in an organic manner ⟨whether the whole of reality is an ~ or a machine —Weston LaBarre⟩ **3** : an individual constituted to carry on the activities of life by means of parts or organs more or less separate in function but mutually dependent : a living being **syn** see SYSTEM

or·ga·nis·mic \¦ȯ(r)gə¦nizmik\ *also* **or·ga·nis·mal** \-məl\ *adj* **1** : of or belonging or relating to an organism esp. as a functional whole **2** : of or relating to organicism or organic mechanism : HOLISTIC ⟨the ~ theory of the state⟩ — **or·ga·nis·mi·cal·ly** \-mək(ə)lē\ *adv*

organismic psychology *n* : the study of man as a psychosomatic unity

or·gan·ist \'ȯ(r)gənəst\ *n* -s [MF or ML; MF *organiste*, fr. ML *organista*, fr. L *organum* organ + *-ista* -ist — more at ORGAN] : a musician who plays an organ : an organ player

or·ga·nis·tic \¦ȯ(r)gə¦nistik\ *adj* [1*organ* + *-istic*] **1** : suitable for performance on an organ **2** : ORGANISMIC 2

or·ga·nis·trum \,ȯ(r)gə'nistrəm\ *n* -s [ML, fr. L *organum* organ — more at ORGAN] : HURDY-GURDY 1

or·gan·ist·ship \'ȯ(r)gənəs(t),ship\ *n* : the position of organist (as of a church)

or·gan·ite \'ȯ(r)gə,nīt\ *n* -s [ISV *organ-* + *-ite*] : ORGANELLE

or·ga·niz·able \'ȯ(r)gə,nīzəbəl, ,=='===\ *adj* : capable of being organized

or·ga·ni·za·tion \,ȯ(r)g(ə)nə'zāshən, ,ȯ(r)gə,nī'z-\ *n* -s *often attrib* [ME *organizacion*, fr. MF or ML; MF *organisation*, fr. ML *organization-*, *organizatio*, fr. *organizatus* (past part. of *organizare*) + L *-ion-*, *-io* -ion] **1 a** : the act or process of organizing ⟨the ~ of his material into an outline⟩ **b** : the formation of fibrous tissue from a clot or exudate by invasion of connective tissue cells and capillaries from adjoining tissues accompanied by phagocytosis of superfluous material and multiplication of connective tissue cells — compare GRANULATION **c** : the unification and harmonizing of all elements of a work of art : COMPOSITION **2** : something organized: **a** : an organic being or system : ORGANISM **b** : a group of people that has a more or less constant membership, a body of officers, a purpose, and usu. a set of regulations ⟨representative of a local business ~⟩ ⟨tax exemption for religious and charitable ~*s*⟩; *specif* : a military command consisting of two or more units **3 a** : a state or manner of being organized : organic structure : purposive systematic arrangement : CONSTITUTION ⟨a group with a high degree of ~⟩ ⟨genius . . . implies an unusually subtle . . . ~ of the personality —E. R.Bentley⟩; *specif* : the administrative and functional structure of an organization (as a business, political party, military unit) including the established relationships of personnel through lines of authority and responsibility with delegated and assigned duties **b** : a body of administrative officials; *specif* : the usu. professional and full-time body of officials directing the affairs of a political party — **or·ga·ni·za·tion·al** \¦ȯ(r)g(ə)nə¦zāshənᵊl, ¦ȯ(r)gə,nī¦z-, -shnəl\ *adj* — **or·ga·ni·za·tion·al·ly** \-ᵊl|ē, -əl|, |i\ *adv*

organization center *n* : the point (as the chordamesoderm of the dorsal lip of the vertebrate blastopore) in a developing embryo that serves as a focus about which the embryo differentiates

organization man *n* : a man who subordinates individualism to conformity with the standards and requirements of an organization

or·ga·nize \'ȯ(r)gə,nīz\ *vb* -ED/-ING/-S *see -ize in Explan Notes* [ME *organysen*, fr. MF or ML; MF *organiser*, fr. ML *organizare*, fr. L *organum* organ + *-izare* -ize — more at ORGAN] *vt* **1 a** : to cause to develop an organic structure ⟨around it the egg is *organized* as a unitary organism —C.H.Waddington⟩ **b** : to make ready for embryonic differentiation and development : act in the manner of an inductor in relation to **2 a** : to arrange or constitute into a coherent unity in which each part has a special function or relation ⟨~ his knowledge in a coherent system of thought —J.S.Schapiro⟩ ⟨these practical proposals are *organized* by a philosophy of natural law —F.S.Cohen⟩ **b** : to unify into a coordinated functioning whole : put in readiness for coherent or cooperative action ⟨paused to ~ his thoughts⟩ ⟨wake and ~ the hikers for the day's climb⟩ ⟨~ a defense before the invasion⟩ : INTEGRATE ⟨was poorly *organized* and revealed an unevenness in logical procedure which is a common identifying mark of schizophrenia —Miriam G. Siegel⟩ : RALLY ⟨active in *organizing* sentiment . . . against the British government —R.E.Moody⟩ **c** (1) : to set up an administrative and functional structure for : provide with or establish as an organization ⟨~ a congregation and erect a church⟩ ⟨~ a company to manufacture his invention⟩ ⟨~ a territory⟩ (2) : to associate in an organization ⟨*organized* the dairymen into a marketing cooperative⟩ (3) : UNIONIZE ⟨~ the white-collar workers⟩ ⟨~ the factory⟩ ⟨~ the garment industry⟩ **3** : to sing the organum to (a cantus firmus) **4** : to arrange by systematic planning and coordination of individual effort ⟨helped to ~ games and entertainment among the passengers —*Current Biog.*⟩ ⟨~ short courses for teacher-librarians —*Times Lit. Supp.*⟩ ⟨~ a traveling art exhibition⟩ ⟨~ a tour of the campus for new students⟩ ⟨~ the attack⟩ ⟨~ a strike⟩ **5** : to put in a state of order ⟨tried to ~ the torrent of emotions . . . seething inside her —Barnaby Conrad⟩ : arrange in an orderly manner ⟨~ the chairs for the rehearsal⟩ ~ *vi* **1** : to sing the organum **2** : to undergo organization ⟨an *organized* clot in the femoral vein⟩ ⟨sometimes the exudate of pneumonia ~*s* instead of being resolved⟩ **3** : to arrange elements into a whole of interdependent parts ⟨began *organizing* for victory by kicking the commander in chief . . . upstairs to the viceroyalty —O.S.J.Gogarty⟩ **4 a** : to form an organization ⟨prohibiting an armed group from *organizing* on its soil —*Collier's Yr. Bk.*⟩ **b** (1) : to establish or found a labor union ⟨that workers had a right to ~⟩ (2) : to persuade workers to join or form a workers group into a union ⟨spent his early years as a union employee *organizing*⟩ **syn** see FOUND, ORDER

organized *adj* **1** : exhibiting the characters of an organism esp. in being differentiated to perform various vital functions ⟨the amoeba is in fact a highly ~ animal⟩ ⟨production of ~ life in an infusion depends chiefly on airborne spores⟩ **2 a** : having a formal organization to coordinate or carry out joint activities ⟨~ baseball⟩ ⟨~ crime⟩ **b** : having a politically defined area and formal governmental institutions usu. as a result of action by a higher authority ⟨~ county⟩ ⟨~ territory of the U. S.⟩ **3** : affiliated by membership in an organization ⟨~ labor⟩ ⟨~ medicine⟩ ⟨an estimated 8 million ~ bowlers in the U. S. —Victor Kalman⟩ **4** *slang* : INTOXICATED

organized militia *n* : a former body of U. S. militia under the concurrent jurisdiction of both the state and the federal governments and now constituted as a National Guard

or·ga·niz·er \'ȯ(r)gə,nīzə(r)\ *n* -s : one that organizes: as **a** : one who travels in various localities for the purpose of establishing new branches of a lodge or similar organization **b** : a union employee who organizes new locals of a particular labor union **c** : something that acts as an inductor in a developing embryo — compare ORGANIZATION CENTER

or·gan·less \'ȯ(r)gənləs\ *adj* : lacking organs

organ meat *n* : any edible part of a slaughter animal that consists of or forms part of an internal organ (as the liver, kidney, heart, or brain) — distinguished from *meat*

organ neurosis *n* : a somatic conversion in which intrapsychic conflict affects or is thought to affect a bodily organ — compare CONVERSION HYSTERIA

organo- — see ORGAN-

or·gano·chlorosilane \¦ȯ(r)gə(,)nō, ȯ(r)¦ganō+\ *n* [*organ-* + *chlorosilane*] : CHLOROSILANE 2

organ of bo·ja·nus \-bō'yänəs\ *usu cap B* [after Ludwig H. *Bojanus* †1827 Ger. anatomist] : one of a pair of nephridial excretory organs of bivalve mollusks situated on each side of the body just below the pericardium

organ of cor·ti \-'kȯrd·ē, -r,tē\ *usu cap C* [after Alfonso *Corti* — more at ARCH OF CORTI] : a complex epithelial structure in the cochlea that in mammals is the chief if not the only part of the ear by which sound is directly perceived and that rests on the internal surface of the basilar membrane and contains two spiral rows of minute rods of Corti which arch over a spiral tunnel of Corti and support on the inner side a single row of columnar hair cells and on the outer side several rows having their bases surrounded by arborizations derived from the ganglion cells of the spiral ganglion of the cochlear nerve

organ of jacobson *usu cap J* : JACOBSON'S ORGAN

organ of johnston *usu cap J* : JOHNSTON'S ORGAN

organ of tö·mös·va·ry \-'tə(r)məsh,värē, -'tēm-\ *usu cap T* [fr. the name *Tömösvary*] : either of a pair of cephalic sensory organs of unknown function in many myriopods

or·gano·gel \ȯ(r)'ganə,jel\ *n* [ISV *organ-* + *gel*] : a gel formed by the coagulation of an organosol

or·gano·genesis \,ȯ(r)gə(,)nō, ȯ(r),ganə+\ *n* [NL, fr. *organ-* + *genesis*] : the origin and development of organs in plants and animals — called also *morphogenesis* — **or·gano·genetic** \"+\ *adj* — **or·gano·genetically** \"+\ *adv*

or·gano·genic \"+¦jenik\ *adj* [*organ-* + *-genic*] : derived from organic substances

or·ga·nog·e·nist \,ȯ(r)gə'näjənəst\ *n* -s : an expert in organogenesis

or·ga·nog·e·ny \-jənē\ *n* -ES [ISV *organ-* + *-geny*] **1** : ORGANOGENESIS **2** : the study of organogenesis

or·gano·graph·ic \¦ȯ(r)gənō¦grafik, ȯ(r)¦ganə¦-\ *adj* : of or relating to organography

or·ga·nog·ra·phy \,ȯ(r)gə'nägrəfē\ *n* -ES [*organ-* + *-graphy*] : description of the organs of animals or plants esp. of the externally recognizable members of the plant body — compare MORPHOLOGY 1

1**or·gan·oid** \'ȯ(r)gə,nȯid\ *adj* [ISV *organ-* + *-oid;* prob. orig. formed in G] : resembling an organ in structural appearance or qualities — used esp. of abnormal masses (as tumors or galls)

2**organoid** \"\ *n* -s **1** : a morphologically differentiated part of a cell (as a Golgi body or a mitochondrion) : ORGANELLE **2** : any of various minute organized body structures (as a stinging hair or a nematocyst) — compare ORGANELLE

or·gano·lep·tic \¦ȯ(r)gənō¦leptik, ȯ(r)¦ganə¦-\ *adj* [F *organoleptique*, fr. *organ-* + Gk *lēptikos* disposed to take or accept, fr. *lēptos*, verbal of *lambanein* to take, seize + *-ikos* -ic — more at LATCH] **1** : affecting or making an impression upon one or more of the organs of special sense **2 a** : of, relating to, or involving the employment of the sense organs — used esp. of subjective testing (as of flavor, odor, appearance) of food and drug products **b** : relating to or determined by organoleptic examination ⟨~ grade of milk⟩ — **organoleptically** *adv*

or·gano·log·ic \-¦läjik\ *or* **or·gano·log·i·cal** \-jəkəl\ *adj* : of or relating to organology

or·ga·nol·o·gy \,ȯ(r)gə'näləjē\ *n* -ES [ISV *organ-* + *-logy*] : the study of the organs of animals and plants; *esp* : SPLANCHNOLOGY

or·gano·mercurial \¦ȯ(r)gə(,)nō, ȯ(r)¦ganō+\ *n* [*organ-* + *mercurial*] : an organic compound or a pharmaceutical preparation containing mercury

or·gano·metallic \"+\ *adj* [ISV *organ-* + *metallic*] : of, relating to, or constituting an organic compound of a metal or sometimes of a metalloid or a nonmetal (as phosphorus) : METALLO-ORGANIC; *esp* : of, relating to, or being a compound in which the metal is attached directly to carbon

or·ga·non \'ȯ(r)gə,nän\ *n* -s [Gk, lit., tool, instrument — more at ORGAN] : an instrument for acquiring knowledge; *specif* : a body of methodological doctrine comprising principles for scientific or philosophic procedure or investigation

or·gano·phil·ic \¦ȯ(r)gənō¦filik, ȯ(r)¦ganə¦-\ *also* **or·gano·phile** \'===,fīl, ='==-\ *adj* [*organ-* + *-philic* or *-phile*] : of, relating to, or having a strong affinity for organic compounds — used esp. of colloids that swell and form solvates in organic liquids commonly used as solvents; compare HYDROPHILIC

or·ganophy·ly \,ȯ(r)gə'näfəlē; 'ȯ(r)gənō,fīlē, ȯ(r)'ganə,-\ *n* -ES [*organ-* + *phyl-* + *-y*] : phylogeny of organs

or·ga·no pie·no \,ȯ(r)gə(,)nōpē'ā(,)nō, -pē'e(-\ *adv* [It] : with full organ — used as a direction in music

or·gano·plas·tic \¦ȯ(r)gə(,)nō¦plastik, ȯ(r)¦ganə¦-\ *adj* [ISV *organ-* + *-plastic;* prob. orig. formed as F *organoplastique*] *biol* : producing organs

or·ga·nos·co·py \,ȯ(r)gə'näskəpē\ *n* -ES [ISV *organ-* + *-scopy*] : examination of the bodily organs

or·gano·silicon \¦ȯ(r)gə(,)nō, ȯ(r)¦ganō+\ *adj* [*organ-* + *silicon*] : of, relating to, or constituting an organic compound of silicon esp. when the silicon is attached directly to carbon (as in silicones)

or·gano·sol \ȯ(r)'ganə,säl, -sȯl\ *n* [*organ-* + *sol*] : a sol in which an organic liquid forms the dispersion medium; *esp* : a dispersion of a powdered thermoplastic resin (as a vinyl resin) in a liquid mixture containing a volatile thinner as well as a plasticizer that is consequently less viscous than a plastisol and is used similarly

or·gano·therapeutic \¦ȯ(r)gə(,)nō, ȯ(r)¦ganə+\ *adj* [*organ-* + *therapeutic*] : of, relating to, or used in organotherapy

or·gano·therapy \"+\ *n* [ISV *organ-* + *therapy*] : a treatment of disease by the administration of animal organs or of their extracts

or·gano·trophic \"+¦träfik, -rōf-\ *adj* [*organ-* + *-trophic*] : relating to the formation and nutrition of living organs

or·gano·trop·ic \"+¦träpik\ *adj* [*organ-* + *-tropic*] : attracted to, localizing in, or entering the body by way of the visceral and abdominal organs or occas. the somatic tissue ⟨an ~ disease⟩ ⟨~ viruses⟩ — compare NEUROTROPIC — **or·gano·trop·i·cal·ly** \-pək(ə)lē\ *adv* — **or·ga·not·ro·pism** \,ȯ(r)gə'nä·trə,pizəm\ *n* -s — **or·ga·not·ro·py** \-‚pē\ *n* -s

organ-pipe cactus *or* **organ cactus** *n* : any of several tall upright cacti of the southwestern U. S. and adjacent Mexico: as **a** : SAGUARO **b** : a cactus (*Lemaireocereus marginatus* or *Pachycereus marginatus*) branching near the base to form several ridged upright stems and bearing 2-inch flowers that are red without and greenish white within

organ-pipe coral *n* : an alcyonarian coral of the genus *Tubipora* having a usu. red or purple skeleton consisting of a mass of parallel cylindrical tubes united at intervals by horizontal plates and being found in tropical parts of the Indian ocean and the Pacific ocean

organ point *n* : PEDAL POINT

organ rest *n* : CLARION 5

organs *pl of* ORGAN, *pres 3d sing of* ORGAN

or·ga·num \'ȯ(r)gənəm, ÷='gan-, ÷='gän-\ *n* -s [ML, fr. L, organ — more at ORGAN] **1** : ORGANON **2 a** : a polyphonic voice part accompanying the cantus firmus note against note in parallel motion, usu. at a fourth, fifth, or octave above or below **b** : part writing or singing of this nature in two, three, or four parts — called also *diaphony*

or·ga·ny \'ȯ(r)gənē\ *n* -ES [modif. of L *origanum* — more at ORIGANUM] : ORIGAN

or·gan·za \ȯ(r)'ganzə\ *n* -s *often attrib* [prob. alter of *Lorganza*, a trademark] : a sheer dress fabric in plain weave usu. made of silk, rayon, or nylon and with more body and stiffness than organdy

or·gan·zine \'ȯ(r)gən,zēn\ *n* -s *often attrib* [F or It; F *or-*

gansin, fr. It *organzino*, prob. fr. *Urgench*, town in Soviet Central Asia where it was first manufactured + It *-ino* -ine] **:** a raw silk yarn formed from two or more twisted strands doubled and twisted in the reverse direction when plied that is used for warp threads in fine fabrics — compare ¹TRAM

or·gasm \ˈȯ(r),gazəm\ *n* -s [NL *orgasmus*, fr. Gk *orgasmos*, fr. *organ* to grow ripe, swell, be lustful; akin to Gk *orgē* impulse, anger, OIr *ferc, ferg* anger, Skt *ūrj, ūrjā* nourishment, power, strength] **1 a :** intense or paroxysmal emotional excitement **b :** an instance or outburst of such excitement **2 a** *obs* **:** a condition of turgescence and physiologic excitement of a body part or organ **b** (1) **:** the climax of sexual excitement typically occurring toward the end of coitus; *specif* **:** the sudden release of tensions developed during coitus usu. accompanied in the male by ejaculation (2) **:** an instance of the occurrence of such a climax

or·gas·mic \(ˈ)ȯ(r)¦gazmik\ *adj* **1 :** like or suggestive of an orgasm **2 :** tending to produce an orgasm

or·gas·tic \-astik\ *adj* [fr. *orgasm*, after such pairs as E *sarcasm: sarcastic*] **:** of, relating to, or being an orgasm

or·geat \ˈȯr,zhä\ *n* -s [F, fr. MF, fr. *orge* barley, fr. L *hordeum* — more at HORDEUM] **1 :** a nonalcoholic drink prepared from the sweetened juice of almonds and other flavorings (as orange blossom essence, rose water) and usu. served cold **2 :** a sweet almond-flavored nonalcoholic syrup used as a cocktail ingredient or food flavoring — called also *sirop d'orgeat*

or·gia \ˈȯ(r)jēə, -)gēə\ *n, pl* **orgia** *also* **orgias** [L, pl. — more at ORGY] **:** ORGY 1, 2

or·gi·ast \ˈȯ(r)jē,ast\ *n* -s [Gk *orgiastēs*, fr. *orgiazein* to celebrate orgies, fr. *orgia* orgies — more at ORGY] **:** one who celebrates orgies

or·gi·as·tic \¦ȯ(r)jē¦astik, -a(a)s,- -tēk\ *also* **or·gi·as·ti·cal** \-təkəl, -tēk-\ *adj* [Gk *orgiastikos*, fr. (assumed) *orgiastos* (verbal of *orgiazein*) + *-ikos*, -ic] **1 :** tending to produce wild emotion ⟨~ music⟩ **2 :** of or having the character or quality of an orgy — **or·gi·as·ti·cal·ly** \-tək(ə)lē, -tēk-, -li\ *adv*

orgn *abbr* organization

or·gone \ˈȯr,gōn\ *n* -s [prob. fr. *orgasm* + *-one* (as in *hormone*)] **:** a vital energy held to pervade nature and to be accumulable for use by the human body by sitting in a specially designed box

orgue \ˈȯ(ə)rg\ *n* -s [F, lit., organ, fr. L *organum* — more at ORGAN] **:** one of a number of long thick timbers pointed and shod with iron and formerly suspended over or in the vaulted passage behind a gateway to be let down in case of attack

or·gui·nette \¦ȯ(r)gə¦net\ *n* -s [irreg. (influence of F *orgue*) fr. ¹*organ* + *-ette*] **:** a small portable reed organ mechanically played by turning a crank

or·gu·lous \ˈȯ(r)g(y)ələs\ *also* **or·gil·lous** \-gəl-\ *adj* [ME *orgeilus, orgulous*, fr. OF *orguilleus, orguilleus*, fr. *orgueil, orguil* pride (of Gmc origin; akin to OHG *urguol* remarkable, distinguished) + *-eus* -ous] **1 :** PROUD, HAUGHTY ⟨such ~ vaunting is best cured by bloodletting —E.G.Bulwer-Lytton⟩ **2 :** SHOWY, SPLENDID ⟨the organ began — an ~ roll — and the academic procession passed slowly down the aisle —J.P. Bishop⟩ — **or·gu·lous·ly** *adv*

or·gy *also* **or·gie** \ˈȯrjē, ˈȯ(ə)j-, -ji\ *n, pl* **orgies** [MF *orgie*, fr. L *orgia*, pl., fr. Gk *orgia*; akin to Gk *ergon* work — more at WORK] **1 :** secret ceremonial rites held in honor of any of various deities (as of ancient Greece) and characterized by ecstatic or frenzied singing and dancing — usu. used in pl. **2 :** a ritual observance or ceremony **3 :** drunken revelry **:** CAROUSAL **4 a :** a manifestation of excessive indulgence in some predilection ⟨an ~ of speechmaking⟩ ⟨indulge in an ~ of destruction⟩ **b :** a riotous display ⟨an ~ of pink stucco⟩

or·ham·wood \ˈȯrəm,=\ *n* [*orham* prob. modif. of F *orme* elm (fr. L *ulmus*) + E *wood* — more at ELM] **:** AMERICAN ELM

ori- *comb form* [MF, fr. LL, fr. L *or-, os* mouth — more at ORAL] **1 :** mouth ⟨*orifice*⟩ **2 :** mouth and ⟨*orifacial*⟩

-oria *pl of* -ORIUM

-o·ri·al \¦ōrēəl,¦ȯr-\ *adj suffix* [ME *-oriale*, fr. L *-orius* -ory + ME *-ale* -al] **:** of, belonging to, or connected with ⟨gress*orial*⟩ ⟨insess*orial*⟩

¹**orib·a·tid** \ōˈribəd·əd, ¦ōrə¦bad-\ *or* **orib·a·toid** \ōˈribə,tȯid, ¦ōrə¦bad-,ȯid\ *adj* [*oribatid* fr. NL *Oribatidae*; *oribatoid* fr. NL *Oribatoidea*] **:** of or relating to the Oribatoidea

²**oribatid** \"\ *n* -s [NL *Oribatidae*] **:** a mite of the superfamily Oribatoidea

ori·bat·i·dae \,ōrəˈbad·ə,dē\ *n pl, cap* [NL, fr. *Oribata*, type genus + *-idae*] *in some classifications* **:** a family of mites coextensive with the superfamily Oribatoidea

ori·ba·toi·dea \,ōrəbəˈtȯidēə\ *n pl, cap* [NL, fr. *Oribata* (perh. fr. Gk *oreibatēs* mountain-ranging, fr. *oros* mountain + *-batēs*, fr. *bainein* to go) + *-oidea* — more at ORIENT, COME] **:** a superfamily of small oval eyeless nonparasitic mites having a heavily sclerotized integument with a leathery appearance

or·i·bi \ˈȯrəbē\ *also* **ou·re·bi** \ˈu̇rə-\ *n* -s [Afrik *oribi*, prob. fr. Hottentot (Nama dial.) *arab*] **:** any of several small antelopes (genus *Ourebia*) of southern and eastern Africa that are tawny yellow above and white below and have straight annulated horns about five inches long

or·i·chalc *or* **or·i·chalch** \ˈȯrə,kalk\ *n* -s [L *orichalcum*, fr. Gk *oreichalkos*, lit., mountain copper, fr. *oros* mountain + *chalkos* copper — more at ORIENT, CHALC-] **1 :** a yellow metallic substance considered precious by the ancient Greeks **2 :** brass rich in zinc

or·i·chal·cum \,ȯrəˈkalkəm\ *n* -s [L] **:** ORICHALC

ori·el \ˈōrēəl, ˈȯr-\ *n* -s [ME, porch, gallery, oriel, fr. MF *oriol* porch, gallery, prob. fr. ML *auleolum* niche, small chapel, dim. of *aula* court, hall, fr. L — more at AULA] **:** a large bay window of semihexagonal or semisquare plan projecting from the face of a wall and supported by a corbel or bracket

ori·en·cy \ˈōrēənsē, ˈȯr-\ *n* -ES [²*orient* + *-cy*] **:** the quality or state of being orient **:** BRILLIANCY

¹**ori·ent** \ˈōrēənt, ˈȯr-, -ē,ent\ *n* -s [ME, fr. MF, fr. L *orient-, oriens*, fr. pres. part. of *oriri* to rise, come forth — more at RISE] **1** *archaic* **:** the part of the firmament or of the world where the sun rises **:** EAST 1 — compare OCCIDENT **2** *usu cap* **:** EAST 2 ⟨sailed for the *Orient*⟩ **3** *archaic* **:** DAWN, SUNRISE **4 a :** a pearl of great luster **b :** the luster or sheen of a pearl **5 :** a moderate to strong blue that is redder than average Prussian blue

oriel

²**orient** \"\ *adj* [ME, fr. MF, *orient*, n.] **1** *archaic* **:** ORIENTAL 1 **2 a :** LUSTROUS, SPARKLING ⟨~ gems⟩ **b** *archaic* **:** GLOWING, RADIANT ⟨with ~ colors waving —John Milton⟩ **3** *archaic* **:** RISING ⟨the ~ moon —P.B.Shelley⟩

³**ori·ent** \-ē,ent *sometimes when no syllable-increasing suffix follows* -ēənt\ *vt* -ED/-ING/-S [F *orienter*, fr. MF, fr. *orient*, n.] **1 a :** to cause to face or point toward the east; *specif* **:** to build (as a church or temple) with the longitudinal axis pointing eastward and the chief altar at the eastern end **b :** to define the position of in relation to the east **c :** to set or arrange in any determinate position in relation to the points of the compass **d :** to ascertain the bearings of ⟨determined to get some distance up the ridge above the hut, to ~ myself with the country —Elyne Mitchell⟩ **2 :** to set right by adjusting to facts or principles **:** put into correct position or relation **:** acquaint with the existing situation ⟨will help freshmen to ~ themselves to college and to life —*advt*⟩ **3 :** to direct toward **:** place in relation to ⟨~ youth to the responsibilities of military service —*Amer. Child*⟩ **4 a :** to direct to a given position in a chemical compound esp. about a nucleus ⟨the ~*ing* effect of the nitro group⟩ **b :** to ascertain the relative positions of atoms or groups in (a compound) **c :** to cause the axes of the molecules of (as a fiber or material) to assume the same direction ⟨~ a fiber by stretching⟩ ⟨highly ~*ed* cellulose⟩ **5 :** to place (a crystal) so that its crystallographic axes lie in conventionally fixed directions **6 :** to rotate (a map attached to a plane table) until the line of direction between any two of its points is parallel to the corresponding direction in nature

¹**ori·en·tal** \,ōrē¦entᵊl, ¦ȯr-\ *adj* [ME, fr. MF, fr. L *orientalis* of or belonging to the East, fr. *orient-, oriens*, n., orient + *-alis* -al] **1** *often cap* **:** of, relating to, or situated in the Orient — compare OCCIDENTAL **2 a :** of superior grade, luster, or value — used of pearls and other precious stones; compare OCCIDENTAL 3 **b :** GLOWING **c** *sometimes cap* **:** being corundum or sapphire but simulating another gem in color ⟨~ amethyst⟩ ⟨~ aquamarine⟩ ⟨~ emerald⟩ **3** *often cap* **:** of, relating to, or having the characteristics of Orientals ⟨maintain . . . an ~ politeness and a set smile which nothing can dispel or penetrate —Joseph Chiari⟩ **4** *usu cap* **:** of, relating to, or constituting the biogeographic realm or region that includes Asia south and southeast of the Himalayas and the Malay archipelago west of Wallace's line — **ori·en·tal·ly** \-ᵊlē,-ᵊli\ *adv*

²**oriental** \"\ *n* -s *usu cap* **1 orientals** *pl, obs* **:** oriental languages **2 :** a member of one of the indigenous peoples of the Orient (as a Chinese, Indian, or Japanese)

³**ori·en·tal** \,ōre,en·ˈtäl\ *n, pl* **ori·en·ta·les** \-ä,lās\ *usu cap* [AmerSp, fr. Sp, adj., easterner, fr. L *orientalis*] **:** URUGUAYAN

oriental arborvitae *n, usu cap O* **:** an Asiatic shrub or small tree (*Thuja orientalis*) having branchlets in vertical planes — compare AMERICAN ARBORVITAE

oriental beetle *n, usu cap O* **:** a small beetle (*Anomala orientalis*) of the family Scarabaeidae now established in the U. S. and having a larva that feeds on the roots of grasses and sugar cane

oriental bezoar *n, usu cap O* **:** a bezoar composed chiefly of resinous organic matter arranged in concentric layers about a hard foreign nucleus and found in the bezoar goat or the gazelle

oriental bittersweet *n* **:** a vigorous European climber (*Celastrus orbiculatus*) naturalized esp. in eastern No. America and having suborbicular to broadly obovate leaves with crenate teeth

oriental blue *n* **:** a strong blue that is redder and darker than Sèvres and redder and duller than cerulean blue (sense 1b) — compare ORIENT BLUE

oriental bole *n* **:** ²BOLE 3

oriental cockroach *also* **oriental roach** *n, sometimes cap O* **:** a dark or blackish brown medium-sized cockroach (*Blatta orientalis*) prob. originating in Asia but now nearly cosmopolitan in warm and temperate areas esp. about dwellings — called also *Asiatic cockroach, blackbeetle*

oriental export porcelain *n, usu cap O* **:** LOWESTOFT WARE 2

oriental fruit fly *n* **:** a trypetid fly (*Dacus dorsalis*) that attacks many fruits, vegetables, and other plants in Hawaii, Formosa, the Philippines, and the Malay archipelago

oriental green *n* **:** a moderate to strong green

ori·en·ta·lia \,ōrēən·ˈtālyə, ,ȯr-, -ē,en-, -lēə\ *n pl, usu cap* [NL, fr. L, neut. pl. of *orientalis* oriental — more at ORIENTAL] **:** materials (as literary, artistic, archaeological products and remains) relating to the Orient

ori·en·tal·ism \-ˈentᵊl,izəm\ *n* -s *often cap* **1 :** a trait, custom, or habit of expression characteristic of oriental peoples **2 :** learning in oriental subjects **3 a :** an oriental turn of thought adopted by a western thinker **b :** a characteristic of oriental art or culture appearing in western practice

ori·en·tal·ist \-ᵊləst\ *n* -s *often cap* [*oriental*ism + *-ist*] **:** a specialist in oriental subjects ⟨a very learned ~ —*Modern Language Notes*⟩

ori·en·tal·i·ty \-ən·ˈtaləd·ē, -,en-\ *n* -ES **:** the quality or state of being oriental

ori·en·tal·iza·tion \-,entᵊlᵊˈzāshən, -ᵊl,īˈz-\ *n* -s *often cap* **:** the act or process of orientalizing or becoming orientalized

ori·en·tal·ize \-ˈentᵊl,īz\ *vb* -ED/-ING/-S *often cap* [¹*oriental* + *-ize*] *vt* **:** to make oriental **:** give oriental qualities or characteristics to ⟨left the West far more *Orientalized* than the East was Hellenized —Elmer Davis⟩ ~ *vi* **1 :** to become oriental **:** adopt oriental traits or attitudes **2 :** to pursue oriental studies

oriental moth *n, usu cap O* **:** an Asiatic moth (*Cnidocampa flavescens*) of the family Eucleidae now established in eastern No. America and having a larva that feeds on fruit and some shade trees

oriental mustard *n* **:** INDIAN MUSTARD

oriental peach moth *or* **oriental fruit moth** *n, sometimes cap O* **:** a small moth (*Grapholitha molesta*) prob. native to Japan but now of nearly cosmopolitan distribution and having a larva that is injurious to the twigs and fruit of orchard trees and esp. to the peach

oriental pearl *n* **1 :** a true or natural marine pearl **2 :** SLATE GRAY

oriental plane *n, usu cap O* **:** a Eurasian shade tree (*Platanus orientalis*) with broad 5- to 7-lobed leaves and globose bristly fruiting heads produced in clusters of 3 to 7

oriental poppy *n, usu cap O* **:** an Asiatic perennial poppy (*Papaver orientale*) commonly cultivated and having stiff coarse heavily haired leaves and bright scarlet, pink, orange, or salmon-colored flowers

oriental rat flea *n* **:** a flea (*Xenopsylla cheopis*) that is widely distributed on rodents and is a vector of plague

oriental red *n* **:** GOYA

oriental rice borer *n* **:** a crambid moth (*Chilo simplex*) with a larva that is destructive to rice in southern and eastern Asia

oriental roller *n, usu cap O* **:** a tumbler pigeon originating in Asia Minor and having a longer head and tail than ordinary tumblers

oriental rug *or* **oriental carpet** *n, usu cap O* **:** a handwoven or hand-knotted one-piece rug or carpet made in the Orient esp. in Asia and usu. having a pile produced by knotting one or several tufts of colored woolen or silk yarn around one or usu. two warps of cotton or wool with a woof shot being passed over each row

oriental sore *n, sometimes cap O* **:** leishmaniasis of the skin caused by a protozoan (*Leishmania tropica*), marked by persistent granulomatous and ulcerating lesions, and distributed widely in the Orient and in tropical regions

oriental spruce *n* **:** an evergreen tree (*Picea orientalis*) of the Caucasus and Asia Minor that is used as an ornamental and has pendulous branchlets with brown pubescence

oriental topaz *n* **:** a yellow corundum used as a gem

orientalwood \,==ˈ==,=\ *or* **oriental walnut** *n, often cap O* **:** AUSTRALIAN WALNUT

ori·en·tate \ˈōrēən·,tāt, ˈȯr-, -ē,en-; ,==ˈen-,tāt; *usu* -ād·+V\ *vb* -ED/-ING/-S [F *orienter* (fr. MF) + E *-ate* — more at ORIENT] *vt* **:** ORIENT ⟨when they come to London, colonials ~ themselves by Piccadilly Circus —Ngaio Marsh⟩ ~ *vi* **:** to face or turn to the east

ori·en·ta·tion \,==ən·ˈtāshən *also* -,en-\ *n* -s **1 a :** the directing or placing of something so as to face the east; *esp* **:** the building of a church or temple on an east-west axis with the chancel and main altar to the east **b :** the placing of a building in any determined relation to the points of the compass **2 a :** the act of determining one's bearings or settling one's sense of direction ⟨witnessed the bee's momentary pause for ~ before it headed back to the hive⟩ **b :** the settling of a sense of direction or relationship in moral or social concerns or in thought or art ⟨reflection conducive to the individual's intellectual and spiritual ~ —*College English*⟩ ⟨America has quite a different ~ toward new music —Ernst Krenek⟩ **3 :** choice or adjustment of associations, connections, or dispositions ⟨development toward a money ~ —W.E.Moore⟩ ⟨nations widely different in their political ~ —J.G.Colton⟩ **4 :** introduction to an unfamiliar situation **:** guidance in experience or activity of a new kind ⟨the ~ program set up for the benefit of new employes —*Dun's Rev.*⟩ **5 :** the change of position exhibited by some protoplasmic bodies within the cell in relation to external influences (as light or heat) or in relation to one another **6 a :** the relative positions of atoms or groups in a chemical compound esp. about a nucleus **b :** the determination of such positions — compare ³ORIENT 4 **7** *psychiatry* **:** awareness of the existing situation with reference to time, place, and identity of persons — **ori·en·ta·tion·al** \¦==(,)=¦tāshənᵊl, -shnəl\ *adj*

ori·en·ta·tor \-ād·ə(r), -ātə-\ *n* -s **:** an apparatus in which a man seated in a partly enclosed box or cage can be subjected to the motions and stresses experienced by an airplane pilot in flight

orient blue *n* **1 :** a grayish blue that is redder and paler than electric, greener than copenhagen, and redder, lighter, and stronger than Gobelin — compare ORIENTAL BLUE **2 :** ORIENT 5

oriented *adj* [fr. past part. of ³*orient*] **1 :** DIRECTED, RELATED ⟨this book, value-*oriented* throughout, associates itself with these more recent tendencies to seek a common human ethics which will be valid for all mankind —Cornelius Krusé⟩ **2 :** having psychological orientation ⟨on the fourth day she was alert and ~ —Milton Rosenbaum⟩

ori·ent·er *or* **ori·en·tor** \ˈ==,entə(r)\ *n* -s **:** one who assists a newcomer in adjusting to a social situation or to the local routine

orienting *pres part of* ORIENT

ori·en·tite \,==ˈen·,tīt; ˈ==ən·,tīt, -,en-\ *n* -s [*Oriente*, province in eastern Cuba, its locality, + E *-ite*] **:** a mineral $Ca_4Mn_4Si_5O_{20}.4H_2O$ consisting of a hydrous calcium manganese silicate occurring in small brown orthorhombic crystals (hardness 4.5-5, sp. gr. 3)

oriently *adv, obs* **:** in an orient manner **:** CLEARLY, LUSTROUSLY

orientness *n* -ES *obs* **:** the quality or state of being orient **:** BRILLIANCY

orient pink *n* **:** a moderate yellowish pink that is yellower and paler than coral pink and yellower and less strong than peach pink

orient red *n* **:** GOYA

orients *pl of* ORIENT, *pres 3d sing of* ORIENT

orient yellow *n* **:** CADMIUM YELLOW 2

-ories *pl of* -ORY

or·i·fice \ˈȯrəfəs, ˈär-\ *n* -s [MF, fr. LL *orificium*, fr. L *or-, os* mouth + *-ficium* (fr. *-ficus* -fic) — more at ORAL] **:** the mouth or opening of something **:** APERTURE, HOLE, VENT ⟨was obviously the ~ of entrance, because its edges were torn and lacerated —Basil Thomson⟩ — see CLAM illustration

orifice box *n* **:** a stilling basin under the inlet to a reservoir

orifice plate *n* **:** a disk containing a calibrated circular hole bolted between two abutting pipe flanges to regulate flow

or·i·fi·cial \¦==¦fishəl\ *adj* **:** of or relating to an orifice

or·i·flamme \ˈȯrə,flam, ˈär-, -laa(ə)m\ *n* -s [ME *oriflamble*, fr. MF *oriflambe, orieflambe*, fr. OF, fr. ML *aurea flamma*, lit., golden flame, fr. L *aurea*, fem. of *aureus* golden (fr. *aurum* gold) + *flamma* flame — more at ORIOLE, FLAME] **:** a banner inspiring lively devotion or courage **:** a bright or glorious ensign or symbol ⟨that gallant and chivalrous spirit that has streamed like an ~ through the storms of centuries —J.L.Lowes⟩

orig *abbr* origin; original; originally

ori·ga·mi \,ȯrəˈgämē\ *n* -s [Jap] **1 :** the art or process of Japanese paper folding **2 :** something (as a representation of a bird, insect, flower) made by origami

or·i·gan \-rəgən\ *also* **or·i·gane** \-,gan, -,gān\ *n* -s [ME *origane*, fr. MF *origan, origane* wild marjoram, fr. L *origanum*] **:** any of various aromatic mints (as wild marjoram)

¹**orig·a·num** \əˈrigənəm, ōˈ-, ȯˈ-\ *or* **oreg·a·no** \əˈregə,nō, ȯˈ-\ *n* -s [*origanum*, fr. ME, fr. L, wild marjoram, fr. Gk *origanon*; *oregano* fr. Sp *orégano*, fr. L *origanum*] **:** any of various fragrant aromatic plants of the families Labiatae and Verbenaceae that are used as seasonings in cookery; *usu* **:** WILD MARJORAM

²**origanum** \"\ *n, cap* [NL, fr. L, wild marjoram] **:** a genus of Eurasian aromatic mints having small erect spikes of flowers arranged in panicles or corymbs and the calyx almost equally 5-toothed — see CRETAN DITTANY, WILD MARJORAM; compare MAJORANA

origanum oil *n* **1 :** an essential oil obtained from various herbs of the genus *Origanum* formerly used in medicine and perfumery **2 :** THYME OIL

¹**or·i·geni·an** \¦ȯrə¦jēnēən, ¦är-, -jen-\ *adj, usu cap* [*Origen* †A.D. 254? Christian writer, teacher, and theologian + E *-an*] **:** of, relating to, or attributed to Origen

²**origenian** \"\ *n* -s *usu cap* **:** an adherent or follower of Origen

or·i·gen·ic \-¦jenik\ *adj, usu cap* [*Origen* †A.D. 254? Christian writer, teacher and theologian + E *-ic*] **:** ORIGENIAN

or·i·gen·ism \ˈ==jə,nizəm, -,je,n-\ *n* -s *usu cap* [*Origen* †A.D. 254? + E *-ism*] **:** the doctrines held by or attributed to the 3d century Christian theologian Origen who sought to work out a complete Christian philosophy based on the Scriptures and developed largely along Platonic lines

¹**or·i·gen·ist** \-nəst\ *n* -s *usu cap* [LL *origenistes*, fr. *Origen* †A.D. 254? Christian writer, teacher and theologian + L *-istes* -ist] **:** an advocate of Origenism

²**origenist** \"\ *or* **or·i·gen·is·tic** \¦==(,)=¦nistik\ *adj, usu cap* [*origen*ism + *-ist* or *-istic*] **:** of or relating to Origen or Origenism

or·i·gin \ˈȯrəjən, ˈär-\ *n* -s [ME *origine*, prob. fr. MF, fr. L *origin-, origo*, fr. *oriri* to rise, come forth — more at ORIENT] **1 :** ANCESTRY, PARENTAGE ⟨was of humble ~⟩ **2 a :** rise, beginning, or derivation from a source ⟨had its ~ . . . when a tramp printer established it as a weekly —*Amer. Guide Series: Pa.*⟩ **b :** primary source or cause **:** FOUNTAIN, SPRING ⟨a letter found on his clothes tells us the ~ of the quarrel —George Meredith⟩ **3 :** the more fixed, central, or larger attachment or part of a muscle — compare INSERTION **4 a :** the intersection of the axes of Cartesian coordinates **b :** any arbitrary zero from which a magnitude is reckoned

syn SOURCE, INCEPTION, ROOT, PROVENANCE, PROVENIENCE, PRIME MOVER: ORIGIN applies to a person, situation, or condition that marks the beginning of a course or development, to the point at which something rises or starts, or, sometimes, to effective causes ⟨it is probable that the *origin* of language is not a problem that can be solved out of the resources of linguistics alone —Edward Sapir⟩ ⟨the exact *origin* of the pain is not definitely known since it might reasonably be expected to appear in any unyielding tissue or it could arise from distention of the joint cavity itself —H.G.Armstrong⟩ ⟨found the *origin* of faith in an undifferentiated feeling of the Infinite and Eternal —W.R.Inge⟩ SOURCE, often interchangeable with ORIGIN, may center attention on a point of ultimate beginning whence something rises, flows, or emanates ⟨this mystery and meaning of freedom, sin, and grace are the perennial *sources* of the religious life —Reinhold Niebuhr⟩ ⟨the *source* of infection was traced to the feeding to hogs of raw garbage from ships from the Orient —*Americana Annual*⟩ ⟨the probable *sources* of civilization, roughly the three great river valleys of the Nile, the Tigris and Euphrates, and the Indus —R.W.Murray⟩ INCEPTION stresses the notion of an initiating, starting, or beginning point without implication about causes ⟨joining the group at its *inception*⟩ ⟨tin miners, who had to bring coal from south Wales, used the Watt engine from the time of its *inception* —S.F.Mason⟩ ⟨has taken part in the United States atomic energy program since its *inception* in 1942 —*Current Biog.*⟩ ROOT may suggest a first, ultimate, or fundamental source, often one not patently evident ⟨several of the large foundations . . . have been spending hundreds of thousands of dollars to get at the *root* of the trouble —J.M.Barzun⟩ PROVENANCE and PROVENIENCE designate the area, sphere, or group in which something has originated or from which it is derived ⟨any layman who is sufficiently interested in the cheese he eats to inquire about its *provenance* must have noticed how much a monastery background improves a cheese —*New Yorker*⟩ ⟨relatively recent words of scientific *provenance*, *e.g.*, appendicitis, iodine, quinine, and so on —H.L.Mencken⟩ ⟨the African *provenience* of northern Negroes —M.J.Herskovits⟩ PRIME MOVER may refer to an ultimate and original source of motive power that sets a thing moving; of personal agents it may refer to an inciter or instigator ⟨wind as the *prime mover* in impelling a sailing ship⟩ ⟨a committee on general education, in the organization of which your headmaster was a *prime mover* —A.W.Griswold⟩ ⟨evidence was also obtained implicating Heath as the *prime mover* in the affair and immediately upon Daniel's return the former was arrested —D.D.Martin⟩

¹**orig·i·nal** \əˈrijənᵊl, -jnəl\ *n* -s [ME, fr. MF, fr. ML *originale*, fr. L *originale*, adj., original, neut. of *originalis*] **1** *archaic* **a :** the source or cause from which something arises **b :** PARENTAGE **c :** AUTHOR, ORIGINATOR **2** *archaic* **:** ORIGIN 2 **3 a :** a model, pattern, or archetype that is copied **b** (1) **:** a primary manuscript from which copies are made (2) **:** a direct impression produced by a typewriter esp. when made simultaneously with one or more carbon copies **c** (1) **:** the person or thing represented in a photograph or an artist's work (2) **:** a picture or work of art from which copies are made **4 :** a work composed firsthand **:** an artist's independent or spontaneous product ⟨caught up on their mail or . . .

wrote an ~ against the rainy season —Budd Schulberg⟩ **5 a :** a person of fresh initiative or inventive capacity : INNOVATOR ⟨an ~ among popular pianists, combining jazz and romantic techniques in an unusually effective manner —Douglas Watt⟩ **b** *archaic* : ECCENTRIC 3 **6 :** a postage stamp from an original issue, as distinguished from a reprint or a reissue

²original \"\ *adj* [ME, fr. MF, fr. L *originalis*, fr. *origin-*, *origo* origin + *-alis* -al] **1 a :** of or relating to a rise or beginning : existing from the start : INITIAL, PRIMARY, PRISTINE ⟨~ plans called for many films to be made simultaneously —Cecile Starr⟩ ⟨the forests were in large part ~ —J.M. Mogey⟩ **b :** constituting a source, beginning, or first reliance ⟨the ~ account of the mutiny . . . as recorded by two of the survivors —F.R.Dulles⟩ **2 a :** taking independent rise : having spontaneous origin : not secondary, derivative, or imitative : FRESH, NEW ⟨gives us, as all good poetry does, an ~ angle of vision —C.D.Lewis⟩ **b :** gifted with powers of independent thought, direct insight, or constructive imagination : CREATIVE, FERTILE, GERMINAL, INVENTIVE ⟨esteemed as an ~ American composer⟩ **c :** constituting the product or model from which copies are made ⟨found the ~ manuscript, of which copies had long been current⟩ **syn** see NEW

original bid *n* : the first bid made in the auction in a card game — called also *opening bid*

original bill *n* : the initial bill of an equity proceeding not already before the court between the same parties standing in the same interests and consisting of a statement of the cause of complaint and petition for relief

original contract *n* : SOCIAL CONTRACT

original cost *n* **1 :** HISTORICAL COST 2 **2** *in public utility practice* : the cost of a property to that owner who first devoted it to public service **3** *in real estate practice* : the cost of a property to a present owner regardless of cost to a prior owner

original gum *n* : the intact adhesive gum on a postage stamp considered as evidence of the stamp's mint condition — abbr. *O.G.;* called also *full gum*

orig·i·nal·i·ty \ə,rijə'naləd·ē, -lətē, -i\ *n* -ES [F *originalité*, fr. *original*, adj. + *-ité* -ity] **1** *archaic* : the quality or state of being authentic or genuine **2 a :** freshness of aspect or design : independence or newness of style or character ⟨modern Brazilian architecture . . . is full of ~ and, above all, vitality —William Tate⟩ **b :** the power of independent thought or perception : capacity for constructive imagination or significant innovation : creative ability ⟨the directness of blunt truth and . . . a bardic ~ and vigor —C.B.Taylor⟩ **3 a** *patent law* : creation of a useful device, design, or process not before known or created **b** *copyright law* : novelty in the form of expression rather than in subject matter

original jurisdiction *n* : jurisdiction of first instance : authority of a court that takes cognizance of a controversy at the inception of legal proceedings therein

orig·i·nal·ly \ə'rijən°lē, -jnəl|, |i\ *adv* **1** *archaic* : by origin or derivation : from the first : INHERENTLY ⟨power ~ the people's⟩ **2 :** in the beginning : in the first place : INITIALLY, PRIMARILY **3 :** in a fresh or original manner ⟨rebinding of single books demanding . . . ~ designed covers —Edith Diehl⟩

original minor scale *n* : NATURAL MINOR SCALE

original package doctrine *n* : a doctrine whereby goods and commodities imported from one state of the U.S. into another or from a foreign country are usu. protected from being subject to the laws of the state of importation until sale is made by the importer so long as they are contained in the original unbroken individual package, container, or receptacle accepted from the shipper by the carrier and delivered in the same form to the importer

original process *n* : an original writ or summons issued by authority of a court as the foundation of and first step in a lawsuit, including always a notice to the defendant when to appear to make his defense and often an order to arrest the defendant, seize or attach his property, or garnishee a claim due from a third person to the defendant or an order that the defendant do or refrain from doing a specified act or that an officer of the court do a specified act in connection with the suit — distinguished from *final process* and *mesne process*

original sin *n* [ME, trans. of ML *peccatum originale*] : hereditary sin or defect often held in Christian theology to be transmitted from one generation to the next and inherited by each person as a consequence of the original sinful choice made by the first man of the human race — compare ACTUAL SIN

original writ *n* [ME, trans. of ML *breve originale*] **1 :** a writ issued under the great seal by which in English law the jurisdiction of the court was laid in beginning personal actions until the summons was substituted by the Judicature Act of 1873 — compare JUDICIAL WRIT, PRAECIPE **2 :** ORIGINAL PROCESS

orig·i·nant \ə'rij(ə)nənt\ *adj* [*origin* + *-ant*] *archaic* : ARISING, ORIGINATING

¹orig·i·nary \-jə,nerē\ *adj* [LL *originarius*, fr. L *origin-*, *origo* origin + *-arius* -ary — more at ORIGIN] **1** *obs* : NATIVE, ORIGINATING **2** *archaic* : constituting a source or cause

²originary *n* -s [LL *originarii* (pl.), fr. pl. of *originarius*, adj.] *obs* : ABORIGINE

orig·i·nate \ə'rijə,nāt, *usu* -ād·+V\ *vb* -ED/-ING/-S [prob. back-formation fr. *origination*] *vt* **1 :** to cause the beginning of : give rise to : INITIATE ⟨have *originated* a mass of legend —*Irish Digest*⟩ **2 :** to start (a person or thing) on a course or journey ⟨freight is *originated* at the dock⟩ ~ *vi* : to take or have origin : be derived : ARISE, BEGIN, START ⟨a retractor muscle that ~s on the body wall⟩ ⟨the train *originated* in Washington⟩ **syn** see SPRING

originating company *n* : DIRECT-WRITING COMPANY 1

originating notice *or* **originating summons** *n, Eng law* : a notice the service of which begins a legal proceeding — see ADJOURNED SUMMONS

orig·i·na·tion \ə,rijə'nāshən\ *n* -s [L *origination-*, *originatio*, fr. *origin-*, *origo* origin + *-ation-*, *-atio* -ation] **1** *obs* : DERIVATION, ETYMOLOGY **2 :** a coming into existence : BEGINNING, RISE ⟨a custom that has its ~ far back in time⟩ **3 :** ORIGIN 3 **4 :** a bringing into existence : CREATION, INVENTION, MAKING, PRODUCTION ⟨a representative legislature with annual meetings and the ~ of laws —C.G.Bowers⟩

orig·i·na·tive \ə'rijə,nād·iv\ *adj* : having ability to originate : CREATIVE, FERTILE, INVENTIVE ⟨the very greatest and most remarkable ~ geniuses —H.S.Hartfield⟩

orig·i·na·tor \ə'rijə,nād·ə(r), -ātə-\ *n* -s : one that originates

or·i·gin·ist \'örəjənəst, 'är-\ *n* -s **1** *obs* : FOUNDER, ORIGINATOR **b :** a historian of origins **2 :** a theorist about origins

origin of coordinates [trans. of F *origine des coordonnées*] : the point of intersection of coordinate axes

ori·hon \'örē,hän\ *n* -s [Jap, prob. fr. *ori* fold + *hon* book, volume] : a strip of paper, papyrus, or vellum that is accordion-folded so as to divide the writing or printing which appears on one side into pages or columns and that sometimes has laced-on covers

oril·lon \ōrēyōⁿ\ *or* **oril·lion** \ə'rilyən\ *n* -s [F *orillon*, lit., little ear, dim. of *oreille* ear, fr. L *auricula*, dim. of *auris* ear — more at EAR] *archaic* : a projection built out at the corner of a bastion between flank and face from which to defend the flank

ori·nasal \¦ōrə, ¦örə, ¦ärə+\ *adj* [*ori-* + *nasal*] **1 :** of or relating to the mouth and nose **2 :** pronounced (as a French nasal vowel) through both mouth and nose

o ring \'ō-\ *n, usu cap O* : a flat ring of synthetic rubber used as a gasket in sealing a joint against high pressures

ori·no·co crocodile \¦ōrə¦nō(,)kō-\ *n, usu cap O* [fr. *Orinoco* river, Venezuela] : a ferocious narrow-snouted crocodile (*Crocodylus intermedius*) of the Orinoco river and drainage basin

ori·ole \'ōrē,ōl, 'ör- *also* -ēəl\ *n* -s [F *oriol*, fr. OF, fr. ML *oryolus*, fr. L *aureolus* golden, dim. of *aureus* golden, fr. *aurum* gold; akin to Lith *auksas* gold, Arm *os-ki* gold and prob. to L *aurora* dawn — more at EAST] **1 :** any of various usu. brightly colored Old World birds constituting the family Oriolidae — see FIG-BIRD, GOLDEN ORIOLE **2 :** any of various American birds of the family Icteridae **3 :** LEATHER 4

ori·ol·i·dae \,==¦ōlə,dē, -'äl-\ *n pl, cap* [NL, fr. *Oriolus*, type genus (fr. ML *oryolus*) + *-idae*] : a family of passerine birds related to the crows and consisting of the Old World orioles most of which inhabit tropical and subtropical regions

ori·on \ə'rīən, ō'-, ö'- *sometimes* 'ōrēən *or* 'örē-\ *n* -s [ME *Orion*, constellation of seven stars located east of Taurus on the equator, fr. L, fr. Gk *Ōriōn*] : HOLLAND BLUE

ori·sha \'ōrə,shä\ *n, pl* **orisha** *or* **orishas** [Yoruba] : a Yoruba deity or spirit

oris·mo·log·i·cal \ə¦rizmə¦läjəkəl\ *or* **oris·mo·log·ic** \-jik\ *adj* [*orismological* fr. *orismology* + *-ical; orismologic* ISV *orismolog-* (fr. *orismology*) + *-ic*] : of or relating to orismology

or·is·mol·o·gy \,örəz'mäləjē, ,är-\ *n* -ES [Gk *horismos* definition (fr. *horizein* to limit, define) + E *-logy* — more at HORIZON] : the science of defining technical terms : TERMINOLOGY

or·i·son \'ōrəsən, 'är-, -rəzən\ *n* -s [ME, fr. OF, fr. LL *oration-*, *oratio*, fr. L, speech, oration — more at ORATION] **1 :** PRAYER ⟨nymph, in thy ~s be all my sins remembered —Shak.⟩ **2 :** mystical contemplation ⟨the steps of the ladder . . . in the art of contemplation are called, in technical terms, the degrees of ~ —Evelyn Underhill⟩

-o·ri·um \'ōrēəm, 'ör-\ *n suffix, pl* **-o·ri·ums** \-ēəmz\ *or* **-o·ria** \-ēə\ [L, fr. neut. of *-orius* -ory] **1 :** place for ⟨*natatorium*⟩ **2 :** thing used for ⟨*haustorium*⟩

ori·ya \ō'rē(y)ə\ *n, pl* **oriya** *or* **oriyas** *usu cap* **1 a :** a chiefly Hindu people of Orissa, India **b :** a member of such people **2 :** the Indic language of Orissa

or·khon turk \'ör,kän-\ *n, usu cap O&T* [fr. *Orkhon* river, northern Mongolia] : one of a Turkish tribe in the 8th century occupying the drainage of the Orkhon river in north central Mongolia, practicing intensive irrigation agriculture and using a runic alphabet derived from Aramaic

ork·ney \'örknē\ *adj, usu cap* [fr. *Orkney* islands, northeastern Scotland] : of or from the Orkney islands constituting the county of Orkney, Scotland : of the kind or style prevalent in the Orkneys : ORKNEYAN

¹ork·ney·an \'örknēən, =¦==\ *adj, usu cap* [*Orkney* islands + E *-an* (adj. suffix)] **1 :** of, relating to, or characteristic of the Orkney islands **2 :** of, relating to, or characteristic of the people of the Orkney islands

²orkneyan \"\ *n* -s *cap* [*Orkney* islands + E *-an* (n. suffix)] : a native or inhabitant of the Orkney islands

orkney skiff *n, usu cap O* : a beamy clinker-built fishing skiff used off the Orkney islands of Scotland

ORL *abbr* owner's risk of leakage

orle \'ör(ə)l\ *n* -s [MF, lit., border, hem, fr. *orler* to put a hem on, fr. (assumed) VL *orulare*, fr. (assumed) VL *orula* border, hem, fr. L *ora* border, rim, coast — more at ORAL] **1** *heraldry* **a :** a number of small charges arranged so as to form a border within the edge of the field ⟨an ~ of martlets⟩ **b :** a border within and parallel to but not touching the edge of the field **c :** the wreath or chaplet surmounting or encircling the helmet of a knight and bearing the crest **2 :** a narrow fillet at the top of a shaft separating it from the bell of the capital or at the bottom above the molding of the base — **in orle** *adv* : in the form of an orle round the escutcheon leaving the middle of the field vacant or occupied by something else — used of bearings on the shield

or·lean \'örlēən, ör'lē(ə)n\ *n* -s [F *orléane*, by folk etymology (influence of *Orléans*, city in north central France) fr. NL *orellana* (specific epithet of *Bixa orellana*), after Francisco de *Orellana* †1549 Span. soldier and explorer who discovered the Amazon on the banks of which annatto is common] : ANNATTO 1a

¹or·lea·nian \(')ö(r)¦lēnyən, -ēnēən\ *adj, usu cap* [New *Orleans*, La. + E *-ian* (adj. suffix)] **1 :** of, relating to, or characteristic of New Orleans, La. **2 :** of, relating to, or characteristic of the people of New Orleans

²orleanian \"\ *n* -s *cap* [New *Orleans* + E *-ian* (n. suffix)] : a native or resident of New Orleans

or·lean·ist \'ö(r)lēənəst, 'ö(r)lyən-, ö(r)'lē(ə)n-\ *n* -s *usu cap* [F *orléaniste*, fr. *Orléans*, cadet branch of the Valois and Bourbon houses of France + *-iste* -ist] : an adherent or supporter of the Orleans family in its claim to the throne of France on the ground of descent from a younger brother of Louis XIV and usu. of the moderate conservative policies associated with it — compare LEGITIMIST

orl fly \'ör(ə)l-\ *n* [E dial. *orl* alder (fr. ME *oryelle*, alter. of *alder, aller*) + E *fly* — more at ALDER] : a British alderfly (*Sialis lutaria*)

or·lo \'ör(,)lō\ *n* -s [It, lit., border, hem, fr. *orlare* to hem, fr. (assumed) VL *orulare*] **1 :** ORLE 2 **2 :** the smooth surface between two flutes of a shaft **3 :** the surface between two grooves of a triglyph **4 :** a flat plinth of any width

or·loff \'ör,läf, -lóf, =¦=\ *n* -s *usu cap* [after Count Aleksei Grigorievich *Orlov* †1808 Russ. nobleman who started the breed] : a Russian breed of trotting horses evolved by interbreeding Dutch, Frisian, and Arabian horses and including a large heavy harness horse that is usu. black and a lighter speedier horse that is commonly gray and is sometimes used for racing

Or·lon \'ör,län, 'ö(ə),l-\ *trademark* **1** — used for an acrylic fiber made in filament or staple form, characterized often by its high bulk and soft warm hand, used esp. in bulky suitings, in knitted goods, and because of its resistance to sunlight in curtains and awnings, and often blended with other fibers in fabrics **2 :** a yarn or fabric made of Orlon fiber

or·lop deck \'ör,läp-\ *n* [*orlop* fr. ME *overlop* deck of a single-decker, fr. MLG *overlōp*, lit., something that overleaps, fr. *over* + *lōp* leap, fr. *lōpen* to leap, run; akin to OHG *ubar* over and to MD *lōpen* to run — more at OVER, LEAP] **1 :** the deck below the lower deck : the lowest continuous deck in a ship having more than three decks — see DECK illustration **2 :** the lowest deck in a ship

or·mer \'örmər\ *n* -s [F dial. (Isle of Guernsey), prob. fr. *or-* (fr. L *auris* ear) + *mer* sea, fr. L *mare;* fr. the shape of the shell — more at EAR, MARINE] : ABALONE

or·mo·lu \'ör(,)mə,lü\ *n* -s *often attrib* [F *or moulu*, lit., ground gold] **1** *archaic* : gold ground for use in gilding; *also* : metal gilded with ground gold **2 :** a brass made to imitate gold and used in mounts for furniture and for other decorative purposes — called also *mosaic gold* **3 :** something pretending to more than its real value or quality : something showy rather than genuine ⟨some ~ vocal numbers —Nat Hentoff⟩ ⟨fiction relating inordinate and ~ violence —*Times Lit. Supp.*⟩

ormolu varnish *n* : a varnish used to give the appearance of gold

or·mo·sia \ö(r)'mōzh(ē)ə\ *n, cap* [NL, fr. Gk *hormos* chain, necklace + NL *-ia;* fr. the use of its berries as beads — more at SERIES] : a genus of shrubs and trees (family Leguminosae) chiefly of So. America and Central America with pink to reddish wood — see JUMBY BEAN, NECKLACE TREE

¹or·na·ment \'ö(r)nəmənt\ *n* -s [ME *ornament, ornement*, fr. OF *ornement*, fr. L *ornamentum*, fr. *ornare* to furnish, embellish + *-mentum* -ment — more at ORNATE] **1** *archaic* : a useful accessory (as of clothing, furniture) : ADJUNCT; *esp* : an article or object used in a church service **2 a :** something that lends grace or beauty : a decorative part or addition : a structural component or applied detail that embellishes ⟨the profiles and the carved ~s of the moldings —D.S.Robertson⟩ **b :** a manner, quality, or trait that adorns or beautifies ⟨the various devices of poetical ~ —*Encyc. Americana*⟩ **3 :** a person whose virtues or graces add luster to his place, time, or society ⟨the greatest teachers and ~s of our species —T.L. Peacock⟩ ⟨the greatest mathematician of his age and an ~ of the academies of Berlin and St. Petersburg —Paul Koelner⟩ **4 :** the act of adorning or beautifying : DECORATION, ORNAMENTATION ⟨indulged in excessive ~⟩ **5 :** an embellishing note or notes (as a trill, appoggiatura, mordent) not belonging to the essential musical harmony or melody and indicated by the composer or esp. in the 16th to 18th centuries introduced by the performer for a decorative effect : GRACE — called also *embellishment, fioritura*

²or·na·ment \-,ment, -,mənt — *see* ²-MENT\ *vt* -ED/-ING/-S : to provide with ornament : DECORATE, EMBELLISH ⟨touched nothing that he did not ~ with his learning and injure with his theories —Harvey Graham⟩ **syn** see ADORN

¹or·na·men·tal \¦ö(r)nə¦ment°l\ *adj* : having decorative quality or value ⟨encourages the useful rather than the ~ public virtues —Ellen Glasgow⟩ — **or·na·men·tal·i·ty** \,==,mən·'taləd·ē, -,men-, -ləd·ē, -i\ *n* -ES — **or·na·men·tal·ly** \¦==¦ment°lē, -°li\ *adv* — **or·na·men·tal·ness** \,=='ment°lnəs\ *n* -ES

²ornamental \"\ *n* -s : a decorative object; *esp* : a plant cultivated for its beauty rather than for use

or·na·men·tal·ism \,=='ment°l,izəm\ *n* -s : a tendency to ornamental display

or·na·men·tal·ist \-°ləst\ *n* -s : one who uses ornamentation freely

or·na·men·ta·tion \,ö(r)nəmən'tāshən, -,men-\ *n* -s [²*ornament* + *-ation*] **1 :** the act or process of ornamenting or the state of being ornamented ⟨an effort at ~ which did little to conceal the poverty of his imagination⟩ **2 :** a decorative device : EMBELLISHMENT; *collectively* : ORNAMENTS **3 :** characteristic markings or sculpture on the body of an animal

or·na·ment·er \'==,mentə(r)\ *n* -s : one that ornaments or decorates

or·na·ment·ist \-,mentəst, -,mən-\ *n* -s : a designer or maker of ornaments

ornaments rubric *n* : a rubric in the Book of Common Prayer concerning objects used in service taken from an act of Elizabeth I directing the retention of usage established in the second year of the reign of Edward VI

ornary *var of* ORNERY

¹or·nate \(')ö(r)¦nāt, (')ö(ə)¦-, *usu* -ād·+V\ *adj* [ME *ornat*, fr. L *ornatus*, past part. of *ornare* to furnish, embellish; akin to L *ordinare* to order, arrange — more at ORDAIN] **1 :** marked by elaborate rhetoric or florid style ⟨~ poems can be more satisfactorily translated than simple ones —Walter Silz⟩ ⟨is clear and simple rather than ~ and pompous —*Times Lit. Supp.*⟩ **2 :** elaborately ornamented : amply or excessively decorated ⟨the most ~ carving and gold of the baroque churches —Lewis Mumford⟩

syn ORNATE, ROCOCO, BAROQUE, FLAMBOYANT, FLORID can mean, in common, elaborately and often pretentiously decorated or designed. ORNATE can apply to anything heavily adorned or ornamented or conspicuously embellished ⟨the extremely *ornate* gingerbread architecture of the eighties and nineties, when fanciful scrollwork trim, cupolas, and brackets were in vogue —*Amer. Guide Series: Ariz.*⟩ ⟨elaborate and *ornate* rituals —A.M.Young⟩ ⟨stately town houses, *ornate* with hand-carved woodwork, sparkling chandeliers, elaborate fireplaces, and imported rugs —*Amer. Guide Series: Ark.*⟩ ⟨a prose simple or *ornate* as the situation demands —William Peden⟩ ROCOCO, applying orig. to an elaborate playful and fanciful 18th century French decorative design, can apply to any similarly elaborate decoration, esp. with an ornateness of design (as of furniture, mirror frames) marked by proliferating curves and scrolls, shellwork, and general fancifulness and often extending to anything regarded as over-elaborately decorated ⟨the long *rococo* halls, giddy with plush and whorled designs in gold, were peopled with Roman fragments, white and disassociated; a runner's leg, the chilly half-turned head of a matron stricken at the bosom —Djuna Barnes⟩ ⟨the extreme refinement and delicacy of 17th century taste is a little saccharine, a little *rococo*, with just a hint of something meretricious verging on the tawdry —T.K. Whipple⟩ ⟨doesn't mind getting caught out with a *rococo* phrase or an overstuffed image —*Los Angeles (Calif.) Times*⟩ BAROQUE, often loosely interchangeable with ROCOCO but from a style of architecture prior to the rococo, suggests more an extravagant massive strength, often grotesqueness, of decorative quality, stressing the ingenious, varied, bizarre, or contorted, often in overintricate interrelationship ⟨a *baroque* style, it has been called by critics who admired this funeral sumptuousness, this glittering bric-a-brac, this aesthetic perversity —Claude Vigée⟩ ⟨a landscape of truly *baroque* invention, richly variegated and unfailing in its calculated surprises —*Times Lit. Supp.*⟩ ⟨*baroque* poetry with its frigid vehemence, its exhibitionistic forcefulness and false dynamism, its arbitrary twisting and distortions, its carefully arranged denaturalizing of living speech into a dead language, its strained mannerisms and calculated artificialities —H.L.Davis⟩ ⟨poetry is *baroque*. Baroque is tragic, massive and mystical. It is elemental. It demands depth and insight —W.S.Maugham⟩ FLAMBOYANT can suggest an ornateness but stresses more an excess of color or bold, daring, conspicuous display ⟨a flair for *flamboyant* clothes, including red slacks —*Time*⟩ ⟨a man of *flamboyant* egotism, given to pomposities of speech and absurdities of prose —*New Yorker*⟩ ⟨he indulges in *flamboyant* gestures and exaggerated strutting —Howard Barnes⟩ ⟨the worker's reaction was characterized more by a serious eagerness than a *flamboyant* enthusiasm —Samuel Liss⟩ FLORID suggests an overelaboration of rich color, figure of speech, ornamental flourish, and so on, implying showiness and conspicuous embellishment ⟨she would put on the *florid* costume, fix the gold circlets into the lobes of her ears, slip the garish imitation topaz onto her forefinger —William Fifield⟩ ⟨*florid* oriental imagery —Douglas Bush⟩ ⟨*florid* verbiage —H.G.Wells⟩ ⟨contrasting with the simplicity of these gardens was the exotic, *florid* display of fruit and vegetable stands —*Buick Mag.*⟩

²ornate *vt* -ED/-ING/-S [ME *ornaten*, fr. L *ornatus*, past part. of *ornare*] *obs* : ADORN

ornate aphid *n* : an aphid (*Myzus ornatus*) widely distributed in northern Europe and now established in California that is a pest of numerous plants

or·nate·ly *adv* [ME *ornatly*, fr. *ornat* ornate + *-ly*] : in an ornate manner

or·nate·ness *n* -ES : the quality or state of being ornate

or·na·ture \'örnə,chù(ə)r, -,chər\ *n* -s [MF, fr. LL *ornatura* ornament, fr. L *ornatus*, past part. + *-ura* -ure] : ORNAMENTATION

or·neri·ness \'ö(r)n(ə)rēnəs, 'än(-, -rinəs\ *n* -ES [*ornery* + *-ness*] : bad temper : PERVERSITY

or·nery *or* **on·ery** *or* **or·na·ry** \'örn(ə)rē, 'ö(ə)n-, 'än-, -ri\ *adj, often* -ER/-EST [alter. of *ordinary*] **1** *chiefly dial* **a :** of inferior quality : COMMON **b :** LAZY, SHIFTLESS **2 a :** having a touchy disposition : inclined to be short-tempered : CANTANKEROUS ⟨he's been ~ all day⟩ ⟨the sorrel was an ~ cuss and threw anybody that tried to ride him⟩ **b :** independent and individualistic sometimes to the point of seeming eccentric ⟨Yankees are an ~ lot, but they're all right at heart⟩ **syn** see CONTRARY

ornify *vt* -ED/-ING/-ES [L *ornare* to embellish + E *-ify*] *obs* : ADORN

or·nis \'örnəs, 'ö(ə)n-\ *n, pl* **orni·thes** \ö(r)'nī(,)thēz\ [G, fr. Gk, bird] : the birdlife of a region : AVIFAUNA

-ornis \"\ *n comb form, pl* **-ornithes** \,ö(r)'nī(,)thēz\ [NL, fr. Gk *ornis* — more at ERNE] : bird ⟨*Heliornis*⟩ ⟨*Archaeornithes*⟩

ornith- *or* **ornitho-** *comb form* [L, fr. Gk, fr. *ornith-*, *ornis*] : bird ⟨*ornith*ichnite⟩ ⟨*ornitho*graphy⟩

or·nith·ic \(')ö(r)¦nithik\ *adj* [Gk *ornithikos*, fr. *ornith-* + *-ikos* -ic] : of, relating to, or characteristic of birds

or·nith·ichnite \¦ö(r)nəth+\ *n* [*ornith-* + *ichnite*] : the fossil footprint of a bird

or·ni·thine \'ö(r)nə,thēn\ *n* -s [ISV *ornith-* (in *ornithuric acid*) + *-ine*] : a crystalline or syrupy basic amino acid $H_2N(CH_2)_3CH(NH_2)COOH$ formed together with urea by hydrolysis of arginine (as by arginase) and in turn converted by reaction with ammonia and carbon dioxide into citrulline and then arginine; α,δ-diamino-valeric acid

or·nith·is·chia \,ö(r)nə'thiskēə\ *n pl, cap* [NL, fr. *ornith-* + *-ischia* (fr. Gk *ischion* hip joint) — more at ISCHIUM] : an order of archosaurian reptiles comprising herbivorous dinosaurs with tetraradiate pelves and including many bizarre forms (as the armored dinosaurs of the suborders Stegosauria and Ankylosauria and the horned dinosaurs of the suborder Ceratopsia) — **or·nith·is·chi·an** \¦==¦skēən\ *adj or n*

or·nitho·ceph·a·lus \¦ö(r)nə(,)thō'sefələs, ö(r),nithə's-\ *n, cap* [NL, fr. *ornith-* + *-cephalus*] : the first discovered and best known genus of pterodactyls (type of the family Ornithocephalidae)

or·nitho·cop·ros \-'käprəs, -,präs\ *n* -ES [NL, fr. *ornith-* + Gk *kopros* dung — more at COPR-] : the dung of birds : GUANO

or·nith·o·delph \ö(r)'nithə,delf\ *or* **or·nith·o·del·phi·an** \=,==delfēən\ *n* -s [*ornithodelph* fr. NL *Ornithodelphia; ornithodelphian* fr. NL *Ornithodelphia* + E *-an*] : MONOTREME

or·nith·o·del·phes \=,==del(,)fēz\ *or* **or·nith·o·del·phia** \-lfēə\ [NL, fr. *ornith-* + *-delphes* or *-delphia* (fr. Gk *delphys* womb) — more at DOLPHIN] *syn of* PROTOTHERIA

or·nith·o·del·phi·an \¦‧‧¦‧fēən\ *or* **or·nith·o·del·phic** \-fik\ *or* **or·nith·o·del·phous** \-fəs\ *adj* [NL *Ornithodelphia* + E *-an* or *-ic* or *-ous*] : MONOTREMATOUS

or·ni·thod·o·ros \ˌȯ(r)nəˈthädərəs\ *n, cap* [NL, fr. *ornith-* + Gk *doros* leather bag; akin to Gk *derma* skin — more at DERM-] : a genus of ticks (family Argasidae) containing forms that act as carriers of relapsing fever as well as Q fever

or·ni·thod·o·rus \"\ [NL] *syn of* ORNITHODOROS

or·ni·tho·fauna \ȯ(r)¦nithə, ¦ȯ(r)nə(ˌ)thō+\ *n* [NL, fr. *ornith-* + *fauna*] : the birds of a region or habitat : AVIFAUNA

or·ni·tho·gae·an *or* **or·ni·tho·ge·an** \"+¦jēən\ *adj, usu cap* [NL, fr. *ornith-* + *-gaea, -gea* + E *-an*] : ¹NEW ZEALAND 2

or·ni·thog·a·lum \ˌȯ(r)nəˈthägələm\ *n* [NL, fr. Gk *ornithogalon* star-of-Bethlehem, fr. *ornith-* + *-galon* (fr. *gala* milk) — more at GALAXY] **1** *cap* : a large genus of Old World bulbous herbs (family Liliaceae) with basal leaves resembling grass and naked scapes bearing clusters of white, yellow, or greenish flowers with spreading perianth segments and flattened filaments — see STAR-OF-BETHLEHEM **2** -S : any plant of the genus *Ornithogalum*

or·ni·thoid \ˈȯ(r)nəˌthȯid\ *adj* [ISV *ornith-* + *-oid*] : resembling a bird : BIRDLIKE

or·ni·tho·les·tes \ȯ(r)ˌnithəˈle(ˌ)stēz, ˌȯ(r)nəthōˈl-\ *n, cap* [NL, fr. *ornith-* + Gk *lēistēs* robber; akin to L *lucrum* gain — more at LUCRE] : a genus of small light-boned carnivorous dinosaurs of the Jurassic with small skull, slender neck, and long slim fingers

or·ni·tho·log·i·cal \ȯ(r)¦nithə¦läjəkəl, ¦ȯ(r)nəthə¦l-, -jēk-\ *or* **or·ni·tho·log·ic** \-jik, -jēk\ *adj* : of or relating to ornithology — **or·ni·tho·log·i·cal·ly** \-jək(ə)lē, -jēk-, -li\ *adv*

or·ni·thol·o·gist \ˌȯ(r)nəˈthäləjəst\ *n* -S : a specialist in ornithology

or·ni·thol·o·gy \-jē,-ji\ *n* -ES [NL *ornithologia*, fr. *ornith-* + *-logia* -logy (fr. L)] **1** : a branch of zoology that deals with birds **2** : a treatise on ornithology

or·nith·o·man·cy \ȯ(r)ˈnithəˌman(t)sē\ *n* -ES [Gk *ornithomanteia*, fr. *ornith-* + *-manteia* -mancy] : divination by observation of the flight of birds : AUGURY

or·ni·tho·mimid \ȯ(r)ˌnithəˈmīməd, ˌȯ(r)nəthōˈm-, -ˈmim-\ *n* -S [NL *Ornithomimidae*, fr. *Ornithomimus* + *-idae*] : a dinosaur of the genus *Ornithomimus* or of the family Ornithomimidae

or·ni·tho·mi·mus \-ˈmīməs\ *n, cap* [NL, fr. *ornith-* + *-mimus*] : a genus (the type of the family Ornithomimidae) of small slender theropod dinosaurs of the Upper Cretaceous having toothless jaws and a birdlike skeleton

or·ni·tho·my·zous \ȯ(r)¦nithə¦mīzəs, ¦ȯ(r)nəthō¦m-\ *adj* [ISV *ornith-* + *myzo-* + E *-ous*] : parasitic on birds

or·ni·thon \ˈȯ(r)nəˌthän, ȯ(r)ˈnīˌth-\ *n* -S [L, fr. Gk *ornithōn*, fr. *ornith-, ornis* bird — more at ERNE] : AVIARY

or·ni·tho·pap·pi \ȯ(r)¦nithəˈpaˌpī, ˌȯ(r)nəthōˈp-, -apē\ [NL, fr. *ornith-* + *-pappi* (fr. Gk *pappos* grandfather) — more at PAPA] *syn of* ARCHAEORNITHES

or·ni·thoph·i·lous \¦ȯ(r)nə¦thäfələs\ *adj* [*ornith-* + *-philous*] **1** : having a fondness for birds : bird-loving **2** : pollinated by birds

or·nith·o·pod \ȯ(r)ˈnithəˌpäd\ *n* -S [NL *Ornithopoda*] : a dinosaur of the suborder Ornithopoda

¹**or·ni·thop·o·da** \ˌȯ(r)nəˈthäpədə\ *n pl, cap* [NL, fr. *ornith-* + *-poda*] : a suborder of the order Ornithischia comprising bipedal dinosaurs having distinctly digitigrade hind limbs usu. with only three functional toes which are blunt and having also hollow limb bones, a fourth trochanter on the femur, and no dermal armor

²**ornithopoda** \"\ [NL, fr. *ornith-* + *-poda*] *syn of* ORNITHISCHIA

or·ni·thop·o·dous \¦‧‧¦‧dəs\ *adj* [NL ²*Ornithopoda* + E *-ous*] : of or relating to the Ornithischia

or·ni·thop·ter \ˈȯ(r)nəˌthäptə(r), ˌ‧‧ˈ‧‧\ *n* -S [ISV *ornith-* + *-pter* (as in *helicopter*)] : a heavier-than-air airplane deriving its chief support and propulsion from flapping wings

or·ni·thop·tera \ˌȯ(r)nəˈthäpt(ə)rə\ *n, cap* [NL, fr. *ornith-* + *-ptera*] : a genus of large butterflies of the Malay archipelago closely related to the genus *Papilio* and having the females much larger and much less brightly colored than the males

or·ni·tho·rhyn·chous \ȯ(r)¦nithə¦riŋkəs, ¦ȯ(r)nəthō¦r-\ *adj* [NL *ornithorhynchus* + E *-ous*] : having a beak like that of a bird

or·ni·tho·rhyn·chus \ȯ(r)ˌnithəˈriŋkəs, ˌȯ(r)nəthōˈr-\ *n* [NL, fr. *ornith-* + *-rhynchus*] **1** *cap* : a genus (coextensive with the family Ornithorhynchidae) of egg-laying mammals including only the platypus **2** -ES : PLATYPUS

or·ni·tho·scop·ic \ȯ(r)¦nithə¦skäpik, ¦ȯ(r)nəthō¦s-\ *adj* : of or relating to ornithoscopy

or·ni·thos·co·pist \ˌȯ(r)nəˈthäskəpəst\ *n* -S : one that practices ornithoscopy

or·ni·thos·co·py \-pē\ *n* -ES [Gk *ornithoskopia*, fr. *ornithoskopos* predicting by observing the flight of birds (fr. *ornith-* + *skopos* observer — fr. *skopein* to view, watch —) + *-ia* -y — more at SPY] **1** : ORNITHOMANCY **2** : BIRD-WATCHING ⟨would alternate ~ with entomology —Rose Macaulay⟩

or·ni·tho·sis \ˌȯ(r)nəˈthōsəs\ *n, pl* **or·ni·tho·ses** \-ōˌsēz\ [NL, fr. *ornith-* + *-osis*] : PSITTACOSIS — used esp. of the form of the disease originating in birds other than psittacines

or·ni·thot·ic \¦‧‧¦thäd·ik\ *adj* [fr. NL *ornithosis* after such pairs as NL *narcosis*: E *narcotic*] : of or relating to ornithosis

or·ni·tho·tom·i·cal \ȯ(r)¦nithə¦täməkəl, ¦ȯ(r)nəthō¦t-\ *adj* [*ornithotomy* + *-ical*] : of or relating to ornithotomy

or·ni·thot·o·mist \ˌȯ(r)nəˈthäd·əməst\ *n* -S : a specialist in ornithotomy

or·ni·thot·o·my \-mē\ *n* -ES [ISV *ornith-* + *-tomy*] : the anatomy or dissection of birds

or·nith·uric acid \¦ȯ(r)nə¦thyu̇rik-\ *n* [*ornithuric* ISV *ornith-* + *-uric*] : a crystalline acid $C_6H_5CONH(CH_2)_3CH(NHCOC_6H_5)COOH$ secreted in the urine of birds and reptiles

¹**oro-** *comb form* [Gk *oros* mountain — more at RISE] : mountain ⟨orography⟩ ⟨orogenesis⟩ ⟨orophyte⟩ : elevation ⟨orometer⟩

²**oro-** *comb form* [L *or-, os* mouth — more at ORAL] : mouth ⟨oropharynx⟩ : mouth and ⟨oroanal⟩ ⟨orofacial⟩

oro·anal \¦ōr(ˌ)ō+\ *adj* [²*oro-* + *anal*] : functioning both as mouth and anus ⟨the ~ orifice of the starfish⟩

oro·ban·cha·ce·ae \ˌōrōˌbaŋˈkāsēˌē\ *n pl, cap* [NL, fr. *Orobanche*, type genus + *-aceae*] : a family of widely distributed brown or yellow leafless root-parasitic herbs (order Polemoniales) with axillary or spicate 2-lipped flowers and a 1-celled ovary

oro·ban·cha·ceous \¦‧‧‚‧¦kāshəs\ *adj* [NL *Orobanchaceae* + E *-ous*] : of or relating to the family Orobanchaceae

oro·ban·che \ˌ‧‧ˈbaŋ(ˌ)kē\ *n, cap* [NL, fr. L, broomrape, fr. Gk *orobanchē* dodder, broomrape, fr. *orobos* bitter vetch, chick-pea + *anchein* to strangle — more at ERS, ANGER] : a large genus (the type of the family Orobanchaceae) of root-parasitic herbs native to the Old World and western America that have fleshy yellowish white and spicate bracted flowers — see BROOMRAPE

oro·bathymetric \¦ōr(ˌ)ō+\ *adj* [¹*oro-* + *bathymetric*] : of or relating to the representation of submerged mountains by depth contours ⟨~ charts of the north Atlantic —*Geog. Jour.*⟩

oro·chi \ōˈrōchē\ *also* **oro·chon** \-ōchən\ *or* **oro·kon** \-ōkən\ *n, pl* **orochi** *or* **orochis** *usu cap* **1** : a Tungus people dwelling near the mouth of the Amur that encoffins its dead on platforms **2** : a member of the Orochi people

oro·crat·ic \¦ōrə¦krad·ik\ *adj* [¹*oro-* + *-cratic*] : of or relating to a degree of roughness of the earth's surface comparable to that now existing

oro·facial \¦ōrō+\ *adj* [²*oro-* + *facial*] : of or relating to the mouth and face ⟨~ abnormalities⟩

oro·gen \ˈōrəjən, -ˌjen\ *also* **oro·gene** \-ˌjēn\ *n* -S [G *orogen*, back-formation fr. *orogenie* orogeny] **1** : a mountain mass that is a unit with respect to origin or uplift **2** : a region of mountain-making disturbance — compare KRATOGEN

oro·gen·ic \¦‧‧¦jenik\ *also* **oro·ge·net·ic** \-jə¦ned·ik\ *adj* [in sense 1, ISV *orogeny* + *-ic* or *-etic*; in sense 2, ISV *orogen* + *-ic* or *-etic*] **1** : of, relating to, or produced by orogeny **2** : of, relating to, or characteristic of an orogen — **oro·gen·i·cal·ly** \-¦jenək(ə)lē\ *adv*

orog·e·ny \ōˈräjənē\ *also* **oro·genesis** \ˌōrō+\ *n, pl* **oro·genies** *also* **orogeneses** [ISV ¹*oro-* + *-geny*] : the process of mountain making esp. by folding of the earth's crust; *also* : a sequence of mountain-making movements closely associated in time and place — compare DIASTROPHISM, EPEIROGENY

oro·graph \ˈōrəˌgraf, -ràf\ *n* [ISV ¹*oro-* + *-graph*] : a machine used in making topographical maps that is operated by being pushed across country and that records both distances and elevations

oro·graph·ic \¦ōrə¦grafik\ *also* **oro·graph·i·cal** \-fəkəl\ *adj* [¹*oro-* + *-graphic, -graphical*] : of or relating to mountains esp. with respect to their location, distribution, and accompanying phenomena — **oro·graph·i·cal·ly** \-fək(ə)lē\ *adv*

orographic rain *n* : the rain produced when a mountain deflects moisture-laden wind upward

orog·ra·phy \ōˈrägrəfē\ *n* -ES [ISV ¹*oro-* + *-graphy*; prob. orig. formed as F *orographie*] : a branch of physical geography that deals with mountains and mountain systems : OROLOGY

oro·hip·pus \ˌōrōˈhipəs\ *n, cap* [NL, fr. ¹*oro-* + *-hippus*] : a genus of very small American Eocene horses having four complete toes in front and three behind and having the tubercles of the molar teeth partially fused into a set of ridges

oro·hydrographic *or* **oro·hydrographical** \¦ōrō+\ *adj* [*orohydrography* ISV *orohydrography* + *-ic*; *orohydrographical* fr. *orohydrography* + *-ical*] : of or relating to orohydrography

oro·hydrography \"+\ *n* [ISV ¹*oro-* + *hydrography*] : a branch of hydrography that deals with the relations of mountains to drainage

oro·hydrologic *or* **oro·hydrological** \"+\ *adj* [¹*oro-* + *hydrologic, hydrological*] : OROHYDROGRAPHIC

oro·hydrology \"+\ *n* [¹*oro-* + *hydrology*] : OROHYDROGRAPHY

oro·ide \ˈōrəˌwīd\ *or* **ore·ide** \-rēˌīd\ *n* -S [F *oréide*, prob. fr. *or* gold (fr. MF) + *-éide* (fr. Gk *eidos* form) — more at OR, WISE] : an alloy chiefly of copper and zinc or tin that resembles gold in color and brilliancy and is used in making cheap jewelry

oro·kai·va \ˌōrəˈkīvə\ *n, pl* **orokaiva** *or* **orokaivas** *usu cap* **1** : a people of Papua **2** : a member of the Orokaiva people

oro·ke \əˈrōkē\ *n, pl* **oroke** *or* **orokes** *usu cap* **1** : a Tungus people of Sakhalin Island related to the Orochi of the Amur river mouth region **2** : a member of the Oroke people

oro·ko·lo \ˌōrəˈkō(ˌ)lō\ *n, pl* **orokolo** *or* **orokolos** *usu cap* **1 a** : a Papuan people of Papua **b** : a member of such people **2** : the language of the Orokolo people

orokon *usu cap, var of* OROCHI

or·o·log·i·cal \¦ōrə¦läjəkəl\ *adj* : of or relating to orology — **or·o·log·i·cal·ly** \-k(ə)lē\ *adv*

orol·o·gist \ōˈräləjəst\ *n* -S : a specialist in orology

orol·o·gy \-jē\ *n* -ES [¹*oro-* + *-logy*] : the science of mountains : OROGRAPHY

orom·e·ter \ōˈrämad·ə(r)\ *n* [¹*oro-* + *-meter*] : an aneroid barometer having a second scale that gives the approximate elevation above sea level of the place where the observation is made

or·o·met·ric \¦ōrə¦me·trik\ *adj* [¹*oro-* + *-metric*] **1** : of or relating to orometry **2** : of or relating to an orometer

orom·e·try \ōˈrämə·trē\ *n* -ES [ISV ¹*oro-* + *-metry*] : the measurement of mountains

oron·chon \ōˈränchən\ *or* **orun·chun** \-rən-\ *n, pl* **oronchon** *or* **oronchons** *or* **orunchun** *or* **orunchuns** *usu cap* **1** : a hunting people dwelling in Siberia and in small numbers over the border in Manchuria **2** : a member of the Oronchon people

oro·no·co *or* **oro·no·ko** \ˌōrəˈnō(ˌ)kō\ *also* **oro·noo·ko** \-nü(-\ *n* -S [perh. fr. *Orinoco* river, Venezuela; fr. the fact that it originated in South America] : a variety of tobacco

or·o·pe·sa \ˌōrəˈpāsə\ *n* -S [fr. *Oropesa*, British trawler that first used it] : one of a pair of torpedo-shaped floats towed one on each side by a minesweeper at a fixed distance to suspend the ends of the steel rope used to tear submerged mines from their moorings

oro·pharyngeal \¦ōr(ˌ)ō+\ *adj* [²*oro-* + *pharyngeal*] **1** : of or relating to the oropharynx **2** : of or relating to the mouth and pharynx

oro·pharynx \"+\ *n* [²*oro-* + *pharynx*] : the lower part of the pharynx that is continuous with the mouth and can be seen by direct vision

oroph·i·lous \(ˈ)ōˈräfələs\ *adj* [¹*oro-* + *-philous*] : preferring or thriving in a subalpine environment

oro·phyte \ˈōrəˌfīt\ *n* -S [¹*oro-* + *-phyte*] : a subalpine plant

oro·sius \ōˈrōzh(ē)əs, -ōsh(ē)əs, -ōzēəs, -ōsēəs\ *n, cap* [NL] : a genus of jassids of the Australian region that includes one (*O. argentatus*) which is a vector of several plant virus diseases

orot·ic acid \(ˈ)ō¦räd·ik-\ *n* [*orotic* prob. fr. *orot-* (fr. Gk *oros* whey) + *-ic* — more at SERUM] : a crystalline acid $C_4H_4N_2O_4$ that was first found in milk, is a growth factor for various microorganisms (as *Lactobacillus bulgaricus*), and is a precursor of the pyrimidines of nucleotides; 4-uracil-carboxylic acid

or·o·ti·ña \ˌōrəˈtēnyə\ *n, pl* **orotiña** *or* **orotiñas** *usu cap* **1** : a Chorotegan people of western Costa Rica **2** : a member of the Orotiña people

oro·tund \ˈōrəˌtənd, ˈär-, ˈȯr-\ *adj* [modif. of L *ore rotundo*, lit., with round mouth] **1** : marked by fullness, strength, and clearness of sound : SONOROUS — used esp. of the human voice ⟨an ~ voice like a preacher's or an actor's —Kenneth Roberts⟩ **2** : unduly full and strong in delivery or style : MAGNILOQUENT, POMPOUS, BOMBASTIC ⟨the surging and ~ utterances of *Leaves of Grass* —J.L.Lowes⟩ ⟨~ speeches about the full dinner pail —F.L.Allen⟩ **syn** see RESONANT

oro·tun·di·ty \ˌ‧‧ˈtəndəd·ē, -ndətē, -i\ *n* -ES : the quality or state of being orotund : orotund mode of intonation ⟨the ~ of the title —Francis Hackett⟩ ⟨orchestral ~ —Virgil Thomson⟩

oroya fever \ōˈrȯiə-\ *n, usu cap O* [*Oroya* fr. La *Oroya*, town in Peru where the disease causing it originally appeared] : the acute first stage of bartonellosis characterized by high fever and severe anemia

orp \ˈȯrp\ *vi* -ED/-ING/-S [prob. back-formation fr. *orpit*] *chiefly Scot* : to fret morosely

¹**or·phan** \ˈȯrfən, ˈȯ(ə)f-, *dial* -nt\ *n* -S [LL *orphanus*, fr. Gk *orphanos*; akin to OE *ierfe* inheritance, OHG *erbi*, ON *arfi*, Goth *arbi*, OIr *orbe* inheritance, L *orbus* orphaned, bereft, Skt *arbha* small, weak] **1 a** : a child deprived by death of both father and mother : parentless child **b** : HALF-ORPHAN **c** : a young animal that has lost its mother by death or desertion ⟨pails for feeding calves, bottles and rubber nipples for feeding ~s —*Better Feeding of Livestock*⟩ **2** : one deprived of some protection or advantage ⟨~s of the storm⟩ ⟨internationalists who are ~s of the . . . national organization —*New Republic*⟩

²**orphan** \"\ *adj* [LL *orphanus* orphan, n.] : that is an orphan ⟨a home for a delicate . . . ~ boy —Flora Thompson⟩ ⟨the ~ pigs . . . drink their synthetic milk —*Farmer's Weekly So. Africa*⟩

³**orphan** \"\ *vt* **orphaned; orphaned; orphaning** \-f(ə)niŋ\ **orphans 1** : to cause to become an orphan : deprive of parents ⟨as a boy on a Texas farm he had been ~*ed* by violence —*Saturday Rev.*⟩ ⟨~*ed* in babyhood, brought up . . . in public institutions —*Times Lit. Supp.*⟩ **2** : to deprive of some protection or advantage ⟨millions were ~*ed* when he died —*New Republic*⟩ ⟨~*ed* of their Primate —*Sunday Independent (Dublin)*⟩

or·phan·age \ˈȯrf(ə)nij, ˈȯ(ə)f-, -fnej\ *n* -S [¹*orphan* + *-age*] **1** : ORPHANHOOD ⟨unemployment, widowhood and ~ —*New Republic*⟩ **2** : an institution for the care of orphans or homeless children : an orphan asylum ⟨the ~ was considered a step forward in treating underprivileged children —N.K.Teeters & J.O.Reinemann⟩

or·phan·cy \-fənsē\ *n* -ES [¹*orphan* + *-cy*] *archaic* : ORPHANHOOD

orphaned mission *n* : a Christian mission cut off by war or some grave world crisis from the assistance of supporting missionary organizations

or·phan·hood \-fənˌhu̇d\ *n* : the quality or state of being an orphan ⟨draw from him the facts . . . including his place of abode, his ~ —Theodore Bonnet⟩

or·phan·ism \-fəˌnizəm\ *n* -S : ORPHANHOOD

or·phan·ize \-nīz\ *vt* -ED/-ING/-S [¹*orphan* + *-ize*] : to make an orphan of

orphans' court *n* : a court existing in some states of the U.S. orig. established to probate wills and grant letters of administration, appoint guardians for minors, and protect orphans and their property and now usu. given additional probate jurisdiction — called also *prerogative court* compare PROBATE COURT

or·phar·i·on \ȯ(r)ˈfa(a)rēən\ *or* **or·phe·o·re·on** \ˌȯ(r)fēˈōrēən\ *or* **or·phe·ri·an** \ȯ(r)ˈfirēən\ *n* -S [*orpharion* prob. fr. *Orpheus*, poet and musician in Greek mythology + *Arion*, 7th cent. B.C. semilegendary Greek poet; *orpheoreon* or *orpherian* alter. of *orpharion* — more at ARION] : an old musical instrument of the cittern family having six to nine pairs of metal strings played with a plectrum

orpharion

or·phe·an \ˈȯ(r)fēən, (ˈ)‧¦‧‧\ *adj, usu cap* [L *Orpheus* (fr. Gk *Orpheios*, fr. *Orpheus*, poet and musician in Greek mythology) + E *-an*] : of, relating to, or resembling Orpheus or his music : ORPHIC 3 ⟨~ lyre⟩

or·phé·on \ȯrfāōⁿ\ *n, pl* **orphéons** \-ōⁿ(z)\ [F, fr. *Orphée* Orpheus, fr. L *Orpheus*] : a French male choral society

or·phe·on·ist \ˈȯ(r)fēənəst\ *n* -S [F *orphéoniste*, fr. *orphéon* + *-iste* -ist] : a member of an orphéon

¹**or·phic** \ˈȯrfik, ˈȯ(ə)f-, -fēk\ *also* **or·phi·cal** \-fəkəl, -fēk-\ *adj* [*orphic* fr. L *Orphicus*, fr. Gk *Orphikos*, fr. *Orpheus*, Thracian poet and musician in Greek mythology who was a favorite of the muses and who symbolized the spirit of music + *-ikos* -ic; *orphical* fr. L *Orphicus* + E *-al*] **1** *usu cap* : of or relating to Orpheus or the literature, rites, or doctrines ascribed to him ⟨the Eleusinian, the Dionysian, and the *Orphic* rites were the most important mystery religions of Greece —G.E.Mylonas⟩ ⟨*Orphic* cults . . . influenced the sublime mysticism of Plato —Nathaniel Micklem⟩ ⟨the *Orphic* brotherhoods, wandering evangelists of a new life —E.D.Soper⟩ **2** *sometimes cap* : ESOTERIC ⟨~ doctrine⟩ ⟨~ expression⟩ : MYSTIC, ORACULAR ⟨~ sayings⟩ ⟨plunged into a sort of youthful ~ response to existence —Louise Bogan⟩ ⟨his critical style is often ~ . . . in its immaculate ardor —*N.Y. Herald Tribune Bk. Rev.*⟩ **3** : resembling the music or song ascribed to Orpheus : ENTRANCING ⟨the imagination sings ~ songs from the center of existence —Stephen Spender⟩ — **or·phi·cal·ly** \-fək(ə)lē, -fēk-, -li\ *adv*

²**orphic** \"\ *n* -S **1** : an Orphic song or hymn **2** [*orphism* + *-ic*] : an adherent of the Orphic rites or doctrines

or·phi·cism \ˈȯ(r)fəˌsizəm\ *n* -S *usu cap* [¹*orphic* + *-ism*] : ORPHISM

¹**or·phism** \ˈȯ(r)ˌfizəm\ *n* -S *usu cap* [*Orpheus*, poet and musician in Greek mythology who was regarded as founder of the mysteries + E *-ism*] : the religion of the Orphic mysteries with its initiating rites, doctrines of original sin and salvation, and belief in the purification of the soul through a cycle of reincarnation

²**orphism** \"\ *n* -S *often cap* [F *orphisme*, fr. *Orphée* Orpheus + *-isme* -ism] : an art movement or practice growing out of cubism about 1912 that is typified by the work of the French painter Delaunay and is characterized by an effort to achieve lyrical emphasis in totally abstract composition by means of brilliant color

or·phist \ˈȯrfəst, ˈȯ(ə)f-\ *n* -S *often cap* [F *orphisme* + E *-ist*] : an adherent or follower of the art theory, method, or practice of Orphism

or·phrey *or* **or·frey** \ˈȯrfrē\ *n* -S [ME *orfrey*, *orfray*, fr. MF *orfreis*, fr. ML *aurifrigium*, fr. *auri-* + L *Phrygium*, neut. of *Phrygius* Phrygian] **1 a** : elaborate embroidery (as of gold) **b** : a piece of such embroidery **2** : an ornamental border or embroidered band esp. on an ecclesiastical vestment

or·pi·ment \ˈȯ(r)pəmənt\ *n* -S [ME, fr. MF, fr. L *auripigmentum*, fr. *auri-* + *pigmentum* pigment — more at PIGMENT] **1 a** : an orange to yellow mineral As_2S_3 consisting of arsenic trisulfide and frequently associated with realgar **b** : artificially produced arsenic trisulfide **2** *or* **orpiment yellow** : a light to brilliant yellow that is darker than empire yellow — called also *king's yellow*, *mineral yellow*, *Montpellier yellow*, *patent yellow*, *quercitron*, *realgar yellow*, *royal yellow*, *Turner's yellow*, *Verona yellow*, *Veronese yellow*, *yellow daisy*

orpiment orange *n* : a strong to vivid orange that is yellower than Big Four yellow

orpiment red *n* : DUTCH ORANGE

or·pine \ˈȯrpən\ *n* -S [ME *orpin*, fr. MF, fr. *orpiment*; prob. fr. the yellow blossoms of a common species (*Sedum acre*)] : a glabrous Eurasian sedum (*Sedum telephium*) having clustered erect stems bearing terminal cymes of reddish purple flowers and numerous fleshy alternate leaves, occurring in No. America in cultivation or locally as an escape, and formerly used in folk medicine; *broadly* : SEDUM 2

orpine family *n* : CRASSULACEAE

orping *pres part of* ORP

or·ping·ton \ˈȯ(r)piŋtən\ *n* [fr. *Orpington*, Kent, England, where the breed originated] **1** *usu cap* : an English breed of large deep-chested broad-backed domestic fowls with short unfeathered legs and usu. single combs that occurs in several color varieties of both standard and bantam types of which the buff is perhaps best known **2** -S *often cap* : a bird of the Orpington breed — usu. used with a qualifying term indicating the color variety

or·pit \ˈȯrpət\ *adj* [origin unknown] *Scot* : FRETFUL

orps *pres 3d sing of* ORP

or·ra *or* **or·row** \ˈärə\ *adj* [origin unknown] **1** *Scot* **a** : ODD, OCCASIONAL ⟨an ~ job here and there⟩ **b** : consisting of odds and ends : MISCELLANEOUS **2** *Scot* : not occupied or employed ⟨your ~ hours⟩ **3** *Scot, of a person* : IDLE, WORTHLESS

orra man *n, Scot* : a farm laborer hired to do odd jobs

or·rery \ˈȯrərē, ˈärə-\ *n* -ES [after Charles Boyle †1731 4th Earl of Orrery] **1** : an apparatus that illustrates the relative positions and motions of bodies in the solar system by rotation and revolution of balls moved by wheelwork **2** : a mechanical device incorporated into a clock to indicate the relative movements of some planets and satellites

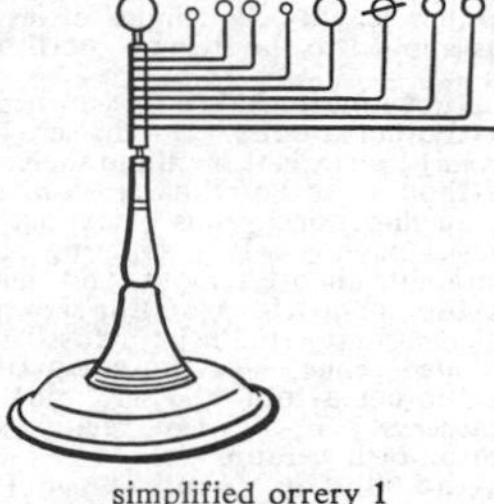

simplified orrery 1

¹**or·ris** \ˈȯrəs, ˈär-\ *n* -ES [prob. alter. of ME *ireos*, fr. OIt, modif. of L *iris* — more at IRIS] **1** : FLORENTINE IRIS **2** : the fragrant rootstock of the Florentine iris

²**orris** \"\ *n* -ES [perh. alter. (influenced by *arras*) of earlier *orfrays*, pl. of *orfray* orphrey] : gold or silver lace or braid used on 18th century clothing; *also* : such lace or braid used as a galloon for upholstery

orris oil *also* **orrisroot oil** *n* : a yellowish semisolid fragrant essential oil containing free myristic acid and irones as its principal components, obtained from the roots of the Florentine iris, and used chiefly as a flavoring material and in perfumes

orrisroot \"‧‚‧\ *n* [¹*orris* + *root*] : the fragrant rootstock of any of several European plants of the genus *Iris* (esp. *I. pallida*) used in pulverized form in perfumery and medicine and as an ingredient of sachet and tooth powders

ors *pl of* OR

-ors *pl of* -OR

ORS *abbr* owner's risk of shifting

or·sat apparatus \ˈȯrsət-, -ˌsat-\ *n, usu cap O* [*orsat* of unknown origin] : an apparatus for gas analysis that consists essentially of a measuring burette, a connected series of pipettes containing selective absorbents, and usu. a combustion pipette

orse *abbr* otherwise

or·seille \(ˈ)ȯrˈsā(ə)l, -sā,-sel\ *or* **or·selle** \-sel,-sā\ *n* -s [F *orseille*] : ARCHIL

or·sel·lin·ic acid \ˌȯ(r)səˈlinik-\ *n* [*orsellinic* ISV *orsellin-* (fr. *orselle* + *-in*, chemical suffix) + *-ic*] : a crystalline acid $C_6H_2(OH)_2(CH_3)COOH$ found chiefly in combination in certain lichens; 4,6-dihydroxy-*ortho*-toluic acid — called also *ortho-orsellinic acid;* compare LECANORIC ACID

[1]**ort** \ˈȯ(ə)rt\ *n* -s [ME, prob. fr. MD *orte*] **1 :** a morsel left at a meal : LEAVING, REFUSE — usu. used in pl. ⟨ate their meals without forks and covered up the ~s with rushes —Frederic Harrison⟩ **2 :** SCRAP, BIT — usu. used in pl. ⟨ideological ~s and fragments —David Daiches⟩

[2]**ort** \"\ *vt* -ED/-ING/-S [prob. fr. MD *orten* to leave over, fr. *orte* leftover, ort] *chiefly Scot* : to select by rejecting what is unsatisfactory

or·tal·i·dae \ȯ(r)ˈtaləˌdē\ [NL, fr. *Ortalis*, type genus + *-idae*] *syn of* OTITIDAE

or·ta·lis \ˈȯ(r)dᵊləs\ *n, cap* [NL, fr. Gk, fowl; akin to Gk *ornis* bird — more at ERNE] : a genus of guans comprising the chachalacas

ort·er·de \ˈȯrd·ˌerdə\ *n* -s [G, fr. *ort* site, place (fr. OHG, point) + *erde* earth (fr. OHG *erda*) — more at ODD, EARTH] : a soil horizon in which there is little or no cementation between the iron and the organic matter

or·tet \ˈȯrˌtet, ⸗ˈ⸗\ *n* -s [L *ortus* origin + E *-et;* akin to L *origin-, origo* origin — more at ORIGIN] : the original plant from which the members of a clone have descended — compare RAMET

orth- *or* **ortho-** *comb form* [ME, fr. MF, straight, right, true, fr. L, fr. Gk, fr. *orthos;* akin to Goth ga*wrisqan* to bring fruit, Skt *ūrdhva* upright, high, *vardhate* he increases] **1 a :** straight : upright : vertical ⟨*ortho*ceras⟩ ⟨*orth*al⟩ ⟨*ortho*grade⟩ ⟨*ortho*symmetric⟩ **b :** exact : parallel ⟨*ortho*diagram⟩ ⟨*ortho*-cousin⟩ ⟨*ortho*dome⟩ **2 :** correct : corrective ⟨*ortho*metry⟩ ⟨*orth*odontia⟩ **3 a :** an acid in the highest hydrated or hydroxylated form known either in the free state or in salts or esters ⟨*ortho*arsenic acid⟩ ⟨*ortho*formic acid⟩ — compare META- 4 c, PYR- 2a **b** (1) **:** the relation of two neighboring positions in the benzene ring (2) *ortho-, usu ital* **:** a derivative in which two substituting groups occupy such positions — abbr. *o-* ⟨*ortho*⸗xylene or *o*-xylene is 1,2-dimethyl-benzene⟩; compare META- 4b, PARA- 2b **4 :** derived from igneous rock — in the name of a metamorphic rock ⟨*ortho*gneiss⟩ ⟨*ortho*site⟩; compare PARA-

or·thal \ˈȯrthəl\ *adj* [*orth-* + *-al*] *of mastication* : effected by vertical motion — compare PALINAL, PROAL, PROPALINAL

or·tha·nil·ic acid \ˌȯ(r)thəˈnilik-\ *n* [*orth-* + sulf*anilic* acid] : a crystalline sulfonic acid $H_2NC_6H_4SO_3H$ isomeric with sulfanilic acid; *ortho*-amino-benzenesulfonic acid

or·the·zia \ȯ(r)ˈthēzh(ē)ə\ *n, cap* [NL, prob. fr. J. A. D*orthes* †1794 Fr. physician + NL *-ia*] : a genus of coccids (the type of the family Ortheziidae) including species that attack greenhouse plants throughout the world

or·thi·an \ˈȯ(r)thēən\ *adj* [Gk *orthios* steep, high-pitched, fr. *orthos* straight + E *-an*] : characterized by high pitch — used of a style of singing or a tune

or·thic \ˈȯrthik\ *adj* [*orth-* + *-ic*] : of or relating to the altitudes of a triangle

or·thi·con \ˈȯ(r)thəˌkän\ *n* -s [ISV *orth-* + *-icon* (fr. *iconoscope*)] : a camera tube similar to but more sensitive than an iconoscope in which the charges are scanned by a low-velocity beam to eliminate the secondary emission that reduces picture quality at low light levels

or·thid \ˈȯrthəd\ *n* -s [NL *Orthidae*, fr. *Orthis* + *-idae*] : a brachiopod of the genus *Orthis* or of the family Orthidae

or·this \-əs\ *n, cap* [NL, fr. Gk *orthos* straight; fr. the valves being hinged along a straight line] : a genus (the type of the family Orthidae) of articulate brachiopods abundant in the Paleozoic

or·thite \-ˌthīt\ *n* -s [G *orthit*, fr. *orth-* + *-it* -ite; fr. the fact that it forms straight radii] : allanite esp. when occurring in slender prismatic crystals — **or·thit·ic** \(ˈ)⸗ˈthid·ik\ *adj*

[1]**or·tho** \ˈȯr(ˌ)thō, ˈȯ(ə)(ˌ)-\ *adj* [*orth-*] **1 :** derived from or being an acid in the highest hydrated or hydroxylated form known — compare ORTH- 3a **2 :** relating to, characterized by, or being two neighboring positions in the benzene ring — compare ORTH- 3b **3 :** of, relating to, or being a diatomic molecule (as of hydrogen) in which the nuclei of the atoms are spinning in the same direction — opposed to *para* ⟨*ortho*⸗para conversion⟩

[2]**ortho** \"\ *adj* [by shortening] : ORTHOCHROMATIC

ortho- — see ORTH-

or·tho·arsenate \ˌȯ(r)(ˌ)thō+\ *n* [*orthoarsenic* (in *orthoarsenic acid*) + *-ate*] : a salt or ester of orthoarsenic acid

or·tho·arsenic acid \"+...-\ *n* [*orth-* + *arsenic acid*] : the arsenic acid $H_3AsO_4 \cdot \frac{1}{2}H_2O$

or·tho·axis \ˌȯ(r)(ˌ)thō+\ *n* [*orth-* + *axis*] : the diagonal or lateral axis that is at right angles with the vertical axis in the monoclinic system of crystallization

or·tho·benzoquinone \"+\ *n* [*orth-* + *benzoquinone*] : QUINONE 1b — written systematically with ital. *ortho-* or *o-*

or·tho·boric acid \"+...-\ *n* [*orth-* + *boric acid*] : BORIC ACID a

or·tho·carbonic acid \ˌȯ(r)(ˌ)thō+...-\ *n* [ISV *orth-* + *carbonic*] : a hypothetical acid H_4CO_4 or $C(OH)_4$ known in the form of its esters

orthocarbonic ester *n* : an ester of orthocarbonic acid; *esp* : the liquid tetraethyl ester $C(OC_2H_5)_4$ of pleasant odor made by reaction of sodium ethoxide with chloropicrin

or·tho·carpus \ˌȯ(r)thə+\ *n, cap* [NL, fr. *orth-* + *-carpus*] : a genus of chiefly Californian herbs (family Scrophulariaceae) having alternate leaves and showy varicolored flowers and having the 4-cleft calyx and bilabiate corolla both tubular — see OWL'S CLOVER

or·tho·center *also* **or·tho·centre** \"+\ *n* [ISV *orth-* + *center, centre*] : the common intersection of the three altitudes of a triangle or of the several altitudes of a polyhedron provided these latter exist and meet in a point

[1]**or·tho·cephalic** \ˌȯ(r)(ˌ)thō+\ *or* **or·tho·ceph·a·lous** \ˌȯ(r)thəˈsefələs\ *adj* [NL *orthocephalus* orthocephalic person (fr. *orth-* + *-cephalus*) + E *-ic*] : having a relatively low head with a length-height index of less than 75 or of less than 63 as applied to the living — **or·tho·ceph·a·ly** \ˌȯ(r)thəˈsefəlē\ *n* -ES

[2]**orthocephalic** \"\ *n* -s : an orthocephalic person

or·tho·cer·a·cone \ˌȯ(r)thəˈserəˌkōn\ *n* [NL *Orthoceras* + E *cone*] : a straight nautiloid shell resembling that of *Orthoceras*

or·thoc·er·as \ȯ(r)ˈthäsərəs\ *n, cap* [NL, fr. *orth-* + *-ceras*] : an ill-defined genus of extinct nautiloid cephalopod mollusks having a long tapering shell that is nearly or quite straight, almost smooth, and many-chambered

or·tho·cer·a·tite \ˌȯ(r)thəˈserəˌtīt\ *n* -s [NL *Orthocerat-, Orthoceras* + E *-ite*] : a fossil nautiloid of *Orthoceras* or a related genus — **or·tho·cer·a·tit·ic** \ˌ⸗⸗ˌ⸗⸗ˈtid·ik\ *adj*

or·tho·cer·a·toid \ˌ⸗⸗ˈserəˌtȯid\ *adj* [NL *Orthocerat-, Orthoceras* + E *-oid*] : of, relating to, or resembling *Orthoceras* or an orthoceratite

or·tho·chlorite \ˌȯ(r)thə+\ *n* [ISV *orth-* + *chlorite*] : a distinctly crystalline form of chlorite (as clinochlore) — opposed to *leptochlorite*

or·tho·chromatic \"+\ *adj* [ISV *orth-* + *chromatic;* prob. orig. formed as F *orthochromatique*] **1 :** of, relating to, or producing tone values of light and shade in a photograph that correspond to the tones in nature **2** *of a photographic material* : sensitive to all colors except red

or·tho·clase \ˈȯ(r)thəˌklās, -āz\ *n* -s [G *orthoklas*, fr. *orth-* + *-klas* -clase] : a mineral $KAlSi_3O_8$ consisting of a monoclinic polymorph of common potassium feldspar with sodium often in place of some of the potassium and occurring usu. colorless to white, cream-yellow, or flesh-red (hardness 6, sp. gr. 2.57) — see FELDSPAR, MOONSTONE

or·tho·clas·tic \ˌ⸗⸗ˈklastik\ *adj* [G *orthoklastisch*, fr. *orth-* + *-klastisch* -clastic] : cleaving in directions at right angles to each other — used orig. of the monoclinic feldspars

ortho-cousin \ˌȯ(r)thə+\ *n* : PARALLEL COUSIN

or·tho·cra·nic \ˌȯ(r)thəˈkrānik\ *adj* [G *orthokran* (fr. *orth-* + Gk *kranion* skull) + E *-ic* — more at CRANIUM] : ORTHOCEPHALIC — **or·tho·cra·ny** \-nē\ *n* -ES

or·tho·cresol \ˌȯ(r)thə+\ *n* [ISV *orth-* + *cresol*] : the ortho isomer of cresol — written systematically with ital. *ortho-* or *o-*

or·tho·diagonal \ˌȯ(r)(ˌ)thō+\ *n* [ISV *orth-* + *diagonal*] : ORTHOAXIS

or·tho·diagram \ˌȯ(r)thə+\ *n* [ISV *orth-* + *diagram*] : a tracing showing the outer contours and exact size of an organ (as the heart) made by illuminating the edge of the organ with parallel X rays through a small movable aperture and marking the outer edge of the shadow cast upon a fluoroscopic screen

or·tho·diagraphic \"+\ *adj* [*orth-* + *diagraphic*] : of, relating to, or by means of orthodiagrams — **or·tho·diagraph·ically** \"+\ *adv*

or·tho·dichlorobenzene \"+\ *n* [*orth-* + *dichlorobenzene*] : a volatile oily liquid compound $C_6H_4Cl_2$ made by chlorination of benzene and used chiefly as a solvent and cleaner, heat⸗transfer medium, and insecticide — written systematically with ital. *ortho-* or *o-*

or·tho·dolichocephalic \ˌȯ(r)(ˌ)thō+\ *adj* [*orth-* + *dolichocephalic*] : having a relatively long head of medium height

or·tho·dome \ˈȯ(r)thəˌdōm\ *n* [ISV *orth-* + *dome*] : the dome of a crystal having planes parallel to the orthoaxis — compare BRACHYDOME, CLINODOME, MACRODOME

or·tho·don·tia \ˌȯ(r)thəˈdänch(ē)ə\ *n* -s [NL, fr. *orth-* + *-odontia*] : ORTHODONTICS

or·tho·don·tic \ˌ⸗⸗ˈdäntik, -tēk\ *adj* [ISV *orthodont-* (fr. NL *orthodontia*) + *-ic*] : of or relating to orthodontics ⟨~ studies⟩ : involving the methods of orthodontics ⟨~ care of facial abnormalities⟩

or·tho·don·tics \ˌ⸗⸗ˈ⸗tiks, -tēks\ *n pl but sing or pl in constr* [NL *orthodont*ia + E *-ics*] : a branch of dentistry that deals with irregularities of the teeth and abnormalities of their relations with surrounding parts and with the correction of these esp. by means of braces and mechanical aids

or·tho·don·tist \ˌ⸗⸗ˈ⸗təst\ *n* -s [NL *orthodont*ia + E *-ist*] : a specialist in orthodontics

[1]**or·tho·dox** \ˈȯ(r)thəˌdäks\ *adj* [MF or LL; MF *orthodoxe*, fr. LL *orthodoxus*, fr. LGk *orthodoxos*, fr. Gk *orthodoxein* to have the right opinion, fr. *ortho-* straight, right, true + *-doxein* (fr. *doxa* opinion, belief, reputation) — more at ORTH-, DOXOLOGY] **1 :** marked by conformity to doctrines or practices esp. in religion that are held as right or true by some authority, standard, or tradition ⟨the simple security of the old ~ assumptions has vanished —A.N.Whitehead⟩: as **a :** conforming to the Christian faith as formulated in the church creeds and confessions ⟨an ~ Christian⟩ **b :** according to or congruous with the doctrines of Scripture as interpreted in some standard (as the creed of a church or decree of a council) ⟨~ belief⟩ ⟨an ~ book⟩ — contrasted with *heretical* and *heterodox* **2** *usu cap* : of, relating to, or characterizing a particular religious organization or group (as the Eastern Orthodox Church, the Sunnites of Islam, Hindus acknowledging the authority of the Vedas, or the conservative Friends as distinguished from the Hicksite Friends) **3 a :** of, relating to, or characterizing the dominant or officially approved form of something ⟨~ Marxism⟩ ⟨the ~ form of a text⟩ ⟨~ economic theory⟩ ⟨the ~ approach⟩ **b :** CONSERVATIVE ⟨very ~ in her belief and practices⟩ ⟨simple, dark, ~ clothes —*English Digest*⟩ **c :** CONVENTIONAL ⟨~ routes to Europe —*Geog. Jour.*⟩ ⟨~ in treatment and subject —Charles Lee⟩ —**or·tho·dox·ness** *n* -ES

[2]**orthodox** \"\ *n, pl* **orthodox** *or* **orthodoxes** [ML *orthodoxus*, fr. LL, orthodox, adj.] **1 :** one that is orthodox **2** *usu cap* : a member of the Eastern Orthodox Church

or·tho·dox·al \ˌ⸗⸗ˈdäksəl\ *adj* [LL *orthodox*us + E *-al*] : ORTHODOX — **or·tho·dox·al·i·ty** \ˌ⸗⸗ˌ⸗ˈsaləd·ē\ *n* -ES — **or·tho·dox·al·ly** \ˌ⸗⸗ˈ⸗səlē\ *adv*

or·tho·dox·ian \ˌ⸗⸗ˈdäksēən\ *n* -s : an adherent of or believer in orthodoxy

or·tho·dox·i·cal \ˌ⸗⸗ˈdäksəkəl\ *adj* [LL *orthodox*us + E *-ical*] : ORTHODOX — **or·tho·dox·i·cal·ly** \-k(ə)lē\ *adv*

or·tho·dox·ism \ˈ⸗⸗ˌdäkˌsizəm\ *n* -s : ORTHODOXY — often used disparagingly

orthodox jew *n, usu cap O&J* : an adherent of Orthodox Judaism

orthodox judaism *n, cap O&J* : Judaism that adheres to Biblical law as interpreted in the authoritative rabbinic tradition as the final and complete revelation of divine law and that seeks to observe all the practices commanded in it — compare CONSERVATIVE JUDAISM, RECONSTRUCTIONISM, REFORM JUDAISM

or·tho·dox·ly *adv* : in an orthodox manner

orthodox sunday *n, usu cap O&S* : FEAST OF ORTHODOXY

or·tho·doxy \ˈȯ(r)thəˌdäksē, -si\ *n* -ES [LL *orthodoxia*, fr. Gk, right opinion, fr. *orthodoxein* to have the right opinion + *-ia* -y] **1 :** the quality or state of being orthodox : conformity to an official formulation of truth esp. in religious belief or practice ⟨make it my object to teach thinking, not ~ —Bertrand Russell⟩ — contrasted with *heresy* and *heterodoxy* **2 :** an orthodox belief or practice ⟨the new astronomy . . . one factor in shaking traditional *orthodoxies* —Douglas Bush⟩ **3** *usu cap* [MGk *orthodoxia*, fr. Gk] : the system of faith, practice, and discipline of the Eastern Orthodox Church

or·tho·drom·ic \ˌ⸗⸗ˈdrämik\ *adj* : of or relating to orthodromy

or·tho·drom·ics \ˌ⸗⸗ˈ⸗miks\ *n pl but sing or pl in constr* [F *orthodromique*, fr. *orthodromie* orthodromy + *-ique* -ic] : ORTHODROMY

or·thod·ro·my \ˈȯ(r)thəˌdrōmē, ȯ(r)ˈthädrəmē\ *n* -ES [F *orthodromie*, fr. *orthodrom-* (fr. Gk *orth-* + *-dromos* -drome) + *-ie* -y] : the act or art of great-circle sailing

or·tho·ep·ic \ˌȯ(r)thəˈwepik\ *also* **or·tho·ep·i·cal** \-pəkəl\ *adj* : of or relating to orthoepy ⟨~ evidence —Harold Whitehall⟩ ⟨the terminology of civic administration seems to abound in ~ pitfalls —J.T.Winterich⟩ — **or·tho·ep·i·cal·ly** \-pək(ə)lē\ *adv*

or·tho·epist \ˈȯ(r)thəˌwepəst, ȯ(r)ˈthōəp-\ *n* -s : a person who is skilled in orthoepy — **or·tho·epis·tic** \ˌȯ(r)thəˌweˈpistik, (ˌ)ȯ(r)ˌthōəˈp-\ *adj*

or·tho·epy \ˈȯ(r)thəˌwepē, ȯ(r)ˈthōəpē\ *n* -ES [NL *orthoepia*, fr. Gk *orthoepeia*, fr. *orth-* + *-epeia* (fr. *epos* word, speech) — more at VOICE] **1 :** the customary pronunciation of a language **2 :** the study of the pronunciation of a language

ortho ester *n* [[1]*ortho*] : an ester of an ortho acid; *esp* : an ester $RC(OR')_3$ (as orthoformic ester) of an ortho-carboxylic acid

or·tho·ferrosilite \ˌȯ(r)(ˌ)thō+\ *n* [*orth-* + *ferrosilite*] : a mineral $FeSiO_3$ consisting of iron silicate in the orthorhombic form — compare CLINOFERROSILITE, FERROSILITE

or·tho·for·mic acid \ˌȯrthəˈfȯrmik-\ *n* [ISV *orth-* + *-form* + *-ic*] : a hypothetical acid $HC(OH)_3$ known in the form of its esters

orthoformic ester *n* : an ester of orthoformic acid; *esp* : the liquid triethyl ester $HC(OC_2H_5)_3$ of pungent odor made by reaction of sodium ethoxide with either chloroform or carbon tetrachloride and used in making acetals

or·tho·genesis \ˌȯ(r)thə+\ *n* [NL, fr. *orth-* + *genesis*] **1 :** variation of organisms in successive generations along some predestined line resulting in progressive evolutionary trends independent of natural selection or other external factors — called also *determinate evolution;* compare ORTHOSELECTION **2 a :** the theory that social evolution takes place in the same direction and through the same stages in every culture despite differing external conditions **b :** variation of culture in a particular direction in accordance with internal predetermining factors rather than through external contact

or·tho·genetic \ˌȯ(r)thə+\ *adj* [ISV *orthogenet-* (fr. NL *orthogenesis*) + *-ic*] : of, relating to, or exhibiting orthogenesis ⟨the theory of ~ evolution —B.R.Redman⟩ — **or·tho·genetically** \"+\ *adv*

or·tho·gen·ic \ˌ⸗⸗ˈjenik\ *adj* [ISV *orthogenesis* + *-ic*] **1 :** ORTHOGENETIC **2** [*orth-* + *-genic*] : of, relating to, or devoted to the rehabilitation of emotionally disturbed mentally retarded children

or·tho·geosyncline \ˌȯ(r)thə+\ *n* [*orth-* + *geosyncline*] : a linear geosyncline between cratons — compare PARAGEOSYNCLINE

or·thog·na·thism \ȯ(r)ˈthägnəˌthizəm\ *or* **or·thog·na·thy** \-nəthē\ *n, pl* **orthognathisms** *or* **orthognathies** [*orthognathism* ISV *orthognathous* + *-ism; orthognathy* ISV *orthognathous* + *-y*] : the quality or state of being orthognathous

or·thog·na·thous \(ˈ)ȯ(r)ˈthägnəthəs\ *also* **or·thognath·ic** \ˌȯ(r)thə(g)ˈnathik, -ˌthägˈn-\ *adj* [*orthognathous* ISV *orth-* + *-gnathous; orthognathic* fr. *orth-* + *gnathic*] : having straight jaws : not having the lower parts of the face projecting

or·tho·gneiss \ˈȯ(r)thə+ˌ-\ *n* [G *orthogneis*, fr. *orth-* + *gneis* gneiss — more at GNEISS] : gneiss derived from an igneous rock

[1]**or·thog·o·nal** \(ˈ)ȯ(r)ˈthägənᵊl\ *adj* [MF, fr. L *orthogonius* orthogonal (fr. Gk *orthogōnios*, fr. *orth-* + *-gōnios*, fr. *gōnia* angle) + MF *-al* — more at -GON] **1 :** lying or intersecting at right angles : RECTANGULAR, RIGHT-ANGLED ⟨wind and sea may displace the ship's center of gravity along three ~ axes —C.C.Shaw⟩ ⟨in ~ cutting, the cutting edge is perpendicular to the direction of tool travel —M.E.Merchant & Hans Ernst⟩ **2 a :** mutually perpendicular ⟨two vector functions the integral of whose scalar product throughout space is zero are ~⟩ **b :** completely independent ⟨two statistical variables having zero correlation are ~⟩ ⟨mental ability may be classified into several ~ . . . factors —O.D.Duncan⟩ — **or·thog·o·nal·ly** \-gənᵊlē, -gnəlē\ *adv*

[2]**orthogonal** \"\ *n* -s : an imaginary line at right angles to wave crests in oceanography

orthogonal functions *n pl* : two mathematical functions such that with suitable limits the definite integral of their product is zero

or·thog·o·nal·i·ty \(ˌ)ȯ(r)ˌthägəˈnaləd·ē\ *n* -ES [ISV *orthogonal-* (fr. [1]*orthogonal*) + *-ity*] : the quality or state of being orthogonal

or·thog·o·nal·ize \⸗ˈ⸗gənᵊlˌīz\ *vt* -ED/-ING/-S [[1]*orthogonal* + *-ize*] : to make orthogonal

orthogonal projection *n* : ORTHOGRAPHIC PROJECTION 1

orthogonal system *n* : a system of curves or surfaces consisting of two families whose components where they intersect are mutually perpendicular (as the lines of force and the equipotential surfaces in an electrostatic field)

orthogonal trajectory *n* : a mathematical curve which cuts every curve of a given set at right angles

or·tho·grade \ˈȯ(r)thəˌgrād\ *adj* [*orth-* + *-grade*] : walking with the body upright or vertical — compare PRONOGRADE

or·tho·graph \-raf,-räf\ *n* [fr. *orthographic*, after such pairs as E *autographic: autograph*] : an orthographic projection plan, elevation, or section esp. of a building

or·thog·ra·pher \ȯ(r)ˈthägrəfə(r)\ *n* -s [LL *orthographus* orthographer (fr. L *orth-* + LL *-graphus* -grapher) + E *-er*] : a person who is skilled in orthography : an expert in spelling

or·tho·graph·ic \ˌȯ(r)thəˈgrafik, -fēk\ *also* **or·tho·graph·i·cal** \-fəkəl, -fēk-\ *adj* [*orthography* + *-ic* or *-ical*] : characterized by perpendicular lines or right angles : ORTHOGONAL **2 a :** of or relating to orthography **b :** correct in spelling : spelled in the traditional way of writing — **or·tho·graph·i·cal·ly** \-fək(ə)lē, -fēk-, -li\ *adv*

orthographic projection *n* **1 :** projection in which the projecting lines are perpendicular to the plane of projection — called also *orthogonal projection* **2 :** a map projection of one half the globe as it would appear to a camera centered on any point desired from an infinite distance being true to scale at the center only

or·thog·ra·phist \ȯ(r)ˈthägrəfəst\ *n* -s : a specialist in orthography

or·thog·ra·phize \-ˌfīz\ *vt* -ED/-ING/-S [*orthography* + *-ize*] **1 a :** to spell correctly or according to usage **b :** to correct in regard to spelling **2 :** to devise a writing system for (a language)

or·thog·ra·phy \ȯ(r)ˈthägrəfē, -fi\ *n* -ES [ME *ortografie*, fr. MF, fr. L *orthographia*, fr. Gk, fr. *orth-* + *-graphia* (fr. *graphein* to write + *-ia* -y) — more at CARVE] **1 a :** the art of writing words with the proper letters according to standard usage : correct spelling — opposed to *cacography* **b :** a method of representing the sounds of a language by written or printed symbols; *also* : a complete set of such symbols **2 :** the part of language study that treats of the letters and of the art of spelling **3** [L *orthographia*, fr. Gk] : ORTHOGRAPHIC PROJECTION

or·tho·hexagonal axes \ˌȯ(r)(ˌ)thō+. . .-\ *n pl* [*orthohexagonal* fr. *orth-* + *hexagonal*] : a set of orthogonal axes with a fixed ratio ($1:\sqrt{3}$) between two of them used occas. in descriptions of and in calculations for hexagonal or trigonal crystals

ortho-hydrogen \ˌȯ(r)thə+\ *n* : molecular hydrogen in which the two hydrogen nuclei are spinning in the same direction — compare PARA-HYDROGEN ⟨ordinary hydrogen gas comprises an equilibrium mixture of three parts of *ortho-hydrogen* (with parallel nuclear spin) to one part of para-hydrogen (with antiparallel nuclear spin) —Otto Reinmuth⟩

or·tho·kinesis \"+\ *n* [NL, fr. *orth-* + *kinesis*] : random movement (as of a planarian) in response to a stimulus

or·tho·metopic \"+\ *adj* [*orth-* + *metopic*] : having or characterized by a vertical forehead

or·tho·metric \"+\ *adj* [ISV *orth-* + *metric*] : ORTHOGONAL

or·thom·e·try \ȯ(r)ˈthämə·trē\ *n* -ES [*orth-* + Gk *-metria* measurement, meter, fr. *metrein* to measure + *-ia* -y — more at MEASURE] : the art of correct versification

or·tho·mor·pha \ˌȯrthəˈmȯrfə\ *n, cap* [NL, fr. *orth-* + *-morpha*] : a genus of millipedes containing the common European greenhouse millipede (*O. gracilis*)

or·tho·mor·phic \ˌ⸗⸗ˈ⸗fik\ *adj* [F *orthomorphique*, fr. *orth-* + *-morphique* -morphic] : CONFORMAL 2

or·tho·mor·phism \ˌ⸗⸗ˈ⸗ˌfizəm\ *n* -s [F *orthomorphisme*, prob. fr. *orthomorphique* + *-isme* -ism] : CONFORMALITY

or·tho·nec·ti·da \ˌ⸗⸗ˈnektədə\ *n pl, cap* [NL, fr. *orth-* + *nect-* + *-ida*] : an order or other division of Mesozoa comprising a number of rare parasites of the tissues and cavities of various invertebrates that alternate between an asexual plasmodial generation and a sexual generation resembling the nematogens of dicyemids but having numerous internal cells — compare DICYEMIDA

ortho nitraniline orange *n, often cap both Os & N* [[1]*ortho*] : an organic pigment — see DYE table I (under *Pigment Orange 2*)

ortho nitroaniline \ˌȯ(r)(ˌ)thō+\ *n* [ISV *orth-* + *nitroaniline*] : NITROANILINE b

or·tho·non \ˈȯ(r)thəˌnän, -ˌnən\ *n* -s [*orth-* + *nonhalation*] : a photographic material sensitive only to violet and blue — compare COLOR-BLIND 2

or·tho·panchromatic \ˌȯ(r)(ˌ)thō+\ *adj* [ISV *orth-* + *panchromatic*] *of a panchromatic material* : having a color sensitivity most nearly matching that of the eye

or·tho·pe·dic *also* **or·tho·pae·dic** \ˌȯ(r)thəˈpēdik, -dēk\ *adj* [F *orthopédique*, fr. *orthopédie* orthopedics (fr. *orth-* + *-pédie* — fr. Gk *paid-, pais* child — + *-ie* -y) + *-ique* -ic — more at FEW] **1 :** of, relating to, or employed in orthopedics **2 :** involving or affected by deformities or crippling ⟨an ~ condition⟩ ⟨~ children⟩

or·tho·pe·dics *also* **or·tho·pae·dics** \ˌ⸗⸗ˈ⸗diks, -dēks\ *n pl but sing or pl in constr* [*orthopedic, orthopaedic* + *-s*] : the correction or prevention of deformities esp. of the skeletal structures in children

or·tho·pe·dist *also* **or·tho·pae·dist** \-dəst\ *n* -s [F *orthopédiste*, fr. *orthopédie* orthopedics + *-iste* -ist] : one that practices orthopedics

or·tho·periodic acid \ˌȯ(r)(ˌ)thō+. . .-\ *n* [*orth-* + *periodic acid*] : PERIODIC ACID a

or·tho·pho·ria \ˌȯ(r)thəˈfōrēə\ *n* -s [NL, fr. *orth-* + *-phoria*] : a normal condition of balance of the ocular muscles of the two eyes in which their visual lines meet at the object toward which they are directed

or·tho·phosphate \ˌȯ(r)thə+\ *n* [*orthophosphoric* acid + *-ate*] : a salt or ester of orthophosphoric acid — called also *phosphate*

or·tho·phosphoric acid \"+. . .-\ *n* [*orthophosphoric* ISV *orth-* + *phosphoric*] : PHOSPHORIC ACID 1a — distinguished from *metaphosphoric acid* and *pyrophosphoric acid*

or·tho·pinacoid \ˌȯ(r)thə+\ *n* [ISV *orth-* + *pinacoid*] : a pinacoid whose planes are parallel to the ortho and vertical axes in a monoclinic crystal

or·thop·nea *also* **or·thop·noea** \ȯ(r)ˈthäpnēə *also* ˌȯ(r)ˌthäpˈnēə *or* ˌȯ(r)thəˈp'n-\ *n* -s [L *orthopnoea*, fr. Gk *orthopnoia*, fr. *orth-* + *-pnoia* -pnea] : inability to breathe except in an upright position (as in congestive heart failure) — **or·thop·ne·ic** *also* **or·thop·noe·ic** \¦=(ˌ)=¦=ik\ *adj*

or·thop·o·da \ȯ(r)'thäpədə\ [NL, fr. *orth-* + *-poda*] *syn of* ORNITHISCHIA

or·tho·praxy \'ȯ(r)thəˌpraksē\ *n* -ES [*orth-* + Gk *praxis* doing, practice + E *-y* (as in *orthodoxy*) — more at PRAXIS] : correctness of practice or a body of practices accepted or recognized as correct ⟨religious ~⟩

or·tho·psychiatric *also* **or·tho·psychiatrical** \¦ȯ(r)(ˌ)thō+\ *adj* : of or relating to orthopsychiatry

or·tho·psychiatrist \"+\ *n* : a specialist in orthopsychiatry

or·tho·psychiatry \"+\ *n* [*orth-* + *psychiatry*] : prophylactic psychiatry concerned esp. with incipient mental and behavioral disorders in childhood and youth — compare MENTAL HYGIENE

or·thop·ter \(ˈ)ȯ(r)¦thäptə(r)\ *n* -S [F *orthoptère*, fr. *orth-* + *-ptère* (as in *hélicoptère* helicopter) — more at HELICOPTER] **1** : a flying machine propelled by flapping of wings : a mechanical bird **2** [F *orthoptère*, fr. NL *Orthoptera*] : ORTHOPTERON

or·thop·tera \ȯ(r)'thäptərə\ *n pl, cap* [NL, fr. *orth-* + *-ptera*; fr. the straight and narrow wings] : an order of Insecta comprising insects with mouthparts fitted for chewing, two pairs of wings or none, and an incomplete metamorphosis: **a** *in some esp. former classifications* : a very large order including the cockroaches, mantises, grasshoppers and crickets, stick insects, and certain related forms and sometimes also the earwigs **b** : an order including the mantises, grasshoppers and crickets, stick insects, and certain related forms and comprising the suborders Manteodea, Grylloblattodea, Saltatoria, and Phasmatodea **c** *in some classifications* : an order coextensive with Saltatoria

or·thop·ter·al \(ˈ)=¦=tərəl\ *or* **or·thop·ter·an** \-rən\ *or* **or·thop·ter·ous** \-rəs\ *adj* : of or relating to the Orthoptera

orthopteran \"\ *n* -S [NL *Orthoptera* + E *-an*] : ORTHOPTERON

or·thop·ter·ist \=ˈ=tərəst\ *n* -S [NL *Orthoptera* + E *-ist*] : ORTHOPTEROLOGIST

¹or·thop·ter·oid \=¦=təˌrȯid\ *adj* [NL *Orthoptera* + E *-oid*] **1** : resembling or related to the Orthoptera **2** [NL *Orthopteroidea*] : of or relating to the Orthopteroidea

²orthopteroid \"\ *n* -S : an orthopteroid insect

or·thop·ter·oi·dea \(ˌ)=ˌ=tə'rȯidēə\ *n pl, cap* [NL, fr. *Orthoptera* + *-oidea*] *in some classifications* : a superorder or other division of Insecta that includes Orthoptera together with various other groups (as Phasmatodea, Dermaptera, and Diploglossata)

or·thop·ter·o·log·i·cal \(ˌ)=¦=tərə¦läjəkəl\ *adj* [*orthopterology* + *-ical*] : of or relating to orthopterology

or·thop·ter·ol·o·gist \(ˌ)=ˌ=ˈrälə̇jəst\ *n* -S : a specialist in orthopterology

or·thop·ter·ol·o·gy \-jē\ *n* -ES [NL *Orthoptera* + E *-logy*] **1** : the study of the Orthoptera **2** : a treatise on the Orthoptera

or·thop·ter·on \=ˈ=tərən, -ˌrän\ *n, pl* **orthoptera** \-ˌrə\ [NL, sing. of *Orthoptera*] : an insect of the order Orthoptera

or·thop·tic \(ˈ)=¦thäptik\ *adj* [ISV *orth-* + *optic*] : of or relating to orthoptics

or·thop·tics \=ˈ=tiks\ *n pl but sing or pl in constr* [*orthoptic* + *-s*] : the treatment or the art of treating defective visual habits, defects of binocular vision, and muscle imbalance (as strabismus) by reeducation of visual habits, exercise, and visual training

or·thop·tist \(ˈ)=¦=təst\ *n* -S [*orthoptics* + *-ist*] : a person who is trained in or practices orthoptics

or·tho·quartzite \¦ȯ(r)thō+\ *n* [*orth-* + *quartzite*] : a quartzite of sedimentary origin

or·tho·quinone \"+\ *n* [*orth-* + *quinone*] **1** : QUINONE 1b **2** : the ortho isomer of a quinone

or·thor·ha·pha *syn of* ORTHORRHAPHA

or·tho·rhombic \¦ȯ(r)thə+\ *adj* [ISV *orth-* + *rhombic*] : of, relating to, or characterized by the orthorhombic system of crystallization : RHOMBIC, PRISMATIC, TRIMETRIC

orthorhombic system *n* : a crystal system characterized by three unequal axes at right angles — see CRYSTAL SYSTEM illustration

or·thor·rha·pha \ȯ(r)'thȯrəfə\ *n pl, cap* [NL, fr. *orth-* + *-rrhapha* (fr. Gk *rhaphē* seam, fr. *rhaptein* to sew together) — more at WRAP] : a large suborder of Diptera that usu. includes the Nematocera and many of the Brachycera but is sometimes restricted to the more primitive families of Brachycera and that is distinguished by a pupal case opening by a T-shaped cleft behind the head or by a transverse slit between the seventh and eighth abdominal segments — **or·thor·rha·phous** \(ˈ)=¦=fəs\ *adj*

or·tho·scope \'ȯ(r)thəˌskōp\ *n* [ISV *orth-* + *-scope*; prob. orig. formed as G *orthoskop*] : an instrument for examining the superficial parts of the eye through a layer of water which neutralizes the corneal refraction

or·tho·scop·ic \¦=¦skäpik\ *adj* [ISV *orth-* + *-scopic*] : giving an image in correct and normal proportions : giving a flat field of view

or·tho·selection \¦ȯ(r)thə+\ *n* [*orth-* + *selection*] : natural selection promoting the progress and continuance of an adaptive trend in biological evolution and thus simulating orthogenesis — **or·tho·selective** \"+\ *adj*

or·tho·silicate \¦ȯ(r)thō+\ *n* [ISV *orth-* + *silicate*] : a silicate containing the group SiO_4 in which the ratio of silicon to oxygen is 1 to 4 : a salt or ester (as ethyl silicate) of orthosilicic acid : NESOSILICATE

or·tho·silicic acid \"+...-\ *n* [*orthosilicic* ISV *orth-* + *silicic*] : a weak acid H_4SiO_4 or $Si(OH)_4$ known only in solution and in the form of salts or esters

or·tho·sis \ȯ(r)'thōsə̇s\ *n, pl* **ortho·ses** \-ōˌsēz\ [NL, fr. Gk *orthōsis* straightening, fr. *orthoun* to straighten, fr. *orthos* straight — more at ORTH-] : corrective treatment of maladjusted or neurotic individuals

or·tho·site \'ȯ(r)thəˌsīt\ *n* -S [F, fr. *orthose* orthoclase (fr. *orth-* + *-ose*) + *-ite*] : a granular igneous rock composed essentially of orthoclase

or·tho·somatic \¦ȯ(r)thō+\ *adj* [*orth-* + *somatic*] : having the body straight ⟨~ insect larvae⟩

or·tho·stat·ic \¦ȯ(r)thə+\ *adj* [ISV *orth-* + *-static* (fr. Gk *statos* — verbal of *histanai* to cause to stand — + *-ikos* -ic) — more at STAND] : of, relating to, or caused by erect posture

orthostatic albuminuria *n* : albuminuria that occurs only when a person is in an upright position and disappears when he lies down for a short time

or·tho·stereoscope \"+\ *n* [*orth-* + *stereoscope*] : a stereoscopic binocular microscope that presents erect images in true perspective — **or·tho·stereoscopic** \"+\ *adj*

or·tho·stereoscopy \¦ȯ(r)(ˌ)thō+\ *n* [*orth-* + *stereoscopy*] : a process of stereoscopic photography for producing a three-dimensional visual image that is a full-sized true-to-scale reproduction of the original object in all three dimensions and that appears at the same distance from the eye as the object

or·thos·ti·chous \(ˈ)ȯ(r)¦thästəkəs\ *adj* [*orthostichy* + *-ous*] : arranged in vertical ranks

or·thos·ti·chy \=ˈ==kē\ *n* -ES [ISV *orth-* + Gk *stichos* row + ISV *-y* — more at STICH] : a hypothetical line passing through the bases of leaves or scales situated directly above one another on an axis; *also* : the arrangement of leaves or scales in such lines — compare PARASTICHY, PHYLLOTAXY

¹or·tho·style \'ȯ(r)thəˌ+ˌ-\ *n* [*orth-* + *-style* (as in *peristyle*)] : an arrangement of architectural columns in a straight row

²orthostyle \"\ *adj* : of or relating to an orthostyle

or·tho·symmetric *or* **or·tho·symmetrical** \¦ȯ(r)(ˌ)thō+\ *adj* [*orth-* + *symmetric, symmetrical*] : ORTHORHOMBIC

or·tho·telluric acid \"+...-\ *n* [*orth-* + *telluric acid*] : TELLURIC ACID a

or·tho·tolidine \¦ȯ(r)(ˌ)thō+\ *n* : TOLIDINE a — written systematically with ital. *ortho-* or *o-*

or·tho·tone \'ȯ(r)thəˌtōn\ *adj* [Gk *orthotonos* with the unmodified accent, fr. *ortho-* orth- + *tonos* accent, tone — more at TONE] : having or retaining an independent accent : not enclitic or proclitic — used esp. of some indefinite Greek pronouns and adverbs when used interrogatively

or·thot·o·nus \ȯ(r)'thät°nəs\ *n* -ES [NL, fr. *orth-* + L *tonus* tension, tone — more at TONE] : tetanic spasm characterized by rigid straightness of the body

or·tho·top·ic \¦ȯ(r)thə¦täpik\ *adj* [*orth-* + *heterotopic*] : of or relating to the grafting of tissue in a natural position ⟨~ transplant⟩ — compare HETEROTOPIA

or·tho·triaene \¦ȯ(r)thō+\ *n* [*orth-* + *triaene*] : a tetraradiate sponge spicule having one long and three short rays

or·tho·trop·ic \¦ȯ(r)thə¦träpik\ *adj* [*orth-* + *-tropic*] : having the longer axis more or less vertical — compare PLAGIOTROPIC — **or·tho·trop·i·cal·ly** \-pə̇k(ə)lē\ *adv*

or·thot·ro·pism \ȯ(r)'thä·trəˌpizəm\ *n* [*orth-* + *tropism*] : the tendency of a plant to have the longer axis more or less vertical

or·thot·ro·pous \(ˈ)ȯ(r)¦thä·trəpəs\ *adj* [ISV *orth-* + *-tropous*] : having the ovule straight so that the chalaza, hilum, and micropyle are in the same axial line — compare AMPHITROPOUS, ANATROPOUS, CAMPYLOTROPOUS

or·tho·type \'ȯ(r)thəˌtīp\ *n* [*orth-* + *type*] : a genotype designated as such in the first publication of a generic name — **or·tho·typ·ic** \¦==¦tipik\ *adj*

or·tho-xylene \¦ȯ(r)thō+\ *n* [*orth-* + *xylene*] : XYLENE 1a — written systematically with ital. *ortho-* or *o-*

or·thros \'ȯrˌthrōs\ *or* **or·thron** \-thrōn\ *n, pl* **orthroses** *or* **orthrons** *often cap* [*orthros* fr. LGk, fr. Gk, dawn, sunrise; *orthron* fr. MGk or NGk, alter. of LGk *orthros*; akin to Gk *orthos* straight, upright — more at ORTH-] : the morning office in the Eastern Orthodox Church somewhat corresponding to the Latin lauds

orting *pres part of* ORT

or·to·lan \'ȯ(r)d·°lən\ *n* -S [F or It; F *ortolan*, fr. It *ortolano* ortolan, gardener, fr. L *hortulanus* gardener, fr. *hortulus* small garden (dim. of *hortus* garden) + *-anus* -an — more at YARD] **1** : a European bunting (*Emberiza hortulana*) that is about six inches long, has a greenish gray head, brown and black wings and back, yellowish breast, and buff abdomen, and is commonly netted and fattened for a table delicacy **2 a** *Brit* : WHEATEAR **b** : SORA **c** : BOBOLINK

orts *pl of* ORT, *pres part of* ORT

ort·stein \'ȯrtˌstīn\ *n* [G, fr. *ort* site, place (fr. OHG, point) + *stein* stone (fr. OHG) — more at ODD, STONE] : HARDPAN

or·ty·gan \'ȯ(r)d·əgən\ *n* -S [Gk *ortyg-*, *ortyx* quail + E *-an*] : one of several East Indian birds of the genus *Turnix*

or·ty·gian \(ˈ)ȯ(r)¦tij(ē)ən\ *adj, usu cap* [in sense 1, fr. *Ortygia* Delos, smallest island of the Cyclades, south Aegean Sea + E *-an*; in sense 2, fr. *Ortygia*, island near the southeastern coast of Sicily + E *-an*] **1** : of or relating to the Greek island of Delos held in antiquity to be the birthplace of Apollo and Artemis ⟨*Ortygian* Artemis⟩ **2** : of or relating to the Sicilian island of Ortygia on which modern Syracuse is built ⟨beneath the *Ortygian* shore —P.B.Shelley⟩

orunchun *usu cap, var of* ORONCHON

orus·si·dae \ō'rəsəˌdē\ *n pl, cap* [NL, fr. *Orussus*, type genus (fr. Gk *oryssein* to dig) + *-idae* — more at ROUGH] : a hymenopterous family including the parasitic wood wasps

or·vi·etan \ˌȯ(r)vē'at°n\ *n* -S [F *orviétan*, fr. It *orvietano*, fr. *Orvieto*, city in central Italy where it was invented + *-ano* -an (fr. L *-anus*)] : a counterpoison formerly in vogue

ORW *abbr* owner's risk of becoming wet

ory \'ō(ə)rē, 'ȯ(-, -ri\ *adj* [¹*ore* + *-y* (adj. suffix)] *archaic* : resembling or containing metallic ore

¹-ory \(ə)rē, -ri, ˌōr-\ *n suffix* -ES [ME *-orie*, fr. L *-orium*, fr. neut. of *-orius*, adj. suffix] : one that relates to or is used for: as **a** : place of or for ⟨reformat*ory*⟩ ⟨observat*ory*⟩ **b** : something that serves for ⟨cremat*ory*⟩

²-ory \"\ *adj suffix* [ME *-orie*, *-oire*, fr. MF & L; MF *-orie* *-oire*, fr. OF, fr. L *-orius*] **1** : of, relating to, or characterized by ⟨observat*ory*⟩ ⟨gustat*ory*⟩ **2** : containing, involving, or conveying ⟨amendat*ory*⟩ ⟨compuls*ory*⟩ **3** : serving for, producing, or maintaining ⟨classificat*ory*⟩ ⟨equilibrat*ory*⟩ ⟨justificat*ory*⟩

oryct- *or* **orycto-** *comb form* [NL, fr. Gk *oryktos* formed by digging, dug, verbal of *orychein*, *oryssein* to dig — more at ROUGH] : fossil : mineral ⟨*orycto*logy⟩ ⟨*orycto*gnosy⟩

oryc·ter·o·pus \əˌrik'terəpəs, ˌōr,i-\ *n, cap* [NL, fr. Gk *oryktēr* miner (fr. *oryssein*, *orychein* to dig) + NL *-pus*] : a genus (coextensive with the family Orycteropodidae and sole recent representative of the order Tubulidentata) that comprises the aardvarks

oryc·tognos·tic \ə¦riktə(g)¦nästik\ *also* **oryc·tognos·ti·cal** \-stəkəl\ *adj* [*oryct-* + *-gnostic*, *-gnostical*] : of or relating to oryctognosy — **oryc·tognos·ti·cal·ly** \-stək(ə)lē\ *adv*

oryc·tog·no·sy \əˌrik'tägnəsē, ˌōr,i-\ *n* -ES [*oryct-* + *-gnosy*] : MINERALOGY

oryc·tol·a·gus \-äləgəs\ *n, cap* [NL, fr. *oryct-* + Gk *lagōs* hare] : a genus comprising the common European rabbits

oryc·to·log·ic \ə¦riktə¦läjik\ *also* **oryc·to·log·i·cal** \-jəkəl\ *adj* : of or relating to oryctology

oryc·tol·o·gist \-ˈäləjəst\ *n* -S : a specialist in oryctology

oryc·tol·o·gy \əˌrik'täləjē, ˌōr,i-\ *n* -ES [prob. fr. (assumed) NL *oryctologia*, fr. Gk *oryktos* formed by digging, dug, verbal of *oryssein* to dig + NL *-logia* -logy] : MINERALOGY

orys·si·dae \ō'risəˌdē\ [NL, fr. *Oryssus* (syn. of *Orussus*) (fr. Gk *oryssein*) + *-idae* — more at ROUGH] *syn of* ORUSSIDAE

oryx \'ōriks, 'ȯr-, 'är-\ *n* [NL, fr. L, a gazelle, fr. Gk, pickax, leucoryx, fr. *oryssein*] **1** *cap* : a genus of large African antelopes having in both sexes long cylindrical nearly straight horns ribbed in their basal half and projecting backward in nearly exact continuation of the plane of the forehead and nose **2** *pl* **oryxes** *also* **oryx** : any antelope of the genus *Oryx*

oryz- *or* **oryzo-** *also* **oryzi-** *comb form* [NL, fr. L *oryza* rice, fr. Gk — more at RICE] : rice ⟨*oryzi*vorous⟩ ⟨*Oryzo*mys⟩

ory·za \ō'rīzə\ *n, cap* [NL, fr. L, rice] : a small genus (family Gramineae) of tropical cereal grasses having perfect flowers with six stamens — see RICE

ory·ze·nin \-zənə̇n\ *n* -S [*oryzen-* (irreg. fr. Gk *oryza* rice) + *-in*] : a glutelin found in the seeds of rice

or·y·ziv·o·rous \¦ōrə¦ziv(ə)rəs\ *adj* [*oryz-* + *-vorous*; prob. orig. formed as F *orizivore*] : feeding on rice

ory·zo·mys \ō'rīzəmə̇s\ *n, cap* [NL, fr. *oryz-* + *-mys*] : a genus of cricetid rodents including the rice rats

or·y·zop·sis \ˌōrə'zäpsə̇s\ *n, cap* [NL, fr. *oryz-* + *-opsis*] : a genus of American tufted grasses with open panicles composed of one-flowered spikelets remotely suggesting rice — see MOUNTAIN RICE, SILK GRASS

ory·zo·ric·tes \ōˌrīzə'rik(ˌ)tēz\ *n, cap* [NL, fr. *oryz-* + Gk *oryktēs* digger, fr. *orychein*, *oryssein* to dig — more at ROUGH] : a genus of Malagasy insectivores that comprises the rice tenrecs

¹os \'äs\ *n, pl* **os·sa** \-sə\ [L *oss-*, *os* — more at OSSEOUS] : BONE

²os \"\ *n, pl* **ora** \'ōrə\ [L *or-*, *os* — more at ORAL] : MOUTH, ORIFICE

³os *also* **ose** \'ōs\ *n, pl* **osar** \'ōˌsär\ *also* **oses** [Sw *ås* mountain ridge, fr. ON *āss* — more at HUMERUS] : ESKER

OS \'ō'es\ *vt* **OSed**; **OSed**; **OSing**; **OSes** [abbr. of *order sheet* or *on sheet*] : to record the time of arrival and departure of (a train) by telegraphing the information prefixed by the signal OS and the office call ⟨turned to the key to ~ his first train out —*Trains*⟩

OS *abbr* **1** [L *oculus sinister*] left eye **2** off stage **3** old school **4** old series **5** old side **6** old style **7** one side **8** only son **9** on sale **10** on sample **11** on schedule **12** on sheet **13** on side **14** ordinary seaman **15** original series **16** out of stock **17** outside **18** outside sentinel **19** outsize **20** outstanding

Os *symbol* osmium

o's *or* **os** *pl of* O

osage \(ˈ)ō¦sāj\ *n, pl* **osage** *or* **osages** *usu cap* [Osage *Wazhazhe*] **1 a** (1) : a Siouan people of the Osage and Missouri river valleys, Missouri (2) : a member of such people **b** : the language of the Osage people **2** : OSAGE ORANGE

osage orange *n, usu cap 1st O* **1 a** *also* **osage apple** : an ornamental American tree (*Maclura pomifera*) of the family Moraceae having dark green glossy leaves, milky sap, hard bright orange-colored wood that yields a dye, and imperfect flowers **b** : the wood of the osage orange **c** : the yellowish green tubercled globular fruit of the osage orange tree consisting of the united fleshy calyxes of the pistillate flowers **2** *usu cap 1st O & often cap 2d O* : the yellow coloring matter that is extracted from the wood of the osage orange tree and is similar to old fustic — see DYE table I (under *Natural Yellow 8*)

osa·gi·an \-jēən\ *adj, usu cap* [*Osage* river, eastern Kansas and western and central Missouri + E *-an*] : of or relating to the division of the Mississippian geologic period between the Kinderhook and the Meramec — see GEOLOGIC TIME table

osa·ka \ō'säkə\ *adj, usu cap* [fr. *Osaka*, city in west central Honshu, Japan] : of or from the city of Osaka, Japan : of the kind or style prevalent in Osaka

OS and D *abbr* over, short, and damaged

osa·zone \'ōsəˌzōn, 'äs-\ *n* -S [ISV ²*-ose* + *az-* + *-one*; prob. orig. formed as G *osazon*] : any of a class of basic compounds that contain two adjacent hydrazone groupings and are made from an alpha-diketone and hydrazine, an alkyl- or aryl-hydrazine, or from an alpha-hydroxy aldehyde or ketone (as glucose or benzoin) and an aryl-hydrazine; *esp* : PHENYLOSAZONE

osc *abbr* oscillate; oscillating; oscillator

os cal·cis \-'kalsə̇s\ *n, pl* **ossa calcis** [L, bone of the heel] : CALCANEUS

os·can \'äskən, 'ōs-\ *n* -S *cap* [L *Oscus* Oscan + E *-an*] **1** : one of a people of ancient Italy occupying Campania **2** : the language of the Oscan people and orig. of the Samnites preserved in inscriptions of various kinds written in an alphabet of Etruscan origin — compare SAMNITE, OSCO-UMBRIAN

¹os·car \=\ *n* [by rhyming slang fr. John S. H. *Oscar* Asche †1936 Australian actor] *Austral* : MONEY, CASH

²oscar \"\ *usu cap* [fr. the name *Oscar*] — a communications code word for the letter *o*

Os·car \'äskə(r), 'ōs-\ *trademark* — used esp. for any of a number of golden statuettes awarded annually by a professional organization for notable achievement in motion pictures

os·cil·late \'äsəˌlāt, *usu* -ād·+V\ *vb* -ED/-ING/-S [L *oscillatus*, past part. of *oscillare* to swing, fr. *oscillum* swing] *vi* **1 a** : to swing backward and forward like a pendulum : move to and fro : VIBRATE ⟨the completed statue . . . was placed upon a turntable base that slowly ~*s*, completing a 90-degree arc every hour —*Amer. Guide Series: Minn.*⟩ ⟨rocker arms on all other overhead valve engines ~ on stationary tubular shafts —H.F.Blanchard & Ralph Ritchen⟩ **b** : to travel back and forth between two points ⟨he ~*s* regularly between his comfortable home . . . and his downtown office-laboratory —Gladwin Hill⟩ **2 a** : to vary the state or condition : FLUCTUATE ⟨the snow line ~*s* with the seasons, descending below ten thousand feet in winter —C.D.Forde⟩ ⟨diaries showing how he *oscillated* between wealth and poverty —E.V.Lucas⟩ **b** : to vary between opposing attitudes, beliefs, feelings, or theories : think or act in a fickle manner : SHILLY-SHALLY ⟨men have *oscillated* in their opinions —W.E.Swinton⟩ **3** : to vibrate or vary above and below a mean value ⟨bank rate oscillating between 2½ percent and 6½ percent —W.M. Dacey⟩ ⟨a polynomial which ~*s* greatly between the observed values —J.G.Kemeny⟩ ~ *vt* : to cause to oscillate ⟨~ the crankshaft slightly to locate dead center —H.F.Blanchard & Ralph Ritchen⟩ **syn** see SWING

oscillating current *n* : electric current consisting of oscillations

oscillating wave *n* : GREGARIOUS WAVE

os·cil·la·tion \ˌäsə'lāshən\ *n* -S [L *oscillation-*, *oscillatio* action of swinging, fr. *oscillatus* (past part. of *oscillare* to swing) + *-ion-*, *-io* -ion] **1** : the action or fact of oscillating : a swinging or moving backward and forward like a pendulum : VIBRATION ⟨stays can be effectively used to prevent aerodynamic ~*s* in new bridges —D.B.Steinman⟩ ⟨vibration in aircraft occurs principally as a result of ~*s* from the motor and propeller —H.G.Armstrong⟩ ⟨a diatomic molecule . . . can absorb vibrational energy by ~ of the atoms within the molecule —F.H.Getman⟩ **2 a** : a periodic variation or fluctuation between conditions ⟨famines due to excessive storminess and violent ~*s* of rain and drought, heat and cold —Ellsworth Huntington⟩ ⟨major prosperities and depressions are not to be explained by the process and mechanism of business cycles (endogenous ~*s*) —Clark Warburton⟩ ⟨men get tired of everything, of heaven no less than of hell; and that all history is nothing but a record of the ~*s* of the world between these two extremes —G.B.Shaw⟩ **b** : the change back and forth between opposing beliefs, opinions, or theories : variation in attitudes, policies, principles, or purposes often for fickle reasons ⟨fruitless ~*s* or the decision to make no decision will destroy his days —J.B.Conant⟩ ⟨a lover's instant ~ from black to white, from hate to love —Clemence Dane⟩ **3** : a flow of electricity changing periodically from a maximum to a minimum or from positive to negative when an electrical system with capacitance and inductance is disturbed from equilibrium **4** : the variation of a mathematical function between limits; *specif* : the difference between the greatest and least values of a function **5 a** : a single swing from one extreme limit to the other of an oscillating body **b** : one of the periodic variations of an oscillating variable (as the electron current in a radio tube) — compare HARMONIC OSCILLATION — **os·cil·la·tion·al** \¦==¦lāshən°l, -shnəl\ *adj*

oscillation circuit *n* : a circuit designed to produce electric oscillations

oscillation ripple *or* **oscillation ripple mark** *n* : a symmetrical ripple on a bedding plane or on a sea or lake floor with sharp crest and broadly rounded trough formed by gregarious waves — compare CURRENT RIPPLE

os·cil·la·tor \'==ˌlād·ə(r), -ātə-\ *n* -S [NL, fr. L *oscillatus* (past part. of *oscillare*) + NL *-or*] : one that oscillates: as **a** : an instrument for measuring rigidity by the torsional oscillations of a weighted wire **b** : a device for producing electric oscillations; *specif* : a radio-frequency or audio-frequency generator esp. of a nonrotating type

os·cil·la·to·ria \ˌäsələ'tōrēə\ *n, cap* [NL, fr. fem. of *oscillatorius* oscillatory] : a genus of blue-green algae that is the type of the family Oscillatoriaceae

os·cil·la·to·ri·a·ce·ae \ˌ==ˌ=ˌtōrē'āsēˌē\ *n pl, cap* [NL, fr *Oscillatoria*, type genus + *-aceae*] : a family of blue-green algae (order Hormogonales) growing as slender filaments often in tangled masses in water or on damp rocks or soil, forming slimy layers on soil, commonly exhibiting oscillating movements, and reproducing only asexually by hormogonia — **os·cil·la·to·ri·a·ceous** \¦==¦==¦āshəs\ *adj*

os·cil·la·to·ri·a·les \ˌ==ˌ==ˈā(ˌ)lēz\ *n pl*, [NL, fr. *Oscillatoria* + *-ales*] *syn of* HORMOGONALES

os·cil·la·to·ry \'äsələˌtōrē, -tōr-, -ri\ *adj* [NL *oscillatorius*, fr. L *oscillatus* (past part. of *oscillare*) + *-orius* -ory] : characterized by oscillation : VIBRATORY

oscillatory circuit *n* : a circuit containing capacity and inductance such that a single voltage impulse would give rise to a damped alternating current

oscillatory current *n* : OSCILLATING CURRENT

oscillatory discharge *n* : an electric discharge in a circuit having sufficient capacitative reactance to result in damped alternating surges of electricity

os·cil·lo·gram \ə'siləˌgram\ *n* [ISV *oscillo-* (fr. L *oscillare*) + *-gram*] : an autographic record made by an oscillograph or a record (as a photograph) of the display on an oscilloscope

os·cil·lo·graph \-ˌraf, -räf\ *n* [F *oscillographe*, fr. *oscillo-* (fr. L *oscillare*) + *-graphe* -graph] : an instrument that produces in the form of a continuous curve a permanent record (as a graph or a photograph) of periodic or irregular variations in an electrical quantity (as voltage) and often indirectly in some related quantity (as sound pressure) by means of a moving element (as a galvanometer needle or a vibrating beam of cathode rays) — compare OSCILLOSCOPE — **os·cil·lo·graph·ic** \=¦==¦grafik\ *adj* — **os·cil·lo·graph·i·cal·ly** \-fə̇k(ə)lē\ *adv* — **os·cil·log·ra·phy** \ˌäsə'lägrəfē\ *n* -ES

os·cil·lom·e·ter \ˌäsə'lämə̇d·ə(r)\ *n* [ISV *oscillo-* (fr. L *oscillare*) + *-meter*] **1** : an instrument for measuring the angle through which a ship rolls or pitches at sea **2** : an instrument for measuring the changes in pulsations in the arteries esp. of the extremities — **os·cil·lo·met·ric** \¦äsəlō¦me·trik\ *adj* — **os·cil·lom·e·try** \ˌäsə'lämə·trē\ *n* -ES

os·cil·lo·scope \ə'siləˌskōp\ *n* [ISV *oscillo-* (fr. L *oscillare*) + *-scope*] : an instrument in which the variations in a fluctuating electrical quantity (as voltage) are not recorded but appear temporarily as a visible wave form on the fluorescent screen of a cathode-ray tube; *broadly* : OSCILLOGRAPH — **os·cil·lo·scop·ic** \=¦==¦skäpik\ *adj*

os·cine \'äsˌīn, 'äˌsīn\ *adj* [NL *Oscines*] : relating to or having the character of the Oscines

os·ci·nel·la \ˌäsə'nelə\ *n, cap* [NL, fr. L *oscin-*, *oscen* singing bird used in divination + *-ella*] : a genus of chloropid flies containing the frit fly

os·ci·nes \'äsəˌnēz\ *n pl, cap* [NL, fr. L, pl. of *oscin-*, *oscen* singing bird used in divination, fr. *os-* (fr. *ob* to, before, against) + *-cin-*, *-cen* (fr. *canere* to sing) — more at EPI-,

CHANT] *in some classifications* **:** a suborder or superfamily of birds equivalent to the suborder Passeres
os·cin·i·dae \ə'sinə,dē\ [NL, fr. *Oscinis* (syn. of *Oscinella*) (fr. L *oscin-*, *oscen* singing bird used in divination) + *-idae*] *syn of* CHLOROPIDAE
os·ci·nine \'äsə,nīn, -,nən\ *adj* [NL *Oscines* + E *-ine*] **:** OSCINE
os·cin·o·so·ma \,äsənō'sōmə\ [NL, fr. L *oscin-*, *oscen* singing bird used in divination + NL *-o-* + *-soma*] *syn of* OSCINELLA
os·ci·tan·cy \'äsəd·ənsē\ *n* -ES [*oscitant* + *-cy*] **1 a :** drowsiness usu. demonstrated by yawns **b :** DULLNESS, SLUGGISHNESS **2 :** the act of gaping or yawning
os·ci·tant \-nt\ *adj* [L *oscitant-*, *oscitans*, pres. part. of *oscitare* to yawn, fr. *os* mouth + *citare* to put in motion — more at CITE] **:** yawning with drowsiness; *also* **:** LAZY, STUPID
os·ci·ta·tion \,äsə'tāshən\ *n* -S [L *oscitation-*, *oscitatio* action of yawning, fr. *oscitatus* (past part. of *oscitare* to yawn) + *-ion-*, *-io* -ion] **1 :** the act of being inattentive **2 :** the condition of being drowsy
os·co-umbrian \,ä(,)skō+\ *n*, *cap O&U* [*osco-* (fr. L *Oscus* Oscan) + *umbrian*] **:** a subdivision of the Italic branch of the Indo-European language family containing the closely related languages of Oscan and Umbrian
os cox·ae \-'käk,sē\ *n*, *pl* **ossa coxae** [L, bone of the hip] **:** INNOMINATE BONE
os·cu·lant \'äskyələnt\ *adj* [NL *osculant-*, *osculans*, fr. L, pres. part. of *osculari* to kiss] **1 :** intermediate in character **:** forming a connecting link between two groups **2 :** adhering closely **:** EMBRACING
os·cu·lar \'äskyələ(r)\ *adj* [NL *oscularis*, fr. L *osculum* little mouth, kiss + *-aris* -ar] **1 :** of, relating to, or concerned with kissing ⟨~ muscles⟩ **2 a :** of or relating to an osculum **b :** of or relating to a mouth — **os·cu·lar·i·ty** \,äskyə'larəd·ē\ *n* -ES
os·cu·late \'äskyə,lāt, *usu* -ād·+V\ *vb* -ED/-ING/-S [L *osculatus*, past part. of *osculari* to kiss, fr. *osculum* little mouth, kiss, dim. of *os* mouth — more at ORAL] *vt* **1 :** KISS **2** *math* **:** to have contact of the second or higher order with ~ *vi* **:** to have characters in common with two groups
os·cu·la·tion \,≈≈'lāshən\ *n* -S [L *osculation-*, *osculatio*, fr. *osculatus* (past part. of *osculari*) + *-ion-*, *-io* -ion] **:** the act of kissing; *also* **:** KISS
¹os·cu·la·to·ry \'äskyələ,tōrē\ *n* -ES [ML *osculatorium*, fr. L *osculatus* (past part. of *osculari*) + *-orium* -ory] **:** PAX 1
²osculatory \"\ *adj* [prob. fr. (assumed) NL *osculatorius*, fr. L *osculatus* (past part. of *osculari*) + *-orius* -ory] **:** of, relating to, or characterized by kissing
os·cule \'ä,skyül\ *n* -S [F, fr. NL *osculum*] **:** OSCULUM
os·cu·lom·e·ter \,äskyə'lämәd·ə(r)\ *n* [*oscul-* (fr. *osculate*) + *-o-* + *-meter*] **:** a graduated series of circular arcs for determining by superposition the curvature at any point on a curve; *also* **:** an instrument used for a similar purpose
os·cu·lum \'äskyələm\ *n*, *pl* **oscula** [NL, fr. L, little mouth, kiss] **:** one of the excurrent orifices of a sponge
¹ose \'ōs\ *n* -S [ISV, fr. ²*-ose*] **:** GLYCOSE
²ose *var of* OS
¹-ose \,ōs, *in some words* ¦ō| *or* 'ō|, *or* |z\ *adj suffix* [ME, fr. L *-osus*] **:** full of **:** having **:** possessing the qualities of ⟨clad*ose*⟩
²-ose \,ōs *also* ,ōz\ *n suffix* -S [F, fr. *glucose*] **1 :** carbohydrate ⟨amyl*ose*⟩; *esp* **:** sugar ⟨fruct*ose*⟩ ⟨pent*ose*⟩ **2 :** primary hydrolysis product ⟨prote*ose*⟩
³-ose \,ōs\ *n suffix* -S [NL *-osis*] **:** -OSIS 4 ⟨chytridi*ose*⟩
osete *cap*, *var of* OSSET
osi·an·dri·an \,ōzē'andrēən, ,ōsē'-\ *also* **osi·an·drist** \-rəst\ *n* -S *usu cap* [Andreas *Osiander* †1552 Ger. Lutheran theologian + E *-an* or *-ist*] **:** an adherent of the doctrine that in justification by faith the believer is actually made righteous by an indwelling of Christ in him and not merely declared righteous by imputation
oside \'ō,sīd, 'ōsəd\ *n* -S [ISV, fr. *-oside*] **:** GLYCOSIDE
-o·side \,ō,sīd; ə,sīd, əsəd\ *n suffix* -S [ISV ²*-ose* + *-ide*] **:** glycoside or similar compound ⟨gangli*oside*⟩ ⟨heter*oside*⟩ — compare -IDE 2b
¹osier \'ōzhə(r)\ *n* -S [ME, fr. MF *osier*, *osiere*, fr. ML *auseria* osier bed] **1 :** any of various willows whose pliable twigs are used for furniture and basketry: as **a :** a European willow (*Salix viminalis*) — called also *velvet osier* **b :** ALMOND WILLOW **c :** GOLDEN WILLOW **d :** PURPLE WILLOW **2 :** an osier rod used in basketry; *esp* **:** a coarse unstripped rod used for making hampers **3 :** any of several American dogwoods
²osier \"\ *adj* **:** made of, covered with, or containing osiers
osi·ered \-(r)d\ *adj* **:** covered or adorned with osiers
osier willow *n* **1 :** OSIER 1 **2 :** a willow used as an osier rod
osiery \-ərē\ *n* -ES **:** an area where osiers are grown; *also* **:** work made of osiers
osi·ri·an \ō'sīrēən\ *adj*, *usu cap* [*Osiris*, Egyptian god of the underworld (fr. L *Osirid-*, *Osiris*, fr. Gk, fr. Egypt *Wsʾr*) + E *-an*] **:** of or relating to the ancient Egyptian god Osiris
osi·ride \ō'sīrəd\ *adj* [L *Osirid-*, *Osiris* Osiris] **:** OSIRIAN — used esp. of a pillar against which is set an image of Osiris
osi·ri·fi·ca·tion \ō,sīrəfə'kāshən\ *n* -S [fr. *osirify*, after such pairs as E *deify: deification*] **:** the act or state of being osirified
osi·ri·fy \ō'sīrə,fī\ *vt* -ED/-ING/-ES [*Osiris* + E *-fy*] **:** to identify as or with Osiris
osi·rism \ō'sī,rizəm\ *n* -S *usu cap* [*Osiris* + E *-ism*] **:** the worship of Osiris
-o·sis \'ōsəs\ *n suffix*, *pl* **-o·ses** \'ō,sēz\ *or* **-o·sis·es** [ME, fr. L, fr. Gk *-ōsis*, fr. *-ō-* (medial vowel characteristic of derivatives of certain verbs) + *-sis*] **1 a :** action **:** process **:** condition ⟨hypn*osis*⟩ **b :** abnormal or diseased condition ⟨leuk*osis*⟩ **2 :** increase **:** formation ⟨leukocyt*osis*⟩ **3 :** arrangement ⟨pteryl*osis*⟩ **4** [NL, fr. L] **:** disease caused by a (specified) fungus ⟨chytridi*osis*⟩
os·lo \'äz(,)lō, 'äs(-\ *adj*, *usu cap* [fr. *Oslo*, Norway] **:** of or from Oslo, the capital of Norway **:** of the kind or style prevalent in Oslo
oslo breakfast *or* **oslo meal** *n*, *usu cap O* **:** a mid-morning or mid-afternoon meal of uncooked protective foods (as whole wheat bread, butter, milk, cheese, raw fruit or vegetable)
os·lo·ite \'äzlō,īt, 'äsl-\ *n* -S *cap* [*Oslo* + E *-ite*] **:** a native or resident of Oslo, Norway
osm- *or* **osmo-** *comb form* [NL, fr. Gk *osm-*, fr. *osmē* — more at ODOR] **1 :** odor **:** smell ⟨*Osm*orhiza⟩ **2 a :** osmium ⟨*osm*ic⟩ **b** *osmo-* **:** osmous ⟨*osmo*cyanide⟩
-os·ma \'äzmə *also* 'äsmə\ *n comb form* [NL, fr. Gk *osmē*] **:** one having (such) an odor — in generic names of plants ⟨Bar*osma*⟩ ⟨Copr*osma*⟩
os·ma·gogue \'äzmə,gäg\ *adj* [*osm-* + *-agogue* (fr. LL *-agogus* promoting the expulsion of) — more at -AGOGUE] **:** stimulating to the sense of smell
os·man·li \äz'manlē, ä'sm-, -mən-\ *also* **os·man** \'äzmən; äz'män, ä'sm-\ *n* -S *cap* [Turk *osmanlı*, fr. *Osman*, *Othman* †1326 founder of the Ottoman Empire] **1 :** a Turk of the western branch of the Turkish peoples **2 :** TURKISH 1
os·man·thus \äz'man(t)thəs\ *n*, *cap* [NL, fr. *osm-* + *-anthus*] **:** a widely distributed genus of evergreen shrubs or trees (family Oleaceae) with inconspicuous bisexual flowers, sometimes foliage resembling holly, and a drupaceous fruit with a hard woody endocarp — see DEVILWOOD
os·mate \'äzmət, -z,māt\ *n* -S [ISV *osmic* + *-ate*] **:** a salt or ester of osmic acid
os·matic \(')äz¦mad·ik\ *or* **os·mic** \'äzmik\ *adj* [*osmatic* fr. *osm-* + *-atic* (as in *aquatic*); *osmic* fr. *osm-* + *-ic*] **:** depending chiefly on the sense of smell for orientation ⟨the dog is a strongly ~ animal⟩ — compare OPTIC
os·mer·i·dae \äz'merə,dē\ *n pl*, *cap* [NL, fr. *Osmerus*, type genus + *-idae*] **:** a family (order Isospondyli) to which the true smelts belong
os·me·rus \äz'mirəs\ *n*, *cap* [NL, fr. Gk *osmēros* odorous, fr. *osmē* odor] **:** a genus of smelts of the type of the family Osmeridae
os·me·sis \äz'mēsəs\ *n* -ES [NL, fr. Gk *osmēsis*, fr. *osmasthai* to smell, perceive by smell (fr. *osmē* odor) + *-sis*] **:** OLFACTION — **os·met·ic** \(')≈¦med·ik\ *adj*
os·me·te·ri·um *also* **os·ma·te·ri·um** \,äzmə'tirēəm\ *n*, *pl* **osmete·ria** *also* **osmate·ria** \-ēə\ [NL, irreg. fr. Gk *osmē* odor] **:** a protrusile forked process that emits a disagreeable odor, is borne on the first thoracic segment of the larvae of many butterflies of the family Papilionidae, and is probably a defensive organ
os·mia \'äzmēə\ *n*, *cap* [NL, fr. *osm-* + *-ia*] **:** a cosmopolitan genus of solitary bees (family Megachilidae) including several that are important pollinators of economic plants
os·mic \'äzmik\ *adj* [ISV *osm-* + *-ic*] **:** of, relating to, or derived from osmium — used esp. of compounds in which this element exhibits a relatively high valence; compare OSMOUS
osmic acid *n* [ISV *osmic* + *acid*] **1 :** a hypothetical acid H_2OsO_4 known esp. in the form of salts (as potassium osmate $K_2OsO_4.2H_2O$) obtainable from osmium tetroxide in alkaline solution **2 :** OSMIUM TETROXIDE
os·mics \'äzmiks\ *n pl but sing in constr* [*osm-* + *-ics*] **:** a science that deals with the sense of smell **:** the study of odors
os·mi·dro·sis \,äzmə'drōsəs\ *n*, *pl* **osmidro·ses** \-ō,sēz\ [NL, fr. *osm-* + *-idrosis*] **:** BROMIDROSIS
os·mio·phil \'äzmēə,fil\ *or* **os·mio·phil·ic** \¦≈≈¦filik\ *also* **os·mio·phile** \'≈≈≈,fīl\ *adj* [*osmium* + *-o-* + *-phil*, *-phile* or *-philic*] **:** reacting specif. to the presence of osmium tetroxide usu. by the formation of a black deposit — **os·mio·phil·ia** \,≈≈≈'filēə\ *n* -S — **os·mi·oph·i·ly** \,äzmē'äfəlē\ *n* -ES
osmious *var of* OSMOUS
os·mi·rid·i·um \,äzmə'ridēəm\ *also* **os·mi·irid·i·um** \-mə,ī'-\ *n* -S [G *osmiridium*, fr. *osm-* + *iridium*, fr. NL] **:** IRIDOSMINE
os·mi·um \'äzmēəm\ *n* -S [NL, fr. Gk *osmē* odor + NL *-ium*; fr. the strong characteristic smell of osmium tetroxide] **:** a hard brittle blue-gray or blue-black high-melting polyvalent metallic element that is one of the platinum metals, that is the heaviest metal known, that occurs in platinum ores principally alloyed with iridium in iridosmine, and that is used chiefly as a catalyst and in hard alloys esp. with platinum or ruthenium (as for pen nibs and phonograph needles) — symbol *Os*; see ELEMENT table
osmium dioxide *n* [ISV *osmium* + *dioxide*] **:** a brown or black solid OsO_2 obtainable by oxidation of osmium or reduction of osmium tetroxide
osmium lamp *n* **:** an incandescent lamp with a filament of osmium or an osmium alloy — compare TUNGSTEN LAMP
osmium oxide *n* [ISV *osmium* + *oxide*] **:** an oxide of osmium: **a :** OSMIUM DIOXIDE **b :** OSMIUM TETROXIDE
osmium tetroxide *n* [ISV *osmium* + *tetroxide*] **:** a crystalline compound OsO_4 that has a poisonous irritating pungent vapor, that is usu. made by oxidizing osmium, and that is used chiefly as a catalyst, as an oxidizing and hydroxylating agent (as in the conversion of olefins to glycols), and as a stain for fatty substances in cytology
¹osmo- *comb form* [¹*osmose*] **:** osmosis **:** osmotic ⟨*osmo*meter⟩
²osmo- — see OSM-
os·mo·graph \'äzmə,graf, -räf\ *n* [¹*osmo-* + *-graph*] **:** an instrument for recording the height of the liquid in an endosmometer or for registering osmotic pressures
os·mom·e·ter \äz'mämәd·ə(r)\ *n* [¹*osmo-* + *-meter*] **:** an apparatus for measuring osmotic pressure
os·mo·met·ric \¦äzmə¦me·trik\ *adj* [*osmometry* + *-ic*] **:** of or relating to osmometry — **os·mo·met·ri·cal·ly** \-rək(ə)lē\ *adv*
os·mom·e·try \äz'mämə·trē\ *n* -ES [ISV ¹*osmo-* + *-metry*] **:** the measurement of osmotic pressure ⟨determination of the molecular weight of proteins by ~⟩
osmond *var of* OSMUND
¹os·mo·phil·ic \¦äzmə¦filik\ *also* **os·mo·phile** \'≈≈,fīl\ *adj* [*osmophilic* fr. ¹*osmo-* + *-philic*; *osmophile* ISV ¹*osmo-* + *-phile*] **:** living or thriving in a medium of high osmotic pressure ⟨~ yeasts that ferment maple syrup⟩
²osmophilic \"\ *also* **osmophile** \"\ *adj* [*osm-* + *-philic* or *-phile*] **:** of, relating to, constituting, or containing cellular lipoids that become blackened with a precipitate of osmium when exposed to osmium tetroxide
os·mo·phore \'äzmə,fō(ə)r\ *n* -S [ISV *osm-* + *-phore*] **:** a group or radical (as hydroxyl, cyanogen, the aldehyde group) to whose presence in a molecule the odor of a compound is attributed — compare CHROMOPHORE — **osmophoric** *adj*
os·mo·receptor \¦äzmō+\ *n* [¹*osmo-* + *receptor*] **:** a sensory endorgan that is stimulated by changes in osmotic pressure
os·mo·regulation \"+\ *n* [ISV ¹*osmo-* + *regulation*] **:** regulation of osmotic pressure esp. in the body of a living organism
os·mo·regulator \"+\ *n* [ISV ¹*osmo-* + *regulator*] **:** a body mechanism concerned with the maintenance of constant osmotic pressure relationships — **os·mo·regulatory** \"+\ *adj*
os·mo·rhi·za \,äzmə'rīzə\ *n*, *cap* [NL, fr. *osm-* + *-rhiza*] **:** a genus of American and Asiatic white-flowered herbs (family Umbelliferae) with decompound leaves and fleshy aromatic roots
¹os·mo·scope \'äzmə,skōp\ *n* [*osm-* + *-scope*] **:** an instrument for detecting and for measuring odors — compare ODOROMETER
²osmoscope \"\ *n* [¹*osmo-* + *-scope*] **:** an apparatus for carrying out osmosis
¹os·mose \'äz,mōs, 'äs,m-\ *n* -S [fr. obs. *endosmose* endosmosis & obs. *exosmose* exosmosis — more at ENDOSMOSIS, EXOSMOSIS] **:** OSMOSIS 1
²osmose \"\ *vb* -ED/-ING/-S *vt* **:** to subject to osmosis **:** DIALYZE ~ *vi* **:** to diffuse by osmosis
os·mo·sis \äz'mōsəs, äs'm-\ *n*, *pl* **osmo·ses** \-ō,sēz\ [alter. (influenced by Gk *-sis*) of ¹*osmose*] **1 :** the flow or diffusion that takes place through a semipermeable membrane (as of a living cell) typically separating either a solvent (as water) and a solution or a dilute solution and a concentrated solution and thus bringing about conditions for equalizing the concentrations of the components on the two sides of the membrane because of the unequal rates of passage in the two directions until equilibrium is reached; *esp* **:** the passage of solvent in distinction from the passage of solute; compare ABSORPTION 1c, DIALYSIS, ELECTROOSMOSIS, ENDOSMOSIS, EXOSMOSIS, IMBIBITION 2 a, SAP, TURGOR **2 :** a process of absorption, interaction, or diffusion suggestive of the flow of osmotic action ⟨owing to the usual mysterious news ~, had already heard about it —Agnes S. Turnbull⟩: as **a :** an interaction or interchange (as of cultural groups or traits) by mutual penetration esp. through a separating medium **b :** a usu. effortless often unconscious absorption or assimilation (as of ideas or influences) by a seemingly general permeation ⟨absorbing democratic habits and ideals as by ~ —H.G.Rickover⟩ ⟨working alongside pupils in higher grades, the bright student gets advanced learning practically by ~ —Gertrude Samuels⟩ ⟨acquired his ideas through thought processes, not through social ~ —Roscoe Drummond⟩ ⟨a kind of cultural ~, the unconscious absorption of Oriental influences through seemingly trivial contacts —Edmond Taylor⟩
os·mo·tac·tic \¦äzmə¦taktik\ *adj* [fr. *osmotaxis*, after such pairs as E *hypotaxis: hypotactic*] **:** of or relating to osmotaxis
os·mo·tax·is \,≈≈'taksəs\ *n* [NL, fr. ¹*osmo-* + *-taxis*] **:** a taxis in which a difference of osmotic pressure is the directing factor
os·mot·ic \(')äz¦mäd·|ik, (')äs¦m-, -ät|, |ēk,\ *adj* [fr. *endosmotic*] **:** of, relating to, or having the property of osmosis — **os·mot·i·cal·ly** \|ək(ə)lē\ *adv*
osmotic pressure *n* **:** the pressure produced by or associated with osmosis and dependent on molar concentration and absolute temperature: as **a :** the maximum pressure that develops in a solution separated from a solvent by a membrane permeable only to the solvent **b :** the pressure that must be applied to a solution to just prevent osmosis — compare OSMOMETRY
os·mous \'äzməs\ *also* **os·mi·ous** \-mēəs\ *adj* [*osmous* fr. *osm-* + *-ous*; *osmious* ISV *osmium* + *-ous*] **:** of, relating to, or derived from osmium — used esp. of compounds in which this element exhibits a relatively low valence; compare OSMIC
¹os·mund *also* **os·mond** \'äzmənd\ *n* -S [ME *osmunde*, fr. OF *osmonde*] **1** *obs* **:** any of various ferns (as the male fern) **2 :** a fern of the genus *Osmunda*; *esp* **:** ROYAL FERN
²osmund *also* **osmond** \"\ *n* -S [ME *osmond*, fr. MLG *osemunt*, fr. OSw *osmunder*] **:** a superior iron formerly imported into England from Sweden and used esp. for making arrowheads, fishhooks, and clockworks; *also* **:** a piece of this iron
os·mun·da \äz'məndə\ *n* [NL, fr. ML, osmund, fr. OF *osmonde*] **1** *cap* **:** the type genus of Osmundaceae comprising rather large ferns with creeping rhizomes, stipes winged at the base, and naked globose sporangia borne on modified pinnae — see CINNAMON FERN, ROYAL FERN **2** -S **:** any fern of the genus *Osmunda*
os·mun·da·ce·ae \,äzmən'dāsē,ē\ *n pl*, *cap* [NL, fr. *Osmunda*, type genus + *-aceae*] **:** a large family of widely distributed ferns with naked sori and brightly stalked annulate sporangia that open longitudinally — **os·mun·da·ceous** \¦≈≈¦dāshəs\ *adj*
osmund brake *n* **:** ROYAL FERN
osmund furnace *n* [²*osmund*] **:** a high forge intermediate in development between the Catalan forge and the blast furnace and formerly used for making a wrought iron for wire
os·mun·dine \äz'mən,dēn\ *n* -S [NL *Osmunda* + E *-ine*] **:** material prepared from the roots of various ferns (primarily *Osmunda cinnamomea* and *O. claytonia*) and used in the potting of orchids
osmund iron *n* [ME *osmonde iren* (trans. of OSw *osmundsiærn*), fr. *osmonde*, *osmond* osmund + *iren* iron] **:** OSMUND; *also* **:** iron made in the osmund furnace
os·na·brück *or* **os·na·bruck** *or* **os·na·brueck** \'äznə,brùk\ *adj*, *usu cap* [fr. *Osnabrück*, city in northwest Germany] **:** of or from the city of Osnabrück, Germany **:** of the kind or style prevalent in Osnabrück
os·na·burg \'äznə,bərg\ *n* -S [irreg. fr. *Osnabrück*, Germany] **:** a rough coarse durable cotton fabric in plain weave made orig. of flax and used in the gray for bagging and industrial purposes and in various finishes usu. for upholstery, sportswear, and curtains
oso·berry \'ōsō- — *see* BERRY\ *n* [Sp *oso* bear (fr. L *ursus*) + E *berry* — more at ARCTIC] **1 :** the blue-black fruit resembling cherries of a shrub (*Osmaronia cerasiformis*) of the family Rosaceae of Oregon and California **2 :** a plant bearing osoberries
osone \'ō,sōn\ *n* -S [ISV ²*-ose* + *-one*; orig. formed as G *oson*] **:** a compound that contains two alpha carbonyl groups and is obtained by hydrolyzing an osazone ⟨xylose ~ $HOCH_2$-$(CHOH)_2COCHO$⟩
oso·triazole \¦ōsə+\ *n* [ISV *oso-* (fr. ²*-ose*) + *triazole*] **:** a vicinal triazole usu. made by boiling an osazone solution with dilute copper sulfate solution and useful in forming crystalline derivatives of carbohydrates
OSP *abbr*, *often not cap* [L *obiit sine prole*] he died without issue
os·phra·di·al \(')äs¦frādēəl\ *adj* [*osphradium* + *-al*] **:** of or relating to the osphradium
os·phra·di·um \≈'≈≈əm\ *n*, *pl* **osphra·dia** \-ēə\ [NL, fr. MGk *osphradion* nosegay, dim. of LGk *osphra* smell; akin to Gk *ozein* to smell — more at ODOR] **:** a single or paired sense organ connected with one of the visceral ganglia and situated near the gill of most aquatic mollusks that is supposed to be olfactory or to test the purity of the water passing to the gills
-os·phre·sia \əs'frēzh(ē)ə, (,)äs-\ *also* **-os·phra·sia** \-rāzh-\ *n comb form* -S [NL, fr. Gk *osphrēsis* sense of smell & Gk *osphrasia* odor; akin to Gk *ozein* to smell] **:** sense of smell ⟨an*osphresia*⟩ ⟨an*osphrasia*⟩
os·phre·sis \äs'frēsəs\ *n* -ES [NL, fr. Gk *osphrēsis*] **:** OLFACTION
os·phret·ic \(')äs¦fred·ik\ *adj* [Gk *osphrētikos*, fr. *osphrētos* capable of being smelled + *-ikos* -ic; akin to Gk *ozein* to smell] **:** OLFACTORY
os·phro·men·i·dae \,äsfrə'menə,dē\ *n pl*, *cap* [NL, fr. *Osphromenus*, type genus (fr. Gk *osphromenos*, aor. part. of *osphrainesthai* to smell, catch the scent of) + *-idae*; fr. a resemblance of certain organs to another supposed by the namer to be an organ of smell; akin to Gk *ozein* to smell] *in some classifications* **:** a family of freshwater fishes of southeastern Asia and Africa including the gouramis and a number of favored aquarium fishes and usu. included in the same family (Anabantidae) as the genus *Anabas*
os·prey \'äsprē, 'ä,sprā\ *n* -S [ME *ospray*, fr. (assumed) MF *osfraie*, fr. L *ossifraga* sea eagle — more at OSSIFRAGE] **1 :** a large harmless hawk (*Pandion haliaetus*) found in most countries of the world that is a dark brown color above and mostly pure white below, builds a bulky nest often occupied year after year, and feeds on fish that it captures by hovering and diving — called also *fish hawk* **2 :** a feather trimming (as an aigrette) used for millinery
ossa *pl of* OS
¹osse *or* **oss** \'äs\ *vb* **ossed; ossed; ossing; osses** [ME *ossen* to prophesy, presage] *dial Eng* **:** ATTEMPT, VENTURE, DARE
²osse *n* -S [obs. *osse*, v., to prophesy, presage, fr. ME *ossen*] *obs* **:** a prophetic or ominous utterance
osse- *or* **osseo-** *comb form* [L *osse-* (in *osseus*)] **1 :** bone ⟨*osse*in⟩ **2 :** osseous and ⟨*osseo*cartilaginous⟩
os·se·in \'äsēən\ *n* -S [ISV *osse-* + *-in*] **:** the chief organic substance of bone tissue that remains as a residue after removal of the mineral matters from cleaned degreased bone by dilute acid and is used in making gelatin **:** the collagen of bones
os·se·let \'äs(ə)lət\ *n* -S [F, lit., small bone, fr. OF, fr. *ossel* bone (fr. *os* bone — fr. LL *ossum*, fr. L *oss-*, *os* — + *-el*) + *-et*] **:** an exostosis on the leg of a horse; *esp* **:** one on the lateral or anterior aspect of the fetlock occurring chiefly in horses subjected to severe strain while young
os·se·ous \'äsēəs\ *adj* [L *osseus*, fr. *oss-*, *os* bone + *-eus* -eous; akin to Gk *osteon* bone, Skt *asthi*] **:** composed of or resembling bone **:** BONY — **os·se·ous·ly** *adv*
osseous fish *n* **:** BONY FISH
osseous labyrinth *n* **:** BONY LABYRINTH
os·set \'äsət\ *also* **os·ete** *or* **os·sete** \'ä,sēt\ *or* **os·se·ta** \'äsəd·ə\ *or* **os·se·tine** \-d·ən\ *or* **os·se·tian** \ə'sēshən\ *n* -S *cap* [*osset*, *osete*, *ossete*, *osseta*, *ossetine* fr. Russ *Osetin*, fr. Georgian *Os*, *Osetʼi*, land of the Ossets; *ossetian* fr. *osset* + *-an*, n. suffix] **:** one of a tall Aryan people of central Caucasus who are possibly immigrants from Persia and are supposed to be descendants of the Alans and who follow a religion that is a mixture of Muhammadanism and Christianity
¹os·set·ic \ə'sed·ik\ *also* **os·se·tian** \-sēshən\ *adj*, *usu cap* [*osset* + *-ic* or *-an*, adj. suffix] **:** of, relating to, or characteristic of the Ossets
²ossetic \"\ *or* **os·sete** \'ä,sēt\ *n* -S *cap* [*ossetic* fr. *ossetic*, adj.; *ossete* fr. *ossete*, var. of *osset*] **:** the Iranian language of the Ossets
ossi- *comb form* [L, fr. *oss-*, *os*] **:** bone ⟨*ossi*fic⟩
os·sia \ō'sēə\ *conj* [It, fr. *o sia* or let it be, fr. *o* or (fr. L *aut*) + *sia* let it be, be it, 3d pers. sing. pres. subj. of *essere* to be, fr. L *esse* — more at EKE, IS] **:** or else — used as a direction in music to indicate an alternative and usu. simpler form of a passage
os·si·an·ic \¦äs(h)ē¦anik\ *adj*, *usu cap* [*Ossian*, 3d cent. A.D. legendary Irish warrior and bard asserted by James Macpherson to be the author of the alleged Gaelic epic poems of which Macpherson's *Fingal* (1762) and *Temora* (1763) are purported to be English translations + E *-ic*] **:** of, relating to, or resembling the legendary Irish bard Ossian, the poems ascribed to him, or the rhythmic prose style used by James Macpherson in his alleged translations
os·si·cle \'äsəkəl\ *n* -S [L *ossiculum*, dim. of *oss-*, *os* bone] **1 :** any of certain small bones: as **a :** the malleus, incus, or stapes of the ear **b :** one of the small plates of bone in the sclerotic of some reptiles and birds **2 :** any of various small calcareous bodies: as **a :** one of the numerous small calcareous pieces of the skeleton of many echinoderms **b :** one of the parts of the gastric mill of the stomach of some crustaceans
os·sic·u·lar \ə'sikyələ(r)\ *adj* [LL *ossicularis*, fr. L *ossiculum* + *-aris* -ar] **:** of, relating to, or resembling ossicles
os·sic·u·late \-yələt, -yə,lāt\ *or* **os·sic·u·lat·ed** \-,lād·əd\ *adj* [*ossiculate* fr. NL *ossiculatus*, fr. L *ossiculum* + *-atus* -ate; *ossiculated* fr. NL *ossiculatus* + E *-ed*] **:** having ossicles
os·si·cu·lec·to·my \,äsəkyə'lektəmē\ *n* -ES [ISV *ossicul-* (fr. L *ossiculum*) + *-ectomy*] **:** the surgical removal of an auditory ossicle
os·si·cu·lot·o·my \-'läd·əmē\ *n* -ES [L *ossiculum* + E *-o-* + *-tomy*] **:** the surgical division of one or more of the auditory ossicles
os·sic·u·lum \ə'sikyələm\ *n*, *pl* **ossicu·la** \-lə\ [L] **:** OSSICLE
os·sif·ic \ə'sifik\ *adj* [prob. fr. (assumed) NL *ossificus*, fr. L *ossi-* + *-ficus* -fic] **:** tending to form bone **:** making bone
os·si·fi·ca·tion \,äsəfə'kāshən\ *n* -S [prob. fr. (assumed) NL *ossification-*, *ossificatio*, fr. (assumed) NL *ossificatus* (past part. of *ossificare* to ossify) + L *-ion-*, *-io* -ion] **1 a :** the process of bone formation usu. beginning at particular centers in each prospective bone and involving the activities of special osteoblasts that segregate and deposit inorganic bone substance about themselves — see ENDOCHONDRAL OSSIFICATION, INTERMEMBRANOUS OSSIFICATION **b :** an instance of this process **2 a :** the condition of being altered into a hard

bony substance ⟨~ of the muscular tissue⟩ **b :** a mass or particle of ossified tissue **:** a calcareous deposit in the tissues ⟨~s in the aortic wall⟩ **3 a :** the process of becoming hardened, indifferent, and insensitive to the feelings of others; *also* **:** a state of callousness ⟨the emotional ~ which the poet must escape —J.M.O'Brien⟩ **b :** the process of becoming molded or set in a conventional pattern; *also* **:** a state of unimaginative conformity ⟨continue its present course of ~ into a new dogmatism —Paul Woodring⟩ ⟨a way of life that . . . might remain in a state of cosy ~ until doomsday —Norman Lewis⟩

os·sif·i·ca·tory \ä'sifəkə,tōrē\ *adj* [fr. *ossification*, after such pairs as E *commendation: commendatory*] **:** of or involving ossification ⟨some ~ processes of the immature skull —E.A. Hooton⟩

ossified *adj* [fr. past part. of *ossify*] **1** *of tissues* **:** changed to bone or something resembling bone **:** hardened by deposits of mineral matter of any kind **2 :** set in a conventional form **:** FIXED, HARDENED, ULTRACONSERVATIVE ⟨bitterly criticized the organization for being ~⟩

os·si·fi·er \'äsə,fī(ə)r\ *n* -s **:** one that ossifies

os·si·frage \'äsəfrij\ *n* -s [L *ossifraga* sea eagle, fr. fem. of *ossifragus* bone-breaking, fr. *ossi-* + *-fragus* (fr. *frangere* to break) — more at BREAK] **1 :** LAMMERGEIER **2 :** OSPREY

os·si·fy \'äsə,fī\ *vb* -ED/-ING/-ES [prob. fr. (assumed) NL *ossificare*, fr. L *ossi-* + *-ficare* -fy] *vi* **1 :** to form or be transformed into bone ⟨additional cartilages ~ with age⟩ **2 :** to become callous or hardened **:** become set in a conventional pattern ⟨so easy for the mind to ~ and generous ideals to end in stale platitudes —John Buchan⟩ ~ *vt* **1 :** to change (as cartilage) into bone ⟨osteoblasts ~ the tissue⟩ **2 :** to make callous, rigid, or inactive **:** mold firmly in a conventional pattern **:** HARDEN ⟨guilds that won freedom by combination and then *ossified* it into monopoly —D.C.Coyle⟩

ossing *pres part of* OSSE

os·su·ary \'äshə,werē, 'äs(y)ə-\ *n* -ES [LL *ossuarium*, fr. L. neut. of *ossuarius* of bones, fr. OL *ossua* (pl. of *oss-*, *os* bone) + L *-arius* -ary — more at OSSEOUS] **1 :** a depository (as a vault, room, urn) for the bones of the dead **2 :** a communal burial place (as of American Indians)

-ost \,äst *also* ,ȯst\ *n comb form* -s [Gk *osteon*] **:** bone ⟨actin*ost*⟩

ost *abbr* osteopathic

OST *abbr, often not cap* ordinary spring tides

o star *n, usu cap O* **:** a star of spectral type O — see SPECTRAL TYPE table

os·tar·i·o·phy·san \ä,sta(a)rēō'fīs³n\ *n* -s [NL *Ostariophysi* + E *-an*] **:** a fish of the order Ostariophysi

os·tar·i·o·phy·se·ae \-īsē,ē\ *or* **os·tar·i·o·phy·si·na** \-īs³nə\ [NL, fr. *ostario-* (fr. Gk *ostarion* small bone) + *-physeae*, *-physina* (fr. Gk *physa* bellows, bladder)] *syn of* OSTARIOPHYSI

os·tar·i·o·phy·si \-ī,sī\ *n pl, cap* [NL, fr. *ostario-* (fr. Gk *ostarion* small bone, dim. of *osteon* bone) + *-physi* (fr. Gk *physa* bellows, bladder) — more at PUSTULE] **:** a large order or other division of teleost fishes (as the characin, carp, catfish) having the anterior four vertebrae strongly modified and often grown together and supporting a chain of small bones which connect the air bladder with the ear — **os·tar·i·o·phys·i·al** \⸗¦⸗⸗⸗¦fizēəl\ *adj* — **os·tar·i·o·phy·sine** \-fī,sīn\ *adj* — **os·tar·i·o·phy·sous** \-fīsəs\ *adj*

oste- *or* **osteo-** *comb form* [NL, fr. Gk, fr. *osteon* — more at OSSEOUS] **:** bone ⟨*oste*al⟩ ⟨*osteo*myelitis⟩

os·te·al \'ästēəl\ *adj* [ISV *oste-* + *-al*] **1 :** sounding like bone under percussion **2 :** of or relating to bone ⟨~ development⟩ **:** like bone ⟨the ~ part of the cartilage⟩ **:** affecting or involving bone or the skeleton ⟨~ lesions in leukemia⟩

os·te·ich·thy·es \,ästē'ikthē,ēz\ *n pl, cap* [NL, fr. *oste-* + Gk *ichthyes*, pl of *ichthys* fish — more at ICHTHUS] *in some classifications* **:** a class or other category of fishes including the lungfishes, crossopterygians, teleosts, and esp. formerly the arthrodires and ostracoderms and distinguished from other forms resembling fish by the presence of true bone in their skeleton — compare CHONDRICHTHYES

os·te·in \'ästēən\ *n* -s [ISV *oste-* + *-in*] **:** OSSEIN

os·te·it·ic \,ästē¦id·ik\ *adj* [*osteitis* + *-ic*] **:** relating to or characterized by osteitis

os·te·i·tis \,⸗⸗'īd·əs\ *n, pl* **os·te·it·i·des** \-'id·ə,dēz\ [NL, fr. *oste-* + *-itis*] **:** inflammation of bone

osteitis de·for·mans \-dē'fȯr,manz\ *n* [NL, deforming osteitis] **:** a chronic disease of bones characterized by their great enlargement and rarefaction with bowing of the long bones and deformation of the flat bones — called also *Paget's disease*

osteitis fi·bro·sa \-fī'brōsə\ *n* [NL, fibrous osteitis] **:** a disease of bone that is characterized by fibrous degeneration of the bone and the formation of cystic cavities and that results in deformities of the affected bones and sometimes in fracture

os·tend \ä'stend\ *vt* -ED/-ING/-S [ME *ostenden*, fr. L *ostendere* to show] **:** to show clearly **:** EXHIBIT, MANIFEST ⟨seemed to me somewhat to ~ his relationship with the . . . household —H.H.Johnston⟩

os·ten·si·bil·i·ty \ä,sten(t)sə'biləd·ē\ *n* -ES **:** the quality or state of being ostensible

os·ten·si·ble \ä'sten(t)səbəl, ə'- *sometimes* ȯ'-\ *adj* [F, fr. L *ostensus* (past part. of *ostendere* to show, fr. *os-* — fr. *ob* to, before, against — + *tendere* to stretch) + F *-ible* -able — more at EPI-, THIN] **1 a :** capable of being shown **:** prepared to be exhibited **:** PRESENTABLE ⟨send me two letters—one confidential, another ~ —Jeremy Bentham⟩ **b :** open to view **:** CONSPICUOUS ⟨the ~ validity of his predictions regarding the past war —S.H.Croog⟩ ⟨have different ~ properties —C.H. Whitely⟩ **2 :** professing genuineness and sincerity but often concealing the real aspects behind a plausible facade ⟨the sketches of Stratford-on-Avon . . . the ~ reason for his trip, duly appeared —F.J.Mather⟩ ⟨organized a company whose ~ purpose was to provide an adequate supply of water —Sidney Warren⟩ **syn** see APPARENT

ostensible authority *or* **ostensible agency** *n* **:** authority or agency by estoppel arising when a principal has intentionally or negligently caused a third person to believe and rely upon the apparent authority of his supposed agent even though it has not been given

ostensible partner *n* **:** one who holds himself out as a member of an actual partnership or one apparently existing or consenting to the partners or apparent partners representing him as such though as between themselves he is no partner **:** a partner by estoppel and liable as such to those relying thereon

os·ten·si·bly \-blē, -li\ *adv* **:** in an ostensible manner **:** to all outward appearances ⟨~ this is a brief statement about a little pale yellow deer —C.S.Kilby⟩ ⟨had been ~ frank as to his purpose while really concealing it —Thomas Hardy⟩

os·ten·sion \ä'stenchən\ *n* -s [ME *ostensioun*, fr. MF *ostension*, fr. L *ostension-*, *ostensio*, fr. *ostensus* (past part. of *ostendere* to show) + *-ion-*, *-io* -ion] **1 :** an act or process of showing, pointing out, or exhibiting **2 :** exposition of the Host

os·ten·sive \-en(t)siv\ *adj* [LL *ostensivus*, fr. L *ostensus* (past part. of *ostendere* to show) + *-ivus* -ive] **1 :** manifestly or immediately demonstrative **:** DEICTIC ⟨the proposition that my pen is falling down is ~ and thus empirical —Stephan Körner⟩ **2 :** OSTENSIBLE 2 — **os·ten·sive·ly** \-səvlē\ *adv*

ostensive definition *n* **:** a definition accomplished by exhibiting and characterizing the thing to be defined or by pointing out and characterizing the cases or instances to be covered

ostensive reduction *n* **:** DIRECT REDUCTION

os·ten·so·ri·um \,ästən'sōrēəm\ *or* **os·ten·so·ry** \ä'sten(t)sərē\ *n, pl* **ostenso·ria** \-ēə\ *or* **ostensories** [ML *ostensorium*, fr. L *ostensus* (past part. of *ostendere* to show) + *-orium* -ory] *Roman Catholicism* **:** MONSTRANCE

os·tent \ä,stent\ *n* -s [in sense 1, fr. L *ostentum*, fr. neut. of *ostentus*, past part. of *ostendere* to show; in other senses, fr. L *ostentus*, n., fr. *ostentus*, past part. of *ostendere* to show] **1 :** a significant sign **:** PORTENT ⟨the night waxed wan, as though with an awed sense of such ~ —Thomas Hardy⟩ **2 :** the act of showing or displaying **:** APPEARANCE, MANIFESTATION ⟨be merry and employ your chiefest thoughts to courtship and such fair ~s of love —Shak.⟩ **3 :** excessive display **:** OSTENTATION 1 a ⟨the city of glorious ~ and vanity —Christopher Morley⟩

os·ten·tate \'ästən·,tāt\ *vt* -ED/-ING/-S [L *ostentatus*, past part. of *ostentare*, fr. *ostentus*, past part. of *ostendere* to show] **:** to display ostentatiously ⟨the front door *ostentated* a brass plate —Israel Zangwill⟩

os·ten·ta·tion \,ä¦stən·'tāshən *sometimes* ,ȯ¦ *or* ¦,sten-\ *n* -s [ME *ostentacioun*, fr. MF *ostentation*, fr. L *ostentation-*, *ostentatio*, fr. *ostentatus* (past part. of *ostentare* to display ostentatiously) + *-ion-*, *-io* -ion] **1 a :** the act of making an ambitious display **:** vain and unnecessary show esp. for the purpose of attracting attention, admiration, or envy **:** PRETENTIOUSNESS ⟨a woman brought up in the traditions of a modesty so proud that it scorns ~ —Arnold Bennett⟩ **b :** overly elaborate embellishment esp. in art **:** FLORIDITY ⟨architecture . . . characterized by ~ and ornamental frills of the Victorian era —*Amer. Guide Series: Texas*⟩ ⟨stepped over the . . . boundary which divides wealth from ~, eloquence from pedantry, art from technique —Gilbert Highet⟩ ⟨interpret the inmost thoughts of the composer, and to reproduce them without sentimentality and ~ —A.E.Wier⟩ **2** *archaic* **:** the act of exhibiting or showing **:** DISPLAY ⟨maintain a mourning ~ —Shak.⟩

os·ten·ta·tious \¦⸗(,)⸗¦tāshəs\ *adj* [fr. *ostentation*, after such pairs as E *contention: contentious*] **:** characterized by, fond of, or evincing ostentation **:** attracting attention often by gaudiness or show **:** overly elaborate or ornate **:** CONSPICUOUS, EXAGGERATED ⟨a very ~ method of gaining her attention —Robertson Davies⟩ ⟨the cold philanthropies, the ~ public charities —Oscar Wilde⟩ ⟨embarrassed by the too ~ piety of our family —R.M.Lovett⟩ ⟨went ahead with plans to build an ~ skyscraper —Christopher Rand⟩ ⟨accumulated an ~ wardrobe of fifty suits —Greer Williams⟩

os·ten·ta·tious·ly *adv* **:** in an ostentatious manner **:** for the purpose of attracting attention **:** PRETENTIOUSLY ⟨crooked ~ picturesque streets —W.B.Yeats⟩ ⟨eccentricity—sometimes ~ cultivated —H.S.Commager⟩

os·ten·ta·tious·ness *n* -ES **:** the quality or state of being ostentatious

ostentative *adj* [*ostentate* + *-ive*] *obs* **:** OSTENTATIOUS

ostentive *or* **ostentous** *adj* [*ostent* + *-ive* or *-ous*] *obs* **:** OSTENTATIOUS

osteo- — see OSTE-

os·teo·arthritic \¦ästēō+,⸗¦⸗⸗\ *adj* [*osteoarthritis* + *-ic*] **:** of, relating to, or affected with degenerative arthritis

os·teo·arthritis \"+,⸗¦⸗⸗\ *n* [NL, fr. *oste-* + *arthritis*] **:** DEGENERATIVE ARTHRITIS

os·teo·arthropathy \"+,⸗¦⸗⸗\ *n* [ISV *oste-* + *arthropathy*; prob. orig. formed as F *ostéoarthropathie*] **:** a disease of joints or bones; *specif* **:** a condition marked by enlargement of the terminal phalanges, thickening of the joint surfaces, and curving of the nails and sometimes associated with chronic disease of the lungs

os·te·o·blast \'ästēə,blast\ *n* [ISV *oste-* + *-blast*; prob. orig. formed in G] **:** a bone-forming cell — see OSSIFICATION 1 a

os·te·o·blas·tic \¦⸗⸗⸗¦blastik\ *adj* [ISV *osteoblast* + *-ic*] **1 :** relating to or involving the formation of bone **2 :** of or relating to osteoblasts

osteochondr- *or* **osteochondro-** *comb form* [ISV *oste-* + *chondr-*] **:** bone and cartilage ⟨*osteochondro*pathy⟩ ⟨*osteochondr*ous⟩

os·te·o·chon·drop·a·thy \,ästēō,kän'dräpəthē\ *n* -ES [*osteochondr-* + *-pathy*] **:** a disease involving both bone and cartilage

os·te·o·chon·dro·sis \-rōsəs\ *n, pl* **osteochondro·ses** \-ō,sēz\ [NL, fr. *osteochondr-* + *-osis*] **:** a disease of children in which an ossification center esp. in the epiphyses of long bones undergoes degeneration followed by calcification — **os·te·o·chon·drot·ic** \¦⸗⸗⸗,⸗¦dräd·ik\ *adj*

os·te·o·chon·drous \¦⸗⸗⸗¦⸗ndrəs\ *also* **os·te·o·chon·dral** \-əl\ *adj* [*osteochondr-* + *-ous* or *-al*] **:** relating to or composed of bone and cartilage

os·te·oc·la·sis \,ästē'äkləsəs\ *n* -ES [NL, fr. *oste-* + *-clasis*] **:** the breaking of a bone as a step in the surgical correction of a deformity

os·te·o·clast \'ästēə,klast\ *n* -s [ISV *oste-* + *-clast*; orig. formed as G *osteoklast*] **1 :** one of the large multinucleate cells in developing bone that are considered to function in the dissolution of unwanted bone (as in the formation of canals or the healing of fractures) **2 :** an instrument for performing osteoclasis — **os·te·o·clas·tic** \¦⸗⸗⸗¦klastik\ *adj*

os·te·o·col·la \,ästēō'kälə\ *n* -s [modif. (influenced by Gk *kolla* glue) of NL *osteocollus*, fr. *oste-* + *-collus* (fr. Gk *kolla* glue); fr. a belief that it could be used to join broken bones — more at PROTOCOL] **:** a cellular incrustation of calcium carbonate on stems and roots of plants

os·te·o·com·ma \-'kämə\ *n* -s [NL, fr. *oste-* + Gk *komma* piece, stamp, clause — more at COMMA] **:** a metameric segment of the vertebrate skeleton

os·teo·cranium \¦ästēō+\ *n* [NL, fr. *oste-* + ML *cranium*] **:** the bony cranium; *esp* **:** the parts of the cranium that arise in membrane bone — distinguished from *chondrocranium*

os·te·o·cyte \'ästēə,sīt\ *n* -s [*oste-* + *-cyte*] **:** a cell that is characteristic of adult bone and isolated in a lacuna of the bone substance

os·teo·dentin *also* **os·teo·dentine** \¦ästēō+\ *n* [*oste-* + *dentin*] **:** a modified dentine approaching true bone in structure and found chiefly in the teeth of fishes — **os·teo·den·tinal** \"+\ *adj*

os·te·o·derm \'ästēə,dərm\ *n* [ISV *oste-* + *-derm*] **:** a bony plate in the skin (as of a crocodile) — **os·te·o·der·mal** \¦⸗⸗⸗¦dərməl\ *adj*

os·te·o·der·ma·tous \¦⸗⸗⸗¦dərməd·əs\ *also* **os·te·o·der·mous** \-məs\ *adj* [*osteodermatous* fr. *oste-* + *-dermatous*; *osteodermous* fr. *osteoderm* + *-ous*] **:** having the skin more or less ossified; *also* **:** having osteoderms

os·teo·dystrophia deformans \¦ästēō+\ *n* [NL, fr. *oste-* + *dystrophia*] **:** OSTEITIS DEFORMANS

osteodystrophia fibrosa *n* **:** OSTEITIS FIBROSA

os·teo·dystrophic \"+(,)⸗¦⸗⸗\ *adj* **:** of, relating to, or marked by osteodystrophy

os·teo·dystrophy \"+\ *also* **os·teo·dystrophia** \"+\ *n* [NL *osteodystrophia*, fr. *oste-* + *dystrophia*] **:** defective ossification of bone usu. associated with disturbed calcium and phosphorus metabolism and renal insufficiency

os·teo·fibrosis \"+,⸗¦⸗⸗\ *n* [NL, fr. *oste-* + *fibrosis*] **:** fibrosis of bone

os·teo·fibrous \"+\ *adj* [*oste-* + *fibrous*] **:** composed of bone and fibrous connective tissue

os·te·o·gen·e·sis \,ästēō'jenəsəs\ *n* [NL, fr. *oste-* + L *genesis*] **:** development and formation of bone **:** OSSIFICATION

osteogenesis im·per·fec·ta \-,impə(r)'fektə\ *n* [NL, imperfect osteogenesis] **:** FRAGILITAS OSSIUM

os·te·o·gen·ic \,ästēə¦jenik\ *also* **os·te·o·ge·net·ic** \-ēōjə¦ned·ik\ *adj* [*osteogenic* ISV *oste-* + *-genic*; *osteogenetic* fr. *oste-* + *-genetic*] **1 :** bone-producing **2 :** originating in bone

os·te·og·e·nous \,ästē¦äjənəs\ *adj* [*oste-* + *-genous*] **:** OSTEOGENIC 1

¹os·te·o·glos·sid \¦ästēə¦gläsəd\ *adj* [NL *Osteoglossidae*] **:** of or relating to the Osteoglossidae

²osteoglossid \"\ *n* -s [NL *Osteoglossidae*] **:** a fish of the family Osteoglossidae

os·te·o·glos·si·dae \,⸗⸗⸗'gläsə,dē\ *n pl, cap* [NL, fr. *Osteoglossum*, type genus + *-idae*] **:** a family of very large tropical freshwater fishes (suborder Osteoglossoidea) consisting of the pirarucu and related forms and having the head naked and largely encased in bone and the scales large, bony, and composed of pieces resembling mosaic

os·te·o·glos·soi·dea \,⸗⸗⸗,glä'sȯidēə\ *n pl, cap* [NL, fr. *Osteoglossum* + *-oidea*] **:** a suborder of Isospondyli comprising the Osteoglossidae and a few related fishes chiefly of the tropical southern hemisphere

os·te·o·glos·sum \,⸗⸗⸗'gläsəm\ *n, cap* [NL, fr. *oste-* + *-glossum* (fr. Gk *glōssa* tongue) — more at GLOSS] **:** a genus of fishes that is the type of the family Osteoglossidae

os·te·og·ra·phy \,ästē'ägrəfē\ *n* -ES [*oste-* + *-graphy*] **:** descriptive osteology

¹os·te·oid \'ästē,ȯid\ *adj* [ISV *oste-* + *-oid*] **1 :** resembling bone **2 :** having a bone skeleton ⟨~ fishes⟩

²osteoid \"\ *n* -s [*oste-* + *-oid*] **:** uncalcified bone matrix

¹os·te·o·lep·id \,ästēō¦lepəd\ *adj* [NL *Osteolepidae*] **:** of or relating to the Osteolepidae

²osteolepid \"\ *n* -s [NL *Osteolepidae*] **:** a fish of the family Osteolepidae

os·te·o·lep·i·dae \,⸗⸗⸗'lepə,dē\ *n pl, cap* [NL, fr. *Osteolepis*, type genus + *-idae*] **:** a widely distributed family of freshwater Paleozoic fishes (order Rhipidistia) having slender elongated bodies, large rhombic scales, and a well-ossified cranium and commonly considered to be on the direct ancestral line of the amphibians

os·te·o·lep·i·form \¦⸗⸗⸗¦lepə,fȯrm\ *adj* [NL *Osteolepiformes*] **:** RHIPIDISTID

os·te·o·lep·i·for·mes \,⸗⸗⸗,⸗⸗'fȯr,mēz\ [NL, fr. *Osteolepis* + *-formes*] *syn of* RHIPIDISTIA

os·te·ol·e·pis \,ästē'äləpəs\ *n, cap* [NL, fr. *oste-* + *-lepis*] **:** the type genus of Osteolepidae comprising fossil fishes chiefly from the Middle Devonian of Scotland

os·te·ol·e·poid \¦⸗⸗¦älə,pȯid\ *adj* [NL *Osteolepis* + E *-oid*] **:** belonging to or like members of the family Osteolepidae

os·te·o·lite \'ästēō,līt\ *n* -s [G *osteolith*, fr. *oste-* + *-lith* -lite] **:** a mineral consisting of a massive impure earthy apatite

os·te·o·log·ic \,ästēə¦läjik\ *or* **os·te·o·log·i·cal** \-jəkəl\ *adj* [*osteologic* ISV *osteology* + *-ic*; *osteological* fr. *osteology* + *-ical*] **:** of or relating to osteology — **os·te·o·log·i·cal·ly** \-jək(ə)lē\ *adv*

os·te·ol·o·gist \,ästē'äləjəst\ *n* -s [*osteology* + *-ist*] **:** a specialist in osteology

os·te·ol·o·gy \-jē\ *n* -ES [NL *osteologia*, fr. Gk, description of bones, fr. *oste-* + *-logia* -logy] **1 :** a branch of anatomy dealing with the bones **2 :** the features comprised in the bony structure and organization of an organism or any of its parts ⟨the ~ of a cat⟩ ⟨the ~ of the head⟩

os·te·ol·y·sis \,ästē'äləsəs\ *n* [NL, fr. *oste-* + *-lysis*] **:** dissolution of bone esp. when associated with resorption

os·te·o·lyt·ic \,ästēō¦lid·ik\ *adj* **:** characteristic of or marked by osteolysis

os·te·o·ma \,ästē'ōmə\ *n, pl* **osteomas** \-məz\ *or* **osteoma·ta** \-məd·ə\ [NL, fr. *oste-* + *-oma*] **:** a benign tumor composed of bone tissue

os·teo·malacia \¦ästēō+\ *n* [NL, fr. *oste-* + *malacia*] **:** a disease of the bones characterized by softening, caused by a deficiency of minerals (as calcium and phosphorus) and of vitamin D, affecting adults of man and domestic animals, and representing the counterpart of rickets in immature animals

os·te·o·ma·toid \,ästē'ōmə,tȯid\ *adj* [NL *osteomat-*, *osteoma* osteoma + E *-oid*] **:** resembling an osteoma

os·te·o·ma·tous \-məd·əs\ *adj* [NL *osteomat-*, *osteoma* osteoma + E *-ous*] **:** of, relating to, or being an osteoma

os·te·o·met·ric \,ästēə¦me·trik\ *or* **os·te·o·met·ri·cal** \-rəkəl\ *adj* **:** of or relating to osteometry

os·te·om·e·try \,ästē'ämə·trē\ *n* -ES [ISV *oste-* + *-metry*; prob. orig. formed as F *ostéométrie*] **:** the measurement of bones; *esp* **:** anthropometric measurement of the human skeleton

os·teo·myelitic \¦ästēō+\ *adj* [*osteomyelitis* + *-ic*] **:** of, caused by, or affected by osteomyelitis

os·teo·myelitis \"+\ *n* [NL, fr. *oste-* + *myelitis*] **:** an inflammatory disease of bone that may involve the marrow, cortex, or periosteum, that is caused by an infectious agent that reaches the site by way of the blood from a source in adjacent tissue or through a penetrating injury (as a laceration or compound fracture), and that produces death of tissue with separation of the devitalized portion from the viable tissue by the formation of a sequestrum

-os·te·on \'ästē,än\ *n comb form* -s [NL, fr. Gk *osteon* bone — more at OSSEOUS] **:** bone **:** bone part ⟨loph*osteon*⟩

os·te·o·path \'ästēə,path\ *n* -s [back-formation fr. *osteopathy*] **:** a practitioner of osteopathy

os·te·o·path·ic \¦⸗⸗⸗¦pathik\ *adj* [*osteopathy* + *-ic*] **:** of, relating to, or by means of osteopathy — **os·te·o·path·i·cal·ly** \-thək(ə)lē\ *adv*

os·te·op·a·thist \,ästē'äpəthəst\ *n* -s [*osteopathy* + *-ist*] **:** OSTEOPATH

os·te·op·a·thy \-thē, -thi\ *n* -ES [NL *osteopathia*, fr. *oste-* + L *-pathia* -pathy] **1 :** a disease of bone **2 :** a system of medical practice based on the theory that diseases are due chiefly to a loss of structural integrity in the tissues and that this integrity can be restored by manipulation of the parts supported by the use of medicines, surgery, proper diet, and other therapy

os·teo·periostitis \¦ästēō+\ *n* [NL, fr. *oste-* + *periostitis*] **:** inflammation of a bone and its periosteum

os·te·o·pe·tro·sis \,ästēōpə'trōsəs\ *n* [NL, fr. *oste-* + *petr-* + *-osis*] **1 :** an abnormal thickening and hardening of bone often with the development of bands of varying density in the long bones and sometimes with partial occlusion of the marrow cavities **2 a :** a hereditary disorder that affects the bones of human beings and that is marked by extreme density and hardness and abnormal fragility — called also *marble bones* **b :** a hereditary bone disease of rabbits that is marked by enlargement and faulty development of the skeletal parts **c :** a disease of the avian leukosis complex of chickens marked by great enlargement and excessive calcification of the long bones esp. of the legs and by more or less complete obliteration of the marrow cavities and varying degrees of anemia — called also *marble bone*

os·te·o·pe·trot·ic \¦⸗⸗⸗⸗¦träd·ik\ *adj* **:** characteristic of or marked by osteopetrosis

os·te·o·phage \'ästēə,fāj\ *n* [ISV *oste-* + *-phage*] **:** OSTEOCLAST 1

os·te·o·pha·gia \,ästēō'fājēə\ *n* -s [NL, fr. *oste-* + *-phagia*] **:** the eating or chewing of bones by herbivorous animals (as cattle) craving phosphorus

os·te·o·phyte \'ästēə,fīt\ *n* -s [ISV *oste-* + *-phyte*] **:** a small pathological bony outgrowth — **os·te·o·phyt·ic** \¦⸗⸗⸗¦fid·ik\ *adj*

os·te·o·plast \'⸗⸗⸗,plast\ *n* -s [ISV *oste-* + *-plast*] **:** OSTEOBLAST

os·te·o·plas·tic \¦⸗⸗⸗¦plastik\ *adj* [ISV *osteoplasty* + *-ic*] **1 :** of, relating to, or being osteoplasty ⟨an ~ operation⟩ **2** [ISV *osteoplast* + *-ic*] **:** OSTEOBLASTIC

os·te·o·plas·ty \'⸗⸗⸗,plastē\ *n* -ES [ISV *oste-* + *-plasty*] **:** plastic surgery on bone; *esp* **:** replacement of lost bone tissue or reconstruction of defective bony parts

os·teo·porosis \¦ästēō+\ *n, pl* **osteoporoses** [NL, fr. *oste-* + *porosis*] **1 :** a condition characterized by decrease in bone mass with decreased density and enlargement of bone spaces producing porosity and fragility and resulting from disturbances of nutrition and mineral metabolism **2 :** a progressive metabolic disease of grazing animals (as horses and mules) marked by withdrawal of mineral matter from the bones causing enlargement, softening, and porosity of the bones esp. of the head

os·teo·porotic \"+\ *adj* [fr. *osteoporosis*, after such pairs as E *narcosis: narcotic*] **:** characteristic of or marked by osteoporosis

os·te·op·sath·y·ro·sis \,ästē,äp,sathə'rōsəs\ *n, pl* **osteopsathyroses** [NL, fr. *oste-* + Gk *psathyros* friable, crumbling + NL *-osis*; akin to Gk *psēphos* pebble — more at SAND] **:** FRAGILITAS OSSIUM

os·teo·radionecrosis \¦ästēō+\ *n* [NL, fr. *oste-* + *radionecrosis*] **:** necrosis of bone following irradiation

os·teo·sarcoma \"+\ *n* [NL, fr. *oste-* + *sarcoma*] **:** a sarcoma derived from bone or containing bone tissue

os·teo·sclereid \"+\ *n* [*oste-* + *sclereid*] **:** one of the sclereids forming the hypodermal layer in many fruits and seeds and occurring also in the leaves of certain xerophytes — called also *bone cell*; compare MACROSCLEREID

os·teo·sclerosis \"+\ *n* [NL, fr. *oste-* + *sclerosis* (fr. ML *sclirosis*) — more at SCLEROSIS] **:** OSTEOPETROSIS 1

os·teo·sclerotic \"+\ *adj* [fr. *osteosclerosis*, after E *sclerosis: sclerotic*] **:** of, relating to, or affected by osteopetrosis

¹os·te·os·tra·can \¦ästē¦ästrəkən\ *adj* [NL *Osteostraci* + E *-an*] **:** of or relating to the Cephalaspida

²osteostracan \"\ *n* -s **:** CEPHALASPID

os·te·os·tra·ci \,⸗⸗'ästrə,sī\ [NL, fr. *oste-* + *-ostraci* (fr. Gk *ostrakon* shell) — more at OYSTER] *syn of* CEPHALASPIDA

os·teo·synthesis \¦ästēō+\ *n* [ISV *oste-* + *synthesis*] **:** the operation of uniting the ends of a fractured bone by mechanical means (as by a metal plate)

os·te·o·tome \'ästēə,tōm\ *n* -s [NL *osteotomus*, fr. *oste-* + *-tomus* -tome] **:** strong nippers or a chisel without a bevel used in surgical and other procedures on bone

os·te·ot·o·my \,ästē'äd·əmē\ *n* -ES [prob. fr. (assumed) NL *osteotomia*, fr. NL *oste-* + *-tomia* -tomy] : a surgical operation of dividing a bone or of cutting a piece out of it to correct a deformity

os·te·o·tribe \'ästēə,trīb\ *n* -S [*oste-* + *-tribe*] : a rasp used for removing carious bone

os·te·ria \,ästə'rēə, ,ōs-\ *n* -S [It, fr. *oste* innkeeper, fr. L *hospit-, hospes* host, stranger, guest — more at HOST] **1** : a wayside inn ⟨stopped for the night at a small ~ —J.H.Shorthouse⟩ **2** : RESTAURANT ⟨a sandwich and wine at an ~ near the job —*N. Y. Times Mag.*⟩

os·ter·ta·gia \,äst(ə)r'tājēə\ *n, cap* [NL, fr. Robert von Ostertag †1940 Ger. veterinarian and parasitologist + NL *-ia*] : a genus of slender brown nematode worms (family Trichostrongylidae) parasitic in the abomasum of ruminants where their presence in numbers is associated with gastritis, scouring, or general unthriftiness

-os·te·us \'ästēəs\ *n comb form* [NL, fr. Gk *osteon* bone — more at OSSEOUS] : one having (such) a bone or bones — in generic names esp. of fishes ⟨Coccosteus⟩

ostiak *usu cap, var of* OSTYAK

os·ti·al \'ästēəl\ *adj* [*ostium* + *-al*] : of or relating to an ostium

os·ti·ary \'ästē,erē\ *n* -ES [L *ostiarius*, fr. *ostium* door, mouth of a river + *-arius* -ary] **1** : DOORKEEPER **2** *obs* : a mouth of a river

os·ti·ate \'ästēət, -ē,āt\ *adj* [*ostium* + *-ate*] : having an ostium

¹os·ti·na·to \,ästə'nä(,)tō, -tē,-, ,ōs-, ,ōs-, -nä(,)tō\ *adj* [It, stubborn, fr. L *obstinatus* obstinate] : relating to any frequently repeated motif or passage in any part of a musical composition or to the use of such repetition

²ostinato \"\ *n* -S **1 a** : a musical figure repeated persistently at the same pitch throughout a composition **b** : the use of such repetition **2** : GROUND BASS

os·ti·o·lar \'ästēələ(r), -ē,ōl-\ *adj* : of, relating to, or being an ostiole

os·ti·o·late \-lət, -,lāt\ *adj* : having ostioles

os·ti·ole \'ästē,ōl\ *n* -S [NL *ostiolum*, fr. L, small door, dim. of *ostium*] : a small aperture, orifice, or pore: as **a** : the mouth of the perithecium or other spore fruit in a fungus or lichen **b** : an orifice of an odoriferous gland in various Hemiptera **c** : the opening of the conceptacle in various fucoid seaweeds **d** : one of the small inhalant orifices of a sponge

os·ti·um \'ästēəm\ *n, pl* **os·tia** \-ēə\ [NL, fr. L, door, mouth of a river; akin to Russ *ust'e* mouth of a river, Skt *oṣṭha* lip, L *or-, os* mouth — more at ORAL] : an entrance or opening: as **a** : either end of a Fallopian tube **b** : one of the lateral slits in the heart of an arthropod by which the blood enters from the pericardium

ostler *var of* HOSTLER

os·tler·ess \'äslərəs\ *n* -ES : a female hostler

ost·men \'ōstmən\ *n pl, cap* [ME, fr. ON *austmenn*, pl. of *austmathr*, fr. *austr* to the east + *mathr* man — more at EAST, MAN] : Scandinavians anciently settled along the east coast of Ireland

¹os·tom·a·tid \ä'stämədəd\ *adj* [NL *Ostomatidae*] : of or relating to the family Ostomatidae

²ostomatid \"\ *n* -S [NL *Ostomatidae*] : a beetle of the family Ostomatidae

os·to·mat·i·dae \,ästə'mad·ə,dē\ *n pl, cap* [NL, fr. *Ostomat-, Ostoma*, type genus (irreg. fr. Gk *osteon* bone) + *-idae*] : a family of beetles most of which are useful predators

-os·to·sis \,ä'stōsəs\ *n comb form, pl* **-osto·ses** *or* **-ostosises** \-ō,sēz\ [NL, fr. Gk *-ostōsis*, fr. *osteon* bone + *-ōsis* -osis] : ossification of a (specified) part or to a (specified) degree ⟨hyperostosis⟩ ⟨ectostosis⟩

ostrac- *or* **ostraco-** *comb form* [NL, fr. Gk *ostrak-, ostrako-*, fr. *ostrakon*] : shell ⟨*Ostracoidea*⟩ ⟨*Ostracophori*⟩

ostraca *pl of* OSTRACON

-os·tra·ca \'ästrəkə *also* 'ōs-\ *n pl comb form* [NL, fr. Gk *-ostraka* (neut. pl. of *-ostrakos*, fr. *ostrakon* shell) — more at OYSTER] : ones having (such) a shell — in names of taxa chiefly of crustaceans ⟨*Arthrostraca*⟩ ⟨*Conchostraca*⟩

os·tra·cea \ä'strāshēə\ [NL, irreg. fr. *Ostrea* + *-acea*] *syn of* OSTRAEACEA

¹os·tra·cean \(')=shən\ *adj* [NL *Ostracea* + E *-an*] : of or relating to the Ostraeacea

²ostracean \"\ *n* -S : an oyster of the suborder Ostraeacea

os·tra·ceous \-shəs\ *adj* [NL *Ostracea* + E *-ous*] : of or relating to the Ostraeacea

os·tra·ci·idae \,ästrə'sīə,dē\ [NL, fr. *Ostracion* + *-idae*] *syn of* OSTRACIONTIDAE

os·tra·ci·on \ä'strās(h)ē,än\ *n, cap* [NL *Ostraciont-, Ostracion*, irreg. fr. Gk *ostrakion* small shell, dim. of *ostrakon* shell] : a genus of boxfishes that is the type of the family Ostraciontidae, is now restricted to forms found chiefly in East Indian waters, and is characterized by a carapace of more or less quadrangular section

os·tra·ci·on·ti·dae \=,==ˈäntə,dē\ *n pl, cap* [NL, fr. *Ostraciont-, Ostracion*, type genus + *-idae*] : a family of marine fishes (order Plectognathi) comprising the boxfishes

os·tra·cism \'ästrə,sizəm *also* 'ōst-\ *n* -S [Gk *ostrakismos*, fr. *ostrakizein* + *-ismos* -ism] **1** : a method of temporary banishment by popular vote and without a trial or special accusation practiced in ancient Greek cities to remove a person considered dangerous to the state **2** : exclusion by general consent from common privileges or social acceptance ⟨met part of her expenses by waiting on tables — a task she thought would mean social ~ —*Current Biog.*⟩

os·tra·cite \'ästrə,sīt\ *n* -S [L *ostracites*, a precious stone, fr. Gk *ostrakitēs* earthen, fr. *ostrakon* earthen vessel, shell] : a fossil oyster

os·tra·cize *also* **os·tra·cise** \'ästrə,sīz *also* 'ōst-\ *vt* -ED/-ING/-S [Gk *ostrakizein* to banish by voting with potsherds, fr. *ostrakon* earthen vessel, potsherd, shell + *-izein* -ize — more at OYSTER] **1 a** : to banish from society : cast out from social or political favor or fellowship ⟨she was ever afterward *ostracized* in her home city —A.F.Harlow⟩ **b** : to get rid of : ABOLISH ⟨when we really become civilized we will certainly ~ smoky cities —C.C.Furnas⟩ **2** : to exile by ostracism : banish temporarily by a popular vote **syn** see BANISH

os·tra·ciz·er \-zə(r)\ *n* -S : one that ostracizes

os·tra·cod \'ästrə,käd\ *also* **os·tra·code** \-,kōd\ *n* -S [NL *Ostracoda*] : one of the Ostracoda

os·tra·co·da \,ästrə'kōdə, ä'strakədə\ *n pl, cap* [NL, fr. Gk *ostrakōdēs* testaceous, fr. *ostrakon* potsherd, shell] : a subclass of crustacea comprising small active mostly freshwater forms having the body enclosed in a bivalve shell composed of right and left valves, the body segmentation obscured, the abdomen rudimentary, and only seven pairs of appendages — **os·tra·co·dan** \-d°n\ *adj* — **os·tra·co·dous** \-dəs\ *adj*

¹os·tra·co·derm \'ästrəkō,dərm\ *adj* [NL *Ostracodermi*] : of, relating to, or having characteristics of the Ostracodermi

²ostracoderm \"\ *n* -S [NL *Ostracodermi*] : one of the Ostracodermi

os·tra·co·der·mi \,===ˈdər,mī\ *n pl, cap* [NL, fr. *ostrac-* + *-dermi* (fr. Gk *derma* skin) — more at DERM-] **1** *in some classifications* : a suborder of the order Plectognathi comprising the boxfishes **2** *in some classifications* : an order or other category comprising the superclass Agnatha except the class Cyclostomi and some members of the class Placodermi that are known only from imperfect remains found in Ordovician, Silurian, and Devonian rocks, that lack jaws and limb girdles as well as paired fins homologous with those of recent fishes, that in most forms show the very broad anterior part of the body to be encased in a bony armor, and that have the slender scaly posterior part ending in an unsymmetrical tail

os·tra·coi·dea \,ästrə'kȯidēə\ [NL, fr. *ostrac-* + *-oidea*] *syn of* OSTRACODA

os·tra·con *or* **os·tra·kon** \'ästrə,kän\ *n, pl* **ostra·ca** *or* **ostra·ka** \-rəkə\ [Gk *ostrakon*] **1** : a potsherd used as a ballot in the ancient Athenian practice of ostracism **2** : a fragment of pottery or limestone containing a written inscription ⟨that the Hebrews . . . wrote freely on papyrus, parchment and potsherds is apparent from large finds of *ostraca* —I.M. Price⟩

os·tra·co·phore \'ästrəkō,fō(ə)r\ *n* -S [NL *Ostracophori*] : one of the Ostracodermi — **os·tra·coph·o·rous** \,ästrə'käf(ə)rəs\ *adj*

os·tra·coph·o·ri \,ästrə'käfə,rī\ [NL, fr. *ostrac-* + *-phori* (fr. Gk *-phoroi*, pl. of *-phoros* -phorous)] *syn of* OSTRACODERMI 2

os·trae·a·cea \,ästrē'āshēə\ *n pl, cap* [NL, irreg. fr. *Ostrea* + *-acea*] : a suborder of the order Eulamellibranchia including the common oysters and related mollusks

ostre- *or* **ostrei-** *or* **ostreo-** *comb form* [L *ostre-*, fr. *ostrea*] : oyster ⟨*ostrei*form⟩ ⟨*ostreo*id⟩ ⟨*ostreo*phagous⟩

os·trea \'ästrēə\ *n, cap* [NL, fr. L, oyster — more at OYSTER] : the type genus of the family Ostreidae including those oysters (as the European oyster) that retain eggs in the parent's gills during early stages of development — compare CRASSOSTREA — **os·tre·a·ceous** \,ästrē'āshəs\ *adj*

os·tre·ger \'ästrəjə(r)\ *n* -S [ME *ostringer*, fr. MF *otrucher, ostricier*, fr. *ostour, ostor* hawk, fr. ML *auceptor*, alter. (influenced by L *avis* bird) of L *acceptor*, alter. (influenced by L *accipere* to take, accept) of *accipiter* — more at ACCIPITER, ACCEPT, AVIARY] : AUSTRINGER

os·trei·culture \'ästrēə+,-\ *n* [ISV *ostre-* + *culture*] : OYSTER CULTURE — **os·trei·culturist** \,===+\ *n*

os·tre·i·dae \ä'strēə,dē\ *n pl, cap* [NL, fr. *Ostrea*, type genus + *-idae*] : a family of bivalve mollusks (suborder Ostraeacea) being usu. attached by the lower valve and including the common edible oysters

os·tre·i·form \'ästrēə,fȯrm, ä's-\ *adj* [ISV *ostre-* + *-form*] : shaped like an oyster

os·treo·dynamometer \¦ästrēō+\ *n* [*ostre-* + *dynamometer*] : a device for detection of the movements of an oyster within its shell and used esp. in connection with water pollution investigations

os·tre·oid \'ästrē,ȯid\ *adj* [ISV *ostre-* + *-oid*] : resembling an oyster

os·tre·oph·a·gous \¦ästrē¦äfəgəs\ *adj* [*ostre-* + *-phagous*] : feeding on oysters

¹os·trich \'ästrich, 'ōs-, -rē| *sometimes* |j\ *n* -ES [ME *ostriche*, fr. OF *ostrusce*, fr. (assumed) VL *avis struthio*, fr. L *avis* bird + LL *struthio* ostrich — more at AVIARY, STRUTHIO] **1 a** : a swift-footed flightless ratite bird of the genus *Struthio* having a downy neck and head, a body covered with soft feathers, thighs nearly bare, two-toed feet, and valuable wing and tail plumes for which it has been domesticated: as (1) : an ostrich (*S. camelus*) of the more arid parts of Africa and Arabia that is the largest of existing birds attaining a height of six or eight feet and a weight of 300 lbs. (2) : an ostrich (*S. c. australis*) of southern Africa (3) : an ostrich (*S. c. molybdophanes*) of eastern Africa **b** : RHEA **2** [so called fr. a popular belief that the ostrich when pursued hides his head and believes himself to be unseen] : a person whose behavior is thought to resemble that ascribed to the ostrich : one having qualities or habits suggesting an ostrich ⟨tried to play ~, pretended not to see —B.H.Williams⟩ ⟨between the positions of the alarmist and the ~ is a broad middle ground —*Scientific Monthly*⟩

²ostrich \"\ *adj* : of, relating to, or resembling an ostrich : OSTRICHLIKE ⟨overcoming the traditional ~ attitude of the public —*Newsweek*⟩ ⟨the uphill fight against . . . ~ isolationism —W.H.Hale⟩

³ostrich \"\ *vi* -ED/-ING/-ES : to hide one's head : deliberately avoid seeing, recognizing, or understanding

ostrich fern *n* : a tall fern of the genus *Pteretis* (*P. struthiopteris*) of the north temperate zone that has graceful arched bipinnatifid fronds growing in a circle from an erect rootstock and pinnate sporophylls having segments like a necklace and resembling ostrich plumes; *broadly* : any fern of the genus *Pteretis*

os·trich·ism \|,chizəm, |,ji-\ *n* -S : the deliberate avoidance or ignorance of conditions as they exist : SELF-DELUSION ⟨~ will not, of course, save one single American —Pearl Buck⟩ ⟨perhaps the lack of fear is a result of what might be called ~ —John Gunther⟩

ostrich leather *n* : strong durable leather from the skins of ostriches readily identified by quill holes and used principally for shoes and handbags

ostrichlike \'==,=\ *adj* : marked or characterized by self-delusion into a sense of security by deliberately refraining from seeing or understanding ⟨our assumptions as to the sources of the criticism have been . . . based upon wishful or ~ thinking —Paul Woodring⟩

ostrich-plume hydroid *n* : a colonial hydroid (genus *Aglaophenia*) characterized by pinnate branching colonies resembling feathers or ferns

os·tro·goth \'ästrə,gäth\ *n, cap* [LL *Ostrogothi, Ostrogothae*, pl., of Gmc origin; prob. fr. a Gothic compound whose first constituent is akin to ON *austr* to the east and whose second constituent is the same as the source of LL *Gothi* Goths — more at EAST, GOTH] : a member of the eastern division of the Goths that conquered Italy toward the end of the fifth century A.D. — called also *East Goth*; compare VISIGOTH — **os·tro·goth·i·an** \¦==¦gäthēən\ *adj, usu cap* — **os·tro·goth·ic** \-thik\ *adj, usu cap*

os·trya \'ästrēə\ *n, cap* [NL, fr. Gk, hop hornbeam; prob. akin to Gk *ostrakon* shell and to Gk *drys* tree — more at OYSTER, TREE] : a small widely distributed genus of trees (family Betulaceae) having fruit resembling cones with membranous inflated bracts — see HOP HORNBEAM

os·ty·ak *also* **os·ti·ak** \'ästē,ak\ *n* -S *cap* [Russ *Ostyak*, fr. Ostyak *ăsyakh* dwellers on the Ob river, fr. *Ăs* Ob river, U. S. S. R.] **1** : a member of any of a group of the Paleo-Asiatic nomadic Finnic peoples of the Ural mountain regions and western Siberia **2** : the Finno-Ugric language of the Ostyak people — see URALIC LANGUAGES table

ostyak samoyed *n, cap O&S* **1** : one of the people of mixed Samoyed and Ostyak stock in Siberia **2** : the Uralic language of the Ostyak Samoyed — see URALIC LANGUAGES table

o substance *n, usu cap O* : an antigen characteristic of red blood cells of persons of blood group O

os·we·go bass \ä'swē(,)gō-\ *n, usu cap O* [*Oswego* river, central New York] **1** : LARGEMOUTH BLACK BASS **2** : SMALLMOUTH BLACK BASS

oswego tea *n, usu cap O* : a No. American mint (*Monarda didyma*) with showy bright scarlet irregular flowers — called also *bee balm, fragrant balm, mountain mint*

ot- *or* **oto-** *comb form* [Gk *ōt-, ōto-*, fr. *ōt-, ous* — more at EAR] : ear ⟨*ot*itis⟩ ⟨*oto*logy⟩ ⟨*oto*scope⟩ ⟨*ot*osteal⟩ : ear and ⟨*oto*laryngology⟩

OT *abbr* **1** occupational therapy **2** oiltight **3** old terms **4** old tuberculin **5** on time **6** on track **7** on truck **8** overtime

ot·acariasis \¦ōd·+\ *n* [NL, fr. *ot-* + *acariasis*] : infestation with or disease caused by ear mites : EAR MANGE, CANKER 7a

¹ot·acoustic \¦ōd·+\ *n* -S [Gk *ōtakoustein* to listen, eavesdrop (fr. *ōt-* ot- + *akoustos* heard, audible) + E *-ic* — more at ACOUSTIC] : an otacoustic instrument

²otacoustic \"\ *adj* [F *otacoustique*, fr. Gk *ōtakoustein* to listen, eavesdrop + F *-ique* -ic] : assisting the sense of hearing

ota·go \ō'tä(,)gō\ *adj, usu cap* [fr. *Otago*, New Zealand] : of or from the provincial district of Otago, New Zealand : of the kind or style prevalent in Otago provincial district

ota·hei·tan \¦ōd·ə¦hāt°n\ *adj or n, usu cap* [fr. *Otaheite* (now Tahiti), island in the southern Pacific + E *-an*] : TAHITIAN

ota·hei·te apple \,==ˈhād·(,)ē-\ *n, usu cap O* [fr. *Otaheite* Tahiti] **1** : a Polynesian tree (*Spondias cytherea*) having a fruit with sweet edible flesh and turpentine-flavored rind **2** : the fruit of the Otaheite apple **3** : MALAY APPLE

otaheite arrowroot *n, usu cap O* : a starch obtained from the root of the pia; *also* : a root or plant yielding such starch

otaheite gooseberry *n, usu cap O* **1** : a tropical African and Asiatic tree (*Phyllanthus acidus*) of the family Euphorbiaceae **2** : the acid edible fruit of the Otaheite gooseberry

otaheite orange *n, usu cap 1st O* : a small shrub (*Citrus taitensis*) sometimes grown as a pot plant and having oblong to elliptic crenulate leaves, flowers colored pink on the outside, and a lemon-shaped fruit

otal·gia \ō'talj(ē)ə\ *n* -S [NL, fr. Gk *ōtalgia*, fr. *ōt-* ot- + *-algia*] : pain in the ear : EARACHE

otal·gic \-jik\ *n* -S [Gk *ōtalgikos*, adj., having an earache, fr. *ōtalgia* + *-ikos* -ic] : a remedy for earache

otar·ia \ō'ta(a)rēə\ *n, cap* [NL, fr. *ot-* + *-aria*] : the type genus of Otariidae comprising the sea lions of the southern So. American coast

ota·ri·idae \,ōd·ə'rīə,dē\ *n pl, cap* [NL, fr. *Otaria*, type genus + *-idae*] : a family of Pinnipedia consisting of the eared seals and sometimes ranked as a subfamily of the family Phocidae — **ota·rine** \'ōd·ə,rēn, -,rən\ *or* **otar·i·ine** \(')ō¦ta(a)rē,īn, -ēən\ *adj* — **otar·i·oid** \-ē,ȯid\ *adj or n*

ota·ru \ō'tä(,)rü\ *adj, usu cap* [fr. *Otaru*, Japan] : of or from the city of Otaru, Japan : of the kind or style prevalent in Otaru

ota·ry \'ōd·ərē\ *n* -ES [NL *Otaria*] : EARED SEAL

ota·te \ō'täd·(,)ā\ *n* -S [Sp, fr. Nahuatl *otlatl*] : a giant grass (*Guadua amplexifolia*) used by Mexicans for making baskets

ota·vite \ō'tä,vīt\ *n* -S [G *otavit*, fr. *Otavi*, town in South-West Africa + G *-it* -ite] : a mineral $CdCO_3$ consisting of the carbonate of cadmium and isostructural with calcite

OTB *abbr* open to buy

otbd *abbr* outboard

OTC *abbr* **1** officer in tactical command **2** officers' training camp; officers' training corps

-ote \,ōt, -,ət\ *n suffix* -S [L & Gk; L *-otes*, fr. Gk *-ōtēs*] : inhabitant : native ⟨*Capriote*⟩

othe·o·scope \'ōthēə,skōp\ *n* [Gk *ōthein* to push + E *-o-* + *-scope* — more at ENDOSMOSIS] : an instrument for exhibiting the pressure exerted by light or other radiation in an exhausted vessel — compare RADIOMETER

¹oth·er \'əthə(r)\ *adj* [ME, adj., n., pron., & adv., fr. OE *ōther*, adj., n., & pron.; akin to OHG *andar* other, ON *annarr*, Goth *anthar*, Skt *antara*, Lith *antras*] **1 a** : being the one (as of two or more) left : not being the one (as of two or more) first mentioned or of primary concern : REMAINING ⟨carrying the load in one hand and holding on with the ~⟩ **b** : being the ones distinct from the one or those first mentioned or understood — used with a plural noun ⟨these cars being somewhat smaller than ~ European cars⟩ **c** : SECOND — now chiefly used with *every* ⟨every ~ day it rained⟩ **2 a** : not the same : DIFFERENT ⟨any ~ man would have done better⟩ **b** : DIFFERENT, DISTINCT — used after the noun and with *than* ⟨all parts of the house ~ than the windows were in good condition⟩ **3** : MORE, ADDITIONAL ⟨thou shalt have no ~ gods before me —Exod 20:3 (AV)⟩ — often used after the noun and with *than* ⟨no clothes ~ than those he was wearing⟩ **4 a** : recently past ⟨the ~ evening⟩ **b** : FORMER ⟨in ~ times⟩

²other \"\ *n* -S [ME] **1 a** : one that remains of two or more ⟨one stayed and the ~ went away⟩ ⟨after he left the ~s played cards⟩ **b** *obs* : second one **2** : a different one ⟨each gust of wind came after the ~ with clocklike regularity⟩ ⟨some businesses survived and ~s went into bankruptcy⟩ **3** : an additional one ⟨some are successful and ~s are not⟩ **4** : something that exists as an opposite of or as excluded by something else ⟨the nonego being the ~ of the ego⟩ ⟨the objective world being the ~ of self-consciousness⟩

³other \"\ *pron, sometimes pl in constr* [ME] **1** *obs* **a** : one of two that remains ⟨priest and people interchangeably pray each for ~ —Anthony Sparrow⟩ **b** : each preceding one **2** *obs* : a different one ⟨every one taketh before ~ his own supper —1 Cor 11:21 (AV)⟩ ⟨I have pleased some and displeased ~ —Robert Wilkinson⟩ **3** : an additional one ⟨hardly a day passes in which we do not have some visitor or ~ —Jane Austen⟩ ⟨~ of the Protestant clergy —F.G.Lee⟩ **4** *chiefly Scot* : one another ⟨we know not ~ — oceans are between —Thomas Campbell⟩

⁴other \"\ *adv* [ME] : OTHERWISE 1 — used with *than* ⟨not being able to sell the product ~ than by reducing the price⟩

¹other-directed \¦===¦==\ *adj* [⁴*other* + *directed*] : determined or motivated by contemporary trends and pressures and not by inner decision ⟨an *other-directed* personality⟩ — **oth·er-di·rect·ed·ness** *n*

²other-directed \"\ *n* -S : an other-directed person

other-direction \¦==¦==\ *n* : a sense of direction based on contemporary trends and pressures

othergates \'==,=\ *adv* [ME, fr. *other* + *gates*, gen. of *gate* way — more at GATE] *chiefly dial* : in another manner : OTHERWISE ⟨he would have tickled you ~ than he did — Shak.⟩

other-group \'==,=\ *n* : OUT-GROUP

otherguess *adj* [alter. of *othergates*, fr. *othergates*, adv.] *archaic* : DIFFERENT

other half *n* **1** : a segment of the population radically different economically and often socially from that to which one belongs or with which a context is associated ⟨see how the *other half* lives⟩; *esp* : PROLETARIAT **2** : SPOUSE

other insurance *n* : DOUBLE INSURANCE

oth·er·ness *n* -ES [¹*other* + *-ness*] **1** : the quality or state of being other; *also* : a thing that is other ⟨externality and ~ —Lionel Stanford⟩ **2** : the quality or state of being different ⟨struck with a sense of ~, of unfamiliarity —A.C.Danto⟩

oth·er·some \'əthə(r)səm\ *pron* [ME *other sum*, fr. *other* + *sum* some — more at SOME] *chiefly dial* : some others ⟨some folks do and ~ don't⟩

otherways \'==,=\ *adv* [ME *other wayes*, fr. *other* + *wayes*, gen. of *way*] *chiefly dial* : OTHERWISE

otherwhere \'==,=\ *adv* : in or to some other place : ELSEWHERE

otherwhile \'==,=\ *also* **otherwhiles** \'==,=\ *adv* [ME *otherwhil, otherwhiles*, fr. *other* + *whil* while *or* *whiles*, gen. of *whil* — more at WHILE] **1** *chiefly dial* : at another time **2** *chiefly dial* : SOMETIMES, OCCASIONALLY

¹oth·er·wise \'əthə(r),wīz\ *adv* [ME, fr. OE (*on*) *ōthre wīsan* in other manner] **1** : in a different way or manner : DIFFERENTLY ⟨he could not act ~⟩ **2** : in different circumstances : under other conditions ⟨~ he might have won⟩ **3** : in other respects ⟨weak but ~ well⟩ **4** : if not ⟨do what I tell you, ~ you'll be sorry⟩ **5** : NOT — paired with an adjective or adverb to indicate its contrary ⟨people whose deeds, admirable or ~ —John Fischer⟩

²otherwise \"\ *adj* **1** : DIFFERENT ⟨if conditions were ~⟩ **2** : under different circumstances ⟨their political enemies were also their ~ friends⟩

oth·er·wise·ness *n* -ES : the quality or state of being otherwise

otherworld \¦==¦=\ *n* [¹*other* + *world*] : a world beyond death or beyond the world of present reality

otherworldliness \¦==¦===\ *n* : the quality or state of being otherworldly; *also* : an otherworldly characteristic

otherworldly \¦==¦==\ *also* **otherworld** \¦==¦=\ *adj* **1 a** : of or relating to a world other than the actual world : TRANSMUNDANE, TRANSCENDENTAL **b** : concerned with the world to come : devoted to preparing for the world to come **c** : morbidly spiritual : selfishly ascetic **2** : devoted to intellectual or imaginative pursuits often to the extent of weakening the hold on or slighting practical everyday living

othman *usu cap, archaic var of* OTTOMAN

othon·na \ō'thänə\ *n, cap* [NL, fr. L, a plant of Syria, fr. Gk] : a genus of southern African herbs or shrubs (family Compositae) with smooth often fleshy leaves and heads of yellow flowers of which the discoid ones are sterile

oti \ō'tē\ *n, pl* **oti** *or* **otis** *usu cap* [Pg *oti, otí*, of AmerInd origin] **1 a** : an extinct group of peoples of southern Brazil — called also *Chavante* **b** : a member of such a group of peoples **2** : the language of the Otí group of peoples

OTI *abbr* official test insecticide

otic \ō|d·|ik, 'ä|, |t|, |ēk\ *adj* [Gk *ōtikos*, fr. *ōt-* ot- + *-ikos* -ic] : of, relating to, or in the region of the ear : AURICULAR, AUDITORY

¹-ot·ic \'äd·|ik, |ät|, |ēk\ *adj suffix* [Gk *-ōtikos*, fr. *-ōtos*, suffix used to form adjectives derived fr. certain verbs & *-ōtēs*, suffix used to form agent nouns derived fr. certain verbs + *-ikos* -ic] **1 a** : of, relating to, or characterized by a (specified) action, process, or condition ⟨holoce*notic*⟩ **b** : having an abnormal or diseased condition of a (specified) kind ⟨aphospho*rotic*⟩ **2** : showing an increase or a formation of (something specified) ⟨leuko*cytotic*⟩ **3** : of, relating to, or characterized by having a disease caused by a (specified) fungus ⟨blasto*mycotic*⟩ — often used to form adjectives corresponding to nouns in *-osis*

²-otic \ō|d·|ik, |ä|, |t|, |ēk\ *adj comb form* [Gk *ōtikos* of the ear] **1** : of or relating to a (specified) part of the ear ⟨epi*otic*⟩ ⟨ent*otic*⟩ **2 a** : of or relating to an area having a (specified) spatial relationship to the ear ⟨par*otic*⟩ ⟨peri*otic*⟩ **b** : of or relating to a bone having a (specified) spatial relationship to the ear ⟨pro*otic*⟩ ⟨sphen*otic*⟩

otic ganglion *n* : a small autonomic ganglion on the mandibular nerve just below the foramen ovale

otic vesicle *n* : the saccular invagination of ectoderm from which the vertebrate ear develops

otid·i·dae \ō'tidə,dē\ *n pl, cap* [NL, fr. *Otid-, Otis*, type genus + *-idae*] : a family of Old World birds comprising the bustards and constituting the suborder Otides, being of the order Gruiformes, and formerly classed with the Charadriiformes

— **otid·i·form** \'⸗⸗,fȯrm\ *adj* — **oti·dine** \'ōd·ə,dēn, -,dən\ *adj*

otid·i·phaps \ō'tidə,faps\ *n, cap* [NL, fr. Gk *ōtid-, ōtis* bustard + NL *-i-* + Gk *phaps* wild pigeon] : a genus of large terrestrial pigeons of New Guinea and adjacent islands

otid·i·um \-dēəm\ *n, pl* **otidia** [NL, fr. *ot-* + *-idium*] : the otocyst of a mollusk

[1]**oti·o·rhyn·chid** \,ōshē(,)ō¦riŋkəd\ *adj* [NL *Otiorhynchidae*] : of or relating to the Otiorhynchidae

[2]**otiorhynchid** \"\ *n* -s : a weevil of the family Otiorhynchidae

oti·o·rhyn·chi·dae \,⸗⸗(,)⸗'riŋkə,dē\ *n pl, cap* [NL, fr. *Otiorhynchus* type genus (fr. Gk *ōtion* ear — dim. of *ōt-, ous* ear — + NL *-rhynchus*) + *-idae* — more at EAR] : an extensive family of weevils often regarded as a subfamily of the family Curculionidae in which the mandibles of the pupa have a deciduous process that leaves a scar in the adult

oti·ose \'ōshē,ōs, 'ōd·ē,ōs\ *adj* [L *otiosus*, fr. *otium* ease, leisure + *-osus* -ose] **1** : being at leisure or ease : IDLE, UNEMPLOYED **2** : without profit : STERILE, FUTILE ⟨an ~ undertaking⟩ **3** : lacking use or effect : FUNCTIONLESS ⟨~ letters in an alphabet⟩ ⟨~ lines in a play⟩ **4** *of a deity* : remote and aloof : not concerned with the details of the world **syn** see VAIN

oti·ose·ly *adv* : in an otiose manner

oti·ose·ness *n* -ES : the quality or state of being otiose

oti·os·i·ty \,⸗⸗'äsəd·ē, -ətē, -i\ *n* -ES [alter. of earlier *ociosity*, fr. MF *ociosité*, fr. LL *otiositat-, otiositas*, fr. L *otiosus* + *-itat-, -itas* -ity] : the quality or state of being otiose

otis \'ōd·əs\ *n, cap* [L, bustard, fr. Gk *ōtis*, fr. *ōt-, ous* ear; fr. its long ear feathers — more at EAR] : a genus of typical bustards that includes the great bustard and is the type of the family Otididae

otit·ic \ō'tid·ik\ *adj* [NL *otitis* + E *-ic*] : of, associated with, or relating to otitis

[1]**otit·id** \(')ō¦tid·əd\ *adj* [NL *Otitidae*] : of or relating to the Otitidae

[2]**otitid** \"\ *n* -s : a fly of the family Otitidae

otit·i·dae \ō'tid·ə,dē\ *n pl, cap* [NL, fr. *Otites*, type genus (origin unknown) + *-idae*] : a family of acalyptrate flies that includes numerous robust flies usu. with spotted or banded wings, frequently with metallic colors, and with larvae which usu. feed on decaying vegetable matter

oti·tis \ō'tīd·əs\ *n, pl* **otit·i·des** \-'tid·ə,dēz\ [NL, fr. *ot-* + *-itis*] : inflammation of the ear

otitis ex·ter·na \-ek'stərnə\ *n* [NL] : inflammation of the external ear

otitis me·dia \-'mēdēə\ *n* [NL] : inflammation of the middle ear marked by pain, fever, dizziness, and abnormalities of hearing — see AERO-OTITIS MEDIA

oto *or* **otoe** \'ōd·(,)ō\ *n, pl* **oto** *or* **otos** *or* **otoe** *or* **otoes** *usu cap* [perh. fr. Iowa-Oto *wat'ota*, lit., lechers; fr. the seduction of one chief's daughter by another chief's son] **1 a** : a Siouan people in the Platte and Missouri river valleys of Nebraska **b** : a member of such people **2** : a dialect of Chiwere

oto- — see OT-

oto·bi·us \ō'tōbēəs\ *n, cap* [NL, fr. *ot-* + *-bius*] *in some classifications* : a genus of argasid ticks that includes the spinose ear tick of southwestern U. S. and Mexico and that is often considered inseparable from *Ornithodoros*

oto·cephalic \'ōd·ə+\ *adj* [ISV *ot-* + *-cephalic*] : of, relating to, or exhibiting otocephaly

oto·ceph·a·ly \,⸗⸗'sefəlē\ *n* -ES [ISV *ot-* + *-cephaly*] : abnormal and deficient development of the head

oto·co·ni·al \¦⸗⸗¦kōnēəl\ *adj* [fr. NL *otoconium* + E *-al*] : of or relating to otoconia

oto·co·ni·um \,⸗⸗'⸗nēəm\ *n, pl* **otoco·nia** \-nēə\ [NL, fr. *ot-* + *-conium* (fr. Gk *konis, konia* ashes, dust — more at INCINERATE] : a vertebrate otolith

oto·cy·on \,⸗⸗'sī,än\ *n, cap* [NL, fr. *ot-* + Gk *kyōn* dog — more at HOUND] : a monotypic genus of the family Canidae that includes only the long-eared fox of southern Africa

oto·cyst \'ōd·ə,sist\ *n* [ISV *ot-* + *-cyst*; orig. formed as F *otocyste*] **1** : one of the supposed auditory organs of many invertebrates that contains a fluid and otoliths : STATOCYST **2** : OTIC VESICLE — **oto·cys·tic** \¦⸗⸗¦sistik\ *adj*

oto·dec·tes \,⸗⸗'dek,tēz\ *n, cap* [NL, fr. *ot-* + *-dectes*] : a genus of mites that have suckers on the legs, live in the ears of dogs, cats, and a few other mammals, and often cause ear mange — **oto·dec·tic** \¦⸗⸗¦dektik\ *adj*

otodectic mange *n* [NL *Otodectes* + E *-ic*] : ear mange caused by mites of the genus *Otodectes*

otog·e·nous \(')ō¦täjənəs\ *or* **oto·gen·ic** \,ōd·ə¦jenik\ *adj* [ISV *ot-* + *-genous, -genic*] : originating in the ear ⟨~ sepsis⟩

oto·laryngological \¦ōd·ə+\ *adj* : of or relating to otolaryngology ⟨a ~ examination⟩ ⟨~ disorders⟩

oto·laryngologist \"+\ *n* : a specialist in otolaryngology

oto·laryngology \"+\ *n* [*ot-* + *laryng-* + *-ology*] : a branch of medicine that deals with the ear, nose, and throat and their disorders and diseases

oto·lite \'ōd·ᵊl,īt\ *n* -s [by alter.] : OTOLITH — **oto·lit·ic** \¦⸗⸗¦id·ik\ *adj*

oto·lith \'ōd·ᵊl,ith\ *n* [F *otolithe*, fr. *ot-* + *lithe* -lith] : a calcareous concretion in the internal ear of a vertebrate or in the otocyst of an invertebrate that is esp. conspicuous in many teleost fishes where they form hard bodies and in most of the higher vertebrates where they are represented by masses of small calcareous otoconia — **oto·lith·ic** \¦⸗⸗¦ithik\ *adj*

oto·lith·i·dae \,ōd·ᵊl'ithə,dē\ [NL, fr. *Otolithus*, type genus (fr. *ot-* + Gk *lithos* stone) + *-idae*] *syn of* SCIAENIDAE

oto·log·ic \¦ōd·ᵊl¦äjik\ *also* **oto·log·i·cal** \-jəkəl\ *adj* : of or relating to otology — **oto·log·i·cal·ly** \-jək(ə)lē\ *adv*

otol·o·gist \ō'täləjəst\ *n* -s : a specialist in otology

otol·o·gy \-jē, -ji\ *n* -ES [ISV *ot-* + *-logy*] : a science that deals with the ear and its diseases — distinguished from *audiology*

oto·mac \,ōd·ə'mäk\ *or* **oto·ma·co** \-ä(,)kō\ *or* **oto·mak** \-äk\ *n, pl* **otomac** *or* **otomaco** *or* **otomak** *or* **otomacs** *or* **otomacos** *or* **otomaks** *usu cap* [Sp *otomaco*, of AmerInd origin] **1 a** : an extinct aboriginal people of southern Venezuela **b** : a member of such people **2** : the language of the Otomac people

oto·man·gue·an \,ōd·ə'mäŋ(,)gāən\ *n* -s *usu cap* [blend of *Otomian* and [2]*Mangue* + *-an*] : a language stock of Mexico and Guatemala comprising the Otomian, Popolocan, Triquean, and Chorotigan language families

oto·mi \,ōd·ə'mē\ *n, pl* **otomi** *or* **otomis** *usu cap* [Sp *otomí*, of AmerInd origin] **1 a** : an Otomian people of the states of Guanajuato, Hidalgo, Querétaro, and México, Mexico **b** : a member of such people **2** : the language of the Otomi people

oto·mi·an \,ōd·ə'mēən, ō'tōmē-\ *n* -s *usu cap* [*Otomi* + *-an*] **1 a** : an Indian people of central Mexico **b** : a member of such people **2** : a language family comprising Otomi, Pame, Mazahua, and Matlatzinca

oto·mycosis \,ōd·ə,mī'kōsəs\ *n* [NL, fr. *ot-* + *mycosis*] : disease of the ear produced by the growth of fungi in the external auditory canal

oto·mycotic \¦⸗⸗+\ *adj* [*ot-* + *mycotic*] : of, relating to, or affected by otomycosis

oto·plas·ty \'⸗⸗,plastē\ *n* -ES [ISV *ot-* + *-plasty*] : plastic surgery of the external ear

oto·rhinolaryngology \¦⸗⸗+\ *n* [ISV *ot-* + *rhin-* + *laryng-* + *-ology*] : OTOLARYNGOLOGY

otor·rhea *also* **otor·rhoea** \,ōd·ə'rēə\ *n* -s [NL, fr. *ot-* + *-rrhea, -rrhoea*] : a discharge from the external ear

oto·salpinx \'ōd·ə+\ *n, pl* **otosalpinges** [NL, fr. *ot-* + *salpinx*] : EUSTACHIAN TUBE

oto·sclerosis \¦⸗⸗+\ *n* [NL, fr. *ot-* + *sclerosis*] : growth of spongy bone in the inner ear where it gradually obstructs the vestibular or cochlear window or both and causes progressively increasing deafness

oto·sclerotic \¦⸗⸗+\ *adj* [*ot-* + *sclerotic*] : of, relating to, or affected by otosclerosis

oto·scope \'ōd·ə,skōp\ *n* [ISV *ot-* + *-scope*] : an instrument fitted with lighting and magnifying lens systems and used to facilitate visual inspection of the auditory canal and ear drum — **oto·scop·ic** \¦⸗⸗¦skäpik\ *adj* — **otos·co·py** \ō'täskəpē\ *n* -ES

oto·sis \ō'tōsəs\ *n, pl* **oto·ses** \-tō,sēz\ [NL, fr. *ot-* + *-osis*] : mishearing or misinterpretation of spoken sounds; *also* : alteration in word forms due to it

oto·sphe·nal \¦ōd·ə¦sfēnᵊl\ *n* -s [*ot-* + *sphen-* + *-al*] : BASIOCCIPITAL

ot·osteal \(')ōd·+\ *adj* [*ot-* + *osteal*] : of or relating to the bones of the ear

otos·te·on \⸗'⸗⸗,än\ *n* -s [NL, fr. *ot-* + *-osteon*] **1** : OTOLITH **2** : any of the auditory ossicles

OTS *abbr* officers' training school

ottar *var of* ATTAR

ot·ta·va \ō'tävə\ *adv (or adj)* [It, octave, fr. ML *octava* — more at OCTAVE] : at an octave higher than written if placed above the staff or lower than written if placed below the staff — abbr. *8va*; used as a direction in music, sometimes as *all' ottava*; compare [5]LOCO

ottava al·ta \-'ältə\ *adj (or adv)* [It, lit., high octave] : intended to be played one octave higher than written — used as a direction in music

ottava bas·sa \-'bäsə\ *adj (or adv)* [It, lit., low octave] : intended to be played one octave lower than written — used as a direction in music

ottava ri·ma \-'rēmə\ *n, pl* **ottava rimas** [It, lit., eighth rhyme] : a stanza of eight lines of heroic verse or sometimes (as in the Italian prototype) hendecasyllabic verse with three rhymes of which the first six lines rhyme alternately and the last two form a couplet (as *a b a b a b c c*)

ot·ta·vi·no \,ōd·ə'vē(,)nō\ *n* -s [It, dim. of *ottava* octave; fr. its playing an octave higher than a flute] : PICCOLO 1

[1]**ot·ta·wa** \'äd·əwə, 'ätə-\ *n, pl* **ottawa** *or* **ottawas** *usu cap* [F *Outouan*, of Algonquian origin; akin to Ojibwa *atâwe* to trade, Cree *atâweu* trader] **1 a** : an Algonquian people of southern Ontario, Canada, and Michigan **b** : a member of such people **2** : a dialect of Ojibwa

[2]**ottawa** \"\ *adj, usu cap* [fr. *Ottawa*, Ontario, Canada] : of or from Ottawa, the capital of Canada : of the kind or style prevalent in Ottawa

ot·ta·wan \-wən\ *n* -s *cap* [*Ottawa*, Ontario + E *-an*] : a native or resident of Ottawa, Canada

[1]**ot·ter** \'äd·ə(r), 'ätə-\ *n, pl* **otter** *or* **otters** *often attrib* [ME *oter*, fr. OE *otor*, *oter*; akin to MD & MLG *otter*, OHG *ottar*, ON *otr* otter, Gk *hydros* water snake, Skt *udra*, an aquatic animal, Gk *hydōr* water — more at WATER] **1 a** : any of several aquatic fish-eating mustelid mammals chiefly of the nearly cosmopolitan genus *Lutra* that are from two to four feet long with the tail long and flattened, the legs short, the feet completely webbed and with claws, the ears small, and the whiskers very bristly and that have dark brown fur highly valued for its beauty and durability and when dressed resembling beaver — compare SEA OTTER **b** : the fur or pelt of an otter **2 a** (1) : fishing tackle consisting of a short plank weighted at one end so as to stand in the water to which flies or bait are attached and whose movements are controlled by lines in the hands of the fisherman ashore (2) : OTTER BOARD **b** : PARAVANE **3** : the larva of a ghost moth (*Hepialus humuli*) that is very injurious to hopvines **4** *or* **otter brown** : a dark grayish yellowish brown that is slightly yellower and deeper than seal and less strong, slightly redder, and darker than sepia brown — called also *loutre, perique, pickaninny*

otter 1 a

[2]**otter** \"\ *vb* -ED/-ING/-s *vi* : to hunt the otter ~ *vt* : to fish with an otter

otter board *n* : one of the two large boards or metal plates that keep the net of an otter trawl spread and that are attached to each side of the mouth of the net and are caused to flare apart by pressure of the water

otter canoe *n* : a long shallow boat used by Alaskans in hunting the sea otter

otter civet *n* : MAMPALON

otterhound \'⸗⸗,⸗\ *n* : a British hound of complex ancestry that in many respects resembles the bloodhound, that has a wiry shaggy coat, long pendulous ears, and a scowling expression, and that is a good water dog with a keen scent although slow and usu. hunted on foot

otter sheep *n* : ANCON SHEEP

otter shell *also* **otter-shell clam** *or* **otter's shell** *n* : any of several bivalve mollusks of the genus *Lutraria* that resemble those of the genus *Mya* but have shells which are more porcelaneous

otter shrew *n* : an African insectivorous mammal (*Potamogale velox*) about the size of a stoat but similar in form and habits to an otter

otter trawl *n* : a trawl using otter boards to spread the net and drawn usu. by trawlers that handle the fish caught

otter trawler *n* : a person or boat fishing with an otter trawl

otto *var of* ATTAR

ot·to cycle \'äd·(,)ō, 'ä(,)tō-\ *n, usu cap O* [after Nikolaus A. *Otto* †1891 Ger. technician and inventor] : a four-stroke cycle for internal-combustion engines of the type used in automobiles wherein the first stroke consists of the suction into the cylinder of the explosive charge (as gas and air), the second stroke consists of the compression, ignition, and explosion of the charge, the third stroke consists of the expansion of the gases, and the fourth stroke consists of the expulsion of the products of combustion from the cylinder

otto engine *n, usu cap O* : an engine using the Otto cycle

[1]**ot·to·man** \'äd·əmən, 'ätə-\ *adj, usu cap* [F, adj. & n., prob. fr. It *ottomano*, fr. Turk *osmanî*, fr. *Osman, Othman* †1326, founder of the Ottoman Empire] : of or relating to the Turks or Turkey : TURKISH ⟨the *Ottoman Empire*⟩

[2]**ottoman** \"\ *n* -s [F *Ottoman*] **1** *cap* : TURK **2** [F *ottomane*, fr. fem. of *ottoman*, adj.] **a** : an upholstered often overstuffed seat or couch usu. without a back **b** : an overstuffed footstool **3** [F *ottoman*, fr. *ottoman*, adj.] : a heavy pliable clothing fabric usu. with a silk or rayon warp covering a cotton or wool weft characterized by pronounced crosswise ribs of regular or varying size

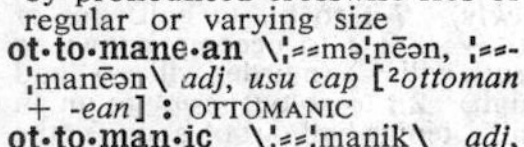

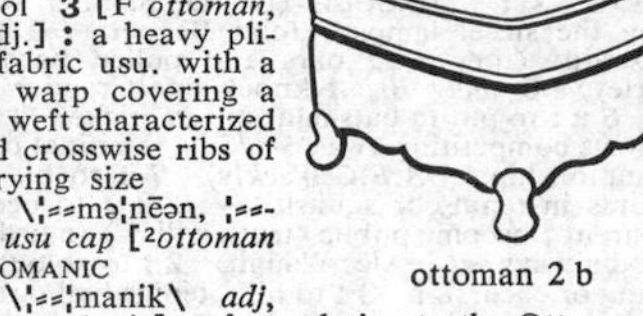

ottoman 2 b

ot·to·mane·an \¦⸗⸗mə¦nēən, ¦⸗⸗¦manēən\ *adj, usu cap* [[2]*ottoman* + *-ean*] : OTTOMANIC

ot·to·man·ic \¦⸗⸗¦manik\ *adj, usu cap* [[2]*Ottoman* + *-ic*] : of or relating to the Ottomans or their empire

ottoman red *n, usu cap O* : vermilion or a color resembling it

ottoman turkish *n, cap O&T* : TURKISH 1

ot·to·ni·an \(')ä¦tōnēən\ *adj, usu cap* [G *Ottonen* Ottos, kings of Germany and Holy Roman Emperors (*Otto* I †973, *Otto* II †983, *Otto* III †1002) + E *-ian*] : of, relating to, or characteristic of the reigns (936–1002) of the first three Ottos of Germany and the Holy Roman Empire or of the arts that flourished in Germany in this period ⟨*Ottonian* bronze doors in Hildesheim and Augsburg —*Art Bull.*⟩

otto of rose *or* **otto of roses** : ATTAR OF ROSES

ot·tre·lite \'ä·trə,līt\ *n* -s [F *ottrélite*, fr. *Ottrez*, Belgium, its locality + F *-lite*] : a gray to black mineral occurring in small scales in certain schists and being a variety of chloritoid

OTU *abbr* operational training unit

otu·ke \¦ōd·ə¦kā\ *n, pl* **otuke** *or* **otukes** *usu cap* [Sp *otuke, otuque, otuki, otuqui*, of AmerInd origin] **1 a** : a people of northern Paraguay **b** : a member of such people **2** : the language of the Otuke people

otu·ki·an \¦ōd·ə¦kēən\ *adj, usu cap* : of, relating to, or constituting a branch of the Bororoan language family

otus \'ōd·əs\ *n, cap* [NL, fr. Gk *ōtos*, fr. *ous* ear — more at EAR] : a genus of rather small-eared owls (family Strigidae) that are usu. predominantly insectivorous and nocturnal — see SCOPS OWL, SCREECH OWL

o-type star \'ō,tīp-\ *n, usu cap O* : a star of spectral type O — see SPECTRAL TYPE table

ou \'ō\ *dial Brit var of* [1]OH

oua·ba·gen·in \,wäbə'jenən; wä'bäjənən, -,nēn\ *n* -s [*ouabain* + *-genin*] : a cardiac hexahydroxy steroidal lactone $C_{23}H_{34}O_8$ obtained by hydrolysis of ouabain

oua·ba·in \wä'bēən, 'wäbəən\ *n* -s [ISV *ouabaio* + *-in*; prob. orig. formed as F *ouabaïne*] : a very toxic crystalline steroidal glycoside $C_{29}H_{44}O_{12}$ obtained from the seeds of an African shrub (*Strophanthus gratus*) or from the wood of trees of the genus *Acocanthera* (as *A. schimperi*) that yields rhamnose and ouabagenin on hydrolysis and that is used similarly to digitalis and in Africa as an arrow poison — called also *g-strophanthin, strophanthin-g*

oua·baio \wä'bī(,)ō\ *n* -s [F *ouabaïo*, fr. Somali *waba yo*] : either of two southern African trees (*Acocanthera ouabaio* and *A. venenata*) from which ouabain is obtained

oua·ga·dou·gou \¦wägə¦dü(,)gü\ *adj, usu cap* [fr. *Ouagadougou*, Upper Volta] : of or from Ouagadougou, capital of the Upper Volta : of the kind or style prevalent in Ouagadougou

oua·ka·ri *or* **ua·ka·ri** \wä'kärē\ *n* -s [Tupi] : any of several So. American monkeys of the genus *Cacajao* that are related to the sakis but have short tails like those of baboons and long silky mostly whitish or yellowish hair

oua·na·niche \¦wänə¦nēsh, -nish\ *also* **ouananiche salmon** *n, pl* **ouananiche** *also* **ouananiche salmon** [CanF *ouananiche*, fr. Montagnais *wananish*, dim. of *wanans* salmon] : a small landlocked salmon of Lake St. John, Canada, and neighboring waters

ouanga *var of* WANGA

ou·bli·ette \,üblē'et\ *n* -s [F, fr. MF, fr. *oublier* to forget (fr. OF *oblider*, fr. — assumed — VL *oblitare*, fr. L *oblitus*, past part. of *oblivisci* to forget) + *-ette* — more at OBLIVION] : a dungeon with an opening only at the top and often a concealed pit below the floor ⟨human animals thrust away in the ~s —V.L.Parrington⟩

[1]**ouch** \'au̇ch\ *n* -ES [ME *ouche*, alter. (resulting from incorrect division of *a nouche*) of *nouche*, fr. MF *nosche, noche, nouche*, of Gmc origin; akin to OS *nuska, nuskia* clasp, brooch, MD *nusche*, OHG *nusca* clasp, brooch; akin to OE *net* — more at NET] **1** *obs* : a clasp or brooch for a garment **2 a** : a bezel or other setting for a precious stone ⟨thou shalt make them to be set in ~*es* of gold —Exod 28:11 (AV)⟩ **b** : a buckle or brooch set with precious stones **3** : a necklace, bracelet, jewel, or other personal ornament ⟨your brooches, pearls, and ~*es* —Shak.⟩ ⟨left her golden chains and ~*es* —Charles Kingsley⟩

[2]**ouch** \"\ *interj* [origin unknown] — used to express sudden pain or displeasure

oucht \'äkt\ *Scot var of* OUGHT

oud \'üd\ *n* -s [Ar *'ūd*, lit., wood] : a musical instrument of southwest Asia and northern Africa resembling a mandolin ⟨hypnotized by the tinkling of an ~ —Truman Capote⟩

oued *var of* WADI

ouf \'au̇f\ *also* **oof** \'üf, 'ůf\ *interj* [origin unknown] — used to express discomfort, aversion, or impatience

ough \'ük, 'ůk\ *interj* [origin unknown] — used to express pain or disgust

[1]**ought** *archaic past of* OWE

[2]**ought** \'ȯt, *usu* -d·+V\ *verbal auxiliary* [ME *aghte, aughten, oughten* to be obliged to, owe, fr. *aghte, aughte, oughte* possessed, owned, owed (past indic. & subj. of *aghen, aughen, owen* to possess, own, owe), fr. OE *āhte*, 1st & 3rd pers. sing. past ind. of *āgan* to possess, own, owe — more at OWE] — used to express moral obligation, duty, or necessity ⟨~ to follow the dictates of our conscience⟩ ⟨~ to pay our debts⟩ or what is correct, advisable, or expedient ⟨you ~ to take care of yourself⟩ ⟨this suit ~ to be pressed⟩ or what is naturally expected or logically sound ⟨~ to be able to understand this book⟩ ⟨if our reasoning is correct, the result ~ to be infinity⟩

syn OUGHT, SHOULD, MUST, and HAVE can all function as verbal auxiliaries meaning to be bound (to do or be or not do or be). HAVE with *got* can be used interchangeably with some of these. OUGHT and SHOULD are often interchangeable and imply the compulsion of obligation, OUGHT more commonly suggesting duty or moral constraint, SHOULD applying more to the obligation of fitness, propriety, or expediency ⟨it *ought* not to be very difficult —Nevil Shute⟩ ⟨*ought* to fulfill our obligations⟩ ⟨the stopper is small enough so that it *ought* to fit in the bottle⟩ ⟨*should* not try to evade responsibilities⟩ ⟨the car *should* be around at noon⟩ ⟨*should* make the five o'clock train⟩ MUST, though sometimes stressing extremely strong obligation, usu. implies the compulsion of necessity, whether physical or moral ⟨number three of my suggestions is that a new federal labor law *must* outlaw unfair bargaining practices —A.E. Stevenson b.1900⟩ ⟨the employees *must* contribute 40 percent of the entire premium for all benefits provided under this plan —*U.S.Code*⟩ ⟨again and again he went to performances of what *must* have been his favorite play —*Time*⟩ ⟨to qualify for a college degree you *must* pass certain examinations⟩ HAVE and *have got* are interchangeable with MUST in meaning although *have got* occurs more frequently in spoken than literary English ⟨to qualify for a college degree you *have* to pass certain examinations⟩ ⟨the man I wished to see *had* to leave before I came⟩ ⟨the speeder *has* got to pay a fine⟩ ⟨we *have* got to come into court — the high court of public opinion — with clean hands —*Newsweek*⟩

[3]**ought** \'äkt\ *vt* -ED/-ING/-s [ME *aghten, aughten, oughten*] **1** *chiefly Scot* : OWE **2** *chiefly Scot* : POSSESS ⟨there's naebody but you and me that ~ the name —R.L.Stevenson⟩

[4]**ought** \'ȯt, *usu* -d·+V\ *n* -s [[2]*ought*] : moral obligation : DUTY ⟨the ethical ~ voices or expresses . . . what would, upon reflection, be regarded as binding upon any normal person within a given social system —H.D.Aiken⟩ — contrasted with *is*

[5]**ought** *var of* AUGHT

ought·lins \'äktlənz\ *adv* [[5]*ought* + *-lins*, alter. of *-lings*] *Scot* : in the least degree

ought·ness *n* -ES [[4]*ought* + *-ness*] : the quality or state of being morally obligatory ⟨to each such duty belongs a feeling of ~ —W.H.Kilpatrick⟩ — contrasted with *isness*

oughtn't \'ȯt·ⁿ(t)\ [by contr.] : ought not

Oui·ja \'wējə, -jē-\ *trademark* — used for a board that has the letters of the alphabet and other signs written on it and that is used together with a planchette to seek messages of spiritualistic or telepathic origin

ouistiti *var of* WISTITI

ouk \'ük\ *n* -s [ME (Sc dial.) *ouke*, alter. of *wouke*, fr. OE *wucu* — more at WEEK] *Scot* : WEEK

oul \'ōl\ *or* **ould** \'ōl(d)\ *Irish var of* OLD

ou·led na·il \ülednäēl, ¦ü,led¦nī(ə)l, ¦ü,led¦nä(ə)l\ *n, pl* **ouled nails** *usu cap O&N* [F, fr. *Ouled Naïl*, a confederation of nomadic peoples in Algeria] : an Arab prostitute and dancing girl of the No. African cities usu. dressed in a brightly colored bespangled costume and ornamental often feathered headdress

[1]**ounce** \'au̇n(t)s\ *n* -s [ME *unce, ounce*, fr. MF *unce*, fr. L *uncia* twelfth part, ounce, inch, fr. *unus* one — more at ONE] **1** : any of various units of weight based on the ancient Roman unit equal to ½ Roman pound: as **a** : a unit equal to $1/12$ troy pound **b** : a unit equal to $1/16$ avoirdupois pound — see MEASURE table **2** : a small portion or quantity ⟨if any of them had used a grain of common sense or an ~ of resolution —Dan Wickenden⟩ **3** : FLUIDOUNCE **4** : ONZA **5** : a unit of thickness for leather equal to $1/64$ inch or 0.397 millimeter

[2]**ounce** \"\ *n* -s [ME *unce, once*, fr. OF *once*, alter. (by false division, the *l* of *lonce* being taken as the definite article, and *lonce* as *l'once* the lynx), of *lonce*, fr. (assumed) VL *lyncea, luncea*, fr. L *lync-, lynx* lynx — more at LYNX] **1** *archaic* : any of various moderate-sized wildcats (as the ocelot or lynx) ⟨tigers, ~s, pards, gamboled before them —John Milton⟩ **2** : SNOW LEOPARD **3** *archaic* : CHEETAH **4** : a heraldic representation of a leopard

ounce metal *n* : an alloy composed of one ounce each of tin, zinc, and lead to one pound of copper

ouph *or* **ouphe** \'au̇f, 'üf\ *n* -s [prob. alter. of *auf*] : ELF

[1]**our** [ME *ure, oure*, fr. OE *ūre* (suppletive gen. of *wē* we); akin to OHG *unsēr* of us, ON *vār*, Goth *unsara* of us, *uns, unsis* us — more at US] *obs possessive of* WE

[2]**our** \(')är, (')au̇(ə)r, (')au̇ə, (')ä(r, *esp in the South* ¦au̇wə(r\ *adj* [ME *ure, oure*, fr. OE *ūre*; akin to OHG *unsēr* our, ON *várr*, Goth *unsar*; derivative fr. the root of E *us*] **1 a** : of or belonging to us or ourselves or ourself as possessors or possessor : due to us : inherent in us : associated or connected with us ⟨bumped ~ heads⟩ ⟨defending ~ rights⟩ ⟨all ~ rela-

tives⟩ **b** : of or relating to us or ourselves as authors, doers, givers, or agents : effected by us : experienced by us as subject : that we are capable of ⟨criticized all ~ words and actions⟩ ⟨kept ~ promise⟩ ⟨was angry because of ~ being late⟩ ⟨did ~ very best⟩ **c** : of or relating to us as object of an action : experienced by us as object ⟨expected ~ being chosen for the job⟩ ⟨~ injuries didn't amount to much⟩ **d** : that we have to do with or are supposed to possess or to have knowledge or a share of or some special interest in ⟨we like golf and we know ~ game⟩ **e** : that is esp. significant for us : that brings us good fortune or prominence — used with *day* or sometimes with other words indicating a division of time ⟨today was really ~ day: everything went fine⟩ **2** : that we have in mind or are speaking of or to ⟨we seem to have digressed from ~ topic⟩ ⟨~ readers will be interested, we feel sure⟩ or that has some other special relation to us ⟨~ man was not so successful⟩

³our \'ō(ə)r, 'ōə\ *dial Eng var of* OVER

ou·ral green \'ürəl-\ *n, often cap O* [*Oural* perh. fr. F, Ural mountains in northwestern Asia] : a light yellowish green to very pale green

ourang *var of* ORANG

ourangoutang *var of* ORANGUTAN

ourebi *var of* ORIBI

ou·ri·cu·ry *also* **ou·ri·cu·ri** \ˌürəkəˌrē\ *or* **ari·cu·ri** \ˌär-\ *n* -ES [Pg *ouricuri, ouricuri, aricuri, aricuri,* fr. Tupi] **1** : a straight-trunked Brazilian palm (*Syagrus coronata*) of the family Palmae having a large thick crown of wax-covered leaves — called also *urucuri iba* **2** : an important Brazilian feather palm (*Attalaea excelsa*) whose large oily nuts are burned for their smoke in curing Para rubber

ouricury oil *n* : a yellowish edible fatty oil obtained from the kernels of the fruit of the ouricury palm

ouricury wax *n* : a hard brown wax exuded by the leaves of the ouricury palm that is similar in properties and uses to carnauba wax — called also *licury wax*

ou·rie \'üri\ *adj* [ME (northern dial.) *ouri,* perh. of Scand origin; akin to ON *ūrigr* wet, fr. *ūr* drizzling rain + *-igr* -y — more at URINE] **1** *chiefly Scot* : DEPRESSING, DISMAL **2** *chiefly Scot* : shivering with cold

our-lady's-bedstraw \ˌ==ˌ=ˌ=\ *n, usu cap O&L* : YELLOW BEDSTRAW

our-lady's-mint \=ˌ==ˌ=\ *n, usu cap O&L* : SPEARMINT

our-lady's-thistle \=ˌ==ˌ==\ *n, usu cap O&L* : MILK THISTLE 1

our lord's candle *n, usu cap O&L* : any of various yuccas with tall spikes of flowers (esp. *Yucca whipplei*)

ourn \'au̇(ə)rn, 'au̇ən, 'är(ə)n, 'au̇wə(r)n\ *pron* [ME *ouren, ourn,* fr. *ure, oure* our + *-n* (as in *min* mine — more at OUR] *dial* : OURS

ou·rou·par·ia \ˌü(ˌ)rü'pa(a)rēə\ [NL, fr. Galibi *y-ourou-pari,* a species of *Uncaria*] *syn of* UNCARIA

-ourous — see -UROUS

ours \'au̇(ə)rz, 'au̇əz, 'ärz, 'äz, 'au̇wə(r)z\ *pron, sing or pl in constr* [ME *ures, oures,* fr. *ure, oure* our + *-s* -'s] **1** : our one or our ones — used without a following noun as a pronoun equivalent in meaning to the adjective *our* ⟨your house is large and ~ is small⟩ ⟨~ is a federal system —Stephen Duggan⟩; often used after *of* to single out one or more members of a class belonging to or connected with a group including the one speaking or writing ⟨a friend of ~⟩ or merely to identify something or someone as belonging to or connected with a group including the one speaking or writing without any implication of membership in a more extensive class ⟨that house of ~⟩ ⟨that indifferent manner of ~⟩ ⟨the tremendous growth that is surely ahead in this country of ~ —C.F.Craig⟩ **2** : something belonging to us : what belongs to us ⟨the victory is ~⟩ ⟨~ is the right to do what we please⟩ ⟨it was all ~⟩

our·sel \ür'sel\ *pron* [by shortening] *Scot* : OURSELF

our·self \='=, ˌ=='=\ *pron* [ME *oure self*] **1** : MYSELF — used to refer to the single-person subject when *we* is used instead of *I* (as in editorial style or as in the formal style often used by heads of state) ⟨we ~ will obey our own law⟩ **2** : the self that each one of us separately possesses : the individual self that each one of us separately is ⟨the being which is ~ —Wallace Fowlie⟩

our·sels \ür'selz\ *pron* [by contr.] *Scot* : OURSELVES

our·selves \='=, ˌ=='=\ *pron pl* [ME *oure selven, our selfs*] **1** : those identical ones that are we : the selves that belong to us : the selves that are ours — used (1) reflexively as object of a preposition or direct or indirect object of a verb ⟨we're doing it solely for ~⟩ ⟨busying ~ only with what concerns us⟩ ⟨we're getting ~ a new home⟩; (2) for emphasis in apposition with *we* or *who* ⟨we ~ will never go⟩ ⟨we can speak with some certainty, we who have ~ had the same experience⟩; (3) for emphasis instead of nonreflexive *us* as object of a preposition or direct or indirect object of a verb ⟨this pleases ~ but no one else⟩; (4) for emphasis instead of *we* or instead of *we ourselves* as predicate nominative ⟨the only ones that want to do it are ~⟩ or in comparisons after *than* or *as* ⟨no one knows more about it than ~⟩ or as part of a compound subject ⟨our children and ~ will be glad to come⟩ or archaically or dialectally as only subject of a verb ⟨~ were country folk —Elizabeth Dye⟩; (5) in absolute constructions ⟨~ hardly able to see what was happening, they shut the door in our face⟩ **2** : our normal, healthy, or sane condition ⟨we were groggy for a moment but quickly came to ~⟩ : our normal, healthy, or sane selves ⟨we had been ill, but today we are again ~⟩

-ous \əs\ *adj suffix* [ME, partly fr. OF *-ous, -os, -eus, -eux,* fr. L *-osus;* partly fr. L *-us* (final portion of the nom. sing. masc. form of adjectives such as *fatuus* foolish, *fuscus* brown)] **1** : full of : abounding in : having : possessing the qualities of ⟨clamor*ous*⟩ ⟨glamour*ous*⟩ ⟨cyst*ous*⟩ ⟨lymph*ous*⟩ **2** : having a valence lower than in compounds or ions named with an adjective ending in *-ic* ⟨ferr*ous* iron⟩ ⟨sulfur*ous* acid⟩ — compare ²-ITE — **-ous·ly** *adv suffix*

ouse \'au̇s\ *chiefly Scot var of* OX

ousel *var of* OUZEL

oushak *var of* USHAK

ou·sia \'üzēə, 'üsēə, 'üzh(ē)ə, 'üsh(ē)ə\ *n* -S [Gk, fr. *ous-* (stem of *ōn,* pres. part. of *einai* to be) + *-ia* -y — more at IS] **1** : true being : ENTITY, ESSENCE, SUBSTANCE **2** : HYPOSTASIS 2a

oust \'au̇st\ *vt* -ED/-ING/-S [AF *ouster* fr. OF *oster,* fr. LL *obstare* to ward off, fr. L, to stand before or against, to thwart, hinder, fr. *ob-* to, toward, against + *stare* to stand — more at OB-, STAND] **1 a** : to put out of possession : eject, dispossess from, or deprive of an inheritance (as land or buildings) ⟨the castles and burghs which had slowly ~*ed* him from his inheritance —W.C.Dickinson⟩ **b** : to take away (as a right or authority) : BAR, REMOVE **2** : to eject from a position or place : turn out : EXPEL ⟨a newfangled apparatus which might ~ them from their jobs —Langston Day⟩ ⟨was ~*ed* from office by a military junta —*Current Biog.*⟩ **3** : to drive out of use : take the place of ⟨must be careful that quantity does not ~ quality —Ralph Vaughan Williams⟩ ⟨colored slides virtually ~*ed* black-and-white —*Geog. Jour.*⟩ **syn** see EJECT

oust·er \-tə(r)\ *n* -S [AF, to oust] **1 a** : a wrongful ejection or dispossession of a person from a freehold or other inheritance or from a right or franchise — compare EVICTION **b** : a judgment removing a public or corporate officer or depriving a corporation of a franchise or right (as a charter) **2** : an ejection from a position or place : EXPULSION ⟨the ~ of the manager failed to stop the team's losing streak⟩ ⟨called for the ~ of the man responsible for the blunder⟩

¹out \'au̇t, *usu* ˈau̇d·+V\ *adv* [ME, fr. OE *ūt;* akin to OHG *ūz* out, ON & Goth *ūt* out, L *us*que continually, Gk *hybris* wantonness, arrogance, insolence, *hys*teros latter, Skt *ud, ut* up, out; basic meaning: up, out] **1 a** : in a direction away from a particular point or place ⟨started ~ from home⟩ ⟨looked ~ across the valley⟩ **b** : away from one's own country or part of the world : ABROAD ⟨went ~ for a short visit and stayed for five years⟩ ⟨was sent ~ as ambassador at a critical time⟩ **c** : away from a particular place, region, or country ⟨said the current storm . . . would move ~ by tonight —*Springfield (Mass.) Daily News*⟩ ⟨left the river with their captives and struck ~ overland —I.B.Richman⟩ **d** : away from one's own control or possession ⟨lent ~ his money on mortgages⟩ ⟨gave ~ the manuscript to be typed⟩ **e** : away from one's usual place of residence, practice, or business ⟨dines ~ once a week⟩ ⟨goes ~ every evening⟩ ⟨~ to lunch⟩ **f** : in a direction away from the shore ⟨the tide is going ~⟩ ⟨they rowed ~ to the ship⟩ **g** : away from a job or task ⟨took time ~ for a cigarette⟩ **2 a** (1) : out of the usual or proper place or position ⟨threw his shoulder ~⟩ ⟨laughing his sides ~⟩ ⟨the time has been that, when the brains were ~, the man would die —Shak.⟩ (2) : out of the necessary or expected place or position ⟨left ~ two lines⟩ ⟨left ~ the most important part of his argument⟩ **b** : away from or contrary to one's normal or usual state of mind or manner of behavior ⟨greatly put ~ by the bad news⟩ ⟨the two friends fell ~ over a trivial matter⟩ **c** : beyond the usual or proper limits ⟨the edge of the house juts ~ over the cliff⟩ ⟨the point of the nail sticks ~⟩ ⟨his shirttails hang ~⟩ **d** : so as to protrude or stick out ⟨~ at elbows⟩ ⟨~ at the knees⟩ **e** : at odds ⟨he is ~ with his friend over a girl⟩ **f** : out of pocket ⟨by the end of the evening, he was $20 ~⟩ **g** : not in accord with the facts ⟨this story is ludicrously ~ in its geography —B.R.Elliott⟩ ⟨the introductory note . . . by an error in arithmetic, is ~ by twenty years —*Times Lit. Supp.*⟩ **h** : not in agreement ⟨the trial balance was ~ $10⟩ **3 a** (1) : in or into the open : out of an enclosed space (as a building or container) ⟨he went ~ about an hour ago⟩ ⟨the whole town turned ~ to greet him⟩ ⟨he took ~ his wallet⟩ ⟨she poured ~ the tea⟩ (2) : out of a place or position tenaciously held to ⟨drag him ~⟩ ⟨smoke him ~⟩ ⟨crowd him ~⟩ (3) : out of a situation or place felt to be confining or unendurable ⟨tried to break ~⟩ ⟨changed his mind afterward and asked to be let ~⟩ **b** : into activity, use, or accessibility ⟨war broke ~⟩ ⟨opened ~ a new route to the West⟩ ⟨the new models are coming ~ next week⟩ **c** : EXTERNALLY ⟨cleaned the house inside and ~⟩ **d** : in the open : OUTDOORS ⟨it was nice ~ . . . with the sky all so blue —J.T.Farrell⟩ ⟨it's a lovely day ~ —James Jones⟩ ⟨camp ~⟩ **e** (1) : in or into active military service or training ⟨the army was ordered ~ —Marjory S. Douglas⟩ ⟨has been ~ on maneuvers⟩ (2) : on a journey or expedition ⟨has been ~ fishing for a week⟩ ⟨has been ~ on a business trip⟩ (3) : in or into active rebellion ⟨he was a bitter rebel, and boasted that his grandfather had been ~ in '98 —G.B. Shaw⟩ (4) : not at work : on strike ⟨ten thousand or more workers are ~ —Warner Bloomberg⟩ **f** : on the exterior or outer side ⟨insulated the roof to keep the heat ~⟩ ⟨closed the windows to keep the rain ~⟩ **g** : to or toward the outside ⟨turned his pockets inside ~⟩ ⟨went to the window and looked ~⟩ **h** : out of jail or prison ⟨he's only been ~ a week, but he's already in trouble⟩ **i** : not on the shelf : in circulation ⟨the book you want is ~⟩ **4 a** : at or to a distance away from a given point ⟨the nearest school is three miles ~⟩ ⟨hit the ball 400 feet ~⟩ **b** : at or to a distance away from land : at sea ⟨when they were three days ~, the weather turned fine⟩ ⟨an island far ~ in the ocean⟩ **c** : at a relatively far distance ⟨motioned to the shortstop to play ~⟩ **d** : around the circuit of the first nine holes of a golf course ⟨he went ~ in 39⟩ **5 a** : from or among a group ⟨sorting operations have selected ~ certain cards —R.S.Casey & J.W.Perry⟩ **b** : into sections or parts ⟨portioned ~ the meat among the five of them⟩ ⟨laid ~ the day's work for his two assistants⟩ **6 a** : FREELY, OPENLY ⟨was too frightened to speak ~⟩ **b** : so as to be audible : ALOUD ⟨cried ~ to attract his friend's attention⟩ ⟨called ~ a greeting⟩ **c** : in or into print or public circulation ⟨the evening paper isn't ~ yet⟩ ⟨there's a warrant ~ against him⟩ **d** : in or into open view ⟨the moon is ~ tonight⟩ ⟨the sun came ~ from behind the clouds⟩ **e** : in or into leaf, blossom, or fruit ⟨the roses are just ~⟩ ⟨the apples are starting to come ~⟩ **f** : in or into society ⟨wear the same clothes and makeup as girls who are already ~ and go to grown-up parties —Helen Eustis⟩ **g** : in an unfurled or extended state ⟨broke ~ the topsail⟩ **7 a** : to a point of exhaustion or depletion ⟨talked herself ~⟩ ⟨cried herself ~⟩ ⟨pumped the well ~⟩ ⟨the cow is milked ~⟩ **b** : to a point of completion or satisfaction ⟨might as well have your sleep ~ —Ellen Glasgow⟩ ⟨deeply satisfied, the way you feel when you have had a chance to say your say all ~ —Dorothy C. Fisher⟩ ⟨fight it ~ on this line if it takes all summer —U.S.Grant⟩ **c** : in or into a state of extinction, inactivity, or nonexistence ⟨the fire is ~⟩ ⟨put ~ the light⟩ ⟨a custom that is going ~⟩ ⟨a species that is on its way ~⟩ **d** : to a solution or result ⟨work ~ the problem in your own way⟩ ⟨the addition comes ~ wrong each time⟩ **e** : to a conclusion (as to adulthood or to a predetermined size or weight) ⟨grow ~ livestock⟩ **8 a** : at an end ⟨before the year is ~⟩ ⟨now that the summer is ~⟩ **b** : in or into an insensible or unconscious state ⟨the glassy eyes and vague expression of a man who was . . . ~ on his feet —S.H.Adams⟩ ⟨after three drinks he was ~ cold⟩ **c** : out of commission : in or into a useless state ⟨only the one plane coming in — actually half a plane — with two of its engines ~ —Saul Levitt⟩ **d** (1) : so as to retire a batter or batsman or so as to be retired ⟨put him ~ on three straight pitches⟩ ⟨bowled him ~⟩ ⟨popped ~ to the infield⟩ (2) : out of participation in a poker pot ⟨count me ~⟩ ⟨deal me ~⟩ (3) : at the winning point of a game (as by having reached or passed the required goal or number of points) **e** : at a stop ⟨the referee called time ~⟩ **f** — used on a two way radio circuit to indicate the end of a communication with no reply expected ⟨over and ~⟩ **9 a** : in an extended manner or to an extended degree ⟨the dog was stretched ~ on the floor⟩ ⟨the last act was terribly drawn ~⟩ **b** : to the fullest possible extent ⟨decked ~ in her best clothes⟩ ⟨clean ~ the attic⟩ ⟨wipe ~ the stain⟩ **c** : in or into competition or determined effort ⟨for class president⟩ ⟨intends to go ~ for the football team next year⟩ ⟨~ to win control of the whole industry⟩ **10 a** : out of office or power ⟨voted ~ at the next election⟩ ⟨turned ~ by the new commissioner⟩ **b** : out of season : no longer in supply ⟨fresh strawberries are ~ now until next spring⟩ **c** : out of vogue or fashion : no longer in request ⟨short skirts are ~⟩ **d** : out of the question : so as to be eliminated from consideration ⟨these last two proposals seem definitely ~ —Tom Fitzsimmons⟩ **11** — used as an intensive with numerous verbs ⟨bait ~ the fish lines⟩ ⟨sketch ~ the plans⟩ ⟨write ~ the speech⟩

²out \'au̇t, *usu* 'au̇d·+V\ *vb* -ED/-ING/-S [ME *outen,* fr. OE *ūtian,* fr. *ūt,* adv.] *vt* **1** : to put out : eject from a place, office, or possession : EXPEL ⟨privately kept ~*ed* vicars as chaplains —Rose Macaulay⟩ **2** *archaic* : to make public : DISCLOSE, REVEAL **3** : EXTINGUISH ⟨the lamplighter went his rounds ~*ing* the street lamps —John Bennett⟩ **4** : to thrust out : EXTEND ⟨they ~*ed* oars and pulled hard —Christopher Morley⟩ **5** *slang Brit* : knock out : render unconscious or kill **6 a** : to put (a batsman) out in cricket **b** : to eliminate in a sports competition ⟨was ~*ed* in a semifinal of the Australian championships —*A.B.C.Weekly*⟩ **7** : to hit (a ball) out of bounds in tennis or squash ~ *vi* **1** : to become known or apparent : become public ⟨truth will ~⟩ ⟨murder will ~⟩ ⟨bad blood always ~*s* —Alec Waugh⟩ **2** : to go out; *esp* : go on an outing or excursion **3** : to hit a tennis ball out of bounds ⟨the Australian ~*ed* and lost the game —*Sydney (Australia) Morning Herald*⟩ — **out with 1** : to bring out ⟨he *outs with* his money⟩ **2** : to make known : UTTER ⟨he *outs with* the whole story⟩

³out \ˌau̇t, *usu* ˌau̇d·+V\ *adj* [ME, fr. *out,* adv.] **1** : situated or lying on the outside of something : EXTERNAL ⟨the ~ edge⟩ **2** : situated or lying at a distance from a center : OUTLYING ⟨the ~ islands⟩ ⟨the ~ parts of the settlement⟩ **3 a** : not in power : having no official position or standing ⟨encourage pirating by ~ unions trying to get in —C.O.Gregory⟩ **b** : not having its inning ⟨the ~ side in cricket⟩ **c** : not successful in reaching base ⟨the batter was ~ at first on a close play⟩ ⟨was ~ trying to steal third⟩ **4** : larger than usual ⟨a dress of an ~ size⟩ **5** : directed outward or serving to direct something outward : OUTGOING ⟨the ~ train⟩ ⟨put the letter in the ~ basket⟩

⁴out \(ˈ)au̇t, *usu* (ˈ)au̇d·+V\ *prep* [ME, fr. *out,* adv.] **1 a** — used as a function word to indicate direction from the inside to the outside ⟨peering ~ his window at the river —Hugh MacLennan⟩ **b** — used as a function word to indicate movement or change of position from the inside to the outside ⟨threw his street clothes and luggage ~ a window onto the platform —Joseph Wechsberg⟩ ⟨put the cat ~ the door⟩ **2** — used as a function word to indicate movement or direction away from a center ⟨drove through the streets of town and ~ the dark, wooded road to his house —Nathaniel Benchley⟩ ⟨lives ~ Elm Street⟩; see OUT OF

⁵out \'au̇t, *usu* 'au̇d·+V\ *n* -S [¹*out* & ³*out*] **1** : OUTSIDE ⟨liking not the inside, locked the ~ —Lord Byron⟩ ⟨the width of the building from ~ to ~⟩ **2** : OUTING **3 a** : one who is without official position or influence : a member of a party or group that is out of power — usu. used in pl. ⟨the ~*s* are invariably more emphatic in their advocacy of principles than the ins —C.J.Friedrich⟩ **b outs** *pl* : the players in a game (as cricket) who are not having their innings **4** : copy matter (as a word) inadvertently omitted in typesetting **5** : SHOWING ⟨makes a poor ~ of it when the hub of the house comes down —H.E. Giles⟩ **6 a** : the retiring of a baseball player during his turn at bat ⟨it was the last ~ of the game⟩ **b** : a player so retired ⟨he was an easy ~⟩ **7 outs** *pl, Brit* : money paid out esp. in taxes **8** : an objectionable feature or circumstance : BLEMISH ⟨despite all the improvement, rubber still has a number of bad ~*s* —Williams Haynes & E.A.Hauser⟩ **9** : a ball hit out of bounds in tennis or squash **10** : an item that is out of stock ⟨the packing list is noted for changes in quantities and ~*s* —D.F.Sellards⟩ **11 a** : a way of avoiding responsibility or escaping from an embarrassing situation : a face-saving device ⟨a discreet retirement may provide the easy ~ —Douglass Cater⟩ ⟨can sometimes serve as an easy ~ in cases that might prove to be politically embarrassing —S.K.Padover⟩ **b** : a way out of a difficulty : SOLUTION ⟨believe the only ~ for the party is to continue the present system of high, rigid supports on basic farm commodities —W.M.Blair⟩ ⟨a possible ~ for big ships would be their use for mass transportation of tourists —*Newsweek*⟩ — **at outs** *or* **on the outs** *adv* : at variance : in a state of opposition ⟨was *at outs* with most of the kids on the block —Verne Athanas⟩ ⟨they are bitterly *on the outs*⟩

out- *prefix* [ME, fr. *out,* adv.] : in a manner that goes beyond, surpasses, or excels ⟨*out*dance⟩ ⟨*out*fight⟩ ⟨*out*run⟩ ⟨*out*bluff⟩ ⟨*out*maneuver⟩

outact \(ˈ)=ˈ=\ *vt* [*out-* + *act*] : to surpass in acting

out·age \'au̇d·ij, 'au̇t|, |ēj\ *n* -S [³*out* + *-age*] **1 a** : a quantity or bulk of something (as of oil or whiskey) lost in transportation or storage **b** : HEADSPACE 3 **2** : a failure or interruption in the use or functioning of something (as of an electric light bulb or a machine) **3** : a period during which the supply of electric energy from a generating station or system is interrupted

out and away *adv* : far and away ⟨*out and away* the best driver I know⟩

out-and-out \ˌ=ˌ=ˈ=\ *adj (or adv)* **1** : free from disguise or concealment : OPEN ⟨an *out-and-out* isolationist⟩ **2** : COMPLETE, THOROUGHGOING ⟨an *out-and-out* fool⟩ ⟨an *out-and-out* attack⟩

out-and-out·er \-ə(r)\ *n* [*out-and-out* + *-er*] **1** : an extreme or outstanding representative of a class or group ⟨the party was split between the moderates and the *out-and-outers*⟩ ⟨an *out-and-outer* as a catcher⟩ **2** : one who goes to an extreme ⟨an *out-and-outer* in everything he does⟩

ou·tarde \ü'tärd\ *n* -S [CanF, fr. F, bustard, fr. (assumed) VL *austarda,* fr. L *avis tarda,* lit., slow bird, fr. *avis* bird + *tarda,* fem. of *tardus* slow — more at AVIARY, TARDY] : CANADA GOOSE

outask \(ˈ)=ˈ=\ *vt* [¹*out* + *ask*] *dial Eng* : to publish the banns of marriage of (a couple) in church for the third time

¹outback \(ˈ)=ˈ=\ *adv* [¹*out* + *back*] : in or in the direction of the outback ⟨the farther ~ toward the deserts you go the larger your station must be —Margaret I. Ross⟩

²outback \ˈ=ˌ=\ *n, sometimes cap, often attrib* : the back-country of Australia or New Zealand : ¹BUSH 2c ⟨~ life⟩ ⟨~ sheep stations⟩ — usu. used with *the* when not attributive ⟨bringing civilization to the ~⟩

out·back·er \-kə(r)\ *n* : a native or resident of the outback

outbalance \(ˈ)=ˈ==\ *vt* [*out-* + *balance*] : OUTWEIGH

outbellow \(ˈ)=ˈ==\ *vt* [*out-* + *bellow*] : to bellow louder than

outbid \(ˈ)=ˈ=\ *vt* [*out-* + *bid*] **1** : to make a higher bid than : offer more than ⟨the rich districts can and do ~ the country school for teachers —W.M.Mason⟩ **2** : to bid more than (another player) in a card game ⟨~ their opponents for the hand⟩

outbirth \ˈ=ˌ=\ *n* [³*out* + *birth*] : something that is brought forth : PROGENY

outblaze \(ˈ)=ˈ=\ *vb* [¹*out* + *blaze*] *vi* : to blaze out ⟨the smouldering fire again *outblazed* within him —William Morris⟩ ~ *vt* [*out-* + *blaze*] : to outdo in brilliance of light : OUTSHINE ⟨*outblazing* the moon —William Sansom⟩

outbloom \(ˈ)=ˈ=\ *vb* [*out-* + *bloom*] *vt* : to exceed in bloom ⟨~*ed* all other flowers in the garden⟩ ~ *vi* [¹*out* + *bloom*] **1** : to come into bloom ⟨~*ed* in glories manifold —Clinton Scollard⟩ **2** : to have finished blooming ⟨her azaleas which were famous but all ~*ed* by the time we got there —Catherine Hutter⟩

outblot \(ˈ)=ˈ=\ *vt* [¹*out* + *blot*] : to blot out

¹outblowing \ˈ=ˌ==\ *adj* [¹*out* + *blowing,* pres. part. of ¹*blow*] : blowing outward ⟨~ winds⟩

²outblowing \"\ *n* [³*out* + *blowing,* gerund of ¹*blow*] : a blowing outward ⟨enormous ~*s* of smoke —Arnold Bennett⟩

outbluff \(ˈ)=ˈ=\ *vt* [*out-* + *bluff*] : to outdo in bluffing ⟨~ the fascist powers —*New Republic*⟩

¹outboard \ˈ=ˌ=\ *adj* [⁴*out* + *board,* n.] **1** : situated or lying outboard ⟨~ rigging⟩ ⟨the ~ walls⟩ **2** : of, relating to, or being a bearing, center, or other support that is used in conjunction with and outside of a corresponding main support usu. in its own independent frame and often on a separate foundation **3** : having, using, or limited to the use of an outboard motor ⟨~ cruiser⟩ ⟨~ classes⟩

²outboard \"\ *adv* [⁴*out* + *board,* n.] **1** : outside the line of a ship's bulwarks or hull : nearer the side than the center : in a lateral direction from the hull or from the keel ⟨swing the davits ~⟩ ⟨stand facing ~⟩ — contrasted with *inboard* **2** : from within outward : to or toward the outside ⟨throw a line ~ and catch a fish —*Harper's*⟩ **3** : in a position closer or closest to either of the wing tips of an airplane : in a lateral direction from the longitudinal axis of an airplane

³outboard \"\ *n* [¹*outboard*] **1** : OUTBOARD MOTOR ⟨a 3 h.p. ~⟩ **2** : a boat with an outboard motor attached ⟨a 16-foot ~⟩

outboarding \ˈ=ˌ==\ *n* [³*outboard* + *-ing*] : the activity or sport of using or racing boats that are equipped with outboard motors

outboard motor *n* : a small internal-combustion engine with propeller integrally attached that is temporarily secured to the stern of a small boat

outbond \ˈ=ˌ=\ *adj* [³*out* + *bond* (connection)] : laid with its longer side parallel to the face of a wall ⟨an ~ brick⟩ — opposed to *inbond*

outbound \ˈ=ˌ=\ *adj* [¹*out* + *bound*] **1** : outward bound ⟨~ traffic⟩ ⟨~ ship⟩ — contrasted with *inbound* **2** : relating to outward or outbound traffic ⟨an ~ station⟩

outbox \(ˈ)=ˈ=\ *vt* [*out-* + *box*] : to surpass in boxing ⟨~*ed* bigger and heavier opponents —Sinclair Lewis⟩

outboard motor

outbranch \(ˈ)=ˈ=\ *vi* [¹*out* + *branch*] : to branch out

outbrave \(ˈ)=ˈ=\ *vt* [*out-* + *brave*] **1** : to face, endure, or resist defiantly ⟨~ defeat⟩ **2** *archaic* : to surpass in beauty or showiness of dress **3** : to exceed in courage ⟨~ the heart most daring on the earth —Shak.⟩

¹outbreak \(ˈ)=ˈ=\ *vi* [ME *outbreken,* fr. OE *ūtbrecan,* fr. *ūt* out + *brecan* to break — more at OUT, BREAK] : to break out ⟨there *outbroke* the blast of a horn —Stephen Graham⟩

²outbreak \ˈ=ˌ=\ *n* [³*out* + *break* (after *break out*)] **1 a** : a bursting forth : a sudden or violent breaking out of activity ⟨the ~ of war⟩ ⟨an ~ of new building⟩ ⟨~*s* of experimentation on group effects among the lower animals —W.C.Allee⟩ **b** : a sudden rise in the incidence of a disease esp. to epidemic or near epidemic proportions ⟨an ~ of flu⟩ **c** : a sudden increase in numbers of a harmful or noxious insect or other organism within a particular area ⟨an ~ of locusts⟩ ⟨an ~ center⟩ **2** : INSURRECTION, REVOLT ⟨a slave ~⟩ ⟨famine conditions led to ~*s* in many cities⟩

outbreaker \ˈ=ˌ==\ *n* [³*out* + *breaker*] : a breaker distant from the shore

outbreaking \ˈ=ˌ==\ *n* [ME *outbreking,* fr. ³*out* + *breking,* gerund of *breken* to break (after *breken out* to break out)] : OUTBREAK

outbreathe \(ˈ)=ˈ=\ *vb* [¹*out* + *breathe*] : EXHALE

out·breathed \ˈ=ˌbretht\ *adj* [*out (of) breath* + *-ed*] **:** out of breath

outbred \ˈ=ˌ=\ *adj* [¹*out* + *bred*] **:** subjected to or produced by outbreeding

outbreed \(ˈ)=ˈ=\ *vt* [¹*out* + *breed*] **1 :** to subject to outbreeding — compare CROSSBREED, INBREED **2** [*out-* + *breed*] **:** to breed faster than ⟨pests sometimes ~ their hosts⟩ **3 :** to breed out **:** eliminate (an unwanted characteristic) through breeding ⟨~ horns⟩

outbreeding \ˈ=ˌ==\ *n* [³*out* + *breeding*] **1 :** a natural mating of relatively unrelated individuals; *esp* **:** the mating of an individual of a particular group (as a tribe, people, or social class) with someone outside the group — compare EXOGAMY **2 :** a selective breeding of animals on the basis of individual excellence and avoidance of close relationship — compare INBREEDING

outbuild \(ˈ)=ˈ=\ *vt* [*out-* + *build*] **1 :** to outdo in building ⟨free societies can ~ . . . societies based on tyrannies —Dean Acheson⟩ **2** [¹*out* + *build*] **:** to build outward or outside of ⟨the fish *outbuilt* her shell —R.W.Emerson⟩

outbuilding \ˈ=ˌ==\ *n* [³*out* + *building*] **:** a building (as a stable or smokehouse) separate from but accessory to a main house ⟨a whitewashed edifice of eight rooms, with ample ~*s* —John Buchan⟩ — called also *outhouse*

outbulk \(ˈ)=ˈ=\ *vt* [*out-* + *bulk*] **:** to surpass in bulk

outburn \(ˈ)=ˈ=\ *vb* [¹*out* + *burn*] *vi* **:** to burn out **:** become consumed in burning ~ *vt* [*out-* + *burn*] **1 :** to outdo in burning **:** burn longer than ⟨stars that have ~*ed* the sun⟩ **2 :** to dissipate by burning ⟨the sun ~*s* the fog⟩

¹**outburst** \(ˈ)=ˈ=\ *vi* [ME *outbersten, outbresten*, fr. *out* + *bersten, bresten* to burst — more at BURST] **:** to burst out

²**outburst** \ˈ=ˌ=\ *n* [³*out* + *burst* (after *burst out*, v.)] **1 :** a bursting out **:** a violent expression or demonstration of intense feeling ⟨an ~ of rage⟩ ⟨an ~ of affection⟩ **2 :** a sudden or intense surge of activity or growth ⟨furious ~*s* of swirling flame —Laurence Binyon⟩ ⟨new ~*s* of creative power —C.E. Montague⟩ ⟨an ~ of vegetative life—Samuel Van Valkenburg & Ellsworth Huntington⟩ **3 a :** ERUPTION ⟨successive volcanic ~*s* which covered the area with dust, pumice, and mudflows —*Biol. Abstracts*⟩ **b :** a cosmic explosion (as of a nova or supernova) ⟨Nova (U) Scorpii has had three ~*s* —*Science*⟩

out·bye *also* **out·by** \ˈau̇tˌbī, ˈüt-\ *adv* [ME (Sc) *out-by*, fr. *out* + *by*] **1** *chiefly Scot* **a :** OUTDOORS, OUTSIDE **b :** a short distance away **c :** far off **:** far away **2** *chiefly Scot* **:** toward the shaft or entry of a mine

outcamp \ˈ=ˌ=\ *n* [³*out* + *camp*] **:** an outlying camp **:** a camp at a distance from a main camp ⟨an ~ which was my base for six weeks —H.H.Finlayson⟩

outcase \ˈ=ˌ=\ *n* [³*out* + *case*] **:** an outer casing (as of a watch)

¹**outcast** \(ˈ)=ˈ=\ *vt* [ME *outcasten*, fr. *out* + *casten* to cast — more at CAST] **:** to cast out

²**outcast** \ˈ=ˌ=\ *adj* [ME, fr. past part. of *outcasten*] **1 :** regarded with contempt **:** DESPISED ⟨afraid lest she should be mixed up with something low, ~, suspected —Rose Macaulay⟩ **2 :** rejected or cast out by society **:** FRIENDLESS ⟨a rebel, feared and ~ —Lewis Dent⟩ ⟨all alone beweep my ~ state —Shak.⟩ **3 :** thrown aside **:** DISCARDED ⟨~ beliefs⟩

³**outcast** \ˈ=ˌ=\ *n* [ME, fr. *outcast*, adj.] **1 a :** one who is cast out or refused acceptance by society **:** a friendless or rejected person **:** CASTAWAY ⟨a social ~⟩ ⟨a political ~⟩ ⟨had no rights and no status and were considered ~*s* —Morris Ploscowe⟩ **b :** something that is cast out ⟨from being a cultural ~ science became a respectable and finally a dominant interest —Douglas Bush⟩ **2** [³*out* + *cast* (after Sc *cast out*)] *Scot* **:** QUARREL ⟨a bitter black ~ —Robert Burns⟩

¹**outcaste** \(ˈ)=ˈ=\ *vt* -ED/-ING/-S [⁴*out* + *caste*, n.] **:** to make an outcaste of ⟨~*s* himself if he eats forbidden food⟩ ⟨his wife's family . . . had *outcasted* him —Ela Sen⟩

²**outcaste** \ˈ=ˌ=\ *n* [⁴*out* + *caste*] **1** *India* **:** one who has been ejected from his caste for violation of its customs or rules **2** *India* **:** one who has no caste **:** one who is considered outside society

³**outcaste** \ˈ=ˌ=\ *adj* **:** belonging to no caste

outclass \(ˈ)=ˈ=\ *vt* [*out-* + *class*, n.] **:** to excel or surpass so decisively as to appear of a higher class ⟨said the players of his generation easily ~*ed* the current crop —Stanley Frank⟩ ⟨these new forms . . . ~*ed* the old flat daggers and axes in effectiveness —Jacquetta & Christopher Hawkes⟩

out-clearing \ˈ=ˌ==\ *n* [³*out* + *clearing* (after *clear out*)] *Brit* **:** the checks sent out by a bank for collection during the process of clearing

outclimb \(ˈ)=ˈ=\ *vt* [*out-* + *climb*] **1 :** to outdo in climbing ⟨~*s* the other children⟩ **2 :** to climb beyond ⟨~*s* the other skyscrapers⟩

out-college \ˈ=ˌ==\ *adj* [⁴*out* + *college*] *chiefly Brit* **:** residing outside a college ⟨an *out-college* student⟩

out·come \ˈau̇tˌkəm\ *n* -S [³*out* + *come* (after *come out*, v.)] **1 a :** something that comes out of or follows from an activity or process **:** CONSEQUENCE, RESULT ⟨this book is the ~ of some 30 years of travel, study and observation —O.S. Nock⟩ ⟨the ~ of the election⟩ ⟨~ of the game⟩ **b :** something that is arrived at on the basis of logic or reason **:** CONCLUSION ⟨if the principles . . . are accepted, certain ~*s* as to post-school and out-of-school education follow —*General Education in a Free Society*⟩ ⟨it has no positive ~ and suffered from a certain cynicism —H.J.Laski⟩ **2 :** OUTLET ⟨offered no ~ for his energy⟩ **syn** see EFFECT

out·com·er \-mə(r)\ *n* [³*out* + *comer*] **:** one who comes from outside **:** FOREIGNER, STRANGER

out·com·ing \-miŋ, -mēŋ\ *n* [³*out* + *coming* (after *come out*)] **:** RESULT, EMANATION

¹**out-country** \ˈ=ˌ==\ *n* [³*out* + *country*] **:** an outlying area or country

²**out-country** \ˈ=ˌ==\ *adj* [in sense 1, fr. ⁴*out* + *country*, in sense 2, fr. ¹*out-country*] **1 :** ALIEN, FOREIGN ⟨looked down upon *out-country* peoples⟩ **2 :** belonging to or characteristic of the country **:** not urban ⟨his clear, healthy, *out-country* look —*Time*⟩

out·cri·er \ˈ=ˌkrī(ə)r, -īə\ *n* [²*outcry* + *-er*] **1 :** one who makes an outcry **2 :** HUCKSTER

¹**outcrop** \ˈ=ˌ=\ *n* [³*out* + *crop* (after *crop out*, v.)] **1 a :** a coming out of bedrock or of an unconsolidated deposit to the surface of the ground **b :** the part of a rock formation that appears at the surface of the ground **2 :** a breaking out **:** a coming to the surface ⟨the recent ~ of unofficial strikes —*Economist*⟩ ⟨recurrent ~*s* of a heavy and pedantic philosophical jargon —*Times Lit. Supp.*⟩

²**outcrop** \(ˈ)=ˈ=\ *vi* **1 :** to come out to the surface of the ground ⟨younger rocks ~ progressively towards the west —A.T.Grove⟩ **2 :** to come to the surface **:** become manifest ⟨originality ~*s* in the course of planning —*Psychiatry*⟩

out·crop·per \ˈ=ˌkräpə(r)\ *n* [¹*outcrop* + *-er*] **:** one who works an outcrop

outcropping *n* -S **:** OUTCROP

¹**outcross** \ˈ=ˌ=\ *n* [³*out* + *cross*] **1 :** a cross between individuals of different strains **2 :** the progeny of an outcross

²**outcross** \(ˈ)=ˈ=\ *vt* **:** to subject to outcrossing

outcrossing *n* [fr. gerund of ²*outcross*] **:** a mating of individuals of different strains but usu. of the same breed

¹**outcry** \ˈ=ˌ=\ *n* [ME, fr. *out* + *cry* (after *crien out* to cry out)] **1 a :** a crying out **:** a loud and excited cry or exclamation **:** CLAMOR, UPROAR ⟨that ~ of despair —P.B.Shelley⟩ ⟨still she made her ~ for the ring —Alfred Tennyson⟩ **b :** a vehement public protest or demand ⟨the ~ against him reverberated throughout the country —Allan Nevins⟩ ⟨an ~ for more and better cottages —G.E.Fussell⟩ **2 a :** AUCTION ⟨the executor's duty to sell it at public ~ —*Southeastern Reporter*⟩ **b :** a calling out of a price (as in a commodity exchange) ⟨a buyer and seller in the ring can by open ~ mutually agree on a price —*Commodities*⟩

²**outcry** \(ˈ)=ˈ=\ *vb* [ME *outcrien*, fr. *out* + *crien* to cry — more at CRY] *vi* **:** to cry out ⟨my every pulse *outcries* for love —Evaleen Stein⟩ ~ *vt* [*out-* + *cry*] **:** to outdo in shouting ⟨~ his competitors⟩

¹**outcurve** \ˈ=ˌ=\ *n* [³*out* + *curve*, n. (after *curve out*, v.)] **1 :** a curving out **2 :** something that curves out; *esp* **:** a curve in baseball in which the ball breaks away from the batter

²**outcurve** \(ˈ)=ˈ=\ *vb* [¹*out* + *curve*, v.] *vt* **:** to cause to curve outward ~ *vi* **:** to bend or curve outward

outdance \(ˈ)=ˈ=\ *vt* [*out-* + *dance*] **:** to outdo in dancing ⟨not only ~ the women, they beat them hands down in the music of castanets —Claudia Cassidy⟩

outdare \(ˈ)=ˈ=\ *vt* [¹*out* + *dare*] **1 :** DEFY ⟨~ any danger⟩ **2** [*out-* + *dare*] **:** to outdo in daring ⟨~*s* all other stuntmen⟩

outdate \(ˈ)=ˈ=\ *vt* [¹*out* + *date*] **:** to make out of date **:** make obsolete ⟨the development of new machinery has *outdated* many plants⟩

outdated \ˈ=ˌ==\ *adj* [¹*out* + *dated*] **:** ANTIQUATED ⟨an ~ directory⟩ ⟨an ~ building⟩

outdazzle \(ˈ)=ˈ==\ *vt* [*out-* + *dazzle*] **:** to surpass in brilliance **:** OUTSHINE ⟨comes close to *outdazzling* the spotlight —Hamilton Basso⟩

outdistance \(ˈ)=ˈ==\ *vt* [*out-* + *distance*] **:** to go far ahead of (as in a race or competition) **:** OUTSTRIP ⟨has *outdistanced* all his rivals for the nomination⟩ ⟨threatens to ~ the highest budget of previous years⟩

outdo \(ˈ)=ˈ=\ *vt* [*out-* + *do*] **1 :** to go beyond in action or performance **:** EXCEL, SURPASS ⟨it took reptiles to ~ amphibians, and it took mammals to surpass reptiles —Weston La Barre⟩ ⟨*outdid* himself to break the record he had set⟩ ⟨*outdid* him in kindness⟩ **2 :** DEFEAT, OVERCOME ⟨*outdid* his enemy by trickery⟩ **syn** see EXCEED

out·done \(ˈ)=ˈ=\ *adj* [fr. past part. of *outdo*] *chiefly South & Midland* **:** PROVOKED, VEXED ⟨grumbled and . . . pretended to be greatly ~ with me —R.P.Warren⟩

out·door \(ˈ)=ˈ=\ *also* **out·doors** \(ˈ)=ˈ=\ *adj* [*out-of-door, out-of-doors*] **1 a :** of, belonging to, or characteristic of the outdoors ⟨the fresh and vigorous complexion of an ~ man —I.A.Gordon⟩ ⟨an ~ setting⟩ ⟨an ~ fragrance⟩ **b :** done or performed outdoors ⟨~ sports⟩ ⟨~ exercise⟩ ⟨an ~ concert⟩ **c :** not enclosed **:** having no roof ⟨an ~ arena⟩ ⟨an ~ theater⟩ **2 :** given or administered outside an institution ⟨~ relief⟩ ⟨~ pensions⟩

¹**outdoors** \(ˈ)=ˈ=\ *adv* [*out (of) doors*] **:** out of a building **:** in or into the open air ⟨stayed ~ until it started to rain⟩ ⟨went ~ to get some fresh air⟩

²**outdoors** \ˈ"\ *n pl but sing in constr* **1 :** the open air ⟨came in from the ~ at dinner time⟩ **2 :** the world away from human habitations ⟨the lure of the great ~⟩ ⟨a man of the ~⟩

out·doors·man \-zmən\ *n, pl* **outdoorsmen 1 :** one who lives or prefers to live in the outdoors ⟨simple *outdoorsmen* without much formal education —C.L.Wirth⟩ **2 :** one who enjoys outdoor activities (as hunting and fishing) ⟨sells equipment for *outdoorsmen*⟩

out·doorsy \-zē, -zi\ *adj* [²*outdoors* + *-y*] **:** belonging to, characteristic of, or devoted to the outdoors or outdoor life ⟨sounded rugged and ~ —*N.Y. Times*⟩ ⟨our least ~ neighbor has succumbed to the popularity of outdoor picnic ovens —*Better Homes & Gardens*⟩

outdraft \ˈ=ˌ=\ *n* [³*out* + *draft*] **:** an outward draft or current

outdraw \(ˈ)=ˈ=\ *vt* [*out-* + *draw*] **1 :** to surpass in drawing power **:** attract a larger audience or following than ⟨basketball ~*s* football in this area⟩ ⟨~*s* all other languages in the city's high schools⟩ **2 :** to draw (a gun) more quickly than ⟨~*s* the villainous gunman in a showdown⟩

outdrink \(ˈ)=ˈ=\ *vt* [*out-* + *drink*] **:** to outdo in drinking alcoholic beverages ⟨she can ~ most men⟩

outdrive \(ˈ)=ˈ=\ *vt* [*out-* + *drive*] **:** to drive (a ball) harder or farther than (as in tennis or golf)

outdrop \ˈ=ˌ=\ *n* [³*out* + *drop*] **:** a drop in which a baseball breaks down and away from a right-handed batter

outdweller \ˈ=ˌ==\ *n* [³*out* + *dweller*] **:** one who dwells outside or remote from (a specified place)

outeat \(ˈ)=ˈ=\ *vt* [*out-* + *eat*] **:** to outdo in eating ⟨~*s* people twice his size⟩

outed *past of* OUT

¹**out·en** \ˈau̇tᵊn\ *prep* [alter. of *out from*] *dial* **:** out of ⟨hand me an egg ~ the icebox —Elizabeth M. Roberts⟩

²**outen** \ˈ"\ *vt* -ED/-ING/-S [¹*out* + *-en*] *chiefly dial* **:** to put out **:** EXTINGUISH ⟨you might ~ the candles there —Hervey Allen⟩

¹**out·er** \ˈau̇d·ə(r), ˈau̇tə-\ *adj* [ME, fr. *out*, adj. + *-er* (comp. suffix) — more at OUT] **1 :** EXTERNAL, OBJECTIVE ⟨~ life⟩ ⟨~ reality⟩ ⟨~ characteristics⟩ — compare INNER **2 a :** situated farther out ⟨~ space⟩ ⟨the ~ line of defense⟩ **b :** away from a center ⟨the satellites of the ~ solar planets—J.T.McIntosh⟩ **c :** situated or belonging on the outside ⟨the two ~ movements of the symphony⟩ ⟨the ~ covering⟩

syn OUTWARD, OUTSIDE, EXTERNAL, EXTERIOR: OUTER may retain comparative suggestion and contrast with *inner* ⟨*outer* garments⟩ ⟨*outer* space⟩ ⟨the *outer* line of defenses⟩ OUTWARD, contrasted with *inward*, may be used in relation to trend, direction, or motion ⟨the *outward* push of tourists in search of strange places is spilling over from the accustomed channels —*N.Y. Times*⟩ Both words may describe a surface semblance in contrast to an inner reality ⟨colorless and grey are the *outer* facts of a monk's life —H.O.Taylor⟩ ⟨these twins were alike in many ways, mostly, however, in their *outer* life or manifest behavior —*Biol. Abstracts*⟩ ⟨to give *outward* and objective form to ideas that bubble inwardly and have a fascinating lure in them —H.L.Mencken⟩ ⟨all *outward* actions, every overt thing we do —J.C.Powys⟩ OUTSIDE describes either a position on the outer side or a location or situation beyond borders, bounds, or limits ⟨these ships are completely air-conditioned and their staterooms are all *outside* —Mary G. Reynolds⟩ ⟨in spite of frequent assertions to the contrary, the monks very seldom taught *outside* pupils —G.G.Coulton⟩ ⟨only a relatively small part of the millions that have come from below the ground have remained in the state and most of the larger present-day properties are owned by *outside* companies —*Amer. Guide Series: Nev.*⟩ Like OUTSIDE, EXTERNAL may describe a position, situation, or sphere beyond or away from a thing under consideration ⟨the slavery which would be imposed upon her by her *external* enemies and her internal traitors —F.D.Roosevelt⟩ ⟨a poet only through the demands of an inner being and compulsion, and not through the *external* circumstances of good fortune or bad —H.V.Gregory⟩ It may imply adventitious appearance or semblance unrelated to or different from inner reality ⟨her heart was breaking with grief in spite of her *external* cheerfulness —D.C.Buchanan⟩ EXTERIOR may describe that which is situated on the outer bounds of something; it may also, like OUTER or OUTWARD, describe that which shows or is made apparent ⟨the *exterior* walls are of Lannon stone, an ivory-toned rock of varied shades and fine texture quarried in Wisconsin —*Amer. Guide Series: Mich.*⟩ ⟨the absence of *exterior* demonstration of affection for my mother had no surprise for me —Dixon Wecter⟩

²**outer** \ˈ"\ *n* -S **:** either of the live outside electric wires of a three-wire system as distinguished from the middle or neutral wire

outer bar *n* **:** the junior counsel who have not yet become Queen's or King's Counsel and are not permitted to plead within the bar of the court — compare INNER BAR

outer closure *n* **:** the outer of the two ends of the chamber formed by a stop articulation ⟨the lips, the tongue and teethridge, the tongue and velum, or the glottis may be the *outer closure*⟩ — compare INNER CLOSURE

outercoat \ˈ=ˌ=\ *n* **:** OVERCOAT

outer-directed \ˈ==+\ *adj* **:** directed in thought and action by external norms **:** conforming to the values and standards of one's group or society ⟨everything well-adjusted and *outer-directed* —Peter Viereck⟩ — compare INNER-DIRECTED

outer-direction \ˈ==+\ *n* **:** a sense of direction based on external norms — compare INNER-DIRECTION

outer ear *n* **:** the part of the typical mammalian ear that is continuous with the external surface of the body, that consists of an outer pinna and an inner meatus separated from the middle ear by the tympanic membrane, and that serves to intercept and direct sound waves toward the sensory receptor

outer form *n* **:** a form that prints the side of a sheet on which the first and last pages appear — called also *outside form;* contrasted with *inner form;* compare SHEET IMPOSITION

¹**out·er·ly** \ˈau̇d·ə(r)lē, ˈau̇t|, |li\ *adv* [ME, fr. *outer* + *-ly* (adv. suffix)] *dial chiefly Eng* **:** UTTERLY

²**outerly** \ˈ"\ *adj* [¹*outer* + *-ly* (adj. suffix)] *dial chiefly Eng* **:** blowing from an outward direction

outer man *n* **:** a person's outward appearance and dress ⟨spent hours in adorning the *outer man*⟩

out·er·most \ˈ==ˌmōst *also chiefly Brit* -ˌməst\ *adj* [¹*outer* + *most*] **:** farthest outward ⟨the ~ corners of the earth —T.D. Durrance⟩

outer planet *n* **:** one of the five principal planets whose orbits are outermost in the solar system ⟨Jupiter, Saturn, Uranus, Neptune, and Pluto are the *outer planets*⟩

outersole \ˈ=ˌ=\ *n* **:** OUTSOLE

outer space *n* **1 :** space immediately outside the earth's atmosphere **2 :** interplanetary or interstellar space

outer table *n* **:** the area of the backgammon board separated by the bar from the inner table

outerwear \ˈ==ˌ=\ *n* **1 :** clothing (as dresses, suits, or sweaters) worn over other clothing **2 :** clothing (as coats or jackets) designed for outdoor wear

outface \(ˈ)=ˈ=\ *vt* [*out-* + *face*] **1 :** to stare down by bold looks **:** force into silence or submission by self-assurance or impudence ⟨she'd *outfaced* angry mothers at amateur hours —James Reaney⟩ **2 :** to confront unflinchingly **:** DEFY ⟨a people who have *outfaced* the terrors of a total war —H.V. Gregory⟩

outfall \ˈ=ˌ=\ *n* [³*out* + *fall* (after *fall out*, v.)] **1 a :** the mouth or outlet of a river, stream, or lake **b :** the lower end of a watercourse or the part of any body of water where it drops away into a larger body **c :** the vent of a drain or sewer **2 :** RAID, SORTIE ⟨storms, onslaughts and ~*s* —Sir Walter Scott⟩

out·fang·thief \ˈau̇tfəŋˌthēf\ *n* [ME *outfangenthef, outfangthef*, fr. OE *ūtfangenetheōf*, fr. *ūt* out + *fangen* (past part. of *fōn* to seize, capture) + *theōf* thief — more at OUT, PACT, THIEF] **:** the right of a lord under medieval English law to try in his manorial court a thief or other felon dwelling in his manor but caught outside it — distinguished from *infangthief*

outfield \ˈ=ˌ=\ *n* [³*out* + *field*] **1 a :** an outlying field **:** a field distant from a farmhouse **b :** land not regularly cultivated or manured and generally used as pasture **2 a** (1) **:** LONG FIELD (2) **:** the area of a cricket field beyond the infield (3) **:** a fielder stationed beyond the infield **b** (1) **:** the area of a baseball field beyond the infield and between the foul lines (2) **:** the defensive positions comprising right field, center field, and left field — contrasted with *infield*

out·field·er \-də(r)\ *n* **1 :** a fielder stationed in the outfield in cricket **2 :** a ballplayer (as in baseball or softball) who covers a position in the outfield

out·field·ing \-diŋ, -dēŋ\ *n* **:** the act or art of playing a position in the outfield

out·fields·man \-l(d)zmən\ *n* **:** an outfielder in cricket

outfight \(ˈ)=ˈ=\ *vt* [*out-* + *fight*] **:** to surpass in fighting **:** defeat in a fight ⟨decisively *outfought* the challenger⟩ ⟨*outfought* superior forces⟩

outfighter \ˈ=ˌ==\ *n* [³*out* + *fighter*] **:** a boxer who fights without closing in or clinching

outfighting \ˈ=ˌ==\ *n* [³*out* + *fighting*] **:** fighting at long range ⟨was no match for the heavier ship in ~⟩ ⟨the first round was all ~⟩

¹**out·fit** \ˈau̇tˌfit, *usu* -id.+V\ *n* -S [³*out* + *fit* (after *fit out*)] **1 :** the act or process of fitting out or equipping (as for a voyage or expedition) ⟨the ~ of the exploring party took several months⟩ **2 a :** the tools, instruments, or materials comprising the equipment necessary for the practice of a trade or profession or for the carrying out of a particular project ⟨a prospector's ~⟩ ⟨a dentist's ~⟩ ⟨a model plane ~⟩ ⟨a shoeshine ~⟩ **b :** wearing apparel with accessories designed to be worn on a special occasion or in a particular situation or setting ⟨an ~ for a bride⟩ ⟨an ~ for graduation⟩ ⟨an ~ for camp⟩ **c :** physical, mental, or moral endowments or requirements ⟨this addition that the dentist has made to my ~ —O.W.Holmes†1935⟩ ⟨perception is only part of our mental ~ —A.S.Eddington⟩ **3 a :** a group of people traveling together ⟨shared our campfire with a packhorse ~ —Joyce R. Muench⟩ **b** (1) **:** a team of ranch hands ⟨the whole ~ was commanded by a trail boss —R.A.Billington⟩ (2) **:** RANCH ⟨almost all the big ~*s* use the stamp iron —S.E.Fletcher⟩ ⟨a dude ~ with a landing field —*Amer. Guide Series: Oregon*⟩ **4 :** a group of people working together as a team: as **a :** a political party or group ⟨a small but influential ~ that has the balance of power in the city⟩ **b :** a military unit (as a division, regiment, or company) ⟨enlisted men in line ~*s* all over the world —*Yank*⟩ ⟨a rear echelon ~ —Gene Baro⟩ **c :** a jazz band or combination ⟨the three-piece troubadour ~ —P.E. Deutschman⟩ ⟨this fifteen piece ~ —*Metronome*⟩ **d :** a Navaho social group based on family relationships that presents a united front toward outsiders **5 :** an organization engaged in a particular industry or activity ⟨a large manufacturing ~⟩ ⟨worked for a publishing ~⟩ ⟨the university employs more people than any other ~ in the city⟩ **syn** see EQUIPMENT

²**outfit** \ˈ"\ *vt* **1 :** to furnish with an outfit ⟨*outfitted* expeditions to far-off places —*Amer. Guide Series: Mich.*⟩ **2 :** FURNISH, SUPPLY ⟨*outfitting* every family with shoes —*Amer. Guide Series: Vt.*⟩ ⟨required . . . the judge to ~ him legally —Francis Hackett⟩ ~ *vi* **:** to acquire an outfit ⟨they *outfitted* for the long journey —*Amer. Guide Series: Texas*⟩ **syn** see FURNISH

outfit car *n* **:** CAMP CAR

out·fit·ter \-ə(r)\ *n* **:** one that outfits: as **a :** HABERDASHER **b :** a dealer in equipment and supplies for expeditions or camping trips **c :** a machinist who installs the machinery and mechanical equipment of ships

outflame \(ˈ)=ˈ=\ *vt* [*out-* + *flame*] **:** to exceed in brilliance ⟨~*s* the cities of the land —Vachel Lindsay⟩

outflank \(ˈ)=ˈ=\ *vt* [¹*out* + *flank*] **1 :** to extend beyond or get around the flank of (an opposing force) ⟨the army retreated when it discovered that the enemy ~*ed* it on the right⟩ ⟨~*ed* and surrounded the enemy troops⟩ **2 :** to get around **:** BYPASS ⟨tries to ~ the opposition to his program by an appeal to the people⟩ — **out·flank·er** \-kə(r)\ *n*

outflaring \ˈ=ˌ==\ *adj* [¹*out* + *flaring*] **:** FLARING 2a

outflash \(ˈ)=ˈ=\ *vb* [*out-* + *flash*] *vt* **:** to outdo in flashing **:** OUTSHINE ~ *vi* [¹*out* + *flash*] **:** to flash out

¹**outflow** \(ˈ)=ˈ=\ *vi* [¹*out* + *flow*] **:** to flow out

²**outflow** \ˈ=ˌ=\ *n* [³*out* + *flow* (after *flow out*, v.)] **1 :** the act or process of flowing out ⟨a dam to stop the ~ of the stream⟩ ⟨the ~ of gold from the country —E.W.Kemmerer⟩ **2 :** something that flows out ⟨a river's ~ is usually expressed in cubic feet per second —F.C.Lane⟩

outflung \ˈ=ˌ=\ *adj* [¹*out* + *flung*, past part. of *fling* (after *fling out*, v.)] **:** flung out **:** thrown wide ⟨~ arms⟩

outflux \ˈ=ˌ=\ *n* [³*out* + *flux*] **1 :** OUTFLOW **2 :** OUTLET

outfly \(ˈ)=ˈ=\ *vt* [*out-* + *fly*] **:** to surpass in speed of flight ⟨in the days when few men even dreamed of ~*ing* the sound of their own voices —Wolcott Gibbs⟩

outfoot \(ˈ)=ˈ=\ *vt* [*out-* + *foot*] **:** to outdo in speed (as in walking, running, or sailing) **:** OUTSTRIP ⟨~*ed* the other yachts⟩ ⟨~*ed* the secondary to race 58 yards to a touchdown —*Time*⟩

outfox \(ˈ)=ˈ=\ *vt* [*out-* + *fox*] **:** to outdo in trickery **:** OUTSMART ⟨learning how to ~ new teachers each year is a liberal education in itself —J.P.McEvoy⟩

out·game \(ˈ)=ˈ=\ *vt* [*out-* + *game*, adj.] **:** to surpass in courage or stamina ⟨could outthink, outfight, and ~ the best the enemy could send against them —Foster Hailey⟩ ⟨will ~ and will finally run down and catch any deer —S.P.McCall⟩

out·gang \ˈüt,gaŋ\ *n* -S [ME, fr. OE *ūtgang*, fr. *ūt* out + *gang* act of going — more at OUT, GANG] *chiefly Scot* **:** DEPARTURE

outgarth \ˈ=ˌ=\ *n* [³*out* + *garth*] **:** an outer yard

outgas \(ˈ)=ˈ=\ *vt* [¹*out* + *gas*, n.] **:** to remove adsorbed or occluded gases from usu. by heating ⟨~ a radio tube⟩

¹**out·gate** \ˈau̇tˌgāt, ˈüt,-\ *n* [ME, fr. *out* + *gate* way, road, act of going — more at GATE (way)] **1** *chiefly Scot* **:** the act of going out **:** EXITING **2** *chiefly Scot* **:** a way out **:** OUTLET

²**outgate** \ˈ=ˌ=\ *prep* [fr. obs. *outgate*, adv., outside, prob. fr. ⁴*out* + *gate* (opening)] *dial* **:** BEYOND, OUTSIDE ⟨run ~ their wits for a woman —Maristan Chapman⟩

outgeneral \(ˈ)=ˈ(=)=\ *vt* -ED/-ING/-S [*out-* + *general*, n.] **:** to surpass in generalship **:** overcome by superior tactics **:** OUTMANEUVER ⟨you've been ~*ed* and outfought —Kenneth Roberts⟩ ⟨if you ~ the bear you may carry off his pelt —John Burroughs⟩

¹**outgiving** \ˈ=ˌ==\ *n* [³*out* + *giving*, gerund of *give* (after *give out*)] **:** something that is given out; *esp* **:** a public statement or utterance ⟨examining these opinions and the ~*s* of eminent bankers —F.L.Allen⟩

²**outgiving** \ˈ=ˌ==\ *adj* [¹*out* + *giving*, pres. part. of *give* (after *give out*)] **:** not holding back **:** free and easy ⟨cocky, confi-

dent, and ~ —Beach Conger⟩ ⟨had an easygoing, ~ personality —Louis Auchincloss⟩

outgliding \ˈ;ˌ;;\ *adj* [¹*out* + *gliding*, pres. part. of *glide* (after *glide out*, v.)] *of a diphthong or triphthong* **:** concluded with the tongue in a position other than that for the central vowel \ə\ (as in *loud, mine, moist*) — compare CENTERING, UPGLIDING

¹outgo \(ˈ)ˌ;ˈ;\ *vb* [ME *outgon, outgan*, fr. OE *ūtgān*, fr. *ūt* out + *gān* to go — more at OUT, GO] *vi* **:** to go out ~ *vt* [*out-* + *go*] **1** *archaic* **:** to surpass in swiftness **:** OUTSTRIP **2 :** to go beyond **:** OUTDO ⟨imprinting an ambition and desire in each of them to ~ his fellow —*Times Lit. Supp.*⟩

²outgo \ˈ;ˌ;\ *n* [³*out* + *go* (after *go out*)] **1 :** something that goes out ⟨income and ~ of radiant solar energy —R.E.Coker⟩ ⟨inflow and ~ of goods —A.F.Chapin⟩; *specif* **:** EXPENDITURE ⟨the cash budget, which lists merely the cash revenues and ~*es* —William Fellner⟩ **2 a :** the act, action, or process of going out ⟨the ~ of his nature to others was something extraordinary —Elizabeth Phelps⟩ **b :** DEPARTURE **3 :** OUTLET

outgoer \ˈ;ˌ;;\ *n* [³*out* + *goer* (after *go out*)] **:** one that goes out ⟨separate ways for ~*s* and incomers —Lew Wallace⟩: as **a :** an outgoing tenant ⟨the ~ could retain use of the farmhouse . . . until the 12th of May —A.D.Rees⟩ **b :** a clay target that is moving away from the shooter

¹outgoing \ˈ;ˌ;;, ;ˈ;;\ *n* [ME, fr. ³*out* + *going*, gerund of *gon, goon* to go (after *gon out* to go out) — more at GO] **1 :** the act or action of going out ⟨the ~ of the tide⟩ ⟨couldn't keep up with her incomings and ~*s*⟩ **2 :** something that goes out **:** ISSUE ⟨a mind whose ~*s* in talk showed her to be warmer and more sympathetic —H.S.Canby⟩ **3 outgoings** *pl* **a :** EXPENDITURES, OUTLAYS ⟨the necessary domestic ~*s* of the week —*Times Lit. Supp.*⟩ **b** *Eng law* **:** expenditures (as for rates and taxes) necessary for the upkeep of a property

²outgoing \ˈ;ˌ;;\ *adj* [¹*out* + *going*, pres. part. of *go* (after *go out*)] **1 a :** going outward **:** DEPARTING ⟨~ correspondence⟩ ⟨an ~ tide⟩ ⟨an ~ ship⟩ **b :** retiring or withdrawing from a place or position ⟨the ~ president⟩ ⟨the ~ sixth grade class⟩ ⟨the ~ generation⟩ **2 :** socially responsive and demonstrative **:** not reserved **:** EXTROVERTED ⟨a boy who was potentially ~ but impeded by fears of his own impulsiveness —Miriam G. Siegel⟩ ⟨as a person he was warm and ~ —E.R.Mowrer⟩ — **out·go·ing·ness** *n* -ES

outgross \(ˈ)ˌ;ˈ;\ *vt* [*out-* + *gross*] **:** to surpass in gross earnings or sales ⟨~*ed* all other pictures for the year⟩

out-group \ˈ;ˌ;\ *n* [³*out* + *group*] **:** a social group that is distinct from one's own and so usu. an object of hostility or dislike — compare INGROUP

outgrow \(ˈ)ˌ;ˈ;\ *vt* [*out-* + *grow*] **1 :** to exceed in rate of growth **:** grow faster than ⟨weeds ~ grass⟩ ⟨mankind is ~*ing* food supplies —R.C.Murphy⟩ **2 :** to grow away from or beyond **:** develop to the point of being able to do without ⟨those whom he had *outgrown* socially —Louis Auchincloss⟩ ⟨teenagers who have *outgrown* children's books —*advt*⟩ **3 :** to grow too large for **:** grow out of ⟨the business *outgrew* the cramped quarters —*Amer. Guide Series: Conn.*⟩ ⟨*outgrew* his new suit⟩

outgrowth \ˈ;ˌ;\ *n* [³*out* + *growth*] **1 :** the process of growing out ⟨the effects of added sugars on the ~ of chick heart fibroblasts —*Biol. Abstracts*⟩ **2 :** something that grows directly out of something else **:** OFFSHOOT ⟨an ~ of hair⟩ ⟨a deformed ~⟩ **3 :** something that results from something else **:** CONSEQUENCE ⟨crime is sometimes an ~ of poverty⟩ ⟨the new program is an ~ of cooperation among the colleges of the area⟩

outguard \ˈ;ˌ;\ *n* [³*out* + *guard*] **:** a guard that forms the line of observation of an outpost

outguess \(ˈ)ˌ;ˈ;\ *vt* [*out-* + *guess*] **:** to anticipate correctly the intentions, actions, or movements of ⟨~ the enemy⟩ ⟨~ the pitcher⟩ ⟨~ the stock market⟩

out guide *n* [³*out*] **:** a card placed in a file to indicate the location of material that has been temporarily removed

outgun \(ˈ)ˌ;ˈ;\ *vt* [*out-* + *gun*] **:** to surpass in firepower ⟨will ~ and outspeed every cruiser in the world —H.W.Baldwin⟩

¹outgush \(ˈ)ˌ;ˈ;\ *vi* [¹*out* + *gush*] **:** to gush out ⟨on either side ~*ed*, with misty spray —John Keats⟩

²outgush \ˈ;ˌ;\ *n* [³*out* + *gush* (after *gush out*, v.)] **:** OUTGUSHING

outgushing \ˈ;ˌ;;\ *n* [³*out* + *gushing*, gerund of *gush* (after *gush out*, v.)] **:** a gushing out **:** a pouring forth ⟨a great ~ of public opprobrium upon his uncalculating head —Donald Davidson⟩

outhalf \ˈ;ˌ;\ *n* [³*out* + *half*] **:** STANDOFF HALF

outhaul \ˈ;ˌ;\ *n* [³*out* + *haul* (after *haul out*, v.)] **:** a rope used to haul a sail taut along a spar

outhauler \ˈ;ˌ;;\ *n* [³*out* + *hauler* (after *haul out*, v.)] **:** a rope or line for hauling something out

outh·er \ˈüthə(r), ˈōth-\ *archaic var of* EITHER

out-her·od \(ˈ)ˌ;ˈherəd\ *vt* -ED/-ING/-S *usu cap H* [*out-* + *Herod* the Great †B.C. 4 ruler of Judea at time of Christ's birth, who was depicted as a blustering despot in medieval mystery plays] **:** to exceed in violent or extravagant ranting — usu. used in the phrase *out-Herod Herod*

outhit \(ˈ)ˌ;ˈ;\ *vt* [*out-* + *hit*] **1 :** to get more hits than ⟨~ the other team but lost the ball game⟩ **2 :** to hit a ball farther than ⟨~ the girls by as much as 50 or 60 yards off the tee⟩

out home *n* [³*out*] **:** OUTSIDE HOME

outhouse \ˈ;ˌ;\ *n* [³*out* + *house*] **1 :** OUTBUILDING ⟨a dwelling house in the middle, with kitchens and ~*s* all detached —C. G.Bowers⟩ **2 :** an outdoor toilet **:** PRIVY

outhousing \ˈ;ˌ;;\ *n* [³*out* + *housing*] **:** a group of outhouses

outhustle \(ˈ)ˌ;ˈ;;\ *vt* [*out-* + *hustle*] **:** to outdo in vigorous and determined effort ⟨it is one thing to be beaten and quite another to be *outhustled* —*Time*⟩

out·ing \ˈau̇d·iŋ, ˈau̇t|, |ēŋ\ *n* -S [¹*out* + *-ing*] **1 :** a trip or stay in the open **:** an excursion usu. with a picnic ⟨the annual company ~⟩ ⟨an ~ at the beach⟩ **2 :** an athletic contest or bout ⟨the team's first victory in three ~*s*⟩ ⟨scored a knockout in his first ~ in over a year⟩

outing flannel *n* **:** a flannelette sometimes having an admixture of wool

out island *n* [³*out*] **:** an island other than the main island of a group (as of the Bahamas)

outjest *vt* [*out-* + *jest*] *obs* **:** to overcome by jesting ⟨labors to ~ his heart-struck injuries —Shak.⟩

outjockey \(ˈ)ˌ;ˈ;;\ *vt* [*out-* + *jockey*] **:** OUTMANEUVER

outjut \(ˈ)ˌ;ˈ;\ *vi* [¹*out* + *jut*] **:** to stick out **:** PROJECT

outkick \(ˈ)ˌ;ˈ;\ *vt* [*out-* + *kick*] **:** to excel (an opponent) in kicking ⟨~*ed* all others in the second half⟩

outkitchen \ˈ;ˌ;;\ *n* [³*out* + *kitchen*] **:** a kitchen housed in a separate building ⟨waddling from kitchen to ~ and back again —Caroline Gordon⟩

¹out·land \ˈau̇t,land, -lənd, -,laa(ə)nd\ *n* [ME, fr. OE *ūtland*, fr. *ūt* out + *land* — more at OUT, LAND] **1** *Old Eng & feudal law* **:** the outlying land not kept in demesne but granted to tenants — compare INLAND **2 :** a foreign land or region ⟨the ~*s* were glutting Europe with novelties —H.B.Alexander⟩ ⟨a vast natural buffer zone between her own centers of population and the vigorous pressure of the ~ —*Time*⟩ **3 outlands** *pl* **:** the outlying regions of a country **:** PROVINCES ⟨the man who brought stars to the ~*s* —R.L.Taylor⟩ ⟨in the ~*s*, the Yankees had been strangers —Oscar Handlin⟩

²outland \"\ *adj* [ME, fr. *outland*, n.] **1 a :** of or relating to a foreign country or region ⟨the chief ~ interests of the Swedish people lay in their eastern colonies —F.M.Stenton⟩ **b :** belonging to a different region or group **:** ALIEN ⟨had taken up with an ~ man —Maristan Chapman⟩ **2 :** of, relating to, or characteristic of the outlying sections of a country **:** PROVINCIAL ⟨one who peregrinated the country for seasonal jobs and could fascinate children with ~ tales —John Buchan⟩

³outland \"\ *adv, South* **:** away from home ⟨on my way ~ — Emmett Gowen⟩

out·land·er \-də(r)\ *n* [¹*outland* + *-er*] **:** one who belongs to another region or culture: **a :** a person from another country ⟨insecure in the presence of ~*s* —T.H.Fielding⟩ ⟨~, a wastrel from Europe —B.T.Cleeve⟩ **b :** a person from another state or section ⟨thousands of Californians and ~*s* crowd the Redwood Highway —Anthony Netboy⟩ ⟨the stranger, the ~, the foreigner from New York —Lionel Trilling⟩

out·land·ish \au̇tˈlandish, -aa(ə)n-, -dēsh\ *adj* [ME, fr. OE *ūtlendisc*, fr. *ūtland* + *-isc* -ish] **1 :** of or belonging to another country **:** not native **:** FOREIGN ⟨the verdict of ~ readers —John Milton⟩ **2 a :** having a foreign or unfamiliar appearance, manner, or quality ⟨an ~ costume⟩ ⟨an ~ way of talking⟩ ⟨an ~ dish⟩ **b :** BIZARRE, FANTASTIC ⟨introduced ~ or unbelievable people and situations into his work —Lincoln Fitzell⟩ **3 :** remote from civilization or familiarly known regions ⟨no other young men foolish enough to offer to go to such an ~ station —*Geog. Jour.*⟩ **syn** see STRANGE

out·land·ish·ly *adv* **:** in an outlandish manner

out·land·ish·ness *n* -ES **:** the quality or state of being outlandish

outlast \(ˈ)ˌ;ˈ;\ *vt* [*out-* + *last*] **:** to last longer than **:** SURVIVE ⟨mummified customs that have long ~*ed* their usefulness —W.R.Inge⟩ **syn** see OUTLIVE

outlaugh \(ˈ)ˌ;ˈ;\ *vb* [ME *outlaughen*, fr. *out* + *laughen* to laugh — more at LAUGH] *vt* **1** *archaic* **:** to make fun of **:** RIDICULE ⟨his apprehensions of being ~*ed* —Benjamin Franklin⟩ **2** [*out-* + *laugh*] **:** to outdo in laughing ⟨though usually solemn, he ~*ed* all the others at the play⟩ ~ *vi* **:** to laugh out loud ⟨in deep derision ~*s* the foeman —Alice Furlong⟩

¹out·law \ˈau̇t,lȯ\ *n* [ME *outlawe, outlage*, fr. OE *ūtlaga*, fr. ON *ūtlagi*, fr. *ūtlagr*, adj., outlawed, fr. *ūt* out + *-lagr* (fr. *lag-, lög* law) — more at OUT, LAW] **1 :** a person or thing excluded from the benefit of the law or deprived of its protection **:** a person against whom outlawry has been pronounced **:** a proscribed person or thing ⟨a hunted ~⟩ ⟨the motor vehicle becomes an ~ on the highways if operated without new registration —*Mass. Registry of Motor Vehicles*⟩ **2 a :** a lawless person or a fugitive from the law **:** a person roving and committing acts of violence ⟨gangs of ~*s* made their hideaways in the inadequately policed Indian territory —C.L. Cannon⟩ **b :** a person or organization under a ban or disability ⟨the union declared that those who had gone on strike against its orders were ~*s*⟩ **3 :** an animal (as a horse) that is wild and unmanageable ⟨spoiled horses are ~*s* — they never can be tamed —S.E.Fletcher⟩

²outlaw \(ˈ)ˌ;ˈ;\ *vt* -ED/-ING/-S [ME *outlawen*, fr. OE *ūtlagian*, fr. *ūtlaga* outlaw] **1 a :** to deprive of the benefit and protection of law **:** declare to be an outlaw ⟨~ the rebels unless they surrendered immediately⟩ **b :** to make illegal ⟨the type of legislation which ~*ed* dueling —Margaret Mead⟩ ⟨has ~*ed* verbal intimidation on the part of employers —*New Republic*⟩ ⟨a proposal to ~ war⟩ **2 :** to place under a ban or disability ⟨it is neither possible nor convenient to ~ the old vocabulary —A.G.N.Flew⟩ ⟨banned in Boston, ~*ed* in Atlanta —Hamilton Basso⟩ **3 :** to remove from legal jurisdiction or enforcement ⟨~ a debt⟩ ⟨~ a claim⟩ ⟨the case was ~*ed* in 1914 by the Supreme Court under the statute of limitations —H.U. Faulkner⟩

³outlaw \ˈ;ˌ;\ *adj* [¹*outlaw*] **1 :** of, relating to, composed of, or dominated by outlaws ⟨an ~ band⟩ ⟨~ country⟩ **2 a :** forbidden by law ⟨an ~ strike⟩ **b :** contrary to the rules of an organization ⟨an ~ baseball league⟩ ⟨playing ~ ball —Oscar Fraley⟩

out·law·ry \-rē, -ri\ *n* -ES [ME *outlagerie, outlagarie, outlawerie*, fr. AF *utlagerie* & ML *utlagaria*, fr. ME *outlage* outlaw + OF *-erie* -ery & L *-aria* -ary respectively] **1 a :** the act of outlawing **:** the act or process of putting a person outside the protection of the law ⟨by proscription and bills of ~ —Shak.⟩ — compare FUGITATION **b :** BANISHMENT, EXILE ⟨on his ~ was allowed five days to leave the country —E.A.Freeman⟩ **c :** the act or process of making something illegal ⟨the ~ of war⟩ ⟨the ~ of atomic weapons⟩ **2 :** the state of living outside the law **:** freedom from legal or conventional restraint ⟨whose gay impudence of ~ had in its time set the underworlds of five continents buzzing —Leslie Charteris⟩ ⟨Quincy . . . was liberty, ~, the endless delight of impressions given by nature for nothing —Henry Adams⟩ **3 :** the act of barring a debt, claim, or right (as by operation of a statute of limitations)

¹outlay \(ˈ)ˌ;ˈ;\ *vt* [¹*out* + *lay*] **1** *archaic* **:** to spread out **:** DISPLAY **2 :** to lay out (money) **:** EXPEND ⟨we *outlaid* 40 billions —*Reader's Digest*⟩

²outlay \ˈ;ˌ;\ *n* [³*out* + *lay* (after *lay out*)] **1 :** the act of laying out or expending ⟨make a great ~ of energy seem worth while —*Collier's Yr. Bk.*⟩ **2 :** something that is laid out **:** EXPENDITURE, PAYMENT ⟨an ~ of $10 for food⟩

¹outleap \ˈ;ˌ;\ *n* [³*out* + *leap* (after *leap out*, v.)] **:** the act of leaping out **:** OUTBURST

²outleap \(ˈ)ˌ;ˈ;\ *vb* [¹*out* + *leap*] *vt* **1 :** to leap beyond ⟨~*s* the barriers of the particular to reach a universal truth — Virgilia Peterson⟩ **2** [*out-* + *leap*] **:** to outdo in leaping ~ *vi* **:** to leap out

outlearn \(ˈ)ˌ;ˈ;\ *vt* [*out-* + *learn*] **:** to surpass in learning ⟨learnt so fast that he *outlearnt* his teacher —Amy Lowell⟩

out·ler \ˈütlər\ *n* -S [prob. alter. of *outlier*] *Scot* **:** an animal left unhoused over the winter

¹out·let \ˈau̇t,le|t, -,lə|t, *usu* |d·+V\ *n* [³*out* + *let* (after *let out*, v.)] **1 a :** a means of exit or escape **:** OPENING, VENT ⟨oxidized impurities are expelled through an ~ in the top —*Amer. Guide Series: Pa.*⟩ ⟨an ~ on the Red sea —*Collier's Yr. Bk.*⟩ ⟨~*s* for the surplus population —B.K.Sandwell⟩ **b :** a means of release or satisfaction for an emotion, impulse, or instinctual need ⟨found an ~ for his anger in chopping wood⟩ ⟨singing provided an ~ for her high spirits⟩ ⟨sexual ~*s*⟩ **c :** a medium of expression or publication ⟨a magazine existed . . . that could provide an ~ for the writers who were appearing on every hand —Van Wyck Brooks⟩ **d :** a radio or television station; *esp* **:** a station that transmits network programs locally **2 a :** a stream flowing out of a lake or pond **b :** the channel through which such a stream flows **c :** the lower end of a watercourse where its water flows into a lake or sea **3 a :** a market for a commodity ⟨the farmer has a choice of several ~*s* for his goods —*Marketing*⟩ ⟨must find new ~*s* for their industries⟩ **b :** a retail store ⟨chain ~*s*⟩ ⟨discount ~*s*⟩ ⟨mass ~*s*⟩ ⟨goods usually bought on impulse are located at high traffic points within the ~ —Bud Wilson⟩ **4 :** one or more pairs of terminals giving access to electric wiring (as for attachment of lamps)

²out·let \ˈau̇t,let, *usu* -ed·+V\ *vt* [¹*out* + *let*] *archaic* **:** to let out

outlet box *n* **:** a terminal box for electric wiring or fittings at which the wires terminate for connection to electric fixtures or appliances

outlie \(ˈ)ˌ;ˈ;\ *vb* [¹*out* + *lie*] *vi* **1 :** to camp out **:** lie outdoors **2 :** to stretch out **:** EXTEND ~ *vt* **:** to lie beyond

out·li·er \ˈau̇t,līə)r\ *n* [³*out* + *lier* (after *lie out*, v.)] **1 a :** one that sleeps outdoors or away from his place of business or duty **b :** an animal outside the fold or enclosure **2 :** something that lies, dwells, or is situated or classed away from a main or related body: as **a :** a minor part of a rock formation separated by erosion from the main body and surrounded by older rocks **b** (1) **:** an outlying island (2) **:** an outlying terrain feature (as a mountain, forest, or plain) **c :** a statistical observation not homogeneous in value with others of a sample

¹out·line \ˈau̇t,līn\ *n* [³*out* + *line*] **1 a :** a line that marks the outer limits of an object or figure **:** BOUNDARY ⟨in good years the ~ of the cultivated area expands —P.E.James⟩ ⟨the rugged ~*s* of the mountains⟩ **b :** CONTOUR, SHAPE ⟨the original ~ of the house is clearly marked —*Amer. Guide Series: La.*⟩ ⟨the sharpening ~ of her face —Willa Cather⟩ **2 a :** a style of representation or drawing in which contours are marked without shading ⟨paint rapidly in ~ on the stone —F.W.Goudy⟩ ⟨drew a dog in ~⟩ **b :** a sketch in outline ⟨prepared several ~*s* of the suggested mural⟩ **c :** ⁴OPEN 4 **d :** a symbol used to represent a word in shorthand writing ⟨learned how to write shorthand ~*s* for every word she heard —Marie M. Stewart⟩ ⟨my hand was so shaky I could hardly make my ~*s* —Dorothy Sayers⟩ **3 a outlines** *pl* **:** the principal features or general principles of a subject of discussion ⟨shall sketch only the ~*s* of some aspects of American education —J.B.Conant⟩ ⟨agreed on the broad ~*s* of a wage settlement⟩ **b :** a relatively brief and condensed treatment of a particular subject ⟨has written a useful ~ of atomic physics⟩ ⟨an ~ of world history in two volumes⟩ **c :** a summary giving the essential content of a written work ⟨the gist of these books was preserved in a series of small ~*s* —R.W.Southern⟩ **4 a :** a preliminary account or sketch of a projected course of action or study ⟨gave his staff an ~ of his proposed strategy in the coming campaign⟩ ⟨gave the class an ~ of the points he intended to cover⟩ **b :** a brief abstract of the principal points to be covered in an argument or exposition often arranged by heads and subheads ⟨such an ~ as would be required of a student in freshman composition —Archer Taylor⟩ **c :** a synopsis of the plot of a projected piece of writing (as a scenario or play) ⟨the producer gave him a sizable advance on the basis of his ~⟩ **5 :** a fishing line set out overnight **:** TROTLINE

syn CONTOUR, PROFILE, SKYLINE, SILHOUETTE: OUTLINE applies to the line marking the outer edge or limit of a thing ⟨the house, built of bricks, was square in *outline* —Elizabeth M. Roberts⟩ ⟨series of natural valleys . . . flanking the western *outlines* of the county —F.S.Williams⟩ ⟨the *outline* of Caprarola palace is a pentagon —George Kish⟩ CONTOUR stresses the shape of a thing, or a visible or particular portion of a thing, as delineated by the outline, esp. involving curving lines ⟨the smooth, though sometimes steep, *contours* of the Coast Range —G.R.Stewart⟩ ⟨glanced up at the pummeled sky and caught sight of a weird, futuristic *contour* —D.B.Dodson⟩ ⟨the chart room, where the changing *contours* of the seabed are automatically recorded —Douglas Willis⟩ PROFILE stresses the sharply outlined shape of something esp. as seen against a lighter background ⟨the beautiful *profile* of the island — William Beebe⟩ ⟨the mountains to the south and east fill the horizon, their *profiles* overlapping one another —*Amer. Guide Series: Vt.*⟩ SKYLINE is the outline or contour of something (as the upper portion of a row of buildings or range of mountains) seen against the sky as background ⟨gracious towers and spires make up the loveliest man-made *skyline* in the world —Sam Pollock⟩ ⟨the region, with its succession of startling contours, jagged *skylines*, sharp pinnacles rising from mountains of solid rock —*Amer. Guide Series: Oregon*⟩ ⟨the *skyline* of Manhattan⟩ SILHOUETTE is the shape of something shadowed, and therefore seen as two-dimensional, with all detail blacked out, blurred, or disregarded ⟨the basilica of Notre Dame de la Garde thrusts a stark *silhouette* in the cobalt sky —Claudia Cassidy⟩ ⟨the *silhouettes* of white sailboats and gray battleships —Jean Stafford⟩ ⟨the ghostly *silhouette* of a submarine gliding under the railway bridge — Stewart Beach⟩

²outline \"\ *vt* **1 a :** to draw the outline of ⟨~ the entire figure before beginning to draw in the features⟩ **b :** to set off the outlines of **:** DEFINE ⟨gnarled stump fences ~ the wide fields —*Amer. Guide Series: Vt.*⟩ ⟨a baffling network of paths *outlined* by a very high hedge —J.C.Swaim⟩ **c :** to discover or trace the outline of ⟨~ the exact limits of the lake⟩ ⟨~ the limits of Assyrian conquest⟩ **2 :** to indicate the principal features or different parts of ⟨*outlining* a plan for a future investigation —J.B.Conant⟩ ⟨*outlined* a five-point program for business —*Current Biog.*⟩ — **out·lin·er** \-nə(r)\ *n*

out·lin·e·ar \(ˈ)au̇t¦linēə(r)\ *adj* [¹*outline* + *-ar* (as in *linear*)] **:** of, relating to, or having the characteristics of an outline

outline map *n* **:** BASE MAP

outline stitch *n* **:** an embroidery stitch used to outline a design; *specif* **:** a stitch made by overlapping backstitches to form a pattern like the twist of a rope

outline stitch

outlive \(ˈ)ˌ;ˈ;\ *vt* [ME *outleven*, fr. *out-* + *leven, liven* to live — more at LIVE] **1 :** to live beyond or longer than **:** OUTLAST, SURVIVE ⟨has *outlived* the century⟩ ⟨has *outlived* all his friends⟩ ⟨a fiction which has *outlived* any usefulness it may have had — —C.S.Lobingier⟩ **2 a :** to survive the effects of **:** live through **:** OVERCOME ⟨the financial support which enabled the small man to ~ a bad harvest —G.G.Coulton⟩ ⟨characters in history whose reputation has *outlived* the vicissitudes of time —*London Calling*⟩ **b :** to live down ⟨repeated the story so often that I have never been able to ~ this joke on myself —David Fairchild⟩

syn OUTLAST, SURVIVE: OUTLIVE stresses the fact of continuing alive or in existence longer than another, sometimes through a marked capacity for enduring and surmounting difficulty, sometimes not ⟨*outlived* his brothers⟩ ⟨universities are among the most persistent of human organizations — they *outlive* many political and social changes —J.B.Conant⟩ OUTLAST differs little from OUTLIVE, although it may stress capacity for endurance to a greater degree ⟨their glory is that they have *outlasted* the conditions they observed —A.T.Quiller-Couch⟩ ⟨the sweet sensations of returning health made me happy for a time; but such sensations seldom *outlast* convalescence —W.H.Hudson †1922⟩ SURVIVE may be used of enduring, continuing in existence, or going on after the demise of something else or after some threatening event ⟨the men *surviving* after the wreck⟩ ⟨*surviving* his wife by several years⟩ ⟨a first marriage did not *survive* the long years of wartime separation —H.H.Martin⟩ ⟨a miracle that H.M.S. Marlborough *survives*, and this is due not only to the courage of the men who *survive* that first explosion, but equally to the attitude of the skipper himself —Peter Forster⟩

¹outlook \(ˈ)ˌ;ˈ;\ *vb* [*out-* + *look*] *vt* **1** *obs* **:** to face down **:** OUTSTARE ⟨~ conquest —Shak.⟩ **2 :** to excel in appearance ⟨a magnificent horse that ~*ed* all the others in the race⟩ ~ *vi* [¹*out* + *look*] **:** to look out ⟨shall be ~*ing*, like a bride newly married —Robert Browning⟩

²outlook \ˈ;ˌ;\ *n* [³*out* + *look* (after *look out*, v.)] **1 a :** a place from which a view can be obtained ⟨has frequent ~*s* affording views of the mountain peaks —*Amer. Guide Series: N.H.*⟩ **b :** a view from a particular place ⟨had as its ~ one of the finest lakes in Europe —Nicholas Monsarrat⟩ **2 :** POINT OF VIEW ⟨a form adapted to the background and ~ of young readers —*Geog. Jour.*⟩ ⟨complete want of sympathy . . . with his entire ~ on life —J.W.Beach⟩ **3 :** the act or state of looking out **:** LOOKOUT ⟨always on the ~ for a better opportunity⟩ **4 :** the prospect for the future ⟨the ~ for steel demand in the U.S. —*Wall Street Jour.*⟩

outlooker \ˈ;ˌ;;\ *n* [³*out* + *looker* (after *look out*, v.)] **1 :** one who looks out ⟨the outlook was not quite the same — or the ~ was changed —Maurice Hewlett⟩ **2 :** a projecting member that supports the portion of a roof extending beyond the face of a gable

out-lot \ˈ;ˌ;\ *n* [³*out* + *lot*] **:** a lot situated outside the corporate limits of a town or city

out loud *adv* **:** ALOUD

outlying \ˈ;ˌ;;\ *adj* [¹*out* + *lying*, pres. part. of *lie* (after *lie out*, v.)] **1 :** lying outside prescribed or accepted limits **:** EXTRANEOUS, EXTRINSIC ⟨~ cattle⟩ ⟨~ facts which might not corroborate the facts already organized by the structural hypothesis —S.C.Pepper⟩ **2 a :** situated or lying at a distance away from a center or main body **:** REMOTE ⟨extending library services to ~ regions and rural areas —Helen T. Geer⟩ **b :** situated or lying at the outer end of something ⟨the ~ parts of the apron —Arnold Bennett⟩ ⟨the two ~ wings connected with the main house —*Amer. Guide Series: N.C.*⟩

¹out·man \ˈau̇tmən\ *n, pl* **outmen** [ME, fr. *out* + *man*] **:** one living or working outside the limits of a medieval English town

²outman \(ˈ)ˌ;ˈ;\ *vt* [*out-* + *man*] **:** OUTNUMBER ⟨our own troops would be dangerously *outmanned* —R.H.Rovere⟩

outmaneuver \ˌ;;ˈ;;\ *vt* [*out-* + *maneuver*] **1 :** to defeat by greater skill in maneuvering ⟨the political resourcefulness to ~ his antagonists —A.L.Funk⟩ **2 :** to surpass in maneuverability ⟨a plane that can ~ anything in the air⟩

¹outmarch \(ˈ)ˌ;ˈ;\ *vt* [*out-* + *march*] **:** to surpass in marching **:** outdo in speed or endurance on the march ⟨he can ~ almost anything for one day —*Cosmopolitan*⟩

²outmarch \ˈ;ˌ;\ *n* [³*out* + *march*] **:** an outward march

outmarriage \ˈ;ˌ;;\ *n* [³*out* + *marriage*] **:** marriage outside one's own family, race, or other grouping **:** EXOGAMY — contrasted with *inmarriage*

outmarry \(ˈ)ˌ;ˈ;;\ *vb* [*out-* + *marry*] *vt* **:** to marry a person superior to (oneself) ⟨my grandfather *outmarried* himself more than any man you ever saw —C.E.Craddock⟩ ~ *vi* [¹*out* + *marry*] **:** to marry outside one's own family, race, or other grouping

outmatch \(ˈ)ˌ;ˈ;\ *vt* [*out-* + *match*] **:** to be superior to **:** OUTDO, SURPASS ⟨can ~ any storyteller in the field —R.M.Dorson⟩

outmeasure \(ˈ)ˌ;ˈ;;\ *vt* [*out-* + *measure*] **:** to surpass in quantity or extent

out-migrant \ˈ⸗ˌ⸗⸗\ *n* [³*out* + *migrant*] **:** a person who outmigrates

out-migrate \(ˈ)⸗¦⸗ˌ⸗\ *vi* [¹*out* + *migrate*] **:** to leave one region or community in order to settle in another esp. as part of a substantial and continuing movement of population — compare IN-MIGRATE — **out-migration** \ˌ⸗¦⸗+\ *n*

outmode \(ˈ)⸗¦⸗\ *vb* -ED/-ING/-S [*out (of) mode*] *vt* **:** to make unfashionable or obsolete ⟨the electric trolley ~*s* the horse car —M.S.Rukeyser⟩ ⟨the machine has *outmoded* human slavery —*Nation*⟩ **~** *vi* **:** to become unfashionable or obsolete ⟨equipment ~*s* quicker than hairdos —J.T.Winterich⟩

out·mod·ed \-dəd\ *adj* [*out (of) mode* + *-ed*] **1 :** left behind by change of fashion **:** not in style ⟨the most ridiculous and ~ fashions —Arnold Bennett⟩ **2 :** no longer acceptable or usable **:** OBSOLETE ⟨an ~ building⟩ ⟨~ ideas⟩ ⟨an ~ textbook⟩

out·most \ˈau̇tˌmōst *also chiefly Brit* -ˌmast\ *adj* [³*out* + *-most*] **:** OUTERMOST ⟨from the centers of fashion to the ~ periphery of the civilized world —Edward Sapir⟩

out·ness *n* -ES [³*out* + *-ness*] **:** the quality or state of being out; *specif* **:** the quality or state of being distinguishable from the perceiving mind by existing in space and possessing materiality **:** EXTERNALITY ⟨are more than thought and have an ~, a reality sui generis —S.T.Coleridge⟩

outnumber \(ˈ)⸗¦⸗⸗\ *vt* [*out-* + *number*] **:** to exceed in number

out of *prep* [ME, fr. OE *ūt of*, fr. *ūt* out (adv.) + *of* — more at OUT, OF] **1 a** — used as a function word to indicate direction or movement from an enclosed space to the outside ⟨fell *out of* the crib⟩ ⟨took his hands *out of* his pockets⟩ ⟨hit the ball *out of* the park⟩ ⟨stomped up the aisle and *out of* the church —James Thurber⟩ **b** — used as a function word to indicate removal or situation outside the bounds of a group, association, belief, or condition ⟨voted him *out of* the club⟩ ⟨married *out of* his faith⟩ ⟨born *out of* wedlock⟩ ⟨*out of* the ordinary⟩ **2 a** — used as a function word to indicate a change in quality, state, or form ⟨the patient is *out of* danger⟩ ⟨translated the play *out of* Latin into English⟩ ⟨woke up *out of* a deep sleep⟩ **b** — used as a function word to indicate a quality or state that is not normal, usual, or correct ⟨the trees grew thicker and lower here . . . and many of them were *out of* the vertical —C.S.Forester⟩ ⟨his prices are *out of* line⟩ ⟨the microscope is *out of* focus⟩ ⟨made some remarks that were *out of* line⟩ **c** — used as a function word to indicate a position or state away from what is familiar or expected ⟨*out of* his depth⟩ ⟨*out of* his sphere⟩ ⟨*out of* his class⟩ **3 a** — used as a function word to indicate direction, motion, or distance from a point regarded as a center or starting point ⟨he has gone *out of* town for two days⟩ ⟨they were ten miles *out of* port before they found the stowaway⟩ ⟨the salesmen operate *out of* New York⟩ **b** — used as a function word usu. with a specified number to indicate distance from a place or limit ⟨a suburb two miles *out of* town⟩ ⟨thousands of miles *out of* the earth's gravitational field⟩ **c** — used as a function word to indicate removal or situation away from the effective action of some faculty or agency ⟨the ships fled *out of* range⟩ ⟨he was soon *out of* sight⟩ ⟨*out of* hearing⟩ ⟨*out of* control⟩ **4 a** — used as a function word to indicate origin or birth ⟨many capable performers have been *out of* mares with below average records —F.A. Wrensch⟩ ⟨a farm boy *out of* the Middle West⟩ **b** — used as a function word to indicate basis or source ⟨a farmer who had done well *out of* strawberries —Roy Lewis & Angus Maude⟩ ⟨has made a fortune *out of* steel⟩ ⟨growth must be financed *out of* saving —W.M.Martin b.1906⟩ **c** — used as a function word to indicate cause or motive ⟨acted *out of* reverence rather than *out of* sensibility —R.M.Weaver⟩ ⟨obeys him *out of* fear⟩ ⟨the inflation arose *out of* many different factors⟩ **5 a** — used as a function word to indicate exclusion from or deprivation of an office or position ⟨was forced *out of* his chairmanship⟩ ⟨turned *out of* his post⟩ **b** — used as a function word to indicate the fact or condition of being without something usu. or formerly possessed ⟨the store was *out of* sugar⟩ ⟨he was all *out of* breath when he ran up⟩ ⟨the car is *out of* gas⟩ **6** — used as a function word to indicate choice or selection from among a group ⟨we must select one policy *out of* the many open to us⟩ ⟨only one *out of* three plants survived the frost⟩ — **out of it :** not part of a group, activity, or fashion **:** not in the swim ⟨he couldn't understand a word they were saying and felt hopelessly *out of it*⟩

out-of-bounds \ˌ⸗⸗¦⸗\ *adv (or adj)* **:** outside the prescribed area of play **:** off the playing field **:** beyond the sidelines or end lines ⟨ran *out-of-bounds*⟩ ⟨kicked the ball *out-of-bounds*⟩ ⟨beyond the line is *out-of-bounds*⟩

out-of-date \ˌ⸗⸗¦⸗\ *adj* **:** OUTMODED — **out-of-date·ness** *n* -ES

out-of-door \ˌ⸗⸗¦⸗\ *or* **out-of-doors** \ˌ⸗⸗¦⸗\ *adj* **:** OUTDOOR

out-of-doors \ˌ⸗⸗¦⸗\ *n pl but sing in constr* **:** OUTDOORS

out of doors *adv* **:** OUTDOORS

out of pocket *adv* **1 :** not in pocket **:** in the position of having lost money ⟨when taxes and drainage rates had been paid, the landlord was *out of pocket* —Henry Williamson⟩ **2 :** out of funds **:** without money ⟨made no effort to order beers, being slightly *out of pocket* —Langston Hughes⟩

out-of-pocket \ˌ⸗⸗¦⸗⸗\ *adj* [*out of pocket*] **1 :** consisting of or requiring an actual cash outlay ⟨*out-of-pocket* expenses⟩ ⟨*out-of-pocket* costs⟩ **2 :** directly attributable to the movement of a particular article of traffic ⟨the *out-of-pocket* cost to the railroad of carrying this freight⟩

out-of-print \ˌ⸗⸗¦⸗\ *n* **:** a title that is out of print

out-of-round \ˌ⸗⸗¦⸗\ *adj* **:** having an imperfectly or unbalanced circular or spherical form or density — **out-of-roundness** \ˌ⸗⸗¦⸗⸗\ *n*

out-of-the-way \ˌ⸗⸗⸗¦⸗\ *adj* **:** off the beaten track **:** rarely frequented, encountered, or experienced ⟨an *out-of-the-way* restaurant⟩ ⟨an *out-of-the-way* plant⟩ ⟨an *out-of-the-way* book⟩

out-of-work \ˌ⸗⸗¦⸗\ *n* [fr. the phrase *out of work*] **:** one who is unemployed ⟨a ragged, shivering *out-of-work*, who could not even provide for his own family —Edward Scouller⟩

outpace \(ˈ)⸗¦⸗\ *vt* [*out-* + *pace*] **1 :** to surpass in speed ⟨can ~ the fastest of your boasted aeroplanes —Leslie Charteris⟩ **2 :** to go beyond **:** OUTDO ⟨the mining industry was for a time *outpaced* by lumbering —*Amer. Guide Series: Mich.*⟩

outpage \ˈ⸗ˌ⸗\ *n* [³*out* + *page*] **:** the first right-hand page of a folded book section

outparish \ˈ⸗ˌ⸗⸗\ *n* [³*out* + *parish*] **:** a parish outside the walls or limits of a town or city; *also* **:** a rural or outlying parish

outparts \ˈ⸗ˌ⸗\ *n pl* [³*out* + *parts*] *archaic* **:** SUBURBS

outpass \(ˈ)⸗¦⸗\ *vt* [*out-* + *pass*] **1 :** to go beyond **:** EXCEED **2 :** to excel in forwardpassing

outpatient \ˈ⸗ˌ⸗⸗\ *n* [³*out* + *patient*] **:** a patient who is not an inmate of a hospital but receives diagnosis or treatment in a clinic or dispensary connected with the hospital — distinguished from *inpatient*

outpayment \ˈ⸗ˌ⸗⸗\ *n* [³*out* + *payment*] **1 :** the act or an instance of paying out **2 :** a payment from — contrasted with *inpayment*

outpeep \(ˈ)⸗¦⸗\ *vi* [¹*out* + *peep*] *archaic* **:** to peep out

outpension \ˈ⸗ˌ⸗⸗\ *n* [³*out* + *pension*] **:** a public pension granted to one not required to live in a charitable institution — **outpensioner** \ˈ⸗ˌ⸗(⸗)⸗\ *n*

outperform \ˌ⸗⸗¦⸗\ *vt* [*out-* + *perform*] **:** to do better than ⟨this stock has consistently ~*ed* the market as a whole⟩ ⟨a machine that ~*s* others⟩

outplace \(ˈ)⸗¦⸗\ *vt* [¹*out* + *place*] **:** DISPLACE ⟨grain sorghums are valuable because of drought resistance and this factor has let the sorghums ~ maize —*Biol. Abstracts*⟩

outplant \(ˈ)⸗¦⸗\ *vt* [¹*out* + *plant*] **:** to transplant from a nursery bed, greenhouse, or other location to an outside area

outplay \(ˈ)⸗¦⸗\ *vt* [*out-* + *play*] **:** to excel in playing a game **:** to play more skillfully than ⟨though he ~*ed* his opponent, a series of bad breaks caused him to lose the match⟩

outpocketing \ˈ⸗ˌ⸗⸗⸗\ *n* -S [³*out* + *pocketing* (after *pocket out* v.)] **:** EVAGINATION

outpoint \(ˈ)⸗¦⸗\ *vt* [*out-* + *point*] **1 :** to sail closer to the wind than **2 a :** to win more points than **b :** to win a decision over (an opponent) in a boxing match by gaining more points **3 :** to get the better of **:** OUTDO

outpoise \(ˈ)⸗¦⸗\ *vt* [*out-* + *poise*] **:** OUTWEIGH

outpoll \(ˈ)⸗¦⸗\ *vt* [*out-* + *poll*] **:** to get more votes than ⟨~*ed* all the other candidates put together⟩

outport \ˈ⸗ˌ⸗\ *n* [³*out* + *port*] **1 a :** a harbor or port outside the limits of a main port or customhouse jurisdiction **b :** a port other than the main port of a country **2 :** a port of export or departure **3 :** a small fishing village in Newfoundland

outporter \ˈ⸗ˌ⸗⸗\ *n* [³*out* + *porter*] **1** *Eng* **:** a luggage porter who plies to or from a station or quay **2** [*outport* + *-er*] **:** a native or resident of a Newfoundland fishing village

¹outpost \ˈ⸗ˌ⸗\ *n* [³*out* + *post*] **1 a :** a security detachment thrown out at some distance from a main body of troops at a halt, in bivouac, or in battle position, to protect it from observation or surprise by the enemy **b :** the post or station of such detachment **c :** a military base established by treaty or agreement in another country ⟨an important U.S. military ~ in the Far East —*Americana Annual*⟩ **2 a :** an outlying settlement ⟨a last-chance ~ at the beginning of the swamp country —B.H.Scott⟩ **b :** the most advanced position or outermost limit of something **:** FRONTIER ⟨at the last ~ of the mind —*Times Lit. Supp.*⟩ ⟨the last ~ of our knowledge of the evolution of man as such —R.W.Murray⟩ ⟨the highest ~ of the trees —G.R.Stewart⟩ **c :** an outlying branch or position of a main organization or group ⟨four Eastern networks, each with an ~ on the West coast —*Time*⟩ **3 :** an oil or gas well near the boundary of an adjoining oil or gas field

²outpost \ˈ"\ *vt* **:** to guard or place under observation by an outpost detachment ⟨~ the road⟩ ⟨~ the farmhouse⟩

outpouching \ˈ⸗ˌ⸗⸗\ *n* -S [³*out* + *pouching*, gerund of *pouch* (after *pouch out*, v.)] **:** EVAGINATION

¹outpour \(ˈ)⸗¦⸗\ *vt* [¹*out* + *pour*] **:** to pour out

²outpour \ˈ⸗ˌ⸗\ *n* [³*out* + *pour* (after *pour out*, v.)] **:** OUTPOURING

outpouring \ˈ⸗ˌ⸗⸗\ *n* -S [³*out* + *pouring*, gerund of *pour* (after *pour out*)] **1 :** the act of pouring out ⟨~*s* of the spirit —L.P. Smith⟩ ⟨a steady ~ of research work —S.M.Spencer⟩ **2 :** something that pours out or is poured out **:** OUTBURST, OUTFLOW ⟨the ~*s* of lava buried the village⟩ ⟨believes that a work of art is not an oracular ~ —Edmund Wilson⟩

outpray \(ˈ)⸗¦⸗\ *vt* [*out-* + *pray*] **:** to surpass in praying

outpreach \(ˈ)⸗¦⸗\ *vt* [*out-* + *preach*] **:** to outdo in preaching

outprize \(ˈ)⸗¦⸗\ *vt* [*out-* + *prize*] **:** to surpass in value or estimation

outproduce \ˌ⸗⸗¦⸗\ *vt* [*out-* + *produce*] **:** to surpass in production

outpull \(ˈ)⸗¦⸗\ *vt* [*out-* + *pull*] **:** to attract a larger audience than ⟨~*s* all other shows in town⟩

¹output \ˈ⸗ˌ⸗\ *n* [³*out* + *put* (after *put out*, v.)] **1 :** something that is put out or produced: as **a :** mineral, agricultural, or industrial production ⟨coal ~⟩ ⟨wheat ~⟩ ⟨new car ~⟩ **b :** mental or artistic production ⟨his enormous symphonic ~⟩ ⟨his small literary ~⟩ ⟨a period of great scientific ~⟩ **c :** the amount produced by a person in a given time ⟨the average daily ~ of coal miners⟩ **d** (1) **:** power or energy delivered by a machine or system for storage (as by a storage battery) or for conversion in kind (as by a mechanically driven electric generator or a radio receiver) or for conversion of characteristics (as by a transformer or electronic amplifier) (2) **:** the terminal for the output on an electrical device **e** (1) **:** the information fed out by a computer or accounting machine (2) **:** the recording or printing device or its product (as magnetic tape, punched cards, or printed records) to which such information is transferred **2 :** the act, process, or an instance of putting out

²output \(ˈ)⸗¦⸗\ *vt* [¹*out* + *put*] **:** to put out **:** PRODUCE

output shaft *n* **:** a shaft that transmits power from the prime mover to the units or parts to be operated

outrace \(ˈ)⸗¦⸗\ *vt* [*out-* + *race*] **:** to run faster than **:** OUTDISTANCE ⟨inflation is *outracing* production —Eliot Janeway⟩

¹out·rage \ˈau̇tˌrāj\ *n* [OE, fr. OF, excess, outrage, fr. *outre* beyond (fr. L *ultra*) + *-age* — more at ULTERIOR] **1 :** an act of violence **:** a brutal attack ⟨arranged ~*s* and assassinations —Anthony West⟩ **2 :** an injury or insult to a person or thing **:** an act or condition that violates accepted standards of behavior or taste ⟨an ~ alike against decency and dignity —John Buchan⟩ ⟨an ~ upon journalism and upon society —F.L.Mott⟩ **3 :** a feeling of anger and resentment aroused by something regarded as an injustice or insult ⟨his sense of ~ overcame his instinct of self-preservation —S.H.Adams⟩ ⟨~ at the harshnesses of the older education —M.B.Smith⟩

²outrage \ˈ"\ *vt* [ME *outragen*, fr. *outrage*, n.] **1 a :** RAPE ⟨seized the unhappy maiden and brutally *outraged* her —T.B. Macaulay⟩ **b :** to subject to violent injury or gross insult **:** do violence to ⟨an act that *outraged* nature and produced the inevitable tragedy of the play —Louis Auchincloss⟩ ⟨this point-blank refusal *outraged* his sense of justice —J.C.Powys⟩ **2 :** to cause a feeling of anger or violent resentment in ⟨*outraged* by the way this whole matter has been handled —Lister Hill⟩ **syn** see OFFEND

out·ra·geous \(ˈ)au̇t¦rājəs\ *adj* [ME, fr. MF *outrageus*, fr. *outrage* + *-eus* -ous] **1 a :** exceeding the limits of what is normal or tolerable ⟨the ~ weather we have been afflicted with —*New Yorker*⟩ **b :** not conventional or matter-of-fact **:** EXTRAVAGANT, FANTASTIC ⟨the text matches the illustrations in this ~ tale —Margaret F. Kieran⟩ ⟨the old ~ gaiety and dash —*Time*⟩ ⟨an ~ scheme⟩ **2 :** violent or unrestrained in action or emotion ⟨know well . . . how formidable a creature you are when you become once ~ —William Cowper⟩ **3 a :** involving or doing violent injury or great harm ⟨an ~ policy of reprisals⟩ ⟨an ~ murder⟩ **b :** extremely offensive **:** showing a disregard for decency or good taste ⟨~ discourtesy⟩ ⟨~ language⟩

syn MONSTROUS, HEINOUS, ATROCIOUS: OUTRAGEOUS describes whatever is so flagrantly bad that one's sense of decency or one's power to suffer or tolerate is violated ⟨*outrageous* treatment of prisoners⟩ ⟨the general conviction that patent and *outrageous* crime would bring divine vengeance —H.O.Taylor⟩ ⟨*outrageous* as it was to open a leaden coffin, to see if a woman dead nearly a week were really dead —Bram Stoker⟩ MONSTROUS applies to what is abnormally or fantastically absurd, wrong, or horrible ⟨remarks of such a *monstrous* nature that Mr. Powell had no option but to accept them for gruesome jesting —Joseph Conrad⟩ ⟨the very horror with which men spoke . . . quite plainly indicates that such a wholesale massacre was exceptional, *monstrous* —A.T.Quiller-Couch⟩ ⟨their faces, which were more horrible to human sight than if they had been creatures of a *monstrous* nightmare —J.C.Powys⟩ HEINOUS describes that which excites extreme hatred, loathing, and horror ⟨a murder, and a particularly *heinous* murder, for it involves the violation of hospitality and of gratitude —R.P.Warren⟩ ATROCIOUS may apply to fierce or barbarous merciless cruelty, violence, or contempt of sanctioned values ⟨an *atrocious* murder of a child⟩ ⟨*atrocious* treatment of displaced persons⟩ ⟨*atrocious* acts which can only take place in a slave country —C.R.Darwin⟩ These words are frequently interchangeable and all lend themselves to hyperbolic descriptions of anything deprecated at the moment ⟨*outrageous* service⟩ ⟨a *monstrous* imposition⟩ ⟨a *heinous* blunder⟩ ⟨*atrocious* weather⟩

out·ra·geous·ly *adv* [ME, fr. *outrageous* + *-ly*] **:** in an outrageous manner or to an outrageous degree

out·ra·geous·ness *n* -ES [ME *oultrageousnes*, fr. *oultrageous*, *outrageous* + *-nes* -ness] **:** the quality or state of being outrageous

out·rag·er \ˈau̇tˌrājə(r)\ *n* **:** one that outrages

ou·trance \ü·ˈträⁿs\ *n* -S [ME *outraunce*, fr. MF *outrance*, fr. *outrer* to pass beyond, overcome, surpass, carry to excess (fr. *outre* beyond) + *-ance* — more at OUTRAGE] **:** the last extremity — used with *at* or *to*; compare À OUTRANCE

outrange \(ˈ)⸗¦⸗\ *vt* [*out-* + *range*] **1 :** to surpass in range ⟨could ~ guns of the average small destroyer —*Ships and the Sea*⟩ **2 :** to go beyond **:** EXCEL ⟨the poets and the philosophers ~ the historians —A.J.Toynbee⟩

outrank \(ˈ)⸗¦⸗\ *vt* [*out-* + *rank*] **1 a :** to have a higher rank than ⟨~*s* most of his colleagues —*Current Biog.*⟩ **b :** to take precedence over ⟨an invitation to the carnival ~*s* one to class day or proms —*Amer. Guide Series: N. H.*⟩ **2 :** to surpass in importance ⟨peaches now ~ cotton as the chief crop —*Amer. Guide Series: Ark.*⟩ ⟨~*ed* all others as a shipping port for coffee —C.L.Jones⟩

ou·tray \ü·ˈtrā\ *vb* [ME *outrayen*, fr. MF *outreer*, fr. *outre*r — more at OUTRANCE] *vt* **1** *archaic* **:** VANQUISH, OVERCOME **2** *archaic* **:** SURPASS, EXCEL **~** *vi*, *archaic* **:** to be immoderate or extravagant **:** commit outrages or excesses

ou·tré \ˌü¦trā\ *adj* [F, fr. past part. of *outrer* to carry to excess — more at OUTRANCE] **:** not conforming to conventional behavior, custom, or style **:** BIZARRE, EXTRAVAGANT ⟨was always so ~ and strange —Samuel Butler †1902⟩ ⟨primitive in style, ~ in pose, and often savage in face —Janet Flanner⟩ — **ou·tré·ness** *n* -ES

¹outreach \(ˈ)⸗¦⸗\ *vb* [*out-* + *reach*] *vt* **1 a :** to surpass in reach ⟨you have to ~ an outfielder to catch a mountain beaver by hand —Irving Petite⟩ **b :** to go beyond **:** EXCEED ⟨the demand for electrical power continues to ~ the supply —*New Republic*⟩ **2 :** to get the better of by trickery **:** OVERREACH ⟨~*ed* his unsuspecting enemies⟩ ⟨~*ed* himself and became tangled in his own plot⟩ **~** *vi* **1 :** to go too far ⟨my foolish and ~*ing* slyness —Owen Wister⟩ **2** [¹*out* + *reach*] **:** to reach out ⟨alert to the ~*ing* trends of his profession —H.A.Overstreet⟩

²outreach \ˈ⸗ˌ⸗\ *n* [³*out* + *reach* (after *reach out*, v.)] **1 :** the act or process of reaching out ⟨the ~ of the human spirit toward beauty of form —C.S.Kilby⟩ **2 :** an extent or length of reach ⟨away from the ~ of the Ohio floods —Clifton Johnson⟩ ⟨his evangelical ~ was already shortened —W.W. Comfort⟩

ou·tre·cuid·ance \ˌüd·ə(r)ˈkwēdᵊn(t)s\ *n* -S [ME *outrecuidaunce*, *utterquidaunce*, fr. MF *outrecuidance*, fr. OF, fr. *outrecuider*, *outrecuidier* to be arrogant, conceited (fr. *outre* beyond + *cuider*, *cuidier* to think, be presumptuous, fr. L *cogitare* to think, think about) + *-ance* — more at OUTRAGE, COGITATE] **:** extreme self-conceit **:** PRESUMPTION

outrelief \ˈ⸗⸗ˌ⸗\ *n* [³*out* + *relief*] *Brit* **:** relief given to persons living outside an institution **:** outdoor relief

¹outride \(ˈ)⸗¦⸗\ *vb* [*out-* + *ride*] *vt* **1 a :** to ride better, faster, or farther than **:** OUTSTRIP ⟨could outwalk them and outdrink them and ~ them —H.W.Van Loon⟩ **2 :** to ride out (a storm) ⟨patience to ~ the intellectual and emotional storms that lie ahead —H.A.Steiner⟩ ⟨a ship strong enough to ~ any storm⟩ **~** *vi* [¹*out* + *ride*] **:** to ride out ⟨*outriding* on the range⟩

²outride \ˈ⸗ˌ⸗\ *n* [³*out* + *ride* (after *ride out*, v.)] **:** an unstressed syllable or group of syllables added to a foot in sprung rhythm but not counted in the scansion because of its lack of effect upon the rhythmical movement

outrider \ˈ⸗ˌ⸗⸗\ *n* [³*out* + *rider* (after *ride out*, v.)] **1 a** (1) **:** an attendant on horseback who rides ahead of or next to a carriage ⟨rode in a six-horse coach with liveried lackeys and ~*s* —*Time*⟩ (2) **:** a mounted attendant who escorts race horses to the starting post **b :** one who clears the way for a vehicle or person ⟨a long black limousine with two motorcycle ~*s* —Albert Hubbell⟩ ⟨swept into the headquarters building with ~*s* brushing reporters . . . out of his path —*Time*⟩ **c :** a member of an advance guard or detachment ⟨she is an advanced ~ of feminism —Christopher Rand⟩ **d :** something that precedes or announces the approach of what is to come **:** HARBINGER, PORTENT ⟨are these shadows on so many of our horizons the ~*s* of another long night —Gilbert Highet⟩ ⟨that sugar maple . . . a flaming torch, an ~ of winter —Margaret A. Barnes⟩ **2** *dial* **:** TRAVELING SALESMAN **3 a :** a cowboy who rides on inspection about the range **b :** SCOUT ⟨a hawk, who was acting as ~, observed a truck coming toward them —James Thurber⟩ **4 :** OUTRIDE

out·rig \ˈau̇ˌtrig, (ˈ)⸗¦⸗\ *vt* [back-formation fr. *outrigger*] **:** to equip with outriggers ⟨a craft *outrigged* with pontoons —Geneva J. Yockey⟩

out·rig·ger \-gə(r)\ *n* [³*out* + *rigger* (after *rig out*, v.)]

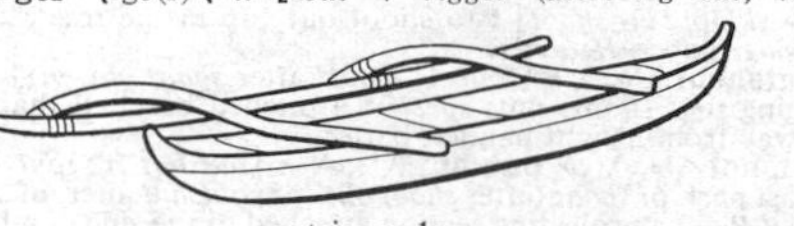

outrigger 1a

1 a : a light projecting spar with a shaped log at the end attached to a seagoing canoe (as in the Pacific or Indian oceans) to prevent it from upsetting **b :** a spar or projecting beam run out from a ship's side to help secure the masts or from a mast to extend a rope or sail **c** (1) **:** a projecting support for an oarlock extended from the side of a rowboat or shell to permit greater leverage for the oar (2) **:** a boat so equipped **2 :** a projecting member run out from a main structure to provide additional stability or to support an extension: as **a :** a projection from a building to support hoisting tackle or to hold a flagpole **b :** a projecting or extended section of the frame of a vehicle (as of a truck) **c** (1) **:** a projecting frame usu. of spars, distance pieces, and braces to support the elevator or tail planes of an airplane (2) **:** a projection from the fuselage of a helicopter to support a rotor or a fan

out·rig·gered \-gə(r)d\ *adj* **:** furnished with an outrigger

¹outright \(ˈ)⸗¦⸗\ *adv* [ME, fr. ¹*out* + *right* (adv.) — more at RIGHT] **1** *archaic* **:** straight ahead **:** DIRECTLY **2 :** in entirety **:** COMPLETELY ⟨efforts to repeal state civil service laws ~ —F.A.Ogg & P.O.Ray⟩ **3 :** UNRESERVEDLY ⟨was crying ~ now —Donn Byrne⟩ **4 :** on the spot **:** INSTANTANEOUSLY ⟨married her ~ there, while he had the chance —George Meredith⟩ ⟨killed thirty people ~ and injured hundreds —F.L. Allen⟩ **5 :** in one transaction ⟨bought ~ or on a "pay later" plan —Morris Gilbert⟩ ⟨one of the few buildings he ever purchased ~ —*Time*⟩

²outright \ˈ"\ *adj* **1 a :** going or carried to the full extent **:** not limited or qualified **:** OUT-AND-OUT, THOROUGHGOING ⟨an ~ lie⟩ ⟨~ dishonesty⟩ ⟨an ~ disaster⟩ **b :** given without reservation ⟨an ~ gift⟩ ⟨an ~ bequest⟩ **2** *archaic* **:** proceeding directly onward **3 :** COMPLETE, ENTIRE ⟨the ~ expense⟩ — **out·right·ly** *adv* — **out·right·ness** *n*

outring \(ˈ)⸗¦⸗\ *vb* [¹*out* + *ring*] *vi* **:** to ring out ⟨the bells ~*ing* from the tower⟩ **~** *vt* [*out-* + *ring*] **:** to sound louder than ⟨~*ing* the noise of the hoofs —Theodore Winthrop⟩

outrival \(ˈ)⸗¦⸗⸗\ *vt* [*out-* + *rival*] **:** to outdo in a competition or rivalry ⟨~*s* her brother in the affections of her parents⟩ ⟨~ other nations in economic development⟩

outroad \ˈ⸗ˌ⸗\ *n* [³*out* + *road*] *archaic* **:** RAID

¹outroar \(ˈ)⸗¦⸗\ *vt* [*out-* + *roar*] **:** to roar louder than ⟨the hurricane ~*ed* them —R.D.Blackmore⟩

²outroar \ˈ⸗ˌ⸗\ *n* [³*out* + *roar* (after *roar out*, v.)] **:** UPROAR

outroll \(ˈ)⸗¦⸗\ *vt* [¹*out* + *roll*] **:** to roll out **:** UNROLL

outroom \ˈ⸗ˌ⸗\ *n* [³*out* + *room*] **:** an outer room

outroot \(ˈ)⸗¦⸗\ *vt* [¹*out* + *root*] **:** ERADICATE

¹outrun \(ˈ)⸗¦⸗\ *vb* [ME *outrennen*, fr. ¹*out* + *rennen* to run — more at RUN] *vi*, *archaic* **:** to run out **~** *vt* [*out-* + *run*] **1 a :** to surpass in running **:** run faster than **:** go ahead of ⟨after a ride lasting all day, the Indians *outran* them —W.S. Campbell⟩ ⟨can ~ any other sub —*Time*⟩ **b :** to increase or develop faster than ⟨believes . . . that saving will chronically tend to ~ investment —W.M.Dacey⟩ ⟨multiplication in numbers must inevitably ~ the food supply —R.E.Coker⟩ **c :** to escape from ⟨we'd ~ my past so far, but it would catch up with us some day —J.B.Benefield⟩ ⟨men who had ~ the established law and all the courts —W.P.Webb⟩ **2 :** to go beyond (a particular point or limit) ⟨scientific theory is *outrunning* common sense —A.N.Whitehead⟩ ⟨fashion never permanently ~*s* discretion —Edward Sapir⟩ **3 :** to receive more votes than ⟨*outran* his party's candidates for other state offices⟩ — **outrun the constable :** to go into debt

²outrun \ˈ⸗ˌ⸗\ *n* [³*out* + *run* (after *run out*, v.)] **1 :** the act of running out ⟨the dog started off in great style on its ~ to collect the sheep —Alastair Robertson⟩ **2 :** a run for cattle or sheep at a distance from the main buildings or head station **3 :** an area into which a skier slides to come to a stop after making a ski jump or run ⟨all steep downhill stretches must have a safe ~ —Walter Prager⟩

outrunner \ˈ⸗ˌ⸗⸗\ *n* [³*out* + *runner* (after *run out*, v.)] **:** one that runs or goes ahead

¹outrush \ˈ⸗ˌ⸗\ *n* [³*out* + *rush* (after *rush out*, v.)] **:** the act or an instance of rushing out **:** OUTFLOW ⟨a great ~ of breath —Liam O'Flaherty⟩

²outrush \(ˈ)⸗¦⸗\ *vt* [*out-* + *rush*] **:** to excel (an opposing team) in rushing ⟨~*ed* 104 yards to 78 —J.M.Sheehan⟩

outs *pres 3d sing of* OUT, *pl of* OUT

outsail \(ˈ)⸗¦⸗\ *vt* [*out-* + *sail*] **:** to surpass in sailing **:** sail faster than **:** OUTSTRIP ⟨~*ed* the earlier Roman ships —G.S.L. Clowes⟩

outscore \(ˈ)⸗¦⸗\ *vt* [*out-* + *score*] **:** to score more points than ⟨*outscored* their opponents by 20 points⟩

outscout \ˈ⸗ˌ⸗\ *n* [³*out* + *scout*] **:** SCOUT

out·scrib·er \(ˈ)au̇tˈskrībə(r)\ *n* [*out*put + tran*scriber*] **:** a device for transferring data recorded on a magnetic wire by an electronic computer to a medium (as a punched tape) that can be used to actuate a machine for printing the data — compare INSCRIBER

outsea \ˈ≈,≈\ *n* [³*out* + *sea*] **:** HIGH SEA

outseam \ˈ≈,≈\ *n* [³*out* + *seam*] **:** PRICKSEAM

outsee \(ˈ)≈¦≈\ *vt* [*out-* + *see*] **1 :** to surpass in power of vision or insight **2** [¹*out* + *see*] **:** to see beyond (a particular point or limit)

outsell \(ˈ)≈¦≈\ *vt* [*out-* + *sell*] **1** *archaic* **:** to sell for a higher price than **:** exceed in worth **2 :** to exceed in number of items sold ⟨nonfiction . . . continues to ~ fiction in the bookstores —*Publishers' Weekly*⟩ **3 :** to surpass in selling or salesmanship ⟨~*s* all other salesmen for the company⟩

outsend \(ˈ)≈¦≈\ *vt* [¹*out* + *send*] *archaic* **:** to send forth **:** EMIT

outsentry \ˈ≈,≈≈\ *n* [³*out* + *sentry*] *archaic* **:** a sentry assigned to an outpost

¹**out·sert** \ˈau̇t,sər|t, -sə̄|, -səi|, *usu* |d·+V\ *n* -S [³*out* + *-sert* (as in *insert*, n.)] **:** a usu. 4-page section (as of a magazine) so imposed and printed that it can be placed outside another signature — compare INSERT

²**out·sert** \(ˈ)au̇tˈsər|t, -sə̄|, -səi|, *usu* |d·+V\ *vt* -ED/-ING/-S [¹*out* + *-sert* (as in *insert*, v.)] **1 :** to place as an outsert ⟨color plates ~*ed* to signatures⟩ **2 :** to add an outsert to ⟨signatures ~*ed* and ready for gathering⟩

outset \ˈ≈,≈\ *n* [³*out* + *set* (after *set out*, v.)] **1** *Scot* **:** an enclosure of land newly placed under cultivation **2 a :** a setting out (as on a journey, career, course of action, or discussion) **:** BEGINNING, START ⟨one must be clear, from the ~, how limited are the author's aims —S.E.Toulmin⟩ ⟨at the ~ of what might have been a great career —E.F.Edgett⟩ **b :** an initial stage of activity or development ⟨the ~ of any investigation must be occupied by asking obvious questions —Edith C. Rivett⟩ **3 :** an outgoing tidal current **4 :** OUTSERT

¹**outsetting** \ˈ≈,≈≈\ *n* [³*out* + *setting*, gerund of *set* (after *set out*, v.)] **:** the act or process of setting out (as on a journey or expedition) ⟨a full description of the ~ from Gravesend of a detachment of Royal Engineers —*Athenaeum*⟩

²**outsetting** \ˈ≈¦≈≈\ *adj* [¹*out* + *setting*, pres. part. of set (after *set out*, v.)] **:** setting or flowing out

outsettlement \ˈ≈,≈≈≈\ *n* [³*out* + *settlement*] **:** an outlying settlement

outsettler \ˈ≈,≈≈\ *n* [³*out* + *settler*] **:** one who lives in an outlying region

outshadow \(ˈ)≈¦≈,≈\ *vt* [*out-* + *shadow*] **:** OVERSHADOW

outsharp \(ˈ)≈¦≈\ *vt* [*out-* + *sharp*] **:** OUTWIT

outshine \(ˈ)≈¦≈\ *vb* [*out-* + *shine*] *vt* **1 a :** to surpass in shining **:** shine brighter than ⟨a star that ~*s* the sun⟩ **b :** to excel in splendor or showiness ⟨seeing another, whom she intended to ~, in a more attractive dress than her own —T.L. Peacock⟩ **2 :** EXCEL, OUTDO ⟨would try to ~ his former disciple in wit —Hesketh Pearson⟩ **~** *vi* [¹*out* + *shine*] **:** to shine out ⟨bright *outshining* beams —Shak.⟩

¹**outshoot** \(ˈ)≈¦≈\ *vb* [*out-* + *shoot*] *vt* **1 :** to surpass in shooting or making shots ⟨a rifle that ~*s* any other model of its type⟩ ⟨won the tennis match by ~*ing* and outrunning his opponent⟩ **2 :** to shoot or go beyond ⟨tell the philosophers of the day, that I have *outshot* them all —William Cowper⟩ **~** *vi* [¹*out* + *shoot*] **:** to shoot out ⟨up in the tree . . . on an ~*ing* limb —*Hearst's*⟩

²**outshoot** \ˈ≈,≈\ *n* [³*out* + *shoot* (after *shoot out*, v.)] **:** something that shoots out; *specif* **:** a pitched baseball that breaks away from a right-handed batter

outshot \ˈ≈,≈\ *or* **outshut** \ˈ≈,≈\ *n* [*outshot* fr. ¹*out* + *shot*, past part. of *shoot* (after *shoot out*, v.); *outshut* alter. of *outshot*] *dial Brit* **:** a projecting section attached to the side of a building **:** LEAN-TO

outshout \(ˈ)≈¦≈\ *vt* [*out-* + *shout*] **:** to shout louder than ⟨acclaimed only so long as he can personally ~ and outthreaten the rest —Margaret Mead⟩

¹**outside** \(ˈ)≈¦≈\ *n* [³*out* + *side*] **1 :** a place or region that is situated beyond an enclosure, boundary, or other limit: as **a :** the world outside an institution ⟨fit an inmate in attitudes and habits for life on the ~ —Garrett Heyns⟩ **b** *Austral* **:** OUTBACK **c** *Alaska* **:** the world outside the territory or state of Alaska **2 a :** an outer side or surface ⟨the ~ of the house needs painting⟩ ⟨the ~ of the door was badly scarred⟩ ⟨walked on the ~ of the path⟩ **b :** the left side of a sword in fencing **c :** the convex aspect of a curve **d :** the side of home plate farther from the batter in baseball ⟨pitched to the batter on the ~⟩ **3 :** an outer manifestation **:** APPEARANCE ⟨he was the fine ~ of a man, the portrait of a gentleman and a soldier —A.W.Long⟩ ⟨the imaginative insides of human reverie can be more thrilling than the heroic ~*s* of action —T.V.Smith⟩ **4 :** the extreme limit of a guess or approximation **:** the utmost extent ⟨the crowd numbered ten thousand at the ~⟩ ⟨estimated that his rate of profit would be ten percent at the ~⟩ ⟨gave him two years to live at the ~⟩ **5 :** one that is without: as **a :** an outside passenger or seat (as in a stagecoach) **b :** a rugby player who is not a forward **6 outsides** *pl* **:** the top and bottom quires of a ream of writing or drawing paper; *broadly* **:** reams made up of such imperfect quires or sheets — compare INSIDE

²**outside** \"\ *adj* **1 a :** of, relating to, or being on the outer side or surface ⟨the ~ edge⟩ ⟨~ qualities⟩ ⟨an ~ lock⟩ **b :** of, relating to, or being on or toward the outer side of a curve or turn ⟨stemming with the ~ ski⟩ ⟨the ~ wheels⟩ **2 a :** situated, belonging, or performed outside a particular place, area, or enclosure ⟨distracted by ~ noises⟩ ⟨take many ~ trips during the school year⟩ ⟨heard little news from the ~ world⟩ **b** *Austral* **:** situated in the outback **c :** connected with or giving access to the outside ⟨asked the switchboard operator for an ~ line⟩ **d** *Eng* **:** done outside a radio or television studio ⟨throughout the summer months the television service specializes in sport and other ~ broadcasts —T.O.Beachcroft⟩ **3 :** MAXIMUM ⟨five millions more than their ~ estimate —F.L.Allen⟩ **4 a :** not included or originating in a particular group or organization **:** EXTRANEOUS ⟨~ influences⟩ ⟨~ pressure⟩ ⟨the ~ public⟩ **b :** not belonging to one's regular occupation, duties, or course of study ⟨~ interests⟩ ⟨~ activities⟩ **c :** done outside of class or class hours ⟨the course demands ten hours a week of ~ preparation⟩ **5 :** barely possible **:** REMOTE ⟨has an ~ chance of scoring an upset and winning the election⟩ **syn** see OUTER

³**outside** \"\ *adv* **1 a :** on or to the outside ⟨waited ~ in the corridor⟩ ⟨carried the lawn furniture ~⟩ **b :** in the open air **:** OUTDOORS **2 :** EXTERNALLY ⟨the car seemed in perfect shape ~⟩

⁴**outside** \"\ *prep* [³*outside*] **1 :** on the outer side of ⟨the American flag ~ my building —William Barrett⟩ ⟨she seemed always ~ her subject —H.J.Laski⟩ **2 :** beyond the limits of ⟨do little of their entertaining ~ their homes —*Amer. Guide Series: Minn.*⟩ ⟨reach ~ the narrow intellectual boundaries imposed by a restricted income in a little village —Flora Rose⟩ ⟨~ the law⟩ **3 :** to the outside of ⟨ran ~ the house⟩ **4 :** EXCEPT 1 ⟨~ these, and a few professional men, there was almost no fancy dress —Arnold Bennett⟩

outside broker *n* **:** a stockbroker who is not a member of an exchange

outside caliper *n* **:** a caliper for measuring outside dimensions

outside car *n, Irish* **:** JAUNTING CAR

outside clinch *n* **:** a clinch knot in which the seized end of a line is outside the noose — compare INSIDE CLINCH

outside finish *n* **:** the final work on the exterior of a building necessary for its completion (as the adding of corner boards and window casings) — compare INSIDE FINISH

outside form *n* **:** OUTER FORM

outside home *n* **:** a lacrosse player whose position is on the right side of the opponents' goal next to inside home — called also *out home*

outside left *n* **:** the outermost forward on the left of the center in a game (as soccer) in which there are five forwards

outside loop *n* **:** a maneuver in which an airplane starting from straight and level flight passes successively through a dive, inverted flight, and a climb and then returns to normal flight

outside market *n* **:** ²CURB 9 b

out·side·ness *n* -ES **:** the quality or state of being outside ⟨my ~ from current affairs —O.W.Holmes †1935⟩

outside of *prep* [³*outside*] **1 :** beyond the limits or compass of ⟨the rapid development of suburban centers *outside of* all our cities —Harrison Smith⟩ **2 :** BESIDES, EXCEPT ⟨*outside of* one servant he is alone in the house⟩

outside quire *n* **:** the top quire or the bottom quire of a ream of handmade or moldmade paper

out·sid·er \(ˈ)au̇tˈsīdə(r)\ *n* -S [²*outside* + *-er*] **1 a :** a person not recognized or accepted as a member of some group, category, or organization ⟨has lived there for 20 years but is still regarded as an ~⟩ ⟨a political ~⟩ **b :** a person who isolates himself or is felt to be isolated from the world around him ⟨the artist ought to be an ~ —E.M.Forster⟩ **2 :** a contender in a sports event that is not favored to win **3 outsiders** *pl* **:** a pair of long-nosed pincers for grasping the point of a key in the keyhole from the outside **4 :** JAUNTING CAR

outside right *n* **:** the outermost forward on the right of the center in a game (as soccer) in which there are five forwards

outside wire *n* **:** OUTER

outsight \ˈ≈,≈\ *n* [³*out* + *sight*] **1 :** the act or capacity of observing **:** the perception of external things ⟨the clear-eyed insight and ~ of the born writer —*New Yorker*⟩ **2** *archaic Scot* **:** movable outdoor goods or property (as plows or cattle)

outsing \(ˈ)≈¦≈\ *vb* [*out-* + *sing*] *vt* **:** to surpass in singing ⟨a violin that will ~ any instrument yet made by man —H.M. Robinson⟩ **~** *vi* [¹*out* + *sing*] **:** to sing out

out sister *n* [³*out*] **:** EXTERN 2

outsit \(ˈ)≈¦≈\ *vt* [*out-* + *sit*] **1 :** to remain sitting longer than the duration of ⟨*outsat* their pleasure in his company⟩ **2 :** to sit longer than ⟨ready to ~ the negotiators for the other side⟩

¹**outsize** \ˈ≈,≈\ *n* [³*out* + *size*] **:** an unusual size (as of an article of clothing); *esp* **:** a size larger than the standard

²**outsize** \ˈ≈\ *also* **outsized** \(ˈ)≈¦≈\ *adj* **1 :** unusually large or heavy ⟨physically he is ~, standing six feet three and weighing 225 pounds —N.M.Clark⟩ ⟨a man whose talent, ego and self-indulgence come in rather ~ proportions —Claudia Cassidy⟩ **2 :** too large ⟨his ~ black homburg resting squarely on both ears —*Newsweek*⟩ ⟨a cheerful rascal in an ~ shirt and undersize pants —J.B.D.Cotter⟩

¹**outskirt** \ˈ≈,≈\ *n* [³*out* + *skirt*] **:** a part remote from the center **:** BORDER, FRINGE ⟨a very thinly settled ~ —Edith Wharton⟩ — usu. used in pl. ⟨showed that our sun was not the center of our galaxy but out toward its ~*s* —B.J.Bok⟩ ⟨the ~*s* of the city⟩ ⟨the ~*s* of consciousness⟩

²**outskirt** \(ˈ)≈¦≈\ *vt* **1 :** BORDER **2 :** to pass along the border of ⟨~*ed* the lawn⟩

outskirter \ˈ≈,≈≈\ *n* **:** one that occupies the outskirts **:** HANGER-ON

outsleep \(ˈ)≈¦≈\ *vt* [*out-* + *sleep*] **1 :** to sleep later than ⟨fear we shall ~ the coming morn —Shak.⟩ **2** [¹*out* + *sleep*] **:** to sleep through or beyond the end of ⟨*outslept* the storm⟩ ⟨*outslept* his opportunity⟩

outslick \(ˈ)≈¦≈\ *vt* [*out-* + *slick* (adj.)] **:** to get the better of by trickery or cunning

outslug \(ˈ)≈¦≈\ *vt* [*out-* + *slug*] **1 :** OUTFIGHT ⟨the trout had *outslugged* him, outwitted him . . . and had got away —Richard Salmon⟩ **2 :** to get more extra-base hits than

outsmart \(ˈ)≈¦≈\ *vt* [*out-* + *smart* (adj.)] **:** to get the better of ⟨is told that existing society will ~ him if given a chance —*Sydney (Australia) Bull.*⟩; *esp* **:** OUTMANEUVER, OUTWIT ⟨a shrewd criminal who fancied he could ~ the whole world —Louis Bromfield⟩

outsmell \(ˈ)≈¦≈\ *vt* [*out-* + *smell*] **:** to smell stronger than ⟨his bear's grease *outsmelt* his primroses —Israel Zangwill⟩

outsoar \(ˈ)≈¦≈\ *vt* [*out-* + *soar*] **:** to soar beyond or above ⟨~ the shadow of war's night —*Times Lit. Supp.*⟩

outsole \ˈ≈,≈\ *n* [³*out* + *sole*] **:** the outside sole of a boot or shoe

¹**outspan** \(ˈ)≈¦≈\ *vb* [¹*out* + *span*; trans. of Afrik *uitspan*] *vi, southern Africa* **:** to unyoke or unharness a draft animal ⟨we *outspanned*, made our beds and then set about preparing supper —*Farmer's Weekly (So. Africa)*⟩ **~** *vt, southern Africa* **:** UNYOKE, UNHITCH

²**outspan** \ˈ≈,≈\ *n, southern Africa* **:** a place publicly set aside for use in outspanning or resting animals

outspeak \(ˈ)≈¦≈\ *vb* [in sense 1, fr. *out-* + *speak*; in other senses, fr. ¹*out* + *speak*] *vt* **1 :** to excel in speaking **:** speak longer, louder, or more forcibly than ⟨though the lawyer for the defense *outspoke* the prosecutor, he lost the case⟩ **2 :** to declare openly or boldly ⟨broke upon him in a loud voice, ~*ing* his contention —Elizabeth M. Roberts⟩ **~** *vi* **:** to speak out ⟨when the rude instinct of our race *outspoke* —Robert Browning⟩

outspeed \(ˈ)≈¦≈\ *vt* [*out-* + *speed*] **1 :** to outdo in speed **:** go faster than ⟨can ~ any other horse over a short distance⟩ **2 :** to go beyond **:** leave behind ⟨no cruelty horrible enough to ~ her pity —Hugh Walpole⟩

outspend \(ˈ)≈¦≈\ *vt* [*out-* + *spend*] **1 :** to exceed the limits of in spending ⟨~*s* his income⟩ **2 :** to outdo in spending ⟨promised to ~ the incumbent administration⟩

outspent \(ˈ)≈¦≈\ *adj* [¹*out* + *spent*] **:** EXHAUSTED

outspin \(ˈ)≈¦≈\ *vt* [¹*out* + *spin*] **:** to spin (a thread) to its full extent ⟨the thread of life *outspun*⟩

outspoken \(ˈ)≈¦≈≈\ *adj* [¹*out* + *spoken*] **1 a :** speaking without fear or reserve **:** direct and open in speech or expression **:** CANDID, FRANK ⟨~ in his assertion of his opinions —H.K. Rowe⟩ ⟨~ in their opposition to slavery —W.L.Sperry⟩ **b :** spoken or expressed without reserve or conventional reticence ⟨won praise for the ~ quality of its language and subject matter —*Current Biog.*⟩ **2** *of a disease* **:** clearly present **:** UNMISTAKABLE ⟨cardiac insufficiency, whether incipient or ~, demands bed rest —R.F.Loeb⟩ — **out·spo·ken·ly** \-nlē, -li\ *adv* — **out·spo·ken·ness** \-n(n)əs\ *n* -ES

outsport *vt* [*out-* + *sport*] *obs* **:** to go beyond (a limit) in sportiveness ⟨let's teach ourselves . . . not to ~ discretion —Shak.⟩

¹**outspread** \(ˈ)≈¦≈\ *vt* [ME *outspreden*, fr. ¹*out* + *spreden* to spread — more at SPREAD] **:** to spread out **:** EXPAND

²**outspread** \"\ *adj* [fr. past part. of ¹*outspread*] **:** spread out **:** EXTENDED ⟨~ arms⟩ ⟨~ hair⟩

³**outspread** \ˈ≈,≈\ *n* [³*out* + *spread* (after *spread out*, v.)] **:** the action or an instance of spreading out ⟨this ~ brought also new problems —D.E.O'Leary⟩

outspring \(ˈ)≈¦≈\ *vi* [ME *outspringen*, fr. ¹*out* + *springen* to spring — more at SPRING] **:** to spring out

outstand \(ˈ)≈¦≈\ *vb* [¹*out* + *stand*] *vt* **1** *dial chiefly Eng* **:** to resist stubbornly **:** CONTRADICT **2 :** to endure beyond ⟨I have *outstood* my time —Shak.⟩ **~** *vi* **:** to stand out clearly ⟨he *outstood* in virtue of being a perfect symbol and emblem of the average —Max Beerbohm⟩

outstanding \ˈ≈¦≈≈\ *adj* **1 :** standing out or projecting ⟨an ~ skirt that strangely resembled the large lampshade in the drawing room —G.K.Chesterton⟩ **2 a :** UNCOLLECTED, UNPAID ⟨left a balance of ten dollars ~ on his account⟩ **b :** continuing in being **:** UNRESOLVED ⟨one of the long ~ problems of astronomy —*Times Lit. Supp.*⟩ ⟨several ~ issues between the two countries⟩ **c** *of stocks and bonds* **:** publicly issued and sold ⟨has 20,000 shares ~⟩ **3 a :** standing out from a group **:** CONSPICUOUS, PROMINENT ⟨cleanliness is an ~ characteristic of the Acadian housewife —*Amer. Guide Series: La.*⟩ ⟨the ~ subject of discussion —Vera M. Dean⟩ **b :** preeminent in a particular quality or activity **:** EXCELLENT ⟨an ~ painter who has received little recognition⟩ ⟨an ~ student⟩ **syn** see NOTICEABLE

out·stand·ing·ly *adv* **:** in an outstanding manner or to an outstanding degree **:** EXTREMELY, REMARKABLY

outstandings \(ˈ)≈¦≈≈\ *n pl* **:** outstanding loans or unsettled accounts ⟨the bank's ~ on real estate mortgages have gone up by over half a million dollars⟩

outstanding term *n, Eng law* **:** an estate for a long term of years granted usu. to trustees to secure regular payments to a beneficiary from the tenant of the estate upon which such payments are charged

outstare \(ˈ)≈¦≈\ *vt* [*out-* + *stare*] **:** to overcome in staring **:** put out of countenance **:** OUTFACE ⟨seem confident that they can ~ the U. S. —*Time*⟩

¹**outstart** \(ˈ)≈¦≈\ *vb* [¹*out* + *start*] *vi* **:** to spring out **:** start forth **~** *vt* [*out-* + *start*] **:** to get the start of

²**outstart** \ˈ≈,≈\ *n* [³*out* + *start* (after *start out*, v.)] **:** BEGINNING, OUTSET

outstate \ˈ≈,≈\ *adj* [³*out* + *state* (n.)] **1 :** of, relating to, or situated in a region of a state outside the principal city or largest center of population ⟨small layoffs here and there in the ~ areas —*Wall Street Jour.*⟩ ⟨lost the governorship because the ~ vote went against him⟩ **2** [*out (of) state*] **:** coming from or resident in an outside state ⟨a gorge of unusual natural beauty which few ~ visitors see —M.W.Fishwick⟩ — **out·stat·er** \ˈ≈ˈstād·ə(r)\ *n*

outstation \ˈ≈,≈≈\ *n* [³*out* + *station*] **:** a station (as a sheep run, diplomatic post, or mission) situated in a remote or sparsely settled region ⟨sit . . . at some lonely ~ and shoot three deer before breakfast —*Sydney (Australia) Bull.*⟩ ⟨three nuns waited . . . for a sister reporting in from an ~ —J.A. Michener⟩

outstay \(ˈ)≈¦≈\ *vt* [*out-* + *stay*] **1 a :** to stay beyond **:** OVERSTAY ⟨~*ed* his welcome⟩ ⟨~*ed* his leave⟩ **b :** to stay longer than ⟨was determined to ~ him —John Buchan⟩ **2 :** to surpass in staying power ⟨~*ed* the favorite by a neck⟩ ⟨a writer who has ~*ed* many who began more brilliantly⟩

outstep \(ˈ)≈¦≈\ *vt* [*out-* + *step*] **:** to step beyond **:** OVERSTEP ⟨~*s* the moderation of his predecessor in office⟩ ⟨program which it would have been almost blasphemy to ~ —J.C. Stobart⟩

outstink \(ˈ)≈¦≈\ *vt* [*out-* + *stink*] **:** to smell worse than **:** have a more powerful stench than ⟨~ a skunk⟩

outstream \(ˈ)≈¦≈\ *vi* [¹*out* + *stream*] **:** to stream out

out·streat \(ˈ)≈¦strēt\ *vi* [¹*out* + obs. *streat* to estreat, short for *estreat* (influenced in meaning by its etymon, obs. F *estrait*, past part. of *estraire* to extract)] — more at ESTREAT] *archaic* **:** EXUDE

¹**outstretch** \(ˈ)≈¦≈\ *vt* [¹*out* + *stretch*] **1 a :** to stretch out ⟨the image of a kitten erect, one paw ~*ed* as if inviting —Lafcadio Hearn⟩ **b :** to spread out **:** EXTEND ⟨began to paint on the ~*ed* canvas⟩ **2** [*out-* + *stretch*] **:** to stretch beyond ⟨this explanation ~*es* common sense⟩ — **outstretcher** \(ˈ)≈¦≈≈\ *n*

²**outstretch** \ˈ≈,≈\ *n* [³*out* + *stretch* (after *stretch out*, v.)] **:** the act or an instance of stretching out ⟨nothing less than poetry's soaring ~ . . . can justify the writing of any novel in verse —*New Republic*⟩

outstride \(ˈ)≈¦≈\ *vt* [*out-* + *stride*] **:** to outdo in striding **:** stride ahead of ⟨on the utilitarian side . . . American education has *outstridden* the rest of the world —F.P.Corson⟩

outstrike *vt* [*out-* + *strike*] *obs* **:** to surpass in striking

outstrip \(ˈ)≈¦≈\ *vt* [*out-* + *strip*] **1 :** to go faster than ⟨a speed far *outstripping* the fastest rocket plane —R.M.Sutton⟩ **2 a :** to leave behind **:** go ahead of **:** EXCEL, SURPASS ⟨in certain countries knowledge had far *outstripped* wisdom —A.L. Guérard⟩ ⟨the central nervous system . . . has *outstripped* all else —Waldemar Kaempffert⟩ **b :** to exceed in quantity or number ⟨fall into ever greater destitution as their numbers ~ their resources —Barbara Ward⟩ ⟨the demand for mortgage money *outstripped* savings —L.H.Olsen⟩ **syn** see EXCEED

outstroke \ˈ≈,≈\ *n* [³*out* + *stroke*] **:** an outward stroke; *specif* **:** a stroke in which the piston in a steam or other engine is moving toward the crankshaft — opposed to *instroke*

outsucken \(ˈ)≈¦≈≈\ *adj* [⁴*out* + *sucken* (n.)] *Scots law* **:** not astricted to a particular mill for the grinding of corn — compare THIRLAGE

outsurge \ˈ≈,≈\ *n* [³*out* + *surge*] **:** an outward surge ⟨other ~*s* of steppe peoples went into Europe —J.R.Smith⟩

outswagger \(ˈ)≈¦≈≈\ *vt* [*out-* + *swagger*] **:** to outdo in swaggering

outswear \(ˈ)≈¦≈\ *vt* [*out-* + *swear*] **1 :** to surpass in swearing ⟨can ~ a trooper⟩ **2 :** to get the better of by swearing ⟨we'll outface them and ~ them too —Shak.⟩

outsweep \(ˈ)≈¦≈\ *vi* [¹*out* + *sweep*] **:** to sweep out ⟨a dress with an ~*ing* skirt⟩

outsweepings \ˈ≈,≈≈\ *n pl* [³*out* + *sweepings*, pl. of *sweeping*, gerund of *sweep* (after *sweep out*, v.)] **:** REFUSE

outsweeten \(ˈ)≈¦≈≈\ *vt* [*out-* + *sweeten*] **:** to surpass in sweetness ⟨~ honey —Robert Browning⟩

outswell \(ˈ)≈¦≈\ *vt* [*out-* + *swell*] **:** to exceed in swelling

outswinger \ˈ≈,≈≈\ *n* [³*out* + *swinger* (after *swing out*, v.)] **:** a bowled cricket ball that swerves in the air from leg to off — compare INSWINGER

outtake \ˈ≈,≈\ *n* [³*out* + *take* (after *take out*, v.)] **1 :** a passage outwards **:** FLUE, VENT ⟨the ~ is at the top of the windows —J.E.Rice & H.E.Botsford⟩ **2 :** a discarded film take ⟨from the ~*s* we made a 100-ft. sound-on-film trailer —A.H.Smith⟩

outtaken \(ˈ)≈¦≈≈\ *prep* [ME, fr. ¹*out* + *taken*, past part. of *taken* to take (after *taken out* to take out) — more at TAKE] *archaic* **:** EXCEPT

outtalk \(ˈ)≈¦≈\ *vt* [*out-* + *talk*] **1 :** to surpass in talking ⟨could outwork and ~ them all —Catherine D. Bowen⟩ **2 :** to get the better of by talking ⟨don't let those swabs ~ you —Kenneth Roberts⟩

outtell \(ˈ)≈¦≈\ *vt* [¹*out* + *tell*] **1 :** to speak out **:** declare openly ⟨all *outtold* their fond imaginations —John Keats⟩ **2 :** to tell completely **3** [*out-* + *tell*] **:** to have more telling effect than ⟨the mere quotation . . . ~*s* all commentary —H. B.Alexander⟩

outthink \(ˈ)≈¦≈\ *vt* [*out-* + *think*] **1 :** to surpass in thinking **:** to go beyond or transcend by thinking ⟨must ~ the world if they are to outlive it —*Religion in Life*⟩ **2 :** to get the better of by thinking more quickly or adroitly **:** OUTWIT ⟨strives to ~ the buyer rather than to outtalk him —*Concrete Products*⟩

¹**outthrow** \(ˈ)≈¦≈\ *vt* [ME *outthrowen*, fr. ¹*out* + *throwen* to throw — more at THROW] **1 :** to throw out ⟨the sheriff grasped one of the *outthrown* arms —Ambrose Bierce⟩ **2** [*out-* + *throw*] **:** to surpass in the length and accuracy of a throw ⟨can ~ any outfielder in the major leagues⟩

²**outthrow** \ˈ≈,≈\ *n* [³*out* + *throw* (after *throw out*, v.)] **1 a :** a throwing out **:** OUTBURST ⟨a creative ~ that lasted only a few years⟩ **b :** the act or process of throwing soil away from the crop by the cultivating gangs of a row-crop cultivator; *also* **:** the amount of soil thrown out **2 :** a waste material (as a rag or piece of paper) so made or treated as to be unsuitable for recovery of fibers — usu. used in pl.

¹**outthrust** \(ˈ)≈¦≈\ *vb* [ME *outthresten*, fr. ¹*out* + *thresten* to thrust — more at THRUST] *vt* **:** to thrust out **~** *vi* **:** to thrust out ⟨the deep roots, ~*ing* far below the plowshare's reach —George Woodbury⟩

²**outthrust** \ˈ≈,≈\ *n* [³*out* + *thrust* (after *thrust out*, v.)] **1 :** a thrusting out **:** an outward pressure **2 :** something that is thrust out **:** PROJECTION ⟨below it was no firm ~ of the mountainside, but eight thousand feet of air —J.R.Ullman⟩

³**outthrust** \ˈ≈¦≈\ *adj* [¹*out* + *thrust*, past part. of *thrust* (after *thrust out*)] **:** thrust out **:** EXTENDED ⟨an ~ jaw⟩ ⟨an ~ hand⟩

outthunder \(ˈ)≈¦≈≈\ *vt* [*out-* + *thunder*] **1 :** to outdo in thundering ⟨in the storm he must ~ the thunder —John Mason Brown⟩ **2 :** to make more noise than **:** overpower in sound ⟨the main thought is ~*ed* by the overtones —J.P. Bishop⟩

outtire \(ˈ)≈¦≈\ *vt* [*out-* + *tire*] **:** to tire out ⟨would ~ ten horses in a tilting-match —C.E.Robinson⟩

outtongue \(ˈ)≈¦≈\ *vt* [*out-* + *tongue*] **:** to exceed in eloquence ⟨my services . . . shall ~ his complaints —Shak.⟩

out-to-out \ˌ≈≈ˈ≈\ *adj* **:** measured from outer edge to outer edge

outtop \(ˈ)≈¦≈\ *vt* [*out-* + *top*] **:** to surpass in height **:** SURMOUNT ⟨far *outtopping* all the other trees of the forest —J.G. Frazer⟩ ⟨~*s* all other composers of the century⟩

outtower \(ˈ)≈¦≈≈\ *vt* [*out-* + *tower*] **:** to tower above **:** surpass in dignity or worth ⟨a moral universe ~*ing* time and passion —H.B.Alexander⟩ ⟨no small man, but ~*ed* by his companion —*Bookman*⟩

outtrade \(ˈ)≈¦≈\ *vt* [*out-* + *trade*] *vt* **:** to get the better of in a trade ⟨if they tried to ~ him, they'd find their pockets full of bad bills of credit —Kenneth Roberts⟩

outtravel \(ˈ)≈¦≈≈\ *vt* [*out-* + *travel*] **1 :** to travel beyond ⟨~ the boundaries of space⟩ **2 :** to travel faster than ⟨~ the news of his coming⟩

out-tray \ˈ≈,≈\ *n* [³*out* + *tray*] **:** a shallow wood or metal basket usu. on a desk for holding outgoing material (as letters to be posted or memoranda) — distinguished from *in-tray*

outtrick \(ˈ)≈¦≈\ *vt* [*out-* + *trick*] **:** to get the better of by trickery ⟨deceived and ~*ed* them⟩

outtrump \(ˈ)≈¦≈\ *vt* [*out-* + *trump*] **:** OUTMANEUVER, OUTPLAY

outturn \'ˌ=,=\ *n* [³*out* + *turn* (after *turn out*, v.)] **1 a :** an amount of something (as of a crop or manufactured item) turned out or produced **:** OUTPUT, YIELD ⟨rice was the chief crop . . . and extensive new irrigation works multiplied the ~ —J.S.Furnivall⟩ **b :** a sampling taken at a paper mill from each run on a paper machine **2 a :** the quality or condition of something turned out or produced ⟨oiling of eggs has resulted in greatly improved ~ in the export pack and winter cold storage —*Poultry Farmer (Australia)*⟩ **b :** the condition in which a shipment arrives at its destination ⟨inaugurated special methods of stowing turpentine barrels, in ships bound on long voyages, in order to assure better ~*s* —*Chem. Markets*⟩

out–turn \'=,=\ *n* [³*out* + *turn* (after *turn out*, v.)] **:** a moving curling stone which is rotating counterclockwise — compare IN-TURN

outvalue \(')=¦=(,)=\ *vt* [*out-* + *value*] **:** to be worth more than ⟨the talk ~*s* many a novel —Thomas Wood †1950⟩

outvie \(')=¦=\ *vt* [*out-* + *vie*] **:** to surpass in a rivalry or competition ⟨*outvying* each other in courtesy⟩

outvote \(')=¦=\ *vt* [*out-* + *vote*] **1 :** to cast more votes than **:** defeat by a majority of votes ⟨these two groups can combine to ~ the other members of the board⟩ ⟨the outstate districts can ~ the city⟩ **2 :** to defeat in a contest or on an issue decided by votes ⟨the cabinet must resign if it is *outvoted* —John Gunther⟩

outwait \(')=¦=\ *vt* [*out-* + *wait*] **:** to remain waiting longer than

outwake \(')=¦=\ *vt* [*out-* + *wake*] **:** to remain awake longer than **:** OUTWATCH

out·wale \'=,wāl\ *n* [³*out* + gun*wale*] **:** the outside piece of a gunwale (as of a canoe)

outwalk \(')=¦=\ *vt* [*out-* + *walk*] **1 :** to outdo in walking ⟨could ~ those not nearly so old as he was —John Mason Brown⟩ **2 :** to walk past or beyond ⟨~*ed* the furthest city light —Robert Frost⟩

outwall \'=,=\ *n* [³*out* + *wall*] **1** *archaic* **:** an outer wall or other enclosure **2** *obs* **:** the outer enclosure of a human being (as clothing or the body) ⟨I am much more than my ~ —Shak.⟩

outwander \(')=¦==\ *vi* [¹*out* + *wander*] **:** to wander out or away ⟨there is little ~*ing* or outgrowth from the tissues —*Science*⟩

¹**out·ward** \'au̇twə(r)d\ *adj* [ME, fr. OE *ūtanweard, ūteweard, ūtweard*, fr. *ūtan* outside, from outside (fr. *ūt* out), *ūte* out, outside (fr. *ūt* out), & *ūt* out + *-weard* -ward — more at OUT] **1 a :** moving, directed, or turned toward the outside or away from a center ⟨the inward or ~ flow of money —*Jour. of Accountancy*⟩ ⟨the gradual ~ slope of the spur ridges —C.B. Hitchcock⟩ ⟨an ~ journey⟩ **b :** of or relating to a movement toward the outside ⟨the cost of returning a parcel includes postage, generally equivalent to the ~ charge —*Great Britain Post Office Guide*⟩ **2 :** situated or lying on the outside of an enclosure or surface **:** EXTERIOR ⟨found the place where I was to lie . . . close and confined . . . and therefore lay all night in an ~ room —Tobias Smollett⟩ **3 :** of or relating to the body and its surface appearance and clothing as opposed to the mind or spirit **:** BODILY, EXTERNAL ⟨~ man⟩ ⟨~ beauty⟩ ⟨~ form⟩ **4 a :** of or relating to an external act, activity, happening, or condition as distinguished from a mental or emotional process ⟨the chief ~ events of his life⟩ ⟨the new job represented a great improvement in his ~ status⟩ ⟨a feverish ~ display of energy⟩ **b :** of or relating to material objects as opposed to ideal concepts ⟨we alone wore ~ shackles —Mary Johnston⟩ **c :** of or relating to form as distinguished from essence ⟨began to find a recognized place in the ~ pattern of church life —*Eastern Churches Quarterly*⟩ **5** *dial Eng* **:** inclined to drink **:** DISSIPATED **syn** see OUTER

²**outward** \"\ *or* **out·wards** \-dz\ *adv* [*outward* fr. ME, fr. OE *ūtanweard, ūteweard, ūtweard*, fr. *ūtanweard, ūteweard, ūtweard*, adj.; *outwards* fr. ME *outwardes*, fr. OE *ūtweardes*, fr. *ūtweard*, adj. & adv. + *-es* -s] **1 a :** toward the outside **:** away from a center or starting point ⟨the eternally ~ moving stars —*N.Y. Times*⟩ ⟨the city stretches ~ for many miles⟩ **b :** from the soul or mind toward external manifestation **2** *obs* **:** on the outside **:** EXTERNALLY ⟨they have a good cover, they show well ~ —Shak.⟩

³**out·ward** \'au̇twə(r)d\ *n* -s [¹*outward*] **1 :** external form or appearance **:** OUTSIDE ⟨so fair an ~ and such stuff within —Shak.⟩ **2 :** the material world ⟨can perceive the ~ and the inward, nature's good and God's —Robert Browning⟩

outward–bound \'==¦=\ *adj* **:** bound in an outward direction or to foreign parts ⟨an *outward-bound* ship⟩ — **outward-bound·er** \-də(r)\ *n*

outward–flow turbine \'==,=-\ *n* **:** a water turbine in which the discharge stage of flow is away from the axis

out·ward·ly *adv* [ME, fr. *outward*, adj. + *-ly*] **1 a :** on the outside **:** EXTERNALLY ⟨~ visible⟩ ⟨~ apparent⟩ **b :** toward the outside **:** in an outward direction ⟨we see ~ and represent the apparent nature of things —Herbert Read⟩ **2 :** in outward state, behavior, or appearance ⟨his ~ more fortunate fellows —Kenneth Fearing⟩ ⟨~ diffident, inwardly dreamy —Jean S. Untermeyer⟩ ⟨~ a placid island —Patrick Smith⟩

out·ward·ness *n* -ES **1 :** the quality or state of being outward **:** EXTERNALITY ⟨the ~ of the world⟩ **2 :** concern with or responsiveness to outward things ⟨hearty showmanship and all-around ~ —F.H.Gervasi⟩

outwash \'=,=\ *n, often attrib* [³*out* + *wash* (after *wash out*, v.)] **1 a :** detritus chiefly consisting of gravel and sand carried by running water from the melting ice of a glacier and laid down in stratified deposits **:** glaciofluvial drift **b :** meltwater from a glacier **2 :** soil material washed down a hillside by rainwater and spread upon the more gently sloping adjacent land

outwash cone *or* **outwash fan** *n* **:** a cone-shaped or fanlike mass of outwash that is ordinarily found at the margin of a dwindling glacier or shrinking ice sheet

outwash plain *also* **outwash apron** *n* **:** a plain constructed of outwash that is ordinarily found on and beyond the distal side of a terminal or recessional moraine and that generally consists of a number of coalescing outwash fans

outwash train *n* **:** VALLEY TRAIN

outwatch \(')=¦=\ *vt* [*out-* + *watch*] **1 :** to surpass in watching **:** maintain a longer vigil than ⟨~ his companions⟩ **2 :** to maintain a vigil till after the disappearance or end of ⟨~ the moon⟩ ⟨~ the night⟩

outwear \(')=¦=\ *vt* [¹*out* + *wear*] **1 :** to wear out or use up **:** consume or destroy by attrition or use **:** EXHAUST ⟨drops of water ~ stone⟩ ⟨the machinery has been *outworn*⟩ ⟨the rowers were *outworn*⟩ **2 a** [*out-* + *wear*] **:** to last longer in use than ⟨a fiber that ~*s* others⟩ **b :** to grow or develop beyond in course of time **:** OUTGROW, OUTLIVE ⟨in cases where tradition is notoriously *outworn* —W.C.Brownell⟩ **3** *archaic* **:** to take up the time of ⟨with sick longing all the night ~ —John Keats⟩

outweep \(')=¦=\ *vt* [¹*out* + *weep*] **1** *archaic* **:** to weep out ⟨like a cloud which had *outwept* its rain —P.B.Shelley⟩ **2** [*out-* + *weep*] **:** to surpass in weeping ⟨can ~ any woman⟩

outweigh \(')=¦=\ *vt* [*out-* + *weigh*] **:** to exceed in weight, value, or importance ⟨an ounce of custom ~*s* a ton of reason —William Hamilton †1856⟩ ⟨no dangers could ~ the advantages of steamboat transportation —*Amer. Guide Series: Ark.*⟩

outwell \(')=¦=\ *vb* [¹*out* + *well*] *vt, obs* **:** to pour out ~ *vi* **:** to well out

outwent *past of* OUTGO

¹**outwick** \'=,=\ *n* [³*out* + *wick*] **:** a shot in curling in which a player's stone is made to hit the outer edge of another stone so as to drive the latter toward the tee — compare INWICK

²**outwick** \"\ *vi* **:** to make an outwick

outwind \'=,=\ *n* [³*out* + *wind*] **:** a wind from the sea

²**outwind** \(')=¦=\ *vt* [¹*out* + *wind*] **:** to put out of breath ⟨an ~*ed* runner⟩

outwing \(')=¦=\ *vt* [*out-* + *wing*] **1 :** to outstrip or pass in flying **2 :** OUTFLANK

outwinter \(')=¦==\ *vb* [¹*out* + *winter*] *vt* **:** to keep (cattle) outdoors in winter ⟨the cost of feeding ~*ed* cattle —T.H. Jackson⟩ ~ *vi* **:** to stay outdoors in winter ⟨the Jersey can ~ provided the climate is not very damp —F.D.Smith & Barbara Wilcox⟩

outwit \(')=¦=\ *vt* [*out-* + *wit*] **1 :** to defeat or get the better of by superior cleverness or ingenuity **:** OVERREACH ⟨how best to ~ the youngster and set him to learning when he is not fully aware of it —G.N.Shuster⟩ ⟨three men, caught *outwitting* an innocent pinball machine with a powerful magnet —*Phoenix Flame*⟩ **2** *archaic* **:** to surpass in wisdom ⟨outsee seers and ~ sages —R.W.Emerson⟩ **syn** see FRUSTRATE

outwith \'=¦=\ *prep* [ME, fr. ¹*out* + *with*] **1** *chiefly Scot* **:** outside of **:** out of **2** *chiefly Scot* **:** EXCEPT

outwore *past of* OUTWEAR

¹**outwork** \(')=¦=\ *vt* [¹*out* + *work*] **1 :** to work out **:** COMPLETE ⟨saw, in web unbroken, its history *outwrought* —Thomas Hardy⟩ **2** [*out-* + *work*] *archaic* **:** to surpass in workmanship **3** [*out-* + *work*] **:** to outdo in working **:** work harder or faster than ⟨~*s* his competitors⟩

²**outwork** \'=,=\ *n* [³*out* + *work*] **1 a :** an outlying point of defense ⟨had been forced to abandon her ~*s* across the Rhine and the Danube —Richard Koebner⟩ ⟨impairs not only the ~*s* but the citadel of personality —Walter Moberly⟩ **b :** a small defensive position constructed outside a fortified area **2 :** work done outside the shop or institution from which it is directed or for which it is performed

outworker \'=,==\ *n* [³*out* + *worker*] **:** one that works outside the institution or shop by which he is employed

outworld \'=,=\ *n* [³*out* + *world*] **:** the outside world

outworn \'=¦=\ *adj* [fr. past part. of *outwear*] **1 :** no longer useful or accepted **:** OUTMODED, OBSOLETE ⟨still attempted to cling to the ~ ethics professed at the dawning of the Gilded Age —J.D.Hart⟩ ⟨an ~ road⟩ **2 :** worn out **:** used up **:** EXHAUSTED ⟨an ~ champion pugilist —Stanley Walker⟩

outwrestle \(')=¦==\ *vt* [*out-* + *wrestle*] **:** to defeat in wrestling **:** grapple with successfully

outwrite \(')=¦=\ *vt* [*out-* + *write*] **1 :** to surpass in ability to write ⟨historian for historian, journalist for journalist, they ~ us —R.H.Rovere⟩ **2** [¹*out* + *write*] **:** to throw off or overcome by writing ⟨*outwrote* his depression⟩

outwrought *past of* OUTWORK

outyell \(')=¦=\ *vt* [*out-* + *yell*] **:** to yell louder than ⟨women quarreling and trying to ~ each other —H.L.Davis⟩

outyield \(')=¦=\ *vt* [*out-* + *yield*] **:** to surpass in yield ⟨fall-sown or winter oats matured earlier and ~*ed* spring oats —*Experiment Station Record*⟩

ouvarovite *var of* UVAROVITE

ou·vert \(')ü¦ve(ə)r\ *adj* [F, lit., open, fr. OF *overt* — more at OVERT] **1** *ballet* **:** having an open stance or movement **2** *card games* **:** OPEN 17b(2)

ou·sel *also* **ou·sel** \'üzəl\ *n* -s [ME *ousel, osel*, fr. OE *ōsle* — more at MERL] **1 :** a European blackbird (*Turdus merula*) **2 :** any of various thrushes or other birds that are related to the ouzel — see RING OUZEL, WATER OUZEL

ou·zo \'ü(,)zō\ *n* -s [NGk *ouzon*] **:** a colorless anise-flavored unsweetened Greek liqueur that turns milk-white when mixed with water and ice

ov- *or* **ovi-** *or* **ovo-** *comb form* [L *ov-, ovi-*, fr. *ovum* — more at EGG] **1 a :** egg ⟨*ov*ejector⟩ ⟨*ovi*form⟩ ⟨*ovo*mucoid⟩ **b :** ovum ⟨*ovo*cyte⟩ ⟨*ovo*genesis⟩ **2 :** ovally ⟨*ovo*-elliptic⟩

ov *abbr* ovum

OV *abbr* **1** oil of vitriol **2** over voltage

ova *pl of* OVUM

¹**oval** \'ōvəl\ *adj* [ML *ovalis*, fr. LL, of an egg, fr. L *ovum* egg + *-alis* -al] **:** having the shape of an oval **:** broadly elliptical ⟨an ~ ball⟩ — often used in combination ⟨an *oval*-faced child⟩ — **oval·ly** \-və(l)lē, -)i\ *adv*

²**oval** \"\ *n* -s **1 :** a body or figure generally in the shape of the longitudinal section of an egg **2 :** an object of oval or ellipsoidal shape: as **a :** a cartouche of an Egyptian king **b** (1) **:** a stadium, arena, or athletic field of oval shape (2) **:** RUNNING TRACK, RACETRACK

oval 1

³**oval** \"\ *vb* **ovaled** *or* **ovalled; ovaled** *or* **ovalled; ovaling** \-v(ə)liŋ\ *or* **ovalling; ovals** *vt* **:** to make oval ~ *vi* **:** to become oval

ov·albumin \(')ōv+\ *n* [*ov-* + *albumin*] **1 :** the principal albumin of white of egg; *esp* **:** the crystalline part of egg albumins — compare CONALBUMIN **2 :** EGG ALBUMIN

ova·le \ō'välē\ *adj* [NL, specific epithet of *Plasmodium ovale*, fr. ML *ovale*, neut. of *ovalis* oval] **:** of, relating to, or caused by a malarial parasite (*Plasmodium ovale*)

oval·i·ty \ō'valədē\ *n* -ES [ISV ¹*oval* + *-ity*] **:** the quality or state of being oval in shape **:** degree of departure from true circularity ⟨~ of a worn gun bore⟩

oval·ness \'ōvəlnəs\ *n* -ES **:** OVALITY

ovalo·cyte \ō'valə,sīt, 'ōvəlō,s-\ *n* -s [ISV ¹*oval* + *-o-* + *-cyte*] **:** an oval red blood cell normal in the camel and occurring as a rare hereditary anomaly in man — **ovalo·cyt·ic** \=¦==¦sid·ik, ¦==-\ *adj*

ovalo·cy·to·sis \=,==,sī'tōsəs, ,==(,)=-\ *n, pl* **ovalocyto·ses** \-ō,sēz\ [NL, fr. ISV *ovalocyte* + NL *-osis*] **:** a hereditary trait in man manifested by the presence in the blood of red blood cells which are oval in shape with rounded ends — compare SICKLE-CELL TRAIT

oval·oid \'ōvə,lȯid\ *adj* [²*oval* + *-oid*] **:** approximately oval

oval window *n* [trans. of NL *fenestra ovalis*] **:** the oval fenestra of the ear

ovari- *or* **ovario-** *also* **ovar-** *comb form* [NL, fr. *ovarium*] **1 :** ovary ⟨*ovar*itis⟩ ⟨*ovari*ectomy⟩ ⟨*ovario*tomy⟩ **2 :** ovarian and ⟨*ovario*-abdominal⟩

ovar·i·al \(')ō¦va(a)rēəl, -ver-,-vär-\ *adj* [prob. fr. (assumed) NL *ovarialis*, fr. NL *ovari-* + L *-alis* -al] **:** of, involving, or affecting an ovary ⟨~ function⟩ ⟨~ poisons⟩

ovar·i·an \-ēən\ *adj* [prob. fr. (assumed) NL *ovarianus*, fr. NL *ovari-* + L *-anus* -an] **:** of or relating to an ovary

ovari·ec·to·mize \(,)ō,va(a)rē'ektə,mīz, ,ovər-\ *vt* -ED/-ING/-s [*ovariectomy* + *-ize*] **:** to remove an ovary surgically from

ovari·ec·to·my \-,mē\ *n* -ES [NL *ovariectomia*, fr. *ovari-* + *-ectomia* -ectomy] **:** the surgical removal of an ovary

ovar·i·ole \ō'va(a)rē,ōl\ *n* -s [*ovari-* + *-ole*] **:** one of the tubes of which the ovaries of most insects are composed

ovar·io·testis \ō¦va(a)rēō+\ *n* [NL, fr. *ovari-* + L *testis*] **:** OVOTESTIS

ovar·i·ot·o·my \(,)ō,va(a)rē'äd·əmē\ *n* -ES [NL *ovariotomia*, fr. *ovari-* + *-tomia* -tomy] **1 :** surgical incision of an ovary **2 :** OVARIECTOMY

ova·ri·tis \,ōvə'rīd·əs\ *n, pl* **ova·rit·i·des** \-rid·ə,dēz\ [NL, fr. *ovari-* + *-itis*] **:** inflammation of an ovary **:** OOPHORITIS

ovar·i·um \ō'va(a)rēəm\ *n, pl* **ovar·ia** \-ēə\ [NL] *archaic* **:** OVARY

ova·ry \'ōv(ə)rē, -ri\ *n* -ES [NL *ovarium*, fr. L *ovum* egg + *-arium* -ary — more at EGG] **1 :** the typically paired essential female reproductive organ that produces eggs and in vertebrates female sex hormones, that occurs in the adult human as an oval flattened body about one inch and one half long suspended from the dorsal surface of the broad ligament of either side, that arises from the Wolffian body, and that consists of a vascular fibrous stroma enclosing developing egg cells which in their later stages with nutricial structures constitute Graafian follicles **2 :** the enlarged rounded usu. basal portion of the pistil or gynoecium of an angiospermous plant that bears the ovules and consists of a single carpel or of several united carpels — see FLOWER illustration

¹**ovate** \'ō,vāt, 'ävət\ *n* -s [modif. of Gk *ouateis*, pl., members of one of three classes of Gaulish bards, prob. of Celt origin; akin to OIr *fáith* seer, poet — more at VATIC] **:** one of a class of bards in Wales graduated in bardic lore and approved by a session of bards

²**ovate** \'ō,vāt, *usu* -ād·+V\ *adj* [L *ovatus*, fr. *ovum* egg + *-atus* -ate] **1 :** shaped like an egg **:** OVAL — often used in combination ⟨*ovate*-oblong⟩ ⟨*ovate*-deltoid⟩ **2 :** having an outline like that of the longitudinal section of an egg with the basal end broader ⟨~ leaves⟩ — see LEAF illustration

¹**ova·tion** \ō'vāshən\ *n* -s [L *ovation-, ovatio*, fr. *ovatus* (past part. of *ovare* to exult, rejoice) + *-ion-, -io* -ion; akin to Gk *euazein* to shout for joy, *euoi*, interjection used in Dionysiac celebrations] **1 :** a ceremony attending the entering of Rome by a general who had won a victory of less importance than that for which a triumph was granted **2** *archaic* **:** EXULTATION **3 :** enthusiastic popular homage or a public expression of it **:** an enthusiastic popular reception or tribute ⟨received an ~ as he entered the hall⟩

²**ovation** \"\ *vt* -ED/-ING/-s **:** to give an ovation ⟨will all be there . . . to ~ you —Barnaby Conrad⟩

ova·tion·al \ō'vāshənᵊl, -shnəl\ *adj* **:** of or relating to an ovation

ovc *abbr* overcast

ov·ejec·tor *also* **ovi·jec·tor** \'ōvə,jektə(r), -vē,j-\ *n* -s [ISV *ov-* + *ejector*; orig. formed as F *ovéjecteur*] **:** the terminal highly muscular part of the oviduct of many nematode worms that forces the egg through the genital pore — **ovejectoral** *adj*

ov·en \'əvən *sometimes* 'əᵛm *or* 'əbᵊm\ *n* -s [ME, fr. OE *ofen*; akin to OHG *ofan* oven, ON *ofn*, Goth *auhns* oven, L *aulla* pot, Gk *ipnos* oven, Skt *ukha* cooking pot] **1** *obs* **:** FURNACE **2 a :** a chamber of brick or stonework used for baking, heating, or drying **b :** a heated enclosure of varying construction used for such purposes: as (1) **:** a chamber in a stove used for baking or roasting (2) **:** a laboratory hot-air sterilizer

ovenbird \'==,=\ *n* [*oven* + *bird*; fr. the shape of their nests] **1 :** any of various S. American passerine birds of the genus *Furnarius* **2 :** an American warbler (*Seiurus aurocapillus*) having olivaceous upper parts with a yellowish brown black-bordered crown, white underparts streaked with black and building a dome-shaped nest placed on the ground

oven dressed *adj* **:** ready for cooking **:** FULL-DRESSED ⟨*oven dressed* poultry⟩

ovendry \'==¦=\ *adj* [*oven* + *dry*, adj.] **:** dried at a temperature at or above that of boiling water (usu. 100 to 110°C or 212 to 230°F)

oven–dry \'==¦=\ *vt* [*oven* + *dry*, v.] **:** to dry in an oven

ovenman \'==,man\ *n, pl* **ovenmen 1 :** a baker who tends an oven **2 :** a worker who bakes parts or products in an oven to harden and strengthen them or to harden their finish

ovenware \'==,=\ *n* **:** dishes used for baking and serving food

oven wood *n* **:** BRUSHWOOD

¹**over** \'ōvə(r)\ *adv* [ME, adv. & prep., fr. OE *ofer*; akin to OHG *ubari, ubiri*, adv., over, *ubar*, prep., over, ON *yfir*, adv. & prep., Goth *ufar*, prep., over, L *super*, adv. & prep., over, Gk *hyper*, adv. & prep., Skt *upari*, adv. & prep., over, OE *ufan* above] **1 a** (1) **:** from one point to another across an intervening space or barrier ⟨sail ~ to England⟩ ⟨throw the ball ~⟩ ⟨galloped ~ to the scene —H.E.Scudder⟩ ⟨the major called the three ~ —C. G. De Van⟩ (2) **:** so as to pass down or forward and down ⟨went too near the edge and fell ~⟩ (3) **:** from inside to outside across the brim ⟨the soup boiled ~⟩ (4) **:** so as to bring the underside to or toward the top ⟨turned himself ~⟩ ⟨roll a stone ~⟩ ⟨turn the page ~⟩ (5) **:** in the opposite direction ⟨gave the order to put the helm ~ —A. A. & Mary Hoehling⟩ (6) **:** over the side of a ship ⟨put a boat ~ to come and look for you —R.F.Mirvish⟩ ⟨put the ladder ~ —Vincent McHugh⟩ (7) **:** from side to side **:** in diameter **:** ACROSS ⟨the mouth of the cave was about 12 feet ~⟩ (8) **:** so as to pass over a target and beyond ⟨the bullets fell short or went ~⟩ (9) **:** away from a vertical to a prone or inclined position ⟨knocked the boy ~⟩ ⟨the wall fell ~⟩ ⟨the ship heeled ~⟩ (10) **:** to one's home ⟨inviting fifteen or twenty of her friends ~ for fun and games —*N.Y.Times*⟩ **b** (1) **:** on the other side of an intervening space ⟨is ~ in England⟩ (2) **:** at some distance from a particular point **:** AWAY ⟨a fellow a couple of counties ~ —Brad Sebstad⟩ ⟨from two blocks ~ he could hear the thin wail —H.M.Brier⟩ ⟨the bomb hit the next pier ~ —R.O.Bowen⟩ **c** (1) **:** so as to pass or transfer from one person, side, activity, or opinion to another ⟨hand ~ the money⟩ ⟨theater orchestras . . . had gone ~ completely to it —*Amer. Guide Series: Wash.*⟩ ⟨endorsed it ~ to the . . . Housing Corporation —Warner Olivier⟩ ⟨turned it ~ to her daughter —*Amer. Guide Series: Ark.*⟩ ⟨went ~ to the opposition⟩ (2) **:** so as to achieve understanding, acceptance, support, or other desired effect — usu. used with *get* ⟨are not getting ~ to those whom we are addressing —A.T.Weaver⟩ ⟨get your effect and your meaning ~ to the orchestra —Warwick Braithwaite⟩ ⟨wants to get his own message ~ —W.F.Hambly⟩ (3) **:** into one's own possession **:** so as to be in control ⟨the university took it ~ —*Amer. Guide Series: Md.*⟩ ⟨took ~ after a revolt⟩ ⟨took ~ from a firm that had gone into liquidation —*Irish Digest*⟩ — compare TAKE OVER **d :** ASIDE ⟨throwing ~ traditional morality⟩ **2 a :** beyond, above, or in excess of some quantity or limit ⟨boys of twelve and ~⟩ **b** (1) **:** in or to excess **:** beyond the norm ⟨she was ~ canvassed —Peter Heaton⟩ ⟨they were seven minutes ~ —Goodman Ace⟩ (2) **:** INORDINATELY, EXCESSIVELY — often used in combination ⟨on his guard against *over*quick deductions —A.E.Duncan-Jones⟩ ⟨just naturally *over*registers emotion —*Current Biog.*⟩ ⟨*over*-conservative traditionalists —John Arlott⟩ **c :** till a later time ⟨leave this new inquiry ~ till Monday —F.W.Crofts⟩ ⟨so glad you can stay ~⟩ **3 a :** ABOVE ⟨the plane was directly ~⟩ **b :** so as to cover, conceal, or affect the whole surface or expanse ⟨the original logs were boarded ~ —*Amer. Guide Series: Ark.*⟩ **4 a :** at an end — often used in the phrase *over with* ⟨hurrying to get the business ~ with⟩ **b** — used on a two-way radio circuit to indicate that a particular sentence or message is complete and that a reply is expected **5 a** (1) **:** from beginning to end **:** THROUGH ⟨read it ~ and let me know what you think⟩ (2) **:** in an intensive or comprehensive manner **:** THOROUGHLY ⟨the issue is worked ~ in the most . . . compelling scene of the play —Leslie Rees⟩ ⟨talk the matter ~⟩ **b** (1) **:** for a second or successive time **:** once more **:** AGAIN ⟨this work will have to be done ~⟩ ⟨read the difficult passage twice ~⟩ — often used in the phrase *over again* ⟨asked to recite the verse ~ again⟩ (2) **:** so as to be transformed or changed from a previous state or condition ⟨a man cannot make himself ~⟩

²**over** \"\ *prep* [ME, adv. & prep., fr. OE *ofer* — more at ¹OVER] **1 a** (1) — used as a function word to indicate position higher up than and usu. directly above another object ⟨~ the elm tops in the west —Lucien Price⟩ ⟨towered ~ his diminutive mother⟩ ⟨leaned ~ the rampart⟩ (2) — used as a function word to indicate a surrounding condition or threatening prospect ⟨an atmosphere of doubt and uncertainty hung ~ the town⟩ (3) — used as a function word to indicate that the author's name is subscribed to a writing ⟨sent a letter to the paper ~ his own signature⟩ (4) **:** above the mental capacity or beyond the comprehension of — usu. used in the phrase *over the head of* ⟨his lecture was way ~ the heads of his audience⟩ **b** (1) — used as a function word to indicate submersion above a specified level ⟨~ his waist in water⟩ (2) — used as a function word to indicate extreme or acute embarrassment or difficulty of a specified kind ⟨~ head and ears in debt⟩ **2 a** — used as a function word to indicate the possession or enjoyment of authority, power, or jurisdiction in regard to some thing or person ⟨installed as minister ~ one of the largest congregations in the city⟩ ⟨unfailing in their service of those ~ them —E.R.Hughes⟩ **b** — used as a function word to indicate a relation of superiority, advantage, or preference to another ⟨the relative importance of the abstract ~ the pictorial —C.J. Bulliet⟩ ⟨taking an unprecedented lead ~ the other teams —*Current Biog.*⟩ ⟨this excess of wealth ~ population —W.P. Webb⟩; often used in the phrase *have it over* or *have it all over* ⟨the Britisher in America has it ~ the anthropologist —V.O. Key⟩ **c** — used as a function word to indicate suppression of or release from a passion, infatuation, or other strong feeling ⟨finally got ~ his mad⟩ ⟨never got ~ his love for the baroque —*Current Biog.*⟩ **d** — used as a function word to indicate someone or something that is overcome, circumvented, or disregarded in achieving an objective ⟨we'll go ~ him —Adrian Bell⟩ ⟨passed ~ the president's veto —*Current Biog.*⟩ **3 a** *archaic* **:** further than **:** BESIDES **b :** more than ⟨cost ~ five dollars⟩ **4 a** (1) **:** upon or down upon so as to rest, cover, or conceal from view ⟨~ which they throw a bridge of flowers —*Amer. Guide Series: La.*⟩ ⟨laid a blanket ~ the sleeping child⟩ ⟨a cap pulled low ~ his eyes⟩ ⟨got some blood ~ your face —Burt Arthur⟩ (2) **:** upon or down upon so as to change or otherwise influence in a pervasive manner ⟨don't know what has come ~ the girl⟩ (3) **:** ON, UPON ⟨bop people ~ the head —Bennett Cerf⟩ ⟨rap a child ~ the knuckles⟩ (4) — used as a function word to indicate change, variation, or difference from some other thing or period ⟨this year's copy contains no innovations ~ those in the past —*Springfield (Mass.) Daily News*⟩ ⟨a drop of three ~ 1956 —*Springfield (Mass.) Daily News*⟩ **b** (1) **:** at or to all the parts of the surface of **:** throughout a specified area ⟨the common toad is found ~ the entire state —*Amer. Guide Series: Minn.*⟩ ⟨packing and shipping concerns who sell the U.S. ~ —*Spokane (Wash.) Spokesman-Rev.*⟩ — often used with intensive *all* ⟨the rumor is all ~ Washington —*New Republic*⟩ ⟨votive chapels sprang up in his honor

all ~ Italy —Norman Douglas⟩ (2) **:** along the length of ⟨~ stony roads that soon wear out the lorries —Michael Barbour⟩ ⟨~ its one-way street system move only the most modern cars —C.B.Hitchcock⟩ (3) — used as a function word to indicate a particular medium or channel of communication ⟨hear one another ~ the air —G.W.Chapman⟩ ⟨spoke to me ~ the telephone⟩ ⟨gave several recitals ~ the . . . network —*Current Biog.*⟩ **c** (1) **:** through every part of **:** all through ⟨the present comtesse . . . showed me ~ it —Ralph Hammond-Innes⟩ (2) — used as a function word to indicate study, review, or examination of something ⟨went ~ his notes in preparation for the quiz⟩ ⟨go ~ the case with the defense attorney⟩ **5 a** — used as a function word to indicate motion that passes above something on the way to the other side or to a place beyond ⟨does a series of tumbles ~ rocky ledges —Y.E.Soderberg⟩ ⟨climb ~ a mountain⟩ ⟨fly ~ a lake⟩ ⟨attack ~ a frontier⟩ ⟨put a boat ~ a ship's side⟩ **b** — used as a function word to indicate position on the other side or beyond ⟨lives in a little shop ~ the way —H.V.Morton⟩ **6 a :** THROUGHOUT, DURING ⟨many times prime minister of his country ~ the past 25 years —Geoffrey Godsell⟩ ⟨lost the use of their eyes through living underground ~ many generations —S.F.Mason⟩ ⟨had written it nights and ~ weekends —*Current Biog.*⟩ **b :** until the end of **:** for a period including ⟨invited us to stay ~ Sunday⟩ ⟨stationed in an isolated post ~ winter⟩ **7 a** — used as a function word to indicate an object of solicitude, interest, consideration, or reference ⟨the Lord watches ~ his own⟩ ⟨laughed ~ my misadventures⟩ ⟨his curiosity ~ the materials and tools —C.D.Gaitskell⟩ ⟨gives way to an intolerable degree of sentimentality ~ some of his women —C.H.Sykes⟩ ⟨am with you ~ this⟩ **b** — used as a function word often with an accompanying concrete word to indicate occupation or activity ⟨spent an hour ~ cards⟩ ⟨deciding to wait ~ a beer —Ralph Ellison⟩ ⟨enjoy an evening with me ~ a bite to eat —Frank O'Leary⟩ **c :** on account of ⟨embittered ~ this fate —L.S.Thompson⟩ ⟨got himself into disgrace ~ some caricatures of military personages —*Times Lit. Supp.*⟩ **8** *card games* **:** next in turn to play after ⟨another card player⟩ — **over a barrel** *adv* **:** at the mercy of one's opponents **:** in a helpless condition ⟨had him *over a barrel*⟩

[3]**over** \"\ *adj* [ME, alter. (influenced by [1]*over*) of *uvere*, fr. OE *uferra*, compar. of *ofer*, adv. — more at [1]OVER] **1 a :** UPPER, HIGHER, SUPERIOR **b :** COVERING, OUTER **c :** EXCESSIVE ⟨too hasty interpretations and ~ imagination —W.E.Swinton⟩ — often used in combination ⟨*over*activity is not recommended for the patient⟩ **2 a :** REMAINING ⟨that didn't leave me much ~ —Albert Halper⟩ ⟨something ~ to provide for unusual requirements —J.A.Todd⟩ **b :** having an excess or surplus ⟨the cash is said to be ~ —*Twentieth Century Bookkeeping & Accounting*⟩ **3 :** fried on both sides ⟨ordered two eggs ~⟩

[4]**over** \"\ *vt* -ED/-ING/-S [[1]*over*] **1** *dial* **:** to get over **:** recover from ⟨whether you ~*ed* a snakebite or not —Conrad Richter⟩ **2** *dial Eng* **:** to bring to an end **:** FINISH **3 :** to leap over **:** CLEAR ⟨~*ed* a stile —A.T.Quiller-Couch⟩ **4** *dial Eng* **:** to be over with ⟨the Sabbath not yet ~*ed* —Charlotte Brontë⟩

[5]**over** *n* -S [[1]*over*] **1** [so called fr. the umpire's cry of "*over*" to declare all play for that series at an end] **:** a series of 6 or 8 cricket balls bowled consecutively by one bowler from one end of the wicket **2 overs** *pl, Brit* **:** extra sheets of paper in a ream to allow for spoilage in printing **3 overs** *pl* **:** LUMBERMEN'S OVERS **4 overs** *pl* **:** material that does not pass through any given screen in the milling process **5 :** a shot which strikes or bursts beyond the target

overabound \¦≈≈¦≈\ *vi* [ME *over abounden*, fr. [1]*over* + *abounden* to abound] **:** to abound too much **:** be too abundant

overabundance \¦≈≈¦≈≈\ *n* [ME, fr. [3]*over* + *abundance*, *abundaunce* abundance] **:** an excessive abundance **:** SURFEIT, EXCESS, PLETHORA ⟨an ~ of experience with totalitarian governments —John Dean⟩

overabundant \¦≈≈¦≈≈\ *adj* [[1]*over* + *abundant*] **:** surpassingly abundant

overaccumulation \¦≈≈,≈¦≈≈\ *n* **:** an undue or excessive accumulation

overact \¦≈¦≈\ *vt* **1 :** to act or perform (as a part) to excess **:** exaggerate in acting **2** *obs* **:** to outdo in acting **3** *obs* **:** to act upon or influence unduly ~ *vi* **1 :** to act more than is necessary **:** go to excess in action ⟨which muscles of the eyes are . . . ~*ing* —H.G.Armstrong⟩ **2 :** to overact a part

overaction \¦≈¦≈\ *n* **:** excessive or abnormal action

overactive \¦≈¦≈\ *adj* **:** excessively or abnormally active ⟨an ~ mind⟩ ⟨~ glands⟩

overactivity \¦≈,≈¦≈≈\ *n* **:** excessive or abnormal activity

over against *prep* **:** as opposed to **:** in contrast with ⟨the failure of Christianity *over against* Islam in successive ages —*Brit. Book News*⟩

[1]**overage** \¦ōvə(r)¦āj\ *adj* [[2]*over* + *age*, n.] **1 :** too old or regarded as too old to be serviceable or useful ⟨~ warships⟩ ⟨an ~ stand of timber⟩ **2 :** older than is normal for one's position, function, or grade ⟨~ students⟩

[2]**over·age** \ˈōvərij\ *n* [[3]*over* + *-age*] **1 :** SURPLUS, EXCESS; *specif* **:** the amount of a product above that recorded as having been shipped or placed in storage **2 :** an excess over a required amount ⟨an ~ was disclosed⟩ — opposed to *shortage* **3 :** the quantity of a pharmaceutical included in a container in excess of the labeled amount (as in an ampul containing a liquid medication intended for injection)

[1]**over·all** \¦ōvə¦r(r)ōl\ *adv* [ME *overal*, fr. OE *ofer eall*, fr. *ofer* over + *eall* all] **1 a :** all over **:** EVERYWHERE ⟨man was ripe for civilization and erupted into it ~ —D.S.Stewart⟩ ⟨ships in the fjord were dressed ~ —*London Calling*⟩ **b :** as a whole **:** IN TOTO, GENERALLY ⟨~, the picture quality was good —Cecil McGivern⟩ ⟨~ and in most of its detail the film has remarkable power —*Time*⟩ **2 :** from one extreme point to another of anything including any projections; *specif* **:** from the extreme forward point to the extreme after point of the deck of a ship including overhangs ⟨the boat's dimensions are 34 feet ~ —*Rudder*⟩

[2]**over·all** \ˈōvə,rōl, *chiefly in substand speech* -və(r),hō- *in sense 1c*\ *n* -S [[2]*over* + *all*, pron.] **1 overalls** *pl* **a** *archaic* **:** loose trousers or leggings worn over regular clothes as a protection from bad weather or dirt **b :** close-fitting trousers worn as part of certain British uniforms or for formal riding **c :** trousers made of strong material usu. with a bib and shoulder straps and worn esp. by workmen **2** *chiefly Brit* **:** an outer garment; *esp* **:** a loose-fitting protective garment like a long coat or a smock worn over regular clothing ⟨a laboratory worker in a white ~⟩

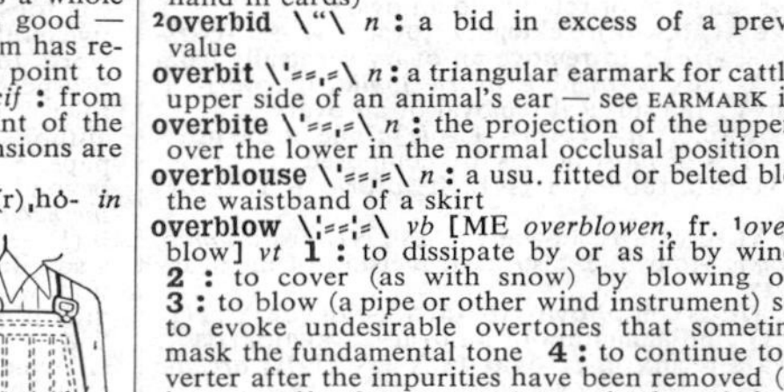
overalls 1c

[3]**over·all** \ˈōvə(r)ōl\ *adj* [[2]*over* + *all*, pron.] **1 :** including everything between the two extreme points ⟨the ~ length of a ship⟩ **2 a :** taking all units into account **:** TOTAL ⟨~ sales of wholesalers . . . increased 10% —*Americana Annual*⟩ ⟨judge what the ~ demand . . . may be —C.F. Craig⟩ ⟨~ industry growth seems well assured —*Brookmire Investment Reports*⟩ **b :** of or relating to something as a whole **:** viewed as a whole **:** GENERAL ⟨liked the ~ composition and design —Levon West⟩ ⟨the ~ picture . . . was bright —*New Englander*⟩ **:** COMPREHENSIVE ⟨an ~ view of the problem⟩ **3 :** placed over or upon other bearings and therefore hiding them in part — used of a heraldic charge

over-alled \-və,rōld, -və(r),hō-\ *adj* **:** wearing overalls ⟨~ women⟩

overall pattern *n* **:** an array of phonetic categories that is necessary and sufficient to account for all phonemes of all dialects of a language

overall watermark *n* **:** SHEET WATERMARK

overambitious \¦≈≈,≈¦≈≈\ *adj* **:** excessively ambitious ⟨a mother ~ for her precocious child⟩

over and above *prep* **:** in addition to **:** BESIDES ⟨provides a financial return *over and above* all direct and indirect costs —R.A.Tybout⟩

over and over *adv* **:** one time after another **:** REPEATEDLY

over-and-under \¦≈≈≈¦≈≈\ *n* -S **:** a 2-barreled firearm whose barrels are fixed one above the other

overanxious \¦≈≈¦≈≈\ *adj* **:** excessively or needlessly anxious

overarch \¦≈≈¦≈\ *vt* **1 :** to form an arch over ⟨dense masses ~*ing* the stream —John Muir †1914⟩ **2 :** to be central or decisive in **:** DOMINATE ⟨an utterance which ~*es* the whole conception of the play —R.O.F.Wynne⟩

overarching *adj* **1 :** forming an arch overhead ⟨the ~ sky⟩ **2 :** subordinating or encompassing all else **:** ALL-IMPORTANT, DOMINANT ⟨the relation of man's freedom to God's ~ power —Liston Pope⟩ ⟨the ~ thesis of this book⟩ ⟨the ~ fact —*Reporter*⟩ ⟨different aspects of an ~ goal —J.R.Butler⟩

[1]**overarm** \ˈ≈≈,≈\ *adj* [[3]*over* + *arm*, n.] **:** done with the arm raised above the shoulder ⟨~ pitching⟩ ⟨~ bowling⟩; *specif* **:** being a swimming stroke in which the arm is lifted out of the water and stretched forward over the shoulder to begin the stroke

[2]**overarm** \"\ *n* [[3]*over* + *arm*, n.] **:** a bar extending parallel to and above the arbor of a milling machine with attachments to provide support for the arbor

overassessment \¦≈≈≈¦≈≈\ *n* **:** the act or an instance of assessing excessively or beyond the norm; *also* **:** the condition of being so assessed

overattachment \¦≈≈¦≈≈\ *n* **:** excessive attachment

overattentive \¦≈≈≈¦≈≈\ *adj* **:** unduly or excessively attentive

overawe \¦≈≈¦≈\ *vt* **:** to make submissive or restrain by awe or fear **:** inspire awe in ⟨~ the English barbarians by his polished Norman manners —Charles Kingsley⟩

[1]**overbalance** \¦≈≈¦≈≈\ *vt* [[1]*over* + *balance*] **1 :** to exceed equality with **:** OUTWEIGH ⟨greatly ~*ed* by their concomitant advantages —T.L.Peacock⟩ **2 :** to cause to lose balance **:** put out of balance ⟨implied that it is desirable to ~ the cash budget —William Fellner⟩

[2]**overbalance** \"\ *n* **1 :** an excess of weight or value **:** something more than an equivalent ⟨an ~ of exports⟩ **2 :** the condition of being out of balance **:** lack of balance **:** INEQUILIBRIUM ⟨keep him from ~, one-sidedness —*Register*⟩

overbanking \¦≈≈¦≈≈\ *n* [[3]*over* + *banking* (gerund of [2]*bank*)] **:** a malfunction in a watch that is caused by premature unlocking of the escape wheel without contact of the fork with the roller jewel and that makes the escapement inoperative — distinguished from *rebanking*

overbear \¦≈≈¦≈\ *vt* **1 :** to bring or carry down by superior weight or force **:** OVERWHELM ⟨rushed forth and . . . *overbore* the white-headed giant —William Beebe⟩ **2 a :** to overcome or bend to one's will by force of argument, domineering manner, or other nonphysical means ⟨*overbore* her protests —Josephine Pinckney⟩ ⟨completely *overborne* by his patient —Osbert Sitwell⟩ **b :** to surpass in importance, cogency, or other quality ~ *vi* **:** to bear fruit or offspring to excess

over·bear·ance \,≈≈ˈba(a)rən(t)s, -ˈber-\ *n* -S **:** domineering action or behavior **:** IMPERIOUSNESS

[1]**overbearing** \,≈≈ˈ≈≈\ *n* [fr. gerund of *overbear*] **:** the behavior of one that overbears another or an instance of such behavior; *esp* **:** dictatorial or arrogant action or conduct ⟨~ and aggression must come to an end —T.E.Goldstein⟩

[2]**overbearing** \"\ *adj* [fr. pres. part. of *overbear*] **1 a :** OVERPOWERING, OVERWHELMING ⟨combine to create an ~ atmosphere —*Irish Digest*⟩ ⟨a grand alliance of European powers against our ~ greatness —J.H.Plumb⟩ ⟨an ~ preoccupation with economic interest —A.W.Gouldner⟩ **b :** decisively important **:** DOMINANT, PREPONDERATING ⟨the ~ problem of basic American relations with the Soviet Union —T.F.Reynolds⟩ ⟨didn't think it was the ~ consideration here —J.S.Cooper⟩ **2 :** aggressively haughty **:** ARROGANT, DOMINEERING ⟨intolerably . . . ~ in his manner —J.C.Snaith⟩

syn see PROUD

over·bear·ing·ly \¦≈≈¦≈≈\ *adv* **:** in an overbearing manner

overbearingness \¦≈≈¦≈≈\ *n* -ES **:** the quality or state of being overbearing

overbed table \¦≈≈-\ *n* [*overbed* fr. [2]*over* + *bed*, n.] **:** a narrow rectangular table designed esp. for hospital patients that spans the bed and is typically fitted with casters and a crank for adjusting the height and tilting the top

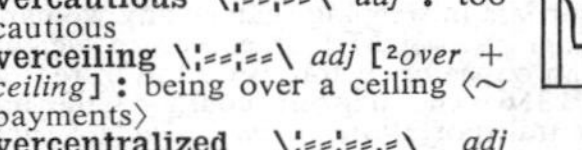
overbed table

overbelief \ˈ≈≈,≈\ *n* [[3]*over* + *belief*] **:** belief that is not verifiable or warranted by the evidence ⟨the ~*s* required by the nature . . . of human knowledge —H.J. Muller⟩

overbend \¦≈≈¦≈\ *vt* **1 a :** to cause to bend over ⟨more *overbent* than ever by his task —Adrian Bell⟩ **b :** to take a bent position over ⟨brooks *overbent* by arching boughs⟩ **2 :** to bend (as a bow) to excess ~ *vi* **:** to bend or stoop over

over·berg \¦≈≈¦≈\ *adj* [[2]*over* + Afrik *berg* mountain — more at BERG] *Africa* **:** being across a berg **:** TRAMONTANE

[1]**overbias** \ˈ≈≈,≈\ *n* [[3]*over* + *bias*] **:** an excessive bias; *specif* **:** an electron-tube grid bias in excess of that required for normal operation

[2]**overbias** \"\ *vt* **:** to apply an overbias to

[1]**overbid** \¦≈≈¦≈\ *vb* [[1]*over* + *bid*] *vi* **1 :** to bid in excess of value ⟨~ for stock⟩ **2 a :** to bid more than the trick-winning or scoring capacity of one's hand **b** *Brit* **:** to make a higher bid than the preceding one **:** OVERCALL ~ *vt* **:** to bid beyond or in excess of; *specif* **:** to bid more than the value of (one's hand in cards)

[2]**overbid** \"\ *n* **:** a bid in excess of a previous bid or of value

overbit \ˈ≈≈,≈\ *n* **:** a triangular earmark for cattle cut out of the upper side of an animal's ear — see EARMARK illustration

overbite \ˈ≈≈,≈\ *n* **:** the projection of the upper anterior teeth over the lower in the normal occlusal position of the jaws

overblouse \ˈ≈≈,≈\ *n* **:** a usu. fitted or belted blouse worn over the waistband of a skirt

overblow \¦≈≈¦≈\ *vb* [ME *overblowen*, fr. [1]*over* + *blowen* to blow] *vt* **1 :** to dissipate by or as if by wind **:** blow away **2 :** to cover (as with snow) by blowing or being blown **3 :** to blow (a pipe or other wind instrument) so vigorously as to evoke undesirable overtones that sometimes completely mask the fundamental tone **4 :** to continue to blow in a converter after the impurities have been removed (as carbon from iron or sulfur from copper) completely or below a proper percentage **5 a :** DISTEND, SWELL ⟨whom stout and high living have much *overblown* —Donagh MacDonagh⟩ **b :** to puff up to inflated proportions **:** give a false pathos or bombastic or flamboyant quality to ⟨would have been easy to ~ the story —C.W.Morton⟩ ~ *vi* **1** *of the wind, archaic* **:** to blow too hard to allow light sails (as topsails) to be carried **2 :** to force wind into a wind musical instrument in such a way as to change its pitch typically producing an overtone instead of its fundamental tone

[1]**overblown** \¦≈≈¦≈\ *adj* [fr. past part. of *overblow*] **1 :** blown over or away **2 a :** marked by excessively large girth or proportions **:** PORTLY ⟨a handsome, ~ creature —S.J.Perelman⟩ ⟨swamps that helped support his ~ body —Jack Breed⟩ **b** (1) **:** puffed up to inflated proportions ⟨the ~ products of propaganda —*Newsweek*⟩ ⟨empty shuffling of ~ memories —*Saturday Rev.*⟩ ⟨the tale becomes ~ and thin —Amy Loveman⟩ ⟨a corrective power to deflate what was ~ —*Listener*⟩ (2) **:** flamboyant, turgid, or bombastic in manner or content **:** PRETENTIOUS ⟨an obsolete and ~ oratory —Bernard De Voto⟩ ⟨as strained, ~, and obvious as a soap opera —Charles Lee⟩ ⟨his climaxes are . . . never maudlin or ~ —*Modern Music*⟩

[2]**overblown** \"\ *adj* [[1]*over* + *blown*, past part. of *blow* (to blossom)] **:** blossomed to excess **:** more than full blown ⟨a rose that already is ~ —C.E.Montague⟩

overboard \ˈ≈≈, *sometimes* ,≈≈ˈ≈\ *adv* [ME *over bord*, fr. OE *ofer bord*, fr. *ofer*, prep., over + *bord* ship's side — more at BOARD] **1 :** over the side of a ship or boat; *esp* **:** from on board a ship into the water ⟨a man fell ~⟩ **2 :** to extremes esp. in approval of someone or something — usu. used in the phrase *go overboard* ⟨tend to go ~ on this subject —*Natural History*⟩ ⟨went ~ for heroes and heroines who don't seem so heroic today —Dwight Macdonald⟩ ⟨go ~ for unattractive girls —J.J.Godwin⟩ ⟨go ~ for passing fads —E.J.Kahn⟩ **3 :** into discard **:** ASIDE ⟨throw theological absolutes ~ —Allan Nevins⟩ ⟨throwing all her moral teachings and inhibitions ~ —Ruth Park⟩

overboil \¦≈≈¦≈\ *vi* **:** to boil over or unduly

overbold \¦≈≈¦≈\ *adj* **:** excessively bold or forward **:** PRESUMPTUOUS, IMPUDENT ⟨a foolish, ~ act —R.L.Stevenson⟩ — **overboldness** \¦≈≈¦≈≈\ *n*

overboot \ˈ≈≈,≈\ *n* **:** OVERSHOE

overbore *past of* OVERBEAR

overborne \¦≈≈¦≈\ *adj* [fr. past part. of *overbear*] **:** held down by superior force **:** OPPRESSED ⟨art, industry, and commerce, so long crushed and ~ —Francis Parkman⟩

overbought *adj* **:** characterized by prices held to be excessively high as a result of heavy buying ⟨price reactions in an ~ market⟩ ⟨an ~ stock⟩ — compare OVERSOLD

overbowed \¦≈≈¦≈\ *adj* [[1]*over* + *bowed* (furnished with a bow)] **:** equipped with a bow whose drawing weight is too great for the archer

overbowl \ˈ≈≈,≈\ *n* **:** a throw at bowls that goes beyond the jack

overbreak \ˈ≈≈,≈\ *n* **:** a caving in of loosened material along the edge of an excavation

overbred \¦≈≈¦≈\ *adj* **:** bred too finely or to excess ⟨an ~ family of the nobility⟩

overbridge \ˈ≈≈,≈\ *n, Brit* **:** OVERPASS

overbrim \¦≈≈¦≈\ *vi* **:** to flow over the brim **:** OVERFLOW ~ *vt* **:** to cause to flow over the brim; *also* **:** to flow over the brim of

overbuild \¦≈≈¦≈\ *vt* **1 a :** to build too much for **:** build beyond the actual demand of ⟨~ capacity in any phase of industry —C.E.Wilson⟩ **b :** to supply with buildings in excess of actual demand ⟨~ a town⟩ **2 :** to erect a building or structure upon ~ *vi* **:** to build houses in excess of demand ⟨claims that the housing industry is ~*ing*⟩

overbuilt \¦≈≈¦≈\ *adj* **:** having too many buildings esp. in relation to the demand ⟨an ~ part of town⟩ **:** faced with an excess of housing in relation to the actual demand ⟨are going to become ~ if we continue to build —*Amer. Builder*⟩

overbulky \¦≈≈¦≈≈\ *adj* **:** excessively bulky

[1]**overburden** \¦≈≈¦≈≈\ *vt* [[1]*over* + *burden*, v.] **:** to place an excessive burden on **:** load to excess **:** weigh down ⟨the pauper class which ~*s* the city asylums —Nels Anderson⟩ ⟨~*ed* . . . by a profusion of ornament —Anny Varron⟩ ⟨tree branches ~*ed* with ice⟩

[2]**overburden** \ˈ≈≈,≈≈\ *n* [in sense 1, fr. [1]*overburden;* in other senses, fr. [3]*over* + *burden*, n.] **1 :** excess of burden **2 a :** consolidated or unconsolidated material overlying a deposit of useful geological materials (as a coal seam or an ore body) esp. where mined by open cuts; *also* **:** sedimentary rock overlying older crystalline rocks **b :** loose soil, sand, gravel, or similar material above a bedrock **3 :** the sterile stratum lying above a cultural level at an archaeological site

over·bur·den·ing·ly \¦≈≈¦≈(≈)≈≈\ *adv* [*overburdening* (pres. part. of [1]*overburden*) + *-ly*] **:** so as to overburden

overburn \¦≈≈¦≈\ *vt* **:** to burn (as clay) too long or at a higher than normal temperature

overbuy \¦≈≈¦≈\ *vb* [ME *overbiggen*, fr. [1]*over* + *biggen, byen* to buy] *vt* **1** *obs* **:** to buy at an excessive price **2 a :** to buy in quantities exceeding needs or demand ⟨found that he had *overbought* fertilizer⟩ **b :** to affect injuriously (as by causing price rises) by too much buying esp. in relation to supply ~ *vi* **:** to make purchases that are in excess of needs or demand or are beyond one's means ⟨~*ing* and then holding for an advance in prices —Jules Backman⟩ ⟨~*ing* . . . is often detected and the subscribers warned —A.F.Chapin⟩

overby \¦≈≈¦≈\ *adv* [[1]*over* + *by*, adv.] *chiefly Scot* **:** a little way over **:** at a short distance ⟨our neighbors ~⟩

[1]**overcall** \¦≈≈¦≈\ *vb* [[1]*over* + *call*] *vt* **1 :** to make a higher card bid than (the preceding bid) **:** bid higher than (the player who last bid) **2** *Brit* **:** OVERBID ~ *vi* **:** to bid over an opponent's bid in bridge when one's partner has not bid or doubled

[2]**overcall** \"\ *n* **1 a :** a bid in bridge usu. showing meager or limited strength made by a player on the side that did not open the bidding **b :** a bid above the preceding bid **2 :** OVERBID

overcanopy \¦≈≈¦≈≈≈\ *vt* **:** to form a canopy over ⟨great white wings ~*ing* the sparkling water —Lilian S. Taylor⟩

overcapacity \¦≈≈(≈)¦≈≈≈\ *n* **:** excessive productive capacity in relation to needs or demand ⟨another industry suffering from ~ —*Newsweek*⟩

overcapitalization \¦ōvə(r)+\ *n* [[3]*over* + *capitalization*] **1 :** the act or an instance of overcapitalizing **2 :** the state of being overcapitalized

overcapitalize \"+\ *vt* [[1]*over* + *capitalize*] **1 :** to put a nominal value on the capital of (a corporation) higher than actual cost or fair market value **2 :** to capitalize (a business enterprise) beyond what the business or the profit-making prospects warrant

overcareful \¦≈≈¦≈≈\ *adj* **:** too careful — **overcarefully** \¦≈≈¦≈(≈)≈\ *adv*

overcarry \¦≈≈¦≈≈\ *vt* **:** to carry too far **:** carry beyond the proper point

[1]**overcast** \¦≈≈¦≈\ *vb* [ME *overcasten*, fr. [1]*over* + *casten* to cast] *vt* **1** *archaic* **:** to cast down **:** OVERTHROW **2 a :** CLOUD, DARKEN, OVERSHADOW ⟨it is the existence of evil . . . which ~*s* life —F.L.Mott⟩ **b :** to cast or cover over **:** OVERSPREAD ⟨the smoke haze that ~ the distant mountains —L.C.Douglas⟩ ⟨something of reverence, ~ with egotism —G.B.Johnson⟩ **3 a** (1) **:** to sew with an overcast stitch from one section of (a book) to the next (2) **:** to reinforce along the back of (a signature) by stitching through half of the leaves (3) **:** to fasten (single leaves) as a group by an overcast stitch at the binding edge **:** WHIPSTITCH **b :** to sew over the edge of; *specif* **:** to sew (raw edges of a seam) with long slanting widely spaced stitches to prevent raveling ~ *vi* **1 :** to become overcast **:** DARKEN **2 :** to make an overbowl at lawn bowls

[2]**overcast** \ˈ≈≈,≈\ *adj* [fr. past part. of [1]*overcast*] **1 a :** clouded over ⟨an ~ night⟩ **b :** DEPRESSED, GLOOMY ⟨his handsome countenance . . . was ~ —Rafael Sabatini⟩ **2** *geol* **:** OVERTURNED ⟨an ~ fold⟩

[3]**overcast** \"\ *n* [[1]*overcast*] **1 :** COVERING ⟨with an ~ of irony —R.M.Coates⟩; *esp* **:** a covering of clouds over the sky ⟨the land rose in pink and violet dales, shading finally into the ~ above the harbor —Norman Mailer⟩ **2 :** an arch or support that carries an overhead passage; *esp* **:** one that carries a passage over another passage in a mine **3 :** sewing that has been overcast

overcaster \ˈ≈≈,≈≈\ *n* **:** one who does overcasting by hand or machine — see SERGER

overcasting \ˈ≈≈,≈≈\ *n* **:** the act of stitching raw edges of fabric to prevent raveling; *also* **:** the stitching so done

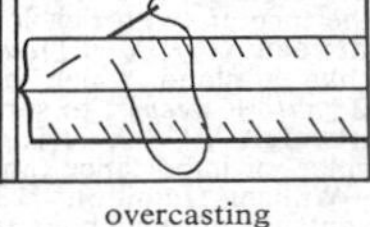
overcasting

overcatch \¦≈≈¦≈\ *vt, chiefly dial* **:** OVERTAKE

overcautious \¦≈≈¦≈≈\ *adj* **:** too cautious

overceiling \¦≈≈¦≈≈\ *adj* [[2]*over* + *ceiling*] **:** being over a ceiling ⟨~ payments⟩

overcentralized \¦≈≈¦≈≈,≈\ *adj* **:** excessively centralized ⟨~ administration⟩

overcertification \¦≈≈,≈≈≈¦≈≈\ *n* [[3]*over* + *certification*] **:** the practice or an instance of overcertifying

overcertify \¦≈≈¦≈≈≈\ *vt* [[1]*over* + *certify*] **:** to certify (a check) for an amount in excess of the balance of the deposit account of the drawer

[1]**overcharge** \¦≈≈¦≈\ *vb* [ME *overchargen*, fr. [1]*over* + *chargen* to charge] *vt* **1 :** to charge excessively or beyond a due rate or price ⟨~ you as much as he likes —G.B.Shaw⟩ **2 :** to fill or load too full **:** CROWD, BURDEN ⟨our language is *overcharged* with consonants —Joseph Addison⟩ ⟨the canvas . . . is rather *overcharged* —Norman Douglas⟩ **3** *obs* **:** to make extravagant accusations against **4 :** EXAGGERATE, OVERDRAW ⟨~ a report⟩ ~ *vi* **:** to make an excessive charge

[2]**overcharge** \ˈ≈≈,≈, ,≈≈ˈ≈\ *n* **1 :** an excessive charge or burden **2 a :** a monetary charge in excess of the proper, legal, or agreed rate or amount **:** an exorbitant charge **b** (1) **:** an act of charging an excessive amount ⟨increase civil penalties for rent ~*s* —*New Republic*⟩ (2) **:** a sum in excess of the just amount ⟨found and corrected a twenty-five-cent ~ —*Atlantic*⟩

overcharge claim *n* : a formal request by a shipper on a carrier for refund of an excess over the lawful charge

¹overcheck \ˈ⸗,⸗\ *n* [³*over* + *check* (checkrein)] : a checkrein passing between the ears of a horse — compare SIDECHECK

²overcheck \"\ *n* [³*over* + *check* (pattern in squares)] : a textile design usu. consisting of two checked patterns of different size or color so made that one is superimposed on the other; *also* : a fabric with such a design

overchurched \ˌ⸗⸗ˈchərcht\ *adj* [¹*over* + *-churched* (fr. *church*, n. + *-ed*)] : having more churches than are needed to serve the population ⟨an ~ community⟩

overchurching \ˌ⸗⸗ˈchərchiŋ\ *n* [¹*over* + *-churching* (fr. *church*, n. + *-ing*)] : the providing of more churches than are needed to serve the population of a community

overchute \ˈ⸗,⸗\ *n* : an overhead flume (as one over a stream or canal)

overcivilized \ˌ⸗⸗ˈ⸗⸗,⸗\ *adj* : too highly civilized ⟨a standardized and ~ minority —Douglas Bush⟩

overclaim \ˈ⸗,⸗\ *n* : an excessive claim ⟨gross and palpable ~s —Raymond Moley⟩

overclothe \ˌ⸗⸗ˈ⸗\ *vt* : to clothe to excess ⟨babies should never be *overclothed* —Morris Fishbein⟩

overclothes \ˈ⸗,⸗\ *n pl* : outer garments

overcloud \ˌ⸗⸗ˈ⸗\ *vt* **1** : to cover or overspread with clouds : OVERCAST, OBSCURE ⟨a dust storm so intense that it ~*ed* the sun⟩ **2 a** : to cast a shadow upon : DARKEN ⟨did much to ~, if they did not embitter, her indulgent husband's early life —Peter Quennell⟩ **b** : to make dim or dull : BECLOUD ⟨if his clear understanding had not been ~*ed* —T.B.Macaulay⟩

¹overcoat \ˈ⸗,⸗\ *n* [³*over* + *coat*, n.] **1** : a coat worn over a suit or other clothing; *esp* : a warm coat for winter wear **2** : a protective coating (as of paint or varnish)

²overcoat \ˌ⸗⸗ˈ⸗\ *vt* [²*over* + *coat*, v.] : to apply an additional coat (as of paint) to

overcoating \ˈ⸗,⸗⸗\ *n* [in sense 1, fr. ¹*overcoat* + *-ing*; in sense 2, prob. fr. ³*over* + *coating*] **1** : heavy material suitable for overcoats **2** : OVERCOAT 2

overcoil \ˈ⸗,⸗\ *n* : the outer coil of a Bréguet hairspring bent over the spring toward the center

overcoiler \"ə(r)\ *n* : a worker who adjusts an overcoil so that it will remain concentric with the balance staff as the spring winds and unwinds

¹overcome \ˌōvə(r)ˈkəm\ *vb* [ME *overcomen*, fr. OE *ofercuman*, fr. *ofer*, adv., over + *cuman* to come] *vt* **1 a** : to get the better of : SURMOUNT, CONQUER, SUBDUE ⟨search out and ~ the difficulties —George Sampson⟩ ⟨finally *overcame* the opposition of the traditionalists —Helen Sullivan⟩ ⟨the difficulty of language had to be ~ —L.S.B.Leakey⟩ **b** : to affect or influence so strongly as to make physically helpless or emotionally distraught (as from exhaustion or agitation) : OVERPOWER, OVERWHELM ⟨were ~ by fear —H.E.Scudder⟩ ⟨too much ~ to notice what was in it —L.A.G.Strong⟩ ⟨~ by the . . . champagne —Kenneth Roberts⟩ **c** *archaic* : to go beyond : EXCEED, OUTSTRIP **d** *obs* : COMPLETE, ACCOMPLISH **2 a** *archaic* : to come or pass over : spread or flow over **b** *obs* : to come over suddenly ~ *vi* **1** : to gain the superiority : WIN ⟨strong in the faith that truth would ~⟩ **2** *chiefly dial* : to regain consciousness after a swoon **syn** see CONQUER

²over·come \ˈō(ə)r,kəm, ˈōvər-, -kŭm\ *n* [³*over* + obs. E *come* action of coming, fr. ME — more at DOWNCOME] **1** *chiefly Scot* : SURPLUS **2** *chiefly Scot* : something (as the burden of a song or a trite phrase) that is often repeated

over·com·er \ˌōvə(r)ˈkəmə(r)\ *n* [ME, fr. *overcomen* to overcome + *-er*] : one that overcomes ⟨they're ~s by nature —Robertson Davies⟩

over·compensate \ˌōvə(r)+\ *vt* : to compensate inordinately or to excess ⟨*overcompensated* the popular teacher and ignored the specialist —H.M.Jones⟩ ~ *vi* : to exhibit overcompensation : overcome through overt behavior a feeling of inferiority ⟨may ~ through disastrous adventures —Jack Weinberg⟩ — **over·compensatory** \"+\ *adj*

over·compensation \"+\ *n* : excessive compensation; *specif* : excessive reaction to a feeling of inferiority, guilt, or inadequacy leading to an exaggerated attempt to overcome the feeling

over·compound \"+\ *vt* : to add series coils to (a compounded dynamo) beyond those required to maintain a constant terminal voltage with the result that the voltage increases with the current load

over·confidence \"+\ *n* : excess of confidence

over·confident \"+\ *adj* : marked by or reflecting overconfidence

overconscientious \ˌ⸗⸗ˈ⸗⸗ˈ⸗⸗\ *adj* : unduly or excessively conscientious

over·conservative \ˌōvə(r)+\ *adj* : unduly or extremely conservative

overcook \ˌ⸗⸗ˈ⸗\ *vt* : to cook too much ⟨threw his chef out of the window for ~*ing* a . . . calf —Quentin Crewe⟩

overcorrect \ˌ⸗⸗⸗ˈ⸗\ *vt* : to apply a correction to in excess of that required (as for satisfactory performance); *specif* : to correct (a lens) beyond the point of achromatism or so that there is aberration of a kind opposite to that of the uncorrected lens — **overcorrection** \ˌ⸗⸗⸗ˈ⸗⸗\ *n*

¹overcover \ˌ⸗⸗ˈ⸗⸗\ *vt* [ME *overcoveren*, fr. ¹*over* + *coveren* to cover] : to cover up : cover completely

²overcover \ˈ⸗,⸗⸗\ *n* : something that covers over or covers completely ⟨beneath a dense ~ of thick jungle trees —G.H. Johnston⟩ ⟨fishing rods in green baize ~s —F.M.Ford⟩

overcritical \ˌ⸗⸗ˈ⸗⸗⸗\ *adj* [¹*over* + *critical*] : HYPERCRITICAL

overcrop \ˌ⸗⸗ˈ⸗\ *vt* [¹*over* + *crop*] : to exhaust the fertility of by excessive production without the application of adequate fertilizer to the soil

overcrossing \ˈ⸗,⸗⸗\ *n* : OVERPASS

overcrow \ˌ⸗⸗ˈ⸗\ *vt* **1** : to crow, exult, or boast over **2** : to triumph over : OVERBEAR, OVERPOWER

overcrowd \ˌ⸗⸗ˈ⸗\ *vt* : to cause to be too crowded : fill to the point of discomfort or disadvantage ⟨there is always danger of ~*ing* the attractive business —*Amer. Guide Series: Mich.*⟩ ~ *vi* : to crowd together too much

overcrowded *adj* : crowded or filled to excess : CONGESTED ⟨an ~ room⟩ : characterized by overcrowding ⟨live in ~ conditions —*Social Services in Brit.*⟩

overcrowding *n* **1** : the act or an instance of crowding too much **2** : the condition of being overcrowded

overcrust \ˌ⸗⸗ˈ⸗\ *vt* : to cover over with a crust

overcup oak \ˈ⸗,⸗⸗-\ *n* [*overcup* fr. ³*over* + *cup*, n.] : any of several oaks (as the bur oak) having the acorn deeply immersed in the cup; *esp* : a timber tree (*Quercus lyrata*) of the southern U. S. that has pale scaly bark and lyrate leaves

overcurious \ˌ⸗⸗ˈ⸗⸗⸗\ *adj* **1** *obs* : too finicky or fastidious **2** : too inquisitive — **overcuriously** \ˌ⸗⸗ˈ⸗⸗⸗⸗\ *adv* — **over·cu·ri·ous·ness** \ˌ⸗⸗ˈ⸗⸗⸗⸗\ *n*

overcurrent \ˈ⸗,⸗⸗\ *n* : an electrical current whose intensity is higher than a specified amount

¹overcut \ˈ⸗,⸗\ *n* [³*over* + *cut*] **1** : excessive cutting; *specif* : cutting of timber in excess of the annual growth of the forest **2** : an absence from class (as in a college) in excess of the number customarily allowed **3** : a cut (as in tennis) made with an overhand stroke

²overcut \ˌ⸗⸗ˈ⸗\ *vb* [¹*over* + *cut*] *vt* : to cut excessively; *specif* : to cut timber from (a forest) in excess of the annual growth or in excess of the annual estimate ~ *vi* : to do excessive cutting; *specif* : to cut timber in excess

overcutter \ˈ⸗,⸗⸗\ *n* [³*over* + *cutter*] : TURRET CUTTER

overcutting \ˌ⸗⸗ˈ⸗⸗\ *n* [³*over* + *cutting* (gerund of *cut*)] : the effect in disc recording of one groove cutting through the intervening wall into the adjacent groove as the result of excessive excursion of the cutting stylus

overdamp \ˌ⸗⸗ˈ⸗\ *vt* : to damp in excess ⟨use of a high sensitivity galvanometer greatly ~*ed* —*Physical Rev.*⟩

overdare *vi* : to dare too much or rashly : become too daring ~ *vt*, *obs* : to surpass in daring

overdaring \ˌ⸗⸗ˈ⸗⸗\ *adj* : too daring : FOOLHARDY — **overdaringly** *adv*

¹overdate \ˈ⸗,⸗\ *n* [³*over* + *date*] **1** : a changed date on a coin that has traces of the original date still showing **2** : a coin having an overdate

²overdate \"\ *vt* [¹*over* + *date*] : to strike (a coin) with an overdate

overdated \ˈ⸗,⸗⸗\ *adj* [in sense 1, fr. ¹*over* + *dated* (past part. of *date*, v.); in sense 2, fr. past part. of ²*overdate*] **1** *archaic* : OUT-OF-DATE : BYGONE **2** : bearing an overdate ⟨~ coins⟩

overdear \ˌ⸗⸗ˈ⸗\ *adj* [ME *over dere*, fr. ¹*over* + *dere* dear] : too dear; *esp* : too costly

overdeck \ˌ⸗⸗ˈ⸗\ *vt* : to adorn extravagantly : adorn excessively

overdecorated \ˌ⸗⸗ˈ⸗⸗,⸗⸗\ *adj* : decorated to excess

overdeepen \ˌ⸗⸗ˈ⸗⸗\ *vt* : to deepen excessively esp. through erosive action (as of water or ice) ⟨the ~*ed* main valleys —A. E.Trueman⟩

overdeepening \ˌ⸗⸗ˈ⸗(⸗)⸗\ *n* : the process or result of deepening excessively ⟨this ~ amounts at most to only a few hundred feet —*Jour. of Geol.*⟩

overdelicate \ˌ⸗⸗ˈ⸗⸗⸗\ *adj* : unduly or extremely delicate

over·den \ˈōvə(r),den\ *n* [PaG *owwerdenn* loft over the threshing floor, fr. *owwer* upper (fr. G *ober*) + *denn* threshing floor, fr. G *tenne*, fr. OHG *tenni* — more at OBERREALSCHULE, DEN] *Northeast* : HAYMOW

overdependent \ˌ⸗⸗⸗ˈ⸗⸗\ *adj* : unduly or extremely dependent

overdetermination \ˌ⸗⸗⸗,⸗⸗ˈ⸗⸗\ *n* [³*over* + *determination*] : the condition of being overdetermined

overdetermined \ˌ⸗⸗⸗ˈ⸗⸗\ *adj* [¹*over* + *determined*] **1** : too determined : too positive or decided ⟨~ insistence that everything . . . can be reduced to sex —Norman Cameron⟩ **2** : having more than one determining psychological factor : affording an outlet for more than a single wish or need ⟨an ~ dream symbol⟩

overdevelop \ˌ⸗⸗⸗ˈ⸗⸗\ *vt* : to develop excessively; *specif* : to subject (as an exposed photographic plate, film, paper) to a developing solution under one or more conditions of excessive time, temperature, agitation, or concentration — **overdevelopment** \ˌ⸗⸗⸗ˈ⸗⸗\ *n*

overdiligent \ˌ⸗⸗ˈ⸗⸗⸗\ *adj* : extremely diligent

¹overdischarge \ˌōvə(r)+\ *vt* [¹*over* + *discharge*] : to discharge excessively; *specif* : to discharge (a battery) beyond the proper point

²overdischarge \"+\ *n* **1** : the act, process, or an instance of overdischarging **2** : the condition of being overdischarged

overdo \ˌ⸗⸗ˈ⸗\ *vb* [ME *overdon*, fr. OE *oferdōn*, fr. *ofer*, adv., over + *dōn* to do] *vt* **1 a** : to do too much : do to excess : carry too far ⟨if she does housework, she will ~ it —H.A.Overstreet⟩ ⟨~ the social side of pregnancy —Morris Fishbein⟩ **b** : to make excessive use or application of ⟨tend to ~ the wisecrack —David Daiches⟩ ⟨quotations are apt to break up a book . . . don't ~ them —J.E.Gloag⟩ **c** : to emphasize unduly : EXAGGERATE ⟨corruption is frequently *overdone* as a cause of national decay —*New Republic*⟩ **2** *archaic* : SURPASS, EXCEL **3 a** : to cook too long **b** : to feed (an animal) to excessive fatness **4** : OVERTAX, FATIGUE, EXHAUST ⟨~ one's strength⟩ ~ *vi* **1** : to do too much : go to extremes in doing ⟨his anxiety that she should not ~ —Ruth P. Randall⟩ **2** : OVERACT ⟨most of her mistakes came from ~*ing* —Claire Sterling & Max Ascoli⟩

overdog \ˈ⸗,⸗\ *n* [³*over* + *dog* (after *underdog*)] : a member of a ruling or privileged class ⟨everybody in the play is stupid, both the ~s and the underdogs —Virgil Thomson⟩

overdone \ˌ⸗⸗ˈ⸗\ *adj* [ME *oferdoon*, fr. OE *oferdōn*, fr. past part. of *oferdōn* to overdo] **1** : done or carried to excess: as **a** : EXAGGERATED ⟨an absent and ~ smile —E.A.Poe⟩ ⟨a courtesy which was a little ~ —Robertson Davies⟩ **b** : cooked too much ⟨an ~ steak⟩ **2** : EXHAUSTED, FATIGUED ⟨looking a bit ~ —Dorothy Sayers⟩ ⟨you're just ~ —Agnes S. Turnbull⟩

overdoor \ˈ⸗,⸗\ *n* [²*over* + *door*] : a picture or carved panel or other decorative member over a doorway or a doorframe

overdosage \ˌ⸗⸗ˈ⸗⸗\ *n* [²*overdose* + *-age*] **1** : the administration or taking of an excessive dose ⟨guard against ~ of this drug⟩ **2** : the condition of being overdosed ⟨the symptoms of acute ~ —Henry Borsook⟩

¹overdose \ˈ⸗,⸗\ *n* [³*over* + *dose*] : too great a dose : an excessive dose ⟨an ~ of exposure to the sun —Morris Fishbein⟩ ⟨an ~ of sweetness and light —C.J.Rolo⟩; *also* : a lethal or toxic amount (as of a drug) ⟨an ~ of sleeping pills⟩

²overdose \"\ *vb* [¹*over* + *dose*] *vt* : to give an overdose or too many doses to ~ *vi* : to take an overdose

overdraft \ˈ⸗,⸗\ *n* [fr. *overdraw*, after E *draw: draft*] **1 a** : an act of overdrawing at a bank or the state of being overdrawn; *also* : the sum overdrawn ⟨an ~ results when a note discounted at a bank is not met when due⟩ **b** : the act, process, or an instance of drawing on or off too much ⟨a mounting ~ in the use of available sweet water —W.A.Ulman⟩ **2** [³*over* + *draft*] : a draft or current of air passing over a fire in a furnace

overdrape \ˈ⸗,⸗\ *also* **overdrapery** \ˈ⸗⸗,⸗(⸗)⸗\ *n* : one of a pair of draperies esp. of heavy fabric that are usu. hung over sheer curtains and are primarily for decoration

overdrapes

overdraw \ˌ⸗⸗ˈ⸗\ *vb* [¹*over* + *draw*] *vt* **1** : to draw checks upon (a bank account) in excess of the deposit balance of the drawer : make a draft upon beyond the proper or authorized amount ⟨*overdrew* his account⟩ **2** : to present or portray with exaggeration or overstatement ⟨has *overdrawn* the dangers —M.H. Swadesh⟩ ⟨have often *overdrawn* their villains —John Mason Brown⟩ ⟨purposely ~ the contrast —A.R.Oxenfeldt & Ernest Van den Haag⟩ **3** : to draw (a bow) beyond the arrow length for which it was designed ~ *vi* : to make an overdraft

overdrawn \ˌ⸗⸗ˈ⸗\ *adj* **1 a** : drawn upon in excess of the deposit balance of the drawer at the bank ⟨an ~ account⟩ **b** : having made an overdraft : having an overdrawn account ⟨was ~ to quite a considerable extent —F.W.Crofts⟩ **2** : EXAGGERATED ⟨claim of having earned a graduate degree . . . appears ~ —Peter Wyden⟩ ⟨all this enthusiasm seems a little ~ —Gladys E. Brown⟩ ⟨particularly ~ comparisons —R.A.Hall b.1911⟩ ⟨like an ~ picture of an English gentleman —John Steinbeck⟩

¹overdress \ˌ⸗⸗ˈ⸗\ *vb* [¹*over* + *dress*] *vt* : to dress or adorn to excess ~ *vi* : to dress oneself to excess

²overdress \ˈ⸗,⸗\ *n* [³*over* + *dress*] : a dress worn over another; *specif* : one designed or draped to show an underdress

overdrifted \ˌ⸗⸗ˈ⸗⸗\ *adj* [¹*over* + *drifted* (past part. of *drift*)] : covered with drifts (as of snow) ⟨steep, snowy, rutty, ~ roads —Stephen Graham⟩

¹overdrive \ˌ⸗⸗ˈ⸗\ *vt* [ME *overdriven*, fr. ¹*over* + *driven* to drive] **1** : to drive too hard or far or beyond strength or a fixed limit ⟨*overdrove* the orchestra —*Current Biog.*⟩ ⟨skeletons of . . . beasts which had been *overdriven* by their anxious owners —Gordon Enders⟩ **2** : to drive (an automotive vehicle) esp. at night at such speed that one cannot stop or guide it safely within the limits of vision or available space

²overdrive \ˈ⸗,⸗\ *n* [³*over* + *drive*] : an automotive transmission gear which transmits to the propeller shaft a speed greater than engine speed

overdriven \ˌ⸗⸗ˈ⸗⸗\ *adj* : driven or worked too hard : EXHAUSTED, OPPRESSED ⟨the tortured and ~ slave —Clive Bell⟩ ⟨I am ~ just now and am trying not to do anything —G.B. Shaw⟩

overdue \ˌ⸗⸗ˈ⸗\ *adj* **1 a** : unpaid after the proper or assigned time of payment ⟨an ~ note⟩ **b** : delayed (as in arrival or presentation) beyond the proper or assigned time ⟨an ~ library book⟩ ⟨an ~ ship⟩ ⟨her gallant was . . . more than an hour ~ —Dorothy Barclay⟩ **c** : being something that fills a need of long standing or that has been long awaited ⟨improvement is long ~ —Stuart Chase⟩ ⟨land reform which was long ~ —Richard Hunt⟩ ⟨the book is ~ —John Berryman⟩ ⟨got an ~ reward —*Time*⟩ **2** : exceeding its merits or what is appropriate : EXCESSIVE ⟨an ~ share of attention —Evelyn Whitehead⟩ ⟨if the tool is built with ~ sturdiness —*Amer. Machinist*⟩ **3** : more than ready or ripe ⟨colonies that are ~ for liberation —David Landman⟩ ⟨announcing that the country was ~ for democracy —*Time*⟩ **syn** see TARDY

overdye \ˌ⸗⸗ˈ⸗\ *vt* **1** : to dye with excess of color **2** : to dye over with another color

overeager \ˌ⸗⸗ˈ⸗⸗\ *adj* : too eager ⟨~ for success⟩ ⟨~ in his pursuit of the girl⟩ — **overeagerly** *adv* — **overeagerness** *n* -ES

overeat \ˌ⸗⸗ˈ⸗\ *vi* : to eat to excess or to the point of surfeit ~ *vt* : to indulge (oneself) in overeating ⟨nearly *overate* myself the other day —Norman Douglas⟩

overeating disease *n* : ENTEROTOXEMIA

overed *past of* OVER

overedger \ˈ⸗⸗,⸗⸗\ *n* [prob. fr. *over edge* (fr. ²*over* + *edge*) + *-er*] : SERGER

overelaborate \ˌ⸗⸗⸗ˈ⸗⸗,⸗\ *vt* [¹*over* + *elaborate*] : to elaborate too far or too much : elaborate beyond the point of need ⟨tended to ~ an intrinsically simple structure —W.A.Paton & A.C.Littleton⟩ — **overelaborately** \ˌ⸗⸗⸗ˈ⸗(⸗)⸗⸗\ *adv*

overelaboration \ˌ⸗⸗⸗,⸗⸗ˈ⸗⸗\ *n* [³*over* + *elaboration*] **1** : the act or an instance of overelaborating ⟨his taste ran to extreme ~ —*Atlantic*⟩ **2** : the condition of being overelaborated ⟨~ characterizes so much of present-day writing —E.S.McCartney⟩

overembellish \ˌ⸗⸗⸗ˈ⸗⸗\ *vt* : to embellish to excess

overemotional \ˌ⸗⸗⸗ˈ⸗(⸗)⸗\ *adj* : abnormally or excessively emotional

overemphasis \ˌ⸗⸗ˈ⸗⸗⸗\ *n* : excessive emphasis

overemphasize \ˌ⸗⸗ˈ⸗⸗,⸗\ *vt* : to give excessive emphasis to ⟨*overemphasizing* detail —*Amer. Guide Series: Pa.*⟩ ~ *vi* : to use too much emphasis ⟨I ~ and exaggerate —B.N.Cardozo⟩

overemployment \ˌ⸗⸗⸗ˈ⸗⸗\ *n* **1** : excessive employment or use ⟨in his case the ~ of the dash seems appropriate —*Jour. of Accountancy*⟩ **2** : a condition in which the demand for labor in a country or region exceeds the available supply ⟨~ caused by inadequacy of labor and other resources compared with all the work needing to be done —*Times Lit. Supp.*⟩

overenthusiastic \ˌ⸗⸗⸗,⸗⸗ˈ⸗⸗\ *adj* : unduly or extremely enthusiastic

overesteem \ˌ⸗⸗⸗ˈ⸗\ *vt* : to esteem too highly

¹overestimate \ˌ⸗⸗ˈ⸗⸗,(,)⸗\ *vt* [¹*over* + *estimate*] : to estimate too highly : OVERVALUE — **overestimation** \ˌ⸗⸗,⸗⸗ˈ⸗⸗\ *n*

²overestimate \"\ *n* : an estimate that is too high

overevaluation \ˌ⸗⸗⸗,⸗⸗ˈ⸗⸗\ *n* : excessive evaluation

overexcite \ˌ⸗⸗⸗ˈ⸗\ *vt* : to excite to an undue or excessive degree

overexcitement \ˌ⸗⸗⸗ˈ⸗⸗\ *n* : undue or excessive excitement

overexert \ˌ⸗⸗⸗ˈ⸗\ *vt* : to exert too much ⟨don't ~ yourself⟩ ~ *vi* : to exert oneself to excess ⟨whenever he ~*ed* or was upset —William Humphrey⟩

overexertion \ˌ⸗⸗⸗ˈ⸗⸗\ *n* : excessive exertion

overexpansion \ˌ⸗⸗⸗ˈ⸗⸗\ *n* : excessive expansion

overexpose \ˌ⸗⸗⸗ˈ⸗\ *vt* : to expose excessively; *specif* : to subject (a light-sensitive material) too long to the action of light or other radiation so that usu. lowered contrast in the developed image results

overexposure \ˌ⸗⸗⸗ˈ⸗⸗\ *n* : excessive exposure

overextend \ˌ⸗⸗⸗ˈ⸗\ *vt* **1** : to extend or expand beyond a safe, proper, or reasonable point ⟨tends to ~ his claim —C.A. Madison⟩ ⟨reduce the peril of ~*ing* our economy —G.A.Sloan⟩ **2** : to spread (as a military force) so thinly or over so large an area as to weaken the total and endanger security ⟨~*ing* the German front lines —Max Werner⟩ **3** : to take upon (oneself) more liabilities, commitments, or risks than are safe ⟨~ themselves through additional land purchases —*Newsweek*⟩ ⟨any users of credit . . . may ~ themselves —C.W.Phelps⟩

overextended *adj* **1** : extended or expanded beyond a safe, proper, or reasonable point ⟨found it ~ and wordy —Philip Hamburger⟩ ⟨this elaborate, ~ vaudeville show —*Newsweek*⟩ **2** : spread too thinly or over too large an area for safety ⟨attacked and routed the ~ German divisions⟩ ⟨pulled back from positions of weakness where we were ~ —Walter Lippmann⟩ **3** : carrying or assuming liabilities, commitments, or risks beyond capacity or what is safe ⟨a speculator ~ in the market⟩ ⟨~ accounts⟩

overextension \ˌ⸗⸗⸗ˈ⸗⸗\ *n* **1** : the act or an instance of overextending **2** : the condition of being overextended

overeye *vt*, *obs* : OVERSEE

overface \ˌ⸗⸗ˈ⸗\ *vt*, *dial chiefly Eng* : OUTFACE, OVERWHELM

overfall \ˈ⸗,⸗\ *n* **1** : a turbulent surface of water caused by strong currents setting over submerged ridges or shoals or by winds opposing a current — usu. used in pl. **2** *obs* : CATARACT, WATERFALL **3** : a place provided for the overflow of surplus water (as from a canal or lock) **4** : a sudden increase of depth in the bottom of the sea or other large body of water

overfastidious \ˌ⸗⸗(,)⸗ˈ⸗⸗⸗\ *adj* : unduly or extremely fastidious

overfed \ˌ⸗⸗ˈ⸗\ *adj* [¹*over* + *fed* (past part. of *feed*)] : fed to excess ⟨shifting her ~ baby from one hip to the other —Evelyn Barkins⟩

¹overfeed \ˌ⸗⸗ˈ⸗\ *vb* [¹*over* + *feed*] *vt* : to feed to excess ⟨~ a child⟩ ~ *vi* : to eat too much ⟨wanders off . . . and ~s —Allan Anderson⟩

²overfeed \ˈ⸗,⸗\ *adj* [¹*over* + *-feed* (fr. *feed*, v.)] : being fed or feeding from above ⟨an ~ stoker⟩ — opposed to *underfeed*

overfertilization \ˌ⸗⸗,⸗⸗(,)⸗⸗ˈ⸗⸗\ *n* : excessive fertilization

overfill \ˌ⸗⸗ˈ⸗\ *vb* [ME *overfillen*, fr. OE *oferfyllan*, fr. *ofer*, adv., over + *fyllan* to fill] *vt* : to fill to excess or overflowing ~ *vi* : to become full to overflowing

overfire \ˌ⸗⸗ˈ⸗\ *vt* : to apply heat treatment to (as a clay ware) beyond maturing ~ *vi* : to become subjected to excessive heat treatment ⟨clays that begin to ~ —Heinrich Ries⟩

overfiring *n* : excessive heat treatment of clay wares causing deformation, bloating, or other defects

overfish \ˌ⸗⸗ˈ⸗\ *vt* : to fish to the detriment of (a fishing ground) or to the depletion of (a kind of fish)

overfleshed \ˌ⸗⸗ˈfleshṭ\ *adj* [¹*over* + *-fleshed* (fr. *flesh*, n. + *-ed*)] : unduly or extremely fleshy : fattened beyond the point of optimum returns ⟨~ hogs⟩

overflew *past of* OVERFLY

overflies *pres 3d sing of* OVERFLY

overflight \ˈ⸗,⸗\ *n* [fr. *overfly*, after E *fly: flight*] : a passage over an area in an airplane ⟨occasional Soviet refusals for ~s —*Internat'l Reference Service*⟩

overfloat *vt* **1** *obs* : OVERFLOW **2** \ˌ⸗⸗ˈ⸗\ *archaic* : to float over

overflood \ˌ⸗⸗ˈ⸗\ *vt* : INUNDATE

¹overflow \ˌ⸗⸗ˈ⸗\ *vb* [ME *overflowen*, fr. OE *oferflōwan*, fr. *ofer*, adv., over + *flōwan* to flow] *vt* **1** : to flow over : cover with or as if with water : INUNDATE ⟨the flooded river ~*ed* the adjacent fields⟩ **2** : to flow over the brim of ⟨a river ~*ing* its banks⟩ **3** : to cause to overflow ~ *vi* **1 a** : to run or flow over bounds ⟨every spring the river ~s⟩ **b** : to fill a space to capacity and spread beyond its limits ⟨the crowd ~*ed* into the street⟩ ⟨we can ~ in pleasant weather into my small garden —Eleanor Roosevelt⟩ **2 a** : to become filled to running over ⟨filled his glass till it ~*ed*⟩ **b** : SUPERABOUND ⟨their soil . . . ~s with wine and oil —H.T.Buckle⟩

²overflow \ˈ⸗,⸗\ *n* **1** : a flowing over (as of water or other fluid) : INUNDATION **2 a** : something that flows over : SURPLUS, EXCESS ⟨territory into which her teeming human ~ can be siphoned —T.H.Fielding⟩ ⟨this year's ~ of applications —Cecile Starr⟩ **b** : the peripheral drift of excess population from a protected habitat to other suitable environments **3** : an outlet or a receptacle for surplus liquid **4** : OVERFLOW PIPE **5 a** : continuance of the sense or extension of a rhetorical unit from one line into the next : ENJAMBMENT **b** : continuance of meter from one line into the next so that a foot begun at the end of a line may be completed at the beginning of the next : SYNAPHEA

³overflow \"\ *adj* [²*overflow*] **1** : constituting an overflow ⟨~ population from central New York —*Amer. Guide Series: Pa.*⟩ ⟨~ patients lie on floors and corridors —Gertrude Samuels⟩ **2** : so large as to exceed capacity and overflow ⟨sang before ~ crowds —*Amer. Guide Series: La.*⟩ ⟨a program with an ~ attendance —W.F.Cunningham⟩

overflow bug *n* : a beetle (*Platynus maculicollis*) of the family Carabidae of the western U.S. that is sometimes locally so numerous as to be a nuisance

overflower \ˌ⸗⸗ˈ⸗⸗\ *vt* **1** : to cover over with flowers **2** : to put forth flowers beyond strength or well-being

¹overflowing \ˌ⸗⸗ˈ⸗⸗\ *adj* [ME, alter. (influenced by *-inge*, *-ing*, n. suffix, *-ing*) of *overflowende*, fr. OE *oferflōwende*, fr. pres. part. of *oferflōwan* to overflow] **1 a** : flowing over the brim : filled too full ⟨raised to his lips the ~ cup⟩ **b** : SUPERABUNDANT ⟨an . . . expanding outlet for the ~ rural population —V.G.Childe⟩ **2** : EBULLIENT, EXUBERANT ⟨breathed with ~ life —E.K.Brown⟩ ⟨the same ~ vitality —Louis Bromfield⟩ — **over·flow·ing·ly** *adv* — **over·flow·ing·ness** *n*

²overflowing \"\ *n* [fr. gerund of ¹*overflow*] **1** : a condition where overflow takes place ⟨full to ~⟩ **2 a** : something that

flows over : EXCESS, SUPERFLUITY **b :** overflowing or exuberant feeling or thought : EBULLITION — usu. used in pl. ⟨the ~s of his full mind —T.B.Macaulay⟩
overflow pipe *n* : a pipe to carry off overflow (as from a cistern)
overflow worm *n* : FALL ARMYWORM
overfly \ˌ==ˈ=\ *vt* [¹*over* + *fly*] **1 a :** to fly over; *esp* : to pass over in an aircraft ⟨will not tolerate that our borders be *overflown* —*Springfield (Mass.) Daily News*⟩ **b :** to fly beyond : OVERSHOOT ⟨~ a landing field⟩ **2 :** to fly better, farther, or higher than **3 :** to fly (as a falcon) too often or too long
¹**overfold** \ˌ==ˈ=\ *vt* [ME *overfolden* to fold over, fr. ¹*over* + *folden* to fold] : to fold over; *specif* : to push over so as to form an overturned anticline
²**overfold** \ˈ==ˌ=\ *n* [¹*overfold;* intended as trans. of G *überfaltung*] **1 :** an overturned anticline **2 :** a sigmoid fold comprising an overturned anticline and a syncline
over frame *adv* [²*over* + *frame*] : outside the frame — used as a direction in television writing to indicate that the source of a sound (as a speaker) is not seen on the screen
overfreight \ˈ==ˌ=\ *n* **1 :** an excessive load or freight **2** *usu* **over freight** \"\ : all or part of a shipment separated from its waybill and without adequate marks
over·fulfill \ˌōvə(r)+\ *vt* : to fulfill and more than fulfill ⟨should the local steel mill ~ its plan —Harry Schwartz⟩ — **over·fulfillment** \"+\ *n*
¹**overfull** \ˌ==ˈ=\ *adj* [ME, fr. OE *oferfull*, fr. *ofer*, adv., over + *full*] : too full ⟨seems ~ of phrases —Clyde Eagleton⟩ — **overfullness** *n* -ES
²**overfull** \"\ *adv* : to excess ⟨having drunk ~ of the human race —*Time*⟩
overfull employment *n* : a state of employment in which employers' demand for labor exceeds the available supply
overgaiter \ˈ==ˌ==\ *n* : GAITER
overgang \ˌ==ˈ=\ *vt* [ME *overgangen*, fr. OE *ofergangan*, fr. *ofer*, adv., over + *gangan* to go — more at GANG] *chiefly Scot* : to go over; *specif* : OVERCOME
overgarment \ˈ==ˌ==\ *n* [ME *over garment*, fr. ³*over* + *garment*] : an outer garment
overgear \ˈ==ˌ=\ *n* : a gear train in which the ultimately driven shaft has greater angular speed than the original driving shaft
overgenerous \ˌ==ˈ=(=)=\ *adj* : unduly or extremely generous
overget \ˌ==ˈ=\ *vt* [ME *overgeten*, fr. ¹*over* + *geten* to get] **1** *dial chiefly Eng* **a :** REACH **b :** OVERTAKE, PASS **2 :** to get beyond : get over : recover from
overgild \ˈ==ˌ=, ˌ==ˈ=\ *vt* [ME *overgilden*, fr. OE *ofergyldan*, fr. *ofer*, adv., over + *gyldan* to gild] : to gild over : VARNISH
¹**overglaze** \ˈ==ˌ=, ˌ==ˈ=\ *vt* [¹*over* + *glaze*, v.] : to glaze over : cover or coat with a glaze or polish : coat so as to conceal
²**overglaze** \ˈ==ˌ=\ *adj* [²*over* + *glaze*, n.] : applied over the glaze after firing; *also* : suitable for so applying — used of some colors; compare UNDERGLAZE
³**overglaze** \"\ *n* [³*over* + *glaze*, n.] : a glaze (as on pottery ware) applied over another
overgloom \ˌ==ˈ=\ *vt* : to make gloomy : OVERSHADOW
overgo \ˌ==ˈ=\ *vt* [ME *overgon*, fr. OE *ofergān*, fr. *ofer*, adv., over + *gān* to go] **1** *dial chiefly Brit* : to cross over or through **2 :** to get the better of : EXCEL, EXCEED; *specif, dial chiefly Eng* : OVERPOWER, OVERBEAR
overgot *past of* OVERGET
overgotten *past part of* OVERGET
overgown \ˈ==ˌ=\ *n* : an outer or upper gown
overgrain \ˌ==ˈ=\ *vt* : to grain over (a grained surface) in painting so as to enrich or emphasize the effect
over·grain·er \"ə(r)\ *n* : a brush used for overgraining
overgraze \ˌ==ˈ=\ *vt* : to graze to excess ⟨overgrazed pastures⟩
overground \ˈ==ˌ=\ *adj* [²*over* + *ground*] : situated over or above ground ⟨operate injuriously to the ~ system —Alvin Johnson⟩
overgrow \ˌ==ˈ=\ *vb* [ME *overgrowen*, fr. ¹*over* + *growen* to grow] *vt* **1 a :** to grow over : cover with growth or herbage ⟨cellar holes, *overgrown* by bushes —*Amer. Guide Series: Maine*⟩ **b** *archaic* : OVERCOME, OVERBURDEN **2 :** to grow beyond or rise above : OUTGROW ⟨has long since *overgrown* the limitations of a coterie —R.U.Johnson⟩ ~ *vi* **1 :** to grow beyond the normal or natural size : grow too large ⟨when a scar ~s into a keloid —Morris Fishbein⟩ **2 :** to become grown over (as with weeds)
overgrown \ˌ==ˈ=\ *adj* [ME *overgrowen*, fr. past part. of *overgrowen* to overgrow] **1 :** covered with overgrowth **2 :** abnormally, disproportionately, or excessively grown
overgrowth \ˈ==ˌ=\ *n* [fr. *overgrow*, after E *grow: growth*] **1 a :** excessive growth or its result : superfluous abundance **b :** HYPERTROPHY, HYPERPLASIA **2 :** something that has grown over a place or thing
overhall *n* [by alter.] *chiefly dial* : OVERALL
¹**overhand** \ˈ==ˌ=\ *n* [ME, fr. ³*over* + *hand*, n.] **1** *chiefly dial* : the upper hand : ADVANTAGE **2** [²*overhand*] : an overhand stroke (as in tennis)
²**overhand** \"\ *adj* [³*over* + *hand*, n.] **1 :** done by grasping with the palm of the hand downward or inward toward the body; *esp* : playing or played with the hand in this position ⟨an ~ stroke in tennis⟩ **2 :** OVERARM
³**overhand** \"\ *adv* : in an overhand manner or style
⁴**overhand** \"\ *vt* [³*overhand*] : to sew (cloth) with short vertical stitches along an edge of a seam, buttonhole, or hem
overhanded \ˈ==ˌ==\ *adv* [³*over* + *-handed* (fr. *hand*, n. + *-ed*)] : OVERHAND ⟨swung ~ with the cornstalk —J.H.Stuart⟩
overhand knot *n* : a small knot (as a stopper knot) often used as a part of other knots esp. as a means of preventing the end of a cord from fraying — called also *thumb knot*

overhand knot

overhand loop knot *n* : LOOP KNOT
overhand stope *n* : an excavation giving access to the under side of an ore body
¹**overhang** \ˌ==ˈ=\ *vb* [¹*over* + *hang*] *vt* **1 a :** to jut, project, or be suspended over : hang over ⟨the wooden raft that *overhung* the iron hull —Fletcher Pratt⟩ **b :** to hang over threateningly : impend over ⟨the threat of death that *overhung* me —R.L.Stevenson⟩ **2 :** to suspend (as a door) from above or from the top ~ *vi* : to project so as to be over something **syn** see BULGE
²**overhang** \ˈ==ˌ=\ *n* : something that overhangs: as **a :** the part of the bow or stern of a ship that projects over the water beyond the water line; *also* : the extent of the projection **b :** a projection of the roof or upper story of a building beyond the wall of the lower part : JETTY **c :** the forward pitch of a pile of lumber **d :** the part of a book cover extending beyond the page edges and forming squares — called also *overlap* **e** (1) : one half the difference in span of any two main supporting surfaces of an airplane, the overhang being positive when the upper of the two main supporting surfaces has the larger span (2) : the distance from the outer strut attachment to the tip of the wings (3) : the part of the balanced-control surface of an aircraft that extends ahead of the hinge

overhang b

overhanging \ˌ==ˈ==\ *adj* **1 :** JUTTING, PROJECTING ⟨crouching miserably under an ~ ledge —F.V.W.Mason⟩ **2 :** hanging over threateningly
overhappy \ˌ==ˈ==\ *adj* : too happy
overhaste \ˌ==ˈ=\ *n* [ME *overhast*, fr. ³*over* + *hast, haste* haste] : excessive haste
overhasty \ˌ==ˈ==\ *adj* [ME, fr. ¹*over* + *hasty*] : too hasty : PRECIPITATE ⟨regarded as an ~ plan for reconversion —*Current Biog.*⟩
¹**over·haul** \ˌōvə(r)ˈhȯl\ *vb* [¹*over* + *haul*] *vt* **1 a :** to light (a ship's rope) along toward the block through which it is being hauled : pull (a ship's rope) through a block or lead so as to ease or slacken : CLEAR, DISENTANGLE **b :** to haul the parts of (a tackle) so as to separate the blocks **2 a :** to subject to strict examination with a view to correction or repair ⟨our systems of education are being constantly ~*ed* —*Saturday Rev.*⟩ ⟨the doctors ... ~*ed* him and found him pretty sound —C.P.Snow⟩ **b :** to repair (as by replacement of worn parts and readjustment) so as to restore to satisfactory working order ⟨~ an engine⟩ **c :** to clean up (a property) after a fire in order to make sure that the fire is extinguished and to prevent further damage (as by weather or falling debris) **3 :** to gain upon in a chase : come up with : OVERTAKE ⟨~*ed* the transport very slowly —W.F.Jenkins⟩ ⟨~*ed* the U.S. in atomic research —*N.Y. Herald Tribune*⟩ ~ *vi* : to run or slack back when the pulling power is removed ⟨an ~*ing* tackle⟩
²**overhaul** \ˈ==ˌ=\ *n* **1 :** OVERHAULING ⟨she had just finished ~ in the Navy Yard —Wirt Williams⟩ ⟨planning a major ~ of its highways —J.N.Robertson⟩ ⟨had an ~, and was treated for sinus trouble —Viola Meynell⟩ **2 a :** the distance for which payment is made for haulage of excavated material that is usu. the excess over a specified distance of free haulage **b :** the number of cubic yards moved through the overhaul distance multiplied by the overhaul distance in units of 100 feet
over·haul·er \ˌ==ˈhȯlə(r)\ *n* : one that overhauls
overhauling \ˌ==ˈ==\ *n* : the action of one that overhauls : an instance of such action ⟨our whole system of taxation needs ... ~ —D.D.Eisenhower⟩
¹**overhead** \ˌ==ˈ=\ *adv* [²*over* + *head*, n.] **1 :** above one's head: as **a :** in the sky : on high : ALOFT ⟨looking up at the stars ~⟩ ⟨~ the terns hovering close —E.A.Weeks⟩ **b :** in the story or on the floor above ⟨making a terrific racket ~⟩ **2 :** so as to be covered head and all ⟨plunged ~ into the water⟩
²**overhead** \ˈ==ˌ=\ *adj* **1 a :** operating or situated above or overhead ⟨gardens ... equipped with ~ irrigation —*Monsanto Mag.*⟩ **b :** passing over the head ⟨an ~ rein⟩ **c :** above the grade of a railway or highway ⟨an ~ crossing⟩ **d :** having the driving part above the part driven ⟨an ~ pulley shaft⟩ **2 :** general, indirect, or undistributed as distinct from particular and direct ⟨~ charges⟩ ⟨~ expenses⟩
³**overhead** \ˈ==ˌ=\ *n* **1 a :** those general charges or expenses in a business which cannot be charged up as belonging exclusively to any particular part of the work or product (as rent, taxes, insurance, lighting, heating, accounting and other office expenses, and depreciation) **b :** a particular charge of such character ⟨there were too many ~s —F.D.Ommanney⟩ **2 :** CEILING ⟨a big room with a low ~ —R.O.Bowen⟩; *esp* : the ceiling of a ship's compartment **3** *North & Midland* : a loft in a barn; *specif* : HAYMOW **4 :** a stroke in a racket game made above head height : SMASH **5 :** the effluent vapor from the top of a distillation column
overhead fire *n* : fire directed over the heads of friendly troops
overhead man *n* **1 :** an electrician in a motion picture studio who plugs lighting, camera, sound, and telephone circuits into the power connection boxes located in the grid of the studio — called also *grid man* **2 :** an operator of an electric bridge crane
overhead railway *n* : one track crossing another by an overhead bridge
overhead valve *n* : an internal-combustion engine valve operated from a camshaft running above the cylinder head
overhear \ˌ==ˈ=\ *vt* : to hear (a speaker or his speech) without the speaker's knowledge or intention ⟨could not help ~*ing* the talk —A.W.Long⟩ ~ *vi* : to overhear something
¹**overheat** \ˌ==ˈ=\ *vb* [ME *overheten*, fr. ¹*over* + *heten* to heat] *vt* **1 :** to heat to excess; *specif* : to heat (a metal) to a temperature so high that the grain structure is coarsened to an undesirable but not irreparable degree **2 :** to excite or agitate to excess or unduly ⟨~*ed* by nationalism —A.T.Bouscaren⟩ ~ *vi* : to become overheated
²**overheat** \"\ *n* : excessive heat or fervor
overheated *adj* **1 :** heated beyond the safe or desirable point ⟨~ metal⟩ ⟨the child became ~⟩ **2 :** marked by or arousing excessive passion, fervor, or excitement ⟨the perennially ~ Malthusian debate —*Economist*⟩ ⟨an occasional ~ adjective —Billy Rose⟩
overheavy \ˌ==ˈ==\ *adj* : unduly or extremely heavy
overhie \ˌ==ˈ=\ *vt* [ME *overhien*, fr. ¹*over* + *hien* to hasten — more at HIE] *archaic* : OVERTAKE
overhook \ˌ==ˈ=\ *vt* : to pass an arm over so as to hook in wrestling
overhung *past of* OVERHANG
overhung door \ˈ==ˌ=-\ *n* : a sliding door suspended from the top (as upon rollers)
overindulge \ˌ===ˈ=\ *vb* [¹*over* + *indulge*] : to indulge to excess
overindulgence \ˌ===ˈ==\ *n* [³*over* + *indulgence*] : excessive indulgence ⟨~ in reading —H.G.Armstrong⟩
overindulgent \ˌ===ˈ==\ *adj* [¹*over* + *indulgent*] : marked by overindulgence : too indulgent : indulging too much
overinform \ˌ===ˈ=\ *vt* **1 :** to actuate or animate excessively **2 :** to furnish with abundant or excessive information
overing *pres part of* OVER
over·insurance \ˌōvə(r)+\ *n* [³*over* + *insurance*] **1 :** insurance that exceeds in amount the actual cash value of the property insured **2 :** insurance in a greater amount than the insured can afford
over·insured \"+\ *adj* [¹*over* + *insured* (past part. of *insure*)] **1 :** insured for more than the real value **2 :** insured in a greater amount than one can afford
over·intricate \"+\ *adj* [¹*over* + *intricate*] : unnecessarily or impractiably intricate ⟨an ~ scheme⟩
¹**overissue** \ˌ==ˈ=(ˌ)=\ *n* [³*over* + *issue*] **1 :** an excessive issue : an issue (as of bonds) exceeding the limit of capital, credit, or authority **2 :** printed matter remaining unsold or undistributed ⟨purchase ~ as wastepaper for pulping⟩
²**overissue** \"\ *vt* [¹*over* + *issue*] : to issue in excess
over·ite \ˈōvəˌrīt\ *n* -S [Edwin *Over* b1903 Am. mineral collector + E *-ite*] : a mineral $Ca_3Al_8(PO_4)_8(OH)_6.15H_2O$ consisting of hydrous basic phosphate of aluminum and calcium
over·jet \ˈ==ˌjet\ *n* [prob. fr. ³*over* + *-jet* (fr. *jet*, v., to jut)] : OVERBITE
overjoy \ˌ==ˈ=\ *vt* : to fill with great joy : cause to rejoice ⟨~*ed* me when I read it —H.J.Laski⟩ ⟨the dealers it failed to ~ —J.M.Conly⟩
overjump \ˌ==ˈ=\ *vt* **1 :** to jump over **2 :** to jump too far over
overkeep \ˌ==ˈ=\ *vt* : to keep too strictly or too long
overkind \ˌ==ˈ=\ *adj* [ME *overkinde*, fr. ¹*over* + *kinde* kind, natural — more at KIND] : excessively kind — **over·kind·ly** *adv* — **over·kind·ness** *n*
overking \ˈ==ˌ=\ *n* [ME, fr. ³*over* + *king*] : a king who has sovereignty over inferior kings or ruling princes
overknee \ˈ==ˌ=\ *adj* [²*over* + *knee*, n.] : extending above the knee ⟨~ boots⟩
overlabor \ˌ==ˈ==\ *vt* : OVERWORK
overlace \ˌ==ˈ=\ *vt* : to lace over : cover with a lacing ⟨*overlaced* with a fantasy of color and sculpture —H.B.Alexander⟩
overlade \ˌ==ˈ=\ *vt* [ME *overladen*, fr. ¹*over* + *laden* to load — more at LADE] : to load with too great a cargo or burden : OVERLOAD ⟨*overladen* with detail and digression —H.S. Bennett⟩
overlaid *past of* OVERLAY
overlain *past part of* OVERLIE
¹**over·land** \ˈ==ˌland, -ˌlaa(ə)nd *also* ˌ==ˈ= *or* ˈ==ˌlənd\ *adv* [ME *overlond*, fr. ²*over* + *lond, land* land] : by, upon, or across land ⟨advantages of transport by river, instead of ~ —G.S.L. Clowes⟩
²**overland** \ˈ==ˌland, -ˌlaa(ə)nd *also* -ˌlənd\ *adj* : going or accomplished over the land instead of by sea ⟨an ~ route⟩ ⟨~ emigrants⟩
³**overland** \ˈ==ˌ=\ *vt, Austral* : to drive (herds or flocks of livestock) overland esp. for considerable distances ~ *vi, Austral* : to make a journey overland esp. while driving livestock
⁴**overland** \ˈ==ˌ=\ *n* [prob. fr. ³*over* + *land*] : land formerly held in the west of England by any of several kinds of local tenure
over·land·er \ˈ==ˌlandə(r), -ˌlaan-\ *n* **1 :** one that travels overland **2** *Austral* : one that drives livestock overland
¹**overlap** \ˌ==ˈ=\ *vb* [¹*over* + *lap*] *vt* **1 :** to extend over and cover a part of : lap over : OVERLIE ⟨the vertical siding has *overlapped* joints —*Amer. Guide Series: N.C.*⟩ ⟨if branches of a tree ~ the boundary of a neighbor —F.D.Smith & Barbara Wilcox⟩ **2 :** to have something in common with : comprehend elements of : coincide in part with ⟨every personality ~s every other personality —*Encyc. Americana*⟩ ⟨the baroque period ~s the rococo⟩ ~ *vi* **1 :** to lap over : occupy the same area in part ⟨the two towns ... now ~ —*Amer. Guide Series: Oregon*⟩ **2 :** to have something in common : coincide in part ⟨the realm where philosophy and psychology ~ —L.W.Beck⟩ ⟨believe that aesthetics partly ~s with ethics —Peter Viereck⟩
²**overlap** \ˈ==ˌ=\ *n* **1 a :** the condition or relationship of things that overlap : an instance of such a condition or relationship ⟨found to have unexpected areas of ~ —*Times Lit. Supp.*⟩ ⟨this incongruous ~ of civilization and savagery —*Time*⟩ **b :** the extent to which or the area in which one thing overlaps another ⟨provide a good ~ between the jacket and trousers —H.G.Armstrong⟩ ⟨a large ~ between emotions and their understanding —S.J.Beck⟩ **c :** a part that overlaps **2 :** OVERHANG d **3 :** the position of two ships when one overtaking the other cannot without dropping astern pass on the other side from that on which she is approaching and when the ships cannot turn toward each other without the risk of fouling **4 :** a geological unconformity in which each successively younger bed within the younger group of strata extends beyond the edge of the next older bed **5 :** an area of deposited metal that is not fused to the parent metal in welding **6 :** a section of railroad track controlled by one signal that extends into territory controlled by another signal
overlap fault *n* : a reversed fault
overlap grip *n* : a grip for holding a golf club in which the little finger of the right hand overlaps the left forefinger
overlapping \ˌ==ˈ==\ *n* **1 :** OVERLAP **2** *prosody* : ENJAMBMENT, SYNAPHEA — **over·lap·ping·ly** *adv*
overlard \ˌ==ˈ=\ *vt* : to lard, line, or cover thickly ⟨a pride ~*ed* with fear —A.H.Raskin⟩
overlarge \ˌ==ˈ=\ *adj* : too large
overlaw \ˈ==ˌ=\ *n* : a higher law ⟨some mystic ~ that it is bound to obey —O.W.Holmes †1935⟩
¹**overlay** \ˌ==ˈ=\ *vt* [ME *overleyen*, fr. ¹*over* + *leyen* to lay] **1 a :** to lay or spread over or across : SUPERIMPOSE, COVER ⟨the whole subject ... is *overlaid* by stratum upon stratum of folklore —C.H.Andrewes⟩ ⟨*overlaid* with a thick veneer —Paul Pickrel⟩ **b** *printing* : to prepare an overlay for ⟨~ a cut⟩ **2 a** *obs* : to crush or overwhelm by massive force : OVERPOWER **b :** to smother (as an infant) by lying upon **c** *archaic* : to weigh down : OVERBURDEN, ENCUMBER **3 :** to hide or obscure by or as if by superimposition
²**overlay** \ˈ==ˌ=\ *n* **1** *Scot* : NECKTIE, CRAVAT **2 :** a covering either permanent or of a temporary and removable kind: as **a :** ornamental work formed by overlaying as with veneer **b :** an ornamental metal covering produced by inserting a decoration made of another metal **c :** a transparent cover on art work or a photograph; *esp* : such a cover carrying instructions to the engraver (as for color breaks or cropping) **d :** material (as paper patches) added to the packing on a printing press to make a stronger impression; *also* : the patched sheet itself — compare INTERLAY, UNDERLAY **e :** a decorative and contrasting design or article placed on top of a plain one ⟨an ~ of lace on a black collar⟩ **f :** a transparent sheet containing graphic matter (as map data) to be superimposed on another sheet (as a map or photograph) **3 :** a betting situation in which the odds on a horse go up beyond those estimated by the track handicapper in the morning line
overlayer \ˈōvə(r)+\ *n* : one that overlays; *esp* : OVERLAY ⟨an ~ of whimsy and of sophistication —Frank Nugent⟩
overleaf \ˌ==ˈ=\ *adv* [²*over* + *leaf*, n.] : on or to the other side of a leaf (as of a book) ⟨data ... tabulated ~ —A.L.Kroeber⟩
overleap \ˌ==ˈ=\ *vt* [ME *overlepen*, fr. OE *oferhlēapan*, fr. *ofer*, adv., over + *hlēapan* to run, jump, leap] **1 a :** to leap over or across ⟨~ing the bars of caste —Douglas Bush⟩ **b :** OMIT, IGNORE ⟨perhaps ~*ed* logic —H.O.Taylor⟩ **2 :** to cause (oneself) to leap beyond one's mark or aim : defeat (oneself) by leaping too far
overlearn \ˌ==ˈ=\ *vt* : to continue to study or practice after reaching a criterion level of performance ⟨~*ed* techniques⟩
overleather *n* [ME *overlether*, fr. ³*over* + *lether* leather] *obs* : upper leather
¹**overleave** \ˌ==ˈ=\ *adv* [²*over* + *leave*, n.] : after the period of leave granted ⟨that time they went back ... ~ —K.M. Dodson⟩
²**overleave** \"\ *adj* : absent beyond the period of leave granted ⟨might simply be ~ —T.O.Heggen⟩
overleaven *vt, obs* : to leaven too much; *also* : to cause to swell excessively
overliberal \ˌ==ˈ=(=)=\ *adj* : too liberal — **overliberality** \ˌ====ˈ===\ *n* — **overliberally** \ˌ==ˈ=(=)==\ *adv*
overlie \ˌ==ˈ=\ *vt* [ME *overliggen, overlien*, fr. ¹*over* + *liggen, lien* to lie, recline] **1 :** to lie over : lie or rest upon ⟨where warm water ~s colder waters —R.E.Coker⟩ ⟨the normal ... granitic layer that ~s it —A.E.Benfield⟩ **2 :** to cause the death of by lying upon ⟨sows that ~ their piglets⟩ ⟨will join the tragedies of the *overlain* —*Times Lit. Supp.*⟩
¹**overlift** \ˌ==ˈ=\ *vt* [¹*over* + *lift*] : to lift too high or too much
²**overlift** \ˈ==ˌ=\ *n* : a device to catch the bolt of a lock when one of the tumblers is overlifted
overlight \ˌ==ˈ=\ *vt* : to subject to or provide with an excess of light ⟨an ~*ed* picture⟩ ⟨garish *overlit* rooms⟩
¹**overline** \ˈ==ˌ=\ *vt* [¹*over* + *line*] : to draw a line or lines over or above
²**overline** \ˈ==ˌ=\ *n* [³*over* + *line*] **1 :** a printed line usu. underlined and of a smaller size or different type face than the headline proper run above a headline and designed to introduce or identify the matter of the story or provoke to read on **2 :** the title or explanatory matter above a picture or cartoon in a newspaper or periodical **3 :** an insertion, correction, or alteration made above the printed or manuscript line it applies to — distinguished from *underline*
overlive \ˌ==ˈ=\ *vb* [ME *overliven*, fr. OE *oferlibban*, fr. *ofer*, adv., over + *libban* to live] *vt, archaic* : OUTLIVE ~ *vi, archaic* : to continue to live : live too long
¹**overload** \ˌ==ˈ=\ *vb* [¹*over* + *load*] *vt* : to load to excess : load with too great a burden ⟨~ a wagon⟩ ⟨~ a ship⟩ ⟨~ a circuit⟩ ~ *vi* : to assume or impose an excessive load ⟨tendency of most women travelers ... to ~ on beauty preparations —T.H. Fielding⟩
²**overload** \ˈ==ˌ=\ *n* : an excessive load : the excess beyond a proper load ⟨issue special permits for ~s —R.R.Ireland⟩
overlock \ˌ==ˈ=\ *vt* **1 :** to interlock or intertwine above **2 :** to shoot (a bolt) beyond its first or normal locking **3 :** to overcast by machine — compare SERGING
¹**overlong** \ˌ==ˈ=\ *adj* [ME, fr. ¹*over* + *long*] : extremely long or too long ⟨thought some of the stories ~ —*Current Biog.*⟩ ⟨this ~ novel —Clifton Fadiman⟩
²**overlong** \"\ *adv* [ME *overlonge*, fr. ¹*over* + *longe* long] : for too long a time ⟨this period ... did not last ~ —J.T.Winterich⟩
¹**overlook** \ˌ==ˈ=\ *vt* [ME *overloken*, fr. ¹*over* + *loken* to look] **1 :** to look over or through : INSPECT, SURVEY, PERUSE ⟨took down a map and ~*ed* it —Eileen Duggan⟩ ⟨most good modern authors, which I have never even ~*ed* —Arnold Bennett⟩ **2 a** *obs* : to regard as inferior or low : SLIGHT **b :** to look down upon from a place that is over or above : look over or view from a higher position ⟨do not like living near water, and prefer not to be ~*ed* —G.W.B.Huntingford⟩ **c :** to rise above or afford a view of : OVERTOP ⟨a house ~*ing* the Pacific —*Current Biog.*⟩ ⟨deep-blue water, ~*ed* by seven volcanoes —Norman Zimmern⟩ ⟨a tower ~*ing* the city —*N.Y.Times*⟩ **3 a :** to look over and beyond so as to fail to see : miss or omit in looking : fail to notice ⟨which would otherwise be entirely ~*ed*, may be seen at night with a flashlight —*Boy Scout Handbook*⟩ ⟨whose sharpened senses ~ nothing —Richard Semon⟩ **b :** to fail to take due note of : pass over : IGNORE, DISREGARD ⟨hungry enough to ~ my scruples —Frank O'Leary⟩ ⟨the editor cannot ~ the problem —Bruce Westley⟩ **c :** to pass over without censure or punishment : EXCUSE ⟨decided to ~ the blank paper he turned in for Latin —*Current Biog.*⟩ ⟨minor misdemeanors may be ~*ed* —*Punch*⟩ **4 :** to watch over : SUPERVISE, OVERSEE ⟨sent ... as her envoy to ~ the conduct of the Kalmucks —Thomas De Quincey⟩ **5 :** to look on with the evil eye : bewitch by looking on ⟨a baby that has been ~*ed* will begin to pine away —F.G. Cassidy⟩ **syn** see NEGLECT
²**overlook** \ˈ==ˌ=\ *n* **1 :** an act of overlooking; *specif* : OVERSIGHT ⟨a slight ~ on my part⟩ **2 :** a place from which one may

look down upon a scene below ⟨plenty of ~*s* and trails —Thelma H. Bell⟩

overlooker \ˌ==ˈ==\ *n* [ME *overloker*, fr. *overloken* to overlook + *-er*] : one that overlooks: as **a** : a superintendent or overseer of workers : FOREMAN **b** : a worker that flips the ends of stacks of newly cut paper in order to discover and remove defective sheets

[1]**overlord** \ˈ==ˌ=\ *n* [ME, fr. [3]*over* + *lord*] **1** : a lord that is lord over other lords or rulers : a lord paramount ⟨when a man died leaving children under age, the ~ took over his land —G.G.Coulton⟩ ⟨the church professed to be . . . ~ of all temporal sovereigns —W.H.Hamilton⟩ **2** : an absolute or supreme ruler ⟨~*s* of the financial world —*Amer. Guide Series: Ind.*⟩ ⟨Asian resentment toward the traditional white ~ —L.S.Feuer⟩

[2]**overlord** \ˌ==ˈ=\ *vt* [[1]*over* + *lord*] : to lord it over : rule domineeringly : TYRANNIZE

over·lord·ship \ˈ==ˌ=ship, ˌ==ˈ=ˌ=\ *n* : the position, power, or authority of an overlord

overloup \ˌ==ˈ=\ *n* [[3]*over* + *loup*] *archaic Scot* : TRESPASS, TRANSGRESSION

overlove \ˌ==ˈ=\ *vt* : to love to excess

overlusty \ˌ==ˈ==\ *adj* : too lusty

[1]**overly** *adj* [ME, fr. [1]*over* + *-ly*, adj. suffix] **1** *obs* : CARELESS, SUPERFICIAL, NEGLIGENT **2** *archaic* : OVERBEARING, SUPERCILIOUS

[2]**over·ly** \ˈōvə(r)lē, -li\ *adv* [ME, fr. [1]*over* + *-ly*, adv. suffix] **1** *archaic* : SUPERFICIALLY, CARELESSLY **2** : EXCESSIVELY, TOO ⟨~ anxious⟩ ⟨~ retiring⟩

overlying *pres part of* OVERLIE

[1]**over·man** *n, pl* **overmen** [ME, fr. [3]*over* + *man*, n.] **1** \ˈōvə(r)mən, -ˌman\ : a man in authority over others : CHIEF; *specif* : FOREMAN **2** \ˈō(ə)rˌman, ˈōvər-\ *Scots law* : an arbiter or umpire appointed to settle a dispute between arbiters **3** \ˈōvə(r)ˌman\ [trans. of G *übermensch*] : SUPERMAN

[2]**over·man** \ˌ==ˈman\ *vt* [[1]*over* + *man*, v.] : to have or get too many men for the needs of ⟨~ a ship⟩

overmantel \ˈ==ˌ==, ˌ==ˈ==\ *n* [[2]*over* + *mantel*] : an ornamental structure (as a painting or a bas-relief) above a mantelpiece

overmast \ˌ==ˈ=\ *vt* [[1]*over* + *mast*, v.] : to furnish (a ship) with too long or too heavy masts

overmaster \ˌ==ˈ==\ *vt* [ME *overmaistren*, fr. [1]*over* + *maistren* to master] **1** : to establish mastery over : SUBDUE, VANQUISH ⟨the sensation ~*ed* me completely —Rudyard Kipling⟩ **2** *obs* : to be master over

overmastering \ˌ==ˈ=(ə)=\ *adj* : having complete or decisive mastery : DOMINANT, OVERRIDING ⟨some ~ motive which he could not guess at —John Buchan⟩ ⟨choking down some ~ emotion —A. Conan Doyle⟩ — **over·mas·ter·ing·ly** *adv*

[1]**overmatch** \ˌ==ˈ=\ *vt* [ME *overmacchen*, fr. [1]*over* + *macchen* to match] **1 a** : to be more than equal to or a match for ⟨a bleakness that ~*ed* his boredom —Booth Tarkington⟩ **b** : VANQUISH, DEFEAT ⟨with the unobtrusive action of an ~*ed* man —Joseph Furphy⟩ ⟨occasionally victorious and usually ~*ed* gladiators —Bennett Cerf⟩ **2** : to match (as a team, a player, a prizefighter) with a superior opponent ⟨does all right . . . until his owner ~*es* him —John McCarten⟩

[2]**overmatch** \ˈ==ˌ=\ *n* **1** : one superior in power ⟨met his ~⟩ **2** : a contest in which one of the opponents is overmatched

overmatter \ˈ==ˌ==\ *n* : overset type matter; *esp* : that portion of the overset that is not used

overmature \ˌ===ˈ=\ *adj* : more than matured : past the age or condition of maturity or of fitness characteristic of maturity — **overmaturity** \ˌ===ˈ===\ *n*

overmeasure \ˈ==ˌ==\ *n* : excessive measure : the excess beyond true or proper measure : SURPLUS

overmodest \ˌ==ˈ==\ *adj* : excessively modest

overmodulation \ˌ==ˌ==ˈ==\ *n* : defective modulation in which the modulating signal is made too strong

over·most \ˈō(ə)rˌmōst, ˈōvər-, -ˌməst\ *adj* [ME, fr. [3]*over* + *-most*] *chiefly Scot* : UPPERMOST, HIGHEST

overmount \ˌ==ˈ=\ *vb* [ME *overmounten*, fr. [1]*over* + *mounten* to mount] *vt, archaic* : to mount over : go higher than : rise above ~ *vi, obs* : to mount too high

overmountain \ˌ==ˈ==\ *adj* [[2]*over* + *mountain*, n.] : situated or residing over the mountains ⟨the ~ farmers —Broadus Mitchell⟩

[1]**overmuch** \ˌ==ˈ=\ *adj* [ME *overmuche*, fr. [1]*over* + *muche*, adj., much] : very great or excessive ⟨does not claim ~ merit —Clifford Leech⟩

[2]**overmuch** \"\ *n* [ME *overmuche*, fr. *overmuche*, adj.] : too great an amount : EXCESS

[3]**overmuch** \"\ *adv* [ME *overmuche*, fr. [1]*over* + *muche*, adv., much] : in too great a degree : too much ⟨do not bother ~ about notes —L.R.McColvin⟩

over·much·ness \ˌ==ˈ=nəs\ *n* : the condition of being overmuch : EXCESS

overname \ˌ==ˈ=\ *vt* : to name over : name in a series

overnet \ˌ==ˈ=\ *vt* : to cover or to snare with a net ~ *vi* : to use nets to excess in fishing

over·nice \ˌōvə(r)+\ *adj* [ME, fr. [1]*over* + *nice*] : excessively nice or particular: **a** : too fastidious **b** : too scrupulous ⟨untroubled by an ~ conscience —V.L.Parrington⟩ — **overnicely** \"+\ *adv* — **overniceness** \"+\ *n* — **overnicety** \"+\ *n*

[1]**overnight** \ˌ==ˈ=\ *adv* [ME *over night*, fr. [2]*over* + *night*, n.] **1 a** : in the evening before ⟨trying to tell a good story he heard ~ —O.S.J.Gogarty⟩ **b** : in the interval between two days ⟨allowing the coarser particles to settle out . . . ~ —*Jour. of Infectious Diseases*⟩ **c** : during the night : till the following morning ⟨stayed with friends ~⟩ **2** : with great or extreme speed or suddenness : very quickly or suddenly : all of a sudden ⟨sprang up ~ in answer to a labor need —*Amer. Guide Series: Maine*⟩ ⟨no such perfected technique is born ~ —L.H. Appleton⟩

[2]**overnight** \ˈ==ˌ=, ˌ==ˈ=\ *n* : the fore part of the night last past : the previous evening ⟨his emotional rapture of the ~ —George Meredith⟩

[3]**overnight** \ˌ==ˈ=\ *adj* **1 a** : of, relating to, or resulting from the previous evening : done or lasting during the night ⟨an ~ carouse⟩ ⟨~ laughter is a commodity that I . . . am always ready to buy —Robert Hatch⟩ **b** : being of the duration of one night ⟨an ~ stop⟩ : staying one night ⟨~ guests⟩ **2** : happening or appearing overnight ⟨became an ~ sensation —*Amer. Guide Series: Ind.*⟩

[4]**overnight** \"\ *vi* : to stay overnight ⟨~*ed* at the official presidential residence —*Wilkes-Barre (Pa.) Record*⟩

overnight bag *or* **overnight case** *or* **over·night·er** \ˌ==ˈnīd·ə(r)\ *n* -s : a traveling bag of a size to carry clothing and personal articles for an overnight trip

overnight race *n* : a horse race for which entries close 72 hours (exclusive of Sundays) or less before the first race of the day on which the race is scheduled to be run

overnumber \ˌ==ˈ==\ *vt, archaic* : OUTNUMBER

overoffice *vt, obs* : to domineer over by virtue of office

overoptimism \ˌ==ˈ==ˌ==\ *n* : excessive optimism

overoptimist \ˌ==ˈ===\ *n* : an excessively optimistic person

overoptimistic \ˌ==ˌ==ˈ==\ *adj* : marked by overoptimism

over·organization \ˌōvə(r)+\ *n* : the act of overorganizing or the state of being overorganized

over·organize \"+\ *vt* : to subject to unduly complex or elaborate organization ~ *vi* : to adopt an unduly complex or elaborate form of organization

over·ornate \ˌōvə(r)+\ *adj* : unduly or excessively ornate

[1]**overpack** \ˌ==ˈ=\ *vt* [[1]*over* + *pack*] : to pack in an overpack

[2]**overpack** \"\ *n* : a wooden or fiber box used over a domestic box for overseas shipments for greater strength and protection

overpaint \ˌ==ˈ=\ *vt* **1** : to paint over : paint out **2** : to color or describe too strongly ⟨heavily ~*ed* the depression of English learning —F.M.Stenton⟩

over·part·ed \ˌōvərˈpärd·əd\ *adj* [[1]*over* + *-parted* (fr. *part*, n. + *-ed*)] : charged with a part or role beyond one's ability

overparticular \ˌōvə(r)+\ *adj* : extremely or unduly particular

[1]**overpass** \ˌ==ˈ=\ *vb* [ME *overpassen*, fr. [1]*over* + *passen* to pass] *vt* **1 a** : to pass or get through : get to the end of ⟨when that six months were ~*ed* —*Ballad Book*⟩ **b** : to manage to get through : SURMOUNT **2** : to pass beyond in quality, value, degree, or amount : SURPASS, EXCEED ⟨so completely had his moral passion ~*ed* his concern for poetry —D.S.Savage⟩ **3 a** : to pass across, over, or beyond : go to the other side of : CROSS ⟨the last American frontier had been ~*ed* —H.J.Laski⟩ **b** : to pass over or beyond the restrictions of : TRANSGRESS ⟨a limit to patience . . . and when that was ~*ed*, then my anger blazed out —W.H.Hudson †1922⟩ ⟨~ the bounds of propriety⟩ **4 a** : to pass over without comment or mention **b** : to pass over in favor of another ⟨colonels who have been ~*ed* for commands —Rudyard Kipling⟩ ~ *vi* : to pass over, by, away, or off

[2]**overpass** \ˈ==ˌ=\ *n* **1** : a grade separation where clearance to traffic on the lower level is obtained by elevating the higher level (as with a bridge or viaduct) — compare UNDERPASS **2** : the upper level of a grade separation — called also *overcrossing*

overpast \ˌ==ˈ=\ *adj* [fr. *overpast*, *overpassed*, past part. of [1]*overpass*] : ENDED, PAST, OVER ⟨all that was ~ —Mary Webb⟩ ⟨the danger was well ~ —Rafael Sabatini⟩

overpay \ˌ==ˈ=\ *vt* : to pay too much to or for : compensate or reward beyond what is due

overpayment \ˌ==ˈ==\ *n* : payment in excess of what is due; *also* : the amount of such excess

overpeer \ˌ==ˈ=\ *vt* **1** *archaic* **a** : to rise or tower above **b** : EXCEL **2** : to peer over : look down on : OVERLOOK ⟨~ the cabin —Maristan Chapman⟩

overpeopled \ˌ==ˈ==\ *adj* : too densely peopled

overperch *vt, obs* : to pass over as if by perching upon

overpersuade \ˌ===ˈ=\ *vt* [[1]*over* + *persuade*] : to persuade to adopt one's side or view : bring over by persuasion ⟨*overpersuaded* her finally —*Manchester Guardian Weekly*⟩

overpersuasion \ˌ===ˈ==\ *n* [fr. *overpersuade*, after E *persuade: persuasion*] : the act of overpersuading ⟨drank two glasses by his ~ —Samuel Richardson⟩

overpester *vt, obs* : to encumber to excess

[1]**overpick** \ˈ==ˌ=\ *adj* [[3]*over* + *pick*, n. (throw of the shuttle)] *of a loom* : having the picking arm or shuttle-driving device over the shuttle boxes — compare UNDERPICK

[2]**overpick** \"\ *n* : an overpick loom

overpicture \ˌ==ˈ==\ *vt* **1** : to surpass nature in the picture or representation of **2** : to cover with pictures

overpitch \ˌ==ˈ=\ *vt* [[1]*over* + *pitch*] : to pitch (a bowled ball) too close to the wicket in cricket

overpitched \ˌ==ˈ=\ *adj* [[1]*over* + *pitched* (past part. of *pitch*)] : having a too great pitch or slope ⟨an ~ roof⟩

overplacement \ˌ==ˈ==\ *n* : SUPERPOSITION

overplaid \ˈ==ˌ=\ *n* [[3]*over* + *plaid*] : a textile design consisting of a plaid pattern superimposed on another plaid or on a textured ground (as of tweed or herringbone); *also* : a fabric with such a design

overplant \ˌ==ˈ=\ *vt* : to plant (a crop) in excess of market demand or of the allotted acreage under a crop control order ~ *vi* : to plant in excess of demand or of the allotted acreage

[1]**overplay** \ˌ==ˈ=\ *vb* [[1]*over* + *play*, v.] *vt* **1 a** : to exaggerate (as a part in a play or an artistic effect) ⟨~ a comic role⟩ ⟨~*ed* every crescendo⟩ **b** : to exaggerate the importance or value of : give undue emphasis or attention to : OVERSTRESS ⟨~ those features of human attention that are peripheral —*Psychological Rev.*⟩ ⟨tends to ~ the intellectual achievement —*Times Lit. Supp.*⟩ ⟨the most ~*ed* newspaper story of 1954 —*Time*⟩ ⟨the present text ~*s* its points of strength —A.R. Turquette⟩ **c** : OVERDO ⟨a theatrical cliché that's ~*ed* —Ethel Merman⟩ **2** : to rely too much upon the strength of : seek to gain too much advantage from — usu. used in the phrase *overplay one's hand* ⟨~*ing* their hands and tending to be greedy —*Sunday Independent (Dublin)*⟩ **3** : to strike a golf ball so that it is driven beyond (a putting green) ~ *vi* : to exaggerate a part or effect ⟨her tendency to ~ —R.A. Hague⟩

[2]**overplay** \ˈ==ˌ=\ *n* [in sense 1, fr. *over* + *play*, n. (after the verb phrase *play over*); in sense 2, fr. [1]*overplay*] **1** : a replay of a hand in duplicate whist **2** : exaggerated or undue emphasis or treatment : OVERSTRESS ⟨~ of highly sensational stories —F.L.Mott⟩

overplot \ˌ==ˈ=\ *vt* : to devise an unduly complex or elaborate plot for (as a novel)

overplow \ˌ==ˈ=\ *vt* : to plow, work, or exploit to excess ⟨Shakespearean commentary is a special and ~*ed* field —Henry Hewes⟩ ⟨grassy hills . . . were ~*ed* —Russell Lord⟩

[1]**over·plus** \ˈōvə(r)ˌpləs\ *n* -ES [ME, part trans. of MF *surplus* — more at SURPLUS] : that which remains above a proper or fit supply or beyond a quantity proposed : SURPLUS ⟨a lack of leaders and an ~ of followers —*Brit. Birds in Colour*⟩ **syn** see EXCESS

[2]**overplus** *adv, obs* : in addition : beyond need

overply \ˌ==ˈ=\ *vt* : to ply to excess : OVEREXERT, OVERWORK

overpoise \ˌ==ˈ=\ *vt* [[1]*over* + obs. E *poise* to weigh, fr. ME *poisen* — more at POISE] *archaic* : OUTWEIGH

overpole \ˌ==ˈ=\ *vt* : to pole (a metal) too long

overpopulate \ˌ==ˈ===\ *vt* : to populate too densely : cause to have too great a population

overpopulation \ˌ==ˌ==ˈ==\ *n* : the condition of being overpopulated; *also* : an excess of population

overpot \ˌ==ˈ=\ *vt* : to plant in too large a pot

overpotential \ˌ===ˈ==\ *n* : OVERVOLTAGE

overpower \ˌ==ˈ==\ *vt* [[1]*over* + *-power* (fr. *power*, n.)] **1** : to get the better of by superior force or power : SUBDUE, VANQUISH ⟨war ~*ed*, dragged out into the open —*Amer. Guide Series: Tenn.*⟩ ⟨by a margin of 15,000 votes . . . was ~*ed* by the winner —*Time*⟩ **2** : to affect overwhelmingly by reason of great power or intensity ⟨when hunger ~*s* him —J.G. Frazer⟩ ⟨the odor ~*ed* him⟩ ⟨his instinct for heroics ~*ed* him —Gerald Beaumont⟩ **3** : to supply with more power than is needed ⟨never ~ your boat —Peter Heaton⟩

syn OVERWHELM, WHELM, ENGULF, DELUGE, SWAMP: OVERPOWER applies to defeating or reducing to submission or ineffectiveness by vastly superior force ⟨a sentry *overpowered* by the attackers⟩ ⟨resistance *overpowered* in a few days⟩ ⟨*overpowered* by the show of wealth around him⟩ OVERWHELM may suggest submerging, overcoming, vanquishing, destroying, or overpowering in the manner of a breaking ocean wave ⟨Scotland was *overwhelmed* by the ice sheets of the great Ice Age —L.D.Stamp⟩ ⟨it was between the inner and outer shoal that disaster *overwhelmed* the lifeboat and her crew —G.G. Carter⟩ ⟨his hopeless endeavor to stem the rising flood of irrationalism and slave-spirit that were soon to *overwhelm* the great Roman world —Norman Douglas⟩ WHELM is a close synonym for OVERWHELM in its dire uses ⟨it seemed as though the entire town might go — as though the sea would *whelm* houses, vessels, and town together —Mary H. Vorse⟩ ⟨this report reached his periwigged Excellency about the time that his own city was being overwhelmed by earthquake; he had little time for ancient ruins when his own was *whelmed* with destruction —V.W. Von Hagen⟩ ENGULF suggests swallowing up as by rushing waters, or catching, burying, entangling, or covering hopelessly so that extrication is impossible ⟨Bonnet thought that periodically the world was *engulfed* by a major catastrophe, the last one being the Mosaic flood —S.F.Mason⟩ ⟨the doom of madness that had *engulfed* her aunt —Edith Sitwell⟩ DELUGE implies a concentrated massing, as of torrential rain, that overwhelms; it is usu. used figuratively ⟨the speaker was *deluged* with questions⟩ ⟨as Yellow Cabs drove up with strikebreakers they were *deluged* with rotten fruit from the trucks —R.M.Lovett⟩ SWAMP, originally in the passive suggesting entanglement or submersion in a swamp, now is close to DELUGE, although it may indicate more hopeless entangling or oppressing ⟨a sea broke over them, and would have *swamped* the *Otter*, had she not been the best of sea boats —Charles Kingsley⟩ ⟨the work rose about him like a tide. It *swamped* his days —Mary Austin⟩ ⟨the mind is *swamped* by the bewildering complexity of directions —R.W. Southern⟩

overpowering *adj* : exercising an irresistible influence : OVERWHELMING ⟨her ~ beauty struck his heart —George Meredith⟩ ⟨both men . . . were ~ personalities —Bernard Smith⟩ — **over·pow·er·ing·ly** *adv*

[1]**overpraise** \ˌ==ˈ=\ *vt* [ME *overpreisen*, fr. [1]*over* + *preisen* to praise] : to praise excessively

[2]**overpraise** \ˈ==ˌ=\ *n* : excessive praise

[1]**overpress** \ˌ==ˈ=\ *vt* [ME *overpressen*, fr. [1]*over* + *pressen* to press] **1** *obs* : AFFLICT, OPPRESS **2** : to load with an excessive burden : OVERBURDEN ⟨all very tired and ~*ed* men —*Economist*⟩ **3** : to press or insist upon unduly : drive or push (as a contention) too far ⟨does not ~ his case —P.R.Levin⟩

[2]**overpress** \ˈ==ˌ=\ *n* : OVERPRESSURE ⟨~ of work⟩

overpressure \ˌ==ˈ==\ *n* : excessive pressure

overprice \ˌ==ˈ=\ *vt* : to set too high a price on : charge too much for

[1]**overprint** \ˌ==ˈ=\ *vt* [[1]*over* + *print*] **1 a** : to print over (matter already printed) with something additional : SURPRINT : IMPRINT **b** : to print too many copies of **2** *photog* **a** : to print too long or with too great an intensity of light **b** : to print (one image) on another **3 a** : to place an overprint on (a stamp) **b** : to mark (a stamp) with a specified overprint ⟨a stamp ~*ed* Samoa⟩ **c** : to make (a specified mark) on a stamp as an overprint ⟨~ a date on a stamp⟩ **4** : to type (typewriter characters) one over another to form a character not on the keys ⟨a star is formed by ~*ing* A and v⟩

[2]**overprint** \ˈ==ˌ=\ *n* **1** : something added by overprinting ⟨road classification is shown by a red ~ —*U. S. Geol. Survey*⟩ **2 a** : a printed marking (as a letter, figure, name, date, inscription) added to a postage or revenue stamp before its sale as a postage or revenue item; *esp* : one that alters the original (as in denomination, locality, or use) or that commemorates a special event — compare SURCHARGE **b** : a stamp bearing an overprint

[3]**overprint** \"\ *adj* : used in overprinting ⟨~ ink⟩ ⟨~ varnish⟩

overprivileged \ˌ==ˈ=(ə)=\ *adj* : privileged to excess; *specif* : endowed with too much of the world's goods

overprize \ˌ==ˈ=\ *vt* **1** : to prize excessively : OVERVALUE **2** *obs* : to exceed in value

overproduce \ˌ===ˈ=\ *vt* : to produce beyond the demand or allotted amount

overproduction \ˌ===ˈ==\ *n* : excessive production : supply beyond the demand at remunerative prices

overpronounce \ˌ===ˈ=\ *vt* : to give an exaggerated, affected, or unnaturally accented pronunciation to (as in \ˈgüdeˌnəf\ instead of \ˈgu̇dᵊnˌəf\ for *good enough*) ~ *vi* : to overpronounce a word, phrase, or other speech element

overpronunciation \ˌ===ˌ=ˈ==\ *n* : the act or an instance of overpronouncing

overproof \ˌ==ˈ=\ *adj* [[2]*over* + *proof*, n.] : containing more alcohol than proof spirit

[1]**overproportion** \ˌ===ˈ==\ *vt* [[1]*over* + *proportion*] : to make of too great proportion : make disproportionately large

[2]**overproportion** \"\ *n* : proportion in excess of the norm

overprotect \ˌ==ˈ=\ *vt* : to protect or shield unduly or excessively ⟨~*ed* children⟩

overprotection \ˌ===ˈ==\ *n* : undue or excessive protection or shielding; *specif* : excessive restriction of a child's behavior allegedly in the interest of his health and welfare by an anxious, insecure, or domineering mother — compare MOMISM

overprotective \ˌ===ˈ==\ *adj* : unduly or excessively protective

overprove \ˌ==ˈ=\ *vt* : to provide more proof of than is needed

overquick \ˌ==ˈ=\ *adj* : too quick or ready — **over·quick·ly** *adv*

over·rank *R & -R* ˈōvə+, *R sometimes* -vər+ *esp for emphasis*\ *adj* : too rank or luxuriant in growth

[1]**overrate** \ˌ==ˈ=\ *vt* [[1]*over* + *rate*] : to rate, value, or estimate too highly ⟨inclined to say that you ~ morality —Havelock Ellis⟩

[2]**overrate** \ˈ==ˌ=\ *n* : an excessive rate; *also* : an extra rate

[1]**overreach** \ˌ==ˈ=\ *vb* [ME *overrechen*, fr. [1]*over* + *rechen* to reach] *vt* **1** : to reach above or beyond : go beyond : OVERTOP ⟨regard anything as vulgar that ~*es* their own attempts —R. P.Warren⟩ **2** : to reach or come up with : OVERTAKE **3** : to defeat or thwart (oneself) by seeking to do or gain too much ⟨one promoter, ~*ing* himself, demanded an exorbitant price —*Amer. Guide Series: Pa.*⟩ ⟨owns a number of . . . properties but has never ~*ed* himself —W.L.Gresham⟩ or by being too crafty ⟨the red prowler's cunning ~*ed* itself —C.G.D.Roberts⟩ **4** : to get the better of esp. by sharp, unfair, tricky, or deceitful means : OUTWIT ⟨never made any bargain without ~*ing* . . . the person with whom he dealt —Henry Fielding⟩ ~ *vi* **1** *of a horse* : to strike the toe of the hind foot against the heel or quarter of the forefoot : GRAB **2 a** : to reach or go too far : go to excess ⟨if at times the argument wears thin, it is because . . . he ~*es* —S.L.A.Marshall⟩ **b** : EXAGGERATE **syn** see CHEAT

[2]**overreach** \ˈ==ˌ=, ˌ==ˈ=\ *n* **1** : the act of overreaching **2 a** : the act of striking the heel of the forefoot with the toe of the hind foot — used of a horse **b** : the injury so caused

over·reach·er \ˌ==ˈrēchə(r)\ *n* : one that overreaches

overreaching \ˌ==ˈ==\ *adj* : tending to overreach; *esp* : CHEATING ⟨are generally poor, greedy, and ~ —Tobias Smollett⟩ — **over·reach·ing·ly** *adv*

overreact \ˌ===ˈ=\ *vi* : to react excessively or too strongly ⟨~*s* to situations which do not entirely please him —A.C. Kinsey⟩

overread *vt* [ME *overreden*, fr. OE *oferrǣdan*, fr. *ofer*, adv., over + *rǣdan* to read] *obs* : to read over or through

overreadiness \ˌ=ˈ===\ *n* : the quality or state of being overready

overready \ˌ==ˈ==\ *adj* : extremely or unduly ready

overreckon \ˌ==ˈ==\ *vt* **1** : OVERESTIMATE **2** : to overcharge in a reckoning

overred \ˌ==ˈ=\ *vt, archaic* : to smear with red

overrefine \ˌ===ˈ=\ *vt* [[1]*over* + *refine*] : to refine to excess

overrefinement \ˌ===ˈ==\ *n* : excessive refinement

overregulate \ˌ==ˈ===\ *vt* : to subject to excessive regulation

overregulation \ˌ==ˌ==ˈ==\ *n* : excessive regulation

overrepresent \ˌ===ˈ=\ *vt* : to give excessive representation to ⟨~*s* the rural counties in the state⟩ — **overrepresentation** \ˌ=ˌ==(ˌ)=ˈ==\ *n*

[1]**override** \ˌ==ˈ=\ *vt* [ME *overriden*, fr. OE *oferrīdan*, fr. *ofer*, adv., over + *rīdan* to ride] **1 a** : to ride over or across ⟨where the beach is steep big waves break directly on it and ~ it —J.A.Steers⟩ ⟨prevent the ship from *overriding* her anchor —*Manual of Seamanship*⟩ **b** : to ride down : trample underfoot ⟨*overrode* the thin line of defenders⟩ **c** : to ride too close to (the hounds) in fox hunting **2** *obs* : to ride beyond : PASS, OUTRIDE **3** : to ride (as a horse) too much or too hard **4 a** : to dominate or prevail over : VANQUISH, CONQUER ⟨panic *overrode* everything else —Marcia Davenport⟩ ⟨a verity of purpose which *override* common domestic trials —P.S.Klein⟩ **b** : to set aside : ANNUL, SUPERSEDE ⟨a rebellious congress *overrode* the president's veto⟩ ⟨the positive law may . . . ~ the law of justice —B.N.Cardozo⟩ ⟨the rights of the individual were being flagrantly *overridden* —C.L.Jones⟩ **5** : to extend or pass over; *esp* : OVERLAP ⟨the lower end of the fractured bone *overrode* the upper⟩ **6** : to pay a commission to (as a general agent or sales manager) on sales made by subordinates

[2]**override** \ˈ==ˌ=, ˌ==ˈ=\ *n* **1** : a commission paid in addition to regular compensation; *esp* : a commission paid to managerial personnel on sales made by subordinates **2** : an auxiliary control that may be temporarily applied by hand to supplant the operation of an otherwise automatic control

over·rid·er \ˌ==ˈrīdə(r)\ *n* [[1]*override* + *-er*] *Brit* : BUMPER GUARD

overriding *adj* [fr. pres. part. of [1]*override*] **1** : DOMINEERING, ARROGANT ⟨in these fits he was the most ~ companion ever known —R.L.Stevenson⟩ **2** : subordinating all others to itself : DOMINANT, PRINCIPAL, PRIMARY ⟨the ~ importance of imponderables in determining human conduct —John Russell b.1872⟩ ⟨a further and ~ reason —Harold Koontz & Cyril O'Donnell⟩ ⟨the ~ danger —*Newsweek*⟩ ⟨the ~ problems of business in the years to come —A.L.Nickerson⟩

overright \ˌ==ˈ=\ *prep* [[2]*over* + *right*, adv.] *dial chiefly Brit* : over against : OPPOSITE ⟨an acre of land ~ the river —Robert Gibbings⟩

overrigid \ˌ==ˈ==\ *adj* : excessively rigid or severe ⟨~ application of a theory⟩ — **overrigidly** \ˌ==ˈ===\ *adv*

overripe \ˌ==ˈ=\ *adj* **1** : too ripe : advanced in development beyond the stage of maturity or ripeness ⟨~ fruit⟩ ⟨hide the flavor of ~ meat —Marjory S. Douglas⟩ **2 a** : advanced to or being a stage of development characterized by loss of vigor, creativity, or originality : DECADENT ⟨belonged to an ~ period of Greek art —Francis Steegmuller⟩ ⟨the relatively drab days of ~ Victorianism —I.J.Suloway⟩ ⟨languid ~ naturalism —Herbert Read⟩ **b** : marked by a fulsome, flabby, or cloying quality : lacking bite or vigor : FLAMBOYANT, ORNATE, SUGARY ⟨the sound is ~ —*Saturday Rev.*⟩ ⟨an early composition . . .

that is just a bit ~ and banal —Douglas Watt⟩ ⟨the atmosphere becomes sententious, the style turns ~ —C.J.Rolo⟩
overroof \¦==¦=\ *vt* **:** to roof over **:** ROOF
overround \¦==¦=\ *vt* **:** to round (as the lips, a vowel) more than usual
¹**overruff** \¦==¦=\ *vb* [¹*over* + *ruff*] **:** OVERTRUMP
²**overruff** \'==,=\ *n* **:** the act or an instance of overtrumping
¹**overrule** \¦==¦=\ *vb* [¹*over* + *rule*] *vt* **1 :** to rule over **:** GOVERN ⟨the guiding presence of the Holy Spirit to assist and ~ the teaching —A.J.Russell⟩ ⟨words plainly force and ~ the understanding —Francis Bacon⟩ **2 a :** to prevail over **:** OVERCOME ⟨tribal customs ~ everything —John Russell b.1872⟩ ⟨a force of attraction which is able to ~ the electrical force —G.W.Gray b.1886⟩ **b :** to bring over by persuasion or other influence **3 a :** to decide or rule against esp. by virtue of superior authority ⟨the chairman *overruled* the point of order⟩ ⟨*overruled* my father —Mary Austin⟩ **b :** to set aside or reverse (as a previous decision or ruling) ⟨the appellate court *overruled* the action of the trial judge⟩ **~** *vi* **1 :** to be supreme or superior in ruling or controlling ⟨the same large mind that ~*s* —Henry Adams⟩ **2 :** to decide or determine by superior authority ⟨all is as God ~*s* —Robert Browning⟩
²**overrule** \'==,=\ *n* **:** the rule of a superior power **:** SUPREMACY
overruler \¦==¦=\ *n* **:** one that overrules; *specif* **:** a supreme ruler
¹**overruling** *adj* [fr. pres. part. of ¹*overrule*] **1 :** serving to overrule ⟨an ~ opinion⟩ **2 :** OVERRIDING ⟨the ~ end of government —J.P.deC.Day⟩ — **over·rul·ing·ly** *adv*
²**overruling** *n* [fr. gerund of ¹*overrule*] **:** the act of one that overrules **:** an instance of such an act
¹**overrun** \¦==¦=\ *vb* [ME *overrinnen, overrennen,* fr. OE *oferyrnan,* fr. *ofer,* adv., over + *yrnan, iernan* to run] *vt* **1 a** (1) **:** to defeat utterly and occupy the positions of **:** OVERWHELM, OVERPOWER, CRUSH ⟨one company of the 25th Division was ~ —*Time*⟩ (2) **:** to invade and occupy or ravage ⟨among the barbarous nations who *overran* the western provinces of the Roman Empire —Adam Smith⟩ ⟨had their own way in *overrunning* the seaboard —Paul Blanshard⟩ **b** *obs* **:** to run over destructively or harmfully **:** run down **c :** to spread or swarm over **:** INFEST ⟨the island was ~ by rats —*Current History*⟩ ⟨a crumbled ruin ~ by the jungle —James Reach⟩ **2 a :** to run faster, further, or better than **:** pass in running **:** OUTRUN **b** (1) **:** to run, go, or extend beyond or past ⟨the plane *overran* the runway⟩ (2) **:** EXCEED ⟨overran by so great a margin any possible gains —C.E.Black & E.C.Helmreich⟩ ⟨warned him not to ~ his time —*Punch*⟩ **c** (1) **:** to readjust (as lines, columns, or pages) by shifting letters or words from one line into another or a line or lines from one column or page to another (2) **:** to print more copies of than were ordered; *also* **:** to print extra copies of (as a section of a magazine containing an article to be available separately) (3) **:** OVERSET **d :** to cause or permit (as an engine) to overrun **e :** to operate (as a lamp or a motor) at higher than normal or rated voltage, pressure, or power **3 :** to flow over ⟨the waves did little else than ~ the beach —J.A.Steers⟩ **~** *vi* **1 :** to run, pass, spread, or flow over or by something **2 :** to go or extend beyond limits **:** be in excess: as **a :** to run too far ⟨an engine operating a winch may ~⟩ **b :** to run at a speed faster than that imparted by the normally driving element of a machine ⟨when the machine stops . . . the bobbin tends to ~ —Albert Thompson & Sigfrid Bick⟩
²**overrun** \'==,=\ *n* **1 :** the act or an instance of overrunning **2 a** (1) **:** the copies printed by overrunning (2) **:** a run in excess of the quantity of a product ordered by a customer **b :** the amount by which lumber actually sawed exceeds that estimated by log scale **c :** the volume increase of a product over the original volume that is accomplished by the incorporation of a worthless substance (as air whipped into a commercial ice cream mix, or water whipped into butter) ⟨2½ gallons ~ in 5 gallons of ice cream⟩ **3 :** a cleared but unpaved area at the end of a runway offering extra landing roll to an airplane in an emergency
overrunner \¦==¦==\ *n* **:** one that overruns
overrunning clutch *n* **1 :** a clutch used in a starter that transmits cranking effort but overruns freely when the engine tries to drive the starter **2 :** a special clutch used in several mechanisms that permits a rotating member to turn freely under some conditions but not under others
overs *pres 3d sing of* OVER, *pl of* OVER
oversail \¦==¦=\ *vb* [¹*over* + obs. E *sail* to project, sally, fr. MF *saillir* to sally, leap, dance — more at SALLY] *vt* **:** to lay (as bricks or stones) so that one projects beyond another upon which it rests; *also* **:** to cover by a roof or arch of such construction **~** *vi* **:** to project or jut out beyond the base
oversanded \¦==¦==\ *adj, of concrete* **:** containing more sand than is needed for normal use and working conditions
oversanguine \¦==¦==\ *adj* **:** too sanguine **:** too hopeful or optimistic
oversaving \¦==¦==\ *n* **:** a process of saving in excess of the amount capable of being absorbed by investment that is regarded by some economists as a major cause of depressions in the modern economy
¹**overscore** \¦==¦=\ *vt* [¹*over* + *score*] **:** to score over **:** obliterate by scoring
²**overscore** \'==,=\ *n* **:** a line drawn over a word, letter, or figure
overscrupulous \¦==¦===\ *adj* **:** unduly or excessively scrupulous
¹**oversea** \'==,=, ,=='=\ *adj* [²*over* + *sea,* n.] **:** OVERSEAS
²**oversea** \¦==¦=\ *adv* [²*over* + *sea,* n.] *chiefly Brit* **:** OVERSEAS
overseal \'==,=\ *n* **:** a secondary closure for bottles, drums, and other containers to prevent tampering and to protect the primary seal
¹**overseam** \'==,=\ *n* [³*over* + *seam,* n.] **:** a seam with raw edges on the outside overcast with short close stitches that is used esp. for gloves
²**overseam** \¦==¦=\ *vt* [¹*over* + *seam,* v.] **:** to seam by overcasting
over·seam·er \¦==¦sēmə(r)\ *n* **1 :** one that seams by overcasting **2 :** SERGER
¹**overseas** \¦==¦=\ *adv* [²*over* + *seas,* pl. of *sea,* n.] **:** beyond or across the sea **:** ABROAD ⟨after serving ~ eight months —W.F. Brantley⟩
²**overseas** \'==,=, ¦=='=\ *adj* **1 :** of or relating to movement, transport, or communication over the sea ⟨some ~ trade in grain arose —Samuel Van Valkenburg & Ellsworth Huntington⟩ ⟨differed from all previous . . . Chinese ~ enterprise —C.P.Fitzgerald⟩ ⟨the importance of ~ broadcasting —*London Calling*⟩ **2 a :** situated, originating in, or relating to lands beyond the sea ⟨American ~ libraries —Malcolm Cowley⟩ ⟨~ markets⟩ ⟨culture was most often defined in terms of some ~ antecedent —Oscar Handlin⟩ ⟨the ~ Chinese⟩ **b :** COLONIAL ⟨changed the designation of France's colonial troops to ~ troops —*N.Y.Times*⟩
³**overseas** \¦==¦=\ *n pl but usu sing in constr* **:** the lands or regions overseas ⟨the . . . route between the Great Lakes and ~ —H.M.Mayer⟩ ⟨visitors from ~⟩
overseas cap *n* **:** a woolen or cotton cap without visor or stiffening **:** GARRISON CAP
oversee \¦==¦=\ *vb* [ME *overseen,* fr. OE *oferséon,* fr. *ofer,* adv., over + *sēon* to see] *vt* **1 :** to look down upon **:** SURVEY, WATCH ⟨from his second-floor window he ~*s* Parliament Hill —T.P.Whitney⟩ **2** *dial* **a :** to fail to observe **:** NEGLECT, DISREGARD **b :** to deceive or delude (oneself) esp. so as to err or blunder **3 a :** to look over **:** INSPECT, EXAMINE **b :** SUPERINTEND, SUPERVISE ⟨~ proofs⟩ ⟨~ workmen⟩ **4 :** to see clandestinely or accidentally ⟨~*ing* . . . the intimate things of common life —John Grierson⟩ **~** *vi* **:** to act as overseer **:** SUPERVISE
over·seen \¦ōvə(r)¦sēn\ *adj* [ME *oversene, overseie,* fr. past part. of *overseen* to oversee, fail to observe] **1** *dial* **:** MISTAKEN, RASH **2** *dial* **:** INTOXICATED, TIPSY **3** *dial* **:** VERSED, LEARNED
over·seer \'==,si(ə)r, -,siə *also* -,sē(ə)r *or* -,sēə *or* ¦=='s-\ *n* [ME, person appointed to assist the executor of a will, fr. *overseen* to oversee + *-er*] **:** a person who oversees: as **a :** a person in charge of a piece of work or of workmen in their labor **:** SUPERINTENDENT, SUPERVISOR ⟨an ~ of a mill⟩ **b :** OVERSEER OF THE POOR **c** *obs* **:** EDITOR, CRITIC **d :** a person selected by a religious body to serve as a local or regional leader; *specif* **:** a Friend selected to manage the pastoral work of a congregation to which he belongs **e :** one of a number of elected or appointed officials forming a governing or supervisory board in a college or university usu. with final responsibility for the management of its affairs — compare TRUSTEE
overseer of the poor : a person who is appointed or elected to take care of or to assist the poor with money, supplies, or services furnished by public authority and whose duties are prescribed by local statutes
over·seer·ship \-,ship\ *n* **:** the office or status of an overseer
oversell \¦==¦=\ *vt* **1 :** to sell more than can be advantageously purchased ⟨sometimes ~ their prospects, thereby laying the foundation for later defaults —H.E.Hoagland⟩ **2 :** to sell beyond means of delivery **3 a :** to make excessive claims for ⟨doesn't pay to ~ an attraction —W.L.Gresham⟩ ⟨opinion research may be *oversold* —J.A.R.Pimlott⟩ ⟨should not seek to ~ psychiatry —Eugene Davidoff⟩ **b :** to cause to have an exaggerated opinion of the value or importance of something ⟨only to find that you have been slightly *oversold* —W.J. Reilly⟩ ⟨permitted the public to be *oversold* on the importance of increasing reading rate —G.D.Spache⟩ **~** *vi* **1 :** to oversell something or someone ⟨great caution must be observed by public relations people not to overstate or ~ —L.A.Appley⟩ **2 :** to be excessively zealous or aggressive in selling something
over·sensitive \¦ōvə(r)+\ *adj* **:** unduly or extremely sensitive — **over·sensitiveness** \¦ōvə(r)+\ *n*
oversentimentalize \,==,=='==,=\ *vt* **:** to treat with excessive sentimentalism **:** consider in an extremely sentimental manner
¹**overset** \¦==¦=\ *vt* [ME *oversetten* to adorn with settings, overthrow, oppress, fr. ¹*over* + *setten* to set] **1 :** to adorn with settings (as of jewels) **2** *dial chiefly Brit* **:** to recover from (an illness) **3 :** to disturb mentally or physically **:** affect so as to cause disorder of body or mind **:** UPSET ⟨~ the delicate organization of the mind —Charles Dickens⟩ **4 :** to turn or tip over from an upright or proper position **:** OVERTURN ⟨so quick he ~ his chair —Helen Eustis⟩ **5 :** to cause to fall or fail **:** SUBVERT ⟨~ a tyranny —John Masefield⟩ **6 :** to set too much type matter for ⟨~ a book⟩ ⟨~ an article⟩; *also* **:** to set too wide ⟨~ a line⟩ **~** *vi* **1 :** to turn or become turned over ⟨the carriage ~⟩ **2 :** to become upset or disordered
²**overset** \'==,=\ *n* [ME, overthrow, fr. *oversetten,* v.] **1 :** an upsetting or overturning ⟨the ~ of a carriage⟩ **2 a :** something that is overset (as type matter or a line of type) **b :** newspaper copy set in type for but not used in a particular edition
oversew \'==,=\ *vt* **1 a :** OVERHAND **b :** OVERCAST **2 :** to sew (books) by machine simulating hand overcasting, the needles and thread passing diagonally through the book section near the binding edge
oversexed \¦==¦=\ *adj* **:** characterized by an inordinate degree of sexual drive or interest ⟨a few ~ egomaniacs —Compton Mackenzie⟩
overshade \¦==¦=\ *vt* **:** to cover with shade **:** OVERSHADOW
overshadow \¦==¦(,)=\ *vt* [ME *overschadewen,* fr. OE *ofersceadwian,* fr. *ofer,* adv., over + *sceadwian* to shadow] **1 a :** to cast a shadow or shade over **:** obscure with shadow ⟨a valley ~*ed* by rugged mountains —*Amer. Guide Series: Tenn.*⟩ **b :** to darken by some calamity or prospective calamity ⟨our lives are ~*ed* now by the threat of impending doom —R.M. Hutchins⟩ ⟨~*ed* by nervous apprehension of a railroad strike —F.L.Paxson⟩ **2 a :** to diminish the relative importance of **:** be more important than **:** tower over ⟨~*ed* his colleagues —D.J.Dallin⟩ ⟨the problem that ~*ed* all others —Vera M. Dean⟩ **b :** OUTWEIGH, EXCEED ⟨the good services of skunks . . . far ~ the harm they do —*Conservation in the U. S.*⟩
¹**overshadowing** *n* [ME *overschadewing,* fr. gerund of *overschadewen*] **:** the act of one that overshadows **:** an instance of such an act
²**overshadowing** *adj* [fr. pres. part. of *overshadow*] **:** serving or tending to overshadow ⟨the ~ event in the baseball world —*Collier's Yr. Bk.*⟩ — **over·shad·ow·ing·ly** *adv*
oversharp \¦==¦=\ *adj* [ME *oversharpe,* fr. ¹*over* + *sharpe, sharp* sharp] **:** too sharp ⟨the ~ distinction between the rich and the poor —*Times Lit. Supp.*⟩
overshifted \¦==¦==\ *adj* **:** marked by an unusual or extreme shift ⟨the unorthodox ~ defense of the opposing team⟩
overshine \¦==¦=\ *vt* **1 :** to shine over or upon **:** ILLUMINE **2 :** to excel in shining **:** OUTSHINE
overship \¦==¦=\ *vt* **:** to ship in excess of ⟨if the restricted areas should ~ their quotas —*Barron's*⟩ **~** *vi* **:** to ship in excess ⟨tendency to . . . ~ during the months of May to October —*Experiment Station Record*⟩
overshirt \'==,=\ *n* **:** a shirt as distinguished from an undershirt
¹**overshoe** *or* **overshoes** \¦==¦=\ *adv* [²*over* + *shoe,* n., or *shoes* (pl. of *shoe,* n.)] **:** beyond the depth to which the shoes cover the feet
²**overshoe** \'==,=\ *n* [³*over* + *shoe,* n.] **:** a shoe that is worn over another (as for extra warmth or for protection from wet); *esp* **:** GALOSH
overshoot \¦==¦=\ *vb* [ME *overshoten, oversheten,* fr. ¹*over* + *shoten, sheten* to shoot] *vt* **1 a :** to pass swiftly beyond or ahead of **:** dart forward over, across, or by ⟨woke to find I'd *overshot* my station —Julian Maclaren-Ross⟩ **b :** to fly beyond (a designated point or area) while attempting to land an airplane **2 a :** to shoot over or beyond **:** miss by shooting too far or too high ⟨~*ing* the target —S.L.Payne⟩ **b :** EXCEED ⟨~ a quota⟩ **3 :** to overreach (oneself) or cause (oneself) to go astray **4 a :** to shoot better than **:** excel in shooting **b :** to deplete of game by too much shooting **5 a :** to shoot down over (as water over a wheel) **b :** to pass swiftly over or above **~** *vi* **1 :** to fly or shoot above or beyond the mark **2 :** to swing or pass beyond the equilibrium point, often with resultant cycling — **overshoot the mark 1 :** to overstate a case **:** assert too much ⟨whose enthusiasm for things Greek may sometimes have *overshot the mark* —Norman Douglas⟩ **2 :** to fall into error **:** go astray ⟨the gossips *overshot the mark* —O.S.J.Gogarty⟩
¹**overshot** \¦==¦=\ *adj* [fr. past part. of *overshoot*] **1** *obs* **:** wide of the mark **:** MISTAKEN, DECEIVED **2 :** carried over on the upper side ⟨an ~ hay stacker⟩ ⟨the ~ cylinder of a thresher⟩ **3 :** having the upper jaw extending beyond the lower (as the mouth or jaw of some dogs)
²**overshot** \"\ *n* **1 :** a pattern or weave featuring filling floats which pass two or more warp yarns before reentering the fabric **2 :** a fishing tool used to recover lost pipe in a drilled well
overshot wheel *n* **:** a vertical waterwheel the circumference of which is covered with cavities or buckets and is turned by water that shoots over the top filling the buckets on the farther side and acting chiefly by its weight

overshot wheel

overshoulder \¦==¦==\ *adv* [²*over* + *shoulder,* n.] **:** over the shoulder ⟨laughing impudently ~ at him —Talbot Mundy⟩
¹**overside** \'==,=, ,=='=\ *adv* [²*over* + *side,* n.] **1 :** over the side of a ship **2 :** on the other side of a phonograph record
²**overside** \"\ *adj* **1 :** done over the side of a ship to a barge alongside ⟨~ delivery of cargo⟩ **2 :** recorded on the other side of a phonograph record ⟨the ~ finale —*Saturday Rev.*⟩
³**overside** \'==,=\ *n* **:** the other side of a phonograph record
oversight \'==,=\ *n* [ME, fr. *overseen* to oversee, after ME *seen* to see: *sight*] **1 :** watchful care **:** general supervision **:** MANAGEMENT ⟨you to whom ~ of the University is entrusted —N.M. Pusey⟩ **2 :** an act of overlooking or something overlooked **:** omission or error due to inadvertence ⟨whether by ~ or intention —G.B.Shaw⟩
oversigned \¦==¦=\ *n* -s [¹*over* + *signed* (fr. past part. of *sign*)] **:** the person whose name appears at the beginning of a report or other writing
oversimplification \¦==,===¦==\ *n* [fr. *oversimplify,* after E *simplify: simplification*] **1 :** the act or an instance of oversimplifying ⟨such a definition . . . errs on the side of ~ —Ralph Linton⟩ **2 :** something that oversimplifies ⟨this theory is an ~⟩
oversimplify \¦==¦==,=\ *vb* [¹*over* + *simplify*] *vt* **:** to simplify to such an extent as to bring about distortion, misunderstanding, or error ⟨seriously *oversimplifies* a complex . . . problem —W.H. Chamberlin⟩ ⟨*oversimplified* their heroes —John Mason Brown⟩ **~** *vi* **:** to engage in undue or extreme simplification ⟨would disagree with their books . . . because they overstate and ~ —F.M.Hechinger⟩
¹**oversize** *vt* [¹*over* + *-size* (fr. *size,* n. — glutinous material)] *obs* **:** to cover with or as if with size
²**oversize** \'==,=\ *n* [³*over* + *size,* n. (magnitude)] **1 :** a size larger than the nominal or normal size (as of a book, shoe, tire) **2 :** fragmental material (as mineral or ore) in pieces too large to pass a given screen or other selector
³**oversize** \¦==¦=\ *adj* **:** being of more than ordinary size ⟨an ~ helping⟩ ⟨~ books⟩ ⟨~ pears⟩
over·sized \¦==¦sīzd\ *adj* [²*oversize* + *-ed*] **:** OVERSIZE
overskip \¦==¦=\ *vt* [ME *overskippen,* fr. ¹*over* + *skippen* to skip] **:** to skip or leap over **:** pass lightly over **:** OMIT
overskirt \'==,=\ *n* **:** a skirt worn over another skirt; *also* **:** an outer skirt draped up to show an underskirt
¹**over·slaugh** \'ōvə(r),slȯ\ *vt* -ED/-ING/-S [D *overslaan* to pass over, omit, fr. MD *overslaen,* fr. *over* + *slaen* to strike; akin to OE *ofer,* adv. & prep., over and to OE *slēan* to strike, beat, slay — more at OVER, SLAY] **1 :** to pass over or remit by overslaugh **2 :** to pass over esp. for an appointment or promotion in favor of another **:** ignore the claims of **3 :** HINDER, OBSTRUCT
²**overslaugh** \"\ *n* -s **:** exemption from a duty in the British armed forces because detailed on a superior duty
oversleep \¦==¦=\ *vb* [ME *overslepen,* fr. ¹*over* + *slepen* to sleep] *vi* **:** to sleep beyond the time for waking **~** *vt* **:** to allow (oneself) to sleep beyond the time for waking ⟨*overslept* herself —Angela Thirkell⟩
oversleeve \'==,=\ *n* **:** a sleeve worn usu. hanging loosely over another sleeve
¹**overslip** *vt* [ME *overslippen,* fr. ¹*over* + *slippen* to slip] **1** *obs* **:** to slip or slide over **:** pass easily or carelessly beyond **:** OMIT, NEGLECT **2** *obs* **:** to slip away from, past, or by **:** ESCAPE
²**overslip** \'==,=\ *n* [³*over* + *slip,* n.] **:** a heavy-duty paper bag enclosing a filled shipping bag for added strength
overslope \'==,=\ *n* **:** an earmark on an animal made by a diagonal cut removing the upper corner of the ear — see EARMARK illustration
overslung \'==,=\ *adj* [¹*over* + *slung* (past part. of *sling*)] **:** supported at a level above that of the wheel axles ⟨an ~ automobile⟩ — opposed to *underslung*
overs·man \'ōvə(r)zmən\ *n, pl* **oversmen** [by alter. (prob. influenced by such words as *kinsman*)] **:** OVERMAN
¹**oversnow** *vt* [¹*over* + *snow,* v.] *obs* **:** to cover with or as if with snow
²**oversnow** \¦==¦=\ *adj* [²*over* + *snow,* n.] **:** used for transport or travel over snow ⟨~ vehicles⟩ ⟨~ equipment⟩
oversoar \¦==¦=\ *vt, archaic* **:** to soar over
oversoft \¦==¦=\ *adj* **:** extremely soft
oversold \¦==¦=\ *adj* [fr. past part. of *oversell*] **:** characterized by prices held to be unjustifiably low as a result of heavy selling ⟨~ stocks⟩ ⟨an ~ market⟩ — compare OVERBOUGHT
over·solicitous \¦ōvə(r)+\ *adj* **:** excessively solicitous
oversophisticated \¦===¦==,==\ *adj* **:** excessively sophisticated
oversoul \¦==¦=\ *n* **:** the absolute reality conceived as a spiritual being in which the ideal nature imperfectly manifested in human beings is perfectly realized and in which our finite and separate existences are grounded
oversound \¦==¦=\ *vi, of an organ pipe* **:** to sound a harmonic instead of the fundamental tone as a result of overblowing
oversow \¦==¦=\ *vt* **1 :** to sow where something has already been sown **2 a :** to scatter seed over **:** SOW **b :** to sow too much
overspan \¦==¦=\ *vt* **1 :** to reach or extend over ⟨~ so many local variations —Ruth Benedict⟩ **2 :** to erect or throw a span over (as a space)
overspeak \¦==¦=\ *vt* **1** *obs* **:** EXAGGERATE **2 :** to exceed or outdo in speaking
over·specialization \¦ōvə(r)+\ *n* **:** excessive specialization
overspeculate \¦==¦==,=\ *vi* **:** to engage in overspeculation
overspeculation \¦==,==¦==\ *n* **:** excessive speculation
¹**overspeed** \'==,=\ *n* [³*over* + *speed,* n.] **:** speed greater than normal or rated speed ⟨subjected to ~*s* —*Time*⟩
²**overspeed** \¦==¦=\ *vb* [¹*over* + *speed,* v.] *vt* **:** to cause (as an engine) to run at an excessive speed **~** *vi* **:** to run at an excessive speed
³**overspeed** \'==,=\ *adj* [¹*overspeed*] **:** operated or operating at greater than normal or rated speed
overspend \¦==¦=\ *vt* **1 :** to spend or use to excess **:** wear out **:** EXHAUST ⟨*overspent* his strength⟩ **2 a :** to spend more than ⟨*overspent* its income by $400 —*Time*⟩ **b :** to permit (oneself) to spend beyond one's means ⟨if we are not to ~ ourselves —Stafford Cripps⟩ **~** *vi* **:** to spend beyond one's means ⟨lived riotously and *overspent* recklessly —G.R.Batho⟩
¹**overspill** \¦==¦=\ *vb* [¹*over* + *spill*] **:** to spill over
²**overspill** \'==,=\ *n* **1 a :** the act or an instance of spilling over ⟨prevent entirely an ~ from a very high surge —J.A.Steers⟩ **b :** something that spills or flows over **2 :** SURPLUS, EXCESS ⟨to provide continued employment . . . we shipped that ~ abroad —Harold Wincott⟩; *esp* **:** surplus population ⟨when the ~ from the cities would go to the land —John Buchan⟩
overspin \'==,=\ *n* **:** TOP SPIN; *esp* **:** forward spin given by a bowler to a bowled ball in cricket
overspray \'==,=\ *n* **:** spray material that does not adhere in spray painting
¹**overspread** \¦==¦=\ *vt* [ME *overspreden,* fr. OE *ofersprǣdan,* fr. *ofer,* adv., over + *sprǣdan* to spread] **:** to spread over or above **:** extend over ⟨a paleness . . . ~ her face —S.M. Crothers⟩
²**overspread** \'==,=\ *n* **:** something spread over
overspring \¦==¦=\ *vt, archaic* **:** to spring over **:** leap over
¹**oversquare** \'==,=\ *n* [³*over* + *square,* n.] **:** an earmark on an animal made by a rectangular cut removing the upper corner of the ear — see EARMARK illustration
²**oversquare** \¦==¦=\ *adj* [¹*over* + *square,* adj.] **:** having a piston diameter greater than the length of stroke — used of a cylinder engine or pump
overstaff \¦==¦=\ *vt* **:** to staff to excess ⟨lest the country be ~*ed* with lawyers —H.J.Carman⟩
overstain \¦==¦=\ *vt* **:** to stain to excess; *specif* **:** to stain (tissue sections) excessively esp. in order to demonstrate selected elements by controlled destaining
overstand \¦==¦=\ *vt* **:** to keep on a navigational course beyond (a mark)
overstate \¦==¦=\ *vt* **:** to state in too strong terms **:** EXAGGERATE
overstatement \¦==¦=\ *n* **1 :** the act of overstating **:** EXAGGERATION **2 :** an exaggerated statement or account
overstay \¦==¦=\ *vt* **1 :** to stay beyond the time or the limits of ⟨~*ed* his leave⟩ **2 :** to carry a transaction in (a market) beyond the point at which the greatest profit would have been made by closing it ⟨~*ed* his market⟩
oversteepen \¦==¦==\ *vt* **:** to make excessively steep (as by glacial erosion)
oversteer \'==,=\ *n* **:** the tendency of an automobile to steer into a sharper turn than the driver intends sometimes with a thrusting of the rear to the outside
overstep \¦==¦=\ *vt* [ME *oversteppen,* fr. OE *ofersteppan,* fr. *ofer,* adv., over + *steppan* to step] **:** to step over or beyond **:** TRANSGRESS ⟨~ the bounds of propriety⟩
overstimulation \¦==,==¦==\ *n* **:** excessive stimulation
¹**overstitch** \'==,=\ *n* [³*over* + *stitch*] **:** any of various stitches now usu. made on a sewing machine with one, two, or three threads for binding a raw edge on cloth or making an ornamental edge, finish, or hem
²**overstitch** \"\ *vt* **:** to edge, finish, or hem with an overstitch
¹**overstock** \¦==¦=\ *vb* [¹*over* + *stock*] *vt* **1 :** to stock beyond requirements or facilities ⟨~ a pasture⟩ ⟨~ merchandise⟩ **2 :** to leave (a cow) unmilked for too long a time **~** *vi* **:** to stock in excess of needs or facilities

2overstock \ˈ⸗⸗ˌ⸗\ *n* **:** an excess of stock; *specif* **:** REMAINDER 3a ⟨publishers' ~ bought and sold —*Publishers' Weekly*⟩
overstoping \ˈ⸗⸗ˌ⸗⸗\ *n* **:** overhand stoping
overstory \ˈ⸗⸗ˌ⸗⸗\ *n* **:** the layer of foliage in a forest canopy; *also* **:** its trees
1overstrain \ˌ⸗⸗ˈ⸗\ *vb* [¹*over* + *strain*] *vt* **1 :** to subject to excessive strain **2 :** to load until the stress exceeds the elastic limit ~ *vi* **:** to subject oneself to excessive strain
2overstrain \ˈ⸗⸗ˌ⸗, ˌ⸗⸗ˈ⸗\ *n* **:** excessive mental or physical strain **:** a condition resulting from overstraining ⟨a serious bout of ~ and overwork —A.L.Rowse⟩
overstream \ˌ⸗⸗ˈ⸗\ *vt* **:** to stream or flow over
1overstrength \ˌ⸗⸗ˈ⸗\ *adj* [²*over* + *strength*, n.] **:** having personnel in excess of that prescribed by a table of organization **:** being in excess of the personnel prescribed by a table of organization ⟨praying fervently some office or other would find some outfit or other ~ —James Jones⟩
2overstrength \ˈ⸗⸗ˌ⸗, ˌ⸗⸗ˈ⸗\ *n* **:** an excess of strength; *specif* **:** the excess of personnel over that prescribed by a table of organization
1overstress \ˌ⸗⸗ˈ⸗\ *vt* [¹*over* + *stress*] **1 :** to stress too much ⟨impossible to ~ the point —*New Republic*⟩ **2 :** to deform (a metal) permanently by a stress greater than the elastic limit
2overstress \ˈ⸗⸗ˌ⸗, ˌ⸗⸗ˈ⸗\ *n* **:** excessive stress
overstretch \ˌ⸗⸗ˈ⸗\ *vt* [ME *overstretchen*, fr. ¹*over* + *stretchen*, *strecchen* to stretch] **1 :** to stretch to excess ⟨strategically ~*ed* around the world —Benjamin Welles⟩ **2 :** to stretch over or across
overstrew \ˌ⸗⸗ˈ⸗\ *vt* **1 :** to strew or scatter about **2 :** to cover here and there
overstrict \ˌ⸗⸗ˈ⸗\ *adj* **:** excessively strict
overstride \ˌ⸗⸗ˈ⸗\ *vt* [ME *overstriden*, fr. ¹*over* + *striden* to stride] **1 a :** to stride over, across, or beyond ⟨~ an obstruction⟩ **b :** BESTRIDE **2 :** to stride faster than or beyond ⟨*overstriding* his little orderly —L.M.Uris⟩
1overstrike \ˌ⸗⸗ˈ⸗\ *vt* [¹*over* + *strike*] **1 :** to impress (a finished coin) with the design of another coin **2 :** to impress (a specified coin design) onto a specified coin of another design ⟨~ an 1827 quarter on an 1806 quarter⟩
2overstrike \ˈ⸗⸗ˌ⸗\ *n* **:** an overstruck coin
overstring \ˌ⸗⸗ˈ⸗\ *vt* **:** to string (a bow) with too short a cord
overstrung \ˌ⸗⸗ˈ⸗\ *adj* **1 :** too highly strung **:** too sensitive ⟨~ nerves⟩ **2** *archery* **:** HIGH-STRUNG
1overstudy \ˌ⸗⸗ˈ⸗⸗\ *vb* [¹*over* + *study*] *vt* **:** to subject to overstudy ~ *vi* **:** to engage in overstudy
2overstudy \"\ *n* **:** excessive study
overstuff \ˌ⸗⸗ˈ⸗\ *vt* **1 :** to stuff too full **2 :** to make or finish (as a chair) with a covering (as of leather or cloth) over a well-sprung and padded base
overstuffed *adj* **1 a :** stuffed too full or to excess **:** padded or overbulky ⟨one of those ~ biographies that have recently become fashionable —Irving Howe⟩ **b :** too fat **:** CORPULENT ⟨the mother was an ~ . . . woman —Truman Capote⟩ **2 :** covered deeply and completely with upholstery ⟨~ furniture⟩
oversubscribe \ˌ⸗⸗⸗ˈ⸗\ *vt* [¹*over* + *subscribe*] **:** to subscribe for more of than is offered for sale ⟨~ an issue of bonds⟩
oversubscription \ˌ⸗⸗⸗ˈ⸗⸗\ *n* [fr. *oversubscribe*, after E *subscribe: subscription*] **:** the act or an instance of oversubscribing ⟨~*s* became the rule —M.S.Kendrick⟩
oversubtle \ˌ⸗⸗ˈ⸗⸗\ *adj* **:** impracticably subtle
oversubtlety \ˌ⸗⸗ˈ⸗⸗⸗\ *n* **:** excessive subtlety
oversum \ˌ⸗⸗ˈ⸗\ *vt, archaic* **:** OVERRATE
oversummer \ˌ⸗⸗ˈ⸗⸗\ *vi* **:** to survive the summer ⟨urediospores may ~ at the high altitudes —*Experiment Station Record*⟩
1oversupply \ˌ⸗⸗⸗ˈ⸗\ *n* [³*over* + *supply*, n.] **:** an excessive supply
2oversupply \"\ *vt* [¹*over* + *supply*, v.] **:** to supply in excess
overswarm \ˌ⸗⸗ˈ⸗\ *vt* **:** to swarm over **:** OVERRUN ~ *vi* **:** to spread out
oversway \ˌ⸗⸗ˈ⸗\ *vt* **1 a :** to hold sway over **:** rule over **:** DOMINATE **b** *obs* **:** to have the upper hand over **:** prevail over **2 :** to induce to change over (as in a matter of opinion) **:** prevail upon **3** *obs* **:** to sway or swing over **:** cause to incline or overturn
oversweep \ˌ⸗⸗ˈ⸗\ *vt* **:** to sweep over or across ⟨the main . . . beach was *overswept* —J.A.Steers⟩
oversweet \ˌ⸗⸗ˈ⸗\ *adj* **:** too sweet **:** CLOYING ⟨~ religious sentiment —Stuart Preston⟩
overswell \ˌ⸗⸗ˈ⸗\ *vt* **1 :** to cause to swell unduly or to excess **2 :** to swell so as to overflow or cover ~ *vi* **:** to rise above the usual level or boundary
overt \(ˈ)ō¦vərt, -ˈvə̄t, -ˈvəit *also* ˈō‚və(r)t; *usu* ˈd· +V\ *adj* [ME, fr. MF, past part. of *ovrir* to open, fr. (assumed) VL *operire*, alter. (influenced by L *cooperire* to cover) of L *aperire* — more at APERTURE, COVER] **:** open to view **:** not concealed **:** publicly observable **:** MANIFEST ⟨rules are maintained only by some form of coercion, ~ or covert —John Dewey⟩ ⟨~ behavior . . . is that which is manifest in motor activity —E.A. Hoebel⟩ ⟨an act of ~ hostility —Mabel R. Gillis⟩
overt act *n* **:** an outward act done in pursuance and manifestation of an intent or design that is not punishable in itself without such act: **a :** an act done in actual preparation for the illegal object and thereby sufficing for conviction **b** *under the treason clause of the U.S. Constitution* **:** an act of such nature as to sustain at least the finding that the accused gave aid and comfort to the enemy
overtake \ˌ⸗⸗ˈ⸗\ *vb* [ME *overtaken*, fr. ¹*over* + *taken* to take] *vt* **1 a** (1) **:** to come or catch up with in pursuit or motion ⟨the next cart they *overtook* —F.V.W.Mason⟩ (2) **:** to catch up with in some course, rivalry, or task ⟨not for several months could the printers ~ the demand —I.M.Price⟩ ⟨already *overtaking* Britain in steel production —Giorgio de Santillana⟩ ⟨*overtaken* and easily passed by Berlin —*Times Lit. Supp.*⟩ (3) *chiefly Brit* **:** to accomplish within a prescribed time or under the pressure of other duties **b :** to catch up with and pass ⟨within four years it *overtook* all other American bands by leaps and bounds —Ann M. Lingg⟩; *specif, chiefly Brit* **:** to go by (another vehicle) ⟨got behind a lorry and could not ~ it for miles⟩ **2 :** to come upon or happen to suddenly or unexpectedly **:** SEIZE, INVOLVE ⟨*overtaken* by a sudden and vicious blizzard —Richard Thruelsen⟩ ⟨a strange adventure *overtook* him —*Brit. Bk. Centre*⟩ ⟨changes and contrasts that have *overtaken* England —S.P.B.Mais⟩ ⟨when calamities ~ the King —Donald Harrington⟩ **3 a** *chiefly Scot* **:** CAPTIVATE, ENSNARE ⟨who married, or rather was *overtaken* —R.M.Macandrew⟩ **b** *archaic* **:** INTOXICATE **4 :** to win a trick by playing a higher card than (one's partner's winning card) ~ *vi, chiefly Brit* **:** to pass another vehicle ⟨never attempt to ~ on the crest of a hill —Noreen Routledge⟩
overtaking *n, chiefly Brit* **:** an act of passing another vehicle ⟨no ~⟩
overtalk \ˌ⸗⸗ˈ⸗\ *vi* **:** to talk too long or too much ⟨would not let him ~ at breakfast and miss the . . . bus —James Jones⟩ ~ *vt* **1 :** to overcome with talking **2 :** to talk too much about
overtalkative \ˌ⸗⸗ˈ⸗⸗⸗\ *adj* **:** abnormally or excessively talkative — **overtalkativeness** *n*
overtax \ˌ⸗⸗ˈ⸗\ *vt* **1 :** to tax too heavily or beyond what is due **2 :** to lay too heavy a burden or demand upon ⟨~ the weakened ability of the body —Morris Fishbein⟩ — **overtaxation** \ˌ⸗⸗ˌ⸗ˈ⸗⸗\ *n*
overteem \ˌ⸗⸗ˈ⸗\ *vt, archaic* **:** to wear out or exhaust by breeding to excess ~ *vi* **:** to teem or breed to excess
overtempt \ˌ⸗⸗ˈ⸗\ *vt* **:** to tempt to excess or beyond the power of resistance
overtheatrical \ˌ⸗⸗⸗ˈ⸗⸗⸗\ *adj* **:** unduly or excessively theatrical
over–the–counter \ˌ⸗⸗⸗ˈ⸗⸗\ *adj* [*over the counter*] **1 a :** not traded on an organized securities exchange **:** traded in direct negotiations between buyers and sellers or their representatives **:** UNLISTED ⟨*over-the-counter* stocks⟩ **b :** not effected on an organized securities exchange ⟨*over-the-counter* transactions⟩ **2 :** capable of being sold legally without the prescription of a physician, dentist, or veterinarian ⟨*over-the-counter* drugs⟩
over–the–road \ˌ⸗⸗⸗ˈ⸗\ *adj* [fr. the phrase *over the road*] **:** used for, being, or relating to transportation between cities or states ⟨*over-the-road* common carriers⟩ ⟨*over-the-road* freight⟩
1overthrow \ˌ⸗⸗ˈ⸗\ *vb* [ME *overthrowen*, fr. ¹*over* + *throwen* to throw] *vt* **1 :** to throw over **:** knock or force over from an accustomed upright or level position **:** OVERTURN ⟨a dozen trees were *overthrown* by the storm⟩ **2 :** to cause the downfall of **:** bring low **:** DEFEAT, DESTROY, RUIN ⟨ancient mechanics were *overthrown* —S.F.Mason⟩ ⟨~ a government⟩ ⟨traditional beliefs which science may ~ —M.R.Cohen⟩ **3** *archaic* **:** DERANGE, DISORDER **4 :** to throw over or past ⟨the passer *overthrew* the receiver⟩; *specif* **:** to throw a baseball over or past (a base) thereby usu. being charged with an error ~ *vi* **:** to throw too far **syn** see CONQUER, OVERTURN
2overthrow \ˈ⸗⸗ˌ⸗\ *n* **1 :** an act of overthrowing or the state of being overthrown **:** DEFEAT, RUIN ⟨its ~ was accomplished simultaneously —S.F.Mason⟩ ⟨the ~ of the monarchy⟩ **2 a :** a high throw made by a fielder in baseball that usu. results in his being charged with an error **b :** a return of the ball by a fielder in cricket that is missed by the wicketkeeper or fielder at the wicket; *also* **:** a run scored on such a missed ball
over·throw·al \ˌ⸗⸗ˈthrōəl\ *n* -S **:** the act or an instance of overthrowing
overthrower \ˌ⸗⸗ˈthrō(ə)r, -ōə\ *n* **:** one that overthrows
overthrust \ˈ⸗⸗ˌ⸗\ *vt* [¹*over* + *thrust*] **:** to thrust over (as a rock mass)
overthrust fault *also* **overthrust** *n* **:** THRUST FAULT
overthrusting \ˌ⸗⸗ˈ⸗⸗\ *n* [³*over* + *thrusting*, gerund of *thrust*] **:** the process of producing an overthrust
1overthwart \ˌ⸗⸗ˈ⸗\ *adv* [ME *overthwart*, *overthwert*, fr. ¹*over* + *thwart*, *thwert*, adv., athwart — more at THWART] *archaic* **:** ACROSS, CROSSWISE, TRANSVERSELY
2overthwart \"\ *adj* [ME *overthwart*, *overthwert*, fr. *overthwart*, *overthwert*, adv.] **1** *archaic* **:** having a crosswise position **:** placed or situated across or over **:** TRANSVERSE **2** *archaic* **:** crossing in kind or disposition **:** ADVERSE, OPPOSING
3overthwart \"\ *prep* [ME *overthwart*, *overthwert*, fr. *overthwart*, *overthwert*, adv.] **1** *archaic* **:** from side to side of **:** ACROSS **2** *archaic* **:** on the opposite side of or opposite to
4overthwart \"\ *vt* [ME *overthwarten*, *overthwerten*, fr. *overthwart*, *overthwert*, adv.] *archaic* **:** to pass or lie athwart **:** CROSS, OBSTRUCT
overtide \ˈ⸗⸗ˌ⸗\ *n* **:** a secondary tide of higher frequency than the principal tide to which it bears a relation analogous to that of a musical overtone to its fundamental
overtilt \ˌ⸗⸗ˈ⸗\ *vt* **:** to tilt over **:** UPSET
1overtime \ˈ⸗⸗ˌ⸗\ *n, often attrib* [³*over* + *time*, n.] **1 :** time beyond or in excess of a set limit ⟨the game went into ~⟩ ⟨played two ~ periods to break the tie⟩; *esp* **:** working time in excess of a minimum total set for a given period ⟨got in a lot of ~ this week⟩ ⟨~ pay⟩ **2 :** an additional payment for overtime ⟨earned some ~ this month⟩
2overtime \"\ *adv* [²*over* + *time*, n.] **:** in excess of a set time limit ⟨the game went ~⟩ or of the regular working time ⟨is working ~ this week⟩ ⟨must work ~ to make our land once again attractive to new ideas —A.E.Stevenson †1965⟩
3overtime \ˌ⸗⸗ˈ⸗\ *vt* [¹*over* + *time*, v.] **:** to exceed the proper limit in timing (as a photographic exposure)
overt·ly *pronunc at* OVERT +lē,li\ *adv* [ME, fr. *overt* + -*ly*] **:** PUBLICLY, OPENLY, MANIFESTLY ⟨~ aggressive behavior —J.H. Masserman⟩
overt·ness \"+nəs\ *n* -ES **:** the quality or state of being overt
overtoil \ˌ⸗⸗ˈ⸗\ *vb* **:** OVERWORK
1overtone \ˈ⸗⸗ˌ⸗\ *n* [³*over* + *tone*, n.; trans. of G *oberton*] **1 :** one of the constituent higher tones that, with the fundamental, comprise a musical tone **:** HARMONIC 1a **2 :** the color of the light reflected (as by a paint or varnish film) **3 :** a secondary or accompanying effect, quality, or meaning usu. of subtle or elusive character **:** IMPLICATION, SUGGESTION ⟨fairy tales with ~*s* . . . meant only for the sophisticated —John Lehmann⟩ ⟨a delicate . . . fantasy with profoundly philosophical ~*s* —John Martin⟩ ⟨an ~, an aftertaste, a flavor that lingers in the mind —Rumer Godden⟩
2overtone \"\ *vt* [¹*over* + *tone*, v.] **1 :** to dominate or drown (a subordinate or discordant tone) with a stronger tone **2 :** to color or produce color effects in by overshadowing the original tone
1overtop \ˌ⸗⸗ˈ⸗\ *vt* [¹*over* + *top*, v.] **1 :** to rise above the top of **:** exceed in height **:** tower above ⟨the unusual height of the surge . . . *overtopped* the wall —J.A.Steers⟩ **2 :** to be superior to in power, station, or importance **:** OVERRIDE ⟨where faith is *overtopped* by prelacy —Ellery Sedgwick⟩ ⟨where cattle raising ~*s* agriculture —*Amer. Guide Series: Va.*⟩ **3 :** to make of less importance or throw into the background by superior excellence **:** SURPASS, OBSCURE ⟨*overtopped* the rest, the giant of them all —H.O.Taylor⟩ **4 :** to cover, flow over, or cast shade over the top of
2overtop \ˌ⸗⸗ˈ⸗\ *adv* [²*over* + *top*, n.] **:** over the top **:** OVERHEAD
overtrade \ˌ⸗⸗ˈ⸗\ *vi* **:** to trade beyond one's capital **:** buy goods beyond the means of paying for or selling them ~ *vt* **:** to do business beyond (as one's capital)
overtrain \ˌ⸗⸗ˈ⸗\ *vt* **:** to train to excess or beyond advantage **:** harm by too much training
overtravel \ˌ⸗⸗ˈ⸗⸗\ *n* **:** amplitude of motion of a machine part or tool beyond that necessary to complete its purpose
overtrick \ˈ⸗⸗ˌ⸗\ *n* **:** a card trick won in excess of the number bid
overtrip *vt, obs* **:** to trip over nimbly
overtrump \ˌ⸗⸗ˈ⸗\ *vt* **:** to trump with a higher trump card than the highest previously played to the same trick ~ *vi* **:** to play a higher trump card than the highest previously played to the same trick
1over·ture *R* ˈōvər¦‚chu̇(ə)r, ¦‚chər, ¦‚tu̇(ə)r, ¦·‚tyu̇(ə)r, *by r-dissimilation* -vəl; -*R* -və‚chu̇ə, -vəchə, -və‚tu̇ə, -və·‚tyu̇ə, +V " *or* -u̇(ə)r *or* -‚chər\ *n* -S [ME, fr. MF, fr. (assumed) VL *opertura*, alter. (influenced by L *cooperire* to cover) of L *apertura* — more at APERTURE, COVER] **1** *obs* **a :** APERTURE, HOLE, OPENING, RECESS **b :** DISCLOSURE, DISCOVERY, REVELATION **c :** an opening or opportunity for action **d :** OVERTURNING, OVERTHROW **2 a :** a formal or informal initiative looking to an agreement, action, or the establishment of a relationship **:** a first move **:** APPROACH, PROPOSAL ⟨making ~*s* to the authorities . . . for a free-trade agreement —*Amer. Guide Series: Maine*⟩ ⟨a very forward girl, who is not afraid to make ~*s* —C.B.Kelland⟩ ⟨received ~*s* from film directors here and abroad⟩ **b :** something that ushers in or introduces what follows **:** COMMENCEMENT, PRELUDE ⟨more often . . . the main thing at supper than it is an ~ to dinner —Jane Nickerson⟩ ⟨the ~ to a sense of panic —Marcia Davenport⟩ ⟨an ~ of speeches —*Time*⟩ **3 a :** a formal proposal or request in Scottish and English Presbyterian churches for legislation made to the highest court of the church **b :** the submission in American Presbyterian churches of a question of doctrine or polity by the highest court to the presbyteries for their judgment on it before formal determination by the court; *also* **:** the question thus submitted **4 a :** an orchestral composition introductory to an oratorio, opera, or other extended musical work consisting usu. of two or more contrasting sections of related material and in later developments esp. in the 19th century comprising a potpourri of melodies or themes of the ensuing work or a free prelude used to establish background or mood for the plot or opening scene **b :** an orchestral concert piece of similar construction or one written as a single movement in sonata form
2overture \", + *suffixal vowel* -u̇r *or* -‚chər\ *vt* **:** to put forward as an overture **:** make or present an overture to
1overturn \ˌ⸗⸗ˈ⸗\ *vb* [ME *overturnen*, fr. ¹*over* + *turnen* to turn] *vt* **1 a :** to turn over **:** tilt or keel over from an upright, level, or proper position esp. with force **:** cause to fall over **:** UPSET ⟨a boat ~*ed* by waves⟩ ⟨~*ed* me in the dust —John Masters⟩ **b :** to tilt beyond a vertical position so that in one limb of an anticline the underside of a fold or of strata contains the younger beds **2 :** to cause the downfall or destruction of **:** bring to nothing **:** RUIN, INVALIDATE ⟨~*ing* the unity of religion —S.M.Crothers⟩ ⟨the degree to which accident could ~ the schemes of wise men —Oscar Handlin⟩ **3** *obs* **:** DERANGE, DISORDER ~ *vi* **1 :** to turn over **2 :** to produce an overturn
syn UPSET, OVERTHROW, SUBVERT, CAPSIZE: OVERTURN, as defined above, has less connotational power and wider range of meaning than others in this set, with which, however, in many uses it is interchangeable. UPSET lends itself to any use involving a tilting, knocking, or keeling over from an accustomed or proper position, and to any figurative use compatible with this notion. It is a simple and familiar word more likely than others in this set to be used in simple and familiar situations ⟨this littlest of carriages could make only a great sweep, and was in danger of *upsetting* at every corner —George Santayana⟩ ⟨wouldn't have believed they could be so *upset* by a hurt woodpecker —Willa Cather⟩ OVERTHROW suggests the same base idea as the preceding but implies more force and is likely to imply more conscious intent and to apply to matters of consequence and importance ⟨I got through about half the work on this scale. But my plans were *overthrown* —C.R. Darwin⟩ ⟨many laws which it would be vain to ask the court to *overthrow* could be shown, easily enough, to transgress . . . the Bill of Rights —O.W.Holmes †1935⟩ SUBVERT, originally a close synonym for the preceding in a literal sense, is now used mostly in reference to governmental systems, established religions, and institutional matters. It now appears more likely to imply insidious impairment than direct force ⟨would do their utmost to *subvert* all religion and all law —Edmund Burke⟩ ⟨and pressure groups will have demonstrated once again that the people's interest can be *subverted* by ruthless lobbyists —*New Republic*⟩ CAPSIZE is likely to involve the picture of a boat keeling over ⟨it may well have been the comedians who restored the theater's balance when the tragedians threatened to *capsize* it into absurdity —W.B.Adams⟩
2overturn \ˈ⸗⸗ˌ⸗\ *n* **1 :** the act of overturning or the state of being overturned ⟨an ideological and political ~ —J.R.Wike & A.Z.Rubinstein⟩ **2 :** the sinking of surface water and rise of bottom water in a lake or sea that results from changes in density due to changes in temperature and that commonly occurs in spring and fall wherever lakes are icebound in winter
over–under \ˈ⸗⸗ˈ⸗⸗\ *n* -S **:** OVER-AND-UNDER
1overuse \ˌ⸗⸗ˈ⸗\ *vt* [¹*over* + *use*] **:** to use to excess
2overuse \ˌ⸗⸗ˈ⸗\ *n* **:** excessive use
1overvalue \ˌ⸗⸗ˈ⸗⸗\ *vt* [¹*over* + *value*] **:** to set too high a value on **:** OVERESTIMATE, OVERPRIZE
2overvalue \"\ *n* **:** an excessive value or estimate
overveil \ˌ⸗⸗ˈ⸗\ *vt* **:** to veil over
overventilation \ˌ⸗⸗⸗⸗ˈ⸗⸗\ *n* **:** excessively deep and rapid breathing; *also* **:** the physiological state resulting from such breathing
1overview *vt* [¹*over* + *view*] **:** SURVEY, INSPECT
2overview \ˈ⸗⸗ˌ⸗\ *n* **:** a general view **:** SURVEY ⟨the best ~ of contemporary psychology for the lay reader —*Key Reporter*⟩ ⟨give a broad ~ of the evidence —C.R.Rogers⟩ ⟨a quick ~ tempts one to make a few generalizations —Frances Spain⟩
overvoltage \ˌ⸗⸗ˈ⸗⸗\ *n* **:** excess voltage; *specif* **:** the excess potential required for the discharge of an ion at an electrode over and above the equilibrium potential of the electrode
overwalk \ˌ⸗⸗ˈ⸗\ *vt* **1** *archaic* **:** to walk over or upon **2 :** to exhaust or injure (oneself) by walking
overwatch \ˌ⸗⸗ˈ⸗\ *vt* **1** *archaic* **:** to weary or exhaust by keeping awake **2 a** *obs* **:** to watch through or throughout (as the night) **b :** to watch over **3 :** to support by fire another element which is moving ⟨tanks ~*ing* an assault battalion⟩
1overwater \ˌ⸗⸗ˈ⸗⸗\ *adv* [²*over* + *water*, n.] **:** over or across a body of water ⟨employed when flying ~ in the daytime —*Official Guide to the Army Air Forces*⟩
2overwater \"\ *adj* **:** situated or occurring over a body of water ⟨the ~ portion . . . had been spanned in four hours —Horace Sutton⟩ ⟨~ flights⟩ ⟨an ~ bridge⟩
overwear \ˌ⸗⸗ˈ⸗\ *vt* **:** to use up or exhaust by wearing **:** wear out
1overweary \ˌ⸗⸗ˈ⸗⸗\ *vt* [¹*over* + *weary*, v.] **:** to weary too much **:** tire out
2overweary \"\ *adj* [¹*over* + *weary*, adj.] **:** wearied to excess
overweathered *adj, obs* **:** WEATHERWORN
over·ween \ˌ⸗⸗ˈwēn\ *vb* [ME *overwenen*, fr. ¹*over* + *wenen* to suppose, think, believe — more at WEEN] *vi, archaic* **:** to regard one's own thinking too highly **:** become egotistic, arrogant, or rash in opinion ~ *vt, obs* **:** to hold in unwarranted esteem
1overweening *n* [ME *overwening*, fr. gerund of *overwenen*] **1** *obs* **:** excessive self-importance, conceit, or arrogance **2** *archaic* **:** excessive esteem or estimation
2overweening *adj* [ME *overwening*, fr. pres. part. of *overwenen*] **1 :** unduly confident **:** ARROGANT, PRESUMPTUOUS, CONCEITED ⟨have no idea how ~ he would be —S.V.Benét⟩ ⟨revolt against an ~ aristocracy —*Encyc. Americana*⟩ **2 :** EXCESSIVE, EXAGGERATED, IMMODERATE, UNRESTRAINED ⟨his ~ ambition . . . has tripped him up —Woodrow Wyatt⟩ ⟨~ greed —H.H. Martin⟩ ⟨an ~ love of power —Helen Howe⟩ — **over·ween·ing·ness** \ˌ⸗⸗ˈ⸗⸗⸗\ *n* -ES
overweigh \ˌ⸗⸗ˈ⸗\ *vt* [ME *overweien*, fr. ¹*over* + *weien*, *weyen* to weigh] **1 :** to exceed in weight **:** OVERBALANCE ⟨sufficient to ~ the less abstract considerations —R.A.Solo⟩ **2 :** to weigh down **:** OPPRESS
1overweight \ˈ⸗⸗ˌ⸗, *in sense 2b usu* ˌ⸗⸗ˈ⸗\ *n* [³*over* + *weight*, n.] **1 :** weight over and above what is required or allowed by law, demand, or custom **2 a :** superabundance of weight **:** PREPONDERANCE **b :** excessive or burdensome weight **3** [³*overweight*] **:** an individual of more than normal weight
2overweight \ˌ⸗⸗ˈ⸗\ *vt* [¹*over* + *weight*, v.] **1 :** to give too much weight or consideration to ⟨said that historians ~ political aspects —A.L.Kroeber⟩ **2 :** to weight excessively ⟨sometimes ~*s* his paragraphs —*Horizon*⟩ **3 :** to exceed in weight **:** OVERBALANCE
3overweight \"\ *adj* [²*over* + *weight*, n.] **:** exceeding normal or proper weight ⟨an ~ individual⟩
overwell \ˌ⸗⸗ˈ⸗\ *adv* [ME *overwel*, fr. ¹*over* + *wel* well] **:** too well
overwelt \ˌ⸗⸗ˈ⸗\ *vb* [¹*over* + *welt*, v. (to roll)] *dial Eng* **:** OVERTURN
over·whelm \ˌ⸗⸗ˈ(h)welm, -eu̇m\ *vt* [ME *overwhelmen*, fr. ¹*over* + *whelmen* to turn over — more at WHELM] **1 :** OVERTHROW, OVERTURN, UPSET **2 a :** to cover over completely (as by a great wave) **:** overflow and bury beneath **:** ENGULF, SUBMERGE ⟨all the rest has been ~*ed* by the desert —Alan Moorehead⟩ **b :** to overcome by great superiority of force or numbers **:** bring to ruin **:** DESTROY, OVERPOWER ⟨~*ed* by the air attack —Sir Winston Churchill⟩ **c :** to overpower in thought or feeling **:** subject to the grip of an overpowering emotion ⟨~*ed* by the death of his loving mother —John McCarten⟩ ⟨unbearable melancholy . . . threatened to ~ him —Christine Weston⟩ **3 :** to project over threateningly or dominatingly ⟨his . . . face, ~*ed* by a monstrous hooked blade of a nose —E.L.Wallant⟩ **syn** see OVERPOWER
overwhelming *adj* **:** tending or serving to overwhelm **:** OVERPOWERING ⟨an ~ happiness⟩ ⟨an ~ majority⟩ — **over·whelm·ing·ly** \ˌ⸗⸗ˈ⸗⸗⸗\ *adv*
over·whelm·ing·ness \ˌ⸗⸗ˈ⸗⸗⸗\ *n* -ES **:** the quality or state of being overwhelming
overwin \ˌ⸗⸗ˈ⸗\ *vt* [ME *overwinnen*, fr. OE *oferwinnan*, fr. *ofer*, adv., over + *winnan* to struggle, fight — more at WIN] *archaic* **:** to win over **:** VANQUISH
overwind \ˌ⸗⸗ˈwīnd\ *vt* **1 :** to wind (as a spring or rope) too tightly or too far **2 :** to wind (as a magnet in a series motor) so that magnetic saturation requires less than normal current
overwing *vt* [¹*over* + -*wing* (fr. *wing*, n.)] *obs* **:** OUTFLANK
overwinter \ˌ⸗⸗ˈ⸗⸗\ *vb* [¹*over* + *winter*, v.; prob. trans. of Norw *overvintre*] *vi* **:** to pass or last through the winter **:** WINTER ~ *vt* **:** to preserve through the winter
overwise \ˌ⸗⸗ˈ⸗\ *adj* **:** too wise
overwit *vt, obs* **:** OUTWIT
overwood \ˈ⸗⸗ˌ⸗\ *n* **:** OVERSTORY
1overword \ˈ⸗⸗ˌ⸗\ *n* [*over-* (fr. ¹*over* — again) + *word*, n.] **:** a word or phrase repeated or said over (as in a song) **:** BURDEN, REFRAIN
2overword \ˌ⸗⸗ˈ⸗\ *vt* [¹*over* + *word*, v.] **:** to compose with an excess of words **:** write too wordily ⟨many of the poems seem to come out ~*ed* —John Ciardi⟩
overwordy \ˌ⸗⸗ˈ⸗⸗\ *adj* **:** too wordy
1overwork \ˌ⸗⸗ˈ⸗\ *vb* [¹*over* + *work*] *vt* **1 a :** to cause to work too hard or too long **:** work to the point of exhaustion ⟨apt to ~ themselves —Adam Smith⟩ **b :** to work upon the mind or feelings of to excess or so as to excite or confuse **2 :** to decorate all over ⟨~*ed* the body with black or red strands —W.G. Fischel⟩ **3 a :** to work too much on **:** OVERDO, OVERELABORATE ⟨~*ing* a design —*Jewelers' Circular - Keystone*⟩ **b :** to make excessive use of **:** employ too frequently ⟨an ~*ed* and sometimes misused term —Charles Ray⟩ ~ *vi* **:** to work too much or too long **:** OVERDO
2overwork \"\ *n* **:** excessively prolonged or severe work
overworld \ˈ⸗⸗ˌ⸗\ *n* **1 :** the world of proper and respectable people ⟨the horizon line where underworld and ~ meet —Frank O'Leary⟩ **2 :** the spiritual or supernatural world ⟨the silent realm of the ~ —Sheldon Cheney⟩

overworn \ˌ⸗⸗ˈ⸗\ *adj* **1** : worn out : SPENT, EXHAUSTED **2 a** : OVERWORKED, STALE **b** *obs* : OBSOLETE

¹overwrap \ˌ⸗⸗ˈ⸗\ *vt* [¹*over* + *wrap*] : to apply a wrapper over

²overwrap \ˈ⸗⸗ˌ⸗\ *also* **overwrapper** \ˈ⸗⸗ˌ⸗⸗\ *n* [²*overwrap* fr. ¹*overwrap*; *overwrapper* fr. ¹*overwrap* + *-er*] : a flexible printed or transparent wrapper applied over a container (as a carton, case tray) or directly over a product

overwrite \ˌ⸗⸗ˈ⸗\ *vt* **1** : to write over the surface of **2** : to write in too literary, diffuse, or labored style ⟨often ~s his speeches —Jack Gould⟩ ~ *vi* : to write too much

over·wrought \ˌ⸗⸗ˈrȯt, *usu* -ȯd+V\ *adj* [fr. past part. of ¹*overwork*] **1** : suffering from or revealing nervous strain : OVEREXCITED, AGITATED ⟨an unsteady ~ voice —Lester Atwell⟩ ⟨tell ~ businessmen to get a hobby —Doyle Smee & Kenneth Smith⟩ **2** : elaborated to excess : OVERDONE ⟨the slightly ~ epigrammatic style —A.L.Guérard⟩

¹overyear \ˌ⸗⸗ˈ⸗\ *vt* [²*over* + *year*, n.] *archaic* : to keep over the year : SUPERANNUATE

²overyear \ˈ⸗⸗ˌ⸗\ *adj* [²*over* + *year*, n.] : kept over one year for use in the next ⟨~ hay⟩

overzealous \ˌ⸗⸗ˈ⸗⸗\ *adj* : too zealous — **overzealously** \ˌ⸗⸗ˈ⸗⸗⸗\ *adv* — **overzealousness** \ˌ⸗⸗ˈ⸗⸗⸗\ *n*

ovhd *abbr* overhead

ovi- — see OV-

ovi·bos \ˈōvə,bäs, -bōs\ *n* [NL, fr. L *ovis* sheep + *bos* ox, cow — more at EWE, COW] **1** *cap* : a genus of arctic ruminant mammals (family Bovidae) that consists of the musk-ox **2** *pl* **ovibos** : MUSK OX

ovi·capsule \ˌōvə+\ *n* [ISV *ov-* + *capsule*] : an egg case : OOTHECA

ovi·cell \ˈōvə+,-\ *n* [*ov-* + *cell*] : a dilatation of the zooecium in many bryozoans serving as a brood pouch — **ovi·cellular** \ˌ⸗⸗+\ *adj*

ovi·ci·dal \ˌōvəˈsīdᵊl\ *adj* : capable of killing eggs : of, relating to, or being an ovicide

ovi·cide \ˈōvə,sīd\ *n* -S [ISV *ov-* + *-cide*] : an agent that kills eggs; *esp* : an insecticide effective against the egg stage

ovic·u·lar \(ˈ)ōˈvikyələ(r)\ *adj* [NL *oviculum* egg (dim. of L *ovum* egg) + E *-ar* — more at EGG] : relating to or like an egg

ovi·cyst \ˈōvə,sist\ *n* -S [*ov-* + *-cyst*] : the pouch in which the eggs develop in some tunicates — **ovi·cys·tic** \ˌ⸗⸗ˈsistik\ *adj*

ovi·dae \ˈōvə,dē\ [NL, fr. *Ovis* + *-idae*] *syn of* CAPRIDAE

ovid·i·an \äˈvidēən, ōˈv-\ *adj*, *usu cap* [*Ovid* (Publius Ovidius Naso) †A.D.17? Roman poet + E *-an*] : of, relating to, or characteristic of Ovid or his poetry which is noted for imaginative vividness and vivacity

ovi·du·cal \ˌōvəˈd(y)ükəl\ *adj* [*ov-* + L *ducere* to lead + E *-al* — more at TOW] : of or relating to an oviduct

ovi·duct \ˈōvə,dəkt\ *n* [NL *oviductus*, fr. L *ov-* + NL *ductus* duct — more at DUCT] : a tube that serves exclusively or esp. for the passage of eggs from an ovary to the exterior of an animal or to some part communicating with the exterior whether directly continuous with the ovary or (as in most vertebrates) distinct from it, that receives the eggs only after their discharge into the body cavity, and that is often modified for secreting a shell or other covering for the eggs or has a part modified to form a uterus in which the eggs or embryos develop — **ovi·duc·tal** \ˌōvəˈdəktᵊl\ *adj*

ovie·do \ˌōvēˈā(ˌ)thō, -)dō; ōv'yā(ˌ)thō\ *adj*, *usu cap* [fr. *Oviedo*, city in northwest Spain] : of or from the city of Oviedo, Spain : of the kind or style prevalent in Oviedo

¹ovi·form \ˈōvə,fȯrm\ *adj* [*ov-* + *-form*] : shaped like an egg

²oviform \"\ *adj* [L *ovis* sheep + E *-form*] : resembling a sheep in shape

ovi·genesis \ˌōvə+\ *n* [*ov-* + *genesis*] : OOGENESIS

ovigenetic \"+\ *adj* [*ov-* + *-genetic*] : OOGENETIC

ovi·ger \ˈōvəjər, -je(ə)r\ *n* -S [prob. back-formation fr. *ovigerous*] : a leg modified for carrying the eggs in some pycnogonids

ovig·er·ous \(ˈ)ōˈvij(ə)rəs\ *adj* [*ov-* + *-gerous*] : bearing eggs or modified for the purpose of bearing them ⟨an ~ leg⟩

ovi·jec·tor \ˈōvə,jektə(r)\ *var of* OVEJECTOR

ovim·bun·du \ˌōvəmˈbün(ˌ)dü\ *n*, *pl* **ovimbundu** *or* **ovimbundus** *usu cap* : MBUNDU 1

ovi·na·tion \ˌōvəˈnāshən\ *n* -S [NL *ovinia* + E *-ation*] : introduction of sheep-pox virus locally into the body as formerly practiced to induce immunity or reduce the severity of the disease — compare INOCULATION a(1)

¹ovine \ˈō,vīn, -vēn\ *adj* [LL *ovinus*, fr. L *ovis* sheep + *-inus -ine*] : of, being, or relating to sheep

²ovine \"\ *n* -S : a sheep or a closely related animal

ovine malaria *n* : ICTEROHEMATURIA

ovin·ia \ōˈvinēə\ *n* -S [NL, fr. LL *ovinus* + NL *-ia*] : SHEEP POX

¹ovip·a·ra \ōˈvipərə\ *n pl* [NL, fr. L, neut. pl. of *oviparus* oviparous] : oviparous animals

²ovipara \"\ *n*, *pl* **ovipa·rae** \-,rē\ [NL, fr. L, fem. of *oviparus* oviparous] : an egg-laying form of an aphid

ovi·par·i·ty \ˌōvəˈparəd·ē\ *n* -ES [prob. fr. (assumed) NL *oviparitat-*, *oviparitas*, fr. L *oviparus* oviparous + *-itat-*, *-itas -ity*] : the quality or state of being oviparous

ovip·a·rous (ˈ)ōˈvipərəs\ *adj* [L *oviparus*, fr. *ov-* + *-parus -parous*] : producing eggs that develop and hatch outside the maternal body; *also* : involving the production of such eggs — compare OVOVIVIPAROUS, VIVIPAROUS — **ovip·a·rous·ly** \(ˈ)⸗ˈ⸗⸗⸗lē\ *adv* — **ovip·a·rous·ness** \⸗ˈ⸗⸗⸗nəs\ *n* -ES

ovi·pos·it \ˈōvə,päzət, ˌ⸗⸗ˈ⸗⸗\ *vi* [*ov-* + *posit*] : to lay eggs — used esp. of insects; compare LARVIPOSIT — **ovi·po·si·tion** \ˌōvəpəˈzishən\ *n* — **ovi·po·si·tion·al** \-shənᵊl, -shnəl\ *adj*

ovi·pos·i·tor \ˈōvə,päzəd·ə(r), ˌ⸗⸗ˈ⸗⸗⸗\ *n* [*oviposit* + *-or*] : a specialized organ for depositing eggs in a position suitable for their development that is frequent in insects, consists of three pairs of unjointed styles at the end of the abdomen of the female, and forms a boring apparatus with which a hole (as in the ground or in a plant) is made where one or more eggs may be placed — see INSECT illustration

ovis \ˈōvəs\ *n*, *cap* [NL, fr. L, sheep — more at EWE] : a genus of Bovidae consisting of the domestic sheep and the majority of the wild sheep most of which inhabit the mountainous regions from western No. America to western Asia and have horns that form a lateral spiral — see ARGALI

ovi·sac \ˈōvə,sak\ *n* -S [ISV *ov-* + *sac*] **1** : an ootheca or other structure that serves to hold eggs (as the distal part of the oviduct of various amphibians) **2** : GRAAFIAN FOLLICLE

ovi·scapt \ˈōvə,skapt\ *n* -S [F *oviscapte*, fr. *ov-* + Gk *skaptein* to dig; akin to Gk *koptein* to smite, cut off — more at CAPON] : OVIPOSITOR

ovism \ˈōvizəm\ *n* -S [ISV *ov-* + *-ism*] : an old theory that the egg contains the whole embryo of the future organism and the germs of all subsequent offspring — compare ANIMALCULISM

ovi·spermary \ˌōvə+\ *n* [*ov-* + *spermary*] : OVOTESTIS

ovist \ˈōvəst\ *n* -S [ISV *ov-* + *-ist*] : one holding the theory of ovism

ovis·tic \(ˈ)ōˈvistik\ *adj* : of or relating to ovism or ovists

ovo- — see OV-

ovo·cyte \ˈōvə,sīt\ *n* -S [ISV *ov-* + *-cyte*] : OOCYTE

ovo·flavin \ˌōvə+\ *n* [*ov-* + *flavin*] : RIBOFLAVIN

ovo·genesis \ˌōvə+\ *n* [NL, fr. L *ov-* + *genesis*] : OOGENESIS

¹ovoid \ˈō,vȯid\ *adj* [F *ovoïde*, fr. *ov-* + *-oïde* -oid] : shaped like an egg : OVATE ⟨an ~ apple⟩; *specif* : egg-shaped with the large end toward the point of attachment ⟨an ~ leaf⟩

²ovoid \"\ *n* -S : an ovoid body

ovoi·dal \(ˈ)ōˈvȯidᵊl\ *adj* [F *ovoïdal*, fr. *ovoïde* + *-al*] : OVOID

ovo·lecithin \ˌō(ˌ)vō+\ *n* [*ov-* + *lecithin*] **1** : lecithin from egg yolk **2** : LECITHIN 2a

ovo·lo \ˈōvə,lō, ˈōv-\ *n*, *pl* **ovo·li** \-,lē\ [It *ovolo*, *uovolo*, dim. of *ovo*, *uovo* egg, fr. L *ovum* — more at EGG] : a rounded convex molding that in Roman work is usu. a quarter circle in section, in Greek work is flatter, and in medieval architecture is not distinguishable from other convex moldings — compare BOLTEL, TORUS

ovolo

ovo·mucin \ˌōvə+\ *n* [*ov-* + *mucin*] : a mucin present in white of egg

ovo·mucoid \"+\ *n* [ISV *ov-* + *mucoid*] : a mucoid present in white of egg

ovo·plasm \ˈōvə,plazəm\ *n* [ISV *ov-* + *-plasm*; orig. formed as G *ovoplasma*] : OOPLASM — **ovo·plas·mic** \ˌōvəˈplazmik\ *adj*

ovo·testicular \ˌō(ˌ)vō+\ *adj* [fr. *ovotestis*, after E *testis*: *testicular*] : of or relating to an ovotestis

ovo·testis \ˌōvō+\ *n* [NL, fr. L *ov-* + *testis*] : a hermaphrodite gonad

ovo·vitellin \ˌō(ˌ)vō+\ *n* [*ov-* + *vitellin*] : VITELLIN

ovo·viviparity \ˌō(ˌ)vō+\ *n* [fr. *ovoviviparous*, after E *oviparous*: *oviparity* and E *viviparous*: *viviparity*] : the condition of being ovoviviparous

ovo·viviparous \"+\ *adj* [prob. fr. (assumed) NL *ovoviviparus*, fr. L *ov-* + *viviparus* viviparous] : producing eggs that develop within the maternal body and hatch within or immediately after extrusion from the parent (as in the case of many reptiles and elasmobranch fishes) — compare OVIPAROUS, VIVIPAROUS — **ovo·viviparously** \"+\ *adv* — **ovo·viviparousness** \"+\ *n*

ovu·la \ˈōvyələ\ *n*, *cap* [NL, fr. L *ovum* egg + *-ula*] : a genus of marine snails related to and sometimes included in the Cypraeidae but now commonly made type of a separate family (Ovulidae)

ovu·lar \ˈävyələ(r) *also* ˈōv-, *in sense 1* " *or* -,vyül-\ *adj* [NL *ovularis*, fr. *ovulum* + L *-aris* -ar] **1** : relating to or being an ovule **2** : of or relating to an ovum

ovu·lar·i·an \ˌävyəˌla(a)rēən *also* ˌōv-\ *adj* [perh. fr. NL *ovulum* ovule of a seed plant, small egg + E *-ary* + *-an*] : resembling an egg

ovu·lary \ˈävyə,lerē *also* ˈōv-\ *n* -ES [*ovule* + *-ary*] : the lower part of a carpel in which the ovules are borne — compare OVARY

¹ovu·late \ˈävyə,lāt; ˈävyələt, -,vyülət; *also* ˈōv-\ *adj* [prob. fr. (assumed) NL *ovulatus*, fr. NL *ovulum* + L *-atus* -ate] : bearing an ovule

²ovu·late \ˈävyə,lāt *also* ˈōv-\ *vi* -ED/-ING/-S [*ovule* + *-ate*, v. suffix] : to produce ovules or discharge them from an ovary — **ovu·la·tion** \ˌävyəˈlāshən *also* ˌōv-\ *n* -S

ovu·la·to·ry \ˈävyələ,tōrē *also* ˈōv-\ *adj* : of, relating to, or involving ovulation

ovule \ˈä(ˌ)vyül, ˈōv-\ *n* -S [NL *ovulum* ovule of a seed plant, small egg, fr. L *ovum* egg + *-ulum*] **1** : a rounded outgrowth of the ovary in seed plants that develops into a seed usu. only after fertilization and that consists of an embryo sac borne centrally within a nucellus, the latter surrounded by one or more integuments **2** : a small egg : an egg in an early stage of growth

ovu·lif·er·ous \ˌävyəˈlif(ə)rəs *also* ˌōv-\ *adj* [*ovule* + *-iferous*] : bearing an ovule

ovu·list \ˈävyələst *also* ˈō-, -,vyül-\ *n* -S [ISV *ovule* + *-ist*; prob. orig. formed in G] : OVIST

ovu·lum \ˈävyələm *also* ˈōv-\ *n*, *pl* **ovu·la** \-lə\ [NL] : OVULE

ovum \ˈōvəm\ *n*, *pl* **ova** \-və\ [NL, fr. L, egg — more at EGG] **1** : a female gamete : MACROGAMETE, EGG CELL: **a** : a mature egg that has undergone reduction, is ready for fertilization, and takes the form of a relatively large inactive gamete providing a comparatively great amount of reserve material and contributing most of the cytoplasm of the zygote — see OOSPHERE; compare CENTROLECITHAL, HOMOLECITHAL, MEGALECITHAL, MICROLECITHAL, OVARY, TELOLECITHAL **b** : an immature ovum (as an oocyte or oogonium) **c** : a fertilized ovum (as a zygote or embryo) — not used technically **2** : an architectural ornament shaped like an egg

ow \ˈau̇, ˈü\ *interj* [ME] — used esp. to express sudden pain or surprise

OW *abbr* oil-in-water

owa·la oil \ōˈwälə\ *n* [*owala* prob. fr. Mpongwe *owala*, *ovala*, *obala* owala tree] : a lubricant oil obtained from the seed of the owala tree

owala tree *n* : a tropical African tree (*Pentaclethra africana*) of the family Leguminosae having pods about two feet long and large flat seeds which yield owala oil

owd \ˈōd, ˈȯd, ˈäd\ *dial var of* OLD

¹owe \ˈō\ *vb*; **owed** \ˈōd\ *or archaic* **ought** \ˈȯt\; **owed** *or archaic* **ought**; **owing**; **owes** [ME *owe*, *ogh* & *oweth*, *ogh* (1st & 3d pers. sing. pres. indic. respectively of *owen* to possess, own, owe, past *owede*, *oughte*), fr. OE *āh* (1st & 3d pers. sing. pres. indic. of *āgan* to possess, own, owe, past *āhte*); akin to OHG *eigun* (1st & 3d pers. pl. pres. indic.) possess, have, ON *ā* (1st & 3d pers. sing. pres. indic.) possess, have, am obliged (infin. *eiga*), Goth *aih* (1st & 3d pers. sing. pres. indic.) possess, have, Skt *īśe* he possesses, owns] *vt* **1 a** *archaic* : POSSESS, OWN **b** *dial Eng* : to claim as one's possession **c** : to have or bear (a specified feeling or relation) to someone or something ⟨~s his master a grudge⟩ **2 a** (1) : to be under an obligation to pay or repay in return for something received : be indebted in the sum of ⟨~s me five dollars⟩ (2) : to be under obligation to render (as duty or service) ⟨the homage which man ~s his Creator —M.W.Baldwin⟩ **b** : to have an obligation to on account of something done or received : be indebted to ⟨~s the grocer for supplies⟩ **3** : to have or possess as something derived or bestowed : be indebted or obliged for ⟨*owed* his wealth to his father⟩ ⟨~s his fame chiefly to his professional activities —Dumas Malone⟩ **~** *vi* **1** : to be in debt ⟨~s for his house⟩ **2** *obs* : to be under obligations to someone

²owe \ˈ(y)ō\ *dial Eng var of* EWE

ow·el·ty \ˈōəltē\ *n* -ES [MF *oelté* equality, fr. L *aequalitat-*, *aequalitas* — more at EQUALITY] **1** : EQUALITY **2 a** : the amount paid or secured by one owner to another to equalize a partition of property in kind **b** : a payment made to achieve equality between those who exchange property

owe·nia \ōˈ(w)ēnēə\ *n*, *cap* [NL, fr. Sir Richard *Owen* †1892 Eng. anatomist and zoologist + NL *-ia*] : a small genus of tropical Australian trees (family Meliaceae) having pinnate leaves, small greenish panicled flowers, and edible acid drupaceous fruits — see NATIVE PLUM

ow·en·ism \ˈōə,nizəm\ *n* -S *usu cap* [Robert *Owen* †1858 Welsh socialist and philanthropist + E *-ism*] : the political and social theories of Robert Owen who advocated a communistic reorganization of society

ow·en·ite \-nīt\ *n* -S *usu cap* [Robert *Owen* + E *-ite*] : an adherent of the political and social theories of Robert Owen

ow·er \ˈō(ə)r, ˈōə\ *dial var of* OVER

ow·er·ance \ˈō(ə)rən(t)s\ *n* -S [*ower* + *-ance*] *chiefly Scot* : MASTERY, CONTROL

OWF *abbr* optimum working frequency

ow·ing \ˈōiŋ, ˈōeŋ\ *adj* [ME *owing*, *owinge*, fr. pres. part. of *owen* to possess, own, owe] **1** *archaic* : INDEBTED, BEHOLDEN **2** : due to be paid or rendered : OWED ⟨sleep ~ to you because of some long vigil —Geoffrey Jefferson⟩ **3** : ATTRIBUTABLE — used with *to* ⟨to whose . . . indulgence the errors of her daughters must be principally ~ —Jane Austen⟩

owing to *prep* : because of ⟨impassable by cars *owing to* soft sand —G.W.Murray⟩

owk \ˈük\ *var of* OUK

¹owl \ˈau̇l, *esp before pause or consonant* ˈau̇əl\ *n* -S [ME *owle*, fr. OE *ūle*; akin to MD *ule* owl, OHG *uwila*, ON *ugla*] **1** : any of numerous widely distributed birds of prey (order Strigiformes) distinguished by their large head and large more or less forwardly directed eyes, short hooked bill, strong talons with reversible outer toe, very soft fluffy usu. mottled plumage, and more or less nocturnal habits, as well as by many anatomical characters **2** : a pigeon of a long-established breed from which the turbits and satinettes are supposed to be derived having a frill on the front of the neck and the bill very short with the upper mandible downwardly curved **3** : a person suggestive of an owl in solemnity of appearance or manner, nocturnal mode of life, or other respect ⟨the ~s who . . . tell us that a dismal period of world history is no time for high musical spirits —Wilder Hobson⟩

²owl \"\ *vi* -ED/-ING/-S *chiefly dial* : to hoot or stare like an owl ⟨~ . . . with hoots that echo eerily down the valley —*Amer. Guide Series: Ark.*⟩

³owl \"\ *adj* : operating or open around or after midnight or all night ⟨the rattle of one of the ~ streetcars —Hamilton Basso⟩

owl butterfly *n* : a large So. American butterfly of the genus *Caligo*; *esp* : a butterfly (*C. eurylochus*) that has a large ocellated spot like an owl's eye on each hind wing

¹ow·ler \ˈau̇lə(r)\ *dial Eng var of* ALDER

²owl·er \ˈau̇lə(r)\ *n* -S [¹*owl* + *-er*; prob. fr. the nocturnal habits of the owl] : a person or ship engaged in owling

owl·ery \ˈau̇lərē\ *n* -ES : an abode or a haunt of owls

owl·et \ˈau̇lət\ *n* -S [¹*owl* + *-et*] **1** : the European little owl or other small owl **2** : a young owl

owlet moth *n* : a moth of the family Noctuidae

owl–fly \ˈ⸗ˌ⸗\ *n* : a neuropterous fly of the family Ascalaphidae

owl·ing \ˈau̇liŋ\ *n* -S [¹*owl* + *-ing*; prob. fr. the nocturnal habits of the owl] : the act of smuggling wool or sheep out of England; *also* : the carrying on of contraband trade of any kind

owl·ish \ˈau̇lish, -lēsh\ *adj* : resembling, characteristic of, or suggestive of an owl ⟨the cigar-smoking man with an ~ look —*Newsweek*⟩ ⟨fluttering his eyelids in ~ bliss —Arline Thomas⟩ — **owl·ish·ly** \-ləshlē, -li\ *adv* — **owl·ish·ness** \-lishnəs -lēsh-\ *n* -ES

owl–light \ˈ⸗ˌ⸗\ *n* : DUSK ⟨the *owl-light* of the deep streets —F.M.Ford⟩

owllike \ˈ⸗ˌ⸗\ *adj* : like that of an owl ⟨an ancient and ~ demeanor —R.L.Stevenson⟩

owl midge *n* : a fly of the family Psychodidae

owl monkey *n* [so called fr. the large yellow eyes] : NIGHT APE

owl moth *n* : a Brazilian moth (*Erebus agrippina*) of the family Noctuidae that is the largest known moth and has a wingspread of 10 inches

owl parrot *n* : KAKAPO

owl's clover *or* **owlclover** \ˈ⸗ˌ⸗⸗\ *n* : a California herb of the genus *Orthocarpus*

owl swallow *n* : a nightjar of the family Podargidae

owly \ˈau̇lē, -li\ *adj* : like an owl

¹own \ˈōn\ *adj* [ME *owen*, fr. OE *āgen*; akin to OHG *eigan* own, ON *eiginn*; derivative fr. the root of OE *āgan* to possess, own — more at OWE] **1** : belonging to oneself or itself — usu. used following a possessive case or pronoun to emphasize or intensify the idea of property, peculiar interest, or exclusive ownership, and usu. with reflexive force ⟨my ~ father⟩ ⟨his ~ composition⟩ **2** — used to specify an immediate or direct relationship ⟨an ~ brother⟩ ⟨an ~ cousin⟩ ⟨~ sister to the queen⟩ **3** — used to indicate or intensify the idea of one's own self as agent or doer ⟨cooked his ~ meal⟩ ⟨acted as his ~ lawyer⟩ — **be one's own man** : to have command of oneself : not to be subject to another ⟨the college president must *be his own man* —Harold Taylor⟩

²own \"\ *vb* -ED/-ING/-S *vt* **1** : to have or hold as property or appurtenance : have a rightful title to, whether legal or natural : POSSESS **2 a** (1) : to acknowledge as one's own ⟨~ a fault⟩ ⟨which the author had once ~*ed* as her habitat —C. W.Ferguson⟩ (2) *of a mother animal* : to acknowledge (offspring) as one's own by nursing and taking care of **b** *archaic* : to acknowledge as an acquaintance : give recognition to **c** *archaic* : to lay claim to : claim for one's own **3** *archaic* : to manifest one's approval or acceptance of : COUNTENANCE **4 a** : to acknowledge (someone or something) to be what is claimed : concede to be true or valid : ADMIT, RECOGNIZE ⟨~ a debt⟩ ⟨~*ed* him to be their master⟩ ⟨would not ~ his mistake⟩ **b** : to acknowledge the supremacy or authority of : yield obedience to **~** *vi* : ADMIT, CONFESS — used with *to* ⟨an old gentleman who ~*ed* to eighty-six years —Osbert Sitwell⟩ ⟨wouldn't ~ to knowin' me these days —Rex Ingamells⟩ **syn** see ACKNOWLEDGE, HAVE — **own the line** *chiefly Brit*, *of a hound* : to get the scent of a fox

³own \"\ *pron*, *sing or pl in constr* : one or ones belonging to oneself — used after a possessive ⟨gave out books so that each student had his ~⟩ — **get one's own back** : to revenge oneself : get even ⟨they're out to *get their own back* —T.C.Worsley⟩ — **into one's own 1** : into possession of that which rightfully belongs to one ⟨the despoiled heir at long last came *into his own*⟩ **2** : into the prosperous or flourishing condition or recognition to which one is entitled or of which one is capable ⟨Italian art poetry . . . now coming for the first time *into its own* —R.A.Hall b.1911⟩ ⟨recognizes that nationalism has rightly come *into its own* in Asia —A.P.Ryan⟩ — **on one's own** : on one's own resources or initiative : for or by oneself ⟨every ship was *on its own* —H.A.Chippendale⟩ ⟨gave the order . . . *on his own* —H.L.Ismay⟩

owned \ˈōnd\ *adj* : held as one's own possession — usu. used in combination ⟨state-*owned* railways⟩

own·er \ˈōnə(r)\ *n* -S [ME *ownere*, fr. *ownen* to possess, take possession of (fr. OE *āgnian* take possession of, assign possession of) + *-ere* -er; akin to MD *eigenen*, *egenen* to take possession of, assign possession of, ON *eigna*; derivatives fr. the word represented by OE *āgen* own] : one that owns : one that has the legal or rightful title whether the possessor or not : PROPRIETOR — **at owner's risk** *adv* : on condition that the owner bear the risk (as of loss, damage or delay)

own·er·less \-ləs\ *adj* : having no owner ⟨~ land⟩

owner's flag *n* : PRIVATE SIGNAL

own·er·ship \-nə(r),ship\ *n* : the state, relation, or fact of being an owner : lawful claim or title : PROPERTY, PROPRIETORSHIP, DOMINIUM

own·hood \ˈōn,hu̇d\ *n* [¹*own* + *-hood*; trans. of G *eigenheit*] : the condition in which one holds oneself or one's own in isolation : reliance upon or desire for one's own way or will : EGOISM, SELFHOOD

own·ness \ˈōnnəs\ *n* -ES : the quality or state of belonging to oneself

own–root \ˈ⸗ˌ⸗\ *or* **own–rooted** \ˈ⸗ˈ⸗⸗\ *adj*, *of a plant* : growing on its own roots rather than on roots obtained from a stock : developing from a seed, cutting, or layer rather than from grafting or budding ⟨*own-root* roses are frequently less vigorous than budded stock⟩ — compare SEEDLING-ROOTED

own up *vi* : to admit or confess frankly and fully ⟨if your ball broke the window . . . you *own up* —*Boy Scout Handbook*⟩

owre \(ˈ)ō(ə)r\ *chiefly Scot var of* OVER — often used in combination as a verbal prefix

owse *chiefly Scot var of* OX

¹owt \ˈōt\ *dial Eng var of* OUGHT

²owt \"\ *dial Eng var of* AUGHT

owy·hee·ite \ōˈwīē,īt\ *n* -S [*Owyhee* county, southwestern Idaho, its locality + E *-ite*] : a mineral $Pb_5Ag_2Sb_6S_{15}$ consisting of a lead silver antimony sulfide occurring in metallic fibrous masses and needlelike crystals

ox \ˈäks\ *n*, *pl* **ox·en** \-ksən\ *also* **ox** *see sense 3* [ME, fr. OE *oxa*; akin to OHG *ohso* ox, ON *oxi*, Goth *auhsa*, W *ych* ox, Skt *ukṣan* ox, bull, *ukṣati* he sprinkles — more at HUMOR] **1** : the domestic bovine (*Bos taurus*); *esp* : an adult castrated male used for a draft animal or for food ⟨pair of *oxen*⟩ ⟨span of *oxen*⟩ ⟨team of *oxen*⟩ ⟨yoke of *oxen*⟩ — compare BULL, BULLOCK, STEER **2** : a member of *Bos* or a closely allied genus ⟨wild ~⟩ ⟨extinct *oxen*⟩ **3** *pl also* **oxes** : a person resembling an ox (as in placidity, stolidity, clumsiness, or strength) ⟨dumb ~⟩ ⟨big ~⟩

¹ox- *or* **oxo-** *comb form* [F, fr. *oxygène* oxygen — more at OXYGEN] **1** : containing oxygen — esp. in the names of various cyclic compounds ⟨*oxazole*⟩ **2** *usu* **oxo-** : containing oxygen in a carbonyl group specif. regarded as formed by replacement of two hydrogen atoms in a methylene group by oxygen — in names of ketones or compounds (as heterocyclic compounds) that are not true ketones because the carbonyl group is not attached to two carbon atoms ⟨*oxo*-acetic acid⟩ ⟨2-*oxo*-indoline⟩ ⟨*oxindole*⟩; distinguished from *oxy-*; compare KET-

²ox- *comb form* [by shortening] : OXAL- ⟨*oxamide*⟩

oxa- *or* **ox-** *comb form* [ISV, fr. ¹*ox-* + *-a-*] : containing oxygen in place of carbon or regarded as in place of carbon usu. in place of the methylene group —CH_2— ⟨10*H*-9-*oxa*anthracene⟩ ⟨*oxa*zacycloheptane⟩ — compare AZA-, THIA-

oxa·diazole \ˌäksə+\ *n* [¹*ox-* + *diazole*] : any of four parent compounds $C_2H_2N_2O$ containing a five-membered ring composed of two carbon atoms, two nitrogen atoms, and one oxygen atom

oxal- *or* **oxalo-** *comb form* [F, fr. (*acide*) *oxalique* oxalic acid] : related to oxalic acid ⟨*oxal*amide⟩ ⟨*oxalo*succinic⟩

ox·al·acetate \ˌäksəl+\ *or* **ox·a·lo·acetate** \ˌäksə(ˌ)lō, äkˈsa(-)+\ *n* [ISV *oxalacetic* (in *oxalacetic acid*) + *-ate*] : a salt or ester of oxalacetic acid

oxalacetic acid \"+ . . . -\ *or* **oxaloacetic acid** \"+ . . . -\ *n* [*oxalacetic*, *oxaloacetic* ISV *oxal-* + *acetic*] : a crystalline acid $HOOCCOCH_2COOH$ formed by reversible oxidation of malic acid (as in the metabolism of fats and carbohydrates) and in reversible transamination reactions (as from aspartic acid) — compare CARBOXYLASE b

ox·al·aldehyde \ˌäksəl+\ *n* [ISV *oxal-* + *aldehyde*] : GLYOXAL

ox·al·amide \ˌäksəˈla,mīd, äkˈsalə,-, -ˌməd\ *n* [ISV *oxal-* + *amide*; orig. formed in F] : OXAMIDE

[1]ox·a·late \'äksə,lāt\ *n* -s [F, fr. *oxal-* (in *acide oxalique* oxalic acid) + *-ate*] : a salt or ester of oxalic acid
[2]oxalate \"\ *vt* -ED/-ING/-s : to treat with an oxalate; *specif* : to add an oxalate to (blood or plasma) to prevent coagulation
ox·a·la·to- \¦äksə¦läd·(,)ō\ *comb form* [[1]*oxalate* + *-o-*] : oxalate — esp. in names of coordination complexes ⟨*oxalato*ferrate (III) ion $Fe(C_2O_4)_3{}^{3-}$⟩
ox·aldehyde \(')äks+\ *n* [[2]*ox-* + *aldehyde*] : GLYOXAL
ox·al·ic acid \(')äk¦salik-, -lēk-\ *n* [*oxalic* fr. F *oxalique*, fr. L *oxalis* garden sorrel + F *-ique* -ic] : a poisonous strong dicarboxylic acid $(COOH)_2$ or $H_2C_2O_4$ that is usu. obtained as the hygroscopic crystalline dihydrate, that occurs in oxalis and other plants in the form of the acid potassium salt or the calcium salt, that is formed by the oxidation or fermentation of carbohydrates but is made industrially chiefly by heating sodium formate and finally acidifying, and that is used esp. as a neutralizing, acidifying, and bleaching agent (as in laundering and in the textile industry), as a cleaning and purifying agent, as a rust and scale remover, in the manufacture of dyes and other chemicals, and in chemical analysis
ox·al·i·da·ce·ae \(,)äk,salə'dāsē,ē\ *n pl, cap* [NL, fr. *Oxalid-, Oxalis*, type genus + *-aceae*] : a family of widely distributed herbs or rarely trees (order Geraniales) having compound leaves and regular pentamerous flowers with monadelphous stamens and five distinct styles — **ox·al·i·da·ceous** \(¦)äk¦salə¦dāshəs\ *adj*
ox·alis \äk'saləs, 'äksələs\ *n* [NL, fr. L, garden sorrel, fr. Gk, sorrel, fr. *oxys* sharp, keen — more at OXY-] **1** *cap* : a large genus (the type of the family Oxalidaceae) of acaulescent herbs mostly of warm or tropical regions having acid foliage, palmately or pinnately compound leaves, and usu. white, pink, or purple flowers with 10 stamens — see OCA **2** -ES : any plant or flower of the genus *Oxalis*
ox·alo·nitrile \¦äksə(,)lō, äk¦salə·+\ *n* [*oxal-* + *nitrile*] : CYANOGEN 2
ox·alo·succinic acid \"+ . . . -\ *n* [*oxal-* + *succinic*] : a tricarboxylic acid $HOOCCOCH(COOH)CH_2COOH$ recognized as an intermediate stage in the metabolism of fats and carbohydrates
ox·al·uria \,äksal'yůrēə, -sə'lůrēə\ *n* -s [NL, fr. *oxal-* + *-uria*] : the presence of oxalic acid or oxalates in the urine esp. in excess
ox·al·uric acid \¦==¦rik-\ *n* [ISV *oxal-* + *-uric*] : a crystalline acid $NH_2CONHCOCOOH$ obtained in the form of salts by the action of alkalies on parabanic acid
ox·a·lyl \'äksə,lil\ *n* -s [ISV *oxal-* + *-yl*] : the bivalent radical —COCO— of oxalic acid
ox·a·lyl·urea \,äksə,lilyů'rēə\ *n* [NL, fr. ISV *oxalyl* + NL *urea*] : PARABANIC ACID
ox·amate \'äksə,māt, äk'samət\ *n* -s [ISV *oxamic* (in *oxamic acid*) + *-ate*] : a salt or ester of oxamic acid
ox·am·ic acid \(')äk¦samik-\ *n* [*oxamic* fr. F *oxamique*, fr. *oxam-* (fr. *oxamide*) + *-ique* -ic] : a high-melting crystalline acid $NH_2COCOOH$ intermediate between oxalic acid and oxamide : the monoamide of oxalic acid
ox·amide \äk'saməd; 'äksə,mīd, -,məd\ *n* [ISV [2]*ox-* + *amide*; orig. formed in F] : a high-melting crystalline amide $(CONH_2)_2$ obtainable by treating ethyl oxalate with ammonia : the diamide of oxalic acid
ox·amine dye \'äksə,mēn-, -,mən; äk'samən-\ *n, usu cap O* [ISV [1]*ox-* + *amine*] : any of several direct dyes — see DYE table I (under *Direct Red 53, Direct Violet 12, Direct Blue 3*)
ox·am·mite \'äksə,mīt, äk'sa,m-\ *n* -s [*oxalate* + *ammonium* + *-ite*] : hydrous ammonium oxalate $(NH_4)_2C_2O_4.1H_2O$ occurring as a crystalline salt in guano
ox·a·nil·ic acid \¦äksə¦nilik-\ *n* [ISV [2]*ox-* + *anilic*] : a crystalline acid $C_6H_5NHCOCOOH$ obtained by heating oxalic acid with aniline; phenyl-oxamic acid
ox·anilide \(')aks+\ *n* [ISV [2]*ox-* + *anilide*] : a crystalline amide $(CONHC_6H_5)_2$ obtainable by heating aniline oxalate and useful as a plasticizer; diphenyl-oxamide
ox·a·zine \'äksə,zēn, -,zən\ *n* -s [ISV [1]*ox-* + *azine*] : any of several parent compounds C_4H_5NO or their derivatives containing a ring composed of four carbon atoms, one oxygen atom, and one nitrogen atom; *esp* : OXAZINE DYE — see AZINE 1; compare MORPHOLINE
oxazine dye *n* : an azine dye containing at least one fused oxazine ring in which the oxygen atom and the nitrogen atom are in the para or 1,4-positions — compare PHENOXAZINE
ox·a·zole \'äksə,zōl\ *n* [ISV [1]*ox-* + *azole*] **1** : a parent compound C_3H_3NO containing a ring composed of three carbon atoms, one oxygen atom, and one nitrogen atom with one carbon atom between the oxygen and nitrogen atoms — compare ISOXAZOLE **2** : a derivative of oxazole
ox·a·zol·i·dine \,äksə'zōlə,dēn, -zäl-\ *n* -s [ISV *oxazole* + *-idine*] : the tetrahydro derivative C_3H_7NO of oxazole; *also* : a derivative of this compound of which some (as trimethadione) are used in the control of convulsions (as in the treatment of epilepsy)
ox ball *n* : a hair ball from an ox's stomach
ox balm *n* : HORSE BALM 1
ox·ber·ry \'äks- — *see* BERRY\ *n, dial Eng* : the fruit of the black bryony
ox bile *n* : OXGALL
oxbird \'=,=\ *n* **1** : DUNLIN **2** *dial Eng* : the sanderling or other small sandpiper **3** : an African weaverbird (*Bubalornis albirostris*) **4** : OXPECKER
oxbiter \'=,==\ *n* **1** : COWBIRD **2** : OXPECKER
oxblood \'=,=\ *or* **oxblood red** *n* : a moderate reddish brown that is yellower, stronger, and slightly darker than roan, stronger than mahogany, redder and stronger than rustic brown, and redder and deeper than russet tan — called also *beef's blood, coptic, Kazak, Malaga red, piccolopasso red, sang de boeuf*
ox bot *or* **ox botfly** *n* : WARBLE FLY
[1]oxbow \'=,=\ *n* [ME *oxbowe*, fr. *ox* + *bowe* bow — more at OX, BOW] **1** : a frame bent into the shape of the letter U and embracing an ox's neck as a kind of collar the upper ends of which pass through the bar of the yoke **2 a** : a river meander with extreme curvature such that only a neck of land is left between two parts of the stream **b** : OXBOW LAKE

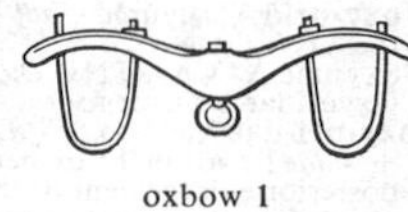
oxbow 1

[2]oxbow \'=,=\ *adj* : having a compound curve with concave center and convex ends — opposed to *serpentine*; used esp. of the front of a piece of cabinet furniture ⟨~ chest⟩
oxbow lake *n* : a crescent-shaped often ephemeral lake formed in the abandoned channel of a meander by the silting up of its ends after the stream has cut through the land within the meander at a narrow point
oxbow stirrup *n* : a large wooden stirrup resembling an oxbow in shape
oxbrake \'=,=\ *n* : a frame in which oxen are shod
oxcart \'=,=\ *n* : a cart drawn by oxen
oxcheek \'=,=\ *n* : an ox's cheek esp. when cut for meat
oxea \'äksēə, äk'sēə\ *n, pl* **oxeas** \-ēəz\ *also* **oxe·ae** \-ē,ē\ [NL, fr. Gk *oxys* sharp — more at OXY-] : a needle-shaped sponge spicule sharp at both ends
[1]oxen *pl of* OX
[2]ox·en \'äksən\ *n* -s [by alter. (influence of [1]*oxen*)] *dial* : OX
oxen dance *n* [trans. of Sw *oxdans*] : a comic Swedish male folk dance representing a mock duel
ox·e·ote \'äksē,ōt\ *also* **ox·e·ate** \-ē,āt\ *adj* [*oxeote* fr. NL *oxea* + E *-ote* (as in *tylote*); *oxeate* fr. NL *oxea* + E *-ate*] : of, relating to, or forming an oxea; *also* : pointed and shaped like a rod
ox·er \'äksə(r)\ *n* -s [*ox* + *-er*] : a hedge with a guardrail running along one side at a distance of two or three feet and often a ditch along the other side to prevent cattle from passing through it — see DOUBLE OXER
oxes *pl of* OX
oxeye \'=,=\ *n* [ME, fr. *ox* + *eye*] **1** : any of several composite plants having heads with both disk and ray flowers: as **a** : DAISY 1b **b** : FIELD CHAMOMILE **c** : a plant of the genus *Buphthalmum* **d** : a plant of the genus *Heliopsis* **e** : BLACK-EYED SUSAN **2 a** *dial Eng* : the dunlin or other small sandpiper **b** *dial Eng* : any of several titmice **c** : LEAST SANDPIPER **d** : BLACK-BELLIED PLOVER **3** : a round or oval window **4** : a small cloud that on the African coasts precedes a storm **5** *or* **oxeye herring** : TARPON 1b
oxeye bean *n* : the large orbicular brown seed of a tall tropical American woody vine (*Mucuna urens*) having flat bristly pods; *also* : the vine producing this seed
ox-eyed \'=;=\ *adj* [trans. of Gk *boōpis*] : having eyes like those of an ox ⟨*ox-eyed* Juno⟩ ⟨*ox-eyed* Hera⟩
oxeye daisy *also* **ox-eyed daisy** *n* **1** : DAISY 1b **2** : OXEYE 1d **3** : BLACK-EYED SUSAN
ox fence *n* : OXER
oxfly \'=,=\ *n* : an ox warble fly or other fly troublesome to cattle
[1]ox·ford \'äksfə(r)d\ *adj, usu cap* [fr. *Oxford*, city in central England] **1** : of or from the city of Oxford, England : of the kind or style prevalent in Oxford : OXONIAN **2** [fr. *Oxford* University, Oxford, England] : of or relating to Oxford University : OXONIAN
[2]oxford \"\ *n* -s **1** *also* **oxford shoe** *sometimes cap O* : a low-cut usu. laced shoe coming to the instep or lower, often being of balmoral or blucher design, and usu. having three or more eyelets **2** *often cap* : OXFORD DOWN **3** *or* **oxford cloth** *sometimes cap O* : a soft durable shirting and general clothing fabric usu. of cotton but sometimes of spun rayon and made in plain weave or basket weaves having two fine warp yarns against one heavier filling yarn

oxford of balmoral design

oxford bag *n, usu cap O* **1** : a bag resembling the Boston bag but larger **2 oxford bags** *pl* : trousers with very large baggy legs
oxford blue *n, often cap O* : a blackish purple that is bluer and darker than average eggplant and bluer and deeper than Burgundy (sense 2b)
oxford chrome *n, often cap O* : YELLOW OCHER
oxford corner *n, usu cap O* : a plain border rule projecting in each outward direction and making a square outside at each corner
oxford dash *n, often cap O* : DOUBLE DASH
oxford down *also* **oxfordshire down** *n* [fr. *Oxford* or *Oxfordshire*, county in central England where the breed originated] **1** *usu cap O&D* : a Down breed of large hornless sheep developed by crossing Cotswolds and Hampshire Downs **2** *usu cap O & often cap D* : a sheep of the Oxford Down breed
oxford frame *n, usu cap O* : a picture frame having sides that cross at the corners and project outward several inches

Oxford frame

oxford gray *also* **oxford** *n* -s *often cap O* : a dark gray that is darker than pelican or Dover gray and lighter than fashion gray
oxford grouper *n, usu cap O&G* : a member of the Oxford Group movement
oxford group movement *n, usu cap O&G* : a life-changing movement stressing personal and social regeneration founded in 1921 at Oxford, England, by Frank Buchman and replaced by Moral Re-Armament in 1938 — called also *Buchmanism*
[1]ox·for·di·an \(')äk¦sfōrdēən\ *adj or n, usu cap* [*Oxford*, England + E *-ian*] : OXONIAN
[2]oxfordian \"\ *adj, usu cap* [Edward de Vere, Earl of *Oxford* †1604 Eng. courtier and lyric poet + E *-ian*] : of or relating to the 17th Earl of Oxford or to the doctrine that he was the author of the dramatic works usu. attributed to Shakespeare
[3]oxfordian \"\ *n* -s *usu cap* : a supporter of the doctrine that the 17th Earl of Oxford was the author of the dramatic works usu. attributed to Shakespeare
oxford india paper *n, usu cap O&I* : INDIA PAPER 2
ox·ford·ism \'äksfə(r)d,izəm\ *n* -s *usu cap* **1** : an Oxonian habit or characteristic **2** : TRACTARIANISM
oxford movement *n, usu cap O & sometimes cap M* : a High Church movement within the Church of England that was started at Oxford in 1833 and that attempted to revive pre-Reformation forms of piety in the interest of an Anglo-Catholicism
oxford ocher *n* **1** *usu cap 1st O* : a yellow ocher found near Oxford, England **2** *often cap 1st O* : YELLOW OCHER
ox·ford·shire \'äksfə(r)d,shi(ə)r, -,shiə, -,shə(r)\ *or* **oxford** *adj, usu cap* [fr. *Oxfordshire* or *Oxford*, county in central England] : of or from the county of Oxford, England : of the kind or style prevalent in the county of Oxford
oxford unit *n, usu cap O* [fr. *Oxford* University, Oxford, England, where it was first adopted] : an international unit of penicillin equivalent to 0.606 micrograms of the crystalline compound
oxford weed *n, usu cap O* : KENILWORTH IVY
oxgall \'=,=\ *n* **1** : the gall of the ox used esp. in medicine, painting, and the marbling of books **2** : LIGHT CHROME YELLOW
ox·gang \'äks,gaŋ\ *or* **ox·gate** \-gāt\ *n* [*oxgang* fr. ME, fr. OE *oxan gang*, fr. *oxan*, gen. of *oxa* ox + *gang* way; *oxgate* fr. *ox* + *gate* (way); fr. its being measured by the work of one ox in a plowing team — more at OX, GANG] : BOVATE
oxgoad \'=,=\ *n* : a goad for driving oxen
oxharrow \'=,(,)=\ *n, archaic* : a large heavy harrow used esp. on clay land
oxheart \'=,=\ *n* **1** : any of various large sweet cherries **2** *or* **oxheart cabbage** : any of various cabbages with oval or conical heads
oxhide \'=,=\ *n* [ME, fr. *ox* + *hide*] **1** : the hide of an ox **2** : leather made from the hide of an ox
oxhorn \'=,=\ *n* **1** : the horn of an ox **2** : a drinking cup made of an ox's horn
ox·i·da·ble \'äksədəbəl\ *adj* [F *oxidable, oxydable*, fr. *oxider, oxyder* to oxidize (fr. *oxide, oxyde*) + *-able* — more at OXIDE] : OXIDIZABLE
ox·i·dant \'äksədənt, -dᵊnt\ *n* -s [F *oxidant* (now *oxydant*), fr. pres. part. of *oxider* (now *oxyder*) to oxidize, fr. *oxide* (now *oxyde*) oxide] : OXIDIZING AGENT — compare REDUCTANT
ox·i·dase \'äksə,dās, -āz\ *n* -s [ISV *oxid-* (fr. *oxidation*) + *-ase*] : any of various enzymes that catalyze oxidation and thus play an important role in biological oxidation-reduction processes; *esp* : a metal-containing enzyme (as cytochrome oxidase or tyrosinase) that differs in general from a dehydrogenase in its ability to react directly with molecular oxygen — compare OXIDOREDUCTASE, PEROXIDASE
ox·i·da·sic \¦==¦dāsik, -āzik\ *adj* : of, like, or relating to an oxidase
ox·i·da·tion \,äksə'dāshən\ *n* -s [F *oxidation* (now *oxydation*), fr. *oxider* (now *oxyder*) to oxidize + *-ation*] **1 a** : the act or process of oxidizing ⟨anodic ~⟩ — compare COMBUSTION 1a, FERMENTATION 1b, RESPIRATION 2 **b** : the state or result of being oxidized **2** : the stage in the firing of clayware in which the organic matter is burned away by the oxygen in the kiln atmosphere
oxidation base *or* **oxidation dye** *n* : any of a small class of dyes (as aniline black) that are formed by oxidation after application to furs or textiles — see DYE table I
oxidation potential *n* : the potential at which oxidation occurs at the anode in an electrochemical cell
oxidation-reduction *n* : a chemical reaction in which one or more electrons are transferred from one atom or molecule to another ⟨the hydrogen—hydrogen-ion system is an *oxidation-reduction* system⟩
oxidation-reduction potential *n* : the potential at which oxidation occurs at the anode and reduction at the cathode in an electrochemical cell; *esp* : the standard potential referred to the standard hydrogen electrode as zero — symbol $E°$; called also *redox potential*; compare ELECTROMOTIVE SERIES, REDUCTION POTENTIAL
oxidation state *or* **oxidation number** *n* : the degree of oxidation of an element or atom (as in a compound) that is usu. expressed as a positive or negative number representing the ionic charge or effective charge of the element or atom ⟨the usual *oxidation state* of hydrogen is +1 and of oxygen −2⟩ — compare VALENCE 1 a
ox·i·da·tive \'äksə,dād·iv\ *adj* : relating to or characterized by oxidation ⟨~ rancidity⟩ : having oxidizing powers ⟨~ catalysts⟩ — **ox·i·da·tive·ly** \-d·əvlē\ *adv*
ox·ide *also* **ox·yde** \'äk,sīd *also* -səd\ *n* -s [F *oxide* (now *oxyde*), fr. *ox-* (fr. *oxygène* oxygen) + *-ide* (fr. *acide* acid) — more at OXYGEN] **1 a** : a binary compound of oxygen with an element ⟨water is hydrogen ~⟩ ⟨~s of iron⟩ — compare OZONIDE, PEROXIDE, RUST 1a, SUPEROXIDE **b** : a compound of oxygen with one or more metallic elements ⟨many minerals (as spinels) are double or multiple ~s⟩ **2** : a compound (as ethylene oxide) of oxygen with an organic radical : ETHER 3b ⟨diphenyl ~⟩ — **ox·id·ic** \(')äk¦sidik\ *adj*
oxide blue *n* : a strong greenish blue to blue
oxide brown *or* **oxide purple** *n* : a moderate reddish brown that is yellower and darker than mahogany or roan, deeper than rustic brown, and yellower and duller than average brick (sense 5a) — called also *purple brown, purple oxide*
oxide of iron : IRON OXIDE
oxide red *n* : any of several colors (as Indian red, Venetian red, or bole) resembling those of ferric oxide under various conditions — compare IRON-OXIDE RED, IRON RED
oxide yellow *n* : YELLOW OCHER
ox·idi·met·ric \¦äksəd¦ə¦me·trik, äk¦sidə¦-\ *adj* : of, relating to, or by means of oxidimetry
ox·i·dim·e·try \,äksə'dimə·trē\ *n* -ES [ISV *oxid-* (fr. *oxidation*) + *-i-* + *-metry*] : quantitative determination in chemical analysis involving oxidation
ox·i·diz·abil·i·ty \,äksə,dīzə'biləd·ē\ *n* : ability to be oxidized
ox·i·diz·able \'äksə,dīzəbəl, ,==¦===\ *adj* : capable of being oxidized
ox·i·di·za·tion \,äksədə'zāshən, -,dī'z-\ *n* -s : OXIDATION
ox·i·dize \'äksə,dīz\ *vb* -ED/-ING/-s [*oxide* + *-ize*] *vt* **1 a** : to combine with oxygen or with more oxygen ⟨~ copper to copper oxide⟩ : add oxygen chemically to (a substance) often by means of a series of reactions ⟨glucose is *oxidized* to carbon dioxide and water with the release of energy during the metabolism of carbohydrates⟩ — compare OXYGENATE **b** : to dehydrogenate esp. by the action of oxygen or other oxidizing agent ⟨~ an alcohol to an aldehyde⟩ **c** : to change (a compound) by increasing the proportion of the electronegative part ⟨~ copper (I) chloride to copper (II) chloride⟩ : change (an element or ion) from a lower to a higher oxidation state ⟨in electrolysis . . . ferrous ions are *oxidized* to ferric ions at the anode —Farrington Daniels & R.A.Alberty⟩ : remove one or more electrons from (an atom, ion, or molecule) ⟨~ metallic copper to ionic copper⟩ — opposed to *reduce* **2** : to produce on (a metallic surface) a decorative film usu. of a compound (as a sulfide) ~ *vi* : to become oxidized; *specif* : RUST 1
oxidized cellulose *n* : an acid degradation product of cellulose that is usu. obtained by oxidizing cotton or gauze with nitrogen dioxide, that is a useful hemostatic (as in surgery), and that is absorbed by body fluids (as when used to pack wounds) — compare OXYCELLULOSE
oxidized oil *n* : an oil that has been treated with air or oxygen; *esp* : BLOWN OIL
ox·i·diz·er \-zə(r)\ *n* -s : one that oxidizes: as **a** : the oxidizing agent (as liquid oxygen) of a rocket propellant **b** : a worker who brushes a special chemical solution on a patterned surface of silver to darken it and make the design stand out after polishing
oxidizing agent *n* : a substance (as oxygen, nitric acid, carbon dioxide) that oxidizes by taking up electrons — called also *oxidant, oxidizer*; compare REDUCING AGENT
oxidizing flame *n* : a flame or the part of a flame having an excess of oxygen (as the outer cone of a gas flame)
oxido- *comb form* [ISV, fr. *oxide*] **1** : oxide; *specif* : EPOXY- — in names of organic chemical compounds ⟨*oxido*ethane⟩ **2** : oxidation ⟨*oxido*reduction⟩
ox·i·do·reductase \¦äksə(,)dō+\ *n* [*oxido-* + *reductase*] : an enzyme that catalyzes oxidation-reduction reactions — compare DEHYDROGENASE, OXIDASE, PEROXIDASE, REDUCTASE
ox·i·do·reduction \"+\ *n* [ISV *oxido-* + *reduction*] : OXIDATION-REDUCTION
ox·id·u·lat·ed \äk'sijə,lād·əd\ *adj* [obs. F *oxidulé* (fr. *oxidule* oxide with lowest degree of oxidation, fr. F *oxide* + *-ule*) + E *-ate* + *-ed*] *archaic* : existing in a lower oxidation state ⟨~ iron Fe_3O_4⟩
ox·i·mate \'äksə,māt\ *vt* -ED/-ING/-s [*oxime* + *-ate*] : to convert into an oxime — **ox·i·ma·tion** \,äksə'māshən\ *n* -s
ox·ime \'ak,sēm, -,səm\ *n* -s [ISV [1]*ox-* + *-ime* (fr. *imide*); orig. formed in G] : any of a class of compounds obtained chiefly by the action of hydroxylamine on aldehydes and ketones and characterized by the grouping >C=NOH in which the isonitroso group replaces the oxygen of the carbonyl group — compare BENZALDOXIME
ox·im·e·ter \äk'siməd·ə(r)\ *n* [[1]*ox-* + *-i-* + *-meter*] : an instrument for measuring continuously the degree of oxygen saturation of the circulating blood — **ox·i·met·ric** \¦äksə¦me·trik\ *adj*
ox·im·e·try \äk'simə·trē\ *n* -ES [ISV [1]*ox-* + *-i-* + *-metry*] : the use of an oximeter
oximino- *also* **oximido-** *comb form* [ISV [1]*ox-* + *imin-* or *imid-*] : ISONITROSO-
ox·in·dole \'äksən,dōl, äk'sin-\ *n* [ISV [1]*ox-* + *indole*] : a crystalline compound C_8H_7NO isomeric with indoxyl and obtainable by reduction of isatin; 2-oxo-indoline
ox·ine \'äk,sēn, -sən\ *n* -s [[1]*ox-* + *-ine*] : a crystalline phenolic base HOC_9H_6N that is used in analysis to form insoluble chelated compounds with ions of metals (as iron, aluminum, titanium, bismuth, zinc) and esp. in the form of its yellow crystalline sulfate in medicine as an antiseptic; 8-hydroxyquinoline
ox·i·rane \'äksə,rān\ *n* -s [[1]*ox-* + *-ir-* (prob. alter. of *tri-*) + *-ane*] : ETHYLENE OXIDE
ox kind *n* : the group of animals comprising the Old World species (*Bos taurus*) and constituting the common bovine domesticated cattle
oxlike \'=,=\ *adj* : resembling, suggestive of, or having the characteristics of an ox
ox·lip \'äk,slip\ *n* [earlier *oxislip, oxelip, oxslip*, fr. OE *oxanslyppe*, fr. *oxan*, gen. of *oxa* ox + *slyppe, slypa* pulp, paste — more at OX, SLIP] **1** : a hybrid primrose **2** : a Eurasian primula (*Primula elatior*) differing from the cowslip chiefly in the flat corolla limb
ox louse *n* : any of several cattle lice (esp. *Haematopinus eurysternus* or *Linognathus vituli*)
ox·man \'äksmən\ *n, pl* **oxmen** : a man who tends or drives oxen
oxo \'äk(,)sō\ *adj* [[1]*ox-*] : containing oxygen ⟨inorganic ~ acids⟩; *esp* : containing oxygen in a carbonyl group ⟨2-*oxo* acids in the sugar series —C.D.Hurd⟩ — compare KETO, [1]OX-2
[1]oxo- — see OX-
[2]oxo- *comb form* [[1]*ox-*] : containing oxygen as a doubly coordinated group ⟨*dioxo*uranium(VI) $UO_2{}^{++}$⟩
[1]ox·o·nian \äk'sōnēən, -ōnyən\ *n* -s *cap* [ML *Oxonia* Oxford + E *-an*] **1** : a native or resident of Oxford, England **2** : a student or graduate of Oxford University
[2]oxonian \(')=¦=(=)=\ *adj, usu cap* : of, relating to, or characteristic of Oxford, England, or its university
ox·on·ic acid \(')äk¦sänik-\ *n* [ISV [1]*ox-* + *-onic* (prob. fr. *carbonic*); orig. formed in G] : ALLANTOXANIC ACID
ox·o·ni·um \äk'sōnēəm\ *n* -s [NL, fr. [1]*ox-* + *-onium*] : the univalent cation H_3O^+ derived from oxygen and known esp. in the form of organic derivatives : the monohydrated hydrogen ion ⟨diethyl-*oxonium* chloride $[(C_2H_5)_2HO]^+Cl^-$⟩ — called also *hydronium*
oxo·phen·ar·sine \,äksəfə'när,sēn, -ärsən\ *n* [[1]*ox-* + *phen-* + *arsine*] : an arsenical used in the form of its white powdery hydrochloride $HOC_6H_3(AsO)NH_2.HCl$ in the treatment of syphilis esp. as an adjuvant to penicillin and Vincent's angina
oxo process *or* **oxo reaction** *n* **1** : a process for synthesizing aldehydes (as propionaldehyde) by the addition of carbon monoxide and hydrogen under pressure to olefins (as ethylene) in the presence of a usu. cobalt catalyst — compare HYDROFORMYLATION **2** : a process for synthesizing alcohols

(as isooctyl alcohol) usu. by producing aldehydes from olefins and hydrogenating the aldehydes to alcohols — compare OXYL PROCESS

ox·pecker \'=,==\ *n* **:** either of two small dull-colored African birds (*Buphagus africanus* and *Buphagoides erythrorhynchus*) that resemble and are closely related to starlings and feed on ticks which they pick from the backs of infested cattle and wild mammals

ox ray *n* **:** DEVILFISH 1

oxshoe \'=,=\ *n* **:** a shoe for an ox often consisting of two pieces one for each side of the hoof

ox·skin \'äk(s),skin\ *n* **:** OXHIDE

oxtail \'=,=\ *n* [ME *ox taill*, fr. *ox* + *taill* tail — more at TAIL] **:** the tail of cattle; *esp* **:** the skinned tail used for soup

oxteam \'=,=\ *n* **:** a team of oxen

¹ox·ter \'äkstər\ *n* -S [OE *ōxta, ōcusta;* akin to OHG *uochsana* armpit, ON *ōstr* hollow of the neck, OE *ōxn* armpit, *eax* axis, axle — more at AXIS] **1** *chiefly Scot & Irish* **a :** the space between the inside upper arm and the body **:** ARMPIT **b :** the armhole of a garment **2** *chiefly Scot & Irish* **:** ARM

²oxter \"\ *vb* -ED/-ING/-S *vi, chiefly Scot* **:** to walk arm in arm ~ *vt* **1** *chiefly Scot* **:** to support at the elbow or by a part of the arm **2** *chiefly Scot* **:** to put or carry under the arm

oxter plate *n* **:** a molded plate used to continue the shell plates immediately above the propeller aperture of a ship

oxtongue \'=,=\ *n* [ME *oxtonge, oxtunge*, fr. *ox* + *tonge, tunge* tongue — more at OX, TONGUE] **:** any of several plants that have rough tongue-shaped leaves: as **a :** BUGLOSS 1 **b :** BUGLOSS 3

ox wagon *n* **:** a heavy wagon drawn by oxen

ox warble *n* **:** the maggot of an ox warble fly

ox warble fly *n* **:** either of two warble flies (*Hypoderma lineata* and *H. bovis*)

¹oxy \'äksē\ *adj* [*ox* + *-y*] **:** of or relating to an ox

²oxy \"\ *adj* [*²oxy-*] **1 :** containing oxygen — compare ²OXY- 1 **2 :** HYDROXY

¹oxy- *comb form* [ME, fr. L, fr. Gk, fr. *oxys;* akin to Gk *achnē* chaff — more at EAR] **1 :** sharp **:** keen **:** pointed **:** acute ⟨*oxyaster*⟩ ⟨*oxycephaly*⟩ ⟨*oxydactyl*⟩ ⟨*oxyrhynchous*⟩ **2 :** quick ⟨*oxytocic*⟩ **3 :** acid ⟨*oxyphytic*⟩ ⟨*oxyphile*⟩

²oxy- *comb form* [F, fr. *oxygène* oxygen — more at OXYGEN] **1 a :** containing oxygen or additional oxygen ⟨*oxycellulose*⟩ ⟨*oxyhemoglobin*⟩ **b :** containing oxygen in the form of an oxide ⟨*oxychloride*⟩ **c :** containing an oxygen atom united to two different atoms — esp. in names of organic compounds; distinguished from *ket-*, ¹*ox-* 2; compare EPOXY- ⟨*oxy*-diacetic acid $O(CH_2COOH)_2$⟩ **2 :** HYDROXY- — not used systematically ⟨*oxynaphthoic*⟩ **3 :** of oxygen and ⟨*oxyhydrogen*⟩

oxy·acan·thine \,äksē'kan,thēn, -an(t)thən\ *n* [ISV *oxyacanth-* (fr. NL *oxyacantha* — specific epithet of the hawthorn *Crataegus oxyacantha* —, fr. Gk *oxyakantha* sharp thorn, fr. *oxy-* ¹oxy- + *akantha* thorn) + *-ine;* prob. orig. formed as G *oxyakanthin* — more at ACANTH-] **:** a bitter crystalline alkaloid $C_{37}H_{40}N_2O_6$ obtained from barberry root

oxy·acetylene \¦äksē+\ *adj* [ISV ²*oxy-* + *acetylene*] **:** of, relating to, or utilizing a mixture of oxygen and acetylene ⟨~ welding⟩

oxyacetylene blowpipe *or* **oxyacetylene torch** *n* **:** a welding

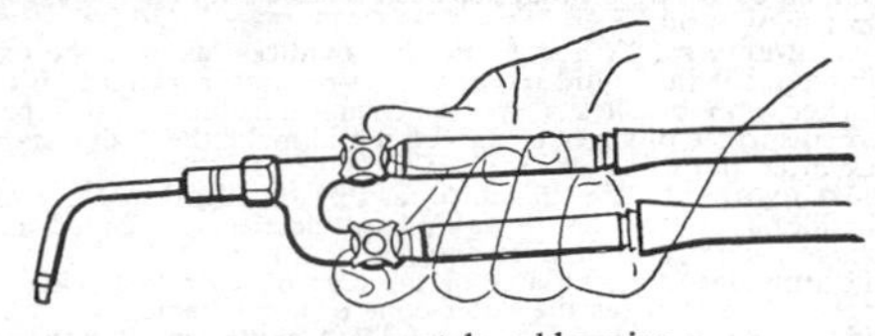

oxyacetylene blowpipe

blowpipe using oxygen and acetylene

oxyacetylene cutting *n* **:** OXYGEN-ACETYLENE CUTTING

oxyacetylene welding *n* **:** OXYGEN-ACETYLENE WELDING

oxy·ae·na \,äksē'ēnə\ *n, cap* [NL, fr. ¹*oxy-* + Gk *-aina*, fem. n. suffix] **:** a genus (the type of the family Oxyaenidae) of long-bodied short-legged plantigrade creodonts from the No. American Eocene

oxy·as·ter \'äksē,astə(r), ,==¦==\ *n* -S [NL, fr. ¹*oxy-* + *-aster*] **:** a stellate sponge spicule having acute rays

ox·yb·e·lis \äk'sibələs\ *n, cap* [NL, fr. Gk *oxybelēs* sharp-pointed, fr. *oxy-* ¹oxy- + *-belēs* pointed, fr. *belos* arrow; akin to Gk *ballein* to throw — more at DEVIL] **:** a genus of slender chiefly arboreal back-fanged snakes (family Colubridae) having slender pointed snouts and being widely distributed in tropical America with one species occurring as far north as Arizona

oxy·bi·o·sis \,äksē,bī'ōsəs\ *n, pl* **oxybio·ses** \-ō,sēz\ [NL, fr. ²*oxy-* + *-biosis*] **:** AEROBIOSIS

oxy·biotic \¦äksē+\ *adj* [²*oxy-* + *-biotic*] **:** AEROBIOTIC

oxy·biotin \¦äksē+\ *n* [ISV ²*oxy-* + *biotin*] **:** a compound $C_{10}H_{16}N_2O_4$ that contains an oxygen atom in place of the sulfur atom in the biotin molecule and that is less active biologically than biotin

oxy·blep·sia \,äksə'blepsēə, -ksē'b-\ *n* -S [NL, fr. MGk, fr. Gk *oxy-* ¹oxy- + *blepsis* sight (fr. *blepein* to see) + *-ia* -y] **:** acuteness of sight

oxy·calcium \¦äksē+\ *adj* [²*oxy-* + *calcium*] **:** of or relating to oxygen and calcium ⟨the ~ light or limelight⟩

oxy·calorimeter \¦äksē+\ *n* [²*oxy-* + *calorimeter*] **:** a calorimeter in which the energy content of a substance is determined by the direct measurement of the oxygen consumed

ox·y·ca·nus \,äksə'kānəs, -ksē'k-\ *n, cap* [NL, fr. ¹*oxy-* + L *canus* white — more at HARE] **:** a genus of moths (family Hepialidae) whose larvae include the subterranean caterpillars of New Zealand

oxy·cellulose \¦äksē+\ *n* [ISV ²*oxy-* + *cellulose*] **:** any of several substances formed by the oxidation of cellulose either naturally (as in wood fiber) or artificially (as in cotton bleached too much) — compare OXIDIZED CELLULOSE

oxy·ce·phal·ic \¦äksēsə¦falik, ¦äksēsə-\ *or* **oxy·ceph·a·lous** \-¦sefələs\ *adj* **:** of, relating to, or exhibiting oxycephaly

oxy·ceph·a·ly \,==¦sefəlē\ *n* -ES [G *oxycephalie*, prob. fr. Gk *oxykephalos* sharp-headed (fr. *oxy-* ¹oxy + *-kephalos* headed, fr. *kephalē* head) + G *-ie* -y — more at CEPHALIC] **:** congenital deformity of the skull due to early synostosis of the parietal and occipital bones with compensating growth in the region of the anterior fontanel resulting in a pointed or pyramidal skull — called also *acrocephaly*

oxy·chloride \¦äksē+\ *n* [ISV ²*oxy-* + *chloride*] **:** a compound of oxygen and chlorine with an element or radical **:** a basic chloride ⟨lead ~s such as $PbCl_2.PbO$ or Pb_2OCl_2⟩

oxychloride cement *n* **:** MAGNESIUM OXYCHLORIDE CEMENT

oxy·chro·mat·ic \¦äksēkrō¦mad·ik\ *or* **oxy·chro·ma·tin·ic** \-,krōmə¦tinik\ *adj* **:** of or relating to oxychromatin

oxy·chromatin \¦äksē+\ *n* [ISV ²*oxy-* + *chromatin;* prob. orig. formed in G] **:** oxyphilic chromatin

oxy·coc·cus \,äksē'käkəs\ *n, cap* [NL, fr. ¹*oxy-* + *-coccus*] *in some classifications* **:** a small genus of trailing or prostrate shrubs consisting of the cranberries — see VACCINIUM

oxy·cyanide \¦äksē+\ *n* [²*oxy-* + *cyanide*] **:** a compound of oxygen and cyanogen with an element or radical ⟨mercuric ~, $Hg_2O(CN)_2$⟩

oxy·dac·tyl \¦äksə¦dakt°l, ¦äksē¦-\ *adj* [¹*oxy-* + *dactyl*] **:** having slender tapered digits

oxyde *var of* OXIDE

oxy·di·act \¦äksə¦dī,akt, ¦äksē¦-\ *adj* [¹*oxy-* + *diact*] **:** having three axes but only two rays developed — used of a sponge spicule

Oxy·di·a·mi·no·gen \ äksē,dīə'mēnəjən, -,jen\ *trademark* —used for a direct dye; see DYE table I (under *Direct Black 80*)

oxy·fluoride \¦äksē+\ *n* [ISV ²*oxy-* + *fluoride*] **:** a compound of oxygen and fluorine with an element or radical

oxy·gas \¦äksē¦+\ *adj* [²*oxy-* + *gas*] **:** of or relating to a mixture of oxygen and fuel gas — compare OXYHYDROGEN

ox·y·gen \'äksəjən, -sēj-\ *n* -S [F *oxygène*, fr. *oxy-* ¹oxy- + *-gène* -gen] **:** a nonmetallic chiefly bivalent element that is normally a colorless odorless tasteless nonflammable diatomic gas slightly soluble in water, that is the most abundant of the elements on earth occurring uncombined in air to the extent of about 21 percent by volume and combined in water, in most common rocks and minerals (as oxides, silicates, carbonates), and in a great variety of organic compounds (as alcohols, acids, fats, carbohydrates, proteins), that has three naturally occurring nonradioactive isotopes of masses 16, 17, and 18 of relative abundance 2494:1:5, that is obtained industrially from liquid air by distilling off the nitrogen or from water by electrolysis or in the laboratory by decomposition by heat of various oxides, peroxides, or salts (as chlorates or permanganates), that combines with all other elements except those of the group of inert gases, and that is used chiefly in oxyacetylene and oxyhydrogen flames in welding and cutting metals, in making steel and in other metallurgical processes, in making glass, in the chemical industry (as in producing synthesis gas), in medicine, aviation, and diving to aid respiration, and usu. in the form of air in many combustion and oxidation processes — symbol *O;* see LIQUID OXYGEN, OZONE; ELEMENT table

oxygen-acetylene cutting *n* **:** gas cutting with oxygen and acetylene

oxygen-acetylene welding *n* **:** gas welding with oxygen and acetylene

oxygen acid *n* **:** an acid (as chloric acid, sulfuric acid) containing oxygen — compare HETEROPOLY ACID, ISOPOLY ACID

ox·y·gen·ate \'äksəjə,nāt, -sēj-; äk'sijə,-; *usu* -ād· +V\ *vt* -ED/-ING/-S [F *oxygéner* (fr. *oxygène* oxygen) + E *-ate*] **:** to impregnate or combine with oxygen **:** treat or supply with oxygen **:** saturate (as blood) with oxygen — compare AERATE, OXIDIZE 1 a — **ox·y·gen·a·tion** \,äksəjə'nāshən, -sēj-; äk,sijə'nāshən\ *n* -S

oxygenated water *n* **1 :** water treated or supplied with gaseous oxygen **2 :** HYDROGEN PEROXIDE

ox·y·gen·a·tor \-ād·ə(r), -ātə-\ *n* -S **:** one that oxygenates (as an apparatus for perfusing an organ or tissue)

oxygen debt *n* **:** the cumulative deficiency of oxygen that develops in the body during periods of intense activity and that must be made good when the bodily activity returns to a normal level

ox·y·gen·er·a·tor \,äksə'jenə,rād·ə(r), -sē'j-\ *n* -S [blend of *oxygen* and *generator*] **:** a machine for making oxygen

oxygen-hydrogen welding *n* **:** gas welding with oxygen and hydrogen at a temperature which is estimated at over 5000° F and which is sufficient to consume the diamond and easily fuse platinum

ox·y·gen·ic \,äksə¦jenik, -sē¦j-, -nēk\ *adj* **:** relating to, consisting of, containing, or resembling oxygen ⟨sheets of ~ paper . . . aid in maintaining color —C.E.Dobbins & R.W.Hoecker⟩ — **ox·y·gen·ic·i·ty** \,==jə'nisəd·ē\ *n* -ES

ox·y·ge·ni·um \,äksə'jēnēəm\ *n* -S [NL, fr. ISV *oxygen* + NL *-ium*] **:** OXYGEN

ox·y·gen·ize \'äksəjə,nīz, -sēj-; äk'sijə,-\ *vt* -ED/-ING/-S [*oxygen* + *-ize*] **:** OXIDIZE, OXYGENATE

oxygen lance *n* **:** an iron pipe that when supplied with oxygen through a hose burns and furnishes heat to cut thick metal

oxygen mask *n* **:** a mask covering esp. the mouth and nose and used in inhaling oxygen from a bottle, tank, or other source of supply

ox·yg·e·nous \(')äk¦sijənəs\ *adj* **:** OXYGENIC

oxygen point *n* **:** the normal boiling point of liquid oxygen which is −182.97°C and which is used as one of the fixed points of the international temperature scale

oxygen ratio *n* **:** ACIDITY COEFFICIENT

oxygen tent *n* **:** a canopy of usu. transparent material which is placed over a bedfast patient and within which a flow of oxygen can be maintained

ox·yg·na·thous \(')äk¦signəthəs\ *adj* [¹*oxy-* + *-gnathous;* fr. the finely lined surface of the jaws] **:** having smooth or nearly smooth jaws ⟨~ land snails⟩ ⟨~ slugs⟩

oxy·halide \¦äksē+\ *n* [²*oxy-* + *halide*] **:** a compound (as an oxychloride) of oxygen and a halogen with an element or radical **:** a basic halide

oxy·hemocyanin \"+\ *n* [²*oxy-* + *hemocyanin*] **:** a blue pigment formed by the combination of hemocyanin with oxygen in the ratio of one molecule of oxygen to two atoms of copper in the hemocyanin

oxy·hemoglobin \"+\ *n* [ISV ²*oxy-* + *hemoglobin*] **:** the bright red crystallizable pigment in the red blood cells chiefly of arterial blood that is formed in the lungs or gills by the combination of hemoglobin with oxygen in the ratio of one molecule of oxygen to each atom of iron in the hemoglobin without oxidation of the iron to the ferric state and that releases its oxygen to the tissues — symbol HbO_2

oxy·hemo·graph \,äksē'hēmə,graf, -hem-, -räf\ *n* [²*oxy-* + *hem-* + *-graph*] **:** OXIMETER

oxy·hexactine \¦äksē+\ *n* [¹*oxy-* + *hexactine*] **:** a hexactinal sponge spicule whose rays end in sharp points

oxy·hexaster \"+\ *n* [¹*oxy-* + *hexaster*] **:** a hexaster whose rays end in sharp points

oxy·hydrogen \"+\ *adj* [²*oxy-* + *hydrogen*] **:** of, relating to, or utilizing a mixture of oxygen and hydrogen

oxyhydrogen blowpipe *or* **oxyhydrogen torch** *n* **:** a welding blowpipe using oxygen and hydrogen

oxyhydrogen light *n* **:** a light produced by the incandescence of some substance (as lime) in the oxyhydrogen flame — compare LIMELIGHT 1

ox·yl·o·phyte \äk'silə,fīt\ *n* -S [²*oxy-* + *-lo-* (prob. fr. *halo-*) *-phyte*] **:** a plant that prefers or is restricted to an acid soil ⟨most heaths are obligatory ~s⟩ — **ox·yl·o·phyt·ic** \=¦==¦fid·ik\ *adj*

ox·yl process \'äksəl-\ *n* [¹*ox-* + *-yl*] **:** a modified Fischer-Tropsch process for synthesizing alcohols from carbon monoxide and hydrogen under pressure in the presence of a usu. iron catalyst — compare OXO PROCESS 2

oxy·luciferin \¦äksē+\ *n* [²*oxy-* + *luciferin*] **:** the product formed by the reversible oxidation of luciferin promoted by luciferase

oxy·luminescence \"+\ *n* [²*oxy-* + *luminescence*] **:** chemiluminescence caused by oxidation

oxy·luminescent \"+\ *adj* **:** marked by oxyluminescence

ox·y·mel \'äksə,mel, -sē,m-\ *n* -S [ME *oximel*, fr. L, fr. Gk *oxymeli*, fr. *oxy-* ¹oxy- + *meli* honey — more at MELLIFLUOUS] **:** a mixture of honey and dilute acetic acid used as an expectorant

ox·y·mo·ron \,äksə'mōr,än, -sē'm-\ *n, pl* **oxymo·ra** \-ōrə\ [Gk *oxymōron*, fr. neut. of *oxymōros* pointedly foolish, fr. *oxy-* ¹oxy- + *mōros* dull, foolish — more at MORON] **:** a combination for epigrammatic effect of contradictory or incongruous words (as *cruel kindness, laborious idleness*) — **oxy·mo·ron·ic** \¦==,mə¦ränik\ *adj*

oxy·muriate \¦äksē+\ *n* [ISV ²*oxy-* + *muriate*] **:** a salt of oxymuriatic acid **:** CHLORIDE ⟨~ of tin⟩ **:** CHLORATE ⟨~ of potash⟩

oxymuriate match *or* **oxymuriated match** \¦äksē+. . .-\ *n, archaic* **:** a match tipped with potassium chlorate

oxy·muriatic \¦äksē+\ *adj* [ISV ²*oxy-* + *muriatic*] **:** relating to or consisting of oxidized hydrochloric acid ⟨chlorine was called ~ acid before it was known to be an element⟩

oxy·myoglobin \"+\ *n* [²*oxy-* + *myoglobin*] **:** a pigment formed by the combination of myoglobin with oxygen

oxy·yn \'äksən\ *n* -S [²*oxy-* + *-in*] **:** a solid product (as linoxyn) formed when a drying oil is oxidized

oxy·naphthoic acid \¦äksē+. . .-\ *n* [ISV ²*oxy-* + *naphthoic*] **:** HYDROXYNAPHTHOIC ACID — not used systematically

oxy·neurine \¦äksē+\ *n* [ISV ²*oxy-* + *neurine;* prob. orig. formed in G] **:** BETAINE 1a

oxy·nitrate \"+\ *n* [²*oxy-* + *nitrate*] **:** a compound of oxygen and the nitrate group with an element or radical ⟨bismuth ~⟩ — compare SUBNITRATE

ox·yn·tic \(')äk¦sintik\ *adj* [Gk *oxynein* to sharpen, make acid (fr. *oxys* sharp, keen) + E connective *-t-* + *-ic* — more at OXY-] **:** secreting acid — used esp. of the parietal cells of the gastric glands

oxy·opia \,äksē'ōpēə\ *also* **oxy·opy** \'äksē,ōpē\ *n, pl* **oxy·opias** *also* **oxyopies** [NL *oxyopia*, fr. ¹*oxy-* + *-opia*] **:** unusual acuteness of sight

oxy·op·i·dae \,äksē'äpə,dē\ *n pl, cap* [NL, fr. *Oxyopes*, type genus (fr. Gk *oxyōpēs* sharp-eyed, fr. *oxy-* ¹oxy- + *-ōpēs* -eyed — fr. *ōps* eye —) + *-idae* — more at EYE] **:** a family of diurnal hunting spiders that have eight eyes and long legs and do not use webs to trap their prey

oxy·petalous \¦äksē+\ *adj* [¹*oxy-* + *-petalous*] **:** having sharp-pointed petals

¹oxy·phile \'äksə,fīl, -sē,f-\ *or* **oxy·phil** \-,fil\ *or* **oxy·phil·ic** \¦==¦filik\ *or* **ox·yph·i·lous** \(')äk¦sifələs\ *adj* [¹*oxy-* + *-phile, -phil* or *-philic* or *-philous*] **:** ACIDOPHILIC

²oxyphile \"\ *adj* [ISV ²*oxy-* + *-phile*] **:** having such an affinity for oxygen that in a molten mass the greatest concentration of an element would be found in the oxide phase (as in the slag of a blast furnace) — compare CHALCOPHILE, SIDEROPHILE

³oxyphile \"\ *also* **oxyphil** \"\ *n* -S [ISV ¹*oxy-* + *-phile, -phil*] **:** ACIDOPHILE

ox·yp·o·lis \äk'sipələs\ *n* [NL, fr. ¹*oxy-* + Gk *polis* city — more at POLICE] **1** *cap* **:** a genus of marsh herbs (family Umbelliferae) having clustered fusiform tuberous roots and leaves only once-pinnate or reduced to slender petioles like rushes — see COWBANE, WATER DROPWORT **2** -ES **:** any plant of the genus *Oxypolis*

oxy·poly·gelatin \,äksē¦pälə, -sē¦pälē +\ *n* [²*oxy-* + *poly-* (fr. *polymerization*) + *gelatin*] **:** gelatin modified by polymerization by means of glyoxal and oxidation with hydrogen peroxide for use as a plasma expander

oxy·quinoline \¦äksē+\ *n* [ISV ²*oxy-* + *quinoline*] **:** HYDROXYQUINOLINE — not used systematically

¹oxy·rhynch \'äksə,riŋk, -sē,r-\ *n* -S [NL *Oxyrhyncha*] **1 :** a crab having a pointed rostrum **:** one of the Oxyrhyncha **2** *also* **oxy·rhyn·chus** \,==¦riŋkəs\ *pl* **oxyrhyn·chi** \-,kī, -(,)kē\ [NL *oxyrhynchus* (specific epithet of *Mormyrus oxyrhynchus*), fr. Gk *oxyrrhynchos*, adj.] **:** a sacred fish (*Mormyrus oxyrhynchus*)

²oxyrhynch \"\ *adj* [Gk *oxyrrhynchos*, fr. *oxy-* ¹oxy- + *rhynchos* snout, beak — more at RHYNCH-] **:** sharp-snouted **:** sharp-billed

oxy·rhyn·cha \,==¦riŋkə\ *n pl, cap* [NL, fr. Gk *oxyrrhyncha*, neut. pl. of *oxyrrhynchos* sharp-snouted] **:** a large superfamily of Brachygnatha comprising crabs that have a distinct rostrum, a more or less triangular carapace, the orbits generally incomplete, nine pairs of gills, and the male genital apertures on the base of the last pairs of legs — compare SPIDER CRAB — **oxy·rhyn·chan** \¦==¦=kən\ *adj or n*

oxy·rhyn·chous \¦==¦=kəs\ *adj* [Gk *oxyrrhynchos*] **1 :** OXYRHYNCH **2 :** of or relating to the Oxyrhyncha

oxy·spi·ru·ra \,äksə,spī'rürə, -ksē,sp-\ *n, cap* [NL, fr. ¹*oxy-* + *spir-* + *-ura*] **:** a genus of spiruroid nematode worms (family Thelaziidae) comprising the eye worms of domestic poultry and other birds

oxy·sto·ma·ta \-'stōməd·ə\ *n pl, cap* [NL, fr. ¹*oxy-* + *-stomata*] **:** a small superfamily or other division of crabs having the buccal area produced anteriorly and more or less acutely triangular and having almost no rostrum — **oxy·stoma·tous** \¦==¦stäməd·əs, -tōm-\ *adj* — **oxy·stome** \'==,stōm\ *adj or n*

oxy·sulfide \¦äksē+\ *n* [ISV ²*oxy-* + *sulfide*] **:** a compound of oxygen and sulfur with an element or radical that may be regarded as a sulfide in which part of the sulfur is replaced by oxygen

oxy·tetracycline \"+\ *n* [²*oxy-* + *tetracycline*] **:** a yellow crystalline antibiotic $C_{22}H_{24}N_2O_9$ produced by a soil actinomycete (*Streptomyces rimosus*) and effective against numerous disease-causing microorganisms; hydroxy-tetracycline

ox·y·to·cia \,äksə'tōsh(ē)ə, -ksē't-\ *n* -S [NL, fr. ¹*oxy-* + Gk *tokos* childbirth + *-ia* -y] **:** quick childbirth

¹ox·y·to·cic \¦==¦tōsik\ *adj* [ISV ¹*oxy-* + *toc-* (fr. Gk *tokos* childbirth) + *-ic;* akin to Gk *teknon* child — more at THANE] **:** hastening parturition; *also* **:** inducing contraction of uterine smooth muscle ⟨an ~ principle of the neurohypophysis⟩

²oxytocic \"\ *n* -S **:** a substance that stimulates contraction of uterine smooth muscle or hastens childbirth

ox·y·to·cin \,==¦tōs°n\ *n* -S [ISV *oxytocic* + *-in*] **:** a polypeptide hormone $C_{43}H_{66}N_{12}O_{12}S_2$ that is secreted together with vasopressin by the posterior lobe of the pituitary, that is also obtained synthetically, and that stimulates esp. the contraction of uterine muscle and the ejection of milk — called also *alpha-hypophamine*

¹ox·y·tone \'äksə,tōn\ *n* [F *oxyton*, adj, & n., fr. Gk *oxytonos* having the acute accent, fr. *oxy-* ¹oxy- + *tonos* tone — more at TONE] **:** an oxytone word

²oxytone \"\ *adj* **1 :** having or characterized by an acute accent on the last syllable of a Greek word **2 :** having or characterized by heavy stress on the last syllable

oxy·ton·ic \¦==¦tänik\ *or* **oxy·ton·i·cal** \-nəkəl\ *adj* **:** of or relating to an oxytone **:** OXYTONE

ox·y·trich \'äksə,trik\ *n* -S [NL *Oxytricha*] **:** a protozoan of the genus *Oxytricha*

ox·yt·ri·cha \äk'si·trəkə\ *n, cap* [NL, fr. ¹*oxy-* + *-tricha*] **:** a widely distributed genus (the type of the family Oxytrichidae) of flexible ellipsoidal hypotrichous ciliates with eight frontal, five ventral, and undeveloped caudal cirri — compare STYLONYCHIA — **ox·yt·ri·chid** \-rəkəd\ *adj or n*

ox·yt·ro·pis \äk'si·trəpəs\ *n, cap* [NL, fr. ¹*oxy-* + Gk *tropis* ship's keel; akin to Gk *trepein* to turn; fr. the pointed keel of the corolla — more at TROPE] **:** a large widely distributed genus of often shrubby herbs (family Leguminosae) having odd-pinnate leaves and racemose or spicate flowers each of which has a pealike corolla with a clawed petal — see LOCOWEED

oxy·tylotate \¦äksē+\ *adj* [*oxytylote* + *-ate*] **:** resembling an oxytylote esp. in shape

oxy·tylote \"+\ *n* [¹*oxy-* + *tylote*] **:** a sponge spicule shaped like a common pin

oxy·uri·a·sis \,äksēyü'rīəsəs\ *n, pl* **oxyuria·ses** \-ə,sēz\ [NL, fr. *Oxyuris* + *-iasis*] **:** infestation with or disease caused by pinworms (family Oxyuridae) — see ENTEROBIASIS

oxy·uric \¦==¦yùrik\ *adj* [NL *Oxyuris* + E *-ic*] **:** of, relating to, or caused by pinworms of *Oxyuris* and related genera

oxy·uri·cide \,==¦yùrə,sīd\ *n* -S [NL *Oxyuris* + E *-cide*] **:** a substance that destroys pinworms

¹oxy·urid \¦==¦yùrəd\ *adj* [NL *Oxyuridae*] **:** of or relating to the Oxyuridae

²oxyurid \"\ *n* -S [NL *Oxyuridae*] **:** a nematode of the family Oxyuridae **:** PINWORM

oxy·uri·dae \,==¦rə,dē\ *n pl, cap* [NL, fr. *Oxyuris*, type genus + *-idae*] **:** a family of nematode worms that have a distinct posterior enlargement of the pharynx, a reduced bursa and no preanal suckers in the male, and meromyarian musculature and that are chiefly parasites of the vertebrate intestinal tract — see ENTEROBIUS, OXYURIS

oxy·uris \-rəs\ *n* [NL, fr. ¹*oxy-* + *-uris* (fr. Gk *oura* tail) — more at -UROUS] **1** *cap* **:** a genus (the type of the family Oxyuridae) of parasitic nematodes with a long slender tail and well-developed pharyngeal bulb **2** -ES **:** any worm of *Oxyuris* or a related genus (as *Enterobius*) **:** PINWORM

oxy·uroid \¦==¦=rȯid\ *adj* [NL *Oxyuris* + E *-oid*] *of a nematode's pharynx* **:** having a bulbous posterior enlargement

oxy·weld·ing \'äksē,==\ *n* [by shortening] **:** OXYGEN-ACETYLENE WELDING

oy *or* **oye** \'ōi\ *n* -S [ME (Sc) *o*, of Celtic origin; akin to OIr *haue, aue* grandson — more at UNCLE] *Scot* **:** GRANDCHILD

oy·a·pock \'ōiə,päk\ *n* -S [fr. *Oyapock, Oyapok*, river between northern Brazil and French Guiana] **:** YAPOCK

oy·er \'ōiər\ *n* -S [ME, fr. AF, fr. OF *oir* to hear, fr. L *audire* — more at AUDIBLE] **1 :** a criminal trial held under a commission of oyer and terminer **2 a :** the hearing of a document read in court; *specif* **:** the hearing of a deed or other instrument read in court by petition of a party to a suit **b :** a copy of the instrument given rather than read to the petitioning party

oyer and ter·mi·ner \,ōiərən'tərmənər\ *n* [ME, fr. AF *oyer et terminer*, lit., to hear and determine] **1 :** COMMISSION OF OYER AND TERMINER **2 :** a high court of criminal jurisdiction in some U.S. states (as Delaware and Pennsylvania)

¹oyez \(')ō¦yā, -yes,-yez\ *v imper* [ME *oyez!*, fr. AF *oyez!* hear ye!, fr. OF *oiez, oyez*, imperative pl. of *oir* to hear] — used by criers of courts as a command to secure silence and attention before a proclamation

²oyez \"\ *n, pl* **oyesses** \-yesəz\ [ME *oyes*, fr. AF *oyez!* hear ye!] **:** a cry of oyez

-o·yl \,əwəl, ə(,)wil, ə,wēl\ *n comb form* -S [ISV *-o-* (as in *-oic*) + *-yl*] **:** acid radical — used in the system of nomenclature adopted by the International Union of Pure and Applied Chemistry in names of radicals derived from acids whose names end in *-oic* ⟨decan*oyl*⟩ and also most other organic acids ⟨ole*oyl*⟩ ⟨phthal*oyl*⟩; compare -YL

oy·let *var of* OILLET

¹**oys·ter** \ˈȯistə(r)\ *n* -S [ME *oistre*, fr. MF, fr. L *ostrea*, fr. Gk *ostreon*; akin to Gk *ostrakon* shell, *osteon* bone — more at OSSEOUS] **1 :** a marine bivalve mollusk (family Ostreidae) having a rough irregular shell closed by a single adductor muscle, the foot small or wanting, and no siphon, living free on the bottom or adhering to stones or other objects in shallow water along the seacoasts or in brackish water in the mouths of rivers, and feeding on minute plants and animals carried to them by the current — see CRASSOSTREA, OSTREA **2 :** any of various bivalve mollusks more or less resembling the true oyster; *esp* **:** a Bermuda mollusk (*Margaritophora radiata*) that is locally important for food — often used with a descriptive adjective ⟨pearl ~*s*⟩ ⟨reef ~⟩ ⟨rock ~⟩ **3 a :** something that is or can be readily attained or made to serve one's personal ends **:** something regarded as belonging to or due one because of one's actual or presumed qualities, abilities, or status ⟨had just married and the world looked like his ~ —*Think*⟩ ⟨the world is the salesman's ~ —D.W.Brogan⟩ ⟨as long as you dressed decently and used acceptable English, and as long as your name could be pronounced, the town was your ~ —Russell Thacher⟩ **b :** CUP OF TEA ⟨aviation is the college girl's ~ —*Mademoiselle*⟩ ⟨youth is conservative, and mild romanticism is its ~ —Virgil Thomson⟩ **4 :** a small mass of muscle contained in a concavity of the pelvic bone on each side of the back of a fowl and usu. regarded as a delicacy **5 :** an extremely taciturn or reserved person **6 :** a usu. sautéed croquette ⟨corn ~⟩ **7** *or* **oyster white a :** a light gray to white **b :** a pale yellow green that is paler and slightly yellower than oyster gray, paler than amber white, and paler and yellower than average Nile

²**oyster** \"\ *vi* **oystered; oystered; oystering** \-t(ə)riŋ\ **oysters :** to gather or dredge oysters

oyster agaric *n* **:** OYSTER MUSHROOM

oys·ter·age \-tərij\ *n* -S [*oyster* + *-age*] **:** OYSTER BED

oyster bar *n* **1** *South* **:** OYSTER BED **2 :** a restaurant that specializes in oysters prepared in various ways and served esp. at a counter

oyster bay *n* **:** a restaurant where oysters and other seafood are served

oyster bay pine *n, usu cap O&B* [fr. *Oyster Bay*, Tasmania, Australia] **:** either of two Australian cypress pines (*Callitris tasmanica* and *C. oblonga*)

oyster bed *n* **:** a place where oysters grow or are cultivated

oysterbird \ˈ==,=\ *n* **1 :** OYSTER CATCHER **2** *Southwest* **:** SANDERLING

oyster catcher *n* **:** any of various wading birds of the widely distributed genus *Haematopus* that are 16 to 20 inches long, have stout legs and a heavy wedge-shaped bill which are usu. pinkish or bright red, and in the common form of Europe, Asia, and northern Africa (*H. ostralegus ostralegus*) and that of the American Atlantic coast (*H. o. palliatus*) have plumage which is chiefly or entirely black and white — see BLACK OYSTER CATCHER

oyster crab *n* **:** a crab (*Pinnotheres ostreum*) that lives as a commensal in the gill cavity of the oyster — compare MUSSEL CRAB, PEA CRAB

oyster cracker *n* **:** a small salted cracker for serving with oyster stew and soups — compare PILOT BISCUIT

oyster culture *n* **:** the cultivation of oysters in prepared beds

oyster-culturist \ˌ=ˈ=(=)=\ *n* **:** one engaged in oyster culture

oyster dredge *n* **:** a dredge having a heavy iron frame with strong teeth along its lower lip and a bag of strong cord and used in taking oysters in deep water

oyster drill *n* **:** ⁵DRILL 4

oys·tered \ˈȯistə(r)d\ *adj* **:** marked by oysterings ⟨~ veneer⟩

oys·ter·er \-tərə(r)\ *n* -S **1 :** a gatherer or seller of oysters **2 :** a boat used in oyster fishing

oyster farm *n* **:** a stretch of sea bottom devoted to oyster culture

oyster-farm \ˈ==,=\ *vi* **:** to culture or grow oysters

oyster farmer *n* **:** one who raises oysters as a crop

oysterfish \ˈ==,=\ *n* **1 :** TAUTOG **2** *also* **oyster-toad** \ˈ==,=\ **:** TOADFISH

oyster fork *n* **:** a long slender 3-tined fork used in eating shellfish

oyster grass *n* **1 :** KELP **2 :** SEA LETTUCE

oyster gray *n* **:** a pale yellow green that is yellower, stronger, and slightly lighter than smoke gray and yellower and paler than average Nile

oystering *n* -S **1 :** the act or business of taking oysters for the market or for food **2 a :** the matching (as on two side-by-side doors of a cabinet) of two oval-grained pieces of wood that are split from one piece **b :** a veneering (as on a table top) consisting of closely fitted pieces of attractively grained wood cut in diagonal section

oyster knife *n* **:** a knife for opening the shells of oysters

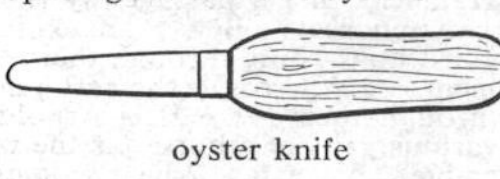

oyster knife

oyster leech *n* **:** a polyclad turbellarian worm (*Stylochus frontalis*) that is barred in brown and flesh and is a pest feeding on oysters along the coast of Florida

oys·ter·ling \ˈȯistə(r)liŋ\ *n* -S [*oyster* + *-ling*] **:** a young or small oyster

oys·ter·man \-mən\ *n, pl* **oystermen 1 :** a gatherer, opener, breeder, or seller of oysters **2 :** OYSTERER 2

oyster mushroom *or* **oyster fungus** *n* **:** an edible agaric (*Pleurotus ostreatus*) growing in shelving masses on dead wood; *also* **:** any of several related species of this genus

oyster nut *n* **:** a climbing plant (*Telfairia pedata*) that is indigenous to East Africa and has large edible nutlike seeds yielding an oil similar to olive oil

oyster plant *n* **1 :** SALSIFY **2 :** SEA LUNGWORT **3 :** a common West Indian herb (*Rhoeo discolor*) of the family Commelinaceae with purplish leaves and showy flower clusters

oyster plover *n* **:** OYSTER CATCHER

oyster rake *n* **:** a long-handled rake usu. with curved teeth for gathering oysters in water of moderate depth

oysters *pl of* OYSTER, *pres 3d sing of* OYSTER

oysterseed \ˈ==,=\ *n, pl* **oysterseed :** the spat of oysters

oystershell \ˈ==,==\ *n* **1 :** crushed or ground oyster shells often used as a mineral supplement in feeding poultry **2 :** OYSTERING 2b

oystershell scale *also* **oystershell bark louse** *n* **:** an abundant widely distributed scale insect (*Lepidosaphes ulmi*) that infests and greatly injures various trees and shrubs — see FIG SCALE

oyster tongs *n pl* **:** a pair of wooden tongs 12 to 20 feet long bearing opposing baskets shaped like rakes and used for gathering oysters

oyster tree *n* [so called fr. the fact that mollusks attach themselves to it] **:** MANGROVE 1

oyster wench *n, archaic* **:** a girl who sells oysters

oyster white *n* **:** OYSTER 7

oysterwife \ˈ==,=\ *n, pl* **oysterwives** *archaic* **:** OYSTERWOMAN

oysterwoman \ˈ==,==\ *n, pl* **oysterwomen :** a woman who sells oysters

oysterwood \ˈ==,=\ *n* **:** OYSTERING 2b

oys·tery \-st(ə)rē\ *adj* [*oyster* + *-y* (adj. suffix)] **:** somewhat resembling the color oyster

oz *abbr* **1** [It *onza*] ounce **2** ooze

ozan·na \ōˈzanə\ [NL] *syn of* HIPPOTRAGUS

ozark \ˈō,zärk, -zák\ *n, pl* **ozark** *or* **ozarks** *usu cap* [prob. alter. of *Aux Arcs*, early French post among the Quapaw in the area of Arkansas Post, Ark., fr. F *aux Arcs* at the Quapaw, prob. by shortening and alter. (influence of *arcs*, pl. of *arc* bow, fr. MF) fr. *aux Arkansas* — more at ARC] **:** an Indian of a division of the Quapaw

ozark·er \-kə(r)\ *n* -S *cap* [*Ozark* mountains + E *-er*] **:** OZARKIAN

¹**ozark·ian** \(ˈ)ōˈzärkēən, -zák-\ *adj, usu cap* [*Ozark* mountains, tableland extending fr. Missouri across Arkansas into Oklahoma + E *-ian* (adj. suffix)] **:** of or relating to the inhabitants or region of the Ozark mountains

²**ozarkian** \"\ *n* -S *cap* [*Ozark* mountains + E *-ian* (n. suffix)] **:** a native or inhabitant of the Ozark mountains ⟨an *Ozarkian's* wealth is mostly dogs —*Chicago Tribune*⟩

oze·na *also* **ozae·na** *or* **ozoe·na** \ōˈzēnə\ *n* -S [L *ozaena*, fr. Gk *ozaina*, fr. *ozein* to smell — more at ODOR] **:** a chronic disease of the nose accompanied by a fetid discharge and marked by atrophic changes in the nasal structures

ozo·brome process \ˈōzə,brōm-\ *n* [*ozobrome* fr. *ozone* + *brom*ide] **:** an early form of the carbro process

ozo·ke·rite \,ōzəˈki,rīt; ōˈzōkə,r-, ōˈzäkə,r-\ *or* **ozo·ce·rite** \,ōzəˈsi,rīt; ōˈzōsə,r-, ōˈzäsə,r-\ *n* -S [G *ozokerit*, fr. *ozo-* (fr. Gk, bad smell, fr. *ozein* to smell) + *ker-* cer- + *-it* -ite] **:** a waxlike mineral that is a mixture of hydrocarbons, is colorless or white when pure but often greenish, yellowish, or brown, has in some varieties an unpleasant odor, and is used in making ceresin, candles, and impressions to be electrotyped — called also *ader wax, earth wax*

ozon- *or* **ozono-** *comb form* [ISV, fr. *ozone*] **:** ozone ⟨*ozon*ize⟩

ozon·ate \ˈō,zō,nāt, -,zə,n-\ *vt* -ED/-ING/-S [*ozon-* + *-ate*] **:** OZONIZE — **ozon·a·tion** \,=(,)=ˈnāshən\ *n* -S

ozon·a·tor \ˈ=(,)=,nād·ə(r)\ *n* -S [*ozon-* + *-ator*] **:** OZONIZER

ozone \ˈō,zōn\ *n* -S [G *ozon*, fr. Gk *ozōn*, pres. part. of *ozein* to smell — more at ODOR] **1 :** an allotropic triatomic form O_3 of oxygen that is normally a faintly blue irritating gas with a characteristic pungent odor but at −112° C condenses to a deep blue magnetic liquid, that occurs in minute amounts in air near the earth's surface and in larger amounts in the stratosphere as a product of the action of ultraviolet light of short wave lengths on ordinary oxygen, that is generated usu. in dilute form by a silent electric discharge in oxygen or air, that decomposes to oxygen (as when heated), that is a stronger oxidizing agent than oxygen, and that is used chiefly in disinfection and deodorization (as in water purification and air conditioning), in oxidation and bleaching (as in the treatment of industrial wastes), and in ozonolysis (as in the manufacture of azelaic acid from oleic acid) **2 :** pure and refreshing air ⟨the fresh crisp ~ of morning —Ashley Halsey⟩

ozon·er \-nə(r)\ *n* -S [*ozon-* + *-er*] *slang* **:** a drive-in theater

ozonic \(ˈ)ōˈzänik, -zōn-\ *adj* [*ozon-* + *-ic*] **:** relating to, like, or containing ozone ⟨the curious ~ smell of the plane —Noel Coward⟩

ozon·ide \ˈō,zō,nīd, -,zə,n-\ *n* -S [ISV *ozon-* + *-ide*; orig. formed as G *ozonid*] **:** any of a class of chemical compounds formed by the addition of ozone to the double or triple bond of an unsaturated organic compound; *esp* **:** such a compound formed from an olefinic compound, characterized by a peroxide-oxide grouping C-O-O-C-O forming a ring, by instability, and often by explosiveness in the pure state but not usu. in solution, and decomposed by water to yield aldehydes or ketones and hydrogen peroxide

ozon·if·er·ous \,ō,zōˈnif(ə)rəs, -,zəˈn-\ *adj* [*ozon-* + *-iferous*] **:** bearing or producing ozone

ozo·ni·fi·ca·tion \ō,zōnəfəˈkāshən\ *n* -S [fr. *ozonify*, after such pairs as E *identify: identification*] **:** OZONIZATION

ozo·ni·fy \ōˈzōnə,fī\ *vt* -ED/-ING/-ES [*ozon-* + *-ify*] **:** OZONIZE

ozo·ni·um \ōˈzōnēəm\ *n, cap* [NL, fr. Gk *ozos* branch + *-onium* (as in *cydonium*); akin to OE *ōst* knot, lump, OHG *ast* branch, Goth *asts*, Arm *ost* branch; prob. all derivative fr. the root of E *sit;* fr. the branching stems] **:** a form genus of fungi of the group Mycelia Sterilia

ozon·iza·tion \,ō,zōnəˈzāshən\ *n* -S **:** the process of ozonizing — compare OZONOLYSIS

ozon·ize \ˈō,zō,nīz, -,zə,n-\ *vb* -ED/-ING/-S *see -ize in Explan Notes* [ISV *ozon-* + *-ize*] *vt* **1 :** to convert (as oxygen) into ozone **2 :** to treat, impregnate, or combine with ozone ⟨*ozonized* air attacks most metals —R.E.Kirk & D.F.Othmer⟩ ~ *vi* **:** to become converted into ozone

ozon·iz·er \-zə(r)\ *n* -S [ISV *ozonize* + *-er;* orig. formed as F *ozoniseur*] **:** an apparatus for converting ordinary oxygen into ozone (as by passing a silent electric discharge through a current of oxygen or air)

ozon·ol·y·sis \,ō,zōˈnäləsəs, -,zəˈn-\ *n, pl* **ozonolyses** \-ə,sēz\ [*ozon-* + *-lysis*] **:** the cleavage of an unsaturated organic compound at the position of unsaturation by conversion to the ozonide followed by decomposition (as by hydrolysis)

ozo·no·sphere \ōˈzōnə,sfi(ə)r\ *n* [*ozon-* + *-sphere*] **:** an atmospheric layer at heights of approximately 20 to 30 miles characterized by high ozone content and relatively high temperature resulting from absorption of ultraviolet solar radiation

ozon·ous \ˈō,zōnəs\ *adj* **:** OZONIC

ozo·sto·mia \,ōzəˈstōmēə\ *n* -S [NL, fr. Gk *ozostomos* having bad breath (fr. *ozo-* bad smell — fr. *ozein* to smell — + *-stomos* -stomous) + NL *-ia* — more at ODOR] **:** foulness of breath

ozo·type \ˈōzə,tīp\ *n* [ISV *ozo-* (prob. fr. *ozone*) + *type*] **:** a modified carbon process in which transfer is obviated

¹p \ˈpē\ *n, pl* **p's** *or* **ps** \ˈpēz\ *often cap, often attrib* **1 a :** the 16th letter of the English alphabet **b :** an instance of this letter printed, written, or otherwise represented **c :** a speech counterpart of orthographic *p* (as *p* in *pill, spill, dip, apt,* or French *puis*) **2 :** a printer's type, a stamp, or some other instrument for reproducing the letter *p* **3 :** someone or something arbitrarily or conveniently designated *p* esp. as the 15th or when j is used for the 10th the 16th in order or class **4 :** something having the shape of the letter P

²p *abbr, often cap* **1** pacer **2** page **3** [L *papa*] pope **4** parallax **5** park **6** part **7** participle **8** [L *partim*] in part **9** past **10** paste **11** pastor **12** [L *pater*] father **13** patrol **14** pawn **15** pengö **16** penny **17** [L *per*] by **18** perch **19** [F *père*] father **20** perforation **21** perimeter **22** period **23** perishable **24** peseta **25** peso **26** pharmacopoeia **27** [It] piano **28** piaster **29** picot **30** pie **31** pint **32** pipe **33** pitch; pitcher **34** [L *pius*] holy **35** planed **36** plate **37** pleasant **38** point **39** polar **40** pole **41** population **42** [L *populus*] people **43** port **44** post **45** postage **46** posterior **47** power **48** predicate **49** present **50** president **51** pressure **52** priest **53** primary **54** prince **55** principal **56** [L *pro*] for **57** proconsul **58** prompter **59** pupil **60** purl **61** pursuit

³p *symbol* **1** *cap* phosphorus **2** *usu cap* parental; parental generation **3** proton **4 a** plaintext — used as a subscript ⟨S_p means the letter S in plaintext or plain component⟩ **b** *usu cap* the numerical value of a plaintext letter when the plain component is serially numbered from 0 to 25 ⟨P+K=C is the Vigenère keying method⟩ **5** *usu cap* priestly code — used in biblical criticism to designate material and redactions belonging to a priestly commentary

p- \ˌparə *also* ˈperə\ *abbr* para-

¹pa \ˈpä, ˈpȯ, ˈpá, ˈpa, ˈpaa\ *n* -s [short for *papa*] **:** FATHER

²pa *or* **pah** \ˈpä\ *n* -s [Maori] **1 :** a fortified and stockaded Maori village usu. located on a hilltop — compare KAINGA **2 :** a Maori village

pa *abbr* **1** paper **2** piaster

PA \ˈpēˈā\ *n, pl* **PA's** *or* **PAs** \-āz\ [fr. *PA,* abbr. of *public address*] **:** the amplifier of a public-address system ⟨the *PA* of each ship had its own peculiar tone —K.M.Dodson⟩

PA *abbr* **1** *often not cap* participial adjective **2** particular average **3** passenger agent **4** *often not cap* per annum **5** post adjutant **6** power amplifier **7** power of attorney **8** prefect apostolic **9** *often not cap* press agent **10** press association **11** private account **12** prothonotary apostolic **13** public address **14** public administration; public assistance **15** purchasing agent

Pa *symbol* protactinium

PABA \ˈpabə\ *n* -s [*para-aminobenzoic acid*] **:** AMINOBENZOIC ACID a

pa·blo \ˈpä(ˌ)blō\ *n* -s [origin unknown] **:** a light brown to yellowish brown that is stronger than bran and lighter and stronger than aloma

Pab·lum \ˈpabləm\ *trademark* — used for a cereal for infants

pab·u·lum \ˈpabyələm\ *n* -s [L, food, fodder — more at FOOD] **1** *archaic* **:** fuel for fire **2 :** a material taken in by a living organism for use in its metabolism as a source of energy or growth **:** FOOD, NUTRIENT; *usu* **:** a more or less fluid medium containing dissolved or suspended nutritive elements in a state suitable for absorption (as through the roots of a plant or into a bacterial cell or a body organ) **3 a :** nourishment for the development of mind or character **:** intellectual sustenance ⟨no two generations need the same mental and emotional ~ —Bonamy Dobrée⟩ ⟨no idea, however freighted with ~ for the brain, is alien . . . to poetry —J.L.Lowes⟩; *esp* **:** a rudimentary or insipid piece of writing ⟨the kind of sentimental ~ which it offered its readers —*Publ's Mod. Lang. Assoc. of Amer.*⟩ **b :** source material for a discussion or document **:** GRIST ⟨never provided that flow of newspaper articles or of interviews which afford ~ to the contemporary biographer —*Times Lit. Supp.*⟩

pac *also* **pack** \ˈpak\ *n* -s [Delaware *paku*] **1 :** SHOEPAC **2 :** a laced heelless sheepskin or felt shoe worn inside a boot or overshoe in cold weather

pac 2

pa·ca \ˈpäkə, ˈpakə\ *n* -s [Pg & Sp, fr. Tupi *páca*] **:** any of several large So. and Central American rodents of a genus (*Cuniculus*) that is closely related to *Dasyprocta; esp* **:** a common rodent (*C. paca*) of northern So. America having a brown coat spotted with white, a hide used locally for leather, and flesh highly esteemed as food — see FALSE PACA, MOUNTAIN PACA

pa·ca·ra·na \ˈpäkəˈränə\ *n* -s [Tupi *pacarana,* fr. *páca* paca + *rana* false] **:** FALSE PACA

pacate *adj* [L *pacatus,* past part. of *pacare* to pacify, fr. *pac-, pax* peace — more at PEACE] *obs* **:** TRANQUIL

pa·cay \pəˈkī\ *n* -s [Sp, fr. Quechua *pa'qay*] **:** a small arboreal guama of uncertain taxonomic identity that is sometimes cultivated in Peru, Ecuador, and Bolivia for ornament and for the white edible pulp of its large pods

pa·ca·ya \pəˈkīə\ *n* -s [AmerSp] **:** any of various Central American palms constituting the genus *Chamaedorea; esp* **:** one having low stems and edible spadices

pac·chi·o·ni·an body \ˌpakēˈōnēən-\ *or* **pacchionian corpuscle** *n, sometimes cap P* [Antonio *Pacchioni* †1726 Ital. anatomist + E *-an*] **:** a small whitish process that is one of the enlarged villi of the arachnoid membrane of the brain protruding into the superior sagittal sinus and into depressions in the neighboring bone

¹pace \ˈpās\ *n* -s [ME *pas,* fr. OF, fr. L *passus* step, pace, fr. *passus,* past part. of *pandere* to spread, unfold — more at FATHOM] **1 a :** rate of locomotion **:** rapidity with which distance is traversed ⟨led off at a good ~ so that they could cover as much ground as possible —Fred Majdalany⟩ ⟨the limousine moved at an easy ~ —John Hersey⟩ ⟨the river broadens, slackening its ~ as it spreads out —Ted Sumner⟩; *esp* **:** an established rate of locomotion ⟨the challenger made the ~ hot from the start —G.E.Odd⟩ **b :** rate of progress **:** rapidity of development ⟨the ~ of developments in science, agriculture, business, politics, international relations . . . is so swift —Lister Hill⟩; *specif* **:** a parallel rate of growth or development ⟨as the demand for livestock . . . grew, the development of shipping facilities kept ~ —*Amer. Guide Series: Minn.*⟩ **c** (1) **:** a rash or headlong course ⟨youth, sped by the ancient dream that seemed so new, . . . went the ~ with a high heart —C.E.Montague⟩ (2) **:** an example to be emulated ⟨one learns to go to church . . . because other members of the community set the ~ for this kind of activity —Edward Sapir⟩; *specif* **:** first place in a competition ⟨three strokes off the ~ —*Time*⟩ **d** (1) **:** rate of performance or delivery **:** TIMING, TEMPO ⟨see the story unwind . . . with an amiable ~ and plenty of time —Stark Young⟩ ⟨housewives, their routine quickened by the ~ of wartime living —*Monsanto Mag.*⟩ ⟨the ease and ~ of his turns and the precision of his beats place him in the line of the great Russian dancers —Caryl Brahms⟩; *specif* **:** SPEED ⟨his stories move at a breathless ~ —Henry Treece⟩ ⟨the ~ at which an audience can absorb ideas differs with the ideas —Henning Nelms⟩ ⟨the pitcher . . . whips the ball, varying ~, swerve and flight —*Dict. of Games*⟩ (2) **:** rhythmic animation **:** FLUENCY ⟨writes with color, with zest, and with ~ —Amy Loveman⟩ **e** (1) **:** the speed of a bowled ball or of bowling ⟨the bowler frequently changed ~⟩ (2) **:** the degree to which a cricket wicket affects the speed of a ball rebounding from it ⟨difference in ~ of matting and turf wickets⟩ **f :** a device in a loom to maintain even tension in pacing the take-up on the woven fabric **g :** ROUTINE ⟨the circus is change of ~ — beauty against our daily ugliness —John Steinbeck⟩ **2 a :** a manner of walking **:** TREAD ⟨walked slowly, with even, unhesitating ~ —Willa Cather⟩ **b** *obs* **:** a route of travel **:** COURSE ⟨we will direct our ~ downward now —James Howell⟩ **3 a :** a movement of the foot over a space to a new position in walking, running, or dancing **:** STEP ⟨took a ~ or two in the room —Guy McCrone⟩ **b** (1) **:** the space traversed by one step — used as an indefinite unit of measure ⟨cannot go five ~*s* without seeing some wretched object —*Irish Digest*⟩ (2) **:** any of various units of distance based on the length of a human step at a specified time (as for quick time 30 inches and for double time 36 inches) — see ROMAN PACE **4 a** (1) **:** a broad step or platform **:** a flat portion in a run of stairs (2) **:** a raised part of a floor (as around an altar) **b** *obs* **:** a narrow passageway **:** DEFILE ⟨making ~*s* through woods and thickets —Meredith Hanmer⟩ **c :** a passageway running the length of a church between seats **5 a :** an exhibition of skills or capacities ⟨bird dogs going through their ~*s* in the most alien environment —J.W.Cross⟩ ⟨the test pilots . . . put the new planes through their ~*s* —H.H.Arnold & I.C.Eaker⟩; *specif* **:** the various gaits of a horse (as the walk, trot, canter, gallop, and amble) **b :** a fast 2-beat gait of the horse and some other quadrupeds in which the legs move in lateral bipeds and support the animal alternately on the right and left pair of legs — compare TROT

²pace \"\ *vb* -ED/-ING/-s *vi* **1 a :** to go with slow or measured tread **:** WALK ⟨a stone platform where meditative persons might ~ to and fro —W.B.Yeats⟩ **b :** to move along **:** PROCEED ⟨they ~ through the obligations of their marriage with . . . cynicism —*Times Lit. Supp.*⟩ **2 :** to move with a lateral gait — usu. used of a horse or dog ⟨*pacing* . . . is characterized by its pistonlike drive with parallel sets of legs traveling together —F.A.Wrensch⟩ ~ *vt* **1 a :** to measure by pacing — often used with *off* ⟨~ off a 10-yard penalty⟩ ⟨had often wondered how far west his land extended, but had never taken the time to ~ it off —O.E.Rölvaag⟩ **b :** to cover at a walk ⟨was slowly *pacing* this narrow enclosure, in his accustomed walk —Sheridan Le Fanu⟩ **2** *archaic* **:** to execute by pacing ⟨~*s* a hornpipe among the eggs —Sir Walter Scott⟩ **3 a** *obs* **:** to train (a horse) to pace **b** *of a horse* **:** to cover (a course) by pacing ⟨*paced* the mile track in 1:55 flat —*Amer. Guide Series: Minn.*⟩ **4 a :** to set or regulate the pace of ⟨traffic, *paced* by clanging cable cars, climbs up and down at cautious speeds —G.W.Long⟩ ⟨advertising must be *paced* so that ads increase in size and frequency as Christmas gets closer —*Nat'l Furniture Rev.*⟩ ⟨must ~ himself, know what his physique will stand —Blair Moody⟩; *specif* **:** to run in advance of (a teammate) as a pacemaker in racing **b :** to let out or take up at regular intervals in weaving ⟨~ the warp⟩ ⟨~ the web⟩ **c** (1) **:** to go before **:** PRECEDE ⟨next in line, *paced* by the scoutmaster⟩ ⟨*paced* by tanks . . . infantrymen were storming a narrow gorge —*Time*⟩; *specif* **:** to draw away from (other competitors) in a race (2) **:** to set an example for **:** excel in accomplishment **:** LEAD ⟨food prices were *pacing* the upsurge —*Newsweek*⟩ ⟨oil advertisers *paced* all other classifications in space gains —*Wall Street Jour.*⟩; *specif* **:** to be high scorer of ⟨*paced* the team with three hits in the sixth game —Robert Shaplen⟩ **d :** to match the progress of **:** keep pace with ⟨schools of porpoises ~ the plodding ship —Tom Marvel⟩ ⟨the speed of the machine may be closely regulated to ~ the packing operation —*Modern Packaging*⟩ ⟨his own growth . . . *paced* that of his science —D.W. Atchley⟩ **5 :** to establish the tempo of **:** control the rhythm and flow of ⟨the dynamic director *paced* the show like a fast 440-yard relay —Henry Hewes⟩ ⟨*paced* the music with . . . sure and tasteful touch —Winthrop Sargeant⟩

³pace \"\ *n, usu cap* [ME (northern dial.) *pase, paas,* fr. MF *pasche,* fr. OF — more at PASCH] *dial chiefly Eng* **:** EASTER

⁴pa·ce \ˈpāsē\ *prep* [L, abl. of *pac-, pax* peace — more at PEACE] **:** with all due respect or courtesy to ⟨I do not, ~ . . . the correspondents, claim to have made any "discovery" —E.M. Almedingen⟩ ⟨~ the feminists, I believe my own sex is largely responsible for this . . . impertinent curiosity —Katharine F. Gerould⟩

paceboard \ˈ=,=\ *n* [¹*pace* + *board*] **:** the footboard of an altar

paced \ˈpāst\ *adj* **1 a :** having a specified speed or gait — usu. used in combination ⟨a fair-*paced* stroke . . . should have the desired effect —A.L.Goundrill⟩ **b :** having the pace set by a pacemaker ⟨a ~ mile⟩ **c :** ACCOMPLISHED ⟨one of the most thorough-*paced* scoundrels —Donn Byrne⟩ **2 :** having a controlled rhythm or tempo ⟨can't recall a better-*paced* performance —Douglas Watt⟩; *specif* **:** MEASURED ⟨in ~ tragic tones —Murray Schumach⟩

pace egg *n, often cap P* [³*pace*] *dial Eng* **:** EASTER EGG

pacemaker \ˈ=,==\ *n* **1 a :** one that sets the pace for another — called also *pacesetter* **b :** one that takes the lead or sets an example ⟨ought to act as ~ of Europe unity —F.E.Hirsch⟩ **2 a :** a body part (as the sinoatrial node of the heart) that serves to establish and maintain a rhythmic activity **b :** an emergency device for stimulating the heart with an alternating current to steady the beat or to reestablish the rhythm of an arrested heart ⟨the time it takes for the electrical impulse to travel from the ~ at the base of the heart —P.D.White⟩

pacemaking \ˈ=,=\ *n* **:** the act or process of serving as a pacemaker

pac·er \ˈpāsə(r)\ *n* -s **1 a :** one that teaches pacing **b :** one that paces; *specif* **:** a horse with a lateral gait — compare TROTTER **2 :** PACEMAKER

paces *pl of* PACE, *pres 3d sing of* PACE

pacesetter \ˈ=,==\ *n* **:** PACEMAKER 1

pachalic *var of* PASHALIC

pacheneg *usu cap, var of* PETCHENEG

pa·chin·ko \pəˈchiŋ(ˌ)kō\ *n* -s [Jap] **:** a Japanese gambling device resembling a pinball machine but with automatic payoff as in a gambling slot machine

pa·chi·si \pəˈchēzē\ *n* -s [Hindi *pacīsī,* fr. *pacīs* twenty-five, fr. Skt *pañca* five + *viṁśati* twenty; fr. twenty-five being the highest throw — more at FIVE, VICENARY] **:** an ancient board game resembling backgammon that is played on a cruciform board with cowries for dice

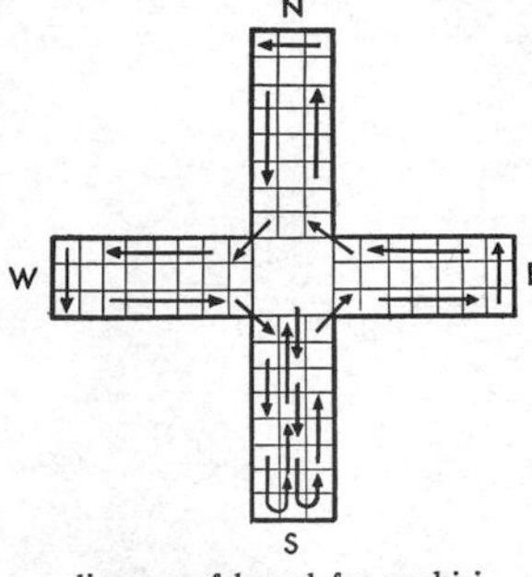

diagram of board for pachisi showing track of one player

pa·chis·ti·ma \pəˈkistəmə\ *n, cap* [NL, prob. irreg. fr. Gk *pachys* thick — more at PACHY-] **:** a genus of No. American dwarf evergreen shrubs (family Celastraceae) having smooth coriaceous serrulate leaves and very small green axillary solitary or fascicled flowers — see MOUNTAIN LOVER, OREGON BOX

pach·no·lite \ˈpaknəˌlīt\ *n* -s [G *pachnolit,* fr. Gk *pachnē* hoarfrost + G *-lit* -lite; akin to Gk *pēgnynai* to fasten together — more at PACT] **:** a mineral $NaCaAlF_6.H_2O$ consisting of a hydrous fluoride of sodium, calcium, and aluminum occurring in colorless to white monoclinic crystals (hardness 3, sp. gr. 3)

pa·cho·mi·an \pəˈkōmēən\ *adj, usu cap* [St. *Pachomius,* 4th cent. A.D. Egyptian monk + E *-an*] **:** of or relating to the cenobitic type of Eastern monasticism originated by St. Pachomius

pachouli *var of* PATCHOULI

pa·chu·ca tank \pəˈchükə-\ *n, usu cap P* [fr. *Pachuca,* Mexico, where it was first used] **:** a high narrow tank with a central cylinder for compressed air used in the agitation and settling of pulp during treatment by the cyanide process

pa·chu·co \pəˈchü(ˌ)kō\ *n* -s [MexSp, prob. fr. El *Paso,* Texas, city from which the pachucos and their families came to California] **:** a young usu. underprivileged Mexican-American of the Los Angeles area having a taste for flashy clothes and fast living, speaking a special jargon, usu. belonging to a neighborhood gang, and often identified by a small tattoo — compare CHOLO 3

pachy- *comb form* [NL, fr. Gk, fr. *pachys;* akin to ON *bingr* heap, Latvian *biezs* dense, thick, Av *bazah* high, deep, Skt *bahu* dense, much, many] **:** thick ⟨*Pachy*dermata⟩ ⟨*pachy*tene⟩ ⟨*pachy*meter⟩

pachy·ceph·a·la \ˌpakəˈsefələ\ *n pl, cap* [NL, fr. *pachy-* + Gk *kephalē* head] **:** a genus of chiefly arboreal and insectivorous birds (family Muscicapidae) that are intermediate in some respects between the typical flycatchers and the shrikes — see WHISTLER

pachy·ce·pha·lia \ˌpakəsəˈfālēə\ *or* **pachy·ceph·a·ly** \ˌpakəˈsefəlē\ *n, pl* **pachycephalias** *or* **pachycephalies** [*pachycephalia* fr. NL, fr. *pachy-* + *cephal-* + *-ia; pachycephaly* ISV *pachy-* + *cephal-* + *-y*] **:** thickness of skull or head

pachy·derm \ˈpakəˌdərm, -dōm, -dəim\ *n* -s [F *pachyderme,* fr. Gk *pachydermos* thick-skinned, fr. *pachy-* + *-dermos* -skinned (fr. *derma* skin) — more at DERM-] **:** one of the Pachydermata (as an elephant or rhinoceros)

pachy·der·mal \ˌ==ˈdərməl\ *adj* **:** PACHYDERMATOUS

pachy·der·ma·ta \ˌ==ˈdərmədə\ *n pl, cap* [NL, fr. *pachy-* + *-dermata*] **:** an artificial assemblage of nonruminant hoofed mammals usu. having a thick skin and including the elephants, hippopotamuses, rhinoceroses, tapirs, horses, pigs, and others

pachy·der·ma·toid \ˌ==ˈdərməˌtȯid\ *adj* [NL *Pachydermata* + E *-oid*] **:** PACHYDERMOID

pachy·der·ma·tous \-mədəs\ *adj* [NL *Pachydermata* + E *-ous*] **1 :** of or relating to the pachyderms **2** [influenced in meaning by F *pachyderme* thick-skinned, fr. Gk *pachydermos*] **a :** THICK, THICKENED — used of skin ⟨the ~ hide that covered the soles of my bare feet —Ben Riker⟩ ⟨~ condition of the skin in elephantiasis⟩ **b :** CALLOUS, INSENSITIVE ⟨that condition of ~ resignation essential to a prolonged residence there —Louis Golding⟩ — **pachy·der·ma·tous·ly** *adv*

pachy·der·mia \ˌ==ˈdərmēə\ *n* -s [NL, fr. *pachy-* + *-dermia*] **:** abnormal thickness of tissue (as of skin or of the laryngeal mucous membrane) — **pachy·der·mi·al** \ˌ==ˈdərmēəl\ *adj*

pachy·der·mic \ˌ==ˈdərmik\ *adj* **:** PACHYDERMATOUS

pachy·der·moid \-rˌmȯid\ *adj* [*pachyderm* + *-oid*] **:** resembling the pachyderms

pachy·der·mous \-rməs\ *adj* [Gk *pachydermos*] **1 :** PACHYDERMATOUS **2 :** having thick walls ⟨a moss with ~ cells⟩

pachyglossal \ˌpakē+\ *or* **pachy·glossate** \"+\ *adj* [*pachy-* + *glossal* or *glossate*] **:** having a thick tongue — used of a lizard

pachygrapsus \"+\ *n, cap* [NL, fr. *pachy-* + *Grapsus*] **:** a genus of common shore crabs (family Grapsidae) widely distributed along the western coast of No. America

pa·chy·ma \pəˈkīmə\ *n, cap* [NL, fr. Gk *pachys* thick — more at PACHY-] **:** a form genus of imperfect fungi based on sclerotial stages of members of the genus *Poria*

pachy·meningitis \ˌpakē+\ *n* [NL, fr. *pachy-* + *meningitis*] **:** inflammation of the dura mater

pachy·meninx \"+\ *n* [NL, fr. *pachy-* + *meninx*] **:** DURA MATER

pa·chym·e·ter \pəˈkimədə(r)\ *n* [ISV *pachy-* + *-meter*] **:** an instrument for measuring thickness (as of paper)

pachy·ne·ma \ˌpakəˈnēmə\ *n* -s [NL, fr. *pachy-* + *-nema*] **:** a postsynaptic meiotic chromosome — compare LEPTONEMA

pachy·o·nych·ia \ˌpakēōˈnikēə\ *n* -s [NL, fr. *pachy-* + *-onychia*] **:** extreme usu. congenital thickness of the nails

pa·chyp·a·sa \pəˈkipəsə\ *n, cap* [NL, prob. fr. *pachy-* + Gk *pas* all; akin to Skt *śaśvat* every, *śvayati* he swells — more at CAVE] **:** a genus of lasiocampid moths including a Syrian silkworm (*P. otus*) reared by the Greeks and Romans for its silk until the introduction of the Chinese silkworm in A.D. 550

pachy·psylla \ˌpakē+\ *n, cap* [NL, fr. *pachy-* + *Psylla*] **:** a genus of plant lice (family Psyllidae) containing several forms that produce galls on hackberry

pachy·rhi·zus \ˌpakəˈrīzəs\ *n, cap* [NL, fr. Gk *pachyrrhizos* having a thick root, fr. *pachy-* + *-rhizos* (fr. *rhiza* root) — more at ROOT] **:** a small genus of tropical herbaceous vines (family Leguminosae) with a tuberous root, trifoliate leaves, and white or purplish flowers — see YAM BEAN

pachy·san·dra \ˌpakəˈsandrə\ *n* [NL, fr. Gk *pachys* thick + NL *-andra* — more at PACHY-] **1** *cap* **:** a genus of evergreen woody herbs (family Buxaceae) having dentate leaves and often used as ground covers — see ALLEGHENY SPURGE, JAPANESE SPURGE **2** -s **:** any plant of the genus *Pachysandra*

pachystima *syn of* PACHISTIMA

pachy·tene \ˈpakəˌtēn\ *n* -s [ISV *pachy-* + *-tene;* orig. formed as F *pachytène*] **:** a stage of the meiotic prophase that immediately follows zygotene and is characterized by the splitting of the paired chromosomes into chromatids — compare DIPLOTENE, LEPTOTENE

pa·chyt·y·lus \pəˈkidᵊləs\ *n, cap* [NL, fr. *pachy-* + Gk *tylos* callus, knob — more at THOLE] **:** a genus of Acrididae that includes several destructive Old World migratory locusts

pac·i·fi·able \ˈpasəˌfīəbəl, ˌ==ˈ===\ *adj* [*pacify* + *-able*] **:** capable of being pacified

pa·cif·ic \pəˈsifik, -fēk\ *adj* [MF *pacifique,* fr. L *pacificus,* fr. *pac-, pax* peace + *-i-* + *-ficus* -fic — more at PEACE] **1 a :** tending to lessen conflict and promote compromise **:** CONCILIATORY ⟨the effect of his ~ policy was that, in his time, no regular troops were needed —T.B.Macaulay⟩ **b :** rejecting the use of force as an instrument of policy **:** PEACEFUL ⟨make recommendations to the parties with a view to a ~ settlement of the dispute —*U.N. Charter*⟩ **2 a :** having a soothing appearance or effect **:** CALM, TRANQUIL ⟨cloud packs pass over it in soft, cumulus, ~ towers —Hugh MacLennan⟩ **b :** characterized by mildness of temper or disposition **:** disinclined to quarrel **:** PEACEABLE ⟨a naturally ~, sociable man —Glenway Wescott⟩ ⟨the polite and ~ . . . cultures of India and China —Lewis Mumford⟩ **3** *usu cap* [fr. *Pacific ocean*] **:** of or relating to the Pacific ocean ⟨*Pacific* barracuda⟩ ⟨ferrying . . . troops to *Pacific* battlefronts—Howell Walker⟩; *specif* **:** POLYNESIAN 3 ⟨the *Pacific* islands, east of Australia —L.F. de Beaufort⟩

syn PEACEABLE, PEACEFUL, PACIFIST, PACIFISTIC, IRENIC: PACIFIC is often used in reference to an individual or group enjoying peace and harboring no desire to arouse contention, strife, or war, more often to those exerting effort and influence to abate strife and attain to peace or to a state of tranquillity ⟨the *pacific* temper, which seeks to settle disputes on grounds of justice rather than by force —Bertrand Russell⟩ ⟨adoption of the convention after three days of fierce dissension —*N.Y. Times*⟩ PEACEABLE stresses enjoyment of peace as a way of life ⟨the primitive state of man, *peaceable,* contented, and sociable —William Bartram⟩ and may be used as the antonym of *forceful* or *warlike* ⟨they told us . . . that if *peaceable* means failed, they would seize little Jule —Herman Melville⟩ PEACEFUL suggests absence of strife or contention as well as of disturbing influences ⟨*peaceful* sisterhood, receive, and yield me sanctuary —Alfred Tennyson⟩ PACIFIST and PACIFISTIC concern peace only as contrasted with war; they refer to efforts to prevent or stop wars and to settle the issues involved by conference and compromise ⟨*pacifist* means have been variously termed "nonviolent coercion", "war without violence", "passive resistance" —M.Q.Sibley⟩ IRENIC concerns peace orig. in connection with religious controversy and may refer to attitudes or measures likely to allay dispute ⟨lived to see his synod adopt a very *irenic* attitude towards its former antagonists —J.M.Rohne⟩

pa·cif·i·cal \-fəkəl\ *adj* [ME, fr. LL *pacificalis,* fr. L *pacificus* + *-alis* -al] *archaic* **:** PACIFIC

pa·cif·i·cal·ly \-fək(ə)lē, -fēk-, -li\ *adv* **:** in a pacific manner **:** AMICABLY, PEACEABLY

pacific athapaskan *n, usu cap P&A* **1 :** a group of Athapaskan peoples occupying a discontinuous territory from southern British Columbia to northern California and including Chastacosta, Chetco, Chilula, Clatskanie, Hupa, Kato, Kwalhioqua, Lassik, Mattole, Whilkut, Sinkyone, Taltushtuntude, Tolowa, Tututni, Umpqua, Wailaki **2 :** a subdivision of the Athapaskan languages including the languages spoken by the Pacific Athapaskan peoples

pac·i·fi·ca·tion \ˌpasəfəˈkāshən\ *n* -s [MF, fr. L *pacification-, pacificatio,* fr. *pacificatus* (past part. of *pacificare* to pacify) + *-ion-, -io* -ion — more at PACIFY] **1 :** the act or process of achieving or restoring peace **:** elimination of disturbance **:** TRANQUILIZATION, SUBDUAL ⟨from the tumult of Hell, through the gradual ~ of Purgatory, to the perfect peace of Paradise —G.G.Coulton⟩ ⟨seven million Arabs and Berbers,

whose ~ had been completed only eight years before —C.R. Codman⟩ **2 :** a treaty of peace ⟨the *Pacification* of Ghent⟩
pa·ci·fi·ca·tor \'ˌ==ˌkād·ə(r), -ātə- *also* pə'sifəˌ-\ *n* -s [L, fr. *pacificatus* + *-or*] **:** one that pacifies **:** ARBITRATOR, PEACEMAKER
pa·cif·i·ca·tory \pə'sifəkəˌtōrē\ *adj* [L *pacificatorius*, fr. *pacificatus* + *-orius* -ory] **:** tending to promote peace **:** CONCILIATORY
pacific blockade *n* **:** a blockade by one country of the ports of another without recourse to war
pacific bonito *n, usu cap P* **:** a bonito that is prob. a northerly strain of the Chile bonito but is often treated as a distinct species (*Sarda lineolata*)
pacific cedar *or* **pacific arborvitae** *n, usu cap P* **:** RED CEDAR 2a
pacific cod *n, usu cap P* **:** ALASKA COD
pacific cultus *n, usu cap P* **:** LINGCOD
pacific dogwood *n, usu cap P* **:** a flowering dogwood (*Cornus nuttallii*)
pacific godwit *n, usu cap P* **:** a large godwit (*Limosa lapponica baueri*) distributed from eastern Siberia to Australia and New Zealand
pacific gull *n, usu cap P* **:** a large black-backed Australian gull (*Gabianus pacificus*) having a black band on the tail at maturity
pacific halibut *n, usu cap P* **:** a halibut (*Hippoglossus stenolepis*) of the northern Pacific ocean
pacific hemlock *n, usu cap P* **1 :** WESTERN HEMLOCK **2 :** the wood of the Pacific hemlock tree
pacific herring *n, usu cap P* **:** a herring (*Clupea pallasii*) of the northern Pacific ocean
pacific iron *n* **:** a metal band or fixture about the end of the yard of a sailing ship — see SAIL illustration
pa·cif·i·cism \pə'sifəˌsizəm\ *n* -s [*pacific* + *-ism*] **:** PACIFISM
pa·cif·i·cist \-fəsə̇st\ *n* -s [*pacific* + *-ist*] **:** PACIFIST
pacific kittiwake *n, usu cap P* **:** a kittiwake (*Rissa tridactyla pollicaris*) of the northern Pacific ocean that is pure white with black feet, a pearl-gray mantle, and broadly black-tipped wings — compare ATLANTIC KITTIWAKE, RED-LEGGED KITTIWAKE
pacific mackerel *n, usu cap P* **:** a common and important food fish (*Pneumatophorus diego*) of the Pacific coast of No. America closely related to and greatly resembling the common mackerel of the Atlantic
pacific madrone *n, usu cap P* **:** MADRONA 1
pacific maple *n, usu cap P* **:** OREGON MAPLE
pacific mite *n, usu cap P* **:** a mite (*Eotetranychus pacificus*) that is a destructive pest of orchard crops and ornamentals along the Pacific coast of the U.S. and southern Canada
pacific plum *n, usu cap P* **:** SIERRA PLUM
pacific rattlesnake *n, usu cap P* **:** a common rattlesnake (*Crotalus viridis oreganus*) of the Pacific slope of No. America
pacific red cedar *n, usu cap P* **:** RED CEDAR 2a
pacific sailfish *n, usu cap P* **:** a sailfish (*Istiophorus greyi* or *I. orientalis*) of the Indian and tropical Pacific oceans that is larger and has a higher dorsal fin than the Atlantic sailfish
pacific salmon *n, usu cap P* **:** a salmon of the genus *Oncorhynchus* — compare BLUEBACK SALMON, DOG SALMON
pacific sardine *n, usu cap P* **:** an extremely abundant small clupeid fish (*Sardinops caerulea*) of the Pacific coast of No. America that is an important commercial fish used for canning and for production of fish meals and fish oils
pacific silver fir *n, usu cap P* **:** AMABILIS FIR
pacific terrapin *n, usu cap P* **:** an aquatic mud turtle (*Clemmys marmorata*) sold as terrapin in West Coast markets
pacific time *or* **pacific standard time** *n, cap P* **:** the time of the 8th time zone west of Greenwich that is based on the 120th meridian, is used in the Pacific coastal region of Canada and the U.S. from the panhandle of Alaska southward, and is three hours slower than eastern time — abbr. *PT, PST*
pacific tree toad *n, usu cap P* **:** a tree toad (*Hyla regilla*) widely distributed in western No. America
pacific yellowtail *n, usu cap P* **:** CALIFORNIA YELLOWTAIL
pacific yew *n, usu cap P* **:** a small or medium irregularly branched evergreen tree (*Taxus brevifolia*) of the Pacific coast yielding a fine hard close-grained wood — called also *California yew, western yew*
pa·cif·id \pə'sifə̇d\ *n* -s *usu cap* [*pacific* + *-id*] **:** an early American Indian of a physical type characterized by moderate stature, broad head usu. with low-vaulted cranium and flattened base, and a broad rugged face — compare CENTRALID, SYLVID
pac·i·fi·er \'pasəˌfī(ə)r, -īə\ *n* -s **:** one that soothes or calms: as **a :** a usu. nipple-shaped device for babies to suck or bite upon **b :** SUGAR-TIT **c :** TRANQUILIZER

pacifier a

pac·i·fism \'pasəˌfizəm\ *n* -s [F *pacifisme*, fr. *pacifique* pacific (fr. MF) + *-isme* -ism — more at PACIFIC] **1 :** opposition to war or violence as a means of settling disputes ⟨their ~ is rooted in their contemplative outlook, and in the fact that they do not desire to change whatever they see —Bertrand Russell⟩ ⟨the fundamental transformation from ~ to full war-mindedness that was necessary to meet the crisis —R. de R. de Sales⟩; *specif* **:** refusal to bear arms because of moral or religious principles ⟨Christian ~ . . . asserts that all warfare is categorically forbidden to followers of Our Lord —T.S.Eliot⟩ **2 :** an attitude or policy of nonresistance **:** PASSIVISM ⟨some assert that . . . ~ should be our aim, and a disarmed neutrality our policy —*Yale Rev.*⟩
¹pac·i·fist \-fə̇st\ *n* -s [F *pacifiste*, fr. *pacifisme* + *-iste* -ist] **:** an adherent to pacifism ⟨~s . . . now found expression for their conviction that war in general is immoral and inexpedient —C.J.H.Hayes⟩; *specif* **:** CONSCIENTIOUS OBJECTOR
²pacifist \"\ *or* **pac·i·fis·tic** \ˌ==ˈfistik\ *adj* **:** of, relating to, or characterized by pacifism ⟨distributing ~ literature⟩
syn see PACIFIC
pac·i·fis·ti·cal·ly \-tə̇k(ə)lē\ *adv* **:** in a pacifistic manner ⟨the ~ inclined liberal —H.D.Lasswell⟩
pac·i·fy \'pasəˌfī\ *vt* -ED/-ING/-ES [ME *pacifien*, fr. L *pacificare*, fr. *pac-, pax* peace + *-ificare* -ify — more at PEACE] **1 a :** to allay anger or agitation **:** PLACATE, SOOTHE ⟨bought the weeping child a lollipop to ~ her⟩ **b :** to make benign or amicable **:** APPEASE, PROPITIATE ⟨such concessions would ~ the Chinese Communist leaders —W.V.Shannon⟩ **2 a :** to restore to a tranquil state **:** QUIET, SETTLE ⟨throws the four of them . . . into a violent emotional upheaval not to be *pacified* until one of them dies —Charles Lee⟩ **b :** to reduce to a submissive state esp. by force of arms **:** SUBDUE ⟨U.S. Marines . . . went in as early as 1910 to ~ the country —*Time*⟩
syn APPEASE, PLACATE, MOLLIFY, PROPITIATE, CONCILIATE: PACIFY indicates a soothing or calming of anger, grievance, or agitation, or the quelling of insurrection esp. by force ⟨seeing his mounting rage, friends did all they could to *pacify* and restrain him⟩ ⟨second-grade troops, useful mainly to occupy parts of the country that have already been *pacified* —Brian Crozier⟩ APPEASE may indicate the quieting of agitation or insistent demand by the making of concessions ⟨open in manner, easy of access, a little quick of temper but readily *appeased* —John Buchan⟩ ⟨he is utterly and absolutely implacable; no prayers, no human sacrifices can ever for one moment *appease* his cold, malignant rage —L.P.Smith⟩ ⟨a frantic effort to *appease* mounting discontent at home —Paul Willen⟩ PLACATE is sometimes interchangeable with APPEASE but may imply a more lasting assuagement of bitter feeling ⟨each and every new route projected was liable to drastic alteration to *placate* local opposition —O.S.Nock⟩ ⟨federal officials who try to *placate* witch-hunting Congressmen —*New Republic*⟩ MOLLIFY stresses softening or abatement of agitation, through mitigating circumstance ⟨*mollified* when they heard that the patio, with its famous cottonwood tree, will be left intact —Green Peyton⟩ PROPITIATE may refer to averting the anger or malevolence or winning the favor of a superior or of one possessing the power to injure greatly ⟨*propitiate* this far-shooting Apollo —George Grote⟩ ⟨Aunty Rosa, he argued, had the power to beat him with many stripes . . . it would be discreet in the future to *propitiate* Aunty Rosa —Rudyard Kipling⟩ ⟨the unlimited power of trustees to abuse their trust unless they are abjectly *propitiated* —H.G.Wells⟩ CONCILIATE may be used of situations in which an estrangement or dispute is settled by arbitration or compromise ⟨policy of *conciliating* and amalgamating conquered nations —Agnes Repplier⟩ ⟨instinctively friendly and wholly free from inflammatory rhetoric, he did much to *conciliate* more stubborn Northern sentiment concerning the South —F.P.Gaines⟩
pacing *n* -s [fr. gerund of ²*pace*] **1 :** an act or instance of executing or controlling a pace ⟨the ~s for a few steps side by side through the crowds —R.M.Coates⟩ ⟨a masterpiece of crisp ~ and refined workmanship —Winthrop Sargeant⟩ ⟨there must be ~ in the introduction of new experiences —C.M.Louttit⟩ **2 :** harness racing for pacers ⟨Little Brown Jug, ~'s biggest race —Gerald Holland⟩
pa·cin·i·an corpuscle \pə'sinēən-\ *also* **pa·ci·ni's corpuscle** \pə'chēnēz-\ *n, sometimes cap P* [Filippo *Pacini* †1883 Ital. anatomist + E *-an* or *-'s* (gen. suffix)] **:** one of the oval bodies serving as terminal capsules of certain sensory nerve fibers esp. in the skin of the hands and feet
¹pack \'pak\ *n* -s *often attrib* [ME *pak, pack*, of LG origin; akin to MLG & MD *pak*, MFlem *pac*] **1 a** (1) **:** a compact bundle of goods or equipment arranged for convenience in carrying esp. on the back of an animal or man ⟨sat on the deck by the bulky aid ~s that the corpsmen had deposited —L.M.Uris⟩ ⟨parachute ~⟩ (2) **:** a knapsack or blanket roll for carrying personal effects ⟨have him roll a full field ~ . . . extra shoes helmet and all —James Jones⟩ (3) **:** a climb or hike with a pack on one's back **b :** a group or pile of related objects: as (1) **:** a shook of cask staves (2) **:** a bundle of sheet-metal plates for rolling simultaneously (3) **:** a number of separate photographic films packed so as to be inserted together into a camera and each attached to a paper tab that on being withdrawn moves the individual exposed film to the back of the lot (4) **:** a set of two or three color films or plates for simultaneous exposure — compare BIPACK, TRIPACK (5) **:** a stack of theatrical flats arranged in sequence **c** (1) **:** a number of individual components packaged as a unit usu. for marketing **:** PACKET ⟨~ of cigarettes⟩ ⟨a fiber drum ~ of dressed chickens —*Recommended Specifications for Poultry & Poultry Products*⟩ ⟨open a ~ of canned goods⟩ (2) **:** CONTAINER ⟨saw the little pilot chute whip out behind him, dragging the silk from the ~ —Howard Hunt⟩; *specif* **:** a package for a commercial product ⟨polyethylene makes ideal individual ~s for catsup, mustard, jelly —*Newsweek*⟩ (3) **:** a compact unitized assembly to perform a specific function (as a power pack to energize a radio set) (4) **:** a container shielded with lead or mercury for holding radium in large quantities esp. for therapeutic application **2 :** a group of people: as **a :** a set of persons with similar aims or background ⟨took her for granted as part of the family ~ —Anne D. Sedgwick⟩; *esp* **:** a hostile or destructive clique ⟨pursued . . . by a ~ of every able-bodied villager, armed with sticks and stones —T.H. White b.1906⟩ ⟨this heedless ~ of curiosity seekers were suffocating him —L.C.Douglas⟩ **b :** the forward line of a rugby team **c :** an organized troop (as of the Boy Scouts) ⟨a cub ~ may be started in any community where a group of interested parents obtain the sponsorship of a responsible institution —*Parents' Mag.*⟩ **3 a :** the contents of a pack **:** any of various units (as a 240-pound measure for wool, a linen yarn measure of 60,000 yards, 20 books of gold leaf) based on the amount in a standard pack **b :** a large amount or number **:** HEAP ⟨a . . . good fellow with ~s of courage —H. J.Laski⟩ ⟨a ~ of lies made up by a vindictive person —Rex Ingamells⟩ **c** (1) **:** a set of cards that is complete for the playing of a given game; *esp* **:** the full deck of 52 cards of 4 suits with all or part of which most card games are played (2) **:** any portion of a set of playing cards remaining undealt at any stage of a card game (3) **:** the discard pile in canasta and similar games (4) **:** a group of cards of special value in a card game because of their number or their high rank **:** a strong card hand **4 a :** an act or instance of packing ⟨field ~ of peaches by migrant workers⟩ ⟨the first experimental ~s were made in Denver in 1908 —M.A.Joslyn&L.A.Hohl⟩ **b :** a method of packing ⟨vacuum ~⟩ ⟨dry sugar ~s are in the proportion of three pounds of fruit to one of sugar —Anne Pierce⟩ **c :** the total amount (as of produce or fish) packed during a specified period ⟨the military requires . . . more than 9 percent of the national ~ of canned fruits and vegetables —R.B.Russell⟩ ⟨supplying the fish for a hundred thousand case ~ —N.C.McDonald⟩ **5 a** (1) **:** a group of domesticated animals trained to hunt or run together ⟨kept a ~ of tiny beagles —E.J.Oates⟩ ⟨led the ~ out of the starting gate —G.F. T.Ryall⟩ (2) **:** a group of usu. wild animals of the same kind congregating in herds, flocks, or schools ⟨baboons . . . ran in ~s of fifty or more —Alan Moorehead⟩ ⟨tunas roving the open sea in ~s —Rachel L. Carson⟩ ⟨prairie chickens congregating in winter ~s⟩; *specif* **:** a group of predatory animals hunting together ⟨wolf ~⟩ **b :** a group of vehicles traveling together ⟨made the freeway and flitted through the slower car ~s —*Motor Life*⟩; *esp* **:** an organized group of combat craft ⟨a submarine ~ that sank twelve ships in two hours —*Fortune*⟩ ⟨the ~ of jets . . . passed overhead on their way to the targets —B.J.Friedman⟩ **6 a :** a concentrated mass ⟨a great ~ of muscle shifting when his shoulder moved —Scott Fitzgerald⟩; *specif* **:** ICE PACK ⟨locked in the antarctic ice until the breakup of the ~ in the summer —Glen Jacobsen⟩ **b :** a supporting wall or pillar in a coal mine built of gob **7 a :** absorbent material saturated with water or other liquid for therapeutic application to the body or a body part — see COLD PACK, HOT PACK, ICE PACK **b :** a folded square or compress of gauze or other absorbent material used esp. to maintain a clear field in surgery, to plug cavities, to check bleeding by compression, or to apply medication **8 a :** MUDPACK **b :** an application or treatment of oils or creams for conditioning the scalp and hair **9 :** material used as packing
²pack \"\ *vb* -ED/-ING/-S [ME *pakken*, prob. fr. MD, fr. *pak* pack, n.] *vt* **1 a :** to stow in or as if in a container **:** make into a compact bundle ⟨~*ed* and unpacked all the gear in traveling —Weston La Barre⟩ ⟨a couple of staff sergeants were ~*ing* film into the combat cameras —Walter Peters⟩ ⟨put on his hat, ~*ed* up his family, and set off —*Atlantic*⟩ ⟨~s an extraordinary amount of information into a few pages —*Times Lit. Supp.*⟩ **b :** to fill completely **:** cram to capacity **:** STUFF, JAM ⟨~ a bag⟩ ⟨~ a stadium⟩ ⟨the whole horizon seemed ~*ed* with their white sails —Kenneth Roberts⟩ ⟨into twelve hours had been ~*ed* the events that well might have filled a lifetime —Rafael Sabatini⟩ ⟨a route . . . ~*ed* with scenes of mountain splendor —O.S.Nock⟩ **c :** to fill with packing: as (1) **:** to fill in (as mine stopes or old workings) with waste rock to support the roof (2) **:** to fill (a fractionating column or tower) with loose pieces of solid material **d** *archaic* **:** to hoist and carry as much (sail) as possible — usu. used with *on* ⟨~*ed* on all sail —William Scoresby †1857⟩ **e :** to load with a pack ⟨~ a mule⟩ **f :** to put in a protective container **:** package or preserve for shipment or marketing ⟨vegetables usually reach Salinas by the truckload and there they are washed, trimmed, inspected and ~*ed* —*Monsanto Mag.*⟩ **2 a :** to crowd together **:** assemble in a compact group ⟨in the yard ~*ed* solid were the farmers, standing silently —Meridel Le Sueur⟩ ⟨in the past all the galaxies now so widely scattered were ~*ed* tightly together —George Gamow⟩ **b :** to increase the density of **:** COMPRESS ⟨~*ed* the lower soil so that capillarity could operate —W.P.Webb⟩ **3 a :** to cause or command to go **:** SEND ⟨saw her ~*ed* back to Holland when the Dutch exiled him —*Time*⟩ — usu. used with *off* ⟨the children are ~*ed* off to Sunday school —*Times Lit. Supp.*⟩ ⟨calmed him down and ~*ed* him off to bed —Clemence Dane⟩; *specif* **:** to dismiss unceremoniously ⟨could neither be tactfully paid off nor summarily ~*ed* off —S.H.Adams⟩ **b :** to bring or come to an end or halt **:** FINISH, STOP — used with *up* or *in* ⟨gossip . . . that he might soon ~ up his assignment and return to the United States —*Springfield (Mass.) Union*⟩ ⟨machine-gun bullets ~*ed* up the airplane's transmitter⟩ ⟨does not mean that . . . a supreme master in the saddle, will ~ in riding —*Irish Digest*⟩ **4 :** to gather into a tight formation **:** make a pack of ⟨hounds well ~*ed* as they close in on their quarry⟩; *specif* **:** to take one's place in (a rugby scrum) ⟨the coach came in and we ~*ed* a scrum for him —A.P.Gaskell⟩ **5 a :** to cover or surround with a pack ⟨~*ed* it away from the operative field with gauze packs —R.P.Parsons⟩; *specif* **:** to envelop (a patient) in a wet or dry sheet or blanket **b :** to caulk or fit by filling or surrounding with material that prevents passage (as of air, water, or steam) ⟨the valve stem is ~*ed* against exhaust pressure only —*Ingersoll-Rand General Catalogue*⟩ **6 a :** to carry or transport on foot ⟨~ a canoe over a portage⟩ ⟨two platoons . . . were ordered to ~ the ammunition to them on foot —*Infantry Jour.*⟩ ⟨~ a suitcase⟩ **b :** to convey usu. on the back of an animal ⟨would pay $20 a day each to be ~*ed* back into the . . . Gorge for trout —Frank Daugherty⟩ ⟨~*ed* guns and ammunition enough to make their horses swaybacked —F.B.Gipson⟩ **c :** to wear or carry as part of one's regular equipment ⟨~ a gun⟩ ⟨~ a union card⟩ ⟨clothes-conscious . . . although they stop somewhere short of ~*ing* a rolled-up umbrella —W.L.Worden⟩ **d :** to be supplied or equipped with **:** POSSESS ⟨the storm . . . ~*ing* winds of eighty to ninety miles —*N.Y. Times*⟩ ⟨these proven weapons . . . ~ nuclear warheads —R.C.Albrook⟩ ⟨few streets in America ~ more history to the square foot —Budd Schulberg⟩ **e** *slang* **:** to be capable of making (an impact) ⟨world's heavyweight champion . . . ~*ed* a wallop —*Springfield (Mass.) Union*⟩ ⟨a book that ~s a man-sized punch —C.J.Rolo⟩ **~** *vi* **1 a :** to go away **:** DEPART ⟨no one simply ~s off and leaves an obligation without first making some explanation —Dorothy Baker⟩; *specif* **:** to consider oneself summarily dismissed ⟨when he refused to work . . . he was calmly told by the youthful manager to ~ up —*Breeder's Gazette*⟩ **b :** to come to a halt **:** cease to function **:** QUIT, STOP — used with *up* or *in* ⟨the motors coughed and ~*ed* up —*Auckland (New Zealand) Weekly News*⟩ ⟨why don't you ~ in, before you kill yourself —Millard Lampell⟩ **2 a :** to stow goods and equipment (as clothes and personal belongings) in luggage or packs for transportation ⟨was given an overseas assignment and sent home to ~⟩ ⟨the company will probably ~ up and move south —*Time*⟩; *specif* **:** to package a product for shipment ⟨the final step in flour manufacture is ~*ing* —*Studies for Flour Salesmen*⟩ **b :** to become adapted for packing ⟨a knit dress ~s well⟩ ⟨air mattresses ~ away into a small space⟩ **c** *archaic* **:** to increase the speed of a ship by crowding on sail ⟨be ready to ~ after them, if they are gone to the bay —Horatio Nelson⟩ **d :** to become filled to capacity ⟨watch the big tarnished grange ~ to the rafters —William Du Bois⟩ **3 a :** to assemble in a group **:** CONGREGATE ⟨snow partridges are wont to ~ like grouse in the autumn —Douglas Carruthers⟩; *specif* **:** to run close together ⟨the dogs followed in fine order, ~*ing* and driving as they went —*Red Ranger*⟩ **b :** to crowd together ⟨excursionists . . . ~ into a bus —Richard Joseph⟩; *specif* **:** to form a rugby scrum ⟨forwards still mostly ~*ed* 3-2-3 —O.L. Owen⟩ **4 a :** to arrange a group of related objects in a compact mass ⟨one man handed up sandbags while the other ~*ed*⟩ **b :** to increase in density ⟨some broken ores tend to ~ in stopes, and must be blasted out —Robert Peele⟩ ⟨ice ~*ed* up against the cab glasses, and visibility was just about nil —O. S.Nock⟩ **5 a :** to carry or convey goods or equipment ⟨domesticated animals . . . used for ~*ing* —J.H.Steward⟩ **b :** to travel with one's baggage by horse or muleback ⟨telling about the summer he ~*ed* into the Big Horn mountains of Wyoming —Hamilton Basso⟩
syn CROWD, CRAM, STUFF, RAM, TAMP: PACK, orig. meaning to form into bundles for convenient handling esp. in transporting, implies also the orderly economical filling of a receptacle or a total often excessive or uncomfortable filling of anything ⟨*pack* a bag for an overnight trip⟩ ⟨*pack* a box until it splits open at the sides⟩ ⟨a play that *packs* the theater every night⟩ CROWD implies a great number of things out of proportion to the space available for them, sometimes suggesting pressing or serious inconvenience ⟨salmon *crowded* both streams —W.L. Worden⟩ ⟨various chapters of the book are *crowded* with references —Paolo Milano⟩ ⟨visitors *crowding* the vacation areas⟩ CRAM suggests more strongly the excessive packing to the point of bruising or squeezing, often implying a disorderly and forcible insertion of something into an inadequately large receptacle or area ⟨into a day that begins each morning at 7:30, Jim *crams* enough work to fill two —*Newsweek*⟩ ⟨the man whose shelves are *crammed* with horticultural books —A.J.P.Taylor⟩ ⟨a man doesn't try to *cram* his feet into his wife's shoes —Constance Foster⟩ STUFF implies a filling to the point of bulging or protrusion, often suggesting also the disorder of cramming ⟨*stuff* a pillow with feathers⟩ ⟨*stuff* a handful of bills into a wallet⟩ ⟨*stuffed* himself with cake⟩ RAM carries the idea of pounding, stamping, or pushing hard to force in ⟨*ram* a bullet into the rifle barrel⟩ ⟨pronging great slices of meat onto his fork and *ramming* them into his mouth —Bruce Marshall⟩ TAMP usu. implies a loose packing in (as of something granular) by the pressure of repeated light blows ⟨*tamping* the gravel back around the ties —Charlton Laird⟩ ⟨*tamp* tobacco in a pipe bowl⟩ ⟨the floors were of *tamped* earth —*Amer. Guide Series: Wash.*⟩
³pack \"\ *vb* -ED/-ING/-S [perh. alter. (influenced by ²*pack*) of ¹*pact*] *vi, obs* **:** to make a secret agreement **:** CONSPIRE ⟨go ~ with him, and give the mother gold —Shak.⟩ **~** *vt* **1** *obs* **a :** to let into a conspiracy **:** make an accomplice of ⟨that goldsmith there, were he not ~*ed* with her, could witness it —Shak.⟩ **b :** to arrange in secret **:** PLOT ⟨had it been a ~*ed* business, they would have been careful not to have differed in a tittle —Francis Bragge⟩ **2 a :** to influence the composition of (as a political agency) so as to bring about a desired result ⟨succeeded . . . in ~*ing* parliament with their adherents —*Publ's Mod. Lang. Assoc. of Amer.*⟩ ⟨could ~ the ballot with dummy candidates to split the vote —*New Republic*⟩ **b** *obs* **:** to manipulate (playing cards) fraudulently **:** STACK **3 :** to add a pack to — used chiefly of the price of an automobile or other item of durable goods ⟨those who sign contracts in blank are making it easy for the unethical dealer to ~ the account —*Facts About Buying Used Cars*⟩ — **pack cards** *archaic* **:** CONSPIRE ⟨she . . . has *packed cards* with Caesars and false played my glory —Shak.⟩
⁴pack \"\ *n* -s **1** *obs* **:** COMPACT, PLOT **2 :** an unjustified surcharge or markup added to a price by a dealer often in collusion with other dealers or with a finance company ⟨many a dealer admitted privately that he added a ~ . . . to allow more room for the discounts his customers expected —*Time*⟩
⁵pack \"\ *adj* [perh. fr. ³*pack*] *chiefly Scot* **:** very friendly **:** INTIMATE ⟨unco ~ and thick thegither —Robert Burns⟩
⁶pack *var of* PAC
pack·abil·i·ty \ˌpakə'bilədē\ *n* **:** the quality or state of being packable
pack·able \'pakəbəl\ *adj* **:** capable of being packed
¹pack·age \'pakij, -kēj\ *n* -s *often attrib* [prob. fr. D *pakkage*, fr. *pak* pack (fr. MD) + *-age* (after *bagage* baggage, fr. MD, fr. ME) — more at PACK, BAGGAGE] **1** [²*pack* + *-age*] *archaic* **:** the act or process of packing ⟨the privileges of the ~ of cloths and certain other outward-bound goods —Patrick Colquhoun⟩ **2 a :** a small or moderate-sized pack **:** BUNDLE, PARCEL ⟨carts, into which ~s were being shot from the warehouses —Virginia Woolf⟩ ⟨before any ~ or parcel is accepted for mailing the sender must . . . endorse the wrapper —*U. S. Official Postal Guide*⟩ **b :** a commodity in its container **:** a unit of a product uniformly processed, wrapped, or sealed for distribution ⟨~ of cigarettes⟩ ⟨handled 6.8 million ~s of fruits and vegetables —C.K.Baker⟩ ⟨the biggest seller was a ~ of four Chinese peel tub chairs —*Retailing Daily*⟩ **c :** a preassembled unit ready for installation or use ⟨with men responsible for the selection and installation of heating units, choice starts with the ~ itself —*Amer. Builder*⟩ ⟨a new self-contained machine gun ~ that is hooked on under the wings —*Science News Letter*⟩ **3 a :** a covering wrapper or container ⟨nature gave the banana a good ~ —*advt*⟩; *specif* **:** a protective unit for storing or shipping a commodity ⟨designing a ~ that attracts the eye of the customer and at the same time protects the merchandise —*Christian Science Monitor*⟩ **b :** any of the various forms (as cheeses, spools, pirns, tubes) in which yarn or thread is wound for processing and handling **4 :** something that resembles a package: as **a :** something organized into or constituting a compact unit ⟨Luxembourg is a diminutive ~ stretching for fifty-seven miles —*N.Y. Times*⟩ ⟨formless procedures that are seldom easy to put in headline ~s —Joseph Alsop⟩ ⟨wry humor, pertinent reflection, and good . . . melodrama, all in one ~ —Phil Stong⟩ **b :** a combination of related elements to be accepted or rejected as a whole ⟨sell them a . . . complete ~ (lot, house, equipment and financing in a

single transaction) —F.A.Gutheim› ‹a series of treaties and agreements forming a single ~ —S.B.Fay› ‹the purchaser is tendered a ~, consisting of a specified amount of common stock with each unit of the senior issue —R.U.Cooper›; *specif* : a complete show or series of shows ready for presentation and usu. bought by a sponsor or network for a lump sum ‹purchasing the entire show as a live-talent or transcribed ~ —Roger Barton› ‹a quarter-hour TV ~ —R.L.Shayon› ‹swung through the Midwest (as part of a jazz concert ~) —*Time*› **c** : a combination of benefits ‹the consumer appeal of a dealer's credit plan depends . . . upon the size and composition of the ~ the consumer gets for what he pays —C.W. Phelps›; *esp* : contract benefits gained through collective bargaining ‹a 10-cent hourly ~ — seven cents to go into a pension fund and three for health and welfare benefits —*Wall Street Jour.*› **d** : a combination of necessaries (as food or tickets) and services usu. offered at a special rate ‹the sports ~ includes accommodations in heated cabins, with or without bath and meals; two sessions at the ski school and unlimited use of the ski lifts —O.R.Geyer› ‹~ vacation› **e** *slang* (1) : COMPOSITE ‹only five feet tall but . . . a ~ of lovely curves —H.D.Osborne› (2) : the police record of a criminal ‹his ~ listed a prison record on a rape charge —Courtney McClendon›

²package \", *esp in pres part* -kəj\ *vt* -ED/-ING/-S **1** : to make into or as if into a package ‹designers showed great ingenuity in constructing and *packaging* these houses —*Americana Annual*› ‹furnished as a *packaged*-type power unit ready to operate —*Air Tools*› ‹neatly ~*s* her findings —James Hilton› ‹his demands for Greece will probably be *packaged* with those for China and Turkey —*New Republic*›; *specif* : to produce as an entertainment package ‹will ~ annually six half-hour TV shows by each writer —Henry Hewes› **2** : to enclose in a package or protective covering ‹there are two ways a designer can ~ this space —*New Yorker*› ‹the car ~*s* its riders like fragile merchandise —A.J.Despagni› ‹airplanes shipped overseas are now *packaged* with a spray of plastic solution —*Aero Products*›; *specif* : to put (a commodity) into a protective wrapper or container for shipment or storage ‹cured hams . . . have been sent out frozen, canned, and otherwise *packaged* —*New Yorker*› ‹the company . . . will ~ about 50% of its beets and 50% of its turnips in these bags —Lee Geist› ‹besides aspirin . . . ~*s* saccharin, eye drops, rubbing alcohol —*Monsanto Mag.*›

pack·age·able \'pakijəbəl\ *adj* : capable of being made into a package

package advertising *n* : advertising placed on the package in which a commodity is sold

package bees *n pl* : bees packaged and sold by weight to constitute the nucleus of a hive

package car *n* : a railroad car for the shipment of goods in less-than-carload lots

package conveyor *n* : a mechanical device for moving packages from one area to another usu. on an endless belt

package deal *n* **1 a** : an offer or agreement to accept or pay a lump sum for a correlated group of goods or services ‹a *package deal*, with all 30 to be leased for four years at a total fee reported somewhat in excess of $1,250,000 —*Wall Street Jour.*› ‹too often parents depend upon *package deals* in children's literature, or on the canned advice of book clubs —F.G.Jennings›; *specif* : a contract involving such an agreement achieved through collective bargaining ‹union-management committees have reportedly worked out a *package deal*, with increased fringe benefits . . . but no flat wage increase —*Time*› **b** : the goods or services supplied through such an agreement ‹offers the franchise operator a complete *package deal*, including ground development, building construction —R.B.Andrews› ‹give the studio a *package deal* — story, star, and director all wrapped up —Bennett Cerf› **2** : an offer or agreement making the acceptance of one proposal or candidate dependent upon the acceptance of another ‹a *package deal* which tied neutralization to a multilateral agreement to share petroleum production —Fred Greene› ‹a *package deal* that would admit all applicants or none —*N. Y. Herald Tribune*›

packaged fuel *n* : fuel sold in bags or briquettes; *specif* : coal or coke briquettes wrapped in paper packages (as of 10 to 15 lb.)

package freight *n* : freight shipped in less-than-carload lots and billed by the piece

package mortgage *n* : a mortgage covering major items of equipment (as kitchen appliances) in addition to the house and lot

package policy *n* : an insurance policy combining coverages for a number of causes of loss or types of property

package powerplant *n* : a small portable steam-electric generating station

pack·ag·er \'pakijə(r), -kēj-\ *n* -S **1 a** : one that packages **b** : an operator of a machine that cuts several pieces of lumber to the same length at the same time **2** : an entrepreneur of complete shows for sale to sponsors or networks ‹an impressively successful radio and television ~ —Gilbert Millstein›

package store *n* : a store licensed to sell alcoholic beverages that may not lawfully be drunk on the premises

package tour *also* **packaged tour** *n* : an all-expense tour ‹*package tours* of the interior of Puerto Rico in five-passenger cars with a guide-driver —M.A.Santin›

packaging *n* -S [fr. gerund of ²*package*] **1** : an act or instance of packing ‹industrial ~ is concerned with transit more than with trade —*Modern Packaging*› ‹the official lot-test number must . . . accompany the dyes through all subsequent ~*s* —*For Instance*› ‹a new ~ of the idea —*Newsweek*› **2** : ¹PACKAGE 3a ‹developing marketable products and their ~*s* —Ben Nash›

pack basket *n* : a basket with shoulder straps designed to be worn on the back

packboard \'=,=\ *n* : a usu. canvas-covered light wood or metal frame with shoulder straps contoured so that only the canvas touches the wearer's back and used for carrying goods and equipment ‹strapped the accordion to his ~ —Robert Lund›

pack drill *n* : a military punishment consisting of marching up and down a beat with full marching equipment

pack basket

packed *adj* [fr. past part. of ²*pack*] **1 a** : CROWDED, STUFFED ‹the characteristic ~ effects are apt to degenerate into cluttered obscurity —F.R.Leavis› — often used in combination ‹crowds his figures into narrow, closely *packed* groups —Roger Fry› ‹his vast and action-*packed* story —Arthur Knight› **b** : COMPRESSED ‹lay on the ~ sand —Hugh MacLennan› — often used in combination ‹ski boots squeak on the hard-*packed* snow —Corey Ford› **2** : filled to capacity ‹played to a ~ house›

packed jury *n* : a jury brought together unfairly or corruptly thereby making it partial or venal

packed out *adj, Brit* : filled to capacity ‹went first to the hotel at which I have frequently put up. *Packed out* —Elizabeth Boyd›

¹pack·er \'pakə(r)\ *n* -S [³*pack* + *-er*] *archaic* : CONSPIRATOR, MANIPULATOR

²packer \"\ *n* -S [²*pack* + *-er*] **1 a** : one that packages goods or equipment for shipment or storage ‹works in the shipping department as a china ~› ‹cans arrive at the automatic ~ in a 4-bank conveyor —*Packaging*›; *specif* : a wholesale dealer ‹tea ~› **b** : one that is processed by a wholesale dealer; *specif* : a dressed hog split down the spine and head with the leaf fat removed **c** : a protective container; *esp* : a usu. wide-mouthed glass bottle **d** : one that loads or fills: as (1) : a specialist in loading pack animals ‹the Missourian was an expert ~ —Theodore Roosevelt› (2) : a worker who loads electrodes into a furnace for graphitizing (3) : a coal miner who fills worked-out rooms with waste material to prevent their collapse and builds rough pillars to support passageways and rooms where mining is being done (4) : a device for packing the space between the wall of an oil well and the pipe or between two strings of pipe in a well (5) : a workman who seals cracks and openings (as in a ship compartment) by packing with paper, canvas, or other caulking materials **2** : one that transports goods or equipment: as **a** : ¹BEARER 2a ‹with eight native guides and ~*s* . . . our men began the march —Clifford Gessler› **b** : one whose business is conveying goods on pack animals ‹knowed more about pack mules than any ~ in his outfit —Ross Santee›; *specif* : a peddler using horses or mules to carry his stock **c** *Austral* : a pack animal **3 a** : one that forms into a compact unit; *specif* : an attachment to a grain binder that forms the grain into sheaves before tying **b** : one that tamps; *esp* : an implement for firming or compacting a plowed and pulverized seedbed

packer hide *n* : a hide usu. of superior quality removed by skilled workmen at a recognized packinghouse in the U. S. or Canada where quantities of hides are uniformly cured and graded — compare COUNTRY HIDE

packers' can *n* : a tin-plated metal can used as a hermetic container for processed foods

pack·ery \'pak(ə)rē\ *n* -ES : PACKINGHOUSE

¹pack·et \'pakət, *usu* -əd·+V\ *n* -S *often attrib* [MF *pacquet*, fr. *pacquer* to pack (fr. *pakke* pack, fr. MD *pak*) + *-et* — more at PACK] **1 a** : a number of letters dispatched at one time ‹the ~*s* kept coming from England, each sheet written to the rim —Virginia Woolf› **b** : a small group or collection ‹~ of rumors› ‹watched little ~*s* of twelve, fifteen, or eighteen tanks approach their positions —Russell Hill› **c** : a small cluster or mass ‹jumbled marl ~*s*, clay balls . . . and pebbles of Alpine origin —*Jour. of Geol.*› ‹a warm ~ of air rises quickly —*Meteorological Abstracts*› **d** : a somewhat cubical cluster of organisms formed as a result of cell division in three planes **2** : a passenger boat carrying mail and cargo on a regular schedule; *specif* : PACKET BOAT **3 a** : a small bundle or parcel ‹a vacuum bottle of coffee and a ~ of sandwiches —B.A.Williams› ‹immobility of the patient, film ~ and X-ray apparatus —Matthew Lozier›; *specif* : ¹PACK 1c(1) ‹~ of cards› **b** (1) : a small thin package (as an envelope or a flat bag) ‹seed ~› ‹~*s*, each of which holds the right amount of powder to make a quart of reconstituted skim milk —*Marketing*› (2) *Brit* : PAY ENVELOPE ‹there wasn't one man in ten took his ~ home —John Morrison› — usu. used with *pay* or *wage* ‹full employment and full pay ~*s* —Sam Pollock› ‹counting of pounds, shillings, and pennies for a weekly wage ~ —H.O. Brayer› **c** (1) *Brit* : SALARY, WAGE — usu. used with *pay* or *wage* ‹the average Irishman is better off, in terms of what his wage ~ will buy —Kevin Devlin› (2) : a considerable amount or number ‹has faced a ~ of trouble since the end of the war —Margaret Stewart› ‹lost a ~ of votes up and down the country —Mollie Panter-Downes› (3) : a sizable sum of money ‹costing a ~, but worth it —Clemence Dane› **d** : something that resembles a packet ‹comes to us in verbal ~*s* —George Eiten› **4** *slang Brit* : severe mental or physical distress; *esp* : the result of illness or of a beating

²packet \"\ *vt* -ED/-ING/-S : to make into or put up in a packet ‹a ~*ed* roll mix —*Packet Foods*›

packet boat *also* **packet ship** *n* **1** : a boat (as orig. a fast sailing ship) chartered by a government to carry mail and dispatches ‹letters . . . conveyed by government *packet boats* or by ordinary sailing ship —Samuel Graveson› **2 a** : a river or coastal steamer usu. of shallow draft carrying mail, passengers, and cargo on a regular run ‹took passage for Boston on the midweek *packet boat* —Kenneth Roberts› **b** : a canalboat designed to carry passengers

packfong *var of* PAKTONG

packhorse \'=,=\ *n* **1** : a horse used to carry loads (as of freight) on a packsaddle or in panniers on the back as distinguished from one used for riding or draft **2** *obs* : one that labors like a beast of burden : DRUDGE ‹I was a ~ in his great affairs —Shak.›

packhouse \'=,=\ *n* **1 a** : WAREHOUSE **b** : a building in which flue-cured tobacco is stored between the end of curing and its preparation for marketing **2** : an establishment for packing produce ‹~ for processing citrus fruit›

pack ice *n* : sea ice formed into a chaotic mass by the crushing together of pans, floes, and brash

pack·ing \'pakiŋ, -kēŋ\ *n* -S [ME *pakking*, fr. gerund of *pakken* to pack — more at PACK] **1 a** : the act or process of preparing goods for shipment or storage ‹planned the trip and had the car serviced but left the ~ to his wife› ‹~ . . . begins when these slabs of curd can be sliced into blocks —L.L. Van Slyke & W.V.Price›; *specif* : the wholesale processing of food for market ‹the first American to give his whole time to the business of ~ —*Story of Meat*› **b** : a method of inserting into a shipping container with appropriate protective covering, cushioning, or bracing ‹typical compression ~: twelve one-quart bottles . . . each wrapped in cushioning material and separated by dividers within the shipping box —*Export Packing*› **c** : the act or process of transporting or being transported on the backs of men or animals ‹the camp is inaccessible by road and ~ is the only way to bring in supplies› **d** : the therapeutic application of a pack ‹hemorrhage . . . could not be controlled by suture or ~ —*Jour. Amer. Med. Assoc.*› **e** : an act or instance of assembling in a compact group or mass ‹~ of runners in a race› **2 a** : a covering, stuffing, or holding apparatus used to protect, cushion, or brace goods packed for shipment or storage ‹excelsior, paper wadding, partitions, chipboard boxes or other types of suitable interior ~ —*Export Packing*› **b** (1) : a thin layer or ring of elastic material (as paper, rubber, asbestos, copper) inserted between the surfaces of a flange joint to make it impervious to leakage — compare GASKET (2) : the material in a stuffing box which prevents leakage (3) : a flexible ring surrounding a piston to maintain a tight fit (as inside a cylinder) (4) : material (as felt, wool, or rope) placed in the sawway of a circular saw to prevent vibration — compare HYDRAULIC PACKING, STEAM PACKING (5) : CAULKING **c** : a masonry filling (as mortar containing small stones) **d** : the material used beneath the drawsheet of a printing press **e** (1) : longitudinal timbers between the hull of a ship and the sliding ways of a launching cradle (2) : a liner between the frame and a raised strake of plating on a ship to make it watertight **f** : the arrangement of several structural members (as I bars or struts) on a single pin forming a truss joint **g** : the filling of a fractionating column consisting usu. of loose pieces of solid material (as glass beads or Raschig rings)

packing box *or* **packing case** *n* **1** : a shipping container; *esp* : a wooden crate for packaged or bulk goods **2** : STUFFING BOX

packing fraction *n* : a measure of the loss or gain of total mass in a group of nucleons when they are brought together to form an atomic nucleus : the ratio multiplied by 10,000 of the mass defect to the mass number

packing gland *n* : ²GLAND 1

packinghouse \'=,=\ *or* **packing plant** *n* **1** : an establishment for the slaughtering, processing, and packing of livestock into meat, meat products, and by-products (as hides, soap, glue) **2** : an establishment for the processing and packing of foodstuffs ‹an apple ~ —A.W.McKay & M.A.Abrahamsen›

pack·ing·less \'pakiŋləs\ *adj* : PACKLESS ‹~ pump›

packing nut *n* : STUFFING NUT

packing press *or* **packing screw** *n* : a press for compressing or packing a substance into a smaller compass

packing radius *n* : half the distance of closest approach of atoms or ions in a crystal

packing ring *n* : PISTON RING

pack·less \'pakləs\ *adj* : using or requiring no packing ‹~ valve›

pack·man \'pakmən\ *n, pl* **packmen** : PEDDLER ‹on hot days a wandering ~ would . . . cool his dusty feet in the burn —Lavinia Derwent›

packmaster \'=,==\ *n* : an officer in charge of a packtrain

pack rat *n* **1** : WOOD RAT; *esp* : a large bushy-tailed rodent (*Neotoma cinerea*) of the Rocky Mountain area having well-developed cheek pouches in which it carries food and the miscellaneous objects it has a tendency to hoard ‹metal buttons and buckles . . . stored nearby by the *pack rats* —J.H. Cook› — called also *trade rat* **2** : one that resembles a pack rat ‹was a *pack rat* and saved everything he got his hands on —Charles Willard›

pack road *n* : a trail suitable for pack animals

packs *pl of* PACK, *pres 3d sing of* PACK

packsack \'=,=\ *n* : a canvas or leather carrying case held on the back by shoulder straps and used to carry gear when traveling on foot

packsaddle \'=,==\ *n* [ME *pakke sadil*, fr. *pakke*, *pak* pack + *sadil*, *sadle* saddle — more at PACK, SADDLE] : any of various saddles (as one with a high frame or a large mat-covered pad stuffed with hay or wool) designed to support loads on the backs of pack animals

packstaff \'=,=\ *n, pl* **packstaves** *archaic* : a staff for supporting a peddler's pack : PIKESTAFF

packsack with tumpline

packthread \'=,=\ *n* [ME *pakthrede*, fr. *pak* pack + *threde* thread — more at THREAD] : strong thread or small twine used for sewing or tying packs or parcels

packtrain \'=,=\ *n* : a string of animals for transporting supplies and equipment ‹a resting place for mule skinners guiding ~*s* across the twisting mountain trails to San Francisco —Hal Nielson›

pack trip *n* : a trip by horseback requiring one or more nights to be spent on the trail

packwax *var of* PAXWAX

packway \'=,=\ *n, Brit* : PACK ROAD

¹pa·co \'pä(,)kō\ *n* -S [Sp, fr. Quechua] : ALPACA

²paco \"\ *n* -S [Sp, fr. Quechua, bay, reddish, prob. fr. *paco* alpaca] : an earthy looking ore consisting of a brown or red iron oxide with minute particles of native silver

pa·cou·ry \pə'kürē\ *also* **pa·cou·ry·uva** \=,=rē'yüvə\ *n, pl* **pacouries** *also* **pacouryuvas** [*pacoury* fr. Galibi; *pacouryuva* fr. Galibi *pacoury* + Tupi *ūva*, *ūba* tree] : BACURY

pact \'pakt\ *n* -S [ME, fr. MF, fr. L *pactum*, fr. neut. of *pactus*, past part. of *pacisci* to agree, contract; akin to OE *fōn* to take, seize, OHG & Goth *fāhan*, ON *fā* to take, seize, L *pangere* to fasten, Gk *pēgnynai* to fix, fasten together, Skt *pāśa* bond] **1** : ⁵COMPACT ‹an unvoiced ~ between us to read him with . . . skepticism —H.V.Gregory› ‹the ~ also grants the broadcasting company exclusive rights —*Wall Street Jour.*›; *specif* : an international treaty ‹~*s* made by mutual consent between states are the foundation of the law of nations —J.H.Hallowell› **2** : PACTUM

¹pac·tion \'pakshən\ *n* -S [MF, fr. L *paction-*, *pactio*, fr. *pactus* (past part. of *pacisci* to agree, contract) + *-ion-*, *-io* -ion] **1** *chiefly Scot* : AGREEMENT, COMPACT, BARGAIN ‹made ~ tween them twa —*Ballad Book*› **2** : a short-term international convention terminating with the execution of a single act or performance — **pac·tion·al** \-shən°l, -shnəl\ *adj*

²paction \"\ *vi* -ED/-ING/-S *Scot* : to make a paction

pactional rent *n, Scots law* : penal rent or liquidated damages stipulated to be paid by a tenant for any breach of the conditions of a lease

pac·to·li·an \(')pak¦tōlēən\ *adj, usu cap* [*Pactolus*, river in Lydia, Asia Minor + E *-ian*] : of or relating to the Pactolus river or its gold-bearing sands : GOLDEN

pac·tum \'pak,tüm\ *also* **pac·tio** \-ktē,ō\ *n, pl* **pac·ta** \-ktə\ *also* **pac·ti·o·nes** \,päktē'ō,nās\ [L] *Roman law* : an informal agreement between two or more persons containing one or more promises and usu. legally unenforceable even when supported by a sufficient consideration except for certain pacta declared enforceable by praetorian edicts and imperial constitutions if arising out of a lawful cause or inducement

pactum de con·sti·tu·en·da do·te \-dā,kän,stid·ə'wendə-'dōtā\ *n* [LL] *Roman law* : an informal agreement to give a dowry

pactum de con·sti·tu·to \-,känstə'tüd·(,)ō\ *n* [LL, pact of settlement] *Roman law* : a pactum vestitum whereby one promises to pay another's debt on a future day or to give security in consideration of the creditor's giving the debtor additional time

pactum do·na·ti·o·nis \-dō,näd·ē'ōnəs\ *n* [LL, donation pact] *Roman law* : a pactum legitimum without legal consideration to make a gratuitous donation enforceable against the donor and his heirs in favor of the prospective donee and his heirs

pactum il·lic·i·tum \-ə'lisə,tüm\ *n, pl* **pacta illici·ta** \-səd·ə\ [L] *civil law* : an unlawful agreement or one contrary to public policy

pactum le·git·i·mum \-lə'gid·ə,müm\ *n, pl* **pacta legiti·ma** \-,mə\ [L, lawful pact] *Roman law* : a pactum vestitum made enforceable by an imperial constitution

pactum prae·to·ri·um \-prī'tōrē,üm\ *n, pl* **pacta praeto·ria** \-ēə\ [L, praetorian pact] *Roman law* : a pactum vestitum made enforceable by praetorian edict

pactum ves·ti·tum \-ve'stē,tüm\ *n, pl* **pacta vesti·ta** \-ēd·ə\ [L, clothed pact] *Roman law* : an informal agreement made legally enforceable by an official act

¹pad \'pad, 'paa(ə)d\ *n* -S [origin unknown] **1 a** : a flat or shaped firm usu. resilient article that is usu. not very thick and that consists typically of dense or closely packed material (as rubber, felt, hair) often enclosed in a casing (as of cloth) and that is used like a mat or cushion to ease contact between two surfaces (as in preventing or lessening friction or pressure or jarring) or for personal comfort (as in sitting or reclining) or protection (as against the impact of blows) or that is used to fill out or expand or emphasize natural outlines or contours (as of the shoulders, hips) or to apparently increase natural size or height: as (1) : a piece of soft often stuffed material like a cushion placed on the back of an animal as a saddle or so as to prevent the animal's back from becoming chafed; *esp* : SADDLE BLANKET (2) : a piece of rubber or cloth shaped to fit a part of the body (as the shoulder) and used to improve the lines of the dressed figure (3) : a protective guard worn in some sports (as ice hockey) to shield parts of the body (as the knees or shins) against impact (4) : a protective cap for the knee of a horse (5) : a usu. square or rectangular piece of often folded typically absorbent material (as gauze) fixed in place over some part of the body as a dressing or other protective covering (6) : a piece of soft material fixed in place (as on the toes) so as to relieve pressure and prevent chafing (7) : a small firm cushion (as of sponge) used for sitting on (8) : a piece of material (as fiberboard) used to separate and protect articles packed for shipment or used as an insert at the top or bottom of a box to protect the contents (9) : a length of thick material often made up of layers used for covering a table top before laying the tablecloth and designed to protect the table top from heat and from marring or scratching (10) : a length of thick material laid over a mattress and under bed sheets to keep the mattress clean and to promote the comfort of one lying on the mattress (11) : a rectangular article resembling a very thin mattress that is laid out (as on a cot or couch) to promote the comfort of one lying on it **b** : a piece of moisture-retaining material typically set in a lidded metal box and saturated with ink for inking the surface of a rubber stamp **c** : a layer of material (as of crushed rock) designed esp. to serve as a cushioning or insulating medium **d** : a small leather cushion that lines the valves of wind instruments (as clarinets) and functions like a washer to prevent an unwanted escape of air **e** : a soft cushiony mass of something ‹the hair falls in heavy ~*s* around the head —G.Montell› ‹a gust of wind blew a snow ~ from the branches overhead —Morley Callaghan› **2** : PALLET 2b **3** : BUNDLE, BUNCH; *esp* : a bundle of cigar wrapper leaves or of binder prepared to be sent to the cigar-making machines **4 a** (1) : the foot of an animal (as a fox, wolf, hare) ‹discovered the mark of a fox's ~ in the mud —Adrian Bell› (2) : one of the footprints made by an animal (3) : PULVILLUS **b** : a part of the body or of an appendage that resembles or is suggestive of a cushion : a thick fleshy resilient part: as (1) : the sole of the foot or underside of the toes of an animal (as a camel, dog) that is typically thickened so as to form a cushion (2) : the underside of the extremities of the fingers; *esp* : the ball of the thumb ‹testing for smoothness with the ~ of her thumb —Elizabeth Bowen› **5** : a floating leaf of a water plant (as a water lily) **6 a** : PADDING **b** : the dye liquor or other liquid used in padding fabrics

pad 1b

7 : a number of sheets of paper (as for writing or drawing) that are grouped together in a stack of varying thickness, that are fastened at one end (as by cementing the extreme edge of each sheet to a cloth strip) so that each sheet may be separately removed, and that are usu. backed by a paperboard stiffener placed below the last sheet **:** TABLET — called also *block* **8 a :** a piece of timber fitted on a beam of a ship to fill out the curve of a deck **b :** a flat plate fixed (as by welding) to a part of the structure of a ship so as to provide an attachment point (as for rigging) or so as to provide a seat to which another part may be fixed **9 a :** a local superimposed deposition of weld metal **b :** a thin adventitious projection that may appear on a casting or forging and that is usu. ground or chipped off **10 :** a nonadjustable attenuator **11 a :** a small area or expanse ⟨in a ~ of green lawn between two heathery steeps —John Buchan⟩ **b** (1) **:** a section of an airstrip or airway used for warming up the motors of a plane before takeoff (2) **:** the section of an airstrip or airway where a plane leaves the ground on takeoff or first touches the ground on landing (3) **:** an area in an airfield or heliport used as the takeoff or landing point of a helicopter **c :** LAUNCHING PAD **12** *slang* **a** (1) **:** APARTMENT (2) **:** ROOM (3) **:** BED **b :** HOVEL, JOINT, DEN **13** *slang* **:** money paid (as to racketeers) for immunity from molestation

2**pad** \"\ *vt* **padded; padded; padding; pads 1 a :** to line or cover or stuff or otherwise equip with or as if with material that serves to cushion or protect or fill out or heighten **:** furnish with a pad or padding ⟨*padded* the box with soft cloth⟩ ⟨his tone was fairly *padded* with caution —Owen Wister⟩ ⟨has a well-*padded* figure⟩ **b :** MUTE, MUFFLE ⟨there was an explosion of muffled coughing *padded* with the whirring of starters —W.W.Haines⟩ ⟨using the flush of water to ~ the sound of movement —Wallace Markfield⟩ **2 a** (1) **:** to expand or lengthen (as a book, magazine article, speech) by the insertion of additional material that is usu. essentially superfluous and often extraneous to the point of being irrelevant and that is usu. used merely to artificially bring the thing so expanded up to some desired size or length or that is used for some other usu. equivocal purpose (as to add impressiveness, suggest intellectual depth, mask an otherwise distasteful theme) **:** INFLATE — often used with *out* ⟨a collection of tourist's notes of the most obvious kind, *padded* out with generalizations that don't bear examining —Honor Tracy⟩ (2) **:** to add purely invented entries to (as an expense account) or fictitious often fraudulent details to (as a request for an allocation of money) ⟨*padded* expense accounts and postage and printing allowances —D.D.McKean⟩ (3) **:** to artificially or fraudulently increase the extent of (as a roster) with real or fictitious names ⟨accused of *padding* his office payroll⟩ ⟨the list of members . . . was heavily *padded* by the inclusion of persons without their knowledge and consent —*Observer*⟩ (4) **:** to artificially or fraudulently increase the numbers of (as an organization) with real or fictitious individuals ⟨*padded* the staff with a lot of unnecessary people⟩ (5) **:** to put fraudulent votes into (as a ballot box) **b :** to state as greater than the actual fact **:** OVERSTATE **:** magnify beyond truth **:** EXAGGERATE ⟨suspected she *padded* her age to work in a cabaret —Jobo Nakamura⟩ **c :** to increase in bulk by the addition of other material ⟨~ a soap⟩ **3 :** to impregnate with a liquid for a special purpose: as **a :** to impregnate (fabric) with dye liquor, mordant, or other liquid by squeezing between rolls **b :** to saturate (leather) with grease **4 :** to fasten (sheets of paper) at one end (as by cementing to a cloth strip) so as to form a pad

3**pad** \"\ *vb* **padded; padded; padding; pads** [perh. fr. MD *paden* to make a path, follow a path, fr. *pad, pat* path] *vt* **1 :** to go along (as a road) on foot ⟨*padding* the streets in search of a job⟩ **2** *dial chiefly Eng* **a :** to tread or trample down by foot travel **b :** to wear (a path) by walking **~** *vi* **1 a :** to go along on foot **:** get from one place to another by walking **:** tramp along **:** TRUDGE ⟨*padding* from one town to the next⟩ **b :** to move along in an easy unhurried way **:** walk in a leisurely nonchalant manner **:** AMBLE ⟨career men-about-town *padded* over to introduce themselves —J.A.Wechsler⟩ **2 a :** to move along usu. steadily with a soft almost noiseless step marked typically by a faint slapping sound or by a light muffled thud ⟨pilgrims hastening to prayers brushed by me, *padding* on brown bare feet —Abdul Ghafur⟩ ⟨~s in her stocking feet to the sofa —Clare B. Luce⟩ ⟨backwards and forwards we *padded* on the soft carpet —John Buchan⟩ ⟨turned and *padded* furtively away —C.G.D.Roberts⟩ ⟨might come *padding* on moccasined feet —J.W.Schaefer⟩ ⟨camels ~ along slowly, with their heads seemingly motionless at the end of their long, undulating necks —Christopher Rand⟩ **b :** to tap softly in such a way as to produce a light muffled sound ⟨he *padded* with his fingers on the tablecloth —Michael McLaverty⟩ — **pad the hoof** *slang chiefly Brit* **:** to travel on foot **:** tramp or trudge along or off or away

4**pad** \"\ *n* [MD or MLG *pad, pat* — more at PATH] **1 a** *dial chiefly Brit* (1) **:** PATH, TRAIL (2) **:** ROAD, ROUTE **b** *dial Eng* **:** CUSTOM, HABIT **2 :** a horse that moves along at an easy pace **3** *archaic* **:** 1FOOTPAD

5**pad** \"\ *n* -s [alter. of 1*ped*] *chiefly dial* **:** BASKET

6**pad** \"\ *n* -s [imit.] **:** a soft light muffled or faintly slapping sound ⟨hear only the ~ of a thousand felt soles on the pavement —James Cameron⟩

7**pad** \"\ *n* -s [prob. fr. obs. E, padlock, fr. ME] **1 a :** the socket of a brace into which the bit is inserted **b :** a tool handle into which tools of various sizes or kinds may be inserted **2 :** a chock or block to space and hold work for tooling

pa·dauk *or* **pa·douk** \pə'dau̇k\ *n* -s [native name in Burma] **1 :** any of several trees of the genus *Pterocarpus* that yield a reddish wood resembling mahogany: as **a :** AFRICAN PADAUK **b :** ANDAMAN PADAUK **c :** BARWOOD **d :** BURMA PADAUK **2 :** the wood of a padauk tree

pa·daung \pə'dau̇ŋ\ *n, pl* **padaung** *or* **padaungs** *usu cap* **:** KARENNI

padcloth \'=,=\ *n* **:** SADDLECLOTH

pad·da \'padə\ *n, cap* [NL, fr. Jav] **:** a genus of birds consisting of the Java sparrow

padded *adj* [fr. past part. of 2*pad*] **:** furnished with or as if with a pad or padding ⟨soundless caravans of camels, swaying with their ~ feet across the desert —L.P.Smith⟩ **:** CUSHIONY ⟨the ~, somber, luxurious hotel we had just left —Christopher Isherwood⟩

padded soap *n* **:** FILLED SOAP

1**pad·der** \'padə(r)\ *n* -s [4*pad* + -*er*] *archaic* **:** 1FOOTPAD

2**padder** \"\ *n* -s [2*pad* + -*er*] **1 :** a person or a machine that pads: as **a** (1) **:** a worker that makes sheets of paper into pads (2) **:** a worker that places ordered tobacco leaves in boxes or on a conveyor for removal of stems (3) **:** a worker that sews padding material into garments (as coats) **b :** a dyeing machine consisting of rolls mounted over a trough for padding fabrics **2 :** a radio set circuit element (as a condenser) used to adjust the tuning of a circuit (as on the local oscillator of a superheterodyne receiver)

paddier *comparative of* PADDY

paddies *pl of* PADDY

paddiest *superlative of* PADDY

padding *n* -s [fr. gerund of 2*pad*] **:** material with which something is padded **:** WADDING, STUFFING

padding stitch *n* **1 :** a stitch used as a foundation for another stitch **2 :** a diagonal basting stitch for holding padding in place

1**pad·dle** \'padᵊl\ *n* -s [ME *padell*] **1** *dial Eng* **:** SPUD 2 **2 a :** a

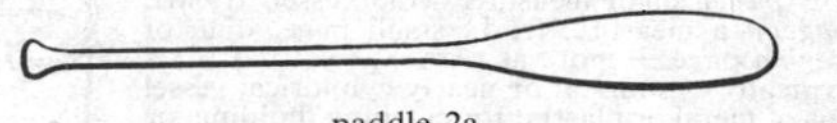
paddle 2a

rather short light wooden pole with a broad fairly flat blade at one end or sometimes at both ends that is used for propelling and steering or stopping a canoe or other similar small light craft, that is not designed for use with an oarlock, and that is grasped and dipped vertically or nearly vertically into the water so that the blade can be pushed against and raised from the water or otherwise manipulated so as to propel or steer or stop **b :** something (as the flipper of a seal) used for propulsion through the water and suggestive of a paddle in appearance or function **c :** the arm or blade of a semaphore signal **3 :** an implement suggestive in shape of a paddle: as **a** (1) **:** a long metal implement used for stirring or mixing something (as molten ore materials in glass manufacture) (2) **:** a small light flat wooden implement used esp. for working butter **b :** an implement of moderate length used for beating clothes being washed by hand **c :** a flat rather heavy usu. wooden instrument used for administering physical punishment **4 a :** one of the broad boards at the circumference of a paddle wheel or waterwheel **b :** PADDLE WHEEL **5 a :** a small gate in a sluice or lock gate to let water in or out **b :** a sliding panel that regulates the quantity of grain running out of a hopper

2**paddle** \"\ *vb* **paddled; paddled; paddling** \-d(ᵊ)liŋ\ **paddles** *vi* **1 a** (1) **:** to go along the surface of water or through water by or as if by using a paddle ⟨*paddling* down the stream in a canoe⟩ (2) **:** to swim along easily or gently or with movements suggestive of one using a paddle **b :** to row a boat easily or gently ⟨were in no hurry so they just *paddled* along⟩ **2 :** to go along the surface of water by means of a paddle wheel ⟨watched the showboat *paddling* slowly toward the shore⟩ **3 :** to throw the feet to the side in running **~** *vt* **1 a :** to propel by or as if by a paddle ⟨*paddled* the little boat closer to shore⟩ **b :** to transport in a canoe or other similar light craft by using a paddle ⟨*paddled* us over to the other side of the river⟩ **2 a :** to beat or stir with a paddle or paddle wheel (as in washing, dyeing, puddling) **b :** to punish by or as if by beating with a paddle **:** THRASH, THWACK, SPANK ⟨her mother *paddled* her for not keeping quiet⟩ **3 :** to treat (hides or skins being processed for leather) in a vat equipped with a paddle wheel — **paddle one's own canoe :** to get along by one's own efforts ⟨told him that he could expect no more help and would have to *paddle his own canoe*⟩

3**paddle** \"\ *n* -s [2*paddle*] **:** the action of paddling ⟨returned to shore after a brief ~ on the lake⟩

4**paddle** \"\ *vb* **paddled; paddled; paddling; paddles** [origin unknown] *vi* **1 :** to move about or dabble (as in shallow water) making light splashes (as with the hands or feet) **:** wade about or play about splashing lightly and dabbling ⟨watched the children gleefully *paddling* in the rain puddles⟩ ⟨sat on the edge of the boat and *paddled* in the water with her feet⟩ **2** *archaic* **:** to keep touching something lightly with the fingers **:** toy with or pat or stroke something in an apparently idle or purposeless way ⟨let her keep *paddling* on with his hand —W.M.Thackeray⟩ **3 :** to walk with short often hesitant or somewhat unsteady steps like those of a child **:** TODDLE ⟨his little daughter *paddled* up to him and kissed him⟩ **4 :** to throw the feet to the side in running; *specif* **:** DISH 2 **~** *vt, dial Eng* **:** to tread upon **:** TRAMPLE

5**paddle** \"\ *n* -s [origin unknown] **:** LUMPFISH

paddle ball *n* **:** a game resembling squash racquets played in a four-wall handball court using a tennis ball and a wooden paddle

paddle beam *n* **:** one of two bracket-shaped beams projecting one before and one abaft the paddle wheel and helping to support the paddle box of a ship

paddleboard \'==,=\ *n* **:** a long narrow extremely buoyant board with rounded bow and pointed stern used esp. for surf-riding or propelled with arm strokes and used in rescuing swimmers

paddle box *n* **:** a structure enclosing the upper part of a paddle wheel of a ship

paddlefish \'==,=\ *n* **:** either of two freshwater relict fishes that are the only surviving members of the family Polyodontidae: **a :** an American fish (*Polyodon spathula*) found in the Mississippi river and its tributaries, having a long spatula-shaped snout, smooth skin, heterocercal tail, and long gill rakers, attaining a length of four feet or more, and having flesh which though coarse is used as food and roe that is made into caviar — called also *duckbill* **b :** a closely related Chinese fish (*Psephurus gladius*) having a narrower snout

paddlefoot \'==,=\ *n, pl* **paddlefeet 1** *slang* **:** INFANTRYMAN **2** *slang* **:** an air force personnel member that lacks distinctive rating and that is usu. occupied with ground duties

pad·dler \'pad(ᵊ)lə(r)\ *n* -s [2*paddle* + -*er*] **1 :** one that paddles **2 :** PADDLE STEAMER

paddle shaft *n* **:** a shaft carrying a paddle wheel

paddle steamer *n* **:** a steamer propelled by a paddle wheel

paddle tennis *n* **:** a game resembling tennis and played with a wooden paddle and sponge rubber ball over a low net on a court whose dimensions are one half those of a lawn tennis court

paddle tumbler *n* **:** a revolving drum fitted inside with paddles or round pins and used to keep a liquid in motion in tanning, dyeing, and other similar processes

paddle-turn \'==,=\ *n* **:** a ballroom step used in turning

paddle wheel *n* **1 :** a wheel used to propel a steamship and orig. having long paddles arranged about a hub or shaft end but later having floats or boards on its circumference and revolving in a vertical plane parallel to the ship's length **2 :** a wheel with paddles that is used in a vat and that revolves and keeps hides or skins in motion while they are soaking in the course of being processed for leather

paddle-wheeler \'==,==\ *n* **:** PADDLE STEAMER

paddlewood \'==,=\ *n* **:** the tough elastic wood of a tropical So. American tree (*Aspidosperma excelsa*) from whose fluted trunk paddles and rollers are made

1**pad·dock** \'padək, -dēk\ *also* **pad·dow** \-də\ *n* -s [ME *paddok*, fr. *pad, pade* toad + -*ok* -ock; akin to ON *padda* toad, MLG *padde, pedde* toad, and perh. to OE *pæth* path — more at PATH] **1** *chiefly dial* **:** FROG **2** *chiefly dial* **:** TOAD

2**paddock** \"\ *n* -s [alter. of *parrock*] **1 a** *chiefly Brit* **:** a small area (as a field) often enclosed and typically adjoining or near a building (as a house or stable) and often used for a pasture **b** *Austral* **:** an often extensive area (as of grassland) usu. fenced in and often used as a pasture **2 a :** a turfed enclosure where horses are kept (as on a stud farm) **b :** an enclosure where racehorses are saddled and paraded before a race **3 :** a space or platform near the mouth of a shaft or excavation for temporary storage of ore or wash dirt

3**paddock** \"\ *vt* -ED/-ING/-S **1 a :** to put (an animal) into an enclosed area (as a field) **b :** to shut up in or as if in an enclosed area **2 :** to store (as ore) temporarily in a space or on a platform near the mouth of a mining shaft or excavation

pad·dock-ride *or* **pad·dock-rod** \'==,=\ *n* [1*paddock* + *ride, rod*, alter. of E dial. *rud* toad spawn] *dial Brit* **:** frog or toad spawn

paddock-stool \'==,=\ *n, chiefly Scot* **:** TOADSTOOL

1**pad·dy** *also* **padi** \'padē, -di\ *n, pl* **paddies** *also* **padis** [Malay *padi*] **1** *or* **paddy rice :** RICE; *esp* **:** threshed unmilled rice **2** *or* **paddy field :** a heavily irrigated or lightly flooded piece of land (as lowland) in which rice is grown **:** a wet field used for growing rice — called also *rice paddy*

2**paddy** \"\ *also* **paddybird** \'==,=\ *n* -ES **1 :** JAVA SPARROW **2 :** one of several small herons of the subcontinent of India **3 :** SHEATHBILL **4** [3*paddy*] **:** RUDDY DUCK

3**paddy** \"\ *n* -ES [fr. *Paddy*, common nickname among the Irish for the name *Patrick*] **1** *usu cap, slang* **:** IRISHMAN **2** *slang* **:** POLICEMAN, COP

4**paddy** \"\ *adj, usu* -ER/-EST [1*pad* + -*y* (adj. suffix)] **:** resembling a pad (as in thickness, firm resiliency)

5**paddy** \"\ *n* -ES [1*pad* + -*y* (dim. suffix)] **:** HAND; *esp* **:** a baby's or child's hand

paddy blast *n* **:** blast (sense 4b) of the rice plant

pad dyeing *n* **:** a process of dyeing fabrics by passing the fabrics between rollers that apply the dyestuff

paddy's hurricane *n, usu cap P* [3*paddy*] **:** a dead calm on the sea

paddy's lucerne *or* **paddy lucerne** *n* [3*paddy*] *Austral* **:** QUEENSLAND HEMP

paddy wagon *n* [prob. fr. 3*paddy*] **:** PATROL WAGON

1**paddywhack** \'==,=\ *n* [3*paddy* + *whack*] **1** *often cap, slang* **:** IRISHMAN **2** *or* **paddy** *dial chiefly Eng* **:** a state of fuming rage **:** FURY, TEMPER ⟨don't be silly and get in a *paddy* about nothing —Compton Mackenzie⟩ **3 :** THRASHING, SPANKING, PADDLING **4 :** RUDDY DUCK

2**paddywhack** \"\ *vt* **:** THRASH, SPANK, PADDLE

pad·e·melon *also* **pad·dy·melon** \'padē,melən\ *n, pl* **pademelon** *also* **paddymelon** *or* **pademelons** [alter. (influence of *melon*) of earlier *paddymalla*, fr. native name in Australia] **:** any of several small usu. more or less reddish or chestnut brown wallabies with extensive distribution in Australia and New Guinea

pad eye *n* [1*pad*] **:** a small usu. round opening that is in an edgewise projection of a plate welded or otherwise fixed to a part of a ship's structure and that is used like an eyebolt as a catch (as for hooks) or other point of attachment (as for rigging); *also* **:** a ring or similar projection forming part of and extending edgewise from a plate on a ship's structure and used in the same way

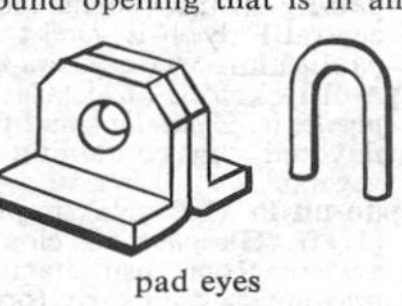
pad eyes

padfoot \'=,=\ *n, pl* **padfeet** [4*pad* + *foot*] **1** *dial Eng* **:** GOBLIN — compare BARGHEST, BOOGEYMAN **2** *dial Eng* **:** 1FOOTPAD

pad foot *r* [1*pad*] **:** CLUB FOOT

padge \'paj\ *also* **padge owl** *n* -s [alter. of *madge*] **:** BARN OWL

pad hook *n* **:** a fishhook having a flattened and enlarged shank instead of an eye

pa·di·na \pə'dīnə\ *n, cap* [NL] **:** a genus of fan-shaped somewhat leathery brown algae (family Dictyotaceae) that are found in warm seas

pa·di·shah \'pädə,shä\ *n* -s [Per *pādshāh*, fr. MPer *pātakhshāh*, fr. OPer *pati* + *xshay-* to rule; akin to Av *xshayeti* he rules — more at CHECK] **1 :** a chief ruler **:** SOVEREIGN; *esp* **:** the shah of Iran **2 :** a powerful important personage **:** MOGUL ⟨a conference of movie ~s⟩

1**pad·lock** \'pad,läk\ *n* [ME *padlok*, prob. fr. *pad* padlock + *lok* lock — more at LOCK] **:** a removable lock with a hinged or pivoted or sometimes sliding shackle that can be opened so as to pass through an eye (as of a staple, ring, link) and then closed so that the entire device hangs suspended and holds something (as a hasp) securely fastened

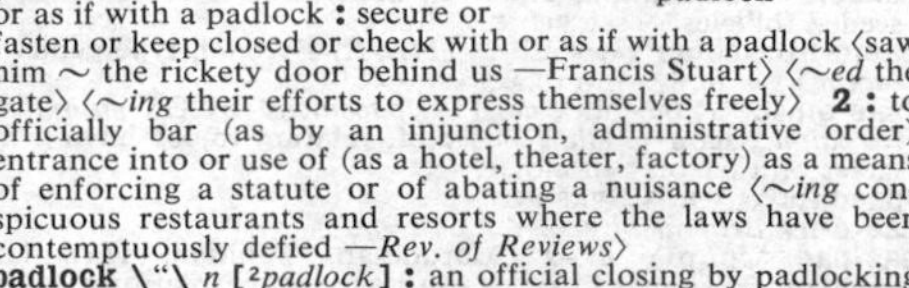
padlock

2**padlock** \"\ *vt* **1 :** to lock with or as if with a padlock **:** secure or fasten or keep closed or check with or as if with a padlock ⟨saw him ~ the rickety door behind us —Francis Stuart⟩ ⟨~*ed* the gate⟩ ⟨~*ing* their efforts to express themselves freely⟩ **2 :** to officially bar (as by an injunction, administrative order) entrance into or use of (as a hotel, theater, factory) as a means of enforcing a statute or of abating a nuisance ⟨~*ing* conspicuous restaurants and resorts where the laws have been contemptuously defied —*Rev. of Reviews*⟩

3**padlock** \"\ *n* [2*padlock*] **:** an official closing by padlocking ⟨the injunction is then carried through to final order and a ~ for one year is attempted —*U.S. Daily*⟩

pad·nag \'pad,nag\ *n* [4*pad* + *nag*] **:** 4PAD 2

padouk *var of* PADAUK

pa·dre \'pä(,)drā, 'pá(-\ *n* -s [Sp or It or Pg, fr. LL *pater* bishop, abbot, fr. L, father — more at FATHER] **1 a :** a Christian clergyman; *esp* **:** PRIEST **b :** a Christian monk usu. ordained to the priesthood — often used as a title or as a mode of address **2 :** a military chaplain

pad roll *n* **:** BLANKET ROLL 2

pa·dro·ne \pə'drōnā\ *n, pl* **padrones** \-āz\ *also* **padro·ni** \-nē\ [It, fr. L *patronus* — more at PATRON] **1 a :** PATRON, MASTER **b :** BOSS, CHIEF ⟨racketeering and shakedowns by the local ~s of the waterfront —*New Republic*⟩ **c :** INNKEEPER, LANDLORD **2 :** one that secures employment often under contract for immigrant usu. unskilled workers esp. of Italian extraction and that also acts as banker and commissary for them with the overall purpose of profit by exploitation

pad room *n* [so called fr. the fact that performing horses used to be padded and rigged in the same room] **:** a dressing room for circus performers

pads *pl of* PAD, *pres 3d sing of* PAD

pad saw *n* [7*pad*] **:** a small compass saw

padstone \'=,=\ *n* **:** a stone template fixed in a wall to support the end of a girder or roof truss

pad·ua \'pajəwə\ *adj; usu cap* [fr. *Padua*, Italy] **:** of or from the city of Padua, Italy **:** of the kind or style prevalent in Padua **:** PADUAN

paduakan *var of* PEDIWAK

1**pad·u·an** \'pajəwən\ *adj, usu cap* [*Padua*, Italy + E -*an* (adj. suffix)] **:** of, relating to, or characteristic of the city of Padua, Italy

2**paduan** \"\ *n* -s *cap* [*Padua*, Italy + E -*an* (n. suffix)] **:** a native or inhabitant of Padua

pad·u·a·soy \'pajəwə,sȯi\ *n* -s [by folk etymology (influence of *Padua*, city in northeast Italy) fr. earlier *poudesoy*, fr. F *pou-de-soie*] **1 :** a rich heavy corded silk fabric for clothing and upholstery **2 :** a garment made of paduasoy

pa·du·ca *or* **pa·du·cah** \pə'd(y)ükə\ *n, pl* **paduca** *or* **paducas** *or* **paducah** *or* **paducahs** *usu cap* [F *Padouca*, of Siouan origin; prob. akin to Dakota *pa-hdó-ka* to pierce, bore] **:** an Amerind people of the southern Great Plains: as **a :** COMANCHE **b :** APACHE

pa·dus \'pādəs\ *n, cap* [NL, fr. Gk *pados*, a tree; prob. akin to Gk *pēdos*, a tree, *pidyein* to gush forth — more at FAT] *in some classifications* **:** a genus of shrubs and trees (family Rosaceae) of the north temperate zone that are now usu. included in the genus *Prunus* from which they are distinguished chiefly by racemose flowers

1**pae·an** *also* **pe·an** \'pēən\ *n* -s [L *paean*, hymn of thanksgiving esp. addressed to Apollo, fr. Gk *paian, paiōn*, fr. *Paian, Paiōn*, epithet by which Apollo was invoked in the hymn] **1 :** a surging joyously exultant song or hymn (as of praise, tribute, thanksgiving, triumph) ⟨unite their voices in a great ~ to liberty —Edward Sackville-West & Desmond Shawe-Taylor⟩ **2 :** an exultant outburst ⟨a great cheer . . . rose in a wild ~ of frenzy —Donn Byrne⟩ **3 :** PAEON

2**paean** \"\ *vt* -ED/-ING/-S **:** to sing or otherwise express in or as if in a paean ⟨~*ed* the virtues of the poor and lowly —S.H. Adams⟩

paed- *or* **paedo-** *or* **ped-** *or* **pedo-** *also* **paid-** *or* **paido-** *comb form* [Gk *paid-, paido-*, fr. *paid-, pais* child, boy — more at FEW] **:** child ⟨*paedo*morphism⟩ ⟨*paedo*baptism⟩ ⟨*pedo*philia⟩ **:** offspring ⟨*paedo*genesis⟩

paedagogy *var of* PEDAGOGY

paederasty *var of* PEDERASTY

paediatric *var of* PEDIATRIC

paedicatio *var of* PEDICATIO

paedobaptism *var of* PEDOBAPTISM

pae·dog·a·mous \pē'dägəməs\ *adj* [*paed-* + *-gamous*] **:** of, relating to, or reproducing by paedogamy

pae·dog·a·my *also* **pe·dog·a·my** \-mē\ *n* -ES [ISV *paed-* + *-gamy*] **:** mutual fertilization of gametes ultimately derived from the same parent cell or gametangium

pae·do·genesis *also* **pe·do·genesis** \,pēdō+\ *n* [NL, fr. *paed-* + *genesis*] **:** reproduction by young or larval animals **:** NEOTENY — compare PROGENESIS

pae·do·ge·net·ic \'==jə'ned·ik\ *or* **pae·do·gen·ic** \'=='jenik\ *adj* [*paedogenesis* + *-etic* or *-ic*] **:** of, relating to, or characterized by paedogenesis

pae·do·mor·phic *also* **pedomorphic** \'=='mȯrfik\ *adj* [*paedomorphosis, pedomorphosis* + E *-ic*] **1 :** of, relating to, or involving paedomorphosis or paedomorphism ⟨~ evolution⟩ **2** [*paed-* + *-morphic*] **:** resembling a child or something characteristic of a child ⟨a ~ outlook⟩

pae·do·mor·phism *or* **pe·do·mor·phism** \,=='=,fizəm\ *n* -s [*paed-* + *-morphism*] **1 :** retention in the adult of infantile or juvenile characters **2 :** PAEDOMORPHOSIS

pae·do·mor·pho·sis *also* **pe·do·mor·pho·sis** \,=='mȯrfəsəs *sometimes* -,mȯr'fōs-\ *n, pl* **paedomorpho·ses** *also* **pedomorpho·ses** \-,sēz\ [NL, fr. *paed-* + *-morphosis*] **:** phylogenetic change involving retention of juvenile characters by adult individuals and typically accompanied by increased capacity for further change and indicative of a potential for further evolution — compare FETALIZATION, GERONTOMORPHOSIS

pae·do·mor·phy \'==,mȯrfē\ *n* -ES [*paed-* + *-morphy*] **:** PAEDOMORPHISM

paedophilia *var of* PEDOPHILIA

pae·do·tribe \'pēdə,trīb\ *n* -s [Gk *paidotribēs*, fr. *paid-* +

-*tribēs* (fr. *tribein* to rub) — more at THROW] **:** a trainer in gymnastics often represented in ancient Greek art as supervising the exercises of young athletes

1pae·lig·ni·an \pē'lignēən\ *n* -s *cap* [L *Paeligni*, a people of central Italy + E *-ian*] **:** a Sabellian dialect

2paelignian \"\ *adj, usu cap* **:** of or relating to Paelignian

pa·el·la \pə'elə\ *n* -s [Catal, lit., metal pot, frying pan, fr. MF *paelle*, fr. L *patella* small pan — more at PATELLA] **:** a saffron-flavored stew containing rice, chicken, seafood, and various vegetables

pae·nu·la \'pēnyələ\ *n, pl* **paenu·lae** \-,lē, -lī\ *or* **paenulas** [L, fr. Gk *phainolē* cloak] **1 :** a long sleeveless cloak of ancient Rome usu. having a hood and sometimes a front opening **2 :** an early form of chasuble

paen·ungulata \(')pēn+\ *n pl, cap* [NL, fr. L *paene* nearly, almost + NL *Ungulata;* so called fr. their position in the evolutionary scale] *in some classifications* **:** a major division of eutherian mammals comprising the extinct orders Pantodonta, Dinocerata, Pyrotheria, and Embrithopoda together with the surviving orders Proboscidea, Hyracoidea, and Sirenia

1paen·ungulate \(')pēn+\ *adj* [NL *Paenungulata*] **:** of or relating to the Paenungulata

2paenungulate \"\ *n* -s **:** a mammal of the Paenungulata

pae·on \'pēən\ *n* -s [L *paeon*, fr. Gk *paiōn* fr. *paian, paiōn*, paean — more at PAEAN] **1 :** a metrical foot of four syllables with one of the syllables long and the other three short (as in classical prosody) or with one of the syllables stressed and the other three unstressed or lesser in stress (as in English prosody) and with the long or stressed syllable varying in position from first to second or third or fourth place — called also respectively (1) *first paeon* — symbol -◡◡◡ also óooo; (2) *second paeon* — symbol ◡-◡◡ also oóoo; (3) *third paeon* — symbol ◡◡-◡ also ooóo; (4) *fourth paeon* — symbol ◡◡◡- also oooó **2 :** a verse written in paeons

pae·o·nia \pē'ōnēə\ *n, cap* [NL, fr. L, peony, fr. Gk *paiōnia*, fr. *Paiōn* Paeon, physician of the gods, its reputed discoverer] **:** a genus of perennial herbs or subshrubs (family Ranunculaceae) that are native chiefly to Europe and Asia and have thickened or tuberous roots, divided leaves, flowers often double in cultivation, and fruit consisting of several many-seeded follicles — see PEONY

pae·o·ni·a·ce·ae \=,==ˈāsē,ē\ [NL, fr. *Paeonia*, type genus + *-aceae*] *syn of* RANUNCULACEAE

1pae·on·ic \(')pē¦änik\ *adj* [LL *paeonicus*, fr. Gk *paiōnikos*, fr. *paiōn* paeon + *-ikos* -ic] **:** of, relating to, or having the meter of a paeon **:** HEMIOLIC

2paeonic \"\ *n* -s **:** PAEON

pae·o·ny *Brit var of* PEONY

pae·pae \'pī,pī\ *n* -s [Marquesan, Tahitian, Hawaiian, Samoan, & Tongan] **1 :** a usu. large stone platform (as of basalt) rising appreciably above ground level and used as the foundation for many native Polynesian houses or other buildings **2 :** a usu. extensive flagged pavement typically used in Polynesia in areas in front of some edifices (as temples)

pa·ez \pä'ez\ *n, pl* **paez** *or* **paezes** *usu cap* **1 a :** a Chibchan people of Colombia in the northwestern part of So. America **b :** a member of such people **2 :** the language of the Paez people

1pa·gan \'pāgən\ *n* -s [ME, fr. LL *paganus*, fr. L, civilian, country dweller, fr. *paganus*, adj., of the country, fr. *pagus* country, village, district; akin to L *pangere* to fix, fasten, *pacisci* to agree, contract — more at PACT] **1 :** HEATHEN 1; *esp* **:** a follower of a polytheistic religion (as in ancient Rome) **2 :** one that has little or no religion and that is marked by a frank delight in and uninhibited seeking after sensual pleasures and material goods **:** an unrestrained irreligious hedonist and materialist ⟨is a ~ of the decadence . . . takes the world with exquisite nonchalance and prefers a well-ordered dinner to a dissertation on the immortality of the soul —T.L.Peacock⟩

2pagan \"\ *adj* **:** of, relating to, or having the characteristics of pagans **:** HEATHENISH ⟨~ customs⟩ ⟨represents the earthy, ~ acceptance of life in all its sensual vulgarity —R.M.Kain⟩ ⟨the ~ concept of death and oblivion as the natural end of life —Cyril Connolly⟩ — **pa·gan·ly** *adv*

pagan cattle *n* **:** half-wild dwarf cattle kept by natives of tropical western Africa

pa·gan·dom \'pāgəndəm\ *n* -s **:** the realm of pagans **:** the pagan world **:** HEATHENDOM

paganic *adj* [LL *paganicus* of a pagan, fr. *paganus* + L *-icus* -ic] *obs* **:** PAGAN

pa·gan·ish \'pāgənish\ *adj* **:** resembling or typical of a pagan **:** rather pagan ⟨a ~ way of life⟩ — **pa·gan·ish·ly** *adv*

pa·gan·ism \-,nizəm\ *n* -s [ME *paganysme*, fr. LL *paganismus*, fr. *paganus* pagan + L *-ismus* -ism] **1 a :** pagan beliefs or practices **:** HEATHENISM ⟨its conflict with modern ~ —C.J.C. Bergendoff⟩ ⟨the rites of ~⟩ ⟨powers which they had ascribed to the gods of ~ —K.S.Latourette⟩ **b :** a particular pagan religion ⟨ancient ~s were all polytheistic, with dozens of gods arranged in complex pantheons —John Bright b.1908⟩ **2 :** the quality or state of being a pagan (as in attitude or outlook) ⟨the natural, joyous ~ of the Greeks —Hunter Mead⟩

pa·gan·i·ty \pā'ganəd·ē\ *n* -ES [LL *paganitas*, fr. *paganus* + L *-itat-, -itas* -ity] *archaic* **:** PAGANISM 2

pa·gan·ization \,pāgənə'zāshən, -,nī'z-\ *n* -s **:** the action of paganizing or condition of being paganized ⟨were shocked by their sudden ~⟩

pa·gan·ize \'==,nīz\ *vb* -ED/-ING/-s *see -ize in Explan Notes* [*pagan* + *-ize*] *vt* **:** to make pagan **:** HEATHENIZE ⟨~s everything with which she comes in contact —*Commonweal*⟩ ⟨the new *paganized* way of life —R.A.Hall b.1911⟩ ⟨denounce such *paganizing* of the faith —G.E.Wright⟩ **~** *vi* [F or ML; F *paganiser*, fr. ML *paganizare*, fr. LL to be a pagan, fr. *paganus* + *-izare* -ize] **:** to become pagan or act in a pagan manner ⟨the *paganizing* Gnostics —W.F.Albright⟩ ⟨spent a riotous week *paganizing*⟩ — **pa·gan·iz·er** \-zə(r)\ *n* -s

pa·gat·pat \pə'gat,pat\ *n* -s [native name in the Philippines] **:** a tree (*Sonneratia apetala*) growing chiefly in mangrove swamps and producing a hard wood that ranges in color from reddish brown to black and is used extensively in construction work and furniture

1page \'pāj\ *n* -s [ME, fr. OF, fr. It *paggio*, perh. fr. Gk *paidion* boy, dim. of *paid-, pais* child, boy — more at PAED-] **1 a** (1) **:** a youth being trained for the medieval rank of knight and attached for this purpose to the personal service of a knight — compare SQUIRE (2) **:** a youth employed as the personal attendant of some person of rank other than a knight esp. in the medieval period and typically holding this position so as to be trained in the usages of good society **b** — used usu. with some qualifying phrase as a title of one of several officers of a royal or princely household ⟨was chosen as a ~ of honor⟩ **c :** a young boy chosen to serve as an honorary attendant at some formal function (as a wedding) and typically acting as a trainbearer **2 a :** one that is employed in a usu. large establishment (as a club, hotel) to deliver messages, assist patrons or visitors esp. with their personal effects (as luggage), serve as a guide, or attend to other similar duties of a usu. routine nature and that is usu. dressed in livery or some similar distinctive formal uniform: as (1) *chiefly Brit* **:** BELLBOY 1 (2) **:** one employed to locate or summon individuals (as for the delivery of personal messages) usu. by walking about in the more frequented spots (as the lobby) while calling out the individual's name at regular intervals (3) **:** a theater attendant who hands out programs and does other small services for the patrons (4) **:** one that serves as a guide to visitors in a radio or television station and attends to miscellaneous light routine duties about the studio **b** (1) **:** an assistant in a library who does messenger duty or attends to other routine duties (as locating, shelving, lettering, and repairing books) (2) **:** a boy or man who does messenger duty and attends to other routine errands for Congress or some other legislative body **3 :** a track along which pallets carrying newly molded bricks are conveyed to the hack

2page \"\ *vt* -ED/-ING/-s **1 :** to wait on or attend or serve in the capacity of a page ⟨chose a new boy to ~ him⟩ **2 :** to try to locate or summon (as for the delivery of a personal message) by repeatedly calling out or relaying the name of ⟨asked the bellboy to ~ her brother⟩ ⟨said they would ~ him over the public-address system⟩

3page \"\ *n* -s [MF, fr. L *pagina;* akin to L *pangere* to fix, fasten — more at PACT] **1 a :** one of the leaves of a book, magazine, newspaper, piece of correspondence, or similar article ⟨tore one of the ~s⟩ ⟨decided to destroy the first ~ of the letter⟩ ⟨turned the ~s idly⟩ ⟨was told to leave one side of the ~ blank⟩ **b** (1) **:** a single side of one of these leaves ⟨found the item on ~ one of the newspaper⟩ ⟨asked the class to turn to the ~ with the picture on it⟩ (2) **:** a page (as in a newspaper) regularly carrying a particular feature ⟨the editorial ~⟩ or devoted to an area of special interest ⟨the amusement ~⟩ ⟨the sports ~s⟩ **c** (1) **:** the matter printed, written, drawn, or otherwise set down or reproduced on a page ⟨rapidly read through the first ten ~s⟩ ⟨could not understand a single ~⟩ (2) **:** the area bounded by the margins or edges of a page ⟨has written enough to fill about three ~s⟩ **d** (1) **:** the original setting (as of type) for a page that has been printed or is to be printed (2) **:** a plate or mold made from such a setting **2 a :** a written record **:** BOOK, WRITING ⟨the ~s of history⟩ **b :** something (as an event or sequence of events) contained in or suitable to be in a written record or report ⟨one of the brightest ~s in his life⟩ ⟨a ~ without parallel in our history⟩ **3 :** a section of a printed or written work ⟨these are among the author's best ~s⟩ ⟨the finale lacks the excitement that is proper to it, especially in the last ~s —Edward Sackville-West & Desmond Shawe-Taylor⟩ ⟨the finest ~s of the four symphonies —Edward Cushing⟩

4page \"\ *vb* -ED/-ING/-s *vt* **1 a** (1) **:** to number or otherwise mark for sequence the pages of (as a book) **:** PAGINATE — compare FOLIATE (2) **:** to check the page numbering of (as a book) so as to verify proper sequence **b :** to make up (as typeset or photocomposed matter) into pages — often used with *up* **2 :** to turn the pages of (as a book) esp. in a steady or a hasty or haphazard manner (as in reading rapidly or examining superficially) **:** riffle through **:** LEAF ⟨*paged* the book without interest⟩ **~** *vi* **:** to turn the pages of a book or magazine or similar article esp. in a steady or a hasty or haphazard manner — usu. used with *through* ⟨*paged* through the magazine impatiently⟩

1pag·eant \'pajənt\ *n* -s [ME *pagyn, pagend, padgeant*, fr. ML *pagina* scene of a play, stage, fr. L *pagina* page] **1 a** (1) *obs* **:** a scene or act of a play (as a medieval mystery play) (2) *archaic* **:** PART, ROLE **b** *obs* **:** STAGE, PLATFORM; *specif* **:** a stage or platform used for the open-air performance of medieval mystery plays and often mounted on wheels so as to be capable of being moved from place to place **2 a :** a falsely impressive display that masks lack of substance and reality **:** a mere show **:** PRETENSE ⟨saw through the hollowness, the sham, the silliness of the empty ~ in which I had always played —Oscar Wilde⟩ **b :** an ostentatious often exhibitionistic display ⟨sympathize profoundly with a poetry that doesn't make a ~ of its bleeding heart —J.L.Lowes⟩ **3 a :** SHOW, SPECTACLE, EXHIBITION ⟨a beauty ~⟩ ⟨the variegated ~ of London life —Douglas Bush⟩; *esp* **:** an elaborate usu. open-air exhibition or spectacle that is marked typically by colorful often gorgeous costuming and scenery and often by vocal and instrumental music, that consists of a series of tableaux (as representations of important events in the history of a community) or of a loosely unified drama with spoken or sung parts or of an often resplendent parade or procession usu. with showy floats and with a loosely dramatic or commemorative theme, and that is usu. presented in celebration of an event or series of events or in honor of some personage or group or of a locality by amateur actors or other amateur performers recruited from or near the locality in which it is presented **b :** a steady continuous movement of things developing or passing by in or as if in a parade or procession ⟨this exciting ~ of events —J.H. Baker⟩ ⟨watch the ~ of the world go by —Ralph Hammond-Innes⟩ **4 :** PAGEANTRY 1 ⟨for ~ of language he has had no equal in English —W.R.Thayer⟩ ⟨lacked the Roman appetite for ~ —John Buchan⟩ ⟨full of stately dignity and somber ~ —Richard Harrison⟩

2pageant \"\ *adj, archaic* **:** of, relating to, or typical of pageants or pageantry ⟨the ~ pomp of such a servile throne —John Dryden⟩

3pageant \"\ *vt* -ED/-ING/-s *archaic* **:** to surround with pageantry

pag·eant·eer \¦pajən¦ti(ə)r, -iə\ *n* -s **1 :** an actor or other performer in a pageant **2 :** one that produces or directs a pageant

pag·eant·ry \'pajən·trē, -ri\ *n* -ES [*pageant* + *-ry*] **1 :** pageants and the presentation of pageants ⟨ritual *pageantries* of the British Crown —R.B.Pearsall⟩ **2 :** colorful, rich, or splendid display **:** grand spectacle **:** gorgeous show **3 :** mere show **:** empty display ⟨was tired of pomp and ~⟩

page boy *n* [*1page*] **1 :** a boy or man serving as a page **2** *usu* **pageboy :** a woman's long often shoulder-length bob with the ends of the hair turned under so as to form a smooth roll

pageboy

page cord *n* [*3page*] **:** cord used to tie up pages of metal type matter

page gauge *n* **:** a device (as a strip of nicked metal or wood or marked paper) for measuring the vertical dimension of a page — compare LINE GAUGE

page paper *or* **page shoe** *n* **:** a strong stiff paper or card on which set and tied-up type is laid for storage

page proof *n* **:** a proof from type that has been made up into a page

pag·er \'pājə(r)\ *n* -s **1 :** one that pages; *specif* **:** an operator of a page-numbering machine **2 :** one that separates and cleans type after it has been taken from the mold

pages *pl of* PAGE, *pres 3d sing of* PAGE

pag·et·oid \'pajə,tȯid\ *adj* [*Paget's* disease + *-oid*] **:** belonging to or typical of Paget's disease ⟨~ symptoms⟩

pag·et process \'pajət-\ *n, usu cap 1st P* [origin unknown] **:** FINLAY PROCESS

paget's disease *n, usu cap P* [after Sir James *Paget* †1899 Eng. surgeon] **1 :** an eczematous inflammatory precancerous condition of the nipple and areola or rarely of other cutaneous areas **2 :** OSTEITIS DEFORMANS

-pagi *pl of* -PAGUS

pag·i·nal \'pajənəl\ *adj* [LL *paginalis*, fr. L *pagina* page + *-alis* -al — more at PAGE] **1 :** of, relating to, or referring to a page (as of a book) ⟨each subject in the index has a ~ reference to the section of the book where it is treated in full⟩ **2 :** consisting of pages; *esp* **:** consisting of one page after another ⟨a pirated edition that is a ~ reprint of the original⟩

pag·i·nary \-,nerē\ *adj* **:** PAGINAL

pag·i·nate \-,nāt, *usu* -ād.+V\ *vt* -ED/-ING/-s [L *pagina* + E *-ate*] **:** 4PAGE 1a(1)

pag·i·na·tion \,pajə'nāshən\ *n* -s [L *pagina* + E *-ation*] **1 :** the action of paging or the condition of being paged ⟨the alphabetical arrangement necessarily involved requires that a considerable number of galleys be available before final ~ —Wheeler Sammons⟩ **2 a :** the numbers or other figures or marks used to indicate the proper sequence of a set of pages (as of a book) **b** (1) **:** the number of numbered pages ⟨a catalog of new books that gives the ~ of each⟩ (2) **:** a statement of such number ⟨the book's title and author are listed but no ~ is given⟩

paging *n* -s [fr. gerund of *4page*] **:** PAGINATION

pa·gi·op·o·da \,pajē'äpədə, ,paj-\ [NL, fr. Gk *pagios* solid, firm + NL *-poda;* akin to Gk *pēgnynai* to fix, fasten — more at PACT] *syn of* CRYPTOCERATA

pa·gle \'pāgəl\ *var of* PAIGLE

pagne \'pän'\ *n* -s [F, fr. Sp *paño* cloth, fr. L *pannus* — more at VANE] **:** a native costume worn esp. in Africa and consisting typically of a long rectangular often brightly colored or decorated piece of cloth that is wrapped tightly about the torso with the ends usu. falling free or that is used as a loincloth or undergarment

pagod \'pagəd, pə'gäd\ *n* -s [Pg *pagode* — more at PAGODA] **1** *archaic* **:** PAGODA **2 a :** an image of a Far Eastern deity **:** IDOL **b** *archaic* **:** 1GOD 1,3,4

pa·go·da \pə'gōdə\ *n* -s [Pg *pagode* oriental idol, temple, fr. a Dravidian source, fr. Skt *bhagavatī*, epithet of Hindu goddesses, fem. of *bhagavat* blessed, possessing good fortune — more at BHAGAVAT] **1 a :** a Far Eastern structure resembling a tower of several stories that is often richly decorated and typically has projecting concavely curved roofs at the division of each story that terminate in sharp points turned upward but sometimes has a simple pyramidal outline and that is erected usu. as a temple or memorial or edifice built out of personal piety either in isolation or as an adjunct to other usu. sacred architecture **b :** a small often ornamental structure (as a summer-house) resembling or suggestive of a pagoda in outline **2 :** a gold or sometimes silver coin used in the subcontinent of India up to the second decade of the 19th century

pagoda 1a

pagoda dogwood *also* **pagoda cornel** *n* **:** a tall shrub (*Cornus alternifolia*) that has the branches arranged in horizontal tiers and flat clusters of white flowers followed by blue fruits

pagoda tree *n* **:** any of several trees of erect habit and conical form suggestive of a pagoda: as **a :** JAPANESE PAGODA TREE **b** *India* **:** BANYAN **c** (1) **:** a frangipani (*Plumeria acutifolia*) of India (2) **:** a frangipani (*Plumeria alba*) of the West Indies

pag·o·dite \'pagə,dīt, pə'gō,dīt\ *or* **pagoda stone** *n* -s [F *pagodite*, fr. *pagode* pagoda (fr. Pg) + *-ite;* so called from its use for carving miniature pagodas] **:** AGALMATOLITE

pag·o·scope \'pagə,skōp\ *n* [Gk *pagos* frost + E *-scope;* akin to Gk *pēgnynai* to fix, fasten together — more at PACT] **:** a device for showing at a glance whether the prevailing dew point is above or below freezing **:** HYGRODEIK

pagri *var of* PUGGAREE

pa·grus \'pāgrəs\ *n* [NL, fr. L, sea bream — more at PARGO] **1** *cap* **:** a genus of sea breams of the family Sparidae **2** -ES **:** PORGY 1a

pa·gu·ma \pə'gyümə\ *n, cap* [NL] **:** a genus of palm civets of southeastern Asia related to civets of the genus *Paradoxurus* but having the tail unmarked by rings

pa·gu·ri·an \pə'gyürēən\ *n* -s [NL *Pagurus* + E *-ian*] **:** a hermit crab of the genus *Pagurus*

pa·gu·ri·dae \-rə,dē\ *n pl, cap* [NL, fr. *Pagurus*, type genus + *-idae*] **:** a cosmopolitan family of anomuran crustaceans that are related to the purse crabs and comprise the typical hermit crabs — compare PARAPAGURIDAE

pa·gu·rus \-rəs\ *n* [NL, fr. L, crab, fr. Gk *pagouros*, fr. *pagos* rock + *-uros* -urus; akin to Gk *pēgnynai* to fix, fasten — more at PACT] **1** *cap* **:** a large cosmopolitan genus (the type of the family Paguridae) of hermit crabs **2** -ES **:** KABURI

-pa·gus \pəgəs\ *n comb form, pl* **-pagi** [NL, fr. Gk *pagos* something fixed, rock, frost — more at PAGOSCOPE] **:** monster with a (specified) type of fixation ⟨craniopagus⟩

1pah *an energetically released p-sound, often followed by any of several vowel or consonant sounds; often read as* 'pä *or* 'pa\ *interj* — used typically to express disdain or contempt or disgust

2pah *var of* PA

pa·ha \pä'hä\ *n, pl* **paha** *or* **pahas** [Dakota *pahá* hill] **:** a hill or ridge of glacial origin with a capping of loess found esp. in the northeastern part of the state of Iowa

pa·ha·ri \pə'härē\ *n, pl* **pahari** *or* **paharis** *usu cap* [Hindi *pahārī* mountaineer, fr. *pahār* mountain] **1 a :** one of several chiefly hill peoples of the northeastern part of the subcontinent of India south and west of the Ganges river **b :** a member of one of these peoples **2 a :** a group of Indic languages or dialects used by the Pahari peoples **b :** one of the languages or dialects of this group

pa·ha·ria \pə'härēə\ *n, pl* **paharia** *or* **paharias** *usu cap* **:** PAHARI 1

pa·hau·tea \,pä,hau̇'tāə\ *n* -s [Maori] **:** a New Zealand cedar (*Libocedrus bidwillii*) with 4-sided ultimate branches

pa·hi \pə'hē\ *n* -s [Tahitian] **:** a large seagoing Polynesian canoe or ship often consisting of two connected hulls

1pah·la·vi \'pälə(,)vē\ *also* **peh·le·vi** \'pele(,)vē\ *n* -s *cap* [Per *pahlawī*, fr. *Pahlav*, fr. MPer, alter. of OPer *Parthava-* Parthia] **1 :** the Iranian language of Sassanid Persia **2 :** a script used for writing Pahlavi

2pahlavi \"\ *or* **pahlevi** \"\ *n, pl* **pahlavi** *or* **pahlavis** *or* **pahlevi** *or* **pahlevis** [Per *pahlawī*, fr. Riza Shah *Pahlawi* (Pahlavi) †1944 Shah of Iran] **1 :** a gold coin of Iran first issued in 1927 with a value of 20 rials and in 1932 with a value of 100 rials **2 :** a unit of value based on the value of one pahlavi

pah·mi \'pämē\ *n, pl* **pahmi** *or* **pahmis** [origin unknown] **1 a :** BOBAC **b :** FERRET-BADGER **2 :** the fur of the bobac or of the ferret-badger

pa·ho \'pä,hō, -hü\ *also* **ba·ho** \'bä-\ *n* -s [Hopi *páaho*] **:** a Hopi Indian plumed prayer stick

pa·hoe·hoe \pə'hōē,hōē\ *n* -s [Hawaiian *pāhoehoe*] **:** cooled hard lava marked by a smooth often billowy shiny surface — contrasted with *aa*

pa·houin \(')pä¦wan\ *n, pl* **pahouin** *or* **pahouins** *usu cap* **:** 4FANG 1

pa·hua \pə'hüə\ *n, pl* **pahua** *or* **pahuas** [Marquesan] **:** GIANT CLAM

pa·hu·tan \pə'hü,tän\ *also* **pa·ho** \'pä(,)hō\ *n* -s [Tag *pahútan, páho*] **:** a Philippine mango (*Mangifera altissima*) with an edible fruit that is often pickled and a dark brown variegated wood used esp. in veneers and cabinetwork

pai·che \'pī(,)chā, -,chē\ *n* -s [AmerSp, prob. fr. AmerInd] **:** PIRARUCU

paid \'pād\ *adj* [fr. past part. of *pay*] **1 a :** receiving pay ⟨is a ~ official of the organization⟩ **b :** marked by the reception of pay esp. in an advance lump sum ⟨has a good job and a ~ vacation⟩ **2 :** that has been cashed ⟨a ~ check⟩ **3 :** that has been or will be paid for ⟨a ~ political announcement⟩

paid- *or* **paido-** — see PAED-

pai·deia \pī'dāə\ *n* -s [G, fr. Gk, education, culture, fr. *paideuein* to educate (fr. *paid-, pais* child) + *-ia* -y — more at FEW] **1 :** training of the physical and mental faculties in such a way as to produce a broad enlightened mature outlook harmoniously combined with maximum cultural development ⟨the long and noble tradition of ~, which made it impossible for a Greek or Roman to write a worthy book merely to record facts —Gilbert Highet⟩ **2 :** the ideal development envisioned or attained by paideia

paid-in surplus \'=¦=-\ *n* [fr. past part. of *pay in*] **:** surplus resulting from sale or exchange of capital stock at amounts in excess of par or stated value — compare CAPITAL SURPLUS

paid-up \'=¦=\ *adj* [fr. past part. of *pay up*] **:** that has satisfied an indicated or implied financial obligation ⟨facilities of the club are granted only to *paid-up* members⟩

paid-up addition *n* **:** addition to an existing insurance policy by using the annual dividend allotment to buy more insurance

paige·ite \'pā,jīt\ *n* -s [Sidney *Paige* b1880 Am. geologist + *-ite*] **:** a mineral $(Fe,Mg)FeBO_5$ consisting of borate of iron and magnesium in fibrous aggregates of coal-black crystals

pai·gle \'pāgəl\ *n* -s [origin unknown] *dial Eng* **:** one of several plants: as **a :** COWSLIP **b :** OXLIP

pai-hua \'bī'hwä\ *n* -s [Chin *pai*² *hua*⁴, lit., plain speech, fr. *pai*² white, plain + *hua*⁴ speech] **:** a form of written Chinese based on modern colloquial — compare WEN-LI, WEN-YEN

paik \'pāk\ *vt* -ED/-ING/-s [origin unknown] *dial Brit* **:** to strike hard and repeatedly **:** PUMMEL

1pail \'pāl, *esp before pause or consonant* -āəl\ *n* -s [ME *payle*, *paille* (infl. by MF *paelle* metal pot), prob. fr. OE *pægel* small measure, wine vessel, fr. ML *pagella* a measure, fr. L, small page, dim. of *pagina* page — more at PAELLA, PAGE] **1 a :** a typically cylindrical or nearly cylindrical vessel (as of metal or plastic) for catching, holding, or carrying liquids or solids and usu. having a bail handle or other handle and sometimes having a removable cover **:** BUCKET — often used in combination with a term suggesting the function ⟨milk ~⟩ ⟨lunch ~⟩ ⟨ice ~⟩ **b :** a usu. tapered or cylindrical shipping container (as of steel or fiber) used esp. for ice cream and other moist foods and having an average capacity of from one to twelve gallons **2 :** the quantity that a pail contains **:** PAILFUL

pail 1a

2pail \"\ *vt* -ED/-ING/-s *North* **:** MILK 1

³**pail** \"\ *vt* -ED/-ING/-S [origin unknown] *dial Eng* : BEAT, THRASH

pail·ful \'ˌ,fu̇l\ *n, pl* **pailfuls** *also* **pails·ful** \-l,fu̇lz, -lz,fu̇l\ : PAIL 2

pail·lasse \(')pal¦(y)as, ¦palē¦as, (')pal¦yas\ *n* -S [F, fr. *paille* straw, fr. L *palea* chaff, straw — more at PALLET] : PALLIASSE

pail·las·son \¦pīə¦sōⁿ\ *n* -S [F, straw mat, fr. *paillasse*] : coarsely woven natural or synthetic straw used for hats

paille finne \(')pī¦fēn, -fin\ *n* [modif. of Amer F *paille fine*, lit., fine straw] : MAIDEN CANE

pail·lette *also* **pai·lette** \(')pī¦(y)et, (')pä¦yet, (')pa¦(y)et, pə'let\ *n* -S [F, fr. *paille* + *-ette*] **1 a** : one of usu. several or many small shiny objects (as spangles, sequins, beads, jewels) applied in small loosely designed clusters as a decorative trimming (as on women's clothing or accessories or on theatrical costumes) **b** : a trimming made of paillettes **2** : a fabric (as of silk) so woven or treated as to give a shiny spangled effect

pail·lett·ed \-ed·əd\ *adj* : trimmed with paillettes ⟨~ gloves⟩

pail·lon \(')pī¦(y)ōⁿ, (')pä¦yōⁿ\ *n* -S [F, metallic foil, handful of straw, fr. *paille*] : a thin sheet of usu. fine metallic foil (as of silver or gold) used esp. in enameling and gilding and often overlaid with a translucent material so as to form a decorative feature

pai-lou *also* **pai-loo** \'pī'lō\ *n, pl* **pai-lou** *or* **pai-lous** [Chin *p'ai²-lou²*, fr. *p'ai²* tablet + *lou²* tower] : a usu. elaborate Chinese commemorative archway erected in honor of someone highly esteemed (as for virtue) and consisting typically of four heavy square pillars topped with horizontal crossbeams and often buttressed with conventionalized lions and having an incised memorial tablet placed against or near the center crossbeam — compare TORAN, TORII

pai-lou

¹**pain** \'pān\ *n* -S [ME *peyne, paine*, fr. OF *peine*, fr. L *poena* penalty, punishment, fr. Gk *poinē* penalty, payment; akin to Gk *tinein* to pay, *tērein* to guard, *timē* price, value, honor, Skt *cayate* he punishes] **1 pains** *pl* : PUNISHMENTS — now used chiefly in the phrase *pains and penalties* ⟨passing acts of attainder and of *pains* and penalties —T.E.May⟩ ⟨there was the principle that civil courts may not add to the *pains* and penalties of crimes —B.N.Cardozo⟩ **2 a** : a state of physical or mental lack of well-being or physical or mental uneasiness that ranges from mild discomfort or dull distress to acute often unbearable agony, may be generalized or localized, and is the consequence of being injured or hurt physically or mentally or of some derangement of or lack of equilibrium in the physical or mental functions (as through disease), and that usu. produces a reaction of wanting to avoid, escape, or destroy the causative factor and its effects ⟨was in constant ~⟩ ⟨her ~, which had been merely a dull ache, was suddenly as keen as if a blade had been driven into her wound —Ellen Glasgow⟩ ⟨perhaps all physical existence is a weary ~ to man —T.E.Lawrence⟩ **b** : a sensation or feeling (as a sharp twinge, dull ache, generalized sense of physical or mental distress) or a complex of sensations or feelings that are produced by such a state or that are produced by some other factor either in isolation or in succession ⟨had no ~⟩ ⟨the ~ of a twisted ankle⟩ ⟨sharp ~s⟩ ⟨dreaded the ~ of separation from them⟩ ⟨his conduct in regard to them caused me the deepest ~ —W.M.Thackeray⟩ ⟨the ~ she had felt at those humiliating words —Morley Callaghan⟩ **c** : a sensation varying in quality from prick to ache that is commonly aroused by a stimulus which injures or nearly injures the skin or tissues, is usu. but not always unpleasant, and leads to avoiding reactions **3 pains** *pl* : the protracted series of involuntary contractions of the uterine musculature that constitute the major factor in parturient labor and that are often accompanied by considerable pain ⟨her ~s had begun⟩ **4** : trouble, care, or effort taken for the accomplishment of something — usu. used in pl. but archaically often as sing. in construction ⟨has obviously taken great ~s to study the practical details —Nancie Matthews⟩ ⟨no ~s were spared in the workmanship —*Amer. Guide Series: N.Y. City*⟩ ⟨lavished their skill and ~s —Willa Cather⟩ ⟨for his ~s he incurred the enmity of the people —*Amer. Guide Series: La.*⟩ ⟨has been at ~s to avoid associating himself with this recommendation —Walter Goodman⟩ ⟨was at ~s to explain away his dangerous subject —Richard Mayne⟩ ⟨goes to ~s to impress —Lucy Crockett⟩ ⟨was at ~s to emphasize the nonpolitical character of the visit —H.J.Morgenthau⟩ ⟨takes that ~s about it —John Locke⟩ **5 a** : something that irks or annoys or that is otherwise troublesome : something provokingly displeasing ⟨she's a real ~⟩ **b** : a reaction of antipathy to something irksome or annoying or provokingly displeasing : a sensation or feeling of annoyance ⟨you give me a ~⟩

syn ACHE, PANG, THROE, TWINGE, STITCH: these nouns all indicate a bodily or mental sensation causing often acute discomfort or suffering. PAIN is the most comprehensive in that it may indicate bodily disturbance ranging from a localized discomfort to a general raging physical agony, although generally it implies a more or less acute sensation as from a cut, burn, or more severe injury ⟨a *pain* in the finger⟩ ⟨chest *pains*⟩ ⟨his face twisted with *pain*⟩ ⟨my craving to hear from her was at times a gnawing *pain* —Kenneth Roberts⟩ ACHE commonly implies a steady, usu. dull, generalized pain ⟨a head*ache*⟩ ⟨an *ache* in the back from bending over all day⟩ ⟨the dull *ache* of his disappointment —Agnes S. Turnbull⟩ PANG suggests a short sharp pain ⟨the *pangs* of toothache⟩ ⟨the *pangs* of grief⟩ THROE is a pain, usu. (and in the plural) intermittent, violent, and convulsive, characteristic of a process as that of labor in childbirth ⟨the *throes* of retching⟩ ⟨the *throes* of civil war —S.W.Chapman⟩ TWINGE is a momentary shooting or darting pain esp. causing muscular contraction ⟨*twinges* of pain in his back and shoulder —Walter O'Meara⟩ ⟨a *twinge* of pity⟩ ⟨a *twinge* of conscience⟩ STITCH suggests a brief sharp pain that runs through a part of the body (usu. the side) like a needle ⟨a *stitch* in the side forced him to drop out of the race⟩ **syn** see in addition EFFORT

— **on pain of** *or* **under pain of** *also* **upon pain of** *prep* : under penalty or punishment of — used with a following specifying word or phrase to indicate that the thing specified is invoked as a threat that will be fulfilled ⟨was told not to leave the country *on pain of* death⟩ ⟨forbidden to pronounce his or her own name, *on pain of* incurring some great evil —J.G.Frazer⟩ ⟨bringing pressure upon the commissioner . . . to appoint to office his favorites *under pain of* meeting his opposition in Congress —R.M.Lovett⟩ or archaically or obsoletely that the thing specified is something that will be forfeited ⟨that every one *upon pain of* life should return to their houses —James Howell⟩ or is a crime or offense with which one will be charged ⟨that every one should open his shop *under pain of* rebellion —James Howell⟩

²**pain** \"\ *vb* -ED/-ING/-S [ME *peynen*, fr. F *pener*, fr. *peine* pain] *vt* **1 a** : to cause to experience pain : inflict pain on : make suffer : cause distress to : HURT ⟨a nagging shoulder injury that ~*ed* him for four months —W.B.Furlong⟩ ⟨it ~*s* me to cast doubt on the competence of my friend —Alfred Burmeister⟩ **b** : to cause a feeling of annoyance in : IRK, PROVOKE ⟨don't ~ me by talking like that —Thomas Hardy⟩ ⟨it ~*s* him to have to go there⟩ **2** *archaic* : to put (oneself) to trouble or exertion for the accomplishment of something ⟨still ~ themselves to write Latin verses —J.R.Lowell⟩ ~ *vi* **1 a** *archaic* : to undergo pain : SUFFER ⟨the patient that so is ~*ing* —*Calisto and Melebea*⟩ **b** *of the body or a bodily part* : to be in a condition that produces a sensation of pain : give or have a sensation of pain : be sore ⟨soaked her feet in hot water because they were ~*ing*⟩ ⟨could hardly think, his head ~*ed* so⟩ **2** : to cause pain ⟨said that it ~*ed* when he moved his arm⟩

pained *adj* [fr. past part. of ²*pain*] **1** : feeling pain : HURT ⟨was quite ~ when you refused her invitation⟩ **2** : showing pain : indicative of pain ⟨the look of ~ attention on the faces of those boys —Robert Birley⟩ ⟨the clerk, lifting a ~ eyebrow, told me that I was in the wrong queue —H.V.Morton⟩ ⟨yawned with ~ boredom⟩

pain·ful \'pānfəl\ *adj, sometimes* **pain·ful·ler**; *sometimes* **pain·ful·lest** [ME *painefull, peynefull*, fr. *paine, peyne* pain + *-full*, -ful] **1 a** : marked by pain : full of pain : having or giving a sensation of pain : affected with pain ⟨a remedy for ~ feet⟩ ⟨a ~ wound⟩ ⟨the ~ awareness that they couldn't go home —Polly Adler⟩ **b** : ANNOYING, IRKSOME, VEXATIOUS ⟨works with ~ slowness⟩ ⟨is so shy that it's ~⟩ ⟨~ righteousness and piety —K.S.Davis⟩ ⟨a provinciality which is ~ —H.J.Laski⟩ **c** : disturbing to one's equilibrium : UPSETTING ⟨would be a ~ anachronism —A.L.Guérard⟩ **d** : extremely disagreeable : most unpleasant ⟨the ~ necessity of renouncing preconceived opinions —Charles Lyell⟩ ⟨received some ~ news⟩ **2 a** : marked by or entailing or requiring much effort or toilsome exertion ⟨a long ~ trip⟩ ⟨wrote the book with ~ care⟩; *esp* : stiff and labored ⟨was uncomfortable in this atmosphere of ~ hospitality⟩ **b** : beset with difficulties : TROUBLESOME ⟨~ problems of rehabilitation —Vera M. Dean⟩ ⟨groping one's ~ way through an imperfectly mastered idiom —A.L.Guérard⟩ **3** *archaic* **a** : done or accomplished or performed with great diligence and care ⟨their virtuous sermons and ~ preaching —Thomas Stapleton⟩ ⟨according to my most ~ discoveries —Ethan Allen⟩ **b** : working with great diligence and care ⟨laws of etymology, which ~ students have discovered —John Peile⟩ — **pain·ful·ly** \-fəlē, -li\ *adv* — **pain·ful·ness** \-lnəs\ *n* -ES

pain-killer \'ˌ,=,==\ *n* : something (as a drug) that relieves pain — **pain-killing** \'ˌ,==\ *adj*

pain·less \'pānləs\ *adj* **1** : not experiencing pain ⟨is a ~ baby suffering from indifference to injury —*Time*⟩ **2** : not causing pain : not accompanied by pain : not painful ⟨~ surgery⟩ ⟨a completely ~ process —D.W.Mitchell⟩ ⟨a ~ solution to the problem⟩ ⟨a ~ transition⟩ — **pain·less·ly** *adv* — **pain·less·ness** *n* -ES

pains *pl of* PAIN, *pres 3d sing of* PAIN

pain spot *n* : one of many small localized areas of the skin that respond to stimulation (as by pricking or burning) by giving a sensation of pain

painstaker *n, obs* : one that takes pains

¹**pains·tak·ing** \'pānz,tāk·iŋ, -n,stā-\ *n* [*pains*, pl. of ¹*pain* + *taking*, gerund of *take*] : the action of taking pains : diligent care and effort ⟨greater ~ to achieve incidental verisimilitude and accuracy of detail —*Times Lit. Supp.*⟩

²**painstaking** \'ˌ,=,==\ *adj* [*pains* + *taking*, pres. part. of *take*] : taking pains or marked by the taking of pains : expending or showing diligent care and effort ⟨a most ~ worker⟩ ⟨the results of scholarly, ~ investigation of historical sources —A.R. Newsome⟩ ⟨will go on painting, with scrupulous, ~ accuracy —D.I.Holman⟩ — **pains·tak·ing·ly** *adv* — **pains·tak·ing·ness** *n* -ES

painsworthy \'ˌ,=,==\ *adj* : worth the expenditure of diligent care and effort ⟨a ~ task⟩

¹**paint** \'pānt\ *vb* -ED/-ING/-S [ME *peynten, painten*, fr. OF *peindre* (past part. *peint*), fr. L *pingere* to paint, embroider, tattoo; akin to OE *fāh* variegated, OHG *fēh*, ON *fā* to paint, Gk *poikilos* variegated, *pikros* pointed, sharp, bitter, Skt *piṁśati* he cuts out, adorns] *vt* **1 a** (1) : to color all or part of (a surface) by or as if by applying a pigment ⟨~*ed* the whole house, inside and out⟩ : apply color to : add color to : coat or touch up with coloring matter ⟨Indians that had ~*ed* their faces with streaks of red and blue⟩; *esp* : to color (a surface) by applying and spreading (as with a brush, spray gun, roller) a liquid or paste composed of a mixture of a pigment and a vehicle (as oil or water) that dries opaque ⟨~*ed* the walls white⟩ (2) : to color with or as if with a cosmetic (as lipstick, rouge, fingernail polish) : apply a cosmetic or something like a cosmetic to ⟨wore blue and, as usual, ~*ed* her mouth —Margaret C. Harriman⟩ **b** (1) : to brush on or swab on or otherwise apply (a liquid) with a movement resembling or suggestive of that used in painting something ⟨~*ed* egg white over the surface of the cake⟩ (2) : to cover or treat or touch up (a localized area) with a liquid by brushing or swabbing or a similar movement ⟨~*ed* the wound with iodine⟩ ⟨savages ~*ing* their arms and legs with henna stain⟩ **2 a** (1) : to make or produce (as a picture, sketch, design) in lines and colors on a surface (as a canvas or wall) by brushing on or similarly applying pigments ⟨~*ed* a picture of his mother⟩ ⟨~*ed* abstract designs on the walls⟩ ⟨~*ed* big black letters on the sign⟩ (2) : to represent to the eye by the use of lines and colors applied in this way : depict or portray by such lines and colors ⟨was especially skillful at ~*ing* animals and birds⟩ ⟨~*ed* a vase of flowers against a dark background⟩ (3) : to depict or portray or delineate as having specified or implied characteristics ⟨is neither as black nor as white as he is ~*ed* —V.S. Pritchett⟩ ⟨~*s* them whiter than the evidence justifies —Oliver La Farge⟩ ⟨wished to ~ their candidate to the South as a free trader —Mary K. Hammond⟩ ⟨are not as unapproachable and unfriendly as a lot of propaganda has ~*ed* them to be —Werner Bamberger⟩ **b** : to decorate, adorn, or variegate by applying lines and colors in this way ⟨an ancient vase that had been ~*ed* with pastoral scenes⟩ **c** : to produce (as a picture, design, color) as if by painting ⟨the campfire ~*ed* queer pictures on the tree trunks and tinted the underbranches with a rosy glow —Myrtle R. White⟩ **3** : to touch up, modify, or cover over by or as if by painting so as to hide defects or so as to deceptively heighten real or apparent attractiveness ⟨the town had been all ~*ed* up in preparation for the event⟩ ⟨difficult to be patient with those who ~ its defects —M.R. Cohen⟩ **4** : to evoke a vivid mental picture or concept of esp. by a colorful or strikingly realistic description : delineate strikingly or colorfully ⟨~*ed* the picture of what would happen after war —F.L.Paxson⟩ ⟨scoured Europe in search of cheap labor, ~*ing* glowing pictures of the promised land across the sea —*Amer. Guide Series: Mass.*⟩ ⟨~*ed* this humanitarian effort so brilliantly —Farley Mowat⟩ ⟨~*s* in vivid words the fresh and free and high spirit of those who conceived the great enterprise —Edith Hamilton⟩ **5 a** : to force (a hearts player) to take a heart by playing it on a trick that must be taken **b** : to deal a face card to (a poker player who is drawing for a low hand) ~ *vi* **1** : to paint things; *esp* : to practice the art of painting pictures or other representations or designs ⟨likes to ~ for relaxation⟩ **2** : to use cosmetics for adding color ⟨is aging rapidly and now ~*s* heavily⟩ **3** *obs* : to become changed in facial color ⟨canst thou ~ pale so quickly —Thomas Middleton⟩ **4** *archaic* : to drink intoxicating liquor — **paint the lily** : to add something artificial or otherwise extraneous (as ornamentation) to something naturally beautiful or otherwise desirable in such a way as actually to lessen or hide or destroy the thing's original qualities — **paint the town red** *also* **paint the town** : to go out and celebrate riotously usu. by much drinking and general dissipation : CAROUSE

²**paint** \"\ *n* -S **1 a** : the action of painting ⟨the car needs a new ~ job⟩ **b** : something produced by painting ⟨portraits which are great pieces of ~ —David Low⟩ **2** : MAKEUP; *esp* : a cosmetic (as lipstick or rouge) designed to add color **3 a** (1) : a mixture of a pigment and a suitable vehicle (as oil, water) that together form a liquid or paste that can be applied and spread (as with a brush, spray gun, roller) to a surface so as to form a thin closely adherent coating that dries opaque and imparts color to the surface and that is often designed to protect the surface (as against weathering) ⟨a can of ~⟩ ⟨a tube of ~⟩ (2) : the dry pigment used in making this mixture; *esp* : a usu. small cake of this dry pigment ⟨a box of ~*s*⟩ **b** : an applied coating of paint esp. when dry ⟨touched the ~ while it was still wet⟩ ⟨the ~ had already begun to chip off⟩ **4** : a usu. antiseptic application (as of iodine) designed to be applied to a localized area (as of the skin) by painting **5** [short for *paint horse*] *chiefly West* : a horse or pony with irregular broad markings of white interspersed with some other solid color

paint·abil·i·ty \,pāntə'biləd·ē\ *n* : the quality or state of being paintable

paint·able \'pāntəbəl\ *adj* : capable of being painted : lending itself well to being painted: as **a** : having arresting qualities (as of color, design, interest) that invite reproduction or interpretation through the art of painting ⟨a highly ~ landscape⟩ **b** : having a surface that takes paint well ⟨made of sturdy eminently ~ wood⟩

paint·able·ness *n* -ES : PAINTABILITY

paint box *n* : a box for paints; *specif* : a box that holds cakes of dry paint (as water colors) or usu. small containers (as jars, tubes) of liquid or semiliquid paint and that typically has one or more small pans for mixing and blending the paints

paint bridge *n* : BRIDGE 3m(2)

paintbrush \'ˌ,=,=\ *n* **1** : a brush for applying paint **2 a** : ORANGE HAWKWEED **b** : MARSH PAINTED CUP **c** : SHRUBBY ST.-JOHN'S-WORT

paintbrushes 1

paint·ed \'pāntəd\ *adj* [ME *peynted, painted*, fr. past part. of *peynten* to paint] **1 a** : produced through the medium of painting ⟨as idle as a ~ ship —S.T.Coleridge⟩ : done in colors that have been applied by painting on a surface ⟨treasured the ~ likeness of her son⟩ **b** : coated or touched up with paint or decorated with painted representations or designs ⟨scratched the ~ woodwork⟩ ⟨the ~ faces of the savages⟩; *esp* : heavily made up with cosmetics ⟨a region not quite used to ~ women⟩ **c** : marked by bright or contrasting colors ⟨the sunlit ~ meadow⟩ **2** : lacking substance and vitality and correspondence with truth : HOLLOW, ARTIFICIAL, SHAM ⟨that ~ hope —Shak.⟩ ⟨enjoying ~ pleasures⟩

painted bat *n* [so called fr. its bright orange fur] : FOREST BAT

painted beauty *n* : an American butterfly (*Vanessa virginiensis*) with dark brown wings marked by large golden orange spots and several white spots

painted bunting *or* **painted finch** *n* **1** : a brightly colored finch (*Passerina ciris*) of the southern part of the U.S. having in the male a deep blue head and neck and bright red rump and underparts with golden green wings and bluish purple tail and in the female green upper parts and yellowish underparts **2** : SMITH'S LONGSPUR

painted cup *n* : INDIAN PAINTBRUSH 1

painted daisy *n* **1** : PYRETHRUM 1b(2) **2** : any of various annual garden chrysanthemums that are prob. largely derived from a Moroccan species (*Chrysanthemum carinatum*) and that have succulent leaves and solitary flower heads with ray flowers brilliantly banded in two or more colors

painted duck *n* **1** : MANDARIN DUCK **2** : HARLEQUIN DUCK

painted enamel *n* : LIMOGES ENAMEL

painted goose *n* : EMPEROR GOOSE

painted grass *n* : RIBBON GRASS

painted horse *or* **painted pony** *n* [trans. of AmerSp *pinto* — more at PINTO] : PAINT 5

painted hyena *n* : AFRICAN HUNTING DOG

painted lady *n* **1** : a migratory butterfly (*Vanessa cardui*) with wings mottled in brown, orange, and white that has a brown or blackish yellow-striped caterpillar often destructive of crop plants **2** : PYRETHRUM 1 b (2) **3** : PAINTED TRILLIUM

painted leaf *n* : MEXICAN FIRE PLANT 1

painted lobster *n* : a large brilliantly marked spiny lobster (*Palinurus fasciatus*) of the Great Barrier reef off the northeastern coast of Queensland, Australia

painted partridge *n* : a francolin (*Francolinus pictus*) of the subcontinent of India

painted pig *n* : a reddish West African river hog (*Koiropotamus porcus*)

painted quail *n* **1** : either of two small bright-plumaged quails: **a** : an African quail (*Coturnix adansonii*) — called also *blue quail* **b** : an Asiatic and Australasian quail (*C. chinensis*) — called also *blue-breasted quail* **2** *Austral* : a button quail (*Turnix varia*)

painted sandgrouse *n* : a sandgrouse (*Pterocles indicus*) of the subcontinent of India

painted snipe *n* : any of several highly colored limicoline birds of the genus *Rostratula* widely distributed in the southern hemisphere

painted tongue *n* : SALPIGLOSSIS 2

painted trillium *or* **painted wake-robin** *n* : a perennial herb (*Trillium undulatum*) of the northeastern part of No. America with three broad stalked leaves and a showy solitary flower with purple-streaked petals

painted turtle *also* **painted terrapin** *or* **painted tortoise** *n* : any of several common freshwater turtles of the genus *Chrysemys* that are found chiefly in the eastern part of the U.S. and that have a greenish black carapace with yellow bands bordering the shields, red markings on the marginal plates, and a yellow plastron

¹**paint·er** \'pāntə(r)\ *n* -S [ME *peynteur, painter*, fr. MF *peinteur, paintre*, fr. (assumed) VL *pinctor*, alter. (influenced by L *pingere*) of L *pictor*, fr. *pictus* (past part. of *pingere* to paint) + *-or* — more at PAINT] : one that paints: as **a** : an artist that paints (as pictures, designs) **b** : one who applies paint (as to buildings, ships, planes, or furniture) esp. as an occupation

²**painter** \"\ *n* -S [ME *paynter*, prob. fr. MF *pentoir, pendoir* clothesline, fr. *pendre* to hang (fr. L *pendēre*) + *-oir* -ory (fr. L *-orium*) — more at PENDANT] : ROPE, LINE; *specif* : a rope or other line attached to the bow of a boat (as a rowboat) and used for securing the boat (as to a pier) or for towing — **cut the painter** : to make a complete and definite break with something : sever all connection ⟨was *cutting the painter* so far as her part was concerned⟩

³**painter** \"\ *n* -S [alter. of *panther*] *chiefly South & Midland* : COUGAR

paint·er·li·ness \'pāntə(r)lēnəs, -lin-\ *n* -ES : the quality or state of being painterly

paint·er·ly \-lē, -li\ *adj* **1** : of, relating to, or typical of a painter : ARTISTIC ⟨a ~ ability of no small order —*N.Y.Times*⟩ ⟨the ~ arts —Joseph Ehreth⟩ ⟨~ attitudes toward color —Matthew Lipman⟩ **2 a** : marked by or tending toward qualities of color or texture or other features that are present or created in a way distinctive of or esp. appropriate to the art of painting ⟨his work is spirited, ~, sensitive as to light and color and ambient surface pattern —Carlyle Burrows⟩ ⟨a free ~ style —Herbert Read⟩ **b** : marked by or tending toward an openness of form which is not linear and in which sharp outlines are wholly or nearly wholly lacking ⟨there was a ~ subtlety in the muted whites and grays —O.W.Larkin⟩

painter's brush *n* : INDIAN PAINTBRUSH 1

painter's colic *n* : LEAD COLIC

painter's cream *n* : a cream made of mastic, nut oil, lead acetate, and water and used to cover a partly finished painting so as to preserve its freshness until resumption of work

painter's naphtha *n* : a petroleum naphtha used as a thinner for paints

paint frame *n* : a large frame usu. suspended at the back of a stage and capable of being raised or lowered that is used for holding a stretched length of canvas on which an entire piece of stage scenery is to be painted

paint horse *or* **paint pony** *n* [trans. of AmerSp *pinto* — more at PINTO] : PAINT 5

paintier *comparative of* PAINTY

paintiest *superlative of* PAINTY

paint·i·ness \'pāntēnəs, -tin-\ *n* -ES : the quality or state of being painty

painting *n* -S [ME *painting, peintunge*, fr. gerund of *painten* to paint] **1** : something produced through the process or art of painting : a product of painting: as **a** : decoration achieved by applying paint to a surface : PAINTWORK ⟨admired the ~ and gilding of his Excellency's carriages —T.B.Macaulay⟩ **b** : a picture or design or other work produced through the art of painting ⟨a ~ done in oils⟩ ⟨a water-color ~⟩ **2** : the art or occupation of painting ⟨studied ~ for some years⟩

painting knife *n* : an artist's tool that consists of a very flexible tapered blade set in a handle and that is used like a small trowel for taking up and applying thick paints

paint·less \'pāntləs\ *adj* : devoid of paint ⟨of the same weathered, ~ church —William Faulkner⟩

paint out *vt* **1** *archaic* : to depict or portray or delineate by or as if by painting **2** : to obliterate by covering over with paint

paintpot \'ˌ,=\ *n* **1** : a receptacle (as a pot, pail, bucket) for holding paint **2** *usu* **paint pot** : an orifice in the earth (as in the vicinity of a volcano, geyser, hot spring) usu. marked by a protruding conical mud rim and containing a liquid mass of thin mud usu. agitated with hot vapors or gases and often vividly colored through chemical reaction induced by heat

paint·ress \'pān·trəs\ *n* -ES [F *peintresse*, fr. *peintre* painter + *-esse* -ess] : a female painter

paint roller *n* **:** a roller that consists typically of a rotating cylinder about two inches in diameter and six inches in length covered with an absorbent material and mounted on a handle so that the cylinder can be dipped into paint or otherwise (as through a hollow feeding center) be supplied with paint and rolled over a flat surface (as a wall) so as to apply the paint

paint roller

paint-root \ˈ=ˌ=\ *n* **:** REDROOT 1

paints *pres 3d sing of* PAINT, *pl of* PAINT

paint shop *n* **1 :** a store where paint and painting supplies are sold **2 :** a room or similar area used for paintwork

painture *n* -s [ME *peynture*, fr. OF *peinture*, fr. (assumed) VL *pinctura*, alter. (influenced by L *pingere* to paint) of L *pictura* — more at PICTURE] *obs* **:** PAINTING

paintwork \ˈ=ˌ=\ *n* **1 a :** the application of paint to a surface ⟨had not yet finished the ~⟩ ⟨decorated with ~⟩ **b :** the quality of work done in the application of paint to a surface ⟨fine ~ was evident in every room⟩ **2 :** paint that has been applied to a surface ⟨was careful not to scratch the ~⟩

painty \ˈpāntē, -ti\ *adj*, *usu* -ER/-EST **1 a :** of, relating to, or suggestive of paint ⟨a ~ odor⟩ **b :** spattered or smeared with paint ⟨after doing the kitchen walls she found that her clothes were all ~⟩ **2 :** marked by or suggestive of an excessive or often crudely obtrusive use of paint ⟨an unskillful ~ portrait⟩ ⟨~ stage scenery⟩

¹pair \ˈpa(a)(ə)r, ˈpe|, |ə\ *n*, *pl* **pairs** *also* **pair** [ME *peire*, *paire*, fr. OF *paire*, fr. L *paria* equal things, fr. neut. pl. of *par* equal; prob. akin to Gk *pernanai* to sell, *pornē* harlot, *poreuein* to convey — more at FARE] **1 a** (1) **:** a set of two separate things designed to be used together that may correspond to each other to the extent of being identical (as in shape, size, color, material) ⟨a ~ of candlesticks⟩ ⟨a ~ of oars⟩ ⟨a ~ of dice⟩ or nearly identical except for differences arising typically out of adaptation to use with or on the right and left sides or parts of something ⟨a ~ of shoes⟩ ⟨a ~ of socks⟩ ⟨a ~ of stirrups⟩ ⟨a ~ of bookends⟩ or with or on the upper or lower parts or levels of something ⟨had arranged a matching ~ of shelves one above the other on the wall⟩ and that may sometimes have only a general correspondence (as in color, design) and otherwise differ markedly (as in shape) while designed to be used together and together forming a single integral unit ⟨a ~ of pajamas⟩ (2) **:** a set of two corresponding bodily parts or members ⟨had a beautiful ~ of eyes⟩ ⟨a ~ of muscular hands⟩ **b :** something made up of two corresponding parts or pieces joined together at or near one end ⟨~ of trousers⟩ ⟨~ of scissors⟩ ⟨~ of tweezers⟩ ⟨~ of pliers⟩ or at some other point ⟨~ of suspenders⟩ ⟨~ of eyeglasses⟩ so as to form a single integral unit **2 a :** a set of two separate things that are identical or similar ⟨a ~ of twins⟩ or that happen to be closely associated without necessarily being identical or similar ⟨the horse and rider made a fine ~⟩ or that in some other way occur together or are brought together or are used together or are viewed as together forming a closely associated couple that is usu. but not necessarily made up of two things that are of the same kind or are identical or similar or that correspond in some other way **:** a group of two ⟨a ~ of brothers⟩ ⟨noticed that some of the plants grew in ~s⟩ ⟨a ~ of champions⟩ ⟨picked up a ~ of greeting cards⟩ ⟨minimal ~s in phonemics⟩: as (1) **:** a mated couple of animals ⟨a ~ of bears⟩ ⟨a ~ of robins⟩ (2) **:** a couple in love; *esp* **:** an engaged or married couple ⟨were a devoted ~⟩ ⟨congratulated the newly married ~⟩ (3) **:** a combination of two playing cards of the same value or denomination ⟨held a ~⟩ (4) **:** a couple of horses harnessed together side by side ⟨a carriage and ~⟩ (5) **:** a couple of partners (as in a game, at a dance, in a business enterprise) ⟨a ~ of bridge players⟩ ⟨enjoyed watching the waltzing ~s⟩ ⟨are a shrewd ~⟩ (6) **:** a couple of individuals that are members of opposite parties or hold opposed opinions in a deliberative body and that mutually agree not to vote on a specific issue during a time (as a period of absence of one or both) agreed on (7) **:** a couple of individuals that are being spoken of or otherwise considered ⟨you'll remember that ~, I think⟩; *esp* **:** a couple of individuals that have something (as specific traits of character) in common ⟨were an honest ~⟩ (8) **:** a combination of two kinematic parts applied to each other in such a way as mutually to constrain relative motion ⟨a cylinder and its piston are a sliding ~⟩ (9) **:** a couple of postage stamps attached to each other (10) **:** a basketry plait made up of two rods woven alternately one over the other **b** (1) **:** PARTNERSHIP ⟨working in ~s⟩; *esp* **:** a partnership of two players (as bridge players) or other contestants engaged in a game or other contest against another such partnership (2) **pairs** *pl* **:** a game, contest, or tournament engaged in by players or other contestants divided up into such partnerships ⟨succeeded in winning the ~s⟩ **c :** an agreement not to vote made by the two members of a pair (sense 2a(6)) **d :** PAIR-OAR ⟨well-trained in sculls, ~s and fours —*Sports Illustrated*⟩ **3** *chiefly dial* **:** an integral whole made up of a set or succession of more than two things (as parts, pieces, sections) that usu. closely resemble each other or belong together for completeness: as **a :** a series of small objects (as beads) strung together (as in a necklace or rosary) **:** STRING **b :** a musical instrument made up of several related parts ⟨a ~ of beautiful old organs —W.M.Thackeray⟩ **c :** a graduated succession of steps **:** FLIGHT ⟨two ~ of stairs —Henry Fielding⟩

²pair \ˈ"\ *vb* -ED/-ING/-S *vt* **1 a :** to make a pair of (as by bringing together, joining, matching, associating, mating) ⟨~*ed* the two films in a double bill⟩ ⟨~*ed* a couple of cards⟩ — often used with *off* or *up* ⟨~*ed* off the animals⟩ **b** (1) **:** to cause to be a member of a pair — often used with *up* ⟨~*ed* him up with an opponent about his equal⟩ (2) **:** to bring into a mutual agreement not to vote on a specific issue during a time agreed on ⟨missed a vote on an important issue . . . by being ~*ed* —*Current Biog.*⟩ **2 :** to arrange in pairs **:** separate into pairs ⟨~*ed* her guests into congenial couples⟩ — often used with *off* ⟨~*ed* off the group into couples for the next dance⟩ ~ *vi* **1 :** to form a matching or equal member of a pair — often used with *off* or *up* ⟨a shoe that doesn't ~ up with the other⟩ **2 a** (1) **:** to become united or closely associated with another so as to form a pair (as by partnership, companionship, mating) — often used with *off* or *up* ⟨~*ed* up with an old friend⟩ ⟨the season when most birds ~ off⟩ (2) **:** to come to a mutual agreement with one of an opposite party or opinion not to vote on a specific issue during a time agreed on ⟨failed to appear, ~, or announce his position —*N.Y.Times*⟩ **b :** to become grouped or separated into pairs — often used with *off* ⟨the happy crowd gradually ~*ed* off⟩ **3 :** to achieve or show a combination of two playing cards of equal value or denomination ⟨on my fourth card I ~*ed*⟩

³pair \ˈ"\ *vb* -ED/-ING/-S [ME *pairen*, short for *apairen*, *apeyren*, *ampayrien*, fr. OF *empeirier* — more at IMPAIR] *chiefly dial* **:** IMPAIR

⁴pair \ˈ"\ *n* -S [F *pair*, adj., even, equal, fr. L *par* equal] **:** the even numbers in roulette when a bet is made on them

pair·age \-rij, -rēj\ *n* -S **:** a quantity of pairs of shoes being manufactured or sold ⟨increased the monthly ~ to reach a new high⟩

pair·er \-rə(r)\ *n* -S **:** one who pairs or matches like or related articles

pair-horse \ˈ=ˈ=\ *adj* **:** drawn by a pair of horses ⟨goes about in a *pair-horse* carriage in the evening —Arnold Bennett⟩

pairing *n* -S [fr. gerund of ²*pair*] **1 a** (1) **:** the action of grouping (as players, other contestants) into pairs (2) **:** a listing of grouped pairs **b** (1) **:** the process of making basketry plaits consisting of two rods woven alternately one over the other (2) **:** a woven row made by this process **2 :** SYNAPSIS

pairle \ˈpa(a)r(ə)l, ˈper-\ *n* -S [F, prob. alter. of OF *paile* mantle, pall, fr. L *pallium* — more at PALL] **:** a heraldic ordinary in the form of a Y extending to the upper corners and the base of the field — called also *pall*; compare SHAKEFORK — **in pairle** *adv* **1 :** in the direction and position of the three arms of a pairle ⟨tierced *in pairle* sable, gules, and azure⟩ **2 :** in such a way that of three heraldic bearings one is bendwise, one bendwise sinister, and one palewise so as to approach or join at a common center ⟨three shields arranged *in pairle* with the points meeting in the center of the escutcheon⟩

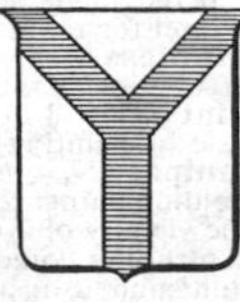

pairle

pair-oar \ˈ=ˌ=\ *n* **:** a boat rowed by two rowers pulling one oar each and seated one abaft the other

pair-oared \ˈ=ˈ=\ *adj* **:** pulled or rigged as a pair-oar

pair of colors 1 *chiefly Brit* **:** the national flag and regimental flag carried by a regiment **2 :** the position or commission of an ensign in the British army until the discontinuance of this rank in 1871

pair of spectacles *Brit* **:** a cricketer's score of nothing in each of his two innings in a single match

pair production *also* **pair formation** *or* **pair creation** *n* **:** the simultaneous and complete transformation of a quantum of radiant energy into an electron and a positron when the quantum interacts with the intense electric field near a nucleus

pair royal *n*, *pl* **pair royal** *or* **pairs royal** [¹*pair* + *royal*, adj.] **:** three of a kind in the game of cribbage

pairs *pl of* PAIR, *pres 3d sing of* PAIR

pairt \ˈpärt\ *chiefly Scot var of* PART

pair·trick \ˈpär·trik\ *chiefly Scot var of* PARTRIDGE

pai·sa *also* **pais·sa** \ˈpīsə\ *n*, *pl* **pai·se** \-(ˌ)sā\ *or* **paisa** *or* **paisas** [Hindi *paisā*] **1 a :** a monetary unit of India, Pakistan, Bangladesh, and Nepal equal to $^1/_{100}$ rupee; *also* **:** a coin representing one paisa — compare NAYA PAISA; see MONEY table **b :** PICE **2 a** (1) **:** an old copper coin of Afghanistan similar to the Indian pice (2) **:** a brass coin issued under Habibullah Khan (1901–19) **b :** an Afghan unit of value equivalent to that of one paisa

pai·sa·no \pīˈzä(ˌ)nō, -ˈsä-\ *n* -S [Sp, fr. F *paysan* — more at PEASANT] **1** *Southwest* **a :** RUSTIC, PEASANT **b :** COMPATRIOT **c :** NATIVE; *esp* **:** a native of the state of California of mixed Spanish and Indian ancestry **2** *Southwest* **:** ROADRUNNER

¹pais·ley \ˈpāzlē, -li\ *adj*, *often cap* [fr. *Paisley*, burgh of southwest Scotland] **1 :** made of soft wool or a similar material resembling cashmere and woven or printed with a colorful usu. elaborate design consisting typically of curved abstract figures ⟨a ~ shawl⟩ **2 :** marked by or consisting of the designs, patterns, or figures typically used in paisley fabrics ⟨a ~ print⟩ ⟨a ~ pattern⟩

²paisley \ˈ"\ *n* -S *often cap* **1 :** a paisley fabric or design **2 :** an article (as a shawl, dress, trimming) made of a paisley fabric

pai·ute *also* **pi·ute** \ˈpī,(y)üt, =ˈ=\ *n*, *pl* **paiute** *or* **paiutes** *usu cap* **1 a :** a Shoshonean people of western Utah, northwestern Arizona, southeastern Nevada, and southeastern California — called also *Southern Paiute* **b :** a member of such people **2 :** the language of the Paiute people — compare NORTHERN PAIUTE

paix·tle \ˈpīchtlē\ *n* -S [MexSp, fr. Nahuatl *paixtli* hay] **:** a fiesta dance of Jalisco, Mexico, performed by men disguised in costumes of hay and representing sorcerers

pa·ja·ma \pəˈjämə, -ja-, -jà-\ *n* -S [Hindi *pāejāma*, *pājāma*, fr. Per *pā(e)* leg + *jāma* garment] **:** PAJAMAS

pa·ja·maed \-məd\ *adj* **:** wearing or fitted out with pajamas

pajama party *n* **:** SLUMBER PARTY

pa·ja·mas \-məz\ *n pl* [pl. of *pajama*] **1 :** loose lightweight trousers formerly much worn by both men and women in some countries of the Near East **2 :** a loosely fitting two-piece or sometimes one-piece lightweight suit in many styles and fabrics designed esp. for sleeping or lounging and consisting typically of trousers and a jacket or pullover top ⟨beach ~⟩

pa·ja·ro·el·lo *or* **pajaroello tick** \ˌpäharəˈwe(ˌ)lō-\ *also* **pa·ja·huel·lo** \ˌ==ˈhwe(ˌ)lō\ *n* -S [origin unknown] **:** a venomous tick (*Ornithodoros coriaceus*) that attacks man and other mammals and some birds and causes painful swellings

paj·i·ta·nian \ˌpajəˈtānēən, -nyən\ *adj*, *usu cap* [origin unknown] **:** of or relating to a Lower Paleolithic culture of Java characterized by choppers, chopping tools, and hand adzes made from cores with one side flat and the other rounded

paj·on·ism \ˈpajəˌnizəm\ *n* -S *usu cap* [F *pajonisme*, fr. Claude *Pajon* †1685 French Protestant theologian + F *-isme* -ism] **:** a theological doctrine according to which the Holy Spirit does not act directly upon an individual but only indirectly (as by influencing intellectual judgments)

pak-a-pu \ˌpäkəˈpü\ *n* -S [Chin *pai²* *ko¹* *p'iao⁴* white pigeon ticket, fr. *pai²* white + *ko¹* pigeon + *p'iao⁴* ticket] **:** a Chinese lottery typically played with sheets of paper carrying columns of characters of which one group is a winning set that entitles the player choosing it to the stakes offered

pa·ka·wan \ˈpäkəˌwän\ *n* -S *usu cap* **:** COAHUILTECAN

pak·choi \ˈbäkˈchȯi\ *n*, *pl* **pakchoi** *or* **pakchois** [Chin (Cantonese) *paāk ts'oi*, fr. *paāk* white + *ts'oi* vegetable] **:** CHINESE CABBAGE

pa·ke·ha \ˈpäkəˌhä, -kēˌä; ˈpakēə\ *n*, *pl* **pakeha** *or* **pakehas** [Maori] *Austral & New Zeal* **:** one that is not of Maori ancestry; *esp* **:** a member of the white race

pakh·pu·luk \ˌpäk(ˌ)pəˈlük\ *n*, *pl* **pakhpuluk** *or* **pakhpuluks** *usu cap* **1 :** a people in the southern part of Kashmir in the subcontinent of India of Indo-Aryan and Turkish ancestry **2 :** a member of the Pakhpuluk people

paki·stan \ˈpakəˌstan, -taa(ə)n *also* ˌ==ˈ=; ˈpäkēˌstän, ˈpäkēˌstän, -kəˈs-\ *adj*, *usu cap* [fr. *Pakistan*, republic in Indian subcontinent] **:** of or from Pakistan **:** of the kind or style prevalent in Pakistan **:** PAKISTANI

¹paki·stani \ˌ==ˈ=ē, -ˈi\ *n*, *pl* **pakistanis** *or* **pakistani** *cap* [Hindustani *Pākistānī*, fr. *Pākistān* Pakistan] **:** a native or inhabitant of West Pakistan or East Pakistan in the northwestern or northeastern part of the Indian subcontinent

²pakistani \ˌ==ˈ=\ *adj*, *usu cap* **:** PAKISTAN

pa·kla·va \ˈpäklə,vä, ˌ==ˈ=\ *n* -S [modif. of Turk *baklava*] **:** BAKLAVA

pak·tong \ˈpakˌtȯŋ\ *also* **pack·fong** \-ˌfȯŋ\ *n* -S [Cantonese *paāk t'ūng*, fr. *paāk* white + *t'ūng* copper] **:** an alloy resembling nickel silver and consisting of nickel, zinc, and copper

¹pal \ˈpal\ *n* -S [Romany (English) *phal* brother, friend, (Continental) *phral*, fr. Skt *bhrātṛ* brother — more at BROTHER] **:** PARTNER: as **a :** ACCOMPLICE **b :** a close friend or boon companion

²pal \ˈ"\ *vi* **palled; palled; palling; pals :** to be or become pals ⟨they *palled* around for years⟩ **:** keep company **:** act as pal to or behave as an intimate with someone

pal *abbr* paleontology

PAL *abbr* prisoner at large

pala *var of* PALLAH

¹pal·ace \ˈpaləs\ *n* -S [ME *palais*, *paleis*, fr. OF, fr. L *palatium*, fr. *Palatium* Palatine Hill in Rome on which the residences of the emperors were built] **1 a :** the official residence of a sovereign **b** *chiefly Brit* **:** the official residence of an archbishop or bishop **2 a :** a large and stately house — used chiefly in translating from French and Italian **b :** a large public building (as for a legislature or superior court) **c :** a gaudy establishment fitted up as a place of public resort (as for amusement or refreshment) ⟨provincial movie ~s —Lewis Mumford⟩ **3** *slang* **:** CABOOSE

²palace \ˈ"\ *adj* **1 :** of or relating to a palace ⟨~ gardens⟩ **2 a :** close to or intimate with a sovereign **:** living at or frequenting the court ⟨~ circles⟩ **b :** of, relating to, involving, or sponsored by the intimates of a sovereign or other chief executive ⟨a ~ revolution⟩ ⟨~ politics⟩ **3 :** showy and luxurious **:** DELUXE ⟨a ~ hotel⟩

³palace \ˈ"\ *vt* -ED/-ING/-S **:** to place or house in or as if in a palace

⁴palace \ˈ"\ *n* -S [prob. fr. Corn *palas* to dig, fr. *pal* spade, fr. L *pala*] **:** an underground storehouse esp. popular in Cornwall for storing fish

palace car *n* **:** a luxuriously or superiorly fitted railway car (as a parlor car or sleeping car)

pal·aced \-st\ *adj* **:** furnished with a palace **:** housed in a palace

palace guard *n* **1 :** a body of men stationed to protect a castle or its inhabitants **2 :** a king's, president's, or other chief executive's inner circle of intimates and advisers ⟨complained that a *palace guard* — made up of men never elected to serve — is running the government —*Springfield (Mass.) Union*⟩

pal·ace·ward \-wə(r)d\ *also* **pal·ace·wards** \-dz\ *adv* **:** toward a palace

pal·a·din \ˈpalədᵊn, -dən\ *n* -S [F, fr. It *paladino*, fr. ML *palatinus* courtier, fr. L, palace official — more at PALATINE, n.] **1 :** a champion of a medieval prince **:** a legendary hero **2 :** a person of outstanding worth or quality who is firm in support of some cause or objective **:** PROTAGONIST ⟨was the ~ of our civil liberties of modern times —Herbert Elliston⟩

palae- — see PALE-

palae·acanthocephala \ˌpālē, ˌpalē+\ *n pl*, *cap* [NL, fr. *pale-* + *Acanthocephala*] **:** an order of Acanthocephala comprising parasites of fishes, birds, and mammals that have spines on the trunk and the proboscis hooks arranged in long rows

palae·an·thro·pi·nae \ˌ==ˌan(t)thrəˈpī(ˌ)nē\ [NL, fr. *pale-* + Gk *anthrōpos* human being + NL *-inae* — more at ANTHROP-] *syn of* PALEOANTHROPINAE

palae·an·thro·pus \ˌ==ˈan(t)thrəpəs, -ˌanˈthrōpəs\ *syn of* PALEOANTHROPUS

palae·arctic *or* **pale·arctic** \ˌ==+\ *adj*, *usu cap* [*pale-* + *arctic*] **:** of, relating to, or being a biogeographic region or subregion that includes Europe, Asia north of the Himalayas, northern Arabia, and Africa north of the Sahara **:** Old World Holarctic

palae·asiatic \ˌ==+\ *adj*, *usu cap* [*pale-* + *asiatic*] **:** PALEO-ASIATIC

palae·echinoidea \ˌ==+\ *n pl*, *cap* [NL, fr. *pale-* + *Echinoidea*] *in some classifications* **:** a division of extinct chiefly Paleozoic sea urchins having the test usu. composed of more than 20 meridional rows of plates that often overlap and jaws always present — compare EUECHINOIDEA — **palae·echinoidean** \ˌ==+\ *adj or n*

palae·eu·dyp·tes \ˌ==yüˈdip(ˌ)tēz\ *n*, *cap* [NL, fr. *pale-* + *Eudyptes*, genus of penguins, fr. *eu-* + Gk *dyptēs* diver, fr. *dyptein* to dive; akin to Gk *dyein* to enter, dive in — more at ADYTUM] **:** a genus of very large fossil penguins of the Eocene of New Zealand

palae·ich·thy·es \ˌ==ˈikthēˌēz\ *n pl*, *cap* [NL, fr. *pale-* + Gk *ichthyes*, pl. of *ichthys* fish — more at ICHTHUS] *in some classifications* **:** a subclass of fishes consisting of the elasmobranchs, ganoids, dipnoans, and crossopterygians — **palaeichthyic** \ˌ==+\ *adj*

pa·lae·mon \pəˈlēˌmän\ *n*, *cap* [NL, fr. L, name of a sea god, fr. Gk *Palaimōn*] **:** a large widely distributed genus (the type of the family Palaemonidae) of prawns with prominently toothed rostrum and three-jointed mandibular palp — **pa·lae·mo·nid** \-ˌmənəd\ *adj or n* — **pa·lae·mo·noid** \-ˌnȯid\ *adj*

pa·lae·mo·ne·tes \ˌ=ˌ=məˈnē(ˌ)tēz\ *n*, *cap* [NL, fr. L *Palaemon*] **:** a genus of prawns related to and resembling those of the genus *Palaemon* but lacking the mandibular palp

palaeo- — see PALE-

palaeo·an·throp·ic \ˌpālēōˌanˈthräpik, ˌpalē-, -pēk\ *also* **pale·anthropic** \ˌpālē, ˌpalē+\ *or* **paleo·anthropic** \ˌpālēō, ˌpalēō+\ *adj* [*pale-* + Gk *anthrōpos* human being + E *-ic* — more at ANTHROP-] **1 :** of or relating to hominids more primitive than those included in the species (*Homo sapiens*) that includes recent man — compare NEOANTHROPIC **2** [NL *Palaeoanthropus* + E *-ic*] **:** of, relating to, or belonging to the genus *Palaeoanthropus*

palaeo·an·thro·pus \ˌpālēōˈan(t)thrəpəs, ˌpalē-, -ˌanˈthrōpəs\ *n*, *cap* [NL, fr. *pale-* + *-anthropus*] *in some classifications* **:** a genus of hominids based on a single lower jaw found at Mauer near Heidelberg, Germany but now often extended to include the entire Neanderthaloid radiation and other primitive men of uncertain affinities (as Solo man and Rhodesian man)

palaeo·ca·ri·da \ˌ===kəˈrīdə, -ˈkarədə\ [NL, fr. *pale-* + Gk *karid-*, *karis* shrimp or prawn] *syn of* GIGANTOSTRACA

palaeo·con·cha \ˌ===ˈkäŋkə\ *n pl*, *cap* [NL, fr. *pale-* + L *concha* conch] *in some classifications* **:** a division of Protobranchia comprising simple extinct bivalve mollusks with thin shells and a primitive hinge and sometimes including also a few recent marine bivalves

¹palaeo·cri·noid \ˌ===ˈkrīˌnȯid, -kri,-\ *adj* [NL *Palaeocrinoidea*] **:** of or relating to the Palaeocrinoidea

²palaeocrinoid \ˈ"\ *n* -S **:** an animal or fossil of the order Palaeocrinoidea

palaeo·crinoidea \ˌ===+\ *n pl*, *cap* [NL, fr. *pale-* + *Crinoidea*] *in some classifications* **:** an order of Paleozoic stalked crinoids of supposedly primitive type having the actinal side of the calyx closed — compare NEOCRINOIDEA

palaeo·dic·ty·op·tera \ˌ===ˌdiktēˈäptərə\ *n pl*, *cap* [NL, fr. *pale-* + *dicty-* + *-ptera*] **:** an order of very primitive extinct insects known only from the Upper Carboniferous and Permian periods and characterized by homonomous segmentation of the thorax and abdomen and by a simple wing venation with a network of cross veins — **palaeo·dic·ty·op·ter·an** \ˌ====ˈ=tərən\ *adj or n* — **palaeo·dic·ty·op·ter·ous** \-rəs\ *adj*

palaeo·dic·ty·op·ter·on \-təˌrän\ *n*, *pl* **palaeodictyoptera** \-tərə\ **:** an insect or fossil of the order Palaeodictyoptera

palaeo·echinoidea \ˌ===+\ *syn of* PALAEECHINOIDEA

palaeo·gae·an *or* **palaeo·ge·an** *also* **paleo·ge·an** \ˌpālēōˈjēən, ˌpal-\ *adj*, *usu cap* [NL *Palaeogaea* eastern hemisphere, lit., old world (fr. *pale-* + *-gaea*) + E *-an*] **:** of, relating to, or being a biogeographic realm consisting of the entire eastern hemisphere

palaeo·genesis *also* **paleo·genesis** \ˌpālē, ˌpalē+\ *n* [NL, fr. *pale-* + L *genesis*] **:** PALINGENESIS c

palaeo·ge·net·ic \ˌ===jəˈned·ik\ *adj* [*pale-* + *genetic*] **:** exhibiting palingenesis **:** of, relating to, or characterized by the retention of ancestral larval characters into or in adulthood

palae·og·na·thae \ˌpālēˈägnəˌthē, ˌpal-\ *n pl*, *cap* [NL, fr. *pale-* + *-gnathae*] *in some esp. former classifications* **:** a superorder of the subclass Neornithes comprising birds with a primitive reptilian type of palate that are now usu. included in Neognathae — **palae·og·nath·ic** \ˌ==ägˈnathik\ *or* **palae·og·na·thous** \ˌ==ˈägnəthəs\ *adj*

palaeo·mastodon \ˌpālēō, ˌpalēō+\ *n*, *cap* [NL, fr. *pale-* + *Mastodon*] **:** a genus of primitive proboscidean mammals of the Oligocene of Egypt that are characterized by a long skull, short tusks, a long lower jaw, 22 molars, and a body about half as large as that of the Indian elephant and are commonly regarded as ancestral to the mastodons

palaeo·nemertea \ˌ===+\ *n pl*, *cap* [NL, fr. *pale-* + *Nemertea*] **:** an order of nemertean worms (class Anopla) that have two layers of body-wall musculature, a proboscis without a stylet, and a brain that is not divided into lobes — **palaeo·nemertean** \ˌ===+\ *adj or n*

palaeo·nemertine \ˌ===+\ *adj or n* [NL *Palaeonemertinea*] **:** PALAEONEMERTEAN

palaeo·nemertinea \ˌ===+\ *or* **palaeonemertini** \ˌ===+\ [NL, fr. *pale-* + *Nemertinea* or *Nemertini*] *syn of* PALAEONEMERTINEA

¹palaeo·nis·cid \ˌ===ˈnisəd\ *adj* [NL *Palaeoniscidae*] **:** of or relating to the Palaeoniscidae

²palaeoniscid \ˈ"\ *n* -S **:** a fish or fossil of the family Palaeoniscidae

palaeo·nis·ci·dae \ˌ===ˈnisəˌdē\ *n pl*, *cap* [NL, fr. *Palaeoniscum*, type genus + *-idae*] **:** a family of extinct primitive ganoid fishes that lived from the Devonian to the Lias and have an elongate body covered usu. with rhombic plates, small pectoral and ventral fins, a single dorsal and anal fin, a heterocercal tail, a skull covered with bony plates, and jaws bearing small teeth

¹palaeo·nis·coid \ˌ===ˈniˌskȯid\ *adj* [NL *Palaeoniscum* + E *-oid*] **:** like or like that of the genus *Palaeoniscum*

²palaeoniscoid \ˈ"\ *n* -S **:** a palaeoniscoid fish or fossil

palaeo·nis·cum \ˌ===ˈniskəm\ *n*, *cap* [NL, fr. *pale-* + Gk *oniskos*, a gadoid fish, dim. of *onos* ass — more at ASS] **:** the type genus of Palaeoniscidae

palaeo·nis·cus \-kəs\ *syn of* PALAEONISCUM

palaeo·phile \ˈpālēəˌfīl, ˈpal-\ *also* **palae·oph·i·list** \ˌ==ˈäfələst\ *n* -S [*pale-* + *-phile*] **:** one fond of or informed about what is ancient **:** ANTIQUARY

pa·lae·o·phis \pəˈlēəfəs\ *n*, *cap* [NL, fr. *pale-* + *-ophis*] **:** a genus of large extinct snakes from the Lower Eocene of England and France that are the earliest known members of the suborder Serpentes sharing many characters with and probably being ancestral to the recent pythons and boas

palaeo·pi·the·cus \ˌpālēōpəˈthēkəs, ˌpal-, -ˈpithəkəs\ *n*, *cap* [NL, fr. *pale-* + *-pithecus*] **:** a genus of extinct Pliocene anthropoids from the Siwalik hills of India that is prob. rather closely related to the recent gorilla

palae·op·tera \ˌ==ˈäptərə\ *n pl*, *cap* [NL, fr. *pale-* + *-ptera*] **:** a major division of Pterygota comprising winged insects that are unable to flex their wings over the abdomen and including the orders Odonata and Plectoptera — **palae·op·ter·ous** \¦==¦t(ə)rəs\ *adj*

palae·op·te·ryg·ii \,==,äptə'rijē,ī\ *n pl, cap* [NL, fr. *pale-* + *-pterygii*] *in some classifications* **:** a subclass of Osteichthyes comprising the primitive orders Cladistia and Chondrostei

palaeo·saur *also* **paleo·saur** \'pālēə,sȯ(ə)r, 'pal-\ *n* -s [NL *Palaeosaurus*] **:** a dinosaur of *Palaeosaurus* or a closely related genus

palaeo·sau·rus \,===ˈsȯrəs\ *n, cap* [NL, fr. *pale-* + *-saurus*] **:** a genus of carnivorous saurischian dinosaurs (suborder Theropoda) of the Upper Triassic of England that is related to *Allosaurus* and *Ceratosaurus*

palaeo·simia \¦pālēō, ¦palēō+\ *n, cap* [NL, fr. *pale-* + L *simia* ape — more at SIMIA] **:** a genus of Miocene fossil apes from the Siwalik hills of India that resemble and are prob. ancestral to the orangutan

palaeo·spondylus \¦===+\ *n, cap* [NL, fr. *pale-* + *-spondylus*] **:** a genus of extinct primitive vertebrates that are known from a single form (*P. gunni*) of the Devonian of Scotland that is usu. about one inch long with a large skull, branchial arches and jaws highly modified or possibly absent, a segmented vertebral column, and the caudal fin and limb girdles well-developed, and that is usu. placed among the Placodermi but sometimes considered a cyclostome — see CYCLIAE

palae·os·tra·ca \,pālē'ästrəkə, ,pal- *also* -'ōs-\ *n pl, cap* [NL, fr. *pale-* + *-ostraca*] *in some classifications* **:** a class of arthropods comprising the king crabs, the eurypterids, and sometimes the trilobites — compare MEROSTOMATA — **palae·os·tra·can** \¦=¦==kən\ *adj or n*

palaeo·then·ti·dae \,==='thentə,dē\ [NL, fr. *Palaeothentes*, genus of marsupials + *-idae*] *syn of* CAENOLESTIDAE

palaeo·there *also* **paleo·there** \'pālēə,thi(ə)r, 'pal-\ *n* -s [NL *Palaeotheriidae*] **:** a mammal or fossil of the family Palaeotheriidae — **palaeo·the·ri·an** \¦==¦thirēən\ *adj*

palaeo·the·ri·idae \,==ōthə'rīə,dē\ *n pl, cap* [NL, fr. *Palaeotherium*, type genus (fr. *pale-* + *-therium*) + *-idae*] **:** a family of extinct perissodactyl mammals of the Eocene and Miocene of Europe and America that are related to the horses but in some respects resemble tapirs

palaeo·the·ri·o·dont \¦===¦thirēə,dänt\ *adj* [NL *Palaeotherium* + E *-odont*] **:** being or having lophodont teeth with the external tubercles longitudinal and the inner united with them by transverse oblique crests

palaeo·trema·ta \,===ˈtremədə, -rēm-\ *n pl, cap* [NL, fr. *pale-* + *-tremata*] **:** a small order of Brachiopoda comprising primitive inarticulate forms known from the Lower Cambrian through the Ordovician — **palaeo·tremate** \¦===¦=mət, -,māt\ *n* -s

palaeo·tropical *or* **paleo·tropical** \¦===+\ *adj, usu cap* [*pale-* + *tropical*] **:** of, relating to, or being a major biogeographic region that includes the Oriental and Ethiopian regions

palaeo·typographist \¦===+\ *n* -s [*palaeotypography* + *-ist*] **:** a student of palaeotypography

palaeo·typography \¦===+\ *n* -ES [*pale-* + *typography*] **:** ancient or early typography

pa·laes·tra *also* **pa·les·tra** \pə'lestrə, *chiefly Brit* -lēs-\ *or* **pa·lais·tra** \-līs-, -lās-\ *n, pl* **palaes·trae** \-e,strē\ *or* **palaes·tras** \-,strəz\ *also* **pales·trae** \-e,strē\ *or* **pales·tras** \-,strəz\ *or* **palais·trae** \-ī,strē, -ā,s-\ *also* **palais·tras** \-,strəz\ [L *palaestra*, fr. Gk *palaistra*, fr. *palaiein* to wrestle; prob. akin to Gk *pallein* to brandish — more at POLEMIC] **1 a :** a place in ancient Greece or Rome for teaching and practicing wrestling and other sports **b :** a gymnasium or stadium **2 :** athletic exercise or practice; *esp* **:** WRESTLING — **pa·laes·tral** *also* **pa·les·tral** \-'lestrəl\ *adj*

pa·lae·ti·o·log·i·cal \pə¦lēd-ēə¦läjəkəl\ *adj* **:** of, relating to, or by means of palaetiology

pa·lae·ti·ol·o·gy *also* **pa·le·ti·ol·o·gy** \=,=='äləjē\ *n* -s [*pale-* + *etiology*] **:** explanation of past events (as in geology) by the laws of causation

pal·a·fitte \'palə,fit, -fēt, ,=='=\ *n, pl* **palafittes** \-ts\ *also* **palafit·ti** \,=='fid-ē, -'fēd-ē\ [F, fr. It *palafitta*, fr. *palo* stake, pile (fr. L *palus*) + *fitto* fixed, past part. of *figgere* to fix, fr. L *figere* to fix, fasten — more at POLE, DIKE] **:** an ancient dwelling built on piles over a lake; *specif* **:** a Neolithic lake dwelling in Switzerland or northern Italy

pa·lag·o·nite \pə'lagə,nīt\ *n* -s [G *palagonit*, fr. *Palagonia*, Sicily + G *-it* -ite] **:** basaltic glass that is more or less altered and devitrified and that occurs with volcanic ash in the form of a basaltic tuff — **pa·lag·o·nit·ic** \=¦==¦nid-ik\ *adj*

pa·la·ic \pə'lāik\ *n, cap* **:** an Anatolian language known from quotations in Hittite documents — see INDO-EUROPEAN LANGUAGES table

pa·laih·ni·han \pə'līnəhən\ *n, pl* **palaihnihan** *or* **palaihnihans** *usu cap* **1 a :** a Shasta people of northeastern California **b :** a member of such people **2 :** a subdivision of the Shastan language family comprising Achomawi and Atsugewi

palaio- — see PALE-

pa·lais \(')pa¦lā\ *n, pl* **palais** \-ā(z)\ *also* **pa·laises** \-āz\ [F, fr. L *palatium* — more at PALACE] **:** PALACE — used esp. of a French public building (as a courthouse) or official residence

palais de danse \-də'däⁿs\ *n, pl* **palais de danse** [F, lit., dance palace] **:** a public dance hall

pa·la·ka \pə'läkə\ *n* -s [Hawaiian, perh. fr. E *block*] **:** a long-sleeved Hawaiian shirt having a simple plaid or cross-striped pattern and usu. worn with the tail out

pal·a·ma \'paləmə\ *n, pl* **pala·mae** \-,mē, -,mī\ [NL, fr. Gk *palamē* palm — more at PALM] **:** the webbing on the feet of aquatic birds

pal·a·mate \-,mət, -,māt, *usu* -d-+V\ *adj* [NL *palama* + E *-ate*] **:** WEB-FOOTED

pal·a·me·dea \,palə'mēdēə\ [NL, fr. Gk *Palamēdēs*, Greek hero of the Trojan war] *syn of* ANHIMA

pal·a·me·de·i·dae \,==mə'dēə,dē\ [NL, fr. *Palamedea* + *-idae*] *syn of* ANHIMIDAE

palamino *var of* PALOMINO

pal·a·mite \'palə,mīt\ *n* -s *usu cap* [Gregorius *Palamas* †1359 Greek mystic and chief apologist for the hesychasts + E *-ite*] **:** HESYCHAST

pal·a·mit·ism \'==,mīd-,izəm, -,mī,ti-\ *n* -s *usu cap* [*palamite* + *-ism*] **:** HESYCHASM

pal·am·pore \'paləm,pō(ə)r\ *also* **pal·am·poor** \-,pu̇(ə)r\ *n* -s [prob. fr. *Palanpur*, town in Rajputana, India] **:** a painted or printed cotton cloth used in India esp. for bedcovers, garments, and prayer rugs

pal·an·der \'paləndə(r)\ *n* -s [It *palandra*] **1 :** a flat-bottomed boat formerly used for horse transport **2** *obs* **:** FIRE SHIP

pa·lan·ka \pə'laŋkə\ *n* -s [Turk *palanka*, fr. It *palanca* fortified place, stake, prob. fr. L *palanga*, *phalanga* carrying pole, roller, fr. Gk *phalang-*, *phalanx* log, roller, phalanx — more at BALK] **:** a former Turkish palisaded camp

¹pal·an·quin \¦palən¦kēn, -¦k(w)in; pə'laŋkwən, -ank-\ *also* **pal·an·keen** \¦palən¦kēn\ *n* -s [Pg *palanquim*, fr. Jav *pĕlaṅki*, fr. Prakrit *pallaṅka*, fr. Skt *palyaṅka*, *paryaṅka*, fr. *pari* around + *añcati* he bends, curves; akin to Skt *aṅka* bend, hook — more at PER, ANGLE] **:** a conveyance that was formerly much used in eastern Asia esp. for the transport of one person, that consists of an enclosed litter usu. in the form of a box with wooden shutters, and that is borne on the shoulders of men by means of projecting poles

palanquin

²palanquin *also* **palankeen** \"\ *vi* -ED/-ING/-S **:** to travel in a palanquin

pa·la·oa \,pälə'ōə\ *n* -s [Hawaiian] **:** an Hawaiian pendant of whale's tooth ivory

pa·la·pa·la \,pälə'pälə\ *n* -s [Hawaiian] *Hawaii* **:** WRITING 2a

pa·la·pa·lai \,päləpə'lī\ *n* -s [Hawaiian] **:** a large fern (*Microlepia hirta*) of the family Polypodiaceae that is widely distributed in tropical Asia and the Pacific islands

pal·ap·ter·yx \pə'laptə(,)riks\ [NL, fr. *pale-* + *Apteryx*] *syn of* DINORNIS

pa·la·qui·um \pə'läkwēəm\ *n, cap* [NL, fr. Tag *palak-palak*] **:** a large genus of East Indian trees (family Sapotaceae) with milky juice, leathery leaves, and hexamerous flowers

pa·lar \'pālə(r)\ *adj* [LL *palaris*, fr. L *palus* stake — more at POLE] **:** of, relating to, or resembling a stake ⟨a ~ line on a heraldic shield⟩

pa·las \pə'läsh\ *or* **palas tree** *also* **pu·las** \pə'l-\ *n* -ES [Hindi *palās*, fr. Skt *palāśa*] **:** DHAK

pal·at·abil·i·ty \,paləd-ə'biləd-ē, -alətə'bilətē, -i\ *n* **:** the quality or state of being palatable

palatability table *n* **:** a tabular scheme for rating the palatability of range plants for grazing animals

pal·at·able \'paləd-əbəl, -ətəb-\ *adj* [¹*palate* + *-able*] **1 :** agreeable to the palate or taste **:** SAVORY **2 :** pleasing or agreeable to the mind **:** ACCEPTABLE

syn PALATABLE, APPETIZING, SAVORY, SAPID, SAPOROUS, TASTY, TOOTHSOME, FLAVORSOME, RELISHING signify, in common, agreeable or pleasant to the taste. PALATABLE usu. implies little more than merely acceptable, often applying to something one would not usu. expect to find pleasant to the taste ⟨the root, when properly cooked, was converted into a *palatable* and nutritious food —W.H.Prescott⟩ ⟨had eaten the raw fish prepared by the Indians of Otaheite, and found it *palatable* when dipped in a sauce of sea water —C.B.Nordhoff & J.N. Hall⟩ APPETIZING implies a whetting of the appetite in some way as by the smell and appearance of food ⟨the *appetizing* odor of roasting turkey⟩ ⟨*appetizing* ways of preparing hamburg⟩ SAVORY applies to foods that have agreeable odor as well as taste, usu. suggesting stimulating and well seasoned as opposed to bland dishes ⟨a *savory* stew⟩ ⟨deer steaks broiled and *savory* —Marjory S. Douglas⟩ ⟨*savory* fried oysters —*Amer. Guide Series: Conn.*⟩ SAPID and SAPOROUS are opposed to *insipid* and imply a marked taste or flavor, usu. keen or exhilarating ⟨roast beef is more *sapid* than roast veal⟩ ⟨a *saporous* onion stew⟩ TASTY implies marked taste and appetizing quality, often of something small and delectable ⟨good, solid, *tasty* food —Della Lutes⟩ ⟨haws, which can be made into a *tasty* jelly —*Amer. Guide Series: La.*⟩ ⟨the smelt — a *tasty* panfish —*Amer. Guide Series: Mich.*⟩ TOOTHSOME heightens the idea of agreeableness in taste and adds the idea of tenderness or daintiness ⟨one of the most *toothsome* chicken dinners you'll ever munch —Gelston Hardy⟩ ⟨venison. Sometimes it was tender and *toothsome;* at other times stringy and strong —Kenneth Roberts⟩ FLAVORSOME is interchangeable with SAVORY though it stresses more a richness of taste ⟨a preserve is made from the Japanese plum, but it is more *flavorsome* eaten raw —*Amer. Guide Series: La.*⟩ ⟨incredibly *flavorsome* wild mushrooms from the forests —Marcia Davenport⟩ RELISHING stresses gusto in enjoyment ⟨plain fare, *relishing* to a hungry boy⟩

pal·at·able·ness \-bəlnəs\ *n* -ES **:** PALATABILITY

pal·at·ably \-blē, -bli\ *adv* **:** so as to be palatable **:** PLEASINGLY

¹pal·a·tal \'paləd-ᵊl, -ətᵊl\ *adj* [F, fr. L *palatum* palate + F *-al* — more at PALATE] **1 :** of or relating to the palate **:** PALATINE **2 a :** formed with the front of the tongue behind the lowered tip near or touching the hard palate (as \k\ in German \ik\ *ich*, as \y\ in *yeast* or *yacht*, as \nʸ\ in French \änʸō\ *agneau*, as \lʸ\ in Italian \lʸē\ *gli*) — compare PALATALIZED, VELAR **b** (1) **:** formed with the blade of the tongue near the hard palate (as the sounds represented by *sh* in *she*, *si* in *vision*, *ch* in *chin*, *j* in *jug*) (2) *of a vowel* **:** FRONT

☞ Because some phoneticians make the hard palate alone their datum of reference, others the combined hard-soft palate, and because some make two subdivisions, others three, compounds of prefix and *palatal* are not consistently used, as indicated in the following rough chart, in which the solid line represents the hard palate, the dotted line the soft:

prepalatal | postpalatal

prepalatal | mediopalatal | postpalatal

antepalatal (= palatal) | postpalatal (= velar)

prepalatal | mediopalatal | postpalatal (= velar)

c *of a vowel in Russian* **:** SOFT 4c **3 :** of, relating to, or situated on the outside of the aperture of a univalve mollusk ⟨a ~ lip⟩ — **pal·a·tal·ly** \-ᵊlē, -ᵊli\ *adv*

²palatal \"\ *n* -s **1 :** PALATINE BONE **2 :** a palatal sound

palatal index *n* **:** the ratio of the length of the hard palate to its breadth multiplied by 100

pal·a·tal·ism \'paləd-ᵊl,izəm, -ətᵊl,i-\ *n* -s **:** palatal character

pal·a·tal·i·ty \,palə'taləd-ē\ *n* -ES **:** PALATALISM

pal·a·tal·iza·tion \,paləd-ᵊlə'zāshən, -lətᵊl-, -,lī'z-\ *n* -s **1 :** the quality or state of being palatalized **2 :** an act or instance of palatalizing an utterance

pal·a·tal·ize \'paləd-ᵊl,īz, -lətᵊl,-\ *vt* -ED/-ING/-S **1 :** to pronounce as or change into a palatal sound **2 :** to modify the utterance of (a nonpalatal sound) by simultaneously bringing the front of the tongue to or near the hard palate

palatalized *adj* [fr. past part. of *palatalize*] *of a vowel in Russian* **:** SOFT 4c

palatal law *n* **:** a statement in historical linguistics: Indo-European guttural consonants become palatals in Indo-Iranian when followed by the palatal vowel *i* or by an *a* which is equivalent to Greek and Latin *e* but remain gutturals when followed by the guttural vowel *u* or by an *a* which is equivalent to Greek and Latin *a* or *o*, thus establishing the *a*, *e*, and *o* found in the European languages as original Indo-European

¹pal·ate \'palət, *usu* -əd-+V\ *n* -s [ME, fr. L *palatum*, perh. of Etruscan origin] **1 :** the roof of the mouth consisting of the structures that separate the mouth from the nasal cavity — see HARD PALATE, SOFT PALATE **2 a :** mental relish **:** intellectual taste **b :** the seat of the sense of taste **3 :** a projection from the base of the lower lip into the throat of a personate corolla

²palate \"\ *vt* -ED/-ING/-S **:** to try with the palate **:** TASTE, RELISH

palate bone *n* **:** PALATINE BONE

pal·ate·ful \'==fəl\ *adj, of a beverage* **:** having body or substance — **pal·ate·ful·ness** *n* -ES

pal·ate·less \'==ləs\ *adj* **:** lacking in delicacy of taste

pa·la·tial \pə'lāshəl\ *adj* [L *palatium* palace + E *-al* — more at PALACE] **1 :** of, relating to, or being a palace ⟨a ~ residence⟩ **2 :** suitable for or used in a palace ⟨~ furnishings⟩ **3 :** MAGNIFICENT, LUXURIOUS ⟨a ~ yacht⟩ — **pa·la·tial·ly** \-shəlē, -li\ *adv* — **pa·la·tial·ness** \-lnəs\ *n* -ES

pa·lat·ic \pə'lad-ik\ *adj* **:** PALATAL

pa·lat·i·nate \pə'latᵊn,ət, -ᵊn,āt\ *usu* |d-+V\ *n* -s [²*palatine* + *-ate*] **1 :** the province or territory of a palatine or count palatine **:** COUNTY PALATINE **2** *cap* **:** a native or inhabitant of a state of the old German Empire that was under the jurisdiction of a count palatine of the Rhine and is now a part of Bavaria

¹pal·a·tine \'palə,tīn\ *adj* [L *palatinus*, fr. *palatium* palace] **1 a :** of or relating to a palace esp. of a caesar or an emperor of Germany **b :** being or suitable for a palace **:** PALATIAL **2** [F *palatin*, fr. L *palatinus*, n. — more at PALATINE, n.] **a :** possessing royal privileges **b :** of or relating to a count palatine or to a palatinate

²palatine \"\ *n* -s [L *palatinus*, fr. *palatinus*, adj.] **1 a :** an officer of an imperial palace: as (1) **:** MAYOR OF THE PALACE (2) **:** an imperial chamberlain or chief minister **b :** a medieval lord having sovereign power in an imperial or royal province or dependency **:** a vassal invested with royal privileges and rights within his domains **c :** a count palatine in England and Ireland **d :** the senior proprietor of a province in an American colony **2** *cap* **:** PALATINATE 2 **3** [F, after Elisabeth Charlotte of Bavaria †1722 Duchess of Orléans, and Princess *Palatine*] **:** a fur cape or stole covering the neck and shoulders

³palatine \"\ *adj* [F *palatin*, fr. (assumed) NL *palatinus*, fr. L *palatum* palate + *-inus* -ine] **:** of, relating to, or lying near the palate

⁴palatine \"\ *n* -s **:** a palatine part; *esp* **:** PALATINE BONE

palatine artery *n* [³*palatine*] **1 :** either of two arteries of each side of the face: **a :** an inferior artery that arises from the facial artery and supplies the soft palate, palatine glands, and tonsils **b :** a superior artery that arises from the internal maxillary and sends branches to the soft palate and one branch to the mucous membrane and glands of the hard palate and gums **2 :** any of the branches of the palatine arteries

palatine bone *n* **:** either of a pair of bones that are situated behind and between the maxillae and in front of the pterygoids and in man are of an extremely irregular form, each consisting of a horizontal plate which joins the bone of the opposite side and forms the back part of the hard palate and a vertical plate which is extended into three processes and helps to form the floor of the orbit, the outer wall of the nasal cavity, and several adjoining parts

palatine canal *n* **:** any of several small openings in the bony palate for the passage of vessels or nerves

palatine gland *n* **:** any of numerous small mucous glands in the palate opening into the mouth

palatine nerve *n* **:** one of the nerves arising from the sphenopalatine ganglion and supplying the roof of the mouth, parts of the nose, and adjoining parts

palatine suture *n* **:** either of two sutures in the hard palate: **a :** a transverse suture lying between the horizontal plates of the palate bones and the maxillary bones **b :** a median suture lying between the two maxillary bones in front and continued posteriorly between the palate bones

palatine tonsil *n* **:** TONSIL 1 a

palating *pres part of* PALATE

pa·la·tion \pə'lāshən\ *n* -s [NL, fr. L *palatum* palate + NL *-ion* (as in *acanthion*, *crotaphion*)] **:** the point where a line tangent to the maxillary tuberosities on the hard palate is bisected by the sagittal plane

pal·a·ti·tis \,palə'tīd-əs\ *n* -ES [NL, fr. L *palatum* + NL *-itis*] **:** inflammation of the palate

palato- *comb form* [L *palatum* palate] **1 :** palate ⟨*palato*gram⟩ ⟨*palato*plegia⟩ **2 :** palatal and ⟨*palato*-dental⟩

pal·a·to-alveolar \¦paləd-ō+\ *adj* [*palato-* + *alveolar*] **:** being in the more alveolar of two positions between alveolar and palatal — compare ALVEOPALATAL

pal·a·to·dental \¦===+\ *adj* [*palato-* + *dental*] **:** relating to or involving both the palate and teeth

pal·a·to·glos·sus \,==='gläsəs, -lȯs-\ *n, pl* **palatoglos·si** \-,sī\ [NL, fr. *palato-* + *-glossus*, (fr. Gk *glōssa* tongue) — more at GLOSS (explanation)] **:** GLOSSOPALATINUS

pal·a·to·gram \'paləd-ə,gram\ *n* [ISV *palato-* + *-gram*] **:** the impression left on a dust-covered artificial palate by the tongue in the articulation of some sounds **:** a reproduction of such an impression

pal·a·to·graphic \¦paləd-ō+\ *adj* **:** of, relating to, or involving palatography

pal·a·tog·ra·phy \,palə'tägrəfē\ *n* -ES [*palato-* + *-graphy*] **:** the making or use of palatograms

pal·a·to·maxillary \¦paləd-ō+\ *adj* [*palato-* + *maxillary* adj.] **:** of, relating to, or involving the palate and maxilla

pal·a·to·pha·ryn·ge·us \,paləd-ōfə'rinjēəs, -,farən'jēəs\ *n* -ES [NL, fr. *palato-* + *pharyngeus* pharyngeal, fr. *pharyng-*, *pharynx*] **:** PHARYNGOPALATINUS

pal·a·to·quadrate \¦===+\ *adj* [*palato-* + *quadrate*] **:** of, relating to, or replacing the palatine and quadrate bones; *esp* **:** constituting a series of bones or a continuous cartilaginous rod that forms part of the upper jaw or roof of the mouth of most vertebrates other than mammals

pal·a·to·velar \¦===+\ *adj* [*palato-* + *velar*] **1 :** of or relating to hard palate and velum **2 :** alternatively, simultaneously, or successively palatal and velar

pa·la·tschin·ken \,pälə'chiŋkən, ,pal-\ *n, pl* **palatschinken** [G, fr. Hung *palacsinta*, fr. Romanian *plăcintă* flat cake, fr. L *placenta* — more at PLACENTA] **:** a thin egg batter pancake stuffed with jam

pa·lau \pə'lau̇\ *also* **pe·lew** \pə'lü\ *n, usu cap* **:** the Austronesian language of the Palau islands

pa·lau·an \pə'lau̇ən\ *n, pl* **palauan** *or* **palauans** *usu cap* [*Palau* islands+ E *-an*] **:** a Micronesian native or inhabitant of the Palau islands

pa·laung \pə'lau̇ŋ\ *n, pl* **palaung** *or* **palaungs** *usu cap* **1 a :** a people of the Shan States, Burma, comprising several tribes **b :** a member of such people **2 :** the Mon-Khmer language of the Palaung people

palaung-wa \='=¦=\ *n, pl* **palaung-wa** *usu cap* [*palaung* + *wa*] **:** a division of the Mon-Khmer language family

¹pa·lav·er \pə'lavə(r), -läv-\ *n* -s [Pg *palavra* word, speech, fr. LL *parabola* speech, parable — more at PARABLE] **1 a :** an often prolonged parley usu. between persons of different levels of culture or sophistication (as between a 19th century European trader and natives of the African west coast) **b :** CONFERENCE, DISCUSSION ⟨a ~ between union leaders⟩ **2 a :** CONVERSATION: as (1) **:** profuse, idle, or worthless talk **:** CHATTER (2) **:** talk intended to deceive **:** misleading or beguiling speech **b :** JARGON 2c, 3a **3 :** AFFAIR, BUSINESS ⟨that's your ~⟩

²palaver \"\ *vb* **palavered; palavered; palavering** \-v(ə)riŋ\ **palavers** *vi* **:** to use palaver: as **a :** to talk profusely or needlessly **b :** PARLEY **c :** to talk idly or beguilingly ~ *vt* **1 a :** to affect in a specified way by palavering ⟨he ~*ed* her into agreeing⟩ **b :** to alter the situation of by palavering ⟨~*ed* himself out of the mess⟩ **2 :** to use palaver to **:** CAJOLE, WHEEDLE ⟨alternately abused and ~*ed* his men⟩

pa·lav·er·er \-v(ə)rə(r)\ *n* -s [²*palaver* + *-er*] **:** one that palavers

pa·lav·er·ous \-v(ə)rəs\ *adj* [¹*palaver* + *-ous*] **:** full of or given to palaver **:** WORDY, VERBOSE

pa·la·wan \pə'läwən\ *n, pl* **palawan** *or* **palawans** *usu cap* [Native name in Palawan] **1 a :** a people of southern Palawan, Philippines **b :** a member of such people **2 :** the Austronesian language of the Palawan people

pa·lay \'pä,lī\ *n* -s [Tag, akin to Malay *padi*] **:** rice at any stage prior to husking — used esp. in the Philippines

pa·lay·an \pə'līən\ *n* -s [Tinggian *palayen*] **:** any of several Philippine oaks (genus *Quercus*)

pa·laz·zo \pə'lät(,)sō\ *n, pl* **palaz·zi** \-(,)sē\ [It, fr. L *palatium* — more at PALACE] **:** a palace or other large imposing residence — used esp. of a building in Italy

pal·berry \'pal- — *see* BERRY\ *n* [by folk etymology fr. *palbri*, native name in Australia] **:** BLUEBERRY 2a(1)

pal·dao \päl'dä(,)ō, -'dau̇\ *n* -s [Tag] **:** DAO

¹pale \'pāl, *esp before pause or consonant* -āəl\ *adj* -ER/-EST [ME, fr. MF, fr. L *pallidus*, fr. *pallēre* to be pale — more at FALLOW] **1 a :** deficient in color or in intensity or depth of color **:** dusky white **:** ASHEN, PALLID, WAN ⟨a ~ face⟩ **b :** having the countenance made pale esp. as a result of emotional or physical disorder ⟨she was ~ with rage⟩ **2 :** not bright or brilliant **:** of a faint luster **:** DIM ⟨a ~ sun shining through fog⟩ **3 :** deficient in intensity or strength **:** WEAK, FEEBLE, FAINT ⟨a ~ imitation of his mighty sire⟩ ⟨~ prose with the faint sweetness of stale lavender⟩ **4** *of a color* **:** deficient in chroma ⟨a ~ pink⟩ **:** deficient in vividness of hue or luster but of high brilliance — compare DULL

²pale \"\ *vb* -ED/-ING/-S [ME *palen*, fr. MF *palir*, fr. *pale*, adj.] *vi* **:** to turn pale **:** lose color or luster **:** BLANCH ⟨she *paled* at the sight⟩ ~ *vt* **:** to make pale **:** diminish the brightness of ⟨illness *paled* her cheek⟩

³pale \"\ *n* -s [¹*pale*] **:** PALENESS, PALLOR

⁴pale \"\ *vt* -ED/-ING/-S [ME *palen*, fr. MF *paler*, fr. *pal* pale (stake)] **1 :** to enclose, provide, or bar with a fence **:** encompass with or as if with pales **:** FENCE, ENCIRCLE **2** *obs* **:** to furnish with vertical stripes by way of adornment **:** STRIPE **3** *pres part* **paleing** [origin unknown] **:** SOLDER ⟨~ an embossed figure on the surface⟩

⁵pale \"\ *n* -s [ME, fr. MF *pal* stake, fr. L *palus* — more at POLE] **1 a** *archaic* **:** a palisade of stakes **:** an enclosing barrier **:** PALING **b** *obs* **:** a restraining boundary **:** DEFENSE **2 a :** a pointed stake driven into the ground in forming a palisade or fence **b :** a slat fastened to a rail at top and bottom for fencing **:** PICKET **3 a :** a space or field having bounds **:** an enclosed or limited region or place **:** ENCLOSURE **b :** a territory or district within certain bounds or under a particular jurisdiction **4 a :** an area (as of conduct) or the limits (as of speech) within which one is privileged or protected esp. by custom (as from censure or retaliation) ⟨conduct that was beyond the ~⟩ **5 a** *obs* **:** a vertical stripe (as on a coat)

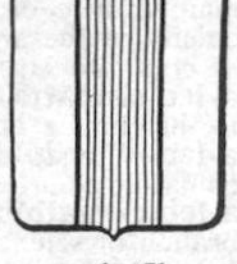

pale 5b

b : a perpendicular stripe in an escutcheon — **in pale** *adv* **1** : in a line in the direction of a pale — used of two or more heraldic charges **2** : PALEWISE 1 — **per pale** : divided in two by a vertical line down the middle — used of heraldic blazons
[6]**pale** \"\ *vt* [origin unknown] *dial Eng* : to beat (barley) to remove the awns
[7]**pale** \"\ *n* -s [NL *palea*] : the palea of a grass
[8]**pale** \"\ *n* -s [L *pala* spade, shovel — more at PALETTE] *Scot* : a cheese scoop
[9]**pale** \"\ *dial Eng var of* PEEL
pale- *or* **paleo-** *or* **palae-** *or* **palaeo-** *also* **palaio-** *comb form* [Gk *palai-*, *palaio-*, fr. *palaios* old, ancient, fr. *palai* long ago; akin to Gk *tēle* far, far off, Skt *carama* last, outermost] **1 a** : remote in point of time ⟨*Paleo*cene⟩ **b** : involving ancient forms or conditions ⟨*paleo*climate⟩ **c** : of ancient origin : ancestral ⟨*Paleo*-Eskimo⟩ **d** : dealing with ancient or fossil forms ⟨*paleo*botany⟩ **2** : early : primitive : archaic ⟨*paleo*anthropic⟩ ⟨*palaeo*typography⟩ **3** : Old World ⟨*Palaeo*tropical⟩ **4** : of pre-Tertiary origin — in names of minerals ⟨*paleo*picrite⟩
pa·lea \ˈpālēə\ *n, pl* **pa·le·ae** \-lē,ē, -lē,ī\ [NL, fr. L, chaff — more at PALLET] **1 a** : one of the chaffy scales on the receptacle subtending the disk flowers in the heads of many composite plants (as sunflowers) **b** : the upper bract that with the lemma encloses the flower in grasses **c** : RAMENTUM **2** : one of the flattened enlarged setae that form the operculum of the tube of polychaete worms of *Sabellaria* and related genera — **pa·le·al** \-lēəl\ *adj*
pa·le·a·ceous \,pālēˈāshəs\ *adj* [NL *palea* + E *-aceous*] : covered with or resembling chaffy scales
pa·le·ac·ri·ta \,==ˈakrəd·ə\ *n, cap* [NL] : a genus of geometrid moths that contains the spring cankerworm
paleanthropic *var of* PALAEOANTHROPIC
paleanthropus *syn of* PALAEOANTHROPUS
palearctic *usu cap, var of* PALAEARCTIC
pa·le·ate \ˈpālēət, -ē,āt\ *adj* [NL *palea* + E *-ate*] : covered with chaffy scales ⟨a ~ rhizome⟩
pale bark *n* [¹*pale*] : cinchona bark from a tree (*Cinchona officinalis*) that contains an exceptionally high percentage of quinine
pale brandy *n* : brandy that has taken up a yellowish tint from the cask in which it is stored
pale broomrape *n* : YELLOW CANCERROOT
pale·buck \ˈpāl,bək\ *n* [prob. of Afrik origin] : ORIBI
pale catechu *n* : GAMBIER
pale corydalis *n* : an annual or biennial corydalis (*Corydalis sempervirens*) of northeastern No. America that has loose panicles of pink flowers with yellow tips
pale crepe *n* : almost white crepe rubber prepared by special treatment usu. with sodium bisulfite
paled \ˈpāld, -āəld\ *adj* [ME, fr. ⁵*pale* + *-ed*] **1** *obs* : having vertical stripes : STRIPED **2** : enclosed with a fence or palisade ⟨a ~ garden⟩ **3** : made with pickets ⟨a ~ gate⟩
pale dock *n* : a tall erect perennial dock (*Rumex altissimus*) that has pale thick oblong-lanceolate leaves and is widely distributed in the better soils of most of No. America
pale dry ginger ale *n* : a pale-colored tart ginger ale suitable for mixing (as in a cocktail or highball)
pa·le·echinoidea \,pālē, ¦pālē+\ *or* **pa·lech·i·noi·dea** \pə-lekəˈnȯidēə\ *syn of* PALAEECHINOIDEA
pa·le·encephalon \,pālē, ¦pālē+\ *n* [NL, fr. *pale-* + *encephalon*] : the phylogenetically older part of the brain consisting of all parts except the cerebral cortex and closely related structures — compare NEENCEPHALON
pa·le·ethnology \¦==+\ *n* [ISV *pale-* + *ethnology*] : ethnology of early prehistoric man
paleface \ˈ=,=\ *n* : a white person : CAUCASIAN
palegold \ˈ=¦=\ *n* : a metallic powder made of a brass alloy and having the appearance of gold when used as a paint pigment
pale goldfinch *n* : a goldfinch (*Spinus tristis pallidus*) of the Rocky mountain area having the male less brilliantly yellow than that of the eastern goldfinches
pale horse *n, usu cap P&H* [fr. the *pale horse* ridden by Death in Rev 6:8] : DEATH — used with *the*
pa·le·ichthyology \,pālē, ¦pālē+\ *n* [*pale-* + *ichthyology*] : the study of fossil fishes
pa·le·i·form \ˈpālēə,fȯrm\ *adj* [L *palea* chaff + *-iform*] : CHAFFY, SCALY
paleing *pres part of* PALE
pale laurel *n* : SWAMP LAUREL 1
paleleaf \ˈ=¦=\ *or* **pale-leaved** \ˈ=¦=\ *adj* : having leaves of an exceptionally light green ⟨~ hickory⟩
pale·ly \ˈpāl(l)ē, -lī\ *adv* : in a pale manner : with an effect of dimness or pallor : DIMLY, FAINTLY
pale·man \ˈ=mən\ *n, pl* **palemen** [⁵*pale* + *man*] : a dweller in a pale (as in the English pale in Ireland)
pa·lem·bang \,päləmˈbäŋ\ *adj, usu cap* [fr. *Palembang*, Indonesia] : of or from the city of Palembang, Indonesia, in Sumatra : of the kind or style prevalent in Palembang
pale·ness *n* -ES [ME *palenesse*, fr. ¹*pale* + *-nesse* -ness] : the quality or state of being pale : PALLOR
paleo- — see PALE-
pa·leo·agrostology \,pālēō, ¦pālēō+\ *n* [*pale-* + *agrostology*] : a branch of paleobotany concerned with the study of fossil grasses
paleo-american \¦===+\ *or* **paleo-amerind** \"+\ *n, usu cap P&A* [*pale-* + *american* or *amerind*] : one of a hypothetical mixed Asian group migrant to No. America before the more typically Mongoloid Asians
paleoanthropic *var of* PALAEOANTHROPIC
pa·leo·an·thro·pi·nae \,===,an(t)thrəˈpī,nē\ *n pl, cap* [NL, fr. *pale-* + Gk *anthrōpos* + NL *-inae* — more at ANTHROP-] : an anthropological subdivision of Hominidae including Neanderthal man and related forms of the genus *Homo* but treated as if comparable to a subfamily — compare ARCHANTHROPINAE, NEOANTHROPINAE — **pa·leo·an·thro·pine** \¦===¦an(t)thrə,pīn\ *adj or n*
pa·leo·anthropologist \¦===+\ *n* : a specialist in paleoanthropology
pa·leo·anthropology \¦===+\ *n* [*pale-* + *anthropology*] : a branch of anthropology dealing with fossil man
paleoanthropus *syn of* PALAEOANTHROPUS
[1]**paleo-asiatic** \¦==+\ *n, usu cap P&A* [ISV *pale-* + *asiatic*] **1** : a member of a group of northeast Asian peoples including the Chukchi, Koryak, and Kamchadal of northeast Siberia and possibly also the Gilyaks of Sakhalin Island and the Ainu of northern Japan **2** *usu* **pa·leo·asiatic** \"\ *usu cap* : PALEOSIBERIAN
[2]**paleo-asiatic** \"\ *adj, usu cap P&A* : of or relating to the Paleo-Asiatics or to Paleosiberian languages
pa·leo·biological \¦==+\ *or* **pa·leo·biologic** \"+\ *adj* : of or relating to paleobiology
pa·leo·biologist \¦==+\ *n* : a specialist in paleobiology
pa·leo·biology \¦==+\ *n* [ISV *pale-* + *biology*] : a branch of paleontology that deals with fossils as organisms rather than as features of historical geology
pa·leo·botanical \¦==+\ *or* **pa·leo·botanic** \"+\ *adj* : of or relating to paleobotany — **pa·leo·botanically** \"+\ *adv*
pa·leo·botanist \¦==+\ *n* : a specialist in paleobotany
pa·leo·botany \¦==+\ *n* [ISV *pale-* + *botany*] : a branch of botany that deals with fossil plants
pa·leo·cene \ˈpālēə,sēn, ˈpal-\ *adj, usu cap* [ISV *pale-* + *-cene*; prob. orig. formed in G] : of or relating to a subdivision of the Tertiary — see GEOLOGIC TIME table
pa·leo·cerebellar \¦==+\ *adj* : of or relating to the paleocerebellum
pa·leo·cerebellum \¦==+\ *n* [NL, fr. *pale-* + *cerebellum*] : a phylogenetically old part of the cerebellum concerned with maintenance of normal postural relationships and made up chiefly of the anterior lobe of the vermis and of the pyramid — compare ARCHICEREBELLUM, NEOCEREBELLUM
pa·leo·climatic \¦==+\ *adj* [*pale-* + *climatic*] : of or relating to the climate of the earth in past ages
pa·leo·climatological \¦==+\ *adj* : of or relating to paleoclimatology
pa·leo·climatology \¦==+\ *n* [ISV *pale-* + *climatology*] : a branch of science dealing with the climate of past ages
pa·leo·cortex \¦==+\ *n* [NL, fr. *pale-* + *cortex*] : the olfactory cortex of the cerebrum
pa·leo·crystallic \¦==+\ *adj* [*pale-* + Gk *krystallos* ice + E *-ic* — more at CRUST] : PALEOCRYSTIC
pa·leo·crys·tic \¦==¦kristik\ *adj* [*pale-* + Gk *krystallos* + E *-ic*] : being, relating to, or characterized by ice that has had prolonged existence ⟨~ sea⟩ ⟨~ ice is several years old; some of it may be dozens of years old —Vilhjalmur Stefansson⟩
pa·leo·dendrology \¦==+\ *n* [*pale-* + *dendrology*] : a branch of paleobotany that deals with fossil trees
pa·leo·ecological \¦==+\ *or* **pa·leo·ecologic** \"+\ *adj* : of or relating to paleoecology
pa·leo·ecologist \¦==+\ *n* : a specialist in paleoecology
pa·leo·ecology \¦==+\ *n* [*pale-* + *ecology*] : a branch of ecology concerned with the identification and interpretation of the relation of ancient plants and animals to their environment and with the characteristics of ancient environments
pa·leo·encephalon \¦==+\ *n* : PALEENCEPHALON
pa·leo·entomological \¦==+\ *adj* : of or relating to paleoentomology
pa·leo·entomology \¦==+\ *n* [*pale-* + *entomology*] : a branch of entomology that deals with fossil insects
pa·leo·ethnic \¦==+\ *adj* [*pale-* + Gk *ethnos* nation, people + E *-ic* — more at ETHNOS] : relating to the earliest human races
pa·leo·ethnography \¦==+\ *n* [*pale-* + *ethnography*] : the ethnography of paleolithic man
paleogean *usu cap, var of* PALAEOGAEAN
[1]**pa·leo·gene** \ˈpālēə,jēn, ˈpal-\ *n, usu cap* [G *paläogen*, fr. *paläo-* pale- + *-gen* (fr. root of Gk *genesthai* to be born) — more at KIN] : the earlier part of the Tertiary including the Paleocene, Eocene, and Oligocene
[2]**paleogene** \"\ *adj, usu cap* : of or relating to the Paleogene
paleogenesis *var of* PALAEOGENESIS
pa·leo·geographer \,pālēō, ¦pālēō+\ *n* : a specialist in paleogeography
pa·leo·geographic \¦==+\ *also* **pa·leo·geographical** \"+\ *adj* : of or relating to paleogeography — **pa·leo·geographically** \"+\ *adv*
pa·leo·geography \¦==+\ *n* [ISV *pale-* + *geography*] : the geography of ancient times or of a particular former geological epoch
pa·leo·geologic \¦==+\ *adj* : of or relating to paleogeology
pa·leo·geology \¦==+\ *n* [*pale-* + *geology*] : a branch of geology concerned with the study of geologic features exposed at the surface during a past epoch or period but now buried beneath rocks formed in subsequent time
pa·leo·geomorphology \¦==+\ *n* [*pale-* + *geomorphology*] : a branch of geomorphology concerned with the study of ancient topographic features now either concealed beneath the surface or removed by erosion
pa·le·og·ra·pher \,pālēˈägrəfə(r), ,pal-\ *n* -s : a specialist in paleography
pa·leo·graphic \,pālēəˈgrafik, ¦pal-, -fēk\ *also* **pa·leo·graph·i·cal** \-fəkəl, -fēk-\ *adj* : of or relating to paleography — **pa·leo·graph·i·cal·ly** \-fək(ə)lē, -fēk-, -li\ *adv*
pa·le·og·ra·phy \,pālēˈägrəfē, ,pal-, -fi\ *n* -ES [NL *palaeographia*, fr. Gk *palaio-* pale- + *-graphia* -graphy] **1 a** : an ancient manner of writing ⟨deciphering early Gaelic ~⟩ **b** : ancient writings **2** : the study of ancient modes of writing including inscriptions : the deciphering and identifying (as by origin or period) of ancient writings
pa·leo·hydrology \,pālēō, ¦pālēō+\ *n* [*pale-* + *hydrology*] : the study of ancient use and handling of water (as in irrigation or urban water supplies)
pa·leo-indian \¦==+\ *n, usu cap P&I* [*pale-* + *indian*] : PALEO-AMERICAN
pa·le·o·la \pəˈlēələ\ *n, pl* **paleo·lae** \-,lē, -lī\ [NL, dim. of *palea*] : a small or secondary palea — **pa·le·o·late** \-,lāt, -lət\ *adj*
pa·leo·lith \ˈpālēə,lith, ˈpal-\ *n* -s [*pale-* + *-lith*] : a Paleolithic implement of unpolished chipped stone
pa·leo·lith·ic \¦==¦lithik, -thēk\ *adj, usu cap* [ISV *pale-* + *-lithic*] : of or relating to the second period of the Stone Age following the Eolithic and preceding the Mesolithic and characterized by rough or chipped stone implements
paleolithic man *n, often cap P* : a man of or peculiar to the Paleolithic period (as the Heidelberg, Neanderthal, or Cro-Magnon)
pa·le·ol·o·gist \,pālēˈäləjəst, ,pal-\ *n* -s : a specialist in paleology
pa·le·ol·o·gy \-jē, -ji\ *n* -ES [*pale-* + *-logy*] : the study or knowledge of antiquities and esp. prehistoric antiquities
pa·leo·mammalogy \,pālēō, ¦pālēō+\ *n* [*pale-* + *mammalogy*] : paleontological mammalogy
pa·le·on·tog·ra·phy \,pālē,änˈtägrəfē, ,pal-, -ēənˈ-, -fi\ *n* -ES [F *paléontographie*, fr. *palé-* + Gk *onta* existing things + F *-graphie* -graphy] : descriptive paleontology
pa·le·on·to·log·i·cal \,==,äntəlˈäjəkəl, -ənt-, -jēk-\ *also* **pa·le·on·to·log·ic** \-jik, -jēk\ *adj* : of or relating to paleontology
paleontologic geology *n* : a branch of geology that deals with the succession and significance of past life
pa·le·on·tol·o·gist \,==,änˈtäləjəst, -ənˈt-\ *n* -s : a specialist in paleontology
pa·le·on·tol·o·gy \-jē, -ji\ *n* -ES [F *paléontologie*, fr. *palé-* pale- + Gk *onta* existing things (fr. neut. pl. of *ont-*, *ōn*, pres. part of *einai* to be) + F *-logie* -logy — more at ONT-] **1** : a science that deals with the life of past geological periods, is based on the study of fossil remains of plants and animals, and gives information esp. about the phylogeny and relationships of modern animals and plants and about the chronology of the history of the earth — compare PALEOBIOLOGY, PALEOBOTANY, PALEOCLIMATOLOGY, PALEOGEOGRAPHY, PALEOZOOLOGY **2 a** : a treatise on paleontology (as of a region or period) **b** : the materials of this science : FOSSILS **c** : the structural attributes of a fossil or extinct organism, type, or group
pa·leo·pal·li·al \¦==ō¦palēəl\ *adj* [NL *paleopallium* + E *-al*] : of, relating to, or mediated by the paleopallium
pa·leo·pallium \¦==+\ *n* [NL, fr. *pale-* + *pallium*] : a phylogenetically old part of the cerebral cortex that develops along the lateral aspect of the hemispheres and gives rise to the olfactory lobes in higher forms
pa·leo·pathology \,pālēō, ¦pālēō+\ *n* [ISV *pale-* + *pathology*] : a branch of pathology concerned with diseases of former times as evidenced esp. in fossil or other remains
pa·leo·pedology \¦==+\ *n* [*pale-* + *pedology*] : a branch of pedology that is concerned with the soils of past geological ages
pa·leo·physiography \¦==+\ *n* [*pale-* + *physiography*] : PALEOGEOMORPHOLOGY
pa·leo·phyt·ic \,pālēəˈfid·ik, ¦pal-\ *adj* [ISV *pale-* + *-phytic*] : PALEOBOTANICAL
pa·leo·plain \¦==+,-\ *n* [*pale-* + *plain*] : an ancient plain of degradation now more or less buried beneath deposits of later times
pa·leo·psychic \,pālēō, ¦pālēō+\ *adj* [*pale-* + *psychic*] : of, relating to, or involving remotely ancestral modes of thought and desire as if still operative in unconscious mentality
pa·leo·psychology \¦==+\ *n* [*paleopsychic* + *-logy*] : the study of paleopsychic phenomena
pa·le·ornithology \,pālē, ¦pālē+\ *n* [*pale-* + *ornithology*] : a branch of paleontology concerned with the study of fossil birds
paleosaur *var of* PALAEOSAUR
[1]**pa·leo·siberian** \,pālēō, ¦pālēō+\ *adj, usu cap* [*pali-* + *siberian*] : PALEO-ASIATIC
[2]**paleosiberian** \"\ *n, usu cap* : a group of language families consisting of Luorawetlan, Yukaghir, Gilyak, and Yeniseian that are spoken by aboriginal peoples in northern and eastern Siberia, are not known to be related, but are conveniently treated together in contrast to the Altaic languages and Russian spoken in the same area
pa·leo·striatal \¦==+\ *adj* [NL *paleostriatum* + E *-al*] : of or relating to the paleostriatum
pa·leo·striatum \¦==+\ *n* [NL, fr. *pale-* + *striatum*] : the phylogenetically older part of the corpus striatum consisting of the globus pallidus
pa·leo·technic \¦==+\ *adj* [*pale-* + *technic*] **1** : belonging to or concerned with ancient art **2** : of, relating to, or constituting a period of industrial development marked by the predominance of hand tools and craft industries or by complex industries based on the use of coal and iron — compare NEOTECHNIC
pa·leo·thalamus \¦==+\ *n* [NL, fr. *pale-* + *thalamus*] : the phylogenetically older part of the thalamus
paleothere *var of* PALAEOTHERE
pa·leo·thermal \,pālēō, ¦pālēō+\ *or* **pa·leo·thermic** \"+\ *adj* [ISV *pale-* + *thermal* or *thermic*] : relating to or characteristic of warm climates of past geological time ⟨a ~ flora⟩
paleotropical *usu cap, var of* PALAEOTROPICAL
pa·leo·volcanic \¦==+\ *adj* [ISV *pale-* + *volcanic*] : of, relating to, or being igneous rocks erupted before the Tertiary
[1]**pa·leo·zo·ic** \¦pālēə¦zōik, ¦pal-, -ōēk\ *adj, usu cap* [*pale-* + *-zoic*] : of or relating to a grand division of geological history from the beginning of the Cambrian to the close of the Permian marked by the culmination of nearly all classes of invertebrates except the insects and in whose later epochs seed-bearing plants, amphibians, and reptiles first appeared — see GEOLOGIC TIME table ⟨many facts in *Paleozoic* stratigraphy —E.O.Ulrich⟩
[2]**paleozoic** \"\ *n* -s *usu cap* : the Paleozoic era or system of rocks
pa·leo·zoological \¦==+\ *adj* : of or relating to paleozoology
pa·leo·zoologist \¦==+\ *n* : a specialist in paleozoology
pa·leo·zoology \¦==+\ *n* [F *paléozoologie*, fr. *palé-* pale- + *zoologie* zoology] : a branch of paleontology that deals with ancient and fossil animals
pale persicaria *n* : a tall erect or decumbent annual persicaria (*Polygonum lapathifolium*) with somewhat glabrous leaves and slender spikes of pink to purplish flowers
pale plantain *n* : RUGEL'S PLANTAIN
[1]**pal·er** \ˈpālə(r)\ *n* -s [⁴*pale* + *-er*] *archaic* : one in charge of palings
[2]**paler** *comparative of* PALE
[1]**pa·ler·mi·tan** \pəˈlərmətᵊn, -ler-\ *adj, usu cap* [It *palermitano*, modif. (influenced by *Palermo* Palermo) of L *panormitanus*, fr. Gk *panormitēs* inhabitant of Palermo (fr. *Panormos* Palermo + *-itēs* -ite) + L *-anus* -an] : PALERMO
[2]**palermitan** \"\ *n* -s *cap* [It *palermitano*, fr. *palermitano*, adj.] : a native or resident of Palermo
pa·ler·mo \pəˈlər(,)mō, -ler-\ *adj, usu cap* [fr. *Palermo*, city in northern Sicily] : of or from the city of Palermo, Italy, in Sicily : of the kind or style prevalent in Palermo
pale rose *n* : CABBAGE ROSE
pales *pres 3d sing of* PALE, *pl of* PALE
palest *superlative of* PALE
pal·es·tine man \ˈpalə,stīn- *sometimes* -,stēn- *or* -,stən-\ *n, pl* **palestine men** *usu cap P* [fr. *Palestine*] : a member of a highly variable early Neanderthaloid population of southwestern Asia that are known chiefly from skulls and other skeletal remains from Palestinian caves, that typically exhibit strong intermixture of Neanderthal and neanthropic characters, and that may represent either transitional forms or hybrids — compare SKHUL MAN, TABUN MAN
[1]**pal·es·tin·ian** \,paləˈstinēən, -inyən *sometimes* -tēn-\ *adj, usu cap* [*Palestine*, country of southwestern Asia + E *-ian*] : of or relating to Palestine
[2]**palestinian** \"\ *n* -s **1** *cap* : a native or inhabitant of Palestine : ISRAELI **2** *usu cap* : PALESTINE MAN
palestra *var of* PALAESTRA
pa·les weevil \ˈpā(,)lēz-\ *n* [NL *pales*, specific epithet of *Hylobius pales*] : a large brown weevil (*Hylobius pales*) that feeds on the bark of white pine and a few other pines frequently girdling and killing young trees
pal·et \(ˈ)pā¦let\ *n* -s [⁷*pale* + *-et*] : PALEA 1a, 1b
paletiology *var of* PALAETIOLOGY
pal·e·tot \ˈpalə,tō, -l(,)tō\ *n* -s [F, fr. MF *paletot*, *paltoke*, fr. ME *paltok* a kind of jacket] **1** : a man's loose outer coat **2** : a man's fitted overcoat; *also* : a woman's fitted jacket worn esp. in the 19th century over a costume with crinoline or bustle
pale touch-me-not *n* : a tall branching jewelweed (*Impatiens pallida*) with glaucous or blue-green foliage and usu. yellow flowers often with reddish brown spots
pal·ette \ˈpalət, *usu* -əd·+V\ *n* -s [F, fr. MF, small shovel, fr. *pale* spade, shovel (fr. L *pala*) + *-ette*; prob. akin to L *pangere* to fix, fasten, plant — more at PACT] **1 a** (1) : a thin oval or rectangular board or tablet in which is a thumbhole near one end for being held horizontally when in use and on which a painter lays and mixes pigments (2) : a surface (as a tabletop or a piece of glass or marble) similarly used **b** : the set or assortment of colors put on the palette (as for a particular picture) **c** (1) : a particular range, quality, or use of color ⟨his ~ predominated in muted tones⟩ (2) : a comparable range, quality, or use of available elements esp. in another art (as music) **2** *Brit* : a curved wooden implement used in transferring a pantile from the mold to the drying shelf

palette 1a (1)

palette cup *n* : a small metal cup for holding vehicle or diluent for paint and equipped with a flange for attachment to an artist's palette
palette knife *also* **pallet knife** *n* : a knife having a very flexible steel blade and no cutting edge that is used esp. by painters to mix colors or spread paint or by printers for distributing ink : SPATULA
pale violet *n* : a leafy-stemmed No. American violet (*Viola striata*) with large white or creamy flowers faintly marked with purple
pale western cutworm *n* : a cutworm that is the larva of a noctuid moth (*Agrotis orthogonia*) and that is a serious pest on grains in central U.S.
pale·wise \ˈpāl,wīz\ *also* **pale·ways** \-wāz\ *adv* [⁵*pale* + *-wise*, *-ways*] **1** *heraldry* : in the direction of a pale : VERTICALLY **2** *heraldry* : in pale
pal·fre·nier \,palfrəˈni(ə)r\ *n* -s [MF *palefrenier*, fr. OProv *palafrenier*, fr. ML *palafrenarius*, alter. (influenced by L *frenum* bridle) of *palafridarius*, fr. *palafredus* + L *-arius* -ary — more at PALFREY] *archaic* : GROOM 2b
pal·frey \ˈpȯlfrē\ *n* -s [ME, fr. OF *palefrei*, fr. ML *palafredus*, fr. LL *paraveredus* post-horse for secondary roads, fr. Gk *para-* beside, subsidiary + L *veredus* post horse, fr. a Gaulish word akin to Welsh *gorwydd* horse, OIr *riadaim* I ride — more at PARA-, RIDE] *archaic* : a saddle horse other than a war-horse; *esp* : a light easy-gaited horse suitable for a lady
palgrave *var of* PALSGRAVE
[1]**pa·li** \ˈpälē\ *n* -s *usu cap* [Skt *pāli* row, line, series, series of Buddhist sacred texts] : an Indic language found in the Buddhist canon and used today as the liturgical and scholarly language of Hinayana Buddhism
[2]**pali** *pl of* PALUS
[3]**pa·li** \ˈpälē\ *n* -s [Hawaiian] *Hawaii* : a steep slope : PRECIPICE
[4]**pali** \"\ *n* -s [Tamil *pālai*] : an Indian timber tree (*Palaquium ellipticum*) of the family Sapotaceae that yields a moderately hard, heavy, and durable reddish to reddish brown straight or wavy grained lumber which is used esp. for joinery, furniture, cooperage, and planking
pali- *comb form* [Gk *palin*, *pali* again, back; akin to Gk *polos* pivot, axis — more at POLE] : pathological state characterized by repetition of a (specified) act ⟨*pali*lalia⟩ ⟨*pali*rrhea⟩
pali buddhism *n, usu cap P&B* [¹*Pali*] : HINAYANA
pal·i·cou·rea \,paləˈkürēə\ *n, cap* [NL] : a large genus of tropical American shrubs (family Rubiaceae) having white or yellow flowers with the tube of the corolla distended within and including several that are cultivated as ornamentals
palier *comparative of* PALY
paliest *superlative of* PALY
pa·li·form \ˈpālə,fȯrm\ *adj* [NL *palus* + E *-iform*] : resembling a palus ⟨the ~ lobes of the septa in corals⟩
pal·i·kar *also* **pal·i·car** \ˈpalə,kär\ *n* -s [NGk *palikari*, *pallēkari* youth, fr. LGk *pallikarion* page, dim. of *pallēk-*, *pallēx* young man or woman] **1** : a Greek or Albanian soldier in the pay of the sultan of Turkey **2** : a soldier of the Greek militia in the war of independence (1821–28) against Turkey
pa·li·la \pəˈlēlə\ *n* -s [Hawaiian] : a Hawaiian honeycreeper (*Psittirostra bailleui*) that resembles a finch
pali·la·lia \,paləˈlālēə, -ālyə\ *n* -s [NL, fr. *pali-* + *-lalia*] : a speech defect marked by abnormal repetition of syllables, words, or phrases

pa·lil·o·gy *or* **pa·lil·lo·gy** \pəˈliləjē\ *n* -ES [LL *palilogia*, fr. Gk *palillogia*, recapitulation, fr. *palin* again, back + *-logia* — more at PALI-] **:** repetition of a word for emphasis (as in Is 38:19 "the living, the living, he shall praise thee")

pal·im·bacchic \ˌpaləm+\ *adj or n* [L *palimbacchius* + E *-ic*] **:** ANTIBACCHIC

pal·im·bacchius \ˌpaləm, ˌpaˌlim, pəˌlim+\ *n, pl* **palimbacchii** *or* **palimbacchiuses** [L, fr. Gk *palimbakcheios*, fr. *palin* back + *bakcheios* bacchius — more at BACCHIUS] **:** ANTIBACCHIUS

¹**pal·imp·sest** \ˈpaləm(p)ˌsest\ *n* -S [L *palimpsestus*, fr. Gk *palimpsēstos* scraped again, fr. *palin* again, back + *-psēstos*, fr. *psēn* to rub, scrape, crumble; akin to Gk *psammos* sand — more at PALI-, SAND] **1** *obs* **:** writing material (as parchment or paper) so prepared that the writing can be erased and the material reused **2 a :** a parchment, tablet, or other portion of writing material that has been used twice or three times after the earlier writing has been erased **b :** a manuscript in which one or two earlier erased writings are found **3 :** a memorial brass having earlier engraving on the side opposite to that which is exposed

²**palimpsest** \"\ *adj* **1** *of a manuscript* **:** having besides its present writing one or two earlier erased writings **2** *of a memorial brass* **:** having earlier engraving on the side opposite to that exposed

pal·imp·ses·tic \ˌ==ˈsestik\ *adj* **1 :** forming or appearing in a palimpsest **2 :** producing palimpsests

pal·i·nal \ˈpalənᵊl\ *adj* [Gk *palin* back + E *-al*] *of mastication* **:** effected by backward motion — compare ORTHAL, PROAL, PROPALINAL

pal·in·drome \ˈpalənˌdrōm\ *n* -S [Gk *palindromos* running back again, fr. *palin* back, again + *-dromos* -drome] **1 a :** a word, verse, or sentence (as "Able was I ere I saw Elba") that reads the same backward or forward **b :** WORD SQUARE 2 **2 :** a number (as 18181) that expressed in arabic numerals has the same value when reversed

pal·in·dro·mia \ˌpalənˈdrōmēə\ *n* -S [NL, fr. Gk *palindromos* + NL *-ia*] **:** recurrence of a disease

pal·in·dromic \ˌpalənˈdrämik, -rōm-\ *adj* [*palindrome* + *-ic*] **1 :** of, relating to, or constituting a palindrome ⟨a ~ sentence⟩ **2** [NL *palindromia* + E *-ic*] **:** RECURRENT ⟨~ rheumatism⟩ — **pal·in·dromi·cal·ly** \-mək(ə)lē\ *adv*

¹**pal·ing** \ˈpāliŋ, -lēŋ\ *pres part of* PALE

²**paling** \"\ *n* -S [ME, fr. gerund of *palen* to pale] **1 :** the act of building a fence or enclosing with pales **2 a :** a fence formed with pales or pickets **b :** wood for making pales **:** a stock of pales **3 :** a pale or picket for a fence

pal·in·ge·ne·sia \ˌpalənjəˈnēzh(ē)ə\ *n* -S [ML, fr. Gk, fr. *palin* again + *-genesia*] **:** PALINGENESIS

pal·in·ge·ne·sian \ˌ===ˈzhən\ *adj* [*palingenesia* + E *-an*] **:** relating to palingenesis

pal·in·gen·e·sis \ˌpalənˈjenəsəs\ *n* [Gk *palin* again + L *genesis* birth — more at GENESIS] **:** renewal by or as if by rebirth: as **a :** Christian baptism **b :** the doctrine of continued rebirths **:** METEMPSYCHOSIS **c** [G, fr. Gk *palin* + L *genesis*] **:** reproduction during development of characters or structures that have been maintained essentially unchanged throughout the phylogeny of a strain **:** RECAPITULATION — opposed to *cenogenesis*; compare RECAPITULATION THEORY **d :** the formation of new rocks by the re-fusion of former rocks deep within the earth

pal·in·gen·e·sist \-səst\ *n* -S **:** a believer in palingenesis

pal·in·gen·e·sy \-nəsē\ *n* -ES [F *palingénésie*, fr. ML *palingenesia*] **:** PALINGENESIS

pal·in·ge·net·ic \ˌpalənjəˈnedˌik\ *adj* [*palingenesis* + *-etic*] **1 :** of or relating to palingenesis **2** *or* **pal·in·gen·ic** \ˌpalənˈjenik\ [*palingenic* fr. *palingenesis* + E *-ic*] **:** produced by or involved in geological or biological palingenesis — **pal·in·ge·net·i·cal·ly** \-jəˈnedək(ə)lē\ *adv*

pal·in·ge·ni·idae \ˌpalənjəˈnīəˌdē\ *n pl, cap* [NL, fr. *Palingenia*, type genus (fr. *palin-* + *-genia* -geny) + *-idae*] **:** a family of mayflies

pal·in·gen·ist \ˌpalənˈjenəst\ *n* -S [*palingenesis* + *-ist*] **:** PALINGENESIST

paling fence *n* **:** PICKET FENCE

¹**pal·in·ode** \ˈpaləˌnōd\ *n* -S [Gk *palinōidia*, fr. *palin* back, again + *-ōidia* (fr. *aeidein* to sing) — more at PALI-, ODE] **1 :** an ode or song recanting or retracting something in a former one **2 :** RETRACTION; *esp* **:** a formal retraction

²**palinode** \"\ *vb* -ED/-ING/-S **:** RECANT, RETRACT

pal·in·odi·al \ˌpaləˈnōdēəl\ *adj* [*palinody* + *-al*] **:** of, relating to, or constituting a palinode

pal·in·odic \-ōdik, -äd-\ *adj* [Gk *palinōidikos*, fr. *palin* + *-ōid-* (fr. *aeidein*) + *-ikos* -ic — more at ODE] **:** of or relating to a form of symmetrical construction found in some ancient odes in which the fourth in a group of four strophes repeats the structure of the first and the third that of the second

pal·in·odist \ˈpaləˌnōdəst, ˌ==ˈ==\ *n* -S **:** one who writes a palinode

pal·in·ody \ˈpaləˌnōdē\ *n* -ES [MF *palinodie*, fr. Gk *palinōidia* — more at PALINODE] **:** PALINODE

pal·in·spas·tic \ˌpalənˈspastik\ *adj* [Gk *palin* back again + *spastikos* drawing — more at SPASTIC] **:** of or relating to the inferred original positions of landmasses prior to extensive diastrophic movements

pal·in·trope \ˈpalənˌtrōp\ *n* -S [Gk *palintropos* turning back, fr. *palin* again + *-tropos* -trope, adj. suffix] **:** the recurved posterior section of either valve of some brachiopod shells

pal·i·nu·ra \ˌpaləˈn(y)ürə\ *n pl, cap* [NL, fr. *Palinurus*] **:** a tribe of decapod crustaceans (suborder Reptantia) usu. having the rostrum and the inner lobes of the second maxillae and first maxillipeds reduced and including the Palinuridae, Scyllaridae, and a few related forms — **pal·i·nu·ran** \ˌ==ˈ=rən\ *adj or n*

pal·i·nu·ri·dae \ˌ==ˈ=rəˌdē\ *n pl, cap* [NL, fr. *Palinurus*, type genus + *-idae*] **:** a family of decapod crustaceans (tribe Palinura) comprising the spiny lobsters — see PALINURUS; compare PANULIRUS

pal·i·nu·rus \-rəs\ *n, cap* [NL, fr. L, name of Aeneas's pilot, understood as fr. Gk *palin* back + *-ouros* -urus] **:** the type genus of Palinuridae comprising the European langouste and other Old World spiny lobsters — compare PANULIRUS

palis *pl of* PALI

¹**pal·i·sade** *also* **pal·li·sade** \ˌpaləˈsād, ˈ==ˌ=\ *n* -S [F *palissade*, fr. OProv *palissada*, fr. *palissa*, fr. (assumed) VL *palicea*, fr. L *palus* stake — more at POLE] **1 a :** a fence of stakes; *esp* **:** a strong fence for defense **b :** a long strong stake pointed at the top and set in the ground vertically or obliquely with others in a close row as a means of defense **2 :** a line of bold cliffs; *esp* **:** one showing a columnar face weathered along vertical joints — usu. used in pl. **3 :** PALISADE PARENCHYMA

²**palisade** \"\ *vt* -ED/-ING/-S **:** to surround, furnish, enclose, or fortify with palisades

palisade cell *n* **:** a cell of palisade parenchyma

palisade layer *n* **1 :** the layer of palisade parenchyma in a leaf **2 :** a sclerenchymatous protective layer inside the epidermis of many hard seeds

palisade parenchyma *n* **:** a layer of columnar or cylindrical cells that are rich in chloroplasts, have small intercellular spaces, and are found typically just beneath the upper epidermis of foliage leaves — compare SPONGY PARENCHYMA

palisade worm *n* **:** any of several comparatively large bloodsucking nematode worms (genus *Strongylus*) that are parasitic in the large intestine of horses and have larvae which wander in the viscera and sometimes lodge in the intestinal blood vessels causing colic or more rarely a fatal aneurysm — called also *bloodworm, red worm*

palisading *n* -S [fr. gerund of ²*palisade*] **:** a row of palisades set in the ground esp. as a protective enclosure

¹**pal·i·sa·do** \ˌpaləˈsā(ˌ)dō\ *n* -ES [Sp *palizada*, fr. OProv *palissada* — more at PALISADE] **:** PALISADE

²**palisado** \"\ *vt* -ED/-ING/-ES **:** PALISADE

pal·i·san·der *also* **pal·is·san·dre** *or* **pal·i·san·dre** \ˈpaləˌsandə(r), ˌ==ˈ==\ *n* -S [F *palissandre, palisandre*, prob. of AmerInd origin] **:** BRAZILIAN ROSEWOOD

pal·ish \ˈpālish, -lēsh\ *adj* [ME, fr. ¹*pale* + *-ish*] **:** rather pale

pal·is·san·dre \ˈpaləˌsandə(r), ˌ==ˈ==\ *n* -S [F, palisander] **:** WALLFLOWER 4

pa·lis·sy ware \pəˈlisē-, ˈpaləˌsē-\ *n, usu cap P* [after Bernard *Palissy* †1589 Fr. potter] **:** a 16th century French pottery decorated with colored glazes laid over embossments and usu. with figures (as of fishes or leaves) in high relief

pal·i·u·rus \ˌpalēˈyürəs\ *n, cap* [NL, fr. L, Christ's-thorn, fr. Gk *paliouros*] **:** a small genus of thorny Eurasian shrubs (family Rhamnaceae) with cymose perfect flowers and dry woody winged fruit — see CHRIST'S-THORN

pal·kee *or* **pal·ki** \ˈpälkē\ *n* -S [Hindi *pālkī*, fr. Prakrit *pallaṅka* — more at PALANQUIN] *India* **:** PALANQUIN

palkee gharry \ˈ==ˌ==\ *n* [Hindi *pālkī-gārī* fr. *pālkī* palkee + *gārī* gharry] **:** a gharry shaped somewhat like a palanquin

¹**pall** \ˈpȯl\ *n* -S [ME, fr. OE *pæll*, fr. L *pallium* pall, Greek mantle; akin to L *palla* women's mantle] **1** *archaic* **:** rich fine cloth used for the outer garments of persons of rank **2 a** *archaic* **:** an outer garment (as a cloak or mantle) esp. when of rich material **b :** PALLIUM 1b **3 a** (1) *archaic* **:** ALTAR CLOTH (2) **:** FRONTAL 2 (3) **:** a linen cloth for covering the chalice; *esp* **:** a square piece of cardboard covered with cloth that is usu. embroidered on the upper side **b** (1) **:** a fine cloth spread over or on something (as a canopy or counterpane); *esp* **:** a heavy cloth draped over a coffin, hearse, or tomb (2) **:** COFFIN; *esp* **:** one holding a body **c** *or* **pall·ing** \-liŋ\ **:** a canvas hatch cover on a ship **4 :** a thing that covers or conceals: as **a** *obs* **:** CLOAK 2c **b :** an overspreading element that produces an effect of gloom ⟨a ~ of smoke⟩ **5 a :** a conventionalized heraldic representation of the front half of an archiepiscopal pallium **b :** PAIRLE — **per pall** \ˌpərˈ=\ **:** divided in three parts by partition lines in the form of a Y **:** tierced in pairle

²**pall** \"\ *vt* -ED/-ING/-S **:** to cover with or as if with a pall **:** CLOAK, DRAPE

³**pall** \"\ *vb* -ED/-ING/-S [ME *pallen*, short for *apallen* to appall] *vi* **1 :** to lose strength **:** fail in vigor or effectiveness **2 a** *obs, of wine or beer* **:** to become flat **b :** to lose in interest or attraction ⟨these occupations ~*ed* —Virginia Woolf⟩ ⟨in the long run ugliness ~*s* almost as much as beauty —George Saintsbury⟩ — often used with *on* or *upon* ⟨smooth, rhetorical mind must have ~*ed* on one who liked sharp edges —John Buchan⟩ **3 :** to become tired of something at first pleasurable ⟨~ of too much music⟩ ~ *vt* **1** *obs* **:** to make faint or fainthearted **:** DAUNT, APPALL **2 a** *obs* **:** to cause (wine or beer) to become flat **b :** to cause (something pleasurable) to become insipid ⟨reason and reflection . . . ~ all his enjoyments —Francis Atterbury⟩ **3 :** to deprive (as a person or his senses) of pleasure in something usu. by cloying or satiating ⟨the choicest delicacies ~ the stomach in time⟩ **syn** see SATIATE

⁴**pall** [³*pall*] *n* -S *obs* **:** NAUSEA, QUALM

⁵**pall** *var of* PAWL

¹**pal·la** \ˈpalə\ *n, pl* **pal·lae** \-ˌlē\ *also* **pallas** [L] **1 :** a loose outer garment formed by wrapping or draping a large square of cloth and worn by women of ancient Rome — compare PALLIUM 1a **2 :** PALL 3a

palla 1

²**palla** *var of* PALLAH

³**pa·lla** \ˈpäyə\ *n* -S [Sp, fr. Quechua] **:** an Incan princess

¹**pal·la·di·an** \pəˈlādēən, (ˈ)paˈl-\ *adj, often cap* [L *palladius*, of Pallas (fr. Gk *palladios*, fr. *Pallad-, Pallas* Pallas, goddess of wisdom) + E *-an*] **:** of or relating to wisdom or learning

²**pal·la·di·an** \pəˈlādēən\ *adj, usu cap* [Andrea *Palladio* †1580 Ital. architect + E *-an*] **:** of, relating to, or being a revived classic style in architecture based on the works of Andrea Palladio — see PALLADIAN WINDOW

pal·la·di·an·ism \-ädēəˌnizəm\ *n* -S *usu cap* [²*palladian* + *-ism*] **:** the Palladian school or style of architecture

palladian window *n, usu cap P* [²*Palladian*] **:** an architectural unit consisting of a central window with an arched head and on each side a usu. narrower window with a square head

Palladian window

pal·lad·ic \pəˈladik, -lād-\ *adj* [NL *palladium* + E *-ic*] **:** of, relating to, or derived from palladium — used esp. of compounds in which this element is tetravalent; compare PALLADOUS

pal·la·dif·er·ous \ˌpaləˈdif(ə)rəs\ *adj* [NL *palladium* + E *-iferous*] **:** bearing palladium

pal·la·di·nize \ˈpalədəˌnīz\ *vt* -ED/-ING/-S [irreg. (influenced by *platinize*) fr. NL *palladium* + E *-ize*] **:** to coat or treat (as charcoal or asbestos) with palladium

pal·la·di·ous \pəˈlādēəs\ *adj* [NL *palladium* + E *-ous*] **:** PALLADOUS

¹**pal·la·di·um** \pəˈlādēəm\ *n, pl* **palla·dia** \-ēə\ *also* **palladiums** [L, fr. Gk *palladion* statue of Pallas on the preservation of which was supposed to depend the safety of Troy, fr. *palladion*, neut. of *palladios* of Pallas, fr. *Pallad-, Pallas* Pallas] **:** something that affords effectual protection or security **:** SAFEGUARD ⟨trial by jury has been called the ~ of our civil rights⟩

²**palladium** \"\ *n* -S [NL, fr. *Pallad-, Pallas* Pallas, the asteroid + *-ium*] **:** a silver-white ductile malleable metallic element that is one of the platinum metals and resembles platinum, that does not tarnish at ordinary temperatures, that occurs usu. with platinum (as in nickel sulfide and gold ores), and that is used chiefly as a hydrogenation and dehydrogenation catalyst because of its ability to occlude large volumes of hydrogen and other gases, as ornamentation in the form of thin leaves esp. on book covers, as electrical contacts in telephone equipment, and in alloys (as with silver or ruthenium) for electrical apparatus and jewelry and in dentistry — symbol *Pd;* see ELEMENT table

palladium process *n* **:** a contact photographic printing process similar to the platinum process except that a palladium salt is used instead of a platinum salt for coating the paper

pal·la·dize \ˈpaləˌdīz\ *vt* -ED/-ING/-S [NL *palladium* + E *-ize*] **:** PALLADINIZE

pal·la·dous \pəˈlādəs, ˈpaləd-\ *adj* [ISV *pallad-* (fr. NL *palladium*) + *-ous*] **:** of, relating to, or derived from palladium — used esp. of compounds in which this element is bivalent; compare PALLADIC

pallae *pl of* PALLA

pal·lah *also* **pal·la** *or* **pala** \ˈpalə\ *n* -S [Tswana *phala*] **:** IMPALA

pal·lall \paˈlal\ *n* -S [origin unknown] *chiefly Scot* **:** HOPSCOTCH

pall·anesthesia \ˌpal+\ *n* [NL, fr. Gk *pallein* to shake, brandish + NL *anesthesia* — more at POLEMIC] **:** loss of sensitivity to vibrational stimulus (as from a tuning fork)

pal·lar \ˈpalə(r)\ *n* -S *usu cap* **:** a member of a depressed caste of India

pallas *pl of* PALLA

pal·las·ite \ˈpaləˌsīt\ *or* **pallas iron** *n* -S [Peter S. *Pallas* †1811 Ger. naturalist and traveler + E *-ite*] **:** a meteorite composed essentially of metallic iron and olivine

pal·las's cat \ˈpaləsəz-\ *or* **pallas cat** *n, usu cap P* [after Peter S. *Pallas*] **:** MANUL

pallas's cormorant *n, usu cap P* [after Peter S. *Pallas*] **:** a large small-winged cormorant (*Phalacrocorax perspicillatus*) of Bering Island that was exterminated by man

pallas's sandgrouse *n, usu cap P* [after Peter S. *Pallas*] **:** a Eurasiatic sandgrouse (*Syrrhaptes paradoxus*) that has long sharply-pointed tail feathers, wings without white markings, and a conspicuous black patch on the belly

pallbearer \ˈ=ˌ==\ *n* **1** *archaic* **:** an attendant at a funeral who holds up a corner of the pall covering the coffin **2 a :** an attendant at a funeral who helps to carry the coffin **b :** a person who attends a funeral esp. as a representative of a fraternal order or other group and serves as a member of the immediate escort or honor guard of the coffin but does not actually assist in carrying it — called also *honorary pallbearer*

palled \ˈpȯld\ *adj* [¹*pall* + *-ed*] **:** covered with or wearing a pall

pal·les·cent \pəˈlesᵊnt, (ˈ)paˈl-, (ˈ)pȯˈl-\ *adj* [L *pallescent-, pallescens* pres. part. of *pallescere* to grow pale, incho. of *pallēre* to be pale — more at FALLOW] **:** growing or becoming pale **:** rather pale

pall·es·the·sia \ˌpaləsˈthēzh(ē)ə\ *n* [NL, fr. Gk *pallein* to shake + NL *esthesia* — more at POLEMIC] **:** awareness or perception of vibration esp. as transmitted through skin and bones

¹**pal·let** \ˈpalət, *usu* -əd·+V\ *n* -S [ME *palet* headpiece, head, fr. MF, fr. *pal* stake, fr. L *palus* — more at POLE] *chiefly Scot* **:** HEAD, PATE

²**pallet** \"\ *n* -S [ME *pailet*, fr. (assumed) MF *paillet*, fr. *paille* straw, fr. L *palea* chaff, straw; akin to Skt *palāla* straw, *palāva* chaff, OSlav *plěva*, and prob. to L *pellis* skin — more at FELL] **1 :** a straw-filled tick or straw mattress **2 a** *or* **pallet bed :** a small, poor, or hard bed often without bedstead or springs ⟨monks retiring to their ~*s*⟩ **b :** a temporary or emergency bed usu. consisting of bedding spread on the ground or floor ⟨do stay, we can fix up a ~ in no time⟩

³**pallet** \"\ *n* -S [MF *palette*, lit., small shovel — more at PALETTE] **1 a :** a wooden instrument consisting of a flat blade or plate with a handle or handhold: as (1) **:** an implement used (as by potters) for forming, beating, or rounding clay work (2) **:** a plasterer's hawk (3) **:** PALETTE 1a(1) **b** (1) *obs* **:** a flat board, plate, or disk (as an oar blade) (2) **:** a flat piece of wood laid in a wall to furnish a means of securing more firmly woodwork that is to be fastened to the wall (3) **:** a board upon which a brick molded in a sanded mold is turned and conveyed from the mold **2 a :** a click or pawl driving or regulating a ratchet wheel **b :** any of various levers or surfaces in a timepiece that receives an impulse from the escape wheel and imparts motion to a balance or pendulum **c :** any of the disks or pistons in a chain pump **d :** a hinged valve on a pipe organ to admit or release compressed air: as (1) **:** a valve opened by a keyboard digital to admit the wind to a groove under the pipes (2) **:** a waste valve to release surplus air from the storage bellows **3 :** a flat brush used in manipulating gold leaves in gilding **4 a :** a usu. brass hand tool for impressing lines and patterns on the covers of books **b :** TYPEHOLDER **5 :** either of a pair of shelly plates borne on the siphon tubes of some bivalve mollusks **6 :** a portable platform of wood, metal, or other material designed for handling by a forklift truck or crane and used for storage or movement of materials and packages in warehouses, factories, or transport vehicles

⁴**pallet** \"\ *n* -S [⁵*pale* + *-et*] **:** a narrow heraldic pale

pallet board *n* [³*pallet*] **1 :** a brickmaker's pallet **2 :** PALLET 6

pal·let·ing \ˈpalədiŋ\ *n* -S [³*pallet* + *-ing*] **:** a light platform raised above the floor of the magazine of a ship to keep powder dry

pal·let·iza·tion \ˌpalədəˈzāshən, -dˌīˈz-\ *n* -S **:** the act or result of palletizing

pal·let·ize \ˈpalədˌīz\ *vt* -ED/-ING/-S [³*pallet* + *-ize*] **1 :** to place on a pallet **:** transport or store by means of pallets **2 :** to alter (the materials-handling system of an organization) by the adoption of pallets and lift trucks

pallet knife *var of* PALETTE KNIFE

pallet stone *n* [³*pallet*] **:** a hard stone or jewel forming the rubbing face of the pallet of a timepiece and serving to diminish friction and wear

pal·lette \ˈpalət\ *n* -S [alter. of *palette*] **:** one of the usu. rounded plates at the armpits of a suit of armor — see ARMOR illustration

pallet truck *n* [³*pallet*] **:** a lift truck for handling pallets

palletwarmer *n* **:** a heat-conducting tool upon which a watch pallet is placed to soften the shellac holding each pallet for readjustment

pallholder \ˈ=ˌ==\ *n, archaic* **:** an attendant at a funeral that holds up a corner of the pall covering the coffin

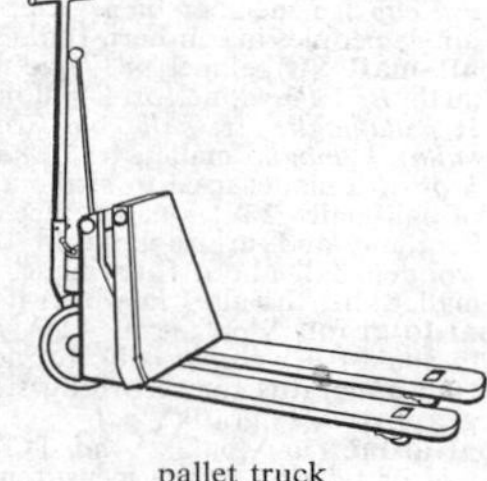

pallet truck

pal·li \ˈpəlē, ˈpälē\ *n* -S [Tamil *palli*] *India* **:** a member of a Sudra caste of field laborers

pallia *pl of* PALLIUM

pal·li·al \ˈpalēəl\ *adj* [NL *pallium* + E *-al*] **1 :** of or relating to the cerebral cortex **2 :** of, relating to, or produced by a mantle of a mollusk ⟨nacre is regarded as a ~ secretion⟩

pallial chamber *n* **:** MANTLE CAVITY

pallial line *also* **pallial impression** *n* **:** a mark on the inner surface of a bivalve shell more or less parallel with the margin caused by the attachment of the mantle

pallial nerve *n* **:** either of a pair of dorsal nerves that innervate the mantle of a mollusk

pallial sinus *n* **1 :** an often conspicuous inward bend in the posterior part of the pallial line of a bivalve mollusk **2 :** any of the branching channels through which fluids circulate in the mantle of a brachiopod

pal·liard \ˈpalyə(r)d\ *n* -S [MF *paillard*, fr. *paille* straw; fr. his sleeping on straw — more at PALLET] *archaic* **:** a low or profligate rascal **:** BEGGAR, VAGABOND, LECHER

pal·li·asse \ˌpalēˈas, (ˈ)palˈyas\ *n* -S [alter. of *paillasse*] **1 :** a usu. thin hard mattress made of a sack of strong fabric (as canvas) stuffed usu. with straw and used as a pallet or sometimes placed under another thicker and softer mattress **2 :** a supporting bed for masonry

palliata, *n, pl* **palliatae** [L (*fabula*) *palliata*, lit., play costumed with the pallium, fr. fem. of *palliatus* wearing a pallium, fr. *pallium* + *-atus* -ate] **:** FABULA PALLIATA

¹**pal·li·ate** \ˈpalēət, -ēˌāt\ *adj* [L *palliatus*] **1 a :** covered with a mantle **b :** HIDDEN, DISGUISED **c :** MITIGATED, ALLEVIATED **2 :** having a pallium

²**pal·li·ate** \ˈpalēˌāt, *usu* -ād·+V\ *vb* -ED/-ING/-S [LL *palliatus*, past part. of *palliare* to cloak, fr. L *pallium*] *vt* **1** *obs* **:** to cover with or as if with a mantle or cloak **:** CLOAK, SHELTER, HIDE, DISGUISE **2 :** to reduce the violence of (a disease) **:** cause to lessen or abate **:** ease without curing **3 :** to cover with excuses **:** conceal or disguise the enormity of by excuses and apologies **:** EXTENUATE, EXCUSE ⟨~ faults⟩ **4 :** to moderate the intensity of **:** LESSEN ⟨~ the boredom of our isolation⟩ ~ *vi, obs* **:** MODERATE, COMPROMISE

syn EXTENUATE, GLOZE, GLOSS, WHITEWASH, WHITEN: PALLIATE may stress disguising or concealing the badness or evil of and mitigating or alleviating their possible effects ⟨resort to coercive force and suppression of civil liberties are readily *palliated* in nominally democratic communities when the cry is raised that "law and order" are threatened —John Dewey⟩ ⟨writers of autobiographies, in so far as they are the chief factors in the action which they portray, *palliate*, embellish, or conceal —S.H.Adams⟩ EXTENUATE may imply intention of lessening seriousness or gravity by excuse, clement consideration of circumstances, or palliation ⟨somewhat overpraised the virtues, and too much *extenuated* the faults —T.S.Eliot⟩ ⟨he did not *extenuate*, he rather emphasized, the criminality of Catiline and his confederates —J.A.Froude⟩ GLOZE may suggest aim to divert attention from the badness, evil, harshness, or unpleasantness of something unpleasant by specious irrelevance or dissembling ⟨the article of January 1878 endeavored to *gloze* over this point as unsuited to the exoteric public addressed —Justus Buchler⟩ ⟨our triangles do not have accurate straight lines for their sides nor exact points at their corners, but this is *glozed* over by saying that the sides are approximately straight and the corners approximately points —Bertrand Russell⟩ GLOSS, often a close synonym for GLOZE, may suggest a distracting of attention from the bad or difficult by artful omission or by explanation that belittles them ⟨when judges mask a change of substance, or *gloss* over its importance —B.N.Cardozo⟩ ⟨rough hard-driving men seeking to *gloss* over the harsh and ugly realities of their calling —Walter O'Meara⟩ WHITEWASH and WHITEN may be used of attempts to cover up, distract attention from, or exculpate by superficial investigation, perfunctory trial, or other rigged procedure ⟨if the police are out to *whitewash* the Mitchell family, I'll call in a bunch of reporters and tell them so —Mary R. Rinehart⟩ ⟨use some family influence to *whitewash* past acts of collusion against the government —James Kelly⟩

pal·li·a·tion \ˌpalēˈāshən\ *n* -s [MF, fr. ML *palliation-, palliatio* cloaking, concealing, fr. LL *palliatus* + L *-ion-, -io* -ion] **1 :** the quality or state of being palliated **2 :** an act of palliating

¹pal·lia·tive \ˈpalēˌād·iv, -lēəd·|, -lyəd·|, |ēv *also* |əv\ *adj* [F *palliatif,* fr. LL *palliatus* + F *-if* -ive] **:** serving to palliate ⟨~ drugs⟩ — **pal·li·a·tive·ly** \|əvlē, -li\ *adv*

²palliative \"\ *n* -s **:** something that palliates **:** a palliative agent or procedure

pal·li·a·tor \-lēˌād·ə(r), -ātə-\ *n* -s **:** one that palliates

pal·lia·to·ry \-lēəˌtōrē, -lyə-, -tȯr-, -ri\ *adj* **:** PALLIATIVE, EXTENUATING ⟨~ circumstances⟩

pal·lid \ˈpaləd\ *adj* [L *pallidus* — more at PALE] **:** deficient in color: as **a :** lacking the normal amount of color **:** WAN — used esp. of the human countenance in illness ⟨a ~ liverish face⟩ **b :** lacking in brightness or intensity **:** PALE—used of a color or a colored object ⟨a ~ sky⟩ **c :** lacking sparkle or liveliness **:** DULL ⟨a ~ entertainment⟩ ⟨~ writings⟩ — **pal·lid·ly** *adv* — **pal·lid·ness** *n* -ES

pal·li·dal \ˈpalədᵊl\ *adj* [NL (*globus*) *pallidus* + E *-al*] **:** of, relating to, or involving the globus pallidus ⟨a severe ~ lesion⟩

pallid bat *n* **:** a large light-colored insectivorous cave bat (*Antrozous pallidus*) of southwestern No. America — called also *desert bat*

pallid cuckoo *n* **:** a slender light-colored Australian cuckoo (*Cuculus pallidus*) with an irritatingly persistent and monotonous call — called also *brain-fever bird*

pallidi- *comb form* [L *pallidus*] **:** pale ⟨*pallidi*florous⟩ ⟨*pallidi*palpate⟩

pal·lid·i·ty \pəˈlidəd·ē, pəˈl-\ *n* -ES [*pallid* + *-ity*] **:** PALLIDNESS, PALENESS

pallido- *comb form* [NL (*globus*) *pallidus* + *-o-*] **1 :** globus pallidus ⟨*pallido*fugal⟩ **2 :** pallidal and ⟨*pallido*hypothalamic⟩

pal·li·dofu·gal \ˌpalə(ˌ)dōˈfyügəl, -ləˈdäfyəg-\ *adj* [*pallido-* + *-fugal*] *of a nerve fiber or impulse* **:** passing out of the globus pallidus

pallid wren-tit *n* **:** a wren-tit of the interior valleys of southern California that constitutes a distinct subspecies (*Chamaea fasciata henshawi*) and is distinguished by pale grayish plumage

¹palling *pres part of* PALL *or of* PAL

²palling *var of* PALL

pall·ing·ly *adv* **:** so as to pall **:** TIRESOMELY

pallio- *comb form* [NL *pallium* + *-o-*] **1 :** pallium **:** sheet ⟨*pallio*stratus⟩ **2 :** pallial and ⟨*pallio*cardiac⟩

pal·lion \ˈpalyən\ *n* -s [origin unknown] **:** a small piece or pellet (as of solder)

pallisade *var of* PALISADE

pal·li·sa·do \ˌpaləˈsā(ˌ)dō-\ *adj* [alter. of *palisade*] **:** VALLARY

pal·li·um \ˈpalēəm\ *n, pl* **pal·lia** \-ēə\ *or* **palliums** [L — more at PALL] **1 a :** a cloak formed by draping a rectangular piece of cloth and worn by men of ancient Greece and Rome—compare PALLA 1 **b :** a circular band of white wool with pendants of the same material in front and back worn in the Latin rite by a pope and conferred by him on archbishops as a symbol of office **c :** ALTAR CLOTH, PALL **2** [NL, fr. L, cloak] **a :** the whole cerebral cortex covering the rest of the brain like a mantle **b :** the mantle of a mollusk, brachiopod, or bird **3 :** an extended sheet of clouds

pallium 1b

pal·li·yan *n, pl* **pal·li·yan** \ˈpalē(y)ən\ *usu cap* **:** a member of a group of negroid jungle peoples in southern India speaking Dravidian languages

pall–mall \(ˈ)pelˈmel *or* (ˈ)palˈmal *or* (ˈ)pōlˈmōl *also* (ˈ)pälˈmäl, *Brit* (ˈ)pelˈmel *or* (ˈ)palˈmal\ *n* -s [MF *pallemaille,* fr. It *pallamaglio,* fr. *palla* ball (of Gmc origin; akin to OHG *balla*) + *maglio* mallet, fr. L *malleus* — more at BALL, MAUL] **1** *obs* **:** a mallet used to strike a ball esp. as used in the game of pall-mall **2 a :** a game once common in Italy, France, and Scotland and in England in the 17th century in which a wooden ball about four inches in diameter is driven with a mallet **b :** the alley in which it is played

pal·lo·graph \ˈpaləˌgraf, -räf\ *n* [ISV *pallo-* (fr. Gk *pallein* to shake) + *-graph;* orig. formed in G — more at POLEMIC] **:** an apparatus for recording steamship vibrations — **pal·lo·graph·ic** \ˌ==ˈgrafik\ *adj*

pal·lo·metric \ˌpalə+\ *adj* [Gk *pallein* + E *-o-* + *metric*] **:** of or relating to the measurement of artificial vibrations of the earth's surface

pal·lo·ne \pəˈlōnē\ *n* -s [It, aug. of *palla* ball — more at PALL-MALL] **:** an Italian game somewhat like tennis played by striking a large leather ball with a cylindrical guard (as of wood, padded metal, or rubber) worn over hand and wrist

pal·lor \ˈpalə(r)\ *n* -s [L, fr. *pallēre* to be pale + *-or* — more at FALLOW] **:** deficiency of color **:** a wan or blanched appearance **:** PALENESS; *esp* **:** abnormal paleness of all or part of the human body

pal·lot·tine \ˈpaləˌtīn, -tēn\ *n* -s *usu cap* [It *pallottino,* fr. Vincenzo Maria *Pallotti* †1850 Ital. secular priest] **:** a member of a Roman Catholic religious society founded in 1835 to aid mission work esp. among immigrants

palls *pl of* PALL, *pres 3d sing of* PALL

pallwise \ˈ=ˌ=\ *adv* **:** in the manner of a pall

pal·ly \ˈpalē\ *adj* -ER/-EST [*pal* + *-y*] **:** sharing the relationship of pals **:** informally intimate

¹palm \ˈpälm, ˈpȧl *also* |lm; *archaic* ˈpam\ *n* -s [In sense 1, fr. ME *palme,* fr. OE *palm, palma, palme;* akin to OHG *palma* palm tree, ON *palmr;* all fr. a prehistoric NGmc-WGmc word borrowed fr. L *palma* palm of the hand, palm tree (fr. the resemblance of its leaves to an outstretched hand); in other senses, fr. ME *paume,* fr. MF, fr. L *palma;* akin to OE *folm* palm of the hand, OHG *folma,* Gk *palamē,* Skt *pāṇi* hand, OE *flōr* floor — more at FLOOR] **1 a :** a plant of the family Palmae — see BETEL PALM, CABBAGE PALM, COCONUT PALM, FAN PALM, FEATHER PALM, PIASSAVA, PALMETTO, PALMYRA, RATTAN, WAX PALM **b** (1) **:** a leaf of the palm borne or worn as a symbol of rejoicing or victory **:** PALM BRANCH (2) **:** a branch of any of various trees or shrubs (as hazel, willow, laurel, yew, larch) used esp. in religious observances as a substitute for symbolic palm; *also* **:** a tree or shrub yielding such palms **c** (1) **:** a symbol or token of superiority, success, or triumph (2) **:** the quality or state of being superior, successful, or triumphant **d :** an addition to a military or other honorary decoration in the form of a palm frond used esp. to indicate that the wearer has a second time merited the basic decoration **2 a** (1) **:** the somewhat concave part of the human hand between the bases of the fingers and the wrist upon which the fingers close when flexed (2) **:** the corresponding part of the forefoot of a lower mammal **b :** MERUS **3 :** a flat expanded part esp. when at the end of a slenderer base or stalk: as **a :** the broad flattened part of an antler (as of a moose) **b :** the blade of an oar or paddle **c :** the end of a bar or pipe flattened to provide a surface for bolting or riveting to a support **d** (1) **:** the flat inner face of an anchor fluke — see ANCHOR illustration (2) **:** ²FLUKE 1 **e :** a flat surface on a shaft strut of a ship's hull or on the end of a deck stanchion **4** [L *palmus,* fr. *palma*] **:** any of various units of length based on the breadth of the hand and varying from around 3 to 4 inches or on the length of the hand from the wrist to the ends of the fingers and varying from around 7 to 10 inches **5 :** something that covers the palm of the hand: as **a :** a piece of leather or heavy canvas fitted to the palm for protection when sewing heavy material (as harness leather or a sail) by hand and often equipped with a metal boss or slug for pushing the needle through the material **b :** the part of a glove that covers the palm ⟨a fabric glove with soft suede ~⟩ **6** [³*palm*] **:** an act of palming (as of cards, dice, or coins) ⟨did a skillful ~ of the extra card⟩

²palm \"\ *adj* **1 :** of or relating to a palm (as the palm plant or the palm of the hand) ⟨~ leaves⟩ ⟨a firm ~ pressure⟩ **2 :** derived from or made of palm ⟨~ fiber⟩

³palm \"\ *vt* -ED/-ING/-S **1 :** to touch with the palm: as **a :** stroke with the palm or hand **b :** to shake hands with **c :** to allow (a basketball) to remain in contact with the hand while moving the hand and arm thus usu. committing a violation **2 a :** to conceal in or with the hand ⟨~ a card⟩ **b :** to abstract by picking up stealthily and concealing ⟨likely to ~ any small thing left lying around⟩ **3 :** to impose by fraud — used with *on* or *upon* ⟨trash fit only to be ~*ed* on the unwary⟩; compare PALM OFF **4 :** BRIBE, TIP

⁴palm *abbr* palmistry

¹pal·ma \ˈpälmə\ *n* -s [Sp, fr. L] **1 a :** ¹PALM 1a **b :** the leaves, fiber, or other part of a palm **2 :** any of various plants (as screw pine and yucca) that resemble palms **3 :** fiber from yucca; *esp* **:** a pale hard fiber from the leaves of a Mexican arborescent yucca (*Samuela carnerosana*)

²palma \"\ *adj, usu cap* [fr. *Palma* de Mallorca, port of Balearic islands] **:** of or from Palma de Mallorca, Spain **:** of the kind or style prevalent in Palma

palma·ce·ae \palˈmāsēˌē, päˈm-\ [NL, fr. L *palma* palm + NL *-aceae*] *syn of* PALMAE

palma·ceous \(ˈ)palˈmāshəs, (ˈ)päˈm-\ *adj* [NL *Palmaceae* + E *-ous*] **:** of or relating to a palm **:** being or resembling a palm

pal·ma chris·ti \ˌpaləˈkristē, -ˌstī\ *also* **palmcrist** *pronunc at* ¹PALM +ˌkrist\ *n, pl* **palmae christi** \-(ˌ)mē-, -ˌmī-\ *also* **palmcrists** *cap Christi* [ML *palma Christi,* lit., palm of Christ] **:** CASTOR-OIL PLANT

palmad \ˈpalˌmad, ˈpäˌm-\ *adv* [¹*palm* + *-ad*] **:** toward the palm

palmae \ˈpalˌmē, ˈpäˌm-, -mī\ *n pl, cap* [NL, pl. of L *palma* palm] **:** a family (coextensive with the order Palmales) of chiefly tropical trees, shrubs, and vines comprising the palms, having a usu. tall columnar trunk that lacks a cambium and is therefore incapable of true secondary growth and bears a crown of very large leaves with stout sheathing and often prickly petioles whose persistent bases often clothe the trunk, and producing small flowers in very large clusters each subtended by a spathe

pal·ma istle \ˈpälmə+\ *n* [AmerSp *palma ixtle*] **:** ISTLE

palma·les \palˈmā(ˌ)lēz, päˈm-\ *n pl, cap* [NL, fr. L *palma* palm + NL *-ales*] **:** a large order of chiefly tropical monocotyledonous plants that is coextensive with the family Palmae and in some classifications includes also the Cyclanthales

palmar \ˈpalmə(r), ˈpäm-\ *adj* [NL *palmaris,* fr. L *palma* palm + *-aris* -ar — more at PALM] **:** of, relating to, situated in, or involving the palm of the hand

palmar arch *n* **:** either of two loops of blood vessels in the palm of the hand: **a :** a deep arch that is formed by the continuation of the radial artery and a branch of the ulnar artery and supplies principally the deep muscles of the hand, thumb, and index finger **b :** a superficial arch that is the continuation of the ulnar artery which anastomoses with a branch derived from the radial artery, its branches mostly going to the fingers

pal·ma re·al \ˌpälmərāˈäl\ *n* [AmerSp, lit., royal palm] **:** any of several large palms esp. of the genus *Roystonea*

palmar fascia *n* **:** a very strong roughly triangular fascia that binds together and protects the structures of the palm of the hand

palmar·i·an \palˈmerēən, päˈm-\ *adj* [L *palmarius* of or deserving the palm + E *-an* — more at PALMARY] **:** bearing or worthy to bear the palm **:** PALMARY

palmar·is \palˈma(a)rəs, päˈm\ *n* -ES [NL, fr. *palmaris* palmar] **:** either of two muscles of the palm of the hand: **a :** a short transverse superficial muscle of the ulnar part of the palm **b :** a frequently absent superficial muscle that arises from the medial epicondyle of the humerus and is inserted into the palmar fascia and annular ligament

palmar nerve *n* **:** any of the branches of the ulnar and median nerves to the palm of the hand

palma·ro·sa oil \ˌpalməˈrōzə, ˌpäm-\ *n* [perh. fr. L *palma* palm + *rosa* rose] **:** a fragrant essential oil obtained from a rosha grass (*Cymbopogon martinii* var. *motia*) esp. of India and Java and used in soaps, cosmetics, and perfumes of the rose type and in the preparation of geraniol — called also *geranium oil*

¹palma·ry \ˈpalmərē, ˈpäm-\ *adj* [L *palmarius* of or deserving the palm, fr. *palma* palm + *-arius* -ary] **:** worthy of praise or notice **:** OUTSTANDING, SUPERIOR ⟨a ~ instance⟩ ⟨his ~ work⟩

²palmary \"\ *adj* [NL *palmaris* palmar] **:** PALMAR

palmat- *or* **palmati-** *comb form* [LL *palmatus* palmate] **1 :** palmate ⟨*palmat*ic⟩ ⟨*palmati*form⟩ **2 :** palmately ⟨*palmati*fid⟩

palma·tae \palˈmāˌtē, päˈm-, -mäˌtī\ *n pl, cap* [NL, fr. LL, fem. pl. of *palmatus*] *in former classifications* **:** a group consisting of the web-footed birds

palmate \ˈpalˌmāt, ˈpäˌm-\ *also* **palmat·ed** \-ād·əd\ *adj* [*palmate* fr. LL *palmatus,* fr. L, marked with the palm of a hand, fr. *palma* palm + *-atus* -ate, *palmated* fr. *palmate* + *-ed* — more at PALM] **:** having the shape of the hand **:** resembling a hand with the fingers spread: as **a :** having lobes radiating from a common point — used orig. only of 5-lobed leaves but now also of other lobed leaves, of leaf venation, and of other plant organs (as the tubers of some orchids); see LEAF illustration, VENATION illustration **b** (1) *of an aquatic bird* **:** having the anterior toes united by a web **:** WEBBED (2) **:** having the distal portion broad, flat, and lobed suggesting a hand with spread fingers — used esp. of the branches of corals or the antlers of a moose — **palmate·ly** *adv*

palmated newt *n* **:** a small European newt (*Triturus palmipes*) with webbed feet

palmately cleft *adj* **:** PALMATIFID

palmat·i·fid \palˈmad·əˌfid, päˈm-\ *adj* [ISV *palmat-* + *-fid*] **:** cleft in a palmate manner ⟨a ~ leaf⟩ — compare PINNATIFID

palma·tine \ˈpalməˌtēn, ˈpäm-\ *n* -s [NL *Jatrorrhiza palmata* plant producing calumba + E *-ine*] **:** an alkaloid $C_{21}H_{23}NO_5$ that occurs esp. in calumba and is related in structure to berberine

palma·tion \palˈmāshən, päˈm-\ *n* -s [³*palm* + *-ation*] **1** *obs* **:** an act of touching with the palm **2** [*palmate* + *-ion*] **a :** the quality or state of being palmate **b :** palmate lobation; *also* **:** a palmate part

pal·ma·to·ria \ˌpalməˈtōrēə\ *n* -s [NL, fr. L *palma* palm of the hand + *-atoria* -atory; fr. its being carried in the hand] **:** BUGIA

palm ball *n* **:** a change of pace pitch in baseball thrown from the palm of the hand with either two or three fingers

palm beetle *n* **:** a beetle that is destructive to palms; *esp* **:** PALM WEEVIL

palm borer *n* **:** any of several beetle larvae that live in palms; *esp* **:** that of a very large bostrychid beetle (*Dinapate wrighti*)

palm branch *n* **:** a palm leaf with its stalk used esp. as an emblem of victory or rejoicing

palm butter *n* **:** PALM OIL

palm cabbage *n* **1 :** CABBAGE PALMETTO **2 :** CABBAGE 2

palm capital *n* **:** an Egyptian capital resembling a spreading group of palm leaves

palm civet *also* **palm cat** *n* **:** any of various arboreal civets: as **a :** any of several black-spotted or black-striped yellowish gray or brownish gray civets of *Paradoxurus* or related genera that are widely distributed in southeastern Asia and the East Indies **b :** an African civet of the genus *Nandinia*

palm cockatoo *n* **:** GREAT BLACK COCKATOO

palm crab *n* **:** PURSE CRAB

palmcrist *var of* PALMA CHRISTI

palm dove *n* **:** any of various doves frequenting palms; *esp* **:** an Egyptian turtledove (*Streptopelia senegalensis aegyptiaca*)

¹palmed \ˈpälmd, ˈpȧl *also* |lmd; *archaic* ˈpamd\ *adj* [ME *pawmed,* fr. *pawme, paume* palm + *-ed*] **1 :** having a palm or palms esp. of a specified kind ⟨horny ~ hands⟩ **2 :** PALMATE

palm capital

²palmed \"\ *adj* [fr. past part. of ³*palm*] **:** held or hidden in the palm

pal·mel·la \palˈmelə\ *n, cap* [NL, fr. Gk *palmos* vibration, quivering (fr. *pallein* to shake) + NL *-ella* — more at POLEMIC] **:** a genus (the type of the family Palmellaceae) comprising terrestrial and freshwater green algae that form large masses of usu. immobile cells embedded in a gelatinous matrix and sometimes including forms generally held to be palmella stages of flagellated algae or plantlike flagellates

pal·mel·la·ce·ae \ˌpalməˈlāsēˌē\ *n pl, cap* [NL, fr. *Palmella,* type genus + *-aceae*] **:** a family of green algae (order Volvocales) — see PALMELLA — **pal·mel·la·ceous** \ˌpalməˈlāshəs\ *adj*

pal·mel·lar \(ˈ)palˈmelə(r)\ *adj* [*palmella* (*stage*) + *-ar*] **:** of or relating to a palmella stage **:** PALMELLOID

palmella stage *also* **palmella form** *n* [so called because orig. thought to be a member of the genus *Palmella*] **:** a colonial aggregate of immobile nonflagellated individuals occurring regularly in the life cycle or in response to increased firmness of medium of some flagellated green algae or plantlike flagellates (as members of the genera *Euglena* and *Chlamydomonas*)

pal·mel·loid \palˈmeˌlȯid\ *adj* [NL *Palmella* + E *-oid*] **:** resembling *Palmella; specif* **:** having a palmella stage in the life history ⟨~ algae⟩

¹palm·er \ˈpä mə(r), ˈpȧl *also* |lm-; *archaic* ˈpam-\ *n* -s [ME *palmere,* fr. MF *palmier, paumier,* fr. ML *palmarius,* fr. L *palmarius,* adj., of palms — more at PALMARY] **1 :** a person wearing two crossed leaves of palm as a sign of his having made a pilgrimage to the Holy Land and its sacred places; *also* **:** a wandering religious votary **2 a** (1) **:** PALMERWORM (2) **:** PALMER FLY **b :** WOOD LOUSE 1

²palmer \"\ *n* -s [ME *palmer, pamere,* fr. MF *paumer,* fr. *paume* palm — more at PALM] **:** a ferule formerly used for punishing schoolboys with blows on the palm of the hand

³palmer \"\ *n* -s [³*palm* + *-er*] **:** one that palms something (as cards or dice) **:** PRESTIDIGITATOR

palmer fly *n* [¹*palmer*] **:** an angler's hackle fly in which the hackle extends along the entire body instead of radiating from the head only

pal·me·rin \ˈpalməˈrēn\ *n* -s *usu cap* [*Palmerin* de Oliva, hero of several 16th cent. Span. romances] *archaic* **:** a medieval knightly hero

palmer moth *n* **:** the adult of a palmerworm

palmer oak *n* [prob. fr. the name *Palmer*] **:** a large evergreen oak shrub (*Quercus palmeri*) of dry sunny areas of the southwestern U. S.

palm·er·sto·ni·an \ˌpä|mə(r)ˈstōnēən, ˌpȧl *also* |lm-\ *adj, usu cap* [Henry John Temple, 3d Viscount *Palmerston* †1865 Eng. prime minister + E *-ian*] **:** of, relating to, or in the manner of Lord Palmerston

palmerworm \ˈ==ˌ=\ *n* [¹*palmer* + *worm*] **:** a caterpillar that suddenly appears in great numbers devouring herbage; *esp* **:** one that is the larva of a No. American moth (*Dichomeris ligulella*) and that is destructive to fruit trees

palm·ery \ˈpä|mərē, ˈpȧl *also* |lm-\ *n* -ES [¹*palm* + *-ery*] **:** a place for growing palms; *also* **:** a collection of growing palms

palm·es·the·sia \ˌpalməsˈthēzh(ē)ə\ *n* -s [NL, fr. Gk *palmos* vibration + NL *esthesia* — more at PALMELLA] **:** PALLESTHESIA

pal·mette \(ˈ)palˈmet\ *n* -s [F, fr. *palme* palm (fr. L *palma*) + *-ette*] **:** a conventional ornament of very ancient origin consisting of radiating petals that spring from a base suggestive of a calyx and being closely related to the Egyptian lotus and Greek anthemion

pal·met·to \palˈmed·(ˌ)ō, -e(ˌ)tō\ *n, pl* **palmettos** *or* **palmettoes** [alter. (influenced by It *-etto* -ette) of ¹*palmito*] **1 :** any of several usu. low-growing fan palms; *esp* **:** CABBAGE PALMETTO — see BLUE PALMETTO, SAW PALMETTO **2 a :** strips of the leaf blade of a palmetto used in weaving ⟨a ~ basket⟩ **b :** a hat woven of palmetto **3** *usu cap* **:** SOUTH CAROLINIAN — a nickname **4 :** a tanning material obtained from the roots of the saw palmetto **5** *or* **palmetto green :** a grayish yellow green that is less strong and very slightly greener and darker than average sage green, greener and deeper than mermaid, and greener and darker than celadon

palmetto weevil *or* **palmetto billbug** *n* **:** a weevil (*Rhynchophorus cruentatus*) that breeds in cabbage palmetto and date palm in the southeastern U. S.

palme·tum \palˈmēd·əm, päˈm-\ *n* -s [L, palm grove, fr. *palma* palm + *-etum*] **:** PALMERY; *esp* **:** an area where palms are grown outdoors for botanical or ornamental purposes

palm family *n* **:** PALMAE

palm fiber *n* **1 :** a fiber (as piassava) obtained from a palm **2 :** the split leaves of a palm used for thatching, weaving, or rope making

palm·ful \ˈ=ˌfu̇l\ *n, pl* **palmfuls** *also* **palms·ful** \-mˌfu̇lz, -mzˌfu̇l\ **:** the quantity that would fill a human palm

palm–grass \ˈ=ˌ=\ *n* **:** a tall perennial Indian grass (*Setaria palmifolia*) that has large showy plicate blades and a long loose panicle and that is often cultivated as an ornamental in warm regions

palm grease *n* [¹*palm* (of the hand)] *slang* **:** money for bribing or tipping

palm green *n* [¹*palm* (tree)] **:** a variable color averaging a dark yellowish green that is yellower, less strong, and very slightly lighter than holly green (sense 1), lighter and stronger than deep chrome green, yellower and duller than golf green, and yellower and paler than average hunter green

palm grub *n* **:** PALM BORER

palm honey *n* **:** a sweet table syrup consisting of the sap of the coquito concentrated by boiling

palm house *n* **:** a greenhouse for growing palms

palmi *pl of* PALMUS

palmi- *comb form* [L, fr. *palma* palm] **1 :** palm tree ⟨*palmi*colous⟩ ⟨*palmi*vorous⟩ **2 a :** palmat- ⟨*palmi*lobate⟩ ⟨*palmi*nerved⟩ **b :** with or on the palms ⟨*palmi*grade⟩

palmier *comparative of* PALMY

pal·mie·rite \ˌpalmēˈeˌrīt, palˈmiˌr-\ *n* -s *often cap* [F *palmiérite,* fr. Luigi *Palmieri* †1896 Ital. meteorologist + F *-ite*] **:** a mineral $(K,Na)_2Pb(SO_4)_2$ that is a sulfate of lead, sodium, and potassium usu. with only a little sodium

palmiest *superlative of* PALMY

palmi·fi·ca·tion \ˌpäməfəˈkāshən, ˈpalm-\ *n* -s [*palmi-* + *caprification*] **:** artificial cross-pollination of the flowers of the date palm as practiced by the Babylonians by suspending clusters from the wild staminate trees among the pistillate blossoms of the cultivated trees

pal·mi·lla \pälˈmē(y)ə\ *n* -s [AmerSp, dim. of Sp *palma* palm — more at PALMITO] **1 :** JIPIJAPA **2** *also* **pal·mi·llo** \-ē(ˌ)(y)ō\ [*palmillo* AmerSp, dim. of Sp *palma*] **:** a soap plant (*Yucca elata*)

palming *pres part of* PALM

¹palmi·ped \ˈpalməˌped, ˈpäm-\ *adj* [L *palmiped-, palmipes,* fr. *palmi-* + *-ped-, -pes* -ped] **:** WEB-FOOTED

²palmiped \"\ *n* -s *archaic* **:** a web-footed bird

palm·ist \ˈpä|məst, ˈpȧl *also* |lm-\ *n* -s [prob. back-formation fr. *palmistry*] **:** one who practices palmistry ⟨current as truths among professional phrenologists and ~*s* —*Educational Rev.*⟩ — called also *palm reader*

pal·miste \(ˈ)palˈmēst\ *n* -s [AmerF, perh. modif. of Sp *palmito*] **:** any of several palms; *esp* **:** CABBAGE PALM 1b

palm·is·ter \ˈpä|məstə(r), ˈpȧl *also* |lm-\ *n* -s [prob. fr. *palmistry,* after such pairs as E *ministry: minister*] *archaic* **:** PALMIST

palm·is·try \-trē, -tri\ *n* -ES [ME *pawmestry,* prob. fr. *paume* palm + *maistrie* mastery — more at PALM, MASTERY] **1 :** the

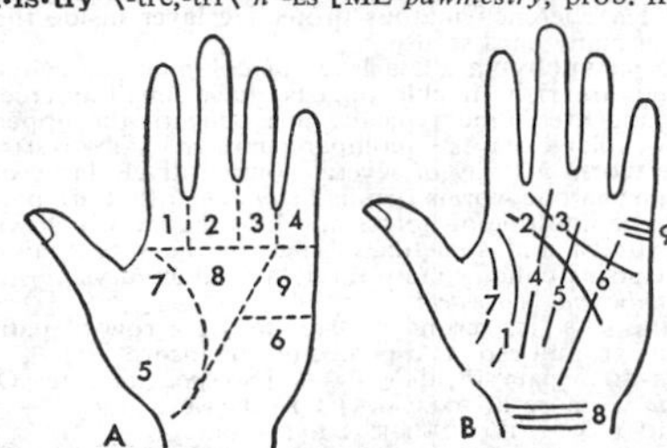

palmistry: diagrams showing Mounts, *A: 1* Jupiter, *2* Saturn, *3* Apollo, *4* Mercury, *5* Venus, *6* Luna, *7* Lower Mars, *8* Plain of Mars, *9* Upper Mars; lines, *B: 1* Life, *2* Head, *3* Heart, *4* Fate, *5* the Sun, *6* Mercury, *7* Mars, *8* rascettes, *9* lines of Affection art or practice of reading a person's character or aptitudes and esp. his past and possible future from the general character and shape of his hands and fingers and the lines, Mounts, and marks on the palms — called also *chirognomy, chiromancy* **2 :** dexterity or trickery (as pocket picking) involving use of the hands

palmi·tate \'palmə,tāt, 'päm-\ *n* -s [ISV *palmit-* (fr. *palmitin*) + *-ate*] **:** a salt or ester of palmitic acid

palmit·ic acid \(')pal¦mid·ik-, (')pä¦m-\ *n* [ISV *palmit-* + *-ic;* orig. formed as F *palmitique*] **:** a waxy crystalline fatty acid $CH_3(CH_2)_{14}COOH$ that occurs both free and combined in the form of glycerides and other esters in palm oil, butter fat, tallow, and most other fats and fatty oils, and also in several essential oils and waxes and that is used chiefly in mixtures with stearic acid — called also *hexadecanoic acid*

palmi·tin \'palmətən, 'päm-\ *n* -s [F *palmitine,* prob. fr. *palmite* pith of the palm tree, fr. *palme* palm tree, fr. L *palma*) + *-ine* -in] **:** an ester of glycerol and palmitic acid; *esp* **:** TRIPALMITIN

¹palmito *n* -s [Sp, dim. of *palma* palm tree, fr. L — more at PALM] *obs* **:** PALMETTO

²palmi·to \pal'mēd·(,)ō, pä'm-\ *n* -s [AmerSp, fr. Sp *palmito* palmetto] **1 a :** CABBAGE 2 **b :** a palm whose terminal bud is used as food **2 :** any of several yuccas of Mexico and the southwestern U. S.

pal·mit·ole·ic acid \¦palməd-ō¦lē¦k-, ¦päm-\ *n* [ISV *palmit-* (fr. *palmatin*) + *oleic* — more at PALMITIN] **:** a crystalline unsaturated fatty acid $C_6H_{13}CH{=}CH(CH_2)_7COOH$ occurring in the form of glycerides esp. in whale, seal, cod, and other marine animal oils and yielding palmitic acid on hydrogenation

palm kernel *or* **palm nut** *n* **:** the seed of any palm that yields palm-kernel oil

palm–kernel oil *n* **:** a white to yellowish edible fat that is obtained from palm kernels esp. of the African oil palm, that resembles coconut oil more than palm oil, and that is used chiefly in making soap and margarine

palm leaf *n* **1 :** the leaf of a palm; *esp* **:** the leaf of a fan palm used for palm fiber or thatching **2 a** *or* **palm–leaf hat :** a hat woven of palm fiber **b** *or* **palm–leaf fan :** a fan made of palm leaf **3** *or* **palm–leaf pattern :** a decorative motif that is common in oriental art and is possibly based on the palm leaf

palmlike \'=,=\ *adj* **:** resembling a palm esp. in habit of growth **:** like that of a palm ⟨~ leaves⟩

palm lily *n* **:** TI 1

palm marten *n* **:** PALM CIVET

pal·mod·ic \(')pal¦mädik\ *adj* [Gk *palmōdēs* throbbing (fr. *palmos* vibration, quivering + *-ōdēs* like) + E *-ic* — more at PALMELLA, -ODE] **:** relating to or resembling palmus **:** JERKY

palm off *vt* [³*palm*] **1 :** to dispose of usu. by trickery or guile in place of something expected or desired ⟨tried to *palm off* the worn-out farm as good bottomland⟩ **2 :** to deceive usu. by trickery or guile ⟨*palmed* his brother *off* with some story or other⟩ **3 :** to present (as oneself) in an untrue light ⟨*palmed* himself *off* as a millionaire sportsman⟩

¹palm oil *n* [¹*palm* (of the hand)] *slang* **:** money given as a bribe or tip

²palm oil *n* [¹*palm* (tree)] **:** a semisolid or solid red or yellowish brown edible fat obtained from the flesh of the fruit esp. of the African oil palm and used chiefly in making soap, candles, and lubricating greases and in coating iron or steel plates to be tinned

pal·mo·spas·mus \¦palmō¦spazməs\ *n* -ES [NL, fr. Gk *palmos* quivering + *spasmos* spasm — more at PALMELLA] **:** clonic spasm

palm play *n* **:** tennis as first played by striking the ball with the palm of the hand

palm print *n* **:** a print of the palm of the hand — compare FINGERPRINT

palm reader *n* **:** PALMIST

palm rest *n* **:** a device often fitted to the stock of a target rifle for supporting the rifle with the hand while firing

palm rhinoceros beetle *n* [¹*palm* (tree)] **:** a reddish brown rhinoceros beetle (*Oryctes rhinoceros*) of tropical Asia

palms *pl of* PALM, *pres 3d sing of* PALM

palmsful *pl of* PALMFUL

palm squirrel *n* **:** a small tree squirrel (*Funambulus palmarum*) of India that is gray with three broad white stripes down the back

palm starch *n* **:** SAGO 2

palm stay *n* [¹*palm* (flat part)] **:** a short boiler stay screwed through a surface into an angle piece riveted to another surface at right angles

palm sugar *n* [¹*palm* (tree)] **:** a usu. moist brown sugar (as jaggery) made from palm sap

palm sunday *n, usu cap P&S* [ME *palmesonday,* fr. OE *palmsunnandaeg,* fr. ¹*palm* + *sunnandaeg* Sunday] **:** the Sunday preceding Easter on which is commemorated Christ's triumphal entry into Jerusalem when the multitude strewed palm branches in his way

palm swift *n* **:** a swift of *Tachornis* or related genera: as **a :** a West Indian bird (*T. phoenicobia*) **b :** an African and Asiatic bird (*Cypsiurus parvus*)

palm–tree cabbage *n* **:** a kale with leafless stems 6 feet or more in height and a terminal cluster of very dark much-curled leaves

palmu·la \'palmyələ, 'päm-\ *n, pl* **palmu·lae** \-,lē, -,lī\ [NL, fr. L, palm of the hand, little palm, dim. of *palma* palm] **:** PULVILLUS

pal·mus \'palməs\ *n, pl* **pal·mi** \-,mī, -,mē\ [NL, fr. Gk *palmos* vibration, quivering — more at PALMELLA] **:** PALPITATION, TWITCHING, JERKINESS

palm vaulting *n* **:** a variation of Gothic rib vaulting in which many ribs of equal length form a palmlike pattern

palm viper *n* **:** any of numerous small arboreal pit vipers (genera *Bothrops* and *Trimeresurus*) of tropical America that are frequently green in color with prehensile tails which help them to move from tree to tree

palm warbler *n* **:** a widely distributed No. American warbler (*Dendroica palmarum*) occurring in a western subspecies (*D. p. palmarum*) chiefly of central Canada and the Mississippi valley that is distinguished by a chestnut crown when adult and yellowish underparts and a more easterly distributed subspecies (*D. p. hypochrysea*) in which the yellow is more marked

palm·ward \'=wə(r)d\ *adv* **:** toward the palm of the hand

palm wax *n* **:** a resinous wax obtained from a wax palm (*Ceroxylon andicolum*) and used in candles

palm weevil *n* **:** any of various weevils of the genus *Rhynchophorus* whose larvae bore in palm trees — compare GRUGRU 2

palm wine *n* **:** the fermented sap of any of various palms used as a beverage esp. in tropical countries

palm wool *n* **:** COIR

palm worm *n* **:** the larva of a palm weevil

¹palmy \'pä(l)mē, 'pȧl, ¦mi *also* ¦lm-\ *adj* -ER/-EST **1 a :** abounding in or bearing palms ⟨a ~ strand⟩ **b :** resembling or derived from a palm ⟨rich ~ suds⟩ ⟨a slender ~ figure⟩ **2** [so called fr. the traditional use of the palm branch as an emblem of triumph] **:** outstanding among members of a class by reason of excellence or superiority **:** constituting an acme **:** notably flourishing or prosperous ⟨not likely to regain that ~ state⟩ ⟨knew her in the *palmier* days⟩

²palmy \'pȧmi\ *n* -ES [MF *palmée* blow with the palm, fr. ML *palmata,* fr. L *palma* palm] *Scot* **:** a blow on the palm of the hand as a punishment

pal·my·ra \pal'mīrə, *attrib* (')=¦==\ *n* -s [alter. (perh. influenced by *Palmyra,* ancient city of Syria) of earlier *palmeira,* fr. Pg, palm tree, fr. *palma,* fr. L] **1** *or* **palmyra palm :** a tall fan palm (*Borassus flabellifer*) that is native to Africa but widely cultivated in India and that yields a very hard moisture-resistant and insect-resistant wood, a sap rich in sugar and important as a source of palm wine and palm sugar, leaves used esp. for thatching and weaving, a coarse fiber similar to piassava, and large edible drupaceous fruits — see BASSINE **2** *or* **palmyra fiber :** BASSINE

¹pal·my·rene \'palmə,rēn, ,==¦=\ *adj, usu cap* [L *palmyrenus,* fr. *Palmyra* ancient city of Syria] **:** of or relating to the ancient city of Palmyra, Syria

²palmyrene \"\ *n* -s *cap* **1 :** a native or resident of Palmyra **2 :** the Aramaic dialect of ancient Palmyra

pa·lo \'pa(,)lō, 'pä(-\ *n* -s [AmerSp, stick, tree, fr. Sp, stick, timber, fr. L *palus* stake — more at POLE] *chiefly Southwest* **:** POLE, STICK — used in names of trees

palo amarillo *n* [MexSp, lit., yellow tree] **:** any of several tropical or western American trees or shrubs with yellowish bark or wood; *esp* **:** OREGON GRAPE

palo blan·co \-'blaŋ(,)kō\ *n* [MexSp, lit., white tree] **:** any of various tropical or western American trees or shrubs with whitish or pale wood or bark: as **a :** a western American hackberry (*Celtis reticulata*), having light-colored bark **b :** a tree (*Lysiloma candida*) of Lower California whose bark is used in tanning

pa·lo·du·ro \,palə'dü(,)rō, ,päl-\ *also* **pa·lo·du·ra** \-ürə\ *n* -s [MexSp *palo duro,* lit., hard tree] **:** PALO BLANCO a

paloe·an·thro·pus \,pālē'an(t)thrəpəs, ,pal-, -,an'thrōp-\ *syn of* PALAEOANTHROPUS

pa·lo·hier·ro \,palō'ye(,)rō, ,päl-\ *or* **pa·lo de hier·ro** \-(,)lōdā'y-, -ōthā-\ *n* -s [MexSp, lit., iron tree] **:** any of several tropical or western American trees or shrubs with very hard strong tough wood; *esp* **:** DESERT IRONWOOD

pa·lo·lo \pə'lō(,)lō\ *or* **palolo worm** *also* **bo·lo·lo** \bə-\ *n* -s [Samoan & Tongan *palolo*] **:** a eunicid worm (*Eunice viridis*) that burrows in the coral reefs of various Pacific islands and swarms in vast numbers at the surface of the sea for breeding a little before the last quarter of the moon in October and November when they are gathered as highly esteemed food

pa·lo·ma \pə'lōmə\ *n* -s [prob. AmerSp, fr. Sp, dove, pigeon, fr. L *palumba, palumbes;* akin to Gk *peleia* dove, pigeon, L *pallēre* to be pale — more at FALLOW] **1** *Southwest* **:** any of several sharks used as food **2** *often cap* **:** a brownish orange to light brown that is redder and lighter than sorrel and redder than caramel

pa·lo ma·ria \,pa(,)lōmə'rēə, ,pä(-\ *n* [PhilSp, lit., Mary tree] *Philippines* **:** POON

pa·lom·bi·no \,päləm'bē(,)nō, ,pal-\ *n* -s [It, lit., of or like a dove, fr. L *palumbinus,* fr. *palumba, palumbes* dove + *-inus* -ine — more at PALOMA] **:** a light gray Italian marble

pal·o·meta \,palə'med·ə\ *n* [Sp, dim. of *paloma* dove — more at PALOMA] **1** -s **:** any of several pompanos (as the longfin pompano and round pompano) **2 a** -s **:** any of various butterfishes (as the California pompano) of the family Stromateidae **b** *cap* **:** a genus of butterfishes that includes the California pompano

pal·o·mi·no *also* **pal·a·mi·no** \,palə'mē(,)nō, -ēnə\ *n* -s [AmerSp *palomino,* fr. Sp, of or like a dove, fr. L *palumbinus*] **:** a slender-legged short-coupled horse of a light tan or cream color with white markings on the face and legs and flaxen or white mane and tail from ancestry largely of Arabian stock

pa·loo·ka \pə'lükə\ *n* -s [origin unknown] **1 :** an inexperienced or incompetent boxer **2 :** a clumsy inept person **:** OAF

pa·lo san·to \,palō'san,tō, ,pälō'sän-\ *n* [AmerSp, lit., holy tree] **:** any of several So. American trees esteemed locally for medicinal or other special properties; *esp* **:** a tree (*Bulnesia sarmienti*) of the family Zygophyllaceae occurring in dry interior regions of Argentina and Paraguay and having a resinous heartwood used for incense — see GUAIAC WOOD

pa·lo·sa·pis \,palō'säpəs, ,päl-\ *n* -ES [Tag] **:** a tall tree (*Anisoptera thurifera*) of the family Dipterocarpaceae that is common in the Philippines and yields a resinous oil and valuable light-colored hard wood used in cabinetwork and paneling

pa·louse \pə'lüs\ *n, pl* **palouse** *or* **palouses** *usu cap* **1 a :** a Shahaptian people in the Palouse river valley, southeastern Washington and northwestern Idaho **b :** a member of the Palouse people **2 :** APPALOOSA

pa·lous·er \pə'lüzə(r)\ *n* -s [*Palouse* + *-er*] **:** an improvised light consisting of candle and a tin can

pa·lo·verde \,pa¦lō¦vərdē, ,pä¦lō¦vərd, ¦äl-\ *n* -s [MexSp, lit., green tree] **:** any of three thorny trees or shrubs (*Cercidium macrum, C. torreyanum,* and *C. microphyllum*) of the family Leguminosae that occur in dry parts of the southwestern U. S. and adjacent Mexico, have smooth light green bark, small transitory leaves, and racemes of bright yellow flowers, and are locally important as wildlife browse and bee pasture

¹palp \'palp, 'paủp\ *vt* -ED/-ING/-S [MF *palper,* fr. L *palpare* to stroke, caress, flatter — more at FEEL] **1 :** to experience a touch sensation from **:** TOUCH, FEEL, HANDLE **2** *obs* **:** to address in a manner designed to please or flatter **:** CAJOLE

²palp \"\ *n* -s [F *palpe,* fr. *palper* or fr. L *palpus* stroking, caress; akin to L *palpare*] **:** PALPUS: as **a :** one of two leaflike fleshy appendages on each side of the mouth of a lamellibranch mollusk **b :** a lobe-shaped sensory process of each side of the head of a chaetopod worm

pal·pa·bil·i·ty \,palpə'biləd·ē, -lətē, -i\ *n* -ES **1 :** the quality or state of being palpable **2 :** something palpable

pal·pa·ble \'palpəbəl\ *adj* [ME, fr. LL *palpabilis,* fr. L *palpare* to stroke, caress + *-abilis* -able — more at FEEL] **1 :** capable of being touched or felt **:** perceptible to the sense of touch **:** TANGIBLE ⟨a barely ~ dust⟩ ⟨an enlarged ~ spleen⟩ **2 :** easily perceptible by one or another of the senses other than touch **:** NOTICEABLE, PATENT **3 :** easily perceptible by the mind **:** PLAIN, DISTINCT, OBVIOUS, MANIFEST ⟨a ~ absurdity⟩ ⟨such ~ impostures⟩ **syn** see EVIDENT, PERCEPTIBLE

pal·pa·ble·ness *n* -ES **:** PALPABILITY 1

pal·pa·bly \-blē, -bli\ *adv* **:** in a palpable manner **:** so as to be palpable ⟨~ untrue⟩

pal·pal \'palpəl\ *adj* [NL *palpalis,* fr. *palpus* + L *-alis* -al] **:** of, relating to, or functioning as a palpus

palpal organ *n* **:** an accessory reproductive organ of a male spider developed on the terminal joint of each pedipalp and used to convey the sperms to the genital orifice of the female

¹pal·pate \'pal,pāt, *usu* -ād·+V\ *vb* -ED/-ING/-S [prob. back formation fr. *palpation*] *vt* **:** to examine by touch **:** explore by palpation **~** *vi* **:** to use the technique of palpation

²palpate \"\ *adj* [NL *palpatus,* fr. *palpus* + L *-atus* -ate] **:** having a palpus or palpi

pal·pa·tion \pal'pāshən\ *n* -s [L *palpation-, palpatio,* fr. *palpatus* (past. part. of *palpare* to stroke) + *-ion-, -io* -ion] **1 :** an act of touching or feeling **2 :** physical examination in medical diagnosis by pressure of the hand or fingers to the surface of the body esp. to determine the condition (as of size or consistency) of an underlying part or organ ⟨~ of the liver⟩ ⟨~ of cervical lymph glands⟩

pal·pa·to·ry \'palpə,tōrē\ *adj* [L *palpatus* (past part. of *palpare*) — E *-ory*] **:** of, involving, or used for palpation

pal·pe·bra \'palpəbrə, pal'pēb-, pal'peb-\ *n, pl* **pal·pe·brae** \-=,brē, -,brī; =¦=(,)brē\ [L; prob. akin to L *palpitare* to palpitate, *palpare* to stroke, caress — more at FEEL] **:** EYELID

pal·pe·bral \-,brəl\ *adj* [LL *palpebralis,* fr. L *palpebra* + *-alis* -al] **:** of, relating to, or located on or near the eyelids

palpebral disk *n* **:** an often transparent complex scale that covers the eyelid of some lizards and is formed by fusion of several palpebral scales

palpebral fissure *n* **:** the space between the margins of the eyelids

pal·pe·brate \'palpə,brat; pal'pēbrət, -pebrət\ *adj* [NL *palpebratus,* fr. L *palpebra* + *-atus* -ate] **:** having eyelids

palped \'palpt, -aủpt\ *adj* [²*palp* + *-ed*] **:** PALPATE

palpi *pl of* PALPUS

pal·pi·fer \'palpəfər, -,fe(ə)r\ *n* -s [NL, fr. *palpus* + *-i-* + *-fer*] **1 :** a lobe of the maxilla of an insect on which the palpus is borne **2 :** PALPIGER — **pal·pif·er·ous** \(')pal¦pif(ə)rəs\ *adj*

pal·pi·form \'palpə,fȯrm\ *adj* [NL *palpus* + E *-iform*] **:** like a palpus

pal·pi·ger \'palpəjər, -,je(ə)r\ *n* -s [NL, fr. *palpus* + L *-i-* + *-ger* bearer (fr. *-ger* -gerous)] **:** the portion of the labium of an insect that bears the palpi — **pal·pig·er·ous** \(')pal¦pij(ə)rəs\ *adj*

pal·pigra·di \pal'pigrə,dī, -,dē; ,palpə'grā,dī\ [NL, fr. *palpus* + L *-i-* + *-gradi* (pl. of *-gradus* -grade)] *syn of* MICROTHELYPHONIDA

pal·pi·tan·cy \'palpəd·ənsē, -lpətən- *also* -t°n-\ *n* -ES [*palpitant* + *-cy*] **:** the quality or state of being palpitant

pal·pi·tant \-nt\ *adj* [F or L; F fr. L *palpitant-, palpitans,* pres. part. of *palpitare* to palpitate] **1 :** TREMBLING, QUIVERING, THROBBING ⟨~ movements rather than violent eruptions —*Amer. Guide Series: Mich.*⟩ **2 :** inducing or likely to induce a palpitant condition ⟨a memorably harsh and ~ record of the nomadic men of the sea —Charles Lee⟩

pal·pi·tate \'palpə,tāt, *usu* -ād·+V\ *vb* -ED/-ING/-S [L *palpitatus,* past part. of *palpitare* freq. of *palpare* to stroke, caress — more at FEEL] *vi* **:** to beat rapidly and strongly **:** THROB **:** bound with emotion or exertion **:** pulsate violently — used esp. of the heart when its pulsation is abnormally rapid **~** *vt* **:** to cause to palpitate **syn** see PULSATE

pal·pi·tat·ing·ly \'==,===, ,==¦===\ *adv* [*palpitating* (pres. part. of *palpitate*) + *-ly*] **:** so as to palpitate or cause palpitation

pal·pi·ta·tion \,palpə'tāshən\ *n* -s [L *palpitation-, palpitatio,* fr. *palpitatus* + *-ion-, -io* -ion] **:** a rapid pulsation **:** THROBBING, QUIVERING; *esp* **:** an abnormally rapid beating of the heart when excited by violent exertion, strong emotion, or disease

palp·less \'palpləs, 'paủp-\ *adj* [²*palp* + *-less*] **:** lacking palpi or palps

pal·po·cil \'palpə,sil\ *n* -s [ISV *palpo-* (fr. NL *palpus*) + *-cil* (fr. NL *cilium*); prob. orig. formed in G] **:** a fine filamentous tactile process (as of some hydroids) **:** TACTILE HAIR

pal·pog·nath \'palpəg,nath\ *n* -s [NL *palpus* + *-o-* + Gk *gnathos* jaw — more at -GNATHOUS] **:** either of the third pair of mouthparts of a centipede

pal·pon \'pal,pän\ *n* -s [prob. fr. ²*palp* + siph*on*] **:** a hollow dactylozooid of some siphonophores that resembles a tentacle

palps *pres 3d sing of* PALP, *pl of* PALP

pal·pu·lus \'palpyələs\ *n, pl* **palpu·li** \-,lī, -,lē\ [NL, dim. of *palpus*] **:** a small palpus; *specif* **:** one of the maxillary palpi of a butterfly or moth

pal·pus \'palpəs\ *n, pl* **pal·pi** \-l,pī, -l,pē\ [NL, fr. L, stroking, caress; akin to L *palpare* to stroke, caress — more at FEEL] **1 :** a segmented process attached to a mouthpart of an arthropod, usu. having a tactile or gustatory function, and occurring in insects usu. in pairs on the maxillae and on the labium **2 :** a process on any of various other invertebrates felt to resemble an insect's palpus — see PALP

pals *pl of* PAL, *pres 3d sing of* PAL

pals·grave \'pȯlz,grāv\ *or* **pal·grave** \-l,g-\ *n* -s [D *paltsgrave;* akin to MHG *pfalzgrave;* both fr. a prehistoric D-G compound whose first element is represented by OHG *pfalanza* (fr. L *palatium* palace) and whose second element is represented by OHG *grāvo* count — more at PALACE, BURGRAVE] **:** COUNT PALATINE

pals·gra·vine \-lzgrə,vēn, ,==ˈ=\ *n* -s [D *paltsgravin,* fr. *paltsgrave* + *-in* -ine] **:** the wife or widow of a count palatine

pal·ship \'pal,ship\ *n* [¹*pal* + *-ship*] **:** the relation existing between pals **:** informal intimacy

pal·sied \'pȯlzēd, -zid\ *adj* [¹*palsy* + *-ed*] **:** affected with palsy **:** PARALYZED, TOTTERING, SHAKY ⟨~ children⟩ ⟨hands weak and ~⟩

pal·stave *also* **pal·staff** \'pȯl+,-\ *n* -s [Dan *paalstav,* fr. ON *pālstafr,* a heavy missile, prob. fr. *pāll* spade, hoe (fr. OE *pāl,* fr. L *pala*) + *stafr* staff — more at PALETTE, STAFF] **:** a usu. bronze celt designed for a split handle

pal·ster \'pȯlztə(r), -l(t)st-\ *n* -s [MD] *archaic* **:** a pilgrim's staff

¹pal·sy \'pȯlzē, -zi\ *n* -ES [ME *palsie, parlesie,* fr. MF *paralisie,* fr. L *paralysis* — more at PARALYSIS] **1 a :** PARALYSIS — used chiefly in combination ⟨shaking ~⟩ ⟨oculomotor ~⟩; compare BELL'S PALSY, CEREBRAL PALSY **b :** a condition that is characterized by uncontrollable tremor or quivering of the body or one or more of its parts ⟨the old man shook with the ~ so he could hardly hold his pipe⟩ — not used technically **2 a :** an enfeebling influence **:** something that causes weakness or uncertainty or impairs activity or effectiveness ⟨a creeping ~ has of late overtaken the liberal mind —*Saturday Rev.*⟩ ⟨the ~ of doubt and distraction hangs . . . upon my energies —Thomas De Quincey⟩ **b :** a weak, enfeebled, or uncertain condition often marked by lack of decisive or effective action ⟨enough to throw the entire diplomatic West into a ~ —*Reporter*⟩ **3 :** VIBRATION ⟨his whole body shook with the ~ of the motor —Kay Boyle⟩

²palsy \"\ *vb* -ED/-ING/-ES *vt* **:** to affect with or as if with palsy **:** deprive of action or energy **:** PARALYZE **~** *vi* **:** to become palsied **:** shake as if with the palsy

palsy–walsy \¦palzē¦walzē\ *adj* [redupl. of *palsy* pally, fr. *pals,* pl. of *pal* + *-y*] *slang* **:** having or giving the appearance of having a high degree of intimacy ⟨got very *palsy-walsy* with the boss all of a sudden⟩ ⟨his *palsy-walsy* attitude⟩

pal·ta \'pältə, 'pȧl-\ *n* -s [AmerSp, fr. Quechua] **:** AVOCADO

pal·ter \'pȯltə(r)\ *vi* **paltered; paltered; paltering** \-t(ə)riŋ\ **palters** [origin unknown] **1 :** to act insincerely or deceitfully **:** play false **:** use trickery **:** EQUIVOCATE **:** play fast and loose ⟨Romans, that have spoke the word, and will not ~ —Shak.⟩ **2 :** to haggle or chaffer in doing business **:** bargain or parley esp. with the intent of delay or compromise **syn** see LIE

pal·ter·er \'pȯltərə(r)\ *n* -s **:** one that palters

pal·ter·ly \'pȯltə(r)lē\ *adj* [alter. (influenced by *palter* & *-ly*) of *paltry*] *archaic* **:** PALTRY, SHABBY

pal·tock \'pal,täk\ *n* -s [ME *paltok*] **:** a man's doublet or tunic worn in the 14th and 15th centuries

pal·tri·ly \'pȯl·trəlē, -əli\ *adv* **:** in a paltry manner **:** so as to be paltry

pal·tri·ness \-rēnəs, -rin-\ *n* -ES **:** the quality or state of being paltry

¹paltry *also* **paultry** *n* -ES [E dial. *palt, pelt* piece of coarse cloth, trash + E *-ry;* akin to MLG *palte* rag, Dan *pjalt,* Sw *palta*] *obs* **:** something useless or worthless **:** RUBBISH, TRASH

²pal·try *also* **paul·try** \'pȯl·trē, -ri\ *adj* -ER/-EST **1 :** INFERIOR, TRASHY, WORTHLESS ⟨building ~ houses unfit for occupancy⟩ **2 :** MEAN, VILE, DESPICABLE ⟨a ~ trick⟩ **3 :** TRIVIAL, PETTY, SLIGHT ⟨a ~ excuse⟩ ⟨these ~ trials⟩ **syn** see PETTY

¹pa·lu \'pä(,)lü\ *n* -s [modif. of Hawaiian *walu* oilfish] **:** ESCOLAR

²palu \"\ *n* -s [of East Indian origin] **:** a hardwood tree (*Mimusops lexandra*) of India and Ceylon with astringent bark used for tanning and red to purplish brown timber resembling bulletwood

pa·lu·dal \pə'lüd°l, 'palyəd°l\ *adj* [L *palud-, palus* marsh + E *-al;* akin to Skt *palvala* pond and perh. to OE *full* — more at FULL] **:** of, relating to, or made up of marshes or fens **:** MARSHY ⟨~ plants⟩ ⟨a ~ environment⟩

pa·lu·da·men·tum \pə,lüdə'mentəm\ *or* **pa·lu·da·ment** \=ˈ== mənt\ *n, pl* **paludamen·ta** \=,=='mentə\ *or* **paludaments** [L *paludamentum;* prob. akin to L *palla* palla] **:** a cloak worn by the rulers and chief military officers of ancient Rome

paludamentum

paludi– *comb form* [LL, fr. L *palud-, palus* marsh — more at PALUDAL] **:** marsh ⟨*paludicole*⟩

pa·lu·di·cel·la \pə,lüdə'selə\ *n, cap* [NL, fr. *paludi-* + *cella* cell] **:** a genus of ectoproctous bryozoans comprising a number of freshwater colonial forms that construct delicate branching tubes with club-shaped zooids and no statoblasts

pal·u·dic·o·lae \,palyə'dikə,lē, -ə,lī\ [NL, pl. of LL *paludicola* marsh dweller, fr. *paludi-* + L *-cola*] *syn of* GRUIFORMES

pal·u·dic·o·lous \,palyə'dikələs\ *or* **pal·u·dic·o·line** \-ə,līn\ *adj* [LL *paludicola* + E *-ous* or *-ine*] **:** PALUSTRINE ⟨~ frogs⟩

¹pal·u·di·na \,palyə'dīnə, -dēnə\ [NL, fr. *paludi-* + *-ina*] *syn of* VIVIPARUS

²paludina \"\ *n* -s [NL *Paludina*] **:** a mollusk of the genus *Viviparus*

pal·u·dism \'palyə,dizəm\ *n* -s [ISV *paludi-* + *-ism*] **:** MALARIA

palu·dous \'palyədəs, pə'lüd-\ *adj* [L *paludosus* marshy, fr. *palud-, palus* marsh + *-osus* -ous — more at PALUDAL] **1 :** PALUSTRINE **2 :** of or relating to marshes or marshland

Pal·u·drine \'palyə,drēn, -,drən; pə'lüdrən\ *trademark* — used for derivatives of biguanide used as antimalarials

pal·ule \'pal(,)yül\ *or* **pal·u·lus** \-lyələs\ *n, pl* **pal·ules** \-yülz\ *or* **pal·u·li** \-yə,lī, -,lē\ [NL *palulus,* dim. of *palus*] **:** PALUS; *esp* **:** one not attached to a septum

pa·lus \'pāləs\ *n, pl* **pa·li** \-,lī\ [NL, fr. L, stake — more at

POLE] : any of several upright slender calcareous processes that surround the central part of the calyculus of some corals

pa·lus·tral \pəˈləstrəl\ *adj* [L *palustris* (fr. *palud-*, *palus* marsh) + E *-al* — more at PALUDAL] : PALUDOUS

pa·lus·trine \pəˈləstrən\ *adj* [L *palustris* + E *-ine*] : living or thriving in a marshy environment ⟨~ plants⟩ : being or made up of marsh ⟨a ~ habitat⟩

¹paly \ˈpālē\ *adj* [ME, fr. MF *palé*, fr. *pal* stake + *-é* -y — more at PALE (fence)] *heraldry* : divided into four or more equal parts by perpendicular lines and of two different tinctures disposed alternately

²paly \"\ *adj* -ER/-EST [¹*pale* + *-y*] : somewhat pale : WAN, PALLID

paly-bendy \ˌ==ˈ==\ *adj*, *heraldry* : divided into lozenge-shaped figures by lines paly and bendy

pal·y·gor·skite \ˌpaləˈgȯrˌskīt\ *n* -S [modif. of G *paligorskit*, fr. the locality in the Ural mountains near which it was found] : a hydrous basic silicate (Mg_3, Al_2)Si_4O_{10}(OH)$_2$.H_2O of magnesium and aluminum that belongs to the family of the clay minerals

pal·y·no·log·i·cal \ˌpalənəˈläjəkəl\ *adj* : of or relating to palynology : concerned with pollen or pollen grains ⟨~ studies⟩ — **pal·y·no·log·i·cal·ly** \-jək(ə)lē\ *adv*

pal·y·nol·o·gy \ˌpaləˈnäləjē\ *n* -ES [Gk *palynein* to strew, sprinkle (fr. *palē* fine meal, dust) + E *-o-* + *-logy* — more at POLLEN] : a branch of science concerned with the study of pollen and spores whether living or fossil

pa·lys·tes \pəˈli(ˌ)stēz\ *n*, *cap* [NL] : a genus of hunting spiders (family Heteropodidae) that includes several large forms which prey on small fish, frogs, and lizards

¹pam \ˈpam, ˈpaa(ə)m\ *n* -S [prob. short for Gk *pamphilos* beloved of all, fr. *pam-* + *philos* beloved] **1** : the jack of clubs in loo played with 5-card hands **2** : a game like napoleon in which the jack of clubs is the highest trump

pam 1

²pam \"\ *vb* **pammed; pammed; pamming; pams** [alter. of ⁸*pan*] : PAN

pam- *comb form* [NL, fr. Gk, alter. of *pan-* — more at PAN-] : PAN-

pam *abbr* pamphlet

PAM *abbr* pulse-amplitude modulation

pa·ma·ka·ni \ˈpäməˌkänē\ *n* -S [Hawaii *pā-makani(haole)*, fr. *pā-makani*, any of several native plants, lit., wind-blown, + *haole* foreign] : a tall tropical American perennial herb (*Eupatorium macrophyllum*) that is sometimes cultivated in the warm greenhouse for its showy corymbs of reddish lilac flower heads

pam·a·quine \ˈpaməˌkwīn, -wēn,-ˌkwən\ *also* **pam·a·quin** \-ˌkwən\ *n* -S [*pent*yl + *a*mino + *m*ethoxyl + connective *-a-* + *-quine*, *-quin* (fr. *quinoline*)] : a toxic antimalarial drug $C_{19}H_{29}N_3O$ derived from an amino-methoxy-quinoline; *also* : PAMAQUINE NAPHTHOATE

pamaquine naphthoate *n* : an insoluble salt $C_{42}H_{45}N_3O_7$ of pamaquine and a derivative of beta-naphthoic acid obtained as a yellow to orange-yellow powder

pa·me \ˈpämā\ *n*, *pl* **pame** *or* **pames** *usu cap* **1 a** : an Otomian people of San Luis Potosí and adjoining states, Mexico **b** : a member of such people **2** : the language of the Pame people

pa·ment \ˈpāmənt\ *or* **pam·ment** \ˈpam-\ *n* -S [ME *pament*, alter. of *pavement*] : tile or brick used for paving a malthouse floor

pa·mi·ri \pəˈmirē\ *n*, *pl* **pamiri** *or* **pamiris** *usu cap* **1** : a moderately tall light-skinned people of the Pamirs **2** : a member of the Pamiri people

pam·li·co \ˈpamləˌkō\ *n*, *pl* **pamlico** *or* **pamlicos** *usu cap* **1 a** : an Indian people of the Pamlico river valley, No. Carolina **b** : a member of such people **2** : an Algonquian language of the Pamlico people

pam·pa \ˈpampə, ˈpaam-, ˈpäm-\ *n*, *pl* **pampas** \-əz, -əs\ [AmerSp, fr. Quechua & Aymara, plain] **1** : an extensive generally grass-covered plain of temperate So. America east of the Andes : PRAIRIE — often used in pl.; compare CAMPO, MONTE **2 a** *usu cap* : an Indian of the pampas; *esp* : ARAUCANIAN **b** : PUELCHE

pam·pan·gan \pämˈpäŋgən\ *also* **pam·pan·ga** \-gə\ *or* **pam·pan·go** \-ŋ(ˌ)gō\ *n*, *pl* **pampangan** *or* **pampangans** *also* **pampanga** *or* **pampangas** *or* **pampango** *or* **pampangos** *usu cap* [*pampangan* modif. of Pampangan *Kapampangan*, fr. *pampang* river bank; *pampanga* prob. alter. of *Pampangan* (taken as adj.); *pampango* fr. Sp, modif. of Pampangan *Kapampangan*] **1 a** : a Christianized people of central Luzon, Philippines **b** : a member of such people **2** : the Austronesian language of the Pampangan people

pampano *var of* POMPANO

pampas cat *n* [*pampas* fr. Sp, pl. of *pampa*] : a small wildcat (*Felis pajeros*) of Argentina and Patagonia that is yellowish gray with dark bands on the legs and tail and brownish stripes running obliquely from the back to the flanks

pampas deer *n* : a deer (*Blastoceros bezoarticus* or *Ozotoceras bezoarticus* syn. *B. campestris*) of southern So. America that is about the size of a roebuck with reddish brown above and white below and with small branched antlers

pampas fox *n* : any of several small mammals of So. America that resemble the fox

pampas grass *n* : a So. American grass (*Cortaderia selloana*) that is extensively cultivated as an ornamental, grows in thick tussocks with basal leaves, and sends up stalks 6 to 12 feet high crowned with ample silky white panicles

pampas hare *n* : MARA

pam·pe·an \ˈpampēən, ˈpäm-, =ˈ==\ *adj* [AmerSp *pampa* + E *-an*] **1** : of or relating to the pampas of So. America **2** *usu cap* **a** : of or relating to the Indian inhabitants of the So. American pampas **b** : ARAUCANIAN

pam·pel·moes \ˈpampəlˌmüs\ *n* -ES [Afrik *pompelmoosje*, fr. *pampelmoose*, *pampelmoes* shaddock, fr. D *pompelmoes*] : a large highly esteemed purplish or bluish butterfish (*Stromateus fiatola*) of the west coast of Africa and the Mediterranean

pam·per \ˈpampə(r), ˈpaam-\ *vt* **pampered; pampered; pampering** \-p(ə)riŋ\ **pampers** [ME *pamperen*, prob. of LG origin; akin to Flem *pamperen* to pamper; perh. akin to Sw dial. *pampen* to blow up, Lith *bámba* navel, Skt *bimba* ball, sphere; basic meaning: stuffing, inflating] **1** *archaic* : to feed luxuriously : GLUT **2 a** : to treat with extreme or excessive care and attention ⟨when cotton is in . . . their days are spent coddling and ~*ing* it —*Amer. Guide Series: Ark.*⟩ **b** : to gratify or humor in one's tastes or desires ⟨the job has enabled him to ~ his wanderlust thoroughly —*New Yorker*⟩ ⟨a desire to ~ the . . . old man in his foibles —T.H.White b. 1915⟩ **syn** see INDULGE

pam·pered·ly *adv* : in a pampered manner

pam·pered·ness *n* -ES : the quality or state of being pampered

pam·per·er \ˈpampərə(r)\ *n* -S : one that pampers

pam·pe·ro \pamˈpe(ˌ)rō\ *n* -S [AmerSp, lit., pampean, fr. *pampa* + *-ero* (n. suffix)] : a strong cold wind from the west or southwest that sweeps over the pampas of So. America from the Andes

pam·phi·li·idae \ˌpam(p)fəˈlīəˌdē\ *n pl*, *cap* [NL, fr. *Pamphilius*, type genus (perh. fr. Gk *pamphilos* beloved of all) + *-idae* — more at PAM] : a family of sawflies whose larvae are usu. gregarious and web together the leaves and twigs of trees on which they feed

pamph·let \ˈpam(p)flət, ÷ -mpl-, *usu* -əd.+V\ *n* -S *often attrib* [ME *pamflet*, fr. *Pamphilet*, fr. *Pamphilus* (*seu De Amore*) Pamphilus or About Love, popular Latin amatory poem of the 12th century + *-et*] **1 a** : a brief treatment of a subject issued as a separate unbound publication ⟨scholarly monographs published as articles or ~*s*⟩ ⟨was first issued in ~ form⟩ ⟨under various names, the ~ . . . tells its readers what to believe, where to travel, what school or college to attend, what candidate to vote for, what cars to ride in and what merchandise to buy —F.F.Bond⟩ **b** : a controversial tract dealing with a religious or political question ⟨the best seller list also includes two books . . . which are fictionized journalistic ~*s* based upon timely situations —Louis Bromfield⟩ ⟨a ~ war⟩ **2 a** : a printed publication having a format with no binding and no cover or with a flush paper cover and often fastened with side or saddle stitches ⟨magazines and catalogs with ~ format⟩ — compare BOOK **b** : an unbound publication other than a periodical having fewer than a fixed number (as 50, 80, 100) of pages — used esp. in library science

pam·phlet·ary \-ləˌterē\ *adj* : of, relating to, or of the character of a pamphlet

¹pam·phle·teer \ˌ==ˈti(ə)r, -iə\ *n* -S [*pamphlet* + *-eer*] : a writer of pamphlets attacking something or urging a cause ⟨interested in the politics of our time but . . . a novelist first, a creator of people and a storyteller, an artist rather than a ~ —Orville Prescott⟩

²pamphleteer \"\ *vi* -ED/-ING/-S **1** : to write and publish pamphlets ⟨lecturing and ~*ing* in favor of free trade⟩ **2** : to attempt to sway opinion on a matter of current interest (as by tracts or through literary works) : engage in partisan argument indirectly in writings ⟨that ~*ing* is . . . a valid aspect of theater —Brooks Atkinson⟩

pam·phlet·ize \ˈ==ˌtīz\ *vb* -ED/-ING/-S [*pamphlet* + *-ize*] *vi* : to write pamphlets ~ *vt* : to write a pamphlet on

¹pam·phyl·i·an \(ˈ)pamˈfilēən\ *adj*, *usu cap* [L *Pamphylius* (fr. *Pamphylia*) + E *-an*] : of or relating to the ancient region and sometime Roman province of Pamphylia in southern Asia Minor

²pamphylian \"\ *n* -S *cap* : a native or inhabitant of ancient Pamphylia

pam·pin·i·form \pamˈpinəˌfȯrm\ *adj* [L *pampinus* tendril, vine-leaf (of non-IE origin) + E *-iform*; akin to the source of Gk *ampelos* vine] : convoluted and like a tendril — used of a venous plexus associated with the spermatic or ovarian veins

pam·poo·tie \pamˈpüd·ē\ *n* -S [perh. alter. of *papoosh*] : a shoe of untanned cowhide worn in the Aran islands, County Galway, Ireland

pam·pre \ˈpampə(r)\ *n* -S [F, fr. L *pampinus* tendril, vine-leaf] : an ornament of vine leaves and grapes

¹pam·pro·dac·tyl \ˌpamprō+\ *or* **pam·pro·dac·ty·lous** \"+\ *adj* [*pam-* + *pro-* + *dactyl* or *dactylous*] : having the toes turned forward ⟨the ~ feet of the colies and some swifts⟩

²pamprodactyl \"\ *n* : a pamprodactyl animal

pam·psy·chism \(ˈ)pam+\ *n* [*pam-* + *psychism*] : PANPSYCHISM

pams *pl of* PAM, *pres 3d sing of* PAM

pa·mun·key \pəˈməŋkē\ *n*, *pl* **pamunkey** *or* **pamunkeys** *usu cap* **1** : an Algonquian people of Virginia formerly part of the Powhatan confederacy **2** : a member of the Pamunkey people

¹pan \ˈpan, ˈpaa(ə)n\ *n* -S [ME *panne*, fr. OE; akin to OFris *panne* pan, OHG *phanna*, ON *panna*; all fr. a prehistoric Gmc word borrowed fr. (assumed) VL *panna* pan, fr. L *patina*, fr. Gk *patanē*; akin to L *patēre* to be open — more at FATHOM] **1 a** : a metal, earthenware, or plastic container (as a warming pan, dustpan, dishpan) for domestic use that is usu. broad, shallow, and open **b** : any of various metal kitchen utensils of different shapes and sizes in which foods are cooked or baked ⟨baking ~⟩ ⟨cake ~⟩ — see FRYING PAN, LOAF PAN, SAUCEPAN, TUBE PAN **c** : any of various other receptacles usu. metal and typically broad, shallow, and open: as (1) *Brit* : BOWL 3c (2) : a vessel for evaporating a liquid (as salt brine, maple sap) (3) : the hollow part of the lock in old guns or pistols that receives the priming (4) : either of the receptacles for the weights or the bodies weighed in a pair of scales or a balance (5) : a round shallow metal container used in placer mining to separate gold or some other metal from waste (as gravel) by washing (6) : a sheet of metal used under the front end of a log while skidding it (7) : a metal or wood form used in constructing a poured concrete floor **2 a** *archaic* : CRANIUM **b** (1) : a natural basin or depression; *esp* : one containing standing water or mud and (as in southern Africa) in the dry season often drying up leaving a salt deposit (2) : an artificial basin (as for evaporating brine) **c** : a fragment typically about 200 feet in diameter of the flat relatively thin ice that forms in bays or fiords or along the shore and then becomes free and drifts about the sea — compare ICE FLOE **d** : the broad posterior part of the lower jawbone of a whale **e** : the round flat disk of metal on a steel trap on which an animal steps to spring the trap **3** : HARDPAN **1 4** *slang* : FACE **5** : a harsh criticism — **on the pan** *adv* (*or adj*) : under criticism ⟨had him *on the pan* for coddling subversives⟩

²pan \"\ *vb* **panned; panned; panning; pans** *vi* **1** : to wash earth, gravel, or other material in a pan in searching for gold or some other precious metal **2** : to yield precious metal (as gold) in the process of panning ⟨gravel that *panned* well⟩ — usu. used with *out* ⟨dirt that ~*s* out 40 ounces of gold to a ton⟩ ~ *vt* **1 a** (1) : to wash (as dirt, gravel) in a pan for the purpose of separating heavy particles (as of gold) (2) : to separate (as gold) by panning **b** : to cook in a pan in a small quantity of fat or water **c** : to extract (salt) or reduce (maple sap) by evaporation in a pan **d** : to place (shaped bread dough) in pans **e** : to steam the leaves of (oolong tea) to stop fermentation **2** : to attack with harsh criticism : criticize severely ⟨whether the critics would praise or ~ the new musical comedy⟩

³pan \"\ *n* -S [ME *panne*, fr. MF *pane*, fr. (assumed) VL *patina*, prob. fr. Gk *pathnē* manger, crib; akin to Gk *peisma* cable — more at BIND] *archaic* : PLATE 5a(1)

⁴pan \"\ *vb* **panned; panned; panning; pans** [origin unknown] *vi*, *chiefly Scot* : to join or fit together : AGREE ~ *vt* : to cause to fit together

⁵pan \ˈpän\ *n* -S [Hindi *pān*, fr. Skt *parṇa* wing, feather, leaf — more at FERN] **1** : the leaf of the betel palm **2** : a preparation of betel nut that is rolled in betel leaf with a little shell lime and is used esp. in India and the East Indies for chewing

⁶pan \ˈpan, ˈpaa(ə)n\ *n* -S [F, fr. MF, pane — more at PANE] : PANEL; *esp* : a structural panel (as of a wall or door) ⟨doors of double ~ construction⟩ ⟨a dormer ~⟩

⁷pan \"\ *n*, *cap* [NL, prob. fr. L *Pan*, ancient Greek god of woods and shepherds, fr. Gk] : a genus of anthropoid apes containing the chimpanzee

⁸pan \"\ *vb* **panned; panned; panning; pans** [short for *panoram*] *vi* **1** : to rotate a motion-picture or television camera in any direction so as to keep an object in the picture or secure a panoramic effect ⟨never ~ if you can avoid it except to follow motion —K.A.Henderson⟩ **2** *of a camera* : to undergo such rotation ⟨the camera ~*s* to the main street of the village —J.P.Marquand⟩ ~ *vt* : to cause (a camera) to pan ⟨the camera is *panned* to follow the action as it moves from one location to another —A.L.Gaskill & D.A.Englander⟩

⁹pan \"\ *n* -S : the process of panning a motion-picture or television camera; *also* : a scene or sequence made by this process

¹⁰pan \"\ *adj* [by shortening] : PANCHROMATIC ⟨ortho film will give greater contrast than ~ film —Aaron Sussman⟩

¹¹pan \"\ — an international radiotelephone signal word introducing an urgent message

¹²pan \"\ *n* -S [¹*pan*] : a tractor-operated scraper that transports the material it collects

¹³pan \ˈpän\ *n* -S [by shortening] : PANGUINGUE

pan- *or* **pano-** *comb form* [Gk, fr. *pan*, neut. of *pas* all, every; akin to Skt *śaśvat* all, every, *śvayati* he swells — more at CAVE] **1 a** : all : completely ⟨*pan*cyclopedic⟩ ⟨*pano*phobia⟩ ⟨*pan*cultural⟩ ⟨*pan*sexualism⟩ ⟨*pan*genesis⟩ ⟨*pan*telegraph⟩ **b** *often cap* : all of a (specified) group — usu. joined to the second element with a hyphen ⟨*pan*-sectarian⟩ ⟨*Pan*-Asian⟩ ⟨*Pan*=Slavism⟩ **2** : whole : general ⟨*pan*atrophy⟩ ⟨*pan*carditis⟩ ⟨*pan*hysterectomy⟩ ⟨*pan*esthesia⟩

pan *abbr* panorama

pan·a·ce \ˈpanəsē\ *n* -S [L *panacea*] *archaic* : a fabulous herb said by the ancients to be a panacea

pan·a·cea \ˌpanəˈsēə\ *n* -S [L, fr. Gk *panakeia*, fr. *panakēs* all-healing, panacea (fr. *pan-* + *-akēs* — fr. *akeisthai* to heal —) + *-ia* -y; akin to Gk *akos* remedy — more at AUTACOID] : a remedy for all ills or difficulties : a universal remedy : CURE-ALL ⟨all con men know that the ~ for all legal troubles is the fix —D.W.Maurer⟩

pan·a·ce·an \ˌ==ˈsēən\ *adj* : having the properties of a panacea

pan·a·chage \ˌpanəˈshäzh\ *n* -S [F, lit., mixture (of colors), fr. *panacher* to variegate, plume (fr. *panache* mixture of colors, bouquet of plumes, tuft, fr. MF *pennache*) + *-age*] : a variation of the list system that permits the voter to redistribute names from several party lists into a list having names in an order of his own choice — compare CROSS-VOTING

¹pa·nache \pəˈnash, -näsh\ *n* -S [earlier *pennache*, fr. MF, fr. OIt *pennacchio*, fr. LL *pinnaculum* small wing — more at PINNACLE] **1** : a tuft (as of feathers) used as a headdress or an ornament on a helmet **2** : dash or flamboyance in style and action : SWAGGER, VERVE ⟨grew progressively more windy and histrionic without ever recapturing the vitality and ~ of the early period —*Times Lit. Supp.*⟩

²pa·na·ché \ˌpanəˈshā\ *adj* [F, fr. past part. of *panacher* to variegate] : comprised of several foods ⟨beans ~— string beans, cooked navy beans, lima beans, flageolets, dressed in butter, cream sauce —J.D.Vehling⟩

panache 1

pa·nached \pəˈnasht\ *adj* [F *panaché* (past part. of *panacher*) + E *-ed*] : variegated with stripes of color

pan·a·chure \ˌpanəˈshu̇(ə)r\ *n* -S [F, fr. *panache* mixture of colors + *-ure*] : MOTTLING

pa·na·da \pəˈnädə, -nādə\ *also* **pa·nade** \-näd, -nād\ *n* -S [Sp, fr. *pan* bread (fr. L *panis*) + *-ada* -ade (fr. LL *-ata*) — more at FOOD] **1** : bread boiled to a pulp in milk, broth, or water **2** : a paste made of flour or bread crumbs and water or stock and used as a base for sauce or for a binder for forcemeat or stuffing

panage *var of* PANNAGE

pan-agglutinability \ˌpan+\ *n* : a condition of red blood cells induced by products of some bacteria or viruses in which they are agglutinable by all human sera

pan-agglutinable \"+\ *adj* [*pan-* + *agglutinable*] *of a red blood cell* : agglutinable by all human sera in the presence of viruses or bacteria

pan-agglutination \"+\ *n* [*pan-* + *agglutination*] : agglutination of panagglutinable red blood cells

pa·na·gia \ˌpänəˈyē(ˌ)ä\ *n* -S [LGk *Panagia* Virgin Mary, fr. fem. of Gk *panagios* all-holy, fr. *pan-* + *hagios* holy] **1** *usu cap* : a ceremony observed in monasteries of the Eastern Church at the first morning meal in honor of the Virgin Mary in which a loaf on a plate is elevated before being shared among participants **2** : ENCOLPION

¹pan·a·ma \ˈpanəˌmä, -má, -mȯ, ˌ==ˈ=\ *adj* [fr. *Panama*, republic in Central America] **1** *usu cap* : of or from the republic of Panama : of the kind or style prevalent in Panama : PANAMANIAN **2** *or* **panama city** *usu cap P&C* [fr. *Panama* City, Panama] : of or from Panama City, the capital of Panama : of the kind or style prevalent in Panama City

²panama \"\ *n* [AmSp *panamá*, fr. *Panama*, Central America, prob. fr. Tupi *panamá* butterfly, migration of butterflies] **1** *also* **panama tree** -S *usu cap P* : a large handsome tree (*Sterculia apetala*) of tropical America having oily edible seeds **2** -S **a** *or* **panama hat** *often cap P* [so called fr. *Panama* being formerly its chief center of distribution] : a fine lightweight hat of natural-colored straw hand-plaited of narrow strips from the young leaves of the jipijapa; *also* : a machine-made imitation of this — compare TOQUILLA **b** : a straw made from jipijapa **3 a** *usu cap* : an American breed of sheep developed by crossing Lincoln rams on Rambouillet ewes **b** -S *often cap* : a sheep of this breed

panama balata *n*, *usu cap P* : gum from a bully tree (*Manilkara darienensis*)

panama bark *or* **panama wood** *n*, *usu cap P* : SOAPBARK

panama disease *n*, *usu cap P* [so called fr. its first occurrence in banana plantations of Panama] : a destructive vascular disease of the banana caused by a fungus (*Fusarium oxysporum cubense*) and characterized by wilting and yellowing of leaves and death of affected shoots

panama hat plant *or* **panama hat palm** *n*, *usu cap 1st P* : JIPIJAPA

panama ipecac *n*, *usu cap P* : CARTAGENA IPECAC

¹pan·a·ma·ni·an \ˌpanəˈmānēən\ *also* **pan·a·man** \ˌpanəˈmän\ *n* -S *cap* [*Panama*, republic in Central America + E *-anian* (as in *Lusitanian*) or *-an*] : a native or inhabitant of Panama

²panamanian \ˌ==ˈ===\ *also* **panaman** \ˌ==ˈ=\ *adj*, *usu cap* : of or relating to Panama or its inhabitants

panama orange *n*, *usu cap P* : CALAMONDIN

panama redwood *n*, *usu cap P* : the hard heavy red wood of a quira (*Platymiscium pinnatum*)

pan-american \ˌpan+\ *adj*, *usu cap P&A* **1** : of or relating to the independent republics of No. and So. America ⟨*Pan*=*American* affairs⟩ **2** : involving or participated in by the Pan-American nations ⟨*Pan-American* congress⟩ ⟨*Pan*=*American* games⟩

pan-americanism \"+\ *n*, *usu cap P&A* : a movement of the late 19th and 20th centuries favoring close cooperation (as mutual protection and the promotion of better commercial and cultural relations) among the Pan-American nations based upon a community of interests stemming largely from geographical proximity ⟨*Pan-Americanism* . . . has none of the spirit of empire in it —Woodrow Wilson⟩

pan·a·mint \ˈpanəˌmint, -ˌmənt\ *n*, *pl* **panamint** *or* **panamints** *usu cap* : KOSO

pan-arabism \ˈpan+\ *n*, *usu cap P&A* : a 20th century movement having as its principal aim the political union of the Arab states

pan·a·ri·ti·um \ˌpanəˈrishēəm\ *n*, *pl* **panari·tia** \-ēə\ [ME *panaricium*, fr. LL, alter. of L *paronychium* — more at PARONYCHIUM] **1** : PARONYCHIA, ³FELON 1 **2** : FOOT ROT 2

pan·arteritis \(ˌ)pan+\ *n* [NL, fr. *pan-* + *arteritis*] : inflammation involving all coats of an artery

pan·arthritis \ˌpan+\ *n* [NL, fr. *pan-* + *arthritis*] : inflammation of all the structures of a joint

pan·a·ry \ˈpanərē\ *adj* [F *panaire*, fr. L *panis* bread + F *-aire* -ary — more at FOOD] : of or relating to bread or breadmaking

pan·a·tela *also* **pan·a·tel·la** *or* **pan·e·tela** *or* **pan·e·tel·la** \ˌpanəˈtelə\ *n* -S [Sp *panatela*, fr. AmerSp, a long thin biscuit, bread pudding, fr. It *panatella*, fr. *panata* panada (fr. *pane* bread — fr. L *panis* — + *-ata* -ade) + *-ella* — more at FOOD] : a long slender cigar that has straight sides that are rounded off at the sealed end

pan·ath·e·naea \ˌpa,nathəˈnēə\ *n pl*, *usu cap* [NL, fr. Gk *panathēnaia*, fr. *pan-* + *Athēna*, *Athēnē*, major Greek deity, goddess of war, fertility, arts, and wisdom] : the annual or quadrennial festivities of ancient Athens in honor of Athena celebrated in their greater form for several days during the third year of each olympiad and including a great procession in which the people marched to the acropolis bearing an embroidered peplos for their tutelary goddess and also athletic, musical, equestrian, and other contests — **pan·ath·e·nae·an** \ˌ=,==ˈnēən\ *adj*, *usu cap*

pan·ath·e·na·ic \ˌ=,==ˈnāik\ *adj*, *often cap* [L *panathenaicus*, fr. Gk *panathēnaikos*, fr. *panathēnaia* + *-ikos* -ic] : of, relating to, or connected with the Panathenaea : PANATHENAEAN ⟨the Parthenon frieze representing the ~ procession⟩ ⟨vases given as prizes in the ~ games⟩

pan·automorphic \(ˌ)pan+\ *adj* [*pan-* + *automorphic*] : PANIDIOMORPHIC

pa·nax \ˈpāˌnaks\ *n* [NL, fr. L, a plant, panacea, fr. Gk *panak-*, *panax*, fr. *panakeia* — more at PANACEA] **1** *cap* : a genus of perennial herbs (family Araliaceae) of eastern No. America and Asia with aromatic tuberous roots, compound verticillate leaves, and a solitary umbel of flowers — see GINSENG **2** -ES : any plant of a genus (*Polyscias*) of trees and shrubs that is related to and sometimes esp. formerly included in *Panax*

pa·nay·an \pəˈnīən\ *n* -S *usu cap* [*Panay*, one of the Visayan islands in the Philippines + E *-an*] : HILIGAYNON

pan bolt *n* : a bolt with the head shaped like an inverted pan

pan-breaking \ˈ=ˌ==\ *n* : the loosening of hardpan or plow sole with a subsoiler, chisel, or similar deep-tillage implement

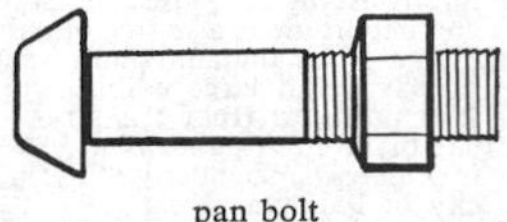
pan bolt

panbroil \ˈ=ˌ=\ *vt* [*pan* + *broil*] : to cook uncovered on a hot metal surface (as a frying pan) with little or no fat

¹pan·cake \ˈpa|n,kāk, ˈpaa| *sometimes* |ŋ,-\ *n*, *often attrib* [ME, fr. *panne* pan + *cake* — more at PAN] **1 a :** GRIDDLE CAKE ⟨~ mix⟩ **b :** a usu. very thin flat cake made of a batter enriched with eggs, milk, or cream, cooked on both sides in a pan or on a griddle and often rolled up with a sweet or savory filling and served in portions as a dessert or appetizer — compare CREPE SUZETTE **2 :** something thin and flat like a pancake; *specif* **:** a fabricated leather made of leather scraps glued together and pressed into sheets and often used in heels

²pancake \"\ *vi* **:** to make a pancake landing ⟨*pancaked* down to a forced landing —F.J.Taylor⟩ ⟨the plane struck . . . an apartment house and *pancaked* down in an orphanage baseball diamond —*N.Y.Times*⟩ ~ *vt* **1 :** to cause (an airplane) to make a pancake landing **2 :** FLATTEN ⟨found his hat had been *pancaked* under a suitcase⟩

Pan-Cake \"\ *trademark* — used for a cosmetic in semimoist cake form used in place of or as a foundation for face powder

pancake bell *n* **:** a bell rung in some English churches about noon on Shrove Tuesday sometimes regarded as a signal to stop work and prepare pancakes

pancake coil *n* **:** a coil having a flat spiral form

pancake day *or* **pancake tuesday** *n, usu cap P&D&T* [so called fr. the custom of having pancakes on that day] **:** SHROVE TUESDAY

pancake engine *n* **:** an engine arranged for compactness by stacking cylinders one above another horizontally or side by side (as for mounting in an airplane wing)

pancake ice *n* **:** thin new ice such as forms in the early fall in polar regions in pieces about one to six feet in diameter resembling pancakes

pancake landing *n* **:** a landing in which the airplane is leveled off higher than for a normal landing causing it to stall and drop in an approximately horizontal position with little forward motion

pancake plant *n* **:** DWARF MALLOW

pancake turner *n* **:** a record operator in a radio or television studio

pan·carditis \¦pan+\ *n* [NL, fr. *pan-* + *carditis*] **:** general inflammation of the heart; *specif* **:** inflammation involving the pericardium, myocardium, and heart valves but not the whole endocardium

pan·cha·ma \ˈpənchəmə\ *n* -s [Skt *pañcama* fifth] **:** a member of the lowest caste group in India **:** HARIJAN, UNTOUCHABLE

pan·chax \ˈpan,chaks\ *n* -ES [NL *Panchax*, former generic name of the panchaxes] **:** any of numerous small brilliantly colored killifishes (genus *Aplocheilus*) of Africa and southeastern Asia that are often kept in the tropical aquarium

pan·cha·yat *also* **pan·cha·yet** *or* **pun·cha·yet** \(ˌ)pən-ˈchäyət, -chīət\ *n* -s [Hindi *pañcāyat*, fr. Skt *pañca* five — more at FIVE] **1 :** a village council in India: **a :** a former group of five influential older men acknowledged by the community as its governing body **b :** an elective council of about five members organized in the republic of India as an organ of village self-government **2 :** a Parsi council of six dasturs and ten mobeds regulating secular affairs

pan·chen lama \ˈpän,chen-\ *n, usu cap P&L* [*panchen* fr. Chin (Pek) *pan¹ ch'an²*] **:** the lama who is the chief spiritual adviser of the Dalai Lama

pan·cheon \ˈpanchən\ *n* -s [prob. alter. (influenced by ¹*pan*) of *puncheon*] **:** a large flaring shallow earthen vessel formerly commonly used in rural England

pan·chromatic \¦pan, ¦paan+(ˌ)¦==\ *adj* [ISV *pan-* + *chromatic*] **:** sensitive to light of all colors in the visible spectrum — used of a photographic emulsion, film, or plate

pan·chro·ma·tize \panˈkrōmə,tīz\ *vt* [*panchromatic* + *-ize*] **:** to make panchromatic ⟨the emulsion must be *panchromatized* —J.S.Friedman⟩

pan conveyor *n* [¹*pan*] **:** a slow-moving chain conveyer in which a series of overlapping plates is attached to continuous chains

pan·cosmic \(ˈ)pan+\ *adj* [*pan-* + *cosmic*] **1 :** affecting or relating to the cosmos as a whole **2** [*pancosmism* + *-ic*] **:** of or relating to pancosmism ⟨pantheism in . . . its ~ or acosmic form —Aldous Huxley⟩

pan·cos·mism \panˈkäz,mizəm\ *n* [*pan-* + Gk *kosmos* order, universe + *-ism*] **:** the theory that the material universe or cosmos in time and space is all that exists

pan·cra·ti·ast \panˈkrāshē,ast\ *or* **pan·cra·tist** \ˈpankrəd·əst\ *n* -s [L *pancratiastes*, fr. Gk *pankratiastēs*, fr. *pankratiazein* to perform the exercises of the pancratium, fr. *pankration* pancratium] **:** a contestant or victor in a pancratium — **pan·cra·ti·as·tic** \ˌpan,krāshēˈastik\ *adj*

pan·crat·ic \(ˈ)panˈkrad·ik\ *adj* [L *pancratium* + E *-ic*] **1 :** of or relating to a pancratium **2** [*pan-* + *-cratic*] **:** marked by or giving mastery of all subjects or matters **3 :** having all or many degrees of power — used esp. of an adjustable eyepiece for a microscope

pan·cra·ti·um \panˈkrāshēəm\ *n* [L, fr. Gk *pankration*, fr. *pankratēs* all-powerful, fr. *pan-* + *kratos* strength, power — more at HARD] **1** *also* **pancration** -s **:** an ancient Greek athletic contest involving both boxing and wrestling **2** [NL, fr. Gk *pankration* sea-daffodil] **a** *cap* **:** a genus of Old World bulbous herbs (family Amaryllidaceae) having mostly pure white umbellate flowers with a funnel-shaped perianth and conspicuous crown — see SEA DAFFODIL **b** -s **:** any plant of the genus *Pancratium*

pancre- *or* **pancreo-** *comb form* [ISV, fr. NL *pancreas*] **:** PANCREAT- ⟨*pancrectomy*⟩ ⟨*pancreozymin*⟩

pan·cre·as \ˈpaŋkrēəs, ˈpank-, ˈpaank-\ *n* -ES [NL, fr. Gk *pankreas*, fr. *pan-* + *kreas* flesh, meat — more at RAW] **:** a large compound racemose gland that in man lies in front of the upper lumbar vertebrae and behind the stomach and is somewhat hammer-shaped and firmly attached anteriorly to the curve of the duodenum with which it communicates through one or more pancreatic ducts and that consists of (1) tubular acini secreting digestive ferments which pass to the intestine and function in the breakdown of proteins, fats, and carbohydrates; (2) modified acinar cells that form islets between the tubules and secrete the hormone insulin; and (3) a firm connective tissue capsule that extends supportive strands into the organ — see BEEF BREAD, ISLET OF LANGERHANS; DIGESTION illustration

pancreat- *or* **pancreato-** *comb form* [NL, fr. Gk *pankreat-*, *pankreas* pancreas] **1 :** pancreas ⟨*pancreat*algia⟩ **:** pancreas and ⟨*pancreato*duodenectomy⟩ **2 :** pancreatic ⟨*pancreatism*⟩

pan·cre·a·tec·to·mize \ˌpaŋkrēəˈtektə,mīz, ˌpankr-\ *vt* -ED/-ING/-S [*pancreatectomy* + *-ize*] **:** to excise the pancreas of

pan·cre·a·tec·to·my \-ektəmē\ *n* -ES [*pancreat-* + *-ectomy*] **:** surgical excision of all or part of the pancreas

pan·cre·at·ic \¦paŋkrē¦ad·ik, ¦pank-, ¦paank-, -at|, |ēk\ *adj* [prob. fr. (assumed) NL *pancreaticus*, fr. *pancreat-* + L *-icus* -ic] **:** of or relating to the pancreas

pancreatic artery *n* **:** any of the branches of the splenic artery that supply the pancreas

pancreatic duct *n* **:** a duct connecting the pancreas with the intestine; *specif* **:** DUCT OF WIRSUNG — distinguished from *duct of Santorini*; see DIGESTION illustration

pancreatic fibrosis *n* **:** MUCOVISCIDOSIS

pancreatic juice *n* **:** a clear alkaline pancreatic secretion that contains at least three different enzymes, trypsin, amylopsin, and lipase, or their precursors and that is poured into the duodenum where when mixed with bile and intestinal juices it furthers the digestion of foodstuffs already partly broken down by salivary and gastric enzymes

pancreatico- *comb form* [ISV, fr. *pancreatic*] **1 :** pancreatic ⟨*pancreatico*gastrostomy⟩ **2 :** pancreatic and ⟨*pancreatico*biliary⟩ ⟨*pancreatico*duodenal⟩

pan·cre·a·tin \ˈpaŋkrēəd·ən, ˈpank-\ *n* -s [ISV *pancreat-* + *-in*] **:** a mixture of enzymes from the pancreatic juice or a preparation containing such a mixture; *esp* **:** a cream-colored amorphous powder containing principally amylase, trypsin, and lipase obtained from the pancreas of the hog or ox and used chiefly in medicine as a digestant and in tanning as a bate

pan·cre·a·tism \-ēə,tizəm\ *n* -s [*pancreat-* + *-ism*] **:** pancreatic activity — used chiefly in combination ⟨*dyspancreatism*⟩

pan·cre·a·ti·tis \ˌpaŋkrēəˈtīd·əs, ˌpank-\ *n, pl* **pancre·ti·ti·des** \-ˈtidə,dēz\ [NL, fr. *pancreat-* + *-itis*] **:** inflammation of the pancreas

pan·cre·o·zy·min \ˌpaŋkrēōˈzīmən, ˌpank-\ *n* [ISV *pancre-* + *zymin*] **:** a hormonal product of the duodenal mucosa that stimulates pancreatic enzyme production — compare SECRETIN

pan·cytopenia \(¦)pan+\ *n* [NL, fr. *pan-* + *cytopenia*] **:** APLASTIC ANEMIA — **pan·cytopenic** \"+\ *adj*

pand \ˈpand\ *n* -s [prob. modif. of MF *pente*, fr. *pendre* to hang — more at PENDANT] *archaic Scot* **:** a narrow drapery hung on a bedstead

¹pan·da \ˈpandə, ˈpaan-\ *n* -s [F, fr. native name in Nepal] **1 :** a long-tailed Himalayan carnivore (*Ailurus fulgens*) that is related to and closely resembles the American raccoon, has long fur, and is basically rusty or chestnut in color with mottling and barring of black and with the muzzle, cheeks and ears conspicuously tufted with white — called also *bear cat*, *cat bear* **2 :** a large mammal (*Ailuropoda melanoleuca*) of western China that somewhat resembles a bear but is related to the raccoons though sometimes placed in a separate family and that is largely white above and black below with black patches about the eyes and black ears — called also *giant panda*

²panda \"\ *n* -s [NL, prob. by shortening & alter. fr. LL *pandura*, *pandurium* three-stringed lute — more at PANDURA] **:** a philodendron (*Philodendron panduriforme*) used as an ornamental and aquarium plant and having fiddle-shaped leaves

³panda \"\ *n* [NL, fr. native name in Gabon and So. Cameroons] **1** *cap* **:** a small West African genus (coextensive with the family Pandaceae and order Pandales) of dicotyledonous trees with drupaceous fruits that are rich in tannin and contain large seeds rich in edible oil **2** -s **a :** a small West African tree (*Panda oleosa*) **b :** the very hard heavy fine-grained brownish yellow to greenish wood of the panda

pandaemonium *var of* PANDEMONIUM

pan·dal \ˈpandᵊl\ *n* -s [Tamil-Malayalam *pantal*] **:** a shelter erected in India of upright poles supporting a roof that is usu. of bamboo matting; *esp* **:** a large open-sided temporary pavilion often used for large meetings

pan·dal·i·dae \panˈdaləˌdē\ *n pl, cap* [NL, fr. *Pandalus*, type genus + *-idae*] **:** a family of deepwater prawns with elongated laterally compressed rostrum armed with spines and the first two pairs of legs slender

pan·da·lus \ˈpandələs\ *n, cap* [NL] **:** a genus of deepwater prawns that includes the common European edible prawn (*P. annulicornis*) and is the type of the family Pandalidae

pan·dan \ˈpandən\ *n* -s [NL *Pandanus*] **:** a plant of the family Pandanaceae; *esp* **:** TEXTILE SCREW PINE

pan·da·na·ce·ae \ˌpandəˈnāsē,ē\ *n pl, cap* [NL, fr. *Pandanus*, type genus + *-aceae*] **:** a family of woody plants (order Pandanales) having rigid leaves and small dioecious flowers without a perianth — see FREYCINETIA, PANDANUS — **pan·da·na·ceous** \¦==¦nāshəs\ *adj*

pan·da·na·les \ˌ==ˈnā(ˌ)lēz\ *n pl, cap* [NL, fr. *Pandanus* + *-ales*] **:** an order of monocotyledonous plants including the families Typhaceae, Sparganiaceae, and Pandanaceae and distinguished by monoecious or dioecious flowers without a perianth that are borne in close spikes or heads and ovules with mealy or fleshy endosperm

pan·da·nus \panˈdānəs\ *n* [NL, fr. Malay *pandan*] **1** *cap* **:** a large genus (the type of the family Pandanaceae) of tropical trees that comprise the screw pines, are native chiefly to Malaysia and naturalized over a wide area, and have slender stems like those of palms, often immense prop roots, and branches with a terminal crown of sword-shaped leaves **2** -ES **a :** any plant of the genus *Pandanus* **b :** a fiber that is made from the leaf of the pandanus and is used for woven articles (as mats)

pandar *var of* PANDER

pan·da·ram \pənˈdärəm\ *n* -s [Tamil *paṇṭāram*] **1 :** a Hindu ascetic mendicant of the Sudra or sometimes a lower caste **2 :** a low-caste Hindu priest of southern India and Ceylon

pan·darc·tos \panˈdärk,täs\ [NL, fr. ¹*panda* + Gk *arktos* bear — more at ARCTIC] *syn of* AILUROPODA

pan·da·rus \ˈpandərəs\ *n, cap* [NL, fr. L *Pandarus*, in Greek mythology leader of the Lycians in the Trojan war, fr. Gk *Pandaros*] **:** a genus of fish lice attacking the skin of marine fishes

P and C *abbr* put and call

P and D *abbr* pickup and delivery

pan·de·an harmonica \ˈpandēən-\ *n, usu cap P* [*pandean* irreg. fr. *Pan*, ancient Greek god of woods and shepherds + E *-an*] **:** a harmonica resembling a panpipe

pandean pipes *n pl, usu cap 1st P* **:** PANPIPE

pan·dect \ˈpan,dekt\ *n* -s [LL *Pandectes*, digest in fifty books of the Roman civil law compiled under the Emperor Justinian in the 6th century, fr. L *pandectes* book that contains everything, fr. Gk *pandektēs* all-receiving, all-containing, fr. *pan-* + *dektēs* receiver, fr. *dechesthai* to receive; akin to Gk *dokein* to seem good, seem, think — more at DECENT] **1 :** a complete code of the laws of a country or system of law **2 :** a treatise covering an entire subject **:** complete digest **3 :** a manuscript containing the whole Bible **syn** see COMPENDIUM

pan·de·mia \panˈdēmēə\ *n* -s [NL, fr. Gk *pandēmia* all the people, fr. *pandēmos* of or belonging to all the people + *-ia* -y] **:** PANDEMIC

¹pan·dem·ic \(ˈ)pan¦demik\ *adj* [LL *pandemus* pandemic (fr. Gk *pandēmos* of or belonging to all the people, fr. *pan-* + *dēmos* deme, populace) + E *-ic* — more at DEM-] **1 a :** occurring over a wide geographic area and affecting an exceptionally high proportion of the population ⟨a ~ outbreak of malaria⟩ **b :** affecting the majority of people in a country or a number of countries ⟨~ alarm⟩ **2** *usu cap* [Gk *pandēmos Erōs* vulgar love (fr. *pandēmos* pandemic + *Erōs*, Greek god of love) + E *-ic* — more at EROS] **:** of or relating to common or sensual love **:** CARNAL **3 :** COSMOPOLITAN 4

²pandemic \"\ *n* -s **:** a pandemic outbreak of a disease **:** an epidemic of unusual extent and severity

pan·de·mo·ni·ac \¦pandə¦mōnē,ak\ *also* **pan·de·mon·ic** \-ˈmänik\ *or* **pan·de·mo·ni·a·cal** \¦pandəmə¦nīəkəl\ *adj* [*pandemonium* + *-ac* (after *demoniac*) or *-ic* (after *demonic*) or *-acal* (after *demoniacal*)] **1 :** of or relating to or resembling Pandemonium **:** INFERNAL **2 :** having the character of a pandemonium **:** RIOTOUS ⟨several hundred thousand hysterical . . . youths roaring ~ approval —J.A.Morris b. 1904⟩

pan·de·mo·ni·um \ˌpandəˈmōnēəm, ˌpaand-\ *n* -s [fr. *Pandaemonium*, capital of Hell in *Paradise Lost* (1667) epic poem by John Milton †1674 Eng. poet, fr. *pan-* + LL *daemonium* evil spirit, fr. Gk *daimonion*, fr. *daimōn* spirit, deity — more at DEMON] **1** *or* **pandaemonium a** *usu cap* **:** the abode of all the demons **:** the infernal regions **:** HELL ⟨a solemn council forthwith to be held at *Pandaemonium* —John Milton⟩ **b :** a center of vice **:** a wicked place **c :** a wildly lawless or riotous place or gathering **2 :** a state of wild uproar **:** tumultuous din ⟨the jubilation grew and grew to a positive ~ —Carolyn Hannay⟩ **syn** see DIN

¹pan·der \ˈpandə(r), ˈpaan-\ *or* **pan·der·er** \-d(ə)rə(r)\ *also* **pan·dar** \-də(r)\ *n* -s [*pander* alter. (influenced by *-er*) of ME *Pandare*, character who procured for Troilus the love of Cressida in *Troilus and Criseyde* (1374) poem by Geoffrey Chaucer †1400 Eng. poet; *panderer* fr. ²*pander* + *-er*; *pandar* fr. ME *Pandare*] **1 a :** a go-between in love intrigues **b :** a man who solicits clients for a prostitute **:** PROCURER **2 :** someone who caters to and often exploits the weaknesses of others

²pander \"\ *vb* **pandered; pandered; pandering** \-d(ə)riŋ\ **panders** *vt* **:** to act as pander for **:** procure for ~ *vi* **:** to act as a pander ⟨~*ing* to the shortcomings of music students —A.E. Wier⟩; *esp* **:** to provide gratification for others' desires (as for sentimentality) ⟨those who ~ to the lower tastes of the young and ignorant —*Britain Today*⟩ ⟨institutions which ~*ed* to the factory workers . . . — a movie house, a quick-lunch wagon —Scott Fitzgerald⟩

pan·der·ism \-də,rizəm\ *n* -s [¹*pander* + *-ism*] **:** the practice of pandering

pan·der·ly \-də(r)lē\ *adj* **:** having the character of a pander

P and I *abbr* protection and indemnity

pan·diagonal \¦pan+,=¦===\ *adj* [*pan-* + *diagonal*] **:** having the same sum along all possible diagonals ⟨~ magic squares⟩

pan·diatonic \(¦)pan+\ *adj* [*pan-* + *diatonic*] **:** marked by the use of the diatonic rather than the chromatic scale as the basic tonal material but without the classical harmonic restrictions ⟨~ style⟩

pan·diatonicism \"+\ *n* **:** the use of pandiatonic harmony

pan·dic·u·la·tion \pan,dikyəˈlāshən\ *n* -s [F, fr. L *pandiculatus* (past part. of *pandiculari* to stretch oneself, fr. *pandere* to spread, unfold) + F *-ion* — more at FATHOM] **:** a stretching and stiffening esp. of the trunk and extremities (as when fatigued and drowsy or after waking from sleep)

pan·di·on \panˈdī,än\ *n, cap* [NL, fr. L, nightingale, fr. *Pandion*, a king of Athens in Greek mythology, fr. Gk *Pandiōn*] **:** a genus (coextensive with the family Pandionidae of the suborder Falcones) of fish-eating hawks comprising the ospreys

pan·dit \ˈpandət, ˈpən-\ *n* -s [Hindi *paṇḍit*, fr. Skt *paṇḍita*] **1 :** a wise or learned man in India — often used before a name as an honorary title **2 :** a Brahman expert in Sanskrit and in the science, laws, and religion of the Hindus **:** SCHOLAR; *broadly* **:** TEACHER **3 :** a Hindu clerk or official in Kashmir

pan·di·ta \pänˈdēd·ə\ *n* -s [Skt *paṇḍita* pandit] **:** a Moro priest

P and L *abbr* profit and loss

¹pan·do·ra \panˈdōrə, paan-, -dȯrə\ *also* **pan·dore** \ˈpan-,dō(ə)r\ *n* -s [*pandora* fr. It *pandora*, *pandura*, fr. LL *pandura*, *pandurium* three-stringed lute; *pandore* fr. F, fr. LL *pandura*, *pandurium* — more at PANDURA] **1 :** BANDORE **2 :** PANDURA 2

²pandora \"\ *n* [NL, after *Pandora* (fr. L, fr. Gk *Pandōra*), the beautiful and gifted first woman of Greek mythology] **1** *cap* **:** a genus (the type of the family Pandoridae) of marine bivalve mollusks of the suborder Anatinacea with largely united siphons, thin equivalve shell, and tongue-shaped foot **2** -s **:** any mollusk of the genus *Pandora* or the family Pandoridae

pandora moth *n* [NL *pandora* (specific epithet of *Coloradia pandora*), fr. L *Pandora*] **:** a saturniid moth (*Coloradia pandora*) the larva of which is a defoliator of pines in western U. S.

pandora's box *n, usu cap P* [fr. *Pandora's box*, a box containing all the ills of mankind and given by Zeus to the mythological Pandora, who opened it against the command of Zeus] **:** something that produces many unforeseen difficulties **:** a prolific source of troubles

pan·do·rea \-rēə\ *n, cap* [NL, prob. fr. L *Pandora*, mythological first woman] **:** a genus of tropical Old World woody vines (family Bignoniaceae) having evergreen compound leaves and white or pink paniculate flowers — see BOWER PLANT, WONGA-WONGA

pan·do·ri·na \ˌpandəˈrīnə\ *n, cap* [NL, prob. fr. *Pandora*, genus of mollusks + *-ina*] **:** a genus of plantlike flagellates closely related to *Volvox* that form a small spherical colony of sixteen cells enclosed in a delicate gelatinous envelope through which the flagella project

pan·dour \ˈpan,dů(ə)r\ *n* -s [F *pandour*, *pandoure*, fr. Hung *pandur*, fr. Croatian, guard, constable, prob. fr. ML *banderius*, *bannerius* guardian of fields, summoner, fr. *bannum* proclamation, summons, ban, prob. of Gmc origin; akin to OHG *ban* command, prohibition, jurisdiction — more at BAN] **1 :** a member of a Croatian regiment in the Austrian army of the 18th century orig. organized as a local militia and having a reputation for cruelty and plundering **2 :** an armed servant or retainer of the nobility or member of a mounted constabulary in and near Croatia

pan·dow·dy \(ˈ)panˈdaůdē, -aůdi\ *n* -ES [origin unknown] **:** a deep-dish apple dessert that is spiced, sweetened with sugar, molasses, or maple syrup and covered with a rich biscuit crust and baked and that is served warm with a sauce or cold with the crust cut into the apples — called also *apple pandowdy*

pands *pl of* PAND

pan dul·ce \ˈpänˈdül(,)sā\ *n* [AmSp, sweet bread] **:** any of various sweet breads; *esp* **:** a raisin bun

pan·du·ra *also* **pan·dou·ra** \panˈd(y)ůrə\ *n* -s [*pandura* fr. It *pandura*, *pandora*, fr. LL *pandura*, *pandurium* three-stringed lute, fr. Gk *pandoura*; *pandoura* fr. Gk] **1 :** BANDORE **2 :** an ancient long-necked small-bodied stringed instrument of the lute class **3 :** BANDURA

pan·du·rate \ˈpand(y)ərət, -ə,rāt\ *also* **pan·du·rat·ed** \-ə,rād·əd\ *adj* [*pandurate* prob. fr. (assumed) NL *panduratus*, fr. LL *pandura* + L *-atus* -ate; *pandurated* prob. fr. (assumed) NL *panduratus* + E *-ed*] **:** resembling a fiddle in outline — see LEAF illustration

pan·du·ri·form \panˈd(y)ůrə,fȯrm\ *adj* [NL *panduriformis*, fr. LL *pandura* + L *-iformis* -iform] **:** PANDURATE

pan·du·ri·na \ˌpand(y)əˈrīnə\ *n* -s [NL, fr. LL *pandura* + L *-ina* (dim. suffix)] **:** a small lute with wire strings

¹pan·dy \ˈpandi\ *n* -ES [prob. fr. L *pande* hold out, extend (the hand), imper. sing. of *pandere* to spread, unfold — more at FATHOM] *dial Brit* **:** a blow on the hand usu. with a cane or stick

²pandy \"\ *vt* -ED/-ING/-ES *dial Brit* **:** to strike (a person) a pandy

³pan·dy \ˈpandē\ *n* -ES *usu cap* [Bengali & Hindi *pāṛe*, one of a subcaste of Brahmans, fr. Skt *paṇḍita* pandit; fr. their enlisting in the Bengal Army] **:** a mutineer in the Sepoy mutiny

¹pane \ˈpān\ *n* -s [ME *pane*, *pan* piece of cloth, strip, section, pane, fr. MF *pan*, fr. L *pannus* cloth, rag, ribbon — more at VANE] **1 :** a piece, section, or side of something: as **a :** one of the compartments of a window or door consisting of one sheet of glass in a frame of wood, lead, or some other metal **b :** one of the sides of a nut or bolt head **2 a :** one of a series of sewn strips or panels often of different colors esp. characteristic of 16th century costumes and curtains **b :** a finished slit in a 16th century garment so slashed in order to show a lining of contrasting color or material — usu. used in pl. **3 a :** one of the sections into which an original plate-sized sheet of postage stamps is cut for distribution to post offices — called also *post-office pane* **b :** a block of stamps forming a page of a stamp booklet — called also *booklet pane*

²pane \"\ *n* -s [prob. by alter.] **:** PEEN

³pane \"\ *vt* -ED/-ING/-S **:** PEEN

paned \-nd\ *adj* **1 :** made of or with panes of cloth **2 :** provided with an often specified number or kind of panes ⟨a small-*paned* window⟩ ⟨a 6-*paned* nut⟩

pan·e·gyr·ic \ˌpanəˈjirik, -jīr-, -rēk\ *n* -s [L *panegyricus*, fr. *panegyricus*, adj., of the nature of a public assembly, festive, fr. Gk *panēgyrikos*, fr. *panēgyris* public festival, public assembly (fr. *pan-* + *agyris*, *agora* assembly) + *-ikos* -ic — more at AGORA] **:** a eulogistic oration or writing **:** a formal or elaborate eulogy or encomium **:** a laudatory discourse; *also* **:** formal or elaborate praise or eulogizing **:** LAUDATION

pan·e·gyr·i·cal \¦==¦jirəkəl, -jīr-, -rek-\ *or* **pan·e·gyr·ic** \¦==-¦=rik, -rēk\ *adj* [*panegyrical* fr. L *panegyricus* panegyric, n. + E *-al*; *panegyric* fr. L *panegyricus* festive] **:** like or constituting a panegyric **:** formally or elaborately eulogistic or encomiastic — **pan·e·gyr·i·cal·ly** \-rək(ə)lē, -rēk-, -li\ *adv*

pa·neg·y·ris \pəˈnejərəs, -nēj-\ *or* **pa·neg·y·ry** \-rē\ *n* -ES [*panegyris* fr. Gk *panēgyris*; *panegyry* fr. Gk *panēgyris* + E *-y* (n. suffix)] **:** an ancient Greek public assembly; *esp* **:** a festival honoring a god

pan·e·gyr·ist \ˌpanəˈjirəst, -jīr-\ *n* -s [LL *panegyrista*, fr. Gk *panēgyristēs* participant in a public festival, fr. *panēgyrizein* to participate in a public festival, deliver a panegyric + *-istēs* -ist] **:** one who writes or delivers a panegyric **:** EULOGIST ⟨a ~ of country simplicity —John Buchan⟩

pan·e·gy·rize \ˈpanəjə,rīz\ *vt* -ED/-ING/-S [Gk *panēgyrizein*, fr. *panēgyris* public festival + *-izein* -ize] **:** to praise highly **:** extol in public **:** write or deliver a panegyric on **:** EULOGIZE

pa·ne·i·ty \pəˈnēəd·ē\ *n* -ES [L *panis* bread + E *-eity* (as in *corporeity*) — more at FOOD] **:** the quality or state of being bread ⟨the ~ of the eucharistic bread⟩

¹pan·el \ˈpanᵊl\ *n* -s *often attrib* [ME, fr. MF, prob fr. (assumed) VL *pannellus*, alter. (influenced by L *-ellus* -el) of L *pannulus* small piece of cloth, fr. *pannus* cloth, rag, ribbon + *-ulus* -ule — more at VANE] **1** *obs* **:** ¹PANNEL **2 a** *obs* **:** a small piece of parchment **b** (1) **:** a schedule containing the names of persons summoned as jurors by a sheriff (2) **:** the whole group of persons so summoned from which the jury is selected (3) **:** JURY 1 **c :** the person or persons arraigned for trial **d :** a list or group of persons selected for some service (as research, investigation, arbitration) ⟨an advisory ~ of experts⟩ ⟨test results . . . accomplished by a ~ of tasters —*Biol.*

panels 3b

Abstracts⟩ **e** (1) **:** a list of physicians from among whom a patient may make a choice in accordance with various British health and insurance plans (2) **:** the patients cared for by a doctor under such a plan **f** (1) **:** a group of three or more people often skilled in various fields who conduct before an audience a discussion on a topic (as of political, economic, or social interest) in order to stimulate interest and to present different points of view rather than to arrive at a single solution or to establish the superiority of one viewpoint (2) *or* **panel discussion :** a discussion conducted by such a panel — compare DEBATE, SYMPOSIUM **g :** a group of three or more entertainers or guests engaged as players in a quiz game or guessing game conducted by a master of ceremonies on a radio or television program **h** (1) **:** a number of persons interviewed as a population sample on two or more occasions for the purposes of a survey (as to ascertain changes in attitude or situation during the interim) ⟨consumer ~⟩ ⟨listener ~⟩ ⟨labor force ~⟩ ⟨~ study⟩ (2) **:** a survey of attitudes, opinions, or objective data using such a panel ⟨a fact-finding ~⟩ **3** [prob. influenced in meaning by L *panis* door panel, table, fr. *panis* food — more at FOOD] **:** a separate or distinct part of a surface ⟨cuts steel sheets into exact sizes for fenders, hoods, and roof ~*s* —*Time*⟩ ⟨the transparent ~ of a window envelope⟩ ⟨the inscription engraved in the ~ of this Royal Medal —P.H.Pettiford⟩: as **a :** a fence section (as the part between two posts in a rail fence) **:** HURDLE **b** (1) **:** a thin usu. rectangular board set sunken in a frame (as in a door, wainscot, or chair back) (2) **:** a usu. sunken or raised section of a surface (as a wall or ceiling) set off by a molding or other margin sometimes of different material or color (3) **:** a flat usu. rectangular piece of construction material (as plywood, metal, concrete, plastic) made usu. in a standard size to form part of a surface (as a wall, ceiling, floor) ⟨quickly put up a wall of prefabricated plywood ~*s*⟩ **c** (1) **:** a compartment of some design in carpet bedding (2) **:** a level expanse of turf (as in a garden) **d** (1) **:** an area on a book cover enclosed by a tooled or stamped border (2) **:** an affixed or inserted label on a book cover on which tooling, stamping, or finishing may be done **e** (1) **:** a vertical section of fabric (as a gore in a skirt) usu. stitched by two or more sides into or onto a garment (2) **:** a length of fabric (as a curtain) allowed to hang freely from its upper edge (3) **:** one of the gores of a parachute canopy **f** (1) **:** BOX 9a, 9c (2) **:** a cartoon consisting of a single picture (3) **:** a space on a postage stamp set off by a border or a tinted ground and containing a value figure, inscription, separate unit of design, or insignia — called also *label, tablet* **g :** a flat-bottomed furrow with sloping or curved sides cut in ornamental glassware **h** (1) **:** any of several units of construction of a wing surface of an airplane (2) **:** any unit piece of fabric of which the envelope or outer cover of an aerostat is made (3) **:** the area in a rigid airship bounded by two adjacent longitudinals and two adjacent transverses **i** (1) **:** any of the flat faces of a box, carton, or case whether separate or in finished form ⟨the trademark printed on the front ~⟩ (2) **:** any flat, smooth, or unmarked area on a container ⟨a ~ on the jar lid for marking in the price⟩ **4 a :** a thin flat piece of wood on which a picture is painted usu. in tempera or oil and tempera combined; *also* **:** a painting on such a surface **b** *or* **panel photograph :** a long narrow photograph; *esp* **:** one about 4 inches by 8½ inches **c :** a picture painted or mounted on a section of wall **d :** a photograph mounted on a stiff backing for display **5 a** *obs* **:** a small portion of coal left uncut **b :** one of the divisions marked by pillars of extra size into which a mine is laid off in one system of extracting coal or ore **6 a :** one of the sections of a folding screen or triptych **b** (1) **:** a book forming part of a series (as a trilogy presenting a subject in historical sequence) (2) **:** a series of such works ⟨this book, the second of a projected ~ of four about the West —*Time*⟩ **7 a :** a section of a switchboard **b :** a flat insulating support for parts of an electrical device usu. with control handles arranged on one face **c :** a usu. vertical mount for controls or dials of instruments of measurement **8** [influenced in meaning by ¹*pane*] **:** a distinctively shaped or colored piece of cloth for display on the ground by troops as a means of signaling to airplanes or of marking front lines or friendly installations or vehicles **9 :** PANEL TRUCK — **in the panel** *or* **on the panel** *or* **upon the panel** *Scots law* **:** arraigned for trial **:** on trial

²**panel** \"\ *vt* **paneled** *or* **panelled; paneled** *or* **panelled; paneling** *or* **panelling; panels 1 :** to furnish or decorate with panels **2 :** to produce flat surfaces in (a container) by distortion or in manufacture

pa·ne·la \pə'nälə\ *n* -s [MexSp, dim. of Sp *pan* bread, fr. L *panis;* fr. the fact that it comes in round chunks that resemble rolls of bread — more at FOOD] **:** low-grade brown sugar

panelboard \'≈,≈\ *n* **1 :** a drawing board with an adjustable outside frame that is forced over paper so as to hold and strain it **2 :** a strong rigid paperboard used for paneling in automobile bodies and in building construction **3 :** an electrical panel containing switches and fuses or circuit breakers controlling branch circuits (as for lights or fan motors) that is enclosed in a metal cabinet and usu. placed in or against a wall — called also *distribution board*

panel door *n* **:** a door having panels framed by stiles and rails of greater thickness — compare FLUSH DOOR

pan·el·er \'panᵊlə(r)\ *n* -s **:** one that makes or fits (as the body of a vehicle) with panels

pane·less \'pānləs\ *adj* [¹*pane* + *-less*] **:** having no pane **:** lacking panes ⟨windows left ~ by the explosion⟩

panel game *n* **:** theft in a panel house

panel heating *n* **:** space heating by means of wall, floor, baseboard, or ceiling panels with embedded electric conductors or hot-air or hot-water pipes — called also *radiant heating*

panel house *n* **:** a house of prostitution in which the rooms have secret entrances (as through sliding panels) to facilitate theft by accomplices of the inmates

paneling *n* -s [fr. gerund of ²*panel*] **:** panels joined in a continuous surface; *esp* **:** a decorative covering for an interior wall or ceiling consisting of usu. wood panels and often framing

pan·el·ist \'panᵊləst\ *n* -s **1 :** a member of a discussion or advisory panel (as for debating a public issue before a forum or for investigating or mediating an industrial controversy) **2 :** a member of a radio or television panel participating in an entertainment program

panel length *n* **:** the distance between two adjacent joints on either the upper or the lower chord of a truss

panel lighting *n* **:** room illumination by means of metal panels electrically heated to emit fluorescence from phosphors embedded between the metal and a glass facing

panel point *n* **:** a point (as on one of the chord members) at which members of a truss intersect

panel radiator *n* **:** a heating radiator set into a wall panel or baseboard

panel saw *n* **:** a handsaw with fine teeth for cutting thin wood (as for panels)

panel stamp *n* **:** a metal plate with which engraved designs or pictorial decorations are mechanically impressed on the sides of leather book covers

panel-stamped \'≈,≈\ *adj, of a leather book cover* **:** stamped with engraved designs or pictorial decorations

panel strip *n* **1 :** a strip of molded wood or metal to cover a joint between two sheathing boards and form a panel **2 :** a strip between a stile and a panel to form a secondary or accessory panel

panel thief *n* **:** the person who performs the robbery in a panel house

panel truck *n* **:** a light motor truck approximately of passenger-car size with a fully enclosed body used principally for delivery

panel wall *n* **:** a nonbearing wall between columns or piers that is supported at each story — compare CURTAIN WALL

pan·endoscope \(')pan+\ *n* [*pan-* + *endoscope*] **:** a cystoscope fitted with an obliquely forward telescopic system that permits wide-angle viewing of the interior of the urinary bladder — **pan·endoscopic** \(ˌ)pan+\ *adj* — **pan·endoscopy** \ˌpan+\ *n* -ES

pan·en·the·ism \pa'nen(t)thē,izəm\ *n* -s [G *panentheismus,* fr. *pan-* + Gk *en* in + G *theismus* theism (fr. Gk *theos* god + G *-ismus* -ism) — more at IN, THE-] **:** the doctrine that God includes the world as a part though not the whole of his being

pan·en·the·ist \-ēəst\ *n* **:** an adherent of panentheism

pan·en·the·is·tic \pa¦nen(t)thē¦istik\ *adj* [*panentheism* + *-istic*] **:** of or relating to panentheism

panes *pl of* PANE, *pres 3d sing of* PANE

pan·es·thia \pa'nesthēə\ *n, cap* [NL, fr. *pan-* + Gk *esthein* to eat + NL *-ia;* akin to Gk (Homeric) *edmenai* to eat; fr. the characteristic of biting off each other's wings — more at EAT] **:** a genus of subsocial burrowing cockroaches

panetela *or* **panetella** *var of* PANATELA

pan·e·tière \,panə'tye(ə)r\ *n* -s [F, fr. MF *panetiere* cupboard for keeping bread, fr. OF, bread sack, irreg. fr. *pan, pain* bread (fr. L *panis*) + *-iere* (fem. of *-ier* -er) — more at FOOD] **:** an ornate French-provincial bread box

pan·et·to·ne \,panə'tōnē\ *n* -s [It, fr. *panetto* small loaf, fr. *pane* bread (fr. L *panis*) + *-etto* -et (fr. LL *-itus*)] **:** a usu. yeast-leavened holiday bread containing raisins and candied fruit peels

pan-europe \'pan+\ *or* **pan-eu·ro·pa** \'panyə'rōpə\ *n* -s *usu cap P&E* [*pan-europa* fr. G *pan-Europa,* fr. *pan-* + *Europa* Europe, continent extending west from Asia] **:** a primarily political union of the countries of Europe excluding Great Britain and the U. S. S. R. projected during the mid-20th century

pan-european \(ˌ)pan+\ *adj, usu cap P&E* **:** of, relating to, or involving all or most of the nations of Europe ⟨a *Pan-European* economic union⟩

pan-fired \'≈,≈\ *adj, of Japanese green tea* **:** steamed and then rolled in metal pans over the fire — compare BASKET-FIRED

¹**panfish** \'≈,≈\ *n* [¹*pan* + *fish;* fr. its being suitable for frying whole in a pan] **:** any of numerous small food fishes (as of the family Centrarchidae) usu. taken with hook and line and not available on the market — compare GAME FISH

²**panfish** \"\ *vi* **:** to angle for panfish

³**panfish** \"\ *n* [¹*pan* + *fish;* fr. its shape] **:** KING CRAB

pan·for·te \pän'fȯrd·(,)ā\ *n* -s [It, fr. *pane* bread + *forte* strong, fr. L *fortis* — more at FORT] **:** a holiday bread that is hard in texture and is made with honey and nuts

pan·fry \'≈¦≈\ *vt* **:** to fry (food) in a pan containing very little fat **:** SAUTÉ — distinguished from *deep fry*

pan·ful \'pan,fu̇l\ *n* -s **:** a quantity that fills a pan

¹**pang** \'paŋ, 'paiŋ\ *n* -s [origin unknown] **1 :** a brief piercing spasm of pain ⟨the ~*s* of childbirth⟩ ⟨a hunger ~⟩ **2 :** a sudden sharp attack of mental pain **:** a feeling of piercing mental anguish ⟨a ~ of remorse⟩ ⟨felt a ~ of conscience⟩ ⟨the ~*s* of love⟩ **syn** see PAIN

²**pang** \"\ *vt* **:** to cause to have pangs **:** pain extremely **:** TORTURE, TORMENT

³**pang** \'paŋ\ *adj* [origin unknown] *Scot* **:** FULL, STUFFED

⁴**pang** \"\ *vt* -ED/-ING/-S *Scot* **:** to fill to capacity **:** CRAM, STUFF

¹**pan·ga** \'päŋgə\ *n* -s [Afrik *panga, pangar,* prob. fr. Tag *panga* jawbone] **:** a small common sparid food fish (*Pterogymnus laniarus*) of southern Africa sometimes congregating in vast schools

²**panga** \"\ *n* -s [native name in East Africa] **:** a large broad-bladed knife used in Africa for heavy cutting (as of brush or bananas) and also as a weapon **:** MACHETE

pan·ga·ne \pän'gä(,)nā\ *n* -s [prob. fr. *Pangani,* river and town in Tanganyika Territory, East Africa] **1 :** an East African bowstring hemp (*Sansevieria kirkii*) **2 :** the strong leaf fiber of the pangane used for cordage

pan·ga·si·nan \pän,gäsē'nän\ *n, pl* **pangasinan** *or* **pangasinans** *usu cap* [Pangasinan *Pangasinán*] **1 a :** a Christianized people in central Luzon, Philippines **b :** a member of such people **2 :** the Austronesian language of the Pangasinan people

pan·gen \'panjən, -,jen\ *also* **pan·gene** \-,jēn\ *n* -s [G *pangen,* fr. *pan-* + *-gen*] **:** a hypothetical heredity-controlling particle of protoplasm — compare PANGENESIS

pan·genesis \(')pan+\ *n* [NL, fr. *pan-* + *genesis*] **:** a hypothetical mechanism of heredity in which the cells throw off pangens that circulate freely throughout the system, multiply by subdivision, and collect in the reproductive products or in buds so that the egg or bud contains pangens from all parts of the parent or parents — opposed to *blastogenesis*

pan·ge·net·ic \¦panjə¦ned·ik\ *adj* **:** of, relating to, or characterized by pangenesis — **pan·ge·net·i·cal·ly** \-d·ək(ə)lē\ *adv*

pan·gen·ic \(')pan¦jenik\ *adj* [NL *pangenesis* + E *-ic*] **:** PANGENETIC

¹**pan-german** \'pan+\ *or* **pan-germanic** \¦pan+(,)¦≈¦≈\ *adj, usu cap P&G* **:** of, relating to, or favoring Pan-Germanism

²**pan-german** \"\ *or* **pan-germanist** \'pan+\ *n, usu cap P&G* **:** an advocate of Pan-Germanism

pan-germanism \'pan+\ *n* -s *usu cap P&G* [F *pangermanisme* (trans. of G *alldeutschtum*), fr. *pan-* + *germanisme* Germanism, fr. *Germanie* Germany (fr. L *Germania* land occupied by the Germanic peoples in western Europe in Roman times) + *-isme* -ism] **1 :** a chiefly 19th century movement having as its principal aim the political union of all Germans **2 :** a 20th century doctrine of German racial superiority and world domination by stages of imperial expansion

pan·gi \'pan,jī\ *n* -s [Bugi] **:** a Malayan tree (*Pangium edule*) having seeds that are edible after long boiling to remove their poisonous principle

pan·gi·um \'panjēəm\ *n, cap* [NL, fr. Bugi *pangi* + NL *-ium*] **:** a genus of Malayan trees (family Flacourtiaceae) having entire or 3-lobed leaves and axillary dioecious flowers with a scale at the base of each petal

pang·less \'paŋləs, 'paiŋ-\ *adj* **:** having or causing no pang — **pang·less·ly** *adv*

pan·gli·ma \pän'glēmə\ *n* -s [Malay *pĕnglima*] **:** a Malay noble of secondary rank **:** a petty raja

pan·gloss·ian \(')pan¦gläsēən\ *adj, usu cap* [*Pangloss,* optimistic tutor of Candide in the satire *Candide* (1759) by Voltaire †1778 Fr. writer (fr. F, fr. *pan-* + Gk *glōssa* tongue) + E *-an* + more at GLOSS] **:** marked by the view that all is for the best in this best of possible worlds ⟨~ economists . . . who had not so much predicted as seen the millenium —*Times Lit. Supp.*⟩

pan·go·la grass \pan'gōlə-\ *n* [*pangola* fr. native name in So. Africa] **:** a rapid-growing perennial grass (*Digitaria decumbens*) of southern Africa introduced into southern U. S. as a pasture grass

pan·go·lin \'paŋgələn, paŋ'gōl-\ *n* -s [Malay *pĕngguling,* fr. *guling* rolling over; fr. its characteristic of rolling itself into a ball] **:** any of several Asiatic and African edentate mammals of *Manis* or related genera of the order Pholidota having the body covered with large flattened reddish brown imbricated horny scales, feeding chiefly on ants, and somewhat resembling in habit and structure the American anteaters

pan grave *n* [¹*pan*] **:** a shallow grave characteristic of an ancient people with Nubian associations included in the inhabitants of Egypt during the Middle Kingdom

pan gravy *n* [¹*pan*] **:** gravy consisting of seasoned but not thickened juices extracted from meat in cooking and often a little water

pangs *pl of* PANG, *pres 3d sing of* PANG

pan·guin·gue \päŋ'geŋgē\ *n* -s [Tag *pangguinggui*] **:** a card game which resembles rummy, which is played with several packs of cards shuffled together, and in which a player tries to meld his whole hand in groups or sequences and bonuses are paid for particular melds

pang·we \'päŋ(,)wā\ *n, pl* **pangwe** *or* **pangwes** *usu cap* [Fang *Mpangwe*] **:** ⁴FANG

¹**panhandle** \'≈,≈≈\ *n* -s [¹*pan* + *handle* (n.)] **:** a comparatively narrow projection of a larger territory (as a state)

²**pan·han·dle** \'pan,handᵊl, 'paan,haan-\ *vb* **panhandled; panhandled; panhandling** \-d(ᵊ)liŋ\ **panhandles** [back-formation fr. *panhandler*] *vi* **:** to stop people on the street and ask for money often telling a hard-luck story **:** BEG ~ *vt* **1 :** to accost on the street and beg from **2 :** to get (as money) by panhandling

pan·han·dler \-d(ᵊ)lə(r)\ *n* [prob. fr. ¹*panhandle* + *-er;* fr. the extended forearm] **:** one that panhandles **:** an able-bodied street beggar

pan·has \'pän,häs\ *also* **pan·haus** \-hau̇s\ *or* **pann·haas** \-häs\ *or* **pann·haus** \-hau̇s\ *n* -ES [PaG *pannhas,* fr. *pann* pan (fr. MHG dial. *panne*) + *has* hare, rabbit, fr. MHG *hase;* akin to OHG *phanna* pan and to OHG *haso* hare — more at PAN, HARE] **:** SCRAPPLE

panhead \'≈,≈\ *n* **:** a head of a rivet or bolt shaped like an inverted cooking pan — **panheaded** \'≈¦≈≈\ *adj*

panhead

pan·hellenic \¦pan+\ *adj, usu cap* [*pan-* + *hellenic*] **1 :** of or relating to all Greece **:** including or representing all Greece or all the Greeks **2 :** of or relating to the Greek-letter sororities or fraternities in American colleges and universities or to an association representing them

pan-hispanism \'pan+\ *n* -s *usu cap P&H* [AmerSp *pan-hispanismo,* fr. Sp *pan-* + *hispanismo* hispanism — more at HISPANISM] **:** a movement in So. and Central America emphasizing the cultural kinship of the Spanish-speaking peoples and opposing Pan-Americanism

panhuman \(')pan+\ *adj* [*pan-* + *human*] **:** of or relating to all humanity ⟨~ values⟩ ⟨a ~ culture⟩

pan·hypopituitarism \(ˌ)pan+\ *n* [*pan-* + *hypopituitarism*] **:** generalized secretory deficiency of the anterior lobe of the pituitary gland **:** SIMMONDS' DISEASE

pan·hypopituitary \"+\ *adj* **:** of or relating to panhypopituitarism

pan·hysterectomy \"+\ *n* [*pan-* + *hysterectomy*] **:** excision of the uterus and uterine cervix

¹**pan·ic** \'panik, -nēk\ *n* -s [ME *panik,* fr. MF or L; MF *panic* Italian millet, fr. L *panicum,* fr. *panus* ear of millet, tuft, swelling, inflammation; akin to L *panic-, pantex* paunch — more at PAUNCH] **1 :** PANIC GRASS **2 :** the edible grain of some panic grasses

²**panic** \"\ *adj* [F *panique,* fr. Gk *panikos,* fr. *Pan,* ancient Greek god of woods and shepherds who was regarded as the cause of the panic among the Persians at Marathon and of any sudden and groundless fear + *-ikos* -ic] **1 :** of, relating to, or resembling the mental or emotional state believed to be induced by the ancient Greek god Pan **:** WILD **:** extreme, sudden, and often groundless — used esp. of fear ⟨driven by a ~ fear that they would be massacred —Alan Moorehead⟩ ⟨no rational fear but a ~ terror —H.G.Wells⟩ **2 :** of, relating to, or coming from a panic ⟨a wave of ~ buying —Mary K. Hammond⟩ ⟨~ haste⟩ ⟨~ conditions⟩ **3 :** of or relating to the god Pan ⟨what old, earthy *Panic* rite came to extinction here —Aldous Huxley⟩ **4 :** being or belonging to hardware securing an exit door that opens readily outward when a bar or lever on the inside of the door is pushed ⟨~ bolts for theater exits⟩ ⟨~ bars for school doors⟩

³**panic** \"\ *n* -s [Gk *panikon,* fr. neut. of *panikos*] **1** *obs* **:** contagious emotion such as was supposed to be due to the ancient Greek god Pan **2 :** a sudden overpowering fright; *esp* **:** a sudden terror often inspired by a trifling cause or a misapprehension of danger and accompanied by unreasoning or frantic efforts to secure safety **3 :** a sudden widespread fright concerning financial affairs and resulting in a depression in values caused by violent measures for protection or for the sale of securities or other property — compare BUSINESS CYCLE **4** *slang* **:** something very funny **syn** see FEAR

⁴**panic** \"\ *vb* **panicked; panicked; panicking; panics** *vt* **1 :** to affect with panic ⟨a brutal murder . . . ~*s* the town —*Publishers' Weekly*⟩ **:** influence by arousing panic ⟨salesmen are attempting to ~ people into buying . . . by threatening a shortage —*Springfield (Mass.) Daily News*⟩ **2 :** to produce demonstrative appreciation on the part of ⟨~ an audience with a gag⟩ ~ *vi* **:** to be stricken with panic **:** lose one's head ⟨~*s* and attempts to flee from the fallout area —R.E.Lapp⟩

pan·i·cal·ly \-nək(ə)lē\ *adv* [obs. E *panical* of panic (fr. E ²*panic* + *-al*) + E *-ly*] **:** in a manner suggesting panic ⟨his voice went up almost ~ at the end —R.M.Coates⟩

panic button *n* [so called fr. the control button or switch for emergency use in an airplane] **:** something setting off a precipitous emergency response

panic grass *n* [¹*panic*] **:** a grass of the genus *Panicum* or of one of several closely related genera (as *Echinochloa*)

pan·ick·i·ness \-nəkēnəs\ *n* -ES **:** the quality or state of being panicky

pan·icky \'panəkē, -ki\ *adj, sometimes* -ER/-EST [³*panic* + *-y*] **1 :** characterized by or resulting from panic ⟨moments of ~ terror at the beginning of each attack —R.H.Newman⟩ **:** groundlessly or extremely fearful ⟨became ~ as the snow deepened —G.R.Stewart⟩ **2 :** inclined to panic ⟨~ sheep⟩

pan·i·cle \'panəkəl, -nēk-\ *n* -s [L *panicula* tuft, swelling, dim. of *panus* ear of millet, tuft, swelling] **1 :** a compound racemose inflorescence that is usu. a raceme in which the secondary branches are themselves racemose (as the inflorescence of yuccas) but sometimes merges into the cymose type (as in the horse chestnut) — called also *compound raceme;* see INFLORESCENCE illustration **2 :** any pyramidal loosely branched flower cluster — **pan·i·cled** \-ld\ *adj*

panic party *n* **:** an extra crew carried on a World War I mystery ship for the purpose of quitting it when attacked and thus leaving it apparently abandoned

panic reaction *also* **panic state** *n* **:** an acute overwhelming attack of fear or anxiety producing personality disorganization that may persist

panic-stricken \'≈¦≈≈\ *or* **panic-struck** \'≈¦≈\ *adj* **:** struck with panic **:** overcome by sudden fear ⟨keeping back the *panic-stricken* crowd —*Blue Bk.*⟩ ⟨a *panic-stricken* urge to hurry the educational process —V.M.Rogers⟩

pa·nic·u·late \pə'nikyələt, -yə,lāt\ *or* **pa·nic·u·lat·ed** \-yə,lād·əd\ *adj* [*paniculate* fr. NL *paniculatus,* fr. L *panicula* tuft + *-atus* -ate; *paniculated* fr. NL *paniculatus* + E *-ed*] **:** arranged or disposed in panicles **:** branching like a panicle — **pa·nic·u·late·ly** *adv*

pan·i·cum \'panəkəm\ *n, cap* [NL, fr. L, Italian millet — more at PANIC (grass)] **:** a large and widely distributed genus of grasses of very diverse habit having 1- to 2-flowered spikelets disposed in a close or open panicle — see MILLET 1a, GUINEA GRASS, PARA GRASS, WITCHGRASS

pan·idiomorphic \(ˌ)pan+\ *adj* [*pan-* + *idiomorphic*] **:** completely idiomorphic

panier *var of* PANNIER

pa·ni·ne·an \,pänə¦nēən\ *adj, usu cap* [*Panini fl*350 B.C. Sanskrit grammarian + E *-an*] **1 :** of or being the grammatical system of the Sanskrit grammarian Panini **2** *of Sanskrit* **:** adhering rigidly to the rules

paning *pres 3d sing of* PANE

pa·ni·ni \pə'nēnē\ *n* -s [Hawaiian, fr. *pa* wall + *nini* fence] *Hawaii* **:** an arborescent prickly pear (*Opuntia megacantha*) introduced from California for its fruits

pa·ni·o·lo \,pänē'ō(,)lō\ *n* -s [Hawaiian, prob. fr. Sp *español* Spaniard, Spanish, fr. (assumed) VL *Hispaniolus,* fr. L *Hispania* Spain + *-olus* -ole] *Hawaii* **:** COWBOY

pan·i·o·ni·an \¦panē¦ōnēən\ *or* **pan·i·on·ic** \-¦änik\ *adj, usu cap* [L *panionium* + E *-an* or *-ic*] **:** of or relating to a Panionium

pan·i·o·ni·um \,≈≈'ōnēəm\ *n, pl* **panio·nia** \-ēə\ *usu cap* [NL, sing. of *panionia,* fr. Gk *paniōnia,* fr. *pan-* + *Iōnia* Ionia — more at IONIAN] **:** a gathering of all the Ionians held on Mycale at which Poseidon was worshiped and political matters were discussed

pan·isc *or* **pan·isk** \'panisk\ *n* -s [L *Paniscus,* fr. Gk *Paniskos,* dim. of *Pan,* Greek god of woods and shepherds] **:** a godling of the forest in Greek mythology that is half man and half goat and is commonly attendant on Pan

pan-islam \¦pan+\ *or* **pan-islamism** \"+\ *n* -s *usu cap P&I* [*pan-* + *islam* or *islamism*] **:** a political movement launched in Turkey at the end of the 19th century by Sultan Abdul-Hamid II for the purpose of combating the process of westernization and fostering the renascence and unification of Islam

pan-islamic \¦pan+\ *adj, usu cap P&I* [*pan-* + *Islamic*] **:** of, relating to, or favoring Pan-Islam ⟨ideal of *Pan-Islamic* union —Alford Carleton⟩

pan-islamist \"+\ *n, usu cap P&I* **:** an advocate of Pan-Islam

pan·i·yan \'panē,yan\ *n, pl* **paniyan** *or* **paniyans** *usu cap* **1 :** one of a number of pre-Dravidian peoples inhabiting the hills and jungles of central India **2 :** one of a Paniyan people

¹**pan·ja·bi** \,pən'jäbē, -bi\ *n* -s [Hindi *pañjābī* — more at PUNJABI] **1 :** PUNJABI 1 **2 a :** an Indic language of Panjab that with Hindi is one of the official languages of East Panjab **b :** LAHNDA

²panjabi \"\ adj, usu cap : PUNJABI
pan·jan·drum \pan'jandrəm\ n -s [fr. Grand Panjandrum, burlesque title of an imaginary personage in some nonsense lines by Samuel Foote †1777 Eng. actor and playwright] : a powerful personage or pretentious official
pank \'paŋk\ vi -ED/-ING/-S [perh. alter. of pant] dial Eng : to breathe hard : PANT
pan·leucopenia also **pan·leukopenia** \(ˌ)pan+\ n [NL, fr. pan- + leucopenia or leukopenia] : an acute usu. fatal viral epizootic disease of cats characterized by fever, diarrhea and dehydration, and extensive destruction of white blood cells — called also *cat distemper, feline distemper, cat typhoid*
pan·logical \(')pan¦läjəkəl\ adj : of or relating to panlogism
pan·lo·gism \'panlə,jizəm\ n -s [G panlogismus, fr. pan- + Gk logos word, reason + G -ismus -ism (fr. L) — more at LEGEND] : the doctrine that the absolute or the absolute reality is of the nature of logos or reason; esp : Hegelian philosophy
¹**pan·lo·gist** \-jəst\ or **pan·lo·gis·tic** \¦==¦jistik\ adj [panlogism + -ist or -istic] : of or relating to panlogism
²**panlogist** \"\ n -s [panlogism + -ist] : an advocate of panlogism
pan·man \'panmən, -,man\ n, pl **pan·men** \-mən, -,men\ [¹pan + man] **1** : one who tends pans **2** : a worker who loads cottonseed cakes into presses for extraction of oil **3** : an operator of a machine that whirls candy in a pan (as of syrup or wax coloring matter) to give it a finishing coat or polish — called also *glazer, grosser*
pan·mer·ism \'panmə,rizəm\ n -s [ISV panmeristic + -ism] : a theory in biology: protoplasm is made up of panmeristic units whose adaptive responses are the ultimate cause of growth and evolutionary change
pan·meristic \¦pan+\ adj [ISV pan- + meristic] : of or involving a hypothetical perfectly adaptable ultimate protoplasmic unit ⟨~ growth⟩
pan·mic·tic \(')pan¦miktik\ adj [pan- + Gk miktos mixed (verbal of mignynai to mix) + E -ic] : of, relating to, or exhibiting panmixia
pan·mix·ia \pan'miksēə\ also **pan·mixy** or **pan·mix·ie** \'pan,miksē\ or **pan·mix·is** \pan'miksəs\ n, pl **panmixias** \-ēəz\ also **panmixies** \-ēz\ or **panmix·es** \-k,sēz\ or **panmixises** [panmixia fr. NL, fr. pan- + Gk mixis act of mingling (fr. mignynai to mix) + NL -ia; panmixy fr. NL panmixia; panmixie ISV, fr. NL, panmixia; panmixis fr. NL, fr. pan- + -mixis — more at MIX] : random or nonselective mating within a breeding population resulting ultimately in a high degree of uniformity if the population is strictly closed — opposed to *apomixy*
pan·mne·sia \pan'nēzh(ē)ə\ n -s [NL, fr. pan- + -mnesia] : the continuance in memory of all mental impression
pan·myelopathy \(ˌ)pan+\ n [pan- + myelopathy] : an abnormal condition of all the blood-forming elements of the bone marrow
pan·myelophthisis \"+\ n [NL, fr. pan- + -myelophthisis] : wasting or degeneration of the blood-forming elements of the bone marrow
pan·nage \'panij\ or **pan·age** n -s [ME pannage, fr. AF pannage, pasnage, fr. OF paasnaige, fr. ML pasnagium, pannagium, alter. of pastionaticum payment for pannage, fr. L pastion-, pastio feeding, grazing (fr. pastus — past part. of pascere to pasture, feed, graze — + -ion-, -io -ion) + -aticum -age — more at FOOD] **1 a** : the act of pasturing swine in a wood or forest (as in medieval England) **b** : the legal right or privilege of such pasturing **c** : the charge or payment made for this privilege **2** : food (as acorns, beechnuts) for swine in a forest
panne \'pan\ n -s [F, fr. OF penne, panne fur used for lining, fr. L pinna feather, wing, alter. of penna — more at PEN] **1** : a finish for velvet or satin produced by heat and roller pressure **2** or **panne velvet** : a silk or rayon velvet with a lustrous pile flattened in one direction **3** or **panne satin** : a heavy silk or rayon satin with a high luster and a waxy smoothness
panned past of PAN
¹**pan·nel** \'panᵊl\ n -s [ME panel — more at PANEL] **1** : a pad or stuffed lining that serves to prevent galling by a saddle **2 a** : a usu. rude pad serving as a saddle **b** : a wooden saddle formerly used for a donkey
²**pannel** \"\ n -s [origin unknown] : the part of the alimentary canal of a hawk below the crop
pan·ner \'panə(r)\ n -s : one that pans or puts in a pan: as **a** : one who pans for gold **b** : a worker who places dough in pans for baking **c** : a worker who places sealed cans from a seamer or conveyor onto pans, racks, or trays — called also *racker*
pan·ne·tier's green \pan·'tyāz-\ n, usu cap P [prob. after Antoine C. Pannetier †1859 Fr. painter and chemist] : GUIGNET'S GREEN 1
pannhaas or **pannhaus** var of PANHAS
pan·nic·u·li·tis \pə,nikyə'līdəs\ n -ES [NL, fr. panniculus + -itis] : inflammation of the subcutaneous layer of abdominal fat
pan·nic·u·lus \pə'nikyələs\ n, pl **pannicu·li** \-yə,lī\ [NL, fr. L, small piece of cloth, dim. of pannus cloth — more at VANE] : a sheet or layer of tissue; esp : a layer of superficial fat-laden fascia
panniculus car·no·sus \-kär'nōsəs\ n [NL, fleshy panniculus] : a thin sheet of striated muscle lying within or just beneath the superficial fascia in many mammals and serving to produce local movement of the skin
¹**pan·nier** or **pan·ier** \'panyə(r), -nēə-\ n -s [ME panier, fr. MF panier, pannier, fr. L panarium, pannarium, fr. panis bread — more at FOOD] **1 a** : a large basket (as for provisions); esp : a wicker basket often used in pairs and carried over the back of a beast of burden or on the shoulders of a person **b** : a pack consisting of two bags or cases for carriage by a pack animal or person **2** : CORBEIL 1 **3 a** : a covered basket holding surgical instruments and medicines for a military ambulance **b** : a conical basket with a pole passing through its axis that can be filled with stones and used as an anchor in bridge and pontoon laying **c** : a shield of basketry set in the ground and formerly used by archers **4 a** : one of a pair of hoops (as of steel or whalebone) formerly used to expand women's skirts at the sides **b** : an overskirt draped or looped at the sides for a similar effect

pannier 1 a

²**pannier** \"\ n -s [prob. short for pannierman] : a table waiter (as formerly at the Inner Temple, London)
pan·niered \-(r)d\ adj [fr. past part. of obs. E pannier to furnish with panniers, fr. E ¹pannier] : bearing or wearing panniers ⟨weary donkeys ~ with heavy baskets—Claudia Cassidy⟩ ⟨wide ~ hoop and pointed bodice —*Fashion Digest*⟩
pan·nier·man \-(r)mən\ n, pl **panniermen** [ME panereman, fr. panere, panier pannier (basket) + man] : an officer (as formerly at the Inns of Court) having various duties connected with the provision and serving of meals
pan·ni·kin \'panəkən\ n -s [¹pan + -kin (after cannikin)] Brit : a small pan or cup often of tin : CANNIKIN ⟨got the ~s out and the tin plates —Mary S. Broome⟩
pannikin boss n, Austral : an overseer of a gang of laborers
panning pres part of PAN
¹**pan·no·ni·an** \pə'nōnēən\ adj, usu cap [L pannonius Pannonian (fr. Pannonia) + E -an] : of or relating to Pannonia, a Roman province in what is now western Hungary, northern Yugoslavia, and eastern Austria, bounded north and east by the Danube
²**pannonian** \"\ n -s cap [L Pannonia + E -an] : a native or inhabitant of ancient Pannonia
pan·non·ic \pə'nänik\ adj, usu cap [L pannonicus, fr. Pannonia, Roman province + -icus -ic] : PANNONIAN
pan·nose \'pa,nōs\ adj [L pannosus ragged, raglike, fr. pannus cloth, rag + -osus -ose — more at VANE] : having the texture or appearance of felt or woolen cloth — **pan·nose·ly** adv
pan·num \'panəm\ n -s [NL] : the dried anthelmintic rootstock of various ferns of the genus *Dryopteris*
pan·nus \'panəs\ n, pl **pan·ni** \-a,nī\ [NL, prob. fr. L, cloth] **1** : a vascular tissue causing a superficial opacity of the cornea and occurring esp. in trachoma **2** : a sheet of inflammatory granulation tissue that spreads from the synovial membrane and invades the joint in rheumatoid arthritis ultimately leading to fibrous ankylosis
pa·no \'pä(,)nō\ n, pl **pano** or **panos** usu cap [AmerSp, a member of the Panoan peoples] **1 a** : an Indian people of the upper Amazon basin **b** : a member of such people **2** : PANOAN
¹**pa·no·an** \'pänəwən\ n -s usu cap [AmerSp Pano + E -an] : a language family including languages spoken by the Panoan peoples
²**panoan** \"\ adj, usu cap : of, relating to, or constituting a group of peoples of western Brazil, Peru, and Bolivia or their language
¹**pa·no·cha** \pə'nōchə\ n -s [MexSp, dim. of Sp pan bread — more at PANELA] : a Mexican raw sugar
²**panocha** or **panoche** var of PENUCHE
pan·o·is·tic \¦panə¦wistik\ adj [pan- + o- (fr. Gk ōion egg) + -istic — more at EGG] : producing ova without nutritive cells — used of the ovaries of insects; compare POLYTROPHIC
pa·no·lia deer \pə'nōlēə-\ n, usu cap P [NL Panolia (genus name of Panolia acuticornis), perh. fr. Gk panōleia all-destructive, fr. panolēs, fr. pan- + ōlēs destroyed, fr. ollysthai to destroy] : THAMIN
pan·om·phe·an or **pan·om·phae·an** \¦pa,näm¦fēən\ also **pan·om·pha·ic** \-fāik\ or **pan·om·phic** \(')pa¦näm(p)fik\ adj [L Panomphaeus Zeus (fr. Gk Panomphaios, fr. panomphaios all-divining, lit., author or sender of divine oracles, fr. pan- + omphē voice, oracle) + E -an or -ic — more at SING] **1** : giving forth all divination **2** : UNIVERSAL
pan·o·pe·us \,panə'pēəs\ n, cap [NL, fr. L Panope, a sea nymph, fr. Gk Panopē] : a genus of crabs (family Xanthidae) comprising the typical mud crabs
pano·phobia \¦panə+\ n [NL, fr. pan- + phobia] : a condition of vague nonspecific anxiety : generalized fear
pan·ophthalmitis \(ˌ)pan+\ n [NL, fr. pan- + ophthalmitis] : inflammation involving all the tissues of the eyeball
pan·o·plied \'panəplēd\ adj : dressed in or having a panoply ⟨no system of law springs into existence full-*panoplied* —P.C. Jessup⟩
pan·o·ply \-lē, -li\ n -ES [Gk panoplia, fr. pan- + hopla armor, arms (pl. of hoplon tool, implement) + -ia -y — more at HOPLITE] **1 a** : a full suit of armor (as of a hoplite or knight) **b** : ceremonial attire ⟨in the ~ of ostrich-feather head-dress, cape, gleaming spear, shield, sword, club, painted face and leg ornaments —G.W.B.Huntingford⟩ : DRESS UNIFORM **2** : something resembling armor in being a protective covering ⟨faces dim in a ~ of smoke —William Baucke⟩ ⟨tradition has become not a sword . . . but a ~ behind which to hide from the world —Max Lerner⟩ **3 a** : a magnificent or impressive array ⟨woods . . . in their full ~ of autumn foliage —S.P.B. Mais⟩ ⟨serving in the endless ~ of jobs for which it is uniquely qualified —*Aero Digest*⟩ : splendid display : POMP ⟨the military ~ of an empire on parade —*Newsweek*⟩ ⟨performed in a grand manner full of ~ and ringing sound —Herbert Weinstock⟩ **b** : a display of all appropriate appurtenances ⟨a colossal land speculation that assumed the full ~ of sovereignty —S.E.Morison & H.S.Commager⟩ ⟨windows . . . behind which the usual ~ of modern mechanical conveniences can brazenly flourish —Lewis Mumford⟩ **4** : a group of pieces of armor forming a collection of trophies, an emblem, or an ornament ⟨sports shirts of a fine lightweight wool printed with . . . *panoplies* of arms and medieval figures —*New Yorker*⟩
pan·op·tic \(')pa¦näptik\ also **pan·op·ti·cal** \-təkəl\ adj [Gk panoptēs all-seeing (fr. pan- + optos visible, verbal of opsesthai to be going to see) + -ic or -ical — more at OPTIC] **1** : comprising all in one view : all-seeing ⟨a ~ study of Soviet nationality —T.G.Winner⟩ **2** : permitting everything to be seen ⟨kinescopic study of tissues treated with a ~ stain⟩
pan·op·ti·con \pa'näptə,kän\ n -s [pan- + Gk optikon, neut. of optikos optic — more at OPTIC] **1** : an optical instrument combining the telescope and microscope **2** : a prison so built radially that a guard at a central position can see all the prisoners
pan·o·ram \'panə,ram\ vb **panoramed** \-amd\ **panoramed** \"\ **panoraming** \-amiŋ\ **panorams** [by shortening fr. panorama] : ⁸PAN
pan·o·ra·ma \,panə'ramə, -rämə, -råmə sometimes '==,==\ n -s [pan- + Gk horama sight, view, fr. horan to see — more at WARY] **1 a** : CYCLORAMA 1 **b** : a picture exhibited a part at a time by being unrolled before the spectator **c** : a building designed to contain and exhibit a panorama **2 a** (1) : an unobstructed or complete and comprehensive view of a region in every direction (2) : a photograph that includes a wide view of a scene or group of people made by a panoramic camera or by joining separate photographs (3) : the process or result of panning in making a motion picture **b** : a complete and comprehensive view or presentation of a subject matter ⟨a ~ of American history⟩ **c** : RANGE ⟨the entire vast ~ of problems which come under the heading of foreign policy —H.H.Lehman⟩ **3** : a scene that passes continuously before one : a mental picture of a series of images or events
pan·o·ram·a·gram \-mə,gram\ n [panorama + -gram] : a method of stereoscopic viewing in which the left-eye and right-eye photographs are divided into narrow juxtaposed strips and viewed through a superimposed ruled or lenticular screen in such a way that each of the observer's eyes is able to see only the correct picture
pan·o·ram·ic \¦==¦ramik, -mēk\ adj [panorama + -ic] : of, relating to, or resembling a panorama ⟨~ novels⟩ ⟨a lookout tower on a summit . . affords a ~ view —*Amer. Guide Series: Pa.*⟩ — **pan·o·ram·i·cal·ly** \-mək(ə)lē, -mēk-, -li\ adv
panoramic camera n : a camera for taking panoramic pictures by revolving a lens so that the film is exposed through a narrow vertical slit or by rotating the camera so that adjacent areas of the film are exposed consecutively
panoramic perspective n : perspective in which objects are represented on a concave cylindrical surface (as in a panorama)
panoramic sight n : a telescopic device for laying an artillery piece for direction that permits the gunner to sight in any direction without moving his head and has an azimuth scale permitting any setting from 0 to 6400 mils
pan·o·ram·ist \¦==¦ramǝst\ n -s [panorama + -ist] : one who paints panoramas
pan·ornithic \¦pan+ ¦=¦==\ adj [pan- + ornithic] : affecting many birds of one kind at the same time — compare EPIDEMIC, EPIZOOTIC
pa·nor·pa \pə'nȯrpə\ n, cap [NL, fr. pan- + Gk horpē, harpē sickle — more at HARPES] : the type genus of the family Panorpidae
pan·or·pa·tae \,panȯ(r)'pā,tē\ [NL, fr. Panorpa + -atae, fem. pl. of L -atus -ate] syn of MECOPTERA
pa·nor·pi·dae \pə'nȯ(r)pə,dē\ n pl, cap [NL, fr. Panorpa, type genus + -idae] : a cosmopolitan family of slender-winged insects (order Mecoptera) that have cylindrical bodies with the male genitalia enlarged into a swollen bulb and that include the typical scorpion flies
pa·nor·pine \pə'nȯr,pīn, -,pən\ adj : of or relating to the Panorpidae : resembling a scorpion fly
pa·nor·poid \-r,pȯid\ adj [NL Panorpa + E -oid] : related to or resembling insects of the order Mecoptera
pan out vi [²pan] : to yield a result : turn out ⟨if things *pan out* as he expects⟩; esp : SUCCEED ⟨considered a genius if his experiments *panned out*⟩
pan·pipe \'pan,pīp\ n, pl **panpipes** but sing or pl in constr [Pan, the ancient Greek god of woods and shepherds who was regarded as its inventor + E pipe] : a primitive wind instrument that consists of a graduated series of short vertical flutes bound together with the mouthpieces in an even row and that is played in the manner of a harmonica — called also *mouth organ, syrinx*

panpipe

pan·pla·na·tion \,panplə'nāshən\ n [pan- + planation] : the process whereby panplanes are formed
pan·plane \'pan,plān\ n [pan- + plane] : a plain resulting from lateral erosion of neighboring streams so extensive that their floodplains coalesce
pan·pneu·ma·tism \pan'n(y)ümə,tizəm\ n [pan- + pneumatism] : a doctrine aiming to synthesize panlogism and panthelism by holding that the world or noumenal reality is both unconscious will and unconscious thought
pan·psychic \(')"+\ adj [panpsychism + -ic] : of or relating to panpsychism
pan·psychism \"+\ n [pan- + psychism] : a theory that all nature is psychical or has a psychic aspect and that every physical happening participates in the mental — compare LEIBNIZIANISM, ORGANIC MECHANISM, WHITEHEADIAN
pan·psychist \"+\ n : an advocate of panpsychism ⟨the metaphysical materialist cannot admit as a real possibility any disembodied spirit, the ~ any absolutely insentient matter —W.P.Alston⟩ — **pan·psy·chis·tic** \¦pan,sī¦kistik\ adj
pans pl of PAN, pres 3d sing of PAN
pan-satanism \'pan+\ n, usu cap P&S [G pansatanismus, fr. pan- + satanismus satanism] : an orig. Gnostic doctrine that the world is the expression of the personality of Satan
pansexual \(')pan+\ adj : of, relating to, or of the character of pansexualism
pan·sexualism \"+\ or **pan·sexuality** \(ˌ)pan+\ n [pansexualism prob. fr. G pansexualismus, fr. pan- + sexualismus sexualism; pansexuality fr. pan- + sexuality] **1** : the suffusion of all experience and conduct with erotic feeling **2** : the view that all desire and interest are derived from the sex instinct
pan·sexualist \(')pan+\ n : an adherent to the theory of pansexualism
pan·sexualize \"+\ vb [pansexualism + -ize] vt : to interpret according to pansexualism ~ vi : to view all phenomena as manifestations, symbols, or derivatives of the sex instinct
panshard \'panshä(r)d\ n [¹pan + shard] dial Eng : POTSHERD
pan shovel n [¹pan] : a scoop excavator
pan·sied \'panzēd\ adj [pansy + -ed] : covered or adorned with pansies
pan·si·fied \-zə,fīd\ adj [pansy + -ify + -ed] : EFFEMINATE, SISSIFIED
pan·sil \'pan(t)səl\ n -s usu cap [Singhalese, fr. Pali pañca sīlāni five precepts, fr. Skt pañca five + śīla custom, moral conduct, moral precept — more at FIVE] : the rite in Hinayana Buddhism of undertaking ceremonially a set of five precepts of morality ⟨~ . . . is taken individually before a Buddhist shrine or collectively at the beginning of a Buddhist meeting of any kind —Christmas Humphreys⟩
pan·sit \'pän(t)sət\ n -s [Tag pansit] : a Chinese noodle dish of the Philippines
pan-slav \'pan+\ adj, usu cap P&S [back-formation fr. pan-slavism] : of, relating to, or favoring Pan-Slavism ⟨the history of Russian Pan-Slav imperialism —Kurt Glaser⟩
pan-slavism \"+\ n, usu cap P&S [G panslavismus, fr. pan- + Slav + -ismus -ism] : a political and cultural movement orig. emphasizing the cultural ties between the Slavic peoples but later associated chiefly with Russian expansionist policies
pan·soph·ic \(')pan¦säfik\ or **pan·soph·i·cal** \-fəkəl\ adj **1** : of or relating to pansophy **2** : OMNISCIENT — **pan·soph·i·cal·ly** \-fək(ə)lē\ adv
pan·so·phism \'pan(t)sə,fizəm\ n [Gk pansophos + E -ism] : universal wisdom or knowledge or pretension thereto
pan·so·phist \-fəst\ n [Gk pansophos all-wise (fr. pan- + sophos wise) + E -ist] : one claiming or pretending to universal knowledge
pan·so·phy \-fē\ n -ES [NL pansophia, fr. pan- + Gk sophia wisdom] **1** : universal wisdom or encyclopedic knowledge; also : a system of universal knowledge **2** : PANSOPHISM
pan·sper·mia \pan'spərmēə\ also **pan·sper·ma·tism** \-mə,tizəm\ n -s [panspermia fr. NL, fr. Gk, mixture of elements, fr. pan- + sperm- + -ia -y; pan- spermatism fr. pan- + spermat- + -ism] : a theory propounded in the 19th century in opposition to the theory of spontaneous generation and holding that reproductive bodies of living organisms exist throughout the universe and develop wherever the environment is favorable
pan's pipes n pl, usu cap 1st P [after Pan, ancient Greek god of woods and shepherds] : PANPIPE
pan·sporoblast \(')pan+\ n [pan- + sporoblast] : a typical cnidosporidian sporont containing two sporoblasts
pan·strongylus \"+\ n, cap [NL, fr. pan- + Strongylus] : a genus of triatomid bugs that contains the conenoses some of which transmit Chagas' disease
pan supari n : ⁵PAN 2
pan·sy \'panzē, 'paan-, -zi\ n -ES [MF pensée, lit., thought, fr. fem. of pensé, past part. of penser to think, fr. L pensare to weigh, ponder — more at PENSIVE] **1** : a garden plant (*Viola tricolor hortensis*), derived chiefly from the wild pansy of Europe by hybridizing the latter with other wild violets and having irregular 5-petaled flowers and lobed or incised leaves with large stipules **2** : a strong violet that is bluer and deeper than clematis and stronger and slightly darker than royal purple (sense 2) — called also *pensée* **3 a** : an effeminate youth **b** : a male homosexual

pansy

pansy orchid n : an orchid of the genus *Miltonia*
pansy purple n : a dark purplish red that is redder, lighter, and stronger than raisin, redgrape, or dahlia purple (sense 1), bluer, lighter, and stronger than Bokhara, and deeper and slightly bluer than Indian purple
pansy violet n **1** : a bird's-foot violet having the two upper petals very dark purple with the lower petals normally lilac-purple **2** : WILD PANSY **3** : a dark reddish purple that is bluer, lighter, and stronger than royal purple (sense 1) and redder, lighter, and stronger than average plum (sense 6a) — called also *Roman violet*
¹**pant** \'pant, 'paa(ə)nt, 'paint\ vb -ED/-ING/-S [ME panten, fr. MF pantiser, pantaisier, fr. (assumed) VL phantasiare to have hallucinations, fr. Gk phantasioun, fr. phantasia appearance, image — more at FANCY] vi **1 a** : to breathe quickly, spasmodically, or in a labored manner (as from exertion, eagerness, or excitement) : respire with heaving of the chest **b** : to run panting ⟨~ed along beside the bicycle⟩ **c** : to move with or make a throbbing or puffing sound ⟨trains ~ing up the hill⟩ **2** : to long eagerly : desire earnestly : YEARN ⟨~ed for immortality, at least the immortality of being recorded —Clifton Fadiman⟩ **3** archaic : PALPITATE, THROB, PULSATE **4** of the sides of a ship : to bulge in and out alternately due to the changes of pressure caused by pitching ~ vt : to utter with panting : GASP ⟨ran up and ~ed out his story⟩
²**pant** \"\ n -s **1 a** : one of a series of short and quick or spasmodic breaths (as after exertion) : a catching of the breath : GASP **b** : the visible physical movement of the chest accompanying such a breath **c** obs : a beat or palpitation of the heart **2** : the throbbing or puffing sound that accompanies each valve cycle of a steam engine
³**pant** sing of PANTS
⁴**pant** adj : of, relating to, or designed for use with pants ⟨~ legs⟩
pant- or **panto-** also **panta-** comb form [MF panto-, fr. L, fr. Gk pant-, panto-, fr. pant-, pas all, every — more at PAN-] : PAN- ⟨pantobase⟩ ⟨pantagraph⟩ ⟨pantophobia⟩ ⟨pantotype⟩
pant abbr pantomime
pan·tag·a·my \pan·'tagəmē\ n -ES [pant- + -gamy] : marriage practiced in some communistic societies in which every man is regarded as the husband of every woman and vice versa
pantagraph var of PANTOGRAPH
pan·ta·gru·el·i·an \¦pantə,grü¦elēən\ also **pan·ta·gru·el·ic** \-lik\ adj, usu cap [pantagruelian fr. Pantagruel, coarsely humorous and gigantic son of Gargantua in the novel Pantagruel (1533) by François Rabelais †1553 Fr. satirist + E -ian; pantagruelic fr. F pantagruélique, fr. Pantagruel + F -ique -ic] : marked by coarse and extravagant satire — **panta·gru·el·i·cal·ly** \-lək(ə)lē\ adv, usu cap
pan·ta·gru·el·ism \,pantə'grüə,lizəm, pan·'tagrüə,l-\ n -s usu cap [F pantagruélisme, fr. Pantagruel + F -isme -ism] : buffoonery or coarse humor with a satirical or serious purpose : cynical humor
pan·ta·gru·el·ist \-ləst\ n -s usu cap [F pantagruéliste, fr. Pantagruel + F -iste -ist] : one who practices pantagruelism

pan·tal·e·on \pan'talē,än\ *also* **pan·ta·lon** \'pantə,län\ *n* -s [G *pantalon, pantaleon*, fr. *Pantaleon* Hebenstreit †1750 Ger. musician, its inventor] **:** a large dulcimer invented about 1700 having from 100 to 250 gut and metal strings struck with wooden mallets

pan·ta·lets *or* **pan·ta·lettes** \,pantᵊl'ets, ,paan-\ *n pl* [*pantalet* fr. *pantaloon* + *-ets* (pl. of *-et*); *pantalettes* fr. *pantaloon* + *-ettes* (pl. of *-ette*)] **1 :** long drawers having an attached or detachable ruffle at the bottom of each leg usu. showing below the skirt and worn by women and children in the first half of the 19th century **2 :** women's drawers **:** BLOOMERS

pantalets 1

pan·ta·loon \,pantᵊl'ün, ,paan-\ *n* -s [MF *Pantalon* stage character wearing pantaloons, fr. OIt *Pantalone, Pantaleone*, fr. San *Pantaleone* 4th cent. A.D. physician and patron saint of physicians formerly often identified with Venice and Venetians] **1 a** *or* **pan·ta·lo·ne** \,päntə'lōnā\ *usu cap* **:** an orig. Venetian character in the commedia dell' arte that is usu. a lean old dotard with spectacles, slippers, and a tight-fitting combination of trousers and stockings **b :** a buffoon in pantomimes; *specif* **:** a vicious old dotard used as the butt of the clown **c** *obs* **:** a feeble or imbecile old man **:** an old dotard **2 a :** BREECHES; *specif* **:** wide breeches worn in England during Charles II's reign — usu. used in pl. **b :** TROUSERS; *specif* **:** close-fitting trousers usu. having straps passing under the insteps and worn esp. in the 19th century — usu. used in pl.

pan·ta·loon·ery \-n(ə)rē\ *n* -ES **:** the character or performance of a pantaloon **:** BUFFOONERY

pan·tarch·ic \(')pan-¦tärkik\ *adj* [Gk *pantarchia* + E *-ic*] **:** of or relating to a pantarchy **:** COSMOPOLITAN

pan·tarchy \'pan,tärkē\ *n* -ES [Gk *pantarchia*, fr. *pant-* + *-archia* -archy] **:** government (as of the world) by all the people

pan·ta·stom·i·na \,pantə'stämənə\ [NL, fr. *panta-* + *stoma* + *-ina*] *syn of* RHIZOMASTIGINA

pan·tech·ni·con \pan'teknəkən, -nə,kän\ *n* [fr. *Pantechnicon*, 19th cent. bazaar in London orig. established for the sale of objects of art, fr. *pan-* + Gk *technikon*, neut. of *technikos* technical, artistic — more at TECHNICAL] **1** *Brit* **:** a large storage warehouse **2** *Brit* **:** ³VAN 1

pan·telegraph \(')pan+\ *n* [ISV *pan-* + *telegraph*; orig. formed as It *pantelegrafo*] **:** a facsimile telegraph using at both ends of the line two isochronously vibrating pendulums

¹**pan·ter** \'pantə(r)\ *or* **pan·ter·er** \-tərə(r)\ *n* -s [*panter* fr. ME *panter, paneter*, fr. OF *panetier*, irreg. fr. *pan, pain* bread (fr. L *panis*) + *-ier* -er; *panterer* fr. ME, fr. ¹*panter* + *-er* — more at FOOD] *archaic* **:** PANTLER

²**panter** *n* -s [ME, fr. MF *pantiere*, fr. L *panther*, fr. Gk *panthēros* supporting all animals, fr. *panthēra* fowler's catch, fr. *pan-* + *thēra* hunt (fr. *thēr* wild animal) — more at FIERCE] *obs* **:** a fowler's net or snare

³**pant·er** \'pantə(r)\ *n* -s [¹*pant* + *-er*] **:** one that pants; *specif* **:** a bovine animal exhibiting failure of the bodily heat-regulating mechanisms esp. as a sequel to foot-and-mouth disease

pan·te·the·ine \,pantə'thē,ēn, -thēən, pan'teth-\ *n* -s [*pantethe-* (by shortening & alter. fr. *pantothenic* — in *pantothenic acid*) + *-ine*] **:** a growth factor $C_{11}H_{22}N_2O_4S$ that is essential for various microorganisms (as *Lactobacillus bulgaricus*) and that is a constituent of coenzyme A; the amide of pantothenic acid and beta-amino-ethyl mercaptan

panth \'pän(t)th\ *n* -s [Skt *patha* way, path, course — more at FIND] *India* **:** a spiritual path or way **:** a religious faith **:** SECT

pan·thay \'pan(t)thā, -n,thā\ *n, pl* **panthay** *or* **panthays** *usu cap* **1 :** a Muslim people of Chinese and Turkic origin inhabiting the Burma-Chinese frontier region **2 :** a member of the Panthay people

pan·the·ism \'pan(t)thē,izəm, 'paan-\ *n* [F *panthéisme*, fr. E *pantheist* + F *-isme* -ism] **1 :** a doctrine that the universe conceived of as a whole is God **:** the doctrine that there is no God but the combined forces and laws that are manifested in the existing universe — compare ACOSMISM, THEISM **2 :** the worship of gods of different creeds, cults, or peoples indifferently; *also* **:** toleration of worship of all gods (as at certain periods in the Roman Empire)

pan·the·ist \-ēəst\ *n* [*pan-* + *theist*] **:** one who holds to pantheism

pan·the·is·tic \¦pan(t)thē¦istik, ¦paan-, -tēk\ *also* **pan·the·is·ti·cal** \-təkəl, -tēk-\ *adj* [*pantheist* + *-ic* or *-ical*] **:** of, relating to, or like pantheism **:** founded in or leading to pantheism — **pan·the·is·ti·cal·ly** \-tək(ə)lē, -tēk-, -li\ *adv*

pan·the·lism \'pan(t)thē,lizəm\ *n* -s [*pan-* + Gk *thelein* to will + *-ism*] **:** the doctrine that the ultimate reality of the universe is will; *specif* **:** the philosophy of Arthur Schopenhauer (1788–1860)

pan·the·on \'pan(t)thē,än, 'paan-, -ēən *sometimes* pan'thēən\ *n* -s [ME *Panteon*, temple at Rome built by the Roman statesman Agrippa †12 B.C. and rebuilt by the Roman emperor Hadrian †A.D.138, fr. L *Pantheon*, fr. Gk *pantheion* temple dedicated to all gods, fr. *pan-* + *theion*, neut. of *theios* of the gods, fr. *theos* god — more at THE-] **1 :** a temple dedicated to all the gods **2 :** a treatise on the pagan gods **3 :** a building serving as the burial place of or containing memorials to the famous dead of a nation **4 a :** the gods of a people; *esp* **:** the gods officially recognized as major or state deities **b :** the persons most highly esteemed by an individual or group ⟨the place which a contemporary writer will occupy in the ~ of letters —Anthony Powell⟩

pan·ther \'pan(t)thə(r), 'paan- *dial* -ntə-\ *n, pl* **panthers** *also* **panther** [ME *panter*, fr. OF *pantere*, fr. L *panthera*, fr. Gk *panthēr*, prob. of non-IE origin; prob. akin to the source of Skt *puṇḍarīka* tiger] **1 :** LEOPARD: as **a :** a leopard of a supposed exceptionally large fierce variety **b :** a leopard of the black color phase **2 :** COUGAR **3 :** JAGUAR

panther cat *n* **:** OCELOT

panther cowrie *n* **:** a spotted East Indian cowrie (*Cypraea pantherina*)

pan·ther·ess \-thərəs\ *n* -ES **:** a female panther

pan·ther·ine \-thə,rīn, -rən\ *adj* [L *pantherinus*, fr. *panthera* panther + *-inus* -ine] **1 :** of or characteristic of a panther **2 :** resembling a panther (as in coloring, markings, or movement) **:** PANTHERISH ⟨a ~ snake⟩ ⟨moved with ~ grace⟩

pan·ther·ish \-thərish\ *adj* **:** resembling or suggestive of a panther ⟨a dark ~ man⟩ ⟨with ~ quickness he leaped for his gun —Zane Grey⟩ — **pan·ther·ish·ly** *adv*

panther lily *n* **:** LEOPARD LILY 1

pant·ie *or* **panty** \'pantē, 'paan-, 'pain-, -ti\ *n, pl* **panties** [*pants* + *-ie* or *-y*] **:** a woman's or child's undergarment covering the lower trunk and made with closed crotch and very short legs — usu. used in pl.

pantie girdle *or* **panty girdle** *n* **:** a woman's girdle with a sewed-in or detachable crotch made with or without garters and boning

pantile \'=,=\ *n* [¹*pan* + *tile*] **1 a :** a roofing tile whose cross section is a dissymmetrical ogee curve **b :** a longitudinally curved roofing tile laid alternately with convex covering tiles **2 :** a Dutch or Flemish flat paving tile **3 :** SEA BISCUIT, HARDTACK — **pantiled** \'=,=\ *adj*

pantiling \'=,==\ *n* -s **:** pantile roofing

pan·tine \'pantən, -n,tīn\ *n* -s [obs. F *pantine* (now *pantin*)] **:** a jointed pasteboard doll representing a well-known living person and carried about for amusement (as by members of the French court) in the 18th century

pantiles 1 a

pant·ing \'pantiŋ\ *n* -s [³*pant* + *-ing*] **:** cloth used in making trousers **:** TROUSERING

pant·ing·ly *adv* **:** in a panting manner ⟨climbed slowly and ~⟩

pant·i·soc·ra·cy \,pantə'säkrəsē, -n,tī'-\ *n* -ES [*pant-* + *isocracy*] **:** a utopian community in which all rule equally

pant·i·so·cra·tic \¦pantəsō¦krad·ik, -n,tī¦-\ *or* **pant·i·soc·crat·i·cal** \-d·əkəl\ *adj* **:** of, relating to, or favoring pantisocracy

pant·i·soc·ra·tist \,pantə'säkrəd·əst, -n,tī'-\ *n* -s **:** an advocate of pantisocracy

pant·ler \'pantlə(r)\ *n* -s [ME *pantelere*, alter. (influenced by *buteler, bottelar* butler) of *panter, paneter* panter — more at PANTER] *archaic* **:** a servant or officer in charge of the bread and the pantry in a great family

pan·to \'pan(,)tō\ *n* -s [by shortening] *Brit* **:** PANTOMIME 3c

panto- — see PANT-

pan·to·chrome \'pantə,krōm\ *or* **pan·to·chro·mic** \¦==-¦krōmik\ *adj* [*pantochrome* back-formation fr. *pantochromism*; *pantochromic* fr. *pantochromism* + *-ic*] **:** relating to or exhibiting pantochromism

pan·to·chro·mism \'==,krō,mizəm\ *n* -s [*pant-* + *-chrome* + *-ism*] **:** the property possessed by some salts of occurring in any of several colors — compare CHROMOISOMERISM

pan·toc·ra·tor \pan'täkrəd·ə(r)\ *n* -s *cap* [ML, fr. Gk *pantokratōr*, fr. *pant-* + *kratōr* ruler, fr. *kratein* to rule (fr. *kratos* strength) — more at HARD] **:** the omnipotent lord of the universe **:** almighty ruler — used esp. of Christ ⟨the typical Byzantine icon presents Jesus as the *Pantocrator* . . . on his heavenly throne —F.B.Artz⟩

pan·to·don \'pantə,dän\ *n* [NL, fr. *pant-* + *-odon*] **1** *cap* **:** a genus (the type of the family Pantodontidae) of freshwater isospondylous fishes of West Africa consisting of the butterfly fish (*Pantodon buchholzi*) **2** *also* **pan·to·dont** \-änt\ -s **:** BUTTERFLY FISH 1e

pan·to·dont \'pantə,dänt\ *n* -s [NL *Pantodonta*] **:** a mammal or fossil of the order Pantodonta

pan·to·don·ta \,==ˈdäntə\ *n pl, cap* [NL, fr. *pant-* + *-odonta*] **:** a small but widely distributed order of primitive ungulate mammals known from the Paleocene to the Oligocene of No. America, Europe, and Asia

pan·tofle *also* **pan·tou·fle** *or* **pan·tof·fle** \'pantəfəl, pan-'täfəl, -'tüf-\ *n* -s [ME *pantufle*, fr. MF *pantoufle*] **1 :** a bedroom slipper **2 :** a chopine having front uppers only and a cork sole and used as an overshoe in the 16th century

¹**pan·to·graph** *also* **pan·ta·graph** \'pantə,graf, -raf\ *n* [F *pantographe*, fr. *pant-* + *-graphe*] **1 a :** an instrument for copying (as a map or plan) on any predetermined scale consisting of four light rigid bars adjustably jointed in parallelogram form so that as one tracing point is moved over the outline to be copied the other makes the desired copy **b :** a linkwork of similar construction or a lazy-tongs device used as a reducing motion for an indicator, a parallel motion for a beam engine, or in a similar function **2 :** an electrical trolley carried by a collapsible and adjustable frame

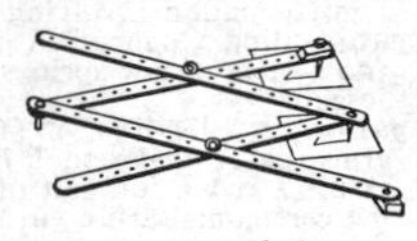

pantograph 1a

²**pantograph** \"\ *vt* **:** to copy with a pantograph ~ *vi* **:** to function by the use of a pantograph

pan·tog·ra·pher \pan'tägrəfə(r)\ *n* -s **:** one that pantographs; *specif* **:** a worker who engraves with a pantograph

pan·to·graph·ic \¦pantə¦grafik\ *adj* **:** of, relating to, or by means of a pantograph ⟨~ reductions⟩ — **pan·to·graph·i·cal·ly** \-fək(ə)lē\ *adv*

pan·to·ic acid \(')pan-¦tōik-\ *n* [*pant-* (fr. *pantothenic acid*) + *-oic*] **:** an unstable dihydroxy acid $HOCH_2C(CH_3)_2CH(OH)COOH$ that is usu. obtained in the form of salts or its crystalline gamma-lactone and that is a constituent of pantothenic acid and used in its synthesis

pan·tol·o·gy \pan'täləjē\ *n* -ES [NL *pantologia*, fr. *pant-* + *-logia* -logy] **:** a systematic view of all knowledge

pan·tom·e·ter \pan'tämǝd·ə(r)\ *n* [F *pantomètre*, fr. *panto-* + *-mètre* -meter] **:** an instrument for measuring all angles (as in determining elevations, distances)

¹**pan·to·mime** \'pantə,mīm, 'paan- *also* -,mēm; ÷ -,mīn\ *n* [L *pantomimus*, fr. Gk *pantomimos* actor, mimic, fr. *pant-* + *mimos* mime — more at MIME] **1** *or* **pan·to·mi·mus** \,=='mīməs\ *pl* **pantomi·mi** \-ī,mī\ **a :** a solo dancer of imperial Rome acting all the characters of a story (as of tragic love) usu. from myth or history by means of steps, postures, and gestures alone with the help of changes of mask and costume, a chorus singing the narrative usu. in Greek, an orchestra, and sometimes an assistant **b :** a performance featuring such a dancer — compare MIME 3 **2** *archaic* **:** PANTOMIMIST 1 **3 a :** an 18th century French or English ballet modeled on the Roman pantomime with subjects from classical mythology **b :** an 18th century English harlequinade orig. burlesquing the pantomime ballet, performed by dancing comedians, and serving as an interlude or afterpiece **c :** a British theatrical extravaganza of the Christmas season based on a story now usu. adapted from a traditional nursery tale, featuring topical songs, tableaux, dances, and similar entertainments in a blend of broad humor, fantasy, melodrama, sentimentality, and morality, and formerly incorporating a harlequinade introduced by a scene in which the persons of the tale are magically transformed into those of the harlequinade — called also *panto*; see DAME 5, PRINCIPAL BOY **4 :** a sequence of movements or actions not accompanied by speech or seen from beyond earshot ⟨her face enacting a vivid ~ of the criticisms passing in her mind —Thomas Hardy⟩ ⟨she strolled up to him . . . and I saw the ~ of the introduction —Mary Deasy⟩ **5 :** expressive bodily movement in drama or dance: **a :** expressive movements (as of the face, hands) of an actor; *esp* **:** silent acting **b :** movement in a ballet that develops a story and is more realistic and less conventionalized than dance movement **c :** expressive movements made by a ballet dancer except with the legs **6 a :** a dramatic performance using no dialogue **b :** a dance that enacts a story esp. by mimed action **:** a ballet mime **7 a :** the art of expressing the action of a story by simplified, exaggerated, and often conventionally symbolic gestures without words **b :** the genre of theatrical entertainment comprising pantomimes

²**pantomime** \"\ *vt* **:** to represent by pantomime ⟨the Butcher's Dance in which he would ~ the killing and carving of an animal —Phyllis Pearsall⟩ ⟨I *pantomimed* the fact that I'd come a long way —Sally Carrighar⟩ ~ *vi* **:** to engage in pantomime

pan·to·mim·ic \¦==¦mimik, -mēk\ *or* **pan·to·mime** \'==,mīm *also* -,mēm; ÷ -,mīn\ *adj* [*pantomimic* fr. L *pantomimicus*, fr. *pantomimus* pantomime + *-icus* -ic; *pantomime* fr. ¹*pantomime*] **1 :** having the characteristics of or constituting a pantomime ⟨a ~ entertainment⟩ ⟨a ~ dance⟩ **2 :** of or relating to a pantomime **3 :** resembling or suggestive of pantomime ⟨the ~ suddenness of the transformation⟩ **4** *dancing* **:** using realistic or symbolic gestures and body movements to suggest a narrative — **pan·to·mim·i·cal·ly** \-mək(ə)lē\ *adv*

pan·to·mimist \'==,mīməst, -,mim-\ *n* -s **1 :** an actor of pantomimes or in pantomime **2 :** a composer of pantomimes

pan·to·mo·rus \,pantə'mōrəs\ *n, cap* [NL, fr. Gk *pantomōros* gluttonous, lit., all-sluggish, fr. *pant-* + *mōros* dull, sluggish, stupid — more at MORON] **:** a genus of weevils containing several (as the white-fringed beetle) that are important plant pests esp. in the southern U. S.

pan·tonal \(')pan+\ *adj* [*pan-* + *tonal*] **:** giving equal importance to each of the 12 semitones of the octave **:** DODECAPHONIC — **pan·to·nal·i·ty** \,pantō'naləd·ē\ *n*

pan·to·nal·ism \pan'tōnᵊl,izəm\ *n* **:** the quality or state of being pantonal

pan·toph·a·gous \(')pan¦täfəgəs\ *adj* [*pant-* + *-phagous*] **:** eating or requiring a variety of foods — distinguished from *polyphagous*

pan·toph·thal·mi·dae \,pan,täf'thalmə,dē\ *n pl, cap* [NL, fr. *Pantophthalmus*, type genus (fr. *pant-* + *-ophthalmus*) + *-idae*] **:** a family of two-winged flies including large flies that are restricted to the American tropics and have larvae which bore in solid wood

pan·top·o·da \pan'täpədə\ [NL, fr. *pant-* + *-poda*] *syn of* PYCNOGONIDA

pan·to·then·ate \,pantə'the,nāt, pan'tänthə,-\ *n* -s [*pantothenic* acid + *-ate*] **:** a salt or ester of pantothenic acid

pan·to·then·ic acid \¦pantə¦thenik-\ *n* [*pantothenic* fr. Gk *pantothen* from every side (fr. *pant-*, *pas* all, every) + E *-ic* — more at PAN-] **:** a viscous oily acid $C_9H_{16}NO_5COOH$ that belongs to the vitamin B complex, occurs usu. combined (as in coenzyme A) in all living tissues esp. liver and elsewhere (as in royal jelly, yeast, and molasses), is made synthetically, and is essential for the growth of various animals and microorganisms; the amide of pantoic acid and beta-alanine

pan·to·there \'pantə,thi(ə)r\ *n* -s [NL *Pantotheria*] **:** a mammal or fossil of the order Pantotheria

pan·to·the·ria \,pantə'thirēə\ *n pl, cap* [NL, fr. *panto-* + *-theria*] **:** an order or other division of generalized mammals widespread during the Jurassic and commonly conceded to be ancestral to the marsupials and placental mammals — **pan·to·the·ri·an** \¦==¦thirēən\ *adj or n*

pantoufle *var of* PANTOFLE

pan·toum \pan-'tüm\ *n* -s [F, fr. Malay *pantun*] **:** a series of quatrains rhyming *abab* in which the second rhyme of a quatrain recurs as the first in the succeeding quatrain, each quatrain introduces a new second rhyme (as *bcbc, cdcd*), and the initial rhyme of the series recurs as the second rhyme of the closing quatrain (*xaxa*)

pan·to·yl \'pantəwəl\ *n* -s [*pant-* (in *pantoic acid*) + *-yl*] **:** the acid radical $HOCH_2C(CH_3)_2CH(OH)CO-$ of pantoic acid

¹**pan·tropic** \(')pan+\ *also* **pan·tropical** \"+\ *adj* [*pan-* + *tropic* or *tropical*] **:** occurring or distributed throughout the tropical regions of the earth ⟨~ plants and animals⟩

²**pantropic** \"\ *adj* [*pan-* + *-tropic*] **:** affecting various tissues without showing special affinity for one of them — used chiefly of viruses; compare DERMOTROPIC, NEUROTROPIC

pan·try \'pan·trē, 'paan-, -ri\ *n* -ES [ME *pantrie, panetrie*, fr. MF *paneterie*, fr. OF, fr. *panetier* pantler + *-erie* -ery — more at PANTER] **1 :** a room or closet adjacent to a kitchen or dining room used for storing provisions or glassware and china or for serving **2 :** a room (as in a hotel, ship, hospital) with refrigerating and other equipment for the preparation of cold foods (as salads, sandwiches, desserts) on order

pan·try·man \'==mən\ *n, pl* **pantrymen :** a man in charge of or working in a pantry (as in a hotel, ship, hospital)

pants \'pants, 'paan-, 'pain-\ *n pl but sometimes sing in constr, often attrib* [short for *pantaloons*, pl. of *pantaloon*] **1** *also* **pant a** (1) **:** PANTALOON 2 (2) **:** TROUSERS, SLACKS **b** *chiefly Brit* **:** men's short underpants **c :** PANTIE **2 pant** *n sing* **:** half or one leg of a pair of pants **3 :** enclosures of streamline shape used to reduce the drag of airplane landing gear — **with one's pants down :** in an embarrassing position (as of being unprepared for an emergency) ⟨caught *with its pants down* by the surprise attack⟩

pan·tun *also* **pan·toun** \pan-'tün\ *n* -s [Malay *pantun*] **:** Indonesian verse consisting of four lines rhyming *abab* of which the first two present a figurative suggestion of what is more directly and clearly stated in the final lines

pan–turanian \¦pan+\ *adj, usu cap P&T* [*pan-* + *turanian*] **:** of, relating to, or being Pan-Turanianism ⟨opposition to Islam in the *Pan-Turanian* movement —*Mohammedan History*⟩

pan–turanianism \"+\ *also* **pan–turanism** \'pan+\ *n, usu cap P&T* [*pan-turanianism* fr. *pan-* + *turanian* + *-ism*; *pan-turanism* fr. *pan-* + *Turan*, ancient desert and steppe region of Central Asia north of Iran corresponding to the regions around the Jaxartes and Oxus in modern Uzbek and Kazakh Republics of the U. S. S. R. + E *-ism*] **:** a political and cultural movement of the early 20th century having as its principal aim the union of all peoples having a common Turkish heritage

panty *var of* PANTIE

¹**pantywaist** \'==,=\ *n* [*panty* + *waist*] **1 :** a child's garment consisting of short pants buttoned to a waist **2 :** SISSY

²**pantywaist** \"\ *adj* **:** CHILDISH, INFANTILE **:** SISSIFIED ⟨the round robin of abuse which enlivened belles lettres before they went ~ in the twentieth century —Richard Hanser⟩

pa·ñue·lo \,pänyə'wā(,)lō\ *n* -s [Sp, dim. of *paño* cloth, fr. L *pannus* — more at VANE] **:** a square cloth folded triangularly and worn in the Philippines like a great ruffle or collar

panulirus *n, cap* [NL, anagram of *Palinurus*] **:** a genus of spiny lobsters comprising the American forms of the group — compare PALINURUS

pa·nung \'pä,nùŋ\ *n* -s [Thai *phā* cloth + *nùŋ* one] **:** a Siamese garment for men and women consisting of a cloth about three yards long draped about the body somewhat in the manner of a loincloth

pan·yan \'pa,nyan\ *n, pl* **panyan** *or* **panyans** *usu cap* **:** a member of a Veddoid people in southern India

¹**pan·zer** \'panzə(r), 'paan, 'päntsə(r)\ *adj* [G, lit., coat of mail, armor, fr. MHG *panzier*, fr. OF *panciere*, fr. L *pantic-*, *pantex* paunch — more at PAUNCH] **:** of, consisting of, or carried out by a panzer division or similar German armored unit **:** ARMORED ⟨~ forces⟩ ⟨the importance of ~ thrusts⟩

²**panzer** \"\ *n* -s **:** a vehicle belonging to a panzer division; *esp* **:** TANK — usu. used in pl.

panzer division *n* [G *panzerdivision*, fr. ¹*panzer* + *division*, fr. F, fr. MF — more at DIVISION] **:** a mechanized unit of the German army (as in World War II) organized for rapid attack

¹**pan·zo·ot·ic** \¦panzō¦äd·ik\ *adj* [*pan-* + *zo-* + *-otic*] **:** affecting animals of many different species; *also* **:** epizootic over wide areas — compare PANDEMIC

²**panzootic** \"\ *n* -s **:** a panzootic disease

pao·lo \'paù(,)lō\ *n, pl* **pao·li** \-(,)lē\ [It, after Pope *Paolo* (Paul) III †1549] **:** a small papal silver coin worth ¹⁄₁₀ scudo struck under Paul III

paon \'päⁿ\ *n* -s [F, fr. L *pavon-*, *pavo* peacock — more at PEACOCK] **:** PEACOCK 3

pao·pao \'paù,paù\ *n* -s [Samoan] **:** a small Samoan outrigger canoe

pao·ting \'baù'diŋ\ *adj, usu cap* [fr. *Paoting* (*Tsingyuan*), China] **:** of or from the city of Paoting, China **:** of the kind or style prevalent in Paoting

¹**pap** \'pap\ *n* -s [ME *pappe*; of imit. origin like Sw dial. & Norw dial. *pappe* pap, L *papilla* nipple, Lith *papas*, Skt *pippalakā*] **1** *chiefly dial* **:** NIPPLE, TEAT **2 :** something shaped like a nipple (as one of two or more hills) ⟨the *Paps* of Jura, Scotland⟩

²**pap** \"\ *n* -s [ME *pap, pape*, prob. fr. L (baby talk) *papa, pappa* food, father] **1 a :** a soft pulpy food (as of bread boiled or softened in milk or water) for infants or invalids **b :** any pulpy or semiliquid substance **:** MASH, PASTE **2 :** political patronage ⟨more concerned about giving honest, efficient, and enlightened government than they are about political ~ and boodle —D.E.Chamberlain⟩ **3 a :** simple discourse or esp. moralistic expression suitable for or felt to be suitable only for the minds of infants **b :** something (as reading matter) that serves only to entertain or is not otherwise intellectually stimulating ⟨persuade people to buy our papers with ~, else we cannot pay for the profound —J.S.C.Butz⟩ ⟨mystery novels and general escapist entertainment ~ —John Roeburt⟩

³**pap** \"\ *vt* **papped; papped; papping; paps :** to feed with pap

⁴**pap** \"\ *Scot & Irish var of* POP

⁵**pap** \"\ *n* -s [by shortening] *dial* **:** PAPA

pap *abbr* **1** paper **2** papyrus

¹**pa·pa** \'päpə, *in sense 2* " *or* pə'pä\ *n* -s [LL (influenced in meaning by LGk *papas, pappas* priest, bishop, pope), fr. Gk (baby talk) *pappa* father, vocative of *papas, pappas*] **1** *usu cap, archaic* **:** the Roman pontiff, bishop of Rome and pope of the Roman Catholic Church **2** [LGk *papas, pappas* (taken as pl.) fr. Gk (baby talk), father] **:** a parish priest of the Eastern Orthodox Church

²**papa** \'päpə, 'pápə, *chiefly Brit* pə'pä\ *n* -s [F, fr. MF; of baby-talk origin like L *papa, pappa* food, father, Gk *papas, pappas* father, *pappos* grandfather] **1 :** FATHER ⟨a promise from ~ to supply more money —A.H.Raskin⟩ **2** *slang* **:** HUSBAND, LOVER

³**papa** *var of* PAPAW

⁴**pa·pa** \'päpə\ *n* -s [AmerSp, fr. Quechua] **:** POTATO

⁵**papa** \"\ *n* -s [Hawaiian, Tahitian, Marquesan, & Maori] **:** a bluish New Zealand clay like indurated pipe clay used for whitening fireplaces

⁶**papa** \"\ *n* -s [Skt *pāpa*; prob. akin to Skt *pāpman* harm, evil — more at PATIENT] *Jainism* **:** EVIL, SIN — compare PUNYA

⁷**papa** *usu cap* — a communications code word for the letter *p*

pa·pa·bi·le \pə'päbə,lā\ *adj* [It, fr. *papa* pope (fr. LL) + *-abile* -able] **:** PAPABLE

pa·pa·ble \'päpəbəl\ *adj* [MF, prob. fr. It *papabile*] **:** qualified for and considered likely to succeed to the papacy

pa·pa·botte *or* **pa·pa·bote** *also* **pa·pa·bot** \,päpə'bōt\ *n* -s [AmerF (Louisiana); prob. of imit. origin] *South* **:** UPLAND PLOVER

pa·pa·cy \'pāpəsē, -si\ *n* -ES [ME *papacie*, fr. ML *papatia*, fr. LL *papa* pope + *-atia* (as in LL *abbatia* abbacy) — more at ABBACY] **1 :** the office of pope **:** papal jurisdiction ⟨under control of the ~⟩ ⟨raised to the ~⟩ **2 :** a succession of popes **:** a papal line ⟨the Avignon ~⟩ ⟨the Roman ~⟩ **3 :** the period of time during which a pope is in office **4** *usu cap* **:** the system of government in the Roman Catholic Church of which the pope is the supreme head

pa·pa·ga·llo \\ˌpäpə'gī(ˌ)ō\\ *n* -s [alter. (prob. influenced by Sp *gallo* cock, fr. L *gallus*) of Sp *papagayo*, lit., parrot; fr. the colored spines of the first dorsal fin that suggest a bird's comb — more at GALLUS] **:** a large brightly colored food fish (*Nematistius pectoralis*) related to the amberfishes and found from southern California to Peru — called also *roosterfish*

pa·pa·ga·yo \\ˌpäpə'gī(ˌ)ō\\ *n* -s *often cap* [fr. Gulf of *Papagayo*, northwestern Costa Rica] **:** a violent often tornadic northerly wind occurring along the Pacific coast of Central America and esp. on the Gulf of Papagayo

papa·go \\'papəˌgō, 'päp-\\ *n, pl* **papago** *or* **papagos** *usu cap* **1 a :** a Piman people of southwestern Arizona and northwestern Sonora, Mexico **b :** a member of such people **2 :** the language of the Papago people

papaia *var of* PAPAYA

pa·pa·in \\pə'pāən, -'pīən\\ *n* -s [ISV *papa-* (fr. *papaya*) + *-in*; orig. formed in G] **:** a crystallizable proteinase in the juice of the green fruit of the papaya obtained usu. as a brownish powder and used chiefly as a tenderizer for meat, in chillproofing beer, and in medicine as a digestant

pa·pa·in·ase \\-əˌnās, -āz\\ *n* -s [*papain* + *-ase*] **:** any of several proteinases (as papain, ficin, bromelin) that are found in plants, are activated by reducing agents (as cysteine, glutathione), and are inactivated by oxidizing agents (as hydrogen peroxide, iodine) toward which other proteinases are stable

pa·pai·pe·ma \\pəˌpī'pēmə\\ *n, cap* [NL, prob. fr. Gk *papai*, exclamation of suffering + *pēma* suffering, calamity — more at PATIENT] **:** a genus of noctuid moths containing several that are pests on corn and other plants in parts of No. America

pa·pal \\'pāpəl\\ *adj* [ME, fr. MF, fr. ML *papalis*, fr. LL *papa* pope + L *-alis* -al] **1 :** of or relating to a pope **:** proceeding from, ordered or uttered by, or subject to a pope ⟨~ edict⟩ **2 :** of, supporting, adhering to, or relating to the Roman Catholic Church — **pa·pal·ly** \\-pəlē, -li\\ *adv*

papal cross *n* **:** a figure of a cross having a long upright shaft and three crossbars with the longest at or somewhat above its middle and the two other successively shorter crossbars above the longest one

papal cross

pa·pa·le \\pə'pä(ˌ)lā\\ *n* -s [Hawaiian] *Hawaii* **:** HAT

papal infallibility *n, Roman Catholicism* **:** the dogma decreed at the Vatican Council, July 18, 1870, that the pope cannot when speaking in his official character of supreme pontiff err in defining a doctrine of Christian faith or rule of morals

pa·pal·ism \\'pāpəˌlizəm\\ *n* -s **1 :** the papal system **2 :** advocacy of papal supremacy

¹pa·pal·ist \\-ləst\\ *n* -s [F *papaliste*, fr. *papal* + *-iste* -ist] **:** an adherent of papalism

²papalist \\"\\ *or* **pa·pal·is·tic** \\ˌ⸗⸗'listik, -tēk\\ *adj* [*papalism* + *-ist* or *-istic*] **:** of or relating to papalism

pa·pal·i·ty \\pə'paləd·ē, pā'-\\ *n* -ES [ME *papalite*, fr. MF or ML; MF *papalité*, fr. ML *papalitas*, fr. LL *papa* pope + L *-itas* -ity — more at POPE] *archaic* **:** PAPACY

pa·pal·ize \\'pāpəˌlīz\\ *vt* -ED/-ING/-S [*papal* + *-ize*] **:** to make papal **:** imbue with papalism ⟨*papalized* sections of the medieval church⟩

papal knight *n* **:** one bearing a title of nobility conferred by the pope in his capacity as temporal sovereign

pa·pa·loi \\ˌpäpəl'wä\\ *n* -s [Haitian Creole *papalwa*, fr. *papa* father + *lwa* loa] **:** a male voodoo priest esp. in Haiti — compare MAMALOI

pa·pa·ni·co·laou test \\ˌpäpə'nēkəˌlaü, ˌpapə'nikəˌlaü-\\ *n, usu cap P* [after George N. *Papanicolaou* b1883 Greco-American medical scientist] **:** a method for the early detection of cancer consisting of the application of a special staining technique to cells exfoliated from diseased tissue

pa·par·chi·cal \\(')pāˌpärkəkəl\\ *adj* **:** of or relating to a paparchy

pa·par·chy \\'pāˌpärkē\\ *n* -ES [LL *papa* pope + E *-archy*] **:** government by a pope

papas *pl of* PAPA

papataci fever *or* **papatasi fever** *var of* PAPPATACI FEVER

pa·paver \\pə'pavə(r), -'päv-\\ *n, cap* [NL, fr. L, poppy — more at POPPY] **:** a genus (the type of the family Papaveraceae) of chiefly bristly hairy herbs or occas. subshrubs with lobed or dissected leaves, long-peduncled often nodding usu. large and showy flowers, and a capsular fruit topped by a radiate disk and dehiscent by pores immediately below — see OPIUM POPPY

pa·pav·er·a·ce·ae \\pəˌpavə'rāsēˌē\\ *n pl, cap* [NL, fr. *Papaver*, type genus + *-aceae*] **:** a family of herbs or shrubs (order Rhoeadales) having milky and often colored juice, regular flowers with caducous sepals and hypogynous stamens, and capsular fruit — compare CHELIDONIUM — **pa·pav·er·a·ceous** \\⸗ˌ⸗⸗'rāshəs\\ *adj*

pa·pav·er·a·les \\⸗ˌ⸗⸗'rā(ˌ)lēz\\ [NL, fr. *Papaver* + *-ales*] *syn of* RHOEADALES

pa·pav·er·ine \\⸗'⸗⸗ˌrēn, -ˌrən\\ *n* -s [ISV *papaver-* (fr. NL *Papaver*) + *-ine*] **:** a crystalline alkaloid $C_{20}H_{21}NO_4$ derived from benzyl-isoquinoline that constitutes about one percent of opium, that is made synthetically from vanillin, and that usu. in the form of its hydrochloride is used chiefly as an antispasmodic because of its ability to relax smooth muscle (as in spasm of blood vessels due to blood clot)

pa·paw *or* **paw·paw** *n* -s [prob. modif. of Sp *papayo* papaya] **1** \\pə'pó, pó'pó\\ **:** PAPAYA **2** \\'pä(ˌ)pó, 'pó(ˌ)pó\\ *also* **pa·pa** \\"\\ **a :** any of several American shrubs or trees of the genus *Asimina*; *specif* **:** a No. American tree (*Asimina triloba*) with large obovate leaves, lurid purple flowers, and a large edible fruit **b :** the oblong yellowish sweet fruit of the No. American papaw

papaw family *n* **:** CARICACEAE

pa·paya *or* **pa·paia** \\pə'pī(y)ə, -'päyə\\ *n* -s [Sp, of AmerInd origin; akin to Otomac *papai*, Carib *ababai*] **1 :** a tree (*Carica papaya*) native to tropical America and having long-petioled palmately 7-lobed leaves, clusters of dioecious yellow flowers, and large oblong yellow fruit that has a pulpy flesh and thick rind and is eaten raw, boiled as a vegetable, pickled, or preserved **2 :** the fruit of the papaya tree — see CARPAINE

pap·a·ya·ce·ae \\ˌpapə'yāsēˌē, ˌpaˌpī'āsēˌē\\ [NL, fr. *papaya* (specific epithet of *Carica papaya*) + *-aceae*] *syn of* CARICACEAE

pa·pay·o·tin \\pə'pīəd·ən\\ *n* -s [*papaya* + *-otin* (as in *picrotin*)] **:** PAPAIN

papboat \\'⸗ˌ⸗\\ *n* [²*pap* + *boat*] **1 :** a boat-shaped dish to hold pap for feeding infants or invalids **2 :** a large spiral East Indian marine shell (*Turbinella rapa*)

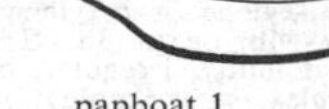

papboat 1

¹pape \\'pāp\\ *Scot var of* POPE

²pape \\'pap\\ *n* -s [AmerF (Louisiana), fr. F, pope, fr. LL *papa* — more at POPE] **:** PAINTED BUNTING

pa·pe·lon \\ˌpäpə'lōn\\ *n* -s [AmerSp *papelón*, fr. Sp, cardboard, aug. of *papel* paper, fr. Catal *paper*, fr. L *papyrus*; fr. its being hardened in cardboard molds — more at PAPER] **:** crude brown sugar produced esp. in northern So. America

pap·e·lon·né \\ˌpapələ'nā\\ *adj* [F, fr. OF *papeillonné*, fr. *papeillon* butterfly, fr. L *papilion-*, *papilio* — more at PAVILION] *heraldry* **:** covered with rows of loops so placed as to suggest the appearance of overlapping scales

¹pa·per \\'pāpə(r)\\ *n* -s [ME *papir*, fr. MF *papier*, fr. L *papyrus* paper, papyrus, fr. Gk *papyros* papyrus] **1 a** (1) **:** a felted sheet of usu. vegetable but sometimes mineral or synthetic fibers laid down on a fine screen from a water suspension (2) **:** paper in sheets 6/1000 inch or thinner — compare BOARD **b :** a sheet or piece of paper **c :** a paper surface ⟨the mind can never resemble a blank ~ —J.H.Newman⟩ ⟨put pen to ~⟩ **d :** something resembling true paper in form and use or in composition: as (1) **:** PAPYRUS (2) **:** PAPIER-MÂCHÉ **2 a :** a piece of paper containing a written or printed statement (as of identity, authority, or ownership) **:** DOCUMENT, INSTRUMENT — usu. used in pl. whether applying to one or to more than one item ⟨naturalization ~*s*⟩ ⟨officer's ~*s*⟩ ⟨pedigree ~*s*⟩ ⟨were both forced to flee the country, separately and without ~*s* —*Current Biog.*⟩ ⟨this policy, including the endorsements and the attached ~*s* —*Mutual of Omaha*⟩ — compare SHIP'S PAPERS, WORKING PAPERS; FIRST PAPERS, SECOND PAPERS **b :** any piece of paper containing writing or print (as a letter or memorandum) — usu. used in pl. ⟨family ~*s*⟩ ⟨the state ~*s* of a president⟩ **c :** a literary composition esp. of brief, occasional, or fragmentary nature — usu. used in pl. ⟨his collected ~*s* — not all previously printed — are too short to be called essays —*Times Lit. Supp.*⟩ **3 a :** a piece of paper shaped to serve as a receptacle or wrapper (as for tacks) ⟨a ~ of peppermints in her pocket —Flora Thompson⟩ **b :** a card or paper folder to which articles (as needles) are attached ⟨the page he had marked with a ~ of matches —Frederick Buechner⟩ ⟨a ~ of pins⟩ **4 a :** NEWSPAPER ⟨daily ~⟩ ⟨his picture would be in the ~*s* —Mary Austin⟩ ⟨~ carrier⟩ ⟨~ route⟩ ⟨~ stand⟩ **b :** PUBLICATION; *esp* **:** one resembling a newspaper in format, content, or frequency of publication ⟨church ~⟩ ⟨school ~⟩ ⟨trade ~⟩ **5 a :** negotiable notes ⟨assets of the bank were shot through with bad ~ —W.A. White⟩ ⟨real-estate portfolios were choked with foreclosed ~ —*Fortune*⟩ ⟨long-term ~⟩ ⟨short-term ~⟩ — compare COMMERCIAL PAPER **b :** PAPER MONEY ⟨with a pocketful of ~ to grab rich mineral and timber lands —*Amer. Guide Series: Minn.*⟩ **6 :** WALLPAPER ⟨pictorial ~*s* printed from wood blocks were imported —H.S.Morrison⟩ **7 :** a piece of written schoolwork: **a :** a written examination — used of either the examiner's questions or the student's answers ⟨candidates may take . . . either (1) a ~ in Latin; or (2) a ~ in Greek —*Edinburgh Univ. Cal.*⟩ **b :** a written assignment done either as an exercise in composition or as a report on an assigned topic ⟨freshman English is a hard course to take because of the many ~*s* coming in weekly⟩ ⟨our history ~ is due next week⟩ ⟨term ~⟩ — compare ESSAY, THESIS **8 a :** a composition of informational nature (as on a scientific or historical topic) for reading before a group ⟨do a ~ for our reading circle —Agnes S. Turnbull⟩; *also* **:** its presentation ⟨all of these ~*s* were extremely well attended and received —*Veterinary Record*⟩ **b :** a similar composition written for publication (as in a journal or in the form of a monograph) or circulation **9 a :** TICKETS ⟨the ~ at the box office is all sold —Barnaby Conrad⟩; *esp* **:** free passes **b :** persons admitted free (as to a theater performance) ⟨most of the first-night audience was ~⟩ ⟨saw at once that the house was filled with ~ —James Joyce⟩ **10 :** CURLPAPER — usu. used in pl. **11** *slang* **:** marked playing cards **12** *slang* **:** bills, posters, or circulars distributed to advertise something (as an appearance of a traveling show) ⟨the circus fell a couple of days behind its ~⟩ **13 :** PAPER WORK ⟨by ~ and red tape —Roy Lewis & Angus Maude⟩ **—off paper** *of a postage stamp* **:** removed from the cover on which it was used **— on paper 1 :** in writing or print ⟨the act of putting ideas *on paper* seems to distort our perspectives —E.S.McCartney⟩ ⟨get the agreement down *on paper*⟩ **2 :** in theory as distinguished from fact, practice, accomplishment, or probable outcome ⟨the plan looks good *on paper*⟩ **3 :** in the planning stage ⟨a project that is still *on paper*⟩ ⟨university, which had existed *on paper* for five years —*Amer. Guide Series: Wash.*⟩ **4 :** figured at face value **:** NOMINALLY ⟨*on paper* he was worth nearly $1,000,000 —Gladwin Hill⟩ **5** *of a postage stamp* **:** remaining on the cover or on a piece of the cover on which it was used

²paper \\"\\ *vt* **papered; papered; papering** \\-p(ə)riŋ\\ **papers 1** *archaic* **:** to put down on paper **:** make a memorandum of **:** describe in writing **2 :** to fold or inclose in or attach to paper ⟨~ butterflies⟩ ⟨~ pins up⟩ **3 :** to affix paper to **:** cover or line with paper; *esp* **:** to furnish with wallpaper ⟨~ a room⟩ **4 :** SANDPAPER ⟨~ down until only sufficient color is left to lighten the wood —C.H.Hayward⟩ **5 :** to supply with an audience augmented by giving out many free tickets ⟨~ a theater for an opening night⟩ **6 :** to cover (an area) with advertising bills, posters, or circulars (as for a circus engagement or a boxing match) **7** *slang* **:** to cover with worthless checks or counterfeit currency ⟨left after ~*ing* the country with bad checks —H.L.Davis⟩ ⟨can get ~*ed* like a circus billboard if you don't know the man you are doing black-market business with —David Dodge⟩ **8 :** to gloss over, explain away, or patch up (major differences) so as to provide a semblance of amity or agreement — used esp. in the phrase *paper over the cracks* ⟨the meeting . . . has done little to ~ over the cracks between the member states —*Economist*⟩ ~ *vi* **:** to hang wallpaper ⟨passion for perpetual painting and ~*ing* —Mary H. Vorse⟩

³paper \\"\\ *adj* **1 a :** made wholly or almost wholly of paper, paperboard, or papier-mâché ⟨~ bag⟩ ⟨~ towel⟩ ⟨~ napkin⟩ ⟨~ mulch⟩ ⟨~ carton⟩ ⟨~ plate⟩ **b :** like paper (as in texture, strength, or thickness) **:** PAPERY **2 a :** carried on by the exchange of written or printed matter **:** consisting of written communications or printed matter ⟨~ friendships⟩ ⟨~ wars⟩ ⟨~ bullets⟩ **b :** involving or involved with paper work **:** CLERICAL, DESK ⟨those ~ procedures by which so much of the business of the Services is transacted —H.W.Dodds⟩ ⟨the fighting navy and the ~ navy —Frederic Wakeman⟩ ⟨the general was transferred to a ~ command⟩ **3 a :** authorized or decreed but not effectively enforced **:** planned but not put into execution **:** proffered but not fulfilled **:** NOMINAL ⟨~ blockade⟩ ⟨~ promises⟩ ⟨the ~ strength of an army⟩ ⟨a project still in the ~ stage⟩ **b** (1) **:** computed or computable as the result of hypothetical business transactions ⟨~ losses from selling the stocks too soon⟩ (2) **:** figured on paper without involving actual money or credit transfers ⟨~ surplus⟩ (3) **:** prospective but unrealized ⟨basing hopes for expansion on ~ profits⟩ **4 :** composed largely of persons admitted by free passes ⟨~ audience⟩ ⟨~ house⟩ **5 :** issued as paper currency ⟨~ mark⟩ ⟨~ peso⟩ **6 :** PAPERBACK ⟨a ~ edition⟩ ⟨~ books⟩ **7** *of thin fabrics* **:** finished with a crisp smooth surface similar to that of paper ⟨~ taffeta⟩

¹paperback \\'⸗⸗ˌ⸗\\ *n* **:** a paperback book — called also *paperbook, paperbound, paper-cover, soft-cover*

²paperback \\ˌ⸗⸗'⸗\\ *also* **paperbacked** \\ˌ⸗⸗'⸗\\ *adj* **1** *of a book* **:** made without rounding, backing, or rigid boards and usu. trimmed flush **:** PAPERBOUND, PAPER-COVER, SOFT-COVER ⟨~ mysteries⟩ ⟨~ reprints⟩ **2 :** of or relating to paperback books ⟨~ storytelling⟩

paper-bag bush *n* [fr. the phrase *paper bag*] **:** a shrub (*Salazaria mexicana*) of the family Labiatae that occurs in the midwestern and southwestern U.S. and has numerous large inflated papery pods

paper bail *n* **:** ⁸BAIL 1f

paperbark \\'⸗⸗ˌ⸗\\ *also* **paperbark tree** *n* [so called fr. the papery bark that peels off in sheets] **:** any of several Australian trees of the genera *Callistemon* and *Melaleuca*; *esp* **:** CAJEPUT

paperbark maple *n* **:** a tree (*Acer griseum*) that is native to China but widely used as an ornamental and that has flaky cinnamon-brown bark and 3-foliolate to 5-foliolate coarsely toothed leaves

paper birch *n* **:** an American birch (*Betula papyrifera*) with peeling white bark often worked into fancy articles (as baskets) — called also *canoe birch*; compare AMERICAN GRAY BIRCH; see TREE illustration

paperboard \\'⸗⸗ˌ⸗\\ *n* **:** a composition board varying in thickness and rigidity according to the purpose for which it is to be used — compare BOARD 6a, CARDBOARD

paper boards *n pl* **:** a style of binding in which the usual board stiffening has a paper covering

paper book *n* **1 :** a book prepared in English legal practice containing copies or abstracts of the pleadings and other papers exchanged between the parties and of the facts necessary to a complete understanding of a case **2 :** a printed booklet containing a legal brief and the record and filed with an appellate court in connection with an appeal

paperbook \\'⸗⸗ˌ⸗\\ *n* [³*paper* + *book*] **:** PAPERBACK

paperbound \\'⸗⸗ˌ⸗\\ *adj or n* **:** PAPERBACK

paper boy *n* [by shortening] **:** NEWSBOY

paper chase *n* **:** the game of hare and hounds when paper is used as scent

paper chromatography *n* **:** chromatography with paper strips or sheets as the adsorbent through which the solution flows by gravity or is sucked up by capillarity — compare CAPILLARY ANALYSIS

paper clip *n* **1 :** a device consisting of a length of wire bent into flat loops that can be separated by a slight pressure to clasp several sheets of paper together — see CLIP illustration **2 :** a spring clamp designed as a clasp for papers

paper coal *n* **:** a variety of lignite splitting into papery layers

paper-cover \\ˌ⸗⸗'⸗⸗\\ *adj or n* **:** PAPERBACK

paper currency *var of* PAPER MONEY

paper curtain *n* **:** an intangible barrier resulting from much red tape ⟨*paper curtain* of passport procedure —*Countryman*⟩

paper cutter *n* **1 :** PAPER KNIFE **2 :** a machine for cutting or trimming sheets of paper to required dimensions

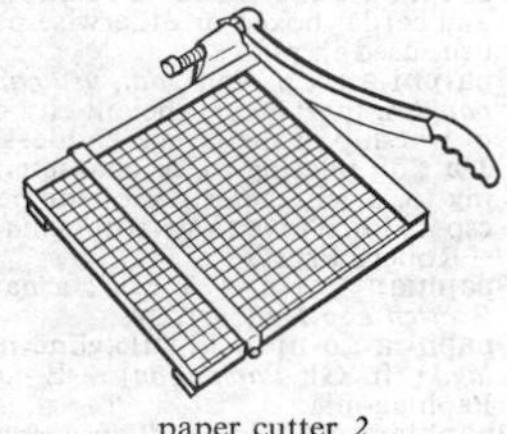

paper cutter *2*

paper doll *n* **:** a paper or cardboard representation of a person usu. in two dimensions for children to play with

papered *past of* PAPER

pa·per·er \\'pāp(ə)rə(r)\\ *n* -s **1 :** one that lines with, wraps in, or fixes on paper **2 :** PAPERHANGER

paper finger *n* **:** one of two movable clamps on some typewriters that are used in place of or in addition to the bail to hold paper firmly against the platen

paperflower \\'⸗⸗ˌ⸗\\ *n* **1 :** STRAWFLOWER **2 :** BOUGAINVILLEA **3 :** a rounded shrub (*Psilostrophe cooperi*) of the family Compositae native to the deserts of the western U.S. and having conspicuous flowers that turn straw-colored and papery with age

paper folding *n* **:** the art or process of folding squares of colored paper into representative shapes — see ORIGAMI

paper foot *n* **:** a foot (as of a dog) with very thin pads

paper-footed \\ˌ⸗⸗'⸗⸗\\ *adj* **:** having paper feet ⟨a *paper-footed* dog⟩

pa·per·ful \\'pāpə(r)ˌfu̇l\\ *n, pl* **paperfuls** *also* **papersful** \\-(r)ˌfu̇lz, -(r)zˌfu̇l\\ **:** as much as will fill a paper ⟨a ~ of pins⟩

pa·per·gram \\'pāpə(r)ˌgram\\ *n* [³*paper* + chromato*gram*] **:** a chromatogram on paper

paper guide *n* **:** a movable attachment on the paper table of a typewriter that can be set at any point to serve as a left-edge guide for inserting paper

paperhanger \\'⸗⸗ˌ⸗⸗\\ *n* **1 :** one that hangs paper or fabric covering on interior walls **:** one that wallpapers **2** *slang* **:** one who passes worthless checks

paperhanging \\'⸗⸗ˌ⸗⸗\\ *n* **1** *usu* **paper hangings** *pl, archaic* **:** WALLPAPER **2 :** the occupation or work of hanging wallpaper

paper hornet *n* [so called fr. the papery nest it builds] **:** WHITE-FACED HORNET

paper hunt *n* **:** PAPER CHASE

pa·per·i·ness \\'pāp(ə)rēnəs, -rin-\\ *n* -ES [*papery* + *-ness*] **:** the condition of being papery ⟨the whole plant is of a dry ~, like the everlastings —M.B.Eldershaw⟩

papering *n* -s [fr. gerund of ²*paper*] **1 :** PAPERHANGING 2 **2 :** wallpaper esp. when covering a wall or ceiling

paper joint *n* **:** a joint by which built-up woodwork is secured to a faceplate for turning and which consists of a layer of paper glued to the faceplate and to the first course of the work

paper knife *n* **1 :** a bladed often ornamental instrument (as of brass or ivory) for slitting envelopes or pages of uncut books **2 :** the knife of a paper-cutting machine

paperlike \\'⸗⸗ˌ⸗\\ *adj* **:** like or suggestive of paper (as in thickness, weight, or texture) ⟨~ walls⟩

paper-mache \\ˌpāpə(r)mə'shā, -ˌma'- *sometimes* -ˌmä'-\\ *n or adj* [by alter.] **:** PAPIER-MÂCHÉ

paper machine *n* **:** a synchronized series of mechanical devices that rapidly and continuously transforms a dilute fibrous stock into a dry sheet of paper — see CYLINDER MACHINE, FOURDRINIER

papermaker \\'⸗⸗ˌ⸗⸗\\ *n* **:** one that makes paper

papermakers' alum *n* **:** ALUMINUM SULFATE

papermaking \\'⸗⸗ˌ⸗⸗\\ *n* **:** the making of paper

paper match *n* **:** a match having a stem made of paperboard **:** BOOK MATCH

paper money *n* **1** *or* **paper currency :** paper documents that circulate instead of metallic money: as **a :** paper forms issued for the purpose of circulation as money (as government notes and bank notes) **b :** paper instruments (as checks and negotiable drafts) that have the effect of replacing money in circulation **2 :** JOSS PAPER

papermouth \\'⸗⸗ˌ⸗\\ *n* [so called fr. the thin membrane of the mouth] **:** WHITE CRAPPIE

paper mulberry *n* [so called fr. the fact that its bark is used in papermaking in China and Japan] **:** an Asiatic tree (*Broussonetia papyrifera* of the family Moraceae) grown as a shade tree in Europe and America — see TAPA

pa·pern \\'pāpə(r)n\\ *adj* [¹*paper* + *-en*] *chiefly dial* **:** made of paper

paper nautilus *n* [so called fr. its delicate white shell] **:** a cephalopod of the genus *Argonauta*

paper office *n, obs* **:** an office where documents (as state or court papers) are kept or recorded

paper patent *n* **:** a patent for an invention never put into manufacture or commercial use

paper plant *or* **paper reed** *or* **paper rush** *n* **:** PAPYRUS

paper pulp *n* **:** PULP 1c

paper rate *n* **:** a railroad freight rate that is believed to be excessive or is otherwise not likely to promote a substantial or regular movement of the type of traffic to which it applies

paper red A *n* **:** an acid dye — see DYE table I (under *Acid Red 137*)

paper release lever *n* **:** a lever on the carriage of a typewriter that releases the pressure on the feed rolls so that paper may be straightened or removed

papers *pl of* PAPER, *pres 3d sing of* PAPER

paper sailor *n* **:** PAPER NAUTILUS

paper shale *n* [so called fr. its layers suggesting sheets of paper] **:** a very thinly laminated shale

papershell \\ˌ⸗⸗'⸗\\ *adj* **:** PAPER-SHELLED ⟨~ pecan⟩ ⟨~ egg⟩

paper-shelled \\ˌ⸗⸗'⸗\\ *adj* **1 :** having a thin fragile shell ⟨*paper-shelled* almond⟩ **2 :** recently shed ⟨*paper-shelled* crab⟩ ⟨*paper-shelled* lobster⟩

paper standard *n* **:** a monetary system based on inconvertible paper money as the standard

paper stock *n* **1 :** any of various plants (as pine, poplar, or grass) from which paper is made **2 :** fibrous material (as waste paper and boards) from which paper pulp may be made

paper table *n* **:** a tilted shelf at the back of the platen of a typewriter for supporting the paper

paper-thin \\ˌ⸗⸗'⸗\\ *adj* **:** so thin as to suggest paper **:** very thin or narrow ⟨*paper-thin* slices of fat salt pork —Della Lutes⟩ ⟨*paper-thin* partitions of the office —*Bookman*⟩ ⟨won only *paper-thin* control of both houses —M.S.Forbes⟩

paper tiger *n* **:** one that is outwardly powerful or dangerous but inwardly weak or ineffectual ⟨claims that the alliance is only a *paper tiger*⟩

paper title *n* **:** a title to real property appearing on the face of a recorded instrument or of a conveyance or document — used chiefly of a title that is defective

paper wasp *n* **:** a wasp (as the yellow jacket and hornet) that makes a nest of papery material

paperweight \\'⸗⸗ˌ⸗\\ *n* **:** an object designed to hold down loose papers by its weight

paper white *n* **:** a yellowish gray to white that resembles the white of good paper and is greener and paler than the colors sand or natural

paper-white narcissus *also* **paper-white** *n* **:** a polyanthus narcissus bearing clusters of small very fragrant pure white blossoms

paper work *n* **:** the writing or reviewing of papers (as records, reports, or examinations); *esp* **:** the procedures necessary in keeping administrative records ⟨the *paper work* involved in running a farm —Christopher Rand⟩ ⟨for meritorious *paper*

work at the Navy Yard —Alva Johnston⟩ ⟨the predictable timing of his *paper work* —D.R.Morris⟩
paperworker \ˈ==,==\ *n* **:** PAPERMAKER
paper worm *n* **:** BOOKWORM 1
pa·pery \ˈpāp(ə)rē, -ri\ *adj* **:** like paper **:** of the thinness or consistency of paper ⟨a skirling of leaves, ~, ephemeral —Elizabeth Enright⟩ ⟨like ~ silk —*Women's Wear Daily*⟩ ⟨a ~ thirty-second of an inch —*Monsanto Mag.*⟩
papery leaf spot *n* **:** a blight and leaf spot of ginseng caused by a fungus (*Alternaria panax*)
papes *pl of* PAPE
pap·e·terie \ˈpapə·trē, -ri\ *n* -s [F *papeterie* paper manufacture, stationery case (fr. *papet-* — irreg. fr. *papier* paper — + *-erie* -ery) + E *-s* — more at PAPER] **1 :** writing papers cut to size for use and boxed **2 :** stationery (as note paper, envelopes, and cards) boxed or otherwise packaged and sold as a unit — usu. used in pl.
¹pa·phi·an \ˈpāfēən\ *adj, usu cap* [L *paphius* Paphian (fr. Gk *paphios*, fr. *Paphos*, ancient city of Cyprus that was the center of worship of the Greek goddess of love Aphrodite) + E *-an*] **1 a :** of, relating to, or characteristic of Paphos **b :** of, relating to, or characteristic of the people of Paphos **2 :** relating esp. to illicit love **:** WANTON ⟨sail for some vague *Paphian* bourn —Robert Frost⟩
²paphian \ˈ"\ *n* -s **1** *cap* **:** a native or inhabitant of Paphos **2** *often cap* **:** PROSTITUTE
¹paph·la·go·nian \ˌpafləˈgōnēən, -nyən\ *n* -s *cap* [L *Paphlagon* (fr. Gk *Paphlagōn*) + E *-ian*] **:** a native or inhabitant of Paphlagonia
²paphlagonian \ˈ"\ *adj, usu cap* [L *paphlagonius* Paphlagonian (fr. *Paphlagonia* ancient country in Asia Minor) + E *-an*] **1 :** of, relating to, or characteristic of Paphlagonia **2 :** of, relating to, or characteristic of the people of Paphlagonia
pa·pia·men·to \ˌpäpyəˈmen·(ˌ)tō\ *n* -s *usu cap* [Sp, fr. Papiamento *papia* talk (prob. fr. Pg *papear* to chatter, of imit. origin) + *-mento* -ment (fr. Sp, fr. L *-mentum*)] **:** a Spanish-based creole language of Curaçao
pa·pier col·lé \ˌpapˌyāˌkōˈlā\ *n, pl* **papiers collés** \-ā(z)\ [F, glued paper] **:** COLLAGE
¹papier-mâché *also* **pa·pier ma·che** *or* **papier-maché** \ˌpāpə(r)məˈshā, -maˈ- *sometimes* ˌpäp,yā,mäˈshā\ *n* -s [F, lit., chewed paper] **:** a light and strong molding material of high plasticity made typically from wastepaper pulped with glue and other additives
²papier-mâché \ˈ==(ˌ)=ˈ=, ˈ=,=ˈ=\ *adj* **1 :** formed of papier-mâché usu. with a lacquered or other decorative surface ⟨*papier-mâché* tray⟩ ⟨*papier-mâché* mask⟩ ⟨*papier-mâché* furniture⟩ **2 :** UNREAL, ARTIFICIAL, FALSE ⟨a real human being and not a *papier-mâché* hero —Leo Gershoy⟩ ⟨a *papier-mâché* crisis⟩ ⟨the *papier-mâché* facade of Allied harmony crumbled —J.P.O'Donnell⟩
pa·pil·io \pəˈpilēˌō, -il(ˌ)yō\ *n* [NL, fr. L, butterfly — more at PAVILION] **1** *cap* **:** a genus (the type of the family Papilionidae) of lepidopterous insects that as orig. formulated included all the butterflies but is now usu. restricted to the typical swallow-tailed butterflies and a few nearly related forms **2** -s **:** any butterfly of the genus *Papilio*
pa·pil·i·o·na·ce·ae \pəˌpilēōˈnāsēˌē\ [NL, fr. L *papilion-*, *papilio* butterfly + NL *-aceae*] *syn of* LEGUMINOSAE
pa·pil·i·o·na·ceous \ˌ=ˌ===ˈnāshəs\ *adj* [L *papilion-*, *papilio* + E *-aceous*] **1 :** resembling a butterfly; *specif* **:** irregular and suggestive of a butterfly in shape ⟨the corolla of many leguminous plants is ~⟩ **2** [NL *Papilionaceae* + E *-ous*] **:** of or relating to the family Leguminosae
¹pa·pil·i·o·nid \pəˈpilēənəd, -lyə-, -ˌnid\ *adj* [NL *Papilionidae*] **:** of or relating to the Papilionidae
²papilionid \ˈ"\ *n* -s [NL *Papilionidae*] **:** a butterfly of the family Papilionidae **:** SWALLOWTAIL
pa·pil·i·on·i·dae \pəˌpilēˈänəˌdē\ *n pl, cap* [NL, fr. *Papilion-*, *Papilio*, type genus + *-idae*] **:** a large family (superfamily Papilionoidea) of butterflies that have all three pairs of legs well developed in both sexes, larvae usu. with osmeteria, and pupae which are angular and typically attached by the anal end and a median loop of silk
¹pa·pil·io·noid \pəˈpilēəˌnȯid, -lyə-,-\ *adj* [NL *Papilionoidea*] **:** of or relating to the Papilionoidea
²papilionoid \ˈ"\ *n* -s [NL *Papilionoidea*] **:** a butterfly of the family Papilionoidea
pa·pil·i·o·noi·dea \=ˌ=ēəˈnȯidēə\ *n pl, cap* [NL, fr. *Papilion-*, *Papilio* + *-oidea*] **:** a superfamily of Lepidoptera including all the typical butterflies — compare HESPERIOIDEA
papill- *or* **papillo-** *comb form* [F *papill-*, fr. L *papilla* nipple — more at PAP] **1 :** papilla ⟨*papilli*ferous⟩ ⟨*papilli*form⟩ **2 :** papillary ⟨*papill*edema⟩ ⟨*papill*oma⟩ ⟨*papill*oretinitis⟩ **3 :** papillomatous ⟨*papillo*carcinoma⟩ ⟨*papillo*sarcoma⟩
pa·pil·la \pəˈpilə\ *n, pl* **papil·lae** \-iˌlē, -ˌlī\ [L] **1** *obs* **:** the nipple of the breast **2** [NL, fr. L, nipple] **:** a small projecting body part similar to a nipple in form: **a :** a vascular process of connective tissue extending into and nourishing the root of a hair, feather, or developing tooth **b :** one of the vascular protuberances of the dermal layer of the skin extending into the epidermal layer and often containing tactile corpuscles **c :** the apex of a Malpighian pyramid of the kidney **d :** one of the small protuberances on the upper surface of the tongue — see CIRCUMVALLATE PAPILLA, FILIFORM PAPILLA, FUNGIFORM PAPILLA
papilla of va·ter \-ˈfät·ə(r), -fāt-\ *usu cap V* [after Abraham *Vater* †1751, Ger. anatomist] **:** AMPULLA OF VATER
pap·il·lar \ˈpapələ(r), pəˈpil-\ *adj* [ISV *papill-* + *-ar*] **:** PAPILLARY
pap·il·lary \ˈpapəˌlerē, pəˈpilərē, -ri\ *adj* [F *papillaire*, fr. *papille* nipple, papilla (fr. L *papilla* nipple) + *-aire* -ary] **:** of, relating to, or resembling a papilla **:** PAPILLOSE
papillary carcinoma *or* **papillary cancer** *n* **:** a carcinoma characterized by a papillary structure
papillary layer *n* **:** the superficial layer of the derma raised into papillae fitting in corresponding depressions on the inner surface of the epidermis
papillary muscle *n* **:** one of the small muscular columns attached at one end to the chordae tendineae and at the other to the wall of the ventricle and that maintain tension on the chordae as the ventricle contracts
pap·il·late \ˈpapəˌlāt, pəˈpilət, *usu* -d·+V\ *or* **pap·il·lat·ed** \ˈpapəˌlād·əd\ *adj* [*papillate* fr. NL *papillatus*, fr. LL, shaped like a bud, fr. L *papilla* nipple, bud + *-atus* -ate; *papillated* fr. NL *papillatus* + E *-ed*] **1 :** covered with or bearing papillae **2 :** resembling a papilla
pap·il·lec·to·my \ˌpapəˈlektəmē, -mi\ *n* -ES [*papill-* + *-ectomy*] **:** the surgical removal of a papilla
pap·il·ledema *also* **pap·il·loedema** \ˌpapəl+\ *n* [NL, fr. *papill-* + *edema*] **:** CHOKED DISK
pap·il·lif·er·ous \ˌpapəˈlif(ə)rəs\ *adj* [NL *papillifer* (fr. *papill-* + L *-ifer*) + E *-ous*] **:** bearing papillae
pa·pil·li·form \pəˈpiləˌfȯrm\ *adj* [prob. fr. (assumed) NL *papilliformis*, fr. *papill-* + L *-iformis*] **:** resembling a papilla
pap·il·li·tis \ˌpapəˈlīd·əs\ *n* -ES [NL, fr. *papill-* + *-itis*] **:** inflammation of a papilla: **a :** inflammation of the optic disk **b :** inflammation of a renal papilla
pap·il·lo·ma \ˌpapəˈlōmə\ *n, pl* **papillo·mas** \-məz\ *or* **papilloma·ta** \-məd·ə, -mətə\ [NL, fr. *papill-* + *-oma*] **1 :** a benign tumor (as a wart or condyloma) resulting from an overgrowth of epithelial tissue on papillae of vascularized connective tissue of skin and other organs that forms projections or ridges **2 :** an epithelial tumor caused by a virus — see PAPILLOMATOSIS
pap·il·lo·ma·to·sis \ˌ==ˌ=məˈtōsəs\ *n, pl* **papillomato·ses** \-ˌsēz\ [NL, fr. *papillomat-*, *papilloma* + *-osis*] **1 :** a condition marked by the presence of numerous papillomas **2 :** a virus disease of various domestic and wild animals characterized by widespread development of warty tumors esp. on the skin or in the mouth ⟨~ of rabbits⟩
pap·il·loma·tous \ˌpapəˈlämad·əs, -lōm-, -mətəs\ *adj* [NL *papillomat-*, *papilloma* + E *-ous*] **1 :** like or being a papilloma **2 :** marked by papillomas **:** having papillomas as a typical symptom
pa·pil·lon \ˌpäpēˈ(y)ōⁿ\ *n* [F, lit., butterfly, fr. L *papilion-*, *papilio*; fr. the shape of its ears — more at PAVILION] **1** *usu cap* **:** a breed of small slender toy spaniels resembling long-haired Chihuahuas, having large usu. obliquely erect ears, and varying in color from brown to white with black spots **2** -s *often cap* **:** any dog of the Papillon breed
pap·il·lose \ˈpapəˌlōs\ *adj* [prob. fr. (assumed) NL *papillosus*, fr. *papill-* + L *-osus* -ose] **:** PAPILLATE — **pap·il·los·i·ty** \ˌ==ˈläsəd·ē\ *n* -ES
pap·il·lote \ˈpapəˌlōt\ *n* -s [F, fr. *papillon* butterfly] **1 :** CURLPAPER **2 :** a greased paper wrapper in which food is cooked and served
pa·pil·lule \pəˈpil(ˌ)yül\ *n* -s [NL *papillula*, fr. *papill-* + L *-ula* -ule] **:** a small papilla
pa·pin·go \ˈpäpənˌgō\ *Scot var of* POPINJAY
¹pa·pio \ˈpāpēˌō\ *n, cap* [NL, fr. ML, baboon, prob. of baby-talk origin like L *papa*, *pappa* food, father — more at PAPA] **:** a genus consisting of the typical baboons
²pa·pio \ˈpä(ˌ)pyō\ *also* **pa·pio·pio** \ˈpäpyōˌpyō\ *n, pl* **papio** *or* **papios** [Hawaiian] *Hawaii* **:** a young ulua
pa·pi·on \ˈpāpēˌän\ *n* -s [ME *papioun*, fr. MF *papion*, fr. ML *papion-*, *papio*] **:** any of several baboons (esp. *Papio sphinx*) of West Africa
¹pa·pish \ˈpāpish, -pēsh\ *adj* [¹*pape* + *-ish*] *dial chiefly Brit* **:** PAPISTIC
²papish \ˈ"\ *n* -ES *often cap, dial chiefly Brit* **:** PAPIST
pa·pism \ˈpāˌpizəm\ *n* -s [MF *papisme*, fr. *pape* pope (fr. LL *papa*) + *-isme* -ism — more at POPE] **:** government by the Roman pope **:** ROMAN CATHOLICISM — usu. used disparagingly
¹pa·pist \ˈ-pəst\ *n* -s *often cap* [MF or NL; MF *papiste*, fr. *pape* pope + *-iste* -ist; NL *papista*, fr. LL *papa* pope + L *-ista* -ist] **:** a Roman Catholic who is a partisan of the pope — usu. used disparagingly
²papist \ˈ"\ *adj, often cap* **:** PAPISTIC — usu. used disparagingly
pa·pis·tic \pəˈpistik, -tēk\ *or* **pa·pis·ti·cal** \-təkəl, -tēk-\ *adj* [*papistic* prob. fr. MF *papistique*, fr. *papiste* + *-ique* -ic; *papistical* prob. fr. MF *papistique* + E *-al*] **:** of or relating to the Roman Catholic Church and its doctrines, ceremonies, or government — usu. used disparagingly — **pa·pis·ti·cal·ly** \-tək(ə)lē, -tēk-, -li\ *adv*
pa·pist·ry \ˈpāpəstrē, -tri\ *n* -ES [*papist* + *-ry*] **:** ROMAN CATHOLICISM — usu. used disparagingly
pa·pize \ˈpāˌpīz\ *vb* -ED/-ING/-S [¹*papa* + *-ize*] *vt, archaic* **:** PAPALIZE ~ *vi* **1** *archaic* **:** to assume authority like a pope **2** *archaic* **:** to conform to the position of the pope or the papacy
pa·poose *also* **pap·poose** \paˈpüs, pəˈ-\ *n* -s [Narraganset *papoòs* child, lit., very small, very young] **:** a young child of No. American Indian parents
papoose board *n* **:** CRADLEBOARD
papooseroot \=ˈ=,=\ *n* [*papoose* + *root*] **:** BLUE COHOSH
pa·poosh \pəˈpüsh, päˈ-\ *n* -ES [earlier *papouch*, fr. F, fr. Per *pāpūsh*] **:** BABOUCHE
pa·pou·la \pəˈpōlə\ *n* -s [Pg, poppy, kenaf, modif., of Ar dial. (Spain) *habapaura* poppy, modif. (influenced by Ar *ḥabba* grain, seed) of L *papaver* poppy — more at POPPY] **:** KENAF
pap·pa·ta·ci fever *also* **pa·pa·ta·ci fever** \ˌpäpəˈtächē-\ *or* **pa·pa·ta·si fever** \-täsē-\ *n* [It *pappataci* sand fly (*Phlebotomus papatasii*), lit., silent eater, fr. *pappare* to eat (fr. L *pappare*, *papare*, fr. *pappa*, *papa* food) + *-taci* (fr. *tacito* — past part. of *tacere* to be silent —, fr. L *tacitus*, past part. of *tacēre* to be silent) — more at PAPA, TACIT] **:** PHLEBOTOMUS FEVER
pap·pea \ˈpapēə\ *n, cap* [NL, fr. Karl W. L. *Pappe*, 19th cent. Ger. botanist] **:** a genus of southern African trees (family Sapindaceae) with regular flowers in panicled racemes and red sometimes edible fruit — see WILD PRUNE
papped *past of* PAP
papping *pres part of* PAP
pap·pose \ˈpaˌpōs\ *also* **pap·pous** \-pəs\ *adj* [L *pappus* + E *-ose* or *-ous*] **:** furnished with a pappus **:** of the nature of a pappus
pap·pus \ˈpapəs\ *n, pl* **pap·pi** \-ˌpī\ [L, fr. Gk *pappos* grandfather, old man, pappus, down of the chin — more at PAPA] **1 a :** an appendage or tuft of appendages crowning the ovary or fruit in various seed plants (as composites), being adapted for dispersal of the fruit by wind or other agencies, and consisting of all or part of the perianth modified into bristles, scales, awns, or short teeth **b :** the group of bristles formed around the fruit by the calyx of members of the Dipsacaceae, Valerianaceae, and Calyceraceae **2** [NL, fr. Gk *pappos*] **:** DOWN; *esp* **:** the early growth of the beard
¹pap·py \ˈpapē, -pi\ *adj* -ER/-EST [²*pap* + *-y*] **:** consisting of pap **:** like pap **:** PULPY, SOFT, SUCCULENT ⟨like corn in a wet harvest — full, but ~, no good —D.H.Lawrence⟩
²pappy \ˈ"\ *n* -ES [²*papa* + *-y* (dim. suffix)] *chiefly South & Midland* **:** PAPA
pa·preg \ˈpāˌpreg\ *n* -s [*paper* + *impregnated*] **:** a material of high tensile strength composed of sheets of resin-impregnated paper bonded together by heat and pressure
pa·pri·ka \pəˈprēkə, paˈ-,päˈ-,pəˈ- *sometimes* -ˈprikə *or* ˈpaprəkə *or* ˈpaprēkə *or* ˈpäp- *or* ˈpȧp-\ *n* -s [Hung, fr. Serb, fr. *papar* pepper, fr. Gk *peperi* — more at PEPPER] **1 :** a condiment consisting of the dried finely ground pods of various cultivated sweet peppers (as the pimientos) — see HUNGARIAN PAPRIKA, KING'S PAPRIKA, SPANISH PAPRIKA **2 :** a sweet pepper that is used for or is suitable for making paprika **3 :** a strong reddish orange that is yellower and slightly darker than poppy, redder and deeper than fire red or scarlet vermilion, and redder and deeper than average coral red
paps *pl of* PAP, *pres 3d sing of* PAP
pap·ua mace \ˈpapyəwə-\ *n, usu cap P* [fr. *Papua* (New Guinea)] **:** MACASSAR MACE
¹pap·u·an \-wən\ *adj, usu cap* [*Papua* (New Guinea), island of the Malay Archipelago, Pacific ocean, and Territory of *Papua*, southeastern New Guinea (fr. Malay *pĕpuah* frizzled) + E *-an*] **1 a** (1) **:** of, relating to, or characteristic of the island of Papua (2) **:** of, relating to, or characteristic of the people of the island of Papua **b** (1) **:** of, relating to, or characteristic of the Territory of Papua (2) **:** of, relating to, or characteristic of the people of the Territory of Papua **2 :** of, relating to, or characteristic of the Negroid native peoples of New Guinea and adjacent areas of Melanesia **3 :** of, relating to, or characteristic of the Papuan languages **4 :** of, relating to, or being a subregion of the Australian biogeographic region that includes New Guinea and the Pacific islands to Wallace's line sometimes with the exception of Celebes
²papuan \ˈ"\ *n* -s *cap* [*Papua* and Territory of *Papua* + E *-an*] **1 a :** a native or inhabitant of the island of Papua **b :** a native or inhabitant of the Territory of Papua **2 :** a member of any of the negroid native peoples of New Guinea and adjacent areas of Melanesia; *specif* **:** a fuzzy-haired prominent-nosed nonpygmy Oceanic Negroid of New Guinea **3 :** the Papuan languages; *also* **:** any of this group of languages
papuan languages *n pl, usu cap P* **:** a heterogeneous group of languages spoken in New Guinea, New Britain, and the Solomon islands that do not belong to the Austronesian family and are not yet capable of classification
papua nutmeg *n, usu cap P* [fr. *Papua* (New Guinea)] **:** MACASSAR NUTMEG
pap·u·la \ˈpapyələ\ *n, pl* **papu·lae** \-ˌlē, -ˌlī\ [in sense 1, fr. L; in other senses, fr. NL, fr. L, pimple] **1 :** PAPULE **2 :** a small papilla **3 :** a dermal branchia of an echinoderm
pap·u·lar \-lə(r)\ *adj* [L *papula* + E *-ar*] **:** consisting of or characterized by papules
pap·u·lat·ed \ˈpapyəˌlād·əd\ *adj* [LL *papulatus* (past. part. of *papulare* to produce pimples, fr. L *papula* pimple) + E *-ed*] **:** covered with papules
pap·u·la·tion \ˌ==ˈlāshən\ *n* -s [LL *papulatus* + E *-ion*] **1 :** a stage in some eruptive conditions marked by the formation of papules **2 :** the formation of papules
pap·ule \ˈpap(ˌ)yül\ *n* -s [L *papula* pimple; akin to L *papilla* nipple — more at PAP] **:** a small solid usu. conical elevation of the skin caused by inflammation, accumulated secretion, or hypertrophy of tissue elements **:** PIMPLE
pap·u·lif·er·ous \ˌpapyəˈlif(ə)rəs\ *adj* [*papule* + *-iferous*] **:** having papules **:** PIMPLY
papulo- *comb form* [NL, fr. L *papula*] **1 :** papula ⟨*papulo*pustular⟩ **2 :** papulous and ⟨*papulo*squamous⟩ ⟨*papulo*vesicular⟩
pap·u·lo·necrotic \ˌpapyəlō+\ *adj* [ISV *papulo-* + *necrotic*] **:** marked by the formation of papules that tend to break down and form open sores ⟨~ tuberculids⟩
pap·u·lose \ˈpapyəˌlōs\ *adj* [NL *papulosus*, fr. L *papula* pimple + *-osus* -ose] **:** covered with papulae
pap·u·lous \-ləs\ *adj* [NL *papulosus*] **1 :** PAPULOSE **2 :** having papules as a characteristic lesion ⟨a ~ eruption⟩
pap·y·ra·ceous \ˌpapəˈrāshəs\ *adj* [L *papyraceus* made of paper, fr. *papyrus* paper + *-aceus* -aceous] **:** resembling papyrus **:** PAPERY
pap·y·rin \ˈpapərən\ *or* **pap·y·rine** \-rən, -ˌrīn\ *n* -s [F *papyrin*, fr. L *papyrus* + F *-in*] **:** VEGETABLE PARCHMENT
papyro- *comb form* [Gk, fr. *papyros* papyrus] **1 :** papyrus ⟨*papyro*logy⟩ **2 :** paper ⟨*papyro*graph⟩
pa·py·ro·logical \pəˌpīrəˌpaˌpirə+\ *adj* **:** of or relating to papyrology
pap·y·rol·o·gist \ˌpapəˈräləjəst\ *n* -s **:** a specialist in papyrology
pap·y·rol·o·gy \-jē, -ji\ *n* -ES [ISV *papyro-* + *-logy*] **:** the study of papyrus manuscripts
pa·py·rus \pəˈpīrəs, ÷ ˈpapər-, ÷ ˈpaper-\ *n, pl* **papyrus·es** \-səz\ *or* **pa·py·ri** \-ˈ=(ˌ)rē, -ˌrī; ˈ==ˌrē, -ˌrī\ *often attrib* [ME *papirus*, fr. ML, fr. L *papyrus* — more at PAPER] **1 :** a tall sedge (*Cyperus papyrus*) of the Nile valley having a smooth triangular stem, a large compound umbel with drooping rays, and fiber that served many uses in historic times — called also *paper reed*, *paper rush* **2 a :** the pith of the papyrus plant **b :** a substance prepared from the pith of the papyrus plant by cutting it in longitudinal strips, arranging them crosswise in two or three layers, soaking them in water, and pressing them into a homogeneous surface and used by the ancient Egyptians, Greeks, and Romans as a writing material esp. between the 4th century B.C. and the 4th century A.D. **c :** a sheet or roll of this material **3 a :** a writing on papyrus **b :** a written scroll made of papyrus
papyrus capital *n* **:** an Egyptian capital resembling a bundle of papyrus buds
papyrus column *n* **:** an Egyptian column resembling a bundle of papyrus stalks

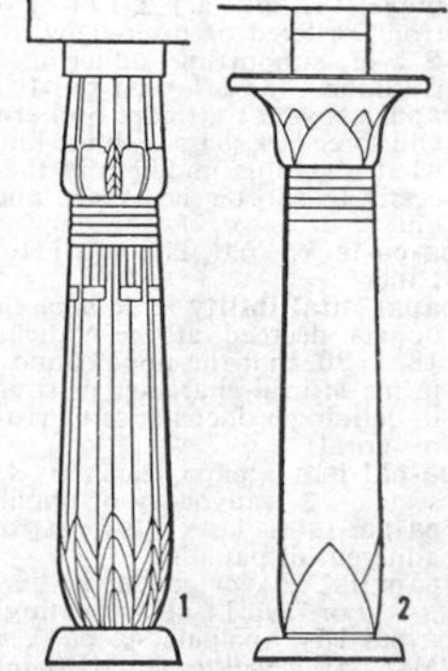

papyrus columns: *1* cluster bud, *2* flower

paque·bot cover \ˈpak(ə)-ˌbō(t)-\ *n* [*paquebot* fr. F, packet boat, fr. E *packet boat*] **:** a philatelic cover bearing a paquebot mail cancellation
paquebot mail *n* **:** mail to a U. S. address that originates on or is carried by a foreign ship outside of regular postal service and that on arrival of the ship in a U. S. port is transmitted by private messenger to the post office where it is canceled and forwarded through the regular mails
¹par \ˈpär, ˈpȧ(r\ *n* -s [L, one that is equal, fr. *par* equal — more at PAIR] **1 a :** the established value of the monetary unit of one country expressed in terms of the monetary unit of another country using the same metal as the standard of value and determined solely on the basis of the relative amounts of precious metal contained in the standard monetary units of the two countries — called also *mint par of exchange*; compare PURCHASING POWER PARITY **b** (1) **:** the nominal value of securities or certificates of value ⟨~ value for bonds in the U. S. is usually $1000⟩ ⟨a security is at ~ when the market price equals the ~ value⟩ — called also *face par*, *nominal par* (2) **:** the value or price at which securities or certificates of value are issued — compare NO-PAR **2 :** equality as to value, condition, or circumstances **:** common level — usu. used with *on* or *upon* ⟨had come out of the war on a ~ with the defeated nations —Osbert Sitwell⟩ ⟨his victories in statecraft and diplomacy were never on a ~ with his soaring ambitions —A.C.Cole⟩ ⟨I and my contemporary bards are by no means upon a ~ —William Cowper⟩ **3 a :** an amount that is taken as an average or mean **b :** a particular value or price taken as the par **c :** an accepted standard or normal level **:** AVERAGE, NORM ⟨novels below ~⟩ ⟨a portrait below ~⟩ ⟨bring a gauge reading up to ~⟩ ⟨keep one's appearance up to ~⟩; *specif* **:** such a level of physical condition or health ⟨not feeling up to ~⟩ **4 :** the score standard set for each hole of a golf course on the basis of the length of the hole allowing two putts for each green; *also* **:** a score equal to par **syn** see AVERAGE
²par \ˈ"\ *adj* **:** of or relating to par or a normal level **:** AVERAGE ⟨the acting is only ~ —Kappo Phelan⟩
³par \ˈ"\ *vt* **parred; parred; parring; pars 1 :** to put on a par **2 :** to make a golf score on (a hole) equal to par
⁴par \ˈ"\ *n* -s [by shortening] *Brit* **:** PARAGRAPH
par *abbr* **1** paragraph **2** parallax **3** parallel **4** parenthesis **5** parish
¹pa·ra \ˈpärə\ *n* -s [Turk, fr. Per *pārah*, lit., piece] **1 a :** a Turkish monetary unit equal in modern Turkey to 1/4000 of a lira **b :** a small orig. silver coin representing one para unit **2 a :** any one of several units of value formerly used in countries at one time under the Turkish Empire (as in Serbia 1/100 dinar and in Montenegro 1/100 perper); *also* **:** one of the corresponding coins **b** *pl* **para** [Serbo-Croatian, fr. Turk] **:** a Yugoslav unit of value equal to 1/100 of a dinar — see MONEY table
²pará \pəˈrä, *attributively as in* "*Para rubber*" *often* ˈparə\ *adj, usu cap* [fr. *Pará* (Belém), Brazil] **:** BELÉM
³para \ˈparə, pəˈrä\ *n* -s *usu cap* **:** PARA RUBBER
⁴para \ˈparə, ˈpärə\ *n* -s [native name in India] **:** HOG DEER
⁵para \ˈparə\ *n, pl* **par·as** *or* **par·ae** \-ˌrē\ [*-para*] **:** a woman delivered of a specified number of children — used in combination with a term or figure to indicate the number ⟨a 36-year-old *para* 5⟩; compare GRAVIDA
⁶para \ˈ"\ *adj* [¹*para-*] **1 :** relating to, characterized by, or being two positions in the benzene ring that are separated by two carbon atoms — compare PARA- 2b **2 :** of, relating to, or being a diatomic molecule (as of hydrogen) in which the nuclei of the atoms are spinning in opposite directions — opposed to *ortho* ⟨ortho-*para* conversion⟩
¹para- *or* **par-** *prefix* [ME, fr. MF, fr. L, fr. Gk, fr. *para*; akin to Gk *pro* before, ahead — more at FOR] **1 a :** beside **:** alongside of ⟨*para*central⟩ ⟨*para*biosis⟩ ⟨*para*synapsis⟩ **b :** parallel ⟨*para*heliotropism⟩ **c :** parasitic ⟨*para*zoon⟩ **d :** associated in a subsidiary or accessory capacity ⟨*para*military⟩ **e :** closely resembling the true form **:** almost — esp. in names of diseases ⟨*para*typhoid⟩ **2 a :** isomeric with, polymeric with, or otherwise closely related to ⟨*par*aldehyde⟩ ⟨*para*casein⟩ ⟨*para*periodic acid⟩ — compare META- 4a **b** (1) **:** the relation of two opposite positions in the benzene ring that are separated by two carbon atoms (2) *para-*, *usu ital* **:** a derivative in which two substituting groups occupy such positions — abbr. *p-* ⟨*para*-xylene or *p*-xylene is 1,4-dimethyl-benzene⟩; compare META- 4b, ORTH- 3b **3 :** beyond **:** outside of ⟨*par*enteral⟩ **4 a :** faulty, irregular, or disordered condition **:** abnormal ⟨*para*lexia⟩ ⟨*para*noia⟩ ⟨*para*phrenia⟩ **b :** perversion ⟨*para*bulia⟩ ⟨*para*canthosis⟩ **c :** abortive ⟨*para*carpium⟩ ⟨*para*style⟩ **5 :** derived from an original sediment — in the name of a metamorphic rock ⟨*para*gneiss⟩; compare ORTH-
²para- *comb form* [*parachute*] **1 :** specially trained or equipped for descent by parachute from airplanes ⟨*para*bomb⟩ ⟨*para*marine⟩ ⟨*para*trooper⟩ **2 :** of, by, or in defense against armed parachutists ⟨*para*spotter⟩
-pa·ra \ˌparə\ *n comb form, pl* **-paras** \-rəz\ *or* **-pa·rae** \-ˌrē, -ˌrī\ [L, fr. *parere* to bring forth, bear (young) — more at PARE] **1 :** woman that has been delivered of (a specified number of) children ⟨nulli*para*⟩ **2 :** female that produces (a specified kind or number of) eggs or gives birth to (a specified kind or number of) young ⟨gyno*para*⟩ ⟨multi*para*⟩
para *abbr* paragraph
para-aminobenzoic acid \ˌparə+. . .-\ *n* [ISV ¹*para-* + *aminobenzoic*] **:** AMINOBENZOIC ACID a — written systematically with ital. *para-* or *p-*
para-aminohippuric acid \ˌparə+. . .-\ *n* [¹*para-* + *amin-*

+ *hippuric*] : a crystalline acid $H_2NC_6H_4CONHCH_2COOH$ used chiefly in the form of its sodium salt in testing kidney function — written systematically with ital. *para-* or *p-*

para-aminophenol \¦parə+\ *also* **par·aminophenol** \¦par+\ *n* [¹*para-* + *aminophenol*] : the para isomer of aminophenol — written systematically with ital. *para-* or *p-*

para-aminosalicylic acid \¦parə+. . .-\ *n* [ISV ¹*para-* + *aminosalicylic*] : the para isomer of aminosalicylic acid — written systematically with ital. *para-* or *p-*

para-analgesia \¦parə+\ *n* [NL, fr. ¹*para-* + *analgesia*] : analgesia of the lower part of the body

para-anesthesia \"+\ *n* [NL, fr. ¹*para-* + *anesthesia*] : anesthesia of both sides of the lower part of the body

par·a·ban·ic acid \¦parə¦banik-\ *n* [part trans. of G *parabansäure*, fr. *paraban-* (fr. Gk *parabainein* to pass over, fr. *para-* ¹*para-* + *bainein* to go) + *säure* acid — more at COME] : a crystalline nitrogenous cyclic diacid $C_3H_2N_2O_3$ made esp. by oxidation of uric acid; imidazole-trione — called also *oxalylurea*

para·basal body \¦parə+. . .-\ *also* **parabasal** *n* [ISV ¹*para-* + *basal*] : a cytoplasmic body closely associated with the kinetoplast of certain flagellates

par·a·ba·sic \¦parə¦bāsik\ *adj* [*parabasis* + *-ic*] : of or relating to parabasis

pa·rab·a·sis \pə'rabəsəs\ *n, pl* **paraba·ses** \-ə,sēz\ [Gk, fr. *parabainein* to go aside, step forward, fr. *para-* ¹*para-* + *bainein* to walk, step, go — more at COME] : an important choral ode in the Old Greek comedy mainly in anapestic tetrameters delivered by the chorus at an intermission in the action while facing and moving toward the audience

para·be·ma \¦parə¦bēmə\ *n, pl* **parabema·ta** \-məd·ə\ [NGk *parabēma*, fr. Gk *para-* ¹*para-* + LGk *bēma* bema — more at BEMA] **1** : PROTHESIS **2** : DIACONICON

para·benzoquinone \¦parə+\ *n* [¹*para-* + *benzoquinone*] : QUINONE 1a — written systematically with ital. *para-* or *p-*

para·bi·ont \¦parə¦bī,änt\ *n* -s [ISV ¹*para-* + *-biont* (modif. of Gk *biount-*, *biōn*, pres. part. of *bioun* to live — more at -BIONT] : either of the organisms joined in parabiosis

para·biosis \¦parə+\ *n, pl* **parabioses** [NL, fr. ¹*para-* + *biosis*] **1 a** : reversible suspension of obvious vital activities (as by suitable drying of a rotifer) **b** : the temporary suppression of excitability in a nerve **2** : the anatomical and physiological union of two organisms either natural (as in Siamese twins) or artificially produced **3** : a condition in which members of two or more species live close to one another without conflict although maintaining separate colonies — used esp. of ants

para·biotic \"+\ *adj* : of, relating to, or marked by parabiosis ⟨~ twins⟩ — **para·biotically** \"+\ *adv*

para·blast \'parə,blast\ *n* [¹*para-* + *-blast*] **1** : the yolk of a meroblastic ovum **2** : MESOBLAST; *esp* : the part of the mesoblast giving rise to vascular structures **3** : blastomeres that give rise to extraembryonic membranes — **para·blas·tic** \¦parə¦blastik\ *adj*

¹**par·a·ble** \'parəbəl *also* 'per-\ *n* -s [ME, fr. MF *parable*, *parabole*, fr. LL *parabola*, fr. Gk *parabolē* juxtaposition, comparison, parable, superposition (in geometry), parabola, fr. *paraballein* to throw or set alongside, compare, superpose (in geometry), fr. *para-* ¹*para-* + *ballein* to throw — more at DEVIL] : COMPARISON, SIMILITUDE; *specif* : a usu. short fictitious story that illustrates a moral attitude or a religious principle ⟨relating the ~ of the prodigal son⟩ **syn** see ALLEGORY

²**parable** *adj* [L *parabilis*, fr. *parare* to get ready, prepare + *-abilis*, -able — more at PARE] *obs* : PROCURABLE

para·blep·sia \,parə'blepsēə\ *also* **para·blep·sis** \-epsəs\ *or* **para·blep·sy** \-epsē\ *n, pl* **parablepsi·as** \-psēəz\ *or* **parablep·ses** \,==blep(,)sēz\ *or* **parablep·sies** \'==,blep,sēz\ [NL *parablepsia* (fr. ¹*para-* + Gk *blepsis* sight — fr. *blepein* to see + *-sis* — + L *-ia* -y) & *parablepsis*, fr. ¹*para-* + Gk *blepsis*] : false or distorted vision

pa·rab·o·la \pə'rabələ\ *n* -s [NL, fr. Gk *parabolē* — more at PARABLE] **1** : a plane curve generated by a point so moving that its distance from a fixed point divided by its distance from a fixed line is equal to 1 : a conic section formed by the intersection of a cone with a plane parallel to an element of the cone **2 a** : a bowl-shaped microphone **b** : a bowl-shaped antenna to receive and transmit radio waves preferentially in one particular direction

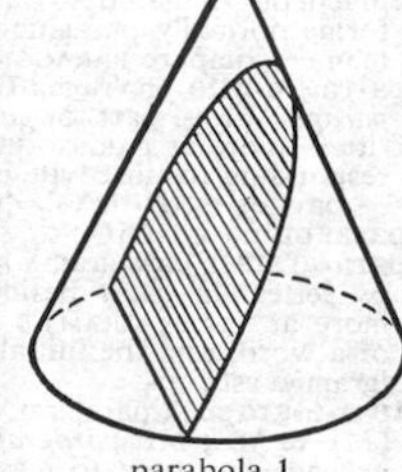

parabola 1

par·a·bo·la·nus \,parəbō'lānəs\ *n, pl* **parabola·ni** \-lā(,)nē\ [LL *parabolanus*, *parabanus*, prob. fr. (assumed) LGk *parabalaneus*, fr. Gk *para-* ¹*para-* + *balaneus* bathhouse servant, fr. *balaneion* bathhouse, hot bath — more at BAGNIO] : an official or a member of a brotherhood in the early church devoted to the care of the sick esp. in infectious or contagious cases

par·a·bol·ic \¦parə¦bälik\ *or* **par·a·bol·i·cal** \-ləkəl\ *adj* [in sense 1, fr. LL *parabola* parable + L *-icus* -ic, -ical; in sense 2, fr. NL *parabola* + E *-ic* — more at PARABLE] **1** : of the nature of or expressed by a parable or figure : ALLEGORICAL ⟨the ~ tradition of the Gospels —*Interpreter's Bible*⟩ ⟨an account in an ancient *parabolical* style of the spiritual life of the race —Helen Keller⟩ **2** : of, having the form of, or relating to a parabola ⟨motion in a ~ curve⟩

par·a·bol·i·cal·ly \-lək(ə)lē\ *adv* **1** : by way of parable : in a parabolic manner **2** : in the form or manner of a parabola

parabolic cylinder *n* : a cylinder whose right section is a parabola

parabolic geometry *n* : EUCLIDEAN GEOMETRY

parabolic reflector *n* **1** *or* **parabolic mirror** : a concave mirror that has the form of a paraboloid of revolution so that rays emanating from the geometrical focus and reflected from the surface are all parallel to each other and to the axis of symmetry and rays from a distant source (as a star) are reflected to the focus and that is used in reflecting telescopes, searchlights, and headlights **2** : a similar device for the directional reflection of microwaves and sound waves

parabolic velocity *n* : the speed at which a body at any point in a central gravitational field must move in order that its orbit be a parabola and which when the gravitational field is due to a spherical mass (as the earth) is equal to the velocity of escape

pa·rab·o·lize \pə'rabə,līz\ *vt* -ED/-ING/-S [in sense 1, fr. LL *parabola* parable + E *-ize*; in sense 2, fr. NL *parabola* + E *-ize*] **1** : to express in fables or explain as parables **2** : to make (as a mirror for a telescope) parabolic or paraboloidal

pa·rab·o·loid \pə'rabə,lȯid\ *n* -s [NL *parabola* + E *-oid*] : a quadric surface for which sections parallel to two of the coordinate planes are parabolas and sections parallel to the third coordinate plane are ellipses, circles, or hyperbolas if proper orientation of the coordinate axes is assumed ⟨an elliptic ~ is dome-shaped⟩ — compare HYPERBOLIC PARABOLOID, PARABOLOID OF REVOLUTION

pa·rab·o·loi·dal \pə¦rabə¦lȯidᵊl\ *adj* : having the shape of, resembling, or relating to a paraboloid ⟨eight hyperbolic ~ domes . . . are used in pairs to form the roof of a textile factory —*Civil Engineering*⟩ ⟨1-meter focus off-axis ~ collimating mirror —*Jour. of Research*⟩

paraboloid of revolution : the surface generated by the rotation of a parabola about its axis ⟨it is a property of a *paraboloid of revolution* . . . that rays from an object at infinity are all imaged at the same point on the axis —F.W.Sears⟩

para·bomb \'parə+,-\ *n* [²*para-* + *bomb*] : a bomb usu. with delayed-action fuze dropped from an airplane by parachute

para·botulism \¦parə+\ *n* [¹*para-* + *botulism*] : FORAGE POISONING

para·brake \'parə+,-\ *n* [²*para-* + *brake*] : a parachute used to assist braking an airplane

para·bran·chia \,parə'braŋkēə\ *n* -s [NL, fr. ¹*para-* + *-branchia*] : the osphradium of a mollusk when it is large and resembles a gill — **para·bran·chi·al** \¦==¦kēəl\ *adj* — **para·bran·chi·ate** \-kēət, -kē,āt\ *adj*

para brown V \-'vē, -'fīv\ *n, usu cap P&B* [⁶*para*] : a direct dye — see DYE table I (under *Direct Brown 151*)

para·bu·lia \,parə'byülēə\ *n* -s [NL, fr. ¹*para-* + *-bulia*] : abnormality or perversion of will power

para·carmine \¦parə+\ *n* [¹*para-* + *carmine*] : a carmine microscopy stain containing calcium chloride and often aluminum chloride

para·casein \"+\ *n* [ISV ¹*para-* + *casein*] : CASEIN c

par·a·cel·sian \¦parə¦sel(t)sēən, -lshən\ *adj, usu cap* [Philippus Aureolus *Paracelsus* (Theophrastus Bombastus von Hohenheim) †1541 Swiss alchemist and physician + E *-ian*] : of, relating to, or conforming to the practice or theories of Paracelsus according to whose teachings the activities of the human body are chemical, health depends on the proper chemical composition of the organs and fluids, and the object of chemistry is to prepare medicines ⟨certain *Paracelsian* medical and alchemical texts —W.A.Murray⟩

para·cen·te·sis \,parə,sen·'tēsəs\ *n, pl* **paracente·ses** \-ē(,)sēz\ [L, fr. Gk *parakentēsis*, fr. *parakentein* to pierce at the side (fr. *para-* ¹*para-* + *kentein* to prick) + *-sis* — more at CENTER] : a surgical puncture of a cavity of the body with a trocar, aspirator, or other instrument to draw off any effused fluid — called also *tapping*

para·central \¦parə+\ *adj* [ISV ¹*para-* + *central*] : lying near a center or central part

¹**para·cen·tric** \¦parə¦sen·trik\ *adj* [¹*para-* + *-centric*] **1** : being a type of key and keyway used with pin-tumbler cylinder locks and having longitudinal ribs and grooves projecting beyond the center to hinder picking **2** : being an inversion that occurs in a single arm of one chromosome and does not involve the chromomere — compare PERICENTRIC

²**paracentric** \"\ *n* -s : a paracentric key or keyway

para·cerebellar \¦parə+\ *adj* [¹*para-* + *cerebellar*] : of or relating to the lateral part of the cerebellum

par·acetaldehyde \(¦)par+\ *n* [¹*para-* + *acetaldehyde*] : PARALDEHYDE

par·a·chor \'parə,kō(ə)r\ *n* -s [¹*para-* + Gk *chōros* space; fr. its indicating volume — more at CHOR-] : an empirical constant for a liquid that relates the surface tension to the molecular volume and that may be used for a comparison of molecular volumes under conditions such that the liquids have the same surface tension and for determinations of partial structure of compounds by adding values obtained for constituent atoms and structural features — called also *molar parachor, molecular parachor*

¹**para·chordal** \"+\ *adj* [ISV ¹*para-* + *chordal*] : situated at the side of the notochord

²**parachordal** \"\ *n* -s : either of a pair of cartilaginous rods that develop on each side of the notochord beneath the posterior part of the embryonic brain and participate in formation of the basilar plate

parachordal plate *n* : BASILAR PLATE

para·chromatin \"+\ *n* [ISV ¹*para-* + *chromatin*] : any of various nonstaining or feebly staining nuclear elements that are a particular kind of protoplasm (as linin or spindle fibers) or are various artifacts

para·chromophorous \"+\ *adj* [¹*para-* + *chromophorous*] : excreting pigment that is insoluble in water and does not diffuse away from a cell wall or capsule — compare CHROMOPAROUS, CHROMOPHOROUS

pa·rach·ro·nism \pə'rakrə,nizəm, pə'r-\ *n* -s [¹*para-* + *chron-* + *-ism*] : a chronological error; *esp* : one by which a date is set later than is correct — compare METACHRONISM

¹**para·chute** \'parə,shüt *also* 'per-; *usu* -üd·+V\ *n, often attrib* [F, fr. *para-* (as in *parasol*) + *chute* fall — more at PARASOL, CHUTE] **1** : a folding umbrella-shaped device usu. made of light fabric for retarding the speed of a body attached to it by offering resistance to the air and used esp. for making a safe descent from an airplane, dropping equipment or supplies from an airplane, or slowing down an airplane upon landing **2** : the patagium of a mammal or reptile **3 a** : a device or structure suggestive of a parachute in form, use, or operation (as to retard the descent of a cage in a mining or to protect the balance wheel of a watch from shock) **b** : the inverted cup acting as the holding part of a mushroom anchor **c** : the tuft of hairs enabling a dandelion seed to float in air **4** : PARACHUTE SPINNAKER — **parachutic** *adj*

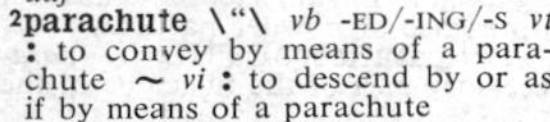

parachute 1: *1* shroud lines, *2* canopy, *3* pilot chute, *4* vent, *5* risers, *6* harness

²**parachute** \"\ *vb* -ED/-ING/-S *vt* : to convey by means of a parachute ~ *vi* : to descend by or as if by means of a parachute

parachute rigger *n* : a person who packs, inspects, and repairs parachutes; *specif* : an enlisted man in the U. S. Navy having such work as his major duties

parachute spinnaker *n* : an exceptionally large spinnaker used esp. on racing yachts

para·chut·ist \-üd·əst, -üt|\ *also* **para·chut·er** \|ə(r)\ *n* -s : one that parachutes; *specif* : a soldier trained and equipped to parachute from an airplane

par·a·clete \'parə,klēt\ *n* -s [ME *Paraclit*, fr. MF *Paraclēt*, *Paraclet*, fr. LL *Paracletus*, *Paraclitus*, fr. Gk *Paraklētos*, lit., intercessor, comforter, fr. *parakalein* to summon, exhort, comfort, fr. *para-* ¹*para-* + *kalein* to call — more at LOW] **1** *cap* : HOLY SPIRIT **2** : one called to aid or support : ADVOCATE

para·colon \¦parə+\ *n, often attrib* [NL, fr. ¹*para-* + *colon*] : any of several bacteria closely related to the genus *Escherichia* but commonly regarded as forming a distinct genus (*Paracolobactrum*) that have been implicated as causative agents of a variety of human gastroenteritides

par·a·col·pi·um \,parə'kälpēəm\ *n* [NL, fr. ¹*para-* + *colp-* + *-ium*] : the vascular and connective tissues alongside the vagina

para·condyloid \¦parə+\ *adj* [¹*para-* + *condyloid*] : being a process of the occipital bone lying on the outer side of each condyle in the skull of some mammals

para·cone \'parə+,-\ *n* [¹*para-* + *cone*] : the anterior of the three cusps of a primitive upper molar that in higher forms is the principal anterior and external cusp

par·aconic acid \¦par+. . .-\ *n* [ISV ¹*para-* + *aconic*] : a white crystalline lactonic acid $C_4H_5O_2COOH$ isomeric with itaconic, citraconic, and mesaconic acids; the beta-carboxy derivative of butyrolactone

para·co·nid \,parə'kōnəd\ *n* -s [*paracone* + *-id*] : the cusp of a primitive lower molar that corresponds to the paracone of the upper molar and that in higher forms is on the anterior internal cusp

para·co·nule \-(,)nyül\ *n* -s [*paracone* + *-ule*] : PROTOCONULE

para·coquimbite \¦parə+\ *n* [F, fr. ¹*para-* + *coquimbite*] : a mineral $Fe_2(SO_4)_3.9H_2O$ consisting of a hydrous ferric sulfate that is rhombohedral in crystallization and dimorphous with coquimbite

para·coto bark \¦parə+. . .-\ *n* [¹*para-* + *coto bark*] : the dried bark of a Bolivian tree (*Ocotea pseudo-coto*) or of an undetermined tree of the family Lauraceae

para·coumarone–indene resin \¦parə+. . .\ *n* [¹*para-* + *coumarone-indene resin*] : COUMARONE-INDENE RESIN

para·cresol \¦parə+\ *n* [ISV ¹*para-* + *cresol*] : the para isomer of cresol — written systematically with ital. *para-* or *p-*

para·crystal \"+\ *n* [¹*para-* + *crystal*] : a solid body with less than the three-dimensional order characteristic of a true crystal ⟨virus . . . in the form of needlelike ~*s* —C.A.Knight⟩ — compare PSEUDOCRYSTAL — **para·crystalline** \"+\ *adj*

par·acu·sia \,parə'k(y)üzh(ē)ə\ *or* **par·acu·sis** \-üsəs\ *n, pl* **paracu·sias** \-üzh(ē)əz\ *or* **paracu·ses** \-ü,sēz\ [NL fr. ¹*para-* + *-acusia* or Gk *akousis* hearing — more at -ACUSIA] : a disorder in the sense of hearing — **par·acu·sic** \¦==¦k(y)üzik, -üsik\ *adj or n*

para·cyanogen \¦parə+\ *n* [ISV ¹*para-* + *cyanogen*] : a polymer of cyanogen obtained as a brown or black amorphous solid (as by heating cyanogen)

para·cyesis \"+\ *n, pl* **paracyeses** [NL, fr. ¹*para-* + *cyesis*] : EXTRAUTERINE PREGNANCY

para·cystitis \"+\ *n, pl* **paracystitides** [NL, fr. *paracystium* + *-itis*] : inflammation of the connective tissue about the bladder

para·cys·ti·um \,parə'sistēəm\ *n, pl* **paracys·tia** \-ēə\ [NL, fr. ¹*para-* + *cyst-* + *-ium*] : the vascular and connective tissues alongside the bladder

¹**pa·rade** \pə'rād, *in rapid speech* 'pr-\ *n* -s [F, fr. MF, fr. *parer* to prepare, adorn + *-ade* — more at PARE] **1 a** : a pompous show : formal display : EXHIBITION ⟨make an important ~ of doing nothing —James Hilton⟩ ⟨could not be restrained from making rather an ostentatious ~ of his liberality —Charles Dickens⟩ ⟨wanted to find people as they always were, not on ~ —Margaret Biddle⟩ ⟨from early spring to late fall there is a constant ~ of gorgeous color —*Amer. Guide Series: Mass.*⟩ ⟨puts human flummery and pretentiousness on ~ in a crowded gallery of portraits —C.J. Rolo⟩ **b** : LISTING, RECITAL ⟨a radio program ~⟩ ⟨the book . . . is a pleasant ~ of the things he has enjoyed most —*Saturday Rev.*⟩ ⟨a ~ of popular songs⟩ **c** *Brit* : a style show or display of fashions by mannequins **2 a** : the ceremonial formation of a body of troops before its commanding or other high officer typically involving exercises in the manual of arms, a report on the numbers of the various units present or accounted for, and the publication of orders and ending with a review; *also* : any of various other ceremonial formations of a body of troops **b** : a place where troops assemble for regular formations or ceremonies **c** : troops that take part in a ceremonial formation **3 a** : an informal march or procession ⟨a ~ of witnesses testified⟩ ⟨a ~ of more outstanding singers than could possibly be cast in a single opera —Miles Kastendieck⟩ **b** : a formal public procession : the movement of any body of people or things marshaled in something like military order ⟨a ~ of firemen⟩ ⟨a circus ~⟩ ⟨a boat ~⟩ **c** : a showy array or succession ⟨a ~ of liniment bottles along the chimneypiece —Elizabeth Bowen⟩ ⟨a ~ of long-distance pipelines —Gardiner Symonds⟩ ⟨slash pockets at the hips, from which a ~ of box pleats starts around the back —Lois Long⟩ ⟨discriminative sensing of the down-the-years ~ of American attitudes —C.L.Carmer⟩ **d** : a movement in favor of a particular policy or action ⟨joined the propaganda ~ —J.B.Reston⟩ ⟨join the UN ~ in accepting the Indian plan —Mark Feer⟩ **4** : a place where people promenade : a public walk, square, or promenade **5 a** : those who parade : an assembly of promenaders **b** : an assembly of people ⟨there have been meets . . . at various places — annual ~*s* —R.E.Meyer⟩ **syn** see DISPLAY

²**parade** \"\ *vb* -ED/-ING/-S *vt* **1** : to assemble (as troops) in formation : cause to maneuver or march ceremoniously : MARSHAL **2** : to promenade (a place) ⟨veiled female had been *parading* the docks —T.B.Costain⟩ **3** : to exhibit in a showy or ostentatious manner : SHOW OFF ⟨the ugly woman does not ~ herself vainly —*Irish Digest*⟩ ⟨lavish floats are *paraded* up and down the river —Green Peyton⟩ ⟨politicians . . . have *paraded* their artistic incapacity as a virtue —*Times Lit. Supp.*⟩ ⟨ladies and gentlemen . . . *paraded* their fine manners, wit, and charm —H.J.Muller⟩ ~ *vi* **1 a** : to march or take part in a procession ⟨this army of penguins would ~ along the beach —H.A.Chippendale⟩ ⟨mob of thousands recently *paraded* through Mustafa Kamal Square in Cairo —H.C. Atyeo⟩ ⟨freighters ~ in and out of the Capes —*Amer. Guide Series: Va.*⟩ **b** : to form a review **2 a** : to walk up and down ⟨~ beneath the balcony —Elizabeth Bowen⟩ ⟨down on the wharf the sentry *paraded* stiffly —K.M.Dodson⟩ **b** : to promenade esp. for showing off ⟨ladies wore black in the morning but in the afternoon *paraded* in dashing silk gowns —C.L. Jones⟩ **3 a** : SHOW OFF ⟨drove so well, so quietly, without making any disturbance, without *parading* to her —Jane Austen⟩ **b** : MASQUERADE ⟨myths which ~ as modern science —M.R.Cohen⟩ ⟨dogmatism *parading* as enlightenment —Eric Partridge⟩ **syn** see SHOW

³**pa·rade** \pə'rād\ *n* -s [F, fr. *parer* to parry + *-ade* — more at PARRY] : PARRY

para·dental \¦parə+\ *adj* [ISV ¹*para-* + *dental*] : adjacent to a tooth

para·den·ti·tis \,parə,den·'tīd·əs\ *n* -ES [NL, fr. *paradentium* + *-itis*] : PERIODONTITIS

para·den·tium \,parə'dentēəm, -nch(ē)əm\ *n, pl* **paraden·tia** \-tēə, -ch(ē)ə\ [NL *para-* + *dent-* + *-ium*] : the paradental tissues including the gums, the alveolar process, and the pericementum

para·den·to·sis \,parə,den·'tōsəs\ *n, pl* **paradento·ses** \-ō,sēz\ [NL, fr. *paradentium* + *-osis*] : PERIODONTOSIS

pa·rad·er \pə'rādə(r)\ *n* -s : one that parades

parade rest \=,=¦=\ *n* : a formal position assumed by a soldier in ranks in which he remains silent and motionless with the left foot 12 inches to the left of the right foot and with the weight resting equally on both feet and when without arms clasps the hands behind the back with the palms to the rear and when with a rifle holds the rifle in the right hand with butt touching the ground and muzzle inclined forward and holds the left hand behind the back — used as a command to assume this position

parade rest

para·dermal \¦parə+\ *adj* [¹*para-* + *dermal*] : lying parallel to the epidermis

para·desmose \"+\ *n* [¹*para-* + *desmose*] : a fibril connecting extranuclear division centers in mitosis (as in many flagellates) — compare CENTRODESMOSE

para·diazine \"+\ *n* [¹*para-* + *diazine*] : a compound containing a diazine ring with the two nitrogen atoms para to each other; *esp* : PYRAZINE

para·dichlorobenzene \"+\ *n* [ISV ¹*para-* + *dichlorobenzene*] : a white crystalline compound $C_6H_4Cl_2$ made by chlorinating benzene that sublimes easily and is used chiefly as a fumigant against clothes moths — called also *PDB*, *p-dichlorobenzene*; written systematically with ital. *para-* or *p-*

par·a·did·dle \¦parə¦didᵊl\ *n* -s [prob. of imit. origin] : a snare-drum stroke characterized by the left-handed and right-handed attack on successive principal beats

para·did·y·mis \¦parə¦didəməs\ *n, pl* **paradidymi·des** \-'didəmə,dēz, -,də'dimə-, -,dī'dimə-\ [NL, fr. ¹*para-* + *-didymis* (fr. Gk *didymos* twin, testicle) — more at DIDYM-] : irregular tubules found among the convolutions of the epididymis and considered to be a remnant of tubes of the mesonephros

par·a·digm \'parə,dīm, -,dim *also* 'per- *sometimes* -,dəm *or* -,dəm\ *n, pl* **paradigms** \-mz\ *also* **paradig·ma·ta** \-dig·məd·ə, -mətə\ [LL *paradigma*, fr. Gk *paradeigma* pattern, model, example, fr. *paradeiknynai* to show side by side, compare, exhibit, fr. *para-* ¹*para-* + *deiknynai* to show — more at DICTION] **1** : EXAMPLE, PATTERN ⟨mistaken the ~ for the theory —Margaret Mead⟩ ⟨a typical conditioned-response ~ —W.N.Kellogg⟩ ⟨regard science as the ~ of true knowledge —G.C.J.Midgley⟩ ⟨~*s* of musical perfection —H.G.Aiken⟩ **2 a** : an example of a conjugation or declension showing a word in all its inflectional forms **b** : a set of forms peculiar to a verb, noun, pronoun, or adjective **3** : a narrative passage in the Gospels that illustrates a saying of Jesus and represents one of the literary patterns distinguished by form criticism ⟨the ~ . . . is represented in its purity by the healing of the paralytic —*Times Lit. Supp.*⟩ **syn** see MODEL

par·a·dig·mat·ic \¦==,dig¦mad·ik\ *also* **par·a·dig·mat·i·cal** \-d·əkəl\ *adj* [LL *paradigmaticos*, fr. Gk *paradeigmatikos* fr. *paradeigmat-*, *paradeigma* + *-ikos* -ic, -ical] **1** : EXEMPLARY, TYPICAL ⟨situation is . . . felt to be not unique but modeled on, or ~ of old situations —*Psychiatry*⟩ ⟨~ analysis of concepts such as space and inertia —Otto Neurath⟩ ⟨a ~ significance for the religious situation of modern man —M.S. Friedman⟩ **2 a** : of or relating to a grammatical paradigm ⟨a ~ set of forms⟩ **b** : INFLECTIONAL — **par·a·dig·mat·i·cal·ly** \-d·ək(ə)lē\ *adv*

paradigmatize *vt* [Gk *paradeigmatizein*, fr. *paradeigmat-*, *paradeigma* + *-izein* -ize] *obs* : to set forth as a model

para·diplomatic \ˌparə+\ *adj* [¹*para-* + *diplomatic*] **:** concerned with or based on evidence apart from strict textual authority

par·a·di·saea \ˌparəˌdīˈsēə, -ˈzēə, ˌ==ˈ=== *also* ˌper-\ *n, cap* [NL, irreg. fr. LL *paradisus* paradise] **:** the type genus of the family Paradisaeidae including various birds of paradise whose males are frequently predominantly brilliant metallic green

par·a·di·sae·i·dae \ˌ==ˌdīˈsēəˌdē, -ˈzē-\ *n pl, cap* [NL, fr. *Paradisaea*, type genus + *-idae*] **:** a family of passerine birds comprising the birds of paradise and often also the bowerbirds

par·a·di·sa·ic \ˌ==ˌ=ˈsāik, -ˌzā-, -āek\ *or* **par·a·di·sa·i·cal** \-āəkəl\ *adj* [*paradise* + *-aic, -aical* (as in *pharisaic, pharisaical*)] **:** PARADISIACAL — **par·a·di·sa·i·cal·ly** \-āək(ə)lē, -li\ *adv*

par·a·di·sal \ˌ==ˈdīsəl, -īzəl\ *adj* [*paradise* + *-al*] **:** PARADISIACAL ⟨a ~ state without work or struggle —*transl*⟩ ⟨vegetation was rich and ~ with flowers —Elinor Wylie⟩ ⟨together in that ~ place —Thomas Cole⟩

par·a·dise \ˈparəˌdīs *also* ˈper- *or* -īz\ *n* -S [ME *paradis*, fr. OF, fr. LL *paradisus*, fr. Gk *paradeisos* enclosed park, garden, orchard, paradise, of Iranian origin; akin to Av *pairi-daēza-* enclosure, fr. *pairi* around + *daēza-* wall; akin to Gk *peri* around and to Gk *teichos* wall — more at PERI-, DOUGH] **1 a :** a place or state in which the souls of the righteous after death enjoy eternal bliss **:** HEAVEN **b :** an intermediate elysium for the souls of the righteous during the interval between death and final judgment **2 a :** a place of bliss **:** a region of supreme felicity or delight ⟨an earthly ~⟩ ⟨a ~ for children⟩; *esp* **:** a place characterized by favorable conditions, special opportunities, or the abundance of something ⟨a tourist's ~⟩ ⟨a gourmet's ~⟩ ⟨a vacation ~⟩ ⟨a ~ for ducks⟩ **b :** a state of happiness ⟨the lost ~ of childhood⟩ **3 a :** a pleasure garden; *esp* **:** an oriental park **b :** a preserve for foreign birds and animals **4 :** an open space in a monastery or next to a church (as in a cloister) or the open court before a basilica **5 :** the plumage (as the long tail feathers) of the male bird of paradise formerly used in millinery **6** *or* **paradise apple** *often cap P* **:** a small Asiatic wild apple (*Malus sylvestris paradisiaca*) used principally as a dwarfing rootstock and the source of several of the Malling rootstocks **7 :** PARADISE FISH

par·a·dise·an \ˌ==ˈdi|sēən, -ˈdī, |zē-\ *adj* [ML *paradiseus* paradisiacal (fr. L *paradisus*) + E *-an*] **:** relating to birds of paradise

paradise bird *n* **:** BIRD OF PARADISE 1

paradise duck *or* **paradise sheldrake** *n* **:** a highly colored New Zealand duck (*Tadorna variegata*) related to the sheldrake

paradise finch *n* **:** PAINTED BUNTING

paradise fish *n* **:** a brilliantly colored freshwater labyrinth fish (*Macropodus opercularis*) of eastern Asia with very large fins often kept in aquariums; *also* **:** a closely related fish (*M. chinensis*) having a rounded tail

paradise flower *n* **:** an arborescent cat's-claw (*Acacia greggii*) with fragrant creamy yellow flowers that is an important browse and wildlife feed in arid parts of the southwestern U.S. and adjacent Mexico

paradise flycatcher *n* **:** any of numerous Asiatic or African flycatchers belonging to the genus *Terpsiphone* in most of which the males have the central tail feathers greatly elongated

paradise grackle *or* **paradise pie** *n* **:** a beautiful long-tailed bird of paradise (*Astrapia nigra*) of New Guinea having dark velvety plumage with brilliant metallic tints

paradise green *n* **:** HIBERNIAN GREEN

paradise grosbeak *n* **:** CUTTHROAT 2

paradise nut *n* **:** SAPUCAIA NUT

paradise plant *n* **:** MEZEREON 1

paradise tree *n* **1 a :** a medium-sized to large-sized tree (*Simarouba glauca*) that occurs from southern Florida to the northern part of So. America and has odd-pinnate leaves and long terminal much branched panicles of small pale yellow flowers borne in early spring and followed by scarlet to dark purple fruits **b :** MARUPA **2 :** CHINABERRY 2

paradise weaver *or* **paradise whydah** *n* **:** a whydah (*Vidua paradiseae*) that is usu. marked with buff or brown and occurs in several distinct subspecies

par·a·di·si·a·cal \ˌ==dəˈsīəkəl, -dīˈ-, -zī- *also* **par·a·dis·i·ac** \ˌ==ˈdisēˌak, -izē-\ *adj* [*paradisiacal* fr. LL *paradisiacus* (fr. *paradisus* paradise) + E *-al*; *paradisiac* fr. LL *paradisiacus*] **:** of, relating to, or resembling paradise ⟨an age of ~ happiness —H.A.Overstreet⟩ ⟨~ innocence⟩ ⟨conception of a ~ state of nature —W.A.Kaufmann⟩ — **par·a·di·si·a·cal·ly** \-ˌdəˈsīək(ə)lē, -dī-, -ˌzī-, -li\ *adv*

par·a·dis·i·al \ˌ==ˈdisēəl, -izē- *also* **par·a·dis·i·an** \-ēən\ *or* **par·a·dis·ic** \-sik, -zik\ *or* **par·a·dis·i·cal** \-səkəl, -zə-\ *adj* [*paradise* + *-ial* or *-ian* or *-ic* or *-ical*] **:** PARADISIACAL ⟨a ~ country⟩ ⟨a ~ people⟩ ⟨~ isles⟩

pa·ra·do \pəˈrä(ˌ)dō, -rā-\ *n* -S [modif. of F *parade* — more at PARADE] **1** *obs* **:** PARADE **2 :** a boastful swaggering air

para·doctor \ˈparə+ˌ-\ *n* [²*para-* + *doctor*] **:** a doctor who reaches isolated areas by parachute

par·a·don·tal \ˌparəˈdäntᵊl\ *adj* [¹*para-* + Gk *odont-, odous* tooth + E *-al* — more at TOOTH] **:** PERIODONTAL 2 ⟨~ disease⟩

par·a·don·to·sis \ˌparəˌdänˈtōsəs\ *n, pl* **paradonto·ses** \-ōˌsēz\ [NL, fr. ¹*para-* + Gk *odont-, odous* + NL *-osis*] **:** PERIODONTOSIS

para·dos \ˈparəˌdäs, -dōs, -dō\ *n, pl* **parados** \-dōz\ *or* **paradoses** \-däsəz, -dōsəz\ [F, fr. *para-* (as in *parasol*) + *dos* back, fr. L *dorsum* — more at PARASOL] **:** a bank of earth behind a fortification trench — compare PARAPET 1

¹**par·a·dox** \ˈparəˌdäks *also* ˈper-\ *n* -ES [L *paradoxum*, fr. Gk *paradoxon*, fr. neut. of *paradoxos* contrary to expectation, incredible, fr. *para-* ¹para + *-doxos* (fr. *dokein* to think) — more at DECENT] **1 :** a tenet or proposition contrary to received opinion **2 a :** a statement or sentiment that is seemingly contradictory or opposed to common sense and yet perhaps true in fact ⟨present-day ~es like "mobilizing for peace" —E.R.May⟩ ⟨~ that the more terrible the prospect of thermonuclear war becomes, the less likely it is to happen —*Blackwood's*⟩ ⟨here is a noble ~: religion tries to satisfy man while its essential purpose is to make him dissatisfied —W.L.Sullivan⟩ **2 b** (1) **:** a statement that is actually self-contradictory and hence false even though its true character is not immediately apparent (2) **:** an argument that apparently derives self-contradictory conclusions by valid deduction from acceptable premises — see LIAR PARADOX, RUSSELL'S PARADOX **3 :** something (as a human being, phenomenon, state of affairs, or action) with seemingly contradictory qualities or phases ⟨she is an interesting ~, an infinitely shy person with an enormously intuitive gift for understanding people —*Current Biog.*⟩ ⟨the colonel . . . is a ~ — a well-known secret agent —John Kobler⟩ ⟨there is ~ in the fact that the artist has come into his own in an age which hates him —W.P.Clancy⟩ ⟨his lectures on mechanical ~es (such as man's lifting himself by his own bootstraps, rolling a barrel uphill by gravity) —C.W.Mitman⟩ ⟨the ~ of impoverished people in a rich land —*Univ. of Minn. Press Cat.*⟩

²**paradox** \"\ *vi* **:** to utter paradoxes

par·a·dox·al \ˌ==ˈdäksəl\ *adj* **:** PARADOXICAL — **par·a·dox·al·i·ty** \ˌ==ˌdäkˈsaləd·ē\ *n* -ES

par·a·dox·er \ˈ==ˌdäksə(r)\ *n* -S **:** one that propounds paradoxes

par·a·dox·i·al \ˌ==ˈdäksēəl, -kshəl\ *or* **par·a·dox·ic** \-ˈdäksik, -sēk\ *adj* **:** PARADOXICAL

par·a·dox·i·cal \ˌ==ˈdäksəkəl, -sēk-\ *adj* **1 a :** of the nature of a paradox ⟨the ~ theory that ice ages occur as the sun gets hotter —R.W.Murray⟩ ⟨in the ~ heart of all of us is the perennial longing to be what we are not —J.L.Lowes⟩ ⟨however ~ it may look at first sight, idealism . . . is actually nearer to common sense than is materialism —C.H.Whiteley⟩ ⟨introvert with a strong and ~ sympathy for his fellowman —J.C.Cort⟩ **b :** inclined to paradoxes **2 :** not being the normal or usual kind ⟨~ embolism⟩ ⟨~ pulse⟩ — **par·a·dox·i·cal·i·ty** \ˌ==ˌ==ˈkaləd·ē, -ətē, -i\ *n* -ES — **par·a·dox·i·cal·ly** \ˌ==ˈdäksək(ə)lē, -sēk-, -li\ *adv* — **par·a·dox·i·cal·ness** \ˌ==ˈsəkəlnəs, -sēk-\ *n* -ES

par·a·dox·i·des \ˌ==ˈdäksəˌdēz\ *n, cap* [NL, fr. L *paradoxum* paradox + *-ides*] **:** a genus of trilobites of the Middle Cambrian having from 17 to 20 free segments, a large cephalic shield, and a very small pygidium and sometimes reaching a length of about two feet

par·a·dox·ist \ˈ==ˌdäksəst\ *n* -S **:** one who deals in paradoxes

par·a·dox·ol·o·gist \ˌ==ˌdäkˈsäləjəst\ *n* -S **:** one who uses or is skilled in the use of paradoxes; *specif* **:** one who stresses the use of paradoxes in theology

par·a·dox·ol·o·gy \-jē\ *n* -ES [Gk *paradoxologia*, fr. *paradoxon* paradox + *-logia* -logy — more at PARADOX] **:** the use of paradoxes

par·a·dox·or·nis \ˌparəˌdäkˈsȯrnəs\ *n, cap* [NL, fr. L *paradoxus* contrary to expectation + NL *-ornis* — more at PARADOX] **:** a genus (the type of the family Paradoxornithidae) of Asiatic large-headed gregarious passerine birds including the typical crow tits

par·a·dox·ure \ˌparəˈdäkshə(r)\ *n* -S [NL *Paradoxurus*] **:** a palm civet of the genus *Paradoxurus*

¹**par·a·dox·u·rine** \-shəˌrīn\ *adj* [NL *Paradoxurus* + E *-ine*] **:** of or relating to the genus *Paradoxurus*

²**paradoxurine** \"\ *n* -S **:** a palm civet of the genus *Paradoxurus*

par·a·dox·urus \ˌparəˌdäkˈshu̇rəs\ *n, cap* [NL, fr. Gk *paradoxos* contrary to expectation + NL *-urus*] **:** a genus of carnivorous mammals (family Viverridae) comprising the typical palm civets

par·a·doxy \ˈ==ˌdäksē\ *n* -ES [Gk *paradoxia*, fr. *paradoxos* + *-ia* -y — more at PARADOX] **:** the quality or state of being paradoxical

para·dromic \ˌparəˈdrämik, -rōm-\ *adj* [Gk *paradromos* paradromic (fr. *para-* ¹para- + *-dromos* -dromous) + E *-ic*] **:** running side by side **:** following a parallel course

para·dro·mism \ˈparəˌdrōˌmizəm, pəˈradrəˌmi-\ *n* -S [*paradromic* + *-ism*] **:** PARALLELISM

¹**para·drop** \ˈparə+ˌ-\ *n* [²*para-* + *drop* (n.)] **:** AIRDROP

²**paradrop** \"\ *vt* [²*para-* + *drop* (v.)] **:** AIR-DROP

parae *pl of* PARA

-parae *pl of* -PARA

pa·raene·sis *also* **pa·rene·sis** \pəˈrēnəsəs, -ren-\ *n, pl* **paraene·ses** *also* **parene·ses** \-nəˌsēz\ [LL *paraenesis*, fr. Gk *parainesis*, fr. *parainein* to advise (fr. *para-* ¹para- + *ainein* to speak of, praise, advise, fr. *ainos* speech, fable) + *-sis*] **:** an exhortatory composition **:** ADVICE, COUNSEL — **par·ae·net·ic** *also* **par·e·net·ic** \ˌparəˈned·ik\ *adj* — **par·ae·net·i·cal** *also* **par·e·net·i·cal** \-d·əkəl\ *adj*

paraesthesia *var of* PARESTHESIA

¹**par·af·fin** \ˈparəfən *also* ˈper-\ *also* **par·af·fine** \" *also* -ˌfēn\ *n* -S [G *paraffin*, fr. L *parum* too little + *affinis* bordering on, related by marriage; akin to *paucus* few, little — more at FEW, AFFINITY] **1 a** *or* **paraffin wax :** a waxy crystalline substance that is white, translucent, odorless, and tasteless when pure, that is obtained esp. from distillates of wood, coal, or now usu. petroleum or shale oil, that is a complex mixture of hydrocarbons principally of the methane series, that is resistant to water and water vapor and is chemically inert, and that is used chiefly in coating and sealing, in making candles, in impregnating matches, in rubber compounding, in electrical insulation, and in pharmaceuticals and cosmetics — called also *hard paraffin;* compare CERESIN, MICROCRYSTALLINE WAX, SCALE WAX, SLACK WAX **b :** any of various mixtures of similar hydrocarbons including mixtures that are semisolid or oily ⟨soft ~⟩ — compare LIQUID PETROLATUM, PETROLATUM **2** *or* **paraffin hydrocarbon :** a hydrocarbon of the methane series **:** ALKANE **3** *chiefly Brit* **:** KEROSENE

²**paraffin** \"\ *vt* -ED/-ING/-S **:** to treat, coat, or saturate with paraffin **:** apply paraffin to

paraffin–base \ˈ===ˌ=\ *adj* **:** containing relatively large amounts of paraffin hydrocarbons **:** yielding paraffin wax on refining — used esp. of crude petroleum; compare ASPHALT-BASE, NAPHTHENE-BASE

paraffin distillate *n* **:** a petroleum fraction that is usu. obtained after most of the gas oil has distilled and that contains chiefly lubricating oils and paraffin wax

par·af·fin·er \ˈ==ˌfənə(r) *also* -ˌfēn-\ *n* -S **:** a worker who pours or sprays melted paraffin into barrels to prevent leakage and contact of stored liquid with wood

par·af·fin·ic \ˌ==ˈfinik\ *adj* **:** of, relating to, or characterized by paraffin hydrocarbons or paraffin wax **:** PARAFFIN-BASE ⟨~ hydrocarbons⟩ ⟨~ crudes⟩ — **par·af·fin·ic·i·ty** \ˌ==ˌfəˈnisəd·ē\ *n* -ES

par·af·fin·ize \ˈ==ˌfəˌnīz\ *vt* -ED/-ING/-S [¹*paraffin* + *-ize*] **:** PARAFFIN

paraffin jelly *n* **:** PETROLATUM a

par·af·fin·oid \ˈ==fəˌnȯid\ *adj* [¹*paraffin* + *-oid*] **:** resembling or related to paraffin **:** belonging to the methane series

paraffin oil *n* **1 :** any of various hydrocarbon oils usu. obtained from petroleum: as **a :** a lubricating oil from paraffin distillate **b** *chiefly Brit* **:** KEROSENE **2 :** LIQUID PETROLATUM

paraffin scale *n* **:** SCALE WAX

paraffin series *n* **:** METHANE SERIES

paraffin test *n* **:** a test in which a paraffin cast of the hand of a person suspected of firing a gun is subjected to chemical analysis to determine the presence of powder particles

para·flocculus \ˌparə+\ *n, pl* **paraflocculi** [NL, fr. ¹*para-* + *flocculus*] **:** a lateral accessory part of the flocculus of the cerebellum

para·follicular \"+\ *adj* [¹*para-* + *follicular*] **:** located in the vicinity of or surrounding a follicle ⟨~ cells of the canine thyroid⟩

para·form \ˈparəˌfȯrm\ *n* [by shortening] **:** PARAFORMALDEHYDE

para·formaldehyde \ˌparə+\ *n* [ISV ¹*para-* + *formaldehyde*] **:** a white solid that is a mixture of hydrated polymers of formaldehyde having the formula $(HCHO)_n.H_2O$ or HO-$(CH_2O)_nH$ in which *n* varies from about 8 to 100, that is usu. made by evaporation of an aqueous solution of formaldehyde, that readily regenerates formaldehyde esp. on heating, and that is used as a source of formaldehyde **:** a mixture of polyoxymethylene glycols

para·fos·sar·u·lus \ˌparəˌfäˈsar(y)ələs\ *n, cap* [NL, fr. ¹*para-* + *Fossarulus* genus of snails, dim. of LL *fossarius* fossor — more at FOSSARIAN] **:** a genus of East Asian freshwater snails (family Bulimidae) including important intermediate hosts of the Chinese liver fluke

para·foulbrood \ˌparə+\ *n* [¹*para-* + *foulbrood*] **:** a bacterial disease of the honeybee

para·foveal \"+\ *adj* [¹*para-* + *foveal*] **1 :** surrounding the fovea ⟨~ regions of the retina⟩ **2 :** dependent on parts of the retina external to the fovea ⟨~ vision⟩ ⟨~ threshold of reaction⟩

para fuchsine *n, often cap P&F* [⁶*para*] **:** the chloride of pararosaniline base — see DYE table I (under *Basic Red 9*)

para·gam·ma·cism \ˌparəˈgaməˌsizəm\ *also* **para·gam·ma·cis·mus** \ˌ==ˌ==ˈsizməs\ *n, pl* **paragammacisms** *also* **paragammacismuses** [NL *paragammacismus*, fr. ¹*para-* + *gammacismus* gammacism — more at GAMMACISM] **:** inability to pronounce the sound of *g* and *k* or difficulty in pronouncing them

para·ganglioma \ˌparə+\ *n* [NL, fr. ¹*para-* + *ganglioma*] **:** a ganglioma derived from chromaffin cells

para·ganglion \"+\ *n* [ISV ¹*para-* + *ganglion*] **:** one of numerous collections of chromaffin tissue associated with the collateral and chain ganglia of the sympathetic nerves and similar in structure to the medulla of the suprarenal glands — **para·ganglionic** \"+\ *adj*

para·gas·ter \ˈparəˌgastə(r), ˌ==ˈ==\ *n* -S [¹*para-* + *-gaster*] **:** a paragastric cavity

para·gastric *also* **para·gastral** \ˌparə+\ *adj* [¹*para-* + *gastric, gastral*] **1 :** situated near the stomach **2 :** being the cavity or one of the cavities of a sponge into which the radial canals open and which opens outwardly through the cloaca

para·gastrula \"+\ *n* [NL, fr. ¹*para-* + *gastrula*] **:** the gastrula formed by the invagination of an amphiblastula (as in many sponges) — **para·gastrular** \"+\ *adj*

parage \ˈparij, pəˈräzh\ *n* -S [ME, fr. OF *parage, perage*, fr. *par, per* equal (fr. L *par*) + *-age* — more at PAIR] **:** equality of condition, blood, or dignity; *specif* **:** equality between persons (as brothers) one of whom holds a part of a fee of the other, does homage to the lord paramount, and is responsible for the whole service of the fee

para·genesis \ˌparə+\ *n* [NL, fr. ¹*para-* + L *genesis*] **1 :** the formation of minerals in contact so as to affect one another's development **2 :** the order in which minerals occurring together in rocks and veins have developed together with the characteristic grouping or association of the minerals — **para·genetic** \ˌparə+\ *adj*

para·geosyncline \ˌparə+\ *n* [¹*para-* + *geosyncline*] **:** a geosyncline within or adjacent to a craton and usu. less elongated, shallower, and less persistent than an orthogeosyncline

par·agglutination \ˌpar+\ *n* [ISV ¹*para-* + *agglutination*] **:** CROSS AGGLUTINATION

para·glossa \"+\ *n, pl* **paraglossae** [NL, fr. *para-* + Gk *glōssa* tongue — more at GLOSS] **:** one of a pair of small appendages of the labium of various insects — **para·glossal** \"+\ *adj*

para·glossate \"+\ *adj* [NL *paraglossa* + E *-ate*] **:** having paraglossae

para·glos·sia \ˌparəˈgläsēə, -lȯs-\ *n* -S [NL, fr. ¹*para-* + *-glossia*] **:** inflammation of the tissues under or about the tongue

para·glycogen \ˌparə+\ *n* [ISV ¹*para-* + *glycogen*] **:** a carbohydrate storage product in protozoa that resembles glycogen of higher animals

par·ag·nath \ˈparəgˌnath\ *n* -S [ISV ¹*para-* + Gk *gnathos* jaw — more at GNATH-] **1 :** one of a pair of foliose lobes of the metastoma lying behind the mandibles in most crustaceans **2 :** one of the paired lobes of the hypopharynx in various insects **3 :** one of the small horny toothlike jaws of various annelids

pa·rag·na·thism \pəˈragnəˌthizəm, paˈr-\ *n* -S [*paragnathous* + *-ism*] **:** the paragnathous condition

pa·rag·na·thous \pəˈragnəthəs, (ˈ)paˌr-\ *adj* [¹*para-* + *-gnathous*] **:** having both mandibles of equal length with the tips meeting — used esp. of a bird

pa·rag·na·thus \pəˈragnəthəs, paˈr-\ *n, pl* **paragna·tha** \-thə\ [NL, fr. ¹*para-* + Gk *gnathos* jaw] **:** PARAGNATH

para·gneiss \ˌparə+\ *n* [ISV ¹*para-* + *gneiss*] **:** gneiss derived from a sedimentary rock

par·a·go·ge \ˌparəˈgōjē *sometimes* -gäjē *or* ˌ==ˈ==\ *n* -S [LL, fr. Gk *paragōgē*, fr. *paragesthai* to be derived, be formed, passive of *paragein* to lead past, change (a letter slightly), fr. *par-* ¹para- + *agein* to lead, drive — more at AGENT] **:** the addition of a sound or syllable to the end of a word either inorganically (as in *against*) or to give emphasis or modify the meaning (as in Hebrew)

par·a·gog·ic \ˌ==ˈgäjik\ *also* **par·a·gog·i·cal** \-jəkəl\ *adj* **:** of, relating to, or constituting a paragoge ⟨a ~ vowel⟩ — **par·a·gog·i·cal·ly** \-jək(ə)lē\ *adv*

¹**par·a·gon** \ˈparəˌgän *also* ˈper- *or* -gən\ *n* -S [MF, fr. OIt *paragone*, lit., touchstone, fr. *paragonare* to compare, test on a touchstone, fr. Gk *parakonan* to rub against, sharpen, fr. *par-* ¹para- + *akonan* to sharpen, fr. *akonē* whetstone, fr. *akē* point — more at EDGE] **1 :** a model of excellence or perfection **:** PATTERN ⟨a ~ of beauty⟩ ⟨a ~ of eloquence⟩ ⟨a ~ of virtue⟩ ⟨these fictional ~s, whose unalloyed happiness depends upon the determination to grin and bear it —W.F.Hambly⟩ ⟨the handsome . . . factory, a ~ in its day —Lewis Mumford⟩ ⟨the French court . . . the ~ of all the lesser courts —Walter Lippmann⟩ **2** *archaic* **a :** COMPANION, MATE **b :** RIVAL **3** *obs* **:** EMULATION, RIVALRY, COMPETITION **4** *obs* **:** a clothing and upholstery fabric of the 17th and 18th centuries similar to camlet **5 a :** a perfect diamond of 100 carats or more **b :** a perfectly spherical pearl of exceptional size **6 :** a black marble **7 :** an old size of type of approximately 20 point and slightly larger than great primer

²**paragon** \"\ *vt* -ED/-ING/-S [MF *paragonner*, fr. *paragon*, n.] **1 :** to compare with **:** PARALLEL **2 :** to put in rivalry **3** *obs* **:** SURPASS ⟨a maid that ~s description —Shak.⟩

par·a·gon·i·mi·a·sis \ˌparəˌgänəˈmīəsəs\ *n, pl* **paragonimiases** \-əˌsēz\ [NL, fr. *Paragonimus* (genus name of *Paragonimus westermanii*) + *-iasis*] **:** infestation with or disease caused by a lung fluke (*Paragonimus westermanii*) that invades the lung where it produces chronic bronchitis with cough and reddish or brownish sputum and that occas. also enters other viscera or the brain

par·a·gon·i·mus \ˌparəˈgänəməs\ *n, cap* [NL, fr. ¹*para-* + Gk *gonimos* productive — more at GONIMOBLAST] **:** a genus of digenetic trematodes (family Troglotrematidae) comprising forms normally parasitic in the lungs of mammals including man — compare PARAGONIMIASIS

pa·rag·o·nite \pəˈragəˌnīt, ˈparəg-\ *n* -S [G *paragonit*, fr. Gk *paragōn* (pres. part. of *paragein* to lead past, mislead) + G *-it* -ite — more at PARAGOGE] **:** a mica $NaAl_3Si_3O_{10}(OH)_2$ corresponding to muscovite but with sodium instead of potassium — **pa·rag·o·nit·ic** \ˌ=ˌ==ˈnid·ik, |===-\ *adj*

paragonize *vt* -ED/-ING/-S [¹*paragon* + *-ize*] *obs* **:** PARAGON

para·gram \ˈparəˌgram\ *n* [Gk (*skōmma*) *para gramma* (joke) by letter, fr. *para* beside, beyond, by + *gramma* letter — more at PARA-, GRAM] **:** a pun made by changing the letters of a word, esp. the initial letter — **para·gram·ma·tist** \ˌ==ˈgraməd·əst\ *n* -S

¹**par·a·graph** \ˈparəˌgraf, -graa(ə)f, -graif, -gräf *also* ˈper-\ *n* [MF & ML; MF *paragraphe* section of writing, fr. ML *paragraphus* sign used to mark a new section of writing, fr. Gk *paragraphos* line used to mark change of persons in a dialogue, fr. *paragraphein* to write alongside, fr. *para-* ¹para- + *graphein* to write — more at CARVE] **1 a :** a distinct section or subdivision of a written or printed composition that consists of from one to many sentences, forms a rhetorical unit (as by dealing with a particular point of the subject or by comprising the words of a distinct speaker), and is indicated by beginning on a new usu. indented line **b :** a usu. numbered article or section of a law or legal document **c :** a short composition consisting of a group of sentences dealing with a single topic **d :** a short article, item, or note in a newspaper or magazine that is complete in one typographical section **2 :** a character (as ¶) used to indicate the beginning of a paragraph (as in manuscripts and printer's proofs) and in printing as the sixth in series of the reference marks

²**paragraph** \"\ *vt* **1 :** to write paragraphs about **:** mention in a paragraph ⟨sneered at by all my acquaintance and ~ed in the newspapers —R.B.Sheridan⟩ **2 :** to divide into paragraphs ⟨the Revised Version is much better ~ed than the Authorized —J.T.Sunderland⟩ ~ *vi* **:** to write paragraphs; *specif* **:** to work as a paragrapher

par·a·graph·er \ˈ==ˌ=ə(r)\ *n* -S **:** a writer of paragraphs esp. for the editorial page of a newspaper

para·graph·ia \ˌ==ˈgrafēə\ *n* -S [NL, fr. ¹*para-* + *-graphia*] **:** a condition in mental disorder or brain injury in which words or letters other than those intended are written

par·a·graph·ic \ˌ==ˈgrafik, -fēk\ *or* **para·graph·i·cal** \-fəkəl, -fēk-\ *adj* **:** of, relating to, or having the characteristics of a paragraph — **par·a·graph·i·cal·ly** \-fək(ə)lē, -fēk-, -li\ *adv*

par·a·graph·ist \ˈ==ˌgrafəst, -raaf-, -raif-, -räf-\ *n* -S **:** PARAGRAPHER

para grass *n, usu cap P* [fr. *Pará*, state and city in Brazil] **1 :** a perennial pasture and green forage grass (*Panicum purpurascens*) grown in tropical countries and esp. suited to soils too wet for other crops **2 :** piassava fiber

par·a·guay \ˈparəˌgwī, -wā *also* ˈper-\ *adj, usu cap* [fr. *Paraguay*, country of So. America] **:** of or from Paraguay **:** of the kind or style prevalent in Paraguay **:** PARAGUAYAN

¹**par·a·guay·an** \ˌ==ˈgwīən, -ˈgwāən\ *adj, usu cap* [Sp *paraguayano*, adj. & n., fr. *Paraguay*, country in So. America + Sp *-ano* -an] **:** of, relating to, or characteristic of Paraguay

²**paraguayan** \"\ *n* -S *cap* [Sp *paraguayano*] **:** a native or inhabitant of Paraguay

paraguay bur *n* **:** SHEEP BUR a

paraguay tea *n, usu cap P* **:** MATÉ

para·hematin \ˌparə+\ *n* [¹*para-* + *hematin*] **:** a combination of a ferriporphyrin with a nitrogen base (as pyridine) — compare HEMOCHROMOGEN 1

para·hemophilia \"+\ *n* [NL, fr. ¹*para-* + *hemophilia*] **:** a tendency to bleed due to the absence of a clotting factor in the blood

para·hepatic \"+\ *adj* [¹*para-* + *hepatic*] **:** adjacent to the liver

para·hilgardite \"+\ *n* [¹*para-* + *hilgardite*] **:** a mineral $Ca_8(B_6O_{11})_3Cl_4.4H_2O$ consisting of a hydrous borate and chloride of calcium dimorphous with hilgardite

para·hippus \ˌparəˈhipəs\ *n, cap* [NL, fr. ¹*para-* + *-hippus*] **:** a genus of Miocene horses intermediate in structure between the genera *Miohippus* and *Merychippus* and having three digits on each foot

para·hopeite \¦parə+\ *n* [¹*para-* + *hopeite*] **:** a mineral $Zn_3(PO_4)_2.4H_2O$ consisting of a hydrous zinc phosphate, being dimorphous with hopeite, and occurring in colorless tabular triclinic crystals (hardness 3.7, sp. gr. 3.3)

para·hormone *or* **para·hormonic** \"+\ *n* [*parahormone* fr. ¹*para-* + *hormone; parahormonic* fr. ¹*para-* + *hormone* + *-ic*] **:** a substance that functions as a hormone but is of relatively nonspecific nature (as carbon dioxide in its effect on the respiratory center in the brain)

para-hydrogen \¦parə+\ *n* [¹*para-* + *hydrogen*] **:** molecular hydrogen in which the two hydrogen nuclei are spinning in opposite directions so that their contribution to the total angular momentum is zero — compare ORTHO-HYDROGEN

para-hydroxybenzoic acid \"+...\ *n* [¹*para-* + *hydroxybenzoic*] **:** HYDROXYBENZOIC ACID a — written systematically with ital. *para-* or *p-*

paraison *var of* PARISON

pa·rai·yan \pə'rī(y)ən\ *n* -s *usu cap* [Tamil *paraiyan* — more at PARIAH] **1 :** a member of the pariah caste **2 :** a Dravidian laboring class

parakeet *var of* PARRAKEET

par·a·ke·lia *also* **par·a·kee·lia** *or* **par·a·kil·ya** \,parə'kēlyə\ *n* -s [native name in Australia] **:** a succulent herb (*Calandrinia balonensis*) that is an important livestock feed in drier parts of interior Australia

para·keratosis \¦parə+\ *n* [NL, fr. ¹*para-* + *keratosis*] **:** an abnormality of the horny layer of the skin resulting in a disturbance in the process of keratinization — **para·keratotic** \"+\ *adj*

para·ki·ne·sia \,parə,kī'nēzh(ē)ə, -,kə'-\ *or* **para·ki·ne·sis** \-ēsəs\ *n, pl* **parakine·sias** \-ēzh(ē)əz\ *or* **parakine·ses** \-ē,sēz\ [NL, fr. ¹*para-* + *-kinesia* or Gk *kinēsis* motion — more at KINESIS] **:** disorder of motor function resulting in strange and abnormal movements — **para·ki·net·ic** \¦==(,)==¦ned·ik\ *adj*

pa·ral·a·brax \pə'ralə,braks\ *n, cap* [NL, fr. ¹*para-* + Gk *labrax* bass] **:** a common genus of Pacific sea basses (family Serranidae) including the kelp bass of California

para·lalia \,parə'lālēə, -'lal-\ *n* -s [NL, fr. ¹*para-* + *-lalia*] **:** a speech disorder marked by distortions of sounds or substitution of letters

para·lambdacism \¦parə+\ *n* [¹*para-* + *lambdacism*] **:** inability to pronounce the sound of *l* or difficulty in pronouncing it with some other sound (as of *t, r,* or *w*) being usu. substituted — compare LAMBDACISM

para·laurionite \"+\ *n* [¹*para-* + *laurionite*] **:** a mineral PbCl(OH) consisting of a basic lead chloride dimorphous with laurionite (sp. gr. 6.1)

par·aldehyde \(')par+\ *n* [¹*para-* + *aldehyde*] **:** a colorless liquid of pleasant odor but disagreeable taste that is a cyclic trimer $C_6H_{12}O_3$ of acetaldehyde formed by adding a drop or two of sulfuric acid to acetaldehyde, that regenerates acetaldehyde on heating with dilute acids, and that is used chiefly as a source of acetaldehyde and as a hypnotic; trimethyl-trioxane — compare METALDEHYDE

par·aldol \"+\ *n* [ISV ¹*para-* + *aldol*] **:** a crystalline cyclic dimer $C_8H_{16}O_4$ of aldol that separates from aldol on standing

para·lectotype \¦parə+\ *n* [¹*para-* + *lectotype*] **:** any of a type series remaining after the designation of the lectotype

para·leip·sis \,parə'līpsəs, -lāp-\ *or* **para·lep·sis** \-lep-\ *or* **para·lip·sis** \-lip-\ *n, pl* **paraleip·ses** *or* **paralep·ses** *or* **paralip·ses** \-p(,)sēz\ [LL & Gk; LL *paraleipsis, paralipsis*, fr. Gk *paraleipsis* neglect, omission, paraleipsis, fr. *paraleipein* to neglect, omit, leave untold (fr. *para-* ¹para- + *leipein* to leave) + *-sis* — more at LOAN] **:** a passing over with brief mention in order to emphasize rhetorically the suggestiveness of what is omitted (as in "I confine to this page the volume of his treacheries and debaucheries")

para·lex·ia \,parə'leksēə\ *n* -s [NL, fr. ¹*para-* + *-lexia*] **:** a disturbance in reading ability marked by the transposition of words or syllables and usu. associated with brain injury — **para·lex·ic** \¦==¦sik\ *adj*

par·algesia \¦par+\ *n* [NL, fr. ¹*para-* + *algesia*] **:** disordered or abnormal sensation — **par·algesic** \"+\ *adj*

pa·ral·ic \pə'ralik\ *adj* [ISV *paral-* (fr. Gk *paralia* seacoast, fr. *para-* ¹para- + *hal-, hals* salt, sea + *-ia* -y) + *-ic* — more at SALT] **:** of, relating to, or being interfingered marine and continental sediments

par·al·ich·thys \,parə'likthəs\ *n, cap* [NL, fr. Gk *paralia* + *ichthys* fish — more at ICHTHUS] **:** a widespread genus of flatfishes that includes the summer flounder, the California halibut, and other important food fishes and that is sometimes made type of a separate family but is usu. included in Bothidae

para·limnetic \¦parə+\ *adj* [¹*para-* + *limnetic*] **:** of, relating to, or constituting a paralimnion

para·limnion \¦parə¦limnē,än, -ēən\ *n* -s [NL, fr. ¹*para-* + *-limnion*] **:** the littoral portion of a lake extending from the margin to the deepest limit of rooted vegetation

para·li·pom·e·na \,parələ'pämənə, -,lī'-\ *n pl* [LL, fr. Gk *paraleipomena*, lit., things left out, fr. neut. pl. of *paraleipomenos*, pres. pass. part. of *paraleipein* to omit — more at PARALEIPSIS] **:** things passed over but added as a supplement ⟨political writings as obvious ~ done merely to make money —H.J.Laski⟩

par·al·lac·tic \¦parə¦laktik\ *adj* [NL *parallacticus*, fr. Gk *parallaktikos*, fr. *parallaxis* parallax — more at PARALLAX] **:** of, relating to, or due to parallax

parallactic angle *n* **:** the spherical angle between the hour circle and the vertical circle passing through a celestial body

parallactic equation *n* **:** a minor inequality of the moon's orbital motion caused by the difference between the sun's perturbing action on the moon when at new and full and used in finding the sun's parallax

parallactic libration of the moon : diurnal libration of the moon caused by the observer's view over the upper limb of the moon when it is rising and setting

parallactic motion *n* **:** the part of the observed proper motion of a star that is caused by the motion of the observer with the solar system as a whole

parallactic orbit *n* **:** the orbit in which a star appears to move once round each year owing to the earth's orbital motion round the sun

par·al·lax \'parə,laks\ *n* -ES [MF *parallaxe*, fr. Gk *parallaxis* change, alternation, parallax, fr. *parallassein* to change, differ, fr. *para-* ¹para- + *allassein* to change, fr. *allos* other, different — more at ELSE] **1 :** the apparent displacement or the difference in apparent direction of an object as seen from two different points not on a straight line with the object ⟨our two eyes are as a rule only about 2¼ inches apart; yet the small ~ caused by the slightly different angle of vision enables us to see three-dimensional, plastic images —Erwin Raisz⟩ **2 a :** GEOCENTRIC PARALLAX **b :** HELIOCENTRIC PARALLAX **c :** STELLAR PARALLAX **d :** HORIZONTAL PARALLAX

¹par·al·lel \'parə,lel *also* 'per- *or* -rələl *sometimes* ,==¦lel\ *adj* [L *parallelus*, fr. Gk *parallēlos*, fr. *para* beside + *allēlōn* of one another, fr. *allos* . . . *allos* one . . . the other — more at PARA-, ELSE] **1 :** extending in the same direction and everywhere equidistant **:** forming a line in the same direction but not meeting ⟨half a dozen ~ scars . . . ran from his forehead into the thickness of his hair —Eric Linklater⟩ ⟨~ rows of tall poplars —*Amer. Guide Series: Wash.*⟩ ⟨the ships steam on ~ courses as close together as feasible —W.D.Leggett⟩ ⟨a long, low house running ~ with the road —G.K.Chesterton⟩ ⟨a line ~ to the edge of a paper⟩ **2 a :** not meeting however far extended — used of lines in the same plane, of planes, or of a line and a plane **b :** everywhere equally distant ⟨concentric circles are ~⟩ ⟨concentric spheres are ~⟩ ⟨involutes of the same space curve are ~⟩ **3 a :** having parallel sides ⟨a ~ file⟩ ⟨a ~ gutter⟩ ⟨a ~ reamer⟩ **b :** being or relating to an electrical circuit having a number of conductors in parallel **4 a :** marked by likeness or correspondence esp. in time, direction, course, tendency, or development **:** similar, analogous, or interdependent in line followed **:** tending toward the same point or result ⟨~ strikes on the railroads, in the gas and electricity services —Percy Winner⟩ ⟨the standing committee systems in the two Houses are reasonably ~ —Harold Zink⟩ **b :** set side by side **:** capable of being matched **:** COMPANION **:** readily compared or contrasted ⟨the marriage rate turned upward . . . the birth rate entered upon a ~ climb —Oscar Handlin⟩ ⟨all sorts of pranks, ~ to the serious exploits performed by the heroes —R.A.Hall b. 1911⟩ **c** (1) **:** having identical syntactic elements in corresponding positions (2) **:** identical in construction to a syntactic element in a corresponding position **d :** keeping at the same distance apart in musical pitch **:** having consecutive motion ⟨~ voice parts⟩ ⟨~ fifths⟩ — compare CONSECUTIVE INTERVALS **5 :** of or in accordance with philosophical parallelism **syn** see LIKE

²parallel \"\ *n* -s **1 a :** a parallel line, curve, or surface **b** (1) **:** one of the imaginary circles on the surface of the earth paralleling the equator and marking the latitude (2) **:** the corresponding line on a globe or map **c :** one of a series of long trenches that is approximately parallel to the face of fortification works attacked and that is constructed by a besieging force as a cover for troops **d :** a character ‖ used in printing as the fifth in series of the reference marks — often used in pl. **2 a :** something equal or similar in all essential details **:** COUNTERPART ⟨progress that is without ~ in the history of mankind —*Current Biog.*⟩ ⟨the situation of modern man . . . has no ~ in the past —Rudolf Allers⟩ ⟨conductor of such genius that he has no exact ~ in reality —Marcia Davenport⟩ ⟨implements from near the end of the old Stone Age find ~s among those of the Eskimo —A.L.Kroeber⟩ **b :** agreement in many or all essential details **:** RESEMBLANCE, SIMILARITY, ANALOGUE ⟨there are ~s in *Grettis Saga* . . . to encounters like this —W.P.Ker⟩ ⟨pre-Columbian cultural ~s found in the two hemispheres —R.W.Murray⟩ **3 :** a comparison to show resemblance **:** a tracing of similarity ⟨many interesting ~s are drawn with the historical plays of Shakespeare —*Times Lit. Supp.*⟩ **4 a :** parallel position or state of being physically parallel **:** PARALLELISM ⟨deviation of the two visual lines from ~ —H.G.Armstrong⟩ **b :** an arrangement of electrical devices in a circuit in which the same potential difference is applied to two or more resistances with each resistance on a parallel branch of the circuit ⟨several generators operated in ~⟩ — called also *multiple*; contrasted with *series* **5 a :** PARALLEL RULE **b :** a block or strip of metal made with two parallel sides and used esp. in machine-shop work (as for a gage block or for setting up work) **6 :** a raised platform that is parallel with the floor, that has a folding base, and that is used esp. for lights or cameras (as in the theater or in a television studio); *also* **:** the folding base **syn** see COMPARISON

³parallel \"\ *vb* -ED/-ING/-S *vt* **1 :** to set up as closely analogous or agreeing in essential qualities or characteristics **:** COMPARE ⟨he ~s the jollity of Christmas at Dingley Dell with the picture of country life in Attica —Lucien Price⟩ **2 a :** to show something equal or parallel to **:** MATCH ⟨~ that stage of national culture —Deems Taylor⟩ ⟨disablement behavior amongst birds may be ~*ed* in human life —E.A.Armstrong⟩ ⟨with a precipitancy only to be ~*ed* by her exit from this mortal scene —T.L.Peacock⟩ ⟨state of affairs is partially ~*ed* in contemporary medicine —A.L.Kroeber⟩ ⟨long head hair in some humans is ~*ed* by that of Angora cats —Weston LaBarre⟩ **b :** to be or form a parallel to **:** correspond to ⟨a piece of fiction ~*ing* a historical incident⟩ ⟨~*ing* this change in artistic practice is a change in the concurrent critical apologia —Bernard Smith⟩ ⟨program which roughly ~*ed* the private school —J.B.Conant⟩ ⟨the career of the principal character ~s the actual life story —Bennett Cerf⟩ **3** *obs* **:** to produce or adduce as a parallel ⟨my young remembrance cannot ~ a fellow to it —Shak.⟩ **4 :** to place so as to be parallel to or to conform in direction with something ⟨machines comb, ~, and blend the fibers —*Story of Twine in Agriculture*⟩ ⟨three rifles were ~*ed* on pegs —Stephen Crane⟩ **5 :** to extend, run, or move in a direction parallel to **:** correspond to or match in direction ⟨an airstrip ~*ing* the highway⟩ ⟨the route ~s the river⟩ ~ *vi* **:** to be parallel ⟨long and narrow farms, crowded by ~*ing* ridges —*Amer. Guide Series: Pa.*⟩

⁴parallel \"\ *adv* **:** in a parallel manner — often used with *with* or *to*

parallel axiom *n* **:** PARALLEL POSTULATE

parallel bars *n pl* **:** a pair of parallel wooden handrails adjustable in height and spacing, connected to metal uprights secured to a common base, and used for gymnastic exercises

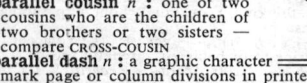

parallel christiania *n, often cap C* **:** a stem christiania executed as close as possible to the fall line and at high speed so as to make the stem preparation indiscernible

parallel cousin *n* **:** one of two cousins who are the children of two brothers or two sisters — compare CROSS-COUSIN

parallel bars

parallel dash *n* **:** a graphic character ═══ sometimes used to mark page or column divisions in printed matter

par·al·lel·epi·ped \,parə,lelə'pīpəd *also* -,lelə'pipəd *or* -,le'lepə,ped *or* -,lə'lepə,ped\ *also* **par·al·lel·e·pip·e·don** \-,lelə'pipə,dän, -,dᵊn\ *or* **par·al·lel·o·piped** \-,lelə'pīpəd *also* -'pip-\ *or* **par·al·lel·o·pip·e·don** \-,lelə'pipə,dän, -,dᵊn\ *n* -s [Gk *parallēlepipedon*, fr. *parallēlos* parallel + *epipedon* plane surface, fr. neut. of *epipedos* level, flat, fr. *epi-* + *pedon* ground — more at PEDION] **:** a six-faced polyhedron all of whose faces are parallelograms lying in pairs of parallel planes — **par·al·lel·e·pip·e·dal** \¦parə,lelə¦pipədᵊl *also* -,le¦lepə¦pedᵊl *or* -lə¦lepə¦pedᵊl\ *or* **par·al·lel·o·pip·e·dal** \¦parə¦lelə¦pipedᵊl\ *adj*

parallelepiped

parallel file *n* **:** BLUNT FILE

parallel forces *n pl* **:** forces acting in parallel lines

parallel induction *n* **:** a hypothetical simultaneous modification of germ plasm and somatoplasm that is due to environmental factors and produces basically similar effects in germ and body cells so that offspring of a modified individual appear to inherit acquired somatic characters

par·al·lel·ism \'parə,le,lizəm, -rələ,li- *also* 'per-\ *n* -s **1 :** the quality or state of being parallel ⟨a lack of ~ of the heads of the testing machine —*Proving Rings for Calibrating Testing Machines*⟩ **2 :** RESEMBLANCE, CORRESPONDENCE, SIMILARITY ⟨~ of interests⟩ ⟨~ in nomenclature between the kinship terms of affinity in English, French, and German —Edward Sapir⟩ ⟨~ between obesity and hypertension —H.M.Marvin⟩ **3 a :** similarity of construction of adjacent word groups equivalent, complementary, or antithetic in sense esp. for rhetorical effect or rhythm **b :** reiteration in similar phrases (as in Hebrew poetry) **4 :** a philosophical theory that mind and matter accompany one another but are not causally related: **a :** a theory that mind and matter are universally coordinate aspects of reality — compare DUALISM, INTERACTIONISM, OCCASIONALISM **b :** PSYCHOPHYSICAL PARALLELISM **5 :** the development or possession of similar new characters by two or more related organisms in response to similarity of environment — compare CONVERGENCE 3 **6 :** the independent development of similar elements or traits in several cultures from a common element — compare CONVERGENCE 4, DIFFUSION 1

par·al·lel·ist \-,leləst *also* -rələ-\ *n* -s **1 :** one who draws a parallel **2 :** an adherent of philosophical parallelism

par·al·lel·is·tic \¦==,le¦listik, ¦==,lə¦li-\ *adj* **1 :** having the nature of or involving a parallelism **2 a :** of or relating to philosophical parallelism or parallelists **b :** resembling or leading to parallelism

par·al·lel·iza·tion \,==,lelə'zāshən, |,lī'z-, ,==,lə|\ *n* -s **:** the process of parallelizing or the state of being parallelized

par·al·lel·ize \'==(,)=,līz\ *vt* -ED/-ING/-S [Gk *parallēlizein*, fr. *parallēlos* parallel + *-izein* -ize — more at PARALLEL] **1 :** to make parallel ⟨~ fibers⟩ **2 :** to place parallel to **:** bring into parallelism with

par·al·lel·ly \'==,lel|lē, '==,lə(l)|lē, |li\ *adv* **:** in a parallel manner

parallel motion *n* **1 :** a jointed link or other mechanism for reproducing motion parallel to itself; *also* **:** a straight-line motion **2 :** melodic progression of two voices moving in same direction by the same intervals

parallel of altitude : ALMUCANTAR 1

parallel of declination : one of the small circles of the celestial sphere that is parallel to the celestial equator

parallel of latitude : PARALLEL 1b

par·al·lelo·gram \,==ˈlelə,gram, -raa(ə)m\ *n* [LL or Gk; LL *parallelogrammum*, fr. Gk *parallēlogrammon*, fr. neut. of *parallēlogrammos* bounded by parallel lines, fr. *parallēlos* parallel + *grammē* line, fr. *graphein* to write — more at PARALLEL, CARVE] **1 :** a quadrilateral with opposite sides parallel — see RECTANGLE, RHOMBOID, RHOMBUS; AREA table **2 :** a four-bar mechanism jointed together in the form of a parallelogram with one link fixed

parallelograms

parallelogram law *n* **:** a law in physics: the resultant of two vector quantities represented in magnitude, direction, and sense by two adjacent sides of a parallelogram both of which are directed toward or away from their point of intersection is the diagonal of the parallelogram through that point

par·al·lelo·gram·mat·ic \¦==¦lelə grə¦mad·ik\ *or* **par·al·lelo·gram·mat·i·cal** \-d·əkəl\ *adj* [*parallelogram* + *-atic* (as in *grammatic, grammatical*)] **:** of, relating to, or like a parallelogram

par·al·lelo·gram·mic \¦==¦==¦gramik\ *or* **par·al·lelo·gram·mi·cal** \-məkəl\ *adj* **:** PARALLELOGRAMMATIC

parallelogram of forces : a parallelogram having two adjacent sides that represent two force vectors and an included diagonal that represents the vector sum

par·al·lel·om·e·ter \,==,le'lämәd·ә(r), ,==,lə'lä-\ *n* [*parallel* + *-o-* + *-meter*] **:** a device that is used to test the parallelism of flat surfaces

parallelopiped *or* **parallelopipedon** *var of* PARALLELEPIPED

parallel perspective *n* **:** linear perspective in which parallel lines of the object that are perpendicular to the drawing surface are represented as meeting at a point on the horizon in line with the common point of intersection of the lines of projection — called also *one-point perspective*

parallel postulate *n* **:** a postulate in geometry: if a straight line incident on two straight lines make the sum of the two angles within and on the same side less than two right angles the two straight lines being produced indefinitely meet one another on whichever side the two angles are less than the two right angles — called also *parallel axiom*

parallel resonance *n* **:** electrical antiresonance accomplished with a capacitance and an inductance in parallel

parallel-resonant \¦==(,)=¦=(=)=\ *adj* **:** marked by parallel resonance

parallel rule *or* **parallel ruler** *n* **:** an instrument for drawing a line parallel to another or a series of parallel lines: as **a :** a flat rule running on a pair of rollers in one of its sides **b :** a pair of straightedges connected by two equal parallel links so that one straightedge can be moved only parallel to the other

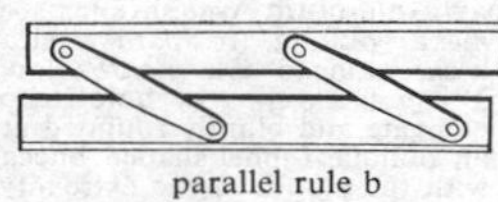

parallel rule b

¹parallels *n pl* [fr. pl. of ²*parallel*] **:** CONSECUTIVES

²parallels *pres 3d sing of* PARALLEL

parallel sailing *n* **:** spherical sailing in which the course is along a parallel and departure is the product of cosine latitude times the difference of longitude — opposed to *meridian sailing*

parallel sphere *n* **:** the celestial sphere seen from either the north or the south pole of the earth where all the celestial bodies seem to move in small circles parallel to the horizon

parallel stance *n* **:** SQUARE STANCE

parallel standard *n* **:** a monetary system in which both gold and silver are freely coined and are legal tender but in which their relative values are not fixed — compare BIMETALLISM

parallel sulcus *n* **:** a sulcus parallel to but some distance below the horizontal limb of the fissure of Sylvius

parallel texture *n, of rock* **:** a texture with tabular or prismatic crystals arranged more or less regularly in parallel positions

parallel turn *n* **:** TEMPO TURN

parallel-veined \¦==(,)=¦=\ *adj, of a leaf* **:** having veins nearly or quite parallel to one another — compare NET-VEINED

parallel vise *n* **:** a vise with jaws so guided as to remain parallel

parallel winding *n* **:** LAP WINDING

par·al·lely *like* PARALLELLY\ *adv* **:** PARALLEL

para·lo·gia \,parə'lōj(ē)ə\ *n* -s [NL, fr. ¹*para-* + *-logia*] **:** a reasoning disorder characterized by inappropriate responses to questioning and based on underlying autistic or dereistic processes (as in schizophrenia)

para·log·i·cal \¦==¦läjəkəl\ *adj* [Gk *paralogos* unexpected, unreasonable + E *-ical*] **:** containing paralogism **:** ILLOGICAL

pa·ral·o·gism \pə'ralə,jizəm\ *n* -s [MF *paralogisme*, fr. LL *paralogismus*, fr. Gk *paralogismos*, fr. *paralogos* unexpected, unreasonable (fr. *para-* ¹para- + *logos* word, reason, speech, account) + *-ismos* -ism — more at LEGEND] **1 :** a reasoning contrary to logical rules or formulas **:** FORMAL FALLACY **2 :** a fallacy of arguing from the empty concept of the ego to its substantiality and eternality

pa·ral·o·gist \-,jəst\ *n* -s [*paralogism* + *-ist*] **:** one who uses reasoning that begs the question **:** one who uses a paralogism

pa·ral·o·gis·tic \=¦==¦jistik\ *adj* **:** utilizing or having the nature of a paralogism **:** FALLACIOUS

pa·ral·o·gize \=ˈ==,jīz\ *vi* -ED/-ING/-S [ML *paralogizare*, fr. Gk *paralogizesthai*, fr. *paralogos* + *-izesthai*, middle & passive form of *-izein* -ize] **:** to reason falsely **:** to draw conclusions not warranted by the premises

pa·ral·y·sis \pə'raləsəs\ *n, pl* **paraly·ses** \-ə,sēz\ [L, fr. Gk, fr. *paralyein* to loosen, disable (fr. *para-* ¹para- + *lyein* to unbind, release, paralyze) + *-sis* — more at LOSE] **1 a :** complete or partial loss of function involving the power of motion or of sensation in any part of the body **:** PALSY — see HEMIPLEGIA, PARAPLEGIA, PARESIS **b :** a disorder of the adult honeybee characterized by trembling **2 :** loss of the ability to move ⟨overcrowded office buildings add to the ~ of traffic —Lewis Mumford⟩ ⟨congestion is increased, sometimes almost to the point of ~, because of the increasing size and number of trucks —*Zoning for Truck-Loading Facilities*⟩ **3 :** a state of powerlessness or inactivity **:** IMPOTENCE ⟨with the ~ of industry will come the surrender of political authority —Louis Wasserman⟩ ⟨a sort of ~ seems to have affected the soldiers when they touched politics —R.C.K.Ensor⟩ ⟨the weakling . . . had succumbed to a ~ of fear —E.S.Miers⟩ ⟨enough idleness to threaten the nation's business . . . with complete ~ —Roger Burlingame⟩

paralysis ag·i·tans \-'ajə,tanz\ *n* [NL, lit., shaking palsy] **:** a chronic progressive nervous disease occurring in advanced life and marked by tremor and weakness of resting muscles, rigidity, masklike facial expression, and a peculiar gait — called also *shaking palsy, Parkinson's disease*

paralysis tick *n* **:** a tick whose bite causes paralysis; *esp* **:** ROCKY MOUNTAIN WOOD TICK

¹par·a·lyt·ic \¦parə¦lid·ik, -lit|, |ēk *also* ¦per-\ *also* **par·a·lyt·i·cal** \|əkəl, |ēk-\ *adj* [*paralytic* fr. ME *peralitik*, fr. MF *paralitique*, fr. L *paralyticus*, fr. Gk *paralytikos*, fr. *paralytos* (verbal of *paralyein*) + *-ikos* -ic; *paralytical* fr. *paralytic* + *-al*] **1 :** affected with or accompanied by paralysis **2 :** of, relating to, or resembling paralysis **:** characteristic of paralysis

²paralytic \"\ *n* -s [ME *paralitik*, fr. MF *paralitique*, fr. *paralitique*, adj.] **1 :** a person affected with paralysis **2 :** a drug used to relieve skeletal muscle and prevent spasm esp. during surgery — compare RELAXANT

par·a·lyt·i·cal·ly \|ək(ə)lē, |ēk-, -li\ *adv* **:** in a paralytic manner

paralytic dementia *n* **:** GENERAL PARESIS

paralytic rabies *n* **:** DUMB RABIES

¹par·a·ly·zant *also* **par·a·ly·sant** \'parə,līzᵊnt, pə'raləzənt\ *adj* [ISV *paralyze, paralyse* + *-ant* (adj. suffix)] **:** causing paralysis

²paralyzant *also* **paralysant** \"\ *n* -s **:** an agent that causes paralysis

par·a·ly·za·tion \,parələ'zāshən, -,lī'z-\ *n* -s **:** paralyzed state ⟨the ~ of the forces of law and order⟩; *also* **:** the act or process of paralyzing

par·a·lyze *also* **par·a·lyse** \'parə,līz *also* 'per-\ *vt* -ED/-ING/-S [F *paralyser*, back-formation fr. *paralysie* paralysis, fr. L *paralysis* — more at PARALYSIS] **1 :** to affect with paralysis

2 : to deprive of strength or activity **:** make powerless **:** make ineffective ⟨a strike that ~*s* an industry⟩ ⟨the atomic bomb . . . can be used to ~ if not destroy a nation —W.O.Douglas⟩ ⟨grand jury could ~ government by indicting a number of important public officials for minor offenses —*N.Y. Times*⟩ ⟨a country economically bankrupt, politically *paralyzed* —W.D.Clark⟩ ⟨discriminating laws *paralyzed* our efforts to lend a helping hand —*Jour. of Internat'l Affairs*⟩ **3 :** UNNERVE ⟨the *paralyzing* thing is the uncertainty —Evelyn Whitehead⟩ ⟨pressure did not ~ the free world but, rather, forged its unity —A.E.Stevenson †1965⟩ **4 :** STUN, STUPEFY, PETRIFY ⟨would ~ the empire with the news —Rudyard Kipling⟩ **5 :** to bring to an end **:** DESTROY, PREVENT ⟨the assertion that principles ~ action —M.R.Cohen⟩ ⟨deadlock *paralyzed* action —F.A.Ogg & Harold Zink⟩ ⟨moral passion . . . has ended by *paralyzing* his aesthetic appreciation —Edmund Wilson⟩ **syn** see DAZE

par·a·lyzed·ly \-z(ə̇)dlē\ *adv* **:** in a paralyzed manner

par·a·lyz·er \-zə(r)\ *n* -s **:** one that paralyzes

par·a·lyz·ing·ly *adv* **:** in a paralyzing manner

para magenta \ˌparə-\ *n, often cap P&M* [pararosaniline] **:** PARA FUCHSINE

para·magnet \ˌparə+\ *n* [back-formation fr. *paramagnetic*] **:** a paramagnetic substance

para·magnetic \"+\ *adj* [ISV ¹*para-* + *magnetic*] **:** being or relating to a magnetizable substance that like aluminum and platinum has small but positive susceptibility varying but little with magnetizing force ⟨~ materials which are but slightly more magnetic than a vacuum, and are therefore attracted weakly by the poles of an electromagnet —R.M. Bozorth & R.A.Chegwidden⟩ — compare DIAMAGNETIC, FERROMAGNETIC

para·magnetism \"\ *n* [ISV ¹*para-* + *magnetism*] **:** the magnetism of a paramagnetic substance

pa·ra·ma·ham·sa \ˌpərəmə'həm(p)sə\ *n* -s [Skt *paramahaṁsa*, fr. *parama* remotest, highest, best (superl. of *parā* away, off) + *haṁsa* swan, goose; akin to Skt *pra-* before, forward — more at FOR, GOOSE] **:** a sannyasi of the highest level of spiritual development in which union with ultimate reality is attained

para·mastoid \ˌparə+\ *adj* [ISV ¹*para-* + *mastoid*] **:** situated beside or adjacent to the mastoid process ⟨the ~ process⟩

par·a·mat·ta *or* **par·ra·mat·ta** \ˌparə'madˌə\ *n* -s [fr. *Parramatta*, Australia] **:** a fine lightweight dress fabric of silk and wool or cotton and wool

par·a·me·cin \ˌparə'mēsᵊn\ *n* -s [NL *paramecium* + E *-in*] **:** a toxic substance secreted into the medium by paramecia that possess the cytoplasmic factor kappa

par·a·me·cium \-mēsh(ē)ləm, -mēsē\ *n* [NL, fr. Gk *paramēkēs* oblong (fr. *para-* ¹para- + *mēkos* length) + NL *-ium*; akin to Gk *makros* long, tall — more at MEAGER] **1** *cap* **:** a genus of holotrichous ciliates having the body elongate and bluntly rounded at the anterior end and having an oblique funnel-shaped buccal groove on the oral surface with the mouth at the extremity **2** *pl* **parame·cia** \|ə\ *or* **parameciums :** a protozoan of the genus *Paramecium*

para·median \ˌparə+\ *adj* [ISV ¹*para-* + *median*] **:** situated adjacent to the midline ⟨a ~ scar on the abdomen⟩

¹para·medic \'parə+,-\ *n* [²*para-* + *medic*] **:** a doctor who parachutes to areas where medical services are needed **:** PARADOCTOR

²para·medic *also* **para·medical** \ˌparə+\ *adj* **:** of or relating to a paramedic or paramedics ⟨a ~ team⟩

para·medical \ˌparə+\ *adj* [¹*para-* + *medical*] **:** concerned with supplementing the work of medical personnel **:** having a secondary relation to medicine ⟨technicians and pharmacists are ~ personnel⟩

para·melaconite \"+\ *n* [¹*para-* + *melaconite*] **:** a tetragonal mineral consisting of cupric and cuprous oxides and occurring in black pyramidal crystals

para·me·nia \ˌparə'mēnēə\ *n* -s [NL, fr. ¹*para-* + *-menia* (fr. *men-* + *-ia*)] **:** disordered menstruation

par·a·ment \'parəmənt\ *n, pl* **paraments** \-ts\ *also* **para·men·ta** \ˌ==ˈmentə\ [ME, fr. ML *paramentum*, fr. *parare* to adorn (fr. L, to prepare, equip) + L *-mentum* -ment — more at PARE] **:** an ornamental ecclesiastical hanging or vestment — usu. used in pl. ⟨~*s* to adorn the altar⟩

para·mer·al \ˌparə'mirəl\ *also* **para·mer·ic** \-merik, -mir-\ *adj* **:** of or relating to a paramere

par·a·mere \'parə,mi(ə)r\ *n* -s [ISV ¹*para-* + *-mere*] **1 :** the right or left half of a bilateral animal or of a somite **2 :** any of several paired structures of an insect and esp. of its ninth abdominal segment

pa·ram·er·on \pə'ramə,rän, -mərən\ *n, pl* **parameron** [NL, fr. ¹*para-* + *-meron* (fr. Gk *meros* part) — more at MERIT] **:** PARAMERE 2

pa·ram·e·ter \pə'ramədˌə(r)\ *n* -s [NL, fr. *para-* + *-meter* (fr. Gk *metron* measure) — more at MEASURE] **1 :** the relative intercept made by a plane on a crystallographic axis, the ratio of the intercepts determining the position of the plane **2 a :** an arbitrary constant characterizing by each of its values some member of a system (as of expressions, curves, surfaces, functions) ⟨we now develop an equation which, for suitable choice of a ~, will represent either a parabola, an ellipse, or a hyperbola —*School Mathematics Study Group*⟩; *specif* **:** a quantity that describes a statistical population ⟨a clear distinction should always be drawn between ~*s* and estimates, i.e. between quantities which characterize the universe, and estimates of these quantities calculated from observations —*Statistical Methods in Research & Production*⟩ ⟨estimation of the values of the ~*s* which enter into the equation representing the chosen relation —Frank Yates⟩ **b :** an independent variable through functions of which other functions may be expressed ⟨four ~*s* are necessary to determine an event, namely the three which determine its position and the one which determines its time —P.W.Bridgman⟩

para·metha·di·one \ˌparə,methə'dī,ōn\ *n* -s [¹*para-* + *trimethadione*] **:** a liquid compound $C_7H_{11}NO_3$ that is a derivative of trimethadione and is also used in the treatment of petit mal epilepsy

para·me·tri·al \ˌparə'mē·trēəl\ *or* **para·me·tric** \-·trik\ *adj* [¹*para-* + *metrial* or *-metric* (fr. *metr-* + *-ic*)] **:** located near the uterus

par·a·met·ric \ˌparə'me·trik\ *also* **par·a·met·ri·cal** \-·trə̇kəl\ *or* **pa·ram·e·tral** \pə'ramə·trəl\ *adj* [*parameter* + *-ic* or *-al*] **:** of, relating to, or in terms of a parameter

par·a·met·ri·cal·ly \ˌparə'me·trə̇k(ə)lē\ *adv* **:** in a parametric manner

para·me·tri·tis \ˌparəmə'trīdˌə̇s\ *n* -ES [NL, fr. *parametrium* + *-itis*] **:** inflammation of the parametrium

para·me·tri·um \ˌparə'mē·trēəm\ *n, pl* **parame·tria** \-·trēə\ [NL, fr. ¹*para-* + *-metrium*] **:** connective tissue and fat adjacent to the uterus

para·military \ˌparə+\ *adj* [¹*para-* + *military*] **1 :** existing where there are no military services or existing alongside the military services and professedly nonmilitary but formed on an underlying military pattern as a potential auxiliary or diversionary military organization ⟨a ~ police force⟩ **2 :** of or relating to a paramilitary organization

para·mim·ia \ˌparə'mimēə\ *n* -s [NL, fr. ¹*para-* + Gk *mimia, mimeia* mimicry, fr. *mimeisthai* to imitate, represent + *-ia* -y — more at MIME] *psychiatry* **:** a misuse of gestures in expressing thought that produces an appearance of inappropriateness of affect

paraminophenol *var of* PARA-AMINOPHENOL — used esp. in photography

pa·ra·mi·ta \pä'rəmə̇tə\ *n* -s [Skt *pāramita*, fr. *pāramita*, adj., crossed, traversed, transcendent, fr. *pāra* bringing across + *ita* gone, past part. of *eti* he goes; akin to Skt *piparti* he brings over — more at FARE, ISSUE] **:** one of the perfect virtues (as morality, charity, patience, wisdom) that must be practiced by one who undertakes the path to Buddhahood

para·mitome \ˌparə+\ *n* [¹*para-* + *mitome*; orig. formed as G *paramitom*] **:** the ground substance of protoplasm as contrasted with mitome

par·amne·sia \ˌpa,ram'nēzhə, ˌparəm'nēzh(ē)ə,ˌparə'nēzh(ē)ə\ *n* [NL, fr. ¹*para-* + *-mnesia*] **:** a disorder of memory: as **a :** a condition in which the proper meaning of words cannot be remembered **b :** the illusion of remembering scenes and events experienced for the first time

pa·ra·mo \'pärə,mō\ *n* -s [AmerSp *páramo*, fr. Sp, wasteland] **:** a high bleak plateau or district (as in the Andes); *specif* **:** alpine meadow of northern and western So. American uplands

par·a·moe·cium *syn of* PARAMECIUM

para·morph \'parə,mȯrf\ *n* [¹*para-* + *-morph*] **1 :** a pseudomorph having the same chemical composition as the original species **2 :** a variant biological form deviating from the mean of the species or other group to which it belongs **:** VARIETY — **para·mor·phic** \ˌ==ˈmȯrfik\ *or* **para·mor·phous** \-fəs\ *adj*

para·morphine \ˌparə+\ *n* [ISV ¹*para-* + *morphine*] **:** THEBAINE

para·mor·phism \ˌparə'mȯr,fizəm\ *n* -s **:** the property of changing from one mineral species to another (as from aragonite to calcite) by a change in internal structure and physical characters but not in chemical composition

¹par·a·mount \'parə,maůnt *also* 'per-; *substand New York City often* -mänt\ *adj* [AF *paramont*, fr. OF *par* by (fr. L *per* through, by) + *amont* above, fr. *a* to (fr. L *ad*) + *mont* mountain — more at FOR, AT, MOUNT] **1 :** having a higher or the highest rank or authority ⟨one of the ~ sheikhs in the desert —*Times Lit. Supp.*⟩ ⟨the ~ king of Yoruba land —J.G.Frazer⟩ ⟨the ~ patriarch of the group —Weston La Barre⟩ **2 :** superior to all others (as in power, position, or importance) **:** CHIEF, SUPREME, PREEMINENT ⟨the need of this people for water is ~ —M.J.Herskovits⟩ ⟨the new constitution should be . . . ~ over all other constitutions —F.A.Ogg & P.O.Ray⟩ ⟨Federal Government's claim of ~ right and dominion over the resources of the marginal sea —*U.S. Code*⟩ ⟨the reporter is the ~ performer —F.L.Mott⟩ ⟨the ~ problem of our time —Cecil Hobbs⟩ ⟨time is of ~ importance —F.D. Roosevelt⟩ **syn** see DOMINANT

²paramount \"\ *n* -s **:** a lord paramount **:** a supreme proprietor or ruler ⟨his cousin . . . the ~ of the tribe —T.E.Lawrence⟩

par·a·mount·cy \-n(t)sē, -si\ *n* -ES **:** the quality or state of being paramount

par·a·mount·ly \-ntlē, -li\ *adv* **:** in a paramount manner

par·amour \'parə,mů(ə)r, -mō(ə)r, -mȯ(ə)r, -ůə, -ōə, -ȯ(ə)\ *n* -s [ME, fr. OF *par amour* through love, by way of love, fr. OF] **:** one who loves or is loved illicitly **:** one taking the place without the legal rights of a husband or wife **:** MISTRESS — called also *lover*

par·am·phis·tome \ˌpa,ram'fi,stōm, ˌparəm-\ *n* -s [NL *Paramphistomum*] **:** a worm of the genus *Paramphistomum* or the family Paramphistomidae

par·am·phis·to·mum \-ˌstəməm\ *n, cap* [NL, fr. ¹*para-* + Gk *amphistomon*, neut. of *amphistomos* with a double mouth — more at AMPHISTOMOUS] **:** a genus (the type of the family Paramphistomidae) of conical digenetic trematodes with a large ventral sucker at the posterior end of the body

par·am·y·lum \(')pa'raməlǝm\ *also* **par·am·y·lon** \-lən, -,län\ *n* -s [NL, fr. ¹*para-* + L *amylum* starch or Gk *amylon* — more at AMYL-] **:** a reserve carbohydrate of various protozoa and algae that resembles starch

para·my·oc·lo·nus mul·ti·plex \ˌparə,mī'äkləno'sməltə,-pleks\ *n* [NL, fr. *paramyoclonus* (fr. ¹*para-* + *myoclonus*) + *multiplex* multiple] **:** a nervous disease characterized by clonic spasms with tremor in corresponding muscles on the two sides

para·myotonia \ˌparə+\ *n* [NL, fr. ¹*para-* + *myotonia*] **:** an abnormal state characterized by tonic muscle spasm

para·nagana \"+\ *n* [¹*para-* + *nagana*] **:** GAMBIA FEVER

par·anal \(')par+\ *adj* [¹*para-* + *anal*] **:** adjacent to the anus ⟨~ glands⟩

pa·ra·ná pine \ˌparə'nä-\ *n, usu cap 1st P* [fr. *Paraná*, river and state in Brazil] **1 :** a timber tree (*Araucaria brasiliana*) of southern Brazil and adjacent regions **2** *also* **parana pine** \" *or* **parana** -s **:** the rather soft yellowish to brown and often rose-streaked wood of paraná pine that is variable in weight and durability, is readily worked and polished, and is used largely in interior finish

para·nasal \ˌparə+\ *adj* [¹*para-* + *nasal*] **:** adjacent to the nasal cavities

paranasal sinus *n* **:** any of various sinuses (as the maxillary and frontal) in the bones of the face and head that are lined with mucous membrane derived from and continuous with the lining of the nasal cavity

pa·ran·dja *also* **pa·ran·ja** \pə'ranjə\ *n* -s [Uzbek] **:** a heavy black horsehair veil worn by women of central Asia

par·an·drus \pə'randrəs\ *n* -ES [NL, fr. ¹*para-* + Gk *-andrus* (fr. *andr-*, *anēr* man) — more at ANDR-] **:** a mythical stag able to change color like the chameleon

par·a·nee \ˌparə'nē\ *n* -s [*paranoid* + *-ee*] **:** the object or victim of paranoid thinking **:** one on whom a paranoiac projects his delusions

para·nephric \ˌparə+\ *adj* [¹*para-* + *nephric*] **1 :** adjacent to the kidney **2 :** relating to or being an adrenal gland

para·nephritis \"+\ *n* [NL, fr. ¹*para-* + *nephritis*] **1 :** inflammation of the adrenal glands **2 :** inflammation of the connective tissue around the kidney

para·neph·ros \ˌparə'nefrəs, -,fräs\ *n, pl* **paranephroi** [NL, fr. ¹*para-* + *-nephros*] **:** ADRENAL GLAND

para·neu·rop·tera \ˌparənyů'räpt(ə)rə\ [NL, fr. ¹*para-* + *Neuroptera* order of insects, fr. *neur-* + *-ptera*] *syn of* ODONATA

pa·rang \pə'räŋ\ *n* -s [Malay] **:** a short sword, cleaver, or machete common in Malaya, British Borneo, and Indonesia

para·ni·tran·i·line red \ˌparə,nī·'tranᵊlən- *sometimes* -ᵊl,īn- *or* -ᵊl,ēn-\ *n* **:** a para red dye produced on the fiber and used as a pigment — see DYE table I (under *Pigment Red 1*)

para–nitro·an·i·line \ˌparə,nī·trō'anᵊlən *sometimes* -ᵊl,īn *or* -ᵊl,ēn\ *or* **para·ni·tran·i·line** \-ī·ˌtran-\ *n* [¹*para-* + *nitr-* + *aniline*] **:** NITROANILINE a

para·noia \ˌparə'nȯi(y)ə *also* ˌper-\ *n* -s [NL, fr. Gk *paranoia* derangement, madness, fr. *paranoos, paranous* demented (fr. *para-* ¹para- + *noos, nous* mind) + *-ia* -y] **1 :** a rare chronic nondeteriorative psychosis characterized chiefly by systematized delusions of persecution or of grandeur that are commonly isolated from the mainstream of consciousness and that are usu. not associated with hallucinations **2 :** a tendency on the part of individuals or of groups toward suspiciousness and distrustfulness of others that is based not on objective reality but on a need to defend the ego against unconscious impulses, that uses projection as a mechanism of defense, and that often takes the form of a compensatory megalomania

¹para·noi·ac \ˌ==ˈnȯi,(y)ak, -ȯi·ik, -ōiēk\ *also* **para·no·ic** \-nōik,-nōēk\ *adj* [NL *paranoia* + E *-ac* (as in *maniac*) or *-ic*] **:** of or relating to paranoia **:** affected with or characteristic of paranoia

²paranoiac \"\ *also* **paranoic** \"\ *n* -s **:** a person who is affected with paranoia

¹para·noid \'==,nȯid\ *also* **para·noi·dal** \ˌ==ˈnȯidᵊl\ *adj* [blend of NL *paranoia* & E *-oid, -oidal*] **1 :** resembling paranoia **2 :** characterized by suspiciousness, persecutory trends, or megalomania ⟨definitely ~ against the army officers with whom he had been associated —Ben Karpman⟩

²paranoid \"\ *n* -s **:** one afflicted with paranoia or paranoid schizophrenia

paranoid schizophrenia *n* **:** a psychosis resembling paranoia but commonly displaying hallucinations, autism, and dereistic thinking and often resulting in marked behavioral deterioration

para·no·mia \ˌparə'nōmēə\ *n* -s [NL, irreg. fr. ¹*para-* + L *nomen* name + NL *-ia* — more at NAME] **:** an aphasia characterized by the incorrect naming of objects

para·normal \ˌparə+\ *adj* [¹*para-* + *normal*] **:** beyond the range of scientifically known or recognizable phenomena **:** RARE, UNUSUAL, SUPERNATURAL — **para·normality** \"+\ *n* — **paranormally** \"+\ *adv*

para·notum \"+\ *n, pl* **paranota** [NL, fr. ¹*para-* + *notum*] **:** one of the paired lateral lobes of the thoracic nota of insects

par·anthelion \ˌpar+\ *n, pl* **paranthelia** [NL, fr. ¹*para-* + *anthelion*] **:** a diffuse image of the sun appearing at the same altitude as the sun and 120 degrees distant on the parhelic circle and caused by reflection from atmospheric ice spicules

par·an·thro·pus \pa'ran(t)thrəpəs, ˌpa,ran'thrōp-\ *n* [NL, fr. ¹*para-* + *-anthropus*] **1** *cap* **:** a genus of australopithecine apes sometimes regarded as synonymous with *Australopithecus* — see KROMDRAAI APE-MAN, SWARTKRANZ APE-MAN **2** -ES **:** a member of the genus *Paranthropus*

para·nuclear \ˌparə+\ *adj* [¹*para-* + *nuclear*] **:** of or relating to a paranucleus

para·nucleus \"+\ *n, pl* **paranuclei** [NL, fr. ¹*para-* + *nucleus*] **1 :** an accessory or additional nucleus or body resembling a nucleus in a cell **2 :** one of the nuclei derived from polar bodies that function in the insect trophamnion

para nut *n, usu cap P* [fr. *Pará*, state and city in Brazil] **:** BRAZIL NUT

para·nymph \'parə+,-\ *n* [LL *paranymphus*, masc., & ML *paranympha*, fem., fr. Gk *paranymphos*, masc. & fem., fr. *para-* ¹para- + *nymphē* bride — more at NYMPH] **1 :** a friend who went with a bridegroom in a chariot to fetch home the bride in ancient Greece; *also* **:** the bridesmaid who conducted the bride to the bridegroom **2 a :** BEST MAN **b :** BRIDESMAID **c :** one who solicits or speaks for another **:** ADVOCATE

par·an·zel·la net *also* **paranzella trawl** \ˌparən'zelə-\ *or* **pa·ran·ze trawl** \pə'ranzə-\ *n* [*paranzella* fr. It, small fishing boat, dim. of *paranza* trawler, fishing boat; *paranze* fr. It *paranza*] **:** a net dragged along the sea bottom between two boats used esp. in fishing for soles and flounders

para·ox·on \ˌparə'äk,sän\ *n* -s [¹*para-* + *ox-* + *-on*] **:** a phosphate ester $(C_2H_5O)_2PO(OC_6H_4NO_2)$ that is formed from parathion in the body and that is a potent anticholinesterase; *O,O*-diethyl *O-para*-nitro-phenyl phosphate

para·paguridae \ˌparə+\ *n pl, cap* [NL, fr. ¹*para-* + *Paguridae*] **:** a family of crustaceans (suborder Macrura) comprising typical hermit crabs — compare PAGURIDAE

para·paresis \"+\ *n* [NL, fr. ¹*para-* + *paresis*] **:** partial paralysis affecting the lower limbs

para·periodic acid \"+ . . . -\ *n* [¹*para-* + *periodic*] **:** PERIODIC ACID a

par·a·pet \'parəpə̇t, -rə,pet, *also* 'per-; *usu* |d·+V\ *n* -s [It *parapetto*, fr. *parare* to shield, guard (fr. L to prepare) + *petto* chest, fr. L *pectus* — more at PARE, PECTORAL] **1 :** a wall, rampart, or elevation of earth or stone to protect soldiers **:** BREASTWORK **:** a rampart raised upon or above the main wall in a permanent fortification **2 :** a low wall or similar barrier; *esp* **:** one to protect the edge of a platform, roof, bridge, or other structure

par·a·pet·ed \-rə,ped·ə̇d, -ˌpə̇|, |tə̇d\ *adj* **:** having a parapet

par·a·pet·less \-rəpə̇tlə̇s, -ˌpet-\ *adj* **:** not having a parapet

paraph \'paraf, pə'raf\ *n* -s [MF *paraffe* paragraph, paraph, fr. L *paragraphus* paragraph — more at PARAGRAPH] **:** a flourish at the end of a signature sometimes used as a sort of rude safeguard against forgery ⟨a blot marred his ~ —V.C.Johnson⟩

paraphase amplifier \'parə,fāz-\ *n* [¹*para-* + *phase*] **:** an amplifier in which by means of a phase inverter the ordinary output of a single amplifier tube is given push-pull characteristics

para·pha·sia \ˌparə'fāzh(ē)ə\ *n* [NL, fr. ¹*para-* + *-phasia*] **:** aphasia in which the patient uses wrong words or words in senseless combinations — **par·a·pha·sic** \ˌ==ˈfāzik\ *adj*

para·phenylenediamine \ˌparə+\ *n* [ISV ¹*para-* + *phenylenediamine*] **:** the para isomer of phenylenediamine — written systematically with ital. *para-*

par·a·pher·na \ˌparə'fərnə\ *n pl* [LL, fr. Gk, fr. *para-* ¹para- + *phernē* dowry; akin to Gk *pherein* to carry — more at BEAR] *Roman & civil law* **:** the property of a woman that on her marriage is not made a part of her dower but remains her own and entirely free from the control of the husband

par·a·pher·nal \ˌ==ˈfərnᵊl\ *adj* [ML *paraphernalis*, fr. LL *parapherna* + L *-alis* -al] **:** being or relating to parapherna or paraphernalia

par·a·pher·na·lia \ˌ*R* ˌparəfə(r)'nālyə, -lēə *also* ˌper-, -*R* -fə'n-\ *n pl but sometimes sing in constr* [ML *paraphernalia* (*bona*), fr. *paraphernalia* (neut. pl. of *paraphernalis*) + L *bona* possessions] **1 :** the separate paraphernal real or personal property of a married woman that she can dispose of by will and sometimes according to common law during her life **2 :** personal belongings (as equipment or finery) ⟨bundled in the ~, down to scarves and woolly caps —Truman Capote⟩ ⟨toy soldiers, little chariot wheels, the entire ~ of a baby —Walter Pater⟩ **3 :** articles of equipment **:** FURNISHINGS, APPARATUS ⟨~ of art⟩ ⟨lighting ~⟩ ⟨~ of war⟩ ⟨ceremonial ~⟩ ⟨~ of a circus⟩ ⟨equestrian ~⟩ **4 :** APPURTENANCES ⟨disguising a naked fact in the ~ of philosophy —Ellen Glasgow⟩ ⟨freedom from the ~ of the modern university —*Rev. of Politics*⟩ ⟨his life . . . has been treated merely as part of the whole ~ of conspiracy and romance —Iris Origo⟩ ⟨the elaborate ~ of our democratic system of popular choice —A.E.Stevenson †1965⟩ ⟨multitude of doctrinal disputes which are part of a lawyer's ~ —R.H.Jackson⟩ **syn** see EQUIPMENT

para·phil·ia \ˌparə'filēə\ *n* -s [NL, fr. ¹*para-* + *-philia*] **:** a preference for or addiction to unusual sexual practices — **para·phil·i·ac** \ˌ==ˈfilē,ak\ *adj or n*

para·phimosis \ˌparə+\ *n* [NL, fr. ¹*para-* + *phimosis*] **:** a condition in which the foreskin is retracted behind the glans penis and cannot be replaced

para·pho·nia \ˌparə'fōnēə\ *n, pl* **paraphonias** \-ēəz\ *also* **paraphoni·ae** \-nē,ē\ [Gk *paraphōnia*, fr. *paraphōnos* sounding beside (fr. *para-* ¹para- + *phōnē* sound) + *-ia* -y — more at BAN] **1** *in Greek & medieval musical theory* **:** a consonance or joint melodic progression of fourths and fifths **2** *pl* **paraphonias** [NL, fr. ¹*para-* + *-phonia* -phony] **:** abnormal change of voice

para·phon·ic \ˌ==ˈfänik\ *adj* **:** of or relating to musical paraphonia — **para·phon·i·cal·ly** \-nə̇k(ə)lē\ *adv*

para·phras·able \'parə,frāzəbəl *also* 'per- *or* ˌ=='===\ *adj* **:** capable of being paraphrased

¹para·phrase \'parə,frāz *also* 'per-\ *n* -s [MF, fr. L *paraphrasis*, fr. Gk, fr. *paraphrazein* to paraphrase (fr. *para-* ¹para- + *phrazein* to point out, show, tell) + *-sis*] **1 a :** a restatement of a text, passage, or work giving the meaning in another form usu. for clearer and fuller exposition **:** a free rendering ⟨a ~ of eternal vigilance is the price of freedom —O.W.Holmes †1935⟩ ⟨plays which are not ~*s* from the Greek —John Buchan⟩ — opposed to *metaphrase* **b :** the use or process of paraphrasing in studying or teaching composition ⟨such subjects as précis, ~, punctuation —*English Language Teaching*⟩ ⟨~, which aims rather at recapturing the general impression of a foreign work —*Times Lit. Supp.*⟩ **2 :** a free or florid musical transcription ⟨a ~ of an ancient Gregorian *Dies Irae* —*Time*⟩ **3 :** an exemplification or an amplification of a theme, idea, or motive **4 :** any of the verses based on passages of Scripture and commonly printed along with the metrical version of the Psalms used in Scottish Presbyterian churches

²paraphrase \"\ *vb* -ED/-ING/-S [F *paraphraser*, fr. MF, fr. *paraphrase*, n.] *vt* **:** to express, interpret, or translate with latitude **:** give the meaning of (a work or passage) in other words **:** make a paraphrase of ⟨~*s* Descartes' famous sentence —Babette Deutsch⟩ ⟨*paraphrased* some of the telegrams —Sir Winston Churchill⟩ ⟨stories will have to be *paraphrased* by Mother —*My Baby*⟩ ⟨work of *paraphrasing* the obscure into the . . . comprehensible —S.E.Hyman⟩ ~ *vi* **1 :** to make a paraphrase **2** *archaic* **:** to comment or expand upon a topic

para·phras·er \-zə(r)\ *n* -s **:** one that paraphrases

para·phra·sia \ˌ=='frāzh(ē)ə\ *n* -s [NL, fr. ¹*para-* + *-phrasia*] **:** speech defect characterized by incoherence in arrangement of words

pa·raph·ra·sis \pə'rafrəsə̇s\ *n, pl* **paraphra·ses** \-ə,sēz\ [L] **:** PARAPHRASE

para·phrast \'parə,frast\ *n* -s [LL *paraphrastes*, fr. Gk *paraphrastēs*, fr. *paraphrazein* to paraphrase — more at PARAPHRASE] **:** PARAPHRASER

para·phras·tic \ˌ==ˈfrastik\ *also* **para·phras·ti·cal** \-tə̇kəl\ *adj* [F *paraphrastique*, fr. MF, fr. ML *paraphrastikos*, fr. (assumed) Gk *paraphrastos* (verbal of Gk *paraphrazein*) + Gk *-ikos* -ic] **:** PARAPHRASING **:** having the nature of paraphrase **:** explaining or translating more clearly and amply an author's meaning — **para·phras·ti·cal·ly** \-tə̇k(ə)lē\ *adv*

para·phre·nia \ˌparə'frēnēə\ *n* -s [NL, fr. ¹*para-* + *-phrenia*] **1 :** the group of paranoid disorders **2 :** any of the paranoid disorders usu. excluding paranoid schizophrenia — **para·phrenic** \ˌ==ˈfrenik *also* -rēn-\ *adj or n*

paraphs *pl of* PARAPH

para·phyl·li·um \ˌparə'filēəm *n, pl* **paraphyl·lia** \-ēə\ [NL, fr. ¹*para-* + *phyll-* + *-ium*] **:** one of the minute branched or stipuliform organs between the leaves of various mosses (as those of the genus *Thuidium*)

pa·raph·y·sate \pə'rafə̇sət, -,sāt\ *adj* [NL *paraphysis* + E *-ate*] **:** bearing or marked by paraphyses

pa·raph·y·se·al \pə¦rafə¦sēəl, -¦zē- *also* ¦parə¦fizē-\ *or* **par·a·phys·i·al** \¦parə¦fizēəl\ *adj* [NL *paraphysis* + E *-eal* (as in *laryngeal*) or *-ial*] **:** of or relating to a paraphysis

para·physical \¦parə+\ *adj* [1*para-* + *physical*] **:** resembling physical phenomena but without recognizable physical cause ⟨~ phenomena as levitation, telekinesis, materialization —Fred Sommers⟩

pa·raph·y·sis \pə'rafəsəs\ *n, pl* **paraphy·ses** \-ə,sēz\ [NL, fr. 1*para-* + Gk *physis* origin, growth, nature — more at PHYSICS] **1 :** one of the slender sterile filaments that are commonly borne among the sporogenous or gametogenous organs in many cryptogamic plants, that may be either unicellular or pluricellular or either simple or branched, and that are often septate **2 a :** a median evagination of the roof of the telencephalon anterior to the epiphysis of certain lower vertebrates **b :** one of several club-shaped chitinous projections near the edge of the pygidium of some scales

pa·raph·y·soid \pə'rafə,sȯid\ *n* -s [NL *paraphysis* + E *-oid*] **:** one of the hyphal threads that are between the asci of various fungi and that resemble paraphyses but lack free ends

pará piassava *n, usu cap 1st P* [fr. *Pará*, state and city in Brazil] **:** PIASSAVA 2

para·pithe·cus \¦parəpə¦thēkəs, -'pithək-\ *n, cap* [NL, fr. 1*para-* + *-pithecus*] **:** a genus of extremely primitive old-world monkeys from the Oligocene of Egypt that are commonly regarded as near the point of divergence of the Cercopithecidae and the higher anthropoid apes and are sometimes made type of a separate family

para·plasm \'parə+,-\ *n* [ISV 1*para-* + *-plasm*] **1 :** HYALOPLASM **2 :** the reserve and waste inclusions of protoplasm in a cell **:** ERGASTOPLASM

para·ple·gia \,parə'plēj(ē)ə *also* ,per-\ *n* -s [NL, fr. Gk *paraplēgiē* hemiplegia, fr. *para-* 1para- + *-plēgiē*, *-plēgia* -plegia] **:** paralysis of the lower half of the body with involvement of both legs usu. due to disease of or injury to the spinal cord

1para·ple·gic \¦==¦plējik, -jēk *sometimes* -lej-\ *adj* [Gk *paraplēgikos*, fr. *paraplēgiē* + *-ikos* -ic] **:** affected with paraplegia

2paraplegic \"\ *n* -s **:** an individual affected with paraplegia

para·pod \'parə,päd\ *n* -s [NL *parapodium*] **:** PARAPODIUM

para·po·di·al \¦==¦pōdēəl\ *adj* [NL *parapodium* + E *-al*] **:** of or relating to a parapodium

para·po·di·um \,=='=dēəm\ *n, pl* **parapo·dia** \-ēə\ [NL, fr. 1*para-* + *podium*] **1 :** one of the short unsegmented processes borne one on each side of most of the body segments in many annelids and serving as locomotive organs and often also as tactile or branchial organs **2 :** a lateral expansion of either side of the foot usu. forming a broad swimming organ in gastropods (as the sea hares and pteropods)

par·apophysis \¦par+\ *n* [NL, fr. 1*para* + *apophysis*] **:** one of the transverse processes that project from the centrum of each vertebra of many lower vertebrates — compare DIAPOPHYSIS

para·prax·ia \,parə'praksēə\ *or* **para·prax·is** \-səs\ *n, pl* **parapraxias** \-ksēəz\ *or* **paraprax·es** \-k,sēz\ [NL, fr. 1*para-* + *-praxia* or Gk *praxis* action] **:** a faulty act (as a slip of the tongue or of memory) **:** BLUNDER, LAPSE

para·proct \'parə,präkt\ *n* -s [1*para-* + Gk *prōktos* anus — more at PROCT-] **:** any of several differentiated lobes or sclerites adjacent to the anus of some insects

para·proc·tium \,=='präktēəm, -ksh(ē)əm\ *n, pl* **paraproc·tia** \-ktēə, -ksh(ē)ə\ [NL, fr. 1*para-* + *proct-* + *-ium*] **:** the connective tissue adjacent to the rectum

pa·rap·si·da \pə'rapsədə\ *n pl, cap* [NL, fr. 1*para-* + *-apsida* (fr. Gk *hapsid-*, *hapsis* arch, loop) — more at APSIS] *in some classifications* **:** a subclass of reptiles in which the skull has two dorsal temporal openings adjoining the parietals and which includes the ichthyosaurs and related extinct forms and sometimes the lizards and snakes — compare DIAPSIDA

pa·rap·si·dal \-dᵊl\ *adj* [NL *parapsid-*, *parapsis* + E *-al*] **:** of or relating to a parapsis

parapsidal furrow *n* **:** one of the longitudinal sutures that separates the parapsides from the median part of the mesonotum in hymenopterans

pa·rap·sis \pə'rapsəs\ *n, pl* **parapsi·des** \-psə,dēz\ [NL, fr. 1*para-* + *apsis*] **:** one of the lateral pieces of the mesoscutum esp. in hymenopterans

para·psychical *also* **para·psychic** \¦parə+\ *adj* [ISV 1*para-* + *psychical*, *psychic*; orig. formed as F *parapsychique*] **:** PARAPSYCHOLOGICAL

para·psychological \"+\ *adj* **:** of or relating to parapsychology

para·psychologist \"+\ *n* **:** a specialist in parapsychology

para·psychology \"+\ *n* [ISV 1*para-* + *psychology*] **:** a science concerned with the investigation esp. by experimental means of events that are apparently not accounted for by natural law and that are considered to be evidence of mental telepathy, clairvoyance, and psychokinesis

pa·rap·ter·um \pə'raptərəm\ *also* **pa·rap·ter·on** \-tə,rän, -,rən\ *n, pl* **parap·tera** \-tərə\ *also* **parapterons** [NL, fr. *para-* + Gk *pteron* wing — more at FEATHER] **1 :** a small sclerite on the side of the mesothorax and metathorax of an insect **2 :** TEGULA 1a

para·quadrate \¦parə+\ *n* [1*para-* + *quadrate*] **:** SQUAMOSAL

para–quinone \¦parə+\ *n* [1*para-* + *quinone*] **1 :** QUINONE 1a **2 :** the para isomer of a quinone

para·rammelsbergite \"+\ *n* [1*para-* + *rammelsbergite*] **:** a mineral $NiAs_2$ consisting of nickel arsenide dimorphous with rammelsbergite

par·arc·ta·li·an \¦pa,rärk¦tālēən\ *adj, usu cap* [NL, fr. *Pararctalia*, temperate marine realm of the northern hemisphere (fr. 1*para-* + *Arctalia*, northern biogeographic realm) + E *-an* — more at ARCTALIAN] **:** of, relating to, or being the temperate marine biogeographic realm that is bounded by the isocrymes of 44 degrees and 68 degrees F and that includes northern seas from the northerly limit of reef-building corals to the southerly limit of floating ice

para·rectus \¦parə+\ *adj* [NL, fr. 1*para-* + *rectus*] **:** situated along the side of the rectus muscle ⟨a ~ incision⟩

para red \¦parə+\ *n* [1*para-*] **1 :** BLOOD RED **2** *also* **para red toner** *sometimes cap P&R* **:** any of a group of brilliant bluish or yellowish red azo dyes or pigments that have fair resistance to light but that may bleed in water and many organic solvents, that are made by coupling diazotized *para*-nitroaniline with beta-naphthol often mixed with a beta-naphthol-sulfonic acid for producing the darker shades of red, and that are used chiefly in paints and printing inks; *esp* **:** PARANITRANILINE RED — compare FIRE RED 2

par·a·re·ka \,parə'rākə\ *n* -s [Maori] **:** POTATO FERN 1

para·rescue \¦parə+\ *n* [2*para-* + *rescue*] **:** rescue of persons (as in a disaster area or an area having inadequate transportation facilities) by parachutists

pará rhatany *n, usu cap P* [fr. *Pará*, state and city in Brazil] **:** rhatany from a Brazilian shrub (*Krameria argentea*)

para·rosaniline \¦parə+\ *n* [ISV 1*para-* + *rosaniline*] **:** a white crystalline base $C(OH)(C_6H_4NH_2)_3$ that is the parent compound of many triphenylmethane dyes (as crystal violet or fuchsine); *also* **:** the red chloride of this base obtainable by oxidation of a mixture of aniline and the para isomer of toluidine and used chiefly in coloring paper, as a biological stain, and in the preparation of other dyes — see DYE table I (under *Basic Red 9*)

para·rosolic acid \"+ . . . -\ *n* [ISV 1*para-* + *rosolic*] **:** AURIN

par·ar·thria \pa'rärthrēə, pə'r-\ *n* -s [NL, fr. 1*para-* + *arthr-* + *-ia*] **:** disorder of speech **:** difficult utterance

para rubber *n, usu cap P* [fr. *Pará*, state and city in Brazil] **1 :** native rubber obtained from So. American trees and usu. exported in dark-colored flat round cakes **2** *or* **para rubber tree :** a So. American euphorbiaceous tree (*Hevea braziliensis*) that is the chief source of Para rubber and is the rubber tree usu. cultivated in plantations

paras *pl of* PARA

-paras *pl of* -PARA

para·sagittal \¦parə+\ *adj* [ISV 1*para-* + *sagittal*] **:** situated alongside of or adjacent to a sagittal location or plane

par·a·sang \'parə,saŋ\ *n* -s [L *parasanga*, fr. Gk *parasangēs*, of Iranian origin; akin to Per *farsang* parasang] **:** any of various Persian units of distance; *esp* **:** an ancient unit equal to about four miles

pará sarsaparilla *n, usu cap P* [fr. *Pará*, state and city in Brazil] **:** a sarsaparilla obtained from a Brazilian plant of the genus *Smilax*

pa·ras·ca·lops \pə'raskə,läps\ *n, cap* [NL, fr. 1*para-* + Gk *skalops* mole — more at HALF] **:** a genus of No. American insectivores comprising the brewer's moles

par·ascaris \(')par, pər+\ *n, cap* [NL, fr. 1*para-* + *Ascaris*] **:** a genus of nematode worms (family Ascaridae) including the large roundworm of the horse (*P. equorum*)

para·sce·ni·um \,parə'sēnēəm *n, pl* **parasce·nia** \-nēə\ [NL, fr. Gk *paraskēnion*, fr. *para-* 1para- + *skēnē* stage — more at SCENE] **:** one of two projecting wings of the skene of an ancient Greek theater flanking and framing the proscenium

par·a·sceve \'parə,sēv\ *n* -s [LL, fr. Gk *paraskeuē*, lit. preparation, fr. *paraskeuazein* to get ready, fr. *para-* 1para- + *skeuazein* to prepare, fr. *skeuos* vessel, implement — more at SKEUOMORPH] **1** *archaic* **:** the day of preparation before the Jewish Sabbath or a feast of similar rank ⟨it was the ~ of the pasch —Jn 19:14 (DV)⟩ **2** *obs* **:** PREPARATION

para·se·le·ne \¦parəsə¦lē(,)nē\ *n, pl* **parasele·nae** \"\ [NL, fr. *para-* 1para- + Gk *selēnē* moon — more at SELENIC] **:** a luminous appearance seen in connection with lunar halos — compare PARHELION — **para·se·len·ic** \-lenik\ *adj*

para·sexuality \¦parə+\ *n* [1*para-* + *sexuality*] **:** PARAPHILIA

pa·ra·shah \'pärə,shä\ *n, pl* **para·shoth** *or* **para·shot** \,pärə'shōt(h)\ *or* **parashi·oth** *or* **parashi·ot** \-,shē'ōt(h)\ *also* **par·shi·oth** \,pärshē'ōt(h)\ *or* **par·shi·ot** [Heb *pārāshāh*, lit., explanation, account] **1 :** one of the weekly portions or lessons that is read from the Pentateuch in the synagogue on the Jewish Sabbath **:** SIDRA — see HAFTARAH **2 :** one of the subsections of the weekly lesson read on Sabbaths, festivals, and on Mondays and Thursdays

para·shoot \'parə+,-\ *vi* [2*para-* + *shoot*] **:** to attack a parachute invader by shooting

para·shot \"+,-\ *n* [2*para-* + *shot*] **:** one trained in parashooting

para·sigmatism *also* **para·sigmatismus** \¦parə+\ *n* [1*para-* + *sigmatism* or *sigmatismus*] **:** inability to pronounce the sound of *s* with some other sound (as of *f*) being usu. substituted for it

parasit- *or* **parasito-** *also* **parasiti-** *comb form* [ISV, fr. 1*parasite*] **:** parasite ⟨*parasit*emia⟩ ⟨*parasito*phobia⟩ ⟨*parasiti*cide⟩

par·a·si·ta \,parə'sīd·ə\ *n pl, cap* [NL, fr. L *parasitus* parasite] *in former classifications* **:** any of several groups of externally parasitic invertebrate animals: as **a :** a group comprising parasitic insects and arachnids **b :** an order or other group coextensive with Anoplura or comprising Anoplura and Mallophaga **c :** ECTOZOA

par·a·si·tal \¦==¦sīd·ᵊl\ *adj* [*parasit-* + *-al*] **:** PARASITIC

par·a·si·ta·ry \¦parə¦sīd·ərē\ *adj* [*parasit-* + *-ary*] **:** PARASITIC

1par·a·site \'parə,sīt *also* 'per-, *usu* -īd·+V\ *n* -s [MF, fr. L *parasitus*, fr. Gk *parasitos*, fr. *para-* 1para- + *sitos* grain, bread, food] **1 a :** one frequenting the tables of the rich or living at another's expense and earning welcome by flattery or diversion **b :** one of a class of assistants in ancient Greek religious rites who dine with the priests after a sacrifice **2 a :** an organism living in or on another living organism, obtaining from it part or all of its organic nutriment, and commonly exhibiting some degree of adaptive structural modification — compare AUTOPHYTE, SAPROPHYTE **b :** such an organism that causes some degree of real damage to its host — compare COMMENSAL, INQUILINE, SYMBIONT **3 :** something that resembles a biological parasite in dependence on something else for existence or support without making a useful or adequate return ⟨resourceful public enemies, ~*s* on the free= press privilege, who thrive on the profits derived from the exploitation of current pornographic materials —*U. S. House of Repr. Report*⟩ ⟨the great city is a ~ on the country —François Bondy⟩ ⟨foiled at one market, they move on to another . . . ~*s* on society, until justice catches up with them —*Irish Digest*⟩ ⟨the young girl is still left incapable of making a living; she can only vegetate as a ~ in her father's home —H.M.Parshley⟩ ⟨new friends who had faith in her ideas, as well as new ~*s* who hoped to profit by them —Havelock Ellis⟩ **4 :** a parasitic sound or letter **5 :** the less perfectly formed twin of a double monster — compare AUTOSITE

syn PARASITE, SYCOPHANT, FAVORITE, TOADY, LICKSPIT, LICKSPITTLE, BOOTLICK, BOOTLICKER, HANGER-ON, LEECH, SPONGE, and SPONGER all signify one that is supported or sustained or seeks support or sustenance, usu. physical but sometimes social or intellectual, from another without right or justification. PARASITE applies to one that as a matter of policy is supported more or less by another and gives nothing in return, extending commonly to anyone who clings to a person of wealth, power, or influence in order to derive personal advantage or who is useless and unnecessary to society ⟨the ones who evade the earth and live upon the others in some way they have devised. They are the *parasites*, and they are the despised —Pearl Buck⟩ ⟨a court society ridden with *parasites*⟩ ⟨as our present society disintegrates, this démodé figure will become clearer; the Bohemian, the outsider, the *parasite*, the rat — one of those figures which have at present no function either in a warring or peaceful world —E.M.Forster⟩ ⟨the poorer citizens were little more than *parasites*, fed with free state bread, amused by free state shows —John Buchan⟩ SYCOPHANT applies to one that clings to a person of wealth, power, or influence and wins or tries to win his favor by fawning, flattery, or adulation ⟨a man who rose in this world because he curried favor, a *sycophant* —Kenneth Roberts⟩ ⟨*sycophants* who kept him from wholesome contact with reality, who played upon his overweening conceit and confirmed him in his persecutional manias —H.A.Overstreet⟩ FAVORITE applies to a close associate or intimate of a king or noble who is unduly favored by him, esp. with power ⟨huge grants of land to court *favorites* —W.C.Ford⟩ ⟨reduced to the ranks every officer who had a good record and appointed scoundrelly *favorites* of his own in their places —Robert Graves⟩ ⟨Pharaoh, his family and his *favorites* —J.E.M.White⟩ TOADY, often interchangeable with SYCOPHANT, stresses more the servility and snobbery of the social climber ⟨he preens himself in the velvet coat, he spies out the land and sees that the Dowager is "the one"; he becomes the perfect *toady* —Stevie Smith⟩ ⟨this induced a sharp distaste for the flagrant political plunder, the obscene scramble for the loaves and fishes by the spoilsmen and their *toadies* —Sidney Warren⟩ LICKSPIT and LICKSPITTLE and BOOTLICK and BOOTLICKER are interchangeable in common speech with SYCOPHANT and TOADY, implying, however, even stronger contemptibleness ⟨characterized those who disagreed as *lickspittles* and toadies of official whiggery —Asahel Bush⟩ ⟨a *lickspittle* humility that went beyond flattery —Alan Moorehead⟩ ⟨*bootlicks* hanging around the mayor's office⟩ ⟨its principal characters were stupid and bemused commanders, or vicious *bootlickers* tainted with homosexuality —Horace Sutton⟩ HANGER-ON applies to anyone who is regarded, usu. contemptuously, as adhering to or depending unduly on another esp. for favors ⟨there were the *hangers-on* who might be called domestics by inheritance —T.R.Ybarra⟩ ⟨a *hanger-on* at Court, waiting for the preferment that somehow eluded him —*Times Lit. Supp.*⟩ ⟨those rather *hangers-on* than friends, whom he treated with the cynical contempt that they deserved —Robert Graves⟩ LEECH stresses the persistence of clinging to or bleeding another for one's own advantage ⟨hatred for the freeloader or deadbeat. Yet, as a student of humanity, he tolerated these *leeches* —H.E.Maule & M.H. Cane⟩ ⟨a *leech* living off his family and friends⟩ SPONGE or SPONGER stress a parasitic laziness, dependence, and indifference to the discomforts caused and usu. a certain pettiness and constant regard for opportunities to cadge ⟨a *sponge* who developed the habit of dropping in for a visit just before mealtimes⟩ ⟨a girl whose disappointment with the world has made her the prey of an unsuccessful crook and *sponger* —*Times Lit. Supp.*⟩

2parasite \"\ *vb* -ED/-ING/-S *vi* **:** to act as a parasite ~ *vt* **:** to cause to act as a parasite **:** PARASITIZE

parasite drag *or* **parasite resistance** *n* **:** the portion of the drag of an airplane that does not include the induced drag of the wings

par·a·sit·emia \,parə,sīd·'ēmēə, -ī'tēm-\ *n* -s [NL, fr. *parasit-* + *-emia*] **:** a condition in which parasites are present in the blood — used to distinguish presence of parasites from clinical state ⟨an afebrile ~ of malaria⟩

parasites *pl of* PARASITE, *pres 3d sing of* PARASITE

parasiti- — see PARASIT-

1par·a·sit·ic \¦parə¦sid·|ik, -sit|, |ēk *also* ¦per-\ *also* **par·a·sit·i·cal** \|əkəl, |ēk-\ *adj* [L *parasiticus*, fr. Gk *parasitikos*, fr. *parasitos* parasite + *-ikos* -ic, -ical — more at PARASITE] **1 a :** having the nature of a parasite **:** fawning for food or favors **:** SPONGING, SYCOPHANTIC ⟨one stable and independent nation . . . is worth a dozen ~ governments that fawn on the U.S. with simulated affection —M.W.Straight⟩ ⟨a ~ desire to thrive on the greatness of others —H.W.Haeusermann⟩ **b :** dependent but contributing or producing little or nothing ⟨a society in which a small class of wealthy people are ~ upon the labor of the masses —H.J.Laski⟩ ⟨criticism of literature and art is ~ and all but futile —Norman Foerster⟩ ⟨~ and unproductive occupations like those of stockbrokers, soldiers, philosophers, economists, and most middlemen —Louis Wasserman⟩ ⟨that religion is . . . intellectually ~ and not creative —M.R. Cohen⟩ **2** *usu parasitic* **a :** relating to or having the habit of a parasite **:** living on another organism **b :** caused by or resulting from the effects of parasites **c** *of a bird* **:** laying eggs in the nest of another **3 :** of, relating to, or constituting an inorganic sound or its orthographic counterpart developed next to another sound (as a liquid or a nasal) through euphony or to facilitate utterance ⟨the \ə\ in \'eləm\ for *elm* or in \'athə,lēt\ for *athlete*, the \t\ in \fents\ for *fence*, and the \b\ and *b* in \'nimbəl\ *nimble* from Middle English *nimel* are ~⟩ **4 a :** being or relating to undesirable component frequencies; *specif* **:** differing from the fundamental frequency that the equipment is designed to generate ⟨a ~ elective oscillation⟩ **b :** consisting of or caused by eddy currents in any conductor within reach of an alternating-current or rotating magnetic field ⟨~ loss in an induction motor⟩ **c :** being part of a radio antenna detached from the main conductor — **par·a·sit·i·cal·ly** \|ək(ə)lē, |ēk, -li\ *adv*

2parasitic \"\ *n* -s **:** a parasitic current or oscillation

1par·a·sit·i·ca \,=='sid·əkə\ [NL, fr. L, neut. pl. of *parasiticus* parasitic] *syn of* ANOPLURA

2parasitica \"\ [NL, fr. L, neut. pl. of *parasiticus* parasitic] *syn of* TEREBRANTIA

parasitic castration *n* **:** inhibition of function or development of gonads by infestation of a host with parasites

par·a·sit·i·ci·dal \¦==¦sid·ə¦sīdᵊl\ *also* **par·a·sit·i·cid·ic** \|idik\ *adj* **:** destructive to parasites ⟨~ action of a substance⟩

par·a·sit·i·cide \,=='sid·ə,sīd\ *n* -s [*parasit-* + *-cide*] **:** a parasiticidal agent

parasitic jaeger *n* **:** a jaeger (*Stercorarius parasiticus*) having moderately long, narrow, and pointed middle tail feathers

parasitic wasp *n* **:** any of numerous hymenopterous insects that are parasitic or parasitoid on other insects; *esp* **:** a member of the division Terebrantia

1par·a·sitid \¦parə¦sīd·əd, -sid·-\ *adj* [NL *Parasitidae*] **:** of or relating to the Parasitidae

2parasitid \"\ *n* -s **:** any mite of the family Parasitidae

par·a·sit·i·dae \,=='sid·ə,dē\ *n pl, cap* [NL, fr. *Parasitus*, type genus (fr. L, parasite) + *-idae* — more at PARASITE] **:** a large family of parasitoid mites with rather short legs, hard body, no eyes, and retractile jaws

par·a·sit·ism \'==,sīd·,izəm, -ī,ti-, -ə,ti-\ *n* -s **1 :** the act or practice of a parasite **:** the parasitic state or condition ⟨abolition of ~ and exploitation of man by man —Upton Sinclair⟩ ⟨countries that let themselves become dependent on the labor of other countries and settle down into a comfortable and ladylike ~ —G.B.Shaw⟩ ⟨economic ~ . . . willingness to live luxuriously at the expense of the poor —E.H.Faulkner⟩ **2 a :** a relationship in which an organism of one kind lives in, on, or in intimate association with an organism of another kind at the expense of which it obtains food and usu. other benefits (as shelter and transportation) causing some degree of overt damage but not usu. killing directly and immediately — compare COMMENSALISM, HELOTISM, PARASITOIDISM, PREDATISM, SYMBIOSIS **b :** a relationship that involves intimate association of organisms of two or more kinds including commensalism, symbiosis, parasitism, and parasitoidism — used esp. when it is not wished or possible to specify the precise relationship **3 :** PARASITOSIS

par·a·sit·iza·tion \,==,sīd·ə'zāshən, -ītə-\ *n* -s **:** the state of being parasitized

par·a·si·tize \'== sə,tīz, -,sīd·,īz, -,sī,tīz\ *vt* -ED/-ING/-S [*parasit-* + *-ize*] **1 :** to infest or live on or with as a parasite **2 :** to lay eggs in the nest of (another kind of bird)

parasito- — see PARASIT-

1par·a·sitoid \¦==¦sīd·,ȯid, -ī,tȯid, '== sə,tȯid\ *adj* [*parasit-* + *-oid*] **1 :** resembling a parasite; *specif* **:** exhibiting or practicing parasitoidism **2 :** of or relating to the Parasitoidea

2parasitoid \"\ *n* -s **:** a parasitoid organism

par·a·si·toi·dea \,==,sīd·'ȯidēə, -,sī'tȯi-, -,sə'tȯi-\ *n pl, cap* [NL, fr. *Parasitus*, genus of mites + *-oidea*] **:** a superfamily of mites that is characterized by a small simple hypostome and the absence of eyes and comprises numerous families including the economically and medically important Dermanyssidae

par·a·sitoid·ism *pronunc at* 1PARASITOID +,izəm\ *n* -s **:** a relation existing between various insect larvae and their hosts in which the larva feeds upon the living host tissues in an orderly sequence such that the host is not killed until the larval development is complete

par·a·si·to·log·i·cal \¦==,sīd·ə¦läjəkəl\ *also* **par·a·si·to·log·ic** \-jək\ *adj* **:** of or relating to parasitology

par·a·sitol·o·gist \,==,sīd·'äləjəst, -,sī'tä-, -,sə'tä-\ *n* -s **:** a specialist in parasitology; *esp* **:** one that deals with the worm parasites of animals

par·a·sitol·o·gy \-jē\ *n* -ES [ISV *parasit-* + *-logy*] **:** a branch of biology that deals with parasites and the parasitic habit and that often is restricted to consideration of animal parasites

par·a·sit·osis \-,sīd·'ōsəs, -,sī'tō-, -,sə'tō-\ *n, pl* **parasito·ses** \-ō,sēz\ [NL, fr. *parasit-* + *-osis*] **:** infestation with or disease caused by parasites

par·a·si·to·trop·ic \¦==¦sīd·ə¦träpik\ *adj* [ISV *parasit-* + *-tropic*] **:** having an affinity for parasites ⟨a ~ drug⟩

para·ske·ni·on \,parə'skēnē|ən, |,än\ *n, pl* **paraske·nia** \|ə\ [Gk *paraskēnion* — more at PARASCENIUM] **:** PARASCENIUM

1par·a·sol \'parə,sȯl *also* 'per- *or* -säl\ *n* -s [F, fr. MF, fr. OIt *parasole*, fr. *parare* to shield, guard (fr. L to prepare) + *sole* sun, fr. L *sol* — more at PARE, SOLAR] **1 :** a lightweight umbrella used as a sunshade esp. by women **2 :** a monoplane with parasol wings

2parasol \"\ *adj* **:** raised above a pilot's head to permit downward vision ⟨~ wings⟩

parasol ant *n* **:** an ant of the genus *Atta*

par·a·soled \-ld\ *adj* **:** carrying a parasol

parasol mushroom *n* **:** a mushroom of the genus *Lepiota; esp* **:** a long-stalked edible mushroom (*L. procera*) that appears in the fall in open woodlands and has white flesh, white gills, and white spores

parasol pine *n* **1 :** STONE PINE 2 **2** *also* **parasol fir :** UMBRELLA PINE 1

para·specific \¦parə+\ *n* [1*para-* + *specific*] **:** a drug or medicinal preparation having other than a specific curative action

1para·sphenoid *also* **para·sphenoidal** \¦parə+\ *adj* [1*para-* + *sphenoid*, *sphenoidal*] **:** of, relating to, or being a bone situated in the base of the skull of many vertebrates and developed in the membrane underlying the basicranial axis

2parasphenoid \"\ *n* **:** a parasphenoid bone

para·spinal \¦parə+\ *adj* [1*para-* + *spinal*] **:** adjacent to the spinal column

para·spore \'parə+,-\ *n* [1*para-* + *spore*] **:** a spore produced by various red algae (as some members of the family Ceramiaceae) that in some cases acts as a tetraspore and in others germinates to produce a triploid generation

par·a·stas \'parə,stas, pə'rastəs\ *n, pl* **pa·ras·ta·des** \pə'rastə,dēz\ [Gk, fr. *paristanai* to place beside, fr. *para-* 1para- + *histanai* to make stand — more at STAND] **:** ANTA; *esp* **:** one of the two large antas enclosing a pronaos in ancient Greek buildings

para·sternal \¦parə+\ *adj* [1*para-* + *sternal*] **:** adjacent to the sternum — **para·sternally** \"+\ *adv*

para·sternum \"+\ *n, pl* **parasternums** *or* **parasterna** [NL, fr. 1*para-* + *sternum*] **:** a bony framework formed by the abdominal ribs in various reptiles

pa·ras·ti·chy \pə'rastəkē\ *n* -ES [ISV 1*para-* + Gk *stichos* row + ISV *-y* — more at STICH] **:** a hypothetical oblique or secondary spiral line joining leaves or scales where the internodes of the axis are short and the members crowded (as in a pine cone); *also* **:** the arrangement of leaves or scales along such lines — compare ORTHOSTICHY

para·style \'parə,stīl\ *n* -S [ISV 1*para-* + *style*] **:** a small cusp lying anterior to the paracone on the cingulum of a molar tooth

par·a·su·chia \,parə'sükēə\ [NL, fr. 1*para-* + Gk *souchos* crocodile + NL *-ia*] *syn of* PHYTOSAURIA

1**para·sympathetic** \¦parə+\ *adj* [ISV 1*para-* + *sympathetic*] **1 :** of or relating to the parasympathetic nervous system ⟨~ fibers of the vascular wall⟩ **2 :** acting on or originating in the parasympathetic nervous system ⟨~ drugs⟩ ⟨~ inhibition⟩

2**parasympathetic** \"\ *n* **1 :** a parasympathetic nerve **2 :** PARASYMPATHETIC NERVOUS SYSTEM ⟨stimulation of the ~ tends to increase smooth muscle tone⟩

parasympathetic nervous system *or* **parasympathetic system** *n* **:** the part of the autonomic nervous system that contains chiefly cholinergic fibers and tends to induce secretion, increase the tone and contractility of smooth muscle, and cause the dilatation of blood vessels and that consists of a cranial part made up of preganglionic fibers leaving and passing the midbrain by the oculomotor nerves and the hindbrain by the facial, glossopharyngeal, vagus, and accessory nerves and passing to the ciliary, sphenopalatine, submaxillary, and otic ganglia of the head or to ganglionated plexuses of the thorax and abdomen and post ganglionic fibers passing from these ganglia to end organs of the head and upper trunk and a sacral part made up of preganglionic fibers emerging and passing in the sacral nerves and passing to ganglionated plexuses of the lower trunk and postganglionic fibers passing from these chiefly to the viscera of the lower abdomen and the external genital organs — compare SYMPATHETIC NERVOUS SYSTEM

para·sym·pa·thet·i·co·mimetic \,parə,simpə¦thed·ə(,)kō+\ *adj* [1*parasympathetic* + *-o-* + *mimetic*] **:** PARASYMPATHOMIMETIC

para·sympatholytic \¦parə+\ *adj* [ISV 1*para-* + *sympatholytic*] **:** tending to oppose the physiological results of parasympathetic nervous activity or of parasympathomimetic drugs — used chiefly of chemical substances and their effects; compare SYMPATHOLYTIC

para·sym·pa·tho·mimetic \,parə¦simpə(,)thō+\ *adj* [ISV 1*para-* + *sympathomimetic*] **:** simulating parasympathetic nervous action in physiological effect — used of chemicals that stimulate secretion and increase smooth muscle activity or of their effects; compare PARASYMPATHOLYTIC, SYMPATHOMIMETIC

para·synapsis \¦parə+\ *n* [NL, fr. 1*para-* + *synapsis*] **:** normal side-by-side union of chromosomes in synapsis in contrast to supposed end-to-end union that is now regarded as purely an observational artifact — compare TELOSYNAPSIS

para·synaptic \"+\ *adj* [1*para-* + *synaptic*] **:** of, relating to, or marked by parasynapsis

para·syndesis \"+\ *n* [NL, fr. 1*para-* + *syndesis*] **:** PARASYNAPSIS — **para·syndetic** \"+\ *adj* — **parasyndetically** \"+\ *adv*

para·synthesis \,parə+\ *n* [NL, fr. 1*para-* + *synthesis*] **:** the formation of words esp. in the Romance languages by composition and derivation jointly **:** the process of word formation by adding a derivative ending and prefixing a particle (as in *denationalize*)

para·synthetic \¦parə+\ *adj* [1*para-* + *synthetic*] **:** of, relating to, or resulting from parasynthesis

para·syn·the·ton \,parə'sin(t)thə,tän\ *n, pl* **parasynthe·ta** \-thəd·ə\ [NL, fr. Gk, neut. of *parasynthetos* formed from a compound, fr. *para-* 1para- + *synthetos* put together, compounded — more at SYNTHETIC] **:** a word formed by parasynthesis

para·syphilitic \¦parə+\ *adj* [ISV 1*para-* + *syphilitic*] *archaic* **:** due indirectly to syphilis — used chiefly of diseases of the nervous system formerly considered indirectly but now known to be directly due to syphilitic infection

par·atacamite \(¦)par+\ *n* [1*para-* + *atacamite*] **:** a mineral that consists of a basic chloride of copper and is dimorphous with atacamite

para·tac·tic \¦parə¦taktik\ *also* **para·tac·ti·cal** \-aktəkəl\ *adj* [fr. *parataxis*, after such pairs as LL *syntaxis* syntax: E *syntactic*, *syntactical*] **:** of, relating to, or exhibiting parataxis — **para·tac·ti·cal·ly** \-tək(ə)lē\ *adv*

para·tax·ic \¦parə¦taksik\ *adj* [NL *parataxis* + E *-ic*] **:** characterized by or relating to a mode of individual experience in which persons, events, and relationships are perceived as discrete phenomena, in which occurrences in the real world are seen as having no sequential or logical relationship, but in which all external stimuli have only idiosyncratic autistic significance — compare PROTOTAXIC

para·tax·is \,==ˈtaksəs\ *n* [NL, fr. Gk, act of placing side by side, fr. *para-* 1para- + *-taxis*] **1 a :** coordinate ranging of clauses, phrases, or words one after another without coordinating connectives (as in "he laughed; she cried") — opposed to *hypotaxis* **b :** the placing of a subordinate clause beside a main clause without a subordinating connective (as in "I believe it is true; there is a man wants to see you") **2 :** the parataxic mode of experience

para·tergite \¦parə+\ *n* [1*para-* + *tergite*] **:** the sclerotized lateral part of the dorsum of an insect

para·tetranychus \"+\ *n, cap* [NL, fr. 1*para-* + *Tetranychus*] **:** a genus of red spiders that in some classifications includes the European red mite

parathesis *n, pl* **paratheses** [NL, fr. Gk, juxtaposition, fr. *paratithenai* to place beside, fr. *para-* 1para- + *tithenai* to place — more at DO] *obs* **:** PARENTHESIS

para·thi·on \,parə'thī,än\ *n* -S [1*para-* + *thio*phosphate + *-on*] **:** a liquid thiophosphate agricultural insecticide ($(C_2H_5O)_2PS(OC_6H_4NO_2)$) of extreme toxicity to mammals as well as insects; *O,O*-diethyl *O-para*-nitro-phenyl thiophosphate

Para–thor–mone \,parə'thȯr,mōn\ *trademark* — used for an aqueous extract of the parathyroid glands of cattle used chiefly in preventing and treating tetanic convulsions

1**para·thyroid** \¦parə+\ *n* [ISV 1*para-* + *thyroid* (n.)] **:** PARATHYROID GLAND

2**para·thyroid** *also* **para·thyreoid** *or* **para·thyroidal** \¦parə+\ *adj* [ISV 1*para-* + *thyroid* (adj.) or *thyreoid* or *thyroidal*] **1 :** adjacent to a thyroid gland **2 :** of, relating to, or produced by the parathyroid glands

para·thyroidectomized \¦parə+\ *adj* **:** having the parathyroid glands removed ⟨~ rats⟩

para·thyroidectomy \"+\ *n* [ISV 1*parathyroid* + *-ectomy*] **:** excision of the parathyroid glands

parathyroid gland *n* **:** any of several usu. four small endocrine glands adjacent to or sometimes embedded in the thyroid gland that are composed of irregularly arranged secretory epithelial cells lying in a stroma rich in capillaries and producing a hormone that functions in maintaining normal calcium balance in the body — compare TETANY

para·thy·ro·pri·val \,parə¦thīrō¦prīvəl\ *also* **para·thy·ro·priv·ic** \-privik\ *adj* [1*parathyro*id + *-prival* (fr. L *privus* single, deprived of + E *-al*) or *-privic* — more at PRIVATE] **:** of, relating to, or caused by functional deficiency of the parathyroid glands ⟨~ tetany⟩

para·thy·ro·trop·ic \-¦träpik\ *adj* [1*parathyro*id + *-tropic*] **:** acting on or stimulating the parathyroid glands ⟨~ hormone⟩

para·tomium \¦parə+\ *n* [NL, fr. 1*para-* + *tomium*] **:** the side of a bird's upper mandible between culmen and tomium

pa·rat·o·my \pə'rad·əmē\ *n* -ES [1*para-* + *-tomy*] **:** reproduction by fission along a special division zone following organization of the structures of a new individual from blastema tissue — compare ARCHITOMY

para·tone brown ZUS \,parə,tōn'brau̇n,zē,yü'es\ *n, usu cap P&B* [1*para-* + *tone*] **:** an organic pigment — see DYE table I (under *Pigment Brown 2*)

para·tonic \¦parə+\ *adj* [ISV 1*para-* + *tonic;* orig. formed as G *paratonisch*] **:** resulting from external stimuli ⟨~ plant growth⟩ — compare AUTONOMIC

para·tracheal \"+\ *adj* [1*para-* + *tracheal*] **:** associated or contiguous with vessels or vascular tracheids ⟨~ parenchyma⟩ — compare APOTRACHEAL, METATRACHEAL, VASICENTRIC

para·trichosis \"+\ *n* [NL, fr. 1*para-* + *trichosis*] **:** abnormal hair or hair growing in an abnormal place

para·troop \'parə+,-\ *adj* [back-formation fr. *paratroops*] **:** of, relating to, or engaged in by paratroops ⟨~ boots⟩ ⟨~ landing⟩ ⟨~ action⟩

para·trooper \'parə+,==\ *n* [2*para-* + *trooper*] **1** *also* **para·troop** [*paratroop* back-formation fr. *paratroops*] **:** a member of the paratroops **2 :** a military person parachuting from an airplane

para·trooping \'parə+,-\ *n* [2*para-* + *trooping*] **:** the action of a paratrooper

para·troops \'parə+,-\ *n pl* [1*para*chute + *troops*] **:** troops trained and equipped to parachute from an airplane

para·troph·ic \¦parə¦träfik\ *adj* **1 :** of or relating to paratrophy **2 :** deriving nourishment parasitically from other organisms ⟨~ pathogenic bacteria⟩

pa·rat·ro·phy \pə'ra·trəfē\ *n* -ES [NL *paratrophia*, fr. 1*para-* + *-trophia* -trophy] **:** DYSTROPHY

para·tuberculosis \¦parə+\ *n, pl* **paratuberculoses** [NL, fr. 1*para-* + *tuberculosis*] **:** JOHNE'S DISEASE — **para·tuberculous** \"+\ *adj*

para·tungstate \"+\ *n* [1*para-* + *tungstate*] **:** a salt in which the ratio of a univalent metal or radical to tungsten may be either 10 to 12 [as in ammonium paratungstate $(NH_4)_{10}W_{12}O_{41}.11H_2O$] or 6 to 7

para·tylenchus \"+\ *n, cap* [NL, fr. 1*para-* + *Tylenchus*] **:** a genus of soil nematodes (family Tylenchidae) that feeds on plant roots

para·type \'parə+,-\ *n* [ISV 1*para-* + *type*] **1 :** a specimen of a type series other than the holotype — usu. used in zootaxy; compare ISOTYPE 1b(1) **2 :** the environmental component of a phenotype — compare GENOTYPE 2

1**para·typhoid** \¦parə+\ *adj* [ISV 1*para-* + *typhoid*] **1 :** resembling typhoid fever **2 :** of, relating to, or involving paratyphoid or its causative organisms ⟨~ infection⟩

2**paratyphoid** \"\ *also* **paratyphoid fever** *n* **:** any of a great variety of infectious enteric diseases of man and animals more or less resembling typhoid fever and commonly contracted by eating food contaminated with bacteria of the genus *Salmonella*; *specif* **:** NECROTIC ENTERITIS — compare SALMONELLOSIS

para·typic *also* **para·typical** \¦parə+\ *adj* **1 :** deviating from type **:** ATYPICAL **2 :** of or relating to a paratype

para·umbilical \"+\ *adj* [ISV 1*para-* + *umbilical*] **:** adjacent to the navel ⟨~ pain⟩

para·urethral \"\ *adj* [ISV 1*para-* + *urethral*] **:** adjacent to the urethra ⟨~ glands that are the female homologue of the prostate⟩

para·vaginal \"+\ *adj* [ISV 1*para-* + *vaginal*] **:** adjacent to the vagina or a vaginal part — **para·vaginally** \"+\ *adv*

par·a·vail \¦parə¦vā(ə)l\ *adj* [AF *paravale*, fr. OF *par aval* below, fr. *par* by + *aval* down, fr. *a* to + *val* valley — more at PARAMOUNT, VALE] *feudal law* **:** being below or at the bottom — used esp. of a tenant who holds of a tenant, esp. the lowest tenant of the fee in immediate possession

para·vane \'parə+,-\ *n* [1*para-* + *vane*] **:** a torpedo-shaped underwater protective device with sawlike teeth in its forward end towed from the bow of a ship in mined areas to sever the moorings of mines — called also *otter*

para·vauxite \¦parə+\ *n* [1*para-* + *vauxite*] **:** a mineral $FeAl_2(PO_4)_2(OH)_2.8H_2O$ consisting of a hydrous basic aluminum phosphate having slightly more water than vauxite

para·vent \'parə,vent\ *n* [F, fr. It *paravento*, fr. *parare* to shield, guard, ward off (fr. L, to prepare) + *vento* wind, fr. L *ventus* — more at PARE, WIND] **:** a screen from the wind

para·vertebral \¦parə+\ *adj* [ISV 1*para-* + *vertebral*] **:** situated beside or adjacent to the vertebral column — **para·vertebrally** \"+\ *adv*

para·vesical \"+\ *adj* [1*para-* + *vesical*] **:** adjacent to the urinary bladder — used chiefly of a peritoneal pouch or recess

para·wollastonite \"+\ *n* [1*para-* + *wollastonite*] **:** a mineral $CaSiO_3$ consisting of calcium silicate dimorphous with wollastonite

par·axial \(ˈ)par+\ *adj* [ISV 1*para-* + *axial*] **1 :** located on each side of the cephalo-caudal axis of the body **2 :** relating to or being the space in the immediate neighborhood of the optical axis of a lens or mirror ⟨~ rays⟩ — **par·axially** \"+\ *adv*

par·axonia \"+\ [NL, fr. 1*para-* + *axonia*] *syn of* ARTIODACTYLA

par·axonic \¦par+\ *adj* [1*para-* + *axonic*] **:** having the axis of the foot between the third and fourth digits ⟨a ~ artiodactyl⟩

para-xylene \¦parə+\ *n* [1*para-* + *xylene*] **:** XYLENE 1b

para·zoa \,parə'zōə\ *n pl, cap* [NL, fr. 1*para-* + *-zoa*] **:** a group of invertebrate animals coextensive with Porifera and comprising multicellular forms that are essentially comparable to a gastrula in organization — compare METAZOA, PROTOZOA

para·zo·ni·um \,parə'zōnēəm\ *n, pl* **parazo·nia** \-ēə\ [L, fr. Gk *parazōnion*, fr. *para-* 1para- + *-zōnion* (fr. *zōnē* belt, girdle) — more at ZONE] **1 :** a small sword or dagger of the ancient Greeks short enough to be worn in the girdle **2 :** a short dagger of medieval times

par·boil \'pär+,-\ *vt* [ME *parboilen* (influenced in meaning by *part*), fr. *parboilen* to boil thoroughly, fr. MF *parboillir*, *parbouillir*, fr. LL *perbullire*, fr. *per-* thoroughly (fr. *per* through) + *bullire* to bubble, boil — more at FOR, BOIL] **1 :** to boil briefly as a preliminary or incomplete cooking procedure ⟨~*ed* it . . . then roasted it —Marjorie K. Rawlings⟩ **2 :** OVERHEAT, SWEAT ⟨work out in the gym and then ~ themselves in steam cabinets⟩ — compare BLANCH, SCALD

parboiled rice *n* **:** rice that has been soaked, steamed, and dried before milling to improve the cooking quality, retain the water-soluble vitamins, and reduce the breakage in milling

1**parbreak** *vb* [by folk etymology fr. older *parbrake*, fr. ME *parbraken*, fr. *par-* thoroughly (fr. OF, fr. L *per-*, fr. *per* through) + *braken* to vomit; akin to D *braken* to vomit, OE *brecan* to break — more at FOR, BREAK] *obs* **:** VOMIT

2**parbreak** *n, obs* **:** VOMIT

1**par·buck·le** \'pär,bəkəl\ *n* [alter. (influenced by *buckle*) of earlier *parbunkel*, of unknown origin] **1 :** a purchase for hoisting or lowering a cylindrical object (as a cask) by making fast the middle of a long rope aloft and looping both ends around the object which rests in the loops and rolls in them as the ends are hauled up or paid out **2 :** a double sling made of a single rope for slinging a cask, gun, or other object

2**parbuckle** \"\ *vt* **:** to hoist or lower by means of a parbuckle

1**par·cel** \'pärsəl, 'pȧs-, *dial except in sense 3* 'pas- *or* 'paas-\ *n* -S [ME, fr. MF *parcelle*, *parcel*, fr. (assumed) VL *particella*, alter. of L *particula* small part — more at PARTICLE] **1 a :** a component part of a whole **:** DIVISION, FRAGMENT, PORTION ⟨nature in all her ~*s* and faculties fell apart —G.M.Hopkins⟩ — often used in the phrase *part and parcel* ⟨part and ~ of a larger tract⟩ **b** *obs* **:** a particular detail **:** ITEM ⟨I will die a hundred thousand deaths ere break the smallest ~ of this vow —Shak.⟩ **2 a :** a continuous tract or plot of land in one possession no part of which is separated from the rest by intervening land in other possession **b :** a tract or plot of land whose boundaries are readily ascertainable by natural or artificial monuments or markers **3 :** a company, collection, or group of persons, animals, or things **:** LOT, PACK — often used as a generalized expression of disapproval ⟨shooing out a ~ of hens —Ida Treat⟩ ⟨a small ~ of cows and a few sheep —Elizabeth M. Roberts⟩ ⟨came to control a whole ~ of maritime companies —E.J.Kahn⟩ ⟨a ~ of giddy young kids —Mark Twain⟩ **4 a :** a wrapped bundle of one or more objects **:** PACKAGE ⟨the box was obviously a diamond ~ —Emily Hahn⟩ ⟨old ladies . . . rustling their luncheon ~*s* —Anthony Carson⟩ ⟨divide science into convenient pedagogic and administrative ~*s* —*Scientific American Reader*⟩ **b :** a unit of salable merchandise **5 :** PARCELING 2 **syn** see PART

2**parcel** \"\ *adv* [ME, fr. *parcel*, n.] *archaic* **:** PARTLY

3**parcel** \"\ *vt* **parceled** *or* **parcelled**; **parceled** *or* **parcelled**; **parceling** *or* **parcelling** \-s(ə)liŋ\ **parcels** [1*parcel*] **1 :** to divide into parts or portions **:** DISTRIBUTE — often used with *out* ⟨small segments of the plantation were ~*ed* out to farmers —W.B.Furlong⟩ **2 :** to make up into a parcel **:** BUNDLE, WRAP ⟨~ his purchase⟩ **3 :** to cover (as a rope or a caulked seam) with strips of canvas **syn** see APPORTION

4**parcel** \"\ *adj* [1*parcel*] **:** PART-TIME, PARTIAL

1**parcel–gilt** \¦==¦=\ *adj* [ME, fr. 2*parcel* + *gilt*] **:** partly gilt (as on the inside only or so as to form ornamental figures)

2**parcel–gilt** \'==,=\ *n* **:** parcel-gilt ware

parceling *or* **parcelling** *n* -S **1 :** an act of dividing and distributing in portions or parts or of wrapping into bundles **2 a :** the covering of a caulked seam with canvas and then tarring it **b :** long narrow slips of canvas usu. daubed with tar and wound about a rope like a bandage to exclude moisture usu. after the interstices between the strands have been wormed to make a smooth surface

par·cel·la·tion \,pärsə'lāshən\ *n* -S **:** division into parcels ⟨endless land ~ and impoverishment —E.M.Kulischer⟩

parcel post *n* **1 :** a mail service handling parcels **2 :** packages handled by parcel post — compare FOURTH CLASS 2

parcenary *n* -ES [AF *parcenarie*, fr. OF *parçonerie*, fr. *parçon* division, distribution, portion (fr. L *partition-*, *partitio* partition) + *-erie* -ery — more at PARTITION] **:** COPARCENARY 1

parcener *n* -S [AF, fr. OF *parçonier*, fr. *parçon* + *-ier* -er] **:** COPARCENER

par·center \(ˈ)pär+\ *vt* [*par-* thoroughly (fr. F, fr. L *per-*, fr. *per* through) + *center* — more at FOR] **:** to align the centers of (optical lenses or diaphragms) along one axis — **par·centricity** \¦pär+\ *n* -ES

1**parch** \'pärch, 'pȧch\ *vb* -ED/-ING/-ES [ME *perchen*, *parchen*, perh. fr. ONF *perchier* to pierce, fr. (assumed) VL *pertusiare* — more at PIERCE] *vt* **1 :** to toast under dry heat **:** burn or roast superficially **:** SCORCH ⟨~*ed* the kernels of sweet corn⟩ **2 :** to dry to extremity **:** shrivel with heat ⟨cheekbones showed clearly under tightly drawn skin, which was tanned and ~*ed* —K.M.Dodson⟩ **3 :** to dry or shrivel with cold ⟨busy restoring complexions that were ~*ed* by winter weather —*New Yorker*⟩ ~ *vi* **:** to lose moisture **:** become dry or scorched ⟨the skin . . . ~*es* and wrinkles early in life —Russell Lord⟩ **syn** see DRY

2**parch** \"\ *n* -ES **:** a drying out ⟨areas hit by the ~ of drought⟩

parched \-cht\ *adj* [ME *parchyd*, fr. past part. of *perchen*, *parchen*] **:** dried out **:** SCORCHED — **parched·ly** \-chədlē, -chtlē\ *adv*

parched·ness \-chədnəs, -ch(t)n-\ *n* -ES **:** the quality or state of being parched

Par·chee·si \pär'chēzē, pȧ'ch- *also* pə(r)'ch-\ *trademark* — used for a board game adapted from pachisi

parching *adj* **:** DRYING, SCORCHING — **parch·ing·ly** *adv*

parch·ment \'pärchmənt, 'pȧch-\ *n* -S [ME *perchement*, *parchement*, alter. (influenced by ML *pergamentum*, alter. of L *pergamena*) of *parchemin*, *perchemin*, fr. OF *parchemin*, alter. (influenced by *parche*, *parge*, a kind of leather, fr. L *Parthica -puellis-*, fr. *Parthica*, fem. of *Parthicus* Parthian + *puellis* leather) of *pargamin*, fr. ML *pergamina*, alter. of L *pergamena*, fr. Gk *pergamēnē*, fr. fem. of *Pergamēnos* of Pergamum, fr. *Perganon* (Pergamum), ancient city in Asia Minor (now Bergama, western Turkey)] **1 a :** the skin of a sheep, goat, or other animal esp. when prepared to receive writing **b :** any of various superior papers of well-beaten rag and wood pulp made to resemble parchment ⟨~ bond⟩ ⟨~ deed⟩ ⟨~ writing⟩ — see VEGETABLE PARCHMENT; compare VELLUM **c :** a document on parchment **:** a parchment manuscript ⟨here's a ~ with the seal of Caesar —*Shak.*⟩; *often* **:** an academic diploma **2 :** the envelope of the coffee bean inside the pulp **3 a :** a variable color averaging a pale yellow green that is greener and paler than average Nile and yellower, lighter, and stronger than oyster gray **b :** a grayish yellow that is duller than chamois and redder and slightly less strong than old ivory

parchment coffee *n* **:** dried but unhulled coffee beans

parch·ment·ed \-məntəd, -,men-\ *adj* **:** having a leathery surface

parch·ment·ize \-_mənt·,īzd, -n·,tī-\ *vt* -ED/-ING/-S **:** to convert (as paper or other cellulosic material) into a substance resembling parchment esp. by treating with sulfuric acid

parchment paper *n* **:** VEGETABLE PARCHMENT

parchment worm *n* **:** a worm of the family Chaetopteridae

parch·menty \-_məntē\ *adj* **:** of, relating to, or resembling parchment ⟨~ cheeks —William Fifield⟩

par·ci·dentate \¦parsə, -sē+\ *adj* [L *parci-* (fr. *parcus* sparing, fr. *parcere* to spare) + E *dentate* — more at PARSIMONY] **:** having few teeth

parcimonious *var of* PARSIMONIOUS

par·ci·ty \'pärsəd·ē\ *n* -ES [L *parcitas*, fr. *parcus* sparing, scanty + *-itas* -ity] **:** FRUGALITY, SCANTINESS

par clearance *n* **:** nationwide clearance of bank checks at face value conducted through the Federal Reserve system

1**par·close** \'pär,klōz\ *also* **per·close** \'pər-\ *n* [ME *parclose*, fr. MF, enclosure, end, fr. fem. of *parclos*, past part. of *parclore* to enclose, end, fr. *par-* thoroughly (fr. L *per-*, fr. *per* through) + *clore* to close — more at FOR, CLOSE] **1** *obs* **:** the end or conclusion of a sentence or discourse **2 :** a screen or railing used esp. to separate a chapel from the main body of a church

2**par·close** \(ˈ)pär¦klōz\ *vt* [obs. F *parclos-*, stem of *parclore*] *archaic* **:** CONCLUDE, ENCLOSE

par·cook \(ˈ)pär+\ *vt* [*par-* (as in parboil) + *cook*] **:** PARBOIL

1**pard** \'pärd\ *n* -S [ME *parde*, fr. OF, fr. L *pardus*, fr. Gk *pardalis*, *pardos*, of non-IE origin like Skt *pṛdāku* leopard, snake, Per *palang* leopard] *archaic* **:** LEOPARD

2**pard** \"\ *n* -S [short for *pardner*] *chiefly dial* **:** PARTNER, CHUM

pardah *var of* PURDAH

pardal *or* **pardale** *n* -S [L *pardalis* female leopard, fr. Gk *pardalis* leopard — more at PARD] *obs* **:** LEOPARD

par·da·lote \'pärdᵊl,ōt\ *n* -S [NL *Pardalotus* genus of birds including the diamond bird, fr. Gk *pardalōtos* spotted like a leopard, fr. *pardalis* leopard] **:** DIAMOND BIRD 1

par·dao \(ˈ)pär¦dau̇, pər'd-\ *n* -S [Pg, fr. Skt *pratāpa* splendor, majesty, fr. *pra-* before, forward + *tapati* it heats; fr. the use of the word *pratāpa* as an epithet of kings on native coins — more at FOR, TEPID] **:** a half rupia coin of Portuguese India

pard·ed \'pärdəd\ *adj, archaic* **:** having spots like those of the leopard

par·des·sus de vi·ole \¦pärdə¦südəvē'ōl\ *n* [F, lit., above the viol] **:** a small viol higher in pitch than the treble viol

par·dhan \'pär,dän\ *n, pl* **pardhan** *or* **pardhans** [Hindi *pardhān*, *pradhān*, fr. Skt *pradhāna* chief, fr. *pra-* before — more at FOR] **:** a bardic minstrel and ritual beggar of the Gond people

par·die *or* **per·die** *or* **par·di** *or* **par·dy** \(,)pər'dē, pär'-\ *interj* [ME *pardee*, fr. OF *par Dé* by God] *archaic* — a mild oath

pard·ine \'pär,dīn, -,dēn\ *adj* [1*pard* + *-ine*] **:** of, relating to, resembling, or spotted like a leopard

pardine lynx *n* [trans. of NL *Lynx pardina*] **:** SPOTTED LYNX

pard·ner \'pärdnər, 'pȧdnə(r\ *n* -S [alter. of *partner*] *chiefly dial* **:** PARTNER, CHUM

par·do \(ˈ)pär¦dō, pər'dō\ *n* -S [by alter.] **:** PARDAO

1**par·don** \'pärdᵊn, 'pȧd-\ *n* -S [ME *pardoun*, fr. OF *pardon*, fr. *pardonner* — more at 2PARDON] **1 a :** the excusing of an offense without exacting a penalty **:** remission of punishment **b :** divine forgiveness **2** *Roman Catholicism* **a :** INDULGENCE **b :** a festival at which an indulgence is granted **3 a :** a release by a sovereign or an officer having jurisdiction from the legal penalties or consequences of an offense or of a conviction **b :** an act of grace of the pardoning authority granted before or after conviction to one person by name or a number (as a class) of persons conditionally or absolutely or in any other form within the power of the pardoning authority — compare AMNESTY 2 **4 :** an official warrant of remission of penalty **5 a :** excuse or forgiveness for a fault, offense, or discourtesy ⟨begged my ~ for his clumsiness⟩ — often used in polite apology or contradiction ⟨I beg your ~, but I think not⟩ **b :** excuse for failure to hear or understand ⟨beg ~⟩

syn AMNESTY, ABSOLUTION: PARDON in the sense here dealt with indicates a remission of punishment or penalty, entirely effective but without indicating exoneration from guilt ⟨a royal *pardon* later freed him from a death sentence —*Amer. Guide Series: Md.*⟩ ⟨decided that a parole wasn't enough — he wanted a full *pardon* —Green Peyton⟩ AMNESTY indicates a general remission of punishment, penalty, retribution, or disfavor to a whole group or class; it may imply a promise to forget ⟨a proclamation of universal *amnesty* . . . finally restored the civil rights of Jefferson Davis and a handful of others —A.D.Kirwan⟩ ⟨issued a general *amnesty* for all those who were imprisoned under the emergency decrees —C.E.

Black & E.C.Helmreich⟩ ABSOLUTION may indicate a formal acquittal in law or a definitive remission of punishment for sin in religion.

²**pardon** \"\ *vb* **pardoned; pardoned; pardoning** \-d(ᵊ)niŋ\ **pardons** [ME *pardonen*, fr. MF *pardoner, pardonner* to give, pardon, fr. LL *perdonare* to give with all one's heart, fr. L *per-*, intensive prefix (fr. *per* through) + *donare* to give — more at FOR, DONATION] *vt* **1 :** to absolve from the consequences of a fault or the punishment of crime **:** free from penalty **2 :** to remit the penalty of (an offense) **:** allow to pass without punishment **:** FORGIVE **3** *obs* **:** to refrain from exacting as a penalty ⟨I ~ thee thy life before thou ask it —Shak.⟩ **4 :** to make allowance for **:** TOLERATE — often used in courteous denial or apology **~** *vi* **:** to grant pardon or forgiveness **syn** see EXCUSE

par·don·able \-d(ᵊ)nəbəl\ *adj* [MF *pardonable, pardonnable*, fr. *pardoner, pardonner* + *-able* — more at PARDON] **:** admitting of being pardoned **:** EXCUSABLE ⟨her heart innocent of the most ~ guile —Joseph Conrad⟩ — **par·don·able·ness** \-nə̇s\ *n* -ES — **par·don·ably** \-blē, -bli\ *adv*

par·don·er \-d(ᵊ)nə(r)\ *n* -S [ME, fr. *pardonen* + *-er*] **1 :** a medieval preacher delegated to raise money for religious works by soliciting offerings and granting indulgences **2 :** one that pardons

pards *pl of* PARD

¹**pare** \ˈpa(a)(ə)r, ˈpe|, |ə\ *vt* -ED/-ING/-S [ME *paren*, fr. MF *parer* to prepare, trim, fr. L *parare* to prepare, procure; akin to OE *fearr* bull, ox, OHG *far, farro*, ON *farri* bull, L *parere* to give birth to, beget, produce, Gk *poris* calf, Skt *pṛthuka* head of cattle, calf, young of an animal, and perh. to OE *faran* to go, travel — more at FARE] **1 a :** to trim off excess, irregular, or surface parts of **:** shave off an outer edge or part of ⟨~ the horse's hoof⟩ **b :** to trim off an outside part (as the skin or rind) of ⟨~ apples for a pie⟩ — usu. used with *off* or *away* **c** *archaic* **:** to remove the turf from (a field) **:** clear a field of (turf) **2 :** to diminish the bulk of by or as if by paring **:** reduce gradually ⟨the navy poker players had *pared* the $70 I brought aboard to $14 —T.W.Lawson⟩ **3 :** to thin (leather, paper, and similar materials) with a knife (as in binding a book) **syn** see SKIN

²**pare** \"\ *chiefly dial var of* PAIR

¹**par·e·gor·ic** \ˌparəˈgȯ|rik, -gä|, |rēk *also* ˈper-\ *also* **par·e·gor·i·cal** \|rə̇kəl, |rēk-\ *adj* [F *parégoreque*, fr. MF *paregorique*, fr. LL *paregoricus*, fr. Gk *parēgorikos*, fr. *parēgorein* to talk over, encourage, soothe (fr. *para-* ¹para- + *agora* assembly, marketplace) + *-ikos* -ic, -ical — more at AGORA] *archaic* **:** assuaging or soothing pain **:** MITIGATING

²**paregoric** \"\ *n* -S **1** *archaic* **:** a medicine that mitigates pain **:** ANODYNE **2 :** camphorated tincture of opium used to relieve pain

pa·reia·saur \pəˈrīəˌsȯ(ə)r\ *n* -S [NL *Pareiasaurus*] **:** a reptile of the family Pareiasauridae

pa·reia·sau·ri·an \pəˌrīəˈsȯrēən\ *adj* [NL *Pareiasaurus* + E *-ian*] **:** of or relating to pareiasaurs

pa·reia·sau·ri·dae \pəˌrīəˈsȯrəˌdē\ *n pl, cap* [NL, fr. *Pareiasaurus*, type genus + *-idae*] **:** a widely distributed family of Permian terrestrial reptiles (order Cotylosauria) — see PAREIASAURUS

pa·reia·sau·rus \ˌ=ˌ==ˈsȯrəs\ *n, cap* [NL, fr. Gk *pareia* cheek + NL *-saurus*] **:** the type genus of the family Pareiasauridae comprising heavily built reptiles from the Karroo formations of southern Africa

pa·rei·ra \pəˈrerə, -rārə\ *n* -S [Pg *parreira (brava)*, lit., wild vine, fr. *parreira* vine, vine on a trellis (fr. *parra* vine (leaf)) + *brava* wild] **1** *or* **pareira brava :** the root of a So. American vine (*Chondodendron tomentosum*) of the family Menispermaceae that is used as a diuretic, tonic, and aperient **2 :** any of several roots of related plants that are sometimes used like pareira — usu. used in combination; see FALSE PAREIRA, WHITE PAREIRA, YELLOW PAREIRA

pa·re·ja \pəˈrā(ˌ)hä\ *n* -S [Sp, lit., pair, fr. (assumed) VL *paricula*, dim. of L *par* pair, fr. *par* equal — more at PAIR] **:** a Spanish trawler using a dragnet that is often worked with the assistance of a second such trawler

parel *n* -S [ME *parail*, short for *apparail, appareil* — more at APPAREL] **1** *obs* **:** APPAREL, CLOTHING, ORNAMENT **2** *obs* **:** a preparation containing eggs and used to refine wine

paremiographer *var of* PAROEMIOGRAPHER

pa·ren \pəˈren\ *n* -S [by shortening] **:** PARENTHESIS 3

pa·ren·chy·ma \pəˈreŋkəmə\ *also* **par·en·chym** \ˈparə̇nˌkim, pəˈreŋkə̇m\ *or* **par·en·chyme** \ˈparə̇nˌkīm\ *n* -S [NL *parenchyma*, fr. Gk, visceral flesh, fr. *parenchein* to pour in beside, fr. *par-* ¹para- + *en-* ²en- + *chein* to pour; fr. the belief that the tissue of internal organs was poured in by the blood vessels of the organ — more at FOUND] **1 :** a tissue of higher plants consisting of thin-walled living cells that remain capable of cell division even when mature, that are agents of photosynthesis and storage, and that make up much of the substance of leaves and roots and the pulp of fruits as well as parts of stems and supporting structures **2 a :** the essential and distinctive tissue of an organ (as a gland) or an abnormal growth (as a tumor) as distinguished from its supportive framework **b :** the soft jellylike connective tissue containing stellate cells and fibers that fills the interstices between the internal organs in the flatworms and some other invertebrates **c :** the endoplasm of a protozoan

pa·ren·chy·mal \pəˈreŋkəməl, ˌparə̇nˈkīm-\ *or* **pa·ren·chy·mous** \-məs\ *adj* [NL *parenchyma* + E *-al* or *-ous*] **:** PARENCHYMATOUS

par·en·chym·a·tous \ˌparə̇nˈkimədəs\ *or* **pa·ren·chy·mat·ic** \pəˌreŋkəˈmad·ik\ *adj* [NL *parenchymat-, parenchyma* + E *-ous* or *-ic*] **:** of, relating to, made up of, or affecting parenchyma — **par·en·chym·a·tous·ly** *adv*

par·en·chym·u·la \ˌparə̇nˈkimyələ\ *n* -S [NL, dim. of *parenchyma*] **:** PLANULA

parenesis *var of* PARAENESIS

pa·rens pa·tri·ae \ˌpa(a)rə̇nzˈpā·trēˌē, -zˈpa·t-; -zˈpä·trēˌī\ *n* [L] **:** the father of the country constituted in law by the state (as in the U. S.) or by the sovereign (as in Great Britain) in the capacity of legal guardian of persons not sui juris and without natural guardians, of heir to persons without natural heirs, and of protector of all citizens or subjects unable to protect themselves ⟨the requirement of escheat to the *parens patriae* —*Harvard Law Rev.*⟩

¹**par·ent** \ˈpa(a)rənt, ˈper-\ *n* -S *often attrib* [ME, fr. MF, fr. L *parent-, parens*, fr. pres. part. of *parere* to give birth to, beget, produce — more at PARE] **1 a :** one that begets or brings forth offspring **:** FATHER, MOTHER **b** *law* (1) **:** a lawful parent (2) **:** a person standing in loco parentis although not a natural parent (3) **:** ANCESTOR — compare PATRIA POTESTAS **2** *obs* **:** RELATIVE 3a **3 a :** an animal or plant regarded in relation to its offspring ⟨the genetic identity of a particular ~ tree —*Farmer's Weekly (So. Africa)*⟩ **b :** the material or source from which something is derived **:** AUTHOR, CAUSE, ORIGIN ⟨means of determining the rate of weathering of the ~ rock —J.P.Minard⟩ ⟨the outermost electrons can be detached from their ~ atoms —Leonard Engel⟩ ⟨while liberty was the ~ of eloquence, eloquence was the stay of liberty —Van Wyck Brooks⟩ **c :** a group (as a society, church, or business) from which another takes its rise and to which it sometimes remains subsidiary ⟨produces shoe linings for its ~ firm —*Amer. Guide Series: Ark.*⟩

²**parent** \"\ *vt* -ED/-ING/-S **1 :** to be or act as the parent of **:** ORIGINATE, PRODUCE **2 :** to provide with a parent or parents **:** trace the derivation of **:** show the real or assumed source of

par·ent·age \-tij, -tēj\ *n* -S [MF, fr. *parent* + *-age* — more at PARENT] **1** *archaic* **:** exercise of a parent's functions or prerogatives **2 :** descent from parents or ancestors **:** BIRTH, FAMILY, LINEAGE ⟨can you tell me anything of the ~ of the lady —Margaret Deland⟩ **3 :** derivation from a source **:** ORIGIN ⟨the ballads about them are of common ~ —G.B.Johnson⟩ ⟨it is sometimes difficult to sort out the ~ of a given idea —*Arctic*⟩ **4** *obs* **:** KINSHIP, KINDRED **5 :** the standing or position of a parent **:** PARENTHOOD

pa·ren·tal \pəˈrentᵊl *sometimes* ˈpa(a)rəntᵊl *or* ˈperən-\ *adj* [L *parentalis*, fr. *parent-, parens* parent + *-alis* -al — more at PARENT] **1 :** of or relating to a parent **:** PATERNAL, MATERNAL ⟨participation in the tests now under way is only upon ~ request —*Monsanto Mag.*⟩ **2 a :** appropriate to, characteristic of, or resembling a parent ⟨maintained a nice balance between ~ authority and ~ affection⟩ ⟨the peculiar and indeed ~ relationship of the author to his work —Stanley Unwin⟩ **b :** of, relating to, or constituting a source or origin ⟨the progenitor of the gold, however, was some ~ magma —A.M. Bateman⟩

parental generation *n* **:** a generation made up of individuals of distinguishable genotypes that are crossed (as in experimental genetics) to produce hybrids — symbol *P;* compare FILIAL GENERATION

par·en·ta·lia \ˌpa(a)rənˈtālēə, ˌper-\ *n pl, usu cap* [L, fr. neut. pl. of *parentalis* parental — more at PARENTAL] **:** the chief annual festival of the dead in ancient Rome from midday February 13 to February 21

pa·ren·tal·ism \pəˈrentᵊlˌizəm\ *n* -S **:** an attitude or the assumption of an attitude of superior authority **:** PATERNALISM

pa·ren·tal·ly \-tᵊlē, -li\ *adv* **:** in a parental manner

parental school *n* **:** a correctional school for truant children

parentate *vi* -ED/-ING/-S [L *parentatus*, past part. of *parentare* to make an offering or sacrifice to the spirits of the family dead, fr. *parent-, parens* parent — more at PARENT] *obs* **:** to perform funeral rites esp. for a parent or relative

par·en·ta·tion \ˌpa(a)rənˈtāshən, ˌper-\ *n* -S [LL *parentation-, parentatio*, fr. L *parentatus* + *-ion-, -io* -ion] **1** *archaic* **:** the celebration of funeral rites for one's parents **2** *archaic* **:** any service memorializing the dead

par·en·te·la \ˌparənˈtēlə\ *n* -S [LL, fr. *parent-, parens* parent + *-ela* (as in *clientela* clientele) — more at CLIENTELE] *law* **:** the line of blood relatives **:** the kin of a person by descent

par·en·tel·ic \ˌ==ˈ==ˈtelik\ *adj, law* **:** of, relating to, or tracing consanguinity through the parentela

¹**par·enteral** \pər+\ *adj* [ISV ¹*para-* + *enteral*] **1 :** not intestinal **:** situated or occurring outside the intestine **:** other than by way of the intestines ⟨~ digestion⟩ **2 :** injected or for injection subcutaneously, intramuscularly, or intravenously ⟨~ glucose⟩ ⟨~ saline⟩ — **par·enterally** \"+\ *adv*

²**parenteral** \"\ *n* -S **:** an agent (as a drug or solution) intended for parenteral administration

pa·ren·the·sis \pəˈren(t)thəsə̇s\ *n, pl* **parenthe·ses** \-əˌsēz\ [LL, fr. Gk, lit., action of inserting or interpolating, fr. *parentithenai* to insert, interpolate, fr. *para-* ¹para- + *entithenai* to put into, fr. *en-* ²en- + *tithenai* to place, set — more at DO] **1 a :** an amplifying or explanatory comment inserted in a passage to which it may be grammatically unrelated and from which it is usu. set off by punctuation (as curved lines, commas, or dashes) ⟨paused, at the end of this ~, to draw breath —Christopher Isherwood⟩ **b :** a remark or passage that constitutes a departure from the theme of a discourse **:** DIGRESSION **2 :** INTERLUDE, INTERVAL ⟨this sandy ~ —Thomas Wood †1950⟩ ⟨the fate of mankind is an irrelevancy, a ~ of no importance —C.I.Glicksberg⟩ **3 a :** one or both of the curved marks ( ) used in writing and printing to enclose a parenthetic expression **:** BRACKET 4c **b :** such a curve used as one of a pair to indicate which operands in a logical or mathematical expression are to be grouped and treated as a unit — compare BRACKET 4a

pa·ren·the·size \-ˌsīz\ *vb* -ED/-ING/-S [*parenthesis* + *-ize*] *vt* **1 :** to make a parenthesis of **:** interject as comment or digression **2 :** to insert a parenthesis in **:** scatter parentheses through ⟨*parenthesized* his address to the point of incoherence⟩ **~** *vi* **:** to say something in parenthesis

par·en·thet·ic \ˌparənˈthed·|ik, -et|, |ēk\ *or* **par·en·thet·i·cal** \-ə̇kəl, -ēk-\ *adj* [fr. *parenthesis*, after such pairs as E *antithesis: antithetic, antithetical*] **1 a :** of or relating to a parenthesis **:** expressed in or as if in a parenthesis **b :** enclosed in parentheses **2 :** containing parentheses **:** using or given to using parenthesis ⟨a ~ style⟩ — **par·en·thet·i·cal·ly** \-ə̇k(ə)lē, -ēk-, -li\ *adv* — **par·en·thet·i·cal·ness** *n* -ES

par·ent·hood \ˈpa(a)rəntˌhu̇d, ˈper-\ *n* **:** the position, function, or standing of a parent

pa·ren·ti·cide \pəˈrentəˌsīd\ *n* -S [¹*parent* + *-i-* + *-cide*] **:** PARRICIDE

parent-in-law \ˈ==ᵊn,=\ *n, pl* **parents-in-law :** the father or mother of one's spouse **:** FATHER-IN-LAW, MOTHER-IN-LAW

par·ent·less \ˈ==lə̇s\ *adj* **:** having no parent ⟨a short wiry stalk of white heath grew, ~ and alone —Eve Langley⟩

parent material *n* **:** the disintegrated rock material usu. unconsolidated and unchanged or only slightly changed that underlies and generally gives rise to the true soil by the natural process of soil development — called also *source material;* compare HORIZON 2, SOLUM

parent metal *n* **:** BASE METAL 4

parents *pl of* PARENT, *pres 3d sing of* PARENT

par·ent·ship \ˈ==ˌship\ *n* **:** PARENTHOOD

parent-teacher association \ˈ==ˈ==-\ *n* **:** an organization of local groups of teachers and the parents of their pupils to work for the improvement of the schools and the benefit of the pupils — abbr. *PTA*

par·e·oe·an \ˌparēˈēən\ *n* -S *usu cap* [¹*para-* + Gk *ēōs* dawn + E *-ean* (as in *European*) — more at EAST] **:** a member of a Mongoloid people having black hair with scant face and body hair, yellowish brown skin, broad face, short flat nose, short stature, and the Mongolian eye fold — called also *Southern Mongol*

parepididymis \(ˌ)par+\ *n* [NL, fr. ¹*para-* + *epididymis*] **:** PARADIDYMIS

parepigastric \(ˌ)par+\ *adj* [ISV ¹*para-* + *epigastric*] **:** adjacent to the epigastric region

par·er \ˈpa(a)rə(r), ˈper-\ *n* -S **:** one that pares: as **a :** a mechanical device for paring vegetables or fruits ⟨potato ~⟩ **b :** one who pares binding leather to proper thickness for use

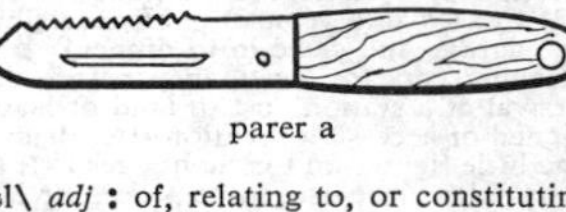

parer a

par·er·gal \(ˈ)paˈrərgəl\ *adj* **:** of, relating to, or constituting a parergon **:** SUBORDINATE

par·er·ga·sia \ˌpar+\ *n* [NL, fr. ¹*para-* + *ergasia*] **:** schizophrenia regarded as a disorder of action

par·er·gon \pəˈrərˌgän\ *n, pl* **parer·ga** \-gə\ [L, fr. Gk, fr. *par-* ¹para- + *ergon* work — more at WORK] **1 :** something subordinate or accessory; *esp* **:** an ornamental accessory or embellishment **2 :** a subordinate activity or work **:** work undertaken in addition to one's main employment ⟨a ~, pondered and written during . . . moments of leisure —J.D. Wilson⟩

pares *pres 3d sing of* PARE, *pl of* PARE

pa·re·sis \pəˈrēsə̇s, ˈparə-\ *n, pl* **pare·ses** \-ˌsēz\ [NL, fr. Gk, action of letting go or slackening, paralysis, neglect, fr. *parienai* to let fall at the side, let fall, fr. *par-* ¹para- + *hienai* to let go, send — more at JET] **1 :** slight or partial paralysis **2 :** GENERAL PARESIS

pa·res·sí \ˌparəˈsē\ *n, pl* **paressí** *or* **paressís** *usu cap* [Pg, of AmerInd origin] **1 a :** a group of Arawakan peoples of central Brazil **b :** a member of any such people **2 :** the language of the Paressí peoples

par·esthesia *also* **par·aesthesia** \ˌpar+\ *n* [NL, fr. *para-* + *esthesia, aesthesia*] **:** a sensation of pricking, tingling, or creeping on the skin having no objective cause and usu. associated with injury or irritation of a sensory nerve or nerve root

par·esthetic *also* **par·aesthetic** \"+\ *adj* **:** of, relating to, or affected with paresthesia

¹**pa·ret·ic** \pəˈre|d·|ik, |t|, |ēk *sometimes* -rē\ *adj* [fr. NL *paresis*, after such pairs as E *antithesis: antithetic*] **:** of, relating to, or affected with paresis — **pa·ret·i·cal·ly** \|ə̇k(ə)lē, |ēk-, -li\ *adv*

²**paretic** \"\ *n* -S **:** an individual affected with paresis

pa·re·to's law \pəˈrād·(ˌ)ōz-\ *n, usu cap P* [after Vilfredo *Pareto* (Marchese di Parigi) †1923 Ital. economist and sociologist] **:** a statement in economics: the distribution of incomes in various countries and in various ages tends to be similar despite differences of governmental policy (as in taxation)

pa·reu \ˈpärāˌü\ *n* -S [Tahitian] **:** a wraparound skirt or loincloth worn throughout Polynesia and usu. made from a rectangular piece of printed cloth

par·eu·nia \pəˈrünēə\ *n* -S [NL, fr. Gk *pareunos* lying beside, bedfellow (fr. *par-* ¹para- + *eunē* bed) + NL *-ia*] **:** COITUS

pa·re·ve \ˈpärəˌvə\ *or* **par·ve** \ˈpärvə\ *adj* [Yiddish *parev*] **:** made without milk, meat, or their derivatives

¹**par ex·cel·lence** \ˌpäˌreksəˈläⁿs, ˌpȧ,(r)e-, -län(t)s, ˌ=ˈ==,=; *sometimes* =ˈ(r)eks(ə)lən(t)s\ *adv* [F, lit. by excellence] **:** PREEMINENTLY

²**par excellence** \"\ *adj* **:** being the best of its kind **:** being an epitome or embodiment ⟨bronze . . . was the metal *par excellence* of the more advanced nations —A.L.Kroeber⟩ ⟨the grassland *par excellence* that accounts for the legendary green of Erin —Samuel Van Valkenburg & Ellsworth Huntington⟩ ⟨the private secretary *par excellence* —John Gunther⟩

par·fait \pärˈfā, pȧˈ-, ˈ=,=\ *n* -S [F, lit., something perfect, fr. *parfait* perfect, fr. L *perfectus* — more at PERFECT] **1 :** a flavored custard containing whipped cream and syrup frozen without stirring **2 :** a cold dessert consisting of alternating layers of fruit, syrup, ice cream, and whipped cream in a parfait glass

parfait amour *n* [F, lit., perfect love] **:** a violet-colored liqueur flavored principally with lemon, vanilla, cloves, and coriander

parfait glass *n* **:** a tall narrow glass with a short stem used for serving a parfait

par·fit \ˈpärfə̇t, ˈpȧf-\ *chiefly dial var of* PERFECT

par·fleche \ˈpärˌflesh, =ˈ=\ *n* -S [CanF *parflèche*, fr. F *parer* to ward off, parry + *flèche* arrow — more at PARRY, FLÈCHE] **1 :** a rawhide (as of buffalo) soaked in lye to remove the hair and dried **2 :** an article (as a box, sack, or saddlebag) made of parfleche

par·focal \(ˈ)pär+\ *adj* [L *par* equal + E *focal* — more at PAIR] **:** having corresponding focal points all in the same plane **:** having sets of objectives or eyepieces so mounted that they may be interchanged without varying the focus of the instrument (as a microscope or telescope) with which they are used

parfait glass

par·focalization \(ˌ)=+\ *n* **:** a rendering parfocal

par·focalize \(ˈ)=+\ *vt* **:** to make parfocal

par·ga·na *or* **per·gun·nah** \pərˈgənə, ˈpərgəˌnä\ *n* -S [Hindi *pargana*, fr. Per] **:** a group of towns in India constituting an administrative subdivision of the zillah

par·gas·ite \ˈpärgəˌsīt\ *n* -S [G *pargasit*, fr. *Pargas*, town in Finland + G *-it* -ite] **:** a green or bluish green hornblende containing sodium

parge \ˈpärj\ *vt* -ED/-ING/-S [by shortening] **:** PARGET

parge coat *n* **:** PARGING

¹**par·get** \ˈpärjə̇t\ *vt* **pargeted** *or* **pargetted; pargeted** *or* **pargetted; pargeting** *or* **pargetting; pargets** [ME *pargetten*, fr. MF *pargeter, parjeter* to throw on top of, fr. *par-*, intensive prefix (fr. L *per-*, fr. *per* through) + *geter, jeter* to throw — more at FOR, JET] **1 :** to coat with plaster; *esp* **:** to apply ornamental plasterwork to **2 :** to decorate with gilding or other ornamental surfacing **3** *archaic* **:** to cover with a fair outward appearance **:** WHITEWASH

²**parget** \"\ *n* -S [ME, fr. *pargetten*, v.] **1 a :** plaster, whitewash, or roughcast for coating a wall **b :** a plaster of cow's dung and lime for lining chimney flues **c :** ornamental pargeting on walls **2** *obs* **:** GYPSUM

par·get·er \-jəd·ə(r)\ *n* -S [¹*parget* + *-er*] *dial Eng* **:** PLASTERER

par·get·ing *or* **par·get·ting** *n* -S [ME, fr. gerund of *pargeten, pargetten* to parget — more at PARGET] **1 :** a decorative plasterwork in raised ornamental figures formerly used for interior and exterior decoration of houses **2 :** the interior plastering of flues intended to give a smooth surface and help the draft

par·get·ry \ˈpärjə·trē, -tri\ *n* -ES [²*parget* + *-ry*] **:** ornamental plaster or stucco relief work applied to a flat surface

pargework \ˈ=,=\ *n* **:** PARGETRY

parging *n* -S [fr. gerund of *parge*] **:** a thin coat of mortar or plaster used to smooth or waterproof the surface of rough brick or stone walls or to line the inside of chimneys

par·go \ˈpär(ˌ)gō\ *n* -S [Sp & Pg, fr. L *pagarus* sea bream, fr. Gk *phagros*, lit., whetstone; akin to Gk *phoxos* pointed, peaked, and perh. to Arm *bark* bitter, sharp-tasting] **1 :** any of various fishes of the family Sparidae; *esp* **:** the European porgy (*Pagrus pagrus*) **2 :** any of various snappers of the family Lutjanidae

par·helic \(ˈ)pär, (ˈ)pȧ+\ *or* **par·heliacal** \ˌ=+\ *adj* **:** of or relating to a parhelion

parhelic circle *or* **parhelic ring** *n* **:** a luminous circle or halo parallel to the horizon at the altitude of the sun

par·helion \"+\ *n, pl* **parhelia** [L *parelion*, fr. Gk *parēlion, parēlios*, fr. *par-* ¹para- + *hēlios* sun — more at SOLAR] **:** any one of several bright spots often tinged with color that often appear symmetrically distributed on the parhelic circle and are intensified parts of halos — called also *mock sun, sun dog;* compare PARASELENE

par·homologous \ˌpär, ˌpȧ+\ *adj* [¹*para-* + *homologous*] **:** exhibiting parhomology

par·homology \"+\ *n* [ISV ¹*para-* + *homology*] **:** apparent or imitative homology esp. between metameres

pari- *comb form* [ME, fr. MF, fr. ML, fr. L *par* — more at PAIR] **:** equal **:** equally ⟨*pari*digitate⟩

pa·ri·ah \pəˈrīə *sometimes* ˈpa(a)rēə\ *n* -S [Tamil *paraiyan*, lit., drummer, fr. *parai* drum] **1 :** a member of a low caste of southern India and Burma that is below Sudra rank and has provided many farm laborers and domestic servants **2 :** a person despised or rejected by society **:** OUTCAST ⟨hundreds of thousands of lepers still exist throughout the world as social ~*s* —V.G.Heiser⟩ ⟨many virile minds dare not speak out for fear of . . . becoming political ~*s* —L.L.Rice⟩ ⟨a ~ to former friends, who were afraid to be seen with me —P.B.Williamson⟩

pariah dog *n* **:** a wild or domesticated native mongrel dog of No. Africa or southern Asia, varying greatly in conformation and important chiefly as a scavenger

pa·ri·ah·dom \-dəm\ *n* -S **:** the condition of a pariah ⟨they walked on together, and I dropped behind suddenly realizing my ~ —W.J.Locke⟩

pa·ri·ah·ism \-əˌizəm\ *n* -S **:** PARIAHDOM

pariah kite *n* **:** a scavenger kite (*Milvus migrans govinda*) of India

¹**pa·ri·an** \ˈpa(a)rēən, ˈper-\ *adj, usu cap* [L *parius* Parian, fr. Gk *parios* (fr. *Paros*, one of the Cyclades islands in the Aegean sea) + E *-an*] **1 :** of or relating to the Cycladic island of Paros, noted for its beautiful marble extensively used for sculptures in ancient times **2 :** of, relating to, or being Parian ware

²**parian** \"\ *n* -S **:** PARIAN WARE ⟨his teeth . . . showed like ~ from his parted lips —Thomas Hardy⟩

parian cement *n, usu cap P* [(*plaster of*) *Paris* + E *-an*] **:** a hard-finish gypsum plaster to which borax has been added

parian ware *n, usu cap P* [*'Parian'*] **:** a relatively low-fired white to pale ivory ceramic body made of feldspar and china clay and used usu. for bisque statuary and ornamental items

pa·ri·ca \ˌparə̇ˈkä\ *n* -S [Pg *paricá*, fr. Tupi] **:** COHOBA

par·i·dae \ˈparəˌdē\ *n, cap* [NL, fr. L *Parus*, type genus + *-idae*] **:** a large family of passerine birds (suborder Oscines) consisting of the titmice, verdins, and bushtits — compare SITTIDAE

pa·ri·es \ˈpa(a)rēˌēz\ *n, pl* **pari·e·tes** \pəˈrīəˌtēz\ [NL, fr. L, wall; akin to OSlav *podŭpora* prop, L *sparus, sparum* short spear — more at SPEAR] **1 :** the wall of a cavity or hollow organ — usu. used in pl. **2 :** the triangular middle part of each segment of the shell of a barnacle

¹**pa·ri·e·tal** \pəˈrīəd·ᵊl\ *adj* [MF, fr. NL *pariet-, paries* + MF *-al*] **1 a :** of or relating to the walls of a part or cavity ⟨~ peritoneum⟩ — compare VISCERAL **b :** of, relating to, or located in the upper posterior part of the head; *specif* **:** relating to either of the pair of bones that form the cranial roof of this part of the skull **2** *of a plant part* **:** peripheral in location or orientation; *esp* **:** attached to the main wall rather than the axis or a cross wall of an ovary — used of an ovule or a placenta **3 :** of or relating to life within college walls or its order and regulation; *esp* **:** of or relating to the visitation regulations for members of the opposite sex in dormitories **4 :** of, relating to, or appearing on a wall ⟨upon the wall . . . some work of ~ art —G.B.Brown⟩

²**parietal** \"\ *n* -S **:** a parietal part (as a bone, scale, or plate)

parietal angle *n* **:** the angle formed by the intersection of lines from the auricular point to the bregma and to the lambda

parietal bone *n* **:** either of a pair of membrane bones of the roof of the skull between the frontals and occipitals that in

man are large and quadrilateral in outline, meet in the sagittal suture, and form much of the top and sides of the cranium
parietal cell *n* **:** any of the large oval acid-secreting cells of the gastric mucous membrane lying between the central cells and the basement membrane — compare CHIEF CELL
pa·ri·e·ta·les \pə,rīə'tā(,)lēz\ *n pl, cap* [NL, fr. *pariet-, paries* + *-ales*] **:** a large order of dicotyledonous plants with spirocyclic or cyclic flowers that have the ovary syncarpous and usu. parietal placentae
parietal eye *n* **:** PINEAL EYE
parietal lobe *n* **:** the middle division of each cerebral hemisphere situated behind the central sulcus, above the fissure of Sylvius, and in front of the parieto-occipital fissure
pa·ri·e·tar·ia \pə,rīə'ta(a)rēə\ *n, cap* [NL, fr. LL, pellitory-of-the-wall, fr. L fem. of *parietarius* of a wall, fr. L *pariet-, paries* wall + *-arius* -ary — more at PARIES] **:** a small genus of widely distributed stingless herbs (family Urticaceae) with alternate entire leaves and small greenish flowers in the leaf axils — see PELLITORY 2
parieto- *comb form* [*parietal*] **:** parietal and ⟨*parieto*frontal⟩
pa·ri·e·to-occipital fissure \pə¦rīəd·,ō+-\ *or* **parieto-occipital sulcus** *n* **:** a fissure near the posterior end of each cerebral hemisphere separating the parietal and occipital lobes
pari-mutuel \parə¦myüch(əw)əl, -chwəl\ *n, pl* **pari-mutuels** \-lz\ *also in sense 1* **par·is-mutuels** \¦parə¦m-\ [F *pari mutuel*, lit., mutual stake] **1 :** a system of betting (as on a horse race) in which those who bet on the winner share the total stakes minus a small percent for the management **2** *or* **pari-mutuel machine :** a machine for registering and indicating the number and nature of bets made (as on a horse race) in the pari-mutuel system of betting
par·i·na·ri \,parənə¦rē\ *n* -s [Galibi] **:** any of several trees of the genus *Parinarium; esp* **:** a tree (*P. rudolphi*) of the Amazonian rain forests that has extremely hard strong yellow wood which is rich in silica and is used in marine construction because of its resistance to borers
par·i·nar·ic acid \¦parə¦narik-\ *n* [ISV *parinar-* (fr. NL *Parinarium*) + *-ic*] **:** a crystalline highly unsaturated fatty acid $CH_3CH_2(CH{=}CH)_4(CH_2)_7COOH$ obtained esp. from seed fats of trees of the genus *Parinarium*
par·i·nar·i·um \,==='na(a)rēəm\ *n, cap* [NL, fr. Galibi *parinari*] **:** a large genus of tropical evergreen shrubs and trees (family Rosaceae) with showy white or pink flowers, drupaceous fruits some of which are edible, and in some larger forms valuable timber — see GINGERBREAD PLUM, PARINARI
pa·rine \'pā,rīn, -,rən\ *adj* [L *parus* titmouse + E *-ine*] **:** of, relating to, or resembling the titmice
paring *n* -s [ME, fr. gerund of *paren* to pare — more at PARE] **1 :** the cutting away of an edge or surface **2 :** something pared off ⟨potato ~*s*⟩ **3 parings** *pl* **:** BOXING 4
paring chisel *n* **:** a long-handled hand chisel having a short thin blade for paring wood surfaces — see CHISEL illustration
paring gouge *n* **:** a woodworker's gouge having a concave blade beveled inside to form the cutting edge
paring iron *n* **:** a knife used for paring a hoof
paring knife *n* **:** a small short-bladed knife for paring fruit and vegetables

paring knife

par·in·tin·tin \,parən·,tin·'tin\ *n, pl* **parintintin** *or* **parintintins** *usu cap* [Pg, of AmerInd origin] **1 a :** a Tupian people of the southern part of the state of Amazonas, Brazil **b :** a member of such people **2 :** the language of the Parintintin people
pa·ri pas·su \,parē'pa(,)sü, -rə'p-; ,pärē'pä(,)sü\ *adv* (*or adj*) [L, with equal step] **:** at an equal rate or pace **:** with identical and simultaneous progression ⟨the rate of development decreased *pari passu* with the density —*Ecology*⟩ ⟨the two made a *pari passu* advance⟩
¹par·is \'parəs *also* 'per-\ *adj, usu cap* [fr. *Paris*, France] **1 :** of or from Paris, the capital of France ⟨the *Paris* scene⟩ ⟨a *Paris* original⟩ **:** of the kind or style prevalent in Paris **:** PARISIAN **2** *of clothing* **:** made in Paris, France, or adapted from designs originating there ⟨girls in *Paris* frocks walked slowly back and forth —J.A.Michener⟩
²paris \"\ *n, cap* [NL, fr. ML or NL (*herba*) *paris* herb Paris — more at HERB PARIS] **:** a small genus of Eurasian herbs (family Liliaceae) not unlike *Trillium* in the whorled leaves and floral parts but having often tetramerous or pentamerous flowers — see HERB PARIS
paris blue *n* [¹*Paris*] **1** *usu cap P* **:** an iron-blue pigment similar to Prussian blue **2** *often cap P* **:** PRUSSIAN BLUE
paris daisy *n, usu cap P* **:** a marguerite (*Chrysanthemum frutescens*)
paris garden *n, usu cap P* [fr. *Paris Garden*, a 16th and 17th cent. bear garden in London, England] *obs* **:** a bear garden **:** a scene of uproar and confusion
paris granite *n, usu cap P* **:** SEMIPORCELAIN
paris green *n* **1** *usu cap P* **:** an insecticide and pigment prepared as a very poisonous bright green powder (as from arsenic trioxide and copper acetate) and consisting of copper acetoarsenite approximately $Cu(C_2H_3O_2)_2.3Cu(AsO_2)_2$ — called also *emerald green, Schweinfurt green* **2** *often cap P* **a :** a variable color averaging a brilliant yellowish green **b :** a moderate yellowish green that is greener, lighter, and stronger than tarragon, lighter and slightly stronger than malachite green, and yellower, lighter, and stronger than verdigris — called also *imperial green*
¹par·ish \'parish, -rēsh *also* 'per-\ *n* -ES [ME *paroche, parosshe, parisshe*, fr. MF *paroche, paroisse*, fr. LL *parochia*, fr. LGk *paroikia*, fr. *paroikos* Christian (fr. Gk, stranger, fr. *par-* ¹para- + *oikos* house) + *-ia* -y; fr. the early Christians' looking upon themselves as strangers on earth, their real home being heaven — more at VICINITY] **1 a :** the ecclesiastical unit of area committed to one pastor; *collectively* **:** the residents of such area or the members of one church **b** *Brit* **:** a subdivision of a county often coinciding with an original ecclesiastical parish and constituting the unit of local government **2 :** a portion of a diocese committed to the pastoral care of one clergyman **3 :** a local church community composed of the members or constituents of a Protestant church **4 :** SOCIETY 3b(2) **5 :** a civil division of the state of Louisiana corresponding to a county in other states **6 :** HOUSE 3d — see CURLING illustration
²par·ish \'parish\ *dial var of* PERISH
parish court *n* **:** a court established for each Louisiana parish and having a jurisdiction similar to that of a county court of common pleas
par·ish·en \'parishən\ *n* -s [ME (northern dial.) *parichin, parishing*, prob. fr. *parisshe* parish + *-ing* — more at PARISH] *Scot* **:** PARISH
parish house *n* **1 :** an auxiliary building belonging to a church and used for its business, social, or extension activities **2 :** the residence of a clergyman (as a Roman Catholic priest)
pa·rish·io·nal \pə'rishənᵊl, -shnəl\ *adj* [*parishioner* + *-al*] *archaic* **:** PAROCHIAL
pa·rish·io·ner \-sh(ə)nə(r) *sometimes* -zh-\ *n* -s [ME *parisshoner*, prob. modif. of MF *parrochien, paroissien* parishioner (fr. *parroche, paroisse* parish + *-ien* -ian) + ME *-er* — more at PARISH] **:** a member or inhabitant of a parish
parish lantern *n, dial chiefly Eng* **:** MOON
parish-pump \¦==¦=\ *adj, chiefly Brit* **:** of local scope or purview **:** having a restricted outlook or limited interest **:** PAROCHIAL ⟨smacked less of a serious schism than of a *parish-pump* quarrel —*Times Lit. Supp.*⟩
parish register *n* **:** a register of the baptisms, marriages, and burials in a parish
parish seat *n* **:** a county seat in Louisiana
¹pa·ri·sian \pə'rizhən, -rēzh- *sometimes* pa'- *or* -rizēən\ *adj, usu cap* [F *parisien*, adj. & n., fr. *Paris*, France, + F *-ien* -ian] **1 a :** of, relating to, or characteristic of Paris, the capital of France **b :** of, relating to, or characteristic of the people of Paris **2 :** of, relating to, or characteristic of the standard French language
²parisian \"\ *n* -s *cap* [F *Parisien*] **1 :** a native or resident of Paris, France **2 a :** the French dialect of Paris **b :** the official and literary language of France based on this dialect **:** standard French
pa·ri·sian·ism \-,nizəm\ *n* -s *usu cap* [F *parisianisme*, fr. *parisien* + *-isme* -ism] **1 :** the traits of a Parisian ⟨his *Parisianism*, grafted upon an imperishable brogue, gave to his utterance a very curious charm —Max Beerbohm⟩ **2 :** a habit or mannerism (as of speech) observable esp. in Parisians
pa·ri·si·enne \pə¦rēzē¦en\ *n* -s *cap* [F, fem. of *Parisien*] **:** a Parisian woman or girl ⟨the 32-year-old *Parisienne* was stopped by . . . border guards —*Springfield (Mass.) Daily News*⟩
par·is·ite \'parə,sīt\ *n* -s [G *parisit*, fr. José *Paris* †1849 Colombian mineowner and philanthropist + G *-it* -ite] **:** a mineral $(Ce,La)_2Ca(CO_3)_3F_2$ consisting of a carbonate and fluoride of calcium, cerium, and lanthanum
paris-mutuels *pl of* PARI-MUTUEL
par·i·sol·o·gy \,parə'säləjē\ *n* -ES [Gk *parisos* almost equal, evenly balanced + *-logy*] **:** the use of equivocal or ambiguous words
¹par·ison \'parə,sän\ *n* -s [Gk, neut. of *parisos* almost equal, evenly balanced, fr. *par-* ¹para- + *isos* equal] **:** even balance between the members of a sentence — **par·ison·ic** \¦==¦sänik\ *adj*
²par·i·son \'parəsən\ *also* **par·ai·son** \", -rə,zān\ *n* -s [F *paraison*, fr. *parer* to prepare — more at PARE] **1 :** a gob of glass that has been partially shaped or molded into an object **2 :** a receptacle in a bottle-making machine from which the exact amount of metal for making a bottle is fed down
par·i·so·sis \,parə'sōsəs\ *n* -ES [Gk *parisōsis*, fr. *parisoun* to make equal (fr. *parisos* almost equal, equally balanced) + *-sis* — more at PARISON] **:** ¹PARISON
paris red *n* **1** *usu cap P* **:** an iron red used as a polishing agent and pigment **2 :** red lead used as a pigment **3** *often cap P* **:** FIRE RED 1
par·isth·mi·on \pa'rismēən, -ē,än\ *n* -s [Gk, fr. *par-* ¹para- + *isthmion* anything belonging to the neck or throat, fr. *isthmos* neck, narrow passage, neck of land — more at ISTHMUS] **:** TONSIL
paris white *n, usu cap P* **:** whiting esp. of good color and very fine particle size used as a pigment or filler
paris yellow *n* **1** *usu cap P* **:** any of various yellow pigments: as **a :** a chrome yellow pigment **b :** CASSEL YELLOW **2** *often cap P* **:** LIGHT CHROME YELLOW
pari·syllabic \¦parə+\ *adj* [*pari-* + *syllabic*] *of a Greek or Latin noun* **:** having the same number of syllables in all inflections
pa·riti \pə'rīd·ē, -rid-ē\ *n, cap* [NL, fr. Malayalam *paritti, parutti* cotton plant, cotton tree] *in some classifications* **:** a small genus of tropical trees (family Malvaceae) with entire cordate leaves and yellow flowers now usu. included in the genus *Hibiscus*
par·i·tor \'parəd·ə(r)\ *n* -s [LL *paritor* servant, attendant, fr. L *paritus* (past part. of *parēre* to come forth, be visible, attend) + *-or* — more at APPEAR] *chiefly dial* **:** APPARITOR
¹pa·ri·ty \'parəd·ē, -ətē, -i *also* 'per-\ *n* -ES [L *paritas*, fr. *par* equal + *-itas* -ity — more at PAIR] **1 :** the quality or state of being equal **:** close equivalence or resemblance **:** equality of rank, nature, or value **:** LIKENESS ⟨~ must exist between authority and responsibility —Harold Koontz & Cyril O'Donnell⟩ **2 a :** equivalence of a commodity price expressed in one currency to its price expressed in another **b :** equality of purchasing power established by law between different kinds of money at a given ratio (as between gold and silver coins of a fixed weight and fineness) **3 :** an equivalence between farmers' current purchasing power and their purchasing power at a selected base period maintained by government support of agricultural commodity prices at a level fixed by law **:** a ratio between agricultural and nonagricultural prices at a specified past time ⟨~ is the price calculated to give the farmer a fair return in relation to the things he must buy —*N.Y.Times*⟩
²parity \"\ *n* -ES [*parous* + *-ity*] **:** parous condition **:** number of children previously borne ⟨the age and ~ of the mother may be a factor —*Jour. Amer. Med. Assoc.*⟩
¹park \'pärk, 'pák\ *n* -s [ME, fr. OF *parc* enclosure, enclosure for animals, park, fr. (assumed) VL *parricus* enclosure (whence ML *parricus*), perh. fr. L *pertica* pole, measuring rod, parcel of land measured off with such a rod — more at PERCH] **1 a** *Eng law* **:** an enclosed piece of ground stocked with beasts of the chase and held by royal prescription or grant — compare ²CHASE 3, FOREST 1 **b** *Brit* **:** a tract of land often including lawns, woodland, and pasture attached to a country house and used as a game preserve and for other purposes of recreation and manorial life **2 :** a tract of land maintained by a city or town as a place of beauty or of public recreation **3 :** a large area often of forested land reserved from settlement and maintained in its natural state for public use (as by campers or hunters) or as a wildlife refuge **4** *dial Eng* **:** HAYFIELD, PASTURE **5 a** (1) **:** a level valley between mountain ranges (2) *chiefly West* **:** an open area surrounded or partly surrounded by woodland and suitable for grazing or cultivation **b :** open grassland interrupted by clumps of trees, forbs, and shrubby vegetation **6 a :** a space occupied by military animals, vehicles, pontoons, or materials of any kind (as ammunition, ordnance stores, hospital stores, or provisions); *also* **:** the objects themselves ⟨a ~ of artillery⟩ **b :** PARKING LOT **7 :** an enclosed basin in which oysters are grown arranged so that the water may be renewed at high tide **:** CLAIRE **8 :** a large enclosed area used for sports; *esp* **:** BALL PARK
²park \"\ *vb* -ED/-ING/-S *vt* **1 a :** to enclose in or as if in a park **b :** to make a park of **2 a** (1) **:** to bring to a stop and keep standing (as a motor vehicle) at the edge of a public way ⟨had never learned to ~ a car properly⟩ (2) **:** to leave temporarily on a public way or in an open space assigned or maintained for occupancy by automobiles ⟨~*ed* his car behind the building⟩ (3) **:** to leave (a vehicle) in an accessible place ⟨~*ed* his car in the garage and came in to dinner⟩ **b :** to set out (a railroad sleeping car) for occupancy before departure from or after arrival at a station **c :** to land or leave an airplane in an assigned or accessible location ⟨flew back to the carrier and ~*ed* the little fighter on the flight deck⟩ **3 a :** to set and leave in a particular place usu. to be picked up later ⟨~*ed* his bag at the club⟩ **b :** to deposit, settle, or establish esp. for a considerable time ⟨~*ed* himself in an easy chair⟩ ⟨the . . . anxiety that they might feel about ~*ing* the baby —J.M.Barzun⟩ **4 :** to assemble (as artillery, vehicles, or stores) in a military dump or park ~ *vi* **1 :** to park a vehicle ⟨after landing on the runway, private owners used to ~ at the far edge⟩ ⟨looked for a place to ~ long enough to run a few errands⟩ **2 :** to stop a vehicle in a secluded place to engage in lovemaking ⟨~*ed* with his girl in a local lovers' lane⟩
par·ka \'pärkə, 'pákə\ *n* -s [Aleut, skin, outer garment, fr. Russ, pelt from a reindeer, dog, or sheep, fr. Samoyed] **1 :** a hooded pullover garment reaching to the thighs or knees that is made usu. of fur and worn by Eskimos and others living in arctic regions **2 :** a garment shorter than the arctic parka but of similar style made of heavy windproof fabric for sports or military wear as either a jacket or a pullover

parka 2

park cattle *n, usu cap P&C* **:** a breed or variety of white long-haired polled or horned cattle with dark points that is maintained in a semidomesticated state on a few English estates and is sometimes considered very close to the wild ancestors from which improved breeds have been derived
parked *adj* **:** laid out with greenery and decorative plantings ⟨~ terraces⟩
park·er \'pärkər, 'pákə(r\ *n* -s [ME, fr. *park* + *-er*] **1** *obs* **:** the keeper of a park **2** [²*park* + *-er*] **:** one that parks a vehicle ⟨facilities already filled by the all-day ~ —Richard Sheddon⟩
parker house roll *n, usu cap P&H* [fr. *Parker House*, hotel in Boston, Mass., where the rolls were introduced] **:** a roll made by folding half of a flat circular piece of dough over the other half
par·ke·ri·a·ce·ae \(,)pärkirē'āsē,ē\ *n pl, cap* [NL, fr. *Parkeria*, type genus (fr. C. S. *Parker*, its 19th cent. discoverer) + *-aceae*] **:** a family of homosporous leptosporangiate ferns that is coextensive with the genus *Ceratopteris* and is sometimes included in Polypodiaceae
par·ker·ite \'pärkə,rīt, 'pák-\ *n* -s [Robert Lüling *Parker* b1893 Swiss mineralogist + E *-ite*] **:** a mineral $Ni_3(Bi,Pb)_2S_2$ consisting of a sulfide of nickel, bismuth, and lead
parkes process \'pärks, 'páks-\ *n, usu cap 1st P* [after Alexander *Parkes* †1890 Eng. chemist] **:** the principal process of desilverizing lead in which zinc is added to molten lead and the silver and gold are absorbed in an alloy of zinc, lead, and silver that rises to the top and is skimmed off
park forest *n* **:** a forest of trees isolated or in groups and interspersed with grass
park green *n* **:** a moderate yellow green that is greener and deeper than average moss green and yellower and deeper than average pea green or apple green (sense 1)
park hack *n* **:** a showy welltrained 3- or 5-gaited saddle horse well-suited for riding
par·kia \'pärkēə\ *n, cap* [NL, fr. Mungo *Park* †1806, Scottish African explorer and surgeon + NL *-ia*] **:** a genus of tropical Old World trees (family Leguminosae) with heads of red or yellow flowers followed by pods that commonly contain edible seeds and pulp — see NITTA TREE
par·kin \'pärkən\ *n* -s [origin unknown] **:** a cake orig. of oatmeal, butter, and molasses now leavened with baking powder and spiced with ginger and esp. popular in Scotland and the border country
park·ing \'pärkiŋ, 'pák-, -kēŋ\ *n* -s **1 a :** ground (as in a park) adorned with trees, lawn, or shrubbery **b** *chiefly North & West* **:** a strip of turf sometimes with trees along the side of a street — compare TREE BELT **2 a :** the leaving of a vehicle in an accessible location **b :** an area in which vehicles may be left ⟨ample ~ is available⟩
parking brake *n* **:** EMERGENCY BRAKE
parking light *n* **:** a small light on an automotive vehicle for use esp. in night parking along a public way
parking lot *n* **:** an outdoor lot for the parking of motor vehicles
parking meter *n* **:** a coin-operated timing device for regulating the parking of motor vehicles
par·kin·so·nia \,pärkən'sōnēə, ,pák-, -nyə\ *n, cap* [NL, fr. John *Parkinson* †1650 Eng. botanist + NL *-ia*] **:** a small genus of spiny shrubs or small trees (family Leguminosae) with minute pinnate early deciduous leaves and racemose yellow flowers with a valvate calyx — see JERUSALEM THORN
par·kin·so·nian \¦==¦sōnēən, -nyən\ *adj* [James *Parkinson* †1824 Eng. physician + E *-ian*] **1 :** of or like that of parkinsonism ⟨~ tremors⟩ **2 :** affected with parkinsonism
par·kin·son·ism \'pärkənsə,nizəm, 'pák-\ *n* -s *sometimes cap* [James *Parkinson* + E *-ism*] **1 :** PARALYSIS AGITANS **2 :** any chronic condition of the nervous system marked by muscle rigidity but without tremor of resting muscles
par·kin·son's disease \'pärkənsənz, 'pákənsənz-\ *n, usu cap P* [after James *Parkinson*] **:** PARALYSIS AGITANS
parkinson's syndrome *n, usu cap P* [after James *Parkinson*] **:** PARALYSIS AGITANS
park·ish \'pärkish, 'pák-, -kēsh\ *adj* **:** resembling a park
parkland \'=,=\ *n* **1 :** land with clumps of trees and shrubs in cultivated condition used as or felt to be suitable for use as a park **2 :** PARK 5b
park·man crab \'pärkmən, 'pákmən-\ *or* **parkman crab-apple** *n, usu cap P* [after Francis *Parkman* †1893 Amer. historian who cultivated it] **:** an ornamental tree (*Malus halliana parkmanii*) with double bright rose-colored flowers
parks *pl of* PARK, *pres 3d sing of* PARK
parkway \'=,=\ *n* **1 a :** a broad landscaped thoroughfare; *esp* **:** one from which trucks and other heavy vehicles are excluded **b :** a roadway in a park **:** a landscaped thoroughfare connecting parks **c :** an expressway located on a strip of land legally constituting a public park and therefore not open to heavy vehicles **2 :** a landscaped strip of land paralleling or running in the center of a thoroughfare **3** *North & Midland* **:** PARKING 1b
parky \'pärkē\ *adj* [¹*park* + *-y*] *dial Brit* **:** COLD
parl *abbr* parliament; parliamentary
par·lance \'pärlən(t)s, 'pál-\ *n* -s [MF, fr. OF, fr. *parler, parlier* to speak, talk + *-ance*] **1 :** an instance of speaking **:** SPEECH; *esp* **:** an instance of formal speaking (as a debate or parley) ⟨battle and not ~ should determine his right and title —John Speed⟩ **2 :** manner or mode of speech **:** DICTION, IDIOM, PHRASEOLOGY ⟨in educational ~, the new school is an activity school —W.H.Kilpatrick⟩ ⟨in movie ~ a junket is a special trip organized by a studio —*Saturday Rev.*⟩
¹par·lan·do \pär'län(,)dō\ *or* **par·lan·te** \-n·(,)tā\ *adj* [*parlando* fr. It, verbal of *parlare* to speak, talk, fr. ML *parabolare*; *parlante* fr. It, pres. part. of *parlare*] **:** delivered or performed in an unsustained style or manner suggestive of speech ⟨the vocal subtlety of the two big ~ solos —Marc Blitzstein⟩ — used as a direction in music
²parlando \"\ *n* -s **1 :** parlando style ⟨singing it in a poker-faced quick ~ —O.J.Gombosi⟩ — contrasted with *cantabile* **2 :** a piece or passage in parlando style
par·la·to·ria \,pärlə'tōrēə, -tór-\ *n* [NL, fr. Filippo *Parlatore* †1877 Ital. botanist + NL *-ia*] **1** *cap* **:** a genus of armored scales distinguished by the presence of very large second exuviae that are widespread in warm regions and include several economically important pests of cultivated plants **2** -s **:** a scale of the genus *Parlatoria*
par·la·to·ry \'==,tōrē, -tór-, -ri\ *n* -ES [ML *parlatorium*, fr. OF *parleor, parlour* parlor — more at PARLOR] **:** a reception room in a convent
¹par·lay \'pär,lā, 'pá,lā *also* -,lē *or* -,li\ *vt* -ED/-ING/-S [alter. of ²*paroli*] **1 :** to bet (as money) in a parlay **2 a :** to increase or otherwise transform into something of much greater value ⟨~ a few beat-up crates into a major airline —*Newsweek*⟩ ⟨~*ed* just four . . . $10 bills into a billion and a quarter dollar fortune —Robert Engler⟩ **b :** to utilize as a means to great gains or a desired objective ⟨100 ways to ~ a good idea and very little cash into a fortune —*advt*⟩ ⟨tried to ~ this Russophobia into a parliamentary career —*Newsweek*⟩
²parlay \"\ *n* -s **1 :** a proposed series of two or more bets in which the bettor selects all contingencies in advance and irrevocably bets the original stake plus any winnings on each successive contingency **2 :** a risking of an original stake plus winnings or of an original investment plus earnings
¹parle \'pär(ə)l\ *vb* -ED/-ING/-S [ME *parlen*, fr. MF *parler* to speak, talk] *archaic* **:** PARLEY
²parle \"\ *n* -s *archaic* **:** PARLEY
par·ley \'pärlē, 'pál-, -li\ *vb* -ED/-ING/-S [MF *parler* to speak, talk, fr. ML *parabolare*, fr. LL *parabola* speech, parable — more at PARABLE] *vt* **1 :** UTTER; *esp* **:** SPEAK 3 ⟨that Yank can't half ~ the lingo —Richard Llewellyn⟩ **2** *archaic* **:** to grant a parley to **:** to hold a conference or discussion with **:** ADDRESS ~ *vi* **:** to speak with another **:** CONFER ⟨the Russian delegations . . . refused to ~ with any Korean parties other than the Leftist —*Current Biog.*⟩; *specif* **:** to hold a parley with or as if with an enemy ⟨the . . . government was forced to ~ with the rebels —Richard Harrington⟩
²parley \"\ *n* -s **1 a :** a conference held usu. for the discussion of points in dispute ⟨the plan of the State Department to sponsor regional ~*s* for its missions throughout the world —*Current Biog.*⟩ ⟨other ~*s* were scheduled Thursday and Friday with the . . . electrical workers —*Retailing Daily*⟩ **b :** an oral and usu. informal conference with an enemy under a truce (as for the discussion of armistice terms or an exchange of prisoners) ⟨details of battle, ~, and further battle —G.B. Saul⟩ ⟨willingness to resume the cease-fire ~*s* —*Current Biog.*⟩ **2 :** mutual discourse **:** CONVERSATION, DISCUSSION ⟨without further ~ she proceeded in the direction indicated —Joseph Hergesheimer⟩ ⟨holding long and interesting ~ with these worthies —*Strand Mag.*⟩
par·ley·er \'pärlēər, 'pálēə(r\ *n* -s **:** one that parleys
¹parley-voo \¦pärlē¦vü\ *n* -s [F *parlez-vous* do you speak (in *parlez-vous français?* do you speak French?)] **1 :** the French language ⟨no words to spell, no sums to do . . . and no *parley-voo* —J.R.Lowell⟩ **2** *usu cap* **:** FRENCHMAN ⟨hardy British tars who had pity on a poor *Parley-voo* —W.S.Gilbert⟩
²parley-voo \"\ *vi* -ED/-ING/-S [F *parlez-vous*] **:** TALK; *esp* **:** to speak French or another language besides English ⟨nice to stop and *parley-voo* a second —Sinclair Lewis⟩
par·lia·ment \'pärləmənt, 'pál-, *chiefly non-British* -lyəm- *or sometimes* -lēəm-\ *n* -s *often attrib* [ME *parliament, parlement*, fr. OF *parlement*, fr. *parler, parlier* to speak, talk + *-ment*] **1 :** a formal conference for the discussion of public affairs; *specif* **:** a general or great council of state summoned by the

sovereign in early medieval England **2 a :** an assemblage of persons (as members of the nobility, clergy, and commons) called together by the British sovereign, sitting for a period of time and then being dissolved, and constituting the supreme legislative body in the United Kingdom ⟨provides for the election and meeting of a new ~ —T.E.May⟩ ⟨sat through three ~*s* —Christopher Hollis⟩ ⟨inspired . . . by the counsel of their elected ~*s* —Elizabeth II⟩ — compare CONGRESS 5 **b :** a similar assemblage in another political unit (as a nation or state) ⟨the third session of Ceylon's second ~ —*London Daily Telegraph*⟩ ⟨elected to Italy's first ~ —J.C.Adams & Paolo Barile⟩ **3 a :** the supreme legislative body of a usu. major political unit (as a nation or state) being a continuing institution comprising a series of individual parliaments ⟨the ~ of the United Kingdom is composed of the Sovereign, the House of Lords and the House of Commons —T.E.May⟩ ⟨reached the committee stage in the French ~ —*N.Y. Times*⟩ ⟨the imperial ~ is the supreme legislature for the whole of His Majesty's dominions —Martin Wight⟩ — compare CONGRESS 3 **b :** the British House of Commons ⟨confer office only upon members of ~ or peers —Ivor Jennings⟩ **4** [MF *parlement*, fr. OF] **:** one of several principal courts of justice existing in France before the revolution of 1789 **5 a :** an assembly representing a group or the members of an organization and usu. convened for the expression of opinion, enactment of policy, and the transaction of other business ⟨the Students' *Parliament* is the official undergraduate organization —*Univ. of Toronto Calendar*⟩ ⟨these general union meetings are . . . the ~*s* of any enterprise or plant —A.R.Williams⟩ **b :** a gathering resembling or held to resemble such a consultative assembly ⟨the rooks called one another to their evening ~ —Archibald Marshall⟩ **6 :** PARLIAMENT CAKE **7 :** FAN-TAN 2

par·lia·men·tal \¦==¦ment³l\ *adj, archaic* **:** PARLIAMENTARY ⟨deriving their ~ authority only from the people —William Prynne⟩

¹par·lia·men·tar·i·an \ˌpärləˌmen·ˈterēən, ˌpäl-, -lyə-, -ˌmən-, -ta(a)r-,-tār-\ *n* -s [*parliament* + *-arian*] **1** *often cap* **:** an adherent of the parliament in opposition to the king during the English Civil War ⟨the civil wars forced both royalists and ~*s* into claims of supremacy —G.H.Sabine⟩ ⟨a ~ who had signed the English king's death warrant —R.C.Garvey⟩ — compare ¹CAVALIER 4, ROUNDHEAD, ROYALIST **2 :** an expert in the rules and usages of a parliament or other deliberative assembly; *specif* **:** an officer of a legislative body acting as adviser to the presiding officer on matters of procedure **3 :** a member of a parliament ⟨a small party . . . which has one ~ —R.C.Bone⟩

²parliamentarian \"\ *adj* **:** PARLIAMENTARY ⟨the ~ major was . . . embarrassed by this proposal —Sir Walter Scott⟩ ⟨a country with a ~ system of government⟩

par·lia·men·tar·i·an·ism \-ēəˌnizəm\ *n* -s **:** PARLIAMENTARISM

par·lia·men·tar·i·ly \-¦terəlē, -li\ *adv* **:** in a parliamentary manner ⟨disliked proceeding ~ in this business —Horace Walpole⟩

par·lia·men·ta·rism \ˌ==ˈmentəˌrizəm\ *n* -s [¹*parliamentary* + *-ism*] **:** the parliamentary system of government **:** PARLIAMENTARY GOVERNMENT

¹par·lia·men·ta·ry \¦==¦mentərē, -n·trē, -ri\ *adj* [*parliament* + *-ary*] **1 a :** of, relating to, or having the nature of a parliament ⟨~ reform⟩ ⟨~ body⟩ ⟨the organizations are largely forensic and ~ —*Amer. Guide Series: N. C.*⟩ **b :** enacted, done, or ratified by a parliament; *specif* **:** enacted, done, or ratified by the British parliament ⟨~ grant of money⟩ ⟨received a ~ title⟩ **c :** according to the procedures, customs, and usages of a parliament; *specif* **:** according to the procedures, customs, and usages of the British parliament ⟨proceed in a ~ way⟩ **d :** permitted or suitable to be permitted to be used in a parliament **:** CIVIL, COURTEOUS, POLITE ⟨two gentlemen politely and in strictly ~ language calling one another incompetent administrators —*Liverpool Daily Post*⟩ **e :** concerned with the business of a parliament ⟨~ correspondent of a newspaper⟩ **f :** taking place in or under the authority of a parliament ⟨proposed a ~ inquiry into the situation⟩ ⟨~ control of expenditures⟩ ⟨~ debate⟩ **2 :** of, belonging to, or adhering to the parliament as opposed to the king during the English Civil War ⟨rendered the ~ armies . . . victorious —David Hume †1776⟩ **3 :** of, relating to, or used on a parliamentary train **4 :** of, based upon, or having the characteristics of parliamentary government ⟨~ institutions in South Africa resemble . . . those in other dominions —Alexander Brady⟩ ⟨~ democracy⟩ ⟨~ socialism⟩ **5 :** of, relating to, or consisting of members of a parliament ⟨the sole object of ~ privilege is to protect the rights . . . of members —*Brit. Parliament*⟩ ⟨have the leader selected by the ~ caucus —*London Times*⟩ **6 :** of, according to, or based upon parliamentary law ⟨~ practice⟩ ⟨~ procedure⟩ ⟨~ inquiry . . . to obtain information from the presiding officer —Alice F. Sturgis⟩

²parliamentary \"\ *n* -ES **1 :** a member of the British parliament **2 :** PARLIAMENTARY TRAIN **3** [modif. of F *parlementaire*, fr. *parlement* negotiation, conference, parliament — more at PARLIAMENT] **:** one sent under a flag of truce to treat with an enemy

parliamentary agent *n* **:** a person professionally employed to represent and look after the interests of parties affected by private legislation of the British parliament

parliamentary borough *n* **:** a borough having the right to return a member to the British parliament **:** a borough forming a constituency

parliamentary burgh *n* **:** a parliamentary borough in Scotland

parliamentary counsel *n* **:** an official attached to the British treasury under whose direction government bills are drafted into the form required by law and custom for introduction into parliament

parliamentary government *n* **:** a system of government characterized by an interdependence of the executive and the legislature and usu. having under a titular chief of state the real executive power vested in a cabinet composed of members of the legislature who are individually and collectively responsible to the legislature **:** CABINET GOVERNMENT ⟨the heart of *parliamentary government* has come to be party responsibility —E.S.Griffith⟩ — compare PRESIDENTIAL GOVERNMENT

parliamentary law *n* **:** the body of rules and precedents used to govern the proceedings of deliberative assemblies and other organizations

parliamentary party *n* **:** the members of a legislative body belonging to a single political party and constituting an entity distinct from the party in the nation as a whole of which they are members

parliamentary system *n* **:** PARLIAMENTARY GOVERNMENT

parliamentary train *n* **:** a train required by a 19th century act of the British parliament to be run daily each way over the entire length of the system of a railway company, to stop at every station, and to provide minimum third-class conveniences at a rate of not over one penny a mile

parliament cake *n* **:** a thin ginger cookie

¹par·lia·men·teer \ˌpärlə(ˌ)men·¦ti(ə)r, ˌpäl-, -lyə-, -ˌmən-, -iə\ *n* -s [*parliament* + *-eer*] **:** PARLIAMENTARIAN 1

²parliamenteer \"\ *vi* -ED/-ING/-s **:** to take an active part in parliamentary affairs

par·lia·men·ter \ˌpärləˈmentər\ *n* -s *Scot* **:** a member of parliament

parliament hinge *n* **:** a hinge with so great a projection (as from a wall or frame) as to allow a door or shutter to swing back flat against the wall

parliament house *n* [ME *parlement-hous*, fr. *parlement* parliament + *hous* house] **:** the building in which a parliament sits

parliament man *n* **:** a member of a parliament; *esp* **:** a member of the British House of Commons

parliament roll *n* [ME *parlement rolle*, fr. *parlement* parliament + *rolle* roll] **:** one of a number of rolls of parchment inscribed by the chancery clerks with the records of the British parliament during the period from 1278 until the beginning of the use of journals by the two houses in 1509

parling *pres part of* PARLE

¹par·lor \ˈpärlər, ˈpálə(r\ *n* -s *see -or in Explan Notes* [ME *parlour*, fr. OF *parleor, parlour* parlor, reception room in a convent, fr. *parler* to speak, talk — more at PARLEY] **1 :** a room used primarily for conversation or the reception of guests: as **a :** an apartment in a monastery or nunnery where the monastics are permitted to meet and converse with each other or with visitors **b :** a room in a private dwelling kept chiefly for the reception of visitors rather than for family use and usu. better furnished than the other rooms in the dwelling — compare LIVING ROOM 1, SITTING ROOM **c :** a room in a large dwelling (as a mansion) or in a public building (as a city hall) used as a conference chamber or private reception room **d :** a room in a public building (as an inn, tavern, hotel, club) designed for conversation, rest, or semiprivacy **e :** one of a suite of rooms (as in a club or hotel) devoted to the general reception of members or guests ⟨the ~*s* of the hotels were lavishly furnished —D.D.Martin⟩ — usu. used in pl. ⟨the annual Christmas supper . . . will be held Monday night in the church ~*s* —*Hartford (Conn.) Courant*⟩ **2** *archaic* **:** DINING ROOM **3 :** something held to resemble an inner or special chamber ⟨the ~ of his heart —George Macdonald †1905⟩ **4 :** a business establishment usu. devoted to a specified service or to the sale of a specified item ⟨funeral ~⟩ ⟨beauty ~⟩ ⟨beer ~⟩ ⟨ice-cream ~⟩

²parlor \"\ *adj, see -or in Explan Notes* **1 :** used in or suitable for a parlor ⟨heard the ~ clock strike twelve —Helen Eustis⟩ ⟨~ trick⟩ ⟨a . . . young woman with a ~ voice —Douglas Watt⟩ ⟨~ furniture⟩ **2 a :** fostered or advocated in comfortable seclusion without consequent action or application to affairs ⟨~ bolshevism⟩ **b :** given to or characterized by fostering or advocating something (as a doctrine) in such a manner ⟨~ pink⟩ ⟨~ socialist⟩

parlor boarder *n* **1 :** a privileged pupil in an English boarding school living with the principal's family **2 :** a person esp. favored in a household

parlor car *n* **:** an extra-fare railroad passenger car for day travel equipped with individual revolving and reclining chairs and providing the services of an attendant — compare CHAIR CAR 1, COACH 1c, LOUNGE CAR, PALACE CAR, PULLMAN

parlor game *n* **:** a game suitable for playing indoors (as in a parlor)

parlor grand *n* **:** a grand piano intermediate in length between a concert grand and a baby grand

parlor house *n* **:** BROTHEL 2; *esp* **:** one having a well-furnished reception room

parlormaid \ˈ==ˌ=\ *n* **1 :** a maid in a private home whose chief duties are to attend to the parlor, the table, and the door **2 :** a maid in a hotel or restaurant who attends to rest rooms and offices — called also *matron*

parlor match *n* **:** a friction match containing little or no sulfur and igniting with less objectionable fumes than a sulfur match

parlor palm *n* **1 :** CAST-IRON PLANT **2 :** a small Mexican palm (*Collinia elegans*) with narrow pinnae and pale yellow flowers in panicles that is often used as a pot plant

¹par·lous \ˈpärləs, ˈpál-\ *adj* [ME *parlous, perlous*, alter. of *perilous*] **1 a :** characterized by uncertainty **:** fraught with danger or risk **:** attended with peril **:** CRITICAL, DANGEROUS, HAZARDOUS ⟨the present ~ state of international relations —Denis Plimmer⟩ ⟨a ~ journey up a ladder —G.E.Fussell⟩ ⟨~ times⟩ **b :** involving risk **:** awkward to deal with ⟨a ~ bird to hit —H.C.Merivale⟩ **2** *obs* **:** shrewd or cunning usu. in a dangerous way — **par·lous·ly** *adv*

²parlous \"\ *adv* **:** to a very great extent **:** EXCEEDINGLY, EXCESSIVELY ⟨it was ~ boggy underfoot —*Strand Mag.*⟩ ⟨she is ~ handsome —J.G.Edgar⟩

¹par·ma \ˈpärmə, ˈpámə\ *n* -s [fr. *Parma*, city in northern Italy] **:** a low anticlinal fold; *esp* **:** one forming a barrier to the migration of marine faunas

²parma \"\ *adj, usu cap* **:** of or from the city of Parma, Italy **:** of the kind or style prevalent in Parma **:** PARMESAN

par·ma·cety \ˌpärməˈsed·ē, -sed·ē\ *n* -ES [by alter.] *archaic* **:** SPERMACETI

parma red *n, often cap P* **:** BLOOD RED

parma violet *n* **1** *usu cap P* **:** a sweet violet widely cultivated for its pale lavender sweet-scented fully double flowers **2** *often cap P* **a :** a moderate violet that is bluer and lighter than damson, bluer and paler than Roman purple, and paler and slightly redder than prelate — called also *Parme, violet Parme* **b** *of textiles* **:** a strong violet that is redder and lighter than pansy, redder, lighter, and stronger than royal purple (sense 2), and lighter, stronger, and slightly redder than clematis

par·ma·zo marble \ˈpärməˌzō-, pär'mä(ˌ)zō-\ *n* [*parmazo* perh. modif. of It *paonazzo, pavonazzo* pavonazzo — more at PAVONAZZO] **:** a marble of northern Italy having a coarse network of dark veins on a white or grayish ground

parme \ˈpärm\ *n* -s *often cap* [F *Parme* Parma, city in northern Italy] **:** PARMA VIOLET 2a

par·me·lia \pärˈmēlēə, -lyə\ *n, cap* [NL, prob. irreg. fr. L *parma* small shield] **:** a large genus (the type of the family Parmeliaceae) of chiefly alpine foliaceous lichens having cortex on both surfaces of a closely appressed thallus and including several that are important sources of purple and brown dyestuffs esp. in Scotland, Wales, and Scandinavia — see CROTTLE

par·me·li·a·ceous \(ˈ)pär¦mēlē¦āshəs\ *adj* [NL *Parmeliaceae* (fr. *Parmelia*, type genus + *-aceae*) + E *-ous*] **:** of or relating to the genus *Parmelia* or the family Parmeliaceae

par·me·li·oid \(ˈ)pär¦mēlēˌȯid\ *adj* [NL *Parmelia* + E *-oid*] **:** like or related to the genus *Parmelia*

par·me·nid·e·an \¦pärmə¦nidēən\ *adj, usu cap* [*Parmenides*, 5th cent. B.C. Greek philosopher + E *-an*] **:** of or relating to Parmenides or to his philosophy which emphasizes a conception of reality as absolute eternal in contrast to the Heraclitean conception of eternal change

par·men·tier \pȧrmäⁿ·tyā\ *also* **par·men·tière** \-yer\ *adj, usu cap* [F *parmentier* (fem. *parmentière*), fr. Antoine A. *Parmentier* †1813 Fr. horticulturist who popularized the cultivation of potatoes in France] **:** prepared or served with potatoes ⟨chipped beef *Parmentier*⟩

par·men·ti·e·ra \ˌpärmənˈtirə\ *n, cap* [NL, fr. Antoine A. *Parmentier*] **:** a small genus of tropical American trees (family Bignoniaceae) having trifoliolate leaves and rather large greenish flowers with a sheathing calyx — see CANDLE TREE

¹par·me·san \ˈpärməˌzan, ˈpám-, -ˌzän, -ˌzaa(ə)n, -ˌzän *sometimes* ˌ==ˈ=; ˈ==zən\ *adj, usu cap* [MF, fr. OIt *parmigiano*] **:** of or relating to Parma, Italy

²parmesan \"\ *or* **parmesan cheese** *n* -s *usu cap P* **:** a very hard dry cheese with a sharp flavor that is cured for several years and used grated to season other foods (as spaghetti and sauces)

par·mi·gia·na \¦pärmē¦jänə, ¦päm-\ *or* **par·mi·gia·no** \-ä(ˌ)nō\ *adj* [*parmigiana* fr. It, fem. of *parmigiano*; *parmigiano* fr. It, Parmesan, fr. OIt, fr. *Parma*] **:** seasoned with Parmesan cheese ⟨eggplant ~⟩

par·mi·gia·no \-ä(ˌ)nō\ *n* -s [It, fr. *parmigiano*, adj.] **:** PARMESAN

par·mone \ˈpärˌmōn\ *n* -s [F, fr. *parm-* (fr. *violette de Parme* Parma violet, fr. *Parme* Parma, city in northern Italy) + *-one*] **:** a terpenoid ketone $C_{13}H_{20}O$ found in oil from violet flowers

par·nas *or* **par·nass** \pärˈnäs, ˈ=ˌ=\ *n, pl* **par·nas·im** *or* **par·nass·im** \ˌ=ˌnäˈsēm, -sim\ [LHeb *parnās* manager] **:** the chief administrative officer of a Jewish congregation

par·nas·sia \pärˈnasēə, -syə\ *n* [NL, fr. L *Parnasus, Parnassus* Parnassus (fr. Gk *Parnasos, Parnassos*) + NL *-ia*] **1** *cap* **:** a genus of smooth bog herbs (family Saxifragaceae) native to arctic and temperate regions and having basal entire leaves and white flowers **2** -s **:** any plant of the genus *Parnassia*

¹par·nas·sian \(ˈ)pär¦nasēən, (ˈ)pá¦n-, -syən\ *adj* [L *parnasius, parnassius* of or belonging to Parnassus (fr. Gk *parnasios*, fr. *Parnasos, Parnassos* Parnassus, mountain in central Greece sacred in ancient times to Apollo and the Muses) + E *-an*] **1** *usu cap* **:** of, relating to, or having the characteristics of poetry ⟨newspaper *Parnassian* columns invited the native muse —H.R.Warfel⟩ **2** *usu cap* [F *parnassien*, fr. *Parnasse* Parnassus (fr. L *Parnasus, Parnassus*, fr. Gk *Parnasos, Parnassos*) + *-ien* -an; fr. the publication in 1866 of an anthology of the work of the Parnassian poets entitled *Le Parnasse contemporain*] **:** of, having the characteristics of, or constituting a school of French poets of the second half of the 19th century emphasizing metrical form and making little use of emotion as poetic material ⟨the *Parnassian* movement⟩ ⟨*Parnassian* poets⟩ ⟨*Parnassian* style⟩ — compare ROMANTIC **3** [NL *Parnassius* + ISV *-an*, adj. suffix] **:** of or relating to the genus *Parnassius*

²parnassian \"\ *n* -s [¹*parnassian*] **1** *usu cap* **:** POET **2** *usu cap* [F *parnassien*, fr. *Parnasse* Parnassus + *-ien* -an] **:** a poet of the Parnassian school **3** [NL *Parnassius* + ISV *-an*, n. suffix] **:** a butterfly of *Parnassius* or a related genus

par·nas·sian·ism \-ˌnizəm\ *n* -s *usu cap* **:** the Parnassian style in poetry ⟨the cradle of both symbolism and *Parnassianism* —K.H.Cornell⟩

par·nas·si·us \pärˈnasēəs\ *n, cap* [NL, fr. L *parnasius, parnassius* of or belonging to Parnassus] **:** a genus of stout-bodied butterflies (family Papilionidae) having short antennae and almost transparent white or yellowish wings marked with black or red ocelli and occurring in the colder parts of the northern hemisphere

par·nell·ite \pärˈneˌlīt *sometimes* ˈpärn³lˌīt\ *adj, usu cap* [fr. Charles Stewart *Parnell* †1891 Irish nationalist leader + E *-ite*] **:** of, relating to, or being an adherent of Parnell esp. in his advocacy of home rule for Ireland during the latter part of the 19th century

¹par·occipital \¦par+\ *adj* [¹*para-* + *occipital*] **:** located at the side of the occipital bone or in the lateral aspect of the occipital region — used chiefly of a bony element or process

²paroccipital \"\ *n* -s **:** a paroccipital part

pa·ro·cheth *or* **pa·ro·chet** *or* **pa·ro·ket** \pä'rōˌket(h)\ *n* -s [Heb *pārokheth* curtain before the holy of holies] **:** a curtain of richly ornamented material hung before the holy ark in a synagogue as a reminder of the curtain used to screen the holy of holies in the tabernacle and the temple

pa·ro·chial \pəˈrōkēəl, -kyəl\ *adj* [ME *parochiell, parochiall*, fr. AF & MF; AF *parochiel* & MF *parochial*, fr. LL *parochialis*, fr. *parochia* parish + L *-alis* -al — more at PARISH] **1 a :** of or relating to a church parish ⟨subordinated the ~ clergy . . . to the authority of the Diocesan —R.C.Mortimer⟩ ⟨~ experience is not required in a bishop —R.G.G.Price⟩ ⟨a ~ church⟩ **b :** controlled by, supported by, or within the jurisdiction of a church parish ⟨construction of a ~ elementary school⟩ **2 :** of or relating to a parish as a unit of local government ⟨supplant the ~ authorities by the central ministry of health —G.B.Shaw⟩ ⟨excluded the able-bodied paupers from the ~ workhouse —G.E.Fussell⟩ **3 :** confined or restricted as if within the borders of a parish **:** limited in range or scope (as to a narrow area or region) **:** NARROW, PETTY, PROVINCIAL ⟨manifestations of national pride or other ~ bigotries —Reinhold Niebuhr⟩ ⟨little sympathy with ~ mentality . . . which would forbid philosophic inquiry —Judah Goldin⟩ ⟨by no means selfishly ~ in outlook —R.H.Pfeiffer⟩ **4 :** of, relating to, or being the charge of a bishop in the early Christian church

parochial church council *n* **:** a governing body of a parish of the Church of England consisting of the vicar, the churchwardens, and elected parishioners

pa·ro·chial·ism \pəˈrōkēəˌlizəm, -kyə-,\ *n* -s **1 :** the quality or state of being parochial; *esp* **:** selfish pettiness or narrowness (as of interests, opinions, or views) ⟨the unconscious and invincible ~ of the specialists —A.L.Guérard⟩ ⟨a tendency to ~ in spite of increasing international contacts —*Brit. Book News*⟩ ⟨unity in an industry . . . hampered by ~ —C.G. Tickle⟩ **2 :** a system of management peculiar to parishes ⟨the fate of these children should no longer . . . rest on ~ or on charity —Marjory G. Allen⟩

pa·ro·chi·al·i·ty \pəˌrōkēˈaləd·ē\ *n* -ES **:** PAROCHIALISM

pa·ro·chial·ize \pəˈrōkēəˌlīz, -kyə-\ *vb* -ED/-ING/-s *vt* **:** to make parochial ~ *vi* **:** to work in a parish

pa·ro·chial·ly \-əlē, -li\ *adv* **1 :** in terms of a church parish **2 :** in a narrow or provincial way ⟨~ British in his political views —F.B.Millett⟩ ⟨a ~ partisan man —*N.Y.Times*⟩

parochial school *n* **:** a school maintained by a religious body usu. for elementary instruction

par·och·in *or* **par·och·ine** \ˈparəkən\ *n* -s [prob. back-formation fr. Sc *parochiner* parishioner, fr. ME (northern dial.) *parochoner, parochanar*, fr. ME *parochien, parochin* parishioner (fr. ML *parochianus*, fr. LL *parochia* parish + L *-anus* -an) + *-er*] *Scot* **:** PARISH

par·o·di·a·ble \ˈparəd·ēəbəl *also* ˈper-\ *adj* **:** capable of being parodied

pa·ro·di·al \pəˈrōd·ēəl\ *adj* **:** PARODIC

pa·rod·ic \pəˈrädik, -dēk\ *also* **pa·rod·i·cal** \-dəkəl, -dēk-\ *adj* **:** having the character of parody

par·o·dist \ˈparəd·əst *also* ˈper-\ *n* -s [F *parodiste*, fr. *parodie* parody (fr. L *parodia*) + *-iste* -ist] **:** one that parodies; *esp* **:** a writer of literary parodies

par·o·dis·tic \¦parə¦distik *also* ¦per-, -tēk\ *adj* **:** of the nature of parody ⟨a ~ effect of singular irony —Ernst Feise⟩

par·o·dize \ˈparəˌdīz\ *vt* -ED/-ING/-s [L *parodia* parody + E *-ize*] **:** PARODY

par·odon·tal \¦parə¦dänt³l\ *adj* [*par-* + *-odont* + *-al*] **:** PERIODONTAL 2

paro·don·ti·tis \ˌparəˌdänˈtēd·əs\ *n* [NL, fr. ¹*para-* + *odontitis*] **:** PERIODONTITIS

par·o·dos \ˈparəˌdäs\ *or* **par·o·dus** \-ˌdəs\ *n, pl* **paro·doi** \-ˌdȯi\ *or* **paro·di** \-ˌdī\ [Gk *parodos* entrance, passage, first choral passage in a drama, fr. *para* beside, beyond, past + *hodos* road, way, journey — more at PARA-, CEDE] **1 :** the first choral passage in an ancient Greek drama recited or sung as the chorus enters the orchestra — compare STASIMON **2 :** a passage in an ancient Greek theater between auditorium and skene by which spectators had access to the theater and actors might come and go during a play — see THEATER illustration

¹par·o·dy \ˈparədē *also* ˈper- *or* -di\ *n* -ES [L *parodia*, fr. Gk *parōidia*, fr. *para* beside + *-ōidia* (fr. *aeidein* to sing) — more at ODE] **1 a :** a writing in which the language and style of an author or work is closely imitated for comic effect or in ridicule often with certain peculiarities greatly heightened or exaggerated ⟨these plays . . . are *parodies* of eighteenth century French farce —Claudia Cassidy⟩ **b :** a literary style characterized by the reproduction of stylistic peculiarities of an author or work for comic effect or in ridicule ⟨the dialogue . . . lapses now and then into inadvertent ~ —Wolcott Gibbs⟩ — compare BURLESQUE 1 **2 :** a form or situation showing imitation that is faithful to a degree but that is weak, ridiculous, or distorted **:** a feeble or ridiculous imitation ⟨a straggling ~ of a military moustache —Fred Majdalany⟩ ⟨the . . . elite who live a ~ of 19th century French culture —Alastair Reid⟩ **3 a :** an imitation of a musical composition in which the original text or music has been altered usu. in a comical manner **b :** PARODY MASS **syn** see CARICATURE

²parody \"\ *vt* -ED/-ING/-ES **1 :** to compose a parody on ⟨~ a poem⟩ ⟨~ a musical composition⟩ **2 :** to imitate in a way resembling or held to resemble a parody ⟨deliberately set out to ~ the . . . technique —Marshall Fishwick⟩ ⟨sounds that ~ rather than imitate the original —Louis Simpson⟩

parody mass *n* **:** a 16th century mass having the text of the mass added to musical material borrowed from an existing composition (as a motet or madrigal)

pa·roe·mia \pəˈrēmēə\ *n* -s [LL, fr. Gk *paroimia* proverb, maxim, incidental remark, fr. *para* beside + *oimos* way, path, path or strain of song; prob. akin to L *vis* strength, force — more at VIM] **:** a rhetorical proverb

¹pa·roe·mi·ac \-mēˌak\ *adj* [Gk *paroimiakos* proverbial, fr. *paroimia*] **:** of, relating to, or constituting a paroemiac

²paroemiac \"\ *n* -s [LL *paroemiacum*, fr. Gk *paroimiakon*, fr. neut. of *paroimiakos*] **:** an anapestic dimeter catalectic

pa·roe·mi·og·ra·pher *or* **pa·re·mi·og·ra·pher** \¦=ˌ==ˈägrəfə(r)\ *n* -s [NL *paroemiographus* (fr. *paroemio-* — fr. LL *paroemia* — + LL *-graphus* one that writes such material or in such a way) + E *-er* — more at -GRAPHER] **:** a writer of proverbs

pa·roe·mi·og·ra·phy \-fē, -fi\ *n* -ES [*paroemio-* (fr. LL *paroemia*) + *-graphy*] **:** the making of collections of proverbs

pa·roe·mi·ol·o·gist \-ˈäləjəst\ *n* -s [*paroemiology* + *-ist*] **:** a student of proverbs

pa·roe·mi·ol·o·gy \jē, -ji\ *n* -ES [*paroemio-* (fr. LL *paroemia*) + *-logy*] **:** the subject of proverbs

par of exchange : the value of the monetary unit of one country expressed in terms of the monetary unit of another country using a given standard of value (as purchasing power); *specif* **:** ¹PAR 1a

pa·roi·cous \pə'rōikəs\ also **pa·roe·cious** \pə'rēshəs\ adj [¹para- + -oicous, -oecious (fr. Gk oikos house + E -ous) — more at VICINITY] : having archegonia and antheridia on the same branch with the antheridia usu. below and around the archegonia — compare AUTOICOUS, HETEROICOUS, MONOICOUS, POLYOICOUS, SYNOICOUS

paroket var of PAROCHETH

¹pa·rol \pə'rōl, 'parəl\ n -s [MF parole word, speech, fr. OF] **1** : an oral declaration or statement : WORD OF MOUTH, UTTERANCE — used in the phrase by parol ⟨open to the defendant to prove by ~ —Gottlieb v. Heyden Chemical Corp.⟩ **2** archaic : the pleadings in a legal action formerly presented by word of mouth

²parol \"\ adj **1** : executed or made by word of mouth or by a writing not under seal ⟨specific performance of an express ~ suit —J.W.Eggleston⟩ **2** : given or expressed by word of mouth : oral as distinguished from documentary ⟨the defendant objected to the introduction of ~ evidence —Jour. Amer. Med. Assoc.⟩

pa·rol·able \pə'rōləbəl\ adj : qualified for parole

parol arrest n : an arrest made in pursuance of a verbal order from a magistrate without written complaint or similar proceedings

parol contract n **1** : a contract made orally or by a writing not under seal : contract not embodied in a judgment of record — called also simple contract **2** : a contract partly or entirely oral and therefore unenforceable under the statute of frauds : contract orig. under seal but modified by an agreement not under seal

¹pa·role \pə'rōl\ n -s [F, word of honor, word, speech, fr. OF, fr. LL parabola speech, parable — more at PARABLE] **1** : WORD OF HONOR : plighted faith; esp : the promise of a prisoner of war upon his faith and honor to fulfill stated conditions (as to return to custody or not to bear arms against his captors) in consideration of special privileges, usu. release from captivity ⟨proposed that officers and men who gave their ~s not to take up arms against the United States be allowed to return to their homes —Virginius Dabney⟩ **2** : the state or period of freedom resulting from a parole ⟨required to report during his ~⟩ ⟨a Federal prisoner . . . may be released on ~ after serving one third of such term —U. S. Code⟩ **3** : a watchword given only to officers of the guard and of the day — distinguished from countersign **4 a** : a conditional and revocable release of a prisoner serving an indeterminate or unexpired sentence in a penal or correctional institution — compare PROBATION **b** : a release under similar conditions of one detained or kept in custody; specif : a release given a patient in a mental hospital enabling him to visit freely and unattended various designated areas on the hospital grounds or beyond its limits **5** : the release of a defendant in a criminal case on his own recognizance or in the custody of his attorney during the period between indictment and trial **6** : a linguistic act : linguistic behavior ⟨~ is from the linguist's point of view the simple raw material for scientific investigation —H.G.Lunt⟩ — contrasted with langue

²parole \"\ vt -ED/-ING/-S : to release on parole ⟨the . . . friend was paroled from the hospital in the custody of her sister —Ruth & Edward Brecher⟩ ⟨when a prisoner is paroled —C.V.Oje⟩

³parole \"\ adj : of or relating to parole or to persons on parole ⟨~ officer⟩ ⟨~ laws⟩ ⟨~ casework⟩

pa·rol·ee \pə,rō'lē, pə'rō(,)lē, ¦parə¦lē\ n -s : one released on parole ⟨a ~ is required to report . . . to a parole officer —N.Y. Times⟩

par·olfactory \¦par+\ adj [¹para- + olfactory] : of, relating to, or constituting an area and a sulcus of the cerebral cortex adjacent to the olfactory trigone

¹par·o·li \,parə'lē, '≈≈(,)≈\ n -ES [F, fr. It (Neapolitan dial.), pl. of parolo, fr. It (Neapolitan dial.) paro equal, fr. L par — more at PAIR] : a system of betting in which the bettor leaves staked money and its winnings as a further stake : PARLAY 1

²paroli \"\ vi -ED/-ING/-ES : to use the paroli in a series of bets

par·o·mo·lo·gia \,pa,rōmə'lōj(ē)ə\ n -s [Gk, fr. para- ¹para- + homologia agreement — more at HOMOLOGY] : a concession made in rhetoric to an adversary in order to strengthen one's own argument

par·ono·masia \,parənō'māzh(ē)ə, pə,ränə'm-\ n -s [L, fr. Gk, fr. paronomazein to call with a slight change of name, fr. para- ¹para- + onomazein to call, name, fr. onoma name — more at NAME] : a play upon words in which the same word is used in different senses or words similar in sound are set in opposition so as to give antithetical force : PUN

par·o·nych·ia \,parə'nikēə\ n [L, fr. Gk parōnychia whitlow, fr. para- ¹para- + onych-, onyx nail of the finger or toe + -ia — more at NAIL] **1** -s : inflammation of the tissues adjacent to the nail of a finger or toe usu. accompanied by infection and pus formation — compare FELON **2** cap [NL, fr. Gk parōnychia, a plant reputed to be a cure for whitlows, fr. parōnychia whitlow] : a genus of small herbs (family Caryophyllaceae) having scarious stipules and small flowers subtended by scarious bracts — see WHITLOWWORT

par·o·nych·i·um \-kēəm\ n [NL, fr. ¹para- + onychium] : a stiff filamentous appendage of the pulvillus of an insect's foot

par·o·nym \'parə,nim\ n -s [LL paronymon, fr. Gk parōnymon, neut. of parōnymos] : a paronymous word

pa·ron·y·mous \pə'ränəməs\ adj [Gk parōnymos, fr. para- ¹para- + -ōnymos, adj. comb. form (as in homōnymos having the same name) — more at HOMONYMOUS] **1** : CONJUGATE 4 **2 a** : formed from a word in another language **b** : having a form similar to a cognate foreign word

par·oophoron \¦par+\ n [NL, fr. ¹para- + oophoron] : a group of rudimentary tubules in the broad ligament between the epoophoron and the uterus that constitutes a remnant of the lower part of the mesonephros in the female corresponding to the paradidymis of the male

paroquet var of PARRAKEET

paroquet auklet n : an auklet (Cyclorrhynchus psittacula) of the northern Pacific having the upper parts dark slate, the underparts white, and the bill orange red

paroquet bur n **1 a** : the bur of a Jamaica plant of the genus Triumfetta **b** : a plant that bears paroquet burs **2** : a yellow-flowered annual weedy herb (Sida rhombifolia) of the southeastern U. S.

par·o·rex·ia \,parə'reksēə\ n -s [NL, fr. ¹para- + -orexia] : an appetite for unusual foods — compare BULIMIA, PICA

par·o·se·la \,parə'sēlə\ [NL, anagram of Psoralea] syn of DALEA

pa·ro·tia \pə'rōsh(ē)ə, -ōd·ēə\ n, cap [NL, fr. L parotis tumor near the ear + NL -ia] : a genus of birds of paradise including several forms distinguished by the presence of three long spatulate feathers on each side of the head

pa·rot·ic \pə'rōd·ik, -räl, |t|, |ēk, (')pa¦r-\ adj [NL paroticus, fr. L para- ¹para- + NL oticus otic, fr. Gk ōtikos] : adjacent to the ear

parotic process n **1** : a process of opisthotic, exoccipital, and prootic elements in the skull of some reptiles **2** : a process formed of pterotic and opisthotic elements articulating with the posttemporal in the skull of some fishes

¹pa·rot·id \pə'räd·əd, -ätəd\ adj [NL parotid-, parotis parotid gland, fr. L, tumor near the ear, fr. Gk parōtid-, parōtis, fr. para- ¹para- + ōtid-, ōtis (fr. ōt-, ous ear) — more at EAR] : of, relating to, being, produced by, or located near the parotid gland

²parotid \"\ n -s [NL parotid-, parotis] : PAROTID GLAND

parotid duct n : STENO'S DUCT

pa·rot·i·dec·to·my \pə,räd·ə'dektəmē\ n -ES [ISV ²parotid + -ectomy] : surgical removal of the parotid gland

parotid gland n : either of a pair of salivary glands situated on the side of the face below and in front of the ear that in man are the largest salivary glands, are of pure serous type, and communicate with the mouth by Steno's duct

pa·rot·i·di·tis \pə,räd·ə'dīd·əs\ n -ES [NL, fr. parotid-, parotis + -itis] : PAROTITIS

parotis n -ES [NL parotid-, parotis] obs : PAROTID GLAND

par·o·tit·ic \¦parə¦tid·ik\ adj [parotitis + -ic] : of, relating to, or having mumps

par·o·ti·tis \,≈≈'tīd·əs\ n -ES [NL, irreg. fr. parotis + -itis] **1** : inflammation and swelling of one or both parotid glands or other salivary glands (as in mumps) **2** : MUMPS — called also epidemic parotitis

par·ous \'parəs\ adj [-parous] **1** : having produced offspring **2** : PREGNANT

-pa·rous \pərəs\ adj comb form [L -parus, fr. parere to give birth to, beget, produce — more at PARE] : giving birth to : bearing : producing ⟨biparous⟩ ⟨fetiparous⟩ ⟨viviparous⟩ ⟨oviparous⟩

par·ou·sia \(')pa¦rüzēə, pə'r-, -üsēə, -üzh(ē)ə, -üsh(ē)ə\ n [Gk, lit., presence, fr. para- ¹para- + ousia substance, being (after pareinai to be present, fr. para- ¹para- + einai to be) — more at OUSIA, IS] **1** usu cap : ADVENT 2b **2** : the presence of a Platonic idea in something

par·o·var·ian \¦parə¦va(a)rēən, -ver-, -vār-\ adj [parovarium + -an] : of or relating to a parovarium

par·o·var·i·um \,≈≈'≈≈əm\ n [NL, fr. L para- ¹para- + NL ovarium] **1** : EPOOPHORON **2** : one of the accessory glands of the female reproductive system of some insects

par·ox·ysm \'parək,sizəm\ n -s [F & ML; F paroxysme, fr. ML paroxysmus, fr. Gk paroxysmos paroxysm, irritation, fr. paroxynein to urge, stimulate, fr. para- ¹para- + oxynein to sharpen, provoke, fr. oxys sharp — more at OXY-] **1 a** : a sudden attack or spasm (as of a disease) ⟨convulsed . . . in the ~s of an epileptic seizure —Thomas Hardy⟩ **b** : a sudden recurrence of symptoms or an intensification of existing symptoms ⟨pain occurred in frequent ~s —Therapeutic Notes⟩ **2 a** : a sudden, violent, and uncontrollable action or occurrence of emotion ⟨threw himself at her feet in a ~ of grief —T. L.Peacock⟩ ⟨burst into a ~ of laughter —Harriet La Barre⟩ **b** : a similar action occurring in nature : a convulsion of physical forces (as an earthquake or the eruption of a volcano) ⟨the first great ~ of alpine orogeny —C.O.Dunbar⟩ ⟨horizontal compression induced by the main tectonic ~s of the mountain ranges —Jour. of Geol.⟩ **3** : an extreme or climactic stage (as of a process, action, or series of developments) ⟨marks the ~ of subtropical conditions —Julia Gardner⟩ ⟨the very moment of fanatical ~ of the French Revolution —John Quincy Adams⟩ **4** obs : a violent and open disagreement or quarrel ⟨the disagreement did proceed so far as to produce a ~ —Cotton Mather⟩

par·ox·ys·mal \¦≈≈¦sizməl\ adj **1** : of, relating to, or of the nature of a paroxysm ⟨~ volcanic eruptions —Arthur Holmes⟩ ⟨~ seizure⟩ **2** : marked or accompanied by paroxysms ⟨whooping cough . . . treated in the early ~ stage —Therapeutic Notes⟩ ⟨the ~ phase in the alpine type of orogeny —P.H.Kuenen & Albert Carozzi⟩

paroxysmal dyspnea n : CARDIAC ASTHMA

paroxysmal tachycardia n : tachycardia that begins and ends abruptly

par·ox·ys·mic \¦parək¦sizmik, -mēk\ adj [ISV paroxysm + -ic] : PAROXYSMAL ⟨the tension . . . made their sleep too desperate and ~ to deserve being called rest —H.L.Davis⟩

par·ox·ys·mist \'≈≈,≈məst\ n -s : CATASTROPHIST

¹par·oxytone \(')par+\ adj [NL paroxytonus, fr. Gk paroxytonos, fr. para- ¹para- + oxytonos oxytone] **1** : having or characterized by an acute accent on the penult of a word in Greek **2** : having or characterized by heavy stress on the penult

²paroxytone \"\ n [NL paroxytonus, fr. paroxytonus, adj.] : a word accented or stressed on the penult

parpen var of PERPEND

¹par·quet \(')pär¦kā\ vt **parqueted** \-ād\ **parqueted; parqueting** \-āiŋ\ **parquets** [F parqueter, fr. parquet, n.] **1** : to furnish (as a room) with a floor of parquetry **2** : to make (as a flooring) of parquetry

²parquet \"\ n -s [F, patterned flooring, branch of the government charged with the prosecution of crime as the representative of the public, (obs.) parquet of a theater or auditorium, fr. MF, small enclosure, judges' section of a courtroom, fr. parc enclosure, enclosure for animals, park + -et — more at PARK] **1 a** : a patterned flooring; esp : one made of parquetry ⟨the front hall where . . . rugs lay on the waxed ~ —Philip Wylie⟩ **b** : PARQUETRY ⟨a . . . very attractive floor is provided by ~ —W.P.Matthew⟩ **2 a** : the lower floor of a theater or auditorium; specif : the part extending from the area in front of the stage used by the orchestra to the parquet circle **b** : the forward part of such an area in a theater or auditorium **3** : the branch of the administrative government in France and other countries having a legal system based on Roman law or the Napoleonic Code that is charged primarily with the prosecution of crime as the representative of the public rather than of the injured party

par·que·tage \'pärkəd·ij, ¦≈kə¦täzh\ n -s [F, fr. parquet + -age] : PARQUETRY

parquet circle n : the part of the lower floor of a theater at the rear of the parquet and beneath the galleries — called also orchestra circle, parterre

par·que·try \'pärkə·trē, 'päk-, -ri\ n -ES [F parqueterie, fr. parquet + -erie -ery] : joinery or cabinetwork consisting of an inlay of geometric or other patterns usu. of different colors and used esp. for furniture and floors

parquetry

par·quette \(')pär¦ket, (')pä¦k-, usu -ed·+V\ n -s [by alter.] : PARQUET 2

parr \'pär, 'pá(r\ n, pl **parr** also **parrs** [origin unknown] **1** : a young salmon in the stage between alevin and smolt when it has parr marks on its sides and is actively feeding in fresh water **2** : the young of any of several fishes other than salmon ⟨a trout ~⟩

par·ra \'parə\ [NL, fr. L, barn owl] syn of JACANA

par·ra·keet or **par·a·keet** \'parə,kēt also 'per- sometimes ,≈≈'≈, usu -ēd·+V\ also **par·o·quet** or **par·ro·quet** \-ket, usu -ed·+V\ n -s [MF & Sp; Sp periquito, fr. MF perroquet, paroquet parrot] **1 a** : any of numerous usu. rather small slender parrots with a long graduated tail — see CAROLINA PARRAKEET, GRASS PARRAKEET **b** : PUFFIN **2** : PARROT GREEN

parramatta var of PARAMATTA

parred past of PAR

¹par·rel or **par·ral** \'parəl\ n -s [ME perell, alter. of parail apparel, equipment — more at PAREL] : a rope loop or sliding collar by which a yard or spar is held to a mast in such a way that it may be hoisted or lowered at pleasure — compare JACKSTAY

²parrel or **parral** \"\ vb -ED/-ING/-S : to fasten by means of a parrel

parrel truck or **parrel ball** n : a ball of hard wood with a hole in the middle that is strung on a parrel

par·rhe·sia \pə'rēzh(ē)ə\ n -s [ML, fr. Gk parrhēsia, fr. para- ¹para- + -rhēsia (fr. rhēsis speech, speaking); akin to Gk eirein to say — more at WORD] : boldness or freedom of speech

par·ri·ci·dal \¦parə¦sīdᵊl\ adj [L parricidalis, fr. parricida + -alis -al] **1** : of, relating to, or having the nature of parricide **2** : guilty of parricide

par·ri·cide \'≈≈,sīd\ n -s [in sense 1, fr. L parricida, parricida killer of a close relative, fr. parri-, pari- (akin to Gk pēos kinsman by marriage) + -cida -cide (killer); in sense 2, fr. L parricidium murder of a close relative, fr. parri-, pari- + -cidium -cide (killing)] **1 a** (1) : one that murders his father (2) : one that murders his mother or another close relative **b** : one that murders a person (as the ruler of his country) who stands in a relationship held to resemble that of a father **c** : one that commits the crime of treason against his country **2** : the act of a parricide

par·ri·cid·i·ous \¦≈≈¦sidēəs\ adj [parricide + -ious] archaic : PARRICIDAL

par·ri·dae \'parə,dē\ n pl, cap [NL, fr. Parra + -idae] syn of JACANIDAE

par·ridge \'parij, -rēj\ chiefly Scot var of PORRIDGE

parring pres part of PAR

par·ritch \'parich, -rēch\ Scot var of PORRIDGE

parr mark n : one of the dark traverse bands on the side of a young salmon

par·rock \'parək\ n -s [ME parrok, fr. OE pearroc fence, enclosure; akin to MD parc, perc, parric enclosure, OHG pfarrih, pferrih; all fr. a prehistoric WGmc word borrowed fr. (assumed) VL parricus enclosure (whence ML parricus) — more at PARK] dial Brit : a small field : PADDOCK

¹par·rot \'parət also 'per-, usu -əd·+V\ n -s [prob. irreg. fr. MF perroquet, paroquet] **1** : any of numerous zygodactyl birds (order Psittaciformes) widely distributed in tropical regions that have a distinctive stout curved cered hooked bill whose upper mandible is movably hinged to the skull, that are often crested and brightly variegated, and that are excellent mimics and often readily learn to simulate laughter and crying and to enunciate words and phrases; esp : an Old World parrot of the genus Psittacus having a rather stout form with a short square tail — see AFRICAN GRAY **2** : a person who repeats the words and sometimes the actions of others mechanically and without understanding ⟨tends to become . . . the ~ of other men's thinking —R.W.Emerson⟩

²parrot \"\ vb -ED/-ING/-S vi : to chatter like a parrot ⟨the idiot clucked and ~ed to herself —Robinson Jeffers⟩; esp : repeat something mechanically in the manner of a trained parrot ⟨it is not praying but ~ing —John Trapp⟩ ~ vt **1** : to repeat mechanically or by rote in the manner of a trained parrot : imitate the form of without understanding the sense or meaning involved ⟨~ obediently what the author expected them to say —John Woodburn⟩ ⟨any school boy . . . can ~ the explanation —D.M.Friedenberg⟩ ⟨a newspaper which ~ed to perfection the imperfections of the home press —Bruce Marshall⟩ **2** : to teach to repeat in the mechanical manner of a parrot ⟨actors ~ed by the stage manager⟩

³parrot \"\ adj **1** : of, resembling, or of the nature of a parrot ⟨~ tongue⟩ **2** : of, characterized by, or resembling the mechanical imitation or repetition of the form of something (as a word) without meaning that characterizes a trained parrot ⟨blatant ignorance and assertive ~ knowledge —A.L. Guérard⟩

parrot-back chair \'≈≈,≈-\ n : a chair having a splat so shaped that the openings on each side suggest two parrots facing each other

parrotbill \'≈≈,≈\ n **1** : CLIANTHUS 2 **2 a** : any of numerous thick-billed Asiatic songbirds of the genus Paradoxornis **b** : a bird of the genus Pyrrhuloxia

parrot blue n : a moderate bluish green to greenish blue that is lighter and stronger than gendarme and stronger than cyan blue

parrot crossbill n : a large European crossbill (Loxia pityopsittacus)

parrot-cry \'≈≈,≈\ n : a cry (as a contention, complaint, or plea) made in stupid imitation or repeated mechanically without understanding ⟨the parrot-cry has gone up that these recommendations must be taken as a whole —Contemporary Rev.⟩

parrot disease or **parrot fever** n : PSITTACOSIS

parrot finch n **1** : one of numerous brilliantly colored weaverbirds of the genus Erythrura found in tropical Asia and Australasia **2** : CROSSBILL

parrot fish n : any of numerous marine percoid fish having the teeth in each jaw fused into a cutting plate or parrotlike beak: **a** : a fish of the family Scaridae **b** : any of various wrasses **c** : a fish of the family Oplegnathidae — called also false parrot fish

parrot green n : a strong yellow green that is yellower and duller than viridine yellow and duller and slightly yellower than love bird — called also parrakeet, perruche, popinjay green, verd gay

par·rot·let \'parətlət also 'per-\ n -s : any of various very small short-tailed So. American parrots constituting the genus Forpus

parrotlike \'≈≈,≈\ adj : resembling a parrot in physical appearance or characteristics ⟨a ~ beak⟩; esp : resembling the mechanical imitation or repetition of the form of something (as a word) without meaning that characterizes a trained parrot ⟨not reading at all but rather a mere ~ word-calling process —A.T.Weaver⟩

parrot mouth or **parrot jaw** n : a congenital anomaly of the mouth of a grazing animal in which the upper incisors project over the lower thus preventing apposition and interfering with normal prehension and mastication of food — **parrot-mouthed** \'≈≈¦≈\ adj

parrot's-beak \'≈≈,≈\ or **parrot's-bill** \'≈≈,≈\ or **parrotbeak** \'≈≈,≈\ n, pl **parrot's-beaks** or **parrot's-bills** or **parrotbeaks** [so called fr. its curved standard] : CLIANTHUS 2; esp : KAKA BEAK

parrot's-feather \'≈≈,≈≈\ or **parrot feather** n, pl **parrot's-feathers** or **parrot feathers** : WATER MILFOIL; esp : a New World plant (Myriophyllum brasiliense) that has trailing stems, feathery pinnately dissected leaves, and minute flowers borne in the leaf axils, and that is often cultivated as an aquarium plant

parrot tulip n : any of various garden tulips usu. considered to constitute a distinct variety (Tulipa gesneriana dracontia) and characterized by ruffled laciniate and often variegated flowers

parrot wrasse n : PARROT FISH; esp : a parrot fish of the genus Scarus

par·roty \'parəd·ē also 'per-\ adj : like or of the nature of a parrot

parrs pl of PARR

¹par·ry \'parē, -ri also 'per-\ vb -ED/-ING/-ES [prob. fr. F parez, imper. of parer to parry, fr. MF, fr. OProv parar, fr. L parare to make ready, prepare — more at PARE] vi **1** : to ward off a weapon or blow by means of a parry ⟨he parried in tierce and his blade continued along his opponent's sword —Frank Yerby⟩ **2** : to evade or turn aside something by a similar defensive technique ⟨can ~ and thrust . . . without losing the thread of his argument —Stewart Cockburn⟩ ~ vt **1** : to ward off or turn aside (as a thrust or blow) by means of a parry ⟨the knife had . . . parried the blow from the traitor's useless sword —W.H.G.Kingston⟩ **2** : to turn aside or otherwise avert ⟨to ~ the encroachment of modifying forces, he made a virtue of his way of life —W.M.Kollmorgen⟩; esp : to avoid (as a question) by a skillful or adroit answer : EVADE ⟨parried every question with plain skill —New Republic⟩ **syn** see DODGE

²parry \"\ n -ES **1** : a defensive action made (as with a blade or glove) to deflect a thrust or blow from an opponent **2** : a defensive movement held to be similar to the parry ⟨skillful in the thrust and ~ of debate —Josiah Royce⟩

parry pinyon or **parry pine** n, usu cap 1st P [after Charles C. Parry †1890 Am. botanist] : a Mexican piñon (Pinus cembroides parryana) having the leaves in fours

pars pl of PAR, pres 3d sing of PAR

parse \'pärs, 'pás, -ärz, -áz\ vb -ED/-ING/-S [L pars part (in pars orationis part of speech) — more at PART] vt **1 a** : to resolve (as a sentence) into component parts of speech and describe them grammatically **b** : to describe (as a word) grammatically by stating the part of speech and explaining the inflection and syntactical relationships **2** : to examine in a minute way : analyze critically : ANATOMIZE 2, DISSECT 2 b ⟨~ problems and solutions —C.B.Marshall⟩ ⟨he excited no interest; he was merely something to ~ —Ben Riker⟩ ~ vi **1** : to give a grammatical description of a word or a group of words ⟨learning to spell and ~⟩ **2** : to admit of being parsed ⟨looked at first reading as if it wouldn't ~⟩

par·sec \'pär,sek, 'pá,s-\ n -s [parallax + second] : a unit of measure for interstellar space equal to a distance having a heliocentric parallax of one second or to 206,265 times the radius of the earth's orbit or to 3.26 light-years or to 19.2 trillion miles

pars·er \'pärsər, 'pásə(r, -ärzər, -ázə(r\ n -s : one that parses

par·set·tens·ite \pär'setᵊn,zīt\ n -s [G parsettensit, fr. Parsettens, mountain in Graubünden canton, Switzerland + G -it -ite] : a mineral $Mn_5Si_6O_{13}(OH)_8$ consisting of a hydrous manganese silicate forming cleavable copper-red masses

par·se·val \'pärzə,väl\ n -s usu cap [after August von Parseval †1942 Ger. engineer] : a nonrigid airship usu. having a car suspended beneath a gas envelope — compare ZEPPELIN

par·shall \'pärshəl\ or **parshall flume** n -s usu cap P [after Ralph L. Parshall b1881 Am. civil and hydraulic engineer] : a device for measuring flow in conduits by observing difference of head on opposite sides of a partial obstruction

parshioth or **parshiot** pl of PARASHAH

par·si also **par·see** \'pär,sē, 'pá,sē, ≈'≈\ n -s usu cap [Per pārsī, fr. Pārs Persia, fr. OPer Pārsa-] **1** : a Zoroastrian of India descended from Persian refugees fleeing Muhammadan persecution in the 7th century and settling principally at

Bombay — compare GABAR **2 :** the Iranian dialect of the Parsi religious literature

par·si·ism \-,izəm\ *or* **par·sism** \'⸗,sizəm\ *or* **par·see·ism** \'⸗,sē,izəm, ⸗'⸗,⸗⸗\ *n* -S *usu cap* [*parsi* + *-ism*] **:** the religious teachings and customs of the Parsis — compare ZOROASTRIANISM

par·sil \'pärsᵊl, 'pås-\ *dial Eng var of* PARSLEY

par·si·mo·nious *also* **par·ci·mo·nious** \,pärsə'mōnēəs, ,pås-, -nyəs\ *adj* [*parsimony* + *-ous*] **:** exhibiting or marked by parsimony: as **a :** excessively frugal **:** PENURIOUS, NIGGARDLY ⟨its ~ thrift, relieved by few generous impulses —V.L.Parrington⟩ ⟨a ~ person⟩ **b :** poor in quality or meager in quantity ⟨gleaned from . . . very ~ scraps of information —S.E. Hyman⟩ ⟨~ fare⟩ **c :** sparing in the use or display of something ⟨~ of editorial material —Allan Nevins⟩ ⟨~ in his use of American journals —D.C.Allen⟩ **syn** see STINGY

par·si·mo·nious·ly *adv* **:** in a parsimonious manner ⟨continued . . . to live most ~ in lodgings —Thomas De Quincey⟩

par·si·mo·nious·ness *n* -ES **:** the quality or state of being parsimonious

par·si·mo·ny \'⸗sə,mōnē, -ni, *Brit usu & US sometimes* -sə̇mən-\ *n* -ES [ME *parcimony*, fr. L *parsimonia*, fr. *parsus* (past part. of *parcere* to spare); perh. akin to Gk *porkēs* hoop around the joint of a spearhead and its shaft, Arm *ors* fishnet] **1 a :** carefulness in the expenditure of money or resources **:** THRIFT ⟨not a single institution appropriate to an economy of ~ will remain unaltered in an economy of surplus —Lewis Mumford⟩ **b :** closeness in such expenditure; *specif* **:** reprehensively excessive frugality **:** NIGGARDLINESS, STINGINESS ⟨despised for their sordid ~ —G.E.Fussell⟩ **2 :** economy in the use of a specific means to an end: **a :** economy of assumption in reasoning or ascription of existence — used chiefly in the phrase *law of parsimony;* compare OCKHAM'S RAZOR **b :** animal or human economy (as of pain or effort) in seeking pleasure or gain

pars in·ter·me·dia \,pär,zintə(r)'mēdēə\ *n* [NL, lit., intermediate part] **:** a thin slip of tissue fused with the neurohypophysis and representing the remains of the posterior wall of Rathke's pouch

pars le·gi·ti·ma \-zlə'jid·əmə\ *n* [NL, lit., legitimate part] **:** LEGITIM

¹pars·ley \'pär|slē, 'pȧ|, |sli| *sometimes* |zl-\ *n* -S [ME *persely, persil*, fr. OE *petersilie* & OF *persil*, both fr. (assumed) VL *petrosilium*, alter. of L *petroselinum*, fr. Gk *petroselinon*, fr. *petros* stone + *selinon* celery] **:** an annual or biennial herb (*Petroselinum crispum*) of southern Europe that is widely cultivated for its finely dissected smooth or closely curled leaves which are extensively used as a culinary herb or garnish; *broadly* **:** any of various plants of the family Umbelliferae — usu. used with a qualifier; see FOOL'S PARSLEY, HAMBURG PARSLEY, HEMLOCK PARSLEY, STONE PARSLEY

²parsley \"\ *adj* **1 :** of, having the characteristics of, or resembling parsley ⟨~ bed⟩ ⟨~ frog⟩ **2 :** dressed or flavored with parsley ⟨~ butter⟩ ⟨~ potatoes⟩

parsley camphor *n* **:** APIOLE 1 a

parsley family *n* **:** UMBELLIFERAE

parsley fern *n* **:** any of several plants with finely cut foliage that suggests that of parsley: as **a :** a tansy (*Tanacetum vulgare*) **b** (1) **:** a lady fern (*Athyrium felix-femina*) (2) **:** a European rock brake (*Cryptogramma crispa*) that has a short creeping or ascending rhizome and densely tufted leaves of which the outer are sterile and the inner fertile and that grows chiefly on acid upland soils in cool regions (3) **:** ROCK FERN c

parsley green *n* **:** a moderate olive green that is lighter, stronger, and slightly yellower than cypress green and greener and stronger than holly green (sense 2) or Lincoln green

parsley haw *n* **:** a hawthorn (*Crataegus marshallii*) of the southern U. S. having pinnately lobed leaves

parsley oil *n* **:** a colorless or yellow viscid essential oil obtained from parsley seeds

parsley piert *n, pl* **parsley pierts** [prob. by folk etymology (influence of ¹*parsley* and of E dial. *piert*, alter. of E *pert*) fr. MF *perce-pierre*, fr. *percer* to pierce + *pierre* stone, fr. L *petra* rock, stone, fr. Gk — more at PIERCE] **1 :** a small European annual herb (*Alchemilla arvensis* or *Aphanes arvensis*) of the family Rosaceae having fan-shaped 3-parted leaves with the divisions 2-cleft to 4-cleft and axillary greenish flowers **2 :** a heath (*Erica aphanes*) of southern Africa **3 :** KNAWEL

parsleyworm \'⸗⸗,⸗\ *n* **:** the caterpillar of the black swallowtail butterfly

parsleywort \'⸗⸗,⸗\ *n* **:** a plant of the family Umbelliferae

pars·lied *or* **pars·leyed** \-lēd, -lid\ *adj* **:** dressed or seasoned with parsley ⟨~ onions⟩ ⟨~ potatoes⟩

pars ner·vo·sa \,pärznər'vōsə\ *n* [NL, lit., nervous part] **:** NEUROHYPOPHYSIS

pars·nip \'pärsnə̇p, 'pås-\ *n* -S [alter. of earlier *pasneppe*, fr. ME *pasnepe*, (influenced by ME *nepe* turnip) modif. of MF *pasnaie*, fr. L *pastinaca* parsnip, carrot, fr. *pastinum* 2-pronged dibble — more at NEEP] **1 :** a European biennial herb (*Pastinaca sativa*) with large pinnate leaves and yellow flowers that is naturalized as a weed in No. America **2 :** the long fusiform root of the parsnip that is somewhat poisonous in the wild state but made palatable and nutritious through cultivation and used for the table — usu. used in pl. **3 :** any of several related or similar plants — used with a qualifier; see COW PARSNIP, MEADOW PARSNIP, SEA PARSNIP, WILD PARSNIP

parsnip swallowtail *n* **:** BLACK SWALLOWTAIL

parsnip webworm *n* **:** the larva of the oecophorid moth (*Depressaria heracliana*) that feeds on parsnips

par·son \'pärsᵊn, 'pås-\ *n* -S [ME *persone*, fr. OF, fr. ML *persona*, lit., person, fr. L — more at PERSON] **1 :** one that represents a parish in its ecclesiastical and corporate capacities; *esp* **:** the rector or incumbent of a parochial church charged with the pastoral care of the persons in the parish **2 :** CLERGYMAN 1; *esp* **:** one belonging to a Protestant denomination **3 :** an animal with a black coat or markings

par·son·age \-s(ᵊ)nij, -nēj\ *n* -S [ME *personage*, fr. MF *personage, personnage*, fr. OF, fr. *persone* + *-age*] **1 :** the benefice under English ecclesiastical law of the parson of a parish: **a :** a parish church and the income attached to it (as from rights, glebes, and tithes) **b :** a certain portion of lands, tithes, and offerings for the maintenance of the parson **2 a :** the house or the house and land provided by a parish or congregation for its pastor's use **b :** a clergyman's residence

parson bird *n* **:** TUI

par·son·ess \-'pärsᵊnəs, 'pås-\ *n* -ES **:** a parson's wife

parson gull *n, dial Eng* **:** GREAT BLACK-BACKED GULL

par·son·ic \(')pär¦sänik\ *also* **par·son·i·cal** \-nə̇kəl\ *adj* **:** of, resembling, or having the characteristics of a parson **:** CLERICAL 1 ⟨a secular as well as a ~ view of life —Edward Peacock⟩ ⟨his rejection of the *parsonical* career —W.J.Locke⟩

parson-in-the-pulpit \'⸗⸗⸗⸗'⸗⸗\ *n, pl* **parson-in-the-pulpits** *or* **parsons-in-the-pulpit :** CUCKOOPINT

par·sons·ite \'pärsᵊn,zīt, 'pås-\ *n* -S [F, fr. Arthur L. *Parsons* †1957 Canadian mineralogist + F *-ite*] **:** a mineral $Pb_2(UO_2)(PO_4)_2.2H_2O$ consisting of a hydrous lead uranyl phosphate found as a brownish powder in Katanga province, Congo

parson's nose *n* **:** POPE'S NOSE

pars ra·ti·o·na·bi·lis \,pärz,rad·ēə'nabələs, ,pärs,r-\ *n* [NL] **:** REASONABLE PART

¹part \'pär|t, 'pȧ|, *usu* |d·+V\ *n* -S [ME, fr. OF & OE, both fr. L *part-, pars;* akin to OIr *rann* part, Skt *pūrta* reward, L *parare* to prepare — more at PARE] **1 a** (1) **:** one of the equal or unequal portions into which something is or is regarded as divided **:** something less than a whole **:** a unit (as a number, quantity, or mass) held to constitute with one or more other units something larger **:** CONSTITUENT, FRACTION, FRAGMENT, MEMBER, PIECE ⟨the greater ~ of the highway . . . is full of sharp curves —*Amer. Guide Series: N.H.*⟩ ⟨the vast ~ of Englishmen who were conscious of a political change —Francis Hackett⟩ ⟨in the early ~ of the summer⟩ ⟨the road was passable only ~ of the year —Samuel Johnson⟩ (2) **:** an essential portion or integral element of something ⟨a Boer's wagon was as much a ~ of him as his bed —Stuart Cloete⟩ ⟨racial prejudice is very much a ~ of the country —B.M.Beck⟩ ⟨as if light and shadow were ~ of her being —Edith Sitwell⟩ **b :** an equal constituent portion **:** one of several or many like units into which something is divided or of which it is composed **:** a proportional division or ingredient ⟨mix the powder with three ~*s* of water⟩ ⟨the compound contained two ~*s* oxygen⟩ **c :** a constituent portion of something in mathematics: as (1) **:** ALIQUOT, SUBMULTIPLE (2) **:** a mathematical aggregate all of whose elements are also elements of another aggregate (3) **:** a line or other element of a geometrical figure **d :** a portion of a plant or animal body: as (1) **:** essential element **:** ORGAN, MEMBER ⟨the chief ~*s* of the digestive system are the esophagus, stomach, intestine, and associated glands⟩ (2) **:** an indefinite area or one lacking or not considered in respect to a natural boundary **:** SPOT, PLACE ⟨bathe the affected ~ with warm water⟩ (3) **:** the external genital and excretory organs — usu. used in pl.; called also *private parts, privy parts* **e** (1) **:** a formal or distinctive division of a literary work ⟨a story in four ~*s*⟩ (2) **:** one of a series of sections of a literary work sold separately and at intervals and designed eventually to be bound into one or more permanent volumes ⟨two volumes sold in ~*s* by subscription⟩ **f** (1) **:** a vocal or instrumental line or melody in concerted music or in harmony (2) **:** a particular voice or instrument in concerted music; *also* **:** the individual score for it ⟨the alto ~⟩ ⟨the viola ~⟩ **g :** a portion of a line in a ship's rigging ⟨standing ~*s*⟩ ⟨hauling ~*s*⟩ **h** (1) **:** a constituent member of a machine or other apparatus ⟨the . . . mechanics had the names for the ~*s* of the planes —Charlton Laird⟩ (2) **:** such a member existing separately apart from a machine ⟨a dealer in automobile ~*s* and accessories⟩ **2 :** something belonging to, assumed by, or falling to one (as in a division or apportionment) **:** SHARE ⟨wanted no ~ of the proposal⟩ ⟨bad men . . . claim as much ~ in God as his best servants —John Milton⟩ **3 :** one's share or allotted task in an action **:** DUTY, FUNCTION, OFFICE ⟨do its ~ in helping persons . . . interested in the field of research —*Bull. of Meharry Med. Coll.*⟩ ⟨it is the ~ of a poet to humor the imagination —Joseph Addison⟩ **4 :** one of the opposing sides in a relationship involving conflict or rivalry (as a contest, question, dispute, contract, or transaction) ⟨he that is not against us is on our ~ —Mk 9:40 (AV)⟩ ⟨make whole kingdoms take her brother's ~ —Edmund Waller⟩ **5 a** *archaic* **:** a side or direction in space ⟨on every ~ walled in —Thomas Hutchinson⟩ **b** *archaic* **:** HAND 3b ⟨on the other ~, I judged that I might lose nearly as much —R.L.Stevenson⟩ **6 a :** a portion of an unspecified territorial area (as of a country or the world) **:** DISTRICT, QUARTER, REGION ⟨go into . . . camp with the other fellows from our ~ —Alice F. Webb⟩ — usu. used in pl. ⟨taking off for ~*s* unknown —Meridel Le Sueur⟩ ⟨Australian soldiers in foreign ~*s* —William Power⟩ ⟨the oddest marker in these ~*s* —S.H. Holbrook⟩ **b** (1) **:** a portion of a specified territorial area ⟨lawyers came from all ~*s* of the state —*Amer. Guide Series: La.*⟩ ⟨no new state shall . . . be formed by the junction of two or more states or ~*s* of states —*U.S.Constitution*⟩ ⟨the central ~ of the eastern section of the state —*Amer. Guide Series: Oregon*⟩ (2) **parts** *pl, usu cap* **:** a territorial area forming one of the three major divisions of the county of Lincoln, England, and now constituting an administrative county ⟨the *Parts* of Holland⟩ ⟨the *Parts* of Kesteven⟩ ⟨the *Parts* of Lindsey⟩ **7 a :** a role or function assumed by a person in real life ⟨he will perform unto thee the ~ of a kinsman —Ruth 3:13 (AV)⟩ **b :** a function or course of action performed **:** a position undertaken ⟨objected to the government's ~ in the strike⟩ **8 a** (1) **:** the words and stage directions assigned to a particular actor in a dramatic production ⟨the actress learned her ~ well⟩ (2) **:** such words and directions set down in written form ⟨the director handed him the ~⟩ **b :** a particular character created by an actor in a dramatic production ⟨the ~ of Ophelia in *Hamlet*⟩ **c :** the role taken by an actor who creates such a character ⟨a speaking ~⟩ **9 a :** a constituent of character or capacity **:** a personal quality **:** a natural or acquired attribute (as an ability or talent) — usu. used in pl. ⟨a steady lad, of good brilliant ~*s* —Walter Besant⟩ ⟨a man of varied ~*s*, learning, and culture —Jossleyn Hennessy⟩ ⟨his natural ~*s* were respectable —V.L.Parrington⟩ **b parts** *pl* **:** such personal qualities of a superior kind (as high intellectual ability, cleverness, talent) ⟨he had ~*s* and his sisters . . . expected him to do great things —W.S.Maugham⟩ ⟨a man of ~*s* and of great culture —Geoffrey Boumphrey⟩ **10** *archaic* **:** a particle of matter **11 :** the line where the hair is parted ⟨the ~ in your hair is a bit crooked⟩ **12 :** a course of conduct ⟨I thought silence the better ~ —H.J.Laski⟩; *specif* **:** one required or suggested by a specified quality ⟨it would be the ~ of prudence . . . to moderate his behavior —G.F.Kennan⟩ ⟨it is the ~ of wisdom to compare different cases —John Dewey⟩

part 11

syn PART, PORTION, PIECE, DETAIL, MEMBER, DIVISION, SECTION, SEGMENT, SECTOR, FRACTION, FRAGMENT, and PARCEL agree in meaning something less than a whole that is considered apart or actually separated from it. PART is the most general and comprehensive, being interchangeable with any of the other terms ⟨a *part* of a machine⟩ ⟨the greater *part* of a square⟩ ⟨a *part* of a year⟩ ⟨a *part* of a statue⟩ PORTION, although it signifies a part, does not necessarily imply an integral or assembled part; it can also suggest an assigned or allotted part (see the synonymy at *fate*) ⟨a *portion* of a diary⟩ ⟨the greater *portion* of a life⟩ ⟨a considerable *portion* of the town was burned —*Amer. Guide Series: Minn.*⟩ ⟨a *portion* of the voting population⟩ PIECE usually applies to a separate or detached part of a whole, often so stressing the idea of independence that the sense of a whole is extremely weak or lacking ⟨a *piece* of pie⟩ ⟨a *piece* of hot pig iron⟩ ⟨a *piece* of furniture⟩ DETAIL applies to a part of a plan or design, esp. in a painting or other art work, often signifying a part or feature that is small but important ⟨the *details* of domestic life on a farm —Havelock Ellis⟩ ⟨the *details* of the landscape dissolved in shadows —*Amer. Guide Series: N.Y.City*⟩ ⟨the most interesting *detail* of the house plan was its ornamentation⟩ MEMBER applies to one of the units of which a body (as a human body, legislative body, club, or construction such as a chair) is composed, implying both association with and separability from the whole ⟨a *member* of a committee⟩ ⟨a loss of an arm or other *member* in an accident⟩ ⟨the design of compression *members* of bridge trusses —*U.S. Nat'l Bureau of Standards Annual Report*⟩ ⟨a mere shell covering the structural *members* —*Amer. Guide Series: N.Y.City*⟩ DIVISION and SECTION apply to a distinct often detached part formed by or as if by cutting, DIVISION often suggesting a larger part than SECTION ⟨the bureaus are subdivided into *divisions* —J.E.Pate⟩ ⟨the *division* of activities arranged by the museum —Ralph Linton⟩ ⟨the New York City Police Department is split into parts, the detective *division* and the uniformed *division* —Walter Arm⟩ ⟨in my *division* of the class were four friends⟩ ⟨a *section* of the country⟩ ⟨a *section* of a circle⟩ ⟨a *section* of a cake⟩ SEGMENT, often interchangeable with SECTION, is often preferred to SECTION in distinguishing a part separated by natural lines of cleavage or determined by the construction of the whole ⟨Berkeley's career in Virginia was divided into two *segments* by the English civil war —G.W.Johnson⟩ ⟨essential raw materials for a broad *segment* of American industry —*Crops in Peace & War*⟩ ⟨the *segments* of an orange⟩ In mathematical use SECTOR signifies any part of a circle bounded by an arc and two radii, and SECTOR in general use can be any section roughly corresponding to this or any section of a whole conceived of as divided like a statistical circle into statistical portions; or, by extension, it can mean any portion cut off or out ⟨we must consider the German problem as a whole and not in *sectors* —A.H.Vandenberg⟩ ⟨the expansion of military production will cut into the civilian *sector* of the economy —L.J.Walinsky⟩ ⟨each society divides its total membership into a series of categories and assigns different *sectors* of the total culture to each category —Ralph Linton⟩ ⟨the tiny *sector* of the puzzle which he has chosen for his own province, finding some new pieces that fit neatly into place and properly rearranging some old ones —R.D.Altick⟩ FRACTION usu. suggests a very small or negligible part of the whole ⟨only a *fraction* of the cost —*Dun's Rev.*⟩ ⟨told him the merest *fraction* of our experiences —Kenneth Roberts⟩ ⟨a reduction of immigration to a mere *fraction* of what it used to be —P.A.Sorokin⟩ FRAGMENT applies to a small part disconnected from the whole esp. by breaking, and often applies to a small piece of a whole remaining after the whole has been almost totally eaten, used, or worn away ⟨the *fragments* of a broken glass⟩ ⟨the artist takes up some *fragment* of that existence, transfigures it, shows it —Havelock Ellis⟩ ⟨they represent only a *fragment* of the dramatic literature that once existed —R.D.Altick⟩ ⟨a *fragment* of an ancient Greek vase⟩ PARCEL in this connection is now used chiefly in law to mean a piece of land or in such a fixed phrase as *part and parcel;* its general sense implies an undetached and undetachable connection with the whole of which it is a part ⟨a number of real estate *parcels* in the downtown area —*Current Biog.*⟩ ⟨Irian has always been part and *parcel* of Indonesia —Cecil Hobbs⟩ ⟨demanded increasing *parcels* of Indian territory —H.M.Hyman⟩ ⟨held a small *parcel* of stock —*Amer. Guide Series: Mich.*⟩

— **for one's part :** as far as the share or interest of the person specified is concerned ⟨*for my part*, I have no intention to dispute her free agency —Tobias Smollett⟩ ⟨*for their part*, the boys . . . gather wood —J.G.Frazer⟩ — **for the most part :** in most cases **:** in the main **:** with regard to the greatest portion ⟨the dunes were . . . *for the most part* protected by seawalls —J.A.Steers⟩ ⟨persons who *for the most part* have some special knowledge —Allan Nevins⟩ ⟨the mafic minerals are *for the most part* hornblende and biotite —*Amer. Jour. of Science*⟩ — **in good part** *adv* **:** without offense **:** FAVORABLY, GRACIOUSLY ⟨took his refusal *in good part* —Archie Binns⟩ ⟨accepted this criticism *in good part* —J.G.Cozzens⟩ — **in part** *adv* **:** with respect to a part rather than a whole **:** in some measure or degree **:** PARTLY ⟨taken his idea *in part* from a picture —Clara Morris⟩ ⟨built *in part* of beams and brick —Philip Brady⟩ — often used with a qualifier ⟨the procedure . . . is the result *in* large *part* of its long struggle —K.B.Smellie⟩ ⟨*in* small *part* . . . the ridge is entirely covered with bracken —C.B.Hitchcock⟩ — **of the part of** *obs* **:** on the side of ⟨what art thou? *of the part of* England —Shak.⟩ — **on the part of 1 :** on the side of **:** with regard to or so far as concerns the one specified ⟨the managers *on the part of* the House at the conference —*U.S.Code*⟩ ⟨vigilance *on our part* —Thomas De Quincey⟩ ⟨incentive for all-out effort *on the part of* every member —A.S.Igleheart⟩ **2 :** as experienced, performed, or shown by ⟨the thoughtfulness of this act *on the part of* these men —*Metronome*⟩

²part \"\ *vb* -ED/-ING/-S [ME *parten*, fr. OF *partir* to divide, go away, fr. L *partire, partiri* to divide, fr. *part-, pars* part — more at ¹PART] *vi* **1 a :** to separate from or take leave of someone — used with *from* ⟨this ring I gave him when he ~*ed* from me —Shak.⟩ or sometimes with *with* ⟨just after I had ~*ed* with him at his lodgings —Matthew Arnold⟩ **b :** to relinquish possession or control of something — used with *with* ⟨sell securities or . . . ~ with some liquid cash —R.B.Westerfield⟩ ⟨willing to ~ with his right to vote —E.H.Collis⟩ or sometimes with *from* ⟨his precious bag which he would by no means ~ from —George Eliot⟩ **2** *obs* **:** to have a part or share **:** PARTAKE ⟨they shall ~ alike —1 Sam 30:24 (AV)⟩ **3 a :** to become separated into distinct parts **:** come apart ⟨saw the curtains ~ . . . on the next act —Winifred Bambrick⟩ **b :** to quit each other's company **:** take leave of one another ⟨they ~*ed* at the door —Irving Bacheller⟩ **4 a :** to go away **:** set out **:** take one's leave **:** DEPART ⟨~*ed* hence to embark for Milan —Shak.⟩ **b :** DIE ⟨~*ed* ev'n just between twelve and one —Shak.⟩ **5 :** to become separated, freed, or detached from something ⟨strips of three-ply that had . . . ~*ed* from the glue —*Sydney (Australia) Bull.*⟩ **6 :** to become divided or broken (as into segments or pieces) ⟨the port cable suddenly ~*ed* —R.B.O'Brien⟩ **7 :** to cause separation, division, or distinction ⟨the lot causeth contentions to cease and ~*eth* between the mighty —Prov 18:18 (AV)⟩ ~ *vt* **1 a** (1) **:** to divide or separate into distinct parts (as by breaking, cutting, cleaving) ⟨thou shalt ~ it in pieces and pour oil thereon —Lev 2:6 (AV)⟩ (2) **:** to divide by assigning or making physical boundaries **b :** to separate (hair) into two portions on each side of a line of demarcation ⟨~*ed* her hair just right of the middle⟩ **c :** to break or suffer the breaking of (as a rope or anchor chain) ⟨the ship ~*ed* her hawser in the gale⟩ **2 a :** to divide into shares and distribute (as among a number of recipients) **:** ALLOT, APPORTION ⟨~*ed* my garments among them —Jn 19:24 (RSV)⟩ **b** *archaic* **:** to share with one or more other persons ⟨~*ed* his breakfast . . . with the child and her grandfather —Charles Dickens⟩ **3 a :** to remove from contact or contiguity **:** cause to go apart **:** DISUNITE, SEPARATE, SUNDER ⟨if aught but death ~ thee and me —Ruth 1:17 (AV)⟩ — often used with *from* ⟨had been ~*ed* from each other years before⟩ ⟨~ animals from a herd⟩ **b :** to keep separate **:** form a boundary or interval between **:** DIVIDE ⟨the narrow seas that ~ the French and English —Shak.⟩ **c :** to hold apart (as combatants) **:** stand between **:** intervene between ⟨~ them! They are incens'd —Shak.⟩ **d :** to separate by a process of extraction, elimination, or secretion ⟨~ gold from silver⟩ **4 :** to bring (as an association) to an end by separating the parties involved ⟨you are . . . come to ~ almost a fray —Shak.⟩ **5 a** *archaic* **:** to take leave of **:** depart from **:** LEAVE, QUIT ⟨since presently your souls must ~ your bodies —Shak.⟩ ⟨loth to ~ his country —Maria Edgeworth⟩ **b** *dial Brit* **:** to give up **:** RELINQUISH **6** *obs* **:** to take sides with **:** espouse the cause of ⟨who ~*ed* our disaffected people and stopped all prosecution of them —Robert Wodrow⟩ **syn** see SEPARATE — **part company 1 a :** to bring a companionship, association, or similar connection between two parties (as individuals, groups, or organizations) to an end ⟨a faint diverging path was reached, where they *parted company* —Thomas Hardy⟩ ⟨held the federal union together . . . when the states might easily have *parted company* —C.A. Herter⟩ **b :** to effect such a separation from someone or something — used with *with* ⟨*parted* legal *company* with his former boss . . . and has hired his own lawyer —Ted Princiotto⟩ **2 a :** to diverge from someone or something (as in opinion, policy, or common purpose) — used with *with* ⟨the Republican Senate leadership *parted company* with the President on this issue —Arthur Krock⟩ and sometimes with *from* ⟨here . . . *parts company* from most of the scholars —*Times Lit. Supp.*⟩ **b :** to diverge in such a way from each other ⟨on the tariff question the two philosophies *parted company*⟩

³part \"\ *adv* [¹*part*] **:** in a measure **:** PARTLY ⟨was at least ~ right⟩ ⟨the rains came down . . . , ~ spoiling the cochineal crop —Oliver La Farge⟩

⁴part \"\ *adj* [¹*part*] **:** PARTIAL ⟨this woman has lived only a ~ life —H.A.Overstreet⟩ ⟨a ~ truth⟩ ⟨~ payments⟩

part *abbr* **1** participating **2** participle; participial **3** particular **4** partner

par·tage \(')pär¦täzh\ *n* -S [ME, fr. MF, portion, division, fr. OF, division, fr. *partir* to divide + *-age* — more at PART] **1 :** something resulting from a division **:** PART, PORTION, SHARE **2 :** the action of dividing or sharing **:** DIVISION, DISTRIBUTION ⟨a bishop made a ~ of money collected —Thomas Fuller⟩

par·take \pär'tāk, pȧ'-, pə(r)'-\ *vb* **par·took** \-tu̇k\ **par·tak·en** \-tākən\ **partaking; partakes** [back-formation fr. *partaker*] *vi* **1 :** to take a part or share in something (as an action or condition) in common with others **:** PARTICIPATE ⟨~ in a common economic and political life —*Amer. Guide Series: N.Y.*⟩ — often used with *of* ⟨their inability to ~ of some of the activities —W.E.Ditmars⟩ **2 a :** to take or receive a portion of something (as food or drink) **:** take some of something — usu. used with *of* ⟨none shall ~ of the meat until the male has had his fill —J.J.Hayward⟩ ⟨invited . . . to ~ of our lowly fare —Charles Dickens⟩ **b :** to consume most or all of something (as a meal) **:** TAKE — usu. used with *of* ⟨her solitary meals she *partook* of in the apartment next the eating room —Emily Clark⟩ **3 :** to have some of the properties, qualities, or attributes of something — usu. used with *of* ⟨these dialects *partook* . . . of the common body of Indo-European vocabulary —Charlton Laird⟩ ⟨the . . . lakes *partook* of the nature of the open sea —*U.S.Code*⟩ ~ *vt* **1 :** to take a part or a share in **:** SHARE ⟨adventurers who were willing to ~ his fortunes —A.W.Kinglake⟩ **2 :** to take some or all of (as food or drink) alone or in company with others ⟨they . . . reclined beside him and his frugal fare *partook* —Robert Southey⟩ **syn** see SHARE

par·tak·er \-kə(r)\ *n* [alter. of earlier *part taker*, fr. ME, fr. ¹*part* + *taker;* intended as trans. of L *particeps* participant] **1 :** one that partakes **:** PARTICIPANT, PARTNER, SHARER ⟨the sacrament . . . by which the Christian is made a ~ of the anointing of the Christ —Donald Allghin⟩ **2** *obs* **:** one that takes the side of another **:** SUPPORTER ⟨the great displeasure . . . of King Henry and his ~s —Edward Hall⟩

par·tan \ˈpärtᵊn\ *n* -s [ME (Sc), of Celt origin; akin to ScGael *partan* crab] **:** a European crab (*Cancer pagurus*) often used as food

part and parcel *n* **:** an essential or constituent portion **:** an integral element ⟨courtesy and geniality are *part and parcel* of the north country makeup —S.P.B.Mais⟩ ⟨thousands of Aramaic words are now *part and parcel* of the language —William Chomsky⟩

partan face *n, Scot* **:** a person whose face wears a sour expression

parted *adj* [fr. past part. of ²*part*] **1 a** *chiefly Scot* **:** ⁴PARTY 2 ⟨a shield ~ per pale —E.S.Holden⟩ **b :** divided into parts (as by a line or space) ⟨~ hair⟩ **c :** cleft so that the divisions reach nearly but not quite to the base — used chiefly in combination ⟨3-*parted* corolla⟩ ⟨5-*parted* calyx⟩ **2** *archaic* **:** departed from earthly life **:** DECEASED ⟨their ~ father's ghost —William Warner⟩ ⟨hymn the departed to his ~ soul —Robert Southey⟩ **3** [¹*part* + *-ed*] *obs* **:** endowed with parts (as abilities or talents) ⟨a man well ~ —Ben Jonson⟩ **4 :** being apart **:** SEPARATED ⟨~ lips⟩

parted and fretted *or* **parted and fretty** *adj* **:** having both arms divided into two separated narrow strips and the four strips interlacing in the form of a fret — used of a heraldic cross

part·er \ˈpär|d·ə(r), ˈpȧ|, |tə-\ *n* -s [ME, one that divides, fr. *parten* to part, divide + *-er* — more at PART] **:** one that parts; *esp* **:** a worker that separates bundles or sheets

par·terre \(ˈ)pär¦te(ə)r, (ˈ)pȧ¦, -eə\ *n* -s [F, fr. MF, fr. *par terre* on the ground, fr. *par* through, along (fr. L *per* through) + *terre* ground, earth, fr. L *terra* — more at FARE, TERRACE] **1 :** a garden having an ornamental and diversified arrangement of beds or plots separated by paths; *esp* **:** one in which flowers are cultivated **2 :** a level space including a building site **3 :** the part of the floor of a theater behind the orchestra; *esp* **:** PARQUET CIRCLE

par terre \"\ *adv (or adj)* [F, lit., on the ground] *ballet* **:** along the ground **:** on the floor — opposed to *en l'air*

par·terred \-e(ə)rd, -eəd\ *adj* **:** laid out in parterres ⟨sundials rose among ~ flowers —H.T.Kane⟩

parthen- *or* **partheno-** *comb form* [Gk, maiden, virgin, fr. *parthenos*] **:** virgin **:** without fertilization ⟨*partheno*genesis⟩ ⟨*parthen*ote⟩

par·then·i·ta \pärˈthenəd·ə\ *n, pl* **partheni·tae** \-nə,tē, -,tī\ [NL, fr. Gk *parthenos* maiden, virgin] **:** a juvenile trematode worm (as a miracidium, sporocyst, or redia) — compare ADOLESCARIA, MARITA

par·the·ni·um \pärˈthēnēəm\ *n, cap* [NL, fr. Gk *parthenion* feverfew, fr. neut. of *parthenios* maidenly, fr. *parthenos* maiden, virgin] **:** a small genus of No. American woody herbs (family Compositae) having small heads of rayed flowers in a terminal panicle — see BASTARD FEVERFEW, GUAYULE

par·the·no·car·pic \ˌpärthənō¦kärpik\ *also* **par·the·no·car·pi·cal** \-pəkəl\ *or* **par·the·no·car·pous** \-pəs\ *adj* [*parthenocarpic* ISV *parthenocarpy* + *-ic*; *parthenocarpical* fr. *parthenocarpy* + *-ical*; *parthenocarpous* fr. *parthen-* + *-carpous*] **:** exhibiting parthenocarpy — **par·the·no·car·pi·cal·ly** \-pək(ə)lē, -li\ *adv*

par·the·no·car·py \ˈ===,pē\ *n* -ES [ISV *parthen-* + *-carpy*; prob. orig. formed as G *parthenokarpie*] **:** the production of fruits without fertilization — compare STENOSPERMOCARPY

par·the·no·cis·sus \ˌ===ˈsisəs\ *n, cap* [NL, fr. *parthen-* + *Cissus*] **:** a genus of Asiatic and No. American woody vines (family Vitaceae) distinguished by disklike tips on the tendrils — see BOSTON IVY, VIRGINIA CREEPER

par·the·no·genesis \ˌ===+\ *n* [NL, fr. *parthen-* + L *genesis*] **1 :** reproduction that involves development of a female or rarely of a male gamete without fertilization, that occurs commonly among lower plants and invertebrate animals but rarely as a natural process among seed plants and vertebrates although it may be induced by artificial mechanical or chemical stimulation of the eggs of some vertebrates and that in nature either constitutes the sole form of sexual reproduction or alternates with bisexual activities in a pattern adapted to the needs and peculiar life circumstances of the organism — distinguished from *asexual reproduction;* compare APOGAMY **2 :** creation or production of something by a process held to resemble biological parthenogenesis ⟨atheism was supposed to have produced revolution by ~ —V.G.Kiernan⟩

par·the·no·genetic \ˌ===+\ *or* **par·the·no·genic** \ˌ===ˈjenik\ *or* **par·the·no·gen·i·tive** \-ˈjenəd·iv, -ətiv\ *or* **par·the·nog·e·nous** \ˌ==ˈnäjənəs\ *adj* [*parthenogenetic* fr. *parthenogenesis*, after E *genesis: genetic; parthenogenic, parthenogenous* fr. *parthenogeny* + *-ic* or *-ous; parthenogenitive* irreg. (influenced by E *-ive* and by L *genitus*, past part. of *gignere* to beget) fr. *parthenogenesis* — more at KIN] **:** of, characterized by, or capable of parthenogenesis **:** produced by parthenogenesis — **par·the·no·genetically** \ˌ===+\ *adv*

par·the·nog·e·ny \ˌ==ˈnäjənē, -ni\ *n* -ES [*parthen-* + *-geny*] **:** PARTHENOGENESIS

par·the·no·gonidium \ˌ==nō+\ *n* [NL, fr. *parthen-* + *gonidium*] **:** an individual or gonidium (as in members of the genus *Volvox*) that can reproduce asexually

par·the·nop·a·rous \ˌ==ˈnäpərəs\ *adj* [*parthen-* + *-parous*] **:** producing living young without fertilization ⟨~ aphids⟩

par·then·o·pe \pärˈthenə(,)pē\ *n, cap* [NL, fr. L *Parthenope*, siren worshiped in Naples in ancient times, fr. Gk *Parthenopē*] **:** a large cosmopolitan genus (the type of the family Parthenopidae) of spider crabs with well-formed orbits and enlarged chelipeds

¹**par·then·o·pid** \-,pəd\ *adj* [NL *Parthenopidae*, fr. *Parthenope*, type genus + *-idae*] **:** of or relating to the Parthenopidae

²**parthenopid** \"\ *n* -s [NL *Parthenopidae*] **:** a spider crab of the family Parthenopidae

par·the·nop·i·dae \ˌpärthəˈnäpə,dē\ *n pl, cap* [NL, fr. *Parthenope*, type genus + *-idae*] **:** a widely distributed family of spider crabs with long heavy chelipeds

par·the·no·spore \ˈpärthənə+,-\ *n* [ISV *parthen-* + *spore*] **:** a spore produced parthenogenetically

par·the·note \ˈpärthə,nōt\ *n* -s [*parthen-* + *-ote* (as in *zygote*)] **:** an individual produced by parthenogenesis

¹**par·thi·an** \ˈpärthēən, ˈpȧth-\ *n* -s *cap* [*Parthia* + E *-an*, n. suffix] **1 :** a native or inhabitant of Parthia, an ancient country to the southeast of the Caspian sea **2 :** an Iranian language or dialect of the Parthian people

²**parthian** \"\ *adj, usu cap* [*Parthia* + E *-an*, adj. suffix] **1 :** of, relating to, or characteristic of ancient Parthia **2 :** of, relating to, or characteristic of the people of ancient Parthia **3 :** suggesting or held to suggest the mode of fighting on horseback with the bow as the only weapon employed by the Parthian people and characterized chiefly by the discharge of arrows while in real or feigned flight **:** delivered in or as if in flight or retreat **:** PARTING ⟨*Parthian* shot⟩

¹**par·ti** \(ˈ)pär¦tē\ *n, pl* **partis** \-ē(z)\ [F, fr. MF, match, party, decision, fr. *parti*, past part. of *partir* to divide, go away — more at PART] **1 :** ¹MATCH 4b ⟨the Englishman whom she naively assumes to be an excellent ~ —*Times Lit. Supp.*⟩ **2 :** a good or desirable match ⟨you don't realize what a ~ he is —Mary Manning⟩

²**parti** \"\ *n* -s [F, fr. MF, match, party, decision] **:** the basic general scheme of an architectural design

¹**parti-** *also* **party-** *comb form* [obs. E *party*, adj., parti-colored, fr. ME *party*, *parti*, fr. MF *parti* striped, party per pale, fr. OF, fr. *parti*, past part. of *partir* to divide, go away] **:** various **:** variegated ⟨*parti*-striped⟩

²**parti-** *comb form* [L, fr. *part-*, *pars* — more at PART] **:** part ⟨*parti*-mortgage⟩

¹**par·tial** \ˈpärshəl, ˈpȧsh-\ *adj* [ME *parcial*, fr. MF *partial* biased, incomplete, fr. ML *partialis*, fr. LL, incomplete, fr. L *part-*, *pars* part + *-ialis* -ial — more at PART] **1 :** inclined to favor one party in a cause or one side of a question more than the other **:** BIASED, PREDISPOSED ⟨loss of the impartiality of the scientific spirit through affiliation with some partisan and ~ interest —John Dewey⟩ ⟨the ~ testimony of friends —H.D. Thoreau⟩ ⟨it is inconsistent with justice to be ~ —J.S.Mill⟩ **2 a** (1) **:** having a predilection for a certain person or thing **:** favorably disposed toward someone or something **:** biased or prejudiced in one's favor (2) **:** inclined to favor a certain person or thing excessively **:** having an unreasonable fondness for something **:** foolishly fond ⟨the ~ father, loving one alone —F.W.Robertson⟩ **b :** having a liking for **:** fond of — used with *to* ⟨the horse is particularly ~ to salt —Henry Wynmalen⟩ ⟨a walk . . . was a marvelous idea for them ~ to it —Richard Llewellyn⟩ **3 :** of, involving, or affecting a part rather than the whole of something **:** not total or entire **:** not general or universal **:** existing to a limited extent only **:** INCOMPLETE ⟨the ~ transfer of sovereignty . . . to a supranational authority —*Current Biog.*⟩ ⟨among ~ men, he stood for the complete man —Van Wyck Brooks⟩ ⟨provides only a ~ solution to the housing problem —D.D.Eisenhower⟩ ⟨~ paralysis⟩

²**partial** \"\ *n* -s **1 :** one of the tones produced by the complex vibrations comprising a musical tone and extending in range from the fundamental upward through the entire overtone series — compare HARMONIC 1 **2 :** PARTIAL SCORE **3 :** PARTIAL DENTURE

partial adjunct *n* **:** a grammatical adjunct that qualifies only a part of the following substantive (as *free* in *free churchman*)

partial cleavage *n* **:** embryonic cleavage in which the division into blastomeres involves only a part of the egg with the rest remaining undivided for a longer or shorter time

partial correlation *n* **:** the correlation between two statistical variables under the condition that all other relevant variables are fixed

partial denture *n* **:** a fixed or removable artificial replacement of one or more teeth in a dental arch

partial derivative *n* **:** the derivative of a function of several variables with respect to one of them and with the remaining variables treated as constants

partial differential equation *n* **:** a differential equation containing at least one partial derivative

partial differentiation *n* **:** the process of finding a partial derivative

partial diphthong *n* **:** a speech sound whose articulation resembles that of an ordinary diphthong in being a transition between two vowel positions but which differs in having a held beginning or ending — called also *imperfect diphthong*

partial disability *n* **:** a condition constituting less than total disability **:** incapacity preventing full performance of duties of an occupation as a result of accident or illness

partial eclipse *n* **:** an eclipse in which one celestial body is not completely obscured by the shadow or body of another

partial fraction *n* **:** one of the fractions into the sum of which a fraction may be decomposed

par·tial·ism \ˈpärshə,lizəm, ˈpȧsh-\ *n* -s [¹*partial* + *-ism*] **1 :** concentration of libidinal interest on one part of the body (as breasts or buttocks) **2 :** a form of fetishism whose object is a part of the body rather than an inanimate symbol

par·tial·ist \-ləst\ *n* -s [MF *partialiste*, fr. *partial* biased + *-iste* -ist] **1 :** one that is partial to one side (as of a controversy or question); *specif* **:** PARTISAN **2** [¹*partial* + *-ist*] **:** a believer in or advocate of imperfect particularism

par·tial·i·ty \ˌpärshēˈaləd·ē, ˌpȧsh-, -lətē, -i *also* =ˈshal-\ *n* -ES [ME *parcialite*, fr. MF *partialité*, fr. ML *partialitat-*, *partialitas*, fr. *partialis* + L *-itat-*, *-itas* -ity] **:** the quality or state of being partial: **a :** the inclination to favor one side (as of a conflict or question) **:** BIAS ⟨difficult . . . to view his work without ~ —A.F.Fforde⟩ **b :** a predilection or fondness for one person or one thing rather than others **:** special taste or liking ⟨his ~ for his old comrades —*Atlantic*⟩ ⟨a huge . . . animal whose ~ for comparatively open country renders it an easy prey —James Stevenson-Hamilton⟩ **syn** see PREDILECTION

par·tial·ize \ˈpärshə,līz, ˈpȧsh-\ *vb* -ED/-ING/-S [MF *partialiser*, fr. *partial* + *-iser* -ize] *vt* **:** to make partial **:** give bias to ⟨his hate will ~ his opinion —Owen Feltham⟩ ~ *vi* **:** to concern oneself with or give emphasis to a part rather than the whole of something

partial lunar eclipse *n* **:** an eclipse in which the moon is not completely immersed in the umbra of the earth's shadow

par·tial·ly \ˈpärsh(ə)lē, ˈpȧsh-, -li\ *adv* [ME *parcially*, fr. *parcial* + *-ly*] **1 :** to some extent **:** PARTLY ⟨a determined but only ~ successful attempt —*Amer. Guide Series: Minn.*⟩ ⟨the scarcity of suitable . . . material ~ explains the trend —*Publishers' Weekly*⟩ ⟨a sharp-featured face with a ~ bald head —Norman Mailer⟩ **2 a** *obs* **:** with inclination or predilection toward one side rather than another **b** *archaic* **:** with affection or favor toward someone or something

partial organ *n* **:** a group of stops in a pipe organ controlled from one keyboard

partial out *vt* **:** to give (a variable) a fixed value while considering the relationship between two related variables

partial rhyme *n* **:** HALF RHYME

partial score *n* **:** PART-SCORE

partial solar eclipse *n* **:** an eclipse of the sun in which the moon does not completely hide the solar surface or photosphere so that some direct rays of sunlight reach the observer **:** all the part of a total solar eclipse outside of the path of totality

partial stop *n* **:** a stop in a pipe organ in which the pipes extend only through a portion of the keyboard — compare FOUNDATION STOP

partial term *n* **:** an undistributed term in logic

partial tone *n* **:** PARTIAL 1

partial veil *n* **:** a membrane of the young sporophore of various mushrooms that initially extends from the margin of the cap to the stem, is ruptured by growth, and is represented in the mature sporophore by an annulus about the stem and sometimes by a cortina on the margin of the cap — compare UNIVERSAL VEIL

partial verdict *n* **1 :** a verdict finding the accused guilty of only part of what is charged **2 :** a verdict covering only a part of the issues in dispute

par·ti·bil·i·ty \ˌpär|d·əˈbiləd·ē, ˌpȧ|, |tə-, -lətē, -i\ *n* -ES **:** the quality or state of being partible **:** DIVISIBILITY, SEPARABILITY ⟨ascribing ~ to God —S.T.Coleridge⟩

par·ti·ble \ˈ==bəl\ *adj* [LL *partibilis*, fr. L *partire*, *partiri* to divide + *-bilis* -able — more at PART] **:** capable of being separated or parted **:** admitting of partition **:** DIVISIBLE, SEPARABLE ⟨~ property⟩ ⟨a ~ inheritance⟩

par·ti·cate \ˈpärtə,kāt\ *n* -s [ML *particata*, *perticata*, fr. L *pertica* pole — more at PERCH] **:** an old Scotch unit of land area equal to about ¼ acre

par·ti·ceps cri·mi·nis \ˌpärd·ə,sepsˈkrimənəs\ *n* [ML] **:** one who has a share in a crime **:** ACCOMPLICE

par·tic·i·pa·ble \pə(r)ˈtisəpəbəl, pärˈt-, pȧˈt-\ *adj* [LL *participabilis*, fr. L *participare* + *-bilis* -able] **:** capable of being participated or shared ⟨the essence of God is . . . ~ by things without —John Norris †1711⟩

¹**par·tic·i·pant** \-pənt\ *adj* [L *participant-*, *participans*, pres. part. of *participare*] **:** having a share or part **:** PARTICIPATING

²**participant** \"\ *n* -s **1 :** one that participates **:** one that takes part or shares in something with others ⟨an active ~ in social work —N.K.Burger⟩ ⟨a dance with the ~s in special costumes —*Amer. Guide Series: Nev.*⟩ ⟨these organs were not ~s in the visual response —F.A.Geldard⟩ **2 :** a tone in an ecclesiastical mode lying between the mediant and either the dominant or the final

participant observation *n* **:** a research technique in anthropology and sociology characterized by the effort of an investigator to gain entrance into and social acceptance by a foreign culture or alien group so as better to attain a comprehensive understanding of the internal structure of the society

participant observer *n* **:** one that is engaged in participant observation

par·tic·i·pate \-,pāt, *usu* -ād.+V\ *vb* -ED/-ING/-S [L *participatus*, past part. of *participare*, fr. *particip-*, *particeps* participant, partaking, fr. *parti-* (fr. *part-*, *pars* part) + *-cip-*, *-ceps* (fr. *capere* to take) — more at PART, HEAVE] *vt* **1 :** PARTAKE 1 ⟨I determined . . . to ~ my amorous flame with a genteel girl —James Boswell⟩ ⟨fit to ~ all rational delight —John Milton⟩ **2** *obs* **:** to impart a share of ⟨who often . . . ~s the profit of his sports with my son —Thomas Kyd⟩; *esp* **:** make known (as information) ⟨I have resolved . . . to write and ~ to you this opportunity —John Freind⟩ ~ *vi* **1 :** to possess some of the properties, qualities, or attributes of something **:** possess something of the nature of a person or thing ⟨both members ~ of harmony —Samuel Johnson⟩ ⟨the individual man ~s in the ideal man —Frank Thilly⟩ **2 a :** to take part in something (as an enterprise or activity) usu. in common with others ⟨three cabinet members from each country . . . would ~ in the Copenhagen meeting —L.B.Burbank⟩ ⟨the metal . . . did not ~ directly in the catalytic activity —Henry Tauber⟩ ⟨residents of this district often ~ in barn dances —*Amer. Guide Series: Conn.*⟩ **b :** to have a part or share in something ⟨your mother ~s in this ambition —Edith Wharton⟩ ⟨another term . . . which ~s in the impulse —R.M.Weaver⟩ ⟨convertible stock . . . ~s with the common stock, share by share alike, in additional dividends —*N. Y. Times*⟩ **syn** see SHARE

participating *adj* **1 :** involving participation by more than one person or agency ⟨~ carrier⟩ ⟨~ sponsorship of a radio program⟩ — see PARTICIPATING MORTGAGE **2 :** sharing in distributions: **a :** entitling the holder to a share in any distribution of surplus by the issuing insurance company ⟨~ policies⟩ ⟨~ insurance⟩ **b :** entitled to a share in additional distributions besides its regular fixed income ⟨~ preference shares⟩ — see PARTICIPATING BOND, PARTICIPATING STOCK

participating bond *n* **:** a bond that besides being entitled to interest at a fixed rate is further entitled to share in additional distributions on a specified basis with the common stock of the issuing company

participating mortgage *n* **:** a mortgage or sometimes a group of mortgages in which two or more persons have fractional equitable interests evidenced by certificates issued by the bank or other fiduciary having legal title to the mortgage and selling the fractional shares to investors or making the investment for the certificate holders

participating stock *n* **:** a preferred stock that besides being entitled to dividends at a fixed rate is further entitled to share in additional distributions on a specified basis with the common stock of the issuing company

par·tic·i·pa·tion \pə(r),tisəˈpāshən, (,)pär,t-, (,)pȧ,t-\ *n* -s [ME *participacioun*, fr. LL *participation-*, *participatio*, fr. L *participatus* (past part. of *participare*) + *-ion-*, *-io* -ion] **1 :** the action or state of participating: as **a :** the action or state of partaking of something (as a substance or quality) ⟨the common ~ of any pleasure —James Boswell⟩ — often used with *in* ⟨~ in the divine nature —K.S.Latourette⟩ ⟨the ~ in meanings and goods . . . effected by communication —John Dewey⟩ **b** (1) **:** association with others in a relationship (as a partnership) or an enterprise usu. on a formal basis with specified rights and obligations ⟨a loan made directly or in ~ with a bank⟩ (2) **:** PROFIT SHARING **c** (1) **:** the action or state of taking part with others in an activity ⟨~ in partisan politics —John Lodge⟩ ⟨active ~ in the field of international affairs —*Current Biog.*⟩ ⟨giving his readers a sense of personal ~ in these explorations —Rachel L. Carson⟩ (2) **:** social interaction in a group (as a family, club, community) esp. as carried on through attendance at and contributions to group activities ⟨measure the intensity of social ~ in a rural community⟩ **2 :** the relation in Platonism of objects in the actual world to the transcendental universal forms or ideas constituting the essential nature of the objects, which are held to be only partial and imperfect embodiments of the ideas — compare IMITATION **3 :** SHARE ⟨the theater . . . came in for a full ~ in the benefit —Tyrone Power †1841⟩ ⟨for a few dollars she buys a ~ in the creative act —*Harper's*⟩ **4 a :** something in which shares are taken by more than one party — compare PARTICIPATING MORTGAGE, PARTICIPATION LOAN **b :** something that results in a share (as of a distribution) — compare PARTICIPATING 2

participation loan *n* **:** a large loan made by a bank or insurance company in which shares are taken by other banks or insurance companies

par·tic·i·pa·tive \=ˈ==,pād·iv, -ät|, |ēv *also* |əv\ *adj* **:** participating or capable of participating ⟨social science is by its nature . . . ~ in human affairs —W.H.Sheldon⟩

par·tic·i·pa·tor \-ād·ə(r), -ātə-\ *n* -s [LL *participator*, fr. L *participatus* (past part. of *participare*) + *-or*] **:** PARTICIPANT ⟨scenes in which she had been such an important ~ —J.D. Beresford⟩ ⟨an observer rather than a ~ —W.E.Collin⟩

par·tic·i·pa·to·ry \-,pə,tōrē, -ȯr-, -ri\ *adj* [*participate* + *-ory*] **:** characterized by or involving participation **:** PARTICIPATING; *esp* **:** providing the opportunity for individual participation ⟨~ democracy⟩

¹**par·ti·cip·i·al** \ˌpär|d·əˈsipēəl, ˌpȧ|, |tə-\ *adj* [L *participialis*, fr. *participium* participle + *-alis* -al] **:** having the characteristics and use of a participle **:** formed with or from a participle — **par·ti·cip·i·al·ly** \-ēəlē, -li\ *adv*

²**participial** \"\ *n* -s *archaic* **:** a verbal derivative having the characteristics of a participle

participial adjective *n* **:** a participle (as *rolling* in *a rolling stone* or *written* in *the written word*) having an adjectival function

par·ti·cip·ial·ize \,līz\ *vt* -ED/-ING/-S **:** to make participial

¹**par·ti·ci·ple** \ˈpär|d·ə,sipəl, ˈpȧ|, |tə- *also* -,səp-, *chiefly Brit* -tsəp-\ *n* -s [ME, fr. MF, modif. of L *participium* (trans. of Gk *metochē* participation, sharing, participle), fr. *particip-*, *particeps* participant, partaking] **1 :** a word having the characteristics of both verb and adjective; *esp* **:** the English verbal adjective ending in *-ing* or in *-ed*, *-d*, *-t*, *-en*, or *-n* that has the function of an adjective and at the same time shows such verbal features as tense and voice and capacity to take an object — see PAST PARTICIPLE, PRESENT PARTICIPLE **2** *obs* **:** one that has the characteristics of two or more different classes ⟨certain ~s in nature which are almost ambiguous to which kind they should be referred —Francis Bacon⟩

²**participle** \"\ *adj* **:** PARTICIPIAL

par·ti·cle \ˈpär|d·əkəl, ˈpȧ|, |tə-, -ēk-\ *n* -s [ME, fr. L *particula*, dim. of *part-*, *pars* part — more at PART] **1** *archaic* **a :** a small part, portion, or division of a whole **b :** a small portion (as a clause or article) of a composition or document **2 a :** one of the minute subdivisions of matter (as a molecule, atom, electron, alpha particle) — see ELEMENTARY PARTICLE **b :** an ideal body that has finite mass but infinitesimal size **3 a :** a very small portion of something material **:** minute quantity **:** tiny fragment ⟨her face was . . . beaded with small ~s of rain —Thomas Wolfe⟩ ⟨each ~ of the tape is magnetized to saturation —*Sound Recording & Reproduction*⟩ ⟨~s of sand⟩ **b :** a very small part of something having an immaterial nature **:** the smallest possible portion or amount of something ⟨there is not a ~ of truth in any of these statements —M.F.A.Montagu⟩ ⟨exertion of every ~ of strength she possessed —C.S.Forester⟩ ⟨a voice from which every ~ of emotion was painfully excluded —Thomas Hardy⟩ **4 a :** a unit of speech serving almost as a loose affix, expressing some general aspect of meaning or some connective or limiting relation, and including the articles, most prepositions and conjunctions, and some interjections and adverbs **b :** an element that resembles a word but that is used only in composition **:** a derivational affix ⟨*un-* in *unfair* and *-ward* in *backward* are ~s⟩ **5 a :** a small-sized host distributed to a member of the laity in a communion service of the Roman Catholic Church **b** *Eastern Church* (1) **:** a portion taken from a loaf of oblation to be consecrated as the Lamb in a communion service (2) **:** one of the small pieces taken from prosphorae but not consecrated in memory of particular living or dead persons (3) **:** a small piece broken from the consecrated Lamb given to a member of the laity in a communion service

particle accelerator *n* **:** ACCELERATOR 1g

particle velocity *n* **:** the velocity with which the individual particles of a medium move when traversed by a wave — compare PHASE VELOCITY

¹**parti-color** \ˈpär|d·ē, ˈpȧ|, |t|, |i+,-\ *adj* [¹*parti-* + *color*, n.] **:** variegated in color **:** PARTI-COLORED 1

²**parti-color** \"\ *n* [¹*parti-* + *color*, n.] **:** variegated color **:** MOTLEY ⟨the *parti-colors* of the atlas —*Spectator*⟩

parti-colored \ˈ==,==\ *adj* [obs. E *party*, adj., parti-colored + E *colored*, adj. — more at PARTI-] **1 :** marked by different colors or tints ⟨*parti-colored* iris⟩ ⟨*parti-colored* cows⟩ ⟨*parti-colored* beach balls⟩ **2 :** characterized by variation or diversity **:** CHECKERED 2 ⟨their delights . . . *parti-colored* and spotted with mixture of sorrow —Samuel Ward⟩ **syn** see VARIEGATED

¹**par·tic·u·lar** *R* pə(r)ˈtikyələr, *-R* pəˈtikyələ(r; pärˈt-, pȧˈt-, ÷ -k(ə)l-\ *adj* [ME *particuler*, fr. MF, fr. LL *particularis*, fr. L *particula* small part, particle + *-aris* -ar] **1 :** of, relating to, or being a single definite person or thing as distinguished from some or all others — opposed to *general* ⟨preferred the general to the ~ approach —F.W.D.Deakin⟩ ⟨claims of the United States or any ~ state —*U. S. Constitution*⟩ ⟨how a ~ piece of land can be put to . . . use —*Wall Street Jour.*⟩ **2** *obs* **:** involv-

ing, affecting, or belonging to a part rather than the whole of something : partial in extent : not universal ⟨the three years drought . . . was but ~ and left people alive —Francis Bacon⟩ **3** : of, relating to, or concerned with the separate parts of a whole; *esp* : describing or setting forth the details of something : MINUTE, PRECISE ⟨a ~ account of the day's events⟩ **4 a** *archaic* : of, relating to, or concerning a single person, class, or thing : PERSONAL, PRIVATE ⟨these domestic and ~ broils are not the question —Shak.⟩ **b** *obs* : not occupying public office : PRIVATE **5 a** : distinctive among others of the same kind : out of the ordinary : markedly unusual : worthy of notice ⟨the . . . selection was the ~ gem of the evening —Douglas Watt⟩ ⟨an attack of ~ severity —*N. Y. Times*⟩ ⟨a rather ~ problem because of the immense size of the timbers —*London Calling*⟩ **b** *obs* : noteworthy as being peculiar, singular, or eccentric **6** : constituting a unit among a number : having a separate status : considered alone : INDIVIDUAL, SEPARATE ⟨each ~ hair to stand an end, like quills —Shak.⟩ ⟨provoked by ~ events in his life —T.S.Eliot⟩ **7 a** : having the character of a particular in logic ⟨all concrete individuals are ~ and all universal individuals are abstract —Nelson Goodman⟩ **b** : affirming or denying a predicate to some part of the subject — used of a proposition in logic; opposed to *universal* ⟨"some men are wise" is a ~ affirmative⟩ **8 a** *archaic* : markedly or esp. attentive to a person : familiar in manner or behavior ⟨never suffer this fellow to be ~ with you —Henry Fielding⟩ **b** : close or intimate in personal relationship ⟨my very ~ friend —Charles Dickens⟩ **9 a** : concerned with or attentive to details : CAREFUL, EXACT, PRECISE, SCRUPULOUS ⟨is very ~ about her housekeeping⟩ **b** : nice in taste : FASTIDIOUS **c** : EXACTING : hard to please : FINICKY, FUSSY ⟨these bacilli are not ~ in their habitats —Justina Hill⟩ ⟨never lost patience with even the most ~ customers⟩ **syn** see CIRCUMSTANTIAL, NICE, SINGLE, SPECIAL

²particular \"\ *n* -S **1** *archaic* : a separate part of a whole : a constituent element, section, or division of something ⟨let us divide the discourse into four ~*s* —Robert Johnson⟩ **2 a** : an individual fact, point, circumstance, or detail ⟨their dissimilarity in every ~ except shape and size —Scott Fitzgerald⟩ ⟨determined that history shall not repeat itself in that melancholy ~ —Dean Acheson⟩ **b** : a specific item of information : a factual detail (as of news, specifications, accounts) — usu. used in pl. ⟨everybody was stirred by the news and wanted to know the ~*s* —H.E.Scudder⟩ ⟨genealogical ~*s* and biographical details are given —*Brit. Book News*⟩; see BILL OF PARTICULARS **3 a** (1) : an individual specific separate thing, instance, or case as distinguished from a whole class ⟨a discussion that attempts to generalize from ~*s* —Harvey Breit⟩ ⟨from moral generalities to business ~*s* —G.B.Shaw⟩ (2) : an individual or a specific subclass in logic falling under some general concept or term : something that can be the subject of an atomic proposition **b** : a particular proposition in logic **4 a** *archaic* : an individual or personal case, business, or interest : special concern or condition ⟨return from the common cause to what concerns our ~ —William Warburton⟩ **b** *obs* : personal profit or advantage : private interest ⟨if the gentleman had kept all the allowance for his own ~ —Edward Nicholas⟩ **5 a** : an individual item or article ⟨a few letters and ~*s* in the possession of the present writer —Richard Garnett †1906⟩ **b** *obs* : an individual person; *esp* : one in private as distinguished from public life ⟨it is the greatest interest of ~*s* to advance the good of the community —Roger L'Estrange⟩ **6** : a statement setting forth the details of a matter ⟨a ~ of premises⟩ ⟨I send you the descriptive ~ —Frederick North⟩ **7** : something constituting a special distinguishing characteristic or feature (as of a place) — see LONDON PARTICULAR **syn** see ITEM — **in particular** *adv* **1** *obs* : one by one : in detail : INDIVIDUALLY ⟨now ye are the body of Christ, and members *in particular* —1 Cor 12:27 (AV)⟩ **2** : as one specific case distinguished from a group, general category, or all cases : in distinction from others : SPECIFICALLY ⟨her belief in the theatre in general and her new play *in particular* —Peter Forster⟩ ⟨the recovery of the Greek world, and of Plato *in particular* —M.R.Cohen⟩ ⟨the shops *in particular* allure the young man —S.P.B.Mais⟩

particular average *n* : a partial loss in marine insurance that must be borne by the interest or goods sustaining it without benefit of contribution from other interests — compare GENERAL AVERAGE

particular baptist *n, usu cap P&B* : a member of a British Baptist body of the 17th to 19th centuries holding Calvinistic doctrines — called also *Calvinistic Baptist;* compare GENERAL BAPTIST

particular custom *n* : a custom prevailing in a local area (as a county, city, town) and generally subject to a determination of its legal existence by a jury on proof rather than by the court — compare GENERAL CUSTOM

particular estate *n* : the smaller estate (as an estate for life, in tail, or for years) created from an inheritance as a precedent estate to a remainder

particular integral *n* : PARTICULAR SOLUTION

par·tic·u·lar·ism \-lə,rizəm\ *n* -S [F *particularisme,* fr. LL *particularis* particular + F *-isme* -ism] **1** : exclusive or special devotion to something particular (as an interest, subject, party, sect) ⟨bourgeois individualism . . . in France took the form of a family ~ —Malcolm Cowley⟩ ⟨an intense ~ that did not welcome outside influences —*Amer. Guide Series: Conn.*⟩ ⟨the forces of ~ are dominant and academic recognition is awarded the specialist —W.W.Stewart⟩ **2** : a theological doctrine that redemption through Christ is provided only for the elect **3** : a political theory or practice advocating a right and freedom for each politically conscious or organized group (as a minority group in a country of several groups or a state in a federation) to promote its own interests and esp. independence without regard to the interests of larger groups ⟨there is no nation . . . only ~ in nine small localities —Nathaniel Peffer⟩ ⟨that country will be hampered . . . by the existence of strong regional ~ —*Current History*⟩ — compare NATIONALISM, STATES' RIGHTS **4** : a tendency to explain complex social phenomena in terms of a single causative factor **5** : a logical system based on particulars

¹par·tic·u·lar·ist \-,rəst\ *n* -S [F *particulariste,* fr. LL *particularis* particular + F *-iste* -ist] : an adherent of particularism

²particularist \"\ *adj* **1** : of, relating to, or having the characteristics of particularism ⟨~ . . . tendencies persisted and seriously complicated national political life —Renzo Sereno⟩ **2** : of, relating to, or being a society in which the family unit is individualized

par·tic·u·lar·is·tic \¦=¦=(=)lə¦ristik, -tēk\ *adj* **1** : of, characterized by, or adhering to particularism ⟨too ~ and too conscious of their historical divisions to unite politically —Robert Strausz-Hupé⟩ ⟨the ~ thesis that the isolation of farm life induces mental breakdown —Kimball Young⟩ ⟨the advancement of ~ and no doubt selfish purposes —Alan Barth⟩ ⟨~ . . . economic pressure groups —Walter Adams⟩ **2** : of, relating to, or characterizing a particularist society ⟨the ~ norms of the immigrants' groups —S.N.Eisenstadt⟩ ⟨~ relationships⟩ **3** : based on concrete spatially or temporally bounded particulars (as physical objects or phenomenal events) ⟨a ~ system⟩ **4** : based upon a particular situation or relationship rather than general principles ⟨a ~ response⟩ — opposed to *universalistic*

par·tic·u·lar·i·ty \=,=='larəd·ē, -rətē, -i\ *n* -ES [MF *particularité* minute detail, particular, fr. LL *particularitat-, particularitas* quality or state of being a part, fr. *particularis* particular + L *-tat-, -tas* -ty] **1** : something particular: as **a** : a special circumstance : a minute detail : PARTICULAR ⟨fixing exclusively on the *particularities* of the current situation —Will Herberg⟩ **b** : an individual characteristic : distinctive quality or feature : special attribute : PECULIARITY ⟨regional life with its *particularities* of outlook and idiom —Roger Manvell⟩ ⟨the *particularities* of French rural society —H.W.Ehrmann⟩ **c** *archaic* : an eccentric or odd distinction : a peculiar action or characteristic : SINGULARITY **2** : the quality or state of being particular: as **a** *archaic* : the fact or quality of being noteworthy : SPECIALITY **b** : the quality or fact of being particular as opposed to universal : quality of being or having a relation to one or some rather than all (as of a class or group) : INDIVIDUALITY ⟨the words . . . when written alone have of course no ~ —*Inland Printer*⟩ ⟨concrete human situations in their complexity and ~ —F.R.Leavis⟩ **c** : attentiveness to detail : precise carefulness (as of description, statement, investigation) ⟨the unimpaired ~ of the compilation —*Times Lit. Supp.*⟩ ⟨after the victim of a theft described with ~ the goods he was seeking —Wayne Morse⟩ ⟨the loving ~ of the essays —Douglas Bush⟩ **d** : preciseness in behavior or expression : FASTIDIOUSNESS **e** *archaic* : attentive or familiar behavior : INTIMACY ⟨this ~ with a young fellow is very indecent —Henry Fielding⟩

par·tic·u·lar·i·za·tion \=,=(=)lərə̇'zāshən, -,rī'z-\ *n* -S [F *particularisation,* fr. MF, fr. *particulariser* + *-ation*] **1** : individualized description or treatment **2** : limitation or application to a particular case

par·tic·u·lar·ize \='=(=)lə,rīz\ *vb* -ED/-ING/-S [MF *particulariser* to give the particulars of, specify, fr. LL *particularis* particular + MF *-iser* -ize] *vt* **1** : to make particular rather than general : apply or limit to a particular case ⟨diocesan laws . . . may ~ or extend this general law in accordance with local needs —P.H.Furfey⟩ **2** : to give the particulars of : describe or state in detail : treat individually : name one by one : SPECIFY ⟨the supplemental answer . . . *particularized* the charges —A.C.Buchanan⟩ **3** : to place apart from others of the same class or group : INDIVIDUALIZE, SEPARATE ⟨woodland and similar landed appendages were common property but pasturage might be *particularized* —S.H.Cross⟩ ~ *vi* : to mention or attend to particulars : go into details (as in a narrative) ⟨even advanced American researchers in science and scholarship tend . . . to ~ excessively —Thomas Munro⟩

par·tic·u·lar·ized \-,rīzd\ *adj* : made particular: as **a** : directed toward a specific object rather than some or all objects ⟨critical ~ thinking as distinct from stereotyped slogan-thinking —David Bidney⟩ ⟨insurance companies were the next corporations on which ~ imposts were laid —M.S. Kendrick⟩ **b** : differentiated from others of the same category : INDIVIDUALIZED ⟨among the American Mongoloids, the Eskimo appear to be the most ~ subvariety —A.L.Kroeber⟩ **syn** see CIRCUMSTANTIAL

particular lien *n* : a lien upon specific property as security for the payment of a debt or the satisfaction of some other obligation arising out of a transaction or agreement involving that property — called also *specific lien;* compare COMMON-LAW LIEN, GENERAL LIEN

par·tic·u·lar·ly \-kyələ(r)lē, -kyəlē, ÷-k(ə)lə(r)lē, ÷-k(ə)lē, -li\ *adv* [ME *particulerly,* fr. *particuler* particular + *-ly*] **1** : in a particular manner: as **a** *archaic* : in the case of each one of a number : one by one : SEVERALLY, SINGLY **b** : in detail : in particulars : item by item : part by part ⟨appurtenances . . . more ~ described —*Act 5 George III*⟩ **c** : in the specific case of one person or thing as distinguished from others : in particular : INDIVIDUALLY, PERSONALLY, SPECIFICALLY ⟨the provision of such facilities, ~ in rural areas —D.D.Eisenhower⟩ ⟨trace major population movements . . . for the Pueblo groups ~, for other southwestern groups incidentally —E.K. Reed⟩ **d** : in a special or unusual degree : to an extent greater than in other cases or towards others : ESPECIALLY ⟨a poison ~ toxic to canines —*Monsanto Mag.*⟩ ⟨a ~ stormy . . . winter voyage —C.H.Grandgent⟩ ⟨the final effect, ~ with modern furniture, could . . . have been barnlike —Betty Pepis⟩ **e** *obs* : in a familiar or intimate way ⟨with whom he was very ~ acquainted —Henry Fielding⟩ **2** : in the manner of a particular (as a term, predication, or proposition) in logic

particular partnership *n* : a partnership formed for a single transaction or enterprise as distinguished from one organized for carrying on a general business

particular solution *n* : the solution of a differential equation obtained by assigning particular values to the arbitrary constants in the general solution

particular synod *n, often cap P&S* : a governing body above a classis and below a general synod in various Reformed Churches

particular tenant *n* : a tenant holding a particular estate

¹par·tic·u·late \-kyələt, -,lāt\ *adj* [L *particula* small part, particle — E *-ate* — more at PARTICLE] **1** : existing in the form of minute separate particles ⟨the transport of ~ matter by the atmosphere —Nelson Dingle⟩ ⟨the application of high-energy beams of . . . ~ radiation —*Nature*⟩ **2** : of or relating to distinct particles ⟨the ~ theory of heredity —Julian Huxley⟩ ⟨the radioactivity in fallout is largely in ~ form —Merril Eisenbud⟩

²particulate \"\ *n* -S : a particulate substance ⟨designed to indicate . . . the presence of airborne radioactive ~*s* —*Tracerlog*⟩ ⟨all cytoplasmic ~*s* remain constant in morphology during division —*Biol. Abstracts*⟩

particulate inheritance *n* : inheritance by the progeny of characters specif. transmitted by genes in the germ cells from one parent or the other or from both in accord with Mendel's laws — opposed to *blending inheritance;* compare QUANTITATIVE INHERITANCE

par·ti·cule \'pärd·ə,kyül, 'pȧl, ¦tə-\ *n* -S [MF, fr. L *particula*] : PARTICLE — used esp. of *de* in French personal names

par·tie car·rée \,pär,tēkä'rā, ,pärd·ē-\ *n* [F, party of two men and two women, fr. *partie* party + *carrée,* fem. of *carré* square] : a party of four persons ⟨as we were a *partie carrée,* you might have your rubber —A.Conan Doyle⟩

partied *past of* PARTY

parties *pl of* PARTY, *pres 3d sing of* PARTY

par·tile \'pär,tīl\ *adj* [LL *partilis* divisible, partial, fr. L *partire, partiri* to divide + *-ilis* -ile — more at PART] **1** *obs* : PARTIAL ⟨a ~ not a total eclipse —John Harvey⟩ **2** : exact to the same degree and minute or to the same degree — used of an astrological aspect

par·ti·men \'pärd·ə,men\ *n* -S [Prov, lit., division, fr. *parti* to divide (fr. L *partire, partiri*) + *-men* -ment (fr. L *-mentum*)] : a lyric poem of dispute composed by Provençal troubadours and characterized by a more limited range of debate than a tenson

par·ti·men·to \,pärd·ə'men·,tō\ *n, pl* **partimen·ti** \-,tē\ [It, lit., division, fr. *partire* to divide, go away (fr. L *partire, partiri* to divide) + *-mento* -ment (fr. L *-mentum*)] : a musical exercise in contrapuntal improvisation of the 17th and 18th centuries, generally played or written on a figured bass

parti-mortgage certificate *or* **parti-mortgage receipt** \'pär¦d·ē, 'pȧ¦, ¦t¦, ¦i +, . . .-\ *n* [*parti-mortgage* fr. *²parti-* + *mortgage*] : a certificate of ownership of a fractional equitable interest in a participating mortgage

¹parting *n* -S [ME *partinge, parting,* fr. gerund of *parten* to part] **1** *archaic* : DEPARTURE ⟨nothing troubled me at my ~ from the island —Daniel Defoe⟩ **2 a** : the action of separating or dividing into parts : the state of being parted ⟨could feel the soft ~ of her lips —Hamilton Basso⟩ ⟨many failures which result in ~ of the drill pipe in the well bore —*Primer of Oil Well Drilling*⟩ **b** : separation of the constituents of alloys; *esp* : the separation of gold from silver (as in refining) **3** : a mutual separation of two or more persons : the action of leaving one another : LEAVE-TAKING ⟨good night, good night! ~ is such sweet sorrow —Shak.⟩ **4** : a part or place where separation occurs: as **a** *chiefly Brit* : PART 11 ⟨wavy black hair, neatly brushed into a ~ —Christopher La Farge⟩ **b** : the joint where one section of a foundry mold meets another **5** : something that serves to separate two or more objects: **a** (1) : a thin depositional layer separating thick deposits (as shale in a coal seam) (2) : a geological joint or fissure **b** : the fine sand or other similar material used to prevent adhesions of the members of a foundry mold **6** : a process of making combs out of flat plates with little or no waste by cutting the combs two at a time so that the teeth of one comb are formed of the material in the interstices between the teeth of the other comb **7** : lamellar separation in a crystallized mineral due to a cause other than cleavage (as the presence of twinning lamellae) — **parting of the ways 1** : the place where a road divides into two or more roads leading in different directions **2 a** : a point of separation or divergence (as for persons traveling together) **b** : a point of decision : a place or time at which a choice must be made **c** : a critical point; *esp* : one at which events will shape the course of future developments

²parting *adj* [fr. pres. part. of *²part*] **1** : being in the process of departing ⟨in the direction of the ~ figure —A.C.Benson⟩; *esp* : DYING 1a ⟨the curfew tolls the knell of ~ day —Thomas Gray⟩ ⟨fortify the ~ soul —J.M.Neale⟩ **2** : given, taken, or performed at parting : FAREWELL, FINAL ⟨he remembered his father's ~ advice —F.V.W.Mason⟩ ⟨added as a ~ shot⟩ **3** : serving to part : constituting a space or boundary between objects : DIVIDING, SEPARATING ⟨a ~ layer of pure flint —Charles Lyell⟩ **4** *archaic* : undergoing division : in the process of dividing : breaking up : BREAKING ⟨the ~ ship that instant is no more —William Falconer⟩ **5** : used in foundry work to prevent adhesion of parts of a mold to each other or of sand to molds ⟨~ compound⟩ ⟨~ dust⟩

parting flask *n* : a flask used for parting in assaying

parting line *n* : the line or plane along which sections of a foundry mold, die, or pattern separate

parting pulley *n* : SPLIT PULLEY

parting stop *n* : a piece of wood separating the top and bottom sashes in a double-hung window

parting strip *or* **parting slip** *n* : a thin piece used to separate two adjoining members in a sash window: **a** *or* **parting bead** : a thin strip of wood let into the pulley stile to keep the sashes apart **b** : a thin piece inserted in the window box to separate the weights

parting tool *n* **1** : a narrow-bladed tool used in turning or

parting tool 1

planing or for cutting a piece in two **2** : a tool used (as in lathe work) for cutting off pieces from the main body of stock being worked on

par·ti pris \,pär,tē'prē\ *n, pl* **partis pris** \"\ [F] : a preconceived opinion : BIAS, PARTIALITY, PREJUDICE ⟨we can read without violent *parti pris* about the things of long ago —G.M. Trevelyan⟩ ⟨valuable workers, with no *parti pris* and a truly broad mind —*Times Lit. Supp.*⟩

¹par·ti·san *or* **par·ti·zan** \'pärd·əzən, 'pȧl, ¦tə-, -əsən *sometimes* -,zaa *or* -aa(ə)n, *chiefly Brit* ,pȧti'zan\ *n* -S [MF *partisan,* fr. OIt *partigiano,* fr. *parte* part, party, faction, fr. L *part-, pars* part — more at PART] **1 a** : one that takes the part of another : an adherent to a party, faction, cause, or person ⟨neither by birth nor breeding . . . a ~ of the imperial cause —G.H.Sabine⟩ **b** : a strong or devoted supporter : a zealous advocate ⟨wrote frankly as a ~ of the liberals —W.A.White⟩ **c** : an adherent characterized by prejudiced, unreasoning, blind, or fanatical allegiance ⟨the chaotic, hysterical feelings of the . . . ~*s* of fascism —*Amer. Scholar*⟩ ⟨a doctrinaire and utopian ~ of democracy —R.A.Dahl⟩ **2 a** (1) : a member of a body of detached light troops engaged in making forays and harassing an enemy (2) : a leader or commander of such a body of light troops **b** : a member of a guerrilla band operating within enemy lines and engaged chiefly in demolition, incendiarism, sabotage, and diversionary attacks ⟨the ~*s* acted in . . . advance of regular army formations —C.P.Fitzgerald⟩ ⟨Polish ~*s* had blown up two trains —*Springfield (Mass.) Union*⟩ **3** [AmerF *partisan* leader of an Indian war party or hunting party, fr. F, member of a body of detached light troops, adherent to a party or person] : the leader of a band of No. American trappers

²partisan *or* **partizan** \"\ *adj* **1** : of, carried on by, or being military partisans ⟨captain of a ~ company of light dragoons —*Amer. Guide Series: Del.*⟩ ⟨~ fighters who . . . use every obscure trick of guerrilla warfare —*New Republic*⟩ ⟨~ warfare⟩ **2** : exhibiting, characterized by, or resulting from partisanship ⟨intensified ~ passions caused one noted duel —*Amer. Guide Series: Va.*⟩ ⟨the principle is that ~ politics stops at the water's edge —Arthur Krock⟩ ⟨criticism conceived in a purely fault-finding or ~ spirit —F.D.Roosevelt⟩ **3** : composed of, based upon, or controlled by a single political party or group ⟨change the Tariff Commission from a nonpartisan to a ~ body —*New Republic*⟩ ⟨giving the governor a greater degree of ~ control over the legislature —*Western Political Quarterly*⟩ — compare BIPARTISAN

³partisan *or* **partizan** \"\ *n* -S [MF *partisane,* fr. OIt *partigiana, partesana,* fem. of *partigiano*] : a military weapon of the 16th and 17th centuries having a long shaft and broad bladed head and resembling in part both a spear and a halberd

par·ti·san·ism \-,nizəm\ *n* -S : partisan spirit or conduct

par·ti·san·ry \-nrē, -ri\ *n* -ES : PARTISANSHIP

par·ti·san·ship *also* **par·ti·zan·ship** \'===,ship\ *n* : the quality or state of being a partisan: as **a** : adherence to a single person or thing (as a cause, group, political party) **b** : a strong or sometimes blind and unreasoning adherence to a single cause or group : BIAS, ONE-SIDEDNESS, PREJUDICE ⟨choose between violent ~ and . . . cool detachment —J.F.Muehl⟩ ⟨seen . . . clearly and in due proportion, freed from the mists of prejudice and ~ —John Galsworthy⟩ **c** : conduct or attitudes resulting from or characterizing such adherence

-par·tism \¦pär¦,tizəm, ¦pȧ¦ *also* ¦d·,izəm\ *n comb form* -S [F *-partisme,* fr. *parti* political party (fr. MF, match, party, decision) + *-isme* — more at PARTI] : tendency toward or active operation of a (specified) number of political parties in a governmental system ⟨multi-*partism*⟩

par·ti–striped \'pär¦d·ē, 'pȧ¦, ¦tē, -i+\ *adj* [¹*parti-* + *striped*] : having stripes of different colors

par·ti·ta \pär'tēd·ə, pȧ't-, -ētə\ *n* -S [It, fr. fem. of *partito,* past part. of *partire* to divide, go away, fr. L *partire, partiri* to divide — more at PART] **1** : a set of musical variations **2** : SUITE 2b(1)

par·tite \'pär¦,tīt, 'pȧ¦ *also* ¦d·,īt, *usu* -īd·+V\ *adj* [L *partitus* divided, past part. of *partire, partiri* to divide] **1** : divided into a usu. specified number of parts or divisions ⟨the rule of four-*partite* military government —*New Republic*⟩ ⟨sex-*partite* vaulting —T.F.Bumpus⟩ **2** : PARTED 1c ⟨a ~ leaf⟩

¹par·ti·tion \pär'tishən, pə(r)'t-, pȧ't-\ *n* -S *often attrib* [ME *particioun,* fr. MF *partition,* fr. L *partition-, partitio,* fr. *partitus* (past part. of *partire, partiri* to divide) + *-ion-, -io* -ion] **1 a** : the action of parting or the state of being parted : DISTRIBUTION, DIVISION, SEPARATION ⟨the exact ~ of power among kings, lords, and commons —T.B. Macaulay⟩ ⟨the ~ of the world into the animate and the inanimate —W.R.Inge⟩ ⟨the ~ of available living space among members of the same . . . species —W.H.Dowdeswell⟩ **b** : the severance voluntarily or by legal proceedings of common or undivided interests esp. in real estate : a division into severalty of property held jointly or in common or the sale of such property by a court and the division of the proceeds **c** (1) : the action of dividing an area forming a single governmental unit into two or more areas under separate authorities ⟨called for the ~ of that country into independent Jewish and Arab states —*Current Biog.*⟩ (2) : the condition or territorial and political organization resulting from such division ⟨the present ~ of Germany into eastern and western regions —*List of Books*⟩ ⟨conceived of a permanent ~ of the continent in terms of the natural boundaries —R.W.Van Alstyne⟩ **d** *logic* : analysis of a class into constituent subclasses **2 a** : something that divides or separates : something by which different things or distinct parts of the same thing are separated; *esp* : an interior wall dividing one part of a structure (as a house, room, or enclosure) from another ⟨a huge space subdivided by light, movable ~*s* —*Current Biog.*⟩ ⟨in banquet halls . . . folding ~*s* are very popular —*Sweet's Catalog Service*⟩ **b** : one of a set of paperboard sheets slotted and assembled in a case to form cells for holding and protecting goods or packages in shipment **3** : one of the parts into which a whole is divided (as a portion, section, or division) ⟨the fruit falls to the ground and splits into ~*s* —*Amer. Guide Series: La.*⟩ ⟨the temple was divided into two noble ~*s* —Frances Brooke⟩ **4** : PARTITUR

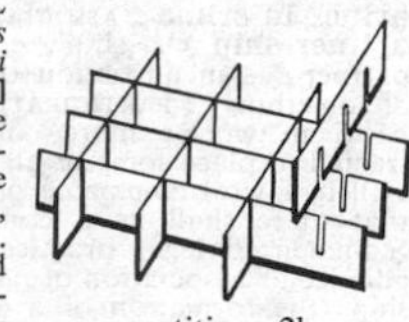

partitions 2b

²partition \"\ *vt* **partitioned; partitioned; partitioning** \-sh(ə)niŋ\ **partitions 1 a** : to divide into parts or shares; *specif* : divide (as an estate) into severalty **b** : to divide (as a country) into two or more territorial units having separate political status ⟨the foreign powers ~*ed* the whole country —Owen & Eleanor Lattimore⟩ ⟨the former German capital was ~*ed* among the . . . allies —*Saturday Rev.*⟩ **2** : to separate or divide into distinct parts by a partition (as a wall) ⟨~*ed* the great hall into many cubicles⟩ — often used with *off* ⟨~ off a closet from the storage area⟩

par·ti·tion·al \-shən°l, -shnəl\ *adj, archaic* **:** of, relating to, or of the nature of a partition

partition chromatography *n* **:** a process for the separation of mixtures in columns or on filter paper based on partition of a solute between two solvents one of which is immobilized by the substance in the column or by the paper

partition coefficient *n* **:** DISTRIBUTION COEFFICIENT

par·ti·tioned \-shənd\ *adj* **:** furnished with or separated by partitions

par·ti·tion·er \-sh(ə)nə(r)\ *n* -s **:** one that partitions ⟨among the enemies and ~*s* of Czechoslovakia —*Times Lit. Supp.*⟩

par·ti·tion·ing \-sh(ə)niŋ, -nēŋ\ *n* -s [¹*partition* + *-ing*] **1 :** work (as in a building) consisting of partitions **2 :** material for partitions

par·ti·tion·ist \-sh(ə)nəst\ *n* -s **:** an advocate of political partition

¹**par·ti·tive** \'pär|d·əd·iv, 'pȧ|, |tətiv\ *adj* [ML *partitivus* serving to indicate that of which a part is specified, fr. L *partitus* (past part. of *partire, partiri* to divide) + *-ivus* -ive] **1 :** serving to part or divide into parts **:** indicating or characterized by partition ⟨~ tendencies in education⟩ ⟨the tragedy of our present ~ social adaptation —W.E.Galt⟩ **2 a** (1) **:** of, relating to, or denoting a part ⟨a ~ construction⟩ (2) **:** serving to indicate that of which a part is specified ⟨~ genitive⟩ **b :** of, relating to, or constituting a grammatical case (as in Finnish) that denotes part of something

²**partitive** \"\ *n* -s **1 :** a word expressing partition or denoting a part **2 a :** the partitive case in a language **b :** a word in the partitive case

par·ti·tive·ly \-əvlē, -li\ *adv* **:** in a partitive way or sense

par·ti·tur \ˌpärd·əˌtu̇(ə)r\ *or* **par·ti·tu·ra** \ˌ==ˈtu̇rə\ *n* -s [*partitur* fr. G, fr. It *partitura*, fr. *partito* (past part. of *partire* to divide, go away, fr. L *partire, partiri* to divide) + *-ura* -ure (fr. L); *partitura* fr. It — more at PART] **:** a full musical score showing each part on a separate line or staff

par·ti·ver·sal \ˌpärd·ē'vərsəl\ *adj* [²*parti-* + *-versal* (as in *quaquaversal*)] *geol* **:** dipping in different directions approximately to the extent of half a circle (as at each end of an anticlinal axis) — contrasted with *quaquaversal*

partizan *var of* PARTISAN

part leading *n* **:** VOICE LEADING

¹**part·let** \'pärtlət, 'pȧt-, *usu* -əd·+V\ *n* -s [alter. of ME (Sc) *patelet*, fr. MF *patelette* band of cloth, dim. of *patte* paw — more at PATTEN] **:** a covering for the neck and shoulders worn chiefly by women in the 16th century and consisting of a separate fill-in for low necklines or of the decorative neckline of an undershirt made usu. of embroidered or plaited gauze or muslin and finished with a small ruff or frill

²**partlet** \"\ *n* -s [*Partlet*, proper name of a hen, fr. ME *Pertelote*, hen that is the favorite wife of Chanticleer (Chaunteclеer) in Chaucer's *Nun's Priest's Tale*] **:** HEN ⟨an ever resounding cackle from his complacent ~*s* —C.G.D.Roberts⟩

part·ly *adv* **:** with respect to a part rather than a whole **:** in some measure or degree **:** PARTIALLY ⟨an interpretation which, while not entirely convincing, is at least ~ true —E.O.Reischauer⟩ ⟨his disease was ~ magical and ~ natural —Robert Burton⟩

part music *n* **1 :** vocal music for several voices in independent parts usu. without accompaniment **2 :** concerted or harmonized music esp. of the vocal type

partn *abbr* partition

¹**part·ner** \'pär|tnər, 'pȧ|tnə(r, *chiefly in substand speech or as a term of address* |dn-\ *n* -s [ME *partener*, alter. (influenced by ¹*part*) of *parcener*, fr. AF, coparcener, partner — more at PARCENER] **1** *archaic* **:** one that shares in the possession or enjoyment of something with another **:** PARTAKER, SHARER ⟨entreated a gentleman . . . to admit me ~ of his bed —Fynes Moryson⟩ **2 a :** one that is associated in any action with another **:** ASSOCIATE, COLLEAGUE ⟨make us ~*s* in the deliberative process —B.N.Cardozo⟩ ⟨a steady military buildup with our ~*s* throughout the world —D.D.Eisenhower⟩ **b** (1) **:** either of a couple who dance together (2) **:** the lady on the right of a man or the man on the left of a lady in a square dance set — compare CORNER 7, CORNER LADY, OPPOSITE LADY, RIGHT-HAND LADY **c :** one of two or more persons who play together in a game against an opposing side **d :** either of two married persons **:** HUSBAND, WIFE **3 a :** one of two or more persons associated as joint principals in carrying on any business with a view to joint profit **:** a member of a partnership — compare GENERAL PARTNER, NOMINAL PARTNER, OSTENSIBLE PARTNER, SECRET PARTNER, SILENT PARTNER, SPECIAL PARTNER **b :** one held to resemble such a partner in having with others joint rights and responsibilities (as in an enterprise) ⟨can men of different races live as ~*s* —Elspeth Huxley⟩ **4 :** one of the heavy timbers forming a framework built around an opening in the deck of a ship to strengthen the deck (as for the support of a mast) — usu. used in pl.

²**partner** \"\ *vb* -ED/-ING/-S *vt* **1 :** to join or associate with another as a partner ⟨British seapower, ~*ed* with the French, beat them off —*Time*⟩ **2 :** to be or act as the partner of ⟨uncle has played alongside nephew and brother has ~*ed* brother —William Morrow⟩ ~ *vi* **:** to be or act as a partner ⟨him and me, we ~*ed* once —A.B.Mayse⟩ ⟨he still ~*ed* with Tom on the piers —R.O.Bowen⟩

partner by estoppel : NOMINAL PARTNER

partner in commendam : a partner in civil law whose liability to creditors of the partnership is restricted to the capital furnished or agreed to be furnished so long as he does not become active and who resembles a limited partner in common law

partner in crime : ASSOCIATE 1

part·ner·ship \'==,ship\ *n* **1 :** the fact or state of being a partner (as in an action or in the possession or enjoyment of something) **:** PARTICIPATION **2 a :** a legal relation existing between two or more competent persons who have contracted to place some or all of their money, effects, labor, and skill in lawful commerce or business with the understanding that there shall be a communion of profit between them ⟨commenced legal practice in ~ with his uncle⟩ **b :** an alliance or association of persons joined together in a partnership ⟨the formation of a ~ is a common-law right —*Jour. of Accountancy*⟩ **c :** the persons joined together in a partnership ⟨the ~ computes its net income . . . in a manner similar to that of an individual —J.K.Lasser⟩ **d :** the contract by which a partnership relation is created **3 :** a relationship resembling a legal partnership and usu. involving close cooperation between parties having specified and joint rights and responsibilities (as in a common enterprise) ⟨an effective working ~ between scientists and military men —Vannevar Bush⟩ ⟨~ in electric power projects between the states and the federal government⟩

partnership life insurance *n* **:** BUSINESS LIFE INSURANCE 1

part of speech [trans. of LL *pars orationis*, trans. of Gk *meros logou*] **1 :** a traditional class of words distinguished according to the kind of idea denoted and the function performed in a sentence **:** MAJOR FORM CLASS — compare ADJECTIVE, ADVERB, CONJUNCTION, INTERJECTION, NOUN, PREPOSITION, PRONOUN, VERB **2 :** a word belonging to a particular part of speech

partook *past of* PARTAKE

part owner *n* **:** one of several owners having no contractual agreement regarding their joint property (as tenants in common or sometimes joint tenants); *specif* **:** a co-owner of a ship

par·trick \'pär·trik\ *Scot var of* PARTRIDGE

¹**par·tridge** \'pär·trij, 'pȧ-, -rēj, *chiefly dial & old-fash* 'pa-\ *n* -s *see sense 1* [ME *partrich, partrik*, modif. of OF *perdris*, modif. of L *perdic-, perdix*, fr. Gk *perdik-, perdix*; perh. akin to Gk *perdesthai* to break wind; fr. the whirring sound of its wings as it takes flight — more at FART] **1** *or pl* **partridge a :** any of various typically medium-sized stout-bodied Old World gallinaceous game birds of *Perdix, Alectoris*, and related genera that have variegated but not gaudily colored plumage, short wings and tail, and rather short legs and neck — see GREEK PARTRIDGE, RED-LEGGED PARTRIDGE **b :** any of numerous gallinaceous birds that are more or less like the Old World partridges in size, habits, or value as game: (1) *chiefly NewEng* **:** RUFFED GROUSE (2) *chiefly South & Midland* **:** BOBWHITE (3) **:** any of several gamebirds belonging to the same subfamily as the bobwhite — usu. used with a qualifying term; see MOUNTAIN PARTRIDGE (4) **:** any of various Asiatic birds (as a bamboo partridge, snow partridge, or hill partridge) **c :** any of several tinamous **d** *Austral* **:** BUTTON QUAIL **2 :** PARTRIDGEWOOD **3 :** RAW UMBER 2

²**partridge** \"\ *adj, usu cap* **:** having a characteristic color pattern resembling that of a partridge — used esp. of poultry ⟨*Partridge* Wyandotte⟩ ⟨Plymouth Rock with *Partridge* plumage⟩

partridgeberry \'==- — *see* BERRY\ *n* **1 :** an American trailing plant (*Mitchella repens*) having roundish evergreen leaves and white fragrant flowers growing in pairs with the ovaries united **2 :** the persistent edible but insipid scarlet fruit of the partridgeberry — called also *checkerberry*

partridgeberry

partridge bronzewing *or* **partridge pigeon** *n* **:** an Australian bronzewing (*Geophaps scripta*) formerly abundant in dry inland parts of western Australia — called also *squatter*

partridge dove *n* **:** a Jamaican quail dove (*Oreopeleia montana*)

partridge pea *n* **:** SENSITIVE PEA

partridge plant *or* **partridge vine** *n* **:** WINTERGREEN 2a

partridge shell *n* **1 :** a large marine gastropod (*Dolium perdix*) **2 :** the varicolored shell of the partridge shell — compare TUN SHELL

partridgewood \'==,=\ *n* **1 a** (1) **:** the hard reddish mottled wood of a tree of the genus *Andira* (esp. *A. americana*) used esp. for walking sticks and cabinetwork — called also *acapu, pheasantwood* (2) **:** a tree yielding such wood **b :** the dark wood of any of several West Indian cabbage palms **c :** GRANADILLA WOOD 4 **d :** the light ornately marked gray wood of an Australian fan palm (*Livistona inermis*) **2 :** wood characteristically speckled as the result of attack by a fungus (*Stereum frustulosum*)

parts *pl of* PART, *pres 3d sing of* PART

part-score \'=ˌ=\ *n* **:** a trick score or contract in bridge that is less than enough for game — called also *partial score*

parts maker *n* **:** a manufacturer producing components for incorporation in assemblies made by another

part-song \'=ˌ=\ *n* **1 :** a 15th century German song for several voice parts **2 :** a homophonic vocal composition usu. in four parts and often unaccompanied; *esp* **:** a choral work of the 19th century

part time *n* **:** an amount of time less than full time ⟨70 percent of the . . . pupils have been on *part time* —*Amer. Guide Series: N.J.*⟩

part-time *adj* [*part time*] **1 :** employed for or working less than the amount of time considered customary or standard ⟨*part-time* worker⟩ ⟨*part-time* student⟩ **2 :** involving or operating less than the amount of time considered customary or standard ⟨continuing their education on a *part-time* basis —L.L.Bethel⟩ ⟨*part-time* schools⟩ ⟨*part-time* jobs⟩

part-timer \'=ˌ==\ *n* **:** one that works or is employed on a part-time basis ⟨the lobstermen sometimes are *part-timers* who hold factory jobs ashore —Thomas Horgan⟩

part title *n* **:** DIVISIONAL TITLE

par·tu·la \'pärchələ\ *n* [NL] **1** *cap* **:** a genus of thin-shelled land and tree snails (suborder Stylommatophora) of the islands of the Pacific that are of great interest to collectors because of their very numerous and highly localized races and species **2** *pl* **partu·lae** \-ə,lē, -,lī\ **:** any snail of the genus *Partula*

parturiency *n* -ES [*parturient* + *-cy*] *obs* **:** the quality or state of being parturient ⟨~ with respect to politics and public counsels —George Berkeley⟩

¹**par·tu·ri·ent** \pär'tu̇rēənt, pȧ|, |·tyu̇-\ *adj* [L *parturient-, parturiens*, pres. part. of *parturire* to be in labor, desiderative of *parere* to give birth to, beget, produce — more at PARE] **1 a :** bringing forth or about to bring forth young **:** engaged in parturition ⟨a ~ heifer⟩ **b :** of or relating to parturition ⟨~ pangs⟩ **c :** typical of parturition ⟨the ~ uterus⟩ **2 :** being at the point of producing something (as an idea, discovery, or literary work)

²**parturient** \"\ *n* -s **:** a parturient individual

parturient paresis *or* **parturient apoplexy** *n* **:** MILK FEVER 2a

par·tu·ri·fa·cient \=ˌ=rəˈfāshənt\ *adj* [L *parturire* to be in labor + E *-facient*] **:** inducing parturition

par·tu·ri·tion \ˌpär|d·əˈrishən, ˌpȧ|, |tə'-, |tü'-, |chə'-, |·tyə'-, |·tyü'-\ *n* -s [LL *parturition-, parturitio*, fr. *parturit-* (fr. L *parturire* to be in labor) + L *-ion-, -io* -ion] **:** the action or process of giving birth to offspring

partway \'=ˌ=\ *adv* **:** to a part of a distance **:** to some extent **:** PARTIALLY, PARTLY ⟨bony shelf . . . extends ~ toward the outer wall —F.A.Geldard⟩ ⟨an even ~ ideal state of human affairs —Charles Merz⟩ ⟨clawing with his feet and getting ~ up —Ernie Pyle⟩

part writing *n* **:** the writing of part music; *specif* **:** the art and science of counterpoint

¹**par·ty** \'pär|d·ē, 'pȧ|, |tē, -i\ *n* -ES [ME *partie* part, portion, party, body of persons forming one side (as in a contest), fr. OF, fr. fem. of *parti*, past part. of *partir* to divide, go away — more at PART] **1** *obs* **:** a part of a whole **:** DIVISION, PORTION, SHARE **2 a :** one (as a person or group) constituting alone or with others one of the two sides in a proceeding ⟨the ~ of the first part and her husband . . . as ~ of the second part entered into a separation agreement —*Southeastern Reporter*⟩ ⟨the two *parties* to a marriage contract⟩ **b** (1) **:** one (as an individual, firm, or corporation) that constitutes the plaintiff or the defendant in a lawsuit **:** LITIGANT (2) **:** one directly disclosed by the record to be so involved in the prosecution or defense of a proceeding as to be bound by the decision or judgment therein (3) **:** one indirectly disclosed by the record as being directly interested in the subject matter of a suit or as having power to make a defense, control the proceedings, or appeal from the judgment **3 a :** a body of persons forming one side (as in a contest) **:** a group united in opinion or action as distinguished from or opposed to a similar or larger group (as the rest of a community or association) **:** a body of partisans or adherents ⟨a war . . . in which both *parties* exerted their utmost strength —William Robertson †1793⟩ **b** (1) **:** a group of persons organized for the purpose of directing the policies of a government esp. by providing the principal political personnel and usu. having as a basis for common action one or more factors (as principle, special interest, or tradition) upon which they have substantial agreement — compare FACTION 1, PRESSURE GROUP (2) **:** an organization constituted a political party under the laws of certain states (as New York) by polling a fixed number or percentage of the total votes cast at an election and thereby possessing the right to appear on the ballot at a succeeding election (3) **:** the political party constituting a principal focus of loyalty or the chief means of operating a governmental system ⟨we may deprecate some of the effects of ~ —Ernest Barker⟩ ⟨compelled . . . to modify his aversion to ~ —Kenneth Mackenzie⟩ **4** *archaic* **:** one of two or more sides (as in a contest, dispute, or contract) **:** CAUSE, INTEREST ⟨many feats of arms were there done on both *parties* —Richard Grafton⟩ **5 :** one (as a person or group) that takes part with others in an action or affair **:** one of several persons engaging or concerned in a transaction **:** PARTICIPANT ⟨should be a ~ in the educational council and participate freely in its deliberation —C.W.Hoff⟩ — usu. used with *to* ⟨Greece and Turkey were brought in as *parties* to the treaty —A.P.Ryan⟩ ⟨the candidate . . . was in no way a ~ to the transaction —S.H. Adams⟩ **6 a :** the individual in question or involved in the case at hand **:** the specific person to whom reference is made ⟨words . . . which generally make the *parties* affected melancholy —Robert Burton⟩ **b :** a particular individual **:** PERSON ⟨he is a shameless and determined old ~ —Winston Churchill⟩ ⟨a rich old ~ who . . . dies and leaves him a fortune —A.H. White⟩ **7** [MF *parti* match, party, decision, fr. *parti*, past part. of *partir* to divide, go away] *obs* **:** a decision on one side or the other **:** RESOLUTION — used chiefly in the phrase *to take a party* ⟨I am not come to ask counsel . . . my ~ is taken —John Vanbrugh⟩ **8 :** a group usu. constituting a detachment from a larger body or company: as **a :** a small number of military personnel dispatched or detailed on special service or duty ⟨infantry . . . repulsed a landing ~ from the British fleet —*Amer. Guide Series: Md.*⟩ ⟨foraging ~⟩ ⟨firing ~⟩ **b :** a group of people working together on a common project or assignment ⟨the men were divided into *parties* of twelve, each ~ to build a hut —H.E.Scudder⟩ ⟨a working ~ on filing systems was . . . appointed —*Library Science Abstracts*⟩ **9** [F *parti* match, party, decision, fr. MF] *archaic* **:** ¹MATCH 4b ⟨try . . . to make him look upon either of your daughters as a desirable ~ for him —Charlotte Smith⟩ **10** [F *partie* social gathering for pleasure, part, portion, party, body of persons forming one side (as in a contest), fr. OF, part, portion, party, body of persons forming one side (as in a contest)] **a :** a social gathering or assembly of persons for entertainment, amusement, or pleasure ⟨asked to cocktail and dinner *parties* —Rose Thurburn⟩ ⟨impulse to gate-crash . . . a private ~ —*Encounter*⟩ ⟨dancing ~⟩ ⟨shooting ~⟩ **b :** something held to resemble (as in appearance or purpose) such a social gathering: as (1) **:** ¹BEE 3 ⟨donation ~⟩ ⟨lynching ~⟩ ⟨scalping ~⟩ (2) **:** a social gathering where the demonstration and sale of articles is the principal feature (3) **:** an occasion on which a specified person is predominant ⟨this is your ~. You're doing the talking —Erle Stanley Gardner⟩ **11** [F *partie* game (as of cards), part, portion, party, body of persons forming one side (as in a contest), fr. OF, part, portion, party, body of persons forming one side (as in a contest)] *archaic* **a :** a game of cards or backgammon **b :** a match in such a game **12 :** PARTISANSHIP ⟨the spirit of ~ which unhappily prevails amongst mankind —Joseph Butler⟩ **13 a :** a group of animals moving or otherwise gathered together ⟨a ~ of over forty hinds with calves . . . passed slowly —Richard Rhodes⟩ ⟨a lively bird seen . . . occasionally in small *parties* —Ernst Mayr⟩ **b :** a company or association of persons ⟨a ~ of visitors from the country —G.B.Shaw⟩; *specif* **:** one formed or gathered together for a particular purpose (as travel, amusement, or attendance at a function) ⟨join a ~ of thirteen American editors to visit Great Britain —Edward Bok⟩ ⟨snowshoeing *parties* . . . visit the snow-clad headland in winter —*Amer. Guide Series: Me.*⟩ **14 :** an act of sexual intercourse

²**party** \"\ *adj* **1 :** being a participating, interested, or otherwise involved party — used with *to* ⟨they refused to be ~ to any arrangement that coerced their employees —Mary K. Hammond⟩ ⟨individuals who are ~ to the relationship —A.J. Vidich⟩ **2 :** characterized by joint ownership or shared use ⟨the ~ fence that divided his backyard from that of his sisters —J.P.Bishop⟩ — see PARTY LINE 2, PARTY WALL **3 a** (1) **:** of, relating to, or associated with a political party ⟨leadership is inherent in ~ organization —C.J.Friedrich⟩ ⟨a conference of rural ~ secretaries —F.C.Barghoorn⟩ ⟨the ~ agent was . . . the sole official tie between the party and municipality —R.H.Wells⟩ (2) **:** in, toward, or favoring a political party ⟨a good ~ paper . . . never published fair news of the opposition —F.L.Mott⟩ ⟨~ membership⟩ ⟨~ loyalty⟩ ⟨~ discipline⟩ **b :** of, between, or based upon political parties ⟨the ~ system has become . . . an integral part of parliamentary democracy —*Brit. Parliament*⟩ ⟨~ alliances⟩ **4 :** suitable for a party or similar social gathering ⟨~ dress⟩ ⟨~ manners⟩ ⟨~ cake⟩ ⟨~ game⟩ **5 :** fond of or addicted to parties and high living ⟨~ boys . . . trying to recapture lost youth —F.J.Taylor⟩

³**party** \"\ *vb* -ED/-ING/-ES *vt* **1** *obs* **:** to side with **:** take the part of ⟨did assist and ~ them in all their enterprises —David Hume †1630?⟩ **2 :** to entertain at or by means of parties ⟨finds himself cocktailed, *partied*, and dined —Ray Josephs⟩ ~ *vi* **:** to attend, take part in, or hold parties and other social gatherings ⟨drinking . . . ~*ing*, or making love —J.W.Aldridge⟩ ⟨this season's . . . social slump on ~*ing* —Alice Dameron⟩

⁴**party** \"\ *adj* [MF *parti* striped, party per pale — more at PARTI-] **1 :** PARTY PER PALE 1 ⟨a silver leopard upon a field ~ gold and gules —W.H. St. John Hope⟩ **2** *heraldry* **:** divided into two or more parts having different tinctures or bearing different coats of arms ⟨arms with ~ fields —W.H. St. John Hope⟩; *esp* **:** divided into parts by a line or lines in the direction and position of one of the ordinaries — followed by a phrase beginning with *per* (as *per bend*) or an adverb in *-wise* or *-ways* (as *bendwise* or *bendways*) indicative of the direction and position of the partition; in modern blazon less usual than a phrase in *per* without preceding adj.

party- — see PARTI-

party-column ballot \ˌ==ˌ==-\ *n* **:** INDIANA BALLOT

party emblem *n* **:** a pictured device (as a gamecock, an eagle, a torch) placed at the head of the party column on a ballot to aid voters in identifying each party

party girl *n* **:** a woman employed to entertain men esp. at parties; *specif* **:** PROSTITUTE ⟨a *party girl* selling a night's pleasure —Luther Robbins⟩

partygoer \'==ˌ==\ *n* **:** one that attends parties and similar social gatherings esp. regularly or frequently ⟨gay clothes . . . for the teen-age ~ —*New Yorker*⟩

party government *n* **:** the direction and control of the processes of government by a single political party usu. by provision of the principal political officials and operation of the formal governmental machinery ⟨in Europe the importance of *party government* has long been recognized —A.N.Holcombe⟩

par·ty·ism *pronunc at* PARTY + ˌizəm\ *n* -s **1 :** devotion to a political party **:** party spirit ⟨the ~ . . . by which the great issue was obscured —Goldwin Smith⟩ **2 :** a party system ⟨cliques and ~ were nonexistent —I.M.Price⟩ — often used in combination ⟨one-*partyism* is on the way out —*Birmingham (Ala.) News*⟩

party jury *n* [obs. E *party*, adj., parti-colored, having a mixed character + E *jury* — more at PARTI-] **:** a jury de medietate linguae

party line *n* **1 :** a line of demarcation held to distinguish a political party in policy or practice or to limit the action of all loyal party members — usu. used in pl. ⟨the house . . . organized quickly along straight *party lines* —W.V.Shannon⟩ ⟨elections . . . not fought on *party lines* —*Scotsman*⟩ ⟨cut across all *party lines* in . . . search for supporters —*Atlantic*⟩ **2** *or* **party wire :** a single telephone circuit connecting two or more subscribers with the exchange **3 :** the bounding line between the properties of two or more parties **4 a :** the complex of policies and attitudes followed or advocated by the Communist party — usu. used with *the* ⟨the *party line* changed from collaboration with the U.S. to antagonism —J.C.Cort⟩ ⟨Communists adhering to the *party line* shifted their stand —J.S.Roucek⟩ **b :** the complex of principles, policies, and attitudes advocated by or associated with an individual, group, or organization ⟨follows closely the official *party line* of organized medicine —H.B.Richardson⟩ ⟨the whole labor *party line* —D.C.Coyle⟩

party-line *adj* [*party line*] **:** characterized by or resulting from adherence to a party line (as of a political party) ⟨*party-line* doctrine⟩ ⟨*party-line* causes⟩

party-liner \ˌ==ˈ==\ *n* **:** one that adheres to a party line; *specif* **:** one that adheres to the Communist party line ⟨a directory of suspected Reds and *party-liners* —*Time*⟩ — compare FELLOW TRAVELER

party man *n* **:** a member or adherent of a political party; *esp* **:** one characterized in cases of conflicting interests by strong loyalty to the party as an institution and to its principles and policies

party per pale *adj* **1** *heraldry* **:** divided into two parts by a line down the middle ⟨three chevrons *party per pale* —A.R. Wagner⟩ **2** *archaic* **:** twofold in character **:** COMPOSITE, HALF-AND-HALF

party politics *n pl but usu sing in constr* **:** politics engaged in by, expressed through the medium of, or considered from the viewpoint of political parties as distinguished from other interests (as geographical sections or economic classes) ⟨a symbol of its unity over and above . . . *party politics* —A.L. Rowse⟩

party question *n* **:** a subject characterized by differences of opinion resulting from party allegiances rather than other factors

party vote *n* **:** a vote (as in a legislature) cast along party lines ⟨strict *party votes* occur . . . on the organization of the House and Senate —Dean Acheson⟩

party wall *n* **:** a wall which divides two adjoining properties usu. having half its thickness on each property and in which each of the owners of the adjoining properties has rights of enjoyment **:** a wall on or near the boundary line between adjoining owners and owned by them in common or in severalty or by one owner alone and providing mutual rights of support for the respective adjacent buildings or structures

par·u·la \'par(y)ələ\ *n, cap* [NL, fr. L *parus* titmouse + *-ula*] **:** the type genus of Parulidae including the parula warblers

parula blue *n* **:** a grayish blue that is redder and paler than electric, greener and paler than copenhagen, and redder and lighter than Gobelin

parula warbler *n* **:** a small grayish blue American warbler (*Parula americana*) of eastern No. America having an olive-green patch on the back

¹paru·lid \'par(y)ələ̇d, pə'rül-\ *adj* [NL *Parulidae*] **:** of or relating to the Parulidae

²parulid *n* -s **:** a bird of the family Parulidae **:** WOOD WARBLER

pa·ru·li·dae \pə'rülə,dē\ *n pl, cap* [NL, fr. *Parula*, type genus + *-idae*] **:** a family of small bright-colored passerine birds containing the American warblers — see WOOD WARBLER

pa·ru·lis \-ləs\ *n, pl* **paruli·des** \-lə,dēz\ [NL *parulid-, parulis*, fr. Gk *paroulid-, paroulis*, fr. *para-* ¹para- + *-oulid-, -oulis* (fr. *oulon* gum); prob. akin to Gk *eilein* to wind, roll — more at VOLUBLE] **:** an abscess in the gum **:** GUMBOIL

par·umbilical \(')par+\ *adj* [ISV ¹*para-* + *umbilical*] **:** near the umbilicus; *specif* **:** being any of several small veins that connect the portal and epigastric veins

pa·rure \pə'rů(ə)r, -ůə\ *n* -s [F, lit., adornment, fr. OF *pareure*, fr. *parer* to adorn, prepare + *-ure* — more at PARE] **:** a matched set of jewelry or other ornaments worn together ⟨a ~ of emeralds including a necklace, bracelets, earrings, and tiara⟩

par·us \'pa(ə)rəs\ *n, cap* [NL, fr. L, titmouse] **:** the type genus of Paridae comprising various common titmice

parv- *or* **parvi-** *also* **parvo-** *comb form* [L *parv-, parvi-*, fr. *parvus;* akin to Gk *pauros* small, slight — more at FEW] **:** small ⟨*parv*animity⟩ ⟨*parvi*folious⟩ ⟨*Parvo*bacteriaceae⟩

par·va \'pärvə, 'pȧvə\ *n* -s [NL, fr. L, fem. of *parvus* small] **:** a late larval stage of shrimps of the tribe Carides

par value *n* **:** ¹PAR 1b

par·va·nim·i·ty \,pärvə'nimədē\ *n* -ES [*parv-* + *-animity* (as in *magnanimity*)] **:** the quality or state of having a little or ignoble mind **:** MEANNESS — opposed to *magnanimity*

parve *var of* PAREVE

¹par·ve·nu \'pärvə,n(y)ü, 'pȧv- *also* ,==ˈ=\ *n* -s [F, fr. *parvenu*, past part. of *parvenir* to arrive, fr. L *pervenire*, fr. *per* through + *venire* to come — more at FARE, COME] **:** one that has risen (as by the acquisition of wealth or power) above the station in life in which he was born; *esp* **:** one that is unaccustomed to his new station or that makes great pretensions because of his acquired wealth **:** UPSTART ⟨loudmouthed ~*s* who took care to obtain great publicity for their charitable works —Leslie Charteris⟩ ⟨the gentry may be the ~*s* of a few generations back —Roy Lewis & Angus Maude⟩

²par·ve·nu *or* **par·ve·nue** \"\ *adj* **:** newly risen to position esp. through the acquisition of wealth or power **:** like or having the characteristics of a parvenu ⟨the threatening power of the ~ middle class —Edmund Wilson⟩ ⟨that vulgar ~ house —Jean Stafford⟩ ⟨there was nothing ~ in the penniless lad —*Harper's*⟩

parvenue \"\ *n* -s [F, fr. *parvenue*, fem. of *parvenu*, past part. of *parvenir* to arrive] **:** a parvenu woman

par·ve·nu·ism \-ü,izəm\ *n* -s **:** parvenu nature or behavior ⟨there is an element of ~ about him —Emily Eden⟩

par·vis *also* **par·vise** \'pärvə̇s\ *n, pl* **parvises** [ME *parvys*, fr. MF *parvis, parevis* parvis, paradise, modif. of LL *paradisus* enclosed park, garden, paradise — more at PARADISE] **1 a :** a court or an enclosed space before a building (as a church or cathedral) often surrounded by a balustrade or parapet or with colonnades or porticos **b :** a single portico or colonnade before a church **:** a church porch **2** *obs* **:** a public and usu. academic conference or debate **3 :** a room over a church porch

par·vi·tude \'pärvə,tüd, -və,tyüd\ *n* -s [*parv-* + *-tude*] **1** *obs* **:** an extremely small or minute thing **:** ATOM **2 :** the quality or state of being little **:** SMALLNESS ⟨differ in magnitude and ~ —Thomas Taylor⟩

parvity *n* -ES [L *parvitat-, parvitas*, fr. *parvus* small + *-itat-, -itas* -ity] *obs* **:** PARVITUDE 2

par·vo·bacteriaceae \¦pärvō+\ [NL, fr. *parv-* + *Bacteriaceae*] *syn of* BRUCELLACEAE

par·vule \'pär(,)vyül\ *n* -s [L *parvulus* very small, fr. *parvus* small] **:** a very small pill

pa·ryph·o·drome \pə'rifə,drōm\ *adj* [*parypho-* (fr. Gk *paryphē* border woven along a robe, fr. *para-* ¹para- + *hyphē* web) + *-drome;* akin to Gk *hyphainein* to weave — more at WEAVE] **:** having a vein that closely follows the margin — used of a form of leaf venation

pas \'pä\ *n, pl* **pas** \'pä(z)\ [F, fr. L *passus* step, pace — more at PACE] **1 :** the right of precedence ⟨when she came in to any full assembly she would not yield the ~ to the best of them —John Arbuthnot⟩ **2 :** a dance step or combination of steps forming a pattern or figure

PAS *abbr* PARA-AMINOSALICYLIC ACID

PA's *or* **PAs** *pl of* PA

pas·a·de·na \¦pasə¦dēnə\ *adj, usu cap* [fr. *Pasadena*, Calif.] **:** of or from the city of Pasadena, Calif. ⟨an annual *Pasadena* event⟩ **:** of the kind or style prevalent in Pasadena

pa·sang *also* **pa·san** \'päzəŋ, -ən\ *n* -s [Per *pāzan* mountain goat, fr. MPer *pāčin*] **1 :** BEZOAR GOAT **2 :** ORYX

pa·sang·gra·han *or* **pas·san·gra·han** \,päsəŋ'grä,hän\ *n* -s [Indonesian *pasanggrahan*, fr. Jav] **:** an Indonesian guesthouse

pa·sa·nia \pə'sānēə\ *or* **pa·sin·ia** \-sin-\ *n* -s [NL *Pasania*, genus of oaks, fr. Sundanese *pasang* oak] **:** the wood of a Formosan oak (*Quercus junghuhnii*) used for joinery and cabinetwork that resembles chestnut but has pronounced medullary rays

pa·sar \pə'sär\ *n* -s [Malay, fr. Per *bāzār* bazaar] **:** an Indonesian public market

pas·cal celery \(')pa¦skal- *also* (')pa¦skäl- *or* 'paskəl-\ *n, often cap P* [perh. fr. the name *Pasqual*] **:** any of several cultivated celeries distinguished by long green firm stalks

pas·cal's law \(')pa¦skalz-, 'paskəlz-\ *n, usu cap P* [after Blaise *Pascal* †1662 Fr. scientist and philosopher] **:** a statement in physics: the component of the pressure in a fluid in equilibrium that is due to forces externally applied is uniform throughout the body of fluid

pascal's triangle *n, usu cap P* [after Blaise *Pascal*] **:** a system of numbers triangularly arranged in rows consisting of the coefficients in the expansion of $(a + b)^n$ for $n = 0, 1, 2, 3,$ etc.

pascal's vases *n pl, usu cap P* [after Blaise *Pascal*] **:** a set of glass containers of various shapes that are used to demonstrate that gravity pressure at a given depth in a liquid is independent of the shape or size of the container

pasch \'pask, 'pȧsk\ *also* **pas·cha** \-kə\ *n* -ES *usu cap* [*pasch* fr. ME *pasch, pasche* Passover, Easter, fr. OF *pasche, pasque*, fr. LL *pascha*, fr. LGk, fr. Gk, Passover, fr. Heb *pesaḥ*, fr. *pāsaḥ* to pass over; *pascha* fr. LL] **1 :** PASSOVER **2 :** EASTER

¹pas·chal \-kəl\ *n* -s *sometimes cap* [ME, fr. MF *pascal*, fr. *pascal* of Easter] **1 :** a paschal candle or candlestick **2 :** the paschal celebration or supper **3 :** PASCHAL LAMB

²paschal \"\ *adj, sometimes cap* [ME, fr. MF *pascal*, fr. LL *paschalis*, fr. *pascha* Passover, Easter + L *-alis* -al] **:** of or relating to Passover or Easter ⟨~ feast⟩

paschal candle *n, sometimes cap P* **:** a large white candle lighted in a church sanctuary on the evening before Easter and kept burning throughout the Easter season

paschal lamb *n, sometimes cap P* [ME] **1 :** a lamb slain and eaten at the Passover **2 :** LAMB OF GOD

paschal letter *n, sometimes cap P* **:** a letter sometimes having the character of a homily and written by patriarchs, archbishops, or bishops of the first six centuries to members of the clergy announcing the date of the next paschal or Easter celebration

paschal moon *n, sometimes cap P* [so called fr. its use in determining the date of Easter] **:** the lunar month whose 14th day falls on or next following March 21 according to ecclesiastical calendar rules employing the golden number and epact of the year

paschal sacrifice *n, sometimes cap P* **:** PASSOVER 2

pa·schen-back effect \¦päshən'bäk-\ *n, usu cap P&B* [after Friedrich *Paschen* †1947 and Ernst *Back* *b*1881 Ger. physicists] **:** a limiting stage of the Zeeman effect which occurs as the magnetic field causing it is greatly increased and in which the extremely fine structure pattern after going through more or less complicated anomalous stages again approaches a normal triplet character

paschen's law *n, usu cap P* [after Friedrich *Paschen*] **:** a statement in electronics: the breakdown voltage between electrodes in a gas is a function of the product of the distance and the pressure so that if the distance is doubled the pressure must be halved

pas·co·ite \'paskō,īt\ *n* -s [Cerro de *Pasco*, mountain in central Peru + E *-ite*] **:** a mineral $Ca_2V_6O_{17}.11H_2O$ consisting of a hydrous calcium vanadate

pas·co·la \pä'skōlə\ *n* -s [MexSp, fr. Yaqui *pahko' ola*, lit., old man of the fiesta] **:** a masked fiesta dancer of the Cahita and Yaqui Indians who provides a ceremonial type of burlesquing and clowning through his ritual dances

pas·cu·al \'paskyüəl\ *adj* [L *pascuum* pasture (fr. *pascere* to feed, pasture) + E *-al* — more at FOOD] **:** of, relating to, or growing in pastures

pas d' ac·tion \¦pädak'syōⁿ\ *n, pl* **pas d' action** [F, lit., action step] **:** a pantomimic dance sequence representing a dramatic scene in a ballet

pas-d'âne \pä'dän\ *n, pl* **pas-d'âne** [F, lit., ass's step] **:** a ring-shaped guard on each side of the blade in rapiers of the 16th and 17th centuries

pas de basque \¦pädə-\ *n, pl* **pas de basque** [F, lit., Basque step] **:** a dance step alternating from side to side in three counts that is characteristic of the Basque national dances

pas de bourrée \¦pädə-\ *n, pl* **pas de bourrée** [F, lit., bourrée step] **:** a sideways ballet step in which one foot crosses behind or in front of the other

pas de chat \¦pädə'sha\ *n, pl* **pas de chat** [F, lit., cat's step] **:** a catlike forward leap in ballet

pas de che·val \-shə'val\ *n, pl* **pas de cheval** [F, lit., horse's step] **:** a ballet step resembling the pawing of a horse

pas de deux \-'də, -'dər, -'dü\ *n, pl* **pas de deux** [F, lit., step for two] **:** a dance or figure for two performers **:** DUET

pas de trois \-'trwä\ *n, pl* **pas de trois** [F, lit., step for three] **:** a dance or figure for three performers **:** TRIO

pa·se \'pä(,)sā\ *n* -s [Sp, lit., pass, feint, fr. *pase* let him pass, 3d sing. pres. subj. of *pasar* to pass, fr. (assumed) VL *passare* — more at PASS] **:** a movement of a cape by a matador in drawing a bull and taking his charge — compare NATURAL, VERONICA

¹pa·se·ar \,päsā'är\ *vi* -ED/-ING/-S [Sp, fr. *paso* step — more at *paso*] *Southwest* **:** to take a walk

²pasear \"\ *n* -s *Southwest* **:** WALK, EXCURSION

pa·seo \pä'sā(,)ō\ *n* -s [Sp, fr. *pasear*] **1 a :** a leisurely stroll **:** PROMENADE ⟨at six in the evening Spanish towns are suddenly reborn: the women are out for the day's ~ —V.S.Pritchett⟩ **b :** EXCURSION ⟨while he was down on a little ~, a rich old don from below the Rio Grande happened to be visiting in the settlement also —J.F.Dobie⟩ **c :** a public walk or boulevard ⟨down its center extends a wide tree-bordered ~ —*Nat'l Geographic*⟩ **2** *or* **paseo de cuadrillas** \-dā-\ **:** a formal entrance march of bullfighters into an arena ⟨formed up for the ~ as soon as the bull had gone through —Ernest Hemingway⟩

¹pash \'pash\ *vb* -ED/-ING/-ES [ME *passhen*, prob. of imit. origin] *vt, dial chiefly Eng* **:** to throw or strike violently **:** SMASH ~ *vi, dial chiefly Eng* **:** to dash or break violently

²pash \"\ *n* -ES **1** *dial chiefly Eng* **:** a crushing or crashing blow **:** a heavy fall **2** *dial Eng* **a :** a heavy fall of rain or snow **b :** a soft or slushy mass

³pash \"\ *n* -ES [origin unknown] *dial Eng* **:** HEAD

⁴pash \"\ *n* -ES [by shortening & alter. fr. *passion*] *slang* **:** a schoolgirl infatuation **:** CRUSH ⟨like a fourteen-year-old with a ~, imitating the gym mistress —Nigel Balchin⟩

pasha \'päshə, 'pȧshə, 'pashə *sometimes* pə'shä\ *also* **ba·shaw** \bə'shȯ, ba'-\ *n* -s *often cap* [Turk *paşa*] **:** a man of high rank or office; *esp* **:** a military commander or provincial governor in Turkey and No. Africa ⟨Mustapha Kemal *Pasha*⟩ ⟨Mohammed El Mokri, *Pasha* of Casablanca⟩ — a title illegal in Turkey since 1934 and abolished in Egypt in 1952

pa·sha·dom \'päshədəm\ *n* -s **:** the rank, estate, or domain of pashas

¹pa·sha·lic *also* **pa·cha·lic** *or* **pa·sha·lik** \pə'shälik\ *n* -s [Turk *paşalık* title or rank of pasha, fr. *paşa*] **:** the jurisdiction of a pasha or the territory governed by him

²pashalic \"\ *adj* [¹*pashalic*] **:** of or relating to a pasha

pash·kov·ist \'päsh,kȯfə̇st\ *n* -s *usu cap* [V.A.*Pashkov* †1902 Russ. religious leader + E *-ist*] **:** a member of a Russian evangelical religious group founded in the 19th century

pashm \'pashəm\ *also* **pash·im** \-,shēm\ *or* **pash·mi·na** \,pəsh'mēnə\ *n* -s [*pashm, pashim* fr. Per *pashm* wool; *pashmina* fr. Per *pashmīn* woolen, fr. *pashm*] **:** the under fleece of upland goats of Kashmir and the Punjab that was formerly used locally for the production of rugs and shawls but is now largely exported

pash·to \'pəsh(,)tō\ *or* **pash·tu** \-tü\ *also* **push·tu** *or* **push·to** \'pəsh-\ *n* -s *cap* [Per *pashtu*, fr. Afghan] **:** the Iranian language of Pathan people and the chief vernacular of eastern Afghanistan, North-West Frontier Province of Pakistan, and northern Baluchistan

pash·toon *or* **pash·tun** \,pəsh'tün\ *n, pl* **pashtoon** *or* **pashtoons** *or* **pashtun** *or* **pashtuns** *usu cap* **1 :** a Moslem people of Afghanistan and the frontier region between Afghanistan and Pakistan **2 :** a member of the Pashtoon people

pas·i·graph·ic \¦pasə¦grafik\ *or* **pas·i·graph·i·cal** \-fə̇kəl\ *adj* **:** of or relating to pasigraphy

pa·sig·ra·phy \pə'sigrəfē\ *n* -ES [Gk *pasi* for all (dat. pl. of *pant-, pas* all) + *-graphy* — more at PAN-] **:** any of various proposed international written languages using signs (as mathematical symbols) to represent ideas rather than words; *broadly* **:** an artificial international written language

pa·si·llo \pə'sē(,)(y)ō\ *n* -s [AmerSp, dim. of Sp *paso* step — more at *paso*] **:** a Latin-American dance for two in triple time

pas·i·mol·o·gy \,pasə'mälәjē\ *n* -ES [prob. fr. Gk *pasi* for all + *sēma* sign + E *-o-* + *-logy* — more at PASIGRAPHY, SEMANTICS] **:** the study of gestures as a means of communication

pa·sin \'pä,sēn\ *n* -s [Thai] **:** a loose straight skirt worn folded snugly about the body (as in Thailand) ⟨dressed like their mothers in ~*s* and white sleeveless blouses —Kathryn Grondahl⟩

pasinia *var of* PASANIA

pas·mo \'paz(,)mō\ *n* -s [AmerSp, fr. Sp, temporary paralysis, lockjaw, fr. L *spasmus* cramp, spasm — more at SPASM] **:** a widespread disease of flax that damages the fibers and reduces the yield of flaxseed and is caused by a fungus (*Mycosphaerella linorum*) which attacks stems, bolls, and leaves and forms characteristic circular brownish lesions on the cotyledons and lower leaves

pa·so \'pä(,)sō\ *n* -s [Sp, lit., step, incident, fr. L *passus* step, pace — more at PACE] **:** ENTREMÉS

paso do·ble \-'dō(,)blā\ *n* [Sp, lit., double step] **:** a Latin-American march step typically associated with bullfighting

pas·pa·lum \'paspələm\ *n, cap* [NL, fr. Gk *paspalos* millet; prob. akin to Gk *palē* fine meal, dust — more at *pollen*] **1 :** a genus of mostly perennial grasses chiefly of warm regions having flat leaves and spikelets in several rows on secund spikes — see DITCH MILLET, JOINT GRASS **2** -s **:** any grass of the genus *Paspalum*

paspy *var of* PASSEPIED

pasque·flow·er \'pask,flaů(ə)r\ *n* [alter. (influenced by MF *pasque* Easter, fr. OF) of earlier *passeflower*, fr. MF *passefleur*, fr. *passer* to pass (fr. OF) + *fleur* flower, fr. L *flor-, flos* — more at PASCH, PASS, BLOW] **1 :** any of several low perennial herbs with palmately compound leaves and large usu. white or purple flowers borne in early spring that form a section of the genus *Anemone* — see AMERICAN PASQUEFLOWER, EUROPEAN PASQUEFLOWER, PULSATILLA **2 :** the blossom of a pasqueflower

pas·quil \'paskwəl\ *n* -s [NL *pasquillus*, fr. It *pasquillo*, fr. *Pasquino*] **:** PASQUINADE

pas·quin \'paskwə̇n\ *n* -s [MF, fr. It *Pasquino*, name given to a statue in Rome on which anonymous lampoons were posted] **:** PASQUINADE ⟨~*s* and pamphlets rained against him —M.A.S.Hume⟩

¹pas·quin·ade \,paskwə'nād\ *n* -s [MF, fr. It *pasquinata*, fr. *Pasquino* + *-ata* -ade] **1 :** an anonymous lampoon posted in a public place **2 :** a lampoon or satire usu. having a political significance ⟨a writer of farce, burlesque and incisive ~ of political criticism —Bonamy Dobrée⟩

²pasquinade \"\ *vt* -ED/-ING/-S **:** LAMPOON, SATIRIZE ⟨been notoriously *pasquinaded* for his pains —E.A.Poe⟩

¹pass \'pas, 'paa(ə)s, 'pais, 'pȧs\ *vb* -ED/-ING/-ES [ME *passen*, fr. OF *passer*, fr. (assumed) VL *passare*, fr. L *passus* step — more at PACE] *vi* **1 a :** to move on **:** PROCEED ⟨from group to group the girls ~, laughing, prattling —Lafcadio Hearn⟩ **b :** to proceed to a specified place or destination ⟨the excess nitrogen ~*es* rapidly into the capillaries —H.G.Armstrong⟩ ⟨could ~ again into his neutral, godlike independence —R.W. Emerson⟩ ⟨all that lives must die, ~*ing* through nature, to eternity —Shak.⟩ **c :** to proceed along a specified route **:** take a particular course ⟨the blood ~*es* through the lungs —H.G.Armstrong⟩ ⟨~*es* between the rolling slopes —*Amer. Guide Series: Ark.*⟩ ⟨~*ed* freely along the great caravan routes —H.J.J.Winter⟩ **d :** to go on with a narrative or discussion ⟨we ~ down the centuries to Anselm —H.O.Taylor⟩ ⟨before I ~ to other matters —J.M.Wordie⟩ **2 a :** to go away from a place, object, or person **:** DEPART, LEAVE ⟨the fright ~*es* almost immediately —Fred Majdalany⟩ **b :** to depart from life **:** DIE ⟨every morning I pray God to let me ~ —Virginia Woolf⟩ ⟨when she ~*ed* there were editorials about her —*N.Y. Herald Tribune Bk. Rev.*⟩ — often used with *on* **3 a :** to go by or move past ⟨the wind ~*ed* again blowing up dust and rain —Greville Texidor⟩ ⟨the mail ~*ed* twice a week —John Burroughs⟩ ⟨the remark ~*ed* unnoticed —T.B.Costain⟩ **b :** to glide by **:** ELAPSE ⟨could not let this moment ~ without a few words of explanation —Gwyn Thomas⟩ ⟨poetical works conceived in the spirit of the ~*ing* time —Matthew Arnold⟩ **c :** to come to an end or finish **:** TERMINATE ⟨the strangeness of his life ~*ed*, and he began to feel that this city was —Pearl Buck⟩ ⟨aid . . . could not be given before the crisis had ~*ed* —C.L.Jones⟩ **d :** to move past another vehicle going in the same direction **:** OVERTAKE ⟨do not ~ on the right⟩ ⟨no ~*ing* permitted⟩ **4 a :** to go or make way through **:** secure a passage through ⟨guarded the door and permitted no one to ~⟩ ⟨better than ordinary glass, since they allowed the sun's actinic rays to ~ —*Amer. Guide Series: Mich.*⟩ **b :** to go uncensured or unchallenged **:** take place or come to view without hindrance or opposition ⟨if malice and vanity wear the coat of philanthropy, shall that ~ —R.W.Emerson⟩ ⟨such behavior cannot ~ in a schoolroom⟩ **c :** to go through a duct or the intestines **5 a :** to move or be transferred from one place to another ⟨from the college he ~*ed* to the novitiate of the order —*Amer. Guide Series: Md.*⟩ ⟨was first a stock clerk, ~*ed* from that to other service departments —*Current Biog.*⟩ **b :** to go from one quality, state, condition, or form to another ⟨a good player on a modern pianoforte can ~ at will . . . from an almost inaudible softness to a thundering loudness —R.V.Williams⟩ ⟨~ from relaxation and refreshment back to the routine of life's clamant duties —W.F.Hambly⟩ ⟨~*es* from a liquid to a gaseous state⟩ **c :** to go from one stage of development to another ⟨~ . . . imperceptibly from youth to age —D.H.Barber⟩ ⟨~*ed* . . . from a primitive, prehistoric stage . . . to the more advanced civilized state —David Bidney⟩ **d :** to go from one activity to another ⟨~*ed* from the study of physiology to the study of psychology —A.N.Whitehead⟩ **6** [AF *passer*, lit., to proceed, fr. OF] **a** *of a jury* (1) **:** to sit in inquest — used with *on* or *upon* (2) **:** to sit in adjudication — usu. used with *between* **b :** to become rendered, given, or done in legal procedure ⟨judgment ~*ed* for the defendant⟩ **c** (1) **:** to render a verdict or judgment **:** pass sentence **:** ADJUDICATE — usu. used with *on* or *upon* ⟨the court did not ~ on the constitutional question⟩ ⟨the jury found it difficult to ~ upon the case because of the conflicting testimony⟩ (2) **:** to give judgment **:** render an opinion or express a point of view — used with *on* or *upon* ⟨our concern here is not to ~ upon the merits of a particular controversy —R.M. Weaver⟩ **d** *of a juryman* **:** SERVE, SIT — used with *on* or *upon* **7 a :** to undergo conveyance or transfer (as by will, deed, or other instrument of conveyance) so as to become vested in another ⟨sold the house . . . the title ~*ed* this afternoon —J.C. Lincoln⟩ **b :** to go from the control or possession of one person, group, or country to that of another ⟨the throne ~*ed* to Darius the Great —W.K.Ferguson⟩ ⟨the institution ~*ed* from parish to state control —*Amer. Guide Series: La.*⟩ **8 a :** to take place **:** HAPPEN, OCCUR ⟨commenting freely on the transactions as they ~ —W.L.Sperry⟩ **b :** to take place as a mutual exchange or transaction (as speech, letters, or lovemaking) ⟨what hath ~*ed* between me and Ford's wife —Shak.⟩ ⟨words ~*ed* and then blows⟩ **c :** to come and go in consciousness **:** exist as ideas or sensations ⟨no one could tell what was ~*ing* within his mind⟩ ⟨visions of the future ~*ed* through his mind⟩ **9 a :** to secure the allowance or approval of a legislature or other body that has power to sanction or reject a bill or proposal ⟨the tax bill ~*ed* by a slim majority⟩ ⟨the proposal to change the date of the dance ~*ed* by unanimous vote of the class council⟩ **b :** to attain the required grade or level of achievement in an examination or course of study ⟨took the scholarship examination and ~*ed*⟩ ⟨did badly in the course and barely ~*ed*⟩ **c :** to go through an inspection or test successfully **:** achieve acceptance ⟨in a day when much that is careless and slipshod ~*es* in the name of realism —Sara H. Hay⟩ ⟨boatmen's skirts with blue stripes and a crew neck ~ nicely too —Horace Sutton⟩ **10 a :** to go from one person to another **:** be current **:** CIRCULATE ⟨bank notes ~ so long as nobody refuses them —William James⟩ **b :** to become falsely held, regarded, or identified — usu. used with *as* or *for* ⟨~ in society not for the person you are, but as a labeled dummy —Stuart Chase⟩ ⟨the doggerel verse that ~*ed* as poetry —*Amer. Guide Series: Minn.*⟩ ⟨~*ed* for being a very devoted couple —Mary Deasy⟩ **c :** to serve as a substitute — usu. used with *for* ⟨dreary lines of shell-like hovels that ~ for dwellings —*Amer. Guide Series: Va.*⟩ ⟨that awful jargon that ~*es* for English —John Hilton⟩ **d :** to identify oneself or accept identification as a white person though having some Negro ancestry ⟨the heroine who has been ~*ing* in the North, comes home to the South . . . to live among and learn to love her people —*Commentary*⟩ **11 a** *obs* **:** to make a pass in fencing ⟨you but dally, I pray you ~ with your best violence —Shak.⟩ **b :** to execute a pass (as in football, basketball, or hockey) ⟨the situation called for a kick but he decided to ~⟩ **12 a** (1) **:** to decline to bid, double, or redouble in a card game (as in bridge) (2) **:** to withdraw from the current poker pot **:** throw up one's hand (as in poker) (3) **:** to transfer a card to another player **b :** to make a winning cast or roll with dice ~ *vt* **1 a :** to go beyond in some degree, measure, or quality **:** SURPASS ⟨the reviews of a few dramatic critics ~ all others in the influence they have⟩ ⟨used to be the largest city in the state, but has now been ~*ed* by several others⟩ **b :** to advance or develop beyond ⟨had ~*ed* the barbaric stage when they invaded Chaldea —Edward Clodd⟩ **c :** to go beyond (a mark or limit) ⟨his drive to provide planetariums for the millions ~*ed* several important milestones —S.M.Spencer⟩ ⟨those who ~ 90 begin to think about reaching 100 —Morris Fishbein⟩ ⟨this information will never ~ my lips⟩ **d :** to go past **:** leave behind in running or racing **:** OUTSTRIP ⟨~*ed* the other runners in the homestretch⟩ **e :** to go beyond or transcend the range or limitations of **:** EXCEED ⟨so new to our experience that it ~*es* comprehension —*Saturday Rev.*⟩ **2 a :** to go by **:** proceed or extend beyond ⟨~*es* the school on his way to work⟩ ⟨an avenue that ~*es* several large churches —*Amer. Guide Series: Ark.*⟩ **b** (1) *obs* **:** NEGLECT, OMIT ⟨could not ~ admiring the great church —John Evelyn⟩ (2) **:** to omit a regularly scheduled declaration and payment of (a dividend) **c :** to leave out in an account or narration ⟨~ the trivial details and get to the heart of the story⟩ **3 a :** to go from one side to the other of **:** proceed across, over, or through **:** CROSS, TRAVERSE ⟨~ the straits and conquer the mountains —Walt Whitman⟩ ⟨nevermore did either ~ the gate —Alfred Tennyson⟩ **b :** to go or live through **:** have experience of **:** ENDURE, SUFFER, UNDERGO ⟨she loved me for the dangers I had ~*ed* —Shak.⟩ **c :** to cause or permit to elapse : abide the passage of : SPEND ⟨you may ~ half an hour pleasantly, even profitably, over an article of his —R.L. Stevenson⟩ ⟨~*ed* the summer at the beach⟩ ⟨~ his life in study⟩ **4 a :** to secure the approval or sanction of : gain the acceptance of ⟨the bill ~*ed* the senate⟩ **b :** to go through successfully or satisfactorily : attain the required standard in : satisfy the requirements of ⟨~*ed* the bar examination⟩ ⟨had ~*ed* a security check —*Time*⟩ **5 a** *obs* : to carry through to completion : EXECUTE, FINISH ⟨where he might hear his father ~ the deed —Ben Jonson⟩ **b** (1) : to cause or permit to proceed : cause or permit to win approval or legal or official sanction : CONFIRM, ENDORSE ⟨the legislature ~*ed* the bill⟩ ⟨the committee ~*ed* the nomination⟩ (2) : to approve as valid, correct, or proper : AUTHORIZE ⟨gave his work perfunctory attention and ~*ed* it without effort or interest —E.T.Bell⟩ ⟨always ~*ed* the final page proofs of the paper personally —*Times Lit. Supp.*⟩ **c :** to let go unnoticed : pass over : OVERLOOK ⟨his commander quietly ~*ed* his likes or dislikes —George Meredith⟩ **d :** to cause or allow to pass an examination or course of study ⟨the examiner ~*ed* him on his written test but failed him on his road test⟩ ⟨the professor ~*ed* most of his students⟩ **6 a :** PLEDGE ⟨had ~*ed* his word that he would repay the debt⟩ **b :** to transfer the right or property in : make over ⟨~ the title to an estate⟩ **7 a :** to place in circulation : give currency to ⟨~*ed* a counterfeit ten-dollar bill⟩ ⟨caught ~*ing* bad checks⟩ ⟨~*es* malicious gossip about her neighbors⟩ **b :** to transfer from one person to another : cause to go from hand to hand ⟨~ the jug⟩ ⟨please ~ the salt⟩ ⟨the problem of ~*ing* prosperity around —Elmer Davis⟩ ⟨signed the attendance sheet and ~*ed* it on⟩ **c :** to cause or make possible to go or proceed : transfer from one place to another : CONVEY, TRANSPORT ⟨waited till the soldiers and wounded were all ~*ed* over —Walt Whitman⟩ **d :** to cause to move in a particular manner or direction or over a specified place or area ⟨~*ed* his hand over his face⟩ ⟨~*ed* the cloth over the top of the desk⟩ **e** (1) : to take a turn with (a line) and make secure ⟨~ a line around a sail in furling⟩ (2) : to take a turn with (a rope or string) around something ⟨~*ed* a rope around the tree⟩ **f :** to transfer to another player on the same team ⟨~*ed* the ball to the left end⟩ ⟨~*ed* the puck to his teammate⟩ **g :** THROW ⟨they'd ~ a ball back and forth or play jackstones —Dorothy C. Fisher⟩ **8 a :** to pronounce judicially ⟨~*ed* sentence on the convicted man⟩ **b :** to give voice to : PRONOUNCE, UTTER ⟨~*ing* a word now and again with the man on the other side of the marble-topped table —Nevil Shute⟩ ⟨~*es* some practical remarks on the present standard locomotive designs —*Brit. Book News*⟩ **9 a :** to cause or permit to go past or through a barrier : cause or allow to gain entrance **b :** to cause to march or go by in order ⟨the general ~*ed* his troops in review⟩ ⟨~*es* rapidly in review the various forms of association between human beings —*Times Lit. Supp.*⟩ **10 :** to emit or discharge from the bowels or other part of the body : EVACUATE, VOID **11 a :** to permit (a batter in baseball) to reach first base by giving a base on balls **b :** to send a ball in a racket game to the side and out of reach of (an opponent) **12 a :** to decline to bid or bet on (one's hand) in a card game **b :** to transfer (a playing card) to another player **13 :** to take (a bull's charge) with a movement of a cape — **pass current :** to circulate freely : be accepted as genuine or valid ⟨now *pass current* as what was always known —F.R.Leavis⟩ — **pass in one's checks :** DIE — **pass muster 1 :** to pass an inspection or examination : be found satisfactory or valid ⟨these excuses will not *pass muster*⟩ **2 :** to pass a routine or casual inspection ⟨the variety of styles and tendencies that all *pass muster* under the name of modern music —Aaron Copland⟩ — **pass the buck :** to shift a responsibility to someone else ⟨inclined to *pass the buck* to some other futile body —Sir Winston Churchill⟩ — **pass the chair :** to complete a term as incumbent of a high office (as in a fraternal organization) — **pass the hat :** to take up a collection of money ⟨*passed the hat* to raise funds for the new youth center⟩ — **pass the time of day :** to exchange greetings or hold a friendly conversation

²pass \"\ *n* -ES [ME *pass, pas,* fr. OF *pas,* fr. L *passus* step — more at PACE] **1 :** an opening, road, channel, or other way that is the only means by which a barrier may be passed or access gained to a particular place: as **a** (1) *archaic* : ROAD, ROUTE (2) : a narrow place in a road or street **b** (1) : a break in a mountain range : an opening between two peaks usu. approached by a steep valley ⟨has the lowest altitude of the three main ~*es* across the Cascades —*Amer. Guide Series: Wash.*⟩ — compare COL, DEFILE, GAP, NOTCH (2) : a narrow road between a mountain and a sea ⟨the *Pass* of Thermopylae⟩ **c** (1) : a place or policy that controls the defense of a country ⟨believe that the government sold the ~ when it abandoned its ally⟩ (2) : a position that must be maintained usu. against odds ⟨our few repertory companies have held the ~ —*Report: (Canadian) Royal Commission on Nat'l Development*⟩ **d** (1) : a navigable channel in a delta ⟨attempts were made to increase the depth of the ~*es* by dredging with buckets —*Amer. Guide Series: La.*⟩ (2) : a narrow opening between two islands or through an obstruction (as a reef) : STRAIT ⟨when the engine that propelled us through the ~ had ceased its clatter, we lay, sails set, rocking in the swell —Ida Treat⟩ (3) : a stretch of open water in a marsh **e** (1) : a crossing over a river (2) : a passage for fish over a dam **2 :** a chute from one level of a mine to another **3 :** an aperture formed between two grooved rolls in a rolling mill through which a bar of metal is passed to be shaped **4 :** DUCK PASS **syn** see WAY

³pass \"\ *n* -ES [partly fr. ME *passe,* fr. MF, fr. *passer* to pass; partly fr. ¹*pass* — more at ¹PASS] **1 a :** the act or an instance of passing : PASSAGE ⟨charming the narrow seas to give you gentle ~ —Shak.⟩ **b** *archaic* : DEATH **2 :** ACCOMPLISHMENT, REALIZATION ⟨the boy's dream comes to ~ —R.W.Emerson⟩ ⟨plot and plan and bring to ~ —Robert Browning⟩ **3 :** a usu. difficult, dangerous, or unfortunate condition or state of affairs ⟨things had come to a pretty ~ when nobody would work for him any more⟩ ⟨a strange ~⟩ ⟨a terrible ~⟩ **4 a :** a written permission to move about freely in a particular area or place or to leave or enter its boundaries or limits ⟨under its provisions vagrancy was no more an offence, and . . . folk were free to move without ~*es* —C.W. de Kiewiet⟩ ⟨obtained a ~ to any port of the Low Countries —Margaret Toynbee⟩ **b :** a written leave of absence from a military post or station for a brief period ⟨if only all of life could be a three-day ~ —James Jones⟩ **c :** a written permission to enter an area or place closed to the general public (as an army post or defense establishment) **d :** a permit, ticket, or order allowing one free transportation (as on a railroad) or free admission (as to a theater) ⟨has a season ~ to the ball park⟩ — called also *free pass* **5 :** a thrust or lunge in fencing **6 a :** a transference of objects by sleight of hand or other deceptive means ⟨one of the most difficult ~*es* for the amateur magician to make⟩ **b :** a gesture or movement of the hands of a juggler or magician ⟨would make ~*es* before the picture, finally making the gesture of picking a grape off the canvas —Victoria Sackville-West⟩ **c :** a shifting of the position of the cards in card tricks ⟨it takes practice to learn to make the ~⟩ **d :** a moving of the hands over or along something : MANIPULATION ⟨a recalcitrant mechanism responded almost instantly to two or three ~*es* of his hands —Ben Riker⟩ **7** *archaic* : a witty or ingenious sally or stroke ⟨a curious ~ of wit —William Hazlitt⟩ **8 :** the passing of an examination or course of study; *also* : the mark or certification of such passing ⟨the examiners may award a ~ with distinction to any candidates who have attained a sufficiently high standard in all subjects —*Durham Univ. Cal.*⟩ ⟨a ~ mark⟩ ⟨a ~ grade⟩ **9 :** a single complete mechanical operation: as **a :** a single passage of a bar, rail, or sheet between the rolls of a rolling mill **b :** a single or multiple passage of the gases from the furnace across the tubes of a steam boiler **c :** a single progression along a joint in welding **d** (1) : a single passage of one or more cards through a punched-card machine (2) : a single sorting or arranging operation with hand-notched punched cards **10 a :** a transfer of a ball (as in football or basketball) or a puck (as in hockey) from one player to another player on the same team ⟨threw a long ~ into the corner⟩ ⟨threw a ~ the length of the court⟩ **b :** PASS STROKE **c :** a passing stroke in tennis **11 :** BASE ON BALLS **12 a :** a refusal to bid, bet, or draw an additional card in a card game **b :** an election not to bid, double, or redouble in bridge **c :** a transfer of a playing card to another player **13 :** a cast or combination of dice that wins the main bet **14 :** a single passage or movement of an airplane or other artificial flying object over a given area or place or in the direction of a given target ⟨made several low ~*es* over the field so the ground crew could inspect the wheel by searchlight —*Time*⟩ ⟨made seven ~*es* at that gun, each time dropping one bomb —Ira Wolfert⟩ ⟨the satellite will make its first ~ over the eastern half of the country at 4 a.m.⟩ **15 a :** EFFORT, TRY ⟨guessed wrong on the crime the first time they made a ~ at it —Erle Stanley Gardner⟩ ⟨told me in French, after a few unsuccessful ~*es* in other languages —A.J.Liebling⟩ **b :** a sexually inviting gesture or approach ⟨was always accusing her of making ~*es* at other men —*Time*⟩ ⟨a girl must be able to recognize a ~ —Bernard De Voto⟩ **16 :** PASE ⟨makes his ~*es* with a stylized, classical grace that catches crowds by the throat —John Stanton⟩ **syn** see JUNCTURE

pass *abbr* **1** passage **2** passenger **3** passim **4** passive

pass·able \'pasəbəl, 'paas-, 'pais-, 'päs-\ *adj* [ME, fr. MF, fr. *passer* to pass + *-able*] **1 a :** capable of being passed, crossed, or traveled on ⟨car owners who needed ~ roads —F.L.Paxson⟩ **b** *archaic* : capable of passing or going through **c :** capable of being freely circulated ⟨counterfeit money so good it was ~ in a bank⟩ **2 :** able to qualify or pass inspection : just good enough : TOLERABLE ⟨there are ~ maps and better summary notes on each territory —*Geog. Jour.*⟩ — **pass·able·ness** *n* -ES

pass·ably \-blē, -li\ *adv* [*passable* + *-ly*] : MODERATELY, TOLERABLY ⟨she was little more than ~ good-looking —Louis Auchincloss⟩

pas·sa·ca·glia \,päsə'kälyə, ,pas-\ *also* **pas·sa·ca·glio** \-l(,)yō\ *n* -S [modif. (influenced by It *passagalia, passagallo,* fr. Sp *pasacalle,* a lively guitar tune) of F *passacaille,* fr. Sp *pasacalle,* fr. *pasar* to pass + *calle* street, fr. L *callis* path — more at PASE] **1 a :** an old Italian or Spanish dance tune **b :** an instrumental musical composition consisting of variations usu. on a ground bass in moderately slow triple time — compare CHACONNE **2 :** an old dance performed to a passacaglia

pas·sa·caille \,päsə'kī\ *or* **passe·caille** \päs'-\ *n* -S [F] : PASSACAGLIA

pas·sade \pə'sād\ *n* -S [F, fr. It *passata,* fr. *passare* to pass (fr. — assumed — VL *passare*) + *-ata* -ade — more at PASS, vb.] **1 :** a turn or course of a horse backward or forward on the same spot **2 :** a passing love affair : FLIRTATION ⟨it describes a ~, a riffle on the surface of life —Anthony West⟩

pas·sa·do \pə'sä(,)dō\ *n, pl* **passados** *or* **passadoes** [modif. of F *passade* or It *passata* — more at PASSADE] : a thrust in fencing with one foot advanced

¹pas·sage \'pasij, -sēj, *in sense 3d* " *or* pə'säzh\ *n* -S [ME, fr. OF, fr. *passer* to pass + *-age*] **1 :** the act or action of passing : movement or transference from one place or point to another, or through or across a space or element : TRANSIT ⟨made the ~ of their domain hazardous to settlers —*Amer. Guide Series: Texas*⟩ ⟨the ~ of the air from the lungs —*Encyc. Americana*⟩ ⟨the ~ of the Red sea —W.L.Sperry⟩ ⟨the ~ of an electric current through the wire⟩ **b** *obs* : DEATH ⟨when he is fit and seasoned for his ~ —Shak.⟩ **c** (1) : the process of passing : a transition from one mode of being, condition, or stage to another ⟨life enlightened is the ~ from irrational passion to reasoned attachment —J.P.Anton⟩ ⟨the indefinable ~ of a season —*Amer. Guide Series: Minn.*⟩ ⟨the ~ from barbarism to civilization —Edward Clodd⟩ (2) : a continuous movement or flow ⟨wounds, illnesses, sorrows were all weakened by the ~ of time —Stuart Cloete⟩ **d :** MIGRATION ⟨the black ducks were on ~ and we could see them coming in high from the north —V.C.Heilner⟩ **2 a :** a means of passing : a road, path, channel, or course through or by which something passes : a way of exit or entrance : PASS ⟨most of the streets were mere alleys, ~*s* between houses and groups of buildings —Edwin Benson⟩ ⟨breathing ~*s*⟩ **b :** a river crossing (as a ford or ferry) ⟨they took him, and slew him at the ~*s* of Jordan —Judg 12:6 (AV)⟩ **c :** a corridor or lobby giving access to the different rooms or parts of a building or apartment ⟨thinking how easy it would be to get lost in this hotel, in all these long ~*s* —Graham Greene⟩ **3 a** (1) : a specific act of traveling or passing from one place to another : a journey esp. by sea or air between two points ⟨the outward ~ was uneventful⟩ ⟨made a swift ~ between New York and Southampton⟩ ⟨the rocket satellite's ~*s* were coming so early they would not show up in the bright sky of sunset —*N. Y. Times*⟩ (2) : a privilege of conveyance as a passenger : ACCOMMODATIONS ⟨was able to secure ~ on the next flight⟩ ⟨took ~ on a freighter⟩ **b :** an obsolete dice game for two played with three dice — compare PASSE-DIX **c :** the passing of a legislative measure or law : ENACTMENT ⟨government leaders bent upon securing ~ of their bills —F.A.Ogg & Harold Zink⟩ **d :** a slow lofty trot with a precise cadence that is often used in traversing **e :** a movement or an evacuation of the bowels **4 a :** the possibility or liberty of passing : a right or permission to pass ⟨attempted to force ~ through the town —C.A.Willoughby⟩ **b :** a toll formerly collected from passengers in England **5 a :** something that happens or is done : OCCURRENCE, ACT, TRANSACTION ⟨our American experience in psychological warfare from 1941 to 1945 was often chaotic and mad; and it had its wholly comic ~*s* —A.M.Schlesinger b.1917⟩ **b :** something that takes place between two persons mutually : a mutual act or transaction (as a negotiation, a quarrel, or lovemaking) ⟨this ~ of arms and wits amused the town —Robert Browning⟩ **6 a :** a usu. brief portion of a written work or speech that is quoted or referred to by itself as relevant to a point under discussion or as noteworthy for content or style ⟨one of the finest ~*s* in the novel⟩ ⟨betrays his inaccuracy in many ~*s*⟩ ⟨this ~ was greeted with laughter by the audience⟩ **b :** a phrase or short section of a musical composition; *esp* : a section demonstrating virtuosity in performance ⟨a scale ~⟩ ⟨the ~ in arpeggios⟩ **c :** a detail of a painting or other work of art ⟨find ~*s* to admire in his best canvases —J.T.Soby⟩ ⟨the picture contains several pretty ~*s* of color —Clive Bell⟩ **7 a :** the act or action of causing something to pass **b** (1) : incubation of a pathogen (as a virus) in a tissue culture, a developing egg, or a living organism to increase the amount of pathogen or to alter its characteristics (2) : an instance of such passage **syn** see WAY

²pas·sage \'pasij, -sēj, pə'säzh\ *vb* -ED/-ING/-S [F *passager,* alter. of *passéger,* fr. It *passeggiare,* fr. *passare* to pass, fr. (assumed) VL — more at PASS] *vi* : to move sideways in riding or being ridden ⟨the horse ~*s* gracefully⟩ ~ *vt* : to cause (a horse) to move sideways

³pas·sage \'pasij, -sēj\ *vb* -ED/-ING/-S [¹*passage*] *vi* **1 :** to engage in a passage of arms or wits **2 :** to go past or across (as in a voyage) : CROSS ⟨*passaged* to Europe last month⟩ ~ *vt* : to subject to passage ⟨the virus has been *passaged* in series seven times —*Jour. Amer. Med. Assoc.*⟩

passage bed *n* [¹*passage*] : a stratum that forms a transition between rocks of two geological systems

passage bird *n* **1 :** BIRD OF PASSAGE **2 :** PASSAGE HAWK

passage boat *n* : a passenger boat plying on regular schedule between two places

passage cell *n* : a thin-walled unsuberized cell found in the endodermis of vascular plants often opposite the protoxylem strands — called also *transfusion cell*

passage grave *n* : a subterranean burial chamber entered through a long passage resembling a tunnel

passage hawk *n* : a haggard hawk

passageway \'=,=\ *n* : a way that allows passage to or from a place or between two points : CORRIDOR, PATH ⟨only one narrow ~ up the steep mountain —Burtt Evans⟩ ⟨outbuildings were connected to the main house by curved ~*s* —H.S.Morrison⟩

passage winds *n pl* : prevailing westerly winds that blow in the belt lying between the horse latitudes and the region of the pole in each hemisphere

passage-work \'=,=\ *n* : a section or part of a musical composition characteristically unimportant thematically and generally consisting of repetitive notes or figures or scale or arpeggio passages

pas·sag·gio \pə'säj(,)jō\ *n* -S [It, lit., passage, fr. *passare* to pass (fr. — assumed — VL) + *-aggio* -age — more at PASS] **1 :** an improvised embellishment or flourish found esp. in 16th century music and usu. excluding plain scale passages or trills **2 :** MODULATION **3 :** PASSAGE-WORK

¹pas·sa·lid \'pasələd\ *adj* [NL *Passalidae*] : of or relating to the Passalidae

²passalid \"\ *n* -S : a beetle of the family Passalidae

pas·sal·i·dae \pə'salə,dē\ *n pl, cap* [NL, fr. *Passalus,* type genus + *-idae*] : a family of rather large usu. black lamellicorn beetles chiefly of tropical countries that live and feed in decaying wood and are sometimes placed in the family Lucanidae — see BESS-BUG, PASSALUS

pas·sa·lus \'pasələs\ *n* [NL, fr. Gk *passalos* peg; akin to Gk *pēssein* to fix, fasten, *pēgnynai* to fix, fasten — more at PACT] **1** *cap* : the type genus of the family Passalidae **2** -ES : any beetle of *Passalus* or a related genus; *esp* : a flat shiny black gregarious bess-bug (*Popilius disjunctus*) of the southern U. S. — called also *horned passalus*

pas·sa·ma·quod·dy \,pasəmə'kwädē\ *n, pl* **passamaquoddy** *or* **passamaquoddies** *usu cap* **1 a :** an Indian people of Maine and New Brunswick, Canada **b :** a member of such people **2 :** a dialect of Malecite

passament *var of* PASSEMENT

pas·sa·mez·zo *or* **pas·se·mez·zo** \,päsə'met(,)sō, -ed(,)zō, -e(,)zō\ *n* -S [It *passamezzo, passo e mezzo,* fr. the phrase *passo e mezzo* step and a half] : an old orig. Italian dance in duple time resembling the pavan but about twice as fast; *also* : the music of this dance

passangrahan *var of* PASANGGRAHAN

pas·sant \'pasᵊnt\ *adj* [MF, fr. pres. part. of *passer* to pass] **1 :** walking with the further forepaw raised — used of a heraldic lion or other beast; compare COUNTERPASSANT **2** *archaic* : having general acceptance or use : CURRENT

pas sauté \,päsō'tā, -sō'-\ *n, pl* **pas sautés** \-ā(z)\ [F] : a jumping step in ballet

pass away *vb* [ME *passen away,* fr. *passen* to pass + *away*] *vi* **1 a :** to go out of existence : come to an end : PERISH, VANISH ⟨when those conditions have *passed away* and history returns to normal —W.P.Webb⟩ **b :** DIE ⟨died of a broken heart soon after his mother *passed away* —David Fairchild⟩ **2** *archaic* : DEPART ⟨saw the damsel *pass away* —Edmund Spenser⟩ **3 :** to slip by : ELAPSE ⟨the evening *passed away* very fairly —Henry Lapham⟩ ~ *vt* **1 :** to let slip by : SPEND ⟨*pass away* the winter⟩ **2** *archaic* : to give away : SURRENDER

passback \'=,=\ *n* -S [¹*pass* + *back,* adv.] : SNAPBACK

passband \'=,=\ *n* : the frequency band (as in a radio circuit or filter) that is transmitted with maximum efficiency and without intentional loss

passbook \'=,=\ *n* **1 :** BANKBOOK **2 :** a customer's book in which a dealer enters articles bought on credit

pass by *vt* [ME *passen by,* fr. *passen* to pass + *by*] : to go past without stopping or noticing : DISREGARD, IGNORE ⟨the sort of writer present-day literary critics *pass by* —Oliver La Farge⟩ ⟨new methods have *passed* them *by* —George Farwell⟩

pass course *n* [³*pass*] : a general undergraduate course at British universities that is taken by all students who are not candidates for honors

pass degree *n* : a bachelor's degree without honors that is taken at a British university

pass door *n* : a door between the stage and the auditorium in a theater

¹pas·sé *or* **pas·sée** \(')pa'sā\ *adj* [F, fr. past part. of *passer* to pass] **1 :** past one's prime : no longer young : FADED ⟨a fine brain in a somewhat ~ body —*Amer. Mercury*⟩ ⟨a somewhat rakish but ~ miss —*Newsweek*⟩ **2 a :** no longer fashionable or in demand : OUTMODED ⟨the work which is spurned as ~ becomes a period piece —A.L.Guérard⟩ ⟨a broad, dark, tree-lined street of ~ frame houses —Lester Atwell⟩ **b :** not up-to-date : behind the times ⟨the clinician without an active experimental laboratory attached to his wards is apt to be called ~ —*Science*⟩

²passé \"\ *n* -S [F, fr. past part. of *passer*] : a ballet movement in which the leg passes from one position to another

³passe \'päs\ *n* -S [F, fr. *passer*] : the high numbers in roulette when a bet is made on them

passecaille *var of* PASSACAILLE

passed *past of* PASS

passed ball *n* [fr. past part. of ¹*pass*] : a pitched ball not hit by the batter that passes the catcher when he should have stopped it and allows a base runner to advance a base ⟨one of his trick pitches shot by the catcher for a *passed ball* —John Drebinger⟩

passe-dix \päs'dēs\ *n, pl* **passe-dixes** [F, fr. *passer* to pass + *dix* ten, fr. L *decem* — more at TEN] : a game played with three dice in which the caster who is the banker bets even money that the pips on his cast of the three dice will total 10 or more

passed master *n* [fr. past part. of ¹*pass* (to go through an inspection successfully)] : a person who has passed as a master : one who is proficient in a particular field or activity ⟨*passed masters* in the use of the cliché —E.H.Criswell⟩ — compare PAST MASTER

passed pawn *n* [fr. past part. of ¹*pass* (to go by)] : a chess pawn having no enemy pawn before it on its own or an adjacent file

passe·garde *or* **pass·guard** \'pas,gärd\ *n* -S [³*pass* (thrust) + *guard*] : a piece fastened on the left elbow in medieval tilting armor; *sometimes* : GARDE-COLLET

pas·sel \'pasəl\ *n* -S [alter. of *parcel*] : a large number : GROUP ⟨a ~ of towheaded kids —Shelby Foote⟩ ⟨a whole ~ of notables —*Time*⟩

pas·se·meas·ure \'pasē,mezhə(r)\ *n* [modif. (influenced by *measure*) of It *passo e mezzo* — more at PASSAMEZZO] : PASSAMEZZO

¹passe·ment \'pasmənt\ *also* **pas·sa·ment** \-sə-\ *n* -S [MF *passement,* fr. *passer* to pass + *-ment*] : an ornamental braid or decorative trimming resembling lace and made of gold, silver, or silk threads

²passe·ment \'pa,sment\ *vt* -ED/-ING/-S : to trim or edge with passement

passe·men·terie \pa'smen·trē\ *n* -S [F, fr. *passement* + *-erie* -ery] : a fancy edging or ornamental trimming made of braid, cord, gimp, beading, or metallic thread in various combinations and used on clothing and upholstery

passemezzo *var of* PASSAMEZZO

pas·sen·ger \'pasᵊnjə(r)\ *n* -S *often attrib* [ME *passyngere, passager,* fr. MF *passager,* fr. *passager, passagier,* adj., passing, fr. *passage* + *-ier* -ary] **1 :** one who passes by : TRAVELER, WAYFARER ⟨the roads are wide, well-kept, and full of ~*s* —Thomas Gray⟩ ⟨foot ~⟩ **2 a :** a traveler in a public conveyance (as a train, bus, airplane, or ship) ⟨carried more ~*s* last year than ever before⟩ **b :** one who is carried in a private conveyance (as an automobile) for compensation or expected benefit to the owner **c :** a rider in an automobile ⟨a six-passenger model⟩ **3 :** a member of a group (as an animal in a herd) that contributes little or nothing to the functioning or productivity of the group ⟨all ~*s* should be eliminated from dairy herds —*Farmer's Weekly (So. Africa)*⟩

passenger car *n* **1 :** a railroad car (as a coach, parlor car, dining car, or sleeping car) for carrying passengers **2 :** an automobile for carrying a limited number of passengers (as no more than nine)

passenger liner *n* : a liner used mainly to carry passengers

passenger list *n* : a list of the passengers on a ship that is submitted by the master to customs officials at ports visited

passenger-mile *n* : a statistical unit denoting one mile traveled by one passenger and used by agencies of public transportation (as railroads, bus lines, or airlines) in measuring the volume of passenger traffic

passenger mileage *n* : the total number of miles traveled by passengers on a given agency of public transportation during a given period

passenger pigeon *n* : an extinct No. American wild pigeon (*Ectopistes migratorius*) of irregularly migratory habits once very abundant esp. in the Mississippi valley and having a long graduated tail, bluish slate upper parts with iridescence on the neck, a vinaceous breast, and a white belly

passenger-train car *n* : a railroad car used in passenger-train service for carrying mail, baggage, or express

¹passe-par·tout \,pa|spə(r)'tü, ,pä|, |,spär'-, |,spä'-\ *n, pl* **passe-partouts** \-ü(z)\ [F, fr. the phrase *passe partout* pass everywhere] **1 :** something that passes or enables one to pass everywhere : MASTER KEY **2 a :** a piece or plate usu. of cardboard or wood that has its central portion cut out for the reception of a picture **b** (1) **:** a method of framing in which a picture, a mat, a glass, and a back (as of cardboard) are held together by strips of paper or cloth pasted over the edges (2) **:** a picture framed in such manner **3 :** a strong paper gummed on one side and commonly used for binding lantern slides and mounting pictures

²passe-partout \"\ *vt* -ED/-ING/-S **:** to frame with a passe-partout

passe-passe \'pä'späs\ *n, pl* **passe-passes** \-s(əz)\ [F, fr. the phrase used by jugglers *passe, passe* pass, pass] **:** a skillful feat of juggling or manipulation ⟨moving divisions from north to south and south to north . . . the kind of *passe-passe* that is a . . . delight —A.J.Liebling⟩

passe-pied \pä'spyā\ *also* **pas·py** \'paspē\ *n, pl* **passepieds** \-ā(z)\ *also* **paspies** \-ēz\ [F *passe-pied*, fr. *passer* to pass + *pied* foot, fr. L *ped-, pes* — more at FOOT] **:** a lively 17th and 18th century dance of French peasant origin resembling the minuet and beginning on the last beat of the measure; *also* **:** the music for this dance typically found in suites

¹pass·er \'pasə(r), 'paas-, 'pais-, 'pȧs-\ *n* -S [ME, fr. *passen* to pass + *-er*] **:** one that passes or causes to pass

²pas·ser \'pasə(r)\ *n, cap* [NL, fr. L, sparrow] **:** a genus consisting of the house sparrow and its near relatives

pass·er·by \'==,=\ *n, pl* **passersby** [¹*passer* + *by*] **:** one who passes by usu. by chance ⟨the robbery had been planned for a day when there would be fewer than the usual number of *passersby* —*N.Y. Times*⟩

passe·relle \päs'rel\ *n* -S [F, fr. *passer* to pass] **:** FOOTBRIDGE

¹pas·ser·es \'pasə,rēz\ [NL, fr. pl. of L *passer* sparrow] *syn of* PASSERIFORMES

²passeres \"\ *n pl, cap* **:** a very large suborder of Passeriformes comprising the typical singing birds that have a specialized vocal apparatus with four or five pairs of diacromyodian syringeal muscles

pas·ser·i·form \'pasərə,fȯrm, pə'serə,-\ *adj* [NL *Passeriformes*] **:** of or relating to the Passeriformes **:** PASSERINE

pas·ser·i·for·mes \,pasərə'fȯr,mēz\ *n pl, cap* [NL, fr. L *passer* + NL *-iformes*] **:** the largest order of birds including more than 5000 species or more than half of all living birds, consisting chiefly of songbirds of perching habits that range in size from the smallest titmice to the ravens and birds of paradise, being usu. divided into the four suborders Eurylaimi, Tyranni, Menurae, and Passeres, and comprising birds that are altricial, lack the ambiens muscle, and have the vomer well developed and truncate anteriorly with its forked posterior end embracing the basisphenoid, three toes in front and one behind and none reversible, 10 primaries of which the first is often rudimentary, and usu. 12 rectrices

pas·ser·i·na \,pasə'rīnə\ *n, cap* [NL, fr. L *passer* sparrow + NL *-ina*] **:** a genus of small No. American bush-loving finches resembling the tanager that are in the male brightly colored in blue or red or variegated and that include the indigo, lazuli, and painted buntings

¹pas·ser·ine \'pasərən, -sə,rīn, -sə,rēn\ *adj* [L *passerinus* of sparrows, fr. *passer* + *-inus* -ine] **:** of or relating to the Passeres or Passeriformes

²passerine \"\ *n* -S **:** a passerine bird

¹passes *pl of* PASS *or of* PASSE, *pres 3d sing of* PASS

²passés *pl of* PASSÉ

pas seul \pä'sǝl\ *n, pl* **pas seuls** \-l(z)\ [F, lit., solo step] **:** a solo performance of a dance or a dance figure

pas·se·wa \pə'sāwə\ *n* -S [Hindi *pasevā* sweat, fr. Skt *prasveda*, fr. *pra-* forth + *svedate* he sweats — more at FOR, SWEAT] **:** a viscous extract from the capsules of the poppy that is obtained after the seeds are removed, hardens on exposure, and is used in making coverings for opium cakes

pass examination *n* **:** an examination for a pass degree or in a pass course

pass·gang \'päs,gäŋ\ *n* -S [G, lit., stepping gait, fr. *pass* step (fr. L *passus*) + *gang* going, gait — more at PACE, GANG] **:** a method of cross-country ski running in which each pole is brought forward simultaneously with the ski on the same side and is thrust so as to produce a glide with the opposite ski

passguard *var of* PASSEGARDE

pas·si·bil·i·ty \,pasə'biləd·ē\ *n* -ES [LL *passibilitas*, fr. *passibilis* passible + *-itat-, -itas* -ity] **:** the quality or state of being passible **:** SENSIBILITY

pas·si·ble \'pasəbəl\ *adj* [ME, fr. MF, fr. ML *passibilis*, fr. L *passus* (past part. of *pati* to suffer) + *-ibilis* -ible — more at PATIENT] **:** capable of feeling or suffering **:** IMPRESSIONABLE ⟨the more nervous, emotional, excitable, and ~ sex —Rose Macaulay⟩

pas·si·flo·ra \,pasə'flōrə\ *n* [NL, fr. *passi-* (fr. L *passion-, passio* passion) + *-flora* (fr. L *flor-, flos* flower) — more at BLOW (bloom)] **1** *cap* **:** a genus (the type of the family Passifloraceae) of mainly tropical American and mostly tendril-bearing vines that have simple or lobed leaves and usu. very showy chiefly red, white, or purple flowers with a short calyx tube, four or five petals, a corona, and numerous stamens monadelphous at base and followed by fruits which are pulpy often edible berries — see GRANADILLA, MAYPOP, PASSIONFLOWER **2** -S **:** any plant of the genus *Passiflora*

pas·si·flo·ra·ce·ae \,pasəflə'rāsē,ē\ *n pl, cap* [NL, fr. *Passiflora*, type genus + *-aceae*] **:** a family of tropical woody tendril-climbing vines or erect herbs (order Parietales) mostly with showy flowers distinguished chiefly by a fringed corona borne on the throat of the calyx and with a fruit that is a berry or capsule — **pas·si·flo·ra·ceous** \¦===¦rāshəs\ *adj*

pas·si·flo·ra·les \,===rā(,)lēz\ *n pl, cap* [NL, fr. *Passiflora* + *-ales*] *in some classifications* **:** an order of dicotyledonous herbs, tendril-bearing vines, shrubs, and trees that have alternate leaves, pentamerous flowers with a superior one-celled ovary, and a fruit which is a berry or capsule and that include plants now usu. placed in Parietales and Cucurbitales

pas·sim \'pasəm\ *adv* [L, fr. *passus* spread about, scattered, past part. of *pandere* to spread out, unfold — more at FATHOM] **:** here and there **:** THROUGHOUT — used esp. with the name of a book or writer to indicate that something (as a word, phrase, or idea) is to be found at many places in the same book or writer's work

pas·sim·e·ter \pə'siməd·ə(r)\ *n* [prob. fr. ¹*pass* + *-i-* + *-meter*] **:** a turnstile operated from inside a change booth that gives access to a public transportation area (as a subway platform)

¹pass·ing \'pasiŋ, 'paas-, 'pais-, 'pȧs-, -sēŋ\ *n* -S [ME, fr. gerund of *passen* to pass] **1 :** the act of one that passes or causes to pass ⟨the ~ of winter⟩ ⟨the ~ of a great man⟩ ⟨the ~ of a major bill⟩ ⟨the ~ of the million dollar mark⟩ ⟨forward ~⟩ **2 :** a means of passing or crossing **:** FORD **3 :** the act of identifying oneself or accepting identification as a white person — used of a person having some Negro ancestry — **in passing** *adv* **:** by the way **:** PARENTHETICALLY

²passing \"\ *adj* [ME, fr. pres. part. of *passen* to pass] **1 :** going by **:** moving past ⟨a ~ youngster called up to him —Judson Philips⟩ ⟨observe with bright-eyed interest the ~ show of the squalid tenement in which they live —*Time*⟩ **2 :** having a brief duration **:** quickly vanishing **:** FLEETING, TRANSITORY ⟨the ~ vogues of the best sellers of the day —J.L.Lowes⟩ ⟨~ interest⟩ ⟨~ sensations⟩ **3** *obs* **:** EXCEEDING, SURPASSING ⟨a ~ traitor, perjured and unjust —Shak.⟩ **4 :** marked by haste, inattention, or inadequacy **:** CURSORY, SUPERFICIAL ⟨a ~ glance⟩ ⟨a few ~ remarks⟩ ⟨has only a ~ acquaintance with the subject⟩ **5 a :** of, relating to, or used in or for the act or process of passing ⟨a ~ place⟩ ⟨a ~ track⟩ **b :** given on satisfactory completion of an examination or course of study ⟨a ~ grade⟩ **syn** see TRANSIENT

³passing \"\ *prep* [ME, fr. ²*passing*] *archaic* **:** BEYOND

⁴passing \"\ *adv* [ME, fr. ²*passing*] **:** to a surpassing degree **:** EXCEEDINGLY, EXTREMELY, VERY ⟨wildflowers or cacti that will prove ~ strange to your eastern eyes —Jack Goodman⟩ ⟨~ fair⟩

passing bell *n* [¹*passing*] **1 :** a bell tolled to announce a death or funeral service — called also *death bell* **2 :** something that announces or marks a death **:** KNELL ⟨a moment's thought is passion's *passing bell* —John Keats⟩

passing duck *n* [²*passing*] **:** KING EIDER

passing hollow *n* **:** CRESCENT 3d

passing light *n* [¹*passing*] **:** a strong red light to warn passing airplanes displayed usu. in the leading edge on an airplane flying after dark

pass·ing·ly *adv* [ME, fr. ²*passing* + *-ly*] **1 a :** TEMPORARILY ⟨were in Cambridge ~ for a few days —Lucien Price⟩ **b :** in passing **:** CURSORILY ⟨he has only studied ~ and is in danger of failing the course⟩ **2** *archaic* **:** EXCEEDINGLY, SURPASSINGLY

pass·ing·ness *n* -ES [²*passing* + *-ness*] **:** the quality or state of being transitory

passing note *or* **passing tone** *n* [¹*passing*] **:** a note or tone foreign to the harmony and usu. unaccented that is interposed for melodic smoothness between essential notes or tones

passing shot *n* **:** a passing stroke in tennis

passing spring *n* **:** GOLD SPRING

passing strake *n* **:** a continuous strake between butts in the same vertical plane in a ship

passing stroke *n* **1 :** a pass stroke in croquet **2 :** a stroke in tennis aimed to drive the ball to one side of and beyond the reach of an opponent at or coming toward the net

passing zone *n* [¹*passing*] **:** a zone 20 yards long in which a baton must be passed to the next runner in a relay race

¹pas·sion \'pashən, 'paash-, 'paish-\ *n* -S [ME *passion, passiun*, fr. OF, fr. LL *passion-, passio*, lit., suffering, fr. L *passus* (past part. of *pati* to suffer) + *-ion-, -io* -ion; in senses 4 & 5 fr. ME, fr. MF, fr. LL *passion-, passio*, trans. of Gk *pathos* — more at PATIENT] **1** *often cap* **a** (1) **:** the sufferings of Jesus on the cross (2) **:** the sufferings of Jesus between the night of the Last Supper and his death including the agony in Gethsemane ⟨places the redeeming ~ of Christ at the heart of revelation —*Times Lit. Supp.*⟩ ⟨the last dark period culminating in the *Passion* —F.J.Rae⟩ **b :** one of the gospel narratives of the passion of Jesus read or sung as the Gospel for the Day on four different days in Holy Week **c :** a musical setting of such a narrative; *esp* **:** an oratorio with narrative, chorales, airs, and choruses based on such a narrative **d :** PASSION PLAY **2 a :** the sufferings of a martyr **:** MARTYRDOM **b :** a narrative of such sufferings **3 a** *obs* **:** SUFFERING ⟨give her what comforts the quality of her ~ shall require —Shak.⟩ **b** *archaic* **:** a bodily disorder causing suffering or distress **4 a :** the state of being subjected to or acted on by what is external or foreign to one's true nature; *esp* **:** a state of desire or emotion that represents the influence of what is external and opposes thought and reason as the true activity of the human mind — contrasted with *action* **b :** a capacity of being affected or acted upon by external agents or influences ⟨moldable and not moldable . . . and many other ~*s* of matter —Francis Bacon⟩ **5 a** (1) **:** EMOTION, FEELING ⟨give me that man that is not ~'*s* slave —Shak.⟩ ⟨his ruling ~ is greed⟩ (2) **passions** *pl* **:** the emotions as distinguished from reason ⟨a study of the ~*s*⟩ **b :** violent, intense, or overmastering emotion **:** depth or vehemence of feeling **:** a state of or capacity for emotional excitement ⟨blue eyes that blazed with ~ as he expounded his favorite theme —Honor Tracy⟩ ⟨with enough ~ to make a great poet —W.B.Yeats⟩ ⟨when the immediate ~*s* of the war recede into the background —C.E.Black & E.C.Helmreich⟩ **c :** an outbreak of anger or a display of bad temper ⟨she flew into a ~ and stabbed him —R.H.Davis⟩ ⟨the grave and stately lady was for once in her life in a towering ~ —William Black⟩ **d** *archaic* **:** a writing or speech marked by intense feeling ⟨here she comes, and her ~ ends the play —Shak.⟩ **e :** a fit of emotional agitation **:** a surrender to a particular feeling **:** an uncontrollable display of emotion ⟨jumped up in a ~ of alarm —Louis Auchincloss⟩ ⟨began to sob and weep like a little boy, in a perfect ~ of emotion —H.G.Wells⟩ **6 a :** ardent affection **:** LOVE ⟨one of the truest ~*s* that ever was inspired by woman was raised in this bosom by that lady —W.M.Thackeray⟩ **b :** a strong liking for or devotion to some activity, object, or concept **:** ENTHUSIASM ⟨became troubled with the ~ for reforming the world —T.L.Peacock⟩ ⟨a ~ for chess⟩ ⟨a ~ for glory⟩ **c :** sexual desire ⟨look with ruffian ~ in her face —John Keats⟩ **d :** an object of desire or interest **:** something that commands one's love or devotion ⟨she is his ~ of the moment⟩ ⟨fishing is his present ~⟩

syn FERVOR, ARDOR, ENTHUSIASM, ZEAL: PASSION applies to intense, overwhelming, or driving emotion, sometimes displayed with agitated vehemence, sometimes indicating intense erotic feeling ⟨with fanatical *passion* he attacked Calvinism and presented Methodism as teaching the only way of salvation —H.E.Starr⟩ ⟨an ungovernable childlike *passion* —W.B.Yeats⟩ ⟨launches into a frenzied oration with the *passion* of Savanarola —C.L.Sulzberger⟩ ⟨the purely physical urges of sex and its gratification can be summed up as *passion* —Lois Pemberton⟩ FERVOR may designate any strong steadily glowing lasting emotion ⟨preached emancipation as a revival in benevolence, with a *fervor* which mobs could not silence —G.H.Barnes⟩ ⟨the man who seizes on one deep-reaching idea, whether newly found or rediscovered, and with single-hearted *fervor* forces it upon the world —P.E.More⟩ ARDOR may differ in suggesting a more demonstrative and excited feeling not so long-lived, although the two words are sometimes interchangeable ⟨the raptures and *ardors* of sudden conversion to any cause —H.V.Gregory⟩ ⟨imperialism left slain behind, she embraced with *ardor* the fantastic ideal of the cleaning up of England —Rose Macaulay⟩ ENTHUSIASM may apply to intense interest or admiration for something, often a matter more objective, tangible, or mundane than those calling forth ardor ⟨whose proposed visit to the U.S. was then stirring *enthusiasm* among Louisiana-French people —*Amer. Guide Series: La.*⟩ ⟨waging the campaign of 1856 with *enthusiasm* —Carol L. Thompson⟩ ZEAL suggests enthusiastic devotion to a cause ⟨missionary *zeal*⟩ ⟨the *zeal* of the Inquisition to burn heretics —M.R.Cohen⟩ ⟨his health was further affected by his *zeal* in public affairs as well as his enthusiasm in study —Havelock Ellis⟩ **syn** see in addition DESIRE, DISTRESS, FEELING

²passion \"\ *vb* -ED/-ING/-S [ME *passionen*, fr. MF *passionner*, fr. *passion*] *vt* **:** to affect or fill with passion ⟨turtles ~ their voices cooingly —John Keats⟩ ~ *vi* **:** to display or become affected by passion ⟨beautiful garden where he had played and ~*ed* in varying moments of grief and glee —George Moore⟩

¹pas·sion·al \-shənᵊl, -shnəl\ *n* -S [ML *passionale*, fr. LL, neut. of *passionalis*, adj.] **:** a book that contains accounts of the sufferings of saints and martyrs to be read on their festivals

²passional \"\ *adj* [LL *passionalis*, fr. *passion-, passio* passion + L *-alis*, -al] **:** of or relating to passion or the passions **:** marked by, filled with, or exciting passion ⟨the emotional and ~ fervor of the evangelist —Adria Langley⟩

pas·sion·ary \'pashə,nerē\ *n* -ES [ML *passionarium*, fr. LL *passion-, passio* passion + L *-arium* -ary] **:** PASSIONAL

¹pas·sion·ate \'pash(ə)nət, 'paash-, 'paish, *usu* -əd·+V\ *adj* [ML *passionatus*, fr. LL *passion-, passio* + L *-atus*, -ate] **1 a :** easily aroused to anger **:** IRASCIBLE, QUICK-TEMPERED ⟨a ~ but not a vicious boy —H.E.Scudder⟩ **b :** filled with or marked by anger **:** ANGRY, ENRAGED ⟨was ~ in defense of her cub, and rage transformed her —G.D.Brown⟩ **2 a :** dominated by strong emotion **:** capable of or affected by intense feeling **:** ARDENT ⟨a ~ and stormy personality⟩ ⟨a ~ and unquestioned faith in the virtue of the cause he served —C.L.Becker⟩ **b :** expressing or communicating violent or intense feeling ⟨a ~ speech⟩ ⟨a ~ performance of the symphony⟩ ⟨a ~ bit of acting⟩ **c :** ENTHUSIASTIC, VEHEMENT ⟨the army was now ~ for an engagement —J.A.Froude⟩ ⟨has become a ~ housekeeper —Joseph Mitchell⟩ **d :** UNRESTRAINED ⟨broke down in a flood of ~ weeping —C.B.Nordhoff & J.N.Hall⟩ **3 :** swayed by or affected with sexual desire ⟨her beauty made an immediate appeal to his ~ temperament⟩ **4 a** *obs* **:** affected with grief **:** SAD, SORROWFUL **b** *chiefly dial* **:** COMPASSIONATE **syn** see IMPASSIONED

²passionate *vt* -ED/-ING/-S **1** *obs* **:** to fill with passion **2** *obs* **:** to express or portray with passion

pas·sion·ate·ly *adv* **:** in a passionate manner **:** with great feeling **:** ARDENTLY, ENTHUSIASTICALLY

pas·sion·ate·ness *n* -ES **:** the quality or state of being passionate

pas·si·o·na·to \¦päsēə¦nä(,)dō, ¦pas-, -syə¦-, ¦pashə¦-\ *adv* (*or adj*) [It, fr. ML *passionatus* passionate] **:** in a passionate manner **:** with passion **:** FERVENTLY — used as a direction in music

passion cross *n* **:** LATIN CROSS

pas·sioned \'pashənd, 'paash-, 'paish-\ *adj* [¹*passion* + *-ed*] **:** affected with or marked by passion **:** PASSIONATE

pas·sionflower \'==,=\ *n* [trans. of NL *flos passionis*, lit., flower of the Passion; fr. the fancied resemblance of parts of the flower to the instruments of Christ's crucifixion] **:** a plant of the genus *Passiflora*

passionflower family *n* **:** PASSIFLORACEAE

passion fruit *n* **:** an edible fruit of a passionflower

pas·sion·ful \'pashənfəl\ *adj* **:** full of or capable of passion **:** PASSIONATE — **pas·sion·ful·ness** *n* -ES

passioning *pres part of* PASSION

pas·sion·ist \'pashənəst\ *n* -S *usu cap* [It *passionista*, fr. *passione* passion (fr. LL *passion-, passio*) + It *-ista* -ist] **:** a member of a Roman Catholic religious order founded by St. Paul of the Cross in 1720 and devoted chiefly to missionary work

pas·sion·less \'pashənləs, 'paash-, 'paish-\ *adj* **1 :** devoid of passion **:** empty of feeling ⟨this ~ girl was like an icicle in the sunshine —Margaret Deland⟩ **2 :** CALM, DETACHED ⟨the same steady impersonal ~ observation of human nature —T.S.Eliot⟩ — **pas·sion·less·ly** *adv* — **pas·sion·less·ness** *n* -ES

passion music *n, usu cap P* **:** PASSION 1c

passion play *n* **1** *often cap 1st P* **:** a dramatic representation of the scenes connected with the passion of Jesus **2 :** a dramatic representation of the sufferings and death of an outstanding religious or spiritual leader

passions *pl of* PASSION, *pres 3d sing of* PASSION

passion sunday *n, usu cap P&S* [ME, trans. of ML *Dominica in Passione*] **:** the fifth Sunday in Lent or the second before Easter

passiontide \'==,=\ *n, usu cap* [¹*passion* + *tide* (time)] **:** the last two weeks of Lent

passion vine *n* **:** PASSIONFLOWER

passion week *n, usu cap P&W* [ME, trans. of ML *hebdomada Passionis*] **1 :** HOLY WEEK **2 :** the second week before Easter occurring between Passion Sunday and Palm Sunday

pas·si·vate \'pasə,vāt\ *vt* -ED/-ING/-S [¹*passive* + *-ate*] **:** to make passive or inactive — **pas·si·va·tion** \,==='vāshən\ *n* -S

pas·si·va·tor \'==,vād·ə(r)\ *n* -S [*passivate* + *-or*] **:** a substance (as a chromate) that passivates esp. by forming a protective film on a metal

¹pas·sive \'pasiv, 'paas-, 'pais-, -sēv *also* -səv\ *adj* [ME, fr. L *passivus*, fr. *passus* (past part. of *pati* to suffer, undergo) + *-ivus* -ive — more at PATIENT] **1 a :** not acting but acted upon **:** subject to or produced by an external agency **:** receptive to outside impressions or influences ⟨nature is neutral and ~ —W.P.Webb⟩ ⟨takes his color from his surroundings, a ~ agent of his environment —Van Wyck Brooks⟩ **b** (1) *of a verb form or voice* **:** asserting that the person or thing represented by the grammatical subject is subjected to or affected by the action represented by the verb ⟨*was hit* in "he was hit by the ball" and *was given* in "he was given a prize" are ~⟩ — compare ACTIVE (2) *of a grammatical construction* **:** containing a passive verb form **c :** lacking in energy or will **:** LETHARGIC ⟨its people are a ~, frustrated, and resigned lot —John Mason Brown⟩ ⟨a vague, ~ girl, content to remain at home and dream —Ruth Blodgett⟩ **d :** induced by an outside agency without either active participation or resistance of the individual affected ⟨neuromuscular reeducation through ~ exercise⟩ **2 a :** not active or operating **:** not moving **:** INERT, QUIESCENT ⟨the faint light from the street lamp outlined the ~ hump he made in the bedclothes —Dorothy Sayers⟩ ⟨engines ~ as great cats —Thomas Wolfe⟩ **b :** existing in a dormant state but capable of being used or brought into play **:** LATENT ⟨has a larger ~ vocabulary than he realizes⟩ **c :** of, relating to, or characterized by a state of chemical inactivity **:** not reacting readily **:** resistant to corrosion ⟨iron and nickel become ~ when treated with fuming nitric acid⟩ **3** *Scots law* **:** of, relating to, or subject to a liability **4 a :** receiving or enduring without resistance **:** PATIENT, SUBMISSIVE, UNRESISTING ⟨there is in her a ~ surrender to the powers of life —P.E. More⟩ ⟨no one has a right explicitly to make of another a mere ~ instrument of his will —G.L.Dickinson⟩ **b :** carried through or expressed by indirect means **:** existing without being active or open ⟨~ support⟩ **syn** see INACTIVE

²passive \"\ *n* -S [ME, fr. ¹*passive*] **1 a :** something (as a person, object, or quality) acted upon by something else — usu. used in pl. **b** *or* **passive bobbin :** HANGER 5 **2 a :** a passive verb **b :** the passive voice of a language or a form in it

passive anaphylaxis *n* **:** anaphylaxis in a normal animal sensitized to a specific substance by injection of serum from an animal sensitized to that substance by direct injection

passive congestion *n* **:** congestion caused by obstruction to the return flow of venous blood

passive defense *n* **:** a defense designed solely to resist in place or minimize the effects of an attack against a specified area, position, or front

passive hyperemia *n* **:** PASSIVE CONGESTION

passive immunity *n* **:** immunity acquired by transfer of antibodies from an actively immune individual

pas·sive·ly \-sȧvlē, -li\ *adv* **1 :** in a passive manner **2 :** in the passive voice **:** in a passive construction

pas·sive·ness \-sivnəs\ *n* -ES **:** the quality or state of being passive

passive noun *n* **:** a noun indicating the recipient of action ⟨*advisee* and *employee* are *passive nouns*⟩

passive obedience *n* **:** absolute obedience or submission of a subject to the authority of a ruler regarded by some political writers as mandatory even when the ruler is bad — compare DIVINE RIGHT

passive resistance *n* **:** resistance (as to a government or an occupying power) that does not resort to violence or active measures of opposition but depends mainly on techniques and acts of noncooperation

passive resister *n* **:** one who practices passive resistance

passive transfer *n* **:** a local transfer of skin sensitivity from an allergic to a normal person by injection of serum from the former used esp. for identifying specific allergens when a high degree of allergic sensitivity is suspected

passive trust *n* **:** a trust in which the trustee has no active duty other than to hold title for the benefit of the designated beneficiary — called also *dry trust*

pas·siv·ism \'pasə,vizəm, 'paas-, 'pais-\ *n* -S **:** a passive attitude, behavior, or way of life ⟨the ~ which has become so much a part of our American recreation —H.A.Block⟩

pas·siv·ist \-,vəst\ *n* -S **1 :** one given to passivism **2 :** PASSIVE RESISTER

pas·siv·i·ty \pa'sivəd·ē, -ətē, -i\ *n* -ES [¹*passive* + *-ity*] **1 a :** the quality or state of being acted upon from without **:** PASSIVENESS ⟨a certain obstinate patient ~, a certain lying back upon life —J.C.Powys⟩ ⟨his aggressive trends were efforts to compensate for his inherent ~ —Charles Anderson⟩ **b :** an instance of passiveness **:** something that is passive ⟨a vast activity of writers, a vast and hungry ~ of readers —Aldous Huxley⟩ **c** (1) **:** chemically inactive state **:** INACTIVITY — used esp. of a metal that has lost its normal chemical activity and is resistant to corrosion (2) **:** inactivity of an electrode due to polarization **2 :** an absence of activity, initiative, or decisiveness **:** INERTIA ⟨what amounts in modern battle to stupid ~ —Tom Wintringham⟩ **3 :** a submission to the will of another or to outside force **:** SUBMISSIVENESS ⟨has emerged from the ~ of defeat to seize and assert its independence —*Time*⟩ **4 :** the construction of the passive voice **:** the meaning expressed by the passive voice

passkey \'=,=\ *n* [¹*pass* + *key*] **1 :** MASTER KEY **2 :** LATCHKEY **3 :** SKELETON KEY

pass·less \'pasləs\ *adj* [¹*pass* + *-less*] **:** IMPASSABLE

pass line *n* [¹*pass*] **:** LINE 13a

pass·man \'pasman, -,maa(ə)n, -,mən\ *n, pl* **passmen :** a student enrolled in a pass course at a British university ⟨they are not educated: they are only college *passmen* —G.B. Shaw⟩

pass master *n* [¹*pass*] **:** an officer under the old English poor laws having the duty of passing vagrant or nonresident paupers on to their own parishes or unions

pass off *vt* **1 :** to make public or offer for sale with intent to deceive **:** present fraudulently ⟨*passed* it *off* as a genuine antique⟩ ⟨*passed off* paste as jewels⟩ **2 :** to give a false identity or character to ⟨*passes* himself *off* as a learned man⟩ ~ *vi* **1 :** to disappear by degrees **:** go away gradually ⟨the numbness will *pass off* in a few hours⟩ **2 :** to last through to completion ⟨the rest of the evening *passed off* badly —Hamilton Basso⟩ ⟨his stay in France *passed off* smoothly —*Times Lit. Supp.*⟩

pas·som·e·ter \pa'sämәd·ә(r)\ *n* [L *passus* step + E *-o-* + *-meter* — more at PACE] **:** an instrument shaped like a watch that is used to count the number of a person's steps — compare PEDOMETER

1passout \'ₛ,ₛ\ *or* **pass–out check** \'ₛ,ₛ-\ *n* -s [fr. the phrase *pass out*] **:** something (as a ticket) that permits one to pass out of or reenter a place (as a theater or ball park) to which admission has usu. been paid

2passout \"\ *n* -s [fr. the phrase *pass out*] **:** draw poker in which a player must either bet or drop out

pass out *vi* **1 a :** to lose consciousness ⟨was pretty well plastered, but he rarely got to the stage where he *passed out* —Myron Brinig⟩ ⟨three men *passed out* from heat exhaustion —F.J.Bell⟩ **b :** to go out of existence **:** DIE ⟨if it was going to *pass out,* I thought it ought to die as it had lived —Edmund Wilson⟩ **2** *Brit* **:** GRADUATE ⟨*passed out* when he was nineteen with a degree in chemistry —Nevil Shute⟩

passover \'ₛ,ₛₛ\ *n* -s [fr. the phrase *pass over;* fr. the exemption of the Israelites from the slaughter of the first-born in Egypt, Exod 12:23–27] **1** *usu cap* **:** an annual religious and spring agricultural festival of the Jews that commemorates the liberation of the Hebrews from slavery in Egypt and that begins on the evening of the 14th day of the month of Nisan and by extension includes the 8 days following or (as orig. and among reform Jews and in modern Israel) the 7 days following — called also *Pesach* **2 :** the sacrifice at the feast of the Passover **:** PASCHAL LAMB ⟨Christ our ~ is sacrificed for us —1 Cor 5:7 (AV)⟩

pass over *vt* **1 :** to ignore in passing **:** deliberately fail to notice ⟨I will *pass over* this aspect of the book in silence⟩ **2 :** to pay no attention to the claims of **:** DISREGARD ⟨though he was next in line for the post, the committee *passed* him *over*⟩

1pass·port \'pas,pō(ә)r|t, 'paas-, 'pais-, -pȯ(ә)r|, -ōә|, -ȯ(ә)|, *usu* |d.+V\ *n* [MF *passeport,* fr. *passer* to pass + *port* port, fr. L *portus* — more at FORD] **1 a :** a formal document issued by a competent officer (as a secretary of state) of a country to a citizen of the country and now usu. necessary for exit from and reentry into the country, that certifies to the identity and citizenship of the bearer, calls upon the officers of foreign governments to extend protection to him when needed, and allows him to travel within the borders of a foreign country when it has been endorsed with a visa by an authorized official of that country **b :** SEA LETTER **c :** a license issued by a country permitting a foreign citizen to pass or take goods through its territory **:** SAFE-CONDUCT **d :** a document of identification required by the laws of a country to be carried by persons residing or traveling within that country ⟨in Germany the labor ~*s* were compulsory only for persons under twenty-one —Manya Gordon⟩ **2 a :** a permission or authorization to go somewhere ⟨held that good works were a ~ to heaven —R.M.Lovett⟩ ⟨the composer managed to write a concerto . . . which proved to be his ~ to Paris —Howard Dietz⟩ **b :** something that introduces or guarantees **:** VOUCHER **c :** something that secures admission or acceptance **:** a means of entry into some group, society, or condition of life ⟨may cultivate art as a culture, as a ~ to more exclusive circles of society —Herbert Read⟩ ⟨trained intellect was henceforth to be a young man's best ~ —G.M.Trevelyan⟩ ⟨a ~ to fame⟩

2passport \"\ *vt* -ED/-ING/-S **:** to provide with a passport

pass·port·less \-tlәs\ *adj* **:** having no passport

pass shooting *n* **:** the shooting of birds (as wild ducks) when they pass over a particular course

pass stroke *n* **:** a stroke in croqueting that sends the player's ball farther in the same direction than the other ball

pass–through \'ₛ,ₛ\ *n* -s [fr. the phrase *pass through*] **:** an opening in a wall between two rooms of a house or apartment (as between a kitchen and dining room) through which something (as dishes) may be passed

passt–mir–nicht \'päst,mi(ә)r'nikt\ *n* -s [G *passt mir nicht* does not suit me] **:** a player's right to reject the first card turned in the game of tournee and let the second card establish the trump suit

pass up *vt* **:** to let go by **:** DECLINE **:** DISREGARD **:** REJECT ⟨*passed up* an invitation to dinner⟩ ⟨*passed up* a chance for promotion⟩

pas·sus \'pasәs\ *n, pl* **passus** *or* **passuses** [ML, passage in a book or document, fr. L, step — more at PACE] **:** a division or part of a narrative or poem

passwalk \'ₛ,ₛ\ *n* [part trans. of G *passgang*] **:** PASSGANG

passway \'ₛ,ₛ\ *n* [*1pass* + *way*] **:** a means of passage **:** PASS

password \'ₛ,ₛ\ *n* **1 a :** a word or phrase that must be spoken by a person before he is allowed to pass a barrier or guard **:** COUNTERSIGN **b :** something that enables one to pass or gain admission ⟨food in any form was the magic ~ to her heart —Evelyn Barkins⟩ **2 :** a secret word or formula used as a sign of greeting or recognition among members of a society or group **:** WATCHWORD ⟨has the usual grips and ~*s* —C.W.Ferguson⟩

passymeasure *n* [modif. (influenced by *measure*) of It *passo e mezzo* — more at PASSAMEZZO] *obs* **:** PASSAMEZZO

1past \'past, 'paa(ә)st, 'paist, 'pȧst\ *adj* [ME *passed, past,* fr. past part. of *passen* to pass] **1 a :** gone by **:** AGO ⟨started working on this project ten years ~⟩ **b :** just gone by or elapsed **:** immediately preceding ⟨the oily swell of the ~ storm —Norman Douglas⟩ ⟨had been sitting in the darkness for nearly an hour ~ —Lucien Price⟩ ⟨the ~ election⟩ ⟨the ~ few months⟩ **c** *archaic* **:** of the past month ⟨your letter of the 30th ~ —Earl of Chesterfield⟩ **2 :** belonging to a former time **:** having existed or taken place in a period before the present **:** BYGONE ⟨in explanation and defense of his own ~ acts —W.C.Ford⟩ ⟨lived in some ~ world, two or three hundred years ago —R.W.Emerson⟩ **3 :** of, relating to, or constituting a verb tense that in English is usu. formed by internal vowel change (as in *sang*) or by the addition of a suffix (as in *laughed*) and that is expressive of time gone by **4 :** having served as a specified officer in a society, order, or organization ⟨~ president⟩ ⟨~ commander⟩ ⟨~ medical director⟩

2past \"\ *prep* [ME *passed, past,* fr. past part. of *passen*] **1 a :** beyond the age for or of ⟨my father was just ~ his first vote —Ben Riker⟩ ⟨~ playing with dolls⟩ **b :** later than **:** AFTER ⟨it was now ~ sunset —Lucien Price⟩ ⟨~ the turn of the year —*Atlantic*⟩ ⟨a quarter ~ two⟩ **c :** older than ⟨is now ~ 60⟩ ⟨is just ~ four⟩ **2 a :** at the farther side of **:** BEYOND ⟨the entrance to the dining room is just ~ the elevators on your right —Hamilton Basso⟩ **b :** in a course going close to and then beyond ⟨women pushed ~ arguing men to reach the counter —Stuart Cloete⟩ ⟨the railroad runs ~ the house⟩ **c :** in a direction going close to and then beyond ⟨standing by the monument and gazing down the grassy aisle ~ the heaps of crumpled chimney stones —Frederick Nebel⟩ **3** *obs* **:** more than ⟨has not ~ three or four hairs on his chin —Shak.⟩ **4 a :** beyond the reach or influence of **:** out of the range, scope, or sphere of **:** incapable of ⟨has declined ~ all help —*Sat. Eve. Post*⟩ ⟨had a way with a horse that was ~ explaining —Gerald Beaumont⟩ ⟨a dilemma ~ solution —Jean Stafford⟩ **b :** beyond the capacity or power of ⟨wouldn't put it ~ him to play a trick like that⟩ **c :** beyond in degree or manner ⟨has gone far ~ other writers in his experiments with language⟩ — **past oneself** *dial Eng* **:** beside oneself

3past \"\ *n* -s [*1past*] **1 a :** former time **:** time gone by ⟨men will turn to the ~ then, as we should now, chiefly to discover the ways of avoiding error —Harlow Shapley⟩ **b :** something that happened or was done in the past ⟨promised to atone for the ~⟩ **2 a :** the past tense of a language **b :** a verb form in the past tense **3 a :** a past life, history, or course of action ⟨for ancient families with chequered ~*s* he had a romantic reverence —John Buchan⟩ **b :** a past life or career that is unknown or deliberately kept secret; *esp* **:** a concealed episode or history of criminal or immoral behavior ⟨his ~ caught up with him when an old prison friend recognized him⟩ ⟨a woman with a ~⟩

4past \"\ *adv* [*2past*] **1 :** so as to reach and go by a point near at hand **:** BY ⟨every moment or so, the trains clank ~ —Hollis Alpert⟩ ⟨counted all eight porters coming ~ —D.L. Busk⟩ **2** *Scot & Irish* **:** ASIDE, AWAY ⟨lay them ~ to rust —William Carleton⟩

pas·ta \'pästә\ *n* -s [It, fr. LL, dough, paste — more at PASTE] **1 :** alimentary paste in processed form (as spaghetti or macaroni) or in the form of fresh dough (as ravioli) **2 :** a dish of cooked pasta

past absolute *n* [*3past* + *absolute,* adj.] **:** PAST TENSE a

pasta fi·la·ta cheese \-fē'läd·ә-\ *n* [It *pasta filata,* lit., spun pasta] **:** a cheese characterized by plasticity of the curd while it is being worked and molded ⟨provolone and mozzarella are *pasta filata cheeses*⟩

pas·tance \'pastәn(t)s\ *n* -s [modif. of MF *passe-temps,* fr. *passer* to pass + *temps* time, fr. L *tempus* — more at TEMPORAL] *archaic* **:** PASTIME

past continuous *n* **:** PAST TENSE b

past descriptive *n* **:** PAST TENSE b

past–due \'ₛ,ₛ\ *adj* **:** OVERDUE

1paste \'pāst\ *n* -s [ME, fr. MF, fr. LL *pasta* dough, paste, perh. fr. Gk *pastē* barley sauce, fr. fem. of *pastos* sprinkled, salted, fr. *passein* to sprinkle — more at QUASH] **1 a** (1) **:** a dough containing a large proportion of fat that is used for pastry crust (2) **:** a dough containing a moderate proportion of fat that is used for fancy rolls (as brioches) **b :** a confection made by evaporating fruit with sugar or by flavoring a gelatin, starch, or gum arabic preparation **c :** a soft or doughy mixture used as bait in fishing **d :** a smooth food product made by evaporation or grinding ⟨almond ~⟩ ⟨tomato ~⟩ ⟨sardine ~⟩ **e** [trans. of It *pasta*] **:** ALIMENTARY PASTE **2 :** a soft plastic mixture or composition**:** as **a** (1) **:** a preparation usu. of flour or starch and water used as a cement for uniting paper or other substances (as in bookbinding) (2) **:** a similar preparation used in calico printing as a vehicle for mordant or color **b :** a moistened clay mixture that is used in making pottery or porcelain — see HARD PASTE, SOFT PASTE **c :** an external medicament that has a stiffer consistency than an ointment but is less greasy because of its higher percentage of powdered ingredients **d :** a mixture of a pigment and a paint vehicle that requires the addition of more vehicle before it can be used **e :** a mixture of cement and water **:** the cement and water portion of mortar or concrete **3 :** MATERIAL, STUFF ⟨a man of a different ~ —Robert Browning⟩ **4 :** a brilliant glass of high lead content used for the manufacture of artificial gems; *also* **:** an imitation gem made of this material — called also *strass*

2paste \"\ *vb* -ED/-ING/-S *vt* **1 a :** to cause to adhere by or as if by means of paste **:** STICK ⟨a poster that had just been *pasted* on a pillar of the general post office —O.S.J.Gogarty⟩ ⟨a wry grin *pasted* onto his dirty face —William Chamberlain⟩ **b :** SPREAD ⟨gave him bread, and *pasted* the butter upon it very thickly —Louis Golding⟩ ⟨the lamps along the river *pasted* long oily golden tracks on the water —R.H.Newman⟩ **2 a :** to cover by or as if by pasting ⟨the ceiling is *pasted* with labels of liquor brands —*This Week in Chicago*⟩ **b :** to repair (a target) for reuse by pasting paper over bullet holes **3 :** to incorporate (as a color in dyeing) with a paste **:** apply paste to **4 :** to convert into a paste ⟨the dry powder is first *pasted* with cold water —*Encyc. of Chem. Technol.*⟩ ~ *vi* **:** to apply paste **:** paste something

3paste \"\ *n* -s [modif. of MF *passe,* part of a woman's hat that shades the face, fr. *passer* to pass] **:** a woman's ornamental headdress of the 16th century

4paste \"\ *vt* -ED/-ING/-S [alter. of *baste* (to beat)] **1 :** to hit hard **:** PUNCH ⟨brutally *pasting* him into a blubbering wreck —Hartley Howard⟩ **2 :** to strike hard at **:** deliver a blow or series of blows against ⟨that time they *pasted* the command post —Fred Majdalany⟩

5paste \"\ *n* -s **:** a hard blow or punch ⟨a ~ in the jaw⟩

1pasteboard \'ₛ,ₛ\ *n* [*2paste* + *board*] **1 :** paperboard made by pasting together two or more sheets or plies; *broadly* **:** paperboard esp. when comparatively thin and stiff **2 a :** VISITING CARD **b :** PLAYING CARD **c :** a railroad ticket or a ticket of admission (as to a theater or ball park) **3** [*1paste* + *board*] **:** a board on which dough is rolled **:** BREADBOARD ⟨a snowy cloth with ~ and rolling pin upon it —Flora Thompson⟩ **4 :** a board on which a paperhanger or a paster lays the paper or work to be pasted

2pasteboard \"\ *adj* **1 :** made of pasteboard ⟨a ~ box⟩ **2 :** of inferior material, construction, or quality **:** FLIMSY, SHAM, UNSUBSTANTIAL ⟨the glittering but ~ life of the palace —F. Tennyson Jesse⟩ ⟨~ romanticism —V.S.Pritchett⟩

pasted *adj* [fr. past part. of *2paste*] **:** fastened or covered with or as if with paste

pastedown \'ₛ,ₛ\ *n* -s **:** the outer leaf of an endpaper that is pasted down to the inside of the front or back cover of a book

paste filler *n* [*1paste*] **:** a compound of silica and drying oil used as a filler for open grain wood (as oak)

paste grain *n* **:** a thin leather (as sheepskin) with an application of paste on the back to stiffen and strengthen it

1pas·tel \(')pa¦stel\ *n* -s [MF, fr. Prov, fr. LL *pastellus* woad, dim. of LL *pasta* paste; fr. the paste made of its twigs in producing the dye] **:** WOAD

2pastel \"\ *n* -s [F, fr. It *pastello,* fr. LL *pastellus*] **1 :** a paste composed of a color ground and compounded with an aqueous binder and used for making crayons; *also* **:** a crayon made of such paste **2 a :** a drawing in pastel **b :** the process or art of drawing with pastels **3 :** a light, brief, and rather formless literary study or sketch **4 :** any of various pale or light colors ⟨its colors lost their infernal intensity, paled to harmless-looking but deadly ~*s* —*Time*⟩

3pastel \"\ *adj* **1 :** of or relating to a pastel **:** made with pastels ⟨a ~ drawing⟩ **2 :** pale and light in color **:** lacking in brilliance or intensity ⟨~ shades⟩ ⟨a ~ prettiness⟩ **3 :** resembling a pastel **:** lacking in body or vigor **:** DELICATE, LIGHT ⟨a ~ and dreamy world — rather thin and bloodless —J.F.Nims⟩ ⟨a tendency to suffuse with a ~ optimism even the dark moments —Leon Edel⟩

pastel blue *n* **1 :** a variable color averaging a pale blue that is redder and stronger than average powder blue and greener, lighter, and stronger than Sistine or average cadet gray **2** *of textiles* **:** a very pale blue that is redder and duller than baby blue (sense 1) and redder and deeper than cloud blue

pastel gray *n* **:** a grayish yellow that is paler and slightly redder than chamois and redder, lighter, and stronger than old ivory

pastel green *n* **:** a variable color averaging a light yellowish green that is paler than apple green (sense 2), greener and paler than pistachio green, and greener and duller than ocean green

pas·tel·ist *or* **pas·tel·list** \-lәst\ *n* -s **:** a maker of pastel drawings

pastel orange *n* **:** a moderate orange that is yellower and duller than honeydew, duller and slightly yellower than Persian orange, and redder and duller than mikado orange

pastel pink *n* **1 :** a moderate yellowish pink that is redder and lighter than coral pink, redder, lighter, and stronger than dusty pink, and redder and stronger than average peach **2** *of textiles* **:** a moderate pink that is yellower and less strong than arbutus pink and bluer and stronger than hydrangea pink

pastel turquoise green *n* **:** a light bluish green that is greener and paler than average turquoise green or average aqua green (sense 1) and bluer and lighter than robin's-egg blue (sense 2)

pastel yellow *n* **:** a variable color averaging a light greenish yellow that is redder and paler than sulphur yellow and redder, darker, and slightly less strong than Martius yellow

paste mold *n* [*1paste*] **:** an iron mold lined with adherent carbon that is used wet to shape a circular glass object as it is blown

paste paper *n* **:** a patterned or textured paper made by applying brushes and hand tools to the surface of a paper that has been coated with thin colored paste and is still wet

pastepot *n* **:** a small container of paste that is ready to use

paste print *n* **:** an impression made in glutinous ink or upon a thick paste from a white-line engraving or metal cut

past·er \'pāstә(r)\ *n* -s **1 :** one that pastes**:** as **a :** a worker who stretches leather for drying by pasting it smoothly on boards or plates **b :** a worker who arranges floor tiles into a form board according to a sketched design and pastes a sheet of paper to the top to preserve the pattern **c :** LUTER **d :** a machine that applies paste **2 :** a slip of paper with a gummed back designed to be pasted on something **:** STICKER

pas·tern \'pastә(r)n\ *n* -s [MF *pasturon,* fr. *pasture* pasture, tether attached to the foot of a horse at pasture, pastern — more at PASTURE] **:** a part of the foot of an equine that lies between the fetlock and the coffin joint; *broadly* **:** a corresponding part of the leg of other animals (as a dog) — see COW illustration

pastern bone *n* **:** either of two bones in the foot of an equine between the cannon bone and the coffin bone

pastern joint *n* **:** the joint between the great and small pastern bones

pastes *pl of* PASTE, *pres 3d sing of* PASTE

paste–up \'ₛ,ₛ\ *n* -s [*2paste*] **1 :** MECHANICAL; *also* **:** the process of preparing mechanicals **2 :** a literary work prepared for publication or production by the piecing together of material previously used ⟨this book is not a new work but a *paste-up* of old magazine articles⟩ **3 :** a picture made by pasting together parts of two or more photographs

pas·teur effect \pa'stәr-\ *n, usu cap P* [after Louis *Pasteur* †1895 Fr. chemist and bacteriologist] **:** the inhibiting effect of oxygen upon a fermentative process (as one carried on by facultative anaerobic organisms)

pas·teu·rel·la \,pastә'relә\ *n* [NL, fr. Louis *Pasteur* + NL *-ella*] **1** *cap* **:** a genus of bacteria (family Brucellaceae) that stain differentially at the poles of the cell and that include several important pathogens of man and domestic animals — see HEMORRHAGIC SEPTICEMIA, PLAGUE, TULAREMIA **2** *pl* **pasteurellas** *or* **pasteurellae :** any bacterium of the genus *Pasteurella*

pas·teu·rel·lo·sis \,pastәrә'lōsәs\ *n, pl* **pasteurello·ses** \-ō,sēz\ [NL, fr. *Pasteurella* + *-osis*] **:** infection with or disease caused by bacteria of the genus *Pasteurella* — see HEMORRHAGIC SEPTICEMIA

pas·teur·ian \pa'stәrēәn\ *adj, usu cap* [Louis *Pasteur* + E *-ian*] **:** of, relating to, or deriving from Pasteur

pas·teur·iza·tion \,pas(h)chәrә'zāshәn, -stәr-, -,rī'-\ *n* -s [*pasteurize* + *-ation*] **1 :** a method devised by Pasteur to check fermentation (as in wine or milk) involving the partial sterilization of a substance (as a fluid) at a temperature and for a length of time that does not greatly change its chemical composition but does destroy many pathogenic organisms and other undesirable bacteria though spores and thermoduric organisms (as lactic acid bacteria) survive **2 :** the use of electricity, hot water, or steam to bring soil (as in a greenhouse bench) to a temperature of 180°F for a period of 30 minutes in order to kill nematodes, weed seeds, and various fungi and bacteria — compare STERILIZATION

pas·teur·ize \'pas(h)chә,rīz, -stә-,-\ *vt* -ED/-ING/-S *see -ize in Explan Notes* [Louis *Pasteur* †1895 Fr. chemist and bacteriologist + E *-ize*] **:** to subject to pasteurization

pas·teur·iz·er \-zә(r)\ *n* -s **:** one that pasteurizes**:** as **a :** an apparatus for pasteurizing fluids **b :** a worker who does pasteurizing

pasteur treatment *n, usu cap P* [after Louis *Pasteur*] **:** a method devised by Pasteur of aborting rabies by stimulating production of antibodies during the long incubation period of the disease through successive inoculations with the virus in attenuated form gradually increasing in strength

paste wash *n* [*1paste* + *wash*] **:** a very thin paste that is applied to the reverse side of leather to shrink and strengthen it, put on the backbone lining of a book to facilitate its removal before rebinding, and sponged on the surface of porous leather to improve the gold tooling

paste–wash \'ₛ,ₛ\ *vt* [*paste wash*] **:** to apply paste wash to

1past future *adj* [*1past* + *future,* adj.] **:** of, relating to, or constituting a verb tense that is traditionally formed in English with *would* or *should* and denotes an action or state as future from a past point of view (as *would write* in "he promised that he would write")

2past future *n* **1 :** the past future tense of a language **2 :** a verb form in the past future tense

1past future perfect *adj* [*1past* + *future perfect,* adj.] **:** of, relating to, or constituting a verb tense that is traditionally formed in English with *would have* or *should have* and denotes an action or state completed at a time formerly in prospect (as *would have finished* in "on Monday I saw that by Friday he would have finished")

2past future perfect *n* **1 :** the past future perfect tense of a language **2 :** a verb form in the past future perfect tense

past historic *n* [*3past* + *historic*] **:** PAST TENSE a

pas·tic·cio \pa'stē(,)chō, pä'-\ *n, pl* **pastic·ci** \-ēchē\ *or* **pasticcios** [It, pasty, hodgepodge, pastiche, fr. ML *pasticius* pasty, fr. LL *pasta* paste] **:** PASTICHE

pas·tiche \(')pa'stēsh, (')pä'-\ *n* -s [F, fr. It *pasticcio*] **1 :** a literary, artistic, or musical work that closely and usu. deliberately imitates the style of previous work ⟨an excellent ~ from European models —H.S.Canby⟩ ⟨will continue to write poetic ~*s* of Euripides and Shakespeare —T.S.Eliot⟩ ⟨any closer approach to their technique would lead us into ~ —C.D.Lewis⟩ **2 a :** a musical composition or piece of writing (as an opera or play) made up of selections from different works **:** POTPOURRI ⟨ending up not with a research paper but a ~, one paragraph drawn from one source, the next section lifted from another source —W.W.Bleifuss⟩ ⟨are rather biblical ~ than biblical material: they are full of biblical phrases and variations upon well-known themes —H.G.G.Herklots⟩ **b :** a usu. incongruous medley of different styles and materials **:** HODGEPODGE ⟨the poem is a ~ of images, tones, and styles —*Western Rev.*⟩ ⟨a ~ of the customs of the developers and of the natural backgrounds —Gilbert McAllister⟩

pas·ti·cheur \,pastē'shәr, ,päs-\ *n* -s [F, fr. *pasticher* to make pastiches (fr. *pastiche*) + *-eur* -or] **:** one who makes pastiches

pastier *comparative of* PASTY

pastiest *superlative of* PASTY

pas·tille \pa'stēl, -til\ *also* **pas·til** *or* **pas·tile** \'pastәl\ *n* -s [F *pastille,* fr. L *pastillus* small loaf, lozenge; akin to L *panis* bread — more at FOOD] **1 :** a small cone or mass made of a paste of gum, benzoin, cinnamon, and other aromatics and used for fumigating or scenting the air of a room **2 :** an aromatic or medicated lozenge **:** TROCHE **3 :** a paper tube filled with combustible material that on ignition causes a pinwheel or other fireworks to revolve

pas·time \'pa,stīm, 'paa,-, 'pai,-, 'pȧ,-\ *n* -s [trans. of MF *passe-temps*] **1 :** something that amuses and serves to make time pass agreeably **:** DIVERSION, RECREATION ⟨would talk ominously for ~ —George Johnston⟩ ⟨indulged a taste for bookish ~ —*Times Lit. Supp.*⟩ **2 :** a specific form of amusement (as a game, hobby, or sport) ⟨gather around the plaza in ~*s* that bring the color of old Spain to the wilderness —*Amer. Guide Series: Oregon*⟩ ⟨the national ~⟩ ⟨defining public relations has been a favorite ~ —J.A.R.Pimlott⟩

pas·ti·na·ca \,pastә'nākә\ *n, cap* [NL, fr. L, parsnip, carrot — more at PARSNIP] **:** a genus of Eurasian mostly biennial herbs (family Umbelliferae) with pinnate leaves, compound umbels of yellow flowers, and very much flattened oval seeds — see PARSNIP

past·i·ness \'pāstēnәs\ *n* -ES **:** the quality or state of being pasty

1pasting *n* -s [fr. gerund of *2paste*] **1 pastings** *pl* **:** thin papers used for facing pasteboard **2 :** a tanning process for setting and drying leather by pasting the damp hide on boards or glass or metal plates **3** *or* **pasting–up** \'ₛₛ'ₛ\ **:** occlusion of the anus of a young chick by pasty masses of feces adherent to the down usu. associated with diarrhea

2pasting *n* -s [fr. gerund of *4paste*] **:** BEATING

past·less·ness \'pastlәsnәs\ *n* -ES **:** the quality or state of being without a past or a sense of the past

past master *n* [*1past* + *master*] **1 :** one who has held the office of worshipful master in a lodge of Freemasons or of master in a guild, club, or other society **2** [alter. (influenced by *1past*) of *passed master*] **:** one who is expert in some art, subject, or activity **:** a thorough master **:** ADEPT ⟨a *past master* at exploiting differences among his opposition —W.G.Hardy⟩

past mistress *n* [*past* (as in *past master*) + *mistress*] **:** a woman who is proficient or thorough in some particular respect **:** ADEPT ⟨a *past mistress* of storytelling —*Newsweek*⟩

past·ness \ˈpas(t)nəs\ *n* -ES **1 :** the quality or state of being past ⟨involves a perception, not only of the ~ of the past, but of its presence —T.S.Eliot⟩ **2 :** the subjective quality of something that is remembered as contrasted with what is currently experienced or anticipated ⟨impressed . . . with the ~ of the old life —Iris Barry⟩

pas·to \ˈpä(,)stō\ *n, pl* **pasto** *or* **pastos** *usu cap* **1 a :** a group of Barbacoan peoples of the province of Carchi, Ecuador **b :** a member of any people of such group **2 :** the language of the Pasto people

pas·to·pho·ri·um \,pastəˈfōrēəm\ *also* **pas·to·pho·ri·on** \-ē,än\ *n, pl* **pastopho·ria** \-ēə\ [LL, apartment of the bearer of the shrine, fr. Gk *pastophorion*, fr. *pastophoros* bearer of the shrine, fr. *pastos* shrine + *-phoros* -phore] **:** either of the two apartments at the sides of the bema that are found in contemporary Greek churches as well as in early Christian churches

¹pas·tor \ˈpastə(r), ˈpaas-, ˈpais-, ˈpås-, *for 1* päˈstȯ(ə)r\ *n* [ME *pastour*, fr. AF, fr. OF *pastur, pastor*, fr. L *pastor*, fr. *pastus* (past. part. of *pascere* to pasture, feed, graze) + *-or* — more at FOOD] **1** -S *chiefly Southwest* **:** HERDSMAN, SHEPHERD **2** -S **a :** a spiritual overseer; *esp* **:** a clergyman serving a local church or parish ⟨the model of an eighteenth-century parish priest, scholar and squire and ~ of souls —Havelock Ellis⟩ **b :** one who gives protection or guidance to a group of people **3 a** *cap* [NL, fr. L] *in some classifications* **:** a genus of starlings that includes only the rose-colored starling and is now usu. incorporated in the genus *Sturnus* **b** -S **:** ROSE-COLORED STARLING **4** -S **:** MAN-OF-WAR FISH

²pastor \"\ *vt* -ED/-ING/-S **:** to serve as pastor to

pas·tor·age \-t(ə)rij\ *n* -S [¹*pastor* + *-age*] **:** PASTORATE

¹pas·to·ral \-rəl\ *n* -S **1 a** [ME, fr. LL *pastoralis* of a pastor (in *Cura Pastoralis*, title of St. Gregory I's work on pastoral care)] **:** a book or treatise on the duties of pastors **b** [²*pastoral*] **:** a letter of a pastor to his charge: as (1) **:** a letter addressed by a bishop to his diocese (2) **:** a letter of the House of Bishops of the Protestant Episcopal Church to be read in each parish **c** *usu cap* **:** PASTORAL EPISTLE — usu. used in pl. with *the* **2** [trans. of L *bucolicum*] **a :** a literary work (as a poem or play) dealing with the life of shepherds or rural life generally in a usu. artificial manner and frequently archaic style, typically drawing a conventional contrast between the innocence and serenity of the simple life and the misery and corruption of city and esp. court life, and often using the characters as vehicles for the expression of the author's moral, social, or literary views ⟨jaded and oversophisticated denizens of towns devote themselves to ~s —J.L.Lowes⟩ — compare IDYLL **b :** pastoral poetry or drama as a literary form or style ⟨the best actors in the world, either for tragedy, comedy, history, ~ —Shak.⟩ **c :** a pastoral or rural picture or scene **d :** PASTORALE **3** *or* **pastoral staff** [prob. fr. It *pastorale*, fr. LL *pastoralis* of a pastor, fr. L, of a shepherd] **:** CROSIER

²pastoral \"\ *adj* [ME, fr. L *pastoralis*, fr. *pastor* herdsman, shepherd + *-alis* -al] **1 a** (1) **:** of, relating to, or composed of shepherds or herdsmen ⟨a ~ people, seminomadic in their habits —J.M.Mogey⟩ ⟨~ simplicity⟩ (2) **:** devoted to or based upon the raising of sheep or cattle ⟨third-class ~ land, having a 10-in. rainfall and all held as sheep stations —T.A. Miles⟩ ⟨a ~ economy⟩ **b :** of or relating to the countryside as contrasted with the city **:** RURAL ⟨charming in its ~ setting amid these cultivated uplands —*Amer. Guide Series: Vt.*⟩ **c :** portraying or expressive of the life of shepherds or country people esp. in an idealized and conventionalized manner ⟨~ poetry⟩ ⟨~ drama⟩ ⟨a ~ symphony⟩ **d :** INNOCENT, IDYLLIC ⟨the ~ legends of America's golden age —August Heckscher⟩ ⟨waiting through a long, ~ afternoon —*Time*⟩ **2 a** (1) **:** of or relating to the spiritual care of a congregation or group of Christians ⟨~ duties⟩ ⟨a ~ letter⟩ (2) **:** of or relating to the pastor of a church ⟨observed that this represented a congregational and not a ~ reluctance to participate —*Episcopal Churchnews*⟩ **b :** of or relating to spiritual care or guidance esp. as carried on through visiting and counseling ⟨a missionary, or at least ~ activity on the part of the teacher —N.G. Fisher⟩ ⟨it was her custom to pay ~ calls at the residences of her pupils —Frances G. Patton⟩ — **pas·to·ral·ly** \-rəlē, -li\ *adv* — **pas·to·ral·ness** *n* -ES

pas·to·rale \,pastəˈräl, -ral *sometimes* -ˈalē\ *n* -S [It, fr. *pastorale* of herdsmen, fr. L *pastoralis*] **1 a :** an opera of the 16th or 17th centuries combining singing and dancing and having a pastoral plot **b :** an instrumental or vocal composition having a pastoral theme **2 :** PASTORAL 2a ⟨a ~, written in homely, muted prose, about life on a farm —*New Yorker*⟩

pastoral epistle *n* -S *usu cap P & E* **:** one of three New Testament letters including two addressed to Timothy and one to Titus and giving advice on matters of church government and discipline

pas·to·ral·ism \ˈpast(ə)rə,lizəm, ˈpaas-, ˈpais-, ˈpås-\ *n* -S **1 :** the quality or style characteristic of pastoral writing **2 a :** HERDING **b :** social organization based upon herding as the primary economic activity

pas·to·ral·ist \-ləst\ *n* -S **1 :** a writer of pastorals **2 a :** a breeder and pasturer of sheep or cattle **b** *chiefly Austral* **:** a station holder who raises livestock and does little or no farming

pas·to·ral·i·ty \,pastəˈraləd·ē\ *n* -ES **:** something pastoral **:** a pastoral object or quality

pas·to·ral·iza·tion \,pastərələˈzāshən\ *n* -S **:** the act or process of making pastoral; *specif* **:** the conversion of an industrial country into a pastoral one ⟨carrying industrial disarmament to the point of ~ —A.O.Wolfers⟩

pas·to·ral·ize \ˈpast(ə)rə,līz\ *vt* -ED/-ING/-S *see -ize in Explan Notes* **1 :** to render pastoral or rural; *specif* **:** to convert to a pastoral economy or social organization ⟨his famous proposal to ~ the country —Robert Lekachman⟩ **2 :** to put into a pastoral or into the pastoral form

pastoral prayer *n* **:** the chief prayer of a church service typically including thanksgiving, supplication, and intercession

pastoral theology *n* **:** the study of the theological bases as well as the practical implications of the professional activities of religious workers

pas·tor·ate \ˈpast(ə)rət, ˈpaas-, ˈpais-, ˈpås-, *usu* -əd·+V\ *n* -S [ML *pastoratus*, fr. LL *pastor* pastor (fr. L, shepherd) + L *-atus* -ate] **1 a :** the office, state, jurisdiction, or tenure of office of a pastor **b :** a body of pastors **2 :** PARSONAGE

pastored *past of* PASTOR

pastoring *pres 3d sing of* PASTOR

pas·to·ri·um \paˈstōrēəm, -tȯr-\ *n* -S [irreg. fr. ¹*pastor* + *-orium*] *chiefly South* **:** a Protestant parsonage

pas·tor·less \ˈpastə(r)ləs\ *adj* **:** having no pastor

pas·tor·ly \-lē\ *adj* **:** of, relating to, or appropriate to a pastor

pastors *pl of* PASTOR, *pres 3d sing of* PASTOR

pas·tor·ship \-(r),ship\ *n* [¹*pastor* + *-ship*] **:** PASTORATE 1

pastos *pl of* PASTO

pas·tose \(ˈ)paˈstōs\ *adj* [It *pastoso* doughy, soft, fr. *pasta* dough, paste (fr. LL) + *-oso* -ose — more at PASTE] **:** painted thickly **:** covered or filled with paint — **pas·tose·ly** *adv* — **pas·tos·i·ty** \paˈstäsəd·ē\ *n* -ES

pas·tou·relle *also* **pas·to·relle** \,pastəˈrel\ *n* -S [F, young shepherdess, shepherdess's song, fem. dim. of OF *pastour* shepherd, fr. L *pastor* — more at PASTOR] **:** a conventional form of poetic pastoral composed in French during the late middle ages and Renaissance and consisting of a love debate between a knight and a shepherdess

past participle *n* **:** a participle that typically expresses completed action, that is traditionally one of the principal parts of the verb, and that is traditionally used in English in the formation of perfect tenses in the active voice and of all tenses in the passive voice and has a perfect active meaning when the verb sense is intransitive (as *arrived* in "the ship, arrived at last, signals for a tug") and usu. a passive meaning when the verb sense is transitive (as *buffeted* in "the ship, buffeted by waves, comes shoreward") and with participial auxiliaries may take a present passive form (as in *being written*), a perfect active form (as in *having written*), or a perfect passive form (as in *having been written*) — called also *perfect participle*

¹past perfect *adj* [¹*past* + *perfect*, adj.] **:** of, relating to, or constituting a verb tense that is traditionally formed in English with *had* and denotes an action or state as completed at or before a past time spoken of (as *had left* in "when he arrived I had left for the city")

²past perfect *n* **1 :** the past perfect tense of a language **2 :** a verb form in the past perfect tense

pas·tra·mi \pəˈsträmē, -mi\ *n* -S [Yiddish, fr. Romanian *pastramă*, fr. *păstra* to preserve, perh. fr. (assumed) VL *parsitare* to spare, fr. L *parsus*, past part. of *parcere* to spare — more at PARSIMONY] **:** a highly seasoned smoked beef prepared esp. from shoulder cuts

pas·try \ˈpāstrē, -ri\ *n* -ES *often attrib* [¹*paste* + *-ry*] **1 a :** sweet baked goods made of dough or having a crust made of enriched dough ⟨French ~⟩ ⟨Danish ~⟩ **b :** a piece of such baked goods ⟨had a ~ and a glass of milk⟩ **c :** PASTE 1a **2** *obs* **:** a place where pastry is made ⟨they call for dates and quinces in the ~ —Shak.⟩

pastry bag *n* **:** a funnel-shaped container for holding soft food mixtures (as mashed potatoes, icing, or whipped cream) from which the foods are forced through a pastry tube at the tip in making ornamental spreads or decorations

pastry blender *n* **:** a device consisting of a handle with wires fastened to each end so that they form a deep curve that is used in cutting fat into flour in pastry making

pastry blender

pastrycook \ˈ=,=\ *n* **1 :** one who is employed (as by a hotel or restaurant) to make pastry **2 :** one who makes pastry for public sale

pastry flour *n* **:** a flour usu. manufactured from soft wheat low in gluten content and milled very fine that is esp. suitable for making pastry and cake

pastry fork *n* **:** a fork with four tines usu. including one with a cutting edge

pastry tube *n* **:** a usu. metal tip that is attached to the opening of a pastry bag and that is often shaped to form a specific pattern (as a star)

pasts *pl of* PAST

past service *n* [¹*past*] **:** the period of a worker's employment prior to the effective date of a pension plan for which credit is given in determining the amount of his pension

past tense *n* **:** a verb tense expressing action or state in or as if in the past: **a :** a verb tense expressive of time gone by (as *wrote* in "on arriving I wrote a letter") — called also *past absolute, past historic* **b :** a verb tense expressing action or state in progress or continuance or habitually done or customarily occurring at a past time (as *was writing* in "I was writing while he dictated" or *loved* in "their sons loved fishing") — called also *past continuous, past descriptive*

pas·tur·able \ˈpas(h)chərəbəl, ˈpaas-, ˈpais-, ˈpås-\ *adj* [partly fr. ¹*pasture* + *-able*, partly fr. ²*pasture* + *-able*] **:** fit for or affording pasture

pas·tur·age \-rij\ *n* -S [MF *pasturer* to pasture + *-age*] **1 a :** grazing land **:** HERBAGE, PASTURE ⟨its promise of fine ~ for sheep —*Amer. Guide Series: Oregon*⟩ **b :** a natural accumulation of food plants ⟨algal ~ of the sea⟩ ⟨bee ~⟩ **2 :** the act or process of pasturing **:** GRAZING ⟨two sample bills, one for irrigation districts, the other for cooperative ~ —Mari Sandoz⟩ **3** *Scots law* **:** the right of pasturing cattle or sheep on a common or another's land

pas·tur·al \-rəl\ *adj* [LL *pastura* pasture + E *-al*] **:** of or relating to pasture

¹pas·ture \-chə(r)\ *n* -S *often attrib* [ME, fr. MF, fr. LL *pastura*, fr. L *pastus* (past part. of *pascere* to pasture, feed, graze) + *-ura* -ure — more at FOOD] **1 a :** grass or other plants grown for the feeding of grazing animals **:** HERBAGE ⟨grows quickly and makes excellent ~ for cattle⟩ **b** *archaic* **:** FOOD, NOURISHMENT **2 a** (1) **:** land that is used for the grazing of animals or is suitable for such use ⟨makes me lie down in green ~s —Ps 23:2 (RSV)⟩ ⟨buffalo ~s on the prairie —R.L. Neuberger⟩ (2) **:** a lot used for grazing ⟨a small, fenced-in holding ~ —John Bird⟩ ⟨his lease was cut into two separate ~s —F.B.Gipson⟩ (3) **:** a large enclosed section of a cattle ranch **b :** FEEDING GROUND ⟨whales, like seals, feed in different ~s at different seasons —*Nat'l Geographic*⟩ **c :** a scene of activity ⟨people in more distant ~s, even in literature and science —Dallas Finn⟩ **d :** a place or state of retirement ⟨eased out and retired to ~ to make room for the younger man —James Jones⟩ **3 :** the feeding of livestock **:** GRAZING ⟨only about 19 percent is used for the ~ of animals —P.E.James⟩

²pasture \"\ *vb* -ED/-ING/-S [ME *pasturen*, fr. MF *pasturer*, fr. *pasture*, n.] *vi* **1 :** to feed on growing grass or herbage **:** GRAZE ⟨men and women holding cows on a rope in a field while the cows *pastured* —Arnold Bennett⟩ **2 :** to feed as if in a pasture ⟨the very early morning when the animals are *pasturing* on the seaweed —*Nautilus*⟩ ~ *vt* **1 :** FEED, NOURISH ⟨a sufficiently unwashed citizen may ~ more than ten thousand lice at one time —Gove Hambidge⟩ **2 a :** to cause or permit to feed on growing grass **:** put out to pasture ⟨*pastured* his cattle on the open range⟩ **b :** to supply growing grass as food for **:** let graze ⟨rich grassland that could ~ many cattle⟩ **3 a :** to eat down in grazing ⟨the field was *pastured* bare⟩ **b :** to put livestock to graze on **:** use as pasture ⟨a conflict between those who wanted to farm the land and those who wanted to ~ it⟩ ⟨some growers ~ young sweet clover as soon as the plants are large enough —D.C.McIntosh & D.M.Orr⟩ **syn** see FEED

pasture bird *n* **1 :** GOLDEN PLOVER **2 :** VESPER SPARROW

pasture breeding *n* **:** uncontrolled mating within a flock or herd — opposed to *hand breeding*

pasture cockchafer *or* **pasture scarab** *n* **:** any of several scarabaeid beetles esp. of the genus *Aphodius*

pasture gooseberry *n* **:** a wild gooseberry (*Ribes cynosbati*)

pasture grub *n* **:** the larva of a pasture cockchafer

pastureland \ˈ=,=,=\ *n* **:** PASTURE 2a(1)

pas·tur·er \-chərə(r)\ *n* -S **:** one that pastures livestock

pasture rose *n* **:** a prickly shrub (*Rosa carolina*) of eastern No. America that has compound leaves, showy pink flowers, and globose sticky hairy fruit

pasture thistle *n* **:** an American thistle (*Cirsium pumilum*) that has large heads of purple flowers

¹pas·ty \ˈpastē, ˈpās-, -ti\ *n* -ES [ME *pastee, paste, pastey*, fr. MF *pasté*, fr. *paste* dough — more at PASTE] **:** a pie consisting of a meat and vegetable mixture or fruit filling wholly surrounded with a crust made of a sheet of paste dough and often baked without a dish — see CORNISH PASTY; compare TURNOVER

²pasty \ˈpāstē, -ti\ *adj, usu* -ER/-EST [¹*paste* + *-y*] **1 :** resembling paste (as in color or consistency); *esp* **:** pallid and unhealthy in appearance ⟨his complexion was always ~, but for the last few nights it had been a chalky white —Agnes S. Turnbull⟩ **2 :** SICKLY ⟨the ~ little books that circulate from beneath the counter —Curtis Bok⟩

pasty-faced \ˈ=,=,=\ *adj* [²*pasty*] **:** having a chalky unwholesome appearance suggestive of lack of exercise or fresh air ⟨the *pasty-faced* indoor cop leading me to jail —Gilbert Millstein⟩

pa·sul \pəˈsül, ˈpō,sül\ *adj* [Heb *pāsūl* disqualified] **:** declared unfit for Jewish ceremonial use according to rabbinic law **:** DEFECTIVE

pa system *n, usu cap P&A* **:** PUBLIC-ADDRESS SYSTEM

¹pat \ˈpat, *usu* -ad·+V\ *n* -S [ME *patte*, prob. of imit. origin] **1 a :** a blow esp. with the hand or a flat or blunt instrument **b :** a light blow or tap given to shape or smooth ⟨a few final ~s around the newly planted flower⟩ **c :** a tap with the hand given in affection or approval ⟨with a quick reassuring ~ on her arm, their hostess left —Harriet La Barre⟩ **2 :** a light tapping sound esp. if rhythmical ⟨the ~ of bare feet⟩ **3 :** something (as butter) shaped into a small flat usu. square piece and served as an individual portion **:** DAB **4 :** a dropping of animal dung ⟨the most satisfactory control measure consists of scattering the cow ~s —Eric Hearle⟩ **5 :** an American Negro dance tune in time with which onlookers often pat their knees or thighs

²pat \"\ *vb* **patted; patted; patting; pats** *vt* **1 :** to hit with a flat or blunt implement **2 a :** to flatten, smooth, or put into place or shape with light strokes (as of the hand) ⟨women *patted* up tortillas by their stalls —G.A.Wagner⟩ **b :** to beat or slap lightly ⟨at 70 miles an hour, pontoons ~ the waves — Jim Wright⟩ **3 :** to stroke or tap gently with the hand to soothe, caress, or show approval ⟨had been *patted* on the head by . . . the city's founder —Alan Carmichael⟩ ~ *vi* **1 a :** to strike or beat gently ⟨snowflakes were *patting* against the windowpane —J.B.Clayton⟩ **b :** to tap lightly and quickly with the soles of the feet (as in dancing a jig) **2 :** to walk or run so as to make a light beating sound ⟨in summer she *patted* away to school —Hamlin Garland⟩ **3** *dial* **:** to keep time to dance music by patting the knee or thigh — **pat juba :** to perform the rhythmic accompaniment to a juba with hands or feet — **pat on the back :** APPLAUD, APPROVE, ENCOURAGE ⟨made speeches to him, *patted* him *on the back*, told him what a priceless fellow he was —H.A.Overstreet⟩

³pat \"\ *adv* **:** in a pat manner **:** APTLY, READILY, PROMPTLY

⁴pat \"\ *adj* **1 a :** exactly suited to the purpose or occasion **:** APT, OPPORTUNE ⟨this ~ tale got a big laugh —Dorothy Barclay⟩ **b :** too exactly suitable **:** CONTRIVED, FACILE, GLIB ⟨his characters flatten out, and his conclusions become annoyingly ~ — Nicolas Monjo⟩ **2 :** learned, mastered, or memorized exactly or with ready or fluent command ⟨didn't say that prayer over twice before he had it ~ —H.G.Wells⟩ **3 :** FIRM, UNYIELDING — usu. used in the phrase *to stand pat* ⟨a major issue on which it has stood ~ since the matter first arose —*Sydney (Australia) Bull.*⟩ **syn** see SEASONABLE

⁵pat \"\ *n* -S *usu cap* [fr. *Pat*, nickname for *Patrick*, a common Irish Christian name] **1 :** IRISHMAN **2** *Austral* **:** CHINESE

pat *abbr* **1** patent; patented **2** patrol **3** pattern

PAT *abbr* point after touchdown

pa·ta·ca \pəˈtäkə\ *n* -S [Pg] **1 :** the basic unit of monetary value in the Portuguese overseas province of Macao — see MONEY table **2 :** a coin of Macao representing one pataca

pat-a-cake \ˈ=,=,=\ *n* [so called fr. the opening words of the rhyme] **:** a nursery play in which a child claps his hands to the words of a rhyme in imitation of another's actions

pa·tache \pəˈtash, -tächā\ *n* -S [Sp, fr. OSp *pataxe*, prob. fr. Ar *baṭash* ship with two masts] **:** a tender to a fleet of sailing vessels

pa·ta·gi·al \pəˈtājēəl\ *adj* [NL *patagium* + E *-al*] **:** of or relating to a patagium

pa·ta·gi·ate \-ēət, -ē,āt\ *adj* [NL *patagium* + E *-ate*] **1 :** having a patagium **2 :** PATAGIAL

pa·ta·gi·um \-ēəm, ,pad·əˈjīəm\ *n, pl* **pata·gia** \-ēə, -īə\ [NL, fr. L *patagium* gold edging or border on a woman's tunic] **1 :** a wing membrane: as **a :** the fold of skin connecting the forelimbs and hind limbs of certain arboreal animals (as flying squirrels and flying lizards) and serving to sustain them in making long leaps **b :** the fold of skin in front of the humeral and radio-ulnar parts of a bird's wing **2 a :** one of a pair of small processes on the back of the prothorax of most Lepidoptera **b :** TEGULA 1a

¹pat·a·go·ni·an \,pad·əˈgōnyən, -atə,-, -nēən\ *adj, usu cap* [*Patagonia*, region in southern So. America belonging partly to Argentina and partly to Chile + E *-an*] **1 :** of, relating to, or characteristic of Patagonia **2 a :** of, relating to, or characteristic of the people of Patagonia **b** *obs* **:** GIGANTIC **3 :** CHILEAN 2

²patagonian \"\ *n* -S **1** *cap* **:** a native or inhabitant of Patagonia; *esp* **:** one of the aboriginal Indian stock — compare TEHUELCHE **2** *usu cap, obs* **:** someone or something that is very large **:** GIANT

patagonian cavy *or* **patagonian hare** *n, usu cap P* **:** MARA

patamar *var of* PATTAMAR

pa·tan \ˈpätən\ *adj, usu cap* [fr. *Patan*, Nepal] **:** of or from the city of Patan, Nepal **:** of the kind or style prevalent in Patan

pa·ta·na \pəˈtänə\ *n* -S [Singhalese] **:** upland grassland of Ceylon that commonly succeeds forest and is maintained by burning

pa·ta·ria \pəˈtärēə\ *n* -S *usu cap* [It, fr. *Pataria*, section of Milan] **:** the party of the Patarines (sense 2) or the movement instituted by them

pat·a·rine \ˈpad·ərən, -ə,rēn\ *or* **pat·a·rene** \-ə,rēn\ *n* -S *usu cap* [ML *Patarinus, Patarenus*, fr. It *Pataria, Patarea*, poor section of Milan, Italy + L *-inus* -ine] **1 :** one of the Manichaean emigrants from Bulgaria who settled in the Pataria quarter of Milan **2 :** a member of a reform party at Milan in the 11th century formed to combat clerical concubinage and simony; *also* **:** one opposed to the marriage of priests **3 :** a Waldensian or one of various Cathari (as the Bogomils or Albigenses)

pa·tas \pəˈtä\ *n, pl* **patas** \-ä(z)\ [F, fr. Wolof *pata*] **:** a reddish colored long-tailed monkey (*Erythrocebus patas*) of West Africa — called also *hussar monkey*

pa·tash·te \pəˈtäshtā\ *n* -S [AmerSp *pataxte, pataste*, fr. Maya] **1 :** a tropical American tree (*Theobroma bicolor*) resembling cacao and yielding a chocolate substitute **2 :** the cocoa obtained from the patashte tree — called also *tiger cocoa*

pat·a·uá oil \,pad·əˈwä-\ *n* [*patauá* fr. Pg, a Brazilian palm, fr. Tupi *batawá, patawá*] **:** a fatty oil similar to olive oil obtained from the fruit of a Brazilian palm (*Oenocarpus bataua*)

pat·a·vin·i·ty \,pad·əˈvinəd·ē\ *n* -ES *usu cap* [L *patavinitas*, fr. *Patavium* (Padua), Italy, birthplace of the Roman historian Livy + L *-itas* -ity] **1 :** the dialectal characteristics of Padua as seen in the writings of Livy **2 :** the use of dialect

pa·ta·yan \,pädəˈyän\ *adj, usu cap* [Walapai *pataya* ancient people + E *-an*] **:** of or belonging to a culture of western Arizona dating from about 700 to 1200 and characterized by crude brush and mud huts, clay pottery, and the cultivation of corn, beans, and cotton **:** YUMAN

pat-ball \ˈ=,=\ *n* [²*pat* + *ball*] **1 :** ROUNDERS **2 :** slow or feeble cricket or lawn tennis

¹patch \ˈpach\ *n* -ES [ME *pacche*, perh. fr. MF *pece, piece, pieche* piece — more at PIECE] **1 :** a piece used to mend or cover a hole, rent, or breach or to reinforce or protect a weak spot ⟨wore a dirty . . . sweater with leather elbow ~es —W.B. Marsh⟩; *esp* **:** a piece of cloth used to repair or reinforce fabric that is torn or worn **2 :** a tiny decorative piece of black silk or court plaster worn on the face or neck esp. by women to hide a blemish or to heighten beauty by contrast **3 a :** a piece of adhesive plaster or other cover applied to a wound **b :** a shield (as of cloth) worn over an injured eye **4 a :** a small piece **:** BIT, SCRAP ⟨on all sides are small ~es of level ground, but nowhere is there a plain —Kenneth Roberts⟩ ⟨slept in ~es, cold and uncomfortable —A.P.Herbert⟩ ⟨the kind of book which in ~es has real interest —H.J.Laski⟩ **b :** a spot of color different from that around it ⟨a ~ of white is noticeable on his dog's head⟩ **c :** a small piece of ground distinct from that about it (as in appearance or in the vegetation it bears) ⟨cabbage ~⟩ ⟨~es of bare earth⟩ **d :** a constricted area of land occupied by mean or impoverished dwellings or farms **5 :** an ornament, badge, or tab of cloth sewed on a garment; *esp* **:** an emblem worn at the shoulder of a military uniform to show the unit to which a serviceman belongs ⟨wears the Third Army ~ —*Westinghouse Mag.*⟩ **6 a :** an irregular small mass of floating cakes of ice **b :** a herd of seals **7 a :** a piece of greased or moistened cloth formerly used as wadding for a rifle ball **b :** a small piece of cotton cloth used for cleaning the bore of small arms **c :** the hard metal covering over the lead core of jacketed bullets **8 :** a circumscribed region (as on the skin or in a section from an organ) differing esp. in color or composition from the tissue normal for that part **9 a :** OVERLAY 2d **b :** a replacement of part of a printing plate (as an electrotype) ⟨a 3-line ~⟩ **10 :** someone or something equal or comparable — usu. used in negative constructions ⟨what the advocates of economic nationalism had accomplished was not a ~ on what they planned —*Time*⟩ ⟨those headlines don't make a ~ against the ones on the front pages —*Newsweek*⟩ **11 :** a temporary connection in a communication system (as a telephone or broadcasting hookup) **12** *chiefly Brit* **:** PERIOD, SPELL ⟨it is not as though we now had large reserves to tide us over a difficult ~ —Donald MacDougall⟩ ⟨poetry is going through a bad ~ —Cyril Connolly⟩ **13 :** a circus lawyer **:** FIXER ⟨if the ~ says you can rip and tear, you can go the limit on anything —D.W.Maurer⟩

²patch \"\ *vt* -ED/-ING/-ES **1 :** to mend, cover, or fill up a hole, rent, breach, or weak spot in **:** apply a patch to ⟨caulked her deck seams, slushed her rigging, and ~ed her sails —Kenneth Roberts⟩ ⟨was trying to get all the fences near the house ~ed —Ellen Glasgow⟩ **2 :** to provide with a patch or patches ⟨neat clearings ~ing the sides of the mountains —Slim Aarons⟩ ⟨went ~ed and darned and shamefaced through the village streets⟩ **3 a :** to make of patches, scraps, or fragments ⟨they possessed only suspicions . . . but out of these they succeeded in ~ing together a mosaic —Louis Bromfield⟩ **b :** to mend, repair, or put together esp. in hasty, insecure, or shabby fashion — usu. used with *up* ⟨was busy ~*ing* up that political disaster —J.P.O'Donnell⟩ ⟨relations between the two men had to be ~*ed* up repeatedly —Ishbel Ross⟩ ⟨sometimes offer a gift, with a view to ~*ing* up a quarrel —W.F.Hambly⟩ ⟨has been since diverted to ~ up the 118-year-old penal slum — Frank O'Leary⟩ **4 :** to apply as a patch ⟨~*ed* new cloth to the old coat until it seemed mere patchwork⟩ **5 :** to cover (a bullet) with a patch **syn** see MEND

³patch \"\ *n* -ES [perh. by folk etymology fr. It dial. (southern Italy) *paccio* fool] **1 :** a domestic fool or jester **2 :** CLOWN, DOLT, NINNY **3** *chiefly dial* **:** CROSSPATCH

patch bolt *n* **:** a bolt used in the repair of boilers and of ships with hulls of steel plate that has a countersunk head with a square knob which is twisted off when the bolt is screwed home

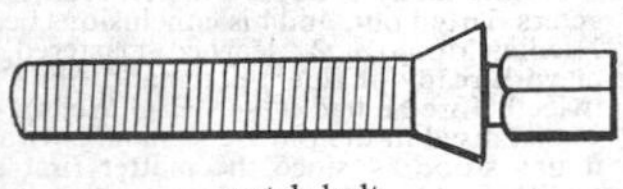

patch bolt

patch box *n* **1 :** a small shallow decorative box formerly used to contain the face patches fashionable in the 17th and 18th centuries **2 :** a recess in the stock of a muzzle-loading rifle for carrying patches, grease, and flints

patch budding *n* **:** plant budding in which a small rectangle of bark bearing a scion bud is fitted into a corresponding opening in the stock

patch cord *or* **patching cord** *n* **:** a wire with plugs at both ends that is used in communications patches

patch·er \ˈpachə(r)\ *n* -S **1 :** a worker who makes repairs to, reinforces, or decorates something by patching **2 :** CEMENTER 2e **3 :** a mine-car brakeman

¹patch·ery \-ch(ə)rē\ *n* -ES [*²patch* + *-ery*] **:** the act of patching **:** clumsy or hasty repairing or making **:** PATCHWORK ⟨a thin sample of poetic ~ —A.C.Swinburne⟩

²patchery *n* -ES [*³patch* + *-ery*] *obs* **:** ROGUERY, KNAVERY

patchhead \ˈ=,=\ *n* [*¹patch* + *head;* fr. the markings on its head] **:** SURF SCOTER

patch·i·ly \ˈpachəlē\ *adv* **:** in a patchy manner **:** in spots

patch·i·ness \-chēnəs\ *n* -ES **:** the quality or state of being patchy

patch·ing \-chiŋ\ *n* -S **1 :** ¹PATCH 7a **2 :** ¹PATCH 10 — usu. used with negative ⟨that boy's not a ~ to his big brother⟩

patch·ou·li *or* **patch·ou·ly** *also* **pach·ou·li** \ˈpachəlē, pəˈchülē\ *n, pl* **patchoulis** *or* **patchoulies** [Tamil *paccuḷi* woolly patchouli] **1 :** an East Indian shrubby mint (*Pogostemon cablin*) that yields a fragrant essential oil **2 :** the perfume made from patchouli ⟨a pleasant perfume of summer flowers rather than a heavy odor of ~ —*Weekly Scotsman*⟩

patchouli oil *also* **patchouly oil** *n* **:** a fragrant brownish yellow to brown essential oil obtained from the leaves of the patchouli and used in perfumes and soaps

patch pocket *n* **:** a flat pocket applied to the outside of a garment

patch-polled coot \ˈpach,pōld-\ *n* [*¹patch* + *poll* (head) + *-ed;* fr. the markings on its head] **:** SURF SCOTER

patch reef *n* **:** a small flat table reef ⟨*patch reefs* . . . are by far the most numerous of the reefs around Australia —*Jour. of Geol.*⟩

patch test *n* **:** a test for determining hypersensitivity made by applying to the unbroken surface of the skin small pads soaked with the allergy-producing substance in question, susceptibility being indicated by the development of irritation at the point of application — compare SCRATCH TEST, SKIN TEST

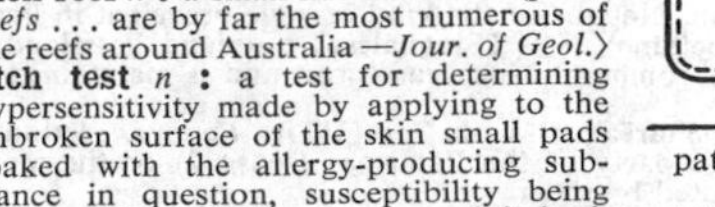

patch pocket

patchwork \ˈ=,=\ *n, often attrib* **1 a :** something composed of ill-assorted, miscellaneous, or incongruous parts **:** HODGEPODGE, JUMBLE ⟨a ~ of four languages laced with gestures and laughter —Claudia Cassidy⟩ ⟨had finished our ~ lunch — Gladys B. Stern⟩ ⟨a ~ report⟩ **b :** work performed in random or unsystematic fashion or confined to patching up ⟨desegregation has been a ~ in Kentucky —J.B.Martin⟩ ⟨argued . . . that economic reform by ~ is illogical and timid —F.L.Allen⟩ ⟨~ efforts⟩ **2 :** pieces of cloth of various colors and shapes sewed together usu. in a pattern to form a covering (as for a bed) ⟨a ~ quilt⟩ ⟨a counterpane of silk ~⟩ — **patchworked** \ˈ=,=\ *adj*

¹patchy \ˈpachē, -chi\ *adj* -ER/-EST [*¹patch* + *-y*] **1 :** marked by or diversified with patches **:** consisting of patches **:** resembling patchwork **:** SPOTTY ⟨~ sunlight shone on the coat of the bay stallion —Ernest Hemingway⟩ **2 :** appearing rough and uneven (as the coat of an animal)

²patchy \ˈpachi\ *adj* [*³patch* + *-y*] *dial Eng* **:** CROSS, TESTY

patd *abbr* patented

¹pate \ˈpāt, *usu* -ād·+V\ *n* -S [ME] **:** the head or part of the head of a person: **a :** the top or crown of the head **b :** the head as containing the brain **c :** BRAIN, BRAINS — used chiefly disparagingly ⟨the nunnish ~ bald as an ant's egg —William Sansom⟩

²pate \"\ *n* -S [perh. fr. *¹pate;* fr. the white spot on the head] *dial Eng* **:** BADGER

³pâ·té \pä'tā\ *n* -S [F, fr. OF *pasté*, fr. *paste* paste, dough — more at PASTE] **1 :** a pie, patty, or pasty containing meat, fish, game, or poultry **2 :** a spread of finely mashed seasoned and spiced meat (as chicken or goose liver)

⁴pâte \ˈpät\ *n* -S [F, lit., paste, fr. OF *paste*] **1 :** the paste or plastic material for pottery or porcelain **2 :** PASTE 1a **3 :** pasty dough

⁵paté *or* **patée** *var of* PATTÉE

pat·ed \ˌpād·əd, ˌpātəd\ *adj* **:** having a pate of a specified kind — usu. used in combination ⟨addle*pated*⟩ ⟨feather*pated*⟩

pâ·té de foie gras \(ˌ)päˌtādəfˈwäˈgrä *also* (ˌ)paˌt- *sometimes* ˌpäd·ēd- *or* ˌpad·ēd-\ *n, pl* **pâ·tés de foie gras** \-ā(z)d-, -ē(z)d-\ [F, goose-liver pastry] **:** a paste of fat goose liver and truffles sometimes with added fat pork

pat·e·fac·tion \ˌpad·əˈfakshən\ *n* -S [L *patefaction-, patefactio*, fr. *patefactus* (past part. of *patefacere*) + *-ion-, -io* -ion] *archaic* **:** DISCLOSURE, MANIFESTATION, REVELATION

patefy *vt* -ED/-ING/-ES [modif. (influenced by E *-fy*) of L *patefacere*, fr. *patēre* to be open, be evident + *facere* to make, do — more at FATHOM, DO] *obs* **:** to make open or manifest **:** DECLARE, REVEAL

pa·tel \pəˈtel\ *n* -S [Hindi *paṭel* & Marathi *pāṭīl*, fr. Prakrit *paṭṭailla*, fr. Skt *paṭṭa* slab, tablet, copper plate for grants] **:** the headman of a village

pa·tel·la \pəˈtelə\ *n* [L, dim. of *patina* pan — more at PATEN] **1** *pl* **pa·tel·lae** \-e,lē, -,lī\ **:** a small dish, pan, or vase of ancient Rome **2** *pl* **patellae** *or* **patellas a :** a thick flat triangular movable bone that forms the anterior point of the knee and protects the front of the joint, increases the leverage of the quadriceps, and is usu. regarded as a sesamoid bone since it is developed in the tendon of the quadriceps and in structure is similar to other sesamoid bones **:** KNEECAP, KNEEPAN **b** [NL, fr. L] **:** the fourth segment in the pedipalpus or in the leg of an arachnid **3** *pl* **patellae** [NL, fr. L] **:** a rounded apothecium in a lichen that has a distinct marginal rim **4** [NL, fr. L] **a** *cap* **:** the type genus of the family Patellidae including the common European limpet (*P. vulgata*) **b** *pl* **patellas** *or* **patellae :** a limpet of the family Patellidae

pa·tel·lar \-lə(r)\ *adj* **:** of, relating to, or involving the patella

patellar ligament *n* **:** the part of the tendon of the quadriceps that extends from the patella to the tibia

patellar reflex *n* **:** KNEE JERK

pa·tel·late \-elət, -e,lāt\ *adj* [*patella* + *-ate*] **:** having a patella or patellula **:** PATELLIFORM

patella ul·na·ris \-,əlˈna(a)rəs\ *n, pl* **patella ulnarises** [NL, lit., elbow patella] **:** a sesamoid at the lower end of the humerus that takes the place of the olecranon process in some birds

¹pa·tel·lid \pəˈteləd\ *adj* [NL *Patellidae*] **:** of or relating to the Patellidae

²patellid \"\ *n* -S **:** a mollusk of the family Patellidae

pa·tel·li·dae \-lə,dē\ *n pl, cap* [NL, fr. *Patella*, type genus + *-idae*] **:** a family of gastropod mollusks (order Aspidobranchia) including numerous typical limpets — **pa·tel·li·dan** \-lədᵊn\ *adj or n*

pa·tel·li·form \-lə,fôrm\ *adj* [*patella* + *-iform*] **1 :** resembling a limpet **:** shaped like a limpet shell **2** *bot* **:** disk-shaped with a narrow rim

pa·tel·line \pəˈte,līn, ˈpad·ᵊl,īn\ *adj* [*patella* + *-ine*] **1 :** PATELLIFORM **2** [NL *Patella* + E *-ine*] **:** of or relating to the Patellidae

pa·tel·lo·femoral \pəˈte(,)lō+\ *adj* [*patella* + *-o-* + *femoral*] **:** of or relating to the patella and femur

pa·tel·loid \pəˈte,lȯid\ *adj* [*patella* + *-oid*] **:** PATELLIFORM

pa·tel·lu·la \pəˈtelyələ\ *n, pl* **patellu·lae** \-yə,lē\ [NL, dim. of L *patella* — more at PATELLA] **:** a cuplike sucker on the tarsus of beetles of the family Dytiscidae

pa·tel·lu·late \-yələt, -yə,lāt\ *adj* [NL *patellula* + E *-ate*] **:** having patellulae

pat·en \ˈpatᵊn\ *n* -S [ME *pateyn, patin, paten*, fr. OF *patene*, fr. ML & L; ML *patina, patena* plate for the Eucharist, fr. L, shallow dish, fr. Gk *patanē;* akin to L *patēre* to be open — more at FATHOM] **1 :** a plate of precious metal used for the bread in the eucharistic service **2 :** PLATE **3 :** a thin metal disk or something resembling one

pat·en·cy \ˈpatᵊnsē, ˈpāt-, -si\ *n* -ES [*¹patent* + *-cy*] **1 :** the quality or state of being patent **:** OBVIOUSNESS **2 :** OPENNESS, UNOBSTRUCTEDNESS ⟨~ of a fistula⟩

pat·en·er \ˈpatᵊnə(r)\ *n* -S **:** an acolyte or priest bearing the paten at mass in the medieval church

¹pat·ent \ˈpatᵊnt, ˈpāt-\ *adj* [ME, fr. MF, fr. L *patent-, patens*, fr. pres. part. of *patēre* to be open, be exposed, be evident — more at FATHOM] **1 a :** open to public inspection — used chiefly in the phrase *letters patent;* opposed to *close* **b** (1) **:** conferred by letters patent ⟨the subject of a ~ privilege —L.H. Edmunds⟩ (2) **:** endowed with a right or privilege by letters patent (as some London theaters) (3) **:** appointed by letters patent **c** *law* **:** appropriated or protected by letters patent **:** secured by letters patent to the exclusive possession and control (as for manufacture) of some person or party **:** PATENTED ⟨~ foodstuffs have acquired an ever-increasing importance —Friedel Strauss⟩ **2 :** of, relating to, or concerned with the granting of patents esp. for inventions ⟨~ attorney⟩ ⟨~ award⟩ ⟨~ law⟩ **3 a :** marketed as a proprietary commodity **:** having patent or trademark protection ⟨a ~ can opener⟩ **b :** making exclusive or proprietary claims or pretensions **:** ostensibly original or superlative ⟨peddled his ~ notions in season and out⟩ **4 :** affording free passage **:** OPEN, UNOBSTRUCTED ⟨the nose ~ with no pathological discharge —*Jour. Amer. Med. Assoc.*⟩ **5** *biol* **:** PATULOUS, SPREADING **6** *archaic* **:** ACCESSIBLE, EXPOSED ⟨a circular temple, ~ to the sun —P.J.Bailey⟩ **7 :** open to view **:** readily visible or intelligible **:** EVIDENT, OBVIOUS ⟨the ~ dissolution of the comfortable scheme of scientific materialism —A.N.Whitehead⟩ ⟨blaze a new trail against ~ stupidity —W.H.Whyte⟩ **8** *archaic* **:** available for public use **syn** see EVIDENT

²pat·ent \ˈpatᵊnt, *chiefly Brit also* ˈpāt-\ *n* -S [ME *patente*, fr. AF, fr. MF (in *lettres patentes* letters patent), fem. of *patent*, adj.] **1 :** an official document; *esp* **:** one issued by a sovereign power conferring a right or privilege ⟨when a prince made a plebeian a noble . . . the ~ of nobility defined what arms he was to bear —T.B.Wigley⟩ **2 a** (1) *U. S. patent law* **:** a government grant of a monopoly right that gives to one who invents or discovers a new and useful process, machine, manufacture, or composition of matter or a new and useful improvement thereof the exclusive right for a specific term of 17 years with certain rights of extension to make, use, or sell his invention or discovery or to assign or license less than the full patent right and that when issued is prima facie evidence of its own validity but may be attacked in a federal court (2) *British patent law* **:** a grant by the sovereign that gives the true and first inventor or certain persons claiming under him the right to exclude for 16 years with certain rights of extension others from the manufacture or use of the inventor's commercially vendible, original, and useful article or method or process of manufacture or of control, improvement, or modification thereof or of any such new and useful method or process of testing such manufacture, control, improvement, or modification, that embraces any substance or material and any plant, machinery, or apparatus, and that is sometimes subject in the public interest to compulsory licenses or to revocation **b :** a monopoly or right granted according to U. S. patent law or British patent law or under similar statutes for the protection of inventions or discoveries that is protected against infringement by remedies provided by such law or statutes and by international conventions executed by the principal nations **:** letters patent for an invention **3 :** something likened to a patent **:** LICENSE, PRIVILEGE ⟨upstarts and outlaws of religion who were infringing its spiritual ~*s* —W.P. Webb⟩ ⟨give her ~ to offend —Shak.⟩ **4 a :** an instrument making a conveyance or grant of public lands **b :** the land or territory so conveyed ⟨gave these obstinate squatters their legal ~*s* —*Amer. Guide Series: Minn.*⟩ ⟨a ~ of 1500 acres —*Amer. Guide Series: N. Y. City*⟩ **5 a :** a patented article, device, or process ⟨one of the inventor's many ~*s*⟩ **b :** an exclusive property or claim **:** sole right of control ⟨the techniques of economic stability and expansion are no longer the ~ of one party —Raymond Aron⟩ ⟨has no ~ on that philosophy —Irving Kolodin⟩ **6 a :** PATENT LEATHER **b patents** *pl* **:** patent leather shoes **7 :** PATENT FLOUR

³patent \"\ *vt* -ED/-ING/-S **1 a :** to grant (someone) a privilege, right, or license by patent **b :** to grant a patent for ⟨~*ed* the device to its inventor⟩ **2 :** to obtain or secure by patent; *esp* **:** to secure by letters patent exclusive right to make, use, and vend (an invention) **3 :** to obtain or grant a patent right to (as land or minerals) **4 :** to heat (an iron-base alloy) above the critical temperature and then cool in air or molten lead at about 700° F.; *esp* **:** to produce a structure desired in wire to be cold-drawn

pat·ent·abil·i·ty \ˌpatᵊntəˈbilədē, -lətē, -i\ *n* **:** the quality or state of being patentable

pat·ent·able \ˈpatᵊntəbəl\ *adj* **:** suitable for patenting **:** capable of being patented — **pat·ent·ably** \-blē, -li\ *adv*

patent ambiguity *n* **:** an ambiguity in a legal document arising from the words themselves — opposed to *latent ambiguity*

patent base *or* **patent block** *n* **:** a base usu. of metal and often in standard interchangeable units to which low-mounted or unmounted letterpress plates are secured in position for printing

patent blue *n, often cap P&B* **:** any of several acid triphenylmethane dyes — see DYE table I (under *Acid Blue 5*)

patent-coated \ˈ=,=\ *adj, of paperboard* **:** vat-lined on one or both sides with an uncoated white liner

pat·en·tee \ˌpatᵊnˈtē\ *n* -S [ME, fr. MF, *patente* patent + *-ee*, *-ee* — more at PATENT] **:** one to whom a grant is made or a privilege secured by patent

patent flour *n* **:** a high-grade wheat flour that is free from bran, embryo, and aleurone and that consists wholly of endosperm of sound wheat grains usu. with outer parts of the endosperm removed

patent hammer *or* **patent ax** *n* **:** BUSHHAMMER

patent insides *n pl* **:** readyprint that comes printed on the inside pages — compare BOILER PLATE, PATENT OUTSIDES

pat·ent leather \ˈpatᵊnt-, *Brit usu* ˈpātᵊnt-\ *n* **1 :** a leather used for shoes, handbags, and belts that is given a hard smooth glossy surface by application of successive coats of daub and varnish with careful drying after each — compare JAPANNED LEATHER **2 patent leathers** *pl* **:** a pair of patent leather shoes

patent log *n* **:** TAFFRAIL LOG

pat·ent·ly *adv* **:** in a patent manner **:** CLEARLY, OBVIOUSLY, PLAINLY ⟨walk a plane that is ~ air —Bernard DeVoto⟩ ⟨all of which is, ~, critical nonsense —Patrick Cruttwell⟩

patent medicine *n* **1 :** a packaged nonprescription drug or medicine of secret composition protected by a trademark and with the name of the medicine, directions for use, and name and business address of the manufacturer on the label or package **2 :** PROPRIETARY 6a

patent note *n* **:** SHAPE NOTE

patent office *n* **:** a government office for examining claims to patents and granting patents

pat·en·tor \ˈpatᵊntə(r)\ *n* -S **1 :** one that grants a patent **2 :** PATENTEE

patent outsides *n pl* **:** readyprint that comes printed on the first and last pages — compare BOILER PLATE, PATENT INSIDES

patent peg *n* **:** a peg for a stringed instrument (as a banjo or guitar) having an internal friction device to prevent slipping

patent plaster *n* **:** CEMENT PLASTER

patent pool *n* **1 :** a pool or combination in which the agreements are enforced by centralized control of essential patent rights **2 :** an arrangement of cross-licensing in which several patent owners join together to make individually held patents available to all members of the group

patent right *n* **:** a right granted by letters patent; *esp* **:** the exclusive right to an invention and the control of its manufacture

patent rolls *n pl* **:** the parchment rolls in which British letters patent are recorded

patents *pl of* PATENT, *pres 3d sing of* PATENT

patent slip *n, chiefly Brit* **:** MARINE RAILWAY

patent theater *n* **:** a theater established or licensed by royal letters patent

patent yellow *n* **1 :** CASSEL YELLOW 1 **2 :** ORPIMENT 2

pa·ter \ˈpa|d·ə(r), ˈpä|, ˈpā|, |tə(r)\ *n* -S [L, father — more at FATHER] **1** *often cap* [ME, by shortening] **:** PATERNOSTER **2 :** the socially acknowledged or legal father among some primitive peoples — compare GENITOR **3** *chiefly Brit* **:** FATHER

pat·era \ˈpad·ərə\ *n, pl* **pater·ae** \-ə,rē\ [L; akin to L *patēre* to lie open — more at FATHOM] **1 :** an earthenware or metal saucer used by the ancient Romans for drinking and libations at sacrifices **2 :** a round or oval disk or medallion bearing an ornamental design in bas-relief or intaglio and often used in decoration of buildings or furniture

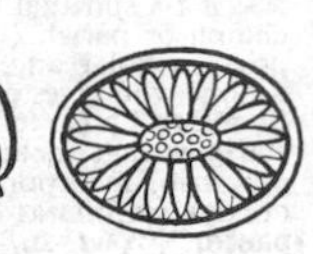

paterae

pa·tera process \pəˈtärə-\ *n, usu cap 1st P* [after Adolf von *Patera*, 19th cent. Ger. metallurgist] **:** extraction of silver from its ores by roasting with salt, leaching out the silver chloride with a solution of sodium thiosulfate, and precipitating the silver as sulfide by means of sodium sulfide

patercove *var of* PATRICO

paterero *var of* PEDRERO

pa·ter·fa·mil·i·as \ˌpa|d·ə(r)fəˈmilēəs, ˌpä|, ˌpā|, |tə(r), -ē,as\ *n* -ES *see sense 1* [L, fr. *pater* father + *familias*, old gen. of *familia* family — more at FATHER, FAMILY] **1** *pl* **pa·tres·fa·mil·i·as** \-a·(ˌ)trēzf-; -ä·,trāsf-, -ā·,-\ *Roman law* **a :** the head of a household **b :** someone who is his own master — compare PATRIA POTESTAS, SUI JURIS **2 :** the father of a family **:** the male head of a household ⟨was rapidly moving into the role of ~, for his own children numbered four —Jean Holloway⟩

pat·er·i·form \ˈpad·ərə,fȯrm\ *adj* [*patera* + *-iform*] **:** formed like a patera

pat·er·is·sa \ˌpad·əˈrisə\ *n* -S [NGk *pateritsa*, fr. MGk *pateriza*, perh. dim. of Gk *pater-, patēr* father — more at FATHER] *Eastern Church* **:** a crosier surmounted by a small cross from whose base issue two serpents

pa·ter·nal \pəˈtərnᵊl, -tə̄n-, -təin-\ *adj* [LL *paternalis*, fr. *paternus* paternal (fr. *pater* father) + *-alis* -al — more at FATHER] **1 :** of or relating to a father **:** evincing a father's care or solicitude **:** FATHERLY ⟨his smile was almost ~ —Kenneth Roberts⟩ **2 :** belonging to or received or inherited from one's father ⟨passed his childhood on the ~ farm —*Current Biog.*⟩ **3 :** related (as an ancestor) through one's father ⟨~ grandfather⟩ — **pa·ter·nal·ly** \-ᵊlē, -ᵊli\ *adv*

pa·ter·nal·ism \-ᵊl,izəm\ *n* -S **:** the care or control of subordinates (as by a government or employer) in a fatherly manner; *esp* **:** the principles or practices of a government that undertakes to supply needs or regulate conduct of the governed in matters affecting them as individuals as well as in their relations to the state and to each other

¹pa·ter·nal·ist \-ᵊləst\ *or* **pa·ter·nal·is·tic** \pəˈtərnᵊlˈistik, -tə̄n-, -təin-, -stēk\ *adj* **:** of, relating to, or practicing paternalism — **pa·ter·nal·is·ti·cal·ly** \-stək(ə)lē, -stēk-, -li\ *adv*

²paternalist \"\ *n* -S **:** a practitioner of paternalism

pat·er·nal·i·ty \ˌpad·ə(r)ˈnaləd·ē\ *n* -S **:** the quality or state of being paternal **:** fatherly conduct or policy

pa·ter·nal·ize \pəˈtərnᵊl,īz\ *vt* -ED/-ING/-S **:** to treat paternalistically

pa·ter·ni·ty \pəˈtərnəd·ē, -tə̄n-, -təin-, -nətē, -i\ *n* -ES [MF *paternité*, fr. LL *paternitat-, paternitas*, fr. L *paternus* paternal + *-itat-, -itas* -ity — more at PATERNAL] **1 :** the quality or state of being a father **:** FATHERHOOD ⟨the cares of ~⟩ **2 :** origin or descent from a father **:** male parentage ⟨provides for citizenship of the child born out of wedlock if ~ is established —William Samore⟩ **3 :** AUTHORSHIP, ORIGINATION ⟨the controversy which has attended the bipartisan policy has extended even to the question of its ~ —Norman Hill & Eugene Hangse⟩

paternity test *n* **:** a test to determine whether a given man could be father to a particular child made by comparison of the blood groups of the mother, child, and suspected man, a negative result proving that the man cannot be the father while a positive result shows only that it is biologically possible that he may be

pa·ter·no·ite \ˌpäd·ə(r)ˈnō,īt\ *n* -S [It, fr. Emanuele *Paternò* †1935 Ital. chemist + It *-ite*] **:** a mineral $MgB_8O_{13}.4H_2O$ consisting of a hydrous magnesium borate

¹pa·ter·nos·ter \ˈpa|d·ə(r),nästə(r), |tə- *also* ˈpā| *or* ˈpä| *or* -nȯs- *or* ˈ=ˌ==; ˌpä|,terˈnȯ,ste(ə)r, ˌpä|, ˌteəˈnȯ,steə(r *or* +V -ste(ə)r, -nä,-\ *n* -S [ME, fr. ML, fr. L *pater noster* our father, the 1st 2 words of the Lord's Prayer] **1** *often cap* **:** a recital of the Lord's Prayer in any language esp. in Latin ⟨say ten ~*s*⟩ **2 a :** one of the large beads of a rosary on which the Lord's Prayer is said **b** *obs* (1) **:** a string with knots or beads for counting the repetitions of the Lord's Prayer (2) **:** ROSARY **3 :** something resembling a rosary: **a :** a beadwork ornament in architectural moldings **b** *or* **paternoster line :** a fishing line with a row of hooks and bead-shaped sinkers **4 :** a repetitious word formula muttered or repeated as a prayer or magical charm ⟨the mystic syllables, O-Mi-T'o Fo . . . the Buddhist ~⟩

²paternoster *pronunc before semicolon at* ¹PATERNOSTER\ *vi* -ED/-ING/-S **:** to fish with a paternoster

paternoster lake *n* **:** one of a series of lakes in a glaciated valley arranged like beads on a string

paternoster while *n* [ME] *archaic* **:** the time required to repeat a paternoster

paters *pl of* PATER

pat·er·son \ˈpad·ə(r)sən, -atə(r)-\ *adj, usu cap* [fr. *Paterson*, N. J.] **:** of or from the city of Paterson, N. J. ⟨*Paterson* silk mills⟩ **:** of the kind or style prevalent in Paterson

pat·er·son's curse \ˈpad·ə(r)sənz-\ *n, usu cap P* [after William *Paterson* †1810 Austral. administrator and botanist] **:** a perennial weed (*Echium plantagineum*) that is particularly troublesome on Australian rangeland

pates *pl of* PATE

pa·te·si \pəˈtäzē\ *n* -S [incorrect reading of Sumerian *ensi*, a title borne by the patesis] **:** a ruler of some of the Sumerian city-states who combined the religious and the secular chieftaincies **:** PRIEST-KING

pâte-sur-pâte \ˌpät,sərˈpät\ *n* [F, lit., paste on paste] **:** a low relief produced in ceramics or sculpture by applying slip in successive layers usu. with a brush

pa·te·ti·co \pəˈtād·ē,kō\ *adv* (*or adj*) [It, pathetic, fr. LL *patheticus* — more at PATHETIC] **:** with feeling **:** MOVINGLY — used as a direction in music

¹path \ˈpa|th, ˈpaa(ə)|, ˈpai|, ˈpá|\ *n, pl* **paths** \|thz *also* |ths\ [ME, fr. OE *pæth, path;* akin to OFris *path*, MD & MLG *pad, pat*, OHG *pfad*] **1 :** a track made by the frequent or habitual use of men or animals **:** a trodden way ⟨a multiplicity of interesting ~*s* crossed the featureless land —E.E.Shipton⟩ **2 :** a track specially constructed for a particular use (as walking or horseback riding) ⟨a garden ~ of flagstones⟩ ⟨touring ~⟩ **3** *dial Brit* **:** a deep cut in a steep road **4 a :** the way or course traversed by something **:** ROUTE ⟨the ~ of a meteor⟩ ⟨a caravan's ~⟩ **b :** a way of life, conduct, or thought ⟨approach for the difficult ~ he must follow —H.M.Parshley⟩ ⟨families and friends put roadblocks on the ~ of romance —Bertha J. Lueck⟩ **c** *sometimes cap* **:** a course of religious duty **:** a prescription of religious obligation **:** a way or method of action prescribed for the devotees of a particular religion ⟨the Sufi ~⟩ **5** *math* **:** the continuous series of positions or configurations assumed in any motion or process of change by any moving or varying system **6 :** a line of communication over interconnecting neurones extending from one organ or center to another ⟨the optic ~ from the retina to the cerebral cortex⟩ **7 a :** the way or course traversed by light or electricity between two points **b :** the iron parts of a magnetic circuit

²path \"\ *vb* -ED/-ING/-S *vt, archaic* **:** go along (as a way or course) **:** TRAVEL, TREAD **~** *vi, obs* **:** MOVE, WALK ⟨for if thou ~, thy native semblance on —Shak.⟩

path- *or* **patho-** *comb form* [NL, fr. Gk, fr. *pathos* experience, emotion, passion, suffering — more at PATHOS] **1 :** pathological ⟨*patho*morphosis⟩ **2 :** pathological and ⟨*patho*histological⟩ **3 :** pathological state **:** disease ⟨*path*ogen⟩ ⟨*path*ergy⟩ **4 :** emotion ⟨*path*ometer⟩

-path \ˌpath, ˌpaa(ə)th, ˌpaith\ *n comb form* -S [in sense 1, fr. G, back-formation fr. *-pathie* -pathy; in sense 2, ISV, fr. Gk *-pathēs*, fr. *pathos*] **1 :** a practitioner of a (specified) system of medicine that emphasizes some one aspect of disease and its treatment ⟨allo*path*⟩ ⟨hydro*path*⟩ ⟨osteo*path*⟩ **2 :** one suffering from a (specified) kind of ailment ⟨psycho*path*⟩ ⟨neuro*path*⟩

path *abbr* pathological; pathology

pa·than \pə'tän, ˌpət'hän\ *n* -S *usu cap* [Hindi *Paṭhān*] **:** a member of an Iranian people who are the principal race of Afghanistan and colonies of whom are scattered throughout Pakistan and India — compare AFGHAN 1

pat hand *n* [⁴*pat*] **1 :** a hand in draw poker on which one stands pat **2 :** a dealt hand in draw poker (as a straight, flush, or full house) that usu. cannot be materially improved by drawing one or two cards

pathbreaking \'ˌ=ˌ==\ *adj* **:** making or pointing a new way **:** TRAILBLAZING ⟨~ scientific discoveries —Maurice Cranston & J.W.N.Watkins⟩

path·e·mat·ic \ˌpathəˈmad·ik\ *adj* [Gk *pathēmatikos*, fr. *pathēmat-*, *pathēma* suffering, emotion (fr. *path-*, stem of *paschein* to experience, suffer) + *-ikos* -ic — more at PATHOS] *archaic* **:** EMOTIONAL — **path·e·mat·i·cal·ly** \-d·ək(ə)lē\ *adv*

pa·thet·ic \pəˈthed·ik, -etl, |ēk\ *also* **pa·thet·i·cal** \|əkəl, |ēk-\ *adj* [MF or LL; MF *pathetique*, fr. LL *patheticus*, fr. Gk *pathētikos* capable of feeling, sensitive, pathetic, fr. *pathētos* subject to suffering, liable to external influence (fr. *path-*, stem of *paschein* to experience, suffer) + *-ikos* -ic, -ical — more at PATHOS] **1** *obs* **a :** exciting or stirring emotion or passion **b :** marked by strong emotion **:** PASSIONATE **2 a :** evoking tenderness, pity, sympathy, or sorrow **:** AFFECTING, PITIABLE ⟨looked old and ~ —Ruth Park⟩ ⟨a ~ confusion between knowledge and guesswork —M.R.Cohen⟩ ⟨~ and misdirected efforts to be one's true self —Sara H. Hay⟩ **b :** marked by sorrow, suffering, or melancholy **:** SAD ⟨mingling playful with ~ thoughts —William Wordsworth⟩ ⟨you may be gentle and ~, or savage and cynical with perfect propriety —W.M.Thackeray⟩ ⟨the eloquent phrases I had arranged, ~ or indignant, seemed out of place —W.S. Maugham⟩ **3 :** of or relating to the superior oblique muscle or the trochlear nerve **syn** see MOVING

pa·thet·i·cal·ly \|ək(ə)lē, |ēk-, -li\ *adv* **:** in a pathetic manner

pathetic fallacy *n* **:** the ascription of human traits or feelings to inanimate nature (as in *cruel sea, pitiless storm, devouring flame*)

pa·thet·ics \|iks\ *n pl* **:** pathetic expression or conduct ⟨our wretched, shameful sentimentalities and ~ go on smouldering —Bernard DeVoto⟩

pa·thet·i·cus \pəˈthed·əkəs\ *n, pl* **patheti·ci** \-d·əˌsī\ [NL, fr. LL, pathetic — more at PATHETIC] **:** TROCHLEAR NERVE

pathfinder \'ˌ=ˌ==\ *n* **1 :** one that discovers a way; *esp* **:** one that explores untraversed or unfrequented regions to mark out a new route **:** TRAILBLAZER ⟨a ~ of the air⟩ ⟨explore so many facets of human knowledge with so many scholars as ~*s* —Paul Fejos⟩ ⟨the average man of today is too gregarious to be a ~ —Hamlin Garland⟩ **2 :** an airplane that precedes the rest, locates the target, and marks it for the main force with flares, smoke bombs, or smoke rockets **3 :** a parachutist who drops into a target area to set up signals for guidance

pathfinding \'ˌ=ˌ==\ *n* **:** the action of a pathfinder

-path·ia \ˈpathēə\ *n comb form* -S [NL — more at -PATHY] **:** -PATHY 2 ⟨hyper*pathia*⟩ ⟨lympho*pathia*⟩

¹path·ic \ˈpathik\ *n* -S [L *pathicus*, fr. (assumed) Gk *pathikos*, fr. Gk *path-* (stem of *paschein* to experience, have something happen to one, suffer) + *-ikos* -ic — more at PATHOS] **1 :** CATAMITE ⟨an elder boy whose ~ he was —W.B.Yeats⟩ **2 :** a passive party **:** SUBJECT, SUFFERER, VICTIM ⟨is at once the "healer" and the ~ who is to be healed —Julian Symons⟩

²pathic \"\ *adj* **1 :** PASSIVE ⟨the genius of the Orient is its discovery and practice of this sort of ~ or affective communion with nature-in-general —V.C.Aldrich⟩ **2 :** DISEASED, MORBID ⟨whether they are healthy or ~ —C.W.Morris⟩

-path·ic \ˈpathik, -thēk\ *adj comb form* [ISV *-pathy* + *-ic*] **1 :** feeling, suffering, or affected in a (specified) way ⟨tele*pathic*⟩ **2 :** affected by disease of a (specified) part or kind ⟨myo*pathic*⟩ **3 :** relating to therapy based on a (specified) unitary theory of disease or its treatment ⟨homeo*pathic*⟩

-pathies *pl of* -PATHY

pathing *pres part of* PATH

path·less \ˈpathləs\ *adj* **:** having no path **:** UNTROD, TRACKLESS ⟨~ woods⟩ — **path·less·ness** *n* -ES

path·let \-lət\ *n* -S **:** a little path

path line *n* **:** LINE OF FLOW

pathmaster \'ˌ=ˌ==\ *n* **:** one whose job it is to care for and maintain public paths and roads

patho- — see PATH-

path·o·don·tia \ˌpathəˈdänch(ē)ə\ *n* -S [NL, fr. *path-* + *-odontia*] **:** a branch of dentistry concerned with diseases of the teeth

path of emergence : the direction of vibration of a particle at the earth's surface during an earthquake

path·o·gen \ˈpathəjən, -ˌjen\ *also* **path·o·gene** \-ˌjēn\ *n* -S [ISV *path-* + *-gen, -gene*] **:** a specific cause of disease (as a bacterium or virus) **syn** see MICROORGANISM

patho·genesis \ˌpathō+\ *n* [NL, fr. *path-* + L *genesis*] **:** the origination and development of a disease

path·o·ge·net·ic \ˌpathōjəˈned·ik\ *adj* [ISV *path-* + *-genetic*] **1 :** of or relating to pathogenesis **2 :** PATHOGENIC

path·o·gen·ic \ˌpathəˈjenik\ *adj* [ISV *path-* + *-genic*] **1 :** PATHOGENETIC ⟨a ~ process⟩ **2 :** causing or capable of causing disease ⟨~ microorganisms⟩ — **path·o·gen·i·cal·ly** \-nək(ə)lē\ *adv*

path·o·ge·nic·i·ty \ˌpathōjəˈnisəd·ē\ *n* -ES **:** the quality or state of being pathogenic **:** degree of pathogenic capacity ⟨~ enhanced by mouse passage⟩

pa·thog·e·ny \pəˈthäjənē, paˈ-\ *n* -ES [*path-* + *-geny*] **:** PATHOGENESIS

path·og·nom·ic \ˌpathə(g)ˈnämik\ *also* **path·og·nom·i·cal** \-mәkəl\ *adj* [contr. of *pathognomonic, pathognomonical*] **1 :** of or relating to pathognomy **2 :** PATHOGNOMONIC

path·og·no·mon·ic \ˌpathə(g)nəˈmänik\ *also* **path·og·no·mon·i·cal** \-nəkəl\ *adj* [Gk *pathognōmonikos* indicating a particular disease, fr. *patho-* path- + *gnōmonikos* fit to judge, fr. *gnōmon-, gnōmōn* one that knows or discerns, interpreter + *-ikos* -ic, -ical — more at GNOMON] **:** specially, distinctively, or decisively characteristic of a particular disease ⟨a ~ symptom⟩ — **path·og·no·mon·i·cal·ly** \-nək(ə)lē\ *adv*

path·og·no·my \pəˈthägnəmē, paˈ-\ *n* -ES [*path-* + *-gnomy*] **:** the study or recognition of emotions and passions through their outward signs or expressions

path·o·log·i·cal \ˌpathəˈläjəkəl, -jēk-\ *or* **path·o·log·ic** \-jik, -jēk\ *adj* [F *pathologique*, fr. MF, fr. Gk *pathologikos* of the study of the passions, fr. *pathologia* study of the passions + *-ikos* -ic, -ical — more at PATHOLOGY] **1 :** of, relating to, for the purposes of, or concerned with pathology ⟨~ laboratory⟩ ⟨~ garden⟩ ⟨a ~ anatomist⟩ **2 :** DISEASED **:** altered by disease ⟨~ tissue⟩ **3 :** caused by pathology ⟨~ changes⟩ **:** being manifestations of disease ⟨~ bodily processes⟩ **4** *Kantianism* **:** of or relating to passion (sense 4); *specif* **:** instinctually or sensuously determined **:** PASSIONAL **syn** see UNWHOLESOME

pathological anatomy *n* **:** a branch of anatomy concerned with structural changes accompanying disease

pathological drinker *n, psychiatry* **:** a person whose characteristic attempt to relieve emotional tension is by excessive consumption of intoxicating liquor

pathological drunkenness *or* **pathological intoxication** *n* **:** acute excitement with confusion and hallucinosis manifested over a short period of time after the drinking of alcohol and by some considered to be an allergic reaction to alcohol

pathological illusion *n* **:** HALLUCINATION 1

pathological liar *n* **:** a person who habitually tells lies so exaggerated or bizarre that they are suggestive of mental disorder

path·o·log·i·cal·ly \-jək(ə)lē, -jēk-, -li\ *adv* **:** in a pathological manner

pathological signalment *n* **:** description of a person's deformities and scars for purposes of identification by the Bertillon system

pathologico- *comb form* [ISV, fr. *pathological*] **:** pathological and ⟨*pathologico*anatomical⟩

pa·thol·o·gist \pəˈthäləjəst, paˈ-\ *n* -S **:** a specialist in pathology; *specif* **:** one who interprets and diagnoses the changes caused by disease in tissues — compare CLINICIAN

pa·thol·o·gy \-jē, -ji\ *n* -ES [NL *pathologia* & MF *pathologie*, fr. Gk *pathologia* study of the passions, fr. *patho-* path- + *-logia* -logy] **1 :** the study of abnormality; *esp* **:** the study of diseases, their essential nature, causes, and development, and the structural and functional changes produced by them **2 :** something abnormal: **a** (1) **:** the anatomic and physiologic deviations from the normal in the tissues of animals and plants that are manifested as disease ⟨the study of human ~⟩ (2) **:** the complex of signs, symptoms, and bodily changes that characterize a particular disease ⟨the ~ of pneumonia⟩ **b :** comparable abnormality of nonliving material ⟨the ~ of steel⟩ ⟨~ of wine⟩ **c :** deviation from propriety or from an assumed normal state of nonmaterial things ⟨the ~ of reaction⟩ ⟨social ~⟩ **3 :** a treatise on or compilation of abnormalities ⟨a new ~ of the eye⟩

pa·thom·e·ter \pəˈthäməd·ə(r), paˈ-\ *n* [*path-* + *-meter*] **:** a lie detector that measures electrical impulses of the body — compare POLYGRAPH

patho·neurosis \ˌpathō+\ *n* [NL, fr. *path-* + *neurosis*] **:** concentration of libido in a bodily organ esp. when the site of previous disease or trauma

path·o·pho·bia \ˌpathəˈfōbēə\ *n* [NL, fr. *path-* + *phobia*] **:** morbid fear of disease **:** HYPOCHONDRIA

patho·physiological \ˌpathō+\ *or* **patho·physiologic** \"+\ *adj* **:** of or relating to pathophysiology

patho·physiology \"+\ *n* [*path-* + *physiology*] **:** the physiology of abnormal states; *specif* **:** the functional changes that accompany a particular syndrome or disease ⟨the ~ of diabetes⟩

pa·thos \ˈpāˌthäs *also* -thōs *or* -thōs *sometimes* ˈpa,- *or* -ˌthəs\ *n* -ES [Gk, experience, emotion, passion, suffering, fr. *path-*, stem of *paschein* to experience, suffer; akin to OIr *cēssaim*, *cēssim* I suffer, Gk *penthos* grief, sorrow, Latvian *ciest* to endure, suffer] **1 a :** an element in experience or in artistic representation evoking pity or compassion ⟨~ she has, the nearest to tragedy the comedian can come —W.B.Yeats⟩ **b :** an emotion of sympathetic pity ⟨felt a stab of ~ —Rex Ingamells⟩ **2 :** the transient or accidental factor in an event or experience as distinguished from that based on personal character — compare ETHOS 2 a (2)

pa·tho·sis \pəˈthōsəs, paˈ-\ *n, pl* **patho·ses** \-ōˌsēz\ [NL, fr. *path-* + *-sis*] **:** a diseased state **:** an abnormal condition ⟨dental ~⟩

path-reversal principle \'==ˈ==-\ *n* **:** a statement in optics: if light traverses a given course it can traverse the same course in the opposite direction and hence it follows that any object point and its real image are interchangeable

paths *pl of* PATH, *pres 3d sing of* PATH

pathway \'ˌ=\ *n* **1 :** a way that is or serves as a path **:** a beaten track **:** COURSE, FOOTPATH ⟨trail drivers forced the ~ for permanent settlement —*Amer. Guide Series: Texas*⟩ ⟨the ~ of the river . . . may sometimes be beset with difficulties —R.E.Janssen⟩ ⟨the ~*s* of pure and applied science are under continuous survey —*Americana Annual*⟩ **2 :** PATH 6 **3 :** the sequence of enzyme-catalyzed reactions by which any energy-yielding substrate is catabolized by protoplasm

pathy \ˈpathē\ *n* -ES [*-pathy*] **:** a system of treating disease — usu. used disparagingly

-pa·thy \pəthē, -thi\ *n comb form* -ES [L *-pathia*, fr. Gk *-patheia*, fr. *path-*, stem of *paschein* to experience, suffer — more at PATHOS] **1 :** feeling **:** suffering ⟨a*pathy*⟩ ⟨tele*pathy*⟩ **2 :** disease of a (specified) part or kind ⟨idio*pathy*⟩ ⟨myo*pathy*⟩ **3 :** therapy or system of therapy based on a (specified) unitary theory of disease or its treatment ⟨homeo*pathy*⟩

¹pat·i·ble \ˈpad·əbəl\ *n* -S [L *patibulum* fork-shaped yoke for the punishment of criminals, fork-shaped gibbet, fr. *patēre* to be open, stretch out + *-ibulum*, suffix used to denote instrumentality — more at FATHOM] **:** the transom of a cross

²patible \"\ *adj* [L *patibilis*, fr. *pati* to bear, undergo + *-ibilis* -ible — more at PATIENT] *archaic* **:** capable of suffering or of being acted on

pa·tib·u·lary \pəˈtibyəˌlerē\ *adj* [ML *patibulum* gallows (fr. L, fork-shaped yoke for punishing criminals, fork-shaped gibbet) + E *-ary* — more at PATIBLE] *archaic* **:** of, relating to, or suggesting the gallows or hanging

¹pa·tience \ˈpāshən(t)s\ *n* -S [ME *pacience*, fr. OF *patience*, *pacience*, fr. L *patientia*, fr. *patient-, patiens*, (pres. part. of *pati* to suffer) + *-ia* -y — more at PATIENT] **1 a :** the capacity or habit of enduring evil, adversity, or pain with fortitude ⟨~, like charity, is long-suffering and kind. It is, moreover, the most practical of the virtues —Irwin Edman⟩ ⟨~ as well as courage — if there be any difference between them — is a necessary mark of the liberal mind —John Dewey⟩ **b :** forbearance under stress, provocation, or indignity **:** toleration or magnanimity for the faults or affronts of others **:** courageous endurance ⟨he conducted himself with ~ and tact, endeavoring to enforce the laws and to check any revolutionary moves —W.E.Stevens⟩ **c :** calm self-possession in confronting obstacles or delays **:** STEADFASTNESS ⟨~ is the capacity to endure all that is necessary in attaining a desired end . . . never forsakes the ultimate goal —Margaret Kennedy⟩ **2** *obs* **:** PERMISSION, LEAVE **3** *also* **patience dock :** a coarse European dock (*Rumex patientia*) formerly used like spinach **4** *chiefly Brit* **:** SOLITAIRE 3a

syn PATIENCE, LONG-SUFFERING, LONG-SUFFERANCE, LONGANIMITY, FORBEARANCE, and RESIGNATION can all signify a power of enduring without complaint what is disagreeable. PATIENCE stresses composure under suffering as in awaiting an unduly delayed outcome or in performing an exacting task ⟨endured with smiling *patience* —Lafcadio Hearn⟩ ⟨by his *patience* in reading manuscript and proofs —E.A.Armstrong⟩ ⟨twigs, which he carried to his basket and later with great *patience* wove into the form of a basket —Sherwood Anderson⟩ ⟨the calm and infinite *patience* of those who have no ambition —G.S.Gale⟩ LONG-SUFFERING (or LONG-SUFFERANCE) and LONGANIMITY imply extraordinary patience under provocation or trial; LONG-SUFFERING sometimes suggests undue meekness or submissiveness; LONGANIMITY more often designates the virtue rather than the capacity of enduring ⟨the earliest heroines in English literature were *long-suffering* creatures. They were subjected to constant masculine persecution —F.A.Swinnerton⟩ ⟨the *long-sufferance* of the army is almost exhausted —George Washington⟩ ⟨the attitude of the officials towards him was one, at first of amused tolerance, then of bored *longanimity*, and finally . . . of irritation —George Antonius⟩ FORBEARANCE adds to LONG-SUFFERING the implication of restraint in expression of feelings or in exaction of penalties, connoting a tolerance of what merits censure ⟨her *forbearance* with her incorrigible husband —Willa Cather⟩ ⟨he dwelt on his *forbearance*, on the concessions which he had offered —J.A.Froude⟩ ⟨show great *forbearance* in the face of insult⟩ RESIGNATION implies submission to or acceptance of something, often connoting stoicism or fatalism ⟨most readers either positively enjoy the snobbery columns of their newspapers, or else accept them with *resignation*, as part of the established order of things —Aldous Huxley⟩ ⟨we need *resignation* to learn to live in a world that is not formed just for our comfort —M.R.Cohen⟩ ⟨notable for their endurance, capacity for suffering and *resignation* —W.C.Huntington⟩

²patience \"\ *vb* -ED/-ING/-S *vi, archaic* **:** to have or practice patience **~** *vt, obs* **:** to make patient

patience plant *n* **:** BALSAM 4

pa·tien·cy \-nsē\ *n* -ES [L *patientia* — more at PATIENCE] *archaic* **:** the quality or state of being patient or passive

¹pa·tient \ˈpāshənt\ *adj, sometimes* -ER/-EST [ME *pacient*, fr. MF *patient, pacient*, fr. L *patient-, patiens*, fr. pres. part. of *pati* to suffer; akin to L *paene* almost, *penuria* want, need, Gk *pēma* suffering, calamity, Skt *pāpman* want, need] **1 :** bearing pains or trials calmly or uncomplainingly **:** exhibiting power to endure hardship or physical or mental distress ⟨love is ~ and kind . . . love bears all things —1 Cor 13:4–7 (RSV)⟩ **2 :** manifesting forbearance under provocation or strain **:** lenient to the shortcomings or offenses of others **:** LONG-SUFFERING ⟨is an orator of great power and persuasiveness; and the most reasonable and ~ negotiator —T.S.Steele⟩ ⟨a ~ teacher⟩ **3 :** exhibiting deliberation or restraint **:** calm in expectation **:** not hasty or impetuous ⟨he had been marvelously ~ and discreet, and he had been miraculously bold —John Buchan⟩ ⟨that means a lot of ~ discussion and consultation —Hugh Gaitskell⟩ **4 :** steadfast despite opposition, difficulty, or adversity **:** UNDAUNTED ⟨the flint miner extracted his stone, and by ~ effort shaped it to his needs —Lewis Mumford⟩ **5 :** able or willing to bear **:** ENDURING — used with *of* ⟨~ of misrepresentations —*Current Biog.*⟩ **6 :** SUSCEPTIBLE, ADMITTING — used with *of* ⟨this passage seems to be ~ of only one interpretation —C.T.Onions⟩ **7** *archaic* **:** acted upon rather than acting **:** PASSIVE — opposed to *agent* — **pa·tient·ly** *adv* — **pa·tient·ness** *n* -ES

²patient \"\ *n* -S [ME *pacient*, fr. MF *pacient, patient*, fr. *pacient, patient*, adj.] **1** *archaic* **:** one that suffers, endures, or is victimized **2 a** (1) **:** a sick individual esp. when awaiting or under the care and treatment of a physician or surgeon ⟨the hospital is equipped to handle 500 ~*s*⟩ (2) **:** a client for medical service (as of a physician or dentist) ⟨a good practice with a large number of ~*s*⟩ **b** (1) **:** the recipient of any of various personal services (as cosmetic care) **:** CUSTOMER, PATRON ⟨found the beauty shop filled with ~*s*⟩ (2) **:** a hypnotist's subject **3 :** one that is subjected to action or external force — opposed to *agent* ⟨are agents as well as ~*s* and observers in the world —C.H.Whiteley⟩

³patient *vt* -ED/-ING/-S [¹*patient*] *obs* **:** to make patient **:** COMPOSE, CALM

pa·tient·less \-tləs\ *adj* **:** having no patients

patimokkha *var of* PRATIMOKSHA

pat·i·na \ˈpad·ənə, -atə-, -at°n-ə, pəˈtēnə\ *n, pl* **patinas** *or* **pati·nae** \-ˌnē, -°nˌē\ [in sense 1, fr. ML, fr. L, shallow dish; in other senses, NL, fr. L — more at PATEN] **1 :** a eucharistic paten **2 :** a usu. green film that is formed naturally on copper and bronze by long exposure esp. to a moist atmosphere or artificially (as by treatment with acids), that is a basic salt (as a carbonate) of copper protecting the metal from further oxidation, and that is often valued aesthetically for its color **3 :** a surface appearance (as a coloring or mellowing) of something grown beautiful esp. with age or use ⟨~ is to sterling what character is to a fine face —Sarah T. Lee⟩ **4 :** a finish or coloration derived from association, habit, or established character **:** the look acquired from long custom or settled use ⟨a ~ of laughter wrinkles around his eyes —H.W.Baldwin⟩ ⟨those old moments have acquired a ~ of value —J.J.Godwin⟩ ⟨takes on for a time the ~ of the international set —*Newsweek*⟩ ⟨it is only I who have coated them with the ~ of my own childhood happiness —Helen Howe⟩

pat·i·naed \-nəd, -°nəd\ *adj* **:** having a patina ⟨a leather snap purse ~ like old silver —William Faulkner⟩

patina green *n* **:** a light to moderate yellowish green

pat·i·nate \ˈpad·əˌnāt\ *vb* -ED/-ING/-S *vt* **:** to coat with a patina **:** cast a patina on ⟨had taken time and pains to ~ them with good manners —Jean Stafford⟩ **~** *vi* **:** to become coated with a patina

pat·i·na·tion \ˌ==ˈnāshən\ *n* -S **1 :** the quality or state of being patinated **2 :** the act or process of patinating

¹pa·tine \pəˈtēn\ *n* -S [F, fr. ML & NL *patina* — more at PATINA] **1 :** PATEN **2 :** PATINA ⟨time has bestowed a ~ of oxidation on these vessels —Dorothy Adlow⟩ ⟨a slight ~ of the ruddiness of youth —Glenway Wescott⟩

²patine \"\ *vt* -ED/-ING/-S **:** PATINATE

pa·tined \-nd\ *adj* [¹*patine* + *-ed*] **:** having a patina

pat·i·nize \ˈpad·əˌnīz\ *vt* -ED/-ING/-S [*patina* + *-ize*] **:** PATINATE

pat·i·nous \-ˌnəs\ *adj* [*patina* + *-ous*] **:** coated with or having a patina

pat·io \ˈpa|d·ēˌō, ˈpä|, ˈpà|, |tēˌō\ *n* -S [Sp, fr. OSp, untilled land, building lot, courtyard enclosed by columns, prob. fr. OProv *patu, pati* rented land, rented pasture, pasture, perh. fr. L *pactum* agreement, contract — more at PACT] **1 a :** the court or courtyard of a house or other building; *esp* **:** an inner court open to the sky **b :** a recreation area adjoining a dwelling, often paved, and adapted esp. to outdoor dining **2 :** a paved yard or floor where ores are cleaned and sorted or reduced

pat·i·oed \-ˌōd\ *adj* **:** having a patio

patio process *n* **:** an amalgamation process of reducing silver ore in which ore crushed to pulp is spread on the patio and mixed with salt, copper sulfate, and mercury by spading the mass and driving horses or mules through it

pa·tis·se·rie \pəˈtisərē\ *n* -S [F *pâtisserie*, fr. MF *pastiserie* pastry (collectively), fr. (assumed) OF *pastis* cake (fr. — assumed — VL *pasticium*, fr. LL *pasta* dough, paste) + OF *-erie* -ery — more at PASTE] **1 :** a shop that sells French pastry **2 :** dessert pastry; *esp* **:** FRENCH PASTRY

patlid *var of* POTLID

patly *adv* [⁴*pat* + *-ly*] **:** in a pat manner **:** APTLY, SUITABLY ⟨the too ~ remembered conversations, and all the other fakeries that have become standard in the "as told to" books —Gilbert Seldes⟩

patmkg *abbr* patternmaking

pat·na \ˈpətnə, ˈpat-\ *adj, usu cap* [fr. *Patna*, India] **:** of or from the city of Patna, India **:** of the kind or style prevalent in Patna

patna rice *n, usu cap P* **:** a rice that originated in the Ganges valley of India and is distinguished by an elongated firm grain of excellent culinary quality which holds its shape well on boiling and is used esp. in commercial soups

pat·ness *n* -ES [⁴*pat* + *-ness*] **:** the quality or state of being pat **:** APTNESS, OPPORTUNENESS, SUITABILITY

pa·to·co \pəˈtō(ˌ)kō\ *n, pl* **patoco** *or* **patocos** *usu cap* **1 :** an Indian people with a language belonging to the Coche language family **2 :** the language of the Patoco people

pa·tois \ˈpaˌtwä, ˈpä-, ˈpà-\ *n, pl* **patois** \-wäz\ [F, fr. OF, peasant speech, prob. fr. *pate*, *patte* paw + *-ois* (as in *françois* French) — more at PATTEN] **1 a :** a dialect other than the standard or literary dialect ⟨the polyglot ~ of a Balkan borderland —*Amer. Guide Series: Minn.*⟩ **b :** illiterate or provincial speech **2 :** the characteristic special language of an occupational or social group or of the followers of a sport or other interest **:** CANT, JARGON ⟨the deportment and language of the gangsters and their "molls" was aped . . . by the "swells", and the ~ of prison yard and call house became the lingua franca of society —Polly Adler⟩ **syn** see DIALECT

¹pa·to·la \pəˈtōlə\ *n* -S [Gujarati *paṭolū*, fr. Skt *paṭola*] **1 :** a silk cloth of India **2 :** a wedding sari woven in Gujarat, India, in chiné technique

²patola \"\ *n* -S [Tag] *Philippines* **:** a dishcloth gourd (*Luffa acutangula*) that is eaten green or cooked

pa·to·lli \pəˈtōl(y)ē\ *n* -S [Sp, fr. Nahuatl] **:** an Aztec board game similar to pachisi

pa·tonce \pəˈtän(t)s\ *adj* [prob. modif. of MF *potencé* having arms like a crutch, fr. *potence* crutch — more at POTENCE] *of a heraldic cross* **:** having the arms concave and expanding toward 3-pointed ends similar to but less recurved than those of a cross fleury — usu. used postpositively; compare FLEURY, PATY; see CROSS illustration

patr- *or* **patri-** *or* **patro-** *comb form* [*patr-* partly fr. L, fr. *patr-, pater*; partly fr. Gk, fr. *patr-, patēr*; *patri-* fr. ME, fr. MF, fr. L, fr. *patr-, pater*; *patro-*, NL, fr. Gk, fr. *patr-, patēr* — more at FATHER] **:** father ⟨*patri*kin⟩ ⟨*patri*lineal⟩ ⟨*patri*stic⟩ ⟨*patro*clinal⟩ ⟨*patro*genesis⟩ ⟨*patro*nomatology⟩

patresfamilias *pl of* PATERFAMILIAS

pa·tria \ˈpä·trēə\ *n* -S [NL, fr. L, native country — more at EXPATRIATE] *biol* **:** natural habitat

¹pa·tri·al \ˈpā·trēəl\ *adj* [ML *patrialis*, fr. L *patria* + *-alis* -al] **1 :** of or relating to one's fatherland **2** *of a word* **:** derived from the name of a country or place and used to denote a native or inhabitant of it

²**patrial** \"\ *n* -s **:** a patrial word

pa·tria po·tes·tas \ˌpä·trēəpō'teˌstäs\ *n* [L, power of a father] **:** the power of the head of a Roman family over his wife, children, agnatic descendants, slaves, and freedmen including orig. the right to punish by death and always embracing complete control over the limited personal and private rights and duties of all members of the family — compare PATERFAMILIAS

pa·tri·arch \'pā·trēˌärk, -ˌȧk\ *n* -s [ME *patriark*, fr. OF *patriarche*, fr. LL *patriarcha*, fr. Gk *patriarchēs*, fr. *patria* lineage, descent, clan, family (fr. *patr-*, *patēr* father) + *-archēs* -arch — more at FATHER] **1 a :** one of the Scriptural fathers of the human race or of the Hebrew people; *specif* **:** one of a group comprising Abraham, Isaac, Jacob, and the twelve sons of Jacob **b :** a man regarded as father or founder (as of a race, science, religion, or class of men) ⟨became one of the great cattlemen of the West, and sheepmen of a later day referred to him as the ~ of their industry —H.J.Peterson⟩ **c** (1) **:** the oldest member or representative of a group ⟨a bullfrog, the ~ of the swamp, blew suddenly on his mighty tuba, "jug-o-rum" —*Springfield (Mass.) Union*⟩ ⟨the cypress of the eastern river courses, growing to heights of 150 feet or more, is the ~ of native trees, going back to the time of the dinosaur —*Amer. Guide Series: Texas*⟩ (2) **:** a venerable old man **:** ELDER, VETERAN ⟨was a whiskered ~, spry for his age —Frank Sullivan⟩ ⟨consultations with the party ~*s* —W.S. White⟩ **2 a** (1) **:** any of the bishops of the ancient or Eastern Orthodox sees of Constantinople, Alexandria, Antioch, and Jerusalem or the ancient and Western see of Rome with authority over other bishops (2) **:** the spiritual head of any of various Eastern churches either autocephalous (as the Russian Orthodox Church) or no longer in communion with the ecumenical patriarch of Constantinople and the Eastern Orthodox Church (as the Syrian or Coptic churches) **b :** an ecclesiastical dignitary next in rank to the pope: (1) **:** a Roman Catholic bishop with purely titular or with metropolitan jurisdiction (2) **:** the active ecclesiastical head of a Uniate body **3 :** the head or president of the Jewish college in Palestine; *sometimes* **:** the head of the Jewish college at Babylon **4 :** one of the Melchizedek priesthood in the Mormon church empowered to perform the ordinances of the church and to invoke and pronounce blessings within a stake or other prescribed jurisdiction **5 :** a dark reddish purple that is bluer and stronger than amaranth, auricula purple, or raisin purple

pa·tri·ar·chal \ˌ==¦ärkəl, -¦ȧk-\ *adj* [LL *patriarchalis*, fr. *patriarcha* patriarch + *-alis* -al] **1 :** of or relating to a patriarch or patriarchs **:** governed by or subject to patriarchs **:** of the nature or rank of a patriarch ⟨political independence was . . . at times preceded by the throwing off of the ~ yoke —K.S.Latourette⟩ **2 :** resembling or suggesting a patriarch **:** ANCIENT, VENERABLE ⟨the long bearded moss festoons the branches . . . a young yellow birch has a venerable, ~ look, and seems ill at ease under such premature honors —John Burroughs⟩ — **pa·tri·ar·chal·ly** \-kəlē\ *adv*

patriarchal cross *n* **:** a chiefly heraldic cross denoting a cardinal's or archbishop's rank and having two crossbars of which the lower is the longer and intersects the upright above or at its center — called also *archiepiscopal cross;* see CROSS OF LORRAINE 2

pa·tri·ar·chal·ism \ˌ==¦ärkəˌlizəm\ *n* -s **1 :** government by a patriarch **2 :** a patriarchal social organization

pa·tri·arch·ate \'==ˌärkət, -ˌkāt\ *n* -s [ML *patriarchatus*, fr. LL *patriarcha* patriarch + L *-atus* -ate — more at PATRIARCH] **1 a :** the office, dignity, jurisdiction, province, or see of a patriarch **b :** the residence or business office of a patriarch **2 :** PATRIARCHY 2

pa·tri·ar·chic \ˌ==¦ärkik, -¦ȧk-, -kēk\ *or* **pa·tri·ar·chi·cal** \-kəkəl, -kēk-\ *adj* [LL *patriarchicus*, fr. Gk *patriarchikos*, fr. *patriarchēs* patriarch + *-ikos* -ic, -ical — more at PATRIARCH] **:** PATRIARCHAL

pa·tri·arch·ism \'==ˌärˌkizəm\ *n* -s **:** patriarchal organization in society or church

pa·tri·arch·ist \-kəst\ *n* -s **:** a supporter of a patriarch or of patriarchy

pa·tri·archy \'==ˌärkē, -ˌȧk-, -ki\ *n* -ES [LGk *patriarchia*, fr. Gk *patriarchēs* patriarch + *-ia* -y] **1** *obs* **:** PATRIARCHATE 1 **2 a :** social organization marked by the supremacy of the father in the clan or family in both domestic and religious functions, the legal dependence of wife or wives and children, and the reckoning of descent and inheritance in the male line **b :** a society so organized — compare MATRIARCHY

pat·ri·centric \ˌpa·trə *sometimes* ¦pā- +\ *adj* [*patr-* + *-centric*] **:** gravitating toward or centered upon the father — compare MATRICENTRIC

patrices *pl of* PATRIX

¹**pa·tri·cian** \pə'trishən\ *n* -s [ME *patricion*, fr. MF *patricien*, fr. L *patricius* (fr. *patres* fathers, senators, pl. of *pater* father) + MF *-en* -an — more at FATHER] **1 :** a member of one of the original citizen families of ancient Rome to whom until about 350 B.C. such offices as those of senator, consul, and pontifex were restricted **2 a :** a member of a noble class created by Constantine and continued by succeeding emperors at Byzantium **b :** an official orig. of this class appointed supreme magistrate of the provinces of Italy and Africa by the Byzantine emperor **c :** a Holy Roman emperor assuming the title of patrician or granted it by the pope **3 a :** a hereditary noble of a medieval Italian city republic **b :** a member of an order of citizens eligible for the senate or council in the German free cities and towns **4 a :** a person of high birth **:** ARISTOCRAT, NOBLEMAN **b :** a person of breeding and cultivation **:** GENTLEMAN ⟨as cultivated a ~ as ever found himself leading the proletariat to Utopia —E.P.Snow⟩

²**patrician** \"\ *adj* [F *patricien*, fr. MF, fr. *patricien*, n.] **1 :** of or relating to the patricians of ancient Rome ⟨the ~ families had the start in the race. Great names and great possessions came to them by inheritance —J.A.Froude⟩ **2 :** of or relating to the patricians of the medieval Italian city republics or the German free cities **3 :** of, relating to, or characteristic of gentle or noble birth or of breeding and cultivation ⟨in the South, ~ landholders and merchants tried to set up a political monopoly —Allan Nevins & H.S.Commager⟩ — **pa·tri·cian·ly** *adv*

pa·tri·cian·ism \-shəˌnizəm\ *n* -s **:** the quality or state of being patrician

pa·tri·ci·ate \-shēət, -ēˌāt\ *n* -s [L *patriciatus*, fr. *patricius* patrician + *-atus* -ate — more at PATRICIAN] **1 :** the position or dignity of a patrician **:** NOBILITY **2 :** the term of office of a patrician **3 :** a patrician class **:** ARISTOCRACY

pat·ri·cid·al \ˌpa·trə¦sīdᵊl *sometimes* ¦pā-\ *adj* **:** of or relating to patricide **:** PARRICIDAL

pat·ri·cide \'==ˌsīd\ *n* -s [in sense 1, fr. L *patricida*, fr. *patri-* patr- + *-cida* -cide (killer); in sense 2, fr. LL *patricidium*, fr. L *patri-* + *-cidium* -cide (killing)] **1 :** one that murders his own father **2 :** the murder of one's own father

pa·trick \'pā·trik\ *chiefly Scot var of* PARTRIDGE

pat·ri·clan \'pa·trəˌklan, 'pā-\ *n* [*patr-* + *clan*] **:** a patrilineal clan — contrasted with *matriclan*

patriclinous *var of* PATROCLINOUS

pat·ri·co \'pa·trəˌkō\ *n* -ES [perh. fr. ML *pater* priest (fr. L, father) + obs. E *co* boy, prob. short for *cove* (man) — more at FATHER] *archaic* **:** HEDGE-PRIEST

pat·ridge sight \'pa·trij-\ *n* [after E. E. *Patridge*, 19th cent. Am. sportsman, its inventor] **:** a gunsight consisting of a square post front sight and a rectangular notch rear sight; *sometimes* **:** the square post front sight

pat·ri·kin \'pa·trəˌkin, 'pā-\ *n* [*patr-* + *kin*] **:** paternal relatives

pat·ri·lateral \¦pa·trə, ¦pā·trə+\ *adj* [*patr-* + *lateral*] **:** on the father's side **:** PATERNAL — contrasted with *matrilateral*

pat·ri·line \'pa·trəˌlīn, 'pā-\ *n* [*patr-* + *line*] **:** an aggregate of patrilineages

pat·ri·lineage \¦pa·trə, ¦pā·trə+\ *n* [*patr-* + *lineage*] **:** lineage based on or tracing descent through the paternal line — contrasted with *matrilineage*

pat·ri·lineal \"+\ *adj* [*patr-* + *lineal*] **:** tracing descent through the father and his ancestry **:** organized on the basis of male descent and inheritance ⟨a ~ society⟩ — contrasted with *matrilineal*

pat·ri·linear \"+\ *adj* [*patr-* + *linear*] **:** PATRILINEAL

pat·ri·li·ny \'pa·trəˌlīnē, 'pā-\ *n* -ES [*patrilineal* + *-y*] **:** the practice of tracing descent through the father's line — contrasted with *matriliny*

pat·ri·local \¦pa·trə, ¦pā·trə+\ *adj* [*patr-* + *local*] **:** located at or centered around the residence of the husband's family or tribe ⟨a ~ marriage⟩ — contrasted with *matrilocal;* compare AVUNCULOCAL, NEOLOCAL

pat·ri·locality \"+\ *n* [*patr-* + *locality*] **:** residence of a couple esp. of the newly married with the husband's family or tribe — contrasted with *matrilocality*

pat·ri·mo·ni·al \ˌpa·trə¦mōnēəl, -nyəl\ *adj* [MF, fr. LL *patrimonialis*, fr. L *patrimonium* patrimony + *-alis* -al] **:** of, relating to, or constituting a patrimony **:** inherited from ancestors **:** HEREDITARY ⟨a ~ estate⟩ — **pat·ri·mo·ni·al·ly** \-əlē, -li\ *adv*

pat·ri·mo·ny \'==ˌmōnē, -ni\ *n* -ES [ME *patrimoine*, *patrimonie*, fr. MF, fr. L *patrimonium*, fr. *patr-*, *pater* father — more at FATHER] **1 a :** an estate inherited from one's father or other ancestor ⟨financially that decision cost him a great share of his ~ —R.J.B.Sellar⟩ **b :** anything derived from one's father or ancestors **:** HERITAGE **c :** an inheritance from the past ⟨man may soon use up his ~ of oil, and after that his inheritance of coal —Leonard Engel⟩ ⟨a most important part of the intellectual ~ of Italy —R.A.Hall b. 1911⟩ **2 a :** an estate or property held by ancient right **b :** an ancient right **c :** an ancient estate or endowment (as of a church)

pat·rin \'pa·trən\ *or* **pat·ter·an** \'pad·ərən\ *n* -s [Romany *patrin*, lit., leaf, fr. Skt *patra* wing, feather, leaf; akin to Skt *patati* he flies — more at FEATHER] **:** a handful of leaves or grass thrown down at intervals by gypsies to indicate their course

pat·ri·o·fe·lis \ˌpa·trēō'fēləs\ *n, cap* [NL, fr. L *patrius* of a father + *-o-* + *felis* cat — more at EXPATRIATE] **:** a genus of creodont mammals (family Oxyaenidae) of the Eocene of Wyoming having a skull as large as that of a lion and teeth like those of a cat

pa·tri·ot \'pā·trēət, -ēˌät, *usu Brit* 'pa-; *usu* -d·+V\ *n* -s *often attrib* [MF *patriote*, fr. LL *patriota*, fr. Gk *patriōtēs*, fr. *patrios* of one's father, of or characteristic of one's forefathers, fr. *patr-*, *patēr* father — more at FATHER] **1** *obs* **:** a fellow countryman **:** COMPATRIOT **2 a :** a person who loves his country and defends and promotes its interests; *esp* **:** a soldier who fights for love of country **b :** an enthusiast for a cause other than national ⟨the South's cotton ~*s* —*Time*⟩ **3** *obs* **:** LOVER, AMATEUR **4 a** *usu cap* **:** an English parliamentary faction opposed to Sir Robert Walpole esp. from 1732-1742 **b :** one who advocates or promotes the independence of his native soil or people from the country or union of countries of which it is a part (as a colony) ⟨immortalized by the illustrious appellation of the ~ army —George Washington⟩ ⟨a band of fiery ~*s* —D.G.Haring⟩ **c :** PATRIOTEER ⟨the most bloodthirsty ~*s* in the safest swivel chairs —Walter Lippmann⟩ **5 a :** one who remains loyal to his country when it is occupied by an enemy **b :** a member of a resistance group

¹**pa·tri·o·teer** \ˌpā·trēə¦ti(ə)r\ *n* -s [*patriot* + *-eer*] **:** one who makes an ostentatious show of patriotism from venal or degraded motives **:** an insincere, misguided, or spurious patriot **:** FLAG-WAVER ⟨they are quick to detect the phony and they can distinguish a patriot from a ~ —Dorothy Thompson⟩ ⟨catchword ~*s* —S.V.Benét⟩ ⟨~*s*, roaring nationalists and reformers with apparently simple devices for making the world better and safer —Stanley Walker⟩

²**patrioteer** \"\ *vi* -ED/-ING/-S **:** to behave as a patrioteer

¹**pa·tri·ot·ic** \ˌpā·trē¦äd·ik, -¦ät|, |ēk, *sometimes & Brit usu* ˌpa-\ *also* **pa·tri·ot·i·cal** \|əkəl, |ēk-\ *adj* [¹*patriot* + *-ic*, *-ical*] **:** inspired by patriotism **:** befitting or characteristic of a patriot **:** actuated by love of one's country **:** devoted to one's country ⟨a ~ statesman⟩ ⟨stirring ~ exercises —*Springfield (Mass.) Union*⟩ — **pa·tri·ot·i·cal·ly** \|ək(ə)lē, |ēk-, -li\ *adv*

²**patriotic** \"\ *n* -s **:** PATRIOTIC COVER

patriotic cover *n* **:** a mailable envelope bearing a patriotic legend, picture, or design and manufactured privately for use in wartime

pa·tri·ot·ics \ˌpā·trē¦äd·iks\ *n pl* **:** patriotic writings, speeches, or activities **:** a display of patriotism

pa·tri·ot·ism \'pā·trēəˌtizəm *also* -əəd·ˌi- *chiefly Brit* 'pa-\ *n* -s **:** love for or devotion to country **:** the virtues and actions of a patriot ⟨the passionate language of ~ —J.A.Froude⟩

patriots' day *n, usu cap P&D* **:** April 19 commemorating the anniversary of the battles of Lexington and Concord in 1775 and observed as a legal holiday in Maine and Massachusetts

pat·ri·pas·si·an \ˌpa·trə'pasēən, ˌpā-\ *n* -s *often cap* [LL *patripassianus*, fr. L *patri-* patr- + *passus* (past part. of *pati* to bear, undergo, suffer) + *-ianus* -ian — more at PATIENT] **:** one who defends or advocates Patripassianism

pat·ri·pas·si·an·ism \-sēəˌnizəm\ *n* -s *usu cap* **:** the doctrine that in the sufferings of Jesus Christ God the Father also suffered — compare SABELLIANISM

pat·ri·pas·si·an·ist \-ˌnəst\ *n* -s **:** PATRIPASSIAN

pat·ri·potestal \¦pa·trə, ¦pā·trə+\ *adj* [*patr-* + *potestal*] **:** marked by the authority of the father or of a council of the father's relatives — contrasted with *matripotestal*

pa·tris·tic \pə'tristik, -stēk\ *or* **pa·tris·ti·cal** \-stəkəl, -stēk-\ *adj* [ISV *patr-* + *-istic*, *-istical*] **1 :** of or relating to the philosophical and theological writings of the early church fathers ⟨the revival of ~ studies in the U.S. —*Times Lit. Supp.*⟩ **2 :** of or relating to the basic early writings of any cult or system ⟨the ~ texts of Soviet Marxism —Daniel Lerner⟩ ⟨Pahlavi ~ literature —A.V.W.Jackson⟩ ⟨the ~ literature of America —D.C.Mearns⟩

patristic greek *n, usu cap P&G* **:** Greek as written by the Greek fathers of the Christian church

pa·tris·ti·cism \-stəˌsizəm\ *n* -s **:** a system based on patristics **:** the theology or mode of thought of the church fathers

patristic latin *n, usu cap P&L* **:** Latin as written by the Western church fathers

patristic philosophy *n* **:** the philosophy developed by the fathers of the Christian church divided with reference to the Nicene Council in A.D. 325 into the ante-Nicene period during which it took the form of defenses of the Christian faith and the post-Nicene period up to St. Augustine with whom it culminates

pa·tris·tics \-ristiks\ *n pl but sing in constr* **:** PATROLOGY

pa·trix \'pā·triks\ *n, pl* **pa·tri·ces** \-rəˌsēz\ [NL, fr. L *patr-*, *pater* father + E *-ix* (as in *matrix*) — more at FATHER] **:** a pattern or die used in typefounding to form a matrix **:** PUNCH 1a(7)

patrizate *vi* -ED/-ING/-S [L *patrizatus*, *patrissatus*, past part. of *patrizare*, *patrissare*, fr. *patr-* + *-issare*, *-izare* -ize] *obs* **:** to imitate one's father or forebears

patro- — see PATR-

pa·troc·i·nate \pə'träsəˌnāt\ *vt* -ED/-ING/-S [L *patrocinatus*, past part. of *patrocinari*, fr. *patrocinium* protection, defense, fr. *patronus* protector, defender — more at PATRON] *archaic* **:** DEFEND, PATRONIZE, SUPPORT — **pa·troc·i·na·tion** \=ˌ==ˈnāshən\ *n* -s

pat·ro·cli·nal \¦pa·trə¦klīnᵊl\ *or* **pat·ro·clin·ic** \-linik\ *also* **pat·ri·cli·nal** \-līnᵊl\ *or* **pat·ri·clin·ic** \-linik\ *adj* [*patr-* + *-clinal*, *-clinic*] **:** PATROCLINOUS

pat·ro·cli·nous *also* **pat·ri·cli·nous** \-līnəs\ *adj* [*patr-* + *-clinous*] **:** derived or inherited from the father or paternal line — compare MATROCLINOUS — **pat·ro·cli·ny** *also* **pat·ri·cli·ny** \'==ˌklīnē\ *n* -ES

pat·ro·genesis \¦pa·trə +\ *n* [NL, fr. *patr-* + L *genesis*] **:** ANDROGENESIS

¹**pa·trol** \pə'trōl, *dial* 'pad·əˌrōl\ *n* -s [F *patrouille*, fr. *patrouiller*] **1 a :** the action of going the rounds along a chain of sentinels or outguards to ensure greater security from attack or to check disorder **b :** the guard or men who go the rounds **c :** a detachment of two or more men employed for reconnaissance, security, or combat **d :** a unit (as of police cars, ships, or airplanes) assigned to any of various patrol duties **2 a :** the perambulation of a district or beat to watch or guard it **b :** the men assigned to this duty ⟨coast ~⟩ ⟨fire ~⟩ **3 a :** a watchful guardianship ⟨lawyers do have peculiar responsibilities for maintaining a vigilant ~ of the domestic scene against infractions of these fundamental constitutional rights —W.O.Douglas⟩ **b :** a routine of regular observation ⟨has discovered three supernovae in extragalactic nebulae in his . . . camera ~ —*American Yr. Bk.*⟩ **4 a :** a subdivision of a boy scout troop made up of two or more boys **b :** a subdivision of a girl scout troop usu. composed of from six to eight girls

²**patrol** \"\ *vb* **patrolled; patrolled; patrolling; patrols** [F *patrouiller*, fr. MF *patouiller*, *patrouiller* to paw or tramp around in the mud, fr. *patte*, *pate* paw, hoof + *-ouiller*, v. suffix — more at PATTEN] *vi* **1 :** to cover the beat of a military, police, or other guard on foot or in a vehicle **2 :** to carry out any of various military, naval, or air patrol missions ⟨carrier-based aircraft *patrolled* above —*Newsweek*⟩ ~ *vt* **:** to carry out a patrol of **:** make routine observations of for purposes of defense or protection ⟨put into service *patrolling* the north Atlantic coast —H.A.Chippendale⟩

patrol judge *n* **:** a horse racing official responsible for detecting fouls committed by the jockeys

pa·trol·ler \-lə(r)\ *n* -s **:** one that patrols **:** a member of a patrol

pa·trol·man \-lmən\ *n, pl* **patrolmen 1 a :** a policeman on patrol duty **b :** a rank-and-file policeman **:** one without supervisory rank or authority **2 :** an inspector of electric power lines **3 :** a fire guard patrolling a section (as of a forest)

pat·ro·log·ic \¦pa·trə¦läjik\ *or* **pat·ro·log·i·cal** \-jəkəl\ *adj* **:** of or relating to patrology

pa·trol·o·gist \pə'träləjəst\ *n* -s **:** a specialist in patrology

pa·trol·o·gy \-jē\ *n* -ES [NL *patrologia*, fr. *patr-* + *-logia* -logy] **1 :** a branch of historical theology treating of the teachings of the fathers of the Christian church — called also *patristics* **2 :** a collection of the writings of the church fathers

patrol wagon *n* **:** an enclosed police wagon or motor truck used to carry prisoners — called also *Black Maria, paddy wagon*

patrol wagon

patrolwoman \=ˈ=,==\ *n, pl* **patrolwomen :** a woman member of a police force without officer's rank

¹**pa·tron** \'pā·trən\ *n* -s [ME *patroun*, fr. MF *patrun*, *patron*, fr. ML & L; ML *patronus* patron of a benefice, patron saint, master, pattern, fr. L, defender, protector, advocate, fr. *patr-*, *pater* father — more at FATHER] **1 a :** a person chosen, named, or honored as a special guardian, protector, or supporter **b :** PATRON SAINT **c :** a wealthy or influential supporter of an artist or writer ⟨a ~ of scholars, a grand seigneur —R.W.Southern⟩ **d :** a social or financial sponsor of an entertainment or other function (as for charity) ⟨included among the ~*s* of the Junior League dance⟩ **2 a :** one who gives of his means or uses his influence to help or benefit an individual, an institution, or a cause **:** BENEFACTOR ⟨philanthropist and ~ of arts —*N.Y.Times*⟩ ⟨widely known as an explorer and a ~ of exploration —W.J.Ghent⟩ **b** *obs* **:** the declared champion of a theory, teaching, or position ⟨a ~ of anarchy —John Locke⟩ **3 :** a steady or regular client: as **a :** an habitual customer of a merchant **b :** a regular client of a physician **c :** a parent or guardian of a child in a private school **d :** one who uses the services of a library and esp. of a public library **4 :** the master or steersman of a galley or of a river boat or coasting ship **5** *obs* **:** an owner of slaves or captives **6** *archaic* **:** a case for pistol cartridges **7 :** the conductor or master of an atelier for the study of architectural design **8 :** the holder of the right of presentation to an English ecclesiastical benefice **:** the owner of the advowson **9 :** a Roman patrician under whose protection a client places himself **10** *Roman law* **:** a master who frees his slave but retains some rights over him — compare OBSEQUIUM **11** \pa'trō⁽ⁿ⁾\ **:** the proprietor of an establishment (as an inn) — compare PATRONNE **12 :** the chief male officer in some fraternal lodges having both men and women members — compare MATRON

²**patron** \"\ *vt* -ED/-ING/-S [prob. fr. F *patronner*, fr. MF, fr. *patron*] *archaic* **:** to serve as patron of **:** PATRONIZE

¹**patron·age** \'pa·trənij, 'pā-\ *n* -s [ME, fr. MF, fr. *patron* + *-age*] **1 :** the right of presentation to an ecclesiastical benefice orig. carrying with it the obligation to protect the rights of the church within the parish **:** ADVOWSON **2 a :** the support or influence of a patron; *esp* **:** a benefactor's provision (as for an artist or institution) ⟨the ~ of science by and through universities is its most proper form —J.R.Oppenheimer⟩ **b** *archaic* **:** DEFENSE, PROTECTION **c** *obs* **:** ADVOCACY **3 :** the tutelary care or guardianship of a deity or saint **4 :** kindness done with an air of superiority **:** condescending favor ⟨accept ~? . . . Never —Marguerite Steen⟩ **5 :** the trade of customers ⟨though it was not yet noon, there was a considerable ~ —C.B.Kelland⟩ **6 :** the right to appoint to government jobs **:** control of political appointments ⟨oust his enemies from office and use the ~ to support his policies —H.K.Beale⟩

²**patronage** *vt* -ED/-ING/-S **:** to act as patron of **:** MAINTAIN, DEFEND

pa·tron·al \'pā·trənᵊl, 'pa-, pə'trōnᵊl\ *adj* [F or LL; F, fr. LL *patronalis*, fr. L *patronus* patron + *-alis* -al — more at PATRON] **:** of or relating to a patron or a patron saint

pa·tron·ate \'pā·trənət, 'pa-, -əˌnāt\ *n* -s [LL *patronatus*, fr. *patronus* patron + *-atus* -ate — more at PATRON] **:** the right, duty, position, jurisdiction, or possession of a patron **:** PATRONAGE

pa·tron·ess \'pā·trənəs\ *n* -ES [ME *patronesse*, fr. *patron*, *patroun* patron + *-esse* -ess — more at PATRON] **:** a female patron: as **a :** a female patron saint **b :** a woman sponsor of a social or charitable affair **c :** a woman who defends or promotes the interests of a protégé

pat·ro·nite \'pa·trəˌnīt\ *n* -s [Antenor Rizo-*Patrona*, 20th cent. Peruvian mineralogist + E *-ite*] **:** a black mixture of vanadium minerals found at Minasragra, Peru, and there mined as an ore of vanadium

pa·tron·iza·tion \ˌpā·trənə'zāshən *also* ˌpa-\ *n* -s **:** the act of patronizing

pa·tron·ize \'pā·trəˌnīz *also* 'pa-\ *vt* -ED/-ING/-S *see -ize in Explan Notes* [MF or ML; MF *patroniser*, fr. ML *patronizare*, fr. L & ML *patronus* patron + L *-izare* -ize — more at PATRON] **1 :** to act as patron of **:** FAVOR, PROTECT, SUPPORT ⟨he did feel real gratitude to the woman who had *patronized* his early ambition —Hilaire Belloc⟩ **2** *obs* **:** DEFEND **3** *obs* **:** to lay responsibility for **:** FATHER — used with *upon* **4 :** to adopt an air of superiority and condescension toward **:** treat haughtily or superciliously ⟨breaks through established formulas to please the judicious without *patronizing* the larger public —*Saturday Rev.*⟩ **5 :** to trade or deal with habitually **:** be a customer or client of **:** USE, FREQUENT ⟨a restaurant . . . *patronized* by democratic folk —P.B.Kyne⟩ ⟨ranchmen ~ stores strung out over a large space —*Amer. Guide Series: Texas*⟩ ⟨we both *patronized* the city library —W.A.White⟩ ⟨introductory astronomy is often a popular undergraduate course, although not as heavily *patronized* as other sciences —F.D.Miller⟩

pa·tron·iz·er \-zə(r)\ *n* -s *archaic* **:** one that patronizes

pa·tron·iz·ing \-zig, -zēŋ\ *adj* **:** CONDESCENDING ⟨her tone was . . . insufferably ~ —P.I.Wellman⟩ — **pa·tron·iz·ing·ly** *adv*

pa·tron·less \'pā·trənləs\ *adj, archaic* **:** having no patron

pa·tronne \pa'trȯn, -'trən\ *n* -s [F, fr. MF, fem. of *patron* — more at PATRON] **1 :** a female patron saint **2 :** the proprietress of an establishment (as an inn)

patrons *pl of* PATRON, *pres 3d sing of* PATRON

patron saint *n* **1 :** a saint to whose protection and intercession a person, a society, a church, or a place is dedicated — compare TITULAR **2 :** an original leader or prime exemplar ⟨a $100-a-plate . . . dinner honoring the party's *patron saints* —*Springfield (Mass.) Union*⟩

¹**pat·ro·nym·ic** \ˌpa·trə'nimik, -mēk\ *n* -s [LL *patronymicum*, fr. neut. of *patronymicus* of a patronymic, fr. Gk *patronymikos*, fr. *patronymia* patronymic (fr. *patr-* + *-onyma* name + *-ia* -y) + *-ikos* -ic] **1 :** a name derived from that of the father or a paternal ancestor usu. by the addition of a prefix or suffix (as in *MacDonald*, son of Donald, or *Ivanovich*, son of Ivan) — contrasted with *matronymic;* compare TEKNONYMY **2 :** a patrilineal surname or family name

²**patronymic** \¦==¦==\ *also* **pat·ro·nym·i·cal** \-məkəl\ *adj*

[*patronymic* fr. LL *patronymicus; patronymical* fr. LL *patronymicus* + E *-al*] **:** of, relating to, or constituting a patronymic — **pat·ro·nym·i·cal·ly** \-mək(ə)lē\ *adv*

pa·troon \pə'trün\ *n* -s [in sense 1, fr. F *patron* & Sp *patrón*, lit., master, fr. ML *patronus;* in sense 2, fr. D, fr. F *patron* patron, master — more at PATRON] **1** *archaic* **:** the captain or officer commanding a ship **2 :** the proprietor of one of the tracts of land with manorial privileges granted to members of the Dutch West India Company under the old Dutch governments of New York and New Jersey

pa·troon·ship \-n,ship\ *n* **:** the rank or estate of a patroon

pats *pl of* PAT, *pres 3d sing of* PAT

¹pat·sy \'patsē, -si\ *n* -ES [perh. fr. It *pazzo* fool, lunatic] **1 :** a butt of ridicule **:** ODDBALL ⟨knew this ~ was a disastrous mistake socially —Elizabeth Janeway⟩ **2 a :** a person on whom blame is foisted **:** FALL GUY ⟨not going to be the ~ for that gang of his —S.H.Adams⟩ **b :** one readily deceived or victimized **:** EASY MARK, SUCKER ⟨a perfect ~ for his enthusiasms —George Sklar⟩

²patsy \"\ *n, pl* **patsys** *usu cap* [fr. *Patsy*, nickname for *Patricia*] **:** any of several awards that are given annually by humane organizations to animals that perform in motion pictures

patt *abbr* pattern

pat·ta·mar *or* **pat·a·mar** \'pad·ə,mär\ *n* -S [Pg *patamar*, fr. Malayalam *pattamāri*] **1** *obs* **:** COURIER, MESSENGER **2 :** a ship used in the coasting trade of Bombay and Ceylon having lateen sails, a keel hollowing upward in the middle, and long overhangs

patted *past of* PAT

pat·tée *also* **pa·té** *or* **pa·tée** \pə'tā\ *adj* [MF *paté, patté* (masc.) & *patee, pattee* (fem.), fr. *pate, patte* paw + *-é, -ee* -ate] *of a cross* **:** FORMÉE

pat·ten \'pat°n\ *n* -S [ME *paten, patin, pateyn*, fr. MF *patin*, fr. *pate, patte* paw, hoof, fr. (assumed) VL *patta*, of imit. origin] **1 :** a clog, sandal, or overshoe often with a wooden sole or metal device to elevate the foot and increase the wearer's height or aid in walking in mud — compare CHOPINE, GETA, PLATFORM, SABOT **2** *Brit* **:** a round wooden plate fastened to the hind feet of horses to prevent their sinking into soft or boggy land that is being plowed or cultivated **3 :** an ice skate of an early variety **4** *archaic* **:** an architectural base, stand, support, foot, bottom plate, or sill

pat·ten·er \'patənə(r)\ *n* -S *dial Eng* **:** SKATER

¹pat·ter \'pad·ə(r), -atə-\ *vb* -ED/-ING/-S [ME *patren, pattern*, fr. *paternoster*] *vt* **1 :** to say or repeat in a rapid or mechanical manner **:** MUTTER ⟨~ the jargon of two different tribes —F.L.Lucas⟩ **2 :** to speak glibly ⟨they're college-reared and can ~ languages —John Buchan⟩ ~ *vi* **1 :** to recite paternosters or other prayers rapidly, mechanically, or perfunctorily ⟨I'd be ~*ing* away with my tongue, in church, like all the rest —Lord Dunsany⟩ **2 :** to talk glibly and volubly usu. without close attention to sense **:** chatter gibberish, jargon, or cant ⟨~*ed*, all smiles, through a soft-voiced colorless recital of events —Lester Atwell⟩ **3 :** to speak or sing the rapid-fire words of a theatrical patter speech or song **4 :** to issue (as words) in staccato fashion ⟨a poem lightly ~*ing* into his ear —Amy Lowell⟩ ⟨jokes . . . ~*ed* regularly from variety comedians —Anthony Glyn⟩

²patter \"\ *n* -S **1 :** a specialized lingo **:** CANT ⟨the sociologist's sometimes useful ~ —Dwight Macdonald⟩ ⟨the ~ of science —Ellen Glasgow⟩ ⟨ad-libbing a sales ~ —*Fortune*⟩ ⟨the silly pseudosophisticated ~ of the most unpleasant smart people —J.C.Powys⟩; *sometimes* **:** the jargon of thieves or other criminals **2 :** the spiel of a street hawker or of a circus barker **3 :** empty chattering talk **:** GABBLE ⟨the incessant ~ of the argument —F.R.Leavis⟩ ⟨nothing's too petty for her to make controversial ~ of —Rex Ingamells⟩ ⟨table talk couched in cliché and ~ —H.R.Warfel⟩ **4 a :** the rapid-fire talk of a comedian or the talk with which any of various performers accompanies his routine **b :** the words of a comic or musical comedy song or of a rapidly spoken usu. humorous monologue introduced into such a song **c :** metrical lines often of nonsense interpolated by a western square dance caller to fill in between commands to the dancers

³patter \"\ *vb* -ED/-ING/-S [freq. of *²pat*] *vi* **1 :** to strike, pat, or tap rapidly usu. so as to make quick light sounds ⟨on the shingled roof the rain was ~*ing* like a multitude of tiny feet —Ellen Glasgow⟩ **2 :** to run with short quick light-sounding steps ⟨~*ed* softly down the stairs —Marcia Davenport⟩ ~ *vt* **:** to cause to patter

⁴patter \"\ *n* -S **:** a quick succession of slight sounds or pats ⟨the ~ of rain⟩ ⟨the ~ of little feet⟩

patteran *var of* PATRIN

pat·ter·er \'pad·ərə(r)\ *n* -S [*¹patter* + *-er*] **:** one that patters; *esp* **:** one that talks patter

¹pat·tern *R* 'pad·ərn, -atə-, *-R* -d·ən, -tən, -t°n; *R* & *-R chiefly substand* -d·ərən *or* -tərən\ *n* -S [ME *patron, patern*, fr. MF, fr. ML *patronus* — more at PATRON] **1 :** a fully realized form, original, or model accepted or proposed for imitation **:** something regarded as a normative example to be copied **:** ARCHETYPE, EXEMPLAR ⟨has been acting like a practically model ~ for a constructive opposition —*New Yorker*⟩ **2 :** something designed or used as a model for making things **:** OUTLINE, PLAN ⟨a dressmaker's ~⟩ **3 a** *obs* **:** a foundry matrix **b :** a model usu. made of varnished or painted wood or of metal for making a mold into which molten metal is poured to form a casting **4 a :** a representative instance **:** a typical example **b :** a specimen offered as a sample of the whole **5 :** an artistic or mechanical design or form: as **a :** the shape or style of a manufactured article ⟨bought a silver service of open stock ~⟩ **b :** a design or figure used in decoration ⟨the simple dignity of ~ of a New England colonial doorframe⟩ ⟨the geometrical ~ of a rug⟩ **c :** form or style in literary or musical composition **:** coherent structure or design ⟨the whole book forms a rich and subtle but highly organized ~ —F.R.Leavis⟩ **d :** the composition or plan of a work of graphic or plastic art **e :** architectural design or style **f :** the tracing made by skate blades by a figure or dance step executed on ice **6 :** a natural or chance configuration (as of markings or of events) ⟨frost ~*s*⟩ **7 a :** a patron saint's day in Ireland **b :** the festivity connected with such a day **c :** a dance on any holiday **8 :** a specimen of a proposed coin or coin design; *esp* **:** one that has not been authorized for regular issue **9 :** a length of fabric sufficient for an article (as a dress) **10 a :** the distribution of the shot from a shotgun or the bullets from an exploded shrapnel on a target perpendicular to the plane of fire **b :** a diagram showing such distribution **c :** the grouping made on a target by rifle or handgun bullets and regarded as a test of marksmanship or of the qualities of the gun **11 :** a reliable sample of traits, acts, or other observable features characterizing an individual ⟨behavior ~⟩ ⟨personality ~⟩ — compare PROFILE **12 :** the approaches, turns, and altitudes prescribed for an airplane that is coming in for a landing **13 :** an established mode of behavior or cluster of mental attitudes, beliefs, and values held in common by the members of a group **14 :** the largest unit of classification in the midwestern system for American archaeology constituting a group of phases having several distinguishing and fundamental features in common — compare ASPECT, COMPONENT, FOCUS **15 :** the manner in which smaller units of language are grouped or groupable into larger units (as sounds into sound classes or into words) ⟨the ~ voiceless stop/voiced stop/nasal seen in the bilabials \p\, \b\, \m\ is paralleled in the alveolars \t\, \d\, \n\ and in the velars \k\, \g\, \ŋ\⟩ **16 :** a standard diagram transmitted for testing television circuits
syn see MODEL

²pattern \"\ *vb* -ED/-ING/-S *vt* **1** *obs* **:** to serve as a pattern for **:** FORESHADOW **2 :** to make, fashion, or design according to a pattern ⟨the . . . chantey was ~*ed* on a salt-water model —*Amer. Guide Series: Mich.*⟩ **3** *chiefly dial Eng* **a :** MATCH, PARALLEL **b :** to use as a pattern or model **:** IMITATE **4 :** to furnish, adorn, or mark with a pattern or design ⟨scarlet, violet, and purple togas ~ the mass of black and brown —Amy Lowell⟩ ~ *vi* **1 :** to form patterns ⟨the dancer is always ~*ing* in space, as well as in time —Ruth A. Radir⟩ **2** *of a firearm* **:** to make a pattern on a target with shot or bullets **3 :** to constitute or fit into a language pattern

pattern bargaining *n* **:** bargaining by a labor union for a number of work contracts based on the example of one that it considers desirable

pattern bombing *n* **:** AREA BOMBING

pattern card *n* **:** any of the perforated cards used in jacquard weaving

pattern chain *n* **:** any of various devices on looms or knitting machines that resemble chains and control the working of the figures or designs in the material by bringing into action or taking out of action various shuttles and harnesses in weaving or various needles and stitches in knitting

pat·terned \-nd\ *adj* **:** arranged in or formed into patterns

pat·tern·ing \-niŋ, -nēŋ\ *n* -S **1 :** decoration, composition, or configuration according to a pattern ⟨the sober ~ of his cravat —Osbert Sitwell⟩ **2 a :** personal conduct illustrating a sociocultural pattern **b :** the characteristic form of a sociocultural custom or institution

pat·tern·ize \-,nīz\ *vt* -ED/-ING/-S **:** to make conform to, reduce to, or arrange in a pattern

pat·tern·less \-nləs\ *adj* **1** *obs* **:** MATCHLESS, PEERLESS **2 :** wanting pattern

patternmaker \'==,==\ *n* **:** one that makes patterns (as for founding, woodworking, sewing, or weaving)

patternmaker's saw *n* **:** a short thin-bladed handsaw with extra sharp teeth and raised handle used for fine work in cabinetmaking and patternmaking

patternmaker's saw

patternmaking \'==,==\ *n* **:** the process of making wood patterns or models for foundry use

pattern mold *n* **:** a mold having depressions or protuberances forming patterns on the interior surface into which a parison of glass is forced or blown — **pattern-molded** \'==;==\ *adj* — **pattern molder** *n*

pattern plate *n* **:** ¹CASTER 1b

patterns *pl of* PATTERN, *pres 3d sing of* PATTERN

patternwood \'==,=\ *n* **1 :** an African tree (*Alstonia congensis*) having light soft even-textured straight-grained wood **2 :** the wood of the patternwood tree used esp. for box making

pattern-word \'==,=\ *n, cryptology* **:** a plaintext idiomorph

pat·terny \-nē\ *adj* **:** conspicuously patterned

patters *pres 3d sing of* PATTER, *pl of* PATTER

patter song *n* [*²patter*] **:** a song (as in musical comedy or comic opera) in which patter is used for humorous effect

patting *pres part of* PAT

pat·tin·son process \'pat°nsən-\ *n, usu cap 1st P* [after Hugh Lee *Pattinson* †1858 Eng. metallurgist] **:** a process for desilverizing and purifying lead

patton's spruce *or* **patton's hemlock** \'pat°nz-\ *n, usu cap P* [after George *Patton*, Lord Glenalmond †1869 Scot. jurist and arboriculturist] **:** MOUNTAIN HEMLOCK

pat·tu *also* **pat·too** *or* **put·too** \'pə(,)tü\ *n* -S [Hindi *paṭṭū*, fr. Skt *paṭṭa* cloth] **1 :** a homespun woolen fabric resembling tweed that is woven usu. of goat hair in northern India **2 :** a blanket or wrap of pattu

pat·ty *also* **pat·tie** \'pad·|ē, -at|, |i\ *n, pl* **patties** [F *pâté* — more at PÂTÉ] **1 :** a little pie or pasty **2 a :** a small flat cake of chopped food (as ground meat) **b :** a small flat candy ⟨peppermint ~⟩ **3 :** PATTY SHELL

patty-cake \'==,=\ *n* [by alter.] **:** PAT-A-CAKE

pattypan \'==,=\ *n* **1 :** a pan for baking patties **:** MUFFIN PAN **2** *or* **pattypan squash :** CYMLING

patty shell *n* **:** a shell of puff paste made to hold a creamed meat, fish, or vegetable filling

pa·tu \'pä(,)tü\ *or* **pa·tu-pa·tu** \-ü'pä(,)tü\ *n* -S [Maori] **:** a short two-edged Maori weapon of stone, wood, or bone resembling a club and tapering in thickness but expanding in width from the butt and designed to give a crushing rather than cutting blow

pat·u·lin \'pachələn\ *n* -S [ISV *patul-* (fr. NL *patulum* — specific epithet of *Penicillium patulum* — fr. L, neut. of *patulus*) + *-in*] **:** CLAVACIN

pat·u·lous \'pachələs\ *adj* [L *patulus*, fr. *patēre* to be open — more at FATHOM] **1 :** spread widely apart **:** wide open **:** DISTENDED ⟨a wound with ~ margins⟩ **2 :** spreading widely from a center **:** loosely or diffusely expanded or spread out ⟨an old apple with ~ branches⟩ — **pat·u·lous·ly** *adv* — **pat·u·lous·ness** *n* -ES

pat·u·ron \'pachə,rän\ *n* -S [F, fr. Gk *patein* to tread, trample on + NL *-uron* (fr. Gk *oura* tail); akin to Gk *patos* path — more at FIND, -UROUS] **:** the basal segment of the arachnid chelicera

¹pa·tux·ent \pə'təksənt\ *n, pl* **patuxent** *or* **patuxents** *usu cap* **1 :** an extinct Algonquian Indian people formerly dwelling in Calvert county, Maryland **2 :** one of the Patuxent people

²patuxent \"\ *adj, usu cap* [*¹Patuxent*] **:** of or relating to a subdivision of the Comanchean — see GEOLOGIC TIME table

pat·wa·ri *or* **put·wa·ri** \(,)pət'wärē\ *n* -S [Hindi *paṭwārī*, fr. Skt *paṭṭa* land grant + Eastern Hindi *-wārī*, agent suffix] **:** a village registrar or accountant in India

pat·win \'pat,win\ *n, pl* **patwin** *or* **patwins** *usu cap* **1 a :** an Indian people of the Sacramento valley, Calif. **b :** a member of such people **2 :** a Copehan language of the Patwin people

paty \'pad·ē\ *adj* [MF *paté, patté* (masc.) & *patee, pattee* (fem.) — more at PATTÉE] *of a heraldic cross* **:** having the ends of the arms splayed or spread out — compare FLEURY, FORMÉE, MOLINE, PATONCE

pau \'paù\ *adj* [Hawaiian] **:** COMPLETED, CONSUMED, FINISHED

pa'u \'pä,ü\ *n* -S [Hawaiian] **:** an Hawaiian sarong formerly made of tapa and now of cotton or silk and worn by women for dancing, horseback riding in parades, and ceremonies

paua \'paùə\ *n* -S [Maori] **:** an abalone of New Zealand

pau bra·sil *also* **pau bra·zil** \,paùbrə'zil\ *n* [Pg *pau Brasil*, lit., Brazil wood] **:** a variety of brazilwood (*Caesalpinia echinata*)

pauci- *comb form* [L, fr. *paucus* little] **:** few ⟨*pauci*foliate⟩ ⟨*pauci*disperse⟩

pau·cil·o·quy \pò'siləkwē\ *n* -ES [L *pauciloquium* fr. *pauci-* + *-loquium* (fr. *loqui* to speak)] *archaic* **:** brevity in speech

pau·ci·spiral \,pòsē+\ *adj* [*pauci-* + *spiral*] **:** spiral with few turns

pau·ci·ty \'pòsəd·ē, -ətē, -i\ *n* -ES [ME *paucite*, fr. MF or L; MF *paucité*, fr. L *paucitat-, paucitas*, fr. *paucus* little + *-itat-, -itas* -ity — more at FEW] **1 :** a small number **:** FEWNESS ⟨the chorus suffered slightly from a ~ of male voices —Douglas Watt⟩ ⟨make up in quality for their ~ of numbers —R.B. Morris⟩ **2 :** smallness of quantity **:** DEARTH, INSUFFICIENCY, SCARCITY ⟨the simplicity that never was ~ —C.D.Lewis⟩ ⟨the ~ of help accorded to me —Rudyard Kipling⟩ ⟨a language now almost unknown because of the extreme ~ of its remains —G.B.Saul⟩

paughty \'pòti, 'päk-\ *adj* [origin unknown] *chiefly Scot* **:** HAUGHTY, HIGHFALUTIN

pauk·pan \'pòk,pan\ *n* -S [Burmese] **1 :** the bast fiber of the sola **2 :** SOLA

¹paul *var of* PAWL

²paul \'pòl\ *n* -S [It *paolo*] **:** PAOLO

paul-bun·nell antibody \'pòl'bən°l-\ *n, usu cap P&B* [after John R. *Paul* †1971 and Walls W. *Bunnell* †1965 Am. physicians] **:** HETEROPHIL ANTIBODY

paul-bunnell reaction *or* **paul-bunnell test** *n, usu cap P&B* [after John R. *Paul* & W. W. *Bunnell*] **:** a test for heterophil antibody used in the diagnosis of infectious mononucleosis

paul bun·yan \'pòl'bənyən\ *n, usu cap P&B* [after *Paul Bunyan*, legendary American lumberjack who was capable of amazing feats of lumbering] **:** a person often of great size who performs unusual often prodigious feats of strength or endurance ⟨a milder *Paul Bunyan* of the coal mines, steel mills, and construction jobs —*N. Y. Herald Tribune Bk. Rev.*⟩

paul·dron \'pòldrən\ *or* **poul·dron** \'pōl-\ *n* -S [ME *polrond*, modif. of MF *espauleron*, fr. *espaule* shoulder, fr. OF — more at EPAULET] **:** a piece of armor covering the shoulder where the body piece and arm piece join — compare EPAULIERE

paul·i·an·ist \'pòlēənəst\ *n* -S *usu cap* [obs. E *paulian* Paulianist (fr. *Paul* of Samosata *fl* A.D.260 bishop of Antioch + E *-ian*) + E *-ist*] **:** a follower of the dynamic Monarchian Paul of Samosata who denied a distinction of persons in God and maintained that Christ was a mere man raised above other men by the indwelling Logos

pau·li·cian \pò'lishən\ *n* -S *usu cap* [ML *Pauliciani*, pl., fr. MGk *Paulikianoi*] **:** a member of a dualistic Christian sect originating in Armenia in the 7th century, influencing the rise of the Bogomils, becoming nearly extinct in the 12th century, and characterized by the belief that matter is evil and that the creator of the material universe is an evil demiurge to be distinguished from the heavenly God who created and rules souls, by denial of the Incarnation, and by rejection of the Old Testament, the cross, and all images — see THONDRAKI

pau·li exclusion principle \'pòlē-\ *also* **pauli principle** *n, usu cap 1st P* [after Wolfgang *Pauli* †1958 Swiss physicist] **:** a principle in physics: no two electrons in an atom or molecule can exist simultaneously in states defined by the same set of quantum numbers — called also *exclusion principle*

pau·lin \'pòlən\ *n* -S [by shortening] **:** TARPAULIN ⟨waterproof material for ~*s* and ponchos —Howell Walker⟩

paul·ine \'pò,līn, -lēn\ *adj, usu cap* [ML *paulinus*, fr. LL *Paulus* Paul †*ab* A.D. 67 Christian saint who was apostle to the Gentiles and author of several epistles in the New Testament + L *-inus* -ine] **:** of, relating to, or characteristic of the apostle Paul or his writings **:** conforming to Paul's teachings

pauline privilege *n, usu cap 1st P* [so called fr. its being based on Paul's doctrine in 1 Cor 7:12–17] **:** the option available to a previously unbaptized person who becomes a Roman Catholic after marriage to another unbaptized person of dissolving the marriage through legal action undertaken with the consent of ecclesiastical authority if the other person refuses to become a Catholic and impedes the convert's practice of religion

¹pau·lin·i·an \pò'linēən\ *adj, usu cap* [L *paulinus* of or pertaining to Paul (fr. *Paulus* Paul) + E *-an*] **:** PAULINE

²paulinian \"\ *n* -S *usu cap* **:** PAULINIST

paul·in·ism \'pòlə,nizəm\ *n* -S *usu cap* [*pauline* + *-ism*] **:** the theological principles taught by or ascribed to the apostle Paul; *esp* **:** Paul's teaching of emancipation from the Jewish law, the indwelling spirit of Christ, and justification by faith

paul·in·ist \-,nəst\ *n* -S *usu cap* [*pauline* + *-ist*] **:** a follower of the apostle Paul or of his teachings

paul·in·ize \-lə,nīz\ *vb* -ED/-ING/-S *often cap* [*pauline* + *-ize*] *vi* **:** to follow the teachings of the apostle Paul ~ *vt* **:** to indoctrinate with Paulinism

paul·ism \'pò,lizəm\ *n* -S *usu cap* [*Paul* †*ab*.A.D.67 Christian apostle and saint + E *-ism*] **:** PAULINISM

paul·ist \-,ləst\ *n* -S *usu cap* [St. *Paul* + E *-ist*] *Roman Catholicism* **:** a member of the Congregation of the Missionary Priests of St. Paul the Apostle

pau·lis·ta \paù'lēstə\ *n* -S *cap* [Pg *Paulista*, fr. São *Paulo*, state and city in Brazil + Pg *-ista* -ist (fr. L)] **1 :** a Brazilian descended from the first Portuguese colonists and from Indian women **2 :** a native or inhabitant of the city of São Paulo, Brazil

paul jones \'pòl'jōnz\ *n, usu cap P&J* [prob. after John *Paul Jones* †1792 Am. naval officer and hero of the American Revolution] **:** a method of changing partners during a dance whereby at a signal the dancers form a circle and execute a grand right and left until at another signal each man resumes the original dance taking as his new partner the lady who is opposite him

paul·lin·ia \pò'linēə\ *n* [NL, fr. Simon *Paulli* †1680 Dan. botanist + L *-inus* -ine + NL *-ia*] **1** *cap* **:** a genus of chiefly tropical American woody vines (family Sapindaceae) with compound leaves, irregular flowers, and pyriform capsules — see GUARANA, SUPPLEJACK **2** -S **:** any vine of the genus *Paullinia*

pau·lo·post \'pòlə,pōst\ *adj* [L *paulo post* a little after] **:** somewhat later; *specif* **:** relating to changes taking place in an igneous rock just after its consolidation

pau·lo·spore \'pòlə,spō(ə)r\ *n* [Gk *paula* rest + E *spore* — more at PAUSE] **:** a specialized growth or development serving as a resting stage in the life of a fungus

pau·low·nia \pò'lōnēə\ *n* [NL, fr. Anna *Paulovna* †1865 Russ. princess and queen of William II of the Netherlands + NL *-ia*] **1** *cap* **:** a small genus of medium-sized deciduous Chinese trees (family Scrophulariaceae) with large opposite trilobate or entire leaves and terminal panicles of whitish to deep violet-purple flowers **2** -S **:** any tree of the genus *Paulownia; esp* **:** a tree (*P. tomentosa*) that is widely cultivated in mild regions for its showy panicles of fragrant violet flowers — see KIRI

paul pry \'pòl'prī\ *n, pl* **paul prys** *usu cap both Ps* [after *Paul Pry* meddlesome hero of the comedy *Paul Pry* (1825) by John Poole †1872 Eng. playwright] **:** an excessively inquisitive person ⟨we don't want any *Paul Prys* in this country at present —John Buchan⟩

pauls *pl of* PAUL

paultry *var of* PALTRY

paul ve·ro·ne·se green \'pòl,varə'nāsā-\ *n, often cap P&V* [after *Paul Veronese* †1588 Ital. painter] **:** EMERALD 2a

paum \'päm\ *dial Brit var of* PALM

pa'u·mo·tu·an \,paù'mōtüən\ *n* -S *usu cap* [*Paumotu* (Tuamotu), archipelago in the south Pacific ocean + E *-an*] **:** TUAMOTUAN

¹paunch \'pònch, 'pänch, 'pánch\ *n* -ES [ME *paunche*, fr. MF *pance, panche*, fr. L *pantic-, pantex*; perh. akin to OSlav *počiti* (sę) to inflate] **1 a :** the belly and its contents **b :** POTBELLY ⟨a comfortable ~ swelled out beneath the buttons of his dinner jacket —Hamilton Basso⟩ **2 a :** RUMEN **b** *chiefly dial* **:** TRIPE — usu. used in pl. **3 a :** PAUNCH MAT **b :** a thin shield of wood on a mast that permits the lower yards to slide easily over the hoops

²paunch \"\ *vt* -ED/-ING/-ES **1 :** to wound in the stomach ⟨with a log batter his skull or ~ him with a stake —Shak.⟩ **2** *obs* **:** to stuff the stomach of with food and drink **3 :** to open the paunch of **:** EVISCERATE ⟨rabbits must not be ~*ed* out of doors in hot weather —F.D.Smith & Barbara Wilcox⟩

paunch·i·ness \-chēnəs\ *n* -ES **:** the quality or state of being paunchy ⟨in cattle it depends upon the condition, ~, type, and quality —F.B.Hadley⟩

paunch mat *n* **:** a thick mat of strands of rope that prevents the yard or rigging from chafing

paunchy \-chē, -chi\ *adj* -ER/-EST [*paunch* + *-y*] **:** having a paunch **:** POTBELLIED

paup \'pòp\ *vi* -ED/-ING/-S [prob. of Scand origin; akin to ON *paufa* to walk slowly, walk stealthily; akin to OE *potian* to push, butt, goad — more at PUT] *dial Eng* **:** to walk about aimlessly

¹pau·per \'pòpə(r)\ *n* -S *often attrib* [L, poor — more at POOR] **1 :** a person destitute of means except such as are derived from charity; *specif* **:** one who receives aid from public poor funds ⟨buried in a ~'s grave⟩ ⟨found his name on the town ~ list⟩ ⟨~ support⟩ **2 :** a very poor person **3 :** one allowed to sue in forma pauperis ⟨~ costs⟩

²pauper \"\ *vt* -ED/-ING/-S **:** PAUPERIZE

pau·per·age \-pərij\ *n* -S [*¹pauper* + *-age*] **:** the condition of being a pauper

pau·per·ism \-pə,rizəm\ *n* -S **:** the quality or state of being a pauper

pau·per·it·ic \;pòpə;rid·ik\ *adj* [*pauper* + *-itic*] **:** appearing to be checked in growth by poor environment **:** STUNTED

pau·per·iza·tion \,pòpərə'zāshən\ *n* -S [*pauperize* + *-ation*] **:** the act or process of being pauperized **:** the state of pauperism ⟨the social restrictions and economic ~ . . . reached a point requiring urgent means of correction —*Collier's Yr. Bk.*⟩

pau·per·ize \'pòpə,rīz\ *vt* -ED/-ING/-S [*¹pauper* + *-ize*] **:** to make a pauper of **:** reduce to abject poverty **:** imbue with the spirit of a pauper **:** BEGGAR, IMPOVERISH ⟨those ragged days when he was only a shaver and his old man was a *pauperized* greenhorn —J.T.Farrell⟩

pau·ra·que \paù'räkā\ *n* -S [MexSp] **:** CUIEJO

pau·ro·me·tab·o·la \,pòrōmə'tabələ\ *n pl, cap* [NL, fr. Gk *pauros* small, slight + NL *metabola*, fr. neut. pl. of Gk *metabolos* changeable — more at FEW, METABOLA] *in some classifications* **:** a group comprising all insects that are paurometabolous

pau·ro·me·tab·o·lism \-bə,lizəm\ *also* **pau·ro·me·tab·o·ly** \-bəlē\ *n* [Gk *pauros* + E *metabolism* or *metaboly*] **:** heterometabolism in which the nymph is fundamentally similar to the adult; *broadly* **:** HETEROMETABOLISM — compare HEMIMETABOLISM — **pau·ro·me·tab·o·lous** \¦≈≈≈¦tabələs\ *adj*

1pau·ro·pod \'pȯrə,päd\ *or* **pau·rop·o·dous** \pȯ'räpədəs\ *adj* [*pauropod* fr. NL *Pauropoda; pauropodous* fr. NL *Pauropoda* + E *-ous*] **:** of or relating to the Pauropoda

2pauropod \"\ *n* -s [NL *Pauropoda*] **:** any arthropod of the class Pauropoda

pau·rop·o·da \pȯ'räpədə\ *n pl, cap* [NL, fr. Gk *pauros* small, slight + NL *-poda*] **:** an obscure class of minute progoneate arthropods with branched antennae, 8 to 10 pairs of legs, and no trachea

pau·ro·pod·i·dae \,pȯrə'pädə,dē\ *n pl, cap* [NL, fr. *Pauropoda* + *-idae*] **:** the largest family of the Pauropoda

pau·ro·pus \'pȯrəpəs\ *n, cap* [NL, fr. Gk *pauros* + NL *-pus*] **:** a genus of arthropods that is the type of the family Pauropodidae

pau ro·xo \,paü'rō(,)shō\ *n, pl* **pau roxos** [Pg, lit., purple wood] **1 :** a purpleheart (esp. *Peltogyne densiflora*) yielding valuable timber **2 :** the wood of pau roxo

pa'us *pl of* PA'U

paus·al \'pȯzəl\ *adj* **1 :** of, relating to, or occurring at a pause (as at the end of a clause or sentence) **2 :** of, relating to, or constituting the form taken by a word or vowel before a pause (as in Hebrew)

pau san·to \,paü'san(,)tō\ *n* [Pg, lit., holy wood] **:** a Brazilian tree (*Kielmeyera coriacea*) of the family Guttiferae having bark that is similar to cork and used for insulation

pau·sa·tion \pȯ'zāshən\ *n* -s [LL *pausation-, pausatio*, fr. *pausatus* (past. part. of *pausare* to halt, pause, fr. L *pausa* pause) + *-ion-, -io* -ion] **:** the act of pausing **:** PAUSE

1pause \'pȯz\ *n* -s [ME *pause*, fr. L *pausa*, fr. Gk *pausis*, fr. *pauein* to stop + *-sis*; akin to Gk *paula* rest and perh. to OSlav *pustŭ* waste, desert] **1 :** a temporary stop **:** intermission of movement or speech **:** brief cessation **:** RESPITE ⟨there is often value in a ~ followed by a fresh start —Leslie Rees⟩ ⟨came to a ~, frowning in concentration —T.S.Stribling⟩ **2 a :** a break in a verse **b :** a brief suspension of the voice to indicate the limits and relations of sentences and their parts ⟨have opened up a new dimension of grammar by listening to its intonations, stresses, and ~s —Richard Braddock⟩ **3 :** temporary inaction often caused by doubt or uncertainty ⟨had my moments of anxious ~ —W.A.White⟩ **4 a :** 1REST 5 **b :** FERMATA 2 **c :** a break or paragraph in writing **d :** a pausal stop or intermission in speaking (as in Hebrew) **e :** the form taken by a word or vowel when occurring before a pausal stop (as in Hebrew) **5 :** a reason for pausing ⟨a thought that should give tremendous ~ —Alistair Cooke⟩

2pause \"\ *vb* -ED/-ING/-S [prob. fr. LL *pausare* to stop, rest, fr. L *pausa* pause] *vi* **1 a :** to cease for a time **:** refrain from acting or speaking for a brief interval **:** stop temporarily ⟨people seemed to ~, listening for a message —Sylvia Berkman⟩ **b :** to become silent **:** wait silently ⟨I ~ for a reply —Shak.⟩ **2 :** to hold for a time **:** LINGER — used with *on* or *upon* ⟨the singer *paused* on the high note⟩ ⟨*paused* upon the threshold to survey the room⟩ **3 :** to stop to consider before proceeding **:** HESITATE ⟨one ought also to ~ and ponder seriously —Lionel Whitby⟩ ⟨*paused* thoughtfully for perhaps two seconds before she consented —G.B.Shaw⟩ **4 :** to delay before going on **:** REMAIN, STAY, TARRY ⟨here hikers ~ to rest —*Amer. Guide Series: Conn.*⟩ ⟨the expedition had to ~ while barges were built —R.A.Billington⟩ ~ *vt* **:** to cause to cease or rest ⟨bad times before . . . had but *paused* him in his climb —Adrian Bell⟩

3pause \"\ *vt* -ED/-ING/-S [origin unknown] *dial Eng* **:** KICK

pause·less \-zləs\ *adj* **:** having no pauses **:** CEASELESS, CONTINUOUS ⟨swung up and veered and kept a ~ speed —William Alfred⟩

pause·less·ly *adv* **:** without pause **:** CEASELESSLY

paus·er \-zə(r)\ *n* -s **:** one that pauses or holds back

pau·ser·na \paü'sernə\ *n, pl* **pauserna** *or* **pausernas** *usu cap* [Pg *Pau Cerne*, fr. *pau cerne* heartwood; fr. the Pauserna living on the upper Guaporé river where heartwood is abundant] **1 :** a division of the Chiriguano people **2 :** a member of the Pauserna people

paus·ing·ly *adv* **:** with hesitation

1paus·sid \'pȯsəd\ *adj* [NL *Paussidae*] **:** of or relating to the Paussidae

2paussid \"\ *n* -s [NL *Paussidae*] **:** any beetle of the family Paussidae

paus·si·dae \-sə,dē\ *n pl, cap* [NL, fr. *Paussus*, type genus + *-idae*] **:** a family of small beetles closely related to the Carabidae that live exclusively in ants' nests and have very thick antennae with the joints fused to form a large club

paut \'pȯt\ *vi* -ED/-ING/-S [origin unknown] **1** *chiefly Scot* **a :** to paw the ground **:** STAMP **b :** FINGER, POKE **2** *chiefly Scot* **:** to walk about slowly

pav·age \'pāvij\ *n* -s [AF, fr. OF *paver* to pave + *-age*] **1 a :** a tax levied to pay for the paving of highways **b :** the right to impose such a tax **2 :** the act of laying a pavement

pavais *var of* PAVIS

pa·vane \pə'vän, -van\ *also* **pav·an** *or* **pav·in** \'pavən\ *n* -s [MF *pavane*, fr. OSp *pavana*, fr. OIt, prob. alter. of *padovana*, fem. of *padovano* of Padua, city in northeastern Italy, fr. *Padova* Padua + *-ano* -an (fr. L *-anus*)] **1 :** a stately court dance by couples in ceremonial costume introduced from southern Europe into England in the 16th century **2 a :** music for the pavane **b :** music having the duple and slow stately rhythm of the pavane

1pave \'pāv\ *vt* -ED/-ING/-S [ME *paven*, fr. MF *paver*, fr. L *pavire* to strike, stamp; akin to OE *fȳran* to castrate, OHG *arfūrian* to castrate, L *putare* to prune, esteem, consider, think, Gk *paiein* to strike, Lith *pjauti* to cut, reap, slaughter] **1 a :** to lay or cover with stone, brick, asphalt, concrete, or other material making a firm, level, or convenient surface for travel **:** floor with brick, stone, or other solid material ⟨the street . . . is *paved* with timeworn cobblestones —Dana Burnet⟩ **b :** to overlie or cover like a pavement ⟨tables inlaid with baskets of many-colored fruit; sideboards *paved* with green marble —Virginia Woolf⟩ **2 :** to cover firmly and solidly as if with paving material ⟨the path of reform was to be *paved* with parliamentary action —Louis Wasserman⟩ ⟨hell is *paved* with good intentions —Samuel Johnson⟩ **3 :** to serve as or provide material for a covering or pavement of ⟨bricks that ~ the cloister⟩ ⟨tons of wire sieves, rolls of sheet lead . . . were used to ~ muddy streets in the rainy season —Julian Dana⟩ — **pave the way :** to prepare a smooth easy way **:** facilitate the means — usu. used with *to* or *for* ⟨alchemy . . . *paved the way* for the modern science of chemistry —*Encyc. Americana*⟩ ⟨the . . . treaty *paved the way* to still closer forms of joint action —Maurice Duverger⟩ ⟨favorable reception by the press *paved the way* for appearance of other verses —G.F.Whicher⟩

2pa·vé \pə'vā, 'pa(,)vā\ *n* -s [F, fr. past part. of *paver* to pave] **:** a paved public road or street **:** PAVEMENT ⟨found stretches of ~ where the horses' hooves struck sparks —Alan Sullivan⟩

3pave \'pāv\ *n* -s [F *pavé*] **:** PAVEMENT ⟨a lantern hung, casting a dim radiance . . . upon the step and ~ below —John Bennett⟩

paved \-vd\ *adj* [ME, fr. past part. of *paven* to pave] **1 :** covered with a pavement ⟨the ~ crest of the central road —Thomas De Quincey⟩ **2** *or* **pa·vé** \pə'vā, 'pa(,)vā\ *also* **pa·véed** \-ād\ [*pavé* fr. *2pavé; pavéed* fr. *2pavé* + *-ed*] *of jewels* **:** set as close together as possible to conceal a metal base ⟨a frosty, half-opened rose, realistically contrived of ~ diamonds —*New Yorker*⟩

pave·ment \'pāvmənt, *in rapid speech sometimes* -ābm-\ *n* -s [ME, fr. OF, fr. L *pavimentum*, fr. *pavire* to strike, stamp + *-mentum* -ment] **1 a :** a paved surface: as (1) **:** the artificially covered surface of a public thoroughfare ⟨stopped his car just off the ~⟩ (2) *chiefly Brit* **:** SIDEWALK ⟨there were crowds on the ~s and roads everywhere —G.W.Talbot⟩ (3) **:** a decorative interior floor of tiles or colored bricks ⟨the tessellated ~ of the hall —G.B.Shaw⟩ (4) **:** a factory floor paved with wood blocks, bricks, or concrete **b :** the material with which something is paved ⟨concrete makes excellent ~⟩ **2 :** something that suggests a pavement (as in flatness, hardness, and extent of surface or in the formation and compact arrangement of its units) ⟨a *pavement*-toothed shark⟩ ⟨~ cells⟩ — see DESERT PAVEMENT

pave·men·tal \pāv'mentᵊl\ *adj* **:** of or relating to a pavement

pavement ant *n* **:** a yellowish ant (*Tetramorium caespitum*) that builds its nests in yards and gardens and often infests houses

pavement artist *n* **:** SIDEWALK ARTIST

pave·ment·ed \'pāvməntəd\ *adj* **:** PAVED ⟨a beautifully ~ staircase⟩

pavement epithelium *n* **:** an epithelium made up of a single layer of flat cells

pavement light *n* **:** a window in a pavement for admitting light into a cellar or storage space beneath

pav·er \'pāvə(r)\ *n* -s [ME, fr. *paven* to pave + *-er*] **1 :** one that lays or sets paving **2 :** a paving stone, brick, or block **3 :** a traveling concrete mixer to which unmixed batches are brought and which deposits the mixture directly in place in the pavement **4 :** the bed stone of a grinding mill

pavestone \'≈,≈\ *n* [*1pave* + *stone*] **:** PAVING STONE

pa·vet·ta \pə'vedə\ *n, cap* [NL, fr. Sinhalese *pāwaṭṭā*] **:** a genus of tropical Old World shrubs (family Rubiaceae) having white corymbose flowers with long-exserted styles and being chiefly of interest for the nitrogen-fixing bacteria found in structures resembling warts on the leaves of various species

pa·via \'pāvēə\ *n, cap* [NL, fr. Petrus *Pavius* (Latinized form of Peter *Paaw*) †1617 Du. botanist + NL *-ia*] *in some classifications* **:** a genus of trees that is now usu. included in the genus *Aesculus* and comprises buckeyes with smooth capsules and four-petaled flowers

pav·id \'pavəd\ *adj* [L *pavidus*, fr. *pavēre* to be frightened, to fear; akin to L *pavire* to strike, stamp — more at PAVE] **:** showing fear **:** TIMID ⟨he was infinitely ~ and stingy —Antonio Barolini⟩ — **pav·id·ly** *adv*

pa·vie \'pāvi\ *n* -s [prob. alter. of *3paw*] *Scot* **:** a quick or deft motion **:** a neat trick

1pa·vil·ion \pə'vilyən\ *n* -s [ME *pavilon*, fr. OF *paveillon*, fr. L *papilion-, papilio* butterfly; akin to OE *fifalde* butterfly, OHG *fifaltra*, ON *fífrildi* butterfly, Lith *petelìške* flighty, *piepala* quail; fr. its spreading out like a butterfly's wings] **1 a :** a large often sumptuous tent ⟨amongst them rose the white ~s of the Turkish irregular cavalry —A.H.Layard⟩ **b :** something resembling a canopy or tent ⟨tree ferns spread their delicate ~s —Blanche E. Baughan⟩ **2 a :** a part of a building usu. having some distinguishing feature and projecting from the rest ⟨rang the bell of the little ~ and was taken into the tiny hall and then into the small dining room —Gertrude Stein⟩ ⟨the country house . . . accented by two-story terminal ~s at the ends —H.S.Morrison⟩ **b :** one of several detached or semidetached units into which a building (as a hospital) is sometimes divided ⟨became supervisor of the dependents' ~ —*Current Biog.*⟩ **3 a :** a light sometimes ornamental structure in a garden, park, or place of recreation that is used for entertainment or shelter ⟨picnicked in ~s —Green Peyton⟩ ⟨the band ~ . . . is the scene of summer concerts —*Amer. Guide Series: Minn.*⟩ ⟨there was a ~, a dance hall up on the highway —Morley Callaghan⟩ **b :** a temporary structure erected at an exposition by an individual exhibitor ⟨the national ~s . . . are the actual property of the nations which display their wares in them —David Sylvester⟩ **4 :** the lower faceted part of a brilliant between the girdle and the culet — compare BEZEL; see BRILLIANT illustration **5 a :** PINNA 2b **b :** INFUNDIBULUM f **6** *chiefly Brit* **:** a permanent structure erected for the use of players and often spectators on a cricket ground

2pavilion \"\ *vt* -ED/-ING/-S [ME *pavilonen*, fr. *pavilion*, n.] **:** to furnish or cover with **:** put, enclose, or shelter in or as if in a pavilion ⟨~*ed* in splendor and girded with praise —Robert Grant †1838⟩

pavilion roof *n* **:** a roof hipped equally on all sides

pa·vil·lon \,pävē'yōⁿ\ *n* -s [F, lit., pavilion, fr. OF *paveillon*] **:** the bell of a wind instrument

pavillon chi·nois \-,shēn'wä\ *n* [F, lit., Chinese pavillon] **:** a showy jingling device that consists of small bells hung from a crescent-shaped crosspiece on a pole or from a hat-shaped canopy surmounting the pole — called also *Chinese crescent, Chinese pavilion, jingling Johnny, Turkish crescent*

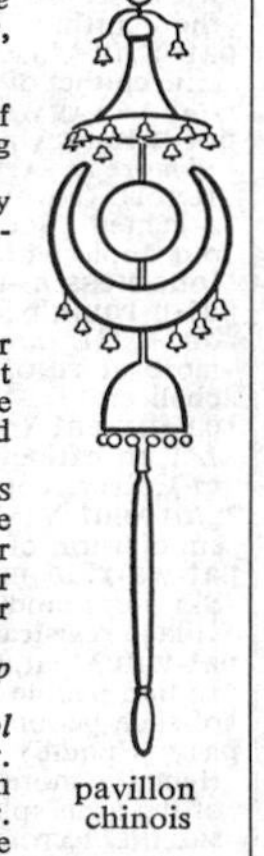

pavillon chinois

pavin *var of* PAVANE

pav·ing \'pāviŋ\ *n* -s [ME, fr. gerund of *paven* to pave] **:** PAVEMENT ⟨hear him coming quiet as anything over the ~s —Kay Boyle⟩

paving brick *n* **:** a vitrified clay brick slightly larger than building brick and used in the construction of pavement surfaces

paving mixer *n* **:** PAVER 3

paving roller *n* **:** ROAD ROLLER

paving stone *n* [ME] **:** a dressed stone used for the wearing surface of a stone-block pavement

paving tile *n* [ME] **:** a glazed decorated tile used for floors, sidewalks, courtyards, and sometimes for walls

pav·ior *or* **pav·iour** *or* **pav·ier** \'pāvyə(r)\ *n* -s [ME *pavier*, fr. *paven* to pave + *-ier* -er — more at PAVE] **1 :** PAVER 1 **2 :** an implement for ramming down paving stones **3 :** a material or a piece of material (as a brick or slab) used for paving **4 :** a hard building brick

pa·vi·o·tso \,pāvē'ōt(,)sō\ *n* -s *usu cap* **:** NORTHERN PAIUTE

pav·is *or* **pav·ise** *also* **pav·ais** \'pavəs\ *n, pl* **pavises** [ME *pavis, pavise*, fr. MF *pavais*, fr. OIt *pavese*, prob. fr. *pavese* of Pavia, city in northeast Italy where pavises were made, fr. *Pavia* + *-ese*] **:** a large shield covering the whole body used esp. in siege operations to protect crossbowmen and sometimes carried by a pavisor before a knight or archer

pavisade *n* -s [F *pavesade*, fr. It *pavesata*, fr. *pavese* pavis + *-ata* -ade (fr. LL)] **:** a continuous defensive screen (as of pavises) joined in a line

pav·i·sor *or* **pav·i·ser** \'pavəsə(r)\ *n* -s **:** a page, varlet, or soldier assigned to carry a pavis in front of a knight or archer

pav·lov·i·an \pav'lōfēən, -lȯl, ¦vē-, '≈,≈≈≈, pav'lōvē-\ *adj, usu cap* [Ivan P. *Pavlov* †1936 Russ. physiologist + E *-ian*] **:** of or relating to the Russian physiologist Ivan Pavlov or to his work and experiments

pav·lov pouch \'pav,lȯ|f-, -lȯl, |v-\ *n, usu cap 1st P* [after Ivan P. *Pavlov* †1936] **:** an isolated portion of the stomach separated by surgical operation from the main part, open to the exterior, and used for study of gastric secretion

pa·vo \'pā(,)vō, 'pä(-\ *n, cap* [NL, fr. L, peacock] **:** a genus of gallinaceous birds (family Phasianidae) consisting of the peacocks

pa·vo·naz·zo \,pävə'nät(,)sō\ *or* **pa·vo·naz·zet·to** \,pävənət'-sed·(,)ō\ *n* -s [*pavonazzo* fr. It, fr. *pavonazzo* peacock-colored, purplish, fr. L *pavonaceus* like a peacock's tail, variegated, fr. *pavon-, pavo* peacock + *-aceus* -aceous; *pavonazzetto* fr. It, fr. *pavonazzo* + *-etto* -et (fr. LL *-itus* & *-ita*)] **1 :** a marble with veins usu. of red, violet, or purple found in ancient Roman buildings and thought to be Phrygian **2 :** a contemporary marble resembling pavonazzo

pa·vo·nia \pə'vōnēə\ *n* [NL, fr. José *Pavon* †1844 Span. botanist + NL *-ia*] **1** *cap* **:** a genus of tropical hairy shrubs or herbs (family Malvaceae) having flowers with an epicalyx of four to eight bracts and aristate carpels **2** -s **:** any plant of the genus *Pavonia*

pa·vo·ni·an \pə'vōnēən\ *adj* [L *pavon-, pavo* peacock + E *-an*] **:** PAVONINE

pav·o·nine \'pavə,nīn, -,nən\ *adj* [L *pavoninus*, fr. *pavon-, pavo* peacock + *-inus* -ine] **1 a :** of, relating to, or resembling the peacock **b :** colored like a peacock's tail or neck **:** IRIDESCENT **2 :** of the color peacock

pav·o·nite \'pavə,nīt\ *n* -s [L *pavon-, pavo* peacock (intended as Latin rendering of Martin A. *Peacock* †1950 Canadian mineralogist) + E *-ite*] **:** a mineral $AgBi_3S_5$ consisting of a sulfide of silver and bismuth

1paw \'pȯ\ *n* -s [ME, fr. MF *poue*] **1 a :** the foot of a quadruped (as the lion, dog, or cat) having claws; *broadly* **:** the foot of an animal **b :** fur taken from the legs and flanks of an animal and sewn together for garments ⟨a coat of mink ~⟩ **2 :** a human hand: as **a :** a large clumsy hand ⟨selected a cigaret with a vast ~ —Ellery Queen⟩ **b :** a child's small often grubby hand ⟨go and wash those ~s before dinner⟩ **3** *archaic* **:** something done by hand (as handwriting) **4 :** the foreleg of an animal depicted in heraldry as couped or erased near the middle joint — distinguished from *gamb*

2paw \"\ *vb* -ED/-ING/-S *vt* **1 :** to stroke with the hand **:** feel or touch clumsily, indelicately, or rudely ⟨he ~*ed* his ear with a doubtful air —Arthur Morrison⟩ ⟨an important man could find more to do than ~ a lady's knees —Kenneth Roberts⟩ **2 :** to touch or strike at with a paw **:** CLAW ⟨barely escaped being ~*ed* by the lion⟩ **3 :** to scrape or beat with or as if with a hoof ⟨long lines of pack mules ~*ed* the dust of the street —*Amer. Guide Series: Oregon*⟩ ⟨the curb where his charger was ~*ing* the gutter —Winston Churchill⟩ **4 :** to handle clumsily or roughly esp. while looking or examining ⟨he ~*ed* the stones hurriedly, searching —Liam O'Flaherty⟩ ⟨don't care to have the critics ~ the book at all —Mark Twain⟩ **5 :** to flail at or grab for wildly ⟨his right hand ~*ed* the steel side ineffectually —R.O.Bowen⟩ **6 :** to struggle to progress ⟨the troops ~*ed* forward gingerly a few hundred yards at a time —Norman Mailer⟩ ⟨walked, stumbled, groped, and ~*ed* our way through the fields —Herbert Passin⟩ ~ *vi* **1 :** to beat or scrape with a hoof ⟨horses . . . begin tossing their heads and ~*ing* and neighing —S.E.Morison⟩ ⟨~*ed* vaguely with his foot for the brass rail —Dorothy Sayers⟩ **2 :** to touch or strike with a paw ⟨the kitten ~*ed* at the mouse⟩ ⟨the dog ~*ed* at the back door begging to come in⟩ **3 :** to feel or touch clumsily or rudely with the hand ⟨his hand ~*ed* about his skull —Liam O'Flaherty⟩ **4 :** to search esp. by handling carelessly or roughly ⟨went back into the woodshed and ~*ed* around for a heavy block of wood —Raymond Chandler⟩ ⟨~*ed* through the bottom of the trunk⟩ **5 :** to flail or grab wildly with the hand ⟨sprang to the door and ~*ed* at the bolt —William Faulkner⟩ ⟨were all on their feet . . . their hands ~*ing* at their daggers —T.B.Costain⟩

3paw \"\ *n* -s [prob. alter. of obs. E (northern dial.) *pawk* trick] *Scot* **:** a quick or deft movement **:** TRICK

4paw \"\ *or* **paw-paw** \'pȯ,pȯ\ *adj* [*paw* prob. alter. of *1pah; paw-paw* redupl. of *paw*] **1 :** childishly improper **:** NAUGHTY **2 :** INDECENT, OBSCENE

paw foot *n* **:** a decorative foot used on a piece of furniture that is usu. in the form of a lion's paw often showing large claws clasping a ball

pawk·ery \'pȯkəri\ *n* -ES [obs. E (northern dial.) *pawk* trick + E *-ery*] *Scot* **:** SLYNESS, TRICKINESS

pawk·i·ly \'pȯkəli\ *adv* **:** in a pawky manner

pawk·i·ness \-kēnəs\ *n* -ES **:** the quality or state of being pawky

pawky \'pȯki\ *adj* [obs. E (northern dial.) *pawk* trick + E *-y*] **1** *chiefly Brit* **:** artfully shrewd **:** CANNY ⟨that favorite of fiction, the ~ rich old lady who incessantly scores off her parasitical descendants —*Punch*⟩ **2** *chiefly Scot* **a :** LIVELY, UNINHIBITED **b :** BOLD, FORWARD ⟨a rude and ~ child⟩ **3** *chiefly Scot* **:** overly fastidious **:** SQUEAMISH

1pawl *also* **pall** *or* **paul** \'pȯl\ *n* -s [perh. modif. of D *pal* pawl] **1 :** a pivoted tongue or sliding bolt on one part of a machine that is adapted to fall into notches or interdental spaces on another part (as a ratchet wheel) so as to permit motion in one direction and prevent it in the reverse (as in a capstan or windlass) **:** CATCH, DETENT — see RATCHET WHEEL illustration **2 :** a part of a poise of a weighing scale shaped to fit into the notches of a beam bar for the definite positioning of the poise

2pawl \"\ *vt* -ED/-ING/-S **:** to check (as a capstan) by a pawl

3pawl \"\ *n* -s [Hindi *pāl* sail, small tent] **:** a small double-poled tent with steep sloping sides used in India

pawl bitt *also* **pawl post** *n* **:** a heavy post set abaft a windlass to receive the strain of pawls which are attached to it

pawl head *n* **:** the part of a capstan usu. the circular base to which the pawls are attached

pawl rim *n* **:** a stationary ring about the base of a capstan with notches for the pawls to catch in

1pawn \'pȯn, 'pän\ *n* -s [ME *paun*, modif. (prob. influenced by MFlem *paen* pawn, fr. MF *pan*) of MF *pan*, prob. fr. *pan* piece of cloth, pane; fr. the practice of holding a garment as security — more at PANE] **1 a :** something delivered to or deposited with another as security for a loan **b :** a person left as a hostage ⟨he must leave behind for ~s, his mother, wife, and son —John Dryden⟩ **2 :** the state of being pledged ⟨the hock shop continued to take into ~ things to charm —John McNulty⟩ **3 a :** something used as a pledge **:** EARNEST, GUARANTY ⟨the new school is the ~ given by the community to its children⟩ **b :** GAGE 2 **4 :** the act of pawning **5 a :** slave held as security for debt **syn** see PLEDGE

2pawn \"\ *vt* -ED/-ING/-S **:** to give or deposit in pledge or as security for the payment of a loan, a debt, or for the performance of some action **:** put in pawn **:** PLEDGE, STAKE, WAGER ⟨in the end he had to ~ that coat —Vicki Baum⟩ ⟨~ my victories, all my honors to you —Shak.⟩ ⟨he now ~*ed* his royal word —T.B.Macaulay⟩ ⟨exploited their own shame, ~*ing* their dignity for profit —Lillian Smith⟩

3pawn \"\ *n* -s [ME *pown, poune*, fr. MF *poon*, fr. ML *pedon-, pedo* foot soldier, fr. LL, one who has broad feet, fr. L *ped-, pes* foot — more at FOOT] **1 a :** one of the chessmen of least value having the power to move only one square forward at a time or at option two on its first move and to capture an enemy only on either of the two squares diagonally forward **b :** a counter in Polish checkers **2 :** one that can be used often to his own disadvantage to further the purposes of another ⟨have become ~s in the hands of those who thrive on agitation and unrest —Elijah Adlow⟩ ⟨innocent-eyed but willing ~ of the family —Leo Gershoy⟩

pawn 1 a

4pawn \"\ *n* -s [ME *poune*, fr. MF *poun, paon*, fr. L *pavon-, pavo* peacock] *archaic* **:** PEACOCK

5pawn \"\ *n* -s [prob. fr. MD *paen* hall, vestibule, fr. MF *pan* pane — more at PANE] **:** a gallery or covered passage esp. in a bazaar

pawn·age \-nij\ *n* -s [*2pawn* + *-age*] **:** an act of pawning

pawnbroker \'≈,≈≈\ *n* [*1pawn* + *broker*] **:** one that loans money on the security of personal property pledged in his keeping

pawn·bro·ker·age \'≈,brōk(ə)rij\ *n* **:** PAWNBROKING

pawn·bro·ker·ing \-riŋ\ *n* -s **:** PAWNBROKING

pawn·bro·kery \-rē\ *n* **1 :** PAWNSHOP **2 :** PAWNBROKING

1pawnbroking \'≈,≈≈\ *adj* [*1pawn* + *broking*] **:** conducting the business of pawnbroking

2pawnbroking \"\ *n* **:** the business of lending money on the security of pawned articles

1pawn·ee \(')pȯ'nē, (')pä'-\ *n* -s [*1pawn* + *-ee*] **:** one to whom a pledge is given as security **:** one who takes something in pawn **:** PLEDGEE

2paw·nee \"\ *n, pl* **pawnee** *or* **pawnees 1** *usu cap* **a** (1) **:** a Caddo confederacy of the Platte and Republican river valleys in Nebraska and Kansas (2) **:** a member of such a confederacy **b :** the language of the Pawnee people **2 :** ALMOND 6a

3paw·nee \"\ *n* -s [Hindi *pānī*, fr. Skt *pānīya* drink, fr. *pāti, pibati* he drinks — more at POTABLE] *India* **:** WATER ⟨brandy-*pawnee*⟩

pawn·er \'pȯnə(r), 'pän- *or* **pawn·or** \(')≈¦nȯ(ə)r, -ō(ə)\ *n* -s [*1pawn* + *-er* or *-or*] **:** one who pawns or pledges something as security

pawn roller *n* **:** an irresistible advance of pawns in a middle game of chess

pawns *pl of* PAWN, *pres 3d sing of* PAWN

pawnshop \'≈,≈\ *n* [*1pawn* + *shop*] **:** a pawnbroker's shop

pawn ticket *n* **:** a pawnbroker's receipt for a pledge

paw-paw *var of* PAWPAW

paw·paw *var of* PAPAW

paws *pl of* PAW, *pres 3d sing of* PAW

1pax \'paks, 'päks\ *n* -ES [ME, fr. ML, fr. L, peace — more at PEACE] **1 :** a tablet or board decorated with a figure or symbol of Christ, the Virgin Mary, or a saint and customarily in medieval times kissed before the communion by the priest and then by the people **2 a :** KISS OF PEACE **b :** a liturgical greeting passed along from the celebrant of the mass shortly before the communion to the other officers of the mass and members of the liturgical choir **3** *usu cap* **:** a period of international history characterized by an absence of major wars and a general stability of international affairs usu. resulting from the predominance of a specified political authority ⟨during the *Pax* Britannica of the nineteenth century a vast empire of trade was built up —E.H.Jacoby⟩ ⟨*Pax* Romana⟩ **4** [L, interj., finished! enough! fr. Gk, adv., very well, enough; akin to Gk *pēgnynai* to fix, fasten together — more at PACT] *Brit* — used as a cry for quarter to end a schoolboy fight

2pax \'paks\ *n* -ES [by alter.] **:** POX

pax·il·la \pak'silə\ *n, pl* **paxil·lae** \-i,lē\ [NL, fr. L *paxillus* peg, dim. of *palus* stake — more at POLE] **:** a spine like a pillar with a flattened summit bearing minute spinules or granules in various starfishes — **pax·il·lar** \-lə(r)\ *adj* — **pax·il·late** \-lət, -,lāt\ *adj* — **pax·il·lif·er·ous** \,paksə'lif(ə)rəs\ *adj* — **pax·il·li·form** \pak'silə,fȯrm\ *adj*

pax·il·lo·sa \,paksə'lōsə\ *n pl, cap* [NL, fr. neut. pl. of (assumed) NL *paxillosus*, fr. NL *paxilla* + L *-osus* -ose] *in some esp. former classifications* **:** an order that comprises starfishes with dorsal paxillae and is sometimes retained as a suborder of Phanerozonia

pax·il·lose \'paksə,lōs\ *adj* [L *paxillus* + E *-ose*] **1 :** resembling a little stake **2** [NL *paxilla* + E *-ose*] **:** bearing paxillae **:** PAXILLATE

pax·il·lus \'paksələs\ *n* [NL, fr. L, peg] **1** *cap* **:** a genus of rusty-spored mushrooms (family Agaricaceae) having a fleshy thallus with no annulus and decurrent gills separating easily from the cap **2** *pl* **paxil·li** \-sə,lī\ *or* **paxilluses :** any fungus of the genus *Paxillus; esp* **:** an edible mushroom (*P. involutus*)

pa·xi·u·ba \,päshē'übə\ *or* **paxiuba palm** *n* -S [*paxiuba* fr. Pg, fr. Tupi] **:** a Brazilian pinnate-leaved palm (*Iriartea exorrhiza*) with remarkable prop roots from which the trunk rises as if on stilts

pax·wax \'pak,swaks\ *or* **paxy·waxy** \'paksē,waksē\ *n* -ES [ME *paxwax*, alter. of *faxwax*, prob. fr. *fax* hair of the head (fr. OE *feax*) + *wax* growth, fr. *waxen* to grow — more at PECTINATE, WAX] *chiefly dial* **:** the nuchal ligament of a quadruped

1pay \'pā\ *vb* **paid** *also in sense 8* **payed** \'pād\ **paid; paying; pays** [ME *payen*, fr. OF *paier*, fr. L *pacare* to pacify, fr. *pac-*, *pax* peace — more at PEACE] *vt* **1** *obs* **:** PACIFY, APPEASE, GRATIFY **2 a :** to satisfy (someone) for services rendered or property delivered **:** discharge an obligation to **:** make due return to ⟨factory hands are *paid* by the hour⟩ ⟨*paid* all his creditors⟩ **b :** to engage for money **:** HIRE ⟨you couldn't ~ me to do that⟩ ⟨have to ~ someone to mow the lawn⟩ **3 a :** to give in return for goods or service ⟨~ high wages⟩ ⟨*paid* a stiff price for the house⟩ ⟨~ interest on borrowed money⟩ **b :** to discharge indebtedness for **:** SETTLE ⟨~ a bill⟩ ⟨~ a tax⟩ ⟨~ a debt⟩ ⟨~ a bet⟩ ⟨~ rent for the house⟩ **c :** to assume the charge of ⟨~ expenses⟩ ⟨*paid* his son's tuition⟩ ⟨~ the freight⟩ **d :** to make any agreed disposal or transfer of (money) ⟨*paid* a few dollars weekly into his savings account⟩ ⟨counting all the contributions actually *paid* in to date⟩ ⟨obliged to ~ out his entire wages every Saturday⟩ ⟨*paid* over a large sum to the lawyer⟩ **4 :** to give or forfeit in expiation or retribution ⟨if he has broken the law he must ~ the penalty⟩ ⟨permanent injury is a high price to ~ for a moment's carelessness⟩ **5 a :** to make compensation for **:** make up for **:** RECOMPENSE ⟨his trouble was well *paid* in the end⟩ **b :** to make retaliation for — usu. used with *back* ⟨*paid* him back blow for blow⟩ **c :** to requite (someone) according to what is deserved **:** get even with — usu. used with *back* ⟨~ back a social obligation⟩ ⟨how can I ~ you back for all your kindness⟩ ⟨cheated me but I'll find some way to ~ him back⟩ **d** *archaic* **:** THRASH, PUNISH **6 :** to give, offer, or make freely or as fitting ⟨~ attention to business⟩ ⟨*paid* no heed to repeated warnings⟩ ⟨~ a visit to the capital⟩ ⟨~*ing* lip service to democratic ideals⟩ ⟨has come to ~ his respects to you⟩ **7 a :** to return value or profit to ⟨it *paid* the store to stay open evenings⟩ **b :** to bring in as a return ⟨the investment *paid* five percent⟩ **8 :** to slacken (as a rope) and allow to run out ⟨wires are *paid* out and their eyes are slipped over the ship's bitts —N.D.Ford & W.J.Redgrave⟩ ⟨*payed* out the line to lower him to the ledge⟩ ~ *vi* **1 :** to give a recompense **:** make payment **:** discharge a debt or obligation ⟨owing doesn't mean ~*ing*, as any butcher or baker or candlestick maker can tell you —Margaret Deland⟩ **2 :** to make suitable return for expense or trouble **:** be worth the effort or pains **:** be profitable ⟨it ~*s* to be careful⟩ ⟨his job ~*s* very little⟩ ⟨justly emphatic against the delusion that persecution never ~*s* —G.G.Coulton⟩ **3 :** to be amiss or afoot — used chiefly in *what's to pay, something is to pay*

syn COMPENSATE, REMUNERATE, SATISFY, REIMBURSE, INDEMNIFY, RECOMPENSE, REPAY: PAY is a general term, usu. lacking particular connotation but sometimes bluntly stressing the purchase of services ⟨*pay* a machinist high wages⟩ ⟨*pay* a person to whom one has lost a bet⟩ In situations involving retaliation or retribution it may connote the bitter or dire ⟨didn't want anything except an opportunity to make somebody *pay* for the injustices, the inhumanities that my father had suffered —Kenneth Roberts⟩ COMPENSATE may indicate the giving of some return felt to be roughly equivalent in value to a service or favor; the extending of some balancing or countering consideration ⟨*compensate* one for his additional trouble⟩ ⟨an epoch in which the immense costs of a war could never be *compensated* by any economic gains that came from it —Max Lerner⟩ ⟨the loss will be far more than *compensated* by the growing tourist business —*Amer. Guide Series: Nev.*⟩ REMUNERATE, generally more formal than PAY, is applicable to rewards generous, not contracted for, or unexpected ⟨the king *remunerated* his retainers with large grants⟩ SATISFY implies payment asked, required, stipulated ⟨the Swedish government bought the shares of the Dutch investors in the New Sweden Company and *satisfied* all Dutch claims —*Amer. Guide Series: Del.*⟩ REIMBURSE applies to the return of an exact equivalent for an expenditure ⟨county charges are admitted, the state *reimbursing* the county in the amount of 75¢ a day for each person; patients financially able to pay are charged $3 a day —*Amer. Guide Series: Mich.*⟩ INDEMNIFY applies to compensations for loss, damage, or injury ⟨the insurance company *indemnified* him for his losses⟩ RECOMPENSE suggests fit return, either in compensation, amends, friendly or loyal repayment, or reward ⟨*recompensed* for unusual services⟩ ⟨from this heritage her writing derives a graciousness and urbanity that *recompense* one, to a degree, for the essential superficiality of her observation and insight —F.B.Millett⟩ REPAY always implies the notion of a return, a paying back, answering, countering, or reprisal ⟨every last one of them eager to *repay* with interest a few of the things that had been done to them —Kenneth Roberts⟩ ⟨the doctor is *repaid* all he wants simply by the interest of your case —Graham Greene⟩ ⟨the region would *repay* investigation —Douglas Carruthers⟩ — **pay as you go 1 :** to pay bills when due **2 :** to limit expenditures to actual income **3 :** to pay taxes on income as it is received — compare WITHHOLDING TAX — **pay for 1 :** to conclude the purchase of by delivering the price ⟨bought and *paid for* the house out of their savings⟩ **2 :** to yield or forfeit an equivalent value for **:** atone for ⟨in life as in business things had to be *paid for* —Louis Bromfield⟩ **3 :** to bear the cost of ⟨willing to *pay for* his son's education⟩ ⟨some improvements *pay for* themselves in increased economy of operation⟩ — **pay home :** to pay back or retaliate in full measure — **pay one's way** *or* **pay one's own way 1 :** to pay expenses as they are incurred **2 :** to yield an income at least equal to operating expenses — **pay the piper 1 :** to bear the cost of something ⟨artists will be chosen . . . supported by the state . . . the people will *pay the piper* and call the tune —Clive Bell⟩ **2 :** to suffer the consequences of or penalty for an act — **pay the shot :** to pay the bill **:** stand the expense — **pay through the nose :** to pay exorbitantly or dearly

2pay \"\ *n* -S [ME *pay*, *paye*, fr. MF *paie*, fr. *paier* to pay] **1** *obs* **:** SATISFACTION, LIKING **2 a :** the act or fact of paying or being paid ⟨no ~, no work⟩ ⟨demanded ~ for overtime work⟩ ⟨long interval between ~*s* . . . to prevent frequent drunkenness among the men —*Times Lit. Supp.*⟩ **b :** the status of being paid by an employer **:** EMPLOY ⟨time when England had not a single battalion in constant ~ —T.B.Macaulay⟩ ⟨suspected of being in the ~ of a foreign power⟩ **3** *archaic* **:** something given in return by way of reward or retaliation ⟨when her lips were ready for his ~ —Shak.⟩ **4 a :** WAGES, SALARY, REMUNERATION ⟨equal ~ for equal work⟩ ⟨stayed just long enough to collect his ~⟩; *esp* **:** money regularly allotted to a member of the armed forces **b :** money paid in addition to basic wages or salary ⟨travel ~⟩ ⟨flying ~⟩ ⟨severance ~⟩ **5 :** a person viewed as to reliability or promptitude in paying debts or bills ⟨business people say the best ~ are Japanese, Filipinos, and Chinese —Joseph Driscoll⟩ **6 a :** earth, rock, or sand that yields metal (esp. gold) in profitable amounts **b :** a zone or stratum (as of sand) that yields oil **syn** see WAGE

3pay \"\ *adj* **1 :** containing or leading to something precious or valuable (as gold, oil) ⟨~ ore⟩ ⟨~ rock⟩ **2 :** equipped with a coin slot for receiving a fee for use ⟨~ telephone⟩ ⟨~ toilet⟩ **3 :** concerned with or used for payment ⟨~ clerk⟩ ⟨~ office⟩ **4 :** requiring payment ⟨~ hospital⟩ ⟨~ TV⟩

4pay \"\ *vt* **payed** *also* **paid; payed** *also* **paid; paying; pays** [obs. F *peier*, fr. OF, fr. L *picare*, fr. *pic-*, *pix* pitch — more at PITCH] **:** to smear or coat (as a spar, caulked seam) with hot tar or pitch or any waterproof composition

paya \'pī(y)ə\ *n, pl* **paya** *or* **payas** *usu cap* **1 a :** an Indian people of northern Honduras **b :** a member of such people **2 :** the language of the Paya

pay·abil·i·ty \,pāə'biləd·ē\ *n* **:** the quality or state of being payable

pay·able \'pāəbəl\ *adj* [ME *paiable*, fr. MF, fr. OF, fr. *paier* to pay + *-able* — more at PAY] **1 a :** requiring to be paid ⟨bills ~⟩ **:** capable of being paid ⟨~ prices⟩ **:** DUE ⟨the interest is ~ in advance⟩ **b** *of a note, bill, or check* **:** specifying payment to a particular payee ⟨~ to John Doe⟩ ⟨~ to cash⟩, at a specified time or occasion ⟨~ on demand⟩, or in a specified manner ⟨~ in monthly installments⟩ **2 :** capable of being profitably worked ⟨~ vein of ore⟩ **:** PROFITABLE, PAYING ⟨~ enterprise⟩ ⟨~ crop of fruit⟩

pay·able·ness *n* -ES **:** the quality or state of being payable

pay·ably \-blē\ *adv* **:** PROFITABLY

paya·guá \,pī(y)ə'gwä\ *n, pl* **payaguá** *or* **payaguás** *usu cap* **1 a :** an extinct Guaicuruan people of the Paraguay river valley including the Agaz **b :** a member of such people **2 :** the language of the Payaguá

payan \'pī(y)ən\ *n* -S *usu cap* [*Paya* + E *-an*] **:** a language family of uncertain relationships comprising the Paya language

payback \'=,=\ *n* -S [fr. *pay back*, v.] **:** return of an amount in profits secured as the result of a capital expenditure such as to offset the expenditure

paybook \'=,=\ *n* **:** an individual pay record of a member of the armed forces

paybox \'=,=\ *n, Brit* **:** a cashier's or ticket seller's booth

paycheck \'=,=\ *n* **1 :** a check in payment of wages or salary ⟨with his first ~ a month off —*Newsweek*⟩ **2 :** WAGES, SALARY ⟨meager, if rising, ~*s* —*Time*⟩

payday \'=,=\ *n* **1 :** the day on which wages or salary is regularly paid **2 :** SETTLEMENT DAY

pay dirt *n* **1 :** earth or ore that yields a profit to a miner **2 :** any useful or remunerative discovery or attained object ⟨after hours of questioning the police struck *pay dirt*⟩ ⟨the *pay dirt* for the fact-seeking reader is there —*Amer. Antiquity*⟩ **3 :** the end zone of a football field

PAYE *abbr* **1** pay as you earn **2** pay as you enter

payed *past of* PAY

pay·ee \(')pā'ē\ *n* -S [2*pay* + *-ee*] **:** the person to whom money is to be or has been paid **:** the person named in a bill of exchange, note, or check as the one to whom the amount is promised or directed to be paid

pa·ye·na \pā'yēnə\ *n, cap* [NL, after Anselme *Payen* †1871 Fr. chemist and botanical writer] **:** a genus of Malayan trees (family Sapotaceae) of medium to very large size having fascicled flowers growing at or near the leaf axils, bearing fruit with one or two endospermous seeds, and yielding gutta-percha

pay envelope *n* **:** an envelope containing one's wages; *often* **:** WAGES, SALARY, STIPEND ⟨hard times affect *pay envelopes*⟩

pay·er \'pāər\ *also* **pay·or** \", (')pā'ȯ(ə)r\ *n* -S [*payer* fr. ME, fr. *payen* to pay + *-er; payor* fr. 1*pay* + *-or* — more at PAY] **:** one that pays: as **a :** the person by whom a bill or note has been or should be paid **b :** a person (as a parent) who agrees to pay the premium on a juvenile policy

payetan *var of* PAYYETAN

pay in *vt* **:** to deposit in an account ~ *vi* **:** to make a deposit into an account

paying *n* -S [fr. gerund of 4*pay*] **:** waterproof material used to pay seams or rigging

paying guest *n* **:** one that pays for board and lodging esp. in a private house; *often* **:** BOARDER

paying-in book \'=='=-\ *n, Brit* **:** BANKBOOK

paying-in slip *n, Brit* **:** DEPOSIT SLIP

paying load *n* **:** PAYLOAD 2

payload \'=,=\ *n* **1 :** the financial burden of the regular payrolls (as in a factory or business) **2 :** the revenue-producing or useful load that a vehicle of transport can carry **:** net load; *also* **:** the explosive charge carried in the warhead of a missile

paymaster \'=,==\ *n* [2*pay* + *master*] **:** an officer or agent of a government, a corporation, or an employer whose duty it is to pay salaries or wages and keep account of them

paymaster general *n, pl* **paymasters general 1 :** a military officer in command of the pay department of an army or navy **2 a :** a government officer in Great Britain formerly making all civil and military payments on the authority of the treasury **b :** a British officer of state whose official duties are nominal but who is often made a member of the cabinet and entrusted with special functions

pay·ment \'pāmənt\ *n* -S [ME *payment*, *payement*, fr. MF *paiement*, fr. OF, fr. *paier* to pay + *-ment* — more at PAY] **1 :** the act of paying or giving compensation **:** the discharge of a debt or an obligation ⟨prompt ~ of debts⟩ ⟨~ of a fine⟩ **2 :** something that is paid **:** something given to discharge a debt or obligation or to fulfill a promise **:** PAY, RETURN, REQUITAL ⟨amortize a debt with monthly ~*s*⟩ ⟨accepted a judgeship as ~ for loyal service to the party⟩ **3** *archaic* **:** PUNISHMENT, CHASTISEMENT

payment bill *n* **:** a bill of exchange under which the drawee can obtain the documents of title only by paying the bill — compare ACCEPTANCE 4

payment by intervention : INTERVENTION 2 a

payment for honor : payment of a protested bill or draft by someone other than the primary debtor made with the purpose of saving the credit of such debtor

payne's gray \'pānz-\ *n, often cap P* [after William *Payne fl* 1800 Eng. artist, its inventor] **:** a grayish to dark grayish blue

pay·nim \'pānəm\ *n* -S [ME *painim*, fr. OF *paienime*, fr. LL *paganismus* heathendom, fr. *paganus* heathen (fr. L, country dweller) + L *-ismus* -ism — more at PAGAN] **1** *archaic* **:** PAGANDOM **2** *archaic* **:** PAGAN, INFIDEL ⟨clasped like a missal where swart ~*s* pray —John Keats⟩; *esp* **:** MUHAMMADAN

pay·nim·ry *or* **pay·nim·rie** \-mrē\ *n* -ES [ME *paynimery*, *paynimrie*, fr. *painim* + *-ery* or *-rie* -ry] *archaic* **:** PAGANDOM

pay off *vt* **1 a :** to give (an employee) all due wages; *esp* **:** to pay in full and discharge (a crew of hands or workmen) **b :** to pay (a debt or a creditor) in full ⟨expects to *pay* all his debts *off* shortly⟩ **c :** BRIBE **2 :** to inflict retribution on **:** get back at **:** settle a grudge with ⟨wanted to *pay* him *off* for stealing his girl⟩ **3 :** to turn the head of (a ship) to leeward **4 :** to allow (a thread, rope) to run off a spool or drum **:** UNWIND ~ *vi* **1** *of a ship* **:** to swing to leeward **2 a :** to yield returns either of profit or loss ⟨the investment *paid off* handsomely⟩ **b :** to reach successful realization ⟨the years of patience and persistence had at last *paid off*⟩ ⟨boldness is the only course that will *pay off* —E.B.George⟩

1payoff \'=,=\ *n* -S [fr. *pay off*, v.] **1 :** the act or occasion of paying employees' wages or gambling winnings or distributing profits, booty, or bribe money **2 a :** PROFIT, REWARD **b :** RETRIBUTION **3 :** the climax of an incident or enterprise; *specif* **:** the denouement of a narrative ⟨now listen to the ~⟩ **4 :** a decisive fact or factor resolving a situation or bringing about a definitive conclusion ⟨the opinion of the tax court on taxability is the ~⟩

2payoff \"\ *adj* **:** yielding results in the final test **:** REWARDING, DECISIVE ⟨gave him the ~ shot —Chester Roth⟩ ⟨maneuvering for a ~ play⟩ ⟨wound up for the ~ pitch⟩

pay·o·la \pā'ōlə\ *n* -S [prob. alter. (influenced by *-ola*, as in *Victrola*) of 1*payoff*] **1 :** an undercover or indirect payment for a commercial favor (as to a disc jockey for plugging a song) **2 :** the practice of engaging in payolas

payor *var of* PAYER

payote *var of* PEYOTE

pay out *vt* **:** to get even with **:** get revenge on ⟨the women did not dare *pay* her *out* for snubbing them —Sherwood Anderson⟩

payout \'=,=\ *n* -S [fr. the phrase *pay out*] **:** the act of paying out **:** EXPENDITURE, DISBURSEMENT ⟨federal ~ for military aircraft —C.J.V.Murphy⟩ ⟨bookmakers had a heavy ~ on the winner —*Sydney (Australia) Bull.*⟩

pay packet *n, Brit* **:** PAY ENVELOPE

payr *abbr* paymaster

payroll \'=,=\ *n* [2*pay* + *roll*] **1 :** a paymaster's or employer's list of those entitled to receive compensation at a given time and of the amounts due to each ⟨make out a ~⟩ **2 :** the sum necessary for distribution to those on a payroll; *also* **:** the money to be distributed ⟨increase the weekly ~⟩ — **on the payroll** *adv* (*or adj*) **:** in the service or employ of someone

pay-roll·er \'=,rōlə(r)\ *n* **:** one receiving pay or periodical stipends; *esp* **:** a state or federal employee

payroll tax *n* **:** a government or state tax levied on employers as a percentage of wages and salaries paid to employees — compare WITHHOLDING TAX

pays *pres 3d sing of* PAY, *pl of* PAY

pay·sage \'pāsij, ,pāē'zäzh\ *n* -S [F, fr. MF, fr. *pays* country (fr. OF *païs*, fr. LL *pagensis* inhabitant of a district, fr. L *pagus* district) + *-age* — more at PAGAN] **:** LANDSCAPE

pay·sa·gist \'pāsəjəst\ *or* **pay·sa·giste** \,pāēzä'zhēst\ *n* -S [F *paysagiste*, fr. *paysage* + *-iste* -ist] **:** a landscape artist

pay·sanne \(')pā'zan\ *adj* [F, fr. *paysanne*, n., fem. of *paysan* rustic, peasant, fr. MF *paisant* — more at PEASANT] **:** prepared (as with diced root vegetables) in country or simple style ⟨~ sauce⟩ ⟨potatoes ~⟩

pay school *n* **:** a school charging tuition **:** PRIVATE SCHOOL

pay sheet *n, Brit* **:** PAYROLL

pay station *n* **:** a public telephone usu. equipped with a slot-machine device for payment of toll

pay streak *n* **:** a stratum of mineral deposit capable of yielding profitable amounts of oil or ore

payt *abbr* payment

pay up *vb* [ME *payen up*, fr. *payen* to pay + *up* — more at PAY] *vt* **:** to pay in full **:** bring (as debts, dues) up to date by paying ~ *vi* **:** to pay what is due or what is demanded ⟨the threat of court action was enough to make him *pay up*⟩

pay·ye·tan *or* **pay·e·tan** \,pīə'tän\ *n, pl* **payyeta·nim** *or* **payeta·nim** \,pīətä'nēm\ [LHeb *payĕṭān*, fr. *piyyūṭ* poem — more at PIYYUT] **:** an author of liturgical poems forming part of the Jewish liturgy on special Sabbaths and festivals — compare PIYYUT — **pay·ye·tan·ic** *or* **pay·e·tan·ic** \'=='tänik\ *adj*

pay station

pa·zend \'pä,zend\ *also* **pa·zand** \-zand\ *n* -S *cap* **:** the language of the transcriptions of Pahlavi texts into the script used for Avestan with substitution of Persian words for the Semitic words in the original; *also* **:** such transcriptions

PB *abbr* **1** passbook **2** passed ball **3** patrol boat **4** patrol bomber **5** permanent bunkers **6** phonetically balanced **7** piebald **8** pocket book **9** prayer book **10** privately bonded

Pb *symbol* [L *plumbum*] lead

PBA *abbr* permanent budget account

PBM *abbr* permanent bench mark

PBX \'pē(,)bē'eks\ *n* -S [*p*rivate *b*ranch e*x*change] **:** a private telephone switchboard

pc *abbr* piece

PC *abbr* **1** past commander **2** *often not cap* percent **3** percentage **4** perpetual curate **5** *often not cap* petty cash **6** pitch circle **7** *often not cap* police constable **8** postcard **9** [L *post cibum*] after meals **10** post commander **11** price current **12** privy council; privy councillor **13** purified concentrate

PCB *abbr* petty cashbook

pce *abbr* piece

PCE *abbr, often not cap* pyrometric cone equivalent

p-celtic \'='==\ *n, cap P&C* **:** those Celtic languages comprising the Gaulish and Brythonic in which the Indo-European labiovelar *qu* has become *p* — compare Q-CELTIC

pchs *abbr* purchase

pcl *abbr* parcel

PCM *abbr* pulse-code modulation

PCO *abbr* pest control operator

pcpn *abbr* precipitation

pcs *abbr* preconscious

PCS *abbr* **1** permanent change of station **2** principal clerk of session

pct *abbr* percent

pd *abbr* **1** paid **2** passed **3** pond **4** pound

PD *abbr* **1** [L *per diem*] by the day **2** pitch diameter **3** point detonating **4** police department **5** port dues **6** port of debarkation **7** position doubtful **8** postage due **9** postal district **10** postdated **11** potential difference **12** prism diopter **13** property damage **14** public domain

Pd *symbol* palladium

PDB *abbr or n* -S paradichlorobenzene

PDF *abbr* point detonating fuse

pdg *abbr* paradigm

PDI *abbr* pilot direction indicator

pdl *abbr* poundal

PDQ *adv, often not cap* [abbr. of *pretty damned quick*] **:** at once **:** IMMEDIATELY

pdr *abbr* **1** pounder **2** powder

1pe *or* **phe** \'pā\ *n* -S [Heb *pē*] **1 :** the 17th letter of the Hebrew alphabet — symbol פ; see ALPHABET table **2 :** the letter of the Phoenician or of any of various other Semitic alphabets corresponding to Hebrew pe

2pe \'pē\ *var of* PEE

-pe- *comb form* [pi*pe*ridine] **:** complete hydrogenation — in names of cyclic bases ⟨lu*pe*tidine⟩ ⟨pi*pe*coline⟩

PE \(')pē'ē\ *abbr or n* -S **:** a petroleum engineer

PE *abbr* **1** *often not cap* photoelectric **2** pinion end **3** port of embarkation **4** post exchange **5** presiding elder **6** *often not cap* printer's error **7** probable error **8** professional engineer **9** pulley end

1pea \'pē\ *n, pl* **peas** *also* **pease** \-ēz\ *often attrib* [back-formation fr. *pease* (taken as a plural), fr. ME *pese*, fr. OE *pise*, *peose*, fr. L *pisa*, pl. of *pisum*, fr. Gk *pisos*, *pison*] **1 a :** a variable annual leguminous vine (*Pisum sativum*) that is of uncertain natural origin and has been cultivated prob. since prehistoric times for its rounded smooth or wrinkled edible seeds which are rich in protein and are borne severally in dehiscent pods — called also *garden pea;* see FIELD PEA **b :** the seed of the pea widely used in its green immature stage as a cooked vegetable or stored in the mature dry stage (as for use in porridges or soups) ⟨a crab-and-*pea* bisque⟩ — usu. used in pl. ⟨steak and fresh buttered ~*s*⟩ **c peas** *pl* **:** the immature pods of the pea with their included seeds ⟨bought a bushel of new ~*s*⟩ **2 a :** any of various leguminous plants related to the pea or felt to resemble it in seed, flower, or use — usu. used with a qualifying term; see BEACH PEA, BLACK-EYED PEA, CHICK-PEA, COWPEA, SWEET PEA **b :** the seed of such a plant **3 :** something resembling a pea usu. in size, shape, or formation: **a :** a small piece or fragment (as of coal, gravel, iron pyrites) **b :** the small object that is hidden in the game of thimblerig

2pea *also* **pee** \"\ *n* -S [by shortening] **:** PEAK 6c

pea aphid *n* **:** a widely distributed aphid (*Acyrthosiphon pisum*) that is a serious pest on legumes (as alfalfa, pea, clover, vetch)

pea bean *n* **:** any of various kidney beans that are cultivated chiefly for their small white seeds which are used dried (as for baking)

pea beetle *n* **:** PEA WEEVIL

pea·ber·ry \'pē- — *see* BERRY\ *n* **:** a coffeeberry with a single round seed resembling a pea

peabird \'=,=\ *n* **1** *dial Eng* **:** WRYNECK **2 :** BALTIMORE ORIOLE

pea·body \'pē,bädē, -,bədē\ *n, sometimes cap* [fr. the name *Peabody*] **:** a fast ballroom dance in open position

peabody bird \"-\ *n, usu cap P* [prob. imit.] **:** WHITE-THROATED SPARROW

pea bug *n* **:** PEA WEEVIL

[1]**peace** \'pēs\ *n* -S *often attrib* [ME *pes, pees, pais,* fr. OF *pes, pais,* fr. L *pac-, pax* peace; akin to L *pacisci* to agree, contract — more at PACT] **1 a :** freedom from civil clamor and confusion **:** a state of public quiet ⟨~ and order were finally restored in the town⟩ **b :** a state of security or order within a community provided for by law, custom, or public opinion — often used with *the* ⟨a breach of the ~⟩ **2 :** a mental or spiritual condition marked by freedom from disquieting or oppressive thoughts or emotions **:** calmness of mind and heart **:** serenity of spirit ⟨the bitter, restless struggling of the last months gave way to ~ —Rose Macaulay⟩ ⟨I have been in perfect ~ and contentment; I never have had one doubt —J.H.Newman⟩ ⟨a ~ of mind because you could no longer be surprised —Stuart Cloete⟩ ⟨farewell and ~ be with you⟩ — compare PEACE OF GOD **3 a :** a tranquil state of freedom from outside disturbance and harassment ⟨decided to accept a year-round post . . . and have ~ to write —*Newsweek*⟩ ⟨now remembered sharply the ~ and quiet of the place —Sherwood Anderson⟩ **b :** eternal repose ⟨may he rest in ~⟩ **4 :** harmony in human or personal relations **:** mutual concord and esteem ⟨he knew that there would never be ~ again while they lived —Graham Greene⟩ **5 a** (1) **:** a state of mutual concord between governments **:** absence of hostilities or war ⟨he had given the world ~, and the world now turned to him for security —John Buchan⟩ (2) **:** the period of such freedom from war ⟨a ~ of 50 years⟩ **b :** a pact or agreement to end hostilities or to come together in amity between those who have been at war or in a state of enmity or dissension **:** a formal reconciliation between contending parties; *esp* **:** a peace treaty ⟨signed ~ in the spring of 1918 —C.E.Black & E.C.Helmreich⟩ ⟨offered the possibility of a negotiated ~ —*N.Y.Times*⟩ **6 :** absence of activity and noise **:** deep stillness **:** QUIETNESS ⟨the ~ of the woods⟩ ⟨the ~ of sky and mountain⟩ **7 :** one that makes, gives, or maintains tranquillity ⟨God is our only ~⟩ — **at peace** *adv* **:** in a state of concord or tranquillity ⟨the problem was settled and his mind was *at peace*⟩ ⟨help man live *at peace* with his unconscious —*Time*⟩

[2]**peace** \"\ *vi* -ED/-ING/-S [ME *peesen,* fr. *pes, pees, pais* peace (n.)] **:** to become quiet or still **:** be, become, or keep silent ⟨when the thunder would not ~ at my bidding —Shak.⟩ — often used interjectionally

peace·abil·i·ty \,pēsə'bilәd·ē, -lətē, -i\ *n* **:** PEACEABLENESS ⟨snore himself to ~ —P.A.Rollins⟩

peace·able \'pēsəbəl\ *adj* [ME *pesible, pesable, paisible,* fr. MF *pesible, paisible,* fr. *pes, pais* peace + *-ible* — more at PEACE] **1 a :** disposed to peace **:** having an amicable disposition disinclined to strife **:** not contentious or quarrelsome ⟨the quiet, humble, modest and ~ person —William Cowper⟩ ⟨his tongue was not always ~ —W.R.Inge⟩ **b :** lacking noisiness or restlessness **:** quietly behaved **:** CALM ⟨was pleased to see how ~ the horse had become⟩ **2 :** marked by freedom from war, strife, hostilities, or disorder ⟨in the most ~ and orderly manner, without the smallest sign of tumult or sedition in the city —J.G.Frazer⟩ ⟨the company . . . in ~ times makes chiefly freight cars —E.D.Kennedy⟩ **syn** see PACIFIC

peace·able·ness *n* -ES [ME *pesiblenesse,* fr. *pesible, pesable, paisible* peaceable + *-nesse* -ness] **:** the quality or state of being peaceable

peace·ably \-blē, -bli\ *adv* [ME *pesibly, paisibly,* fr. *pesible, paisible* + *-y*] **1 :** in a peaceable and friendly manner **:** without contention or strife ⟨possible for more than one religion to survive comparatively ~ in the same state —Alfred Cobban⟩ **2 :** without subjection to annoyance or confusion **:** in peace **:** QUIETLY ⟨disturb him not; let him pass ~ —Shak.⟩

peace belt *n* **:** a wampum belt used to symbolize peace among No. American Indians

peacebreaker \'=,==\ *n* **:** a violator of peace or of the peace **:** a perpetrator of strife ⟨international obligations to repress ~*s* —*Contemporary Rev.*⟩

peacebreaking \'=,==\ *n* **:** the action of violating peace **:** the commission of a breach of the peace

peace democrat *n, usu cap P&D* **:** a Democrat in the northern states advocating peaceful measures as opposed to prosecution of the Civil War; *esp* **:** COPPERHEAD 2a

peace dollar *n* **:** a silver dollar of the U.S. struck from 1921 to 1928 and in 1934 and 1935

peace·ful \'pēsfəl\ *adj, sometimes* **peacefuller;** *sometimes* **peacefullest** [ME *paisful, pesful,* fr. *pais, pes, pees* peace + *-ful* — more at PEACE] **1 :** PEACEABLE 1 ⟨the ~ comportment of the seals had quieted my alarm —Jack London⟩ ⟨the modest man becomes bold . . . or the impetuous prudent and ~ —W.M.Thackeray⟩ **2 :** marked by, conducive to, or enjoying peace, quiet, or calm **:** untroubled by conflict, agitation, or commotion ⟨the feeling . . . that we as neighbors could settle any disputes in ~ fashion —F.D.Roosevelt⟩ ⟨rocky promontories shelter ~ bays —Samuel Van Valkenburg & Ellsworth Huntington⟩ **3 :** of or relating to a state or time of peace ⟨a bomb material as well as a ~ fuel —Oliver Townsend⟩ **4 :** devoid of violence or force **:** without recourse to warlike methods ⟨all the political groups . . . employed ~ tactics —*Collier's Yr. Bk.*⟩ ⟨~ procedures . . . mediation, investigation and conciliation —*Current History*⟩ **syn** see CALM, PACIFIC

peace·ful·ly \-fəlē, -li\ *adv* **:** in a peaceful manner ⟨cattle which ~ browse —Tom Marvel⟩ ⟨a ~ inclined and responsible government —Vera M. Dean⟩

peace·ful·ness \-fəlnəs\ *n* -ES **:** the quality or state of being peaceful ⟨the ~ and neighborliness of the parish is proverbial —*Amer. Guide Series: La.*⟩

peace-keeper \'=,==\ *n* **:** a maintainer of peace or of the peace **:** a pacific country or person

peace·less \'pēsləs\ *adj* **:** having no peace — **peace·less·ness** *n* -ES

peacemaker \'=,==\ *n* [ME *peace maker,* fr. *pease, pes, pees, pais* peace + *maker*] **:** one that makes or seeks to make peace esp. by reconciling parties or persons at variance

[1]**peacemaking** \'=,==\ *n* **:** the action of bringing about peace

[2]**peacemaking** \"\ *adj* **:** bringing about peace or done in an effort to bring about peace

peacemonger \'=,==\ *n* **:** PEACEMAKER; *esp* **:** one making or seeking peace unrealistically or at the expense of honor — usu. used disparagingly

peacemongering \'=,=(=)=\ *adj* **:** PEACEMAKING — usu. used disparagingly

peace offensive *n* **:** a campaign designed to serve the interests of a nation by the expression of wishes to end a war or of intentions to resolve conflicts peacefully and thus cause hostile or unfriendly nations to relax their efforts or become less vigilant

peace offering *n* **1 :** an ancient Hebrew votive, freewill, or thank offering **2 :** a gift or service to procure peace or reconciliation

peace officer *n* **:** a civil officer (as a sheriff, constable, policeman) whose duty it is to preserve the public peace

peace of god 1 *cap G* **:** the peace of heart which is the gift of God **2** *usu cap P & cap G* **:** an exemption from attack in feudal warfare urged by the church beginning in the latter part of the 9th century for all consecrated persons and places and later for all who claimed the protection of the church (as pilgrims, the poor) — compare TRUCE OF GOD

peace pipe *n* **:** CALUMET

peaces *pl of* PEACE, *pres 3d sing of* PEACE

peacetime \'=,=\ *n, often attrib* **:** a time when a nation is not at war ⟨as anxious to save lives in ~ as . . . in wartime —*Tomorrow*⟩

[1]**peach** \'pēch\ *n* -ES [ME *peche,* fr. MF (the fruit) fr. LL *persica,* fr. L *persicum,* fr. neut. of *Persicus* Persian] **1 a :** a low spreading freely branching tree (*Prunus persica*) that is native to China but cosmopolitan in cultivation in temperate areas and often found as an escape and that has drooping lanceolate leaves, sessile usu. pink flowers borne on the naked twigs in early spring, and a fruit which is a drupe with a single seed enclosed in a hard endocarp, a pulpy white or yellow mesocarp, and a thin firm downy epicarp — compare CHERRY 1a, PLUM **b :** the sweet juicy edible fruit of the peach which is widely used as a fresh or cooked fruit, in preserves, or dried **2 :** the quandong of Australia **3 :** any of various trees or shrubs or their edible fruits resembling the peach **4 :** a variable color averaging a moderate yellowish pink that is yellower, less strong, and slightly darker than peach pink, yellower and paler than coral pink, and yellower, lighter, and stronger than dusty pink **5 :** peach brandy **6 :** one likened to a peach in sweetness, beauty, or excellence **:** something particularly good in its class ⟨is a ~ to work with —*Atlantic*⟩ ⟨should be a ~ of a game —*Holiday*⟩ ⟨she's got a studio with a ~ of an English girl —A.H.Gibbs⟩

[2]**peach** \"\ *vb* -ED/-ING/-ES [ME *pechen,* short for *apechen* to appeach — more at APPEACH] *vt* **:** to inform against **:** BETRAY ⟨the woman was about to play false, and to ~ the rest —George Borrow⟩ ~ *vi* **:** to turn informer **:** BLAB, TATTLE ⟨the vilest of all sins — is to ~ to the headmaster —F.M.Ford⟩

pea chaparral *n* **:** CHAPARRAL PEA

peach aphid *n* **:** an aphid destructive to the peach — see BLACK PEACH APHID, GREEN PEACH APHID

peach bark beetle *n* **:** a scolytid beetle (*Phloeotribus liminaris*) the larvae of which feed on the inner bark of cherry and other stone-fruit trees

peach-bark borer *n* **:** PEACH TREE BORER

peach bell *n* **:** a perennial European bellflower (*Campanula persicifolia*) with racemose white or blue flowers — usu. used in pl.

peach bisque *n* **:** a light reddish brown that is redder and slightly deeper than copper tan and darker than monkey skin

peach blight *n* **1 :** a brown rot of stone fruits characterized by blighting of the twigs, leaves, or flowers **2 :** CALIFORNIA BLIGHT

peach blister *n* **:** LEAF CURL a

peach bloom *n* **1 :** a moderate yellowish pink that is yellower and paler than coral pink, less strong and slightly redder and darker than peach pink, and redder, less strong, and slightly darker than average peach — called also *rose morn* **2 :** a reduced copper glaze that is used esp. on Chinese porcelain and is mottled pinkish red often streaked with russet and green

peachblossom \'=,==\ *n* **1** *also* **peachblossom pink** *or* **peachblossom red :** a moderate to strong pink that is yellower and lighter than hermosa pink or nymph pink **2** *of textiles* **:** a deep pink to moderate purplish red that is bluer and stronger than rambler rose

peachblossom ore *n* **:** ERYTHRITE 2

peachblow \'=,=\ *n* **1 :** a pale orange yellow that is slightly redder, lighter, and stronger than sunset and redder and stronger than freestone — called also *fakir* **2 :** PEACH BLOOM 2 **3 :** *or* **peachblow glass :** a late 19th century opaque and often satinized art glass of graduated color which shades from red or rose to yellow or pale blue or white

peach borer *n* **1 :** PEACH TREE BORER **2 :** the larva of a large beetle (*Dicerca divaricata*) of the family Buprestidae which bores esp. in the peach, cherry, and maple

peach canker *n* **:** a disease of peaches characterized by production of cankers (as those caused by fungi of the genera *Valsa* and *Sclerotinia*) — compare BROWN ROT 1a

peach curl *n* **:** LEAF CURL a

peach·er·i·no \,pēchə'rē(,)nō\ *n* -S [prob. irreg. fr. [1]*peach* + It *-ino,* dim. suffix] *slang* **:** PEACH 6

peach family *n* **:** ROSACEAE

peachick \'=,=\ *n* **:** the chick of the peafowl

peachier *comparative of* PEACHY

peachiest *superlative of* PEACHY

peach-kernel oil *n* **:** either of two oils obtained from peach kernels that are very similar in properties and uses to the true almond oils: **a :** a colorless or straw-colored nondrying fatty oil obtained by expression — called also *persic oil* **b :** a colorless to yellow aromatic toxic essential oil obtained by steam distillation — called also *bitter almond oil*

peach leaf curl *n* **:** LEAF CURL a

peachleaf willow \'=,=-\ *or* **peach-leaved willow** \'=,=-\ *n* **:** a willow (*Salix amygdaloides*) of the western U. S. with leaves like those of the peach or almond — called also *almond-leaved willow*

peach lecanium *n* **:** TERRAPIN SCALE

peach melba *n, sometimes cap M* [trans. of F *pêche Melba*] **:** PÊCHE MELBA

peach mildew *n* **:** a powdery mildew of peaches caused by a fungus (*Sphaerotheca pannosa*)

peach moth *n* **:** a moth having larvae that attack the peach; *esp* **:** ORIENTAL PEACH MOTH

peach oak *n* **1 :** WILLOW OAK **2 :** TANBARK OAK a

peach palm *n* **1 :** a So. American pinnate-leaved palm (*Bactris gasipaes*) with thorny stems and edible fruit **2 :** a spiny So. American palm (*Guilielma utilis*) that is prized for its hard wood and edible fruit

peach pink *n* **:** a moderate yellowish pink that is yellower and lighter than coral pink, yellower, lighter, and stronger than dusty pink, and redder, stronger, and slightly lighter than average peach

peach red *n* **:** a strong yellowish pink that is redder and darker than salmon pink, redder and deeper than melon, and yellower than madder scarlet

peach rosette *n* **:** a very destructive virus disease attacking peach, plum, and almond trees and characterized by the growth of dense rosettes of dwarfed leaves at the ends of the branches and by the failure to bear fruit

peach rust *n* **:** a fungous disease of stone fruits caused by rust fungi of the genus *Tranzschelia* (as *T. discolor* and *T. pruni-spinosae*) and attacking the peach, plum, apricot, and cherry

peach scab *n* **:** a fungous disease of the peach and related plants (as cherry and plum) caused by a scab (*Cladosporium carpophilum*) producing freckles on the fruit and small brown spots on the leaves and twigs — called also *cherry scab, plum scab*

peach scale *n* **:** any of several scales infesting peach trees: as **a :** a large dark-colored hemispherical scale (*Lecanium persicae*) **b :** a flatter and lighter-colored scale (*Pseudaulacaspis pentagona*)

peach silver mite *n* **:** an eriophyid mite (*Aculus cornutus*) that is a pest on peach trees

peach tan *n* **:** a light reddish brown that is lighter, stronger, and slightly redder than copper tan and yellower, lighter, and stronger than monkey skin or peach bisque

peach tip moth *n* **:** an olethreutid moth (*Carpocapsa molesta*) having a larva that damages twigs and fruit of cherry, peach, and some other fruit trees

peach tree bark beetle *n* **:** PEACH BARK BEETLE

peach tree borer *n* **:** any of several moth larvae that are destructive to peach trees, boring in the wood usu. near ground level; *esp* **:** a white brown-headed grub that is the larva of a blue-black orange-marked clearwing moth (*Sanninoidea exitiosa*) and that attacks peach and other stone fruit trees in much of eastern No. America — see LESSER PEACH TREE BORER, WESTERN PEACH BORER

peach twig borer *n* **:** the larva of a small gelechiid moth (*Anarsia lineatella*) that bores into the smaller twigs of the peach and other fruit trees

peach wart *n* **:** a virus disease of the peach characterized by leathery or hard outgrowths of fruit tissue that at first are bleached and later tan or reddish, that appear esp. near the style end where they frequently form patterns like rings or are clustered, and that may exhibit russeting

peach weevil *n* **:** a large curculio (*Ithycercus noveboracensis*) that attacks the buds and twigs of the peach and oak

peachwood \'=,=\ *n* **:** a brazilwood (*Caesalpinia echinata*)

peachy \'pēchē, -chi\ *adj, sometimes* -ER/-EST **1 :** resembling a peach ⟨~ cheeks and slender figure —Edmund Wilson⟩ **2 :** unusually fine **:** DANDY ⟨airedales were ~ dogs —J.T. Farrell⟩ ⟨thinks things are pretty ~ as they are —J.R.Newman⟩

peach yellows *n pl but usu sing in constr* **:** a destructive virus disease of the peach producing yellowing or browning and curling up of the leaves, dwarfing of the branches, the growth of willowlike sterile shoots, dwarfing and premature ripening of fruit, and in a few years death

pea coal *n* **:** anthracite coal of a small size — see ANTHRACITE table

pea coat *n* [*pea* (as in *pea jacket*) + *coat*] **:** PEA JACKET

[1]**pea·cock** \'pē,=\ *n* [ME *pecok, pocok,* fr. *pe-* (fr. OE *pēa* peafowl) & *po-* (fr. OE *pāwa* peafowl) + *cok* cock; akin to Fris *pau* peafowl, OS *pāo,* OHG *pfāwo,* ON *pāi;* all fr. a prehistoric WGmc-NGmc word borrowed fr. L *pavon-, pavo* peacock, prob. of imit. origin like Gk *taōs* peacock — more at COCK] **1** *pl also* **peacock :** a male peafowl distinguished by a crest of upright plumules and by greatly elongated loosely webbed upper tail coverts that are mostly tipped with ocellate spots and are erected and spread at will in a fan shimmering with iridescent color; *broadly* **:** PEAFOWL — see INDIAN PEACOCK, JAPANNED PEACOCK, JAVAN PEACOCK **2 :** one making a proud or arrogant display of himself ⟨the poodles were the ~*s* of the local dog show⟩; *esp* **:** a vainglorious person ⟨would take the young ~ down a peg —Marguerite Steen⟩ **3** *or* **peacock blue :** a variable color averaging a moderate greenish blue that is greener and deeper than Brittany or average colonial blue and deeper and slightly greener than larkspur — called also *paon* **4 :** PEACOCK BUTTERFLY

[2]**peacock** \"\ *vb* -ED/-ING/-S *vt* **1 :** to cause to be like a peacock (as in vainglorious display) ⟨he may have ~*ed* it a bit, he supposed he did —William Humphrey⟩ ⟨attempted to ~ his way through the world —C.S.Bluemel⟩ **2** *slang Austral* **:** to pick out or buy the choicest pieces of (land) esp. by the use of dummies ~ *vi* **:** to make a vainglorious display (as in gait, dress, speech) **:** POSE, STRUT ⟨all the girls . . . were ~*ing* in their bustles —Flora Thompson⟩ ⟨my father ~*ing* about on the lawn —Osbert Sitwell⟩

peacock bittern *or* **peacock heron** *n* **:** SUN-GREBE

peacock blue *n* **:** any of several bright blue pigments; *esp* **:** a clear fugitive lake made from Azure Blue AEG and used chiefly in printing inks — see DYE table I (under *Pigment Blue 24*); compare PEACOCK 3

peacock butterfly *n* **:** any of several butterflies having ocellate spots on the wings: as **a :** a widespread European butterfly (*Nymphalis io*) **b :** BUCKEYE 4

peacock coal *n* **:** coal (as anthracite) with iridescent films on broken surfaces

pea·cock·ery \'=,=ərē\ *n* **:** the dress or mannerism of a fop **:** ostentatious display ⟨his vanity is extreme but . . . he has no ~ —John Gunther⟩ ⟨designs ranged from elaborate ~ to sexy sheaths of black sequins —*Time*⟩

peacock flounder *n* **:** a large West Indian flounder (*Platophrys lunatus*) that is dark olive covered with bright blue spots

peacock flower *n* **1 :** ROYAL POINCIANA **2 :** PRIDE OF BARBADOS

peacock green *n* **:** a moderate yellowish green that is greener and stronger than tarragon, deeper than malachite green, and deeper and slightly yellower than verdigris

peacock iris *n* **:** an ornamental South African herb (*Moraea pavonia*) having orange-red flowers with a black spot at the base of each perianth segment

pea·cock·ish \'=,=ish\ *adj* **:** resembling a peacock **:** FLAMBOYANT, OSTENTATIOUS — **pea·cock·ish·ly** *adv* — **pea·cock·ish·ness** *n* -ES

peacock moth *n* **:** EMPEROR MOTH

peacock ore *n* **:** a mineral consisting of an iridescent variety of copper ore: as **a :** BORNITE **b :** CHALCOPYRITE

peacock pheasant *n* **:** any of several showy Asiatic pheasants of the genus *Polyplectron* having in the male two or three spurs on the leg, erectile tail coverts, and brilliantly ocellated plumage

peacock's-tail \'=,=,=\ *n, pl* **peacock's-tails :** a widely distributed tropical alga (*Padina pavonia*) with fan-shaped fronds

pea·cocky \'pē,käkē\ *adj* -ER/-EST **1 :** PEACOCKISH ⟨a decidedly ~ horse in the ring⟩ **2 :** exhibiting a showy air

pea comb *n* **:** a comb of a gallinaceous bird (as a Brahma fowl) consisting of three low weakly serrated and usu. partly fused crests side by side of which the middle one is the highest — see COMB illustration

pea crab *n* **:** a minute commensal crab of the family Pinnotheridae living in bivalve mollusks; *esp* **:** a European crab (*Pinnotheres pisum*) found in mussels and cockles and regarded as a great delicacy — compare OYSTER CRAB

pea dove *n* **:** the zenaida dove of Jamaica

pea family *n* **:** LEGUMINOSAE

pea finch *n, Brit* **:** CHAFFINCH

pea flower *n* **1 :** the flower of the pea **2 :** any flower of the papilionaceous type

peafowl \'pē,=\ *n* [*pea-* (as in *peacock*) + *fowl*] **:** a very large terrestrial pheasant (genus *Pavo*) of southeastern Asia and the East Indies that occurs chiefly in the open woodland and at the margins of cultivated areas and is often reared as an ornamental fowl — see PEACOCK, PEAHEN

peag *also* **peage** \'pēg\ *or* **peak** \-ēk\ *n* -S [Narraganset *wampompeag* — more at WAMPUM] **:** WAMPUM

pea-gall \'=,=\ *n* **:** a small gall on rosaceous plants caused by gall wasps of the genus *Rhodites*

pe·age \'pāij\ *n* -S [ME *payage,* fr. MF *paiage,* fr. ML *pedaticum, pedagium,* fr. L *ped-, pes* foot + *-aticum* -age or ML *-agium* (alter. of L *-aticum*) — more at FOOT] *archaic* **:** toll for passage

pea·goose \'pē,=\ *or* **peak·goose** \'pēk,=\ *n* [obs. E *peke* simpleton + *goose*] *obs* **:** a poor simpleton **:** NINNY

pea green *n* **:** a variable color averaging a moderate yellow-green that is greener, lighter, and stronger than average moss green, greener and lighter than mosstone, and lighter and slightly stronger than spinach green

pea grit *n* **:** PISOLITE

peahen \'pē,=\ *n* [ME *pehenne, pohenne,* fr. *pe-* (fr. OE *pēa* peafowl) & *po-* (fr. OE *pāwa* peafowl) + *henne* hen — more at PEACOCK, HEN] **:** a female peafowl

pea huller *n* **:** VINER 1

pe·ai \pē'ī\ *or* **pe·ai·man** \-īmən\ *n, pl* **peais** *or* **peaimen** [*peai* fr. Galibi *piaye; peaiman* fr. *peai* + *man*] **:** a medicine man of the Indian peoples of northeastern So. America

pea jacket \'pē,=\ *n* [by folk etymology fr. D *pijjekker,* fr. *pij,* a kind of coarse cloth, a coat made of this material (fr. MD *pie*) + *jekker* jacket] **:** a heavy woolen double-breasted jacket that is straight-hanging and hip-length and is worn chiefly by sailors — called also *pea coat*

pea jacket

[1]**peak** \'pēk\ *vi* -ED/-ING/-S [origin unknown] **1** *obs* **:** to go about quietly or dejectedly **:** be spiritless ⟨I, a dull and muddy-mettled rascal ~ . . . and can say nothing —Shak.⟩ **2 :** to acquire sharpness of figure or features **:** grow thin **:** look wan or sickly ⟨the new baby was due next month, and its mother inclined to ~ —Margery Sharp⟩ **3 :** to dwindle away **:** FADE, PETER — often used with *out* ⟨before long the game began to ~ —T.A.G.Hungerford⟩ ⟨the little business they had started finally ~*ed* out⟩

[2]**peak** \"\ *n* -S [prob. alter. (perh. influenced by *beak*) of [1]and [3]*pike*] **1 :** a pointed or projecting part of a garment: as **a** *obs* **:** the pointed front of a woman's headdress **b :** the visor of a cap or hat **:** BILL ⟨by way of salutation, jerked the ~ of his cap —George Seddon⟩ **2 :** a jut of land **:** PROMONTORY **3 :** a sharp or pointed end **:** a projecting point ⟨the ~*s* of the roof —Fiske Kimball⟩ **4** *obs* **:** a pointed beard **5 a** (1) **:** the top of a hill or mountain **:** one of the crests of a mountain or mountain range **:** SUMMIT ⟨where pines . . . look out towards ~*s* that tower in the distance —Laurence Binyon⟩ ⟨the fog hung . . . heavily on the ~ of the hill—H.D.Skidmore⟩ (2) **:** a whole hill or mountain esp. when isolated **b :** something resembling a mountain peak ⟨the clouds are piled . . . in frothy white ~*s* —Claudia Cassidy⟩ ⟨beat steadily . . . until the frosting will form ~*s* when the beater is lifted —Marjorie M. Heseltine & Ula M. Dow⟩ **6 a** (1) **:** the upper aftermost corner of a fore-and-aft sail esp. when extended by a gaff (2) **:** the upper end of the gaff **b** (1) **:** AFTERPEAK (2) **:** FOREPEAK **c :** the bill of an anchor **7 a :** the very top **:** PINNACLE **:** the highest level or greatest degree (as of efficiency or excellence) **:** ULTIMATE ⟨his vocal control was at its ~ when he did the recording —Paul Hume⟩ ⟨the illusion of setting and atmosphere was carried to its ~ —W.P.Eaton⟩ ⟨none of them attained the highest ~*s* of the Greek genius —G.A.L.Sarton⟩ **b :** a high point in a course of development esp. as represented or capable of representation on a graph ⟨the community prospered . . . reaching its ~ of prosperity and population about 1840 —*Amer. Guide Series: Maine*⟩ ⟨regularize employment and reduce ~*s* and

valleys —*N.Y.Times*⟩ ⟨here for the ~ of the season —A.L. Himbert⟩ **c :** the highest point to which prices rise in a given period **8 :** a point formed by the hair on the forehead — called also *widow's peak* **9 :** the maximum value of a periodically varying quantity during a cycle (as of voltage or current): as **a :** the strongest part of an electronic communications signal **b :** the maximum signal recorded on a volume indicator in a broadcasting studio **10 :** the most sonorous part of a syllable (as a vowel or a syllabic consonant)

³peak \"\ *vb* -ED/-ING/-S *vi* **1 :** to rise or extend to a peak or point **:** form or appear as a peak ⟨beat egg whites until they ~ —D.L.Bolinger⟩ **2 :** to reach a maximum (as of capacity, value, or activity) ⟨a firm whose business ~*s* from July to December —*N.Y.Times*⟩ ~ *vt* **1 :** to cause to come to a peak or point ⟨pursed her pretty lips and ~*ed* her eyebrows —Marcia Davenport⟩ **2 :** to bring to a maximum ⟨stores ~ spring stocks too late —*Women's Wear Daily*⟩ **3 :** to adjust (as an electronic communication circuit) so as to cause a signal to have a maximum or a higher value

⁴peak \"\ *adj* **:** reaching the maximum of capacity, value, or activity ⟨the factories of all countries giving at ~ productivity —*Current Biog.*⟩ ⟨the street at ~ hours is congested with traffic —*Amer. Guide Series: La.*⟩

⁵peak \"\ *vt* -ED/-ING/-S [*apeak*] **1 :** to set nearer the perpendicular (as a gaff or yard) **2** *of a whale* **:** to raise (as tail or flukes) straight up in the air in diving vertically ⟨the interesting motion known as ~*ing* flukes —R.L.Cook⟩ **3 :** to tilt up to a perpendicular or nearly perpendicular position; *esp* **:** to hold (oars) with blades well raised

⁶peak \"\ *dial var of* PIQUE

⁷peak *var of* PEAG

peak arch *n* **:** a pointed or Gothic arch

peak crest *n* **:** a pointed crest on the head (as of various pigeons) — distinguished from *shell crest*

¹peaked \'pēkt, -kəd, *dial* 'pikəd\ *adj* [ME *peked*, alter. of *piked* — more at PIKED] **:** having a peak **:** rising to or ending in a peak **:** POINTED ⟨pointed to the ~ ceiling —Erle Stanley Gardner⟩ ⟨the ~ hills of the islands —William Black⟩

²peak·ed \'pēkəd, *dial* 'pikəd\ *adj* [fr. past part. of ¹*peak*] **:** looking pale and wan **:** SICKLY, THIN ⟨the boy looked sallow and ~, slept uneasily —Aldous Huxley⟩ ⟨they were smiling, but . . . both looked a little ~ —Ellery Queen⟩

peaked·ness \'pēk(t)nəs, -kədn-\ *n* -ES **:** the quality or state of being peaked; *specif* **:** the degree to which conditions that constitute a peak in a frequency curve are present

peaked roof *n* **:** a roof of two or more slopes rising to a ridge

peak·er \'pēkə(r)\ *n* -S **1 :** a load of logs narrowing toward the top **2 :** the top log of a load

peak-fresh \'⸗'⸗\ *adj* **:** having reached but not passed the optimum stage of maturity for use — used of fruits and vegetables

peakgoose *var of* PEAGOOSE

peaking *adj* [fr. gerund of ¹*peak*] **1** *dial Eng* **:** MEAN, SNEAKING **2** *dial Eng* **:** ²PEAKED

peak load *n* **:** the maximum load carried during a given period (as by a railroad, telegraph line, power plant, pumping station) ⟨the person who uses the highways only on such days as . . . Labor Day makes a marginal contribution to the *peak load* —W.H.Anderson⟩

peaks *pres 3d sing of* PEAK, *pl of* PEAK

peak voltmeter *n* **:** an instrument for measuring the maximum voltage during an alternating current cycle — called also *crest voltmeter*

¹peaky \'pēkē\ *adj* -ER/-EST [²*peak* + *-y*] **1 :** having a peak or peaks **:** marked by peaks ⟨crossed the ~ ridge⟩ **2 :** POINTED, SHARP ⟨a ~ face⟩

²peaky \"\ *adj* -ER/-EST [²*peaked* + *-y*] **:** PEAKED, SICKLY ⟨he was a small boy, nine at most, and ~ —Margery Allingham⟩

³peaky \"\ *var of* PECKY

¹peal \'pēl, *esp before pause or consonant* -ēəl\ *n* -S [ME *pele* appeal, summons to church by bell-ringing, short for *appel, apel, apele* appeal — more at APPEAL] **1 a :** the loud ringing of bells ⟨the ~ of victory won —*Bull. of Bates Coll.*⟩ **b** (1) **:** a complete set of changes on a given number of bells; *esp* **:** the series on seven bells usu. with the tenor struck at the end of each change ⟨each tower ~ took three hours —*Christian Science Monitor*⟩ — compare TOUCH 12 (2) **:** a shorter performance than a full peal **c :** a set of bells tuned to the tones of the major scale for change ringing ⟨the original bells . . . will be melted down and recast into another ~ —Sylvia Gray⟩ **2 :** a loud sound or succession of sounds ⟨send him into ~*s* of laughter —H.A.Overstreet⟩ ⟨heavy ~*s* of thunder —W.J.Humphreys⟩ ⟨the loud ~ of the doorbell —Agnes S. Turnbull⟩ — **in peal** *adv* **:** in rhythmic and melodic order in change ringing

²peal \"\ *vb* -ED/-ING/-S *vi* **:** to utter or give out peals **:** RESOUND ⟨silvery laughter ~*ed* against the ceiling —Frank Yerby⟩ ⟨the bells in the parish churches . . . began ~*ing* —*Saturday Rev.*⟩ ~ *vt* **1** *obs* **:** to assail or din (as the ear) with sound ⟨nor was his ear less ~*ed* with noises loud and ruinous —John Milton⟩ **2 :** to utter or give forth loudly **:** sound forth in a peal **:** noise abroad ⟨~*ed* his ideas through all the neighborhood⟩ ⟨~*ed* a high C on the trumpet⟩

³peal \"\ *vb* -ED/-ING/-S [ME *pelen*, short for *apelen, appelen* to appeal — more at APPEAL] *dial Eng* **:** APPEAL

⁴peal \"\ *n* -S [origin unknown] *Brit* **:** GRILSE

pea leaf miner *n* **:** a leaf miner that is the larva of an agromyzid fly (*Liriomyza bryoniae*) and that tunnels in celery, spinach, and similar plants esp. in California

peale's falcon \'pē(ə)lz-\ *n, usu cap P* [after Titian R. *Peale* †1885 Am. naturalist] **:** a medium-sized hawk of western No. America that constitutes a dark variety (*Falco peregrinus pealei*) of the duck hawk — compare PEREGRINE FALCON

pealike \'⸗,⸗\ *adj* **1 :** resembling a garden pea esp. in size, firmness, and shape ⟨a palpable ~ mass under the skin⟩ **2 a :** resembling a plant of the genus *Lathyrus* or that of such a plant ⟨a ~ pod⟩ ⟨~ vines⟩ **b** *of a flower* **:** showy and papilionaceous

peal ringing *n* [¹*peal*] **:** CHANGE RINGING

peameal \'⸗,⸗\ *n* **:** meal made from ground dried peas and used to coat cured meats ⟨~ bacon⟩

pea mildew *n* **1 :** either of two fungous diseases attacking peas: **a :** one caused by a powdery mildew (*Erysiphe polygoni*) **b :** one caused by a downy mildew (*Peronospora viciae*) **2 :** a fungus causing pea mildew

pea moth *n* **:** a small dark moth (*Laspeyresia nigricana*) of the family Olethreutidae whose larva feeds in pea pods destroying the seeds and that is native to Europe but is now a major pest in No. American commercial plantings

¹pean *var of* PAEAN

²pean \'pēn\ *n* -S [MF *pene*, lit., feather, fr. L *penna* — more at PEN] **:** a heraldic fur consisting of ermine spots of gold on a black field

³pean \"\ *adj* **:** of the heraldic fur pean

⁴pean *var of* PEEN

¹pea·nut \'pē(,)nət, *usu* -əd·+V\ *n* [¹*pea* + *nut*] **1 a :** a low branching annual herb (*Arachis hypogaea*) that has slightly hairy stems, bijugate leaves, and showy yellow flowers initially sessile but with a hypanthium which elongates and bends into the soil where the ovary ripens into a reticulated usu. constricted indehiscent pod containing one to three edible seeds and that is prob. native to Brazil but is cultivated in most tropical and many mild temperate regions for its oily seeds and as forage **b :** the seed of the peanut either enclosed in its papery husk and outer pod or freed from these — see PEANUT BUTTER, PEANUT OIL **2 :** FLAX 3 **3 :** an insignificant, petty, or tiny person ⟨shows a lot of strength for such a ~⟩ — often used disparagingly **4 peanuts** *pl* **a :** something small, inconsequential, or of little value ⟨the rush of westward traffic was ~*s* to what the roads will be handling late this summer —*Time*⟩ ⟨total volume of business . . . is so small that I used to call it ~*s* —W.M.Mason⟩ **b :** a very petty sum of money usu. in comparison to the total amount involved ⟨compared to present prices . . . I was getting ~*s* —John Lardner⟩ ⟨persuading big names to appear for ~*s* in his productions —Al Hine⟩

²peanut \"\ *adj* **:** characterized by smallness or insignificance **:** MEAN, PETTY ⟨~ politicians —*New Republic*⟩ ⟨no time for congress to be dawdling over ~ legislation —*Newsweek*⟩ ⟨I haven't got all day for this ~ case — Douglass Welch⟩

peanut butter *n* **:** a paste made by grinding roasted, skinned, and degermed peanuts

peanut cactus *n* **:** a cactus (*Chamaecereus silvestrii*) of So. America that forms clumps of cylindrical joints resembling a peanut in shape and is used as an ornamental

peanut gallery *n* **:** the upper balcony of a theater

peanut oil *n* **:** a colorless to yellow nondrying fatty oil obtained from peanuts and used chiefly as a salad oil, in margarine, in soap, and as a vehicle in pharmaceutical preparations and cosmetics — called also *arachis oil*

peanut shaker *n* **:** an implement attached to a tractor for freeing the vines from soil as peanuts are dug

peanut tube *n* **:** a small vacuum tube

peanut worm *n* **:** SIPUNCULID

pea ore *n* **:** limonite occurring in round grains about the size of a pea

peapod \'⸗,⸗\ *n* **:** a clinker-built open double-ended boat used for fishing in Maine

¹pear \'pa(a)(ə)r, 'pe|, |ə\ *n* -S [ME *pere*, fr. OE *pere, peru*, fr. L *pirum*, of non-IE origin; akin to the source of Gk *apios* pear tree, *apion* pear] **1 :** the fleshy oblong pome fruit of a tree of the genus *Pyrus* (esp. *P. communis*) that is generally larger at the apical end and has grit cells throughout the flesh — compare APPLE **2 :** a tree that bears pears

²pear \'pi(ə)r, -iə\ *vi* -ED/-ING/-S [ME *peren*, short for *aperen, apperen* — more at APPEAR] *now dial* **:** APPEAR

pear bark beetle *n* **:** a small beetle (*Scolytus rugulosus*) whose larva bores under the bark of the pear and other fruit trees (as the peach, plum, apple)

pear blight *n* **1 :** FIRE BLIGHT **2 a** *also* **pear blight beetle :** a minute beetle (*Anisandrus pyri*) whose larvae bore in the twigs of pear and other hardwood trees **b :** a mealybug (*Pseudococcus adonidum*)

pear blister mite *n* **:** PEAR LEAF BLISTER MITE

pear borer *n* **1 :** the larva of a small clearwing moth (*Thamnosphecia pyri*) that is similar to the peach-tree borer but smaller and that bores beneath the bark of the pear **2 :** the larva of a beetle (*Chrysobothris femorata*) of the family Buprestidae that attacks apple, pear, oak, and maple trees **3 :** the larva of a related European beetle (*Agrilus sinuatus*) that bores under the bark making zigzag galleries

pearce·ite \'pir,sīt\ *n* -S [Richard *Pearce* †1927 Eng. metallurgist + E *-ite*] **:** a mineral $Ag_{16}As_2S_{11}$ consisting of a monoclinic silver and arsenic sulfide

pear drop *n* **:** a drop (as a jewel or a candy) that is shaped like a pear

pear-drop \'⸗,⸗\ *adj* [*pear drop*] **:** having the shape of a pear — used of handles on furniture and also of supports for small arches employed in place of pillars in the 18th century

pear fruit chafer *n* **:** BUMBLE FLOWER BEETLE

pear haw *or* **pear hawthorn** *n* **:** any of several American hawthorns (as *Crataegus tomentosa*) with somewhat pyriform fruit

pea rifle *n, chiefly dial* **:** a muzzle-loading rifle having a thick barrel and firing a ball about the size of a pea

¹pearl \'pərl, *esp before pause or consonant* 'pər·əl; 'pəl, 'pəil\ *n* -S [ME *perle*, fr. MF, fr. (assumed) VL *pernula*, dim. of L *perna* haunch, ham, sea mussel attached to the ocean floor by a peduncle shaped like a ham; akin to OE *fyrsn, fiersn* heel, OS *fersna*, OHG *fersana*, Goth *fairzna* heel, Gk *pternē* heel, hip, Skt *pārṣṇi* heel] **1 a** (1) **:** a dense concretion that is formed in various mollusks by deposition of thin concentric layers of nacre about a foreign particle within or beneath the mantle and is free from or attached to the shell, that occurs in various forms but is typically more or less round, that exhibits various colors but is usu. white or light-colored, and that has various degrees of luster — see CULTURED PEARL (2) **:** SIMULATED PEARL **b pearls** *pl* **:** a necklace of pearls **2 :** MOTHER-OF-PEARL **3 :** one that is very choice or precious **:** the finest or noblest of its kind **:** a supreme rarity ⟨enunciated this ~ of wisdom —J.C.Snaith⟩ ⟨learned from him one tale which is a ~ of price —H.J.Laski⟩ **4 :** something resembling a pearl intrinsically or physically: as **a** *dial Eng* **:** a whitish film on the eye **:** CATARACT **b :** a small round globule (as a teardrop or dewdrop) ⟨~*s* of dew glistened on the grass⟩ **c :** one of the tubercles forming the burr on an antler — usu. used in pl. **d :** white shining teeth ⟨a red lip, with two rows of ~ beneath —Lord Byron⟩ **e :** one of several small white or silver balls on a coronet **f :** a small piece, fragment, or size esp. of coal or of molten metal cooled by being dropped in water **g :** a small white circle on a colored ground (as on a postage stamp) **h :** ¹PERLE **i :** one of a succession of beads or small bosses used ornamentally (as on the edge of a piece of furniture) **5 :** an old size of type (approximately 5 point) between diamond and agate **6 a :** SHELL TINT **b** *or* **pearl blue** *or* **pearl white :** a nearly neutral slightly bluish medium gray that is lighter than battleship gray — called also *granite blue, moonbeam* **7 :** TALL OAT GRASS **8** *dial Eng* **:** TERN **9 :** one of the rounded concentric masses of squamous epithelial cells characteristic of certain tumors

²pearl \"\ *vb* -ED/-ING/-S [ME *perlen*, fr. *perle*, n.] *vt* **1 :** to set or adorn with pearls or with mother-of-pearl **2 :** to sprinkle or bead with pearly drops ⟨sweat ~*ed* his forehead —William DuBois⟩ ⟨morning dew ~*ed* the garden⟩ **3 :** to form esp. by machine into small round grains ⟨~ barley⟩ **4 :** to give a pearly color, luster, or radiance to ⟨his mind was still ~*ed* with . . . roseate ideals —Francis Hackett⟩ ~ *vi* **1 :** to form drops or beads like pearls ⟨rain ~*ed* down the window⟩ **2 :** to fish or search for pearls ⟨tried gold mining, ~*ing*, and fur trapping —*Current Biog.*⟩ **3** *of hot syrup* **:** to form small or large bubbles in boiling usu. at 220° F or a long thread without breaking when dropped from a spoon

³pearl \"\ *adj* [¹*pearl*] **1 :** of, relating to, or resembling pearl **:** made of or adorned with pearls or mother-of-pearl **:** having the color or luster of pearl **:** PEARLY **2 :** having grains or particles of medium size — compare PEARL BARLEY, PEARL HOMINY, PEARL TAPIOCA

⁴pearl \"\ *n* -S [alter. of *purl*] **1** *Brit* **:** one of a series of tiny loops forming a decorative edging usu. on ribbon or lace **:** PICOT **2 :** ¹PURL 5

⁵pearl \"\ *vt* -ED/-ING/-S *Brit* **:** to finish (an edge) with picot

pearl ash *n* **:** POTASSIUM CARBONATE a; *esp* **:** an impure product obtained by partial purification of potash from wood ashes

pearl barley *n* **:** barley ground into small round pellets

pearl blush *n* **:** a brownish pink to light grayish brown — called also *rosetan*

pearlbush \'⸗,⸗\ *n* **:** a Chinese ornamental shrub (*Exochorda racemosa*) with lanceolate leaves and racemes of white flowers

pearl-coated \'⸗'⸗⸗\ *adj* **:** coated to resemble a pearl usu. in whiteness or smoothness — used esp. of pills

pearl cotton *n* **:** a mercerized cotton yarn for needlework (as embroidery)

pearl crescent *n* **:** a nymphalid butterfly (*Phyciodes tharos*) common in eastern No. America

pearl danio *n* **:** a small lustrous cyprinid fish (*Brachydanio albolineatus*) that is often kept in the tropical aquarium

pearl disease *n* **:** tuberculosis of serous membranes (as the pleura or peritoneum) with lesions in small rounded grayish elevations and appearing chiefly in cattle — called also *pearly disease*

pear leaf blister mite *n* **:** an eriophyid mite (*Eriophyes pyri*) that attacks the young leaves of pear trees — called also *pear blister mite*

pearled \-ld\ *adj* [ME *perled*, fr. past part. of *perlen* to pearl — more at PEARL] **1 :** set or adorned with pearls or mother-of-pearl ⟨the fancy vest, the ~ revolver —A.B.Guthrie⟩ **2 :** formed into, covered, or filled with drops ⟨the gossamer . . . ~ with the morning cew —Sir Walter Scott⟩ ⟨a ~ sea-mist —William Sansom⟩ ⟨~ with women's tears —J.G.Neihardt⟩ **3 :** formed into grains like pearls **4 :** resembling a pearl in color or luster **:** PEARLY ⟨the ~ splendor of the moonlit scene⟩

pearl edge *n* [⁴*pearl*] **:** a very narrow edging or ribbon with tiny loops on one or both sides

pearl·er \-lə(r)\ *n* -S **1 a :** a person that dives for pearls **b :** one that employs pearl divers **c :** a boat used in pearl fishing **2 :** BARLEY PEARLER **3 :** a worker that uses a special tool on a vertical lathe to decorate watch pillar plates with an interlocking ring design

pearl·es·cent \,pər'les°nt\ *adj* [¹*pearl* + *-escent*] **:** having the appearance of mother-of-pearl ⟨our swanlike necks should be swathed in ~ beads and other glitter —Lois Long⟩

pearl essence *n* **1 :** a translucent substance containing guanine and constituting the silvery coloring matter of the scales of various fish (as the bleak or herring) that is used in making artificial pearls and also lacquers and plastics — compare ESSENCE D'ORIENT **2 :** a synthetic translucent substance (as crystallized mercuric chloride)

pearl·et \,pər'let, 'pərlət\ *n* -S [¹*pearl* + *-let*] **:** a small pearl

pearl eye *n* **1 :** PEARLY EYE **2 :** a bird's eye (as of a pigeon) suggestive of a pearl — **pearl-eyed** *adj*

pearlfish \'⸗,⸗\ *n* **1** [so called fr. its inhabiting the mantle cavity of the pearl oyster] **:** a fish of the family Carapidae and esp. of the genus *Carapus* **2 :** PEARLSIDES **3 :** any of various cyprinoid and clupeoid fishes having scales which yield pearl essence

pearl glue *n* **:** glue in the form of beads or pellets

pearl grain *n* **:** CARAT GRAIN

pearl gray *n* **1 :** a yellowish gray to light gray **2 :** a variable color averaging a pale blue that is redder and paler than Sistine or average powder blue and redder and lighter than baby blue (sense 2)

¹pearl harbor \,⸗'⸗⸗\ *n, usu cap P&H* [fr. *Pearl Harbor*, Oahu, Hawaii, Am. naval station attacked without warning by the Japanese on Dec. 7, 1941] **:** a sneak attack usu. with devastating effect ⟨remove the possibility of atomic *Pearl Harbors* —Bertrand Russell⟩

²pearl harbor \"\ *vt, usu cap P&H* [¹*Pearl Harbor*] **:** to attack suddenly without warning and usu. with devastating effect ⟨got to thinking of the danger of being *Pearl Harbored* —*Time*⟩

pearl hominy *n* **:** hominy milled to pellets of medium size

pearlies *pl of* PEARLY

pearl·i·ness \'pərlēnəs, 'pəl-,'pəil-, -lin-\ *n* -ES **:** the quality or state of being pearly ⟨that faint blue haze . . . that almost imagined ~ against the distant hills —S.E.White⟩

pearl·ing *or* **pearl·in** \'pərlən, -liŋ\ *n* -S [⁴*pearl* + *-ing* or *-in* (alter. of *-ing*)] **1** *chiefly Scot* **:** a lace of silk or thread **2 pearlings** *pl, chiefly Scot* **a :** trimmings made of pearling **b :** clothes trimmed with pearling **c :** PEARLS 1b

pearl·ite \'pər,līt\ *n* -S [F *perlite*, fr. *perle* pearl + *-ite* — more at PEARL] **1 :** the lamellar mixture of ferrite and cementite in the microstructure of slowly cooled iron-carbon-base alloys occurring normally as a principal constituent of both steel and cast iron **2 :** PERLITE — **pearl·it·ic** \,⸗'lid·ik\ *adj*

pearl·ized \'pər,līzd\ *adj* **:** having the appearance of mother-of-pearl ⟨a tiara of ~ orange blossoms —*Springfield (Mass.) Daily News*⟩ ⟨hats . . . of white ~ straw with straight brims —*New Yorker*⟩

pearl kite *n* **:** WHITE-TAILED KITE

pearl lamp *n* **:** an electric lamp having the inside of the glass frosted

pearl millet *n* **1 :** a tall cereal grass (*Pennisetum glaucum*) that is prob. of East Indian origin, is grown in Africa and Asia for its seeds and in the U.S. chiefly for forage, and has long broad leaves and dense round spikes like those of the cattail — called also *bulrush millet, cattail millet* **2 :** COMMON SORGHUM

pearl moss *n* **:** CARRAGEEN

pearl mussel *n* **:** a freshwater mussel producing pearls or mother-of-pearl

pearl onion *n* **:** a very small onion resembling a pearl in size and used pickled in appetizers and as a garnish

pearl opal *n* **:** CACHOLONG

pear louse *n* **:** PEAR PSYLLA

pearl oyster *n* **:** any of several large marine bivalve mollusks of the genera *Avicula* and *Pinctada* (esp. *P. margaritifera*) that often produce pearls, differ from the ordinary oyster in having a byssus, and are found chiefly in the East Indies (as at Ceylon), in the Persian gulf, on the northern coasts of Australia, and on the Pacific coast of America

pearl perch *n* **:** EPAULET FISH

pearl pink *n* **:** a variable color averaging a pale yellowish pink

pearl plant *n* **1 :** GROMWELL **2 :** CORN GROMWELL

pearls *pl of* PEARL, *pres 3d sing of* PEARL

pearl shell *n* **:** a nacreous or pearl-bearing shell **:** PEARL OYSTER

pearl shell·er \'⸗,shelə(r)\ *n* **:** a fisher for pearl shells

pearlsides \'⸗,⸗\ *n, pl* **pearlsides :** a small silvery isospondylous fish (*Maurolicus pennanti*) with several rows of luminous organs like pearls on the head and body that is widely distributed in the North Atlantic

pearl sinter *n* **:** geyserite of pearly luster

pearlspar *n* **:** a dolomite with a pearly luster

pearlstone \'⸗,⸗\ *n* **:** PERLITE

pearl tapioca *n* **:** tapioca formed during processing into pellets that retain their shape in cooking but swell

pearl-twist \'⸗,⸗\ *n* **:** an orchid of the genus *Spiranthes* — usu. used in pl.

pearl ware *n* **:** an improved white variant of queensware introduced by Josiah Wedgwood in 1779

pearl white *n* **1 :** any of several white or pearly white substances: as **a :** bismuth subnitrate esp. when used in cosmetics or ceramics **b :** bismuth oxychloride esp. when used as a pigment or in cosmetics **c :** a nacreous preparation (as of mother-of-pearl or pearl essence) used in imitating pearls **2 :** PEARL 6b

pearlwort *also* **pearlweed** \'⸗,⸗\ *n* **:** a plant of the genus *Sagina* resembling chickweed

¹pearly \'pərlē, 'pəl-,'pəil-, -li\ *adj* -ER/-EST [ME *peerly*, fr. *perle* pearl + *-y* — more at PEARL] **1 :** having the appearance of a pearl or of mother-of-pearl (as in luster, shape, texture) ⟨a ~ complexion that was the envy of her companions⟩ **2 :** containing a pearl or mother-of-pearl ⟨~ oyster⟩ **3 :** adorned or set with pearls or mother-of-pearl ⟨loved her ~ Juliet cap⟩ **4 :** highly precious **:** rare and beautiful ⟨in the delicate etching with which he makes the daughter shine with a kind of ~ virginity —Marjory S. Douglas⟩ **5 :** having the color of pearl ⟨his teeth of a ~ whiteness —Mary W. Shelley⟩ **6 :** having a pear-shaped tone ⟨crooning ~ high notes —*Time*⟩

²pearly \"\ *adv* **:** in a way suggesting a pearl (as in luster, color, texture) ⟨~ white satin⟩

³pearly \"\ *n* -ES *Brit* **1 :** clothing heavily ornamented or sometimes nearly covered with pearl buttons and worn by costermongers on special occasions **2 :** COSTERMONGER

pearly disease *n* **:** PEARL DISEASE

pearly everlasting *n* **:** an American everlasting (*Anaphalis margaritacea*) having floccose-woolly herbage and small corymbose heads with pearly white scarious involucres

pearly eye *n* **1 :** any of several satyrid butterflies of the genus *Lethe* (esp. *L. portlandia*) **2 :** ocular lymphocytomatosis of poultry — called also *pearl eye*

pearly gate *n* **:** one of the 12 gates of heaven — usu. used in pl. and in allusion to Rev 21:21

pearly nautilus *n* **:** NAUTILUS 1a

pearly tumor *n* **:** CHOLESTEATOMA

pear midge *n* **:** a minute gall midge (*Contarinia pyrivora*) which lays its eggs in the flower buds of the pear and whose larvae destroy the developing fruits

pear molding *n* **:** KEEL MOLDING

pearmonger *n, obs* **:** a pear seller ⟨you are as pert as a ~ this morning —Jonathan Swift⟩

pear oil *n* **:** either of two esters: **a :** ISOAMYL ACETATE **b :** AMYL ACETATE a

pear psylla *also* **pear tree psylla** *n* **:** a yellowish or greenish jumping plant louse (*Psylla pyricola*) that is often destructive to the pear — called also *pear louse*

pears *pl of* PEAR, *pres 3d sing of* PEAR

pear sawfly *n* **:** PEAR SLUG

pear scab *n* **:** a disease of the pear caused by a fungus (*Venturia pyrina*) that is similar to apple scab but produces lesions more frequently on the twigs

pear scale *n* **:** any of several scales which infest pear trees

pear-shaped \'⸗,⸗\ *adj* **1 :** having an oval shape markedly tapering at one end **2** *of a vocal tone* **:** free from harshness, thinness, or nasality **:** FULL, MELLOW, ROUNDED

pear shell *n* **:** FIGSHELL 1

pear slug *n* **:** a sluglike caterpillar that is the larva of a sawfly (*Caliroa cerasi*), that feeds on the foliage of the pear and cherry trees, and that has a wide distribution in both New and Old Worlds

pearsonian coefficient of correlation \(')pir'sōnēən-\ *usu cap P* [*pearsonian* fr. Karl *Pearson* †1936 Eng. scientist + E *-an*] **:** CORRELATION COEFFICIENT

peart \'pi(ə)r|t, -ə|, *usu* |d.+V\ *adj, sometimes* -ER/-EST [alter. of *pert*] *chiefly South and Midland* : LIVELY, CHIPPER ⟨sleep well and wake up ~ —Ellen Glasgow⟩ — **peart·ly** *adv*

peart·en \|tᵊn\ *vb* -ED/-ING/-S *vt, chiefly dial* : to make peart or cheerful — usu. used with *up* ~ *vi, chiefly dial* : to become peart or cheerful — usu. used with *up* ⟨when he ~*ed* up, we all took fresh heart —H.E.Giles⟩

pear thrips *n* : a destructive thrips (*Taeniothrips inconsequens*) native to Europe that attacks the buds and young fruits of prune, cherry, pear, and almond trees

pear tomato *n* : a tomato with pear-shaped fruit that is usu. considered to constitute a distinct variety (*Lycopersicon esculentum pyriforme*)

pearwood \'ˌ=,=\ *n* : the wood of any pear; *esp* : the wood of a white pear (*Pterocelastrus rostratus*)

peas *pl of* PEA

¹peas·ant \'pezᵊnt\ *n* -S [ME *paissaunt*, fr. MF *paisant*, fr. OF *paisant*, fr. *païs* country — more at PAYSAGE] **1** : one of a chiefly European class that tills the soil as small free landowners or hired laborers ⟨burgesses, ~*s* . . . have borne arms indistinguishable from those of the nobility —D.L.Galbreath⟩ **2** *obs* : a rascally person : SCAMP ⟨thou shalt know I will predominate over the ~ —Shak.⟩ **3** : a rather uneducated uncouth person in the low income group ⟨nobody gave a thought to the rest of us ~*s* —Bernard Taper⟩ ⟨she was a complete ~ when she came here —Margery Allingham⟩

²peasant \"\ *adj* **1 a** : of or relating to peasants : having the status of a peasant ⟨the conservative ~ ideas of . . . immigrants —Oscar Handlin⟩ ⟨most . . . were ~ stock whose descendants today hold important positions —*Amer. Guide Series: Minn.*⟩ **b** : based upon and characterized by a simple agricultural economy ⟨Asian ~ societies⟩ **2** : of or resembling the designs in the clothing of peasants ⟨a very pretty girl in a ~ blouse —Calvin Tompkins⟩ **3** : relating to native culture or art : produced by native craftsmen ⟨lacking . . . any marked tradition of decorative ~ art —Charles Marriott⟩ ⟨~ wares were often so cheap —W.E.Cox⟩

peasant blue *n* : a grayish blue that is redder and darker than electric, greener and deeper than copenhagen or old china, and redder and deeper than Gobelin

peas·ant·ize \-ᵊnt,īz\ *vt* -ED/-ING/-S : to make peasants of : cause to resemble peasants ⟨you cannot ~ a common people who have been educated in their vocations —*Rev. of Reviews*⟩

peasantlike \'==,=\ *adj* : of, relating to, or characteristic of a peasant

peasantly *adj, obs* : of, relating to, or characteristic of a peasant ⟨their ~ throats —Sir Walter Scott⟩

peasant proprietor *n* : a peasant who owns the soil he cultivates

peas·ant·ry \'pezᵊntrē, -ri\ *n* -ES **1** : PEASANTS : a body of peasants ⟨the ~ of this unhappy country have never been much more than slaves —Darrell Berrigan⟩ ⟨the rich ~ of that region rose —F.M.Stenton⟩ **2** : the state, position, or rank of a peasant : the quality or behavior of a peasant ⟨as a gentleman, you could have never descended to such ~ of language —Samuel Butler †1680⟩

peas·anty \-ᵊntē, -ti\ *adj* : having or suggesting a peasant manner or style ⟨the ~ English countryside of the Georgian short story —Naomi Lewis⟩ ⟨a small crowd . . . garishly dressed in ~ clothes —Ann Bridge⟩

¹pease \'pēz\ *n, pl* **peases** [ME *pese* — more at PEA] *chiefly Brit* : PEA — archaic except in attrib. use

²pease \"\ *pl of* PEA

peasecod *or* **peascod** \'=,=\ *n* [ME *pesecod*, fr. *pese* pea + *cod* — more at PEA, COD (husk)] **1** : a pea pod **2** : the stuffed or quilted front of a 16th century doublet extending to a point below the waistline

pease crow *n, dial Eng* : TERN

peas·en *also* **peas·on** \'pēzᵊn\ *dial chiefly Brit pl of* PEASE

pease porridge *n* [¹*pease*] : PEA SOUP

pease pudding *n* [¹*pease*] : a pudding made of cooked and strained split peas and eggs boiled in a cloth or mold

peaseweep *or* **peasweep** *var of* PEESWEEP

pea·sey hut \'pēzē-\ *n* [*peasey* alter. of *pisé*] : a construction of rammed earth

pea–shoot \'=,=\ *vb* [back-formation fr. *peashooter*] *vt* : to shoot peas at ⟨*pea-shooting* pigeons from an attic window⟩ ~ *vi* : to shoot with a peashooter

peashooter \'=|==\ *n* [¹*pea* + *shooter*] **1** : a toy blowgun for shooting peas **2** *slang* : a small caliber pistol ⟨a burglar carrying a little ~ like that —William Norsworthy⟩

pea shrub *n* : PEA TREE

pea soup *n* **1** : a thick soup made of dried green or yellow peas usu. pureed **2** *or* **pea–souper** : a heavy dull yellow fog ⟨a wall of the thickest *pea soup* I had ever seen —H.A.Chippendale⟩

pea–soupy \'=|==\ *adj* [*pea soup* + *-y*] : resembling pea soup ⟨the *pea-soupy* January evening —Robert Benton⟩

peas porridge *n* [alter. of *pease porridge*] : PEA SOUP

peas pudding *n* [by alter.] : PEASE PUDDING

pea–stick \'=,=\ *n* : a long stake or branch upon which garden peas are trained ⟨cutting down the green young branches for *pea-sticks* —Georgianna Bruce⟩

peastone \'=,=\ *n* : PISOLITE

¹peat \'pēt, *usu* -ēd.+V\ *n* -S *often attrib* [ME *pete*, fr. ML *peta*, perh. of Celt origin; akin to W *peth* thing — more at PIECE] **1** : a piece of turf cut for use as fuel ⟨in a moment he had the ~*s* in the grate blazing —Elizabeth Goudge⟩ **2** : a mass of partially carbonized vegetable tissue formed by partial decomposition in water of various plants and esp. of mosses of the genus *Sphagnum*, widely found in many parts of the world, varying in consistency from a turf to a slime, and used as a fertilizer, as stable litter, as a fuel, and for making charcoal

²peat \"\ *n* -S [origin unknown] : a bold gay woman ⟨a pretty ~ —Shak.⟩ ⟨you were always a proud, undaunted ~ of a lass —Henrietta Keddie⟩

peat bank *n* : a place from which peat is cut

peat bog *or* **peat moor** *n* : a bog containing peat : an accumulation of peat

peat coal *n* **1** : a natural product intermediate between peat and lignite **2** : an artificial fuel made by carbonizing peat

peat·ery \'pēd·ərē\ *n* -ES **1** : PEAT BANK **2** : PEAT BOG

peat fiber *n* : finely chopped roots and rootstocks of various wild ferns used for potting orchids

peat gas *n* : gas made by carbonizing peat

peat hag *n* : ground from which peat has been cut

peat machine *n* : a machine for grinding and briquetting peat

peat·man \'pētmən\ *n, pl* **peatmen** : a digger or seller of peat

peat moss *n* **1** : any moss from which peat has formed or may form; *specif* : SPHAGNUM **2** *chiefly Brit* : PEAT BOG

pea tree *n* : any of several plants of the family Leguminosae; *esp* : an Asiatic tree of the genus *Caragana* (as Chinese pea tree)

peat–reek \'=,=\ *n* **1** : the smoke of burning peat ⟨when I get a sniff of wood smoke it makes me sick with longing for *peat-reek* —John Buchan⟩ **2 a** : the peculiar flavor of whiskey distilled over peat as fuel **b** : whiskey made in this manner

peat scours *n pl* : acute copper-deficiency disease of New Zealand sheep and cattle marked by severe persistent diarrhea and occurring esp. in animals pastured on peaty land

peat soil *n* : a soil consisting largely of peat and consequently rich in humus and of acid reaction

peat spade *n* : a spade with an L-shaped blade for cutting out peat in blocks

peatwood *or* **peatweed** \'=,=\ *n* : SWAMP LOOSESTRIFE

peaty \'pēd·ē\ *adj* -ER/-EST : of, resembling, or containing peat

peau d'ange \(')pō¦dänzh\ *n* [F, lit., angel skin] **1** : a dull waxy smooth finish usu. used for crepes, satins, and lace **2** : a fabric with a finish of peau d'ange

peau de soie \ˌpōdə¦swä\ *n* [F, lit., skin of silk] : a silk or rayon dress fabric with a smooth satiny texture and a fine ribbed or grained surface

pea·vey *or* **pea·vy** *or* **pee·vy** *or* **pe·vy** \'pēvē\ *n, pl* **peaveys** *or* **peavies** *or* **peevies** *or* **pevies** [prob. fr. the name *Peavey*] : a stout lever used in lumbering that is like a cant hook but has the end armed with a strong sharp spike

peavey

peavine \'=,=\ *n* : any of various usu. twining American herbaceous leguminous plants: as **a** : the vine of the common edible pea or of the cowpea esp. when stripped of pods and used for hay **b** : AMERICAN VETCH **c** : a locoweed (*Astragalus emoryanus*) of the Big Bend area of Texas

peavine clover *n* : ZIGZAG CLOVER

pea weevil *n* **1** : a small weevil (*Bruchus pisorum*) that destroys peas by eating out the interior **2** : a European weevil (*Sitona lineatus*) that feeds on the leaves of peas

peba \'pebə\ *n* -S [Pg, fr. Tupi *tatupeba*, fr. *tatu* armadillo + *peba* flat] : a small armadillo (*Dasypus novemcinctus*) having nine movable bands of scutes and ranging from Texas to Paraguay

¹peb·ble \'pebəl\ *n* -S [ME *pibbil, puble, pobble*, fr. OE *papolstān*, fr. *papol-* (prob. of imit. origin) + *stān* stone] **1 a** : a small usu. round stone esp. when worn and rounded by the action of water **b** : one of the pieces in a mass of material obtained in a form resembling pebbles ⟨lime ~*s*⟩ **2 a** : transparent and colorless quartz : ROCK CRYSTAL ⟨Brazilian ~⟩ **b** : a rough gem sometimes found in a stream ⟨delighted to find a small ~ of agate⟩ **3** : PEBBLEWARE **4 a** *also* **pebble leather** (1) : leather that has been pebbled (2) : the surface on the leather produced by pebbling **b** : an irregular, crinkled, or grainy surface on a fabric produced by fancy weaves or finishing processes **c** : a formation of tiny protuberances produced on the surface of a curling rink by sprinkling water on the ice **5** : FLAX 3

²pebble \"\ *vt* **pebbled; pebbled; pebbling** \-b(ə)liŋ\ **pebbles 1** : to pelt with or as if with pebbles ⟨teased the dog by *pebbling* it with acorns⟩ **2** : to pave or cover with pebbles or something resembling pebbles ⟨cookies . . . fat ones with white sugar *pebbling* the surface —Warren Eyster⟩ **3** : to grain (as leather or paper) so as to produce a rough and irregularly indented surface **4** : to produce pebble on (a curling rink)

pebble cast *n* : a cast or casting of pebbles esp. from the sea

peb·bled \-bəld\ *adj* [¹*pebble* + *-ed*] : containing, covered, or strewn with pebbles or something resembling pebbles ⟨areas of sandstone . . . as well as ~ plains —W.G.East⟩

pebble dash *n* : ROCK DASH

pebble gravel *n* : gravel with pebbles between 4 and 64 millimeters in diameter

pebble mill *n* : a rotating cylinder in which usu. hard rounded stones or flint pebbles grind ceramic materials to extreme fineness

pebble powder *n* : gunpowder or black powder pressed and cut into large cubical grains so as to make it slow-burning

peb·bler \-b(ə)lə(r)\ *n* -S **1** : one who pebbles leather by hand or by machine **2** : one who pebbles a curling rink

pebblestone \'==,=\ *n* [ME *pibbil ston, publestone*, fr. OE *papolstān* — more at PEBBLE] : PEBBLE 1

pebbleware \'==,=\ *n* : a variety of Wedgwood ware having a mottled surface produced by mingling colored pastes in the body of the pottery

peb·bly \-b(ə)lē, -li\ *adj, sometimes* -ER/-EST : containing or resembling pebbles ⟨chuckled over its ~ bed or plunged down in little waterfalls —Margaret Deland⟩ ⟨done in ~ navy wool —Lois Long⟩

pé·brine \(')pā¦brēn\ *n* -S [F, fr. Prov *pebrino*, fr. *pebre* pepper, fr. L *piper* — more at PEPPER] : a contagious disease of the silkworm and other caterpillars produced by a microsporidian protozoan (*Nosema bombycis*) — **peb·ri·nous** \'pebrənəs\ *adj*

PEC *abbr, often not cap* photoelectric cell

pe·can \pə'kän, -'kan,-'kaa(ə)n,-'kän, (')pē¦k-; *sometimes* 'pēkən\ *n* -S [fr. earlier *paccan*, of Algonquian origin; akin to Ojibwa *pagân* any hard-shelled nut, Abnaki *pagann*, Cree *pakan*] **1** : a hickory (*Carya illinoensis*) of the south central U.S. having roughish bark and hard but brittle wood, sometimes attaining great size, and producing an edible nut **2** : the wood of the pecan tree **3** : the smooth oblong thin-shell nut of the pecan tree

pecan brown *n* : GOLDEN CHESTNUT

pecan carpenter worm *n* : a worm that is the larva of a cossid moth (*Cossula magnifica*) and that bores in the twigs, branches, and trunk of pecan, oak, and hickory

pecan nut casebearer *n* : a grub that is the larva of a moth (*Acrobasis caryae*) and that feeds on various hickories and walnuts

pecan scab *n* : a disease of the pecan caused by a fungus (*Cladosporium effusum*) and characterized by the smoky superficial growth of the fungus on leaves, twigs, and nuts

pecan weevil *n* : a weevil (*Curculio caryae*) that attacks hickory and pecan nuts esp. in the southern U.S.

pec·a·ri \'pekərē\ [NL, fr. F *pécari* peccary, of Cariban origin like E *peccary* — more at PECCARY] *syn of* TAYASSU

pec·ca·bil·i·ty \ˌpekə'biləd·ē, -lətē, -i\ *n* : the quality or state of being peccable : capability of sinning ⟨the common ~ of mankind —Henry More⟩

pec·ca·ble \'pekəbəl\ *adj* [MF, fr. L *peccare* to sin + MF *-able* — more at PECCANT] : liable or prone to sin : susceptible to temptation ⟨a frail and ~ mortal —Sir Walter Scott⟩

pec·ca·dil·lo \ˌpekə'di(ˌ)lō\ *n, pl* **peccadilloes** *or* **peccadillos** [Sp *pecadillo*, dim. of *pecado* sin, fr. L *peccatum*, fr. neut. of *peccatus*, past part. of *peccare* to sin] : a slight offense : a petty fault ⟨lapses and ~*es* —Herbert Askwith⟩ ⟨the sexual ~*es* of a popular hero —Edmund Fuller⟩

peccan *or* **peccane** *archaic var of* PECAN

pec·can·cy \'pekənsē, -nsi\ *n* -ES [LL *peccantia*, fr. L *peccant-*, *peccans* (pres. part. of *peccare*) + *-ia* -y] **1** : the quality or state of being peccant ⟨horrible exultation at the universal ~ of husbands —George Meredith⟩ **2** : OFFENSE, FAULT ⟨his trivial *peccancies* —Carl Van Vechten⟩

pec·cant \'pekənt\ *adj* [L *peccant-*, *peccans*, pres. part. of *peccare* to stumble, commit a fault, sin, prob. fr. (assumed) L *peccus* having an injured foot, stumbling, fr. L *ped-*, *pes* foot — more at FOOT] **1** : guilty of a moral offense : SINNING, CORRUPT ⟨~ humanity —*Saturday Rev.*⟩ ⟨imposing severe . . . discipline in public on ~ parishioners —*Times Lit. Supp.*⟩ ⟨~ corporations —*Times Lit. Supp.*⟩ **2** : violating a principle or rule (as of taste or propriety) : FAULTY ⟨intervene to save the ~ poet —George Saintsbury⟩ **3** : DISEASED, UNWHOLESOME ⟨by the lopping of a ~ member the body is saved from decay —John Austin⟩ ⟨capable of sloughing off its ~ parts —K.L. Bates⟩

pec·ca·ry *also* **pec·a·ri** *or* **pec·a·ry** \'pekərē\ *n, pl* **peccaries** *also* **pecaris** *or* **pecaries** [of Cariban origin; akin to Chayma *paquera* peccary, Apalai *pakĭrā*] : either of two more or less nocturnal gregarious wild swine (genus *Tayassu*) ranging from Texas to Paraguay and resembling small pigs — see COLLARED PECCARY, WHITE-LIPPED PECCARY **2** *or* **peccary leather** : leather tanned from skins of wild peccary boars of So. and Central America and used chiefly for gloves

peccary

pec·ca·vi \pe'kä(ˌ)vē *sometimes* -kā,vī\ *n* -S [L, I have sinned] : a humble acknowledgment of sin or error : CONFESSION ⟨chanting their ~*s* —*Saturday Rev.*⟩

pech *var of* PEGH

pech·an \'pekən\ *n* -S [origin unknown] *dial Scot* : STOMACH, GULLET

pechay *n* -S [Sp, fr. Tag *petsay*, fr. Chin *peʼtsʼai⁴*] : CHINESE CABBAGE

pêche mel·ba \'pēch'melbə, 'pesh-,'pāsh-\ *n, pl* **pêches melba** \ˌpēchəz'm-, 'pesh'm-, 'pāsh'm-\ *usu cap M* [F, lit., Melba peach] : half a peach filled with cream set on a bed of vanilla ice cream and covered with raspberry sauce

pecheneg *usu cap, var of* PETCHENEG

¹peck \'pek\ *n* -S [ME *pek*, fr. OF] **1 a** : either of two units of dry capacity equal to ¼ bushel: (1) : a U.S. unit equivalent to 537.605 cubic inches (2) : a British unit equivalent to 554.84 cubic inches — see MEASURE table **b** : the quantity measured by a peck **c** : a container used as a peck measure **2** : a large quantity or number ⟨a ~ of trouble⟩ ⟨a ~ of dirt⟩ ⟨a ~ of uncertainties and doubts —John Milton⟩

²peck \"\ *vb* -ED/-ING/-S [ME *pecken*, alter. of *piken* to pierce — more at PICK] *vt* **1 a** : to strike, pierce, or make holes in (as wood) with or as if with quick movements of the beak ⟨~*ed* the tree all morning⟩ **b** : to kiss in a quick perfunctory fashion ⟨she ~*ed* his forehead —John Galsworthy⟩ **2** : to pick up (as food) with the beak ⟨give the hens a feed of whole grain . . . to ~ and pick over —Emily Holt⟩ — often used with *up* ⟨watching hens . . . ~ up the pulps from the sand —Lillian Smith⟩ **3 a** : to make or produce by repeated strokes of the beak or of a pointed tool ⟨the group of elk were ~*ed* out . . . on a rocky monolith —W.D.Hartley⟩ ⟨figures . . . ~*ed* into the rock —F.H.H.Roberts⟩ **b** : to shape (stone) by striking or abrading with a hammerstone ⟨stone was . . . ~*ed* and ground into cylindrical pestles —A.C.Spaulding⟩ ~ *vi* **1 a** : to strike, pierce, or pick up something with repeated small blows or movements with or as if with a beak — often used with *at* ⟨a hen that ~*s* all day⟩ ⟨~*ed* at the hard ground with a pickaxe⟩ **b** : to deliver a series of petty and repeated blows — usu. used with *at* ⟨left hand ~*ed* . . . at the old fighter's eyes —Donn Byrne⟩ ⟨there wasn't any use just ~*ing* at them —J.P.Marquand⟩ **c** : CARP, SCOLD, NAG — usu. used with *at* ⟨my wife keeps *peckin'* at me —H.L.Davis⟩ **d** : to strike the keys esp. of a typewriter or piano with quick downward thrusts of the fingers — usu. used with *at* ⟨started ~*ing* at the keys —Eleanor Bayer⟩ ⟨~*ing* away at the yellowed keys —Frank Brookhouser⟩ **2 a** : EAT ⟨wants to know if you'll ~ with us —Richard Dehan⟩ **b** : to bite daintily : NIBBLE — usu. used with *at* ⟨~*ed*, without enthusiasm, at a lamb chop —P.B.Kyne⟩

³peck \"\ *n* -S **1** : FOOD, GRUB 3 **2** : an impression or hole made by pecking **3 a** : an act of pecking : a quick sharp stroke (as with the beak of a bird or a pointed instrument) **b** : a kiss like a bird's peck ⟨leaned down to give her a brief ~ on the cheek —Louis Auchincloss⟩ **4** : PECKINESS

⁴peck \"\ *vb* -ED/-ING/-S [alter. of *pick* (to pitch)] *vt, chiefly dial* : PITCH, FLING, JERK ~ *vi, of a horse* : to stumble as a result of landing on the toe after taking a jump ⟨~*ed* badly, but recovered and won by a head —Adrian Bell⟩

⁵peck *dial var of* PICK

peck·ed \'pekəd, -kət\ *adj* [by alter.] *chiefly dial* : PEAKED

peck·er \'pekə(r)\ *n* -S [²*peck* + *-er*] **1** : one that pecks: as **a** : an instrument for pecking (as a pick) **b** : WOODPECKER **c** : a bird's bill **2 a** : NOSE **b** *chiefly Brit* : COURAGE, SPIRITS — used chiefly in the phrase *keep one's pecker up* ⟨one thing . . . helped to *keep the pecker up* during the journey —P.G. Wodehouse⟩ **3** : PENIS — often considered vulgar

peck·er·wood \'pekə(r),wu̇d\ *n* [inversion of *woodpecker*] **1** *South* : WOODPECKER **2** *South & Midland* : CRACKER 5a **3** : PECKERWOOD MILL

peckerwood mill *or* **peckerwood sawmill** *n, chiefly South* : a small usu. portable sawmill characterized by slipshod equipment and operation

peck horn *n* [prob. fr. the name *Peck*] : MELLOPHONE

peck·i·ness \'pekēnəs, -kin-\ *n* -ES [*pecky* + *-ness*] : any of several diseases of the heartwood of trees caused by polypores and related fungi and characterized by lens-shaped or finger-shaped pockets of decay running with the grain — called also *dry rot, pocket dry rot*; compare PIN ROT

peck·ish \-kish,-kēsh\ *adj* [²*peck* + *-ish*] **1** *chiefly dial* : ready to eat : having a keen appetite : HUNGRY ⟨pork pies and what all, case they come over a bit ~ —Richard Llewellyn⟩ ⟨their swim had made them ~ —*Harper's*⟩ **2** : inclined to peck : NAGGING, IRRITABLE ⟨the old woman, in constant pain, was spiteful and ~ —Jean Stafford⟩

¹peck·le \'pekəl\ *n* -S [alter. of *speckle*, n.] *dial Brit* : SPOT, SPECK

²peckle \"\ *vt* -ED/-ING/-S [by alter.] *dial Brit* : SPECKLE

peckled *adj* [by alter.] *chiefly dial* : SPECKLED

peck order *also* **pecking order** *n* [trans. of G *hackordnung*] **1** : the basic pattern of social organization within a flock of poultry in which each bird is permitted to peck another lower in the scale without fear of retaliation and is expected to submit to pecking by one of higher rank and in which separate peck orders usu. exist for each sex with all the males normally dominating all the females — compare HOOK ORDER **2** : a hierarchy of social dominance, prestige, or authority ⟨got to the top of the *pecking order* in their own town —Margaret Mead⟩ ⟨the *peck order* in women's clubs, faculty groups, families, or churches —W.C.Allee⟩

pecks *pl of* PECK, *pres 3d sing of* PECK

peck·sniff·ery \'pek,snifərē\ *or* **peck·sniff·ian·ism** \pek'snifēə,nizəm\ *n, pl* **pecksnifferies** *or* **pecksniffianisms** *often cap* [*pecksniffery* fr. Seth *Pecksniff*, character in *Martin Chuzzlewit* (1843–44) by Charles Dickens †1870 Eng. novelist + E *-ery*; *pecksniffianism* fr. *pecksniffian* + *-ism*] : the quality or state of being pecksniffian ⟨the national ~ —H.L.Mencken⟩

peck·sniff·ian \(')pek¦snifēən\ *adj, often cap* [Seth *Pecksniff* + E *-ian*] : marked by unctuous hypocrisy : selfish and corrupt behind a display of seeming benevolence : SANCTIMONIOUS, HOLIER-THAN-THOU ⟨~ cant⟩ ⟨legislation designed to correct injustice and to translate ~ phrases into living realities —*Nation*⟩ ⟨a censorship that is . . . ~ suppression —*Springfield (Mass.) Union*⟩

pecky \'pekē\ *also* **peaky** \'pēkē\ *adj* -ER/-EST [³*peck* + *-y*] **1** : marked by peckiness — used esp. of lumber; see PECKY CYPRESS **2** : containing discolored and shriveled grains ⟨~ rice⟩

pecky cypress *n* : cypress lumber affected by peckiness that is very durable in damp ground and is much used in greenhouse benches and in ornamental work (as paneling)

pecky dry rot *n* : PECKINESS

pe·cop·ter·is \pə'käptərəs\ *n, cap* [NL, fr. Gk *pekein* to comb + NL *-pteris* — more at FEE] : a genus of Carboniferous fossil ferns characterized by a regular arrangement of the leaflets resembling a comb

pe·cop·ter·oid \-,rȯid\ *adj* [NL *Pecopteris* + E *-oid*] : like or related to the genus *Pecopteris*

pec·o·ra \'pekərə\ *n pl, cap* [NL, fr. L, cattle, pl. of *pecor-*, *pecus* cattle, herd; akin to L *pecu* cattle, *pecud-*, *pecus* head of cattle, Gk *pekos* fleece — more at FEE] : a division of Artiodactyla equivalent to the suborder Ruminantia with the chevrotains and their extinct related forms excluded

pec·o·ri·no \ˌpekə'rē(ˌ)nō, *attrib* ¦==¦=(ˌ)= *or* **pecorino cheese** *n, pl* **pecorinos** *also* **pecori·ni** \ˌ==¦=(ˌ)nē\ *often cap P* [It, fr. *pecorino* of ewes, fr. *pecora* ewe, sheep (fr. L *pecora* cattle) + *-ino* -ine] : romano cheese made of ewe's milk

pe·cos \'pākəs\ *n, pl* **pecos** *usu cap* **1** : a Tanoan people formerly occupying a pueblo in New Mexico **2** : a member of the Pecos people

pec·tase \'pek,tās, -āz\ *n* -S [ISV *pect-* (fr. *pectin*) + *-ase*; prob. orig. formed in F] : PECTINESTERASE

pec·tate \-āt\ *n* -S [ISV *pect-* (fr. *pectic*) + *-ate*; prob. orig. formed in F] : a salt or ester of a pectic acid

pec·ten \'pektən\ *n* [NL *pectin-*, *pecten*, fr. L, comb, pubic hair, pubic bone, scallop — more at PECTINATE] **1** *pl* **pectens** \-tənz\ *also* **pecti·nes** \-tə,nēz\ : any of various animal body parts resembling a comb in structure: as **a** : a vascular pigmented membrane in the eyes of nearly all birds and many reptiles that has parallel plications suggesting the teeth of a comb and that projects into the vitreous humor of the eye from the point of entrance of the optic nerve **b** *archaic* : PUBIS **c** : one of a pair of appendages of a scorpion that are located on the underside of the body behind the legs and are thought to be sensory organs **d** : an arrangement of bristles on the respiratory tube of a mosquito larva resembling a comb **e** : a series of modified bristles forming a part of the stridulating organ of some spiders **2 a** *cap* : a genus (the type of the family Pectinidae) of marine bivalve mollusks including the common market scallops — see BAY SCALLOP, SEA SCALLOP **b** -S : any mollusk of this genus; *broadly* : a mollusk of the suborder Pectinacea

pec·tic \'pektik\ *adj* [F *pectique*, fr. Gk *pēktikos* coagulating, fr. *pēktos* coagulated (fr. *pēgnynai* to fix, coagulate) + *-ikos* -ic — more at PACT] : of, relating to, or derived from pectin

pectic acid *n* [F *acide pectique*] : any of the pectic substances composed mostly of colloidal polymeric galacturonic acids and essentially free from methyl ester groups

pectic substance *n* : any of a group of complex colloidal carbohydrate derivatives of plant origin containing a large proportion of units derived from galacturonic acid and subdivided into protopectins, pectins, pectinic acids, and pectic acids

pec·tin \ˈpektən\ *n* -s [F *pectine*, fr. *pect*ique pectic + *-ine* -in] **1 :** any of the group of colorless amorphous methylated pectic substances occurring in plant tissues or obtained by restricted treatment of protopectin (as with protopectinase or acids) that are found in or obtained esp. from fruits or succulent vegetables, that yield viscous solutions with water and when combined with acid and sugar in proper concentration yield a gel constituting the basis of fruit jellies, and that on hydrolysis yield pectic acids and methanol; *esp* **:** a pectinic acid containing at least 7 to 8 percent methyl ester groups expressed as methoxyl **2 :** a product containing mostly pectin obtained as a powder or syrup (as by extraction with acid of citrus peels, dried apple pomace, or dried sugar beet slices) and used chiefly in making jelly and other foods, in pharmaceutical products, and in cosmetics

pectin- *or* **pectini-** *comb form* [NL *pectin-, pecten* pecten] **:** comb **:** pecten ⟨*pectin*oid⟩ ⟨*pectini*form⟩ ⟨*Pectini*branchia⟩

pec·ti·na·cea \ˌpektəˈnāshēə\ *n pl, cap* [NL, fr. *Pectin-, Pecten*, type genus + *-acea*] **:** a suborder of Filibranchia comprising active bivalve mollusks that have a fan-shaped shell and no siphons including the typical pectens and related forms — **pec·ti·na·cean** \ˌpektəˈnāsh(ē)ən\ *n* -s

pec·ti·na·ceous \ˌpektəˈnāshəs\ *adj* **1** [*pectin* + *-aceous*] **:** of, relating to, or containing pectin **2** [NL *Pectinacea* + E *-ous*] **:** of or relating to the Pectinacea

pec·ti·nal \ˈpektənəl\ *adj* [LL *pectinalis*, fr. L *pectin-, pecten* comb, pubic bone + *-alis* -al — more at PECTINATE] **1 :** PECTINEAL **2** *obs* **:** of, relating to, or resembling a comb

pec·tin·ase \ˈpektəˌnās, -āz\ *n* -s [ISV *pectin* + *-ase*] **:** an enzyme or complex of enzymes that catalyzes the hydrolysis of pectic substances; *esp* **:** the polygalacturonase that is active toward pectic acid

¹pec·ti·nate \ˈpektəˌnāt\ *also* **pec·ti·nat·ed** \-ād·əd\ *adj* [L *pectinatus*, fr. *pectin-, pecten* comb + *-atus* -ate; akin to L *pectere* to comb, Gk *kten-, kteis* comb, Skt *pakṣman* eyelashes, OE *feax* head of hair — more at FEE] **:** shaped like a comb **:** having narrow parallel projections, teeth, or divisions suggestive of the teeth of a comb ⟨a ~ leaf⟩ ⟨a ~ antenna⟩ — see ANTENNA illustration — **pec·ti·nate·ly** *adv*

²pectinate \"\ *n* -s [*pectinic* acid + *-ate*] **:** a salt or ester of a pectinic acid

pectinate claw *n* **:** a claw found in some birds that has a serrate edge and is believed to be used in cleaning the feathers

pec·ti·na·tel·la \ˌpektəˌnāˈtelə, -nəˈt-\ *n, cap* [NL, fr. L *pectinatus* pectinate + *-ella*] **:** a common genus of freshwater colonial bryozoans forming large lobate gelatinous colonies with circular or subquadrangular statoblasts having a single row of marginal hooks

pec·ti·na·tion \ˌpektəˈnāshən\ *n* -s [*pectinate* + *-ion*] **1 :** the quality or state of being pectinate **2 :** a pectinate part or structure

pec·tin·e·al \(ˈ)pekˈtinēəl\ *adj* [NL *pectineus* + E *-al*] **:** of, relating to, or located near the pubic bone

pectineal line *n* **:** ILIOPECTINEAL LINE

pec·tin·esterase \ˈpektən+\ *n* [*pectin* + *esterase*] **:** an enzyme that catalyzes the hydrolysis of pectins into pectic acids and methanol and that occurs esp. in higher plants — called also *pectase*

pec·tin·e·us \pekˈtinēəs\ *n, pl* **pectin·ei** \-ēˌī, -ēˌē\ [NL, fr. *pectineus* of the pubic bone, fr. *pectin-, pecten* pecten + L *-eus* -eous] **:** a flat quadrangular muscle of the upper front and inner aspect of the thigh that arises mostly from the iliopectineal line of the pubis and is inserted between the lesser trochanter and a marked posterior ridge on the femur

pec·tini·bran·chia \ˌpektənəˈbraŋkēə, pekˌtin-\ *n pl, cap* [NL, fr. *pectin-* + *-branchia*] **:** a large order of Gastropoda (subclass Streptoneura) comprising univalve mollusks that have a single kidney, have typically a single ctenidium which resembles a comb and is usu. attached to the mantle throughout its length, and have a heart with only one auricle

pec·tini·bran·chi·a·ta \-ˌbraŋkēˈād·ə, -ˈäd·ə\ [NL, fr. *pectin-* + *branchia* + *-ata*] *syn of* PECTINIBRANCHIA

¹pec·tini·bran·chi·ate \ˌ⸗⸗⸗ˈbraŋkēət, ⸗ˌ⸗⸗-, -ēˌāt\ *also* **pec·tini·bran·chi·an** \-ēən\ *adj* [NL *Pectinibranchia* + E *-ate* or *-ian*] **:** of, relating to, or resembling the Pectinibranchia **:** having gills that resemble combs

²pectinibranchiate \"\ *also* **pectinibranchian** \"\ *n* -s **:** a mollusk of the order Pectinibranchia

pec·tin·ic acid \(ˈ)pekˈtinik-\ *n* [*pectin* + *-ic*] **:** any of the colloidal polysaccharides of acidic nature that are obtained by partial hydrolysis of protopectins and are intermediate in methyl ester content between pectic acids and the usual pectin

¹pec·ti·nid \ˈpektənəd\ *adj* [NL *Pectinidae*] **:** of or relating to the Pectinidae

²pectinid \"\ *n* -s **:** a mollusk of the family Pectinidae **:** SCALLOP

pec·tin·i·dae \pekˈtinəˌdē\ *n pl, cap* [NL, fr. *Pectin-, Pecten*, type genus + *-idae*] **:** a family of bivalve mollusks having a single adductor muscle, comprising the pectens, and belonging to and formerly being coextensive with the suborder Pectinacea

pec·tini·form \pekˈtinəˌfȯrm, ˈpektən-\ *adj* [L *pectin-, pecten* comb + E *-iform* — more at PECTINATE] **1 :** PECTINATE **2** [*pectin-* + *-form*] **:** resembling a scallop shell

pectiniform septum *n* **:** a fibrous septum between the corpora cavernosa

pec·ti·nite \ˈpektəˌnīt\ *n* -s [*pectin-* + *-ite*] **:** a fossil scallop shell

pec·tin·o·gen \pekˈtinəjən, -ˌjen\ *n* -s [*pectin* + *-o-* + *-gen*] **:** PROTOPECTIN

pec·ti·no·lyt·ic \ˌpektənōˈlid·ik\ *adj* [*pectin* + hydro*lytic*] **:** producing hydrolysis of pectins

pec·ti·noph·o·ra \ˌpektəˈnäf(ə)rə\ *n, cap* [NL, fr. *pectin-* + *-o-* + *-phora*] **:** a genus of gelechiid moths containing the pink bollworm

pec·tin·ous \ˈpektənəs\ *adj* [*pectin* + *-ous*] **:** of, relating to, or containing pectin

pec·tiz·able \ˈpekˌtīzəbəl\ *adj* **:** capable of being pectized

pec·ti·za·tion \ˌpektəˈzāshən\ *n* -s **:** the act or process of pectizing

pec·tize \ˈpekˌtīz\ *vb* -ED/-ING/-S [Gk *pēktos* coagulated + E *-ize* — more at PECTIC] *vt* **:** to change from a sol to a gel — compare PEPTIZE ~ *vi* **:** to undergo a change from a sol to a gel

pec·to·cellulose \ˌpek(ˌ)tō+\ *n* [*pectic* + *-o-* + *cellulose*] **:** any of several protopectins formerly regarded as combinations of pectic substances and cellulose

pec·to·lite \ˈpektəˌlīt\ *n* -s [G *pektolith*, fr. Gk *pēktos* compacted (fr. *pēgnynai* to fix, fasten) + G *-lith* -lite — more at PACT] **:** a whitish or grayish monoclinic mineral $NaCa_2Si_3O_8(OH)$ consisting of a basic sodium calcium silicate occurring in crystal aggregates or fibrous masses (hardness 5, sp. gr. 2.68–2.78)

pec·to·lyt·ic \ˌpektəˈlid·ik\ *adj* [*pectic* + hydro*lytic*] **:** producing hydrolysis of pectic substances

¹pec·to·ral \ˈpekt(ə)rəl\ *n* -s [ME, fr. MF, fr. L *pectorale* breastplate, fr. neut. of *pectoralis* of the breast] **1 :** something worn on the breast for protection or ornament: as **a :** a breastplate or cloth worn as an ecclesiastical vestment **b :** a breastplate worn as armor **c :** PECTORAL CROSS **d** *obs* **:** ²HOUSING **2** [²*pectoral*] **:** a pectoral part or organ: as **a :** PECTORAL FIN **b** *or* **pectoral muscle :** PECTORALIS **c :** a pectoral scale, plate, or shield

²pectoral \"\ *adj* [MF, or L; MF, fr. L *pectoralis*, fr. *pector-, pectus* breast + *-alis* -al; akin to Toch A *pāśśäm* (dual) the two breasts, and perh. to OIr *hucht* breast, Skt *pakṣas* side, wing] **1 :** of, relating to, situated or occurring in or on, or worn on the chest ⟨~ arch⟩ ⟨the ~ plates of a turtle's plastron⟩ **2 :** relating to or good for diseases of the respiratory tract ⟨a ~ syrup⟩ **3 :** coming from the breast or heart as the seat of emotion or spiritual inspiration **:** SUBJECTIVE, FERVENT ⟨wildly implausible tale . . . conforms to every ~ rule of historical fiction without ever quite spinning an illusion —James Kelly⟩ ⟨the genre of the ~ historical romance —*New Yorker*⟩

pectoral cross *n* **:** a cross worn on the breast by various ecclesiastics as a mark of office

pectoral fin *n* **:** either of the fins of a fish that correspond to the forelimbs of a quadruped — see FISH illustration

pectoral girdle *also* **pectoral arch** *n* **:** the bony or cartilaginous arch supporting the forelimbs of a vertebrate that corresponds to the pelvic girdle of the hind limbs but is usu. not attached to the spinal column and that consists primitively of a single cartilage on each side which in higher forms becomes ossified, divided into the scapula above and the precoracoid and coracoid below, and complicated by the addition or substitution of one or more membrane bones and which in man is highly modified with the scapula alone of the original elements well developed, the coracoid being represented only by a process, and the precoracoid being replaced by the clavicle that connects the scapula with the sternum and is the only bony connection of the arm bones with the rest of the skeleton

pec·to·ra·lis \ˌpektəˈraləs, -rāl-, -räl-\ *or* **pectoralis muscle** *n, pl* **pectora·les** \-(ˌ)lēz\ [NL, fr. L *pectoralis* pectoral] **:** one of the muscles that connect the ventral walls of the chest with the bones of the upper arm and shoulder, in man being two in number on each side: (1) a larger that arises from the clavicle, the sternum, the cartilages of most or all of the ribs, and from the aponeurosis of the external oblique muscle, and is inserted by a strong, flat tendon into the posterior bicipital ridge of the humerus and (2) a smaller that lies beneath the larger, arises from the third, fourth, and fifth ribs, and is inserted by a flat tendon into the coracoid process of the scapula — called also respectively (1) *pectoralis major*, (2) *pectoralis minor*

pectoral limb *n* **:** either member of the anterior of the two pairs of limbs characteristic of a vertebrate (as an arm, forelimb, wing, or pectoral fin)

pectoral ridge *n* **:** a ridge on the upper ventral part of the humerus

pectoral sandpiper *n* **:** a rather small sandpiper (*Erolia melanotos*) with a thickly streaked breast that breeds in Arctic America and migrates through most of No. and So. America — called also *grass snipe, jacksnipe*

pec·to·ril·o·quy \ˌpektəˈriləkwē\ *n* -ES [F *pectoriloquie*, fr. L *pector-, pectus* breast + *-loquium* speaking (fr. *loqui* to speak) — more at PECTORAL] **:** the sound of words heard through the chest wall and usu. indicating a cavity or consolidation of lung tissue — compare BRONCHOPHONY

pec·tose \ˈpekˌtōs, -ōz\ *n* -s [ISV *pect-* (fr. *pectic*) + *-ose*] **:** PROTOPECTIN

pec·tous \ˈpektəs\ *adj* [*pectic* or *pectin* + *-ous*] **1 :** of, relating to, or consisting of protopectin or pectin **2 :** resembling a jelly esp. in consistency

pec·tun·cu·late \(ˈ)pekˈtəŋkyələt, -ˌlāt\ *adj* [L *pectunculus* small scallop (dim. of *pectin-, pecten* comb, scallop) + E *-ate* — more at PECTINATE] **:** minutely pectinate

pec·tus \ˈpektəs\ *n, pl* **pec·to·ra** \-tərə\ [NL, fr. L, breast — more at PECTORAL] **1 :** the breast of a bird **2 :** the lower surface of the thorax or of the prothorax of an insect

pecul *var of* PICUL

¹peculate *n* -s [L *peculatus*, fr. past part. of *peculari* to embezzle] *obs* **:** PECULATION

²pec·u·late \ˈpekyəˌlāt\ *vb* -ED/-ING/-S [L *peculatus*, past part. of *peculari* to embezzle, fr. *peculium* private property — more at PECULIAR] *vt* **:** to steal or appropriate wrongfully to one's own use (as public money entrusted to one's care) **:** EMBEZZLE ⟨a large sum *peculated* from the treasury⟩ ~ *vi* **:** to engage in the wrongful appropriation of money committed to one's charge ⟨the . . . chef began to ~ —Arnold Bennett⟩

pec·u·la·tion \ˌpekyəˈlāshən\ *n* -s [LL *peculation-, peculatio*, fr. L *peculatus* + *-ion-, -io* -ion] **:** the act or practice of peculating **:** EMBEZZLEMENT ⟨the ~ of state revenue —Owen Lattimore⟩

pec·u·la·tor \ˈpekyəˌlād·ə(r)\ *n* -s [L, fr. *peculatus* + *-or*] **:** one who peculates **:** EMBEZZLER

¹pe·cu·liar \pəˈkyülyə(r), pēˈk-\ *adj* [ME *peculier*, fr. L *peculiaris* of private property, owned privately, special, extraordinary, fr. *peculium* private property, peculium (fr. *pecu* cattle) + *-aris* -ar; akin to L *pecus* cattle — more at FEE] **1 a :** belonging exclusively or esp. to a person or group ⟨a ~ garb of their own⟩ ⟨a mystic belief in a ~ soil —M.R.Cohen⟩ **b** *obs* **:** owned or used privately rather than publicly or in common ⟨~ fields are turn'd to common roads —William Davenant⟩ ⟨groping for trouts in a ~ river —Shak.⟩ **2 a** *archaic* **:** SEPARATE, INDEPENDENT **b :** of or relating to an ecclesiastical jurisdiction not subject in English canon law to the ordinary of the diocese ⟨the *Peculiar* Jurisdiction of the Dean of Sarum —H.W.Jones⟩ **3 :** tending to be characteristic of one only **:** DISTINCTIVE ⟨the ~ character of the Government of the U.S. —R.B.Taney⟩ ⟨the ~ responsibility of the junior college —L.L.Medsker⟩ — often used postpositively with *to* ⟨a drowsy fervor . . . quite ~ to her —Thomas Hardy⟩ ⟨problems . . . ~ to particular segments of the engineering profession —H.A. Wagner⟩ **4 a :** different from the usual or normal **:** SINGULAR, SPECIAL, PARTICULAR ⟨a matter of ~ interest⟩ ⟨this truth comes to us with ~ shock —R.B.Heilman⟩ ⟨a man still feels it a ~ insult to be taunted with cowardice by a woman —Virginia Woolf⟩ **b :** STRANGE, CURIOUS ⟨a ~ situation⟩ ⟨said in a ~ tone —Guy Fowler⟩ ⟨feel a bit ~ —Richard Joseph⟩ **c :** ECCENTRIC, QUEER ⟨her ~ behavior⟩ ⟨all great writers have been . . . ~ —*Time*⟩ **syn** see CHARACTERISTIC, STRANGE

²peculiar \"\ *n* -s **1 :** something (as an office or place) exempt from ordinary jurisdiction **:** INDEPENDENT: as **a :** a church or parish exempt from the jurisdiction of the ordinary in whose territory it lies ⟨the Deanery . . . one of the three *Peculiars* in the Province —*Manchester Guardian Weekly*⟩ — compare ROYAL PECULIAR **b :** a piece of land, precinct, or district in the New England colonies not in any town and not constituting a town **2 :** something peculiarly one's own: as **a** *obs* **:** an exclusive quality **:** PECULIARITY **b** *obs* **:** a private or special interest **c :** an exclusive property or privilege **:** PREROGATIVE **3** *usu cap* **:** one of a religious group called the Peculiar People

peculiar institution *n* **:** Negro slavery — used formerly of slavery as an institution peculiar to the South

pe·cu·liar·ism \-yəˌrizəm\ *n* -s **1** *sometimes cap* **:** the teachings or practices of Peculiars **2 :** the cult of peculiarity ⟨library ~⟩

pe·cu·liar·i·ty \⸗ˌkyülˈyarəd·ē, -lēˈa-, -rətē, -i *also* -yer- *or* -ēˈer-\ *n* -ES [LL *peculiaritat-, peculiaritas*, fr. L *peculiaris* peculiar — *-itat-, -itas* -ity] **1 :** the quality or state of being peculiar **:** DISTINCTIVENESS ⟨that sweet ~ of manner . . . so much a part of herself —Jane Austen⟩ **2 :** partiality in interest or affection ⟨his regard for her seemed to have lost all its ~ —Fanny Burney⟩ **3 :** something peculiar in a person or thing **:** a distinguishing characteristic **:** a distinctive feature ⟨the intrusion of his personal *peculiarities* —Matthew Arnold⟩ ⟨all her shoes had this ~ —Ruth Park⟩ **4 :** ODDITY, QUIRK ⟨for all their tribal *peculiarities* . . . a happy people —Patrick Smith⟩

pe·cu·liar·ize \⸗ˈkyülyəˌrīz\ *vt* -ED/-ING/-S **1** *obs* **:** to assign or appropriate as exclusive **2 :** to make peculiar or distinctive **:** INDIVIDUALIZE

pe·cu·liar·ly *adv* **:** in a peculiar manner: as **a :** UNIQUELY, EXCLUSIVELY ⟨a ~ French phenomenon —D.W.Brogan⟩ ⟨dowered with some . . . combination of gifts ~ his own —W.F. Hambly⟩ **b :** CHARACTERISTICALLY, DISTINCTIVELY ⟨bar associations . . . ~ fitted to protect the individual —W.O. Douglas⟩ ⟨the ~ metaphysical problems . . . involved —J.E. Smith⟩ **c :** PARTICULARLY, UNUSUALLY ⟨under ~ tragic circumstances —Allen Johnson⟩ ⟨a ~ indecent form of rudeness —W.L.Alden⟩ **d :** ODDLY, STRANGELY ⟨taught ordinary subjects ~ —Richard McLaughlin⟩ ⟨~, the key to the room was under the bed —E.D.Radin⟩

peculiar motion *n* **:** the actual motion of a star after its observed proper motion and radial velocity are corrected for the effect of the sun's motion

peculiar people *n pl* [ME *peculier people*, fr. *peculier* peculiar] **1 :** God's own chosen people — used by various Christians to emphasize their nonconformity to the world **2** *cap both Ps* **:** an Evangelical Christian organization founded in England in the 19th century that holds to essentially fundamentalist doctrines and practices divine healing to the extent of refusing medical aid

pe·cu·li·um \⸗ˈk(y)ülēəm\ *n, pl* **pecu·lia** \-ēə\ [L — more at PECULIAR] **1 :** the property held by a person (as a wife, child, slave) under the potestas, manus, or mancipium of another as his own private property either by the permission of the paterfamilias or master or by the rules of law but becoming with certain exceptions the property of the paterfamilias or master at his pleasure — compare BONA ADVENTITIA **2 :** a fund or property held by one as his own exclusive possession or for his own private use (as the salary of a Roman soldier or the separate personal property of a wife in Scotland)

peculium ad·ven·ti·ci·um \-ˌadˌvenˈtikēəm, -ˌvən-, -tishē-\ *n* [LL] **:** BONA ADVENTITIA

pe·cu·niar·i·ly \pəˈkyünēˌerəlē, pēˈk-, -ünˈye-, -li\ *adv* **:** in a pecuniary manner **:** with respect to money ⟨~ profitable —*Times Lit. Supp.*⟩

pe·cu·niary \pəˈkyünēˌerē, pēˈk-, -ri *also* -nyər-\ *adj* [L *pecuniarius*, fr. *pecunia* money + *-arius* -ary — more at FEE] **1 :** taking the form of or consisting of money ⟨the chief . . . entitled to certain regular gifts, ~ or in kind —*Notes & Queries on Anthropology*⟩ ⟨a system of ~ mulcts —J.M. Kemble⟩ **2 :** of or relating to money **:** MONETARY ⟨~ gain⟩ ⟨~ needs⟩ ⟨the ~ aims and class animosities of capitalist production —Lewis Mumford⟩ ⟨the medieval cathedrals were not built with any ~ motive —Bertrand Russell⟩

pecuniary unit *n* **:** MONETARY UNIT

¹ped \ˈped\ *n* -s [ME *pedde*] *dial chiefly Eng* **:** a covered basket **:** HAMPER

²ped \"\ *n* -s [Gk *pedon* ground, earth — more at PEDION] **:** a natural soil aggregate — compare CLOD

¹ped- *or* **pedi-** *or* **pedo-** *comb form* [*ped-, pedi-* fr. L, fr. *ped-, pes* foot; *pedo-* fr. *ped-* + *-o-* — more at FOOT] **1 :** foot **:** feet ⟨*pedi*form⟩ ⟨*pedi*gerous⟩ ⟨*pedi*cure⟩ **2 :** a creature or object (specified) having feet or footlike projections ⟨*Pedi*astrum⟩ ⟨*ped*rail⟩ **3 :** something (specified) involving the feet ⟨*pedo*motor⟩

²ped- *or* **pedo-** *comb form* [Gk *pedon* ground, earth — more at PEDION] **:** soil ⟨*pedo*genesis⟩ ⟨*pedo*geography⟩

³ped- — see PAED-

¹-ped \ˌped\ *adj comb form* [L *-ped-, -pes*, fr. *ped-, pes* foot — more at FOOT] **:** having (such or so many) feet ⟨scuti*ped*⟩

²-ped \"\ *or* **-pede** \ˌpēd\ *n comb form* -s [L *ped-, pes*] **:** foot ⟨maxilli*ped*⟩ ⟨maxilli*pede*⟩

ped *abbr* **1** pedal **2** pedestal **3** pedestrian

ped·age \ˈpedij\ *n* -s [ME, fr. ML *pedagium* — more at PEAGE] *archaic* **:** toll for passage

ped·a·gese *or* **ped·a·guese** \ˌpedəˈgēz, -gēs\ *n* -s [*pedagogue* + *-ese*] **:** gobbledygook in the speeches or writings of educationists ⟨reads like a Fourth-of-July oration in ~ —R.M. Hutchins⟩ ⟨turgid ~ —H.M.Kallen⟩ ⟨convert ~ into lucid and workmanlike English —*Amer. Scholar*⟩

ped·a·gog·ic \ˌpedəˈgäjik, -gōj, -gäg|, |ēk *sometimes* -gōg-\ *or* **ped·a·gog·i·cal** \|əkəl, |ēk-\ *also* **paed·a·gog·ic** \ˌpedə-\ *adj* [*pedagogic* fr. Gk *paidagōgikos*, fr. *paidagōgos* pedagogue + *-ikos* -ic; *pedagogical* fr. Gk *paidagōgikos* + E *-al*] **1 :** of, relating to, or befitting a pedagogue or teacher ⟨~ zeal⟩ ⟨the ~ mind⟩ ⟨tends to give a ~ tone to his discourse that makes me shrink from it —O.W.Holmes †1935⟩ **2 :** of or relating to teaching or pedagogy **:** EDUCATIONAL ⟨~ innovations⟩ ⟨the material selected . . . must have regard to our own ~ techniques —C.F.Strong⟩ ⟨contemporary . . . ~ thinking —Alfred Kähler & Ernest Hamburger⟩ — **ped·a·gog·ically** \|ək(ə)lē, |ēk-, -li\ *adv*

ped·a·gog·ics \|iks, |ēks\ *n pl but sing in constr* [*pedagogy* + *-ics*] **:** the science or art of teaching **:** PEDAGOGY ⟨~ is the most revolutionary of all sciences —Alice Balint⟩ ⟨an ultramodern school of ~ —Rudolf Hirschberg⟩

ped·a·gog·ist \ˈ⸗⸗ˌgäjəst, -gōj-, ˌ⸗⸗ˈ⸗⸗\ *n* -s [perh. fr. F *pédagogiste*, fr. *pédagogie* pedagogy + *-iste* -ist] **:** a specialist in pedagogy

ped·a·gogue *also* **ped·a·gog** *or* **paed·a·gogue** \ˈ⸗⸗ˌgäg *sometimes* -gōg\ *n* -s [ME *pedagoge*, fr. MF *pedagogue, pedagogue*, fr. L *paedagogus*, fr. Gk *paidagōgos*, fr. *paid-* paed- + *agōgos* leader, escort, fr. *agein* to lead, drive — more at AGENT] **1 :** a teacher of children or youth **:** SCHOOLMASTER ⟨the opinion of . . . experienced ~s —Virgil Thomson⟩ ⟨a fine ~ —A.J.Liebling⟩ ⟨the mere ~ —W.S.Deffenbaugh⟩ ⟨a wooden and perfunctory ~ —John Dewey⟩ **2 a :** one (as a slave) having charge of a boy chiefly on the way to and from school in classical antiquity **b :** a youth's tutor and often traveling companion esp. in the Renaissance

ped·a·gogy *also* **paed·a·gogy** \ˈ⸗⸗ˌgäj|ē, -gōj|, -gäg|, |i *sometimes* -gōg|\ *n* -ES [MF *pedagogie*, fr. Gk *paidagōgia* training, instruction, fr. *paidagōgos* pedagogue + *-ia* -y] **1 :** INSTRUCTION ⟨knowledge . . . not as ~ but as gossip in the marketplace —A.W.Griswold⟩ **2 :** the art, science, or profession of teaching; *esp* **:** the study that deals with principles and methods in formal education **:** EDUCATION 4 ⟨convinced . . . that ~ should be recognized as one of the major "disciplines" —J.L.Childs⟩ **3** [prob. fr. L *paedogogium*, fr. Gk *paidagōgeion*, fr. *paidagōgos* pedagogue] **:** a place of instruction in medieval times **:** SCHOOL

¹ped·al \ˈpedᵊl\ *n* -s [MF *pedale*, fr. It, organ pedal, tree trunk, plant stem, fr. L *pedalis* of the foot] **1 :** a lever acted on by the foot in the playing of musical instruments: as **a** (1) **:** any of the keys of an organ keyboard played upon with the feet; *broadly* **:** PEDAL KEYBOARD (2) **:** a foot lever for drawing or shutting off one or more organ stops, for opening or shutting the swell box, or for coupling two keyboards **b :** one of the foot levers functioning as stops on a harpsichord **c** (1) **:** any of the levers used to alter the quality of or to sustain the tone of a piano (2) **:** any of the keys of a pedalier **d :** one of the seven foot levers by which the strings of a harp are stopped to raise their pitch either one or two half steps — see HARP illustration **e :** a foot lever or treadle used to pump the bellows of a reed organ **f** (1) **:** a foot lever used to change the pitch of a kettledrum quickly (2) **:** a foot lever used to beat a bass drum in a jazz orchestra **2 :** PEDAL POINT **3 :** a foot lever or treadle by which a part is activated in a mechanism (as a bicycle, loom, or sewing machine) — see BICYCLE illustration, HYDRAULIC BRAKE illustration **4** [It. *pedale*] *or* **pedal straw a :** the light straw from the lower portion of wheat stalks **b :** a plait made of this straw and used esp. for millinery

²ped·al \", ˈpēdᵊl\ *adj* [L *pedalis*, fr. *ped-, pes* foot + *-alis* -al — more at FOOT] **1 :** of or relating to the foot **2 :** of, relating to, or involving a pedal

³ped·al \ˈpedᵊl\ *vb* **pedaled** *also* **pedalled; pedaled** *also* **pedalled; pedaling** *also* **pedalling** \-d(ə)liŋ\; **pedals** [¹*pedal*] *vi* **1 :** to use or work a pedal (as of an organ, piano, or bicycle) ⟨complimenting a pianist upon the accuracy of his . . . ~*ing* —Dudley Fitts⟩ **2 :** to ride a bicycle **:** CYCLE 2 ⟨~*ed* off . . . to summon a mason —Ida Treat⟩ ~ *vt* **:** to work the pedals of ⟨~*ing* a bicycle⟩ ⟨~*s* the garbage can —Herbert Gold⟩

pedal board *or* **pedal clavier** *n* [¹*pedal*] **:** a pedal keyboard esp. of a pipe organ

pedal boat *n* **:** a boat propelled like a bicycle by pedaling — see SWAN BOAT

pedal bone *n* [²*pedal*] **:** COFFIN BONE

pedal clarinet *n* **:** CONTRABASS CLARINET

pedal coupler *n* [¹*pedal*] **:** a coupling mechanism in the pipe organ to make a manual stop sound when the pedals are played

pedal disk *n* [²*pedal*] **:** the broad base by which most sea anemones attach themselves to the substrate

ped·al·er *also* **ped·al·ler** \ˈped(ᵊ)lə(r)\ *n* **:** one that pedals

pe·dal·fer \pəˈdalfə(r)\ *n* -s [²*ped-* + *alumen* + L *ferrum* iron — more at FARRIER] **:** a soil that lacks a hardened layer of accumulated carbonates — compare PEDOCAL — **ped·al·fer·ic** \ˌpeˌdalˈferik\ *adj*

pedal ganglion *n* [²*pedal*] **:** either of a pair of ganglia in most mollusks that supply nerves to the muscles of the foot and that correspond to the subesophageal ganglia of many other invertebrates but are often far removed from the esophagus and joined to the central ganglia by long nerves

pedal gland *n* **:** any of the unicellular or syncytial glands that occur in the foot of many rotifers and secrete an adhesive substance

pe·da·li·a·ce·ae \pəˌdālēˈāsēˌē\ *n pl, cap* [NL, fr. *Pedalium*, type genus + *-aceae*] **:** a family of annual or perennial hairy tropical herbs (order Polemoniales) with opposite leaves and zygomorphic flowers having bilabiate corollas and 4-loculate ovaries with two carpels — **pe·da·li·a·ceous** \⸗ˌ⸗⸗ˈāshəs\ *adj*

ped·a·lier \ˌpedᵊlˈi(ə)r, -iə\ *n* -s [F *pédalier*, fr. *pédale*, fr. MF *pedale* — more at PEDAL, n.] **1 a :** the pedal keyboard of an organ **b :** one attached to a harpsichord or piano **2 :** an independent pedal keyboard for practice

ped·al·ine \ˈpedᵊlˌēn, ˌ⸗⸗ˈ⸗\ *n* -s [¹*pedal* + *-ine*] **:** a strawy material that has usu. a hemp or cotton core covered with a cellulose mixture or cellophane and that is made into a braid and used for millinery and ribbon

pe·dal·i·ter \pə'daləd·ə(r)\ *adv* [NL, fr. L *pedalis* of the foot + *-ter*, adv. suffix] **:** on the pedal keyboard — used as a direction in organ music; compare MANUALITER

pe·da·li·um \pə'dalēəm, -lyəm\ *n, cap* [NL, fr. Gk *pēdalion* rudder, fr. *pēdon* oar blade; akin to Gk *pod-, pous* foot — more at FOOT] **:** a genus (the type of the family Pedaliaceae) of smooth annual musky Indian or tropical African herbs having dentate leaves, axillary yellow flowers, and mucilaginous seeds

pedal key *n* [¹*pedal*] **:** any of the keys of the pedal keyboard of an organ

pedal keyboard *n* **:** a keyboard of pedals (as in a pipe organ)

pedal–note \'==,=\ *n* **1 :** PEDAL POINT **2 :** a tone produced by depressing a pedal; *also* **:** its notation **3 :** one of the lowest tones sounded by a brass wind instrument being an octave below the normal usable range, and representing the fundamental of the harmonic series

pedal organ *n* **:** the portion of a pipe organ that is controlled from the pedal keyboard

pedal piano *n* **:** a piano with a pedal keyboard attached

pedal point *n* **1 :** a single tone usu. the tonic or dominant that is normally sustained in the bass and sounds against changing harmonies in the other parts — called also *organ point;* compare DRONE BASS **2 :** the phrase or passage in which a pedal point occurs

pedal pushers *n pl* **:** women's and girls' calf-length trousers for sportswear

ped·ant \'ped°nt\ *n* -s [MF *pedant*, fr. It *pedante*, perh. fr. L *paedagogant-, paedagogans*, pres. part. of *paedagogare* to instruct, fr. *paedagogus* pedagogue] **1** *obs* **a :** a household tutor **b :** a male schoolteacher ⟨like a ~ that keeps a school in the church —Shak.⟩ **2 a :** one who parades his learning esp. book learning ⟨a pompous ~ —T.B.Macaulay⟩ ⟨the polysyllabic obscurantist style of the . . . ~ —Marvin Lowenthal⟩ **b :** one who is uninspired, unimaginative, or narrowly academic or who unduly emphasizes minutiae in the presentation or use of knowledge ⟨some dusty college of ~*s*, their noses buried in . . . bibliographical data —Herbert Read⟩ ⟨a scholar, yet surely no ~ —Oliver Goldsmith⟩ **c :** a formalist or precisionist in teaching ⟨the great musicians of the past were not ~*s* —Irving Babbitt⟩

pe·dan·tic \pə'dantik, -daan-, -tēk\ *adj* [*pedant* + *-ic*] **:** marked by pedantry: as **a :** ostentatiously learned ⟨the ~ style, the profuse classical quotations —J.R.Green⟩ **b :** narrowly academic ⟨the intellectual life that remained came to be ~ . . . rather than humane and broad —J.T.Adams⟩ **c :** UNIMAGINATIVE, PEDESTRIAN ⟨dull ~ minds —Lewis Mumford⟩ **d :** excessively meticulous ⟨a ~ speaker —G.A.Kennedy⟩ **e :** FORMALISTIC ⟨the living Bach as opposed to the dry and ~ Bach —A.E.Wier⟩ — **pe·dan·ti·cal·ly** \-tək(ə)lē, -tēk-, -li\ *adv*

pe·dan·ti·cal \-təkəl, -tēk-\ *adj, archaic* **:** PEDANTIC

pe·dan·ti·cism \-tə,sizəm\ *or* **ped·ant·ism** \'ped°n·,tizəm\ *n* -s [*pedanticism* fr. *pedantic* + *-ism*; *pedantism* fr. *pedant* + *-ism*] **:** PEDANTRY

ped·an·toc·ra·cy \,ped°n·'täkrəsē\ *n* -ES [F *pédantocratie*, fr. *pédant* pedant (fr. MF *pedant*) + *-o-* + *-cratie* -cracy] **:** a government of pedants

pe·dan·to·crat \pə'dantə,krat\ *n* -s [*pedant* + *-o-* + *-crat*] **:** one who rules according to a pedantic system — **pe·dan·to·crat·ic** \=;==;krad·ik\ *adj*

ped·ant·ry \'ped°ntrē, -ri\ *n* -ES [F or It; F *pédanterie*, fr. It *pedanteria*, fr. *pedante* pedant + *-eria* -ry] **1 :** pedantic presentation or application of knowledge or learning esp. by a teacher or scholar ⟨the book . . . is a demonstration of scholarship without ~ —W.S.Woytinsky⟩ ⟨to correct popular speech according to formal canons is sheer ~ —A.L.Guérard⟩ **2 :** an instance of pedantry ⟨methods of study may involve . . . specialized *pedantries* —G.W.Sherburn⟩

pe·da·ta \pə'dād·ə, -ād·ə\ *n pl, cap* [NL, fr. L, neut. pl. of *pedatus* footed] *in some classifications* **:** a division of Holothurioidea comprising forms that have tube feet either in longitudinal rows or scattered over the surface of the body and including the orders Aspidochirota and Dendrochirota or broadly all holothurians except the Apoda

ped·ate \'pe,dāt, -,dət, *usu* -d·+V\ *adj* [L *pedatus* footed, fr. *ped-, pes* foot + *-atus* -ate — more at FOOT] **1 a :** having a foot **b :** having tube feet ⟨many holothurians are ~⟩ **2** [NL *Pedata*] **:** of or relating to the Pedata **3 :** palmate with the lateral lobes cleft into two or more segments ⟨~ leaves⟩ — see LEAF illustration — **ped·ate·ly** *adv*

pedati- *comb form* [L *pedatus*] **:** pedate ⟨*pedati*form⟩ **:** pedately ⟨*pedati*sect⟩

ped·der \'pedə(r)\ *n* -s [ME *peddere*, prob. fr. *pedde* covered basket + *-ere* -er] *dial chiefly Brit* **:** PEDDLER, HAWKER

ped·dle \'ped°l\ *vb* **peddled; peddled; ped·dling** \-d(°)liŋ\ **peddles** [back-formation fr. *peddler*] *vi* **1 :** to travel about with wares for sale **:** pursue the occupation of a peddler ⟨~ without a license⟩ ⟨have been *peddling* on the corner for . . . weeks —John O'Hara⟩ **2 :** to be busy with trifles **:** PIDDLE ⟨no science *peddling* with the names of things —J.R.Lowell⟩ ~ *vt* **1 :** to sell or offer for sale from place to place **:** HAWK ⟨*peddled* fish from a pushcart —Phil Stong⟩ ⟨tried to ~ their wares to smart shops —Martha McDowell⟩ ⟨*peddled* his unwanted manuscripts —*Amer. Guide Series: N.Y. City*⟩ **2 :** to deal out or seek to disseminate (as ideas or opinions) **:** RETAIL, CIRCULATE ⟨*peddling* personal advice —G.F.Kennan⟩ ⟨*peddling* secondhand truths and undigested truisms to popular audiences —William Phillips b. 1907⟩

ped·dler *or* **ped·lar** *or* **ped·ler** \'ped(°)lə(r)\ *n* -s [ME *pedlere*, prob. alter. of *peddere* peddler] **1 :** one that peddles: as **a :** one that offers merchandise (as fruit or vegetables) for sale along the street or from door to door usu. carrying his goods in a pushcart, wagon, or truck as distinguished from a canvasser who takes orders for future delivery — called also *arab, hawker, huckster, vendor* ⟨an itinerant ~ crying his wares⟩ **b :** one that retails or offers for sale something intangible (as an idea or personal asset) ⟨a ~ of dreams⟩ ⟨~*s* of race hatred⟩ ⟨influence ~*s*⟩ **2 :** the larva of various leaf beetles of the genus *Cassida* and related forms **3 :** a local or way freight train

peddler car *n* **:** a freight car carrying less-than-carload shipments from one consignor over a specified route with deliveries direct to consignees

peddler truck *n* **:** a truck carrying less-than-truckload shipments from one consignor over a specified route with deliveries direct to consignees

ped·dlery *or* **ped·lary** \'pedlərē, -ri\ *n* -ES [*peddler* + *-y*] **1 :** peddlers' merchandise **2 :** the trade of a peddler

ped·dling \'ped(°)liŋ, -lēŋ\ *adj* [alter. of *piddling*] **:** PETTY, PIDDLING ⟨a ~ and pettifogging view of morality —George Saintsbury⟩ — **ped·dling·ly** *adv*

-pede — see -PED

pede cloth \'pēd-\ *n* [L *ped-, pes* foot — more at FOOT] **:** an altar carpet

¹**pedee** *n* -s [origin unknown] *obs* **:** a serving boy **:** FOOTBOY

²**pe·dee** \'pē,dē\ *n, pl* **pedee** *or* **pedees** *usu cap* **1 :** a Siouan people of the Pee Dee river valley in So. Carolina **2 :** a member of the Pedee people

ped·er·ast *also* **paed·er·ast** \'pedə,rast, 'pēd-\ *n* -s [Gk *paiderastēs*, lit., lover of boys, fr. *paid-* paed- + *erastēs* lover, fr. *erasthai* to love] **:** one that practices pederasty — **ped·er·as·tic** \;==;rastik, -tēk\ *adj* — **ped·er·as·ti·cal·ly** \-tək(ə)lē, -tēk-, -li\ *adv*

ped·er·as·ty *also* **paed·er·as·ty** \'==,rastē, -ti\ *n* -ES [Gk *paiderastia* love of boys, fr. *paiderastēs* + *-ia* -y] **:** anal intercourse esp. with a boy as the passive partner

pederero *var of* PEDRERO

pe·der·sen device \'pedə(r)sən-\ *n, usu cap P* [after J. D. *Pedersen*, 20th cent. Amer. inventor] **:** a device consisting of a special bolt and magazine for converting a slightly modified version of the bolt action Springfield rifle into a semiautomatic firearm

pedes *pl of* PES

pe·de·sis \pə'dēsəs\ *n, pl* **pede·ses** \-,sēz\ [NL, fr. Gk *pēdēsis* leaping, fr. *pēdan* to leap; akin to L *ped-, pes* foot — more at FOOT] **:** BROWNIAN MOVEMENT

¹**ped·es·tal** \'pedəst°l\ *n* -s *often attrib* [MF *piedestal*, fr. OIt *piedestallo*, fr. *pie di stallo* foot of a stall] **1 a :** the support or foot of a late classic or neoclassic column consisting of base, dado, and surbase moldings **b :** the base of an upright structure (as a statue, vase, lamp, harp) ⟨a ~ worthy of a storyteller's statue —Van Wyck Brooks⟩ **c :** a supporting part (as of a table or kneehole desk) **d :** PIVOT STAND **e :** a cone or column of ice that supports or has supported a boulder or block of rock **:** PEDESTAL ROCK **2 a :** the supporting base or foundation of something intangible ⟨pedigree was the ~ of the British constitution —Wilfrid Lawson⟩ **b :** an elevated plane **:** position of esteem ⟨places him . . . on a ~ —E.V.Buckholder⟩ ⟨shown off his ~ . . . as the members of his family group saw him —Dorothy C. Fisher⟩ **3 a :** a guide in the frame or truck of a car or locomotive that slides against the sides of the journal box and holds it in place as the body rides on the springs **b** *Brit* **:** an axle guard of a railroad car **4 a :** a separate bearing or pillow block; *also* **:** a housing for a bearing or pillow block **b :** a metal support that carries one end of a bridge truss or girder and transmits the load it receives to the top of a pier or abutment **5 :** the strength of the television signal on which the synchronizing signal is superimposed corresponding to black or slightly blacker than black in the picture

²**pedestal** \"\ *vt* **pedestaled** *or* **pedestalled; pedestaled** *or* **pedestalled; pedestaling** *or* **pedestalling; pedestals 1 :** to place on or furnish with a pedestal ⟨the pride of the . . . collection stands *pedestalled* in an alcove —Aldous Huxley⟩ **2 :** to elevate in position **:** EXALT ⟨desired not to be . . . *pedestalled*, but to sink into the crowd —John Buchan⟩

pedestal box *n* **:** JOURNAL BOX

pedestal desk *n* **:** a kneehole desk with the top supported by one or two pedestals containing cupboards or drawers

pedestal mount *n* **:** a gun mount having its pivot stand in the general form of a truncated cone

pedestal pile *n* **:** a concrete pile that is cast in place with a bulb-shaped enlargement at its lower end

pedestal ring *n* **:** the element or part of a packing gland that applies pressure to the packing **:** a stepped ring

pedestal rock *n* **:** a residual or erosional rock mass balanced upon a relatively slender neck or pedestal

pedestal table *n* **:** a table having a central supporting column or pillar

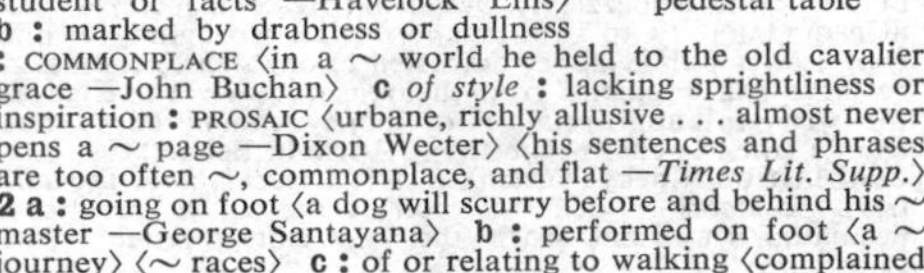
pedestal table

pedestrial *adj* [L *pedestr-*, *pedester*, *pedestris* going on foot + E *-al*] *obs* **:** PEDESTRIAN 2

¹**pe·des·tri·an** \pə'destrēən\ *adj* [L *pedestr-, pedester, pedestris* going on foot, prosaic (fr. *pedes* one going on foot, fr. *ped-, pes* foot) + E *-an* — more at FOOT] **1 a :** having the characteristics of a drudge or plodder **:** UNIMAGINATIVE ⟨a dry laborious ~ student of facts —Havelock Ellis⟩ **b :** marked by drabness or dullness **:** COMMONPLACE ⟨in a ~ world he held to the old cavalier grace —John Buchan⟩ **c** *of style* **:** lacking sprightliness or inspiration **:** PROSAIC ⟨urbane, richly allusive . . . almost never pens a ~ page —Dixon Wecter⟩ ⟨his sentences and phrases are too often ~, commonplace, and flat —*Times Lit. Supp.*⟩ **2 a :** going on foot ⟨a dog will scurry before and behind his ~ master —George Santayana⟩ **b :** performed on foot ⟨a ~ journey⟩ ⟨~ races⟩ **c :** of or relating to walking ⟨complained about the ~ distances —Lewis Mumford⟩

²**pedestrian** \"\ *n* -s **:** a person who travels on foot **:** WALKER: as **a :** one who walks for pleasure, sport, or exercise **:** HIKER ⟨an indefatigable ~⟩ ⟨he liked company on a walk . . . and most of his guests were not ~*s* —R.M.Lovett⟩ **b :** one walking as distinguished from one travelling by car or cycle ⟨signalled traffic to halt to allow ~*s* to cross the street⟩

pe·des·tri·an·ate \-,nāt\ *or* **pe·des·tri·nate** \-trə,nāt\ *vi* -ED/-ING/-S **:** PEDESTRIANIZE

pedestrian island *n* **:** a space between roadways where pedestrians can await a break in vehicular traffic

pe·des·tri·an·ism \pə'destrēə,nizəm\ *n* -s **1 a :** the practice of walking ⟨a feat of ~⟩ **b :** addiction to walking for exercise or recreation **2 :** the quality or state of being pedestrian **:** BANALITY ⟨the latest mass medium to bewitch the multitude with canned ~ —Jack Gould⟩ — used esp. of literary style ⟨a ~ which may defeat the heaven-sent chance to deal fully and splendidly with a mighty subject —Oliver La Farge⟩

pe·des·tri·an·ize \-,nīz\ *vi* -ED/-ING/-S **:** to do some walking **:** go afoot

pe·de·tes \pə'dēd·(,)ēz\ *n, cap* [NL, fr. Gk *pēdētēs* leaper, fr. *pēdan* to leap — more at PEDESIS] **:** a genus (the type and sole recent representative of the family Pedetidae) of rodents that consists of the jumping hare

¹**pe·det·id** \-'ded·əd\ *adj* [NL *Pedetidae*] **:** of or relating to the genus *Pedetes* or the family Pedetidae

²**pedetid** \"\ *n* -s **:** a rodent of the genus *Pedetes* or the family Pedetidae

pede window \'pēd-\ *n* [L *ped-, pes* foot — more at FOOT] **:** a window placed at the foot of a cross (as in the west end of a cruciform church)

¹**pedi-** — see ¹PED-

²**pedi-** *or* **pedio-** *comb form* [Gk, fr. *pedion* — more at PEDION] **:** flat surface **:** plain ⟨*Pedio*ecetes⟩ **:** sole of the foot ⟨*pedi*algia⟩ ⟨*Pedio*coccus⟩

pedia *pl of* PEDION

ped·i·al \'pedēəl, 'pēd-\ *adj* [NL *pedion* + E *-al*] **:** of or relating to a pedion **:** ASYMMETRIC d

ped·i·as·trum \,pedē'astrəm, ,pēd-\ *n, cap* [NL, fr. ²*pedi-* + Gk *astron* star — more at STAR] **:** a genus of free-floating green algae (family Hydrodictyaceae) that have flat platelike colonies of two or more polygonal cells with the marginal cells usu. differing in shape and having usu. two projections of the cell wall

pe·di·at·ric *also* **pae·di·at·ric** \,pēdē;a·trik, ;ped-, -rēk\ *adj* [*paed-* + *-iatric*] **:** of or relating to the care and medical treatment of children ⟨an effective ~ service⟩ **:** belonging to or concerned with pediatrics

pe·di·a·tri·cian \,pēdēə'trishən, ,ped-\ *also* **pe·di·at·rist** \,==a·trəst, pə'dīə·trəst\ *n* -s [*pediatrician* fr. *pediatric* + *-ian*; *pediatrist* fr. *paed-* + *-iatrist*] **:** a specialist in pediatrics

pe·di·at·rics *also* **pae·di·at·rics** \,pēdē'a·triks, ped-\ *n pl but sing or pl in constr* [*paed-* + *-iatrics*] **:** a branch of medicine that deals with the child, its development, care, and diseases

ped·i·cab \'pedə, 'pedē+ ,-\ *n* [¹*ped-* + *cab*] **:** a light 3-wheeled pedaled or sometimes motorized vehicle used esp. in the Orient for transporting passengers for hire ⟨boys who used to pull rickshaws now pedal . . . ~*s* —G.W.Long⟩

ped·i·ca·tio *also* **paed·i·ca·tio** \,pedə'kāshē,ō, -kād·ē-\ *n* -s [NL *paedicatio*, *paedicatio*, fr. L *paedicatus* (past part. of *paedicare* to engage in pederasty, fr. Gk *paidika* boy favorite, fr. neut. pl. of *paidikos* of boys, fr. *paid-, pais* boy + *-ikos* -ic) + *-ion-, -io* -ion — more at PAED-] **:** anal intercourse

ped·i·cel \'pedə,sel\ *n* -s [NL *pedicellus*, dim. of L *pediculus* little foot, footstalk — more at PEDICLE] **1 a :** a slender plant stalk; *esp* **:** one that supports a fruiting or spore-bearing organ ⟨the ~ of a sporangium⟩ **b (1) :** one of the ultimate single flower-bearing divisions of a common peduncle **(2) :** a peduncle esp. if slender or delicate that bears a single flower — see FLOWER illustration **2 a :** a small or short stalk or stem in an animal body **:** a narrow basal part by which a larger part or body is attached (as the outgrowth of the frontal bone that supports the antler of a deer or the pedicle of a vertebra) **:** PEDUNCLE, FOOTSTALK **b :** a small foot or footlike organ (as a tube foot of an echinoderm) **c :** the second joint of the antenna of an insect between the scope and funicle **d :** the nodiform basal segment of the abdomen of an ant **e :** the narrow anterior portion of the abdomen of a spider that links abdomen and cephalothorax

ped·i·celed *or* **ped·i·celled** \-,seld\ *adj* **:** PEDICELLATE

ped·i·cel·la·ria \,pedəsə'la(a)rēə\ *n, pl* **pedicellar·i·ae** \-rē,ē\ [NL, fr. *pedicellus* pedicel + *-aria*] **:** any of various peculiar minute organs resembling forceps that are borne in large numbers on the external integument of sea urchins and starfish and also often on the spines of the latter and that have as their probable function keeping the body clear of small parasites and other foreign objects — compare FORCIPULATE

ped·i·cel·late \;==;selət, -,lāt, *usu* -d·+V\ *also* **ped·i·cel·lat·ed** \-,lād·əd\ *adj* [NL *pedicellus* pedicel + E *-ate*] **:** having or attached by a pedicel

ped·i·cel·li·form \;==;selə,fȯrm\ *adj* [NL *pedicellus* + E *-iform*] **:** having the form of a pedicel

ped·i·cel·li·na \,==sə'līnə\ *n, cap* [NL, fr. *pedicellus* + *-ina*] **:** a genus (the type of the family Pedicillinidae) of colonial bryozoans in which the zooids have a bell-shaped body on a slender pedicel

ped·i·cel·lin·i·dae \,==sə'linə,dē\ *n pl, cap* [NL, fr. *Pedicellina*, type genus + *-idae*] **:** a family of small noncalcareous usu. solitary and hermaphroditic bryozoans

ped·i·cle \'pedəkəl\ *n* -s [L *pediculus* little foot, footstalk, dim. of *ped-, pes* foot — more at FOOT] **:** PEDICEL: as **a :** the basal part of each side of the neural arch of a vertebra connecting the laminae with the centrum **b :** the narrow basal part by which various organs (as a kidney or spleen) are continuous with other body structures **c :** the narrow base of a tumor **d :** the part of a skin or tissue graft left attached to the original site during preliminary stages of union

ped·i·cled \-kəld\ *adj* [*pedicle* + *-ed*] **:** having or having the form of a pedicle

pe·dic·u·lar \pə'dikyələ(r)\ *adj* [L *pedicularis*, fr. *pediculus* louse, dim. of *pedis* louse; perh. akin to L *pedere* to break wind — more at PETARD] **:** of or relating to lice **:** PEDICULOUS, LOUSY

pe·dic·u·lar·is \pə,dikyə'la(a)rəs\ *n, cap* [NL, fr. L (*herba*) *pedicularis* lousewort] **:** a large genus of hemiparasitic herbs (family Scrophulareaceae) found in temperate or alpine regions that have pinnate or pinnatifid leaves and variously colored bilabiate flowers in terminal spikes — see LOUSEWORT

¹**pe·dic·u·late** \=;==,lət, -,lāt, *usu* -d·+V\ *adj* [NL *pediculatus*, fr. L *pediculus* footstalk + *-atus* -ate — more at PEDICLE] **1 :** PEDICELLATE **2** [NL *Pediculati*] **:** of or relating to the Pediculati

²**pediculate** \"\ *n* -s [NL *Pediculati*] **:** a fish of the order Pediculati

pe·dic·u·lat·ed \=;==;lād·əd\ *adj* [L *pediculus* footstalk + E *-ate* + *-ed*] **:** PEDICELLATE, PEDUNCULATE

pe·dic·u·la·ti \=,==·'lād·,ī\ *n pl, cap* [NL, fr. pl. of *pediculatus* pediculate] **:** an order of highly specialized marine teleost fishes including the anglers and batfishes that have the ventral fins on the throat and the pectoral fins at the end of a process suggesting a wrist or arm and consisting of the elongated and modified hypercoracoid and hypocoracoid and that have the anterior portion of the dorsal fin modified into a movable structure which stands out from the protectively colored body as a lure attracting prey within reach of the very large mouth

ped·i·cule \'pedə,kyül\ *n* -s [F *pédicule*, fr. L *pediculus* footstalk] **:** PEDICEL

pe·dic·u·li·ci·dal \pə;dikyələ;sīd°l\ *adj* **:** of, relating to, or being a pediculicide

pe·dic·u·li·cide \=;===,sīd\ *n* -s [L *pediculus* louse + E *-i-* + *-cide* — more at PEDICULAR] **:** an agent for destroying lice

¹**pe·dic·u·lid** \=;==ləd, -,lid\ *adj* [NL *Pediculidae*] **:** of or relating to the Pediculidae

²**pediculid** \"\ *n* -s **:** a louse of the family Pediculidae

ped·i·cu·li·dae \,pedə'kyülə,dē\ *n pl, cap* [NL, fr. *Pediculus*, type genus + *-idae*] **:** a family of true lice (order Anoplura) including the human lice and related forms

pe·dic·u·li·na \pə,dikyə'līnə\ *n pl, cap* [NL, fr. *Pediculus* + *-ina*] *in some classifications* **:** a group of lice: as **a :** a group coextensive with Anoplura **b :** a group coextensive with Pediculidae

pe·dic·u·line \=;==,līn, -lən\ *adj* [NL *Pediculina*] **:** of, relating to, or resembling the Pediculina

pe·dic·u·loid \-,lȯid\ *adj* [NL *Pediculus* + E *-oid*] **:** resembling or related to the common lice

pe·dic·u·loi·des \=,==·'lȯi(,)dēz\ [NL, fr. L *pediculus* louse + *-oides*] *syn of* PYEMOTES

pe·dic·u·lo·sis \-'lōsəs\ *n, pl* **pediculo·ses** \-ō,sēz\ [NL, fr. L *pediculus* louse + *-osis* — more at PEDICULAR] **:** infestation with lice esp. of the genus *Pediculus*

pe·dic·u·lous \=;==ləs\ *adj* [L *pediculosus*, fr. *pediculus* louse + *-osus* -ous — more at PEDICULAR] **:** infested with lice **:** LOUSY

pe·dic·u·lus \"\ *n* [NL, fr. L, louse] **1** *cap* **:** the type genus of Pediculidae including common lice infesting man **2** *pl* **pediculi** \-,lī\ *or* **pediculus :** any louse of the genus *Pediculus*

ped·i·cure \'pedə,kyü(ə)r, 'pedē,-, -üə\ *n* [F *pédicure*, fr. *péd-* ped- + L *curare* to take care of, fr. *cura* care — more at CURE] **1 :** CHIROPODIST **2 a :** care of the feet, toes, and nails **b :** a single treatment of these parts ⟨she had a ~ today⟩

ped·i·form \'==,fȯrm\ *adj* [F *pédiforme*, fr. *péd-* ped- + *-iforme* -iform] **:** resembling a foot — used chiefly of segmental appendages of insects and other arthropods that are not characteristically of this form ⟨~ antennae⟩

pe·dig·er·ous \pə'dijərəs\ *adj* [¹*ped-* + *-gerous*] **:** having feet **:** FOOTED ⟨the three ~ segments of the adult insect⟩

¹**ped·i·gree** \'pedə,grē\ *n* -s [ME *pedegru*, fr. MF *pie de grue* crane's foot; fr. the shape made by the lines of a genealogical chart] **1 :** a register (as a table or chart) recording a line of ancestors **:** a genealogical tree **:** STEMMA ⟨drawing up a family ~⟩ **2 a :** an ancestral line **:** LINEAGE, DESCENT ⟨the dowager scrutinized his ~ and background⟩ **b (1) :** the origin and the history (as of the developmental stages or the successive states or owners) of something ⟨the ~ of a document⟩ ⟨~*s* of ideas or influences —*Times Lit. Supp.*⟩ ⟨the ~ of the house we lived in —Mary A. Allen⟩ **(2) :** the sequence of owners of a work of art (as a painting) ⟨the condition of the pictures . . . their ~, the subjects represented —*Times Lit. Supp.*⟩ **(3) :** the history of a collector's coin or stamp including facts about its original issuance, its rarity, and the sales in which it has changed hands **3 a :** distinguished ancestry ⟨actions spoke louder than ~*s* in the trenches —Dixon Wecter⟩ **b :** recorded purity of breed (as of horses or plant strains) ⟨vouch for a horse's ~⟩ **4 :** a long line of succession (as of persons holding an office or continuing a tradition) ⟨the whole ~ of club presidents⟩ **syn** see ANCESTRY

²**pedigree** \"\ *adj* **:** having a pedigree **:** PUREBRED ⟨a ~ cocker spaniel⟩ ⟨a four-year-old ~ Guernsey bull —*Veterinary Record*⟩

³**pedigree** \"\ *vt* **pedigreed; pedigreed; pedigreeing; pedigrees :** to breed or propagate so that descent is known and can be recorded **:** provide with a pedigree

pedigree theory *n* **:** FAMILY-TREE THEORY

ped·i·lan·thus \,pedə'lan(t)thəs\ *n, cap* [NL, fr. Gk *pedilon* sandal + NL *-anthus;* akin to L *ped-, pes* foot — more at FOOT] **:** a genus of tropical American shrubby plants (family Euphorbiaceae) resembling cactus and differing from members of the genus *Euphorbia* chiefly in having an irregular involucre with a short spur on the upper side containing the glands

pe·dim·a·na \pə'dimənə; pedə'manə, -änə\ *n pl* [NL, fr. ¹*ped-* + *-mana*, fr. L *manus* hand — more at MANUAL] **1** *cap, in former classifications* **:** a division of Marsupialia equivalent to Didelphidae **2 :** QUADRUMANA

ped·i·mane \'pedə,mān\ *n* -s [NL *Pedimana*] **:** a mammal of the group Pedimana — **pe·dim·a·nous** \pə'dimənəs\ *adj*

ped·i·ment \'pedəmənt\ *n* -s [alter. of obs. E *periment*, prob. alter. of E *pyramid*] **1 a :** the triangular space forming the gable of a 2-pitched roof in classic architecture **b :** a similar form used as a decoration (as over porticoes, doors, windows) **c :** a rounded or broken frontal having a similar position and use **2 :** a part in decorative art resembling or suggestive of an architectural pediment in form and position **3** [perh. fr. It *pedamento* flooring, fr. L *pedamentum* vine prop, fr. *pedare* to supply with feet (fr. *ped-, pes* foot) + *-mentum* -ment — more at FOOT] **:** BASE 1a, PAVEMENT **4 :** a broad gently sloping bedrock surface with low relief that is situated at the foot of a much steeper mountain slope in an arid or semiarid region, is usu. covered with a thin veneer of alluvial gravel and sand, and is an erosional surface in contrast to a depositional piedmont plain

pediments 1

ped·i·men·tal \\ ⸗⸗ˈment³l\\ *adj* : of, relating to, or resembling a pediment
ped·i·men·ta·tion \\ˌpedəmənˈtāshən, -(ˌ)men-\\ *n* -s : the action or process that produces a geological pediment; *also* : the formation resulting from such an action or process
ped·i·ment·ed \\ˈ⸗⸗ˌmentəd\\ *adj* [*pediment* + *-ed*] : having or resembling a pediment ⟨a ~ gable was used —H.S.Morrison⟩
pedio- — see ²PEDI-
ped·io·coc·cus \\ˌpedēəˈkäkəs\\ *n* [NL, fr. ²*pedi-* + *-coccus*] **1** *cap, in some classifications* : a genus of micrococci (family Micrococcaceae) that grow in beer and wort producing clouding and acid **2** *pl* **pediococ·ci** \\-ˈkäˌkē, -ä(ˌ)kē, -äkˌsē, -äk(ˌ)sī\\ : any member of the genus *Pediococcus*
ped·i·oe·ce·tes \\ˌ⸗⸗ēˈsēd·(ˌ)ēz\\ *n, cap* [NL, fr. ²*pedi-* + Gk *oikētēs* dweller, fr. *oikein* to dwell, fr. *oikos* house — more at VICINITY] : a genus of birds (family Tetraonidae) consisting of the sharp-tailed grouse
ped·i·on \\ˈpedēˌän, ˈpēd-\\ *n, pl* **ped·ia** \\-dēə\\ [NL, fr. Gk, plain, flat surface, fr. *pedon* ground; akin to L *oppido* thoroughly, ON *fet* step, Skt *pada* step, track, L *ped-, pes* foot — more at FOOT] : a form of crystal having only a single face and belonging to the rare asymmetric class of the triclinic system
ped·i·on·o·mus \\ˌpedēˈänəməs\\ *n, cap* [NL, fr. Gk *pedionomos* plain-dweller, fr. *pedi-* + *-nomos* (fr. *nemein* to inhabit, pasture) — more at NIMBLE] : a monotypic genus of Australian birds (family Turnicidae) consisting of the plain wanderer and closely related to the button quails
ped·i·palp \\ˈpedəˌpalp, ˈpēdē-\\ *n* -s [NL *pedipalpus*] **1** : PEDIPALPUS **2** [NL *Pedipalpida*] : an arachnid of the order Pedipalpida
ped·i·pal·pal \\ˌ⸗⸗ˈpalpəl\\ *adj* [*pedipalp* + *-al*] : of or relating to a pedipalpus
ped·i·pal·pate \\-ˌpāt, -ˌpə̇t\\ *adj* [NL *pedipalpus* + E *-ate*] : having pedipalpi
ped·i·pal·pi \\ˌ⸗⸗ˈ⸗ˌpī\\ [NL *pedipalpus*] *syn of* PEDIPALPIDA
¹**ped·i·pal·pid** \\ˌ⸗⸗ˈ⸗pəd\\ *adj* [NL *Pedipalpida*] : of or relating to the Pedipalpida
²**pedipalpid** \\"\\ *n* -s : an arachnid of the order Pedipalpida
ped·i·pal·pi·da \\ˌ⸗⸗ˈ⸗pədə\\ *n pl, cap* [NL, fr. *pedipalpus* + *-ida*] : an order of Arachnida limited to warm or tropical regions that includes the whip scorpions and other moderate-sized arachnids having an unsegmented cephalothorax and a segmented flattened abdomen, small often retractile 2-segmented chelicerae, large usu. chelate pedipalps, and a slender many-jointed first pair of legs
ped·i·pal·pous \\ˌ⸗⸗ˈpalpəs\\ *adj* [NL *Pedipalpida* + E *-ous*] : of, relating to, or resembling the Pedipalpida
ped·i·pal·pus \\ˌ⸗⸗ˈ⸗pəs\\ *n, pl* **pedipal·pi** \\-ˌpī\\ [NL, fr. ¹*ped-* + *palpus*] : one of the second pair of appendages of an arachnid that lie on each side of the mouth and are variously developed in the different orders, that in spiders are small and resemble legs, in the scorpions are the largest appendages and end in pincers, and in the solpugids are long and resemble the four pairs of walking legs
ped·i·plain *or* **ped·i·plane** \\ˈpedəˌ+-\\ *n* [*pediment* + *plain*] : an extensive geological pediment or a plain resulting from the coalescence of two or more pediments
ped·i·pla·na·tion \\ˌ⸗⸗(ˌ)plāˈnāshən\\ *n* -s [*pediplane* + *-ation*] : pedimentation on a regional scale
ped·i·wak \\ˈpedəˌwak\\ *also* **pa·duak·an** \\pəˈdwakən\\ *n* -s [native name in Celebes] : a decked sailing boat of northern Celebes in the Malay archipelago
pedlar *or* **pedler** *var of* PEDDLER
¹**pedo-** — see PED-
²**pedo-** — see PAED-
pe·do·baptism *also* **pae·do·baptism** \\ˈpēdō+\\ *n* [*paed-* + *baptism*] : infant baptism
pe·do·baptist \\"+\\ *n* : one who advocates or practices infant baptism
ped·o·cal \\ˈpedəˌkal\\ *n* -s [²*ped-* + L *calc-, calx* lime — more at CHALK] : a soil that includes a definite hardened layer of accumulated carbonates — compare PEDALFER
pe·do·don·tia \\ˌpēdōˈdänch(ē)ə\\ *n* -s [NL, fr. *paed-* + *-odontia*] : PEDODONTICS
pe·do·don·tic \\ˌ⸗⸗ˈdäntik\\ *adj* [NL *pedodontia* + E *-ic*] : of or relating to pedodontics ⟨~ procedures⟩
pe·do·don·tics \\ˌ⸗⸗ˈ⸗tiks\\ *n pl but sing or pl in constr* : a branch of dentistry that is concerned with the dental care of children
pe·do·don·tist \\ˌ⸗⸗ˈdäntəst, ˈ⸗⸗ˌ⸗⸗\\ *n* -s [NL *pedodontia* + E *-ist*] : a specialist in pedodontics
pedogamy *var of* PAEDOGAMY
¹**pedogenesis** *var of* PAEDOGENESIS
²**ped·o·genesis** \\ˌpedō+\\ *n* [NL, fr. ²*ped-* + L *genesis*] : the formation and development of soil
ped·o·gen·ic \\ˌ⸗⸗ˈjenik\\ *adj* [²*ped-* + *-genic*] : of, relating to, or involved in soil formation ⟨~ agents⟩ ⟨~ processes⟩
ped·o·geography \\ˌ⸗⸗+\\ *n* [²*ped-* + *geography*] : the geography of soils
pedo·log·ic \\ˌpedōˈläjik, *in sense 2* ˌpēd-\\ *or* **pedo·log·i·cal** \\-jəkəl\\ *adj* **1** : of or relating to soil science **2** : of or relating to child study
¹**pe·dol·o·gist** \\pəˈdäləjəst\\ *n* -s [¹*pedology* + *-ist*] : a specialist in child study
²**pedologist** \\"\\ *n* -s [²*pedology* + *-ist*] : a soil scientist
¹**pe·dol·o·gy** \\-jē, -ji\\ *n* -ES [*paed-* + *-logy*] : the science and study of the life and development of children
²**pedology** \\"\\ *n* -ES [ISV ²*ped-* + *-logy;* prob. orig. formed as Russ *pedologiya*] : a science that treats of soils — called also *soil science*
pe·dom·e·ter \\pəˈdäməd·ə(r), -mətə-\\ *n* [F *pédomètre,* fr. *péd-* ped- + *-mètre* -meter] : an instrument usu. in watch form that records the distance a walker covers by responding to his body motion at each step — compare PASSOMETER
pedo·met·ri·cal \\ˌpedəˈmetrəkəl\\ *also* **pedo·met·ric** \\-ˈmetrik\\ *adj* : of, relating to, or functioning as a pedometer — **pedo·met·ri·cal·ly** \\-trək(ə)lē, -li\\ *adv*
pe·dom·e·tri·cian \\pəˌdäməˈtrishən\\ *n* -s [*pedometer* + *-ician*] : a pedometer maker
pedo·motive \\ˈpedə, ˈpēdə+\\ *adj* [¹*ped-* + *motive*] : moved by foot power (as of a velocipede)
pedo·motor \\ˈ⸗⸗+\\ *n* [¹*ped-* + *motor*] **1** : a machine (as a bicycle) driven by foot power **2** : a device (as a treadle) for applying foot power
pe·do·phil·ia *or* **pae·do·phil·ia** \\ˌpēdəˈfilēə\\ *n* -s [NL, fr. *paed-* + *-philia*] : paraphilia in which children are the preferred sexual object — **pe·do·phil·i·ac** \\ˌ⸗⸗ˈfilēˌak\\ *or* **pe·do·phil·ic** \\-ˈfilik\\ *adj*
pedo·sphere \\ˈpedə+ˌ-\\ *n* [²*ped-* + *sphere*] : a part of the earth's surface that contains the soil layer
ped·rail \\ˈped+ˌ-\\ *n* [¹*ped-* + *rail*] **1** : a tractor wheel with circular feet fastened about its periphery so that they come successively in contact with the road **2** : a vehicle (as a traction engine) having pedrails
pe·dre·ro \\pəˈdrə(ˌ)rō\\ *also* **pa·te·re·ro** \\ˌpäd·əˈre(ə)(ˌ)rō\\ *or* **pe·de·re·ro** \\ˌpädəˈre-\\ *n* -s [Sp *pedrero,* fr. ML *petraria,* fr. L, fem. of *petrarius* of stones, fr. *petra* stone (fr. Gk, rock, stone) + *-arius* -ary] : a piece of chambered ordnance used for throwing chiefly stones and scraps of iron
pe·dro \\ˈpē(ˌ)drō\\ *n* -s [Sp *Pedro* Peter] **1** : the five of trumps in card games of the all fours family **2** : a card game (as cinch) of the all fours family
pedro sancho *n* : SANCHO PEDRO
pe·dro xi·me·nez \\ˌpā(ˌ)drōhēˈmā(ˌ)nās\\ *n, usu cap P&X* [Sp *pedroximenes, pedrojimenez,* perh. fr. the name *Pedro Ximenes* or *Pedro Jimenez*] : a rich usu. sweet sherry from Pajarete near Arcos in Spain sometimes used for blending with and flavoring other wine
peds *pl of* PED
-peds *pl of* -PED
ped·ule \\ˈpeˌdyül\\ *n* -s [LL *pedulis,* fr. L, of the foot, fr. *ped-, pes* foot — more at FOOT] : a long socklike boot made of leather or cloth and worn esp. by ancient and early medieval Gauls
pe·dun·cle \\ˈpēˌdəŋkəl, ⸗ˈ⸗⸗\\ *n* -s [NL *pedunculus,* dim. of L *ped-, pes*] **1 a** : a stalk that bears a flower or a flower cluster — see PEDICEL 1b **b** : the stalk supporting the fructification in some thallophytes **2** : a narrow part by which some larger part or the whole body of an organism is attached (as the footstalk of a brachiopod or the petiole joining the abdomen of an ant or wasp to the thorax) : STEM, STALK, PEDICEL, PEDICLE — see BARNACLE illustration **3** : a band of white matter joining different parts of the brain ⟨the ~s of the pineal body pass from its base to the pillars of the fornix⟩ — see CEREBELLAR PEDUNCLE, CEREBRAL PEDUNCLE **4** : a narrow stalk by which a tumor or polyp is attached to an organ
pe·dun·cled \\-kəld\\ *adj* [*peduncle* + *-ed*] : pedunculate or as if pedunculate
pe·dun·cu·lar \\(ˈ)pēˈdəŋkyələ(r)\\ *adj* [NL *pedunculus* + E *-ar*] : of or relating to a peduncle
pe·dun·cu·late \\-lət, -ˌlāt, *usu* -d.+V\\ *or* **pe·dun·cu·lat·ed** \\-ˌlād·əd\\ *adj* [NL *pedunculus* + E *-ate* or *-ate* + *-ed*] : having a peduncle : growing on or from a peduncle ⟨a ~ flower⟩; *esp* : being attached by a peduncle ⟨a ~ tumor⟩
pedunculate barnacle *n* : a barnacle (as the goose barnacle) attached to the substrate by the base of a fleshy foot or stalk — compare SESSILE BARNACLE
pedunculate body *n* : a group of association neurones or their fibers in the insect forebrain
pedunculate oak *n* : ENGLISH OAK
pe·dun·cu·la·tion \\(ˌ)pēˌdəŋkyəˈlāshən\\ *n* -s [*pedunculate* + *-ion*] : the quality or state of being pedunculate
pe·dun·cu·lus \\⸗ˈ⸗⸗ləs\\ *n, pl* **peduncu·li** \\-ˌlī\\ [NL — more at PEDUNCLE] : PEDUNCLE
¹**pee** *also* **pe** \\ˈpē\\ *n* -s : the letter *p*
²**pee** \\ˈpē\\ *vi* **peed; peed; peeing; pees** [euphemism fr. the initial letter of *piss*] : URINATE — not often in polite use
³**pee** \\"\\ *n* -s **1** : URINE — not often in polite use **2** : an act of urination — often used with *take;* not often in polite use
⁴**pee** *var of* PEA
pee·bles·shire \\ˈpēbəl(z)ˌshi(ə)r, -lzh,-,-,shiə, -ˌshə(r)\\ *or* **pee·bles** \\ˈpēbəlz\\ *adj, usu cap* [fr. *Peeblesshire, Peebles,* county in southeast Scotland] : of or from the county of Peebles, Scotland : of the kind or style prevalent in Peebles
pee·gee hydrangea \\ˈpēˌjē-\\ *n* [*peegee* prob. fr. the initial letters of NL *paniculata* (specific epithet of *Hydrangea paniculata grandiflora*), fem. of *paniculatus* paniculate, and NL *grandiflora* (varietal epithet of *Hydrangea paniculata grandiflora*), fem. of *grandiflorus* large-flowered, fr. L *grandis* large, great + LL *-florus* -florous — more at PANICULATE, GRAND] : a shrub (*Hydrangea paniculata grandiflora*) having large panicles of white flowers that turn pink as the flowers mature
¹**peek** \\ˈpēk\\ *vi* -ED/-ING/-S [ME *piken*] **1** : to look slyly or furtively : peer through a crack or hole or from a place of concealment : PEEP ⟨~*ing* around the corner of the chair is a little girl —H.E.Salisbury⟩ — often used with *in* or *out* ⟨~*ed* in through a window —J.M.Flagler⟩ ⟨~ out at us from behind the curtains —Winifred Bambrick⟩ **2** : to take a brief look : GLANCE — usu. used with *at* ⟨~*ed* at his flashlight —Herbert Gold⟩
²**peek** \\"\\ *n* -s **1** : a surreptitious look : PEEP ⟨an investigatory ~ through the side window —S.H.Adams⟩ ⟨newest ~ into the royal boudoir —*Saturday Rev.*⟩ **2** : a brief look : GLANCE, GLIMPSE ⟨exclusive ~ at new products —*Modern Industry*⟩ ⟨a ~ inside the laboratory gives you some idea . . . of the future —*Dun's Rev.*⟩
¹**peek·a·boo** \\ˈpēkəˌbü\\ *n* [¹*peek* + connective *-a-* + *boo,* interj.] : a game for amusing a baby in which one repeatedly hides his face or body and pops back into view exclaiming "Peekaboo!"
²**peekaboo** \\ˌ⸗⸗ˈ⸗\\ *adj* **1** : trimmed with eyelet embroidery ⟨a ~ blouse⟩ **2** : made of sheer or transparent fabric ⟨dons a ~ negligee —S.J.Perelman⟩
¹**peel** \\ˈpēl, *esp before pause or consonant* -ēəl\\ *n* -s [ME *pele,* fr. OE *pyle* — more at PILLOW] *dial Eng* : PILLOW
²**peel** \\"\\ *vb* -ED/-ING/-S [ME *pelen* to rob, peel, fr. MF *peler* to peel, remove the hair from, fr. L *pilare* to remove the hair from, make bald, fr. *pilus* hair — more at PILE] *vt* **1** *obs* : ²PILL 1 **2 a** : to strip off the outer layer of : PARE, DECORTICATE ⟨~ an apple⟩ ⟨~*ing* potatoes⟩ ⟨machine automatically ~*s* . . . shrimp —*Time*⟩ **b** : to remove (the outer layer or covering) by stripping, tearing off, or rolling back — usu. used with *off* or *from* ⟨~*ing* off the skin of a banana⟩ ⟨~*ing* the white bark from his . . . trees —E.W.Smith⟩ ⟨stamps should never be ~*ed* from the paper —H.M.Ellis⟩ ⟨~*ed* the . . . shirt off over his head —Kay Boyle⟩ ⟨the canvas coverings were ~*ed* back —R.F.Mirvish⟩ **c** : to remove part of the bran from (the grains of wheat or rice) by abrasion **3** : to cause (a ball other than one's own) to pass through a wicket in croquet ⟨~*ed* his partner's ball through the last wicket⟩ ~ *vi* **1 a** : to become detached : come off : scale off : DESQUAMATE ⟨sunburned skin ~*s*⟩ ⟨the paint was ~*ing* off⟩ ⟨the . . . roof from which shingles were ~*ing* —Ellen Glasgow⟩ **b** : to lose the outer layer of skin ⟨his face is ~*ing*⟩ **2** : to take off one's clothes ⟨it got hotter . . . you had to ~ to get relief —L.M.Uris⟩ **syn** see SKIN
³**peel** \\"\\ *n* -s **1 a** : the skin or rind of a fruit ⟨letting the ~*s* drop on the floor —Truman Capote⟩ **b** : such rind candied ⟨orange ~⟩ **2** : a thin layer of organic material embedded in a film of collodion and stripped from the surface of an object (as a plant fossil) for microscopic study
⁴**peel** \\(ˈ)\\ *also* **peel tower** *n* -s [ME *pel, pele* castle, stockade, stake, fr. AF *pel, pele* stockade & MF *pel* stake, fr. L *palus* stake — more at POLE] : a medieval small massive fortified tower along the Scottish-English border having a usu. vaulted ground floor for confining and protecting cattle and a floor above for the family dwelling place reached by outside movable stairs or a ladder
⁵**peel** \\"\\ *n* -s [ME *pele* shovel, oven peel, fr. MF, shovel, fr. L *pala* spade, oven peel; prob. akin to L *pangere* to fix, fasten, plant — more at PACT] **1 a** : SHOVEL **b** *dial Eng* : a fire shovel **2** : a usu. long-handled spade-shaped instrument used chiefly by bakers (as for getting loaves and pies into and out of an oven) **3** : a T-shaped implement formerly in use by printers and papermakers for hanging up sheets of paper to dry
⁶**peel** *dial var of* PEAL
⁷**peel** \\ˈpēl, *esp before pause or consonant* -ēəl\\ *vt* -ED/-ING/-S [origin unknown] *Scot* : to equal : MATCH
⁸**peel** \\"\\ *n* -s **1** *chiefly Scot* : EQUAL, MATCH **2 peels** *pl, chiefly Scot* : an even game in curling : tie score ⟨it was ~*s* at 8 to 8 in the tenth head —*Time*⟩
⁹**peel** \\"\\ *Scot var of* POOL
¹⁰**peel** \\"\\ *chiefly dial var of* PAIL
peeled *adj* [ME (Sc) *peilit,* fr. past part. of *pelen* to peel] : BALD, TONSURED ⟨my ~ head and . . . white whiskers —Mark Twain⟩ ⟨~ priest —Shak.⟩
¹**peel·er** \\ˈpēlə(r)\\ *n* -s [ME *peler* pillager, plunderer, fr. *pelen* to rob, peel + *-er* — more at PEEL] **1** : one that peels : PARER, STRIPPER as **a** : one whose work it is to peel a specified thing ⟨potato ~ in a restaurant⟩ **b** : a worker who peels bark from felled trees or logs — called also *rosser, spudder* **c** : an instrument or machine that performs an operation of peeling, paring, or stripping ⟨the swivel-blade ~ . . . for fruit and vegetable paring —*Tools for Food Preparation & Dishwashing*⟩ ⟨electric paint ~⟩ **d** : STRIPTEASER **2** : a crab that has begun to shed its shell **3** : a log of softwood (as Douglas fir) having a diameter of 24 or more inches and suitable for cutting into veneer that is peeled cylindrically from the log by a lathe **4 a** : long-staple cotton orig. from the Delta region of northwestern Mississippi **b** : yarn spun from such cotton **5** : an energetic industrious person : HUSTLER ⟨a real ~ for work —Esther Forbes⟩ **6** : a cowhand who specializes in breaking horses
²**peeler** \\"\\ *n* -s [origin unknown] *dial Eng* : an iron bar used to make holes in the ground esp. for hop poles
³**peeler** \\"\\ *n* -s [Sir Robert *Peel* †1850 Eng. statesman who instituted the Irish constabulary + E *-er*] *Brit* : POLICE OFFICER; *specif* : a policeman of the lowest rank ⟨an officious ~ arrested him as a vagabond —W.B.Yeats⟩
peelgarlic *var of* PILGARLIC
peel·ing \\ˈpēliŋ, -ēŋ\\ *n* -s **1** : a peeled-off piece or strip (as of skin or rind) : PEEL **2** *archaic* : a thin dress material **3** : a defect in a ceramic glaze or enamel caused by high contraction
peel·ite \\ˈpēˌlīt\\ *n* -s *usu cap* [Sir Robert *Peel* + E *-ite*] : one of a group of 19th century British Tories supporting Peel in the repeal of the Corn Laws and later maintaining a position between the protectionist Tories and the Liberals until eventually merging with the Liberals
peel off *vi* **1** : to veer away from in a wingover to the outside of a flight formation esp. from the bottom of an echelon for a steep dive or for a landing **2** : to veer away from ships in convoy (as for an attack upon a submarine)
peels *pl of* PEEL, *pres 3d sing of* PEEL
¹**peen** *also* **pean** \\ˈpēn\\ *vt* -ED/-ING/-S [prob. of Scand origin; akin to Norw *penne* to hammer out thin, fr. *penn,* n., peen] **1** : to draw, bend or flatten (as metal or leather) by hammering with a peen **2** : to work the surface of (metal) by a stream of shot ⟨great improvement has been brought about in the service life of springs by shot ~*ing* —D.K.Bullens⟩
²**peen** *or* **pein** *also* **pean** \\ˈpēn\\ *n* -s [prob. of Scand origin; akin to Norw *penn* peen, Sw *pen*] : the hemispherical, wedge-shaped, or otherwise formed end of the head of a hammer opposite the face, used for bending, indenting, or cutting the material being struck — compare BALL PEEN, CROSS PEEN

peens: *1* straight peen; *2* cross peen; *3* ball peen

peenge \\ˈpēnzh, -nj\\ *vi* -ED/-ING/-S [prob. imit.] *chiefly Scot* : to complain : GRUMBLE
peening rammer *n* : PEGGING RAMMER
peen-to \\ˈpēnˌtō\\ *n* -s [Chin (Pek) *pien³ t'ao²,* fr. *pien³* flat + *t'ao²* peach] : any of several peaches with a flattened shape; *esp* : a peach of Chinese origin grown in the southern U.S.
pee·oy \\pēˈōi\\ *n* -s [prob. imit.] *Scot* : a cone of damp gunpowder used for fireworks
¹**peep** \\ˈpēp\\ *vi* -ED/-ING/-S [ME *pepen,* of imit. origin] **1** : to utter a feeble shrill sound as of a bird hatching or newly hatched : CHEEP, CHIRP ⟨a brood of chickens ~*ed* in a coop —*Harper's*⟩ **2** : to speak with a small weak voice : utter the slightest sound ⟨every time he ~*s,* she jumps to see what's the matter —Benjamin Spock⟩
²**peep** \\"\\ *n* -s [ME *pepe,* fr. *pepen* to peep, chirp] **1** : a feeble shrill sound (as by a young chicken or mouse) : CHEEP, CHIRP, SQUEAK **2** : a slight utterance esp. of complaint or protest ⟨don't let me hear another ~ out of you⟩ **3 a** : any of several small sandpipers: as (1) : LEAST SANDPIPER (2) : SEMIPALMATED SANDPIPER **b** *Brit* : MEADOW PIPIT
³**peep** \\"\\ *vb* -ED/-ING/-S [ME *pepen,* perh. alter. of *piken* to peek] *vi* **1 a** : to peer through or as if through a crevice ⟨~*ing* . . . out from chinks and knotholes —George Orwell⟩ **b** : to look cautiously or slyly : PEEK, SPY ⟨~ behind the scenes⟩ ⟨would never . . . ~ under her bed —Oliver Goldsmith⟩ **2** : to begin to emerge from or as if from concealment : become partly evident : show slightly — usu. used with *through, out,* or *from* ⟨crocuses ~*ing* through the grass⟩ ⟨the ancient belief . . . keeps ~*ing* out in unexpected quarters —C.W.Cunnington⟩ ⟨his brown curls ~*ed* from the edges of his cap —Marcia Davenport⟩ ~ *vt* : to put forth or cause to protrude slightly (as the head of one peeping) — usu. used with *out* ⟨not a dangerous action can ~ out his head —Shak.⟩
⁴**peep** \\"\\ *n* -s **1** : the first glimpse or faint appearance ⟨at the ~ of dawn⟩ **2 a** : a slight or brief look : GLANCE ⟨take a quick ~ at the past —*London Calling*⟩ **b** : a furtive look through or as if through a crevice or from or into a hiding place : PEEK ⟨a ~ at the neighbors through the blinds⟩ **3** : PEEP SIGHT **4** : PEEKABOO
⁵**peep** *n* -s [obs. E *peep* one of the dots used on dice and dominoes to indicate numerical value, of unknown origin] *obs* : STEP, DEGREE
⁶**peep** \\ˈpēp\\ *n* -s [by alter.] : JEEP
peep-bo \\ˈ⸗ˌbō\\ *n* -s [³*peep* + *boo,* interj.] : PEEKABOO
¹**peep·er** \\ˈpēpə(r)\\ *n* -s [¹*peep* + *-er*] **1** : one (as a young chicken or pigeon) that peeps or chirps **2** : any of various frogs (esp. of the family Hylidae) that make peeping sounds; *specif* : SPRING PEEPER ⟨the sound of ~*s* in springtime pools —*Sat. Eve. Post*⟩
²**peeper** \\"\\ *n* -s [³*peep* + *-er*] **1** : one that peeps; *specif* : PEEPING TOM, VOYEUR **2** : EYE — usu. used in pl. ⟨let his ~*s* roll over towards our table —Ring Lardner⟩
peep frog *n* : ¹PEEPER 2
peep hawk *n, Irish* : KESTREL
peephole \\ˈ⸗ˌ⸗\\ *n* : a hole or crevice (as in a furnace, oven, or door) through which one may peep ⟨a ~ was uncovered, an eye peered at me, the door was opened —Joseph Wechsberg⟩
peeping tom *n* -s *often cap P&T* [after *Peeping Tom,* legendary 11th cent. tailor of Coventry supposed to have been struck blind for peeping at Lady Godiva as she rode naked through the town in order to win relief for its inhabitants from burdensome taxation] : a pruriently prying person : VOYEUR, PEEPER ⟨*peeping toms* . . . who spy on spooning couples —Morris Ploscowe⟩
peep show *n* : a small show or object exhibited that is viewed through an orifice or a magnifying glass ⟨a carnival with *peep shows* and flea acts —Stanley Walker⟩ ⟨sexual exhibitions reminiscent of the modern . . . *peep show* —Ralph Linton⟩
peep sight *n* : a rear sight having an adjustable metal piece pierced with a small hole to peep through in aiming
peepul *also* **peepal** *var of* PIPAL
peepy \\ˈpēpē, -pi\\ *adj* -ER/-EST [³*peep* + *-y*] *dial Eng* : SLEEPY ⟨the potboy, very tousled and ~ —Ngaio Marsh⟩
¹**peer** \\ˈpi(ə)r, -iə\\ *n* -s [ME *peer, peere,* fr. OF *per,* fr. *per,* adj., equal, fr. L *par* — more at PAIR] **1 a** : one that is of the same or equal standing (as in law, rank, quality, age, ability) with another : EQUAL ⟨scholars of the first rank welcomed him as their ~ —B.W.Bond⟩ ⟨an electrode material without ~ —B.W.Gamson⟩ ⟨boys and girls in their teens . . . form groups of their ~*s* —Martha M. Eliot⟩ **b** : a fellow citizen ⟨a jury of his ~*s*⟩ **2** *archaic* : COMPANION, FELLOW **3 a** : a member of one of the five ranks of the British peerage (as a duke, marquess, earl, viscount, or baron) **b** : a man of high rank or position in any country or organization that recognizes different orders : NOBLE ⟨high capital of Satan and his ~*s* —John Milton⟩
²**peer** \\"\\ *vt* -ED/-ING/-S [ME *peeren, peren,* fr. *peer, peere,* n.] *archaic* : to equal in rank : be the peer of : RIVAL, MATCH
³**peer** \\"\\ *adj* [¹*peer*] : belonging to the same group in society esp. when membership is determined by age, grade, or status ⟨a ~ group of adolescents⟩ ⟨school children oriented to ~ culture values, rather than adult ones⟩
⁴**peer** *obs var of* PIER
⁵**peer** \\ˈpi(ə)r, -iə\\ *vi* -ED/-ING/-S [perh. by shortening & alter. fr. *appear*] **1** : to look intently or curiously : STARE ⟨the natives . . . were ~*ing* from behind trees —Francis Birtles⟩ ⟨~*ing* impudently into your face —L.C.Douglas⟩; *esp* : to look searchingly at something difficult to discern ⟨~*ing* into the distance⟩ ⟨drove . . . and began to ~ at the signs on street corners —Raymond Chandler⟩ **2** : to come slightly into view : emerge partly : peep out ⟨when daffodils begin to ~ —Shak.⟩ ⟨a vast white cloud, through which the sun ~*ed* —Francis Kingdon-Ward⟩ **3** *archaic* : APPEAR ⟨darkly a project ~*s* upon my mind —John Home⟩ **syn** see GAZE
⁶**peer** \\ˈpēr\\ *Scot var of* POOR
peer·age \\ˈpirij, -rēj\\ *n* -s [ME *perage,* fr. *peer, peere* peer + *-age*] **1** : the body of peers : NOBILITY ⟨Charlemagne with all his ~ —John Milton⟩ **2** : the rank or dignity of a peer ⟨the prime minister submitted the industrialist's name for a ~⟩ **3** : a book containing a list of the peers with their genealogy, history, and titles ⟨his name is in the ~⟩
peer·ess \\-rəs\\ *n* -ES **1** : the wife or widow of a peer **2** : a woman who holds in her own right the rank of a peer
¹**peer·ie** *or* **peery** \\ˈpērī\\ *n, pl* **peeries** [perh. irreg. fr. ¹*pear* + *-ie;* fr. its shape] *chiefly Scot* : PEG TOP 1
²**peerie** \\"\\ *adj* [origin unknown] *Scot* : SMALL ⟨a ~ lad⟩
peer·ing·ly *adv* [*peering* (pres. part. of ⁵*peer*) + *-ly*] : in a peering manner
peer·less \\ˈpi(ə)rləs, ˈpiəl-\\ *adj* [ME *pereles,* fr. *pere, peer, peere* peer + *-les* -less] : MATCHLESS, INCOMPARABLE ⟨~ among women —H.O.Taylor⟩ ⟨his ~ readings —Margaret Rutherford⟩ — **peer·less·ly** *adv* — **peer·less·ness** *n* -ES
peert \\ˈpi(ə)r|t, -iə|, *usu* |d.+V\\ *var of* PEART
peery \\ˈpirē, -ri\\ *adj* -ER/-EST [⁵*peer* + *-y*] : INQUISITIVE, SUSPICIOUS ⟨~ envious eyes —Bruce Marshall⟩
pees *pl of* PEE, *pres 3d sing of* PEE
pees·weep *or* **peese·weep** \\ˈpēzˌwēp\\ *also* **pee·weep** \\ˈpē-

,wēp\ *n* -s [imit.] 1 *dial Brit* : LAPWING 2 *dial Brit* : GREENFINCH

peet·weet \'pē,twēt, *usu* -wēd·+V\ *n* -s [imit.] : SPOTTED SANDPIPER

¹peeve \'pēv\ *vt* -ED/-ING/-S [back-formation fr. *peevish*] : to make peevish or resentful : ANNOY ⟨don't believe you'll ever be able to ~ that boy —H.L.Wilson⟩ ⟨was very *peeved* about being left out —C.B.Palmer b. 1910⟩ **syn** see IRRITATE

²peeve \"\ *n* -s 1 : a peevish mood : a feeling of resentment ⟨in a ~ over it⟩ ⟨the atmosphere . . . charged with ~ —R.L. Taylor⟩ 2 : a particular grievance : GRUDGE ⟨grumbling their pet ~s as they go —R.L.Smith⟩

peev·er \'pēvər\ *n* -s [origin unknown] 1 *Scot* : a stone used in hopscotch 2 **peevers** *pl* : HOPSCOTCH

pee·vish \'pēvish, -vēsh\ *adj* [ME *pevish* spiteful] 1 : morose or querulous in temperament or mood : hard to please : IRRITABLE, FRETFUL ⟨had never known her so ~ —W.M. Thackeray⟩ ⟨rather ~ with waiting —Edmund Wilson⟩ 2 : perversely obstinate : CONTRARY ⟨the forwardness of ~ children —Edmund Burke⟩ ⟨a frequently ~ struggle against the universal spirit of innovation —Daniel Aaron⟩ 3 : marked by ill temper (as actions or words) ⟨with a ~ gesture she slapped over the rest of the notes —A.J.Cronin⟩ ⟨her accent was ~ —Jane Austen⟩ ⟨that ~ sort of criticism —*Times Lit. Supp.*⟩ **syn** see IRRITABLE

pee·vish·ly \-vəshlē, -vēsh-, -li\ *adv* : in a peevish manner ⟨everybody ordered him around, he complained to himself ~ —John Dos Passos⟩

pee·vish·ness \-vishnəs, -vēsh-\ *n* -ES [ME *pevyshnesse* spitefulness, fr. *pevysh, peyish* spiteful + *-nesse* -ness] : the quality or state of being peevish : PETULANCE ⟨mumbled with childish ~ —Richard Blaker⟩

peevit *var of* PEWIT

peevy *var of* PEAVEY

¹pee·wee *or* **pe·wee** \'pē,wē\ *n* -s [imit.] 1 a *usu* **pewee** : any of various small olivaceous flycatchers; *esp* : WOOD PEWEE b *Scot* : LAPWING c *Austral* : MAGPIE LARK 2 : something diminutive or tiny: as a : a small child b : an abnormally small animal : RUNT c *dial* : a small marble usu. of poor quality d : an egg of the smallest size e : a low-topped cowboy boot

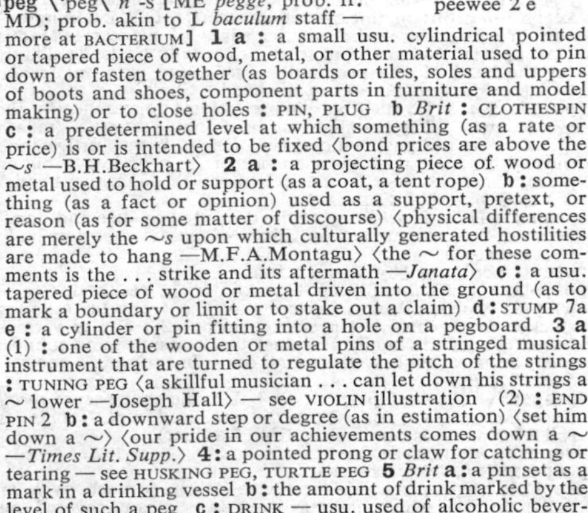
peewee 2 e

²peewee \"\ *adj* : DIMINUTIVE, TINY ⟨the ~ doorman —Earle Birney⟩ ⟨a little ~ vial of vinegar —Kenneth Roberts⟩ ⟨league of ~ players⟩

peewit *var of* PEWIT

peff \'pef\ *dial Eng var of* PEGH

¹peg \'peg\ *n* -s [ME *pegge*, prob. fr. MD; prob. akin to L *baculum* staff — more at BACTERIUM] 1 a : a small usu. cylindrical pointed or tapered piece of wood, metal, or other material used to pin down or fasten together (as boards or tiles, soles and uppers of boots and shoes, component parts in furniture and model making) or to close holes : PIN, PLUG b *Brit* : CLOTHESPIN c : a predetermined level at which something (as a rate or price) is or is intended to be fixed ⟨bond prices are above the ~s —B.H.Beckhart⟩ 2 a : a projecting piece of wood or metal used to hold or support (as a coat, a tent rope) b : something (as a fact or opinion) used as a support, pretext, or reason (as for some matter of discourse) ⟨physical differences are merely the ~s upon which culturally generated hostilities are made to hang —M.F.A.Montagu⟩ ⟨the ~ for these comments is the . . . strike and its aftermath —*Janata*⟩ c : a usu. tapered piece of wood or metal driven into the ground (as to mark a boundary or limit or to stake out a claim) d : STUMP 7a e : a cylinder or pin fitting into a hole on a pegboard 3 a (1) : one of the wooden or metal pins of a stringed musical instrument that are turned to regulate the pitch of the strings : TUNING PEG ⟨a skillful musician . . . can let down his strings a ~ lower —Joseph Hall⟩ — see VIOLIN illustration (2) : END PIN 2 b : a downward step or degree (as in estimation) ⟨set him down a ~⟩ ⟨our pride in our achievements comes down a ~ —*Times Lit. Supp.*⟩ 4 : a pointed prong or claw for catching or tearing — see HUSKING PEG, TURTLE PEG 5 *Brit* a : a pin set as a mark in a drinking vessel b : the amount of drink marked by the level of such a peg c : DRINK — usu. used of alcoholic beverages ⟨poured himself out a stiff ~ —Dorothy Sayers⟩ 6 a : something felt to resemble a peg (as a foot, leg, tooth, kernel of corn) b : a wooden leg c : the elongated hypanthium of the peanut flower that bends over and forms the subterranean stem on which the pod is borne 7 : PEG TOP 8 [²*peg*] : THROW; *esp* : one made in baseball by a fielder or a baseman ⟨scooped up hot grounders with one hand . . . and made lightning ~s to first —Edwin Corle⟩

²peg \"\ *vb* **pegged**; **pegged**; **pegging**; **pegs** *vt* 1 a : to put a peg into : pin, attach, fasten together, plug, or block with a peg ⟨~ a notice to a post⟩ ⟨~ shoes⟩ ⟨~ seedlings⟩ ⟨a wooden plank . . . *pegged* to the ground —J.G.Frazer⟩ ⟨articles should be *pegged* to a workboard —F.J.Christopher⟩ b *Brit* : to pin or hang (laundry) on a clothesline — usu. used with *up* ⟨in the garden *pegging* up the clothes⟩ c : to keep in place : pin down : RESTRICT — usu. used with *down* ⟨set on *pegging* him safely down —Clemence Dane⟩ d : to fix or hold (as prices, wages, rate of exchange) at a constant or predetermined point or level ⟨*pegging* the price of grapefruit —*New Republic*⟩ ⟨the ruble was *pegged* at four to the dollar —Horace Sutton⟩ e : to place in a definite category : nail down : IDENTIFY ⟨had you *pegged* for one of these ladies with fainting spells —Wallace Stegner⟩ ⟨*pegging* it as the cause of vast future unemployment —D.S.Harder⟩ f : to give (something) support, reason, or relevance by attaching it to or making it depend on something else ⟨~ your sales talk to some recent happening⟩ ⟨broadcasts . . . *pegged* to themes that reflect a continuing propaganda compaign —H.R.Lieberman⟩ 2 *obs* : HAMMER 3 : to strike or pierce (as a turtle, lobster, shellfish) with a thrown peg 4 : to score (a specified number of points) in cribbage esp. by advancing a peg on the board 5 : to mark (as a boundary) by pegs — usu. used with *out* ⟨~ out a certain patch for the hose —*Gadgets Annual*⟩; *specif* : to mark out (a miner's claim or an agricultural selection) at the four corners by pegs bearing the claimant's name ⟨had got in first . . . had *pegged* out a claim —Eleanor Dark⟩ 6 *of a hunting dog* : POINT 7 a : to throw (as a baseball) esp. low and fast ⟨the shortstop *pegged* the ball to the first baseman⟩ ⟨*pegged* stones at the trains —Rosemary V. Donatelli⟩ b : to retire (a batter or base runner) in baseball by a throw to a base or to home plate ⟨*pegged* the runner at third⟩ — often used with *out* ⟨*pegged* the runner out⟩ ~ *vi* 1 : to throw, cast, or let fly with a missile (as a peg) or ball; *specif* : to cast a fly in fishing 2 : to work steadily and diligently : PLOD, PLUG — usu. used with *away, at, on* ⟨*pegging* away at his writing —Brooks Atkinson⟩ ⟨find it terribly hard to ~ at things —*Atlantic*⟩ 3 : to move along vigorously or hastily : HUSTLE ⟨*pegging* down the stairs —Elizabeth Bowen⟩ 4 : to make a score (as in cribbage) esp. when the score is recorded on a pegboard

³peg \"\ *or* **pegged** \'pegd\ *adj* : PEG-TOP ⟨had on a black coat and black ~ pants —Thurston Scott⟩

PEG *abbr* prior endorsement guaranteed

pe·ga \'pägə\ *or* **peg·a·dor** \,pegə'dō(ə)r, -ō(ə)\ *n* -s [*pega* fr. Sp, lit., act of sticking, fr. *pegar* to stick, paste, cling, fr. L *picare* to daub with pitch, fr. *pic-, pix* pitch; *pegador* fr. Sp, fr. *pegar* — more at PITCH] : REMORA

peg and eye *n* : LOOP HINGE

peg-and-socket \¦==¦=\ *adj* : of, relating to, or constituting the method of jointing of the scales in ganoid fishes by which processes suggestive of pegs on the anterior end of a scale fit into corresponding depressions in the posterior end of the one in front of it

peg·a·num \'pegənəm\ *n, cap* [NL, fr. Gk *pēganon* rue; prob. akin to Gk *pēgnynai* to fix, fasten together — more at PACT] : a widely distributed genus of herbs (family Zygophyllaceae) having alternate leaves and large white solitary flowers with 12 to 15 stamens — see AFRICAN RUE

peg·a·se·an \,pegə¦sēən, pə'gāsēən\ *also* **pe·ga·si·an** \pə'gāsēən\ *adj, usu cap* [*pegasean* fr. L *pegaseus* pegasean (fr. *Pegasus*, mythological winged horse + *-eus* -eous) + E *-an*; *pegasian* alter. of *pegasean*] 1 : of, relating to, or resembling the mythological winged horse Pegasus; *esp* : SWIFT 2 : of or relating to poetic inspiration : highly imaginative : POETIC

peg·a·sid \'pegəsəd, -,sid\ *n* -s [NL *Pegasidae*] : a fish of the family Pegasidae

pe·gas·i·dae \pə'gasə,dē\ *n pl, cap* [NL, fr. *Pegasus*, type genus + *-idae*] : a small family (order Hypostomides) of marine fishes — see PE-TSAI

peg·a·soid \'pegə,sȯid\ *adj* [NL *Pegasus* + E *-oid*] : like or related to the Pegasidae

peg·a·sus \'pegəsəs\ *n* [L *Pegasus*, mythological winged horse fabled to have created by a blow of his hoof the fountain Hippocrene that was supposed to be a source of poetic inspiration, fr. Gk *Pēgasos*] 1 *pl* **pegasi** \-ə,sī\ *or* **pegasuses** *often cap* a : a fabulous winged horse ⟨many interesting figures of . . . griffins, *pegasi* —G.W.Eve⟩; *esp* : the winged steed thought of as bearing a poet in his flights of fancy b : poetic inspiration ⟨each spurs his jaded *Pegasus* apace —Lord Byron⟩ 2 [NL, fr. L *Pegasus*, mythological winged horse] a *cap* : a genus (the type and best known genus of the family Pegasidae) of small chiefly tropical Indo-Pacific marine fishes having a long snout, a small toothless mouth, a body wholly covered with bony plates, pelvic fins of only two rays, and pectoral fins spread horizontally like a pair of wings b -ES : any fish of the genus *Pegasus* : SEA MOTH

pegboard \'=,=\ *n* 1 : a small usu. about 6 in. x 6 in. board perforated with a pattern of holes into which pegs are stuck in playing certain games (as solitaire) 2 : an educational toy consisting of a board with holes into which a child hammers or thrusts pegs

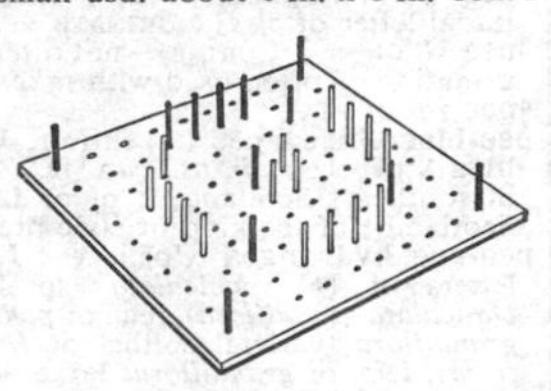
pegboard 2

pegbox \'=,=\ *n* : the open part of the head in a stringed musical instrument in which pegs are set

peg float *also* **peg cutter** *n* : a short knife set at an angle across the end of a shaft that is inserted into finished pegged shoes to cut off the protruding peg ends

pegged *adj* [fr. past part. of ²*peg*] 1 : maintained at or near a predetermined level, rate, or price ⟨~ rate of exchange⟩ ⟨buying at the present ~ prices⟩ 2 : PEG-TOPPED ⟨sharply ~ pants with deep pleats —Irving Shulman⟩

pegged boot *also* **peg boot** *n* : a boot having soles fastened on by wooden pegs

pegged shoe *also* **peg shoe** *n* : a shoe having soles fastened on by wooden pegs

pegged splint *n* : a splint or exostosis on the back of the cannon bone of a quadruped that lies beneath the flexor tendons and frequently interferes with their movement causing lameness

pegging *pres part of* PEG

pegging rammer *n* : a rammer used in a foundry for soft open sand courses that consists of an oblong piece of iron varying usu. from a quarter of an inch to an inch in thickness which is secured to the end of a piece of tubing or bar iron

cross section of a pegged shoe: *1* lining, *2* upper, *3* insole, *4* outsole, *5* lasting tack, *6* peg

peg graft *n* : a side graft in which a scion of leafless dormant wood with wedge-shaped base is driven into an opening cut in the stock and sealed with wax or other material

¹peg·gy \'pegē, -gi\ *n* -ES [fr. *Peggy*, nickname fr. the name *Margaret*] *dial Eng* : any of several small birds: as a : WHITETHROAT b : BLACKCAP c : CHIFFCHAFF d : WILLOW WREN

²peggy \"\ *adj* [by alter.] : PECKY 1

¹pegh \'pef, 'pek\ *vi* -ED/-ING/-S [ME (northern dial.) *pechen*, prob. of imit. origin] *dial chiefly Scot* : to breathe hard after bodily exercise : PANT

²pegh \"\ *n* -s *dial chiefly Scot* : a breath taken with difficulty : PANT

peg in the ring : a game of spinning a peg top within the bounds of a marked-out circle

¹peg leg *n* [¹*peg* + *leg*] 1 : an artificial leg; *esp* : one fitted to the bent knee 2 : a person wearing such a leg ⟨tale . . . concerns a choleric British ex-soldier and *peg leg* —Anthony West⟩

²peg leg *vi* : to strike bottom only intermittently or on alternate strokes — used of a cable tool in drilling

pegma *also* **pegme** *n* -s [L *pegmat-, pegma*, fr. Gk *pēgmat-, pēgma* framework, stage or scaffold in theaters, fr. *pēgnynai* to fix, fasten together — more at PACT] 1 *obs* : a movable theatrical structure used esp. in pageants 2 *obs* : an inscription on a pegma

peg·man \'=mən\ *n, pl* **pegmen** : a man who attends to a peg (as one blocking a power hammer)

peg·ma·tite \'pegmə,tīt\ *n* -s [F, fr. Gk *pēgmat-, pēgma* something fastened together, framework + F *-ite*] 1 : GRAPHIC GRANITE 2 a : a natural igneous rock formation consisting of a variety of granite that occurs in dikes or veins and is usu. characterized by extremely coarse texture caused by crystallization from an exceptionally fluid magma rich in mineralizers containing rare elements that frequently form unusual minerals (as tourmaline spodumene, beryl) b : a similar formation in a rock other than granite ⟨syenite ~⟩ ⟨diorite ~⟩

peg·ma·tit·ic \¦==¦tid·ik\ *adj* [ISV *pegmatite* + *-ic*] : having a texture like that of pegmatite

peg·ma·tit·ization \,==,tīd·ə'zāshən, -d·,ī'z-\ *n* -s [*pegmatite* + *-ization*] : the formation of pegmatite from other rocks

peg·ma·tize \'==,tīz\ *vt* -ED/-ING/-S [*pegmatite* + *-ize*] : to convert into pegmatite

¹peg·ma·toid \-,tȯid\ *adj* [*pegmatite* + *-oid*] : PEGMATITIC

²pegmatoid \"\ *n* -s 1 : a pegmatite containing a feldspathoid as an essential constituent 2 : a coarse-grained pegmatite of normal habit as distinguished from graphic granite

peg·mat·o·phyre \peg'mad·ə,fī(ə)r\ *n* -s [*pegmatite* + *-o-* + *-phyre*] : a granite porphyry with micropegmatitic groundmass

peg organ *n* : an insect sense organ that is basically an innervated hair

peg out *vt* 1 : to put out of the game in croquet by making (a rover ball) hit the stake 2 : to toss out or allow to run out (as a line) : pay out ~ *vi* 1 a : to end one's play by pegging out one's ball in croquet b : to score the winning point in a cribbage game 2 a : to give out : FAIL b : DIE ⟨you only pretend to care because you thought I was going to *peg out* —Miles Franklin⟩

pegs *pl of* PEG, *pres 3d sing of* PEG

peg shoe *var of* PEGGED SHOE

peg switch *n* : PLUG SWITCH

peg tankard *n* : a tankard with a vertical row of pegs set at equal distances on the inner surface to mark the quantity of drink permitted each person at the passing of the cup

peg tooth *n* 1 : a sawtooth shaped like a peg 2 : a cylindrical or conical gear-wheel tooth projecting axially or radially from the rim of the wheel

peg-tooth harrow *n* : a harrow consisting of a set of horizontal transverse wooden or iron bars fitted with wooden or iron teeth

peg top *n* 1 : a pear-shaped wooden top that ends in a sharp metal peg and that is made to spin by the unwinding of a string wound round its center 2 : a game played with peg tops 3 **peg tops** *pl* : peg-top trousers

peg-top \'=¦=\ *or* **peg-topped** \'=¦=\ *adj* [*peg-top* fr. *peg top*; *peg-topped* fr. *peg top* + *-ed*] : wide at the top and narrow at the bottom — used esp. of trousers, skirts, and pockets with pleated or draped fullness at the top

¹pe·gu·an \pe'güən\ *adj, usu cap* [*Pegu*, town, district, division, and river in south central Burma + E *-an*] : of, relating to, or characteristic of Pegu, Burma

²peguan \"\ *n* -s *cap* : a native or resident of Pegu, Burma : MON

pe·gu catechu \pe'gü-\ *n, usu cap P* : CATECHU 1 a

pegwood \'=,=\ *n* 1 : a spindle tree (*Euonymus europaeus*) 2 : wood used in splints whittled to a point for cleaning out pivot holes in watchmaking

pehlevi *cap, var of* PAHLAVI

peh-tsai *var of* PE-TSAI

peign·oir *R* pān'wä(r), '=,= *also* -wȯ(ə)r; *–R* -wå(r *also* -wȯ(ə)(r\ *n* -s [F, peignoir, garment worn over the shoulders while combing the hair, fr. MF, garment worn over the shoulders while combing the hair, fr. *peigner* to comb the hair, fr. L *pectinare* to comb, fr. *pectin-, pecten* comb — more at PECTINATE] : a woman's loose negligee or dressing gown

pein *var of* PEEN

pei·ping \'pā¦piŋ, 'bā¦-\ *adj, usu cap* [*Peiping* (name used by the Nationalist government of China) (fr. Chin — Pek — *Pe⁴ p'ing²*, fr. *pe⁴* north + *p'ing²* peace), *Peking* (name used up to 1928 by the imperial and republican governments of China and since 1949 by the Communist government) (fr. Chin — Pek — *Pe⁴ ching¹*, fr. *pe⁴* north + *ching¹* capital), city in northeast China that was the capital up to 1928 and has been the capital of the Communist government of China since 1949] : PEKING

pei·ram·e·ter \pī'ramədə(r), -ətə-\ *n* [Gk *peira* trial, attempt + E *-meter*; akin to Gk *peiran* to attempt — more at FEAR] : a dynamometer of the kind used to indicate the power necessary to haul a truck or carriage over a road or track

pei·ras·tic \(')pī¦rastik, -tēk\ *also* **pei·ras·ti·cal** \-təkəl, -tēk-\ *adj* [Gk *peirastikos*, fr. *peiran* to attempt] : fitted for trial : EXPERIMENTAL, TENTATIVE — **pei·ras·ti·cal·ly** \-tək(ə)lē, -tēk-, -li\ *adv*

peirc·e·an \'pərsēən *also* 'pirs-\ *adj, usu cap* [Charles S. *Peirce* †1914 Am. physicist, mathematician, and logician + E *-an*] : of, relating to, or resembling Charles Sanders Peirce or his philosophical teachings (as pragmatism, metaphysical realism) — compare FIRSTNESS, SECONDNESS, THIRDNESS

pei·res·kia \pə'reskēə, pē'-\ *n, cap* [NL, fr. Nicolas-Claude Fabri de *Peiresc* †1637 Fr. antiquarian and naturalist + NL *-ia*] : a genus of shrubby spinose tropical American plants (family Cactaceae) having slender branches, broad flat leaves, and large pyramidal flowers — see BARBADOS GOOSEBERRY

¹peise \'pāz, 'pēz\ *n* -s [ME *peis*, fr. ONF, fr. L *pensum* — more at POISE] 1 *dial Brit* : WEIGHT 2 *dial Brit* : BALANCE, POISE

²peise \"\ *vb* -ED/-ING/-S [ME *peisen*, fr. ONF *peser* (3d pers. sing. pres. indic. *peise*), fr. L *pensare* to weigh (something) — more at PENSIVE] *vi* 1 *dial Brit* : to have weight : WEIGH 2 *dial Brit* : to bear down with weight ~ *vt* 1 *dial Brit* : to estimate the weight of : weigh (as in the hand) 2 *dial Brit* : to exert weight or force upon : open or lift by force

peishwa *var of* PESHWA

pei·xe re *or* **pei·xe-rei** *or* **pei·xe·rey** \,pāshə'rā\ *n* -s [Pg *peixe-rei* silversides, fr. *peixe* fish (fr. L *piscis*) + *rei* king, fr. L *reg-, rex* — more at FISH, ROYAL] : any of several silversides (as the jacksmelt of California)

pej·er·rey \,pāhə'rā\ *n, pl* **pejerre·yes** \-(,)yās\ *or* **pejerreys** [Sp, silversides, fr. Sp dial. *peje* fish (fr. L *piscis*) + Sp *rey* king, fr. L *reg-, rex*] : any of various silversides of the So. American coasts; *esp* : any of several relatively large silversides that resemble mackerel and are important as food

pej·i·ba·ye \,pāhē'bäyə\ *also* **pe·ji·ba·ve** \-və\ *n* -s [AmerSp *pejibaye, pijibay*, perh. fr. Arawak] : PEACH PALM

pe·jo·rate \'pejə,rāt, 'pēj-, *usu* -ād·+V\ *vt* -ED/-ING/-S [LL *pejoratus*, past part. of *pejorare* to become worse, make worse] : to make worse : DEPRECIATE

pe·jo·ra·tion \,==='rāshən\ *n* -s [ML *pejoration-, pejoratio*, fr. LL *pejoratus* (past part. of *pejorare* to become worse, make worse) + L *-ion-, -io* -ion] : a change for the worse : DEPRECIATION; *specif* : an historical process by which the semantic and connotative status of a word tends to decline — compare MELIORATION

¹pe·jo·ra·tive \pə'jȯrəd·iv; 'pej(ə)rəd·-, -jə,rād·-, 'pēj-\ *adj* [prob. fr. (assumed) NL *pejorativus*, fr. LL *pejoratus* (past part. of *pejorare* to become worse, make worse, fr. L *pejor* worse) + L *-ivus* -ive; akin to L *pessimus* worst, Skt *padyate* he falls, goes, L *ped-, pes* foot — more at FOOT] : having a tendency to make or become worse : DEPRECIATORY, DISPARAGING ⟨resort to ~ epithets as their argument —M.R. Cohen⟩ ⟨the ~ sense given the word "scholasticism" by the Renaissance —Frank Thilly⟩ — often used of words whose basic meaning is depreciated either by a suffix or by semantic application or association ⟨the ~ "poetaster" for a mere versifier⟩ ⟨we use the neutral word "paranormal" in preference to "abnormal" which is faintly ~ —A.G.N.Flew⟩ — **pe·jo·ra·tive·ly** \-əvlē, -li\ *adv*

²pejorative \"\ *n* -s : a pejorative word

pek·an \'pekən\ *n* -s [CanF *pékan, pécan*, of Algonquian origin; akin to Abnaki *pékané*] : FISHER 2

peke \'pēk\ *n* -s *often cap* [by shortening & alter.] : PEKINGESE 2

peke-faced \'=¦=\ *adj* : having a short wrinkled muzzle like that of a Pekingese dog — used esp. of a long-haired show cat

¹pe·kin \'pē'kin\ *n* -s [F *pékin*, fr. *Pékin* Peking, city in northeast China, fr. Chin (Pek) *Pe⁴ ching¹*] *often cap* a clothing fabric orig. of silk that is usu. characterized by wide vertical stripes in contrasting colors or weaves

²pekin \"\ *n, usu cap* [*Peking, Pekin*, city in northeast China] 1 : a breed of large active creamy white ducks of Chinese origin that is the breed chiefly used for commercial meat duck production in the U. S. 2 -s : a duck of the Pekin breed

¹pe·king \'pē¦kiŋ\ *also* **pe·kin** \-¦kin\ *adj, usu cap* [*peking* fr. *Peking* (name used up to 1928 by the imperial and republican governments of China and since 1949 by the Communist government), city in northeast China that was the capital up to 1928 and has been the capital of the Communist government of China since 1949, fr. Chin (Pek) *Pe⁴ ching¹*, fr. *pe⁴* north + *ching¹* capital; *pekin* fr. *Pekin* Peking, fr. F *Pékin*, fr. Chin (Pek) *Pe⁴ ching¹*] : of or from the city of Peking, China : of the kind or style prevalent in Peking

²peking \"\ *or* **peking duck** *n, usu cap P* : PEKIN

peking blue *n, often cap P* : a dark blue that is greener, lighter, and stronger than Japan blue or Majolica blue and stronger and slightly greener than Flemish blue

peking cotoneaster *n, often cap P* : a deciduous spreading shrub (*Cotoneaster acutifolia*) that is native to China but is used elsewhere as an ornamental esp. for hedges and that has the young branchlets pubescent, the leaves dull green above and pale and more pubescent below, and the flowers pink and in 2- to 5-flowered clusters

¹pe·king·ese \¦pēkiŋ¦ēz, -kə¦nēz, -ēs\ *or* **pe·kin·ese** \¦pēkə¦nēz, -ēs\ *n, pl* **pekingese** *or* **pekinese** [*Peking, Pekin*, city in northeast China + E *-ese*, n. suffix] 1 *cap* a : a native or resident of Peking b : the Chinese dialect of Peking 2 a *usu cap* : a breed of very small dogs originating in China over 2000 years ago that have a flat face, a broad skull flat between the ears, bowed forelegs, a deep stop, prominent eyes, and a long soft coat with profuse coarser mane and thick undercoat, that are of all colors (as red, fawn, black, and parti-color) with the lighter-colored dogs often having a black mask, and that may weigh up to 14 pounds b *often cap* : a dog of the Pekingese breed

²pekingese \"\ *or* **pekinese** \"\ *adj, usu cap* [*Peking, Pekin*, city in northeast China + E *-ese*, adj. suffix] : of, relating to, or characteristic of Peking, China

peking man *also* **pekin man** *n, usu cap P* : an extinct man that is known from fragmentary skulls and parts of skeletons found in Pleistocene cave deposits at Choukoutien, China, that is more advanced in some details than Java man but nearer to him than to other fossil hominids or to recent man, and that though orig. set apart as a distinct species (*Sinanthropus pekinensis*) is now often made congeneric with Java man in a species (*Pithecanthropus pekinensis*) or even congeneric with recent man in a species (*Homo erectus*)

peking nightingale *n, usu cap P* : JAPANESE NIGHTINGALE

pe·koe \'pē,kō *also chiefly Brit* 'pe,-\ *n* -s *sometimes cap* [Chin (Amoy) *pek-ho*, fr. *pek* white + *ho* down] 1 : a tea made from the first three leaves on the spray 2 : any tea of India or Ceylon made from leaves of approximately the same size obtained by screening fired tea

pel- or **pelo-** comb form [ISV, fr. Gk pēl-, pēlo-, fr. pēlos; perh. akin to L pallēre to be pale — more at FALLOW] : clay : mud ⟨pelite⟩ ⟨Pelomyxa⟩

pe·la \'pālə\ n -s [Chin (Pek) pe² la⁴, fr. pe² white + la⁴ wax] **1** : CHINESE WAX **2** : a scale (Ericerus pela) that secretes Chinese wax

pe·la·do \pä'lä(,)dō\ n -s [AmerSp, fr. pelado, adj., penniless, fr. Sp, bare, bald, fr. past part. of pelar to cut (the hair), pluck, skin, fr. L pilare to make bald, fr. pilus hair — more at PILE] Southwest : a Mexican peon — usu. used disparagingly

pelag- or **pelago-** comb form [L pelag-, fr. Gk pelag-, pelago-, fr. pelagos — more at FLAKE] : sea ⟨pelagial⟩

pel·age \'pelij, -lēj\ n -s [F, fr. MF, fr. poil hair (fr. L pilus) + -age] : the hairy covering of a mammal ⟨color variation of the . . . hare's ~ —R.E.Trippensee⟩

pe·la·gi·al \pə'lājēəl\ adj [pelag- + -ial] : PELAGIC

¹pe·la·gian \-j(ē)ən\ n -s usu cap [LL pelagianus, adj. & n., fr. Pelagius †A.D.420? Brit. monk and theologian + L -anus -an] : an advocate of or believer in Pelagianism

²pelagian \"\ adj, usu cap [LL pelagianus] : of or relating to Pelagius or Pelagianism

³pelagian \"\ adj [pelag- + -an] : PELAGIC

⁴pelagian \"\ n -s : a pelagic animal

pe·la·gian·ism \-ə,nizəm\ n -s usu cap [¹Pelagian + -ism] : the teachings of Pelagius condemned as heretical in A.D.431 and marked by the denial of original sin, the assertion that each individual has freedom of the will to choose not to sin, and the avowal that each person's freedom of the will includes the unassisted initiating power to move toward salvation and to appropriate the divine grace necessary thereto

pe·la·gian·ize \-,nīz\ vb -ED/-ING/-S often cap [¹Pelagian + -ize] vi : to become Pelagian ~ vt : to make Pelagian — **pe·la·gian·iz·er** \-zə(r)\ n -s often cap

pe·lag·ic \pə'lajik, -jēk\ adj [L pelagicus, fr. Gk pelagikos, fr. pelagos sea + -ikos -ic] **1** : of, relating to, or living in the open sea : OCEANIC **2** : of, relating to, or constituting a biogeographic realm consisting of the open sea and esp. those portions beyond the outer border of the littoral zone which are above the abyssal zone and to which light penetrates — compare BATHYPELAGIC, NERITIC

pelagic deposits n pl : sedimentary deposits in the abyssal parts of the ocean composed largely of the remains of pelagic organisms, volcanic dust, and meteoritic particles

pelagic sealing n : the act or occupation of killing, capturing, or pursuing fur seals in the ocean as distinguished from killing them at their breeding places on land

pel·a·go·thu·ria \,peləgō'thùrēə\ n, cap [NL, fr. pelag- + -thuria (as in Holothuria)] : a genus (the type of the family Pelagothuriidae) of free-swimming pelagic holothurians totally lacking skeletal plates

pel·a·myd \'peləməd, -,mid\ n -s [L pelamyd-, pelamys, fr. Gk pēlamyd-, pēlamys] : a young tuna

pe·lar·gi \pə'lär,jī\ n pl, cap [NL, fr. Gk pelargoi, pl. of pelargos stork, prob. fr. pela- (akin to Gk polios gray) + argos white — more at FALLOW, ARGENT] in some classifications : a group of birds coextensive with or including the Ciconiidae

pe·lar·gic \-jik\ adj [Gk pelargikos, fr. pelargos stork + -ikos -ic] : of or relating to the stork

pe·lar·go·morph \pə'lärgə,mȯrf\ n -s [NL Pelargomorphae] : a bird of the division Pelargomorphae — **pe·lar·go·mor·phic** \-;==;mȯrfik\ adj

pe·lar·go·mor·phae \=,==;mȯr(,)fē\ n pl, cap [NL, fr. pelargo- (fr. Gk pelargos stork) + -morphae] in some esp former classifications : a major division of birds comprising the storks, herons, and ibises or these together with the remainder of the Ciconiiformes, the Anseriformes and Falconiformes

pel·ar·gon·aldehyde \¦pe,lär,gän+\ n [ISV pelargonic + aldehyde] : a liquid aliphatic aldehyde $CH_3(CH_2)_7CHO$ that occurs in many essential oils (as of orrisroot, cinnamon, or lemongrass) and is used in perfumes and flavors; nonanal

pel·ar·go·nate \pe'lärgə,nāt\ n -s [ISV pelargonic + -ate] : a salt or ester of pelargonic acid

pel·ar·gon·ic acid \¦pe,lär'gänik, -gōnik-\ n [pelargonic ISV pelargon- (fr. NL Pelargonium) + -ic] : an oily fatty acid $CH_3(CH_2)_7COOH$ found esp. in fusel oil and rancid fats, obtained in the form of esters esp. from the leaves of pelargoniums and related plants, and usu. made synthetically along with azelaic acid by oxidation of oleic acid — called also nonanoic acid

pel·ar·gon·i·din \,=,=;gänədən\ n -s [ISV pelargonic + -idin] : an anthocyanidin pigment obtained in the form of its red= brown crystalline chloride $C_{15}H_{11}ClO_5$ by hydrolysis of pelargonin and also made synthetically

pel·ar·go·nin \,=,=;gōnən\ n -s [ISV pelargonic + -in] : an anthocyanin that is extracted from the dried petals of red pelargoniums or blue cornflowers or various dahlias in the form of its red crystalline chloride $C_{27}H_{31}ClO_{15}$, that changes to the blue sodium salt $C_{27}H_{29}O_{15}Na$ if made alkaline, and that is a diglucoside of pelargonidin

pel·ar·go·ni·um \,pe,lär'gōnēəm, -,lə(r)'g-\ n [NL, fr. pelargo- (fr. Gk pelargos stork) + -nium (as in Geranium); fr. the resemblance of the capsules to the bill of a stork] **1** cap : a large genus of southern African herbs (family Geraniaceae) with showy flowers of various shades of red or white distinguished by the spurred calyx and irregular corolla — compare GERANIUM **2** -s : any plant of the genus Pelargonium; esp : one that is cultivated

pelargonium oil n : GERANIUM OIL 1

pelas pl of PELA

pe·las·gi \pə'laz,jī\ n pl, usu cap [L, fr. Gk Pelasgoi] : PELASGIANS

¹pe·las·gi·an \-jēən, -gē-\ n -s usu cap [Gk pelasgios, adj., Pelasgian (fr. Pelasgoi) + E -an, n. suffix] **1** : one of an ancient people or group of peoples mentioned by classical writers as earlier inhabitants of Greece and the eastern islands of the Mediterranean — compare MINOAN, MYCENAEAN, PHILISTINE **2** : a putative Indo-European language of the Pelasgians

²pelasgian \"\ adj, usu cap [Gk pelasgios, adj., Pelasgian + E -an, adj. suffix] **1** : of, relating to, or characteristic of the Pelasgians **2** : of, relating to, or characteristic of the Pelasgian language

pe·las·gic \-jik, -gik\ adj, usu cap [Gk pelasgikos, fr. Pelasgoi + -ikos -ic] : PELASGIAN

pe·le·an \pə'lēən, -'lā-\ adj [Mount Pelée, volcano in Martinique + E -an] : of, relating to, or resembling volcanic eruptions characterized by violent expulsion of clouds or blasts of incandescent volcanic ash

pel·e·can·i·dae \,pelə'kanə,dē\ n pl, cap [NL, fr. Pelecanus, type genus + -idae] : a family formerly held to be nearly coextensive with Pelecaniformes but now restricted to the pelicans and constituting with the boobies, cormorants, and snakebirds a suborder of Pelecaniformes

pel·e·can·i·for·mes \,==,==;fȯr,mēz\ n pl, cap [NL, fr. Pelecanus + -iformes] : an order of swimming birds having all four toes united by a broad web and including the pelicans, gannets, cormorants, tropic birds, snakebirds, and frigate birds

pel·e·ca·noi·des \,==,kə'nȯi(,)dēz\ n, cap [NL, fr. LL pelecanus pelican + L -oides -oid] : a genus (the type of the family Pelecanoididae) comprising the diving petrels

pel·e·ca·nus \,==;kānəs\ n, cap [NL, fr. LL, pelican — more at PELICAN] : a genus of aquatic birds (family Pelecanidae) comprising the pelicans

pel·e·cin·i·dae \,==;sinə,dē\ n pl, cap [NL, fr. Pelecinus, type genus (fr. Gk pelekinos, pelekan pelican) + -idae — more at PELICAN] : a New World family of large parasitic wasps

pe·lec·y·pod \pə'lesə,päd\ adj or n [NL Pelecypoda] : LAMELLIBRANCH

pel·e·cyp·o·da \,pelə'sipədə\ [NL, fr. Gk pelekys ax, battle= ax + NL -poda] syn of LAMELLIBRANCHIA

pel·e·cyp·o·dous \;==;sipədəs\ adj [NL Pelecypoda + E -ous] : LAMELLIBRANCHIATE

pe·le·lith \pə'lā,lith\ n -s [Mount Pelée, volcano in Martinique + E -lith] : a plug or spine of vesicular or pumiceous lava thrust upward in the throat of a volcano

pêle-mêle \'pel¦mel\ archaic var of PELL-MELL

pel·er·ine \,pelə'rēn, '==,=, '==,rən\ n -s [obs. F, neckerchief, fr. F pèlerine, fem. of pèlerin pilgrim, fr. LL pelegrinus — more at PILGRIM] : a woman's narrow cape of fabric or fur usu. with long ends hanging down in front

pe·le's hair \,pälāz-, ,pēlēz-\ n, usu cap P [trans. of Hawaiian lauoho-o-Pele, fr. Pele, Hawaiian volcano goddess] : glass threads or fibers blown by the wind from frothy lava, the tips of lava jets, or drops of liquid lava thrown into the air that often collect in thick masses resembling tow

pele's tears n pl, usu cap P [after Pele, Hawaiian volcano goddess] **1** : small drops of volcanic glass **2** Hawaii : a clear chalcedony or opal in cabochon cut

pel·e·thite \'pelə,thīt, 'pēl-\ n -s usu cap [Heb pělēthī Pelethite + E -ite] : a member of a group of ancient Philistines forming part of the bodyguard of David, King of Israel

pelew cap, var of PALAU

pelf \'pelf\ n -s [ME, fr. MF pelfre booty] **1 a** archaic : PROPERTY, BELONGINGS ⟨providing them weapon and other like ~ —Thomas Tusser⟩ **b** : MONEY, RICHES, WEALTH ⟨let him disenslave himself from the ~ of the world —Robert South⟩ ⟨looked on him as an asset to earn us ~ or glory —John Galsworthy⟩ **2** chiefly Brit **a** : TRASH, REFUSE **b** dial chiefly Brit : COMPOST **3** dial Brit : GOOD-FOR-NOTHING

pel·ham \'peləm\ n -s usu cap [prob. fr. the name Pelham] : a horse's bit with a bar mouthpiece and double rings commonly used in riding bridles and designed to combine the function of curb and snaffle — see BIT illustration

pel·i·can \'pelə̇kən, -lēk-\ n -s [ME pelican, pellican, fr. OE pellican, fr. LL pelicanus, pelecanus, fr. Gk pelekan; akin to Gk pelekys ax, battle-ax, prob. of non-IE origin; akin to the source of Skt paraśu ax] **1** : any of various large totipalmate birds of the genus Pelecanus with a very large bill and distensible gular pouch in which fish are caught and with very long wings — see BROWN PELICAN, CALIFORNIA BROWN PELICAN, SPECTACLED PELICAN, WHITE PELICAN; BILL illustration **2** : a representation of a pelican in heraldry or art **3** : a retort or still with curved tubes leading from the head to the body for continuous condensation and redistillation **4** : a dark gray that is lighter than fashion gray, Oxford gray, or Dover gray — called also charcoal gray, dove, light gunmetal, pigeon's-neck **5** : a device that consists of a pocket attached to a long wooden handle and that is used for sampling a stream of falling grain in an elevator or on a loading ship

pelican fish or **pelican eel** n : a deep-sea fish (Eurypharynx pelecanoides) of the order Lyomeri that is black in color and has a head very long in proportion to the trunk, an enormous mouth, and a body ending in a tapering tail

pelican flower n : any of several tropical vines of the genus Aristolochia (esp. A. grandiflora) the shape of whose flowers suggests a pelican

pelican hook n : a hinged hook held closed by a ring and used (as on boat gripes and cargo gear) to provide instantaneous release

pel·i·can·ry \-rē, -ri\ n -ES [pelican + -ry] : a breeding place of pelicans

pelican's-foot \'==;=,=\ n, pl **pelican's-foots** **1** : a European marine gastropod (Aporrhais pespelecani) having fingerlike processes at the edge of the shell **2** : the shell of the pelican's-foot

pel·id·no·ta \,pelə̇d'nōd·ə\ n [NL, fr. Gk pelidnos, pelitnos livid; akin to Gk polios gray — more at FALLOW] **1** cap : a genus of American scarabaeoid beetles related to the goldsmith beetles **2** -s : any beetle of the genus Pelidnota — see SPOTTED PELIDNOTA

pelican hook: 1 open, 2 closed

pel·i·got's blue \'pelə,gōz-\ n, often cap P [prob. after Eugène Melchior Péligot †1890 Fr. chemist] : BREMEN BLUE

pe·li·ke \'pelə̇kē\ n -s [Gk pelikē wooden bowl, pitcher — more at PELVIS] : an ancient Greek amphora with a wide mouth, little or no neck, and the body set plump on the base

pe·lisse \pə'lēs, pe'-\ n -s [F, fr. LL pellicia cloak, fr. fem. of pellicius made of skin, fr. L pellis skin — more at FELL] **1** : a long cloak or coat made of fur or lined or trimmed with fur and worn by men and women **2** : a woman's loose lightweight cloak with wide collar and fur trimming

pe·lite \'pē,līt\ n -s [ISV pel- + -ite] : a rock composed of fine particles of clay or mud — compare PSAMMITE, PSEPHITE — **pe·lit·ic** \pə'lid·ik\ adj

¹pell \'pel\ vb -ED/-ING/-S [ME pellen] vi, dial chiefly Eng : HASTEN, HURRY ~ vt, obs : BEAT, PELT

²pell \"\ n -s [ME pel skin, roll of parchment, fr. MF, fr. L pellis skin] : a roll of parchment; specif : one formerly used in the English Exchequer to record receipts and expenditures ⟨appointed . . . his second brother clerk of the ~s —G.O. Trevelyan⟩

pel·laea \pə'lēə, pe'-\ n, cap [NL, fr. LGk pellaia, fem. of pellaios dark-colored; fr. the dark leaves; akin to Gk polios gray — more at FALLOW] : a genus of mostly small rock-loving ferns (family Polypodiaceae) having pinnate or pinnatifid often evergreen fronds and intramarginal sori with the indusium formed by the reflexed margins of the fertile segments

pel·la·gra \pə'lagrə, -lag-\ n -s [It, fr. pelle skin (fr. L pellis) + -agra (as in podagra, fr. L)] : a disease marked by dermatitis, inflammation of mucous membranes, gastrointestinal disorders, and central nervous symptoms and associated with a diet deficient in niacin and protein — compare KWASHIORKOR

pel·la·gra·gen·ic \=;==;jenik\ adj : producing pellagra

pellagra-preventive factor n : either of the two members of the vitamin B complex nicotinic acid or nicotinamide — called also PP factor

pel·lagric \=;=grik\ adj [pellagra + -ic] : of, relating to, or causing pellagra

pel·lagrin \-grən\ n -s [irreg. fr. pellagra] : a person having pellagra

pel·lagroid \-,grȯid\ adj [ISV pellagra + -oid] : resembling pellagra

pel·lagrous \-grəs\ adj [NL pellagrosus, fr. pellagra (fr. It) + L -osus -ose] : of, relating to, or affected with pellagra ⟨~ insanity⟩ ⟨~ symptoms⟩ ⟨~ patients⟩

¹pel·let \'pelə̇t, usu -əd·+V\ n -s often attrib [ME pelet, pelote, fr. MF pelote, fr. (assumed) VL pilota, dim. of L pila ball — more at PILL] **1 a** : a usu. small round or spherical body : a little ball **b** : a small cylindrical chunk of compressed feeding stuffs used for livestock, poultry, or pets to avoid waste and to increase the attractiveness of the food **c** : a small cylindrical or ovoid compressed mass (as of a hormone) for implantation in muscular tissues **d** : a wad or bolus of indigestible material (as bones and other resistant remains of prey) regurgitated by a carnivorous bird **e** : a small firm mass of dung (as that dropped by a mouse or rabbit) **2 a** : a usu. stone ball used as a missile (as in a mangonel) during later medieval times **b** : CANNONBALL **c** : a ball for firearms : BULLET **d** (1) : one of a charge of small shot ⟨~s of buckshot⟩ (2) : a piece of small shot fired singly (as from a BB gun) ⟨~ gun⟩ **e** : an imitation bullet (as of cork, paper, wax) for use in a popgun **3** heraldry : a roundel sable : OGRESS, GUNSTONE **4 a** : a circular boss in decorative work **b** : BEAD 4g

²pellet \"\ vt -ED/-ING/-S **1 a** : to form into pellets **b** : to coat (seeds) with soluble adhesive material mixed with plant foods and protective substances to facilitate planting and promote growth **2** : to strike with pellets : throw pellets at

pel·let·er \'pelə̇d·ə(r)\ n -s : one that pellets

pel·le·tier·ine \,pelə'ti,rēn, -,rən\ n -s [ISV pelletier- (fr. Pierre Joseph Pelletier †1842 Fr. chemist) + -ine] **1** : a liquid alkaloid $C_8H_{15}NO$ derived from piperidine and found in the bark of the pomegranate **2** : a mixture of alkaloids from the bark of the pomegranate used esp. in the form of the tannate against tapeworm

pel·let·i·za·tion \,pelə̇d·ə̇'zāshən, -d·,ī'z-\ n -s : the process of pelletizing

pel·let·ize \'pelə̇d·,īz\ vt -ED/-ING/-S : to make into pellets ⟨~ foodstuffs for animals and fowl⟩ ⟨~ ore⟩

pel·let·iz·er \-zə(r)\ n -s : one that pelletizes; specif : an operator of a machine for compressing plastics powder into pellets from which plastic objects are molded

pel·lett clover \'pelə̇t-\ n [after Frank C. Pellett †1951 Am. apiculturist] : KURA CLOVER

pel·let·é or **pel·let·ée** \¦pelə̇d·¦ā,-ə¦tā; 'pelə̇d·ē,-i\ or **pel·lety** \'pelə̇d·ē, -i\ adj [¹pellet + -y] : charged with heraldic pellets

-pel·lic \'pelik, -lēk\ adj comb form [Gk pella wooden bowl + E -ic — more at PELVIS] : having (such) a pelvis ⟨dolichopellic⟩

pel·li·cle \'pelə̇kəl, -lēk-\ n -s [MF pellicule, fr. ML pellicula, fr. L, small skin, dim. of pellis skin — more at FELL] **1 a** : a thin skin or membrane **b** : a semipermeable membrane; esp : PLASMA MEMBRANE **2** : a film on a liquid; specif : a bacterial growth in the form of a sheet on the surface of a liquid medium **3** : a semitransparent partially reflecting thin membrane used in cameras for color photography to divide a light beam and form two optical images of a single subject

pel·lic·u·la \pə'likyələ\ n -s [ML] : PELLICLE

pel·lic·u·lar \-lə(r)\ adj [prob. fr. (assumed) NL pellicularis, fr. ML pellicula + L -aris -ar] : of, relating to, or having the characteristics of a pellicle : MEMBRANOUS, FILMY

pel·lic·u·lar·ia \=,==la(a)rēə\ n, cap [NL, fr. ML pellicula + NL -aria] : a genus of fungi (family Thelephoraceae) having the hymenium in the form of a crust

pellicularia disease n : a disease of coffee and some other tropical plants caused by a fungus (Pellicularia koleroga) and producing leaf spots and effects similar to those of thread blight

pellicular water n : ground water suspended above the water table in films that adhere to the surface of solid particles or the walls of cavities

pel·lic·u·late \-lə̇t, -,lāt\ adj [prob. fr. (assumed) NL pelliculatus, fr. ML pellicula + L -atus -ate] : characterized by or covered with a pellicle : PELLICULAR

pel·li·cule \'pelə,kyül\ n -s [ME, fr. ML pellicula] : PELLICLE

pelling pres part of PELL

pel·li·to·ry \'pelə,tōrē, -tȯr-, -ri\ n -ES [alter. of earlier peletyr, fr. ME peletre, modif. of MF piretre, fr. L pyrethrum — more at PYRETHRUM] **1 a** or **pellitory-of-spain** \'==,===;=\ usu cap S : a southern European plant (Anacyclus pyrethrum) resembling yarrow **b** : the root of this plant formerly used as a sialagogue and as a constituent of dentifrice **2** or **pellitory-of-the-wall** \'==,====;=\ [alter. of earlier paritory, fr. ME paritorie, modif. of MF paritaire, fr. LL parietaria — more at PARIETARIA] : any plant of the genus Parietaria (as P. officinalis, P. pennsylvanica) **3** : any of various plants resembling the southern European pellitory: as **a** : FEVERFEW **b** : a yarrow (Achillea millefolium) **c** : MASTERWORT a

pellitory bark n : PRICKLY ASH 1a

¹pell-mell \'pel'mel\ adv [MF pelemele, fr. OF pesle mesle, prob. redupl. of mesle, imper. sing. of mesler to mix, mingle — more at MEDDLE] **1** : in mingled confusion or disorder ⟨the infantry followed pell-mell —W.H.Prescott⟩ ⟨piles of volumes that were heaped pell-mell around him —Christopher Morley⟩ **2** : without distinction or discrimination : INDISCRIMINATELY ⟨so that you will not simply read everything pell-mell and without judgment —N.N.Glatzer⟩ **3** : in or as if in confused haste : HEADLONG ⟨hesitated to barge ahead pell-mell as he had done in previous years —Clay Blair⟩

²pell-mell \"\ adj : marked by confusion, disorder, or haste : HELTER-SKELTER ⟨the pell-mell rush of magnitudinous events —Marian E. Wagner⟩ ⟨a shelf that contained a pell-mell assortment of French novels —Nicolas Nabokov⟩

³pell-mell \"\ n -s **1** : an indiscriminate medley ⟨five setters . . . came down the drive in a pell-mell of welcome —James Reynolds⟩ **2** : CONFUSION, DISORDER ⟨the pell-mell of life's disorganized and casual happenings —J.C.Powys⟩

⁴pell-mell \"\ vb -ED/-ING/-S vt : to mix up in an indiscriminate manner ⟨they pell-mell the dead with the living all in one kirk —William Birnie⟩ ~ vi : to hurry in a confused or disorderly manner : RUSH ⟨they all pell-melled out of that river —Esther Forbes⟩

pel·lock \'pelək\ n -s [ME (Sc) pelok] Scot : PORPOISE

pello·te \pə'lōd·ə, pə'yō-\ n -s [modif. of MexSp peyote — more at PEYOTE] : PEYOTE

pel·lo·tine \'pelə,tēn, -ət³n, -ətə̇n, -əd·ə̇n\ also **pel·lo·tin** \-ət³n, -ətə̇n, -əd·ə̇n\ n -s [ISV pellote + -ine] : a crystalline narcotic alkaloid $C_{13}H_{19}NO_3$ derived from isoquinoline and obtained from mescal and other cacti of the genus Lophophora

pells pres 3d sing of PELL, pl of PELL

pel·lu·cid \pə'lüsə̇d, pel'yü-\ adj [L pellucidus, fr. per through + lucidus lucid — more at FARE, LUCID] **1** : admitting maximum passage of light without diffusion or distortion : permitting one to see through to a remarkable degree : TRANSLUCENT, TRANSPARENT ⟨water in a white glass beaker, clear, ~, without shadow —W.J.Turner⟩ **2** : pleasing in appearance: **a** : pure in color and pleasing as genuine or appropriate ⟨the fresh green blade of corn is . . . so ~, so clear —Richard Jefferies⟩ **b** : reflecting light evenly from all surfaces : SHINING, IRIDESCENT ⟨~ as a pearl —Robert Browning⟩ **3** : extremely easy to understand : readily intelligible or comprehensible : completely lacking in ambiguity or turgidity ⟨apposite quotations from the classics . . . grace the ~ flow of his English —V.L.Parrington⟩ ⟨the chiseled ~ beauty of many an image . . . lends distinction to the best work of the new school —J.L. Lowes⟩ ⟨the firm, round ~ handwriting which was so great a contrast to his wife's temperamental scrawl —Margaret Cole⟩ **syn** see CLEAR

pel·lu·cid·i·ty \,pelyə'sidəd·ē, -ətē, -i\ n -ES [L pelluciditat-, pelluciditas, fr. pellucidus + -itat-, -itas -ity] : the quality or state of being pellucid

pel·lu·cid·ly adv : in a pellucid manner

pel·lu·cid·ness n -ES : PELLUCIDITY

pel·man·ism \'pelmə,nizəm\ n -s usu cap [Pelman Institute, institution for training of the mind founded in London 1898 + E -ism] **1** : a system of training held to develop the mind **2** : CONCENTRATION 5

pel·mat·o·gram \pel'mad·ə,gram, -raa(ə)m\ n -s [pelmato- (fr. Gk pelmat-, pelma sole of the foot) + -gram] : an impression of the sole of the foot

pel·ma·to·zoa \,pelməd·ə'zōə\ n pl, cap [NL, fr. pelmato- (fr. Gk pelmat-, pelma sole of the foot) + -zoa] : a subphylum or other division of Echinodermata comprising the crinoids, cystoids, blastoids, and edrioasteroids — compare ELEUTHEROZOA — **pel·ma·to·zo·an** \;===;zōən\ adj or n — **pel·ma·to·zo·ic** \-zōik\ adj

pel·met \'pelmə̇t, usu -ə̇d·+V\ n -s [prob. modif. of F palmette — more at PALMETTE] : a short valance or small cornice for concealing curtain fixtures

-pel·mous \¦pelməs\ adj comb form [Gk pelma sole of the foot + E -ous — more at FELL] : having (such) a sole ⟨heteropelmous⟩

pelo- — see PEL-

pel·o·bat·id \,pelō'bad·ə̇d, ,pēl-\ n -s [NL Pelobatidae] : an amphibian of the family Pelobatidae

pel·o·bat·i·dae \-bad·ə,dē\ n pl, cap [NL, fr. Pelobates, type genus (fr. pel- + -bates) + -idae] : a large widely distributed family of anomocoelous amphibians including the spadefoot toads

pel·o·bat·oid \¦==¦bad·,ȯid\ adj [NL Pelobates + E -oid] : related to or resembling the Pelobatidae

pe·loc·o·ris \pə'läkərə̇s\ n, cap [NL, fr. pel- + -coris (fr. Gk koris bedbug) — more at COREIDAE] : a No. American genus of nepid bugs

pe·lod·y·tes \pə'lädəd·(,)ēz\ n, cap [NL, fr. pel- + -dytes] : a genus of Eurasian frogs (family Pelobatidae) distinguished from the spadefoot toads by their slender build and unmodified tarsus — **pel·o·dyt·id** \,pelō'did·ə̇d\ n -s — **pel·o·dyt·oid** \¦==¦di,tȯid\ adj

pel·oid \'pe,lȯid\ n -s [ISV pel- + -oid] : mud prepared and used for therapeutic purposes ⟨remedies . . . at spas include natural mineral waters, ~s, and climate —W.S.McClellan⟩

pel·ok \'pelək\ also **pel·og** \-ləg\ n -s [Jav] : a Javanese pentatonic scale approximately equal to the tones G♯, A, C♯, D, E, G♯

pel·o·me·du·si·dae \,pelōmə'd(y)üsə,dē\ n pl, cap [NL, fr. Pelomedusa, type genus (fr. pel- + L Medusa, one of the three Gorgons) + -idae — more at MEDUSA] : a family of freshwater pleurodiran tortoises of Africa, Madagascar, and So. America

pel·o·myxa \-'miksə\ n, cap [NL, fr. pel- + -myxa] : a genus of large sluggish multinucleate freshwater amoebas (family Amoebidae) with the cytoplasm obscured by metabolic and other inclusions

pel·o·pae·us \,pelə'pēəs\ [NL, modif. of LGk pēlopoios potter, fr. Gk pēlos clay, mud + -poios (fr. poiein to make) — more at PEL-, POET] syn of SCELIPHRON

[1]**pel·o·pon·ne·sian** \ˌpeləpəˈnēzhən, -shən\ *adj, usu cap* [L *peloponnesius* Peloponnesian (fr. Gk *peloponnēsios*, fr. *Peloponnēsos* Peloponnesus, peninsula forming southern part of the mainland of Greece) + E *-an*] **1 :** of or relating to the southern peninsula of Greece **2 :** of or relating to the people of the southern peninsula of Greece

[2]**peloponnesian** \"\ *n* -s *cap* **:** a native or inhabitant of the southern peninsula of Greece

pe·lo·ria \pəˈlōrēə, -lȯr-\ *n* -s [NL, fr. Gk *pelōros* monstrous (fr. *pelōr* portent, monster) + NL *-ia*; akin to Gk *terat-, teras* portent, monster — more at TERAT-] **:** an abnormal often hereditary regularity of structure occurring in normally irregular flowers — see IRREGULAR PELORIA, REGULAR PELORIA

pe·lor·ic \-ōrik, -är-\ *or* **pe·lo·ri·an** \-ōrēən, -ȯr-\ *or* **pe·lo·ri·ate** \-ēət, -ēˌāt\ *adj* [*peloric* fr. NL *peloricus*, fr. *peloria* + L *-icus* -ic; *pelorian* fr. *peloria* + *-an; peloriate* prob. fr. (assumed) NL *peloriatus*, fr. NL *peloria* + L *-atus* -ate] *of a flower* **:** having peloria **:** abnormally regular or symmetrical

pel·o·ri·za·tion \ˌpelərəˈzāshən, -ˌrīˈz-\ *n* -s [ISV *pelorize* + *-ation*] **:** the process of pelorizing

pel·o·rize \ˈpeləˌrīz\ *vt* -ED/-ING/-S [ISV *peloria* + *-ize*] **:** to affect with peloria

pe·lo·rus \pəˈlōrəs, -lȯr-\ *n* -ES [origin unknown] **:** a navigational instrument resembling a mariner's compass without magnetic needles and having two sight vanes by which bearings are taken

portable pelorus

pe·lo·ta \pəˈlōd·ə\ *n* -s [Sp, ball, ball game, fr. OF *pelote* little ball — more at PELLET] **1 :** any of various Basque, Spanish, or Spanish-American games played in a court with a ball and a wickerwork racket; *specif* **:** JAI ALAI **2 :** the ball used in pelota

pelo·therapy \ˌpelō, ˌpēlō+\ *n* [*pel-* + *therapy*] **:** the therapeutic use of mud; *specif* **:** treatment by mud baths

pel·o·ton \ˌpeləˈtän, *F* plȯtōⁿ\ *n* -s [F, platoon, ball, fr. MF, ball, fr. *pelote* little ball] **1 :** a small body of soldiers **:** PLATOON **2 :** an endotrophic mycorrhiza characterized by coiled masses of hyphae in the host cells

[1]**pelt** \ˈpelt\ *n* -s [ME, perh. back-formation fr. *peltry* — more at PELTRY] **1 a :** a usu. undressed skin with its hair, wool, or fur **b :** a skin (as of a sheep or goat) stripped of hair or wool for tanning **2 :** the human skin **3 :** the dead body of a hawk's quarry

[2]**pelt** \"\ *vb* -ED/-ING/-S *vt* **:** to remove the skin or pelt from (an animal) ~ *vi* **:** to remove the skin or pelt from animals

[3]**pelt** \"\ *vb* -ED/-ING/-S [ME *pelten*] *vt* **1 a :** to strike with a succession of blows or missiles ⟨the chidden billow seems to ~ the clouds —Shak.⟩ ⟨boys . . . ~*ed* the girls with green apples —Sherwood Anderson⟩ **b :** to assail repeatedly and usu. forcefully with words **:** BESET ⟨~*ing* him with ridicule and vilification —Walter O'Meara⟩ ⟨the crowd ~*ed* him with questions while he slid from his saddle —*Everybody's Mag.*⟩ **2 :** to drive by means of a succession of blows or missiles ⟨lads . . . ~*ing* through the gloaming their sheep and goats —Sir Richard Burton⟩ **3 :** to throw a succession or stream of (as missiles) ⟨the rout followed and ~*ed* stones —Anthony Wood⟩ **4 :** to fall upon or dash against with a succession of vigorous impacts ⟨~*ed* the sides of houses like hailstones —R.A.Billington⟩ ~ *vi* **1 a :** to deliver a succession of strokes or blows ⟨the smith . . . ~*ing* away at his hot iron —James Hogg⟩ **b** *obs* **:** to utter a succession of angry words **2 :** to throw a succession of missiles ⟨filled their pockets full of pebblestones and . . . ~ so fast at one another's pate —Shak.⟩ **3 :** to fall or dash with a succession of vigorous impacts **:** beat incessantly ⟨listening to the rain ~ and rattle on the tin roof —Marcia Davenport⟩ **4 :** to move rapidly and vigorously **:** HURRY ⟨riding low . . . as hard as the mare could ~ —H.L.Davis⟩ ⟨imagine the whole crowd ~*ing* to the telephones —C.W.Morton⟩

[4]**pelt** \"\ *n* -s **1 :** a blow with or as if with something thrown **:** WHACK ⟨gave him . . . a good ~ on the head with his crutch —Tobias Smollett⟩ **2** *dial chiefly Eng* **:** a fit of rage **3 :** a rapid vigorous pace **:** SPEED ⟨the tug going by, full ~, down the river —Joseph Conrad⟩ **4 :** a persistent falling or beating (as of rain) **:** a pelting storm ⟨the swish and ~ of the rain were heard in pauses —D.C.Murray⟩

pel·ta \ˈpeltə\ *n, pl* **pel·tae** \-ˌtē, -ˌtī\ [L, small shield, fr. Gk *peltē*; perh. akin to L *pellis* skin — more at FELL] **1 :** a small light shield used by the ancient Greeks and Romans **2** [NL, fr. L] **:** a body of unknown function found in association with the blepharoplast of a flagellate

pel·tan·dra \pelˈtandrə\ *n, cap* [NL, fr. L *pelta* + NL *-andra*] **:** a genus of aquatic or marsh herbs (family Araceae) of the eastern U.S. having large hastate or sagittate leaves and elongated spathes

pel·tast \ˈpelˌtast\ *n* -s [Gk *peltastēs*, fr. *peltē* pelta] **:** a soldier of ancient Greece armed with a pelta

pel·tate \ˈpelˌtāt\ *adj* [prob. fr. (assumed) NL *peltatus*, fr. L *pelta* + *-atus* -ate] **:** SCUTIFORM; *specif* **:** having the stem or support attached to the lower surface instead of at the base or margin ⟨a ~ leaf⟩ — see LEAF illustration — **pel·tate·ly** *adv*

[1]**pelt·er** \ˈpeltə(r)\ *vb* -ED/-ING/-S [freq. of [3]*pelt*] **:** PELT

[2]**pelter** \"\ *n* -s [[2]*pelt* + *-er*] **1 :** one that pelts **2 :** an old slow horse **3 :** SKEET

[3]**pelter** \"\ *n* -s [[2]*pelt* + *-er*] **1 :** one that pelts small animals **2 :** an animal raised for pelting

pel·ter·er \-tərə(r)\ *n* -s [[1]*pelt* + *-erer* (as in *fruiterer*)] **:** a dealer in pelts or peltry

pel·tier effect \ˈpelˌtyā-\ *n, usu cap P* [after Jean C. A. *Peltier* †1845 Fr. physicist who discovered it] **:** the production or absorption of heat at the junction of two metals on the passage of a current

pel·ti·form \ˈpeltəˌfȯrm\ *adj* [NL *peltiformis*, fr. *pelti-* (fr. L *pelta*) + L *-formis* -form] **:** PELTATE

pel·tig·era \pelˈtijərə\ *n, cap* [NL, fr. *pelti-* (fr. *pelta*) + *-gera* (fr. L, fem. of *-ger*, fr. *gerere* to bear, wage, cherish) — more at CAST] **:** a large genus (the type of the family Peltigeraceae) of foliaceous lichens with shield-shaped or tooth-shaped apothecia

pel·tig·er·ous \(ˈ)=ˌtijərəs\ *adj* [*pelti-* (fr. NL *pelta*) + *-gerous*] **:** bearing a pelta or peltate part ⟨a ~ lichen⟩

[1]**pelt·ing** \ˈpeltiŋ, -tēŋ\ *adj* [prob. fr. E dial. *palt, pelt* piece of coarse cloth, trash + E *-ing* — more at PALTRY] *archaic* **:** PALTRY, INSIGNIFICANT ⟨flourishing cities . . . dwindled into ~ villages —R.C.Trench⟩

[2]**pelting** \"\ *adj* [fr. pres. part. of [3]*pelt*] *chiefly dial* **:** RAGING, FURIOUS

pel·to·gas·ter \ˌpeltōˈgastə(r)\ *n, cap* [NL, fr. *pelto-* (fr. L *pelta*) + *-gaster*] **:** a genus of parasitic cirripedes order Rhizocephala

pel·ton wheel \ˈpeltᵊn *also* -tən-\ *n, usu cap P* [after Lester Allen *Pelton* †1908 Am. engineer who invented it] **:** an impulse turbine or waterwheel consisting of a row of double cup-shaped buckets arranged around the rim of a wheel and actuated by one or more jets of water playing into the cups at high velocity

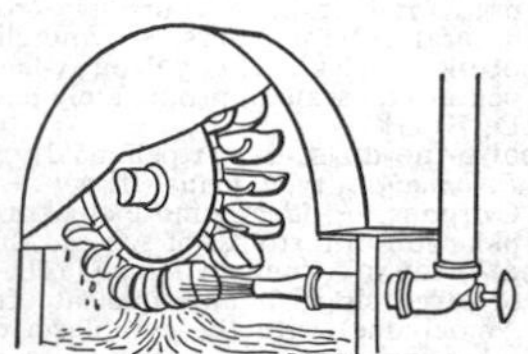
Pelton wheel

pel·try \ˈpel·trē, -ri\ *n* -ES [ME, fr. AF *pelterie*, fr. OF *peleterie*, fr. *peleter*, *peletier* furrier (prob. fr. assumed OF *pelet* small skin — fr. OF *pel* skin, fr. L *pellis* + OF *-et* — + OF *-er, -ier* -er) + *-ie* -y — more at FELL] **:** PELTS, SKINS, FURS; *esp* **:** raw undressed skins

pelts *pl of* PELT, *pres 3d sing of* PELT

pelt wool *n* **1 :** a short skin wool from the pelt of a sheep that has been killed within about three months after shearing **2 :** wool that has been removed from the pelt of a dead sheep

pe·lu \ˈpāˌlü\ *n* -s [Sp *pelú*, fr. Araucanian *pùlu*] **:** KOWHAI

pe·lu·do \pəˈlü(ˌ)dō\ *n* -s [AmerSp, fr. Sp, hairy, fr. *pelo* hair, fr. L *pilus* — more at PILE] **1 :** an Argentine armadillo (*Euphractus sexcinctus*) having six movable bands and hairy underparts **2 :** any of several armadillos similar to and congeneric with the peludo

pe·lure paper \pəˈlü(ə)r, pelˈyü(ə)r, -üə-\ *n* [*pelure* fr. F, lit., peel, fr. OF *peleure*, fr. *peler* to peel, remove the hair from (fr. L *pilare* to remove the hair from, make bald, fr. *pilus* hair) + *-ure*] **:** a crisp hard thin paper sometimes used for postage stamps

pe·lu·si·os \pəˈlüsēˌäs\ *n, cap* [NL, irreg. fr. Gk *pēlos* clay, mud — more at PEL-] **:** a genus of African and Malagasy freshwater turtles of the family Pelomedusidae

pelv- *or* **pelvi-** *or* **pelvo-** *comb form* [ISV, fr. NL *pelvis* — more at PELVIS] **1 :** pelvis ⟨*pelvic*⟩ ⟨*pelviscope*⟩ **2 :** pelvic and ⟨*pelvisacral*⟩ ⟨*pelvorenal*⟩

pelves *pl of* PELVIS

pel·ve·tia \(ˈ)pelˈvēsh(ē)ə\ *n, cap* [NL, fr. *Pelvet*, 19th cent. Fr. naturalist and physician + NL *-ia*] **:** a genus of rockweeds (family Fucaceae) having a cylindrical branched thallus — see CHANNELED WRACK

[1]**pel·vic** \ˈpelvik, -vēk\ *adj* [*pelv-* + *-ic*] **:** of, relating to, or located in or near the pelvis ⟨~ arteries⟩ ⟨deep ~ pain⟩

[2]**pelvic** \"\ *n* -s **:** a pelvic part (as a bone or fin)

pelvic brim *n* **:** the bony ridge that marks the boundary between the upper and lower parts of the cavity of the pelvis

pelvic cavity *n* **:** PELVIS 2

pelvic colon *n* **:** the sigmoid flexure of the colon

pelvic diaphragm *or* **pelvic floor** *n* **:** the muscular floor of the pelvis

pelvic fascia *n* **:** the fascia lining the cavity of the pelvis

pelvic fin *n* **:** one of the paired fins of a fish homologous with the hind limbs of a quadruped — called also *ventral fin;* see FISH illustration

pelvic girdle *also* **pelvic arch** *n* **:** a bony or cartilaginous arch that supports the hind limbs of a vertebrate, that corresponds to the pectoral girdle of the forelimbs but is usu. more rigid and firmly attached to the vertebral column, and that consists primitively of a single cartilage which is replaced in higher forms by paired innominate bones articulating solidly with the sacrum dorsally and with one another at the pubic symphysis

pelvic index *n* **:** the ratio of the transverse to the dorsoventral diameter of the brim of the pelvis opening multiplied by 100

pelvic limb *n* **:** either member of the posterior of the two pairs of limbs characteristic of vertebrates **:** a leg, hind limb, or pelvic fin

pelvic outlet *n* **:** the irregular bony opening bounded by the lower border of pelvis and closed by muscle and other soft tissues through which the terminal parts of the excretory, reproductive, and digestive systems pass to communicate with the surface of the body

pelvic plexus *n* **:** the inferior hypogastric plexus

pel·vi·form \ˈpelvəˌfȯrm\ *adj* [ISV *pelv-* + *-form*] **:** having the shape of a basin

pel·vi·graph \-ˌgraf\ *n* [ISV *pelv-* + *-graph*] **:** a recording pelvimeter

pel·vim·e·ter \pelˈvimәd·ə(r)\ *n* [ISV *pelv-* + *-meter*] **:** an instrument for measuring the dimensions of the pelvis

pel·vim·e·try \-ə·trē, -tri\ *n* -ES [ISV *pelv-* + *-metry*] **:** measurement of the pelvis (as by a pelvimeter or by X-ray examination)

pel·vis \ˈpelvəs\ *n, pl* **pelvis·es** \-vəsəz\ *or* **pel·ves** \-ˌvēz\ [NL, fr. L, basin; akin to OE & ON *full* cup, Gk *pella* wooden bowl] **1 a :** a basin-shaped structure in the skeleton of many vertebrates that is formed by the pelvic girdle together with the sacrum and often various coccygeal and caudal vertebrae and that in man is composed of the two innominate bones bounding it on each side and in front while the sacrum and coccyx complete it behind — see BAT illustration **b :** the bones of the pelvic girdle viewed as a structural unit in vertebrates in which these bones are not arranged in a basin-shaped structure **c :** the enlarged basipterygial bones that in teleost fishes replace the pelvic bones and support the pelvic fins **2 :** the cavity of the bony pelvis comprising in man a broad upper and a more contracted lower part — called also respectively *false pelvis* and *true pelvis* **3 :** the main cavity of the kidney into which the nephrons discharge urine

pel·vi·sacral \ˌpelvē+\ *adj* [*pelv-* + *sacral*] **:** of or relating to the pelvis and the sacrum

pel·vi·scope \ˈpelvəˌskōp\ *n* [*pelv-* + *-scope*] **:** an instrument that is equipped with lighting and optical systems and that permits direct and oblique visualization of the pelvis through the vagina — compare CULDOSCOPE

pelvo- — see PELV-

pel·vo·renal \ˌpelvō+\ *adj* [*pelv-* + *renal*] **:** of, relating to, or involving the pelvis of the kidney

pel·y·co·saur \ˈpeləkōˌsȯ(ə)r\ *n* -s [NL *Pelycosauria*] **:** one of the Pelycosauria

pel·y·co·sau·ria \ˌ===ˈsȯrēə\ *n pl, cap* [NL, fr. *pelyco-* (fr. Gk *pelyk-, pelyx* wooden bowl) + *-sauria*] **:** an order of primitive Permian reptiles (subclass Synapsida) that resemble mammals and often have extreme development of the dorsal vertebral processes — compare DIMETRODON, EDAPHOSAURUS — **pel·y·co·sau·ri·an** \ˌ===ˈsȯrēən\ *adj or n*

pem·bi·na \ˈpemˈbēnə, ˈpembənə\ *n* -s [CanF *pimbina*, perh. modif. of Cree *nipiminân*, lit., berry growing by the water] **:** CRANBERRY TREE

pem·broke \ˈpemˌbrůk, -rōk\ *n* -s *usu cap* [fr. *Pembroke*, Wales, where it was orig. bred] **:** a Welsh corgi of a variety that is characterized by pointed erect ears, straight legs, and short tail

pem·broke·shire \-kˌshi(ə)r, -ˌshiə, -ˌshə(r)\ *or* **pembroke** *adj, usu cap* [fr. *Pembrokeshire* or *Pembroke*, county in Wales] **:** of or from the county of Pembroke, Wales **:** of the kind or style prevalent in Pembroke

pembroke table *also* **pembroke** *n* -s *usu cap P* [prob. fr. *Pembroke*, English family of noblemen] **:** a small often profusely ornamented four-legged table originating in the Georgian period and having a drawer and on each side a narrow leaf supported by a swinging bracket

Pembroke table

pem·mi·can *also* **pem·i·can** \ˈpemәkən\ *n* -s [Cree *pimikân*, fr. *pimii* grease, fat] **1 a :** a concentrated food used by No. American Indians consisting essentially of lean buffalo meat or venison cut in thin slices, dried in the sun, pounded fine, mixed with melted fat, and packed in sacks of hide **b :** a similar preparation (as of dried beef, flour, molasses, suet) used for emergency rations (as by explorers) **2 :** information or thought condensed into little compass

pem·phi·goid \ˈpem(p)fəˌgȯid\ *adj* [NL *pemphigus* + E *-oid*] **:** resembling pemphigus

[1]**pem·phi·gus** \-gəs, pemˈfīgəs\ *n, pl* **pemphiguses** \-səz\ *or* **pem·phi·gi** \-fəˌjī, -ˌjī\ [NL, fr. Gk *pemphig-, pemphix* breath, drop, storm, pustule; akin to Gk *pomphos* blister, *bembix* buzzing insect, top, whirlpool, cyclone — more at BEMBIX] **:** a disease of unknown cause characterized by the formation of successive crops of large blisters on apparently normal skin and mucous membranes often in association with sensations of itching or burning and with constitutional symptoms

[2]**pemphigus** \"\ *n, cap* [NL, fr. Gk *pemphig-, pemphix*] **:** a genus of gall-making aphids (family Eriosomatidae) with both primary hosts (as trees and woody shrubs) and secondary hosts (as roots of sugar beets and lettuce)

pem·phre·don·i·dae \ˌpem(p)frəˈdänəˌdē\ *n pl, cap* [NL, fr. *Pemphredon*, type genus (fr. Gk *pemphrēdōn*, a wasp) + *-idae;* akin to Skt *bambhara* bee] **:** a family of small wasps that provision their nests with aphids and other small homopterous insects

[1]**pen** \ˈpen\ *n* -s [ME, fr. OE *penn*] **1 a :** a small enclosure for animals; *also* **:** the animals in one such enclosure ⟨erected a ~ for the calves⟩ or enough to fill one ⟨stole a whole ~ of sheep⟩ **b :** a specified number of animals entered in an exhibition as a unit ⟨a ~ of one cock and four hens⟩ **c :** a number of animals regarded as a suitable breeding unit whether kept together or not ⟨start with a ~ of one buck and 10 does⟩ **2 :** a device to dam the water in a stream **:** DAM **3 :** any small place of confinement or storage: as **a :** BULLPEN 1 **b :** PLAYPEN **4** *Jamaica* **:** a farm where livestock is bred and raised **5 a :** a berthing area for small ships or boats formed by enclosing piers or jetties **b :** a dock or slip for reconditioning submarines that is protected against aerial bombs by a superstructure of thick concrete **6 :** a hollow square crib of pulpwood stacked for storage

[2]**pen** \"\ *vt* **penned; penned; penning; pens** [ME *pennen*, fr. OE *-pennian*, fr. *penn* pen] **1 :** to shut in or as if in a pen **:** place in an enclosure to prevent straying **:** confine in a restricted location ⟨~*s* the sheep in the barnyard⟩ ⟨a convalescent child *penned* up in a house⟩ ⟨the individual's being so bafflingly *penned* within himself —W.M.Frohock⟩ **2 :** to exhibit (as rabbits, poultry) in pens **:** arrange a show of penned animals **syn** see ENCLOSE

[3]**pen** \"\ *n* -s *often attrib* [ME *penne*, fr. MF, feather, wing, pen, fr. L *pinna*, alter. of *penna* feather, wing; akin to Gk *pteron* wing, feather — more at FEATHER] **1** *archaic* **a :** FEATHER **b pens** *pl* **:** PINIONS, WINGS **c :** QUILL 2a(1) **2 :** an implement for writing or drawing with ink or a similar fluid: **a :** QUILL 3a **b :** a small thin convex metal device tapering to a split point and fitting into a holder for writing and drawing with ink or a similar fluid — called also *nib;* see STUB **c :** a penholder (as of wood) containing a pen **d :** any of various similar implements (as a fountain pen, ball-point pen, ruling pen) **3 a :** a writing instrument regarded as a means of expression (as of thoughts, feelings) ⟨lived by his ~⟩ ⟨verses from her ~ had been published in the . . . newspapers —H.E.Starr⟩ ⟨enlisted the ~*s* of the best writers —F.H.Chase⟩ ⟨such a scene as no ~ can describe —*Irish Digest*⟩ **b :** a manner of style of writing ⟨his vivid ~ gave a truthful picture of the Southern capital —J.S.Wilson b. 1880⟩ **c :** WRITER **4 :** PINFEATHER **5 :** the internal horny feather-shaped shell of a squid — called also *gladius*

[4]**pen** \"\ *vt* **penned; penned; penning; pens** [ME *pennen*, fr. *penne* pen] **:** WRITE: **a :** to record in writing in proper form ⟨a minute was *penned* that the Corporation might pay . . . the cost —*Crompton & Royton Chronicle*⟩ **b :** to compose and commit to paper ⟨~ a letter⟩ ⟨the best novel he ever *penned*⟩ **c :** to write with a pen ⟨Salesman A ~*s* angular letters —H.O. Teltscher⟩

[5]**pen** \"\ *n* -s [origin unknown] **:** a female swan — compare [3]COB 2

[6]**pen** \"\ *n* -s [by shortening] *slang* **:** PENITENTIARY

[1]**pen-** — see PENE-

[2]**pen-** — see PENTA-

pen *abbr* **1** penetration **2** peninsula **3** penitent

pe·naea \pəˈnēə\ *n* [NL, fr. Pierre *Pena* 16th cent. Fr. botanist] **1** *cap* **:** a genus (the type of the family Penaeaceae) of southern African shrubs with small sessile leaves and spicate yellowish or reddish flowers **2** -s **:** any plant of the genus *Penaea*

pen·ae·a·ce·ae \ˌpenēˈāsēˌē\ *n pl, cap* [NL, fr. *Penaea*, type genus + *-aceae*] **:** a family of small heathlike evergreen shrubs (order Myrtales) with solitary red, apetalous flowers with 4-valvate calyx lobes and 4 stamens — **pen·ae·a·ceous** \ˌ==ˈāshəs\ *adj*

penaeid *var of* PENEID

pe·nae·us \pəˈnēəs\ *syn of* PENEUS

[1]**pe·nal** \ˈpēnᵊl\ *adj* [ME, fr. MF, fr. L *poenalis*, fr. *poena* penalty, punishment + *-alis* -al — more at PAIN] **1 :** designed to impose punishment **:** prescribing, enacting, or threatening punishment **:** PUNITIVE ⟨the ~ clause⟩ **2 :** liable or subject to punishment or a penalty **:** incurring punishment ⟨a ~ offense⟩ **3 :** inflicted as or constituting punishment or penalty or used as a means of punishment ⟨marks for any infraction of the rules . . . were worked off in ~ study —A.W.Long⟩ **4 a :** forfeitable or payable as a penalty **b :** involving or imposing a pecuniary penalty — see PENAL SUM **5 :** of or relating to punishment, penalty, penal laws, or penal servitude ⟨~ reform⟩ **6 :** used as a place of confinement and punishment ⟨a ~ colony⟩ ⟨a ~ farm⟩ **7 :** inflicting a penalty **:** severely disadvantageous ⟨terms decidedly ~ to those who . . . put their money into steel —*Economist*⟩

[2]**penal** \"\ *adj* [*penis* + *-al*] **:** PENIAL

penal action *or* **penal suit** *n* **:** an action under a penal statute

penal code *n* **:** a code of laws concerning crimes and offenses and their punishment

pe·nal·i·ty \pēˈnalәd·ē\ *n* -ES [ML *poenalitas*, fr. L *poenalis* penal + *-itas* -ity] **:** liability to punishment

pe·nal·iz·able \ˈpēnᵊlˌīzəbəl, ˈpen-, ˌ==ˈ===\ *adj* **:** capable of or subject to being penalized

pe·nal·iza·tion \ˌpēnᵊləˈzāshən, ˌpen-, -ᵊlˌīˈ-\ *n* -s **1 :** the act of penalizing **2 :** the state of being penalized

pe·nal·ize \ˈpēnᵊlˌīz, ˈpen-\ *vt* -ED/-ING/-S *see -ize in Explan Notes* [[1]*penal* + *-ize*] **1 :** to inflict a penalty on ⟨~ unlicensed drivers⟩ ⟨~ the team 10 yards for unnecessary roughness⟩ **:** put at a serious disadvantage ⟨following his initial triumph he was bound to be *penalized* by his own achievement —John Mason Brown⟩ **2 :** to make (an action) legally punishable

penal law *n* **1 a :** a law imposing a penalty (as of fine, imprisonment, loss of civil rights) on persons who do or forbear a certain act or acts **b :** the body of such laws **:** CRIMINAL LAW **2 :** PENAL STATUTE 2

pe·nal·ly \ˈpēnᵊlē\ *adv* **:** in a penal manner

penal servitude *n* **:** imprisonment with hard labor in a prison orig. in lieu of transportation

penal statute *n* **1 :** PENAL LAW 1 a **2 :** a statute that provides for the use of the state or a private person wronged a forfeiture or penalty and not compensatory damages against the wrongdoer committing an offense against the state by violating the provisions of the statute and that is distinguished from a statute awarding a civil remedy for compensatory damages against a wrongdoer in favor of the person wronged

penal sum *n* **1 :** a sum of money payable under a statute as a forfeiture for wrongdoing by the wrongdoer to the person wronged **2 :** a sum of money or penalty agreed upon in a bond or in a contract to be paid to one party in case there is a breach of the condition of the bond or in case the other fails to perform his contract in some respect specified

penal theory *n* **:** a development of the satisfaction theory of the atonement introduced by the Protestant reformers and prevalent in Lutheran and Reformed orthodoxy that holds that Christ reconciled man to God by participating in human life to the extent of taking on himself without corruption the status of sinner and bearing in his soul the penal torment and desolation

[1]**pen·al·ty** \ˈpenᵊltē, -ti\ *n* -ES [modif. (influenced by *-ty*) of ML *poenalitas*, fr. L *poenalis* penal + *-itas* -ity] **1 a :** the suffering in person, rights, or property which is annexed by law or judicial decision to the commission of a crime or public offense **:** punishment for crime or offense **:** penal retribution ⟨where a life sentence is the extreme ~⟩ ⟨trespassing forbidden under ~ of imprisonment⟩; *specif* **:** a fine or mulct imposed as such a punishment **b :** a sum of money made recoverable in a civil action by the state or an informer for the less serious offenses not mala in se — compare FINE **2 :** the suffering or the sum to be forfeited to which a person subjects himself by covenant or agreement in case of nonfulfillment of stipulations and which is if imposed in good faith as liquidated damages in general recoverable and enforceable in equity **:** FORFEITURE, FINE **3 :** disadvantage, loss, or hardship due to some action (as transgression or error) **4 :** a disadvantage (as loss of yardage, time, or possession of the ball) imposed for violation of the rules of a contest **5 a** *usu pl* **:** points scored in bridge by a side that defeats the opposing contract **b :** ROYALTY 6

[2]**penalty** \"\ *adj* **1 a** *of government free mail* **:** imprinted with the penalty clause ⟨a ~ envelope⟩ ⟨~ labels⟩ ⟨~ mail⟩ **b :** of or relating to the use of penalty mail ⟨the ~ privilege⟩

2 : involving or received in compensation for hardship ⟨~ taxation⟩ ⟨~ cargo⟩ ⟨~ overtime⟩ ⟨~ pay⟩ ⟨a ~ throw⟩ 3 a : imposed as a penalty ⟨~ time⟩ ⟨a ~ charge⟩ b : used in determining or carrying out a penalty ⟨crossed the ~ line⟩ ⟨~ spot⟩ 4 : being or containing a clause specifying a penalty for violation of an agreement or regulation ⟨a ~ bond⟩ ⟨contained certain ~ provisions⟩

penalty area *n* : an area 44 yards wide and 18 yards deep in front of each goal on a soccer field within which an infringement of given rules by a defending player causes a penalty kick to be awarded to the opposing team

penalty box *n* 1 : a box adjoining an ice-hockey rink for seating penalized players, timekeepers, and scorers 2 : a desk to which a lacrosse player reports when suspended from the game

penalty bully *n* : a penalty in field hockey that is awarded when a member of the defending team fouls inside the striking circle and thus prevents a goal and that consists of a bully five yards in front of the goal between the offending player and any member of the attacking team

penalty card *n, bridge* : a card that has been illegally exposed and must be left faceup on the table and played at the first legal opportunity

penalty clause *also* **penalty indicia** *n* : the statement printed on the cover of a piece of government free mail giving notice of the penalty for private use to avoid payment of postage — compare FRANK *vt* 1

penalty corner *n* : a hit awarded an attacking player in field hockey from any point on the goal line not less than 10 yards from the nearest goalpost when the defending team fouls in its own striking circle — called also *short corner*

penalty double *n* : a double made for the purpose of increasing a bridge score if the opponents' contract is defeated

penalty goal *n* 1 : a goal in rugby or soccer that results from a penalty kick 2 : a goal in field hockey resulting from a penalty bully 3 : an automatic goal in ice hockey awarded an attacking team if an opponent throws his stick at the puck in his own defense zone

penalty kick *n* 1 : a free kick allowed in rugby because of some violation of the rules by the opponents 2 : a free kick allowed in soccer for certain infringements of the rules within the penalty area and made from a mark 12 yards in front of the center of the goal with all players of both sides except the player making the kick and the opposing goalkeeper barred from the penalty area

penalty pass *n, bridge* : a pass of a double that one's partner intended to be taken out

penalty shot *n* 1 : a shot at the goal in ice hockey awarded a team for certain violations by the opposing defense 2 : a free throw in basketball

penalty stroke *n* : a stroke in golf added to the score of a side under certain rules (as when a ball has been lost or hit out of bounds or is deemed unplayable)

1**pen·ance** \'penən(t)s\ *n* -s [ME *penaunce*, fr. OF *penance*, fr. ML *paenitentia* penitence — more at PENITENCE] 1 a : an act of self-abasement, mortification, or devotion either voluntarily performed to show sorrow or repentance for sin or imposed as a punishment for sin by a church official ⟨required to do ~⟩ b : a sacrament in the Roman Catholic and Eastern Churches consisting in repentance or contrition for sin, confession to a priest, satisfaction as imposed by the confessor, and absolution 2 : sorrow or contrition for sin : REPENTANCE, PENITENCE 3 : consequent or compensating hardship or suffering 4 *obs* a : punishment or sufferings after death (as in Hades or purgatory) in expiation of sin b : PUNISHMENT; *specif* : PEINE FORTE ET DURE 5 : PAIN, SORROW, DISTRESS

2**penance** \"\ *vt* -ED/-ING/-S : to impose penance on

1**pen-and-ink** \ˌ=ˌ=ˌ=\ *adj* [fr. the phrase *pen and ink*] : executed with pen and ink ⟨a *pen-and-ink* sketch⟩

2**pen-and-ink** \"\ *n, pl* **pen-and-inks** : a pen-and-ink drawing

penang *var of* PINANG

pe·nang-lawyer \pə'naŋ-\ *n* [*penang* fr. *Penang*, Federation of Malaya] 1 : a walking stick having usu. a bulbous head and made of the stem of an East Asiatic palm (*Licuala acutifida*) 2 : the palm from which a penang-lawyer is made

pen·annular \(')pen+\ *adj* [*pene-* + *annular*] : having the form of a ring with a small break in the circumference ⟨~ silver brooch used to fasten . . . the Highlander's dress —Ian Finlay⟩

pe·na·tes \pə'nād·(ˌ)ēz, -näd-\ *n pl* [L — more at PENETRATE] 1 : the Roman gods of the household and primarily of the storeroom worshiped in close connection with Vesta, goddess of the hearth, and with the lares and household genius 2 : treasured household furnishings

pen-cancel \'pen'kan(t)səl\ *vt* [back-formation fr. *pen cancellation*] : to cancel (a stamp) by hand with a pen

pen cancellation *n* : a stamp cancellation made by hand with a pen (as on a revenue stamp or on a postage stamp) prior to the general use of the handstamp and canceling machine

pence \'pen(t)s\ *pl of* PENNY

pen·cel *or* **pen·cil** *also* **pen·sil** \'pen(t)səl\ *n* -s [ME *pencel, pensil*, modif. of OF *penoncel* — more at PENNONCEL] : PENNONCEL

pence·less \'pen(t)sləs\ *adj* : having no pence : PENNILESS

pench·ant \'penchənt *sometimes* (')pä̃ⁿshäⁿ\ *n* -s [F, fr. pres. part. of *pencher* to incline, bend, fr. (assumed) VL *pendicare*, fr. L *pendere* to weigh — more at PENDANT] : a strong leaning or attraction : strong and continued inclination; *broadly* : LIKING ⟨a ~ for sharp criticism that often offended⟩ : decided taste ⟨a ~ for art⟩ **syn** see LEANING

pen·ché \(')pä̃ⁿ¦shā\ *adj* [F, leaning, stooped, fr. past part. of *pencher* to incline, bend] *ballet* : LEANING, FLEXED

1**pen·cil** \'pen(t)səl\ *n* -s *often attrib* [ME *pensel, pencel*, fr. MF *pincel*, fr. (assumed) VL *penicellus*, fr. L *penicillus* brush, pencil, lit., little tail, dim. of *penis* tail, penis — more at PENIS] 1 : a brush of hair or bristles used to lay on colors; *esp* : a small brush for fine art work 2 : the individual style or technique of an artist or descriptive writer 3 : a tufted growth (as of hair or feathers) 4 a : an implement for writing, drawing, or marking made of or containing a slender rod or strip of a solid marking substance: (1) : a stick of marking substance (as chalk, slate) often encased in paper — see GREASE PENCIL (2) : a wooden rod containing a core of marking substance exposed at one end by sharpening and often having an eraser on the other end ⟨corrected with a red ~⟩ ⟨a ~ sketch⟩ — see LEAD PENCIL (3) : a mechanical device consisting of a cylinder of metal or plastic containing a lead projected by means of a screw b : a small medicated or cosmetic roll or stick for local applications ⟨a menthol ~⟩ c : a writing or marking device resembling a pencil that uses another means of marking ⟨etched by a hot electric ~⟩ 5 a : an aggregate of rays of light or other radiation esp. when diverging from or converging to a point b : the lines passing through a given point and lying on a plane 6 : something long and thin like a pencil ⟨the flashlight sent a long, white ~ of illumination stabbing through the darkness —Erle Stanley Gardner⟩ 7 : PENCIL DIAMOND 8 : graphite used as the marking substance in pencils ⟨written in ~ rather than in ink⟩ ⟨a page half typewritten and half ~⟩

2**pencil** \"\ *vb* **penciled** *or* **pencilled**; **penciled** *or* **pencilled**; **penciling** *or* **pencilling** \-s(ə)liŋ\ **pencils** *vt* 1 a : to paint, draw, shade, write, or mark with or as if with a pencil ⟨a typewritten manuscript with corrections ~*ed* in⟩ : SKETCH ⟨~ in a cartoon with rapid strokes⟩ b : to make a tentative plan of : write (as an assignment) subject to change ⟨had been ~*ed* in for the lead —Budd Schulberg⟩ 2 : to treat (as a wound) by means of a medicated pencil ~ *vi* : to take the shape of a pencil : form into pencils ⟨rays of light ~*ing* through the darkness⟩ ⟨the pale smoke from the cottage chimneys ~ up —William Sansom⟩

3**pencil** *var of* PENCEL

pencil and pearl *n* : BEAD AND REEL

pencil beam *n* : a sharp-focus radar beam nearly round in its axis used to pick up an intruder located by a search radar beam and give it better definition on the radar screen

pencil cedar *n* 1 a : any of several junipers with wood suitable for or used for making pencils: as (1) : RED CEDAR 1 a (2) : EAST AFRICAN CEDAR (3) : a rather small densely pyramidal tree (*Juniperus bermudiana*) that is grown in warm regions as an ornamental b : INCENSE CEDAR 2 *Austral* a : RED BEAN b : SHE-PINE 1 3 : the wood of a pencil cedar

pencil compass *n* : a compass with a pencil on one leg for use in drawing

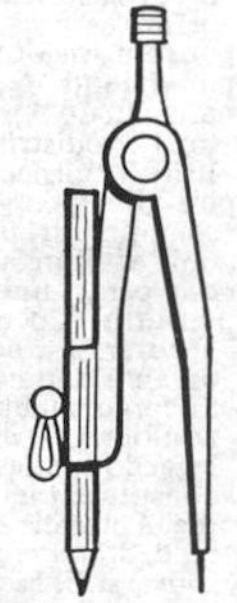
pencil compass

pencil diamond *n* : a chip diamond set in a wooden handle for cutting glass

penciled *adj* [fr. past part. of 2*pencil*] : marked with narrow usu. transverse or concentric lines — used of a feather esp. of a domestic fowl; compare 1BARRED

pencil fish *n* : a small slender So. American topminnow (*Poecilobrycon auratus*) that is sometimes kept in the tropical aquarium and is golden brown with gold, brown, and black stripes running the length of the body and a red spot on the anal fin

pencil flower *n* : a plant of the genus *Stylosanthes*

penciling *n* -s [fr. gerund of 2*pencil*] 1 : the work of the pencil or brush or a product of this ⟨delicate ~ in a picture⟩ 2 : the narrow linear markings of penciled feathers 3 : lines of white or other color drawn along a mortar joint in a brick wall

pen·cil·ler \'pen(t)s(ə)lə(r)\ *n* -s 1 : one that pencils 2 : one that makes or removes pencil marks 3 *Brit* : BOOKMAKER

pencillike \'==ˌ=\ *adj* : having the shape of a pointed rod : STYLOID

pencil orchid *n* : an Australian orchid (*Dendrobium teretifolium*) with terete fleshy leaves

pencil pusher *n* : a person (as a writer, clerk, or bookkeeper) whose work involves writing : INKSLINGER

pencil rod *n* : a round steel rod with a diameter of ¼ inch

pencils *pl of* PENCIL, *pres 3d sing of* PENCIL

pencil sharpener *n* : a device for sharpening the point of a lead pencil by pressure against a rotating blade or cutting edges

pencil sharpener

pencil stone *n* : a compact pyrophyllite used for making slate pencils

pencil stripe *n* : a textile design of fine warp stripes in white or pastel against a dark ground; *also* : a fabric with such a design

pencilwood \'==ˌ=\ *n* : a moderate brown to reddish brown that is lighter than Tuscan brown — called also *mordoré*

pencraft \'=ˌ=\ *n* [3*pen* + *craft*] 1 : skill in using the pen : PENMANSHIP 2 : the use of the pen 3 : the business of writing or of a writer : AUTHORSHIP

1**pend** \'pend\ *vi* -ED/-ING/-S [in sense 1, short for *depend*; in sense 2, fr. obs. F *pendre* to lean, fr. MF, fr. (assumed) VL *pendere*] 1 *chiefly dial* : DEPEND 2 *chiefly dial* : INCLINE, LEAN

2**pend** \"\ *n* -s [obs. E *pend* to arch over, vault, fr. ME *penden*, prob. fr. MF *pendre* to overhang, hang] 1 *Scot* : ARCH, ARCHWAY 2 *Scot* : a covered passage

3**pend** \"\ *n* -s [prob. fr. obs. E *pend* to pen, confine, fr. ME *penden*, prob. alter. of *pennen* to pen — more at PEN] *dial Eng* : PRESSURE, EMERGENCY

pen·da \'pendə\ *n* -s [native name in Australia] : an Australian timber tree (*Xanthostemon oppositifolium*) of the family Myrtaceae with exceptionally heavy hard wood

1**pen·dant** *also* **pen·dent** \'pendənt, *in sense 4* 'penənt\ *n* -s [ME *pendaunt*, fr. MF *pendant*, fr. pres. part. of *pendre* to hang, fr. (assumed) VL *pendere*, fr. L *pendēre*; akin to L *pendere* to weigh, estimate, pay, *pondus* weight, pound, OSlav *pędi* span, *spandyti* to span, Gk *span* to pull, draw — more at SPAN] 1 : something suspended : a hanging object: as a : an ornament that is attached by its upper edge and allowed to hang free ⟨a jeweled ~ on a chain⟩ ⟨ear ~*s*⟩ ⟨a crystal chandelier with 40 ~*s*⟩ b : an electrical fixture (as a droplight or cord switch) suspended from the ceiling 2 a : the often decoratively carved terminal of a vertical member of a structure projecting below another member attached to it: as (1) : a boss formed on the base of a keystone extended below the junction of ribs in late Gothic vaulting (2) : the sculptured lower end of a newel post at the angle of a stair (3) : the end of a vertical timber projecting below the overhanging second floor of an early American colonial house — called also *drop, pendill* b : a carved or molded often bas-relief ornament (as a representation of fruit or flowers) attached to a ceiling or wall in a hanging position 3 *naut* a : a short rope or wire rope hanging from a spar and having at its free end a block or spliced thimble — called also *pennant* b : a length of rope or wire rope with eyes, blocks, or hooks spliced in the ends — often used with a qualifier specifying position or purpose ⟨a centerboard ~⟩ ⟨a mooring ~⟩ — see SHIP illustration 4 : PENNANT 2 a — used chiefly by the British navy 5 : the part of a pocket watch from which the chain is suspended; *specif* : the shank on the watch stem to which the bow attaches 6 a : something (as a picture) forming a match, companion piece, or counterpart to another b : something forming a supplement (as to a book) ⟨publishes the present book frankly as a ~ to his earlier one —Lionel Stevenson⟩ **syn** see FLAG

2**pendant** *var of* PENDENT

pendant post *n* : a part of the framing of an open-timbered roof that consists of a post set against the wall, resting on a corbel or other solid support, and supporting the ends of a collar beam or any part of the roof

pendant-set \ˌ=ˌ=ˌ=\ *adj, of a watch* : set by pulling out the stem

pendant switch *n* : CORD SWITCH

pendant tackle *n* : a tackle attached to a pendant (as on a masthead) for hoisting, tautening, or staying purposes

pendant-winding \ˌ=ˌ=ˌ=ˌ=\ *adj* : STEM-WINDING

pend d'o·reille \ˌpändəˌrā\ *n, pl* **pend d'oreille** *or* **pend d'oreilles** *or* **pends d'oreille** \-ä(z)\ *usu cap P&O* [modif. of F *pendant d'oreille* earring; prob. fr. the fact that members of the tribe used to wear large shell earrings] : KALISPEL

pen·de·loque \ˌpäⁿdᵊ'lōk\ *n* -s [F, blend of obs. F *pendeler* to dangle (dim. of F *pendre* to hang) and F *breloque* charm, breloque] 1 : a diamond or other gemstone cut in the form of a pear-shaped brilliant with a table — compare BRIOLETTE; see CUT illustration 2 : a usu. pear-shaped glass pendant used for ornamenting a lamp or chandelier

pen·den·cy \'pendənsē, -si\ *n* -ES [1*pendent* + *-cy*] : the state of being pending ⟨during the ~ of a suit at law⟩ ⟨during the ~ of the war⟩

1**pen·dent** *or* **pen·dant** \'pendənt\ *adj* [ME *pendaunt* — more at PENDANT] 1 a : supported from above : SUSPENDED ⟨vines bearing ~ bunches of grapes⟩ ⟨a plant with a ~ blossom⟩ ⟨icicles ~ from the eaves⟩ b *archaic* : hanging without visible support : FLOATING ⟨blown . . . round about the ~ world —Shak.⟩ 2 : sloping steeply down ⟨a ~ hillside⟩ 3 : jutting or leaning over : OVERHANGING ⟨a ~ cliff⟩ 4 : remaining undetermined : PENDING ⟨a claim still ~⟩ 5 : marked by incomplete grammatical construction

2**pendent** *var of* PENDANT

pen·den·te lite \pen'dentē'līt̬ē\ *adv* [NL] : during the suit : while litigation continues ⟨the granting of an injunction *pendente lite* —Benjamin Werne⟩

1**pen·den·tive** \pen'dentiv, -tēv *also* -təv\ *n* -s [F *pendentif*, fr. L *pendent-, pendens* (pres. part. of *pendēre* to hang) + F *-if* -ive] 1 : one of the triangular spherical sections of vaulting that spring from the corners of a rectangular ground plan and serve to allow the room enclosing it to be covered by a cupola of rounded or polygonal plan 2 : any supporting member at the corner of a square or polygonal plan for making transition to a circular or octagonal plan — compare SQUINCH 3 : the part of a groined vault that springs from a single pier or corbel

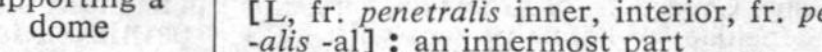
pendentives 1 supporting a dome

2**pendentive** \(')=ˌ=\ *adj* 1 : of, relating to, or having pendentives 2 : formed like a pendentive

pen·dent·ly *adv* : in a pendent manner

pen·di·cle \'pendəkəl\ *n* -s [ME, prob. fr. ML *pendiculum* appendage, fr. LL *pendiculus* cord, noose, fr. L *pendere* to weigh — more at PENDANT] 1 : a pendent ornament 2 *Scot* : a property forming part of a large estate; *esp* : one rented separately

pen·dill \'pendᵊl\ *n* -s [earlier *pendle* overhanging part, pendant, prob. modif. of MF *pendisel*, dim. of *pendre* to hang — more at PENDANT] : PENDANT 2 a (3)

1**pending** *pres part of* PEND

2**pend·ing** \'pendiŋ, -dēŋ\ *prep* [F *pendant* (fr. pres. part. of *pendre* to hang, suspend, after L *pendente*, abl. of *pendent-, pendens*, pres. part.) + E *-ing*] 1 : through the period of continuance or indeterminacy of : DURING ⟨their opportunity to develop trade ~ the laborious and fruitless negotiations —Theodore Hsi-En Chen⟩ 2 : until the occurrence or completion of : while awaiting ⟨military rule . . . prevailed ~ the adoption of a new constitution —*Amer. Guide Series: N.C.*⟩ ⟨four withholding a vote ~ further information —*Jour. of Accountancy*⟩

3**pending** \"\ *adj* [F *pendant* + E *-ing*] 1 : not yet decided : in continuance : in suspense ⟨the drafting of opinions and decisions on cases ~ before the Commission —*Current Biog.*⟩ ⟨that on all important ~ problems he be given . . . also minority views —Dorothy Fosdick⟩ 2 : IMPENDING, IMMINENT ⟨the war scare in Europe, with the ~ strife between communism and fascism —Leon Halden⟩

pen·dle \'pendᵊl\ *n* -s [F *pendille*, fr. *pendiller* to hang, fr. MF, fr. *pendre*] *chiefly dial* : a pendent object (as an earring or a pendulum)

pen·drag·on \pen'dragən\ *n* -s [ME, fr. W, fr. *pen* chief + *dragon* leader, fr. L *dracon-, draco* dragon; fr. the figure of a dragon on the leader's standard — more at DRAGON] *often cap* : a chief leader among the ancient British chiefs (as in time of war) : head of all the chiefs : KING

pends *pres 3d sing of* PEND, *pl of* PEND

pen·du·lant *or* **pen·du·lent** \'penjələnt, -nd(y)əl-\ *adj* [L *pendulus* hanging, pendent (fr. *pendere* to weigh) + E *-ant* or *-ent*] : PENDULOUS

pen·du·lar \-lə(r)\ *adj* [F *pendulaire*, fr. *pendule* pendulum (fr. L *pendulus*) + *-aire* -ar] : being or resembling the movement of a pendulum : swinging or undulating back and forth ⟨public opinion has moved in violent ~ swings between optimism and pessimism —*New Republic*⟩ ⟨~ vibrations produce the sine wave —C.S.Myers⟩ ⟨the ~ movements of the isolated rat intestine —Gilles Papineau-Couture⟩

pen·du·late \-ˌlāt\ *vi* -ED/-ING/-S [NL *pendulum* + E *-ate*] 1 : to swing as a pendulum 2 : FLUCTUATE, UNDULATE **syn** see SWING

pen·du·la·tion \ˌ==ˈlāshən\ *n* -s [NL *pendulum* + E *-ation*] : a pendular movement : OSCILLATION

pen·dule \'penˌjül\ *n* -s [F, fr. L *pendulus* hanging, pendent] : a timepiece having a pendulum; *specif* : an ornate French chamber clock of the late 18th century sometimes with escutcheons, shields, masts, and historical or mythical figures

pen·du·lette \ˌpenjə'let\ *n* -s [F, fr. *pendule* + *-ette*] : a small table clock with short fast-moving pendulum

1**pen·du·line** \'penjələn, -ˌlīn\ *adj* [NL *pendulinus* (specific epithet of *Anthoscopus pendulinus*, genus of titmice), fr. L *pendulus* hanging, pendent + *-inus* -ine] : constructing hanging nests

2**penduline** \"\ *n* -s [NL *Pendulinus*, a genus of titmice (Aegithalos) in former classifications, fr. L *pendulus* + *-inus* -ine] : a penduline bird

penduline titmouse *n* : a titmouse (*Remiz pendulinus*) of southern Europe that builds an ovoid nest suspended in the twigs of a bush or tree

pen·du·los·i·ty \ˌpenjə'läsəd·ē\ *n* -ES : the quality or state of being pendulous

pen·du·lous \'penjələs, -nd(y)əl-\ *adj* [L *pendulus*, fr. *pendēre* to hang — more at PENDANT] 1 a *obs* : suspended or projecting so as to overhang b *archaic* : poised without visible support 2 a : suspended so as to swing freely ⟨branches hung with ~ vines⟩ b : inclined or hanging downward : DROOPING ⟨a ~ ovule on the upper part of a carpel⟩ ⟨a corpulent old man with flabby, ~ jowls⟩ 3 : WAVERING, VACILLATING ⟨a state of ~ uncertainty⟩ — **pen·du·lous·ly** *adv* — **pen·du·lous·ness** *n* -ES

pendulous crop *n* : a greatly dilated crop occurring esp. in strains of the turkey as a permanent deformity following initial distention by heavy liquid intake during hot weather — called also *drop crop*

pen·du·lum \-ləm\ *n* -s *often attrib* [NL, fr. L, neut. of *pendulus* hanging, pendent] 1 a : a body suspended from a fixed point so as to swing freely to and fro under the action of gravity and commonly used to regulate the movements of clockwork and other machinery b : a suspended body that vibrates not by swinging but by rotating, with alternate twisting and untwisting (as the balance wheel of a watch) — called also *torsion pendulum* 2 : something that alternates between opposites ⟨the ~ of public opinion⟩ 3 : a technique used in mountain climbing to accomplish a difficult traverse by swinging across on a rope

pendulum gun *n* [so called fr. its motion when fired] : a mechanism for obtaining certain ballistic data for given shotshell loadings that consists of a tube fitted with a breech and a firing mechanism and moving freely on its four supporting wires and that by means of attached and coordinated instruments determines velocity, time required for shot charge to pass through barrel, chamber pressure, energy of recoil, and shot pattern

pendulum level *n* : PLUMB LEVEL

pendulum press *n* : a small foot-operated punch press with a swinging treadle

pendulum saw *n* : a circular saw arranged to swing in a vertical arc for crosscut work

pendulum watch *n* : a late 18th century watch with a mock pendulum attached to a concealed balance wheel and showing through a curved slit in the dial

pene- *also* **pen-** *prefix* [L *paene-, pene-*, fr. *paene, pene* almost — more at PATIENT] : almost ⟨*pene*plain⟩ ⟨*pen*acute⟩

pe·ne·contemporaneous \ˌpēnē+\ *adj* [*pene-* + *contemporaneous*] : of, relating to, or being a geological phenomenon originating or effectuated during or soon after the formation of the rocks in which it is displayed ⟨a ~ mineral⟩ ⟨~ structures⟩ — **pe·ne·con·tem·po·ra·ne·ous·ly** *adv*

1**pe·ne·id** *also* **pe·nae·id** \pə'nēəd\ *adj* [NL *Peneidae*] : of or relating to the Peneidae

2**peneid** *also* **penaeid** \"\ *n* -s : a prawn of the family Peneidae

pe·ne·idae \-ēəˌdē\ *n pl, cap* [NL, fr. *Peneus*, type genus + *-idae*] : a family of chiefly warm water and tropical prawns (tribe Peneides) including several edible prawns — see PENEUS

pe·ne·ides \-ˌdēz\ *n pl, cap* [NL, fr. *Peneus* + *-ides*] : a tribe of decapod crustaceans (suborder Natantia) comprising shrimps and prawns in which the lateral plates of the second abdominal segment do not overlap those of the first segment

pe·nel·o·pe \pə'neləpē\ *n, cap* [NL, fr. L *Penelope*, faithful wife of Ulysses in Greek legend, fr. Gk *Pēnelopē*] : a genus of guans

pe·nel·o·pine \-ləˌpīn, -ˌpən\ *adj* [NL *Penelope* + E *-ine*] : of or relating to the genus *Penelope*

1**pe·ne·plain** *also* **pe·ne·plane** \ˌpēnē, ˌpēnə+\ *n* [*pene-* + *plain* or *plane*] : an erosion surface of considerable area and slight relief — called also *endrumpf*; compare BASELEVEL PLAIN

2**peneplain** *or* **peneplane** \"\ *vt* -ED/-ING/-S : to erode to a peneplain

pe·ne·pla·na·tion \ˌpēnəplə'nāshən\ *n* : the process of peneplaining a land surface : erosion to a peneplain

penes *pl of* PENIS

pe·ne·seismic \ˌpēnē+\ *adj* [ISV *pene-* + *seismic*] : being or relating to a region rarely affected by earthquakes

pen·e·tra·bil·i·ty \ˌpenə·trə'biləd·ē, -lətē, -i\ *n* [F *pénétrabilité*, fr. *pénétrable* penetrable (fr. L *penetrabilis*) + *-ité* -ity] : the quality or state of being penetrable

pen·e·tra·ble \'penə·trəbəl\ *adj* [L *penetrabilis*, fr. *penetrare* to penetrate + *-abilis* -able] : capable of being penetrated — **pen·e·tra·ble·ness** *n* -ES — **pen·e·tra·bly** \-blē, -li\ *adv*

pen·e·tra·le \ˌpenə·'trālē\ *or* **pen·e·tral** \'penə·trəl\ *n* -s [L, fr. *penetralis* inner, interior, fr. *penetrare* to penetrate + *-alis* -al] : an innermost part

pen·e·tra·lia \ˌpenə·'trālēə\ *n pl* [L, pl. of *penetrale*] 1 : the innermost or most private parts of some thing or place (as a temple or palace) ⟨explored the shuddery ~ of caves —Spencer Brown⟩ **2 :** hidden things or secrets **:** PRIVACY, SANCTUARY ⟨admitted to the inmost ~ of affairs —A.C.Benson⟩

pen·e·tram·e·ter \ˌpenəˈtraməd·ə(r)\ *n* [*penetration* + *-meter*] **:** a device for measuring the penetrating power of X rays or other radiation by comparing transmission through different absorbers — called also *penetrometer*

pen·e·trance \ˈpenətrən(t)s\ *n* -s [ISV *penetrant* + *-ance*] **:** the relative ability of a gene to produce its specific effect in any degree whatever in the organism of which it is a part sometimes measured as the percentage of individuals that detectably manifest the effect in a group in which the gene is present — compare EXPRESSIVITY

¹pen·e·trant \-rənt\ *adj* [MF or L; MF *penetrant*, fr. L *penetrant-, penetrans*, pres. part. of *penetrare* to penetrate] **:** that penetrates **:** PENETRATING ⟨a ~ wind⟩ ⟨a ~ fumigant⟩

²penetrant \"\ *n* -s **:** one that penetrates or is capable of penetrating: as **a :** a large barbed nematocyst designed to pierce the body of the prey and inject a paralyzing substance **b :** a penetrating agent **:** a surface-active agent having high penetrating power — compare WETTING AGENT

pen·e·trate \ˈpenəˌtrāt, *usu* -ād·+V\ *vb* -ED/-ING/-S [L *penetratus*, past part. of *penetrare* to penetrate; akin to L *penitus* inward, inwardly, *penes* with, in the possession of, *penus* food provisions, innermost part of a house, *Penates* household gods, Lith *peneti* to nourish, fatten and perh. to Goth *fenea* pearl barley] *vt* **1 a :** to pass into or through: (1) **:** to extend into the interior of ⟨this route . . . ~*s* the leading resort and lake areas —*Amer. Guide Series: Minn.*⟩ (2) **:** to enter or go through by overcoming resistance ⟨nails . . . of sufficient length to pass through the insulation and ~ the roof boards at least ¾ of an inch —P.D.Close⟩ ⟨it required a long time for an idea to ~ the heads of this stubborn people —V.G.Heiser⟩ **:** PIERCE ⟨the salt rain driven by the wind ~*s* the thickest coat —Richard Jefferies⟩ ⟨a smooth voice that *penetrated* the mighty vibrations of the falls —C.G.D.Roberts⟩ ⟨the doctor's words of encouragement finally *penetrated* my despair —Herbert King⟩ (3) **:** to gain entrance to ⟨an apartment I now *penetrated* for the first time —Osbert Lancaster⟩ ⟨youngsters under 21 who, 10 years ago, could never have *penetrated* the underworld circles where they now circulate freely —D.W.Maurer & V.H. Vogel⟩ **b :** to see into or through ⟨their keen eyes can ~ the water to a depth of . . . forty feet —L.K.Porritt⟩ **c :** to insert the penis into the vagina of in copulation **2 a :** to pierce into with the mind **:** discover the inner contents or meaning of ⟨a scientific secret which will eventually be *penetrated* by other countries —Vera M. Dean⟩ **:** perceive or recognize the precise nature of ⟨~ his disguise and expose his true identity⟩ **:** UNDERSTAND, FATHOM ⟨the seer who ~*s* the underlying principles of men and things —C.H.Grandgent⟩ **b :** to affect profoundly through the senses or feelings **:** touch with feeling **:** move deeply ⟨men may still be *penetrated* with awe by the divine righteousness —R.W.Dale⟩ **3 a :** to diffuse through **:** PERMEATE ⟨the cold began to ~ his bones —E.K.Gann⟩ ⟨corruption *penetrated* . . . the country's mercantile class —T.E. Ennis⟩ **:** INFILTRATE ⟨the Communist plan to ~ political parties and unions⟩ **b :** to cause to be diffused (as with a feeling) **:** IMBUE, STEEP ⟨choose a fitting action, ~ yourself with the feeling of its situations —Matthew Arnold⟩ **~** *vi* **1 a** (1) **:** to pass, extend, pierce, or diffuse into or through something ⟨fishes . . . which enter tidal rivers and ~ almost to fresh water —J.L.B.Smith⟩ ⟨fjords . . . ~ more than 300 kilometers inland —Valter Schytt⟩ ⟨an acid that ~*s* into the tissues⟩ ⟨time for the news to ~ to all the distant country places —Mary Austin⟩ (2) **:** to get (as by force or resolution) past an obstacle or boundary ⟨*penetrated* . . . beyond the Rhine, the Alps, and the Pyrenees —Alfred Cobban⟩ ⟨circumnavigated the southern ice region . . ., *penetrating* beyond lat. 67 S. —*Encyc. Americana*⟩ (3) **:** to gain admittance (as to an exclusive group) ⟨women who ~ to the upper levels of the bureaucracy⟩ ⟨secret Communist agents had *penetrated* into high government circles —T.R. Fyvel⟩ **b :** to pierce something with the eye or mind **:** see or enable to see into or through something hidden or obscure ⟨strained his eyes to ~ beyond the thick cloud of dust⟩ ⟨a telescope that ~*s* to the remote parts of the universe⟩ ⟨insight that ~*s* to the very heart of some . . . problem —W.F.Hambly⟩ **2 :** to affect deeply the senses or feelings ⟨the suggestion might ~ deeply enough . . . to make her a good deal more wary —H.A.Overstreet⟩ **syn** see ENTER, PERMEATE

penetrating *adj* **1 :** having the power of entering, piercing, or pervading **:** PENETRATIVE ⟨a ~ oil⟩ ⟨a ~ shriek⟩ ⟨a ~ odor⟩ **2 :** quick to discover **:** ACUTE, DISCERNING ⟨a ~ mind⟩ — **pen·e·trat·ing·ly** *adv* — **pen·e·trat·ing·ness** *n* -ES

pen·e·tra·tion \ˌpenəˈtrāshən\ *n* -s [L *penetration-, penetratio*, fr. *penetratus* (past part. of *penetrare*) + *-ion-, -io* -ion] **1 :** the act or process of penetrating ⟨Indian groups . . . angered by the constant ~*s* of whites into their new territories —P.W.Gates⟩ ⟨the ~ of the theater by scholarship and taste —R.W.Speaight⟩: as **a :** the act (as of a foreign diplomatic or commercial body) of entering a country so continued or repeated that actual establishment of influence is accomplished **b :** an attack that drives a wedge into or through the enemy's front ⟨when the situation does not favor an envelopment, the main attack is directed toward a ~ —C.E.Welsh⟩ **c :** flight in air warfare over enemy territory and through enemy air defenses to attack ground targets ⟨a shallow ~ mission⟩ ⟨~ tactics⟩ ⟨a ~ fighter⟩ **2 a :** the depth to which something penetrates; *specif* **:** the depth to which a projectile sinks into any substance at which it is fired **b :** the power or ability to penetrate or its manifestation **:** PENETRATIVENESS ⟨used a lighter oil for its superior ~⟩ ⟨the human eye aided by telescopes and microscopes of ever greater ~⟩; *specif* **:** the ability to discern acutely the inner nature or meaning of something or the resulting perceptive quality of expression (as in a written work) ⟨a writer who analyzes the underlying causes with great ~⟩ ⟨good little novels, full of Gallic irony and ~ —*Time*⟩ **c :** depth of field (as of a microscope) **d :** the extent to which a commercial product or agency is familiar or sells in a market ⟨the manufacturer's view of the dealer's performance is based on ~ of the market —Hartley Howe⟩ **3 :** the intersection of a minor architectural form and a major one ⟨the ~ of a minor vault with a main vault⟩ **4 :** the penetrability of a bituminous material expressed as the distance that a standard needle vertically penetrates a sample of the material under known conditions of loading, time, and temperature

penetration gland *n* **:** one of the anterior glands of some cercarias that actively invade the skin of the definitive host and are believed to produce a histolytic secretion

penetration path *n* **:** the course taken by the sperm in entering the egg — compare COPULATION PATH

penetration twin *n* **:** a twin crystal in which the two parts are joined along a complex surface so that they appear to penetrate through one another — see TWIN illustration

pen·e·tra·tive \ˈpenəˌtrād·|iv, -trə|, |t|, |ēv *also* |əv\ *adj* [ME, fr. MF or ML; MF *penetratif*, fr. ML *penetrativus*, fr. L *penetratus*, past part. + *-ivus* -ive] **1 :** tending to penetrate **:** of a penetrating quality **:** PIERCING ⟨applying a toxic ~ spray to the bark surface —F.C.Craighead b. 1890 & J.M.Miller⟩ **2 :** ACUTE ⟨stimulate in the reader intuitive faculties more ~ than formal reasoning —C.E.Montague⟩ ⟨frequent ~ observations —J.C.Ireson⟩ **3 :** IMPRESSIVE ⟨~ lecturers . . . sent the hearer home with an idea, or a fact, or an enthusiasm firmly and usefully planted —H.S.Canby⟩ — **pen·e·tra·tive·ly** \|əvlē, -li\ *adv* — **pen·e·tra·tive·ness** \|ivnəs\ *n* -ES

pen·e·tra·tiv·i·ty \ˌpenəˈtrāˈtivəd·ē\ *n* -ES **:** the quality or state of being penetrative **:** PENETRATIVENESS

pen·e·tra·tor \ˈpenəˌtrād·ə(r)\ *n* -s [LL, fr. L *penetratus* (past part. of *penetrare* to penetrate) + *-or* — more at PENETRATE] **:** one that penetrates

pen·e·trom·e·ter \ˌpenəˈträməd·ə(r)\ *n* [ISV *penetro-* (fr. L *penetrare* + *-o-*) + *-meter*] **:** an instrument for determining penetrability or ability to penetrate: as **a :** an instrument for measuring the consistency of semisolids (as pitch, grease) from the depth to which a needle penetrates under given conditions **b :** PENETRAMETER

pe·ne·us \pəˈnēəs\ *n, cap* [NL, prob. fr. L *Peneus*, river in northwestern Peloponnesus, Greece, fr. Gk *Pēneios*] **:** a genus (the type of the family Peneidae) of edible prawns with well-developed rostrum and exopodites on all but the last pair of legs

pen feather [³*pen*] *n* **:** a quill feather

pen·field·ite \ˈpenˌfēlˌdīt\ *n* -s [Samuel L. *Penfield* †1905 Am. mineralogist + E *-ite*] **:** a mineral $Pb_2(OH)Cl_3$ consisting of a basic lead chloride and occurring in white hexagonal prisms

penfold *var of* PINFOLD

pen-friend \ˈ=ˌ=\ *n* **:** PEN PAL

peng·hu·lu \ˈpeŋˈü(ˌ)lü\ *n* -s [Malay *pĕnghulu*, fr. *hulu* head, top] **:** a district or village headman in Indonesia, Malaya, or British Borneo

pen·gö \ˈpenˌgə̄\ *n, pl* **pengö** *or* **pengös** [Hung *pengő*, lit., sounding, fr. *pengeni* to sound, jingle] **1 :** the basic monetary unit of Hungary from 1925 to 1946 **2 :** a coin representing one pengö unit

pen·guin \ˈpengwən, -eŋg-\ *n* -s [perh. fr. W *pen gwyn* white head, fr. *pen* head + *gwyn* white; perh. fr. a white promontory on an island near Newfoundland where great auks were found in large numbers in the 16th century — more at ARPENT, FINNOCK] **1** *archaic* **:** GREAT AUK **2 :** any of various short-legged flightless aquatic birds of the southern hemisphere that constitute the family Spheniscidae, are most numerous about the Antarctic continent, the Falkland islands, and New Zealand, stand erect on land but walk clumsily, are covered with short, stiff, scalelike feathers many of which are simple shafts without barbs, have wings resembling flippers, bearing only rudimentary scalelike quills, being used for swimming and incapable of flexure but moved with a rotary motion by specially developed muscles, and feed chiefly on crustaceans, mollusks, and fish — see EMPEROR PENGUIN, JACKASS PENGUIN, KING PENGUIN, ROCK HOPPER

penguin duck *n* **:** INDIAN RUNNER

pen·guin·ery *also* **pen·guin·ry** \-ən(ə)rē\ *n* -ES **:** a breeding place of penguins

pengun \ˈ=ˌ=\ *n* [³*pen* + *gun*; fr. its being orig. made from quills] *Scot* **:** POPGUN

penholder \ˈ=ˌ==\ *n* **1 :** a holder or handle for a pen **2 :** a rack for holding pens

-pe·nia \ˈpēnēə\ *n comb form* -s [NL, fr. Gk *penia* poverty, lack] **:** deficiency of ⟨erythro*penia*⟩ ⟨thrombo*penia*⟩ ⟨eosino*penia*⟩

penholder 2

pe·ni·al \ˈpēnēəl\ *adj* [F *pénial*, fr. *pénis* penis, fr. L *penis* — more at PENIS] **1 :** PENILE **2 :** functioning as a penis ⟨~ setae⟩

pen·i·cil·la·mine \ˌpenəˈsiləˌmēn\ *n* [*penicillin* + *amine*] **:** an amino acid $(CH_3)_2C(SH)CH(NH_2)COOH$ obtained by acid hydrolysis of the penicillins; β-mercapto-valine or β,β-dimethyl-cysteine

pen·i·cil·lary \ˌpenəˈsilərē\ *adj* [NL *penicillus* + E *-ary*] **:** of, relating to, or being a penicillus

pen·i·cil·late \ˌpenəˈsilət, -ˌlāt\ *adj* [prob. fr. (assumed) NL *penicillatus*, fr. L *penicillus* brush + *-atus* -ate] **:** furnished with a tuft of fine hairs **:** ending in a tuft of hairs like a camel's-hair brush **:** PENICILLIFORM ⟨a grass with ~ stigmas⟩ ⟨the ~ ear of the squirrel⟩ — **pen·i·cil·late·ly** *adv* — **pen·i·cil·la·tion** \ˌpenəsəˈlāshən\ *n* -s

pen·i·cil·lat·ed \ˌ==ˈsiˌlād·əd\ *adj* **:** PENICILLATE

pen·i·cil·lic acid \ˌ==ˈsilik-\ *n* [NL *Penicillium* + E *-ic*] **:** a crystalline antibiotic unsaturated keto acid $CH_2{=}C(CH_3)COC(OCH_3){=}CHCOOH$ or the tautomeric hydroxy lactone produced by several molds of the genera *Penicillium* and *Aspergillus*

pen·i·cil·li·form \ˌ==ˈsiləˌfȯrm\ *adj* [prob. fr. (assumed) NL *penicilliformis*, fr. L *penicillus* brush + *-iformis* -iform] **:** PENICILLATE

pen·i·cil·lin \ˌpenəˈsilən\ *n* -s [*penicill-* (fr. NL *Penicillium*) + *-in*] **1 :** a mixture of antibiotic relatively nontoxic acids produced esp. by molds of the genus *Penicillium* (as *P. notatum* or *P. chrysogenum*) and having a powerful bacteriostatic effect against various bacteria (as staphylococci, gonococci, pneumococci, hemolytic streptococci, or some meningococci) **2 :** any of numerous often hygroscopic and unstable amido acids that have the general formula $RCONH(C_7H_9NOS)COOH$ and contain fused thiazolidine and beta-lactam rings in their structures and that are components of the penicillin mixture or are produced biosynthetically by the use of different strains of molds or different media or are synthesized chemically: as **a** *or* **penicillin F** *also* **penicillin I :** the first penicillin $C_5H_9CONH(C_7H_9NOS)COOH$ isolated in Britain; 2-pentenyl-penicillin **b** *or* **penicillin G** *also* **penicillin II :** the penicillin $C_6H_5CH_2CONH(C_7H_9NOS)COOH$ that constitutes the principal or sole component of most commercial preparations and is used chiefly in the form of stable salts (as the crystalline sodium salt or the crystalline procaine salt) — called also benzylpenicillin **c** *or* **penicillin V :** a crystalline nonhygroscopic acid $C_6H_5OCH_2CONH(C_7H_9NOS)COOH$ that is produced biosynthetically and synthetically and that is similar to penicillin G in antibacterial action but is better absorbed by the gastrointestinal tract — called also *phenoxymethylpenicillin* **3 :** a salt or ester of a penicillin acid or a mixture of such salts or esters

pen·i·cil·lin·ase \-əˌnās\ *n* -s [*penicillin* + *-ase*] **:** an enzyme that inactivates the penicillins by hydrolyzing them and that is found esp. in bacteria

pen·i·cil·lin·ic acid \ˌpenəsəˈlinik-\ *n* [*penicillin* + *-ic*] **:** PENICILLIN 2

pen·i·cil·li·o·sis \ˌpenəˌsilēˈōsəs\ *n, pl* **penicillio·ses** \-ōˌsēz\ [NL, fr. *Penicillium* + *-osis*] **:** infection with or disease caused by molds of the genus *Penicillium*

pen·i·cil·li·um \ˌpenəˈsilēəm\ *n* [NL, fr. L *penicillus* brush + NL *-ium*] **1** *cap* **:** a genus of fungi (family Moniliaceae) comprising the blue molds found chiefly on moist nonliving organic matter (as decaying fruit), characterized by the erect branching conidiophores ending in tufts of club-shaped cells from which conidia are formed in chains, and including molds useful in economic fermentation — compare CAMEMBERT CHEESE, PENICILLIN **2** *pl* **penicil·lia** \-ēə\ **:** any mold of the genus *Penicillium*

pen·i·cil·lo·ic acid \ˌpenəsəˈlōik-\ *n* [*penicillin* + *-oic*] **:** an amido dicarboxylic acid that has the general formula $RCONH(C_6H_{10}NS)(COOH)_2$ and is obtained from a penicillin by hydrolytic opening of the lactam ring (as by mild treatment with alkali or by the action of a penicillinase)

pen·i·cil·lus \ˌpenəˈsiləs\ *n, pl* **penicil·li** \-iˌlī\ [NL, fr. L, brush, pencil — more at PENCIL] **1 :** one of the small straight arteries of the red pulp of the spleen **2 :** the branching penicillate conidiophore in fungi of *Penicillium* or similar genera

pe·ni·el mission \pəˈnīəl-, ˈpenēəl-\ *n, usu cap P&M* [*peniel* prob. fr. Heb *Pĕnīel, Pĕnuel*, lit., face of God, place on the Jabbok river in Jordan where Jacob wrestled with a stranger and received a blessing (Gen 32: 30 AV)] **:** one of a number of religious groups centering in California that carry on a program of mass evangelism on city streets

pe·ni·form \ˈpēnəˌfȯrm\ *adj* [*penis* + *-form*] **:** resembling a penis ⟨~ setae⟩

¹penile *n* -s [*pene-* + obs. *ile* isle, fr. ME — more at ISLE] *obs* **:** PENINSULA

²pe·nile \ˈpēnᵊl, -ēˌnīl\ *adj* [*penis* + *-ile* (adj. suffix)] **:** of, relating to, by means of, or affecting the penis

pe·nil·lion \pəˈnilyən\ *n pl* [W, pl. of *penill* verse] **:** orig. improvised but now usu. traditional Welsh verses and melody sung (as in an eisteddfod) in counterpoint to a familiar tune played on the harp

pe·nin·su·la \pəˈnin(t)s(ə)lə, -inchələ, -inshələ *sometimes* -insyələ\ *n* -s [L *paeninsula*, fr. *paene-* pene- + *insula* island — more at ISLE] **1 a :** a portion of land nearly surrounded by water and connected with a larger body by an isthmus — distinguished from *mainland* **b :** a piece of land jutting out into the water whether with or without a well-defined isthmus ⟨the Italian ~⟩ **2 :** something that juts out in the manner of a peninsula ⟨the ~ of land at the angle of the two roads⟩ ⟨a cooking ~ projecting from one wall and dividing the working and eating areas⟩

peninsula pine *n* **:** JEFFREY PINE

¹pe·nin·su·lar \-lə(r)\ *adj* [L *paeninsula* + E *-ar*] **1 :** of, belonging to, forming, or like a peninsula ⟨the many beaches of the ~ region⟩ **2** *often cap* **:** of, relating to, or characteristic of the Iberian peninsula ⟨the Spanish Civil War . . . worked out with a peculiar ~ glory and despair —*Newsweek*⟩

²peninsular \"\ *n* -s **:** an inhabitant of a peninsula

pe·nin·su·lar·i·ty \pəˌnin(t)səˈlarəd·ē\ *n* -ES **1 :** the state of being a peninsula **2 :** adherence to local ideas and customs (as due to peninsular isolation) **:** PROVINCIALISM

pe·nin·su·late \pəˈnin(t)səˌlāt\ *vt* -ED/-ING/-S [L *paeninsula* + E *-ate*] **:** to form into a peninsula

pe·nis \ˈpēnəs\ *n, pl* **pe·nes** \-ēˌnēz\ *or* **penises** [L, penis, tail; akin to Gk *peos, posthē* penis, Skt *pasas* penis, OE *fæsl* fetus, offspring, OHG *faselt* penis, *fasel* fetus, offspring, ON *fösull*] **1 :** the copulatory organ of the male of a higher vertebrate animal that in mammals usu. provides also the channel by which urine leaves the body and is typically a cylindrical organ made up of a broad root by which it is suspended from the pubic arch, an elongated cylindrical body consisting chiefly of a pair of large lateral corpora cavernosa and a smaller ventromedial corpus cavernosum containing the urethra, and a terminal glans enclosing the ends of the corpora cavernosa, covered by mucous membrane, and sheathed by a foreskin continuous with the skin covering the body of the organ **2 :** any of various male copulatory organs that are not homologous with the vertebrate penis (as the aedeagus of an insect or the copulatory setae of some worms)

penis bone *n* **:** BACULUM

penis envy *n* **:** the unverbalized longing of a girl or woman to be a boy or man

pen·i·ston *also* **pen·i·stone** \ˈpenəstən\ *n* -s *often cap* [fr. *Penistone*, town in Yorkshire, England, where it was first made] **:** a coarse woolen cloth used for clothing from the 16th into the 19th century

pen·i·tence \ˈpenəd·ən(t)s, -ətən- *also* -ətᵊn-\ *n* -s [ME, fr. OF, fr. ML *poenitentia*, alter. (influenced by L *poena* penalty, pain) of L *paenitentia* regret, fr. *paenitent-, paenitens* (pres. part. of *paenitēre* to be sorry, cause to be sorry) + *-ia* -y; akin to L *paene* almost — more at PAIN, PATIENT] **1 :** PENANCE **2 :** the quality or state of being penitent **:** sorrow for sins or faults ⟨forgiveness following true ~⟩

syn REPENTANCE, CONTRITION, ATTRITION, REMORSE, COMPUNCTION: PENITENCE describes the state of mind of one who acknowledges and deeply regrets his wrongs and is determined to amend ⟨that no sin is beyond forgiveness if it is followed by true *penitence* —K.S.Latourette⟩ REPENTANCE emphasizes the change of mind of one who not only regrets specific faults or errors but has abandoned his former way of life and is following a new standard ⟨for godly grief produces a *repentance* that leads to salvation —2 Cor 7: 10 (RSV)⟩ ⟨without *repentance* . . . man is too much his own god to feel the need of . . . knowing the true God —Reinhold Niebuhr⟩ CONTRITION stresses a sense of unworthiness; in general use it implies penitence that is manifest in signs of pain or grief ⟨you must — whether you feel it or not — present an appearance of *contrition* —George Meredith⟩; in theological use, CONTRITION implies sorrow arising out of love of God and one's failure to respond to his graces; in this sense, it is contrasted with ATTRITION, which means sorrow over one's sin due to a lower motive, such as fear of punishment ⟨most Christian churches hold that *attrition* is imperfect contrition and is not sufficient for salvation⟩; ATTRITION, in this sense, is limited to theological use. All these terms imply an authority, religious or secular, to which one submits; this implication is absent from REMORSE and COMPUNCTION, both of which denote a painful sting of conscience, without necessarily connoting humility or hope of forgiveness; but REMORSE emphasizes mental anguish and often intense suffering for consequences which cannot be escaped, not necessarily accompanied by any resolve to reform ⟨*remorse* that makes one walk on thorns —Oscar Wilde⟩ ⟨chronic *remorse*, as all the moralists are agreed, is a most undesirable sentiment —Aldous Huxley⟩ COMPUNCTION, the least powerful of these terms, usu. suggests a momentary reaction, not only for something done, but also for something being done or about to be done ⟨would not hurt a gnat unless his party . . . told him to do so, and then only with *compunction* —Sir Winston Churchill⟩

pen·i·ten·cy \-nsē\ *n* -ES [ME *penitencie*, fr. ML *poenitentia*] **:** PENITENCE 2

¹pen·i·tent \-nt\ *adj* [ME, fr. MF, fr. L *paenitent-, paenitens*, pres. part. of *paenitēre* to be sorry, cause to be sorry] **:** feeling or expressing pain or sorrow for sins or offenses **:** sincerely affected by a sense of guilt and resolved on amendment of life ⟨saw him lose his temper . . . for a second and he was ~ about it for a day or two —W.A.White⟩ ⟨wrote a ~ letter apologizing for her hasty words⟩

²penitent \"\ *n* -s [ME, fr. *penitent* (adj.)] **1 :** a person who repents of sin **:** one sorrowful because of his transgressions **2 :** a person under church censure but admitted to penance esp. under the direction of a confessor **3** *often cap* **:** a member of one of many confraternities of lay persons bound to penitential exercises and works of charity very numerous from the 13th to the 16th centuries and often named from their garb ⟨blue ~*s*⟩ ⟨white ~*s*⟩

pen·i·ten·te \ˌpenəˈtentā, -tē\ *n, pl* **penitentes** \-ās, -ēz\ *usu cap* [AmerSp, lit., penitent, sing. of *Penitentes* Penitents, short for *Los Hermanos Penitentes* The Penitent Brothers, religious society that originated in Mexico] **:** a member of a religious society of Flagellants in Spanish-American communities of the southwestern U.S. (as New Mexico) who practice self-whipping and other forms of penitential torture particularly during Holy Week

penitent-form \ˈ===ˌ=\ *n* **:** the bench at which salvation seekers kneel at a Salvation Army meeting

¹pen·i·ten·tial \ˌpenəˈtenchəl\ *adj* [ML *poenitentialis*, fr. *poenitentia* penitence + L *-alis* -al] **:** of or relating to penitence or penance **:** expressing penitence **:** of the nature of penance ⟨~ tears⟩ ⟨the Day of Atonement which is the great ~ day of the Hebrew calendar —Nathaniel Micklem⟩ ⟨collections of the penances which he had appointed . . . came to influence the whole ~ system of the West —F.M.Stenton⟩ — **pen·i·ten·tial·ly** \-chəlē, -li\ *adv*

²penitential \"\ *n* -s [in sense 1, fr. ML *poenitentiale*, fr. *poenitentialis* penitential, adj.; in other senses, fr. *penitential*, adj.] **1 :** a manual of ecclesiastical rules for the imposition of penances suitable to different sins **2 :** PENITENT **3 penitentials** *pl* **:** penitential garb; *also* **:** garments of black

penitential psalm *n* **:** one of a group of seven liturgical psalms including psalms 6, 32, 38, 51, 102, 130, 143 in the RSV or 6, 31, 37, 50, 101, 129, 142 in the DV

¹pen·i·ten·tia·ry \ˌpenəˈtench(ə)rē, -ri *sometimes* -chēˌer-\ *n* -ES [ME *penitenciary*, fr. ML *poenitentiarius*, fr. *poenitentia* penitence + L *-arius* -ary — more at PENITENCE] **1 a :** an officer in some Roman Catholic dioceses vested with power from the bishop to absolve in cases reserved to him **b** [ML *poenitentiaria*, fem. of *poenitentiarius*] **:** a tribunal of the Roman curia dealing with cases concerning the private spiritual good of individuals esp. in relation to the sacrament of penance, presided over by a cardinal priest, granting absolutions, dispensations, commutations, ratifications of impediments, and condonations, regulating the use and granting of indulgences, and deciding questions of conscience referred to the Holy See **2** *obs* **a :** a place for penitents **b :** PENITENT **3 :** a place of refuge for reformation of prostitutes in 19th century England **4 :** a public institution in which offenders against the law are confined for detention or for punishment, discipline, and reformation and in which they are generally compelled to labor; *specif* **:** a state or federal prison in the U.S. — compare HOUSE OF CORRECTION, REFORMATORY

²penitentiary \ˈ==ˈ=(=)=, ˈ==ˈ===\ *adj* [ML *poenitentiarius*] **1 a :** of or relating to penance **:** prescribing or doing penance **b :** of or expressing penitence **2 a :** used for punishment, discipline, and reformation **b :** making one liable to a term in a penitentiary ⟨a ~ offense⟩ **c :** of, relating to, or confined in a penitentiary ⟨improve ~ conditions⟩ ⟨~ inmates⟩

pen·i·tent·ly *adv* **:** in a penitent manner ⟨returned ~ to beg their pardon⟩

penk *dial Eng var of* ⁴PINK 1

penkeeper \ˈ=ˌ==\ *n* [¹*pen* + *keeper*] **:** a person engaged in breeding and raising livestock in Jamaica **:** RANCHER

pen-keeping \ˈ=ˌ==\ *n* **:** stock raising in Jamaica

penknife \ˈ=ˌ=\ *n* [ME *penneknif*, fr. *penne* quill, feather + *knif* knife — more at PEN, KNIFE] **1 :** a small knife used for making and mending quill pens **2 :** a small pocketknife usu. with only one blade

penlight \'=,=\ *or* **pen·lite** \-,līt\ *n* [*penlight* fr. ³*pen* + *light* (as in *flashlight*); *penlite* alter. of *penlight*] **:** a small flashlight resembling a fountain pen in size or shape

pen·lop \'penləp\ *n* -s *often cap* [native name in Bhutan] **:** the feudal ruler of one of the provinces of Bhutan **:** CHIEF, GOVERNOR

pen machine *n* [³*pen*] **:** a machine for ruling with pens

¹**pen·man** \'penmən\ *n, pl* **penmen** [³*pen* + *man*] **1 a :** a person who writes or copies (as documents) for another **:** CLERK, SCRIBE **b :** a person with a specified quality or kind of handwriting ⟨a poor ~⟩ ⟨a swift ~⟩ ⟨a good shorthand ~⟩ **c :** one who is expert in penmanship — called also *calligrapher* **2 :** AUTHOR

²**penman** \"\ *n, pl* **penmen** [¹*pen* + *man*] **:** a stockyard worker who drives hogs to and from weighing pens and tattoos identification marks on them

pen·man·ship \'penmən,ship\ *n* [¹*penman* + *-ship*] **1 :** the art or practice of writing with the pen ⟨skills in ~, spelling, and sentence structure —*Education Digest*⟩ **2 :** the action of writing with a pen ⟨shading . . . involves no extra ~ —*Pitman Shorthand*⟩ **3 :** quality or style of handwriting **:** writing of an often specified kind or quality ⟨drills to improve your ~⟩ ⟨written in his best ~⟩ ⟨deciphers the awful ~ of the captain —Elbridge Colby⟩

pen-mate \'=,=\ *vt* [¹*pen*] **:** to breed (poultry) as a pen consisting of one male with a selected group of females — compare FLOCK-MATE, STUD-MATE

pen·na \'penə\ *n, pl* **pen·nae** \-e,nē\ [L, feather, wing — more at PEN] **:** a normal contour feather as distinguished esp. from down or plume feathers

pen·na·ceous \pə'nāshəs\ *adj* [NL *pennaceus*, fr. L *penna* + *-aceus* -aceous] **:** of, being, or resembling a penna

pen·na·cook \'penə,kůk\ *n, pl* **pennacook** *or* **pennacooks** *usu cap* [of Algonquian origin; akin to Abnaki *pĭnâkuk* downhill] **1 :** a confederacy of Algonquian peoples of southwestern Maine, northeastern Massachusetts, and New Hampshire **2 :** a member of the Pennacook confederacy

pen·na·les \pə'nā(,)lēz\ *n pl, cap* [NL, fr. L *penna* feather + NL *-ales*] **:** an order of diatoms having a raphe or pseudoraphe and ornamentation of the valves always bilaterally arranged in relation to a line rather than to a point — compare CENTRALES

pen name *n* **:** an author's pseudonym **:** NOM DE PLUME ⟨writes both under his own name and under a *pen name*⟩

pen·nant \'penənt\ *n* -s [alter. (influenced by *pennon*) of ¹*pendant*] **1 :** PENDANT 3 **2 a :** any of various nautical flags tapering usu. to a point or swallowtail and used for identification or signaling: as (1) **:** LONG PENNANT (2) **:** BROAD PENNANT (3) *Brit* **:** a long tapering flag cut off at the outward end by a line parallel to the staff and used esp. as a signal flag (4) **pennants** *pl* **:** a visual call sign of a British naval vessel consisting of an alphabetical flag above two or more numbered pennants (5) **:** a signal flag longer in the fly than in the hoist and tapering to a point ⟨flags and ~*s* used for international signals⟩ **b :** a flag or banner that tapers toward the fly ⟨a new filling station decorated with lines of fluttering ~*s*⟩; *esp* **:** one that tapers to a point **3 :** a flag emblematic of championship (as in a league of professional baseball clubs) ⟨the team that won the ~⟩ — called also *flag* **4 :** ⁵FLAG 3a **5 :** PENNON 1a **syn** see FLAG

pennant fish *n* [so called fr. the appearance of the fins] **:** THREADFISH 1

pen·nant·ite \'penənt-,īt\ *n* -s [Thomas *Pennant* †1798 Welsh naturalist + E *-ite*] **:** a mineral $Mn_9Al_6Si_5O_{20}(OH)_{16}$ of the chlorite group consisting of basic silicate of manganese and aluminum isomorphous with thuringite

pennant's marten \'penənts-\ *n, usu cap P* [after Thomas *Pennant* †1798] **:** FISHER 2

pennant-winged nightjar \'==,=-\ *n* **:** either of two African nightjars: **a :** a bird (*Macrodipteryx longipennis*) that has second primary in the male with a very long almost naked shaft and a broad racketlike web at the tip **b :** a bird (*Semeiophorus vexillarius*) that has the second to fifth primaries more or less lengthened and the ninth extremely so although the shaft is not bare for any portion of its length

pen·nar·ia \pə'na(a)rēə\ *n, cap* [NL, perh. fr. L *penna* feather, wing + NL *-aria*] **:** a genus (the type of the family Pennaridae) comprising gymnoblastic hydroids in which the hydranth has a basal whorl of ten to twelve tentacles with a number of short knobbed tentacles on the hypostome

pen·na·tae \pə'nā,tē\ *n pl, cap* [NL, fr. L *penna* feather + NL *-atae* (fem. pl. of L *-atus* -ate)] *in some classifications* **:** a group equivalent to the order Pennales

pen·nate \'pe,nāt\ *also* **pen·nat·ed** \-ād·əd\ *adj* [*pennate* fr. L *pennatus* winged, fr. *penna* feather, wing + *-atus* -ate; *pennated* fr. L *pennatus* + E *-ed* — more at PEN] **1 :** PINNATE **2 :** WINGED, FEATHERED **3 :** having the shape of a wing **4** [*penna-* (fr. NL *Pennales*) + *-ate*] **:** of or resembling the Pennales

pen·nat·u·la \pə'nachələ\ *n* [NL, fr. LL, fem. of *pennatulus* winged, fr. L *pennatus* winged + *-ulus* -ule] **1** *cap* **:** a common genus (the type of the family Pennatulidae) of sea pens **2** *pl* **pennatu·lae** \-chə,lē\ *or* **pennatulas :** SEA PEN — **pen·nat·u·lid** \-ləd\ *adj or n*

pen·nat·u·la·cea \pə,nachə'lāshēə\ *n pl, cap* [NL, fr. *Pennatula* + *-acea*] **:** an order of Alcyonaria including the sea pens, sea pansies, and related forms that develop a colony which usu. resembles a feather, leaf, or club, is often more or less bilaterally symmetrical with the polyps arranged along the distal part of a central axis or on lateral branches and has the basal end of the axis destitute of polyps and embedded in the mud of the sea bottom — **pen·nat·u·la·cean** \=,=='lāshən\ *adj or n* — **pen·nat·u·la·ceous** \-shəs\ *adj*

¹**pen·nat·u·lar·i·an** \=,=='la(a)rēən\ *adj* [NL *Pennatularia*, former family of sea pens (fr. *Pennatula* + *-aria*) + E *-an*] **:** of or relating to the Pennatulacea

²**pennatularian** \"\ *n* -s **:** a member of the Pennatulacea

pen·na·tu·li·da \,penə'tüləda, -ə'tyü-\ [NL, fr. *Pennatula* + *-ida*] *syn of* PENNATULACEA

pen·nat·u·loid \pə'nachə,lȯid\ *adj* [NL *Pennatula* + E *-oid*] **:** of, relating to, or resembling the Pennatulacea

penned *past of* PEN

pen·neech *also* **pen·neeck** \pə'nēk\ *n* -s [origin unknown] **:** an old game that is played with hands of seven cards and that has a card turned up before each trick in order to determine trumps

¹**pen·ner** \'penər\ *n* -s [ME, fr. *penne* pen + *-er* — more at PEN] *chiefly Scot* **:** a case worn at the waist for holding pens

²**pen·ner** \'penə(r)\ *n* -s [⁴*pen* + *-er*] **:** one that pens a document **:** WRITER

³**penner** \"\ *n* -s [²*pen* + *-er*] **:** one that pens animals or attends to their pens

pen·ni \'penē\ *n, pl* **pen·nia** \-ēə\ *or* **pennis** [Finn, prob. fr. G *pfennig* penny (fr. OHG *pfenning*) — more at PENNY] **1 :** a unit of value of Finland equal to ¹⁄₁₀₀ markka — see MONEY table **2 :** a coin representing one penni unit

penni- *also* **penno-** *comb form* [L *penni-*, fr. *penna* feather, wing — more at PEN] **1 :** feather ⟨*penno*plume⟩ ⟨*penni*form⟩ **2 :** pinnately ⟨*penni*nerved⟩ ⟨*penni*veined⟩

pen·nied \'penēd\ *adj* **:** having pennies

pennies *pl of* PENNY

pen·ni·less \'penələs, -nəl-\ *adj* [ME *peniles*, fr. *peni* penny + *-les* -less] **:** destitute of money **:** extremely poor ⟨in one day the rich man . . . saw himself ~, landless, a bankrupt among creditors —J.G.Lockhart⟩ **syn** see POOR

pen·ni·less·ly *adv* **:** in a penniless condition

pen·ni·less·ness *n* -ES **:** the quality or state of being penniless

penning *pres part of* PEN

pen·ni·nite \'penə,nīt\ *also* **pen·nine** \'penən, -,nīn\ *n* -s [*penninite* fr. G *pennin* (fr. *Pennine* Alps) + E *-ite*; *pennine* fr. G *pennin*] **:** a mineral approximately $(Mg,Fe,Al)_6(Si,Al)_4O_{10}(OH)_8$ of the chlorite group consisting of a basic aluminosilicate of magnesium, iron, and aluminum, that is monoclinic and is commonly emerald or olive green (hardness 2–2.5, sp. gr. 2.6–2.85)

pen·ni·se·tum \,penə'sēd·əm\ *n, cap* [NL, fr. *penni-* + L *seta* bristle — more at SINEW] **:** a large genus of Old World grasses having a bristly involucre surrounding the jointed pedicels of the spikelet — see FOUNTAIN GRASS, PEARL MILLET

pen·non *also* **pen·on** \'penən\ *n* -s [ME, fr. MF *penon*, aug. of *penne* feather, wing — more at PEN] **1 a :** a long usu. triangular or swallow-tailed streamer typically attached to the head of a lance: as (1) **:** one borne as the ensign of a knight bachelor in the middle ages (2) **:** one borne as the ensign of a modern regiment of lancers **b :** PENNANT 2a **2 :** a flag of any shape **:** BANNER **3 :** WING, PINION **4 :** a retractor muscle of the septa of a zooantharian — called also *muscle pennon* **syn** see FLAG

pen·non·cel *or* **pen·on·cel** *also* **pen·non·celle** \'penən,sel\ *n* -s [ME *penoncelle*, *penouncell*, fr. MF *penoncel*, dim. of *penon* pennon] **1 :** a small narrow flag or streamer borne by a man-at-arms in late medieval or Renaissance times; *esp* **:** such a flag borne at the head of a lance **2 :** a flag borne by a ship in the later middle ages and similar in shape to but smaller than a long pennant

pen·no·pluma \,penə'plümə\ *or* **pen·no·plume** \'==,plüm\ *n* [*pennopluma* fr. NL, fr. *penno-* + L *pluma* down; *pennoplume* fr. *penno-* + *plume* — more at FLEECE] **:** SEMIPLUME

pen·north \'penə(r)th\ *n* -s [by contr.] **:** PENNYWORTH

penn·syl·va·nia \,pen(t)səl'vānyə, -ānēə\ *adj, usu cap* [fr. *Pennsylvania*, middle Atlantic state of the U.S., fr. NL, fr. Sir William *Penn* †1670 Eng. naval commander and father of William Penn †1718 founder of the colony of Pennsylvania + NL *-sylvania* (fr. L *silva*, *sylva* wood, forest)] **:** of or from the state of Pennsylvania ⟨*Pennsylvania* coal⟩ **:** of the kind or style prevalent in Pennsylvania **:** PENNSYLVANIAN

pennsylvania dutch *n, usu cap P&D* **1 pennsylvania dutch** *pl* **:** people living mostly in eastern Pennsylvania whose characteristic cultural traditions go back to the German migrations of the 18th century **2** *or* **pennsylvania german** *usu cap P&G* **:** a dialect of High German spoken in parts of Pennsylvania and Maryland by descendants of 17th and 18th century immigrants from southwest Germany and Switzerland **3 :** the architectural and decorative style associated with the Pennsylvania Dutch

pennsylvania dutchman *n, usu cap P&D* **:** a member of the Pennsylvania Dutch

¹**penn·syl·va·nian** \-nyən, -nēən\ *adj, usu cap* [*Pennsylvania*, state of the U.S. + E *-an*] **1 :** of, relating to, or characteristic of Pennsylvania or Pennsylvanians **2 a :** of or relating to the Paleozoic period between the Mississippian and Permian **b :** of or relating to the system formed during this period which contains most of the coal of the U.S. east of the Great Plains — see GEOLOGIC TIME table

²**pennsylvanian** \"\ *n* -s **1** *cap* **:** a native or resident of the state of Pennsylvania **2** *usu cap* **:** the Pennsylvanian period or system

pennsylvania system *n, usu cap P* **:** a system of prison discipline introduced in Pennsylvania in the late 18th century and characterized by solitary confinement of prisoners convicted of serious offenses

pennsylvania truss *n, usu cap P* **:** a truss developed from the Pratt truss esp. for bridges with long spans and having subdivided panels, curved top chords for through trusses, and curved bottom chords for deck spans

pen·ny \'penē, -ni\ *n, pl* **pennies** \-ēz, -iz\ *or* **pence** \'pen(t)s\ *often attrib* [ME *penny*, *peny*, fr. OE *penig*, *penning*; akin to OHG *pfenning*, *pfenting* coin, penny, ON *penningr*] **1 a :** a British monetary unit equal to ¹⁄₂₄₀ pound or ¹⁄₁₂ shilling — see MONEY table **b :** a British coin representing one penny, orig. made of silver but after the 18th century except for the silver maundy money made of copper or of bronze **2 :** any of various coins of small denomination or the monetary units they represent: as **a** (1) **:** a Roman denarius ⟨three measures of barley for a ~ —Rev 6:6 (AV)⟩ ⟨they brought unto him a ~ —Mt 22:19 (AV)⟩ (2) *pl pennies* **:** a Roman quadrans **:** FARTHING ⟨are not two sparrows sold for a ~ —Mt 10:29 (RSV)⟩ **b** *pl pennies* **:** a cent of the U.S. or Canada ⟨~ candy⟩ **3 a** *archaic* **:** the part of an amount of money indicated by a specified ordinal ⟨interest was reduced from the twentieth to the fiftieth ~ or from five to two percent —Adam Smith⟩ **b :** the sum exacted by a specified tax or customary payment ⟨earnest ~⟩ — often used in combination ⟨ale*penny*⟩ ⟨fish*penny*⟩ **4 :** a trivial amount **:** the least bit ⟨never a ~ the worse⟩ **5 :** a piece or sum of money ⟨make an honest ~⟩ ⟨saved every ~ he earned⟩ **6** *pl pennies* **:** a token or good-luck piece worth or resembling a cent or a penny — **pennies from heaven :** something had without effort or payment **:** an unexpected benefit

pen·ny-a-lin·er \'penēə'līnə(r)\ *n* [fr. *penny-a-line*, adj. (fr. the phrase *a penny a line*) + *-er*] **:** a hack writer or journalist

penny ante *n* **1 :** poker played for very low stakes (as pennies) **2 :** any dealings on a small scale or with picayune sums involved

penny arcade *n* **:** an amusement center where each device for entertainment may be operated for a penny

penny bank *n* **1 :** a savings bank setting no minimum limit on a deposit **2 :** a small, often slotted, box or safe designed to receive deposits of pennies

pennycress \'==,=\ *n* [prob. alter. (influenced by *cress*) of *penny grass*] **:** a plant of the genus *Thlaspi*; *esp* **:** a Eurasian herb (*T. arvense*) having round flat pods — called also *fanweed, field pennycress, French weed, penny grass*

penny dreadful *n, pl* **penny dreadfuls 1 :** a novel of violent adventure or crime esp. popular in late Victorian England and costing orig. one penny — compare DIME NOVEL, SHILLING SHOCKER **2 :** a story or periodical characterized by sensationalism and violence

penny-farthing \'=='==\ *n, Brit* **:** a bicycle with a large front wheel and a small rear wheel common from about 1870 to 1890

pennyflower \'==,=\ *n* [so called fr. its round flat pods] **:** HONESTY 3

penny gaff *n, Brit* **:** ⁵GAFF

penny grass *n* [ME *penygres*, fr. *peny* penny + *gres*, *gras* grass; fr. the round flat pods — more at PENNY, GRASS] **:** PENNYCRESS

pennyland \'==,=\ *n* **:** a small piece of land in Orkney and Shetland once taxed about a penny a year

penny mountain *n* **:** WILD THYME

pen·ny-pinch \'penē,pinch\ *vt* [back-formation fr. *penny pincher*] **:** to give out money to in a niggardly manner ⟨takes a sinister but fascinating kind of joy in . . . *penny-pinching* his own family —James Yaffe⟩ **:** deprive of funds by petty economy ⟨*penny-pinched* himself out of . . . millions of dollars —S.N.Behrman⟩

penny pincher *n* **:** a niggardly or parsimonious person

penny-pinching \¦==¦==\ *adj* **:** given to or marked by mean and petty economy and miserliness ⟨*penny-pinching* cuts in appropriations crippling the project⟩ **syn** see STINGY

penny-plain \¦==¦=\ *adj, Brit* **:** having no decorative or pretentious features ⟨can have it *penny-plain* and no nonsense —Rose Macaulay⟩

penny post *n* **1 a :** a postal system carrying a letter for a penny: (1) **:** a system established in London about 1680 (2) **:** the former system of Great Britain established in 1840 (3) **:** a local mail service in colonial America carrying letters from post office to addressee **b :** a mail carrier in such a system **2 :** a common American marsh pennywort (*Hydrocotyle americana*)

pen·ny·prick \'penē,prik\ *n* [ME *penyprike*, fr. *peny* penny + *prike* prick — more at PENNY, PRICK] *archaic* **:** an old game of throwing at a penny

penny rent *n* **:** a nominal rent

pen·ny·roy·al \¦penē¦rȯi(y)əl, -nə¦-, -ȯil, *dial* ¦penə¦rīl\ *n* [prob. by folk etymology (influence of *pennywort* and *royal*) fr. MF *poullieul*, *poliol*, modif. of L *puleium*, *pulegium* fleabane, fleawort, pennyroyal] **1 :** a European perennial mint (*Mentha pulegium*) with small pungently aromatic leaves **2 :** a plant of the genus *Hedeoma*; *esp* **:** an erect hairy branching American herb (*H. pulegioides*) that yields an essential oil and is sometimes used in folk medicine as an emmenagogue and diaphoretic — called also *American pennyroyal*; see PENNYROYAL OIL **3 :** any of several western No. American aromatic herbs of the genus *Monardella*; *esp* **:** an herb (*M. villosa*) of California

pennyroyal oil *n* **:** either of two yellowish essential oils obtained from pennyroyal: **a :** the oil obtained from European pennyroyal that has an odor like mint and is used chiefly in soaps **b :** the aromatic oil from an American pennyroyal (*Hedeoma pulegioides*) — called also *hedeoma oil*

pennysiller \'==,=\ *n* -s [*penny* + *siller*] *Scot* **:** MONEY, CASH

penny stock *n* **:** stock selling under one dollar a share and quoted in cents

pennystone \'==,=\ *n* [ME *penystan*, fr. *peny* penny + *stan* stone — more at STONE] *Scot* **:** a flat circular stone used as a quoit

pennystones \'==,=\ *n pl but usu sing in constr, Scot* **:** a game resembling quoits

penny wedding *n* **:** a wedding paid for by money collected from the guests and formerly common in Scotland

pennyweight \'==,=\ *n* [ME *penyweight*, fr. *peny* penny + *weight* — more at WEIGHT] **:** a unit of troy weight equal to 24 grains or ¹⁄₂₀ troy ounce — see MEASURE table

pen·ny·weight·er \'penē,wād·ə(r)\ *n* -s [fr. obs. E *pennyweight* jewelry (fr. E *pennyweight*, weight unit) + E *-er*] **:** a thief that steals jewelry by substituting a fake for a valuable piece

penny whistle *n* **1 :** a small fipple flute — called also *tin whistle* **2 :** a simple toy whistle

pen·ny·win·kle \'penē,wiŋkəl\ *n* [by alter.] *dial* **:** PERIWINKLE

penny-wise \¦==¦=\ *adj* **:** wise or prudent only in small matters **:** excessively sparing in expenditure — used chiefly in *penny-wise and pound-foolish*

pennywort \'==,=\ *n* [ME *penywort*, fr. *peny* penny + *wort* — more at PENNY, WORT] **:** any of several round-leaved plants: as **a :** NAVELWORT **b :** any of various umbelliferous plants of the genera *Hydrocotyle* and *Centella* — called also *marsh pennywort* **c :** KENILWORTH IVY **d :** a leafless perennial (*Obolaria virginica*) of the family Gentianaceae with white or purplish flowers

pennyworth \'==,=\ *n, pl* **pennyworth** *or* **pennyworths** [ME *penyworth*, fr. OE *penigwurth*, fr. *penig* penny + *wurth* worth — more at PENNY, WORTH] **1 :** the amount that a penny buys **:** a penny's worth ⟨sold fruit . . . by the ~ —*Commonweal*⟩ ⟨two ~ of bread⟩ ⟨more ~*s* of birdseed — Richard Llewellyn⟩ **2 :** value for money expended **:** BUY, BARGAIN ⟨seemed a ~ at that price⟩ ⟨a good ~⟩ **3 :** a small quantity **:** MODICUM

pe·nob·scot \pə'näbzkət, -bsk-, -bz,kät, -b,skät\ *n, pl* **penobscot** *or* **penobscots** *usu cap* **1 a :** an Indian people of the Penobscot river valley and Penobscot Bay region **b :** a member of such people **2 :** a dialect of Abnaki

penoche *var of* PENUCHE

pe·no·correctional \¦pēnō+\ *adj* [*penology* + *correctional*] **:** combining correctional treatment with penal confinement ⟨an institution offering a ~ program⟩

pe·no·log·i·cal \¦pēn°l¦äjəkəl\ *adj* **:** of or relating to penology ⟨~ methods⟩

pe·nol·o·gist \pē'näləjəst, pə'-\ *n* -s **:** a specialist in penology

pe·nol·o·gy \-jē, -ji\ *n* -ES [*peno-* (fr. Gk *poinē* penalty) + *-logy* — more at PAIN] **:** the study of punishment for crime; *specif* **:** a branch of criminology dealing with prison management and the treatment of offenders esp. with regard to their rehabilitation

penon *var of* PENNON

penoncel *var of* PENNONCEL

pe·nor·con \pə'nȯrkən\ *n* -s [NL] **:** an obsolete 17th century cittern

pen pal *n* [³*pen*] **:** a person with whom one carries on a friendly correspondence usu. without ever meeting

pen palsy *or* **pen paralysis** *n* **:** WRITERS' CRAMP

pen picture *or* **pen portrait** *n* **1 :** a picture drawn with a pen **2 :** a written description **:** SKETCH

pen pot *n* [¹*pen*] **:** a fisherman's pot for keeping crabs or lobsters

pen-pusher \'=,==\ *n* **:** PENMAN; *esp* **:** a clerical worker

pen·rose·ite \'pen,rō,zīt\ *n* -s [Richard A. F. *Penrose* †1931 Am. geologist + E *-ite*] **:** a mineral $(Ni,Cu,Pb)Se_2$ structurally like pyrite consisting of a selenide of lead, copper, and nickel and occurring in lead gray radiating columnar masses (hardness 3, sp. gr. 6.9)

pens *pl of* PEN, *pres 3d sing of* PEN

pen·sa·co·la \,pen(t)sə'kōlə\ *n, pl* **pensacola** *or* **pensacolas** *usu cap* [modif. of Choctaw *panshiokla*, fr. *panshi* hair + *okla* people] **1 :** a Muskogian people near Pensacola Bay, Fla. **2 :** a member of the Pensacola people

pensacola snapper *n, usu cap P* [fr. *Pensacola* Bay, inlet of Gulf of Mexico] **:** GRAY SNAPPER

penscript \'=,=\ *n* **:** matter written with a pen

pen·sée \päⁿ'sā\ *n* -s [in sense 1, fr. F, fr. *Pensées* (1670), literary work by Blaise Pascal †1662 Fr. scientist and philosopher; in sense 2, fr. F, fr. MF — more at PANSY] **1 :** a thought expressed in literary form ⟨not a system of ethics at all but simply a collection of maxims and ~*s* —J.C.Ransom⟩ **2 :** PANSY 2

pen shell *n* **:** a bivalve mollusk of the family Pinnidae having the shell resembling a quill pen in outline — compare PINNA

pensil *var of* PENCEL

pen·sile \'pen(t)səl\ *adj* [L *pensilis*, fr. *pensus* (past part. of *pendēre* to hang) + *-ilis* -ile — more at PENDANT] **1 a :** suspended from above **:** HANGING, PENDENT **b :** set or poised on a declivity **:** OVERHANGING **2 :** having or building a hanging nest

¹**pen·sion** \'penchən, *in sense 3* (')päⁿs¦yōⁿ *or* ¦päⁿsē¦ōⁿ\ *n* -s *often attrib* [ME *pensioun*, fr. MF & ML; MF *pension*, fr. ML *pension-*, *pensio*, fr. L, payment, fr. *pensus* (past part. of *pendere* to weigh, estimate, pay) + *-ion-*, *-io* -ion — more at PENDANT] **1 a :** a fixed sum of money charged annually upon the revenues of a benefice by an ecclesiastical superior and paid to a cleric for any just cause (as the work of the church, reward for services, support of a former incumbent) **b** *obs* **:** a payment required of a person or group; *specif* **:** the dues payable by a member of a society (as a guild or Inn of Court) — often used in pl. **2 :** a fixed sum paid regularly to a person: **a** *archaic* **:** one paid to an employee for current services **:** WAGE **b :** one paid for secret service or for a claim upon assistance when needed **c :** a gratuity granted (as by a government) as a favor or reward or as a subsidy to a person of recognized merit in art, literature, or science **d** (1) **:** one paid under given conditions to a person following his retirement from service (as due to age or disability) or to the surviving dependents of a person entitled to such a pension (2) **:** the portion of an employee's retirement income provided by the employer's contributions under a contributory plan — compare ANNUITY **3 a** (1) **:** payment for board and room ⟨strolled to the inn where he paid his ~ —Robert Hichens⟩ (2) **:** accommodations at a European hotel or boardinghouse **:** ROOM AND BOARD ⟨charges $3 a day for . . . full ~ or $2.50 for half-pension, breakfast and one meal —Horace Sutton⟩ **b** *also* **pen·si·o·ne** \,pen(t)sē'ōnē\ [*pensione* fr. It, pension, fr. OIt, fr. MF] **:** a boardinghouse in continental Europe or Latin America

²**pen·sion** \'penchən, *in vi sense* (')päⁿs¦yōⁿ *or* ¦päⁿsē¦ōⁿ\ *vb* -ED/-ING/-S *vi* **:** to receive board and lodging at a fixed rate ⟨the small country house where we ~*ed* —W.J.Cory⟩ ~ *vt* **:** to grant or pay a pension to **:** dismiss or retire from service with a pension ⟨the present nizam . . . is ~*ed* by the new State Government and has withdrawn from politics —*Jewelers' Circular*⟩ — often followed by *off* ⟨finally ~*ed* off his faithful old servant⟩

pen·sion·able \'penchənəbəl\ *adj* **1 :** qualified to receive a pension ⟨a ~ employee⟩ **2 :** that qualifies a person to receive a pension ⟨the post is ~ after three years' probation —*Nature*⟩ ⟨~ disabilities⟩ ⟨a ~ age⟩ **3** *chiefly Brit* **:** connected with or affecting a pension ⟨for ~ purposes⟩ ⟨a ~ salary⟩ — **pen·sion·ably** \-blē\ *adv*

pen·si·o·na·do \,pen(t)sēə'nä(,)dō\ *n* -s [PhilSp, fr. Sp, pensioned, fr. past part. of *pensionar* to pension, fr. *pensión* pension, fr. L *pension-*, *pensio* payment] **:** a Philippine student whose expenses are paid by the government while he studies abroad

¹**pen·sion·ary** \'penchə,nerē, -ri\ *n* -ES [MF & ML; MF *pensionnaire*, fr. ML *pensionarius*, fr. *pension-*, *pensio* pension + *-arius* -ary] **1 :** PENSIONER; *esp* **:** HIRELING ⟨those who predicted ill success for France in the cafes were suspected of being *pensionaries* . . . of the . . . English chargé d'affaires —Evelyn G. Cruickshanks⟩ **2** [trans. of MD *pensionarijs*, *pensionaris*] **:** an official of the province of Holland or one of its cities

during the 17th and 18th centuries giving legal counsel, representing the city or province in the provincial or general legislature, and in the case of the provincial pensionary presiding over the provincial legislature

²**pensionary** \"\ *adj* [ML *pensionarius*] **1 :** receiving a pension **:** serving as a pensionary **2 :** consisting of a pension

pen·sion·er \'pench(ə)nə(r)\ *n* -s [ME, fr. MF *pensionnier*, fr. ML *pensionarius* pensionary] **1 :** a former officer in the Inns of Court responsible for collecting and recording pensions **2 :** a student at Cambridge University who pays for his own board, room, and tuition instead of being dependent on a foundation — compare COMMONER **3 :** a person who receives a pension ⟨payments to ~s of the Spanish-American War⟩ **:** one subsisting on a pension ⟨the diet of our low-income families, ~s, unemployed and the institutionalized —C.C. Mitchell⟩ **4** *obs* **a :** GENTLEMAN-AT-ARMS **b :** a member of a bodyguard **:** RETAINER **5** [modif. (influenced by *pensioner* in earlier senses) of D *pensionaris*, fr. MD *pensionarijs*, *pensionaris*, fr. ML *pensionarius* pensionary] *archaic* **:** ¹PENSIONARY 2 **6** [F *pensionnaire*, fr. MF] **:** a boarder in a pension or institution (as a continental school)

pen·sion·less \'penchənləs\ *adj* **:** having no pension

pen·sion·naire \ˌpäⁿˌsyȯ'na(a)(ə)r\ *n* -s [MF] **1 :** PENSIONER; *esp* **:** BOARDER **2 :** one of a junior class of actors appointed annually at the Comédie Française — compare SOCIÉTAIRE

pen·sion·nat \-'nä\ *n* -s [F, fr. *pension*, fr. MF — more at PENSION] **:** a European boarding school

pension plan *n* **:** systematic provision by an employer for definitely determinable periodic incomes to employees upon retirement with or without funding; *specif* **:** one financed exclusively by the employer — compare RETIREMENT PLAN

pensions *pl of* PENSION, *pres 3d sing of* PENSION

pension trust *n* **:** a trust established to provide financial administration of a pension or retirement fund

pen·sive \'pen(t)siv, -sēv *also* -sȧv-\ *adj* [ME *pensif*, fr. MF, fr. *penser* to think (fr. L *pensare* to weigh, ponder, consider, fr. *pensus*, past part. of *pendere* to weigh, estimate, pay) + *-if* -ive — more at PENDANT] **1 :** absorbed or engrossed in or given to sober thoughtfulness; *esp* **:** musingly or dreamily occupied with grave, mildly regretful, or melancholy meditations often with contriving or anxiety for the future ⟨as she gazed at the view . . . she would grow ~ —Owen Wister⟩ ⟨a ~ mood⟩ **2 :** expressing or suggesting thoughtfulness with sadness ⟨her face had the ~ mournfulness of a seraph in an old sad painting —Herman Wouk⟩ **3 :** conducive or favorable to or fostering serious thoughtfulness or melancholy — **pen·sive·ly** \-sȧvlē, -li\ *adv* — **pen·sive·ness** \-sivnəs, -sēv- *also* -sȧv-\ *n* -ES

pen sketch *n* **1 :** a sketch made with a pen **2 :** a literary sketch

pen–stabling \'ˌ=(=)=\ *n* **:** stabling (as of dairy cattle) in a loafing barn — compare LOOSE-HOUSING SYSTEM

pen staff *n, dial* **:** PENHOLDER

¹**pen·ste·mon** \pen'stēmən, 'pen(t)stəm-\ *n, cap* [NL, fr. *penta-* + Gk *stēmōn* warp, thread — more at STAMEN] **:** a genus of chiefly American herbs or rarely shrubs (family Scrophulariaceae) having opposite or verticillate leaves and showy blue, purple, red, yellow, or white flowers, four perfect stamens, and one sterile stamen

²**penstemon** *var of* PENTSTEMON

pen·ster \'penztə(r), -n(t)st-\ *n* -s [³*pen* + *-ster*] **:** WRITER; *esp* **:** a hack writer

penstick \'=ˌ=\ *n* [³*pen* + *stick*] **:** PENHOLDER

penstock \'=ˌ=\ *n* [¹*pen* + *stock*] **1 :** a sluice gate, or valve for restraining, deviating, or otherwise regulating a flow (as of water or sewage) **2 :** PENTROUGH **3 :** a closed conduit or pipe for conducting water to a waterwheel

pen·sum \'pen(t)səm\ *n* -s [NL, fr. L, duty, charge, something weighed out, fr. neut. of *pensus*, past part. of *pendere* to weigh, estimate, pay] **:** a task assigned in school often as a punishment

pen·sy \'pen(t)sē\ *adj* [ME *pensie*, *pensey*, prob. fr. MF *pensif* pensive] **1** *dial* **:** PENSIVE, THOUGHTFUL **2** *dial Eng* **:** SQUEAMISH **3** *chiefly Scot* **:** SELF-IMPORTANT, CONCEITED

¹**pent** \'pent\ *adj* [prob. fr. past part. of obs. E *pend* to pen, confine, fr. ME *penden* — more at PEND] **:** shut up **:** PENNED, CONFINED — often used with *up* or *in* ⟨slow-moving vehicles can turn aside to allow *pent*-up traffic . . . in the rear to proceed onward —*N.Y. Times*⟩ ⟨she listened until her ~ breath tore itself from her lungs —John Faulkner⟩ ⟨famous Quarter . . . ~ in a sliver of space, seven blocks long, three wide —*Saturday Rev.*⟩

²**pent** *n* -s *obs* **:** a place containing pent-up water **:** RESERVOIR

³**pent** \'pent\ *n* -s [by shortening] **:** PENTHOUSE 1

penta- *or* **pent-** *or* **pen-** *comb form* [ME *pent-*, fr. Gk *pent-*, *penta-*, fr. *pente* — more at FIVE] **1 :** five ⟨*penta*cyclic⟩ ⟨*penta*hedron⟩ ⟨*penta*lobate⟩ ⟨*pent*ode⟩ **2 :** containing five atoms, groups, or equivalents ⟨*penta*hydrate⟩ ⟨*pent*amine⟩ ⟨*penta*acetate⟩ ⟨*pen*thiophene⟩

pen·ta·basic \ˌpentə+\ *adj* [*penta-* + *basic*] **1 :** having five hydrogen atoms capable of replacement by basic atoms or radicals — used of acids **2 :** containing five atoms of a univalent metal or their equivalent — used of salts

pen·ta·carbonyl \"+\ *n* [*penta-* + *carbonyl*] **:** a compound containing five carbonyl groups esp. combined with a metal

pen·ta·chloride \"+\ *n* [*penta-* + *chloride*] **:** a chloride containing five atoms of chlorine in the molecule

pen·ta·chlo·ro·phe·nate \ˌpentəˌklōrə'fēˌnāt\ *n* [*pentachlorophenol* + *-ate*] **:** a salt of pentachlorophenol — not used systematically

pen·ta·chlorophenol \ˌpentə+\ *n* [*penta-* + *chlorophenol*] **:** a crystalline compound C_6Cl_5OH made by reaction of hexachlorobenzene with sodium hydroxide or of chlorine with phenol and used chiefly as a wood preservative, fungicide, and disinfectant usu. in solution in hydrocarbon oils or in a water solution of its sodium salt

pen·ta·chord \'pentəˌkȯrd\ *n* [Gk *pentachordon*, fr. neut. of *pentachordos* five-stringed, fr. *penta-* + *-chordos* stringed (fr. *chordē* string) — more at CORD] **1 :** an ancient musical instrument with five strings **2 :** a diatonic system of five tones

pent·acid \(')pent+\ *adj* [*penta-* + *acid*] **1 :** able to react with five molecules of a monobasic acid (as to form a salt) — used esp. of bases **2 :** containing five hydrogen atoms replaceable by basic atoms or radicals — used esp. of acids

pen·ta·cle \'pentəkəl\ *n* -s [OIt *pentacol*, *pentacolo*, fr. (assumed) ML *pentaculum*, prob. fr. L *penta-* + (fr. Gk) *-culum* -cle] **1 :** a 5-pointed star having points formed by extension of the sides of a usu. regular pentagon, producible by one continuous line, and used as a magical or talismanic symbol — called also *pentagram*, *pentalpha*, *pentangle* **2 :** any of several occult symbols resembling the true pentacle (as in being producible by a continuous line); *esp* **:** HEXAGRAM

pentacle 1

pen·ta·con·tane \ˌpentə'känˌtān\ *n* -s [Gk *pentēkonta* fifty + E *-ane* — more at PENTECOST] **:** a paraffin hydrocarbon $C_{50}H_{102}$; *esp* **:** the normal hydrocarbon $CH_3(CH_2)_{48}CH_3$

pen·ta·co·sane \-'kōˌsān\ *n* -s [ISV *penta-* + *eicosane*] **:** a paraffin hydrocarbon $C_{25}H_{52}$; *esp* **:** the crystalline normal hydrocarbon $CH_3(CH_2)_{23}CH_3$

pen·tac·ri·nite \pen'takrəˌnīt\ *n* -s [NL *Pentacrinus* + E *-ite*] **1 :** a fossil of the genus *Pentacrinus* **2 :** a Jurassic crinoid with star-shaped columnals

pen·tac·ri·noid \-ˌnȯid\ *n* -s [NL *Pentacrinus* + E *-oid*] **:** a larval form of some crinoids (as members of the genus *Antedon*) resembling crinoids of the genus *Pentacrinus*

pen·tac·ri·nus \-ˌnəs\ *n, cap* [NL, fr. *penta-* (fr. Gk) + *-crinus*] **:** a genus (the type of the family Pentacrinidae) comprising large stalked Jurassic crinoids having a small bowl-shaped calyx, strong numerously branched and pinnulate arms, and a pentangular stalk

pen·tact \'penˌtakt\ *adj* [*penta-* + *-act*] **:** having five rays

pen·tac·tu·la \pen'takchələ\ *n* -s [NL, fr. *penta-* + *-act-* (fr. Gk *aktis* ray) + *-ula* — more at ACTIN-] **:** a late larval echinoderm having five tentacles

pen·ta·cyclic \ˌpentə+\ *adj* [*penta-* + *cyclic*] **:** containing five usu. fused rings in the molecular structure

pen·tad \'penˌtad\ *n* -s [Gk *pentad-*, *pentas*, fr. *pente* five — more at FIVE] **1 a :** a group of five **b :** a period of five days **2 :** a pentavalent element, atom, or radical

pen·ta·dac·tyl \ˌpentə'daktəl\ *also* **pen·ta·dac·ty·late** \-ktələt, -ktəˌlāt\ *adj* [*pentadactyl* fr. L *pentadactylus*, fr. Gk *pentadaktylos*, fr. *penta-* + *daktylos* finger; *pentadactylate* fr. *pentadactyl* + *-ate*] **:** having five digits to the hand or foot or five fingerlike parts

pen·ta·dac·tyl·ism \ˌ==='daktəˌlizəm\ *n* -s **:** the condition of being pentadactyl

pentadeca- *or* **pentadec-** *comb form* [L Gk *pentadeka-*, fr. Gk *pentekaideka*, lit., five and ten, fr. *penta-* + *kai* and + *deka* ten — more at TEN] **:** fifteen ⟨*pentadeca*hydrate⟩

pen·ta·dec·a·gon \ˌpentə'dekəˌgän\ *n* -s [*pentadeca-* + *-gon*] **:** a polygon of 15 sides

pen·ta·deca·hydrate \ˌpentəˌdekə+\ *n* [*pentadeca-* + *hydrate*] **:** a chemical compound with 15 molecules of water

pen·ta·dec·ane \ˌpentəˌdeˌkān\ *n* -s [ISV *pentadeca-* + *-ane*] **:** any of numerous paraffin hydrocarbons $C_{15}H_{32}$ one of which has been obtained from petroleum; *esp* **:** the oily liquid normal hydrocarbon $CH_3(CH_2)_{13}CH_3$

pen·ta·decyl \ˌpentə+\ *n* [*penta-* + *decyl*] **:** an alkyl radical, $C_{15}H_{31}$ derived from a pentadecane; *esp* **:** the normal radical $CH_3(CH_2)_{13}CH_2$—

pen·ta·del·phous \ˌpentəˌdelfəs\ *adj* [*penta-* + *-adelphous*] **:** having the stamens in five sets or clusters with the filaments in each cluster more or less united

pen·ta·diene \ˌpentə+\ *n* [*penta-* + *-diene*] **:** any of several straight-chain liquid diolefins C_5H_8; *esp* **:** PIPERYLENE — compare CYCLOPENTADIENE

pen·ta·erythritol \"+\ *n* [*penta-* + *erythritol*] **1 :** a crystalline tetrahydroxy alcohol $C(CH_2OH)_4$ derived from neopentane that is made by reaction of formaldehyde and acetaldehyde in the presence of an alkaline condensing agent (as a slurry of calcium hydroxide) and that is used chiefly in making alkyd resins and other synthetic resins, synthetic drying oils, and explosives **2 :** a polyhydroxy ether alcohol formed by condensation usu. of two or three molecules of pentaerythritol in the synthesis of pentaerythritol

pentaerythritol tetranitrate *n* **:** a crystalline ester $C(CH_2ONO_2)_4$ made by nitrating pentaerythritol and used as a powerful high explosive and in the treatment of angina pectoris — called also *penthrite*, *pentrite*, *PETN*

¹**pen·ta·gon** \'pentəˌgän, -tē,- *sometimes* -tə̇gən *or* -tēg-\ *n* -s [LL *pentagonum*, fr. Gk *pentagōnon*, fr. neut. of *pentagōnos* five-angled, fr. *penta-* + *-gōnos* (fr. *gōnia* angle) — more at -GON] **:** a polygon having five sides — see AREA table

pentagons: *1* regular, *2* irregular

²**pentagon** \"\ *adj, usu cap* [fr. the *Pentagon*, pentagonal building (erected 1943) in Arlington, Va., that is the headquarters of the U. S. Dept. of Defense and other government offices] **:** of or relating to the Pentagon building esp. as symbolizing the U.S. military, naval, and air force leadership concentrated there

pen·tag·o·nal \(')pen'tagənᵊl, -taig-\ *adj* [MF, fr. ML *pentagonalis*, fr. LL *pentagonum* + *-alis* -al] **1 :** having five angles and five sides **:** five-sided **:** divided into pentagons ⟨a ~ dodecahedron⟩ **2 :** having a pentagon as section or base ⟨a ~ column⟩ ⟨a ~ pyramid⟩ **3 :** relating or belonging to a pentagonal system — **pen·tag·o·nal·ly** \-ᵊlē -ᵊli\ *adv*

pentagon crab *n* [so called fr. its shape] **:** a small dully colored angular parthenopid crab (*Heterocrypta granulata*) living at moderate depths along the eastern coast of No. America

pen·ta·gon·ese \ˌpentəˌgä'nēz, -tē,-, -nēs\ *n* -s *usu cap* [*Pentagon*, headquarters of the U.S. Dept. of Defense + E *-ese*] **:** a style of writing characteristic of the Pentagon bureaucracy

pen·tag·o·noid \(')pen'tagəˌnȯid\ *adj* [¹*pentagon* + *-oid*] **1 :** somewhat pentagonal **2** *of a skull* **:** resembling a pentagon as viewed from the inferior aspect

pen·ta·gram \'pentəˌgram\ *n* [Gk *pentagrammon*, fr. *penta-* + *-grammon* (akin to Gk *gramma* letter) — more at GRAM] **:** PENTACLE 1

pen·ta·graph \'pentəˌgraf, -rȧf\ *n* [*penta-* + *-graph*] **:** a cluster of five successive letters — **pen·ta·graph·ic** \ˌ==-'grafik\ *adj* — **pen·ta·graph·i·cal·ly** \-fə̇k(ə)lē\ *adv*

pen·ta·grid \'pentəˌgrid\ *adj* [*penta-* + *grid*] **:** having five grids ⟨a ~ converter⟩

pen·ta·gyn·ia \ˌpentə'jinēə\ *n pl, cap* [NL, fr. *penta-* + *-gynia*] *in former classifications* **:** a group of plants comprising those having flowers with five styles or pistils

pen·ta·he·dral \ˌpentə'hēdrəl\ *adj* [NL *pentahedron* + E *-al*] **:** having five faces

pen·ta·he·dron \ˌ=='hēdrən\ *n* -s [NL, fr. *penta-* + *-hedron*] **:** a solid bounded by five faces

pen·ta·hydrate \ˌpentə+\ *n* [*penta-* + *hydrate*] **:** a chemical compound with five molecules of water — **pen·ta·hydrated** \"+\ *adj*

pen·ta·hy·dric \ˌpentə'hīdrik\ *adj* [*penta-* + *-hydric*] **:** PENTAHYDROXY — used esp. of alcohols and phenols

pen·ta·hy·drite \ˌpentə'hīˌdrīt\ *n* -s [*penta-* + *hydr-* + *-ite*] **:** a mineral $MgSO_4.5H_2O$ consisting of hydrous sulfate of magnesium isostructural with chalcanthite and containing less water than epsomite

pen·ta·hy·droxy \ˌpentəˌhī'dräksē\ *adj* [*pentahydroxy-*] **:** containing five hydroxyl groups in the molecule

pentahydroxy- *comb form* [*penta-* + *hydroxy-*] **:** containing five hydroxyl groups — in names of chemical compounds

pentail \'=ˌ=\ *n* [³*pen* + *tail*] **1** *also* **pen–tailed tree shrew** \'==ˌ=-\ **:** a tree shrew (genus *Ptilocercus*) of Malaysia and adjacent islands that is dark brown above and white below and has a naked tail bilaterally fringed with long stiff hairs on its distal third **2** *also* **pen–tailed phalanger :** a small New Guinea phalanger (genus *Distoechurus*) related to the mouse opossums but distinguished by a tail fringed with long hairs **3** [by alter.] **:** PINTAIL 1

pen·tal·o·gy \pen'taləjē\ *n* -ES [*penta-* + *-logy* (as in *trilogy*)] **:** a series of five closely related published works

pen·ta·lo·nia \ˌpentə'lōnēə\ *n, cap* [NL] **:** a genus of aphids containing forms which transmit bunchy top disease to some bananas

pen·tal·pha \pen'talfə\ *n* [Gk, fr. *penta-* + *alpha*; fr. its presenting the form of an A on each of its five corners — more at ALPHA] **:** PENTACLE 1

pen·ta·mer \'pentəmə(r)\ *n* -s [*penta-* + *-mer*] **:** a polymer formed from five molecules of a monomer

pen·tam·e·ra \pen'tamərə\ *n pl, cap* [NL, fr. *penta-* + Gk *meros* part — more at MERIT] **:** an artificial division of beetles including those normally having five-jointed tarsi and embracing about half of all the known beetles — **pen·tam·er·an** \-rən\ *n* -s

pen·tam·er·al \(')=ˌ=rəl\ *adj* [*penta-* + *mer-* + *-al*] **:** PENTAMEROUS

pen·tam·er·id \pen'tamərəd\ *n* -s [NL *Pentameridae*, family of brachiopods, fr. *Pentamerus*, type genus + *-idae*] **:** a brachiopod of *Pentamerus* or related genera

pen·tam·er·ism \pen'taməˌrizəm\ *n* -s **:** the state of being pentamerous

pen·tam·er·ous \(')pen'tamərəs\ *adj* [NL *pentamerus*, fr. *penta-* (fr. Gk) + *-merus* -merous] **:** divided into or consisting of five parts **:** arranged in five sets of parts; *specif* **:** having each floral whorl consisting of five or a multiple of five members — often written *5-merous*

pen·tam·er·us \pen'tamərəs\ *n, cap* [NL, fr. *penta-* (fr. Gk) + *-merus* -merous] **:** a genus (the type of the family Pentameridae) comprising Paleozoic brachiopods of the order Protremata abundant in the Silurian and having the shell rostrate and oval or somewhat pentagonal with its cavity divided by two internal vertical ridges and a spondylium in each valve

¹**pen·tam·e·ter** \(')pen'tamәd·ә(r)\ *also* **pen·ta·met·ric** \ˌpentə'me·trik\ *adj* [*pentameter* fr. MF *pentametre*, fr. Gk *pentametros*, fr. *penta-* + *-metros* (fr. *metron* measure, meter); *pentametric* fr. *pentameter*, n. + *-ic* — more at MEASURE] **:** having five metrical feet

²**pentameter** \"\ *n* [L, fr. Gk *pentametros*] **:** a line of five metrical feet: *as* **a :** ELEGIAC PENTAMETER **b :** HEROIC VERSE 3

pen·ta·methine \ˌpentə+\ *n* [*penta-* + *methine*] **:** DICARBOCYANINE

pen·ta·methyl \ˌpentə+\ *adj* [*penta-* + *methyl*] **:** containing five methyl groups in the molecule

pen·ta·methylene \"+\ *n* [ISV *penta-* + *methylene*] **1 :** CYCLOPENTANE **2 :** the bivalent radical $-CH_2CH_2CH_2CH_2CH_2-$ derived from normal pentane by removal of one hydrogen atom from each end carbon atom

pen·ta·methylene·diamine \"+\ *n* [*pentamethylene* + *diamine*] **:** CADAVERINE

pen·tam·e·trist \pen'tamə·trəst\ *n* **:** a writer of pentameters

pent·am·i·dine \pen'taməˌdēn, -ˌdən\ *n* [*penta-* + *amidine*] **:** a diamidine used chiefly in the form of its bitter crystalline isethionate salt $C_{23}H_{36}N_4O_{10}S_2$ in the treatment of early stages of African sleeping sickness

pent·am·mine \pen'taˌmēn, -ˌmȯn, 'pentəˌmēn\ *n* [*penta-* + *ammine*] **:** an ammine containing five molecules of ammonia

pen·tan·dria \pen·'tandrēə\ *n pl, cap* [NL, fr. *penta-* (fr. Gk) + *-andria*] *in former classifications* **:** a class comprising all plants having five stamens

pen·tan·drous \(')pen'tandrəs\ *adj* [NL *pentandrus*, fr. *penta-* + *-andrus* -androus] *of a flower* **:** having five stamens

pen·tane \'penˌtān\ *n* -s [ISV *penta-* + *-ane*] **:** any of three isomeric paraffin hydrocarbons C_5H_{12} found in petroleum and natural gas: **a :** the volatile flammable liquid normal hydrocarbon $CH_3CH_2CH_2CH_2CH_3$ used chiefly in gasoline, in organic synthesis, and as a solvent — called also *n-pentane*, *normal pentane* **b :** ISOPENTANE **c :** NEOPENTANE

pen·tane·dione \ˌpenˌtān'dīˌōn\ *n* -s [*pentane* + *-dione*] **:** a diketone derived from normal pentane; *esp* **:** ACETYLACETONE

pentane lamp *n* **:** a lamp having an Argand burner that burns pentane vapor and formerly being used as a photometric standard developing about ten candles

pen·tan·gle \'penˌtaŋgəl\ *n* [*penta-* + *angle*] **:** PENTACLE 1

pen·tan·gu·lar \(')pen'taŋgyələ(r)\ *adj* [*penta-* + *angular*] **:** having five angles **:** PENTAGONAL

pen·ta·no·ic acid \ˌpentə'nōik-\ *n* [*pentane* + *-oic*] **:** VALERIC ACID a — used in the system of nomenclature adopted by the International Union of Pure and Applied Chemistry

pen·ta·nol \'pentəˌnȯl, -nōl\ *n* -s [*pentane* + *-ol*] **:** any of three pentyl alcohols derived from normal pentane; *esp* **:** PENTYL ALCOHOL a

pen·ta·none \'pentəˌnōn\ *n* -s [*pentane* + *-one*] **:** either of two isomeric flammable liquid ketones derived from normal pentane: **a :** the unsymmetrical compound $CH_3CH_2CH_2COCH_3$ — called also *methyl propyl ketone*, *2-pentanone* **b :** the symmetrical compound $(C_2H_5)_2CO$ obtainable from propionic acid — called also *diethyl ketone*, *3-pentanone*, *propione*

pen·ta·phyl·a·ca·ce·ae \ˌpentəˌfilə'kāsēˌē\ *n pl, cap* [NL, fr. *Pentaphylac-*, *Pentaphylax*, type genus + *-aceae*] **:** a family of plants (order Sapindales) coextensive with the genus *Pentaphylax*

pen·taph·y·lax \pen·'tafəˌlaks\ *n, cap* [NL, fr. *penta-* + Gk *phylax* guard] **:** a genus of Chinese and Malayan shrubs comprising the family Pentaphylacaceae and having alternate leathery leaves and racemose pentamerous flowers

¹**pen·ta·ploid** \'pentəˌplȯid\ *also* **pen·ta·ploi·dic** \ˌ==ˌplȯidik\ *adj* [*pentaploid* fr. *penta-* + *-ploid*; *pentaploidic* fr. ²*pentaploid* + *-ic*] **:** fivefold in appearance or arrangement **:** having or being a chromosome number that is five times the basic number — **pen·ta·ploi·dy** \'==ˌplȯidē\ *n* -ES

²**pentaploid** \"\ *n* -s **1 :** a pentaploid chromosome number **2 :** something (as an individual or generation) characterized by the pentaploid chromosome number

pen·tap·o·dy \pen·'tapədē\ *n* -ES [*penta-* + *-pody* (as in *dipody*)] **:** a metrical unit or verse consisting of five feet

pen·tap·o·lis \pen·'tapələs\ *n* -ES [LL, a district of five towns on the Dead Sea, fr. Gk, group of five cities, fr. *penta-* + *polis* city — more at POLICE] **:** a union, confederacy, or group of five cities

pen·ta·pol·i·tan \ˌpentə'pälətᵊn\ *adj* [LL *pentapolitanus*, fr. *pentapolis*, after such pairs as LL *metropolis*: *metropolitanus* metropolitan] **:** of or relating to a pentapolis

pen·ta·prism \'pentə+ˌ-\ *n* [*penta-* + *prism*] **:** a pentagonal prism having one angle 90° and the others 112° 30′, producing a constant deviation of 90° for any wavelength, and used as a reflector in range finders

pen·ta·quine *also* **pen·ta·quin** \'pentəˌkwēn, -ˌkwə̇n\ *n* -s [*penta-* + *quinoline*] **:** a liquid basic antimalarial $C_{18}H_{27}N_3O$ that is an amino-methoxy-quinoline derivative and is used chiefly in the form of its pale yellow crystalline phosphate

¹**pen·tarch** \'penˌtärk\ *n* -s [*pent-* + *-arch*] **:** one of five joint rulers

²**pentarch** \"\ *adj* [ISV *pent-* + *-arch*] **:** having five protoxylem groups

pen·tarchy \-kē\ *n* -ES [Gk *pentarchia*, fr. *penta-* + *-archia* -archy] **1 :** a government by five persons **:** five joint rulers **2 :** a union of five powers

pen·tas \'pentəs\ *n* [NL, irreg. fr. Gk *pente* five — more at FIVE] **1** *cap* **:** a genus of chiefly African herbs or subshrubs (family Rubiaceae) that are grown as ornamentals esp. in mild regions or in greenhouses and have opposite leaves, tubular flowers with a hairy throat, and capsular fruit **2** *pl* **pentas :** any plant of the genus *Pentas*

pen·ta·stich \'pentəˌstik\ *n* -s [LGk *pentastichos* of five verses, fr. Gk *penta-* + *stichos* verse, line — more at STICH] **:** a unit, stanza, or poem consisting of five lines

pen·tas·ti·chous \(')pen'tastəkəs\ *adj* [NL *pentastichus*, fr. *penta-* (fr. Gk) + *-stichus* -stichous] **:** arranged in five orthostichies in such a manner that each leaf diverges from the preceding by an angle equal to two fifths of the circumference of the stem so that the sixth leaf stands above the first ⟨~ arrangement of leaves⟩ — **pen·tas·ti·chy** \=''==kē\ *n* -ES

pen·ta·stome \'pentəˌstōm\ *or* **pen·tas·to·mid** \pen'tastəməd\ *or* **pen·tas·to·moid** \-əˌmȯid\ *n* -s [*pentastome* ISV, fr. NL *Pentastomum*; *pentastomid* ISV, fr. NL *Pentastomidae*, family of tongue worms, fr. *Pentastomum* + *-idae*; *pentastomoid* fr. NL *Pentastomum* + E *-oid*] **:** TONGUE WORM

pen·ta·stom·i·da \ˌpentə'stäməda\ [NL, fr. *Pentastomum* + *-ida*] *syn of* LINGUATULIDA

pen·tas·to·mum \pen·'tastəməm\ *n, cap* [NL, fr. neut. of *pentastomus* having five stomata, fr. *penta-* + *-stomus* -stomous] **:** a genus of tongue worms that are chiefly parasitic in carnivorous mammals

pen·ta·style \'pentəˌstīl\ *adj* [*penta-* + *-style*] **:** marked by columniation with five columns across the front — compare DISTYLE

pen·ta·sty·los \ˌ=='stīˌläs\ *n* -ES [NL, fr. *penta-* + *-stylos* -style] **:** a pentastyle building

pen·ta·sulfide \ˌpentə+\ *n* [*penta-* + *sulfide*] **:** a sulfide containing five atoms of sulfur in the molecule

pen·ta·syllabic \"+\ *adj* [LL *pentasyllabus* (fr. Gk *pentasyllabos*, fr. *penta-* + *syllabē* syllable) + E *-ic* — more at SYLLABLE] **:** having five syllables

pen·ta·syllable \"+\ *n* [*penta-* + *syllable*] **:** a word of five syllables

pen·ta·teu·chal \ˌpentəˌtükəl, -əˌtyü-\ *adj, usu cap* [*Pentateuch*, the first five books of the Old Testament (fr. LL *Pentateuchus*, fr. Gk *Pentateuchos*, fr. *penta-* + *teuchos* tool, implement, roll of writing material) + E *-al*; akin to Gk *teuchein* to build — more at DOUGHTY] **:** of or relating to the first five books of the Old Testament

pen·ta·thionic acid \ˌpentə+ˌ=ˌ==-\ *n* [ISV *penta-* + *thionic*] **:** the thionic acid $H_2S_5O_6$ containing five atoms of sulfur in the molecule

pen·tath·lete \pen'tathˌlēt\ *n* [LGk *pentathlētēs*, fr. Gk *pentathlein* to practice the pentathlon, fr. *pentathlon*, *pentaethlon*] **:** an athlete participating in a pentathlon

pen·tath·lon \pen·'tathlən, -thˌlän\ *n* -s [Gk *pentathlon*, *pentaethlon*, fr. *penta-* + *athlon*, *aethlon* prize, contest — more at ATHLETE] **1 :** an ancient Greek athletic contest in which each contestant participates in five different events (as leaping, foot racing, wrestling, throwing the discus, and throwing the spear) **2 :** an athletic contest involving participation by each contestant in five different events (as formerly in the Olympic games a running broad jump, a javelin throw, a 200-meter flat race, a discus throw, and a 1500-meter flat race) **3 :** a contest in the modern Olympic games involving participation by each contestant in horseback riding, shooting, fencing, swimming, and running — see MODERN PENTATHLON

pen·ta·tom·ic \ˌpentəˈtämik\ *adj* [ISV *penta-* + *atomic*] **1 :** consisting of five atoms **2 :** having five replaceable atoms or radicals

¹pen·ta·tom·id \ˌpentəˈtämə̇d\ *adj* [NL *Pentatomidae*] **:** of or relating to the Pentatomidae

²pentatomid \"\ *n* -s [NL *Pentatomidae*] **:** a bug of the family Pentatomidae

pen·ta·tom·i·dae \ˌ=ˈtäməˌdē\ *n pl, cap* [NL, fr. *Pentatoma*, type genus (fr. *penta-* + *-toma*) + *-idae*] **:** a large and widely distributed family of terrestrial bugs (order Hemiptera) usu. flattened and angular in form and often brilliantly colored that live mainly on the juices of plants and fruits though some are important predators of caterpillars and other insect pests — compare HARLEQUIN BUG

pen·ta·tone \ˈpentəˌtōn\ *n* [*penta-* + *tone*] **:** PENTATONIC SCALE

pen·ta·tonic \ˌpentə+\ *adj* [*penta-* + *tonic*] **1 :** consisting of five musical tones **2 :** relating to a pentatonic scale — **pen·ta·ton·i·cism** \ˌpentəˈtänəˌsizəm\ *n* -s

pentatonic scale *n* **:** a musical scale of five tones in which the octave is reached at the sixth tone; *specif* **:** a scale in which the tones are arranged like a major scale with its fourth and seventh tones omitted

pentatonic scale

pen·ta·triacontane \ˌpentə+\ *n* [ISV *penta-* + *triacontane*] **:** a paraffin hydrocarbon $C_{35}H_{72}$; *esp* **:** the normal hydrocarbon $CH_3(CH_2)_{33}CH_3$

pen·ta·trichomonas \"+\ *n, cap* [NL, fr. *penta-* (fr. Gk) + *Trichomonas*] **:** a genus of flagellates related to *Trichomonas* but possessing five anterior flagella and often regarded as indistinguishable from or a subgenus of *Trichomonas*

pen·ta·valent \ˌpentə+\ *adj* [*penta-* + *valent*] **:** having a valence of five **:** QUINQUEVALENT

pen·te·con·ter \ˈpentēˈkäntə(r)\ *n* -s [Gk *pentēkonteros*, fr. *pentēkonta* fifty] **:** an early Hellenic galley characterized by decks fore and aft and carrying fifty rowers

pen·te·cost \ˈpentəˌkȯst, -tē,-, -ˌkäst\ *n* -s *usu cap* [ME *Pentecost*, fr. OE *Pentecosten*, fr. LL *Pentecoste*, fr. Gk *pentēkostē* fiftieth day, Pentecost, fr. *pentēcostos* fiftieth, fr. *pentēkonta* fifty, fr. *penta-* + *-konta* (akin to L *-ginti* in *viginti* twenty) — more at VICENARY] **1 :** SHABUOTH **2 :** a Christian church festival on the 7th Sunday after Easter commemorating the descent of the Holy Spirit on the apostles — called also *Whitsunday*

¹pen·te·cos·tal \ˌ==ˈkȯstᵊl, -kä̇s-\ *n* -s *usu cap* [NL *pentecostalia* (pl.), fr. LL, neut. pl. of *pentecostalis*, adj.] **1** *obs* **:** an offering given in the Church of England by parishioners to the parish priest or by a subordinate church to the cathedral church at the celebration of Pentecost **2** *also* **pen·te·cos·tal·ist** \-stələ̇st\ **:** a member of a Pentecostal religious body

²pentecostal \ˌ==ˈ==\ *adj, usu cap* [LL *pentecostalis*, fr. *Pentecoste* Pentecost + *-alis* -al] **1 :** of, relating to, or resembling Pentecost or the descent of the Holy Spirit described in Acts 2 **2 :** of, relating to, or being one of various Christian religious bodies that employ revivalistic methods typically including the generating of great emotionalism within the congregation, that stress the individual attainment of holiness, perfection, and a regenerative experience comparable to the Pentecostal experience of the first Christian disciples, that particularly seek the gift of tongues and observe such other practices as foot washing, divine healing, and spirit baptism, and that are generally fundamentalist in outlook

pen·te·cos·tal·ism \ˌ==ˈ=stəˌlizəm\ *n* -s *sometimes cap* **:** the doctrines and practices of Pentecostal religious bodies; *esp* **:** religious excitement or emotionalism accompanied by ecstatic utterances interpreted as the gift of tongues

pen·te·cos·ta·ri·on \ˌ==ˌkōˈsta(a)rēˌän, -kä-\ *n* -s [LGk *pentēkostarion*, fr. *pentēkostē* Pentecost] **:** a liturgical book in the Eastern Church containing offices for the period from Easter Sunday to the first Sunday after Pentecost

pen·te·cos·tys \ˌpentəˈkästə̇s\ *n, pl* **pentecosty·es** \-ˌästēˌēz\ [Gk *pentēkostys* body of fifty, fr. *pentēkostos* fiftieth] **:** a troop of 50 soldiers in the Spartan army

pen·tel·ic \(ˈ)penˈtelik\ *adj, usu cap* [L *pentelicus*, fr. Gk *pentelikos*, fr. *Pentelē*, area near Athens, Greece + *-ikos* -ic] **:** of or from Mount Pentelicus, Greece ⟨*Pentelic* marble⟩

pen·tene \ˈpenˌtēn\ *n* -s [ISV *penta-* + *-ene*] **:** either of the two normal amylenes obtained from gasoline: **a :** the alpha or 1-isomer $CH_3CH_2CH_2CH{=}CH_2$ — called also *alpha-n-amylene, 1-pentene* **b :** the beta or 2-isomer CH_3CH_2-$CH{=}CHCH_3$ — called also *beta-n-amylene, 2-pentene*

pen·te·nyl \ˈpentəˌnil\ *n* -s [*pentene* + *-yl*] **:** any of four univalent radicals C_5H_9 derived from the pentenes by removal of one hydrogen atom

pen·the·mim·er \ˌpen(t)thəˈmimə(r)\ *n* -s [LL *penthemimeres*, *penthemimeris*, fr. Gk *penthēmimerēs*, fr. *penta-* + *hēmimerēs* halved, fr. *hēmi-* hemi- + *meros* part — more at MERIT] **:** a group of five half feet in Greek and Latin prosody **:** a catalectic colon of two and a half feet — **pen·the·mim·er·al** \ˌ==ˈmimərəl\ *adj*

penthemimeral caesura *n* **:** a caesura in classical verse occurring after the fifth half foot

pen·thes·tes \penˈtheˌstēz\ [NL, prob. fr. Gk *penthein* to mourn (akin to Gk *penthos* grief, sorrow) + *esthēs* clothing; fr. its including the black-capped variety — more at PATHOS, WEAR] *syn of* PARUS

pen·tho·rum \ˈpen(t)thərəm\ *n, cap* [NL, fr. *penta-* (fr. Gk) + *-horum* (fr. Gk *horos* boundary, limit)] **:** a genus of herbs (family Crassulaceae) with thin leaves and greenish pentamerous flowers — see DITCH STONECROP

¹pent·house \ˈpentˌhau̇s\ *n* [by folk etymology (influence of MF *pente* slope — fr. *pendant* — and E *house*) fr. ME *pentis*, fr. MF *appentis*, prob. fr. ML *appenticium* appendage, fr. L *appendic-, appendix* appendage, supplement, fr. *appendere* to append — more at PENDANT, APPEND] **1 a :** a shed or roof attached to and sloping from a wall or building (as to shelter a passage, door, window) **b :** a smaller structure joined to a building **:** ANNEX **2 a :** a structure built on the roof of a building to cover a stairway, elevator shaft, water tank, or ventilating or other equipment — called also *bulkhead* **b :** a dwelling built on a roof **c :** a corridor with a sloping roof surrounding a court-tennis court on three sides

²penthouse \"\ *vt* **:** to furnish with or as if with or to make like a penthouse

pen·thrite \ˈpenˌthrīt\ *n* -s [*pentaerythritol tetranitrate*] **:** PENTAERYTHRITOL TETRANITRATE

pen·tice \ˈpentə̇s\ *archaic var of* PENTHOUSE

pen·ti·men·to \ˌpentəˈmen(ˌ)tō\ *n, pl* **pentimen·ti** \-(ˌ)tē\ [It, repentance, correction, fr. *pentire* to repent (fr. L *paenitere*) + *-mento* -ment — more at PENITENCE] **:** a reappearance in a painting of a design which has been painted over

pent·it \ˈpentə̇t\ *adj* [prob. alter. (influenced by ¹*pent*) of obs. E *pended*, past. part. of *pend* to pen, confine, fr. ME *penden* — more at PEND] **1** *chiefly Scot* **:** PENT, CONFINED **2** *chiefly Scot* **:** COMFORTABLE, SNUG

pen·ti·tol \ˈpentəˌtōl, -tōl\ *n* -s [*penta-* + *-itol*] **:** any of the pentahydroxy alcohols $HOCH_2(CHOH)_3CH_2OH$ obtainable by reducing the corresponding pentoses

pent·land·ite \ˈpentlənˌdīt\ *n* -s [F *pentlandite*, fr. Joseph B. *Pentland* †1873 Irish traveler & scientist + F *-ite*] **:** a mineral $(Fe,Ni)_9S_8$ consisting of an isometric nickel iron sulfide that is found in pale bronze-yellow masses and that is the principal ore of nickel (hardness 3.5–4, sp. gr. 4.60)

pentlatch *usu cap, var of* PUNTLATSH

pen·to·barbital \ˌpentō+\ *n* [*penta-* + *-o-* + *barbital*] **:** a granular barbiturate $C_{11}H_{18}N_2O_3$ used chiefly in the form of its sodium or calcium salt as a sedative, hypnotic, and antispasmodic; 5-ethyl-5-(1-methyl-butyl)barbituric acid

pen·tode \ˈpenˌtōd\ *n* -s [ISV *penta-* + *-ode*] **:** a vacuum tube with five electrodes including a cathode, an anode, a control grid, and two additional grids or other electrodes

pen·to·lite \ˈpentəˌlīt\ *n* -s [*penta-* + *-ol* + *-ite*] **:** a high-explosive mixture of pentaerythritol tetranitrate and trinitrotoluene

pen·tom·ic \(ˈ)penˈtämik\ *adj* [*penta-* + atomic] **1** *of an army division* **:** made up of five battle groups **2 :** organized into pentomic divisions ⟨a ~ army⟩

pen·to·san \ˈpentəˌsan\ *n* -s [ISV *pentose* + *-an*] **:** any of a class of polysaccharides (as xylan or araban) that yield only pentoses on hydrolysis and that are widely distributed in plants (as in corncobs, oat hulls, wood, straw, mesquite gum, gum arabic) — compare FURFURAL, HEMICELLULOSE

pen·tose \ˈpenˌtōs *also* -ōz\ *n* -s [ISV *penta-* + *-ose*] **:** any of a class of monosaccharides $C_5H_{10}O_5$ (as xylose or ribulose) containing five carbon atoms in the molecule that are obtained esp. from pentosans, nucleic acids, or nucleosides by hydrolysis or from hexoses by degradation — compare DEOXYPENTOSE, METHYLPENTOSE

pentose nucleic acid *n* **:** any of various nucleic acids yielding a pentose on hydrolysis; *esp* **:** RIBONUCLEIC ACID

pen·to·side \-təˌsīd\ *n* -s [ISV *pentose* + *-ide*] **:** a glycoside that yields a pentose on hydrolysis

pen·tos·uria \ˌpentəˈs(h)u̇rēə, -təsˈyu̇-\ *n* -s [NL, fr. ISV *pentose* + NL *-uria*] **:** the excretion of pentoses in the urine; *specif* **:** a rare hereditary anomaly characterized by regular excretion of pentoses

Pen·to·thal \ˈpentəˌthȯl\ *trademark* — used for thiopental

pent·oxide \(ˈ)pent+\ *n* [ISV *penta-* + *oxide*] **:** an oxide containing five atoms of oxygen in the molecule

pen·tre·mi·tes \ˌpenˌtrəˈmīˌtēz\ *n, cap* [NL, fr. *penta-* (fr. Gk) + Gk *trēma* hole + NL *-ites* — more at THROW] **:** a genus (the type of the family Pentremitidae) comprising Mississippian blastoid echinoderms having an ovate or pyriform calyx with five ambulacral areas suggestive of petals

¹pen·tre·mit·id \ˌ==ˈmidə̇d\ *adj* [NL *Pentremitidae*, family of echinoderms, fr. *Pentremites*, type genus + *-idae*] **:** of or relating to the genus *Pentremites* or the family Pentremitidae

²pentremitid \"\ *n* -s [NL *Pentremitidae*] **:** an echinoderm or fossil of the genus *Pentremites* or the family Pentremitidae

pen·trite \ˈpenˌtrīt\ *n* -s [*pentaerythritol tetranitrate*] **:** PENTAERYTHRITOL TETRANITRATE

pent road *n* [¹*pent*] *NewEng* **:** a public road that may be barred or enclosed by gates or bars esp. at its terminal points

pent roof *n* [*pent* short for *penthouse*] **:** a roof sloping one way only — called also *shed roof*

pentrough \ˈ=ˌ=\ *n* [¹*pen* + *trough*] **:** an open usu. planked or boarded trough or tank from which water falls onto a waterwheel

pen·tryl \ˈpen·trəl\ *n* -s [*penta-* + *-ryl* (as in *tetryl*)] **:** an explosive $C_8H_6(NO_2)_4ONO_2$ that is derived from nitramide, picric acid, and ethyl nitrate and that is somewhat more sensitive to friction than tetryl and much more sensitive than picric acid or trinitrotoluene

pents *pl of* PENT

pent·ste·mon *or* **pen·ste·mon** \pen(t)ˈstēmən, ˈpen(t)stəm-\ *n* -s [*pentstemon* fr. NL, alter. (influenced by *penta-*) of *penstemon; penstemon* fr. NL — more at PENSTEMON] **:** a plant or flower of the genus *Penstemon*

pen·tu·lose \ˈpenchəˌlōs\ *n* -s [*penta-* + *-ulose* (as in *ribulose*)] **:** a ketose $C_5H_{10}O_5$ (as ribulose or xylulose) containing five carbon atoms in the molecule

pen·tyl \ˈpentᵊl\ *n* -s [ISV *penta-* + *-yl*] **:** any of eight isomeric alkyl radicals C_5H_{11} derived from the three pentanes by removal of one hydrogen atom: as **a :** the normal radical $CH_3(CH_2)_3CH_2$— — called also *amyl, n-amyl, n-pentyl* **b :** ISOPENTYL **c :** NEOPENTYL

pentyl alcohol *n* **:** any of eight isomeric liquid alcohols C_5H_{11}-OH used chiefly as solvents and in making esters: as **a :** the normal primary alcohol $CH_3(CH_2)_3CH_2OH$ that in vapor form is irritating to the eyes and respiratory tract and that is used in organic synthesis; 1-pentanol — called also *amyl alcohol, n-amyl alcohol, n-pentyl alcohol* **b :** ISOPENTYL ALCOHOL **c :** ACTIVE AMYL ALCOHOL **d :** TERTIARY AMYL ALCOHOL

pen·tyl·ene \-təˌlēn\ *n* -s [*pentyl* + *-ene*] **:** AMYLENE

pen·tyl·ene·tet·ra·zol \ˌpentəˌlēnˈteˈtrəˌzōl, -zōl\ *n* -s [*pentamethylene-tetrazole*] **:** a white crystalline drug $C_6H_{10}N_4$ used as a respiratory and circulatory stimulant and for producing a state of convulsion in treating certain mental disorders; pentamethylene-tetrazole

pen·tyli·dene \penˈtiləˌdēn\ *n* -s [*pentyl-* + *-idene*] **:** the bivalent radical $CH_3CH_2CH_2CH_2CH$< derived from normal pentane by removal of two hydrogen atoms from an end carbon atom — called also *amylidene*

pen·tyne \ˈpenˌtīn\ *n* -s [*penta-* + *-yne*] **:** either of two normal isomeric hydrocarbons C_5H_8 of the acetylene series

pentz·ia \ˈpentsēə\ *n, cap* [NL, fr. Charles J. *Pentz*, 18th cent. Swedish student + NL *-ia*] **:** a small genus of southern African hoary shrubs (family Compositae) having small wedge-shaped leaves, yellow flowers in small heads, and achenes crowned with a cleft and cuplike pappus

pe·nu·che \pəˈnüchē\ *also* **pa·no·cha** \-nōchə\ *or* **pa·no·che** \-chē\ *or* **pe·nu·chi** \-nüchē\ *or* **pi·no·che** *or* **pi·no·chi** *or* **pe·no·che** \-nōchē\ *n* -s [MexSp *panocha* raw sugar — more at PANOCHA] **:** fudge made usu. of brown sugar, butter, cream or milk, and nuts

penuchle *var of* PINOCHLE

pe·nult \ˈpēˌnəlt\ *also* **pe·nul·ti·mate** \pə̇ˈnəltəmə̇t\ *or* **pe·nul·ti·ma** \-mə\ *n* -s [*penult* fr. *penult*, adj.; *penultimate* fr. *penultimate*, adj.; *penultima* fr. L *paenultima* penult, fr. fem. of *paenultimus, penultimus*] **:** the next to the last member of a series; *esp* **:** the next to the last syllable of a word

penultimate *also* **penult** *adj* [*penultimate* fr. *pene-* + *ultimate*; *penult* fr. L *paenultimus, penultimus*, fr. *paene-, pene-* pene- + *ultimus* last — more at ULTIMATE] **1 :** next to the last ⟨the ~ chapter of a book⟩ ⟨the ~ phase of a war⟩ **2 :** of or relating to a penult ⟨a ~ accent⟩ — **pe·nul·ti·mate·ly** *adv*

pe·num·bra \pə̇ˈnəmbrə\ *n, pl* **penumbrae** \-mˌbrē, -rī\ *or* **penumbras** [NL, fr. L *pene-* + *umbra* shadow — more at UMBRAGE] **1 :** a shadow cast (as in an eclipse) where the light is partly but not wholly cut off by the intervening body **:** a space of partial illumination between the perfect shadow on all sides and the full light **2 :** the shaded region surrounding the dark central portion of a sunspot **3 a :** a surrounding or adjoining region in which something exists in a lesser degree **:** a marginal area **:** FRINGE ⟨the ~ of consciousness⟩ ⟨Thracian existed in a sort of cultural ~ on the border line of the civilized world —Jaan Puhvel⟩ ⟨the seventeenth century lay in the ~ of the middle ages —Edward Eggleston⟩ ⟨the few sure findings remain surrounded by a much larger ~ of uncertainties —A.L. Kroeber⟩ **b :** a surrounding atmosphere (as of obscurity, emotion, meaning) **:** AURA, NIMBUS ⟨love . . . has been stripped of its mystical ~ —J.W.Krutch⟩ ⟨symbols carrying with them vital ~s of meaning —M.R.Cohen⟩ **c :** an area containing things of obscure classification **:** an uncertain middle ground between fields of thought or activity **:** BORDERLAND, NO-MAN'S-LAND ⟨orthodoxy and heterodoxy have too large a ~ of doubt —*New Republic*⟩ **4 :** a part of a picture where shade gradually blends with light — **pe·num·bral** \-rəl\ *adj*

penumbral lunar eclipse *n* **:** an eclipse of the moon caused when the moon passes through the penumbra of the earth's shadow but not into the umbra

pe·nu·ri·ous \pə̇ˈn(y)u̇rēəs\ *adj* [ML *penuriosus*, fr. L *penuria* want, need + *-osus* -ose] **1 :** marked by or suffering from penury ⟨actually saved money in these ~ times —R.V.Mills⟩ **2 :** given to or marked by extreme stinting frugality ⟨as keen on the penny as a ~ weaver —G.D.Brown⟩ **syn** see STINGY — **pe·nu·ri·ous·ly** *adv* **:** in a penurious manner ⟨incurred a few modest liabilities, and then lived ~ till next term — Samuel Butler †1902⟩ — **pe·nu·ri·ous·ness** *n* -ES **:** the quality or state of being penurious

pen·ury \ˈpenyərē, -ri\ *n* -ES [ME, fr. L *penuria* want, need — more at PATIENT] **1 a :** extreme poverty **:** PRIVATION **b :** absence of resources **:** SCANTINESS **2 :** PENURIOUSNESS

pe·nu·tian \pəˈnüdēən\ *n* -s *usu cap* [Wintun & Maidu *pen* two + Miwok & Costanoan *uti* two + E *-an*] **1 :** a language stock of California comprising the Copehan, Costanoan, Mariposan, Moquelumnan, and Pujunan families **2 :** a language phylum comprising the Penutian stock plus Chinookan, Kalapooian, Kusan, Shahaptian, and Takilman centering in Oregon and Tsimshian of British Columbia to which some add other families extending into Central America

penwoman \ˈ=ˌ=\ *n, pl* **penwomen** [³*pen* + *woman*] **:** a female writer **:** AUTHORESS

penwrite \ˈ=ˌ=\ *vt* [³*pen* + *write* (as in *typewrite*)] **:** to write with a pen ⟨puts both *penwritten* and typewritten signatures on his letters⟩

pen·za \ˈpenzə\ *adj, usu cap* [fr. *Penza*, U.S.S.R.] **:** of or from the city of Penza, U.S.S.R. **:** of the kind or style prevalent in Penza

pe·on \ˈpēˌän, ˈpēən, *in sense 2c usu* päˈōn\ *n, pl* **peons** \-nz\ *or* **peo·nes** \-ōˌnās\ *see numbered senses* [Pg *peão* & F *pion*, fr. ML *pedon-, pedo* foot soldier — more at PAWN] **1 :** any of several Indian or Ceylonese workers: **a :** FOOT SOLDIER **b :** CONSTABLE **c :** an office attendant or messenger **2 :** a member of the usu. landless laboring class in Spanish America: as **a :** an agricultural worker or miner of native Indian or mixed blood forced to serve virtually in bondage to creditors **b :** an unskilled laborer **c** *pl usu* **peones :** a bullfighter's attendant **3** *pl* **peons a :** a person held in a state of compulsory servitude to a master (as in the southwestern states formerly part of Mexico) for the working out of an indebtedness **b :** a convict laborer in parts of the southeastern U.S. **4** *pl* **peons :** a person occupying a position of subordination or drudgery esp. through stupidity or lack of initiative

pe·on·age \ˈpēənij\ *n* -s **1 :** the condition of a peon **2 a :** the use of peon labor; *esp* **:** the use of laborers bound in servitude because of debt or a penal sentence **b :** the system of convict labor by which convicts are leased to contractors in parts of the southeastern U.S. **3 a :** compulsory or involuntary servitude in working out indebtedness to a master **b :** a scheme effecting coercion for such servitude

pe·on·i·din \pēˈänədə̇n\ *n* -s [*peon-* (in *peonin*) + *-id* + *-in*] **:** an anthocyanidin obtained by hydrolysis of peonin usu. in the form of its reddish brown chloride $C_{16}H_{13}ClO_6$ **:** a monomethyl ether of cyanidin

pe·o·nin \ˈpēənə̇n\ *n* -s [*peony* + *-in*] **:** an anthocyanin pigment that is the coloring matter esp. of violet red peonies and is usu. obtained in the form of its reddish violet crystalline chloride $C_{28}H_{33}ClO_{16}$

pe·on·ism \ˈpēəˌnizəm\ *n* -s *archaic* **:** PEONAGE 2a

pe·on·ize \-ˌnīz\ *vt* -ED/-ING/-S **:** to reduce to the status of a peon ⟨*peonized* farm labor —*Atlantic*⟩

pe·o·ny \ˈpēənē, -ni, *dial* pēˈōn- *or* ˈpī(ə)n- *or* ˈpēn-\ *n* -ES [ME *piony, pione, pioine*, fr. OE & OF; OE *peonie* & OF *peone, pioine*, fr. L *paeonia*, fr. Gk *paiōnia*] **1 :** an herbaceous or shrubby plant of the genus *Paeonia* including numerous chiefly hybrid plants that are widely cultivated for their showy single or double red, pink, or white flowers — see TREE PEONY **2 :** a dark red that is less strong and slightly yellower and darker than cranberry and bluer, lighter, and stronger than average garnet or average wine — called also *Burmese ruby*

peony-flowered \ˈ===ˌ==\ *or* **peony-flowering** \ˈ===ˌ==ˌ=\ *adj* **:** having a flower resembling that of a peony ⟨a *peony-flowering* camellia⟩

peony-flowered dahlia *also* **peony dahlia** *n* **:** any of numerous showy cultivated dahlias having open-centered flowers with not more than four rows of functional ray flowers and with smaller curled or twisted ray flowers around the disk

peony red *n* **:** a dark to deep red — compare PEONY

¹peo·ple \ˈpēpəl\ *n, pl* **people** *or* **peoples** *see numbered senses* [ME *peple, poeple*, fr. OF *pueple*, fr. L *populus* — more at POPULAR] **1** *people pl* **a :** human beings not individually known or considered as individuals ⟨~ say⟩ ⟨tell ~ about his luck⟩ **b** (1) **:** human beings who form a segment of humanity usu. sharing a common characteristic ⟨stupid ~⟩ ⟨met all sorts of ~ on the trip⟩ ⟨~ who live in glass houses⟩ (2) **:** human beings distributively as individuals or constituting a numerable group ⟨we saw many ~ on our walk⟩ ⟨shelter for thousands of ~⟩ **c :** human beings as distinguished from the lower animals ⟨diseases that ~ catch from their pets⟩ ⟨it is hard to avoid thinking of some dogs as ~⟩ ⟨we heard cows lowing but saw no ~⟩ **2 a** *people pl* **:** human beings making up a group or assembly **:** persons linked by a common factor: as (1) **:** the members of a geographically distinct community ⟨the ~ of the next town⟩ (2) **:** persons who share in common a point of origin or residence ⟨city ~⟩ ⟨mountain ~⟩ (3) **:** members of a racial or national group or of a common ancestry ⟨Chinese ~⟩ ⟨the Slavic ~ in the U.S.⟩ ⟨Negro ~⟩ (4) **:** the members of a caste, class, or other isolable or identifiable group ⟨illiterate ~ of the community⟩ (5) **:** persons sharing a common occupation or interest ⟨academic ~⟩ (6) **:** the members of an organization (as a society or congregation) ⟨the ~ of the new synagogue⟩ **b** *pl* **peoples**, *obs* **:** a concourse of persons **:** THRONG, MULTITUDE **3** *people pl* **a :** human beings that constitute an organized body subordinate to a superior: as (1) **:** the subjects of a ruler ⟨a king's duty to his ~⟩ (2) **:** a body of retainers, servants, or followers ⟨the family and the ~ of the household⟩ (3) **:** the crew of a ship as distinguished from the officers **b :** the members of a family or kinship **:** ANCESTORS ⟨his ~ have been farmers for generations⟩ ⟨her ~ are all dead⟩ **4** *people pl* **a :** the mass of a community as distinguished from a special class: as (1) **:** the common crowd **:** COMMONALTY, POPULACE ⟨disputes between the ~ and the nobles⟩ (2) **:** LAITY 2 ⟨the priest shall say to the ~⟩ **b :** plain-mannered persons of unassuming and friendly nature **:** FOLKS ⟨real ~, kind and unpretentious⟩ **c** *usu cap* **:** the common people of a country as distinguished from a privileged minority — used esp. by Communists to distinguish Communists or those under Communist control from other people ⟨if one compares the situation in the *People's* Democracies . . . with that in the capitalist countries —Hilary Minc⟩ ⟨in other Communist states . . . justice is administered by *People's* Courts —N.D.Palmer⟩ ⟨the Bulgarian *People's* Republic was proclaimed by the national assembly —*Statesman's Yr. Bk.*⟩ **5** *pl* **peoples a :** a body of persons that are united by a common culture, tradition, or sense of kinship though not necessarily by consanguinity or by racial or political ties and that typically have common language, institutions, and beliefs ⟨many European nations are populated by several distinct ~s⟩ ⟨primitive ~s⟩ ⟨each ~ builds a culture adapted to its peculiar needs⟩ **b :** a body of persons constituting a ¹politically organized or consanguineous group (as a tribe, nation, or race) ⟨the ~s of Europe⟩ ⟨the Caucasian ~ gradually populated Europe and much of northern Africa⟩ ⟨the military genius of the German ~⟩ **6 a :** lower animals usu. of a specified kind or situation ⟨squirrels, mice, and other mischievous little ~s of field and forest⟩ ⟨the clever bee ~⟩ **b :** supernatural beings that are thought of as similar to humans in many respects ⟨the little ~⟩ ⟨kobolds, trolls, and such ~s are not to be trusted⟩ **7 :** the body of enfranchised citizens of a state **:** ELECTORATE; *broadly* **:** the body of persons in whom is vested the sovereignty of a nation or who are capable of expressing their general wish — usu. used with *the* and pl. in constr. **8** *slang* **:** a human being **syn** see RACE

²people \"\ *vb* **peopled; peopled; peopling** \-p(ə)liŋ\ **peoples** [MF *peupler*, fr. OF, fr. *peuple*, n.] *vt* **1 :** to supply, stock, or fill with or as if with people ⟨settlers were *peopling* the new lands⟩ *also* **:** to represent or picture as full of inhabitants **2 :** to be the inhabitants of **:** dwell in **:** INHABIT ⟨dreams that ~ idle hours⟩ ⟨a winter sky *peopled* with stars⟩ ~ *vi* **:** to become inhabited ⟨the drier lands *peopled* slowly⟩

peopled *adj* **:** POPULATED

peopledom *n* -s **1** *obs* **:** an ancient Grecian community or province **2** *obs* **:** a democratic rule

peo·ple·hood \ˈpēpəlˌhu̇d\ *n* **:** the quality or state of constituting a people; *also* **:** awareness of the underlying unity that makes the individual a part of a people ⟨tried to weld the groups together on a broad basis of ~ rather than theological doctrine —*Time*⟩

peo·ple·ize \-pəˌlīz\ *vt* -ED/-ING/-S **:** POPULARIZE

people-king \ˈ==ˌ=\ *n* [trans. of F *peuple-roi*, trans. of L *populus rex*] **:** a people as sovereign

peo·ple·less \ˈpēpəllə̇s\ *adj* **:** void of people **:** UNPOPULATED

people of god *usu cap P&G* **:** members of a Russian Christian sect developed in reaction to the extreme ritualism of the official church probably during the 17th century and characterized by disbelief in inspiration of written scriptures and absence of any formal ritual

people of the book *usu cap P&B* **:** KITABIS

peo·pler \-p(ə)lə(r)\ *n* -s **:** one that peoples **:** SETTLER, INHABITANT

peoples *pl of* PEOPLE, *pres 3d sing of* PEOPLE

people's bank *n* **:** any of various chiefly European cooperative financial institutions (as a credit union)

people's party *n* **:** a political party representing or claiming to represent the great majority of the inhabitants of a territorial unit (as a nation) as opposed to a particular class or group ⟨attempted to transform themselves from a class party into a *people's party*⟩ ⟨the Austrian *People's Party* . . . represents farmers, industrialists, and merchants, as well as some labor and many white-collar workers —Hans Kohn⟩

peo·plet \'pēplət\ *n* -s [*people* + *-et*] **:** a people small in numbers or very local in distribution

peopling *n* -s [fr. gerund of ²*people*] **:** POPULATING, SETTLING

peo·plish \'pēp(ə)lish\ *adj* [ME, fr. ¹*people* + *-ish*] **:** POPULAR 4

¹**pe·o·ria** \pē'ōrēə, -'ȯr-\ *n, pl* **peoria** *or* **peorias** *usu cap* [F, fr. Peoria *Piwarea*] **1 a :** an Indian people of Illinois and Iowa associated with the Illinois confederacy **b :** a member of such people **2 :** a dialect of Illinois

²**peoria** \"\ *also* **pe·o·ri·an** \-ən\ *adj, usu cap* [*peoria* fr. *Peoria*, Ill.; *peorian* fr. *Peoria*, Ill. + E *-an*] **:** of or from the city of Peoria, Ill. ⟨a *Peoria* industry⟩ **:** of the kind or style prevalent in Peoria

¹**pep** \'pep\ *n* -s [short for ¹*pepper*] **:** brisk energy or initiative usu. accompanied by high spirits **:** animated activity **:** LIVELINESS, DASH, GO ⟨a progressive tiredness and malaise, a loss of ~, an inability to work effectively —H.C.Hopps⟩

²**pep** \"\ *vt* **pepped; pepped; pepping; peps :** to inject pep into **:** quicken or stimulate to greater alertness or brightness — usu. used with *up*

pep·er·ek \'peperək\ *n* -s [fr. native name in Indonesia] **:** SAPSAP

pep·er·o·mia \,pepə'rōmēə\ *n* [NL, fr. Gk *peperi* pepper + *homoios* like, same + NL *-ia* — more at SAME] **1** *cap* **:** a very large genus of tropical fleshy often epiphytic climbing herbs (family Piperaceae) having flowers with two stamens and confluent anther cells and being often cultivated for their showy variegated leaves **2** -s **:** any plant of *Peperomia* or a closely related genus

peperoni *var of* PEPPERONI

pep·ful \'pepfəl\ *adj* [¹*pep* + *-ful*] **:** PEPPY, VIGOROUS

pe·pi·no \pə'pē(,)nō\ *n* -s [AmerSp, fr. Sp, cucumber, fr. L *pepon-, pepo*, a melon] **:** a bushy somewhat woody perennial plant of temperate uplands of Peru that is sometimes cultivated for its ovoid purple-marked edible yellow fruits which have a juicy aromatic yellow pulp

pep·lis \'pepləs\ *n, cap* [NL, fr. L, a plant, fr. Gk, wild purslane] **:** a genus of chiefly aquatic herbs (family Lythraceae) that have opposite leaves and minute solitary greenish flowers in the axils and are sometimes used as aerators in the balanced aquarium — see WATER PURSLANE

pep·los *also* **pep·lus** \'pepləs\ *n* -ES [L *peplus*, fr. Gk *peplos*; prob. akin to L *pellis* skin — more at FELL] **:** a garment worn by women of ancient Greece consisting of a rectangular cloth folded and draped on the upper body and clasped usu. with a brooch at the shoulder — compare HIMATION

pep·losed \-st\ *adj* **:** having or clothed with a peplos

pep·lum \'pepləm\ *n, pl* **peplums** \-mz\ *also* **pep·la** \-lə\ [L, fr. Gk *peplos*] **1** *obs* **:** PEPLOS **2 :** a short skirtlike section usu. attached to the waistline of a blouse, jacket, dress, and made usu. with a flared, pleated, or ruffled design — **pep·lumed** \-md\ *adj*

peplum 2

pe·po \'pē(,)pō\ *n* -s [L, a melon — more at PUMPKIN] **1 :** an indehiscent fleshy 1-celled or falsely 3-celled many-seeded berry usu. with a hard rind (as a pumpkin, squash, melon, and cucumber) that is the characteristic fruit of the family Cucurbitaceae — see FRUIT illustration **2 :** the dried ripe seed of the cultivated pumpkin used as an anthelmintic and a source of oil

¹**pep·per** \'pepə(r)\ *n* -s *often attrib* [ME *peper*, fr. OE *pipor*; akin to OHG *pfeffar* pepper, ON *piparr*; all fr. a prehistoric Gmc word borrowed fr. L *piper* pepper, fr. Gk *peperi*, prob. fr. Skt *pippali* long pepper] **1 a :** a pungent product obtained from the fruit of an East Indian plant (*Piper nigrum*), used as a condiment and sometimes as a carminative or stimulant, and prepared in a form (1) consisting of the entire dried berry or (2) consisting of the dried seeds divested of all membranes and pulp with both forms being usu. ground into powder before use — called also (1) *black pepper*, (2) *white pepper* **b :** any of several somewhat similar products obtained from other plants of the genus *Piper* — often used with a qualifying term; see LONG PEPPER **c :** any of various pungent condiments obtained from plants other than those of the genus *Piper* — used with a qualifying term ⟨paprika is sometimes known as Hungarian ~⟩; see CAYENNE PEPPER **2 a :** a plant of the genus *Piper*; *esp* **:** a woody vine (*Piper nigrum*) with ovate leaves and spicate flowers that is native to the oriental tropics but widely cultivated in tropical regions for its red berries from which pepper is prepared **3 a :** a plant of the genus *Capsicum* (esp. *C. frutescens*) **b :** the many-seeded berry enclosed in a thickened integument like an indehiscent pod that is the fruit of any of these plants, varies greatly in shape and size in different varieties, is usu. red or yellow when ripe, and includes numerous cultivated forms used in the preparation of condiments and relishes and as vegetables — see BIRD PEPPER, CHERRY PEPPER, CONE PEPPER, LONG PEPPER; HOT PEPPER, SWEET PEPPER **4 :** any of numerous plants other than members of the genera *Piper* and *Capsicum* that have pungent or aromatic qualities — usu. used with a qualifying term ⟨African ~⟩ **5 :** PEPPERBOX 1 **6** *or* **pepper trash :** finely broken leaf present as an impurity in raw cotton **7 :** PEPPER GAME

²**pepper** \"\ *vb* **peppered; peppered; peppering** \-p(ə)riŋ\ **peppers** *vt* **1 a :** to sprinkle or season with pepper ⟨~ a stew⟩ **b :** to sprinkle as if with pepper **:** cover with small dots, marks, or injuries ⟨~*ed* with freckles⟩ ⟨the bees ~*ed* him with stings⟩ **c :** to shower with or as if with shot or other missiles ⟨~ the boys with bird shot⟩ ⟨~*ing* them with questions⟩ **2 :** to make (as writing) spicy or provocative **3 a :** to thrash or beat thoroughly with or as if with rapid repeated blows ⟨~*ed* his opponent with short lefts⟩ **b** *obs* **:** to conquer or ruin by or as if by beating **4** *archaic* **:** to infect with a venereal disease **:** POX **5 :** to sprinkle as pepper is sprinkled **:** strew in or as if in grains ⟨~*ing* classical quotations right and left⟩ ⟨the wind ~*ed* stinging sleet into our faces⟩ ~ *vi* **1 a :** to shower in small particles and usu. briskly ⟨the rain came ~*ing* down⟩ ⟨shot ~*ed* among the leaves⟩ **b** *archaic* **:** to shower flattery or fulsome praise **2 :** to apply pepper esp. as a seasoning ⟨don't ~ so heavily⟩

¹**pepper-and-salt** \'⁼⁼⁼'⁼\ *n* **1 :** a suiting or other fabric woven with flecks of dark and light (as black and white or dark gray and light gray) **2 :** a pepper-and-salt color **3** [so called fr. the effect of dark stamens against white petals] **:** HARBINGER-OF-SPRING

²**pepper-and-salt** \"\ *adj* **:** having black and white or dark and light color intermingled in small flecks giving an irregular gray or grayed effect

pepper-and-salt cat *n* [so called fr. its color] **:** a small active diurnal grizzled gray mongoose (*Mungos pulverulentus*) of southern Africa

pepper-and-salt moth *n* [so called fr. the sprinkling of dark brown on black on its dull white wings] **:** a geometrid moth (*Biston cognataria*) having a larva that feeds on various deciduous plants (as willow, apple, and black currant)

pepperbox \'⁼⁼,⁼\ *n* **1 :** a small box or bottle with a perforated top used for sprinkling ground pepper on food **2 :** something resembling a pepperbox in shape or contents: as **a :** a small cylindrical tower or turret **b :** a temperamental person **:** SPITFIRE **c :** a pistol developed in the late 18th century having five or six barrels revolving upon a central axis and fired individually by a single striker **d :** a prepared military position (as of concrete) sheltering a machine gun and its crew

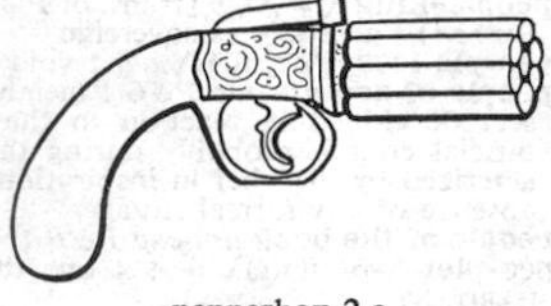
pepperbox 2 c

pepperbush *n* **:** SWEET PEPPERBUSH

pepper caster *n* **:** a caster or bottle for pepper **:** PEPPERBOX

¹**pep·per·corn** \'pepər,kȯrn, -pə,kȯ(ə)n\ *n* [ME *pepercorn*, fr. OE *piporcorn*, fr. *pipor* pepper + *corn* — more at CORN] **1 :** a dried berry of the black pepper **2 :** a trifling return by way of acknowledgment — compare PEPPERCORN RENT

²**peppercorn** \"\ *adj* **1 :** consisting of a peppercorn **:** TRIVIAL **2** *of hair* **:** woolly and closely spiraled into twisted clumps or knots ⟨the ~ hair of the Hottentots⟩

peppercorn rent *n* **1 :** a rent formerly often stipulated in deeds and consisting in supplying a certain amount (as a pound) of black peppercorns at stated intervals **2 :** a merely nominal rent in kind operating to keep alive a title

pepper cress *n* **:** PEPPERGRASS

pepper dulse *n, chiefly Scot* **:** a pungent edible red alga (*Laurencia pinnatifida*) with fine feathery fronds

peppered moth *n* **:** a European geometrid moth (*Biston betularia*) having white wings with small black specks

pep·per·er \'pep(ə)rə(r)\ *n* -s [¹*pepper* + *-er*] *archaic* **:** a dealer in pepper **:** GROCER

pepper family *n* **:** PIPERACEAE

pep·per game \'pepə(r)-\ *n* [*pepper* fr. ²*pep* + *-er*] **:** a group warm-up usu. preceding a baseball or softball game consisting of short quick throws bunted in return by a single batter

peppergrass \'⁼⁼,⁼\ *n* [¹*pepper* + *grass*; fr. the pungent flavor] **1 :** a cress of the genus *Lepidium*; *esp* **:** GARDEN CRESS **2 :** SHEPHERD'S PURSE

peppergrass beetle *n* **:** a beetle (*Galerucа browni*) of the family Galerucidae that feeds on turnips and other plants in western U. S. and Canada

pepper green *n* **:** a strong green that is very slightly bluer than mintleaf (sense 1) and yellower and less strong than primitive green

pep·per·idge \'pep(ə)rij\ *also* **pip·per·idge** *or* **pip·er·idge** \'pip-\ *n* -s [origin unknown] **1 :** BLACK GUM 1 a **2** *dial Eng* **:** COMMON BARBERRY

pep·per·i·ly \'pepərəlē\ *adv* **:** in a peppery manner

pep·per·i·ness \-rēnəs\ *n* -ES **:** the quality or state of being peppery

peppering *pres part of* PEPPER

pep·per·ish \'pep(ə)rish\ *adj* **:** somewhat peppery — **pep·per·ish·ly** *adv*

pepper maggot *n* **:** a maggot that is the larva of a trypetid fly (*Zonosternata electa*) and that infests pepper plants in various parts of the U. S.

pepper mill *n* **:** a hand mill for grinding peppercorns

pep·per·mint \'pepə(r),mint, -p,m-, -,mənt, -pᵊm,i-, -pᵊmə-\ *n* [¹*pepper* + *mint*] **1 a :** a pungent and aromatic mint (*Mentha piperita*) with dark green lanceolate leaves and whorls of small pink flowers in spikes **b :** any of several related mints (as *M. arvensis*) **2 a :** PEPPERMINT OIL **b :** PEPPERMINT SPIRIT **c :** a preparation consisting of the dried leaf and flowering top of peppermint **3 :** candy flavored with peppermint **4** *Austral* **a :** PEPPERMINT GUM **b :** WILLOW MYRTLE

peppermint camphor *n* **:** MENTHOL

peppermint gum *n* **:** any of various Australian eucalypts with aromatic leaves (as *Eucalyptus piperita, E. amygdalina, E. microcorys*, and *E. stuartiana*)

peppermint oil *n* **:** either of two essential oils obtained from mints: as **a :** an oil that has a strong peppermint odor and produces a cooling sensation in the mouth, is obtained from peppermint, and is used chiefly as a flavoring agent and as a carminative **b :** JAPANESE MINT OIL

peppermint spirit *n* **:** an alcoholic solution of peppermint oil that is green if made from the leaves of peppermint

peppernut \'⁼⁼,⁼\ *n* [by trans.] **:** PFEFFERNUSS

pepper oil *n* **:** a volatile oil that has an odor like that of pepper but no pungency, is obtained from the fruit usu. of black pepper, and is used chiefly in flavoring

pep·per·o·ni *also* **pep·er·o·ni** \,pepə'rōnē\ *n* -s [It *peperoni* chilies, pl. of *peperone* chili, aug. of *pepe* pepper, fr. L *piper* — more at PEPPER] **:** a highly seasoned beef and pork sausage

pepper plant *n* **1 :** a plant yielding pepper **2 :** any of several pungent plants: as **a :** SHEPHERD'S PURSE **b :** an Australian plant (*Alpinia caerulea*) with a pungent edible rootstock **c :** a widely distributed smartweed (*Polygonum hydropiper*)

pepper pot *n* **1 :** PEPPERBOX **2 a :** a stew of vegetables, meat or fish, cassareep, and other condiments common in the West Indies **b :** a thick soup of tripe, meat, dumplings, and vegetables highly seasoned esp. with crushed peppercorns — called also *Philadelphia pepper pot*

pepper red *n* **:** a moderate red that is yellower and paler than cerise, Harvard crimson (sense 1), or Turkey red and yellower and less strong than claret (sense 3a) or average strawberry (sense 2a) — called also *bronze red*

pepperroot \'⁼⁼,⁼\ *n* [so called fr. its pungent flavor] **:** TOOTHWORT 2

peppers *pl of* PEPPER, *pres 3d sing of* PEPPER

pepper sauce *n* **:** vinegar in which small hot peppers are steeped and which is used as a condiment at table

pepper trash *n* **:** PEPPER 6

pepper tree *n* **1 :** a Peruvian evergreen tree (*Schinus molle*) with broad rounded head, graceful pinnate leaves, and panicles of greenish flowers succeeded by small red drupes **2** *also* **pepper shrub :** a small often shrubby New Zealand tree (*Wintera colorata*) with foliage conspicuously blotched with red and yellow and small blackish fruits

pepper turnip *n* **:** JACK-IN-THE-PULPIT

pepper vine *n* **1 :** PEPPER PLANT 1 **2 :** a woody vine (*Ampelopsis arborea*) of the southern U. S. with bipinnate leaves and pungent black berries

pepperweed \'⁼⁼,⁼\ *n* **1 :** a plant of the genus *Peperomia* **2 :** PEPPERGRASS

pepper weevil *n* **:** a small black weevil (*Anthonomus eugenii*) that is a serious pest on pepper plants in warmer parts of the New World

pepperwood \'⁼⁼,⁼\ *n* **1 :** HERCULES'-CLUB 1 a **2 :** CALIFORNIA LAUREL

pepperwort \'⁼⁼,⁼\ *n* **1 :** PEPPERGRASS 1 **2 a :** a water fern of the family Marsileaceae 1 **b :** TOOTHWORT 2

pep·pery \'pep(ə)rē, -ri\ *adj* **1 :** of or relating to pepper **:** having the qualities of pepper **:** HOT, PUNGENT, PIQUANT **2 :** easily moved to anger or irascibility **:** HOT-TEMPERED, TOUCHY; *also* **:** SPIRITED, PASSIONATE **3 :** FIERY, STINGING ⟨~ words⟩ ⟨a ~ satire⟩

pep pill *n* [¹*pep*] **:** any of various stimulant drugs (as amphetamine) dispensed in pill or tablet form

pep·pin \'pepən\ *dial var of* PIPPIN

pep·pi·ness \'pepēnəs, -pin-\ *n* -ES **:** the quality or state of being peppy

pepping *pres part of* PEP

pep·py \'pepē, -pi\ *adj* -ER/-EST **:** full of pep **:** KEEN, ALERT, LIVELY ⟨the members responded to the ~ and interesting program —*Nat'l Miller*⟩

pep rally *n* **:** a mass meeting (as of students before an athletic contest) usu. featuring songs, cheers, and inspiring talks

peps *pl of* PEP, *pres 3d sing of* PEP

-pep·sia \'pepshə, -psēə\ *n comb form* -s [L, fr. Gk, fr. *pepsis* digestion] **:** digestion ⟨brady*pepsia*⟩

pep·si·gogue \'pepsə,gäg *also* -gȯg\ *adj* [*pepsin* + *-agogue*] **:** inducing the secretion of pepsin

pep·sin \'pepsən\ *n* -s [G, fr. Gk *pepsis* digestion (fr. *peptein, pessein* to cook, digest) + G *-in*] **1 :** a crystallizable proteinase that in an acid medium digests most proteins to polypeptides (as by dissolving coagulated egg albumin or causing casein to precipitate from skim milk), that is secreted by glands in the mucous membrane of the stomach of higher animals, and that in combination with dilute hydrochloric acid is the chief active principle of gastric juice **2 :** a preparation containing pepsin obtained as a powder or scales from the stomach esp. of the hog and used chiefly as a digestant, in making peptones, and in digesting gelatin for the recovery of silver from photographic film

pep·sin·if·er·ous \,pepsə'nif(ə)rəs\ *adj* [*pepsin* + *-iferous*] **:** producing or yielding pepsin

pepsino- *comb form* [ISV, fr. *pepsin*] **:** pepsin ⟨*pepsino*genic⟩

pep·sin·o·gen \pep'sinəjən, -,jen\ *n* -s [ISV *pepsino-* + *-gen*] **:** a crystallizable zymogen occurring in the form of granules in the peptic cells of the gastric glands and readily converted into pepsin in a slightly acid medium

pep·sis \'pepsəs\ *n, cap* [NL, fr. Gk, digestion] **:** a genus of large spider-hunting wasps (family Pompilidae) comprising the tarantula hawks

pep·si·ten·sin \,pepsə'ten(t)sən\ *n* -s [*pepsin* + *-tensin* (as in *hypertensin*)] **:** a vasoconstrictor pressor polypeptide similar to hypertensin formed by the action of pepsin on hypertensinogen

-pep·sy \'pepsē, -si\ *n comb form* -ES [L *-pepsia*] **:** -PEPSIA

pept- *or* **pepto-** *comb form* [ISV, fr. *peptone*] **:** peptone ⟨*pept*ide⟩ ⟨*pepto*genic⟩

pep talk *n* [¹*pep*] **:** a usu. brief, high-pressure, and emotional utterance designed to influence or encourage an audience (as to some outstanding effort or sacrifice)

peptalk \'⁼,⁼\ *vi* **:** to give a pep talk ~ *vt* **:** to influence with a pep talk

pep·tic \'peptik, -tēk\ *adj* [L *pepticus*, fr. Gk *peptikos*, fr. *peptos* cooked (fr. *peptein, pessein* to cook, digest) + *-ikos* -ic — more at COOK] **1 :** relating to digestion **:** promoting or aiding digestion **:** DIGESTIVE ⟨~ sauces⟩ **2 :** able to digest **3 :** of, relating to, or resembling pepsin ⟨a ~ secretion⟩ **:** containing pepsin or a substance of similar properties ⟨the ~ glands⟩ **:** involving or like that produced by pepsin ⟨~ digestion⟩ **4 :** connected with or to some degree caused by the action of digestive juices — see PEPTIC ULCER

peptic gland *n* **:** a cardiac gland of the stomach

pep·tics \-ks\ *n pl* **:** the digestive organs

peptic ulcer *n* **:** an ulcer in the wall of the stomach or duodenum resulting from the digestive action of the gastric juice on the mucous membrane when the latter is rendered susceptible to its action (as by psychosomatic or local factors)

pep·ti·dase \'peptə,dās\ *n* -s [ISV *peptide* + *-ase*] **:** any of a group of enzymes that hydrolyze simple peptides or their derivatives containing free amino or carboxyl groups **:** EXOPEPTIDASE — distinguished from *proteinase*

pep·tide \'pep,tīd\ *n* -s [ISV *pept-* + *-ide*; prob. orig. formed as G *peptid*] **:** any of a class of amides that are derived from two or more amino acids by combination of the amino group of one acid with the carboxyl group of another, that yield these acids on hydrolysis, that are classified according to the number of component amino acids, and that are obtained by partial hydrolysis of proteins or by synthesis (as from alpha-amino acids or their derivatives) — compare DIPEPTIDE, POLYPEPTIDE

peptide bond *or* **peptide linkage** *n* **:** the bond between carbon and nitrogen in the amide group —CO—NH— that unites the amino acid residues in a peptide

pep·tiz·able \(')pep¦tīzəbəl\ *adj* **:** capable of being peptized

pep·ti·za·tion \,peptə'zāshən\ *n* -s **:** the process of peptizing

pep·tize \'pep,tīz\ *vt* -ED/-ING/-S [prob. fr. Gk *peptein* to cook, digest + E *-ize*] **:** to bring into colloidal solution **:** convert into a sol — **pep·tiz·er** \-zə(r)\ *n* -s

pepton- *comb form* [ISV, fr. *peptone*] **:** PEPT- ⟨*pepton*uria⟩ ⟨*pepton*ize⟩

pep·to·nate \'peptə,nāt\ *n* -s [ISV *pepton-* + *-ate*] **:** a combination of pepsin with a metallic salt

pep·tone \'pep,tōn\ *n* -s [G *pepton*, fr. Gk, neut. of *peptos* cooked] **1 :** any of various protein derivatives that are formed by the partial hydrolysis of proteins (as by enzymes of the gastric and pancreatic juices or by acids or alkalies), that are not coagulated by heat, and that are soluble in water but unlike proteoses are not precipitated from solution by saturation with ammonium sulfate **2 :** a complex water-soluble product containing proteoses as well as peptones that is obtained by digesting protein (as meat) with an enzyme (as pepsin or trypsin) and is used chiefly in nutrient media in bacteriology

pep·to·nephridium \¦peptō+\ *n* [NL, fr. *pept-* + *nephridium*] **:** a nephridium that opens into the alimentary canal and is regarded as having a digestive function

pep·to·ni·za·tion \,peptənə'zāshən, -,nī'z-\ *n* -s [ISV *peptonize* + *-ation*] **:** the process of peptonizing **:** PROTEOLYSIS

pep·to·nize \'peptə,nīz\ *vt* -ED/-ING/-S [*pepton-* + *-ize*] **1 :** to convert into peptone **:** digest or dissolve by a proteolytic enzyme **2 :** to combine with peptone ⟨*peptonized* iron⟩

pep·to·noid \'peptə,nȯid\ *n* -s [ISV *pepton-* + *-oid*] **:** a substance resembling peptone

pepys·i·an \'pēpsēən\ *adj, usu cap* [Samuel *Pepys* †1703 Eng. official in navy office and diarist + E *-ian*] **:** of or relating to Samuel Pepys or his diary

pe·quot \'pē,kwät\ *n, pl* **pequot** *or* **pequots** *usu cap* [prob. modif. of Narraganset *paquatanog* destroyers] **1 a :** an Indian people of southeastern Connecticut **b :** a member of such people **2 :** an Algonquian language of the Pequot people

¹**per** *R* ,pər, ¦pər, +V ¦pər·; *-R* ,pə(r, ¦pə, +V ¦pər· *or* ¦pə *also* ¦pər\ *prep* [L, through, by means of, for the sake of, for each — more at FOR] **1 :** by the means or agency of **:** by way of **:** THROUGH ⟨~ bearer⟩ ⟨wealth . . . of a nation could increase only ~ medium of an expanded consumption —*Economica*⟩ ⟨enter through the mouth lining and ~ the bloodstream to the stomach —*Sydney (Australia) Bull.*⟩ **2 :** with respect to every member of a specified group or series **:** for each ⟨miles ~ hour⟩ ⟨income ~ person⟩ ⟨greater number of trout ~ cubic foot than any other Vermont stream —H.E.McDaniel⟩ ⟨capital investment abroad ~ dollar stimulates no more production or development than . . . consumption expenditure at home —T.J.Kreps⟩ **3 :** as indicated by **:** as directed or stated in **:** according to ⟨~ list price⟩ ⟨employers paid their quota . . . ~ the number of employees working for them —C.P.Curtis⟩ ⟨mats are moistened as ~ his specifications —G.A.Kubler⟩ ⟨calling in his coach as ~ family arrangement —*Times Lit. Supp.*⟩ **4 :** in the direction of — used in heraldry to indicate division of the field or a charge into parts by a line or lines having the direction and unless otherwise specified the customary position of one of the ordinaries ⟨~ fess⟩ ⟨~ saltire⟩ ⟨~ pale or and sable is borne by the English family of Serle —John Woodward⟩

²**per** \'⁼\ *adv* **1** *slang* **a :** for each of an implied unit (as of time) ⟨swung crazily down the road at sixty-five ~ —Glenn Scott⟩ **b :** APIECE ⟨back numbers two-fifty ~ —Susan Glaspell⟩ **2** *slang* **:** in the usual manner **:** CUSTOMARILY ⟨she was by herself, as ~, reading —Richard Llewellyn⟩

³**per** \'pər(·), 'pe(ə)r\ *adj* [*per-*] **1 :** containing a chemical element in its highest or relatively high oxidation state **2 :** PEROXY — not used systematically

per- *prefix* [in sense 1, fr. L, throughout, thoroughly, completely, deviating from (also, used as verbal prefix with the meanings "through", "throughout", "thoroughly", "detrimentally", and to denote completion or perfection or intensification), fr. *per* through, by; in sense 2, fr. *per* through, by — more at FOR] **1 a :** throughout ⟨*per*dominant⟩ **b** (1) **:** containing the largest possible or a relatively large proportion of a (specified) chemical element esp. as a result of exhaustive substitution for hydrogen or of exhaustive addition in an organic compound or group ⟨*per*chloroethylene⟩ ⟨*per*hydronaphthalene $C_{10}H_{18}$⟩ — compare PEROXIDE 1, PROT- 2a (2) **:** containing an element in its highest or a high oxidation state ⟨*per*chloric acid⟩ (3) **:** PEROXY- — not used systematically ⟨*per*sulfate⟩ ⟨*per*benzoic acid⟩ **2 :** through ⟨*per*radius⟩ **:** by means of ⟨*per*lingual⟩ ⟨*per*rectal⟩

per *abbr* **1** perdendosi **2** perennial **3** period **4** person

pera·car·i·da \,perə'karədə\ *n pl, cap* [NL, fr. Gk *pēra* pouch, bag + NL *-carida* (fr. L *carid-, caris*, a kind of sea crab) — more at -CARIS] **:** a division of Malacostraca including among others the amphipods and isopods all having the first thoracic segment fused with the head, the thoracic legs flexed between the fifth and sixth segments, and the young developed in a brood pouch from which they escape at a late stage

per ac·ci·dens \,pə'raksə,denz, ,pər·'a-, pe'ra-\ *adv* [LL] **1 :** by chance or extraneous circumstance **:** ACCIDENTALLY ⟨he is not learned, except *per accidens* —Walter Moberly⟩ **2 :** in accidental or nonessential character

per·acetic acid \¦pər·, ¦per+...-\ *n* [ISV *per-* + *acetic*] **:** a corrosive toxic strongly oxidizing unstable pungent liquid acid CH_3COOOH made usu. by oxidation of acetaldehyde or by reaction of hydrogen peroxide with acetic acid or acetic anhydride and used chiefly in a solution in acetic acid or an inert solvent in bleaching, in organic synthesis, and as a fungicide and disinfectant — called also *peroxyacetic acid;* not used systematically

per·acid \ˌpər·, ˌper+\ *n* [ISV *per-* + *acid*] **1 :** an acid (as perchloric acid or permanganic acid) derived from the highest oxidation state of an element **2 :** PEROXY ACID

per·act \pəˈrakt\ *vt* -ED/-ING/-S [L *peractus,* past part. of *peragere,* fr. *per-,* prefix denoting completion or perfection + *agere* to drive, act, do — more at PER-, AGENT] *archaic* **:** PERFORM, ACCOMPLISH

per·acute \ˌpər, ˌper+\ *adj* [L *peracutus,* fr. *per-* + *acutus* acute — more at ACUTE] *of disease* **:** very acute and violent ⟨anthrax occurs in four forms: ~, acute, subacute and chronic —G.W.Stamm⟩

[1]per·adventure \ˌpər·, ˌper+\ *adv* [ME *per aventure,* fr. OF *per aventure, par aventure,* fr. *per, par* by (fr. L *per* through, by) + *aventure* chance — more at FOR, ADVENTURE] *archaic* **:** PERHAPS, POSSIBLY ⟨~ I will with you to the court —Shak.⟩ ⟨it may ~ be thought there was never such a time —Thomas Hobbes⟩

[2]peradventure \"\ *n* **1 :** a possibility of error or uncertainty **:** DOUBT, CHANCE ⟨the foregoing facts establish beyond ~ the conclusion —E.H.Wilkins⟩ ⟨put federal credit beyond ~ of a doubt —B.M.Baruch⟩ **2 :** an opinion based on guesswork **:** SURMISE ⟨beyond the reach of ~ —H.J.Laski⟩

peraeon *var of* PEREION

peraeopod *var of* PEREIOPOD

per aes et li·bram \ˌpeˌrīˌsetˈlēˌbrăm\ [L] **:** with bronze and balance — used to designate the formal ceremony by which mancipatory contracts were made in ancient Rome

peragration *n* -S [L *peragration-, peragratio* action of wandering or traversing, fr. *peragratus* (past part. of *peragrare* to wander, traverse, fr. the phrase *per agros* through fields, fr. *per* through + *agros,* acc. pl. of *agr-, ager* field) + *-ion-, -io* -ion — more at FOR, ACRE] *obs* **:** an act of traversing; *specif* **:** a sidereal revolution of the moon

per·alkaline \ˌpər·, (ˈ)per+\ *adj* [*per-* + *alkaline*] **:** having a molecular proportion of alumina less than that of soda and potash combined — used of an igneous rock

per·aluminous \ˌpər·, ˌper+\ *adj* [*per-* + *aluminous*] **:** having a molecular proportion of alumina greater than that of soda and potash combined — used of an igneous rock

per·am·bu·lant \pəˈrambyələnt, -ˈraam-\ *adj* [L *perambulant-, perambulans,* pres. part. of *perambulare*] **:** PERAMBULATORY

per·am·bu·late \-ˌlāt, *usu* -ād·+V\ *vb* -ED/-ING/-S [L *perambulatus,* past part. of *perambulare,* fr. *per-* through + *ambulare* to walk — more at PER-, AMBLE] *vt* **1 a :** to travel over or through esp. on foot **:** TRAVERSE ⟨~ the park or . . . bask and loiter and gossip on its benches —Virginia Woolf⟩ **b :** to push in a perambulator ⟨mothers, with toddlers and *perambulated* infants in tow —*Time*⟩ **2 :** to make an official inspection of (a boundary) on foot ⟨according to tradition, selectmen . . . are required by law to ~ the bounds every five years —*Springfield (Mass.) Daily News*⟩ **~** *vi* **1 a :** to cover ground at a leisurely pace **:** STROLL, PROMENADE ⟨when woman was a *perambulating* clothes closet —H.A.Overstreet⟩ **b :** to follow a meandering course **:** RAMBLE ⟨the road, winding about in the *perambulating* style of all mountain roads —N.H.Fulbright⟩ **2 :** to walk a boundary for purposes of inspection

per·am·bu·la·tion \=ˌ==ˈlāshən, ˌpər·ˌa- *also* pə̄ˌra-\ *n* -S [ME *perambulacion,* fr. ML *perambulation-, perambulatio,* fr. L *perambulatus* (past part. of *perambulare*) + *-ion-, -io* -ion] **1 a :** an act of walking about **:** a tour on foot **:** STROLL ⟨his ~ to the river for his midday bath is a progress in the grand manner —Alan Moorehead⟩ **b :** an official act or ceremony of walking around an area (as a town, parish, forest) to assert and record its boundaries and thereby maintain the rights of possession **c :** an act of traveling through and inspecting an area ⟨spent his whole reign . . . in a ~ or survey of the Roman Empire —Francis Bacon⟩ **2 :** a written account of a perambulation **3 :** the boundary or extent of an area as determined by walking its perimeter ⟨enlarged the ~*s* of what they had —Edmund Hickeringill⟩ **4** *obs* **:** a comprehensive account **:** SURVEY ⟨a . . . ~ of learning —Francis Bacon⟩

per·am·bu·la·tor \=ˈ==ˌlād·ə(r), -ātə-\ *n* -S [ML, fr. L *perambulatus* (past part. of *perambulare*) + *-or*] **1 a** *archaic* **:** an inveterate rambler **:** TRAVELER **b :** one that inspects a boundary on foot **2 :** ODOMETER 2 **3** *chiefly Brit* **:** BABY CARRIAGE

per·am·bu·la·to·ry \=ˈ==_ləˌtōrē, -tȯr-, -ri\ *adj* [*perambulate* + *-ory*] **1 :** inclined to move about **:** ITINERANT **2 :** of, relating to, or characterized by perambulation

Pera·mel·i·dae \ˌperəˈmeləˌdē\ *n pl, cap* [NL, fr. *Perameles,* type genus (fr. Gk *pēra* pouch, bag + L *meles* marten, badger) + *-idae*] **:** a family of marsupials consisting of the bandicoots

Pe·ra·mi·um \pəˈrāmēəm\ *n, cap* [NL, fr. L *pera* bag, pouch (fr. Gk *pēra*) + NL *-amium* (origin unknown)] *in some classifications* **:** a small genus of No. American orchids comprising a few rattlesnake plantains more commonly included in *Goodyera*

per·a·na·kan \ˌperəˈnäkən\ *n* -S *often cap* [Jav] **:** an old established Chinese immigrant of West Java

per an·num \pəˈranəm\ *adv* [L] **:** in or for each year **:** ANNUALLY

Pe·ra·tes \pəˈrāˌtēz\ *n, pl* **pera·tae** \-ˌtē\ *or* **perates** *usu cap* [LL *Peratae,* pl., fr. LGk *Peratai,* fr. pl. of Gk *peratēs* one that crosses over, fr. *peran* to cross over, pass through — more at FARE] **:** a member of a Gnostic school venerating the serpent as a powerful being intermediary between God the Father and unformed matter

per·bend \ˈpərbənd\ *n* -S [by alter.] **:** PERPEND

per·borate \ˌpər, (ˈ)per+\ *n* [ISV *per-* + *borate*] **1 :** a salt containing the anion BO_3– formed by the action of hydrogen peroxide on a borate — called also *true perborate* **2 :** a salt (as sodium perborate) that is a compound of a borate with hydrogen peroxide

per·bromide \"+\ *n* [*per-* + *bromide*] **:** a bromide containing a relatively high proportion of bromine

Per·bu·nan \ˌpərˌb(y)ünən, (ˈ)perˈb-\ *trademark* — used for a nitrile rubber

perc *abbr* percussion

Per·ca \ˈpərkə\ *n, cap* [NL, fr. L *perca* perch — more at PERCH] **:** the type genus of Percidae formerly including numerous perches and related fishes but now restricted to the typical perches — see YELLOW PERCH

per·cale \pə(r)ˈkā(ə)l, ˈpərˌkā-, ˈpə̄ˌkā-, ˈpəiˌkā-, *esp in the southern U S* _pə(r)ˈkal\ *n* -S *often attrib* [Per *pargālah*] **:** a firm smooth cotton cloth closely woven in plain weave and variously finished for clothing, sheeting, and industrial uses

per·ca·line \ˌpərkəˌlēn\ *n* -S [F, fr. *percale* (fr. Per *pargālah*) + *-ine*] **:** a lightweight cotton fabric made in plain weave, given various finishes (as glazing, moiré), and used esp. for clothing and linings; *esp* **:** a glossy fabric usu. of one color used for bookbindings

per cap·i·ta \pə(r)ˈkapəd·ə, ˌpərˈk-, pə̄ˈk-, -pətə\ *adv (or adj)* [L by heads] **1 :** per unit of population **:** by or for each person ⟨the heaviest debt *per capita* and in proportion to wealth in the union —D.Y.Thomas⟩ ⟨*per capita* consumption⟩ ⟨*per capita* tax⟩ **2 :** equally to each individual — used of the sharing of an inheritance; compare PER STIRPES

per cap·ut \-pət\ *adv (or adj)* [L, by the head] **:** PER CAPITA

per·carbonate \ˌpər, (ˈ)per+\ *n* [*per-* + *carbonate*] **:** a salt or ester of a percarbonic acid — called also *peroxycarbonate*

per·carbonic acid \ˌpər, ˌper+...-\ *n* [*per-* + *carbonic*] **:** any of three peroxy acids derived from carbonic acid and known only in the form of their salts and esters; *esp* **:** the peroxy-di-carbonic acid $H_2C_2O_6$ — called also *peroxycarbonic acid;* not used systematically

per·ceant \ˈpərsᵊnt\ *adj* [ME *persaunt,* fr. MF *perçant,* pres. part. of *percer* to pierce — more at PIERCE] *archaic* **:** PENETRATING, PIERCING ⟨~ was his spright —Edmund Spenser⟩

per·ceiv·able \pə(r)ˈsēvəbəl\ *adj* [ME *perceyvable,* fr. *perceyven, perceiven* to perceive + *-able*] **:** PERCEPTIBLE, INTELLIGIBLE — **per·ceiv·ably** \-blē,-bli\ *adv*

per·ceiv·ance \-vən(t)s\ *n* -S *dial* **:** PERCEPTION, NOTICE

per·ceive \pə(r)ˈsēv\ *vt* -ED/-ING/-S [ME *perceiven,* fr. OF *perceivre, percevoir,* fr. L *percipere* to take possession of, obtain, receive, perceive, fr. *per-,* prefix denoting completion or perfection + *-cipere* (fr. *capere* to seize, take) — more at PER-, HEAVE] **1 a :** to become conscious of **:** DISCERN, REALIZE ⟨the reasoning process which ~*s* divergence among authorities —H.O.Taylor⟩ ⟨*perceiving* the uselessness of further resistance, surrendered —Marquis James⟩ **b :** to recognize or identify esp. as a basis for or as verified by action ⟨goes beyond simple observation and begins to ~ things like causal principle —R.M.Weaver⟩ **2 :** to become aware of through the senses **:** NOTE, OBSERVE ⟨~ roughness and smoothness —R.S.Woodworth⟩ ⟨the length of the interval determines whether the delayed sound is *perceived* as completely merged with the first —R.D.Darrell⟩; *esp* **:** to look at ⟨people have become so used to the sight of ruins that they hardly ~ them any more —Norbert Mühlen⟩ **3** *obs* **:** GET, RECEIVE ⟨I could ~ nothing at all from her; no, not so much as a ducat for delivering your letter —Shak.⟩ **syn** see SEE

per·ceiv·er \-və(r)\ *n* -S **:** one that perceives

perceiving *adj* [ME, fr. gerund of *perceiven* to perceive] **:** OBSERVANT, DISCERNING

[1]per·cent \pə(r)ˈsent\ *adv* [fr. *per cent.,* abbr. for *per centum,* fr. L] **:** in the hundred **:** of each hundred ⟨a rate of . . . 1 shilling 3 pence ~ —W.D.Winter⟩ ⟨cannot recover if he is even one ~ responsible for the accident —S.H.Hofstadter⟩ ⟨agreed with her suggestions a hundred ~ —Sally Benson⟩

[2]percent \"\ *n, pl* **percent** *or* **percents** **1 a :** one part in a hundred **:** HUNDREDTH ⟨while they are laboring with tenths of a ~, the rest of us are letting tens of ~*s* slip through our fingers —S.L.Payne⟩ ⟨come upon stars which can not have spent more than a few ~ of their hydrogen —G.W.Gray b. 1886⟩ ⟨provided forty ~ of Europe's requirements — Harold Butler⟩ — symbol % **b :** PERCENTAGE ⟨a large ~ of the hotel's income . . . stems from convention visitors —G.T.Hellman⟩ ⟨manufacturing and mercantile rates are both ~*s* of the fire insurance rate —Robert Riegel & J.S.Miller⟩ **2** *percents pl, Brit* **:** securities bearing a specified rate of interest ⟨invested in three ~*s*⟩

[3]percent \"\ *adj* **1 :** reckoned on the basis of a whole divided into one hundred parts ⟨a five ~ increase⟩ ⟨harvested 50 ~ more wheat because of timely rains⟩ ⟨another 100 ~ result —*Manchester Guardian Weekly*⟩ **2 :** paying interest at a specified percent ⟨a 3½ ~ government bond⟩

per·cent·age \pə(r)ˈsentij, -tēj\ *n* -S *often attrib* [[1]*percent* + *-age*] **1 a :** a part of a whole expressed in hundredths **:** rate in percent ⟨the higher the income, the larger is the ~ saved —George Soule⟩ **b :** the result obtained by multiplying a number by a percent **2 a :** a share of winnings or profits **:** COMMISSION, CUT ⟨some of my troupe of clients . . . brought me thick slices of ~ —Christopher Morley⟩ **b :** ADVANTAGE, PROFIT ⟨no ~ in going around looking like an old sack of laundry —Wallace Stegner⟩ ⟨there must be some ~ in this for the kid —J.A.MacEwen⟩ **3 :** an indeterminate part or number **:** PROPORTION ⟨a high ~ of textbook publishers are themselves former school teachers —*Textbooks in Education*⟩ **4 a :** a likelihood based on cumulative statistics **:** PROBABILITY ⟨more use is made of the ~ today, such as playing the hitter where he hits the ball most of the time —Ted Williams⟩ **b :** the mathematical odds in favor of success ⟨chooses his career, his connections, his mistresses . . . solely on the ~*s* —Isaac Rosenfeld⟩; *specif* **:** the degree by which a gambler's expectancy of winning exceeds that of his opponent

percentage bridge *n* **:** a variation of bridge played with a pack of 60 cards comprising 5 suits in which tricks taken with cards of the 5th suit count an additional 10 percent of trick value

percentage composition *n* **:** composition expressed by percentages of constituents

percentage error *n* **:** RELATIVE ERROR

percentage lease *n* **:** a lease of business property at a base rental plus a specified percent of receipts from the business

percentage shop *n* **:** a shop in which by agreement between union and management a specified percentage of the work force must be union members

percentage tare *n* **:** tare computed as a percentage of the gross weight

per·cent·age·wise \=ˈ==ˌwīz\ *adv* [*percentage* + *-wise*] **:** in terms of percentage ⟨this college ranked second in the nation ~ in the production of scientists —W.K.Hicks⟩

per·cent·ile \=ˈsen·ˌtīl, -nt·ˌīl, -ntᵊl\ *n* -S *often attrib* [prob. fr. [1]*percent* + *-ile* (as in *quartile,* n. — quartile aspect — and *sextile,* n.)] **:** the value of the statistical variable that marks the boundary between any two consecutive intervals in a distribution of 100 intervals each containing one percent of the total population — called also *centile*

per cen·tum \pə(r)ˈsentəm\ *n* [L] **:** PERCENT

per·cept \ˈpərˌsept\ *n* -S [back-formation fr. *perception*] **1 :** an object perceived **2 :** the meaningful impression of an object obtained by use of the senses **:** SENSE-DATUM

percepta *pl of* PERCEPTUM

per·cep·ti·bil·i·ty \pə(r)ˌseptəˈbiləd·ē, -lətē, -i\ *n* -ES **:** capability of being perceived

per·cep·ti·ble \pə(r)ˈseptəbəl\ *adj* [LL *perceptibilis,* fr. L *perceptus* (past part. of *percipere* to perceive) + *-ibilis* -ible — more at PERCEIVE] **1** *archaic* **:** able to perceive **:** PERCEPTIVE, SENSITIVE ⟨the soul . . . becomes more ~ of happiness or misery —Thomas Green⟩ **2 :** capable of being perceived **:** DISCERNIBLE, RECOGNIZABLE ⟨rotating . . . discs, driven at speeds sufficiently high to eliminate all ~ flicker —F.A. Geldard⟩ ⟨something strange was in the air, ~ to a little boy but utterly beyond his understanding —H.G.Wells⟩ ⟨a ~ trend . . . away from dairying —E.C.Higbee⟩

syn SENSIBLE, PALPABLE, TANGIBLE, APPRECIABLE, PONDERABLE: PERCEPTIBLE applies to that which may be discerned by the senses even to the smallest extent ⟨out of the stillness, little scarcely *perceptible* noises began to emphasize themselves —Mark Twain⟩ ⟨the traces left by ages of slaughter and pillage were still distinctly *perceptible* —T.B.Macaulay⟩ or recognized by the intellect ⟨greeted the idea with a *perceptible* lack of enthusiasm⟩ SENSIBLE in its earlier senses applies to what is discerned by the senses as opposed to the intellect ⟨our true ideas of *sensible* things do indeed copy them —William James⟩ ⟨the distinction between some elements of subject matter as rational and others as *sensible* —John Dewey⟩ PALPABLE applies to that which has physical substance ⟨touch beauty as though it were a *palpable* thing —W.S.Maugham⟩ or is obvious or unmistakable ⟨carry, besides their *palpable* meaning, another which is veiled and more spiritual —H.O.Taylor⟩ TANGIBLE stresses tactile quality or utilitarian value ⟨free negative electricity, released from dense matter, disconnected from atoms, and finer and subtler substance than any which is *tangible* —K.K.Darrow⟩ ⟨a summer job at a national park offers many *tangible* advantages, such as fresh air and scenery⟩ ⟨a cloud, a pillar of fire, a *tangible* physical something —Jack London⟩ APPRECIABLE refers to that which is distinctly discernible esp. by the senses, or definitely measurable ⟨the temperature of even a single day plays an *appreciable* and measurable part in determining the general health of the community —Ellsworth Huntington⟩ ⟨an *appreciable* pause fell . . . a pause that must have lasted fully a minute —Jack London⟩ PONDERABLE suggests esp. what is bulky, massive, or of weighty importance ⟨energy, at any rate kinetic energy, resists motion in the same way as *ponderable* masses —Albert Einstein & Leopold Infeld⟩ ⟨*ponderable* and powerful reasons peculiarly his own for feeling as he did —Hervey Allen⟩

per·cep·ti·bly \-blē,-bli\ *adv* **:** in a perceptible manner **:** to a perceptible extent **:** VISIBLY, DISCERNIBLY

per·cep·tion \pə(r)ˈsepshən\ *n* -S [L *perception-, perceptio* act of taking possession, obtaining, receiving, perceiving, fr. *perceptus* (past part. of *percipere* to take possession of, obtain, receive, perceive) + *-ion-, -io* -ion — more at PERCEIVE] **1 :** the receipt or collection of profits, rents, or crops — used chiefly in civil law ⟨the lessee had the benefit of . . . the ~ of the profits for the whole term —C.G.Addison⟩ **2** *obs* **:** power of apprehension ⟨matter hath no life nor ~, and is not conscious of its own existence —Richard Bentley †1742⟩ **3 a :** a result of perceiving **:** OBSERVATION, DISCERNMENT ⟨it is a film bristling with sharp ~*s* but lacking in coherence —Arthur Knight⟩ **b :** a mental image **:** CONCEPT ⟨lyric ~*s* of friendship, of love and lust —Edward Hubler⟩ ⟨endeavor to correct their ~ of what is beautiful by the opinions of other people —A.C. Benson⟩ **4 a :** awareness of the elements of environment through physical sensation **:** reaction to sensory stimulus ⟨color ~⟩ ⟨depth ~⟩ ⟨since smell is a chemical sense, a contact is necessary for ~ —R.N.Shreve⟩ ⟨some sensation of ~ of the extremity after amputation is felt by 98% of patients —*Orthopedics & Traumatic Surgery*⟩ **b :** physical sensation as interpreted in the light of experience **:** the integration of sensory impressions of events in the external world by a conscious organism esp. as a function of nonconscious expectations derived from past experience and serving as a basis for or as verified by further meaningful motivated action **5 a :** direct or intuitive recognition **:** intelligent discernment **:** APPRECIATION, INSIGHT ⟨a clear ~ of the uncertain boundary which exists between the liberties freely permitted to the press and the area in which there are bound to be limitations —F.L. Mott⟩ ⟨renewed ~ into the heart of human activity —H.V. Gregory⟩ **b :** a capacity for comprehension **:** intellectual grasp ⟨persecutors were ordinary, reasonably well-intentioned people lacking in keen ~ —C.H.Sykes⟩

per·cep·tion·ism \-shəˌnizəm\ *n* -S **:** the theory that all knowledge is relative to sense perception

per·cep·tion·ist \-_nəst\ *n* -S **:** an advocate or adherent of perceptionism

per·cep·tive \pə(r)ˈseptiv, -tēv\ *adj* [*perception* + *-ive*] **1 :** responsive to sensory stimulus **:** SHARP, DISCERNING ⟨a ~ eye⟩ ⟨the children developed a taste that was as ~ as her own —S.N.Behrman⟩ **2 a :** capable of or exhibiting keen perception **:** OBSERVANT, KNOWING ⟨here the moralist . . . has overcome the artist who can be so ~ —M.D.Geismar⟩ ⟨a wise and ~ scholar who knows how to relate the past to the present —L.C.Eiseley⟩ **b :** characterized by sympathetic understanding or insight **:** SENSITIVE, PENETRATING ⟨effective music and . . . ~ staging —*Time*⟩ ⟨one of the most ~ essays by one of our poets about another —F.O.Matthiessen⟩ ⟨an eloquent and warmly ~ exploration . . . of intimate human relationships —John Nerber⟩ — **per·cep·tive·ly** \-tə̇vlē, -li\ *adv*

per·cep·tive·ness \-tivnə̇s, -tēv-\ *n* -ES **:** the quality or state of being perceptive

per·cep·tiv·i·ty \pə(r)ˌsepˈtivəd·ē, ˌpərˌs-, ˌpə̄ˌs-, ˌpəiˌs-, -vətē, -i\ *n* -ES **:** PERCEPTIVENESS

per·cep·tu·al \pə(r)ˈsepch(əw)əl, -psh-\ *adj* [L *perceptus* (past part. of *percipere* to perceive) + E *-al* — more at PERCEIVE] **:** of or relating to sensory stimulus as opposed to abstract concept ⟨the greater part of our knowledge may in fact be ~; we learn about . . . our total environment principally through the senses —C.W.Shumaker⟩; *specif* **:** of, relating to, or characterized by physical sensation as conditioned by experience ⟨personal preference is always an element of ~ response to a work of art⟩ ⟨the ~ pattern . . . selects, rejects, and distorts sense stimuli in such a way as to maintain its own integrity —J.W.Woodard⟩ — compare IDEATIONAL

per·cep·tu·al·ly \-əlē,-əli\ *adv* **:** in a perceptual manner

per·cep·tum \pə(r)ˈseptəm\ *n, pl* **percep·ta** \-tə\ [NL, fr. L, neut. of *perceptus,* past part. of *percipere*] **:** PERCEPT

Perc·es·o·ces \(ˈ)pərˌkesəˌsēz, -ˌse-\ *n pl, cap* [NL, fr. L *perca* perch + *esoces,* pl. of *esox* pike — more at PERCH, ESOX] *in some classifications* **:** a suborder of Percomorphi or sometimes a separate order including the gray mullets (Mugilidae), the barracudas, the silversides, and other related fishes — **perc·es·o·cine** \-esəˌsīn\ *adj or n*

[1]perch \ˈpərch, -ə̄-,-əi-\ *n* -ES [ME *perche,* fr. OF, fr. L *pertica* pole, staff, measuring stick; prob. akin to Gk *ptorthos* young branch, shoot, Arm *ortʻ* vine, grapevine] **1 a** *obs* **:** a wooden prop or pole **b** (1) **:** a frame of uprights with a horizontal bar for holding cloth at full width during inspection (2) **:** a textile machine with a similar frame **c :** a pole used esp. to mark a buoy, shoal, or rock ⟨the end of the channel . . . where two iron ~*es* stood —J.O.Hannay⟩ **d :** the main shaft connecting the front and rear axles of a coach or other vehicle **:** REACH **e :** a long pole used by an acrobat for climbing and balancing feats ⟨his celebrated headstand atop a swaying forty-foot ~ —R.L.Taylor⟩ **2 :** a bar or peg on which something is hung ⟨spotlights . . . hung from ~*es* in a forest of pipes above the stage —Winthrop Sargeant⟩; *specif* **:** a horizontal pole to which a skin is attached while being scraped with a moon knife in the hand softening of leather **3 a :** a roost for a bird **b :** something that resembles a roost: as (1) **:** a small usu. elevated seat for a liveryman on a coach or carriage (2) **:** a short nonretractable trapeze on an airship **c :** a resting place or vantage point **:** SEAT, STATION ⟨our favorite ~ . . . was the roof of the wheelhouse —J.W. Brown⟩ ⟨from my ~ in an attic window —Jan Valtin⟩ **d :** a secure or prominent position **:** EMINENCE ⟨his new ~ as president of one of the most important concert managements in the country —Helen Howe⟩ **e :** a pad on the axle of an automotive vehicle on which the spring is mounted — called also *spring chair* **4 a** *chiefly Brit* **:** [1]ROD 3 **b :** any of various units of measure (as 24¾ cubic feet representing a pile 1 rod long by 1 foot by 1½ feet, or 16½ cubic feet, or 25 cubic feet) for stonework

[2]perch \"\ *vb* -ED/-ING/-ES [ME *perchen,* fr. MF *percher,* fr. *perche,* n. — more at [1]PERCH] *vt* **1 :** to place on or as if on a perch, a height, or other precarious spot **:** SET, STATION ⟨~ a pullet at three months⟩ ⟨~ a hat on his head⟩ ⟨red brick buildings with carved white sandstone demons ~*ed* on their entrance gates —Faubion Bowers⟩ ⟨a cottage . . . ~*ed* on a wild sea cliff —Van Wyck Brooks⟩ ⟨islands ~*ed* on the edge of Europe —Jacquetta & Christopher Hawkes⟩ ⟨~*ed* himself on the table, his hands gripping the edges of it —Rafael Sabatini⟩ **2 :** to examine (cloth from the loom) for imperfections by placing on a perch **~** *vi* **1 :** to come to rest often uneasily or precariously on or as if on a perch **:** settle oneself **:** ALIGHT, SIT ⟨flew off to ~ on their eyries —C.G.D.Roberts⟩ ⟨the pianist ~*es* on a small suitcase to make his chair high enough —Claudia Cassidy⟩ ⟨~ happily on a hillside and watch the sea —M.P.O'Connor⟩ **2 :** to occupy a usu. precipitous location ⟨tall apartment buildings ~ on the top of rocky cliffs —*Amer. Guide Series: N.Y. City*⟩

[3]perch \"\ *n, pl* **perch** *or* **perches** [ME *perche,* fr. MF, fr. L *perca,* fr. Gk *perkē;* akin to OE *forn* trout, OHG *forhana* trout, *faro* colored, Sw *färna* whiting, L *porcus,* a spiny fish, Gk *perknos* dusky, dark, Skt *pṛśni* speckled, and perh. to Gk *prēthein* to blow up — more at FROTH] **1 a :** a rather small European freshwater spiny-finned fish (*Perca fluviatilis*) **b :** a closely related fish (*P. flavescens*) of the eastern and central U.S. inhabiting lakes and streams and well known as a sport and food fish — see YELLOW PERCH **2 a :** any of numerous marine or freshwater teleost fishes more or less resembling the European perch and mostly belonging to Percidae, Centrarchidae, Serranidae, and related families — usu. used in combination; compare BLACK PERCH, WHITE PERCH **b** *West* **:** SURF FISH

percha *n* -S [by shortening] **:** GUTTA-PERCHA

per·chance _pə(r)+\ *adv* [ME *perchaunce, parchaunce,* fr. MF *per chance, par chance,* fr. *per, par* by (fr. L *per* by, through) + *chance* — more at FOR, CHANCE] **:** PERHAPS, POSSIBLY ⟨~ he is not drowned —Shak.⟩ ⟨if ~ what they know of you is not to their liking —H.J.Johnson⟩ ⟨come to obtain vacation travel data or ~ to brush up on their geography —H.H.Baetjer⟩

perched *adj* [fr. past part. of [2]*perch*] **:** seated on or as if on a perch ⟨~ on the seat of a bright red peddler's wagon —Lucy M. Montgomery⟩

perched block *or* **perched rock** *n* **:** a perched boulder esp. when notably angular

perched boulder *n* **:** a boulder transported and deposited by a glacier in a conspicuous and relatively unstable position — compare BALANCED ROCK

perched water *or* **perched groundwater** *n* **:** groundwater occurring in a saturated zone separated from the main body of groundwater by unsaturated rock

perched water table *n* **:** the upper surface of a body of perched groundwater

perch·er \ˈpərchə(r), ˈpə̄ch-,ˈpəich-\ *n* -S [[2]*perch* + *-er*] **:** one that perches: as **a :** a bird having feet adapted for perching **b :** a textile worker who inspects cloth **c :** a tannery worker who softens hides — called also *staker*

per·che·ron \ˈpərchəˌrän, -rsh-\ *n, usu cap* [F, fr. *Perche,* region in northern France] **1 :** a breed of powerful rugged usu. dapple-gray or black draft horses originating in the Perche region of France but now much used in America and other countries **2** -S **:** a horse of the Percheron breed

perching *adj* [fr. pres. part. of [2]*perch*] **1 :** coming to rest usu. on an elevated perch (as a twig or bough) — used of a wild

bird **2 :** old enough to roost on a perch — used of poultry ⟨the small flock is often better started with ~ pullets⟩
perchlor- *or* **perchloro-** *comb form* [ISV *per-* + *chlor-*] **:** containing a relatively large amount of chlorine esp. in place of hydrogen ⟨*perchloro*ethylene⟩ ⟨*perchloro*methyl CCl_3⟩
per·chlorate \ˌpər, (ˈ)pər+\ *n* [ISV *per-* + *chlorate*] **:** a salt or ester of perchloric acid — compare AMMONIUM PERCHLORATE, LITHIUM PERCHLORATE
per·chloric acid \"+ . . . -\ *n* [*per-* + *chloric*] **:** a fuming liquid strong acid $HClO_4$ that is the highest oxygen acid of chlorine, that is a powerful oxidizing agent when heated, is corrosive, and is explosive in contact with combustible material, that is usu. made by treating a perchlorate (as sodium perchlorate) with acid, and that is used chiefly in chemical analysis, in electroplating, and as a catalyst
per·chloride \ˌpər, (ˈ)pər+\ *n* [ISV *per-* + *chloride*] **:** a chloride containing a relatively high proportion of chlorine
per·chlorinate \ˈ;pər, ˈ;pər+\ *vt* [*per-* + *chlorinate*] **:** to combine with the maximum amount of chlorine esp. in place of hydrogen
per·chlorination \ˈ;pər, ˈ;pər+\ *n* **:** the process of perchlorinating
per·chlo·ro·ethane \ˈ;pər,klōrō, ˈ;pər-+\ *n* [ISV *perchlor-* + *ethane*] **:** HEXACHLOROETHANE
per·chlo·ro·ethylene \"+\ *also* **per·chlor·ethylene** \ˈ;pər-,klōr, ˈ;pər-+\ *n* [*perchlor-* + *ethylene*] **:** TETRACHLOROETHYLENE
per·chlo·ryl \ˌpərˈklōrəl, pər-\ *n* [*perchlor-* + *-yl*] **:** the univalent ion ClO_3^+ or radical ClO_3 of perchloric acid
perch pole *n* **:** [1]PERCH 1e
per·chromate \ˈ;pər, (ˈ)pər+\ *n* [ISV *perchromic* (in *perchromic acid*) + *-ate*] **:** a salt of a perchromic acid formed by the action of hydrogen peroxide on a chromate — called also *peroxychromate*
per·chromic acid \"+. . .-\ *n* [ISV *per-* + *chromic*] **:** any of several peroxy compounds of chromium known esp. in the form of salts — called also *peroxychromic acid;* not used systematically
[1]**per·cid** \ˈpərsəd\ *adj* [NL *Percidae*] **:** of or relating to the Percidae
[2]**percid** \"\ *n* -s **:** a fish of the family Percidae
per·ci·dae \-sə,dē\ *n pl, cap* [NL, fr. *Perca*, type genus + *-idae*] **:** a family of vigorous active percoid fishes that is now usu. restricted to freshwater forms of the northern hemisphere including the true perches, pike perches, and a few related forms (as the zingel) but that formerly also included the sand darters or was sometimes made nearly coextensive with Percoidea — see PERCA
[1]**per·ci·form** \-sə,fȯrm\ *adj* [NL *Perciformes*] **1 :** resembling a perch **2 :** of or relating to the Perciformes or Percoidea
[2]**perciform** \"\ *n* -s **:** a perciform fish
per·ci·for·mes \ˌ==ˈfȯr(ˌ)mēz\ *n pl, cap* [NL, fr. L *perca* perch + NL *-iformes* — more at PERCH] *in some classifications* **:** a group of fishes nearly or exactly equivalent to Percoidea
per·ci·pi \ˈperkə,pē; ˈpərsə,pī, -ə,pē\ *n* -s [L, to be perceived, pres. pass. inf. of *percipere* to perceive — more at PERCEIVE] **:** the condition of being perceived — see ESSE EST PERCIPI
per·cip·i·ence \pə(r)ˈsipēən(t)s\ *n* -s **:** capacity to perceive **:** perceptive quality **:** PERCEPTION ⟨a mood of exaltation which combined intense ~ with intense benevolence —John Connell⟩ ⟨their informal style, ~ and urbane charm endear them to every generation —*Brit. Book News*⟩
per·cip·i·en·cy \-nsē, -nsi\ *n* -ES **:** PERCIPIENCE
[1]**per·cip·i·ent** \-nt\ *n* -s [L *percipient-, percipiens*, pres. part. of *percipere* to perceive — more at PERCEIVE] **1 :** one that perceives **2 :** a person on whose mind a telepathic impulse or message is held to fall — compare AGENT 2b
[2]**percipient** \"\ *adj* [L *percipient-, percipiens*, pres. part. of *percipere*] **:** capable of or characterized by perception **:** DISCERNING ⟨~ critic⟩ ⟨five ~, satirical and compassionate tales —Anne Fremantle⟩
perclose *var of* PARCLOSE
perc·no·some \ˈpərknə,sōm\ *n* -s [Gk *perknos* dusky, dark + E *-some* — more at PERCH] **:** a small body occurring in the androcyte of a fern
[1]**per·coid** \ˈpər,kȯid\ *or* **per·coi·de·an** \(ˌ)pərˈkȯidēən\ *adj* [*percoid* fr. NL *Percoidea; percoidean* fr. NL *Percoidea* + E *-an*] **:** of or relating to the Percoidea
[2]**percoid** \"\ *or* **percoidean** \"\ *n* -s **:** a fish of the suborder Percoidea
per·coi·dea \(ˌ)pərˈkȯidēə\ *n pl, cap* [NL, fr. *Perca* + *-oidea*] **:** a suborder of Percomorphi of uncertain limits that includes Percidae, Centrarchidae, Serranidae, Sparidae, and numerous other families and constitutes even in its least extensive application one of the largest natural groups of fishes
[1]**per·co·late** \ˈpərkə,lāt, ˈpəːk-, ˈpəik-, *chiefly in substand speech* -kyə-; *usu* -ād·+V\ *vb* -ED/-ING/-S [L *percolatus*, past part. of *percolare*, fr. *per-* through + *colare* to filter, strain, sieve — more at PER-, COLANDER] *vt* **1 a :** to cause (a liquid) to pass through a permeable substance **:** FILTER, STRAIN **b** (1) **:** to cause a liquid to pass through (as coffee) in order to extract the essence (2) **:** to prepare (coffee) by percolation **c :** to ooze or drain slowly through (a porous medium) **2 :** to be diffused through **:** PENETRATE ⟨events . . . *percolated* the censorships and reached the cables —F.L.Paxson⟩ **~** *vi* **1 :** to ooze or trickle through a permeable substance **:** SEEP ⟨rainwaters . . . ~ between the loose sands and gravels that fill the buried valley —R.E.Janssen⟩ **2 a :** to undergo percolation ⟨waited for the coffee to ~ —Willa Cather⟩ **b :** to be or become lively or effervescent **:** show animation ⟨once his voice is *percolating* to his satisfaction —Joseph Wechsberg⟩ ⟨keep college football spirit *percolating* —F.J.Taylor⟩ **3 :** to become diffused **:** spread gradually ⟨allow the sunlight to ~ into our rooms —Norman Douglas⟩ ⟨soldiers and political police had already *percolated* into Bulgaria —Sir Winston Churchill⟩
[2]**per·co·late** \"; -,lət, *usu* -əd+V\ *n* -s **:** a product of percolation ⟨no increase in nitrite in the soil ~ —*Biol. Abstracts*⟩
percolating filter *n* **:** TRICKLING FILTER
per·co·la·tion \ˌ==ˈlāshən\ *n* -s [L *percolation-, percolatio*, fr. *percolatus* + *-ion-, -io* -ion] **1 a :** the slow passage of a liquid through a filtering medium **:** LEACHING, SEEPAGE ⟨~ of water downward through the soil —Russell Lord⟩ **b :** a method of extraction or purification by means of filtration ⟨decolorization of lubricating oils by ~⟩ **c :** the process of brewing coffee by causing hot water to pass through it in a percolator **d :** the process of extracting the soluble constituents of a powdered drug by passage of a liquid through it **2 :** diffusion by gradual spreading or penetration ⟨a gradual ~ of Scandinavian motives into sculpture —O. Elfrida Saunders⟩ ⟨the ~ downward through the whole middle class of the sense of freedom —Roy Lewis & Angus Maude⟩
per·co·la·tive \ˈ==,lād·iv\ *adj* [[1]*percolate* + *-ive*] **:** of, relating to, or permitting percolation **:** POROUS
per·co·la·tor \-,lād·ə(r), -ātə-\ *n* -s [*percolate* + *-or*] **:** one that percolates: as **a :** a coffeepot in which boiling water rising through a tube is repeatedly deflected downward through a perforated basket containing ground coffee beans to extract their essence **b :** an apparatus for the extraction of a drug with a liquid solvent by downward displacement
[1]**per·co·morph** \ˈpərkə,mȯrf\ *adj* [NL *Percomorphi*] **:** of or relating to the Percomorphi
[2]**percomorph** \"\ *n* -s **:** a fish of the order Percomorphi
per·co·mor·phi \ˌ==ˈmȯr,fī\ *n pl, cap* [NL, fr. L *perca* perch + NL *-o-* + *-morphi* (fr. Gk *morphē* form) — more at PERCH, FORM] **:** the largest order of teleost fishes comprising typically small or moderate-sized more or less streamlined or fusiform fishes with the ventral fin possessing not more than one spine and five rays and the first dorsal fin always spinose, being divided into a number of suborders, and including the perches, basses, gobies, mackerels, blennies, and numerous related forms — **per·co·mor·phous** \ˌ==ˈ;=fəs\ *adj*
percomorph liver oil *n* **:** a fatty oil obtained from the fresh livers of percomorph fishes and administered to infants as a source of vitamins A and D
per·con·ta·tion \ˌpər,kän-ˈtāshən\ *n* -s [L *percontation-, percontatio*, fr. *percontatus* (past part. of *percontari* to inquire, lit., to sound with a punting pole, fr. *per* through, by means of, + *contus* pole, punting pole, fr. Gk *kontos*) + *-ion-, -io* -ion; akin to Gk *kentein* to prick — more at FOR, CENTER] *archaic* **:** an act or process of questioning **:** INQUIRY

per con·tra \(ˌ)pərˈkän-trə, per-, -kōn·(ˌ)trä, -kōn·(ˌ)trä\ *adv* [L] **1 a :** on the contrary ⟨*per contra* I don't ask you to forget but to remember —J.H.Wheelwright⟩ **b :** on the other hand **:** by way of contrast ⟨the female is generally drab . . . the male, *per contra*, brilliant —Julian Huxley⟩ **2 :** as an offset — compare [3]CONTRA 2
[1]**per·cop·sid** \(ˌ)pərˈkäpsəd\ *adj* [NL *Percopsidae*] **:** of or relating to the Percopsidae
[2]**percopsid** \"\ *n* -s **:** a fish of the family Percopsidae
per·cop·sis \-psəs\ *n, cap* [NL, fr. L *perca* perch + NL *-opsis* — more at PERCH] **:** a small genus (the type of the family Percopsidae) of trout-perches much resembling young walleyed pikes and in many respects intermediate between typical isospondyls and the percoids — compare PIRATE PERCH
per cu·ri·am \per ˈkūrē,äm\ *adv (or adj)* [ML, lit., by the court] **:** summarily or immediately and usu. by unanimous action of the court
per curiam decision *or* **per curiam opinion** *n* **:** a very brief usu. unanimous opinion or decision of a court rendered without elaborate discussion of the principles or reasons therefor — compare MEMORANDUM DECISION
per·current \ˈ;pər, (ˈ)pər+\ *adj* [L *percurrent-, percurrens*, pres. part. of *percurrere* to run through, fr. *per-* through + *currere* to run, hasten — more at PER-, CURRENT] **:** extending from the base to the apex — used of the midrib of a leaf
per·cuss \pə(r)ˈkəs\ *vb* -ED/-ING/-ES [L *percussus*, past part. of *percutere*] *vt* **:** to strike on or against **:** RAP; *esp* **:** to tap (a body part) repeatedly to elicit evidence (as sounds) of use in medical diagnosis ⟨a healthy tooth ~*ed* with a metal instrument . . . gives a metallic sound —K.H.Thoma⟩ **~** *vi* **:** TAP; *esp* **:** to percuss a body part ⟨~*ing* with the ends of our fingers over the lungs —Robert Chawner⟩
[1]**per·cus·sion** \pə(r)ˈkəshən\ *n* -s [L *percussion-, percussio*, fr. *percussus* (past part. of *percutere* to beat, strike, fr. *per-*, intensifying prefix + *-cutere*, fr. *quatere* to shake, strike, beat) + *-ion-, -io* -ion — more at PER, QUASH] **1 :** a forcible impact **:** BLOW, STROKE: as **a :** an act or process of striking together ⟨use flint and steel in making fire by ~⟩ **b** (1) **:** the beating or striking of a musical instrument ⟨a drum is played by ~⟩ (2) **:** the sounding of a dissonant tone or chord — compare RESOLUTION 1d **c :** the setting off of an explosive charge by forcible contact; *specif* **:** the striking of a gun hammer on fulminating powder **d** (1) **:** the act of tapping or striking the surface of a body part (as chest or abdomen) to learn the condition of the parts beneath by the resultant sound — compare AUSCULTATION (2) **:** massage consisting of the striking of a body part with light rapid blows **:** TAPOTEMENT **2 :** a sharp auditory impact **:** vibratory shock ⟨a long, quasi-narrative poem . . . which has ~, if not much distinction as poetry —*New Yorker*⟩ **3 :** the edge of the palm below the fourth finger — used chiefly by palmists **4 a :** the section of a band or orchestra consisting of percussion instruments ⟨enough strings to balance the brass and ~ —Virgil Thomson⟩ **b :** percussion instruments ⟨big orchestras, with their brasses, woodwinds, and ~ —Joseph Wechsberg⟩ **syn** see IMPACT
[2]**percussion** \"\ *adj* **1 a :** of, relating to, or produced by percussion ⟨classification of the ~ note into resonant, dull, and tympanitic —*Medical Physics*⟩ **b :** actuated or operating by percussion ⟨~ rifle⟩; *specif* **:** PNEUMATIC ⟨a ~ drill for drilling holes in rock⟩ **2 :** of or relating to percussion instruments ⟨members of the ~ choir are the tympani, the bass drum, the snare drum, the cymbals —Henry Melnik⟩
per·cus·sion·al \-shənᵊl, -shnəl\ *adj* **:** PERCUSSION
percussion cap *n* **:** [1]CAP 8a
percussion drilling *n* **:** ROPE DRILLING
percussion figure *n* **:** the figure formed by cracks started in a cleavage plate of a crystal by a blow from a dull-pointed instrument
percussion flaking *n* **:** the shaping of a stone implement by striking or chipping off flakes with another stone or a piece of wood, bone, or antler — compare PRESSURE FLAKING
percussion fuse *n* **:** [1]FUSE 2
percussion instrument *n* **:** a musical instrument (as a piano) on which the tone is produced by striking; *specif* **:** an instrument (as kettledrum, bass drum, triangle, bells) belonging to the choir of band and orchestral percussion instruments as distinguished from the string or wind choirs and having both definite and indefinite pitch
per·cus·sion·ist \-sh(ə)nəst\ *n* -s **:** one skilled in the playing of percussion instruments
percussion lock *n* **:** the lock of a gun fired by percussion — compare FLINTLOCK
percussion mark *n* **:** a crescentic scar on a pebble (as of chert or quartzite) caused by impact
percussion stop *n* **1 :** a draw-knob in the reed organ by which a mechanism is made to strike a reed as it is sounded to give promptness and force to its tone **2 :** a pipe-organ stop (as the xylophone) whose tone is produced by striking
percussion table *n* **:** an inclined table suspended on springs and used as an apparatus for sorting particles of ore according to specific gravity by running the ore in a thin sheet of water over the table and jarring it to effect separation
percussion wave *n* **:** a shock wave esp. from a blow or an explosion
per·cus·sive \-ˈkəsiv, -sēv *also* -səv\ *adj* [*percussion* + *-ive*] **1 a** (1) **:** characterized by percussion or featuring percussion instruments ⟨the occurrence . . . of inexplicable noises, usually ~ — thuds, taps, drumbeats, raps —A.G.N.Flew⟩ ⟨~, furious, this wind sweeps down the mountain —Barbara Howes⟩ ⟨~ rhythms⟩ (2) *dancing* **:** staccato and vigorous with suddenly checked impulse ⟨a solemn minuet . . . interrupted by tropical drumbeats and ~ primitive movement —*Dance Observer*⟩ **b :** having powerful impact **:** STRIKING, SHOCKING ⟨the stark dramatic power of the scenes is ~ and stabbing —William Goyen⟩ **2 :** PERCUSSION ⟨~ drill⟩ — **per·cus·sive·ly** \-səvlē, -li\ *adv*
per·cus·sive·ness \-sivnəs, -sēv- *also* -səv-\ *n* -ES **:** the quality or state of being percussive ⟨to his harpsichord style he carries over a pianistic ~ —*Saturday Rev.*⟩
percussive welding *or* **percussion welding** *n* **:** resistance welding in which a hammer blow is applied simultaneously with or immediately following a sudden discharge of current across the contact area of the parts to be united
per·cus·sor \-sə(r)\ *n* -s [NL, fr. L, one that strikes or beats, fr. *percussus* (past part. of *percutere* to strike, beat) + *-or* — more at PERCUSSION] **:** PLEXOR
per·cutaneous \ˈ;pər, ˈ;pər+\ *adj* [*per-* + *cutaneous*] **:** effected or performed through the skin ⟨~ absorption⟩ — **per·cutaneously** \"+\ *adv*
per·cy·lite \ˈpərsē,līt, -sə,l-\ *n* -s [John *Percy* †1889 Eng. metallurgist + E *-lite*] **:** a mineral $PbCuCl_2(OH)_2$(?) consisting of a rare basic chloride of lead and copper
per·den·do \pə(r)ˈden(ˌ)dō\ *adj (or adv)* [It (verbal of *perdere* to lose), fr. L *perdendum*, gerund of *perdere* to destroy, lose — more at PERDITION] **:** PERDENDOSI
per·den·do·si \-ˌdō,sē\ *adj (or adv)* [It, lit., losing itself] **:** dying away — used as a direction in music
per·di·cine \ˈpərdə,sīn\ *adj* [NL *Perdic-, Perdix* + E *-ine*] **:** of or relating to the genus *Perdix*
perdie *var of* PARDIE
[1]**per di·em** \ˌpə(r)ˈdēəm, ˌpərˈ-, pə̄ˈ- *also* -dīəm\ *adv* [L] **:** by the day **:** for each day ⟨computed the total of man-hours saved *per diem* —C.D.Lewis⟩
[2]**per diem** \"; ˈ=,==\ *adj* **1 :** based on use or service by the day **:** DAILY ⟨*per diem* allowance⟩ ⟨a large firm can establish hourly or *per diem* rates for various levels of performance —R.E. Witschey⟩ ⟨the fee is charged on a *per diem* basis —Jules Backman⟩ ⟨when *per diem* costs are high, fast turnarounds become increasingly important —Daniel Marx⟩ **2 :** paid by the day ⟨a *per diem* assignment⟩ ⟨Hawaii uses a *per diem* referee —*Comparison of State Unemployment Insurance Laws*⟩
[3]**per diem** \(ˌ)ˈ==\ *n, pl* **per diems 1 :** a daily allowance ⟨given a fixed *per diem* for each day he was away from . . . his home base —Linda Braidwood⟩ — compare CAR MILEAGE 2 **2 :** a daily fee ⟨a detective works day and night for a measly *per diem* —Erle Stanley Gardner⟩ **3 :** the daily rental paid by one railroad for the use of cars of another
per·di·tion \pə(r)ˈdishən, ˌpərˈ-, pəˈ-, pəiˈ-\ *n* -s [ME *perdicioun*, fr. LL *perdition-, perditio*, fr. L *perditus* (past part. of *perdere*) to destroy, squander, lose, fr. *per-* destructively, detrimentally + *-dere*, fr. *dare* to give) + *-ion-, -io* -ion — more at PER-, DATE] **1 a** *archaic* **:** utter destruction **:** complete ruin ⟨certain tidings . . . importing the mere ~ of the Turkish fleet —Shak.⟩ **b** *obs* **:** LOSS, DIMINUTION ⟨not so much ~ as an hair betid to any creature in the vessel —Shak.⟩ **c** *obs* **:** something that causes loss or destruction ⟨revelings, carnivals and balls which are the ~ of precious hours —Jeremy Taylor⟩ **2 a :** utter loss of the soul or of final happiness in a future state **:** eternal damnation ⟨reserved unto fire against the day of judgment and ~ of ungodly men —2 Pet 3: 7 (AV)⟩ **b :** the place of eternal damnation **:** HELL ⟨send a soul straight to ~, dying frank an atheist —Robert Browning⟩
per·dix \ˈpərdiks\ *n, cap* [NL, fr. L, partridge — more at PARTRIDGE] **:** a once extensive genus of birds (family Phasianidae) now limited to the European partridge and near related forms
per·dominant \ˈ;pər, (ˈ)pər+\ *n* [*per-* + *dominant*] **:** a plant widely distributed in a climax and usu. a dominant in at least some of the constituent associations
[1]**per·du** *or* **per·due** \(ˌ)pərˈd(y)ü, per-\ *adj* [MF *perdu* (masc.) & *perdue* (fem.), fr. past part. of *perdre* to lose, fr. L *perdere* to destroy, lose — more at PERDITION] **1 a** *obs* (1) **:** keeping covert watch in a hazardous military outpost or ambush ⟨so many . . . desire to enter upon breaches, lie sentinel ~, give the first onset —Robert Burton⟩ (2) **:** being in a desperate plight **b :** remaining out of sight **:** CONCEALED ⟨seek shelter in a cavern, stay there ~ for three days —Thomas Carlyle⟩ **2 :** withdrawn from the public eye **:** OBSCURED, UNNOTICED ⟨the evidence has been lying ~ . . . in the preface —I.A.Shapiro⟩ ⟨suffered from . . . lack of appreciation, remaining ~ in Italy —*Publ's Mod. Lang. Assoc. of Amer.*⟩
[2]**perdu** *or* **perdue** \"\ *n* -s **1** *obs* **a :** a soldier assigned to extremely hazardous duty **b :** FORLORN HOPE 1 **2** *obs* **:** one that guards or reconnoiters **:** WATCH, SPY
per·du·el·lion \ˌpərd(y)üˈelyən\ *n* -s [L *perduellion-, perduellio*, fr. *perduellis* enemy, fr. *per* by + OL *duellum* war — more at DUEL] *Roman law* **:** TREASON, SUBVERSION
per·durability \(ˌ)pər+, *archaic* ˌpərjərəˈbiləd·ē\ *n* **:** the quality or state of being perdurable **:** PERSISTENCE, PERMANENCE
per·durable \(ˌ)pər+, *archaic* ˈpərjərəbəl\ *adj* [ME, fr. OF *perdurable, pardurable*, fr. LL *perdurabilis*, fr. L *perdurare* to endure, last long + *-abilis* -able — more at PERDURE] **1 :** very durable **:** lasting a very long time or indefinitely ⟨the ~ granite of the ancient Appalachian spine of the eastern continent —Marjory S. Douglas⟩ ⟨our literature is going to be our most ~ claim on man's remembrance —A.T.Quiller-Couch⟩ **2 :** ETERNAL — **per·du·ra·bly** \-blē\ *adv*
per·durableness \(ˌ)pər+, *archaic* ˈpərjərəbəlnəs\ *n* -ES *archaic* **:** PERDURABILITY
per·dur·ance \(ˌ)pərˈd(y)ürən(t)s\ *n* -s [*perdure* + *-ance*] **:** PERMANENCE, PERSISTENCE
per·dur·ant \-nt\ *adj* [L *perdurant-, perdurans*, pres. part. of *perdurare* to endure, last — more at PERDURE] **:** PERDURABLE
per·duration \ˌpər+\ *n* [LL *perduration-, perduratio*, fr. L *perduratus* (past part. of *perdurare*) + *-ion-, -io* -ion] *archaic* **:** PERDURANCE
per·dure \(ˌ)pərˈd(y)ü(ə)r\ *vi* -ED/-ING/-S [ME *perduren*, fr. L *perdurare*, fr. *per-*, intensifying prefix + *durare* to endure, last — more at PER-, DURE] **:** to continue to exist **:** LAST
perduring *adj* [fr. pres. part. of *perdure*] **:** long lasting **:** PERSISTENT — **per·dur·ing·ly** *adv*
perea *var of* APEREA
père da·vid's deer \ˌperdäˈvēdz-, (ˈ)perˈdävədz-\ *n, usu cap P & 1st D* [after *Père* Armand *David* †1900 French Catholic missionary and naturalist] **:** a large grayish deer (*Elaphurus davidianus*) having long slender antlers and prob. originating in northern China but known only from domesticated herds
per·e·gri·na \ˌperəˈgrēnə\ *n* -s [AmerSp, fr. Sp, woman pilgrim, fr. ML, fem. of *peregrinus* male pilgrim — more at PILGRIM] **:** a Cuban shrub (*Adenoropium hastatum*) of the family Euphorbiaceae having showy cymes of scarlet or rose-colored flowers
[1]**per·e·gri·nate** \ˈperəgrə,nāt, *usu* -ād·+V\ *vb* -ED/-ING/-S [L *peregrinatus*, past part. of *peregrinari* to travel in foreign lands, fr. *peregrinus* foreigner — more at PILGRIM] *vi* **:** to travel on foot **:** WALK, TOUR ⟨a land bridge . . . which enabled prehistoric man to ~ from North Africa —Hendrik de Leeuw⟩ **~** *vt* **:** to walk over **:** TRAVERSE ⟨*peregrinated* the country for seasonal jobs —John Buchan⟩
[2]**peregrinate** \"\ *adj* [L *peregrinatus*, past part of *peregrinari*] **:** having the air of one who has traveled or lived abroad **:** FOREIGN ⟨too affected, too odd, as it were, too ~ —Shak.⟩
per·e·gri·na·tion \ˌ===ˈnāshən\ *n* -s [MF or L; MF, fr. L *peregrination-, peregrinatio*, fr. *peregrinatus* (past. part. of *peregrinari*) + *-ion-, -io* -ion] **1 a :** an act of traveling or traversing ⟨stopped a moment in his ~ of the room —J.C.Snaith⟩; *esp* **:** foreign travel **b :** an excursion esp. on foot or to a foreign country **:** JOURNEY, TRAVEL — usu. used in pl. ⟨his anthropological ~*s* took him into the hylean Amazon⟩ ⟨desire to promote national sentiment through the ~*s* of the Supreme Court justices maintained the circuit riding system —Felix Frankfurter⟩ ⟨built great boats for his posthumous ~*s* —J.D. Hillaby⟩ **c** *obs* (1) **:** a stay in a foreign country **:** SOJOURN, EXILE (2) **:** the period of man's life on earth ⟨pray that God would pour down upon us graces for our ~ here —John Donne⟩ **2 :** a widely ranging discourse or treatment ⟨an unevenly rambling intellectual ~ —Jacob Hammer⟩
per·e·gri·na·tor \ˈ===,nād·ə(r)\ *n* -s [L, fr. *peregrinatus* + *-or*] *archaic* **:** TRAVELER, WANDERER
[1]**per·e·grine** \ˈ==grən, -,grēn, -,grīn\ *adj* [in sense 1, fr. L *peregrinus;* in other senses, fr. ML *peregrinus*, fr. L — more at PILGRIM] **1** *archaic* **:** of or from a foreign country **:** ALIEN, IMPORTED **2** *archaic* **:** engaged in or traveling on a pilgrimage ⟨~ Christians going to visit the Holy Sepulchre —Matthew Carter⟩ **3 a :** having a tendency to wander **:** ROVING ⟨believes the profession of ~ typist has a happy future —*Saturday Rev.*⟩ **b** *also* **per·e·grin·ic** \ˈ;perəˈ;grinik\ [*peregrinic* fr. ML *peregrinus* + E *-ic*] **:** widely distributed **:** found in many parts of the world ⟨*Allolobophora* is a markedly ~ genus of earthworms⟩
[2]**peregrine** \"\ *n* -s [in sense 1, fr. ML *peregrinus*, fr. L, stranger; in sense 2, fr. L *peregrinus;* in sense 3, fr. (*falcon*) *peregrine* — more at PILGRIM] **1** *obs* **:** TRAVELER, PILGRIM **2 :** a sojourner in a foreign country; *specif* **:** an alien resident of ancient Rome **3 :** PEREGRINE FALCON
peregrine falcon *n* [ME *faucon peregrin*, trans. of ML *falco peregrinus*] **:** a swift falcon (*Falco peregrinus*) much used in falconry that is of almost cosmopolitan distribution and has adult plumage which is dark bluish ash on the back, nearly black on the head and cheeks, white beneath, and barred with black below the throat — compare DUCK HAWK 1, PEALE'S FALCON
per·e·grin·ism \-,grə,nizəm, -,grēn-\ *n* -s **:** tendency to wander
per·e·grin·i·ty \ˌ==ˈgrinəd·ē\ *n* -ES [MF or L; MF *peregrinité*, fr. L *peregrinitat-, peregrinitas*, fr. *peregrinus* foreign + *-itat-, -itas* -ity — more at PILGRIM] **:** the quality or state of being peregrine
pe·rei·on \pəˈrī,än, -rəl, -rēl\ *or* **pe·re·on** \-rē,län\ *also* **pe·rae·on** \-rē\ *n, pl* **pe·reia** \|ə\ [NL, fr. Gk *peraiōn*, pres. part. of *peraioun* to transport, carry over, fr. *peraios* situated beyond, fr. *pera* beyond; fr. the walking appendages; akin to Skt *para* further, ulterior, Gk *peran* to pass through — more at FARE] **:** the thorax or the 7 metameres constituting the thorax of some crustaceans (as a decapod or a copepod)
pe·reio·pod \-īə,päd, -ēə-, -ēə-\ *or* **pe·reo·pod** \-ēə,päd\ *n* -s [NL *pereion* + E *-pod*] **:** an appendage of the pereion **:** THORACIC LIMB
pe·rei·ra bark \pəˈrerə-, -ˈrārə-\ *or* **pereira** *n* -s [after Jonathan *Pereira* †1853 Eng. pharmacologist.] **1 :** a Brazilian tree (*Geissospermum vellosii*) of the family Apocynaceae **2 :** the bark of the pereira tree used in Brazil as a tonic and febrifuge
perempt *vt* [L *peremptus*, past part. of *perimere* — more at PEREMPTORY] *obs* **:** QUASH
pe·remp·tion \pəˈrem(p)shən\ *n* -s [LL *peremption-, peremptio*, fr. L *peremptus* + *-ion-, -io* -ion] **:** the act or process of quashing
pe·remp·tive \-m(p)tiv\ *adj* **:** of, relating to, or marked by peremption
pe·remp·to·ri·ly \pəˈrem(p)t(ə)rəlē, -li *sometimes* pəˌrem(p)ˈtōr- *or* ˈ;perəm(p)ˈ;tōr- *or* -tȯr-\ *adv* **:** in a peremptory manner **:** HAUGHTILY, IMPERATIVELY

pe·remp·to·ri·ness *pronunc at* ¹PEREMPTORY +nəs\ *n* -ES **:** the quality or state of being peremptory

¹**pe·remp·to·ry** \pə'rem(p)t(ə)rē, -)ri *sometimes* 'perəm(p)-,tōr- *or* 'perəm(p),tȯr-; *substand* prē'em-\ *adj* [LL & L; LL *peremptorius* final, decisive, fr. L, destructive, fr. *peremptus* (past part. of *perimere* to take away entirely, destroy, kill, fr. *per-* detrimentally, destructively + -*imere*, fr. *emere* to buy, obtain, acquire) + -*orius* -ory — more at PER-, REDEEM] **1 a :** putting an end to or precluding a right of action, debate, or delay **b** *obs* **:** admitting no contradiction **:** ABSOLUTE, FINAL ⟨a mathematician's conclusions ought to be ~ and grounded in . . . infallible evidence —Edward Reynolds⟩ **2 a :** expressive of urgency or command **:** IMPERATIVE ⟨knew only a few words of practical, ~ Greek —Glenway Wescott⟩ ⟨the brassy, ~ shout of the ship's siren —R.B.Robertson⟩ **b** *archaic* **:** of an indispensable nature **:** ESSENTIAL ⟨find this law of one to one ~ for conversation —R.W.Emerson⟩ **3 a** (1) **:** marked by self-assurance **:** CONFIDENT, POSITIVE ⟨is a man of conviction . . . and requires no excessive prodding to let fly a ~ speech —*New Yorker*⟩ (2) **:** DOGMATIC ⟨has clear and ~ ideas about right and wrong —W.C.Brownell⟩ **b** (1) **:** marked by determination **:** DECISIVE, RESOLUTE ⟨the ~ use of force, if needed —*Time*⟩ (2) **:** OBSTINATE ⟨~ lack of interest in commercial affairs —Brooks Atkinson⟩ **4 :** of an arrogant or imperious nature **:** HAUGHTY, DICTATORIAL ⟨ordered around in the most ~ terms —Frank Oliver⟩ ⟨asserting their ~ claim to a grander knowledge —J.D.Adams⟩ **syn** see MASTERFUL

²**peremptory** \"\ *adv, archaic* **:** PEREMPTORILY

³**peremptory** \"\ *n* -ES *obs* **:** a case, circumstance, document, or command that cannot be ignored ⟨two or three afternoons he allotted every week to hear *peremptories* —John Hacket⟩ ⟨went up with my father's ~ . . . to my sister —Samuel Richardson⟩

peremptory challenge *n* **:** a challenge (as of a juror) made as of right without assigning any cause

peremptory exception *or* **peremptory plea** *n* **:** a legal exception or plea attacking the cause of action or defense on its merits

peremptory instruction *n* **:** an instruction charging a jury that if they agree to the truth of certain stated facts they must find for a designated party

peremptory mandamus *n* **:** a final and absolute mandamus to enforce the court's judgment

peren·nate \'perə,nāt, pə're,n-\ *vi* -ED/-ING/-S [L *perennatus*, past part. of *perennare*, fr. *perennis* perennial] **:** to live over from season to season **:** be perennial **:** PERSIST ⟨a *perennating* rhizome from which flowering shoots arise annually —Clarence Sterling⟩ — **peren·na·tion** \,perə'nāshən, ,pe,re'n-, pə,re'n-\ *n* -S

¹**pe·ren·nial** \pə'renēəl, -nyəl\ *adj* [L *perennis* perennial (fr. *per-* throughout + -*ennis*, fr. *annus* year) + E -*al* — more at PER-, ANNUAL] **1 a** *obs* **:** EVERGREEN ⟨where round the scene ~ laurels bloom —William Falconer⟩ **b :** present at all seasons of the year ⟨~ stream⟩ ⟨the ~ snow fields are of such great depth that glacial ice forms —W.W.Atwood †1949⟩ **2 a :** continuing or lasting for several years — used specif. of a plant (as delphinium) that dies back seasonally and produces new growth from a perennating part; compare ANNUAL, BIENNIAL **b :** existing for more than one season ⟨~ insect⟩ ⟨~ colony of bees⟩ **3 a :** lasting indefinitely **:** impervious to change **:** PERMANENT, ENDURING ⟨the ~, elemental processes of nature —J.L.Lowes⟩ ⟨the family and the church have proved ~ in the experience of man —*Political Science Quarterly*⟩ ⟨the ~ value of this comparative study —*Digest of Neurology & Psychiatry*⟩ **b :** continuing without interruption **:** invariably present **:** CONSTANT, PERPETUAL ⟨a ~ twinkle in his eye —F.W.Crofts⟩ ⟨the ~ conflict among the services over the question of defense organization —*Atlantic*⟩ ⟨a ~ problem of the land, erosion —Leslie Rees⟩ ⟨the ~ quest for certainty —D.A.Wells⟩ **:** unfailingly popular ⟨as ~ as *Uncle Tom's Cabin* —*New Republic*⟩ **c :** regularly repeated **:** RECURRENT ⟨has begun to locate the ~ problems of man in the ordinary affairs of the men of his own time —Vincent Buckley⟩ ⟨~ efforts . . . to stipulate the requirements demanded of their discipline —R.C.Hinkle⟩ **syn** see CONTINUAL

²**perennial** \"\ *n* -S **1 :** a plant (as a tree or shrub, or an herb renewing the top growth seasonally) that lives for an indefinite number of years — compare ANNUAL, BIENNIAL **2 a :** a permanent fixture or continuing question ⟨hardy ~ among independent producers —Budd Schulberg⟩ ⟨that vexatious ~ of Southern politics, the status of the Negro —W.G.Carleton⟩; *specif* **:** a stock item ⟨a hardy ~ in the book trade —A.L. Guérard⟩ **b :** a recurrent topic or item ⟨certain to become fiery ~*s* on the assembly agenda —W.R.Frye⟩ ⟨infantile paralysis, that hardy summer ~ on magazine covers —Edith M. Stern⟩

perennial canker *n* **:** a canker that lives over from one season to the next; *specif* **:** a serious disease of apples caused by a fungus (*Gloeosporium perennans*) and characterized by cankers on the trunk and limbs

perennial european sow thistle *n, usu cap E* **:** a perennial sow thistle (*Sonchus arvensis*) that is native to Europe but widely naturalized as a weed, spreads by creeping underground rhizomes, and has clasping spiny leaves and heads of yellow flowers on long peduncles — called also *field sow thistle*

pe·ren·nial·ly \-əlē, -əli\ *adv* **:** in a perennial manner **:** REPEATEDLY, PERPETUALLY

perennial pea *n* **:** EVERLASTING PEA

perennial peppercress *n* **:** a European peppergrass (*Lepidium latifolium*) introduced into No. America and esp. troublesome as a weed in the southwestern U.S. having extensive rhizomes and leaves distinctly tapered to the base

perennial peppergrass *n* **:** HOARY CRESS

perennial philosophy *n* **:** the philosophical tradition of the world's great thinkers from Plato, Aristotle, and Aquinas to their modern successors dealing with problems of ultimate reality (as the nature of being) and sometimes emphasizing mysticism — opposed to *skepticism;* compare RATIONALISM

perennial phlox *n* **:** any of various garden phlox derived chiefly from a No. American species (*Phlox paniculata*) and having erect stems 2 to 4 feet high, leaves 3 to 5 inches long and all opposite, and flowers that are distinctly stalked — compare ANNUAL PHLOX

perennial ragweed *n* **:** WESTERN RAGWEED

perennial ryegrass *n* **:** a European perennial grass (*Lolium perenne*) with erect culms and spikelets borne in a zigzag spike that is widely cultivated for pasture and hay and as a lawn grass — called also *English ryegrass;* compare ITALIAN RYEGRASS

perennial teeth *n pl* **:** teeth (as those of rodents) that grow continuously at the root as they are worn away at the crown

pe·ren·ni·branch \pə'renə,braŋk\ *n or adj* [NL *Perennibranchia* (syn. of *Perennibranchiata*), fr. L *perennis* perennial + NL -*branchia* — more at PERENNIAL] **:** PERENNIBRANCHIATE

pe·ren·ni·bran·chi·a·ta \⸗,⸗⸗,braŋkē'ād-ə, -'ād-ə\ *n pl, cap* [NL, fr. L *perennis* perennial + NL *branchi-* + -*ata*] *in former classifications* **:** a division of Caudata comprising amphibians (as salamanders of the genus *Necturus*) that retain their gills through life — compare CADUCIBRANCHIATA

¹**pe·ren·ni·bran·chi·ate** \⸗¦⸗⸗¦⸗kēət\ *adj* [NL *Perennibranchiata*] **:** having permanent gills **:** of or relating to the Perennibranchiata

²**perennibranchiate** \"\ *n* -S **:** an amphibian of the division Perennibranchiata

pe·ren·ni·chor·da·ta \⸗,⸗⸗,kȯ(r)'dād-ə, -'dād-ə\ [NL, fr. L *perennis* + NL *chord-* + -*ata*] *syn of* LARVACEA

pe·res·kia \pə'reskēə\ [NL, irreg. fr. N.C. de Fabre de *Peiresc* †1637 French scientist and author + NL -*ia*] *syn of* PEIRESKIA

pere·zone \'perə,zōn\ *n* [L *peresus* (past part. of *peredere* to eat up, consume, waste away, fr. *per-*, prefix denoting completion + *edere* to eat) + E *zone* — more at EAT] **:** the zone of deposition along low coastal lands lying chiefly between low tide and land undergoing active erosion and including lagoons and brackish-water bays with the accumulated sediments being usu. nonfossiliferous but sometimes containing terrestrial or brackish water forms

perf *abbr* **1** perfect **2** perforate; perforated; perforation **3** performance; performed; performer

¹**per·fect** \'pərfikt, 'pə̄f-,'pəif-, -fēkt\ *adj, sometimes* -ER/-EST [alter. (influenced by L *perfectus*) of ME *perfit*, *parfit*, fr. OFr *parfit*, fr. L *perfectus* perfect, fr. past part. of *perficere* to carry out, complete, perfect, fr. *per-*, prefix denoting completion or perfection + -*ficere* (fr. *facere* to do, make) — more at PER-, DO] **1 :** accomplished in knowledge or performance **:** EXPERT, PROFICIENT ⟨men more ~ in the use of arms —Shak.⟩ — used chiefly in the phrase *practice makes perfect* **2 a :** entirely without fault or defect **:** meeting supreme standards of excellence **:** FLAWLESS ⟨a ~ technique⟩ ⟨a ~ gem⟩ ⟨a ~ crime⟩ ⟨must be ~ as your heavenly Father is perfect —Mt 5:48 (RSV)⟩ ⟨a starched shirtfront . . . if it is not ~ is nothing —Robert Lynd⟩ **b :** satisfying all requirements: as (1) **:** having precision of form or identity of relationship **:** ACCURATE, EXACT ⟨~ circle⟩ ⟨only the stronger and more ~ parts of his music reach me —John Burroughs⟩ ⟨its cleavage is in ~ parallel with the base —*Encyc. Americana*⟩ (2) **:** corresponding to an archetype **:** having all the proper characteristics **:** IDEAL ⟨a ~ gentleman⟩ ⟨the ~ Christmas gift⟩ ⟨~ money should be . . . endowed with unchanging purchasing power —Ludwig Von Mises⟩ ⟨we, the people of the United States, in order to form a more ~ union —*U.S. Constitution*⟩ (3) **:** conforming in every particular to an abstract concept ⟨a gas thermometer containing a ~ gas . . . would give readings directly on Kelvin's thermodynamic scale of temperature —L.C.Jackson⟩ (4) **:** faithfully reproducing the original ⟨a ~ likeness⟩ ⟨record engineers . . . finally succeeded in giving us music that was acoustically ~ —E.T.Canby⟩; *specif* **:** LETTER-PERFECT (5) **:** free from any valid legal objection **:** valid and effective in law ⟨a ~ title⟩ **3 a :** free from admixture or limitation **:** PURE, TOTAL ⟨the dim trees below me were in ~ stillness —John Galsworthy⟩ **b :** lacking in no essential detail **:** fully developed **:** COMPLETE, WHOLE ⟨have a ~ baby⟩ ⟨the memory of that night remained intact and ~ —Elinor Wylie⟩ ⟨complete justification of belief does not depend on . . . ~ knowledge —W.F.Hambly⟩ **c** *obs* **:** possessing all one's mental faculties **:** SANE ⟨I fear I am not in my ~ mind —Shak.⟩ **d :** being without qualification **:** ABSOLUTE, UNEQUIVOCAL ⟨God possesses ~ power —Charles Hartshorne⟩ ⟨has a ~ right to use this division —James Jeans⟩ ⟨treats him like a ~ stranger⟩ ⟨looks like a ~ angel in her organdy pinafore⟩ **e :** of an extreme kind **:** UNMITIGATED ⟨a ~ little snob —Eugene Walter⟩ ⟨a ~ tirade of abuse —S.H.Holbrook⟩ ⟨the dog had been in a ~ frenzy, trying to get out —Erle Stanley Gardner⟩ **4** *obs* **:** fully grown or legally competent **:** MATURE ⟨sons at ~ age —Shak.⟩ **5** [LL *perfectus*, fr. L] **:** of, relating to, or constituting a form of the verb or verbal that expresses an action or state completed at the time of speaking or at a time spoken of — compare FUTURE PERFECT, PAST PERFECT, PRESENT PERFECT **6** *obs* **a :** CERTAIN, SURE ⟨thou art ~ then, our ship hath touched upon . . . Bohemia —Shak.⟩ **b :** SATISFIED, CONTENT ⟨then comes my fit again: I had else been ~ —Shak.⟩ **7 a** *of an interval* **:** belonging to the consonances (as unison, fourth, fifth, and octave) that retain their character when inverted and when raised or lowered by a half step become augmented or diminished — compare MAJOR **b** (1) **:** of or relating to a note (as a large) in mensural notation equaling three rather than two of the next lower denomination (as a long) (2) *of a rhythmic mode* **:** being in triple time **8 a :** having its distinctive characters fully developed **:** TYPICAL ⟨a ~ lesion⟩ ⟨a ~ jellyfish⟩ **b :** sexually mature and fully differentiated — used esp. of an insect in the imago stage ⟨the click beetle (the ~ stage of the wireworm) —*Farming*⟩ **c :** MONOCLINOUS

²**per·fect** \pə(r)'fekt *sometimes* 'pərfikt *or* 'pə̄f- *or* 'pəif-\ *vt* -ED/-ING/-S [alter. (influenced by L *perfectus*) of ME *perfiten*, *parfiten*, fr. *perfit*, *parfit*, adj.] **1 :** to bring to a state of supreme excellence **:** rid of faults or drawbacks **:** IMPROVE, REFINE ⟨art must be selective; nature must be ~*ed* —G.C. Sellery⟩ ⟨rhetoric . . . seeks to ~ men by showing them better versions of themselves —R.M.Weaver⟩ ⟨laboratory methods for examining foods had been still further ~*ed* —V.G. Heiser⟩ **2 a :** to plan or carry out to the last detail **:** bring to a successful conclusion **:** FINISH ⟨arrangements we're ~*ing* to keep newspaper reporters from bothering you —Erle Stanley Gardner⟩ ⟨youthful learners who desired to . . . ~ their education —H.O.Taylor⟩ **b :** to complete or put in final form in conformity with law ⟨to defeat the federal priority a lien . . . must be both specific and ~*ed* —*Harvard Law Rev.*⟩ **c :** to print the second side of (a sheet already printed on one side) **:** back up **3 :** to instruct or inform fully ⟨the object of this society is . . . to ~ its members practically and scientifically —G.B.Cummings⟩ **syn** see UNFOLD

³**perfect** *like* ¹PERFECT\ *adv* [alter. (influenced by L *perfectus*) of ME *perfit*, *parfit*, fr. *perfit*, *parfit*, adj.] *chiefly dial* **:** PERFECTLY

⁴**perfect** *like* ¹PERFECT\ *n* -S [¹*perfect*] **1 :** one that is perfect ⟨the ~*s* go into one bag and the rejects into another —*Listener*⟩ **2 a :** the perfect tense of a language **b :** a verb form in the perfect tense

per·fect·abil·i·ty *like* PERFECTIBILITY\ *n* [by alter.] **:** PERFECTIBILITY

per·fect·able *like* PERFECTIBLE\ *adj* [by alter.] **:** PERFECTIBLE

perfect binder *n* **:** a machine for producing perfect-bound books and pamphlets

perfect binding *n* **:** a bookbinding in which single leaves are held together with a backbone adhesive

perfect-bound \¦⸗⸗¦⸗\ *adj* **:** produced by perfect binding ⟨*perfect-bound* books⟩

perfect cadence *n* **:** a cadence consisting of a dominant to tonic harmony with the root of the tonic appearing in both the bass and the soprano — called also *full cadence;* compare IMPERFECT CADENCE; see CADENCE illustration

perfect cocktail *n* **:** a cocktail consisting of equal parts of French vermouth, Italian vermouth, and gin shaken with ice and strained before serving

perfect competition *n* **:** COMPETITION 4b

perfect correlation *n* **:** correlation for which the Pearsonian coefficient or its equivalent for multiple correlation is 1

perfected *adj* [fr. past part. of ²*perfect*] **:** brought to a state of perfection **:** COMPLETED, REFINED — **per·fect·ed·ly** *adv*

perfect engine *n* **:** IDEAL ENGINE

¹**per·fect·er** *pronunc at* ¹PERFECT + ə(r)\ *comparative of* PERFECT

²**per·fect·er** *pronunc at* ²PERFECT + ə(r)\ *n* -S **1 :** one that perfects **2 :** PERFECTING PRESS

perfectest *superlative of* PERFECT

perfect flower *n* **:** a monoclinous flower

perfect form *n* **:** PERFECT STAGE

perfect fungus *n* **:** a fungus known to produce sexual spores (as zygospores, ascospores, basidiospores)

perfect game *n* **:** a no-hit no-run baseball game in which no batter reaches first base ⟨a pitcher has to be . . . doubly fortunate to pitch a *perfect game* —Vic Wall⟩

perfect gas *n* **:** IDEAL GAS

per·fec·ti \pə(r)'fek,tī, -,tē\ *n pl* [ML, fr. L, pl. of *perfectus* perfect — more at PERFECT] **:** members of the most extreme and ascetic class constituting the elite of various religious sects (as the Cathari or the Manichaeans)

per·fect·ibil·ian \(,)pər,fektə'bilēən, ,pərfik-, -lyən\ *n* -S [*perfectibility* + -*an*] **:** PERFECTIONIST

per·fect·ibil·ism \pər'fektəbə,lizəm, 'pərfik-\ *n* -S [*perfectibility* + -*ism*] **:** PERFECTIONISM

per·fect·ibil·ist \pər'fektəbələst\ *n* -S [*perfectibility* + -*ist*] **1 :** a believer in perfectibility **:** PERFECTIONIST **2 perfectibilists** *pl, usu cap* **:** ILLUMINATI 1b **3** *usu cap* **:** ALUMBRADO

per·fect·ibil·i·tar·i·an \pər,fektə,bilə'terēən, ,pərfik-\ *n* -S [*perfectibility* + -*arian*] **:** PERFECTIONIST 1

per·fect·ibil·i·ty \pər,fektə'biləd-ē *sometimes* ,pərfik-\ *n* -ES [F *perfectibilité*, fr. *perfectible* + -*ité* -ity] **1 a :** a capacity for progress or improvement esp. in the attainment of moral excellence ⟨believed in rationalism, progress, and the infinite ~ of the human race —J.G.Colton⟩ **b :** PERFECTIONISM 1 ⟨the New England mind turned from ~ . . . to intellectual progress —H.S.Canby⟩ **c :** a belief advanced by Lessing that religion is rooted in humanitarian morality rather than dogmatic creed and is therefore subject to improvement **2 :** PERFECTION ⟨ever the craftsman seeking ~ in . . . art —*Saturday Rev.*⟩

per·fect·ible \pər'fektəbəl *sometimes* 'pərfik-\ *adj* [F, fr. ML *perfectibilis*, fr. L *perfectus* perfect + -*ibilis* -ible — more at PERFECT] **:** capable of being improved or attaining to perfection ⟨if men are not perfect, they are at least indefinitely ~ —M.R.Cohen⟩

perfect induction *n* **:** ENUMERATIVE INDUCTION

perfecting *n* -S [fr. gerund of ²*perfect*] **:** an act or instance of completion or refinement ⟨man seems not to be evolving at all . . . except in minor ~*s* of his vertical posture —Weston La Barre⟩

perfecting press *n* **:** a press that prints paper on both sides at the same time

¹**per·fec·tion** \pə(r)'fekshən\ *n* -S [ME *perfeccioun*, fr. OF *perfection*, fr. L *perfection-*, *perfectio*, fr. *perfectus* (past part. of *perficere* to complete, perfect) + -*ion-*, -*io* -ion — more at ¹PERFECT] **1 a** *obs* **:** the quality or state of being finished **:** COMPLETION, WHOLENESS **b :** the condition of having reached full development **:** MATURITY, RIPENESS ⟨Greek civilization, as it slowly flowered to ~ —Agnes Repplier⟩ **c :** an exemplification of supreme moral or physical excellence ⟨her figure was ~ —Max Peacock⟩ **2 a :** freedom from fault or defect **:** correspondence with or approximation to an ideal concept **:** FLAWLESSNESS ⟨the diminutive ~ and wonder of leaf, berry, sand whorl —E.B.Garside⟩ ⟨collection . . . noteworthy for its ~ of preparation and mounting —*City Library Bull. Springfield (Mass.)*⟩ ⟨postulated a progressive evolution in human history toward . . . ~ —Allen Johnson⟩; *specif* **:** SAINTLINESS ⟨the grand aim of the Buddhist is to attain a ~ like Buddha's —A.M.Fairbairn⟩ **b :** an unsurpassable degree of accuracy or excellence **:** CULMINATION ⟨difficult to find solitude to such ~ upon earth nowadays —Richard Semon⟩ **3 :** the act or process of freeing from faults or drawbacks **:** IMPROVEMENT, REFINEMENT ⟨worked toward the ~ of the fountain pen⟩ ⟨charity will be the foremost virtue in the active ~ of a Christian —D.J.Unger⟩ **4 a :** skillful execution **:** complete mastery of technique **:** PROFICIENCY, VIRTUOSITY ⟨~ is what we strive for constantly in the ballet —Moira Shearer⟩ ⟨ancient rock drawings of amazing ~ and complexity —*Geog. Jour.*⟩ **b** *archaic* **:** a trait or skill acquired by education or practice **:** ACCOMPLISHMENT ⟨I am not master of any of those ~*s* —John Dryden⟩ **5 :** triple time in mensural notation **syn** see EXCELLENCE

²**perfection** \"\ *vt* -ED/-ING/-S **:** PERFECT

per·fec·tion·ate \-shə,nāt\ *vt* -ED/-ING/-S [¹*perfection* + -*ate*] *archaic* **:** PERFECT

per·fec·tion·ism \-shə,nizəm\ *n* -S **1 :** a belief in perfectibility: as **a :** the ethical doctrine that self-realization or the perfection of moral character constitutes man's highest good **b :** the theological doctrine that a state of freedom from sin is attainable or has been attained in the earthly life **c** *usu cap* **:** the utopian principles governing the 19th century Christian communist community at Oneida, N.Y. **2 :** a disposition to regard anything short of perfection as unacceptable ⟨~ no less than isolationism . . . may obstruct the paths to international peace —F.D.Roosevelt⟩

¹**per·fec·tion·ist** \-sh(ə)nəst\ *n* -S [¹*perfection* + -*ist*] **1 :** an adherent of perfectionism: as **a :** one who believes in the ethical or spiritual perfectibility of mankind ⟨a Puritan ~ —*Saturday Rev.*⟩ **b** *usu cap* **:** a member of the original Oneida Community practicing perfectionism **c :** one who claims to have attained moral perfection or sinlessness **2 :** one that demands or works to achieve perfection ⟨they are ~*s* and will either have the best or nothing at all —Nancy Mitford⟩ ⟨a ~, he rehearsed one scene . . . 50 times —*Time*⟩

²**perfectionist** \"\ *also* **per·fec·tion·is·tic** \pə(r)'feksh-ə,nistik, -tēk\ *adj* **:** of, relating to, or characterized by perfection or perfectionism

per·fec·tion·ize \⸗'⸗shə,nīz\ *vt* -ED/-ING/-S [¹*perfection* + -*ize*] *archaic* **:** PERFECT

perfection loop knot *n* **:** a knot used by anglers to tie a fixed loop in a leader or spinning line

per·fec·tion·ment \-shənmənt\ *n* -S [²*perfection* + -*ment*] **:** the act or process of bringing to perfection **:** IMPROVEMENT, REFINEMENT

per·fect·ist \pər'fektəst, 'pərfik-\ *n* -S [¹*perfect* + -*ist*] **1 :** one of the perfecti **2 :** PERFECTIONIST

¹**per·fec·tive** \pər'fektiv, 'pərfik-\ *adj* [ML *perfectivus*, fr. L *perfectus* (past part. of *perficere* to complete, perfect) + -*ivus* -ive — more at PERFECT] **1** *archaic* **a :** tending to make perfect **b :** being in the process of improvement **:** becoming better **2 :** expressing action as complete or as implying the notion of completion, conclusion, or result — used of a form or aspect of the verb; opposed to *imperfective* — **perfectively** *adv* — **perfectiveness** *n* -ES — **perfectivity** *n* -ES

²**perfective** \"\ *n* -S **1 :** the perfective aspect of a language **2 :** a verb form in the perfective aspect

per·fec·tiv·iza·tion \pər,fektəvə'zāshən, -,vī'z-\ *n* -S **:** the act or process of perfectivizing

per·fec·tiv·ize \⸗'⸗⸗,vīz\ *vt* -ED/-ING/-S [¹*perfective* + -*ize*] **:** to make perfective

per·fect·ly \'pərfik(t)lē, 'pə̄f-,'pəif-, -fēk-, -li\ *adv* [alter. (influenced by L *perfectus* perfect) of ME *perfitly*, *parfitly*, fr. *perfit*, *parfit* perfect + -*ly* — more at PERFECT] **1 a :** to the fullest extent **:** COMPLETELY, THOROUGHLY ⟨a ~ deliberate measure —Ralph Linton⟩ ⟨a ~ straight face⟩ ⟨poems . . . ~ suited to an occasion —J.D.Hart⟩ **b :** to a precise degree **:** ACCURATELY ⟨breadboard, which is ~ round —*New Yorker*⟩ ⟨~ predictable electronic reactions —Robert Bendiner⟩ **c :** to an adequate extent **:** QUITE ⟨most parents . . . manage to raise ~ good children —B.M.Beck⟩ **d** *dial* **:** EXACTLY ⟨~ as if she were back on her own porch —Maristan Chapman⟩ **2 :** in a flawless manner **:** FAULTLESSLY, IDEALLY ⟨attractive churches, ~ kept parks, playgrounds —*Amer. Guide Series: Minn.*⟩ ⟨sang ~ —Virgil Thomson⟩

per·fect·ness \-k(t)nəs\ *n* -ES [alter. (influenced by L *perfectus*) of ME *perfitnesse*, *parfitnesse*, fr. *perfit*, *parfit* + -*nesse* -ness] **:** PERFECTION; *esp* **:** moral excellence

perfect number *n* **:** an integer (as 6) the sum of whose divisors including 1 but excluding itself is equal to itself ⟨28, which = 1 + 2 + 4 + 7 + 14, is a *perfect number*⟩ — compare IMPERFECT NUMBER

per·fec·to \pə(r)'fek(,)tō\ *n* -S [Sp, perfect, fr. L *perfectus* — more at PERFECT] **:** a cigar that is thick in the middle and tapers almost to a point at each end

per·fec·tor \pər'fektə(r), 'pərfik-\ *n* -S [L, fr. *perfectus* (past part. of *perficere* to complete, perfect) + -*or* — more at PERFECT] **1 :** one that perfects **2** *or* **perfector press :** PERFECTING PRESS

perfect participle *n* **:** PAST PARTICIPLE

perfect radiator *n* **:** an ideal black body absorbing all the radiation falling upon it and therefore constituting the best possible radiator

perfect ream *n* **:** PRINTER'S REAM

perfects *pres 3d sing of* PERFECT, *pl of* PERFECT

perfect square *n* **:** a number or expression that is the square of a number or expression of the class under consideration; *esp* **:** an integral rational term that is the square of an integral rational term ⟨9 is a *perfect square* because it is the square of 3⟩ or a trinomial that is the square of a binomial ⟨$a^2 + 2ab + b^2$ is the *perfect square* of $a + b$⟩

perfect stage *n* **:** the stage in the life cycle of a fungus at which sexual spores are produced — compare PERFECT FUNGUS

per·fec·tum \pə(r)'fektəm\ *n* -S [NL, fr. neut. of L *perfectus* perfect — more at PERFECT] **:** an aspectual category of tenses in Latin that includes all which indicate that action or state is completed in contrast with those tenses which indicate that action or state is in progress — compare INFECTUM

perfect usufruct *n* **:** a usufruct whose subject matter is not destroyed by its normal use and enjoyment though it may be subject to depreciation or gradual deterioration

perfect year *n* **:** a common year of 355 days or a leap year of 385 days in the Jewish calendar — see YEAR table

per·fervid \¦pər, (')per+\ *adj* [NL *perfervidus*, fr. L *per-* thoroughly + *fervidus* fervid — more at PER-, FERVID] **:** extremely or excessively fervent **:** ZEALOUS, IMPASSIONED ⟨the ~ beliefs of religious converts —Edward Glover⟩ ⟨a ~ patriot —R.A.Austen-Leigh⟩ ⟨~ adolescent sexuality—John Farrelly⟩ ⟨~ screams from the press about freedom of the press —J.W. Albig⟩ **syn** see IMPASSIONED

per·fi·cient \pə(r)'fishənt\ *adj* [L *perficient-*, *perficiens*, pres. part. of *perficere* to complete, perfect — more at PERFECT] *archaic* **:** having decisive influence or authority **:** EFFECTIVE

per·fid·i·ous \pə(r)ˈfidēəs\ *adj* [L *perfidiosus*, fr. *perfidia* perfidy + *-osus* -ous — more at PERFIDY] **:** of, relating to, or characterized by perfidy **:** DECEITFUL, TREACHEROUS ⟨that common but most ~ refuge of men of letters . . . the profession of teaching —Matthew Arnold⟩ **syn** see FAITHLESS

per·fid·i·ous·ly *adv* **:** in a perfidious manner ⟨~ playing one side against the other⟩

per·fid·i·ous·ness *n* -ES **:** PERFIDY

per·fi·dy \ˈpərfədē, ˈpə̄f-,ˈpəif-, -di\ *n* -ES [L *perfidia*, fr. *perfidus* faithless, dishonest (fr. *per-* deviating from + *fides* faith) + *-ia* -y] **1 :** the quality or state of being dishonest or disloyal **:** DECEIT, TREACHERY ⟨such obvious liars that their ~ palled after it ceased to be amusing —W.A.White⟩ ⟨the name of Judas has become a byword of covetousness and ~ —Samuel Cox⟩ **2 :** an act or instance of deception or betrayal ⟨tirades of a slighted lover against the beloved object's *perfidies* —C.E. Montague⟩

per·filo·graph \(ˌ)pərˈfīləˌgraf, -fil-, -râf\ *n* [L *per filum* by means of a cord (fr. *per* by means of, through + *filum* cord, thread) + E *-o-* + *-graph* — more at FOR, FILE] **:** an instrument for recording undulations in the bottom of a river or harbor channel

perf·ins \ˈpərˌfinz\ *n pl* [*perf*orated *in*itial*s*] **:** PERFORATED INITIALS

per·fit \ˈpərfət, ˈpärfət, (ˌ)pərˈfēt\ *dial var of* PERFECT

per·flate \pə(r)ˈflāt\ *vt* -ED/-ING/-S [L *perflatus*, past part. of *perflare*, fr. *per-* + *flare* to blow — more at BLOW] *archaic* **:** VENTILATE 3

perflatile *adj* [L *perflatilis*, fr. *perflatus* + *-ilis* -ile] *obs* **:** open to the wind

per·fla·tion \pə(r)ˈflāshən\ *n* -S [LL *perflation-*, *perflatio*, fr. L *perflatus* + *-ion-*, *-io* -ion] **:** VENTILATION

per·flu·ent \(ˌ)pərˈflüənt, ˈpərˌflüə-, ˈpərfləwə-\ *adj* [L *perfluent-*, *perfluens*, pres. part. of *perfluere* to flow through, fr. *per-* + *fluere* to flow — more at FLUENT] *archaic* **:** flowing through **:** FLOWING

perfluor- *or* **perfluoro-** *comb form* [ISV *per-* + *fluor-*] **:** containing a relatively large amount of fluorine esp. in place of hydrogen ⟨*perfluoro*octane C_8F_{18}⟩

per·fluorinate \ˌpər, (ˈ)per+\ *vt* [*per-* + *fluorinate*] **:** to combine with the maximum amount of fluorine esp. in place of hydrogen

per·foliate \ˌpər, (ˈ)per+\ *adj* [NL *perfoliata*, an herb having leaves pierced by the stem, fr. L *per* through + *foliata*, fem. of *foliatus* foliate — more at FOR, FOLIATE] **1 :** having the basal part naturally united around the stem — used of a leaf (as of many honeysuckles) apparently perforated by the stem or petiole **2 :** having the terminal joints expanded into flattened plates and encircling the stalk which connects them — used of the antenna of an insect (as a lamellicorn beetle) — **per·folia·tion** \ˌpər, ˌper+\ *n*

per·fo·ra·ble \ˈpərf(ə)rəbəl, ˈpə̄f-,ˈpəif-\ *adj* [*perforate* + *-able*] **:** capable of being perforated

per·fo·ra·ta \ˌ==fəˈrädə, -rād-ə\ *n pl, cap* [NL, fr. L, neut. pl. of *perforatus* — more at PERFORATE] **1 :** a division of corals including those (as members of the genus *Porites*) whose skeleton has a porous texture — opposed to *Aporosa* **2 :** a division of Foraminifera including those having shells with small perforations for the protrusion of pseudopodia

¹per·fo·rate \ˈpərfəˌrāt, ˈpə̄f-,ˈpəif-, *usu* -ād·+V\ *vb* -ED/-ING/-S [L *perforatus*, past part. of *perforare* to bore through, fr. *per-* + *forare* to bore — more at BORE] *vt* **1 a :** to make a hole through **:** PIERCE, PUNCTURE ⟨~ a jar top to give a captured butterfly air⟩ ⟨tarpaulins liberally *perforated* by small V-shaped rents —I.T.Sanderson⟩ ⟨~ a stamp in making a cut cancellation⟩ ⟨an ulcer ~*s* the duodenal wall⟩; *specif* **:** to make a line of holes or small incisions in (as a sheet of stamps or coupons) to facilitate separation **b :** to make a hole or opening in **:** PIT, INDENT ⟨gopher holes ~ the range⟩ ⟨scenic fjords ~ the coastline⟩ **c :** to enter or extend through ⟨divisions of the eighth nerve . . . again ~ the dura mater through smaller openings —G.V.Ellis⟩ **2 :** to make (a hole or design) by boring or piercing ⟨tools for *perforating* thousands of different patterns —*Industrial Equipment News*⟩ **~** *vi* **1 :** to penetrate a surface ⟨occasionally an ulcer ~*s* . . . just when it seems to be well under control —Frank Forty⟩ **2 :** to pierce the casing of an oil well at a desired depth to allow the oil to seep in

syn PERFORATE, PUNCTURE, PUNCH, PRICK, BORE, and DRILL mean, in common, to pierce so as to leave a hole. PERFORATE, though it can mean to pierce, now applies chiefly to the making, usu. by machine, of a series of small holes in a line or pattern for ornamentation, identification, or ease of separation ⟨boat stones, resembling canoes and sometimes *perforated* to be worn as pendants —*Amer. Guide Series: N.J.*⟩ ⟨a monogram *perforated* on each title page⟩ ⟨a set of pins that *perforates* an entire sheet at one operation —Al Burns⟩ PUNCTURE implies the passing of a sharp pointed instrument into or through a tissue, substance, or material, often carrying also the added connotation of deflation ⟨the dark green blind that was *punctured* here and there, admitting starlike bits of light —Jean Stafford⟩ ⟨today we have holes that *puncture* the earth's shell as much as three miles —*Lamp*⟩ ⟨*puncture* a balloon or a tire⟩ PUNCH is often interchangeable with PERFORATE esp. when a mechanical device is used ⟨a bullet an inch and a half in diameter was formerly big enough to *punch* holes in a tank —G.R.Harrison⟩ ⟨an army captain had invented a system of dot-and-dash symbols which could be *punched* out on thick paper and read by touch at night —*Time*⟩ ⟨cement mixer . . . crashed through a buried septic tank early yesterday afternoon, *punching* a large crater in the earth —*Springfield (Mass.) Union*⟩ ⟨a machine for *punching* cards for automatic computing machines⟩ PRICK implies a piercing with a sharp fine point to make a small hole or inflict a superficial wound ⟨*prick* a finger with a needle⟩ ⟨urged the laggards along by *pricking* them with the point of his bayonet⟩ ⟨seedlings were *pricking* through the soil —Anne Dorrance⟩ BORE suggests excavation or the use of a rotating cutting tool, as an auger or broach; in figurative use, as distinguished from DRILL, BORE suggests a slow continuous penetrating by force ⟨three tunnels were *bored* —Tom Marvel⟩ ⟨holes *bored* in the beach by small reddish crabs —J.G.Frazer⟩ ⟨*bore* one's way patiently through a dense crowd of spectators⟩ DRILL commonly implies the use of a pointed or sharp rotating tool for boring holes in hard substances; in figurative use, as distinguished from BORE, DRILL suggests a forced penetration through repetitive persistence ⟨*drill* a hole through a plank⟩ ⟨*drill* a sheet of metal in several places⟩ ⟨it is firmly *drilled* into the minds of ministers by their officials that in red tape can security be found in war —E.H.Collis⟩

²per·fo·rate \-f(ə)rət, -fəˌrāt, *usu* |d·+V\ *adj* [L *perforatus*, past part. of *perforare*] **1 :** PERFORATED **2 a :** having a permanently open umbilicus at the origin of the whorls **:** UMBILICATE — used of a spiral shell; compare IMPERFORATE **b :** of or relating to the Perforata

perforated *adj* **:** having a hole or series of holes **:** PIERCED, PUNCTURED ⟨~ eardrum⟩ ⟨~ answer sheet for correcting tests⟩ ⟨cream cheese, made of clabber drained in ~ molds —*Amer. Guide Series: La.*⟩ ⟨~ cancellation⟩; *specif* **:** having a (specified) number of perforations in 20 millimeters ⟨the stamps are ~ 13 —Yoshitsugu Mishima & Helen K. Zirkle⟩

perforated ax *n* **:** a prehistoric stone ax head pierced by a hole for the insertion of a handle

perforated initials *n pl* **1 :** a set of initials (as a business monogram) or other design pierced into a postage stamp as a means of identification or as a safeguard against theft **2 :** stamps having perforated initials

perforated space *also* **perforate space** *n* **:** any of three small areas on the lower surface of the brain that are perforated by many small openings for blood vessels and that are situated two anteriorly at the commencement of the fissure of Sylvius and one posteriorly between the mammillary bodies in front and the cerebral peduncles laterally

perforating *n* -S [fr. gerund of ¹*perforate*] **:** PERFORATION

perforating rule *n* **:** a notched steel or brass printer's rule a little more than type high used for making perforations

per·fo·ra·tion \ˌpərfəˈrāshən, ˌpə̄f-, ˌpəif-\ *n* -S [NL, fr. L *perforatus* + NL *-orium* — more at PERFORATE] **1 :** the act or process of perforating ⟨a machine for the ~ of a sheet of stamps at one stroke⟩; *specif* **:** the penetration of a body part through accident or disease ⟨spontaneous ~ of the sigmoid colon in the presence of diverticulosis —*Jour. Amer. Med. Assoc.*⟩ **2 a** (1) **:** a hole or pattern made by piercing or boring ⟨~*s* on the edge of the film engage sprockets in the projector⟩ ⟨mark all ~*s* which indicate seams, darts . . . and buttonhole locations —*Needlecraft for the Home*⟩ ⟨overprints gave way to ~*s* —Gordon Ward⟩; *specif* **:** a series or one of a series of holes made in a shoe upper for ornament or ventilation (2) **:** a series of small incisions to facilitate tearing along a predetermined line **b** (1) **:** one of the series of holes made between rows of postage stamps in a sheet — compare PIN PERFORATION, ROULETTE (2) **:** one of the teeth on the edge of a detached stamp resulting from tearing along the series of holes (3) *or* **perforation number :** a philatelic classification based on the number of perforations along the edge of a stamp per 20 millimeters **c :** a rupture in a body part caused by accident or disease **d :** a natural opening in an organ or body part ⟨small ~*s* opening at the bottom of the sulci —Ferdinand Canu & R.S.Bassler⟩

perforation gauge *n* **:** a calibrated strip of cardboard, celluloid, or metal for determining the perforation number of a stamp

perforation tooth *n* **:** TOOTH 3e

per·fo·ra·tor \ˈ==ˌrād·ə(r), -ātə-\ *n* -S **:** one that perforates: as **a :** a prehistoric stone or bone implement for drilling or boring holes **b :** a mechanical device for punching holes or designs through or into a flat surface ⟨check ~⟩ ⟨hand ~ that punches up to 12 sheets without tearing⟩ ⟨railroads use ~*s* for dating tickets —*Office Appliance Manual*⟩; *specif* **:** a telegraphic apparatus that perforates a continuous tape according to code (as for use in a tape transmitter) **c :** an operator of a machine that makes perforations (as in paper or leather) **d :** a device resembling a gun for puncturing an oil well casing at the oil stratum

per·fo·ra·to·ri·um \ˌpərf(ə)rəˈtōrēəm\ *n, pl* **perforato·ria** \-ēə\ [NL, fr. *perforator* + *-ium*] **:** ACROSOME

per·force \pə(r)+\ *adv* [ME *par force*, fr. MF, fr. *par* by (fr. L *per* through, by) + *force* — more at FOR, FORCE] **1** *obs* **:** by physical coercion **:** FORCIBLY ⟨he rushed into my house and took ~ my ring away —Shak.⟩ **2 :** by force of circumstances or of necessity **:** WILLY-NILLY ⟨steppe folk must . . . dwell ~ in skin tents or in subterranean shelters —V.G.Childe⟩ ⟨antistatism and the distrust of governmental power have been ~ swept away in a world in which only the cohesive civilization can survive —Max Lerner⟩

per·form \R pə(r)ˈfō(ə)rm, *-R* pəˈfō(ə)m\ *vb* -ED/-ING/-S [ME *parformen*, *performen*, fr. AF *parformer*, *performer*, alter. (influenced by OF *forme*, *fourme* form) of OF *parfournir*, *perfournir*, fr. *par-*, *per-* thoroughly (fr. L *per-*) + *fournir* to complete, carry out, accomplish — more at FORM, PER-, FURNISH] *vt* **1 a :** to adhere to the terms of **:** treat as an obligation **:** IMPLEMENT, FULFILL ⟨~ a contract⟩ ⟨when she promised a thing she was . . . scrupulous in ~*ing* it —Jane Austen⟩ **b** *obs* **:** to effect as an agent **:** ACTUATE, ENACT ⟨hast thou, spirit, ~*ed* to point the tempest that I bade thee —Shak.⟩ **c :** to bring to a finished state **:** COMPLETE ⟨passenger miles ~*ed* by Class I railways —*Yrbk. of Railroad Information*⟩ ⟨a student who . . . fails to ~ satisfactorily the work of his course —*Univ. of Toronto Cal.*⟩ **2 a :** to carry out or bring about **:** ACCOMPLISH, EXECUTE ⟨~ a function⟩ ⟨~ calculations with astronomical speed —Stuart Chase⟩ ⟨figurines which once ~*ed* amusing antics actuated by power from a waterwheel —*Amer. Guide Series: Conn.*⟩ ⟨imaginative editing can ~ miracles in creating interest —F.L.Mott⟩ ⟨dissections were ~*ed* on monkeys —Benjamin Farrington⟩ **b :** to make available or do in line of duty **:** PROVIDE ⟨the university ~*s* more than 50 distinct services to the state —*Amer. Guide Series: Mich.*⟩ ⟨services ~*ed* by New Zealand forces in Korea —*Americana Annual*⟩ **3 a :** to construct or give aesthetic form to **:** DESIGN ⟨a ship . . . may be as well ~*ed* as such large buildings —William Sutherland⟩ **4 a :** to do in a formal manner or according to prescribed ritual ⟨~ a marriage ceremony⟩ ⟨dramatic satisfaction . . . in a High Mass well ~*ed* —T.S.Eliot⟩ **b :** to give a rendition of **:** PRESENT, PLAY ⟨~*ed* a hula . . to entertain the passengers —Horace Sutton⟩ ⟨guest conductors ~*ed* certain new scores on tolerance —Virgil Thomson⟩ ⟨two of his plays had been ~*ed* by the dramatic club —Gilbert Millstein⟩ **~** *vi* **1 :** to carry out an action or pattern of behavior **:** fulfill a threat or promise **:** ACT, FUNCTION ⟨not only promised but ~*ed* —V.L.Albjerg⟩ ⟨about one third of one's time must be spent in sleep if one is to ~ effectively —Webb Garrison⟩ ⟨the car ~*ed* beautifully except on a short incline —M.M.Musselman⟩ **2 :** to give a performance **:** put on a show **:** PLAY ⟨~ under a circus tent⟩ ⟨experience as a composer helps him understand the problems of ~*ing* —*Time*⟩

syn EXECUTE, DISCHARGE, ACCOMPLISH, ACHIEVE, EFFECT, FULFILL: PERFORM usu. implies an act for which a process or pattern of movement has already been established, esp. one calling for skill or precision, or for the assignment or assumption of responsibility ⟨*perform* a dance⟩ ⟨*perform* drill work in rhythm⟩ ⟨*perform* a miracle⟩ ⟨*perform* an experiment⟩ ⟨*perform* one's duties⟩ ⟨they examine patients and *perform* simple forms of treatment under supervision —*Bull. of Meharry Med. Coll.*⟩ ⟨*perform* such courtesies as writing letters of thanks to those who assisted —W.T.Gruhn⟩ ⟨there were certain important functions which it was expected to *perform* —W.B.Graves⟩ EXECUTE, similar to PERFORM, stresses more the completion, esp. the skillful completion, of the process or pattern of movement ⟨*execute* a dance step⟩ ⟨*execute* maneuvers⟩ ⟨*execute* a difficult task⟩ ⟨the escape was planned meticulously and *executed* boldly —Edmond Taylor⟩ ⟨*executed* a precise and calculated campaign —V.L.Albjerg⟩ DISCHARGE is generally used of the execution, esp. in full, of duties or obligations ⟨*discharge* a debt to society⟩ ⟨*discharge* a monetary obligation⟩ ⟨before setting sail he *discharged* all arrears of business and heard last-minute petitions and appeals —P.J.Phelan⟩ ACCOMPLISH emphasizes the idea of successful, often triumphant, completion of an act or attainment of an objective, esp. one involving some difficulty ⟨society enabled them to *accomplish* difficult enterprises —H.M.Parshley⟩ ⟨this project was so vast and so quickly *accomplished* that it has no parallel —Lou Stoumen⟩ ⟨elementary education . . . has tried to *accomplish* something when it should merely have tried to begin something —George Sampson⟩ ⟨help a man to *accomplish* his destiny —W.J.Locke⟩ ACHIEVE emphasizes the notion of a difficult end gained or of honor acquired in the process ⟨*achieve* distinction⟩ ⟨*achieved* a long-hoped-for dream —*Americana Annual*⟩ ⟨the heights he has since *achieved* —Alec Bishop⟩ EFFECT, like ACHIEVE, emphasizes the notion of a difficult end gained but focuses the mind more on the force of the effective agent ⟨were imprisoned until Aug. 6, when friends *effected* their release —*Amer. Guide Series: Del.*⟩ ⟨a chance to *effect* a compromise —*Amer. Guide Series: N. C.*⟩ ⟨done more than perhaps any other modern critic to *effect* a revaluation of English literature —Edmund Wilson⟩ FULFILL implies a full realization of what exists potentially, or hitherto in conception, or in the nature or sense of responsibility of the agent ⟨*fulfill* a promise⟩ ⟨*fulfilled* his last duty —C.S.Forester⟩ ⟨*fulfill* human hopes —A.E.Stevenson b.1900⟩ ⟨*fulfill* the whole purpose of language —A.L.Guérard⟩

per·form·able \-məbəl\ *adj* **:** capable of being performed

per for·mam do·ni \ˌperˈfórˌmämˈdōˌnē\ *adv* [L, through the form of a gift] **:** in accordance with the terms of the gift — used of the disposition of an estate as designated by the donor rather than by operation of the law

per·form·ance \R pə(r)ˈfórmən(t)s, *-R* pəˈfō(ə)m-\ *n* -S **1 a :** the act or process of carrying out something **:** the execution of an action ⟨a repetitive act the ~ of which is facilitated by repetition —D.W.Maurer & V.H.Vogel⟩ ⟨satisfactory ~ on achievement tests —S.C.Brownstein & Mitchel Weiner⟩ **b :** something accomplished or carried out **:** ACCOMPLISHMENT, FEAT ⟨could entertain in his own house — a difficult if not impossible ~ in the present dearth of domestic help —E.H.Collis⟩ **c :** a literary or artistic composition **:** WORK ⟨for a new writer this novel would be rated a brilliant ~ —E.C.Wagenknecht⟩ **2 :** the fulfillment of a claim, promise, or request **:** IMPLEMENTATION ⟨contracts whose ~ would violate the act are unenforceable —*Harvard Law Rev.*⟩ **3 a :** the action of representing a character in a dramatic work ⟨congratulated him on his daughter's ~ in the play⟩ **b :** a public presentation or exhibition ⟨his current collection of sculpture and paintings . . . is a truly handsome ~ —R.M.Coates⟩ ⟨the play ran for 285 ~*s*⟩ ⟨the orchestra gave a benefit ~⟩ ⟨the first ~ of a new symphony⟩ **c :** something resembling a dramatic representation ⟨get the child to a place where you both can get over the effects of such a ~ —H.R.Litchfield & L.H.Dembo⟩ ⟨looking to see if anyone caught them going through such a silly ~ —G.E. & Nettie MacGinitie⟩ **4 a :** the ability to perform **:** capacity to achieve a desired result **:** EFFICIENCY ⟨senescence represents a marked decline in function and ~ —George Lawton⟩ ⟨a good power-weight ratio not only improves ~ but lowers fuel consumption —Grenville Manton⟩ **b :** the factors (as speed, rate of climb, ceiling) influencing such capacity in an airplane **c :** the acceleration, power, and speed of an automobile **5 :** the manner of reacting to various stimuli **:** BEHAVIOR ⟨variation in the ~ of the skin structures⟩ ⟨the ~ of the stock market⟩; *specif* **:** the rate of sale of a product ⟨the bookseller enters the Christmas and spring selling seasons . . . with hundreds of unknown books whose ~ he must watch —*Canadian Forum*⟩

performance bond *n* **:** a surety bond guaranteeing faithful performance of a contract — compare CONTRACT BOND

performance test *n* **:** a test of capacity to achieve a desired result; *esp* **:** an intelligence test (as by a form board, maze, or picture completion) requiring little use of language

per·form·ato·ry \-məˌtōrē, -tȯr-, -ri\ *adj* [*perform* + *-atory*] **:** of, relating to, or based on performance ⟨"I'll do it" is a ~ utterance⟩

per·form·er \-mə(r)\ *n* -S **:** one that performs ⟨~ of a contract⟩ ⟨the common stock . . . has not been a vigorous ~ —*Brookmire Investment Reports*⟩; *specif* **:** ENTERTAINER ⟨the ~*s* would have kept on with unabated zest as long as any audience remained —V.G.Heiser⟩

performing *adj* **1 :** of, relating to, or capable of giving a performance ⟨~ rights of a lyric —*Westminster Gazette*⟩ ⟨~ seals⟩ **2 :** of, relating to, or constituting an art (as drama) that involves public performance ⟨project an image of the U.S. through displays, films, publications, fine arts, and the ~ arts —Virginia Krepela⟩

perfricate *vt* -ED/-ING/-S [L *perfricatus*, past part. of *perfricare*, fr. *per-* throughout, thoroughly + *fricare* to rub — more at PER-, FRICTION] *obs* **:** to rub thoroughly

per·fri·ca·tion \ˌpərfrəˈkāshən, ˌper-\ *n* -S [LL *perfrication-*, *perfricatio*, fr. L *perfricatus* + *-ion-*, *-io* -ion] *archaic* **:** thorough rubbing

per·fum·ato·ry \(ˌ)pərˈfyüməˌtōrē\ *adj* [¹*perfume* + *-atory*] *obs* **:** of or relating to perfumes

¹per·fume \ˈpərˌfyüm, ˈpə̄ˌf-, ˈpəiˌf-, ˌpə(r)ˈf-, ˌpə̄ˈf-, pəiˈf-\ *n* [MF *parfum*, *perfum*, prob. fr. OProv *perfum*, fr. *perfumar* to perfume, fr. *per-* thoroughly (fr. L) + *fumar* to smoke, expose to fumes, fr. L *fumare* to smoke — more at PER-, FUME] **1 a** *obs* **:** the fumes generated by burning (as to fumigate a room or to fill it with an agreeable odor) **b :** the scent of something usu. sweet-smelling ⟨~ of violets⟩ ⟨a house fragrant with the ~ of freshly baked cookies —June Platt⟩ ⟨~ of the stockyards —Francis Hackett⟩ **c :** a distinctive atmosphere or pleasurable quality **:** AURA ⟨the literary ~ . . . in the grand salons of the nineteenth century —Frederic Morton⟩ **2 :** a substance that emits a pleasant odor; *esp* **:** a fluid preparation (as one containing essences of flowers, synthetics, and a fixative) used for scenting **syn** see FRAGRANCE

²per·fume \(ˌ)=ˈ=, ˈ=ˌ=, (ˌ)=ˈ=\ *vb* -ED/-ING/-S [MF *parfumer*, *perfumer*, prob. fr. OProv *perfumar*] *vt* **1 a** *obs* **:** FUMIGATE **b :** to fill or impregnate with the pleasantly odorous fumes of a burning substance **2 a :** to fill or impregnate with an odor (as of flowers) **:** SCENT ⟨the heavy odor of the frangipani . . . ~*s* the air —Tom Marvel⟩ **b :** to pervade with an aura ⟨subtly to ~ an art nominally concerned with the aspects of earth and sky —Laurence Binyon⟩ **~** *vi* **:** to emit a sweet odor

per·fumed \ˈ=ˌ=, ˈ=ˌ=, (ˌ)=ˈ=\ *adj* **1 a :** filled or impregnated with perfume **:** SCENTED ⟨~ boudoir⟩ ⟨~ stationery⟩ ⟨breathing the . . . ~ air of June —A.W.Long⟩ **b :** having a natural fragrance ⟨thick drops of their ~ gums oozed through the . . . branches —Edith Sitwell⟩ **2 :** gracious or refined often to excess **:** DELICATE, SACCHARINE ⟨rapid, rather ~ playing —E.T.Canby⟩ ⟨elegant, ~, lyric, but largely . . . unconvincing works —P.H. Lang⟩

perfumed cherry *n* **:** MAHALEB

per·fume·less \ˈ=ˌ=ləs, (ˌ)=ˈ=-\ *adj* **:** lacking perfume

per·fum·er \R pə(r)ˈfyümər, ˈpərˌf-, ˌpərˈf-; *-R* ˌpəˈfyümə(r, ˈpə̄ˌf-, ˈpəiˌf-, pə̄ˈf-, pəiˈf-\ *n* -S [¹*perfume* + *-er*] **1 a :** one that makes or sells perfumes **b :** a specialist in blending new perfumes **2** [²*perfume* + *-er*] *obs* **:** one who is hired to fumigate or scent a room

per·fum·ery \-m(ə)rē, -ri\ *n* -ES [¹*perfume* + *-ery*] **1 a :** the art or process of making perfume **b :** the products made by a perfumer **2 :** a perfume establishment

per·fumy *pronunc at* ¹PERFUME +ē *or* i\ *adj* [¹*perfume* + *-y*] **:** SCENTED, FRAGRANT

per·func·to·ri·ly \pə(r)ˈfəŋ(k)t(ə)rəlē, -li\ *adv* **:** in a perfunctory manner **:** CARELESSLY, APATHETICALLY

per·func·to·ri·ness \-t(ə)rēnəs, -rin-\ *n* -ES **:** the quality or state of being perfunctory **:** CARELESSNESS, INDIFFERENCE

per·func·to·ri·ous \ˌpərˌfəŋ(k)ˈtōrēəs\ *adj* [LL *perfunctorius*] *archaic* **:** PERFUNCTORY — **per·func·to·ri·ous·ly** *adv, archaic*

per·func·to·ry \pə(r)ˈfəŋ(k)t(ə)rē, -)ri\ *adj* [LL *perfunctorius*, fr. L *perfunctus* (past part. of *perfungi* to accomplish, perform, get through with, fr. *per-*, prefix denoting completion + *fungi* to perform) + *-orius* -ory — more at PER-, FUNCTION] **1 :** characterized by routine or superficiality **:** done merely as a duty **:** CURSORY, MECHANICAL ⟨gave a ~ smile and became again immersed in the folder —Ethel Wilson⟩ ⟨a speech more lifeless and ~ than most of its mechanical type —S.H.Adams⟩ ⟨the subject of eternal life is a ~ addendum to the last chapter —Walter Lowrie⟩ **2 :** lacking in interest or enthusiasm **:** APATHETIC, INDIFFERENT ⟨a wooden and ~ pedagogue —John Dewey⟩

per·fus·ate \(ˌ)pərˈfyüˌzāt, -ˌzət\ *n* -S [*perfuse* + *-ate*] **:** a fluid (as a solution pumped through the heart) that is perfused

per·fuse \-üz\ *vt* -ED/-ING/-S [L *perfusus*, past part. of *perfundere* to pour over, fr. *per-* through, throughout + *fundere* to pour — more at PER-, FOUND] **1 :** SUFFUSE ⟨rubbing of ice over the skin . . . permitted the cold skin to be *perfused* by blood from which heat was extracted —*Yr. Bk. of Physical Medicine & Rehabilitation*⟩ **2 :** to cause to flow or spread **:** DIFFUSE; *specif* **:** to force a fluid through (an organ or tissue) esp. by way of the blood vessels ⟨~ a liver with salt solution⟩

per·fu·sion \-üzhən\ *n* [L *perfusion-*, *perfusio* act of pouring over, fr. *perfusus* + *-ion-*, *-io* -ion] **:** an act or instance of perfusing: as **a :** baptism by affusion **b :** the pumping of a fluid through an organ or tissue ⟨believes that intermittent injection . . . is better and safer than continuous ~ —*Yr. Bk. of Urology*⟩

per·ga·mene \ˈpərgəˌmēn, ˌ==ˈ=\ *adj, usu cap* [L *Pergamenus*, fr. Gk *Pergamēnos*, fr. *Pergamos*, *Pergamon* (Pergamum), ancient city in Asia Minor] **:** of or relating to the ancient city of Pergamum

per·ga·me·ne·ous \ˌpərgəˈmēnēəs\ *adj* [L *pergamena* parchment + E *-eous* — more at PARCHMENT] **:** resembling parchment

per·gel·i·sol \ˌpərˈjeləˌsȯl, -säl\ *n* -S [*per*manent + L *gel*are to freeze + E *-i-* + L *sol*um ground — more at COLD, SOIL] **:** permanently or perennially frozen ground **:** PERMAFROST

per·go·la \ˈpərgələ, ÷ (ˌ)pərˈgōlə\ *n* -S [It, fr. L *pergula* projecting roof, vine arbor] **1 a :** an openwork arch or covering for a walk or passageway over which climbing plants are trained **:** ARBOR, TRELLIS **b :** a usu. vine-covered openwork shelter in a garden **:** BOWER **c :** a small usu. circular structure consisting of a roof supported by columns ⟨policemen in Panama have . . . pillared ~*s* from which to direct traffic —Flora Lewis⟩ **2 :** a structure usu. consisting of parallel colonnades supporting an open roof of girders and cross rafters ⟨at the end of the ~ are the industrial exhibits —*Architectural Rev.*⟩

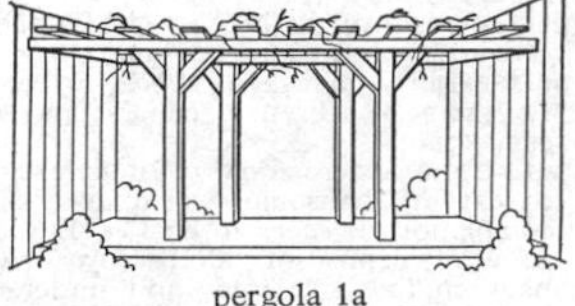

pergola 1a

pergunnah *var of* PARGANA

per·halide \ˌpər, (ˈ)per+\ *n* [*per-* + *halide*] **:** a halide containing a relatively high proportion of halogen

per·halogen \"+\ *adj* [*per-* + *halogen*] **:** containing a relatively high proportion of halogen

¹per·haps \pə(r)ˈhaps, pəˈra-, ˈpra- *also chiefly –R* ˈpa- *sometimes –R* pəˈa-\ *adv* [*per* + *haps*, pl. of *hap* (chance)] **:** possibly but not certainly **:** MAYBE ⟨drove on . . . for ~ fifty yards —William Faulkner⟩ ⟨~ this is true, but it is certainly debatable —R.H.Walker⟩ ⟨here ~ I ought to say —James Gray⟩

²perhaps \"\ *n* -ES **1 :** something open to doubt or conjecture **:** SPECULATION, SUPPOSITION ⟨make ourselves uncomfortable to any extent with ~*es* —John Ruskin⟩ **2** *usu cap* **:** the postulate of a life after death ⟨a belief in the great *Perhaps* —Thornton Wilder⟩

perhydr- *or* **perhydro-** *comb form* [ISV *per-* + *hydr-*] **:** combined with the maximum amount of hydrogen ⟨*perhydro*anthracene $C_{14}H_{24}$⟩

per·hydrogenate \ˌpər, (ˌ)per+\ *vt* [*per-* + *hydrogenate*] **:** to hydrogenate to the fullest extent — **per·hydrogenation** \"+\ *n*

per·hydrogenize \"+\ *vt* [*per-* + *hydrogenize*] **:** PERHYDROGENATE

pe·ri \ˈpirē\ *n* -S [Per *perī* fairy, genius, fr. MPer *parīk*, modif. of Av *pairikā* seducing sorceress, witch; akin to L *paelex* concubine, Gk *pallax* boy, girl, *pallakis* concubine] **1** *Persian folklore* **:** a male or female supernatural being like an elf or fairy but formed of fire, descended from fallen angels and excluded from paradise until penance is accomplished, and orig. regarded as evil but later as benevolent and beautiful — compare HOURI **2 :** a beautiful and graceful girl or woman

peri- *prefix* [L, fr. Gk, fr. *peri*; akin to Gk *peran* to pass through — more at FARE] **1 :** all around **:** about **:** round ⟨*Peri*arctic⟩ ⟨*peri*center⟩ ⟨*peri*cyclone⟩ ⟨*peri*scope⟩ **2 :** near ⟨*peri*helion⟩ **3 a :** enclosing or surrounding ⟨*peri*neurium⟩ ⟨*peri*proct⟩ ⟨*peri*sinuous⟩ **b :** tissue surrounding (a specified part) — in terms in *-itis* ⟨*peri*arthritis⟩ **4** *usu ital* **:** having substituents in or relating to positions 1 and 8 in two fused 6-membered rings (as in naphthalene)

peri *abbr* perigee

peri acid \ˈperē+\ *n* [*peri* fr. *peri-*] **:** a crystalline naphthylaminesulfonic acid $H_2NC_{10}H_6SO_3H$ used as a dye intermediate; 8-amino-1-naphthalenesulfonic acid

peri·aci·nal \ˌperēˈasənᵊl, -ēəˈsīn-\ *also* **peri·acinous** \ˌperē+\ *adj* [*periacinal* fr. *peri-* + NL *acinus* + E *-al*; *periacinous* fr. *peri-* + *acinous*] **:** located about or surrounding an acinus

peri·ac·tus \ˌperēˈaktəs\ *n, pl* **periac·ti** \-ˌtī, -ˌtē\ [NL, fr. Gk *periaktos* — more at PERIAKTOS] **:** PERIAKTOS

per·i·a·gua \ˌperē; "-*agua*" *as in* PIRAGUA\ *archaic var of* PIRAGUA

peri·ak·tos \ˌperēˈaktəs\ *n, pl* **periak·toi** \-ˌtȯi\ [Gk, fr. *periaktos* revolving, fr. *periagein* to lead around, turn around, fr. *peri-* + *agein* to lead, drive — more at AGENT] **:** a 3-sided revolving apparatus painted with scenery and used at each side of the stage in ancient Greek theaters

peri·anal \ˌperē+\ *adj* [ISV *peri-* + *anal*] **:** located about or surrounding the anus

peri·anth \ˈperēˌan(t)th\ *n* -S [NL *perianthium*, fr. *peri-* + *anth-* + *-ium*] **1 :** the external envelope of a flower **:** floral leaves esp. when not differentiated into calyx and corolla — see FLOWER illustration **2 :** the protective envelope that surrounds the archegonium or group of archegonia of various mosses

peri·aortal *or* **peri·aortic** \ˌperē+\ *adj* [*peri-* + *aortal* or *aortic*] **:** about or surrounding the aorta

peri·apical \"+\ *adj* [*peri-* + *apical*] **:** about or surrounding the apex of the root of a tooth — **peri·apically** \"+\ *adv*

per·i·apt \ˈperēˌapt\ *n* -S [MF or Gk; MF *periapte*, fr. Gk *periapton*, fr. neut. of *periaptos* hung around (one), fr. *periaptein* to fasten around (oneself), fr. *peri-* + *haptein* to fasten — more at APSIS] **:** a charm worn esp. as a protection against disease or mischief **:** AMULET

peri·arctic \ˌperē+\ *adj, usu cap* [*peri-* + *arctic*] **:** HOLARCTIC

peri·ar·ter·i·tis no·do·sa \ˌperēˌärd·əˈrīd·əsnōˈdōsə\ *n* [NL, fr. *periarteritis* (fr. *peri-* + *arteritis*) + L *nodosa*, fem. of *nodosus* knotty, nodose — more at NODOSE] **:** an acute inflammatory disease that involves all layers of the arterial wall and is characterized by degeneration, necrosis, exudation, and the formation of inflammatory nodules along the outer layer

peri·arthritis \ˌperē+\ *n* [NL, fr. *peri-* + *arthritis*] **:** inflammation of the structures (as the muscles, tendons, and bursa of the shoulder) around a joint

peri·articular \"+\ *adj* [ISV *peri-* + *articular*] **:** about or surrounding a joint

peri·as·tron \ˌperēˈastrən, -ˌsträn\ *n, pl* **perias·tra** \-strə\ [NL, fr. *peri-* + Gk *astron* star — more at STAR] **:** the point in the orbit of a star or other celestial body where it is nearest to the primary star with reference to which it is revolving ⟨the ~ of a comet⟩ — compare APASTRON

per·i·au·ger \ˌperēˈȯgə(r)\ *archaic var of* PIRAGUA

peri·blast \ˈperəˌblast\ *n* [ISV *peri-* + *-blast*] **1 :** the nucleated cytoplasmic layer surrounding the blastodisc of an egg undergoing discoidal cleavage **2 a :** CYTOPLASM **b :** PERIPLASM — **peri·blas·tic** \ˌ⁼⁼ˈblastik\ *adj*

peri·blastula \ˌperə+\ *n* [NL, fr. *peri-* + *blastula*] **:** a blastula resulting from superficial segmentation of a centrolecithal egg

peri·blem \ˈperəˌblem\ *n* -S [G, fr. Gk *periblēma* garment, fortification, fr. *periballein* to throw around, encompass, put on, fr. *peri-* + *ballein* to throw — more at DEVIL] *according to the histogen theory* **:** a primary meristem that gives rise to the cortex and is located between plerome and dermatogen **:** the cortical region of the root tip

pe·rib·o·los \pəˈribələs, -ˌläs\ *or* **pe·rib·o·lus** \-ləs\ *n, pl* **peribo·loi** \-ˌlȯi\ *or* **peribo·li** \-ˌlī, -ˌlē\ [LL & Gk; LL *peribolus*, fr. Gk *peribolos*, fr. *peribolos*, adj., encompassing, fr. *periballein* to throw around, encompass] **:** an enclosed court esp. about a temple of classical times; *also* **:** the wall of such a court

peri·branchial cavity \ˌperə+ . . . -\ *n* [*peri-* + *branchial*] **:** ATRIUM 4

peri·cambium \ˌperə+\ *n* [NL, fr. *peri-* + *cambium*] **:** PERICYCLE

peri·capillary \"+\ *adj* [*peri-* + *capillary*] **:** lying or occurring in the vicinity of the capillaries of a part or organ ⟨~ infiltration⟩

pericardi- *or* **pericardio-** *or* **pericardo-** *comb form* [NL *pericardium*] **1 :** pericardium ⟨*pericardi*ectomy⟩ ⟨*pericardio*symphysis⟩ ⟨*pericardo*tomy⟩ **2 :** pericardial and ⟨*pericardio*phrenic⟩ ⟨*pericardio*pleural⟩

peri·cardial *also* **peri·cardiac** \ˌperə+\ *adj* [NL *pericardium* + E *-al* or *-ac* (as in *cardiac*)] **:** of, relating to, or affecting the pericardium **:** situated around the heart

pericardial cavity *n* **1 :** the fluid-filled space between the two layers of the vertebrate pericardium **2 :** PERICARDIUM 2

pericardial cell *n* **:** one of many cells along the sides of the insect heart usu. occurring in strands

pericardial fluid *n* **:** the serous fluid that fills the pericardial cavity and protects the heart from friction

pericardial septum *n* **:** a membrane separating the pericardium of an insect from the main body cavity and formed in part by the alary muscles

pericardial sinus *or* **pericardial space** *n* **:** PERICARDIUM 2

peri·car·dit·ic \ˌperəˌkärˈdid·ik\ *adj* [NL *pericarditis* + E *-ic*] **:** of or relating to pericarditis

peri·car·di·tis \ˌperəˌkärˈdīd·əs\ *n, pl* **pericar·dit·i·des** \-rˈdid·əˌdēz\ [NL, fr. *pericardi-* + *-itis*] **:** inflammation of the pericardium

peri·car·di·um \ˌperəˈkärdēəm\ *n, pl* **pericar·dia** \-ēə\ [NL, fr. Gk *perikardion*, neut. of *perikardios* around the heart, fr. *peri-* + *kardia* heart — more at HEART] **1 :** the conical sac of serous membrane that encloses the heart and the roots of the great blood vessels of vertebrates and consists of an outer fibrous coat that loosely invests the heart and is prolonged on the outer surface of the great vessels except the inferior vena cava and a double inner serous coat of which one layer is closely adherent to the heart while the other lines the inner surface of the outer coat, the intervening space being filled with pericardial fluid **2 :** a cavity or space that contains the heart of an invertebrate and in arthropods is a part of the hemocoele and contains blood which passes directly from it into the heart through the ostia in the walls of the latter

peri·carp \ˈperəˌkärp\ *n* -S [NL *pericarpium*, fr. Gk *perikarpion* pod, husk, fr. *peri-* + *-karpion* -carp] **:** the ripened and variously modified walls of a plant ovary that are thin and foliaceous or membranous (as in the legume and most capsules), fleshy (as in berries), or hard and bony (as in nuts) and are more or less homogeneous or consist of up to three distinct layers — see EPICARP, MESOCARP; ENDOCARP illustration — **peri·car·pi·al** \ˌ⁼⁼ˈkärpēəl\ *or* **peri·car·pic** \-pik\ *adj*

peri·car·pi·um \ˌperəˈkärpēəm\ *n, pl* **pericar·pia** \-ēə\ [NL] **:** PERICARP

peri·car·poi·dal \ˌperəˌkärˈpȯidᵊl\ *adj* [*pericarp* + *-oid* + *-al*] **:** resembling a pericarp

pericaryon *var of* PERIKARYON

peri·cellular \ˌperə+\ *adj* [*peri-* + *cellular*] **:** PERICYTIAL 1

peri·ce·ment·al \ˌperəsə̇ˈmentᵊl\ *adj* [NL *pericementum* + E *-al*] **1 :** around the cement layer of a tooth **2 :** of, relating to, or involving the pericementum

peri·ce·men·ti·tis \ˌperəˌsēˌmenˈtīd·əs\ *n* -ES [NL, fr. *pericementum* + *-itis*] **:** PERIODONTITIS

peri·cementum \ˌperə+\ *n* [NL, fr. *peri-* + *cementum*] **:** the connective-tissue membrane covering the cement layer of a tooth

peri·center \ˈperə+ˌ-,⁼⁼ˈ⁼⁼\ *n* [*peri-* + *center*] **:** the point in the orbit of a revolving body nearest the center of gravity about which the body moves — compare PERIGEE, PERIHELION

peri·central cell \ˌperə+ . . . -\ *n* [*peri-* + *central*] **:** any of various cells surrounding the central cells of the thallus in many red algae (as of the genus *Polysiphonia*) and in some cases acting as the apical cells of laterals or in others producing an outer cortical layer or branches

peri·cen·tric \ˌperəˈsen·trik\ *adj* [NL *pericentricus*, fr. *peri-* + ML *-centricus* -centric] **:** of, relating to, or involving the centromere of a chromosome ⟨~ inversion⟩ — compare PARACENTRIC

peri·chaete *or* **peri·chete** \ˈperəˌkēt\ *n* -S [NL *perichaetium*] **:** PERICHAETIUM

peri·chae·ti·al \ˌ⁼⁼ˈkēd·ēəl\ *adj* [NL *perichaetium* + E *-al*] **:** of or relating to the perichaetium

peri·chae·tine \ˌ⁼⁼ˈkēˌtīn\ *adj* [NL *Perichaeta*, genus of earthworms (fr. *peri-* + *-chaeta*) + E *-ine*] **:** having numerous setae arranged about each segment in a ring usu. interrupted dorsally and ventrally and in a distribution characteristic of a common genus (*Perichaeta*) of earthworms — compare LUMBRICINE

peri·chae·ti·um \ˌ⁼⁼ˈkēd·ēəm\ *n, pl* **perichae·tia** \-d·ēə\ [NL, fr. *peri-* + Gk *chaitē* flowing hair, mane, foliage + NL *-ium* — more at CHAETA] **:** an enveloping sheath in a bryophyte; *esp* **:** a cluster of modified leaves surrounding the sex organs or later the seta of mosses

peri·chon·dral \ˌperəˈkändrəl\ *adj* [*peri-* + *chondr-* + *-al*] **:** occurring about or surrounding cartilage — used chiefly of bone and bone formation occurring peripherally beneath the perichondrium of a cartilage; compare ENDOCHONDRAL

peri·chon·dri·al \-drēəl\ *also* **peri·chon·dral** \-drəl\ *adj* [NL *perichondrium* + E *-al*] **:** of or relating to the perichondrium

peri·chon·dri·um \ˌperəˈkändrēəm\ *n, pl* **perichon·dria** \-ēə\ [NL, fr. *peri-* + *chondr-* + *-ium*] **:** the membrane of fibrous connective tissue investing a cartilage except at joints

peri·chord \ˈperəˌkȯrd\ *n* -S [*peri-* + *notochord*] **:** the sheath of the notochord — **peri·chord·al** \ˌ⁼⁼ˈkȯrdᵊl\ *adj*

peri·cho·re·sis \ˌperəkəˈrēsə̇s\ *n, pl* **perichore·ses** \-ēˌsēz\ [Gk *perichōrēsis* rotation, fr. *perichōrein* to go around, rotate (fr. *peri-* + *chōrein* to make room, give way) + *-sis* — more at ANCHORITE] **:** a doctrine of the reciprocal inherence of the human and divine natures of Christ in each other; *also* **:** CIRCUMINCESSION

peri·clase \ˈperəˌklās, -āz\ *or* **peri·cla·site** \ˌperəˈklāˌsīt, pəˈriklə|, |ˌzīt\ *n* -S [*periclase* fr. G *periklas*, modif. of It *periclasia*, fr. Gk *periklasis* act of twisting or breaking around (fr. *periklan* to twist around, break around — fr. *peri-* + *klan* to break — + *-sis*) + *-ia* -y (fr. L); *periclasite* fr. *periclase* + *-ite* — more at HALT (lame)] **:** native magnesia MgO in granular forms or isometric crystals (hardness 6, sp. gr. 3.67–3.90)

Per·i·cle·an \ˌperəˈklēən\ *adj, usu cap* [*Pericles* †429 B.C. Athenian statesman + E *-an*] **:** of or relating to Pericles or his age when Athens was at its highest material and intellectual state

peri·cli·nal \ˌperəˈklīnᵊl\ *adj* [Gk *periklinēs* sloping on all sides (fr. *peri-* + *-klinēs*, fr. *klinein* to lean, slope) + E *-al* — more at LEAN] **1 :** parallel to the surface or circumference of an organ — compare ANTICLINAL **2 :** QUAQUAVERSAL **3** *of a plant chimera* **:** having tissue of one kind completely surrounded by another kind — compare SECTORIAL — **peri·cli·nal·ly** \-ᵊlē\ *adv*

peri·cline \ˈperəˌklīn\ *n* -S [Gk *periklinēs*, adj., sloping on all sides] **1 :** a variety of albite occurring in white opaque crystals elongated in the direction of the macro-axis and often twinned with this axis as twinning axis **2 :** one of the layers making up a periclinal chimera **3 :** a periclinal cell wall

peri·clin·i·um \ˌperəˈklinēəm\ *n, pl* **periclin·ia** \-ēə\ [NL, fr. *peri-* + *clin-* + *-ium*] **:** the involucre of a composite plant

pe·ric·li·tate \pəˈrikləˌtāt\ *vb* -ED/-ING/-S [L *periclitatus*, past part. of *periclitari*, fr. *periclum*, *periculum* danger, trial — more at PERIL] *vt* **:** to expose or put in a perilous situation **:** IMPERIL ~ *vi* **:** to be in a perilous situation — **pe·ric·li·ta·tion** \pəˌrikləˈtāshən\ *n* -S

pe·ri·cón \ˌperəˈkōn\ *n, pl* **peri·co·nes** \-kō(ˌ)nās\ [AmerSp, prob. fr. Sp, large fan, aug. of *perico* parrakeet, large fan, dim. of the name *Pero*, alter. of *Pedro* (Peter)] **:** a group circle dance of the Uruguayan and Argentine pampas with shouting and rugged movements expressive of the gaucho

pe·ric·o·pal \pəˈrikəpəl\ *or* **peri·cop·ic** \ˌperəˈkäpik\ *adj* **:** of, relating to, or constituting a pericope

pe·ric·o·pe \pəˈrikə(ˌ)pē\ *n, pl* **pericopes** \-ēz\ *also* **pericopae** \-(ˌ)pē, -ˌpī\ [LL, section of a book, fr. Gk *perikopē* act of cutting around, section, fr. *peri-* + *kopē* action of cutting; akin to Gk *koptein* to smite, cut off — more at CAPON] **1 :** a selection or extract from a book; *esp* **:** a selection from the Bible appointed to be read in church or used as a text for a sermon **2** [Gk *perikopē* section (as in the phrase *kata perikopēn anomoiomerē* of unlike parts as far as the section is concerned — used to describe such a group of strophes)] *Greek & Latin prosody* **:** a group of strophes in choral lyric each of which has a different structure corresponding to another such group in which each will have similarly differentiated structures

peri·coronal \ˌperə+\ *adj* [*peri-* + *coronal*] **:** occurring about or surrounding the crown of a tooth ⟨~ infection⟩

peri·coronitis \"+\ *n, pl* **pericoronitides** [NL, fr. *peri-* + *coronitis*] **:** inflammation of the gum about the crown of an unerupted tooth

peri·crane \ˈperəˌkrān\ *n* -S [MF, fr. NL *pericraneum*, *pericranium*] *archaic* **:** PERICRANIUM

peri·cranial \ˌperə+\ *adj* [NL *pericranium* + E *-al*] **1 :** surrounding the head **2 :** of or relating to the pericranium

peri·cranium \ˌperə+\ *n, pl* **pericrania** [NL, fr. Gk *perikranion*, neut. of *perikranios* around the skull, fr. *peri-* + *kranion* skull — more at CRANIUM] **1 :** the external periosteum of the skull **2** *archaic* **:** the head or brain esp. as the seat of thought

per·i·cu \ˈperəˌkü\ *n, pl* **pericu** *or* **pericus** *usu cap* [Sp *pericú*, of AmerInd origin] **1 a :** an Indian people of southern Lower California, Mexico **b :** a member of such people **2 :** the language of the Pericu people

pe·ric·u·lous \pəˈrikyələs\ *adj* [L *periculosus*, fr. *periculum* danger + *-osus* -ous] **:** PERILOUS

peri·cycle \ˈperə+\ *n* [F *péricycle*, fr. Gk *perikyklos*, adj., spherical, extending all around, fr. *peri-* + *kyklos* circle, wheel — more at WHEEL] **:** a layer of parenchymatous or sclerenchymatous cells from one to a few cells thick and in some cases discontinuous that sheathes the stele esp. of the root of most vascular plants and in roots is associated with the formation of vascular cambium, phellogen, and lateral roots — called also *pericambium*

peri·cyclic \ˌperə+\ *adj* **:** relating to, consisting of, or located adjacent to or in the pericycle ⟨~ cell⟩ ⟨~ fiber⟩

peri·cyclone \ˌperə+\ *n* [*peri-* + *cyclone*] **:** the boundary line or ring of slightly rising pressure that usu. precedes and partly surrounds a cyclonic storm area — **peri·cyclonic** \"+\ *adj*

peri·cyst \ˈperəˌsist\ *n* [*peri-* + *cyst*] **:** the enclosing wall of fibrous tissue laid down by the host about various parasites (as a hydatid)

peri·cys·tic \ˌperəˈsistik\ *adj* [in sense 1, fr. *peri-* + *cystic*; in sense 2, fr. NL *pericystium* + E *-ic*] **1 :** occurring about or surrounding a cyst or bladder **2 :** of, relating to, or being a pericystium

peri·cys·ti·um \ˌperəˈsistēəm\ *n, pl* **pericys·tia** \-ēə\ [NL, fr. *peri-* + *cyst-* + *-ium*] **:** the vascular and connective tissues surrounding a cyst or bladder

peri·cyte \ˈperəˌsīt\ *n* -S [ISV *peri-* + *-cyte*] **:** an adventitious cell of the connective tissue about capillaries or other small blood vessels that is variously regarded as a macrophage or a contractile element

peri·cy·tial \ˌperəˈsīd·ēəl, -sish(ē)əl, -sid·ēəl\ *adj* [in sense 1, fr. *peri-* + *cyt-* + *-ial*; in sense 2 fr. *pericyte* + *-ial*] **1 :** situated around or enveloping a cell **2 :** of, relating to, or being a pericyte

peri·dental \ˌperə+\ *adj* [*peri-* + *dental*] **:** PERIODONTAL

peri·den·ti·tis \ˌperəˌdenˈtīd·əs\ *n* -ES [NL, fr. *peridentium* + *-itis*] **:** PERIODONTITIS

peri·den·ti·um \ˌperəˈdenchēəm, -ntēəm\ *n, pl* **periden·tia** \-ēə\ [NL, fr. *peri-* + *dent-* + *-ium*] **:** PERIODONTIUM

peri·derm \ˈperəˌdərm\ *n* -S [NL *peridermis*, fr. *peri-* + *-dermis*] **1 :** a protective layer of secondary tissue that develops first in the epidermis or subepidermal layers of many stems, roots, and other plant organs, is usu. continuous and followed by similar but only partial deeper-lying layers, and in full development consists of an initiating layer, an inner parenchymatous layer, and an outer cork layer — compare PHELLEM, PHELLODERM, PHELLOGEN **2 :** the perisarc of a hydroid **3 :** the outer layer of the epidermis of the skin esp. of an embryo — **peri·der·mal** \ˌ⁼⁼ˈdərməl\ *or* **peri·der·mic** \-mik\ *adj*

peri·der·mi·um \ˌ⁼⁼ˈdərmēəm\ *n, cap* [NL, fr. *peri-* + *derm-* + *-ium*] **:** a form genus of rust fungi having only the pycnial and aecial stages, characterized by the irregularly split or torn peridium, and formerly including many fungi that have since the discovery of their telial stages been placed in various other genera (as *Cronartium* and *Coleosporium*)

peri·desm \ˈperəˌdezəm\ *n* -S [ISV *peri-* + *-desm* (fr. Gk *desmē* bundle, fr. *dein* to bind — more at DIADEM] **:** the conjunctive tissue about a vascular bundle in astelic stems — **peri·des·mic** \ˌ⁼⁼ˈdezmik\ *adj*

pe·rid·i·al \pəˈridēəl\ *adj* [NL *peridium* + E *-al*] **:** of or relating to a peridium

peri·diastole \ˌperə+\ *n* [*peri-* + *diastole*] **:** the interval between the systole and the diastole of the heart

peri·did·y·mis \ˌperəˈdidəmə̇s\ *n, pl* **perididymi·des** \-ˈdidəməˌdēz, -ˌdə̇ˈdimə-, -ˌdīˈdimə-\ [NL, fr. *peri-* + *-didymis* (as in *epididymis*)] **:** the tunica albuginea of the testicle

pe·rid·i·i·form \pəˈridēəˌfȯrm\ *adj* [NL *peridium* + E *-iform*] **:** of the form of a peridium

peri·din·i·a·ce·ae \ˌperəˌdinēˈāsēˌē\ *n pl, cap* [NL, fr. *Peridinium*, type genus + *-aceae*] **:** a family of nearly unicellular algae (order Peridiniales) that was formerly nearly coextensive with the zoological family Peridiniidae but is now often restricted to *Peridinium* and a few closely related marine forms — **peri·din·i·a·ceous** \ˌ⁼⁼ˌ⁼⁼ˈāshəs\ *adj*

peri·din·i·a·les \ˌ⁼⁼ˌ⁼⁼ˈā(ˌ)lēz\ *n pl, cap* [NL, fr. *Peridinium* + *-ales*] **:** an order of algae (class Dinophyceae) that is coextensive with or somewhat more inclusive than the zoological family Peridiniidae

¹peri·din·i·an \ˌ⁼⁼ˈdinēən\ *or* **peri·din·i·al** \-inēəl\ *adj* [NL *Peridinium* + E *-an* or *-al*] **:** of or relating to the Peridiniidae

²peridinian \"\ *n* -S **:** a dinoflagellate of the family Peridiniidae; *broadly* **:** DINOFLAGELLATE

peri·di·ni·idae \ˌperədə̇ˈnīəˌdē\ *n pl, cap* [NL, fr. *Peridinium*, type genus + *-idae*] **:** a family of marine and freshwater dinoflagellates that have a thick test composed of plates and well-marked flagellar grooves — compare CERATIUM, GONYAULAX, PERIDINIACEAE

peri·din·i·um \ˌperəˈdinēəm\ *n* [NL, fr. Gk *peridinēs* whirled around (fr. *peridinein* to whirl around, fr. *peri-* + *dinein* to whirl, rotate) + NL *-ium*; akin to Gk *dinos* rotation, whirling — more at DINO-] **1** *cap* **:** the type genus of Peridiniidae comprising marine and freshwater dinoflagellates that are typically subspherical to ovoid in outline and that sometimes have the test prolonged into short horns — compare CERATIUM **2** *pl* **peridiniums** \-ēəmz\ *or* **peridinia** \-ēə\ **:** any flagellate of the genus *Peridinium*

pe·rid·i·ole \pəˈridēˌōl\ *n* -S [NL *peridiolum*, dim. of *peridium*] **:** any of the lenticular bodies situated either free or attached within the peridium of fungi of the family Nidulariaceae and containing the spores

pe·rid·i·o·lum \⁼ˌ⁼⁼ˈōləm\ *n, pl* **peridio·la** \-lə\ [NL] **:** PERIDIOLE

pe·rid·i·um \pəˈridēəm\ *n, pl* **perid·ia** \-ēə\ *also* **peridiums** [NL, fr. Gk *pēridion* small leather bag, dim. of *pēra* leather bag, wallet] **:** the outer envelope of the sporophore of many fungi: as **a :** the tough often two-layered cortical investment of the gleba of a gasteromycete **b :** the layer of sterile hyphae that surrounds an aecium of a rust fungus

per·i·dot \ˈperəˌdō, -dät\ *n* -S [F *péridot*, fr. OF *peritot*] **1** *also* **per·i·dote** \-dōt\ **:** a deep yellowish green transparent variety of olivine used as a gem **2 :** WOODBINE GREEN

per·i·dot·ic \ˌperəˈdäd·ik\ *adj* [F *péridotique*, fr. *péridot* + *-ique* -ic] **:** of or relating to peridot

pe·rid·o·tite \pəˈridəˌtīt\ *n* -S [F *péridotite*, fr. *péridot* + *-ite*] **:** any of a group of granitoid igneous rocks composed of olivine and usu. other ferromagnesian minerals but with little or no feldspar and usu. occurring in dikes or small intrusive bodies — **pe·rid·o·tit·ic** \⁼ˌ⁼⁼ˈtid·ik\ *adj*

peri·dural \ˌperə+\ *adj* [*peri-* + *dural*] **:** occurring or applied about the dura mater — used chiefly of anesthesia in which the anesthetic agent is injected along the spinal column so as to act on spinal nerves as they emerge from the dura

peri·ege·sis \ˌperēəˈjēsə̇s\ *n, pl* **periege·ses** \-ēˌsēz\ [LL, fr. Gk *periēgēsis* act of leading or showing around, geographical description, fr. *periēgeisthai* to show around, describe, fr. *peri-* + *hēgeisthai* to lead — more at SEEK] **:** a description of a region ⟨a ~ of the Italian peninsula⟩

peri·enteric \ˌperē+\ *adj* [in sense 1, fr. *peri-* + *enteric*; in sense 2, fr. NL *peri enteron* + E *-ic*] **1 :** around the intestine **2 :** of or relating to the perienteron

peri·enteron \ˌperē+\ *n* [NL, fr. *peri-* + *enteron*] **:** the space between the inner and outer gastrular walls of an embryo **:** the primitive body cavity — distinguished from *archenteron*

peri·focal \ˌperə+\ *adj* [ISV *peri-* + *focal*] **:** occurring about or surrounding a focus ⟨~ proliferation of fibroblasts⟩

peri·follicular \"+\ *adj* [*peri-* + *follicular*] **:** occurring about or surrounding a follicle

peri·ge·an \ˌperəˈjēən\ *also* **peri·ge·al** \-ēəl\ *adj* [*perigee* + *-an* or *-al*] **:** of or relating to perigee

perigean tide *n* **:** any of the spring tides that occur soon after the moon passes her perigee

peri·gee \ˈperə(ˌ)jē, -əjē\ *n* -S [MF & NL; MF, fr. NL *perigaeum*, *perigeum*, fr. Gk *perigeion*, fr. neut. of *perigeios* near the earth, fr. *peri-* + *-geios* (fr. *gē* earth)] **:** the point in the orbit of a satellite (as the moon or an artificial body) of the earth that is nearest to the center of the earth — opposed to *apogee*; compare APSIS, PERICENTER, PERIHELION

peri·glacial \ˌperə+\ *adj* [ISV *peri-* + *glacial*] **:** of or relating to the area marginal to a frozen or ice-covered region (as an ice sheet or glacier) esp. with respect to its climate or the influence of its climate upon geological processes ⟨~ topography⟩ ⟨~ weathering⟩ ⟨~ wind action —*Jour. of Geol.*⟩

peri·gloea \ˌperəˈglēə\ *n* [NL, fr. *peri-* + *gloea*] **:** the gelatinous covering of a diatom

peri·glottis \ˌperə+\ *n* [Gk *periglōttis*, fr. *peri-* + *glōttis* glottis — more at GLOTTIS] **:** the mucous membrane covering the tongue

peri·gon \ˈperəˌgän\ *n* -S [*peri-* + *-gon*] **:** an angle obtained by rotating a half line in the same plane once around the point from which it extends

peri·gone \-gōn\ *n* -S [F & NL; F *périgone*, fr. NL *perigonium*] **:** PERIGONIUM

peri·go·ni·al \¦==¦gōnēəl\ *or* **peri·go·nal** \¦==¦gōnᵊl, pə'rigən-\ *adj* [NL *perigonium* + E *-ial* or *-al*] **:** of or relating to a perigonium

peri·go·ni·um \,perə'gōnēəm\ *n, pl* **perigo·nia** \-ēə\ [NL, fr. *peri-* + *gon-* + *-ium*] **1 :** a perianth esp. of a liverwort — compare PERICHAETIUM **2 :** a sac surrounding the generative bodies in the gonophore of a hydroid

per·i·gor·di·an \¦perə¦gȯ(r)dēən\ *adj, usu cap* [*Périgord*, region in southwestern France + E *-ian*] **:** of or belonging to a Paleolithic culture epoch of western Europe including the Châterperronian and Gravettian phases and characterized by narrow pointed flint knife blades and the art of Lascaux Cave

peri·gyn·i·al \¦perə¦jinēəl, -¦gi-\ *adj* [NL *perigynium* + E *-al*] **:** of or relating to the perigynium

peri·gyn·i·um \¦==¦=nēəm\ *n, pl* **perigyn·ia** \-ēə\ [NL, fr. *peri-* + *-gynium* (fr. Gk *gynē* woman, wife, pistil + NL *-ium*) — more at QUEEN] **1 :** a fleshy cup or tube that surrounds the archegonium of various bryophytes (as of the liverwort group) and that is formed either from the stem apex or from the thallus **2 :** the saclike bract that subtends the pistillate flower of sedges of the genus *Carex* and that in fruit becomes a flask-shaped envelope investing the achene

pe·rig·y·nous \pə'rijənəs\ *adj* [NL *perigynus*, fr. *peri-* + *-gynus* -gynous] **1 :** borne on a ring or cup of the receptacle surrounding a pistil ⟨~ petals⟩ ⟨~ stamens⟩ **2 :** having stamens and petals borne on a ring or cup of the receptacle surrounding a pistil and usu. adnate to the calyx although appearing to be situated upon it — compare EPIGYNOUS

pe·rig·y·ny \-nē\ *n* -ES [*peri-* + *-gyny*] **:** the quality or state of being perigynous

peri·he·li·al \¦perə¦hēlēəl\ *adj* [NL *perihelion* + E *-al*] **:** of or relating to perihelion

peri·he·lion \¦perə¦hēlyən, -lēən\ *n* -S [NL *perihelium, perihelion*, fr. *peri-* + *-helium, -helion* (fr. Gk *hēlios* sun) — more at SOLAR] **:** periastron in the solar system **:** the point in the path of a planet, comet, meteor, artificial planetoid, passing star, or other celestial body that is nearest to the sun — opposed to *aphelion*; compare APSIS, PERICENTER, PERIGEE; see APHELION illustration

peri·hepatitis \¦perə+\ *n* [NL, fr. *peri-* + *hepatitis*] **:** inflammation of the peritoneal capsule of the liver

peri·jove \'perə,jōv\ *n* -S [F *périjove*, fr. *péri-* peri- (fr. Gk *peri-*) + *Jove* (Jupiter), 5th planet from the sun] **:** the point in the orbit of a satellite of Jupiter nearest the planet's center — compare APOJOVE

peri·kar·y·al \¦perə¦karēəl\ *adj* [NL *perikaryon* + E *-al*] **:** of or relating to a perikaryon

peri·karyon \¦perə+\ *also* **pericaryon** \"\ *n, pl* **perikarya** [NL, fr. *peri-* + Gk *karyon* nut, kernel — more at CAREEN] **:** the cytoplasmic body of a nerve cell

[1]**per·il** \'perəl *sometimes* -(,)ril\ *n* -S [ME, fr. OF, fr. L *periculum, periclum* trial, attempt, danger — more at FEAR] **1 :** the situation or state of being in imminent or fearful danger **:** exposure (as of one's person, property, health, or morals) to the risk of being injured, destroyed, or lost **:** a position of jeopardy ⟨in constant ~ of death⟩ ⟨a time of moral ~⟩ **2 a :** something that imperils **:** a source of danger or possible cause of loss **:** RISK ⟨to lessen the ~*s* of the streets⟩ ⟨the ~*s* of a turgid rhetoric —Van Wyck Brooks⟩ ⟨a ~ is marine if it threatens a waterborne vessel —H.L.Haehl⟩ **b :** conduct subjecting one to possible civil or criminal liabilities **3** *archaic* **:** risk of incurring a penalty or of suffering unhappy consequences in saying or doing something that is prohibited — used as an imprecation ⟨by my soul's ~⟩ ⟨that I speak the truth, my ~ be my proof —Lord Byron⟩ **syn** see DANGER — **at one's peril :** being responsible for any harmful or destructive consequences ⟨a new order in party politics, which party leaders will disregard *at their peril* —A.N.Holcombe⟩ ⟨a person who uses fire is bound to keep it under control *at his peril* —F.D.Smith & Barbara Wilcox⟩

[2]**peril** \"\ *vt* **periled** *also* **perilled; periled** *also* **perilled; periling** *also* **perilling; perils :** to expose to danger **:** HAZARD, RISK ⟨and ~*ed* his life daily to find out what would happen if you pulled a Mountain Baltery mule's tail—Rudyard Kipling⟩

peri·lampidae \,perə'lampə,dē\ *n pl, cap* [NL, fr. *Perilampus*, type genus (fr. Gk *perilampein* to shine around, fr. *peri-* + *lampein* to give light, shine) + *-idae* — more at LAMP] **:** a small family of Hymenoptera comprising insects that are mostly secondary parasites on other insects (as of the orders Diptera and Hymenoptera)

pe·ril·la \pə'rilə\ *n, cap* [NL, perh. dim. of *pera* leather bag, wallet, fr. Gk *pēra*] **:** a genus of Asiatic mints having four didynamous stamens, a bilabiate fruiting calyx, and rugose nutlets — see BEEFSTEAK PLANT

per·ill·aldehyde \¦perəl+\ *n* [*perilla* (*oil*) + *aldehyde*] **:** a liquid compound $C_3H_5C_6H_8CHO$ found esp. in the essential oil of an Asiatic mint (*Perilla frutescens* var. *nankinensis*) and yielding an *anti*-oxime that is about 2000 times sweeter than sucrose; 4-isopropenyl-3,4,5,6-tetrahydro-benzaldehyde

perilla oil *n* **:** a light yellow drying oil obtained from the seeds of mints of the genus *Perilla* and used chiefly in varnish, printing ink, and linoleum and in the Orient as an edible oil

perilla purple *n* **:** a dark purplish red that is paler and slightly bluer than pansy purple, redder and paler than raisin, and bluer and paler than Bokhara

per·il·less \'perəlləs *sometimes* -(,)rill-\ *adj* **:** free from peril

per·il·ous \'perələs *sometimes* -eril-\ *adj* [ME, fr. OF *perilleus*, fr. L *periculosus*, fr. *periculum* danger + *-osus* -ous — more at FEAR] **1 :** full of, attended with, or involving peril **:** beset by perils **:** HAZARDOUS ⟨perpetual struggle for the preservation of a ~ and precarious existence —T.L.Peacock⟩ ⟨feel that ~ fascination which haunts the brow of precipices —Nathaniel Hawthorne⟩ ⟨if crossing the parkway was ~ for them on weekends, it was risky at all times —E.J.Kahn⟩ **2 :** capable of inflicting harm or injury **:** DREADFUL ⟨foam of ~ seas —John Keats⟩ ⟨a ~ stone cliff high above the river —*Amer. Guide Series: Pa.*⟩ **3 :** subject to the possibility of destruction, damage, loss, or grave change at any moment ⟨never lose a sense of the whimsical and ~ charm of daily life —L.P. Smith⟩ ⟨old man who trots along under a ~ tower of painted straw chairs —Gertrude Diamant⟩ **syn** see DANGEROUS

per·il·ous·ly *adv* [ME, fr. *perilous* + *-ly*] **:** in a manner or to a degree involving peril ⟨~ close to defeat⟩

per·il·ous·ness *n* -ES **:** the quality or state of being perilous

peril point *n* **:** the rate in tariff legislation at or below which imports of a commodity reach a volume that endangers business or employment

perils of the sea : perils resulting from dangers peculiar to sea navigation **:** MARINE PERILS; *specif* **:** perils to a ship or her cargo causing damage to or loss of ship or cargo in the course of navigation on the high seas or navigable waters that in admiralty law is not attributable to latent defects in ship or cargo, to an unseaworthy ship, or to unskillful seamanship

perils of war : the war hazards specif. assumed under a policy of insurance

peri·lymph \'perə+,-\ *n* [ISV *peri-* + *lymph*] **:** the fluid between the membranous and bony labyrinths of the ear — compare ENDOLYMPH

peri·lymphatic \¦perə+\ *adj* [*perilymph* + *-atic* (as in *lymphatic*)] **:** relating to or containing perilymph

perimedullary zone \¦perə+...-\ *n* [ISV *peri-* + *medullary*] **:** MEDULLARY SHEATH

pe·rim·e·ter \pə'rimәd·ə(r)\ *n* -S *often attrib* [F *périmètre*, fr. L *perimetros*, fr. Gk, fr. *peri-* + *metron* measure — more at MEASURE] **1 a** (1) **:** the boundary of a closed plane figure ⟨the ~ of a circle⟩ (2) **:** the measure of the boundary of a closed plane figure; *specif* **:** the sum of the lengths of the line segments forming a polygon **b :** a line or strip bounding or protecting an area ⟨small cities on the ~ of the reservation —Zdenek Salzmann⟩ ⟨digging in behind a barbed-wire ~ with antitank guns —Barrett McGurn⟩ ⟨the ~ of a shopping district⟩ **c :** outer limits ⟨criticism which attempts to bring to literature insights found outside its ~ —C.W.Shumaker⟩ ⟨the ~ of possible excursions was reduced —André Maurois⟩ ⟨House of Representatives report described the ~ of the legislation —*U. S. Code*⟩ **2 a :** an instrument for examining the discriminative powers of different parts of the retina often consisting of an adjustable semicircular arm with a fixation point for the eye and variable stations for the visual stimuli **b :** a similar instrument used in studying auditory space perception — **peri·met·ric** \¦perə¦me·trik\ *or* **peri·met·ri·cal** \-·trəkəl\ *adj* — **peri·met·ri·cal·ly** \-·trək(ə)lē\ *adv* — **pe·rim·e·try** \pə'rimə·trē\ *n* -ES

peri·me·tri·um \,perə'mē·trēəm\ *n, pl* **perime·tria** \-·trēə\ [NL, fr. *peri-* + *-metrium*] **:** the peritoneum covering the fundus and ventral and dorsal aspects of the uterus

peri·morph \'perə,mȯrf\ *n* [ISV *peri-* + *-morph*] **:** a crystal of one species enclosing one of another species

per im·pos·si·bi·le \¦pe,rimpə'sibə,lā, ¦pər-,impə'sibə(,)lē\ *adv* [L, lit., through the impossible] **:** as is impossible ⟨if, *per impossibile*, stones could reason⟩

peri·my·si·al \¦perə¦miz(h)ēəl\ *adj* [NL *perimysium* + E *-al*] **:** of, relating to, or being perimysium

peri·my·si·um \¦==¦miz(h)ēəm\ *n, pl* **perimy·sia** \-ēə\ [NL, irreg. fr. *peri-* + Gk *mys* mouse, muscle + NL *-ium* — more at MOUSE] **:** the connective-tissue sheath that surrounds a muscle and sends partitions inward which form sheaths for the bundles of muscle fibers; *often* **:** the portion sheathing the bundles — distinguished from *epimysium*

peri·natal \¦perə+\ *adj* [ISV *peri-* + *natal*] **:** occurring at about the time of birth ⟨~ mortality⟩

per·ine \'pe,rēn, -rīn\ *n* -S [prob. fr. G, fr. NL *perinium*] **:** PERINIUM

per·i·ne·al \¦perə¦nēəl\ *adj* [NL *perineum* + E *-al*] **:** of or relating to the perineum

perineo- *comb form* [NL *perineum*] **1 :** perineum ⟨*perineo*cele⟩ ⟨*perineo*plasty⟩ ⟨*perineo*tomy⟩ **2 :** perineum and ⟨*perineo*-vaginal⟩

per·i·ne·or·rha·phy \,perənē'ȯrəfē\ *n* -ES [ISV *perineo-* + *-rrhaphy*] **:** suture of the perineum usu. to repair a laceration occurring during labor

peri·nephric \¦perə+\ *adj* [NL *perinephrium* + E *-ic*] **1 :** of or relating to the perinephrium **2 :** occurring about or surrounding the kidney

peri·nephritic \"+\ *adj* [ISV *perinephrit-* (fr. NL *perinephritis*) + *-ic*] **:** PERINEPHRIC; *also* **:** of or affected with perinephritis

peri·nephritis \"+\ *n* [NL, fr. *perinephrium* + *-itis*] **:** inflammation of the perinephric tissue

peri·neph·ri·um \,perə'nefrēəm\ *n, pl* **perineph·ria** \-ēə\ [NL, fr. Gk *perinephros* fat about the kidneys (fr. *peri-* + *nephros* kidney) + NL *-ium* — more at NEPHRITIS] **:** the capsule of connective and fatty tissue about the kidney

per·i·ne·um *also* **per·i·nae·um** \,perə'nēəm\ *n, pl* **per·i·nea** \-ēə\ [NL, fr. LL *perinaion, perineon*, fr. Gk *perinaion, perineos*, fr. *peri-* + *-inaion, -ineos* (fr. *inan, inein* to empty out, defecate) — more at IRE] **:** an area of tissue marking externally the approximate boundary of the outlet of the pelvis and as usu. demarked giving passage to the urinogenital ducts and the rectum; *sometimes* **:** the area between the anus and the posterior part of the external genitalia esp. in the female

peri·neural \¦perə+\ *adj* [ISV *peri-* + *neural*] **:** occurring about or surrounding nervous tissue or nerves

peri·neu·ri·al \¦perə¦nyu̇rēəl\ *adj* [NL *perineurium* + E *-al*] **1 :** of or relating to perineurium **2 :** PERINEURAL

peri·neu·ri·um \,perə'nyu̇rēəm\ *n, pl* **perineu·ria** \-ēə\ [NL, fr. *peri-* + *neur-* + *-ium*] **:** the connective-tissue sheath that surrounds a bundle of nerve fibers

pe·rin·i·um \pə'rinēəm\ *n, pl* **perin·ia** \-ēə\ [NL, fr. *peri-* + *ᵊin-* + *-ium*] **:** the sculptured outer coat of a pollen grain

peri·ocular \¦perē+\ *adj* [*peri-* + *ocular*] **:** surrounding the eyeball but within the orbit ⟨~ space⟩

[1]**pe·ri·od** \'pirēəd, 'pēr-\ *n* -S [ME *pariode*, fr. MF *periode*, fr.

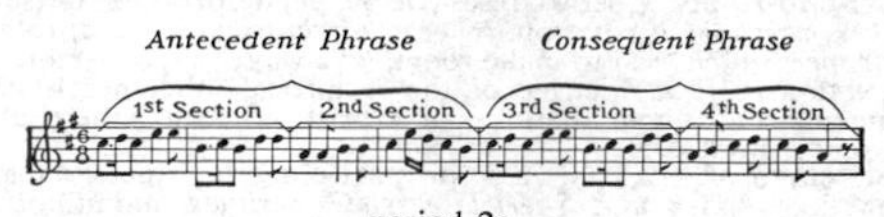

period 2c

ML, L, & Gk; ML *periodus* period of time, punctuation mark, fr. L & Gk; L, rhetorical period, fr. Gk *periodos* way around, circuit, period of time, rhetorical period, fr. *peri-* + *hodos* way, journey — more at CEDE] **1 a** *obs* **:** customary or ordained length of existence **:** LIFETIME ⟨make plants more lasting than their ordinary ~ —Francis Bacon⟩ **b :** the half-life of a radioactive element **2 a :** an utterance from one full stop to another **:** SENTENCE; *esp* **:** a well-proportioned sentence of several clauses ⟨rounded ~*s*⟩ ⟨stately ~*s*⟩ **b :** PERIODIC SENTENCE **c :** a musical structure or melodic section usu. of eight or sixteen measures and of two or more contrasting or complementary phrases and ending with a cadence **3 a :** the full pause with which the utterance of a sentence closes **b :** a point of time marking a termination of a course or an action **:** END, STOP, CESSATION ⟨progress . . . towards the perfection of nature without arriving at a ~ in it —S.F.Mason⟩ ⟨worries, together with . . . disease put a ~ to his honorable life —C.G.Bowers⟩ **4 a** *obs* **:** final outcome **:** CONSUMMATION **b** *obs* **:** the goal of an action or a journey **c** *obs* **:** a particular point in a progress **:** MOMENT, OCCASION **d** *obs* **:** the highest point **:** CULMINATION **e :** PERORATION ⟨to hear the admiral's ~ to the piece —Lee Rogow⟩ **5 a :** a point . used to mark the end of a declarative sentence, the end of an abbreviation (as *Eng., Mr.*), or the end of a paragraph heading or outline heading — often used interjectionally at the end of a statement to indicate and emphasize that the statement is finished and complete without further qualification or discussion ⟨private profit by public servants at the expense of the general welfare is corrupt, ~ —Estes Kefauver⟩ ⟨conclusion that we fought the war to win, ~ —H.W.Baldwin⟩ ⟨not just unlucky in love, but unlucky, ~⟩ **b :** a division of time in a rhythmic series **:** a temporal unit of measure; *specif* **:** a rhythmical unit in Greek verse composed of a series of two or more cola **6 :** the completion of a cycle, a series of events, or a single action **:** CONCLUSION ⟨certain cheeses . . . serve as a brilliant ~ for a gay, well-ordered meal —*This Week Mag.*⟩ **7 a :** a portion of time determined by some recurring phenomenon **:** a division of time in which something is completed and ready to commence and go on in the same order ⟨~ of the earth's orbit⟩ ⟨~ of a flashing beacon⟩ **b :** the interval of time required for a cyclic motion or phenomenon to complete a cycle and begin to repeat itself ⟨the ~ of a pendulum⟩ ⟨~ of an alternating current⟩ being equal to one divided by the frequency **c :** a single cyclic occurrence of menstruation — called also *menstrual period* **8 a :** a chronological division (as of a life, a development) **:** STAGE ⟨~ of infancy⟩ ⟨~ of preparation and training⟩ ⟨~ of incubation of a disease⟩ **b :** an extent of time that is an epoch or era in the history of civilization ⟨the Reformation ~⟩ ⟨art in the Victorian ~⟩ ⟨furniture of the Empire ~⟩ **c :** a time often of indefinite length but of distinctive or specified character **:** SPELL ⟨~ of laziness⟩ ⟨~*s* of anxiety⟩ ⟨a ~ of wet weather⟩ ⟨~*s* of rising prices⟩ **d :** a division of geologic time longer than an epoch and included in an era **e :** a stage of culture having a definable place in time and space; *specif* **:** the length of time a pottery style is maintained in a certain area **9 :** a number *k* that does not change the value of a periodic function *f* when added to the independent variable: $f(x+k)=f(x)$; *esp* **:** the smallest such number **10 :** a sequence of elements of increasing atomic numbers as represented usu. in horizontal rows in the periodic table from one inert gas to the next and that may be short (as from helium through fluorine or from neon through chlorine) or long (as from argon through bromine) **11 a :** one of the divisions of the academic day **:** the time appointed for a recitation or lecture or for study, physical training, luncheon, assembly, or other activity **:** a class hour **b :** one of the portions usu. of equal duration into which the playing time of a game (as hockey, polo) is divided

syn EPOCH, ERA, AGE, AEON: PERIOD, the most general of these terms, can designate any extent of time ⟨a *period* of a few seconds⟩ ⟨the *period* of five thousand years prior to recorded history⟩ EPOCH often designates the beginning of a period, esp. a striking or remarkable beginning ⟨this is an *epoch* . . . the end and the beginning of an age —H.G.Wells⟩, but more often designates a period set off by some significant or striking quality, event, or series of related events ⟨an *epoch* in the annals of printing —*Encyc. Americana*⟩ ⟨the Renaissance *epoch* —G.C.Sellery⟩ ERA, often interchangeable with EPOCH in its more frequent meaning, is a period, usu. of history, marked by some new or characterizable order of things ⟨the Victorian *era*⟩ ⟨the Christian *era*⟩ ⟨an *era* of singular crisis and upheaval —J.W.Aldridge⟩ AGE, usu. interchangeable with but possibly more definite than ERA, is used frequently of a period dominated by a central figure or clearly marked feature ⟨the atomic *age*⟩ ⟨the *age* of Shakespeare⟩ ⟨the *age* of Reason⟩ AEON is an immeasurable or indefinitely long period ⟨Mars is a planet which has rusted away, its oxygen having been used up *aeons* ago —J.G.Vaeth⟩ ⟨the hour of waiting seemed an *aeon* to the impatient child⟩

[2]**period** \"\ *adj* **1 :** relating or belonging to an historical period **:** deriving from or fashioned after the style prevalent in a particular period ⟨~ furniture⟩ ⟨~ costume⟩ **2 :** representing realistically a particular historical period; *esp* **:** depending largely on evocation of a period for effect ⟨~ play⟩ ⟨~ novel⟩ ⟨an amusing ~ study of manners —*Time*⟩ ⟨~ film⟩

per·iodate \¦pər, (')per+\ *n* -S [ISV *periodic* (*acid*) + *-ate*] **:** a salt of a periodic acid

pe·ri·od·ic \¦pirē¦ädik, ¦pēr-, -dēk\ *adj* [F *périodique*, fr. L *periodicus*, fr. Gk *periodikos*, fr. *periodos* period + *-ikos* -ic — more at PERIOD] **1 a :** characterized by periods **:** occurring at regular intervals ⟨~ phases of the moon⟩ ⟨~ municipal elections⟩ **b :** occurring repeatedly from time to time **:** RECURRENT, INTERMITTENT ⟨~ epidemics⟩ ⟨~ drinking sprees⟩ **:** FREQUENT ⟨one of Bermuda's ~ power failures —*Time*⟩ **2 :** consisting of a series of stages or processes that is regularly repeated **:** CYCLIC ⟨~ vibration⟩ **3 :** of or relating to a period ⟨house was pleasant and comfortable, they were too sophisticated to be ~ —*Scribner's*⟩ **4 a :** of or relating to a form of construction found in some Greek odes in which the second and third in a group of four strophes are alike in structure and the first and fourth differ from these and from each other **b :** expressed in or characterized by periodic sentences ⟨~ style⟩

per·iod·ic acid \¦pər-|,ī¦ädik-, ¦per|\ *n* [ISV *per-* + *iodic*] **:** any of a series of strongly oxidizing acids that are the highest oxygen acids of iodine and may be regarded as derived from a hypothetical iodine heptoxide I_2O_7 by union with varying amounts of water: as **a :** a hygroscopic crystalline acid H_5IO_6 obtainable by electrolytic oxidation of iodic acid — called also *orthoperiodic acid, paraperiodic acid* **b :** an unstable acid HIO_4 that forms stable salts and is obtained as a white residue by dehydration of orthoperiodic acid by heat — called also *metaperiodic acid*

[1]**pe·ri·od·i·cal** \¦pirē¦ädəkəl, ¦pēr-, -dēk-\ *adj* [L *periodicus* + E *-al*] **1 :** PERIODIC 1 ⟨when the bookmobile pulls in for its ~ call —*Saturday Rev.*⟩ **2 a :** published with a fixed interval usu. longer than a day between the issues or numbers ⟨newspapers and ~ publications⟩ ⟨keeping up with the ~ literature on the arts⟩ **b :** published in, characteristic of, or connected with a periodical ⟨~ book reviews⟩ ⟨~ room in a library⟩

[2]**periodical** \"\ *n* -S **:** a magazine or other publication of which the issues appear at stated or regular intervals — usu. used of a publication appearing more frequently than annually but infrequently used of a newspaper

periodical cicada *n* **:** SEVENTEEN-YEAR LOCUST

pe·ri·od·i·cal·ly \¦pirē¦ädək(ə)lē, -dēk-, -li\ *adv* **1 :** at regular intervals of time **2 :** from time to time **:** RECURRENTLY, FREQUENTLY

PERIODIC TABLE

This is a common long form of the table. Roman numerals and letters heading the vertical columns indicate the groups (there are differences of opinion regarding the letter designations, those given here being probably the most generally used). The horizontal rows represent the periods, with two series removed from the two very long periods and represented below the main table. Atomic numbers are given above the symbols for the elements, and atomic weights or (in square brackets) mass numbers of the isotopes of longest known half-life are given below the symbols. Compare ELEMENT table

IA	IIA	IIIB	IVB	VB	VIB	VIIB	VIII	VIII	VIII	IB	IIB	IIIA	IVA	VA	VIA	VIIA	Zero
1 H 1.008																1 H 1.008	2 He 4.003
3 Li 6.940	4 Be 9.013											5 B 10.82	6 C 12.011	7 N 14.008	8 O 16.000	9 F 19.00	10 Ne 20.183
11 Na 22.991	12 Mg 24.32											13 Al 26.98	14 Si 28.09	15 P 30.975	16 S 32.066	17 Cl 35.457	18 Ar 39.944
19 K 39.100	20 Ca 40.08	21 Sc 44.96	22 Ti 47.90	23 V 50.95	24 Cr 52.01	25 Mn 54.94	26 Fe 55.85	27 Co 58.94	28 Ni 58.71	29 Cu 63.54	30 Zn 65.38	31 Ga 69.72	32 Ge 72.60	33 As 74.91	34 Se 78.96	35 Br 79.916	36 Kr 83.80
37 Rb 85.48	38 Sr 87.63	39 Y 88.92	40 Zr 91.22	41 Nb 92.91	42 Mo 95.95	43 Tc [99]	44 Ru 101.1	45 Rh 102.91	46 Pd 106.4	47 Ag 107.88	48 Cd 112.41	49 In 114.82	50 Sn 118.70	51 Sb 121.76	52 Te 127.61	53 I 126.91	54 Xe 131.30
55 Cs 132.91	56 Ba 137.36	57 *La 138.92	72 Hf 178.50	73 Ta 180.95	74 W 183.86	75 Re 186.22	76 Os 190.2	77 Ir 192.2	78 Pt 195.09	79 Au 197.0	80 Hg 200.61	81 Tl 204.39	82 Pb 207.21	83 Bi 209.00	84 Po 210	85 At [210]	86 Rn 222
87 Fr [223]	88 Ra 226.05	89 #Ac 227															

Series														
*LANTHANIDE SERIES	58 Ce 140.13	59 Pr 140.92	60 Nd 144.27	61 Pm [145]	62 Sm 150.35	63 Eu 152.0	64 Gd 157.26	65 Tb 158.93	66 Dy 162.51	67 Ho 164.94	68 Er 167.27	69 Tm 168.94	70 Yb 173.04	71 Lu 174.99
#ACTINIDE SERIES	90 Th 232.05	91 Pa 231	92 U 238.07	93 Np [237]	94 Pu [244]	95 Am [243]	96 Cm [248]	97 Bk [247]	98 Cf [251]	99 Es [254]	100 Fm [253]	101 Md [256]	102 No [253]	

pe·ri·od·i·cal·ness \ˌ⸗⸗ˈädəkəlnəs, -dēk-\ *n* -ES : PERIODICITY
periodical year *n* : ANOMALISTIC YEAR
periodic comet *n* : a comet that moves about the sun in a closed orbit
periodic current *n* **1** : an electric current whose strength or direction varies periodically **2** : a current caused by the tide-producing forces of moon and sun
periodic curve *n* : a curve formed by the continued repetition of some part of itself : the graph of a periodic function
periodic decimal *n* : REPEATING DECIMAL
periodic function *n* : a function any value of which recurs at regular intervals
pe·ri·o·dic·i·ty \ˌpirēəˈdisəd·ē, ˌpēr-, -sətē, -i\ *n* -ES [F *périodicité*, fr. L *periodicus* + F *-ité* -ity] : the quality, state, or fact of being regularly recurrent: as **a** : the tendency of a plant to exhibit rhythmical changes in such vital functions as nyctitropic movements, root pressure, flowering, and fruiting **b** : the position of an element in the periodic table **c** : electrical frequency
periodic key *n* : a cryptographic keying sequence consisting of a repeated series
periodic kiln *n* : a kiln operated in periods or cycles of loading, firing, cooling, and drawing ware
periodic law *n* **1** : a law in chemistry according to Mendeléeff: the physical and chemical properties of the elements are periodic functions of their atomic weights **2** : a law in chemistry: the physical and chemical properties of the elements are dependent on the structure of the atom and are for the most part periodic functions of the atomic numbers
periodic motion *n* : a recurrent motion in which the intervals of time required to complete each cycle are equal
periodic ophthalmia *n* : ophthalmia that recurs at approximately regular intervals; *specif* : moon blindness of the horse
periodic sentence *n* : a usu. complex sentence in which the principal clause comes last or which has no subordinate or trailing elements following full grammatical statement of the essential idea (as in "yesterday while I was walking down the street, I saw him") — compare LOOSE SENTENCE
periodic table *n* : an arrangement of chemical elements based on the periodic law and proposed in various forms that are usu. either short with only short periods (as in Mendeléeff's original table) or long with long as well as short periods (as in most modern tables) *(see previous page for table)*
per·iodide \ˌpər·, (ˈ)per+\ *n* [*per-* + *iodide*] : an iodide containing a relatively high proportion of iodine ⟨potassium ~ KI_3⟩
pe·ri·od·iza·tion \ˌpirēədəˈzāshən, ˌpēr-, -ˌdīˈz-\ *n* -S : division of history in periods ⟨the easy ~ of history into ancient, medieval, and modern —Herbert Weisinger⟩ ⟨a ~ of the material which permits the author to convey a sense of continuity —K.W.Kapp⟩
period key *n* : the set of cryptographic key details which are kept unchanged during an agreed time — compare SPECIFIC KEY
period-luminosity law *n* : a law in astronomy: the period of light variation of a Cepheid variable is in direct relation with its absolute magnitude whereby intrinsically fainter stars have the shorter periods
period of reverberation : REVERBERATION TIME
pe·ri·od·ogram \ˌpirēˈädəˌgram, ˈpirēədə-\ *n* [ISV ¹*period* + *-o-* + *-gram*] : a curve exhibiting graphically the periodicity of any natural or physical phenomenon
pe·ri·od·o·graph \-ˌraf, -ˌrȧf\ *n* [ISV ¹*period* + *-o-* + *-graph*] : HARMONIC ANALYZER
peri·odon·tal \ˌperēōˈdäntᵊl\ *adj* [*peri-* + *odont-* + *-al*] **1** : investing or surrounding a tooth : PERICEMENTAL **2** : of or affecting periodontal tissues or regions ⟨~ infection⟩
periodontal disease *n* : PERIODONTOSIS
periodontal membrane *n* : PERICEMENTUM
peri·odon·tia \ˌperēōˈdänch(ē)ə\ *n* -S [NL, fr. *periodontium* + *-ia*] : PERIODONTICS — **peri·odon·tic** \ˌ⸗⸗⸗ˈdäntik\ *adj*
peri·odon·tics \ˌ⸗⸗⸗ˈdantiks\ *n pl but sing or pl in constr* [NL *periodontium* + E *-ics*] : a branch of dentistry that is concerned with diseases of the supporting structures of the teeth
peri·odon·tist \-ntəst\ *n* -S [*periodontics* + *-ist*] : a specialist in periodontics
peri·odon·ti·tis \-(ˌ)ōˌdänˈtīd·əs\ *n* -ES [NL, fr. *periodontium* + *-itis*] : inflammation of the pericementum
peri·odon·ti·um \-ˌōˈdänch(ē)əm\ *n, pl* **periodon·tia** \-)ə\ [NL, fr. *peri-* + *-odont-* + *-ium*] : the periodontal tissue; *specif* : PERICEMENTUM
peri·odon·to·cla·sia \-ˌōˌdäntəˈklāzh(ē)ə\ *n* -S [NL, fr. *periodontium* + *-o-* + *-clasia*] : inflammatory and degenerative disease of the periodontal tissues characterized by resorption of alveolar bone with consequent loosening of the teeth and often with shrinking of the gums
peri·odon·tol·o·gy \-(ˌ)ōˌdänˈtäləjē\ *n* -ES [NL *periodontium* + E *-o-* + *-logy*] : PERIODONTICS
peri·odon·to·sis \-(ˌ)ōˌdänˈtōsəs\ *n, pl* **periodonto·ses** \-tōˌsēz\ [NL, fr. *periodontium* + *-osis*] : disease involving the supporting structures of the teeth (as the gums and periodontal membranes)
pe·ri·od·o·scope \ˌpirēˈädəˌskōp\ *n* [¹*period* + *-o-* + *-scope*] : a table or dial for calculating the probable date of parturition
period piece *n* : a piece (as of fiction, art, furniture, music) whose special or chief value lies in its characterization or evocation of an historical period
periods *pl of* PERIOD
peri·oe·ci \ˌperēˈēˌsī\ *n pl* [NL, fr. Gk *perioikoi*, lit., neighbors, fr. pl. of *perioikos* neighboring, fr. *peri-* + *oikos* dwelling, house — more at VICINITY] **1** : those who live on the same parallel of latitude but on opposite meridians so that it is noon in one place when it is midnight in the other — compare ANTOECI **2** *usu cap* : free citizens without political rights constituting the subject class of ancient Sparta who carried on the trade and industry of the country and served in the armed forces — compare HELOT 1, SPARTIATE — **peri·oe·cic** \ˌ⸗⸗ˈēsik\ *or* **peri·oe·cid** \-səd\ *adj*
peri·oe·cian \ˌperēˈēshən\ *n* -S [NL *perioeci* + E *-an*] : one of the perioeci
perioecus *sing of* PERIOECI
per·i·ogue \ˈperēˌōg\ *archaic var of* PIROGUE
peri·onych·ia \ˌperēōˈnikēə\ *n* -S [NL, fr. *perionychium* + *-ia*] : inflammation of the perionychium
peri·onych·i·um \-kēəm\ *n, pl* **perionych·ia** \-ēə\ [NL, fr. *peri-* + *onych-* + *-ium*] : the tissue bordering the root and sides of a fingernail or toenail
peri·on·yx \ˌperēˈäniks\ *n* [NL, fr. *peri-* + Gk *onyx* fingernail, claw — more at NAIL] : the persistent layer of stratum corneum at the base of a fingernail or toenail
peri·ople \ˈperēˌōpəl, ˌ⸗⸗ˈ⸗⸗\ *n* -S [F *périople*, fr. *péri-* peri- + Gk *hoplē* hoof] : the thin waxy outer layer of a hoof — **peri·op·lic** \ˌperēˈäplik\ *adj*
peri·optic \ˌperē+\ *adj* [*peri-* + *optic*] : situated about or surrounding the eyeball
peri·optometry \"+\ *n* [*peri-* + *optometry*] : the measurement of the limits of the visual field
peri·orbital \"+\ *adj* [*peri-* + *orbital*] : situated about, surrounding, or lining the orbit of the eye; *also* : constituting or belonging to a structure having a periorbital location
peri·orchitis \"+\ *n* [NL, fr. *peri-* + Gk *orchis* testicle + *-itis* — more at ORCHIS] : inflammation of the tissue around the testis
peri·orificial \"+\ *adj* [*peri-* + *orificial*] : situated about or surrounding an opening
peri·ost \ˈperēˌäst\ *n* -S [NL *periosteum*] : PERIOSTEUM
periost- *or* **perioste-** *or* **periosteo-** *comb form* [NL *periosteum*] **1** : periosteum ⟨*periosteo*myelitis⟩ ⟨*periost*eoma⟩ ⟨*periost*itis⟩ **2** : periosteal and ⟨*periosteo*alveolar⟩
peri·os·te·al \ˌperēˈästēəl\ *adj* [*periost-* + *-al*] **1** : situated around bone or produced external to existing bone **2** : of, relating to, or involving the periosteum
peri·os·te·o·ma \ˌperēˌästēˈōmə\ *n, pl* **periosteomas** \-məz\ *or* **periosteoma·ta** \-məd·ə\ [NL, fr. *periost-* + *-oma*] : a tumor on the outer surface of a bone
peri·os·te·um \ˌperēˈästēəm\ *n, pl* **perios·tea** \-ēə\ [NL, fr. LL *periosteon*, fr. Gk, neut. of *periosteos* around the bones, fr. *peri-* + *osteon* bone — more at OSSEOUS] **1** : the membrane of connective tissue that closely invests all bones except at the articular surfaces and is made up of an outer fibrous layer that furnishes attachment for muscles and an inner layer that furnishes osteoblasts and contains blood vessels by which the bone is nourished **2** : the vascular areolar tissue lining the marrow cavity of a bone — called also *internal periosteum*
peri·os·tit·ic \ˌperēˌäˈstid·ik\ *adj* [NL *periostitis* + E *-ic*] : of or relating to periostitis
peri·os·ti·tis \ˌperēˌäˈstīd·əs\ *n* -ES [NL, fr. *periost-* + *-itis*] : inflammation of the periosteum
peri·os·tra·cal \ˌperēˈästrəkəl\ *adj* [NL *periostracum* + E *-al*] : of, relating to, or being the periostracum
peri·os·tra·cum \ˌperēˈästrəkəm\ *n, pl* **periostra·ca** \-kə\ [NL, fr. *peri-* + Gk *ostrakon* shell — more at OYSTER] : a chitinous layer covering the exterior of the shell in many mollusks, being usu. well developed in freshwater forms, and serving to protect the shell from corrosion
¹**peri·otic** \ˌperē+\ *adj* [*peri-* + *-otic*] : situated around the ear; *specif* : being, relating to, or composed of the typically three bony elements that surround the internal ear and form or help to form its capsule
²**periotic** \"\ *n* -S : one of the periotic bones or cartilages that in man form the petrous and mastoid portions of the temporal bone on each side
¹**peri·pa·tet·ic** \ˌperəpəˈted·ik, -et|, |ēk\ *n* -S [ME *perypatetik*, fr. L *peripateticus*, fr. *peripateticus*, adj.] **1** *usu cap* : a follower of the philosophy of Aristotle : ARISTOTELIAN **2** : PEDESTRIAN, ITINERANT **3 peripatetics** *pl* : movements or journeyings hither and thither ⟨the kind of mixed bag of travelogues and ~s to which publishers accustomed us —Maurice Richardson⟩
²**peripatetic** \ˌ⸗⸗⸗ˈ⸗⸗\ *adj* **1** [MF & L; MF *peripatetique*, fr. L *peripateticus*, fr. Gk *peripatētikos*, irreg. fr. *peripatos* place for walking, covered walk in the Lyceum where Aristotle taught — more at PERIPATUS] *usu cap* : of or relating to the philosophy of Aristotle or of his followers : ARISTOTELIAN **2** [Gk *peripatētikos*, fr. *peripatein* to walk around, fr. *peri-* + *patein* to walk; akin to Gk *patos* path — more at FIND] : of or relating to walking or moving from place to place : performed or performing while moving about : ITINERANT ⟨~ habits⟩ ⟨~ teaching⟩ ⟨a ~ fruit stand which he pushed about on a cart —W.D. Howells⟩ ⟨his camera is never aimlessly ~ —Arthur Knight⟩ ⟨~ candidates⟩
peri·pa·tet·i·cal·ly \ˌ⸗⸗⸗ˈted·ək(ə)lē, -et|, |ēk-, -li\ *adv* : in the manner of a peripatetic; *esp* : while walking ⟨walking, sobering, and ~ conscious of the world outside him —Thomas Wolfe⟩ ⟨philosophized ~ in its orientally luxuriant gardens —Mary Lindsay⟩
peri·pa·tet·i·cism \|əˌsizəm\ *n* -S **1** *usu cap* : the doctrines or philosophy of the Peripatetics **2** : peripatetic exercise : the habit of being peripatetic ⟨interrupted his slovenly ~ long enough to remark —*Amer. Mercury*⟩
peri·pa·tid·ea \ˌperəpəˈtidēə\ [NL, fr. *Peripatus* + *-idea*] *syn of* ONYCHOPHORA
pe·rip·a·toid \pəˈripəˌtȯid\ *adj* [NL *Peripatus* + E *-oid*] **1** : of or relating to the genus *Peripatus* **2** : resembling a peripatus
pe·rip·a·top·sis \pəˌripəˈtäpsəs\ *n* [NL, fr. *Peripatus* + *-opsis*] **1** *cap* : a genus (the type of the family Peripatopsidae) of chiefly palaeotropical onychophorans — compare PERIPATUS **2** *pl* **peripatop·ses** \-äpˌsēz\ : an arthropod of the genus *Peripatopsis*
pe·rip·a·tus \pəˈripəd·əs\ *n* [NL, fr. Gk *peripatos* act of walking, place for walking, fr. *peri-* + *patos* path — more at FIND] **1** *cap* : a genus (the type of the family Peripatidae) comprising chiefly neotropical onychophorans or in former classifications made coextensive with the class Onychophora — compare PERIPATOPSIS **2** -ES : any arthropod of the genus *Peripatus; broadly* : ONYCHOPHORAN
peri·pe·teia \ˌperəpəˈtē(y)ə, -tīə\ *also* **peri·pe·tia** \-tīə\ *n* -S [Gk *peripeteia*, fr. (assumed) Gk *peripetos* (verbal of Gk *peripiptein* to fall around, fall into, change suddenly, fr. *peri-* + *piptein* to fall) + Gk *-eia* -y — more at FEATHER] : a sudden or unexpected reversal of circumstances or situation in a literary work ⟨a thrilling nick-of-time ~ —F.R.Leavis⟩; *also* : a similar change in actual affairs ⟨participating in the major intellectual ~ of the past eighty years —Hugh Kenner⟩
pe·rip·e·ty \pəˈripəd·ē, ˈperəp-\ *n* -ES [F *péripétie*, fr. Gk *peripeteia*] : PERIPETEIA ⟨simply that ~ in either direction is a law of dramatic interest —W.H.Auden⟩
peri·pha·ci·tis \ˌperəfəˈsīd·əs\ *n* -ES [NL, fr. *peri-* + *phac-* + *-itis*] : inflammation of the capsule around the crystalline lens of the eye
peri·pharyngeal \ˌperə+\ *adj* [*peri-* + *pharyngeal*] : surrounding the pharynx; *specif* : being or relating to two bands of cilia encircling the inside of the pharynx of an ascidian at the oral end
peripher- *or* **periphero-** *comb form* [*periphery*] **1** : periphery ⟨*peripher*ad⟩ : peripheral ⟨*periphero*neural⟩ **2** : peripheral and ⟨*periphero*central⟩
pe·riph·er·ad \pəˈrifəˌrad\ *adv* [*peripher-* + *-ad*] : toward the periphery ⟨the region of the rete ~ —L.B.Arey⟩
pe·riph·er·al \pəˈrif(ə)rəl\ *also* **peri·pher·ic** \ˌperəˈferik, pəˈrifər-\ *adj* [*peripher-* + *-al* or *-ic*] **1** : of, relating to, or forming a periphery : originating in a periphery : MARGINAL ⟨rotary boiler . . . was run at various speeds up to a ~ speed of 830 ft./sec. —G.G.Smith⟩ ⟨~ parking space⟩ ⟨~ wars⟩ ⟨rather ~ criticisms of a fine book —Paul Pickrel⟩ ⟨security programs which are ~ to the main business of democratic living —Sidney Hook⟩ ⟨such retarded cultures are often spoken of as ~ whether their situation be on the edges or in the interiors of land masses —A.L.Kroeber⟩ **2** : located away from a center or central portion : EXTERNAL; *esp* : located at or near the surface of the body ⟨~ nerve endings⟩ **3** : of, relating to, or involving the surface of the body ⟨~ vascular disorders⟩ **4** : of or relating to the peripheral field ⟨~ acuity⟩ ⟨~ vision⟩
peripheral field *n* : the outer part of the field of vision; *specif* : the part that lies more than 30 degrees from the line of sight
pe·riph·er·al·ism \-rəˌlizəm\ *n* -S : emphasis on sensory motor processes rather than cognitive or other central processes as determinants of behavior
pe·riph·er·al·ly \-rəlē, -li\ *also* **peri·pher·i·cal·ly** \-rək(ə)lē, -li\ *adv* : in a peripheral position or relationship : at, near, or from a periphery : in a peripheral role or function : MARGINALLY
peripheral neuritis *n* : inflammation of one or more peripheral nerves
peripheral vascular disease *n* : vascular disease involving peripheral blood vessels (as thromboangiitis obliterans)
pe·riph·ery \pəˈrif(ə)rē, -ri\ *n* -ES [MF *peripherie*, fr. LL *peripheria*, fr. Gk *periphereia*, fr. *peripherēs* moving around (fr. *peripherein* to carry around, turn around, fr. *peri-* + *pherein* to carry) + *-eia* -y — more at BEAR] **1** : the perimeter of a circle, ellipse, or other closed curvilinear figure; *also* : the perimeter of a polygonal figure **2** : the external boundary or surface of any body ⟨the ~ of an orange⟩ ⟨the ~ of a tire⟩ **3 a** : the outward bounds of something as distinguished from its internal regions or center : encompassing limits : CONFINES ⟨the drift toward the ~ of the great metropolitan districts —Oscar Handlin⟩ ⟨the ~ of the retina —F.A. Geldard⟩ ⟨the fixed stars at the ~ of the universe were stationary —S.F.Mason⟩ ⟨an exploration of the ~ of logic —M.R.Cohen⟩ **b** : surrounding space : an area lying beyond the strict limits of a thing ⟨around each of these states was a ~ of mixed populations that made exact boundaries on racial lines hopeless —Herbert Hoover⟩ **4** : the regions (as the sense organs, the muscles, and the viscera) in which nerves terminate
peri·phlebitis \ˌperə+\ *n* [NL, fr. *peri-* + *phlebitis*] : inflammation of the outer coat of a vein or of tissues around a vein
¹**peri·phrase** \ˈperəˌfrāz\ *n* [MF, fr. L *periphrasis*] : PERIPHRASIS
²**periphrase** \"\ *vb* [F *périphraser*, fr. MF *periphraser*, fr. *periphrase*] *vt* : to express by periphrasis ~ *vi* : to use periphrasis
pe·riph·ra·sis \pəˈrifrəsəs\ *n, pl* **periphra·ses** \-əˌsēz\ [L, fr. Gk, fr. *periphrazein* to express periphrastically (fr. *peri-* + *phrazein* to point out, show, declare) + *-sis*] **1** : the use of a longer phrasing (as in naming by descriptive epithet, introduction of abstract general terms) in place of a possible shorter and plainer form of expression : the use of a negative, passive, or inverted construction in place of a positive, active, or normal construction : a roundabout or indirect way of speaking : CIRCUMLOCUTION **2** : an instance of periphrasis ("the answer is in the negative" is a ~ for "no" —*Time*)
peri·phras·tic \ˌperəˈfrastik, -raas-, -tēk\ *adj* [Gk *periphrastikos*, fr. (assumed) Gk *periphrastos* (verbal of Gk *periphrazein*) + Gk *-ikos* -ic] **1** : of, relating to, or characterized by periphrasis : CIRCUMLOCUTORY **2** : formed by the use of function words or auxiliaries instead of by inflection ⟨*more fair* is a ~ comparative⟩ ⟨*of man* is a ~ phrase⟩ ⟨*does go* is a ~ verb⟩ — **peri·phras·ti·cal·ly** \-tək(ə)lē, -tēk, -li\ *adv*
pe·riph·y·sis \pəˈrifəsəs\ *n, pl* **periphy·ses** \-əˌsēz\ [NL, fr. Gk, overgrowth, fr. *periphyein* to grow around, grow over (fr. *peri-* + *phyein* to grow, bring forth) + *-sis* — more at BE] : one of the sterile filaments that line the ostiole of many perithecia and other fruiting structures — compare PARAPHYSIS
peri·phyt·ic \ˌperəˈfid·ik\ *adj* [NL *periphyton* + E *-ic*] : of, relating to, or forming part of the periphyton ⟨~ organisms⟩
pe·riph·y·ton \pəˈrifəˌtän\ *n* [NL, fr. *peri-* + Gk *phyton* plant — more at PHYT-] : organisms that live attached to underwater surfaces ⟨rotifers that browse on bacteria and other ~⟩
peri·pla·ne·ta \ˌperəpləˈnēd·ə\ *n, cap* [NL, fr. *peri-* + Gk *planētēs* wanderer — more at PLANET] : a genus of large cockroaches including the American cockroach (*P. americana*) and the Australian cockroach (*P. australasiae*) which are two common cosmopolitan species
peri·plasm \ˈperə+ˌ-\ *n* -S [ISV *peri-* + *-plasm*] : a peripheral layer of protoplasm (as of a yolk-filled egg or an oogonium) — compare OOPLASM
peri·plasmodium \ˌperə+\ *n* [NL, fr. *peri-* + *plasmodium*] : a multinucleate mass of protoplasm in various anthers that surrounds the sporocytes and pollen grains and is formed by fusion of tapetal cells following breakdown of their walls
peri·plast \ˈperəˌplast\ *n* -S [*peri-* + *-plast*] **1** : STROMA 1a **2 a** : CYTOPLASM **b** : PERIPLASM **c** : a cell membrane — **peri·plas·tic** \ˌ⸗⸗ˈplastik\ *adj*
pe·rip·lo·ca \pəˈripləkə\ *n, cap* [NL, fr. Gk *periplokē* action of twining round, interlacing, fr. *peri-* + *plokē* action of twisting or turning, fr. the stem of *plekein* to plait, twine — more at PLY] : a genus of woody vines (family Asclepiadaceae) found in warm regions of the Old World and having opposite entire leaves, cymose flowers with a rotate corolla, and cylindrical follicles — see SILK VINE
peri·plus \ˈperə(ˌ)pləs, -rəˌplüs\ *n, pl* **peri·pli** \-ˌplī, -ˌplē\ [L & Gk; L, circumnavigation, fr. Gk *periplous* circumnavigation, account of a coasting voyage, fr. *periplein* to sail around, fr. *peri-* + *plein* to sail — more at FLOW] **1** : a voyage or a trip around something (as an island or a coast) : CIRCUIT, CIRCUMNAVIGATION **2** : an account of a circumnavigation
per·ip·neus·tic \ˌperəpˈn(y)üstik\ *adj* [ISV *peri-* + Gk *pneustikos* of breathing, fr. *pneust-* (fr. *pnein* to breathe) + *-ikos* -ic — more at SNEEZE] : having spiracles in a row on each side of the body ⟨~ insects⟩
peri·portal \ˌperə+\ *adj* [*peri-* + *portal*] : situated about or surrounding a portal vein
peri·printer \ˈperə+ˌ-\ *n* [*peri-* + *printer*] : a grooved inking roller that is used to force plastic ink through a stencil in a special method of printing solid tangible braille points on paper
peri·proct \ˈperəˌpräkt\ *n* -S [ISV *peri-* + Gk *prōktos* anus — more at PROCT-] : the well-defined area surrounding the anus of various invertebrates (as a sea urchin) — **peri·proc·tal** \ˌ⸗⸗ˈpräktᵊl\ *or* **peri·proc·tic** \-ktik\ *or* **peri·proc·tous** \-ktəs\ *adj*
pe·rip·ter·al \pəˈript(ə)rəl\ *adj* [L *peripteros* peristylar (fr. Gk, flying around, peristylar, fr. *peri-* + *pteron* feather, wing, row of columns) + E *-al* — more at FEATHER] **1** : having a row of columns on all sides : PERISTYLAR — see COLUMNIATION illustration **2** : relating to or characterized by the motions of the air surrounding a moving body
pe·rip·ter·os \-təˌräs\ *n, pl* **peripter·oi** \-ˌrȯi\ [NL, fr. L, adj., peristylar] : a peripteral building
pe·rip·tery \pəˈript(ə)rē\ *n* -ES [L & Gk *peripteros* + E *-y*] **1** : PERIPTEROS **2** : the region surrounding a moving body (as the wing of a bird or a gliding airplane) within which cyclic or vortical motions of the air occur
peri·py·lea \ˌperəˌpīˈlēə\ *n pl, cap* [NL, fr. *peri-* + *-pylea* (fr. Gk *pylē* gate) — more at PYLON] : a suborder of Radiolaria comprising mostly spherical protozoans without skeletons or with simple spicules and with the central capsule uniformly perforated
pe·rique \pəˈrēk\ *n* -S [LaF *périque*, prob. fr. *Périque*, nickname of Pierre Chenet, Am. pioneer tobacco grower who introduced it] **1** : a strong-flavored tobacco with tough and gummy fiber raised in St. James parish, Louisiana, cured in its own juices, and used chiefly in smoking mixtures **2** : OTTER 4
peris *pl of* PERI
peri·sarc \ˈperəˌsärk\ *n* -S [ISV *peri-* + *-sarc*] : the outer usu. chitinous integument of a hydroid — **peri·sar·cal** \ˌ⸗⸗ˈsärkəl\ *or* **peri·sar·cous** \-rkəs\ *adj*
pe·ris·cho·ech·i·noi·da \pəˌris(ˌ)kōˌekəˈnȯidə\ *n pl, cap* [NL *perischo-* (fr. Gk *perischesis* surrounding, fr. *periechein*, *perischein* to surround — fr. *peri-* + *echein*, *schein* to have, hold — + *-sis*) + *echin-* + *-oida* — more at SCHEME] : a large order of regular Paleozoic Echinoidea
¹**pe·ris·cian** \pəˈrisēən, -ish(ē)ən\ *adj* [NL *periscii* + E *-an*] : of or relating to the periscii
²**periscian** \"\ *n* -S : one of the periscii
pe·ris·cii \pəˈrisēˌī, -ishēˌī\ *n pl* [NL, fr. Gk *periskioi*, pl. of *periskios* throwing a shadow all around, fr. *peri-* + *skia* shadow — more at SCENE] : those who live within a polar circle and whose shadows during some summer days will therefore move entirely round and fall toward every point of the compass
peri·scope \ˈperəˌskōp\ *n* [ISV *peri-* + *-scope*] : an optical instrument by which an observer (as on a submerged submarine or in work with highly radioactive materials) looks through or as if through an eyepiece into a mirror or totally reflecting prism attached at an angle of 45 degrees to one end of a tube containing a system of lenses and obtains an otherwise obstructed field of view from another mirror or prism correspondingly attached to the other end of the tube

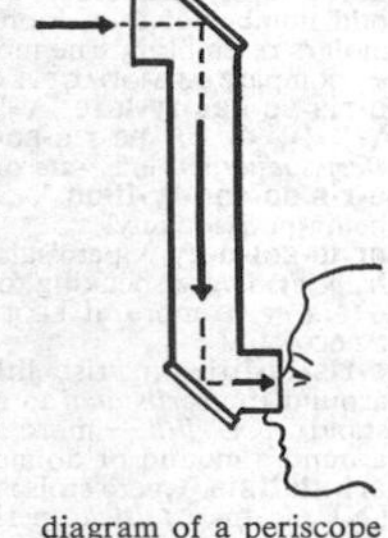

diagram of a periscope

peri·scop·ic \ˌperəˈskäpik, -ēpēk\ *adj* [Gk *periskopein* to look around (fr. *peri-* + *skopein* to look, view) + E *-ic* — more at SPY] **1** : viewing all around or on all sides : giving a distinct image of objects viewed obliquely as well as those in a direct line — used esp. of various compound lenses for the microscope or camera and of spectacles having meniscus lenses with the concave surface toward the eye **2** : of, relating to, by means of, or resembling a periscope
¹**per·ish** \ˈperish, -rēsh, *esp in pres part* -rəsh\ *vb* -ED/-ING/-ES [ME *perissen, perisshen*, fr. OF *periss-*, stem of *perir*, fr. L *perire* to pass away, be destroyed, perish, fr. *per-* detrimentally, destructively + *ire* to go — more at PER-, ISSUE] *vi* **1** : to become destroyed or ruined : come to an esp. violent or untimely end : pass away completely (as by disintegration) : DIE ⟨~*ed* by the tomahawk —*Amer. Guide Series: N.H.*⟩ ⟨many elephants were known to have ~*ed* of their wounds —Stuart Cloete⟩ ⟨their skeletons have ~*ed* —Ruth Benedict⟩ ⟨recollection of a past already long since ~*ed* —Philip Sherrard⟩ ⟨that the great human energy which manifests itself in free thought will not ~ —M.R.Cohen⟩ — formerly often used in imprecations but now so used chiefly with *thought* ⟨guard

against your mistakes or your attempts (~ the thought) to cheat —C.B.Davis› **2 :** to suffer spiritual or moral death **:** become spiritually lost ‹~ in one's sins› ‹nations ~*ing* for want of religious teachers› **3** *chiefly dial* **:** to deteriorate or decay to the point of being unserviceable or useless **:** SPOIL ‹window frames . . . cannot be left bare of paint indefinitely without the woodwork ~*ing* —*Country Life*› ‹belts should then be carefully examined for any signs of ~*ing* —*Fire Service Drill Bk.*› **~** *vt* **1** *chiefly dial* **:** to cause to die, be lost, spoiled, hurt, or ruined **:** DESTROY ‹the boots I get nowadays wholly ~ my feet —Adrian Bell› ‹this process has a tendency to ~ the straw —Beryl Fegan› **2** *chiefly Scot* **:** to cause to vanish **:** SQUANDER, WASTE

²perish \"\ *n* -ES *Austral* **:** a state of privation in the bush — **do a perish** *Austral* **:** to come near to dying esp. from hunger, thirst, or exposure

per·ish·abil·i·ty \,perəshə'biləd·ē, -rēsh-, -lətē, -i\ *n* -ES **:** the quality or condition of being perishable

¹per·ish·able \'perəshəbəl, -rēsh-\ *adj* [¹*perish* + *-able*] **1 :** liable to perish **:** subject to destruction, death, decay, or deterioration **:** not durable ‹human life on this minute and ~ planet is but a mock episode —L.P.Smith›; *esp* **:** subject to quick deterioration or spoilage except under proper conditions (as of temperature or moisture content) ‹~ foods such as butter and fruit› **2 :** that cannot be conserved indefinitely **:** highly consumable ‹no art is so ~ as music —P.H.Lang› ‹jazz is ~, ephemeral, elusive —Whitney Balliett› ‹news is one of the ~ products that can lose much or all of its value by delays —*Modern Industry*› ‹estimates for ~ tools and tool grinding —R.E.Cross› ‹skills are highly ~ . . . unless practice keeps pace with technological improvements —*Newsweek*›

²perishable \"\ *n* -S **:** something subject to death, destruction, or esp. rapid decay or deterioration — usu. used in pl. (as of foodstuffs) ‹~*s* such as dairy products, meats, and fruits›

per·ish·able·ness *n* -ES **:** PERISHABILITY

per·ish·ably \-blē, -bli\ *adv* **:** in a perishable manner or degree

perished *adj* [fr. past part. of ¹*perish*] **1** *chiefly dial* **a :** injuriously affected esp. by exposure or age **b :** feeling the effects of exposure or deprivation of necessities ‹blowing on their ~ fingers —Lawrence Durrell› **2 :** deadened or weakened by exposure (as to weather or heat) ‹~ staple› ‹~ cotton›

per·ish·er \-rishə(r), -rēsh-\ *n* -S [¹*perish* + *-er*] *Austral* **:** BOUNDER, CHAP, FELLOW — **do a perisher** *Austral* **:** do a perish

perishing *adj* [ME *perissing, perisshing*, fr. pres. part. of *perissen, perisshen* to perish — more at PERISH] **1 :** that perishes **:** that causes extreme discomfort, pain, or hardship; *specif* **:** FREEZING ‹~ cold› **2 :** CONFOUNDED ‹the ~ old blighter wouldn't have it —Margery Allingham› ‹a ~ amateur —J.M. Barzun› ‹a ~, jerky little town —James Reynolds›

per·ish·ing·ly *adv* **:** in a manner or to a degree causing extreme discomfort or hardship **:** BITTERLY, EXTREMELY, VERY ‹~ humid in the fall —Alan Moorehead› ‹a half-a-gale of ~ cold wind —Llewellyn Howland› ‹promises all kinds of miracles in his person — and delivers ~ few of them —Weston La Barre›

per·ish·less \-rishləs, -rēsh-\ *adj* [¹*perish* + *-less*] **:** IMPERISHABLE

per·ish·ment \-shmənt\ *n* -S **:** the act of perishing; *also* **:** something that perishes (another thing)

peri·sin·u·ous \¦perə¦sinyəwəs\ *adj* [*peri-* + *sinus* + *-ous*] **:** surrounding a venous sinus (as of the brain)

peri·som·al \¦perə¦sōməl\ *or* **peri·so·mi·al** \-¦sōmēəl\ *or* **peri·so·mat·ic** \-.sō'mad·ik\ *adj* [*perisomal, perisomial* fr. *perisome* + *-al* or *-ial*; *perisomatic* fr. NL *perisomat-, perisoma* + E *-ic*] **:** of, relating to, or being a perisome

peri·some \'perə,sōm\ *also* **peri·so·ma** \,==¦sōmə\ *n* -S [NL *perisoma*, fr. *peri-* + *-soma*] **:** the body wall of an invertebrate; *esp* **:** the body wall of an echinoderm

peri·sperm \'perə,spərm\ *n* [F *périsperme*, fr. *péri-* peri- + *-sperme* -sperm] **1 :** nutritive tissue of a seed derived from the nucellus and deposited external to the embryo sac — distinguished from *endosperm* **2 :** nutritive tissue of a seed that includes both endosperm and perisperm — not used technically — **peri·sperm·al** \¦==¦spərməl\ *or* **peri·sper·mic** \-mik\ *adj*

peri·sphinc·tes \,perə'sfiŋ(k)(,)tēz\ *n, cap* [NL, fr. *peri-* + *-sphinctes* (fr. Gk *sphinktos* tightly bound, fr. *sphingein* to bind fast) — more at SPHINCTER] **:** a genus (the type of the family Perisphinctidae) comprising discoidal ammonites having bifurcating ribs not interrupted on the ventral side and being characteristic of the Upper Jurassic — **peri·sphinc·toid** \¦==¦sfiŋ(k),tȯid\ *adj*

peri·spome·non \,perə'spämənən, -pōm-, -mə,nän\ *n, pl* **perispomena** [Gk *perispōmenon* neut. of *perispōmenos*, pres. passive part. of *perispan* to pronounce with a circumflex accent, draw off from around, fr. *peri-* + *span* to draw — more at SPAN] **:** a word having the circumflex accent on the last syllable

peri·spore \'perə+,-\ *n* [F *périspore*, fr. NL *perisporum*, fr. *peri-* + *-sporum* -spore (fr. Gk *spora* seed) — more at SPORE] **:** the covering of a spore — compare EPISPORE

peri·spo·ri·a·ce·ae \,perə,spōrē'āsē,ē\ *n pl, cap* [NL, fr. *Perisporium*, type genus (fr. *peri-* + *-sporium*) + *-aceae*] **1** *in some classifications* **:** a family of fungi placed in the order Perisporiales and characterized by dark-colored mycelium **2** *in some classifications* **:** a family coextensive with or including Erysiphaceae — **peri·spo·ri·a·ceous** \¦==¦==¦āshəs\ *adj*

peri·spo·ri·a·les \-'ā(,)lēz\ *n pl, cap* [NL, fr. *Perisporium* + *-ales*] *in some classifications* **:** an order of parasitic or saprophytic fungi nearly coextensive with the order Erysiphales

pe·ris·sad \pə'risəd, -i,sad\ *n* -S [Gk *perissos* beyond the regular number or size, superfluous, excessive, uneven (fr. *peri* around, beyond) + E *-ad*] **1** *obs* **:** an element or radical of odd valence **2 :** an element of odd atomic number — contrasted with *artiad*

¹pe·ris·so·dac·tyl \pə¦risə¦daktᵊl\ *also* **pe·ris·so·dac·tyle** \",-,tīl\ *adj* [NL *Perissodactyla*] **:** having the toes in odd numbers or unevenly disposed in relation to the axis of the foot **:** relating to Perissodactyla

²perissodactyl \"\ *n* -S **:** one of the Perissodactyla

pe·ris·so·dac·ty·la \-==='daktələ\ *n pl, cap* [NL, fr. MGk *perissodaktyla*, neut. pl. of *perissodaktylos* having more than the usual number of fingers or toes, fr. Gk *perissos* beyond the regular number or size, extraordinary, excessive, uneven (fr. *peri* around, beyond) + *daktylos* finger, toe — more at PERI-] **:** an order of nonruminant ungulate mammals including the horse, tapir, rhinoceros, and related forms and usu. having an odd number of toes, lophodont teeth with the posterior premolars resembling true molars, and 23 dorsolumbar vertebrae — compare ARTIODACTYLA

pe·ris·so·dac·ty·late \=¦==¦==lət\ *or* **pe·ris·so·dac·tyl·ic** \=¦==¦=¦==\ *or* **pe·ris·so·dac·ty·lous** \=¦==¦===\ *adj* [NL *Perissodactyla* + E *-ate* or *-ic* or *-ous*] **:** PERISSODACTYL

pe·ris·so·dac·ty·lism \=,==¦==,lizəm\ *n* -S **:** the condition of being perissodactyl

per·is·sol·o·gy \,perə'säləjē\ *n* -ES [LL *perissologia*, fr. Gk, fr. *perissologos* speaking too much (fr. *perissos* + *logos* speech) + *-ia* -y — more at LEGEND] *archaic* **:** superfluity of words **:** PLEONASM

pe·ris·ta·lith \pə'ristə,lith\ *n* -S [Gk *peristatos* standing around (fr. *periistanai* to stand around, fr. *peri-* + *histanai* to stand) + E *-lith* — more at STAND] **:** a ring of upright stones around a mound or dolmen **:** STONE CIRCLE

peri·stal·sis \,perə'stȯlsəs, -tal-\ *n, pl* **peristal·ses** \-l,sēz\ [NL, fr. *peristalticus* peristaltic (fr. Gk *peristaltikos*), after such pairs as LL *antitheticus: antithesis*] **:** successive waves of involuntary contraction passing along the walls of the intestine or other hollow muscular structure and forcing the contents onward — compare SEGMENTATION

peri·stal·tic \¦==¦==tik\ *adj* [Gk *peristaltikos*, fr. (assumed) Gk *peristaltos* (verbal of Gk *peristellein* to wrap around, fr. *peri-* + *stellein* to set, place, send) + Gk *-ikos* -ic — more at STALL] **:** of, relating to, resulting from, or being peristalsis

peri·stal·ti·cal·ly \-tək(ə)lē\ *adv* **:** in a peristaltic manner **:** with peristaltic action

peri·stal·toid \¦==¦=,tȯid\ *adj* [*peristaltic* + *-oid*] **:** resembling peristalsis

peri·stele \'perə,stēlē, ,==¦=; 'perə,stēl\ *n* [*peri-* + Gk *stēlē* block of stone, slab — more at STELA] **:** a stone in a peristalith

pe·ris·te·rite \pə'ristə,rīt\ *n* -S [Gk *peristera* dove, pigeon + E *-ite*] **:** a gem variety of albite resembling moonstone and showing internal reflections of blue, green, and yellow

pe·ris·te·ro·mor·phae \pə,ristərō'mȯr(,)fē, -,fī\ *n pl, cap* [NL, fr. *peristero-* (fr. Gk *peristera* dove, pigeon) + *-morphae*] *in former classifications* **:** a superfamily of birds consisting of the pigeons — **pe·ris·te·ro·mor·phic** \=¦==¦=¦==fik\ *adj*

pe·ris·te·ron·ic \=,==¦ränik\ *adj* [Gk *peristera* dove, pigeon + E *-onic* (as in *demonic*)] **:** of or relating to pigeons

pe·ris·te·ro·pod \pə'ristərō,päd\ *or* **pe·ris·te·ro·pode** \-,pōd\ *n* -S [NL *Peristeropodes*] **:** a bird of the group Peristeropodes

pe·ris·te·rop·o·des \=,==¦räpə,dēz\ *n pl, cap* [NL, fr. *peristero-* (fr. Gk *peristera* dove, pigeon) + *-podes* (fr. Gk *pod-, pous* foot) — more at FOOT] *in former classifications* **:** a group of birds comprising the curassows and megapodes and having feet with the hind toe inserted low down (as in pigeons) — **pe·ris·te·rop·o·dous** \=¦=¦==dəs\ *adj*

peri·stethi·um \,perə'stēthēəm, -steth-\ *n, pl* **peri·stethia** \-thēə\ [NL, fr. *peri-* + *steth-* + *-ium*] **:** the mesosternum of an insect

peri·stom·al \¦perə¦stōməl\ *or* **peri·sto·mat·ic** \-.stō¦madik\ *adj* [*peristomal* fr. *peristome* + *-al*; *peristomatic* fr. NL *peristomat-, peristoma* + E *-ic*] **:** PERISTOMIAL

peri·stome \'perə,stōm\ *n* -S [NL *peristoma*, fr. *peri-* + *-stoma*] **1 :** the fringe of teeth surrounding the orifice of a moss capsule **2 :** the region around the mouth in various invertebrates: as **a :** the lip of a spiral shell **b :** the membranous area around an echinoderm's mouth **c :** the margin of the mouth opening of an insect formed by the skeleton of the head **d :** the area surrounding the mouth or cytostome of a protozoan

peri·sto·mi·al \¦perə¦stōmēəl\ *adj* **:** of or relating to the peristome

peri·sto·mice \¦perə¦stōməs, pə'ristəm-\ *n* -S [*peristome* + *orifice*] **:** the opening of a chamber of a bryozoan colony

peri·sto·mi·um \,perə'stōmēəm\ *n, pl* **peristo·mia** \-ēə\ [NL, fr. *peri-* + *stom-* + *-ium*] **:** PERISTOME; *esp* **:** the foremost true segment of an annelid worm usu. bearing the mouth

peri·sty·lar \¦perə¦stīlə(r)\ *adj* [*peri-* + *-stylar*] **:** marked by columniation consisting of a row of free columns completely encircling the structure or an area of the structure — compare PSEUDOPERIPTERAL

peri·style \'perə,stīl\ *n* [F *péristyle*, fr. L *peristylum*, fr. Gk *peristylon, peristylos*, fr. neut. & masc. respectively of *peristylos*, adj., surrounded by a colonnade, fr. *peri-* + *stylos* pillar — more at STEER] **1 :** a colonnade surrounding a building or court; *specif* **:** a range of roof-supporting columns together with their entablature on all sides of a building (as the cella of a temple) or an inner court **2 :** an open space enclosed by a colonnade (as the larger and inner court of a Roman dwelling) — compare ATRIUM

peri·styli·um \,perə'stīlēəm, -til-\ *n, pl* **peri·stylia** \-ēə\ [L, fr. Gk *peristylion*, dim. of *peristylon*] **:** PERISTYLE

peri·sty·los \,perə'stīləs, -,läs\ *n, pl* **peristy·loi** \-l,ȯi\ [Gk] **:** a building with a peristyle

per·it \'perət\ *n* -S [origin unknown] **:** a former moneyers' unit of weight equal to ¹⁄₂₀ droit or ¹⁄₉₆₀₀ grain

pe·rite \pə'rīt\ *adj* [L *peritus*; akin to L *periculum* danger — more at FEAR] *archaic* **:** SKILLED

peri·tec·tic \¦perə¦tektik\ *adj* [*peri-* + Gk *tēktikos* able to dissolve, fr. *tēktos* molten, capable of being dissolved (fr. *tēkein* to melt) + *-ikos* -ic — more at THAW] **:** taking place between the solid phases and the still unsolidified portions of the liquid melt

peri·ten·din·e·um \,perə,ten'dinēəm\ *n, pl* **peritendin·ea** \-ēə\ [NL, fr. *peri-* + ML *tendin-, tendo* tendon + L *-eum*, neut. of *-eus* -eous — more at TENDON] **:** the connective tissue sheath of a tendon

peri·ten·on \¦perə¦tenən, pə'ritᵊn,än\ *n* -S [NL, fr. *peri-* + LL *tenon* tendon, fr. Gk *tenōn* — more at TENDON] **:** PERITENDINEUM

peri·the·cial \¦perə¦thēsh(ē)əl, -thēsēəl\ *adj* [NL *perithecium* + E *-al*] **:** of, relating to, or being a perithecium ‹~ wall›

peri·the·ci·um \,perə'thēs(h)ēəm\ *n, pl* **perithe·cia** \-)ēə\ [NL, fr. *peri-* + *-thecium*] **:** a spherical, cylindrical, or flask-shaped hollow fruiting body in various ascomycetous fungi that contains the asci, usu. opens by a terminal pore, and sometimes includes the cleistothecium — compare APOTHECIUM

peri·the·li·al \¦perə¦thēlēəl\ *adj* [NL *perithelium* + E *-al*] **:** of, relating to, or made up of perithelium

peri·the·li·o·ma \-,thēlē'ōmə\ *n, pl* **peritheliomas** \-məz\ *or* **perithelioma·ta** \-məd·ə\ [NL, fr. *perithelium* + *-oma*] **:** a sarcomatous tumor originating from adventitious connective tissue around a blood vessel or from the surrounding lymphatics

peri·the·li·um \,perə'thēlēəm\ *n, pl* **perithe·lia** \-lēə\ [NL, fr. *peri-* + *-thelium* (as in *epithelium*)] **:** a layer of connective tissue surrounding a small vessel (as a capillary)

periton- *or* **peritone-** *or* **peritoneo-** *comb form* [LL *peritoneum*] **1 :** peritoneum ‹*peritonealgia*› ‹*peritoneoplasty*› ‹*peritonitis*› **2 :** peritoneal and ‹*peritoneomuscular*› ‹*peritoneopericardial*›

peri·to·ne·al *also* **peri·to·nae·al** \¦perətə¦nēəl, -rətᵊn¦ē-, -rəd·ə¦nē-\ *adj* [LL *peritoneum, peritonaeum* + E *-al*] **:** of, relating to, or affecting the peritoneum — **peri·to·ne·al·ly** *also* **peri·to·nae·al·ly** \-ēəlē\ *adv*

peri·to·ne·al·ize \-ēə,līz\ *vt* -ED/-ING/-S **:** to cover (a surgical surface) with peritoneum

peri·to·neo·scope \,perətə'nēə,skōp\ *n* [*periton-* + *-scope*] **:** a tubular instrument with an optical and lighting system used to examine the abdominal and pelvic cavities through an opening in the abdominal wall — **peri·to·neo·scop·ic** \¦===¦=¦skäpik\ *adj*

peri·to·ne·os·co·pist \-,nē'äskəpəst\ *n* -S **:** a specialist in peritoneoscopy

peri·to·ne·os·co·py \-ᵊpē\ *n* -ES [*periton-* + *-scopy*] **:** the study of the abdominal and pelvic cavities by means of the peritoneoscope

peri·to·ne·um *also* **peri·to·nae·um** \,perətə'nēəm, -rətᵊn'ē-, -rəd·ə'nē-\ *n, pl* **peritoneums** *or* **perito·nea** *also* **perito·naea** \-ēə\ [LL, fr. Gk *peritonaion*, neut. of *peritonaios*, stretched across, fr. *peritonos* stretched over, fr. *peri-* + *-tonos* (fr. *teinein* to stretch) — more at THIN] **1 :** the smooth transparent serous membrane that lines the cavity of the abdomen of a mammal, is reflected inward over the abdominal and pelvic viscera, and consists of (1) an outer layer closely adherent to the walls of the abdomen except in some places along the back where it extends forward to form (2) an inner layer that folds to invest the viscera — called also (1) *parietal peritoneum*, (2) *visceral peritoneum*; compare MESENTERY **2 :** PLEUROPERITONEUM **3 :** the membranous lining of the body cavity of certain invertebrates

peri·to·nit·ic \¦===¦nid·ik, ¦===¦id-\ *adj* [NL *peritonitis* + E *-ic*] **:** of, relating to, or belonging to peritonitis ‹~ symptoms›

peri·to·ni·tis \,perətə'nīd·əs, -rətᵊn'ī-, -rəd·ə'nī-, -ītəs\ *n* -ES [NL, fr. *periton-* + *-itis*] **:** inflammation of the peritoneum

peri·tonsillar abscess \¦perə+. . -\ *n* [ISV *peri-* + *tonsillar*] **:** an abscess in the connective tissue around a tonsil usu. resulting from acute infection of a tonsil and extension of pus through the tonsil capsule into the surrounding tissue and being accompanied by fever, pain, and swelling — called also *quinsy*

peri·tre·ma \,perə-'trēmə\ *n* -S [NL] **:** PERITREME

peri·tre·mal \¦==¦=məl\ *adj* **:** being or functioning as a peritreme

peri·trema·tous \-·¦tremədəs, -rēm-\ *adj* [NL *peritremat-, peritrema* + E *-ous*] **:** of or relating to a peritreme

peri·treme \'perə,trēm\ *n* -S [NL *peritrema*, fr. *peri-* + *-trema*] **1 :** a rounded plate that surrounds the spiracles in some insects **2 :** the edge of the aperture of a shell

peri·trich \'perə,trik\ *n* -S [NL *Peritricha*] **:** a ciliate of the order Peritricha

pe·rit·ri·cha \pə'ri·trəkə\ *n pl, cap* [NL, fr. *peri-* + *-tricha* (fr. Gk *trich-, thrix* hair) — more at TRICHINA] **:** an order of Ciliophora comprising euciliate protozoans with an enlarged disklike ciliated anterior end leading to the cytostome via a counterclockwise adoral zone and with reduced body ciliation and often being attached to the substrate by a contractile stalk

pe·rit·ri·chate \-kət, -,kāt\ *adj* [*peri-* + *trich-* + *-ate*] **:** PERITRICHOUS 1

peri·trich·ic \¦perə¦trikik\ *adj* [*peri-* + *trich-* + *-ic*] **:** PERITRICHOUS

peri·trich·i·da \,==¦=kədə\ [NL, fr. *peri-* + *trich-* + *-ida*] *syn of* PERITRICHA

pe·rit·ri·chous \pə'ri·trəkəs\ *adj* [*peri-* + *-trichous*] **1 :** having flagella uniformly distributed over the body — used chiefly of bacteria **2 :** having a spiral line of modified cilia around the oral disc — used of various protozoa — **pe·rit·ri·chous·ly** *adv*

peri·troch \'perə,träk\ *n* -S [*peri-* + *-troch*] **1 :** an embryo or larva surrounded by a band of cilia **2 :** a band of cilia — **pe·rit·ro·chal** \pə'ri·trəkəl\ *adj*

peri·troph·ic membrane \¦perə-¦träfik-\ *n* [ISV *peri-* + *-trophic*] **:** a tubular chitinous sheath inside the midgut of many insects that is continuously secreted at the anterior end of the midgut

perits *pl of* PERIT

peri·typhl·ic \¦perə¦tiflik\ *adj* [*peri-* + *typhl-* + *-ic*] **:** surrounding the cecum

peri·typhlitis \,perə+\ *n* -ES [NL, fr. *peri-* + *typhl-* + *-itis*] **:** inflammation of the connective tissue about the cecum and appendix **:** APPENDICITIS

peri·umbilical \¦perē+\ *adj* [*peri-* + *umbilical*] **:** situated about or in the neighborhood of the navel

peri–urban \"+\ *adj* [*peri-* + *urban*] **:** of or relating to an area immediately surrounding a city or town ‹154,000 urban and *peri-urban* houses were required —Leo Marquard› ‹occupying land in urban or *peri-urban* areas —*African Abstracts*› ‹undaunted *peri-urban* hyenas —Isabel Talbot›

peri·vacuolar layer \"+. . .-\ *n* [*peri-* + *vacuolar*] *bot* **:** TONOPLAST

peri·vascular \¦perə+\ *adj* [ISV *peri-* + *vascular*] **:** situated about or surrounding a blood vessel **:** occurring in the neighborhood of a blood vessel

peri·visceral \¦perə+\ *adj* [*peri-* + *visceral*] **:** situated about, surrounding, or enclosing the viscera

peri·vitelline space \"+. . .-\ *n* [*peri-* + *vitelline*] **:** the fluid-filled space between fertilization membrane and ovum after the entry of a sperm into the egg

¹peri·wig \'perə,wig, -rē,-\ *n* [alter. of earlier *perwyke*, modif. of MF *perruque* — more at PERUKE] **:** PERUKE

²periwig \"\ *vt* **:** to dress or supply with or as if with a periwig

peri·wig·pat·ed \¦==,=¦pād·əd\ *adj* **:** PERIWIGGED

¹peri·win·kle \'perə,wiŋkəl, -rē,-\ *n* -S [alter. (prob. influenced by ²*periwinkle*) of ME *pervenke, pervinke, perwynke*, fr. OE *perfince, perwince*, fr. L *pervinca, pervica*, (*vinca*) *pervinca*, perh. fr. *per* through + *-vinca, -vica* (fr. *vincire* to bind) — more at FOR, VETCH] **1 :** any of several plants of the genus *Vinca*: as **a :** a trailing evergreen herb (*V. minor*) with solitary blue or white flowers often cultivated and frequently escaping — called also *myrtle* **b :** a trailing foliage plant (*V. major*) often variegated and used for window boxes — called also *large periwinkle* **c :** a commonly cultivated woody herb (*V. rosea*) of the Old World tropics having opposite entire leaves and large white, pinkish, or rosy flowers often with a red eye — called also *Cape periwinkle, Madagascar periwinkle, red periwinkle* **2** *or* **periwinkle blue :** a variable color averaging a light purplish blue that is redder and deeper than lupine or zenith

²periwinkle \"\ *n* -S [fr. (assumed) ME, alter. (influenced by ME *pervenke, perwynke*) of (assumed) ME *pinewinkle* (whence E dial. *pennywinkle*), fr. OE *pinewincle*, fr. L *pīna*, a mussel (fr. Gk *pinē, pina*) + OE *-wincle* (akin to Dan *vinkel* snail shell); akin to OE *wincel* corner, OFris *winkel*, OHG *winkil* corner, OE *wincian* to wink — more at WINK] **:** any of various gastropod mollusks: as **a :** any of numerous edible shallow-water or littoral marine snails (genus *Littorina*) having the shell thick, solid, and conical without an umbilicus and the foot longitudinally divided; *also* **:** the shell of such a mollusk **b :** any of various other marine snails or their shells similar or related to those of *Littorina* (as various American members of *Thais* or in Australia some of the Trochidae) **c :** any of several No. American freshwater snails

³periwinkle \"\ *vi* -ED/-ING/-S **:** to gather periwinkles ‹go *periwinkling* on the beach›

peri·win·kler \-k(ə)lə(r)\ *n* -S **:** one who gathers or sells periwinkles

peri·zo·ni·um \,perə'zōnēəm\ *n, pl* **perizo·nia** \-ēə\ [NL, fr. *peri-* + Gk *zōnē* girdle + NL *-ium* — more at ZONE] **:** the thin membrane that invests the young auxospore in diatoms

periz·zite \'perə,zīt, pə'ri,z-\ *n* -S *usu cap* [Heb *pěrizzī* Perizzite + E *-ite*] **:** a member of an ancient people of Palestine before its conquest by the Israelites

per·jink \pər'jiŋk\ *adj* [origin unknown] *Scot* **:** PRECISE, NEAT

per·jure \'pərjər, 'pəjə(r, 'pəijə(r\ *vb* **perjured; perjured; perjuring** \-j(ə)riŋ\ **perjures** [MF *parjurer, perjurer*, fr. L *perjurare*, fr. *per-* detrimentally + *jurare* to swear — more at PER-, JURY] *vi, archaic* **:** to violate one's oath, vow, or sworn promise **:** take an oath with the intention of breaking it **:** commit perjury ‹resolved to abjure and ~, as occasion might serve —Edward Gibbon› **~** *vt* **1** *obs* **:** to cause to commit perjury ‹want will ~ the ne'er touched vestal —Shak.› **2 :** to make a perjurer of (oneself) esp. by telling what is false when sworn or swearing to tell the truth **:** to be involved in or proved guilty of perjury or falsely swearing ‹claimed that the witness *perjured* himself› ‹thanked her, with as much enthusiasm as he could muster without actually *perjuring* himself —Archibald Marshall›

perjured *adj* **1 :** guilty of perjury **:** FORSWORN ‹O ~ woman! thou dost stone my heart —Shak.› **2 :** marked by perjury **:** PERJURIOUS ‹a conviction manifestly based on ~ testimony —O.K.Fraenkel›

per·jur·er \-j(ə)rə(r)\ *n* -S **:** a person guilty of perjury ‹a self-confessed ~›

per·ju·ri·ous \pə(r)'jurēəs, ¦pər¦j-, (')pə¦j-, (')pəi¦j-, -jür-\ *adj* [L *perjuriosus* fr. *perjurium* perjury + *-osus* -ous] **:** marked by perjury ‹~ divorce court testimony› — **per·ju·ri·ous·ly** *adv* — **per·ju·ri·ous·ness** *n* -ES

per·jur·ous \'pərj(ə)rəs\ *adj* [L *perjurus*, fr. *perjurare*] **:** PERJURIOUS

per·ju·ry \'pərj(ə)rē, 'pəj-,'pəij-, -ri\ *n* -ES [ME *perjurie, parjurie*, fr. AF *parjurie*, fr. L *perjurium*, fr. *perjurus*] **1 :** the voluntary violation of an oath or vow either by swearing to what is untrue or by omission to do what has been promised under oath **:** false swearing; *specif* **:** a willfully false statement of fact material to the issue made by a witness under oath in a competent judicial proceeding or under statute law so made on affirmation and in some jurisdictions any case including one that is extrajudicial of willful false statement made under an oath authorized to be administered by law ‹convicted of ~› ‹subornation of ~› **2 :** an instance of false swearing or willful breach of oath ‹at lovers' *perjuries*, they say, Jove laughs —Shak.› ‹brazen it out . . . in the box by absurd and silly *perjuries* —Oscar Wilde›

¹perk \'pərk, 'pək, 'pəik\ *vb* -ED/-ING/-S [ME *perken*, perh. fr. ONF *perquer* to perch, fr. *perque* perch, fr. L *pertica* pole — more at PERCH] *vi* **1 a :** to thrust up the head, stretch out the neck, or carry the body in a bold, self-assertive, or insolent manner ‹a file of geese ~*ing* down the roadway —Ellen Glasgow› **b :** to stick up or out jauntily ‹a . . . sand-colored handkerchief with monogram in brown ~*ed* from his breast pocket —Adria Langley› **2 :** to wear or assume an air of superiority or condescension **:** become presumptuous **:** exalt oneself ‹~*ing* over her neighbors› **3 :** to gain or assume an appearance of vigor, animation, or cheerfulness esp. after a period of weakness or depression — usu. used with *up* ‹had ~*ed up* considerably . . . the morale had plainly stiffened —P.G.Wodehouse› **~** *vt* **1 :** to make smart, trim, or spruce in appearance **:** make brisk or acute **:** FRESHEN ‹~ the taste and lift the spirit —Irving Kolodin› — often used with *up* ‹~ up their jaded zest in life —Dorothy C. Fisher› ‹denims are ~*ed up* with . . . embroidery —*Woman's Wear Daily*› ‹a giveaway . . . helps ~ up sales —*Sales Management*› **2 :** to lift or thrust quickly, assertively, or impudently ‹~*s* his tail up and challenges the world —Richard Jefferies›

²perk \"\ *adj* [prob. fr. ¹*perk*] **:** proud or jaunty in bearing **:** SELF-CONFIDENT, BRISK ‹~ as a peacock›

³perk \"\ *n* -S [ME *perke*, fr. ONF *perque* — more at ¹PERK] *n, dial* **:** PERCH

⁴perk \"\ *vb* -ED/-ING/-S **:** PERCH

[5]**perk** \"\ *n* -s [by shortening & alter.] *chiefly Brit* : PERQUISITE — usu. used in pl. ⟨as pay and ~s go, it's a good job —Ian Scott⟩

[6]**perk** \"\ *vi* -ED/-ING/-S [by shortening & alter.] : PERCOLATE ⟨smelled and heard the coffee ~*ing* —Vance Packard⟩

perk·i·ly \-kəlē, -li\ *adv* : in a perky manner : IMPUDENTLY, SAUCILY ⟨stuck ~, like a bustle on a woman's skirt —Kenneth Roberts⟩

perk·i·ness \-kēnəs, -kin-\ *n* -ES : the quality or state of being perky : JAUNTINESS ⟨kept his . . . ~ of spirit —Richard Church⟩ ⟨his ~ and his occasional irascibility have marked him out as an average man —*London Daily Mail*⟩

perking *adj* [fr. pres. part. of [1]*perk*] : PERKY

per·kin reaction *also* **perkin synthesis** \'pərkə̇n-\ *n, usu cap P* [after Sir William Henry *Perkin* †1907 Eng. chemist] : a reaction for making an unsaturated aromatic acid (as cinnamic acid) by heating an aromatic aldehyde with an acid anhydride (as acetic anhydride) in the presence of a base (as sodium acetate or potassium carbonate)

per·kin·si·el·la \,pərkə̇nzē'elə, (,)pər,kin-\ *n, cap* [NL, fr. Robert C.L.*Perkins* †1955 Brit. entomologist + NL *-i-* + *-ella*] : a genus of leafhoppers that includes some which are vectors of Fiji disease of sugarcane in Fiji and Samoa

per·kin's purple *or* **perkin's violet** \'pərkə̇nz-\ *n, often cap 1st P* [after Sir W. H. *Perkin*] : MAUVE 2

perky \'pərkē, 'pə̄k-,'pəik-, -ki\ *adj* -ER/-EST [[1]*perk* + *-y*] **1** : briskly self-assured : COCKY ⟨the common barnyard rooster . . . every step ~ —*Atlantic*⟩ ⟨a short, ~ woman with . . . the agile, inquisitive appearance of a monkey —Edwin O'Connor⟩ **2** : JAUNTY, SPRIGHTLY, CHIPPER ⟨from ~ jeeps to leviathan trailer trucks —*Amer. Fabrics*⟩ ⟨a ~ . . . waltz —*New Yorker*⟩ ⟨always in good health, always ~ —*Listener*⟩ **3** : standing up, away, or out from a garment to which it is attached ⟨caps are . . . of velvet with a ~ little fence of trimming around the edges —Lois Long⟩

per·la \'pərlə\ *n, cap* [NL, fr. ML, pearl, fr. OF *perle* — more at PEARL] : a genus (the type of the family Perlidae) of stone flies

per·la·ceous \,pər'lāshəs\ *adj* [ML *perla* pearl + E *-aceous*] : resembling pearl : PEARLY

per·lar·ia \,pər'la(a)rēə\ [NL, fr. *Perla* + *-aria*] *syn of* PLECOPTERA

[1]**per·la·tive** \pər'lād·iv, 'pərləd·-\ *adj* [L *perlatus* (suppletive past part. of *perferre* to carry through, convey; *perlatus* fr. *per-* through + *latus*, suppletive past part. of *ferre* to carry) + E *-ive* — more at PER-, BEAR, TOLERATE] : of, relating to, or constituting a grammatical case that signifies the means of transportation

[2]**perlative** \"\ *n* -s : the perlative case of a language or a form in the perlative case

[1]**perle** *like* PEARL\ *n* -s [F, lit., pearl — more at PEARL] **1** : a soft gelatin capsule for enclosing volatile or unpleasant tasting liquids intended to be swallowed **2** : a fragile glass ampul that contains a liquid (as amyl nitrite) and that is intended to be crushed and the vapor inhaled

[2]**perle** \"\ *n* -s [fr. *purl*] : PICOT

per·lèche \(')per¦lesh\ *n* -s [F, fr. F dial. *perlicher* to lick one's lips, fr. *per-* thoroughly (fr. L) + *licher* to lick, of Gmc origin; akin to OS *likkon* to lick — more at LICK] : a superficial inflammatory condition of the angles of the mouth often with fissuring that is caused esp. by infection, avitaminosis

perle cotton *n* [by alter. (influenced by F *perle*)] : PEARL COTTON

[1]**per·lid** \'pərlə̇d\ *adj* [NL *Perlidae*] : of or relating to the Perlidae

[2]**perlid** \"\ *n* -s : a stone fly of the family Perlidae

per·li·dae \-lə,dē\ *n pl, cap* [NL, fr. *Perla*, type genus + *-idae*] : a large family of stone flies

per·lingual \,pər, (')per+\ *adj* [ISV [1]*per-* + *lingual*] : through or by way of the tongue ⟨~ administration of a drug⟩ ⟨~ medication⟩ — **per·lingually** \"+\ *adv*

per·lite \'pər,līt\ *n* -s [F, fr. *perle* pearl + *-ite* — more at PEARL] : volcanic glass that has a concentric shelly structure, appears as if composed of concretions, is usu. grayish and sometimes spherulitic, and when expanded by heat forms insulating material and a lightweight aggregate used esp. in concrete and plaster

per·lit·ic \,pər¦lid·ik\ *adj* [ISV *perlite* + *-ic*] : of, relating to, or having a texture like perlite

per·loir \,pərl'wär\ *n* -s [F, fr. *perler* to make in the shape of pearls, fr. *perle*] : a steel punch of half-bead form used esp. for modeling balls on metal and for cutting foil to be inserted in enamel

Per·lon \'pər,län\ *trademark* — used for either of two synthetic polyamide fibers similar to nylon

per·lus·trate \(,)pər'lə,strāt\ *vt* -ED/-ING/-S [L *perlustratus*, past part. of *perlustrare*, fr. *per-* through + *lustrare* to traverse, survey, lustrate, brighten — more at PER-, LUSTRATE] : to go through and examine thoroughly : SURVEY ⟨~ a building⟩

per·lus·tra·tion \,pər,lə'strāshən\ *n* -s : the act or process of perlustrating

[1]**perm** \'p(y)e(ə)rm\ *adj, usu cap* [*Perm*, city near the Ural mountains, U.S.S.R.] : of or from the city of Perm, U.S.S.R. : of the kind or style prevalent in Perm

[2]**perm** \'pərm\ *n* -s [by shortening] : PERMANENT WAVE

perm *abbr* permanent

per·ma·frost \'pərmə+,-\ *n* [*permanent* + *frost*] : a permanently frozen layer of soil, subsoil, or other deposit sometimes including the bedrock and occurring at variable depth below the earth's surface in arctic or subarctic regions : PERGELISOL

Perm·al·loy \'pərmə,lȯi\ *trademark* — used for an easily magnetized and demagnetized alloy composed of about 80 percent nickel and 20 percent iron

per·ma·nence \'pərmənən|(t)s, 'pə̄m-,'pəim- *also* -mnən|\ *n* -s [ME, fr. MF, fr. ML *permanentia*, fr. L *permanent-, permanens* + *-ia* *-y*] **1** : the quality or state of being permanent : DURABILITY ⟨a pioneer town . . . that has not yet acquired an air of ~ —Ivor Jones⟩ ⟨the ~ of his achievement —Hilaire Belloc⟩ ⟨the degree of ~ of different ruling inks —*Ruling Inks & Dyes*⟩ **2** : two adjacent like signs in a series of positive and negative signs in mathematics — opposed to *variation* ⟨in the series of coefficients of the polynomial $3x^3-x^2-8x+7$ there is one ~⟩

per·ma·nen·cy \|sē, |si\ *n* -ES [ML *permanentia*] **1** : the quality or state of being permanent : DURATION, FIXEDNESS ⟨old homes and churches have about them an air of . . . ~ —L.O. Warner⟩ **2** : one that is permanent ⟨the visit developed into a ~ —Humphrey Bullock⟩ ⟨the *permanencies* of the human heart —Clifton Fadiman⟩

[1]**per·ma·nent** \|t\ *adj* [ME, fr. MF, fr. L *permanent-, permanens*, pres. part. of *permanēre* to endure, remain, fr. *per-* through, throughout + *manēre* to remain — more at PER-, MANSION] : continuing or enduring (as in the same state, status, place) without fundamental or marked change : not subject to fluctuation or alteration : fixed or intended to be fixed : LASTING, STABLE ⟨literature of ~, not ephemeral, value⟩ ⟨likely to cause ~ injury⟩ ⟨the paintings in the ~ collection⟩ ⟨elected ~ chairman of the convention⟩ — **per·ma·nent·ness** *n* -ES

[2]**permanent** *n* -s **1** : one that is permanent; *specif* : something (as a quality, element, entity) conceived of as abiding or eternal ⟨the ~s of existence —D.W.Gotshalk⟩ **2** : PERMANENT WAVE ⟨an unbecoming ~ —Ruth Domino⟩

permanent alimony *n* : alimony decreed after a hearing on the merits of a divorce, separate support, or separation case — compare ALIMONY PENDENTE LITE

permanent assets *n pl* : CAPITAL ASSETS

permanent axis *n* : the axis about which a free rigid body can rotate in equilibrium being in general the axis of greatest moment of inertia through the center of mass — compare PRINCIPAL AXIS

permanent blue *n* : FRENCH BLUE

permanent bordeaux FRR \-,e,fä'rär\ *n, usu cap P&B* : an organic pigment — see DYE table I (under *Pigment Red 12*)

permanent capital *n* : capital that does not require replacement but is in continuous existence

permanent carmine FB \-,ef'bē\ *n, usu cap P&C* : an organic pigment — see DYE table I (under *Pigment Red 5*)

permanent fast yellow NCG \,en,sē'jē\ *n, usu cap P&F&Y* : an organic pigment — see DYE table I (under *Pigment Yellow 16*)

permanent gas *n* **1** : a gas (as hydrogen, nitrogen, carbon monoxide) believed to be incapable of liquefaction **2** : a substance that remains gaseous under normal conditions; *esp* : one whose critical temperature is far below room temperature — compare VAPOR

permanent green *n* : TERRE VERTE 2

permanent hardness *n* : the part of the total hardness of water that persists after boiling — distinguished from *temporary hardness*

per·ma·nent·ly *adv* [ME, fr. *permanent* + *-ly*] : in a permanent manner

permanent magnet *n* : a magnet that retains its magnetism after removal of the magnetizing force — see MAGNETO illustration

permanent magnetism *n* : magnetism that remains after the exciting force has been removed : stable residual magnetism

permanent mold *n* : a metal mold into which liquid metal is poured by gravity for the production of many successive castings of the same shape

permanent oil *n* : NONDRYING OIL

permanent pasture *also* **permanent meadow** *n* : natural or seeded grassland that remains unplowed for many years

permanent red *n* **1** : BLOOD RED **2** *often cap P&R* : any of several organic pigments — see DYE table I (under *Pigment Orange 5* and *Pigment Red 2, 7, 10, 48*)

permanent red R \-'är\ *n, usu cap P&R* : FIRE RED 2 — see DYE table I (under *Pigment Red 4*)

permanent set *n* : the amount by which a material stressed beyond its elastic limit fails to return to its original size or shape when the load is removed

permanent strain *n* : a strain that develops within a body upon rapid or nonuniform solidification and that may be removed by careful annealing

permanent tissue *n* : a tissue that has completed its growth and differentiation and is generally incapable of meristematic activity — compare MERISTEM

permanent tooth *n* : one of the second set of teeth of a mammal that follow the milk teeth, typically persist into old age, and in man are 32 in number including 4 incisors, 2 canines, and 10 premolars and molars in each jaw

permanent violet *n* : MANGANESE VIOLET

permanent wave *n* : a long-lasting hair wave produced by winding hair on curlers and applying chemicals or chemicals and heat — compare COLD WAVE

permanent way *n, Brit* : the roadway of a railroad

permanent white *n* : a durable white pigment that does not darken on exposure: as **a** : BLANC FIXE **b** : ZINC WHITE **c** : TITANIUM WHITE

permanent wilting *n* : wilting from which a plant will recover only upon addition of moisture to the soil

permanent yellow *n* : YELLOW OCHER 2

per·manganate \,pər, (')per+\ *n* -s [ISV *permanganic* + *-ate*] : a salt of permanganic acid; *esp* : POTASSIUM PERMANGANATE

per·manganic acid \,pər, ¦per+ . . .\ *n* [ISV *per-* + *manganic*] : an unstable strong acid $HMnO_4$ known only in purple-colored strongly oxidizing aqueous solutions (as those prepared by dissolving manganese heptoxide in water) and in the form of purple salts

permanganic anhydride *n* : MANGANESE HEPTOXIDE

per·man·sive \pə(r)'man(t)siv\ *adj* [L *permansus* (past part. of *permanēre* to endure, remain) + E *-ive* — more at PERMANENT] : of, relating to, or constituting an aspect of the verb (as in Akkadian) denoting that the action is a continuous procedure

per·ma red \,pərmə-\ *n* [*permanent red*] : BLOOD RED

per·ma·tron \'pərmə-,trän\ *n* -s [*permanent* + *-tron*] : a vacuum tube in which the electron flow is controlled by a magnetic field

per·me·abil·i·ty \,pərmēə'bilə̇d·ē, ,pə̄m-, ,pəim-, -lə̇tē, -i\ *n* **1** : the quality or state of being permeable ⟨the ~ of protective films⟩ ⟨the ~ of a membrane⟩ ⟨the water vapor ~ of leather is inherently high —*Technical News Bull.*⟩ **2** : the property of a porous material that is measured by the rate by volume at which a fluid of unit viscosity passes through unit cross section of the material under unit pressure gradient; *specif* : a measure of the ease of fluid flow through rocks — compare DARCY, DARCY'S LAW **3** : the measure of the rate of diffusion of gas through intact balloon fabric usu. expressed in liters per square meter of fabric per 24 hours under standard conditions **4** : the property of a magnetizable substance that determines the degree in which it modifies the magnetic flux in the region occupied by it in a magnetic field; *specif* : the ratio of the induction to the magnetizing force in the substance

per·me·able \'==əbəl\ *adj* [LL *permeabilis*, fr. L *permeare* to permeate + *-abilis* -able — more at PERMEATE] : capable of being permeated : PASSABLE, PENETRABLE, PERVIOUS ⟨class lines are moderately ~ in a democratic society —Abram Kardiner⟩ — used esp. of a substance that allows the passage of fluids ⟨a ~ membrane⟩ ⟨white limestone . . . extremely ~ to water —*Jour. of Geol.*⟩ — **per·me·able·ness** *n* -ES — **per·me·ably** \-blē, -bli\ *adv*

per·meame·ter \'pərmēə,mēd·ər, ,pərmē'aməd·-\ *n* [*permeability* + *-meter*] **1** : an instrument for measuring magnetic permeability — compare PERMEABILITY 4 **2** : an apparatus for measuring porous permeability — compare PERMEABILITY 2

per·me·ance \'pərmēən(t)s, 'pə̄m-,'pəim-\ *n* -s [fr. [1]*permeant*, after such pairs as E *abundant: abundance*] **1** : PERMEATION **2** : the reciprocal of magnetic reluctance

[1]**per·me·ant** \-nt\ *adj* [L *permeant-, permeans*, pres. part. of *permeare* to pass through, permeate — more at PERMEATE] : PERMEATING

[2]**permeant** \"\ *n* -s : an animal influent that ranges widely within the ecological community of which it is a part

per·me·ate \-ē,āt, *usu* -ād.+V\ *vb* -ED/-ING/-S [L *permeatus*, past part. of *permeare*, fr. *per-* through + *meare* to go, pass; akin to MW *mynet* to go, OSlav *minǫti* to go past, pass] *vi* : to diffuse through or penetrate something ⟨liquid *permeating* through the porous substance⟩ ~ *vt* **1** : to spread or diffuse through ⟨the air is *permeated* by the pungent scent of tobacco —*Amer. Guide Series: N.C.*⟩ ⟨an atmosphere of distrust . . . has been allowed to ~ the government —Vannevar Bush⟩ **2** : to pass through the pores or interstices of : penetrate and pass through without causing rupture or displacement — used esp. of a fluid that passes through substances of loose texture ⟨water ~s sand⟩

syn PERMEATE, PERVADE, PENETRATE, IMPENETRATE, INTERPENETRATE, IMPREGNATE, and SATURATE can mean, in common, to pass or cause to pass through every part of a thing, literally or figuratively. PERMEATE implies diffusion through the total or all the pores or interstices of a substance or entity ⟨a green dye *permeating* a garment⟩ ⟨a pleasant smell which *permeated* the shop from morning till night —Ben Riker⟩ ⟨the entire Divine Comedy is *permeated* with the spirit of courtly love —R.A. Hall b.1911⟩ ⟨how deeply the sense of beauty had *permeated* the whole nation —Laurence Binyon⟩ ⟨their tribes gradually became *permeated* with a good deal of Chinese culture —Owen & Eleanor Lattimore⟩ PERVADE, close to PERMEATE, stresses a spreading diffusion throughout every part of a whole ⟨I want kindness and tolerance to *pervade* the earth —F.A.Swinnerton⟩ ⟨an eerie silence *pervades* the place —Lewis Mumford⟩ ⟨the artistry of this first chapter . . . *pervades* and illumines the entire novel —G.H.Genzmer⟩ ⟨the influence of Descartes *pervades* economics even today —Phoebe T. Danière⟩ PENETRATE in this context implies the entrance of something that goes deep and transmits its characteristic or efficient force throughout ⟨a commanding significance, which *penetrates* the whole, informing and ordering everything —F.R.Leavis⟩ ⟨the whole poem is *penetrated* with religion —G.G.Coulton⟩ ⟨the remains of the aristocratic society . . . are *penetrated* not only with an aristocratic but with a political spirit —Walter Bagehot⟩ IMPENETRATE is an intensive of PENETRATE, often throwing more stress on the idea of diffusion than of entrance ⟨some coloring substance with which the liquid was *impenetrated*⟩ INTERPENETRATE, an intensive of PENETRATE, can also apply to the mutual penetration of two substances or entities ⟨it overlaps and *interpenetrates* every other major field of human enterprise —Thomas Munro⟩ ⟨the way in which the Bible — and the *Book of Common Prayer* — have *interpenetrated* English life —Douglas Bush⟩ ⟨the . . . the earth *interpenetrated* in the warm gusts of spring; the soil was full of sunlight, and the sunlight full of red dust —Willa Cather⟩ ⟨the organization of the sonnet often demands that the discourse and the moral should *interpenetrate* —Iain Fletcher⟩ IMPREGNATE can strongly imply a causative power and stress a strong influence or effect on a thing or diffusion of something within it to the point of pervasion of all parts of the whole ⟨the water is *impregnated* with magnesia —Aldous Huxley⟩ ⟨the air is *impregnated* with a sort of frigid clamminess —E.A.Robinson⟩ ⟨from his environment the boy had been thoroughly *impregnated* with what was to become the prevailing American doctrine —Harriot B. Barbour⟩ SATURATE in this context implies impregnation, usu. by something obvious or overabundant, to the point where nothing more may be taken up or absorbed ⟨the air is warm, thick, sticky, and . . . *saturated* with vegetable odours —E.J.Banfield⟩ ⟨the air is *saturated* with golden light —Gertrude Diamant⟩ ⟨grew up in an atmosphere *saturated* by the strictest Puritan dogma and doctrine —David Fairchild⟩ ⟨verse that is *saturated* with emotion —J.L.Lowes⟩ ⟨the lugubrious vigilance that *saturates* the whole document —J.V. Kelleher⟩

per·me·ation \,==='āshən\ *n* -s **1** : the quality or state of being permeated : PERVASION ⟨the ~ of this theme . . . in all the areas of communication —J.D.Adams⟩ **2 a** : the act or process of permeating : PENETRATION ⟨the sands are so compacted . . . there is no more space for ~ —*Oil*⟩ ⟨assisted in the ~ of the principles of mental hygiene in all agencies —*U.S. Dept. of Labor Bull.*⟩ **b** : IMPREGNATION 2a

per·me·ative \'==,ād.|iv, -,āt|, |ēv *also* |əv\ *adj* : PERMEATING ⟨armed with ~ irony . . . he punctures affectations —James Kelly⟩

permed \'pərmd\ *adj, chiefly Brit* [[2]*perm* + *-ed*] : having a permanent wave ⟨an exquisitely ~ . . . blonde with delicate features —Phelim Brady⟩

per men·sem \(,)pər'men(t)səm, per-, -n,sem\ *adv* [L] : by the month : MONTHLY ⟨salary . . . *per mensem* —*Scotsman*⟩ ⟨the number of men transported . . . *per mensem* —*Times Hist. of the War*

per·miak *or* **per·myak** \'pərmē,ak, 'per-, -m,yak\ *n* -s *usu cap* [Russ *Permyak*, fr. *Perm'* (Perm), region in eastern Russia] : a member of a Russian-Finnish people northeast of Perm in the U.S.S.R. that are part of the Komi or Zyrians — called also *Permian*

[1]**per·mi·an** \'pərmēən\ *adj, usu cap* [*Perm*, region in eastern Russia (fr. Russ *Perm'*) + E *-ian*] : of or relating to the last major division of the Paleozoic marked by extensive glaciation in India, So. Africa, So. America, and Australia, by decline of the amphibians and increase of primitive reptiles, and by rocks consisting largely of red sandstone and shale — see GEOLOGIC TIME table

[2]**permian** \"\ *n* -s *usu cap* **1** : the Permian period or system of rocks **2 a** : PERMIAK **b** : the Finno-Ugric languages of the Permiaks, Votyaks, and Zyrians

per mill *also* **per mil** \(,)pər'mil\ *adv* [*mill, mille, mil* fr. L *mille* thousand — more at MILE] : by the thousand : per thousand

per·mil·lage \(,)pər'milij\ *n* -s [*per mill* + *-age*] : rate or proportion per thousand

per·mis·si·bil·i·ty \pə(r),misə'biləd·ē, -lətē, -i\ *n* -ES : the quality or state of being permissible ⟨a greater emotional ~, a greater readiness to welcome tears or laughter —Irving Howe & Eliezer Greenberg⟩

[1]**per·mis·si·ble** \pə(r)'misəbəl\ *adj* [ME, fr. ML *permissibilis*, fr. L *permissus* (past part. of *permittere* to permit) + *-ibilis* -ible — more at PERMIT] **1** : that may be permitted : ALLOWABLE, ADMISSIBLE ⟨~ error⟩ ⟨~ dose⟩ ⟨maximum ~ exposure to radiation⟩ ⟨always ~ in a crisis but now a regular practice —John Buchan⟩ **2 a** *of an explosive* : permitted by law to be owned, purchased, or sold **b** : approved by the Federal Bureau of Mines for use in gaseous coal mines — **per·mis·si·ble·ness** *n* -ES

[2]**permissible** \"\ *n* -s : a permissible explosive ⟨sales of ~s and other high explosives —*U.S.Daily*⟩

per·mis·si·bly \-blē,-bli\ *adv* : in a permissible manner

per·mis·sion \pə(r)'mishən\ *n* -s [ME, fr. MF, fr. L *permission-, permissio*, fr. *permissus* (past part. of *permittere* to permit) + *-ion-, -io* -ion — more at PERMIT] **1** : the act of permitting : formal consent : AUTHORIZATION ⟨by the gracious ~ of the party in power —J.B.Priestley⟩ ⟨had asked her ~ —Willa Cather⟩ ⟨obtain written ~s from the holders of the copyrights —*Publisher to Author*⟩

per·mis·sive \pə(r)'misiv, -sēv *also* -səv\ *adj* [F *permissif*, fr. MF, fr. L *permissus* (past part. of *permittere* to permit) + MF *-if* -ive] **1** *archaic* : granted on sufferance : TOLERATED ⟨with what ~ glory since his fall —John Milton⟩ **2** : granting permission : allowing freedom (as of choice, development, behavior) : TOLERANT, INDULGENT ⟨a ~ environment⟩ ⟨the ~ tendencies of the age —C.A.Tonsor⟩ ⟨a cordial ~ pat —Marjorie Brace⟩ ⟨~ parents⟩ **3** : allowing discretion : OPTIONAL ⟨a ~ standard⟩ — used often of legislation enacted by a higher body to be put into effect or not at the option of local authorities ⟨direct primary legislation is largely ~ rather than prescriptive —V.O.Key⟩ — **per·mis·sive·ly** \-səvlē, -li\ *adv* — **per·mis·sive·ness** \-sēvnəs, -siv-\ *n* -ES

permissive blocking *n* : BLOCK SYSTEM

permissive waste *n* : waste arising from a tenant's neglect to repair, take reasonable care of, or keep in proper order or condition an estate or freehold

[1]**per·mit** \pə(r)'mit, *usu* -id·+V\ *vb* **permitted; permitted; permitting; permits** [L *permittere* to let through, allow, permit, fr. *per-* through + *mittere* to let go, send — more at PER-, SMITE] *vt* **1** : to consent to expressly or formally : grant leave for or the privilege of : ALLOW, TOLERATE ⟨~ smoking⟩ ⟨~ an appeal⟩ ⟨~ access to records⟩ **2** : to give (a person) leave : AUTHORIZE ⟨obliged to ~ others to use his patent —Tris Coffin⟩ ⟨one must ~ oneself . . . a certain margin of misstatement —B.N.Cardozo⟩ ⟨~ me to offer my congratulations⟩ **3** *archaic* : to give over : COMMIT ⟨to the gods ~ the event of things —Joseph Addison⟩ **4** : to make possible ⟨building has been divided . . . to ~ an unobstructed view —*Amer. Guide Series: Conn.*⟩ ~ *vi* **1** : to give an opportunity ⟨if time *permitted* I could go on —H.G.Doyle⟩ ⟨made himself as comfortable as the hard rock *permitted* —Fred Majdalany⟩ **2** : ADMIT — usu. used with *of* ⟨the distance . . . was too great to ~ of frequent social intercourse —Martha T. Stephenson⟩

syn see LET

[2]**per·mit** \'pər,mit, 'pə̄,m-, 'pəi,m-, pə(r)'m-, *usu* -id·+V\ *n* -s **1** : a written warrant or license granted by one having authority ⟨a building ~⟩ ⟨a work ~⟩ ⟨a fishing ~⟩ **2** : PERMISSION, ALLOWANCE ⟨had their ~ to proceed⟩ **3** *or* **permit indicia** : postal indicia giving notice that postage has been paid under a special permit (as for bulk mailing)

[3]**permit** \"\ *n* -s [by folk etymology fr. Sp *palometa* — more at PALOMETA] **1** : a large up to three feet long blue and silver pompano (*Trachinotus goodei*) found esp. off the West Indies and Florida — called also *great pompano* **2** : ROUND POMPANO

permit bond *n* : a surety bond required by law as a condition precedent to the enjoyment of some privilege granted by governmental permit

permit card *n* : a card issued by a union to a nonmember allowing him to work on a temporary basis on a union job

per·mit·tance \pə(r)'mit°n(t)s\ *n* -s [[1]*permit* + *-ance*] : PERMISSION

permitted *adj* : ALLOWED

permitted explosive *n, Brit* : a permissible explosive

per·mit·tee \,pərmə¦tē, pər'mid·(,)ē\ *n* -s : one to whom a permission or permit is given ⟨the ~ should begin drilling operations within six months —W.F.Cloud⟩

per·mit·tiv·i·ty \,pərmə'tivəd·ē\ *n* -ES [[1]*permit* + *-ive* + *-ity*] : DIELECTRIC CONSTANT

permix *vt* [back-formation fr. obs. *permixt* mixed thoroughly, fr. ME, fr. L *permixtus*, past part. of *permiscēre* to mix thoroughly, fr. *per-* thoroughly + *miscēre* to mix — more at PER-, MIX] *obs* : to mix thoroughly

permo- *comb form, usu cap* [ISV, fr. [1]*Permian*] : Permian and — esp. in the names of geologic strata ⟨*Permo*carboniferous⟩ ⟨*Permo*pennsylvanian⟩ ⟨*Permo*triassic⟩

per·mono·sulfuric acid \,pər,mänō, -mō+ . . . -\ *n* [*per-* + *mon-* + *sulfuric*] : an unstable crystalline strong monobasic acid H_2SO_5 obtained by acid hydrolysis of persulfates or by the action of hydrogen peroxide on chlorosulfonic acid or sulfuric acid — called also *Caro's acid, peroxymonosulfuric acid*

perm·selective \ˌpərm+\ *adj* [*perm*eable + *selective*] : of, relating to, or being a semipermeable membrane that is also an ion exchanger

per·mu·tate \ˈpərmyəˌtāt, (ˌ)pərˈmyüˌtāt\ *vt* -ED/-ING/-S [L *permutatus*, past part. of *permutare* to change thoroughly, exchange — more at PERMUTE] : CHANGE, INTERCHANGE; *esp* : to arrange in a different order

per·mu·ta·tion \ˌpərmyəˈtāshən, ˌpēm-, ˌpəim-, -myüˈt-\ *n* -S [ME *permutacioun*, fr. MF *permutation*, fr. L *permutation-, permutatio*, fr. *permutatus* + *-ion-, -io* -ion] **1** : exchange of one thing for another as distinguished from a sale for money : BARTER **2** : a thorough change (as in character or condition) : TRANSMUTATION, TRANSFORMATION ⟨the ∼*s* . . . taking place in the physical world —Henry Miller⟩ **3 a** : the act or process of changing the lineal order of a set of objects arranged in a group **b** : an arrangement of a given number of objects ⟨∼*s* of the three items *a*, *b*, and *c*: *abc, acb, bac* . . . —A.K.Kurtz & H.A.Edgerton⟩ — compare COMBINATION 1b(3) — **per·mu·ta·tion·al** \ˌ==ˈtāshənᵊl, -shnəl\ *adj*

permutation lock *n* : a lock having tumblers that may be changed to require different keys or setting combinations

permutation table *n* : a synoptic chart governing the construction of the code groups of a particular code and serving to facilitate correction of garbles

per·mu·ta·tor \ˈ==ˌtād·ə(r)\ *n* -S : a rotary converter with stationary commutator and rotating brushes that has the exciting field induced by the alternating current in a short-circuited magnetic core instead of produced by an external magnet

per·mute \pə(r)ˈmyüt\ *vt* -ED/-ING/-S [ME *permuten* (also, to exchange), fr. MF or L; MF *permuter*, fr. L *permutare*, fr. *per-* thoroughly + *mutare* to change — more at PER-, MUTABLE] **1** *obs* : to change thoroughly : TRANSFORM **2** : to change the order or arrangement of; *esp* : to arrange (objects in a series) in all the possible ways in which they can be arranged

permyak *usu cap*, *var of* PERMIAK

[1]pern *chiefly Brit var of* PIRN 1

[2]pern \ˈpərn\ *n* -S [NL *Pernis*] : HONEY BUZZARD

per·nam·bu·co \ˌpərnəmˌb(y)ü(ˌ)kō, ˌpernəmˌbü-\ *adj, usu cap* [fr. *Pernambuco* (Recife), Brazil] : RECIFE

pernambuco cotton *n, usu cap P* : KIDNEY COTTON

pernambuco jaborandi *n, usu cap P* : JABORANDI 1a

pernambuco rubber *n, usu cap P* : MANGABEIRA RUBBER

pernambuco wood *n, usu cap P* : a brazilwood from a leguminous tree (*Caesalpinia echinata*)

per·nan·cy \ˈpərnənsē\ *n* -ES [AF *pernance* (alter. of OF *prenance*, fr. *prendre* to take — fr. L *prehendere* to seize, grasp — + *-ance*) + E *-y* — more at GET] : a taking or receiving of something (as profits or rents or tithes in kind)

per·net·tia \pə(r)ˈned·ēə\ [NL, fr. Antoine J. *Pernetty* †1796 Fr. traveler and naturalist + NL *-ia*] *syn of* PERNETTYA

per·net·tya \"\ *n, cap* [NL, after A.J.*Pernetty*] : a genus of chiefly American evergreen shrubs (family Ericaceae) having small serrate leaves and usu. solitary axillary flowers

[1]per·ni·cious \pə(r)ˈnishəs\ *adj* [MF *pernicieus*, fr. L *perniciosus*, fr. *pernicies* ruin, destruction (fr. *per* through + *-nicies*, fr. *nec-, nex* violent death) + *-osus* -ous — more at FOR, NOXIOUS] **1** : highly injurious or destructive : tending to a fatal issue : DEADLY ⟨a ∼ influence⟩ ⟨∼ habits⟩ ⟨∼ nonsense⟩ ⟨a ∼ practice⟩ ⟨∼ disease⟩ ⟨emphasis on fixed order frequently results in ∼ restraints against growing and vital movement —M.R.Cohen⟩ ⟨no excuse for allowing our children to be taught a morality which we ourselves believe to be ∼ —Bertrand Russell⟩ **2** *archaic* : intending or doing evil : WICKED, VILLAINOUS ⟨two ∼ daughters —Shak.⟩
syn BANEFUL, NOXIOUS, DELETERIOUS, DETRIMENTAL: PERNICIOUS describes that which harms exceedingly or irreparably by evil or insidious corrupting or enervating ⟨*pernicious* social institutions which stifle the nobler impulses and encourage the baser —V.L.Parrington⟩ ⟨addiction, on the other hand, carries with it a certain stigma which is not unjustified; it suggests the connotation of a *pernicious* or harmful repetitive act which gets out of the control of the individual —D.W.Maurer & V.H.Vogel⟩ BANEFUL may describe anything malevolent or malignant that is likely to kill, poison, or destroy ⟨the *baneful* influence of this narrow construction on all the operations of the government —John Marshall⟩ ⟨seen to be the outward projections of *baneful* subconscious elements and add up to a fearful indictment of the man —*Times Lit. Supp.*⟩ NOXIOUS may refer to what is at once harmful and unwholesome, corrupting, or noisome ⟨the primitive plumbing of the 1870s, by conveying *noxious* odors into the rooms, was often a threat to the family health —A.M.Schlesinger b.1888⟩ ⟨when the educator shall have been educated, the air cleared of *noxious* fallacies, and a sound and virile conception of learning restored —C.H.Grandgent⟩ DELETERIOUS describes whatever has a harmful effect, often in some concealed or unguessed way ⟨it was obvious that lime juice adulterated with five percent sulphuric acid, jellies with formaldehyde, peas with copper, cheap flavoring extracts with wood alcohol, and coloring matter with arsenic or mercury were highly *deleterious* to health —V.G.Heiser⟩ ⟨heroin and other *deleterious* drugs —H.L.Ickes⟩ DETRIMENTAL is a general adjective for anything that harms ⟨neutralizing or eliminating those influences in military aviation which are *detrimental* to the efficiency, health, or life of flying personnel —H.G.Armstrong⟩ ⟨the wheat is cleaned and scrubbed and the fine hairs, *detrimental* to color and quality, removed —*Amer. Guide Series: Minn.*⟩

[2]pernicious \"\ *adj* [L *pernic-, pernix* swift (fr. *perna* haunch, ham) + E *-ious* — more at PEARL] *archaic* : QUICK, SWIFT

pernicious anemia *n* **1** : a severe hyperchromic anemia characterized by a progressive decrease in number and increase in size of the red blood cells and by pallor, weakness, and gastrointestinal and nervous disturbances resulting from absence from the gastric juice of hydrochloric acid and the intrinsic factor necessary for the intestinal absorption of vitamin B_{12} **2** : INFECTIOUS ANEMIA

per·ni·cious·ly *adv* : in a pernicious manner

pernicious malaria *n* : FALCIPARUM MALARIA

per·ni·cious·ness *n* -ES : the quality or state of being pernicious

pernicious scale *n* : SAN JOSE SCALE

per·nick·e·ti·ness \pə(r)ˈnikəd·|ēnə̇s, -kət|, |in-\ *n* -ES : the quality or state of being pernickety : FINICALITY, FASTIDIOUSNESS ⟨∼ and refinement, resulting in a sterile preciosity —Michael Williams⟩

per·nick·e·ty \|ē, |i\ *adj* [perh. alter. of *particular*] **1** : having extremely exacting standards : FINICAL, FUSSY, METICULOUS ⟨dons who can be . . . obstinate and ∼ —R.F.Harrod⟩ **2** : requiring great precision : TICKLISH ⟨his ∼, very nasty job —Paul de Kruif⟩ **syn** see NICE

per·nine \ˈpərˌnīn\ *adj* [NL *Pernis* + E *-ine*] : of or relating to the genus *Pernis*

per·nio \ˈpərnēˌō\ *n, pl* **perni·o·nes** \ˌ==ˈō(ˌ)nēz\ [L, fr. *perna* haunch, ham + *-io* -ion — more at PEARL] : CHILBLAIN

per·ni·o·sis \ˌpərnēˈōsə̇s\ *n, pl* **pernio·ses** \-ōˌsēz\ [NL, fr. L *pernio* + NL *-osis*] : a skin abnormality resulting from cold

per·nis \ˈpərnə̇s\ *n, cap* [NL, modif. of Gk *pternis*, a hawk] : a genus of hawks (family Falconidae) consisting of the honey buzzards

per·nitric acid \ˌpər+. . .-\ *n* [ISV *per-* + *nitric*] : an explosive acid HNO_4 held to be obtained as a liquid or in the form of salts (as by oxidation of nitrogen pentoxide with anhydrous hydrogen peroxide) — called also *peroxynitric acid;* not used systematically

per·noc·tate \(ˌ)pərˈnäkˌtāt\ *vi* -ED/-ING/-S [L *pernoctatus*, past part. of *pernoctare*, fr. *per-* through + *noct-, nox* night — more at PER-, NIGHT] : to stay up or out all night; *esp* : to pass the night in vigil or prayer ⟨I *pernoctated* with the . . . students once —J.C.Ransom⟩

per·noc·ta·tion \ˌpərˌnäkˈtāshən\ *n* -S [LL *pernoctation-, pernoctatio*, fr. L *pernoctatus* + *-ion-, -io* -ion] : the act of pernoctating; *esp* : an all-night vigil

Per·nod \(ˈ)perˌnō\ *trademark* — used for an aromatic French liqueur that is used as an aperitif and has a flavor somewhat like that of anisette

per·nor \ˈpərnər, -ˌnȯ(ə)r\ *n* -S [ME *pernour*, fr. AF, alter. of OF *preneor, preneur* taker, fr. *prendre* to take + *-eor, -eur* -or — more at PERNANCY] : a taker or receiver esp. of income (as from rents) or profits

per·not furnace \(ˈ)perˌnō-\ *n, usu cap P* [after Charles *Pernot*, its inventor] : a reverberatory furnace with a circular revolving hearth used in making steel

perns *pl of* PERN

per·nyi moth \ˈpərnēˌī-, ˈpernēˌē-\ *n* [NL *pernyi* (specific epithet of *Antheraea pernyi*), after Paul H. *Perny* †1907 French missionary and Chinese scholar] : a Chinese silk-producing moth (*Antheraea pernyi*)

pernyi silkworm *n* : a caterpillar that is the larva of the pernyi moth, feeds on oak leaves, and produces pongee silk

pe·ro·ba \pəˈrōbə\ *n* -S [Pg, fr. Tupi *iperoba, peroba*] : any of several important Brazilian timber trees: as **a** *or* **peroba rosa** : a tree (*Aspidosperma polyneuron*) with very hard rose-yellow wood common in the state of São Paulo **b** : a tree (*Paratecoma peroba*) of the family Apocynaceae with yellowish brown wood found along the coast of So. America — called also *ipé peroba*

perofskite *var of* PEROVSKITE

pe·rog·na·thus \pəˈrägnəthəs\ *n, cap* [NL, fr. Gk *pēro-* (fr. *pēra* pouch, wallet) + *-gnathus*] : a genus of sciuromorph rodents (family Heteromyidae) consisting of the pocket mice

pero·medusae \ˌperō+\ *n pl, cap* [NL, fr. Gk *pēro-* (fr. *pēra* pouch) + *medusae*, pl. of *medusa*] *in some classifications* : a division of Scyphozoa that is characterized by the presence of four interradial tentaculocysts and is approximately equal to the order Coronatae

[1]pero·medusan \"+\ *adj* [NL *Peromedusae* + E *-an*] : of or relating to the Peromedusae

[2]peromedusan \"\ *n* -S : a coelenterate of the division Peromedusae

pe·rom·e·la \pəˈrämələ\ [NL, fr. Gk *pēromelēs* with maimed limbs, fr. *pēros* maimed + *melos* limb; akin to Gk *pēma* suffering, calamity — more at PATIENT, MELODY] *syn of* AISTOPODA

pero·mys·cus \ˌperəˈmiskəs\ *n, cap* [NL, fr. Gk *pēros* maimed + *myskos* small mouse, dim. of *mys* mouse — more at MOUSE] : a genus of rodents (family Cricetidae) comprising the white-footed mice of No. America

pero·nate \pəˈrōnə̇t, ˈperəˌnāt\ *adj* [L *peronatus* having boots of untanned leather, fr. *peron-, pero* hide boot (prob. fr. *pera* leather sack, pouch, fr. Gk *pēra*) + *-atus* -ate] : having a mealy or woolly covering resembling a boot or stocking — used of the stipe of a mushroom

per·o·ne·al \ˌperəˌnēəl\ *adj* [NL *perone*us peroneal (fr. *perone* fibula, fr. Gk *peronē* pin, fibula) + E *-al;* akin to Gk *peran* to pass through — more at FARE] **1** : of or relating to the fibula **2** : near the fibula; *esp* : being a body part so located **3** : of, relating to, or involving a peroneal part ⟨∼ spasm⟩

peroneal artery *n* : a deeply seated artery running along the back part of the fibular side of the leg to the heel, arising from the posterior tibial, and giving off or dividing near the ankle into an anterior and posterior branch

peroneal atrophy *n* : wasting of the muscles of the calf

peroneal nerve *n* : the smaller of the popliteal nerves passing obliquely outward and downward from the popliteal space and to the neck of the fibula where it divides into deep and superficial branches that supply certain muscles and skin areas of the leg and foot

peroneo- *comb form* [*peroneal*] : peroneal and ⟨*peroneo*calcaneal⟩

per·o·ne·us \ˌperəˌnēəs\ *n, pl* **pero·nei** \-ēˌī\ [NL, fr. *peroneus* peroneal — more at PERONEAL] : any of several muscles (as the peroneus longus) of the lower leg that arise from the fibula and are inserted on one of the metatarsal bones of the foot

pe·ro·ni·al \pəˈrōnēəl\ *adj* [NL *peronium* + E *-al*] : of or relating to a peronium

pero·nism \pəˈrōˌnizəm *sometimes* ˈperəˌn-\ *or* **pe·ro·nis·mo** \ˌperəˈniz(ˌ)mō, -nēz-\ *n* -S *usu cap* [Sp *peronismo*, fr. Juan Domingo *Perón* †1974 Argentine politician + Sp *-ismo* -ism] : the political, economic, and social principles and policies associated with Perón and his regime and usu. regarded as fascist ⟨a . . . factual indictment of the aims and methods of *Peronism* —*Times Lit. Supp.*⟩

[1]pero·nist \pəˈrōnə̇st *sometimes* ˈperən-\ *or* **pe·ro·nis·ta** \ˌperəˈnistə, -nēs-\ *n* -S *usu cap* [Sp *peronista*, fr. J. D. *Perón* + Sp *-ista* -ist] : a follower of Perón : an adherent of Peronism

[2]peronist \"\ *or* **peronista** \"\ *adj, usu cap* [Sp *peronista*, fr. *peronista*, n.] : of, relating to, or having the characteristics of Peronism or Peronists ⟨free the economy from strangling *Peronist* controls —*Time*⟩ ⟨efforts to build a *Peronista* bloc in South America —*New Republic*⟩

pe·ro·ni·um \pəˈrōnēəm\ *n, pl* **pero·nia** \-ēə\ [NL, fr. Gk *peronion*, small pin, dim. of *peronē* pin, fibula — more at PERONEAL] : a tract of modified epithelium between the margin of the umbrella and the base of a tentacle in some Hydromedusae

perono- *comb form, cap* [NL, fr. *perone* fibula — more at PERONEAL] : pin : fibula ⟨*Perono*spora⟩ — in the names of taxa

per·o·nos·po·ra \ˌperəˈnäspərə\ *n, cap* [NL, fr. *perono-* + *-spora*] : a genus (the type of the family Peronosporaceae) of destructive downy mildews having the sporangiophores dichotomously branched and with pointed tips — see ONION MILDEW, TOBACCO BLUE MOLD

per·o·no·spo·ra·ce·ae \ˌperənōspəˈrāsēˌē\ *n pl, cap* [NL *Peronospora*, type genus + *-aceae*] : a family of parasitic fungi (order Peronosporales) in which the conidiophores form outside the epidermis of the host and develop conidia or sporangia singly or in clusters but never in chains — see DOWNY MILDEW — **per·o·no·spo·ra·ceous** \ˌ====ˌrāshəs\ *adj*

per·o·nos·po·ra·les \ˌperəˌnäspəˈrā(ˌ)lēz\ *n pl, cap* [NL, fr. *Peronospora* + *-ales*] : an order comprising chiefly parasitic lower fungi (subclass Oomycetes) that have equally biflagellate zoospores and conidia which either germinate directly or act as sporangia and contain the families Albuginaceae, Peronosporaceae, and Pythiaceae

pe·rop·o·dous \pəˈräpədəs\ *adj* [Gk *pēros* maimed + E *-podous* — more at PEROMELA] : having rudimentary hind limbs — used of a snake (as a boa, python)

peropus *n* -ES [origin unknown] *obs* : a 17th century fabric resembling paragon

per·oral \ˌpər·, (ˈ)per+\ *adj* [ISV *per-* + *oral*] : occurring through or by way of the mouth ⟨∼ administration of a drug⟩ ⟨∼ infection⟩ — **per·orally** \"+\ *adv*

per·orate \ˌper|əˌrāt, |ōˌr- *also* ˌpər·| *sometimes* ˌpər|; *usu* -ād·+V\ *vb* [L *peroratus*, past. part. of *perorare*, fr. *per-*, prefix used to denote completion + *orare* to speak — more at ORATION] *vi* **1** : to deliver an oration esp. in a grandiloquent style : speak at length **2** : to make a peroration : conclude or sum up a speech ∼ *vt* : to utter in a declamatory manner

per·ora·tion \-ˌrāshən\ *n* -S [ME *peroracyon*, fr. L *peroration-, peroratio*, fr. *peroratus* + *-ion-, -io* -ion] **1** : the concluding part of a composition or discourse (as an oration) : a final usu. formal summing up of the argument (as in a speech) ⟨concludes, in a moving ∼ —Alice S. Morris⟩ ⟨framing . . . the ∼ of his powerful maiden speech —Harold Nicolson⟩ **2** : a flowery highly rhetorical speech ⟨what means this passionate discourse? this ∼ with such circumstance —Shak.⟩ — **per·ora·tion·al** \-shənᵊl,-shnəl\ *adj*

per·ora·tive \ˈ==ˌrād·iv\ *adj* : of, relating to, or suitable for a peroration ⟨∼ examples —John Caffrey⟩

per os \peˈrōs, ˌpər·ˈōs, ˌpər·ˈäs\ *adv* [L] : by way of the mouth

pe·ro·sis \pəˈrōsə̇s\ *n, pl* **pero·ses** \-ōˌsēz\ [NL, fr. Gk *pēros* maimed + NL *-osis* — more at PEROMELA] : a disorder of chicks, turkey poults, and young swans characterized by enlargement of the hock, twisted metatarsi, and slipped tendons and largely eliminable by additions of choline to the diet

pe·rot·ic \pəˈräd·ik\ *adj* [fr. NL *perosis*, after such pairs as NL *narcosis:* E *narcotic*] : of or relating to perosis

pe·rov·skite \pəˈrävzˌkīt, -äfˌsk-\ *or* **pe·rof·skite** \-äfˌ-\ *n* -S [G *perowskit*, fr. Count L. A. *Perovski* †1856 Russian statesman + G *-it* -ite] : a mineral $CaTiO_3$ consisting of calcium titanate, sometimes having also cerium and other rare-earth metals, and occurring in yellow, brown, or grayish black crystals of cubic habit or in reniform masses (hardness 5.5, sp. gr. 4.02–4.04)

per·ox·i·dase \pəˈräksəˌdās, -āz\ *n* -S [ISV *peroxide* + *-ase*] : an enzyme occurring esp. in plants, milk, and leukocytes and consisting of a protein complex with hematin groups that catalyzes the oxidation of various substances (as diphenols or aromatic amines) by peroxides — compare CATALASE

per·ox·i·date \pəˈräksəˌdāt\ *vb* [[1]*peroxide* + *-ate*] : PEROXIDIZE

peroxidatic \pəˌräksəˌdad·ik\ *adj* [fr. *peroxidase*, after such pairs as E *catalase: catalatic*] : of or relating to peroxidase

per·ox·i·da·tion \=ˌ==ˈdāshən\ *n* : the process of peroxidizing

[1]per·ox·ide \pəˈräkˌsīd\ *n* [ISV *per-* + *oxide*] **1** : an oxide containing a relatively high proportion of oxygen — not used systematically **2 a** : a compound (as sodium peroxide or benzoyl peroxide) characterized by the bivalent group or anion -O-O- consisting of two oxygen atoms united to each other and yielding a solution of hydrogen peroxide when treated with acid — compare SUPEROXIDE **b** : HYDROGEN PEROXIDE

[2]peroxide \"\ *vt* -ED/-ING/-S : to treat with a peroxide; *esp* : to bleach (hair) with hydrogen peroxide

peroxide blonde *n* : a woman with bleached hair ⟨doting on a *peroxide blonde* . . . a brazen gold digger —Ngaio Marsh⟩

per·ox·i·dize \pəˈräksəˌdīz\ *vb* [[1]*peroxide* + *-ize*] *vt* : to oxidize to the utmost or so as to form a peroxide ∼ *vi* : to become oxidized to the utmost or so as to form a peroxide

peroxo- *comb form* [ISV *per-* + *ox-*] : PEROXY- — in names of coordination complexes ⟨hex-oxo-*peroxo*-disulfate $S_2O_8^{--}$⟩

per·oxy \pəˈräksē\ *adj* [*peroxy-*] : containing the group -O-O-

peroxy- *comb form* [ISV *per-* + *oxy-*] : containing the group -O-O- characteristic of a peroxide ⟨*peroxy*disulfate⟩ ⟨*peroxy*benzoic acid⟩

per·oxy·acetic acid \pəˌräksē+...-\ *n* [*peroxy-* + *acetic*] : PERACETIC ACID

peroxy acid *n* : an acid (as persulfuric acid) containing the peroxide group

per·oxy·carbonate \pəˌräksē+\ *n* [*peroxy-* + *carbonate*] : PERCARBONATE

per·oxy·carbonic acid \"+...-\ *n* [*peroxy-* + *carbonic*] : PERCARBONIC ACID

per·oxy·chromate \pəˌräksē+\ *n* [*peroxy-* + *chromate*] : PERCHROMATE

per·oxy·chromic acid \"+...-\ *n* [*peroxy-* + *chromic*] : PERCHROMIC ACID

per·oxy·disulfate \pəˌräksē+\ *n* [*peroxy-* + *disulfate*] : a persulfate of the acid $H_2S_2O_8$

per·oxy·disulfuric acid \"+...-\ *n* [*peroxy-* + *disulfuric*] : PERSULFURIC ACID a

per·oxygen \(ˌ)pər+\ *adj* [*per-* + *oxygen*] : PEROXY

per·oxy·mono·sulfuric acid \pəˌräksēˌmänō, -mōnō+...-\ *n* [*peroxy-* + *mon-* + *sulfuric*] : PERMONOSULFURIC ACID

per·oxy·nitric acid \pəˌräksē+...-\ *n* [*peroxy-* + *nitric*] : PERNITRIC ACID

peroxy salt *n* : a salt (as ammonium persulfate) of a peroxy acid

per·oxy·sulfate \pəˌräksē+\ *n* [*peroxy-* + *sulfate*] : PERSULFATE 2

per·oxy·sulfuric acid \"+...-\ *n* [*peroxy-* + *sulfuric*] : PERSULFURIC ACID

perp *abbr* **1** perpendicular **2** perpetual

per pais *or* **per pays** \ˌpərˈpā\ *adv* [AF] : by the country : by a jury or by matter triable by a jury ⟨trials *per pais*⟩

per pa·res \perˈpäˌrās, ˌpərˈpa(a)rēz\ *adv* [L] : by one's peers

[1]per·pend \pə(r)ˈpend\ *vb* -ED/-ING/-S [L *perpendere*, fr. *per-* thoroughly + *pendere* to weigh — more at PER-, PENDANT] *vt* : to weigh carefully in the mind : reflect on : PONDER ⟨∼ my words —Sir Walter Scott⟩ ⟨found himself . . . ∼*ing* it as an experiment in realism —Leonard Merrick⟩ ∼ *vi* : to be attentive : REFLECT, CONSIDER ⟨∼, my princess, and give ear —Shak.⟩ ⟨∼, and do not compel me to use violence —Benjamin Jowett⟩

[2]per·pend \ˈpərpənd\ *or* **per·pent** \-nt\ *or* **par·pen** \ˈpärpən\ *n* -S [ME *perpend, perpoynt*, fr. MF *perpain, parpain*] **1** : a brick or large stone reaching through a wall so as to appear on both sides of it and acting as a binder **2** : PERPEND WALL

[1]per·pen·dic·u·lar \ˌpər|pənˌdikyələr, ˌpə̄|...lə(r, ˌpəi|...lə(r, |pᵊmˌd-\ *adj* [alter. (influenced by L *perpendicularis*) of ME *perpendiculer*, fr. MF, fr. L *perpendicularis*, fr. *perpendiculum* plumb line (fr. *per-* through + *pendēre* to hang + *-iculum*, suffix denoting an instrument) + *-aris* -ar — more at PER-, PENDANT] **1 a** : standing at right angles to the plane of the horizon : pointing to the zenith : exactly vertical or upright ⟨measure the ∼ height⟩ **b** : being or set at right angles to a given line or plane ⟨the lines are ∼ to each other⟩ ⟨an almost ∼ rise in share prices —*U.S. News & World Report*⟩ **2** *obs* : leading directly to : IMMEDIATE ⟨∼ cause⟩ **3** : extremely steep : PRECIPITOUS ⟨a lofty ∼ cliff —E.V.Lucas⟩ **4** *of a person* **a** : erect in bearing ⟨a ∼ retired colonel⟩ **b** : standing up ⟨a bus . . . its platform weighed down with ∼ men —Bruce Marshall⟩ **5** : of, relating to, or in a medieval English Gothic style of architecture in which vertical lines predominate **6** : relating to, uniting, or consisting of individuals of dissimilar type or on different levels ⟨∼, in the sense of providing a strand that will run through both high school and college, uniting different ages —*General Education in a Free Society*⟩ **syn** see VERTICAL

[2]perpendicular \"\ *n* -S **1 a** : a line at right angles to another line or plane **b** : a line through a vertex at right angles to the opposite side or face in a triangle or tetrahedron **2** : an instrument for indicating the vertical line from any point **3 a** : a line at right angles to the plane of the horizon : a vertical line or direction **b** : a vertical plane **c** : an extremely steep or precipitous face (as of a mountain)

per·pen·dic·u·lar·i·ty \ˌ==ˌ==ˈlarəd·ē, -rətē, -i *also* -ˈler-\ *n* -ES [ML *perpendicularitas*, fr. L *perpendicularis* + *-itas* -ity] : the quality or state of being perpendicular

perpendicularly *adv* : in a perpendicular manner

perpendicular separation *n* : the distance between the two dislocated parts of an orig. continuous surface (as the top of a stratum) measured normal to the plane — called also *stratigraphic separation*

perpend wall *n* [[2]*perpend*] : a wall built of perpends : a thin wall

per·pen·sion \pə(r)ˈpenchən\ *n* -S [LL *perpension-, perpensio*, fr. L *perpensus* (past part. of *perpendere* to perpend) + *-ion, -io* -ion — more at PERPEND] : careful weighing in the mind : REFLECTION, CONSIDERATION ⟨give me the results of your ∼*s* —R.L.Stevenson⟩

per·per \ˈperpə(r)\ *n, pl* **perpers** \-(r)z\ *or* **per·pera** \-ərə\ [Serbo-Croatian] : the basic unit of monetary value of Montenegro from 1908 to 1919 equivalent to the Austrian krone

per·pe·trate \ˈpərpə·ˌtrāt, ˈpə̄p-, ˈpəip-, *usu* -ād·+V\ *vt* -ED/-ING/-S [L *perpetratus*, past part. of *perpetrare*, fr. *per-*, prefix denoting completion + *-petrare* (fr. *patrare* to carry out, accomplish — prob. orig. "to perform a ritual" — fr. *patr-, pater* father, religious leader) — more at PER-, FATHER] **1 a** : to be guilty of (as a crime, an offense) : COMMIT ⟨*perpetrated* the . . . massacre —*Amer. Guide Series: Pa.*⟩ ⟨the horrors . . . their former rulers had *perpetrated* —F.E.Hirsch⟩ ⟨that the press . . . should ∼ this calumny —Stephen Spender⟩ **b** : to carry through (a deception) ⟨had *perpetrated* a delightful fraud —L.P.Smith⟩ ⟨∼*s* a successful practical joke —J.A. Morris b. 1904⟩ — often used with *on* or *upon* ⟨a huge hoax *perpetrated* on a band of solemn votaries —C.H.Grandgent⟩ **2** : to produce, perform, or execute badly or in a manner held to be execrable or shocking ⟨∼ such an ungainly sentence⟩ ⟨∼ a pun⟩ ⟨the simpering family groups *perpetrated* on canvas —Dixon Wecter⟩

per·pe·tra·tion \ˌ==·ˈtrāshən\ *n* -S [ME *perpetracionne*, fr. LL *perpetration-, perpetratio*, fr. L *perpetratus* + *-ion-, -io* -ion] **1** : the act or process of perpetrating : COMMISSION ⟨the ∼ of a series of thefts⟩ ⟨the effective ∼ of sabotage —J.J.McCarthy⟩ **2** : something perpetrated : an evil or offensive act ⟨savage ∼*s* —J.H.Newman⟩

per·pe·tra·tor \ˈ==·ˌtrād·ə(r), -ātə-\ *n* -S [LL, fr. L *perpetratus* + *-or*] : one that perpetrates esp. an offense or crime ⟨war is a crime, for which its instigators and ∼*s* can be tried —Vera M. Dean⟩

[1]per·pet·u·al \pə(r)ˈpech(əw)əl, -chwəl\ *adj* [ME *perpetuel*, fr. MF, fr. L *perpetualis*, fr. *perpetuus* continuous, perpetual (fr. *perpet-, perpes*, fr. *per* through, by means of + *-pet-, -pes*, fr. *petere* to go to or toward, seek) + *-alis* -al — more at FOR, FEATHER] **1 a** : continuing forever : EVERLASTING, ETERNAL, UNCEASING ⟨∼ torment after death —H.O.Taylor⟩ ⟨dedicated to a life of ∼ virginity —J.G.Frazer⟩ ⟨the song of the minstrel moved through a ∼ Maytime —J.R.Green⟩ **b** (1) : granted to be valid for all time ⟨was awarded a ~ right-of-way⟩ ⟨granted a ~ charter by the national government —C.W. Ferguson⟩ (2) **:** holding (as an office) for life or for an unlimited time ⟨~ curate⟩ ⟨~ president of a club⟩ ⟨elected ~ fellow —A.G.Chester⟩ **2 :** occurring continually **:** indefinitely long-continued **:** not intermittent **:** CONSTANT ⟨a ~ source of amusement —Havelock Ellis⟩ ⟨the ~ struggle to maintain standards in a democracy —F.N.Robinson⟩ ⟨~ quarreling between one parish and the next —Dorothy Sayers⟩ **3 a :** PERENNIAL 2a **b :** blooming more or less continuously throughout the season **:** REMONTANT ⟨a hybrid ~ rose⟩ **syn** see CONTINUAL

²**perpetual** \"\ *adv* [ME *perpetuel*, fr. *perpetuel*, adj.] *archaic* **:** PERPETUALLY

³**perpetual** \"\ *n* -s [¹*perpetual*] **1 :** PERENNIAL 1 **2 :** a hybrid perpetual rose

perpetual adoration *n* **:** unceasing adoration of the consecrated Host as practised in the convents of several Roman Catholic orders of that name

perpetual calendar *n* **1 :** a table for finding the day of the week for any one of a wide range of dates

PERPETUAL CALENDAR (1781-2011)

DAY OF THE MONTH					Jan. Oct.	Apr. July *Jan.* *	Sept. Dec.	June	Feb. Mar. Nov.	Aug. *Feb.* *	May	DAY OF WEEK
1	8	15	22	29	a	b	c	d	e	f	g	Mon.
2	9	16	23	30	g	a	b	c	d	e	f	Tues.
3	10	17	24	31	f	g	a	b	c	d	e	Wed.
4	11	18	25		e	f	g	a	b	c	d	Thurs.
5	12	19	26		d	e	f	g	a	b	c	Fri.
6	13	20	27		c	d	e	f	g	a	b	Sat.
7	14	21	28		b	c	d	e	f	g	a	Sun.
					1781	1782	1783	1789	*1784*	1785	1786	
					1787	1793	*1788*	1795	1790	1791	1797	
					1792	1799	1794	1801	1802	*1796*	1809	
					1798	1805	1800	1807	1813	1803	1815	
					1804	1811	1806	*1812*	1819	*1808*	*1820*	
					1810	*1816*	1817	1818	*1824*	1814	1826	
					1821	1822	1823	1829	1830	1825	1837	
					1827	1833	*1828*	1835	1841	1831	1843	
					1832	1839	1834	*1840*	1847	*1836*	*1848*	
					1838	*1844*	1845	1846	*1852*	1842	1854	
					1849	1850	1851	1857	1858	1853	1865	
					1855	1861	*1856*	1863	1869	1859	1871	
					1860	1867	1862	*1868*	1875	*1864*	*1876*	
					1866	*1872*	1873	1874	*1880*	1870	1882	
					1877	1878	1879	1885	1886	1881	1893	
					1883	1889	*1884*	1891	1897	1887	1899	
					1888	1895	1890	*1896*	1909	*1892*	1905	
					1894	1901	1902	1903	1915	1898	1911	
					1900	1907	1913	*1908*	*1920*	*1904*	*1916*	
					1906	*1912*	1919	1914	1926	1910	1922	
					1917	1918	*1924*	1925	1937	1921	1933	
					1923	1929	1930	1931	1943	1927	1939	
					1928	1935	1941	*1936*	*1948*	*1932*	*1944*	
					1934	*1940*	1947	1942	1954	1938	1950	
					1945	1946	*1952*	1953	1965	1949	1961	
					1951	1957	1958	1959	1971	1955	1967	
					1956	1963	1969	*1964*	*1976*	*1960*	*1972*	
					1962	*1968*	1975	1970	1982	1966	1978	
					1973	1974	*1980*	1981	1993	1977	1989	
					1979	1985	1986	1987	1999	1983	1995	
					1984	1991	1997	*1992*	*2004*	*1988*	*2000*	
					1990	*1996*	2003	1998	2010	1994	2006	
					2001	2002	*2008*	2009		2005		
					2007				2011			

To find the day of the week corresponding to any date, find the small letter directly under the name of the month and opposite the number of the day of the month; then find the column containing the number of the year and follow up to where that same letter appears at the top of the year column; then, following out to the right, find the day of the week. Thus, to find the day on which March 18, 1930, fell, from the date and month columns find the letter *b* in the fifth letter column, then finding the year 1930 in the third year column follow up to the letter *b* above it and then to the right to the day, Tuesday.

*For dates occurring in Jan. or Feb. of a leap year (indicated by italics), use *italic* names of months, above.

2 : a mechanical calendar for keeping track of current dates over a period of many years **3 :** a calendar in which the years are uniform in the correspondence of days and dates (as in the proposed World Calendar of equal quarter-years and uniform months)

perpetual calendar 2

perpetual canon *n* **:** CIRCULAR CANON 1

perpetual check *n* **:** an endless succession of checks to which the opponent's king in chess may sometimes be subjected to force a draw; *also* **:** a situation involving such an attack

perpetual day *n* **:** the period of nearly six months alternately at the earth's north and south poles when the sun does not set — compare PERPETUAL NIGHT

perpetual inventory *n* **:** a book record of inventory kept continuously up to date by detailed entries for all incoming and outgoing items — compare BOOK INVENTORY

per·pet·u·al·ism \-ə,lizəm\ *n* -s **:** a doctrine of the everlastingness or perpetuation of something (as a system, creed, natural state)

per·pet·u·al·ist \-ələst\ *n* -s **:** an advocate of perpetualism; *specif* **:** one advocating the perpetuation of Negro slavery in the U.S. — **per·pet·u·al·is·tic** \=¦=(=)=¦listik\ *adj*

per·pet·u·al·i·ty \pə(r),pechə'waləd·ē\ *n* -ES [L *perpetualitas*, fr. *perpetualis* perpetual + *-itas* -ity — more at PERPETUAL] **:** PERPETUITY

perpetual lease *n* **:** a lease renewable forever at the lessee's option

per·pet·u·al·ly \pə(r)'pechəlē, -ch(ə)wəlē, -li\ *adv* [ME *perpetuelly*, fr. *perpetuel* perpetual + *-ly*] **1 :** EVERLASTINGLY, FOREVER ⟨an annuity for life or ~⟩ ⟨rays . . . streaming ~ from the sun —Stuart Chase⟩ **2 :** CONSTANTLY, INCESSANTLY ⟨claims people were ~ making on him —Mary Deasy⟩

perpetual motion *n* **1 :** the motion of an ideal mechanism that could continue to operate indefinitely without drawing upon an external source of energy **2** *obs* **:** PERPETUAL MOTION MACHINE

perpetual motion machine *n* **:** a device inherently impossible under the law of conservation of energy that can continue to do work indefinitely without drawing energy from external sources

per·pet·u·al·ness *n* -ES **:** the quality or state of being perpetual

perpetual night *n* **:** the period of nearly six months alternately at the earth's north and south poles when the sun does not rise — compare PERPETUAL DAY

perpetuals *pl of* PERPETUAL

perpetual succession *n* **1 :** the capacity of a corporation to have continuous enjoyment of its property so long as it is legally in existence **2 :** the perpetual existence of a corporation

perpetual trust *n* **:** a trust estate bearing no specific limitation as to its duration — compare PERPETUITY 3b

per·pet·u·a·na \pə(r),pechə'wänə\ *n* -s [L *perpetuus* continuous, perpetual + *-ana*, fem. of *-anus* -an] **:** a durable usu. wool or worsted fabric made in England from the late 16th through the 18th centuries

per·pet·u·ate \pə(r)'pechə,wāt, *usu* -ād·+V\ *vt* -ED/-ING/-S [L *perpetuatus*, past part. of *perpetuare*, fr. *perpetuus* perpetual — more at PERPETUAL] **:** to make perpetual **:** preserve from extinction **:** cause to last indefinitely ⟨~ the species⟩ ⟨~ his memory⟩ ⟨*perpetuating* a defunct tradition —Herbert Read⟩ ⟨~ their absolute control —W.E.McManus⟩

per·pet·u·a·tion \=,=='wāshən\ *n* -s [ME *perpetuacioun*, fr. ML *perpetuation-*, *perpetuatio*, fr. L *perpetuatus* + *-ion-*, *-io* -ion] **:** the act or process of perpetuating **:** PRESERVATION ⟨~ of the culture —A.L.Kroeber⟩ ⟨the ~ of social inequalities —George Sampson⟩

per·pet·u·a·tor \='==,wād·ə(r), -ātə-\ *n* -s **:** one that perpetuates

per·pe·tu·ity \,pər|pə'tüəd·ē, ,pə̄|, ,pəi|, |pə·'tyü-, -üətē, -i\ *n* -ES [ME *perpetuite*, fr. MF *perpetuité*, fr. L *perpetuitat-*, *perpetuitas*, fr. *perpetuus* continuous, perpetual + *-itat-*, *-itas* -ity — more at PERPETUAL] **1 :** endless time **:** ETERNITY ⟨so lost to ~ —John Milton⟩ ⟨his companions are playing for ~ —Sacheverell Sitwell⟩ **2 :** the quality or state of being perpetual ⟨a path to ~ of fame —Lord Byron⟩ — often used with *in* ⟨bequeathed them to the nation in ~ —S.P.B.Mais⟩ **3 a :** duration without limitations as to time **b :** the condition of an estate limited so that it will not take effect or vest within the period fixed by law or so limited as to be or have a possibility of being inalienable either perpetually or beyond the bounds fixed by law **c :** an estate so limited — see RULE AGAINST PERPETUITIES **4 a :** a perpetual annuity **b :** the number of years in which simple interest equals the principal **c :** the number of years' purchase to be given for an annuity to continue forever

per·pet·u·um mo·bi·le \pə(r)¦pechəwəm'mōbə,lē, -,lā\ *n* [NL, lit., perpetual moving (thing)] **1 :** perpetual motion **2 :** a musical composition having the same rapid motion from beginning to end — called also *moto perpetuo*

per·plex \pə(r)'pleks\ *vt* -ED/-ING/-ES [obs. E *perplex*, adj., perplexed, involved, fr. L *perplexus*, fr. *per-* thoroughly + *plexus* involved, fr. past part. of *plectere* to plait, braid, interweave — more at PER-, PLY] **1 :** to disturb mentally esp. so as to make impossible clear or decisive thinking on the matter at hand **:** fill with doubt, uncertainty, or confusion **:** BEWILDER, NONPLUS ⟨~*ed* by many cares⟩ ⟨such contradictions ~ the historian⟩ ⟨questions that have ~*ed* men since time began —C.F.Strubbe⟩ **2 a :** to make intricate, involved, or difficult to understand **:** COMPLICATE, CONFUSE ⟨no attempts at wit obscure or ~ his matter —Earl of Chesterfield⟩ **b :** INTERWEAVE, ENTANGLE ⟨brambles . . . ~*ed* and interwoven with one another —Joseph Addison⟩ **3** *obs* **:** PLAGUE, VEX, TORMENT **syn** see PUZZLE

per·plexed \-kst\ *adj* [L *perplexus* + E *-ed*] **1 a** *archaic* **:** emotionally disturbed by the intricacy or difficulty of a situation **:** ANXIOUS, TROUBLED, DISTRAUGHT ⟨undaunted . . . though wearied and ~ —William Cowper⟩ **b :** filled with doubt or uncertainty **:** PUZZLED, BEWILDERED ⟨the ~ person who . . . no longer trusts the sources of information —E.C.Lindeman⟩ **2 :** full of difficulty **:** COMPLICATED ⟨~ language⟩ ⟨this ~ age of the world —Bliss Perry⟩ **3 :** ENTANGLED ⟨~ with thorn —Alexander Pope⟩

per·plexed·ly \-ksədlē, -kstlē, -li\ *adv* **:** in a perplexed manner

per·plexed·ness \-ksədnəs, -ks(t)n-\ *n* -ES *archaic* **:** PERPLEXITY

per·plex·ful \-ksfəl\ *adj* [*perplex* + *-ful*] **:** full of perplexity **:** PERPLEXING

perplexing *adj* **:** that causes perplexity **:** PUZZLING, BEWILDERING ⟨the situation was most ~ —J.A.Froude⟩ ⟨~ problems . . . had led to the violations of law —T.W.Arnold⟩ — **per·plex·ing·ly** *adv*

per·plex·i·ty \pə(r)'pleksəd·ē, -sətē, -i\ *n* -ES [ME *perplexite*, fr. OF *perplexité*, fr. LL *perplexitat-*, *perplexitas*, fr. L *perplexus* + *-itat-*, *-itas* -ity] **1 :** an agitated or confused mental condition caused by a disturbing or puzzling situation or state of affairs **:** BEWILDERMENT ⟨the look of ~ on his face⟩ ⟨in bitter ~ she kneeled down and prayed —D.H.Lawrence⟩ **2 :** something that perplexes ⟨beset with *perplexities*⟩ **3 :** ENTANGLEMENT ⟨the dense ~ of vines⟩

per pri·mam \per'prē,mäm, ,pər-, -ēməm\ *adv* [NL *per primam (intentionem)*] **:** by first intention ⟨a wound that heals *per primam* usually leaves little scarring⟩

per pro·cu·ra·ti·o·nem \,per,präkə,räd·ē'ō,nem\ *also* **per procuration** \,pər+\ *adv* [L *per procurationem*] **:** by agency **:** by the authority of an agent **:** by proxy

per·qui·site \'pərkwəzət, 'pə̄k-,'pəik-, *usu* -əd·+V\ *n* -s [ME, fr. ML *perquisitum*, fr. neut. of *perquisitus*, past part. of *perquirere* to obtain, acquire, fr. L, to ask about diligently, to make diligent search for, fr. *per-* thoroughly + *-quirere* (fr. *quaerere* to seek, gain, obtain, ask) — more at PER-] **1** *obs* **:** CONQUEST 5 **2 a :** casual income or profits (as from heriots, escheats, reliefs) accruing to the lord of a feudal manor **b :** a privilege, gain, or profit incidental to an employment in addition to regular salary or wages; *esp* **:** one expected or promised ⟨the ~s of the college president include a home and car⟩ ⟨the easy profits of a navy purser's ~s —*Times Lit. Supp.*⟩ **3 :** GRATUITY, TIP; *esp* **:** one expected or claimed by custom for a service ⟨a servant's wages and ~s⟩ **4 :** something held or claimed as an exclusive right or possession ⟨concepts . . . not the ~s of any particular groups —Gilbert Ryle⟩ **syn** see RIGHT

per·qui·si·tion \,pərkwə'zishən\ *n* -s [F, fr. LL *perquisition-*, *perquisitio*, fr. L *perquisitus* + *-ion-*, *-io* -ion] **:** a thorough search; *specif* **:** a search by warrant

per·quis·i·tor \(,)pər'kwizəd·ə(r)\ *n* -s [ML & L; ML, one that obtains or acquires, fr. L, one that searches diligently, fr. *perquisitus* + *-or*] **1 :** the original owner or first purchaser of an estate **2 :** one who makes a perquisition

per·radial \¦pər, (')per+\ *adj* [NL *perradius* + E *-al*] **:** of, relating to, or involving a perradius — **per·radially** \"+\ *adv*

per·radius \"+\ *n* [NL, fr. *per-* + *radius*] **:** any one of the usu. four primary radii of a medusa that pass through radial canals

per·rectal \"+\ *adj* [*per-* + *rectal*] **:** entering through or by way of the rectum ⟨~ feeding⟩ — **per·rectally** \"+\ *adv*

per·rhenate \(,)pər, ˌpə, pe+\ *n* -s [*perrhenic* + *-ate*] **:** a salt of perrhenic acid; *esp* **:** a salt of metaperrhenic acid

per·rhenic acid \¦pər, ˌpə, (')per+. . .-\ *n* [*per-* + NL *rhenium* + E *-ic*] **:** either of two acids formed by the oxidation of rhenium or rhenium compounds of lower valence states and known only in solution or in the form of salts: **a :** the monobasic acid $HReO_4$ analogous to permanganic acid that forms colorless stable salts — called also *metaperrhenic acid* **b :** the tribasic acid H_3ReO_5 that forms yellow salts turning red when heated and hydrolyzed in water to salts of metaperrhenic acid — called also *mesoperrhenic acid*

per·ri·er \'perēə(r)\ *n* -s [ME *perrerer*, fr. MF *perrier*, fr. *pierre* stone, rock (fr. L *petra*) + *-ier* -er — more at PETROUS] **1 :** a medieval engine for throwing stones **2 :** a short mortar formerly used on ships for throwing stones and light shot **:** PEDRERO

per·rine lemon \pə'rīn-\ *n* [after Henry *Perrine* †1840 Am. physician and naturalist] **:** a hybrid produced by crossing the lime and the lemon

per·rin·ist \'perənəst\ *n* -s *usu cap* [F *Perriniste*, fr. Ami *Perrin*, 16th cent. Swiss political leader + F *-iste* -ist] **:** LIBERTINE 2a

per·ron \'perən, pə'rōⁿ\ *n* -s [F, fr. OF, large block of stone, aug. of *perre*, *pierre* stone, rock — more at PERRIER] **1 :** an outdoor stairway leading up to an entrance to a large building (as a church or a mansion) **2 :** a platform at the top of a perron

per·ruche \pə'rüsh\ *n* -s [F, lit., a kind of parrot, alter. of *perroquet* parrot] **:** PARROT GREEN

perruque *var of* PERUKE

perruquier *var of* PERUKIER

per·ry \'perē\ *n* -ES [ME *pereye*, *peirrie*, *perre*, fr. MF *peré*, fr. (assumed) VL *piratum*, fr. L *pirum* pear + *-atum* -ate — more at PEAR] *chiefly Brit* **:** the expressed juice of pears often made alcoholic by fermentation and sometimes effervescent by carbonation or by fermentation in a closed container

pers *abbr* **1** person; personal; personally **2** personnel

per·sae \'pər,sē, 'per,sī\ *n pl*, *usu cap* [L, fr. Gk *Persai*, pl. of *Persēs* Persian] **:** PERSIAN 5

per·salt \'pər, 'per+,-\ *n* [⁶*per* + *salt*] **1 a :** a salt containing a relatively large proportion of the acidic element or group ⟨ferric salts are *persalts* of iron⟩ **b :** a salt (as sodium perchlorate) of a per acid **2 :** PEROXY SALT

per sal·tum \(¦)pər¦sȯltəm, (')per¦säl-\ *adv* (*or adj*) [L] **:** by a leap, spring, or bound **:** at a single bound; *specif* **:** without intermediate stages ⟨*per saltum* evolution⟩

per·scru·ta·tion \,pər,skrü'tāshən\ *n* -s [F, fr. MF, fr. L *perscrutation-*, *perscrutatio*, fr. *perscrutatus* (past part. of *perscrutari* to examine thoroughly, fr. *per-* thoroughly + *scrutari* to search, examine) + *-ion-*, *-io* -ion — more at SCRUTINY] **:** a thorough examination **:** careful investigation

perse \'pərs\ *adj* [ME *pers*, fr. MF, fr. ML *persus*, prob. fr. L *Persa* Persian] **1** *obs* **:** light or pale blue and grayish **2 :** dark grayish blue resembling indigo

per se \¦pər'sā, ¦pə̄'sā *also* ˌpə(r)'sā *or* (')pe(ə)r'sā *or* (')peə'sā *or* ¦pər'sē *or* (')pə̄'sē *or* ˌpə(r)'sē\ *adv* [L] **:** by, of, or in itself or oneself or themselves **:** as such **:** INDEPENDENTLY, INTRINSICALLY ⟨a lover of language *per se* —W.T.Scott⟩ ⟨not a scientist *per se* and so he had none of the inhibitions of the scientist —W.L.Howard⟩ ⟨his manufactory of fireworks was *per se* a public nuisance —*McDade vs. City of Chester (Pa.)*⟩ ⟨the mathematician is not interested in the truth, *per se*, of his postulates —Harry Lass⟩ ⟨money is evil *per se* and must be apologized for —Dwight Macdonald⟩ ⟨natural environment cannot *per se* cause forms of culture —A.L.Kroeber⟩ ⟨egoistic or altruistic dispositions . . . are *per se* neither rational nor irrational —W.M.Sibley⟩

per·sea \'pərsēə\ *n* [NL, fr. L, a tree growing in Egypt and Persia, fr. Gk] **1** *cap* **:** a large genus of chiefly tropical trees and shrubs (family Lauraceae) having thick alternate leaves, small panicled flowers with nine stamens, and a fleshy one-seeded fruit and in some kinds yielding superior cabinet woods — see AVOCADO **2** -s **:** any tree or fruit of the genus *Persea*

per second per second *adv* **:** per second every second — used of a rate of acceleration over an indefinite period ⟨the value of the acceleration of gravity is . . . about 32 feet *per second per second* —N.H.Black & H.N.Davis⟩

per·se·cute \'pərsə,kyüt, 'pə̄s-,'pəis-, -sē,k-, *usu* -üd·+V\ *vt* -ED/-ING/-S [MF *persecuter*, back-formation fr. *persecuteur* persecutor — more at PERSECUTOR] **1** *obs* **a :** to follow with the intent of killing, capturing, or harming **:** hunt down **:** PURSUE **b :** to follow up with vigor or to the end **2 :** to harass in a manner to injure, grieve, or afflict usu. because of some difference of outlook or opinion **:** set upon with cruelty or malignity **:** OPPRESS; *specif* **:** to cause to suffer or put to death because of belief (as in a religion) **3** *chiefly dial* **:** to prosecute at law **4 :** to afflict, harass, or annoy with persistent or urgent approaches (as attacks, pleas, importunities) **:** PESTER, VEX **syn** see WRONG

per·se·cut·ee \¦==,kyüd·¦ē, -ü¦tē\ *n* -s **:** a victim of persecution

per·se·cut·ing·ly *adv* **:** in a persecuting manner **:** so as to constitute persecution ⟨flies buzzed ~ about our faces⟩

per·se·cu·tion \,=='kyüshən\ *n* -s [ME *persecucioun*, fr. MF *persecution*, fr. LL *persecution-*, *persecutio*, fr. L, action of pursuing, fr. *persecutus* (past part. of *persequi* to continue to follow, pursue, fr. *per-*, prefix denoting completion or perfection + *sequi* to follow) + *-ion-*, *-io* -ion — more at PER-, SUE] **1 a :** the act or practice of persecuting: as (1) **:** the infliction of sufferings, harm, or death on those who differ (as in origin, religion, or social outlook) in a way regarded as offensive or meriting extirpation (2) *obs* **:** a carrying out (as of an aim or course of action) **:** PROSECUTION **b :** a campaign having for its object the subjugation or extirpation of the adherents of a religion or way of life ⟨pogroms and ~*s* in imperial Russia⟩ **2 :** the condition of being persecuted, harassed, or annoyed ⟨live through ~ and exile⟩

per·se·cu·tion·al \¦==¦kyüshənᵊl, -shnəl\ *adj* **:** of or relating to persecution ⟨a ~ mania⟩

persecution complex *n* **:** the feeling of being persecuted esp. without basis in reality

per·se·cu·tive \'==,kyüd·iv\ *adj* **:** marked by or tending toward persecution ⟨~ views⟩

per·se·cu·tor \-üd·ə(r), -ütə-\ *n* -s [MF *persecuteur*, fr. LL *persecutor*, fr. *persecutus* (past part. of *persequi* to persecute, fr. L, to continue to follow, pursue) + L *-or* — more at PERSECUTION] **:** one that persecutes

per·se·cu·to·ry \'==ˌkyə,tōrē, '==,kyüd·ərē, pə(r)'sekyə,tōrē\ *adj* [*persecute* + *-ory*] **:** of or relating to persecution **:** PERSECUTIVE

per·se·cu·tress \'pərsə,kyü·trəs, 'pə̄s-,'pəis\ *n* -ES [*persecutor* + *-ess*] **:** a female persecutor

per·se·cu·trix \¦==¦kyü·triks\ *n*, *pl* **persecutri·ces** \,=='kyü·trə,sēz, -ˌkyü·'trī(,)sēz\ [LL, fr. L *persecutor*] **:** PERSECUTRESS

per·se·id \'pərsēəd\ *n* -s *usu cap* [*Perseus*, a constellation (fr. L, fr. Gk fr. *Perseus*, a hero of ancient Greek mythology) + E *-id*] **:** one of a group of meteors appearing annually about August 11

per·se·i·tol \'pərsēə,tȯl, ˌpər's-, -tōl\ *n* -s [ISV *perse-* (fr. NL *Persea*, genus name of *Persea gratissima*) + *-itol*] **:** a crystalline polyhydric alcohol $CH_2OH(CHOH)_5CH_2OH$ found in the fruit and leaves of avocados

per·se·i·ty \(,)pər'sāəd·ē, -sēə-\ *n* -ES [ML *perseitas*, fr. L *per se* + *-itas* -ity] **:** the quality or state of being per se **:** self-inclusive or self-sufficient being

per·se·pol·i·tan \¦pərsə¦pälət'n\ *adj*, *usu cap* [fr. *Persepolis*, ancient capital of Persia situated about 30 miles northeast of present-day Shiraz, Iran, after such pairs as E *metropolis: metropolitan*] **:** of or relating to the ancient city of Persepolis

per·se·quent \'pərsəkwənt\ *adj* [L *persequent-*, *persequens*, pres. part. of *persequi* to pursue — more at PERSECUTION] **:** PURSUING

per·se·ulose \'pərsēyə,lōs, ˌpər'sē-\ *n* -s [ISV *perseitol* + *-ulose*] **:** the heptulose sugar $C_7H_{14}O_7$ obtained by bacterial oxidation of perseitol

per·se·ver·ance \,pərsə'virən(t)s, ,pə̄s-, ,pəis-, *archaic* pə(r)'sevər-\ *n* -s [ME *perseveraunce*, fr. MF *perseverance*, fr. L *perseverantia*, fr. *perseverant-*, *perseverans* (pres. part. of *perseverare* to persevere) + *-ia* -y — more at PERSEVERE] **1 :** the action or fact or an instance of persevering **:** continued or steadfast pursuit or prosecution of an undertaking or aim ⟨owing to an obstinate ~ in error —Edmund Burke⟩ **2 :** the condition or power of persevering **:** persistence in the pursuit of objectives or prosecution of any project **:** STEADFASTNESS ⟨the king-becoming graces as justice, verity . . . ~ —Shak.⟩ **3 :** continuance in a state of religious or spiritual grace until it is succeeded by a state of glory ⟨final ~⟩ ⟨the ~ of the saints⟩

per·se·ver·ant \-nt\ *adj* [ME *perseveraunt*, fr. MF *perseverant*, fr. L *perseverant-*, *perseverans*, pres. part. of *perseverare*] **:** able or willing to persevere **:** ENDURING ⟨with hope ~ —Coventry Patmore⟩

per·sev·er·ate \pə(r)'sevə,rāt\ *vi* -ED/-ING/-S [L *perseveratus*, past part. of *perseverare* to persevere] **1 :** to manifest the phenomenon of perseveration ⟨the *perseverating* tendency in stutterers in sensorimotor tasks —*Quarterly Jour. of Speech*⟩ **2 :** to repeat or recur persistently ⟨the tune ~*s* in my mind⟩ **:** go back over previously covered ground ⟨a careful scholar who ~*s* unhesitatingly to reevaluate and incorporate new data⟩

per·sev·er·a·tion \=,=='rāshən\ *n* -s [L *perseveration-*, *perseveratio* perseverance, fr. *perseveratus* + *-ion-*, *-io* -ion] **:** continuation of something (as an activity or pursuit) usu. to an exceptional degree or beyond a desired point: as **a :** continual repetition of a mental act usu. evidenced by speech or by some other form of overt behavior esp. as a mechanism of defense **b :** spontaneous and persistent recurrence of something (as an idea, mental image, tune, or word)

per·sev·er·a·tive \='==,rād·iv\ *adj* **:** characterized by perseveration

per·se·vere \¦pərsə¦vi(ə)r, ¦pə̄s-, ¦pəis-, -iə, *archaic* pə(r)'sevə(r)\ *vb* -ED/-ING/-S [ME *perseveren*, fr. MF *perseverer*, fr. L *perseverare*, fr. *per-*, intensive prefix + *-severare* (fr. *severus* serious, severe) — more at PER-, SEVERE] *vi* **1 :** to persist in a state of life, in the pursuit of an end, or esp. in an enterprise undertaken in spite of counter influences, opposition, or discouragement **:** pursue steadily any project or course begun **2 a** *archaic* **:** to continue either actively or passively **:** REMAIN, ABIDE **b :** to continue in a state of religious or spiritual grace **3 :** to be persistent (as in arguing) **:** INSIST ~ *vt* **:** to give continued existence or assistance to **:** make steadfast

syn PERSIST: PERSEVERE and PERSIST are often interchangeable in indicating continuing in the face of difficulty, opposition, and discouragement ⟨I do not intend to take that cowardly course, but, on the contrary, to stand to my post and *persevere* in accordance with my duty as I see it —Sir Winston Churchill⟩ ⟨this is the poetry within history, this is what causes mankind to *persist* beyond every defeat —Jean S. Untermeyer⟩ ⟨*persisted* long after I was willing to abandon the search and to try to get some sleep —Mary R. Rinehart⟩ PERSIST may be more likely than PERSEVERE to imply stubborn obstinacy in an ill-advised course or to lead to a regrettable outcome ⟨the eyes become tired if they *persist* in the work —Morris Fishbein⟩ ⟨it is hard to see how they can have *persisted* so long in inflicting useless misery —Bertrand Russell⟩ ⟨old savage customs have been allowed to *persevere* too long in many parts of the continent —C.L.Sulzberger⟩

per·se·ver·er \-irə(r)\ *n* -s : one that perseveres : a persistent person

persevering *adj* : of or characterized by perseverance : PERSISTENT — **per·se·ver·ing·ly** *adv*

persh *abbr* perishable

per·sia \ˈpər|zhə, ˈpə̄|, ˈpəi| *sometimes* |shə\ *adj, usu cap* [fr. *Persia* (Iran), country in southwestern Asia] : IRAN

¹**per·sian** \|zhən *sometimes* |shən\ *n* -s [ME *Persien*, fr. MF, adj. & n., fr. *Persie* Persia (fr. L *Persia*, fr. Gk *Persis* + L *-ia* -y) + MF *-ien* -ian] **1** *cap* : one of the people of Persia: as **a** : one of the ancient Iranian Caucasians who under Cyrus and his successors became the dominant Asiatic race **b** : a member of one of the peoples forming the modern Iranian nationality **2** *cap* **a** : any of several Iranian languages dominant in Persia at different periods — compare AVESTAN, MIDDLE PERSIAN, OLD PERSIAN, PAHLAVI **b** : the modern language of Iran and western Afghanistan that is used also in Pakistan and by Indian Muslims as a literary language **3** *usu cap* : a thin soft plain or printed silk in plain weave formerly used esp. for linings (as of women's clothing) **4 persians** *or* **persian blinds** *pl, usu cap P* : PERSIENNES **5** *usu cap* : a male figure replacing a column in the Persian style — usu. used in pl.; compare ATLAS **4 6** *or* **persian leather** *usu cap P* : leather from India-tanned hair sheepskins **7** *usu cap* **a** : PERSIAN CAT **b** : PERSIAN LAMB **c** : BLACKHEAD PERSIAN

²**persian** \ˈ"\ *adj, usu cap* [ME *percynne*, fr. MF *persien*] **1** : of or relating to Persia, the Persians, or their language **2** : relating to or consisting of Persian lamb **3** : constituting an order and a style of ancient art in which architectural columns are replaced by male figures in oriental costume or are adorned by such figures

per·si·ana \ˌpərz(h)ēˈanə, -rs(h)ē-, -ˈänə\ *n* -s [by alter.] : PERSIENNE 1

persian ammoniac *n, usu cap P* : AMMONIAC 1

persian apple *n, usu cap P* : CITRON 1a, 1b

persian berry *n, usu cap P* : any of several buckthorn berries from southern Europe, Asia Minor, and Iran that are used esp. in textile dyeing — compare AVIGNON BERRY

persian blue *n, often cap P* **1** : a pale blue that is redder and lighter than average powder blue and redder and paler than Sistine **2** : REGIMENTAL 2

persian buttercup *n, usu cap P* : TURBAN BUTTERCUP

persian cat *n, usu cap P* : a cobby round-headed domestic cat with long and silky fur that is the long-haired cat of shows and fanciers

persian clover *n, usu cap P* : a winter annual Asiatic clover (*Trifolium resupinatum*) sometimes used as a pasture and fodder crop in regions of mild winter

persian daisy *n, usu cap P* : a perennial chrysanthemum (*Chrysanthemum roseum*) with solitary flower heads borne on long peduncles and flesh-colored to rosy-red ray flowers

persian date *n, usu cap P* : any of several rather large light-skinned soft-fleshed dates grown in southwestern Asia

persian deer *n, usu cap P* **1** : a fallow deer (*Dama dama mesopotamiae*) of western Asia **2** : MARAL

persian earth *n, usu cap P* : INDIAN RED 2b

persian gazelle *n, usu cap P* : a gazelle (*Gazella gutturosa*) of central Asia

persian green *n, often cap P* : a dark grayish green that is bluer, lighter, and stronger than average ivy and yellower and lighter than hemlock green — called also *sea moss*

persian gulf oxide *n, usu cap P & G* [fr. the *Persian Gulf*, arm of the Arabian sea between Arabia and Iran] : INDIAN RED 1a

persian insect powder *n, usu cap 1st P* : pyrethrum derived from an Asiatic pyrethrum

persian iris *n, usu cap P* : a bulbous iris (*Iris persica*) that is native to Asia Minor and is cultivated for its pale lilac-colored flowers with small often minute deflexed falls

per·sian·ized \ˈpərzhəˌnīzd *sometimes* -rsh-\ *adj, usu cap* : rendered Persian in orientation or culture

persian lamb *n, usu cap P* **1** : the young of the karakul sheep esp. of Bokhara and other parts of central Asia that furnishes skins used in furriery — compare BROADTAIL **2** : a pelt obtained from karakul lambs older than those yielding broadtail and characterized by very silky tightly curled fur — compare ASTRAKHAN 1, BOKHARA

persian lawn *n, usu cap P* : a very fine usu. white cotton fabric of plain weave that resembles a sheer linen

persian lilac *n* **1** *usu cap P* **a** : CHINABERRY 2 **b** : a showy Asiatic shrub (*Syringa persica*) cultivated for its terminal panicles of fragrant lilac-colored flowers **2** *often cap P* : a dark purplish pink that is redder than clover pink and bluer and stronger than rhodonite pink

persian lime *n, usu cap P* : a vigorously growing lime that has a large oval to elliptical light yellow or slightly orange acid fruit, is possibly of hybrid origin, and was introduced into the southern U.S. from Tahiti — called also *Tahiti orange*

persian lynx *n, usu cap P* : CARACAL

persian melon *n* **1** *usu cap P* : a large globular muskmelon having a netted unribbed greenish outer surface and orange-colored flesh that is considered superior for freezing **2** *often cap P* : a grayish reddish orange that is redder and lighter than Etruscan red or hyacinth red and redder and paler than light persimmon

persian morocco *n, usu cap P&M* **1** : a fine leather made orig. from Persian goatskin and later from skins of various hair sheep and used chiefly in bookbinding **2** : an imitation leather resembling Persian Morocco

persian nightingale *n, usu cap P* : BULBUL 1a

persian orange *n, often cap P* : a moderate orange that is yellower, stronger, and slightly darker than honeydew, redder and lighter than ocher brown, and redder and deeper than average apricot

persian red *n* **1** *usu cap P* **a** : INDIAN RED 1a **b** : CHROME RED 1 **2** *often cap P* **a** : INDIAN RED 2b **b** : vermilion or a color resembling it

persian rose *n, often cap P* : a vivid purplish red that is bluer and lighter than rubellite and bluer and paler than Indiana

persian rug *or* **persian carpet** *n, usu cap P* : an Oriental rug made in Persia

persians *pl of* PERSIAN

persian stonecrop *n, often cap P* : a somewhat woody Asiatic stonecress (*Aethionema grandiflorum*) that is sometimes cultivated for its racemes of showy rose-colored flowers

persian tick *n, usu cap P* : CHICKEN TICK

persian violet *n, often cap P* : CYCLAMEN 2a

persian walnut *n, usu cap P* : ENGLISH WALNUT

persian wheat *n, usu cap P* : a hardy productive Eurasian wheat with short stems and heavy heads regarded as a variety of the common wheat or as a distinct species (*Triticum persicum*)

persian wheel *n, usu cap P* : an undershot waterwheel adapted for raising water and occurring in several varieties all fitted with radial floats

per·sic \ˈpərsik, -rzik\ *adj, usu cap* [L *Persicus*, fr. *Persia* + *-icus* -ic — more at PERSIAN] : of or relating to Persia or the Persian language

per·si·car·ia \ˌpərsəˈka(a)rēə\ *n* [ML, fr. L *persicum* peach + *-aria* -ary — more at PEACH] **1** -s : a plant of the genus *Polygonum* that has flowers in spicate racemes (as the lady's thumb or water pepper) **2** *cap* [NL, fr. L] *in some classifications* : a genus of herbs (family Polygonaceae) having flowers in spicate racemes and being now usu. included in the genus *Polygonum*

per·si·cary \ˈpərsəˌkerē\ *n* -ES [ME *persicarie*, fr. ML *persicaria*] : PERSICARIA 1

per·si·co *also* **per·si·cot** \ˈpərsəˌkō\ *n* -s [F *persicot*, fr. L *persicum* peach — more at PEACH] : a liqueur made from brandy or rectified spirit flavored with peach or apricot kernels, parsley, bitter almonds, and cloves

per·sic oil \ˈpərsik-, -rzik-\ *n* [*persic* fr. NL *persica* (specific epithet of *Prunus persica*), fr. L, fem. of *Persicus* Persian, fr. Gk *Persikos* fr. *Persis* Persia + *-ikos* -ic] : either of two fatty oils: **a** : APRICOT-KERNEL OIL **a b** : PEACH-KERNEL OIL **a**

per·si·enne \ˌpərzēˈen, -rsē-\ *n* -s [F, fr. fem. of adj. *persien* Persian — more at PERSIAN] **1** : painted or printed cotton or silk orig. made in Persia and later imitated in Europe **2 a** : an exterior window shutter having adjustable horizontal slats or louvers fixed at an angle so as to admit light but exclude sun and rain — usu. used in pl. **b** : VENETIAN BLIND — usu. used in pl.

per·si·flage \ˈpərsəˌfläzh, ˈper-, ˌ==ˈ=\ *n* -s [F, fr. *persifler* to banter (fr. *per-*, intensive prefix — fr. Latin — + *siffler* to whistle, hiss, boo) + *-age* — more at SIFFLE] : frivolous bantering talk : a frivolous and somewhat derisive manner of treating a subject : light raillery

per·si·flate \ˈ==ˌflāt\ *vi* -ED/-ING/-S [*persiflage* + *-ate*] : to indulge in persiflage

per·si·fleur \ˈ==flər(·), ˌ==ˈ=\ *n* -s [F, fr. *persifler* + *-eur* -or] : a person who indulges in persiflage : one given to frivolous banter esp. about matters usu. given serious consideration ⟨this indolent sceptic; this ~ who . . . posed as a martyr of remorse because he had driven his mistress out of his house —J.C. Powys⟩

per·silicic \ˌpər, ˌper+\ *adj* [*per-* + *silicic*] *of a rock* : containing much silica : ACID — distinguished from SUBSILICIC

per·sil·lade \ˌpersēˈäd, -səˈyäd\ *adj* [F, fr. *persil* parsley + *-ade* — more at PARSLEY] : dressed with or containing parsley ⟨~ potatoes⟩

per·sim·mon \pə(r)ˈsimən\ *n* -s [of Algonquian origin; akin to Cree *pasiminan* dried fruit, Del *pasimĕnan*] **1** : a tree or shrub of the genus *Diospyros*: as **a** : a medium-sized tree (*D. virginiana*) of the southern and eastern U.S. with hard fine-grained wood, oblong leaves, and greenish yellow or greenish white bell-shaped flowers followed by a pale orange to reddish orange several-seeded berry that is edible when fully ripe but usu. extremely astringent when unripe **b** : JAPANESE PERSIMMON **2** : the fruit of a persimmon **3 a** : a variable color averaging a moderate reddish orange that is yellower and duller than crab apple or flamingo **b** : a strong brown that is redder and deeper than average russet and redder and duller than rust

per·sis \ˈpərsə̇s\ *also* **per·sio** \-rsēˌō\ *n, pl* **persises** *also* **persios** [G] : archil in a dry paste form : CUDBEAR

per·sist \pə(r)ˈsist *also* -ˈzi-\ *vb* -ED/-ING/-S [MF *persister*, fr. L *persistere*, fr. *per-*, intensive prefix + *sistere* to stand firm; akin to L *stare* to stand — more at PER-, STAND] *vi* **1** : to go on resolutely or stubbornly despite opposition, importunity, or warning : continue firmly or obstinately ⟨~ in a bad habit⟩ **2** *obs* : to remain unchanged or fixed in a usu. specified character, condition, or position : continue to be ⟨but for thee, I had ~*ed* happy —John Milton⟩ **3** : to be insistent in the repetition or pressing of an utterance (as a question, an excuse, or an opinion) **4** : to continue to exist or endure (as beyond a normal period or after the removal of a cause) : recur constantly ⟨characteristics that ~ through generations⟩ ⟨a melody that ~*s* in the mind⟩ ~ *vt* : to repeat or press (an utterance) insistently : continue saying : URGE **syn** see CONTINUE, PERSEVERE

per·sist·ence \-tən(t)s\ *n* -s [MF, fr. *persister* + *-ence*] **1** : the action or fact of persisting : determined or stubborn continuance (as in a course of action) in spite of opposition ⟨their ~ in pressing the invitation⟩ ⟨annoyed by the salesman's ~⟩ **2** : the quality or state of being persistent: as **a** : continued existence ⟨the ~ of a fever⟩ **b** : power or capacity of continuing in a course in the face of difficulties : PERSEVERANCE ⟨developing ~ in children⟩ **c** : continuance of an effect after its cause is removed ⟨~ of smoke in the air⟩ ⟨~ of sounds⟩; *esp* : AFTERIMAGE — see PERSISTENCE OF VISION

persistence of vision : a visual phenomenon that is responsible for the apparent continuity of rapidly presented discrete images (as in motion pictures or television) consisting essentially of a brief retinal persistence of one image so that it is overlapped by the next and the whole is centrally interpreted as continuous — compare FUSION 2d(2)

per·sist·en·cy \-nsē, -nsi\ *n* -ES [MF *persistence* + E *-y*] : the quality or state of being persistent: as **a** : the continuance of an insurance policy in full force until death of the insured or completion of the term of the policy **b** : capacity (as of an animal) for long-continued production of a valuable product ⟨a cow milking heavily but lacking ~⟩

per·sist·ent \-nt\ *adj* [L *persistent-, persistens*, pres. part. of *persistere* to persist — more at PERSIST] **1 a** : continuing in a course of action without regard to opposition or previous failure : tenacious of position or purpose : inclined to persist ⟨~ in good works⟩ ⟨this ~ suitor⟩ ⟨a ~ effort⟩ **b** : continuing to exist in spite of interference or treatment ⟨a ~ cancer⟩ : tending to recur ⟨a ~ cough⟩ **2** : existing for a long or longer than usual time or continuously : ENDURING, LINGERING ⟨a ~ odor of boiling cabbage⟩: as **a** (1) *of a plant corolla* : retained beyond the period of anthesis — opposed to *caducous* (2) *of a leaf* : clinging all winter even though withered ⟨some oaks and beeches have ~ leaves⟩ — opposed to *deciduous*; compare HALF-EVERGREEN **b** : continuing without change in function or structure — used chiefly of animal structures that are characteristic of some ancestral type or of a larval or young stage ⟨~ gills⟩; opposed to *deciduous* **c** *of a chemical warfare agent* : effective in the open for an appreciable time (as at least 2 to 10 minutes) : volatilizing relatively slowly ⟨mustard gas is a ~ gas⟩ — **per·sist·ent·ly** *adv*

per·sist·er \-tə(r)\ *n* -s : one that persists

persisting *adj* : inclined to persist : tenacious of purpose : PERSISTENT, ENDURING — **per·sist·ing·ly** *adv*

per·sis·tive \-tiv\ *adj* : tending to persist : PERSISTENT

per·snick·e·ti·ness \pə(r)ˈsnikəd·|ēnə̇s, -kət|, |in-\ *n* -ES : the quality or state of being persnickety

per·snick·e·ty *also* **per·snick·i·ty** \|ē, |i\ *adj* [alter. of *pernickety*] **1 a** : excessively meticulous : FINICAL, FUSSY ⟨approached native food and drink pretty much like a ~ peacetime tourist —Ernie Pyle⟩ **b** : having the characteristics of a snob ⟨have no manners, . . . they're stuck up, uppity, ~ —Carl Withers⟩ **2** : indicative of or requiring great precision, delicacy, or punctiliousness

per·son \ˈpərsᵊn, ˈpə̄s-, ˈpəis-\ *n* -s [ME *persone, person, persoun*, fr. OF *persone, persoune*, fr. L *persona* mask (esp. one worn by an actor), actor, role, character, person, prob. fr. Etruscan *phersu* mask] **1 a** : an individual human being ⟨a very interesting ~⟩ ⟨any ~ present⟩ **b** *archaic* : PERSONAGE 3 **c** : a human being as distinguished from an animal or thing ⟨only ~*s* can inherit under a will⟩ **d** : an inferior human being ⟨people in our position could scarcely know a ~ in trade socially⟩ ⟨the young ~ I mentioned in my letter⟩ **2** *archaic* : a character or part in or as if in a play : a particular manifestation of individual character whether real or fictional : GUISE, SEMBLANCE **3** *sometimes cap* **a** : one of the three modes of being in the Godhead as understood by Trinitarians : HYPOSTASIS **b** : the unitary personality of Christ that unites the divine and human natures **4 a** (1) *archaic* : bodily appearance ⟨had a goodly ~⟩ (2) : an individual having a specified kind of bodily appearance ⟨a fairer ~ lost not heaven —John Milton⟩ **b** : the body of a human being as distinguished from the mind ⟨pure in mind and ~⟩ **c** : the body of a human being as presented to public view usu. with its appropriate coverings and clothing ⟨an unlawful search of the ~⟩ **5 a** : the individual personality of a human being : SELF ⟨a very touchy ~⟩ ⟨in his proper ~⟩ **b** : bodily presence — usu. used in the phrase *in person* ⟨a well-known comedian appearing in ~⟩ **6** : a human being, a body of persons, or a corporation, partnership, or other legal entity that is recognized by law as the subject of rights and duties — see JURISTIC PERSON **7** : any one of the three relations underlying discourse that are distinguished by certain pronouns and in many languages by inflected forms of the verb — see FIRST PERSON, SECOND PERSON, THIRD PERSON **8 a** : a being characterized by conscious apprehension, rationality, and a moral sense **b** : a being possessing or forming the subject of personality **9** : a living individual unit; *specif* : a single zooid in a compound animal (as a colonial hydrozoan or coral) — **in the person of 1** : in the character of **2** : in the place of : acting for

per·sona \pə(r)ˈsōnə, ˌpərˈs-, pə̄ˈs-, pəiˈs- *sometimes* -säna\ *n, pl* **per·sonae** *see sense 2* \-(ˌ)nē, -ˌnī\ [L — more at PERSON] **1** personae *pl* : the characters of a fictional presentation (as a novel or play) ⟨comic *personae*⟩ **2** *pl* **personas** \-nəz\ : the social front, facade, or mask an individual assumes to depict to the world at large the role in life that he is playing — often contrasted with *anima* in the analytic psychology of C. G. Jung; compare EGO 3 **3** [ML, fr. L] : a parson or rector of a parish **4** [LL, fr. L] : JURISTIC PERSON **5** : PERSON 9

per·son·abil·i·ty \ˌpərs(ᵊ)nəˈbiləd·ē, ˌpə̄s-, ˌpəis-, -lətē, -i\ *n* : the quality or state of being personable

per·son·able \ˈpərs(ᵊ)nəbəl, ˈpə̄s-, ˈpəis-\ *adj* [ME, fr. *persone* + *-able*] **1** : pleasing in person : well-favored esp. in body or person : COMELY, SHAPELY, ATTRACTIVE **2** : having the legal status of a person with a right to maintain pleas in court and to take anything granted; *also* : SUI JURIS — **per·son·able·ness** *n* -ES

per·son·age \-s(ᵊ)nij, -nēj\ *n* -s [ME, fr. MF *personnage*, fr. *persone, personne* person + *-age* — more at PERSON] **1 a** *archaic* : the physical form or appearance of a person : form, bearing, and stature of one's body **b** *obs* : a person of specified bodily form or makeup **2 a** *obs* : a representation of a human being **b** : the human figure as an element in design (as for a tapestry) **3** : a person of rank, note, or distinction : an eminent man or woman; *esp* : one distinguished for presence and personal power ⟨fast becoming a ~⟩ **4** *obs* : one's self, personality, or personal identity : one's character or status as an individual **5** : a dramatic, fictional, or historical character; *also* : a character as assumed or represented : IMPERSONATION **6** : a human individual : a person not meriting specific identification

person aggrieved *n, pl* **persons aggrieved** : a person sufficiently harmed by a legal judgment, decree, or order to have standing to prosecute an appellate remedy

persona grata \see PERSONA NON GRATA\ *n, pl* **personae gratae** *or* **persona grata** [L] : an acceptable person ⟨informed the . . . ambassador that these two officers were no longer *persona grata* —*Christian Science Monitor*⟩ — compare PERSONA NON GRATA

persona gra·tis·si·ma \=,==grəˈtisəmə\ *n, pl* **personae gratissi·mae** \-(ˌ)mē, -ˌmī\ [L] : a highly favored person

¹**per·son·al** \ˈpərs(ᵊ)nəl, ˈpə̄s-, ˈpəis-\ *adj* [ME, fr. MF *personnel, personel, personal*, fr. LL *personalis*, fr. L *persona* person + *-alis* -al — more at PERSON] **1** : of or relating to a particular person : affecting one individual or each of many individuals : peculiar or proper to private concerns : not public or general ⟨~ allegiance⟩ ⟨~ baggage⟩ ⟨~ correspondence⟩ **2 a** : done in person without the intervention of another : direct from one person to another ⟨a ~ inquiry⟩; *also* : originating in or proceeding from a single person ⟨a ~ ultimatum⟩ ⟨~ government⟩ **b** *obs* : engaged or present in person **c** : carried on between individuals directly ⟨a ~ interview⟩ **3** : relating to the person or body : BODILY ⟨~ appearance⟩ ⟨~ liberty⟩ **4 a** : relating to an individual, his character, conduct, motives, or private affairs esp. in an invidious and offensive manner ⟨~ reflections⟩; *also* : relating to oneself ⟨~ vanity⟩ **b** : making or given to making personal reflection ⟨very ~ in his comments⟩ **5 a** : relating to or characteristic of human beings as distinct from things **b** : rational and self-conscious ⟨a ~ God⟩ **6** : exclusively for a given individual ⟨a ~ letter⟩ **7** *substand* : PERSONABLE 1 **8** : of, relating to, or constituting personal property ⟨a ~ estate⟩ ⟨~ interests⟩ — compare REAL 1a **9 a** : denoting grammatical person ⟨a ~ suffix⟩ **b** *of a verb* : inflected for all three persons — compare IMPERSONAL

²**personal** \ˈ"\ *n* -s : something of which the relation to a human individual is a basic attribute: as **a personals** *pl, archaic* : personal property : CHATTELS **b** (1) : a personal remark (2) : a short newspaper item giving information about the social or other activities of a local person, family, or group (3) : a short personal or private communication printed in a special column of the classified ads section of a newspaper or periodical — compare AGONY COLUMN **c** *archaic* : PERSONNEL **d** : PERSONAL PRONOUN **e** : a personal foul in a sports contest

³**personal** \ˈ"\ *adv, substand* : PERSONALLY

personal account *n* : DRAWING ACCOUNT

personal action *n* **1** : an action under a civil law system for the enforcement of an obligation which therefore must be brought against the person obligated **2** : an action under the common law not brought for the recovery of or involving rights in lands, tenements, or hereditaments : an action brought to enforce or recover a debt or personal duty or damages in lieu of it or damages for an injury to person or property or for the specific recovery of or enforcement of a lien upon goods or chattels — compare REAL ACTION

personal covenant *n* : a legal covenant that does not run with the property but is binding upon the covenantor and his personal representatives — compare REAL COVENANT

personal effects *n pl* : effects of a personal character: as **a** : property esp. appertaining to one's person and having a close relationship thereto — used in legal contexts (as wills, tariff laws) **b** : such property as is usu. or normally carried by a traveler for his use and comfort — used esp. in connection with insurance **c** : personal property other than that employed in business — used esp. in a residuary clause of a will

personal equation *n* **1** : a constant or systematic deviation from an assumed correct observational result depending on personal qualities of the observer: **a** : ABSOLUTE PERSONAL EQUATION **b** : RELATIVE PERSONAL EQUATION **2** : variation of judgment or method occasioned by individual bias or limitation or temperamental qualities of individuals ⟨eliminating the *personal equation* in historical writing⟩

personal estate *n* : all of a person's property not coming under the denomination of real estate including corporeal tangibles and incorporeal intangibles, movables, chattels, choses in action, or rights : PERSONAL PROPERTY

personal finance company *n* : a company primarily or solely engaged in making loans of 300 dollars or less to private individuals

personal flag *n* : a flag indicative of the command rank of an officer (as in the U.S. Navy) and flown by a ship or station to which he is attached and present — compare DISTINGUISHING FLAG, FLAG OFFICER

personal foul *n* : a foul in a game (as basketball or lacrosse) involving usu. personal contact with or deliberate roughing of an opponent

personal freedom *n* : freedom of the person in going and coming, equality before the courts, security of private property, freedom of opinion and its expression, and freedom of conscience subject to the rights of others and of the public — compare PERSONAL LIBERTY

personal holding company *n* : a corporation more than one half of whose stock is owned by not more than five persons and the more than 80 percent of whose income is from investments

per·so·na·lia \ˌpərsᵊnˈālyə, -lēə\ *n pl* [NL, fr. LL, neut. pl. of *personalis* personal — more at PERSONAL] **1** : biographical or personal anecdotes or notes **2** : personal belongings or concerns

personal idealism *or* **personalistic idealism** *n* : PERSONALISM 2a

personal identity *n* : the persistent and continuous unity of the individual person normally attested by continuity of memory with present consciousness

personal income *n* : the current income received by persons from all sources excluding transfers among persons — used esp. in national income accounting

personal injury *n* **1** : an injury affecting one's physical and mental person as contrasted with one causing damage to one's property **2** : an injury giving rise to a personal action at law

personal insurance *n* **1** : insurance of human life values against the risks of death, injury, illness or against expenses incidental to the latter **2** : insurance purchased for personal or family protection purposes as contrasted with insurance of business property or interests

per·son·al·ism \ˈpərs(ᵊ)nəˌlizəm\ *n* -s **1** : personal quality or state : individuality of character or influence : INDIVIDUALISM **2** : a doctrine, theory, or school of thought emphasizing the significance, uniqueness, and inviolability of personality: as **a** : the philosophical theory developed in America principally by Borden P. Bowne and George H. Howison but foreshadowed in Walt Whitman and Bronson Alcott holding that ultimate reality consists of a plurality of spiritual beings or independent persons ⟨~ is a modern title used particularly to indicate a break, not only with absolutisms of every kind and with fundamental monisms, but also to distinguish its system from those personal idealisms and theisms which retain a hidden Absolute treated as a person —R.T.Flewelling⟩ **b** : a theory that psychology is properly concerned with the person or self

¹**per·son·al·ist** \-ˌlə̇st\ *n* -s [¹*personal* + *-ist*] **1** : a writer of personalia **2** : an advocate of personalism

²**personalist** \ˈ"\ *adj* : concerned with or oriented toward personalism ⟨a ~ theme⟩

per·son·al·is·tic \¦=(=)=¦listik\ *adj* **1 :** PERSONAL, INDIVIDUAL **2 :** of or relating to personalism **:** PERSONALIST

personalistic psychology *n* **:** organismic psychology that emphasizes the self or the individual personality

per·son·al·i·ty \ˌpərsᵊn'aləd·ē, ˌpə̄s-, ˌpəis-, -lətē, -i\ *n* -ES [ME *personalite,* fr. LL *personalitas,* fr. *personalis* personal + L *-itas* -ity — more at PERSONAL] **1 a :** the quality or state of being a person and not an abstraction, thing, or lower being **:** the fact of being an individual person **:** personal existence or entity **:** capacity for the choices, experiences, and liabilities of an individual person ⟨questions which must be answered by man not as part of nature but as a ~ —Christian Gauss⟩ ⟨the proper moral relation between the individual and society, or . . . between ~ and community —J.A.Hobson⟩ **b :** the distinctive quality or state of a spiritual entity ⟨the three *Personalities* of the Trinity⟩ **2 :** the qualities of a person that constitute or fix his legal status or general legal capacity **3 :** a personal being **:** a single individual **4 a :** the condition or fact of relating to a particular person; *specif* **:** the condition of referring directly to or being aimed at an individual esp. disparagingly or hostilely **b :** an utterance that refers to the person, conduct, or other aspect of some individual usu. disparagingly or offensively **:** personal remark — usu. used in pl. ⟨indulgence in *personalities*⟩ **5 a :** the complex of characteristics that distinguishes a particular individual or individualizes or characterizes him in his relationships with others ⟨the organization flourished under her administration, for she had a winning ~ and a capacity for hard work —Marie A. Kasten⟩ ⟨a pious and good man, but an utterly negligible ~ —Compton Mackenzie⟩ **b :** a comparable complex characteristic of a group or nation ⟨southeast Asia had now attained a diplomatic ~ of its own —Virginia M. Thompson & Richard Adloff⟩ **c :** the total of distinctive traits and characteristics ⟨the ~ of the English countryside —S.W.Wooldridge⟩ **d** (1) **:** the totality of an individual's emergent tendencies to act or behave esp. self-consciously or to act on, interact with, perceive, react to, or otherwise meaningfully influence or experience his environment (2) **:** the organization of the individual's distinguishing character traits, attitudes, or habits — compare EGO, SELF **6 a :** distinction or excellence of personal and social traits **:** the social characteristic of commanding notice, admiration, respect, or influence through personal characteristics ⟨a superior in charm, in experience, in knowledge of the world and in force of ~ —Arnold Bennett⟩ **b :** a person having such quality; *also* **:** a person of importance, prominence, renown, or notoriety ⟨an able speaker, a strong and positive character, and a gentle and lovable ~ —F.T.Persons⟩ **syn** see DISPOSITION

personality disorder *n* **:** a psychopathological condition or group of conditions in which an individual's entire life pattern is considered deviant or nonadaptive although he shows neither neurotic symptoms nor psychotic disorganization

personality test *n* **:** any of several tests consisting of standardized tasks designed to determine various aspects of the personality type or the emotional status of the person examined

per·son·al·iza·tion \ˌpərs(ᵊ)nələ'zāshən, ˌpə̄s-, ˌpəis-, -ˌlī'z-\ *n* -S **1 :** the quality or state of being personalized ⟨the ~ of natural forces in myth and religion⟩ **2 :** the act or process of personalizing ⟨~ of propaganda⟩

per·son·al·ize \'=(=)=ˌlīz\ *vt* -ED/-ING/-S *see -ize in Explan Notes* [¹*personal* + *-ize*] **1 :** to ascribe personality to **:** invest or endow with human qualities **:** ANTHROPOMORPHIZE ⟨death *personalized* as a man with a scythe⟩ **2 :** to realize or embody in one's personality **:** TYPIFY ⟨~ the genius of his age⟩ ⟨a man who *personalized* an ideal of our childhood⟩ **3 :** to make personal or individual: as **a :** to take (as a remark) personally **b :** to mark so as to identify as the property of a particular person ⟨*personalized* luggage⟩ **c :** to direct or adjust to the individual ⟨*personalizing* sales techniques⟩

personal law *n* **:** law that applies to a particular person or class of persons only wherever situated — distinguished from *territorial law*

personal liberty *n* **:** the freedom of the individual to do as he pleases limited only by the authority of politically organized society to regulate his action to secure the public health, safety, or morals or of other recognized social interests

per·son·al·ly \-s(ᵊ)nəlē, -li\ *adv* [ME, fr. *personal* + *-ly*] **:** so as to be personal **:** in a personal manner; *often* **:** as oneself **:** on or for one's own part ⟨~ I don't want to go⟩

personal name *n* **:** a name (as the praenomen or the forename) by which an individual is intimately known or designated and which may be displaced or supplemented by a surname, a cognomen, or a royal name

per·son·al·ness *n* -ES **:** the quality or state of being personal; *esp* **:** appeal to the individual ⟨the ~ of this message⟩

personal pronoun *n* **:** a pronoun (as *I, you, they*) expressing a distinction of person

personal property *n* **:** estate or property other than real property consisting in general of things temporary or movable including intangible property **:** property recoverable by a personal action **:** CHATTELS

personal representative *n* **:** a person (as an executor or administrator for a deceased person, heir, or next of kin for an ancestor, a devisee or legatee for a testator, a receiver for an absent or insolvent person or a guardian or conservator or committee for an incompetent) who stands in the place of another or who represents his legal interests

personal rights *n pl* **:** rights (as of personal security, personal liberty, and private property) appertaining to the person

personals *pl of* PERSONAL

personal service *n* **1 :** service of a legal process by delivering it or a copy thereof to the defendant or by statute to an agent of the defendant authorized to receive service in the case in issue **2 :** economic service involving the either intellectual or manual personal labor of the server rather than a salable product of his skill ⟨physicians, architects, and garbage collectors equally sell *personal service*⟩

personal servitude *n* **:** a servitude (as use, usufruct, or habitation) due to a particular person for his lifetime under civil law as distinguished from praedial or real servitudes due to a tract of land

personal shopper *n* **:** a person (as a store employee) who assists shoppers to choose their purchases or who personally selects merchandise to fill telephone or written orders

personal staff *n* **:** the military aides of a general officer or flag officer — distinguished from *general staff* and *special staff*

personal standard *n* **:** a flag (as the royal banner of Great Britain) that is the emblem of a particular person (as a sovereign)

personal tithe *n* **:** a tithe arising entirely from the personal industry of man (as fish caught in the sea) — compare MIXED TITHE, PRAEDIAL TITHE

personal treaty *n* **:** a treaty that relates only to the persons of the contracting parties — compare REAL TREATY

personal trust *n* **:** a trust in which the beneficiary is an individual or individuals — opposed to *corporate trust*

per·son·al·ty \-s(ə)nəltē, -ti\ *n* -ES [AF *personalte,* fr. LL *personalitat-, personalitas* personality — more at PERSONALITY] **:** PERSONAL PROPERTY

personal union *n* **:** a union of two states consituted by their becoming subject to the same personal ruler without loss of independent sovereignty

per·sona non gra·ta \pə(r),sōnə,nän'gra|d·ə, -grā|, -grä|, |tə *also* -ˌnōn'g- *or* -grā| *sometimes* -sän-\ *n, pl* **per·sonae non gratae** \-(ˌ)nē . . . |d·(ˌ)ē, |(ˌ)tē; -ˌnī . . . |d ,t, |ˌtī\ *or* **persona non grata** [L] **:** an unacceptable person; *specif* **:** a diplomatic official who is personally not acceptable to the government of the foreign country to which he is accredited

personas *pl of* PERSONA

¹**per·son·ate** \'pərsᵊnət, -ᵊnˌāt\ *adj* [L *personatus* masked, counterfeited, fr. *persona* mask + *-atus* -ate — more at PERSON] **1 a** *archaic* **:** PERSONATED, FEIGNED, COUNTERFEIT **b :** MASKED, DISGUISED; *esp* **:** having a form differing from the typical adult form ⟨a ~ larva⟩ **c** *of a bilabiate corolla* **:** having the throat nearly closed by a palate; *also* **:** having such a corolla ⟨a ~ flower⟩ **2** *obs* **:** having personality or personal existence **:** embodied in a person

²**per·son·ate** \'pərsᵊnˌāt, 'pə̄s-,'pəis-, *usu* -ād·+V\ *vb* -ED/-ING/-S [*person* + *-ate*] *vt* **1 :** to impersonate or represent as an actor, pretender, or masquerader **:** act the part of **:** pretend or represent oneself to be ⟨I do not ~ the stage-play emperor to entrap applause —John Keats⟩ **2 :** PERSONALIZE: as **a :** to invest with personality or with personal characteristics **:** represent as a person ⟨in fable, hymn, or song, so *personating* their gods ridiculous, and themselves past shame —John Milton⟩ **b :** to serve as a representative, embodiment, or symbol of **:** TYPIFY **3 :** to give the appearance of possessing (as a quality, emotion) **:** FEIGN **4 a :** to give an imitation of (as a person's manner or speech) **:** MIMIC **b :** to pretend without authority to be **:** create a wrongful appearance of being (someone other than oneself whether fictitious or real) **:** assume without authority and with criminal or fraudulent intent (some character or capacity) ⟨~ an officer of the law⟩ **~** *vi* **:** to play or assume a character

per·son·ate·ly *adv* **:** in a personate manner or arrangement **:** so as to be personate

personating *n* -S **:** the act of one that personates **:** IMPERSONATION

per·son·a·tion \ˌ==ˈāshən\ *n* -S **1 :** IMPERSONATION **2 :** PERSONIFICATION, EMBODIMENT

per·son·ative \'==ˌād·iv\ *adj* **:** of or relating to personation; *esp* **:** employing dramatic representation

per·son·ator \-ˌād·ə(r)\ *n* -S **:** one that personates

per·son·eity \ˌ==ˈēəd·ē\ *n* -ES [*person* + *-eity* (as in *corporeity*)] **1 :** PERSONALITY 1b **2** *archaic* **:** ANIMISM **3 :** PERSONAGE 3

per·son·i·fi·able \pə(r)'sänəˌfīəbəl, =ˌ==ˈ===\ *adj* **:** capable of being personified

per·son·i·fi·ca·tion \pə(r)ˌsänəfə'kāshən\ *n* -S [fr. *personify,* after such pairs as E *amplify: amplification*] **:** an act of personifying or something that personifies: as **a :** attribution of personal qualities (as of form, character) **:** representation of a thing or abstraction as a person or by the human form **b :** rhetorical representation of an inanimate object or abstract idea as a personality or as endowed with personal attributes **:** PROSOPOPOEIA; *also* **:** an instance of this ⟨"the floods clap their hands" is a ~⟩ **c :** a divinity or imaginary being thought of as representing a thing or abstraction ⟨Aeolus is the ~ of wind⟩ **d :** EMBODIMENT, INCARNATION ⟨be the ~ of pride⟩ **e :** a dramatic or literary representation of a character ⟨a series of excellent readings and ~s⟩

per·son·i·fi·ca·tive \=ˈ===ˌkād·iv\ *adj* [*personification* + *-ive*] **:** tending or serving to personify ⟨a ~ principle in primitive social organizations⟩

per·son·i·fi·ca·tor \-ˌād·ə(r)\ *n* -S [*personification* + *-or*] **:** PERSONIFIER

per·son·i·fi·er \pə(r)'sänəˌfī(ə)r, -īə\ *n* -S **:** one that personifies

per·son·i·fy \pə(r)'sänəˌfī\ *vb* -ED/-ING/-ES [F *personnifier,* fr. *personne* person + *-ifier* -ify — more at PERSON] *vt* **1 :** to conceive of or represent as a person or as having human qualities or powers **:** impute personality to ⟨~ justice as a blindfolded woman⟩ **2 :** to be the embodiment or personification of **:** INCARNATE ⟨*personifies* the law⟩ ⟨courage *personified*⟩ **~** *vi* **:** to employ personification **:** make personifications

per·son·ize \'pərsᵊnˌīz\ *vt* -ED/-ING/-S [*person* + *-ize*] **:** PERSONIFY 1

per·son·nel \¦pərsᵊn¦el, ¦pə̄s-, ¦pəis-\ *n, pl* **personnel** *or* **personnels** *often attrib* [F, modif. (influenced by *personnel,* adj., personal) of G *personal,* alter. of *personale,* fr. LL, neut. of *personalis* personal — more at PERSONAL] **1 a :** a body of persons employed in some service (as the army or navy, a factory, office, airplane) — distinguished from *matériel* **b** *personnel pl* **:** persons of a particular (as professional or occupational) group ⟨military ~⟩ ⟨missionary ~⟩ ⟨34,000 ~ in the expanded operation⟩ ⟨the changing ~ of the theater⟩ **2 a :** a body of employees that is a factor in business administration esp. with respect to efficiency, selection, training, service, and health **b :** the division of an organization concerned primarily with the selection, placement, and training of employees and with the formulation of policies, procedures, and relations with employees or their representatives

personnel administration *or* **personnel management** *n* **:** the phase of management concerned with the engagement and effective utilization of manpower to obtain optimum efficiency of human resources

personnel carrier *n* **:** a usu. armored motor vehicle for transporting military personnel and their equipment

person of color **1 :** NEGRO **2 :** a person of partially Negro ancestry

person of incidence : a person against whom a legal right may be enforced by another or upon whom a correlative duty falls

person of inherence : a person having a legal right enforceable against another

person-to-person \¦===¦==\ *adv* (*or adj*) **:** from one person to another ⟨the inoculum was transferred *person-to-person*⟩ ⟨made a *person-to-person* call⟩

persp *abbr* perspective

per·spec·tiv·al \pə(r)'spektivəl\ *adj* **:** exhibiting or concerned with perspective **:** marked by the use of perspective

¹**per·spec·tive** \pə(r)'spektiv, -tēv *also* -təv\ *n* -S [ME; in sense 1, fr. ML *perspectiva,* fr. fem. of *perspectivus* of sight, optical, fr. L *perspectus* (past part. of *perspicere* to look through, look at, examine, fr. *per-* through + *-spicere,* fr. *specere* to look) + *-ivus* -ive; in sense 2, fr. ML *perspectivum,* fr. neut. of *perspectivus* — more at PER-, SPY] **1** *or* **perspectives** *pl, obs* **:** OPTICS **2 :** an optical glass: as **a :** a telescope that shows objects in the right position **b :** any of various optical devices for producing a fantastic effect or optical illusion

²**perspective** \"\ *adj* [ME, fr. ML *perspectivus*] **1** *obs* **:** of or relating to vision **:** OPTICAL **2 a** *obs, of an optical glass* **:** aiding the vision **:** used for seeing, viewing, or looking **b :** seen in mental perspective — **per·spec·tive·ly** \-tə̇vlē, -tēv-, -li\ *adv*

³**perspective** \"\ *n* -S [MF, prob. modif. (influenced by *perspective* optics, fr. ML *perspectiva*) of OIt *prospettiva,* fr. *prospetto* view, prospect (fr. L *prospectus*) + *-iva* n. suffix (fr. L, fr. fem. of *-ivus* -ive) — more at ¹PERSPECTIVE, PROSPECT] **1 a :** the technique of representing on a plane or curved surface the space relationships of natural objects as they appear to the eye **b :** the technique of adjusting the apparent sources of sounds (as on a radio program) into a natural-seeming and integrated whole **c :** a picture or figure that looks distorted except when viewed from some particular point **2 a :** the interrelation in which parts of a subject are mentally viewed **:** the aspect of an object of thought from a particular standpoint **:** CONFIGURATION ⟨thrown into a fresh ~⟩ ⟨time and experience, which alter all ~s —Henry Adams⟩ **b :** capacity to view things in their true relations or relative importance ⟨some folks cannot see the wood for the trees, while others have ~⟩ **3 a** (1) **:** a visible scene; *esp* **:** one giving a distinctive impression of distance **:** VISTA (2) **:** a mental view or prospect **b :** a picture in linear perspective; *specif* **:** a scenic picture giving an effect of extension of the vista (as on a stage) **4 :** the appearance to the eye of objects in respect to their relative distance and positions **5 :** HOMOLOGY 4 ⟨two geometric configurations in ~⟩ ⟨center of ~⟩ **6 a :** a perceptible appearance **b :** appearance of a thing at a given place and time conceived (as by Bertrand Russell) as something actually existing at that place and time even when no perceiver is present and as being a constituent of the object whose appearance it is — **in perspective 1 :** as viewed in the mind **:** in prospect **:** ANTICIPATED **2 a :** represented according to the principles of perspective **b :** viewed with a proper pattern of relationships as to value, importance, or other basic quality ⟨keeping the temporary advantage strictly *in perspective*⟩

perspective formula *n* **:** a structural formula representing three dimensions and used primarily to distinguish among optical isomers — compare PROJECTION FORMULA

COOH, C, CH₂OH, H, NH₂ — **D-serine**; COOH, C, CH₂OH, H₂N, H — **L-serine**

perspective formula

per·spec·tive·less \-tivlə̇s, -tēv- *also* -təv-\ *adj* **:** lacking perspective

perspective transformation *n* **:** the collineation set up in a plane by projecting on it the points of another plane from two different centers of projection

per·spec·tiv·ic \ˌpərspek¦tivik\ *or* **per·spec·tiv·is·tic** \pərˌspektə̇¦vistik\ *adj* **:** of, relating to, or concerned with perspectivism

per·spec·tiv·ism \pə(r)'spektə̇ˌvizəm\ *n* -S [ISV ³*perspective* + *-ism;* orig. formed as G *perspektivismus*] **1 :** a concept in philosophy: the world forms a complex of interacting interpretive processes in which every entity views every entity and event from an orientation peculiar to itself **2 :** consciousness of or the process of using different points of view (as in literary criticism or artistic representation)

¹**per·spec·tiv·ist** \-ˌvə̇st\ *n* -S [³*perspective* + *-ist*] **:** an advocate or user of perspectivism

²**perspectivist** \"\ *adj* **:** of, relating to, or based on perspectivism ⟨~ theories⟩ ⟨a ~ outlook⟩

per·spec·tiv·i·ty \ˌpərˌspek'tivəd·ē\ *n* -ES [ISV ³*perspective* + *-ity*] **:** the correspondence between the points, lines, or planes of two geometric configurations in perspective

per·spec·to·graph \pə(r)'spektəˌgraf, -rȧf\ *n* [L *perspectus* (past part. of *perspicere* to look through) + E *-o-* + *-graph* — more at PERSPECTIVE] **:** an instrument used as an aid to drawing in perspective by fixing in the picture the positions of some of the points or outlines of the objects to be represented

per·spec·tom·e·ter \ˌpərˌspek'tämədˌər\ *n* [L *perspectus* (past part. of *perspicere*) + E *-o-* + *-meter*] **:** PERSPECTOGRAPH

Per·spex \'pərˌspeks\ *trademark* — used for an acrylic plastic consisting essentially of polymerized methyl methacrylate

per·spi·ca·cious \¦pərspə¦kāshəs, ¦pə̄s-, ¦pəis-\ *adj* [L *perspicac-, perspicax* clear-sighted, (fr. *perspicere* to see through) + E *-ious* — more at PERSPECTIVE] **1** *archaic* **:** CLEAR-SIGHTED, QUICK-SIGHTED, SHARP-SIGHTED **2 :** of acute mental vision or discernment **:** KEEN **3** *substand* **:** PERSPICUOUS **syn** see SHREWD

per·spi·ca·cious·ly *adv* **:** in a perspicacious way **:** with perspicacity

per·spi·ca·cious·ness *n* -ES **:** PERSPICACITY

per·spi·cac·i·ty \ˌ==ˈkasəd·ē, -sətē, -i\ *n* -ES [LL *perspicacitas,* fr. L *perspicac-, perspicax* perspicacious + *-itas* -ity — more at PERSPICACIOUS] **:** the quality or state of being perspicacious; *esp* **:** acuteness of discernment

perspicil *n* -S [NL *perspicillum,* fr. L *perspicere* to look through + *-illum,* suffix denoting an instrument — more at PERSPECTIVE] *obs* **:** an optical glass (as a telescope)

per·spi·cu·ity \ˌpərspə'kyüəd·ē, ˌpə̄s-, ˌpəis-, -üətē, -i\ *n* -ES [L *perspicuitas,* fr. *perspicuus* perspicuous + *-itas* -ity] **1** *obs* **:** TRANSPARENCY, TRANSLUCENCY **2 :** the quality or state of being clear to the understanding **:** lucidity in expression or development of ideas **3** *obs* **:** the quality or state of being distinctly visible **4 :** PERSPICACITY

per·spic·u·ous \pə(r)'spikyəwəs\ *adj* [L *perspicuus,* fr. *perspicere* to look through — more at PERSPECTIVE] **1** *obs* **:** capable of being seen through **:** not opaque **:** TRANSPARENT, TRANSLUCENT **2 :** capable of being clearly and readily understood **:** plain to the understanding ⟨~ in meaning⟩: as **a :** clear in presentation and expression of thought and free from obscurity or ambiguity ⟨a ~ argument⟩ **b :** speaking or writing clearly **:** precise and intelligible in utterance ⟨try to be ~⟩ **3** *archaic* **:** easily seen **:** distinctly visible **:** CONSPICUOUS, MANIFEST **4 :** PERSPICACIOUS **syn** see CLEAR

per·spic·u·ous·ly *adv* **:** in a perspicuous manner **:** with perspicuity

per·spic·u·ous·ness *n* -ES **:** PERSPICUITY

per·spir·able \pə(r)'spīrəbəl\ *adj* [F, fr. MF, fr. *perspirer* to perspire + *-able* — more at PERSPIRE] **1 :** capable of perspiring or being perspired **2** *obs* **:** permitting circulation of air or wind **:** DRAFTY, BREEZY, AIRY

per·spi·rate \'pərspəˌrāt\ *vi* -ED/-ING/-S [back-formation fr. *perspiration*] *archaic* **:** PERSPIRE

per·spi·ra·tion \ˌpərspə'rāshən, ˌpə̄s-, ˌpəis-, *substand* ˌpres-\ *n* -S [F, fr. MF, fr. *perspirer* to perspire + *-ation* — more at PERSPIRE] **1 :** the act or process of perspiring **2 :** a saline fluid that is secreted by the sweat glands, that consists chiefly of water containing sodium chloride and other salts, nitrogenous substances (as urea), carbon dioxide, and other solutes, and that serves both as a means of excretion and as a body temperature regulator through the cooling effect of its evaporation **:** SWEAT **3 :** vigorous effort such as might be expected to cause sweating ⟨more is usually accomplished by ~ than by inspiration⟩

per·spira·tive \pər'spīrəd·iv, 'pərspəˌrād·-\ *adj* [*perspiration* + *-ive*] **:** causing perspiration

per·spir·a·to·ry \pə(r)'spīrəˌtōrē\ *adj* [*perspiration* + *-ory*] **:** of, relating to, secreting, or inducing perspiration ⟨~ glands⟩

per·spire \pə(r)'spī(ə)r, -īə\ *vb* -ED/-ING/-S [F *perspirer,* fr. MF, fr. *per-* through (fr. L) + *-spirer* (fr. L *spirare* to blow, breathe) — more at PER-, SPIRIT] *vi* **1 :** to pass off by evaporation or exhalation esp. through the pores of a substance ⟨beads of moisture *perspiring* through the porous walls of a clay water jug⟩ **2 :** to emit matter through the skin; *specif* **:** to secrete and emit perspiration **3 :** to expend effort (as in thought) to such a degree as might be expected to cause sweating **~** *vt* **1 :** to emit, exhale, or evacuate through pores ⟨firs . . . ~ a fine balsam of turpentine —Tobias Smollett⟩ **2 :** to emit (a substance) as or in perspiration ⟨whooped and drank and *perspired* beer —Christopher Isherwood⟩

perspired *adj* **:** covered with perspiration **:** SWEATY

perspiring *adj* **1 :** that perspires esp. as a result of effort; *also* **:** laboring diligently ⟨this aspiring and ~ young man⟩ **2 :** likely to cause sweating **:** hot and sticky ⟨a ~ atmosphere⟩ ⟨~ weather⟩

per·spir·ing·ly *adv* **:** in a perspiring manner

per·spiry \pə(r)'spīrē\ *adj* **:** SWEATY ⟨put on his coat for a ~ luncheon talk —*Newsweek*⟩

per stir·pes \per'stirˌpās, ˌpər'stər(ˌ)pēz\ *adv* (*or adj*) [L] **:** by familial stocks **:** as representatives of the branches of the descendants of a person — used of a mode of reckoning the rights or liabilities of descendants in which the children of any one descendant have or take only the share that their parent would have taken if living — compare PER CAPITA

per·stringe \pə(r)'strinj\ *vt* -ED/-ING/-S [L *perstringere* to bind up, graze, touch upon, censure, fr. *per-,* intensive prefix + *stringere* to draw tight, bind, touch upon — more at PER-, STRAIN] **1 :** to find fault with **:** CENSURE, CRITICIZE **2** *obs* **:** to dull the vision of **3** *archaic* **:** to touch upon lightly or in passing

per·suad·abil·i·ty \pə(r)ˌswādə'biləd·ē, -lətē, -i\ *n* **:** the quality or state of being persuadable

per·suad·able \pə(r)'swādəbəl\ *adj* [*persuade* + *-able*] **1 a :** capable of persuading **b :** subject to being persuaded **2** *obs* **:** commendable to the judgment — **per·suad·able·ness** \-nə̇s\ *n* -ES — **per·suad·ably** \-blē, -bli\ *adv*

per·suade \pə(r)'swād\ *vb* -ED/-ING/-S [L *persuadēre,* fr. *per-,* prefix denoting completion + *suadēre* to advise, urge — more at PER-, SUASION] *vt* **1 :** to induce by argument, entreaty, or expostulation into some mental position (as a determination, decision, conclusion, belief) **:** win over by an appeal to one's reason and feelings (as into doing or believing something) **:** bring (oneself or another) to belief, certainty, or conviction **:** argue into an opinion or procedure ⟨he ~s his friend to study law⟩ ⟨*persuaded* us that we were wrong⟩ ⟨~ yourself that you cannot fail⟩ **2 :** to use persuasion upon **:** plead with **:** URGE ⟨even now at my elbow, *persuading* me not to kill the duke —Shak.⟩ **3 :** to demonstrate or prove (something) to be true, credible, essential, commendable, or worthy (as of belief, adoption, practice) **:** bring about by argument and persuasion the doing, practicing, or believing of ⟨hadst thou thy wits, and didst ~ revenge —Shak.⟩ **4 :** to obtain or get with difficulty (as by coaxing) ⟨finally *persuaded* an answer out of him⟩ **~** *vi* **1 :** to use or to prevail by persuasion **:** plead movingly or successfully — sometimes formerly used with *with* **2 :** to become persuaded ⟨he ~s easily⟩ **syn** see INDUCE

per·suad·er \-də(r)\ *n* -S **1 :** one that persuades **2 :** something (as a gun or whip) used in compelling

per·suad·ing·ly *adv* **:** in a persuading manner **:** so as to persuade ⟨spoke ~ and at length⟩

per·sua·si·bil·i·ty \pə(r)ˌswāzə'biləd·ē, -āsə-, -lətē, -i\ *n* -ES **:** PERSUADABILITY

per·sua·si·ble \-ˈ=zəbəl, -səb-\ *adj* [MF, fr. L *persuasibilis* persuasive, fr. *persuasus* + *-ibilis* -ible] : PERSUADABLE

per·sua·sion \pə(r)ˈswāzhən\ *n* -S [ME *persuasioun*, fr. MF or L; MF *persuasion*, fr. L *persuasion-*, *persuasio*, fr. *persuasus* (past part. of *persuadēre* to persuade) + *-ion-*, *-io* -ion — more at PERSUADE] **1 a :** an act or the action of influencing the mind by arguments or reasons offered or by anything that moves the mind or passions or inclines the will to a determination **b :** something that serves to persuade : a persuading argument : INDUCEMENT ⟨if none of these ~*s* move you⟩ **c :** ability to persuade : PERSUASIVENESS ⟨there is an inherent ~ in some voices⟩ **2 :** the condition of having the mind influenced (as to decision, acceptance, or belief) from without : the quality or state of being persuaded **3 :** something of which one is persuaded: as **a :** a notion or opinion receiving full credence : a view held with complete assurance ⟨holding the ~ that they could not fail⟩; *esp* : a system of religious or other beliefs ⟨the several Protestant ~*s*⟩ **b :** a group, faction, sect, or party that adheres to a particular system of beliefs or ideas or promotes a particular view, theory, or cause ⟨composers of all different ~*s* —Arthur Berger⟩ ⟨the Tory ~⟩ **4 :** KIND, SORT, DESCRIPTION ⟨persons of the male ~⟩ **5 :** an act of persuading by force; *also* : compulsive force **6 :** a method of treating the neuroses consisting essentially in rational conversation and reeducation **syn** see OPINION, RELIGION

[1]**per·sua·sive** \-ˈāsˌiv, ˌēv *also* -āz| *or* |əv\ *adj* [MF *persuasif*, fr. ML *persuasivus*, fr. L *persuasus* (past part. of *persuadēre* to persuade) + *-ivus* -ive — more at PERSUADE] : tending to persuade : having the power of persuading ⟨~ eloquence⟩ ⟨a most ~ speaker⟩ — **per·sua·sive·ly** \|əvlē, |ēv-, -li\ *adv* — **per·sua·sive·ness** \|ivnəs, |ēv- *also* |əv-\ *n* -ES

[2]**persuasive** \"\ *n* -S : something that persuades or is intended to persuade : INDUCEMENT, INCENTIVE ⟨bribes and other ~*s*⟩

persuasive definition *n* : a definition that seeks to influence the attitude of the hearer to something by redefining its name ⟨that jazz is really classical music free of artificial constraints is a typical *persuasive definition*⟩

per·sua·so·ry \pə(r)ˈswāzərē, -āsə-\ *adj* [ML *persuasorius*, fr. L *persuasus* + *-orius* -ory] *archaic* : PERSUASIVE

per·sulfate \ˌpər, (ˈ)per+\ *n* [ISV *per-* + *sulfate*] **1 :** a sulfate in which the metal has a relatively high valence ⟨~ of iron $Fe_2(SO_4)_3$⟩ **2 :** a salt of persulfuric acid; *esp* : a salt (as potassium persulfate) of the acid $H_2S_2O_8$

per·sulfuric acid \ˌpər, ˌper+ . . . -\ *n* [ISV *per-* + *sulfuric*; prob. orig. formed as F *persulphurique*] : either of two peroxy acids of sulfur: **a :** a crystalline strongly oxidizing acid $H_2S_2O_8$ obtained usu. by electrolysis of sulfuric acid and used chiefly in making hydrogen peroxide and in the form of salts — called also *peroxydisulfuric acid*; not used systematically **b :** PERMONOSULFURIC ACID

[1]**pert** \ˈpər|t, ˈpə̄|, ˈpəi|, *usu* |d·+V\ *adj, usu* -ER/-EST [ME, modif. of OF *apert* — more at APERT] **1** *obs* : CLEVER, SHARP ⟨the ~*est* operations of wit —John Milton⟩ **2 a :** marked by a saucy freedom and forwardness : flippantly cocky and self-assertive : IMPUDENT, IMPERTINENT ⟨children were ~, disobedient, irreverent at home —Dixon Wecter⟩; *esp* : mischievously or heedlessly aggressive and rather disrespectful ⟨was amused by the boy's ~ answer⟩ ⟨with a ~ toss of her head —W.M.Thackeray⟩ ⟨~ little girls in short frocks —Siegfried Sassoon⟩ **b :** marked by a smart crisp jauntiness : trim and chic ⟨the ~ little hat —F. Tennyson Jesse⟩ ⟨bought a ~ little business suit for herself⟩ ⟨stories about ~ young career girls and junior executives —J.D.Adams⟩ **c :** piquantly stimulating ⟨is a ~ notion and one to fascinate the attention —G.J.Nathan⟩ ⟨a ~ turn in the end of a sentence —O.W. Holmes †1935⟩ **3 a (1) :** full of good spirits and vitality : chipper and frisky : full of pep ⟨felt ~ and relaxed after their long vacation⟩ **(2) :** LIVELY, BRISK, SPRY ⟨were moving along at a ~ pace⟩ **b :** brightly vivacious : PERKY ⟨was as rosy and ~ as a schoolgirl —Vera Caspary⟩ ⟨finds fun in ~, informal chatter —Flora Lewis⟩

[2]**pert** \"\ *adv* [ME, fr. *pert*, adj.] : PERTLY

pert *abbr* pertaining

per·tain \pə(r)ˈtān\ *vi* -ED/-ING/-S [ME *parteinen*, *partenen*, *perteinen*, *pertenen*, fr. MF *partenir*, fr. (assumed) VL *partenēre*, alter. of L *pertinēre* to reach to, belong, fr. *per-*, intensive prefix + *-tinēre* (fr. *tenēre* to hold) — more at PER-, THIN] **1 a (1) :** to belong to something as a part or member or accessory or product ⟨those who ~*ed* to the Christian tradition —J.D.Conway⟩ **(2) :** to belong to something as an attribute or adjunct or attendant feature or function ⟨the destruction and havoc ~*ing* to war⟩ ⟨a job that ~*s* to one man alone⟩ **(3) :** to belong to something as a care or concern or duty ⟨responsibilities that ~ to fatherhood⟩ **(4) :** to belong to something by inherent character, right, assignment, or established association ⟨privileges that ~*ed* only to the wealthier class⟩ **b :** to be appropriate to something : be right or proper or suitable ⟨trades ~*ing* to military activities —*Amer. Guide Series: Minn.*⟩ : be pertinent ⟨the criteria for their appointments will be different from those that ~ elsewhere in the faculty —J.B.Conant⟩ **2 :** to have some connection with or relation to something : have reference : RELATE ⟨in matters ~*ing* to man and his environment —*Current Biog.*⟩ ⟨his intention to translate some historical documents ~*ing* to Christopher Columbus —Saxe Commins⟩ ⟨the enormous stress which women lay on everything ~*ing* to clothes —P.M. Gregory⟩

perth \ˈpərth\ *adj, usu cap* **1** [fr. *Perth*, burgh and county in Scotland] **a :** of or from the burgh of Perth, Scotland : of the kind or style prevalent in Perth **b :** PERTHSHIRE **2** [fr. *Perth*, Western Australia] : of or from Perth, the capital of Western Australia : of the kind or style prevalent in Perth

perth·ite \ˈpərˌthīt\ *n* -S [*Perth*, Ontario, Canada + E *-ite*] : a feldspar rock consisting of orthoclase or microcline in which is interlaminated albite — **per·thit·ic** \ˌpərˈthid·ik\ *adj* — **per·thit·i·cal·ly** \-d·ək(ə)lē\ *adv*

per·tho·phyte \ˈpərthəˌfīt\ *n* -S [Gk *perthein* to destroy + E *-o-* + *-phyte*; akin to L *ferire* to strike — more at BORE] : a plant (as a fungus) that lives on dead or decaying tissue forming part of a living plant — compare SAPROPHYTE

perth·shire \ˈpərth,shi(ə)r, -,shər\ *adj, usu cap* [fr. *Perthshire*, Scotland] : of or from the county of Perth, Scotland : of the kind or style prevalent in Perth

per·ti·na·cious \ˌpərtᵊnˈāshəs, ˌpə̄t-, ˌpəit-\ *adj* [L *pertinac-*, *pertinax* (fr. *per-* thoroughly, completely + *-tinac-*, *-tinax*, fr. *tenac-*, *tenax* tenacious) + E *-ious* — more at PER-, TENACIOUS] **1 :** marked by an unyieldingly persistent fixedness (as of opinion, purpose, action) that is often annoyingly perverse in fact or in appearance : stubbornly inflexible ⟨a ~ opponent⟩ ⟨~ opinions⟩ **2 :** hard to get rid of : doggedly tenacious: as **a :** that resolutely or obstinately continues to last : not easily dislodged or dismissed or brought to an end ⟨many years of ~ advertising —Berton Roueché⟩ ⟨the theater . . . is a ~ institution, always confounding the prophets who announce from time to time that it is about to die —John Brophy⟩ ⟨~ curiosity⟩ **b :** that resolutely or obstinately persists in asking or demanding : refusing to be put off or denied : IMPORTUNATE ⟨a ~ beggar⟩ ⟨~ creditors⟩ **c :** stubbornly unshakable ⟨when the danger was so obvious that all but the most ~ optimists or partisans were silent —D.W.Brogan⟩ **d :** that resists treatment ⟨a ~ fever⟩ **syn** see OBSTINATE

per·ti·na·cious·ly *adv* : in a pertinacious manner : with pertinacity

per·ti·na·cious·ness *n* -ES : PERTINACITY

per·ti·nac·i·ty \ˌ==ˈasəd·ē, -ˈaas-, -sətē, -i\ *n* -ES [MF *pertinacité*, fr. LL *pertinacitas*, fr. L *pertinac-*, *pertinax* pertenacious + MF *-ité* -ity — more at PERTINACIOUS] : the quality or state of being pertinacious

pertinacy *n* -ES [ME *pertinacie*, fr. L *pertinacia*, fr. *pertinac-*, *pertinax* pertinacious + *-ia* -y] *obs* : PERTINACITY

per·ti·nence \ˈpər|t(ᵊ)nən(t)s, ˈpə̄|, ˈpəi| *also* |d·ənə- *or* |tənə-\ *n* -S [ME, fr. MF, fr. *pertinent*] : PERTINENCY

per·ti·nen·cy \-ənsē, -si\ *n* -ES [MF *pertinence* + E *-y*] : the quality or state of being pertinent : RELEVANCE ⟨the ~ of the evidence —Sidney Hyman⟩

[1]**per·ti·nent** \-ənt\ *adj* [ME, fr. MF, fr. L *pertinent-*, *pertinens*, pres. part. of *pertinēre* to reach, belong — more at PERTAIN] : that has some connection or relation with something (as a matter under discussion) : that is to the point : that is relevant or applicable ⟨the message of the book is as ~ today as at the time it was written —*Forth*⟩ ⟨had some ~ comments —Cormac Philip⟩ ⟨a ~ question⟩ ⟨~ facts⟩ ⟨~ information⟩ ⟨data ~ to such federal aid —*Collier's Yr. Bk.*⟩ **syn** see RELEVANT

[2]**pertinent** \"\ *n* -S [ME, fr. ML *pertinentia*, fr. L, pl. of *pertinent-*, *pertinens*] *chiefly Scots law* : APPURTENANCE; *specif* : something belonging to an estate and passing with ownership of the estate to any new owner ⟨the dignity . . . was territorial and a part and ~ of the lands —F.J.Grant⟩ — usu. used in pl. ⟨conveying the land with parts and ~*s*⟩

per·ti·nen·tia \ˌpərtᵊnˈenchēə\ *n pl* [ML] *civil & Scots law* : appurtenances belonging to real or personal property and passing with ownership of the property to any new owner

per·ti·nent·ly *adv* : in a pertinent way : with pertinency

pert·ly *adv* [ME, fr. *pert* + *-ly*] : in a pert manner : with pertness

pert·ness *n* -ES : the quality or state of being pert

per tout et non per my \pə(r)ˈtüā,nänpə(r)ˈmē\ [AF] : by the whole and not by a share, moiety, or divisible part — used esp. in property law with reference to concurrent ownership by two or more persons

per·turb \pərˈtərb; pəˈtə̄b, -tәib\ *vt* -ED/-ING/-S [ME *perturben*, fr. MF *perturber*, fr. L *perturbare*, fr. *per-*, intensive prefix + *turbare* to throw into disorder, disturb, make turbid — more at PER-, TURBID] **1 :** to disturb considerably in mind : make quite uneasy : cause to be upset or worried or alarmed : DISQUIET, UNSETTLE ⟨was ~*ed* by the news⟩ ⟨had not expected this development and it rather ~*ed* him⟩ **2 :** to put into considerable disorder or confusion : throw out of kilter : DERANGE ⟨~*ing* good social order with their lies and propaganda⟩ **3 a :** to cause (a planet or other celestial body) to deviate from a theoretically regular orbital motion usu. as a result of interposed or otherwise extraordinary gravitational pull **b :** to disturb or interfere with or modify the usual or expected motion or course or arrangement of (as atoms) ⟨interaction between a hydrogen atom ~*ed* by a passing ion —*Physical Rev.*⟩ **4 :** to subject to tonal perturbation **syn** see DISCOMPOSE

[1]**per·tur·bate** \ˈpərd·ərˌbāt\ *vt* -ED/-ING/-S [L *perturbatus*, past part. of *perturbare*] *archaic* : PERTURB

[2]**perturbate** \"\ *adj* [L *perturbatus*, past part.] *archaic* : PERTURBED

per·tur·ba·tion \ˌpərd·ərˈbāshən, ˌpərtər'-, ˌpərˌtər'-; ˌpə̄d·ə'-, ˌpə̄tə'-, ˌpə̄ˌtə̄'-, ˌpəiˌtəi'-\ *n* -S [ME *perturbacioun*, fr. MF *perturbation*, fr. L *perturbation-*, *perturbatio*, fr. *perturbatus* + *-ion-*, *-io* -ion] **1 :** the action of perturbing or condition of being perturbed : COMMOTION ⟨the ~*s* of the period of revolution —Ernest Barker⟩; *esp* : mental or emotional disturbance or agitation ⟨was in great ~ of mind⟩ **2 :** irregular variation in or alteration of or deviation from what is usual or expected (as in the orbital motion of a celestial body affected by extraordinary gravitational pull) **3 :** alternation of tone conditioned by phonetic environment — **per·tur·ba·tion·al** \ˌ=(ˌ)=ˈbāshənᵊl, -shnəl\ *adj*

per·tur·ba·tive \ˈpərd·ərˌbād·iv, ˌpərˈtərbəd·-\ *adj* [LL *perturbativus*, fr. L *perturbatus* (past part. of *perturbare* to perturb) + *-ivus* -ive — more at PERTURB] *archaic* : tending to perturb : PERTURBING

per·tur·ba·tor \ˈpərd·ərˌbād·ə(r)\ *n* -S [LL, fr. L *perturbatus* + *-or*] *archaic* : one that perturbs

per·turbed *pronunc at* PERTURB + d\ *adj* : DISTURBED, AGITATED, UPSET ⟨was . . . so ~ as to forget the convention of the usual greetings —Joseph Conrad⟩ — **per·turbed·ly** \-bədlē, -bdlē\ *adv*

perturbing *adj* : DISTURBING, UPSETTING ⟨a revelation that was most ~⟩ — **per·turb·ing·ly** *adv*

per·tu·sar·ia \ˌpərd·əˈsa(a)rēə\ *n, cap* [NL, fr. L *pertusus* (past part. of *pertundere* to bore through) + NL *-aria* — more at PIERCE] : a large widely distributed genus (the type of the family Pertusariaceae) of crustose lichens that have the fruiting bodies in structures resembling knobs and that are one of the sources of litmus and archil — compare ROCCELLA

per·tus·sal \pə(r)ˈtəsəl\ *adj* [NL *pertussis* + E *-al*] : of or relating to whooping cough

per·tus·sis \-səs\ *n* [NL, irreg. fr. L *per-* thoroughly + *tussis* cough] : WHOOPING COUGH

pe·ru \pəˈrü *sometimes* piˈ- *or* pēˈ- *or* pāˈ- *or* peˈ-\ *adj, usu cap* [fr. *Peru*, country in So. America] : of or from Peru : of the kind or style prevalent in Peru : PERUVIAN

peru balsam *n, usu cap P* : BALSAM OF PERU

[1]**pe·ru·gian** \pəˈrüj(ē)ən, pāˈ-\ *adj, usu cap* [*Perugia*, city in Umbria, Italy + E *-an*] : of or relating to Perugia, Italy

[2]**perugian** \"\ *n* -S *cap* : a native or inhabitant of Perugia

pe·ru·gi·nesque \ˌpā(ˌ)rüjəˈnesk, ˌpe(-, pāˌrü-, peˌrü-, pəˌrü-\ *adj, usu cap* [F *péruginesque*, fr. *Perugino* (Pietro Vannucci) †1523 Ital. painter + F *-esque*] : resembling or suggestive of the paintings of the early Renaissance Italian artist Perugino

pe·ruke *also* **pe·ruque** *or* **per·ruque** \pəˈrük\ *n* -S [MF *perruque*, fr. OIt *parrucca*, *perrucca* head of hair, wig] : WIG; *specif* : one of several wigs popularly worn in the period extending from the 17th century to the early 19th century

pe·ruk·er \pəˈrükə(r)\ *or* **peru·kier** *or* **per·ru·quier** \pəˈrükēə(r); ˌperəˈki(ə)r, -rəkˈyā\ *n* -S [F *perruquier*, fr. *perruque* + *-ier* -er] : WIGMAKER

pe·ru·lar·ia \ˌper(y)əˈla(a)rēə\ *n, cap* [NL, fr. L *perula* scale of a leaf bud (fr. L, small wallet, dim. of *pera* wallet, fr. Gk *pēra*) + NL *-aria*] : a genus of leafy-stemmed greenish flowered terrestrial orchids with fibrous roots and a bracted spicate inflorescence

pe·rus·able \pəˈrüzəbəl\ *adj* : that may be perused

pe·rus·al \-zəl\ *n* -S [*peruse* + *-al*] : the action of perusing ⟨had not finished his ~ of the evening papers⟩ ⟨a magazine article that deserves careful ~⟩

peru saltpeter *n, usu cap P* : CHILE SALTPETER

pe·ruse \pəˈrüz\ *vb* -ED/-ING/-S [ME *perusen*, prob. fr. L *per-* completely, thoroughly + ME *usen* to use — more at PER-, USE] *vt* **1 :** to examine or consider or survey with some attention and typically for the purpose of discovering or noting one or more specific points : look at or look through fairly attentively : go through : STUDY ⟨applicants should ~ the lists carefully —*Official Register of Harvard Univ.*⟩ ⟨as we ~ the course of history of civilized man —Sumner Welles⟩ ⟨people who began by beholding him ended by *perusing* him —Thomas Hardy⟩ ⟨*perused* the terms of the contract⟩ **2 :** READ ⟨evenings spent in *perusing* the world's masterpieces —L.P.Smith⟩ ⟨*perusing* the newspaper⟩; *specif* : to read through or read over with some attention and typically for the purpose of discovering or noting one or more specific points ⟨thought something more might be learned by carefully *perusing* the letter she had written⟩ ⟨*perused* the book in the hope of getting needed material for further research⟩ ~ *vi* **1 :** to spend time in perusal : peruse something ⟨have tried to ~ and learn all my life —Thomas Hardy⟩ ⟨sat there *perusing* until he was ready to speak⟩ **2** *chiefly dial* : to proceed somewhere and take a look around ⟨let's go ~ down that draw —C.T.Jackson⟩ — **peruser** *n* -S

[1]**pe·ru·vi·an** \pəˈrüvēən\ *adj, usu cap* [NL *Peruvia* Peru (fr. Sp *Perú*) + E *-an*] **1 :** of, relating to, or characteristic of Peru in So. America **2 :** of, relating to, or characteristic of the people of Peru

[2]**peruvian** \"\ *n* -S *cap* : a native or inhabitant of Peru

peruvian balsam *n, usu cap P* : BALSAM OF PERU

peruvian bark *n, usu cap P* : CINCHONA 3

peruvian coca *n, usu cap P* : COCA 2b

peruvian cotton *n, usu cap P* : a cotton with long rough hairy fibers that is derived from a Peruvian plant (*Gossypium peruvianum*)

peruvian cypress *n, usu cap P* : MING TREE

peruvian daffodil *n, usu cap P* : any of several Peruvian herbs of the genus *Hymenocallis*

peruvian lily *n, usu cap P* : an Andean herb (*Alstroemeria pelegrina*) that resembles a lily and has showy pinkish purple umbellate flowers and that is used as an ornamental

peruvian mastic tree *n, usu cap P* : PEPPER TREE 1

peruvian nutmeg *n, usu cap P* : the aromatic fruit of a So. American tree (*Laurelia aromatica*) of the family Monimiaceae

peruvian rhatany *n, usu cap P* : a rhatany obtained from an American shrub (*Krameria triandra*) and used as an astringent — called also *knotty rhatany*

peruvian saltpeter *n, usu cap P* : CHILE SALTPETER

peruvian yellow *n, often cap P* : a moderate reddish orange that is stronger than burnt ocher and yellower, darker, and slightly less strong than crab apple

per·vade \pə(r)ˈvād\ *vb* -ED/-ING/-S [L *pervadere*, fr. *per-* through + *vadere* to go — more at PER-, WADE] *vt* **1** *archaic* : to move along through : TRAVERSE ⟨*pervaded* Westminster Hall and looked into most of the courts —A.K.H.Boyd⟩ **2 :** to become diffused throughout every part of : spread throughout : PERMEATE ⟨that heavy, still, musty odor that ~*s* all railroad waiting rooms —Thomas Whiteside⟩ ⟨an air of Sunday boredom ~*s* the streets —S.J.Roche⟩ ⟨the lassitude that ~*s* most of our prisons —Frank O'Leary⟩ ~ *vi* : to become diffused throughout every part of something ⟨it is pleasant to live in a locality where this spirit ~*s* —*Railway Gazette*⟩ **syn** see PERMEATE

pervading *adj* : prevalent or dominant by reason of having become widely diffused or diffused through every part of something ⟨reflects the crisis in the world and its ~ sense of insecurity —Walter Moberly⟩ — **per·vad·ing·ly** *adv*

per·valvar axis \ˌpər, (ˈ)per+...-\ *n* [*per-* + *valvar*] : the longitudinal axis of the frustule of a diatom

per·vap·o·rate \(ˌ)pərˈvapəˌrāt\ *vt* -ED/-ING/-S [*per-* + *evaporate*] : to subject to pervaporation

per·vap·o·ra·tion \(ˌ)pərˌvapəˈrāshən\ *n* -S : the concentration of a colloidal solution whose colloid will not pass through a semipermeable membrane by placing the solution in a bag made of the membrane material and blowing warm air against the surface of the bag

per·va·sion \pə(r)ˈvāzhən\ *n* -S [LL *pervasion-*, *pervasio*, fr. L *pervasus* (past part. of *pervadere* to pervade) + *-ion-*, *-io* -ion — more at PERVADE] : the action of pervading or condition of being pervaded : PERMEATION

per·va·sive \pə(r)ˈvās|iv, |ēv *also* |əv *sometimes* -āz|\ *adj* [L *pervasus* + E *-ive*] : that pervades or tends to pervade esp. in such a way as to be or become prevalent or dominant : PERVADING ⟨a ~ odor that clings stubbornly to clothes —M.M. Gassman⟩ ⟨the ~ dampness of the stone-flagged floor —Elinor Wylie⟩ ⟨an age in which large-scale catastrophe and ~ anxiety have overshadowed the triumphs of individual men —C.J.Rolo⟩ — **per·va·sive·ly** \|əvlē, |ēv-, -li\ *adv* — **per·va·sive·ness** \|ivnəs, |ēv- *also* |əv-\ *n* -ES

per·venche \ˈpər,vänch, -,vinch\ *n* -S [F, lit., periwinkle (plant), fr. L *pervinca* — more at PERIWINKLE] : a grayish purplish blue that is duller than average delft, bluer, lighter, and stronger than regimental, and lighter and stronger than average navy blue

per ver·ba de prae·sen·ti \ˌperˌverbəˌdāˌprīˈsentē\ *adv* [L] : by words of the present tense

per·verse \pərˈvərs, pəˈvə̄s, pəˈvəis, ˈpərˌv-, ˈpə̄ˌv-, ˈpəiˌv-\ *adj* [ME *pervers*, fr. L *perversus*, fr. past part. of *pervertere* to turn the wrong way, destroy, corrupt, pervert — more at PERVERT] **1 a :** turned away from what is right or good : CORRUPT, WICKED ⟨the only righteous in a world ~ —John Milton⟩ **b :** contrary to accepted standards or practice : INCORRECT, IMPROPER ⟨felt it ~ that a bondman's son should be made a bishop —G.G.Coulton⟩ **c** *of a verdict* : contrary to the evidence or the direction of the judge on a point of law **2 a :** stubborn, obstinate, and persistent by temperament and disposition in opposing what is right, reasonable, correct, or accepted : WRONGHEADED ⟨a dual nature, one half positive, and passionate to yearning, one half negative, satirical, and really ~ —H.S.Canby⟩ ⟨certain matters of fact which not even the most ~ of . . . clerks could disguise —F.M.Stenton⟩ **b :** arising from or indicative of stubbornness or obstinacy ⟨will gain nothing by keeping it except a possible ~ satisfaction in doing so —Hervey Allen⟩ **3** *obs* : ADVERSE, UNFAVORABLE **4 :** marked by peevishness or petulance : CRANKY ⟨if thou thinkest I am too quickly won, I'll frown and be ~ —Shak.⟩ **5 a :** relating to, characterized by, or resulting from a perverted disposition or inclination ⟨the last ~ whim which has taken possession of the debauchee —J.W.Krutch⟩ **b :** suffering from a perversion **syn** see CONTRARY

per·verse·ly *adv* : in a perverse manner : with perverseness

per·verse·ness *n* -ES : PERVERSITY

per·ver·sion \pərˈvər|zhən, pəˈvə̄|, pəˈvəi| *also* |shən\ *n* -S [ME, fr. L *perversion-*, *perversio*, fr. *perversus* (past part. of *pervertere* to pervert) + *-ion-*, *-io* -ion — more at PERVERT] **1 a :** the action of perverting **b :** the condition of being perverted **2 :** a perverted form of something; *esp* : some form of sex gratification (as fellatio, exhibitionism) preferred to heterosexual coitus and habitually sought after as the primary or only form of sex gratification desired

per·ver·si·ty \|səd·ē, -ətē, -i\ *n* -ES [L *perversitas*, fr. *perversus* perverse + *-itas* -ity — more at PERVERSE] **1 :** the quality or state of being perverse ⟨some sort of ~ in our souls —D.H. Lawrence⟩ **2 :** an instance of perversity ⟨in spite of a hundred *perversities* —C.E.Montague⟩ ⟨one of the ironic *perversities* that often attend the course of affairs —John Dewey⟩

per·ver·sive \|s|iv, |ēv *also* |z| *or* |əv\ *adj* [L *perversus* (past part. of *pervertere* to pervert) + E *-ive* — more at PERVERT] : that perverts or tends to pervert : marked by perversion ⟨illegitimate sex drives, ~ behavior —Ben Karpman⟩

[1]**per·vert** \pərˈvər|t, pəˈvə̄|, pəˈvəi|, ˈpərˌv-, ˈpə̄ˌv-, ˈpəiˌv-, *usu* |d·+V\ *vt* -ED/-ING/-S [ME *perverten*, fr. MF *pervertir*, fr. L *pervertere* to turn the wrong way, destroy, corrupt, pervert, fr. *per-*, prefix denoting deviation + *vertere* to turn — more at PER-, WORTH] **1 a (1) :** to cause to turn aside or away from what is viewed as good or true or morally right : lead astray : CORRUPT ⟨was accused of ~*ing* youth⟩; *esp* : to make a moral pervert of **(2) :** to cause to turn aside or away from what is generally done or generally accepted : divert into what is wrong or incorrect or not normal or usual : MISDIRECT ⟨~*ed* the course of justice⟩ ⟨were deliberately ~*ing* to their ends essentially the same techniques —*New Republic*⟩ **b (1) :** to make use of usu. willfully in a wrong or improper way : divert to a wrong end or purpose : MISUSE ⟨the idea is one that may easily deteriorate or be ~*ed* —Lionel Trilling⟩ **(2) :** to twist the meaning or sense of usu. willfully : MISINTERPRET, MISCONSTRUE, MISAPPLY ⟨~*s* some evidence and omits the rest —Norman Douglas⟩ **2 :** to effect a symmetric exchange between the right and left parts of ⟨an object as viewed in a plane mirror is ~*ed* from its actual appearance⟩ **syn** see DEBASE

[2]**per·vert** \ˈpərˌvər|t, ˈpə̄ˌvə̄|, ˈpəiˌvəi| *sometimes* pə(r)ˈv-; *usu* |d·+V\ *n* -S : one that has been perverted or that manifests or is given to some form of perversion esp. sexual

perverted *adj* **1 :** that has been perverted : TWISTED, CORRUPT, VICIOUS ⟨a custom as ~ as any ever recorded⟩ **2 :** marked by perversion esp. sexual ⟨a still more ~ form of behavior⟩ — **per·vert·ed·ly** *adv* — **per·vert·ed·ness** *n* -ES

per·vert·er *pronunc at* [1]PERVERT + ə(r)\ *n* -S : one that perverts

per·vert·i·ble \-d·əbəl, -təb-\ *adj* [F, fr. MF, fr. *pervertir* to pervert + *-ible* — more at PERVERT] : capable of being perverted ⟨incompetent and therefore easily ~ —James Bryce⟩

per·vi·ca·cious \ˌpərvəˈkāshəs\ *adj* [L *pervicac-*, *pervicax* pervicacious (fr. *per-* thoroughly + *-vicac-*, *vicax*, fr. the stem of *vincere* to prevail, win a point, conquer) + E *-ious* — more at PER-, VICTOR] : very obstinate : WILLFUL, REFRACTORY — **per·vi·ca·cious·ly** *adv*

per·vi·ca·cious·ness *n* -ES : the quality or state of being pervicacious : great obstinacy or willfulness

per·vi·cac·i·ty \ˌpərvəˈkasəd·ē\ *n* -ES [ML *pervicacitas*, fr. L *pervicac-*, *pervicax* + *-itas* -ity] : PERVICACIOUSNESS

pervicacy *n* -ES [L *pervicacia*, fr. *pervicac-*, *pervicax* + *-ia* -y] *obs* : PERVICACIOUSNESS

per·vi·ous \ˈpərvēəs, ˈpə̄v-,ˈpəiv-\ *adj* [L *pervius*, fr. *per* through + *-vius* (fr. *via* way, road) — more at FOR, VIA] **1 a** *archaic* : lying open to the understanding : INTELLIGIBLE **b :** being of such a kind as to permit access to something indicated ⟨~ to reason and the logic of facts —*Scotsman*⟩ **2 a :** being of a substance that can be penetrated or permeated ⟨a ~ rock⟩ ⟨~ soil⟩ or that allows passage through ⟨a metal especially ~ to heat⟩ : not impervious **b** *archaic* : that is passable (as by a traveler) **c :** PERFORATE 2a **3** *archaic* : PERVADING — **per·vi·ous·ness** *n* -ES

per·wits·ky \pə(r)ˈwitskē\ *n* -ES [prob. modif. of Russ *perevyazka*] **1 :** a tiger weasel (*Vormela peregusna*) of eastern Europe and northern Asia that is mottled reddish and white above and black below **2 :** the fur of the perwitsky

per·y·lene \ˈperəˌlēn\ *n* -S [*peri-di-naphthylene*] : a yellow crystalline aromatic hydrocarbon $C_{20}H_{12}$ that is constituted of two naphthalene residues joined to each other through the peri-positions, that is found in small amounts in coal tar, and that can be made from naphthalene by the action of aluminum chloride

pes \ˈpēz\ *n, pl* **pe·des** \ˈpē(ˌ)dēz, ˈpeˌ-\ [NL *ped-, pes*, fr. L, foot — more at FOOT] **1 :** the distal segment of the hind limb of a vertebrate including the tarsus and foot **2 :** a part resembling a foot: as **a :** the diverging branches of the facial nerve in and near the parotid gland **b :** the enlarged lower extremity of the hippocampus major **c :** the crusta of either of the cerebral peduncles **3** [ML *ped-, pes*, fr. L, foot] **a :** a neume indicating an ascending motion **b :** the tenor in medieval choral music **c :** the ground bass of a canon

pes *abbr* peseta

pe·sach *or* **pe·sah** \ˈpāsäk\ *n* -S *usu cap* [Heb *Pesaḥ*] **:** PASSOVER

pe·sade \pəˈsäd, -zäd, -zād\ *n* -S [F, alter. (influenced by *peser* to weigh, fr. L *pensare*) of obs. F *posade*, fr. MF, fr. OIt *posata*, fr. *posare* to put, rest, pause, fr. LL *pausare* to stop, rest, fr. L *pausa* pause — more at PAUSE, PENSIVE] **:** a dressage maneuver in which a horse is made to raise his forequarters while keeping his hind feet on the ground without advancing

pe·san·te \pāˈsän·(ˌ)tā\ *adv (or adj)* [It, heavy, fr. pres. part. of *pesare* to weigh, fr. L *pensare* to weigh (something) — more at PENSIVE] **:** in a heavy manner — used as a direction in music

pes·cha·ni·ki \pesˈchänəkē\ *also* **pes·cha·nik** \pesˈchänik\ *n* -S [Russ *peschanik* sandstone, fr. *pesok* sand; prob. akin to Skt *pāṁsu* sand] **:** the fur of a suslik (*Citellus fulvus*)

pes·cod \ˈpeˌskäd\ *dial Eng var of* PEASECOD

pe·se·ta \pəˈsād·ə, peˈ-, ·sed·ə\ *n* -S [Sp, dim. of *peso*] **1 a :** an old Spanish silver coin worth ¼ of the piece of eight **b :** a corresponding unit of value **2 a :** the basic monetary unit of Spain since 1868 — see MONEY table **b :** a coin or note representing this unit

pe·sha·war \pəˈshäwər, -shau̇(ə)r\ *adj, usu cap* [fr. *Peshawar*, city in northwest Pakistan] **:** of or from the city of Peshawar, Pakistan **:** of the kind or style prevalent in Peshawar

pesh·wa *or* **peish·wa** \ˈpāshwə\ *n* -S [Hindi & Marathi *peśvā*, fr. Per *peshwā* leader, guide, fr. *pesh* before] **:** the chief minister of a Maratha prince

pes·ki·ly \ˈpeskəlē, -li\ *adv* **:** in a pesky manner

pes·ki·ness \-kēnəs, -kin-\ *n* -ES **:** the quality or state of being pesky

¹**pes·ky** \ˈpeskē, -ki\ *adj* -ER/-EST [prob. irreg. fr. *pest* + *-y*] **:** giving rise to annoyance or vexation **:** TROUBLESOME ⟨how to dress the wall behind the range is a ~ decorating problem —Marion Mayer⟩ ⟨tired after that ~ train —Jean Stafford⟩

²**pesky** \"\ *adv* **:** EXTREMELY, VERY — used as an intensive ⟨those who are so ~ mean as to destroy library books —*Star of Hope*⟩

pe·so \ˈpā(ˌ)sō, ˈpe(-\ *n* -S [Sp, lit., weight, fr. L *pensum* — more at POISE] **1 a :** a former unit of value in Spain and Spanish America equal to 8 reales **:** the Spanish dollar **b :** a coin (as a gold ½ escudo) equal in value to one peso **2 a :** the basic monetary unit in Bolivia, Chile, Colombia, Cuba, Dominican Republic, Guinea-Bissau, Mexico, and Uruguay **b :** a coin or note representing one of these units — see MONEY table **3 a :** the basic monetary unit in the Republic of the Philippines **b :** a coin or note representing this unit —see MONEY table **4 :** a monetary unit of value equal to ¹⁄₁₀₀ austral — see MONEY table

pes·sa·ry \ˈpesərē, -ri\ *n* -ES [ME *pessarie*, fr. LL *pessarium*, fr. *pessum, pessus* pessary (fr. Gk *pessos* pessary, oval stone for playing checkers or backgammon) + L *-arium* -ary] **1 :** a vaginal suppository **2 :** an instrument or device to be introduced into and worn in the vagina to support the uterus, remedy a malposition, or prevent conception

pes·si·mal \ˈpesəməl\ *adj* [*pessimum* + *-al*] **:** of, relating to, or constituting a pessimum **:** WORST ⟨a ~ environment⟩

pes·si·mism \ˈpesəˌmizəm, ˈpez-\ *n* -S [F *pessimisme* inclination to put the least favorable construction on actions and happenings, fr. L *pessimus* + F *-isme* -ism — more at PEJORATIVE] **1 :** the worst possible or conceivable state ⟨an age when public criticism is . . . at the very point of ~ —Robert Southey⟩ **2 :** an inclination to put the least favorable construction on actions and happenings, to emphasize adverse aspects, conditions, and possibilities, or to anticipate the worst possible outcome ⟨the ~ with which some of us view the prospect of establishing . . . brotherhood among the human race —Elmer Davis⟩ **3 a :** the philosophical doctrine or opinion that reality is essentially evil, completely evil, or as evil as it conceivably can be **b :** the philosophical doctrine that the evils of life overbalance the happiness it affords and that life is preponderantly evil — compare OPTIMISM

pes·si·mist \-ˌməst\ *n* -S *often attrib* [F *pessimiste*, fr. *pessimisme*, after such pairs as F *déisme* deism: *déiste* deist] **:** one given to pessimism; *esp* **:** an adherent of philosophical pessimism — compare OPTIMIST

pes·si·mis·tic \ˌ≈≈ˈmistik, -tēk\ *also* **pes·si·mis·ti·cal** \-təkəl, -tēk-\ *adj* **:** of, relating to, or characterized by pessimism **:** marked by disbelief, distrust, or a lack of confidence, hope, or joy **:** GLOOMY, DESPAIRING **syn** see CYNICAL

pes·si·mis·ti·cal·ly \-tək(ə)lē, -tēk-, -li\ *adv* **:** in a pessimistic manner

pes·si·mum \ˈpesəməm\ *n* -S [L, neut. of *pessimus* worst] **:** the least favorable environmental condition under which an organism can survive

pes·su·lar \ˈpes(y)ələ(r)\ *adj* [*pessulus* + *-ar*] **:** of, relating to, or resembling the pessulus

pes·su·lus \-ləs\ *n, pl* **pessu·li** \-ˌlī\ [L, bolt, modif. of Gk *passalos* peg, stake; akin to Gk *pēgnynai* to fix, fasten together — more at PACT] **:** a bony or cartilaginous bar crossing the lower end of the windpipe of a bird dorsoventrally at its division into bronchi

pest \ˈpest\ *n* -S *often attrib* [MF *peste*, fr. L *pestis*] **1 :** an epidemic disease associated with high mortality; *specif* **:** PLAGUE **2 :** something resembling a pest esp. in destructiveness or noxiousness; *esp* **:** a plant or animal detrimental to man or to his interests **3 :** one that pesters or annoys **:** NUISANCE ⟨gave the greatest encouragement to those ~s of society, mercenary informers —Edmund Burke⟩

pes·ta·loz·zian \ˌpestəˈlätsēən, -syən\ *adj, usu cap* [Johann H. *Pestalozzi* †1827 Swiss educational reformer + E *-an*] **:** of, relating to, or constituting a system of education in which the sense perceptions are first trained and the other faculties are then developed in what is held to be natural order

¹**pes·ter** \ˈpestə(r)\ *vt* **pestered; pestered; pestering** \-st(ə)riŋ\ **pesters** [modif. of MF *empestrer* to hobble (an animal), impede, embarrass, fr. (assumed) VL *impastoriare* to hobble (an animal), fr. L *in-* ²in- + (assumed) VL *pastoria*, n., hobble, fr. L, fem. of *pastorius* of or belonging to a herdsman, fr. L *pastor* herdsman, shepherd + *-ius* -ious — more at PASTOR] **1** *obs* **a :** OBSTRUCT, IMPEDE ⟨seeing him ~*ed* in a narrow passage —Henry Holcroft⟩ **b :** ENCUMBER, OVERBURDEN ⟨shall not ~ my account . . . with descriptions of places —Daniel Defoe⟩ **c :** to crowd together ⟨men . . . confined and ~*ed* in this pinfold —John Milton⟩ **2** [influenced in meaning by *pest*] *archaic* **:** INFEST ⟨is rich and fertile but ~*ed* with green adders —Jedidiah Morse⟩ **3** [influenced in meaning by *pest*] **:** to harass with petty and repeated irritations **:** ANNOY, BOTHER, VEX ⟨~*ed* him . . . so that he could not keep his mind on reading —Jean Stafford⟩ ⟨would ~ people with irritating questions —Elsa Maxwell⟩ **syn** see WORRY

²**pester** \"\ *n* -S **:** one that obstructs, encumbers, or annoys

pes·ter·er \-t(ə)rə(r)\ *n* -S **:** one that pesters

pes·ter·ing·ly *adv* **:** in a pestering manner

pes·ter·ment \-tə(r)mənt\ *n* -S *dial chiefly Brit* **:** ANNOYANCE

pes·ter·ous \-t(ə)rəs\ *adj* **:** inclined to pester **:** TROUBLESOME

pest·ful \ˈpestfəl\ *adj* **:** PESTIFEROUS

pesthole \ˈ≈,≈\ *n* **:** a place subject or liable to epidemic disease

pesthouse \ˈ≈,≈\ *n* **:** a shelter or hospital for those infected with a pestilential or contagious disease

pes·ti·ci·dal \ˌpestəˈsīdᵊl\ *adj* **:** of, relating to, or constituting a pesticide

pes·ti·cide \ˈ≈≈,sīd\ *n* -S [*pest* + *-i-* + *-cide*] **:** an agent (as a chemical) used to destroy a pest **:** ECONOMIC POISON

pes·tif·er·ous \(ˈ)peˈstif(ə)rəs\ *adj* [ME, fr. L *pestifer*, *pestiferus* pestilential, noxious, fr. *pestis* plague + *-fer, -ferus* (fr. *ferre* to bear, carry) — more at BEAR] **1 :** dangerous to society **:** PERNICIOUS, EVIL ⟨one of the most ~ forms of calumny —Gilbert Burnet⟩ **2 a :** carrying or propagating infection **:** destructive of health **:** PESTILENTIAL ⟨~ vermin⟩ **b :** infected with a pestilential disease ⟨poor ~ creatures begging alms —John Evelyn⟩ **3 :** causing annoyance, irritation, or vexation ⟨a ~, high-principled, gimlet-eyed old gentleman —*Today*⟩ — **pes·tif·er·ous·ly** *adv* — **pes·tif·er·ous·ness** *n* -ES

pes·ti·lence \ˈpestələn(t)s\ *n* -S [ME, fr. MF, fr. L *pestilentia*, fr. *pestilent-, pestilens* + *-ia* -y] **1 :** a contagious or infectious epidemic disease that is virulent and devastating; *specif* **:** BUBONIC PLAGUE **2 :** something that is destructive or pernicious ⟨I'll pour this ~ into his ear —Shak.⟩

pes·ti·lent \-lənt\ *adj* [ME, fr. L *pestilent-, pestilens*, fr. *pestis* plague] **1 :** destructive of life **:** FATAL, DEADLY ⟨a ~ land where people died like flies —Maurice Carr⟩ **2 :** injuring or endangering society **:** PERNICIOUS ⟨grew impatient with such ~ heresies —V.L.Parrington⟩ **3 :** giving rise to annoyance **:** VEXING, IRRITATING ⟨~ outsiders . . . assailing the reputation of the neighborhood —Arthur Morrison⟩ **4** *archaic* **:** INFECTIOUS, CONTAGIOUS — **pes·ti·lent·ly** *adv*

pes·ti·len·tial \ˌpestəˈlenchəl\ *adj* [ME *pestilencial*, fr. ML *pestilentialis*, fr. L *pestilentia* pestilence + *-alis* -al] **1 a :** causing or tending to cause pestilence **:** DEADLY ⟨a ~ malignancy in the air —Jonathan Swift⟩ **b :** of, relating to, or having the characteristics of a pestilence ⟨~ diseases⟩ **2 :** morally harmful or injurious **:** PERNICIOUS ⟨blow up the blind rage of the populace with a continued blast of ~ libels —Edmund Burke⟩ **3 :** giving rise to vexation or annoyance **:** IRRITATING ⟨the ~ nuisances who write for autographs —W.S.Gilbert⟩ — **pes·ti·len·tial·ly** \-chəlē, -li\ *adv*

pestilentious *adj* [MF or LL; MF *pestilencieux*, fr. LL *pestilentiosus*, fr. L *pestilentia* + *-osus* -ose] *obs* **:** PESTILENTIAL

pes·tis \ˈpestəs\ *n* -ES [L] **:** PLAGUE

¹**pes·tle** \ˈpesəl *also* -stᵊl\ *n* -S [ME *pestel*, fr. MF, fr. L *pistillum*; akin to MLG *vīsel* pestle, L *pilum* pestle, javelin, *pinsere* to pound, crush, Gk *ptissein* to crush, Skt *pinaṣṭi* he pounds, crushes] **1 a :** a usu. club-shaped implement for pounding or grinding substances esp. in a mortar **b :** any of various devices for pounding, stamping, or pressing **2** *dial chiefly Eng* **:** the leg or a part of the leg of an animal used for food

²**pestle** \"\ *vb* **pestled; pestled; pestling** \-s(ə)liŋ *also* -st(ᵊ)l-\ **pestles** [ME *pestelen*, fr. MF *pesteler*, fr. OF, fr. *pestel*, n.] *vt* **:** to beat, pound, or pulverize with or as if with a pestle ~ *vi* **:** to work with a pestle **:** use a pestle

pes·to \ˈpe(ˌ)stō\ *n* -S [It, fr. *pesto*, adj., pounded, fr. *pestare* to pound, fr. LL *pistare*, freq. of L *pinsere* to pound, crush] **:** a green spaghetti sauce made of green herbs, garlic, and olive oil

pes·tol·o·gy \peˈstäləjē, -ji\ *n* -ES [*pest* + *-o-* + *-logy*] **:** a branch of science dealing esp. with insect pests

pest pear *n* **:** an American prickly pear (*Opuntia inermis*) introduced into Australia where it is a troublesome weed

pests *pl of* PEST

¹**pet** \ˈpet, *usu* -ed·+V\ *n* -S [perh. back-formation fr. obs. E *petty* small, fr. ME *pety* — more at PETTY] **1 a :** a domesticated animal kept for pleasure rather than utility **b** *dial Brit* **:** a pet lamb **2 a :** a pampered and usu. spoiled child **b :** a person who is treated with unusual kindness or consideration **:** DARLING ⟨the spoilt ~ of America's idle rich —Bernard Smith⟩ ⟨teacher's ~⟩ **3 :** something having marked popularity **:** current favorite ⟨enormous buttons put together like cuff links are another . . . ~ —Lois Long⟩ **4** *South & Midland* **:** BOIL, SORE

²**pet** \"\ *adj* **1 a :** kept or treated as a pet ⟨~ dogs⟩ **b :** treated with unusual kindness or consideration **:** CHERISHED, INDULGED ⟨~ students⟩ **2 :** expressing fondness or endearment ⟨a ~ name⟩ **3 :** inspiring a special interest or liking **:** FAVORITE ⟨~ theories⟩ ⟨~ stories⟩

³**pet** \"\ *vb* **petted; petted; petting; pets** *vt* **1 a :** to make a pet of **:** treat as a pet ⟨died . . . in the newest and largest of hospitals *petted* by all her nurses —Randall Jarrell⟩ **b :** to stroke in a gentle or loving manner **:** CARESS ⟨*petted* the seat with his fingers as though that would mend it —John Steinbeck⟩ **c :** to treat with unusual kindness and consideration **:** PAMPER, INDULGE ⟨that a man whom he had *petted* and favored . . . should go back on him was more than he could endure —John Buchan⟩ **2 :** to embrace and kiss (a member of the opposite sex) in sexual play **:** NECK ~ *vi* **:** to engage in embracing, caressing, and kissing a member of the opposite sex ⟨a girl is . . . more popular with boys if she ~*s* —Valeria H. Parker⟩

⁴**pet** \"\ *n* -S [origin unknown] **1 :** OFFENSE, UMBRAGE ⟨take the ~ in a case of failure and go off in disgust —R.H.Elliot⟩ **2 :** a fit of peevishness, sulkiness, or anger ⟨resigned in a ~, went off to improve his mind by travel —*Time*⟩

⁵**pet** \"\ *vi* **petted; petted; petting; pets :** to take offense **:** SULK

pet *abbr* **1** petrolatum **2** petroleum

pe·ta \ˈpād·ə\ *n* -S [Pali, fr. Skt *preta* — more at PRETA] **:** PRETA

¹**pet·al** \ˈped·ᵊl, ˈpetᵊl\ *n* -S [NL *petalum*, fr. Gk *petalon* leaf; akin to Gk *petannynai* to spread out — more at FATHOM] **1 :** one of the usu. leaf-shaped members that comprise the corolla of a flower — compare SEPAL **2 :** the expanded part of a petaloid ambulacrum in an irregular sea urchin of the order Exocycloida

²**petal** \"\ *vb* **petaled** *or* **petalled; petaled** *or* **petalled; petaling** *or* **petalling; petals** *vi* **:** to put forth petals ~ *vt* **:** to cover with or as if with petals

-pe·tal \-ˌpəd·ᵊl, -ˌpətᵊl, *esp Brit also* ˌpēt-\ *adj comb form* [NL *-petus* -petal (fr. L *petere* to go toward, seek) + E *-al* — more at FEATHER] **:** going toward **:** seeking ⟨acro*petal*⟩

petala *pl of* PETALON

-pet·a·lae \ˈped·ᵊlˌē\ *n pl comb form* [NL, fr. fem. pl. of *-petalus* -petalous] **:** ones having (such or so many) petals — in names of botanical groups ⟨Chori*petalae*⟩

pet·al·age \ˈped·ᵊlij, ˈpetᵊl-, -lēj\ *n* -S **:** the petals of a flower

pet·aled *or* **pet·alled** \ˈped·ᵊld, -etᵊld\ *adj* **1 :** having petals — often used in combination ⟨crimson-*petaled*⟩ **2 :** resembling a petal esp. in shape

petal fall spray *n* **:** CALYX SPRAY

pe·ta·lia \pəˈtālēə\ [NL, fr. *petalum* petal + *-ia*] *syn of* NYCTERIS

pet·al·ine \ˈped·ᵊlˌīn, -ˌən\ *adj* [NL *petalinus*, fr. *petalum* petal + L *-inus* -ine] **:** relating to, attached to, or resembling a petal

pet·al·ism \-lˌizəm\ *n* -S [Gk *petalismos* banishment by voting with olive leaves, fr. *petalon* leaf + *-ismos* -ism] **:** an ancient Syracusan method of banishing for five years a citizen suspected of having dangerous influence or ambition — compare OSTRACISM

pet·al·ite \-ˌīt\ *n* -S [G *petalit*, fr. Gk *petalon* leaf + G *-it* -ite] **:** a usu. white mineral $LiAl(Si_2O_5)_2$ consisting of a lithium aluminum silicate occurring in foliated cleavable masses or in monoclinic crystals (hardness 6–6.5, sp. gr. 2.39–2.46)

pet·al·less \ˈped·ᵊl(l)əs, -etᵊl-\ *adj* **:** having no petals

petallike \ˈ≈,≈\ *adj* **:** resembling a petal

pet·a·loc·er·ous \ˌped·ᵊlˈäsərəs\ *adj* [NL *Petalocera* (syn. of *Lamellicornia*) (fr. *petalo-* — fr. Gk *petalon* leaf — + *-cera*) + E *-ous*] **:** having the joints of the antennae lamellate or leaf-shaped

pet·al·odont \ˈped·ᵊləˌdänt\ *n* -S [NL *Petalodontidae*] **:** an elasmobranch of the family Petalodontidae

pet·al·o·don·ti·dae \ˌ≈≈≈ˈdäntəˌdē\ *n pl, cap* [NL, fr. *Petalodont-, Petalodus*, type genus + *-idae*] **:** a family of Carboniferous and Permian elasmobranchs (subclass Holocephali) related to the rays and having peculiar flattened petaloid teeth and greatly enlarged pectoral fins — see PETALODUS

pet·a·lo·dus \ˌ≈≈ˈōdəs\ *n, cap* [NL *Petalodont-, Petalodus*, fr. *petal-* (fr. Gk *petalon* leaf) + *-odont-, -odus* -odus] **:** the type genus of the family Petalodontidae known only from fossil teeth

pet·a·lo·dy \ˈ≈≈ˌōdē\ *n* -ES [ISV *petal* + *-ody*] **:** the metamorphosis of various floral organs (as stamens) into petals

pet·al·oid \ˈ≈≈ˌȯid\ *adj* [prob. fr. (assumed) NL *petaloides*, fr. NL *petalum* petal + L *-oïdes* -oid] **1 :** resembling a flower petal in form, appearance, or texture **2 :** consisting of petaloid elements ⟨a ~ perianth⟩

petaloid ambulacrum *n* **:** an ambulacrum in which the apical portion is expanded to form an area petaloid in outline on the aboral surface of the test (as in most irregular sea urchins)

pet·a·lon \ˈped·ᵊlˌän\ *n, pl* **peta·la** \-ᵊlə\ [Gk, petalon, leaf, leaf of metal — more at PETAL] **1 :** a plate of gold fastened to the front of the Jewish high priest's miter

pet·a·lo·ste·mon \ˌped·əˈlōˈstēˌmän\ *n, cap* [NL, fr. *petalo-* (fr. Gk *petalon* leaf) + Gk *stēmōn* warp, thread — more at STAMEN] **:** a genus of perennial glandular herbs (family Leguminosae) of the central and western U. S. and Mexico having pinnately compound leaves and pink, purple, or white pealike flowers in close heads or spikes and exhibiting a superficial resemblance to clover — see PRAIRIE CLOVER

pet·al·ous \ˈped·ᵊləs, -etᵊl-\ *adj* [*-petalous*] **:** having petals **:** PETALED

-pet·al·ous \ˈ≈≈≈\ *adj comb form* [NL *-petalus*, fr. *petalum* petal — more at PETAL] **:** having (such or so many) petals ⟨apo*petalous*⟩

petal pink *n* **:** a light yellowish pink that is redder and paler than light apricot and lighter than opera pink

petals *pl of* PETAL, *pres 3d sing of* PETAL

petar *obs var of* PETARD

pe·tard \pəˈtärd, -tȧd\ *n* -S [MF, fr. *peter* to break wind (fr. *pet* expulsion of intestinal gas, fr. L *peditum*, fr. neut. of *peditus*, past part. of *pedere* to break wind) + *-ard*; akin to Gk *bdein* to break wind silently, Russ *bzdet'*] **1 :** a metal or wood case containing an explosive for use in breaking down a door or gate or in breaching a wall **2 :** a firework that explodes with a loud report

pet·ar·dier \ˌped·ərˈdi(ə)r\ *n* -S [F *pétardier*, fr. *pétard* petard (fr. MF *petard*) + *-ier*] **:** a soldier who manages a petard

pe·ta·ry \ˈpēd·ərē\ *n* -ES [ML *petaria*, fr. *peta* peat + L *-aria* -ary — more at PEAT] **:** PEATERY

pet·a·si·tes \ˌped·əˈsīd·(ˌ)ēz\ *n, cap* [NL, fr. Gk *petasitēs*, *petasitis* butterbur, fr. *petasos* broad-brimmed hat; prob. fr. the shape of the leaves; akin to Gk *petannynai* to spread out — more at FATHOM] **:** a genus of herbs (family Compositae) that are native to temperate and subarctic regions, have thick rootstocks, large basal leaves, and radiate white or purplish flowers, and possess medicinal properties similar to those of the true coltsfoot — see BUTTERBUR

pe·tas·ma \pəˈtazmə\ *n* -S [NL, fr. Gk, something spread out; akin to Gk *petannynai* to spread out] **:** a membranous modified endopodite of the first abdominal appendage in a male decapod crustacean

pet·a·sos *or* **pet·a·sus** \ˈped·əsəs\ *n* -ES [L & Gk; L *petasus*, fr. Gk *petasos*] **:** a broad-brimmed low-crowned hat worn by ancient Greeks and Romans; *esp* **:** the winged hat of Hermes or Mercury as represented in art

pe·ta·te \pəˈtäd·ē\ *n* -S [Sp, fr. Nahuatl *petlatl*] **:** a mat or matting made of dried palm leaves or grass

pe·tau·rine \pəˈtȯˌrīn, -ˌrən\ *adj* [NL *Petaurina* group of mammals in some classifications consisting of the flying phalangers, fr. *Petaurus* + *-ina*] **:** of, relating to, or resembling a flying phalanger

pe·tau·rist \-ˌrəst\ *n* -S [NL *Petaurista* (syn. of *Petaurus*), fr. L *petaurista* ropedancer] **:** FLYING PHALANGER

pet·au·ris·ta \ˌped·ȯˈristə\ *n, cap* [NL, fr. L *petaurista* ropedancer, fr. *petaurum* stage or springboard used by ropedancers (modif. of Gk *petauron* platform, roost) + *-ista* -ist; akin to Gk *petesthai* to fly — more at FEATHER] **:** a genus of large Asiatic flying squirrels some of which may reach a length of 18 inches excluding the long bushy tail

pet·au·ris·ti·dae \-təˌdē\ *n pl, cap* [NL, fr. *Petaurista* + *-idae*] *in some classifications* **:** a family of rodents comprising the flying squirrels but now usu. regarded as constituting a subfamily of Sciuridae

pet·au·roi·des \-ˈrȯiˌdēz\ [NL, fr. *Petaurus* + L *-oïdes* -oid] *syn of* SCHOINOBATES

pe·tau·rus \pəˈtȯrəs\ *n, cap* [NL, alter. of L *petaurista* ropedancer] **:** a genus of flying phalangers

pet bank *n* **:** any of a group of state banks selected as depositories of federal funds removed from the U. S. Bank during the first Jacksonian administration

pe·tchary \pəˈcha(a)rē\ *n* -ES [imit.] **:** GRAY KINGBIRD

petch·e·neg *or* **pech·e·neg** \ˈpechəˌneg\ *also* **pach·e·neg** \ˈpach-\ *n* -S *usu cap* [Russ *Pecheneg*] **:** a member of a Turkish people invading the South Russian, Danubian, and Moldavian steppes during the early middle ages

petcock \ˈ≈,≈\ *n* **:** a small cock, faucet, or valve set in a water pipe or pump to let air out, at the end of a steam cylinder or in a radiator or water jacket to drain it, or at the end of an internal-combustion-engine cylinder to release compression — called also *draw cock*

pet day *n, chiefly Scot* **:** an unseasonably fine or pleasant day

pete \ˈpēt, *usu* -ēd·+V\ *n* -S [short for ¹*peter*] *slang* **:** SAFE 1b ⟨could size up a ~ at a glance and tell instantly whether to drill it or draw the spindle —W.M.Swann⟩

¹**pe·te·ca** \pəˈtekə\ *n* -S [modif. of It *petecchia*] **:** a disease of the lemon characterized by deep pitting of the surface of the rind

²**peteca** \"\ *n* -S [Pg] **1 :** a large feathered shuttlecock with a rubber or leather base **2 :** a net game in which a peteca is batted with the palm of the hand

pe·te·chia \pəˈtēkēə, -tek-\ *n, pl* **petechi·ae** \-kēˌē\ [NL, fr. It *petecchia*, perh. fr. (assumed) VL *peticula*, short for (assumed) VL *impeticula*, fr. L *impetic-, impetix* impetigo (alter. of *impetigo*) + *-ula* — more at IMPETIGO] **:** one of the minute hemorrhages or purpuric spots that appear on the skin or mucous and serous membranes or within an organ esp. in some infectious diseases (as typhus or typhoid) — compare ECCHYMOSIS

pe·te·chi·al \-kēəl\ *adj* [NL *petechialis*, fr. *petechia* + L *-alis* -al] **:** giving rise to petechiae ⟨~ hemorrhage⟩ **:** marked by petechiae ⟨a ~ rash⟩ **:** relating to petechiae or petechiation ⟨a ~ index⟩

petechial fever *also* **petechial typhus** *n* **:** purpura hemorrhagica of the horse

pe·te·chi·ate \-kēət, -ēˌāt\ *or* **pe·te·chi·at·ed** \-ēˌād·əd\ *adj* [*petechiate* fr. *petechia* + *-ate*; *petechiated* fr. *petechiate* + *-ed*] **:** marked by petechiae ⟨a severely ~ heart⟩

pe·te·chi·a·tion \≈ˌ≈≈ˈāshən\ *n* -S **:** the state of being petechiate

pete·man \ˈpētmən\ *n, pl* **petemen** *slang* **:** SAFECRACKER

¹**pe·ter** \ˈpēd·ə(r), -ētə-\ *n* -S [fr. the name *Peter*] **1** *slang* **a :** SAFE 1b **b :** a prison cell **2 :** PENIS — often considered vulgar

²**peter** \"\ *vi* **petered; petered; petering** \-əriŋ *also* -ē·triŋ\ **peters** [origin unknown] **1 a :** to diminish gradually and cease **:** run out and disappear **:** give out ⟨when the rain had ~*ed* to a misty drizzle —Hugh Fosburgh⟩ — usu. used with *out* ⟨the stream ~*s* out between the rocks⟩ ⟨when the rich copper deposits ~*ed* out —Harold Griffin⟩ **b :** to come to an end ⟨broad daylight song ~*s* to diminuendo —Lee Anderson⟩ — usu. used with *out* ⟨that all the old American families are ~*ing out* —*N. Y. Times Mag.*⟩ **2 :** to become exhausted ⟨after a long desert journey the oxen became much ~*ed* —*Overland Monthly*⟩ — usu. used with *out* ⟨raked half the lawn before he ~*ed* out⟩

³**peter** \"\ *n* -S [fr. *blue peter*] **:** a signal given by a whist player to his partner to play trumps

⁴**peter** \"\ *vi* **petered; petered; petering** \-əriŋ *also* -ē·triŋ\ **peters :** to signal to a whist partner to play trumps

⁵**peter** \"\ *usu cap* [fr. the name *Peter*] — a communications code word for the letter *p*

peter boat *n, often cap P* [prob. fr. *peterman* + *boat*] **:** a small double-ended half-decked fishing boat used on some English rivers

peter funk \ˈ≈≈ˈfəŋk\ *n, usu cap P&F* [fr. the name *Peter Funk* (not necessarily in reference to any real person)] **1 :** SWINDLER **2 :** BY-BIDDER

peter·man \ˈ≈≈mən\ *n, pl* **petermen** [ME, fr. St. *Peter* †A.D.67? disciple of Jesus + ME *man*; fr. the fact that St. Peter was a fisherman (Mt. 4:18)] **1 :** FISHERMAN **2** [¹*peter* + *man*] *slang* **:** SAFECRACKER

peter pan \ˈ≈≈ˈpan, -aa(ə)n\ *n, usu cap both Ps* [after *Peter Pan*, boy hero of the play *Peter Pan, or the Boy who wouldn't grow up* (1904), by Sir James M. Barrie †1937 Scot. novelist & dramatist] **1 :** a person who retains in mature years the naturalness, simplicity of spirit, and charm associated with childhood ⟨we could all remain perpetual children, clean, happy, epicene *Peter Pans* —Dwight Macdonald⟩ ⟨you're married to a

peter pan 2

Peter Pan who absolutely will refuse to escape from the comfortable irresponsible stage of childhood —Dorothy Dix⟩ **2 :** a small flat close-fitting collar usu. with rounded ends meeting in front used on women's and children's clothing

peter's cress *n* [*Peter's* (gen. of the name *Peter*) + E *cress*] **:** SAMPHIRE 1

pe·ter·sen coil \ˈpēd·ə(r)sən-\ *n, usu cap P* [prob. after Waldemar *Petersen b*1880 Ger. electrical engineer] **:** a ground-fault neutralizer for high-voltage power circuits

peter's fish *n, usu cap P* **:** SAINT PETER'S FISH

pe·ter·sham \ˈpēd·ə(r),sham, -shəm\ *n* -s [after Charles Stanhope, Lord *Petersham* †1851 Eng. colonel] **1 a :** a rough nubby woolen cloth used chiefly for men's coats **b :** a coat made of such material **2 :** a heavy corded ribbon used for belts and hatbands

peter's pence *n pl but usu sing in constr, usu cap 1st P* [ME *Peteres pens*, pl. of *Peteres peny* (trans. of ML *denarius Sancti Petri*), fr. *Peteres* (gen. of *Peter* St. Peter †A.D.67? disciple of Jesus) + ME *peny* penny; fr. the Roman Catholic tradition that St. Peter founded the papal see] **1 :** an annual tax or tribute of a penny formerly paid by each householder in England to the papal see **2 a :** a voluntary annual contribution made by Roman Catholics to the pope **b :** the collection in a Roman Catholic Church at which such contributions are made

petes *pl of* PETE

pether *var of* PEDDER

peth·i·dine \ˈpethə,dēn, -,dən\ *n* -s [perh. blend of *piperidine* and *ethyl*] **:** meperidine or its hydrochloride

pé·til·lant *or* **pe·til·lant** \pātē(ʸ)äⁿ\ *adj* [F *pétillant*, pres. part. of *pétiller* to effervesce with a crackling sound, fr. MF *petiller* to crackle, fr. *peter* to break wind — more at PETARD] *of wine* **:** mildly and slowly effervescing

pet·i·o·lar \ˈped·ē,ōlə(r), ,==ˈ==\ *adj* [NL *petiolaris*, fr. *petiolus* petiole + L *-aris* -ar] **:** of, relating to, or proceeding from a petiole **:** growing or supported upon a petiole ⟨a ~ tendril⟩ ⟨a ~ gland⟩

pet·i·o·lary \ˈ==,ə,lerē\ *adj* [*petiole* + *-ary*] **:** PETIOLAR

pet·i·o·la·ta \,===ˈläd·ə, -ād·ə\ [NL, fr. *petiolus* petiole + *-ata*] *syn of* CLISTOGASTRA

pet·i·o·late \ˈ===,lāt, *usu* -ād·+V\ *also* **pet·i·o·lat·ed** \-ād·əd\ *adj* [*petiolate* fr. NL *petiolatus*, fr. *petiolus* + L *-atus* -ate; *petiolated* fr. *petiolate* + *-ed*] **:** having a stalk or petiole

pet·i·ole \ˈ==,ōl\ *n* -s [NL *petiolus*, fr. L, small foot, fruitstalk, spelling in some MSS of *peciolus*, irreg. fr. *pediculus* small foot, fruitstalk, dim. of *ped-, pes* foot — more at FOOT] **1 :** a slender stem that supports the blade of a foliage leaf and that is usu. cylindrical but sometimes flattened or even winged — called also *leafstalk* **2 :** a part resembling the stalk of a plant **:** PEDUNCLE; *specif* **:** the slender abdominal segment joining the rest of the abdomen to the thorax in an insect

pet·i·oled \-ld\ *adj* **:** PETIOLATE

pet·i·o·li·ven·tres \,ped·ē,ōlə'ven·,trēz\ [NL, fr. *petioli-* (fr. *petiolus*) + *-ventres* (fr. L *venter* belly) — more at VENTER] *syn of* CLISTOGASTRA

pet·i·ol·u·lar \¦ped·ē¦älyələ(r)\ *adj* [prob. fr. (assumed) NL *petiolularis*, fr. NL *petiolulus* petiolule + L *-aris* -ar] **:** of or relating to a petiolule

pet·i·ol·u·late \-,lāt, -lət, *usu* -d·+V\ *adj* [prob. fr. (assumed) NL *petiolulatus*, fr. NL *petiolulus* petiolule + L *-atus* -ate] **:** having a petiolule

pet·i·o·lule \ˈ==ə,lül, -əl,yül; ,==ˈäl,yül\ *n* -s [NL *petiolulus*, fr. *petiolus* petiole + *-ulus*] **:** a stalk of a leaflet or other segment of a compound leaf

pet·it \ˈped·|ē, ˈpet|, |i, |ət; pə'tēt\ *adj* [ME, fr. MF, fr. OF] **1** *archaic* **:** SMALL ⟨a really handsome man . . . with . . . an erect though somewhat ~ figure —Hugh Miller †1856⟩ **2** *obs* **:** INSIGNIFICANT, TRIFLING ⟨he hated every thing ~ —W.H. Dilworth⟩ **3** *archaic* **:** SECONDARY, SUBORDINATE ⟨tried all ~ cases relating to the inhabitants —*Genealogical Mag.*⟩

pe·tit battement \pə'tē-\ *n* [F, lit., small battement] **:** a battement with the free foot lifted slightly usu. without taking the toes from the floor

pe·tit bourgeois \"-\ *n* [F, lit., small bourgeois] **:** a member of the petite bourgeoisie

pet·it ca·pe \ˈped·|ē, ˈpet|, |iˈkä(,)pē, -ˈkä(,)pā\ *n* [AF (part trans. of ML *cape parvum*), fr. *petit* small + *cape* any of several writs including the grand cape and the petit cape — more at GRAND CAPE] **:** a writ formerly used in English real actions for the recovery of land

¹pe·tite \pə'tēt, *usu* -ēd·+V\ *adj* [F, fem. of *petit*] **:** small and trim of figure **:** LITTLE — usu. used of a woman ⟨a bit incongruous that such a ~ woman should write such huge tomes —Vardis Fisher⟩ **syn** see SMALL

²petite \"\ *n* -s **:** a clothing size for short women

petite bourgeoisie *n* [F, lit., small bourgeoisie] **:** the least affluent or influential class of the bourgeoisie **:** lower middle class

petite marmite *n* [F, lit., small kettle] **1 :** a soup of brown stock made with a few large pieces of vegetable, fowl, or beef and served in a marmite with slices of French bread **2 :** MARMITE 1b

pe·tite·ness *n* -ES **:** the quality or state of being petite

petite no·blesse \-nō'bles\ *n* [F, lit., small nobility] **:** the lesser nobility of France; *esp* **:** rural landowners of noble ancestry

pe·tites perceptions *n pl* \pə'tēt-\ [F, lit., small perceptions] **:** vague or unconscious perceptions

pe·tit four \pə,tē'fō(ə)r, -fȯ(ə)r, ¦ped·ē¦= *sometimes* -fü(ə)r\ *n, pl* **petits fours** *or* **petit fours** \-ō(ə)rz, -ȯ(ə)rz, -ü(ə)r(z)\ [F, lit., small oven] **:** a small cake cut in a fancy shape from pound or sponge cake, decoratively frosted, and ornamented with sugar flowers or crystallized fruit

pet·it·grain \ˈped·ē,grān\ *n* [F *petit grain* unripe bitter orange, fr. *petit* small + *grain* seed] **:** PETITGRAIN OIL

petitgrain oil *n* **:** a fragrant yellowish essential oil obtained from the leaves and twigs of the sour orange and other trees of the genus *Citrus* and used chiefly in perfumes, soaps, and cosmetics

¹pe·ti·tion \pə'tishən\ *n* -s [ME *peticioun*, fr. MF *petition*, fr. L *petition-, petitio*, fr. *petitus* (past part. of *petere* to go to or toward, seek, request) + *-ion-, -io* -ion — more at FEATHER] **1 a :** an earnest request **:** ENTREATY, SUPPLICATION ⟨listens with a vinegar aspect to your ~ for shelter —C.E.Montague⟩ **b** (1) **:** a solemn prayer to God ⟨our ~ in the litany against sudden death —John Ruskin⟩ (2) **:** a single clause in such a prayer **2 a :** a formal written request addressed to an official person or organized body: (1) **:** a bill in the form of a request by which Parliament formerly presented measures for the king's granting (2) **:** a formal written request addressed to a sovereign or political superior for a particular grace or right (3) **:** a formal written request addressed to a magistrate or court praying for preliminary, incidental, or final specific relief and setting forth the facts or reasons therefor (4) **:** a formal statement of a cause of action that is addressed to a court or magistrate and is based on a statute or on an extraordinary remedy for which common-law declarations cannot be invoked or is founded on equity, probate, or ecclesiastical jurisdiction (5) *civil law* **:** COMPLAINT **b :** a document embodying a formal written request **3 :** the act or action of formally asking or humbly requesting ⟨an ancient right guaranteed by the early state constitutions . . . is that of ~ —Harvey Walker⟩ **4 :** something asked or requested ⟨I make thee promise, . . . thou receivest thy full ~ —Shak.⟩ **syn** see PRAYER

²petition \"\ *vb* **petitioned; petitioned; petitioning** \-sh(ə)niŋ\ **petitions** *vt* **1 :** to make a request to **:** ENTREAT; *esp* **:** to make a formal written request to ⟨the right of the people . . . to ~ the government for a redress of grievances —*U.S.Constitution*⟩ **2 :** to make a request for **:** SOLICIT ⟨all that I hope, ~, or expect —George Crabbe †1832⟩ **~** *vi* **:** to make a request; *esp* **:** to make a formal written request ⟨she neither ~ed for her right nor claimed it —George Meredith⟩

pe·ti·tion·al \-shənᵊl, -shnəl\ *adj* **:** of, relating to, or having the characteristics of a petition ⟨a ~ prayer⟩

pe·ti·tion·ary \-shə,nerē, -ri\ *adj* **1 :** of, relating to, or containing a petition ⟨the ~ procedure . . . had a certain immanent quality of indecisiveness —J.G.Edwards⟩ **2** *archaic* **:** SUPPLIANT ⟨say no to a poor ~ rogue —Charles Lamb⟩

pe·ti·tion·ee \=¦==¦nē\ *n* -s **:** a person cited to answer or defend against a petition

pe·ti·tion·er \-sh(ə)nə(r)\ *n* -s [ME *peticioner*, fr. *peticion*, *peticioun* petition + *-er*] **1 :** one that petitions **2** *usu cap* **:** one of those signing petitions to Charles II in 1679 for an assembling of Parliament — compare ABHORRER

petition for intervention : a petition in which a person seeks to be permitted to intervene in a lawsuit involving other parties so that his own rights and interests may be protected by a judgment or decree binding all

petition in bankruptcy : a written application by a debtor for the benefit of the Bankruptcy Act or by creditors to have a debtor adjudicated a bankrupt

petition in error : an application for a hearing to reverse action in a lower court that is a statutory substitute in some jurisdictions for the common-law writ of error — compare APPEAL

petition of right [ME] **:** a legal petition formerly used to obtain redress (as possession or restitution of property) from the British Crown for breach of contract or to remedy manifest injustice

pe·ti·tio prin·ci·pii \pə¦tid·ē,ō,prin'kipē,ē, pə¦tishē,ō,prin'sipē,ī, pā¦tētsē,ō,prin'chēpē,ē\ *n* [ML, lit., postulation of the beginning] **:** a logical fallacy in which a premise is assumed to be true without warrant or in which what is to be proved is implicitly taken for granted

pet·it juror \ˈped·|ē, ˈpet|, |i-\ *n* [fr. *petit jury*, after E *jury: juror*] **:** one that serves on a petit jury

petit jury *n* [ME, lit., small jury] **:** a jury of twelve men or in some jurisdictions twelve men and women that is guaranteed by constitutional rights and that is impaneled to try and decide finally upon the facts at issue in causes for trial in a court — compare GRAND JURY

petit larceny \"-\ *n* **:** PETTY LARCENY

petit-maître \pətēmātrᵊ, -ā·tr, -ā·trə, -āt\ *n, pl* **petits-maîtres** *or* **petit-maîtres** \"\ [F, lit., small master] **:** DANDY, FOP ⟨the most finished gentleman in every sense of the word . . . without an atom of frippery or a shade of the *petit-maître* —W.G.Hammond⟩

petit mal \pə¦tē¦mål, -mal, -mål\ *n* [F, lit., small illness] **:** epilepsy due to an inborn usu. inherited dysrhythmia of the electrical pulsations of the brain and characterized by attacks of mild convulsive seizures with transient clouding of consciousness without amnesia and with or without slight movements of the head, eyes, or extremities — compare GRAND MAL

petit-nègre \pə,tē'negrə, -g(rᵊ)\ *n, usu cap P&N* [F *petit nègre*, lit., small Negro] **:** a French-based Creole language of West Africa

pet·i·to·ry \ˈped·ə,tōrē\ *adj* [L *petitorius*, fr. *petitus* (past part. of *petere* to go to or toward, seek, request) + *-orius* -ory — more at FEATHER] **1** *archaic* **:** PETITIONARY, SUPPLICATORY **2 a :** of or relating to an admiralty or civil law action or suit in rem as distinguished from one in personam **b :** of or relating to a civil law action to adjudge title to and ownership of real estate as distinguished from one to try merely the right of possession **c :** of or relating to a suit in Scots law in which the plaintiff claims ownership of property or damages or money due from the defendant **3 :** of or relating to a petitio principii

petitory action *n* **1** *civil & admiralty law* **:** an action in rem to establish a right or title in or ownership of specific property — compare POSSESSORY ACTION **2** *Scots law* **:** an action in which property, money, or damages are demanded from the defendant

pet·it point \ˈped·|ē, ˈpet|, |i-\ *n* [F, lit., small point] **1 :** canvas work made with small tent stitches each of which crosses one vertical and one horizontal thread — compare GROS POINT **2 :** TENT STITCH

pe·tits che·vaux \pə'tēshə'vō\ *n pl but sing in constr* [F, lit., small horses] **:** a gambling machine on which eight toy horses are spun on a circular track and bets are made on which horse will reach the finish line first

pet·it sergeanty \ˈped·|ē, ˈpet|, |i-\ *n* [AF *petit serjeanty*, lit., small sergeanty] **1 :** the rendering of an implement of war (as a bow, sword, lance) annually to the king in accordance with English feudal law **2 :** the right to or the duty of petit sergeanty

petits fours *pl of* PETIT FOUR

pe·tits pois \pə,tēp'wä\ *n pl* [F, small peas] **:** very small green peas

pet·it treason \ˈped·|ē, ˈpet|, |i-\ *n* [alter. (influenced by *petit*) of *petty treason*] *Eng law* **:** the crime committed by a servant in killing his master, by a wife in killing her husband, or by an ecclesiastic in killing his superior

pet·i·ve·ria \,ped·ə'virēə\ *n, cap* [NL, fr. James *Petiver* †1718 Eng. botanist and entomologist + NL *-ia*] **:** a genus of tropical American garlic-scented herbs (family Phytolaccaceae) with small greenish spicate flowers

petn *abbr* petition

PETN *n* -s [*p*entaerythritol *te*tra*n*itrate] **:** PENTAERYTHRITOL TETRANITRATE

pe·to \ˈpād·(,)ō\ *n* -s [AmerSp, fr. Sp, breastplate, fr. It *petto* breast, breastplate, fr. L *pectus* breast — more at PECTORAL] **:** ³WAHOO

petr- *or* **petri-** *or* **petro-** *comb form* [MF *petr-, petri-* & L *petr-* & NL *petro-*, fr. Gk *petr-, petro-*, fr. *petros* stone & *petra* rock] **1 a :** stone **:** rock ⟨*petr*escent⟩ ⟨*Petri*cola⟩ ⟨*petro*genesis⟩ **b :** petroleum ⟨*petro*porphyrins⟩ **2 :** of or relating to the petrous portion of the temporal bone and ⟨*petro*hyoid⟩

pe·tra·le sole \pə'trälē-\ *n* [*petrale* perh. fr. It. dial., a flatfish] **:** a large brown brill (*Eopsetta jordani*) of the Pacific coast of No. America that is an important market flatfish highly esteemed as food — called also *English sole*

¹pe·trar·chan \(ˈ)pē¦trärkən, (ˈ)pe-, -räk- *sometimes* (ˈ)pā-\ *also* **pe·trar·chi·an** \-kēən\ *adj, usu cap* [*Petrarch* (Francesco *Petrarca*) †1374 Ital. poet + E *-an*] **:** of, relating to, or having the characteristics of Petrarch **:** imitative of the style of Petrarch

²petrarchan \"\ *n* -s *usu cap* **:** PETRARCHIST

petrarchan sonnet *n, usu cap P* **:** a sonnet composed of an octave rhyming *abba abba* and a sestet with two or three rhymes (as *cdc dcd* or *cde cde*) — called also *Italian sonnet*; compare ENGLISH SONNET

pe·trar·chi·an·ism \-kēə,nizəm\ *or* **pe·trarch·ism** \ˈ=,=-,kizəm\ *n* -s *usu cap* **:** the poetic style characteristic or imitative of Petrarch

pe·trarch·ist \ˈ=,=,kəst\ *n* -s *usu cap* **:** a poet writing in a manner characteristic or imitative of Petrarch; *specif* **:** one of the poets of the English Renaissance whose sonnets reflect the influence of Petrarch in their conceits, play upon words, and involved structure

pe·trarch·ize \-,kīz\ *vi* -ED/-ING/-S *usu cap* [MF *petrarchiser*, fr. Francesco *Petrarca* + MF *-iser* -ize] **:** to write in a manner characteristic or imitative of Petrarch

pet·ra·ry \ˈpe·trərē\ *n* -ES [ML *petraria* — more at PEDRERO] **:** PEDRERO

pe·trea \ˈpē·trēə\ *n, cap* [NL, fr. Robert James, Baron *Petre* †1743 Eng. patron of botany] **:** a genus of tropical American woody vines (family Verbenaceae) having large blue or purple flowers in long racemes with the colored sepals enlarging in fruiting — see PURPLE WREATH

pe·trel \ˈpe·trəl *sometimes* ˈpē-\ *n* -s [alter. of earlier *pitteral*, perh. irreg. fr. St. *Peter* †A.D.67? disciple of Jesus; fr. the gospel account of St. Peter's walking on the sea (Mt 14:29)] **1 :** any of numerous sea birds constituting the families Procellariidae and Hydrobatidae; *esp* **:** any of various small to medium-sized long-winged birds that fly far from land, feed on small surface-swimming creatures and refuse from ships, breed in burrows and crevices in rocks and cliffs usu. on islands, and have a plumage chiefly dark but sometimes with white areas near the rump — see DIVING PETREL, GIANT PETREL, MOTHER CAREY'S CHICKEN, STORM PETREL **2 :** STORM PETREL

pe·tres·cent \pə'tresᵊnt\ *adj* [*petr-* + *-escent*] *archaic* **:** having the quality of petrifying **:** causing petrifaction

petri- — see PETR-

pe·tric·o·la \pə'trikələ\ *n, cap* [NL, fr. *petr-* + *-cola*] **:** a genus (the type of the family Petricolidae) of bivalve mollusks living in holes that they excavate in rocks, clay, or mud and having an oval shell slightly gaping behind, a large mantle, and a small foot

pet·ri·col·i·dae \,pe·trə'käla,dē\ *n pl, cap* [NL, fr. *Petricola*, type genus + *-idae*] **:** a family of bivalve mollusks (suborder Veneracea) having an elongated shell with which they burrow in soft rock or clay

pe·tric·o·lous \-ləs\ *adj* [*petr-* + *-colous*] **:** living in rocks

pe·tri dish \ˈpē·trē- *sometimes* ˈpā| *or* ˈpe|\ *or* **petri plate** *n, often cap 1st P* [after Julius R. *Petri* †1921 Ger. bacteriologist] **:** a small shallow dish of thin glass with a loosely fitting overlapping cover used esp. for plate cultures in bacteriology

petri dish

pet·ri·fac·tion \,pe·trə'fakshən\ *n* -s [fr. *petrify*, after such pairs as E *satisfy: satisfaction*] **1 :** the process of petrifying; *specif* **:** the conversion of organic matter into stone or a substance of stony hardness through the infiltration of water containing dissolved mineral matter (as calcium, carbonate, silica) that replaces the organic material particle by particle with the original structure sometimes retained — compare CAST **2 :** something that is petrified; *specif* **:** an organic body infiltrated with mineral matter and preserving more or less clearly its original form or structure — compare FOSSIL **3 :** the quality or state of being petrified ⟨a ~ . . . of the artist's soul —G.E.Woodberry⟩

pet·ri·fac·tive \¦==¦faktiv\ *adj* [fr. *petrify*, after such pairs as E *putrefy: putrefactive*] **:** having the quality of converting organic matter into stone **:** PETRIFYING

pe·trif·ic \pə'trifik\ *adj* [ML *petrificus*, fr. L *petra* rock, stone + *-ficus* -fic] **:** PETRIFACTIVE

pet·ri·fi·ca·tion \,pe·trəfə'kāshən\ *n* -s [F *pétrification*, fr. MF *petrification*, fr. *petr-* + *-fication*] **:** PETRIFACTION

pet·ri·fier \ˈ==,fī(ə)r\ *n* -s **:** one that petrifies

pet·ri·fy \ˈ==,fī\ *vb* -ED/-ING/-ES [MF *petrifier*, fr. *petr-* + *-fier* -fy] *vt* **1 :** to convert into stone; *specif* **:** to convert (organic matter) into stone or a substance of stony hardness through the infiltration of water containing dissolved mineral matter **2 :** to make hard, rigid, or inert like or as if like stone: **a :** to make lifeless or inactive **:** DEADEN ⟨slogans are apt to ~ a man's thinking —*Saturday Rev.*⟩ ⟨his independence had not *petrified* his sympathies —*Times Lit. Supp.*⟩ **b :** to confound with fear, amazement, or awe **:** PARALYZE, STUPEFY ⟨the original purpose of the aborigine's objects was to ~ uninitiated members of the tribe —T.H.Robsjohn-Gibbings⟩ ⟨is *petrified* of talking in public —Alan Frank⟩ **~** *vi* **1 :** to become stone or a substance of stony hardness **2 :** to become hard, rigid, or inert like or as if like stone ⟨principles and rules . . . have *petrified* with the accumulated weight of precedent on precedent —B.N.Cardozo⟩ ⟨her face had *petrified* into the fearsome pioneer resolution of unremitting housewifery —Nigel Dennis⟩ **syn** see DAZE

pe·trine \ˈpē,trīn, -,trən\ *adj, usu cap* [LL *Petrus* St. Peter †A.D.67? disciple of Jesus (fr. Gk *Petros*) + E *-ine*] **:** of, relating to, or having the characteristics of the apostle Peter, his teachings, or the doctrines associated with his name ⟨the *Petrine* tradition⟩

pe·trin·ism \ˈpē·trə,nizəm\ *n* -s *usu cap* **:** the theological principles taught by or ascribed to the apostle Peter

pe·trin·ist \-,nəst\ *n* -s *usu cap* **:** a follower of the apostle Peter **:** an adherent of Petrinism

pe·tris·sage \¦pā·trə¦säzh\ *n* -s [F *pétrissage*, lit., kneading, fr. *pétriss-* (stem of *pétrir* to knead, fr. ML *pistrire*, fr. L *pistrix* female baker, fem. of *pistor* baker, miller) + *-age*; akin to L *pinsere* to pound, crush — more at PESTLE] **:** massage in which the muscles are kneaded

pe·tro·bia \pə'trōbēə\ *n, cap* [NL, perh. fr. *petr-* + *-bia*] **:** a genus of mites containing the brown wheat mite

pet·ro·bru·sian \¦pe·trō¦brüzhən, -shən\ *n* -s *usu cap* [ML *petrobrusianus*, fr. *Petrus Brusius* Pierre de Bruys †*ab*1126 Fr. religious reformer who founded the sect of the Petrobrusians + L *-anus* -an] **:** a member of a 12th-century French sect rejecting infant baptism, the mass, prayers for the dead, and the veneration of the cross and opposing the construction of churches

pet·ro·chel·i·don \,pe·trō'kelə,dän\ *n, cap* [NL, fr. *petr-* + Gk *chelidōn* swallow — more at CELANDINE] **:** a genus of swallows consisting of the American cliff swallows

¹pe·tro·chemical \¦pe·trō+\ *adj* [*petr-* + *chemical*, adj.] **1 :** of or relating to the chemistry of rocks ⟨a thorough ~ study of certain weathering profiles —F.J.Pettijohn⟩ **2 a :** of or relating to the production of petrochemicals ⟨the ~ industry⟩ **b :** produced as a petrochemical ⟨~ acetone⟩

²petrochemical \"\ *n* [*petr-* + *chemical*, n.] **:** a chemical isolated from petroleum or natural gas or a derivative produced from such a substance by chemical reaction — used chiefly commercially ⟨chemicals derived from petroleum and natural gas, such as ammonia, carbon black, and thousands of organic chemicals, are classified as ~s —*Chemical & Engineering News*⟩

pe·tro·chemistry \"+\ *n* [*petr-* + *chemistry*] **1 :** the chemistry of rocks **2 :** the chemistry of petroleum; *esp* **:** a branch of chemistry dealing with the production of petrochemicals

pet·ro·cole *or* **pet·ri·cole** \ˈpe·trə,kōl\ *n* -s [*petr-* + *-cole* (fr. NL *-cola*)] **:** an organism that inhabits or prefers rocky terrain

pet·ro·fabric \¦pe·trō+\ *adj* [*petr-* + *fabric*, n.] **:** of or relating to the analysis of rock fabric in contrast to rock composition

petrofabric diagram *n* **:** a diagram showing spatial distribution of fabric features of a rock (as crystal axes, twin planes, or fracture surfaces)

pet·ro·fabrics \¦==+\ *n pl but sing in constr* **:** the investigation of rock fabric with particular emphasis on the microscopic features

pe·trog·a·le \pə'trägə,lē\ *n* [NL, fr. *petr-* + Gk *galē* weasel, ferret — more at GALEA] **1** *cap* **:** a genus of marsupial mammals consisting of the rock wallabies **2** -s **:** ROCK WALLABY

pet·ro·genesis \¦pe·trō+\ *n* [NL, fr. *petr-* + L *genesis*] **:** the origin of rocks

pet·ro·genetic \¦==+\ *adj* [fr. *petrogenesis*, after E *genesis: genetic*] **:** PETROGENIC

pet·ro·gen·ic \¦==¦jenik\ *adj* [*petr-* + *-genic*] **:** of or relating to the origin or formation of rocks and esp. of igneous rocks

pe·trog·e·ny \pə'träjənē, -ni\ *n* -ES [*petr-* + *-geny*] **:** the science of the origin of rocks

pet·ro·glyph \ˈpe·trə,glif\ *n* -s [F *pétroglyphe*, fr. *pétr-* petr- + *-glyphe* (as in *hiéroglyphe* hieroglyph)] **:** a carving or inscription on a rock — compare PICTOGRAPH

pet·ro·glyph·ic \¦==¦glifik\ *adj* [*petroglyph* + *-ic*] **:** of or relating to a petroglyph or to petroglyphy

pe·trog·ly·phy \pə'trägləfē, -fi\ *n* -ES [*petroglyph* + *-y*] **:** the art or operation of carving figures or inscriptions on rock or stone

pet·ro·graph \ˈpe·trə,graf\ *n* [*petr-* + *-graph*] **:** PETROGLYPH

pe·trog·ra·pher \pə'trägrəfə(r)\ *n* -s [*petrography* + *-er*] **:** a specialist in petrography

pet·ro·graph·ic \,pe·trə¦grafik, -fēk\ *or* **pet·ro·graph·i·cal** \-fəkəl, -fēk-\ *adj* [*petrographic* prob. fr. (assumed) NL *petrographicus*, fr. NL *petrographia* petrography + L *-icus* -ic; *petrographical* fr. NL *petrographia* + E *-ical*] **:** of or relating to petrography — **pet·ro·graph·i·cal·ly** \-fək(ə)lē, -fēk-, -li\ *adv*

petrographic province *n* **:** a region in which the various igneous rocks are so related as to indicate origin from a common magma

pe·trog·ra·phy \pə'trägrəfē, -fi\ *n* -ES [NL *petrographia*, fr. *petr-* + L *-graphia* -graphy] **:** the description and systematic classification of rocks usu. based on microscopic study — compare PETROLOGY

pet·ro·hyoid \¦petrō+\ *adj* [*petr-* + *hyoid*] **:** connecting the petrous region of the skull and the hyoid

pe·troi·ca \pə'trȯikə, -rōəkə\ *n, cap* [NL] **:** a genus of flycatchers (family Muscicapidae) of Australia and the Pacific islands that are usu. dark above with pale underparts and pink to scarlet breasts

pet·rol \ˈpe·trəl, -,träl\ *n* -s [MF *petrole*, fr. ML *petroleum*] **1** *archaic* **:** PETROLEUM **2** [F *pétrole* petroleum (in the term *essence de pétrole* gasoline), fr. MF *petrole*] *Brit* **:** petroleum motor fuel **:** GASOLINE

pet·ro·lage \ˈpe·trəlij\ *n* -s [ISV *petrol* + *-age*] **:** the treatment of stagnant water with petroleum so as to exterminate mosquitoes

pet·ro·la·tum \,pe·trə'lād·əm, -lād-\ *n* -s [NL, fr. ML petroleum + NL -*atum* -ate] **:** a neutral unctuous substance that is practically odorless and tasteless and is insoluble in water, that is obtained from petroleum and differs chemically from paraffin wax in containing unsaturated hydrocarbons or naphthenes as well as hydrocarbons of the methane series, and that is produced in several forms: as **a :** a yellowish to light amber semisolid mass obtained in various ways (as by purifying the residue from the distillation of petroleum or by dewaxing heavy lubricating oils) and used chiefly as a base for ointments and cosmetics, as a protective dressing (as for burns), and in lubricating greases — called also *petroleum jelly, yellow petrolatum, yellow soft paraffin;* compare MICROCRYSTALLINE WAX, MINERAL JELLY **b :** a white or faintly yellowish mass obtained by decolorizing yellow petrolatum and used similarly to it — called also *white petrolatum, white petroleum jelly, white soft paraffin* **c :** LIQUID PETROLATUM

pet·ro·lene \ˈpe·trə,lēn, ,==ˈ=\ *n* -s [G *petrolen*, irreg. fr. *petroleum*, fr. ML] **:** the part of asphalt soluble in paraffin naphtha or hexane and free from asphaltenes and carbenes

pe·tro·le·ous \pə̇ˈtrōlēəs\ *adj* [*petroleum* + *-ous*] **:** containing petroleum

pe·tro·leum \pə̇ˈtrōlēəm, -lyəm\ *n* -s *often attrib* [ML, fr. L *petr-* + *oleum* oil — more at OIL] **1 :** an oily flammable bituminous liquid that in the crude state often has a very disagreeable odor and may vary from almost colorless to black but is usu. of a dark brown or greenish hue and sometimes fluorescent, that occurs in many places in the upper strata of the earth either in seepages or in reservoir formations from which it is obtained by drilling and pumping if necessary, that is essentially a complex mixture of hydrocarbons of different types with small amounts of other substances (as oxygen compounds, sulfur compounds, nitrogen compounds, resinous and asphaltic components, and metallic compounds), that is sometimes classed as paraffin-base, asphalt-base or naphthene-base, or mixed-base, and that is subjected to various refining processes (as fractional distillation, cracking, catalytic re-forming, hydroforming, alkylation, polymerization) for producing useful products (as gasoline, naphtha, kerosine, fuel oils, lubricants, waxes, asphalt, coke, and chemicals) — called also *mineral oil, rock oil* **2 :** any of various substances (as natural gas or shale oil) similar in composition to petroleum

petroleum asphalt *n* **:** ARTIFICIAL ASPHALT

petroleum benzin *n* **:** a flammable petroleum distillate boiling between 35° and 80°C, containing largely pentanes, hexanes, and heptanes, and used chiefly as a solvent esp. in pharmacy

petroleum coke *n* **:** a solid nonvolatile residue which is obtained as the final still product in the distillation of crude petroleum and whose purity makes it desirable for metallurgical processes, for carbon electrodes, and as a fuel

petroleum engine *n* **:** GASOLINE ENGINE

petroleum ether *n* **:** a volatile flammable petroleum distillate (as ligroin or petroleum benzin)

petroleum fly *n* **:** an ephydrid fly (*Psilopa petrolei*) that breeds in pools of waste petroleum

petroleum gas oil *n* **:** GAS OIL

petroleum geologist *n* **:** a specialist in petroleum geology

petroleum geology *n* **:** a branch of economic geology that deals with the origin, occurrence, and exploitation of oil and gas

petroleum grease *n* **:** a grease made from a petroleum product (as still bottoms)

petroleum hexane *n* **:** a mixture of hexanes that occurs in petroleum and is separated therefrom by distillation in the range 50° to 70°C and that is used as a solvent — compare LIGROIN

petroleum jelly *n* **:** PETROLATUM a, b

petroleum naphtha *n* **:** NAPHTHA 3a

petroleum pentane *n* **:** a mixture essentially of pentane and isopentane that occurs in petroleum and is separated therefrom by distillation below 50°C and that is used as a low-boiling solvent

petroleum spirit *n* **:** a flammable petroleum distillate that boils lower than kerosine and is suitable for use as a solvent and thinner esp. for paints and varnishes — usu. used in pl.; compare NAPHTHA 3

petroleum sulfonate *n* **:** any of various sulfonic acid derivatives of petroleum (as mahogany acids or green acids)

petroleum wax *n* **:** a wax obtained from petroleum — compare CERESIN, MICROCRYSTALLINE WAX, PARAFFIN 1

pe·trol·ic \pə̇ˈträlik\ *adj* [*petroleum* + *-ic*] **1 :** of or relating to petroleum or gasoline **2 :** of or relating to gasoline engines or motor cars

pet·ro·lif·er·ous \¦pe·trə¦lif(ə)rəs\ *adj* [ISV *petroleum* + *-i-* + *-ferous*] **:** containing or producing petroleum

pet·ro·lif·ic \¦==¦lifik\ *adj* [*petroleum* + *-i-* + *-fic*] **:** PETROLIFEROUS

pet·ro·lith·ic \¦==¦lithik\ *adj* [*petr-* + *lithic*] **1 :** of, relating to, or constituting a road surface consolidated to a rocklike firmness **2 :** of, relating to, or constituting the tampers and other apparatus used to harden a road surface

pet·ro·li·za·tion \,==,lə̇ˈzāshən, -,līˈz-\ *n* -s **:** the act or process of petrolizing

pet·ro·lize \ˈpe·trə,līz\ *vt* -ED/-ING/-S [*petroleum* + *-ize*] **1 :** to ignite by means of petroleum **2 :** to treat or impregnate with petroleum or a petroleum product **3 :** to cover the surface of (as water) with petroleum for mosquito control

pet·ro·log·ic \¦pe·trə¦läjik, -jēk\ *or* **pet·ro·log·i·cal** \-jə̇kəl, -jēk-\ *adj* [*petrology* + *-ic* or *-ical*] **:** of or relating to petrology — **pet·ro·log·i·cal·ly** \-jə̇k(ə)lē, -jēk-, -li\ *adv*

pe·trol·o·gist \pə̇ˈträləjə̇st\ *n* -s [*petrology* + *-ist*] **:** a geologist who specializes in petrology

pe·trol·o·gy \-jē, -ji\ *n* -ES [ISV *petr-* + *-logy*] **1 :** a science that deals with the origin, history, occurrence, structure, chemical composition, and classification of rocks — compare PETROGRAPHY **2 :** the materials of petrology ⟨the ~ of New England⟩ **3 :** a treatise on petrology

petrols *pl of* PETROL

pet·ro·my·zon \,pe·trōˈmī,zän\ *n* [NL *Petromyzont-*, *Petromyzon*, fr. *petr-* + *-myzont-*, *-myzon* -myzon] **1** *cap* **:** a genus (the type of the family Petromyzontidae) of cyclostomes comprising the typical lampreys **2** -S **:** any cyclostome of the genus *Petromyzon*

pet·ro·my·zon·i·dae \,==,mīˈzänə,dē\ *syn of* PETROMYZONTIDAE

pet·ro·my·zont \,==ˈmī,zänt\ *n* -s [NL *Petromyzontidae*] **:** a cyclostome of the family Petromyzontidae **:** LAMPREY

pet·ro·my·zon·tes \,==mīˈzän,tēz\ [NL, pl. of *Petromyzont-*, *Petromyzon*] *syn of* HYPEROARTIA

pet·ro·my·zon·ti·dae \-mīˈzäntə,dē\ *n pl, cap* [NL, fr. *Petromyzont-*, *Petromyzon*, type genus + *-idae*] **:** a family of cyclostomes (order Hyperoartia) comprising elongated animals that resemble eels or hagfishes, have no barbels and seven pairs of circular gill openings, and feed on the blood of fishes which they obtain by rasping the flesh with their toothed circular mouth — see PETROMYZON; compare LAMPREY — **pet·ro·my·zon·toid** \¦==¦zän,tȯid\ *adj or n*

pet·ro·nel \ˈpe·trənəl\ *n* -s [perh. modif. of MF *petrinal*, alter. of *poitrinal*, fr. *poitrinal*, adj., of the chest, fr. *poitrine* chest, breast (fr. assumed VL *pectorina*, fr. fem. of assumed VL *pectorinus*, adj., of the breast, fr. L *pector-*, *pectus* breast + *-inus* -ine) + *-al* — more at PECTORAL] **:** a portable firearm resembling a carbine of large caliber and fired with the butt resting against the chest

pet·ro·nel·la \,==ˈnelə\ *n* -s [perh. fr. the feminine name *Petronella*] **:** a Scottish country-dance of the 19th century

pe·tro·nian \pə̇ˈtrōnēən, -nyən\ *adj, usu cap* [Gaius *Petronius*, 1st cent. A.D. Rom. director of entertainments at Nero's court + E *-an*] **:** of, relating to, or reminiscent of Petronius or his writings

pe·troph·i·lous \pə̇ˈträfələs\ *adj* [ISV *petr-* + *-philous*] **:** attached to or living on rock — used esp. of algae and crustaceans

pe·tro·sa \pə̇ˈtrōsə\ *n, pl* **petro·sae** \-ō,sē, -,sī\ [NL, fr. L, fem. of *petrosus* rocky] **:** the petrous part of the temporal bone

pe·tro·sal \-,səl\ *adj* [NL *petrosa* + E *-al*] **:** PETROUS, HARD, STONY; *specif* **:** of, relating to, or situated in the region of the petrous portion of the temporal bone or capsule of the internal ear

petrosal bone *also* **petrosal** *n* -s **1 :** a bone corresponding to the petrous portion of the temporal bone of man **2 :** a bone forming more or less of the capsule of the internal ear and composed of one or more periotic bones

petrosal ganglion *n* **:** the lower and larger of two sensory ganglia on the glossopharyngeal nerve

petrosal nerve *n* **:** any of several small nerves passing through foramina in the petrous portion of the temporal bone

petrosal sinus *n* **:** any of four venous sinuses at the base of the brain: **a :** a small superior sinus on each side that connects the cavernous and lateral sinuses of the same side **b :** a larger inferior sinus on each side that extends from the end of the cavernous sinus into the jugular foramen and there joins the lateral sinus to form the corresponding jugular vein

pet·ro·se·li·num \,pe·trōsəˈlīnəm\ *n, cap* [NL, fr. L, parsley — more at PARSLEY] **:** a small genus of European glabrous herbs (family Umbelliferae) having slender stems, bracts that are not reflexed, and oval fruits — see PARSLEY

pet·ro·sphere \ˈpe·trə,-\ *n* [*petr-* + *sphere*] **:** LITHOSPHERE

pet·ro·stearin *or* **pet·ro·stearine** \¦pe·trō+\ *n* [*petr-* + *stearin*] **:** MINERAL WAX, OZOKERITE

pet·ro·tympanic \¦==+\ *adj* [*petr-* + *tympanic*] **:** of or relating to the petrous and tympanic portions of the temporal bone

petrotympanic fissure *n* **:** a narrow transverse slit dividing the mandibular fossa of the temporal bone — called also *Glaserian fissure*

pet·rous \ˈpe·trəs, ˈpē-\ *adj* [MF *petreux*, fr. L *petrosus* rocky, fr. *petra* rock (fr. Gk) + *-osus* -ose] **:** resembling stone esp. in hardness **:** ROCKY; *specif* **:** of, relating to, or constituting the exceptionally hard and dense portion of the temporal bone of man that contains the internal auditory organs, corresponds chiefly to the periotic bones of many vertebrates, and is a pyramidal process wedged in at the base of the skull between the sphenoid and occipital bones with its lower half exposed on the surface of the skull and pierced by the external auditory meatus

petrous ganglion *n* **:** PETROSAL GANGLION

pe·trox·o·lin \pə̇ˈträksələn\ *n* -s [*petroleum* + Gk *oxys* sharp, acid + E *-ol* + *-in* — more at OXY-] **:** a mixture of liquid petrolatum and ammonia soap medicated and perfumed for use by inunction

pets *pl of* PET, *pres 3d sing of* PET

pe–tsai *or* **peh–tsai** \ˈbāˈtsī\ *n* -s [Chin (Pek) *pe²* *ts'ai⁴*, fr. *pe²* white + *ts'ai⁴* vegetable, greens] **:** CHINESE CABBAGE

pet·ta·ble \ˈped·əbəl, ˈpetə-\ *adj* [³*pet* + *-able*] **:** capable of, fit for, or worthy of being petted

pet·tah \ˈped·ə\ *n* -s [Tamil *pēṭṭai*, Malayalam *pēṭṭa*, & Kanarese *pēṭe*] **:** a village or suburb outside a fort in India or Ceylon

pet·ted \ˈped·əd, ˈpetəd\ *adj* [⁴*pet* + *-ed*] **:** marked by peevishness, sulkiness, or anger ⟨poverty brought on a ~ mood and a sore temper —William Wordsworth⟩ — **pet·ted·ly** *adv* — **pet·ted·ness** *n* -ES

pet·ter \ˈped·ə(r), -etə-\ *n* -s [³*pet* + *-er*] **:** one that pets

pet·ti·au·ger \,ped·ēˈōgə(r)\ *n* -s [by alter.] **:** PIRAGUA

pet·ti·chaps \ˈped·ē,-\ *n pl but sing or pl in constr* [perh. fr. obs. E *petty* small (fr. ME *pety*) + E *chaps*, pl. of *chap* (jaw)] **:** any of several European warblers: as **a :** CHIFFCHAFF **b :** GARDEN WARBLER

¹**pet·ti·coat** \ˈped·|ē|,kōt, ˈpet|, |ə|, *usu* -ōd·+V\ *n* [ME *petycote*, lit., small coat, fr. *pety* small + *cote* coat — more at PETTY] **1 :** a skirt worn by women, girls, or young children: as **a :** an outer skirt usu. constituting part of a dress formerly worn by women and small children **b :** a fancy skirt made to show below a draped-up overskirt **c :** a skirt on its own waistband that is usu. a little shorter than outer clothing, is often made with a ruffled, pleated, or lace edge, and is worn by women and girls as underwear **d** *archaic* **:** the skirt of a woman's riding habit **2 a :** a garment characteristic or typical of women — often used in the phrase *in petticoats* **b :** WOMAN ⟨a little nervous lest ~*s* in a government office might demoralize the male staff —Langston Day⟩ **3 :** the skirt of a garment worn by men or boys: as **a :** KILT **b :** FUSTANELLA **4 a :** the space outside the white ring of an archery target **b :** a hit in such a space **5 :** something resembling a petticoat: as **a :** a gathered or pleated skirt of cloth concealing the lower part of a table, bed, or chair **b :** the flaring base of a lamp or tankard **c :** a sheeting hung about a yacht before launching to hide its outline **d** (1) **:** any of the sleeves or cups forming part of a petticoat insulator (2) **:** PETTICOAT INSULATOR **e :** PETTICOAT PIPE

petticoat 1c

²**petticoat** \"\ *adj* **:** of, relating to, or exercised by women **:** FEMALE ⟨~ rule⟩ ⟨~ government⟩ ⟨~ influence⟩

petticoat breeches *n pl* **:** elaborate breeches with legs resembling skirts worn by Englishmen in the late 17th century

pet·ti·coat·ed \ˈ==,kōd·əd\ *adj* **:** wearing or furnished with a petticoat ⟨the ~ girls⟩ ⟨a ~ table⟩

petticoat insulator *n* **:** an insulator made in the form of superposed inverted cups and used for high insulation

petticoat·less \ˈ==,ləs\ *adj* **:** having or wearing no petticoat

petticoat pipe *n* **:** a short flaring pipe around the blast nozzle in the smokebox of a steam locomotive to equalize the draft

petticoat tails *n pl but sing or pl in constr, chiefly Scot* **:** a small cake

petticoat trousers *n pl* **:** trousers with very wide legs that resemble skirts

petties *pl of* PETTY

pet·ti·fog \ˈped·ē,fäg, -etē-, -fȯg\ *vb* **pettifogged; pettifogged; pettifogging; pettifogs** [back-formation fr. *pettifogger*] *vi* **1 :** to engage in legal chicanery **2 :** to quibble over insignificant details **:** CAVIL, BICKER ~ *vt* **:** to plead (as a case) with legal chicanery

pet·ti·fog·ger \-g(ə)r\ *n* -s [prob. fr. *petty* + obs. E *fogger* pettifogger, perh. irreg. fr. *Fugger*, 15th & 16th cent. Ger. family of financiers and merchants] **1 :** a lawyer whose methods are petty, underhanded, or disreputable **:** SHYSTER ⟨a gentleman of the law — there was nothing of the ~ about him —George Borrow⟩ **2 :** one given to quibbling over insignificant details ⟨a ringing indictment of all the proud and cautious ~*s* who could agree only on what could not be done —*Time*⟩

pet·ti·fog·gery \-g(ə)rē, -ri\ *n* -ES **:** the practice of a pettifogger **:** CHICANERY ⟨are apt to fall victims to . . . ~ on a huge scale —Howard Cosell⟩

pet·ti·fog·ging *adj* **1 :** having the characteristics of a pettifogger **:** marked by pettifoggery ⟨this curious combination of the masterfulness of the man of action with the ~ lawyer's mind —G.G.Coulton⟩ **2 :** having little or no significance or importance **:** PETTY, TRIVIAL ⟨all the complex ~ little quirks of doctrine —A.J.Cronin⟩

pet·ti·ly \ˈped·|ᵊlē, -et|, |əlē, -li\ *adv* **:** in a petty manner

pet·ti·ness \|ēnə̇s, |in-\ *n* -ES **1 :** the quality or state of being petty ⟨seeking . . . freedom from the ~ he found everywhere —Peggy Bennett⟩ **2 :** something petty **:** TRIVIALITY ⟨life was made up of innumerable little ~*es* —Sherwood Anderson⟩

petting *pres part of* PET

pet·tish \ˈped·|ish, -et|, |ēsh\ *adj* [prob. fr. ⁴*pet* + *-ish*] **:** marked by ill temper **:** FRETFUL, PEEVISH **syn** see IRRITABLE

pet·tish·ly \-ə̇shlē, -ēsh-, -li\ *adv* **:** in a pettish manner

pet·tish·ness \-ishnə̇s, -ēsh-\ *n* -ES **:** the quality or state of being pettish

pet·ti·skirt \ˈped·ē+,-\ *n* [*petticoat* + *skirt*] **:** PETTICOAT 1c

pet·ti·toes \ˈ==,tōz\ *n pl* [pl. (influenced in meaning by *toes*, pl. of *toe*) of obs. E *pettytoe* offal, fr. MF *petite oye*, fr. *petite* (fem. of *petit* small) + *oye* goose, fr. LL *auca* — more at OCARINA] **1 :** the feet of a pig used as food **2 :** TOES, FEET ⟨a child's ~⟩

pet·tle \ˈpetᵊl\ *vb* [³*pet* + *-le*] *vt, chiefly Scot* **:** FONDLE, CARESS ~ *vi* **1** *chiefly Scot* **:** NESTLE, CUDDLE **2** *chiefly Scot* **:** TRIFLE, POTTER

¹**pet·ty** \ˈped·|ē, -et|, |i\ *adj* -ER/-EST [ME *pety* small, minor, alter. of *petit*] **1 :** having secondary rank or importance **:** MINOR, SUBORDINATE ⟨the mountainous character of Greece explains its division into a crowd of ~ states —Edward Clodd⟩ ⟨a primarily agrarian society of ~ producers —R.H.Hilton⟩ **2 :** having little or no importance or significance **:** FUTILE ⟨defend with our lives the ~ principles which divide us —Henry Miller⟩ ⟨the ~ cares and vexations that absorb life's energies —M.R.Cohen⟩ **3 a :** marked by narrow interests and sympathies **:** SMALL-MINDED ⟨thought that little colleges are woefully circumscribed and ~ places —A.C.Benson⟩ ⟨suffering . . . makes men ~ and vindictive —W.S.Maugham⟩ **b :** reflecting small-mindedness or meanness **:** unnecessarily harsh or severe ⟨revealed to us the ~ cruelty of men, not the large injustice of the gods —Virginia Woolf⟩

syn PETTY, PUNY, TRIVIAL, TRIFLING, PALTRY, MEASLY, PICAYUNISH, and PICAYUNE can mean little or insignificant, esp. contemptibly so. PETTY applies to what is very small or unimportant and often contemptible by comparison to other things of its kind ⟨giants beside whom we seem *petty* —Sinclair Lewis⟩ ⟨the universe of our fathers shrinks to a *petty* compass, not much larger than the snug little state of Connecticut —V.L. Parrington⟩ ⟨*petty* courts⟩ ⟨fruit dealers, chestnut roasters, cigar venders, and other people, whose *petty* and wandering traffic is transacted in the open air —Nathaniel Hawthorne⟩ ⟨the contrast between a dying way of life which is spacious and noble and a new way which is *petty* and crude —E.K.Brown⟩ ⟨the *petty*, quibbling type of lawyer —Kenneth Roberts⟩ PUNY applies to what is small or slight enough to seem feeble or ineffectual ⟨a man of *puny* frame⟩ ⟨the streams, often *puny* and insignificant during dry weather, become raging torrents during a storm —C.L.White & G.T.Renner⟩ ⟨he was a *puny* eater —Lenard Kaufman⟩ ⟨his *puny* accomplishments and his many failures —F.G.Slaughter⟩ TRIVIAL applies to what is petty and commonplace, esp. not worth any special notice, extending to apply to persons or activities marked by concern for mainly trivial matters ⟨philosophy is at once the most sublime and the most *trivial* of human pursuits —William James⟩ ⟨had seemed to him *trivial* and of no import —Oscar Wilde⟩ ⟨the incessant hurry and *trivial* activity of daily life —C.W.Eliot⟩ ⟨light, *trivial* conversation over tea⟩ TRIFLING applies to what is so small or unimportant as to have little if any value or significance ⟨their estimate of her very *trifling* merits: and their wonder that their brothers could find any charms in her —W. M.Thackeray⟩ ⟨a considerable sum was paid to Egmont and a *trifling* one to the Prince —J.L.Motley⟩ ⟨most accidents are of *trifling* extent, and involve nothing more than the loss of time —*Amer. Guide Series: N. Y. City*⟩ PALTRY applies to what is ridiculously or contemptibly small esp. by comparison with what it should be ⟨how unsubstantial then appear our hopes and dreams, our little ambitions, our *paltry* joys —A.C.Benson⟩ ⟨*paltry* personal details prevail over world problems and cosmic questions —O.W.Holmes † 1935⟩ ⟨a little equipment costing a *paltry* amount —F.T.Williams⟩ MEASLY applies to what is contemptibly small or petty ⟨snatch at a little *measly* advantage and miss the big one —Sherwood Anderson⟩ ⟨a *measly* portion of pie⟩ ⟨a *measly* stingy individual⟩ PICAYUNISH and PICAYUNE usu. apply to the petty and insignificant, or to what is paltry in outlook or interests ⟨a lifetime of *picayunish* drudgery in the company of louts —H.L.Davis⟩ ⟨weed out dishonest or *picayunish* government employees⟩ ⟨a narrow, *picayune* mind —Felix Lazarus⟩ ⟨the obvious futility, the *picayune*, question-begging character, of such ethical analyses —Asher Moore⟩

²**petty** \"\ *n* -ES **1** *archaic* **:** a boy in a lower form of an English school **:** a small schoolboy **2** *dial Eng* **:** PRIVY

petty average *n* **:** AVERAGE 2b

petty bag *or* **petty–bag office** *n* [*petty bag* fr. obs. E *petty* small (fr. ME *pety*) + E *bag*; fr. the fact that the record of each case was kept in a small bag] *n* **:** a former office of the common-law side of the English Chancery Court having jurisdiction in suits for and against solicitors and officers of the court, in proceedings by extents on statutes, recognizance, scire facias, certiorari, and in other cases closely affecting the interests of the subject

petty bourgeois *or* **petty bourgeoisie** *n* [*petty bourgeois* alter. (influenced by ¹*petty*) of *petit bourgeois*; *petty bourgeoisie* alter. (influenced by ¹*petty*) of *petite bourgeoisie*] **:** PETIT BOURGEOIS

petty cash *n* **1 :** money expended or received in small items or amounts **2 :** a cash fund kept on hand for the payment of minor items

petty constable *n* **:** an officer of a British parish or township formerly appointed to act as keeper of the peace and to perform various minor administrative duties

pettygod *n, obs* **:** a minor deity **:** DEMIGOD

petty jury *n* [by alter. (influenced by ¹*petty*)] **:** PETIT JURY

petty larceny *n* [alter. (influenced by ¹*petty*) of *petit larceny*] **1** *common law* **:** larceny of property having a value of less than a shilling **2** *statutory law* **:** larceny of property having a value ranging in the U.S. from $10 to $200 — compare GRAND LARCENY

petty morel *n* **1 :** BLACK NIGHTSHADE **2 :** SPIKENARD 2a

petty offense *n* **1 :** a minor offense for which one may be tried at common law without a jury or for which there is no constitutional right to trial by jury **2 :** MISDEMEANOR; *esp* **:** one that may not be the subject of an indictment

petty officer *n* **:** a person belonging to one of three classes of lowest rating among noncommissioned naval officers ⟨a *petty officer* second class rates just below one of the first class and above one of the third class⟩

petty sergeanty *n* [by alter. (influenced by ¹*petty*)] **:** PETIT SERGEANTY

petty sessions *n pl* **:** the sessions of magistrates or justices that require no jury and that are held in exercise of summary jurisdiction and similar minor matters

petty spurge *n* **:** an Old World devil's milk (*Euphorbia peplus*) that is an introduced weed in the eastern U.S.

petty treason *n* [ME, fr. *petty*, *pety* small, minor + *treason*, *tresoun* treason — more at PETTY] **:** PETIT TREASON

petty whin *n* **1 :** NEEDLE FURZE **2 :** RESTHARROW

pet·u·lance \ˈpechələn(t)s\ *n* -s [F *pétulance*, fr. L *petulantia* impudence, fr. *petulant-*, *petulans* impudent + *-ia* -y] **1 :** the quality or state of being petulant: **a** *archaic* **:** wantonness or insolence in speech or behavior **:** RUDENESS ⟨the ~ with which obscure scribblers . . . treat men of the most respectable character —James Boswell⟩ **b :** temporary or capricious ill humor **:** PEEVISHNESS ⟨the ~ and crankiness of an old man who has been at the head of affairs all his life —Robert Graves⟩ **2 :** a petulant expression ⟨his dexterous ~*s* making the air all like needles round you —Thomas Carlyle⟩

pet·u·lan·cy \-nsē, -si\ *n* -ES [L *petulantia* impudence] *archaic* **:** PETULANCE

¹**pet·u·lant** \-lənt\ *adj* [L or MF; MF *petulant* impudent, fr. L *petulant-*, *petulans*; akin to L *petere* to go to or toward, seek — more at FEATHER] **1** *archaic* **a :** wanton or immodest in speech or behavior ⟨corrupted . . . amongst lascivious and ~ men and women —Thomas Tryon⟩ **b :** insolent or rude in speech or behavior ⟨as fair a mark as factious animosity and ~ wit could desire —T.B.Macaulay⟩ **2** [influenced in meaning by ⁴*pet*] **:** characterized by temporary or capricious ill humor **:** PEEVISH ⟨grew moody and ~ and would not eat —Pearl Buck⟩ ⟨developed a ~ and fussy disposition —E.L. Pearson⟩ **syn** see IRRITABLE

²**petulant** \"\ *n* -s **:** a person who is petulant

pet·u·lant·ly *adv* **:** in a petulant manner

pe·tun \pəˈtün\ *n* -s [MF *petun*, *petum*] *archaic* **:** TOBACCO

pe·tune \pəˈtün, pə̇ˈtyün\ *vt* -ED/-ING/-S [perh. fr. obs. F *petuner* to smoke tobacco, fr. obs. F *petun* tobacco, fr. MF *petun*, *petum*] **:** to heighten the flavor and aroma of (tobacco) by dipping in or spraying with a thick infusion of tobacco stems of the best quality or a liquid of other materials

pe·tu·nia \pə̇ˈtünyə, pə̇ˈtyü-, -nēə\ *n* [NL, fr. obs. F *petun* tobacco (fr. MF *petun*, *petum*, fr. Tupi *petyn*, *petyma*) + NL *-ia*] **1 a** *cap* **:** a genus of branching and often straggling annual or perennial So. American herbs (family Solanaceae) that have viscid and pubescent stems and foliage, bear abundant flowers with funnel-form or salver-shaped flowers, and are widely cultivated as ornamentals **b** -s **:** any plant of the genus *Petunia* **2** -s **:** a dark purple that is bluer, lighter, and stronger than average prune, bluer and stronger than plum (sense 6b) and bluer and duller than mulberry (sense 2a)

petunia 1b

petunia violet *n* **:** a deep purple that is redder and slightly lighter than hyacinth violet, redder and lighter than pontiff, paler than dahlia purple (sense 2), and bluer, lighter, and stronger than imperial purple (sense 2)

pe·tun·tse *also* **pe·tun·se** *or* **pe·tun·tze** \pə'tủntsə, bī-'dəndzə\ *n* -s [Chin (Pek) *pe*² *tun*¹ *tzŭ*³, fr. *pe*² white + *tun*¹ *tzŭ*³ mound of earth, fr. *tun*¹ mound, heap + *tzŭ*³ son, child] : CHINA STONE

pet·wood \'pe‚twủd\ *also* **pet·wun wood** \-‚twən-\ *n* [Burmese *phetwŭn*] : TRINCOMALI WOOD

petz·ite \'pet‚sīt\ *n* -s [G *petzit*, fr. W.K.*Pecz* †1873 Hung. geologist who analyzed it + G *-it* -ite] : a mineral $Ag_3 Au Te_2$ consisting of a silver gold telluride that is steel gray to iron black (hardness 2.5–3, sp. gr. 8.7–9.0)

petz·val lens \'pets‚väl-\ *n*, *usu cap P* [after Joseph *Petzval* †1891 Austrian mathematician and optician] : a two-element highly achromatized camera objective having low transmission loss

peu·ced·a·num \pyə'sedᵊnəm\ *n*, *cap* [NL, fr. L, sulphurweed, fr. Gk *peukedanon*, prob. fr. neut. of *peukedanos* sharp, piercing — more at PUNGENT] : a genus of Old World tall branching herbs (family Umbelliferae) characterized by a conical stylopodium and solitary oil tubes

peul *or* **peuhl** \'p(y)ül\ *n* -s *usu cap* : FULANI

peu·mus \'pyüməs\ *n*, *cap* [NL, fr. Sp *peumo* boldo, fr. Mapuche *péumo*] : a genus of Chilean evergreen shrubs (family Monimiaceae) with elliptic or ovate revolute coriaceous leaves

pevy *var of* PEAVEY

¹**pew** \'pyü\ *n* -s *often attrib* [ME *pue, pewe, puwe*, fr. MF *puie* balcony, fr. L *podia*, pl. of *podium* balcony, fr. Gk *podion* small foot, base, dim. of *pod-*, *pous* foot — more at FOOT] **1 a** : a compartment in the auditorium of a church providing seats for several persons: (1) : a compartment esp. in an old English church raised on a footpace, separated by partitions, furnished with a long seat or when square with seats facing each other, and designed for the use of a family (2) : one of the benches with backs and sometimes doors fixed in rows in a church **b** : the persons occupying such pews : CONGREGATION **2** *obs* : station in life : allotted place or position **3 a** *obs* : a raised place for a speaker in a church; *esp* : a preacher's stall or desk **b** *archaic* : a raised seat or bench for a person (as a judge) sitting in an official capacity

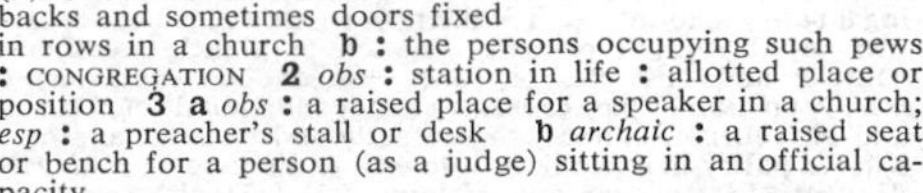
pew 1a

²**pew** \"\ *vt* -ED/-ING/-S [ME *puyen*, fr. *pue, pewe, puwe*, n.] **1** : to furnish with pews ⟨they ~ their churches and sometimes lock them —E.A.Freeman⟩ **2** : to enclose in or as if in a pew ⟨men who were as willingly ~*ed* in the parish church as their sheep were in night folds —*Examiner*⟩

³**pew** \a sound made by blowing or whistling through rounded lips, often with the tongue moving from the front to the back of the mouth in the process; often read as 'pyü\ *interj* [origin unknown] — used to express contempt or disgust (as at an odor)

⁴**pew** \'pyü\ *n* -s *Scot* : a thin stream of air or smoke

⁵**pew** \"\ *n* -s [F *pieu* stake, fr. L *palus* — more at POLE] : a long-handled hooked prong for pitching fish (as on a cannery wharf)

pew·age \'pyüij, -ēj\ *n* -s **1** : the amount paid for the use of a pew in a church **2** : the pews in a church

pew chair *n* : a seat hinged against the end of a pew to afford accommodation when needed in the aisle

pew·dom \'pyüdəm\ *n* -s : the system or prevalence of pews in churches

pewee *var of* PEEWEE

pew·ful \'pyü‚fủl\ *n*, *pl* **pewfuls** \-ü‚fủlz\ *or* **pews·ful** \-üz‚fủl\ [¹*pew* + *-ful*] : as many as a pew will hold

pewholder \'⸗‚⸗⸗\ *n* : a renter or owner of a church pew

pewing *n* -s [fr. gerund of ²*pew*] : PEWAGE 2

pe·wit *or* **pee·wit** \'pēwət, -ē‚wit, 'pyüət *usu* -d·+V\ *also* **pee·vit** \'pēvət, -‚vit\ *n* -s [imit.] **1** : LAPWING **2** *also* **pewit gull** : LAUGHING GULL **1 3** : PEEWEE 1a

pew·less \'pyüləs\ *adj* : having no pews

pew rent *n* : the rent for a pew or for sittings in a church

pews *pl of* PEW, *pres 3d sing of* PEW

pew·ter \'pyüd·ə(r), -ütə-\ *n* -s *often attrib* [ME *pewtre*, fr. MF *peutre, peautre;* akin to OProv *peltre* pewter, It *peltro*] **1** : any of various alloys having tin as their principal component: as **a** : a dull alloy with lead used formerly for domestic utensils **b** : a bright alloy hardened with antimony and copper and used esp. for artware — compare BRITANNIA METAL **2** : utensils or vessels made of pewter: as **a** : a pewter tankard or mug **b** *Brit* : a prize cup **3** : MONEY **4 a** : a grayish blue that is redder and paler than electric or Gobelin, paler than copenhagen, and paler and slightly greener than old china **b** : a nearly neutral slightly bluish dark gray that is darker than mole

pew·ter·er \-ərə(r)\ *n* -s [ME *peautrer, peuterer*, fr. MF *peautrier*, fr. *peutre, peautre* pewter + *-ier* -er] : one that makes pewter utensils or vessels

pewter mill *n* : a lapidary's wheel used for stones of the hardness of amethyst or agate

-pexy \‚peksē, -si\ *n comb form* -ES [NL *-pexia*, fr. Gk *-pēxia* solidity, fr. *pēxis* solidity, freezing, putting together (fr. *pēgnynai* to fix, fasten together) + *-ia* -y — more at PACT] : fixation : making fast ⟨colloido*pexy*⟩ ⟨gastro*pexy*⟩

pey·e·ri·an gland \(')pī¦irēən-\ *n*, *usu cap P* [*peyerian* fr. Johann K. *Peyer* †1712 Swiss physician and anatomist + E *-an*] : PEYER'S PATCH

pey·er's patch \'pī(ə)rz-\ *also* **peyer's gland** *n*, *usu cap 1st P* : any of numerous large oval patches of closely aggregated lymph follicles in the walls of the small intestines esp. in the ileum that partially or entirely disappear in advanced life and in typhoid fever become the seat of ulcers which may perforate the intestines

pe·yo·te \pā'(y)ōd·ē\ *also* **pe·yotl** \-d·ᵊl\ *or* **pa·yo·te** \-d·ē\ *n* -s [MexSp *peyote*, fr. Nahuatl *peyotl*] **1** : any of several cacti (genus *Lophophora*) of the southwestern U.S. and northern Mexico; *esp* : MESCAL **2** : a stimulant drug derived from mescal buttons and used in religious ceremonials by some Indian peoples

peyote cult *n*, *often cap P* **1** : an American Indian religious society or form of worship centering around the sacramental use of peyote **2** : PEYOTISM

peyote dance *n* : an ecstatic fertility dance of the Huichol and Tarahumara Indians of northern Mexico with visions induced by eating the mescal button

pe·yo·tism \pā'yōd·‚izəm\ *n* -s : an intertribal American Indian religion adapting Christian elements to traditional tribal beliefs and practices and distinguished by the sacramental use of peyote

pe·yo·tist \-d·əst\ *n* -s : an adherent of peyotism : a member of a peyote cult

pey·ro·nie's disease \¦pārə¦nēz-\ *n*, *usu cap P* [prob. after François Gigot de La *Peyronie* †1747 Fr. surgeon] : the formation of fibrous plaques in one or both corpora cavernosa of the penis resulting in distortion or deflection of the erect organ

pey·tral *or* **pey·trel** \'pā·trəl\ *n* -s [ME *peytrel*, fr. MF *peitral, poitral* — more at POITREL] : POITREL

pe·zi·za \pə'zīzə\ *n* [NL, alter. of L *pezica* puffball, modif. of Gk *pezis;* perh. akin to L *pedere* to break wind — more at PETARD] : the type genus of Pezizaceae comprising cup fungi with sessile usu. dull tan or brown apothecia that lack external hairs or bristles — see PLECTANIA

pez·i·za·ce·ae \‚pezə'zāsē‚ē\ *n pl*, *cap* [NL, fr. *Peziza*, type genus + *-aceae*] : a large and widely distributed family of fungi (order Pezizales) comprising many typical cup fungi — see PEZIZA

pe·zi·zae·form *also* **pe·zi·zi·form** \pə'zīzə‚fȯrm\ *adj* [*pezizaeform* irreg. fr. NL *Peziza* + E *-form; peziziform* fr. NL *Peziza* + E *-iform*] : having the shape of a fungus of the genus *Peziza*

pez·i·za·les \‚pezə'zā(‚)lēz\ *n pl*, *cap* [NL, fr. *Peziza* + *-ales*] : an order of epigeal mostly saprophytic fungi (subclass Euascomycetes) having asci borne in a hymenium that is usu. exposed before maturity and on or in a fleshy or horny apothecium often colored and typically shaped like a cup, saucer, or disc — see HELVELLACEAE, PEZIZACEAE

pe·zi·zoid \pə'zī‚zȯid, 'pezə‚z-\ *adj* [ISV *peziz-* (fr. NL *Peziza*) + *-oid*] : resembling a fungus of the genus *Peziza* : cup-shaped

pez·o·graph \'pezə‚graf\ *n* [perh. fr. Gk *pezis* puffball + E *-o-* + *-graph*] : any of various small pits suggestive of the imprints of finger tips that are common on meteorites

pez·o·phaps \-‚faps\ *n*, *cap* [NL, fr. Gk *pezos* walking, on foot + *phaps* wild pigeon; akin to L *ped-*, *pes* foot — more at FOOT] : a genus of birds (family Rhaphidae) constituted by the extinct solitaire

pf *abbr* **1** perfect **2** pfennig **3** preferred

pF *symbol* — used when *p* denotes logarithm and *F* indicates free energy to express logarithmically the water-holding energy of soil that is usu. measured by the height in centimeters of a column of water which produces a tension of equal force ⟨a tension of 40 centimeters equals ~ 1.6⟩

PF *abbr* **1** *often not cap* pianoforte **2** *often not cap* picofarad **3** *often not cap* [It *più forte*] a little louder **4** *often not cap* power factor **5** procurator fiscal **6** pro forma

pfc \¦pē‚ef¦sē\ *abbr or n* -s *often cap P* private first class

pfce *abbr* performance

pfd *abbr* preferred

pfef·fer·ku·chen \'fefə(r)‚kükən, *G* '(p)fefər‚kükən\ *n* [G, fr. *pfeffer* pepper (fr. OHG *pfeffar*) + *kuchen* cake, fr. OHG *kuocho* — more at PEPPER, CAKE] : GINGERBREAD

pfef·fer·nuss \'fefə(r)‚nüs, -nủs, *G* '(p)fefər‚nủs\ *n*, *pl* **pfef·fernues·se** \-nüsə‚-nủsə, *G* -nœsə\ [G, fr. *pfeffer* + *nuss* nut, fr. OHG *nuz* — more at NUT] : a small hard highly spiced cookie made traditionally for the Christmas holidays

pfeif·fer·el·la \‚fīfə'relə\ [NL, fr. Richard F. J. *Pfeiffer* †1945? Ger. bacteriologist + NL *-ella*] *syn of* ACTINOBACILLUS

pfeif·fer's bacillus \'fīfə(r)z-\ *also* **pfeiffer's influenza bacillus** *n*, *usu cap P* [after Richard F. J. *Pfeiffer*] : a minute bacillus (*Hemophilus influenzae*) associated with acute respiratory infections and meningitis — compare KOCH-WEEKS BACILLUS

pfen·nig \'fenig, -ik, *often (by persistence of the nasality of the* n) -iŋ; *G* '(p)fenik\ *n*, *pl* **pfennigs** \-igz, -iks, -iŋz\ *or* **pfenni·ge** \-nigə, -niyə\ [G, fr. OHG *pfenning* — more at PENNY] **1** *in Germany before 1871* : any of several units of value or their corresponding coins (as, in Bavaria, ¼ kreuzer; in Lübeck, ¹⁄₁₂ schilling) **2** *in Germany after 1871* : a unit of value equal to ¹⁄₁₀₀ mark; *also* : a coin representing this value — see MONEY table

pfg *abbr* pfennig

PFI *abbr* physical fitness index

pfit·zer's juniper \'fitsə(r)z-\ *or* **pfitzer juniper** *n*, *usu cap P* [after Ernst *Pfitzer* †1906 Ger. botanist] : a low-growing evergreen shrub (*Juniperus chinensis pfitzeriana*) that has spreading chiefly horizontal branches and gray green foliage and is extensively used in landscaping

pflei·der·er \'flīdərə(r)\ *or* **pflei·der·ing machine** \-dəriŋ-\ *n* -s [perh. fr. the name *Pfleiderer*] : a machine for shredding cellulose sheets to bits in rayon manufacturing

pfte *abbr* pianoforte

pfx *abbr* prefix

pg *abbr* page

PG *abbr* **1** Paris granite **2** paying guest **3** postgraduate **4** proving ground **5** public gaol

PGA \¦pē¦jē¦ā\ *n* -s [pteroylglutamic acid] : FOLIC ACID 1

pgn *abbr* pigeon

PGR *abbr* psychogalvanic reaction or response

PGT *abbr*, *often not cap* per gross ton

ph *abbr* **1** phase **2** phone **3** pharmacopoeia **4** phosphor **5** phot

pH *symbol* the negative logarithm of the effective hydrogen-ion concentration or hydrogen-ion activity in gram equivalents per liter determined in various ways (as by means of a hydrogen electrode or a glass electrode) and used for convenience in expressing both acidity and alkalinity usu. on a scale of 0 to 14 on which 7 represents the value for pure water at 25°C or neutrality, values less than 7 represent increasing hydrogen-ion concentration and increasing acidity (as 3.1 for vinegar, 2.3 for lemon juice, and 1.04 for tenth-normal hydrochloric acid), and values greater than 7 represent decreasing hydrogen-ion concentration and increasing alkalinity (as 8.2 for one percent sodium bicarbonate solution, 10.7 for one percent sodium carbonate solution, 13 for tenth-normal sodium hydroxide) ⟨instead of saying that the concentration of hydrogen ion in pure water is 1.00×10^{-7}, it is customary to say that the ~ of pure water is 7 —Linus Pauling⟩ ⟨soils may vary in ~ from about 3.5 to 9, but the general range most favorable for ordinary crops is from 6.0 to 7.5 —E.G.Davies⟩ — compare PK, RH

PH *abbr* public health

Ph *symbol* phenyl

phac- *or* **phaco-** *or* **phak-** *or* **phako-** *comb form* [Gk *phak-*, *phako-*, fr. *phakos* lentil, object shaped like a lentil, mole, wart] **1** : lentil : thing shaped like a lentil ⟨*Phaco*choerus⟩ ⟨*phaco*lith⟩ ⟨*Phac*ops⟩ **2 a** : lens ⟨*phaco*meter⟩ **b** *usu phak-* : crystalline lens of the eye ⟨*phak*oma⟩

pha·ce·lia \fə'sēlēə\ *n* [NL, fr. Gk *phakelos* bundle, faggot + NL *-ia*] **1** *cap* : a genus of American herbs (family Hydrophyllaceae) with usu. pinnatifid or dissected leaves and blue, purple, or white flowers in scorpioid cymes — see CALIFORNIA BLUEBELL **2** -s : any plant of the genus *Phacelia*

pha·cel·la \fə'selə\ *also* **phacel·lus** \-ləs\ *n*, *pl* **phacel·lae** \-‚lē, -‚lī\ *also* **phacel·li** \-‚lī\ [NL, fr. Gk *phakellos*, MS var. of *phakelos* bundle, faggot] : one of the rows of filaments usu. bearing nematocysts on the inner surface of the gastric cavity of some scyphozoan jellyfishes

pha·cid·i·a·ce·ae \fə‚sidē'āsē‚ē\ *n pl*, *cap* [NL, fr. *Phacidium*, type genus (fr. Gk *phakos* lentil + NL *-idium*) + *-aceae*] : a family of fungi (order Phacidiales) having a thin hypothecium and ascocarps that are embedded in the host tissue or in a stroma

pha·cid·i·a·les \-'ā(‚)lēz\ *n pl*, *cap* [NL, fr. *Phacidium* genus of fungi + *-ales*] : an order of fungi (subclass Euascomycetes) having the hymenium covered by a membrane until the ascospores mature following which the membrane breaks up into stellate or irregular fragments

phac·o·choere *or* **phac·o·chere** \'fakə‚ki(ə)r\ *n* -s [NL *Phacochoerus*] : WARTHOG

phac·o·choe·rus \‚⸗⸗'kirəs, -kēr-\ *n*, *cap* [NL, fr. *phac-* + *-choerus*] : a genus of mammals that comprises the warthogs and was formerly made the type of a separate family but is now placed in the family Suidae near the genus *Sus*

phac·o·lith \'⸗⸗‚lith\ *n* -s [*phac-* + *-lith*] : a lens-shaped mass of igneous rock intruded in folded sedimentary beds with which it is approximately concordant and having its greatest thickness along the axes of synclines or anticlines — **phac·o·lith·ic** \¦⸗⸗¦lithik\ *adj*

pha·com·e·ter \fə'kämәd·ə(r)\ *n* [ISV *phac-* + *-meter*] : an instrument for measuring the focal power of lenses

pha·cops \'fā‚käps\ *n*, *cap* [NL, fr. *phac-* + *-ops*] : a genus (the type of the family Phacopidae) comprising Silurian and Devonian trilobites with a large rounded glabella and a large pygidium

phae·dra·nas·sa \‚fēdrə'nasə\ *n*, *cap* [NL, fr. Gk *phaidros* bright + *anassa* queen] : a small genus of chiefly Andean bulbous herbs (family Amaryllidaceae) with tall hollow scapes bearing umbels of showy drooping usu. red or rose green-marked flowers — see QUEEN LILY

phae·ism \'fē‚izəm\ *n* -s [Gk *phaios* dusky, gray + E *-ism;* akin to Gk *phaidros* bright, Lith *giedras* bright, clear, Latvian *gàiss* air, weather] : incomplete melanism in a butterfly

phaen- *or* **phaeno-** — see PHEN-

phaeo- *or* **pheo-** *comb form* [Gk *phaio-*, fr. *phaios* dusky, gray] : dun-colored ⟨*phaeo*derm⟩ ⟨*Phaeo*phyceae⟩ — often in names of compounds related to chlorophyll ⟨*pheo*phytin⟩

phae·och·rous \fē'äkrəs\ *adj* [*phaeo-* + *-chrous*, irreg. fr. Gk *-chroos, -chrous* -colored — more at -CHROOUS] : DUSKY

phaeo·derm \'fēə‚dərm\ *n* -s [*phaeo-* + Gk *derma* skin — more at DERM-] : a person with a grayish brown skin

phaeo·melanin \¦fēō+\ *n* [*phaeo-* + *melanin*] : a reddish or yellowish brown animal pigment related to melanin and common in animals of arid areas

phaeo·phy·ce·ae \¦⸗⸗'fisē‚ē, -fis-\ *n pl*, *cap* [NL, fr. *phaeo-* + *-phyceae*] *in some classifications* : a class comprising the brown algae and being coextensive with the division Phaeophyta — **phaeo·phy·cean** \¦⸗⸗¦fishən\ *adj or n* — **phaeo·phy·ceous** \-shəs\ *adj*

phae·oph·y·ta \fē'äfəd·ə\ *n pl*, *cap* [NL, fr. *phaeo-* + *-phyta*] : a division or other category of algae that have the chlorophyll masked by brown pigments, are mostly marine, diverse in form, often of gigantic size, and anchored by holdfasts to the substrate, and are usu. divided among the classes Isogeneratae, Heterogeneratae, and Cyclosporeae — see BROWN ALGA

phaeophytin *var of* PHEOPHYTIN

phae·o·plast \'fēə‚plast\ *n* -s [ISV *phaeo-* + *-plast*] : one of the brownish chromatophores occurring in the brown algae — compare RHODOPLAST

phaeoporphyrin *var of* PHEOPORPHYRIN

phaeo·spo·ra·les \‚fēōspə'rā(‚)lēz\ *n pl*, *cap* [NL, fr. *phaeo-* + *spora* spore + *-ales*] *in some classifications* : an order of brown algae orig. equivalent to Phaeosporeae but later excluding the Laminariales

phaeo·spore \'fēə‚spō(ə)r\ *n* [*phaeo-* + *spore*] : a spore (as a zoospore) containing phaeoplasts

phaeo·spo·re·ae \‚fēə'spōrē‚ē\ *n pl*, *cap* [NL, fr. *phaeo-* + *spora* spore + *-eae*] *in some classifications* : an order or other group of brown algae characterized by the production of asexual swarm spores and usu. comprising all the Phaeophyceae except the Dictyotales and Fucales — compare CYCLOSPOREAE — **phaeo·spor·ous** \¦⸗⸗¦spōrəs, (')fē¦äspərəs\ *adj*

phaeo·tham·ni·on \‚fēə'thamnē‚än\ *n*, *cap* [NL, fr. *phaeo-* + Gk *thamnion* little bush, dim. of *thamnos* bush — more at THAMN-] : a genus (the type of the family Phaeothamniaceae) of rare yellow green algae growing upon other algae and having a definite central axis and ascending lateral filaments made up of cylindrical to subovoid cells

pha·ë·thon \'fāəthən, -‚thän\ *n*, *cap* [NL, fr. L, name of son of Helios] : a genus (the type of the family Phaëthontidae) of tropical sea birds of the order Pelecaniformes — see TROPIC BIRD — **pha·ë·thon·ic** \¦⸗⸗¦thänik\ *or* **pha·ë·thon·tic** \-ntik\ *adj*

pha·e·ton \'fāətᵊn *also* -āt-\ *n* -s [L *Phaethon*, son of Helios who attempted to drive the chariot of the sun with the result of setting the earth on fire, fr. Gk *Phaethōn*] **1** *archaic*, *usu cap* **a** : one who drives a chariot or coach esp. at a reckless or dangerous speed **b** : one that would or may set the world on fire **2** : any of various light four-wheeled horse-drawn vehicles usu. having no sidepieces in front of the seats **3** : TOURING CAR

phag- *or* **phago-** *comb form* [Gk, fr. *phagein* to eat — more at BAKSHEESH] **1** : eating : feeding ⟨*phag*edena⟩ ⟨*phago*mania⟩ **2** : phagocyte ⟨*phago*lysis⟩

-pha·ga \fəgə\ *n comb form*, *pl* **-phaga** \"\ [NL, fr. Gk *phagein*] : eater : eaters — in taxonomic names in zoology ⟨Ento*mophaga*⟩ ⟨Litho*phaga*⟩ ⟨Xylo*phaga*⟩ ⟨Glosso*phaga*⟩

phage \'fāj *sometimes* 'fäzh *or* 'fȧzh\ *n* -s [by shortening] : BACTERIOPHAGE

-phage \‚fāj *sometimes* ‚fäzh *or* ‚fȧzh\ *also* **-phag** \‚fag, -aa(ə)g, -aig\ *n comb form* -s [Gk *-phagos*, fr. *phagein*] **1** : one that eats ⟨ostreo*phage*⟩ ⟨xylo*phage*⟩ **2** : cell (as a phagocyte) that destroys cells ⟨bacterio*phage*⟩

phag·e·de·na *also* **phag·e·dae·na** \‚fajə'dēnə\ *n* -s [L, fr. Gk *phagedaina*, fr. *phagein* to eat — more at BAKSHEESH] : rapidly spreading destructive ulceration of soft tissue

phag·e·den·ic *also* **phag·e·daen·ic** \¦⸗⸗¦denik, -dēn-\ *adj* **1** *of a lesion* : being or marked by phagedena **2** : of, like, or resembling phagedena ⟨the ~ form of chancroid⟩

phage type *n* : the phages to which a particular bacterium is susceptible

phage-typing *n* : determination of the phage type of a bacterium

-pha·gia \'fāj(ē)ə\ *n comb form* -s [NL, fr. Gk — more at -PHAGY] **1** : -PHAGY ⟨hemo*phagia*⟩ **2** : desire for food ⟨hyper*phagia*⟩

pha·gin·e·ae \fə'jinē‚ē\ *n pl*, *cap* [NL, fr. *phag-* + *-ineae*] *in some classifications* : a suborder of Virales comprising the bacteriophages

phago·cyt·able \¦fagə¦sīd·əbəl\ *adj* [*phagocyt*osis + *-able*] : susceptible to phagocytosis

phago·cy·ta·ry \¦⸗⸗¦sīd·ərē\ *adj* [ISV *phagocyte* + *-ary*] : functioning or supposed to function as a phagocyte

¹**phago·cyte** \'fagə‚sīt\ *n* -s [ISV *phag-* + *-cyte*] : any cell that characteristically engulfs foreign material, is typically a leukocyte or reticuloendothelial cell and often amoeboid, and functions in the body to remove and consume debris and foreign bodies (as degenerating tissue or bacteria) — compare ATHROCYTE

²**phagocyte** \"\ *vt* -ED/-ING/-S : PHAGOCYTIZE

phago·cyt·ic \¦⸗⸗¦sid·ik\ *adj* : having the ability to phagocytize : capable of functioning as phagocytes

phagocytic index *n* : a measure of phagocytic activity determined by counting the number of bacteria ingested per phagocyte during a limited period of incubation of a suspension of bacteria and phagocytes in serum

phago·cyt·ize \'⸗⸗‚sīd·‚īz, -‚sə‚tīz\ *vt* -ED/-ING/-S : to consume by phagocytosis

phago·cy·tose \'⸗⸗‚sī‚tōs, -ōz\ *also* **phago·cy·toze** \-ōz\ *vt* -ED/-ING/-S [back-formation fr. *phagocytosis*] : PHAGOCYTIZE

phago·cy·to·sis \‚fagə‚sī'tōsəs\ *n*, *pl* **phagocyto·ses** \-ō‚sēz\ [NL, fr. ISV *phagocyte* + NL *-osis*] : the process of ingestion and usu. of isolation or destruction of particulate material by cells that in vertebrates is a characteristic function of various leukocytes and reticuloendothelial cells and serves as an important bodily defense mechanism against infection by microorganisms and against occlusion of mucous surfaces or tissues by foreign particles and tissue debris

phago·cy·tot·ic \¦⸗⸗⸗¦täd·ik\ *adj* : of or relating to phagocytosis

phago·dynamometer \¦⸗⸗+\ *n* [*phag-* + *dynamometer*] : an instrument for measuring the force that may be exerted by the jaws in bringing the teeth together (as in chewing)

pha·gol·y·sis \fə'gäləsəs\ *n*, *pl* **phagoly·ses** \-ə‚sēz\ [NL, fr. *phag-* + *-lysis*] : destruction of phagocytes

phago·lyt·ic \¦fagə¦lid·ik\ *adj* : of or relating to phagolysis

-pha·gous \fəgəs\ *adj comb form* [Gk *-phagos*, fr. *phagein* to eat — more at BAKSHEESH] : feeding esp. on a (specified) kind of food ⟨anthropo*phagous*⟩ ⟨creo*phagous*⟩ ⟨cyto*phagous*⟩ ⟨sapro*phagous*⟩

pha·gun \'pägủn, 'fä-\ *n* -s *usu cap* [Hindi *phāgun*, fr. Skt *phālguna*] : a month of the Hindu year — see MONTH table

-pha·gus \fəgəs\ *n comb form* [NL, fr. Gk *-phagos*] : eater : one that eats an indicated thing or in an indicated way — in generic names of animals ⟨Melo*phagus*⟩

-pha·gy \fəjē, -ji\ *n comb form* -ES [Gk *-phagia*, fr. *phagein* to eat + *-ia* -y — more at BAKSHEESH] : eating of a (specified) type or substance — esp. in biological and medical terms ⟨anthropo*phagy*⟩ ⟨bio*phagy*⟩ ⟨cyto*phagy*⟩ ⟨geo*phagy*⟩

phai·no·pep·la \fā‚inō'peplə, ‚fīn-\ *n* [NL, fr. Gk *phaeinos* shining + *peplos* robe; akin to Gk *phaos, phōs* light — more at FANCY, PEPLOS] **1** *cap* : a monotypic genus of passerine birds of Mexico and southwestern U.S. of which the male is uniform glossy blue-black with a white spot on each primary and the female is brownish **2** -s : any bird of the genus *Phainopepla*

phai·us \'fīəs\ *n*, *cap* [NL, fr. Gk *phaios* dusky — more at PHAEISM] : a genus of Asiatic orchids that are locally naturalized in tropical America and are sometimes cultivated for their large plicate leaves and showy racemose flowers

pha·jus \'fājəs\ [NL, fr. Gk *phaios*] *syn of* PHAIUS

phak- *or* **phako-** — see PHAC-

phal·a·cro·cor·a·cine \¦falə‚krō¦kȯrə‚sīn, -‚sən\ *adj* [NL *Phalacrocorac-*, *Phalacrocorax* + E *-ine*] : of or relating to the genus *Phalacrocorax*

phal·a·cro·co·rax \‚⸗⸗'krōkə‚raks\ *n*, *cap* [NL, fr. L, coot, cormorant, fr. Gk *phalakros* bald + *korak-*, *korax* raven — more at RAVEN] : a genus consisting of the cormorants and constituting a family of the order Pelecaniformes

phal·a·cro·sis \ˌfalə'krōsəs\ *n, pl* **phalacro·ses** \-ˌsēz\ [NL, fr. Gk *phalakrōsis*, fr. *phalakros* bald (fr. *phalos* white + *akron* top) + *-ōsis* -osis; akin to Gk *phalios* having a white spot, and to Gk *akmē* point — more at BALD, EDGE] **:** BALDNESS, ALOPECIA

pha·lae·ce·an \ˌfalə'sēən\ *n* -S *usu cap* [Gk *phalaikeion* phalaecean (fr. *Phalaikos* Phalaecus, Greek poet) + E *-an*] **:** a hendecasyllabic verse in Greek and Latin prosody that is a glyconic with three additional syllables forming a single bacchius or an iambic dipody catalectic **:** a logaoedic verse of five feet the first of which is indeterminate, the second a dactyl, and the last three trochees

pha·laen·i·dae \fə'lenəˌdē\ [NL, fr. *Phalaena*, genus of moths (fr. Gk *phalaina*, *phallaina* whale, moth) + *-idae* — more at BALAENA] *syn of* NOCTUIDAE

phal·ae·nop·sid \ˌfalə'näpsəd, -ˌsid\ *n* -S [NL, fr. *Phalaenopsis*] **:** an orchid of the genus *Phalaenopsis*

phal·ae·nop·sis \-ˌsəs\ *n, cap* [NL, fr. Gk *phalaina* moth + *-opsis*] **:** a genus of ornamental epiphytic orchids that are natives of India and the Malay archipelago and have fleshy leaves with persistent sheathing bases and large flowers of various colors with broad lateral petals — see BUTTERFLY PLANT 2, MOTH ORCHID

pha·lange \'fāˌlanj, fə'l-, -aa(ə)nj\ *n* -S [F, fr. NL *phalang-, phalanx* — more at PHALANX] **1 :** PHALANX 2 **2 :** one of the segments of an insect's tarsus

pha·lan·ge·al \fə'lanj(ē)əl, fā'-\ *adj* [L *phalang-, phalanx* + E *-al*] **1 :** of or relating to a phalanx **2** [NL *phalang-, phalanx* + E *-al*] **:** of or relating to the phalanges

phalangeal bone *n* **:** PHALANX 2

pha·lan·ger \fə'lanjə(r), fā'-\ *n* [NL, fr. *phalang-, phalanx* — more at PHALANX] **1** -S **:** any of various marsupial mammals of the family Phalangeridae ranging in size from a mouse to a large cat, having soft thick fur and a long and usu. prehensile tail, and being chiefly nocturnal, arboreal, and frugivorous or insectivorous — see FLYING PHALANGER **2** *cap* **:** a genus (the type of the family Phalangeridae) comprising the cuscuses

phal·an·ger·i·dae \ˌfalən'jerəˌdē\ *n pl, cap* [NL, fr. *Phalanger*, type genus + *-idae*] **:** a family of marsupial mammals (suborder Diprotodontia) consisting of the phalangers, the flying phalangers, the koala, and related forms

phalanges *pl of* PHALANX

phal·an·gette \ˌfalən'jet\ *n* -S [F, fr. *phalange* phalanx (fr. NL *phalang-, phalanx*) + *-ette*] **:** a distal phalanx of a finger or toe

-pha·lan·gia \fə'lanj(ē)ə, fā'-\ *n comb form* -S [NL, fr. *phalang-, phalanx* + *-ia*] **:** condition of the phalanges ⟨brachy*phalangia*⟩

pha·lan·gi·an \fə'lanj(ē)ən, fā'-\ *adj or n* [NL *Phalangium* + E *-an*] **:** PHALANGID

¹pha·lan·gid \-jəd, -ˌjid\ *adj* [NL *Phalangida*] **:** of or relating to the Phalangida

²phalangid \"\ *n* -S **:** an arachnid of the order Phalangida

pha·lan·gi·da \-jədə\ *n pl, cap* [NL, fr. *Phalangium* + *-ida*] **:** a cosmopolitan order of Arachnida comprising the harvestmen

pha·lan·gi·dan \-jədən, -dᵊn\ *or* **phal·an·gid·e·an** \ˌfalən'jidēən\ *adj* [*phalangidan* fr. NL *Phalangida* + E *-an; phalangidean* fr. NL *Phalangidea* + E *-an*] **:** ¹PHALANGID

phal·an·gid·ea \ˌfalən'jidēə\ [NL, fr. *Phalangium* + *-idea*] *syn of* PHALANGIDA

phal·an·gid·e·an \-dēən\ *n* -S [NL *Phalangidea* + E *-an*] **:** ²PHALANGID

pha·lan·gi·des \fə'lanjəˌdēz, fā'-\ [NL, fr. *Phalangium*] *syn of* PHALANGIDA

pha·lan·gi·form \-jəˌfȯrm\ *adj* [ISV *phalangi-* (fr. NL *phalang-, phalanx*) + *-iform*] **:** resembling a phalanx ⟨a ~ bone⟩

pha·lan·gi·gra·da \ˌ==='grādə\ [NL, fr. neut. pl. of *phalangigradus* phalangigrade] *syn of* TYLOPODA

pha·lan·gi·grade \fə'lanjəˌgrād, fā'-\ *adj* [NL *phalangigradus*, fr. *phalang-, phalanx* phalanx + *-gradus* -grade] **:** walking on the phalanges

pha·lan·gist \fə'lanjəst, fā'-\ *n* -S [by alter.] **:** FALANGIST

phal·an·gis·ta \ˌfalən'jistə\ [NL, fr. *phalang-, phalanx* + *-ista* -ist] *syn of* PHALANGER

phal·an·gis·ti·dae \-təˌdē\ [NL *Phalangista* + *-idae*] *syn of* PHALANGERIDAE

phal·an·gi·ta \-'jēd·ə\ [NL *Phalangium*] *syn of* PHALANGIDA

phal·an·gite \'falənˌjīt\ *n* -S [Gk *phalangitēs*, fr. *phalang-, phalanx* phalanx + *-itēs* -ite] **:** a soldier of a phalanx

pha·lan·gi·um \fə'lanjēəm, fā'-\ *n* [NL, fr. Gk *phalangion*, a spider, fr. *phalang-, phalanx* phalanx] **1** *pl* **phalan·gia** \-jēə\ *obs* **:** a venomous spider **2** *cap* **:** a genus (the type of the family Phalangiidae) of harvestmen

¹phal·an·ste·ri·an \ˌfalənˌstirēən\ *adj* [F *phalanstérien*, fr. *phalanstère* phalanstery + *-ien* -ian] **:** of or relating to a phalanstery, to phalansterianism, or to a system of phalansteries

²phalansterian \"\ *n* -S **1 :** a member of a phalanstery **2 :** one who favors the system of phalansteries proposed by Fourier **:** FOURIERIST

phal·an·ste·ri·an·ism \-ˌnizəm\ *n* -S **:** FOURIERISM

phal·an·stery \'falənˌsterē, -ri\ *n* -ES [F *phalanstère* dwelling of a Fourierite community, fr. *phalange* phalanx (fr. L *phalang-, phalanx*) + *monastère* monastery (fr. LL *monasterium*) — more at PHALANX, MONASTERY] **1 a :** an association or community organized on the plan of Fourier **b :** the dwelling or buildings of such an association — compare FOURIERISM **2 a :** a group or association of persons who live together more or less cooperatively **b :** the dwelling of such a group

¹pha·lanx \'fāˌlaŋks, 'fa,-, -aiŋks\ *n, pl* **phalanx·es** \-ksəz\ *or* **pha·lan·ges** \fə'lanˌjēz, fā'-\ *see numbered senses* [L *phalang-, phalanx* line of battle, fr. Gk, log, line of battle, bone of the finger or toe — more at BALK] **1 a :** a body of heavily armed infantry in ancient Greece formed in close deep ranks and files with joined shields and long lances ⟨the Macedonian ~, formed by Philip, was first 8 ranks, later from 12 to 16 ranks, deep⟩ **b :** any of various compact orders of battle like the Greek phalanx (as the parallelogrammatic one of the ancient Gauls and Germans); *broadly* **:** a body of troops in close array **2** [NL, fr. Gk] *pl phalanges* **:** one of the digital bones of the hand or foot beyond the metacarpus or metatarsus of a vertebrate that in man are three to each finger and toe with the exception of the thumb and great toe which have but two each, in many other vertebrates vary slightly in numbers, and are greatly increased in some aquatic forms with paddle-shaped limbs **3** *pl usu phalanxes* **a :** a group or body in close formation **:** a massed arrangement of persons, animals, or things ⟨a ~ of umbrellas —Betty W. Powers⟩ **b :** an organized or closely united body of persons (as for aggressive or defensive action) ⟨police locked and barred all but one door, and formed a solid ~ in front of it —Green Peyton⟩ ⟨a solid ~ of orthodoxy against which the revolutionaries shatter themselves —Sheldon Cheney⟩ **4 :** chess pawns of one player placed side by side **5 :** a rarely used taxonomic category to which various ranks have been assigned **6** [trans. of F *phalange*] **:** a Fourierist community **:** PHALANSTERY

²phalanx \"\ *vt* -ED/-ING/-ES **:** to form into a phalanx ⟨back of him the graduating class was ~*ed* —J.T.Farrell⟩ ⟨whose homes are in the ~*ed* apartment buildings and hotels nearby —*Amer. Guide Series: N.Y. City*⟩

phal·a·ris \'falərəs\ *n, cap* [NL, fr. L, canary-grass, fr. *phalaros* having a white spot; akin to Gk *phalios* having a white spot — more at BALD] **:** a genus of American and European grasses with broad leaves and a dense head or spike of flowers — see CANARY GRASS 1, RIBBON GRASS

phal·a·rope \-ˌrōp\ *n* -S [F, fr. NL *phalaropus*, fr. Gk *phalaris* coot (fr. *phalaros* having a white spot) + NL *-o-* + *-pus*] **:** a bird of the family Phalaropodidae — see NORTHERN PHALAROPE, RED PHALAROPE, WILSON'S PHALAROPE

phal·a·ro·pod·i·dae \ˌfalərō'pädəˌdē\ *n pl, cap* [NL, fr. *Phalaropod-, Phalaropus* type genus, fr. *phalaropus* phalarope] **:** a family of small shorebirds that resemble sandpipers but have lobate toes and are good swimmers, breed in the arctic, winter in the tropics, and often occur in large flocks far out at sea, and are distinguished by having the female perform the courtship and the dully colored male the incubation

phal·era \'falərə\ *n, pl* **phaler·ae** \-əˌrē, -ˌrī\ [L, fr. Gk *phalara*, pl.; akin to Gk *phalos* horn of a helmet and prob. to Skt *hvarate* he bends, *hruṇāti* he gets lost — more at FAIL] **:** a metal boss or disk (as of bronze or silver) worn in ancient times on the heads or breasts of horses or sometimes by men as signs of military rank; *also* **:** a cameo worn as an ornament

phal·gun \'pälˌgün, 'fä-\ *n, usu cap* [Skt *phālguna*] **:** PHAGUN

phall- *or* **phallo-** *comb form* [Gk *phallos* — more at BLOW] **:** penis ⟨*phall*algia⟩ ⟨*phallo*plasty⟩ ⟨*phallo*rrhagia⟩

phal·la·ce·ae \fə'lāsēˌē\ *n pl, cap* [NL, fr. *Phallus* type genus + *-aceae*] **:** a family of fungi (order Phallales) comprising the true stinkhorns and distinguished from Clathraceae by having the gleba external to the tubular receptacle — see PHALLUS — **phal·la·ceous** \-shəs\ *adj*

phal·la·les \fə'lā(ˌ)lēz\ *n pl, cap* [NL, fr. *Phallus* + *-ales*] **:** an order of fungi (subclass Homobasidiomycetes) comprising the stinkhorns and related forms whose hymenium is on an elongated or enlarged receptacle that is slimy and fetid at maturity — see CLATHRACEAE, PHALLACEAE

phal·lic \'falik, -lēk\ *adj* [Gk *phallikos*, fr. *phallos* phallus + *-ikos* -ic] **1 :** of or relating to phallicism ⟨~ cult⟩ ⟨~ fertility symbol⟩ **2 :** of, relating to, or being a phallus ⟨~ eroticism⟩ **3 :** resembling or symbolizing a phallus ⟨~ tree trunks⟩ **:** PHALLOID

phal·li·cism \-ləˌsizəm\ *n* -S [*phallic* + *-ism*] **:** the worship of or reverence for the generative principle in nature as symbolized esp. by the phallus

phal·lism \'faˌlizəm\ *n* -S [ISV *phall-* + *-ism*] **:** PHALLICISM

phal·lo·base \'faləˌbās\ *n* [*phall-* + *base*] **:** the proximal part of the phallic organ

¹phal·loid \'faˌlȯid\ *adj* [ISV *phall-* + *-oid*] **:** resembling a penis; *specif* **:** relating to or resembling fungi of the genus *Phallus* or the family Phallaceae

²phalloid \"\ *n* -S [NL *Phallus* + E *-oid*] **:** a fungus of the genus *Phallus* or the family Phallaceae

phal·loi·dine \fa'lȯidᵊn, 'faˌlȯiˌdīn\ *also* **phal·loi·din** \fa'lȯidᵊn\ *n* -S [NL *phalloides* (specific epithet of the death cup *Amanita phalloides*) (fr. *phall-* + *-oides* -oid) + E *-ine* or *-in*] **:** a very toxic crystalline peptide $C_{35}H_{46}N_8O_{10}S.H_2O$ obtained from the death cup mushroom

phal·lo·mere \'faləˌmi(ə)r\ *n* -S [*phall-* + *-mere*] **:** any of various lobes formed at the sides of the gonopore of many insects and commonly fusing to form the phallus

phal·lo·some \-ˌsōm\ *n* -S [*phall-* + *-some*] **:** a chitinized tube enclosing the penis of some mosquitoes and other insects

phal·lo·steth·i·dae \ˌfalō'stethəˌdē\ *n pl, cap* [NL, fr. *Phallostethus*, type genus (fr. *phall-* + Gk *stēthos* breast) + *-idae*] **:** a family of small freshwater and brackish-water fishes of southeastern Asia and the Philippines that are of very uncertain systematic position and are sometimes isolated in a suborder of Percomorphi and regarded as related to the Atherinidae or are made a separate order and held to have affinities chiefly with the Microcyprini

phal·lus \'faləs\ *n* [L, fr. Gk *phallos* penis, representation of the penis — more at BLOW] **1** *pl* **phal·li** \-aˌlī\ *or* **phalluses** **:** a symbol or representation of the male organ of generation — compare LINGAM, YONI **2** *pl* **phalli** *or* **phalluses** [NL, fr. Gk *phallos*] **a** (1) **:** a vertebrate intromittent organ **:** PENIS, CLITORIS (2) **:** an embryonic or primitive organ homologous with a penis or clitoris **b :** any of various structures of a male invertebrate that play a specific part in copulation; *esp* **:** a median intromittent organ of the ninth abdominal segment of a male insect **3** [NL, fr. Gk *phallos* penis] *cap* **:** a genus of fungi (family Phallaceae) with the pileus hanging free around the stem — see DICTYOPHORA, STINKHORN

phal·lu·sia \fə'l(y)üzh(ē)ə\ *n, cap* [NL, irreg. fr. Gk *phallos* + NL *-ia*] *in some classifications* **:** a genus of simple ascidians — see ASCIDIA

pha·nar·i·ot *or* **fa·nar·i·ot** \fə'na(a)rēət, -ēˌät\ *n* -S *usu cap* [NGk *phanariōtēs*, lit., inhabitant of the Fanar, fr. *Phanari* Fanar, chief Greek quarter in Constantinople under the Turks + Gk *-ōtēs* -ote] **:** one of the Greeks of Constantinople who became powerful in clerical and other offices under Turkish patronage

phanatron *var of* PHANOTRON

-phane \ˌfān\ *n comb form* -S [Gk *-phanēs* appearing, shining, fr. *phainein* to show — more at FANCY] **:** substance having a (specified) form, quality, or appearance ⟨cymo*phane*⟩ ⟨glauco*phane*⟩ ⟨hydro*phane*⟩

phaner- *or* **phanero-** *comb form* [Gk, fr. *phaneros*, fr. *phainein* to show] **:** visible **:** manifest **:** open ⟨*phanero*cryst⟩ ⟨*phanero*gam⟩

phan·er·ite \'fanəˌrīt\ *n* -S [ISV *phaner-* + *-ite*] **:** a rock having grains that are large enough to be seen with the unaided eye

phan·er·it·ic \ˌ=='ridik\ *adj* **:** of, relating to, or characteristic of phanerite

phan·er·o·car·pae \ˌfanərō'kärˌpē\ [NL, fr. *phaner-* + Gk *karpos* fruit — more at HARVEST] *syn of* ACRASPEDA

phan·er·o·ceph·a·la \-'sefələ\ *n pl, cap* [NL, fr. *phaner-* + *-cephala*] *in some classifications* **:** a division of Polychaeta distinguished by the well-developed prostomium corresponding to Errantia together with many Sedentaria — **phan·er·o·ceph·a·lous** \ˌ==='sefələs\ *adj*

phan·er·o·co·don·ic \ˌ==='kōˌdänik\ *adj* [*phaner-* + Gk *kōdōn* bell + E *-ic*] **:** developing an umbrella and becoming detached — used of the sexual zooids of hydroids; compare ADELOCODONIC

phan·er·o·cryst \'===ˌkrist\ *n* -S [*phaner-* + *crystal*] **:** a crystal visible megascopically

phan·er·o·crystalline \'===+\ *adj* [ISV *phaner-* + *crystalline*] **:** megascopically crystalline — compare CRYPTOCRYSTALLINE

phan·er·o·gam \'===ˌgam\ *n* -S [F *phanérogame*, fr. NL *Phanerogamia*] **:** a seed plant or flowering plant **:** SPERMATOPHYTE — compare CRYPTOGAM

phan·er·o·gam·ia \ˌ==='gamēə, -gām-\ *n, cap* [NL, fr. *phaner-* + *-gamia* (fr. Gk *-gamia* -gamy)] *in some esp former classifications* **:** a division of plants comprising all the seed plants — compare CRYPTOGAMIA — **phan·er·o·gam·i·an** \ˌ==='gamēən, -gām-\ *or* **phan·er·o·gam·ic** \-'gamik\ *or* **phan·er·og·a·mous** \ˌ=='rägəməs\ *adj* — **phan·er·og·a·my** \ˌ=='rägəmē\ *n* -ES

phan·er·o·gen·ic \ˌfanərō'jenik\ *also* **phan·er·o·genetic** \ˌ===+\ *adj* [*phanerogenic* fr. *phaner-* + *-genic; phanerogenetic* fr. *phaner-* + *genetic*] **:** of known origin — opposed to *cryptogenic*

phan·er·o·glos·sa \ˌ==='gläsə, -lȯsə\ *n pl, cap* [NL, fr. *phaner-* + *-glossa*] *in former classifications* **:** a division of Amphibia comprising frogs and toads with tongues and being equivalent to Lingusta and Costata of other classifications — **phan·er·o·glos·sal** \ˌ==='gläsəl, -lȯs-\ *adj* — **phan·er·o·glos·sate** \ˌ===—\ *adj or n*

phan·er·o·mania \ˌ===+\ *n* [NL, fr. *phaner-* + L *mania*] **:** a persistent or obsessive picking at some superficial body growth (as in habitual nail-biting)

phan·er·o·phyte \'===ˌfīt\ *n* -S [ISV *phaner-* + *-phyte*] **:** a perennial plant that bears its overwintering buds well above the surface of the ground — compare CHAMAEPHYTE, GEOPHYTE

phan·er·os·co·py \ˌfanə'räskəpē\ *n* -ES [*phaner-* + *-scopy*] **:** the formal analysis of appearances apart from the questions of to whom they appear and of their material content that discovers broad classes of appearances, describes their features, proves that a short list of classes is exhaustive, and enumerates the principal subdivisions of the categories

phan·er·o·sis \ˌfanə'rōsəs\ *n, pl* **phanero·ses** \-ōˌsēz\ [NL, fr. *phaner-* + *-osis*] **:** the attaining of visibility — used chiefly of intercellular lipoids that become visible fatty droplets as the cells degenerate

phan·er·o·zo·ic \ˌfanərō'zōik\ *adj* [*phaner-* + *-zoic*] **1 :** living unconcealed esp. in daylight — compare CRYPTOBIOTIC **2 :** PHANEROZOITIC **3** *of a geologic eon* **:** of or relating to the Paleozoic, Mesozoic, and Cenozoic eras taken together — compare CRYPTOZOIC 2

phan·er·o·zo·ite \ˌ==='zōˌīt\ *n* -S [*phaner-* + *-zoite* (as in *sporozoite*)] **:** an exoerythrocytic malaria parasite found late in the course of an infection

phan·er·o·zo·it·ic \ˌ===zō'id·ik\ *adj* **:** of, relating to, or being a phanerozoite ⟨~ stage⟩

phan·er·o·zo·nate \ˌ==='zōˌnāt\ *adj* [NL *Phanerozonia* + E *-ate*] **:** of or relating to the Phanerozonia

phan·er·o·zo·nia \ˌ==='zōnēə\ *n pl, cap* [NL, fr. *phaner-* + Gk *zōnē* girdle + NL *-ia* — more at ZONE] **:** an order of starfishes bordered by large marginal plates

phano \'fa(ˌ)nō\ *n* -S [alter. of *fanon*] **:** FANON

phan·o·tron *also* **phan·a·tron** \'fanəˌträn\ *n* -S [perh. fr. Gk *phano-* showing (fr. *phainein* to show) + E *-tron* — more at FANCY] **:** a low-pressure diode filled with mercury vapor or an inert gas and used as a rectifier for radio transmitters and industrial direct current power

phan·si·gar \'pän(t)sēˌgär, 'fä-\ *n* -S [Hindi *phãsīgār*, fr. *phãsī* snare, noose + Per *-gār* doer, doing] **:** an East Indian robber and assassin **:** THUG

phan·ta·si·ast \fan'tāzēˌast, -ˌəst\ *n* -S *usu cap* [LGk *phantasiastēs*, fr. Gk *phantasia* appearance, image, imagination + *-astēs* -ast; fr. the belief that Christ's body was only a phantom — more at FANCY] **:** JULIANIST — **phan·ta·si·as·tic** \ˌ=;==ˌastik\ *adj, usu cap*

phan·tasm *or* **fan·tasm** \'fanˌtazəm\ *n* -S [ME *fantasme*, fr. OF, fr. L *phantasma*, fr. Gk, fr. *phantazein* to present to the mind — more at FANCY] **1 :** a product of phantasy: as **a :** delusive appearance **:** ILLUSION, DECEPTION ⟨a fleeting ~, born and gone, intangible as a flash of lightning —Heinrich Zimmer⟩ **b :** GHOST, SPECTER, SPIRIT ⟨~*s* of the dark⟩ **c :** a figment of the imagination, fancy, or disordered mind **:** an imaginative conception **:** FANTASY, DREAM, DELUSION ⟨twilight ~*s*, and deep noonday thought —P.B.Shelley⟩ ⟨husband who is "an utter coward" about the ~*s* of his own imagination —Scott Fitzgerald⟩ ⟨now first the cloud of ~*s* cleared away: he beheld his real life —George Meredith⟩ **2 :** a mental image or representation of a real object **:** a sensuous idea or impression — compare SPECIES 2b ⟨all of the sensible qualities are but ~*s* of the observer, not properties of the object —Douglas Bush⟩ **3 a** *obs* **:** one that counterfeits the real or true **b :** a deceptive or illusory appearance of a thing **:** SHADOW, ADUMBRATION ⟨follow ~*s* of truth⟩ ⟨grasping at every ~ of hope⟩ **4 :** an apparition of a living or dead person in a place where his body is known not to be **syn** see FANCY

phan·tas·ma \fan'tazmə\ *n, pl* **phantas·mas** \-məz\ *or* **phantas·ma·ta** \-məd·ə\ [L] **:** PHANTASM 1 ⟨the ice runs surrealistically riot in a ~ of frozen sculpture —Glen Jacobsen⟩

phan·tas·ma·go·ria \(ˌ)=ˌ=mə'gōrēə, -gȯr-\ *also* **phan·tas·ma·go·ry** \=ˈ==ˌgōrē, -gȯr-, -ri\ *n, pl* **phantasmagorias** *also* **phantasmagories** [modif. of F *phantasmagorie* production of images appearing to be phantoms, fr. *phantasme* phantasm (fr. L *phantasma*) + *-agorie* (prob. fr. Gk *ageirein* to assemble, collect) — more at GREGARIOUS] **1 a** (1) **:** an optical effect by which figures on a screen appear to dwindle into the distance or to rush toward the observer with enormous increase of size (2) **:** any of various similar optical effects **b :** an apparatus for producing the effect of phantasmagoria consisting of a magic lantern arranged to be moved toward and from a screen and having an automatic device for keeping the correct focus **2 a :** a constantly shifting, complex succession of things seen or imagined (as in a dream or fever state) ⟨a simple view of the ~ of life —C.E.Norton⟩ ⟨supernatural visions which reveal past, present, and future under the guise of a ~ of symbolic persons and animals, divine and diabolical beings, celestial and infernal phenomena —Edmund Wilson⟩ **b :** a scene that constantly changes or fluctuates ⟨lowlands under the hills became an undulating ~ as mirages flickered endlessly —Farley Mowat⟩ ⟨streets were a nightmarish *phantasmagory* —Van Wyck Brooks⟩

phan·tas·ma·gor·ic \=ˌ=='gȯrik, -gär-\ *also* **phan·tas·ma·gor·i·cal** \-rəkəl\ *adj* **:** of, relating to, or like a phantasmagoria ⟨the ~ armorial trophies which rattled as I strode —E.A. Poe⟩ ⟨a great concourse of ~ shadows —J.C.Powys⟩

phan·tas·mal \(')fan'tazməl\ *adj* **:** of, relating to, or like a phantasm **:** transitory as a phantasm **:** ILLUSIVE, SPECTRAL, UNREAL ⟨his fear of the last few hours looked thin and ~ in the presence of so much light —Walter Gilkyson⟩ ⟨coastline of frozen ~ peaks —Marguerite Young⟩ ⟨the moon's ~ fire —Walter de la Mare⟩ — **phan·tas·mal·i·ty** \ˌ=ˌ='maləd·ē, -ətē, -i\ *n* -ES — **phan·tas·mal·ly** \(')=;=məlē, -li\ *adv*

phan·tas·mic \(')=;=mik, -mēk\ *adj* **:** PHANTASMAL ⟨seemed, for all his bulk, ~ —D.C.Loughlin⟩ ⟨farewell, your lost ~ truth —John Erskine †1951⟩

phantasy *var of* FANTASY **syn** see FANCY

¹phan·tom *also* **fan·tom** \'fantəm, 'faan-\ *n* -S [ME *fantosme, fantome, fantom* fr. MF *fantosme*, fr. L *phantasma* — more at PHANTASM] **1** *obs* **:** mere appearance or seeming **:** ILLUSION **2 a :** something (as a specter or an optical illusion) that is apparent to the sight or other sense but has no actual or substantial existence **:** APPARITION, FIGMENT ⟨is not all that I see a lie — a deceitful ~ —George Borrow⟩ **b :** something elusive or visionary **:** WILL-O'-THE-WISP ⟨the glittering ~*s* of wealth and fashion, the whole pageantry of the metropolis, were dissolved by the suicide —M.D.Geismar⟩ **c :** an object of continual dread or abhorrence **:** BOGEY, BUGBEAR ⟨the ~ of a Holy War has been exorcised —A.L.Guérard⟩ ⟨the ~*s* of disease and want⟩ **3 :** one that is something in appearance but not in reality **:** a mere show **:** SHADOW ⟨only a ~ of a king⟩ ⟨maintain but the ~ of authority⟩ **4 :** a representation or shadowing forth of something abstract, ideal, or incorporeal ⟨she was a ~ of delight —William Wordsworth⟩ **5 a :** a manikin or a model of the body or one of its parts **b :** a body of material resembling a body part in mass, composition, and dimensions and used to measure absorption of radiations **6 :** PHANTOM CIRCUIT **7 :** GHOST 14 **8 :** a halftone or drawing having certain details shown as though transparent or translucent so as to indicate various esp. internal parts of a machine in their working position

²phantom \"\ *adj* [ME *fantom*, fr. *fantom*, n.] **1 :** being a phantom **:** of the nature of or suggesting a phantom ⟨headless blacksmiths, ~ black dogs, haunted houses —*Amer. Guide Series: Md.*⟩ ⟨a ~ ship⟩: **a :** ILLUSORY ⟨~ pain⟩ ⟨~ pregnancy⟩ ⟨amputee's illusion of a ~ organ —*Psychological Abstracts*⟩ ⟨conjuring up ~ dangers of feudal aristocracy —V.L.Parrington⟩ — compare PHANTOM LIMB **b :** operating or placed so as to seem or to be invisible **:** UNEMBODIED, ELUSIVE ⟨proved again that they are a ~ army —W.O.Douglas⟩ ⟨his ~ crew miles away on the ground —*Time*⟩ ⟨~ voices⟩ **c :** FICTITIOUS, DUMMY ⟨~ voters⟩ ⟨a ~ regime⟩ **2 :** of or relating to a phantom circuit ⟨~ wire⟩ **3 :** showing certain details as though transparent or translucent so as to indicate various esp. internal parts of a machine in their working position ⟨~ drawing⟩ ⟨~ halftone⟩ ⟨~ view⟩ — compare EXPLODED

phantom circuit *n* **:** the equivalent of an additional circuit or wire that in reality does not exist obtained by certain arrangements of real circuits (as in some telephone and multiplex telegraph systems)

phantom crane fly *n* **:** a fly of the family Ptychopteridae

phantom freight *n* **:** a transportation charge included in the delivered price of a commodity (as an automobile) that is in excess of the charge for service actually performed

phan·tom·ist \-məst\ *n* -S *usu cap* [*phantom* + *-ist*] **:** JULIANIST

phantom larva *n* **:** the colorless transparent aquatic larva of any of the small flies of the family Chaoboridae

phantomlike \'==ˌ=\ *adv* (*or adj*) **:** like a phantom (as in appearance or elusiveness) ⟨swans which glided ~ across the pond —*Current History*⟩ ⟨escaped ~ from jail —*Springfield (Mass.) Daily News*⟩

phantom limb *n* **:** an often painful sensation of the presence of a limb that has been amputated

phantom orchid *or* **phantom orchis** *n* **:** a saprophytic white orchid (*Cephalanthera austinae*) of the western U.S.

phantom tumor *n* **:** a swelling (as of the abdomen) suggesting a tumor and occurring in hysterical persons

phan·to·scope \'fantəˌskōp\ *n* [Gk *phantos* visible (fr. *phainein* to show) + E *-scope* — more at FANCY] **:** a kaleidoscope into which small objects may be introduced to vary the design

-pha·ny \fənē, -ni\ *n comb form* -ES [LGk *-phania, -phaneia*, fr. Gk *phainein* to show — more at FANCY] **:** appearance **:** manifestation ⟨pneumato*phany*⟩ ⟨Satano*phany*⟩

phar *abbr* **1** pharmaceutical; pharmacist; pharmacy **2** pharmacopoeia

phar·aoh \'fe(ə)(ˌ)rō, 'fa(a)(ˌ), 'fā\ *sometimes* |ˌrēˌō\ *n* -S *often cap* [LL *Pharaon-, Pharao*, fr. Gk *Pharaō*, fr. Heb *par'ōh*, fr. Egypt *pr-'ꜣ*] **1 a :** a ruler of ancient Egypt **b :** TYRANT ⟨they tell me he's a regular *Pharaoh* —John Cheever⟩ ⟨that tough old *Pharaoh* of a captain —*Theatre Arts*⟩ **2** [trans. of F *pharaon* or It *faraone*] *archaic* **:** FARO

pharaoh ant *or* **pharaoh's ant** *n, often cap P* **:** a little red ant (*Monomorium pharaonis*) that is a common household pest

pharaoh's chicken *or* **pharaoh's hen** *n, usu cap P* **:** EGYPTIAN VULTURE

pharaoh's fig *n, usu cap P* **:** SYCAMORE 1

pharaoh's mouse *or* **pharaoh's rat** *n, usu cap P* **:** the common ichneumon of Egypt and adjacent regions

pharaoh's serpent *or* **pharaoh's serpents** *or* **pharaoh's serpents' eggs** *n, usu cap P* **:** a firework consisting of pelleted mercury thiocyanate that on burning expands greatly to yield a porous serpentine ash

phar·a·on·ic \¦ferā¦änik, ¦fa(a)r-, ¦fār-, -rē¦-\ *adj, usu cap* [F *pharaonique*, fr. *pharaon* pharaoh, fr. LL *Pharaon-, Pharao*] **:** of, relating to, or characteristic of a pharaoh or the pharaohs

phare \'fa(a)(ə)r, 'fe(ə)r\ *n* -S [F, fr. L *pharus*, fr. Gk *pharos* — more at PHAROS] **:** PHAROS ⟨afternoons I walk to the ~ —Archibald MacLeish⟩ ⟨a lightship, or some ~ —William Beebe⟩

pha·re·o·dus \fə'rēədəs\ *n, cap* [NL, prob. fr. Gk *phare-, pharos* cloth, mantle + NL *-odus* — more at BRAT] **:** a genus of fossil fishes (family Osteoglossidae) widely distributed in Eocene formations

¹**phar·e·trone** \'farə‚trōn\ *adj* [NL *Pharetrones*] **:** of or relating to the Pharetrones

²**pharetrone** \"\ *n* -S **:** a sponge of the group Pharetrones

phar·e·tro·nes \‚==-'trō(‚)nēz\ *n pl, cap* [NL, fr. L *pharetra* quiver, fr. Gk, fr. *pherein* to bear + *-tra*, suffix denoting instrument — more at BEAR] **:** a group of sponges (class Calcispongiae) that are thick-walled and have the spicules united in a rigid network — **phar·e·tro·nid** \¦==¦=nəd\ *adj*

¹**phar·i·an** \'fa(a)rēən\ *adj, usu cap* [L *pharius* (fr. Gk *pharios*, fr. *Pharos* Egyptian island) + E *-an*] **1 :** of or relating to the peninsula or ancient island of Pharos **2** *archaic* **:** EGYPTIAN 1

²**pharian** \"\ *n* -S *cap, archaic* **:** EGYPTIAN 1

phar·i·sa·ic \¦farə¦sāik, -āēk *also* ¦fer-\ *adj* [LL *pharisaicus*, fr. LGk *pharisaikos*, fr. Gk *pharisaios* Pharisee + *-ikos* -ic] **1** *usu cap* **:** of or relating to the Pharisees **2** *sometimes cap* **:** PHARISAICAL ⟨the ~ voice of a society wholly absorbed in barricading itself against the unpleasant —Edith Wharton⟩

phar·i·sa·i·cal \-āəkəl, -ēk-\ *adj, sometimes cap* [LL *pharisaicus* + E *-al*] **:** resembling the Pharisees esp. in strictness of doctrine and in rigid observance of forms and ceremonies **:** making an outward show of piety and morality but lacking the inward spirit **:** censorious of others' morals or practices **:** FORMAL, SANCTIMONIOUS, SELF-RIGHTEOUS, HYPOCRITICAL ⟨censure of any sort is apt to sound ~, I suppose —P.A.Hope-Wallace⟩ ⟨in this process of reeducation we should be ~ if we did not include ourselves —Llewellyn Woodward⟩ — **phar·i·sa·i·cal·ly** \-ək(ə)lē, -ēk-, -li\ *adv* — **phar·i·sa·i·cal·ness** \-əkəlnəs, -ēk-\ *n* -ES

phar·i·sa·ism \'==‚sā‚izəm\ *n* -S [NL *pharisaismus*, fr. Gk *pharisaios* Pharisee + L *-ismus* -ism] **1** *usu cap* **:** the doctrines or practices of the Pharisees ⟨the path of withdrawal, separation, and dedication, which is the path of *Pharasaism* —Maurice Samuel⟩ **2** *often cap* **:** pharisaical character, spirit, or attitude **:** SELF-RIGHTEOUSNESS, SANCTIMONIOUSNESS, HYPOCRISY ⟨~, stupidity, and despotism reign not in merchants' houses and prisons alone —J.T.Farrell⟩

phar·i·se·an \¦==¦sēən\ *adj, usu cap* [LL *pharisaeus* Pharisee + E *-an*] **:** PHARISAIC 1

phar·i·see \'farə‚sē *also* 'fer- *or* -‚sē *or* -si\ *n* -S [ME *pharise*, fr. OE *farise*, fr. LL *pharisaeus*, fr. Gk *pharisaios*, fr. Aram *pĕrīshayyā*, pl. of *pĕrīshā*, lit., separated; akin to Heb *pārūsh* separated, distinct] **1** *usu cap* **:** a member of a school or party among the ancient Jews who were noted for strict and formal observance of rites and ceremonies of the written law and for insistence on the validity of the traditions of the elders, who differed from the Sadducees in traditionalism and in their teachings concerning the immortality of the soul, the resurrection of the body, future retribution, and a coming Messiah, and whose interpretation provided the standard of observance and belief for the great majority of Jews from the 1st century A.D. **2** *often cap* **:** a pharisaical person

phar·i·see·ism \'==(‚)=‚izəm\ *n* -S *usu cap* [*pharisee* + *-ism*] **:** PHARISAISM

phar·ma·cal \'färməkəl, 'fām-, -mēk-\ *adj* [Gk *pharmakon* drug + E *-al* — more at PHARMACY] **:** PHARMACEUTICAL

phar·ma·ceu·tic \¦=mə¦süd·ik, -üt¦, ¦ēk\ *adj or n* [LL *pharmaceuticus*, fr. Gk *pharmakeutikos*, fr. (assumed) *pharmakeutos* (verbal of *pharmakeuein* to administer drugs, fr. *pharmakon* drug) + *-ikos* -ic] **:** PHARMACEUTICAL

¹**phar·ma·ceu·ti·cal** \¦əkəl, ¦ēk-\ *adj* [LL *pharmaceuticus* + E *-al*] **:** of or relating to pharmacy or pharmacists — **phar·ma·ceu·ti·cal·ly** \-ək(ə)lē, -ēk-, -li\ *adv*

²**pharmaceutical** \"\ *n* -S **:** a pharmaceutical preparation **:** medicinal drug

pharmaceutical chemist *n* **1** *Brit* **:** DRUGGIST **2 :** one engaged in research in medicinal chemistry or in the production thereof

phar·ma·ceu·tics \‚==-'süd·iks, -ütiks, -ēks\ *n pl but sing in constr* [*pharmaceutic* + *-s*] **:** the science of preparing, using, or dispensing medicines **:** PHARMACY

phar·ma·ceu·tist \‚==-'süd·əst, -ütə-\ *n* -S [*pharmaceutic* + *-ist*] **:** PHARMACIST

pharmacies *pl of* PHARMACY

phar·ma·cist \'färməsəst, 'fām-\ *n* -S [*pharmacy* + *-ist*] **:** one skilled in pharmacy **:** one engaged in the practice of pharmacy — compare APOTHECARY, DRUGGIST

phar·ma·co- *in pronunciations below*, ¦====¦färmə(‚)kō *or* 'fāmə(‚)kō *or* -‚kə\ *comb form* [Gk *pharmako-*, fr. *pharmakon* — more at PHARMACY] **:** medicine **:** drug ⟨*pharmaco*mania⟩ ⟨*pharmaco*phobia⟩ ⟨*pharmaco*therapy⟩

phar·ma·co·dynamic \¦===+\ *adj* [*pharmacodynamics*] **:** of, relating to, or used in pharmacodynamics ⟨responses of the autonomic nervous system to various ~ substances —*Psychosomatic Medicine*⟩ — **phar·ma·co·dynamically** \"+\ *adv*

phar·ma·co·dynamics \"+\ *n pl but sing in constr* [*pharmaco-* + Gk *dynamis* power (fr. *dynasthai* to be able) + E *-ics*] **:** a branch of pharmacology dealing with the reactions between drugs and living structures; *specif* **:** the experimental study of the action and fate of drugs in the animal organism ⟨the ~ of magnesium sulfate⟩ ⟨the ~ of streptomycin in man⟩

phar·ma·cog·no·sist \‚färmə'kägnəsəst, ‚fām-\ *n* -S [*pharmacognosy* + *-ist*] **:** a specialist in pharmacognosy

phar·ma·cog·nos·tic \¦==(‚)käg¦nästik, -tēk\ *adj* [ISV *pharmaco-* + *-gnostic*] **:** of or relating to pharmacognosy

phar·ma·cog·no·sy \‚=='kägnəsē, -si\ *also* **phar·ma·cog·no·sia** \-‚käg'nōzh(ē)ə\ *n, pl* **pharmacognosies** *also* **pharmacognosias** [*pharmacognosy*, ISV *pharmaco-* + *-gnosy; pharmacognosia*, NL, fr. *pharmaco-* + *-gnosia*] **:** a science dealing with the composition, production, use, and history of drugs of plant and animal origin — compare PHARMACOLOGY

phar·mac·o·lite \fär'makə‚līt, fā'm-; '=‚makə-\ *n* -S [G *pharmakolith*, fr. *pharmako-* pharmaco- + *lith* -lite] **:** a monoclinic mineral $CaH(AsO_4).2H_2O$ that is a hydrous acid calcium arsenate occurring in silky fibers of a white or grayish color (hardness 2–2.5, sp. gr. 2.64–2.73)

phar·ma·co·logical \¦=== *at* PHARMACO- +\ *or* **phar·ma·co·logic** \"+\ *adj* **:** of, relating to, or determined by pharmacology ⟨~ action⟩ ⟨~ methods⟩ — **phar·ma·co·logically** \"+\ *adv*

phar·ma·col·o·gist \‚färmə'käləjəst, ‚fām-\ *n* -S **:** a specialist in pharmacology

phar·ma·col·o·gy \-jē, -ji\ *also* **phar·ma·co·logia** \‚=== *at* PHARMACO- + -lōj(ē)ə\ *n, pl* **pharmacologies** *also* **pharmacologias** [*pharmacology* fr. *pharmaco-* + *-logy; pharmacologia* NL, fr. *pharmaco-* + *-logia*] **1 :** the science of drugs including materia medica, toxicology, and therapeutics; *specif* **:** PHARMACODYNAMICS **2 :** the materials of the science of pharmacology **:** the properties and reactions of drugs esp. with relation to their therapeutic value

phar·ma·con \'färmə‚kän, 'fām-\ *n* -S [NL, fr. Gk — more at PHARMACY] **:** MEDICINE, DRUG, POISON

pharmaco-oryctology \¦=== *at* PHARMACO- +\ *n* [*pharmaco-* + *oryctology*] **:** the science of mineral drugs

phar·ma·co·pe·dia \‚färməkə'pēdēə, ‚fām-\ *n* -S [NL, fr. *pharmaco-* + Gk *paideia* education — more at ENCYCLOPEDIA] **:** information concerning drugs and medicinal preparations

phar·ma·co·pe·dic \¦===¦pēdik, -dēk\ *adj* **:** of or relating to pharmacopedia or to pharmacopedics

phar·ma·co·pe·dics \‚===¦=diks, -dēks\ *n pl but sing in constr* [NL *pharmacopedia* + E *-ics*] **:** the scientific study of drugs and medicinal preparations

phar·ma·co·poe·ia *also* **phar·ma·co·peia** \-'pē(y)ə\ *n* -S [NL, fr. LGk *pharmakopoiia* preparation of drugs, fr. Gk *pharmakopoios* preparing drugs (fr. *pharmako-* pharmaco- + *-poios* making, fr. *poiein* to make) + *-ia* -y — more at POET] **1 :** a book containing a selected list of drugs, chemicals, and medicinal preparations with descriptions of them, tests for their identity, purity, and strength, and formulas for making the preparations; *esp* **:** one issued by official authority and recognized as a standard **2 :** a collection or stock of drugs

phar·ma·co·poe·ial \¦===¦pē(y)əl\ *adj* **:** of or relating to a pharmacopoeia **:** according to the pharmacopoeia

phar·ma·co·poe·ist \‚==='pēəst\ *n* -S **:** a compiler of a pharmacopoeia

phar·ma·cop·o·list \‚färmə'käpələst, ‚fām-\ *n* -S [L *pharmacopola* seller of drugs (fr. Gk *pharmakopōlēs*, fr. *pharmako-* pharmaco- + *-polēs* seller, fr. *pōlein* to sell) + E *-ist* — more at MONOPOLY] *archaic* **:** one who sells drugs **:** APOTHECARY

phar·ma·co·siderite \¦=== *at* PHARMACO- +\ *n* [G *pharmakosiderit*, fr. *pharmako-* + *siderit* siderite] **:** a mineral $Fe_3(AsO_4)_2(OH)_3.5H_2O$ consisting of a hydrous basic iron arsenate commonly occurring in green or yellowish green cubic crystals (hardness 2.5, sp. gr. 2.9–3)

phar·ma·co·therapeutic \"+\ *or* **phar·ma·co·therapeutical** \"+\ *adj* [*pharmaco-* + *therapeutic*] **:** relating to the use or value of drugs in the treatment of disease

phar·ma·co·therapeutics \"+\ *n pl but sing or pl in constr* [*pharmaco-* + *therapeutics*] **:** the therapeutic aspect of pharmacology

phar·ma·co·therapy \"+\ *n* [ISV *pharmaco-* + *therapy*] **:** the treatment of disease with drugs

phar·ma·cy \'färməsē, 'fām-, -si\ *n* -ES [ME *fermacie*, fr. MF *farmacie*, fr. LL *pharmacia*, fr. Gk *pharmakeia*, fr. *pharmakon* drug, medicine, poison, magic potion, charm; akin to Lith *burti* to practice divination or magic] **1 :** the administering of drugs **:** treatment by drugs **2 :** the art or practice of preparing, preserving, compounding, and dispensing drugs, of discovering new drugs through research, and of synthesizing organic compounds of therapeutic value **3 :** a place where medicines are compounded or dispensed ⟨a hospital ~⟩; *broadly* **:** DRUGSTORE 1 — compare DISPENSARY **4 :** PHARMACOPOEIA 2 ⟨never traveled without a complete family ~ —Edith Wharton⟩

phar·ma·kos \'färmə‚käs\ *n, pl* **pharma·koi** \-‚kȯi\ [Gk, prob. irreg. fr. *pharmakon* medicine, charm + *-ikos* -ic] **:** a person often already condemned to death sacrificed in ancient Greece as a means of purification or atonement for a city or community

phar·mic \'färmik, 'fām-, -mēk\ *adj* [*pharmacy* + *-ic*] **:** relating to drugs or pharmacy

pharo fig \'fa(a)(‚)rō, 'fe, fā-\ *n, usu cap P* [alter. of *pharaoh's fig*] **:** SYCAMORE 1

phar·o·mach·rus \‚farə'makrəs\ *n, cap* [NL, fr. Gk *pharos* cloth, mantle + *makros* long — more at BRAT, MEAGER] **:** a genus of trogons consisting of the quetzal and related birds

pha·ros \'fa‚räs, 'fa(a)r-\ *n* -ES [Gk, fr. *Pharos*, island in the bay of Alexandria, Egypt, famous for its lighthouse] **1 :** a lighthouse or beacon to guide seamen **2 a :** a conspicuous light; *specif* **:** a ship's lantern **b :** CANDELABRUM

pharyng- *or* **pharyngo-** *comb form* [Gk, fr. *pharyng-, pharynx*] **1 :** pharynx ⟨*pharyng*algia⟩ ⟨*pharyng*itis⟩ **2 :** pharyngeal and ⟨*pharyngo*nasal⟩

pha·ryn·gal \fə'riŋgəl\ *adj or n* [NL *pharyng-, pharynx* + E *-al*] **:** PHARYNGEAL

¹**pha·ryn·ge·al** \fə'rinj(ē)əl, ¦farən¦jēəl\ *adj* [NL *pharyngeus* pharyngeal (fr. *pharyng-, pharynx* pharynx) + E *-al*] **1 :** relating to or found in the region of the pharynx **2** *of a sound* **:** formed with the base of the tongue near the back of the pharynx and with the pharynx walls strongly constricted

²**pharyngeal** \"\ *n* -S **1 :** a pharyngeal part (as a bone) **2 :** a pharyngeal sound

pharyngeal aponeurosis *n* **:** the middle or fibrous coat of the walls of the pharynx

pharyngeal arch *n* **:** BRANCHIAL ARCH

pharyngeal basket *n* **:** a circle of trichites that reinforces and stiffens the gullet of various predaceous ciliates

pharyngeal bone *n* **:** one of the bones of the pharynx of a fish — compare HYPOPHARYNGEAL, PHARYNGOBRANCHIAL

pharyngeal bursa *n* **:** a crypt in the pharyngeal tonsil thought to represent the communication that exists during fetal life between the pharynx and the hypophysis

pharyngeal cleft *or* **pharyngeal slit** *n* **:** VISCERAL CLEFT

pharyngeal gland *n* **:** a gland in the pharynx of an insect; *esp* **:** one of those that produce royal jelly in the honeybee

pha·ryn·ge·al·iza·tion \fə‚rinj(ē)ələ'zāshən, ‚farən‚jēə-‚-‚lī'z-\ *also* **pha·ryn·gal·iza·tion** \fə‚riŋgələ'zāshən, -‚lī'z-\ *n* -S **:** the action of pharyngealizing or the state of being pharyngealized

pha·ryn·ge·al·ize \fə'rinj(ē)ə‚līz, ‚farən'jēə-\ *also* **pha·ryn·gal·ize** \fə'riŋgə‚līz\ *vb* -ED/-ING/-S [¹*pharyngeal, pharyngal* + *-ize*] *vt* **:** to produce (a sound) by strong constriction of the pharynx ~ *vi* **:** to acquire or to be regularly accompanied by strong constriction of the pharynx

pharyngeal membrane *n* **:** STOMODAEUM

pharyngeal plexus *n* **1 :** a plexus formed by branches of the glossopharyngeal, vagus, and sympathetic nerves supplying the muscles and mucous membrane of the pharynx and adjoining parts **2 :** either of a pair of small venous plexuses at the side of and behind the pharynx

pharyngeal pouch *n* **:** any of a series of outpocketings of ectoderm on either side of the pharynx that meet the corresponding visceral furrows and give rise to the visceral clefts of the vertebrate embryo

pharyngeal tonsil *n* **:** a mass of lymphoid tissue at the back of the pharynx between the eustachian tubes that is usu. best developed in young children, is commonly atrophied in the adult, and is markedly subject to hypertrophy and adenoid formation esp. in children

pharyngeal tooth *n* **:** one of the teeth developed on the pharyngeal bones and esp. on the hypopharyngeals in many fishes

pharynges *pl of* PHARYNX

phar·yn·gis·mus \‚farən'jizməs\ *n, pl* **pharyngis·mi** \-‚mī\ [NL, fr. *pharyng-* + L *-ismus* -ism] **:** spasm of the pharynx

phar·yn·gi·tis \‚farən'jīd·əs, -ītəs *also* ‚fer-\ *n, pl* **pharyn·git·i·des** \-'jid·ə‚dēz, -jitə-\ [NL, fr. *pharyng-* + *-itis*] **:** inflammation of the pharynx

pha·ryn·gob·del·lae \fə‚riŋ'gäb'de(‚)lē\ [NL, fr. *pharyng-* + *-bdellae* (fr. Gk *bdella* leech)] *syn of* PHARYNGOBDELLIDA

phar·yn·gob·del·li·da \-'deləd·ə\ *n pl, cap* [NL, fr. *pharyng-* + *bdell-* + *-ida*] **:** an order or other division of Hirudinea sometimes regarded as a subdivision of Gnathobdellida and comprising leeches lacking both proboscis and jaws

¹**pha·ryn·go·branchial** \fə¦riŋ(‚)gō+\ *adj* [NL, fr. *pharyng-* + *-branchii* (fr. L *branchia* gill) — more at BRANCHIA] **:** of or relating to the pharynx and the gills; *specif* **:** of, relating to, or constituting the dorsal bony elements in the branchial arches of fishes that in teleosts form four pairs two or more of which may be provided with teeth opposed to those of the hypopharyngeals

²**pharyngobranchial** \"\ *n* -S **:** a pharyngobranchial element; *esp* **:** one of the pharyngobranchial bones of a teleost fish — called also *superior pharyngeal, upper pharyngeal*

pha·ryn·go·branchii \¦=¦=(‚)=+\ [NL, fr. *pharyng-* + *branchia*] *syn of* LEPTOCARDII

pha·ryn·go·glos·sus \=¦=¦(‚)='gläsəs, -lȯs-\ *n, pl* **pharyngo·glos·si** \-‚sī\ [NL, fr. *pharyng-* + *-glossus* (fr. Gk *glōssa* tongue) — more at GLOSS] **:** a part of the superior constrictor muscle of the pharynx inserting in the base of the tongue

¹**pha·ryn·gog·nath** \fə'riŋgəg‚nath\ *adj* [NL *Pharyngognathi*] **:** of or relating to the Pharyngognathi

²**pharyngognath** \"\ *n* -S **:** a fish of the order Pharyngognathi

phar·yn·gog·na·thi \‚farən'gägnə‚thī\ *n pl, cap* [NL, fr. *pharyng-* + *-gnathi* (fr. Gk *gnathos* jaw) — more at -GNATHOUS] *in some classifications* **:** an order or other division of teleost fishes comprising forms (as scaroid and labroid fishes and formerly cichlid and embiotocid fishes) in which the lower pharyngeal bones are united and which are now usu. placed in Percoidea — **phar·yn·gog·na·thous** \¦==¦=nəthəs\ *adj*

pha·ryn·go·log·i·cal \fə¦riŋgə¦läjəkəl\ *adj* **:** of or relating to pharyngology

phar·yn·gol·o·gy \‚farən'gäləjē, -ji *also* ‚fer-\ *n* -ES [*pharyng-* + *-logy*] **:** a branch of medical science treating of the pharynx and its diseases

pha·ryn·go·palatine arch \fə¦rin(‚)gō + -\ *n* [NL *pharyngopalatinus*] **:** either of the posterior pillars of the fauces; *also* **:** the arch formed by both

pha·ryn·go·pal·a·ti·nus \fə‚riŋgō‚palə'tīnəs\ *n, pl* **pharyngopalati·ni** \-ī‚nī\ [NL, fr. *pharyng-* + *palatinus* palatine] **:** one of the longitudinal muscles of the pharynx arising from the soft palate and inserting into the thyroid cartilage

pha·ryn·go·scope \fə'riŋgə‚skōp\ *n* [F, fr. *pharyng-* + *-scope*] **:** an instrument for inspecting the pharynx

phar·ynx \'fariŋ(k)s, -rēŋ- *also* 'fer-, *substand* 'färniks *or* 'fān- *or* -nēks\ *n, pl* **pha·ryn·ges** \fə'rin(‚)jēz\ *also* **pharynxes** [NL *pharyng-, pharynx*, fr. Gk, throat, pharynx; akin to ON *barki* throat, windpipe, L *frumen* larynx, throat, Gk *pharanx* gully, chasm, L *forare* to bore — more at BORE] **1 a :** the part of the alimentary canal between the cavity of the mouth and the esophagus that is in man a conical musculomembranous tube about four and a half inches long, continuous above with the mouth and nasal passages, communicating through the eustachian tubes with the ears, and extending downward past the opening into the larynx to the lower border of the cricoid cartilage where it is continuous with the esophagus **b :** the corresponding part of the alimentary canal in which the gills of water-breathing vertebrates are lodged **2 :** a differentiated part of the alimentary canal in many invertebrates that is commonly thickened and muscular or in some worms eversible and toothed or adapted as a suctorial organ

phas·al \'fāzəl\ *adj* [²*phase* + *-al*] **:** PHASIC

phas·cog·a·le \fa'skägə(‚)lē\ *n, cap* [NL, irreg. fr. Gk *phaskōlos* pouch + *galē* weasel — more at GALEA] **:** a genus of small ratlike chiefly arboreal polyprotodont marsupials comprising the broad-footed pouched mice of Australia

phas·co·larc·tos \‚faskō'lärktəs\ *n, cap* [NL, fr. Gk *phaskōlos* pouch + *arktos* bear — more at ARCTIC] **:** a genus comprising the koala and formerly regarded as the type of a distinct family but now usu. referred to the Phalangeridae

phas·co·lom·i·dae \‚faskə'lämə‚dē\ *n pl, cap* [NL, fr. *Phascolomis*, type genus + *-idae*] **:** a family of stockily built partially fossorial Australian marsupials that comprise the wombats and related extinct forms and have strong five-toed forefeet with digging claws and a very short tail

phas·co·lo·mis \-'lōməs\ *n, cap* [NL, irreg. fr. Gk *phaskōlos* pouch + NL *-mys*] **:** a genus (the type of the family Phascolomidae) comprising the common Australian wombats

phas·co·lo·my·i·dae \‚faskələ'mīə‚dē\ [NL, fr. *Phascolomys* + *-idae*] *syn of* PHASCOLOMIDAE

phas·co·lo·mys \‚=='lōməs\ [NL, fr. Gk *phaskōlos* pouch + NL *-mys*] *syn of* PHASCOLOMIS

phas·col·o·nus \fa'skälənəs\ *n, cap* [NL, fr. Gk *phaskōlos* + *onos* ass — more at ASS] **:** a genus of Pleistocene Australian diprotodont marsupials related to the wombats and as large as tapirs

phas·co·lo·so·ma \fa‚skōlə'sōmə\ *n, cap* [NL, fr. Gk *phaskōlos* + NL *-soma*] **:** a cosmopolitan genus of sipunculid worms

phas·cum \'faskəm\ *n, cap* [NL, fr. Gk *phaskon* tuft of moss] **:** a small genus of terrestrial cleistocarpous mosses having costate leaves covering subglobose or ovate-oblong capsules and included in the Tortulaceae or made type of a separate family

¹**phase** \'fāz\ *n* -S *usu cap* [LL, fr. Gk *phasech, phasek*, fr. Heb *pesaḥ* — more at PASCH] **:** PASSOVER — so translated in the Douay Version of the Bible

²**phase** \"\ *n* -S [NL *phasis*, fr. Gk, appearance of a star, phase of the moon, fr. *phainein* to show — more at FANCY] **1** *astron* **:** a particular appearance or state in a regularly recurring cycle of changes with respect to quantity of illumination or form of illuminated disk (as of a planet, the moon) **2 a :** a stage or interval in a development or cycle **:** a subdivision or an activity or operation on the basis of time, place, or accomplishment ⟨the assembly ~ of production —*advt*⟩ ⟨the way children develop and the different ~*s* they go through —Dorothy Barclay⟩ ⟨the final ~ of a war⟩ ⟨addition of a left-turn ~ to the . . . intersection traffic light —*Amarillo (Texas) Sunday News-Globe*⟩ **b :** an aspect or part (as of a situation or activity) being subjected to consideration ⟨the moral ~ of the problem —John Dewey⟩ ⟨engaged in several ~*s* of transportation in the course of his career —*Current Biog.*⟩ ⟨monographs which take up special ~*s* of life within the localities —C.L.Jones⟩ **3 :** the point or stage in a period in uniform circular motion, simple harmonic motion, or the periodic changes of any magnitude varying according to a simple harmonic law (as sound vibrations, alternating currents, or electric oscillations) to which the rotation, oscillation, or variation has advanced considered in its relation to a standard position or assumed instant of starting and expressed in angular measure with one cycle or period being 360 degrees **4 a :** a homogeneous, physically distinct, and mechanically separable portion of matter that is present in a nonhomogeneous physical-chemical system and that may be either a single compound or a mixture — compare STATE 2a ⟨water exists in the solid ~ as ice, in the liquid as water, and in the gaseous as water vapor or steam⟩ **b :** a part of a soil unit or type varying slightly from the normal in the characteristics used in its classification **5 :** an individual or subgroup distinguishably different in appearance or behavior from the norm of the group to which it belongs ⟨the gregaria ~ of a grasshopper⟩; *also* **:** the distinguishing peculiarity ⟨the silver ~ of the red fox⟩ ⟨an avirulent ~ of *Brucella abortus*⟩ — compare COLOR PHASE **6 :** a unit of classification in the Midwestern system for American archaeology constituting a group of aspects having in common a significant number of those features determinative of type — see PATTERN; compare COMPONENT, FOCUS

syn ASPECT, SIDE, FACET, ANGLE: PHASE may apply to a manifestation of change or to a stage in growth or development ⟨the *phases* of the moon⟩ ⟨the red fox shows various color *phases*⟩ ⟨another war, he explained recently, would be likely to start with an opening *phase* of unparalleled intensity —A.P. Ryan⟩ ⟨felt that one *phase* of his poetic development was completed —Douglas Cleverdon⟩ ASPECT may also suggest an appearance showing a change or stage, sometimes a minor or superficial one; it is frequently used to indicate changes in the observer's point of view or specific compartmenting of his notions ⟨the lower part of the basin of the Tweed takes on a kindly *aspect* of ploughed land, grass fields —L.D.Stamp⟩ ⟨from a certain *aspect* it is acceptable for the artist to ignore his public —Huntington Hartford⟩ ⟨only the military side of European defense will be considered, leaving the economic *aspects* for a later article —S.B.Fay⟩ SIDE in this sense may be interchangeable with PHASE and ASPECT but is likely to suggest more forcefully the existence of an opposed or tangential point of view ⟨I have shown you only one *side*, or rather one phase, of her —Edith Wharton⟩ ⟨asked to be allowed to tell his own *side* of the story⟩ ⟨the history as a whole is deficient on the economic *side* —Allen Johnson⟩ FACET implies a multiplicity of other faces or sides comparable to the one singled out for attention ⟨the *facets* of a cut diamond⟩ ⟨his talk revealed every *facet* of his glittering, bizarre personality, his wit, his scholarship, his quick, penetrating intellect, his delight in the use of decorative, high-sounding words, his love of the ornate and picturesque —Alvin Redman⟩ ⟨conferences of the chief departmental officers of the railways are regularly held, including accounts, advertising, engineering, traffic, stores — in fact every conceivable *facet* of railway operation —O.S.Nock⟩ ANGLE may suggest concentration on one restricted specific viewpoint ⟨much safer from the technical *angle*, but terrible for the actors —Denis Johnston⟩ ⟨views these developments from a fresh *angle* —Dumas Malone⟩

— **in phase** *adv* **1 :** in or of the same phase **:** of magnitudes whose maximum values are simultaneous ⟨this voltage must be *in phase* with the primary antenna voltage —*Proceedings of the Institute of Radio Engineers*⟩ **2 :** in a synchronized or correlated manner ⟨sure that at least one propeller was moving *in* and out of *phase* —E.K.Gann⟩ — **out of phase** *adv* **1 :** in or of different phases : of magnitudes whose maximum values are not simultaneous **2 :** in an unsynchronized manner : not in step-by-step correspondence : not in correlation ⟨windshield wipers were *out of phase* —Ralph Robin⟩ ⟨the cultural evolution of man has got *out of phase*, and armaments have developed faster than inhibitions —Marston Bates⟩ ⟨occasionally the Latin and the English are *out of phase* on the opposing pages —*Times Lit. Supp.*⟩

³phase \"\ *vt* -ED/-ING/-S **1 :** to adjust so as to be in phase ⟨the *phasing* of the recorder to the incoming signals —M.G. Artzt⟩ **2 a :** to conduct or carry out by esp. planned phases ⟨a *phased* advance, with coordination between units —*Time*⟩ ⟨fundamental approach in the *phased* march toward "socialized agriculture" —H.R.Lieberman⟩ ⟨drastic plan for *phased* disarmament in all weapons —M.W.Straight⟩ **b :** to schedule (as operations) or contract for (as goods or services) to be performed or supplied as required ⟨guiding industry to ~ its development programs —Barbara Ward⟩ ⟨could talk their language — production *phasing*, subcontracting —*Time*⟩ ⟨construction power was *phased* along with combat power —J.L.Collins⟩ **3 :** to introduce (as into a system, plan, or operation) in stages ⟨the new weapons and methods will be *phased* into the system —*Sydney* (*Australia*) *Bull.*⟩ ⟨~ . . . the establishment of a neutral zone —H.W.Baldwin⟩ — often used with *in* ⟨~ in reinforcements in accordance with tactical plans⟩ ⟨new-model autos are now being *phased* in⟩

⁴phase *var of* FAZE

phase advancer *n* [²*phase*] **:** a synchronous or asynchronous machine for supplying leading reactive volt amperes to the system to which it is connected

phase angle *n* **1 :** the angle between the earth and the sun as seen from a planet **2 :** an angle expressing phase or phase difference

phase-contrast \'=¦=,=\ *adj* **:** of or employing the phase microscope ⟨*phase-contrast* microscopy⟩

phase converter *n* **:** a machine for converting an alternating current into an alternating current of a different number of phases and the same frequency

phase diagram *n* **:** a diagram composed of equilibrium curves between different phases of the same substance ⟨the *phase diagram* of the gold-uranium system —*Jour. of Research*⟩

phase distortion *n* **:** change of wave form of a composite wave due to change of relative phase of its component harmonics

phase inverter *n* **:** a communications circuit in which the phase of a signal is reversed

phase·less \'fāzləs\ *adj* **:** having no phases

phase line *n* **:** a line (as a terrain feature extending across the zone of action) used to control and coordinate a military advance or withdrawal ⟨the regimental commander may prescribe any *phase lines* —*Infantry Jour.*⟩ ⟨reach a *phase line* one mile inland by 1600 hours —Irwin Shaw⟩ — abbr. *PL*

phasemeter \'=,=,=\ *n* [*phase* + *-meter*] **:** a device for measuring the difference in phase of two alternating currents or electromotive forces

phase microscope *also* **phase-contrast microscope** *or* **phase-difference microscope** *n* **:** a microscope that translates differences in phase of the light transmitted through or reflected by the object into differences of intensity in the image and thus provides contrast among parts and with the background

phase modulation *n* **:** modulation of the phase of a radio carrier wave by voice or other signal

pha·se·my bean \'fāsəmē-\ *also* **phasemy** *n* -ES [irreg. blend of *phas-* and *semi-* in NL *Phaseolus semierectus*, binomial designation of a species of bean] **:** an erect tropical American herb (*Phaseolus lathyroides*) sometimes cultivated in warm regions for forage or green manure

pha·se·o·lin \fə'sēələn\ *n* -S [NL *Phaseolus* + ISV *-in*] **:** a crystalline globulin found esp. in the kidney bean

pha·seo·lu·na·tin \,fāzē(,)ōlü'nātᵊn\ *n* -S [ISV *phaseolunat-* (fr. NL *Phaseolus lunatus*, binomial designation of a species of bean) + *-in*] **:** LINAMARIN

pha·se·o·lus \fə'sēələs\ *n, cap* [NL, fr. L, dim. of *phaselus*, a bean, fr. Gk *phasēlos*] **:** a genus of herbs (family Leguminosae) which are widely distributed throughout warm regions, which include most of the true American beans, and whose flowers are in axillary racemes or panicles with the corolla having a spirally twisted keel — see BEAN 1b, LIMA BEAN, MUNG BEAN, SIEVA BEAN

phase out *vt* **1 :** to eliminate as a phase of an operation or system **2 :** to discontinue the practice, production, or use of by phases **3 :** to complete (as an operation or activity) by planned phases ⟨*phase out* an advertising campaign⟩ ~ *vi* **1 :** to stop production or operation by phases (as by discontinuing the manufacture of component parts exceeding the quantity required for the assembling of items scheduled for completion) ⟨the company has *phased out* of the truck manufacturing business⟩ **2 :** to pass from one phase into another ⟨groups have *phased out* into a new command⟩

phase plate *n* **:** a transparent plate of doubly refracting material that changes the relative phase of the components of polarized light

phas·er \'fāzə(r)\ *n* -S **:** one that phases

phase rule *n* **:** a law in physical chemistry: the number of degrees of freedom of a system in equilibrium is equal to the number of components minus the number of phases plus the constant two (as in the system ice –liquid water– water vapor consisting of the one chemical component water and its three physical phases there are no degrees of freedom and the system can exist at only one temperature and pressure)

phases *pl of* PHASE, *pres 3d sing of* PHASE

phase shift *n* **:** change of phase of an oscillation or a wave train

phase space *n* **:** an ideal often multidimensional space of which the coordinate dimensions represent the variables required to specify the phase or state of a system or substance — see COORDINATE SPACE

phase splitter *n* **:** a device by which a single-phase current is split into two or more currents differing in phase and which is used in starting a single-phase induction motor

phase transformer *n* **:** PHASING TRANSFORMER

phase velocity *n* **:** the velocity of a wave motion as determined by the product of the wavelength and frequency — called also *wave velocity*; compare GROUP VELOCITY, PARTICLE VELOCITY

phase-wound \'=¦=\ *adj, of an induction motor* **:** having the secondary wound — compare SQUIRREL CAGE

phas·go·nu·rid \,fazgə'n(y)ürəd\ *adj or n* [NL *Phasgonuridae*] **:** TETTIGONIID

phas·go·nu·ri·dae \,==='n(y)ürə,dē\ [NL, fr. *Phasgonura*, type genus, fr. Gk *phasganon* sword + NL *-ura*] *syn of* TETTIGONIIDAE

-pha·sia \'fāzh(ē)ə\ *also* **-pha·sy** \.fəsē, -si\ *n comb form, pl* **-phasias** *also* **-phasies** [*-phasia*, NL, fr. Gk, speech, fr. *phasis* utterance, statement, fr. *phanai* to say, speak; *-phasy* fr. NL *-phasia* — more at BAN] **:** speech disorder (of a specified type esp. relating to the symbolic use of language) ⟨*dysphasia*⟩ ⟨tachy*phasia*⟩ — compare -LALIA, -PHEMIA, -PHONY 2

pha·si·a·nel·la \,fāzēə'nelə, -āsē-\ *n, cap* [NL, fr. L *phasianus* pheasant + *-ella* — more at PHASIANUS] **:** a genus (the type of the family Phasianellidae) of marine rhipidoglossate snails having intricately patterned porcelaneous shells

pha·si·an·ic \,=='anik\ *adj* [NL *Phasianus* + E *-ic*] **:** of or relating to the genus *Phasianus*

pha·si·an·id \,=='anəd, -'ān-\ *n* -S [NL *Phasianidae*] **:** a bird of the family Phasianidae

pha·si·an·i·dae \-'anə,dē\ *n pl, cap* [NL *Phasianus*, type genus + *-idae*] **:** a large family of gallinaceous birds including the Asiatic pheasants, domestic fowls, jungle fowls, argus pheasants, Old World partridges, often also the turkeys and guinea fowls, and sometimes the grouse — see COTURNIX

pha·si·a·noid \'==,ə,nȯid\ *adj* [NL *Phasianus* + E *-oid*] **:** resembling or related to the genus *Phasianus*

pha·si·a·nus \,=='ānəs\ *n, cap* [NL, fr. L, pheasant — more at PHEASANT] **:** a genus (the type of the family Phasianidae) containing the typical pheasants

pha·sic \'fāzik, -zēk\ *adj* [ISV ²*phase* + *-ic*] **:** of, relating to, or of the nature of a phase **:** having phases **:** functioning by phases ⟨~ alternation of excitability and inexcitability —*Encyc. Britannica*⟩

phasing *pres part of* PHASE

phasing current *n* [fr. pres. part. of ³*phase*] **:** the momentary current between two alternating-current generators when juxtaposed in parallel and not agreeing exactly in phase or period

phasing transformer *also* **phase transformer** *n* **:** a transformer whose purpose is to produce a secondary current differing in phase from the primary current

pha·sis \'fāsəs\ *n, pl* **pha·ses** \-,sēz\ [NL — more at PHASE] **:** PHASE ⟨direct our survey chiefly to that religious ~ of the matter —Thomas Carlyle⟩

pha·si·tron \'fāzə,trän\ *n* -S [²*phase* + *-i-* + *-tron*] **:** a vacuum tube used for frequency modulation of a signal and having a cathode, deflector electrodes, two anodes, and an external inductor

phasm \'fazəm\ *n, pl* **phasms** \-zəmz\ *or* **phas·ma·ta** \-zməd·ə\ [Gk *phasmat-, phasma*, fr. *phainein* to show — more at FANCY] **1** *archaic* **:** an extraordinary appearance (as of light) **:** METEOR **2** *archaic* **:** APPARITION, PHANTOM

phas·ma \'fazmə\ *n, cap* [NL *Phasmat-, Phasma* fr. Gk, apparition] **:** the type genus of Phasmatidae

phas·ma·tid \'fazməd·əd, -mətəd\ *n* -S [NL *Phasmatida*] **:** ²PHASMID

phas·mat·i·da \faz'mad·əd·ə\ *or* **phas·ma·toi·dea** \,fazmə'tȯidēə\ *or* **phas·mi·da** \'fazmədə\ [*Phasmatida, Phasmida*, NL, fr. *Phasmat-, Phasma* + *-ida; Phasmatoidea*, NL, fr. *Phasmat-, Phasma* + *-oidea*] *syn of* PHASMATODEA

phas·mat·i·dae \faz'mad·ə,dē\ *n pl, cap* [NL, fr. *Phasmat-, Phasma*, type genus + *-idae*] **:** a family of cursorial insects (suborder Phasmatodea) with long antennae and the abdomen simple and cylindrical or expanded laterally through part of its length

phas·ma·to·dea \,fazmə'tōdēə\ *n pl, cap* [NL, fr. *Phasmat-, Phasma* + *-odea*] **:** a suborder of Orthoptera often considered a separate order, comprising large, cylindrical or sometimes flattened, chiefly tropical insects with long strong legs, strictly phytophagous habits, and very slight metamorphosis and including the stick insects and leaf insects

¹phas·mid \'fazməd\ *adj* [NL *Phasmida*] **:** of or relating to the Phasmatodea

²phasmid \"\ *n* -S **:** an insect of the suborder Phasmatodea (as a leaf insect or a stick insect)

³phasmid \"\ *n* -S [origin unknown] **:** either of the paired lateral postanal organs characteristic of most parasitic nematodes and usu. regarded as chemoreceptors — see PHASMIDIA — **phas·mid·i·al** \(')faz¦midēəl\ *adj*

phas·mi·dae \'fazmə,dē\ [NL, fr. *Phasma*, type genus + *-idae*] *syn of* PHASMATIDAE

phas·mid·ia \faz'midēə\ *n pl, cap* [NL, fr. ISV *phasmid* + NL *-ia*] *in many classifications* **:** a subclass of Nematoda comprising worms having phasmids, simple amphids like pores, usu. deirids, and sensory organs that are typically papillose or, rarely, setose — compare APHASMIDIA — **phas·mid·i·an** \-dēən\ *n* -S

phaso- *comb form* [²*phase*] **:** phase ⟨*phaso*geneous⟩

pha·so·ge·neous \¦fāzō¦jēnyəs, -nēəs\ *adj* [*phaso-* + chrono*geneous*] **:** appearing synchronously with a particular phase of development ⟨a ~ engram and its ecphoria⟩ — compare CHRONOGENEOUS

pha·sor \'fāzə(r) *also* -,zō(ə)r *or* -ō(ə)\ *n* -S [²*phase* + *vector*] **:** a vector (as one representing an alternating current or voltage) whose vectorial angle represents a phase or phase difference

-phasy *— see* -PHASIA

¹phat *or* **fat** \'fat, *usu* -ad·+V\ *adj* [alter. of *fat*] *of copy or type matter* **:** susceptible of easy and rapid setting (as because of plentiful white space or the existence of standing type) — contrasted with *lean*

²phat *or* **fat** \"\ *n* -S **:** phat matter

³phat *or* **fat** \"\ *vt* **phatted** *or* **fatted; phatted** *or* **fatted; phatting** *or* **fatting; phats** *or* **fats :** to keep (type) standing in hope of a further order

phat·ic \'fad·ik, -atik, -ēk\ *adj* [Gk *phatos* spoken (fr. *phanai* to speak, say) + E *-ic* — more at BAN] **:** employing or involving speech for the purpose of revealing or sharing feelings or establishing an atmosphere of sociability rather than for communicating ideas ⟨greetings, bromides, ~ communion —I.A. Richards⟩ ⟨indulged in a little ~ communion and were about to part —M.J.Maloney⟩ ⟨transition from the symbolic level to the ~ —Arthur Minton⟩ — **phat·i·cal·ly** \-ək(ə)lē, -ēk-, -li\ *adv*

PhD \¦pē,ā̇ch¦dē\ *abbr or n* -S [L *philosophiae doctor*] **:** a doctor of philosophy

phe *var of* PE

pheas·ant \'fezᵊnt\ *n, pl* **pheasant** *or* **pheasants** [ME *fesaunt*, fr. AF, fr. OF *fesan*, fr. L *phasianus*, fr. Gk *phasianos*, fr. *phasianos* of the Phasis river, fr. *Phasis*, river in Colchis] **1 :** any of numerous large, often long-tailed, and brilliantly colored Old World gallinaceous birds that constitute *Phasianus* and related genera of the family Phasianidae, are most abundant in Asia and the adjacent islands, and include many forms raised in semidomestication as ornamentals and one widely distributed species (*P. colchicum*) which has been naturalized in many parts of the world — see ARGUS 2, BLOOD PHEASANT, GOLDEN PHEASANT, KALIJ, LADY AMHERST'S PHEASANT, MONAL, MONGOLIAN PHEASANT, RING-NECKED PHEASANT, SILVER PHEASANT, TRAGOPAN **2 :** any of various birds having real or fancied resemblance to a pheasant: as **a** *South & Midland* **:** RUFFED GROUSE **b** *Austral* **:** LEIPOA **c** *Austral* **:** LYREBIRD **d** *Brit* **:** MAGPIE **e :** any of various guans **f :** a francolin (as *Francolinus capensis* or *Pternistis afer*) of southern Africa **3** *pl pheasants* **:** a moderate orange to light brown

pheasant cuckoo *n* **:** COUCAL

pheasant duck *n* **1 :** a pintail (*Anas acuta*) **2 :** MERGANSER

pheasant finch *n* **:** a small African waxbill (*Estrilda astrild*)

pheas·ant·ry \'fezᵊntrē, -ri\ *n* -ES [*pheasant* + *-ry*] **:** a place for keeping and rearing pheasants

pheasant's-eye \'==¦=\ *n, pl* **pheasant's-eyes 1 :** a plant of the genus *Adonis*; *esp* **:** a Eurasian herb (*A. annua*) often cultivated for its deep red dark-centered flowers **2 :** PHEASANT'S-EYE PINK **3 :** POET'S NARCISSUS

pheasant's-eye pink *n* **:** a ring-marked cottage pink

pheasant shell *n* **:** a tropical gastropod mollusk of the family Phasianellidae or its smooth shell having a moderately high spire and an intricate pattern suggesting the plumage of a pheasant

pheasant-tailed jacana *n* \'==¦=-\ **:** a jacana (*Hydrophasianus chirurgus*) of India and the East Indies having no frontal plate and the four middle tail feathers much elongated — called also *Indian jacana*

pheasant-tailed widgeon *n* **:** a pintail duck (*Anas acuta*)

pheasantwood \'==,=\ *n* **:** PARTRIDGEWOOD 1a

phebe *var of* PHOEBE

phe·gop·ter·is \fə'gäptərəs\ [NL, fr. Gk *phēgos* oak + *pteris* fern — more at BEECH, PTERIS] *syn of* DRYOPTERIS

phei·do·le \'fīdᵊlē\ *n, cap* [NL, fr. Gk *pheidōlē*, fem. of *pheidōlos* thrifty, fr. *pheidesthai* to spare, be sparing; prob. akin to Skt *bhedati* he splits — more at BITE] **:** a large and widely distributed genus of seed-storing ants having highly polymorphic workers

phel·lan·dral \fə'lan,dral, -,drəl\ *n* -S [fr. NL *phellandrium* (specific epithet of *Oenanthe phellandrium*) + ISV *-al*] **:** a liquid aldehyde $C_3H_7C_6H_8CHO$ that is related to alpha-phellandrene and is found esp. in eucalyptus oils and water-fennel oil

phel·lan·drene \-,drēn\ *n* -S [NL *phellandrium* + ISV *-ene*] **:** either of two isomeric aromatic oily liquid terpene hydrocarbons $C_{10}H_{16}$ occurring in many essential oils: **a :** the terpene $C_3H_7C_6H_6CH_3$ occurring in the dextrorotatory form esp. in bitter fennel oil and ginger-grass oil and in the levorotatory form esp. in eucalyptus oils (as from *Eucalyptus phellandra*); 1,5-*para*-menthadiene — called also *alpha-phellandrene* **b :** the terpene $C_3H_7C_6H_7{=}CH_2$ occurring in the dextrorotatory form esp. in water-fennel oil and in the levorotatory form esp. in turpentine; 1(7),2-*para*-menthadiene — called also *beta-phellandrene*

phel·lem \'feləm, -,lem\ *n* -S [*phello-* + *-em* (as in *phloem*)] **:** a layer of usu. suberized cells produced outwardly by a phellogen — called also *cork*; compare PHELLODERM

phello- *comb form* [Gk, cork, fr. *phellos*; prob. akin to Gk *phloos* bark — more at PHLOEM] **:** cork **:** bark ⟨*phello*derm⟩ ⟨*phello*gen⟩

phel·lo·den·dron \,felə'dendrən\ *n, cap* [NL, fr. *phello-* + *-dendron*] **:** a genus of aromatic deciduous trees (family Rutaceae) of eastern Asia that have handsome compound leaves turning yellow in autumn, dioecious yellowish green flowers, and black persistent drupes — see CORK TREE

phel·lo·derm \'felə,dərm\ *n* -S [ISV *phello-* + *-derm*] **:** a layer of parenchyma produced inwardly by a phellogen — compare PHELLEM — **phel·lo·der·mal** \¦==¦dərməl\ *adj*

phel·lo·gen \'feləjən, -,jen\ *n* -S [ISV *phello-* + *-gen*] **:** a secondary meristem that initiates phellem and phelloderm in the periderm — called also *cork cambium* — **phel·lo·gen·et·ic** \¦==jə¦ned·ik\ *adj* — **phel·lo·gen·ic** \¦==¦jenik\ *adj*

phel·lon·ic acid \fə'länik-, fe'l-\ *n* [*phellonic* ISV *phellon-* (fr. Gk *phellos* cork) + *-ic*] **:** a crystalline hydroxy acid $HOCH_2(CH_2)_{20}COOH$ that is isolated esp. from cork by alkaline cleavage and extraction **:** 22-hydroxy-behenic acid — see SUBERIN

phe·lo·ni·on \fə'lōnēən\ *n* -S [LGk *phelōnion, phailonion*, alter. of *phainolion*, fr. L *paenula* cloak — more at PAENULA] **:** a priest's vestment of the Eastern Orthodox Church that is similar to a western chasuble

-phe·mia \'fēmēə\ *n comb form* -S [NL, fr. Gk *-phēmia* speech, fr. *-phēmos* speaking (fr. *phēmē* speech, fr. *phanai* to speak, say) + *-ia* -y — more at BAN] **:** speech disorder (of a specified type esp. relating to the articulation or fluency of speech sounds) ⟨a*phemia*⟩ ⟨brachy*phemia*⟩ — compare -LALIA, -PHASIA, -PHONY 2

phen- *or* **pheno-** *comb form* [Gk *phain-, phaino-*, fr. *phainein* to show — more at FANCY] **1** *also* **phaen-** *or* **phaeno- a :** showing ⟨*pheno*cryst⟩ **b :** PHANER- ⟨*phaeno*gam⟩ **2** [*phene*] **a :** related to benzene ⟨*phen*ol⟩ **:** containing phenyl ⟨*phen*ethyl⟩ ⟨*pheno*barbital⟩; *esp* **:** containing two benzene rings ⟨*phen*azine⟩ ⟨*pheno*thiazine⟩ **b :** phenol (sense 1) ⟨*phen*oxide⟩

phena·caine *or* **pheno·cain** \'fēnə,kān, 'fen-\ *n* -S [*phenacaine* prob. fr. *phen*etidine + acet- + *-caine*; *phenocain* prob. irreg. fr. *phen-* + *-caine*] **:** a crystalline base $C_{18}H_{22}N_2O_2$ or its hydrochloride used chiefly for producing local anesthesia in the eye

phen·acetin \(')fēn, fən+\ *n* [ISV *phen-* + *acetin*] **:** ACETOPHENETIDIN

phen·aceturic acid \(¦)fēn, (¦)fen+ . . . -\ *n* [ISV *phen-* + *acetyl* + *hippuric*] **:** a crystalline amido acid $C_6H_5CH_2CONHCH_2COOH$ found in the urine of the horse and sometimes in that of man and also made synthetically; *N*-(phenyl-acetyl)-glycine

phe·nac·odus \fə'nakədəs\ *n, cap* [NL, fr. Gk *phenak-, phenax* deceiver + NL *-odus*] **:** a genus (type of the family Phenacodontidae) of condylarths of the Eocene of Europe and America

phe·nac·o·mys \fə'nakə,mis\ *n, cap* [NL, fr. Gk *phenak-, phenax* + NL *-mys*] **:** a genus of chiefly arboreal No. American voles — see LEMMING MOUSE 2, RED TREE MOUSE

phen·a·cyl \'fenə,sil, -sēl\ *n* -S [ISV *phen-* + *acetyl*] **:** the univalent radical $C_6H_5COCH_2$– derived from acetophenone

phenacyl chloride *n* **:** CHLOROACETOPHENONE

phenagle *var of* FINAGLE

phen·a·kis·to·scope \,fenə'kistə,skōp\ *n* [modif. of F *phénakisticope*, fr. Gk *phenakistēs* deceiver (fr. *phenakizein* to deceive, fr. *phenak-, phenax* deceiver + *-izein* -ize) + F *-scope*] **:** an optical toy resembling the zoetrope in principle and use and in one form consisting of a disk with the figures arranged about the center and having near the edge radial slits through which the figures are viewed by means of a mirror

phenakistoscope

phen·a·kite \'fenə,kīt\ *or* **phen·a·cite** \-,sīt\ *n* -S [Sw *phenakit*, fr. Gk *phenak-, phenax* deceiver + Sw *-it* -ite; fr. its being easily mistaken for quartz] **:** a colorless, wine-yellow, rose-red, or brown glassy mineral that is a beryllium silicate Be_2SiO_4, occurs in rhombohedral crystals, and is sometimes used as a gem (hardness 7.5–8, sp. gr. 2.97–3.00)

phenanthr- *or* **phenanthro-** *or* **phenanthra-** *comb form* [*phenanthrene*] **:** phenanthrene ⟨*phenanthr*idine⟩ ⟨*phenanthro*furan⟩ ⟨*phenanthra*quinone⟩

phen·an·threne \fə'nan,thrēn\ *n* -S [ISV *phen-* + *-anthrene*; prob. orig. formed as G *phenanthren*] **:** a crystalline tricyclic aromatic hydrocarbon $C_{14}H_{10}$ that is isomeric with anthracene, that is obtained chiefly from the anthracene oil fraction of coal tar and is also made synthetically, and that provides the ring system in whole or in part for many complex naturally occurring compounds (as resin acids, morphine, codeine, steroids) — compare STRUCTURAL FORMULA

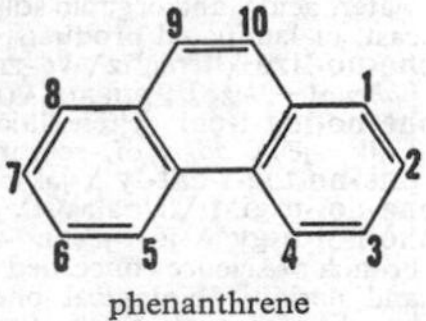

phenanthrene

phen·an·thri·dine \fə'nan(t)thrə,dēn, -,dən\ *n* -S [ISV *phenanthr-* + *pyridine*; prob. orig. formed in G] **:** a crystalline base $C_{13}H_9N$ isomeric with acridine; 3,4-benzquinoline; 5-aza-phenanthrene

phe·nan·thri·din·i·um \fə,nan(t)thrə'dinēəm\ *n* -S [NL, fr. ISV *phenanthridine* + *-ium*] **:** the ion $[C_{13}H_9NH]^+$ derived from phenanthridine and occurring in substituted form in quaternary salts used as trypanocides

phe·nan·thri·done \fə'nan(t)thrə,dōn\ *n* -S [ISV *phenanthridine* + *-one*] **:** a crystalline lactam $C_{13}H_9NO$ obtainable from phenanthridine by oxidation

phe·nan·thro·line \fə'nan(t)thrə,lēn, -,lən\ *n* -S [ISV *phenanthr-* + *quinoline*] **:** any of three crystalline nitrogen bases $C_{12}H_8N_2$ related to phenanthrene and derivable from *ortho-*, *meta-*, and *para*-phenylenediamine; di-aza-phenanthrene; *esp* **:** the ortho or 1,10-isomer that forms a red coordination complex with ferrous ions useful as an oxidation-reduction indicator (as with potassium permanganate as oxidizing agent) because it becomes faint blue in the oxidized form

phe·nan·thryl \fə'nan(t)thrəl\ *n* -S [*phenanthr-* + *-yl*] **:** a univalent radical $C_{14}H_9$ derived from phenanthrene

phen·ar·sa·zine chloride *n* \fə'närsə,zēn-\ [*phen-* + *ars*enic + *azine*] **:** ADAMSITE

phe·nate \'fē,nāt, 'fe,-\ *n* -S [ISV *phen-* + *-ate*] **:** PHENOXIDE

phen·azine \'fenə,zēn, -,zən\ *n* -S [ISV *phen-* + *azine*] **:** a yellowish crystalline tricyclic nitrogen base $C_6H_4N_2C_6H_4$ that is the parent compound of many azine dyes (as the safranines) and a few antibiotics (as pyocyanin); 9,10-di-aza-anthracene

phen·a·zone \'fenə,zōn\ *n* -S [ISV *phen-* + *az-* + *-one*] **:** ANTIPYRINE

phene \'fēn\ *n* -S [F *phène*, fr. Gk *phainein* to show; from its occurrence in illuminating gas — more at FANCY] **:** BENZENE — used esp. in names of derivatives; compare PHEN-

phen·ethyl \(')fēn+\ *n* [*phen-* + *ethyl*] **:** the phenylethyl radical $C_6H_5CH_2CH_2$–

phenethyl alcohol *n* **:** PHENYLETHYL ALCOHOL

phe·net·i·dine \fə'ned·ə,dēn, -,dən\ *n* -S [ISV *phenet*ole + *-idine*] **:** any of three isomeric liquid basic amino derivatives $C_6H_4(NH_2)OC_2H_5$ of phenetole of which the ortho and para isomers are used in the manufacture of dyes and pharmaceuticals

phen·e·tole \'fenə,tōl, -,täl\ *n* -S [ISV *phen-* + *-et-* + *-ole*] **:** an aromatic liquid $C_6H_5OC_2H_5$ that is the ethyl ether of phenol

phen·gite \'fen,jīt\ *n* -S [G *phengit*, fr. L *phengites*, fr. Gk, fr. *phengos* light, moonlight + *-itēs* -ite] **1 :** a transparent or translucent stone prob. selenite or crystallized gypsum used by the ancients for windows **2 :** a variety of muscovite with substitution of aluminum for magnesium and silicon — **phen·git·ic** \(ˈ)fen¦jid·ik\ *adj*

phe·nic acid \ˈfēnik, ˈfenik-\ *n* [F *acide phénique*, fr. *phén-* phen- + *-ique* -ic] **:** PHENOL — not used systematically

phenician *usu cap, var of* PHOENICIAN

phenicochroite *var of* PHOENICOCHROITE

pheni·cop·ter \ˌfenə̇ˈkäptə(r), ¦fēn-, -ne¦k-\ *n* -S [MF *phoenicoptere*, fr. L *phoenicopterus*, fr. Gk *phoinikopteros*, lit., red-feathered, fr. *phoinik-*, *phoinix* red, purple, crimson + *-pteros* -feathered (fr. *pteron* feather, wing) — more at PHOENICIAN, FEATHER] **:** FLAMINGO

phen·mi·azine \ˌfen,mī+\ *n* -S [G *phenmiazin*] **:** QUINAZOLINE

pheno- — see PHEN-

phe·no·barbital \¦fē(ˌ)nō+\ *n* [*phen-* + *barbital*] **:** a crystalline barbiturate $C_{12}H_{12}N_2O_3$ that is used as a hypnotic and sedative esp. in grand mal epilepsy; 5-ethyl-5-phenyl-barbituric acid

pheno·barbitone \"+\ *n* [*phen-* + *barbitone*] *Brit* **:** PHENOBARBITAL

phenocain *var of* PHENACAINE

pheno·clast \ˈfēnə,klast, ˈfen-\ *n* -S [*phen-* + *-clast*] **:** a large fragment in sediment composed of various sizes of material

pheno·coll \-,käl\ *n* -S [ISV *phen-* + glycocoll] **:** a crystalline base $C_{10}H_{14}N_2O_2$ used in the form of a salt (as the hydrochloride) as an antipyretic and analgesic

phe·no·contour \¦fēnə+\ *n* [*phenotype* + *contour*] **:** a line that shows the geographic distribution of a particular phenotype

phe·no·cop·ic \¦==¦käpik\ *adj* [*phenocopy* + *-ic*] **:** of or relating to a phenocopy

phe·no·copy \"+\ *n* [*phenotype* + *copy*] **:** a phenotypic variation due to modifying environmental influences that mimics the expression of a genotype other than its own

phe·no·critical period \"+-\ *n* [*phenotype* + *critical*] **:** a period in the development of an organism when a particular gene effect can be most readily modified by environmental factors

pheno·cryst \ˈfēnə,krist, ˈfen-\ *n* -S [F *phénocryste*, fr. *phéno-* phen- + *-cryste* (fr. *crystal*)] **:** one of the prominent embedded crystals of a porphyry — **pheno·crys·tic** \¦==¦kristik\ *adj*

phe·no·genesis \¦fēnə+\ *n* [NL, fr. *phenotype* + *genesis*] **:** DEVELOPMENT; *specif* **:** differentiation of the phenotype

phe·no·genetic \¦==+\ *adj* **:** of or pertaining to phenogenetics or to phenogenesis — **pheno·genetically** \"+\ *adv*

phe·no·genetics \"+\ *n pl but sing in constr* [*phenotype* + *genetics*] **:** developmental genetics **:** the part of genetics that deals with the mechanisms of development and the differentiation of the concrete qualities controlled by the genes

phe·nol \ˈfē,nōl, -,nȯl, -,näl, fēˈnōl\ *n* -S [ISV *phen-* + *-ol*] **1 :** a soluble crystalline acidic compound C_6H_5OH that turns pinkish on exposure to light and air and has a characteristic odor, that is present in coal tar and wood tar, occurs in urine esp. of herbivorous animals, and is synthesized by various methods (as from sodium benzenesulfonate by alkaline fusion, from chlorobenzene by hydrolysis, or from cumene by oxidation to cumene hydroperoxide and treatment with sulfuric acid) that is a powerful caustic poison and in dilute solution is a useful disinfectant and that is used otherwise chiefly in making resins and plastics, dyes, pharmaceuticals (as aspirin), and other products (as *picric acid* 2,4-D) and as a solvent for refining lubricating oils; hydroxy-benzene — called also *carbolic acid* **2 :** any of a class of acidic compounds (as the cresols or resorcinol) analogous to phenol in constitution and regarded as hydroxyl derivatives of aromatic hydrocarbons in which one or more hydroxyl groups are attached directly to the aromatic ring — see NAPHTHOL 2, TAR ACID; compare ALCOHOL 4

phe·no·lase \ˈfēnə,lās, -lāz\ *n* -S [*phenol* + *-ase*] **:** PHENOL OXIDASE

¹phe·no·late \-,lāt, -lət, *usu* -d·+V\ *n* -S [ISV *phenol* + *-ate*, n. suffix] **:** PHENOXIDE

²phe·no·late \-,lāt, *usu* -ād·+V\ *vt* -ED/-ING/-S [*phenol* + *-ate*, vb. suffix] **:** to treat, mix, or impregnate with phenol

phenol coefficient *n* **:** a number relating the germicidal efficiency of a compound to phenol regarded as having an arbitrarily assigned value of 1 toward specified bacteria (as typhoid bacteria) under specified conditions ⟨if disinfectant X has a *phenol coefficient* of 2 that means that . . . X is twice as strong as phenol —H.C.Wood †1920 & Arthur Osol⟩

phenol-formaldehyde \¦=,==¦=,=\ *n* **:** a condensation product, resin, or plastic made from phenol itself or another phenol and formaldehyde

¹phe·no·lic \fēˈnōlik, fəˈn-, -näl-, -lēk\ *adj* [ISV *phenol* + *-ic*] **1 a :** of, relating to, or having the characteristics of phenol or a phenol **b :** containing or derived from phenol or a phenol **2 :** of, relating to, or containing phenolic resin

²phenolic \"\ *n* -S **1 :** PHENOLIC RESIN **2 :** PHENOLIC PLASTIC

phenolic plastic *n* **:** a plastic consisting of a phenolic resin

phenolic resin *n* -S **:** any of various usu. thermosetting resins of high mechanical strength and electrical resistance that are made by condensation of a phenol with an aldehyde (as formaldehyde), are characterized generally by resistance to water, acids, and organic solvents, and are used esp. in molded, cast, or laminated products, as adhesives, or in coatings

phe·no·lize \ˈfēnə,līz\ *vt* -ED/-ING/-S *see -ize in Explan Notes* [*phenol* + *-ize*] **:** PHENOLATE

phe·no·log·i·cal \¦fēnə¦läjəkəl, -jēk-\ *also* **phe·no·log·ic** \-jik, -jēk\ *adj* **:** of, relating to, or involving phenology — **phe·no·log·i·cal·ly** \-jək(ə)lē, -jēk-, -li\ *adv*

phe·nol·o·gist \fəˈnäləjəst\ *n* -S **:** a specialist in phenology

phe·nol·o·gy \-jē, -ji\ *n* -ES [*phenomena* + *-logy*] **1 :** a branch of science concerned with the relations between climate and periodic biological phenomena (as the migrations and breeding of birds or the flowering and fruiting of plants) ⟨a student of ~⟩ **2 :** the relation between climate and periodic biological phenomena (as of a kind of organism) ⟨studies in nest ~⟩ ⟨the ~ of Tasmanian lichens⟩

phenol oxidase *n* **:** any of various copper-containing enzymes (as one from potatoes) that promote the oxidation of phenols — called also *phenolase;* compare POLYPHENOL OXIDASE

phe·nol·phthalein \¦==+\ *n* [ISV *phenol* + *phthalein*] **:** a white or yellowish white crystalline compound $C_{20}H_{14}O_4$ formed by condensation of phthalic anhydride and phenol and used in medicine as a laxative and in analysis as an indicator because its solution is brilliant red in alkalies and is decolorized by even weak acids — compare PHTHALEIN

phenol red *n* **:** PHENOLSULFONEPHTHALEIN

phe·nol·sulfonate \¦=,=+\ *n* [ISV *phenolsulfonic* (in *phenolsulfonic acid*) + *-ate*] **:** a salt or ester of a phenolsulfonic acid

phenolsulfonephthalein *or* **phenolsulfonphthalein** \¦=,=-¦=,=(=)=\ *n* [ISV *phenol* + *sulfonephthalein* or *sulfonphthalein*] **:** a red crystalline compound $C_{19}H_{14}O_5S$ formed by condensation of the anhydride of *ortho*-sulfobenzoic acid and phenol and used chiefly as a test of kidney function and as an acid-base indicator — called also *phenol red*

phe·nol·sulfonic acid \¦=,=+-\ *n* [*phenolsulfonic* ISV *phenol* + *sulfonic*] **:** a sulfonic acid derived from phenol; *esp* **:** a crystalline monosulfonic acid $HOC_6H_4SO_3H$ (as the para isomer) used chiefly as an intermediate for dyes and pharmaceuticals

phe·nom \fəˈnäm\ *n* -S [by shortening] **:** PHENOMENON; *esp* **:** a person of phenomenal ability or promise ⟨a prep ~ whom major-league scouts are battling to sign —Robert Cromie⟩

¹phe·nom·e·nal \fəˈnämənᵊl\ *adj* [*phenomenon* + *-al*] **:** relating to or being a phenomenon or phenomena: as **a :** known through the senses and immediate experience rather than through thought or intuition **:** SENSIBLE ⟨the ~ world⟩ **b :** concerned with phenomena rather than with hypotheses ⟨~ science⟩ **c :** EXTRAORDINARY, REMARKABLE ⟨his influence over juries was ~ —H.W.H.Knott⟩ ⟨crop yields are ~ —*Americana Annual*⟩ ⟨claimed for himself one talent: a ~ memory for places —James Stern⟩ ⟨a ~ sandstorm —W.B.Fisher⟩ ⟨book enjoyed a ~ sale⟩ **syn** see MATERIAL

²phenomenal \"\ *n* -S **:** that which is known through observation; *also* **:** PHENOMENA

phe·nom·e·nal·ism \-nᵊl,izəm\ *n* -S [¹*phenomenal* + *-ism*] **1 :** a theory that limits positive or scientific knowledge to phenomena only **2 :** a theory that we know only phenomena and that there is no existence except the phenomenal **3 :** a theory that any statements containing names of things or physical objects can be expressed in terms of statements containing the names of sense-data to the exclusion of names of physical objects

¹phe·nom·e·nal·ist \-ləst\ *n* -S **:** an advocate or proponent of phenomenalism

²phenomenalist \"\ *adj* **:** of or relating to phenomenalism or phenomenalists

phe·nom·e·nal·is·tic \=¦===¦istik, -tēk\ *adj* **:** of or relating to phenomena or phenomenalism ⟨a ~ system . . . is one that takes some perceptible physical individuals as its basic units —Nelson Goodman⟩ — **phe·nom·e·nal·is·ti·cal·ly** \-tək(ə)lē, -tēk-, -li\ *adv*

phe·nom·e·nal·i·ty \=,==ˈnaləd·ē\ *n* -ES **:** the quality or state of being phenomenal

phe·nom·e·nal·ize \=ˈ==nᵊl,īz\ *vt* -ED/-ING/-S *see -ize in Explan Notes* [¹*phenomenal* + *-ize*] **1 :** to treat or view as phenomenal **2 :** to interpret phenomenalistically

phe·nom·e·nal·ly \-nᵊlē, -li\ *adv* [¹*phenomenal* + *-ly*] **1 :** in relation to phenomena ⟨view that man is normally free although ~ determined —*Times Lit. Supp.*⟩ **2 :** EXTRAORDINARILY, REMARKABLY ⟨~ successful classes —*N. Y. Times Bk. Rev.*⟩ ⟨a ~ dull and tasteless comedy —Wolcott Gibbs⟩

phen·o·men·ic \¦fenə¦menik\ *adj* [*phenomenon* + *-ic*] **:** PHENOMENAL 1 ⟨such reality was for them not ~ —Giorgio de Santillana⟩

phe·nom·e·nism \fəˈnämə,nizəm\ *n* -S [*phenomenon* + *-ism*] **:** PHENOMENALISM

phe·nom·e·nist \-nəst\ *n* -S **:** PHENOMENALIST

phe·nom·e·nis·tic \=¦==¦nistik\ *adj* **:** PHENOMENALISTIC

phe·nom·e·nize \=ˈ==,nīz\ *vt* -ED/-ING/-S *see -ize in Explan Notes* [*phenomenon* + *-ize*] **:** PHENOMENALIZE

phe·nom·e·no·logical \fə¦nämənə+\ *also* **phe·nom·e·no·logic** \"+\ *adj* **1 :** of, relating to, or advocating phenomenology **2 :** of or relating to phenomena — **phe·nom·e·no·logically** \"+\ *adv*

phe·nom·e·nol·o·gist \=,==ˈnäləjəst\ *n* -S **:** an advocate of phenomenology

phe·nom·e·nol·o·gy \-jē, -ji\ *n* -ES [*phenomenon* + *-logy*] **1 :** a branch of a science dealing with the description and classification of phenomena **2** [G *phänomenologie*, fr. *phänomenon* phenomenon (fr. LL *phaenomenon*) + *logie* -logy] **a** *Kantianism* **:** a division of metaphysics that treats of motion and rest as predicables of things **b** *Hegelianism* **:** a doctrine of the growth of science or knowledge **:** the progress of mind from the lowest to the highest stages **c :** PHANEROSCOPY **d** *Husserlian philos* **:** a discipline endeavoring to lay foundations for all sciences by describing the formal structures of phenomena or of both actual and possible material essences that are given through a suspension of the natural attitude in pure acts of intuition — compare EPOCHE

phe·nom·e·non \fəˈnämə,nän, -,nən\ *n, pl* **phenome·na** \-,nä, -nə\ *or* **phenomenons** *see numbered senses* [LL *phaenomenon*, fr. Gk *phainomenon*, fr. neut. of pres. pass. part. of *phainein* to show — more at FANCY] **1** *pl phenomena* **:** an observable fact or event **:** an item of experience or reality ⟨studied capitalism, not mankind, and reduced economics to the *phenomena* of price —H.J.Muller⟩ ⟨from the moment of its birth surrealism was an international ~ —Herbert Read⟩ **2** *pl phenomena* **a :** a fact or event in the changing and perceptible forms as distinguished from the permanent essences of things: as (1) **:** a mutable, caused, or developing aspect of things as contrasted with their fixed and substantial natures (2) **:** a perceptible aspect or appearance of things as contrasted with their true or ideal being (3) **:** an object of sense perception as distinguished from an ultimate reality (4) [G *phänomenon*, *phänomen*, fr. LL *phaenomenon*] *Kantianism* **:** an object of experience in space and time as distinguished from a thing-in-itself (5) **:** a sense impression or sense-datum as distinguished from a thing ⟨*phenomena*, not only physical things, have spatial and temporal aspects —Nelson Goodman⟩ **b :** a fact or event of scientific interest susceptible of scientific description and explanation — in common usage retaining the implication of change or mode of being esp. illustrating the operation of some general law **3 a :** a rare fact or event **:** a fact or event of special or unique significance ⟨authorities explained the fiery light as an optical ~ —Fred Zimmer⟩ **b** *pl usu phenomenons* **:** an exceptional, unusual, or abnormal thing or occurrence ⟨the annual is . . . something of a publishing ~: selling for $3.95, it has a circulation of 40,000 —Harvey Breit⟩ **c** *pl phenomenons* **:** an extraordinary or remarkable person esp. in ability **:** PRODIGY ⟨a ~ at tennis⟩ **syn** see WONDER

phe·nom·ic \fəˈnämik, -mēk\ *adj* [prob. fr. *phenomenon* + *-ic*] **:** PHENOTYPIC

phenoms *pl of* PHENOM

-phe·none \fəˈnōn, ˈfē,nōn\ *n comb form* -S [*phen-* + *-one*] **:** aromatic ketone containing a phenyl or substituted phenyl group attached to a (specified) acyl group ⟨aceto*phenone*⟩ ⟨benzo*phenone*⟩ ⟨resaceto*phenone*⟩

phe·no·plast \ˈfēnə,plast\ *n* -S [ISV *phen-* + *-plast*] **:** PHENOLIC RESIN — **phe·no·plas·tic** \¦==¦plastik\ *adj*

phe·no·quinone \¦fēnō +\ *n* [ISV *phen-* + *quinone*] **:** a deep red crystalline complex $C_6H_4O_2.2C_6H_5OH$ formed by the union of phenol with quinone

phe·no·safranine \¦==+\ *n* [ISV *phen-* + *safranine*] **:** a simple red safranine dye made by oxidation of a 1:2 mixture of *para*-phenylenediamine and aniline and used chiefly as a desensitizer in photography

phe·no·sper·my \ˈfēnə,spərmē\ *n* -ES [¹*phen-* + *-spermy*] **:** the production with or without pollination of empty or abortive seeds

phe·no·thiazine \¦fēnō+\ *n* [ISV *phen-* + *thiazine*] **:** a greenish yellow crystalline compound $C_{12}H_9NS$ that is formed by heating diphenylamine with sulfur, that is an anthelmintic and insecticide, and that is used chiefly in veterinary practice to rid farm animals of internal parasites — called also *thiodiphenylamine;* compare STRUCTURAL FORMULA

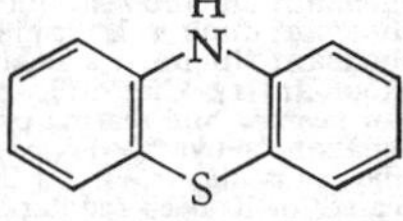

phenothiazine

phe·no·type \ˈfēnə,tīp, ˈfen-\ *n* [G *phänotypus*, fr. *phäno-* phen- + *typus* type, character, fr. L — more at TYPE] **1 a :** the detectable expression of the interaction of genotype and environment **b :** the visible characters of an organism **2 :** a group of organisms sharing a particular phenotype — compare GENOTYPE

phe·no·typ·ic \¦==¦tipik\ *or* **phe·no·typ·i·cal** \-pəkəl\ *adj* [G *phänotypisch*, fr. *phänotypus* + *-isch* -ic, -ical] **:** of, relating to, or constituting a phenotype ⟨~ pigmentation combinations —*Science*⟩ — **phe·no·typ·i·cal·ly** \-pək(ə)lē\ *adv*

phen·ox·azine \(ˈ)fēn, (ˈ)fen+\ *n* [ISV *phen-* + *oxazine*] **:** a crystalline compound $C_{12}H_9NO$ that is analogous in structure to phenothiazine with oxygen in place of sulfur and that is the parent of oxazine dyes (as gallocyanine)

phen·oxide \fə̇n+\ *n* [*phen-* + *oxide*] **1 :** a salt of phenol in its capacity as a weak acid ⟨sodium ~ C_6H_5ONa⟩ **2 :** a salt of any phenol

phe·noxy \fəˈnäksē\ *adj* [*phenoxy-*] **:** containing the radical C_6H_5O-

phenoxy- *comb form* [*phen-* + *oxy-*] **:** containing the univalent radical $C_6H_5(-)$ composed of phenyl united with oxygen — in names of chemical compounds ⟨*phenoxy*acetic acid $C_6H_5OCH_2COOH$⟩

phe·noxy·methylpenicillin \fə¦näksē+\ *n* [*phenoxy-* + *methyl* + *penicillin*] **:** PENICILLIN 2c

phenyl \ˈfenᵊl, ˈfēn-\ *n* -S [ISV *phen-* + *-yl;* orig. formed as F *phényle*] **:** a univalent radical C_6H_5 derived from benzene by removal of one hydrogen atom — compare BIPHENYL

phenyl·acetaldehyde \¦==+\ *n* [ISV *phenylacetic* + *aldehyde*] **:** a liquid compound $C_6H_5CH_2CHO$ of hyacinth odor used in perfumes

phenyl·acetamide \¦==+\ *n* [ISV *phenyl* + *acetamide*] **:** ACETANILIDE

phenyl·acetic acid \¦==+-\ *n* [*phenylacetic* ISV *phenyl* + *acetic*] **:** a crystalline acid $C_6H_5CH_2COOH$ obtained usu. by hydrolyzing benzyl cyanide and used chiefly in the manufacture of penicillin and in the form of esters with odor like honey in perfumes (as for soap); alpha-toluic acid

phenyl·alanine \¦==+\ *n* [ISV *phenyl* + *alanine*] **:** a crystalline alpha-amino acid $C_6H_5CH_2CH(NH_2)COOH$ that is obtained in its levorotatory L form by the hydrolysis of proteins (as lactalbumin), that is essential in the nutrition of man and lower animals, and that is converted in the normal body to tyrosine; α-amino-beta-phenyl-propionic acid — compare PHENYLKETONURIA, PHENYLPYRUVIC ACID

¹phenyl·ate \ˈfenᵊl,āt, ˈfēn-, -nᵊlət, *usu* -d·+V\ *n* -S [ISV *phenyl* + *-ate*, n. suffix] **:** PHENOXIDE 1

²phenyl·ate \-nᵊl,āt, *usu* -ād·+V\ *vt* -ED/-ING/-S [*phenyl* + *-ate*, v. suffix] **:** to introduce the phenyl group into (a compound) — **phenyl·a·tion** \,==ˈāshən\ *n* -S

phenyl·bu·ta·zone \,==ˈbyüd·ə,zōn\ *n* -S [*phenyl* + *but-* + *pyrazolone*] **:** a white or light yellow powder $C_{19}H_{20}N_2O_2$ derived from pyrazolone and used for its analgesic and antipyretic effects

phenyl·carbamate \¦==+\ *n* [*phenylcarbamic* + *-ate*] **:** CARBANILATE

phenyl·carbamic acid \¦==+-\ *n* [ISV *phenyl* + *carbamic*] **:** CARBANILIC ACID

phenyl chloride *n* **:** CHLOROBENZENE

phenyl cyanide *n* **:** BENZONITRILE

phenyl·ene \ˈfenᵊl,ēn, ˈfēn-\ *n* -S [ISV *phenyl* + *-ene*] **:** any of three bivalent radicals $-C_6H_4-$ derived from benzene by removal of two hydrogen atoms from the ortho, meta, or para positions

phenyl·ene·diamine \¦==,=+\ *n* [ISV *phenylene* + *diamine*] **:** any of three toxic isomeric crystalline compounds $C_6H_4(NH_2)_2$ that are ortho, meta, and para diamino derivatives of benzene of which the ortho and para isomers are used as photographic developers and the meta and para isomers in dye manufacture

phenyl·eph·rine \,==ˈe,frēn, -frən\ *n* -S [*phenyl* + epine*phrine*] **:** a basic compound $C_9H_{13}NO_2$ related chemically to epinephrine and ephedrine and used in the form of the hydrochloride as a vasoconstrictor to the nasal mucosa, a mydriatic in ophthalmology, and by injection to raise the blood pressure

phenyl ether *n* **1 :** a low-melting crystalline compound $(C_6H_5)_2O$ of geranium odor used chiefly in perfumes (as for soaps) and in a mixture with biphenyl as a heat-transfer medium — called also *diphenyl ether, diphenyl oxide* **2 :** an ether in which one of the radicals united to oxygen is phenyl

phenyl·ethyl \¦==+\ *n* [ISV *phenyl* + *ethyl*] **:** either of two univalent radicals derived from ethylbenzene by removal of one hydrogen atom from the side chain; *esp* **:** the beta or 2-derivative $C_6H_5CH_2CH_2$—

phenylethyl alcohol *n* **:** a fragrant liquid alcohol $C_6H_5CH_2CH_2OH$ that is found in rose oil and neroli oil but is usu. made synthetically and that is used chiefly in perfumes of the rose type — called also *beta-phenylethyl alcohol, phenethyl alcohol, 2-phenylethyl alcohol*

phenyl·ethylene \¦==+\ *n* [ISV *phenyl* + *ethylene*] **:** STYRENE

phenyl·glycine \¦==+\ *n* [ISV *phenyl* + *glycine*] **:** a phenyl derivative of glycine; *esp* **:** the crystalline synthetic acid $C_6H_5NHCH_2COOH$ containing a phenyl group attached to nitrogen and used in the manufacture of indigoid dyes

phenylglyoxylic acid \¦==+-\ *n* [ISV *phenyl* + *glyoxylic*] **:** a crystalline keto acid $C_6H_5COCOOH$ obtained esp. by oxidizing styrene or mandelic acid; benzoyl-formic acid

phenyl·hydrazide \¦==+\ *n* [ISV *phenyl* + *hydrazide*] **:** a hydrazide $RCONHNHC_6H_5$ formed from phenylhydrazine by reaction usu. with an ester, acid chloride, or acid anhydride

phenyl·hydrazine \¦==+\ *n* [ISV *phenyl* + *hydrazine;* orig. formed as G *phenylhydrazin*] **:** a toxic liquid nitrogen base $C_6H_5NHNH_2$ that is made by reduction of benzenediazonium chloride and that reacts with aldehydes, ketones, acids, and related compounds to form hydrazides, hydrazones, and osazones useful in the identification of such compounds esp. as sugars

phenyl·hydrazone \¦==+\ *n* [ISV *phenyl* + *hydrazone*] **:** a hydrazone derived from phenylhydrazine

phe·nyl·ic \fəˈnilik\ *adj* [ISV *phenyl* + *-ic*] **:** relating to, derived from, or containing phenyl

phenyl iodide *n* **:** IODOBENZENE

phenyl isocyanate *n* **:** a colorless liquid ester C_6H_5NCO of acrid odor made usu. by the action of phosgene on aniline and used in identifying alcohols and amines by the formation of phenylurethans and phenyl-ureas respectively

phenyl·ketonuria \¦==+\ *n* [NL, fr. *phenyl* + *ketonuria*] **:** a rare genetic anomaly in man marked by inability to oxidize phenylpyruvic acid and by severe mental deficiency — called also *phenylpyruvic amentia, phenylpyruvic oligophrenia*

phenyl·ke·to·nu·ric \,==,kēd·ə¦n(y)ùrik\ *n* -S **:** one affected with phenylketonuria

phenyl mercaptan *n* **:** THIOPHENOL 1

phenyl·mercuric acetate \¦==+-\ *n* [*phenyl* + *mercuric*] **:** a crystalline salt $C_6H_5HgOOCCH_3$ made by reaction of benzene with mercuric acetate in alcoholic solution and used chiefly as a fungicide and herbicide

phenylmercuric nitrate *n* [*phenyl* + *mercuric*] **:** a crystalline basic salt approximately $C_6H_5HgNO_3.C_6H_5HgOH$ used chiefly as a fungicide and external antiseptic

phenyl methyl ketone *n* **:** ACETOPHENONE

phenyl·osazone \¦==+\ *n* [*phenyl* + *osazone*] **:** an osazone (as glucose phenylosazone) derived from phenylhydrazine that is usu. yellow and crystalline and that is useful esp. in the study of carbohydrates

phenyl·propanolamine \¦==+\ *n* [*phenyl* + *propanol* + *amine*] **:** NOREPHEDRINE

phenyl·pyruvic acid \¦==+-\ *n* [*phenyl* + *pyruvic*] **:** a crystalline keto acid $C_6H_5CH_2COCOOH$ found in the urine as a metabolic product of phenylalanine esp. in phenylketonuria

phenylpyruvic amentia *or* **phenylpyruvic oligophrenia** *n* **:** PHENYLKETONURIA

phenyl salicylate *n* **:** a crystalline ester $HOC_6H_4COOC_6H_5$ used chiefly as a stabilizer for cellulosic plastics and vinyl plastics and as an ingredient of suntan preparations because of its ability to absorb ultraviolet light and also esp. formerly as an internal antiseptic

phenyl·thiocarbamide \¦==+\ *n* [*phenyl* + *thiocarbamide*] **:** PHENYLTHIOUREA

phenyl·thiourea \¦==+\ *n* [NL, fr. *phenyl* + *thiourea*] **:** a crystalline compound $C_6H_5NHCSNH_2$ that is made from aniline, carbon disulfide, and ammonia and is tasteless to many persons and extremely bitter to others — called also *phenylthiocarbamide*

phenyl·urethan \¦==+\ *or* **phenyl·urethane** \¦==+\ *n* [ISV *phenyl* + *urethan*] **1 :** an aromatic crystalline ester $C_6H_5NHCOOC_2H_5$ made usu. by addition of ethyl alcohol to phenyl isocyanate **2 :** any ester of carbanilic acid

phe·nyt·o·in \fəˈnid·əwə̇n\ *n* -S [diphenylhydant*oin*] **:** DIPHENYLHYDANTOIN

pheo- — see PHAEO-

pheo·chrome \ˈfēə,krōm\ *adj* [ISV *phaeo-* + *-chrome*] **:** CHROMAFFIN

pheo·chro·mo·blast \¦fēō+\ *also* **pheo·chro·mo·cy·to·blast** \,fēō,krōmōˈsīd·ə,blast\ *n* [*pheochromoblast* fr. *pheochrome* + *-o-* + *-blast; pheochromocytoblast* fr. *pheochromocyte* + *-o-* + *-blast*] **:** an embryonic cell destined to give rise to chromaffin tissue esp. of the adrenal medulla

pheo·chromocyte \¦fēō+\ *n* [ISV *phaeochrome* + *-o-* + *-cyte*] **:** a chromaffin cell

pheo·chro·mo·cy·to·ma \,==,krōmōsīˈtōmə\ *n, pl* **pheochromocytomas** \-məz\ *or* **pheochromocytoma·ta** \-məd·ə\ [NL, fr. ISV *phaeochromocyte* + NL *-oma*] **:** a tumor derived from chromaffin cells and usu. associated with paroxysmal or sustained hypertension

phe·on \ˈfē,än\ *n* -S [ME *feon*] **1 :** a conventional heraldic representation of the head of a javelin, dart, or arrow point downward with two long barbs engrailed on the inner edge **2 :** a head of an arrow borne as a heraldic charge

pheon

pheo·phor·bide \,fēəˈfȯr,bēd, -,bəd\ *n* -S [ISV *phaeo-* + *phorb-* (fr. Gk *phorbē* pasture, fodder) + *-ide;* akin to Gk *pherbein* to feed and prob. to OE *byrgan* to taste, eat, ON *bergja*] **:** a blue-black crystalline acid obtained from chlorophyll or pheophytin by treatment with hydrochloric acid

pheo·phy·tin *or* **phaeo·phy·tin** \,fēəˈfīd·ən\ *n* [ISV *pheo*phorbide + *phytyl* + *-in*] **:** a bluish black waxy pigment that is olive-brown in solution, that is obtained from chlorophyll by mild treatment with acid (as oxalic acid), and that differs from chlorophyll structurally only by the replacement of the magnesium atom in the molecule by two hydrogen atoms; the phytyl ester of pheophorbide

pheo·porphyrin *or* **phaeo·porphyrin** \ˌfēō+\ *n* [*pheophorbide* + *porphyrin*] : a crystalline isomer of pheophorbide that is obtained from pheophorbide by treatment with hydriodic acid and that is not of typical porphyrin structure but is a substituted dehydro-phorbin

-pher \fə(r)\ *n comb form* -s [Gk *pherein* to carry — more at BEAR] : one that carries ⟨chronopher⟩ ⟨telpher⟩

pher·e·crat·ic \ˌferəˈkrad·ik\ *also* **pher·e·cra·te·an** \-krādēən\ *or* **pher·e·cra·tian** \-āshən\ *n* -s *sometimes cap* [*pherecratic* fr. *Pherecrates*, 5th cent. B.C. Greek poet (fr. Gk *Pherekratēs*) + E -*ic*; *pherecratean* alter. of *pherecratian*, fr. LL *pherecratius* of Pherecrates (fr. Gk *pherekrateios*, fr. *Pherekratēs*) + E -*an*] **1** : a classical verse or rhythmic system of the form –∪∪–∪–⏑ — called also *aristophanic, first pherecratic* **2** : a classical verse or rhythmic system of the form ⏑⏑–∪∪–⏑ — called also *second pherecratic*

phew *voiceless whistling breath emitted through rounded lips & usu followed by a voiceless* (y)ü *or* ue *sound; often read as* ˈfyü\ *interj* [imit. of a whistling sound] — used to express discomfort caused usu. by heat or humidity; compare PHOO

phi \ˈfī\ *n* -s [MGk, fr. Gk *phei*] : the 21st letter of the Greek alphabet — symbol Φ or φ; see ALPHABET table

phi *abbr* philosophy

phi·al \ˈfī(ə)l\ *n* -s [ME *fiole*, fr. MF, fr. OProv *fiola*, fr. L *phiala*, fr. Gk *phialē*] : a container for liquids; *esp* : a small glass bottle for medicines : VIAL

phi·a·le \ˈfīəlē\ *n, pl* **phia·lae** \-əˌlē\ [Gk *phialē*] **1** : a shallow Greek bowl resembling a Roman patera usu. made with a boss in the center and used in ancient times for drinking or pouring libations **2** : a fountain or laver in a church (as at the entrance)

phi·a·lide \ˈfīəˌlīd\ *n* -s [F, fr. Gk *phialidion*, dim. of *phialē* bowl] : STERIGMA; *esp* : one that is flask-shaped or constricted just below the apex and in some forms is the end cell of the phialophore

phi·a·lid·i·um \ˌfīəˈlidēəm\ *n, cap* [NL, prob. fr. Gk *phialidion*] : a widely distributed genus of hydrozoan medusae

phi·a·loph·o·ra \ˌfīəˈläf(ə)rə\ *n, cap* [NL, fr. Gk *phialē* + NL -*phora*] : a form genus of imperfect fungi (family Dematiaceae) which are characterized esp. by spores borne on phialides and some forms of which are important in mycotic infections of man (as chromoblastomycosis)

phi·a·lo·pore \ˈfīələˌpō(ə)r\ *n* [Gk *phialo-* (fr. *phialē* bowl) + E -*pore*] : the aperture through which the hollow asexual daughter colony of a volvox inverts itself

phi be·ta kap·pa \ˈfīˌbād·əˈkapə, ˌtə- *sometimes* -bē\ *n, usu cap P&B&K* [so called fr. the initials of the society's Greek motto, *philosophia biou kybernētēs* philosophy the guide of life] : a person winning high scholastic distinction usu. in course in an American college or university and being elected to membership in a national honor society founded in 1776 — called also *Phi Bete*

phi bete \ˈfīˈbāt\ *n, usu cap P&B* [by shortening & alter.] : PHI BETA KAPPA

phid·i·an \ˈfidēən\ *adj, usu cap* [*Phidias*, 5th cent. B.C. Greek sculptor + E -*an*] : of, relating to, or characteristic of the Greek sculptor Phidias or his school

phil *abbr* **1** philharmonic **2** philological; philologist; philology **3** philosopher; philosophical; philosophy

phil- *or* **philo-** *comb form* [ME, fr. OF, fr. L, fr. Gk, fr. *philein* to love, fr. *philos* beloved, dear, loving — more at -PHILOUS] : loving : having an affinity for ⟨*phil*ydraceous⟩ ⟨*philo*-Celticism⟩ ⟨*philo*graph⟩

¹-phil \ˌfil\ *or* **-phile** \ˌfīl\ *n comb form* -s [F *-phile*, fr. Gk *-philos*, fr. *philos* beloved, dear, loving] : one that loves : lover : one having a fondness or affinity for or a strong attraction to ⟨acido*phil*⟩ ⟨hemo*phile*⟩ ⟨biblio*phile*⟩ ⟨Anglo*phile*⟩

²-phil \"\ *or* **-phile** \"\ *adj comb form* [NL *-philus*, fr. L, fr. Gk *philos* beloved, dear, loving] : loving : having a fondness or affinity for ⟨hemo*phile*⟩ ⟨Franco*phil*⟩ ⟨negro*phile*⟩ ⟨organo*phile*⟩

-phi·la \fələ\ *n comb form, pl* **-phila** [NL, fr. L, fem. sing. and neut. pl. of *-philus*] : one or ones attracted to or living or growing by preference in — in names of biological taxa ⟨Ammo*phila*⟩ ⟨Antho*phila*⟩

philabeg *var of* FILLEBEG

phil·a·del·phia \ˌfiləˈdelfyə, -fēə\ *adj, usu cap* [fr. *Philadelphia*, Pa.] : of or from the city of Philadelphia, Pa. ⟨*Philadelphia* department stores⟩ : of the kind or style prevalent in Philadelphia : PHILADELPHIAN

philadelphia chair *n, usu cap P* : WINDSOR CHAIR

philadelphia chippendale *n, usu cap P&C* : a style of 18th century furniture made in Philadelphia and characterized by rich ornamental carving

philadelphia fleabane *n, usu cap P* : SKEVISH

philadelphia ice cream *n, usu cap P* : ice cream made from flavored cream without eggs or other thickening

philadelphia lawyer *n, usu cap P* : an exceptionally competent lawyer ⟨language that . . . cannot be correctly and definitely interpreted even by a *Philadelphia lawyer* —*Jour. of Accountancy*⟩; *esp* : a shrewd lawyer versed in the intricacies of legal phraseology and adept at exploiting legal technicalities ⟨involves . . . a murder syndicate, blackmail, and enough complicated talk to require the services of a dozen *Philadelphia lawyers* —Charles Lee⟩

¹phil·a·del·phian \-fyən, -fēən\ *adj, usu cap* [Gk *philadelphia* brotherly love (fr. *philadelphos* brotherly — fr. *phil-* + *adelphos* brother — + -*ia* -y) + E -*an*] **1** : of or relating to the Philadelphian Society of Boehmenists **2** [*Philadelphia*, Pa. + E -*an*] : PHILADELPHIA

²philadelphian \"\ *n* -s [Gk *philadelphia* brotherly love + E -*an*] **1** *usu cap* : a member of the Philadelphian Society founded in London in 1670 as a sect of Boehmenism **2** *cap* [*Philadelphia*, Pa. + E -*an*] : a native or resident of Philadelphia, Pa.

philadelphia pepper pot *n, usu cap 1st P* : PEPPER POT 2 b

philadelphia vireo *n, usu cap P* : a vireo (*Vireo philadelphicus*) of eastern No. America with a grayish green back and yellowish underparts

phil·a·del·phus \ˌfiləˈdelfəs\ *n* [NL, fr. Gk *philadelphos* brotherly] **1** *cap* : a genus of ornamental shrubs (family Saxifragaceae) of wide distribution in temperate regions that are distinguished by the numerous stamens and the inferior ovary — see MOCK ORANGE **2** -ES : any plant of the genus *Philadelphus*

phil·a·mot \ˈfiləˌmät\ *n* -s [obs. *fieulamort*, adj., of the color of faded leaf, fr. F *feuille morte* philamot] : FEUILLE MORTE

¹phi·lan·der \fəˈlandə(r), -laan-\ *n* [Gk *philandros* loving men, fr. *phil-* + *andr-*, *anēr* man — more at ANDR-] **1** -s **a** : PHILANDERER **b** : FLIRTATION **2** [alter. of *filander*] **a** -s : any of several medium-sized woolly opossums of So. and Central America **b** *cap* : a genus of marsupials including the woolly opossums

²philander \"\ *vi* **philandered; philandered; philandering** \-d(ə)riŋ\ **philanders** : to make love frivolously or in a trifling or fickle way : DALLY, FLIRT ⟨belles and beaux ~*ed* in the big hotels —Van Wyck Brooks⟩ ⟨his penchant for ~*ing* with pretty stenographers finally drove his wife to sue for divorce⟩

phi·lan·der·er \-d(ə)rə(r)\ *n* -s [²*philander* + -*er*] : one that plays at courtship : a fickle lover : FLIRT ⟨"like all ~*s* you're afraid you've never been in love," she said sharply —Louis Auchincloss⟩

¹phi·lan·thid \fəˈlan(t)thəd\ *n* -s [NL *Philanthidae*] : a wasp of the family Philanthidae

²philanthid \"\ *adj* [NL *Philanthidae*] : of or relating to the Philanthidae

phi·lan·thi·dae \-thəˌdē\ *n pl, cap* [NL, fr. *Philanthus*, type genus + -*idae*] : a family of digger wasps that are usu. black with conspicuous yellow markings

phil·an·thrope \ˈfilənˌthrōp\ *n* -s [F, fr. Gk *philanthrōpos* loving mankind] *archaic* : PHILANTHROPIST

phil·an·throp·ic \ˌ;thräpik, -pēk\ *also* **phil·an·throp·i·cal** \-pəkəl, -pēk-\ *adj* [*philanthropic* fr. F *philanthropique*, fr. Gk *philanthrōpos* + F -*ique* -ic; *philanthropical* fr. *philanthropy* + -*ical*] **1** : of, relating to, or characterized by philanthropy : BENEVOLENT, HUMANITARIAN ⟨~ sympathy for the cause of the slave —V.L.Parrington⟩ ⟨found time to devote to church, civic, and ~ affairs —Marian Silveus⟩ **2** : dispensing or receiving aid from funds set aside for humanitarian purposes : ELEEMOSYNARY ⟨~ foundation⟩ ⟨the need for books at nearby hospitals and ~ homes —*Wonderful World of Books*⟩ — **phil·an·throp·i·cal·ly** \-pək(ə)lē, -pēk-, -li\ *adv*

phi·lan·thro·pism \fəˈlan(t)thrəˌpizəm, -laan-\ *n* -s [*philanthropy* + -*ism*] : PHILANTHROPY

phi·lan·thro·pist \-pəst\ *n* -s [*philanthropy* + -*ist*] : one characterized by or practicing philanthropy : ALTRUIST, HUMANITARIAN — **phi·lan·thro·pis·tic** \ˌ;ˈpistik\ *adj*

phi·lan·thro·py \fəˈlan(t)thrəpē, -laan-, -pi\ *n* -ES [LL *philanthropia*, fr. Gk *philanthrōpia*, fr. *philanthrōpos* loving mankind (fr. *phil-* + *anthrōpos* man) + -*ia* -y — more at ANTHROP-] **1** : goodwill toward one's fellowmen esp. as expressed through active efforts to promote human welfare : HUMANITARIANISM ⟨~ . . . is civic, social, and amply beneficial —J.A.Franquiz⟩ — contrasted with *misanthropy* **2 a** : an act or instance of deliberative generosity : a contribution made in a spirit of humanitarianism ⟨among his *philanthropies* were full tuition scholarships for deserving students⟩ **b** (1) : an organization distributing funds for humanitarian purposes ⟨funds for the new rehabilitation center came from two of the big *philanthropies*⟩ (2) : an institution or agency supported by such contributions ⟨community chest funds are distributed among various *philanthropies*⟩

phi·lan·thus \fəˈlan(t)thəs\ *n, cap* [NL, fr. *phil-* + -*anthus*] : a genus of digger wasps that is the type of the family Philanthidae

phil·an·tom·ba \ˌfilənˈtämbə\ *n* -s [origin unknown] : a West African duiker (*Cephalophus maxwelli*)

phil·a·tel·ic \ˌfiləˈtelik, -lēk\ *adj* [*philately* + -*ic*] **1** : of or relating to philately ⟨~ data⟩ ⟨~ organizations⟩ ⟨~ accessories⟩ **2** : of interest or value to philatelists ⟨~ features of a stamp⟩ — **phil·a·tel·i·cal·ly** \-lək(ə)lē, -lēk-, -(ə)li\ *adv*

philatelic mail *n* : mail whose primary purpose is the acquisition of special stamps or postal markings

phi·lat·e·list \fəˈlat͟ələst, ˌtᵊl- *also* -ˈlā\ *n* -s [F *philatéliste*, fr. *philatélie* + -*iste* -ist] : a specialist in philately : one that collects or studies stamps ⟨the primary motive which actuates collectors (as opposed to ~*s*) is cash value —A.E.Hopkins⟩

phi·lat·e·ly \-lē, -ᵊli\ *n* -ES [F *philatélie*, fr. *phil-* + Gk *ateleia* tax exemption, immunity, fr. *atelēs* free from tax or tribute, immune from public duties (fr. *a-* ²a- + *telos* tax) + -*ia* -y; akin to Gk *telein* to pay, *tlēnai* to bear; fr. the fact that the postage stamp exempted the recipient from paying the mailing charge or tax — more at TOLERATE] **1** : the collection and study of postage stamps and of postal stationery that has passed through the mail : stamp collecting ⟨it is with adhesive postage stamps that ~ is primarily concerned —R.H.P.Curle⟩ **2** : stamp collectors : PHILATELISTS ⟨surprised and delighted ~ by his early announcement of . . . commemorative stamps —K.B.Stiles⟩

-phile — see -PHIL

phil·e·nor butterfly \fəˈlēnə(r)-\ *n* [NL *philenor* (specific epithet of *Papilio philenor*, species of swallowtails) fr. Gk *philēnōr* conjugal] : PIPE-VINE SWALLOWTAIL

phil·e·pit·ta \ˌfiləˈpid·ə\ *n, cap* [NL] : a genus of Madagascan birds related to the pittas but constituting a distinct family

phil·e·tai·rus \ˌfiləˈtīrəs\ *n, cap* [NL, fr. *phil-* + Gk *hetairos* companion] : a monotypic genus of passerine birds consisting of the sociable weaverbird of southern Africa

¹phil·har·mon·ic \ˌfilə(r)ˈmänik, -ilˌhär;-, -iˌlär;-, -ilˌhä;-, -iˌlä;-, -nēk *sometimes* -ilhə(r);-\ *n* [F *philharmonique*, fr. It *filarmonico*, adj., fr. *fil-* phil- + *armonico* harmonic, fr. L *harmonicus* — more at HARMONIC] **1** *archaic* : a lover of music **2** *often cap* : a musical concert or musical organization (as a society or orchestra) ⟨served as guest conductor for the ~⟩

²philharmonic \"\ *adj* [F *philharmonique*, fr. It *filarmonico*] **1** *archaic* : of or relating to a lover of music ⟨the most ~ ear is at times deeply affected by a simple air —*New Monthly Mag.*⟩ **2** : of or relating to a musical organization, esp. a symphony orchestra ⟨a ~ pace is slower than the pace set by a . . . pit band —Ethel Merman⟩

philharmonic pitch *n* : a tuning standard of English origin of approximately 450 vibrations per second for A above middle C — contrasted with *new philharmonic pitch*

¹phil·hel·lene \(ˈ)filˌheˌlēn\ *adj* [Gk *philellēn*, fr. *phil-* + *Hellēn* Hellene] : venerating Greece or the Greeks ⟨more ~ than the Greeks themselves —J.H.Moulton⟩

²philhellene \"\ *n, often cap* : an admirer or supporter of Greece or of the Greeks ⟨an almost fanatical ~, fluent in both ancient and modern Greek —Alistair MacLean⟩

phil·hel·len·ic \ˌfilheˈlenik\ *adj* **1** : PHILHELLENE **2** : supporting the Greek struggle for independence from Ottoman domination ⟨~ dispositions of the satrap —George Grote⟩

phil·hel·len·ism \filˈheləˌnizəm\ *n* : veneration of Greece or the Greeks ⟨literary ~ from Shakespeare to Byron —Terence Spencer⟩

phil·hel·len·ist \-ˌnəst\ *n* [Gk *philellēn* + E -*ist*] : PHILHELLENE

phil·ia \ˈfilēə\ *n* -s [NL, fr. Gk, friendship, fr. *philos* loving, friendly + -*ia* -y — more at -PHILOUS] : love of friends or of one's fellowman : social sympathy — compare AGAPE, EROS

-philia \"\ *n comb form* -s [NL, fr. Gk *philia*, fr. *philos* loving — more at -PHILOUS] **1** : tendency toward ⟨chromato*philia*⟩ ⟨spasmo*philia*⟩ **2** : abnormal appetite or liking for ⟨alcoholo*philia*⟩ ⟨copro*philia*⟩

phil·i·a·ter \ˌfilēˌad·ə(r), ˌ;ˈ;\ *n* -s [Gk *philiatros*, fr. *phil-* + *iatēr* healer, doctor] : one interested in medical science

philibeg *var of* FILLEBEG

-phil·ic \ˈfilik, -lēk\ *adj comb form* [*phil-* + -*ic*] : having an affinity for : loving : attracted by : adapted to : ⟨electro*philic*⟩ ⟨helio*philic*⟩ ⟨lyo*philic*⟩ — opposed to -*phobic*

-philies *pl of* -PHILY

phi·li·ne \fəˈlīnē\ *n* -s [NL] : a bubble shell of the family Philinidae

phi·lin·i·dae \fəˈlinəˌdē\ *n pl, cap* [NL, fr. *Philine* + -*idae*] : a small but widely distributed family of marine bubble shells with the shell wholly concealed in the mantle

phil·ip \ˈfiləp\ *n* -s [fr. the name *Philip*; prob. fr. the name resembling the sound of their chirps] **1** *dial Eng* : HEDGE SPARROW **2** *dial Eng* : HOUSE SPARROW

philippan *adj, usu cap* [*Philippi*, town in ancient Macedonia, Greece + E -*an*] *obs* : used at Philippi ⟨while I wore his sword ~ —Shak.⟩

¹phi·lip·pi·an \fəˈlipēən\ *adj, usu cap* [*Philippi* + E -*an*] : of, relating to, or characteristic of Philippi, a city of ancient Macedonia

²philippian \"\ *n* -s *cap* [*Philippi* + E -*an*] : a native or inhabitant of Philippi

phi·lip·pic \fəˈlipik, -pēk\ *n* -s [MF *philippique*, fr. LL & Gk; LL (*orationes*) *philippicae*, speeches of the Greek orator Demosthenes †322 B.C. against Philip II †336 B.C. king of Macedon and speeches of the Roman orator Cicero †43 B.C. against Mark Antony †30 B.C. Roman orator, triumvir, and soldier, fr. L, fem. pl. of *philippicus* of Philip, fr. Gk *philippikos* of or against Philip; Gk *philippikoi* (*logoi*), speeches of Demosthenes against Philip II, fr. masc. pl. of *philippikos* of Philip, fr. *Philippos* Philip + -*ikos* -ic] : a discourse or declamation full of acrimonious invective : TIRADE ⟨a ~ so withering that it roused a lethargic Senate —S.H.Adams⟩

²philippic *adj, obs* : characterized by acrimony : ABUSIVE

philippina *or* **philippine** *var of* PHILOPENA

phil·ip·pine \ˈfiləˌpēn, ˌ;ˈ;\ *adj, usu cap* [fr. the *Philippine* islands, north Malay archipelago, southeast Asia] : of or from the Philippines : of the kind or style prevalent in the Philippines : FILIPINO

philippine cedar *n, usu cap P* : a Philippine timber tree (*Toona calantas* syn *Cedrela toona*) with red or pale red hard fragrant wood used esp. for cigar boxes and interior finish — called also *kalantas*

philippine fowl disease *n, usu cap P* : NEWCASTLE DISEASE

philippine mahogany *n, usu cap P* **1** : any of several Philippine timber trees with wood resembling that of the true mahoganies: as **a** : PHILIPPINE CEDAR **b** : NARRA **c** : LUMBAYAO **d** : RED LAUAN **e** : TANGUILE **f** : ALMON **2** : the wood of a Philippine mahogany; *esp* : BAGTIKAN

phil·ip·pism \ˈfiləˌpizəm\ *n* -s *cap* [F *philippisme*, fr. *Philipp* Melanchthon (Schwarzert) †1560 Ger. scholar and religious reformer + F -*isme* -ism] : the doctrines of the Lutheran theologian Philipp Melanchthon or his followers marked by a conciliatory policy toward both the Calvinists and the Roman Catholic Church

phil·ip·pist \-pəst\ *n* -s *usu cap* [F *philippiste*, fr. *Philipp* Melanchthon †1560 + F -*iste* -ist] : an adherent to or supporter of Philippism — **phil·ip·pis·tic** \ˌ;ˈpistik\ *adj, usu cap*

phil·ip·pize \ˈfiləˌpīz\ *vi* -ED/-ING/-S *often cap* [Gk *Philippizein* to be on Philip's side, fr. *Philippos* Philip (of Macedon) + -*izein* -ize] : to speak in support of a cause under the influence of a bribe

phi·lip·pus \fəˈlipəs\ *n, pl* **philip·pi** \-ˌpī\ [L] **1** : a gold stater of Philip II of Macedon **2** : any of several gold or silver 15th or 16th century coins of France, Spain, and Burgundy issued by rulers named Philip

phil·ip·stad·ite \ˈfiləpˌstäˌdīt\ *n* -s [*Philipstad*, Sweden, its locality + E -*ite*] : a mineral approximately $Ca_2(Fe, Mg)_5(Si, Al)_8O_{22}(OH)_2$ consisting of silicate of calcium, iron, magnesium, and aluminum and belonging to the amphibole group

phi·lis·tia \fəˈlistēə\ *n pl, often cap* [NL, fr. LL *Philistaea*, ancient country in southwestern Palestine that was the land of the Philistines] : cultural Philistines as a class : the Philistine world ⟨the perennial tendency of ~ to suspect what it does not understand —Mary McCarthy⟩ ⟨fierce . . . refusal to compromise with ~ which she shared with writers to whom she was in no other way allied —*New Republic*⟩

¹phil·is·tine \ˈfiləˌstēn, fəˈlistən, fəˈliˌstēn *sometimes* ˈfiləˌstīn *or* -stən\ *n* -s [ME, fr. LL *Philistinus*, fr. Gk *Philistinos*, fr. Heb *Pelishtī*] **1** *cap* : a native or inhabitant of ancient Philistia in the coastal regions of southwest Palestine **2** *usu cap, archaic* : someone (as a bailiff, a critic) regarded as a natural or traditional enemy because belonging to a despised class **3** [trans. of G *Philister*] *often cap* **a** : a crass prosaic often priggish individual guided by material rather than intellectual values : ⁴BABBITT, BOURGEOIS ⟨it is only the *Philistine* who seeks to estimate a personality by the vulgar test of production —Oscar Wilde⟩ ⟨the *Philistine* wants to talk about morals, not to understand what is morally wrong —J.T.Farrell⟩ **b** (1) : one deficient in originality or aesthetic sensitivity ⟨the *Philistine's* sturdy preference for reproduction of the familiar —John Dewey⟩ ⟨irresponsible ~*s* will bring about the disfigurement of Trinity's front greens and the walled banks of the Liffey —*Dublin Sunday Independent*⟩ (2) : one uninformed in a special area of knowledge : IGNORAMUS, OUTSIDER ⟨a course . . . designed to bring ~*s* to like literature —L.A.King⟩ ⟨the history . . . makes fascinating reading even for philatelic *Philistines* —Mollie Panter-Downes⟩

²philistine \"\ *adj* **1** *usu cap* : of or relating to the people of ancient Philistia **2** *often cap* : of, relating to, or characteristic of a Babbitt : BOURGEOIS, MATERIALISTIC ⟨a slightly missionary flavor as of one bringing the gospel of culture to a *Philistine* world —*Yale Rev.*⟩ — compare BIEDERMEIER **3** *often cap* **a** : oblivious to aesthetics : INSENSITIVE ⟨the old familiar theme of the misunderstood genius at war with ~ society —Henry Miller⟩ **b** : displaying or marked by indifference or lack of specialized knowledge : UNINFORMED ⟨my attitude toward the ballet, which is *Philistine* and ignorant —John Woodburn⟩

phil·is·tin·ic \ˌfiləˈstinik\ *also* **phil·is·tin·ish** *pronunc at* PHILISTINE + ish\ *adj, often cap* [¹*philistine* + -*ic* or -*ish*] : PHILISTINE

phil·is·tin·ism *pronunc at* PHILISTINE +ˌizəm\ *n* -s *often cap* : the attitudes, beliefs, and conduct characteristic of the modern philistine : MATERIALISM, BARBARISM ⟨his protest against the ~ of bourgeois values, emphasizes that art should be appreciated for its own sake —Bernard Smith⟩ ⟨what he called the cant of the great middle part of the English nation, what we call its *Philistinism* —Matthew Arnold⟩

phil·li·lew \ˈfiləˌlü\ *n* -s [prob. imit.] *Irish* : OUTCRY, UPROAR

phil·lips code \ˈfiləps-\ *n, cap P* [after Walter P. *Phillips* †1920 Am. telegrapher and journalist] : a code of abbreviations formerly used for telegraphic messages and esp. for press dispatches

phil·lips·ite \ˈfiləpˌsīt\ *n* -s [William *Phillips* †1828 Eng. mineralogist and geologist + E -*ite*] : a white or reddish mineral approximately $(K_2,Na_2,Ca)Al_2Si_4O_{12}.4\frac{1}{2}H_2O$ consisting of a hydrous silicate of potassium, calcium, and aluminum, belonging to the zeolite family, and commonly occurring in complex often cruciform crystals (hardness 4–4.5, sp. gr. 2.2)

Phillips Screws *trademark* — used for screws having a special head with a cross slot for use with a special screwdriver

phil·ly \ˈfilē, -li\ *adj, usu cap* [fr. *Philly*, nickname for *Philadelphia*, Pa.] *slang* : of or relating to the city of Philadelphia, Pa. ⟨*Philly* sportswriters⟩

phil·lyr·ea \fəˈlirēə\ *n, cap* [NL, fr. Gk *philyrea* mock privet] : a genus of evergreen shrubs (family Oleaceae) of the Mediterranean region with small greenish white flowers and fruit resembling olives

philo- — see PHIL-

phil·o·bib·list \ˌfiləˈbibləst, -ˈbīb-\ *n* -s [Gk *philobiblos* (fr. *phil-* + *biblos* book) + E -*ist* — more at BIBLE] : a lover of books : BIBLIOPHILE

philo-celticism \ˌfi(ˌ)lō+\ *n, cap C* : a fondness for Celtic expressions or idioms ⟨dismissed his entire essay as another example of crackpot *philo-Celticism* —J.V.Kelleher⟩

phil·o·den·dron \ˌfiləˈdendrən\ *n* [NL, fr. Gk, neut. of *philodendros* loving trees, fr. *phil-* + *dendron* tree — more at DENDR-] **1** *cap* : a genus of tropical American climbing aroids with prominent sheathing leafstalks, fleshy spathes of various colors, and flowers in a dense spadix **2** *pl* **philodendrons** \-nz\ *or* **philoden·dra** \-rə\ **a** : any plant of the genus *Philodendron* grown commonly as a house plant often in water alone **b** : any of various other aroid plants (as the ceriman) that are cultivated for their showy foliage

phil·o·di·na \ˌfiləˈdīnə\ *n, cap* [NL, fr. *phil-* + Gk *dinos* rotation, whirling] : a genus (the type of the family Philodinidae of the order Bdelloidea) comprising rotifers with a corona made up of two nearly circular disks on short stalks

phi·log·e·ny \fəˈläjənē\ *n* -ES [by alter. (influence of *phil-*)] : PHYLOGENY

phil·o·graph \ˈfiləˌgraf, -ràf\ *n* -s [*phil-* + -*graph*] : an apparatus with a transparent plane (as of glass or celluloid) on which to trace a facsimile of a view or object seen through an adjustable eyepiece — **phil·o·graph·ic** \ˌ;ˈgrafik\ *adj*

phi·log·y·nous \fəˈläjənəs\ *adj* [*philogyny* + -*ous*] : fond of women

phi·log·y·ny \-nē\ *n* -ES [Gk *philogynia*, fr. *phil-* + *gyn-* + -*ia* -y] : fondness for women

phi·lo·he·la \fəˈlōhələ\ *n, cap* [NL, fr. *phil-* + Gk *helē* sun's heat, fr. *hēlios* sun — more at SOLAR] : a genus of birds (family Scolopacidae) consisting of the American woodcock

phi·lol·o·gas·ter \fəˈläləˌgastə(r), ˌ;ˈ;\ *n* -s [*philologist* + -*aster*] : an incompetent philologist : dabbler in philology — **phi·lol·o·gas·try** \-trē\ *n* -ES

phi·lol·o·ger \fəˈläləjə(r)\ *n* -s [MF *philologie* philology + E -*er*] : PHILOLOGIST ⟨primarily a ~ and only secondarily a prosodist —T.S.Omond⟩

phil·o·lo·gi·an \ˌfiləˈlōjēən\ *n* -s [L *philologia* philology + E -*an*] : PHILOLOGIST 2

phil·o·log·i·cal \ˌfiləˈläjəkəl, -jēk-\ *also* **phil·o·log·ic** \-jik, -jēk\ *adj* [*philological* fr. L *philologia* philology + E -*ical*; *philologic* fr. F *philologique*, fr. MF *philologie* philology + -*ique* -ic] : of, relating to, or dealing with philology ⟨~ studies⟩ ⟨a ~ society⟩ ⟨a date based chiefly on ~ evidence⟩ — **phil·o·log·i·cal·ly** \-jək(ə)lē, -jēk-, -li\ *adv*

phi·lol·o·gist \fəˈläləjəst\ *n* -s **1** : one that loves learning or literature : a learned or literary man : a scholar esp. of classical antiquity **2** : LINGUIST 2; *esp* : one that concerns himself with human speech as the vehicle of literature and as a field of study that sheds light on cultural history

phi·lol·o·gize \ˌ;ˈ;ˌjīz\ *vb* -ED/-ING/-S [*philology* + -*ize*] *vt* : to render by philological investigation ~ *vi* : to study or make investigations in philology

phil·o·logue *or* **phil·o·log** \ˈfiləˌläg *also* -ˌlōg\ *n* -s [MF, fr. L *philologus* lover of learning, fr. Gk *philologos* lover of words and learning, fr. *phil-* + *logos* word, reason, speech — more at LEGEND] : PHILOLOGIST

phi·lol·o·gy \fə'läləjē, -ji\ *n* -ES [F *philologie*, fr. MF, fr. L *philologia* love of talk, speech, or argument, fr. Gk, love of argument, learning, and literature, fr. *philologos* love of words and learning + *-ia* -y] **1 :** study of literature that includes or may include grammar, criticism, literary history, language history, systems of writing, and anything else that is relevant to literature or to language as used in literature **:** literary or classical learning **2 a :** LINGUISTICS; *esp* **:** historical and comparative linguistics **b :** the study of human speech esp. as the vehicle of literature and as a field of study that sheds light on cultural history

phi·lom·a·chus \fə'läməkəs\ *n, cap* [NL, fr. Gk *philomachos* loving fighting, warlike, fr. *phil-* + *machē* battle, fight (fr. *machesthai* to battle, fight)] **:** a genus of shorebirds (family Scolopacidae) consisting of the ruff

phil·o·math \'filə,math\ *n* -S [Gk *philomathēs*, fr. *phil-* + *-mathēs* (fr. *mathein*, *manthanein* to learn) — more at MATHEMATICAL] **:** a lover of learning **:** SCHOLAR; *esp* **:** a student of mathematics — **phil·o·math·e·an** \¦==¦mathēən\ *adj*

phil·o·math·ic \¦==¦mathik\ *or* **phil·o·math·i·cal** \-thəkəl\ *adj* **:** of or relating to a philomath or to love of learning

phil·o·mel \'filə,mel\ *n* -S *usu cap* [ME *philomene*, fr. ML *philomena*, modif. of L *philomela*, fr. *Philomela*, Athenian princess in Greek mythology who was changed into a nightingale, fr. Gk *Philomēla*] **:** NIGHTINGALE ⟨clear was the song from *Philomel's* far bower —John Keats⟩

philomela \,filə'mēlə\ *n* -S [L, nightingale] **1** *usu cap* **:** PHILOMEL **2 a :** a large-scale solo Doppelflöte organ stop **b :** a high-pitched small-scale pipe-organ stop of sweet tone

phi·lo·ni·an \fə'lōnēən, (')fī¦l-\ *or* **phi·lon·ic** \-länik\ *adj, usu cap* [LL *philonianus*, fr. *philon-*, *Philo* Judaeus *fl* late 1st century B.C. and early 1st century A.D. Hellenistic Jewish philosopher + L *-ianus* -ian] **:** of or relating to the Alexandrian Jewish philosopher Philo Judaeus or based on his system of philosophy consisting of a combination of Judaism and Platonism and being a precursor of Neoplatonism

phi·lo·nism \'fīlə,nizəm\ *n* -S *usu cap* [LL *philon-*, *Philo* + E *-ism*] **:** the Philonian philosophy

phi·lo·nist \-,nəst\ *n* -S *usu cap* [LL *philon-*, *Philo* + E *-ist*] **:** a supporter of Philonism

phi·lo·ni·um \fə'lōnēəm\ *n* -S [LL, after L *Philon-*, *Philo*, 1st cent. A.D. Greek physician] **:** an ancient remedy for colic containing opium, saffron, euphorbium, henbane, spikenard, and honey

phi·lon·o·tis \fə'länətəs, fī'l-\ *n, cap* [NL, fr. *phil-* + Gk *notis* moisture; akin to Gk *noteros* damp — more at NOURISH] **:** a genus of acrocarpous mosses (order Eubryales) that is related to *Bartramia* and includes the fountain mosses

phil·o·pe·na *or* **phil·ip·pi·na** \,filə'pēnə\ *or* **phil·ip·pine** \-ēn\ *n* -S [modif. (influenced by Gk *philos* loving and L *poena* penalty) of G *vielliebchen*, lit., much loved; perh. fr. the idea that the gift was a penalty of friendship or love — more at PAIN] **1 :** a game in which a man and woman who have shared the twin kernels of a nut each try to claim a gift from the other as a forfeit at their next meeting by fulfilling certain conditions (as by being the first to exclaim "philopena") — called also *fillipeen* **2 a :** a nut with two kernels **b :** a gift given as a forfeit

phil·o·po·tam·i·dae \,filəpə'tamə,dē\ *n pl, cap* [NL, fr. *Philopotamus*, type genus (fr. *phil-* + Gk *potamos* river, stream) + *-idae*] **:** a small but widely distributed family of caddis flies

phil·o·pro·ge·ne·i·ty \,filō,prōjə'nēəd·ē\ *n* -ES [*phil-* + *progeny* + *-ity*] **:** PHILOPROGENITIVENESS

philo·progenitive \¦fi(,)lō+\ *adj* [*phil-* + *progenitive*] **1 :** tending to produce offspring **:** PROLIFIC ⟨younger writers . . . have been more ~, and some of them will end by having four or five children —Malcolm Cowley⟩ **2 :** of, relating to, or characterized by love of offspring ⟨the ~ drive is less powerful in men than in women —*Jour. Amer. Med. Assoc.*⟩

philoprogenitiveness *n* -ES **:** love of offspring

[1]**phi·lop·ter·id** \fə'läptərəd\ *adj* [NL *Philopteridae*] **:** of or relating to the Philopteridae

[2]**philopterid** \"\ *n* -S [NL *Philopteridae*] **:** a louse of the family Philopteridae

phil·op·ter·i·dae \,fi,läp'terə,dē\ *n pl, cap* [NL, fr. *Philopterus*, type genus (fr. *phil-* + *-pterus*) + *-idae*] **:** a family of bird lice (order Mallophaga) having the tarsi fitted with two claws for clinging to the feathers of their host

philo·samia \¦filə+\ *n, cap* [NL, fr. *phil-* + *Samia*] **:** a genus of large silk-spinning saturniid moths

phi·los·o·phas·ter \fə¦läsə¦fastə(r)\ *n* -S [LL, fr. L *philosophus* philosopher + *-aster*] **:** a pretender or dabbler in philosophy

phi·los·o·phas·ter·ing \-t(ə)riŋ\ *adj* **:** acting the philosopher **:** philosophizing in a shallow or pretentious manner

phi·los·o·phas·try \-trē\ *n* -ES [*philosophaster* + *-y*] **:** spurious or pretended philosophy

philosophate *vi* -ED/-ING/-S [L *philosophatus*, past part. of *philosophari* to philosophize, fr. *philosophus* philosopher] *obs* **:** PHILOSOPHIZE

phil·o·sophe *also* **phil·o·soph** \'filə,säf, ,=='zäf\ *n* -S [F *philosophe*, fr. MF] **1 :** PHILOSOPHER; *esp* **:** one of the popular quasi-philosophers of the 18th century French Enlightenment **2 :** PHILOSOPHASTER

phi·los·o·pheme \fə'läsə,fēm\ *n* -S [LL *philosophema*, fr. Gk *philosophēma*, fr. *philosophein* to love or pursue knowledge, fr. *philosophos* lover of wisdom] **:** a philosophical formulation or principle **:** PROPOSITION

phi·los·o·pher \fə'läs(ə)fə(r) *sometimes* -äzəf-\ *n* -S [ME *philosopher*, *philosophre*, modif. (influenced by *-er*) of MF *philosophe*, fr. L *philosophus*, fr. Gk *philosophos*, fr. *phil-* + *-sophos* (fr. *sophia* wisdom, fr. *sophos* wise + *-ia* -y)] **1 a :** one who seeks wisdom or enlightenment **:** reflective thinker **:** SCHOLAR, INVESTIGATOR ⟨the ~, traditionally, is thought of as a person whose chief interest is in attempting to discover the innermost essence of reality —Theodore Brameld⟩ **b :** a specialist in the synthesis of knowledge ⟨a ~ . . . must attempt to give us a comprehensive account of human values and a plausible theory of human destiny —Eliseo Vivas⟩ — compare PHILOSOPHY 2d **c :** a student of philosophy **2** *obs* **:** one versed in an occult science; *specif* **:** ALCHEMIST **3 a :** one whose life is governed by reason **:** a person whose philosophical perspective enables him to meet trouble with equanimity **:** RATIONALIST ⟨to a ~ there is some compensation for blindness in the increased acuity of the other senses⟩ **b :** the expounder of a theory in a particular area of experience ⟨he is no ~ of freedom, but he is certainly a fighter for freedom —C.P. Romulo⟩ **c :** PHILOSOPHIZER ⟨Bowery Thespian and ~ —*Amer. Guide Series: N.Y. City*⟩

philosophers' egg *n* **1 a :** the first matter of the philosophers' stone composed of salt, sulfur, and mercury **b :** GRIPE'S EGG **2 :** a medicine made of saffron and the yolk of an egg and once considered a cure for plague and poison

philosopher's game *or* **philosopher's table** *also* **philosophy**

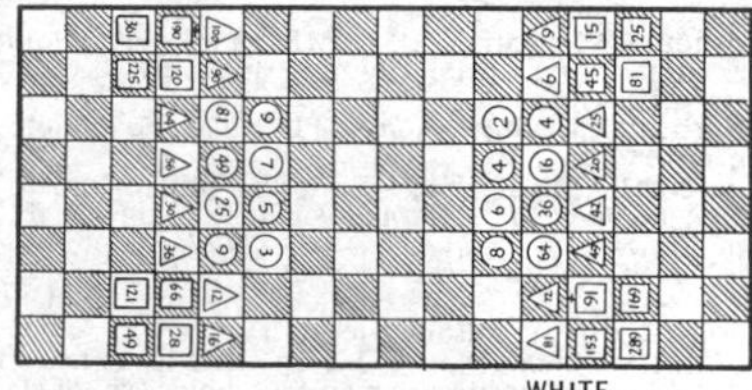

board for philosopher's game with men arranged as at beginning of a game

game *n* **:** an old form of chess or checkers played on a double board each side having 24 numbered men cut into circles, triangles, and squares

philosophers' oil *n* **:** a remedy described in old pharmacopoeias and consisting of linseed oil and powdered brick

philosophers' stone *also* **philosopher's stone** *n* [ME *philosophres stoon*, prob. trans. of ML *lapis philosophorum*] **1 :** an imaginary stone, substance, or chemical preparation believed to have the power of transmuting the baser metals into gold, much sought for by alchemists, and by some identified with elixir **2 :** a principle or concept capable of achieving the spiritual regeneration of man ⟨exuded confidence that Turkey possessed the political *philosopher's stone* in its policies of modernization —William Clark⟩

philosopher's wool *n, archaic* **:** FLOWERS OF ZINC

phil·o·so·phia pe·ren·nis \,filə'sōfēəpə'renəs\ *n, sometimes cap both P's* [NL, lit., perennial philosophy] **:** a group of universal philosophical problems, principles, and ideas (as concepts of God, freedom, and immortality) that perennially constitutes the primary subject matter of philosophical thought **:** the foundations of Roman Catholic Christian principles esp. as philosophically formulated by St. Thomas Aquinas and Neothomists ⟨some *Philosophia Perennis* which would be agreed on in advance as a sort of intellectual base of operations —H.D.Aiken⟩

philosophia pri·ma \-'prēmə, -'prīmə\ *n* [L] **:** FIRST PHILOSOPHY

phil·o·soph·ic \¦filə¦säfik, -fēk *also* -¦zä-\ *adj* [L *philosophicus*, fr. Gk *philosophikos*, fr. *philosophos* philosopher + *-ikos* -ic] **1 a :** of or relating to philosophers or philosophy ⟨the very ~ dogma that God is everywhere —George Santayana⟩ ⟨a considerable knowledge of ~ terminology —Paul Woodring⟩ **b :** based on philosophy ⟨a doctrine of ~ anarchism —Benjamin Farrington⟩ **2 :** imbued with or characterized by the attitude of a philosopher ⟨that breadth of outlook which distinguishes the ~ mind —*Manchester Guardian Weekly*⟩ ⟨papers of a more ~ temper —G.N.Shuster⟩; *specif* **:** meeting trouble with level-headed detachment **:** TEMPERATE ⟨this ~, long term attitude towards life —B.K.Sandwell⟩ **3** *of a hand* **:** long and angular with bony fingers having developed joints and long nails usu. held by palmists to indicate a studious and analytical nature and a love of mystery in all things — **phil·o·soph·i·cal·ly** \-fək(ə)lē, -fēk-, -li\ *adv*

phil·o·soph·i·cal \-fəkəl, -fēk-\ *adj* [L *philosophicus* + E *-al*] **1** *archaic* **:** characterized by learning or the spirit of inquiry **:** SCHOLARLY ⟨a ~ chemist would probably make a very unprofitable business of farming —Humphry Davy⟩ **2** *archaic* **:** of or relating to the physical sciences ⟨a manufacturer of ~ instruments⟩ **3 :** PHILOSOPHIC ⟨no ~ system is ever final, for life itself is never final —*Time*⟩ ⟨a ~ resignation toward disaster —Harrison Smith⟩

philosophical existentialism *n* **:** EXISTENTIALISM a

philosophical grammar *n* **:** GENERAL GRAMMAR

philosophical induction *n* **:** BACONIAN INDUCTION

phil·o·soph·i·cal·ness *n* -ES [*philosophical* + *-ness*] **:** the quality or state of being philosophic

philosophical pitch *n* **:** a theoretical tuning standard of 427 vibrations per second for A above middle C used for convenience in scientific calculations

philosophical radical *n, usu cap P&R* **:** one of a group of early 19th century English liberals characterized chiefly by a belief in Benthamite utilitarianism and advocating legal, economic, and social reforms including free trade and reform of Parliament and the judiciary

philosophical radicalism *n, usu cap P&R* **:** the doctrines of the Philosophical Radicals

phi·los·o·phism \fə'läsə,fizəm\ *n* -S [F *philosophisme*, fr. MF, fr. OF *philosophie* philosophy + *-isme* -ism] **1 :** spurious philosophic argument **:** SOPHISTRY **2 :** SOPHISM

phi·los·o·phist \-,fəst\ *n* -S [F *philosophiste*, fr. *philosophie* + *-iste* -ist] *archaic* **:** SOPHIST, PHILOSOPHIZER — **phi·los·o·phis·ti·cal** \=¦==¦fistəkəl\ *adj*

phi·los·o·phize \fə'läsə,fīz *sometimes* -äzə,-\ *vb* -ED/-ING/-S [*philosophy* + *-ize*] *vi* **1 :** to reason as or as if a philosopher **:** seek a rational basis for fact and experience **:** REFLECT, THEORIZE ⟨one can draw conclusions about behavior; about instinct one can only ~ —Abram Kardiner⟩ **2 :** to expound a philosophy often superficially ⟨songs that ~, like "Love Thy Neighbor" and "Count Your Blessings" —Mitch Miller⟩ ~ *vt* **:** to consider from or bring into conformity with a philosophic point of view ⟨the course should be history, but history *philosophized*, a history of ideas as well as of events —W.C. DeVane⟩ ⟨tried to ~ himself out of his sense of social maladjustment —H.S.Canby⟩

phi·los·o·phiz·er \-īzə(r)\ *n* -S **:** one that philosophizes; *esp* **:** one that expounds a superficial philosophy

philosophizing *n* -S [fr. gerund of *philosophize*] **:** an inquiry into the essence and value of some aspect of life ⟨Plato's ~*s* on art —*Publishers' Weekly*⟩; *specif* **:** MORALIZING ⟨in explaining why she had to be in at 11, the girl's mother chose a middle course between admonition and ~⟩

phi·los·o·phy \fə'läs(ə)fē, -fi *sometimes* -äzəf-\ *n* -ES [ME *philosophie*, fr. OF, fr. L *philosophia*, fr. Gk, fr. *phil-* + *sophia* wisdom, fr. *sophos* wise + *-ia* -y] **1 a :** a love or pursuit of wisdom **:** a search for the underlying causes and principles of reality **:** INVESTIGATION, INQUIRY ⟨~ is a natural function of the human mind —Stuart Hampshire⟩ — see FIRST PHILOSOPHY **b :** a quest for truth through logical reasoning rather than factual observation ⟨every advance in knowledge robs ~ of some problems which formerly it had —Bertrand Russell⟩ **c :** a critical examination of the grounds for fundamental beliefs and an analysis of the basic concepts employed in the expression of such beliefs ⟨the job of ~ is the study and statement of the logic, informal and formal, of the employment of expressions —V.C.Aldrich⟩ **d :** a synthesis of learning ⟨it is the primary aim of ~ to unify completely . . . all departments of rational thought —Henry Sidgwick⟩ **2 a** *archaic* **:** the study of natural phenomena **:** PHYSICAL SCIENCE — see SECOND PHILOSOPHY **b :** the study of the principles of human nature and conduct **:** ETHICS **c :** a science that comprises all learning exclusive only of technical precepts and practical arts **d :** the coordinate disciplines of sciences and liberal arts exclusive only of medicine, law, and theology ⟨the ~ of the medieval universities⟩ ⟨the academic degree doctor of ~⟩ ⟨an English bachelor of ~⟩ **e :** a science that comprises logic, ethics, aesthetics, metaphysics, and epistemology **3 a :** a system of motivating beliefs, concepts, and principles ⟨the ~ of a culture determines the general pattern of its . . . institutions —David Bidney⟩ ⟨three *philosophies* contending for dominance in contemporary politics —*Times Lit. Supp.*⟩ ⟨the changing ~ of the courts with regard to many questions —Margaret Nicholson⟩ ⟨set the . . . ~ and the basic course of the museum —Roger Angell⟩ **b :** a basic theory concerning a particular subject, process, or sphere of activity ⟨design ~ in chemical plants —D.E.Pierce⟩ — usu. used with *of* ⟨~ of religion⟩ ⟨~ of education⟩ ⟨the whole ~ of the bill is to ignore the realities —*New Republic*⟩ ⟨a chance to prove my ~ of flying the mail —C.A.Lindbergh b.1902⟩ ⟨automation is a completely new ~ of production —John Diebold⟩ **4 a :** the sum of an individual's ideas and convictions **:** personal attitude ⟨lived by the plain ~ . . . do your best, be loyal to your friends, never forget your enemies —*Time*⟩ ⟨every writer has not one but two *philosophies* — his more or less conscious artistic credo and . . . his often unconscious vision of life and scheme of values —Max Lerner & Edwin Mims⟩ **b :** calmness of temper and judgment befitting a philosopher **:** mental serenity or equanimity ⟨this is the place that calls out all a composer's self-control; it's a moment for ~ —Aaron Copland⟩

philosophy of organism : a theory advanced by A. N. Whitehead that the ultimate entities of nature though governed by mechanical principles are not inert but are enduring structures of activity and that the nature of each reflects its organic relations with the larger structures of nature into which it enters — called also *organic mechanism*

philosophy of the garden *usu cap G* [so called fr. the fact that Epicurus taught in a garden in Athens] **:** EPICUREANISM 1a

phi·lo·tria \fə'lō·trēə\ [NL, irreg. fr. Gk *phyllon* leaf + *tria* three — more at BLADE, THREE] *syn of* ELODEA

-phi·lous \f(ə)ləs\ *adj comb form* [Gk *philos* beloved, dear, loving; prob. akin to OE *bile-* simple, innocent, OHG *bil-*, *bila-* good-natured, friendly, MIr *bil* good] **:** loving **:** having an affinity for ⟨dendro*philous*⟩ ⟨litho*philous*⟩ ⟨acido*philous*⟩

-phils *pl of* -PHIL

[1]**phil·ter** *or* **phil·tre** \'filtə(r)\ *n* -S [MF *philtre*, fr. L *philtrum*, fr. Gk *philtron*, fr. *philein* to love, fr. *philos* loving] **1 :** a potion, drug, or charm supposedly having the power to excite sexual passion esp. toward a particular person — called also *love-philter*, *love-potion* **2 :** a potion credited with magical power

[2]**philter** *or* **philtre** \"\ *vt* -ED/-ING/-S *archaic* **:** to bewitch by the use of a philter **:** EXCITE, FASCINATE

phil·trum \'fil·trəm\ *n, pl* **phil·tra** \-rə\ [NL, fr. Gk *philtron* philter, charm, dimple in the upper lip] **:** the vertical groove on the median line of the upper lip

-phi·lus \f(ə)ləs\ *n comb form* [NL, fr. L, loving, fr. Gk *philos*] **:** creature attracted to (such) a food or habitat — in generic names ⟨Campe*philus*⟩ ⟨Spermo*philus*⟩

-phi·ly \f(ə)lē, -li\ *n comb form* -ES [NL *-philia*] **1 :** fondness for ⟨toxo*phily*⟩ **2 :** affinity for ⟨hydro*phily*⟩ ⟨photo*phily*⟩ ⟨zoo*phily*⟩ — chiefly in biological and chemical terms

phil·y·dra·ce·ae \,filə'drāsē,ē\ *n pl, cap* [NL, fr. *Philydrum*, type genus (fr. *phil-* + Gk *hydōr* water) + *-aceae* — more at WATER] **:** a family of Asiatic and Australian perennial herbs (order Xyridales) with sheathing narrow leaves and spicate flowers resembling orchids — **phil·y·dra·ceous** \¦==¦drāshəs\ *adj*

phi·mosed \'fī,mōzd, -ōst\ *adj* [NL *phimosis* + E *-ed*] **:** affected with phimosis

phi·mo·sis \fī'mōsəs, fə'-\ *n, pl* **phimo·ses** \-ō,sēz\ [NL, fr. Gk *phimōsis* muzzling, stopping up of an orifice, contraction of the prepuce, fr. *phimos* muzzle] **:** tightness or constriction of the orifice of the prepuce arising either congenitally or from inflammation, congestion, or other postnatal causes and making it impossible to bare the glans

phi·mot·ic \(')fī¦mäd·ik, fə¦m-\ *adj* **:** of, relating to, or marked by phimosis

phi·o·mia \fī'ōmēə\ *n, cap* [NL, fr. Copt *ph-iom* the sea, the lake (fr. Egypt *ym* sea, fr. a Canaanite word akin to Heb *yām*) + NL *-ia;* fr. its discovery in the Faiyum, lake province of Egypt] **:** a genus of long-jawed mastodons (family Gomphotheriidae) found in the Oligocene of Egypt

phi phenomenon *n, sometimes cap 1st P* **:** the apparent motion of lines, pictures, or other objects shown in a rapid succession of different positions without any actual motion being presented to the eye

phis *pl of* PHI

phi tong luang \'fē'täŋlü'äŋ\ *n, pl* **phi tong luang** *or* **phi tong luangs** *usu cap P&T&L* **1 :** a nomadic food-gathering people of southeast Asia believed to be the most primitive discovered in that area and showing signs of early extinction **2 :** a member of the Phi Tong Luang people

phiz \'fiz\ *n* -ES [by shortening & alter. fr. *physiognomy*] **:** FACE ⟨he'd never dare show his ~ again —S.H.Adams⟩

phleb- *or* **phlebo-** *comb form* [ME *fleb-*, fr. MF, fr. LL *phleb-*, fr. Gk, fr. *phleb-*, *phleps* blood vessel, vein; akin to Gk *phlyein*, *phlyzein* to boil over — more at FLUID] **:** vein ⟨*phleb*itis⟩ ⟨*phlebo*gram⟩

phle·bit·ic \flə'bid·ik, flē'-, fle'-\ *adj* [NL *phlebit*is + E *-ic*] **:** of or relating to phlebitis

phle·bi·tis \-bīd·əs, -bītəs\ *n, pl* **phle·bit·i·des** \-bid·ə,dēz, -bitə,-\ [NL, fr. *phleb-* + *-itis*] **:** inflammation of a vein

phlebo·clysis \¦flebō+\ *n* [NL, fr. *phleb-* + *clysis*] **:** administration of a large volume of fluid intravenously

phle·bo·di·um \flə'bōdēəm\ *n, cap* [NL, fr. Gk *phlebōdēs* full of veins, with large veins, veinlike (fr. *phleb-* + *-ōdēs* -ode) + NL *-ium*] **:** a genus of mostly epiphytic tropical ferns (family Polypodiaceae) having the areolae of the fronds each with two or more free veinlets bearing sori — see SERPENT FERN

phleb·oe·de·sis \,flebē'dēsəs\ *n* -ES [NL, fr. *phleb-* + Gk *oidēsis* swelling] **:** the condition of having the terminal parts of the vascular system so expanded as to largely obliterate the coelom which is replaced by a hemocoel (as in arthropods and mollusks)

phleb·o·gram \'flebə,gram\ *n* [ISV *phleb-* + *-gram*] **:** a figure of a vein or a record of its movements (as by roentgenography following injection of a radiopaque substance)

phleb·o·graph·ic \¦==¦grafik\ *adj* [ISV *phlebography* + *-ic*] **:** of or relating to phlebography

phle·bog·ra·phy \flə'bägrəfē\ *n* -ES [ISV *phleb-* + *-graphy*] **:** the art of making phlebograms

phleb·oid \'fle,bȯid\ *also* **phle·boi·dal** \flə'bȯidᵊl\ *adj* [*phleb-* + *-oid*] **:** having the properties of or characterized by veins

phleb·o·lith \'flebə,lith\ *n* -S [ISV *phleb-* + *-lith*] **:** a calculus in a vein usu. resulting from the calcification of an old thrombus

phlebo·sclerosis \¦flebō+\ *n* [NL, fr. *phleb-* + *sclerosis*] **:** sclerosis of the wall of a vein esp. of its inner coats

phlebo·sclerotic \"+\ *adj* **:** of, relating to, or affected by phlebosclerosis

phlebo·thrombosis \"+\ *n* [NL, fr. *phleb-* + *thrombosis*] **:** venous thrombosis accompanied by little or no inflammation — compare THROMBOPHLEBITIS

phleb·o·tom·ic \¦flebə¦tämik\ *also* **phleb·o·tom·i·cal** \-məkəl\ *adj* [*phlebotomic* fr. F *phlébotomique*, fr. MF *phlebotomie* phlebotomy + *-ique* -ic; *phlebotomical* fr. *phlebotomy* + *-ical*] **1 :** of or relating to phlebotomy **2 :** BLOODSUCKING — used of insects — **phleb·o·tom·i·cal·ly** \-mək(ə)lē\ *adv*

phle·bot·o·mist \flə'bäd·əməst, flē'-, fle'-, -ätəm-\ *n* -S [*phlebotomy* + *-ist*] **:** one that practices phlebotomy

phle·bot·o·mize \-ə,mīz\ *vb* -ED/-ING/-S [MF *phlebotomiser*, fr. ML *flebotomizare*, fr. LL *phlebotomia*, *flebotomia* phlebotomy + *-izare* -ize] *vt* **:** to draw blood from **:** BLEED ~ *vi* **1 :** to practice phlebotomy **2 :** to submit to phlebotomy **:** undergo bleeding

phle·bot·o·mus \flə'bäd·əməs\ *n* [NL, fr. LL, lancet, fleam — more at FLEAM] **1** *cap* **:** a genus of small delicate bloodsucking sand flies (family Psychodidae) including one (*P. papatasii*) that is the carrier of phlebotomus fever and others suspected of carrying other human diseases **2** *pl* **phleboto·mi** \-d·ə,mī\ *also* **phlebotomuses :** a fly of the genus *Phlebotomus*

phlebotomus fever *n* **:** a virus disease of brief duration characterized by fever, headache, pain in the eyes, malaise, and leukopenia and transmitted by the bite of a sand fly (*Phlebotomus papatasii*) — called also *sand-fly fever*

phle·bot·o·my \flə'bäd·əmē, flē'-, fle'-, -ätə-, mi\ *n* -ES [ME *fleobotomie*, fr. MF *flebotomie*, fr. LL *phlebotomia*, *flebotomia*, fr. Gk *phlebotomia*, fr. *phleb-* + *-tomia* (fr. *temnein* to cut) — more at TOME] **:** the letting of blood in the treatment of disease **:** VENESECTION

phleg·e·thon·tal \¦flegə¦thäntᵊl, -ejə¦-\ *or* **phleg·e·thon·tic** \-tik\ *adj, usu cap* [L *phlegethont*is phlegethontal (fr. *Phlegethon*, principal river of Hades that ran with fire instead of water, fr. Gk *Phlegethōn*, fr. *phlegethein* to blaze, fr. *phlegein* to burn) + E *-al* or *-ic*] *archaic* **:** of, relating to, or resembling a river of fire **:** BURNING

phlegm \'flem\ *n* -S [ME *fleem*, *fleume*, fr. MF *fleume*, fr. LL *phlegma*, *flegma*, fr. Gk *phlegma* flame, inflammation, phlegm, fr. *phlegein* to burn — more at BLACK] **1 :** the one of the four humors of early physiology that was supposed to be cold and moist and to cause sluggishness **2 :** MUCUS; *usu* **:** viscid mucus secreted in abnormal quantity in the respiratory passages and discharged through the mouth **3** *archaic* **:** a watery distillation that in early chemistry is one of the five principles of bodies **:** WATER, MOISTURE **4 :** temperament or conduct supposedly associated with abundance of the humor phlegm: **a :** dull or apathetic coldness or indifference **b :** intrepid coolness or calm fortitude ⟨a lofty ~, a detachment in the midst of action, a capacity for watching in silence and commanding without excitement —Edmund Wilson⟩ **syn** see EQUANIMITY

phleg·ma \'flegmə\ *n* -S [LL, phlegm] **:** a watery distilled liquor as distinguished by distillers from a spirituous liquor

phleg·ma·sia \fleg'māzh(ē)ə, -āzēə\ *n, pl* **phlegmasiae** \-āz(h)ē,ē\ [Gk, fr. *phlegma*] **:** INFLAMMATION

phlegmasia al·ba do·lens \-'albə'dō,lenz\ *n* [NL, lit., painful white inflammation] **:** MILK LEG

[1]**phleg·mat·ic** \(')fleg¦mad·|ik, -at|, |ēk\ *or* **phleg·mat·i·cal** \|əkəl, |ēk-\ *adj* [*phlegmatic* fr. ME *flaumatike*, fr. MF *flaumatique*, fr. LL *phlegmaticus*, fr. Gk *phlegmatikos*, fr. *phlegmat-*, *phlegma* flame + *-ikos* -ic; *phlegmatical* fr. [2]*phlegmatic* + *-al*] **1 a :** like or consisting of the humor phlegm ⟨~ matter⟩ **:** abounding in or producing phlegm ⟨a ~ constitution⟩ **b** *obs* **:** MUCOID, VISCOUS, WATERY **2 :** having or

showing the character or temperament formerly associated with a predominance of the humor phlegm : marked by slowness and stolidity : CALM, COMPOSED, UNDEMONSTRATIVE ⟨was ~ in the way of a man who accepts all things, and accepts them in the spirit of cool bravery —Bram Stoker⟩ **syn** see IMPASSIVE

2**phlegmatic** \"\ *n* -s : a person of phlegmatic constitution or temperament

phleg·mat·i·cal·ly \|ək(ə)lē, |ēk-, -li\ *adv* [*phlegmatical* + *-ly*] : in a phlegmatic manner

phleg·ma·tous \'flegmәdәs\ *adj* [Gk *phlegmat-, phlegma* + E *-ous*] : PHLEGMATIC

phleg·mon \'fleg,män\ *n* -s [ME *flegmone*, fr. L *phlegmone*, *phlegmon*, fr. Gk *phlegmonē* inflammation, boil, fr. *phlegein* to burn — more at PHLEGM] : purulent inflammation and infiltration of connective tissue — compare ABSCESS

phleg·mon·ic \(')fleg¦mänik\ *adj* [ML *phlegmonicus*, fr. Gk *phlegmonikos*, fr. *phlegmon* + *-ikos* -ic] : PHLEGMONOUS

phleg·mon·ous \'flegmәnәs\ *adj* [F *phlegmoneux*, fr. *phlegmon* (fr. L *phlegmone, phlegmon*) + *-eux* -ous] : of, relating to, or constituting a phlegmon : accompanied or characterized by phlegmons — **phleg·mon·ous·ly** *adv*

phlegmy \'flemē\ *adj* -ER/-EST [*phlegm* + *-y* (adj. suffix)] : of, constituting, characterized by, or due to phlegm ⟨a ~ cough⟩ : PHLEGMATIC; *sometimes* : WATERY

phlep·si·us \'flepsēәs\ *n, cap* [NL, fr. Gk *phleps* blood vessel, vein — more at PHLEB-] : a large and widely distributed genus of leafhoppers

phle·um \'flēәm\ *n, cap* [NL, prob. fr. Gk *phleōs* wool-tufted reed] : a genus of grasses that are natives of temperate regions and have dense oblong or terete spike and long mucronate empty glumes — see TIMOTHY

phlob·a·phene \'fläbә,fēn\ *n* -s [ISV *phlobaph-* (fr. Gk *phloos, phloios* bark + *baphē* dye — fr. *baptein* to dip, dye —) + *-ene* — more at BAPTIZE] **1** : a reddish brown complex substance found in oak bark and also formed by heating quercitannin with dilute acids **2** : any of several substances that are similar to phlobaphene and are obtained esp. from barks or from condensed tannins

phloba·tannin \¦fläbә+\ *n* [*phlobaphene* + *tannin*] : a tannin that with hot dilute acids yields a phlobaphene

phlo·em \'flō,em\ *n* -s [G, fr. Gk *phloios, phloos* bark; akin to Gk *phallos* penis — more at BLOW] : a complex tissue in the vascular system of higher plants consisting mainly of sieve tubes and companion cells and usu. also of fibers and parenchyma cells and functioning chiefly in translocation but also in support and storage — called also *bast, sieve tissue*

phloem fiber *n* : a fiber found in or associated with the phloem that is often commercially useful (as in flax) because of its great tensile strength and pliability and that differs from the xylem fiber in that its pits are usu. small and simple — called also *bast fiber*

phloem necrosis *n* : any pathological state in a plant characterized by brown discoloration and disintegration of the phloem: as **a** : a phase of potato leaf roll in which such changes occur **b** : a virus disease of tea **c** : a fatal virus disease of the American elm widespread in the U.S. characterized by yellowish often black-flecked discoloration and degeneration of the phloem and resulting in death of the root system through lack of food followed by wilting, yellowing, and loss of leaves

phloem parenchyma *n* : the nonspecialized vertically arranged parenchyma of the phloem — called also *bast parenchyma;* compare WOOD PARENCHYMA

phloem ray *n* : a vascular ray or part of a vascular ray that is located in phloem — called also *bast ray;* compare XYLEM RAY

phloe·o·thrip·i·dae \,flēō'thripә,dē\ *n pl, cap* [NL, fr. *Phloeothrips*, type genus (fr. Gk *phloios, phloos* bark + *thrips*) + *-idae*] : a widely distributed family of thrips many of which are serious pests on a great variety of plants

phlo·gis·tian \flō'jis(h)chәn\ *n* -s [NL *phlogiston* + E *-an*] : PHLOGISTONIST

phlo·gis·tic \flō'jistik, -tēk\ *adj* [in sense 1, prob. fr. (assumed) NL *phlogisticus*, fr. *phlogiston* + L *-icus* -ic; in sense 2, fr. Gk *phlogistos* inflammable + E *-ic*] **1** *archaic* : of or relating to phlogiston or the phlogiston theory **2** : of or relating to inflammations and fevers : INFLAMMATORY **3** *archaic* **a** : BURNING, FIERY **b** : IMPASSIONED, HEATED

phlo·gis·ti·cate \-tә,kāt\ *vt* -ED/-ING/-S [*phlogistic* + *-ate*] : to combine phlogiston with ⟨highly *phlogisticated* substances⟩ — **phlo·gis·ti·ca·tion** \=,==¦kāshәn\ *n* -s

phlogisticated air *n* **1** *archaic* : air exhausted of oxygen by burning a combustible (as charcoal or phosphorus) in it and therefore composed chiefly of nitrogen **2** *archaic* : hydrogen regarded as inflammable air

phlo·gis·ton \flō'jistәn\ *n* -s [NL, fr. Gk, neut. of *phlogistos* burnt, inflammable, fr. *phlogizein* to set on fire, fr. *phlog-, phlox* flame, fr. *phlegein* to burn — more at BLACK] : the hypothetical principle of fire or inflammability regarded by the early chemists as a material substance ⟨metals were supposed to be prepared from their calxes by the union of the latter with ~ —M.C.Sneed & J.L.Maynard⟩ ⟨what manner of substance or principle could ~ be that when it was added to another material the total mass or weight diminished? —J.B.Conant⟩

phlo·gis·ton·ism \-ә,nizәm\ *n* -s : the phlogiston theory or the system of chemistry built upon it

phlo·gis·ton·ist \-.nәst\ *n* -s : an adherent of the phlogiston theory

phlogiston theory *n* : a theory in 18th century chemistry disproved by Lavoisier: every combustible substance is a compound of phlogiston and the phenomena of combustion are due to the liberation of phlogiston with the other constituent left as a residue ⟨the *phlogiston theory* thus provided a general explanation of the chemical processes of oxidation and reduction: oxidation was taken to be the liberation of phlogiston, and reduction combination with phlogiston —Linus Pauling⟩

phlog·o·ge·net·ic \¦flägōjә¦ned·ik\ *adj* [Gk *phlog-, phlox* flame + *-genetic*] : PHLOGOGENIC

phlo·go·gen·ic \¦flägә¦jenik\ *also* **phlo·gog·e·nous** \flō'gäjәnәs\ *adj* [Gk *phlog-, phlox* flame + E *-genic* or *-genous*] : producing inflammation

phlog·o·pite \'flägә,pīt\ *n* -s [G *phlogopit*, fr. Gk *phlogōpos* fiery-looking, flaming red (fr. *phlog-, phlox* flame + *ōps* eye) + G *-it* -ite — more at EYE] : a usu. yellowish brown to brownish red or copper form of mica that is typically a silicate of potassium, magnesium, and aluminum with some fluorine or hydroxyl and that is grouped with biotite

phlog·o·pi·ti·za·tion \,==,pīd·ә'zāshәn\ *n* -s [*phlogopite* + *-ization*] : the development of phlogopite in a solid rock

phlo·ic \'flōik\ *adj* [*phloem* + *-ic*] : relating to, consisting of, or located in the phloem

phlo·i·on·ic acid \¦flōē¦änik-\ *n* [*phloionic* fr. Gk *phloios* bark + E *-onic*] : a crystalline hydroxy acid $[-CH(OH)(CH_2)_7COOH]_2$ that is among the acidic products formed by alkaline hydrolysis of cork; 9,10-dihydroxy-octadecanedioic acid — see SUBERIN

phlo·mis \'flōmәs\ *n* [NL, fr. L *phlomis, phlomos* mullein, fr. Gk] **1** *cap* : a genus of Old World mints having rugose often woolly leaves and whorls of white, yellow, or purple flowers with bilabiate corolla **2** -ES : a plant of the genus *Phlomis*

phlor- *or* **phloro-** *comb form* [F, fr. ISV *phlorizin*] **1** : related to phlorizin ⟨*phlor*etin⟩ ⟨*phloro*glucin⟩ **2** : related to phloroglucinol ⟨*phloro*-acetophenone $CH_3COC_6H_4(OH)_3$⟩

phlor·e·tin \'flōrәd·әn, 'flär-, flә'rēd·әn\ *n* -s [F *phlorétine*, fr. *phlor-* (in *phlorizin*) + Gk *rhētinē* resin] : a crystalline phenolic ketone $C_{15}H_{14}O_5$ derived from phloroglucinol and phenol and obtained esp. by hydrolysis of phlorizin

phlor·i·zin \'flōrәzәn, 'flär-, flә'rīzᵊn\ *or* **phlo·rhi·zin** *or* **phlo·rid·zin** \flә'ridzәn\ *also* **phlor·rhi·zin** \'flōrәzәn, 'flär-, flә'rīzᵊn\ *n* -s [ISV *phlo-* (fr. Gk *phloios, phloos* bark) + *-riz-* or *-rhiz-* or *-ridz-* or *-rrhiz-* (fr. Gk *rhiza* root) + *-in;* perh. orig. formed as F *phlorizine* — more at ROOT] : a bitter crystalline glucoside $C_{21}H_{24}O_{10}$ that is extracted from root bark or bark esp. of the apple, pear, cherry, or plum, that on hydrolysis yields glucose and phloretin, and that produces glycosuria if injected hypodermically and is used chiefly in producing experimental diabetes in animals

phlor·i·zin·ize \'flōrәzә,nīz, 'flär-, flә'rīzᵊn,īz\ *also* **phlo·rhi·zin·ize** *or* **phlo·rid·zin·ize** \flә'ridzә,nīz\ *vt* -ED/-ING/-S : to administer phlorizin to

phlor·o·glu·cin \¦flōrә¦glüsᵊn, ¦flär-\ *n* -s [ISV *phlor-* + *gluc-* + *-in*] : PHLOROGLUCINOL

phlor·o·glu·cin·ol \-sᵊn,ōl, -,ōl\ *n* -s [*phloroglucin* + *-ol*] : a sweet crystalline phenol $C_6H_3(OH)_3$ that occurs in combined form in glycosides (as phlorizin), in resins, and in tannins, that is usu. made from trinitrotoluene by a series of steps, and that is used chiefly as a developer in black-and-white reproduction; 1,3,5-trihydroxy-benzene

phlox \'fläks\ *n* [NL, fr. L, a flower, fr. Gk, wallflower, flame, fr. *phlegein* to burn — more at BLACK] **1** *cap* : a genus of American herbs (family Polemoniaceae) having red, purple, white, or variegated flowers, the corolla salver-shaped with the stamens on its tube, and a 3-valved capsular fruit — see ANNUAL PHLOX, MOSS PINK **2** *pl* **phlox** *or* **phloxes** : any plant of the genus *Phlox* **3** -ES : a dark purplish red that is bluer and less strong than pansy purple and bluer, lighter, and stronger than raisin, Bokhara, dahlia purple (sense 1), or redgrape

phlox family *n* : POLEMONIACEAE

phlox·ine \'fläk,sēn, -,sәn\ *n* -s *often cap* [Gk *phlox* flame + E *-ine*] : either of two acid dyes or their sodium salts that are chloro derivatives of eosine and are used chiefly as biological stains and organic pigments: **a** *or* **phloxine B** : the dichloro derivative **b** : the tetrachloro derivative — see DYE table I (under *Acid Red 92, Solvent Red 48*)

phlox pink *n* : a pale purple that is redder and paler than average lavender, redder and darker than wistaria (sense 2a), and redder and stronger than flossflower blue

phlox purple *n* : a strong reddish purple that is bluer, lighter, and stronger than average fuchsia purple and redder and paler than purple orchid

phlyc·te·na *or* **phlyc·tae·na** \flik'tēnә\ *n, pl* **phlyc·te·nae** *or* **phlyc·tae·nae** \-ē,nē\ [NL, fr. Gk *phlyktaina* blister, fr. *phlyein, phlyzein* to boil over — more at FLUID] : PHLYCTENULE

phlyc·te·noid \-ē,nȯid\ *adj* [NL *phlyctena* + E *-oid*] : resembling a phlyctenule

phlyc·ten·u·la *or* **phlyc·taen·u·la** \-'tenyәlә, -tēn-\ *n, pl* **phlyc·ten·u·lae** *or* **phlyc·taen·u·lae** \-yә,lē\ [NL, fr. *phlyctena*, *phlyctaena* + *-ula* (fem. of *-ulus*)] : PHLYCTENULE

phlyc·ten·u·lar \-'tenyәlә(r)\ *adj* [NL *phlyctenula* + E *-ar*] : marked by or associated with phlyctenules ⟨~ conjunctivitis⟩

phlyc·ten·ule \-n,yül\ *n* -s [NL *phlyctenula*] : a small vesicle or pustule; *esp* : one on the conjunctiva or cornea of the eye

pho *abbr* photographer

phob- *or* **phobo-** *comb form* [LL, fr. Gk, fr. *phobos*] : fear : avoidance ⟨*phob*ism⟩ ⟨*phobo*phobia⟩ ⟨*phobo*taxis⟩

-phobe \,fōb\ *n comb form* -s [Gk *-phobos* -fearing, fr. *phobos* fear, flight] : one having a (specified) phobia ⟨Anglo*phobe*⟩ ⟨chromo*phobe*⟩ ⟨helio*phobe*⟩ ⟨photo*phobe*⟩

pho·bia \'fōbēә\ *n* -s [NL, fr. LL *-phobia* fear of something, fr. Gk, fr. *phobos* fear, flight + *-ia* -y; akin to Gk *phebesthai* to flee, be frightened, Lith *bėgti* to run, flee] : an exaggerated and often disabling fear usu. inexplicable to the subject, having occas. a logical but usu. an illogical or symbolic object, and serving to protect the ego against anxiety arising from unexpressed aggressive impulses — compare COMPULSION, OBSESSION

pho·bi·ac \-ē,ak\ *n* -s [*phobia* + *-ac* (as in *maniac*)] : one that exhibits a phobia

1**pho·bic** \'fōbik, -bēk *also* 'fäb-\ *adj* [NL *phobia* + E *-ic*] **1** : of, relating to, characterized by, or arising from phobia **2** *of a taxis* : based on withdrawal from an unpleasant rather than movement toward a pleasing stimulus

2**phobic** \"\ *n* -s : PHOBIAC

-pho·bic \¦fōbik, -bēk *also* ¦fäb-\ *or* **-pho·bous** \fәbәs\ *adj comb form* [*-phobic* fr. F *-phobique*, fr. LL *-phobicus*, fr. Gk *-phobikos*, fr. *-phobos* fearing + *-ikos* -ic; *-phobous* fr. LL *-phobus*, fr. Gk *-phobos*] **1** : exhibiting a phobia: having an aversion for ⟨Anglo*phobic*⟩ ⟨calci*phobous*⟩ ⟨helio*phobous*⟩ **2** *chem* : lacking or relating to lack of strong affinity for (such) a substance — opposed to *-philic*

phobic reaction *n* : a psychoneurosis in which the principal symptom is a phobia

pho·bism \'fō,bizәm *also* 'fä,-\ *n* -s [*phobia* + *-ism*] : the state of one affected by a phobia

pho·bo·tac·tic \¦fōbә¦taktik\ *adj* [*phob-* + *-tactic*] : of or relating to phobotaxis : involving random trial and error

pho·bo·tax·is \,==¦taksәs\ *n* [NL, fr. *phob-* + *-taxis*] : a random avoiding reaction in response to a distasteful stimulus

pho·by cat \'fōbē-\ *n* [*phoby* by shortening and alter. fr. *hydrophobia;* fr. the belief that its bite causes hydrophobia] *West* : LITTLE SPOTTED SKUNK

pho·ca \'fōkә\ *n, cap* [NL, fr. L, seal, fr. Gk *phōkē*] : a genus of seals formerly nearly coextensive with the family Phocidae but now restricted to the harbor seal and a few closely related forms

pho·ca·cean \fō'kāshәn\ *or* **pho·ca·ceous** \-shәs\ *adj* [NL *Phoca* + E *-acean* or *-aceous*] : PHOCINE

1**pho·cae·an** \fō'sēәn\ *adj, usu cap* [L *Phocaea* (fr. Gk *Phōkaia*) + E *-an*] **1** : of, relating to, or characteristic of the ancient Ionian city of Phocaea in Asia Minor **2** : of, relating to, or characteristic of the people of Phocaea

2**phocaean** \"\ *n* -s *cap* : a native or inhabitant of Phocaea

pho·cae·na \fō'sēnә\ *n, cap* [NL, fr. Gk *phōkaina* porpoise] : a widely distributed genus of porpoises that includes the harbor porpoise and other common porpoises

1**pho·cae·nid** \-nәd\ *adj* [NL *Phocaenidae*] : of or relating to porpoises

2**phocaenid** \"\ *n* -s [NL *Phocaenidae*] : PORPOISE

pho·cae·ni·dae \-nә,dē\ *n pl, cap* [NL, fr. *Phocaena*, type genus + *-idae*] *in some classifications* : a small family of toothed whales that comprises the porpoises and is now usu. included in Delphinidae

pho·cal \'fōkәl\ *adj* [NL *Phoca* + E *-al*] : PHOCINE

1**pho·cian** \'fōshәn\ *adj, usu cap* [L *Phocis* (fr. Gk *Phōkis*) + E *-an*] **1** : of, relating to, or characteristic of the ancient Greek state of Phocis between Boeotia and Locris **2** : of, relating to, or characteristic of the people of Phocis

2**phocian** \"\ *n* -s *cap* : a native or inhabitant of Phocis

1**pho·cid** \'fōsәd\ *adj* [NL *Phocidae*] : of or relating to the Phocidae

2**phocid** \"\ *n* -s [NL *Phocidae*] : a seal of the family Phocidae

pho·ci·dae \-sә,dē\ *n pl, cap* [NL, fr. *Phoca*, type genus + *-idae*] : a family of mammals (suborder Pinnipedia) comprising the hair seals and lacking external ears — **pho·ci·form** \-sә,fȯrm\ *adj* — **pho·coid** \'fō,kȯid\ *adj or n*

pho·cine \'fō,sīn, -,sәn\ *adj* [NL *Phoca* + E *-ine*] : of, relating to, or resembling seals

pho·coe·na \fō'sēnә\ [NL] *syn of* PHOCAENA

pho·co·me·lia *also* **pho·ko·me·lia** \,fōkә'mēlēә\ *n* -s [NL, fr. Gk *phōkē* seal + NL *-melia*] : the condition of having the limbs extremely shortened so that feet or hands arise close to the trunk (as in creeper fowls) — **pho·co·me·lic** \¦==¦mēlik\ *adj*

pho·com·e·lus \fō'kämәlәs\ *n* -ES [NL, fr. Gk *phōkē* seal + NL *-melus*] : an individual affected with phocomelia

1**phoe·be** \'fēbē, -bi\ *or* **phoebe bird** *also* **phe·be** \"\ *n* -s [alter. (influenced by the name *Phoebe*) of *pewee*] : any of several American flycatchers of the genus *Sayornis; esp* : a flycatcher (*S. phoebe*) of the eastern U.S. that has a slight crest, is plain grayish brown above and yellowish white below, and often places its nest built of mud and grass about old buildings

2**phoebe** \"\ *n* -s *usu cap* [prob. fr. the name *Phoebe*] *slang* : a throw of five in the game of craps

phoe·be·an \'fēbēәn, =¦==\ *adj, usu cap* [L *phoebeus* Phoebean (fr. Gk *phoibeios*, fr. *Phoibos* Phoebus, Greco-Roman god of the sun and of poetry) + E *-an*] : of, relating to, or characteristic of Phoebus Apollo

Phoebe lamp

phoebe lamp *n, usu cap P* [prob. fr. the name *Phoebe*] : a shallow early American fat-burning or grease-burning lamp of metal, pottery, or stone with a spout to hold the wick and often a cup attached to catch drippings — compare BETTY LAMP

1**phoe·ni·cian** *also* **phe·ni·cian** \fә'nishәn, fē'-, fә'nēshәn\ *n* -s *cap* [ME *phenicien*, fr. L *phoenicius* (fr. *Phoenice* Phoenicia, fr. Gk *Phoinikē*, fr. *phoinik-, phoinix* Phoenician, phoenix, date palm, purple, crimson) + ME *-ien* -ian; akin to Gk *phoinos* bloodred, *phonos* murder and perh. to Gk *theinein* to strike — more at DEFEND] **1** : a native or inhabitant of ancient Phoenicia **2** : the Semitic language of ancient Phoenicia differing only dialectically from Hebrew

2**phoenician** *also* **phe·ni·cian** \"\ *adj, usu cap* **1 a** : of, relating to, or characteristic of the ancient land of Phoenicia on the coast of Syria **b** : of, relating to, or characteristic of the people of Phoenicia **2** : of, relating to, or characteristic of the Phoenician language

3**phoe·ni·cian** \fē'nishәn\ *n* -s *cap* [*Phoenix*, Ariz. + E *-an*] : a native or resident of Phoenix, Ariz.

phoenician alphabet *n, usu cap P* **1** : an extinct northern Semitic alphabet used by the Phoenicians of Syria and their Carthaginian colonists from the 13th century B.C. and the immediate ancestor of the Greek alphabet **2** : the ancestor of the alphabets used by the Phoenicians and other contemporary Semitic inhabitants of western Syria that is held to be the earliest system of alphabetic writing **3** : the oldest Hebrew alphabet as distinguished from the square Hebrew or Aramaic alphabet

phoe·ni·cite \'fēnә,sīt, 'fen-\ *n* -s [G *phönikit*, contr. of *phönikochroit*] : PHOENICOCHROITE

phoe·ni·coch·ro·ite *or* **phe·ni·coch·ro·ite** \,fēnә'käkrә,wīt\ *n* -s [G *phönikochroit*, fr. Gk *phoinik-, phoinix* purple, crimson + *-chroia* + G *-it* -ite] : a mineral $Pb_3(CrO_4)_2O$(?) consisting of a basic lead chromate in red crystals and masses

phoenicopter *var of* PHENICOPTER

phoe·ni·cop·teri \,fēnә'käptә,rī\ *n pl, cap* [NL, fr. pl. of *Phoenicopterus*] : a small suborder of Ciconiiformes comprising the flamingos and related extinct birds

phoe·ni·cop·ter·i·dae \,fēnә,käp'terә,dē\ *n pl, cap* [NL, fr. *Phoenicopterus*, type genus + *-idae*] : a family of large showy wading birds that comprises the flamingos, usu. constitutes a suborder of the order Ciconiiformes, but was formerly considered to form a distinct order — **phoe·ni·cop·ter·oid** \¦==¦käptә,rȯid\ *adj or n* — **phoe·ni·cop·ter·ous** \-tәrәs\ *adj*

phoe·ni·cop·ter·i·for·mes \,==,käptәrә'fȯr,mēz\ *n pl, cap* [NL, fr. *Phoenicopterus* + *-iformes*] *in some esp. former classifications* : an order of wading birds coextensive with the family Phoenicopteridae

phoe·ni·cop·ter·us \,==¦käptәrәs\ *n, cap* [NL, fr. L, flamingo — more at PHENICOPTER] : a genus (the type of the family Phoenicopteridae) comprising the European flamingos and some New World forms including the one (*P. ruber*) that ranges into the southern U.S.

phoe·nic·u·lus \fē'nikyәlәs\ *n, cap* [NL, fr. *phoenic-, phoenix* (fr. L *phoenix*) + *-ulus*] : an African genus (coextensive with the family Phoeniculidae of the suborder Coracii) comprising the wood hoopoes and having a long decurved bill, a long wedge-shaped tail, and no crest

1**phoe·nix** \'fēniks, -nēks\ *n* -ES [ME *fenix*, fr. OE, fr. L *phoenix*, fr. Gk *phoinix* phoenix, Phoenician, date palm, purple, crimson — more at PHOENICIAN] **1** : a legendary bird represented by the ancient Egyptians as living five or six centuries in the Arabian desert, being consumed in fire by its own act, and rising in youthful freshness from its own ashes and often regarded as an emblem of immortality or of the resurrection **2** : a person or thing likened to the phoenix: as **a** : a paragon of excellence or beauty ⟨concerned at seeing the ~ of modern culture throw herself away on a man unworthy of her —G.B.Shaw⟩ **b** : one that experiences a restoration, renewal, or seeming rebirth after ruin or destruction ⟨natural law is the ~ of legal speculation; however often it is criticized to extinction, it rises again, an old spirit in a new and vigorous body —Glenn Negley⟩ **3** : a representation of the phoenix (as in heraldry) **4** : FENG HUANG

2**phoenix** \"\ *n, cap* [NL, fr. Gk *phoinix* date palm] : a large genus of pinnate-leaved palms distributed throughout tropical Asia and Africa and having dioecious flowers and an ovary with three carpels only one of which matures — see 1DATE

3**phoenix** \"\ *adj, usu cap* [fr. *Phoenix*, Ariz.] : of or from Phoenix, the capital of Arizona ⟨a *Phoenix* motel⟩ : of the kind or style prevalent in Phoenix

phoenix brown *n, often cap P&B* : a basic dye — see DYE table I (under *Basic Brown 2*)

phoenix fowl *n* : JAPANESE FOWL

phoe·nix·i·ty \fē'niksәd·ē\ *n* -ES [1*phoenix* + *-ity*] : the quality or state of being a phoenix; *esp* : UNIQUENESS ⟨she —poor girl!—cannot appreciate even her own ~ —G.B.Shaw⟩

phoenix tree *n* : CHINESE PARASOL TREE

phokomelia *var of* PHOCOMELIA

1**pho·lad** \'fō,lad\ *n* -s [Gk *phōlad-, phōlas* stone-boring mollusk] : a mollusk of the family Pholadidae : PIDDOCK — **pho·la·di·an** \fō'lādēәn\ *adj or n*

2**pholad** \"\ *adj* : of, relating to, or due to a pholad

pho·la·da·cea \,fōlә'dāshēә\ *n pl, cap* [NL, fr. *Pholad-, Pholas* + *-acea*] *in some classifications* : a suborder of Eulamellibranchia comprising the piddocks and shipworms

1**pho·la·did** \'fōlәdәd\ *adj* [NL *Pholadidae*] : of or relating to the Pholadidae

2**pholadid** \"\ *n* -s [NL *Pholadidae*] : a mollusk of the family Pholadidae

pho·lad·i·dae \fō'ladә,dē\ *n pl, cap* [NL, fr. *Pholad-, Pholas*, type genus + *-idae*] : a family of bivalve mollusks (order Eulamellibranchia) comprising the piddocks and related borers — **pho·la·doid** \'fōlә,dȯid\ *adj*

pho·las \'fōlәs\ *n* [NL, fr. Gk *phōlas* stone-boring mollusk, lit., lying in a hole; akin to Gk *phylē* tribe, clan — more at PHYSIC] **1** *cap* : a large genus of bivalve usu. marine mollusks (family Pholadidae) with an elongate-oval rough shell having no hinge ligament, gaping at the end, and having two accessory valves to protect the dorsal margin that with the foot serves as a rasp to bore in wood and stone **2** *pl* **pho·la·des** \-lә,dēz\ : any mollusk of the genus *Pholas* or of the family Pholadidae : PIDDOCK

1**phol·cid** \'fälsәd\ *adj* [NL *Pholcidae*] : of or relating to the Pholcidae

2**pholcid** \"\ *n* -s [NL *Pholcidae*] : a spider of the family Pholcidae

phol·ci·dae \-sә,dē\ *n pl, cap* [NL, fr. *Pholcus*, type genus + *-idae*] : a family of spiders having very long slender legs and weaving irregular webs in which they rest with the back downward — **phol·coid** \'fäl,kȯid\ *adj or n*

phol·cus \'fälkәs\ *n, cap* [NL, fr. Gk *pholkos* bowlegged] : a genus of spiders that is the type of the family Pholcidae

pholid- *or* **pholido-** *comb form* [NL, fr. Gk, fr. *pholid-, pholis* scale of a reptile; akin to Gk *phloos* bark — more at PHLOEM] : scale ⟨*pholid*osis⟩ ⟨*pholido*lite⟩

phol·i·do·sis \,fälә'dōsәs\ *n, pl* **pholido·ses** \-ō,sēz\ [NL, fr. *pholid-* + *-osis*] : LEPIDOSIS 2

phol·i·do·ta \,fälә'dōd·ә\ *n pl, cap* [NL, fr. Gk *pholidōtos* covered with scales, fr. *pholid-, pholis*] : an order of toothless scaly eutherian mammals comprising the pangolins that in many respects resemble true edentates and were formerly included in Edentata

phol·i·o·ta \,fälē'ōd·ә\ *n, cap* [NL, fr. Gk *pholis* scale of a reptile + *ōt-, ous* ear — more at EAR] : a genus of brown-spored agarics of Europe and No. America having an annulus and growing on open ground or decaying wood

-pho·lis \fәlәs\ *n comb form* [NL, fr. Gk *pholis* scale of a reptile] : organism having a (specified) kind of scale — in generic names ⟨*Conopholis*⟩

pho·ma \'fōmә\ *n, cap* [NL, fr. Gk *phōis* blister] : a large form genus of imperfect fungi (family Sphaeropsidaceae) typically stem-inhabiting but some causing destructive rots of fruits or roots and having nonseptate hyaline ovate to elongate pycnospores in pycnidia — compare PHOMOPSIS

pho·mop·sis \fō'mäpsәs\ *n, cap* [NL, fr. *Phoma* + *-opsis*] : a form genus of imperfect fungi (family Sphaeropsidaceae) producing pycnospores and also filiform scolecospores

phon \'fän\ *n* -s [ISV, fr. Gk *phōnē* sound, voice] : the unit of loudness level on a scale beginning at zero for the faintest audible sound and corresponding to the decibel scale of sound intensity with the number of phons of a given sound being equal to the decibels of a pure 1000-cycle tone judged by the listener to be equally loud

phon- *or* **phono-** *comb form* [L, fr. Gk *phōn-, phōno-,* fr. *phōnē* — more at BAN] **:** sound **:** voice **:** speech **:** tone ⟨*phon*al⟩ ⟨*phono*graph⟩ ⟨*phono*logy⟩

phon *abbr* **1** phonetics **2** phonology

pho·nal \ˈfōnᵊl\ *adj* [*phon-* + *-al*] **:** of, relating to, or producing speech sounds

phon·as·the·nia \ˌfōnəsˈthēnēə\ *n* [NL, fr. *phon-* + *asthenia*] **:** weakness or hoarseness of voice

pho·nate \ˈfōˌnāt\ *vi* -ED/-ING/-S [*phon-* + *-ate*] **:** to produce speech sounds **:** use the voice

pho·na·tion \fōˈnāshən\ *n* -S [ISV *phon-* + *-ation*] **:** the act or process of producing speech sounds

pho·na·to·ry \ˈfōnəˌtōrē\ *adj* **:** of or relating to phonation

phon·au·to·graph \fōˈnȯd·əˌgraf, -rȧf\ *n* [*phon-* + *aut-* + *-graph*] **:** an instrument by which a sound can be made to produce a visible record of itself — **phon·au·to·graph·ic** \ˌ≈ˌ≈ˈgrafik\ *adj* — **phon·au·to·graph·i·cal·ly** \-fək(ə)lē\ *adv*

[1]**phone** \ˈfōn\ *n* -S [short for *telephone*] **:** EARPHONE, TELEPHONE, TELEPHONE RECEIVER

[2]**phone** \"\ *vb* -ED/-ING/-S **:** TELEPHONE ⟨if I didn't ~ the office, she would close up at 5 p.m. —Christopher Morley⟩

[3]**phone** \"\ *n* -S [Gk *phōnē* sound, voice] **1 :** ALLOPHONE **2 :** a speech sound considered as a physical event without regard to how it fits into the structure of a language — compare PHONEME

-phone \ˌfōn\ *n comb form* -S [LL *-phona,* fr. LGk *-phōna,* fr. Gk, neut. pl. of *-phōnos* -sounding, fr. *phōnein* to sound] **:** sound **:** voice — in names of musical instruments and sound-transmitting devices ⟨saxo*phone*⟩ ⟨ear*phone*⟩ ⟨radio*phone*⟩

pho·ne·mal \fəˈnēməl\ *adj* [*phoneme* + *-al*] **:** PHONEMIC

pho·ne·mat·ic \ˌfōnəˈmad·ik\ *adj* [ISV *phonemat-* (fr. Gk *phōnēmat-, phōnēma* sound) + *-ic*] **:** PHONEMIC; *esp* **:** of or relating to segmental phonemes

pho·ne·mat·ics \ˌ≈≈ˈmad·iks\ *n pl but sing in constr* [Gk *phōnēmat-, phonēma* sound + E *-ics*] **:** PHONEMICS; *esp* **:** segmental phonemics

pho·neme \ˈfōˌnēm\ *n* -S [F *phonème,* fr. Gk *phōnēma* sound, fr. *phōnein* to sound] **1 :** the smallest unit of speech that distinguishes one utterance from another in all of the variations that it displays in the speech of a single person or particular dialect as the result of modifying influences (as neighboring sounds and stress) ⟨the *p* of English *pin* and the *f* of English *fin* are two different ~*s*⟩ — compare ALLOPHONE, PHONE **2** [G *phonem,* fr. Gk *phōnēma* sound] **:** an auditory hallucination of voices and spoken words

pho·ne·mic \fōˈnēmik, fəˈ-, -mēk\ *adj* **1 :** of, relating to, or having the characteristics of a phoneme ⟨~ analysis⟩ **2 a** *of speech sounds* **:** constituting members of different phonemes ⟨Welsh *l* and *ll* are ~⟩ **b :** DISTINCTIVE 3 ⟨must regard length . . . as being significant or ~ —A.L.James⟩ — **pho·ne·mi·cal·ly** \-mək(ə)lē, -mēk-, -li\ *adv*

phonemic change *n* **:** a phonological development that causes an alteration in the distribution of phoneme constituents of a language

pho·ne·mi·cist \fōˈnēməsəst\ *n* -S **:** a specialist in phonemics

pho·ne·mic·i·ty \ˌfōnəˈmisəd·ē\ *n* -ES **:** the quality or state of being phonemic

pho·ne·mi·ci·za·tion \fōˌnēməsəˈzāshən\ *n* -S [*phonemicize* + *-ation*] **:** analysis into phonemes

pho·ne·mi·cize \fōˈnēməˌsīz\ *vt* -ED/-ING/-S **:** to analyze into or reduce to phonemes **:** represent by or convert into phonemic symbols **:** treat as a phoneme **:** make (a phonetic distinction) phonemic rather than allophonic

phonemicness *n* -ES **:** the quality or state of being phonemic

pho·ne·mics \fōˈnēmiks, fəˈ-, -mēks\ *n pl but sing in constr* [*phoneme* + *-ics*] **1 :** a branch of linguistic analysis that consists of the study of phonemes and often includes a study of their allophones **2 a :** the structure of a language in terms of phonemes **b :** a statement of such structure in terms of phonemes

pho·nen·do·scope \fōˈnendəˌskōp\ *n* [ISV *phon-* + *end-* + *-scope*; prob. orig. formed as It *fonendoscopio*] **:** a stethoscope for intensifying auscultatory sounds

phon·es·theme \fōˈnesˌthēm\ *n* -S [blend of *phoneme* and *esthetic*] **:** the common feature of sound occurring in a group of symbolic words

[1]**pho·net·ic** \fōˈned·|ik, fəˈ-, -et|, |ēk\ *adj* [NL *phoneticus,* fr. Gk *phōnētikos,* fr. *phōnētos* to be spoken (fr. *phōnein* to sound, speak, fr. *phōnē* sound, voice) + *-ikos* -ic — more at BAN] **1 a :** of or relating to spoken language or speech sounds ⟨~ developments in English since Chaucer's time⟩ ⟨~ differences between ancient and modern Greek⟩ **b :** of or relating to the science of phonetics ⟨~ texts⟩ ⟨~ laboratory apparatus⟩ **2 :** representing the sounds and other phenomena (as stress, pitch) of speech ⟨~ symbols⟩: **a :** constituting an alteration of the ordinary orthographic spelling that better represents its value in the spoken language, that employs only characters of the regular alphabet, and that is used in a context of conventionally spelled orthographies ⟨*thru* and *nite* are fairly common ~ spellings⟩ **b :** constituting those characters in some ancient writings (as Egyptian) that represent speech sounds as distinguished from such as are ideographic or pictorial **c :** representing speech sounds by means of symbols that have one value only ⟨in this ~ system *g* always has the value of *g* in *go,* never of *g* in *gem*⟩ **d :** employing for speech sounds more than the minimum number of symbols necessary to represent the significant differences in a speaker's speech ⟨the minutely ~ transcriptions of this linguistic atlas⟩ — contrasted with *phonemic*

[2]**phonetic** \"\ *n* -S **:** a Chinese character used with a radical to form a new character whose pronunciation it suggests

pho·net·i·cal \|əkəl\ *adj* [[1]*phonetic* + *-al*] **:** PHONETIC

pho·net·i·cal·ly \|ək(ə)lē\ *adv* **:** in a phonetic manner **:** in a phonetic sense or from a phonetic point of view ⟨words spelled ~⟩ ⟨~ similar⟩

phonetic alphabet *n* **1 :** a set of symbols used for phonetic transcription **2 :** any of various systems of identifying letters of the alphabet by means of code words in voice communication (as radio) ⟨*Alfa* and *Bravo* represent *a* and *b* in one *phonetic alphabet*⟩

phonetic change *n* **:** a phonological development in a language that affects one or more allophones of a phoneme but causes no alteration in the phoneme constituents

pho·ne·ti·cian \ˌfōnəˈtishən *sometimes* ˌfän-\ *n* -S **:** a specialist in phonetics

pho·net·i·cism \fōˈned·əˌsizəm\ *n* -S **1 :** the quality or state of being phonetic **2 :** phonetic representation

pho·net·i·cist \-səst\ *n* -S **1 :** PHONETIST 2 **2 :** PHONETICIAN

pho·net·i·ci·za·tion \fōˌned·əsəˈzāshən\ *n* -S **:** phonetic representation

pho·net·i·cize \fōˈned·əˌsīz\ *vt* -ED/-ING/-S **:** to make phonetic **:** spell phonetically

phonetic law *n* **:** a formula deduced from observed uniformity in the development under given conditions of a sound or combination of sounds within a linguistic area at or during a given time

pho·net·ics \fōˈned·|iks, fəˈ-, -et|, |ēks\ *n pl but sing in constr* **1 a :** the study and systematic classification of the sounds made in spoken utterance as they are produced by the organs of speech and as they register on the ear and on instruments **b :** the practical application of this science to the understanding and speaking of languages **2 :** the system of speech sounds of a language or group of languages ⟨reads Portuguese with some ease but finds its ~ difficult⟩ **3 :** a written representation other than conventional spelling ⟨*thru* is pretty fair ~⟩

pho·ne·tism \ˈfōnəˌtizəm\ *n* -S [[1]*phonetic* + *-ism*] **:** alteration of orthography for better agreement with pronunciation

pho·ne·tist \-nəd·əst, -nətəst\ *n* -S [[1]*phonetic* + *-ist*] **1 :** PHONETICIAN **2 :** one who advocates or uses phonetic spelling

Phone·vi·sion \ˈfōnˌvizhən\ *trademark* — used for a system of television transmission over telephone lines designed to make possible the distribution of television programs for paying subscribers

phoney *var of* PHONY

phongyi *var of* PONGYI

-phonia — see -PHONY

pho·ni·at·ric \ˌfōnēˈa·trik\ *adj* [*phon-* + *-iatric*] **:** of or relating to the treatment of speech defects

phon·ic \ˈfänik, -nēk *sometimes* ˈfōn-\ *adj* [*phon-* + *-ic*] **1 :** of, relating to, or producing sound **:** ACOUSTIC **2 a :** of or relating to the sounds of speech **:** PHONETIC **b :** of or relating to phonics — **phon·i·cal·ly** \-nək(ə)lē\ *adv*

phon·ics \-ks\ *n pl but sing in constr* [*phon-* + *-ics*] **1 :** the science of sound **:** ACOUSTICS **2 :** a method of teaching beginners to read and pronounce words by learning the phonetic value of letters and letter groups

phonic wheel *n* **:** either of two wheels one of which is at the receiving and the other at the transmitting station that rotate synchronously in some synchronous multiplex telegraph systems

phonied *past of* PHONY

phonier *comparative of* PHONY

phonies *pl of* PHONY, *pres 3d sing of* PHONY

-phonies *pl of* -PHONY

phoniest *superlative of* PHONY

pho·ni·ly \ˈfōnᵊlē\ *adv* **:** in a phony manner **:** SPURIOUSLY ⟨~ flamboyant amours and impossible deeds of derring-do —C.J.Rolo⟩

pho·ni·ness *also* **pho·ny·ness** \-nēnəs\ *n* -ES **:** the quality or state of being phony **:** FALSITY, SPURIOUSNESS ⟨describes vicious, idle, and deliriously acquisitive sides of American life — the eccentric cruelties, the lack of standards, the scintillating ~ —Alfred Kazin⟩

pho·nism \ˈfōˌnizəm\ *n* -S [*phon-* + *-ism*] **:** a synesthetic auditory sensation

phono *abbr* phonograph

phono- — see PHON-

pho·no·camp·tic \ˌfōnəˈkam(p)tik\ *adj* [*phon-* + *campt-* (fr. Gk *kamptein* to bend) + *-ic*; akin to Gk *kampē* bend — more at CAMP] *archaic* **:** reflecting sound

pho·no·cardiogram \ˌfōnō+\ *n* [ISV *phon-* + *cardiogram*] **:** a graphic record of heart sounds made by means of a microphone, amplifier, and galvanometer

pho·no·cardiography \"+\ *n* [*phon-* + *cardiography*] **:** the graphic recording of the sounds of the heart by phonocardiogram

pho·no·deik \ˈfōnəˌdīk\ *n* -S [*phon-* + *-deik* (fr. Gk *deiknynai* to show) — more at DICTION] **:** an instrument for making photographic records of sound waves in air by means of a tiny mirror that is oscillated in a rotary manner by sound waves agitating a glass diaphragm and that by its reflections of a ray of light traces corresponding paths on a moving film

pho·no·gen·ic \ˌfōnəˈjenik\ *adj* [ISV *phon-* + *-genic*] **:** adapted to or suitable for successful production or reproduction of sound ⟨some scores are more ~ than others —*Saturday Rev.*⟩ ⟨their wonderfully ~ hall —J.M.Conly⟩

pho·no·gram \ˈfōnəˌgram\ *n* [ISV *phon-* + *-gram*] **1 :** a character or symbol used to represent a word, syllable, or phoneme — compare IDEOGRAM **2 :** a succession of orthographic letters that occurs with the same phonetic value in several or many words (as the *ight* of *bright, fight, flight, light*) ⟨~*s* are used in teaching phonics⟩ **3 :** a compound character in Chinese writing consisting of a radical and a phonetic — **pho·no·gram·mic** *or* **pho·no·gram·ic** \ˌ≈≈ˈgramik\ *adj* — **pho·no·gram·mi·cal·ly** *or* **pho·no·gram·i·cal·ly** \-mək(ə)lē\ *adv*

pho·no·graph \ˈfōnəˌgraf, -raa(ə)f, -raif, -rȧf\ *n* [*phon-* + *-graph*] **:** an instrument for reproducing sounds by means of the vibration of a stylus or needle following a spiral groove on a revolving circular disc or cylinder

pho·nog·ra·pher \fōˈnägrəfə(r), fōˈ-\ *n* -S [*phonography* + *-er*] **:** a specialist in phonography

pho·no·graph·ic \ˌfōnəˈgrafik, -fēk\ *adj* [in sense 1, fr. *phonography* + *-ic*; in sense 2, fr. *phonograph* + *-ic*] **1 :** of or relating to phonography **2 :** of, relating to, or resembling the phonograph ⟨a witness of almost ~ fidelity —*Atlantic*⟩ — **pho·no·graph·i·cal·ly** \-fək(ə)lē, -fēk-, -li\ *adv*

pho·nog·ra·phy \fəˈnägrəfē, fōˈ-\ *n* -ES [*phon-* + *-graphy*] **1 :** spelling based on pronunciation **2 :** a system of shorthand writing based on sound

pho·no·lite \ˈfōnəˌlīt\ *n* -S [F, fr. G *phonolith,* fr. *phon-* + *-lith*; fr. the fact that a slab of the fresh compact rock gives a ringing sound when struck] **:** a gray or green volcanic rock consisting essentially of orthoclase and nepheline — called also *clinkstone* — **pho·no·lit·ic** \ˌ≈≈ˈlid·ik\ *adj*

pho·no·log·i·cal \ˌfōnᵊlˈäjəkəl, -jēk- *also* **pho·no·log·ic** \-jik, -jēk\ *adj* **:** of or relating to phonology — **pho·no·log·i·cal·ly** \-jək(ə)lē, -jek-, -li\ *adv*

pho·nol·o·gist \fəˈnäləjəst, fōˈ-\ *n* -S **:** a specialist in phonology

pho·nol·o·gi·za·tion \fəˌnäləjəˈzāshən\ *n* -S **:** the act or process of phonologizing or the state of being phonologized

pho·nol·o·gize \fəˈnäləˌjīz\ *vt* -ED/-ING/-S [*phonology* + *-ize*] **:** to transform (an allophonic distinction) into a phonemic distinction

pho·nol·o·gy \fōˈnäləjē, fəˈ-, -ji\ *n* -ES [*phon-* + *-logy*] **1 :** the science of speech sounds including esp. the history and theory of sound changes in a single language or in two or more related languages considered together for comparative purposes **2 :** the phonetics and the segmental and suprasegmental phonemics of a language at a particular time

pho·no·ma·nia \ˌfōnəˈmānēə\ *n* [NL, fr. *phono-* (fr. Gk *phonos* murder) + *mania* — more at PHOENICIAN] **:** homicidal mania

pho·nom·e·ter \fəˈnäməd·ə(r)\ *n* [prob. fr. F *phonomètre,* fr. *phon-* + *-mètre* -meter] **:** an instrument for measuring the intensity of sound or the frequency of its vibration

pho·no·met·ric \ˌfōnəˈme·trik\ *adj* [F *phonométrique,* fr. *phonomètre* + *-ique* -ic] **:** of, relating to, or measured by a phonometer

pho·nom·e·try \fəˈnämə·trē\ *n* -ES [F *phonométrie,* fr. *phonomètre* + *-ie* -y] **:** the measurement of sounds by a phonometer

pho·no·mo·tor \ˌfōnəˈmōd·ə(r)\ *n* [*phon-* + *motor*] **:** an instrument in which the motion produced by the vibrations of a sounding body is communicated to a small wheel

pho·non \ˈfōˌnän\ *n* -S [*phon-* + *-on*] **:** one of the quanta into which compression-wave energy is assumed to be divided and which like photons are supposed to have individual identity and mean free path — compare SECOND SOUND

pho·nop·a·thy \fəˈnäpəthē\ *n* -ES [*phon-* + *-pathy*] **:** a disorder of phonation

pho·no·phile \ˈfōnəˌfīl\ *n* -S [*phon-* + *-phil*] **:** a collector or connoisseur of phonograph records

pho·no·pho·bia \ˌfōnəˈfōbēə\ *n* [NL, fr. *phon-* + *phobia*] **:** pathological fear of sound, voice, or speaking aloud

pho·no·phore \ˈfōnəˌfō(ə)r\ *n* -S [ISV *phon-* + *-phore*] **1 a :** a device that enables telephone messages to be sent over a telegraph line simultaneously with the use of ordinary currents operating code instruments **b :** a system using this apparatus **2 :** a device to enable the deaf to hear by conducting vibrations from the speaker's larynx to the hearer's teeth — **pho·no·phor·ic** \ˌ≈≈ˈfōrik\ *adj*

pho·noph·o·rous \fəˈnäf(ə)rəs\ *adj* **:** capable of transmitting sound waves

pho·no·photogram \ˌfōnō+\ *n* [*phon-* + *photogram*] **:** a record made by phonophotography

pho·no·photograph \"+\ *n* [*phon-* + *photograph*] **:** PHONOPHOTOGRAM

pho·no·photography \"+\ *n* [*phon-* + *photography*] **:** the art or process of recording sound-vibration curves photographically (as by means of the phonodeik)

pho·no·pro·jec·to·scope \ˌfōnōprəˈjektəˌskōp\ *n* [*phon-* + *project* + connective *-o-* + *-scope*] **:** an instrument for projecting sound-vibration curves directly on a screen without first recording them photographically

pho·no·reception \ˌfōnō+\ *n* [*phon-* + *reception*] **:** the perception of vibratory motion of relatively high frequency; *specif* **:** HEARING

pho·no·receptor \"+\ *n* [*phon-* + *receptor*] **:** an animal organ for phonoreception; *esp* **:** OTOCYST

pho·no·scope \ˈfōnəˌskōp\ *n* [*phon-* + *-scope*] **:** an instrument for observing or exhibiting motions or properties of sounding bodies; *esp* **:** a device for testing the quality of musical strings

pho·no·telemeter \ˌfōnō+\ *n* [*phon-* + *telemeter*] **:** a device for estimating the distance of firearms in action by measuring the interval between the flash and the arrival of the sound from the discharge

Pho·no·vi·sion \ˈfōnəˌvizhən\ *trademark* — used for a Phonevision system

pho·nus bo·lo·nus \ˈfōnəsbəˈlōnəs\ *n* [alter. of *phony baloney*] **1 :** pretentious falsity **:** PIFFLE, TRIPE ⟨all the stylish humbug he is fond of calling *phonus bolonus* —*N.Y.Times*⟩ **2 :** CHICANERY, SKULDUGGERY, TRICKERY ⟨it was owing to some *phonus bolonus* on his part that the conflagration had been unleashed —P.G.Wodehouse⟩

[1]**pho·ny** *or* **pho·ney** \ˈfōnē, -ni\ *adj* **phonier; phoniest** [origin unknown] **:** marked by empty pretension **:** FALSE, SPURIOUS ⟨a perpetually ~ front of good fellowship is assumed —V.A.Young⟩ **syn** see COUNTERFEIT

[2]**phony** *or* **phoney** \"\ *n, pl* **phonies** *or* **phoneys :** one that is fraudulent or spurious **:** FAKE, SHAM ⟨this political issue — absenteeism — is a ~ if there ever was one —T.R.Ybarra⟩ ⟨he who writes or composes without the true inner fire . . . will always be a ~ —H.W.Van Loon⟩

[3]**phony** *or* **phoney** \"\ *vt* **phonied** *or* **phoneyed; phonied** *or* **phoneyed; phonying** *or* **phoneying; phonies** *or* **phoneys :** COUNTERFEIT, FAKE ⟨no one could ~ a list like that —Frances Lindley⟩

-pho·ny \fənē, -ni\ *also* **-pho·nia** \ˈfōnēə\ *n comb form, pl* **-phonies** *also* **-phonias** [ME *-phonie,* fr. OF, fr. L *-phonia,* fr. Gk *-phōnia,* fr. *-phōnos* -sounding (fr. *phōnein* to sound) + *-ia* -y — more at PHONETIC] **1 :** sound ⟨acro*phony*⟩ ⟨caco*phony*⟩ **2** *usu* **-phonia :** speech disorder (of a specified type esp. relating to phonation) ⟨dys*phonia*⟩ ⟨bary*phony*⟩ — compare -LALIA, -PHASIA, -PHEMIA

phony disease *also* **phony peach** *n* [*phony* alter. (influenced by [1]*phony*) of [1]*pony*; fr. the dwarfing effect of the disease] **:** a serious virus disease of the peach that causes dwarfing, abnormally dark green leaves, and a light crop of small but highly colored fruit, makes the trees stop bearing after a few years, and is of lesser importance on almond, apricot, nectarine, and plum

phonyness *var of* PHONINESS

phoo \ˈfü\ *interj* — used to express contempt, repudiation, or astonishment; compare PHEW

phoo·ey \ˈfüē, -üi\ *interj* [*phoo* + *-y*] — used to express repudiation or disgust ⟨but an American garden suburb ~ —Sinclair Lewis⟩ ⟨~ on this fellow —John & Ward Hawkins⟩

phooka *var of* POOKA

pho·ra \ˈfōrə\ *n, cap* [NL, fr. Gk *phōr* thief; akin to L *fur* thief — more at FURTIVE] **:** a genus of small flies that is the type of the family Phoridae

[1]**-pho·ra** \f(ə)rə\ *n comb form, pl* **-phora** [NL, fr. fem. sing. & neut. pl. of *-phorus*] **:** organism bearing a (specified) structure ⟨Clado*phora*⟩ **:** organisms bearing a (specified) structure ⟨Cteno*phora*⟩

[2]**-phora** *pl of* -PHORUM

pho·ra·den·dron \ˌfōrəˈdendrən\ *n, cap* [NL, fr. Gk *phōr* thief + *dendron* tree; fr. the parasitic habit — more at DENDR-] **:** a genus of American hemiparasitic plants (family Loranthaceae) having erect and vertically 2-celled anthers — see MISTLETOE 2a

-pho·rae \fəˌrē\ *n pl comb form* [NL, fr. fem. pl. of *-phorus*] **:** organisms carrying a (specified) structure ⟨Disco*phorae*⟩ ⟨Physo*phorae*⟩

phor·bide \ˈfōrˌbīd\ *n* -S [*phorbin* + *-ide*] **:** PHORBIN 2

phor·bin \-rbən\ *n* -S [ISV *phorb-* (GK *phorbē* pasture, fodder) + *-in* — more at PHEOPHORBIDE] **1 :** a magnesium-free compound $C_{22}H_{18}N_4$ that is the parent of chlorophyll in that it contains the unsubstituted ring structure of chlorophyll consisting of one carbocyclic ring in addition to the porphin ring system **2 :** any of several magnesium-free derivatives of chlorophyll (as pheophytin) that contain its characteristic ring structure — compare CHLORIN

-phore *or* **-phor** \ˌfō(ə)r, ˌfȯ(ə)r, -ōə, -ȯ(ə)\ *n comb form* -S [NL *-phorus,* fr. Gk *-phoros,* fr. *pherein* to carry — more at BEAR] **:** carrier ⟨chromo*phore*⟩ ⟨cteno*phore*⟩ ⟨gameto*phore*⟩ ⟨lumino*phor*⟩ ⟨sema*phore*⟩

pho·re·sis \fəˈrēsəs\ *also* **pho·re·sia** \-ēzēə\ *n, pl* **phoreses** *also* **phoresias** [*phoresis* fr. NL, fr. Gk *phorēsis* being carried; *phoresia* fr. NL] **:** PHORESY

-pho·re·sis \fəˈrēsəs, fōˈ-\ *n comb form, pl* **-phore·ses** \-ēˌsēz\ [NL, fr. Gk *phorēsis* being carried] **:** transmission ⟨electro*phoresis*⟩ ⟨ionto*phoresis*⟩

phor·e·sy \ˈfōrəsē\ *n* -ES [NL *phoresia,* fr. Gk *phorēsis* being carried (fr. *phorein* to carry along, wear, freq. of *pherein* to carry) + L *-ia* -y] **:** the nonparasitic association of one kind of animal (as a larval insect) with another in order to obtain transportation

pho·ret·ic \fəˈred·ik\ *adj* [fr. *phoresy,* after such pairs as E *heresy: heretic*] **:** of, relating to, or exhibiting phoresy

pho·ria \ˈfōrēə\ *n* -S [NL, fr. *-phoria*] **:** any of various tendencies of the lines of vision to deviate from the normal

-pho·ria \ˈfōrēə, ˈfȯr-\ *n comb form* -S [NL, fr. Gk, act of carrying, fr. *-phoros* -phorous + *-ia* -y] **:** bearing **:** state **:** tendency ⟨eu*phoria*⟩ ⟨idea*phoria*⟩ ⟨hetero*phoria*⟩

-phor·ic \ˈfōrik, ˈfär-, -rēk\ *adj comb form* [*-phore* + *-ic*] **:** having (such) a bearing or tendency ⟨eccoproticо*phoric*⟩

[1]**phor·id** \ˈfōrəd, ˈfȯr-\ *adj* [NL *Phoridae*] **:** of or relating to the Phoridae

[2]**phorid** \"\ *n* -S [NL *Phoridae*] **:** a fly of the family Phoridae

phor·i·dae \ˈfōrəˌdē\ *n pl, cap* [NL, fr. *Phora,* type genus + *-idae*] **:** a family of small two-winged flies of hunchbacked appearance with short apparently one-jointed antennae and without crossveins in the wing

phor·mia \ˈfȯrmēə\ *n, cap* [NL, prob. irreg. fr. Gk *phōr* thief — more at PHORA] **:** a genus of calliphorid flies some of which are parasitic as larvae on sheep

phor·minx \ˈfȯrˌmiŋks\ *n, pl* **phormin·ges** \fȯ(r)ˈminˌjēz\ [Gk, lyre] **:** CITHARA 1

phor·mi·um \ˈfȯ(r)mēəm\ *n* [NL, fr. Gk *phormion,* a plant, small mat, dim. of *phormos* mat, basket for carrying corn, fr. *pherein* to carry] **1** *cap* **:** a genus of herbs (family Liliaceae) with rigid sword-shaped leaves and red or yellow flowers on a leafless scape — see NEW ZEALAND FLAX **2** -S **:** a hard fiber from New Zealand flax used for bagging and cordage

phoro- *comb form* [NL, fr. ML, fr. Gk, fr. *phorein* to carry along, freq. of *pherein* to carry — more at BEAR] **:** carrying on **:** having motion **:** direction ⟨*phoro*zooid⟩ ⟨*phoro*nomy⟩ ⟨*phoro*metry⟩

pho·rom·e·ter \fəˈräməd·ə(r)\ *n* [*phoro-* + *-meter*] **:** any of various instruments for measuring the strength, deviation, and direction of the extrinsic muscles of the eyes and for inducing exercise to correct defects in their functioning

phor·o·met·ric \ˌfōrəˈme·trik\ *adj* **:** of or relating to phorometry

pho·rom·e·try \fəˈrämə·trē\ *n* -ES [*phoro-* + *-metry*] **:** the science or practice of testing and correcting the action of the extrinsic muscles of the eyes in order to cure strabismus and to produce stereoscopic vision

pho·rone \ˈfōˌrōn\ *n* -S [ISV cam*phor* + *-one*] **:** a yellowish green unsaturated open-chain ketone $[(CH_3)_2C{=}CH]_2CO$ that is isomeric with camphorone and isophorone, is obtained by condensation of acetone, and is used chiefly as a solvent

[1]**pho·ro·nid** \fəˈrōnəd\ *adj* [NL *Phoronidea*] **:** of or relating to the Phoronidea

[2]**phoronid** \"\ *n* -S [NL *Phoronidea*] **:** one of the Phoronidea

pho·ron·i·da \-ränədə\ [NL, fr. *Phoronis* + *-ida*] *syn of* PHORONIDEA

pho·ro·nid·ea \ˌfōrəˈnidēə\ *n pl, cap* [NL, fr. *Phoronis* + *-idea*] **:** a group (coextensive with the genus *Phoronis*) of marine animals of uncertain systematic position that has at various times been associated with the Molluscoidea, the Gephyrea, or the Hemichordata or treated as a separate phylum

pho·ro·nis \fəˈrōnəs\ *n, cap* [NL, prob. fr. L *Phoronis* (Io, mythical priestess of Argos who was loved by Zeus)] **:** a genus of small marine tubicolous unsegmented wormlike animals that have the mouth, anal opening, and nephridial apertures at one end of the body close together and surrounded by a horseshoe-shaped lophophore bearing numerous tentacles, a closed system of blood vessels containing red blood, and free-swimming larvae which pass through a complex metamorphosis — see ACTINOTROCHA, PHORONIDEA

pho·ron·o·my \fə'ränəmē\ *n* -ES [NL *phoronomia*, fr. Gk *phoro-* (fr. *phorein* to carry along) + NL *-nomia* (fr. Gk, fr. *nomos* law) — more at NIMBLE] **:** a Kantian theory of motion deducible from a priori conceptions — compare KINEMATICS

Pho·rop·tor \fə'räptə(r)\ *trademark* — used for an instrument used to determine the corrective eyeglass lenses needed by an individual

phor·o·rhac·i·dae \,fōrə'rasə,dē\ *n pl, cap* [NL, fr. *Phororhacos*, type genus + *-idae*] **:** a family of gigantic flightless birds of the order Gruiformes from the Miocene of Patagonia

pho·ro·rha·cos \fə'rōrə,käs\ *n, cap* [NL, fr. Gk *phōr* thief + *rhakos* rag — more at *phora*] **:** a genus of prehistoric birds that is the type of the family Phororhacidae

-pho·rous \f(ə)rəs\ *adj comb form* [Gk *-phoros*, fr. *pherein* to carry — more at BEAR] **:** carrying **:** -FEROUS ⟨ascophorous⟩ ⟨phyllophorous⟩ ⟨androphorous⟩

phoro·zooid \¦fōrə+\ *n* [*phoro-* + *zooid*] **:** a zooid of the sexual generation of some free-swimming tunicates which though it becomes free-swimming does not mature sexually

-pho·rum \f(ə)rəm\ *n comb form, pl* **-pho·ra** \-rə\ [NL, fr. Gk *-phoron*, neut. of *-phoros* -phorous] **:** -PHORE ⟨hymenophorum⟩

-pho·rus \f(ə)rəs\ *n comb form* [NL, fr. Gk *-phoros* -phorous] **:** carrier — in generic names in zoology ⟨Istiophorus⟩

phos- *comb form* [Gk *phōs*-, fr. *phōs* — more at FANCY] **:** light ⟨*phos*acid⟩ ⟨*phos*nitric⟩

phose \'fōz, -ōs\ *n* -S [Gk *phōs* light] **:** a subjective visual sensation (as of light or color)

phos·gene \'fäz,jēn\ *n* -S [*phos-* + *-gene;* fr. its being orig. obtained by exposing equal volumes of chlorine and carbon monoxide to the sun's rays] **:** a colorless gaseous compound $COCl_2$ of unpleasant sour odor that condenses to a liquid at the temperature of ice, is usu. made from carbon monoxide and chlorine in the presence of a catalyst, causes severe and often fatal edema of the lungs some hours after inhalation (as used as a poison gas in World War I), and is now used chiefly as an intermediate (as in the manufacture of organic isocyanates, polyurethanes, and carbonic esters) — called also *carbon oxychloride, carbonyl chloride*

phos·gen·ic \(')fäz¦jenik\ *adj* [*phos-* + *-genic*] **:** PHOTOGENIC

phos·gen·ite \'fäz,jē,nīt, -,jə,n-\ *n* -S [G *phosgenit*, fr. *phosgen* phosgene + *-it* -ite] **:** a mineral $Pb_2Cl_2CO_3$ consisting of lead chloroformate occurring in tetragonal crystals of a white, yellow, or grayish color and adamantine luster (hardness 3, sp. gr. 6.0–6.3)

phosph- *or* **phospho-** *comb form* [F, fr. *phosphorique* phosphoric (in *acide phosphorique* phosphoric acid) — more at PHOSPHORIC] **1 :** phosphoric acid **:** phosphate ⟨*phosph*ergot⟩ ⟨*phospho*arginine⟩ **2 :** phosphorus ⟨*phospho*ferrite⟩

phos·pha·gen \'fäsfəjən, -,jen\ *n* -S [ISV *phosphate* + *-gen* (as in *glycogen*)] **:** any of several organic phosphate compounds (as phosphocreatine or phosphoarginine) occurring esp. in muscle and releasing energy on hydrolysis of the phosphate

phos·pham·ic acid \(')fä¦sfamik-\ *n* [*phosphamic* fr. *phosph-* + *amidogen* + *-ic*] **:** AMIDOPHOSPHORIC ACID

phos·pha·tase \'fäsfə,tās, -āz\ *n* -S [ISV *phosphate* + *-ase*] **:** any of a large group of widely occurring enzymes that accelerate the hydrolysis and synthesis of organic esters of phosphoric acid and the transfer of phosphate groups to other compounds and that are active (1) in alkaline media in many instances (as the phosphomonoesterases from blood plasma, milk, intestinal mucosa, or bone) and (2) in acid media in other instances (as the phosphomonoesterase from the prostate gland) — called respectively (1) *alkaline phosphatase*, (2) *acid phosphatase;* compare PYROPHOSPHATASE ⟨~s play an important role in bone formation, muscle metabolism, lactation, and alcoholic fermentation —Henry Tauber⟩

phosphatase test *n* **:** a test for the efficiency of pasteurization of milk and other dairy products based on a determination of the activity of the phosphatase that is present in raw milk and is inactivated by proper pasteurization

[1]**phos·phate** \'fä,sfāt, *usu* -ād·+V\ *n* -S [F, fr. *phosphorique* phosphoric (in *acide phosphorique* phosphoric acid) + *-ate*] **1 a :** a salt of a phosphoric acid classified often as primary, secondary, or tertiary according to the number of hydrogen atoms replaced in the acid; *esp* **:** ORTHOPHOSPHATE — called also *inorganic phosphate;* see CALCIUM PHOSPHATE, SODIUM PHOSPHATE **b :** an ester of a phosphoric acid that often plays an important role in metabolism — called also *organic phosphate* — compare ADENOSINE DIPHOSPHATE, ADENOSINE TRIPHOSPHATE, ADENYLIC ACID, GLUCOSE PHOSPHATE, NUCLEIC ACID, PHOSPHOGLYCERIC ACID **c :** an organic compound of phosphoric acid in which the acid unit is bound to nitrogen (as in phosphocreatine) or to a carboxyl group (as in acetyl phosphate) in such a manner that useful energy is released on hydrolysis during metabolism — called also *organic phosphate* **2 :** an effervescent drink of carbonated water with a small amount of phosphoric acid or of an acid phosphate of potassium, magnesium, sodium, or calcium or a mixture of them flavored with fruit syrup ⟨orange ~⟩ **3 :** a phosphatic material used for fertilizers — see SUPERPHOSPHATE

[2]**phosphate** \"\ *vt* -ED/-ING/-S **:** to treat with phosphoric acid or a phosphate (as in coating iron)

phosphated flour *n* **:** flour made from soft wheat to which monocalcium phosphate is added to improve the baking qualities

phos·pha·te·mia \,fäsfə'tēmēə, -,sfād·'ēm-\ *n* -S [NL, fr. *phosphate* + *-emia*] **:** the occurrence of phosphate in the blood esp. in excessive amounts

phosphate rock *n* **:** a rock that consists of calcium phosphate largely in the form of apatite or carbonate-apatite usu. together with calcium carbonate and other minerals, that is useful in fertilizers and is a source of phosphorus compounds, and that occurs in large beds in the southeastern U. S. and in extensive deposits in Arkansas and the northwestern U. S. — compare SUPERPHOSPHATE

phos·phat·ic \(')fä¦sfad·ik, -fād-\ *adj* [[1]*phosphate* + *-ic*] **:** of, relating to, or containing phosphoric acid or phosphates

phosphatic slag *n* **:** BASIC SLAG

phos·pha·tide \'fäsfə,tīd\ *n* -S [ISV *phosphate* + *-ide*] **:** any of a class of complex phosphoric ester lipids (as the lecithins, cephalins, sphingomyelins, lipositol) that are found in all living cells in association with depot fats esp. in active tissues (as nerve tissue) and that on hydrolysis yield phosphoric acid, fatty acids, a polyhydric alcohol (as glycerol or inositol), and usu. a nitrogen base (as choline or ethanolamine) — called also *phospholipid* — **phos·pha·tid·ic** \¦fäsfə¦tidik\ *adj*

phosphatidic acid *n* [*phosphatidic* fr. *phosphatide* + *-ic*] **:** any of several acids $(RCOO)_2C_3H_5OPO_3H_2$ that are formed from phosphatides by partial hydrolysis (as by removal of the nitrogen base), that are glycerides of glycerophosphoric acids, and that yield on hydrolysis two fatty-acid molecules RCOOH and one molecule each of glycerol and phosphoric acid

phos·phati·dyl \,fäsfə¦tīd³l, fä'sfad·əd-\ *n* -S [*phosphatidic* acid + *-yl*] **:** any of several univalent radicals $(RCOO)_2C_3H_5$-$OPO(OH)$— derived from the phosphatidic acids ⟨*phosphatidyl*-serine is one of the cephalins⟩

phos·pha·tion \fä'sfāshən\ *n* -S [*phosphate* + *-ion*] **:** PHOSPHATIZATION

phos·pha·ti·za·tion \,fäsfəd·ə'zāshən, -sfə,tī'z-, -,sfād·ə'z-\ *n* -S **:** the process of phosphatizing

phos·pha·tize \'fäsfə,tīz\ *vt* -ED/-ING/-S [ISV *phosphate* + *-ize*] **1 :** to convert to a phosphate or phosphates **2 :** PHOSPHATE

phosphato- *comb form* [fr. *phosphate*] **:** containing the phosphate group PO_4 — esp. in names of coordination complexes ⟨*phosphato*-ferrates(III)⟩

phos·pha·tu·ria \,fäsfə'tu̇rēə, -sfə-'tyu̇-\ *n* -S [NL, fr. ISV [1]*phosphate* + NL *-uria*] **:** the excretion of phosphates in urine esp. in excessive amounts — **phos·pha·tu·ric** \¦==¦=rik\ *adj*

phosphazo- *comb form* [*phosph-* + *az-*] **:** containing the bivalent unsaturated group —P=N— consisting of phosphorus and nitrogen

phos·phene \'fä,sfēn\ *n* -S [ISV *phos-* + *-phene* (fr. Gk *phainein* to show) — more at FANCY] **:** a luminous impression due to excitation of the retina of the eye by some cause other than the impingement of rays of light (as by pressure on the eyeball when the lids are closed) — compare AFTERIMAGE

phos·phide \'fä,sfīd, -,sfəd\ *n* -S [ISV *phosph-* + *-ide*] **:** a binary compound of phosphorus usu. with a more electropositive element or radical

phos·phi·nate \'fäsfə,nāt\ *n* -S [*phosphinic* acid + *-ate*] **:** a salt or ester of a phosphinic acid

phos·phine \'fä,sfēn, -,sfən\ *n* -S [ISV *phosph-* + *-ine*] **1 :** a colorless very poisonous gaseous compound PH_3 that may ignite spontaneously when mixed with air or oxygen, that is a weaker base than ammonia but forms phosphonium salts with strong acids, and that is made in various ways (as by decomposing metallic phosphides with water) **2 :** any of a class of organic compounds derived from phosphine that are analogous to amines but are much weaker bases **3 :** an orange-yellow basic dye consisting essentially of a nitrate of chrysaniline — see DYE TABLE I (under *Basic Orange 15*)

phosphine oxide *n* **:** any of a series of oxides having the general formula R_3PO that are obtained by oxidation of trisubstituted phosphines

phos·phin·ic acid \(')fä¦sfinik-\ *n* [*phosphinic* ISV *phosphine* + *-ic*] **:** any of a series of monobasic organic acids RR'PO-(OH) [as diphenyl-phosphinic acid $(C_6H_5)_2PO(OH)$] obtainable from disubstituted phosphines by oxidation — compare PHOSPHONIC ACID

phos·phite \'fä,sfīt\ *n* -S [F, fr. *phosph-* + *-ite*] **:** a salt or ester of phosphorous acid

phospho- — see PHOSPH-

phos·pho·ami·no·lipid *also* **phos·pho·ami·no·lipide** \¦fä-(,)sfōə,mēnō.-sfō,amə(,)nō+\ *n* [*phosph-* + *amino* + *lipid, lipide*] **:** a phosphatide containing a nitrogen base

phos·pho·arginine \¦fä(,)sfō+\ *n* [*phosph-* + *arginine*] **:** a compound $C_6H_{13}N_4O_2PO_3H_2$ of arginine and phosphoric acid that functions in various invertebrates (as crustaceans) in a way similar to that of phosphocreatine in vertebrates

phos·pho·creatine \"+\ *n* [ISV *phosph-* + *creatine*] **:** a compound $C_4H_8N_3O_2PO_3H_2$ of creatine and phosphoric acid occurring esp. in the muscles of vertebrates where its enzymatic hydrolysis releases phosphate and available energy for the work of muscular contraction — called also *creatine phosphate;* see ADENOSINE DIPHOSPHATE

phos·pho·di·es·ter·ase \,fä(,)sfō,dī'estə,rās, -'dī,e-, -āz\ *n* [*phosph-* + *diester* + *-ase*] **:** a phosphatase (as from snake venom) that acts on diesters (as some nucleotides) to hydrolyze only one of the two ester groups — compare PHOSPHOMONOESTERASE

phos·pho·enol·pyruvic acid \,fäs,fōə,nōl, ,fäsfō,ē,nōl, -nōl+\ *n* [*phosph-* + *enol* + *pyruvic*] **:** PHOSPHOPYRUVIC ACID

phos·pho·ferrite \,fäsfō+\ *n* [*phosph-* + *ferrous* + *-ite*] **:** a mineral $(Fe,Mn)_3(PO_4)_2.3H_2O$ consisting of a manganese ferrous hydrous phosphate and occurring in white or greenish crystalline masses (hardness 4–5, sp. gr. 3.2)

phos·pho·glu·co·mutase \,fäsfō,glükō+\ *n* [*phosph-* + *gluc-* + *mutase*] **:** an enzyme found in all plant and animal cells and obtained crystalline from rabbit-muscle extracts that catalyzes esp. the acylal-ester interconversion of glucose phosphates

phos·pho·glycerate \,fäsfō+\ *n* [ISV *phosphoglycer-* (in *phosphoglyceric acid*) + *-ate*] **:** a salt or ester of a phosphoglyceric acid

phos·pho·glyceric acid \¦fä(,)sfō+...-\ *n* [*phosphoglyceric* ISV *phosph-* + *glyceric*] **:** either of two isomeric mono-phosphates $HOOCC_2H_3(OH)OPO_3H_2$ of glyceric acid formed as intermediates in photosynthesis and in carbohydrate metabolism

phos·pho·glycerol \,fäsfō+\ *n* [*phosph-* + *glycerol*] **:** GLYCEROPHOSPHORIC ACID

phos·pho·lipase \¦fäsfō+\ *n* [*phosph-* + *lipase*] **:** LECITHINASE

phos·pho·lipid *also* **phos·pho·lipide** \"+\ *n* [*phosph-* + *lipid, lipide*] **:** PHOSPHATIDE

phos·pho·lipin \"+\ *n* [*phosph-* + *lipin*] **:** PHOSPHATIDE

phos·pho·molybdate \¦fä(,)sfō+\ *n* [ISV *phosphomolybd-* (in *phosphomolybdic acid*) + *-ate*] **:** a salt of a phosphomolybdic acid — called also *molybdophosphate*

phos·pho·molybdic acid \"+...-\ *n* [ISV *phosph-* + *molybdic*] **:** any of several heteropoly acids obtainable from solutions of phosphoric acid and molybdic acid and used chiefly as precipitants (as for alkaloids and for basic dyes for organic pigments); *esp* **:** the yellow crystalline acid $H_3PMo_{12}O_{40}.xH_2O$ containing twelve atoms of molybdenum in the molecule — called also *molybdophosphoric acid*

phos·pho·mono·es·ter·ase \,fä(,)sfō,mänō'estə,rās, -'mänō-, -mōnō-, -āz\ *n* [*phosph-* + *monoester* + *-ase*] **:** a phosphatase that acts on monoesters (as a beta-glycerophosphate or glucose phosphate)

phos·pho·nate \'fäsfə,nāt\ *n* -S [*phosphonic* acid + *-ate*] **:** a salt or ester of a phosphonic acid

phos·phon·ic acid \(')fä¦sfänik-\ *n* [*phosphonic* alter. (influenced by *-onic*) of *phosphinic*] **:** any of a series of dibasic organic acids $RPO(OH)_2$ [as phenyl-phosphonic acid $C_6H_5PO(OH)_2$] obtainable from monosubstituted phosphines by oxidation — compare PHOSPHINIC ACID

phos·pho·nitrile \¦fäsfō+\ *n* [*phosph-* + *nitrile*] **:** a bivalent ion PN^{++} or radical PN consisting of phosphorus and nitrogen and known in the form of polymeric compounds esp. halides [as phosphonitrile chloride $(PNCl_2)_n$] — **phos·pho·nitrilic** \"+\ *adj*

phos·pho·ni·um \fä'sfōnēəm\ *n* -S [NL, fr. *phosph-* + *-onium*] **:** a univalent ion PH_4^+ or radical PH_4 analogous to ammonium that is derived from phosphine and is known esp. in the form of salts (as phosphonium iodide PH_4I) and organic derivatives [as tetraphenyl-phosphonium iodide $(C_6H_5)_4PI$] — compare QUATERNARY AMMONIUM COMPOUND

phos·pho·phyllite \,fäsfō+\ *n* [*phosph-* + *phyllite*] **:** a mineral $Zn_2(FeMn)(PO_4)_2.4H_2O$ consisting of a hydrous phosphate of zinc, ferrous iron, and manganese and forming colorless or pale blue monoclinic crystals with perfect micaceous cleavage (hardness 3–4, sp. gr. 3.1)

phos·pho·protein \¦fä(,)sfō+\ *n* [*phosph-* + *protein*] **:** any of a class of proteins containing combined phosphoric acid (as casein or phosvitin)

phos·pho·pyruvic acid \"+...-\ *n* [*phosph-* + *pyruvic*] **:** the phosphate $CH_2{=}O(OPO_3H_2)COOH$ of the enol form of pyruvic acid formed as an intermediate in carbohydrate metabolism (as from phosphoglyceric acid by reversible dehydration) — called also *phosphoenolpyruvic acid*

phos·phor \'fäsfər, -,sfō(ə)r\ *n* -S [F *phosphore*, fr. NL *phosphorus* — more at PHOSPHORUS] **1 :** anything that exhibits phosphorescence ⟨her eyes . . . flashed ~ and sharp sparks —John Keats⟩ **2** *also* **phos·phore** \-,sfō(ə)r\ **:** any of various phosphorescent or fluorescent materials (as zinc sulfide activated with silver or copper or zinc silicate activated with manganese) that may occur as minerals (as wurtzite or willemite) but are now usu. produced synthetically and are used chiefly in fluorescent lamps, in cathode-ray tubes (as for television and radar), in instruments for detecting various radiations, and in luminous paints and inks

phosphor- *or* **phosphoro-** *comb form* [NL *phosphorus*] **:** phosphorus ⟨*phosphor*ate⟩ **:** phosphoric acid ⟨*phosphor*amidic acid⟩ ⟨*phosphoro*thioic acid⟩

phos·phor·amidic acid \¦fäsfər+...\ *n* [*phosphor-* + *amidic*] **:** AMIDOPHOSPHORIC ACID

phos·pho·rate \'fäsfə,rāt\ *vt* -ED/-ING/-S [*phosphor-* + *-ate*] **1 :** to impregnate or combine with phosphorus or a compound of phosphorus **2 :** to make phosphorescent **:** cause to phosphoresce

phosphorated oil *n* **:** a one percent solution of phosphorus in almond oil formerly used as a nerve stimulant and tonic

phosphor bronze *n* **:** a bronze of great hardness, elasticity, and toughness whose superiority is due to the introduction of a small amount of phosphorus

phosphor copper *n* **:** a crude alloy of copper and phosphorus used to deoxidize copper and to make phosphor bronze

phos·pho·re·al *also* **phos·pho·ri·al** \(')fä¦sfōrēəl\ *adj* [prob. fr. (assumed) NL *phosphoreus* phosphorous (fr. NL *phosphorus*) + E *-al* or *-ial*] **:** of, relating to, or having the characteristics of phosphorus

phos·pho·resce \,fäsfə¦res\ *vi* -ED/-ING/-S [prob. back-formation fr. *phosphorescent*] **:** to exhibit phosphorescence **:** glow esp. in the dark

phos·pho·res·cence \,fäsfə'res³n(t)s\ *n* -S [*phosphorescent* + *-ence*] **1 :** luminescence that is perceptible with characteristic rate of decay after the exciting cause ceases to act — compare FLUORESCENCE **2 :** an enduring luminescence (as bioluminescence or the chemiluminescence of phosphorus)

phos·pho·res·cent \¦==¦res³nt\ *adj* [*phosphor* + *-escent*] **:** exhibiting or characterized by phosphorescence ⟨the ~ glow of decaying wood —Nathaniel Hawthorne⟩ — **phos·pho·res·cent·ly** *adv*

phos·pho·ret·ed *or* **phos·pho·ret·ted** \'fäsfə,red·əd\ *adj* [alter. of *phosphureted*] **:** impregnated or combined with phosphorus ⟨~ hydrogen⟩

phosphori *pl of* PHOSPHORUS

phos·phor·ic \(')fä¦sfōrik, -sfär-, -rēk; 'fäsfərik\ *adj* [F *phosphorique*, fr. *phosphore* phosphor (fr. NL *phosphorus*) + *-ique* -ic — more at PHOSPHORUS] **1 :** PHOSPHORESCENT **2 :** of, relating to, or resembling phosphorus — used esp. of compounds in which this element has a valence higher than in phosphorous compounds

phosphoric acid *n* [F *acide phosphorique*] **1 a :** a syrupy or deliquescent crystalline tribasic acid H_3PO_4 that is obtained by hydration of phosphorus pentoxide or by decomposition of phosphates (as phosphate rock) by leaching with sulfuric acid, that is converted to pyrophosphoric acid when heated above 150°C and to metaphosphoric acid when heated until dense white fumes appear, and that is used chiefly in making fertilizers and other phosphates, in rust-proofing metals, in sugar refining, and as a flavoring agent in soft drinks — called also *orthophosphoric acid* **b :** a compound (as pyrophosphoric acid or metaphosphoric acid) consisting of phosphate groups linked directly to each other by oxygen **2 :** phosphorus pentoxide in combined form as determined by analysis esp. in soils and fertilizers

phosphoric anhydride *n* **:** PHOSPHORUS PENTOXIDE

phosphoric oxide *n* **:** PHOSPHORUS PENTOXIDE

phos·pho·rif·er·ous \¦fäsfə¦rif(ə)rəs\ *adj* [*phosphor-* + *-iferous*] **:** bearing or yielding phosphorus

phos·pho·rism \'fäsfə,rizəm\ *n* -S [ISV *phosphor-* + *-ism*] **:** a poisoning by phosphorus esp. when chronic

phos·pho·rite \'fäsfə,rīt\ *n* -S [*phosphor-* + *-ite*] **1 :** a fibrous concretionary apatite **2 :** PHOSPHATE ROCK — **phos·pho·rit·ic** \¦==¦rid·ik\ *adj*

phos·pho·rize \'fäsfə,rīz\ *vt* -ED/-ING/-S [F *phosphoriser*, fr. *phosphore* phosphor + *-iser* -ize] **:** PHOSPHORATE

phosphoro- — see PHOSPHOR-

phos·pho·ro·clas·tic \¦fäsfərō¦klastik\ *adj* [*phosphor-* + *-clastic*] **:** of, relating to, or inducing a reaction in which a phosphate is involved in the splitting of a compound (as pyruvic acid)

phos·pho·ro·fluoridic acid *n* \¦fäsfə(,)rō+...-\ [*phosphor-* + *fluoride* + *-ic*] **:** the fluorophosphoric acid H_2PO_3F

phos·phor·o·gen \fä'sfōrəjən, -,jen\ *n* -S [ISV *phosphor-* + *-gen;* perh. orig. formed as F *phosphorogène*] **:** a substance or group that produces or helps to produce phosphorescence or luminescence

phos·pho·ro·gen·ic \¦fäsfərō¦jenik\ *adj* [ISV *phosphor-* + *-genic*] **:** generating phosphorescence

phos·phoro·graph \fä'sfōrə,graf, -räf\ *n* [*phosphor-* + *-graph*] **:** a photographic impression made by laying a phosphorescent body directly upon the photographic film in order to detect phosphorescence too feeble to be observed visually — **phos·pho·ro·graph·ic** \¦fäsfərə¦grafik\ *adj* — **phos·pho·rog·ra·phy** \,fäsfə'rägrəfē\ *n* -ES

phos·pho·rol·y·sis \,fäsfə'räləsəs\ *n* [NL, fr. *phosphor-* + *-lysis*] **:** a reversible reaction analogous to hydrolysis in which phosphoric acid functions in a manner similar to that of water with the formation of a phosphate; *esp* **:** the reaction of a glycoside (as sucrose, starch, or glycogen) with phosphate in the presence of a phosphorylase to yield a phosphate of a monosaccharide (as glucose) — compare PHOSPHORYLATION — **phos·pho·ro·lyt·ic** \¦fäsfərō¦lid·ik\ *adj*

phos·phoro·scope \fä'sfōrə,skōp\ *n* [ISV *phosphor-* + *-scope;* orig. formed in F] **:** an apparatus for observing phosphorescence and esp. for studying its rate of decay

phos·pho·ro·thio·ic acid \¦fäsfə(,)rō¦thī¦ōik-\ *n* [*phosphorothioic* fr. *phosphor-* + *-thioic*] **:** the thiophosphoric acid H_3PO_3S

phos·pho·rous \'fäsf(ə)rəs\ *adj* [prob. fr. (assumed) NL *phosphoreus*, fr. *phosphorus*] **1 :** PHOSPHORESCENT ⟨the overlapping waves shiny and ~ —R.V.Cassill⟩ **2 :** of, resembling, or containing phosphorus — used of compounds in which this element has a valence lower than in phosphoric compounds

phosphorous acid *n* **:** a deliquescent crystalline usu. dibasic acid H_3PO_3 made esp. by hydrolysis of phosphorus trichloride and used chiefly as a reducing agent and in making phosphites

phosphorous anhydride *n* **:** PHOSPHORUS TRIOXIDE

phos·phor·roesslerite \¦fäsfə(r)+\ *n* -S [G *phosphorrösslerit*, fr. *phosphor-* + *rösslerit* roesslerite] **:** a mineral $MgH(PO_4).7H_2O$ consisting of an acid hydrous phosphate of magnesium

phosphors *pl of* PHOSPHOR

phos·pho·rus \'fäsf(ə)rəs\ *n, pl* **phospho·ri** \-sfə,rī, -,rē\ [NL, fr. Gk *phōsphoros* light-bearing, fr. *phōs*- phos- + *-phoros* -phorous] **1 :** a phosphorescent substance or body; *esp* **:** one that shines or glows in the dark **2 :** a nonmetallic multivalent element of the nitrogen family that occurs widely in combined form esp. as inorganic phosphates in minerals (as the apatites), soils, natural waters, bones, and teeth and as organic phosphates in all living cells and that exists in several allotropic forms including (1) a low-melting distillable corrosive poisonous white or yellowish soft waxy crystallizable solid which glows faintly in air and ignites readily in warm moist air giving off dense white smoke, which is manufactured usu. from phosphate rock, sand, and coke in an electric furnace, and which is used chiefly in making phosphorus pentoxide, phosphoric acid, phosphates, and other phosphorus compounds, in incendiaries and screening smokes, and in roach and rat poisons, (2) a violet to red nonpoisonous less reactive powder obtained by heating white phosphorus with a catalyst (as iodine) at temperatures usu. around 250°C and used chiefly in the abrasive surfaces on which safety matches are to be scratched and in pyrotechnics, and (3) a black electrically conducting solid resembling graphite and obtained by heating white phosphorus to high temperatures under high pressure — symbol *P;* see ELEMENT table

phosphorus chloride *n* **:** a chloride of phosphorus: as **a :** PHOSPHORUS TRICHLORIDE **b :** PHOSPHORUS PENTACHLORIDE

phosphorus hep·ta·sulfide \-¦heptə+\ *n* [*heptasulfide* fr. *hepta-* + *sulfide*] **:** a yellow crystalline compound P_4S_7 made by heating a mixture of phosphorus and sulfur in a ratio of about 4 to 7 equivalents, regarded formerly as a trisulfide, and used chiefly in the synthesis of organic sulfur compounds (as thiophene); tetra-phosphorus heptasulfide

phosphorus oxide *n* **:** an oxide of phosphorus: as **a :** PHOSPHORUS TRIOXIDE **b :** PHOSPHORUS PENTOXIDE

phosphorus oxychloride *n* **:** a volatile fuming liquid compound $POCl_3$ made usu. by oxidation of phosphorus trichloride or by reaction of phosphorus pentachloride with phosphorus pentoxide and used chiefly in making phosphoric esters (as tricresyl phosphate) — called also *phosphoryl chloride*

phosphorus pentachloride *n* **:** a fuming irritating white or yellowish crystalline compound PCl_5 made by reaction of phosphorus or phosphorus trichloride with chlorine and used much like phosphorus trichloride

phosphorus pentasulfide *n* **:** a light-yellow hygroscopic crystalline compound P_2S_5 or P_4S_{10} used chiefly in making organic sulfur compounds, flotation reagents, and additives for lubricating oils; di-phosphorus pentasulfide

phosphorus pentoxide *n* **:** a compound known in various polymeric forms $(P_2O_5)_x$ (as the dimer P_4O_{10} in the vapor and one crystalline modification) that is obtained usu. by burning phosphorus in an excess of dry air and occurs as a white powder that reacts vigorously and sometimes explosively with water to form phosphoric acids irritating to the skin and mucous membranes, and is used chiefly as a drying agent, as a condensing agent in organic synthesis, and in making phosphoric acids and derivatives; di-phosphorus pentoxide — called also *phosphoric anhydride*

phosphorus sesquisulfide *n* **:** a flammable yellow crystalline compound P_4S_3 used chiefly in the manufacture of matches; tetra-phosphorus trisulfide — not used systematically

phosphorus sulfide *n* **:** any of several compounds of phosphorus and sulfur obtained by heating these elements: as **a :** PHOSPHORUS SESQUISULFIDE **b :** PHOSPHORUS PENTASULFIDE

phosphorus 32 \-ˌthərd·ēˈtü\ *n* **:** a heavy radioactive isotope of phosphorus having a mass number of 32 and a half-life of 14.3 days that is produced in nuclear reactors and used chiefly in tracer studies (as in biology and in chemical analysis) and in medical diagnosis (as in location of tumors) and therapy (as of polycythemia vera) — symbol P^{32} or ^{32}P; called also *radiophosphorus*

phosphorus trichloride *n* **:** a volatile fuming liquid compound PCl_3 made usu. by reaction of phosphorus with chlorine and used chiefly in chlorinating organic compounds and in making organic phosphorus compounds

phosphorus trioxide *n* **:** a deliquescent volatile crystalline compound P_4O_6 that is made by burning phosphorus in a limited supply of air or oxygen, that reacts with cold water to form phosphorous acid, and that decomposes with hot water; tetra-phosphorus hexoxide — called also *phosphorous anhydride*

phos·pho·ryl \ˈfäsfərəl\ *n* -s [ISV *phosphor-* + *-yl*] **:** the usu. trivalent radical PO consisting of phosphorus and oxygen

phos·pho·ryl·ase \fäsˈfȯrəˌlās, -ˈfär-, -lāz\ *n* -s [*phosphoryl* + *-ase*] **:** any of a group of enzymes that catalyze phosphorolysis and act through the formation of organic phosphates (as glucose phosphate in the breakdown and synthesis of glycogen and other carbohydrates) and that occur widely in animal and plant tissues — compare KINASE 2; TRANSPHOSPHORYLASE

phos·pho·ryl·ate \fäsˈfȯrəˌlāt, -ˈfär-\ *vt* -ED/-ING/-S [*phosphoryl* + *-ate*] **:** to convert (an organic compound) into an organic phosphate

phos·pho·ryl·ation \ˌ=ˌ==ˈlāshən\ *n* -s [*phosphoryl* + *-ation*] **:** the process of phosphorylating either by reaction with inorganic phosphate or by transfer of phosphate from another organic phosphate; *esp* **:** the enzymatic conversion of carbohydrates into their phosphoric esters in metabolic processes (as of glucose to glucose 6-phosphate by adenosine triphosphate and the enzyme hexokinase) ⟨it was shown that oxidative ~ was the link between fermentation and respiration on the one hand, and life on the other —V.R.Potter⟩ — compare PHOSPHOROLYSIS, TRANSPHOSPHORYLATION

phos·pho·ryl·ative \ˈ===ˌlād·iv\ *adj* [*phosphorylate* + *-ive*] **:** of, relating to, or characterized by phosphorylation

phosphoryl chloride *n* **:** PHOSPHORUS OXYCHLORIDE

phos·pho·silicate \¦fä(ˌ)sfō+\ *n* [*phosph-* + *silicate*] **:** a combined phosphate and silicate

phos·pho·tungstate \"+\ *n* [*phosphotungstic* + *-ate*] **:** a salt of a phosphotungstic acid — called also *tungstophosphate*

phos·pho·tungstic acid \"+. . .-\ *n* [*phosph-* + *tungstic*] **:** any of several heteropoly acids obtainable from solutions of phosphoric acid and tungstic acid and used chiefly as precipitants (as for alkaloids and for basic dyes for pigments) and in analytical reagents; *esp* **:** the greenish yellow crystalline acid $H_3PW_{12}O_{40}.xH_2O$ containing twelve atoms of tungsten in the molecule — called also *tungstophosphoric acid*

phos·phu·ran·yl·ite \ˌfäsfyəˈranᵊlˌīt\ *n* -s [*phosph-* + *uranyl* + *-ite*] **:** a mineral $(UO_2)_3(PO_4)_2 6H_2O$ consisting of a hydrous uranyl phosphate and occurring as a deep lemon-yellow powdery substance that exhibits phosphorescence upon exposure to radium emanations

phos·phu·ret·ed *or* **phos·phu·ret·ted** \ˈfäsfyəˌred·əd\ *adj* [obs. E *phosphuret* something combined with phosphorus (modif. — influenced by F *phosphure* something combined with phosphorus — of NL *phosphoretum* phosphuret, fr. *phosphorus*) + E *-ed*] **:** PHOSPHORETED

phos·sy jaw \ˈfäsē-\ *n* [*phossy* fr. *phos* (short for NL *phosphorus*) + *-y*] **:** a jawbone destroyed by chronic phosphorus poisoning

phos·vi·tin \ˈfäsˌvītᵊn, -svətən\ *n* -s [*phos-* (fr. *phosphoprotein*) + *vit-* + *-in*] **:** a phosphoprotein obtained from egg yolk

phot \ˈfōt, ˈfät\ *n* -s [ISV, fr. Gk *phōt-*, *phōs* light] **:** the cgs unit of illumination equal to one lumen per square centimeter and therefore to 10,000 luxes or about 929 footcandles

phot *abbr* photograph; photographer; photographic; photography

phot- *or* **photo-** *comb form* [Gk *phōt-*, *phōto-*, fr. *phōt-*, *phōs* — more at FANCY] **1 :** light ⟨*phot*eolic⟩ ⟨*phot*on⟩ ⟨*photo*graphy⟩ ⟨*photo*period⟩ **2 :** photograph **:** photographic ⟨*photo*finish⟩ ⟨*photo*album⟩ ⟨*photo*film⟩ **3 :** photoelectric ⟨*photo*cell⟩ ⟨*photo*current⟩ **4 :** photon ⟨*photo*meson⟩ **5 :** photochemical ⟨*photo*chlorination⟩ ⟨*photo*product⟩

phot·eol·ic \¦fōd·ē¦älik\ *adj* [*phot-* + *eol-* (fr. Gk *aiolos* quick-moving) + *-ic;* prob. akin to Skt *āyus* life — more at AYE] **:** NYCTITROPIC

pho·tian \ˈfōsh(ē)ən\ *adj, usu cap* [*Photius* †A.D. 891 Patriarch of Constantinople + E *-an*] **:** of or relating to the patriarch Photius noted for precipitating an early schism between the Eastern and Western churches by challenging the claim of the Roman see to supremacy and charging the Latin churches with heretical innovations (as the credal phrase "and the son")

pho·tic \ˈfōd·ik\ *adj* [*phot-* + *-ic*] **1 a :** of, relating to, or caused by light **b :** of or relating to the reaction to or the production of light by living organisms **2 a :** penetrated by light esp. of the sun ⟨~ layers⟩ **b :** of, relating to, or constituting the part of the oceanic waters of the seas that light is able to penetrate — compare ABYSSAL — **pho·ti·cal·ly** \-k(ə)lē\ *adv*

photic region *or* **photic zone** *n* **:** the uppermost layer of the sea or other body of water receiving sufficient light from the sun to affect living organisms esp. by permitting the occurrence of photosynthesis

pho·tics \-ks\ *n pl but usu sing in constr* [*photic* + *-s*] **:** a science that deals with light — compare OPTICS

pho·tin·ia \fōˈtinēə\ *n, cap* [NL, fr. Gk *phōteinos* shining, bright (fr. *phōt-*, *phōs* light) + NL *-ia*] **:** a genus of small trees and shrubs (family Rosaceae) of eastern Asia including the toyon and other plants that have shining green leaves, showy white paniculate or corymbose flower clusters, and red fruits and that are widely cultivated as ornamentals — compare HETEROMELES

pho·tism \ˈfōd·ˌizəm\ *n* -s [ISV, fr. Gk *phōtismos* illumination, light, fr. *phōtizein* to shine, give light (fr. *phōt-*, *phōs* light) + *-ismos* -ism] **:** a synesthetic visual sensation

1**pho·to** \ˈfōd·(ˌ)ō, ˈfō(ˌ)tō\ *n* -s [by shortening] **:** PHOTOGRAPH

2**photo** \"\ *vb* -ED/-ING/-S [by shortening] **:** PHOTOGRAPH

3**photo** \"\ *adj* [*phot-*] **:** PHOTOGRAPHIC

pho·to·activate \¦fōd·(ˌ)ō+\ *vt* [*phot-* + *activate*] **:** to activate (a substance) by means of radiant energy (as light) **:** subject (a reaction) to photocatalysis

pho·to·activation \"+\ *n* [*photoactive* + *-ation*] **:** the process of photoactivating — opposed to *photoinactivation*

pho·to·active \"+\ *adj* [*phot-* + *active*] **:** physically or chemically responsive to radiant energy and esp. to light: as **a :** susceptible to photoelectric stimulation **b :** photochemically sensitive — **pho·to·activity** \"+\ *n*

pho·to·allergy \"+\ *n* [*phot-* + *allergy*] **:** an allergic sensitivity to light

pho·to·aquatint \"+\ *n* [*phot-* + *aquatint*] **:** an aquatint made by a photomechanical process resembling photogravure

pho·to·autotrophic \"+\ *adj* [*phot-* + *autotrophic*] **:** autotrophic and obtaining energy from light ⟨green plants and various photosynthetic bacteria are ~⟩ — compare CHEMOAUTOTROPHIC — **pho·to·autotrophically** \"+\ *adv*

pho·to·biography \"+\ *n* [*phot-* + *biography*] **:** a history of a person's life in photographs

pho·to·biologic *or* **pho·to·biological** \"+\ *adj* [*phot-* + *biologic* or *biological*] **:** of or relating to photobiology

pho·to·biology \"+\ *n* [ISV *phot-* + *biology*] **:** a branch of biology that deals with the effects on living beings of light and other forms of radiant energy

pho·to·biotic \"+\ *adj* [*phot-* + *biotic*] **:** requiring light in order to live or thrive ⟨~ cells⟩

pho·to·catalysis \¦fōd·(ˌ)ō+\ *n* [NL, fr. *phot-* + *catalysis*] **:** the acceleration of a chemical reaction by radiant energy (as light) acting either directly or by exciting a substance that in turn catalyzes the main reaction — opposed to *photoinactivation*

pho·to·catalyst \"+\ *n* [*phot-* + *catalyst*] **:** a substance that catalyzes the main reaction in photocatalysis

pho·to·catalytic \"+\ *adj* **:** of or relating to photocatalysis

pho·to·catalyze \"+\ *vt* [NL *photocatalysis* + E *-ize*] **:** to subject to photocatalysis

pho·to·cathode \"+\ *n* [ISV *phot-* + *cathode*] **:** a cathode (as in a photoelectric cell) that emits electrons when exposed to light or other radiation

pho·to·cell \ˈfōd·ōˌsel\ *n* [ISV *phot-* + *cell*] **:** PHOTOELECTRIC CELL

pho·to·ceramics \¦fōd·(ˌ)ō+\ *n pl but usu sing in constr* [*phot-* + *ceramics*] **:** the art or process of decorating pottery with photographically prepared designs

Pho·to·charger \ˈfōd·(ˌ)ō+ˌ-\ *trademark* — used for a camera that uses rolls of paper negative for making a record of library books being borrowed

pho·to·chemical \"+\ *adj* [*phot-* + *chemical*] **1 :** of, relating to, or produced by the chemical action of radiant energy and esp. of light **2 :** relating to photochemistry — **pho·to·chemically** \"+\ *adv*

pho·to·chemigraphy \"+\ *n* [ISV *phot-* + *chemigraphy*] **1 :** the process of making zinc etchings from line drawings by the aid of chemistry and photography **2 :** any of various photomechanical engraving processes

pho·to·chemist \"+\ *n* [*phot-* + *chemist*] **:** a specialist in photochemistry

pho·to·chemistry \"+\ *n* [*phot-* + *chemistry*] **1 :** a branch of chemistry that deals with the effect of radiant energy (as light) in producing chemical changes (as in photography) — compare RADIATION CHEMISTRY **2 a :** the photochemical properties of a substance ⟨~ of gases⟩ **b :** photochemical processes ⟨the ~ of vision⟩

pho·to·chlorination \"+\ *n* [*phot-* + *chlorination*] **:** photochemical chlorination

pho·to·chrome \ˈfōd·əˌkrōm\ *n* [ISV *phot-* + *-chrome*] **:** a photograph in colors

pho·to·chromoscope \¦fōd·(ˌ)ō+\ *n* [ISV *phot-* + *chromoscope*] **:** a device for combining three color-separation positives optically according to the additive principle and viewing them as a color photograph

pho·to·chro·my \ˈfōd·əˌkrōmē\ *n* -ES [ISV *phot-* + *-chromy*] **:** a formerly used process of color photography in which a silver chloride emulsion layer assumes approximately the color of the exposing light

pho·to·chronograph \¦fōd·(ˌ)ō+\ *n* [ISV *phot-* + *chronograph;* perh. orig. formed in F] **1 :** CHRONOPHOTOGRAPH; *also* **:** an apparatus for taking chronophotographs **2 :** an instrument for the photographic recording of star transits **3 :** an instrument for recording minute intervals of time photographically

pho·to·chronography \"+\ *n* **1 :** the art of recording or measuring intervals of time by the photochronograph **2 :** CHRONOPHOTOGRAPHY

photocinesis *var of* PHOTOKINESIS

pho·to·compose \¦fōd·(ˌ)ō+\ *vt* [*phot-* + *compose*] **:** to compose (as reading matter) by photocomposition — **pho·to·composer** \"+\ *n*

pho·to·composition \"+\ *n* [*phot-* + *composition*] **:** composition of reading matter directly on film or photosensitive paper for reproduction

pho·to·conductance \"+\ *n* [*phot-* + *conductance*] **:** PHOTOCONDUCTIVITY

pho·to·conducting \"+\ *adj* [*phot-* + *conducting*] **:** PHOTOCONDUCTIVE

pho·to·conduction \"+\ *n* [*phot-* + *conduction*] **:** variation of current in a circuit due to the photoconductivity of some part of it under varying illumination

pho·to·conductive \"+\ *adj* [*phot-* + *conductive*] **:** of, having, or relating to photoconductivity

photoconductive cell *n* **:** a photoelectric cell utilizing photoconductivity (as in a layer of selenium) so that an increase in illumination causes a decrease in electrical resistance and permits the flow of a greater electrical current

pho·to·conductivity \"+\ *n* [*phot-* + *conductivity*] **:** electrical conductivity of a substance (as selenium) as affected by exposure to light or other radiation ⟨the increase in conductivity induced by light is termed ~ —T.H.James & G.C.Higgins⟩

pho·to·conductor \"+\ *n* [*phot-* + *conductor*] **:** a photoconductive substance

pho·to·copier \"+\ *n* [1*photocopy* + *-er*] **:** one that makes photocopies

1**pho·to·copy** \ˈfōd·ō+ˌ-\ *n* [ISV *phot-* + *copy*] **:** a negative or positive photographic reproduction of graphic matter (as a drawing or printing)

2**photocopy** \"\ *vt* **:** to make a photocopy of ~ *vi* **:** to make a photocopy

pho·to·current \¦fōd·(ˌ)ō+\ *n* [short for *photoelectric current*] **:** a stream of electrons produced by photoelectric or photovoltaic effects

pho·to·decomposition \"+\ *n* [*phot-* + *decomposition*] **:** chemical decomposition by means of radiant energy (as light) **:** PHOTOLYSIS

pho·to·degradation \"+\ *n* [*phot-* + *degradation*] **:** chemical degradation by means of radiant energy (as light)

pho·to·disintegration \"+\ *n* [*phot-* + *disintegration*] **:** a disintegration of the nucleus of an atom produced by absorption of radiant energy — compare ELECTRODISINTEGRATION

pho·to·dissociation \"+\ *n* [*phot-* + *dissociation*] **:** a dissociation (as of a chemical compound) produced by the absorption of radiant energy (as light)

pho·to·drama \ˈfōd·ō+ˌ-\ *n* [*phot-* + *drama*] **:** MOTION PICTURE; *esp* **:** one based upon a serious plot and characterized by sustained action and exciting incident

1**pho·to·duplicate** \¦fōd·(ˌ)ō+\ *vb* [*phot-* + *duplicate*] **:** PHOTOCOPY

2**pho·to·duplicate** \"+\ *n* **:** PHOTOCOPY

pho·to·duplication \"+\ *n* [*phot-* + *duplication*] **1 :** the process of making photocopies **2 :** PHOTOCOPY

pho·to·dynamic \"+\ *adj* [ISV *phot-* + *dynamic*] **:** of, relating to, or having the property of intensifying or inducing a toxic reaction to light and esp. sunlight in living systems — used of a chemical (as a fluorescent dye or a hemoglobin derivative) or of its action or effect ⟨a ~ pigment⟩ ⟨~ action in fagopyrism⟩ ⟨~ disorders in sheep⟩ — **pho·to·dynamically** \"+\ *adv*

photoed *past of* PHOTO

pho·to·effect \"+\ *n* [ISV *phot-* + *effect*] **1 :** PHOTOELECTRIC EFFECT **2 :** the effect of high-energy radiation (as gamma rays) on an atomic nucleus; *esp* **:** PHOTODISINTEGRATION

pho·to·elastic \"+\ *adj* [*phot-* + *elastic*] **:** of, relating to, or exhibiting photoelasticity — **pho·to·elastically** \"+\ *adv*

pho·to·elasticity \"+\ *n* [ISV *phot-* + *elasticity*] **:** the property exhibited by transparent isotropic solids of becoming doubly refracting when subjected to either tensile or compressive stress making possible a detailed study of the stress distribution from the patterns observed when the solid is examined in a polariscope

pho·to·electric \¦fōd·(ˌ)ō+\ *adj* [ISV *phot-* + *electric*] **:** relating to or utilizing any of various electrical effects due to the interaction of light or other radiation with matter — compare PHOTOCONDUCTIVE, PHOTOEMISSIVE, PHOTOVOLTAIC — **pho·to·electrically** \"+\ *adv*

photoelectric cell *n* **:** a photoelectric device: **a :** PHOTOTUBE **b :** PHOTOCONDUCTIVE CELL **c :** PHOTOVOLTAIC CELL

photoelectric current *n* **:** PHOTOCURRENT

photoelectric effect *n* **:** the effect of light falling upon metal surfaces and causing them to give out electrons, to generate an electromotive force, or to undergo a change in resistance

photoelectric emission *n* **:** PHOTOEMISSION

pho·to·electricity \"+\ *n* [ISV *photoelectric* + *-ity*] **1 :** electricity produced by the action of light **2 :** a branch of physics that deals with the electrical effects of light

photoelectric threshold *n* **:** the least quantum energy or the lowest frequency that will enable incident radiation to release photoelectrons from a surface

photoelectric tube *n* **:** PHOTOTUBE

pho·to·electron \"+\ *n* [ISV *phot-* + *electron*] **:** an electron released in photoemission (as in a phototube)

pho·to·element \"+\ *n* [ISV *phot-* + *element*] **:** PHOTOVOLTAIC CELL

pho·to·emission \"+\ *n* [*phot-* + *emission*] **:** the release of electrons from a metal (as cesium) by means of energy supplied by incidence of light or other radiation — compare FIELD EMISSION

pho·to·emissive \"+\ *adj* [*phot-* + *emissive*] **:** emitting or capable of emitting electrons when exposed to light or other radiation of suitable wavelength

photoemissive cell *n* **:** PHOTOTUBE

pho·to·engrave \¦fōd·(ˌ)ō+\ *vt* [back-formation fr. *photoengraving*] **:** to make a photoengraving of

pho·to·engraver \"+\ *n* [*photoengrave* + *-er*] **:** one that makes photoengraved plates; *also* **:** a worker who performs one or more of the operations of photoengraving

pho·to·engraving \"+\ *n* [*phot-* + *engraving*] **1 :** a photomechanical process for making linecuts and halftone cuts by photographing an image on a metal plate and then etching **2 a :** a plate made by photoengraving **b :** a print made from such a plate

pho·to·etch \"+\ *vt* [*phot-* + *etch*] **:** PHOTOENGRAVE

pho·to·etching \"+\ *n* [fr. gerund of *photoetch*] **:** PHOTOENGRAVING

photo finish *n* **1 :** a finish in which racing contestants are so close that a photograph of them as they cross the finish line has to be examined to determine the winner **2 :** a close contest (as in an election) ⟨newsmen who covered the campaign . . . foresaw a *photo finish* —*Newsweek*⟩

pho·to·finisher \"+\ *n* [*phot-* + *finisher*] **:** one that engages in photofinishing

pho·to·finishing \"+\ *n* [*phot-* + *finishing*] **:** the commercial development and printing of films exposed usu. by amateur photographers

pho·to·fission \"+\ *n* [*phot-* + *fission*] **:** nuclear fission produced by the absorption of radiant energy (as gamma rays)

pho·to·flash \ˈfōd·ō+ˌ-\ *or* **photoflash lamp** *also* **photoflash bulb** *n* [*phot-* + *flash*] **:** an electrically operated flash lamp; *esp* **:** FLASHBULB

photoflash bomb *n* **:** FLASH BOMB

pho·to·flood \"+ˌ-\ *or* **photoflood lamp** *also* **photoflood bulb** *n* [*phot-* + *flood*] **:** an electric lamp using excess voltage to give intense sustained illumination for taking photographs

pho·to·flu·o·ro·gram \¦fōd·(ˌ)ō¦flu̇(ə)rəˌgram, -lōr-,-lȯr-\ *n* [*phot-* + *fluor-* + *-gram*] **:** a photograph made by photofluorography

pho·to·fluorographic \¦fōd·(ˌ)ō+\ *adj* [*photofluorography* + *-ic*] **:** of, used in, or relating to photofluorography

pho·to·fluorography \"+\ *n* [*phot-* + *fluorography*] **:** the photography of the image produced on a fluorescent screen by X rays — called also *photoradiography*, *photoroentgenography*

pho·to·fluorometer \"+\ *n* [*phot-* + *fluorometer*] **:** a photoelectric fluorometer — **pho·to·fluorometric** \"+\ *adj* — **pho·to·fluorometrically** \"+\ *adv*

pho·to·fluoroscopy \"+\ *n* [*phot-* + *fluoroscopy*] **:** PHOTOFLUOROGRAPHY

pho·tog \fəˈtäg, fōˈ-\ *n* -s [by shortening] **1 :** PHOTOGRAPH **2 :** PHOTOGRAPHER **3 :** PHOTOGRAPHY

pho·to·galvanic \¦fōd·(ˌ)ō+\ *adj* [*phot-* + *galvanic*] **:** PHOTOVOLTAIC

pho·to·gelatin process \"+. . .-\ *n* [*phot-* + *gelatin*] **:** COLLOTYPE 1

pho·to·gene \ˈfōd·əˌjēn\ *n* -s [ISV *phot-* + *-gene;* prob. orig. formed in F] **:** an afterimage or retinal impression

pho·to·genic \¦fōd·ə¦jenik, -ōtə-, -jēn-, -nēk\ *adj* [*phot-* + *-genic*] **1 a :** produced or precipitated by light ⟨~ epilepsy⟩ ⟨~ dermatitis⟩ **b :** marked by a tendency to darken on exposure to sunlight ⟨the ~ property of a pigment⟩ **2 :** PHOTOGRAPHIC **3 :** producing or generating light **:** PHOSPHORESCENT ⟨~ bacteria⟩ ⟨~ organs of a firefly⟩ **4 :** eminently suitable for being photographed esp. from the aesthetic point of view ⟨~ hands⟩ — **pho·to·geni·cal·ly** \-nək(ə)lē, -nēk-, -li\ *adv*

pho·to·geologic *also* **pho·to·geological** \¦fōd·(ˌ)ō+\ *adj* [*photogeology* + *-ic* or *-ical*] **:** of or relating to photogeology

pho·to·geology \"+\ *n* [*phot-* + *geology*] **:** the geologic interpretation of aerial photographs; *esp* **:** the identification of geologic structures by studying such photographs

pho·to·gram \ˈfōd·əˌgram\ *n* [ISV *phot-* + *-gram*] **1 :** a photograph usu. of a pictorial nature **2 :** a shadowlike picture made by placing opaque, translucent, or transparent objects between light-sensitive paper and a light source and developing the latent photographic image

pho·to·gram·met·ric \¦==grə¦me·trik\ *also* **pho·to·gram·met·ri·cal** \-·trəkəl\ *adj* [*photogrammetric* ISV *photogrammetry* + *-ic; photogrammetrical* fr. *photogrammetry* + *-ical*] **:** of, made by, or relating to photogrammetry ⟨~ methods⟩ — **pho·to·gram·met·ri·cal·ly** \-ək(ə)lē\ *adv*

pho·to·gram·me·trist \ˌ=='gramə·trəst\ *n* -s [*photogrammetry* + *-ist*] **:** a specialist in photogrammetry

pho·to·gram·me·try \-·trē\ *n* -ES [ISV *photogram* + *-metry;* orig. formed as G *photogrammetrie*] **:** a science of making reliable measurements by the use of usu. aerial photographs in surveying and mapmaking

1**pho·to·graph** \ˈfōd·əˌgraf, -ōtə-, -raa(ə)f, -raif, -räf\ *n* [*phot-* + *-graph*] **1 :** a picture, image, or likeness obtained by photography **2 :** a portrayal, description, or mental picture or image characterized by great truth of representation or minute detail in reproduction

2**photograph** \"\ *vb* -ED/-ING/-S *vt* **1 :** to take a photograph of **2 :** to depict vividly in words ⟨verse ~*ed* the human ruins —*Time*⟩ ⟨editorial . . . ~*s* the upper layer of my mind —W.A. White⟩ **3 :** to impress on the mind ⟨a man may see your signal, ~ it in his mind's eye —H.A.Calahan⟩ ~ *vi* **1 :** to practice photography **:** take photographs **2 :** to undergo being photographed

pho·to·graph·able \-əbəl, ˌ=='===\ *adj* **1 :** capable of being photographed **2 :** PHOTOGENIC 4

pho·tog·ra·pher \fəˈtägrəfə(r), fōˈ-, *in rapid speech often* -gəf- *by* r-*dissimilation*\ *n* -s **:** one who practices or is skilled in photography; *esp* **:** one who makes a business of taking photographs

pho·to·graph·ic \¦fōd·ə¦grafik, -ōtə-, -fēk\ *adj* **1 :** of or relating to photography **:** obtained by or used in photography **2 :** representing nature and human beings with the exactness, fidelity, and minuteness of a photograph **:** concerned only with accurate presentation of external objective details ⟨~ paintings⟩ ⟨~ realism in literature⟩ **3 :** capable of retaining vivid impressions ⟨a ~ mind⟩ ⟨a few detectives have ~ memories which enable them to carry a whole rogues' gallery right under their hats —D.W.Maurer⟩ — **pho·to·graph·i·cal·ly** \-fək(ə)lē, -fēk-, -li\ *adv*

photographic magnitude *n* **:** the magnitude of a celestial body as determined by observations with an ordinary blue-sensitive photographic plate

photographic paper *n* **:** light-sensitive photographic printing paper

pho·tog·ra·phist \fəˈtägrəfəst, fōˈ-\ *n* -s **:** PHOTOGRAPHER

pho·tog·ra·phy \-rəfē, -fi\ *n* -ES [*phot-* + *-graphy*] **1 :** an art or process of producing a negative or positive image directly or indirectly on a sensitized surface by the action of light or other form of radiant energy **2 :** extremely faithful, minutely detailed, or mechanically accurate reproduction or representation

1**pho·to·gra·vure** \¦fōd·əgrə¦vyu̇(ə)r, -ōtə-, -grā¦v-, -u̇ə\ *n* [F, fr. *phot-* + *gravure*] **1 :** any of several printing processes in which an intaglio usu. copper printing plate is prepared by photographing an image through a screen onto the sensitized surface that after development is etched **2 :** a print produced by photogravure

2**photogravure** \"\ *vt* **:** to reproduce by photogravure

photogs *pl of* PHOTOG

pho·to·halide \¦fōd·(ˌ)ō+\ *n* [*phot-* + *halide*] **:** any of a series of variously colored products formed by the action of radiant energy on silver halide or obtained by the introduction of colloidal silver into silver halide during its preparation

pho·to·heliograph \"+\ *n* [*phot-* + *heliograph*] **:** a telescope adapted for photographing the sun

pho·to·impose \"+\ *vt* [*phot-* + *impose*] **:** to arrange (matter from which a printing surface is to be made by a photographic process) in final form

pho·to·inactivation \"+\ *n* [*phot-* + *inactivation*] **1 :** the retardation or prevention of a chemical reaction by radiant energy (as light) — opposed to *photocatalysis* **2 :** the inactivation of a substance by radiant energy (as light) — opposed to *photoactivation*

pho·to·induction \"+\ *n* [*phot-* + *induction*] **:** the action of light on an organism (as when the length of day affects the flowering of a plant) — **pho·to·inductive** \"+\ *adj*

photoing *pres part of* PHOTO
pho·to·intaglio \ˌfōd·(ˌ)ō+\ *n* [*phot-* + *intaglio*] **:** an intaglio printing surface produced photographically
photo interpretation *n* **:** a science of identifying and describing objects in photographs (as for military or topographic significance)
photo interpreter *n* **:** a specialist in photo interpretation
photo–ionization \ˌfōd·(ˌ)ō+\ *n* **:** ionization by the action (as in the ionosphere) of radiant energy (as light)
pho·to·ist \ˈfōd·əwəst\ *n* -s [¹*photo* + *-ist*] **:** PHOTOGRAPHER
pho·to·journalism \ˌfōd·(ˌ)ō+\ *n* [*phot-* + *journalism*] **:** journalism in which written copy is subordinate to pictorial usu. photographic presentation of news stories or in which a high proportion of such pictorial presentation is used
pho·to·journalist \"+\ *n* [*photojournalism* + *-ist*] **:** a news photographer whose work is photojournalism or whose photographs serve or are extremely suitable to photojournalism
pho·to·kinesis *or* **pho·to·cinesis** \"+\ *n* [NL, fr. *phot-* + *-kinesis*] **:** motion or activity induced by light ⟨~ (locomotion in a variable direction with respect to the light source) is seen in lampreys, hagfishes, and blinded catfish —Norman Millott⟩ — **pho·to·kinetic** \"+\ *adj*
pho·to·kymograph \"+\ *n* [*phot-* + *kymograph*] **:** a kymograph in which the record is made photographically — **pho·to·kymographic** \"+\ *adj*
pho·to·labile \"+\ *adj* [*phot-* + *labile*] **:** susceptible of change under the influence of radiant energy and esp. of light **:** unstable in the presence of light — opposed to *photostable*
pho·to·lability \"+\ *n* **:** the quality or state of being photolabile
pho·to·lettering \"+\ *n* [*phot-* + *lettering*] **:** lettering produced photomechanically from alphabets on film made from original drawings or existing type designs
¹**pho·to·lith** \ˈfōd·əˌlith\ *adj* [by shortening] **:** PHOTOLITHOGRAPHIC
²**photolith** \"+\ *vt* -ED/-ING/-S [by shortening] **:** PHOTOLITHOGRAPH
¹**pho·to·litho** \ˌfōd·əˈli(ˌ)thō\ *adj* [by shortening] **:** PHOTOLITHOGRAPHIC
²**photolitho** \"\ *n* [by shortening] **:** PHOTOLITHOGRAPH
¹**pho·to·lithograph** \ˌfōd·(ˌ)ō+\ *n* [*phot-* + *lithograph*] **:** a print made by photolithography
²**photolithograph** \"\ *vt* **:** to make a photolithograph of
pho·to·lithographer \ˌfōd·(ˌ)ō+\ *n* **:** a specialist in photolithography
pho·to·lithographic \"+\ *adj* [ISV *photolithograph* + *-ic*] **:** of, made by, or used in photolithography
pho·to·lithography \"+\ *n* [ISV *phot-* + *lithography*] **:** lithography in which photographically prepared plates are used
¹**pho·to·lithoprint** \"+\ *n* [*phot-* + *lithoprint*] **:** PHOTOLITHOGRAPH
²**photolithoprint** \"\ *vt* **:** PHOTOLITHOGRAPH
pho·to·lofting \ˌfōd·(ˌ)ō+\ *n* [*phot-* + *lofting*] **:** the production of full-scale templates or patterns of large objects by the use of a photographic process
pho·to·luminescence \"+\ *n* [ISV *phot-* + *luminescence*] **:** luminescence in which the excitation is produced by visible or invisible light — **pho·to·luminescent** \"+\ *adj*
pho·tol·y·sis \fōˈtäləsəs\ *n, pl* **photoly·ses** \-ləˌsēz\ [NL, fr. *phot-* + *-lysis*] **:** chemical decomposition or dissociation by the action of radiant energy (as light)
pho·to·lyt·ic \ˌfōd·əlˈid·ik\ *adj* [*phot-* + *-lytic*] **:** of, relating to, or formed by photolysis — **pho·to·lyt·i·cal·ly** \-d·ək(ə)lē\ *adv*
pho·to·lyze \ˈfōd·əlˌīz\ *vt* -ED/-ING/-S [NL *photolysis* + E *-ize*] **:** to subject to photolysis
pho·to·ma \fəˈtōmə, fōˈ-\ *n, pl* **photoma·ta** \-məd·ə\ [NL, fr. *phot-* + *-oma*] **:** a rudimentary subjective visual sensation (as of sparks or flashes of light or color)
pho·to·macrograph \ˌfōd·(ˌ)ō+\ *n* [*phot-* + *macrograph*] **1 :** a photograph in which the object is either unmagnified or slightly magnified up to a limit of magnification often of about 10 diameters **:** a macrograph made by photography **2 :** a photomicrograph of very low magnification
pho·to·macrographic \"+\ *adj* [*photomacrograph* + *-ic*] **:** of or relating to photomacrography
pho·to·macrography \"+\ *n* [*phot-* + *macrography*] **:** the making of photomacrographs
pho·to·magnetic \"+\ *adj* [ISV *phot-* + *magnetic*] **1 :** of or relating to the direct effect of light upon the magnetic properties of substances **2 :** of or relating to interactions between the magnetic component of electromagnetic radiation (as gamma rays) and the magnetic dipole moments of nuclear particles
¹**pho·to·map** \ˈfōd·əˌmap\ *n* [*phot-* + *map*] **:** a photograph or series of matched photographs taken vertically from an airplane upon which a grid and data pertinent to maps (as scale and place names) have been added
²**photomap** \"\ *vt* **:** to make a photomap of ~ *vi* **:** to make a photomap
pho·to·mechanical \ˌfōd·(ˌ)ō+\ *adj* [ISV *phot-* + *mechanical*] **:** relating to or being any process of printing mechanically from a photographically prepared surface — **pho·to·mechanically** \"+\ *adv*
pho·to·mechanics \"+\ *n pl but usu sing in constr* [*photomechanical* + *-ics*] **:** the technique of photomechanical methods
pho·to·meson \"+\ *n* [*phot-* + *meson*] **:** a meson ejected from an atomic nucleus as a result of the incidence of a gamma ray or other high energy photon
pho·to·meteor \"+\ *n* [ISV *phot-* + *meteor*] **:** a temporary luminous phenomenon (as lightning, a rainbow, a halo) in the sky
¹**pho·tom·e·ter** \fōˈtäməd·ə(r)\ *n* [NL *photometrum*, fr. *phot-* + *-metrum* -meter] **:** an instrument for measuring luminous intensity, luminous flux, illumination, or brightness by comparison of two unequal lights from different sources usu. by reducing the illumination of one (as by varying the distance of the source or using a polarizing device) until the two lights appear equal, the amount of adjustment serving as the basis of comparison and the equality of illumination being judged by various means
²**photometer** \"\ *vt* **:** to examine with a photometer
pho·to·met·ric \ˌfōd·əˈme·trik\ *also* **pho·to·metrical** \-rəkəl\ *adj* [*photometric* ISV *photometer* + *-ic*; *photometrical* fr. *photometer* + *-ical*] **:** of or relating to photometry or the photometer — **pho·to·met·ri·cal·ly** \-rək(ə)lē\ *adv*
pho·tom·e·try \fōˈtämə·trē\ *n* -ES [NL *photometria*, fr. *phot-* + *-metria* -metry] **:** a branch of science that deals with measuring the intensity of light; *also* **:** the practice of using a photometer
pho·to·microgram \ˌfōd·(ˌ)ō+\ *n* [*phot-* + *microgram*] **:** PHOTOMICROGRAPH
¹**pho·to·micrograph** \"+\ *n* [*phot-* + *micr-* + *-graph*] **:** a photograph of a magnified image of a small object **:** a micrograph made by photography — compare MICROPHOTOGRAPH, PHOTOMACROGRAPH
²**photomicrograph** \"\ *vt* **:** to make a photomicrograph of
pho·to·micrographer \ˌfōd·(ˌ)ō+\ *n* **:** one who makes photomicrographs
pho·to·micrographic *also* **pho·to·micrographical** \"+\ *adj* [*photomicrographic* ISV *photomicrograph* + *-ic*; *photomicrographical* fr. *photomicrograph* + *-ical*] **:** of or relating to photomicrography — **pho·to·micrographically** \"+\ *adv*
pho·to·micrography \"+\ *n* [ISV *photomicrograph* + *-y*] **:** the making of photomicrographs
pho·to·microscope \ˌfōd·(ˌ)ō+\ *n* [*phot-* + *microscope*] **:** a combined microscope, camera, and suitable light source

photomicroscope

pho·to·microscopy \"+\ *n* [*phot-* + *microscopy*] **:** PHOTOMICROGRAPHY
pho·to·montage \"+\ *n* [ISV *phot-* + *montage*] **1 :** montage in which photographic images are used (as in making a number of exposures on the same negative, projecting a number of negatives to make a composite print, or copying a picture consisting of cut and pasted prints) **2 :** a picture made by photomontage
pho·to·mosaic \"+\ *n* [*phot-* + *mosaic*] **:** a photographic mosaic; *esp* **:** one composed of aerial photographs
pho·to·multiplier \"+\ *also* **pho·tomultiplier tube** *n* [*phot-* + *multiplier*] **:** an electron multiplier in which the first stage consists of photoelectric emission from a suitable cathode — called also *multiplier phototube*
pho·to·mural \"+\ *n* [*phot-* + *mural*] **:** an enlarged photograph usu. several yards long used on walls esp. as decoration
pho·ton \ˈfōˌtän\ *n* -S [*phot-* + *-on*] **1 :** a massless elementary particle with one quantum unit of spin that is the carrier of radiant energy (as light or X rays) **2 :** a unit of intensity of light at the retina equal to the illumination received per square millimeter of a pupillary area from a surface having a brightness of one candle per square meter — called also *troland*
pho·to·nas·tic \ˌfōd·ōˈnastik\ *adj* [*photonasty* + *-ic*] **:** of relating to, or caused by photonasty — **pho·to·nas·ti·cal·ly** \-tək(ə)lē\ *adv*
pho·to·nas·ty \ˈ==ˌnastē\ *n* -ES [ISV *phot-* + *-nasty*; prob. orig. formed as G *photonastie*] **:** a nastic movement that is associated with changes in light intensity
pho·to·negative \ˌfōd·(ˌ)ō+\ *adj* [*phot-* + *negative*] **:** exhibiting negative phototropism or phototaxis
pho·to·neutron \"+\ *n* [*phot-* + *neutron*] **:** a neutron released as a result of photodisintegration
pho·ton·ic \(ˈ)fōˈtänik\ *adj* [ISV *photon* + *-ic*] **:** of or relating to a photon ⟨~ nature of the incoming rays —R.A.Millikan⟩
pho·ton·o·sus \fōˈtänəsəs\ *n, pl* **photono·si** \-nəˌsī\ [NL, fr. *phot-* + Gk *nosos* disease] **:** an abnormality (as snow blindness) caused by exposure to light
pho·to·nuclear \ˌfōd·(ˌ)ō+\ *adj* [ISV *phot-* + *nuclear*] **:** relating to or caused by the incidence of radiant energy (as X rays or gamma rays) upon atomic nuclei ⟨~ reaction⟩
photo–offset \"+\ *n* **:** offset using a photolithographic printing plate
pho·to·oxidation \"+\ *n* [*phot-* + *oxidation*] **:** oxidation under the influence of radiant energy (as light) **:** photochemical oxidation ⟨~ of polyethylene, nylon and cellulose esters . . . causes crazing, cracking, embrittlement —B.S.Biggs⟩ — **pho·to·oxidative** \"+\ *adj*
pho·to·oxidize \"+\ *vb* [*photooxidation* + *-ize*] *vi* **:** to undergo photooxidation ~ *vt* **:** to subject to photooxidation
pho·to·path·ic \ˌfōd·əˈpathik\ *adj* [*photopathy* + *-ic*] **:** of or relating to photopathy
pho·top·a·thy \fōˈtäpəthē\ *n* -ES [*phot-* + *-pathy*] **1 :** pronounced and usu. negative phototaxis or phototropism **2 :** any diseased condition caused by light esp. through overexposure
pho·to·period \ˌfōd·(ˌ)ō+\ *n* [*phot-* + *period*] **:** the relative lengths of alternating periods of lightness and darkness as they affect the growth and maturity of an organism (as in the effect upon the flowering of plants and the breeding of animals) — compare THERMOPERIOD — **pho·to·periodic** *or* **pho·to·periodical** \"+\ *adj* — **pho·to·periodically** \"+\ *adv*
pho·to·pe·ri·od·ism \ˌfōd·(ˌ)ōˈpirēəˌdizəm\ *also* **pho·to·periodicity** \ˌfōd·(ˌ)ō+\ *n, pl* **photoperiodisms** *also* **photoperiodicities** [*photoperiodism* ISV *phot-* + *period* + *-ism*; *photoperiodicity* fr. *photoperiodic* (fr. *phot-* + *periodic*) + *-ity*] **:** capacity to respond to the photoperiod
pho·to·phil·ic \ˌfōd·əˈfilik\ *also* **pho·toph·i·lous** \(ˈ)fōˈtäfələs\ *or* **pho·to·phile** \ˈfōd·əˌfīl\ *adj* [*photophilic* fr. *phot-* + *-philic*; *photophilous* ISV *phot-* + *-philous*; *photophile* fr. *phot-* + *-phile*] **:** thriving in full light **:** requiring abundant light for complete and normal development **:** light-loving ⟨~ grasses⟩ — **pho·toph·i·ly** \(ˈ)fōˈtäfəlē, -li\ *n* -ES
pho·to·phobe \ˈfōd·əˌfōb\ *n* -S [*phot-* + *-phobe*] **:** an organ or organism that thrives best in the dark or turns away from light
pho·to·pho·bia \ˌ==ˈfōbēə\ *n* [NL, fr. *photo-* + *phobia*] **:** intolerance to light; *esp* **:** painful sensitiveness to strong light
pho·to·phobic \ˌ==ˈfōbik *also* -ˈfäb-\ *also* **pho·to·phobe** \ˈ==ˌfōb\ *adj* [*photophobic* fr. NL *photophobicus*, fr. *phot-* + *-phobicus* -phobic; *photophobe* fr. *phot-* + *-phobe*] **1 a :** shunning or avoiding light **:** exhibiting negative phototropism ⟨the bedbug and other ~ insects⟩ **b :** growing best under reduced illumination **2 :** of or relating to photophobia
pho·to·phone \ˈ==ˌfōn\ *n* [*phot-* + *-phone*] **:** a device whereby a sound signal (as a voice) is transmitted by causing it to modulate a beam of visible or infrared light which is received by a photoelectric cell, amplified, and reconverted into sound
pho·to·phore \-ˌfō(ə)r\ *n* -S [ISV *phot-* + *-phore*; prob. orig. formed in F] **:** a light-emitting organ; *specif* **:** one of the luminous spots on various marine mostly deep-sea fishes
pho·to·pho·re·sis \ˌfōd·əfəˈrēsəs\ *n, pl* **photophore·ses** \-ēˌsēz\ [NL, fr. *phot-* + *-phoresis*] **:** movement of small particles (as dust particles) under the influence of radiant energy (as light) that is considered positive when the movement is away from the source of energy and negative when toward it — compare MAGNETOPHOTOPHORESIS — **pho·to·pho·ret·ic** \ˌ===ˈred·ik\ *adj*
pho·to·phosphorescence \ˌfōd·(ˌ)ō+\ *n* [*phot-* + *phosphorescence*] **:** phosphorescence excited by visible or invisible light — **pho·to·phosphorescent** \"+\ *adj*
pho·toph·y·gous \(ˈ)fōˈtäfəgəs\ *adj* [*phot-* + Gk *phygē* flight (fr. *pheugein* to flee) + E *-ous* — more at FUGITIVE] **:** preferring or thriving in shade ⟨a ~ plant⟩
pho·to·pia \fōˈtōpēə\ *n* -S [NL, fr. *phot-* + *-opia*] **:** vision in bright light with light-adapted eyes believed to be mediated by the cones of the retina — opposed to *scotopia* — **pho·topic** \(ˈ)fōˈtōpik, -täpik\ *adj*
pho·to·play \ˈfōd·ə, -d·ō+ˌ-\ *n* [*phot-* + *play*] **:** a motion picture of a story or play
pho·to·polymerization \ˌfōd·(ˌ)ō+\ *n* [*phot-* + *polymerization*] **:** polymerization under the influence of radiant energy (as light) **:** photochemical polymerization
pho·to·positive \"+\ *adj* [*phot-* + *positive*] **:** exhibiting positive phototropism or phototaxis
pho·to·print \ˈfōd·ō+ˌ-\ *n* [*phot-* + *print*] **:** an image formed on paper or other sensitive material by photographic means **:** a photographic print
pho·to·printing \+ˌ-\ *n* [*photoprint* + *-ing*] **:** the making of photoprints
pho·to·product \+ˌ-\ *n* [*phot-* + *product*] **:** a product of a photochemical reaction
pho·to·production \ˌfōd·ō+\ *n* [*phot-* + *production*] **:** the production of mesons as a result of the action of high energy photons on atomic nuclei
pho·to·proton \"+\ *n* [*phot-* + *proton*] **:** a proton ejected from an atomic nucleus as a result of photodisintegration
phot·optometer \ˌfōd·+\ *n* [*phot-* + *optometer*] **:** an instrument for studying visual impressions
pho·to·radio \ˌfōd·(ˌ)ō+\ *n* [*phot-* + *radio*] **:** the process of transmitting photographs or pictures by radio
pho·to·radiogram \"+\ *n* [fr. *Photoradiogram*, a trademark] **:** a picture or image reproduced at a distance by radio transmission
pho·to·radiograph \"+\ *n* [*phot-* + *radiograph*] **:** PHOTOFLUOROGRAM
pho·to·radiographic \"+\ *adj* [*photoradiography* + *-ic*] **:** PHOTOFLUOROGRAPHIC
pho·to·radiography \"+\ *n* [*phot-* + *radiography*] **:** PHOTOFLUOROGRAPHY
pho·to·reaction \"+\ *n* [ISV *phot-* + *reaction*] **:** a chemical reaction brought about by radiant energy (as light) **:** a photochemical reaction
pho·to·reception \"+\ *n* [*phot-* + *reception*] **:** perception of waves in the range of visible light; *specif* **:** VISION — **pho·to·receptive** \"+\ *adj*
pho·to·receptor \"+\ *n* [*phot-* + *receptor*] **:** a receptor for light stimuli
pho·to·reconnaissance \"+\ *n* [*phot-* + *reconnaissance*] **:** reconnaissance in which aerial photographs are taken
pho·to·record \ˈfōd·ō+ˌ-\ *n* [*phot-* + *record*] **:** a photographic record
pho·to·recorder \ˌfōd·(ˌ)ō+\ *n* **:** an apparatus (as a camera) for making photorecords
pho·to·recording \"+\ *n* **:** the making of photorecords
pho·to·reduction \"+\ *n* [*phot-* + *reduction*] **:** chemical reduction under the influence of radiant energy (as light) **:** photochemical reduction
pho·to·report \"+\ *n* [*phot-* + *report*] **:** a sequence of photographs (as of an event or phenomenon) combined with a minimum of text in such a way that the words and pictures supplement each other
pho·to·reproduction \"+\ *n* [*phot-* + *reproduction*] **:** the process of reproducing (as pictures or printed matter) by photographic means; *also* **:** a photographic reproduction
pho·to·resistance \"+\ *n* [*phot-* + *resistance*] **:** PHOTOCONDUCTIVITY
pho·to·resistive \"+\ *adj* [*phot-* + *resistive*] **:** of, having, or relating to photoconductivity
pho·to·roentgen *or* **pho·to·roentgenographic** \ˌfōd·(ˌ)ō+\ *adj* [*photoroentgen* fr. *phot-* + *roentgen*; *photoroentgenographic* fr. *photoroentgenography* + *-ic*] **:** PHOTOFLUOROGRAPHIC
pho·to·roentgenogram \"+\ *n* [*phot-* + *roentgenogram*] **:** PHOTOFLUOROGRAM
pho·to·roentgenography \"+\ *n* [*phot-* + *roentgenography*] **:** PHOTOFLUOROGRAPHY
photos *pl of* PHOTO, *pres 3d sing of* PHOTO
pho·to·scope \ˈfōd·əˌskōp\ *n* [ISV *phot-* + *-scope*] **:** a photofluorographic screen and camera
pho·to·sculpture \ˈfōd·ō+ˌ-\ *n* [F, fr. *phot-* + *sculpture*] **:** a method of sculpture whereby one or more cameras are used to produce photographs that are processed and combined in one of various ways to make either a bas-relief or a solid sculpture
pho·to·sensitive \ˌfōd·(ˌ)ō+\ *adj* [*phot-* + *sensitive*] **:** sensitive chemically, electrically, or otherwise to the action of radiant energy (as light) — **pho·to·sensitivity** \"+\ *n*
pho·to·sensitization \"+\ *n* [*phot-* + *sensitization*] **1 :** the process of photosensitizing **2 :** the condition of a cell, tissue, or organism acted upon by a substance (as a dyestuff) that renders it sensitive to a particular region of the spectrum to which it was previously insensitive **3 :** the development in light-colored skin of an abnormal capacity to react to sunlight typically by edematous swelling and dermatitis that in grazing animals results from ingestion of toxic substances (as porphyrins) that cause the body to absorb ultraviolet rays to an excessive degree where these are not screened out by skin pigments — compare BIGHEAD, FAGOPYRISM, HYPERICISM **4 :** a chemical change through the agency of a substance excited by the absorption of radiant energy (as light)
pho·to·sensitize \"+\ *vt* [*phot-* + *sensitize*] **1 :** to make photosensitive by means of chemical or optical sensitizers **2 :** to induce (as a chemical reaction) by means of an intermediary substance that absorbs radiant energy (as light)
pho·to·sensitizer \"+\ *n* **:** a substance (as a dye) capable of sensitizing a material (as photographic film or paper) to rays to which it is not normally sensitive
pho·to·sensory \"+\ *adj* [*phot-* + *sensory*] **:** relating to the perception of light in animals
pho·to·set \ˈfōd·ō+ˌ-\ *vt* [*phot-* + *set*] **:** PHOTOCOMPOSE — **pho·to·setter** \"+ˌ-\ *n*
pho·to·shock \"+ˌ-\ *n* [*phot-* + *shock*] **:** a method of treating psychosis by exposing the patient to a flashing light while he is under the influence of a sensitizing drug
pho·to·sphere \"+ˌ-\ *n* [*phot-* + *sphere*] **1 :** a sphere of light or glory **2 :** the luminous surface of the sun or a star beneath which it is completely opaque to the visible region of the spectrum — **pho·to·spheric** \ˌfōd·ō+\ *adj*
pho·to·stability \ˌfōd·(ˌ)ō+\ *n* **:** the property of being photostable
pho·to·stable \"+\ *adj* [*phot-* + *stable*] **:** resistant to change under the influence of radiant energy and esp. of light — opposed to *photolabile*
pho·to·stage \ˈfōd·ō+ˌ-\ *n* [*phot-* + *stage*] **:** a phase of plant development during which light exerts a dominant effect
pho·to·stat \ˈfōd·əˌstat, -ōd·ōˌs-, *usu* -ad·+V\ *vb* **photostated; photostated; photostating; photostats** [*Photostat*] *vt* **:** to make a Photostat copy of ~ *vi* **:** to photostat graphic matter
Photostat \"\ *trademark* **1** — used for a device for making a photographic copy of graphic matter **2 :** a copy made by a Photostat machine
pho·to·stationary \ˌfōd·(ˌ)ō+\ *adj* [*phot-* + *stationary*] **:** of, relating to, or being a stationary state in which the rate of photochemical dissociation of reactants is equaled by the rate of recombination
pho·to·stereograph \"+\ *n* [*phot-* + *stereograph*] **:** a double photograph mounted for use with a stereoscope — **pho·to·stereographic** \"+\ *adj*
pho·to·syn·thate \ˌfōd·ōˈsinˌthāt\ *n* -S [NL *photosynthesis* + E *-ate*] **:** a product of photosynthesis
pho·to·synthesis \ˌfōd·ō+\ *n* [NL, fr. *phot-* + *synthesis*] **:** synthesis of chemical compounds with the aid of light sometimes including the near infrared or near ultraviolet; *esp* **:** the formation of carbohydrates from carbon dioxide and a source of hydrogen (as water) in chlorophyll-containing cells (as of green plants) exposed to light involving a photochemical release of oxygen through the decomposition of water followed by various enzymatic synthetic reactions that usu. do not require the presence of light
pho·to·synthesize \ˌfōd·ō+\ *vi* [*photosynthesis* + *-ize*] **:** to engage in photosynthesis
pho·to·synthetic \ˌfōd·ō+\ *adj* **:** using, relating to, or formed by photosynthesis ⟨the direct or indirect source of free energy for all living organisms is the sunlight utilized by ~ organisms —S.L.Miller & H.C.Urey⟩ — **pho·to·synthetically** \"+\ *adv*
photosynthetic ratio *also* **photosynthetic quotient** *n* **:** the ratio of the volume of oxygen given off to the volume of carbon dioxide absorbed by a plant during photosynthesis, this ratio being theoretically near 1 when the primary product of photosynthesis is a simple carbohydrate
pho·to·tac·tic \ˌfōd·əˈtaktik\ *adj* [ISV *phot-* + *-tactic*] **:** of, relating to, or exhibiting phototaxis — **pho·to·tac·ti·cal·ly** \-k(ə)lē, -li\ *adv*
pho·to·taxis \"+\ *also* **pho·to·taxy** \ˈfōd·əˌtaksē\ *n, pl* **phototax·es** \-ˌtakˌsēz\ *or* **phototax·ies** \-ˌtakˌsēz\ [NL, fr. *phot-* + *-taxis*] **:** a taxis in which light is the directive factor (as in the movement of an infusorian toward the lighted side of a vessel); *also* **:** the orientation of various chloroplasts to light
pho·to·telegraph \ˌfōd·(ˌ)ō+\ *n* [ISV *phot-* + *telegraph*] **:** a picture received by phototelegraphy; *also* **:** the apparatus used for transmitting such a picture — **pho·to·telegraphic** \"+\ *adj*
pho·to·telegraphy \"+\ *n* [ISV *phot-* + *telegraphy*] **1 :** telegraphy by means of light (as by the heliograph) **2 :** the transmission of photographs or pictures by telegraphy
pho·to·theodolite \"+\ *n* [ISV *phot-* + *theodolite*] **:** an instrument consisting of a theodolite mounted on a camera which can take at each of several stations of known position and elevation (as determined by transit survey) a series of photographs used in terrestrial photogrammetry
pho·to·therapeutics \"+\ *n pl but sing or pl in constr* [*phot-* + *therapeutics*] **:** PHOTOTHERAPY
pho·to·therapy \"+\ *n* [ISV *phot-* + *therapy*] **:** the application of light for therapeutic purposes
pho·to·thermal *also* **pho·to·thermic** \"+\ *adj* [*phot-* + *thermal* or *thermic*] **:** of or relating to both light and heat
pho·to·timer \ˈfōd·ō+ˌ-\ *n* [*phot-* + *timer*] **1 :** a photoelectric device that automatically controls photographic exposures (as to X rays or light) **2 :** an electrically operated camera for photographing the finish of a race and the record of the elapsed time from start to finish
phot·o·nus \fōˈtätᵊnəs\ *n* [NL, fr. *phot-* + *tonus*] **:** tonic condition (as of musculature) resulting from exposure to particular conditions of lighting ⟨~ in plants usu. results in curvature towards a source of light⟩
pho·to·topography \ˌfōd·(ˌ)ō+\ *n* [ISV *phot-* + *topography*] **:** PHOTOGRAMMETRY
pho·to·transistor \"+\ *n* [*phot-* + *transistor*] **:** a transistor that acts as a photoconductive cell
pho·to·trope \ˈfōd·əˌtrōp\ *n* [*phot-* + *-trope*] **1 :** a phototropic organism or organ **2 :** a substance that changes color when exposed to radiant energy (as light)
pho·to·troph·ic \ˌfōd·əˈträfik\ *adj* [*phot-* + *-trophic*]

: capable of utilizing carbon dioxide in the presence of light as a source of metabolic carbon ⟨a ~ organism⟩

pho·to·trop·ic \-ˈäpik\ *adj* [ISV *phototrope* + *-ic*] **:** of, relating to, or capable of undergoing phototropism ⟨study . . . was confined to ~ dyes —*Chem. & Engineering News*⟩

pho·tot·ro·pism \fōˈtä·trə,pizəm\ *n* [ISV *phot-* + *-tropism*] **1 :** a tropism in which light is the orienting stimulus (as in the turning toward a light of a plant shoot or a tube worm and in the creeping away from a light of a blowfly larva) — compare HELIOTROPISM **2 :** the reversible change in color of a substance produced by the formation of an isomeric modification when exposed to radiant energy (as light)

pho·tot·ro·py \-,pē\ *n* -ES [ISV *phot-* + *-tropy*] **:** PHOTOTROPISM 2

pho·to·tube \ˈfōd·ō+,-\ *n* [*phot-* + *tube*] **:** an electron tube having a photoemissive cathode whose released electrons are drawn to the anode by reason of its positive potential

pho·to·typesetting \ˈfōd·(,)ō+\ *n* [*phot-* + *typesetting*] **:** PHOTOCOMPOSITION; *esp* **:** photocomposition done on a keyboard composing machine

pho·to·typographic *or* **pho·to·typographical** \"+\ *adj* [*phototypographic* ISV *phot-* + *typographic; phototypographical* fr. *phototypography* + *-ical*] **:** producing matter used in phototypography ⟨a ~ composing machine⟩

pho·to·typography \"+\ *n* -ES [ISV *phot-* + *typography*] **:** a photomechanical process producing matter resembling that done by typographical printing

pho·to·visual \"+\ *adj* [*phot-* + *visual*] **:** having the same focal length for actinic rays and for the brightest of the visual rays — used of an achromatic lense

photovisual magnitude *n* **:** the magnitude of a celestial body that is determined by observations with a photographic plate and filter combination giving nearly the same yellow-green sensitivity as the human eye and that is nearly equal to the visual magnitude

pho·to·voltage \"+\ *n* [*phot-* + *voltage*] **:** electromotive force developed by a photosensitive device as a result of the incidence of radiant energy

pho·to·voltaic \"+\ *adj* [ISV *phot-* + *voltaic*] **:** of, utilizing, or relating to the generation of an electromotive force when radiant energy (as light) falls on the boundary between certain dissimilar substances in close contact (as cuprous oxide and copper or an electrode and an electrolyte) ⟨produced the ~ effect in the sample under investigation —Kurt Lehovec⟩

photovoltaic cell *n* **:** a cell having a photovoltaic element mounted for exposure to light and provided with terminals for connection with a sensitive current meter

¹pho·to·zincograph \"+\ *n* [*phot-* + *zincograph*] **:** a print made by photozincography

²photozincograph \"\ *vt* -ED/-ING/-S **:** to produce by photozincography

pho·to·zincography \ˈfōd·(,)ō+\ *n* [ISV *phot-* + *zincography*] **:** zincography using photographically prepared plates

pho·to·zin·co·typy \"+ˈziŋkə,tīpē\ *n* -ES [ISV *phot-* + *zinco-* + *-typy*] **:** PHOTOZINCOGRAPHY

Pho·tron·ic \(ˈ)fōˈtränik\ *trademark* — used for a photoelectric cell in which the action of light upon the contact between two dissimilar metals causes generation of an electromotive force

phous·dar \ˈfau̇z·,där\ *archaic var of* FAUJDAR

PHP *abbr* **1** packing-house products **2** pump horsepower

phr *abbr* **1** phrase **2** phraseology

phrag·ma \ˈfragmə\ *n, pl* **phragma·ta** \-məd·ə, -mətə\ *also* **phragmas** [NL, fr. Gk *phragma* fence, fr. *phrassein, phrattein* to enclose, fence in — more at FARCE] **1 :** a septum or partial diaphragm; *esp* **:** an infolded part or inwardly extending process of the walls of the thorax of an insect or other arthropod **2 :** a false dissepiment in a plant ovary

phrag·mid·i·um \fragˈmidēəm\ *n, cap* [NL, fr. Gk *phragma* fence + NL *-idium*] **:** a genus of rust fungi of the family Pucciniaceae having teliospores of more than three cells lineally arranged — see ROSE RUST

phrag·mi·tes \fragˈmīd·(,)ēz\ *n, cap* [NL, fr. Gk *phragmitēs* growing in hedges, fr. *phragma* fence, hedge + *-itēs* -ite] **:** a genus of widely distributed reedlike grasses with tall stems and large showy panicles resembling plumes — see DITCH REED

phrag·mo·cone *also* **phrag·ma·cone** \ˈfragmə,kōn\ *n* -S [*phragmocone* ISV *phragmo-* (fr. Gk *phragmos* fence, fencing in, fr. *phrassein, phrattein* to enclose, fence in) + *cone; phragmacone* ISV *phragma-* (fr. Gk *phragma* fence) + *cone*] **:** the thin conical chambered internal shell of a belemnite that is either straight or curved, is produced in front into a very thin process resembling a blade or leaf, and fits behind into a deep cavity in the anterior end of the guard — **phrag·mo·con·ic** \¦==¦känik\ *adj*

phrag·mo·cyt·ta·rous \¦fragmō¦sid·ərəs\ *adj* [*phragmo-* (fr. Gk *phragmos* fence, fencing in) + Gk *kyttaros* cell of a honeycomb; akin to Gk *kytos* hollow vessel — more at HIDE] **:** of, relating to, or being a type of nest of social wasps (family Vespidae) in which the layers of brood comb are attached by the periphery to the envelope — compare POECILOCYTTAROUS

phrag·moid \ˈfrag,mȯid\ *adj* [Gk *phragma* fence + E *-oid*] *bot* **:** septate at right angles to the long axis ⟨the ~ conidia of various fungi⟩

phrag·moph·o·ra \fragˈmäf(ə)rə\ *n pl, cap* [NL, fr. *phragmo-* (fr. Gk *phragmos* fence) + *-phora*] *in some classifications* **:** a suborder of Decapoda comprising the fossil belemnites and the surviving genus *Spirula*

phrag·mo·plast \ˈfragmə,plast\ *n* -S [ISV *phragmo-* (fr. Gk *phragmos* fence) + *-plast*] **:** the enlarged barrel-shaped spindle characteristic of the later stages of plant mitosis within which the cell plate forms

phrag·mo·sis \fragˈmōsə̇s\ *n* -ES [NL, fr. Gk *phragmos* fence, fencing in + NL *-osis*] **:** a method of closing the burrow or nest by means of some specially adapted part of the body (as the flattened head in some ants)

phrag·mo·some \ˈfragmə,sōm\ *n* -S [*phragmo-* (fr. Gk *phragmos* fence) + *-some*] **:** a differentiated cytoplasmic diaphragm that develops from the strands of parietal cytoplasm during cell division in plant cells and forms a medium in which the phragmoplast and cell plate develop

phrag·mo·spore \ˈ==+,-\ *n* [*phragmo-* (fr. Gk *phragmos* fence) + *spore*] **:** a plant spore having two or more septa — **phrag·mo·spor·ous** \¦==¦spōrəs, (ˈ)fragˈmäspərəs\ *adj*

phras·able *or* **phrase·able** \ˈfrāzəbəl\ *adj* **:** capable of being phrased

phras·al \ˈfrāzəl\ *adj* **:** of, relating to, or consisting of a phrase ⟨~ felicity⟩ ⟨the danger of ~ hypnosis —J.M.Mitchell⟩ ⟨~ rhythm —J.L.Lowes⟩ ⟨a ~ modifier⟩ — **phras·al·ly** \-zəlē, -li\ *adv*

¹phrase \ˈfrāz\ *n* -S [L *phrasis*, fr. Gk, fr. *phrazein* to point out, show, explain] **1 :** a characteristic manner of style or expression **:** a mode or form of speech **:** DICTION, PHRASEOLOGY ⟨writes in a stilted, self-conscious ~⟩ ⟨a welcome occasional crack of American ~ —Sean O'Faolain⟩ ⟨half past one — three bells in the sea ~ —R.L.Stevenson⟩ **2 a :** a brief expression; *esp* **:** one that is pithy, telling, or memorable **:** CATCHWORD ⟨sum the matter up in a ~⟩ ⟨good at turning a ~⟩ ⟨a fine ~⟩ ⟨a hackneyed ~⟩ **b :** WORD ⟨denounced . . . as socialistic, a ~ they evidently never get tired of —A.E.Stevenson b.1900⟩ ⟨"accommodated" . . . a good ~ —Shak.⟩ **3** *also* **phraise** \"\ *chiefly Scot* **a :** smooth unmeaning talk **:** FLATTERY **b :** FUSS, COMMOTION ⟨an honest lad . . . though he made little ~ about it —Sir Walter Scott⟩ **4 :** a short musical thought that is typically two to four measures long and that closes with a cadence ⟨a cymbal crash followed immediately by a low ~ in the bassoon —*Saturday Rev.*⟩ **5 :** a group of two or more words that form a sense unit expressing a thought either fragmentarily without a complete predication (as in *Good for you!*) or with a weakened form of predication (as in *God willing*) or as a sentence element not containing a predication but having the force of a single part of speech (as in *could have been found*) and that bear to one another either the modifying relation (as in *faithful dog*) or the coordinate or multiple relation (as in *dogs and cats*) or the composite relation (as in *might have been found*) — often used with a qualifying grammatical term indicating structure ⟨participial ~⟩ ⟨infinitive ~⟩ ⟨prepositional ~⟩ ⟨verb ~⟩ or syntactical relation ⟨adverbial ~⟩ ⟨appositive ~⟩ ⟨noun ~⟩ ⟨verbal ~⟩ **6 :** a continuous series of attacks and parries in fencing ⟨during a single ~, the attack may pass back and forth between the two fencers several times —Jeanette Schlottmann⟩ **7 :** a frequently occurring group of words written in shorthand without lifting the pencil ⟨the common ~s consisting of two or three words should be written with the same facility as an ordinary word form —J.R.Gregg⟩ **8 :** a series of dance movements comprising a section of a pattern ⟨learning to move in terms of ~s rather than in steps⟩

²phrase \"\ *vb* -ED/-ING/-S *vt* **1 a :** to express in words **:** formulate in appropriate or telling terms **:** WORD, PUT ⟨unable to ~ his idea⟩ ⟨a thought . . . imperishably *phrased* —J.L.Lowes⟩ ⟨a poor but proud family, as he ~s it⟩ **b :** to designate by a descriptive word or phrase **:** TERM, STYLE ⟨these suns — for so they ~ 'em —Shak.⟩ **2** *also* **phraise** \"\ *Scot* **:** FLATTER **3 :** to divide (a musical composition) into melodic phrases ⟨the job before her, that of *phrasing* and rephrasing a fugue of Bach's —Osbert Sitwell⟩ **4 :** to write (a frequently occurring group of words) in shorthand without lifting the pencil ⟨have the student insert hyphens in the text between words which the teacher desires to have *phrased* —E.H.Eldridge⟩ ~ *vi* **:** to group notes or tones into a musical phrase **:** perform music so as to show its melodic phrasing ⟨they sang with ease and confidence . . . and *phrased* with the subtlety of master musicians —*Time*⟩

phrase book *n* **:** a book containing idiomatic expressions of a foreign language and their translation

phrasemaker \ˈ=,==\ *n* **1 :** one that coins telling phrases ⟨was a born ~ —G.W.Johnson⟩ ⟨a humorist, a wit, a vivid ~, a superb paradoxer —*Outlook*⟩ **2 :** one given to making fine-sounding but often hollow and meaningless phrases ⟨shame the demagogue ~ and the smart heckler into discomfited silence —*World's Work*⟩ — compare PHRASEMONGER

phrasemaking \ˈ=,==\ *n* **:** the art or practice of making vivid striking phrases ⟨lavishes his own power of ~ alike on king, abbot . . . and mendicants —*Irish Statesman*⟩

phrase·man \ˈfrāzmən\ *n, pl* **phrasemen :** PHRASEMONGER

phrasemonger \ˈ=,==\ *n* **:** one habitually using fine-sounding but often empty phrases usu. not of his own invention — called also *phraseman*; compare PHRASEMAKER 2

phra·se·o·gram \ˈfrāzēə,gram, -aa(ə)m\ *n* [*phraseo-* (as in *phraseology*) + *-gram*] **:** a symbol for a phrase **:** a conventional combination of signs or letters representing a phrase in certain shorthand systems **:** PHRASE ⟨described the . . . pleasure he experienced on seeing the first ~ in a letter —*Pitman's Phonographic Phrase Bk.*⟩

phra·se·o·graph \-,graf, -räf\ *n* [*phraseo-* (as in *phraseology*) + *-graph*] **:** PHRASEOGRAM — **phra·se·o·graph·ic** \¦===¦grafik\ *adj*

phra·se·og·ra·phy \,frāzēˈägrəfē, -fi\ *n* -ES [*phraseo-* (as in *phraseology*) + *-graphy*] **:** representation of word phrases by phraseograms

phra·se·o·log·i·cal \¦frāzēə¦läjəkəl, -jēk-\ *adj* **1 a :** expressed in formal often sententious phrases ⟨her father professed an elaborate ~ love for her —William Black⟩ **b :** marked by the frequently insincere use of such phrases ⟨would be only a ~ liberal and a practicing conservative —Roscoe Drummond⟩ **2 :** of or relating to phraseology ⟨~ annotations —C.J. Ellicott⟩; *esp* **:** of or relating to the phraseology characteristic of a language, a writer, or a work ⟨a ~ peculiarity of these tracts —H.G.Graham⟩ — **phra·se·o·log·i·cal·ly** \-jək(ə)lē, -jēk-, -li\ *adv*

phra·se·ol·o·gist \,==ˈäləjəst\ *n* -S **:** PHRASEMAKER, PHRASEMONGER

phrase·ol·o·gy \,frāzēˈäləjē, -ji *also* frāˈzā-\ *n* -ES [NL *phraseologia*, fr. *phraseo-* (fr. L *phrasis* phrase) + L *-logia* -logy] **1 :** a manner of organization of words into phrases and of phrases into longer elements of expression **:** idiomatic or peculiar phrasing **:** STYLE ⟨meetings . . . characterized by religious singing, biblical ~, and prayer —*Current Biog.*⟩ **2 :** choice of words **:** VOCABULARY ⟨called a flapper in the ~ of the twenties⟩

phras·er \ˈfrāzə(r)\ *n* -S **:** PHRASEMAKER, PHRASEMONGER

phrasey *also* **phrasy** \ˈfrāzē, -zi\ *adj* **:** marked by an excessive use of phrases ⟨~ fellow —John Galsworthy⟩

-phra·sia \ˈfrāzh(ē)ə, -zēə\ *n comb form* -S [NL, fr. L *phrasis* diction + NL *-ia* — more at PHRASE] **:** speech disorder (of a specified type) ⟨embolo*phrasia*⟩

phrasing *n* -S [fr. gerund of ²*phrase*] **1 :** style of expression **:** PHRASEOLOGY, WORDING ⟨the great artists of that age knew that without ~ dramatic verse was a dead thing —Lytton Strachey⟩ ⟨the exquisite ~ in which we feel that every word is in its place —Edmund Wilson⟩ **2 :** the act, method, or result of grouping notes so as to form distinct musical phrases ⟨critics were wondering at the sureness of his ~ and rhythmic pulse —*Time*⟩

phra·tor \ˈfrād·ə(r), -ātə- *also* -,tȯ(ə)r *or* -ȯ(ə)\ *n* -S [Gk *phratōr*; akin to Gk *phratēr* member of the same clan] **:** a member of a phratry ⟨at important funerals the ~s of the dead person mourned while the other phratry conducted the ceremonies —E.R.Embree⟩

phra·tric \ˈfrā·trik\ *or* **phra·tral** \-trəl\ *adj* [*phratric* fr. Gk *phratrikos*, fr. *phratra, phratria* phratry + *-ikos* -ic; *phratral* fr. *phratry* + *-al*] **:** of or relating to a phratry ⟨~ exogamy⟩

phra·try \ˈfrā·trē, -ri\ *n* -ES [Gk *phratria*, fr. *phratēr* member of the same clan, member of a phratry — more at BROTHER] **1** *also* **phra·tria** \ˈfrā·trēə\ -S **:** a kinship group forming a subdivision of a Greek phyle and serving to give religious recognition to the citizenship of its members ⟨no deme coincided with a *phratria* or with any subdivision of a *phratria* —*Athenaeum*⟩ — compare CLAN, DEME **2 :** a social tribal subdivision; *specif* **:** an exogamous group typically comprising several totemic clans ⟨the ~ overruled its clans in many ways —Diamond Jenness⟩

phre·at·ic \frēˈad·ik\ *adj* [Gk *phreat-*, *phrear* well + E *-ic* — more at BOURN] **:** of or relating to a well — used of underground waters reachable or probably reachable by drilling wells ⟨survival . . . in deep ~ waters —*Biol. Abstracts*⟩

phre·at·o·phyte \frēˈad·ə,fīt\ *n* -S [Gk *phreat-*, *phrear* well + E *-o-* + *-phyte*] **:** a deep-rooted plant that obtains its water from the water table or the layer of soil just above it — **phre·at·o·phyt·ic** \(ˈ)¦=¦==¦fid·ik\ *adj*

phren \ˈfren, ˈfrēn\ *n, pl* **phre·nes** \ˈfrē(,)nēz\ [NL, fr. Gk *phren-, phrēn* diaphragm, mind] **:** DIAPHRAGM 1

phren- *or* **phreni-** *or* **phreno-** *comb form* [L *phren-*, fr. Gk *phren-, phreno-, phren-, phrēn* diaphragm, mind — more at FRENETIC] **1 :** mind ⟨*phreno*logy⟩ **2 a :** diaphragm ⟨*phren*ic⟩ **b :** diaphragmatic and ⟨*phreno*cardiac⟩ **3 :** phrenic nerve ⟨*phreni*clasia⟩

phren·em·phrax·is \,fre,nemˈfraksə̇s\ *n, pl* **phrenemphrax·es** \-k,sēz\ [NL, fr. *phren-* + Gk *emphraxis* stoppage, fr. *emphrassein, emphrattein* to stop up, block, fr. *em-* ²en- + *phrassein, phrattein* to enclose, fence in — more at FARCE] **:** crushing of the phrenic nerve for therapeutic reasons

¹phre·net·ic \frə̇ˈned·ik, -etik\ *also* **phre·net·i·cal** \-ə̇kəl\ *adj* [L *phreneticus* — more at FRENETIC] **:** FRENETIC

²phrenetic \"\ *n* -S *archaic* **:** one who is phrenetic **:** MADMAN

-phrenia \ˈfrēnēə *sometimes* -ren-\ *n comb form* -S [NL, fr. Gk *phren-, phrēn* diaphragm, mind + NL *-ia*] **:** disordered condition of mental functions ⟨hebe*phrenia*⟩

phrenic \ˈfrenik, -rēn-\ *adj* [NL *phrenicus*, fr. *phren-* + L *-icus* -ic] **1 :** of or relating to the diaphragm **:** DIAPHRAGMATIC **2 :** of or relating to the mind **:** MENTAL

phrenic artery *n* **:** any of the arteries supplying the diaphragm and consisting of a superior pair that arise from the thoracic aorta and are distributed over the upper surface of the diaphragm and an inferior pair from the abdominal aorta that pass to the under surface

phren·i·cec·to·my \,frenə̇ˈsektəmē, -mi\ *n* -ES [ISV *phrenic* + *-ectomy*] **:** surgical removal of part of a phrenic nerve to secure collapse of a diseased lung — compare PHRENICOTOMY

phren·i·cla·sia \-ˈklāzh(ē)ə\ *or* **phren·i·cla·sis** \,==ˈklāsə̇s; frə̇ˈnikləsə̇s, freˈ-\ *n, pl* **phreniclasi·as** \-əz\ *or* **phrenicla·ses** \-,sēz\ [NL, fr. *phren-* + *-clasia* or *-clasis*] **:** PHRENEMPHRAXIS

phrenic nerve *n* **:** a nerve of each side of the body arising chiefly from the fourth cervical nerve, passing down through the thorax to the diaphragm, and giving branches to the pericardium and pleura but distributed mostly over the lower surface of the diaphragm

phren·i·cot·o·my \,frenə̇ˈkäd·əmē, -mi\ *n* -ES [ISV *phrenic* + *-o-* + *-tomy*] **:** surgical division of a phrenic nerve to secure collapse of a diseased lung — compare PHRENICECTOMY

phrenic vein *n* **:** any of the veins accompanying the phrenic arteries

phren·o·cardiac \¦frenō+\ *adj* [*phren-* + *cardiac*] **:** of, relating to, or constituting the region between the heart and the diaphragm

phren·o·log·i·cal \¦frenᵊl¦äjəkəl, -jēk-\ *also* **phren·o·log·ic** \-jik, -ēk\ *adj* [*phrenology* + *-ical* or *-ic*] **:** of or relating to phrenology — **phren·o·log·i·cal·ly** \-jək(ə)lē, -jēk-, -li\ *adv*

phre·nol·o·gist \frə̇ˈnäləjəst, freˈ-\ *n* -S [*phrenology* + *-ist*] **:** one versed in phrenology

phre·nol·o·gy \-jē, -ji\ *n* -ES [*phren-* + *-logy*] **:** the study of the conformation of the skull as indicative of mental faculties and traits of character esp. according to the hypothesis of F. J. Gall (1758–1828); *also* **:** the system of faculties and their localization based on this hypothesis

phren·o·sin \ˈfrenəsə̇n\ *n* -S [ISV *phren-* + *-ose* + *-in*] **:** a crystalline cerebroside that yields cerebronic acid on hydrolysis

phren·o·sin·ic acid \¦==¦sinik-\ *n* [*phrenosinic* ISV *phrenosin* + *-ic*] **:** CEREBRONIC ACID

phrensy *var of* FRENZY

phren·zy \ˈfrenzē, -zi\ *archaic var of* FRENZY

phron·i·ma \ˈfränəmə\ *n, cap* [NL, fr. Gk *phronimos* sane, sensible; prob. akin to Gk *phren-, phrēn* diaphragm, mind — more at FRENETIC] **:** a genus (the type of the family Phronimidae) of pelagic amphipod crustaceans having one known member (*P. sedentaria*) that lives in a barrel-shaped case made from the swimming bell of a siphonophore or the test of a tunicate

phron·tis·tery \ˈfräntə,sterē\ *n* -ES [Gk *phrontistērion*, fr. *phrontistēs* philosopher, deep thinker, person with intellectual pretensions, fr. *phrontizein* to reflect, take thought, fr. *phrontid-, phrontis* reflection, thought; akin to Gk *phren-, phrēn* diaphragm, mind] **:** a place for thinking or study

phry·ga·nea \friˈgānēə\ *n, cap* [NL, fr. Gk *phryganon* dry stick; akin to Gk *phrygein* to roast — more at FRY] **:** a genus (the type of the family Phryganeidae) of caddis flies

¹phryg·a·ne·id \¦frigə¦nēə̇d\ *adj* [NL *Phryganeidae*] **:** of or relating to the Phryganeidae

²phryganeid \"\ *n* -S [NL *Phryganeidae*] **:** a caddis fly of the family Phryganeidae

phryg·a·ne·i·dae \,==ˈnēə,dē\ *n pl, cap* [NL, fr. *Phryganea*, type genus + *-idae*] **:** a family of caddis flies containing rather large insects whose larvae live in still water and construct portable cases of very regular form

phry·ga·ne·oid \friˈgānē,ȯid\ *adj* [NL *Phryganea* + E *-oid*] **:** resembling or related to the Phryganeidae

¹phryg·i·an \ˈfrijēən\ *adj, usu cap* [L *phrygianus*, fr. *Phrygia*, ancient country in west central Asia Minor + L *-anus* -an] **1 :** of, relating to, or characteristic of the ancient country of Phrygia **2 :** of, relating to, or characteristic of the Phrygians

²phrygian \"\ *n* -S **1** *cap* **:** a native or inhabitant of ancient Phrygia **2** *cap* **:** the language of the Phrygians that is generally assumed to be Indo-European but of uncertain position within the family **3** *usu cap* **:** MONTANIST

phrygian cap *n, usu cap P* **:** a close-fitting cap represented in Greek art as conical and identified in modern art with the liberty cap — compare BONNET ROUGE

Phrygian cap

phrygian marble *n, usu cap P* **:** a marble from Phrygia noted in antiquity — see PAVONAZZO

phrygian mode *n, usu cap P* **1 :** one of seven diatonic octave species in ancient Greek music consisting of two disjunct tetrachords represented on the white keys of the piano by a descending diatonic scale from D to D — see GREEK MODE illustration **2 :** an authentic ecclesiastical mode consisting of a pentachord and an upper conjunct tetrachord represented on the white keys of the piano by an ascending diatonic scale from E to E — see MODE illustration

phrygian stone *n, usu cap P* **:** a stone used by the ancients in dyeing and believed to have been a sort of pumice

phrygian tetrachord *n, usu cap P* **:** a descending tetrachord in Greek music consisting of a whole step and a half step followed by a whole step

phry·ma \ˈfrīmə\ *n, cap* [NL] **:** a genus of plants constituting the family Phrymaceae and having opposite leaves and small purplish spicate flowers reflexed in fruit — see LOPSEED

phry·ma·ce·ae \frīˈmāsē,ē\ *n pl, cap* [NL, fr. *Phryma*, type genus + *-aceae*] **:** a family of plants (order Polemoniales) coextensive with the genus *Phryma*

phryn·i·dae \ˈfrinə,dē\ [NL, fr. *Phrynus*, genus of whip scorpions (fr. Gk *phrynos, phrynē* toad) + *-idae*] *syn of* TARANTULIDAE

phry·nin \ˈfrīnə̇n\ *n* -S [Gk *phrynos, phrynē* toad + E *-in*] **:** a poisonous substance secreted from the glands of various toads that resembles digitalin in its physiologic action — compare BUFOTOXIN

phry·no·der·ma \,frīnəˈdərmə\ *n* -S [NL, fr. *phryno-* (fr. Gk *phrynos, phrynē* toad) + *-derma*] **:** a rough dry skin eruption marked by keratosis and usu. associated with vitamin A deficiency

phry·no·so·ma \-ˈsōmə\ *n, cap* [NL, fr. *phryno-* (fr. Gk *phrynos, phrynē* toad) + *-soma* — more at BROWN] **:** a genus comprising the horned toads

phthal- *or* **phthalo-** *comb form* [ISV, fr. *phthalic* (in *phthalic acid*)] **:** phthalic acid **:** related to phthalic acid ⟨*phthal*amic acid⟩ ⟨*phthalo*nitrile⟩

phtha·lam·ic acid \thəˈlamik-\ *n* [ISV *phthal-* + *amide* + *-ic*] **:** a crystalline compound $HOOCC_6H_4CONH_2$ formed by reaction of phthalic anhydride and ammonia; the half amide of phthalic acid

phthal·anilic acid \ˈthal+-\ *n* [ISV *phthal-* + *anilic*] **:** a crystalline amido acid $HOOCC_6H_4CONHC_6H_5$ prepared by reaction of phthalic anhydride and aniline

¹phthal·ate \ˈtha,lāt\ *n* -S [ISV *phthal-* + *-ate*, n. suffix] **:** a salt or ester of phthalic acid

²phthalate \"\ *vt* -ED/-ING/-S [*phthal-* + *-ate*, v. suffix] **:** to treat with or combine with phthalic acid or phthalic anhydride

phthal·azine \(ˈ)thal+\ *n* [ISV *phthal-* + *azine*] **:** a crystalline base $C_8H_6N_2$ that is the azine of the dialdehyde related to phthalic acid; 2,3-di-aza-naphthalene — compare HYDRALAZINE, LUMINOL

phthalein \ˈthalēə̇n, -āl-, -,lēn\ *also* **phthalein dye** *n* -S [ISV *phthal-* + *-ein*] **:** any of a group of xanthene dyes (as phenolphthalein, fluorescein, rhodamine) that are intensely colored in alkaline solution and are obtained by condensation of phenols with phthalic anhydride

phthalic acid \ˈthalik-, ˈthālik-\ *n* [*phthalic* ISV, short for *naphthalic* (in *naphthalic acid*)] **:** any of three isomeric dicarboxylic acids $C_6H_4(COOH)_2$ obtained by oxidation of various benzene derivatives: **a :** a crystalline acid made usu. by hydration of phthalic anhydride that regenerates the anhydride on heating and is used chiefly in making esters, benzoic acid, dyes, and intermediates; *ortho*-benzene-dicarboxylic acid **b :** ISOPHTHALIC ACID **c :** TEREPHTHALIC ACID

phthalic anhydride *n* **:** a crystalline cyclic acid anhydride $C_6H_4(CO)_2O$ made usu. by hot vapor-phase oxidation of naphthalene or *ortho*-xylene over a vanadium pentoxide catalyst and used chiefly in making alkyd resins and other polyester resins, phthalate esters for use as plasticizers and solvents, dyes, and intermediates

phthalide \ˈtha,līd, ˈthā-, -lə̇d\ *n* -S [ISV *phthal-* + *-ide*] **:** a crystalline lactone $C_8H_6O_2$ made usu. by reduction of phthalic anhydride

phthal·imide \(ˈ)thal+\ *n* [ISV *phthal-* + *imide*] **:** a crystalline weakly acidic cyclic compound $C_6H_4(CO)_2NH$ made usu. by action of ammonia on phthalic anhydride and used chiefly in the synthesis of amines and amino acids, anthranilic acid, and formerly of indigo

phthal·in \ˈthalə̇n\ *n* -S [ISV *phthal-* + *-in*] **:** any of a group of colorless compounds obtained by reduction of the phthaleins into which they are easily reconverted by oxidation; *esp* **:** the compound $C_{20}H_{16}O_4$ from phenolphthalein

phthal·o·cyanine \¦thalō+\ *n* [ISV *phthal-* + *cyanine*] **1** *or* **phthalocyanine blue G :** a bright greenish blue crystalline compound $C_{32}H_{18}N_8$ related to porphin — called also *metal-free phthalocyanine*; see DYE TABLE I (under *Pigment Blue 16*) **2 :** any of various derivatives of phthalocyanine that in the case of the metal derivatives are brilliant fast blue to green dyes or pigments made usu. by heating phthalonitrile with a metal (as copper powder) or metallic salt

phthalocyanine blue *or* **phthalocyanine blue B** *n* **:** a blue pigment used chiefly in printing ink esp. for outdoor use, in roofing shingles, and in paint for automobiles; the copper derivative of phthalocyanine — see DYE table I (under *Pigment Blue 15*)

phthalocyanine green *or* **phthalocyanine green G** *n* **:** a green pigment that is made by passing chlorine into a melt containing the copper derivative of phthalocyanine and aluminum chloride until it is almost completely chlorinated and that is used similarly to phthalocyanine blue — see DYE table I (under *Pigment Green 7*)

phthal·o·gen brilliant blue IF3G \ˈthaləjən-\ *n, usu cap P & both Bs* [*phthalogen* fr. *phthal-* + *-gen*] **:** an ingrain dye — see DYE table I (under *Ingrain Blue 2*)

phthal·o·nitrile \ˌthalō+\ *n* [ISV *phthal-* + *nitrile*] **:** a crystalline compound $C_6H_4(CN)_2$ made usu. by heating phthalic anhydride and ammonia under dehydrating conditions and used chiefly in making phthalocyanines

phthal·o·yl \ˈthalə,wil\ *n* -s [*phthal-* + *-oyl*] **:** the bivalent radical $C_6H_4(CO—)_2$ of phthalic acid

phthal·yl·sulfathiazole \ˌtha,lil, -ˌlēl+\ *n* [*phthal-* + *-yl* + *sulfathiazole*] **:** a crystalline compound $C_{17}H_{13}N_3O_5S_2$ derived from phthalamic acid and sulfathiazole and used in the treatment of intestinal infections

phthar·tol·a·trae \thärˈtälə,trē\ *n pl, usu cap* [NL, fr. LGk *phthartolatrai*, pl. of *phthartolatrēs* worshiper of the corruptible, fr. Gk *phthartos* destructible + *-latrēs* -later — more at APHTHARTODOCETAE] **:** SEVERIANS — compare APHTHARTODOCETAE

phthi·o·col \ˈthīə,kōl, -kōl\ *n* -s [prob. fr. *phthisis* + connective *-oc-* + *-ol*] **:** a yellow crystalline quinone $C_{11}H_8O_3$ with vitamin K activity that is isolated from the human tubercle bacillus and also made synthetically; 2-hydroxy-3-methyl-1,-4-naphthoquinone

phthi·o·ic acid \thīˈōik-\ *n* [*phthioic* fr. *phthisis* + *-oic*] **:** a branched-chain optically active fatty acid or mixture of such acids isolated from the human tubercle bacillus that causes the formation of tubercular lesions on injection into animals

phthir·a·car·i·dae \ˌthirəˈkarə,dē\ *n pl, cap* [NL, fr. *Phthiracarus*, type genus (fr. Gk *phtheir* louse + NL *Acarus*) + *-idae*] **:** a family of oribatid mites

phthi·ri·a·sis \thīˈrīəsəs\ *n, pl* **phthiria·ses** \-ˌsēz\ [L, pediculosis, fr. Gk *phtheiriasis*, fr. *phtheir* louse + *-iasis*; akin to Gk *phtheirein* to destroy, corrupt, defile, Skt *kṣarati* it flows, perishes] **:** PEDICULOSIS; *esp* **:** infestation with crab lice **:** pubic pediculosis

phthir·i·us \ˈthirēəs\ *n, cap* [NL, fr. Gk *phtheir* louse] **:** a genus (the type of the family Phthiriidae) containing the crab louse

phthi·roph·a·gous \thīˈräfəgəs\ *adj* [prob. fr. (assumed) NL *phthirophagus*, fr. Gk *phtheir* louse + NL *-o-* + *-phagus* -phagous] **:** eating lice

phthi·rus \ˈthīrəs\ *syn of* PHTHIRIUS

¹**phthisic** \ˈtiz|ik, |ēk *also* ˈthīs| *or* ˈtīs|\ *n* -s [alter. (influenced by *phthisis*) of earlier *ptisique*, *ptisicke*, fr. ME *ptisike*, alter. (influenced by L *phthisicus*, adj., phthisic) of *tisike*, fr. MF *tisique*, fr. OF, fr. *tisique*, adj.] **1 a :** pulmonary tuberculosis **b :** a tubercular person **2** *obs* **:** any of various throat or lung conditions (as asthma)

²**phthisic** \ˈ"\ *or* **phthisi·cal** \|əkəl, |ēk-\ *adj* [*phthisic* alter. (influenced by *phthisis*) of earlier *ptisicke*, alter. (influenced by L *phthisicus*) of ME *tisike*, fr. MF *tisique*, fr. OF, fr. L *phthisicus*, fr. Gk *phthisikos*, fr. *phthisis* + *-ikos* -ic; *phthisical* alter. (influenced by *phthisis*) of earlier *ptisicall*, alter. (influenced by L *phthisicus*) of earlier *tizicall*, *tysicall*, fr. (assumed) obs. E *tisike*, adj., phthisic (fr. ME) + E *-al*] **1 :** TUBERCULAR, TUBERCULOUS **2 :** ENFEEBLED, WEAK, DEBILITATED

phthis·icky \ˈtizəkē, -zēk-, -ki\ *adj* [¹*phthisic* + *-y*] **:** PHTHISIC, ASTHMATIC, WHEEZY

phthisio- *comb form* [ISV, fr. *phthisis*] **:** phthisis ⟨*phthisio*therapy⟩

phthis·io·genesis \ˌthizēō, ˌtizēō+\ *n* [NL, fr. *phthisio-* + L *genesis*] **:** the development of pulmonary tuberculosis

phthis·io·genic \¦==+ˈjenik\ *adj* [*phthisio-* + *-genic*] **:** of or relating to phthisiogenesis

phthis·i·ol·o·gist \ˌ==ˈäləjəst\ *n* -s **:** a physician who specializes in phthisiology

phthis·i·ol·o·gy \-jē\ *n* -ES [ISV *phthisio-* + *-logy*] **:** the care, treatment, and study of tuberculosis

phthis·io·therapy \ˌthizēō, ˌtizēō+\ *n* [ISV *phthisio-* + *therapy*] **:** the treatment of pulmonary tuberculosis

phthi·sis \ˈthīsəs, ˈtī-\ *n, pl* **phthi·ses** \-(ˌ)sēz\ [L, fr. Gk; akin to Gk *phthiein*, *phthinein* to decay, wane, Skt *kṣiṇāti*, *kṣiṇoti* he destroys, and prob. to L *sitis* thirst] **:** a progressively wasting or consumptive disease; *usu* **:** pulmonary tuberculosis **:** CONSUMPTION

phthisis bul·bi \-ˈbəl,bī\ *n* [NL] **:** wasting and shrinkage of the eyeball following destructive diseases of the eye (as panophthalmitis)

phthor \ˈthȯ(ə)r, -ō(ə)\ *n* -s [F *phthore*, fr. Gk *phthora*] *archaic* **:** FLUORINE

-phtho·ra \fthərə\ *n comb form* [NL, fr. Gk *phthora* destruction, death, fr. *phtheirein* to destroy — more at PHTHIRIASIS] **:** destroyer — in generic names of fungi ⟨Entomo*phthora*⟩

phu·goid \ˈfyü,gȯid\ *adj* [irreg. fr. Gk *phygē* act of fleeing, avoidance, flight + E *-oid*; akin to Gk *pheugein* to run away, flee — more at FUGITIVE] **:** of, relating to, or representing variations in the longitudinal motion or course of the center of mass of an airplane in flight

phugoid chart *n* **:** a chart showing a complete series of phugoid curves corresponding to different starting conditions

phugoid curve *also* **phugoid** *n* -s **:** a curve showing the motion of the center of mass of an airplane during a phugoid oscillation

phugoid oscillation *n* **:** a long-period oscillation in the longitudinal motion of an airplane

phugoid theory *n* **:** the theory dealing with the longitudinal stability and the form and equations of the flight path of a glider

phul·ka·ri \ˈpül,kärē\ *n* -ES [Hindi *phulkārī*, lit., flowered] **1 :** a flower pattern embroidery made in India **2 :** a cloth embroidered with phulkari; *esp* **:** a Punjabi peasant's chador

phul·wa butter \ˈfülwə-\ *also* **phul·wa·ra butter** \fülˈwärə-\ *n* [Beng *phulwāra* Himalayan butter tree] **:** INDIAN BUTTER

phut \ft, ˈfət\ *n* -s [imit.] **:** a dull sound of impact (as of a bullet or distant shell) **:** a light thud ⟨~ of a tennis ball against a racket —H.V.Morton⟩ — often used interjectionally to express a feeling of hopelessness ⟨otherwise — ~ —S.H.Adams⟩

phu·teng *or* **pu·teng** \ˈpü,teŋ\ *n, pl* **phuteng** *or* **phutengs** *or* **puteng** *or* **putengs** *usu cap* **1 :** a mountain people of Laos occupying the intermediate slopes between the plains and the higher mountain lands of the Miao people **2 :** a member of the Phuteng people

phyc- *or* **phyco-** *comb form* [ISV, fr. Gk *phyk-*, *phyko-* seaweed, fr. *phykos* — more at FUCUS] **:** seaweed **:** algae ⟨*phyc*itol⟩ ⟨*phyco*chrome⟩

-phyce·ae \ˈfīsē,ē, ˈfis-\ *n pl comb form* [NL, fr. Gk *phykos* seaweed] **:** seaweed **:** algae — in names of major groups of algae ⟨Chloro*phyceae*⟩ ⟨Myxo*phyceae*⟩

phy·ci·o·des \fiˈsīə,dēz\ *n, cap* [NL, prob. fr. Gk *phykion* seaweed, rouge (fr. *phykos* seaweed) + NL *-odes*] **:** a large genus of small butterflies (family Nymphalidae) that are usu. fulvous with black markings

¹**phyc·i·tid** \ˈfisəd·əd\ *adj* [NL *Phycitidae*] **:** of or relating to the Phycitidae

²**phycitid** \"\ *n* -s [NL *Phycitidae*] **:** a moth of the family Phycitidae

phy·cit·i·dae \fīˈsid·ə,dē\ *n pl, cap* [NL, fr. *Phycita*, type genus (perh. fr. Gk *phykos* seaweed, rouge) + *-idae*] **:** a family of small moths that are related to and sometimes placed among the Pyralididae, include the Mediterranean flour moth and other pests having larvae which feed in stored cereals, and are usu. mottled gray and brown with long narrow fore wings

phy·co·bilin \ˌfīkōˈbīlən, -bil-\ *n* -s [*phyc-* + *bil-* (fr. L *bilis* bile) + *-in* — more at BILE] **:** any of a class of pigments that occur in the cells of algae, are active in photosynthesis, and are proteins combined with pyrrole derivatives related to the bile pigments — compare PHYCOCYANIN, PHYCOERYTHRIN

phy·co·chro·ma·ce·ae \ˌfīkōkrōˈmāsē,ē\ [NL, fr. ISV *phycochrome* + NL *-aceae*] *syn of* MYXOPHYCEAE

phy·co·chrome *also* **phy·co·chrom** \ˈfīkə,krōm\ *n* -s [ISV *phyc-* + *-chrome*] **1 :** a mixture of chlorophyll and phycocyanin that is the characteristic coloring matter of blue-green algae **2 :** BLUE-GREEN ALGA

phy·co·chro·mo·phyce·ae \ˌfīkō,krōməˈfīsē,ē, -fisē,ē\ [NL, fr. ISV *phycochrome* + NL *-o-* + *-phyceae*] *syn of* MYXOPHYCEAE

phy·co·colloid \¦==+\ *n* [*phyc-* + *colloid*] **:** any of several polysaccharide hydrocolloids from brown or red seaweeds

phy·co·cyanin \¦fīkō+\ *or* **phy·co·cy·an** \ˌ==ˈsī,an, -ən\ *n* -s [*phycocyanin* ISV *phycocyan* + *-in*; *phycocyan* ISV *phyc-* + *-cyan*] **:** any of the bluish green protein pigments in the cells of blue-green algae

phy·co·cyanogen \¦==+\ *n* -s [*phyc-* + *cyan-* + *-gen*] **:** PHYCOCYANIN

phy·co·drom·i·dae \ˌfīkōˈdrämə,dē\ [NL, fr. *Phycodroma*, genus of Diptera (fr. *phyc-* + *-droma*, fr. fem. of *-dromus* -dromous) + *-idae*] *syn of* COELOPIDAE

phy·co·er·y·thrin \ˌ==ˈerəthrən, -ˌəˈrith-\ *n* -s [ISV *phyc-* + *erythr-* + *-in*] **:** any of the red protein pigments in the cells of red algae

phy·co·log·i·cal \ˌfīkəˈläjəkəl\ *adj* **:** ALGOLOGICAL

phy·col·o·gist \fīˈkäləjəst\ *n* -s [ISV *phycology* + *-ist*] **:** ALGOLOGIST

phy·col·o·gy \-jē, -ji\ *n* -ES [ISV *phyc-* + *-logy*] **:** ALGOLOGY

phy·co·my·ces \ˌfīkōˈmī,sēz\ *n, cap* [NL, fr. *phyc-* + *-myces*] **:** a genus of fungi (family Mucoraceae) forming a metallic mycelium with large, simple, stiffly erect, and often very tall sporangiophores

phy·co·my·ce·tae \ˌ==ˌmīˈsēd·ē\ *or* **phycomyce·te·ae** \-ēd·ē,ē\ *syn of* PHYCOMYCETES

phy·co·my·cete \¦==ˈmī,sēt, ¦==ˌ=ˈ=\ *n* -s [NL *Phycomycetes*] **:** a fungus of the class Phycomycetes

phy·co·my·ce·tes \ˌ==ˌmīˈsēd·(ˌ)ēz\ *n pl, cap* [NL, fr. NL *phyc-* + *-mycetes*] **:** a large class of fungi having a plant body that ranges from an undifferentiated mass of protoplasm to a well-developed and much-branched coenocytic mycelium in which septations commonly occur in age or where reproductive structures develop and having reproduction that is mainly asexual by the formation of conidia or sporangia but includes every form of transition from this method through simple conjugation to sexual reproduction by the union of egg and sperm in the higher forms — see OOMYCETES, ZYGOMYCETES — **phy·co·my·ce·tous** \ˌ==ˌ=¦sēd·əs\ *adj*

phy·co·phae·in *or* **phy·co·phe·in** \ˌ==ˈfēən\ *n* -s [ISV *phyc-* + *-phaein*, *-phein* (fr. Gk *phaios* dusky + ISV *-in*)] **:** a brown pigment in the cells of brown algae (as the kelps) now believed to be no more than a postmortem oxidation product of fucosan

phy·co·xanthin \¦==+\ *n* -s [ISV *phyc-* + *xanth-* + *-in*] **:** DIATOMIN

phyl- *or* **phylo-** *comb form* [L *phyl-*, fr. Gk *phyl-*, *phylo-*, fr. *phylē* tribe, clan, phyle & *phylon* tribe, race; both akin to Gk *phyein* to bring forth — more at BE] **1 :** tribe **:** race ⟨*phylo*graphy⟩ **2 :** phylum ⟨*phylo*geny⟩ ⟨*phyl*ar⟩

phy·la *pl of* PHYLUM

phyl·a·co·bi·o·sis \ˌfiləkō,bīˈōsəs\ *n, pl* **phylacobioses** [NL, fr. *phylaco-* (fr. Gk *phylak-*, *phylax* guard) + *-biosis*] **:** a mixobiosis in which ants of a particular species live in a termite nest and appear to replace functionally the nasute or soldier caste of the termite — **phyl·a·co·bi·ot·ic** \ˌ===,bīˈäd·ik -ˌbēˈ-\ *adj*

phy·lac·ter·ied \fəˈlakt(ə)rēd, -rid\ *adj* **:** wearing or furnished with a phylactery

phy·lac·tery \-t(ə)rē, -ri\ *n* -ES [alter. (influenced by LL *phylacterium*) of earlier *philatery*, fr. ME *philaterie*, fr. ML *philaterium*, alter. of LL *phylacterium*, fr. Gk *phylaktērion* phylactery, amulet, safeguard, fr. *phylak-*, *phylax* guard] **1 :** either of two small square leather boxes with leather straps attached that contain parchment slips inscribed in Hebrew with the four scriptural passages Deuteronomy 6: 4–9 and 11: 13–21 and Exodus 13: 1–10 and 11–16 and that are worn fastened in a prescribed manner one on the left arm and one on the forehead by orthodox and conservative Jewish males during morning weekday prayers as reminders of their obligation to keep the Law **2 :** a case or chest enclosing a holy relic **3** [by confusion of the phylacteries (sense 1) mentioned in Mt 23: 5 with the zizith mentioned in Num 15: 38–39] **:** a distinctive fringe or border **4 :** something worn as a charm or preservative against danger or disease **:** AMULET **5 a :** an inscribed scroll that in medieval art is made to appear as if held or coming from the mouth to show what is being said; *broadly* **:** RECORD **b :** an infula of a miter

phy·lac·tic \fəˈlaktik\ *adj* [ISV, fr. Gk *phylaktikos* preservative, fr. *phylassein* to guard, preserve, fr. *phylak-*, *phylax* guard] **:** of or relating to defense **:** COUNTERACTIVE ⟨~ power against infection⟩ — compare PROPHYLACTIC

phy·lac·to·carp \fəˈlaktə,kärp\ *n* -s [Gk *phylaktos* (verbal of *phylassein* to guard, preserve) + E *-carp*] **:** a branch of a plumularian hydroid modified to protect the gonothecae — **phy·lac·to·car·pal** \ˌ=¦==ˈkärpəl\ *adj*

phy·lac·to·lae·ma *or* **phy·lac·to·le·ma** \ˌ=ˌ==ˈlēmə\ *or* **phy·lac·to·lae·ma·ta** \-məd·ə\ *syn of* PHYLACTOLAEMATA

phy·lac·to·lae·ma·ta \-məd·ə\ *n pl, cap* [NL, fr. *phylacto-* (fr. Gk *phylaktos*, verbal of *phylassein* to guard, preserve) + *laem-* (fr. Gk *laimos* throat, gullet) + *-ata* — more at GYMNOLAEMATA] **:** a class or other division of Bryozoa comprising freshwater forms having the tentacles arranged on a horseshoe-shaped lophophore and the mouth covered by an epistome — compare GYMNOLAEMATA — **phy·lac·to·lae·ma·tous** \ˌ=¦==ˌ=ˈmed·əs\ *adj*

phy·lad \ˈfī,lad\ *n* -s [*phyl-* + *-ad*, n. suffix] **:** a small group of closely related species presumably of common origin

phy·lar \ˈfīlə(r)\ *adj* [*phyl-* + *-ar*] **:** of or relating to a phylum

phy·larch \ˈfī,lärk\ *n* -s [L *phylarchus*, fr. Gk *phylarchos*, fr. *phylē* + *archos* ruler — more at ARCHI-] **1 a :** the chief ruler of an ancient Grecian phyle **b :** the commander of the cavalry furnished by each ancient Athenian tribe **2 :** the magistrate or head of a recognized tribal division of any of the Asiatic provinces of the Roman empire — **phy·lar·chic** \(ˈ)fīˈlärkik\ *or* **phy·lar·chi·cal** \-kəkəl\ *adj*

phy·le \ˈfīlē\ *n, pl* **phy·lae** \-ˌlē\ [Gk *phylē* — more at PHYL-] **1 :** the largest political subdivision among the ancient Athenians and a principal division of the army — see DEME 1, PHRATRY 1 **2 :** any of the four orders into which the population of Egypt was divided during the Old and Middle Kingdoms

phyl·ephe·bic \¦fil+\ *adj* [*phyl-* + *ephebic*] **:** being or relating to the phase of maximum vigor of a race

phy·le·sis \fīˈlēsəs\ *n, pl* **phyle·ses** \-ˌsēz\ *also* **phylesises** [NL, fr. *phyl-* + *-esis*] **:** the course of evolutionary or phylogenetic development (as of a natural group of organisms)

phy·let·ic \fīˈled·ik\ *adj* [ISV, fr. NL *phylesis*, after such pairs as LL *antithesis: antitheticus* antithetical] **:** of or relating to a line of descent or to phylesis **:** PHYLOGENETIC, RACIAL — **phy·let·i·cal·ly** \-ək(ə)lē\ *adv*

phy·le·tism \ˈfīləd·ˌizəm\ *n* -s [NGk *phyletismos*, fr. Gk *phyletēs* fellow tribesman (fr. *phylē* tribe, clan, phyle) + *-ismos* -ism] **:** nationalism applied to ecclesiastical affairs; *specif* **:** a doctrine that a nationality should be served by its own independent ecclesiastical administration even on the territory of another church

phy·lic \ˈfilik\ *adj* [*phyl-* + *-ic*] **1 :** of or relating to a Grecian phyle **2 :** being or viewed as a member of a group ⟨man as a ~ organism⟩

phyll- *or* **phyllo-** *comb form* [NL *phyllo-*, fr. Gk *phyll-*, *phyllo-*, fr. *phyllon* — more at BLOW] **1 :** leaf ⟨*phyllo*morphous⟩ **2 :** part or thing resembling a leaf ⟨*phyll*idium⟩ **3 :** chlorophyll ⟨*phyll*in⟩

-phyll \ˌfil\ *n comb form* -s [F *-phylle*, fr. Gk *phyllon* leaf] **1 :** coloring matter occurring in plants ⟨chryso*phyll*⟩ **2** [NL *-phyllum*, fr. Gk *phyllon* leaf] **:** leaf ⟨sporo*phyll*⟩

-phylla *pl of* -PHYLLUM

phyl·lac·o·ra \fəˈlakərə\ *n, cap* [NL, fr. *phyll-* + *-acora* (fr. Gk *achōr* dandruff, scurf)] **:** a genus of fungi (order Dothideales) that have the perithecia embedded in flattened black stromata and that include economically important parasites of grasses — see TAR SPOT 2

phyl·lac·tin·ia \ˌfi,lakˈtinēə\ *n, cap* [NL, fr. *phyll-* + *actin-* ray + *-ia* — more at ACTIN-] **:** a genus of powdery mildews having perithecia with several asci and rigid pointed appendages swollen at the base and occurring on the leaves of various trees and shrubs

phyl·lade \ˈfi,lād\ *n* -s [irreg. fr. *phyll-*] **:** CATAPHYLL; *specif* **:** one of the reduced leaves in a quillwort

phyl·lan·thus \fəˈlan(t)thəs\ *n, cap* [NL, fr. *phyll-* + *-anthus*] **:** a very large genus of tropical plants (family Euphorbiaceae) with alternate leaves and small monoecious flowers succeeded by polycarpellary capsules

phyl·la·ry \ˈfilərē, -ri\ *n* -ES [NL *phyllarium*, fr. Gk *phyllarion* small leaf, dim. of *phyllon* leaf] **:** one of the involucral bracts subtending the flower head of a composite plant

phyl·li·dae \ˈfilə,dē\ *n pl, cap* [NL, fr. *Phyllium*, type genus + *-idae*] **:** a family of insects (order Orthoptera) that includes the leaf insects

phyl·lid·i·um \fəˈlidēəm\ *n, pl* **phyllid·ia** \-ēə\ [NL, fr. *phyll-* + *-idium*] **:** any of two or four complex muscular usu. leaf-shaped or cuplike outgrowths from the lateral wall of the scolex of some tapeworms

phyl·li·form \ˈfilə,fȯrm\ *adj* [*phyll-* + *-iform*] **:** having the shape of a leaf

phyl·lin \ˈfilən\ *n* -s [*phyll-* + *-in*] **:** a complex magnesium derivative of a porphyrin or a phorbin ⟨the ~ formed from etioporphyrin⟩

phyl·line \ˈfi,lēn, -ˌlən\ *adj* [*phyll-* + *-ine*] **:** LEAFLIKE

phyl·lite \ˈfi,līt\ *n* -s [*phyll-* + *-ite*] **:** a foliated rock that is intermediate in composition and fabric between slate and schist — **phyl·lit·ic** \fəˈlid·ik\ *adj*

phyl·li·tis \fəˈlīd·əs\ *n, cap* [NL, fr. Gk *phyllitis* hart's-tongue, fr. *phyllon* leaf] **:** a small genus of ferns (family Polypodiaceae) with large oblong or strap-shaped fronds and linear elongated sori contiguous in pairs that give the appearance of a double indusium — see HART'S-TONGUE 1

phyl·li·um \ˈfilēəm\ *n, cap* [NL, fr. *phyll-* + *-ium*] **:** a genus of Asiatic leaf insects

phyl·lo·both·ri·oi·dea \ˌfilō,bäthrēˈȯidēə\ [NL, fr. *phyll-* + *bothri-* + *-oidea*] *syn of* TETRAPHYLLIDEA

phyl·lo·bran·chia \ˌ==ˈbraŋkēə\ *n* [NL, fr. *phyll-* + *-branchia*] **:** a crustacean gill composed of lamellae — **phyl·lo·bran·chi·al** \¦==ˈbraŋkēəl\ *or* **phyl·lo·bran·chi·ate** \-ēət, -ē,āt\ *adj*

phyl·lo·caline \¦filō+\ *n* [*phyll-* + *caline*] **:** a hormone or hormonoid substance distinct from auxin that is held to play a role in the development of mesophyll parts of a leaf

¹**phyl·lo·car·id** \¦filō¦karəd\ *adj* [NL *Phyllocarida*] **:** of or relating to the Phyllocarida

²**phyllocarid** \"\ *n* -s [NL *Phyllocarida*] **:** a crustacean of the group Phyllocarida

phyl·lo·car·i·da \ˌ==ˈkarədə\ *n pl, cap* [NL, fr. *phyll-* + *-carida* (fr. Gk *karid-*, *karis* shrimp, prawn); perh. akin to Gk *kara* head — more at CEREBRAL] **:** a group of Malacostraca comprising forms with the head and thorax enclosed in a chitinous or calcareous bivalve carapace and including Nebaliidae and related extinct families — **phyl·lo·car·i·dan** \-ədən\ *adj or n*

phyl·loc·er·as \fəˈläsərəs\ *n, cap* [NL *Phyllocerat-*, *Phylloceras*, fr. *phyll-* + *-cerat-*, *-ceras* -ceras] **:** a genus (the type of the family Phylloceratidae) comprising smooth involute compressed ammonites with complex sutures that occur first in the Triassic and are believed to have been ancestral to most Jurassic and Cretaceous ammonites

phyl·lo·cer·a·tid \ˌfilōˈserəd·əd, -ətəd\ *n* -s [NL *Phylloceratidae*, family of ammonites, fr. *Phyllocerat-*, *Phylloceras*, type genus + *-idae*] **:** an ammonite of the genus *Phylloceras* or family Phylloceratidae

phyl·lo·clade \ˈfilə,klād\ *also* **phyl·lo·clad** \-,klad\ *n* -s [NL *phyllocladium*] **:** a flattened stem or branch (as a joint of a cactus or a cladophyll) that functions as a leaf — compare PHYLLODE

phyl·lo·cla·di·oid \¦==ˈklādē,ȯid\ *adj* [NL *phyllocladium* + E *-oid*] **:** being or resembling a phylloclade ⟨a ~ stem⟩

phyl·lo·cla·di·um \¦==ˈdēəm\ *n, pl* **phyllocla·dia** \-dēə\ [NL, fr. *phyll-* + *clad-* + *-ium*] **:** PHYLLOCLADE

phyl·loc·la·dous \fəˈläklədəs\ *adj* [*phylloclade* + *-ous*] **:** having phylloclades

phyl·lo·cop·tes \ˌfiləˈkäp,tēz\ *n, cap* [NL, fr. *phyll-* + *-coptes* (fr. Gk *koptein* to cut off) — more at CAPON] **:** a genus of eriophyid mites containing several that attack various economically important plants

phyl·lo·cop·tru·ta \ˌ==ˌkäpˈtrüd·ə\ *n, cap* [NL, fr. *phyll-* + *-coptruta* (prob. fr. Gk *koptein* to cut off)] **:** a genus of eriophyid mites that includes the citrus rust mite

phyl·lo·cyst \ˈfilə,sist\ *n* -s [*phyll-* + *-cyst*] **:** the cavity of a hydrophyllium — **phyl·lo·cys·tic** \¦==ˈsistik\ *adj*

phyl·lode \ˈfi,lōd\ *n* -s [NL *phyllodium*, fr. Gk *phyllōdēs* like leaves (fr. *phyllon* leaf) + NL *-ium*] **1 :** a flat expanded petiole that replaces the blade of a foliage leaf, fulfills the same functions, and is analogous to but not homologous with a cladophyll — compare PHYLLOCLADE **2 :** the expanded and more or less depressed oral end of an ambulacrum in some sea urchins — **phyl·lo·di·al** \fəˈlōdēəl\ *adj*

phyl·lo·din·e·ous \ˌ==ˈdinēəs\ *or* **phyl·lod·i·nous** \fəˈläd°nəs\ *adj* [*phyllodineous* prob. fr. (assumed) NL *phyllodineus*, irreg. fr. NL *phyllodium* phyllode + L *-eus* -eous; *phyllodinous* alter. of *phyllodineous*] **:** relating to or having phyllodes

phyl·lo·di·um \fəˈlōdēəm\ *n, pl* **phyllo·dia** \-dēə\ [NL] **:** PHYLLODE 1

phyl·lod·o·ce \fəˈlädə,sē\ *n, cap* [NL, fr. L *Phyllodoce*, one of the Nereids] **1 :** a small genus of arctic and alpine shrubs (family Ericaceae) with linear evergreen leaves and nodding umbellate flowers having an ovoid pink, blue, or purple corolla — see MOUNTAIN HEATH **2 :** a genus of polychaete worms that is the type of the family Phyllodocidae

phyl·lo·doc·i·dae \ˌfiləˈdäsə,dē\ *n pl, cap* [NL, fr. *Phyllodoce*, type genus + *-idae*] **:** a cosmopolitan family of elongated active polychaete worms with broad leaflike cirri, several prostomial tentacles, and one or two pairs of eyes

phyl·lo·dro·mi·idae \ˌfilōdrəˈmīə,dē\ *n, pl, cap* [NL, fr. *Phyllodromia*, type genus (fr. *phyll-* + *drom-* + *-ia*) + *-idae*] **:** a family of cockroaches that includes the croton bug

phyl·lo·dy \ˈfilədē, -di\ *n* -ES [ISV *phyll-* + *-ody*] **:** metamorphosis of a specialized plant organ (as a flower petal) into a foliage leaf (as by the action of a virus)

phyl·lo·er·y·thrin \ˌfilōˈerəthrən, -ˌəˈrith-\ *n* -s [ISV *phyll-* + *erythr-* + *-in*] **:** a rose-red photosensitizing porphyrin pigment formed as a degradation product of chlorophyll in the digestive tract of herbivorous animals and normally excreted esp. in the bile but absorbed by the blood in pathological conditions (as geeldikkop)

phyl·lo·genetic \¦filō+\ *adj* [*phyll-* + *-genetic*] **:** relating to or concerned with the development of leaves

¹**phyl·loid** \ˈfi,lȯid\ *also* **phyl·loi·dal** \fəˈlȯid°l\ *adj* [*phylloid* fr. NL *phylloides*, fr. *phyll-* + L *-oides* -oid; *phylloidal* fr. *phylloid* + *-al*] **:** resembling a leaf **:** FOLIACEOUS

²**phylloid** \"\ *n* -s **:** a plant part functioning as or of similar origin to a leaf; *esp* **:** a leaf or leaflike structure organogenetically derived by fusion of a system of orig. dichotomizing telomes — used in connection with the telome theory

phyl·lo·man·cy \ˈfilə,man(t)sē, -si\ *n* -ES [MGk *phyllomanteia*, fr. Gk *phyll-* + *manteia* divination — more at -MANCY] **:** divination by means of leaves

phyl·lo·mania \¦==+\ *n* [NL, fr. *phyll-* + LL *mania*] **:** an abnormal or excessive production of leaves — **phyl·lo·ma·ni·ac** \¦==+\ *adj*

phyl·lome \ˈfi,lōm\ *n* -s [ISV *phyll-* + *-ome*] **:** a plant part that is a leaf or is phylogenetically derived from a leaf **:** a foliar organ (as a leaf, petal, or phylloid) — **phyl·lo·mic** \fəˈlämik, -lōm-\ *adj*

phyl·lo·morph \ˈfilə,mȯrf\ *n* [*phyll-* + *-morph*] **:** a detail in art resembling a leaf — **phyl·lo·mor·phic** \¦==ˈmȯrfik\ *adj*

phyl·lo·mor·pho·sis \ˌ==ˈmȯrfəsəs *sometimes* -ˌmȯrˈfōs-\ *n* [NL, fr. *phyll-* + *-morphosis*] **1 :** succession and variation of leaves during different seasons **2 :** PHYLLODY

phyl·lo·mor·phous \¦==ˈmȯrfəs\ *adj* [*phyll-* + *-morphous*] **:** resembling a leaf in appearance ⟨a ~ insect⟩

phyl·lo·mor·phy \ˈ==ˌmȯrfē\ *n* -ES [ISV *phyll-* + *-morphy*] **:** PHYLLODY

phyl·lo·nite \ˈfilə,nīt\ *n* -s [*phyll*ite + *mylo*nite] **:** a phyllite of cataclastic origin

phyl·loph·a·ga \fə'läfəgə\ *n, cap* [NL, fr. *phyll-* + *-phaga*] **:** a large genus of beetles (family Scarabaeidae) including the common june beetles of the northern U. S. — **phyl·loph·a·gan** \-gən\ *adj*

phyl·lo·phag·ic \¦filə¦fājik\ *adj* [*phyll-* + *phag-* + *-ic*] *of a green plant* **:** deriving nutritive material from foliar activities

phyl·loph·a·gous \fə'läfəgəs\ *adj* [prob. fr. (assumed) NL *phyllophagus*, fr. NL *phyll-* + *-phagus* -phagous] **:** feeding on leaves

phyl·lo·phore \'filə,fō(ə)r\ *n* -s [*phyll-* + *-phore*] **:** a leaf-bearing axis; *specif* **:** the apex of a palm stem

phyl·loph·o·rous \fə'läf(ə)rəs\ *adj* [Gk *phyllophoros*, fr. *phyll-* + *-phoros* -phorous] **:** producing leaves **:** leaf-bearing ⟨~ plants⟩

phyl·lo·pod \'filə,päd\ *also* **phyl·lop·o·dan** \fə'läpədən\ *n* -s [*phyllopod* fr. NL *Phyllopoda; phyllopodan* fr. NL *Phyllopoda* + E *-an*, n. suffix] **:** a phyllopodous crustacean

phyl·lop·o·da \fə'läpədə\ *n pl, cap* [NL, fr. *phyll-* + *-poda*] *in some esp former classifications* **:** a group comprising entomostracan crustaceans with leaflike swimming appendages that serve as gills, mandibles without palpi, and reduced maxillae: as **a :** BRANCHIOPODA 1 **b :** an order or suborder coextensive with the combined orders Anostraca, Notostraca, and Conchostraca

phyl·lo·pod·ic \¦filə¦pädik\ *adj* [*phyll-* + *pod-* + *-ic*] **:** having a leafy base ⟨a ~ culm⟩

phyl·lo·po·di·um \,==='pōdēəm\ *n, pl* **phyllopo·dia** \-dēə\ [NL, fr. *phyll-* + *-podium*] **1 :** a primordial leaf or leaf axis **:** a leaf in the undifferentiated state — compare EPIPODIUM **2 a** *chiefly Brit* **:** the basal portion of a mature leaf which is sometimes inconspicuous or absent or modified into a sheath (as in grasses) **b :** a stem or axis made up of the expanded and fused bases of leaves

phyl·lop·o·dous \fə'läpədəs\ *or* **phyl·lo·pod** \'filə,päd\ *also* **phyl·lop·o·dan** \fə'läpədən\ *adj* [*phyllopodous* fr. NL *Phyllopoda* + E *-ous; phyllopod* fr. NL *Phyllopoda; phyllopodan* fr. NL *Phyllopoda* + E *-an*, adj. suffix] **:** of or relating to the Phyllopoda

phyl·lo·porphyrin \¦filō+\ *n* [ISV *phyll-* + *porphyrin;* prob. orig. formed in G] **:** a dark red crystalline porphyrin $C_{20}H_6N_4$-$(CH_3)_5(C_2H_5)_2CH_2CH_2COOH$ with a violet luster obtained by degradation of chlorophyll or pheophytin

phyl·lop·ter·yx \fə'läptə(,)riks\ *n, cap* [NL, fr. *phyll-* + *-pteryx*] **:** a genus of syngnathid fishes comprising several Australian sea dragons

phyl·lo·pyrrole \¦filō+\ *n* [ISV *phyll-* + *pyrrole*] **:** a crystalline homologue $C_9H_{15}N$ of pyrrole formed during reduction of hemin, chlorophyll, or phylloporphyrin with hydriodic acid; 2,3,5-trimethyl-4-ethyl-pyrrole

phyl·lo·quinone \¦==+\ *n* [ISV *phyll-* + *quinone*] **:** VITAMIN K 1a

phyl·lo·rhine \'filə,rīn, -,rən\ *adj* [NL *Phyllorhina* (syn. of *Hipposideros*), fr. *phyll-* + *-rhina*] **1 :** LEAF-NOSED **2 :** of or relating to leaf-nosed bats or to the genera they belong to

phyl·los·co·pus \fə'läskəpəs\ *n, cap* [NL, fr. *phyll-* + *-scopus*] **:** a genus of Old World warblers including the chiffchaff and the willow warbler

phyl·lo·silicate \¦filō+\ *n* [*phyll-* + *silicate*] **:** a mineral of a class of polymeric silicates in which the silicon-oxygen tetrahedral groups are linked by sharing three of every four oxygen atoms so as to form sheets of indefinite extent, in which the ratio of silicon to oxygen is 2:5, and in which some silicon atoms may be replaced by aluminum (as in mica, chlorite, kaolinite) — called also *sheet-silicate;* compare CYCLOSILICATE, INOSILICATE, NESOSILICATE, SOROSILICATE, TECTOSILICATE

phyl·lo·siphon \"+\ *n, cap* [NL, fr. *phyll-* + Gk *siphōn* siphon, tube] **:** a genus (the type of the family Phyllosiphonaceae of the order Siphonales) of filamentous green algae that live as intracellular parasites of plants of the family Araceae (as the jack-in-the-pulpit) and cause yellowing and discoloration of the leaves and stems

phyl·lo·siphonic \"+\ *adj* [*phyll-* + *siphonic*] *of a pteropsid plant* **:** possessing leaf gaps ⟨ferns, gymnosperms, and angiosperms are ~⟩

phyl·lo·so·ma \,filə'sōmə\ *n* [NL, fr. *phyll-* + *-soma*] **:** a flat transparent long-legged larva that is typical of various spiny lobsters and was formerly supposed to constitute a distinct genus

phyl·lo·spon·dy·li \,filō'spändə,lī\ *n pl, cap* [NL, fr. *phyll-* + *-spondyli*] *in some esp former classifications* **:** an order of extinct amphibians with phyllospondylous vertebrae that are now usu. regarded as larval labyrinthodonts — compare BRANCHIOSAURUS

phyl·lo·spon·dy·lous \¦==¦==,ləs\ *adj* [NL *Phyllospondyli* + E *-ous*] **:** being or having vertebrae with a hypocentrum but no pleurocentra, the neural arch extending down to enclose the notochord and form transverse processes to support the ribs — used esp. of a larval labyrinthodont amphibian

phyl·los·ta·chys \fə'lästəkəs\ *n, cap* [NL, fr. *phyll-* + Gk *stachys* spike of grain — more at STING] **:** a genus of Chinese and Japanese bamboo grasses having slender cylindrical culms used esp. for walking sticks and bamboo furniture

phyl·lo·stic·ta \,filə'stiktə\ *n, cap* [NL, fr. *phyll-* + *-sticta* (fr. Gk *stiktos* tattooed, spotted, fr. *stizein* to tattoo) — more at STICK] **:** a very large form genus of imperfect fungi (family Sphaeropsidaceae) that are characterized by hyaline ovate to elongate nonseptate pycniospores produced typically in leaf spots within dark globose leathery or carbonaceous pycnidia and that include forms causing leaf blights of economically important plants — see BLOTCH 2a

phyl·lo·stic·ta·ce·ae \,==(,)='tāsē,ē\ [NL, fr. *Phyllosticta* + *-aceae*] *syn of* SPHAEROPSIDACEAE

phyl·lo·stic·ta·les \,==,='tā(,)lēz\ [NL, fr. *Phyllosticta* + *-ales*] *syn of* SPHAEROPSIDALES

phyl·los·to·ma \fə'lästəmə\ [NL *Phyllostomat-, Phyllostoma*, fr. *phyll-* + *-stomat-, -stoma* -stoma] *syn of* PHYLLOSTOMUS

phyl·lo·stom·a·tid \,filə'stämәd-әd\ *adj* [NL *Phyllostomatidae*] **:** of or relating to the Phyllostomatidae

phyl·lo·sto·mat·i·dae \,filəstō'mad·ə,dē\ *n pl, cap* [NL, irreg. fr. *Phyllostomus*, type genus + *-idae*] **:** a large family of leaf-nosed bats that range from the southern U. S. to Paraguay and are distinguished from the Old World horseshoe bats by the well-developed tragus — see SPEARNOSE BAT

phyl·lo·stoma·tous \¦==¦stämәd·әs, -stōm-\ *adj* [NL *Phyllostomat-, Phyllostoma* + E *-ous*] **1 :** LEAF-NOSED **2 :** belonging to the Phyllostomatidae

phyl·lo·stome \'filə,stōm\ *n* -s [NL *Phyllostomus*] **:** a bat of the family Phyllostomatidae; *broadly* **:** LEAF-NOSED BAT

phyl·los·to·mid \fə'lästəməd, -,mid\ *n* -s [NL *Phyllostomidae*] **:** a bat of the family Phyllostomatidae

phyl·lo·stom·i·dae \,filə'stämə,dē\ [NL, fr. *Phyllostomus* + *-idae*] *syn of* PHYLLOSTOMATIDAE

phyl·los·to·mine \fə'lästə,mīn, -,mən\ *adj* [NL *Phyllostomus* + E *-ine*] **:** LEAF-NOSED

phyl·los·to·mous \-,məs\ *adj* [NL *Phyllostomus* + E *-ous*] **:** PHYLLOSTOMATOUS

phyl·los·to·mus \-məs\ *n, cap* [NL, fr. *phyll-* + *-stomus*] **:** the type genus of Phyllostomatidae — see JAVELIN BAT

phyl·lo·tac·tic \¦filō¦taktik\ *or* **phyl·lo·tac·ti·cal** \-təkəl\ *adj* [*phyllotactic* fr. *phyll-* + *-tactic; phyllotactical* fr. *phyllotactic* + *-al*] **:** of or relating to phyllotaxy

phyl·lo·tax·ic \-¦taksik\ *adj* [*phyllotaxy* + *-ic*] **:** PHYLLOTACTIC

phyl·lo·taxy \¦filə¦taksē, -si\ *or* **phyl·lo·tax·is** \-ksəs\ *n, pl* **phyllotax·ies** \-sēz, -siz\ *or* **phyllotax·es** \-,sēz\ [NL *phyllotaxis*, fr. *phyll-* + *-taxis*] **1 :** the arrangement of leaves on a stem and in relation to one another ⟨decussate ~⟩ ⟨alternate ~⟩ — compare GENETIC SPIRAL, ORTHOSTICHY, PARASTICHY **2 :** the study of phyllotaxy and of the laws that govern it

phyl·lo·tre·ta \,filə'trēd·ə\ *n, cap* [NL, fr. *phyll-* + *-treta* (fr. Gk *trētos* perforated, fr. *tetrainein* to perforate, pierce) — more at THROW] **:** a genus of chrysomelid beetles that includes flea beetles which are serious pests on garden plants and which transmit a mosaic disease to cabbage and other plants of the genus *Brassica*

-phyl·lous \¦filəs\ *adj comb form* [NL *-phyllus*, fr. Gk *-phyllos*, fr. *phyllon* leaf — more at BLOW] **1 :** having (such or so many) leaves, leaflets, or leaflike parts ⟨iso*phyllous*⟩ ⟨oligo*phyllous*⟩ ⟨macro*phyllous*⟩ **2 :** being in (such) a position in relation to a leaf ⟨epi*phyllous*⟩

phyl·lox·era \,fi,läk'sirə, -,lək-; fə'läksərə\ *n* [NL, fr. *phyll-* + *-xera* (fr. Gk *xēros* dry) — more at SERENE] **1** *cap* **:** the type genus of Phylloxeridae comprising plant lice that differ from the aphids in wing structure, in being continuously oviparous, in lacking honey tubes, and in their extreme polymorphism and that are very destructive to many plants (as grapes) **2** -s **:** any plant louse of the genus *Phylloxera* or family Phylloxeridae — **phyl·lox·er·an** \fə'läksərən\ *adj or n* — **phyl·lox·er·ic** \¦fi,läk¦serik\ *adj*

phyl·lox·er·i·dae \,fi,läk'serə,dē\ *n pl, cap* [NL, fr. *Phylloxera*, type genus + *-idae*] **:** a small family of destructive plant lice in which the wings when present are laid flat upon the abdomen when at rest — see PHYLLOXERA

phyl·lo·zooid \¦filō+\ *n* [*phyll-* + *zooid*] **:** HYDROPHYLLIUM

-phylls *pl of* -PHYLL

-phyl·lum \'filəm\ *n comb form* [NL, fr. Gk *phyllon* leaf] **1 :** one having (such) leaves or leaflike parts — in generic names of animals ⟨Cyatho*phyllum*⟩ and esp. plants ⟨Brachy*phyllum*⟩ ⟨Podo*phyllum*⟩ **2** *pl* **-phyl·la** \-lə\ **:** leaf ⟨meso*phyllum*⟩ **3 :** fossil resembling a plant of a (specified) group — in generic names ⟨Sapindo*phyllum*⟩

phylo- — see PHYL-

phy·lo·genesis \¦filō+\ *n* [NL, fr. *phyl-* + L *genesis*] **:** PHYLOGENY 2

phy·lo·ge·net·ic \¦fīlōjə¦ned·ik\ *adj* [ISV, fr. NL *phylogenesis*, after such pairs as LL *antithesis: antitheticus* antithetical] **1 :** of or relating to phylogeny ⟨~ studies⟩ **2 :** based on natural evolutionary relationships ⟨a ~ system of classification⟩ **3 :** acquired in the course of phylogenetic development **:** RACIAL ⟨a ~ trait⟩ ⟨the hypothetical ~ drive and the actual social behavior —I.Atkin⟩ — **phy·lo·ge·net·i·cal·ly** \-ək(ə)lē\ *adv*

phy·lo·genetics \¦filō+\ *n pl but sing or pl in constr* **:** a branch of science that deals with phylogeny

phy·lo·gen·ic \¦filə¦jenik\ *adj* [ISV *phylogeny* + *-ic*] **:** PHYLOGENETIC

phy·log·e·nist \fī'läjənəst\ *n* -s **:** a specialist in phylogeny

phy·log·e·ny \-nē, -ni\ *n* -ES [ISV *phyl-* + *-geny*] **1 :** the racial history of a specified kind of organism **2 :** the evolution of a race or genetically related group of organisms (as a species, family, or order) as distinguished from the development of the individual organism — compare ONTOGENY **3 :** the history or course of the development of an immaterial thing (as a word or custom) ⟨we cannot hope ~ will explain the morphology of philosophies —W.P.Kent⟩

phy·lon \'fī,län\ *n, pl* **phy·la** \-lə\ [NL, fr. Gk, tribe, race] **:** a genetically related group **:** TRIBE, RACE

phy·lum \'fīləm\ *n, pl* **phy·la** \-lə\ [NL, fr. Gk *phylon* tribe, race — more at PHYL-] **1 a :** a direct line of descent within a group presumably from a single point of origin ⟨the various evolutionary *phyla* of plants⟩ **b :** a group that constitutes or has the unity of such a phylum ⟨whole *phyla* of resentments —W.H.Auden⟩ ⟨a family of birds containing three *phyla* of subfamilial rank⟩ **2 :** a major taxonomic unit comprising organisms sharing a fundamental pattern of organization and presumably a common descent: **a :** one of the usu. primary divisions of the animal kingdom ⟨the ~ Arthropoda⟩ ⟨the ~ Chordata⟩ — called also *branch* **b** (1) **:** DIVISION (2) **:** any of several major categories of plants; *esp* **:** CLASS **3 :** a group of languages related more remotely than those of a family or stock

phy·ma \'fīmə\ *n, pl* **phymas** \-məz\ *or* **phyma·ta** \-məd·ə, -mətə\ [L *phymat-, phyma*, fr. Gk, swelling, tumor, fr. *phyein* to bring forth, grow — more at BE] **:** an external nodule or swelling **:** a skin tumor — **phy·matic** \(')fī¦mad·ik, -atik, -ēk\ *adj*

phy·ma·ta \'fīməd·ə, -mətə\ *n, cap* [NL, fr. L *phymat-, phyma*] **:** the type genus of the family Phymatidae

¹phy·mat·id \fī'mad·əd\ *adj* [NL *Phymatidae*] **:** of or relating to the Phymatidae

²phymatid \"\ *n* -s [NL *Phymatidae*] **:** a bug of the family Phymatidae **:** AMBUSH BUG

Phy·mat·i·dae \fī'mad·ə,dē\ *n pl, cap* [NL, fr. *Phymata*, type genus + *-idae*] **:** a family of short stocky carnivorous bugs that have strong thick forelegs, live chiefly in or about flowers, and feed on other insects — see AMBUSH BUG

phy·ma·to·des \,fīmə'tō(,)dēz\ *n, cap* [NL, fr. L *phymat-, phyma* + NL *-odes*] **:** a genus of tropical ferns (family Polypodiaceae) in general resembling members of *Polypodium* but having fronds with many areolae, irregularly anastomosing veins, and free veinlets

phy·ma·to·rhy·sin \,fīmə'tōrəsən\ *n* -s [*phymato-* (fr. L *phymat-, phyma*) + *-rhysin* (fr. Gk *rhysis* flow — fr. *rhein* to flow — + E *-in*) — more at STREAM] **:** a melanin pigment found in certain melanotic tumors in man and in the urine of persons affected with them

phy·ma·to·sis \,fīmə'tōsəs\ *n, pl* **phymato·ses** \-ō,sēz\ [NL, fr. L *phymat-, phyma* + NL *-osis*] **:** skin disease marked by phymas

phy·ma·tot·ri·chum \,fīmə'tä·trəkəm\ *n* [NL, fr. *phymato-* (fr. L *phymat-, phyma*) + *-trichum* (fr. Gk *trich-, thrix* hair) — more at TRICHINA] **1** *cap* **:** a genus of imperfect fungi (order Moniliales) including a species (*P. omnivorum*) that causes cotton root rot and similar rots of various other plants **2** -s **:** any fungus of the genus *Phymatotrichum*

phy·mo·sis \fī'mōsəs, fə'-\ *n, pl* **phymo·ses** \-ō,sēz\ [NL, modif. of Gk *phimōsis* stopping up of an orifice — more at PHIMOSIS] **:** PHIMOSIS

-phyre \,fī(ə)r, ,fīə\ *n comb form* -s [F *-phyre*, fr. *porphyre* porphyry, fr. ML *porphyrium* — more at PORPHYRY] **:** porphyritic rock ⟨aphano*phyre*⟩

-phyric \¦firik, -īrik, -rēk\ *adj comb form* [ISV *-phyre* + *-ic*] **:** porphyritic ⟨a*phyric*⟩

phys *abbr* **1** physical **2** physician **3** physicist; physics **4** physiological

phys- *or* **physo-** *comb form* [NL, fr. Gk *physa* bellows] **1 a :** marked by the presence of gas ⟨*physo*cele⟩ **b :** swollen **:** bladdery ⟨*Physo*cephalus⟩ ⟨*Phys*opsis⟩ **2 :** air bladder ⟨*Physo*stomi⟩

phy·sa \'fīsə\ *n* [NL, fr. Gk *physa* bellows — more at PUSTULE] **1 a** *cap* **:** a widely distributed genus (the type of the family Physidae) of freshwater air-breathing snails, having a sinistral, ovate, usu. rather short-spired shell and slender nonretractile tentacles with the eyes at their bases **b** -s **:** any snail of the genus *Physa* **2** *pl* **phy·sae** \-,sē, -,sī\ *also* **physas :** the lower often retractile part of the body of some anthozoans

phy·sa·lia \fī'sālēə, -lyə\ *n* [NL, modif. of Gk *physallis* bladder, bubble; akin to Gk *physa* bellows] **1** *cap* **:** a genus (the type of the family Physaliidae) of large oceanic siphonophores including the Portuguese man-of-war **2** -s **:** any member of the genus *Physalia* — **phy·sa·lian** \-ən\ *adj or n*

phy·sa·lis \'fīsələs, 'fis-; fī'saləs\ *n* [NL, modif. of LGk *physallis* Chinese lantern plant, fr. Gk, bladder, bubble] **1** *cap* **:** a large genus of low-growing chiefly American annual or perennial herbs (family Solanaceae) that have an angled campanulate corolla and an inflated and sometimes brightly colored calyx enclosing a fruit which is a greenish or yellow 2-celled globular berry and that include several plants which are cultivated for their edible fruit or their showy calyxes — see CAPE GOOSEBERRY, CHINESE LANTERN PLANT, GROUND-CHERRY, STRAWBERRY TOMATO **2** -ES **:** any plant of the genus *Physalis*

physa·lop·tera \,fīsə'läptərə, ,fis-\ *n, cap* [NL, fr. *physalo-* (irreg. fr. Gk *physallis* bladder, bubble) + *-ptera*] **:** a large genus (the type of the family Physalopteridae) of spiruroid nematode worms parasitic in the digestive tract of various vertebrates including man

physa·lop·ter·oid \¦==¦=tə,rōid\ *adj* [NL *Physaloptera* + E *-oid*] *of a nematode worm* **:** resembling worms of the genus *Physaloptera*

physa·los·po·ra \,=='läspərə\ *n, cap* [NL, fr. *physalo-* (irreg. fr. Gk *physalles* bladder, bubble) + *-spora*] **:** a genus of fungi (family Mycosphaerellaceae) with hyaline ovoid to oblong nonseptate ascospores including some species that were formerly placed in the form genus *Sphaeropsis* — see BLACK ROT

phy·sap·o·da \fī'sapədə\ [NL, fr. Gk *physa* bellows + NL *-poda*] *syn of* THYSANOPTERA

phy·sar·ia \fī'sa(a)rēə\ *n, cap* [NL, fr. *phys-* + *-aria*] **:** a small genus of herbs (family Cruciferae) of western No. America having racemose yellow flowers and inflated pods — see BLADDERPOD

physa·rum \'fīsərəm, 'fis-\ *n, cap* [NL, modif. of Gk *physarion* small bellows, dim. of *physa*] **:** a large genus of slime molds (subclass Myxogastres) that have violet to brownish spores and a sporangium covered with fine granules of lime

phy·scia \'fish(ē)ə, -isēə\ *n, cap* [NL, fr. Gk *physkē* large intestine, sausage + NL *-ia;* akin to Gk *physa* bellows] **:** a genus (the type of the family Physciaceae) of usu. foliaceous grayish ascolichens with brown 2-celled ascospores and a distinct cortical tissue of short closely united and interwoven filaments — **phy·sci·oid** \-ē,ȯid\ *adj*

phys·co·mit·ri·um \,fiskō'mi·trēəm\ *n, cap* [NL, fr. *physco-* (fr. Gk *physkē* large intestine, sausage) + *mitr-* (fr. L *mitra* headband, turban) + *-ium* — more at MITER] **:** a genus of mostly minute mud-inhabiting mosses (family Funariaceae) having globose to pyriform erect capsules with no peristome — see URN MOSS

phy·se·ter \fī'sēd·ə(r)\ *n, cap* [NL, fr. L, sperm whale, fr. Gk *physētēr* bellows, blowhole of a whale, sperm whale; akin to Gk *physa* bellows] **:** the type genus of the family Physeteridae comprising the sperm whales

¹phy·se·ter·id \-d·ərəd\ *adj* [NL *Physeteridae*] **:** of or relating to the Physeteridae

²physeterid \"\ *n* -s [NL *Physeteridae*] **:** a whale of the family Physeteridae

phys·e·ter·i·dae \,fisə'terə,dē\ *n pl, cap* [NL, fr. *Physeter*, type genus + *-idae*] **:** a family of whales that includes the sperm whales, pygmy sperm whale, various related extinct forms, and formerly also the beaked whales — compare PHYSETEROIDEA

phy·se·ter·oid \fī'sēd·ə,rȯid\ *n* -s [NL *Physeteroidea*] **:** a member of the superfamily Physeteroidea **:** BEAKED WHALE, SPERM WHALE

phys·e·ter·oi·dea \,fisəd·ə'rȯidēə\ *n pl, cap* [NL, fr. *Physeter* + *-oidea*] **:** a superfamily of toothed whales comprising the beaked whales and the sperm whales

phys·harmonica \,fis+\ *n* [G *physharmonika*, fr. Gk *physa* bellows + L *harmonica*, fem. of *harmonicus* musical — more at HARMONIC] **:** a small reed organ that is a precursor of the harmonium

phys·har·mon·i·ka \"\ *n* -s [G, lit., physharmonica] **:** a set of harmonium reeds incorporated into a pipe organ

physi- *or* **physio-** *comb form* [L *physio-*, fr. Gk *physi-, physio-*, fr. *physis* nature] **1 a :** nature **:** natural **:** belonging to or concerned with the natural order ⟨*physi*theism⟩ **b :** of, relating to, or concerned with the body esp. as distinct from the mind ⟨*physio*genic⟩ **2 :** physical ⟨*physio*therapy⟩ **:** physical and ⟨*physio*psychic⟩ **3 :** physiological ⟨*physio*psychology⟩ **:** physiological and ⟨*physio*pathologic⟩

phys·i·an·thro·py \,fizē'an(t)thrəpē\ *n* -ES [*physi-* + *anthrop-* + *-y*] **:** the study of the constitution of man and his diseases and their remedies

phys·i·at·rics \,fizē'a·triks, -rēks\ *n pl but sing or pl in constr* [ISV *phys-* (fr. Gk *physis* nature) + *-iatrics*] **1** *also* **phys·i·at·ric** \¦=='a·trik, -rēk\ **:** a system of medicine based on utilization of the healing powers of nature **2 a :** PHYSICAL MEDICINE **b :** PHYSICAL THERAPY

phys·i·at·rist \,=='a·trəst, '==,==\ *n* -s [*physiatrics* + *-ist*] **:** a physician who specializes in physical medicine

¹physic *var of* PHYSICS

²phys·ic \'fizik, -zēk, *chiefly in pres part* -zək\ *vt* **physicked; physicked; physicking; physics** *or* **physicks** [ME *phisiken*, fr. *phisik, fisike* medical science — more at PHYSICS] **1 :** to treat with medicine **:** administer medicine to; *esp* **:** PURGE **2 :** RELIEVE, HEAL, CURE

³physic \"\ *adj* [in sense 1, fr. ME *fisike*, fr. ML *physicus*, fr. L, natural, of or relating to natural philosophy, fr. Gk *physikos;* in other senses, fr. L *physicus* — more at PHYSICS] **1** *obs* **:** MEDICAL, MEDICINAL **2** *archaic* **:** NATURAL, PHYSICAL **3 :** of or relating to natural philosophy

¹phys·i·cal \'fizəkəl, -zēk-\ *adj* [ME *phisycal*, fr. ML *physicalis* medicinal, physical, fr. L *physica* study of nature + *-alis* -al — more at PHYSICS] **1 a** *archaic* **:** of or relating to medicine or the practice of medicine **b** (1) *obs* **:** curing or alleviating ill health **:** beneficial to health (2) *archaic* **:** used in medicine **c** *obs* **:** needing or having medical treatment **:** ILL **d** *archaic* **:** practicing medicine **2 a :** of or belonging to all created existences in nature **:** relating to or in accordance with the laws of nature **b :** of or relating to natural or material things as opposed to things mental, moral, spiritual, or imaginary **:** MATERIAL, NATURAL ⟨labor, in the ~ world, is . . . employed in putting objects in motion —J.S.Mill⟩ **3 a :** of, relating to, concerned with, or devoted to natural science **b :** of or relating to physics **:** characterized or produced by the forces and operations of physics **:** employed in the processes of physics ⟨~ changes⟩ ⟨~ laws⟩ ⟨~ forces⟩ **4 a :** of or relating to the body ⟨~ strength⟩ — often opposed to *mental* **b :** concerned or preoccupied with the body and its needs **:** CARNAL, LUSTY ⟨a purely ~ person⟩ **syn** see BODILY, MATERIAL

²physical \"\ *n* -s **:** PHYSICAL EXAMINATION

physical anthropologist *n* **:** an anthropologist specializing in physical anthropology

physical anthropology *n* **:** a branch of anthropology primarily concerned with the comparative study of human evolution, variation, and classification esp. through measurement and observation — distinguished from *cultural anthropology*

physical astronomy *n* **:** CELESTIAL MECHANICS

physical chemistry *n* **:** a branch of science applying physical methods and theory to the study of chemical systems

physical culture *n* **:** the systematic care and development of the physique

physical culturist *n* **:** an exponent or practicer of physical culture

physical double star *also* **physical double** *n* **:** BINARY STAR — compare OPTICAL DOUBLE STAR

physical education *n* **:** education in methods designed to promote the development and care of the body and usu. involving instruction in hygiene and systematic exercises and in various sports and games

physical environment *n* **:** the part of the human environment that includes purely physical factors (as soil, climate, water supply)

physical examination *n* **:** an examination of the bodily functions and condition of an individual: as **a :** an examination to determine the fitness of an individual for a particular purpose (as military service, participation in a strenuous sport, driving a locomotive) **b :** an examination by a physician under direction from a judge or court of the body and sometimes the mental state of a party to an action usu. before trial and chiefly in actions for damages for personal injury but also in some divorce proceedings and in some criminal causes

physical geography *n* **:** a branch of geography that deals with the exterior physical features and changes of the earth in land, sea, and air

physical geology *n* **:** a branch of geology made up of structural geology and dynamic geology

physical inventory *n* **:** an actual count of all stock or equipment or both of a manufacturing or mercantile concern — distinguished from *book inventory*

phys·i·cal·ism \'fizəkə,lizəm, -zēk-\ *n* -s [G *physikalismus*, fr. ML *physicalis* physical + G *-ismus* -ism] **:** a thesis that the descriptive terms of scientific language are reducible to terms which refer to spatiotemporal things or events or to their properties

phys·i·cal·ist \-ləst\ *n* -s [¹*physical* + *-ist*] **1 :** one who holds human thoughts and acts to be determined by physical laws **2 :** an advocate of physicalism

phys·i·cal·is·tic \¦===¦listik, -tēk\ *also* **phys·i·cal·ist** *adj* **1 :** of or relating to the physical **2 a :** constituting, marked by, or based on physicalism **b :** advocated by physicalists — **phys·i·cal·is·ti·cal·ly** \-tək(ə)lē, -tēk-, -lī\ *adv*

phys·i·cal·i·ty \,fizə'kaləd·ē, -zēk-, -lətē, -i\ *n* -ES **:** intensely physical orientation **:** predominance of the physical usu. at the expense of the mental, spiritual, or social **:** preoccupation with the body ⟨alert attitudes and nervous silhouettes of the beasts have an intense ~ —*New Republic*⟩ ⟨a vigorous earthy man with strong appetites and great ~⟩

physical jerks *n pl, Brit* : CALISTHENICS

physical language or **physicalistic language** *n* : the language of physics : a language that employs in addition to the terms of a thing-language those needed for quantitative descriptions

physical libration *n* : the oscillation of the moon's body with respect to the earth caused by gravitational stresses on the former's unsymmetrical shape

phys·i·cal·ly \'fizək(ə)lē, -zēk-, -li\ *adv* **1 a** : in a physical manner : in accord with physical laws ⟨~ impossible to go⟩ **b** : in respect to the body ⟨~ adapted to cold⟩ **2** *archaic* : as a natural or intrinsic quality : ESSENTIALLY, FUNDAMENTALLY

physical medicine *n* : a branch of medicine that deals with the diagnosis and treatment of disease and disability by physical means (as radiation, heat, cold, electricity) — compare PHYSICAL THERAPY

physical metallurgy *n* : a branch of metallurgy that deals with the physical properties and structure of metals and alloys

physical mixture *n* : a mixture in which the constituent substances are not chemically combined though they may be so intimately mingled (as by solution or diffusion) as to be impossible to separate by simple mechanical means

phys·i·cal·ness \'fizəkəlnəs, -zēk-\ *n* -ES : the quality or state of being physical

physical oceanography *n* : a branch of oceanography that deals with the physical and chemical properties of ocean water and the topography and composition of the ocean bottom

physical optics *n pl but usu sing in constr* : a branch of optics that deals with the description and explanation of all optical phenomena in terms of physical theories (as undulatory theory, electromagnetic phenomena, or quantum mechanics)

physical pendulum *n* : a rigid body so mounted on a horizontal axis through its center of suspension that when the body is displaced it vibrates freely about its position of equilibrium — distinguished from *simple pendulum*

physical poetry *n* : poetry (as imagist poetry) that is primarily concerned with the projection of a descriptive image of material things

physical property *n* : a property (as color, hardness, boiling point) of matter not involving in its manifestation a chemical change

physical punishment *n* : CORPORAL PUNISHMENT

physicals *pl of* PHYSICAL

physical science *n* : the natural sciences (as mineralogy, astronomy, meteorology, geology) that deal primarily with nonliving materials — compare BIOLOGY

physical sign *n* : an indication of bodily condition that can be directly perceived (as by sight or hearing) by an examining physician — compare SIGN 7d(1)

physical therapist *n* : one skilled in the methods of physical therapy and qualified to use these methods in the treatment of disease or disability usu. under the supervision of a physician

physical therapy *n* : the treatment of disease by physical and mechanical means (as massage, regulated exercise, water, light, heat, electricity) — compare PHYSICAL MEDICINE

physical valuation *n* : the use of reproduction cost of physical property as a basis for calculating the investment on which stockholders in railroads or public-utility companies are entitled to a reasonable return

physical value *n* : the cost of reproduction of physical property less depreciation and other allowances as of a given date

physic garden *n* : a botanical garden devoted to the cultivation and display of medicinal plants

phy·si·cian \fə'zishən\ *n* -S [ME *fisicien*, fr. OF, fr. *phisike, fisique* medical science — more at PHYSICS] **1** : a person skilled in the art of healing : one duly authorized to treat disease : a doctor of medicine — often distinguished from *surgeon* **2** : one who restores (as a troubled spirit or the body politic) : one exerting a remedial or salutary influence ⟨a ~ of the soul⟩ ⟨nature as a ~⟩ **3** *obs* : NATURAL PHILOSOPHER, PHYSICIST

phy·si·cian·er \-sh(ə)nə(r)\ *n* -S *archaic* : PHYSICIAN 1

phy·si·cian·less \-shənləs\ *adj* : lacking a physician : having no physician in attendance

phy·si·cian·ly *adj* : suitable to or typical of a physician ⟨a ~ attitude⟩

phy·si·cian·ship \-,ship\ *n* : the condition or position of a physician; *esp* : a particular appointment as physician ⟨appointed to the municipal ~⟩

phys·i·cism \'fizə,sizəm\ *n* -S : a physical view or explanation of the universe : a materialistic doctrine or theory

phys·i·cist \'fizəsəst, *in rapid speech* -zsəst\ *n* -S **1 a** : a specialist in physics **b** *archaic* : a person skilled in one or more branches of natural science **2** : a believer in physicism : MATERIALIST; *esp* : HYLOZOIST

phys·ick \'fizik, -zēk\ *archaic var of* PHYSIC

physicked *past of* PHYSIC

physicking *pres part of* PHYSIC

physicks *pres 3d sing of* PHYSIC

phys·icky \'fizəkē, -ki\ *adj* [[1]*physic* + *-y*] : like physic in a specified way : resulting from physic ⟨~ cramps⟩

physic nut *n* **1** : the seed of a small tropical American tree (*Jatropha curcas*) containing a strongly purgative oil that is poisonous if taken in large quantities **2** : the tree that bears the physic nut and yields a purple dye and a tanning extract

physic-nut oil *n* : CURCAS OIL

physico- *comb form* [NL, fr. L *physicus* natural, of or relating to natural philosophy, fr. Gk *physikos* — more at PHYSICS] **1** : natural : based on the study of nature ⟨*physico*theology⟩ **2** : physical ⟨*physico*optics⟩ : physical and ⟨*physico*mental⟩ **3** : combined with physics ⟨*physico*chemistry⟩ : relating to physics and ⟨*physico*mathematical⟩

phys·i·co·chemical \¦fizə(,)kō, -zē(-+\ *adj* [alter. of earlier *physicochymical*, fr. NL *physicochymicus* physicochemical (fr. *physico-* + *-chymicus* — fr. *chimicus*, n., alchemist) + E -al — more at CHEMIC] **1** : physical and chemical ⟨~ properties⟩ **2** : relating to physical chemistry ⟨~ experiments⟩ — **phys·i·co·chemically** \"+\ *adv*

phys·i·co·geographical \"+\ *adj* : of or relating to physical geography

phys·i·co·morph \'=≈(,)=,mȯrf\ *n* [*physico-* + *-morph*] : a detail in art resembling something in inanimate nature

phys·i·co·mor·phism \,=≈(,)='mȯr,fizəm\ *n* -S [*physico-* + *-morphism*] : a representation or conceptualization of nonphysical things (as deity or spiritual realities) in terms of physical categories

phys·i·co·theological \¦fizə(,)kō, -zē(-+\ *adj* **1** : of, relating to, or based on physicotheology ⟨~ argument⟩ **2** : TELEOLOGICAL ⟨the ~ argument for the existence of God⟩

phys·i·co·theology \"+\ *n* : theology illustrated or enforced by evidences of purpose in nature

physic root *n* : CULVER'S ROOT

[1]**phys·ics** \'fiziks, -zēks\ *n pl but usu sing in constr* [*physics* pl. of *physic* (intended as trans. of L *physica*, neut. pl., natural science, fr. Gk *physika*, fr. neut. pl. of *physikos* natural); *physic* fr. ME *phisik, fisike* medical science, natural science, fr. OF *phisike, fisique*, fr. L *physica*, fem. sing., study of nature, fr. Gk *physikē*, fr. fem. of *physikos* natural, fr. *physis* nature + *-ikos* -ic; akin to Gk *phylē* tribe, clan, *phyein* to bring forth — more at BE] **1 physic** *n sing* **a** : the art or practice of healing diseases : the science of therapeutics : the practice or profession of medicine; *also, archaic* : medical science : the theory of diseases and their treatment **b** *obs* : medical treatment; *also* : a health-giving or curative practice or regimen **c** (1) : a remedy for disease : a medicinal agent or preparation; *esp* : a medicine (as a laxative) that purges (2) *obs* : a mental, moral, or spiritual medicine **syn** see REMEDY **2** *also* **physic** *archaic* : NATURAL SCIENCE **3 a** : a science that deals with matter and energy and their interactions in the fields of mechanics, acoustics, optics, heat, electricity, magnetism, radiation, atomic structure, and nuclear phenomena **b** : a particular system or branch of physics ⟨classical ~⟩ ⟨nuclear ~⟩ **4** : a treatise or manual of physics ⟨left his ~ on the bench⟩ **5 a** : physical processes and phenomena (as of a particular system) ⟨~ of the living cell⟩ **b** : the physical properties and composition of something ⟨the ~ of different soils⟩ ⟨the study of marine ~⟩

[2]**physics** *pres 3d sing of* PHYSIC

[1]**physid** \'fisəd, 'fis-\ *adj* [NL *Physidae*] : of or relating to the Physidae

[2]**physid** \"\ *n* -S [NL *Physidae*] : a snail of the family Physidae

physi·dae \'fisə,dē, 'fis-\ *n pl, cap* [NL, fr. *Physa*, type genus + *-idae*] : a family of freshwater pulmonate snails (suborder Basommatophora) including *Physa* and related genera

phy·sig·na·thus \fə'zignəthəs\ *n, cap* [NL, fr. *physi-* + *-gnathus*] : a genus of lizards closely related to *Draco* — see WATER DRAGON

physio- — see PHYSI-

phys·i·o·chemical \¦fizēə+\ *adj* [*physi-* + *chemical*] : of or relating to physiological chemistry — **phys·i·o·chemically** \"+\ *adv*

phys·i·oc·ra·cy \,fizē'äkrəsē, -si\ *n* -ES [F *physiocratie*, fr. *physi-* + *-cratie* -cracy] **1** : government according to supposed natural order **2** : a physiocratic doctrine or system

phys·i·o·crat \'fizēə,krat\ *n* -S [F *physiocrate*, fr. *physi-* + *-crate* -crat] : a follower of a French physician and economist François Quesnay who in the 18th century founded a system of political and economic doctrines based on the supremacy of natural order and emphasizing the powers of nature as the source of public wealth and national prosperity and the only proper source of public revenue and the necessity for governing so as not to interfere with the natural laws which affect the relations and processes of society and industry — **phys·i·o·crat·ic** \¦=≈=¦krad·ik, -atik\ *adj*

phys·i·oc·ra·tism \,=≈'äkrə,tizəm\ *n* -S [*physiocrat* + *-ism*] : PHYSIOCRACY 2

phys·io·gen·ic \¦fizēə¦jenik\ *adj* [ISV *physi-* + *-genic*] **1** : of bodily origin : SOMATOGENIC — often opposed to *psychogenic* **2** *of a plant disease* : due to environmental or physiological abnormalities rather than parasites

phys·i·og·nom·ic \¦fizēə(g)¦nämik, -mēk\ *also* **phys·i·og·nom·i·cal** \-məkəl, -mēk-\ *adj* [*physiognomic* fr. LL *physiognomicus*, fr. LL *physiognomia* physiognomy + L *-icus* -ic; *physiognomical* fr. LL *physiognomicus* + E *-al*] **1 a** : of, relating to, pertaining to, or characteristic of physiognomy or the physiognomy **b** : relating to or depending upon anthropometric landmarks that are present on the living or the cadaver but not on the skeleton — compare MORPHOLOGICAL **2** : according with the theories of physiognomy ⟨~ laws⟩; *also* : skilled in or treating of physiognomy ⟨~ treatises⟩ — **phys·i·og·nom·i·cal·ly** \-mək(ə)lē, -mēk-, -li\ *adv*

phys·i·og·nom·ics \,=≈=¦miks, -mēks\ *n pl but usu sing in constr* : PHYSIOGNOMY 1

phys·i·og·no·mist \,fizē'ä(g)nəməst\ *n* -S [*physiognomy* + *-ist*] : one skilled in physiognomy; *esp* : one who professes to tell character through physiognomy

phys·i·og·no·mize \,=≈'=nə,mīz\ *vt* -ED/-ING/-S [*physiognomy* + *-ize*] : to observe and study the physiognomy of : deduce the character or qualities of from the physiognomy

phys·i·og·no·mon·ic \¦=≈,nə¦mänik\ *also* **phys·i·og·no·mon·i·cal** \-nəkəl\ *adj* [*physiognomonic* fr. Gk *physiognōmonikos*, fr. *physiognōmonia* physiognomy + *-ikos* -ic; *physiognomonical* fr. Gk *physiognōmonikos* + E *-al*] : PHYSIOGNOMIC

phys·i·og·no·my \,fizē'ä(g)nəmē, -mi\ *n* -ES [alter. (influenced by LL *physiognomia*) of earlier *phisnami*, fr. ME *fysnamye, phisnomye, phisonomie*, fr. MF *phisonomie*, fr. LL *physiognomia*, fr. Gk *physiognōmia*, alter. of *physiognōmonia*, fr. *physi-* + *gnōmon-, gnōmōn* interpreter, discerner + *-ia* -y — more at GNOMON] **1 a** : the technique or art of discovering temperament and character from outward appearance (as from facial features) **b** : divination by means of facial features : fortune-telling or a fortune told by one reading a face **2 a** : the facial features that show the qualities of mind or character by peculiarities of configuration or cast or characteristic expression ⟨a stern ~ indicative of great pride⟩; *broadly* : characteristic facial appearance or type (as of a race or group) ⟨a Grecian ~⟩ ⟨slender aristocratic ~⟩ **b** *obs* : a representation of a human face **3** : external aspect : characteristic or peculiar contour; *also* : inner character or quality as revealed outwardly ⟨the ~ of a mountain⟩ ⟨~ of a political party⟩ **syn** see FACE

phys·i·og·o·ny \,fizē'ägənē, -ni\ *n* -ES [*physi-* + *-gony*] : a theory of natural origins

phys·i·og·ra·pher \,=≈'ägrəfə(r)\ *n* -S [*physiography* + *-er*] : a specialist in physiography

phys·io·graph·ic \¦fizēə¦grafik, -fēk\ *also* **phys·io·graph·i·cal** \-fəkəl, -fēk-\ *adj* [prob. fr. (assumed) NL *physiographia* physiography + E *-ic* or *-ical*] : of, relating to, or employing the methods of physiography ⟨~ studies⟩ ⟨~ features⟩ — **phys·io·graph·i·cal·ly** \-fək(ə)lē, -fēk-, -li\ *adv*

physiographic climax *n* : an ecological climax that develops in association with a particular physiographic situation and persists only while the physiographic component remains stable — compare EDAPHIC CLIMAX

physiographic geology *n* : a branch of geology that deals with topography

physiographic province *n* : a region having a particular pattern of relief features or land forms that differs significantly from that of adjacent regions

phys·i·og·ra·phy \,fizē'ägrəfē, -fi\ *n* -ES [prob. fr. (assumed) NL *physiographia*, fr. NL *physi-* + L *-graphia* -graphy] **1 a** : description of nature or natural phenomena in general : phenomenal as distinguished from theoretical or etiological natural science — sometimes used of the descriptive part of a particular science **2 a** : PHYSICAL GEOGRAPHY **b** : the description and genetic interpretation of the relief features of the earth's surface : GEOMORPHOLOGY

phys·i·ol·a·ter \,fizē'äləd·ə(r)\ *n* -S [fr. *physiolatry*, after such pairs as E *idolatry: idolater*] : a nature worshiper

phys·i·ol·a·trous \,=≈'älə·trəs\ *adj* [fr. *physiolatry*, after such pairs as E *idolatry: idolatrous*] **1** : of or relating to nature worship **2** : constituting physiolatry ⟨~ behavior⟩

phys·i·ol·a·try \,=≈'älə·trē, -ri\ *n* -ES [*physi-* + *-latry*] : nature worship

phys·i·ol·o·ger \-ləjə(r)\ *n* -S [*physiology* + *-er*] **1** *archaic* : NATURAL PHILOSOPHER **2** *archaic* : a student of vital phenomena : PHYSIOLOGIST

phys·i·o·log·i·cal \,fizēə¦läjəkəl, -jēk-\ *or* **phys·i·o·log·ic** \-jik, -jēk\ *adj* [*physiological* fr. LL *physiologicus* physiological (fr. Gk *physiologikos* relating to natural science, fr. *physiologia* natural science + *-ikos* -ic) + E *-al*; *physiologic* fr. LL *physiologicus*] **1** : of or relating to physiology **2** : characteristic of or appropriate to an organism's healthy or normal functioning — contrasted with *pathological* **3** : differing in reactions or functional properties rather than in morphological features ⟨a ~ strain of a bacterium⟩ — see PHYSIOLOGIC RACE **4** : of, relating to, associated with, or caused by disorganization of functions or of metabolism — used in plant pathology and sometimes opposed to *infectious* ⟨a ~ rather than an infective disorder⟩ ⟨a ~ destruction of tissue⟩ — **phys·i·o·log·i·cal·ly** \-jək(ə)lē, -jēk-, -li\ *adv*

physiological assay *or* **physiological standardization** *n* : BIOASSAY

physiological chemistry *n* : a branch of science dealing with the chemical aspects of physiological and biological systems : BIOCHEMISTRY

physiological psychology *n* : a branch of psychology that deals with the effects of normal and pathological physiological processes on mental life

physiological saline *or* **physiological saline solution** *or* **physiological salt solution** *n* : a solution of a salt or salts that is essentially isotonic with tissue fluids or blood; *esp* : an approximately 0.9 percent solution of sodium chloride — compare RINGER'S SOLUTION

physiological spray *n* : a spray applied primarily to the foliage of plants to supply nutrient elements

physiological zero *n* : a temperature that is felt by the skin as neither warm nor cold and that under ordinary conditions usu. falls at about 85° to 90° F

physiologic race *also* **physiologic form** *n* : a biotype or group of biotypes within a taxonomic group distinguished by some physiological peculiarity (as host preference, chemical dependence, or pathogenicity) — used esp. of economically important fungi, insects, or bacteria

physiologic specialization *n* : the presence or development of physiologic races within a taxonomic group

phys·i·ol·o·gist \,fizē'äləjəst\ *n* -S [*physiology* + *-ist*] : a specialist in physiology

phys·i·ol·o·gize \-,jīz\ *vb* -ED/-ING/-S [*physiology* + *-ize*] *vi* **1** *archaic* : to enquire into or theorize on natural phenomena **2** : to formulate theories or explanations in accord with physiology ~ *vt, archaic* : to explain (as a phenomenon) in terms of natural laws

phys·i·ol·o·giz·er \-zə(r)\ *n* -S : one that physiologizes

phys·i·ol·o·goi \,fizē'älə,gȯi\ *n pl* [Gk, pl. of *physiologos*, fr. *physi-* + *logos* word, speech — more at LEGEND] : the ancient Greek nature philosophers

phys·i·o·logue \'fizēə,lȯg *also* -läg\ *n* -S [LL *physiologus*, fr. Gk *physiologos*] : a natural philosopher : PHYSIOLOGIZER

phys·i·ol·o·gy \,fizē'äləjē, -ji\ *n* -ES [L *physiologia*, fr. Gk, fr. *physi-* + *-logia* -logy] **1** *obs* **a** : NATURAL SCIENCE, NATURAL PHILOSOPHY 1 **b** : a particular theory or view of nature **2** : a branch of biology dealing with the processes, activities, and phenomena incidental to and characteristic of life or of living organisms : the study of the functions and activities of living matter (as of organs, tissues, or cells) as such and of the physical and chemical phenomena involved — distinguished from *anatomy*; compare PSYCHOLOGY **3** : the organic processes and phenomena of an organism or any of its parts or of a particular bodily process ⟨the ~ of the jellyfish⟩ ⟨~ of the thyroid gland⟩ ⟨~ of a rust fungus⟩ ⟨the ~ of digestion⟩ **4** : a treatise on physiology

phys·i·om·e·try \,=≈'ämə·trē, -ri\ *n* -ES [*physi-* + *-metry*] : the measurement of bodily functions esp. as a feature of anthropometric studies — compare PSYCHOMETRICS

phys·io·neurosis \¦fizēō+\ *n* [NL, fr. *physi-* + *neurosis*] : the somatic component of a psychosomatic ailment

phys·i·on·o·trace \,fizē'änə,trās\ *n* -S [F, fr. *physiono-* (fr. *physionomie* facial features, fr. MF *phisonomie, physionomie* facial features, physiognomy) + *-trace* (fr. *tracer* to trace, draw) — more at PHYSIOGNOMY, TRACE] : a device used in the late 18th and early 19th centuries to trace the profile of a sitter with chalk or white crayon on a red paper, the image being then completed in black or white crayon

phys·io·pathologic \¦fizēō+\ *also* **phys·io·pathological** \"+\ *adj* [*physi-* + *pathologic, pathological*] **1** : of or relating to both physiology and pathology **2** : involving pathological alteration of bodily function — **phys·io·pathology** \"+\ *n*

phys·io·philosophy \"+\ *n* [*physi-* + *philosophy*; intended as trans. of G *naturphilosophie*] : a system of natural philosophy expounded by Lorenz Oken (1779–1851) and designed to set forth a natural system of universal relations

phys·io·plastic \"+\ *adj* [*physi-* + *plastic*] : following or being in accord with nature ⟨a ~ representation⟩

phys·io·psychic \"+\ *adj* [*physi-* + *psychic*] : of, relating to, or involving the physical and the psychical or their interrelations

phys·io·psychological \"+\ *adj* : of or relating to physiological psychology

phys·io·psychology \"+\ *n* [*physi-* + *psychology*] : PHYSIOLOGICAL PSYCHOLOGY

phys·io·sociological \"+\ *adj* [*physi-* + *sociological*] : of or relating to both physiology and sociology

phys·i·os·o·phy \,fizē'äsəfē\ *n* -ES [*physi-* + *-sophy*] : wisdom about nature

phys·io·therapeutic \¦fizēō+\ *adj* [*physi-* + *therapeutic*] : of or relating to physical therapy

phys·io·therapeutics \"+\ *n pl but usu sing in constr* [*physi-* + *therapeutics*] : PHYSICAL THERAPY

phys·io·therapist \"+\ *n* [*physiotherapy* + *-ist*] : PHYSICAL THERAPIST

phys·io·therapy \"+\ *n* [NL *physiotherapia*, fr. *physi-* + *therapia* therapy] : PHYSICAL THERAPY

phy·sique \fə'zēk\ *n* -S [F, fr. *physique*, adj., physical, bodily, fr. L *physicus* natural, fr. Gk *physikos* — more at PHYSIC] **1** : bodily makeup or type : the structure, constitution, appearance, or strength of the human body ⟨a muscular ~⟩ ⟨a race of slender ~ and notable alertness⟩ **2** : physical form or construction (as of a geographic area) ⟨the ~ of the Alps is such as to make access from the north . . . easier than movement northwards from Italy —W.G.East⟩

syn BUILD, CONSTITUTION, HABIT: PHYSIQUE designates the total bodily or physical construction or qualities of an individual ⟨tall of stature, slender in *physique* —H.W.H.Knott⟩ ⟨his five-foot-nine-inch *physique* —*Current Biog.*⟩ BUILD, usu. interchangeable with PHYSIQUE, often stresses the geometrically determinable qualities of the physique ⟨a man of rather square *build*⟩ ⟨leisure and heredity gave me a husky *build*⟩ CONSTITUTION is the overall makeup of an individual comprising both mental and physical qualities ⟨extremely high-spirited, my greatest advantage was that my *constitution* did not allow me to be depressed —Osbert Sitwell⟩ ⟨a frail *constitution* necessitated his living in the South —H.E.Starr⟩ ⟨wealthy by inheritance but saving by *constitution* —Ellen Glasgow⟩ HABIT, usu. occurring with a qualifier, is generally confined to characteristic mental or moral quality, makeup, or disposition ⟨the country is where he has gone to indulge a contemplative *habit* —L.J.Halle⟩ ⟨an educated person . . . was one who possessed a certain intellectual *habit* —H.A.Overstreet⟩ ⟨a girl of frivolous *habit*⟩

phy·siqued \-kt\ *adj* : having a specified physique

phy·sis \'fīsəs\ *n, pl* **phy·ses** \-ī,sēz\ [Gk, nature — more at PHYSIC] : the source of growth or change inherent in or construed as nature : something that grows or becomes

phys·i·theism \¦fizə+\ *n* [*physi-* + *theism*] **1** : ascription of physical form to deity **2** : veneration of the physical powers of nature

phys·i·urgic \¦fizē¦ərjik\ *adj* [*physi-* + *-urgic* (as in *theurgic*)] : effected or brought about by natural as distinguished from divine or human influences

physo- — see PHYS-

phy·so·car·pous \¦fīsə¦kärpəs\ *adj* [*phys-* + *-carpous*] : having a bladdery fruit

phy·so·car·pus \,=≈'=pəs\ *n, cap* [NL, fr. *phys-* + *-carpus*] : a genus of chiefly No. American shrubs (family Rosaceae) with palmately lobed leaves and corymbose white flowers — see NINEBARK

phy·so·ceph·a·lus \,=≈'sefələs\ *n, cap* [NL, fr. *phys-* + *-cephalus*] : a genus of nematode worms (family Thelaziidae) including a common parasite (*P. sexalatus*) of the stomach and small intestine of swine

[1]**phy·so·clist** \'fīsə,klist\ *n* -S [NL *Physoclisti*] : a teleost fish lacking a duct between the air bladder and the alimentary canal

[2]**physoclist** \"\ *also* **phy·so·clis·tous** \¦=≈¦klistəs\ *or* **phy·so·clis·tic** \-tik\ *adj* [*physoclist* fr. NL *Physoclisti*; *physoclistous, physoclistic* fr. NL *Physoclisti* + E *-ous* or *-ic*] **1** : of or relating to a physoclist or to the Physoclisti **2** : lacking a duct between the air bladder and alimentary canal

phy·so·clis·ti \,=≈'kli,stī\ *n pl, cap* [NL, fr. *phys-* + *-clisti* (fr. Gk *kleistos* closed) — more at CLEIST-] *in some classifications* : an order of fishes comprising the physoclists — compare PHYSOSTOMI

phy·sode \'fī,sōd\ *n* -S [G, fr. Gk *physōdēs* full of wind, fr. *physa* bellows — more at PUSTULE] : any of various vesicular intracellular inclusions of brown algae that are of uncertain constitution and function

phy·so·der·ma \,fīsə'dərmə\ *n, cap* [NL, fr. *phys-* + *-derma*] : a genus of parasitic fungi (order Chytridiales) that have an intracellular thallus of fine fibrils and usu. extracellular sporangia — see BROWN SPOT

physoderma disease *n* : BROWN SPOT

phy·so·gas·tric \¦fīsə¦gastrik\ *adj* [*physogastry* + *-ic*] *of an insect* : having the abdomen greatly distended

phy·so·gas·try \,=≈,gastrē\ *also* **phy·so·gas·trism** \,=≈'ga,strizəm\ *n, pl* **physogastries** *also* **physogastrisms** [*physogastry* ISV *phys-* + *gastr-* + *-y*; *physogastrism* fr. *phys-* + *gastr-* + *-ism*] : the condition (as of some termitophiles) of having the abdomen greatly distended — compare STENOGASTRY

phy·so·nec·tae \,=≈'nek,tē, -,tī\ *n pl, cap* [NL, fr. *phys-* + *-nectae*] : a group of siphonophores having a float and usu. a series of swimming bells — **phy·so·nec·tous** \¦=≈¦nektəs\ *adj*

phy·soph·o·rae \fī'säfə,rē\ [NL, fr. *phys-* + *-phorae*] *syn of* PHYSOPHORIDA

phy·so·phore \'fīsə,fō(ə)r\ *n* -S [NL *Physophorae*] : a siphonophore of the suborder Physophorida

phy·so·phor·i·da \,=≈'fȯrədə\ *n pl, cap* [NL, fr. *Physophora*, included genus (fr. *phys-* + *-phora*) + *-ida*] : a suborder of siphonophores characterized by possession of a pneumatophore

phy·so·pod \ˈfīsə,päd\ *or* **phy·sop·o·dan** \(ˈ)fīˈsäpədən\ *adj or n* [*physopod* fr. NL *Physopoda; physopodan* fr. NL *Physopoda* + E *-an*] : THYSANOPTERAN, THRIPID

phy·sop·o·da \fīˈsäpədə\ [NL, fr. *phys-* + *-poda*] *syn of* THYSANOPTERA

phy·sop·sis \fīˈsäpsəs\ *n, cap* [NL, fr. *phys-* + *-opsis*] : a genus of Old World freshwater pulmonate snails (family Bulinidae) including important intermediate hosts of the schistosome (*Schistosoma haematobium*) and other trematodes of medical or veterinary significance

phy·so·ste·gia \,fīsəˈstējēə\ *n* [NL, fr. *phys-* + Gk *stegē* roof + NL *-ia;* akin to Gk *stegein* to cover, shelter — more at THATCH] **1** *cap* : a genus of No. American perennial herbs (family Labiatae) having sessile linear to oblong leaves and showy white, rose, or lavender flowers with an inflated 5-toothed calyx — see FALSE DRAGONHEAD **2** -s : any plant of the genus *Physostegia*

phy·so·stigma \ˌ≈≈+\ *n* [NL, fr. *phys-* + L *stigma* mark — more at STIGMA] **1** *cap* : a genus of African woody vines (family Leguminosae) whose fruit is the Calabar bean **2** -s : CALABAR BEAN

phy·so·stig·mine \ˌ≈≈ˈstig,mēn, -mən\ *n* -s [ISV *physostigm-* (fr. NL *Physostigma*) + *-ine;* orig. formed as G *physostigmin*] : a crystalline tasteless tricyclic alkaloid $C_{15}H_{21}N_3O_2$ that is the chief alkaloid of the Calabar bean and is used in medicine esp. in the form of its salicylate as a myotic; eseroline methylcarbamate — called also *eserine*

¹phy·so·stome \ˈfīsə,stōm\ *n* -s [NL *Physostomi*] : a teleost fish having a duct between the air bladder and the alimentary canal; *broadly* : one of the Physostomi

²physostome \ˈ"\ *adj* [NL *Physostomi*] : PHYSOSTOMOUS

phy·sos·to·mi \fīˈsästə,mī\ *n pl, cap* [NL, fr. *phys-* + *-stomi*] *in some classifications* : an order of teleost fishes comprising those in which the air bladder when present is joined with the esophagus by an open duct and the ventral fins when present are abdominal, including the salmons, herrings, carps, catfishes, and others, and being more or less nearly equivalent to Isospondyli — compare MALACOPTERYGII, PHYSOCLISTI

phy·sos·to·mous \(ˈ)≈ˈ≈≈məs\ *also* **phy·so·stoma·tous** \ˌfīsōˈstämədəs, -stōm-\ *adj* [*physostomous* fr. NL *Physostomi* + E *-ous; physostomatous* fr. *phys-* + *-stomatous*] **1** : of or relating to a physostome or the Physostomi : ISOSPONDYLOUS **2** : having a duct between the air bladder and alimentary canal

phyt- *or* **phyto-** *comb form* [NL, fr. Gk, fr. *phyton;* akin to Gk *phyein* to bring forth — more at BE] : plant ⟨*phyto*bacteriology⟩ ⟨*phyt*osis⟩

-phy·ta \fədə, fətə\ *n pl comb form* [NL, fr. Gk *phyta,* pl. of *phyton*] : plants — in names of taxa ⟨Bryo*phyta*⟩ ⟨Cormo*phyta*⟩

phyt·albumose \(ˈ)fīd·+\ *n* [*phyt-* + *albumose*] : a vegetable albumose

phy·tase \ˈfī,tās, -āz\ *n* -s [ISV *phytin* + *-ase*] : an esterase present in grains, alfalfa, molds, and kidneys that accelerates the hydrolysis of phytin or phytic acid into inositol and phosphoric acid

phy·tate \ˈfī,tāt\ *n* -s [ISV *phytin* + *-ate*] : a salt or ester of phytic acid

-phyte \,fīt, *usu* -īd.+V\ *n comb form* -s [ISV, fr. Gk *phyton* plant] **1** : plant having a (specified) characteristic or habitat ⟨xero*phyte*⟩ ⟨micro*phyte*⟩ **2** : pathological growth ⟨osteo*phyte*⟩

phy·tel·e·phas \fīˈteləˌfas\ *n, cap* [NL, fr. *phyt-* + Gk *elephas* elephant, ivory — more at ELEPHANT] : a small genus of So. American pinnate-leaved palms having simple drooping flower spikes with many stamens and syncarpous fruit — see IVORY NUT

phyter·al \ˈfīdərəl, ˈfīd-\ *n* -s [*phyt-* + *-eral* (as in *mineral*)] : recognizable plant forms and fossils in coal as distinguished from the organic coal substance

phythrpst *abbr* physiotherapist

-phyt·ic \ˈfid|ik, -it|, |ēk\ *adj comb form* [ISV *-phyte* + *-ic*] : like a plant ⟨holo*phytic*⟩

phytic acid \ˈfī|d|ik-, ˈfi|, |t|, |ēk-\ *n* [*phytic* fr. *Phytin* + *-ic*] : an acid $C_6H_6(OPO_3H_2)_6$ obtained on acidification of Phytin salt that yields inositol and phosphoric acid on hydrolysis; inositol hexa-phosphoric acid ester

Phy·tin \ˈfītᵊn\ *trademark* — used for a calcium magnesium salt of phytic acid that occurs as a reserve material esp. in seeds or tubers and is obtained usu. by processing corn steepwater and that is used chiefly as a source of inositol

phy·tiv·o·rous \fīˈtiv(ə)rəs\ *adj* [*phyt-* + *-i-* + *-vorous*] : PHYTOPHAGOUS

phy·to·bacteriology \ˌfīd·(ˌ)ō, ˌfī(ˌ)tō+\ *n* [*phyt-* + *bacteriology*] : a branch of bacteriology that deals with organisms associated with or pathogenic for plants

phy·to·bezoar \ˌ≈≈+\ *n* [ISV *phyt-* + *bezoar*] : a bezoar composed chiefly of undigested compacted vegetable fiber

phy·to·biology \ˈ"+\ *n* [ISV *phyt-* + *biology*] : plant ecology

phy·to·cecidium \ˈ"+\ *n* [NL, fr. *phyt-* + *cecidium*] : a gall caused by the presence of a plant (as a parasitic bacterium or fungus) — compare CROWN GALL

phy·to·chlore \ˈfīdə,klō(ə)r\ *n* -s [*phyt-* + Gk *chlōros* greenish yellow — more at YELLOW] *archaic* : CHLOROPHYLL

phy·to·ci·dal \ˌfīdəˈsīdᵊl\ *adj* [*phyt-* + *-cide* + *-al*] : killing or tending to kill plants

phy·to·cide \ˈ≈≈,sīd\ *n* -s [*phyt-* + *-cide*] : a substance (as a herbicide) used to kill unwanted plants

phy·to·climatology \ˌ≈≈+\ *n* [ISV *phyt-* + *climatology*] : the bioclimatology of plants

phy·to·coe·no·sis \ˌfīd·(ˌ)ōsēˈnōsəs\ *n, pl* **phytocoeno·ses** \-,sēz\ [NL, fr. *phyt-* + *coen-* + *-osis*] : the whole body of plants occupying a particular habitat

phy·to·concretion \ˌ≈≈+\ *n* [*phyt-* + *concretion*] : PHYTOBEZOAR

phy·to·flagellata \ˌfīdə+\ [NL, fr. *phyt-* + *Flagellata*] *syn of* PHYTOMASTIGINA

phy·to·flagellate \ˌ≈≈+\ *n* [NL *Phytoflagellata*] : PLANTLIKE FLAGELLATE

phy·to·flu·ene \ˌ≈≈ˈflü,ēn\ *n* -s [prob. fr. *phyt-* + *flu-* (fr. *fluorescent*) + *-ene*] : a polyene hydrocarbon $C_{40}H_{64}$ occurring with carotenoids in plants

phy·tog·a·my \fīˈtägəmē\ *n* -ES [ISV *phyt-* + *-gamy*] : CROSS-FERTILIZATION

phy·to·genesis \ˌfīd·ō+\ *n* [NL, fr. *phyt-* + L *genesis*] : the origin and developmental history of plants

phy·to·genetical \ˈ"+\ *also* **phy·to·genetic** \ˈ"+\ *adj* [fr. *phytogenesis,* after E *genesis: genetic, genetical*] : of or relating to phytogenesis or to the phylogeny of plants — **phy·to·genetically** \ˈ"+\ *adv*

phy·to·gen·ic \ˌ≈≈ˈjenik\ *adj* [*phyt-* + *-genic*] : of plant origin ⟨a ~ skin lesion⟩; *esp* : of, relating to, or constituting an organic deposit directly attributable to the presence of plants ⟨~ rocks⟩

phy·tog·e·ny \fīˈtäjənē\ *n* -ES [*phyt-* + *-geny*] : PHYTOGENESIS

phy·to·geographer \ˌfīd·(ˌ)ō+\ *n* [*phytogeography* + *-er*] : a specialist in phytogeography

phy·to·geographical \ˈ"+\ *or* **phy·to·geographic** \ˈ"+\ *adj* [*phytogeographical* fr. *phytogeography* + *-ical; phytogeographic* ISV *phytogeography* + *-ic*] : of or relating to phytogeography — **phy·to·geographically** \ˈ"+\ *adv*

phy·to·geography \ˈ"+\ *n* [ISV *phyt-* + *geography*] : the biogeography of plants

phy·to·globulin \ˈ"+\ *n* [ISV *phyt-* + *globulin*] : a plant globulin

phy·to·graph \ˈfīdə,graf, -ràf\ *n* [*phyt-* + *-graph*] : a diagram expressing measurements of lines crossing each other istics by means of various plant characteristics

phy·tog·ra·phy \fīˈtägrəfē, -fi\ *n* -ES [NL *phytographia,* fr. *phyt-* + L *-graphia* -graphy] : descriptive botany sometimes including plant taxonomy

phy·to·hormone \ˌfīd·(ˌ)ō, ˌfī(ˌ)tō+\ *n* [ISV *phyt-* + *hormone*] : PLANT HORMONE

phy·toid \ˈfī,tȯid\ *adj* [ISV *phyt-* + *-oid*] : resembling a plant

phy·tol \ˈfī,tȯl, -ōl\ *n* -s [ISV *phyt-* + *-ol*] : an oily aliphatic diterpenoid primary alcohol $C_{20}H_{39}OH$ obtained by hydrolysis of chlorophyll (as by means of chlorophyllase), also made synthetically, and used in synthesizing vitamin E and vitamin K_1

phy·to·lac·ca \ˌfīdəˈlakə\ *n, cap* [NL, fr. *phyt-* + *lacca* lac — more at LACCA] : a genus (the type of the family Phytolaccaceae) of mostly tropical perennial herbs or occasionally trees having a 5- to 15-celled berry — see POKEWEED, UMBRA TREE

phy·to·lac·ca·ce·ae \ˌ≈≈laˈkāsē,ē\ *n pl, cap* [NL, fr. *Phytolacca,* type genus + *-aceae*] : a family of chiefly tropical herbs, shrubs, and trees (order Caryophyllales) with racemose flowers and fruit of many carpels — **phy·to·lac·ca·ceous** \ˌ≈≈≈ˈkāshəs\ *adj*

phy·tol·a·try \fīˈtälətrē\ *n* -ES [*phyt-* + *-latry*] : worship of plants

phy·to·lite \ˈfīdə,līt\ *or* **phy·to·lith** \-,lith\ *n* -s [*phyt-* + *-lite* or *-lith*] : a plant fossil

phy·to·log·ic \ˌfīdəˈläjik, -jēk\ *or* **phy·to·log·i·cal** \-jəkəl, -jēk-\ *adj* [*phytologic* ISV *phytology* + *-ic; phytological* fr. *phytology* + *-ical*] : BOTANICAL

phy·to·log·i·cal·ly \-jək(ə)lē, -jēk-\ *adv* : BOTANICALLY

phy·tol·o·gist \fīˈtäləjəst\ *n* -s [*phytology* + *-ist*] : BOTANIST

phy·tol·o·gy \-jē, -ji\ *n* -ES [NL *phytologia,* fr. *phyt-* + L *-logia* -logy] : BOTANY

phy·to·mas·tig·i·da \ˌfīdō,maˈstijədə\ *or* **phy·to·mas·ti·go·da** \-,mastəˈgōdə\ *or* **phy·to·mas·ti·go·ta** \-ōd·ə\ *syn of* PHYTOMASTIGINA

phy·to·mas·ti·gi·na \-,mastəˈjīnə\ *n pl, cap* [NL, fr. *phyt-* + *mastig-* + *-ina*] : a subclass of Mastigophora comprising the plantlike flagellates that are often regarded as unicellular algae, have chromatophores which contain chlorophyll, usu. secrete a covering of cellulose, and have a pigmented eyespot — compare ZOOMASTIGINA

phy·to·mer \ˈfīdəmə(r)\ *n, pl* **phytomers** \-mə(r)z\ *also* **phy·tom·er·on** \fīˈtämərən\ [NL *phytomeron,* fr. *phyt-* + *-meron* (fr. Gk *meros* part) — more at MERIT] : one of the individual structural units that in serial arrangement make up the body of a plant ⟨a bud-bearing node is a typical ~⟩

phy·tom·e·ter \fīˈtämədə(r), -mətə-\ *n* [*phyt-* + *-meter*] : a plant or group of plants grown usu. under controlled conditions and used as a measure of the physiological responses to various environmental factors

phy·to·met·ric \ˌfīdəˈme·trik\ *adj* : of or relating to phytometry

phy·tom·e·try \fīˈtämə·trē, -ri\ *n* -ES [*phyt-* + *-metry*] : the measurement of the physiological responses of a plant or group of plants to various environmental factors

¹phy·tom·o·nad \fīˈtämə,nad\ *adj* [NL *Phytomonadina*] : of or relating to the Phytomonadina

²phytomonad \ˈ"\ *n* -s [NL *Phytomonadina*] : a flagellate of the order Phytomonadina

phy·to·mon·a·di·na \ˌfīd·(ˌ)ō,mänəˈdīnə\ *n pl, cap* [NL, fr. *Phytomonad-, Phytomonas* (genus of flagellates) + *-ina*] : an order of small green plantlike flagellates (subclass Phytomastigina) comprising solitary forms (as *Polytoma uvella*) and complex colonial forms (as members of the genus *Volvox*) — compare VOLVOCALES

phy·tom·o·nas \fīˈtämənəs, -,nas\ *n, cap* [NL, fr. *phyt-* + *-monas*] **1** : a genus of flagellates (family Trypanosomatidae) that are morphologically similar to members of the genus *Leptomonas* but alternate between a hemipterous insect and a latex plant as hosts **2** [NL, fr. *phyt-* + *-monas*] *in some esp former classifications* : a large genus of plant-pathogenic bacteria (family Pseudomonadaceae) the members of which are now usu. divided between the genera *Pseudomonas* and *Xanthomonas*

phy·to·morph \ˈfīd·ə,mȯrf\ *n* [*phyt-* + *-morph*] : a conventionalized representation of a plant — used esp. of primitive art

phy·to·mor·phic \ˌ≈≈ˈmȯrfik\ *adj* [ISV *phyt-* + *-morphic*] : having or represented with the attributes of a plant ⟨~ bryozoans⟩

phy·to·myx·i·nae \ˌfīd·(ˌ)ō,mikˈsī,nē\ *n pl, cap* [NL, fr. *phyt-* + *myx-* + *-inae*] *in some classifications* : a class of fungi coextensive with the order Plasmodiophorales

phy·to·my·za \ˌfīd·əˈmīzə\ *n, cap* [NL, fr. *phyt-* + *-myza*] : a genus of two-winged flies having larvae that are leaf miners in corn, sugarcane, and related plants

phy·ton \ˈfī,tän\ *n* -s [NL, fr. Gk, plant — more at PHYT-] **1** : a structural unit of a plant consisting of a leaf and its associated portion of stem : PHYTOMER **2** : the smallest part of a stem, root, or leaf that when severed may grow into a new plant : a potential cutting — **phy·ton·ic** \(ˈ)fīˈtänik\ *adj*

phy·to·na·di·one \ˌfīd·ōnəˈdī,ōn\ *n* -s [*phyto-* (fr. *phytyl*) + *na-* (fr. *napthoquinone*) + *-dione*] : VITAMIN K 1a — used in the U. S. Pharmacopoeia

phy·to·parasite \ˌfīd·(ˌ)ō+\ *n* [*phyt-* + *parasite*] : a parasitic plant

phy·to·pathogen \ˌ≈≈+\ *n* [*phyt-* + *pathogen*] : an organism parasitic on a plant host — **phy·to·pathogenic** \ˌ≈≈+\ *adj* — **phy·to·pathogenicity** \ˌ≈≈+\ *n*

phy·to·pathologic \ˌ≈≈+\ *or* **phy·to·pathological** \ˌ≈≈+\ *adj* [*phytopathologic* ISV *phytopathology* + *-ic; phytopathological* fr. *phytopathology* + *-ical*] : of or relating to plant pathology

phy·to·pathologist \ˌ≈≈+\ *n* [ISV *phytopathology* + *-ist*] : a plant pathologist

phy·to·pathology \ˌ≈≈+\ *n* [ISV *phyt-* + *pathology*] **1** : PLANT PATHOLOGY **2** : an abnormal condition caused by parasitic plants

¹phy·toph·a·ga \fīˈtäfəgə\ *n pl, cap* [NL, fr. *phyt-* + *-phaga*] : any of several groups of vegetable-feeding animals: as **a** : a very large division of Coleoptera comprising beetles that have all the tarsi apparently 4-jointed, the head not rostrate, the labrum exposed, and the palpi never wholly occluded in the mouth and including the families Bruchidae, Chrysomelidae, and Cerambycidae or being made coextensive with Chrysomelidae **b** : a division of Hymenoptera comprising forms (as the sawflies) with larvae that feed on plants **c** : a group of Edentata including the sloths

²phytophaga \ˈ"\ *n, cap* [NL, fr. *phyt-* + *-phaga*] : a genus of gall midges

phy·toph·a·gan \-gən\ *also* **phy·to·phage** \ˈfīd·ə,fāj\ *n* -s [*phytophagan* fr. NL *¹Phytophaga* + E *-an; phytophage* fr. NL *¹Phytophaga*] : a phytophagous animal; *esp* : one of the Phytophaga

phy·to·phag·ic \ˌfīd·əˈfajik\ *adj* [*phyt-* + *-phagic* (fr. *-phagy* + *-ic*)] : PHYTOPHAGOUS 1

phy·to·pha·gin·e·ae \ˌ≈≈,fəˈjinē,ē\ *n pl, cap* [NL, fr. *phyt-* + *phag-* + *-ineae*] *in some classifications* : a suborder of Virales comprising plant-parasitic viruses

phy·toph·a·gous \fīˈtäfəgəs\ *adj* [*phyt-* + *-phagous*] **1** : feeding on plants — used esp. of a lower animal (as an insect); distinguished from *herbivorous* and *vegetarian* **2** [NL *¹Phytophaga* + E *-ous*] : of or relating to the Phytophaga

phy·toph·a·gy \-jē\ *n* -ES [*phytophagous* + *-y*] : the condition of being phytophagous

phy·to·pharmacology \ˌfīd·(ˌ)ō+\ *n* [*phyt-* + *pharmacology*] : the study of the influences of drugs on the physiological processes of plants

phy·toph·i·lous \fīˈtäfələs\ *adj* [*phyt-* + *-philous*] : fond of plants : living or feeding on plants — **phy·toph·i·ly** \-əlē\ *n* -ES

phy·toph·tho·ra \fīˈtäfthərə\ *n* [NL, fr. *phyt-* + *-phthora*] **1** *cap* : a genus of destructive parasitic fungi (family Pythiaceae) having conidia that usu. act as sporangia esp. under moist cool conditions and sporangiophores that are simple or branched — see LATE BLIGHT, PYTHIACYSTIS **2** -s **a** : any fungus of the genus *Phytophthora* **b** : a disease (as late blight) caused by such a fungus

phy·to·plankter \ˈfīd·ə+\ *n* [*phyt-* + *plankter*] : a planktonic plant ⟨diatoms and other ~s⟩

phy·to·plankton \ˌ≈≈+\ *n* [ISV *phyt-* + *plankton*] : plankton consisting of plant life — **phy·to·planktonic** \ˌ≈≈+\ *adj*

phy·to·plasm \ˈfīd·ə,plazəm\ *n* -s [ISV *phyt-* + *-plasm*] : plant protoplasm

¹phy·top·tid \fīˈtäptəd\ *adj* [NL *Phytoptidae*] : of or relating to the Phytoptidae

²phytoptid \ˈ"\ *n* -s [NL *Phytoptidae*] : a mite of the family Phytoptidae

phy·top·ti·dae \-təˌdē\ *n pl, cap* [NL, fr. *Phytoptus,* type genus + *-idae*] : a family of minute plant-parasitic mites that includes various destructive bud mites and blister mites and is often treated as a subfamily of Eriophyidae

phy·top·tus \-təs\ *n, cap* [NL, fr. *phyt-* + *-ptus* (fr. Gk *ptoia* terror, flight); akin to Gk *petesthai* to fly — more at FEATHER] : the type genus of Phytoptidae

phy·to·saur \ˈfīd·ə,sȯ(ə)r\ *n* -s [NL *Phytosauria*] : a reptile of the suborder Phytosauria

phy·to·sau·ria \ˌ≈≈ˈsȯrēə\ *n pl, cap* [NL, fr. *phyt-* + *-sauria*] : a suborder of Thecodontia comprising Triassic reptiles similar to long-snouted crocodiles but having narial openings far back on the head — **phy·to·sau·ri·an** \ˌ≈≈ˈsȯrēən\ *adj or n*

phy·to·serology \ˌfīd·ō+\ *n* [*phyt-* + *serology*] : a branch of serology that deals with plants and plant products esp. in respect to identification, determination of relationships, and study of plant viruses

phy·to·sis \fīˈtōsəs\ *n, pl* **phyto·ses** \-ō,sēz\ [NL, fr. *phyt-* + *-osis*] : an infection with or a disease caused by parasitic plants

phy·to·sociological \ˌfīd·(ˌ)ō+\ *also* **phy·to·sociologic** \ˌ≈≈+\ *adj* : of or relating to phytosociology : pertinent to or involved in floral interrelations ⟨~ factors⟩ — **phy·to·sociologically** \ˌ≈≈+\ *adv*

phy·to·sociologist \ˌ≈≈+\ *n* : a specialist in phytosociology

phy·to·sociology \ˌ≈≈+\ *n* [*phyt-* + *sociology*] : a branch of ecology that deals with the interrelations among the flora of particular areas and esp. with plant communities

phy·tos·te·rol \fīˈtästə,rȯl, -rōl\ *n* [ISV *phyt-* + *-sterol* (as in *cholesterol*)] : any of a group of sterols (as ergosterol, sitosterol, stigmasterol) derived from plants

phy·to·succivorous \ˌfīd·(ˌ)ō+\ *adj* [*phyt-* + *succivorous*] : feeding on the sap of plants — used esp. of an insect

phy·to·therapy \ˌfīd·ō+\ *n* [ISV *phyt-* + *therapy*] **1** : the use of vegetable drugs in medicine **2** : the treatment of disease or parasitism in the individual plant

phy·to·tom·i·dae \ˌfīd·əˈtäməˌdē\ *n pl, cap* [NL, fr. *Phytotoma,* type genus (fr. *phyt-* + Gk *tomē* action of cutting, fr. *temnein* to cut) + *-idae* — more at TOME] : a family of So. American passerine birds that resemble finches but have serrated bills with which they nip off the young shoots and buds of plants

phy·tot·o·my \fīˈtäd·əmē\ *n* -ES [ISV *phyt-* + *-tomy*] : the anatomy of plants

phy·to·toxic \ˌfīd·ə+\ *adj* [*phyt-* + *toxic*] **1** : of or relating to a phytotoxin **2** : poisonous to plants — **phy·to·toxicity** \ˌ≈≈+\ *n*

phy·to·toxin \ˌ≈≈+\ *n* [ISV *phyt-* + *toxin*] : a toxin (as ricin) produced by a plant

phy·to·zo·on \ˌfīd·əˈzō,än\ *n, pl* **phyto·zoa** \-ōə\ [NL, fr. *phyt-* + *-zoon*] : ZOOPHYTE

phy·tyl \ˈfīdᵊl\ *n* -s [*phytol* + *-yl*] : the univalent radical $C_{20}H_{39}$ derived from phytol

¹pi \ˈpī\ *n* -s [MGk, fr. Gk *pei,* of Sem origin; akin to Heb *pē*] **1** : the 16th letter of the Greek alphabet — symbol Π or π; see ALPHABET table **2 a** : the symbol π denoting the ratio of the circumference of a circle to its diameter **b** : the ratio itself : a transcendental number having a value to eight decimal places of 3.14159265

²pi *also* **pie** \ˈ"\ *n, pl* **pies** [origin unknown] **1 a** : type or type matter that is spilled, mixed, or incorrectly distributed ⟨when . . . a disaster occurs and the type falls or collapses, the resulting disordered heap is the famous printer's ~ —Seán Jennett⟩ **b** : the condition of pi ⟨a great deal of what he has set up is often thrown into ~ —John Southward⟩ **2** : a pi character or matrix **syn** see CONFUSION

³pi \ˈ"\ *adj* **1** : not intended to appear in final printing because improperly set or containing a temporary instruction to the printer — used of a line of type or print **2** : not carried in a keyboard-controlled channel and therefore insertable only by hand — used of a typesetting-machine matrix

⁴pi *also* **pie** \ˈ"\ *vb* **pied; pied; pi·ing** *or* **pie·ing; pies** *vt* : to spill or throw (type or type matter) into disorder ⟨~ a case⟩ ⟨~ a form⟩ ⟨~ a galley⟩ ~ *vi* : to become pied ⟨some display matter ~*es* easily⟩

⁵pi \ˈ"\ *adv* [*³pi*] : as a pi character ⟨border matrices always run ~ but can have special combinations cut to run in magazine —*Intertype Faces*⟩

⁶pi \ˈ"\ *adj* [short for *pious*] *Brit* : MORALIZING, PREACHY, GOODY-GOODY

pi *abbr* piaster

PI *abbr* **1** paper insulated **2** photo interpreter; photo interpretation

¹pia \ˈpīə\ *n* -s [by shortening] : PIA MATER

²pia \ˈpēə\ *n* -s [Hawaiian] : a perennial herb (*Tacca pinnatifida*) of East India, Australasia, and Polynesia cultivated for its large starch-yielding root — see OTAHEITE ARROWROOT

pia–arach·noid \ˌ≈≈ˈ≈,≈\ *or* **pi·a·rach·noid** \ˌpīəˈrak,nȯid\ *n* [*¹pia*] : the pia mater and the arachnoid regarded as a single membrane investing the brain and spinal cord — **pia–arachnoidal** \ˌ≈≈ˈ≈,≈\ *adj*

pia·ce·vo·le \pyäˈchāvə,lā\ *adv* (*or adj*) [It, fr. LL *placibilis* fr. L *placēre* to please + *-ibilis* -ible — more at PLEASE] : PLEASANTLY, AGREEABLY — used as a direction in music

pi·a·cle \ˈpīəkəl\ *n* -s [L *piaculum,* fr. *piare* to appease, atone for — more at PIOUS] **1** *archaic* : a sacrificial offering : PIACULUM **2** *archaic* : OFFENSE, SIN, CRIME

pi·ac·u·lar \(ˈ)pīˈakyələ(r)\ *adj* [L *piacularis,* fr. *piaculum* + *-aris* -ar] **1** : SACRIFICIAL, EXPIATORY ⟨required to make a ~ offering for their sins⟩ **2** : requiring expiation : SINFUL, HEINOUS ⟨~ offense⟩ — **pi·ac·u·lar·ly** *adv* — **pi·ac·u·lar·ness** *n* -ES

pi·ac·u·lum \pīˈakyələm\ *n, pl* **piacu·la** \-lə\ [L] : a sacrificial rite by which communion is reestablished between a god and worshiper : an expiatory offering

pia family *n* [*²pia*] : TACCACEAE

¹piaffe \ˈpyaf\ *vi* **piaffed; piaffed; piaffing; piaffes** [F *piaffer,* lit., to strut] *of a horse* : to execute a piaffe

²piaffe \ˈ"\ *n* -s : a dressage movement consisting of a collected trot executed in place

piaffer *vi* -ED/-ING/-S [F] *obs* : PIAFFE

pi·al \ˈpīəl\ *adj* [*¹pia* + *-al*] : of or relating to the pia mater ⟨a ~ artery⟩

pia ma·ter \ˌpīəˈmād·ə(r), -ātə-\ *n* [ME, fr. ML, fr. L, tender mother] : the delicate and highly vascular membrane of connective tissue investing the brain and spinal cord, lying internal to the arachnoid and dura mater, dipping down between the convolutions of the brain, and sending an ingrowth into the anterior fissure of the cord

pia-ma·tral \ˌpīəˈmā·trəl\ *adj* [*pia mater* + *-al*] : of or relating to the pia mater : PIAL

pi·an \pēˈan, ˈpyän\ *n* -s [F, fr. Tupi & Guarani] : YAWS

pi·a·nette \ˌpēəˈnet\ *n* -s [*³piano* + *-ette*] : PIANINO

pian·gen·do \(ˈ)pyänˈjen(ˌ)dō\ *adv* (*or adj*) [It, fr. L *plangendum,* gerund of *plangere* to lament — more at PLAINT] : PLAINTIVELY — used as a direction in music

pi·a·ni·no \ˌpēəˈnē(ˌ)nō\ *n* -s [It, dim. of *piano*] : a small upright piano

pi·a·nism \ˈpēə,nizəm, pēˈa,-\ *n* -s [*³piano* + *-ism*] **1** : the art or technique of piano playing **2** : the composition or adaptation of music for performance on the piano

¹pi·a·nis·si·mo \ˌpēəˈnisə,mō\ *adv* (*or adj*) [It, fr. *piano* softly + *-issimo,* suffix denoting a high degree of (fr. L *-issimus,* superl. suffix)] : very softly — used as a direction in music; abbr. *pp, ppp*

²pianissimo \ˈ"\ *n, pl* **pianissi·mi** \-sə(ˌ)mē\ *or* **pianissimos** : a passage played, sung, or spoken very softly ⟨whispering *pianissimi*⟩

pi·an·ist \pēˈanəst, ˈpēən-\ *n* -s [F *pianiste,* fr. It *pianista,* fr. *piano* + *-ista* -ist] : one who plays the piano; *esp* : a skilled or professional performer on the piano

pi·a·niste \ˌpēəˈnēst\ *n* -s [F] : PIANIST; *often* : a female pianist

pi·a·nis·tic \ˌpēəˈnistik\ *adj* [*³piano* + *-istic*] **1** : relating to or characteristic of the piano **2** [*pianist* + *-ic*] : skilled in or adapted to piano playing — **pi·a·nis·ti·cal·ly** \-tək(ə)lē\ *adv*

pi·a·nis·tics \ˌ≈≈ˈnistiks\ *n pl but sometimes sing in constr* : the art or practice of performing on the piano; *esp* : display of virtuosity in piano playing

pianist's cramp *n* : painful spasm of the muscles of the forearm caused by excessive piano playing

pi·an·ka·shaw *or* **pi·an·ke·shaw** \pīˈaŋkə,shȯ\ *n, pl* **piankashaw** *or* **piankashaws** *or* **piankeshaw** *or* **piankeshaws** *usu cap* **1** : an Indian people of southwestern Indiana associated with the Miami **2 :** a member of the Piankashaw people

pi·an·net *or* **pi·a·net** \ˈpīə,net\ *n* -s [prob. fr. ¹*pie* + *Annet*, fr. *Ann*, feminine name + *-et*] **:** MAGPIE 1a

¹pi·a·no \pēˈä(,)nō, -ˈa(-\ *adv* (*or adj*) [It, fr. LL *planus* smooth, graceful] **:** SOFTLY, QUIETLY — used as a direction in music; opposed to *forte;* abbr. *p*

²piano \"\ *n* -s **:** a softly performed passage or tone (as in a voice or instrument)

³pi·ano \pēˈa(,)nō, -_nə *sometimes* -ˈä(-\ *n* -s [It, short for *pianoforte*, fr. *piano e forte* soft and strong, fr. *piano* soft (fr. LL *planus* smooth, graceful, fr. L, even, level, flat) + *e* and (fr. L *et*) + *forte* loud, strong (fr. L *fortis* strong); fr. the fact that its tones can be varied in loudness — more at FLOOR, FORT] **1 :** a stringed percussion instrument structurally derived from the dulcimer but historically from the clavichord and harpsichord and having steel wire strings stretched over a sounding board that sound when struck by felt-covered hammers operated from a keyboard and pedals that alter or modify the quantity and quality of sound produced — called also *pianoforte;* see GRAND PIANO, UPRIGHT PIANO **2 :** a machine operated by a keyboard for perforating the cards for a jacquard apparatus

piano accordion *n* **:** an accordion with a keyboard for the right hand resembling and corresponding to the middle register of a piano keyboard

piano accordion

piano as·sai \-əˈsī\ *adv* (*or adj*) [It] **:** very softly — used as a direction in music

pi·ano·forte \pēˈanə,fōr|d·(ē), |t(ē), -fȯr|, -fōə|, -fȯ(ə)|, ≈,≈≈ˈ≈; *in the 4-syllable pronunc,* |d· *does not occur before consonants other than* ᵊl\ *n* -s [It] **:** PIANO 1

pi·an·o·fort·ist \pēˈanə,fōrd·əst\ *n* -s **:** PIANIST

pi·an·o·graph \pēˈanə,graf, -rȧf\ *n* [³*piano* + *-graph*] **:** a melograph applied to a piano

piano hinge *n* **:** a hinge having a thin pin joint and extending along the full length of the turning part — called also *continuous hinge*

pi·a·no·la \,pēəˈnōlə\ *n* -s [*Pianola*] **1 :** a deal or hand (as in contract) that offers no difficulty in the play **2 :** something easy to perform or accomplish **:** CINCH

Pianola \"\ *trademark* — used for an automatic piano player

piano legs *n pl* **:** fat or disproportionately thick legs ⟨some were bowlegged and some were knock-kneed, some had pipestems and some *piano legs* —Esther Forbes⟩

pi·an·o·logue \pēˈanᵊl,ȯg *also* -,äg\ *n* -s [³*piano* + *-logue*] **:** a comic monologue accompanied by piano playing

pia·no no·bi·le \pyä(,)nōˈnōbē,lā\ *n* [It]**:** the principal story of a house

piano organ *n* **:** a mechanical piano built like a barrel organ and operated like a hand organ **:** STREET PIANO

piano player *n* **1 :** PIANIST **2 :** a mechanism for reproducing the playing of piano music usu. housed in a portable cabinet and consisting of an electropneumatic apparatus for turning a perforated roll representing the composition to be played and for actuating a series of levers which operate the piano keys

piano quartet *n* **:** a musical composition written for piano, violin, viola, and cello; *also* **:** the performers for such a composition

piano score *n* **:** a musical score having the separate instrumental parts condensed upon two staffs

piano-violin \≈ˈ≈(,)≈,≈≈ˈ≈\ *n* **:** a sostinente pianoforte producing tones resembling those of the violin

piano wire *n* [so called fr. its being used for the strings of pianos] **:** steel wire of high tensile strength and evenness of thickness containing 0.75 to 0.85 percent carbon

pi·a·po·co *n, pl* **piapoco** *or* **piapocos** *usu cap* **1 a :** an Arawakan people of the lower Guaviar river in Colombia, So. America **b :** a member of such people **2 :** the language of the Piapoco people

piarachnoid *var of* PIA-ARACHNOID

pi·a·rist \ˈpīərəst\ *n* -s *usu cap* [prob. fr. (assumed) NL *piarista*, fr. *piarum* (in the phrase *patres scholarum piarum* fathers of the religious schools) + *-ista* -ist] **:** a member of a religious teaching institute founded at Rome early in the 17th century by St. Joseph of Calasanza

pias *pl of* PIA

pias *abbr* piaster

pi·as·sa·va *also* **pi·as·sa·ba** *or* **pi·a·sa·va** *or* **pi·a·sa·ba** \,pēəˈsävə, -äbə\ *n* -s [Pg *piassaba*, fr. Tupi *piaçaba*] **1 a :** a coarse brown fiber that invests the bases of the leaf sheaths of a Brazilian palm and is used in making ropes, mats, and brushes; *also* **:** the palm (*Attalea funifera*) that bears this fiber and yields the coquilla nut **2 :** a fiber from a Brazilian palm (*Leopoldinia piassaba*) common along the Amazon river; *also* **:** the tree yielding this fiber **3 :** the stiff coarse bast fiber of an African palm (*Raphia vinifera*) **4 :** coarse fiber derived from any of several palms (as tucum, gomuti, and hemp palm)

piast \ˈpyäst\ *n* -s *usu cap* [after *Piast*, legendary peasant who was believed to be the founder of the dynasty in the 9th century] **1 :** a member of the first dynasty of Polish rulers that ended with the death of Casimir III in 1370 **2 a :** a member of the native Polish nobility **b :** a man of purely Polish descent

pi·as·ter *or* **pi·as·tre** \pēˈastə(r)\ *n* -s [F *piastre*, fr. It *piastra* thin metal plate, coin, fr. OIt, fr. L *emplastra*, *emplastrum* plaster — more at PLASTER] **1 a :** a Spanish dollar **:** PIECE OF EIGHT — see MONEY table **b :** a coin or note representing one piaster **2 a** (1) **:** any of several monetary units of some Middle Eastern countries (as Turkey, Egypt, or Syria) equal to $\frac{1}{100}$ pound — see MONEY table (2) **:** a former Saudi Arabian unit equal to $\frac{1}{22}$ rial **b :** a coin representing one of these units **3 a :** a monetary unit of Cyprus equal to $\frac{1}{9}$ shilling or $\frac{1}{180}$ pound sterling **b :** a coin representing this unit **4 a :** the basic monetary unit of French Indochina and (1956–75) of the Republic of Vietnam **b :** a coin or note representing one piaster

pi·at \ˈpī,at\ *n* -s [*projector infantry antitank*] **:** a short-range antitank gun used in the British and Canadian armies weighing 33 pounds and firing a 2.75-pound projectile that explodes on impact with force sufficient to penetrate four inches of tempered armor plate

piat·ti \ˈpyäd·ē\ *n pl* [It, fr. pl. of *piatto* plate, fr. *piatto* flat, fr. (assumed) VL *plattus* — more at PLATE] **:** CYMBALS

pi·az·za \pēˈazə, *in sense 1 usu* -atsə\ *n, pl* **piazzas** \-əz\ *or* **piaz·ze** \-t(,)sā\ [It, fr. L *platea* street, courtyard — more at PLACE] **1** *pl* **piazze :** an open square in an Italian or other European town **:** a town square or open market **2 a :** an arcaded and roofed gallery that often surrounds an open court; *also* **:** a portico or single colonnade before a building **b** *dial* **:** VERANDA, PORCH **syn** see BALCONY

pi·az·zaed \-əd\ *adj* **:** furnished with a piazza ⟨long-*piazzaed* summer hotel⟩

pib·ble \ˈpibəl\ *dial var of* PEBBLE

pib·gorn \ˈpib,gȯrn\ *also* **pib·corn** \-,kȯrn\ *n* -s [W, fr. *pib* pipe + *corn* horn] **:** an obsolete Welsh single-reed woodwind instrument similar to the hornpipe

pi·blok·to *or* **pi·block·to** \pəˈbläk(,)tō\ *n* -s [Esk *piblokto*] **:** a hysteria among Eskimos characterized by excitement and sometimes by mania, usu. followed by depression, and occurring chiefly in winter and usu. to women

pi·broch *or* **piob·aireachd** \ˈpē,bräk\ *n* -s [ScGael *piobaireachd* pipe-music, fr. *piobair* piper, fr. *pìob* pipe] **:** elaborate variations for the Scottish Highland bagpipe on a traditional theme

pibgorn

¹pic \ˈpēk\ *n* -s [F, prob. fr. Sp *pico*, fr. *picar* to prick, pierce, prob. fr. (assumed) VL *piccare* — more at PIKE (weapon)] **:** PEAK 5a

²pic \"\ *n* -s [F, fr. MF *picq*, fr. *piquer* to prick — more at PIKE] **:** ³PIQUE

³pic *var of* PIK

⁴pic \ˈpik\ *n, pl* **pics** *or* **pix** \-ks\ [short for *picture*] **1 :** PHOTOGRAPH ⟨these ~*s* tell the story —*Springfield (Mass.) Republican*⟩ **2 :** MOTION PICTURE

⁵pic \"\ *n* -s [Sp *pica*, fr. *picar* to prick] **1 :** the picador's lance **2** [by shortening] **:** PICADOR

⁶pic \"\ *vt* **pic·ed** \-kt\ **pic·ed; pic·ing** \-kiŋ\ **pics** \-ks\ **:** to prod or thrust at (a bull) with a pic

¹pi·ca \ˈpīkə\ *n* -s [prob. fr. ML, collection of church rules, prob. fr. L, magpie; perh. fr. its use in printing the service book and its resemblance to the colors of the bird] **1 :** an old size of type between small pica and english **2 a :** a size of type equivalent to 12 point **b :** a unit equal to 12 point or about ⅙ inch used in measuring composing materials, line and cut widths, and type-page dimensions — compare EM, LINE 9c, POINT SYSTEM **3 :** a size of typewriter type with 10 characters to the linear inch and six lines to the vertical inch

²pica \"\ *n* [NL, fr. L, magpie — more at ¹PIE] **1** *cap* **:** the genus containing the magpies **2** -s [prob. fr. the fact that the magpie is omnivorous] **:** a craving for and eating of unnatural substances (as chalk, ashes, or bones) that occurs in nutritional deficiency states (as aphosphorosis) in man or animals or in hysteric or insane conditions in man **:** GEOPHAGY — called also *depraved appetite;* compare LICKING DISEASE, WOOL EATING

pi·ca·cho \pəˈkä(,)chō\ *n* -s [Sp, fr. *pico* peak + *-acho* (fr. L *-aceus* -aceous)] **:** a large pointed isolated hill

pic·a·dor \ˈpikə,dȯ(ə)r, -ō(ə)\ *n, pl* **picadors** \-rz, -(ə)z\ *or* **picado·res** \,≈≈ˈdō,rēz, -dō,-, -rās\ [Sp, fr. *picado* (past part. of *picar* to prick, pierce) + *-or*] **:** a mounted member of the bullfighting cuadrilla who prods the bull with a lance in order to weaken the neck and shoulder muscles — compare TORERO

pic·a·du·ra \,pikəˈdu̇rə\ *n* -s [Sp, fr. *picado* (past part. of *picar*) + *-ura* -ure (fr. L)] **:** cut tobacco for cigarettes

pi·cae \ˈpī,sē\ *n pl, cap* [NL, fr. L *pica* magpie] *in former classifications* **:** an order of birds including most of the recent order Coraciiformes together with the parrots, cuckoos, and various passerine birds

pic·ail·lon \,pikəlˈyōn\ *n* -s [F — more at PICAYUNE] **:** PICAYUNE 1

picaninny *var of* PICKANINNY

¹pic·ard \ˈpikərd, -i,kärd\ *n* -s *cap* [F, fr. MF, fr. *Picardie* Picardy, province of northern France] **1 :** a native or inhabitant of Picardy in northern France **2 :** the French dialect of Picardy

²picard \"\ *adj, usu cap* [F, fr. *Picardie*] **:** of, relating to, or coming from Picardy

³picard \"\ *n* -s *usu cap* [ML *Picardus*, fr. *picardus* inhabitant or native of Picardy, fr. MF *picard;* fr. the fact that the group was founded by Picards who were accused of heresy and driven out of France] **:** one of a religious group active in Bohemia around the 15th century

pic·ar·dy third \ˈpikə(r)dē-\ *n, sometimes cap P* [trans. of F *tierce de Picardie;* fr. its being chiefly practiced in the church music of Picardy] **:** the major third as introduced into the final chord of a musical composition written in a minor key

pic·a·rel \,pikəˈrel\ *n* -s [F] **:** a small European marine fish (*Spicara smaris*) of the family Maenidae

¹pic·a·resque \ˈpikəˈresk *sometimes* ˈpēk-\ *adj* [Sp *picaresco*, fr. *picaro* rogue + *-esco* -esque] **:** of, relating to, or characteristic of rogues or rascals; *specif* **:** relating to or being a type of prose fiction of Spanish origin in modern literature in which the principal character is a rogue or vagabond and the narrative is a series of incidents or episodes connected chronologically but with little or no motivation or complication of plot ⟨~ novel⟩ ⟨~ career⟩ ⟨waifs of the ~ tradition —Asher Brunes⟩

²picaresque \"\ *n* -s **:** someone or something that is picaresque ⟨forming a kind of children's ~ of loosely connected episodes —Irving Howe⟩

pi·car·i·ae \pəˈka(a)rē,ē\ *n pl, cap* [NL, irreg. fr. L *picus* woodpecker — more at PIE] *in former classifications* **:** an order of birds nearly equivalent to the Coraciiformes but often including the parrots and cuckoos

pi·car·i·an \-rēən\ *adj* [NL *Picariae* + E *-an*] **:** of or relating to the Picariae

pi·carii \-rē,ī\ *n pl, cap* [NL, prob. alter. of *Picariae*] *in former classifications* **:** a group of birds practically equivalent to the Picariae together with the Clamatores

pic·a·ro \ˈpikə,rō\ *n* -s [Sp *picaro*] **:** ROGUE, TRAMP, VAGABOND, BOHEMIAN

¹pic·a·roon *or* **pick·a·roon** \ˈpikəˈrün\ *n* -s [Sp *picarón*, aug. of *picaro*] **1 :** PICARO **2 :** PIRATE, CORSAIR — used of a man or a ship

²picaroon \"\ -ED/-ING/-S *vi* **:** to act as a pirate or brigand watching or searching for a prize or victim

picas *pl of* PICA

¹pic·a·yune \,pikēˈyün, -kəˈ-\ *n* -s [F *picaillon* old copper coin of Piedmont, halfpenny, fr. Prov *picaioun*, fr. *picaio* money, fr. *pica* to strike, prick, sound, jingle (fr. — assumed — VL *piccare* to prick, pierce) + *-aio* -al (fr. L *-alia*) — more at PIKE (weapon)] **1 a :** a Spanish half real piece formerly current in Louisiana and other southern states **b :** HALF DIME **2 :** something of very small or of the least value ⟨not worth a ~⟩

²picayune \ˈ≈≈ˈ≈\ *adj* **1 :** of little value **:** PALTRY, MEASLY ⟨not more than two or three countries are carrying on any sort of forest research, and these programs are ~ —William Vogt⟩ ⟨compared to the total number of people employed, such cutbacks were still ~ —*Time*⟩ **2 :** concerned with trifling matters **:** petty, narrow, or small-minded in point of view ⟨within the limits of a short review it would seem ~ to be critical —W.F.Stolper⟩ **syn** see PETTY

pic·a·yun·ish \-nish, nēsh\ *adj* [¹*picayune* + *-ish*] **:** PICAYUNE ⟨a lifetime of ~ drudgery in the company of louts —H.L. Davis⟩ **syn** see PETTY

pic·ca·dil·ly \ˈpikəˈdilē\ *n* -ES [F *picadilles*, pl. of *picadille* pickadil — more at PICKADIL] **1 :** PICKADIL **2 :** a high wing collar worn by men in the late 19th century

piccage *var of* PICKAGE

pic·ca·lil·li \ˈpikəˈlilē\ *n* -s [earlier *piccalillo*, prob. alter. (perh. influenced by Sp *picadillo* hash) of ¹*pickle*] **:** a relish of chopped vegetables and pungent spices

pic·ca·nin \ˈpikə,nin\ *n* -s [Afrik, short for *piccaninny*, fr. E — more at PICKANINNY] *southern Africa* **:** PICKANINNY

pic·ca·nin·ny \ˈpikə,ninē\ *Brit var of* PICKANINNY

¹pic·co·lo \ˈpikə,lō\ *n* -s [It, lit., small, prob. fr. It dial. *picca* little] **1 :** a small shrill flute pitched an octave higher than the ordinary flute **2 :** a two-foot labial pipe-organ stop with a high piercing tone **3 :** an apprentice waiter in a European restaurant **:** BUSBOY **4** *South* **:** JUKEBOX

piccolo 1

²piccolo \"\ *adj* [It] *of a musical instrument* **:** smaller than ordinary size ⟨~ banjo⟩ ⟨~ cornet⟩ ⟨~ piano⟩

pic·co·lo·ist \-lōəst\ *n* -s **:** a piccolo player

pic·co·lo·pas·so red \ˈpikəlōˈpä(,)sō-\ *n* [*piccolopasso* fr. It *piccolo* small + *passo* raisin wine] **:** OXBLOOD

piccotah *var of* PICOTAH

pice \ˈpīs\ *n, pl* **pice** [Hindi *paisā*] **1 a :** a unit of value of India equal before 1955 to ¼ of an anna or $\frac{1}{64}$ rupee **b :** PAISA 1 **2 :** a bronze or copper coin representing one pice

pic·ea \ˈpisēə, ˈpīs-\ *n, cap* [NL, fr. L, pitch pine, fr. *pic-, pix* pitch] **:** a genus of temperate and arctic evergreen trees (family Pinaceae) having acicular leaves that are keeled on both surfaces and borne individually on persistent peg-shaped bases and cones that become pendulous and have reflexed scales — see SPRUCE

pic·e·in \ˈpisēən, ˈpīs-\ *n* -s [NL *Picea* (genus name of the Norway spruce *Picea abies*) + ISV *-in*] **:** a bitter crystalline glucoside $C_{14}H_{18}O_7$ obtained esp. from the needles of the Norway spruce and from the barks of willows

¹pi·cene \ˈpī,sēn\ *adj, usu cap* [L *picenus* of Picenum, fr. *Picenum*, ancient Roman province in eastern central Italy] **:** PICENIAN

²picene \"\ *n* -s *cap* **:** a native or inhabitant of ancient Picenum

³picene \"\ *n* -s [ISV *pic-* (fr. L *pic-, pix* pitch) + *-ene*] **:** a fluorescent crystalline hydrocarbon $C_{22}H_{14}$ obtained from the pitchy residue of petroleum or lignite tar; benzo-chrysene

¹pi·ce·ni·an \(ˈ)pīˈsēnēən\ *adj, usu cap* [L *picenus* Picenian + E *-an*] **:** of or relating to Picenum, the Picenes, or their language — compare SABELLIAN

²picenian \"\ *n* -s *cap* **1 :** PICENE **2 :** the Italic language of the Picenian people

pic·e·ous \ˈpisēəs, ˈpīs-\ *adj* [L *piceus*, fr. *pic-, pix* pitch + *-eus* -eous — more at PITCH] **:** of, relating to, or resembling pitch **:** PITCHY; *esp* **:** glossy brownish black in color

¹pi·chi \ˈpēchē\ *n* -s [AmerSp *pichi*, *piche*, fr. Araucan *pichi*, *pichin* small thing] **:** a small armadillo (*Zaedyus pichiy* syn. *Z. minutus*) of southern So. America

²pichi \"\ *n* -s [AmerSp *pichi*, *piche*, fr. Araucan *pichi*, *pichin*] **:** a Peruvian shrub (*Fabiana imbricata*) the herbage of which yields a tonic and diuretic

pich·i·ci·a·go \,pichēsēˈä(,)gō, |ā(-\ *also* **pich·i·cha·go** \-chēˈchā\ *n* -s [perh. fr. Allentiac] **:** a small burrowing So. American armadillo (*Chlamyphorus truncatus*) armored with many bands of plates that are laterally replaced by thick hair; *also* **:** a larger but very similar form that constitutes a separate genus (*Burmeisteria*)

pich·u·rim \ˈpishərəm\ *or* **pichurim bean** *n* -s [Pg *pichurim*, fr. Tupi *pechurim*] **:** one of the thick strongly aromatic cotyledons of a tropical American tree (*Nectandra pichurim*) used as a substitute for nutmegs and as a flavoring agent and stimulant tonic

pi·ci \ˈpī,sī\ *n pl, cap* [NL, fr. L, pl. of *picus* woodpecker — more at ¹PIE] **:** a group of birds formerly coextensive with or more extensive than the order Piciformes but now usu. made a suborder of Piciformes comprising the woodpeckers and piculets

pic·i·dae \ˈpisə,dē, ˈpīs-\ *n pl, cap* [NL, fr. *Picus*, type genus + *-idae*] **:** a family of birds (suborder Pici) comprising the woodpeckers, the piculets, and the wrynecks

pic·i·form \ˈpisə,fȯrm, ˈpīs-\ *adj* [prob. fr. (assumed) NL *piciformis*, fr. L *picus* woodpecker + *-iformis* -iform] **1 :** like a woodpecker **2** [NL *Piciformes*] **:** of or relating to the Piciformes

pic·i·for·mes \,≈≈ˈfȯr,mēz\ *n pl, cap* [NL, fr. *Picus* + *-iformes*] **:** an order of nonpasserine birds formerly restricted to the woodpeckers but now usu. including also the jacamars, puffbirds, barbets, honey guides, and toucans

pi·cine \ˈpī,sīn, -,sən\ *adj* [L *picus* woodpecker + E *-ine*] **:** of or relating to woodpeckers **:** PICIFORM

¹pick \ˈpik\ *vb* -ED/-ING/-S [ME *piken*, partly fr. MF *piquer* to prick, pick, pluck, strike & partly fr. (assumed) OE *pician* to prick (whence OE *picung* pricking); akin to MD *picken*, *pecken* to prick, hoe, pick, ON *pikka* to peck, hack — more at PIKE (weapon)] *vt* **1 :** to pierce, penetrate, or break up with a pointed instrument ⟨~*ing* the hard clay⟩ ⟨~ the surface of a millstone⟩ **2 :** to remove covering or adhering matter from bit by bit ⟨~*ed* the bones clean⟩; *specif* **:** to remove feathers from ⟨~ a goose⟩ **3 a :** to separate and remove with the fingers or fingertips **:** PLUCK ⟨~*ing* flowers for the table⟩ **b :** to take lightly, neatly, or selectively **:** CULL ⟨~*ing* only the ripest berries⟩ **c :** to gather one by one or bit by bit ⟨~ apples⟩ ⟨~ rags⟩ **d :** to take needed sorts from (standing type) ⟨if you ~ this form chalk the chase⟩ **4 :** to select from among a group **:** CHOOSE, NAME ⟨attempts to ~ an exact synonym —Johnson O'Connor⟩ ⟨tried to ~ the shortest route⟩ ⟨~*ed* his way cautiously through the swamp⟩ ⟨~*ed* a winner in the next race⟩ **5 :** to take the contents of (as a pocket) by stealth ⟨suspected of ~*ing* pockets⟩ ⟨skilled at ~*ing* the brains of his associates⟩ **6 :** to seek and find occasion for **:** provoke deliberately ⟨~ a quarrel⟩ **7 a :** to dig into or pull lightly at with fingertips or fingernails or a pointed instrument ⟨~*ing* his teeth with a knife⟩ ⟨~*ed* the shoestring until it came untied⟩ **b :** to pluck (the strings of a stringed musical instrument) with a plectrum or with the fingers to cause vibrations; *also* **:** to play music on (a stringed instrument) ⟨reputed to ~ a mighty mean guitar —G.S.Perry⟩ **c :** to loosen or pull apart with a sharp point ⟨~ wool⟩ ⟨~ oakum⟩ **8 :** to turn (a lock) with a wire or a pointed tool instead of the key esp. with intent to steal **9 a** *of a bird* (1) **:** to strike with the bill ⟨cruelly ~*ed* by the stronger chicks⟩ (2) **:** to take up (food) with the bill **b :** to eat sparingly or mincingly **10 :** to cause (bits of the surface of paper) to stick to type and be pulled off — used of ink **11 :** to finish (an edge of cloth) with a line of fine running stitches parallel to the edge ⟨pocket flaps ~*ed* by hand⟩ **~** *vi* **1 :** to use or work with a pick or pickax **2 :** to gather something from a plant **:** HARVEST ⟨the ~*ing* season⟩ ⟨fruit ripe for ~*ing*⟩ **3 :** PILFER, FILCH — used chiefly in the phrase *picking and stealing* **4 a** *of a bird* **:** to strike or take things up with the bill ⟨chickens ~*ing* about the yard⟩ **b :** to eat sparingly or mincingly **:** eat with little appetite ⟨~*ing* listlessly at his dinner⟩ **5 :** to lose bits of the surface by adhesion to the inked form during printing — used of paper — **pick a hole in :** to find or reveal a flaw in (as an argument) or blemish in (as a reputation) — **pick and choose :** to select with care and deliberation or with notable fastidiousness ⟨*picking and choosing*, dillying and dallying; not a man to have straightforward love for a woman —Virginia Woolf⟩ — **pick at 1 :** to try to pull or seize with the fingertips ⟨*picking at* the bedclothes⟩ **2 :** to find fault with continually **:** pick on **:** NAG, PESTER — **pick on 1 :** to pick at **:** HARASS, NAG, TEASE ⟨felt that he was *picked on* because he was better than the others —Robertson Davies⟩ **2** *or* **pick upon :** to single out for special attention **:** choose for a particular purpose or reason ⟨they had *picked on* a poor camping site⟩

²pick \"\ *n* -s **1 :** a blow or stroke with a pointed instrument **2 a :** the act of choosing or selecting **:** right or privilege of selection **:** CHOICE ⟨had the ~ of several jobs⟩ ⟨here are several brands, take your ~⟩ **b :** something that is or would be chosen first **:** the best or choicest part or member ⟨the ~ of the herd⟩ ⟨the ~ of the rebel forces⟩ **3** *dial* **a :** the taking of a bit of food **:** PECK **b :** a scanty meal **c :** a little bit **:** SCRAP **4 :** the portion or quantity of a crop gathered at one time **:** PICKING ⟨biggest berry ~ in several years⟩ ⟨the first ~ of peaches⟩ **5 :** something that is picked in with a point or pointed pencil **6 a :** a particle (as of hardened ink, dirt, or paper) embedded in the hollow of a letter and causing a spot on a printed sheet; *also* **:** the spot so caused **b :** a burr on the face of a plate or cut or of newly cast type **c :** the tendency of paper to pick **7 :** a maneuver (as in basketball) for cutting off a player from the play **:** SCREEN

³pick \"\ *adj* [²*pick*] **:** PICKED, BEST ⟨handed out the new guns to the ~ rifle shots of his crew —F.B.Gipson⟩

⁴pick \"\ *vb* -ED/-ING/-S [ME *pykken*, alter. of *picchen* pitch, v.] *vt* **1** *obs* **:** to set up or fix in place (as a tent) **2 a** *chiefly dial* **:** to throw or thrust with effort **:** HURL ⟨high as I could ~ my lance —Shak.⟩ **b :** PITCH ⟨time to ~ the hay⟩ **3** *dial* **:** to give birth to prematurely **4 :** to throw (a shuttle) across the loom **~** *vi* **1** *dial Eng* **:** to fall or topple forward **2 :** to throw the shuttle across the loom

⁵pick \"\ *n* -s **1** *dial Eng* **a :** the act of pitching or throwing **:** CAST **b :** something that is thrown **2 a :** a throw of the shuttle — used esp. in calculating the speed of a loom ⟨so many ~*s* per minute⟩ **b :** one filling thread — used esp. in describing the fineness of a fabric ⟨so many ~*s* to an inch⟩

⁶pick \"\ *n* -s [ME *pik*, *pek*, prob. alter. of ¹*pike*] **1** *obs* **a :** PIKE **b :** a sharp point **:** SPIKE **2 :** a heavy iron or steel tool pointed at one or both ends and often curved, wielded by means of a wooden handle inserted in an eye between the ends, and used by quarrymen, roadmakers, miners, and stonecutters **3** *dial Brit* **:** any of various pointed or pronged implements: as **a :** PITCHFORK **b :** GAFF **4 :** a sharp-pointed instrument for picking: as **a :** TOOTHPICK **b :** PICKLOCK **c :** PLECTRUM 1 **5** *dial Eng* **:** a diamond in playing cards **6 :** one of the points on the forepart of a figure skate blade

⁷pick \"\ *dial var of* PIQUE

pickaback *also* **pickback** *or* **pickapack** *var of* PIGGYBACK

pickaback plant \ˈ≈≈,≈-\ *also* **piggyback plant** \ˈ≈≈,≈-\ *n* **:** a glandular pubescent perennial herb (*Tolmiea menziesii*) of the family Saxifragaceae that is native to western No. America, has young plants borne at the junction of leaf blade and petiole, and is used as a foliage plant — called also *youth-on-age*

pick·able \'pikəbəl\ *adj* [[1]*pick* + *-able*] **:** able or suitable to be picked — **pick·able·ness** *n* -ES

pick·a·dil \'pikə,dil\ *or* **pick·a·dil·ly** \¦==¦dilē\ *n, pl* **pickadils** *or* **pickadillies** [F *picadille*, prob. fr. Sp *picado* pierced, cut (fr. past part. of *picar* to prick, pierce) + F *-ille*, dim. suffix — more at PIC] **1 :** a decorative trimming of cutwork that is scalloped, tabbed, or pointed and used as an edging on doublets, collars, and other garments of the late 16th and early 17th centuries **2 :** a ruff or standing collar trimmed with cutwork **3 :** a stiff support for a ruff or standing collar

pick·age *or* **pic·cage** \'pikij\ *n* -S [ME *pikage*, fr. *piken* to pick + *-age*] **:** a toll paid at fairs for leave to break ground for booths

pick-and-pick \¦==¦=\ *adj* [[5]*pick*] **:** capable of weaving a succession of different filling yarns into a fabric ⟨*pick-and-pick* loom⟩; *also* **:** woven with such yarns

pick-and-shovel \¦==¦==\ *adj* **:** done with or as if with a pick and shovel **:** LABORIOUS, DRUDGING ⟨*pick-and-shovel* routine⟩

pick·a·nin·ny *or* **pic·a·nin·ny** \'pikə,ninē, -ni\ *n* -ES [prob. modif. of Pg *pequenino* very little, fr. *pequeno* little, small + *-ino*, dim. suffix] **1 a :** a Negro child **b** *Africa* **:** a child of any of various native peoples (as Kaffirs or Zulus) **c** *Australia* **:** a child of one of the aboriginal peoples **2 :** OTTER 4

[1]**pickaroon** *var of* PICAROON

[2]**pick·a·roon** \¦pikə¦rün\ *n* -S [prob. fr. obs. F *piqueron* spur, prickle, fr. F *piquer* to prick, fr. MF — more at PIKE] **:** a piked pole with a hook used by lumbermen in river driving and by tracklayers in aligning railroad ties — called also *hookaroon*

pickaroons

pickaternie *var of* PICTARNIE

pick·a·way anise \'pikə,wā-\ *n* [*pickaway* perh. fr. *Pickaway* county, Ohio] **:** HOP TREE

[1]**pick·ax** *or* **pick·axe** \'pi,kaks\ *n* [alter. (influenced by *ax*, *axe*) of ME *pikois*, *pikeis* pickax, fr. OF *picois*, fr. *pic* pick, fr. L *picus* woodpecker — more at PIE] **:** [6]PICK 2

[2]**pickax** *or* **pickaxe** \"\ *vt* **:** to break up or dig with a pickax ~ *vi* **:** to work with a pickax

pickax sheldrake *n* **:** HOODED MERGANSER

pickax team *n* **:** UNICORN 4

pick-can \'=,=\ *n* [[1]*pick*] **:** a metal container holding water in which the stems of flowers are placed as they are cut

pick clock *or* **pick counter** *n* [[5]*pick*] **:** a device installed on a loom to determine the number of picks woven and thus the length of cut and amount of weaver's pay at a rate per thousand picks

pick dressing *n* [[2]*pick*] **:** a facing in cut stonework made by a pointed tool that leaves the surface in little pits

[1]**picked** \'pikt\ *adj* [ME *piked*, fr. past part. of *piken* to pick — more at PICK] **1 a** *obs* **:** ADORNED, TRIM **b** *obs* **:** DAINTY, FASTIDIOUS **2 :** selected as being the best obtainable or best for the purpose ⟨a ~ crew⟩ ⟨a raiding party of ~ men⟩

[2]**pick·ed** \'pikəd, -kt\ *adj* [ME, fr. [6]*pick* + *-ed*] *chiefly dial* **:** POINTED, PEAKED

picked dogfish *n* **1 :** SPINY DOGFISH **2 :** a sand shark (*Carcharias littoralis*)

pickedevant *n* -S [earlier *pique de vant*, prob. fr. F *pique* point, tip (fr. *piquer* to prick, puncture) + E *de vent*, modif. of F *devant* in front — more at DEVANT] *obs* **:** VANDYKE BEARD

pickeer *vi* -ED/-ING/-S [prob. modif. of F *picorer* to maraud, lit., to steal sheep, fr. MF, alter. (influenced by *piquer* to pick, prick) of *pecore* sheep, fr. OIt *pecora*, fr. L, neut. pl. of *pecor-*, *pecus* cattle — more at PIKE, FEE] **1** *obs* **:** to engage in piracy **:** PRIVATEER, MARAUD **2 a** *obs* **:** to skirmish in advance of an army **b** *obs* **:** SCOUT, RECONNOITER

pickeerer *n* -S *obs* **:** SKIRMISHER

pick·el \'pikəl\ *n* -S [prob. alter. of *pikel*] **:** ICE AX

pick·el·hau·be \'pikəl,haübə\ *n, pl* **pickelhau·ben** \-bən\ *or* **pickelhaubes** [G, alter. (influenced by *pickel* pickax) of MHG *beckelhūbe*, *beckenhūbe*, fr. *becken* basin (fr. OHG *beckīn*, fr. LL *bacchinon*) + *hūbe* cap (fr. OHG *hūba*); akin to OE *hȳf* hive — more at BASIN, HIVE] **:** a spiked helmet worn by German soldiers

[1]**pick·er** \'pikə(r)\ *n* -S [[1]*pick* + *-er*] **1 :** one that picks: as **a :** one that uses a pickax **b :** one that picks the fruit of agricultural crops **c :** a worker who selects material or articles suitable to a given purpose or one who picks out foreign matter **d :** one that operates a picking machine **2 :** any of various tools or devices: as **a :** a tool for clearing out small openings **b :** a machine for picking fibrous materials to pieces so as to loosen and separate the fiber; *specif* **:** a machine that precedes the card in textile manufacturing **c** *or* **picking machine :** a mechanical device consisting essentially of a revolving drum with numerous rubber fingers for the removal of feathers from table poultry

[2]**picker** \"\ *n* -S [[4]*pick* + *-er*] **:** the hard leather piece of a picker stick that hits the shuttle in a loom

pick·er·el \'pik(ə)rəl\ *n, pl* **pickerel** *or* **pickerels** [ME *pikerel*, dim. of *pik*, *pike* pike (fish) — more at PIKE] **1 a** *dial chiefly Brit* **:** a young or small pike **b :** any of several comparatively small fishes of the genus *Esox* — usu. used with a qualifying term; see CHAIN PICKEREL, GRASS PICKEREL, REDFIN PICKEREL **2 :** WALLEYE 4

pickerel frog *n* **:** a meadow frog (*Rana palustris*) of eastern No. America very similar to the leopard frog but distinguished by squarish dark spots on the back

pickerelweed \'=(=)=,=\ *n* **1 :** a plant of the genus *Pontederia; esp* **:** an American aquatic herb (*P. cordata*) growing in shallow water of streams and ponds and having spikes of blue flowers and cordate or sagittate leaves **2 :** any of various still-water species of the genus *Potamogeton*

pickerelweed family *n* **:** PONTEDERIACEAE

pick·er·ing \'pik(ə)riŋ\ *n* -S [alter. (prob. influenced by *herring*) of *pickerel*] **1 :** PICKEREL **2 :** SAUGER

pick·er·ing governor \'pik(ə)riŋ-\ *n, usu cap P* [after Thomas R. *Pickering* Am. engineer] **:** a governor in which the revolving balls act against curved flat springs

pick·er·ing·ite \'pik(ə)riŋ,īt\ *n* -S [John *Pickering* †1846 Am. scientist + E *-ite*] **:** a mineral $MgAl_2(SO_4)_4.22H_2O$ composed of a hydrous magnesium aluminum sulfate occurring in white to faintly colored fibrous masses

pickering's tree frog *n, usu cap P* [after Charles *Pickering* †1878 Am. naturalist] **:** SPRING PEEPER

picker stick *n* [[2]*picker*] **:** a lever that transmits the crank action of a loom motion into the thrust which drives the shuttle across the loom

picker-up \'=='=\ *n, pl* **pickers-up :** one who picks up (as bits of information or articles to be transported or cleared away); *specif* **:** one who picks up a fleece from the shearer and tosses it on the sorting table

pick·ery \'pik(ə)ri\ *n* -ES [[1]*pick* + *-ery*] *Scots law* **:** petty theft

[1]**pick·et** *also* **pi·quet** \'pikət, *usu* -əd·+V\ *n* -S [F *piquet*, fr. MF, fr. *piquer* to prick, pierce + *-et* — more at PIKE] **1 :** a pointed or sharpened stake, post, peg, or pale: as **a :** a pale used in making fences **b :** a stake used in constructing revetments, obstacles, and fences **c :** PICKET PIN 1 **d :** a peg for a tent rope **e :** RANGE POLE **f :** a stake on which in a former mode of military punishment the offender was forced to stand with one foot; *also* **:** this punishment **2 a :** a detached body of soldiers serving to guard an army from surprise and to oppose reconnoitering parties of the enemy — called also *outlying picket* **b :** a detachment kept ready in camp for such duty — called also *inlying picket* **c :** a detail to bring in those who have overstayed leave **d :** SENTINEL **e :** the duty of serving as a picket **f :** PICKET SHIP **3 :** a person posted by a labor organization at an approach to the place of work affected by a strike to ascertain the workmen going and coming and to persuade or otherwise influence them to quit working there; *also* **:** one posted similarly in a demonstration as a protest against a policy of government **4 :** an elongated bullet of cylindroconical form

[2]**picket** \"\ *vb* -ED/-ING/-S *vt* **1 :** to enclose, fasten, fence, or fortify with pickets **:** PALISADE **2 a :** to guard (as a camp or road) by an outlying picket **b :** to post as a picket **3 :** TETHER **4 a :** to post pickets at (a place of employment) **b :** to walk or stand in front of as a picket ~ *vi* **:** to take up the station and duties of a military or labor picket **:** do or go on picket duty

[3]**picket** \"\ *n* -S [origin unknown] **:** TERN

picketboat \'==,=\ *n* [[1]*picket* + *boat*] **:** a craft used (as by the Coast Guard) for harbor patrol

pick·et·er \'pikəd·ə(r), -ətə-\ *n* -S **:** PICKET 3

picket fence *n* **:** a fence made of pickets

picket line *n* **1 :** a position held by a line of pickets **2 :** a rope to which horses or mules are secured by halter shanks esp. while being groomed **3 :** a line of workers picketing a place of employment

picket pin *n* **1 :** a short stake driven into the ground for tethering a horse **2** *West* **:** any of several species of small ground squirrels of the genus *Citellus* which when sitting erect and motionless resemble a stake at a short distance

picket ship *n* **:** a ship or airplane stationed outside a formation of ships or a geographical area as a rescue or warning unit

picket fence

pick·fork \'pik,fȯrk\ *n* [ME *pikfork* — more at PITCHFORK] *dial Eng* **:** PITCHFORK

pick glass *n* [[5]*pick*] **:** a magnifying glass for comparing and counting yarns in fabrics

pick hammer *n* **:** a pick with one end sharp and the other blunt

pickier *comparative of* PICKY

pickiest *superlative of* PICKY

pick in *vt* [[1]*pick*] **:** to work (as a shadow) into a painting with a pointed tool

picking *n* -S [fr. gerund of [1]*pick*] **1 pickings** *pl* **:** something that is picked or picked up: as **a :** gleanable or eatable fragments esp. from refuse **:** SCRAPS ⟨the dogs have scanty ~*s* in that house⟩ **b :** share of spoils **c :** yield or return for effort expended ⟨the U-boats . . . shifted to fields where the ~*s* were easier —J.P.Baxter⟩ **2 :** a soft brick or one not fully burned

pick hammer

picking machine *n* **:** PICKER 2c

pick key *n* [[1]*pick*] **:** SKELETON KEY

[1]**pick·le** \'pikəl\ *n* -S [ME *pekille*, prob. fr. MD *pekel*, *peekel;* perh. akin to MD *picken*, *pecken* to prick, pick — more at PICK] **1 a :** a salt-and-water solution for preserving or corning fish or meat **:** BRINE **b :** plain or spiced vinegar for preserving vegetables, fruit, fish, eggs, oysters **c :** a bath usu. of sulfuric acid and salt for treating skins after bating in chrome tanning **d :** a bath of dilute sulfuric or nitric acid used to cleanse or brighten the surface of castings or other articles of metal **e :** a solution of caustic soda or other antiseptic used for cleaning wort or beer pipes **f :** any of various solutions (as of alcohol or formaldehyde) in which organic substances are soaked for preservation **2 a :** an unpleasant or difficult situation or condition **:** PLIGHT, PREDICAMENT, TROUBLE **b** *chiefly Brit* **:** a state of disorder **:** MESS ⟨small boy who had . . . left a bathroom in a ~ —C.S.Lewis⟩ **3 a :** an article of food (as a cucumber) that has been preserved in brine or in vinegar ⟨sour as a ~⟩ **b** *dial* **:** a fresh cucumber **4 a** *Brit* **:** a mischievous or troublesome person **b :** a person with a forbidding face or unsociable disposition — **in pickle :** in reserve or use on occasion **:** saved up **:** in readiness ⟨there's a rod *in pickle* for bad boys like you⟩ **syn** see PREDICAMENT

[2]**pickle** \"\ *vt* **pickled; pickled; pickling** \-k(ə)liŋ\ **pickles 1 a :** to steep in a solution of salt or vinegar for preservation ⟨~ herring⟩ ⟨~ fruit in syrup and vinegar⟩ **b :** to soak in a chemical solution in order to cleanse ⟨~ steel castings⟩ or condition ⟨*pickled* leather⟩ ⟨*pickled* seeds to induce sprouting⟩ **c :** to steep or soak (as seed) in a fungicide for the control of seed-borne diseases **d :** to hold (cut flowers) under refrigeration for an extended period of time with or without the use of a material in order to lengthen the life **2 a :** to give an antique appearance to — used of copies or imitations of paintings by the old masters **b :** to give a light finish to (as a piece of furniture) by bleaching or painting and wiping ⟨paneled in *pickled* pine⟩ **3 :** to rub salt or salt and vinegar on (a wound made by flogging)

[3]**pickle** \"\ *vb* [ME *pikelen*, fr. *piken* to pick + *-len* -le] **1** *chiefly Scot* **:** to pick a little at a time **:** eat sparingly or mincingly **2** *chiefly Scot* **:** TRIFLE, DAWDLE **3** *chiefly Scot* **:** PILFER

[4]**pickle** \"\ *n* -S [perh. fr. [3]*pickle*] **1 :** GRAIN, KERNEL **2** *dial* **:** a small quantity or amount — usu. with no preposition following ⟨get my ~ meal —Sir Walter Scott⟩

pickle-cured \¦==¦=\ *adj* **:** preserved in pickle

pickled *adj* [fr. past part. of [2]*pickle*] **1 :** preserved in or cured with pickle **2** *slang* **:** DRUNK ⟨seldom gets thoroughly ~ before dinner —*New Yorker*⟩

pickled brood *or* **pickle brood** *n* [prob. so called fr. the fact that the dead brood develops a sour smell] **:** a disease of honeybees caused by a fungus (*Aspergillus pollinis*)

pickle grass *or* **pickle plant** *n* **:** GLASSWORT 1

pickle-herring \'==,==\ *n* [obs. D *pekel-haerinck* (now *pekelharing*), fr. D *pekel* pickle + obs. D *haerinck* herring (fr. MD *harinc*, *herinc*) — more at HERRING] **1 :** a pickled herring **2** [D *pekelharing*, fr. G *pickelhering*, fr. *Pickelhering*, droll comic character of the 17th cent. German stage] **:** BUFFOON

pick·le·man \'pikəlmən\ *n, pl* **picklemen 1 :** one who makes or deals in pickles **2 :** one who prepares pickling solution

pick·ler \'pik(ə)lə(r)\ *n* -S **1 :** a vegetable (as a cucumber or onion) of a suitable size or quality for pickling **2 :** one that prepares or uses pickling solution for the preservation of food or hides or the cleaning of metal

pickleweed \'==,=\ *n* [[1]*pickle* + *weed*] **1 :** IODINE BUSH **2 :** GLASSWORT 1

pickleworm \'==,=\ *n* [[1]*pickle* + *worm*] **:** the larva of a brown-and-yellow moth (*Diaphania nitidales*) of the family Pyralididae that attacks the vines of cucurbits in No. and So. America

pickling cabbage *n* **:** any of various cabbages (as the red-leafed cabbage) that are esp. suitable for pickling

pickling cucumber *n* **:** any of various cucumbers grown primarily for pickling and characterized by the production of large crops of uniform rather small fruits with few spines

[1]**picklock** \'=,=\ *n* [[1]*pick* + *lock*] **:** one that picks a lock: as **a :** a tool for picking locks **b :** BURGLAR, THIEF

[2]**picklock** \"\ *adj* **:** resembling or relating to a picklock

pick·man \'pikmən\ *n, pl* **pickmen 1 :** a laborer who uses a pick or pickax **2 :** one in charge of picks (as in a mine)

pick-mattock \'='==\ *n* **:** a digging tool with a head having a point at one end and a transverse blade at the other

pickmaw \'=,=\ *n* [[1]*pick* + *maw*] *dial Eng* **:** BLACK-HEADED GULL

pick-me-up \'==,=\ *n* -S [fr. *pick* (*me*) *up*, v.] **1 :** something that stimulates or restores **:** TONIC, BRACER **2 :** KITTIWAKE

pick·nick *var of* PICNIC

pick off *vt* **1 :** to remove by plucking ⟨*picked* the dog hairs *off* his coat⟩ **2 a :** to shoot or bring down singly or selectively ⟨*picked off* his pursuers as they emerged from the pass⟩ ⟨wolves trailed the herd to *pick off* stragglers⟩ ⟨had time to reload and *pick off* first one single, then the other —W.G. Means⟩ **b :** to catch (a base runner) off base with a quick throw by either the pitcher or the catcher that often results in a put-out

[1]**pick-off** \'=,=\ *n* -S [*pick off*] **1 :** a baseball play in which a base runner is caught off base by a quick throw from the catcher or pitcher **2 :** electrical means for automatic correction of flight stability by means of impulses from a gyro

[2]**pick-off** \"\ *adj* [*pick off*] **:** REMOVABLE ⟨*pick-off* gears for changing speeds of a lathe⟩

pick out *vt* [ME *piken out*, fr. *piken* to pick + *out* — more at PICK] **1 a :** to take out or remove by picking **:** peck out **b :** to play the notes of (a melody) by ear or one by one **2 a :** SELECT, CHOOSE ⟨bright students are *picked out* at the age of 10 or 11 and brought along on scholarships —Douglas Bush⟩ **b :** to make out or distinguish with the senses or the understanding ⟨many famous summits can be *picked out* on a clear day —O.S.Nock⟩ **3 a :** to relieve (a plain surface) or accentuate (a pattern or outline) with lines or flecks of color **b :** to cause to stand out clearly **:** make distinct or emphatic ⟨help to *pick out* morals which have already been hinted —G.N.Flew⟩ ⟨in snow-white gaucho costume, *picked out* by the spotlights —Winifred Bambrick⟩

pickout \'=,=\ *n* -S [*pick out*] **:** cannibalistic attack of young fowls on the extruded tissues of individuals in the flock afflicted with prolapse of the cloaca or oviducts

pick over *vt* [[1]*pick*] **:** to examine (a collection of objects or mass of material) in order to select the best or remove unwanted bits ⟨*pick over* a junkpile⟩ ⟨*picked* the berries *over* for stems and leaves⟩

pickover \'=,==\ *n* -S [*pick over*] *archaic* **:** FLOAT 10

pickpocket \'=,==\ *n* **1 :** one who steals money or valuables that someone is carrying in his pockets or on his person **2 :** SHEPHERD'S PURSE

pickpole \'=,=\ *n* [[6]*pick* + *pole*] **:** PIKE POLE

pickproof \'=¦=\ *adj* [[1]*pick* + *proof*] **:** designed to prevent picking ⟨~ lock⟩

pick·purse \'pik,pərs\ *n* [ME *pikepurs*, *pikepors*, fr. *piken* to pick + *purs*, *pors* purse — more at PURSE] **1** *archaic* **:** PICKPOCKET **2 :** SHEPHERD'S PURSE

picks *pres 3d sing of* PICK, *pl of* PICK

pick sack *or* **picker sack** *n* **:** a deep cloth bag suspended from the shoulder with a wide band and dragged between cotton rows to receive the cotton picked by hand

[1]**pick's disease** \'piks-\ *n, usu cap P* [after Arnold *Pick* †1924 Czech psychiatrist] **:** a condition marked by progressive impairment of intellect and judgment and transitory aphasia, caused by progressive atrophic changes of the cerebral cortex, and found chiefly in elderly women

[2]**pick's disease** *n, usu cap P* [after Friedel *Pick* †1926 Ger. physician] **:** pericarditis with adherent pericardium resulting in circulatory disturbances with edema and ascites

picks·man \'piksmən\ *n, pl* **picksmen** [*picks* (poss. of [6]*pick*) + *man*] **:** a workman who uses a pickax

pick·some \'piksəm\ *adj* [[1]*pick* + *-some*] **:** PARTICULAR, FASTIDIOUS, CHOOSY

pickthank \'=,=\ *n* [fr. the phrase *pick a thank* "to seek someone's favor"] *archaic* **:** one who tries to curry favor by flattery, sycophancy, or talebearing ⟨smiling ~*s* and base newsmongers —Shak.⟩

pickthatch *n* [contr. of obs. E *picked-hatch*, fr. E [2]*picked* + [1]*hatch;* fr. the fact that the entrance would usu. be guarded by iron pikes] *obs* **:** BROTHEL

pick tongs *n pl* [[6]*pick*] **:** tongs for handling hot metal

[1]**picktooth** \'=,=\ *n* [[1]*pick* + *tooth*] **:** TOOTHPICK

[2]**picktooth** \"\ *adj* **:** LEISURELY, INDOLENT

pick tree *n* [[6]*pick*] **:** HERCULES'-CLUB 3

pick up *vb* [ME *piken up*, fr. *piken* to pick + *up* — more at PICK] *vt* **1 a :** to take up or lift from the ground or a low surface ⟨*picking up* sticks for firewood⟩ **:** lift or recover something dropped or fallen ⟨bent to *pick up* his hat⟩ ⟨tripped and fell, *picked* himself *up* and ran on⟩ **b :** to take or accept with the purpose of paying ⟨offered to *pick up* the bill for all expenses of the trip⟩ **c :** to do over (a dropped stitch) **d :** to start (a knitting or crochet stitch) by inserting the needle into a loop of a finished stitch **2 a :** to take (passengers or freight) into a vehicle or ship **b :** to rescue from the water ⟨*picked up* by a passing freighter⟩ **3 a** (1) **:** to get by bits **:** acquire or gain as occasions offer **:** acquire casually ⟨*picked up* a few dollars doing odd jobs⟩ (2) **:** to learn informally ⟨*pick up* a trade⟩ ⟨where do you *pick up* such expressions⟩ **b :** to gather in or up one by one ⟨time to *pick up* tools and go home⟩ **c :** to tidy up **:** put in order ⟨this room must be *picked up* before the company comes⟩ **4 a :** to happen upon or catch sight of ⟨*picked up* the harbor lights⟩ **b :** to bring within the range of vision or audition (as by a telescope or radio) **:** discover or receive (as a radio wave or signal) by ear **5 a :** to enter informally into conversation or companionship with ⟨had a brief affair with a girl he *picked up* in a bar⟩ **b :** to find or come upon and take into custody ⟨*picked up* by the police for questioning⟩ **6 a :** to come to and follow ⟨*picked up* the trail of the fugitives⟩ **b :** to respond promptly to (an acting cue) ⟨if he *picks up* his cue and speaks promptly he will kill the laugh —Henning Nelms⟩ **c :** to move in conjunction with in an athletic contest: as (1) **:** to move into position to guard (an opponent) (2) **:** to move so as to gain the protection of (a teammate) **7 :** PILFER ⟨didn't bother to *pick up* any other valuables —*N.Y.Times*⟩ **8 :** to prepare (a meal) from materials at hand or already cooked **9 a :** to brace up **:** revive the spirits of ⟨a bite of something might *pick* you *up* as well as me —Ellen Glasgow⟩ **b :** to increase the speed or tempo of ⟨urging the band to *pick* it *up*⟩ **10 :** to resume (a narrative, an activity, or a relation) after a break ⟨narrative switches back . . . to *pick up* its major characters —Eichard Sullivan⟩ **11 :** LIFT 12 ~ *vi* **1 :** to recover speed, vigor, or activity (as after a check or setback) ⟨business began to *pick up* towards summer⟩ **:** IMPROVE **2 :** to gain speed **:** ACCELERATE ⟨to see how fast they can *pick up* from a standing start —*Lamp*⟩ **3 :** to strike up an acquaintance **:** enter informally on a relationship ⟨the danger of *picking up* with anyone who happens to come along —Erle Stanley Gardner⟩ **4 :** to gather up or pack up one's belongings ⟨many other Georgians had *picked up* and gone to Texas —Laura Krey⟩

[1]**pickup** \'=,=\ *n* -S [*pick up*] **1 :** the act or process of picking up: as **a :** the taking aboard of passengers, freight, or mail by a carrier **b :** the taking on of a railway car by a train or of a barge by a tow **c :** revival of activity (as after a business slump) **:** IMPROVEMENT **d :** ACCELERATION **e :** ARREST **f :** the act of making a chance acquaintance **g :** the fielding or hitting of a ball just after it strikes the ground; *specif* **:** HALF VOLLEY **2 a :** translation of mechanical movements into electrical impulses in the reproduction of sound **b :** the reception of sound in a radio transmitting apparatus for conversion into electrical energy **c :** the conversion of the image of a scene into electrical energy in the transmitting apparatus **3 a :** a dance step consisting of a hop with a pullback **b :** a progressive accumulation of the other couples by the leading couple in square dancing **4 :** something that is picked up: as **a :** an article (as a golf ball) found by chance **b :** an article or consignment taken up for shipment by a carrier **c :** a railway car, barge, trailer added to a train, tow, or tractor **d :** type matter saved for reuse with new copy **e** (1) **:** a sum or balance brought forward on accounts or records esp. in machine bookkeeping (2) **:** the receipts collected from a single cash register or the total collected for a certain period **f :** material to be broadcast or telecast that originates outside the studio or station ⟨the program was a live ~ from the theater⟩ **g :** an unaccented note or group of notes preceding the strong beat of the measure and beginning a musical phrase or composition **:** ANACRUSIS **5 :** someone who is picked up: as **a :** HITCHHIKER **b :** a chance and usu. temporary companion or acquaintance ⟨may pass the disease along to ~, prostitute, or wife —H.V.Tooker⟩ **6 :** something that picks up or is used for picking up: as **a :** [3]BRUSH 3a **b :** a device (as a microphone or a thermocouple) that serves as a transducer between the source of vibrations (as of sound or heat) to be detected or measured and the part of the system that translates the collected signals into observable form; *esp* **:** a device for converting record groove undulations into corresponding electrical voltages which may be amplified in an electrical phonograph **c :** the electrical system or arrangements for connecting to a broadcasting station or studio a radio or television program produced outside the studio **d :** the apparatus used for picking up images and sound for television transmission ⟨the field ~ included four cameras⟩ **e :** an attachment to a harvester used for picking up grain or hay left in windrows by a swather for curing **7** *or* **pickup truck :** a light truck having an open body with low sides and tailboard mounted usu. on a passenger car chassis

pickup 7

²pickup \"\ *adj* **1 :** picking up or used in picking up ⟨~ station⟩ ⟨~ tongs⟩ **2 :** utilizing the available or convenient without prior planning ⟨a ~ ballgame⟩ ⟨leftovers enough for a ~ meal⟩
pickup arm *n* **:** TONE ARM
pick-up baler \'ˌ=-\ *n* **:** a hay baler that gathers hay from a windrow and compresses it into bales
pickup cartridge *n* **:** a usu. removable portion of a phonograph pickup containing the stylus and the mechanism for converting stylus motion into an electrical voltage
pickup current *or* **pickup voltage** *n* **:** the current or voltage at which a magnetic contactor starts to close under normal operating temperature
pick–up man *n* **:** a mounted attendant in a rodeo who lifts a bucking horse rider from his mount when the time limit has expired
pickup service *n* **:** the collection of small shipments from a customer's door by trucks acting for railroads, truck lines, or airlines
pickup tube *n* **:** CAMERA TUBE
pick·wick·i·an \(')pik¦wikēən\ *adj, usu cap* [Samuel *Pickwick*, benevolent and simple-minded character in the novel *Pickwick Papers* (1836–37) by Charles Dickens †1870 Eng. novelist + E *-an*] **1 :** marked by simplicity and generosity of character or by an appearance and manner suggesting these qualities ⟨struck one as an almost *Pickwickian* old gentleman —Louis Auchincloss⟩ ⟨welcomed by a *Pickwickian* headmaster, a jolly, rotund man —Norris Houghton⟩ **2** [so called fr. the peculiar sense given to common words by Mr. Blotton and Mr. Pickwick, characters in the novel *Pickwick Papers*] **:** intended or taken in a sense other than the obvious or literal one **:** specially or whimsically limited or distorted in intended meaning ⟨injustice . . . is merely a *Pickwickian* expression for what human beings do not like —*Nation*⟩ ⟨evidently England is starving to death, if at all, only in a strictly *Pickwickian* sense —*Economist*⟩
picky \'pikē, -ki\ *adj* -ER/-EST [¹*pick* + *-y*] **:** overly fastidious **:** FUSSY, CHOOSY, FINICKY ⟨a ~ eater⟩ ⟨a tedious day of ~ objections to the agriculture appropriations bill —*Time*⟩
¹pic·nic *also* **pick·nick** \'pik,nik\ *n* -S *often attrib* [G or F; G *picknick*, fr. F *pique-nique*, prob. redupl. (influenced by obs. F *nique* trifle, of imit. origin) of *piquer* to pick, peck, prick — more at PIKE] **1 a :** a social entertainment at which each person contributes food to a common table **b :** an excursion or outing with food usu. provided by members of the group and eaten in the open **2 a :** a pleasant or amusing experience **:** a time free of ordinary cares and responsibilities ⟨I don't expect being married to be a ~ like you seem to —Josephine Pinckney⟩ **b :** an easy task or feat ⟨as the fight started . . . any thoughts . . . that this was to be a ~ for him were dissipated —*Ring*⟩ **3 a :** a standard size of container for canned food **b :** a standard size of cheddar cheese **4** *or* **picnic ham** *or* **picnic shoulder :** a shoulder of pork with much of the butt removed commonly smoked and often boned — see PORK illustration
²picnic \"\ *vb* **picnicked; picnicked; picnicking; picnics** *vi* **:** to go on or hold a picnic *vt* **:** to entertain with a picnic ~ *vi* **:** to go on or hold a picnic **:** eat in picnic fashion — **pic·nick·er** \-kə(r)\ *n* -S
pic·nicky \-kē\ *adj* [¹*picnic* + *-y*] **:** relating to or characteristic of picnics
picnometer *var of* PYCNOMETER
pico- *comb form* [ISV, perh. fr. It *piccolo* small — more at PICCOLO] **:** one trillionth (10^{-12}) part of ⟨*pico*farad⟩ ⟨*pico*gram⟩
pi·coid \'pī,kȯid\ *adj* [*pic-* (fr. NL *Picidae*) + *-oid*] **:** resembling or related to the Picidae
picol *var of* PICUL
pic·o·line \'pikə,lēn, -,lən\ *n* -S [ISV *pic-* (fr. L *pic-, pix* pitch) + *-ol* + *-ine* — more at PITCH] **:** any of the three liquid pyridine bases $CH_3C_5H_4N$ that are monomethyl derivatives of pyridine, are found in coal tar, ammonia liquor, and bone oil, and are used chiefly as solvents and in organic synthesis: **a :** the flammable alpha derivative that has an odor resembling that of pyridine — called also *2-picoline* **b :** the beta derivative that has a sweetish odor and is used in making nicotinic acid — called also *3-picoline* **c :** the gamma derivative used in making isonicotinic acid — called also *4-picoline*
pic·o·lin·ic acid \¦==¦linik-\ *n* **:** a crystalline acid $C_5H_4N(COOH)$ obtained by oxidation of 2-picoline; 2-pyridinecarboxylic acid
pi·co·pi·co·gram \'pīkō'pīkō,gram\ *n* [*pico-* + *pico-* + *-gram*] **:** a unit of mass equal to 10^{-24} gram — abbr *ppg*
picory *n* -ES [MF *picoree*, fr. *picorer* to maraud + *-ee -y* — more at PICKEER] *obs* **:** PILLAGE, FORAGING
¹pi·cot \'pē(,)kō\ *n* -S *often attrib* [F, lit., small point, fr. MF, fr. *pic* peak, point, prick, fr. *piquer* to prick] **1 :** one of a series of small ornamental loops forming an edging on ribbon or lace **2 :** an edge finish made by cutting through the center of a line of machine hemstitching or folding on a line of open stitches in hosiery **3 :** one of the small loops used for tatting and lace patterns
²picot \"\ *vt* -ED/-ING/-S **:** to finish with a picot
pi·co·tah *or* **pi·cot·tah** *or* **pic·co·tah** \pə'kōd·ə, -kŭd·ə\ *n* -S [Pg *picota*, lit., post, pillory, fr. *pico* point, peak, fr. *picar* to prick, pierce, fr. (assumed) VL *piccare* — more at PIKE] **:** a counterpoised sweep used in India for raising water from wells
pic·o·tee \,pikə'tē\ *n* -S [modif. of F *picoté* furnished with points, fr. past part. of *picoter* to mark with points or pricks, fr. *picot* small point, prick; fr. a variety of carnation that had a white ground marked with specks of color] **:** a flower (as carnation, tulip, rose) having one basic color with a margin of another color ⟨~ pattern⟩ ⟨~ edging⟩
pic·o·tite \'pikə,tīt\ *n* -S [F *picotite*, fr. *Picot*, Baron de la Peyrouse †1818 Fr. botanist + F *-ite*] **:** a dark brown variety of spinel containing chromium and iron
¹pic·quet *var of* PIQUET
²pic·quet \'pikət\ *chiefly Brit var of* PICKET
pic·quet·er \'pikəd·ə(r)\ *n* -S [F *piquet (de fleurs)* spray of flowers, spade, post, pointed object (fr. *piquer* to prick + *-et*) + E *-er* — more at PIKE] **:** one who bunches artificial flowers
picr- *or* **picro-** *comb form* [F, fr. Gk, fr. *pikros* bitter — more at PAINT] **1 :** bitter ⟨*Picr*amnia⟩ ⟨*Picro*dendron⟩ **2 :** picric acid ⟨*picr*yl⟩ ⟨*picro*carmine⟩ **3 :** containing magnesium ⟨*picro*merite⟩
pic·ram·ic acid \(')pi¦kramik-\ *n* [*picramic* ISV *picr-* + *amic* (acid)] **:** a red crystalline acid $C_6H_2(NO_2)_2(NH_2)OH$ obtained by reducing picric acid and used chiefly in making azo dyes
pic·ram·ide \pik'ra,mīd, 'pikrə,-, -məd\ *n* [*picr-* + *amide*] **:** a yellow crystalline compound $C_6H_2(NO_2)_3NH_2$ made from picryl chloride and ammonia; 2,4,6-trinitro-aniline
pic·ram·nia \pik'ramnēə\ *n, cap* [NL, irreg. fr. *picr-* + Gk *thamnos* shrub + NL *-ia* — more at THAMN-] **:** a genus of tropical American shrubs or trees (family Simaroubaceae) with alternate pinnate leaves, small dioecious flowers, and baccate fruit — see BITTERBUSH
pic·ras·min \pik'razmən\ *n* -S [NL *Picrasma* (genus name of the bitterwood *Picrasma excelsum* — fr. Gk *pikrasmos* bitterness, fr. *pikros* bitter) + ISV *-in*] **:** a bitter crystalline principle $C_{22}H_{28}O_6$ occurring in Jamaica quassia
pic·rate \'pi,krāt\ *n* -S [ISV *picr-* + *-ate*] **1 :** a salt or ester of picric acid **2 :** a molecular complex formed by addition of picric acid to another compound (as a bicyclic or polycyclic aromatic hydrocarbon)
pic·ric acid \'pikrik-, -rēk-\ *n* [*picric* ISV *picr-* + *-ic*] **:** a bitter toxic explosive yellow crystalline strong acid $C_6H_2(NO_2)_3OH$ made usu. by nitration of phenolsulfonic acids or chlorobenzene and used chiefly in high explosives, as a dye or biological stain, as an antiseptic, and as a precipitant for organic bases and polycyclic hydrocarbons; 2,4,6-trinitrophenol
-pic·rin \'pikrən\ *n suffix* -S [ISV *-picr-* (fr. Gk *pikros* bitter) + *-in*] **1 :** bitter substance ⟨*genti*opicrin⟩ **2 :** substance related to picric acid ⟨*chloro*picrin⟩
pic·ris \'pikrəs\ *n, cap* [NL, fr. L, bitter lettuce, a salad, fr. Gk *pikris* oxtongue, fr. *pikros* bitter] **:** a genus of weedy herbs (family Compositae) chiefly of the Old World having leafy stems, large yellow ray flowers, and linear achenes
pic·rite \'pi,krīt\ *n* -S [F, fr. *picr-* + *-ite*] **1 :** a variety of olivine-diabase without feldspar **2 :** a variety of often porphyritic peridotite composed of either augite or hornblende and olivine
pic·ro·carmine \¦pikrō+\ *n* [ISV *picr-* + *carmine*] **:** a stain for tissue sections made by mixing solutions of carmine and picric acid
pic·ro·chromite \"+\ *n* [*picr-* + *chromite*] **:** MAGNESIOCHROMITE
pic·ro·crocin \¦pikrō+\ *n* [*picr-* + *crocin*] **:** a bitter crystalline terpene-glucoside $C_{16}H_{26}O_7$ from saffron (sense 2)
pic·ro·den·dra·ce·ae \,pikrōden'drāsē,ē\ *n pl, cap* [NL, fr. *Picrodendron*, type genus + *-aceae*] *in some classifications* **:** a family of plants coextensive with the genus *Picrodendron*
pic·ro·den·dron \,pikrō'dendrən\ *n, cap* [NL, fr. *picr-* + *-dendron*] **:** a small genus of West Indian trees and shrubs (family Simaroubaceae) with bitter wood, 3-foliolate leaves, and dioecious flowers — see JAMAICA WALNUT
pic·ro·lite \'pikrə,līt\ *n* -S [G *pikrolith*, fr. *picr-* + *-lith* -lite] **:** a dark green, gray, or brown fibrous variety of serpentine
pic·ro·lon·ic acid \¦pikrə¦länik-\ *n* [*picrolonic* fr. *picr-* + *-olon-* (in *pyrazolone*) + *-ic*] **:** a yellow crystalline acidic compound $C_{10}H_8N_4O_5$ made by nitration of methyl-phenylpyrazolone that yields yellow solutions with alkalies and is used as a precipitant for organic bases (as alkaloids)
pic·rom·er·ite \pi'krämə,rīt\ *n* -S [ISV *picr-* + *mer-* + *-ite*; orig. formed in It] **:** a mineral $K_2Mg(SO_4)_2.6H_2O$ consisting of a hydrous magnesium potassium sulfate and occurring as a white crystalline incrustation
pic·ro·pharmacolite \¦pikrō+\ *n* -S [G *pikropharmakolith*, fr. *pikr-* picr- + *pharmakolith* pharmacolite — more at PHARMACOLITE] **:** a mineral $(Ca,Mg)_3(AsO_4)_2.6H_2O$ composed of a hydrous arsenate of calcium and magnesium
pic·ro·podophyllin \"+\ *n* [ISV *picr-* + *podophyllin*] **:** a bitter crystalline compound obtained from podophyllin
pic·ro·rhi·za \,pikrə'rīzə\ *n* -S [NL, fr. *picr-* + *-rhiza*] **:** the dried rhizome of a Himalayan herb (*Picrorhiza kurrooa*) of the family Scrophulariaceae that is used in India as a bitter tonic and antiperiodic
pic·ro·tin \'pikrəd·ən\ *n* -S [ISV *picrotoxin* + *-in*] **:** a nonpoisonous bitter crystalline compound $C_{15}H_{18}O_7$ obtained from picrotoxin
pic·ro·tox·in \,pikrə'täksən\ *n* [ISV *picr-* + *tox-* + *-in*; orig. formed as F *picrotoxine*] **:** a poisonous bitter crystalline principle $C_{30}H_{34}O_{13}$ found esp. in cocculus indicus that is an equimolecular compound of picrotoxinin and picrotin and is a stimulant and convulsant drug administered intravenously as an antidote for poisoning by overdoses of barbiturates
pic·ro·tox·in·in \-sənən\ *n* -S [*picrotoxin* + *-in*] **:** a poisonous bitter crystalline compound $C_{15}H_{16}O_6$ obtained from picrotoxin
pic·ry \'pikrē\ *n* -ES [perh. fr. *picr-* + *-y*] **:** POISON IVY
pic·ryl \'pikrəl\ *n* -S [ISV *picr-* + *-yl*] **:** the univalent radical $C_6H_2(NO_2)_3$— derived from picric acid by removal of the hydroxyl group; 2,4,6-trinitro-phenyl
pics *pl of* PIC
pict \'pikt\ *n* -S *usu cap* [ME *Pictes*, pl., Picts, fr. LL *Picti*] **:** one of a possibly non-Celtic people older than the Gaelic and Brythonic peoples who once occupied Great Britain, were in many places displaced by the Britons, carried on continual border wars with the Romans, and about the 9th century became finally amalgamated with the Scots
pict *abbr* pictorial
pic·tar·nie \'pik,tärnī\ *also* **pick·a·ter·nie** \'pikə,tərnī\ *n* -S [origin unknown] **1** *chiefly Scot* **:** BLACK-HEADED GULL **2** *chiefly Scot* **:** COMMON TERN
pic·ta·vi \pik'tä,vī\ *n pl, usu cap* [LL] **:** PICTONES
¹pict·ish \'piktish, -tēsh\ *adj, usu cap* [*Pict* + *-ish*] **:** of or relating to the Picts **:** resembling a Pict
²pictish \"\ *n* -ES *usu cap* **:** the language of the Picts that is known only from a few proper names, glosses, and inscriptions
picto- *comb form* [L *pictus* (past part. of *pingere* to paint) + E *-o-* — more at PAINT] **:** picture ⟨*picto*graph⟩
pic·to·gram \'piktə,gram\ *n* [ISV *picto-* + *-gram*] **:** PICTOGRAPH
pic·to·graph \-raf, -raa(ə)f, -raif, -räf\ *n* [*picto-* + *-graph*] **1 :** an ancient or prehistoric drawing or painting on a rock wall (as of a cave, cliff) — compare PETROGLYPH **2 a :** a pictorial representation of some object used to symbolize that object in pictography or in writing that includes elements of pictography **b :** a record in such symbols **3 :** one of the symbols belonging to any graphic system the characters of which are to a considerable extent pictorial in appearance regardless of whether the symbols serve a pictographic, ideographic, or phonetic function **4 :** a diagram representing statistical data by pictorial forms which can be varied in color, size, or number to indicate change
pic·to·graph·ic \¦==¦grafik\ *adj* [ISV *picto-* + *-graphic*] **1 :** consisting of or characterized by use of pictographs ⟨a ~ script⟩ ⟨the ~ stage in the development of writing⟩ **2 :** being a pictograph ⟨a ~ character⟩ **3 :** displaying the characteristics of a pictograph ⟨a character in its primitive ~ form⟩
pic·to·graph·i·cal·ly \-fək(ə)lē\ *adv* **:** by means of or in the manner of pictographs
pic·tog·ra·phy \pik'tägrəfē\ *n* -ES [ISV *picto-* + *-graphy*] **:** use of pictographs **:** PICTURE WRITING 1 a
pic·to·nes \'piktə,nēz\ *n pl, usu cap* [L] **:** an ancient people of western Gaul
¹pic·to·ri·al \(')pik¦tōrēəl, -tȯr-\ *adj* [LL *pictorius* pictorial (fr. L *pictor* painter + *-ius* -ious) + E *-al* — more at PICTURESQUE] **1 :** of or relating to a painter, a painting, or the painting or drawing of pictures ⟨~ perspective⟩ ⟨~ invention⟩ **2 a :** consisting of pictures **:** being in the form of a picture or pictograph ⟨~ records⟩ **b :** illustrated by or adorned with pictures ⟨~ weekly⟩ **c :** PICTOGRAPHIC **3 :** having the qualities of a picture **:** suggesting or conveying visual images ⟨~ imagination⟩ ⟨~ poetry⟩ — **pic·to·ri·al·ly** \-əlē, -li\ *adv* — **pic·to·ri·al·ness** *n* -ES
²pictorial \"\ *n* -S **1 :** a periodical employing a high proportion of pictorial matter **2 :** a postage stamp having a picture as the central feature of its design
pic·to·ri·al·ism \pik'tōrēə,lizəm\ *n* -S **:** the use or creation of pictures or visual images ⟨development from his original level of illustration into full ~ —Virgil Barker⟩
pic·to·ri·al·ist \-,ləst\ *n* -S **:** one who produces a picture esp. by photography for its own sake or as an end in itself ⟨interesting both to the ~ and the professional is the article on architectural photography —*Photography Yr. Bk.*⟩
pic·to·ri·al·iza·tion \pik,tōrēələ'zāshən\ *n* -S [*pictorialize* + *-ation*] **:** the act or process of representing by a picture or illustrating with pictures ⟨detailed ~ of the . . . coronation —*Newsweek*⟩
pic·to·ri·al·ize \pik'tōrēə,līz\ *vt* -ED/-ING/-S [¹*pictorial* + *-ize*] **:** to make pictorial **:** represent in or as if in a picture ⟨each of the stories . . . recreated . . . with a *pictorialized* concept by the finest . . artists —*advt*⟩
pic·tor·ic \(')pik¦tōrik\ *adj* [LL *pictor*ius + E *-ic*] **:** PICTORIAL — **pic·tor·i·cal·ly** \-rək(ə)lē\ *adv*
pic·tou disease \'pik(,)tü-\ *n, usu cap P* [fr. *Pictou*, Nova Scotia] **:** WINTON DISEASE
picts *pl of* PICT
picts' house *n, usu cap P* [so called fr. being attributed to the Picts] **:** one of the prehistoric dwellings in Scotland consisting of subterranean chambers with convergent stone walls
pic·tun \'pik,tün\ *n* -S [Maya, fr. *pic* 8000 + *tun* year of 360 days] **:** a period of 400 katuns or 8000 tuns in the Maya calendar — compare BAKTUN
pic·tur·abil·i·ty \,pikchərə'bilədē\ *n* **:** the quality or state of being picturable
pic·tur·able \'pikchərəbəl\ *adj* **:** capable of or suited for being represented by a picture or visual image ⟨~ objects of everyday experience⟩ — **pic·tur·able·ness** *n* -ES — **pic·tur·ably** \-blē\ *adv*
pic·tur·al \'pikchərəl\ *adj* [L *pictura* + E *-al*] **:** PICTORIAL
¹pic·ture \'pikchə(r), -ksh-\ *n* -S *often attrib* [ME, fr. L *pictura*, fr. *pictus* (past part. of *pingere* to paint) + *-ura* -ure — more at PAINT] **1** *obs* **a :** the act, process, or art of painting **:** representation by painting **b :** pictorial representations **2 a :** a representation (as of a person, landscape, building) on canvas, paper, or other surface produced by painting, drawing, engraving, or photography ⟨old ~*s* of the family⟩ ⟨~*s* of the wedding⟩; *esp* **:** such representation as a work of art ⟨walls hung with ~*s*⟩ ⟨~ dealer⟩ **b** *obs* **:** STATUE, MODEL **3 :** a description so vivid or graphic as to suggest a mental image or give an accurate idea of the thing described ⟨he hath drawn my ~ in his letter —Shak.⟩ ⟨language, our most faithful and indispensable ~ of human experience —Susanne K. Langer⟩ ⟨horn and trumpet become parts of a musical ~⟩ **4 a :** something that by its likeness vividly suggests some other thing **:** COPY ⟨the boy is the ~ of his father⟩ **b :** a concrete embodiment of an abstraction **:** ILLUSTRATION, SYMBOL ⟨she was the very ~ of grief⟩ ⟨the ~ of health⟩ **5 a :** a transitory visible image or reproduction due to the working of physical laws or made by utilizing such laws (as with a lens) ⟨adjusting the television set for a brighter ~⟩ **b :** MOTION PICTURE ⟨a Western ~⟩ **c pictures** *pl, chiefly Brit* **:** MOVIES ⟨have a few drinks with their friends, and a grill, and then perhaps the ~*s* —Nevil Shute⟩ **6 :** a mental image ⟨shocks of corn were dotted about in her mind ~*s* —Elizabeth M. Roberts⟩ **7 :** a picturesque person or thing ⟨the ship was really a ~ with all her sails unfurled⟩ **8 :** TABLEAU 1 ⟨created a world with his words, and his fine image is never lost because of unnecessary stage ~*s* —Virginia B. Slaughter⟩ **9 a :** a scene or a set of facts or circumstances immediately present to the attention **:** a field of observation ⟨in all matters artistic, personal taste enters into the ~ —John Gutman⟩ **b :** verbal or graphic presentation of a problem or situation ⟨drew an alarming ~ of the economic future⟩ **c :** PATTERN, CONFIGURATION ⟨need more details to understand the full ~⟩ **d :** SITUATION ⟨in the spring the employment ~ will change⟩
²picture \"\ *vt* **pictured; pictured; picturing** \-chəriŋ, -sh(ə)r-\ **pictures** [ME *picturen*, fr. ¹*picture*] **1 a :** to paint or draw a representation, image, or visual conception of **:** form a likeness of on a surface **:** DEPICT ⟨*pictured* holding a banner aloft⟩ **b :** to show a picture of ⟨the room they finished for him is *pictured* on this page —Kathryn Larson⟩ **c :** to present (as a narrative) in pictures or provide with pictures **:** ILLUSTRATE ⟨printing, airing, and *picturing* the news —F.L. Mott⟩ **2 :** to represent (something abstract or imperceptible) in visible or symbolic form **:** PORTRAY ⟨illustrated his letters as he did, *picturing* what he couldn't put so well into words —J.K.Hutchens⟩ **3 :** to describe graphically **:** describe vividly in words ⟨likes to ~ the triumph of well-born Nordics over the Canadian wilderness —Malcolm Cowley⟩ **4 :** to form a mental image or definite impression of **:** IMAGINE ⟨the children . . . were *picturing* a beautiful, sad face, and the figure of a noble lady moving among her soldiers —Grace Kinnicut⟩ **5 :** to photograph for showing as a motion picture
syn see REPRESENT
picture book *n* **:** a book that consists wholly or chiefly of pictures
picture bride *n* **:** a bride in a picture marriage
picture card *n* **1 :** FACE CARD **2 :** PICTURE POSTCARD
pic·ture·dom \-(r)dəm\ *n* -S [¹*picture* + *-dom*] **:** FILMDOM
pic·ture·drome \'pikchə,drōm\ *n* -S [¹*picture* + *-drome*] *Brit* **:** a movie theater
pictured-wing fly \'==,=-\ *n* **:** a member of the dipterous family Otitidae
picture element *n* **:** the smallest subdivision into which a television picture is divided in scanning
picture frequency *n* **:** the number of complete images sent or received per second in television transmission
picture gallery *n* **:** a large room for the exhibition of pictures; *also* **:** a collection of pictures
pic·ture·go·er \'pikchə,gōə(r\ *n, Brit* **:** one who goes regularly or frequently to see motion pictures
picture hat *n* **:** a woman's dressy broad-brimmed hat usu. for afternoon wear
picture house *or* **picture palace** *n, chiefly Brit* **:** a motion-picture theater
pic·ture·less \'pikchə(r)ləs\ *adj* **:** being without pictures
picturelike \'==,=\ *adj* **:** PICTURESQUE
picture marriage *n* **:** a marriage (as between persons living in different countries) contracted after acquaintance only by an exchange of photographs; *specif* **:** such a marriage effected by a ceremony in the absence of the groom for the purpose of entitling the bride to enter the country of the groom's residence
picture mirror *n* **:** a mirror having a picture painted on the back of a glass framed with and immediately above the looking glass
picture molding *or* **picture mold** *n* **:** a narrow molding fastened to the walls of a room near the ceiling to support pictures hung by hooks
picture ore *n* **:** ore in which gold or silver can be seen before processing
picture paper *n, chiefly Brit* **:** an illustrated newspaper
picture plane *n* **:** the surface of a picture drawn in linear perspective regarded as a transparent plane perpendicular to the lines of sight on which the points of objects in the scene may be considered as projected by straight lines drawn from these points to the eye
picture postcard *n* **:** a postcard bearing a picture typically of a scene or place of interest
picture puzzle *n* **:** JIGSAW PUZZLE
pic·tur·er \'pikchərə(r)\ *n* -S **:** one that makes pictures **:** PAINTER
picture rail *n* **:** PICTURE MOLDING
pictures *pl of* PICTURE, *pres 3d sing of* PICTURE
picture show *n* **1 :** an exhibition of paintings **2 :** MOTION PICTURE **3 :** a motion-picture theater
picture signal *n* **:** the electrical signal derived from the television camera — called also *video signal*
¹pic·tur·esque \¦pikchə¦resk, -ksh-\ *adj* [modif. (influenced by ¹*picture*) of F & It; F *pittoresque*, fr. It *pittoresco*, fr. *pittore* painter (fr. L *pictor*, fr. *pictus* — past part. of *pingere* to paint — + *-or*) + *-esco* -esque — more at PAINT] **1 a :** like a picture **:** resembling or suggesting a painted scene **:** suitable as a subject for painting ⟨~ village⟩ ⟨~ fishing fleet⟩ ⟨discovered grouped in ~ attitudes about the stage —W.S. Gilbert⟩ **b :** pleasing or charming by reason of quaintness **:** creating informal patterns of shape, light, and color ⟨a pleasantly ~ style of architecture⟩ ⟨venerable family mansion in a highly ~ state of semidilapidation —T.L.Peacock⟩ **c :** unusual, primitive, or markedly characteristic in appearance **:** QUAINT ⟨modern touches without sacrificing its ~ French colonial charm —Mary R. Johnson⟩ ⟨pioneering conditions that are ~ to look back upon but were rather trying to live through —Marquis James⟩ **2 :** characterized by an interest in what is picturesque ⟨easy for a ~ historian to lay side by side the most glaring contrasts —Virginia Woolf⟩ **3 :** evoking mental images **:** VIVID ⟨~ epithets⟩ ⟨gave a ~ account of his adventure⟩ — **pic·tur·esque·ly** *adv* — **pic·tur·esque·ness** *n* -ES
²picturesque \"\ *n* -S **:** picturesque quality **:** PICTURESQUENESS; *esp* **:** esthetic quality that evokes the atmosphere of another age, environment, or mode of existence — used with *the* ⟨the novelist of contemporary manners needs to be saturated with a sense of the ~ in modern things —Arnold Bennett⟩
picture tube *n* **:** KINESCOPE 1
picture window *n* **:** an outsize window (as in a living room) placed to frame or as if to frame a desirable exterior view and often between two narrower windows

picture window

picture writing *n* **1 a :** the act or art of recording events or expressing messages by pictures representing actions or facts **b :** the record or message so represented **2 :** a graphic system of symbols that are to a considerable extent pictorial in appearance regardless of whether they serve pictographic, ideographic, or phonetic functions
pic·tur·iza·tion \,pikchərə'zāshən\ *n* -S [*picturize* + *-ation*] **:** the act or fact of presenting in pictures
pic·tur·ize \'pikchə,rīz\ *vt* -ED/-ING/-S *see -ize in Explan Notes* [¹*picture* + *-ize*] **:** to make a picture of **:** present in pictures; *esp* **:** to make into a motion picture

pic·u·cule \ˈpikyə,kyül\ *n* -s [F, prob. fr. *pic* woodpecker (fr. L *picus*) + L *cuculus* cuckoo — more at CUCKOO] **:** WOODHEWER 1

pi·cu·da \pəˈküdə\ *n* -s [AmerSp, fr. Sp, fem. of *picudo* beaked, pointed, sharp, fr. *pico* beak, modif. of L *beccus* beak, fr. Gaulish] **:** GREAT BARRACUDA

pic·u·dil·la \,pikyəˈdilə\ *n* -s [AmerSp, dim. of *picuda*] **:** a small West Indian and tropical Atlantic barracuda (*Sphyraena picudilla*)

pi·cu·do \pəˈkü(,)dō\ *n* -s [AmerSp, fr. Sp, sharp] **:** BOLL WEEVIL

pic·ul *or* **pic·ol** *also* **pik·ol** \ˈpikəl\ *or* **pec·ul** \ˈpek-\ *n* -s [Malay *pikul* to carry a heavy load (i.e. as much as an ordinary man can lift)] **:** any of various units of weight used in China and southeast Asia; *esp* **:** a Chinese unit equal to 133.33 pounds

pic·u·let \ˈpikyələt\ *also* **pic·ule** \ˈpi,kyül\ *n* -s [*piculet* fr. L *picus* woodpecker + E *-let*; *picule* fr. L *picus* + E *-ule*] **:** any of numerous small woodpeckers that form a distinct subfamily of Picidae, have the tail feathers soft and rounded, and are widely distributed in So. America, Africa, and the East Indies

pi·cun·che \pəˈkünchē\ *n, pl* **picunche** *or* **picunches** *usu cap* **1 a :** an Araucanian people of central Chile **b :** a member of such people **2 :** the language of the Picunche people

pi·cu·ris \ˈpikərəs\ *n, pl* **picuris** *or* **picurises** *usu cap* **1 a :** a Tanoan people occupying a pueblo in New Mexico **b :** a member of such people **2 :** the language of the Picuris people

pi·cus \ˈpīkəs\ *n, cap* [NL, fr. L, woodpecker — more at PIE] **:** a genus formerly including all woodpeckers but now usu. restricted to the green woodpecker (*P. viridis*) of Europe and western Asia and its related forms

pi·dan \pēˈdän\ *n* -s [Chin (Pek) *p'i²tan⁴*, lit., covered eggs] **:** duck eggs preserved in a brine to which lime, ashes, and an infusion of tea are added and after several months coated with rice hulls

pid·dle \ˈpidᵊl\ *vi* **piddled; piddled; piddling** \-d(ᵊ)liŋ\ **piddles** [origin unknown] **1 :** to deal or work in trifling or petty ways **:** act idly or inefficiently **:** waste time **:** TRIFLE, PUTTER, DAWDLE **2 :** to pick at one's food **3 :** URINATE — not often in polite use

pid·dler \-d(ᵊ)lə(r)\ *n* -s **:** one that piddles **:** TRIFLER, PUTTERER

pid·dling *adj* **:** TRIFLING, TRIVIAL, PALTRY ⟨~ profits⟩ ⟨wore my patience . . . with her endless and ~ detail —U.P.Hass⟩

pid·dock \ˈpidək\ *n* -s [origin unknown] **:** a bivalve mollusk of the genus *Pholas* or family Pholadidae characterized by boring holes in wood, clay, peat, and rocks

pi·ded \ˈpīdəd\ *adj* [by alter.] *dial* **:** PIED

pid·gin *also* **pi·geon** \ˈpijən\ *n* -s [*Pidgin English*] **1 :** a form of speech that usu. has a simplified grammar and a limited often mixed vocabulary and is used principally for intergroup communication: as **a :** BÊCHE-DE-MER 2 **b :** WEST AFRICAN PIDGIN **c :** PIDGIN ENGLISH **2 :** PIGEON 5

pidgin english *n, usu cap P&E* [*pidgin* fr. Pidgin English, business modif. of E *business*] **:** an English-based pidgin orig. used in Chinese ports

pid·gin·iza·tion \,pijənəˈzāshən\ *n* -s **:** the process of pidginizing

pid·gin·ize \ˈpijə,nīz\ *vt* -ED/-ING/-S [*pidgin* + *-ize*] **:** to cause (a language) to develop pidgin **:** adapt to pidgin ⟨a *pidginized* variety of English —R.A.Hall b.1911⟩

pi–dog *var of* PYE-DOG

pid·yon ha·ben \,pidyənhəˈben\ *n, pl* **pidyon habens** *or* **pidyon habonin** [LHeb *pidyōn habēn*, lit., redemption of the son] **:** a traditional Jewish ceremonial rite observed on the 30th day after the birth of a first-born male child of one not a Cohen or a Levite in which the father symbolically relieves the child of ritual responsibilities by redeeming him from a Cohen for a certain sum

¹pie \ˈpī\ *n* -s [ME, fr. OF, fr. L *pica*; akin to L *picus* woodpecker, OHG *speh, speht*, ON *spætr* and perh. to Skt *pika* cuckoo] **1 a :** MAGPIE 1 **b** *dial chiefly Brit* **:** MAGPIE 2 **2 a** *obs* **:** a cunning or wily person **b** *archaic* **:** a voluble, talkative, or impudent person **3 :** a pied or parti-colored animal

²pie \"\ *n* -s [ME, perh. fr. ¹*pie*] **1 a :** a food usu. consisting of meat or fruit baked in or under dough esp. in a dish or pan lined with pastry or topped with pastry or both ⟨deep-dish ~⟩ ⟨apple ~⟩ **b :** a layer of cake split in half horizontally and spread with a custard, cream, or jam filling — see BOSTON CREAM PIE, WASHINGTON PIE **2 :** something resembling a pie ⟨mud ~⟩ **3 :** a heap or pile: as **a** *dial Eng* **:** a pile of potatoes or other root crop stored in a pit and covered with straw **b** *dial Eng* **:** a manure pile **4 :** something easy or much desired ⟨caught him, and the rest was ~ —G.F.T.Ryall⟩ ⟨we can get four million dollars, easy as ~ —Nancy Rutledge⟩ ⟨if there is going to be any ~, they want to be in —*New Republic*⟩ **5 a :** AFFAIR, BUSINESS, UNDERTAKING ⟨she wanted her finger . . . in every possible social ~ —Mary Deasy⟩ **b :** a whole regarded as divisible into shares ⟨industry is getting its share of the prosperity ~ —A.H.Raskin⟩

³pie \"\ *or* **pye** \"\ *n* -s [ME, prob. fr. ¹*pie*] **1 :** a table or collection of ecclesiastical rules used in England before the Reformation to ascertain the proper service or office for the day **2** *obs* **:** an alphabetical index or catalog (as of court records)

⁴pie \"\ *var of* PI

⁵pie \"\ *n* -s [Hindi *pāī*, fr. Skt *pādikā* quarter, fr. *pāda* foot, leg, quarter — more at FOOT] **1 :** a former monetary unit of India and Pakistan equal to ¹⁄₁₉₂ rupee **2 :** a coin representing one pie unit

¹pie·bald \ˈ⸗,⸗\ *adj* [¹*pie* + *bald*] **1 :** marked by or with usu. two different colors: **a :** spotted or blotched with black and white **b :** SKEWBALD **2 :** composed of incongruous parts **:** HETEROGENEOUS, MIXED, MOTLEY ⟨this ~ jargon —Sir Walter Scott⟩ **syn** see VARIEGATED

²piebald \"\ *n* -s **1 :** a piebald animal (as a horse) **2 :** a person or animal of mixed blood or qualities

pie·bald·ly \-ōl(d)lē\ *adv* **:** in a piebald manner

pie·bald·ness \-ōl(d)nəs\ *n* -ES **:** the quality or state of being piebald

pie–bed \ˈ⸗,⸗\ *n* [by shortening] **:** APPLE-PIE BED

¹piece \ˈpēs\ *n* -s [ME *pece, piece*, fr. OF, fr. (assumed) VL *pettia*, fr. (assumed) Gaulish; akin to Bret *pez* piece, W *peth* part, thing, OIr *cuit* part] **1 :** a part of a whole **:** FRAGMENT, PORTION ⟨the besieging forces would try to mine under a ~ of wall —Tom Wintringham⟩ **2 a** *obs* **:** MAN — usu. used disparagingly **b :** GIRL, WOMAN, BAGGAGE **3 :** an object or individual regarded as a unit of a kind or class **:** EXAMPLE ⟨handsome teak tables copied . . . from antique ~s —*New Yorker*⟩ ⟨each ~ of ripe fruit . . . has to be picked by hand —*Sat. Eve. Post*⟩: as **a :** a person exemplifying a particular quality ⟨thy mother was a ~ of virtue —Shak.⟩ **b :** a period of time esp. if brief ⟨sat thinking for a ~⟩ **c :** an interval of space regarded as part of a longer distance ⟨had gone a fair ~ of the way —A.J.Liebling⟩ **d :** an individual instance or specimen ⟨a ~ of impudence⟩ ⟨a ~ of news⟩ **4 a :** a length varying from 40 to 120 yards of cloth suitable for processing and esp. for dyeing and finishing **b** *archaic* **:** a standard or customary quantity or length of merchandise (as wallpaper, wine) made up for sale or use **c :** a pair, block, strip, or sheet of stamps or a single stamp considered as a single unit for sale as philatelic material **5 :** a product of creative work: as **a :** a literary composition ⟨a collection of mostly out-of-the-way ~s — a biography, a fictional biography, horror stories, adventure stories, and long short stories —*Saturday Rev.*⟩ **b :** a product of graphic or plastic art **:** PAINTING, PICTURE, SCULPTURE ⟨images of the Buddha are made to certain conventional patterns and there is often great difficulty in determining the origin of any ~ on stylistic grounds —C.P. Fitzgerald⟩ **c :** a theatrical production **:** DRAMA, PLAY ⟨the series of psychological ~s —Leslie Rees⟩ **d :** a musical composition ⟨has played four American ~s in a row —Virgil Thomson⟩ **e :** a passage to be recited **:** DECLAMATION ⟨spoke his ~ at the school graduation⟩ **6 :** a projectile weapon (as a rifle, revolver, or artillery big gun) ⟨ceased to debate the question of his ~ being loaded —Stephen Crane⟩ **7 a :** a coin of a specified metal ⟨gold ~⟩ ⟨~ of silver⟩ or denomination ⟨shilling ~⟩ ⟨10-cent ~⟩ **b** *obs* **:** any of several 17th and early 18th century English gold coins (as the unite, sovereign, or guinea) **c :** TOKEN, COUNTER ⟨good-luck ~⟩ **8** *chiefly dial* **:** a light simple lunch esp. when not eaten as a regular meal ⟨a ~ in our pockets, so that mealtimes didn't matter —Margaret Aitken⟩ **9** *obs* **:** a fortified city or other stronghold **10 :** a strip of leather inserted in a panel or affixed between bands on the backbone of a book and lettered **11 :** FLOOR 10 **12 a :** a man used in playing a board game; *specif* **:** any of the 16 chessmen of superior rank as distinguished from the pawns — see BISHOP, KING, KNIGHT, QUEEN, ROOK **b** *slang* **:** PLAYING CARD ⟨a ~ of trump⟩ **13 :** LOG 1a **14 :** a chunk of whole blubber **15 pieces** *pl* **:** portions picked out of the skirtings as suitable to be included with better grade wools **16** *archaic* **:** an inferior crystallized sugar obtained as one of the products of a now obsolete manufacturing process **17 :** OPINION, VIEWPOINT, MIND ⟨you have to know your ~ to get by them —H.J.Laski⟩ ⟨just about every accredited Republican spokesman has said his ~ —R.H.Rovere⟩ **18 a :** an act of copulation — usu. considered vulgar **b :** a partner in sexual intercourse — usu. considered vulgar **19 :** something composed of a specified material ⟨fur ~⟩ ⟨floral ~⟩ **20 :** part ownership of an enterprise or property ⟨had a ~ of a nearby automobile dealership⟩ **syn** see PART — **by the piece** *adv* **:** at a piecework rate ⟨paid *by the piece*⟩ — **of a piece :** of uniform kind or quality **:** CONSISTENT — sometimes used with *with* ⟨his performance under stress was *of a piece* with his honorable record⟩ — **on piece :** on a piece of cover — used of an adhesive stamp — **piece of one's mind :** TONGUE-LASHING ⟨was giving his jockey a *piece of his mind* —*Irish Digest*⟩ — **to pieces** *adv* **1 :** THOROUGHLY, COMPLETELY ⟨love you *to pieces*⟩ — often used with *all* **2 a :** into fragments **:** to bits **:** APART ⟨an elaborate toy fell *to pieces*⟩ — often used with *all* **b :** out of control **:** out of command — often used with *all* ⟨went *all to pieces* when the news came⟩

²piece \"\ *vb* -ED/-ING/-S [ME *pecen*, fr. *pece* piece, n.] *vt* **1 :** to repair, renew, or complete by adding pieces **:** PATCH ⟨*pieced* from scrap a locomotive —A.F.Harlow⟩ ⟨*pieced* out a set of china⟩ **2 :** to join into a whole **:** unite the parts of **:** combine out of pieces ⟨had been *piecing* a quilt all afternoon⟩ — often used with *together* ⟨his new book . . . has been *pieced* together from talks —Merle Miller⟩ **3 a :** FOOT 8 ⟨~ an arrow⟩ **b :** to splice (a stele) with other wood **c :** to splice (new wood) in a bow where a defect has been cut out ~ *vi* **1** *obs* **:** to come or fit together **:** coalesce from parts **:** AGREE, ASSEMBLE **2** *chiefly dial* **:** to eat between meals **:** nibble at snacks ⟨there he was, *piecing* on the ham —Eudora Welty⟩ **3 :** to join broken threads, slivers, or rovings in spinning or other textile manufacturing operations — **piece up :** to raise the temperature of mash in brewing by putting hot water into the mash tun under the false bottom

piece accent *n* **:** an accent cast by itself on a separate type body ⟨*piece accents* are available for the diacritics ˊ ˋ ¨ ˜ ˆ ⟩ — called also *floating accent, loose accent*

piece bag *n* **:** a bag of cloth scraps suitable for quilting or for patches ⟨silk and ribbon from her *piece bag* —Amy Lowell⟩

piece broker *n, archaic* **:** a dealer in cloth remnants

piece by piece *adv* **:** bit by bit

pièce de ré·sis·tance \pē,esdərəˈzēˈstäⁿ(t)s, -(,)rāˈz-, -ziˈs-, -äⁿs *sometimes* ,pēsd- *or* -,rəˈzistən(t)s *or* -,rēˈzistən(t)s\ *n, pl* **pièces de résistance** \"\ [F, lit., piece of resistance] **1 :** the chief dish of a meal ⟨the official *pièce de résistance*, labeled fried chicken on toast, proved after careful examination to be sea gull —*Textile World*⟩ **2 :** the showpiece of a collection **:** the outstanding item of a group **:** the prize piece or main exhibit ⟨the *pièce de résistance* — a Christmas mummers' play —Angelica Gibbs⟩ ⟨the *pièce de résistance* appears in a luxurious black antelope coat —*Women's Wear Daily*⟩

piece–dye \ˈ⸗,⸗\ *vt* **:** to dye after weaving or knitting — distinguished from *yarn-dye*

piece fraction *n* **:** a fraction set in type on two separate type bodies (as ¹⁷⁄₃₂ by juxtaposing ¹⁷ and ⁄₃₂) — called also *built-up fraction, split fraction*

piece goods *n pl* **:** cloth fabrics that are sold from the bolt at retail in lengths specified by the customer — called also *yard goods*

piece mark *n* **:** ASSEMBLY MARK

¹piece·meal \ˈpēˈsmē(ə)l\ *adv* [ME *pece-mele*, fr. *pece* piece + *-mele* -meal] **1 :** one piece at a time **:** by degrees **:** little by little **:** GRADUALLY ⟨has achieved the real substance of independence gradually and ~ —H.R.Lieberman⟩ **2 :** in pieces or fragments **:** APART ⟨the beasts will tear thee ~ —Alfred Tennyson⟩

²piecemeal \"\ *n* **:** FRAGMENT — usu. used with *by* ⟨we know . . . by ~ and accumulation —J.H.Newman⟩

³piecemeal \"\ *adj* **:** done, made, or accomplished piece by piece or in a fragmentary way **:** GRADUAL ⟨engaged in ~ attacks upon discrimination —*Collier's Yr. Bk.*⟩

⁴piecemeal \"\ *vt* **:** to divide piecemeal **:** separate into pieces

piece mold *n* **:** a sculptor's mold (as of plaster of paris) that can be removed from the cast in pieces

piec·en \ˈpēsᵊn\ *vt* -ED/-ING/-S [¹*piece* + *-en*] *dial Eng* **:** to piece together **:** SPLICE

piece of eight : an old Spanish peso of eight reals

piece of perspective 1 *obs* **:** a picture painted so as to appear distorted or confused except when viewed from a single viewpoint **2** *obs* **:** PEEP SHOW

piece of water : LAKE, POND

piece price *n* **:** PIECE RATE

piece price system *n* **:** a convict labor system in which a private contractor furnishes the raw materials and pays the government a stipulated price for the work done on each piece or article produced

piec·er \ˈpēsə(r)\ *n* -s **1 :** one that pieces **:** PATCHER **2 :** one that joins or collects pieces; *esp* **:** a textile worker who pieces threads

piece rate *n* **:** the price per unit of production paid to a pieceworker

piece–root grafting *n* **:** propagation in which the root of a seedling is cut into two or more parts and each is used as a stock

pieces *pl of* PIECE, *pres 3d sing of* PIECE

piecework \ˈ⸗,⸗\ *n* **:** work done by the piece and paid for at a standard rate for each unit produced — compare TIMEWORK

piece·work·er \"ə(r)\ *n* [*piecework* + *-er*] **:** a worker engaged on piecework

pie chart *n* [²*pie*] **:** a circle divided by several radii into sectors showing by their relative areas the relative magnitudes of quantities or the relative frequencies of items of a frequency distribution

pie chart

piec·ing *n* -s [ME *pecing*, fr. gerund of *pecen* to piece] **1 :** the uniting of pieces **:** MENDING, PATCHING **2 :** an arrow footing or any piece of wood set in an arrow or bow

pie–counter \ˈ⸗,⸗⸗\ *n* [²*pie*] **:** political patronage or spoils esp. when regarded as venal or corrupt ⟨has been kept away from the *pie-counter* for these four long years —*Los Angeles (Calif.) Times*⟩

piecrust \ˈ⸗,⸗\ *n* **1 :** paste for pies **2 :** the pastry shell of a pie

piecrust table *n* **:** a tip-top table of the Chippendale style and period with raised and decoratively carved edge

piecrust table

¹pied \ˈpīd\ *adj* [ME, fr. ¹*pie* + *-ed*] **:** of two or more colors in blotches (as black and white) **:** PARTI-COLORED, PIEBALD, VARIEGATED ⟨a ~ coat⟩; *also* **:** wearing or having a parti-colored coat ⟨a ~ horse⟩ **syn** see VARIEGATED

²pied *past of* PI *or of* PIE

pied antelope *n* [¹*pied*] **:** BONTEBOK

pied–à–terre \pē,ād·əˈte(ə)r, ,pyā-\ *n, pl* **pieds–à–terre** \-ād·ə-\ [F, lit., foot to the ground] **:** a temporary or second lodging (as a city apartment maintained by a country dweller)

pied–billed grebe \ˈ⸗,⸗-\ *n* [¹*pied*] **:** a medium-sized No. American grebe (*Podilymbus podiceps*) that is largely dark grayish brown above and whitish below and has a whitish bill encircled by a black band — called also *dabchick, hell-diver*

pied brant *n* **:** WHITE-FRONTED GOOSE

pied dishwasher *n* **:** PIED WAGTAIL

pied duck *n* **:** LABRADOR DUCK

pied·ed \ˈpīdəd\ *adj* [¹*pied* + *-ed*] *dial* **:** PIED

pied finch *n* **1 :** CHAFFINCH **2** *dial Eng* **:** a snow bunting in immature plumage

pied flycatcher *n* **:** a common European flycatcher (*Muscicapa hypoleuca*) having the male black and white

pied·fort *or* **pie·fort** \pēˈāˈfō(ə)r, (ˈ)pyā-\ *n* -s [F *pied-fort*, fr. *pied* foot (fr. L *ped-, pes*) + *fort* strong, fr. L *fortis* — more at FOOT, FORT] **:** a coin struck on an unusually thick flan (as some pattern pieces and multiple coins of France, Bohemia, and the Low Countries)

pied goose *n* [¹*pied*] **1 :** WHITE-FRONTED GOOSE **2 :** MAGPIE GOOSE

piedish \ˈ⸗,⸗\ *n* [²*pie* + *dish*] *Brit* **:** a pie plate or deep baking dish

pied lemming *n* [¹*pied*] **:** any of various No. American lemmings (genus *Dicrostonyx*) that have some claws much enlarged and a white winter coat — compare COLLARED LEMMING

¹pied·mont \ˈpēd,mänt\ *adj* [fr. *Piedmont*, region of northwest Italy] **:** lying or formed at the base of mountains

²piedmont \"\ *n* -s **:** a piedmont district, plain, or glacier

¹pied·mon·tese \ˈpēdmən-ˈtēz, -ēs\ *n, pl* **piedmontese** *cap* [*Piedmont*, region in northwest Italy + E *-ese*] **:** a native or inhabitant of Piedmont, Italy

²piedmontese \"\ *adj, usu cap* **1 :** of, relating to, or characteristic of Piedmont, Italy **2 :** of, relating to, or characteristic of people of Piedmont

piedmont glacier *n* **:** a glacier formed by convergence of the ends of valley glaciers at the base of mountains

pied·mont·ite \ˈpēd,mänt-,īt\ *n* -s [modif. of G *piemontit*, fr. It *Piemonte* Piedmont + G *-it* -ite] **:** a reddish brown or black mineral allied to epidote and containing manganese

pied·ness *n* -ES **:** the quality or state of being pied **:** VARIEGATION

pie–dog *var of* PYE-DOG

pied pip·er \ˈpīdˈpīpə(r)\ *n, usu cap both Ps* [fr. the *Pied Piper of Hamelin*, title and hero of poem (1842) by Robert Browning †1889 Eng. poet] **:** one that offers strong but delusive enticement **:** a leader who makes irresponsible promises

pie·dra \pēˈādrə, ˈpyā-\ *n* -s [AmSp, fr. Sp, stone, fr. L *petra* rock, stone, fr. Gk] **:** a fungus disease of the hair marked by the formation of small stony nodules along the hair shafts

pied starling *n* [¹*pied*] **:** a large crested gray-and-white starling (*Fregilupus varius*) of Réunion Island now extinct

pied stilt *n* **:** WHITE-HEADED STILT

pied wagtail *n* **:** a water wagtail (*Motacilla alba yarrellii*) having chiefly black-and-white plumage that is the commonest wagtail in the British Isles

pied widgeon *n* **1 :** GARGANEY **2 :** GOOSANDER

pied–winged coot \ˈ⸗,wiŋd-\ *n* **:** VELVET SCOTER

pied–winged curlew *n* **:** WILLET

pied woodpecker *n* **:** GREAT SPOTTED WOODPECKER

piedy \ˈpīdē\ *adj* [¹*pied* + *-y*] *chiefly Midland* **:** PIED

pie–eyed \ˈ⸗ˈ⸗\ *adj* [²*pie*] **:** INTOXICATED ⟨can a grown man get *pie-eyed* on beer —Maxwell Anderson⟩

pie–faced \ˈ⸗ˈ⸗\ *adj* **:** having a round, smooth, or blank face ⟨a pair of *pie-faced* louts —A.J.Liebling⟩

piefort *var of* PIEDFORT

pie·gan \pēˈgan\ *n, pl* **piegan** *or* **piegans** *usu cap* **1 a :** an Indian people of the Blackfoot confederacy **b :** a member of the Piegan people **2 :** the language of the Piegan people

pieing *pres part of* PIE

pie in the sky [fr. *You'll get pie in the sky when you die*, line in *The Preacher and the Slave* (*ab*1906), song by Joe Hill] **:** a prospect or promise of deferred happiness or prosperity ⟨good, solid, efficient government is more palatable than *pie in the sky* —Gordon Harrison⟩

pie·man \ˈpīmən\ *n, pl* **piemen 1 :** a baker or cook who specializes in making pies **2 :** a pie vendor

piemarker \ˈ⸗,⸗⸗\ *n* [so called fr. the use of its pods for stamping pie crust] **:** an Indian mallow (*Abutilon theophrasti*)

pien *or* **piend** \ˈpēn(d)\ *n* -s [perh. alter. of *peen*] **:** ARRIS

pien check *n* **:** a rabbet cut out of a pien (as in the upper of two consecutive stone steps) as a partial means of support

pien niu \pē,ennēˈ(y)ü\ *n* [prob. fr. Chin *pien¹* frontier + *niu²* ox, cow] **:** a hybrid between Chinese domestic cattle and the yak

pieplant \ˈ⸗,⸗\ *n, chiefly dial* **:** RHUBARB

pie plate *n* **:** a metal, ceramic, or glass plate for baking pies

pie·pou·dre *or* **pie·pow·der** \ˈpī,paüdə(r)\ *n* -s [ME *pipoudre* itinerant trader — more at COURT OF PIEPOUDRE] **:** TRAVELER, WAYFARER; *esp* **:** an itinerant merchant — see COURT OF PIEPOUDRE; compare DUSTYFOOT

pieprint \ˈ⸗,⸗\ *n* [so called fr. the use of its pods for stamping pie crust] **:** an Indian mallow (*Abutilon theophrasti*)

pier \ˈpi(ə)r, -iə\ *n* -s [ME *pere, per*, fr. OE *per*, fr. ML *pera*] **1 :** an intermediate support for the adjacent ends of two bridge spans — distinguished from *abutment* **2 a :** a breakwater, groin, or mole extending into navigable water for use as a landing place or promenade or to protect or form a harbor **b :** a structure built out into the water on piles for use as a landing place or pleasure resort **c** *obs* **:** HAVEN **3 :** a vertical structural support: as **a :** the wall between two windows, doors, or other openings **b :** PILLAR, PILASTER; *esp* **:** one that carries a major load (as at a church crossing) **c :** a pillar, post, or other vertical member that supports the end of an arch or lintel **:** DOORPOST, GATEPOST, BUTTRESS **d :** an auxiliary mass of masonry used to stiffen a wall **e :** a vertical layer of ashlars in a rubble wall **4 :** a structural mount (as of a large telescope) usu. of stonework, concrete, or steel **syn** see WHARF

pier·age \ˈpirij\ *n* -s [*pier* + *-age*] **:** WHARFAGE

pier arch *n* **:** an arch supported by piers; *esp* **:** a side arch of the nave of a basilican church

pier buttress *n* **:** the pier that receives the thrust of a flying buttress

¹pierce \ˈpi(ə)rs, -iəs\ *vb* -ED/-ING/-S [ME *percen*, fr. OF *percer, percier*, perh. fr. (assumed) VL *pertusiare*, fr. L *pertusus*, past part. of *pertundere* to pierce, fr. *per* through + *tundere* to beat, pound — more at FOR, STUTTER] *vt* **1 a :** to run into or through as a pointed instrument or weapon does **:** make a thrust into or through **:** STAB ⟨the needle *pierced* an ear lobe⟩ ⟨argued that the meaty edges of steak neither should be gashed or *pierced* with a fork —Jane Nickerson⟩ ⟨*pierced* his side with a spear⟩ ⟨the rigid, eternal obelisk *piercing* the mist like a sword —Louis Bromfield⟩ **b :** to penetrate sharply or painfully ⟨the cold *pierced* him to the bone⟩ ⟨tight-lipped whistles *pierced* the din —Darrell Berrigan⟩ ⟨bullets *pierced* his flesh⟩ **2 :** to make a hole in or through **:** BORE, PERFORATE, TUNNEL ⟨cylinders *pierced* by three or more . . . longitudinal perforations —*Encyc. Americana*⟩ ⟨the marble walls are *pierced* with four doors —*Amer. Guide Series: N.J.*⟩ ⟨the railway tunnel . . . ~s the rolling uplands —Guy McCrone⟩ **3 :** to force or make a way into or through **:** break into or through ⟨wanted to get swiftly through the field of fire and ~ and overthrow the enemy lines —Tom Wintringham⟩ ⟨the market . . . has already made new lows for the year and the question in the minds of technical followers is whether it will ~ the lows of last October —C.N.Stabler⟩ **4 :** to penetrate with the eye or mind **:** see through **:** COMPREHEND, DISCERN ⟨stood hidden in the doorway of an old empty house, *piercing* the darkness with wild eyes —Liam O'Flaherty⟩ ⟨a Shakespeare, *piercing* and developing the springs of passion —T.L.Peacock⟩ ⟨the curious and indiscreet who might wish to ~ the mystery that is taking place in the temple —J.G.Frazer⟩ **5 :** to penetrate so as to move or touch the emotions of **:** affect poignantly ⟨the remembrance of all that made life dear *pierced* me to the core —W.H.Hudson †1922⟩ ~ *vi* **:** to make a way into or through something as a pointed instrument does **:** break through **:** ENTER, PENETRATE ⟨tried to ~ into the enigma of her conduct for some sort of meaning⟩ **syn** see ENTER

²pierce \"\ *n* -s **1 :** PIERCING, STAB **2 :** a pierced hole **:** PERFORATION

pierce·able \-səbəl\ *adj* **:** capable of being pierced **:** PENETRABLE

pierced *adj* [ME *perced,* fr. past part. of *percen* to pierce] **1 :** having holes; *esp* **:** perforated so as to form an ornamental design **:** decorated with perforations ⟨beautiful creations in ~ brass —*New Yorker*⟩ ⟨porcelain with lattice-*pierced* borders⟩ **2** *heraldry* **:** perforated (as a cross) with the tincture of the field showing through the hole **3 :** having the earlobe punctured for an earring ⟨~ ears⟩

pierced dollar *n* **:** HOLEY DOLLAR

pierced nose *n, pl* **pierced nose** *or* **pierced noses** *usu cap P&N* [trans. of F *Nez Percé*] **:** NEZ PERCÉ

pierc·er \-sə(r)\ *n* -s [ME *percer, persour,* fr. AF *perceour, persour,* fr. OF *percer* to pierce + AF *-our, -eour* -er — more at PIERCE] **:** one that pierces: as **a** *archaic* **:** a keen eye **b :** an instrument (as an auger, gimlet, or stiletto) for boring or making holes **c :** a worker that pierces by hand or machine **d :** the ovipositor or the sting of an insect

pierce's disease \ˈpir|səz-, -iə\ *n, usu cap P* [after Newton B. *Pierce* †1917 Am. plant pathologist] **:** a virus disease of grapes marked by delay in leafing out and interveinal mottling and spotting followed by scalding and blighting of the leaves, premature defoliation, early ripening and withering of the fruit, reduced growth, and eventual death of the vines — called also *Anaheim disease, California vine disease;* see ALFALFA DWARF

¹piercing *n* -s [ME *percing,* from gerund of *percen* to pierce] **:** the act or process of perforating or the perforations made by it; *esp* **:** openwork design (as in metalwork)

²piercing *adj* [ME *percing,* fr. pres. part. of *percen* to pierce] **:** PENETRATING: as **a :** LOUD, SHRILL ⟨~ cries⟩ **b :** seeing clear or deep **:** DISCERNING, PERCEPTIVE, SHREWD ⟨an alert and enthusiastic face, with clear, ~ eyes and tender mouth —Walter Hough⟩ **c :** penetratingly cold **:** BITING ⟨a bitter ~ winter wind⟩ **d :** CUTTING, INCISIVE, KEEN ⟨~ sarcasm⟩ ⟨a ~ conviction⟩ ⟨looked through her with ~ wisdom —Zane Grey⟩ — **pierc·ing·ly** *adv* — **pierc·ing·ness** *n* -ES

piercing punch *n* **:** a metal-perforating punch that is often part of a stamping die

pier dam *n* **:** a pier built from shore to deepen a channel or to divert logs — called also *wing dam*

pier glass *n* **:** a large high mirror; *esp* **:** one designed to occupy the wall space between windows — see PIER TABLE illustration

pierhead \ˈ=,=\ *n* **:** the outer end of a wharf

pierhead line *n* **:** a line beyond which no structure may extend out into navigable waters

pi·eri·an \(ˈ)pīˈirēən, -iˈer-\ *adj, usu cap* [L *pierius* Pierian (fr. Gk *Pieria,* region of ancient Macedonia) + E *-an*] **1 :** of or relating to the region of Pieria in ancient Macedonia or to the Muses as early worshiped there **2 :** of or relating to learning or poetry

¹pi·er·id \ˈpīərəd, (ˈ)pīˈerəd\ *adj* [NL *Pieridae*] **:** of or relating to the Pieridae

²pierid \"\ *n* -s **:** a butterfly of the family Pieridae

pi·er·i·dae \pīˈerə,dē\ *n pl, cap* [NL, fr. *Pieris,* type genus + *-idae*] **:** a very large and almost cosmopolitan family of butterflies formerly regarded as a subfamily of Papilionidae that comprises the cabbage butterflies, sulphur butterflies, and others having three pairs of well-developed legs in both sexes and being usu. of medium size and white or yellow color with dark markings esp. on the edges of the wings

¹pi·er·ine \ˈpīə,rīn, (ˈ)pīˈerən\ *adj* [NL *Pieris* + E *-ine*] **:** of or relating to the genus *Pieris*

²pierine \"\ *n* -s **:** a member of the genus *Pieris*

pi·er·is \ˈpīərəs\ *n cap* [NL, fr. Gk, Pierian Muse fr. *Pieria* — more at PIERIAN] **1 :** a small genus of American and Asiatic evergreen shrubs (family Ericaceae) having white flowers in bracted racemes and a cylindrical or urn-shaped corolla — see JAPANESE ANDROMEDA, MOUNTAIN FETTERBUSH **2 :** the type genus of Pieridae containing the common cabbage butterflies

pier·less \ˈpi(ə)rləs, -iəl-\ *adj* **:** having no pier

pierre \ˈpi(ə)r, -iə\ *adj, usu cap* [fr. *Pierre,* capital of So. Dakota] **:** of or from Pierre, the capital of So. Dakota ⟨a *Pierre* merchant⟩ **:** of the kind or style prevalent in Pierre

pierre–perdue \pēˈer,perˈd(y)ü\ *n* -s [F *pierre perdue,* lit., lost stone] **:** blocks of stone or concrete heaped loosely in the water to make a foundation (as for a seawall)

pier·rette \ˌpēəˈret, (ˈ)piˈr-\ *n* -s *often cap* [F, fem. dim. of *Pierre* Peter] **:** a female pierrot

pier·rot \ˌpēə,rō, ˈpiə,rō\ *n* -s *often cap* [F, dim. of *Pierre* Peter] **1 a :** a standard comic character of old French pantomime usu. with whitened face and loose white clothes **b :** BUFFOON, CLOWN, MINSTREL **2 :** a masked carnival reveler dressed as a pierrot

pier·ro·tage \pēˈerəˈtäzh\ *n* -s [F, collection of small stones, fr. (assumed) *pierrot* (dim. of *pierre* stone, fr. L *petra*) + *-age*] **:** a stone and mortar filler used between framing members in southern colonial architecture

pier·rot·ic \ˌpēəˈrōd·ik, -ˈräd·ik, (ˈ)piˈr-\ *adj* [*pierrot* + *-ic*] **:** of, relating to, or resembling a pierrot or the pierrot tradition in pantomime and clowning

piers *pl of* PIER

pier table *n* **:** a table to be placed against a wall between two windows and usu. under a pier glass

pies *pl of* PI *or of* PIE, *pres 3d sing of* PI *or of* PIE

pi·es·ma \pēˈezmə, pīˈez-\ *n, cap* [NL, fr. Gk, pressed mass, pulp, fr. *piezein* to squeeze, press — more at PIEZO-] **:** a genus of tingid bugs including several that transmit virus diseases of sugar beets

pi·et \ˈpīət\ *n* -s [alter. of ME *piot,* dim. of ¹*pie*] *archaic* **:** MAGPIE 1

pie·tà \ˌpēāˈtä\ *n* -s *often cap* [It, lit., pity, fr. L *pietat-, pietas* piety, pity — more at PIETY] **:** a representation in painting or sculpture of the Virgin Mary mourning over the dead body of Christ often held on her knees

pier table under a pier glass

pi·etism \ˈpīə,tizəm\ *n* -s [G *pietismus,* fr. *pietist* + *-ismus* -ism] **1** *usu cap* **:** a 17th century religious movement originating in Germany that emphasized the need for a revitalized evangelical Christianity over against an excessive formalism and intellectualism, and stressed informal devotional meetings, Bible study, and personal religious experience **2 a :** emphasis on devotional experience and practices **b :** affectation of devotion **:** RELIGIOSITY

pi·etist \ˈpīəd·əst, -ətə-\ *n* -s [G, fr. L *pietat-, pietas* piety + G *-ist*] **1** *usu cap* **:** an adherent of Pietism **2 a :** a devoutly religious person **b :** an affectedly or excessively religious person

pi·etis·tic \ˌpīəˈtistik\ *or* **pi·etis·ti·cal** \-stəkəl\ *adj* [*pietist* + *-ic, -ical*] **1 :** of or relating to Pietism **2 a :** of or relating to religious devotion or devout persons **b :** affectedly or excessively religious **syn** see DEVOUT

pi·etis·ti·cal·ly \-stək(ə)lē\ *adv* **:** in a pietistic manner

pieto·so \ˌpēəˈtō(,)sō, pyāˈt-, -)zō\ *adv (or adj)* [It, fr. ML *pietosus,* fr. L *pietas* + *-osus* -ous] **:** with pity or sympathy **:** COMPASSIONATELY — used as a direction in music

pi·e·ty \ˈpīəd·ē, -ətē, -i\ *n* -ES [F *pieté* piety, pity, fr. L *pietat-, pietas,* fr. *pius* dutiful, kindly — more at PIOUS] **1 :** the quality or state of being pious: as **a :** fidelity to natural obligations **:** devoted loyalty to parents, family, or race **b :** dutifulness in religion **:** habitual reverence for God or accepted deities **:** zeal in religious service or worship **:** DEVOUTNESS ⟨a man noted for his ~ and devotion to the Church —R.P.Casey⟩ **c :** religious simplicity and devotion **:** PIETISM ⟨was sympathetic to the ~ of the revivalists —J.C.Brauer⟩ **2 :** an act inspired by piety **:** an instance of devotion ⟨the *pieties* of a simple life justly and charitably lived⟩ **3 :** the moral or spiritual resources of an individual or a group ⟨has achieved the broadest, most harmonious synthesis of living writers, but only after a drastic cross-examination of his deepest *pieties* —H.J. Muller⟩ **4 :** a conventional belief or standard **:** ORTHODOXY, SANCTION ⟨massed social *pieties* ... were invested in the established economic order —David Riesman⟩ **syn** see FIDELITY

pie wagon *n* [²*pie*] **:** PATROL WAGON

pie wool *n* [¹*pie*] *Austral* **:** inferior wool obtained from scraps and pieces of sheepskin sweated in heaps to loosen the fibers from the skin

pi·ezo \pēˈā(,)zō, pēˈāt(,)sō, pīˈē(,)zō\ *adj* [by shortening] **:** PIEZOELECTRIC

piezo- *comb form* [Gk *piezein* to squeeze, press; akin to Skt *pīḍayati* to squeeze, press; both fr. an IE compound whose first constituent is akin to Gk *epi* on and whose second constituent is akin to Gk *hezesthai* to sit — more at EPI-, SIT] **:** pressure ⟨*piezo*meter⟩

pi·ezo·chemistry \pēˈāzō, pēˈātsō, pīˈēzō+\ *n* [ISV *piezo-* + *chemistry*] **:** a science dealing with the effect of pressure on chemical phenomena

piezo crystal *n* **:** a piezoelectric crystal used in an oscillating electric circuit

pi·ezo·crystallization \=ˈ=(,)=+\ *n* [ISV *piezo-* + *crystallization*] **:** crystallization under pressure caused by orogenic forces

pi·ezo·electric \"+\ *adj* [ISV *piezo-* + *electric*] **:** of, relating to, or marked by piezoelectricity — **pi·ezo·electrically** \"+\ *adv*

pi·ezo·electricity \"+\ *n* [ISV *piezo-* + *electricity*] **:** electricity or electric polarity due to pressure esp. in a crystalline substance (as quartz or Rochelle salt)

piezoelectric oscillator *n* **:** a vacuum-tube circuit that contains a plate of piezoelectric material and is used as a generator of electric oscillations of a particular frequency

pi·ezo·luminescence \"+\ *n* [*piezo-* + *luminescence*] **:** TRIBOLUMINESCENCE

pi·ezom·e·ter \ˌpēəˈzäməd·ə(r), ˌpīə-\ *n* [*piezo-* + *-meter*] **1 :** an instrument for measuring pressure; *specif* **:** a gage joined to a main for indicating the pressure of liquid or gas inside **2 :** an apparatus for determining the compressibility of materials; *specif* **:** a vessel for measuring the change in volume of a solid, liquid, or gas when subjected to hydrostatic pressure

pi·ezo·met·ric \pēˈāzōˈme·trik, pēˈātsō-, pīˈēzō-\ *adj* [*piezometry* & *piezometer* + *-ic*] **:** of or relating to pressure or the piezometer

piezometric surface *n* **:** the imaginary surface to which groundwater rises under hydrostatic pressure in wells or springs

pi·ezom·e·try \ˌpēəˈzämə·trē, ˌpīə-\ *n* -ES [ISV *piezo-* + *-metry*] **:** the measurement of hydrostatic pressure affecting the occurrence and movements of groundwater

piezo resonator *n* **:** PIEZOELECTRIC OSCILLATOR

piff·er \ˈpifə(r)\ *n* -s *usu cap* [*Punjab Irregular Frontier Force* + *-er*] **:** a member of the Punjab Irregular Frontier Force or of a successor regiment

pif·fe·ro *or* **pif·e·ro** *also* **pif·fa·ro** \ˈpifə,rō\ *n* -s [It *piffero, piffaro,* fr. MHG *pfīfer* piper, fr. *pfīfe* pipe, fife (fr. OHG *pfīfa*) + *-er* — more at PIPE] **1 :** one of various old Italian wind instruments used by shepherds (as the bagpipe or oboe) **2 :** FIFE

¹pif·fle \ˈpifəl\ *vi* -ED/-ING/-S [perh. blend of *piddle* and *trifle*] **:** to talk or act in a trivial, inept, or ineffective way **:** TRIFLE, TWADDLE

²piffle \"\ *n* -s **:** trivial nonsense or ineptitude **:** empty gabble ⟨has written ~ —Geoffrey Grigson⟩

pif·fler \ˈpif(ə)lə(r)\ *n* -s **:** one that piffles

pif·fling \-f(ə)liŋ\ *adj* [fr. pres. part. of ¹*piffle*] **:** TRIVIAL ⟨brushed aside this ~ bit of legalistic hairsplitting —Ernest Cuneo⟩

pif paf \ˈpif,paf, ˈpēf,päf\ *n* -s [Pg] **:** a card game played like rummy and bet on like poker

¹pig \ˈpig\ *n* -s *often attrib* [ME *pigge*] **1 :** a young swine of either sex that has not reached sexual maturity; *broadly* **:** a wild or domestic swine — see HOG 1a **2 a :** pig's flesh as food **:** BACON, HAM, PORK **b :** the dressed carcass of a young swine weighing less than 130 pounds **c :** PIGSKIN **3 :** one thought to resemble or suggest a pig in habits or behavior (as in dirtiness, greediness, selfishness) ⟨profit by such a lesson and not make such a gorging ~ of himself —F.S.Anthony⟩ ⟨feel a ~ for having allowed a fortnight to go by without a letter —H.J.Laski⟩ **4 :** an animal likened to the pig (as a guinea pig or bushpig) — usu. used in combination or with a qualifying word **5** [so called fr. the resemblance of the arrangement of the molds in the pig bed to suckling pigs] **a :** a crude casting of metal (as iron or lead) convenient for storage, transportation, or melting; *esp* **:** one of standard size and shape for marketing run directly from the smelting furnace — compare INGOT **b :** a mold or channel in the pig bed **c :** PIG IRON, PIG LEAD **6 a :** a small iron or steel car pulled by a cable on a narrow-gage track and used for handling a railway freight car on an incline too steep for a locomotive **b** *slang* **:** a railroad locomotive **7 :** a flask having two or more tubulures to which smaller flasks may be attached and used esp. to collect fractions during fractional distillation **8 :** a brush, swab, or scraper pushed or pulled through a pipe or duct to clean it **9 :** a simple card game in which as cards are passed one at a time from player to player the first player to hold four of a kind lays his hand on the table and puts a finger against his nose and the last to notice and do likewise becomes the pig **10** *slang* **:** an immoral woman — **in pig :** PREGNANT — used of a sow

²pig \"\ *vb* **pigged; pigged; pigging; pigs** *vi* **1 :** to bring forth in the manner of pigs **:** FARROW **2 :** to huddle, lie together, or live in a way attributed to pigs ⟨a rare collection of human animals ... *pigging* together in mean huts —V.L. Parrington⟩ ~ *vt* **1 :** LITTER **2 :** to crowd like pigs ⟨they love fighting and they get more chance when they're all *pigged* in together —J.N.Hall⟩ — **pig it 1** *chiefly Brit* **:** to live in a way attributed to pigs **2** *chiefly Brit* **:** to exist in very poor circumstances or under considerable hardship ⟨had a whole house ... and did not have to *pig it* in one room —Flora Thompson⟩

³pig \"\ *n* -s [ME *pygg*] *chiefly Scot* **a :** an earthenware vessel **b :** CROCK

pig-a-back *var of* PIGGYBACK

pig bed *n* **1 :** PIGSTY **2 :** a bed of sand in which iron is cast into pigs

pigboat \ˈ=,=\ *n* [¹*pig* + *boat;* fr. the resemblance of submarines nosed against a tender to suckling pigs] *slang* **:** SUBMARINE ⟨the boys ... who'd been in ~s —Frederic Wakeman⟩

pig deer *n* **:** BABIRUSA

¹pi·geon \ˈpijən\ *n* -s [ME *pejon, pijon, pigeon,* fr. MF *pijon* young bird, pigeon, fr. LL *pipion-, pipio* young bird, fr. L *pipire* to chirp; akin to L *pipare* — more at PIPE] **1 :** a bird of the widely distributed family Columbidae (order Columbiformes) having a stout body with rather short legs, a bill horny at the tip but with a soft cere at the base, and smooth and compact plumage; *esp* **:** a member of one of the many domesticated varieties derived from the rock pigeon (*Columba livia*) of the coasts of Europe — see BILL illustration **2 :** a young girl ⟨he was taking out a very pretty ~⟩ **3 :** one who is an easy mark **:** DUPE **4 :** CLAY PIGEON **5** [alter. of *pidgin*] **:** an object of special concern **:** accepted business or interest ⟨she's not our ~ unless she's an accessory —Ngaio Marsh⟩ ⟨tennis was not his ~⟩ **6 :** the final card received in a deal of stud poker when it makes the hand a winner **7 :** a pari-mutuel ticket that is counterfeit or has been canceled **8 :** a dark purplish gray that is redder and paler than slate, redder, lighter, and stronger than charcoal, and redder and lighter than taupe gray

²pigeon \"\ *adj* **:** of or characteristic of pigeons **:** made of or for pigeons ⟨~ roost⟩ ⟨~ pie⟩

³pigeon \"\ *vt* -ED/-ING/-S **:** to fleece esp. by tricks in gambling **:** make a pigeon of **:** GULL ⟨sit down with him in private to cards and ~ him —W.M.Thackeray⟩

⁴pigeon *var of* PIDGIN

pigeonberry \ˈ== — *see* BERRY\ *n* **1 a :** POKEWEED **b :** the berry of the pokeweed **2 :** JUNEBERRY **3 :** a dogwood (*Cornus alternifolia*) **4 :** any of several No. American buckthorns (as cascara buckthorn or California coffee) **5 :** PARTRIDGEBERRY **6** *West Indies* **:** GOLDEN DEWDROP **7** *Austral* **:** either of two timber trees (*Litsea ferruginea* and *L. dealbata*) **8 :** BRISTLY SARSAPARILLA

pigeon blood *or* **pigeon's blood** *n* **:** a dark red that is yellower and duller than cranberry, yellower, lighter, and stronger than average garnet, and yellower and stronger than average wine — called also *Spanish wine*

pigeon breast *n* **:** a deformity of the chest that is marked by sharp projection of the sternum and that occurs esp. in rickets — opposed to *funnel chest* — **pigeon–breasted** \ˈ==ˈ==\ *adj*

pigeon cherry *n* **:** PIN CHERRY

pi·geon·dom \ˈ==,dəm\ *n* -s [¹*pigeon* + *-dom*] **:** the world of pigeons or of pigeon fanciers ⟨prominently associated with pigeons and ~ ever since it became a hobby —*Amer. Pigeon Jour.*⟩

pigeon–dropper \ˈ==,==\ *n* **:** one who practices pigeon-dropping

pigeon–dropping \ˈ==,==\ *n* **:** a confidence game

pi·geon·eer \ˌpijəˈni(ə)r\ *n* -s [¹*pigeon* + *-eer*] **1 :** a person who cares for and manages pigeons; *esp* **:** one in military service who has charge of the breeding, training, housing, and care of homing pigeons **2 :** one who kills or captures unwanted pigeons

pigeon fly *n* **:** a hippoboscid fly (*Pseudolynchia canariensis*) that is an ectoparasite of pigeons esp. in the southern U.S. and a vector of pigeon malaria

pigeon flying *n* **:** the sport of racing homing pigeons

pigeonfoot \ˈ==,=\ *n, pl* **pigeonfoots :** DOVE'S-FOOT

pi·geon·gram \ˈ==,gram\ *n* [¹*pigeon* + *-gram*] **:** a message carried by a pigeon

pigeon grape *n* **:** SUMMER GRAPE

pigeon grass *n* **1 :** YELLOW FOXTAIL **2 :** GREEN FOXTAIL **3 :** BUR BRISTLEGRASS **4 :** CRABGRASS 1a

pigeon guillemot *n* **:** a guillemot (*Cepphus columba*) of the north Pacific

pigeon hawk *n* **:** any of several small hawks: as **a :** a small American falcon (*Falco columbarius*) related to the European merlin **b :** SHARPSHINNED HAWK

pigeonhearted \ˈ==ˈ==\ *adj* **:** marked by timidity **:** CHICKEN-HEARTED ⟨don't talk sniveling and ~ like you —Conrad Richter⟩

¹pigeonhole \ˈ==,=\ *n* [¹*pigeon* + *hole*] **1 a :** a hole or small recess for pigeons to nest **b :** an excessively small room **:** CUBBYHOLE ⟨hated the little ~ where she had to work⟩ **2 a :** one of a series of holes usu. in a wall or door for the passage of pigeons **b :** one of a set of holes for passage (as of gases in a furnace arch) **3 pigeonholes** *pl, obs* **:** ¹STOCK 4 **4 :** excessive space between printed words **5 :** a seat in the upper gallery of a theater or in the top row of the gallery **6 :** a small open compartment usu. in a desk, case, or cabinet esp. for keeping letters or documents **7 :** a storing place in the mind for a classified item or topic **8 :** a place in a rigidly conventional pattern **:** a neat category ⟨they label or ticket our public men too patly, putting them into ~s —*Kiplinger Washington Letter*⟩

²pigeonhole \"\ *vt* -ED/-ING/-S **1 :** to provide with or divide into pigeonholes ⟨the cabinet was conveniently *pigeonholed* for the tiny glass figures she collected⟩ **2 a :** to place in or as if in the pigeonhole of a desk ⟨accepted the papers and *pigeonholed* them in his desk —C.G.Norris⟩ **b :** to put away as if in a place readily accessible or for future reference **:** to lay aside indefinitely **:** SHELVE ⟨find some polite formula for *pigeonholing* the whole idea —Denis Healey⟩ ⟨any new projects and plans ... will inevitably be *pigeonholed* to await better times —Grenville Manton⟩ **3 :** to assign to a proper class or category **:** arrange according to a logical scheme **:** analyze and classify **:** LABEL ⟨life was neatly *pigeonholed* into compartments —Alan Moorehead⟩ ⟨attempted to ~ the new knowledge in the light of his experience⟩

³pigeonhole \"\ *adj* [¹*pigeonhole*] **:** based on a rigid system of classification ⟨~ theories of art —John Dewey⟩ ⟨combat the static thinking that derives from ~ diagnosis —E.A. Strecker⟩

pigeon horntail *or* **pigeon tremex** *n* **:** a large American horntail (*Tremex columba*) having a burrowing larva that is preyed upon by a large ichneumon fly (*Thallesa lunator*)

pigeon house *n* **:** DOVECOTE 1

pigeoning *pres part of* PIGEON

pi·geon·ite \ˈpijə,nīt\ *n* -s [*Pigeon* Point, northeast Minn. + E *-ite*] **:** a monoclinic mineral $(Mg_1Fe_1Ca)_2Si_2O_6$ consisting of pyroxene with rather low calcium, little or no aluminum or ferric iron, and less ferrous iron than magnesium

pigeon–livered \ˈ==ˈ==\ *adj* [¹*pigeon* + *livered*] **:** GENTLE, MILD ⟨it cannot be but I am *pigeon-livered* and lack gall to make oppression bitter —Shak.⟩

pigeon louse *n* **:** any of several philopterid bird lice that are parasitic on wild and domestic pigeons

pigeon louse fly *n* **:** PIGEON FLY

pigeon pea *n* **1 :** a tropical woody herb (*Cajanus cajan*) with trifoliate leaves, showy yellow flowers, and flattish pods much cultivated esp. in the tropics **2 :** the small highly nutritious seed of the pigeon pea

pigeon plover *n* **:** BLACK-BELLIED PLOVER

pigeon plum *n* **1 a :** the edible drupaceous fruit of any of several tropical American plants of the genus *Coccoloba* (esp. *C. laurifolia*) **b :** the edible fruit of an African tree (*Chrysobalanus ellipticus*) **2 :** a tree that bears pigeon plums

pigeon post *n* **1 :** a postal or private communications system using pigeons as carriers **2 :** letters or messages carried by pigeons **:** mail carried by pigeons

pigeon pox *n* **:** a virus disease of pigeons which is closely related to fowl pox and the virus of which is often used to produce a vaccine against fowl pox that is safer though less lastingly effective than that prepared with fowl pox virus

pi·geon·ry \ˈpijənrē\ *n* -ES [¹*pigeon* + *-ry*] **:** DOVECOTE ⟨picturesque villages with their *pigeonries* —H.H.Johnston⟩

pigeons *pl of* PIGEON, *pres 3d sing of* PIGEON

pigeon's blood *var of* PIGEON BLOOD

pigeon's–foot \ˈ==,=\ *n, pl* **pigeon's–foots :** DOVE'S-FOOT

pigeon's–grass \ˈ==,=\ *n, pl* **pigeon's–grasses** [so called fr. its attractiveness to pigeons] **:** a common vervain (*Verbena officinalis*)

pigeon's milk *or* **pigeon milk** *n* **:** a milky fluid with solid particles resembling cheese that is produced by the breaking down and discharge of the cells lining the crop and regurgitated by pigeons for their young

pigeon's–neck \ˈ==,=\ *n, pl* **pigeon's–necks :** PELICAN 4

pigeontail \ˈ==,=\ *n* **:** PINTAIL 1

pigeon tick *n* **:** an argasid tick (*Argas reflexus*) that is an ectoparasite on various birds and mammals

pigeon–toe \ˈ==ˈ=\ *vb* [back-formation fr. *pigeon-toed*] *vi* **:** to walk with toes turned in ⟨will go *pigeon-toeing* off —J.A. Phillips⟩ ~ *vt* **:** to go along with toes turned in ⟨*pigeon-toed* his way into the new editor's presence —Eugene Field⟩

pigeon–toed \ˈ==ˈ=\ *adj* [¹*pigeon* + *toed*] **:** having the toes turned in ⟨a *pigeon-toed* boy⟩

pigeon tree *n* **:** HERCULES'-CLUB 3

pigeonweed \ˈ==,=\ *n* **:** CORN GROMWELL

pigeon–wheat \ˈ==,=\ *also* **pigeon–wheat moss** *n* **:** a moss of the genus *Polytrichum* in which the capsules resemble small grains of wheat

¹pigeonwing \ˈ==,=\ *n* **1 a :** a wing of a pigeon **b :** a wing resembling that of a pigeon **2 a :** a fancy dance step executed by jumping and striking the legs together ⟨performing capers ... and ~s around each other —H.L.Davis⟩ **b :** a fancy figure in skating **3 :** a style of dressing men's side hair in waves or curls resembling pigeon's wings **4 :** a brown dappled with purple that comes between dark brown and light blue in the table of colors in tempering of hardened steel

²pigeonwing \"\ *vt* **:** to move by doing pigeonwings ⟨~*ed* himself across the floor⟩ ~ *vi* **:** to dance a pigeonwing ⟨~*ed* in the middle of the dance floor⟩

pigeonwood \ˈ==,=\ *n* **:** any of various tropical trees with marked or mottled wood: as **a :** BLOLLY **b :** BUSTIC **c :** a West Indian tree (*Diospyros tetrasperma*) **d :** ZEBRAWOOD 1b **e :** ZEBRAWOOD 1a **f :** a tree of the genus *Coccoloba*

pigeon woodpecker *n* **:** FLICKER

pig–eyed \ˈ=ˈ=\ *adj* **:** having small deep-set eyes

pigface \ˈ=,=\ *n* [¹*pig* + *face*] *Austral* **:** the fruit of the beach apple

pigfish \ˈ=,=\ *n* [so called fr. the grunting sound it makes when taken from the water] **:** any of various fishes: as **a :** any of several salt-water grunts; *esp* **:** a food fish (*Orthopristis* *chrysopterus*) of the U.S. from Long Island southward **b** : PINFISH a **c** *Austral* : any of several wrasses (esp. of the genera *Diastodon* and *Verreo*) of the family Labridae

pigfoot \ˈ=,=\ *n, pl* **pigfoots** : a mottled reddish brown marine fish (*Scorpaena porcus*) of southern Europe; *also* : a fish of a related species

pig-footed bandicoot \ˈ=¦==-\ *n* : a large-eared herbivorous bandicoot (*Chaeropus ecaudatus* syn. *C. castanotis*) formerly abundant in much of Australia, with two functional toes resembling hooves on each foot

pigged *past of* PIG

¹pig·gery \ˈpig(ə)rē, -ri\ *n* -ES [¹*pig* + *-ery*] **1 a** : a pig breeding or rearing establishment **b** : PIGSTY **2** : PIGS

²piggery \"\ *n* -ES [³*pig* + *-ery*] *Scot* : CROCKERY

pig·gin \ˈpigə̇n\ *n* -S [origin unknown] **1 a** : *chiefly dial* : a wooden vessel shaped approximately like a pail and often having one stave extended upward for use as a handle **b** : a dish shaped like a piggin, often made of glass or silver, and used usu. for butter or sugar **2 a** *dial Eng* : a one-handled wooden drinking vessel **b** *chiefly Midland* : a milking pail

piggin 1a

pigging *pres part of* PIG

pig·gin' string \ˈpigə̇n-\ *n* [origin unknown] *West* : a small rope used by cowhands for tying cattle by the feet

pig·gish \ˈpigish, -gēsh\ *adj* : of, relating to, or resembling those characteristics thought to be typical of a pig : DIRTY, GREEDY, MEAN, STUBBORN ⟨a somewhat ~ material happiness —Paul de Kruif⟩ ⟨~ obstinacy —Louis Bromfield⟩ ⟨his sharp ~ eyes and . . . piercing voice —Vincent Sheean⟩ — **pig·gish·ly** *adv*

¹pig·gy \ˈpigē, -gi\ *n* -ES [¹*pig* + *-y*, dim. suffix] : a little pig

²piggy \"\ *adj* -ER/-EST [¹*pig* + *-y*, adj. suffix] **1** : having qualities felt to resemble those attributed to a pig ⟨plump, with round ~ cheeks —L.K.Liang⟩ **2** *of a sow* : appearing to be in pig

¹pig·gy·back *or* **pick-a-back** *also* **pig-a-back** \ˈpig¦ē,bak, ¦i,b- *sometimes* -ik¦ *or* ¦ə,b-\ *adv* [alter. of earlier *a pick pack, a pickback*, of unknown origin] **1** : up on the back and shoulders ⟨had her child with her . . . astraddle on her hip, or ~ —John Bennett⟩ ⟨shows a flood victim being carried from his home ~ —*Altoona (Pa.) Mirror*⟩ **2** : on a railroad flatcar ⟨the trailer rode ~ from coast to coast⟩

²piggyback *or* **pickaback** *also* **pig-a-back** \"\ *n* **1** : the act of carrying piggyback : the state of being carried piggyback ⟨beg daddy for a ~ —*Parents' Mag.*⟩ **2** : the process of loading, transporting, and unloading truck trailers on railroad flatcars or cars of special design ⟨estimate the cost of shipping by ~⟩

³piggyback *or* **pickaback** *also* **pig-a-back** \"\ *adj* **1** : marked by being up on the shoulders and back ⟨a child needs hugging, tussling, and ~ rides —Benjamin Spock⟩ **2** : of or relating to the hauling of truck trailers on railroad flatcars ⟨~ service⟩ ⟨~ cars⟩

⁴piggyback \"\ *vt* **1** : to carry up on the shoulders and back ⟨swum with them and ~*ed* them and attended them —R.P. Smith⟩ ⟨~*ing* a crippled classmate to school for a whole year —*Saturday Rev.*⟩ **2** : to haul (as a truck trailer) by railroad car ~ *vi* : to haul truck trailers usu. loaded with commodities on railroad cars ⟨the railroad has been ~*ing* for quite a number of years⟩

piggyback plant *var of* PICKABACK PLANT

piggy bank *n* [¹*piggy*] : a bank often in the shape of a pig and usu. used by children for saving small coins

piggy bank

pigheaded \ˈ=¦==\ *adj* [¹*pig* + *headed*] : stupidly perverse : STUBBORN, WILLFUL : refusing to yield **syn** see OBSTINATE

pig·head·ed·ness \(ˈ)=ˈ==nə̇s\ *n* -ES : the quality or state of being pigheaded ⟨thanks to their ~ —Kenneth Roberts⟩

pig hickory *n* : PIGNUT 2

pight [ME *pihte*, past of *pichen* to pitch] *archaic past of* PITCH

pigh·tle *or* **pigh·tel** \ˈpīd·ᵊl\ *n* -S [origin unknown] *dial* : a small field or enclosure usu. near or surrounding a building (as a house, barn, shed); *specif* : BARNYARD

pig in a poke : something offered in such a way that the one to whom it is offered does not know exactly what the thing is nor what its real value is ⟨was too shrewd ever to buy a *pig in a poke*⟩

pig iron *n* [¹*pig*] : crude iron that is the direct product of the blast furnace and that is either refined to produce steel, wrought iron, or ingot iron or is remelted and cast into special shapes — compare CAST IRON

pig islander \ˈ=ˈ===\ *n, usu cap P&I* [so called from the introduction of pigs into New Zealand by Captain Cook] *Austral* : NEW ZEALANDER

pig latin *n, often cap L* : a jargon that is made by systematic mutilation of English (as *amscray the ointjay* for *scram the joint*)

pig lead *n* : lead cast in pigs

pig·let \ˈpiglə̇t\ *n* -S [¹*pig* + *-let*] : a small usu. young hog

piglike \ˈ=,=\ *adj* [¹*pig* + *-like*] : resembling a pig

pig lily *n* : CALLA LILY

pig·ling \ˈpigliŋ\ *n* -S [¹*pig* + *-ling*] : PIGLET

pig louse *n* : HOG LOUSE

pigmaker \ˈ=,==\ *n* [¹*pig* + *maker*] : a manufacturer of pig iron

pig·man \ˈpigmən\ *n, pl* **pigmen** : one who takes care of pigs

pig meat *n* [¹*pig* + *meat*] *Brit* : PORK

¹pig·ment \ˈpigmənt\ *n* -S [L *pigmentum* pigment, paint, fr. *pingere* to paint + *-mentum* -ment — more at PAINT] **1 a** : a natural or synthetic inorganic or organic substance that imparts a color including black or white to other materials; *esp* : a powder or easily powdered substance mixed with a liquid in which it is relatively insoluble and used in making paints, enamels, and other coating materials, inks, plastics, and rubber and also for imparting opacity and other desirable properties as well as color **b** : a compounding ingredient (as a filler or reinforcing agent) used in the manufacture of rubber or plastics — compare ¹DYE 2 **2 a** : any of various coloring matters in animals and plants; *esp* : solid or opaque coloring matter in a cell or tissue **b** : any of various related colorless substances (as various respiratory enzymes)

²pig·ment \-mənt, -,ment — *see* ²-MENT\ *vb* -ED/-ING/-S *vt* : to color or imbue with or as if with pigment ⟨wished to ~ the photograph⟩ ~ *vi* : to acquire pigment : become colored or imbued ⟨those who ~*ed* well gave about the same values as those who did not ~ well —*Experiment Station Record*⟩

pig·men·tal \(ˈ)pig¦mentᵊl\ *adj* [¹*pigment* + *-al*] : PIGMENTARY — **pig·men·tal·ly** \-ᵊlē\ *adv*

pig·men·tary \ˈpigmən,terē\ *adj* [L *pigmentarius*, fr. *pigmentum* + *-arius* -ary] : of, relating to, or producing or containing pigment : furnished with or characterized by pigment

pig·men·ta·tion \,pigmənˈtāshən, -,men-\ *n* -S [LL *pigmentatus* painted, colored (fr. L *pigmentum* + *-atus* -ate) + E *-ion*] : coloration with, compounding with, or deposition of pigment; *esp* : an excessive deposition of pigment in body tissues

pigment black B *n, usu cap P & 1st B* : an organic pigment — see DYE table I (under *Pigment Black 1*)

pigment blue WNL *n, usu cap P&B* : an organic pigment — see DYE table I (under *Pigment Blue 25*)

pigment bordeaux N *n, usu cap P&B* : an organic pigment — see DYE table I (under *Pigment Red 40*)

pigment cell *n* : a cell containing a deposition of coloring matter — compare CHROMATOPHORE 1

pig·ment·ed \-,mentə̇d, -mən-\ *adj* [¹*pigment* + *-ed*] : dulled by adding a pigment to the spinning solution — used esp. of rayon yarn

pigment finish *n* : leather finished with coating containing pigment or other opaque substance

pigment green B *n, usu cap P&G* : an organic pigment — see DYE table I (under *Pigment Green 8*)

pig·ment·ize \ˈpigmənt,īz, -n,tīz\ *vt* -ED/-ING/-S [¹*pigment* + *-ize*] : PIGMENT

pigmento- *comb form* [L *pigmentum* — more at PIGMENT] : pigment ⟨*pigmento*genic⟩

pig·men·to·phage \pigˈmentə,fāj\ *n* [ISV *pigmento-* + *-phage*; prob. orig. formed in F] : a cell that ingests pigment

pigment orange R *n, usu cap P&O* : an organic pigment — see DYE table I (under *Pigment Red 22*)

pigment process *n* : a photographic printing process in which the image consists of a black or colored pigment distributed in a colloidal medium (as gelatin)

pigment purple A *n, usu cap both Ps* : a solvent dye — see DYE table I (under *Solvent Red 1*)

pigment scarlet 3B *n, usu cap P&S* : an organic pigment — see DYE table I (under *Pigment Red 60*)

pigment volume *n* : the space occupied by pigment in paint or ink expressed as a percent of the total nonvolatile volume

pig metal *n* : metal cast in pigs

pigmy *var of* PYGMY

pigmy blue *n* : any of the several small butterflies of the lycaenid genus *Brephidium*

pigmy deer *n* : KEY DEER

pi·gnet index \(ˈ)pēn¦yā-\ *n, usu cap P* [after M. C. J. *Pignet* b1871 Fr. physician] : a measure of the type of body-build obtained by subtracting the sum of the weight in kilograms and the chest circumference in centimeters from the stature in centimeters

pi·gno·lia \pēnˈyōlēə\ *or* **pi·gno·li** \-lē\ *n* -S [It *pignolo*, fr. (assumed) VL *pineolus*, dim. of L *pineus* of the pine, fr. *pinus* pine] : the edible seed of the nut pine

pi·gnon \ˈpēn,yän\ *n* -S [F, fr. (assumed) VL *pineon-, pineo*, fr. L *pineus* of the pine] **1** : the nutlike seed of any of several pines (as the European stone pine) **2** : PHYSIC NUT

¹pig·no·rate \ˈpignərə̇t\ *adj* [L *pigneratus, pignoratus*, past part. of *pignerare, pignorare* to pledge — more at PIGNORATION] **1** : given or taken in pledge : PLEDGED **2** : of or relating to something pledged or to a contract of pignus : PIGNORATITIOUS

²pig·no·rate \-,rāt\ *vt* -ED/-ING/-S [L *pigneratus, pignoratus*] **1** : to give over (as a pledge) : PAWN **2** : to take in pawn

pig·no·ra·tion \,pignəˈrāshən\ *n* -S [LL *pigneration-, pigneratio, pignoration-, pignoratio*, fr. L *pigneratus, pignoratus* (past part. of *pignerare, pignorare* to pledge, fr. *pigner-, pignor-, pignus* pledge, stake) + *-ion-, -io* -ion] **1** : the act of pledging or pawning **2** : a civil-law process answering in general to common-law distraint

pig·no·ra·ti·tious \¦pignərə¦tishəs\ *adj* [LL *pigneraticius, pignoraticius*, fr. L *pigneratus, pignoratus* + *-icius* -itious] : of or relating to pignoration

pig·no·ra·tive \ˈpignə,rād·iv\ *adj* [F *pignoratif*, fr. L *pigneratus, pignoratus* + F *-if* -ive] **1** : giving in pledge **2** : PIGNORATITIOUS

pig·nus \ˈpignəs\ *n, pl* **pigno·ra** \-nərə\ [L *pigner-, pignor-, pignus* pledge, stake] *Roman & civil law* : a pledge or pawn arising where a creditor has power of sale and takes possession for security

pignus ju·di·ci·a·le \-,yü,dikēˈä(,)lā, -,jü,dishēˈālē\ *or* **pignus prae·to·ri·um** \-,prīˈtōrēəm, -,prē'-\ *n* [*pignus judiciale* fr. NL, lit., judge's pledge; *pignus praetorium* fr. LL, lit., praetor's pledge] : the right or lien that a judgment creditor has in the property of the judgment debtor

pignus le·ga·le \-,läˈgä(,)lā, -lə'gālē\ *n* [L] : a pledge or lien arising by operation of law (as in case of a landlord)

pignut \ˈ=,=\ *n* [¹*pig* + *nut*] **1** : EARTHNUT **2 a** : any of several bitter-flavored hickory nuts **b** *also* **pignut hickory** : a hickory (as *Carya glabra, C. ovalis*, or *C. cordiformis*) bearing pignuts **3** : JOJOBA

pigpen \ˈ=,=\ *n* **1** : PIGSTY **2** : a place that is dirty or littered up

pig potato *n* **1** : GROUNDNUT 2a **2** : COWBANE b **3** : a small or inferior potato suitable for pig feed

pig rat *n* : BANDICOOT 1

pigs *pl of* PIG, *pres 3d sing of* PIG

pigs and whistles *n pl* [³*pig*] *Scot* : RUIN ⟨poor girl, gone to *pigs and whistles*⟩

pig's-face \ˈ=,=\ *n, pl* **pig's-faces** [¹*pig*] : PIGFACE

pigs' feet *n pl* : the feet of swine used as an article of food esp. after boiling and pickling

pigs in blankets : oysters, chicken livers, or other choice morsels wrapped in thin slices of bacon, fastened with skewers, and broiled or sautéed

pigs in clover [¹*pig*] : a game played by tilting a small box containing holes and marbles so that every marble will roll into a hole

¹pigskin \ˈ=,=\ *n* **1 a** : the skin of a swine or leather made of it used typically in bookbindings, saddles, shoes, and wallets **b** : leather for gloves made chiefly from skins of capybaras and peccaries **2 a** : a jockey's saddle **b** : FOOTBALL 2a

²pigskin *adj* : having dimpled depressions like pigskin — used of the skin over a malignant tumor esp. of the breast

pigs·ney \ˈpigznē\ *n* -S [ME *piggesnye*, lit., pig's eye, fr. *pigges* (gen. of *pigge* pig) + *nye* eye, alter. (resulting from incorrect division of *an ye, an eye*) of *ye, eye* eye] **1** : DARLING, SWEETHEART **2** : a little eye

pigstick \ˈ=,=\ *vi* [back-formation fr. *pigsticking* action of hunting the wild boar with a spear, fr. *pig* + *sticking*, fr. gerund of *stick*] : to hunt the wild boar on horseback with a spear

pigsticker \ˈ=,==\ *n* [¹*pig* + *sticker*] : ¹STICKER 1a(1)

pigsty \ˈ=,=\ *n* [¹*pig* + *sty*] **1** : an enclosure with covered shed or area for pigs **2** : a dirty dwelling or room thought to resemble a pigsty ⟨you would end up in some dark ~ over a smelly stable —T.B.Costain⟩ **3** : a timber crib often filled with rock used to support a roof in a mine working

pigsty daisy *n* : MAYWEED 1

pig's-wash \ˈ=,=\ *n, pl* **pig's-washes** [¹*pig*] : SWILL 1a

pigtail \ˈ=,=\ *n* [so called from its resemblance to the tail of a pig] **1** : tobacco in small twisted ropes or rolls **2** : a tight braid of hair — compare QUEUE 1 **3** : a device used in logging that is usu. driven into a stump for supporting a rope or wire **4** : a cleavers (*Galium aparine*) **5** : a short flexible band or lead of stranded or braided copper wire used for electrical connections **6** : a spirally twisted wire or ceramic used as a guide in yarn manufacturing

pig-tailed \ˈ=,tāld\ *adj* [¹*pig* + *tailed*] **1** : having a tail like a pig's **2** [*pigtail* + *-ed*] : having or wearing a pigtail ⟨a *pig-tailed* little girl⟩

pig-tailed ape *or* **pig-tailed macaque** *or* **pig-tailed monkey** *n* : a macaque (*Macaca nemestrina*) of the Malay peninsula and the East Indies with a short slender tail which is held in the shape of a letter S when the animal is excited

pig-tailed langur *n* : a large dark snub-nosed langur (*Simias concolor*) of Sumatra distinguished by a very short nearly naked tail

pig tin *n* [¹*pig*] : tin cast in pigs

pig typhoid *or* **pig typhus** *n* : NECROTIC ENTERITIS

pigwash \ˈ=,=\ *n* [¹*pig* + *wash*] : SWILL 1a

pigweed \ˈ=,=\ *n* [¹*pig* + *weed*] : any of various strongly growing weedy plants: as **a** : any of several plants of the genus *Amaranthus* (as *A. retroflexus* and *A. hybridus*) that are sometimes used as potherbs, have edible seeds for which they have been cultivated locally, and produce pollen that is an important hay fever allergen **b** : GOOSEFOOT 1; *esp* : LAMB'S-QUARTERS 1 **c** *Austral* : a purslane (*Portulaca oleracea*)

pigweed family *n* : CHENOPODIACEAE

pig·wid·geon *also* **pig·wid·gin** \ˈpig,wijə̇n\ *n* [origin unknown] : an insignificant or simple person

piing *pres part of* PI

pi-jaw \ˈ=,=\ *n* [⁶*pi* + *jaw*] *Brit* : pious or moralizing talk or cant ⟨millions of hours under schoolroom discipline, reading the Bible, listening to *pi-jaws* —Aldous Huxley⟩

pik *also* **pic** *or* **pike** \ˈpik, ˈpēk\ *n* -S [F *pic*, fr. Gk *pēchys* forearm, cubit — more at BOUGH] : any of various units of length used in Mediterranean countries (as Greece, Turkey, Egypt, Algeria) equal to between 18 and 30 inches

pi·ka \ˈpīkə, ˈpēkə\ *n* -S [Tungusic *piika*] : any of various small lagomorph mammals of the family Ochotonidae inhabiting rocky parts of high mountains in Asia and western No. America that are closely related to the rabbits, but have small ears, the tail rudimentary, and the hind legs relatively short — called also *mouse hare*; see LITTLE CHIEF HARE

pi·ka·ke \ˈpēkə,kā\ *n* -S [Hawaiian *pikake*] : ARABIAN JASMINE

¹pike \ˈpīk\ *n* -S [ME, fr. OE *pic*, prob. of Celt origin; akin to ScGael *pic* pickax, Bret *pik*, IrGael *pice* pitchfork, W *pig* point, beak] **1** *dial chiefly Eng* : PICK 2 **2** : PIKESTAFF 1 **3** : a sharp point, pointed tip, or spike (as in the center of a buckler) : the tip of a spear **4** : the long pointed toe of a shoe worn in the 14th and 15th centuries : POULAINE **5** *dial Eng* : one of various sharp-pointed tools or implements (as a pitchfork) ⟨the windrows are loaded on a wagon by hand with a ~ —F.D.Smith & Barbara Wilcox⟩

²pike \"\ *vi* -ED/-ING/-S [ME *pyken* to pike (oneself), perh. fr. ¹*pike* pikestaff] **1** : to leave abruptly : take off : DEPART ⟨get lonely and sore, and ~ out —Sinclair Lewis⟩ **2** : to make one's way — used with *along* ⟨should he begin in a small way and ~ along —Theodore Dreiser⟩

³pike \"\ *n* -S [ME, perh. of Scandinavian origin; akin to Norw dial. *pīk* pointed mountain] **1** *dial Eng* : a mountain or hill having a peaked summit — used esp in place names **2** : a pile of hay or grain having a pointed top **3** [Sp *pico*, fr. *picar* to prick, pierce, fr. (assumed) VL *piccare* — more at ⁶PIKE] *archaic* : ²PEAK

⁴pike \"\ *n, pl* **pike** *or* **pikes** [ME, fr. ¹*pike*, fr. the shape of its head] **1 a** : an elongate long-snouted voracious teleost fish (*Esox lucius*) that reaches a length of four feet, is valued for food and sport, and is widely distributed in cooler parts of the northern hemisphere — called also *northern pike* **b** : a fish of the family Esocidae: as (1) : MUSKELLUNGE (2) : PICKEREL **2** : any of various fishes of families other than Esocidae that are felt to resemble the pike in appearance or habits: as **a** : SNOOK **b** : BARRACUDA 1 **c** : WALLEYE 4 **d** : SAUGER **e** : SQUAWFISH

⁵pike \"\ *chiefly dial var of* PICK

⁶pike \"\ *n* -S [MF *pique*, fr. *piquer* to prick, pierce, nettle, pique, fr. (assumed) VL *piccare*, fr. (assumed) *piccus* woodpecker, fr. L *picus* — more at PIE] **1** : a weapon consisting of a long wooden shaft with a pointed steel head sometimes having a hook or pick on the side and used by the foot soldier until superseded by the bayonet **2** *obs* : PIKEMAN **3** : the sharp-tipped staff on which a flag is carried ⟨carried on a ~ 9 feet, 10 inches long including the spear tip —W.F.Harris⟩

⁷pike \"\ *vt* -ED/-ING/-S **1** : to pierce, kill, or wound with or as if with a pike **2** : to thrust with or as if with a pike

⁸pike *var of* PIK

⁹pike \ˈpīk\ *n* -S [short for *turnpike*] **1 a** (1) : a guarded entrance for the collection of tolls for the use of a road (2) : a toll paid for the use of a road **b** (1) : a usu. publicly maintained road for direct travel from one place to another ⟨water transportation was outmoded by railroads and good ~*s* —*Amer. Guide Series: Tenn.*⟩ (2) : TURNPIKE 3 ⟨ridden the ~*s* enough to know the price of dozing off at the wheel —P.W. Kearney⟩ **2** : a railroad or model railroad line or system ⟨railroading on . . . backwoods ~*s* —F.P.Donovan⟩

¹⁰pike \"\ *n* -S [fr. *Pike* county, Missouri, whence they were first believed to have come to California] *West* : a migratory farmer — usu. used disparagingly

¹¹pike \"\ *n* -S : a body position used in diving and gymnastics in which the hips are bent, the knees are straight, the head is pressed forward, and the hands touch the toes or clasp the legs behind and just above the knees — compare JACKKNIFE, TUCK

piked \ˈpīkə̇d, -kt\ *adj* [ME, fr. ¹*pike* + *-ed*] : having a pike, sharp point, or spine : PEAKED, POINTED

piked dogfish *n* : SPINY DOGFISH

piked whale *n* : a small north Atlantic finback whale (*Balaenoptera acutorostrata*) having a prominent dorsal fin

pikel \ˈpīkəl, ˈpik-\ *n* -S [prob. fr. ¹*pike* + *-el* (as in *shovel*)] *dial chiefly Eng* : PITCHFORK

¹pike·let \ˈpīklə̇t\ *n* -S [by shortening and alter. fr. earlier *bara-picklet*, fr. W *bara pyglyd* pitchy bread] : a small round thick pancake baked on a griddle and traditionally served on Christmas day in Great Britain : CRUMPET

²pikelet \"\ *n* -S [⁴*pike* + *-let*] : a small usu. young pike

pikelike \ˈ=,=\ *adj* [⁴*pike* + *like*] : resembling a pike

¹pike·man \ˈpīkmən\ *n, pl* **pikemen** [⁶*pike* + *man*] : a soldier armed with a pike

²pikeman \"\ *n, pl* **pikemen** [¹*pike* + *man*] : PICKMAN

³pikeman \"\ *n, pl* **pikemen** [⁹*pike* + *man*] : a keeper of a turnpike gate or entrance

pike perch *n* [⁴*pike*] : any of various perches of the family Percidae that are felt to resemble pikes: as **a** : any of several large vigorous sport fishes of the Old World genus *Lucioperca* **b** : a fish of the genus *Stizostedion* (as a sauger or a walleye)

pike pole *n* [¹*pike*] **1** : a pole usu. 12 to 20 feet long with a pike in one end used in directing floating logs or to hold utility poles upright while they are being raised or removed **2** : a fire hook having a head with a sharp point at the tip

¹pik·er \ˈpīkə(r)\ *n* -S [⁹*pike* + *-er*] : TRAMP, VAGRANT

²pik·er \"\ *n* -S [*Pike* county, Missouri (thought to be the original home of many shiftless farmers who migrated to California) + E *-er*] **1** *usu cap* : MISSOURIAN — used as a nickname **2** *slang* : one who gambles or speculates with small amounts of money **3** : one who does things in a small way : a niggard in money or effort : TIGHTWAD

³piker \"\ *n* -S [¹*pike* + *-er*] : a user of a pike

pikes *pl of* PIKE, *pres 3d sing of* PIKE

pikestaff \ˈ=,=\ *n* [ME, fr. ¹*pike* + *staff*] **1** : a staff or walking stick with a spike at the end to guard the user from slipping **2** [⁶*pike* + *staff*] : ⁶PIKE 3

pike whale *n* [¹*pike*] : PIKED WHALE

pi·ki \ˈpēkē\ *n* -S [Hopi] : maize bread baked in thin sheets by the Indians of the southwestern U. S.

pik·ing \ˈpīkiŋ\ *n* -S [⁴*pike*] : fishing for pike

pi·kle \ˈpikəl\ *var of* PIGHTLE

pikol *var of* PICUL

piks *pl of* PIK

pil *abbr* **1** [L *pilula*] pill **2** pilot

¹pil- *or* **pili-** *or* **pilo-** *comb form* [L *pilus* — more at PILE] : hair ⟨*pil*osis⟩ ⟨*pili*fer⟩ ⟨*pilo*cystic⟩

²pil- *or* **pilo-** *comb form* [Gk, fr. *pilos* — more at PILE (hair)] : felt ⟨*Pilo*carpus⟩

¹pila *pl of* PILUM

²pi·la \ˈpīlə\ *n, cap* [NL, fr. L *pila* ball — more at PILE (hair)] : the type genus of the family Pilidae comprising apple snails with dextral shells

³pi·la \ˈpēlə\ *n* -S [AmSp, fr. Sp, basin, font, fr. L, pillar] : a communal fountain

pi·laf *or* **pi·laff** *or* **pi·lau** *also* **pi·lav** *or* **pi·law** \pə̇ˈläf, pē'-, -laf, -laa(ə)f, -láf, -laů, -lò, -lō, ˈpē,l-, ˈpi,l-, *in southern U S often* ˈpə̄(,)lü *or* ˈpəi(,)lü *or* -lō\ *n* -S [Per & Turk *pilāu, palāu*] : rice usu. combined with meat and vegetables, fried in oil, steamed in stock, and seasoned with any of numerous herbs (as saffron or curry) ⟨chicken ~⟩ ⟨Turkish ~⟩

pi·la·gá \,pēləˈgä\ *n, pl* **pilagá** *or* **pilagás** *usu cap* **1 a** : a Guaicuruan people of the Gran Chaco, Argentina **b** : a member of such people **2** : the language of the Pilagá people

pi·lar \ˈpīlə(r)\ *adj* [NL *pilaris*, fr. L *pilus* hair + *-aris* -ar — more at PILE] : of or relating to the hair or a hair : HAIRY

pi·la·ry \-ərē\ *adj* [¹*pil-* + *-ary*] : PILAR

pi·las·ter \pə̇ˈlastə(r), -laas-\ *n* -S [MF *pilastre*, fr. It *pilastro*, prob. modif. (influenced by L *pila* pillar & *-aster*, suffix denoting partial resemblance) of L *parastata*, fr. Gk *parastatēs*, lit., one that stands beside, fr. *paristanai* to stand beside, fr. *para* beside + *histanai* to stand — more at PARA-, STAND] **1** : an upright architectural member that is rectangular in plan and is structurally a pier but architecturally treated as a column, that with capital, shaft, and base usu. projects one third of its width or less from the wall, and that may be load-bearing or merely applied as surface decoration **2** : a member in furniture resembling the architectural pilaster but always purely decorative and often elaborately carved **3** : an elongated hardened ridge; *esp* : a longitudinal bony ridge on the back of the femur

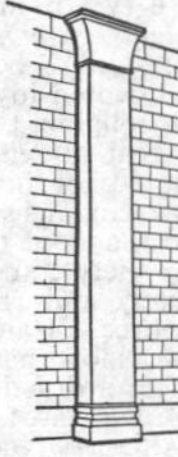
pilaster 1

pi·las·tered \-(r)d\ *adj* [*pilaster* + *-ed*] : having or borne on pilasters

pilasterlike \=ˈ==,=\ *adj* **:** resembling a pilaster

pilaster mass *n* **:** a pier projecting from but usu. built with a wall and differing from the anta and parastas in that it does not form the termination of the projecting wall but usu. stiffens it (as between two windows)

pilaster strip *n* **:** a pilaster mass of slight projection or of slender proportions

pil·as·trade \ˌpiləˈstrād\ *n* -s [It *pilastrata*, fr. *pilastro* — more at PILASTER] **:** a row or series of pilasters — **pil·as·trad·ed** \-dəd\ *adj*

pi·las·tric \pəˈlastrik\ *adj* [*pilaster* + *-ic*] **:** characterized by or like pilasters

pi·lau *also* **pilav** *or* **pilaw** *var of* PILAF

pilch \ˈpilch\ *n* -ES [ME *pilche*, fr. OE *pylce*, *pylece*, fr. ML *pellicea*, fem. of LL *pelliceus*, *pellicius* made of skin, fr. L *pellis* skin — more at FELL] **1 :** an outer garment made orig. of skin or fur and later of leather or wool **2 a** *obs* **:** a saddle cover **b :** a light child's saddle **3 :** an infant's wrapper covering the diaper

pil·chard \ˈpilchə(r)d\ *n* -s [origin unknown] **1 :** a clupeid fish (*Sardinia pilchardus* or *Sardinella pilchardus*) that resembles the herring, occurs in great schools along the coasts of Europe, attains a length of 8 or 10 inches, and that is extensively used for food — see SARDINE **2 :** any of several fishes (family Clupeidae) related to the European pilchard: as **a :** CALIFORNIA SARDINE **b :** a sardine (*Sardinops sagax* or *Arengus sagax*) of the west coast of So. America and the coast of southern Africa that may be identical with the California sardine **c :** an Australian sardine (*Sardinops neopilchardus*)

pilchard oil *n* **:** a pale yellow drying oil obtained from pilchards (as *Sardinops caerulea*) — compare SARDINE OIL

¹pil·cher \ˈpilchə(r)\ *archaic var of* PILCHARD

²pilch·er \ˈ"\ *n* -s [alter. of *pilch*] **:** SCABBARD ⟨will you pluck your sword out of his ~ by the ears —Shak.⟩

³pilcher *n* -s [perh. fr. *pilch* + *-er*] *obs* **:** a contemptible person

pil·crow \ˈpil,krō\ *n* -s [prob. alter. of ME *pylcrafte*, modif. of LL *paragraphus* — more at PARAGRAPH] **:** a paragraph mark ¶

¹pile \ˈpīl, *esp before pause or consonant* -īəl\ *n* -s [ME, dart, pointed shaft, stake, fr. OE *pīl*; akin to OHG *pfīl* dart, arrow, stake; both fr. a prehistoric WGmc word borrowed fr. L *pilum* heavy javelin, pestle — more at PESTLE] **1 :** a long slender member usu. of timber, steel, or reinforced concrete driven into the ground to carry a vertical load, to resist a lateral force, or to resist water or earth pressure — see BATTER PILE, BEARING PILE, SHEET PILE **2 :** a wedge-shaped heraldic charge usu. placed palewise with the broad end up **3 :** a pointed blade of grass **4 a :** a target-shooting arrowhead without cutting edges that is usu. cylindrical or conoidal in shape and either pointed or blunt — called also *point*, *tip* **b** [L *pilum*] **:** an ancient Roman foot soldier's heavy javelin

pile 2

²pile \ˈ"\ *vt* -ED/-ING/-S [ME *pilen*, fr. ¹*pile*] **:** to drive piles into **:** fill, support, or strengthen with piles

³pile \ˈ"\ *adj* [¹*pile*] **:** relating to or used as a pile **:** formed of or supported on piles ⟨a ~ road⟩

⁴pile *n* -S [ME] *obs* **:** a small fortified tower; *esp* **:** PEEL

⁵pile \ˈpīl, *esp before pause or consonant* -īəl\ *n* -s [ME, fr. MF, fr. L *pila* pillar, pier, mole of stone] **1** *obs* **:** a pier of a bridge **2 a :** a quantity of things heaped together or laid one on top of the other ⟨a ~ of dishes⟩ ⟨a small ~ of clothes on a chair —Arnold Bennett⟩ ⟨a ~ of wood by the fireplace⟩: as (1) *obs* **:** a series of weights fitting together and forming a solid figure usu. a cone (2) **:** a heap usu. of wood for burning a corpse or a sacrifice **:** PYRE (3) **:** a stack of arms (4) **:** FAGOT 3 **b :** any great number or large quantity **:** HEAP, LOT ⟨had had a ~ of troubles in his lifetime⟩ ⟨anyone who wants to teach has to take ~s of their education courses —W.L.Miller⟩ ⟨~s of good things to eat, fish, meat, fowls, vegetables —Stringfellow Barr⟩ **3 a :** the lower die of an old English apparatus for striking coins by hand with a hammer — compare TRUSSELL **b :** the reverse of a coin **4 :** a large often imposing building or group of buildings ⟨a Gothic ~⟩ ⟨contrast between the vast ~ of the cathedral and the pigmy men in the street —H.J. Laski⟩ ⟨a great ~ of houses, inhabited by a great number of people —Charles Dickens⟩ **5 a :** a great amount of money **:** FORTUNE ⟨one went to the city . . . made one's ~ and married —Van Wyck Brooks⟩ **b :** all the money or chips a player has available for play in a particular game or at a particular juncture in a game **6 a :** a vertical series of alternate disks of two dissimilar metals (as copper and zinc) with disks of cloth or paper moistened with an electrolyte between them for producing a current of electricity — called also *voltaic pile*, *Volta's pile* **b :** a battery made up of cells similarly constructed ⟨a dry ~⟩ **7 :** REACTOR

⁶pile \ˈ"\ *vb* -ED/-ING/-S [ME *pilen*, fr. ⁵*pile*] *vt* **1 a :** to lay or place in or as if in a pile **:** put or throw on top of a heap **:** STACK — often used with *on* or *up* ⟨sand dunes *piled* up by the winds —Samuel Van Valkenburg & Ellsworth Huntington⟩ ⟨her black hair cut in a straight fringe . . . and *piled* up on top of her head —Edith Sitwell⟩ **b :** to place (as weapons) so as to be easily available ⟨outside the station we *piled* arms and waited —John Sommerfield⟩ **c :** to form a fagot of (lengths of iron) **2 :** to heap in abundance **:** LOAD ⟨*piled* . . . the salad on her plate —Hamilton Basso⟩ **3 a :** to add to esp. for an intensified effect **:** INCREASE ⟨I do think he *piled* the agony up a little too high in that last scene —Frederick Marryat⟩ **b :** to build or gather together **:** AMASS — usu. used with *up* ⟨*piled* up a wealth of information on the American Indian —Ruth Underhill⟩ ⟨forebears were early settlers . . . and quickly *piled* up fortunes —*Amer. Guide Series: Md.*⟩ ⟨hunting down and *piling* up quantities of knowledge —E.M.Burns⟩ ~ *vi* **1 :** to form a pile **:** ACCUMULATE — usu. used with *up* ⟨found the yield of this crop *piling* up on its hands —C.L. Jones⟩ ⟨office work which had *piled* up for months —D.A. Howarth⟩ **2 a :** to move or press forward in or as if in a mass **:** CROWD ⟨pushing one another . . . they *piled* out of the restaurant —Morley Callaghan⟩ ⟨our whole party *piled* into one . . . compartment —O.S.Nock⟩ **b :** to get in, off, or out ⟨he *piled* quickly into bed⟩ **3 :** to thicken and accumulate (as ink on printing plates, rollers, or blankets or paint on a brush) instead of transferring or spreading properly

⁷pile \ˈ"\ *n* -S [ME, fr. L *pila* ball — more at ⁸PILE] **1 :** a single hemorrhoid **2 piles** *pl* **:** HEMORRHOIDS; *also* **:** the condition of one affected with hemorrhoids ⟨is suffering terribly from ~s⟩

⁸pile \ˈ"\ *n* -S [ME, fr. L *pilus* hair; akin to L *pilleus*, *pilleum*, *pileus* felt cap, Gk *pilos* felt, felt cap, ball, L *pila* ball] **1 a :** HAIR; *esp* **:** a growth of short fine hair like fur **:** DOWN **b :** a thick undercoat (as of certain dogs) **c :** a velvety surface of fine hairs on various insects; *collectively* **:** the hairs making up such a surface **2 :** a mass of raised loops or tufts covering all or part of a fabric or carpet that is formed by extra warp or weft yarns during the weaving and that produces a soft even compact furry or velvety surface **3 :** a quality possessed by bread when the crumb is silky in appearance and texture **4 a :** yellowish red coloration on wingbows, neck, saddle, back, and flight feathers of various white domestic fowls that is a disqualification in standard breeds but characteristic of some game types **b :** a bird colored in this manner

¹pi·lea \ˈpīlēə, ˈpil-\ *n, cap* [NL, fr. L *pileus*, *pilleus* felt cap; fr. the shape of a section of the perianth] **:** a genus of chiefly tropical smooth stingless herbs (family Urticaceae) with opposite leaves and greenish axillary flowers

²pilea *pl of* PILEUM

pi·le·a·ta \ˌpīlēˈād·ə, ˌpil-\ *adj* [NL, fr. L, fem. of *pileatus*, *pilleatus*] *of an organ pipe* **:** STOPPED

pi·le·ate \ˈpīlēət, ˈpil-, -ē,āt\ *or* **pi·le·at·ed** \-ē,ād·əd\ *adj* [L *pilleatus*, *pileatus*, fr. *pilleus*, *pileus* felt cap + *-atus* -ate — more at PILE (hair)] **:** having a pileus; *specif* **:** having a crest covering the pileum

pileated woodpecker *n* **:** a No. American woodpecker (*Dryocopus pileatus*) that is black with a red crest and white on the wings and sides of the neck and that inhabits dense forests

pile bent *n* [¹*pile*] **:** the part of a trestle that carries the adjacent ends of timber stringers or concrete slabs and consists of a row of timber or concrete bearing piles and a timber or concrete cap

pile bridge *n* **:** a bridge supported by pile bents

pile cap *n* **1 :** a member passing over and connecting the heads of a row of piles **2 :** a block used to protect the head of a pile and to hold it in the leads while being driven in the ground

¹piled \ˈpīld, *esp before pause or consonant* -īəld\ *adj* [ME, fr. ⁸*pile* + *-ed*] **1 :** having pile **:** covered with hair or down **2 :** having a pile ⟨~ textiles⟩ ⟨~ bread⟩

²piled \ˈ"\ *adj* [fr. past part. of ⁶*pile*] **:** heaped in or into a pile or piles

³piled \ˈ"\ *adj* [¹*pile* + *-ed*] **:** built on piles

pile drawer *n* [¹*pile*] **:** a machine for withdrawing piles

pile driver *n* **1** *or* **pile engine :** a machine for driving down piles usu. consisting of a high frame with appliances for raising and dropping a pile hammer or for supporting and guiding a steam or air hammer **2 :** an operator of a pile driver

pile dweller *n* **:** LAKE DWELLER

pile dwelling *or* **pile house** *n* **:** LAKE DWELLING

pile hammer *n* **:** the heavy weight of the pile driver whose impact forces a pile into the earth

pi·le·i·form \pīˈlēə,fȯrm, ˈpīl-, ˈpil-\ *adj* [NL *pileiformis*, fr. *pileus* + *-iformis* -iform] **:** having the form of a pileus

pile·less \ˈpīlləs\ *adj* **:** having no pile ⟨~ carpet⟩

pi·le·o·lat·ed warbler \ˈpīlēə,lād·əd-\ *n* [*pileolated* capped, fr. L *pilleolus*, *pileolus* small cap (dim. of *pilleus*, *pileus* felt cap) + E *-ate* + *-ed* — more at PILE (hair)] **:** a northwestern warbler that is a variety (*Wilsonia pusilla pileolata*) of Wilson's warbler distinguished by a brighter olive green on the upper parts and a deeper yellow beneath

pi·le·o·lus \pīˈlēələs\ *n, pl* **pileo·li** \-ə,lī\ [NL, dim. of *pileus*] *biol* **:** a small pileus

pi·le·ous \ˈpīlēəs, ˈpil-\ *adj* [¹*pil-* + *-eous*] **:** HAIRY, PILOSE

pile perch *n* [¹*pile*] **1 :** a common surf fish (*Rhacochilus vacca*) dusky with a silvery luster above fading to silver below that is common along sandy shores of the Pacific coast of No. America and is a leading market fish of the area **2 :** RUBBERLIP PERCH

pile plank *n* **:** a thick plank used as a pile in sheetpiling

pil·er \ˈpīlə(r)\ *n* -s [⁶*pile* + *-er*] **:** one that piles or heaps up; *esp* **:** one whose work is piling materials or products for storage, transportation, or processing

piles *pl of* PILE, *pres 3d sing of* PILE

pile saw *n* [¹*pile*] **:** a saw for cutting piles under water

pile start *n* **:** a pintail (*Anas acuta*)

pi·le·um \ˈpīlēəm, ˈpil-\ *n, pl* **pi·lea** \-ēə\ [NL, fr. L *pilleum*, *pileum* felt cap, fr. *pilleus*, *pileus*] **:** the top of the head of a bird from the bill to the nape

pile up *vi* [⁶*pile*] **1 :** to get into a tangle or confused mass ⟨angry horn blasts from cars that had *piled up* in the intersection⟩ **2 :** to run aground **:** become stranded ⟨that difficult coast where the wrecks still *piled up* —Marjory S. Douglas⟩ ⟨*piled up* on a reef just off a lovely island —*Time*⟩ **3 a :** to become involved in a pileup of vehicles; *broadly* **:** to wreck one's car **:** crack up **b :** to crash an airplane

pileup \ˈ=,=\ *n* -s [⁶*pile* + *up*] **:** a collision involving usu. several objects and causing damage or injury ⟨was instantly killed in an automobile ~ —*Springfield (Mass.) Union*⟩

pi·le·us \ˈpīlēəs, ˈpil-\ *n, pl* **pi·lei** \-ē,ī\ [NL, fr. L *pilleus*, *pileus* felt cap — more at PILE (hair)] **1 :** an umbrella-shaped upper cap of many fungi (as the mushrooms and other basidiomycetes) **2** [L *pilleus*, *pileus*] **a :** a pointed or close-fitting cap worn by ancient Romans **b :** a cap worn by some ecclesiastics **3 :** the umbrella of a jellyfish **4 :** a cloud resembling a cap that sometimes appears above and partially obscures the bulging top of a cumulus cloud

pilework \ˈ=,=\ *n* [¹*pile* + *work*] **1 :** work consisting of piles **2 :** a structure of piles (as in lake dwellings)

pileworm \ˈ=,=\ *n* [¹*pile* + *worm*] **:** SHIPWORM

pilewort \ˈ=,=\ *n* [⁷*pile* + *wort*; fr. its use in treating piles] **1 :** LESSER CELANDINE **2 :** a coarse hairy erect but much branched perennial figwort (*Scrophularia marilandica*) of the eastern and central U.S. that was formerly believed useful in the treatment of scrofula **3 :** a very variable fireweed (*Erechtites hieracifolia*) chiefly of damp woodlands of eastern No. America that has heads of straw-colored tubular flowers **4 :** PRINCE'S-FEATHER 1

piley \ˈpīlē\ *adj* [⁸*pile* + *-y*] **:** having pile; *esp* **:** having a strong development of pile

¹pil·fer \ˈpilfə(r)\ *n* -s [ME *pilfre*, fr. MF *pelfre*] *archaic* **:** something that is pilfered; *also* **:** the act of pilfering **:** PILFERAGE

²pilfer \ˈ"\ *vb* **pilfered; pilfered; pilfering** \-f(ə)riŋ\ **pilfers** [MF *pelfrer*, fr. *pelfre* booty] *vi* **:** PLUNDER, ROB; *esp* **:** to steal little by little or by taking articles of small value **:** commit or practice petty theft ⟨~*ed* from his fellow students —*Times Lit. Supp.*⟩ ~ *vt* **1 :** to steal in small quantities **:** FILCH ⟨~*ed* his roommate's stamps and writing paper⟩ **2 :** to take (as ideas or thoughts) and use as one's own **:** CRIB ⟨able to ~ all the new ideas of industrial construction —Emil Lengyel⟩ **syn** see STEAL

pil·fer·age \-f(ə)rij\ *n* -s [²*pilfer* + *-age*] **1 a :** the act of pilfering **b :** something that is pilfered **2** *insurance law* **:** the theft of insured property by one not in possession

pilferage hazard *n* **:** the risk of loss to cargo when specifically covered by marine insurance through theft committed by the ship's crew, stevedores, or others having access to the insured subject matter

pil·fer·er \-f(ə)rə(r)\ *n* -s **:** one that pilfers **:** a petty thief

pil·fery \-rē\ *n* -ES [prob. alter. of earlier *pelfery* booty, fr. (assumed) ONF *pelferie*, fr. the source of MF *pelfre* booty] **:** petty theft

pil·gar·lic \pilˈgärlik\ *also* **peel·gar·lic** \pēl-\ *n* -s [*pilgarlic* fr. *pilled garlic*, fr. ²*pill*; *peelgarlic*, alter. (influenced by ²*peel*) of *pilgarlic*] **1 a :** a bald head **b :** a bald-headed man **2 :** a man looked upon with humorous contempt or mock pity **:** a poor creature

¹pil·grim \ˈpilgrəm\ *n* -s *except sense 6a* [ME, fr. OF *peligrin*, fr. LL *pelegrinus*, alter. of L *peregrinus* foreigner, fr. *peregre* abroad, fr. *pereger* being abroad, fr. *per* through + *agr-*, *ager* land, field — more at FARE, ACRE] **1 a :** one who journeys esp. in alien lands **:** TRAVELER, WAYFARER **b :** a person who passes through life as if in exile from a heavenly homeland or in search of it or of some high goal (as truth) **2 :** one who travels to visit a shrine or holy place as a devotee ⟨realizes the ideal of every devout ~ and journeys to the Holy Land —R.M.French⟩ **3 a** *usu cap* **:** one of the Pilgrim Fathers **b :** a first settler ⟨trace their line back to the original . . . ~*s* —*Amer. Guide Series: Md.*⟩ **4 :** a recent immigrant or settler **:** one that is new or strange in a locality **5 :** FASHION GRAY **6 a** *usu cap* **:** an American breed of rather small domestic geese distinguished by having the male white and the female gray **b** *sometimes cap* **:** a bird of this breed

²pilgrim \ˈ"\ *vi* -ED/-ING/-S **:** to be or act as a pilgrim **:** PILGRIMAGE ⟨they had ~*ed* for that peace —R.O.Bowen⟩

¹pil·grim·age \ˈpilgrəmij\ *n* -s [ME *pelrimage*, *pilgrimage*, fr. OF *pelerinage*, fr. *pelerin*, *peligrin* pilgrim + *-age*] **1 a :** a journey of a pilgrim; *esp* **:** one to a shrine or a sacred place ⟨Arabs make ~*s* to worship at his tomb —Robert Hichens⟩ **b :** the act of making such a journey ⟨~ had . . . been adopted by the church as a form of canonical penance —M.W.Baldwin⟩ **2 :** a trip taken to visit a place of historic or sentimental interest or to participate in a specific event or for a definite purpose ⟨American writers, artists and composers have made ~*s* to France —G.W.Chapman⟩ ⟨every spring the rhododendron inspires . . . ~*s* —*Amer. Guide Series: Wash.*⟩ **3 a :** the course of life on earth ⟨prosperity . . . came to him during his earthly ~ —V.L.Parrington⟩ **b :** a particular part of the life course of an individual ⟨my ~ from prep school to University —Osbert Lancaster⟩ **4 :** a search for mental and spiritual values ⟨the pursuit of knowledge was no mere intellectual search, but a ~ —H.O.Taylor⟩

²pilgrimage \ˈ"\ *vi* -ED/-ING/-S **:** to go on or as if on a pilgrimage ⟨all . . . had *pilgrimaged* to the capital —Walter Goodman⟩

pilgrimage festival *n* **:** any of three great festivals in the Jewish calendar orig. celebrated in part by a pilgrimage to Jerusalem — compare PASSOVER, SHABUOTH, SUKKOTH

pilgrim bottle *also* **pilgrim's bottle** *n* **:** a flat usu. circular bottle with a small spout and with rings to hold a cord for slinging it over the shoulder

pilgrim brown *n* **:** a grayish brown to dark grayish brown — called also *friar*, *mandalay*

pil·grim·er \-rəmə(r)\ *n* -s [²*pilgrim* + *-er*] **:** PILGRIM

pil·grim·ess \-məs\ *n* -ES [¹*pilgrim* + *-ess*] **:** a female pilgrim

pilgrim father *n, usu cap P&F* **:** one of the English colonists who under the dominant religious motivation of a minority of Separatists from the Church of England sailed to America in 1620 aboard the *Mayflower* and founded the first permanent settlement in New England

pil·grim·ize \-rə,mīz\ *vb* -ED/-ING/-S *vi* **:** to go or act as a pilgrim ~ *vt* **:** to make a pilgrim of

pilgrim psalm *n, usu cap both Ps* **:** SONG OF ASCENTS

pilgrim scallop *or* **pilgrim's scallop shell** *also* **pilgrim's shell** *n* **:** a scallop shell or something resembling it worn as a pilgrim sign

pilgrim sign *n* **:** a symbol or badge (as palm leaves, a catherine wheel, a Canterbury bell) carried by a pilgrim to indicate the shrine he sought or had visited and believed to preserve him against molestation

¹pili *pl of* PILUS

²pi·li \pēˈlē\ *or* **pili nut** *n* -s [Tag *pili*] **1 :** the nut of any of various trees of the genus *Canarium*; *esp* **:** the edible nut of a Philippine tree (*Canarium ovatum*) **2 :** JAVA ALMOND

³pi·li \ˈpēlē\ *or* **pili grass** *n* -s [Hawaiian, lit., to adhere, cling] *Hawaii* **:** TANGLEHEAD

pili- — see PIL-

pi·li·bezoar \ˌpīlə+\ *n* [¹*pil-* + *bezoar*] **:** HAIR BALL

pi·li·dae \ˈpilə,dē\ *n pl, cap* [NL, fr. *Pila*, type genus + *-idae*] **:** a family of oviparous freshwater snails having the respiratory cavity modified to permit breathing in either air or water — see APPLE SNAIL, PILA

pi·lid·i·um \pīˈlidēəm\ *n, pl* **pilid·ia** \-ēə\ [NL, fr. Gk *pilidion*, dim. of *pilos* felt cap — more at PILE (hair)] **:** the free-swimming hat-shaped larva of various nemertean worms in whose interior the young worm develops

pilier *comparative of* PILY

piliest *superlative of* PILY

pi·li·fer \ˈpiləfə(r)\ *n* -s [NL, fr. ¹*pil-* + *-fer*] **:** a lateral hairy process of the labrum in Lepidoptera formerly regarded as the vestige of the mandible

pi·lif·er·ous \(ˈ)pīˈlif(ə)rəs\ *adj* [¹*pil-* + *-ferous*] **:** bearing or producing hairs — compare PILOSE

pi·li·gan \ˈpēlē,gän\ *n* -s [NL *Piligena*, genus of Lycopodiaceae, fr. ²*pil-* + *-gena* -gen] **:** a club moss (*Lycopodium saururus*) of Brazil and Argentina with cathartic properties

pili gum *n* [²*pili*] **:** BREA 1 a (2)

pi·li·kia \ˌpēlēˈkēə\ *n* -s [Hawaiian] *Hawaii* **:** TROUBLE

pi·line \ˈpī,līn, -ˌlən\ *adj* [¹*pil-* + *-ine*] **:** HAIRY

piling *n* -s [ME, fr. gerund of ²*pile*] **1 :** pile driving **:** the formation (as of a foundation) with piles **2 :** a structure of piles **:** PILEWORK; *collectively* **:** PILES **3 :** logs suitable for or ready to be made into piles

piling strip *n* **:** a narrow piece of lumber used to separate the courses in a pile

¹pill \ˈpil\ *n* -s [earlier *pille*, fr. (assumed) ME, fr. OE *pyll*, alter. of *pull* pool, creek, prob. of OW origin] **1** *dial Eng* **:** POOL **2** *dial Eng* **:** a running stream **:** CREEK

²pill \ˈ"\ *vb* -ED/-ING/-S [ME *pilen*, *pillen*, partly fr. OE *pilian* to peel (prob. fr. L *pilare* to depilate, fr. *pilus* hair), partly fr. MF *piller* to plunder — more at PILE, PILLAGE] *vi*, *dial chiefly Eng* **:** PEEL **:** come off esp. in flakes or scales ~ *vt* **1 a** *archaic* **:** to subject to depredation or extortion **:** DESPOIL, ROB ⟨the commons hath he ~*ed* with grievous taxes and quite lost their hearts —Shak.⟩ **b** *obs* **:** to seize by violence **:** EXTORT ⟨hear me, you wrangling pirates, that fall out in sharing that which you have ~*ed* from me —Shak.⟩ **2** *dial* **:** to peel or strip off (as bark) ⟨took him rods of green poplar . . . and ~*ed* white streaks in them —Gen 30:37 (AV)⟩ **3** *obs* **:** to deprive of hair **:** remove hair from

³pill \ˈ"\ *n* -s [ME *pile*, fr. *pilen* to pill] *dial* **:** the peel or rind of fruit **:** the shell or skin of fruits and bulbous roots **:** the bark of a tree

⁴pill \ˈ"\ *n* -s [L *pilula*, lit., little ball, dim. of *pila* ball — more at PILE (hair)] **1 :** a medicine in the form of a little ball or small rounded mass that may be coated or uncoated and is to be swallowed whole — compare TABLET **2 :** something offensive, repugnant, or unpleasant that must be accepted or endured ⟨the loss of the promotion was a bitter ~ to swallow⟩ **3 :** something resembling a pill usu. in size or shape: as **a :** PELLET 1a ⟨kneading his bread into little white ~*s* —Robin Maugham⟩ **b** (1) **:** CANNONBALL (2) **:** a musket ball ⟨thirty thousand muskets flung their ~*s* like hail —Lord Byron⟩ **c** *slang* (1) **:** BASEBALL (2) **:** GOLF BALL **d :** a small ball of textile fibers often formed by the balling of nap when subject to friction **e :** a compressed mass of a plastic material for use in a mold **:** PREFORM **4 :** a disagreeable or tiresome person ⟨she was considered in some circles a vast ~ —Alma Stone⟩ **5 a** *slang* **:** CIGARETTE **b :** a portion of opium prepared for smoking

⁵pill \ˈ"\ *vb* -ED/-ING/-S *vt* **1 :** to dose with pills **2 :** BLACKBALL **3 :** to make or form into or as if into pills ~ *vi* **:** to form balls ⟨sweaters made of wool yarns may have a tendency to ~ —*Chicago Daily Drovers Jour.*⟩

¹pil·lage \ˈpilij, -lēj\ *n* -s [ME, fr. MF, fr. *piller* to plunder (fr. *peille* rag, fr. L *pilleum* felt cap) + *-age* — more at PILL (hair)] **1 a :** the act of stripping of money and goods esp. during war **:** SACK ⟨the painting may have been ruined in a ~ or massacre —Willa Cather⟩ ⟨plan for the ~ and enslavement of the earth —Calvin Coolidge⟩ **b :** the unlawful taking of property **:** ROBBERY **2** *archaic* **:** something taken as booty **:** SPOIL ⟨robbed all the country there about and brought the ~ home —Edmund Spenser⟩

²pillage \ˈ", *esp in pres part* -ləj\ *vb* -ED/-ING/-S *vt* **1 :** to strip of money or goods by open violence **:** LOOT, SACK ⟨pirates *pillaged* the coasts —C.L.Jones⟩ **2 :** to acquire by stealing **:** take possession of unlawfully **:** PURLOIN ⟨gradually deserted, *pillaged* for building material, so that little marble remains —Claudia Cassidy⟩ ⟨the thought process which leads to the *pillaging* of an idea —L.P.Beth⟩ ⟨tobacco *pillaged* from a tin-full which his father had bought —Arthur Morrison⟩ ~ *vi* **:** to take booty **:** PLUNDER ⟨swept down . . . burning and *pillaging* —Mary Smith⟩ **syn** see RAVAGE

pil·lag·er \-jə(r)\ *n* -s **:** one that pillages

¹pil·lar \ˈpilə(r)\ *n* -s [ME *piler*, *piller*, fr. OF *piler*, fr. ML *pilare*, fr. L *pila* pillar, pier] **1 a :** a firm upright support for a superstructure **:** POST **b :** a column or shaft standing alone esp. for a monument **2 :** a natural pillar-shaped formation or mass ⟨to follow in the wake of another vehicle . . . was to move in a ~ of dust —Rose Macaulay⟩ ⟨little ~*s* of sand rose here and there —Norman Douglas⟩ **3 :** one that is a mainstay **:** a chief supporter **:** PROP ⟨a rough-hewn ~ of the . . . Church —Ben Riker⟩ ⟨the middlemen, . . . the ~*s* of society, the cornerstone of convention —Roy Lewis & Angus Maude⟩ **4 :** any of various vertical supporting members: as **a :** the central support of a table **:** PEDESTAL **b :** BEDPOST **c :** STANCHION **d :** the vertical hollow post of a harp frame — see HARP illustration **5 :** something regarded as a chief support **:** a fundamental fact, idea, principle, or practice ⟨science and criticism had eaten away the ~*s* of superstition and unreasoning faith —W.P.Webb⟩ ⟨there are five compulsory practices, or ~*s* of Islam —A.C.Bouquet⟩ **6 :** any of the brass posts between the two plates of a watch or clock movement that serve to keep the plates in their proper positions **7 :** a solid mass of coal, rock, or ore left standing to support the roof **8 :** the center of the volt, ring, or manege ground around which a horse turns **9 :** a body part likened to a pillar or column (as the columella of a snail shell or the margin of the external abdominal ring); *specif* **:** PILLAR OF THE FAUCES **10 :** a mailbox shaped like a pillar **11 :** a frame on which clay pipes rest while being baked in a kiln — **from pillar to post :** from one place or one situation to another **:** HITHER AND THITHER ⟨the library . . . forced to move *from pillar to post* needed a home —*Saturday Rev.*⟩

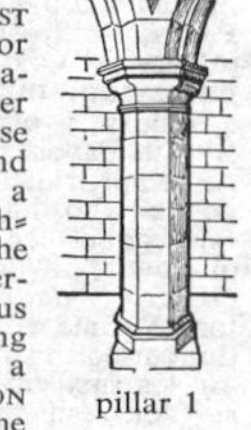

pillar 1

²pillar \ˈ"\ *vb* -ED/-ING/-S *vt* **1 :** to support or strengthen with or as if with a pillar **2 :** to embody in or represent in the form of a pillar ~ *vi* **:** to be supported by pillars

pillar-and-breast \ˈ≈≈ˌ≈\ *adj* **:** BORD-AND-PILLAR
pillar and scroll *n* **:** an early American shelf clock designed with slender pillars and scrolled cresting and ornamented with turned wood finials
pillar bolt *n* **:** a projecting stud bolt intended to support a part near its outer end
pillar–box \ˈ≈ˌ≈\ *n, Brit* **:** a pillar-shaped mailbox
pillar crane *n* **:** a crane the mechanism of which can be rotated about a fixed pillar
pillar dollar *n* **:** the old Spanish-American peso having on its reverse two pillars with a ribbon about them
pillar drawing *n* **:** PILLAR ROBBING
pil·lared \ˈpilə(r)d\ *adj* [ME *pilered*, fr. *piler* pillar + *-ed*] **:** having pillars **:** resembling or formed into a pillar ⟨the ~ portico —Osbert Lancaster⟩

pillar and scroll

pil·lar·et \ˈpiləˌret\ *n* -s [¹*pillar* + *-et*] **:** a little pillar
pillar file *n* **:** a usu. double-cut file that is rectangular in section, parallel in width with one safe edge, and tapered in thickness from the middle both ways and that is esp. suitable for narrow work
pil·lar·ing \ˈpilərıŋ\ *n* -s [¹*pillar* + *-ing*] **:** a series of pillars; *collectively* **:** PILLARS
pil·lar·ist \ˈpilərəst\ *n* -s [¹*pillar* + *-ist*] *relig* **:** STYLITE
pillar light *n* **:** a light mounted on the pillar between doors of an automobile
pillar lip *n* **:** the inner or columellar portion of the border of the orifice of a spiral shell
pillar mount *n* **:** a mount or support in the form of a pillar for a gun in a fortification
pillar of fire *adj, usu cap P&F* [fr. *Pillar of Fire*, bulletin published by the founder of the sect] **:** of, relating to, or being a fundamentalist holiness premillenarian church beginning as an offshoot of U.S. Methodism in 1901, retaining Methodist polity, and emphasizing sanctification as a second work of grace following justification
pillar of the diaphragm : any of the crura of the diaphragm
pillar of the fauces : one of the lateral bounding folds of the fauces
pillar of the fornix : either of the anterior and posterior diverging extensions of the fornix of the brain
pillar plate *n* **:** the plate in watchworks that is nearest to the dial
pillar press *n* **:** a punch press with a frame of two parallel uprights through which the driving shaft passes and within which the slide works
pillar robbing *n* **:** the mining and removal of pillars after the main coal or ore body has been removed — called also *pillar drawing*
pillar root *n* **:** PROP ROOT
pillar rose *n* **:** any of various climbing roses growing to a moderate height and esp. adapted for use on low fences and walls
pillars *pl of* PILLAR, *pres 3d sing of* PILLAR
pillar saint *n* **:** STYLITE
pillar shaper *n* **:** a shaper whose reciprocating toolhead is mounted on a pillar, the feeding being obtained by a movement of the table to which the work is secured
pillar–stone \ˈ≈≈ˌ≈\ *n* **1 :** a pillar-shaped monument or memorial of stone **2 :** CORNERSTONE
pil·lary \ˈpilərē\ *adj* [¹*pillar* + *-y*] **:** PILLARED
pill–bearing spurge \ˈ≈ˌ≈≈-\ *n* [⁴*pill*] **:** a dried herb (*Euphorbia pilulifera*) used esp. in folk medicine in the treatment of asthma
pillbox \ˈ≈ˌ≈\ *n* **1 :** a box for pills; *esp* **:** a shallow round box of pasteboard **2 :** a small low emplacement for machine guns and antitank weapons that is usu. made of reinforced concrete with overhead cover and forms part of a defensive position **3 :** a small round brimless hat; *specif* **:** a woman's shallow hat with a flat crown and straight sides
pill bug *n* **:** WOOD LOUSE
pilled \ˈpild\ *adj* [ME *piled, pilled*, fr. past part. of *pilen, pillen* to pill] *dial* **:** having a bald or shaven head **:** TONSURED
pil·ler \ˈpilə(r)\ *dial var of* PILLOW
pil·let \ˈpilət\ *n* -s [ME, alter. of *pelet* pellet] **:** a small pill **:** PELLET
pil·li·cock \ˈpiləˌkäk\ *n* [E dial. *pillie* penis (of Scand origin, the source of Norw dial. *pill* penis) + *cock*] **1** *obs* **:** PENIS **2** *obs* **:** a fine lad
pilling *pres part of* PILL
¹pil·lion \ˈpilyən\ *n* -s [ScGael or IrGael; ScGael *pillean*, dim. of *peall* covering, couch; IrGael *pillín*, dim. of *peall* covering, couch; ScGael & IrGael *peall* fr. a prehistoric Goidelic word borrowed fr. L *pellis* skin, hide — more at FELL] **1 a :** a light saddle for women consisting chiefly of a cushion or pannel **b :** a pad or cushion put on behind a man's saddle chiefly for a woman to ride on **2 :** a motorcycle or bicycle riding saddle for a passenger
²pillion \ˈ"\ *vt* -ED/-ING/-S **:** to seat on a pillion
³pillion \ˈ"\ *adv* **:** on or as if on a pillion ⟨ride ~ behind their sleek and slender cavaliers —Frances P. Keyes⟩
⁴pillion \ˈ"\ *n* -s [Corn *pylyon*, pl. of *pyl* peel, stripping, prob. fr. E *peel*] **:** tin left in the slags after the first smelting — compare PRILLION
pil·li·winks \ˈpiləˌwiŋks\ *n pl but sing or pl in constr* [ME *pyrwykes, pyrewinkes*] **:** an old instrument of torture for the thumbs and fingers
pill masser *n* [⁴*pill*] **:** a machine that mixes the ingredients for pills
pill millipede *n* **:** PILLWORM
pil·lor \ˈpilə(r)\ *vt* -ED/-ING/-S [back-formation fr. ¹*pillory*] **:** PILLORY
pil·lor·ize \-ləˌrīz\ *vt* -ED/-ING/-S [¹*pillory* + *-ize*] **:** PILLORY
¹pil·lory \ˈpilərē, -ri\ *n* -ES [ME, fr. OF *pilori*] **1 :** a device for publicly punishing offenders consisting of a frame of adjustable boards erected on a post and having holes through which the head and hands of the offender were thrust — compare STOCK 4 **2 :** a means by which to expose to public scorn or ridicule ⟨~ by publicity today is nationwide —R.H. Paul & Philip Mandel⟩
²pillory \ˈ"\ *vt* **pilloried; pilloried; pillorying; pillories 1 :** to set in a pillory **:** punish with the pillory **2 :** to expose or hold up to public contempt, ridicule, or scorn ⟨a demagogue who has risen to power by ~*ing* good men —*Newsweek*⟩

pillory

¹pil·low \ˈpi(ˌ)lō, -lə; -ləw *or* -lō+V\ *n* -s [ME *pilwe*, fr. OE *pyle, pylu*; akin to OHG *pfuliwi* pillow; both fr. a prehistoric WGmc word borrowed fr. L *pulvinus* pillow] **1 a :** something used to support the head of a person resting or sleeping; *esp* **:** a sack or bag made typically of cloth and filled with a soft or resilient material (as feathers, down, hair, sponge rubber) **:** CUSHION **b :** something resembling a pillow ⟨the hemlock tree . . . let its ~ of new snow slip to the ground —*New Yorker*⟩ **2 :** a block or support used esp. to equalize or distribute pressure **:** PILLOW BLOCK **3 :** a cushion or pad tightly stuffed and used as a support for the design and tools in making bobbin lace
²pillow \ˈ"\ *vb* -ED/-ING/-S *vt* **1 :** to rest or lay on or as if on a pillow ⟨his head ~*ed* on a sack —Kenneth Roberts⟩ **2 :** to serve as a pillow for ⟨her arm gently ~*ed* the sleeping child⟩ **3 :** to support by means of a pillow or something resembling a pillow **:** CUSHION ⟨~*ed* his back comfortably in the big chair⟩ **4 :** to furnish or equip with pillows ⟨fine lounging chairs of bamboo and reed handsomely ~*ed* in bright blocked linen —Adria Langley⟩ ~ *vi* **:** to lay or rest one's head on or as if on a pillow
pillowback \ˈ≈≈ˌ≈\ *adj* [¹*pillow* + *back*] *of a chair* **:** having an oval-turned section in the center of the top rail suggesting a pillow in shape
pil·low·beer \ˈpilōˌbi(ə)r\ *n* [ME *pilwe beer*, fr. *pilwe* pillow + *beer, bere* covering; akin to MD *-buur* covering] *chiefly dial* **:** PILLOWCASE
pillow block *n* **:** a block or standard to support a journal (as of a shaft) **:** BEARING
pillowcase \ˈ≈≈ˌ≈\ *n* **:** a removable covering for a pillow usu. of white linen or cotton cloth
pillow fight *n* **1 :** a sham battle with pillows esp. among children ready for bed **2 :** a sham fight or trivial argument
pillow lace *n* **:** BOBBIN LACE
pillow lava *n* **:** lava commonly basaltic in type that is congealed in rounded masses suggestive of pillows and is believed by most geologists to be indicative of submarine eruption or flow
pillow sham *n* **:** a decorative covering enclosing or laid over a pillow on a bed or couch
pillow slip *n* **:** PILLOWCASE
pillow structure *n* **:** PILLOW LAVA
pillowwork \ˈ≈≈ˌ≈\ *n* **:** decorative treatment of surfaces using projections resembling pillows **:** PULVINATION
pil·lowy \ˈpiləwē\ *adj* **:** of, relating to, or resembling a pillow
pill pipe *n* [⁴*pill*] **:** a thin rod that is formed by rolling the mixture from a pill masser on a pill tile and is then cut into pieces of the proper size for pills
pillroller \ˈ≈ˌ≈≈\ *n* **:** ²MEDIC ⟨~ had missed on the diagnosis —N.C.McDonald⟩
pills *pl of* PILL, *pres 3d sing of* PILL
pill tile *n* **:** a flat slab of porcelain or glass on which the mixture from a pill masser is placed and rolled
pillular *var of* PILULAR
pillule *var of* PILULE
pillwillet *var of* PILWILLET
pill wood louse *n* [⁴*pill*] **:** WOOD LOUSE 1
pillworm \ˈ≈ˌ≈\ *n* [⁴*pill* + *worm*] **:** a millepede that curls up to protect itself
pillwort \ˈ≈ˌ≈\ *n* [⁴*pill* + *wort*; fr. its small globose sporocarps] **:** a water fern of the genus *Pilularia*; *esp* **:** a widely but locally distributed European plant (*P. globulifera*) occurring chiefly about the margins of bodies of water or in wet acid soil
pilm \ˈpilm\ *n* -s [origin unknown] *dial Eng* **:** DUST
pilo- — see PIL-
pi·lob·o·lus \pīˈläbələs\ *n, cap* [NL, fr. Gk *pilos* felt cap, ball + *-bolos* throwing (fr. *ballein* to throw) — more at PILE (hair), DEVIL] **:** a genus of saprophytic fungi (order Mucorales) notable for the forcible ejection of the entire ripe sporangium
pi·lo·car·pi·dine \ˌpīləˈkärpəˌdēn, ˌpil-, -dən\ *n* -s [ISV *pilocarp-* (fr. NL *Pilocarpus*) + *-idine*] **:** a liquid alkaloid $C_{10}H_{14}N_2O_2$ closely related to pilocarpine and occurring with it in the leaves of jaborandi (*Pilocarpus jaborandi*)
pi·lo·car·pine \-rˌpēn, -rpən\ *n* -s [ISV *pilocarp-* + *-ine*] **:** an alkaloid $C_{11}H_{16}N_2O_2$ derived from imidazole and butyrolactone that is obtained from jaborandi as an oily syrup crystallizing when quite pure, that is a strong sialagogue and diaphoretic, and that is used chiefly in the form of its hydrochloride or nitrate as a miotic in glaucoma or in counteracting mydriasis caused by atropine
pi·lo·car·pus \ˌpīləˈkärpəs, ˌpil-\ *n* [NL, fr. ²*pil-* + *-carpus*] **1** *cap* **:** a small genus of tropical American shrubs (family Rutaceae) having small greenish flowers in long racemes with versatile anthers and one-seeded loculi in the ovary **2** -ES **:** JABORANDI 1
pi·lo·cystic \ˌpīlō+\ *adj* [¹*pil-* + *cystic*] *of a dermoid tumor* **:** encysted and containing hair
pi·lo·erection \"+\ *n* [¹*pil-* + *erection*] **:** involuntary erection or bristling of hairs due to a sympathetic reflex usu. triggered by cold, shock, or fright or due to a sympathomimetic agent
pi·lo·motion \"+\ *n* [¹*pil-* + *motion*] **:** movement of cutaneous hair
pi·lo·motor \"+\ *adj* [ISV ¹*pil-* + *motor*] **:** moving or tending to cause movement of the hairs of the skin ⟨~ nerves⟩
pilomotor muscle *n* **:** ERECTOR PILI
pilomotor nerve *n* **:** an autonomic nerve supplying an erector pili
pi·lon \pēˈlōn\ *n* -s [MexSp *pilón*, fr. Sp, mortar, sugar loaf, fr. L *pila* mortar; akin to L *pilum* pestle — more at PESTLE] *Southwest* **:** a bonus given with a large purchase, a trade, or a cash payment **:** LAGNIAPPE
pi·lon·ci·llo \ˌpēlōnˈsē(ˌ)(y)ō\ *n* -s [MexSp, dim. of Sp *pilón* — more at PILON] **:** unrefined sugar esp. when molded into cones or sticks
pi·lo·ni·dal \ˌpīləˈnīdᵊl\ *adj* [¹*pil-* + L *nidus* nest + E *-al* — more at NEST] **1 :** containing hair nested in a cyst — used of congenitally anomalous cysts in the sacrococcygeal area that often become infected and discharge through a channel near the anus **2 :** of, relating to, involving, or for use on pilonidal cysts, tracts, or sinuses
pi·lo·ri *or* **pilori rat** \pəˈlōrē\ *n* -s [perh. of Arawakan or Cariban origin] **:** a Cuban hutia (*Capromys pilorides*)
pi·lo·sa \pəˈlōsə\ *n pl, cap* [NL, fr. L, neut. pl. of *pilosus* hairy] **:** a division of edentate mammals comprising the sloths, anteaters, and extinct related forms
pi·lose \ˈpīˌlōs\ *adj* [L *pilosus*, fr. *pilus* hair + *-osus* -ose — more at PILE] **:** covered with hair esp. of soft texture **:** HAIRY
pi·lo·sebaceous \ˌpīlō+\ *adj* [¹*pil-* + *sebaceous*] **:** of or relating to hair and the sebaceous glands
pi·lo·sine \ˈpīləˌsēn, -sən\ *n* -s [ISV *pil-* (fr. *pilocarpine*) + *-ose* + *-ine*] **:** a crystalline alkaloid $C_{16}H_{18}N_2O_3$ occurring in the leaves of jaborandi (*Pilocarpus microphyllus*)
pi·lo·sis \pīˈlōsəs\ *n* -ES [NL, fr. ¹*pil-* + *-osis*] **:** the condition of abnormal or excessive growth of hair
pi·lo·sism \ˈpīləˌsizəm\ *n* -s [L *pilosus* + ISV *-ism*] **:** abnormal hairiness
pi·los·i·ty \pīˈläsəd·ē\ *n* -ES [ML *pilositat-, pilositas*, fr. L *pilosus* hairy + *-itat-, -itas* -ity — more at PILOSE] **:** the state of being pilose **:** HAIRINESS
¹pi·lot \ˈpīlət, *usu* -əd·+V\ *n* -s *often attrib* [MF *pilote*, fr. It *pilota*, alter. of *pedota*, fr. (assumed) MGk *pēdōtēs*, fr. Gk *pēda* steering oars, rudder, pl. of *pēdon* oar; akin to Gk *pod-, pous* foot — more at FOOT] **1 a :** one employed to steer a ship **:** HELMSMAN **b :** a person who is duly qualified and usu. licensed to conduct a ship into and out of a port or in special waters, often for fixed fees and who while in charge has the whole conduct of her navigation **c :** a book giving detailed navigational information of a body of water and the adjacent coastline **2 :** a guide who leads along a difficult or unknown course **:** one who takes charge during dangerous or unsettled times **:** a leader who inspires **3 :** MENOMINEE WHITEFISH **4 a :** an inclined triangular frame on the front of a railroad locomotive for removing obstacles from the track — called also *cowcatcher* **b :** a locomotive engineer assigned to assist in operating a train over track with which the regular engineer is unfamiliar **5 :** one who flies or is qualified to fly an airplane — see COMMERCIAL PILOT, TRANSPORT PILOT **6 a :** a cylindrical projection at the end of a tool (as a counterbore, countersink, boring rod) to guide it **b :** a bar or simple element acting as a guide or relay for another mechanical element **c :** an auxiliary mechanism that actuates, energizes, governs, or regulates another mechanism ⟨a *pilot*-operated sliding disk valve⟩ **7 :** the relatively small heading or excavation first made in the driving of a larger tunnel **8 :** the manager of a baseball team

1 pilot 4a

²pilot \"\ *vt* -ED/-ING/-S **1 a :** to guide along strange paths or through dangerous places ⟨a mountain man ~*ed* them through the Blackfoot country —R.H.Billington⟩ **b :** CONDUCT, ESCORT ⟨were ~*ed* . . . up to the capitol to pay our respects to the governor —A.W.Long⟩ ⟨~*s* the customers to their tables —Joseph Wechsberg⟩ **2 :** to steer or set the course of (a ship) **:** serve as a pilot on, for, or over ⟨~*ing* ships through the canal⟩ ⟨all were charged with ~*ing* raiding parties from a British fleet —*Amer. Guide Series: Md.*⟩ **3 :** to direct or lead in a straight course esp. under difficult circumstances ⟨~*ed* through the House the government's elaborate education bill —*Newsweek*⟩ **4 a :** to fly or act as pilot of (an airplane) ⟨~*ed* the huge transport plane to the west coast⟩ **b :** to drive or act as operator of (as a motor vehicle) ⟨through little lanes between huts in the village, the jeep was ~*ed* —M.R.Masani⟩ ⟨fresh as a daisy after ~*ing* a big tractor-trailer —*Motor Transportation*⟩ **5 :** to lead as though showing the way to **:** COACH, MANAGE ⟨each dog is . . . ~*ed* by his handler and observed by the judges —W.F.Brown b.1903⟩ ⟨~*ed* the baseball team to a league pennant⟩ **syn** see GUIDE
³pilot \"\ *adj* **:** serving on a small scale as a guiding or tracing device, an activating or auxiliary unit of a full-scale contrivance, or as a trial unit in experimenting or in testing apparatus, or in checking technique or cost preparatory to full-scale activity ⟨~ studies are being made to determine the most effective ways in which local health departments can function —Thomas Parran⟩ ⟨the ~ plant provides the surest and quickest way of transmuting laboratory investigations . . . into commercial application —*Mellon Institute Report*⟩
pi·lot·age \ˈpīləd·ij\ *n* -s [F, fr. *piloter* to pilot (fr. MF *pilote* pilot) + *-age*] **1 a :** the act or business of piloting **:** employment of a pilot **:** guidance by a pilot **b** (1) **:** the technical knowledge or skill of a pilot **:** the charting or steering of a course (as for a ship) (2) **:** navigation of a ship or airplane by observation of landmarks directly or by means of radar — compare CONTACT FLYING **2 :** the compensation made or allowed to a pilot
pi·lo·tax·it·ic \ˌpīlōˌtakˈsid·ik\ *adj* [ISV ²*pil-* + *taxis* + *-itic*] **:** having the form of or characterized by a rock structure composed of a glass-free felted mesh of slender plagioclase strips between which are enclosed the other constituent minerals in minute grains and commonly observed in finely crystallized andesites and basalts
pilot balloon *n* **:** a small unmanned balloon sent up to show the direction and speed of the wind
pilot bird *n* **1 :** BLACK-BELLIED PLOVER **2 :** an Australian bird (*Pycnoptilus floccosus*) of uncertain affinity but similar to the babbling thrushes
pilot biscuit *also* **pilot cracker** *n* **:** hardtack baked in biscuit form and served with seafood chowders and stews
pilot black snake *n* **:** a large No. American colubrid snake (*Elaphe obsoleta*) that is lustrous black with some scales edged in white — called also *mountain black snake*
pilot boat *n* **:** a strong fast seaworthy boat in which pilots meet incoming ships usu. at the mouth of rivers and harbors
pilot bread *n* **:** HARDTACK
pilot burner *n* **:** a small burner kept lighted to rekindle the principal burner (as in a flash boiler)
pilot cell *n* **:** a selected cell whose temperature, voltage, and specific gravity of electrolyte are assumed to indicate the state of charge of the entire storage battery of which the cell forms a part
pilot chart *n* **:** a chart for a navigator showing direction and strength of prevailing winds, temperature, storm paths, positions of rocks, shoals, and other information helpful to navigators
pilot chute *n* **:** a miniature parachute that is several feet in diameter and is attached to the peak of a parachute and whose function is to draw the parachute out of its pack and extend it in position for opening — see PARACHUTE illustration
pilot cloth *n* **:** a heavy twilled woolen overcoating with a thick nap used esp. for seamen's blue uniforms
pilot coat *n* **:** PEA JACKET
pilot engine *n* **:** a locomotive going in advance of a train to make sure that the way is clear
pilot film *n* **:** a sample film of a proposed television series made to induce sponsorship
pilot fish *n* **1 :** a pelagic carangid fish (*Naucrates ductor*) that often swims in company with a shark **2 :** BANDED RUDDERFISH **3 :** MENOMINEE WHITEFISH
pilot flag *n* **:** a flag hoisted at the fore by a ship desiring a pilot (as the union jack in the U.S., the British union jack with a white border in Great Britain)
pilot flame *n* **:** PILOT BURNER
pilothouse \ˈ≈≈ˌ≈\ *n* **:** a deckhouse on a ship located forward near the bridge containing the steering wheel, compass, charts and navigating equipment, and communication systems to the engine room and other parts of the ship — called also *wheelhouse*
piloting *n* -s [fr. gerund of ²*pilot*] **:** the part of navigation concerned with directing the movement or determining the position of a ship or airplane by reference to landmarks, aids to navigation, or soundings
pi·lot·ism \ˈpīləˌtizəm\ *n* -s [¹*pilot* + *-ism*] **:** the practice or skill of piloting
pilot jack *n* **:** PILOT FLAG
pilot ladder *n* **:** JACK LADDER
pi·lot·less \ˈpīlətləs\ *adj* **:** having no pilot ⟨~ aircraft⟩
pilot light *n* **1** *also* **pilot lamp :** an electric light usu. used to indicate the position of a switch or circuit breaker, that a motor is in operation, or that the power is on **2 :** a small permanent flame used to ignite gas at a burner
pilot method *n* **:** the method of excavating a tunnel by driving a small tunnel ahead and then enlarging its dimensions
pilot motor *n* **:** a small motor used in the automatic control of an electric circuit
pilot nut *n* **:** a tapered steel nut temporarily screwed on a bridge pin to serve as guide while the pin is being driven through the pinholes of the members it is to join
pilot officer *n* **:** an air force officer (as in the British Royal Air Force) who is equivalent in rank to a second lieutenant in the army
pilot pin *n* **:** a pin to locate a center or bearing
pilot plow *n* **:** a snowplow on a locomotive's pilot
pi·lot·ry \ˈpīlətrē\ *n* -ES [¹*pilot* + *-ry*] **:** PILOTISM
pilots *pl of* PILOT, *pres 3d sing of* PILOT
pi·lot·ship \-tˌship\ *n* [¹*pilot* + *-ship*] *archaic* **:** the function or office of a pilot
pilot's luff *n* **:** HALF BOARD
pilot snake *n* **1 :** PILOT BLACK SNAKE **2 :** BULL SNAKE **3 :** COPPERHEAD 1a
pilot train *n* **:** a train that precedes another to ensure that the roadway is safe and free of obstructions
pilot truck *n* **:** LEADING TRUCK
pilot valve *n* **:** a relay valve that controls the operation of another valve
pilotweed \ˈ≈≈ˌ≈\ *n* [¹*pilot* + *weed*] **:** COMPASS PLANT a
pilot whale *n* [so called fr. the fact that the largest male acts as pilot or leader for the rest of the school] **:** BLACKFISH 2
pilot wheel *n* [so called fr. its resemblance to the wheel used in steering ships] **:** a wheel usu. with handles projecting from the rim for traversing the saddle of a machine tool or for operating any of the feeds by hand
pi·lous \ˈpīləs\ *adj* [L *pilosus* — more at PILOSE] **:** PILOSE
pil·pul \ˈpilˌpül\ *n* -s [Aram & Heb *pilpūl*, fr. *pilpēl* to search, argue] **:** critical analysis and hairsplitting **:** casuistic argumentation esp. among Jewish scholars on talmudic subjects **:** rabbinical dialectic
pil·pul·ist \-ləst\ *n* -s **:** one who practices talmudic dialectic **:** a subtle reasoner — **pil·pul·is·tic** \ˌpilˌpüˈlistik\ *adj*
pil·sen \ˈpilzən, -lsən\ *or* **plzen** \ˈpəlˌzen, -nʸ, (ˌ)≈ˈ≈\ *adj, usu cap* [fr. *Pilsen, Plzeň*, city of Czechoslovakia] **:** of or from the city of Pilsen, Czechoslovakia **:** of the kind or style prevalent in Pilsen
pil·sner *also* **pil·sen·er** \ˈpilz(ə)nə(r), -ls(ə)-\ *n* -s *often cap* [G *pilsner*, fr. *Pilsner* of Pilsen, fr. *Pilsen*, city of Czechoslovakia] **1 a :** a light Bohemian beer with a strong hop flavor **b :** a beer of a similar type **2** *or* **pilsner glass :** a tall slender footed glass usu. used for beer
pilt·down man \ˈpiltˌdau̇n-\ *n, usu cap P* [fr. *Piltdown*, East Sussex, England] **:** a supposedly very early primitive modern man based on skull fragments uncovered in a gravel pit at Piltdown and used in combination with comparatively recent skeletal remains of various animals (as ape, beaver, hippopotamus, elephant) in the development of an elaborate fraud
pil·u·lar *or* **pil·lu·lar** \ˈpilyələ(r)\ *adj* [*pilule* + *-ar*] **:** of, relating to, or characteristic of a pill ⟨~ mass⟩
pil·u·la·ria \ˌpilyəˈla(a)rēə\ *n, cap* [NL, fr. L *pilula* little ball + NL *-aria*] **:** a widely distributed genus of small aquatic pteridophytic plants (family Marsileaceae) having filiform fronds and globose sporocarps — see PILLWORT

pilsner 2

pil·ule *or* **pil·lule** \ˈpilˌyül\ *n* -s [MF, fr. L *pilula* little ball, pill, dim. of *pila* ball — more at PILE (hair)] **:** a little pill

pi·lum \'pīləm\ *n, pl* **pi·la** \-lə\ [L, pestle, heavy javelin] **1 :** the heavy javelin of a Roman foot soldier **2 :** PESTLE

pi·lus \'pīləs\ *n, pl* **pi·li** \-ī,lī\ [NL, fr. L — more at PILE] **:** a hair or a structure resembling a hair

pil·wil·let *or* **pill·wil·let** \pil'wilət\ *n* [imit.] **1 :** WILLET **2 :** an American oyster catcher (*Haematopus ostralegus palliatus*)

¹pily \'pīlē\ *adj* -ER/-EST [⁸*pile* + -*y*] **:** having a pile **:** resembling pile

²pily \"\ *adj* [¹*pile* + -*y*] *heraldry* **:** divided into piles

¹pi·ma \'pēmə\ *n, pl* **pima** *or* **pimas** *usu cap* **1 a :** a people of southern Arizona and northern Mexico **b :** a member of such people **2 :** the Uto-Aztecan language of the Pima people

²pima \" *sometimes* 'pimə\ *or* **pima cotton** *n* -s *sometimes cap P* [*Pima* county, southern Arizona] **1 :** a cotton with fiber of exceptional strength and firmness developed in the southwestern U.S. by selection and breeding of Egyptian cottons **2 :** a cloth made from pima

pi·man \'pēmən\ *adj, usu cap* [¹*pima* + -*an*] **1 :** constituting or relating to a language family of the Uto-Aztecan phylum containing the Pima, Tepehuan, and Papago languages **2 :** of or relating to the Pima

pim·an·threne \pə'man,thrēn\ *n* -s [*pimaric* (in *pimaric acid*) + -*anthrene*] **:** a crystalline aromatic tricyclic hydrocarbon $(CH_3)_2C_{14}H_8$ obtained by dehydrogenation of various bicyclic or tricyclic diterpenes and by synthesis; 1,7-dimethylphenanthrene

pi·mar·ic acid \pə'mar|ik, (')pī¦m|\ *n* [*pimaric* ISV *pimar*- (fr. NL *Pinus maritima* — syn. of *Pinus pinaster*, species name of the cluster pine —, fr. *Pinus* + *maritima*, fr. L, fem. of *maritimus* maritime) + -*ic*] **:** either of two isomeric crystalline acids occurring esp. in oleoresins from pine trees and formerly regarded as stereoisomeric: **a :** DEXTROPIMARIC ACID **b :** LEVOPIMARIC ACID

pim·bi·na \pim'bēnə, 'pimbənə\ *n* -s [CanF — more at PEMBINA] **:** any of several plants of the genus *Viburnum; esp* **:** CRANBERRY BUSH 2

pim·e·late \'piməˌlāt, -ˌlət\ *n* -s [ISV *pimelic* (in *pimelic acid*) + -*ate*] **:** a salt or ester of pimelic acid

pi·me·lea \pə'mēlyə *also* -lēə\ *n* [NL, fr. Gk *pimelē* lard — more at FAT] **1** *cap* **:** a genus of shrubs (family Thymelaeaceae) of Australia and New Zealand having small opposite leaves and clustered white, yellow, or pink flowers with two stamens succeeded by berrylike fruits — see RICE FLOWER **2** -s **:** any plant of the genus *Pimelea*

pi·mel·ic acid \pə'melik, pī'-, -mēl-, -lēk-\ *n* [*pimelic* ISV *pimel*- (fr. Gk *pimelē* lard) + -*ic*] **:** a crystalline dicarboxylic acid $HOOC(CH_2)_5COOH$ obtained usu. by oxidation of unsaturated fats, castor oil, or cycloheptanone

pim·e·lo·met·o·pon \ˌpiməlō'med·əˌpän\ *n, cap* [NL, fr. *pimelo*- (fr. Gk *pimelē* lard) + Gk *metōpon* forehead — more at METOPION] **:** a genus of Pacific wrasses closely related to *Bodianus* but distinguished by smaller scales that include the sheepshead of the California coast

pi·ment *also* **py·ment** \pə'ment\ *n* -s [ME, fr. OF *piment* piment, aromatic spice, fr. LL *pigmentum* plant juice] **:** wine flavored with spice and honey

pi·men·ta \pə'mentə\ *n, cap* [NL, fr. Pg, pepper, fr. LL *pigmenta*, pl. of *pigmentum* plant juice] **:** a genus of tropical American aromatic trees (family Myrtaceae) having large coriaceous pinnately veined leaves, small cymose flowers, and 1 to 6 pendulous ovules — see ALLSPICE, BAYBERRY

pi·men·to \pə'ment·(ˌ)ō, -en·(ˌ)tō\ *n, pl* **pimentos** *or* **pimento** [Sp *pimienta* pepper, allspice, fr. LL *pigmenta*, pl. of *pigmentum* plant juice, fr. L, pigment — more at PIGMENT] **1 a** *obs* **:** a small hot pepper (as a cayenne or Guinea pepper) **b :** PIMIENTO 1 **2 a :** ALLSPICE **b** *or* **pimento tree :** ALLSPICE TREE **c :** the fine-grained tough heavy pinkish wood of the allspice tree that is used chiefly for small specialty articles (as canes and umbrella handles) **3 :** a vivid red that is yellower, lighter, and slightly stronger than apple red, yellower, lighter, and stronger than carmine, yellower and darker than Castilian red, yellower and lighter than madder crimson, and yellower, stronger, and slightly lighter than scarlet

pimento cheese *also* **pimiento cheese** *n* **:** a Neufchâtel, club, cream, or occas. cheddar cheese to which ground pimientos have been added

pimento grass *n* [so called fr. its often being found under allspice trees] **:** SAINT AUGUSTINE GRASS

pi·men·ton \ˌpē,men·'tōn\ *n* -s [Sp *pimentón*, aug. of *pimiento*] **:** SPANISH PAPRIKA 2

pimento oil *or* **pimenta oil** *n* **:** a colorless to yellow or reddish pungent essential oil obtained from allspice and used chiefly in flavoring — called also *allspice oil*

pi–meson \'=¦=,=\ *n* [¹*pi* + *meson*] **:** a short-lived meson that is primarily responsible for the nuclear force and that exists in three charge states of which the positive and negative have mass 273.2 times the electron mass and the neutral has mass 264.2 times the electron mass

pi·mien·to \pə'ment·(ˌ)ō, -en·(ˌ)tō, ˌpimē'e-, pəm'ye-\ *n* -s [Sp, fr. *pimienta*] **1 :** any of various bluntly conical thick-fleshed sweet peppers of European origin with a distinctive mild sweet flavor that are much used as a garnish, as a stuffing for olives, and as a source of paprika **2 :** a plant that bears pimientos **3 :** PIMENTO 2 — not used technically

pim·li·co \'pimlə,kō, -lē,-\ *also* **pim·pli·coe** \'pimpl-\ *n* -s [imit.] **1 :** FRIARBIRD 1 **2 :** AUDUBON'S SHEARWATER

¹pimp \'pimp\ *n* -s [origin unknown] **1 a :** one who panders or procures; *esp* **:** a man who solicits for a prostitute or a house of prostitution and receives compensation therefor from the prostitute or the patron **b :** a man who cohabits with a prostitute, lives off her earnings, and often solicits for her — called also *cadet* **2 a :** a person who lends himself to some corrupting or corrupt activity **:** SCOUNDREL **b** *Austral* **:** SNEAK, INFORMER **3** *dial Eng* **:** a small bundle of kindling wood **:** FAGOT

²pimp \"\ *vi* -ED/-ING/-S **1 :** to engage in the business or practices of a pimp **2** *Austral* **:** to act as an informer

¹pim·per·nel \'pimpə(r)ˌnel, -ˌnəl\ *n* -s [ME *pympernele*, fr. MF *pimprenelle*, *pimpinelle*, fr. LL *pimpinella*, a medicinal plant, perh. irreg. fr. L *piper* pepper — more at PEPPER] **1 :** SALAD BURNET **2 :** an herb of the genus *Anagallis; esp* **:** SCARLET PIMPERNEL

²pimpernel \"\ *n* -s *usu cap* [fr. *The Scarlet Pimpernel*, rescuer of aristocrats from the French revolutionists in the novel *The Scarlet Pimpernel* (1905) by Baroness Emmuska Orczy †1947 Eng. novelist] **:** a gallant dashing resourceful man given to remarkable feats of bravery and derring-do in liberating victims of tyranny and injustice ⟨lined up solidly with the *Pimpernels* and with the persecuted —Hal Lehrman⟩

pimpernel root *n* **:** the dried rhizome and roots of the burnet saxifrage formerly used as a diaphoretic and diuretic

pimp·ery \'pimp(ə)rē, -ri\ *n* -ES **:** the occupation of a pimp

pim·pi·nel·la \ˌpimpə'nelə\ *n, cap* [NL, fr. LL, a medicinal plant] **:** a genus of herbs (family Umbelliferae) having narrow-ribbed fruit and no calyx teeth — see BURNET SAXIFRAGE, ANISE

pimp·ing \'pimpiŋ, -pēŋ\ *adj* [origin unknown] **1 :** PETTY, PALTRY, INSIGNIFICANT **2** *chiefly dial* **:** PUNY, WEAK, SICKLY

pim·pla \'pimplə\ *n, cap* [NL, perh. fr. L *Pimplea*, fountain in Macedonia, fr. Gk *Pimpleia*] **:** a common and widespread genus of ichneumon flies

¹pim·ple \'pimpəl\ *n* -s [ME *pinple*] **1 :** a small prominent inflamed elevation of the skin **:** PAPULE; *esp* **:** PUSTULE **2 a :** a swelling or protuberance like a pimple ⟨reproduces the ~*s* on an orange —Olive Bell⟩ **b :** a slight elevation of the ground ⟨a nameless ~ in the middle of nowhere —Fred Majdalany⟩

²pimple \"\ *vt* **pimpled; pimpled; pim·pling** \-p(ə)liŋ\ **pimples :** to spot or cover with or as if with pimples ⟨surfaces *pimpled* with rivet heads —G.W.Gray b. 1886⟩

pim·pled \-pəld\ *adj* **:** having or marked by pimples

pimple metal *n* [so called fr. the appearance of its surface] **:** matte containing 77–79 percent copper

pim·pli·ness \'pimp(ə)lēnəs, -lin-\ *n* -ES **:** the condition of being pimply

pim·ply \-p(ə)lē, -li\ *adj* -ER/-EST **:** covered with pimples **:** PIMPLED ⟨a ~ face⟩

pimply gut *n* **:** NODULAR DISEASE

pimply gut worm *n* **:** NODULAR WORM

¹pin \'pin\ *n* -s [ME, fr. OE *pinn;* akin to MD *pin*, *pinne* pin, peg, OHG *pfinn* peg, and perh. to MIr *benn* peak, horn] **1 a :** a usu. cylindrical piece of wood, metal, or other material used esp. for fastening separate articles together or as a support by which one article may be suspended from another **:** PEG, BOLT **b** *obs* **:** a peg or similar object in the center of a target; *also* **:** the center itself **c** (1) **:** one of the wooden pieces constituting the target in bowling, skittles, and similar games (2) **:** the peg at which a quoit is pitched (3) **:** the staff of the flag marking a hole on a golf course (4) **:** one of the small upright posts on a board or billiard table used in playing bagatelle, pinball, and related games **d :** a peg for regulating the tension of the strings of a musical instrument (as a piano or harp) **:** WREST PIN **e :** one of a row of pegs in the side of an ancient drinking cup to mark how much each man should drink **f** (1) **:** DRILL PIN (2) **:** the part of a key stem esp. if solid that enters a lock (3) **:** the part of a cylinder lock that prevents turning unless the proper key is inserted — see SPOOL PIN **g** *chiefly Scot* **:** the latch or handle of a door ⟨gently tirled the ~ —*Ballad Book*⟩ **h** (1) **:** THOLEPIN (2) **:** BELAYING PIN **i :** the tenon of a dovetail joint **j :** a triangular rod of refractory clay that is thrust into the wall of a sagger to support glazed flatware **k** (1) **:** a small axle, gudgeon, or spindle on which to journal (2) **:** a slender post or peg acting as a stop for motion of a pointer or lever (3) **:** a slender post or peg that is used to locate two parts in proper relative position **l** (1) **:** a long slender piece of metal that is used to fasten together the ends of broken bone (2) **:** a metal peg that is used to fasten the artificial crown of a tooth to a prepared root **m :** the part of the bedding mortar that is forced into the holes extending through the brick **2 a** (1) **:** a small pointed and headed piece of brass or other wire commonly tinned and used for fastening clothes, attaching papers, and similar purposes (2) **:** something very small **:** a thing of small value **:** TRIFLE ⟨doesn't care a ~ for her⟩ **b** (1) **:** a decorative fastener in the form of a straight pointed wire with a plain or ornamented head (as a tiepin or hatpin) or a small ornamental plaque often jeweled with a fastening device on the back (as a breastpin or bar pin) (2) **:** an ornament (as a brooch) having a pin fastener on the back **c** (1) **:** BOBBY PIN (2) **:** HAIRPIN (3) **:** SAFETY PIN **d :** a needlelike device typically one of a series of perforators whose puncture in a printed sheet serves as a reference point for accurate positioning and correct folding — called also *point* **3** *archaic* **:** frame of mind **:** MOOD — usu. used in such phrases as *on a merry pin, in a merry pin* **4 a** *chiefly dial* **:** POINT, PINNACLE, APEX **b** *chiefly Scot* **:** the projecting part of the hipbone esp. of a horse **5 :** LEG — usu. used in pl. ⟨pretty wobbly on his ~*s*⟩ **6 :** a very small knot in a bow or bow stave **7 :** a cask of ½ firkin capacity; *also* **:** this capacity as a unit of measure **8 :** a handled knife with a blade of triangular section used esp. to remove the bloom from freshly tanned leather — called also *striking pin* **9** [²*pin*] **:** a fall in wrestling **10 :** a fabric with designs as small and fine as the point, head, or width of a pin

²pin \"\ *vb* **pinned; pinned; pinning; pins** [ME *pinnen*, fr. ¹*pin*] *vt* **1 a** (1) **:** to fasten, join, or secure with a pin, peg, or bolt ⟨~ joists and girders⟩ ⟨~ a rose to a dress⟩ ⟨~ a fractured hip with steel needles⟩ (2) **:** to transfix with a pin or other sharp-pointed instrument ⟨an entomologist *pinning* a butterfly —Coleman Rosenberger⟩ **b :** to secure (hair) in place with a pin used for arranging or setting **c :** to fit (a garment) by securing adjustments of width or length with pins — usu. used with *in, out,* or *up* ⟨~ up a hem⟩ **d :** to present (a girl) with a fraternity pin as a pledge of affection ⟨she is *pinned* to the captain of the football team⟩ **2** [ME *pinnen*, perh. alter. of *pinden* to put in a pound — more at PIND] **:** ENCLOSE, CONFINE, PEN, IMPOUND ⟨held twice their number *pinned* within their works —J.A.Froude⟩ **3 a** *obs* **:** UNDERPIN **b :** to fill in (as a rubble wall) with small wedges or spalls of stone mortar **c** *obs* **:** to face esp. with marble **4 a :** to make absolutely dependent or contingent **:** attach firmly or bindingly — used with *on* or *to* ⟨~ their hope of universal salvation on some cause —M.R.Cohen⟩ ⟨*pinning* its destiny to a weak ally —*New Republic*⟩ **b :** to assign the blame or responsibility for **:** fix by proof or strong presumption — usu. used with *on* ⟨~ a murder on an innocent woman —*Sydney (Australia) Bull.*⟩ ⟨~*s* all the woes of the world on grog —John Lardner⟩ **5 a :** to hold or keep esp. as to a line of conduct or debate **:** keep from evading an issue — usu. used with *down* ⟨~ philosophy down and make it talk sense —Charles Frankel⟩ ⟨~ the author . . . down to a definite statement —Deems Taylor⟩ ⟨impossible to ~ him down to anything —D.G. Gerahty⟩ **b :** to define clearly or unequivocally **:** FIX, ESTABLISH — usu. used with *down* ⟨cannot ~ down the essence of poetry —C.I.Glicksberg⟩ ⟨the subject is not easy to ~ down —Stuart Chase⟩ **6 :** to make (a chess opponent's man) unable to move without exposing the king to check or a valuable piece to capture **7 a :** to hold fast or immobile in a spot or position ⟨*pinned* his arms to his sides⟩ ⟨*pinned* an enemy to his ground by powerful infantry attacks —Tom Wintringham⟩ ⟨*pinned* down by fallen rock⟩ ⟨*pinned* down by heavy enemy shelling⟩ **b** *of a wrestler* **:** to secure a fall over (an opponent) **c** *of a bird dog* **:** to detect and show (game) ~ *vi, of a file* **:** to become clogged so that the adhering filings scratch the work — **pin one's ears back 1 :** to administer a sound thrashing or defeat to ⟨announced that he could *pin back* the *ears* of any animal in the world —James Thurber⟩ **2 :** to give a tongue-lashing to ⟨the blouse buyer had *her ears* . . . *pinned back* —*Women's Wear Daily*⟩

³pin \"\ *adj* [¹*pin*] **1 :** of or relating to a pin **2** *of leather* **:** having a grain suggesting pinheads — see PIN SEAL

pi·na \'pēnyə, 'pīnə\ *or* **pi·ña** \'pēnyə\ *n* -s [Sp *piña* residuary cone of spongy silver left after retorting, pinecone] **1 :** a cone of silver amalgam prepared for retorting **2 :** the residuary cone of spongy silver left after retorting

pi·na·be·te \ˌpēnə'bād·ē\ *n* -s [AmerSp, fr. Sp, silver fir, fr. Catal *pinavet*, fr. *pin*-, *pi* pine (fr. L *pinus*) + *avet* fir, fr. L *abiet*-, *abies* silver fir] **:** a Central American fir (*Akies religiosa*) having young shoots that are furrowed and olive green on the lower side during the first year and brown and downy later

pinac- *or* **pinaco-** *also* **pinak-** *comb form* [L *pinaco*- picture, fr. Gk *pinak*-, *pinako*- board, tablet, picture, fr. *pinak*-, *pinax;* akin to OHG *witufīna* heap of wood, Russ *pen'* stump, stub, and prob. to Skt *pināka* staff] **:** tablet ⟨*pinacoid*⟩ ⟨*pinacocyte*⟩

pi·na·ca·te bug \ˌpēnə¦käd·ē-\ *n* [MexSp *pinacate*, fr. Nahuatl *pinacatl*] **:** any of several clumsy wingless beetles of the genus *Eleodes* (family Tenebrionidae) found in arid regions of the Pacific states

pi·na·ce·ae \pī'nāsē,ē\ *n pl, cap* [NL, fr. *Pinus*, type genus + -*aceae*] **:** a family of coniferous trees and shrubs (order Coniferales) comprising plants with needle-shaped or scalelike leaves, cones with woody, fleshy, or membranous scales, and fine-grained wood that is often of great economic value and being often divided into four or more smaller families (as Araucariaceae, Taxodiaceae, and Cupressaceae) — compare TAXACEAE — **pi·na·ceous** \(')=¦nāshəs\ *adj*

pin·a·chrome \'pinəˌkrōm\ *n* [ISV *pina*- (irreg. fr. Gk *pinak*-, *pinax* board, tablet, picture) + -*chrome*] **:** an isocyanine dye used in photography sensitizing to the green and orange-red regions of the spectrum

pi·ña cloth \'pēnyə-\ *n* [Sp *piña* piña cloth, pineapple, pinecone, fr. L *pinea* pinecone — more at PINEAL] **:** a lustrous transparent cloth of Philippine origin that is woven of fine silky unspun fibers from the pineapple plant and used esp. for decorative handkerchiefs and trimmings

pin·a·coc·er·as \ˌpinə'käsərəs\ *n, cap* [NL, fr. *pinac*- + -*ceras*] **:** a genus (the type of the family Pinacoceratidae) of compressed involute ammonites with the most highly complicated suture known

pin·a·co·cyt·al \¦pinəkō¦sīd·ᵊl\ *adj* **:** of or relating to a pinacocyte

pin·a·co·cyte \'===,sīt\ *n* -s [*pinac*- + -*cyte*] **:** one of the flat cells covering the external surface and lining the incurrent and excurrent canals of sponges

pin·a·coid *also* **pin·a·koid** \'pinəˌkȯid\ *n* -s [ISV *pinac*- + -*oid*] **1 :** a crystal form consisting of two parallel and opposite faces **2 :** a crystal form whose faces are parallel to two crystal axes

pin·a·coi·dal *also* **pin·a·koi·dal** \¦==¦kȯid·ᵊl\ *adj* [ISV *pinacoid* + -*al*] **:** having only a center of symmetry — used of one class in the triclinic system; see CRYSTALLIZATION, SYMMETRY

pin·a·col \'pinəˌkȯl, -kōl\ *n* -s [ISV *pinac*- + -*ol;* fr. the fact that it unites with water to form tabloid-shaped crystals] **1 :** a liquid glycol $(CH_3)_2C(OH)C(OH)(CH_3)_2$ that forms a crystalline hexahydrate $C_6H_{12}(OH)_2.6H_2O$ and that is usu. made from acetone by reduction with amalgamated magnesium followed by hydrolysis of the intermediate magnesium derivative; 2,3-dimethyl-2,3-butanediol **2 :** any of a series of tetrasubstituted derivatives of ethylene glycol obtained by reduction of ketones other than acetone — **pinacolic** *adj*

pi·nac·o·late \pə'nakəˌlāt, ˌpinə'kōlət\ *n* -s [*pinacol* + -*ate*] **:** a metallic derivative of pinacol — compare ALCOHOLATE

pi·nac·o·lin \pə'nakələn, ˌpinə'kōlən\ *also* **pi·nac·o·line** \-ˌlēn, -ˌlən\ *n* -s [ISV *pinacolone* + *ol*- (fr. L *oleum* oil) + -*in* — more at OIL] **:** PINACOLONE

pi·nac·o·lone \-ˌlōn\ *n* -s [*pinacol* + -*one*] **1 :** a liquid ketone $(CH_3)_3COCH_3$ of peppermint odor formed from pinacol by treatment with acid to cause loss of water and molecular rearrangement; 3,3-dimethyl-2-butanone **2 :** any of a series of ketones R_3CCOR formed like pinacolone from other pinacols

pin·a·cone \'pinəˌkōn\ *n* -s [ISV *pinac*- + -*one*] **:** PINACOL

pin·a·co·the·ca \ˌpinəkō'thēkə\ *n* -s [L, fr. Gk *pinakothēkē*, fr. *pinako*- (fr. *pinak*-, *pinax* board, tablet, picture) + *thēkē* case, chest; akin to Gk *tithenai* to put, place — more at PINAC-, DO] **:** PICTURE GALLERY

pi·nac·u·lum \pə'nakyələm\ *n, pl* **pinacu·la** \-lə\ [NL, fr. *pinac*- + -*ulum*] **:** one of the small chitinized plates on the integument of a caterpillar to which the body setae are attached

Pin·a·cy·a·nol \ˌpinə'sīəˌnȯl, -nōl\ *trademark* — used for a carbocyanine dye derived from quinoline and used in photography as a sensitizer for the red portion of the spectrum

¹pin·a·fore \'pinəˌfō(ə)r, -ó(ə)r, -ōə, -ó(ə)\ *n* -s [²*pin* + *afore*] **:** a covering garment worn to protect clothes from soil, made variously as an apron with or without a bib **:** a sleeveless low-necked wraparound garment tied or buttoned at the back

²pinafore \"\ *vt* -ED/-ING/-S **:** to dress in a pinafore

pinak- — see PINAC-

pi·nak·i·o·lite \pə'nakēəˌlīt\ *n* -s [G *pinakiolith*, fr. Gk *pinakion* small tablet (dim. of *pinak*-, *pinax* board, tablet) + G -*lith* -lite] **:** a magnesium and manganese borate $Mg_3Mn_3B_2O_{10}$ occurring in small black tabular crystals

pinakoid *var of* PINACOID

pi·nal \pē'nal\ *n, pl* **pinal** \"\ *or* **pi·na·les** \-ä(ˌ)lās\ *usu cap* **1 :** a band of San Carlos Apaches **2 :** a member of the Pinal band

pi·na·les \pī'nā(ˌ)lēz, pə'-\ *n pl, cap* [NL, fr. *Pinus* + -*ales*] *in some classifications* **:** an order of gymnospermous trees and shrubs coextensive with the order Coniferales

pi·nane \'pīˌnān\ *n* -s [ISV *pin*- (fr. L *pinus* pine) + -*ane* — more at PINE] **:** a liquid saturated bicyclic hydrocarbon $C_{10}H_{18}$ occurring in stereoisomeric forms of which pinene and nopinene are unsaturated derivatives; 1,3,3-trimethyl-2,4-methylene-cyclohexane

pi·nang *also* **pe·nang** \pə'naŋ\ *n* -s [Malay *pinang*] **1 :** BETEL PALM **2 :** the fruit of the betel palm

pi·nard \(')pē¦när\ *n* -s [F, fr. *pineau*, *pinot* any of several vinifera grapes used esp. for wine-making (fr. MF, fr. *pine* pinecone, fr. *pin* pine, fr. L *pinus*) + -*ard* — more at PINE] **:** a red French table wine sometimes issued to French soldiers

pinard yellow *n, often cap P* **:** a light yellow that is greener and paler than average maize or jasmine and paler than popcorn

pi·nas·ter \(')pī¦nastə(r)\ *n* -s [L, wild pine, fr. *pinus* pine + -*aster*] **:** CLUSTER PINE

pi·ña·ta *or* **pi·na·ta** \pēn'yäd·ə, pin-\ *n* -s [Sp *piñata*, lit., pot, fr. It *pignatta*, fr. *pigna* pinecone, fr. L *pinea* — more at PINEAL] **:** a decorated pottery jar filled with candies, fruits, toys, or other gifts and usu. suspended from the ceiling that blindfolded children try to break with a stick esp. as a traditional part of Mexican Christmas festivities

pin·a·type \'pinəˌtīp\ *n* [ISV *pina*- (irreg. fr. Gk *pinak*-, *pinax* board, tablet, picture) + -*type*] **:** HYDROTYPE

pin·a·ver·dol \ˌpinə'vərˌdōl, -dōl\ *n* -s [ISV *pina*- (irreg. fr. Gk *pinak*-, *pinax* board, tablet, picture) + *verd*- (fr. F *verd*, *vert* green) + -*ol* — more at VERDURE] **:** an isocyanine dye formerly used in photography as a sensitizer for the green and yellow portions of the spectrum

pinball \'=,=\ *n* **1 :** a ball-shaped pincushion **2 :** the globular flower head of the buttonbush **3 :** any of various forms of bagatelle in which pins or upright posts are set in the board or table; *esp* **:** any of various games that are played on pinball machines

pinball machine *or* **pinball game** *n* **:** an amusement device that consists of a glass-topped cabinet in which a ball propelled by a plunger rolls down a slanting surface among an arrangement of pins and targets with each contact between ball and target scoring a number of points indicated by a system of electric lights

pinbefore \'==,=\ *n* -s [²*pin* + *before*, adv.] *dial Eng* **:** PINAFORE

pin birch *n* **:** POPLAR BIRCH

pin block *n* **:** a wooden block or plank in a piano into which the wrest pins are driven — called also *wrest plank*

pinboard \'=,=\ *n* **:** a board set with numerous pegs on which yarn bobbins or spools may be placed for transportation and use

pinbone \'=,=\ *n* **:** the hipbone esp. of a quadruped

pinbone steak *n* **:** a small sirloin steak that contains the pinbone — see BEEF illustration

pin borer *n* **:** any of various small beetles that bore minute holes into trees; *esp* **:** an ambrosia beetle (*Monarthrum mali*) that attacks apple trees

pinboy \'=,=\ *n* **:** PINSETTER

pin bush *n* [¹*pin* + *bush* (bushing)] **:** a tool for reaming or polishing small pinholes

pinbush \'=,=\ *n* [¹*pin* + *bush* (shrub)] **:** an Australian needlebush (*Hakea leucoptera*)

pin buttock *n, obs* **:** a thin sharp buttock

pince-nez \(')pan(t)¦snā, (')paⁿ¦snā, (')pin(t)¦snā *sometimes* ÷(')pin(t)¦snez\ *n, pl* **pince-nez** \-ā(z), -ezəz\ [F, fr. *pincer* to pinch (fr. OF *pincier*) + *nez* nose, fr. L *nasus* — more at PINCH, NOSE] **:** eyeglasses clipped to the nose by a spring

pince-nezed \-ād, -ezd\ *adj* **:** wearing pince-nez

pin·cer \'pinchə(r), -n(t)sə-; -n(t)sə- *is chiefly Brit in senses 1&2*\ *n* -s *often attrib* [ME *pynsour*, *pynceour*, prob. fr. (assumed) MF *pinceour*, fr. MF *pincier* to pinch + -*our* -or (fr. OF -*eor*, -*eur*)] **1 pincers** *pl but sometimes sing in constr* **:** an instrument having two short handles and two grasping jaws working on a pivot and used for gripping things — often used in the phrase *pair of pincers* **2 a pincers** *pl but sometimes sing in constr* **:** a grasping apparatus (as on the anterior legs of the lobster) resembling a pair of pincers **:** CHELA **b :** one of the central incisors of a horse or other equine **3 :** one part of a double envelopment in which two forces are driven one on each side of an enemy position so as to be able by converging like the jaws of pincers to isolate and crush it ⟨caught in a ~ movement, they do not know where to turn —*Survey Graphic*⟩

pincers 1

²pincer \"\ *vt* -ED/-ING/-S **:** to pinch, nip, or torture with or as if with pincers

pincerlike \'==,=\ *adj* **:** like a pincer or a pair of pincers in appearance or action ⟨executing a ~ maneuver in an effort to wipe out the insurgents —*N.Y. Times*⟩ ⟨the ~ claw of the lobster⟩

pin·cette \(')pan¦set, (')paⁿ¦-\ *n* -s [MF, fr. *pincier* to pinch + -*ette*] **:** a small pair of pincers, tweezers, or forceps used in surgery

¹pinch \'pinch\ *vb* -ED/-ING/-ES [ME *pinchen*, fr. (assumed) ONF *pinchier;* akin to OF *pincier* to pinch, Sp *pinchar* to prick] *vt* **1 a :** to press hard between the ends of the finger and thumb, between teeth or claws, or between the jaws of an instrument **:** SQUEEZE ⟨~*ed* and patted my cheek —W.F. De Morgan⟩ **b** (1) **:** to bring into a specified state or position by pinching ⟨mountains come gradually together, and the coastal lowland is ~*ed* out —P.E.James⟩ (2) **:** to nip off or prune the tip of (a young shoot or bud) usu. to induce branching or to bring into flower at a definite time the shoots which develop after the pinching — usu. used with *out, off,* or *back* **c :** to squeeze or compress painfully ⟨complained the shoe

~*ed* his toes⟩ **d :** to cause physical or mental pain to **:** HURT, NIP ⟨how that knowledge would have ~*ed* their pride —R.P.Warren⟩ ⟨the air was so cold that it ~*ed* ... nostrils —Marcia Davenport⟩ ⟨the tobacco hunger ~*ed* me sore —William Baucke⟩ **e** (1) **:** to cause to appear thin, shrunken, drawn, or haggard (as with pain, hunger, or strain) ⟨cruelty ~*ed* his face about the mouth —Elizabeth M. Roberts⟩ ⟨face ... was ~*ed* with disquiet —Marcia Davenport⟩ (2) **:** to cause to shrivel or wither up ⟨a heavy frost had ~*ed* the flowers⟩ **2 a :** to subject to strict rationing or economy or severe shortage **:** STRAITEN, STINT ⟨were ready to ~ themselves for years —Samuel Butler †1902⟩ ⟨so ~*ed* for money that he often had only tea for dinner —W.A.Swanberg⟩ ⟨would be ~*ed* for supplies —*N.Y. Times*⟩ **b :** to cause distress or embarrassment to **:** VEX, HARASS; *esp* **:** to cause economic distress to ⟨the debtor who found himself ~*ed* by the shrinking supply of currency —V.L.Parrington⟩ ⟨industries like textiles ... will be seriously ~*ed* as their contracts drop —*Market Report*⟩ ⟨is ... true that inflation is ~*ing* some of our people now —M.G.Dilke⟩ **c :** to confine or limit narrowly **:** CONSTRICT ⟨will ~ their operating irrigation projects —Raymond Moley⟩ ⟨local prices and sales are being drastically ~*ed* by foreign imports —*Christian Science Monitor*⟩ **d :** to squeeze out (money) **:** EXTORT, WRING **3 :** to urge (a horse) to the limit **4 a :** STEAL ⟨~*ed* that box and ... got caught —Claud Cockburn⟩ **b :** ARREST ⟨~*ed* for speeding —*Springfield (Mass.) Daily News*⟩ **5 :** to move by prying with a pinch bar **6 :** to sail (a boat) too close to the wind **7 a :** to press (the cue ball) against a billiard table with a downward stroke of the cue held more or less vertically **b :** to propel (the ball) by such a stroke **~** *vi* **1 :** to press or encroach so as to hem in or confine — used with *in* ⟨the hills ~ in from either side of the river —*Amer. Guide Series: Conn.*⟩ ⟨could have ~*ed* in on him at any time —Williams Forrest⟩ **2 :** to be economical **:** be miserly or closefisted ⟨~*ed* on everything, even necessities⟩ ⟨couldn't ~ and be shabby —Willa Cather⟩ **3 :** to cause pain by pressing or squeezing **:** press painfully ⟨this shoe ~*es*⟩ **4 :** NARROW, TAPER — often used with *out* ⟨a calcareous sandstone ... which ~*es* out to the south —M.A.Clement⟩ **5 :** to form a pinch **syn** see STEAL — **pinch pennies :** to practice strict economy ⟨there weren't any *pennies pinched* when it was furnished —F.B.Gipson⟩

2pinch \"\ *n* -ES **1 a :** a critical point or juncture **:** EMERGENCY, STRAIT ⟨a good man to have when it comes to a ~⟩ — usu. used in the phrases *in a pinch* ⟨in a ~ it could carry half again as much —N.M.Clark⟩ and *at a pinch* ⟨at a ~, it could be supplied by sea —Richard Dimbleby⟩ **b** *obs* **:** mental or spiritual pain or distress **c** (1) **:** painful impact **:** PRESSURE, STRESS ⟨felt the ~ of chronic hunger —Dixon Wecter⟩ ⟨when the ~ of foreign competition came at last —G.M.Trevelyan⟩ ⟨again felt the ~ of blockade —F.A.Southard⟩ (2) **:** condition of hardship or privation ⟨feeling a ~ this year in that house —Pearl Buck⟩ **d :** SHORTAGE ⟨a labor ~ may be in the making —*Newsweek*⟩ ⟨the essential facts of the ammunition ~ —Elie Abel⟩ **2 a :** an act of pinching **:** NIP, SQUEEZE ⟨gave me a ~ in the leg —Margaret Deland⟩ **b :** as much as may be taken between the finger and thumb **:** a very small quantity ⟨a ~ of snuff⟩ ⟨a ~ of salt⟩ **3 :** PINCH BAR **4 :** a marked thinning of a vein or bed **5 :** a faint superficial line of crushed fibers running transversely across the belly of a bow or less commonly across part of an arrow **6 a :** THEFT **b :** a police raid **:** ARREST **7 :** pressure of the cue ball against a billiard table caused by a downward stroke of the cue **syn** see JUNCTURE — **with a pinch of salt :** with reservations

3pinch *adj* **1 :** SUBSTITUTE ⟨a ~ runner⟩ **2 :** made by a pinch hitter ⟨a two-run ~ single —*Springfield (Mass.) Union*⟩

pinch·able \ˈpinchəbəl\ *adj* **:** capable of being pinched

pinchback \ˈ=,=\ *adj* [*1pinch* + *back*, n.] *of a coat or jacket* **:** having a close-fitting or pleated back

pinch bar *n* **:** a lever having a pointed projection at one end and used esp. to roll heavy wheels — compare CROWBAR

1pinch·beck \ˈpinch,bek\ *n* -S [after Christopher *Pinchbeck* †1732 Eng. watchmaker who invented it] **1 :** an alloy of copper and zinc used esp. to imitate gold in cheap jewelry and ordinarily containing 10 to 15 percent of zinc **2 :** something that is counterfeit or spurious

2pinchbeck \"\ *adj* **1 :** made of pinchbeck **2 :** SHAM, CHEAP, SPURIOUS ⟨a ~ throne —J.A.Symonds⟩ **syn** see COUNTERFEIT

pinchbeck brown *n* **:** BURNISHED GOLD

pinchbottle \ˈ=,=\ *n* **:** a bottle with pinched or indented sides

pinch bug *or* **pinching bug** *n* **1 :** STAG BEETLE **2 :** HELLGRAMITE

pinch clamp *n* **:** PINCHCOCK

pinchcock \ˈ=,=\ *n* **:** a clamp used on a flexible tube to regulate the flow of a fluid through the tube — compare HOFFMAN CLAMP, MOHR PINCHCOCK

pin·che \ˈpēn(,)chā\ *n* -S [F *piché*, fr. AmerSp *pinche*] **:** a So. American tamarin (*Leontocebus oedipus*) having a tufted head

pincheck \ˈ=,=\ *n* **1 :** a fine check made with different colored yarns, end-and-end, and smaller than the shepherd's check **2 :** a fabric having a pattern of pinchecks — **pinchecked** \ˈ=¦=\ *adj*

pinchbottle

pinched \ˈpincht\ *adj* [fr. past part. of *1pinch*] **1 :** COMPRESSED, SQUEEZED, CONTRACTED ⟨the ~ attic —Sinclair Lewis⟩ ⟨the valleys become ~ —Richard Joseph⟩ ⟨feel the effect on the consumer's ~ purse —*Wall Street Jour.*⟩ **2 :** drawn thin (as from hunger or cold) **:** WASTED, HAGGARD ⟨a small, ~ face —T.B.Costain⟩ ⟨thought he looked ~ and cold —G.G.Carter⟩ **3 :** being in straitened circumstances **:** hard up ⟨throve ... when all their neighbors were ~ —Samuel Butler †1902⟩ — **pinched·ly** \ˈpinchədlē, -chtl-, -li\ *adv* — **pinched·ness** \-chədnəs, -ch(t)n-\ *n* -ES

pinch effect *n* **:** the tendency of a linear solid or fluid electrical conductor (as a rod or a column of ionized gas) to be compressed due to the action of its own magnetic field

pinch·er \ˈpinchə(r)\ *n* -S [ME *pynchar*, fr. *pynchen*, *pinchen* to pinch + *-ar*, *-er*, *-ere* -er] **1 :** one that pinches **2 pinchers** *pl* **:** PINCERS

pin cherry *n* **1 :** a small often shrubby shallow-rooted American wild cherry (*Prunus pensylvanica*) with small white flowers in short clusters **2 :** the bright red acid fruit of the pin cherry

pinches *pres 3d sing of* PINCH, *pl of* PINCH

pinchfist \ˈ=,=\ *n* [*1pinch* + *fist*, n.] **:** NIGGARD — **pinchfisted** \ˈ=¦=\ *adj*

pinchgut \ˈ=,=\ *n* [*1pinch* + *gut*, n.] *archaic* **:** a miserly person who starves himself or others

pinchgut money *or* **pinchgut pay** *n*, *archaic* **:** a money allowance made to sailors when food is scarce

pinch-hit \ˈ=¦=\ *vb* [back-formation fr. *pinch hitter*] *vi* **1 :** to go to bat in the place of another player esp. in an emergency when a hit is particularly needed — usu. used with *for* ⟨sent up to *pinch-hit* for the pitcher —*Scholastic Coach*⟩ **2 :** to act or serve in place of another ⟨might have to *pinch-hit* as naval officers —Sydney Connor⟩ — usu. used with *for* ⟨would *pinch-hit* for the president in the entertainment of foreign visitors —*Newsweek*⟩ **~** *vt* **:** to make (a hit) while acting as a pinch hitter ⟨*pinch-hit* a home run in the 7th inning⟩

pinch hit *n* [*pinch-hit*] **:** a hit made while pinch-hitting

pinch hitter *n* [*2pinch* + *hitter*] **1 :** a player who is sent in to bat in the place of another esp. in an emergency **2 :** a person who acts or serves in the place of another **:** SUBSTITUTE ⟨asked to fill in as a *pinch hitter* —Bernard Kalb⟩

1pinch·ing \ˈpinchiŋ, -chēŋ\ *n* -S [ME *pinchinge*, fr. gerund of *pinchen* to pinch] **:** the act of one that pinches; *specif* **:** the practice of severe economy or self-denial ⟨the difference between ~ and prodigality —G.B.Shaw⟩

2pinching *adj* [fr. pres. part. of *1pinch*] **1 :** COMPRESSING, SQUEEZING ⟨~ shoes⟩ **2 :** causing physical or mental pain ⟨achieved at the cost of ~ self-sacrifice —*Sydney (Australia) Bull.*⟩ **3 :** NIGGARDLY, PARSIMONIOUS — **pinch·ing·ly** *adv*

pinching bar *n* **:** PINCH BAR

pinchpenny \ˈ=¦=\ *adj* [fr. obs. E *pinchpenny*, n., stingy person, fr. ME *pynchepeny*, fr. *pynchen*, *pinchen* to pinch + *peny* penny] **:** NIGGARDLY ⟨~ economy⟩

pinch pleat *n* **:** a narrow short pleat usu. used in groups in the heading of curtains for controlling fullness

pinch pleats

pinch roller *n* **:** a roller of flexible material which presses the tape or wire in a magnetic recorder against the capstan for drive purposes

pinch-spotted *adj*, *obs* **:** spotted with bruises caused by pinching

pinck·neya \ˈpiŋknēə, piŋkˈnēyə\ *n*, *cap* [NL, fr. Charles C. *Pinckney* †1825 Am. statesman] **:** a genus of trees (family Rubiaceae) having showy pink and purple flowers with large colored bracts — see GEORGIA BARK

pin cloth *n*, *dial Eng* **:** PINAFORE

pin clover *n* **:** ALFILARIA

pinc·ta·da \piŋkˈtādə\ *n*, *cap* [NL] **:** a genus of bivalve mollusks (family Pteriidae) containing the principal pearl oysters

pin curl *n* **:** a curl made usu. by dampening a strand of hair with water or lotion, coiling it smoothly, and securing it in place by a hairpin or clip

pincushion \ˈ=,==\ *n* **1 :** a small cushion in which pins may be stuck ready for use **2 a :** SCABIOUS **b :** GUELDER ROSE **c :** a common No. American everlasting (*Antennaria plantaginifolia*) **d :** a plant of the genus *Chaenactis*

pincushion cactus *n* **:** a cactus of the genus *Mammillaria*

pincushion distortion *n* **:** distortion (as by an optical instrument or television receiver) in which the image of a straight line appears to be curved convexly toward the axis — compare BARREL DISTORTION

pincushion flower *n* **:** SCABIOUS 1

pind \ˈpind, ˈpīnd\ *vt* -ED/-ING/-S [ME *pinden* to put in a pound, dam up, fr. OE *pyndan* to dam up, fr. *pund-* enclosure, pound] *chiefly Scot* **:** to put (stray cattle) in a pound

pin·da·ri \pinˈdärē\ *n* -S *usu cap* [Marathi *peḍārī*, *peḍhārī* & Hindi *pinḍārā*] **:** one of the marauding mercenaries frequently making disastrous raids in British territory in India in the 18th century

1pin·dar·ic \(ˈ)pinˈdarik, -rēk\ *adj* [L *pindaricus*, fr. Gk *pindarikos*, fr. *Pindaros* Pindar †443 B.C. Greek lyric poet + Gk *-ikos* -ic] **1** *usu cap* **a :** of or relating to the poet Pindar **b :** written in the manner or style characteristic of or believed to be characteristic of Pindar **2** *obs* **:** marked by irregularity or lack of restraint ⟨the beauteous strife 'twixt their cool writings and ~ life —Edward Young⟩

2pindaric \"\ *n* -S *usu cap* **1 :** a Pindaric ode **2 pindarics** *pl* **:** loose irregular verses that are similar to those used in Pindaric odes

pindarical *adj* [*1pindaric* + *-al*] *obs* **:** PINDARIC

1pin·der \ˈpində(r)\ *n* -S [ME *pynder*, fr. *pynden*, *pinden* to put in a pound + *-er*] *Brit* **:** POUNDMASTER

2pin·der \ˈpində(r)\ *or* **pin·da** \-də\ *or* **pin·dar** \-də(r)\ *n* -S [Kongo *mpinda*] *chiefly South* **:** PEANUT

pin·dling \ˈpind(ᵊ)lən, -liŋ, ˈpin(ᵊ)lən\ *adj* [perh. alter. of *spindling*] **1** *dial* **:** PUNY, DELICATE, FRAIL ⟨one ... ~ little girl —Della Lutes⟩ **2** *dial* **:** PEEVISH, FRETFUL

pin·do palm \ˈpin(,)dō-\ *n* [AmerSp *pindo*, fr. Guarani *pindó*] **:** a Paraguayan coconut palm (*Cocos australis*) widely cultivated in northern greenhouses for its feathery graceful foliage

pindot \ˈ=,=\ *n* **:** a dot of the smallest size used in textiles — **pindotted** \ˈ=¦==\ *adj*

pin drafter *n* **:** a machine used in yarn manufacturing for combining and drafting sliver or top

pin drill *n* **:** a drill with a central pin or projection to fit into a hole to act as a guide while the hole is being enlarged or countersunk

pin·dy \ˈpindi\ *adj* [origin unknown] *dial Eng* **:** gone bad

1pine \ˈpīn\ *n* -S [ME, fr. (assumed) OE *pīn* punishment, torment, fr. L *poena* — more at PAIN] **1** *archaic* **:** mental suffering **:** ANGUISH, GRIEF, SORROW **2** *obs* **:** PRIVATION, WANT, FAMINE **3** *also* **pine disease :** a dietary deficiency disease of sheep or cattle marked by anemia, malnutrition, and general debility; *specif* **:** such a disease due to cobalt deficiency

2pine \"\ *vb* -ED/-ING/-S [ME *pinen*, fr. OE *pīnian*, fr. (assumed) OE *pīn* punishment, torment] *vt* **1 a** *obs* **:** to inflict pain upon **:** TORMENT, TORTURE **b** *chiefly dial* **:** to waste, wear out, consume, or exhaust by suffering or in grieving ⟨*pined* his flesh —Edmund Spenser⟩ **c** *archaic* **:** to grieve or mourn for **2 :** to shrink or dry (fish) esp. in curing **~** *vi* **1 :** to lose vigor, health, or flesh (as through grief, anxiety, or hunger) **:** become wasted (as through sorrow) **:** LANGUISH, FADE ⟨so she *pined*, and so she died forlorn —John Keats⟩ — often used with *away* ⟨sickens immediately, ~*s* away, and is soon dead —Bill Beatty⟩ **2 :** to languish with desire **:** yearn intensely — used with *for* ⟨*pined* for his native hills⟩ **3** *archaic* **:** REPINE, LAMENT **syn** see LONG

3pine \"\ *n* -S [ME, fr. OE *pīn*, fr. L *pinus*; akin to Gk *pitys* pine, Skt *pitu* drink, food — more at PIP] **1 :** a tree of the genus *Pinus* **2 a :** the straight-grained white or yellow usu. very durable often highly resinous wood of a pine varying from extreme softness in the white pines to hardness in the longleaf pine and related forms — compare FIR **b** *Midland & South* **:** KINDLING WOOD **3 a :** any of numerous coniferous trees of Australia: as (1) **:** a tree of the genus *Callitris* **:** CYPRESS PINE (2) **:** a tree of various other genera (as *Agathis*, *Podocarpus*, *Araucaria*, *Cupressus*, and *Dacrydium*) **b :** the wood of an Australian pine **4 a :** PARANÁ PINE **b :** the wood of the Paraná pine **5 :** PINEAPPLE

4pine \"\ *adj* **1 :** of or relating to the pine — often used in combination ⟨*pine*-clad hills⟩ **2 :** made of pine wood

pine·al \ˈpinēəl, ˈpīn-\ *adj* [F *pinéal*, fr. MF *pineal*, fr. L *pinea* pinecone (fr. fem. of *pineus* of the pine, fr. *pinus* pine + *-eus* -eous) + MF *-al*] **1 :** relating to or resembling a pinecone **2 :** of, relating to, or being the pineal body

pineal body *n* **:** a small body arising from the roof of the third ventricle and enclosed by the pia mater in all craniate vertebrates that in man and most existing vertebrates is conical, reddish gray, and suggestive of a gland or in larval lampreys and a few reptiles is raised on a stalk toward the upper surface of the head and has the essential structure of an eye, that functions in some birds as part of a time-measuring system, and that is variously postulated to be a vestigial third eye, an endocrine organ, or the seat of the soul — called also *pineal gland*, *pineal organ*; see BRAIN illustration

pineal eye *n* **:** the pineal body when eyelike in form with distinguishable lens and retina — see SPHENODON

pin·e·a·lo·ma \pinēəˈlōmə\ *n*, *pl* **pinealo·mas** \-məz\ *or* **pinealoma·ta** \-mədə\ [NL, fr. *pineal-* (fr. F *pinéal*) + *-oma*] **:** a tumor of the pineal body

pine aphid *n* **:** any of several plant lice that feed on pine; *specif* **:** PINE LEAF CHERMID

pine·ap·ple \ˈpī,napəl\ *n*, *often attrib* [ME *pinappel* pinecone, fr. *pin*, *pine* pine + *appel* apple, fruit] **1 :** an ornament (as a finial on furniture) representing either a pinecone or a true pineapple **2 a :** a plant (*Ananas comosus*) native to tropical So. America but now widely cultivated in the tropics that has rigid spiny-margined recurved leaves and a short stalk with a dense oblong head of small abortive flowers **b :** the fruit of the pineapple that consists of the succulent fleshy inflorescence and that ripens into a solid mass invested with the tough persistent floral bracts and crowned with a tuft of small leaves **3 a :** a dynamite bomb **b :** HAND GRENADE

pineapples 1

pineapple cheese *also* **pineapple** *n* **:** a cheddar type of cheese molded in the shape of a pineapple and hung in a net to give characteristic diamond-shaped markings to the outside

pineapple cloth *n* **:** PIÑA CLOTH

pineapple family *n* **:** BROMELIACEAE

pineapple flower *n* **:** a southern African plant of the genus *Eucomis* (family Liliaceae); *esp* **:** a bulbous plant (*E. punctata*) having a greenish fragrant flower

pineapple guava *n* **:** a feijoa (*Feijoa sellowiana*)

pineapple mealybug *n* **:** a mealybug (*Dysmicoccus brevipes*) that feeds on pineapple and other hosts chiefly in Hawaii and So. America

pineapple oil *or* **pineapple essence** *n* **:** an alcoholic solution of ethyl butyrate

pineapple weed *n* **:** an annual aromatic herb (*Matricaria matricarioides*) native to the Pacific coast of No. America but widely naturalized and having much-dissected leaves and rayless yellow flowers

pine bark *n* **:** the dried inner bark of a white pine (*Pinus strobus*) used in the preparation of cough syrups

pine bark aphid *n* **:** a plant louse (*Pineus strobi*) that lives on the bark of the white pine and produces a white flocculent deposit

pine barren *n* **:** a tract of sandy or peaty soil wooded with pine trees esp. in the southern U.S. with the longleaf pine or further north with a pitch pine (*Pinus rigida*)

pine-barren sandwort *n* **:** a white-flowered very deep-rooted perennial herb (*Arenaria caroliniana*) of the southeastern U.S. — called also *longroot*

pine beetle *n* **:** any of several buprestid beetles esp. of the genus *Dendroctonus* the larvae of which bore in pine trees in No. America

pine borer *n* **:** an insect larva that bores in pine timber: as **a :** the larva of various beetles esp. of the families Cerambycidae and Buprestidae **b :** a larval horntail

pine bud gall *n* **:** a gall on pine caused by the larva of a gall midge (*Contarina coloradensis*)

pine butterfly *n* **:** a black-and-white pierid butterfly (*Neophasia menapia*) whose larva is very injurious to young pines in western No. America

pine cheat *n* [so called fr. its fancied resemblance to a pine needle] **:** the leaf of a common spurry (*Spergula arvensis*)

pine co·las·pis \-kəˈlaspəs\ *n* [*3pine* + NL *Colaspis* (genus name of *Colaspis pini*)] **:** a chrysomelid beetle (*Colaspis pini*) having larvae that feed on pine needles in the southern U.S.

pinecone \ˈ=,=\ *n* **1 :** the cone of a pine **2 :** SOOT BROWN

pinecone fish *n* **:** a small sluggish berycoid fish (*Monocentris japonicus*) that has the body enclosed in a boxlike case made up of firmly fused large bony scales and is widely distributed in shallow waters of warm parts of the Indo-Pacific

pinecone willow gall *also* **pinecone gall** *n* **:** an oval imbricated gall resembling a pinecone formed on the twigs of willow by a gall midge (*Rhabdophaga strobiloides*)

pine crab *n* **:** a small green grapsoid crab (*Metapaulias depressus*) living in water accumulating at the leaf base of the broad-leaved pine in Jamaica

pine creeper *or* **pine creeping warbler** *n* **:** PINE WARBLER

pined *adj* [fr. past part. of *2pine*] *archaic* **:** wasted esp. by suffering or hardship **:** GAUNT, PINCHED

pinedrops \ˈ=,=\ *n pl but sing or pl in constr* **1 :** a purplish brown leafless saprophytic plant (*Pterospora andromedea*) of the family Pyrolaceae with racemose drooping white flowers **2 :** BEECHDROPS

pine engraver *n* **:** any of several beetles of the genus *Ips* having larvae that attack pines esp. in the western U.S.; *esp* **:** a common destructive beetle (*Ips pini*)

pine family *n* **:** PINACEAE

pine finch *or* **pine linnet** *n* **:** PINE SISKIN

pine gall weevil *n* **:** a weevil (*Podapion gallicola*) that forms galls on pitch, scrub, and red pines

pine grass *n* **1 :** a bunchgrass (*Calamagrostis rubescens*) of Oregon and Washington where it forms valuable forage **2 :** a sedge (*Carex pensylvanica*) furnishing pasturage for cattle in the pine barrens of the southern U.S.

pine green *n* **:** a variable color averaging a dark green that is yellower and lighter than evergreen or average bottle green and bluer and paler than forest green (sense 1)

pine grosbeak *also* **pine bullfinch** *n* **:** a large grosbeak (*Pinicola enucleator*) of coniferous forests of northern America, Europe, and Asia that is chiefly gray with the crown, rump, and breast strongly suffused with rosy red in the adult male and yellow in the female

pine grouse *n* **:** DUSKY GROUSE

pine gum *n* **1 :** Australian sandarac **2 :** oleoresin from various pines

pine hyacinth *n* **:** an erect perennial herb (*Viorna baldwinii*) of Florida that is cultivated for its solitary urn-shaped pink or purplish flower

pine knot *n* **:** a joint of pine wood; *esp* **:** one used for fuel

pineland \ˈ=,=\ *n* **:** land naturally predominantly forested with pine

pineland three-awn *n* **:** a tufted erect perennial grass (*Aristida stricta*) that is native to the southeastern U.S. pineland and useful for grazing and has a slender panicle and appressed spikelets with long awns

pine leaf chermid *n* [*chermid* fr. NL *Chermidae*] **:** a pine aphid (*Pineus pinifoliae*) of western No. America — called also *pine leaf aphid*, *pine leaf chermes*

pine-leaf scale \ˈ=,=-\ *or* **pine needle scale** *n* **:** a long narrow white scale (*Phenacaspis pinifoliae*) common esp. on the leaves of pine in No. America

pine lily *n* **1 :** a lily (*Lilium catesbaei*) chiefly of the southeastern U.S. having flowers and narrow leaves erect **2 :** SQUAW GRASS

pine lizard *n* **:** a small very active iguanid lizard (*Sceloporus undulatus*) varieties of which occur in most of the U.S. and north to British Columbia — see SWIFT

pine looper *n* **:** any of several geometrid moths having larvae that attack pines in parts of both Europe and No. America

pine marten *n* **1 :** a European marten (*Martes martes*) larger than the stone marten **2 :** an American marten (*Martes americana*) closely related to the sable of Europe

pine moth *n* **:** any of several moths having caterpillars that feed on the leaves or bore in twigs or trunks of pine trees — compare PINE PEST

pine mouse *n* **:** a short-tailed glossy-furred burrowing meadow mouse (*Pitymys pinetorum*) of the eastern U.S.

pi·nene \ˈpī,nēn\ *n* -S [ISV *pin-* (fr. L *pinus* pine) + *-ene* — more at PINE] **:** either of two liquid isomeric unsaturated bicyclic terpene hydrocarbons $C_{10}H_{16}$ derived from pinane and found in turpentine oils: **a :** the isomer having the ethylenic double bond as part of the ring system, occurring in many essential oils (as juniper oil and eucalyptus oil), constituting in either its dextrorotatory or levorotatory form the principal component of various turpentines, and used chiefly as a solvent and chemical intermediate (as in making camphor or terpineol) — called also *alpha-pinene*, *2-pinene* **b :** NOPINENE

pine needle *n* **1 :** one of the slender needle-shaped leaves of a pine tree **2 :** ALFILARIA

pine needle gall *n* **:** a gall on pitch pine caused by the larva of a gall midge (*Itonida pinirigidae*)

pine-needle oil *n* **:** an essential oil obtained from the needles and twigs of various pines or other conifers: as **a :** the colorless or yellowish bitter aromatic oil from the mugho pine used chiefly in medicine as an expectorant and inhalant **b :** the oil from the Siberian fir used chiefly in insecticides, soaps, and perfumes and as an inhalant

pine nut *n* [ME *pinnote*, fr. OE *pinhnutu*, fr. *pīn* pine + *hnutu* nut] **1 :** PINECONE **2 :** the edible seed of any of several pines (as the neoza pine, the stone pine, or the piñon)

pine oil *n* **:** any of various essential oils obtained from pines or other conifers or oils similar to these oils in composition: as **a :** a colorless to light-amber liquid with an aroma of pine that contains principally terpineols and other terpenoid alcohols, is obtained from the wood esp. of the longleaf pine, boils higher than wood turpentine, and is used chiefly as a solvent, in disinfectants, deodorants, insecticides, wetting and emulsifying agents, and detergents, and in ore flotation **b :** a synthetic oil made by hydrating terpene hydrocarbons to form alcohols

pine pandora moth *n* : PANDORA MOTH
pine pest *n* : a phycitid moth (*Dioryctria zimmermani*) whose larva bores into pine trees causing exudation of pitch
¹pin·er \'pīnə(r)\ *n* -s [ME *pynour*, fr. MD *piner*, fr. *pinen* to punish, suffer pain, work hard, fr. *pine* punishment, torment, fr. L *poena* — more at PAIN] *archaic* : LABORER
²piner \"\ *n* -s [²*pine* + -*er*] : one that pines; *specif* : an animal that suffers from pine
³piner \"\ *n* -s [³*pine* + -*er*] *Austral* : a pine-forest lumberman
pine reproduction weevil *n* : a weevil (*Cylindrocopturus eatoni*) that is a serious pest in plantations of ponderosa and Jeffrey pine in California
pine root–collar weevil *n* : a weevil (*Hylobius radicis*) having a larva that feeds in the cambium at crown level of various pines in the U. S.
pin·ery \'pīn(ə)rē, -ri\ *n* -ES [³*pine* + -*ery*] **1** : a hothouse or area where pineapples are grown **2 a** : a pine forest ⟨the ruthless destruction of the Michigan *pineries*⟩ **b** : a grove of pine trees
pines *pl of* PINE, *pres 3d sing of* PINE
pinesap \'⸗,⸗\ *n* : any of several parasitic or saprophytic herbs of the genus *Monotropa* of the north temperate zone resembling the Indian pipe but being yellowish or reddish; *esp* : a fleshy tawny or reddish usu. pubescent saprophytic herb (*M. hypopithys*) growing in woodland humus of eastern No. America — called also *false beechdrops*
pine sawfly *n* : any of several sawflies (family Diprionidae) having larvae that feed on pine needles
pine sawyer *n* : any of several large beetles of the genus *Monochamus* (family Cerambycidae) whose larvae bore into the trunks of dead or dying pine trees
pine–shoot moth *n* : a small gaily colored moth (*Rhyacionia buoliana*) of the family Olethreutidae having a larva that damages pines by feeding in the young buds and shoots
pine siskin *n* : a small No. American finch (*Spinus pinus*) similar to the American goldfinch but having the plumage streaked, that breeds in the north and migrates irregularly southward in flocks in winter
pine snake *n* : BULL SNAKE
pine spittlebug *n* : a cercopid bug of the genus *Aphrophora* that attacks pines in many parts of No. America
pine squirrel *n* : FREMONT'S SQUIRREL
pine straw *n, chiefly Midland* : dried pine needles
pine sugar *n* : PINITOL
pine swift *n* : PINE LIZARD
pine tag *n, chiefly Midland* : the dried needle of the pine — usu. used in pl.
pine tar *n* : tar obtained by destructive distillation of pinewood that is a viscid dark brown phenolic liquid of empyreumatic odor and used chiefly in roofing, in rubber and plastics as a softener and plasticizer, in paints and varnishes, in soaps, and in the treatment of skin diseases
pine–tar oil *n* : a dark brown phenolic liquid of empyreumatic odor obtained by distillation of pine tar and used chiefly as a deodorant, antiseptic, and parasiticide and in ore flotation
pine–tip moth \'⸗,⸗-\ *n* **1** : PINE PEST **2** : a moth (*Rhyacionia frustrana*) of the family Olethreutidae with larvae that bore in the twigs of pine
pine tortoise scale *n* : a scale (*Toumeyella numismaticum*) that feeds on pines esp. in the eastern U. S.
pine tree *n* [ME *pine tre*, fr. OE *pīntrēow*, fr. *pīn* pine + *trēow* tree] **1** : PINE **2** : DUCK GREEN
pine–tree lizard *n* : PINE LIZARD
pine tree shilling *n* [so called fr. the representation of a pine tree on the coin] : a silver shilling coined in Massachusetts in the 17th century
pine–tube moth \'⸗,⸗-\ *n* : a moth (*Argyrotaenia pinatubana*) with larvae that feed within a tube of pine needles webbed together
pine tulip *n* : PIPSISSEWA
pi·ne·tum \pī'nēd·əm\ *n, pl* **pine·ta** \-d·ə\ [L, pine grove, fr. *pinus* pine + -*etum*] **1** : a plantation of pine trees; *esp* : a scientific collection of living coniferous trees **2** : a treatise on pines
pi·ne·us \'pīnēəs\ *n, cap* [NL, fr. L *pineus*, adj., of the pine — more at PINEAL] : a genus of aphids (family Psyllidae) including several that feed on coniferous trees — see PINE BARK APHID
pine warbler *n* : a large plainly colored warbler (*Dendroica pinus*) of the eastern U. S. usu. inhabiting pinewoods
pine webworm *n* : a webworm that is the larva of a small dull-colored moth (*Tetralopha robustella*) and that attacks various pines in eastern U. S.
pineweed \'⸗,⸗\ *n* : ORANGE GRASS
pine weevil *n* : any of several weevils that attack pines; *esp* : a brightly metallic weevil (*Scythropus elegans*) of western No. America — called also *elegant pine weevil*
pinewood \'⸗,⸗\ *n* **1** : a wood of pines ⟨this dank, dreary ~ —Christopher Isherwood⟩ — often used in pl. but sing. or pl. in constr. ⟨a ~s I was very fond of —Jean Stafford⟩ **2** : the wood of the pine tree
pinewoods grape \'⸗,⸗-\ *n* : POST-OAK GRAPE
pine worm *n* : a larval pine sawyer
¹pi·ney \'pīnē, -ni\ *n* -s [ME *piony* — more at PEONY] *dial* : PEONY
²piney \'pīnē, -ni\ *adj, usu* **pinier**; *usu* **piniest** [³*pine* + -*y*] : PINY ⟨~ smell of my bath soap —Gladys Schmitt⟩ ⟨the ~ hills —Dillon Anderson⟩
piney dammar *or* **piney resin** *or* **piney varnish** *n* [*piney* prob. by folk etymology (influence of ²*piney*) fr. Malayalam *payin* piney tree] : a pellucid fragrant acrid resin that exudes from the piney tree when wounded and is used as a varnish, in making candles, and as a substitute for incense and for amber
pin eye *n* : a primula flower in which the pistil stands above the stamens
pin–eyed \'⸗¦⸗\ *adj* : having very small eyes or spots suggesting eyes; *specif* : having the stigma visible at the throat of a gamopetalous corolla while the stamens are concealed in the tube — used of dimorphous flowers; compare THRUM-EYED
piney tallow *n* [*piney* (as in *piney dammar*) + *tallow*] : a solid fatty substance obtained from seeds of the piney tree and used in making candles
piney tree *or* **piney varnish tree** *n* [*piney tree* fr. *piney* (as in *piney dammar*) + *tree*; *piney varnish tree* fr. *piney varnish* + *tree*] : an East Indian tree (*Vateria indica*) that has panicles of showy white flowers and yields timber, resin, and oil
piney woods *n pl* : woodland of the southern U. S. in which pines are the dominant tree
pinfall \'⸗,⸗\ *n* : the total score made by a player or side in bowling
¹pinfeather \'⸗,⸗⸗\ *n* [¹*pin* + *feather*] : a feather not fully developed; *esp* : a young feather just emerging through the skin and still enclosed for most of its length in a cylindrical horny sheath which is afterwards cast off — **pinfeathered** \'⸗¦⸗⸗\ *adj* — **pinfeathery** \'⸗,⸗(⸗)⸗\ *adj*
²pinfeather \'⸗,⸗⸗\ *vt* : to pluck the pinfeathers from — **pin-featherer** \'⸗,⸗⸗⸗\ *n*
¹pinfire \'⸗¦⸗\ *adj* [¹*pin* + *fire*, v.] **1** *of a cartridge* : having a movable pin projecting from the rim that when struck by a hammer explodes a cap encased in the cartridge **2** *of a fire-arm* : using a pinfire cartridge
²pinfire \"\ *n* : a pinfire firearm
pinfish \'⸗,⸗\ *n* : any of several fishes having sharp dorsal spines: as **a** : a small compressed dark green grunt (*Lagodon rhomboides*) of the Atlantic coast from Cape Cod to Cuba **b** : a related fish (*Diplodus holbrooki*)
¹pin·fold \'pin,fōld\ *also* **pen·fold** \'pen,-\ *n* [*pinfold* fr. ME *pynfold*, *pyndefolde*, alter. (influenced by *pinden* to put in a pound and prob. by *pinnen* to enclose) of *pundfald*, fr. OE, fr. *pund-* enclosure, pound + *fald* fold, pen; *penfold* alter. (influenced by ¹*pen*) of *pinfold* — more at PIND, PIN (v.)] **1** : a pound for animals **2** : a place of restraint : CONFINE
²pinfold \"\ *also* **penfold** \"\ *vt* : to enclose or confine in or as if in a pinfold
¹ping \'piŋ\ *n* -s [imit.] **1** : a sharp metallic sound like or suggestive of that made by a rifle bullet striking an obstruction ⟨heard the ~ of a slingshot —Frank O'Connor⟩ ⟨a bell . . . rang with a ~ —Bruce Marshall⟩ **2** : an abnormal sound made by a gas engine usu. due to advanced spark or excessive carbon accumulation : KNOCK **3** : the pulse of sound waves reflected from or emitted by a submerged object in submarine signaling or detection and heard by special apparatus
²ping \"\ *vi* -ED/-ING/-S : to make a sharp metallic sound like or suggestive of that made by a rifle bullet striking an obstruction : sound a ping ⟨a few mosquitoes . . . ~*ing* shrilly —John Onslow⟩ ⟨a bullet ~*ed* into the water —Henriette Roosenburg⟩
pin game *n* : PINBALL 3
pinging *n* -s : the act of one that pings; *specif* : DETONATION
¹pin·gle \'piŋ(g)əl\ *vi* -ED/-ING/-S [origin unknown] **1** *chiefly Scot* : STRIVE, STRUGGLE **2** *chiefly Scot* : to dawdle or trifle esp. with one's food
²pingle \"\ *n* -s *Scot* : STRUGGLE, EFFORT
³pingle \"\ *n* -s [origin unknown] *dial chiefly Eng* : a small enclosed field
⁴pingle \"\ *n* -s [origin unknown] *Scot* : a long-handled cooking pot or pan
pin·go \'piŋ(,)gō\ *n* -s [Esk] : a small low mound of earth or gravel presumably due to frost action (as in arctic regions)
Ping–Pong \'piŋ,päŋ, -,pòŋ\ *trademark* — used for table tennis
pin grass *n* : ALFILARIA
pin·gue *also* **pin·guay** \'pēŋ(,)gwā, 'piŋ-\ *n* -s [Sp *pingüe* fat, fr. L *pinguis*; akin to Gk *pimelē* lard — more at FAT] : a perennial glandular herb (*Actinea richardsoni*) of the family Compositae of the southwestern U. S. yielding an inferior rubber and causing poisoning of livestock
pin·guec·u·la \piŋ'gwekyələ\ *also* **pin·guic·u·la** \-'gwik-\ *n, pl* **pinguecu·lae** \-,lē, -,lī\ *also* **pinguicu·lae** \-,lē, -,lī\ [*pinguecula* fr. NL, alter. of *pinguicula*; *pinguicula* fr. NL, fr. L, fem. of *pinguiculus* fattish] : a small yellowish elevation situated near the inner or outer margins of the cornea and occurring esp. in people of advanced age
pin·gue·fy \'piŋgwə,fī\ *vb* -ED/-ING/-ES [L *pinguefacere*, fr. *pingue-* (as in *pinguescere* to grow fat) + *facere* to make — more at DO] *archaic* : FATTEN
pin·gues·cent \(')piŋ¦gwes°nt\ *adj* [L *pinguescent-*, *pinguescens*, pres. part. of *pinguescere* to grow fat, fr. *pinguis* fat] *archaic* : FATTENING
pin·guic·u·la \piŋ'gwikyələ\ *n, cap* [NL, fr. L, fem. of *pinguiculus* fattish, fr. *pinguis* fat] : a large genus of acaulescent bog herbs (family Lentibulariaceae) having showy solitary purple, yellow, or white flowers on naked scapes and leaves that capture insects in the viscid secretion on the leaf surface and digest them
pin·guid \'piŋgwəd\ *adj* [L *pinguis* fat + E -*id* (as in *languid*)] : FAT, FATTY ⟨a ~ bullfrog —Carl Van Vechten⟩
pin·guid·i·ty \piŋ'gwidəd·ē\ *n* -ES : FATNESS
pin·guin \'piŋgwən\ *n* -s [native name in the West Indies] : a tropical American plant (*Bromelia pinguin*) that is used in the tropics for hedges, has spiny leaves resembling aloes, reddish panicled flowers, and plum-shaped edible fruit, and yields a cordage fiber
pin·gui·nus \'piŋgwənəs, piŋ'gwīn-\ *n, cap* [NL, fr. F *pingouin* great auk, fr. E *penguin*] : a genus of very large extinct flightless seabirds (family Alcidae) containing solely the great auk
pin·gui·tude \'piŋgwə,tüd, -ə,tyüd\ *n* -s [L *pinguitudo*, fr. *pinguis* fat + -*tudo* -tude] *archaic* : FATNESS, OBESITY, OILINESS
¹pinhead \'⸗,⸗\ *n* **1 a** : the head of a pin **b** : something very small or insignificant **2 a** : a microcephalic idiot **b** : a very dull or stupid person : FOOL ⟨seems an awful ~ —Wolcott Gibbs⟩ **3** : a part of a plow containing pinholes for a pin the position of which regulates the depth of furrow **4** : a small minnow
²pinhead \'⸗¦⸗\ *adj* : PINHEADED ⟨~ philosophy . . . and abysmal ignorance —James Kelly⟩
pinheaded \'⸗¦⸗⸗\ *adj* **1** : lacking intelligence or understanding : DULL, STUPID ⟨a ~ young man⟩ **2** : PIN-EYED — **pin-head·ed·ness** *n* -ES
pin hinge *n* : a hinge that uses a pin as a pivot as opposed to a loop hinge
pinhole \'⸗,⸗\ *n* **1** : a hole made by or for a pin : PINPRICK **2** : a small aperture or perforation resembling a hole made by a pin: as *a archery* : the center of the gold **b** : a hole through which a pin passes (as in a truss) **c** : a transparent spot on a developed photographic film or plate often caused by dust on the surface during exposure **d** : a defect in a glaze or enamel consisting of a tiny area of the body or metal that is not covered **e** : a hole in lumber caused by beetles **f** : a minute froth pit in a coated paper
pinhole borer *n* : any of various minute larval beetles (as of an ambrosia beetle) whose larvae excavate long slender burrows in timber
pinhole camera *n* : a photographic camera having a minute aperture and no lens
pinhole pupil *n* : a pupil of the eye contracted (as in opium poisoning) to the size of a pinhole
¹pinhook \'⸗,⸗\ *n* [¹*pin* + *hook*, n.] : a fishhook made from a pin
²pinhook \"\ *vi* [back-formation fr. *pinhooker*] : to act as a pinhooker
pin·hook·er \-kə(r)\ *n* [prob. fr. ¹*pinhook* + -*er*] : a small speculator in tobacco at a local market
pi·nic acid \'pīnik, 'pinik-\ *n* [*pinic* fr. F *pinique*, fr. *pin* pine (fr. L *pinus*) + -*ique* -ic — more at PINE] : a crystalline dicarboxylic acid $HOOCC_6H_{10}CH_2COOH$ formed by oxidation of pinonic acid
pinier *comparative of* PINEY *or of* PINY
pinies *pl of* PINY
piniest *superlative of* PINEY *or of* PINY
¹pin·ing \'pīniŋ, -nēŋ\ *n* -s [ME *pininge*, *pining*, fr. OE *pīnung* torment, punishment, fr. *pīnian* to torture + -*ung* -ing — more at PINE] **1** : the act or condition of one that pines **2** *also* **pining disease** : ¹PINE 3
²pining *adj* [fr. pres. part. of ²*pine*] **1** *archaic* : CONSUMING, WASTING **2** : LANGUISHING ⟨a ~ lover⟩ — **pin·ing·ly** *adv*
¹pin·ion \'pinyən\ *n* -s [ME *pynyon*, fr. MF *pignon*, fr. OF, prob. fr. *pignon*, *penon* pennon — more at PENNON] **1 a** : the distal part of a bird's wing including the carpus, metacarpus, and phalanges **b** : WING **c** : FLIGHT FEATHER, QUILL; *also* : the flight feathers **2** : the anterior border of an insect's wing
²pinion \"\ *vt* -ED/-ING/-S **1** : to restrain (a bird) from flight: **a** : to bind or confine the wings of **b** : to confine by binding the wings of **c** : to cut off the distal joint of one wing of **2 a** : to disable or restrain by binding the arms usu. to the body ⟨bodyguards had ~*ed* his attacker —Hodding Carter⟩ **b** : to disable or restrain a person by so binding (the arms) **3** : to bind fast : SHACKLE ⟨this frame . . . which now is ~*ed* with mortality —George Herbert⟩
³pinion \", (')pēn¦yōn\ *n* -s [Sp *piñón* pine nut, physic nut — more at PIÑON] **1** : PHYSIC NUT **2** [AmerSp *piñón*, fr. Sp] : PIÑON
⁴pinion \"\ *n* -s [F *pignon*, fr. MF, alter. of *peignon*, fr. *peigne* comb, fr. L *pecten* — more at PECTINATE] **1** : a gear with a small number of teeth designed to mesh with a larger wheel or rack **2** : the smaller wheel of a pair or the smallest of a train or set of gear wheels
¹pin·ioned \-nd\ *adj* [ME *pynyonyd*, fr. *pynyon* pinion + -*yd*, -*ed* -ed] : having wings or pinions
²pinioned *adj* [fr. past part. of ²*pinion*] : BOUND, FETTERED
pinion end *n* [obs. E *pinion* gable (fr. ME, fr. OF *pignon*, fr. assumed VL *pinnion-*, *pinnio*, fr. L *pinna* battlement, feather — alter. of *penna* feather — + -*ion-*, -*io* -ion) + E *end* — more at PEN] : GABLE END

pinion: *1* gear, *2* pinion

¹pi·nite \'pē,nīt\ *n* -s [G *pinit*, fr. the *Pini* mine, Saxony, Germany + G -*it* -ite] : a compact mineral of a dull grayish, green, or brownish color that is essentially muscovite derived from the alteration of other minerals (as cordierite)
²pi·nite \'pī,nīt\ *n* -s [NL *Pinites*, form genus of fossil pines, fr. *Pinus* + -*ites*] : a fossil wood referred to the family Pinaceae (as to the form genera *Pinites* and *Pinoxylon*) and usu. resembling that of the recent pines
pi·ni·tol \'pīnə,tȯl, -tōl\ *n* -s [obs. E *pinite* pinitol (fr. F, fr. *pin* pine — fr. L *pinus* — + -*ite*) + E -*ol* — more at PINE] : a sweet crystalline compound $C_6H_6(OH)_5OCH_3$ that is extracted esp. from the heartwood of the sugar pine and is found also in legumes and other plants; *dextro*-inositol monomethyl ether
¹pink \'piŋk\ *vt* -ED/-ING/-S [ME *pynken* to make holes with a pointed instrument] **1 a** (1) : to pierce with a sword or other pointed instrument : STAB ⟨~*s* him neatly in the arm —*Life*⟩ (2) : to wound with a bullet ⟨~*ed* three times by an assassin —*Time*⟩ (3) : to hit with a missile ⟨gets ~*ed* so often because he crowds the plate —W.B.Furlong⟩ **b** : to wound (as pride) by insensitivity : wound with the weapons of irony, criticism, or ridicule ⟨television, advertising, and urban gullibility . . . are rather easily ~*ed* —John McCarten⟩ ⟨~*ed* by the small darts of political enemies —W.S.White⟩ **2 a** : to cut or perforate (cloth, leather or paper) in an ornamental pattern that often shows an underlay of a contrasting color **b** : to cut a saw-toothed edge on (cloth, paper, leather) esp. with pinking shears **3 a** : ADORN, DECORATE, DECK **b** *obs* : TATTOO
²pink *n* -s *obs* : a hole or eyelet made with or as if with a pinking iron
³pink \'piŋk\ *n* -s [ME *pynk*, fr. MD *pinke*] **1** : a small Dutch fishing craft characterized by a full forebody narrowing to an almost pointed stern with an overhanging false counter **2** : any of various ships having a narrow overhanging stern — called also *pinkie*
⁴pink \"\ *n* -s [alter. of earlier *penk*, fr. ME] **1** *dial Eng* : the European minnow **2** *Brit* : a newly hatched salmon or grayling
⁵pink \"\ *vi* -ED/-ING/-S [prob. fr. D *pinken* to wink, blink] **1** *chiefly dial* : to peer or peep with half-closed eyes : WINK, BLINK **2** *chiefly dial* : to gleam faintly : DIMINISH, FADE
⁶pink \"\ *adj, dial chiefly Brit, of an eye* : half shut : WINKING
⁷pink \"\ *n* -s *chiefly Scot* : a small gleam of light — **pink of the evening** *dial* : late afternoon : early evening ⟨enjoy the *pink of the evening* with my friends —Marie Campbell⟩
⁸pink \"\ *n* -s [origin unknown] **1** : a plant of the genus *Dianthus*: as **a** : COTTAGE PINK **b** : CHINA PINK **2 a** : the very embodiment : PARAGON ⟨your new doctor is the ~ of politeness —*Encore*⟩ ⟨the ~ and pattern of a soldier —Thomas Wood †1950⟩ **b** : a member of the elite : a person dressed in the height of fashion : SWELL, EXQUISITE; *also* : ELITE ⟨the ~ of Victorian propriety appeared —C.W.Cunnington⟩ **c** : highest degree possible : HEIGHT, EXTREME ⟨dressed in the ~ of fashion —G.E. Fussell⟩ ⟨keep their house in the ~ of repair —Rebecca West⟩ — **in the pink** *or* **in the pink of condition** : in the best of health : in splendid physical condition ⟨delighted to see you . . . *in the pink* —James Reynolds⟩ ⟨the plants were *in the pink of condition* —Anne Dorrance⟩
⁹pink \"\ *adj* [⁸*pink*] **1** : resembling the garden pink in color : being of the color pink ⟨tallish man with ~ wrinkly face —R.W.Brown †1956⟩ — often used in combination ⟨his fat *pink*-haired wife —Maeve Brennan⟩ **2** : holding or believed to hold advanced liberal or moderately radical political or economic views **3** : MOVED, ANGERED, EXCITED ⟨would get quite ~ on the subject —Graham Greene⟩ — often used as an intensive ⟨ought to be thrilled ~ that you know an aristocrat like me —Calder Willingham⟩ ⟨flattered ~ at the charge —T.O.Heggen⟩ ⟨scared ~ of . . . friends with marriage in their eye —Ethel Wilson⟩ — **pink·ness** *n* -ES
¹⁰pink \"\ *n* -s [⁹*pink*] **1** : any of a group of colors bluish red to red in hue, of medium to high lightness, and of low to moderate saturation **2 a** (1) : the scarlet color of a fox hunter's coat (2) : a fox hunter's coat of this color (3) : a fox hunter **b** : pink-colored clothing ⟨dressed in ~⟩ **c pinks** *pl* : light-colored trousers worn with a winter semidress uniform by army officers **3** : a person who holds advanced liberal or moderately radical political or economic views — compare RED **4** : HUMPBACK SALMON
¹¹pink \"\ *vb* -ED/-ING/-S [⁹*pink*] *vi* : to turn pink ⟨when the eastern sky was beginning to ~ —T.W.Duncan⟩ ⟨~*ing* up just a little —Victoria Case⟩ ~ *vt* **1** : to cause to turn pink ⟨~*ed* his ears with pleased embarrassment —J.H.Wheelwright⟩ **2** : to change the color of (a topaz) to pink by heating
¹²pink \"\ *vi* -ED/-ING/-S [imit.] : to make a tinkling or pinging noise : PING ⟨~*ing* like a hundred tiny coins —Gerald Durrell⟩ ⟨when the mixture is too rich . . . the engine ~*s* —Cyril Connolly⟩
¹³pink \"\ *n* -s [imit.] : CHAFFINCH
pink–and–white shower \¦⸗⸗¦⸗-\ *n* : an ornamental leguminous tree (*Cassia javanica*) from Java and Sumatra bearing masses of pink and white flowers and having pods like those of the golden shower but ridged transversely
pink bollworm *n* : the pinkish larva of a small dark brown moth (*Pectinophora gossypiella* syn. *Gelechia gossypiella*) which bores into the flowers and bolls of cotton and is a very widespread destructive pest occurring in most cotton-growing countries including the U. S.
pink bud stage *n* : PINK STAGE
pink calla *n* : a calla (*Zantedeschia rehmannii*) that is native to southern Africa and used as an ornamental and that has lanceolate leaves and rose-colored spathes
pink cockatoo *n* : a white Australian cockatoo (*Kakatoe leadbeateri*) with the plumage flushed roseate and a large showy barred crest
pink coral *n* : a deep pink to strong yellowish pink
pink curlew *n* : ROSEATE SPOONBILL
pink disease *n* **1** : a serious bark disease of rubber, cacao, citrus, coffee, and many other trees that is caused by a fungus (*Corticium salmonicolor*) and is marked by a pink covering of hyphae on the stems and branches **2** : ACRODYNIA
pink dogwood *n* : a pink flowering dogwood
pink–eared duck \'⸗¦⸗-\ *n* : an Australian duck (*Malacorhynchus membranaceus*) with a bill superficially resembling that of the shoveler
pinked *past of* PINK
pink·een \(')piŋ¦kēn\ *n* -s [⁴*pink* + -*een*] **1** *Irish* : MINNOW **2** *Irish* : an insignificant person
pink elephants *n pl* : any of various hallucinations arising from heavy drinking, use of narcotics, or other cause — usu. used in the phrase *see pink elephants* ⟨what a drunk would see who is too pleasant to see *pink elephants* or snakes —John Mason Brown⟩
pink·en \'piŋkən\ *vi* -ED/-ING/-S : to become pink ⟨~*ed* with anger —Audrey Barker⟩ ⟨his body ~*ed* from a shower —Maritta Wolff⟩
pinkeny *n* -ES [alter. of earlier *pink nye*, fr. ⁶*pink* + obs. E *nye* eye, fr. ME — more at PIGSNEY] **1** *obs* : a small blinking or peering eye **2** *obs* : PET, DARLING
pink·er \'piŋkə(r)\ *n* -s : one that does pinking
pin·ker·ton \'piŋkə(r)t°n, -)tən *or* -)d·°n\ *n* -s *usu cap* [after Allan *Pinkerton* †1884 Am. detective] : PRIVATE DETECTIVE
pinkeye \'⸗,⸗\ *n* [⁹*pink* + *eye*] **1** : an acute highly contagious conjunctivitis of man and various domestic animals (as sheep and cattle) **2** : SHIPPING FEVER 2c **3** : PINK-EARED DUCK
pink family *n* : CARYOPHYLLACEAE
pinkfish \'⸗,⸗\ *n* : a blind goby (*Typhlogobius californiensis*) of southern California found under stones on the beaches
pink gin *n, chiefly Brit* : a mixed drink of gin and bitters
¹pin·kie \'piŋkē, -ki\ *adj* [prob. fr. ⁶*pink*] *chiefly Scot* : SMALL
²pinkie \"\ *or* **pin·ky** \"\ *n, pl* **pinkies** [prob. fr. D *pinkje*, dim. of *pink* little finger] : LITTLE FINGER ⟨caught his ~ in the spring mechanism —S.J.Perelman⟩
³pinkie *also* **pinky** \"\ *n, pl* **pinkies** [prob. fr. D *pinkje* small pink, dim. of *pink*, fr. MD *pinke* — more at PINK (fishing craft)] : ³PINK 2
⁴pinkie \"\ *n* -s [origin unknown] : RABBIT BANDICOOT
pink·ify \'piŋkə,fī\ *vt* -ED/-ING/-ES : to make pink
pink·i·ly \'piŋkəlē, -li\ *adv* : in a pinky manner : with a touch of pink
pink·i·ness \-kēnəs, -kin-\ *n* -ES : the quality or state of being pinky ⟨his shaven face, scarcely ruffled by the lines of his fifty years, had the same shell-like ~ —W.J.Locke⟩
pinking *n* -s [fr. gerund of ¹*pink* & ¹²*pink*] : the act or condition of one that pinks: as **a** : a method of decorating, cutting, or finishing cloth, leather, or paper with a pinking iron or pinking shears; *also* : the work so done **b** *Brit* : DETONATION, KNOCK ⟨too much ignition advance leads to . . . ~ —B.C.MacDonald⟩
pinking iron *n* : a metal instrument for cutting or perforating designs on cloth, leather, or paper

pinking shears *n pl* **:** shears with a saw-toothed inner edge on the blades used chiefly for cutting cloth or finishing garments with a nonraveling zigzag edge

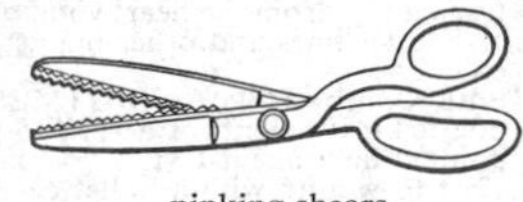
pinking shears

pink·ish \'piŋkish, -kēsh\ *adj* **:** somewhat pink; *esp* **:** tending to be pink in politics — **pink·ish·ness** *n* -ES

pink lady *n* **:** a cocktail consisting of gin, brandy, fresh lemon juice, grenadine, and white of egg shaken with cracked ice and strained before serving

pink lady's-slipper *also* **pink lady slipper** *n* **:** a moccasin flower (*Cypripedium acaule*)

pink laver *n* **:** RED LAVER

pink·ly *adv* **:** in a pink manner **:** with a pink hue ⟨neon signs shining ~ on the snow —Morley Callaghan⟩

pink madder *n* **:** MADDER ROSE

pink mahogany *n* **:** a large evergreen West African tree (*Guarea cedrata*) with pale pinkish cedar-scented wood; *also* **:** the wood of this tree

pink meadowsweet *n* **:** either of two No. American spireas: **a :** HARDHACK 1 **b :** a small erect mat-forming spirea (*Spiraea densiflora*) of the western U.S. with glabrous leaves and lavender flowers

pink needle *n* [¹*pink* + *needle;* fr. the long tapering points of the carpels] **:** ALFILARIA

pin knot *n* **:** a sound knot in lumber not over ½ inch in diameter

pinko \'piŋ(,)kō\ *n* -s [⁹*pink* + *-o*] **:** ¹⁰PINK 3 ⟨pledged to purge the ~s —Addison Burbank⟩

pink patch *n* **:** a disease of turf grasses caused by a fungus (*Corticium fuciforme*) that mats the leaves together with reddish mycelial threads

pink pearl *n* **:** ROSE HERMOSA

pink pill *n* **:** a pink-coated pill; *also* **:** such a pill used as a proprietary medicine

pink rhododendron *n* **:** any pink-flowered rhododendron; *esp* **:** CALIFORNIA ROSEBAY

pinkroot \'=,=\ *n* [⁸*pink* + *root*] **:** any of several plants of the genus *Spigelia* used as anthelmintics: as **a :** a perennial woodland herb (*S. marilandica*) of the U.S. that is sometimes cultivated for its showy red and yellow flowers — called also *Indian pink* **b :** a tropical American annual herb (*S. anthelmia*) with purplish white flowers

pink root *n* [⁹*pink* + *root*] **:** a disease of onion and garlic characterized by a red coloration of the roots and caused by any of several fungi esp. of the genera *Phoma* and *Fusarium*

pink rot *n* **1 :** a destructive disease of potato tubers caused by a fungus (*Phytophtora erythroseptica*) characterized by a wet rot and pinkish color of the cut tuber surfaces when exposed to the air **2 :** a rot of apples caused by a saprophytic fungus (*Tricothecium roseum*) **3 :** a watery soft rot of celery caused by a fungus (*Sclerotinia sclerotiorum*)

pinks *pres 3d sing of* PINK, *pl of* PINK

pink salmon *n* [⁹*pink* + *salmon*] **:** HUMPBACK SALMON

pink salt *n* **:** a white crystalline salt $(NH_4)_2SnCl_6$ used formerly as a mordant in dyeing for producing pink colors with madder and cochineal; ammonium chloro-stannate

pink shower *also* **pink shower tree** *n* **:** a tropical American tree (*Cassia grandis*) used as an ornamental having rose-colored flowers in lateral racemes

pink slip *n* **:** a notice from an employer that a recipient's employment is being terminated

pink spray *n* **:** a spray applied to fruit trees (as apple) when the flower buds are in the pink stage — compare PREPINK SPRAY

pink stage *n* **:** a stage in the development of the flower of an apple or other fruit tree in which the buds show pink color but are only beginning to open ⟨the *pink stage* of blossom growth⟩ — called also *pink bud stage*

pink·ster *or* **pinx·ter** \'piŋ(k)stə(r), -ŋzt-\ *n* -s *usu cap* [D *pinkster* fr. MD *pinxter*, alter. of *pinxten;* akin to OFris *pinxtera* Whitsuntide, OS *pinkoston*, MHG *pfingesten;* all fr. a prehistoric continental WGmc word borrowed fr. Goth *paintekuste* Pentecost, fr. Gk *pentēkostē* — more at PENTECOST] **:** WHITSUNTIDE

pinkster flower *var of* PINXTER FLOWER

pink-stockings \'=,=\ *n pl but sing or pl in constr* **:** BLACK-NECKED STILT

pink tea *n* **1 :** a formal afternoon tea usu. marked by a high degree of decorum **2 :** a decorous or namby-pamby affair or proceeding ⟨do not find press relations anybody's *pink tea* —F.L.Mott⟩

pink tint *n* **:** a pinkish white

pink vine *n* **:** a climbing Mexican vine (*Antigonon leptopus*) cultivated for its racemes of coral pink flowers and its bright-colored veined fruits

pink wax scale *n* **:** a scale (*Ceroplastes rubens*) that attacks mandarins in Australia

pinkweed \'=,=\ *n* **:** any of several knotgrasses with pink flowers; *esp* **:** a knotgrass (*Polygonum aviculare*) common throughout the northern U.S. and southern Canada

pinkwood \'=,=\ *n* [⁸*pink* & ⁹*pink* + *wood*] **1 :** any of several trees and shrubs: as **a :** a Brazilian tree (*Dicypellium caryophyllatum*) of the family Lauraceae with carnation-scented bark used as a substitute for cinnamon and cloves **b :** a tree (*Physocalymma scaberrimum*) of the family Lythraceae of central So. America having hard rose-colored wood **c :** an Australian tree (*Eucryphia billardieri*) yielding cabinet wood **d :** WALLABY BUSH **2 :** the wood of a pinkwood

pinkwort \'=,=\ *n* [⁸*pink* + *wort*] **:** a plant of the family Caryophyllaceae

¹**pinky** \'piŋkē, -ki\ *adj* -ER/-EST [⁹*pink* + *-y*] **:** being of a pink cast **:** tinged with pink ⟨~ beige wool —Lois Long⟩

²**pinky** *var of* PINKIE

pin·less \'pinləs\ *adj* **:** being without a pin

pinlock \'=,=\ *n* **:** a lock having a pin over which the pipe of the key fits

pinmaker \'=,==\ *n* **:** one who makes pins

pin·man \'pinmən, -,man, -aa(ə)n\ *n, pl* **pinmen :** BOWLER

pin mark *n* **1 :** a slight indentation in the side of a piece of foundry type made by the pin that pushes the type from the mold **2 :** the mark on the bottom of a piece of ceramic ware made by a pin supporting it during firing

pin money *n* **1 a :** money allotted by a man to his wife, daughter, or sister for her personal expenses esp. for clothes ⟨this man provides *pin money* in plenty for his daughter —W. J.Weston⟩ **b :** money used or set aside for the purchase of incidentals **:** POCKET MONEY ⟨selling . . . jam and things for *pin money* —Alice S. Rivoire⟩ **2 :** a trifling sum of money ⟨worked feverishly for what would look like *pin money* to modern . . . men —D.W.Maurer⟩

pinn- *or* **pinni-** *comb form* [L, fr. *pinna* feather, wing, fin] **:** feather **:** fin ⟨*pinnal*⟩ ⟨*Pinnipedia*⟩

¹**pin·na** \'pinə\ *n, pl* **pin·nae** \-,nē, -,nī\ *or* **pinnas** [NL, fr. L, feather, wing, alter. of *penna*] **1 :** a leaflet or primary division of a pinnate leaf or frond **2 a :** a feather, wing, or fin or some similar part **b :** the largely cartilaginous projecting portion of the external ear — called also *auricle;* see EAR illustration

²**pinna** \"\ *n* [NL, fr. L *pinna*, *pina* pen shell, fr. Gk *pinē*] **1** *cap* **:** the type genus of Pinnidae comprising large wedge-shaped bivalves that have thin shells with a toothless hinge and linear ligament and are attached to the substrate by a long silky byssus **2** *pl* **pinnas** *or* **pinnae :** PEN SHELL

pin·nace \'pinəs\ *n* -s [MF *pinace*, prob. fr. OSp *pinaza*, fr. *pino* pine, fr. L *pinus* — more at PINE] **1 a :** a light sailing ship that is often schooner-rigged but sometimes is propelled by oars and is used largely as a tender for a warship or other large craft **b :** a doublebanked boat of a warship; *also* **:** any of various ship's boats (as a man-of-war's steam launch) **2** *obs* **a :** WOMAN **b :** PROSTITUTE, MISTRESS

¹**pin·na·cle** \'pinəkəl, -nēk-\ *n* -s [ME *pinacle*, fr. MF, fr. LL *pinnaculum* gable, small wing, dim. of L *pinna* battlement, feather, wing, alter. of *penna* feather, wing — more at PEN] **1 :** an upright architectural member generally ending in a small spire and used esp. in Gothic construction to give additional weight to a buttress or an angle pier **:** FINIAL **2 :** a structure or formation suggesting a pinnacle's height and tapering slenderness; *specif* **:** a lofty peak ⟨these silent ~s of aged snow —Alfred Tennyson⟩ **3 :** the highest point of development or achievement **:** ACME ⟨men who . . . reached the ~ of their profession —*advt*⟩ ⟨on a ~ of happiness —Van Wyck Brooks⟩

²**pinnacle** \"\ *vt* **pinnacled; pinnacled; pinnacling** \-k(ə)liŋ\ **pinnacles 1 :** to surmount with a pinnacle ⟨~ a pediment⟩ **2 :** to raise or rear on or as if on a pinnacle ⟨desired not to be *pinnacled* . . . but to sink into the crowd —John Buchan⟩

pin·na·globin \,pinə+\ *n* [NL ²*Pinna* + E *globin*] **:** a brown respiratory pigment in the blood of a mollusk of the genus *Pinna* that is apparently similar to hemocyanin but contains manganese in place of copper

pin·nal \'pinᵊl\ *adj* [ISV *pinn-* + *-al*] **:** relating to a pinna

pin·nate \'pi,nāt, -,nət, *usu* -d·+V\ *adj* [NL *pinnatus*, fr. L, feathered, winged, fr. *pinna* + *-atus* -ate] **1 :** resembling a feather esp. in having similar parts arranged on opposite sides of an axis like the barbs on the rachis of a feather — used esp. of compound leaves; see LEAF illustration **2 :** characterized by pinnate arrangement of parts ⟨~ veining⟩ — see VENATION illustration

pin·nat·ed \-,nād·əd\ *adj* [*pinnate* + *-ed*] **:** PINNATE — **pin·nat·ed·ly** *adv*

pinnated grouse *n* **:** PRAIRIE CHICKEN

pin·nate·ly *adv* **:** in a pinnate manner

pinnati- *comb form* [NL, fr. *pinnatus* pinnate] **:** pinnately ⟨*pinnatisect*⟩

pin·nat·i·fid \pə'nad·ə,fid\ *adj* [NL *pinnatifidus*, fr. *pinnati-* + L *-fidus* -fid] **:** cleft in a pinnate manner ⟨a ~ leaf⟩ — compare PALMATIFID — **pin·nat·i·fid·ly** *adv*

pin·na·tion \pə'nāshən\ *n* -s **:** the state of being pinnate

pin·nati·sect \pə'nad·ə,sekt\ *adj* [*pinnati-* + *-sect*] **:** cleft pinnately to or almost to the midrib

pinned \'pind\ *adj* [partly fr. ¹*pin* + *-ed*, partly fr. past part. of ²*pin*] **:** having or fastened with a pin

¹**pin·ner** \'pinə(r)\ *n* -s [ME, fr. ¹*pin* + *-er*] *archaic* **:** PINMAKER

²**pinner** \"\ *n* -s [²*pin* + *-er*] *Brit* **:** POUNDMASTER

³**pinner** \"\ *n* -s [²*pin* + *-er*] **1 :** a woman's cap with long lappets worn in the 17th and 18th centuries; *also* **:** one of these lappets **2 :** one whose work is inserting or removing pins, placing on pins, or fastening with pins: as **a :** a hat assembler who cuts and pins brims **b :** a worker who sticks cookies on pins of a wire rack before dipping them into icing **c :** one who rivets the pins by which knife blades are attached to handles **3** [prob. by shortening & alter.] *dial* **:** PINAFORE **4 :** a small stone used to support a large stone in masonry construction

pinni- — see PINN-

pin·ni·dae \'pinə,dē\ *n pl, cap* [NL, fr. *Pinna*, type genus + *-idae*] **:** a family of chiefly tropical marine bivalve mollusks (suborder Ostreacea) that live in bottom sediment — see PINNA

pin·ni·gra·da \,pinə'grād·ə\ [NL, fr. *pinn-* + *-grada* (fr. L, neut. pl. of *-gradus* going) — more at -GRADE] *syn of* PINNIPEDIA

¹**pin·ni·grade** \'==,grād\ *adj* [NL *Pinnigrada*] **:** walking by means of fins or flippers

²**pinnigrade** \"\ *n* -s [NL *Pinnigrada*] **:** a pinnigrade animal

pin·ning \'piniŋ, -nēŋ\ *n* -s [ME *pynnynge* action of fastening with pegs, fr. gerund of *pynnen*, *pinnen* to pin] **1 a :** a pin or peg for fastening; *also* **:** a fastening made by pins **b :** small stones for filling masonry interstices **c :** FOUNDATION, PROP, UNDERPINNING **2 :** adhesion of the tail of the young lamb to the body due to pasting up with sticky meconium preventing passage of feces **3 :** clogging of the teeth of a file by abraded material

pinning block *n* [*pinning* fr. gerund of ²*pin*] **:** a metal or wooden block with pinholes used as an aid in pinning and mounting insects

pinning end *n* [by alter. (influence of *pinning*, gerund of ²*pin*)] **:** GABLE END

pinning forceps *n* **:** small forceps usu. resembling dental forceps used for inserting insect pins in boxes

¹**pin·ni·ped** \'pinə,ped\ *adj* [NL *Pinnipedia*] **:** of or relating to the Pinnipedia

²**pinniped** \"\ *n* -s [NL *Pinnipedia*] **:** a mammal of the family Pinnipedia **:** SEAL, WALRUS

pin·ni·pe·dia \,==='pēdēə\ *n pl, cap* [NL, fr. *pinn-* + *ped-* + *-ia*, n. pl. suffix] **:** a suborder of aquatic carnivorous mammals including all the seals and the walruses

pin·nock \'pinək\ *n* -s [origin unknown] *dial Eng* **:** a small bridge

pin·no·ite \'pinə,wīt\ *n* -s [G *pinnoit*, fr. *Pinno*, 19th cent. Ger. mining official + G *-it* -ite] **:** a hydrous magnesium borate $Mg(BO_2)_2.3H_2O$ usu. occurring in yellow nodular masses with a radiating fibrous structure (hardness 3–4, sp. gr. 2.3)

pin·no·the·res \,pinə'thi(,)rēz\ *n, cap* [NL, fr. L *pinoteres*, *pinotheres* crab living in the mantle cavity of the pen shell, fr. Gk *pinotērēs*, fr. *pino-* (fr. *pinē* pen shell) + *-tērēs* (fr. *tērein* to guard) — more at PAIN] **:** a genus (the type of the family Pinnotheridae) of small crabs (as the oyster crab and the pea crab) having usu. a thin membranous covering and living as commensals in the mantle cavity of various bivalve mollusks or in some similar cavity in other marine animals

¹**pin·no·therid** \;=='thirəd, -ther-\ *adj* [NL *Pinnotheridae*] **:** of or relating to the genus *Pinnotheres* or the family Pinnotheridae

²**pinnotherid** \"\ *n* -s [NL *Pinnotheridae* family of crabs, fr. *Pinnotheres*, type genus + *-idae*] **:** a crab of the genus *Pinnotheres* or the family Pinnotheridae

pin·nu·la \'pinyələ\ *n, pl* **pinnu·lae** \-,lē, -,lī\ [NL, fr. L, small feather, small fin, fr. *pinna* feather, wing, fin, alter. of *penna* feather, wing — more at PEN] **1 :** PINNULE 2, 3 **2 :** a barb of a feather — **pin·nu·lar** \-lə(r)\ *adj*

pin·nu·late \-,lāt, *usu* -ād·+V\ *or* **pin·nu·lat·ed** \-,ād·əd\ *adj* [*pinnulate* fr. *pinnule* + *-ate; pinnulated* fr. *pinnulate* + *-ed*] **:** having pinnules

pin·nule *also* **pin·ule** \'pin(,)yül\ *n* -s [NL *pinnula*, fr. L, small feather, small fin] **1 :** a small plate (as in an alidade) pierced with a peephole **2 a :** one of the secondary branches of a plumelike organ; *specif* **:** one of the lateral parts of the arm of a crinoid or of the tentacle of an alcyonarian polyp **b :** a small detached fish fin (as behind the dorsal and anal fins of the mackerel) **:** FINLET **3 :** a secondary pinna **:** one of the ultimate divisions of a bipinnate or twice-pinnate leaf

¹**pin·ny** \'pinē, -ni\ *adj* -ER/-EST [¹*pin* + *-y*] **1 :** containing hard specks — used esp. of metal **2 :** PINNED — used of a file **3 :** matted together — used of wool

²**pinny** \"\ *n* -ES [by shortening & alter.] **:** PINAFORE

pin oak *n* [so called fr. the persistence of the bases of dead branches which resemble pins driven into the trunk] **:** any of several American oaks (as a bastard oak or laurel oak); *esp* **:** a large symmetrical pyramidal oak (*Quercus palustris*) that is native to the northeastern U. S. but widespread in cultivation and has deeply pinnatifid leaves which turn brilliant red in the fall and rather small almost hemispherical acorns — called also *swamp oak*

pin oat *n* **:** a very slender oat kernel that is usu. borne as the higher secondary or tertiary grain in the spikelet

pi·no·cam·phe·ol \,pīnō'kam(p)fē,ōl, -,ōl\ *n* -s [*pinane* + *-o-* + *camph-* + connective *-e-* + *-ol*] **:** a crystalline bicyclic terpenoid alcohol $C_{10}H_{17}OH$ occurring in hyssop oil; 3-pinan-ol

pinoche *or* **pinochi** *var of* PENUCHE

pi·noch·le *also* **pi·noc·le** \'pē,nəkəl *sometimes* -nēk-\ *or* **pe·nuch·le** \'pē,nək-\ *n* -s [perh. modif. of G dial. (Swiss) *binokel*, fr. F dial. (Swiss) *binocle*, fr. F *binocle* pince-nez, lorgnette, fr. obs. F *binocle*, adj., binocular, fr. NL *binoculus*, fr. *bin-* + L *oculus* eye — more at EYE] **:** a card game for two, three, four or sometimes more players played with a 48-card pack containing two each of A, K, Q, J, 10, 9, in which points are scored by melding combinations of cards and by taking cards in tricks; *also* **:** the meld of queen of spades and jack of diamonds scoring 40 points in this game

pinochle rummy *n* **:** FIVE HUNDRED RUM

pino·cytosis \;pinō, ;pīnō+\ *n, pl* **pinocytoses** [NL, fr. *pino-* (fr. Gk *pinein* to drink) + *cyt-* + *-osis* — more at POTABLE] **:** the taking up of fluid by living cells

pi·no·ki \pə'nōkē\ *n* -s *usu cap* **:** a dialect of Chiquitoan

pi·nol *or* **pi·nole** \'pī,nōl, -nōl\ *n* -s [ISV *pin-* (fr. *pinene*) + *-ole*] **:** a liquid cyclic ether $C_{10}H_{16}O$ that is obtained by oxidation of alpha-pinene

pi·no·le \pə'nōlē\ *n* -s [AmerSp, fr. Nahuatl *pinolli*] **1 :** a finely ground meal made from parched corn **2 :** any of various flours resembling pinole and ground from the seeds of other plants (as mesquite beans or chia)

pi·no·lin *also* **pi·no·line** \pī'nōlən; 'pīnᵊl,ēn, -ᵊlən\ *n* -s [ISV *pin-* (fr. L *pinus* pine) + *-ol* + *-in* or *-ine* — more at PINE] **:** ROSIN SPIRIT

pi·ñon \(')pēn¦yōn, 'pinyən\ *n, pl* **piñons** \-ōnz,-ənz\ *or* **piño·nes** \pēn'yōnēz\ [AmerSp *piñón*, fr. Sp, pine nut, fr. *piña* pinecone, fr. L *pinea* — more at PINEAL] **1** *or* **piñon pine a :** any of various low-growing nut pines (as *Pinus parryana*, *P. cembroides*, *P. edulis*, and *P. monophylla*) of western No. America **b :** the nut pine of Europe **2 :** the nutlike seed of a piñon pine used esp. in confectionery

piñon bird *or* **piñon jay** *n* **:** a bluish corvine bird (*Gymnorhinus cyanocephalus*) of western No. America that feeds on piñon nuts

pi·non·ic acid \pə'nänik-\ *n* [*pinonic* ISV *pin-* (fr. *pinene*) + *-one* + *-ic*] **:** a crystalline keto acid $CH_3COC_6H_{10}CH_2COOH$ derived from dimethyl-cyclobutane and obtained by oxidation of alpha-pinene

pi·no·syl·vin \,pīnō'silvən\ *n* -s [ISV *pino-* (fr. NL *Pinus* — genus name of the Scotch pine *Pinus sylvestris* —, fr. L *pinus* pine) + *sylv-* (fr. NL *sylvestris* — specific epithet of the Scotch pine *Pinus sylvestris* —, fr. L *silvestris* of a forest, fr. *silva* forest) + *-in* — more at PINE] **:** a toxic phenolic compound $C_6H_5CH{=}CHC_6H_3(OH)_2$ related to stilbene that is found in the heartwood of Scotch pine and that gives protection to the wood against fungi, insects, and chemicals (as calcium bisulfite); 5-styryl-resorcinol

pi·not \(')pē¦nō\ *n* -s *usu cap* [F — more at PINARD] **1 :** any of several purple or white vinifera grapes grown chiefly in California and used esp. for wine-making **2 :** a wine made from Pinot grapes

pinot blanc \(,)=¦='blä͞n\ *n, usu cap P&B* [F, white Pinot] **:** a white table wine of Chablis type produced in California from a white Pinot grape

pinot chardonnay *n, usu cap P&C* [F, Chardonnay Pinot] **:** CHARDONNAY

pinot noir \(,)=,nōn(ə)'wär\ *n, usu cap P&N* [F, black Pinot] **:** a dry red table wine of Burgundy type produced in California from a purple Pinot grape

pin pallet *n* **:** an alarm clock lever escapement in which the pallet has upright pins instead of horizontally set jewels

pinpatch \'=,=\ *n, dial Eng* **:** PERIWINKLE

pin perforation *n* **:** a roulette on a stamp made of pinpricks

¹**pinpoint** \'=,=\ *n* [¹*pin* + *point*, n.] **1 a :** the point of a pin ⟨left impaled upon the ~ —Marcia Davenport⟩ **b :** a very small, infinitesimal, or very sharp point ⟨a ~ of rock —Wynford Vaughan-Thomas⟩ ⟨above the town ~s of light twinkled —Eric Ambler⟩ **2 a :** something that is relatively of very small size, scope, or importance ⟨at this one ~ in the heart of the wilderness —Walter O'Meara⟩ ⟨not a ~ of difference —*Irish Digest*⟩ ⟨his interests and ideals shrink to the ~s of the commonplace —H.A.Overstreet⟩ **b** (1) **:** a precisely identified point that locates a relatively small target, a place for rendezvous, or other strategic position or locality **:** the coordinates that define such a point ⟨fussy to a fault about anchoring on the precise ~ assigned —K.M.Dodson⟩ (2) **:** a target, installation, or other place on the ground thus located **:** a pinpoint target ⟨hit his ~⟩

²**pinpoint** \"\ *vt* **1 a :** to locate with great precision or accuracy ⟨can ~ the position of his aircraft within two miles —*Time*⟩ **b :** to make (something) a specific target of bombing, shelling, or air photography by means of precision instruments ⟨~*ed* oil refineries and other strategic installations⟩ **c :** to aim or direct with great precision or accuracy ⟨~ very heavy bombs on the most vulnerable point —J.W.Angell⟩ **2 a :** to fix, determine, or identify with precision ⟨hope to ~ promising young engineers by psychometric methods —W.H. Hale⟩ ⟨~ and define the procedural rights of a citizen —*New Republic*⟩ **b :** to cause to stand out conspicuously **:** HIGHLIGHT, EMPHASIZE ⟨~*ed* the obvious fact —Nona B. Brown⟩ ⟨scenes that were supposed to ~ delicate emotional balances —Cecile Starr⟩ **3 :** to punctuate with pinpoints of light ⟨the lights of their cigarettes ~*ed* the darkness —Robert De Vries⟩

³**pinpoint** \'=¦=\ *adj* **1 a :** extremely fine or precise ⟨functions with ~ accuracy —*Progress Thru Research*⟩ ⟨~ localization of the foreign body —*Jour. Amer. Med. Assoc.*⟩ **b :** located or fixed with great precision or accuracy ⟨~ targets⟩ **c :** directed with extreme precision ⟨~ bombardment⟩ **d :** extremely detailed or specific ⟨a revulsion against ~ planning —A.M. Schlesinger b. 1917⟩ ⟨opposed to ~ price control —*N.Y. Herald Tribune*⟩ **2 :** small as a pinpoint ⟨little ~ creatures —Anthony Standen⟩ ⟨millions of ~ holes —T.R.Ybarra⟩

pin-point clover *n* **:** an annual clover (*Trifolium gracilentum*) of western No. America having long-peduncled heads of reddish purple or pink flowers

pin pool *n* **:** any of several varieties of billiards in which small wooden pins are used; *specif* **:** a game played with two white balls, one red ball, and five small pins that are set up in diamond fashion at the center of the table and have a value according to position

¹**pinprick** \'=,=\ *n* [¹*pin* + *prick*, n.] **1 :** a small puncture made by or as if by a pin **2 :** a petty irritation or annoyance; *specif* **:** a small, irritating, and antagonistic action or statement that is often repeated for the purpose of annoying ⟨the action was viewed as another ~ —Walter Sullivan⟩

²**pinprick** \"\ *vt* **:** to administer pinpricks to ⟨~*ed* and heckled the socialist leaders —John Gunther⟩ **~** *vi* **:** to administer pinpricks

pin punch *n* **:** a punch used to dislodge rivets and pins

pinrail \'=,=\ *n* **:** a rail or strip fitted with pins or for holding pins: as **a :** a rail that holds belaying pins; *esp* **:** one along the bulwarks **b :** a beam at one side of a theater stage through which wooden or metal pins are driven and to which lines from the flies are fastened

pin rod *n* **:** a rod or plate with turned ends for connecting two parts (as brake shoes on the opposite sides of a locomotive) so that they act kinematically as one part

pin rot *n* **:** a rot of the heartwood of incense cedar caused by a pore fungus (*Polyporus amarus*) — called also *peckiness*

pins *pl of* PIN, *pres 3d sing of* PIN

pins and needles *n pl* **:** a pricking tingling sensation in a limb recovering from numbness — **on pins and needles :** in a very nervous or jumpy state esp. as a result of some suspense-provoking situation ⟨*on pins and needles* while awaiting the doctor's verdict⟩

pin seal *n* [³*pin*] **:** leather made from a very young seal

pinsetter \'=,==\ *n* **1 :** an employee of a bowling alley who clears away deadwood, sets up pins, and returns balls to players **2 :** a mechanical device in a bowling alley for spotting the pins simultaneously

pinson *n* -s *obs* [ME *pynson*, perh. fr. (assumed) MF *pinçon* pincers, fr. MF *pincier* to pinch — more at PINCH] **:** a thin shoe **:** SLIPPER

pin·sons \'pin(t)sənz\ *n pl* [ME *pynsons*, perh. fr. (assumed) MF *pinçons*, pl. of (assumed) MF *pinçon* pincers] *dial chiefly Eng* **:** PINCERS

pin spanner *n* **:** PIN WRENCH

pinspot \'=,=\ *n* **:** each of the spots like pinheads often forming a pattern on a textile

pinspotter \'=,==\ *n* **:** PINSETTER

pinstripe \'=,=\ *n, often attrib* **:** a fine stripe on a fabric; *also* **:** a fabric made with such stripes

¹**pint** \'pīnt\ *n* -s *often attrib* [ME *pinte*, fr. MF, fr. ML *pincta*, fr. (assumed) VL *pincta*, fem. of (assumed) VL *pinctus* painted, alter. of L *pictus*, past part. of *pingere* to paint; prob. fr. the use of a painted mark on a container to point out its capacity — more at PAINT] **1 :** any of various units of capacity equal to ½ quart: as **a :** a U. S. unit for liquids equivalent to 28.875 cubic inches **b :** a U. S. dry unit equivalent to 33.600 cubic inches **c :** a British liquid or dry unit equivalent to 34.678 cubic inches — see MEASURE table **2 a :** a pint pot or vessel **b** *chiefly Brit* **:** a pint pot of ale, beer, or other beverage

²**pint** \"\ *dial var of* POINT

pin·ta \'pintə, 'pēn-\ *n* -s [AmerSp, fr. Sp, spot, mark, fr. (assumed) VL *pincta*, fem. of (assumed) VL *pinctus* painted]

: a chronic skin disease endemic in tropical America that occurs successively as an initial papule, a generalized eruption of pintids, and a patchy loss of pigment, that chiefly affects dark-skinned people, and that is caused by a spirochete (*Treponema carateum*) morphologically indistinguishable from the causative agent of syphilis
pin table *n, Brit* : PINBALL MACHINE
pin·ta·do \pin·'tä(,)dō\ *n, pl* **pintados** *or* **pintadoes** [Pg, fr. past part. of *pintar* to paint, fr. (assumed) VL *pinctare,* fr. (assumed) VL *pinctus* painted] **1** : a painted or printed chintz formerly made in India **2** *or* **pintado petrel** : CAPE PIGEON **3** *or* **pin·ta·da** \-·də\ [*pintado* fr. AmerSp, fr. Sp, past part. of *pintar* to paint, fr. (assumed) VL *pinctare; pintada* fr. AmerSp, fr. Sp, fem. of *pintado,* past part. of *pintar*] : CERO
pin·ta·do·ite \-dō,īt\ *n* -s [*Pintado* Canyon, San Juan county, southeast Utah + E *-ite*] : a hydrous calcium vanadate $Ca_2V_2O_7.9H_2O$ occurring in a green incrustation
pintail \'=,=\ *n, pl* **pintails** *or* **pintail** **1 a** *or* **pin-tailed duck** : a river duck (*Anas acuta*) of Europe, Asia, and No. America having central tail feathers markedly elongated in the male and the head and neck brown, the breast white, and the upper parts grayish **b** : RUDDY DUCK **2 a** *or* **pin-tailed chicken** : SHARP-TAILED GROUSE **b** : PIN-TAILED SANDGROUSE
pin-tailed \'=;=\ *adj* **1** : having a tapered tail with the middle feathers longest **2** : having the tail feathers spiny
pin-tailed sandgrouse *or* **pin-tailed grouse** *n* : a sandgrouse (*Pterocles alchata*) of Europe and Africa having elongated middle tail feathers
pin·ta·no \pin·'tä(,)nō\ *n* -s [AmerSp] : SERGEANT MAJOR 4
pin thorn *n* : COCKSPUR THORN
pin·tid \'pintəd\ *n* -s [*pinta* + *-id*] : one of many initially reddish, then brown, slate blue, or black patches on the skin characteristic of the second stage of pinta
pin·tle \'pintᵊl\ *n* -s [ME *pintel* pintle, penis, fr. OE, penis; akin to OFris & MLG *pint* penis, OE *pinn* pin, peg — more at PIN] **1** : a usu. upright pivot pin (as of a hinge or a rudder) on which another part turns **2** : a hook at the rear of a limber to receive the lunette of a gun trail, caisson, or other vehicle when the gun is limbered
pintle chain *n* : a chain for sprocket wheels consisting of links fastened together by pintles
pintle valve *n* : a short extension of the needle-valve tip to facilitate control of fluid through the valve
¹pin·to \'pin·(,)tō, 'pēn·(,)-\ *n, pl* **pintos** *also* **pintoes** *often attrib* [AmerSp, fr. *pinto,* adj., spotted, mottled, fr. obs. Sp, fr. (assumed) VL *pinctus* painted — more at PINT] *chiefly West* : a spotted or calico horse or pony
²pinto \"\ *n* -s [AmerSp (esp. in the expression *mal del pinto* pinta), fr. *pinto,* adj., spotted, mottled] : PINTA
pinto bean *also* **pinto** *n* [AmerSp *pinto,* fr. *pinto,* adj., spotted, mottled] : a mottled bean that resembles the kidney bean in size and shape and is grown extensively in Colorado and in other southwestern states as a field bean for food and for stock feed
pintoes \'=,=\ *n pl* [¹*pin* + *toes,* pl. of *toe*] : toes that turn inward ⟨a horse with ~ is never liable to strike himself —Henry Wynmalen⟩
pinto leaf *n* : a virus disease of some cherries characterized by a blotchy mosaic pattern on the leaves
pint pot *n* : a pint-measure pot or drinking vessel usu. of pewter; *also* : such a pot full of beer, ale, or other beverage
pints *pl of* PINT
pintsch gas \'pinch-\ *n, usu cap P* [after Julius *Pintsch* †1884 Ger. manufacturer] : a compressed oil gas obtained from gas oil, consisting chiefly of hydrocarbons and hydrogen, and formerly used in lighting railroad cars and buoys
pint-size \'=;=\ *or* **pint-sized** \'=;=\ *adj* : SMALL, DIMINUTIVE ⟨a *pint-size* but highly efficient adding machine —*New Yorker*⟩ ⟨horse carts drawn by *pint-sized* horses —R.A.Gunnison⟩
pin tuck *n* : a very narrow tuck
pin tumbler *n* : the part of a cylinder lock that in conjunction with others prevents motion unless the proper key is used — compare LEVER TUMBLER
pin·tu·ra \pin·'tùrə\ *n* -s [Sp, painting, fr. (assumed) VL *pinctura,* alter. (influenced by assumed VL *pinctus* painted) of L *pictura* — more at PICTURE] : a symbolic or hieroglyphic manuscript of Mexico with colored characters and figures
pi·ñue·la \,pēnyə'wālə\ *n* -s [AmerSp, fr. Sp *piña* pineapple, pinecone, fr. L *pinea* pinecone — more at PINEAL] : any of several bromeliads or aroids (as the pineapple and the pinguin) that are often epiphytic
pin·u·late \'pinyə,lāt, -,lət\ *adj* [*pinulus* + *-ate*] : being or having the form of a pinulus
pinule *var of* PINNULE
pin·u·lus \'pinyələs\ *n, pl* **pinu·li** \-ə,lī\ [NL *pinulus, pinnulus,* alter. of *pinnula*] : a usu. pentact sponge spicule of which one ray projects either internally or externally from the sponge and develops numerous small spines
¹pinup \'=,=\ *n* -s [fr. *pin up,* v., fr. ²*pin* + *up,* adv.] : something that is fastened to a wall: as **a** : a photograph of a pinup girl ⟨sprinkled with blond ~s on the walls —A.W. Baum⟩ ⟨magazine ~s⟩ **b** : a lamp or other accessory that is attached to a wall
²pinup \'=;=\ *adj* **1** : of or relating to pinup girls ⟨those pictures . . . give producers the idea that I am the ~ type —*Irish Digest*⟩ **2** : designed for hanging upon a wall of a room ⟨a ~ lamp⟩
pinup girl *n* **1** : a girl whose physical charms, attractive personality, or other glamorous qualities make her a suitable subject of a photograph pinned up on an admirer's wall ⟨the worship of the movie hero and the *pinup girl* —J.M.Barzun⟩ ⟨has been the *pinup girl* of libidinous . . . undergraduates —Bennett Cerf⟩ **2** : PINUP a
pi·nus \'pīnəs\ *n, cap* [NL, fr. L, pine — more at PINE] : a large and economically important genus (the type of the family Pinaceae) of coniferous trees chiefly of north temperate regions, in former classifications including pines, firs, spruces, larches and hemlocks, now restricted to the true pines, and comprising trees with primary leaves that are early deciduous, secondary needlelike leaves that are borne usu. in fascicles of one to seven, and cones that consist of imbricated woody scales enclosing winged seeds
pin valve *n* : NEEDLE VALVE
pin vise *n* : a hand vise used (as by jewelers) for holding fine work
pinwale \'=,=\ *adj, of a fabric* : made with extremely narrow wales
pinweed \'=,=\ *n* **1** : an herb of the genus *Lechea* **2** : ALFILARIA
¹pinwheel \'=,=\ *n, often attrib* [¹*pin* + *wheel,* n.] **1** : a contrate gear wheel in which the teeth are cylindrical pins **2 a** : a toy consisting of lightweight vanes (as of paper or plastic) attached loosely to the end of a stick so that they revolve in a breeze **b** : a fireworks device in the form of a small wheel which when the fuse is lighted is made to spin by spouts of colored fire that shoot out tangentially at various points on the wheel **3** : a revolvable cylindrical box with pins on its inner surface used for washing and softening hides in warm water or other liquid

pinwheel 2 a

²pinwheel \"\ *vt* : to wash and soften (hides) in a pinwheel ~ *vi* : to revolve rapidly in the manner of a pinwheel
pin-wing \'=,=\ *vt* : PINION
pin wire *n* : wire from which pins are made
pinworm \'=,=\ *n* **1** : any of numerous small nematode worms that have the tail of the female prolonged into a sharp point, infest the intestines esp. the cecum of various vertebrates, and belong to the family Oxyuridae — see ENTEROBIASIS, OXYURIASIS **2** : any of several rather slender insect larvae that burrow in plant material; *specif* : TOMATO PINWORM
pin wrench *n* : a wrench having a projecting pin to enter a hole (as in a nut or cylinder) to make a hold
pinxter *usu cap, var of* PINKSTER
pinxter flower *also* **pinxter bloom** *or* **pinxter** *or* **pinkster flower** *n* [*pinxter, pinkster* fr. D *pinkster* Whitsuntide — more at PINKSTER] : a deciduous pink-flowered azalea (*Rhododendron nudiflorum*) native to rich moist woodlands of eastern No. America — called also *wild honeysuckle*
¹pi·ny \'pīnē, -ni\ *n* -ES [ME *piony* — more at PEONY] *dial* : PEONY
²piny \'pīnē, -ni\ *adj* -ER/-EST [³*pine* + *-y*] **1** : abounding in pines ⟨~ woods⟩ **2** : of, relating to, or characteristic of pine ⟨a ~ odor⟩
pin·yo·ca \pēn'yōkə\ *n* -s *usu cap* : a dialect of Chiquitoan
pi·nyon \(')pēn,yōn, 'pinyən\ *n* -s [AmerSp *piñón* — more at PIÑON] : PIÑON
pinyon jay *n* : PIÑON BIRD
pinz·gau \'pin(t)s,gaù\ *or* **pinz·gau·er** \-aù(ə)r\ *n* -s *usu cap* [*pinzgau* fr. *Pinzgau,* valley in western Austria; *pinzgauer* fr. G, lit., one that is of or comes from Pinzgau, fr. *Pinzgau* + G *-er*] : an Austrian breed of heavy draft horse; *also* : a horse of this breed
PIO *abbr* public information office; public information officer
piobaireachd *var of* PIBROCH
pi·o·let \,pēə'lā\ *n* -s [F, fr. F dial. (Valais canton, Switzerland & Piedmont), dim. of *piola* small ax, fr. (assumed) MF dial., fr. OProv, dim of *apcha, abcha* battle-ax, of Gmc origin; akin to OHG *hāppa* sickle, pruning knife — more at HASH] : a two-headed ice ax used in mountaineering (as in Switzerland)
¹pion *vi* -ED/-ING/-S [MF *pioner, pionner,* fr. *peon, pion* foot soldier, pioneer — more at PIONEER] *obs* : to dig or excavate as a pioneer
²pi·on \'pī,än\ *n* -s [by contr.] : PI-MESON
¹pi·o·neer \,pīə'ni(ə)r, -iə\ *n* -s [MF *pionier, pionnier,* fr. OF *peonier* foot soldier, fr. *peon, pion* foot soldier (fr. ML *pedon-, pedo*) + *-ier* -er — more at PAWN] **1 a** : a member of a military unit usu. of engineers equipped and trained esp. for road building, temporary bridging, demolitions **b** *obs* : one that excavates or undermines **2** : one that begins or helps develop something new and prepares a way for others to follow: **a** : a person or group that originates or helps open up a new line of thought or activity or a new method or technical development ⟨broke decidedly with the prevailing theological views and became the ~ of a new order —C.A.Dinsmore⟩ ⟨a ~ in oceanography⟩ ⟨a ~ in the development of radar⟩ **b** : one of the first to settle in a primitive territory : an early settler **3** *usu cap* : a member of the Russian Communist youth organization for boys and girls in the 10 to 16 year age group — compare KOMSOMOL, OCTOBRIST **4** : a plant or animal capable of establishing itself in a bare or barren area (as after a burn) and initiating a new ecological cycle **5** *or* **pioneer publisher** *usu cap both Ps* : a full-time worker of the Jehovah's Witnesses
²pioneer \"\ *adj* **1** : first of a kind : EARLIEST, ORIGINAL ⟨a ~ model improved by later inventions⟩ ⟨one of the ~ institutions in America for the education of young women —S.P. Chase & J.K.Snyder⟩ **2** : of or relating to a pioneer; *esp* : of, relating to, or characteristic of early settlers or their time ⟨~ days⟩ ⟨a ~ village⟩ ⟨~ conditions⟩ **3** : being a pioneer ⟨settled on the frontier as a ~ merchant⟩ ⟨the ~ exponent of ballet on ice —*Current Biog.*⟩ **4** *usu cap* : of or relating to a culture in the southwestern U. S. about the beginning of the Christian era characterized by a squarish semisubterranean house having an entrance passage and a roof supported by four posts, the beginning of agriculture and pottery, and cremation
³pioneer \"\ *vb* -ED/-ING/-S *vi* : to act as a pioneer : lead the way ⟨group which ~*ed* in the development of the modern art movement —*Current Biog.*⟩ ~ *vt* **1** : to open or prepare (as a way or region) for others to follow : EXPLORE ⟨Portugal, which had done so much to ~ the outer ocean —Marjory S. Douglas⟩; *also* : SETTLE ⟨an important distributing center for the farmers who ~*ed* the region⟩ **2** : to originate or take part in the development of (as a new enterprise, course of action, or style) ⟨~ some of the first big natural-gas developments in north Texas —T.H.White b. 1915⟩ ⟨she ~*ed* the short haircut for women⟩ **3** : to lead safely : GUIDE
pioneer day *n, usu cap P&D* **1** : July 24 observed as a legal holiday in Utah in commemoration of the arrival of Brigham Young on the present site of Salt Lake City in 1847 **2** : June 15 formerly observed as a legal holiday in Idaho as the anniversary of the acceptance of the Oregon treaty by the president and the senate in 1846
pioneer gold *n* : PRIVATE GOLD
pioneer tunnel *or* **pioneer bore** *n* : a small tunnel parallel to a main tunnel and well in advance of the completed main tunnel so that by crosscuts to the line of the main tunnel several headings can be exposed and work expedited
pioner *obs var of* PIONEER
pi·on·no·tal \;pīə;nōdᵊl\ *adj* : producing pionnotes
pi·on·no·tes \,pīə'nōd·ēz\ *n pl but sing or pl in constr* [NL, prob. irreg. fr. Gk *piōn* fat + *nothos* spurious] : a smooth or tuberculate gelatinous layer of spores (as in fungi of the genus *Fusarium*)
pi·o·ny \'pīənē, pē'ōnē\ *archaic var of* PEONY
¹pi·oph·i·lid \(')pī;äfələd\ *adj* [NL *Piophilidae*] : of or relating to the Piophilidae
²piophilid \"\ *n* -s : a fly of the family Piophilidae
pi·o·phil·i·dae \,pīə'filə,dē\ *n pl, cap* [NL, fr. *Piophila,* type genus (fr. *pio-* fat — fr. Gk *piōn-* — + *-phila*) + *-idae;* akin to Gk *pimelē* lard — more at FAT] : a family of two-winged flies including the cheese fly
pi·os·i·ty \pī'äsəd·ē\ *n* -ES [fr. *pious,* after such pairs as E *religious: religiosity*] : an exaggerated or superficial piousness : an obvious manifestation of devoutness
pi·o·tine \'pīə,tēn\ *n* -s [G *piotin,* fr. Gk *piotēs* fattiness (fr. *piōn* fat, fatty) + G *-in* -ine] : SAPONITE
piou·piou \pyüpyü\ *n* -s [F, fr. F (baby talk), small chicken, of imit. origin] *slang* : a French infantryman
pioury *var of* PIURI
pi·ous \'pīəs\ *adj* [L *pius;* akin to L *piare* to appease, atone for, Oscan *pihatu* appeased, and perh. to L *purus* pure — more at PURE] **1 a** : marked by or showing reverence for deity and zealous devotion to the duties and rites of religion : DEVOUT ⟨the ~ Jewish historian, who saw in Israel's exile God's punishment for sin —J.G.Frazer⟩ ⟨one society is genuinely ~, another is worldly-minded —A.L.Kroeber⟩ ⟨~ practices such as attendance at daily mass —T.F.McNally⟩ **b** : marked by conspicuous religiosity **c** : of, relating to, or suggesting the sacred or devotional as distinct from the profane or secular : RELIGIOUS ⟨~ papers devoted to the publication of . . . offerings made at sacred shrines —D.H.Wiest⟩ ⟨a ~ opinion⟩ ⟨a ~ hush in the atmosphere —Mary McCarthy⟩ **2** : marked by or showing loyal reverence for and faithfully performing the duties owed to a person or thing (as a family, school, cause) : DUTIFUL ⟨undertaking the ~ task of writing the life of an ancestor —*Times Lit. Supp.*⟩ ⟨took me to pay a ~ visit to my old school —A.T.Quiller-Couch⟩ ⟨hangs on to his ~ Marxianism —H.A.Overstreet⟩ **3** : perpetrated for a supposed good end ⟨often the gap between the old rule and the new was bridged by a ~ fraud of a fiction —B.N.Cardozo⟩ **4** : being or relating to a use that is legally a charitable use **5 a** : characterized by pretense at propriety, virtue, benevolence, or devotion : given to or intended for the concealment of real feelings or intentions : marked by sham or hypocrisy ⟨a world of arrogant acts accompanied by ~ disclaimers —Rosemond Tuve⟩ ⟨~ noble phrases about ideals which serve only to cover up . . . iniquity —M.R.Cohen⟩ **b** : marked by politic or self-conscious virtue : VIRTUOUS ⟨sick of your ~ penny-pinching —Marcia Davenport⟩ ⟨put on ~ expressions and were altogether very superior, if not stuffy —Edison Marshall⟩ **6** : deserving commendation : COMMENDABLE, WORTHY ⟨the ~ practice of sifting the past twelve months' new books for gold —W.T.Scott⟩; *specif* : displaying an ideal, a benevolent wish, or a good intention ⟨international law was scoffed at as ~ but impotent —W.E.Jackson b. 1919⟩ ⟨a ~ hope⟩ ⟨~ platitudes⟩ **syn** see DEVOUT
pi·ous·ly *adv* : in a pious manner : with a pious motive or intention ⟨~ reminded them of their duty⟩ ⟨knelt ~ at the shrine⟩
pi·ous·ness *n* -ES : the quality or state of being pious
¹pip \'pip\ *n* -s [ME *pippe,* fr. MD *pip, pippe* nasal mucus, slime, pip; akin to OHG *pfiffiz, pfiffiz* pip; both fr. a prehistoric WGmc word borrowed fr. (assumed) VL *pipita,* alter. of L *pituita* nasal mucus, phlegm, pip; akin to OIr *ith* grain, Skt *pitu* drink, food, L *opimus* fat, fertile — more at FAT] **1 a** : the formation of a scale or crust on the tip and dorsal surface of the tongue of a bird often associated with respiratory diseases **b** : the scale or crust itself **2 a** : any of various ailments formerly or locally identified as syphilis, dyspepsia, a slight cough, or other ailment **b** : a fit of peevishness or feeling out of sorts : a slight nonspecific disorder : mild malaise — usu. used with *the* ⟨gives me the ~, the way some of them make a fuss about it —Dorothy Sayers⟩
²pip \"\ *n* -s [alter. of earlier *peep,* of unknown origin] **1 a** : one of the dots used on dice and dominoes to indicate numerical value **b** : SPOT 3c(1) **2 a** : SPOT, SPECK, PROTUBERANCE **b** : an image in the form of an inverted V or a spot of light on a radarscope or sonar screen indicating the return of radar or sound waves reflected from an object : BLIP **c** : an inverted V on the line of a graph **3 a** : the individual rootstock of the lily of the valley producing leaves and a flower stalk **b** : any of various other dormant roots or rootstocks (as of peonies and anemones) **4** : one of the segments forming the surface of a pineapple **5** : a diamond-shaped insignia worn to indicate rank (as by a second lieutenant, lieutenant, or captain) in the British army ⟨the three ~s of a captain⟩
³pip \"\ *vb* **pipped; pipped; pipping; pips** *vt* **1** *Brit* : BLACKBALL **2** *Brit* : DEFEAT ⟨*pipped* his opponent in the race⟩ **3** *Brit* : KILL ~ *vi* : DIE — sometimes used with *out*
⁴pip \"\ *n* -s [short for *pippin*] **1** : a small fruit seed; *esp* : a seed of a fleshy fruit (as the orange, apple, pear) having several seeds **2** *slang* : something extraordinary of its kind : PIPPIN ⟨the gal's a ~ and I'm going to marry her —Ring Lardner⟩ ⟨created a traffic jam that was a ~ —Emmett Kelly⟩
⁵pip \"\ *vb* **pipped; pipped; pipping; pips** [imit.] *vi* **1** : PEEP 1 **2 a** *of a hatching bird* : to break through the shell of the egg **b** *of an egg* : to break open from pipping ~ *vt* : to break open (the shell of an egg) in hatching
⁶pip \"\ *n* -s [imit.] : a short high-pitched tone produced as a signal ⟨broadcast six ~s as a time signal⟩
pi·pa \'pēpə\ *n* [D, fr. Galibi] **1** -s : SURINAM TOAD **2** *cap* [NL, fr. D *pipa*] : a genus of toads comprising solely the Surinam toad
pi-pa \'pē'pä\ *n* -s [Chin (Pek) *p'i² p'a¹*] : a 4-stringed Chinese musical instrument plucked like a guitar and having a large body resembling a lute and a neck with 12 or more frets that leads into the body
pip·able \'pīpəbəl\ *adj* : capable of being piped
pip·age *or* **pipe·age** \'pīpij\ *n* -s [¹*pipe* + *-age*] **1 a** : the transportation of natural gas, petroleum, or water by means of pipes **b** : the charge for such transportation **2** : PIPING, PIPES
pi·pal tree *or* **pipal** *or* **pi·pul** *also* **pee·pul** \'pēpəl\ *n* -s [Hindi *pīpal,* fr. Skt *pippala*] : a fig (*Ficus religiosa*) of India remarkable for its great size and longevity, useful as a source of lac, and distinguished from the banyan by the absence of prop roots — called also *sacred fig*
pip card *n* : SPOT CARD 2
¹pipe \'pīp\ *n* -s *often attrib* [ME, fr. OE *pīpa;* akin to OFris *pipe* pipe, OS *pīpa,* OHG *pfīfa,* all fr. a prehistoric WGmc word derived fr. (assumed) VL *pipa,* back-formation fr. L *pipare* to peep, chirp, of imit. origin like Gk *pipos, pippos* young bird, Skt *pippakā,* a kind of bird] **1 a** (1) : a wind instrument consisting of a tube of straw, reed, wood, or metal (as a flageolet, oboe) — compare PANPIPE, PITCH PIPE, SHEPHERD'S PIPE; *specif* : a small fipple flute held in and played by the left hand leaving the right hand free for beating a tabor — called also *tabor pipe* (2) : one of the open or closed tubes comprising the stops of a pipe organ — compare FLUE PIPE, REED PIPE (3) : BOATSWAIN'S PIPE (4) : BAGPIPE — usu. used in pl. **b** (1) : VOICE, VOCAL CORD — usu. used in pl. ⟨a soloist with a powerful set of ~s⟩ (2) : PIPING 1 ⟨their voices came in a shallow unison ~ —*Time*⟩ ⟨helped him with his first ~s on the flute —H.S. Canby⟩ **2 a** : a long hollow cylinder (as of metal, clay, concrete, plastic) used for conducting a fluid, gas, or finely divided solid and for structural purposes; *typically* : metal tubing in standard diameters and lengths threaded at the ends for joining and used for water, steam, and other conduits **b** *chiefly dial* : a canal or vessel of the body (as of the respiratory organs) — usu. used in pl. ⟨cleared her ~s and began to sing⟩ **c** *slang* : a coaxial cable used to transmit television or telephone signals **3 a** : a tubular or cylindrical object, part, or passage: as (1) : the tubular stem of a plant — compare PIPE TREE (2) : BURROW (3) : the hollow part of a pipe key (4) : BLOWPIPE 4 (5) : isinglass dried in the form of long hollow pieces (6) : PLAYPIPE **b** : a roughly cylindrical and vertical geological formation ⟨a firn ~⟩ ⟨a sand ~⟩: as (1) : an elongated vertical or steeply inclined body of ore (2) : one of the vertical cylindrical masses of volcanic agglomerate in which diamonds occur in So. Africa (3) : the eruptive channel opening into the crater of a volcano; *also* : the filling of such a channel (4) : the vent of a geyser **c** : a cavity in a casting (as an ingot of steel) due to unequal contraction on solidifying **d** : a small rounded molder's trowel for dressing up concave surfaces **4** : a former department of the British Exchequer charged with drawing up the pipe rolls **5** [ME, fr. MF, pipe, cask, fr. (assumed) VL *pippa,* alter. of *pipa*] **a** : a large cask of varying capacity used esp. for wine and oil **b** : any of various units of liquid capacity based on the size of a pipe; *esp* : a unit equal to 2 hogsheads **6 a** : a device usu. consisting of a tube having a bowl at one end and a mouthpiece at the other and used for smoking ⟨tobacco ~⟩ **b** : PIPEFUL **7** : any of the channels of a decoy **8 a** : a distance (as three quarters of a mile) customarily traveled in colonial New York while smoking one pipeful **b** : a distance (as six miles) customarily traveled by voyageurs or dogsledders between rests **9** *slang* **a** : PIPE DREAM ⟨might turn in a story about a sea serpent . . . but I haven't got the nerve to try 'em with a ~ like this —O.Henry⟩ **b** : something easy : SNAP ⟨both think acting on the show is a ~ —*Newsweek*⟩ **c** : something sure : CINCH ⟨a play . . . that is at least a ~ and as certain to make a fortune for anyone who invests in it as anything reasonably can be —G.S.Kaufman⟩

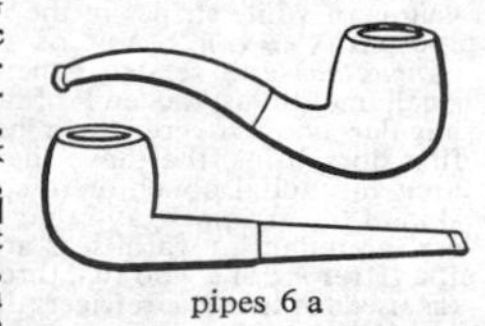

pipes 6 a

²pipe \"\ *vb* -ED/-ING/-S [partly fr. ME *pipen* to play on a pipe, fr. OE *pīpan,* fr. *pīpe,* n.; partly fr. ¹*pipe*] *vi* **1 a** : to play on a pipe (as a bagpipe) ⟨we *piped* to you, and you did not dance —Mt 11:17 (RSV)⟩ **b** : to convey orders by signals on a boatswain's pipe **2 a** : to speak in a high or shrill voice ⟨a thin call *piped* from the house, and he turned to wave —Ellen Glasgow⟩ ⟨his shrill voice *piped* above the hot volume of American jazz —Scott Fitzgerald⟩ **b** : to emit or have a shrill sound like that of a pipe : WHISTLE ⟨wind began to ~ around the stacks, not loud —Warren Eyster⟩ ⟨tree frogs ~ . . . before rain —Marjory S. Douglas⟩ **3** *slang* : WEEP **4** : to become pipy **5** : to develop cavities in the interior during solidification — used esp. of cast steel ~ *vt* **1 a** : to play (a tune) on a pipe (as a bagpipe) **b** : to utter in the shrill tone of a pipe ⟨a robin . . . *piping* a few querulous notes —Washington Irving⟩ **2 a** : to cause to go or be with pipe music ⟨men of Scotland who've *piped* their men into battle —Wynford Vaughan-Thomas⟩ **b** (1) : to call or direct by the boatswain's pipe ⟨*piped* all hands on deck⟩ (2) : to receive aboard or attend the departure of from a naval vessel with side boys and piping the side ⟨~ the admiral aboard⟩ **3** : to make slips or cuttings of for propagation **4** : to trim with piping ⟨the edge of the white jacket was *piped* with navy⟩ **5** : to throw water upon from a hydraulic pipe : wash with a pipe **6** : to furnish or equip (as a building) with pipes **7 a** : to convey by means of pipes ⟨~ water from the standpipe into every house⟩ **b** : to convey as if by pipes ⟨every bit of talk in that town is *piped* into his ears —W.L.Gresham⟩; *specif* : to transmit (as current, a radio or television program) by wire or coaxial cable ⟨~ electricity from the dam to the cities⟩ ⟨~ music into restaurants, stores, and factories⟩ ⟨~ the telecast to all network stations⟩ **8** *slang* : to look at : NOTICE ⟨slapped their wrists when they *piped* the red long johns —H.D.Schwartz⟩ **9** : to put (cookie dough, frosting) on a cookie sheet or baked goods by forcing through a pastry tube **10** : to make cavities in (as an ingot of steel) during casting — **pipe one's eye** *Brit* **:** WEEP — **pipe the side :** to sound on a boatswain's pipe a ceremonial signal when a commissioned officer or high official comes aboard or leaves a naval vessel

pipeage *var of* PIPAGE

pipe amygdule *n* **:** an elongated nodule resembling a tube in an amygdaloid

pipe–band \ˈ=,=\ *n* **:** a band of bagpipers ⟨a Scottish *pipe-band*⟩

pipe beetle *n* **:** SNOUT BEETLE

pipe berth *or* **pipe cot** *n* **:** a berth of canvas in a pipe frame that can swing up or down when not in use

pipe clay *n* **:** highly plastic and fairly pure clay of a grayish white color used in making tobacco pipes, in calico printing, for marking and scouring, and for whitening leather — called also *ball clay*

pipe–clay \ˈ=,=\ *vt* -ED/-ING/-S [*pipe clay*] **1 :** to whiten or clean with pipe clay ⟨*pipe-clay* shoes or helmets⟩ **2 :** to put in order **:** clean up ⟨*pipe-clay* accounts⟩

pipe–clay·ey \ˈ=,=ē, -i\ *adj* [*pipe clay* + *-y*] **:** PIPE-CLAYISH

pipe–clay·ish \-ish,-ēsh\ *adj* [*pipe clay* + *-ish*] **1 :** manifesting cleanliness or spruceness **2 :** formally and stiffly military (as in appearance, manner)

pipe cleaner *n* **:** something used to clean the inside of a pipe; *specif* **:** a device made of flexible wire with which tufted fabric is twisted and used to clean the stem of a tobacco pipe

pi·pec·o·line \pīˈpekə,lēn, pə̇ˈp-, -,lən\ *n* -S [ISV, blend of *picoline* and *-pe-*] **:** any of the three liquid monoethyl derivatives $CH_3C_5H_9NH$ of piperidine

pipe covering *n* **:** insulating material applied around a pipe to prevent heat exchange between contents and the surroundings

pipe cutter *n* **:** a tool or machine for cutting pipe; *specif* **:** a hand tool comprising a grasping device and three sharp-edged wheels forced inward by screw pressure that cut into the pipe as the tool is rotated

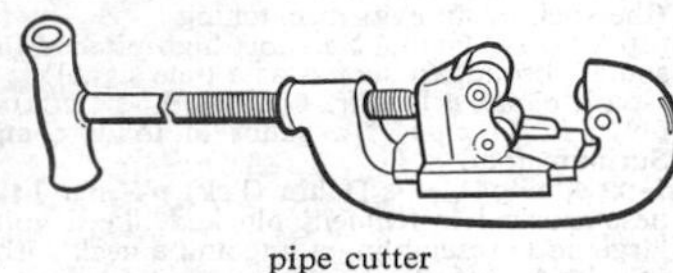
pipe cutter

piped \ˈpīpt\ *adj* [¹*pipe* + *-ed*] **1** *of leather* **:** having small pipelike wrinkles when flexed **2** *of a tailored seam* **:** finished with a binding to prevent raveling **3** *slang* **:** INTOXICATED

pipe dance *n* **:** CALUMET DANCE

pipe die *n* **:** a screw-thread die for cutting pipe threads

pipe down *vi* **1 :** to dismiss sailors from an activity by a pipe call **2 :** to become quiet **:** stop talking

pipe dream *n* [so called fr. the fantasies brought about by the smoking of opium] **:** an illusory or fantastic plan, hope, or story

piped rot *n* **:** a decay of oak and chestnut caused by a fungus (*Stereum hirsutum*) and characterized by the appearance of yellow or white stripes in the wood

pipefish \ˈ=,=\ *n* **:** any of various long slender fishes of *Syngnathus* and related genera that are distinguished by a small mouth at the end of an elongate tubular snout, an angular body covered with bony plates, and no pelvic and first dorsal fins, that have the eggs hatched by the male in a long subcaudal pouch or in some cases in depressions in the skin of the abdomen, and that are nearly cosmopolitan but are esp. abundant in warm seas among seaweeds

pipe fitter *n* **:** one who fits, threads, installs, and repairs piping (as used for heating, refrigerating, or air-conditioning systems)

pipe fitting *n* **1 :** a piece (as a coupling or an elbow) used for connecting pipe lengths or as accessory to a pipe **2 :** the work of a pipe fitter

pipe·ful \ˈpīp,fu̇l\ *n* -S **:** a quantity of tobacco smoked in a pipe at one time

pipe grip *n* **1 :** PIPE WRENCH **2 :** CHAIN TONGS

pipe hanger *n* **:** a bracket, clamp, clip, or loop used to suspend pipes (as from ceilings, overhead beams)

pipe in *vi* **:** to put in a word

pipe–joint cement *n* **:** a cement (as a mixture of red lead with linseed oil in a thick paste) for making a pipe joint impervious to leakage — compare DIAMOND CEMENT

pipe key *n* **:** a bit key having a hollow barrel that fits over a stem in the lock — called also *barrel key*

pipelayer \ˈ=,==\ *n* **:** one that lays conducting pipe (as for water or gas)

pipe·less \ˈpīplə̇s\ *adj* **:** having no pipe

pipeless furnace *n* **:** a furnace with but a single short pipe to connect it with the space to be heated

pipe light *n* **:** a twisted or folded paper used to light a pipe

pipelike \ˈ=,=\ *adj* **:** resembling a pipe or piping

¹**pipeline** \ˈ=,=\ *n* [¹*pipe* + *line*] **1 :** a line of pipe connected to pumps, valves, and control devices for conveying liquids, gases, or finely divided solids **2 :** a direct channel for receiving information from an inside source or for conveying messages ⟨a news ~ from the mayor's office⟩ **3 :** the processes (as of transportation) through which supplies pass between the source and the user ⟨the Army estimates it will take . . . five months to activate its equipment ~ —*Newsweek*⟩

²**pipeline** \"\ *vt* **:** to convey by a pipeline ~ *vi* **:** to construct a pipeline

pipe·lin·er \ˈ=,=ə(r)\ *n* **1 :** one of a crew who build and maintain pipelines and pumping stations **2 :** a leader in the pipeline industry

pipeline run *n* **1 :** the quantity of oil transported from one point to another by a pipeline **2 :** the quantity of oil delivered by a producer to the pipeline **3 :** the quantity of oil delivered by a pipeline

pipe major *n* **:** the principal player in a band of bagpipes

pipe·man \ˈpīpmən\ *n, pl* **pipemen 1 :** one whose work is installing or repairing conduit pipes **2 :** one who holds the nozzle of a hose or pipe and directs its play **3 :** one who inspects and repairs the air brakes of railroad cars

pipe metal *n* **:** an alloy of tin and lead and sometimes zinc for making organ pipes

pip em·ma \(ˈ)pipˈemə\ *adv* [fr. Brit. signalmen's telephone pronunc. of *P.M.*] *Brit* **:** after noon

pipe of peace : CALUMET

pipe–opener \ˈ=,=(=)=\ *n* **1** *Brit* **:** a walk or other exercise in the open to get fresh air in the lungs **2 :** a practice game or trial preliminary to a contest

pipe organ *n* **:** ORGAN 1b (1) — compare REED ORGAN

pipe plant *n* **:** INDIAN PIPE

¹**pip·er** \ˈpīpə(r)\ *n* -S [in sense 1, fr. ME, one that plays a pipe, fr. OE *pīpere*, fr. *pīpan* to play a pipe + *-ere* -er; in other senses, partly fr. ¹*pipe* + *-er*; partly fr. ²*pipe* + *-er* — more at PIPE] **1 a :** one that plays on a pipe (as a bagpipe) **b :** a young pigeon **c** [so called fr. the piping sound it makes when caught] **:** a European gurnard (*Trigla lyra*) having a large head with prominent nasal projections **2 :** a maker, layer, or repairer of pipes ⟨a water ~⟩ **3 :** a caddisworm that lives in a piece of reed **4 :** a mine fissure from which gas is discharged **5 a :** a sewing machine attachment for applying piping **b :** a worker who pipes garments, shoes, or other articles

²**piper** \ˈpīpə(r), ˈpip-\ *n, cap* [NL, fr. L, pepper — more at PEPPER] **:** a very large genus (the type of the family Piperaceae) of tropical plants comprising the true peppers and being mostly climbing jointed shrubs with entire stipulate leaves and baccate fruit — see BETEL, BLACK PEPPER

piper·a·ce·ae \,pipəˈrāsē,ē, ,pīp-\ *n pl, cap* [NL, fr. *Piper*, type genus + *-aceae*] **:** a family of tropical plants (order Piperales) having aromatic herbage, minute naked spicate flowers, and one-celled ovary — **piper·a·ceous** \ˈ;==ˈrāshəs\ *adj*

pipe rack *n* **1 :** a rack for pipes **2 :** a rack (as for garments in a store) made of piping

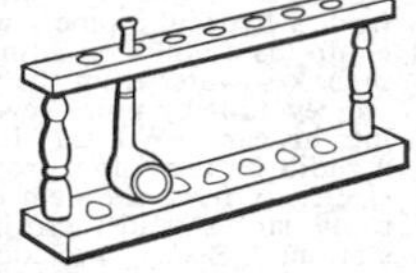
pipe rack 1

piper·a·les \,==ˈrā(,)lēz\ *n pl, cap* [NL, fr. *Piper* + *-ales*] **:** an order of apetalous dicotyledonous plants constituting the families Piperaceae, Sauruaceae, and Chloranthaceae and having simple leaves and minute flowers in spikes with the perianth simple or lacking

piper·a·zine \pīˈperə,zēn, pə̇ˈp-, ˈpipər-\ *n* -S [ISV, blend of *piperidine* and *az-*] **1 :** a crystalline heterocyclic base $C_4H_{10}N_2$ or $C_4H_{10}N_2.6H_2O$ obtained usu. by the action of ammonia on ethylene dibromide or ethylene dichloride or by reduction of pyrazine and used in medicine esp. as an anthelmintic; hexahydro-pyrazine **2 :** a derivative of piperazine — compare DIKETOPIPERAZINE

pipe reamer *n* **:** a fluted conical tool for beveling or removing burrs from pipe ends

pi·per·ic acid \(ˈ)pī;ˈperik-, pə̇ˈ|\ *n* [ISV *piper-* (fr. L *piper* pepper) + *-ic* — more at PEPPER] **:** a crystalline unsaturated acid $(CH_2O_2)C_6H_3(CH{=}CH)_2COOH$ formed by hydrolysis of piperine

pip·er·idge \ˈpipərij\ *var of* PEPPERIDGE

pi·per·i·dide \pīˈperə,dīd, pə̇ˈp-, -rədə̇d\ *n* -S [*piperidine* + *-ide*] **:** an amide of which piperidine is the amine constituent **:** an *N*-acyl derivative of piperidine

pi·per·i·dine \-,dēn, -dᵊn\ *n* -S [ISV, blend of *piperine* and *-ide*] **:** a liquid heterocyclic base $C_5H_{10}NH$ having a peppery ammoniacal odor that is obtained usu. by hydrolysis of piperine or by reduction of pyridine; hexahydro-pyridine — compare CONHYDRINE, CONIINE

pip·er·ine \ˈpipə,rēn, -,rən\ *n* -S [ISV *piper-* (fr. L *piper* pepper) + *-ine* — more at PEPPER] **:** a crystalline alkaloid $C_{17}H_{19}NO_3$ that is an active constituent of various kinds of pepper and that on hydrolysis yields piperidine and piperic acid

pi·per·i·tone \pīˈperə,tōn, pə̇ˈp-\ *n* -S [ISV *piperit-* (fr. NL *piperita* — specific epithet of *Eucalyptus piperita* —, fr. L *piper* pepper + *-ita*, fem. of *-itus* -ite) + *-one* — more at PEPPER] **:** a liquid unsaturated cyclic ketone $C_{10}H_{16}O$ of camphoraceous odor found in various essential oils and used chiefly in making menthol and thymol; 1-*p*-menthen-3-one

pip·er·ly \ˈpipə(r)lē\ *adj* **:** resembling or befitting a strolling piper **:** TRIVIAL, WORTHLESS

pi·per·o·caine \pīˈperə,kān, pə̇ˈp-\ *n* -S [*piperidine* + *cocaine*] **:** a base $C_6H_5COO(CH_2)_3(NC_5H_9)CH_3$ derived from piperidine and benzoic acid and used in the form of its crystalline hydrochloride as a topical, infiltration, and spinal anesthetic

pipe–rock \ˈ=,=\ *n* **:** sedimentary rock containing scolites

pip·er·oid of ginger \ˈpipə,rȯid-\ [L *piper* pepper + E *-oid*] **:** an oleoresin prepared by extracting ginger with ether and removing the solvent by evaporation

pipe roll *n* **1 :** one of the annual rolls containing the statements of the accounts of the king's revenue and various expenses and other matters affecting the British public treasury and dating from 1131 to 1833 **2 :** a roller for supporting a pipe without restraining its longitudinal movement caused by expansion and contraction

piper·o·nal \pīˈperə,nal, pə̇ˈp-, ˈpipər-\ *n* -S [ISV *piperine* + *-one* + *-al*] **:** a crystalline aldehyde $(CH_2O_2)C_6H_3CHO$ that has an odor like that of the heliotrope, that is obtained usu. by oxidation of piperic acid or isosafrole, and that is used chiefly in perfumery, cosmetics, and soaps; 3,4-methylenedioxybenzaldehyde — called also *heliotropin*

piper·o·nyl \pīˈperənᵊl, pə̇ˈp-; ˈpipərə,nil\ *n* -S [ISV *piperonal* + *-yl*] **:** the univalent radical $(CH_2O_2)C_6H_3CH_2$ of piperonyl alcohol; 3,4-methylenedioxy-benzyl

piperonyl alcohol *n* **:** a crystalline alcohol $(CH_2O_2)C_6H_3$-CH_2OH obtained by reduction of piperonal

piperonyl butoxide *n* **:** an insecticide $C_{19}H_{30}O_5$ derived from piperonyl alcohol and the butyl ether of diethylene glycol; *also* **:** an oily liquid containing this compound and related compounds used chiefly as a synergist (as for pyrethrum insecticides)

piperonyl cyclonene *n* **:** an insecticide containing as its principal components two ketones derived from cyclohexenone and related to piperonyl alcohol and used chiefly as a synergist

piper·o·nyl·ic acid \(;)pī;per|ə;nilik-, pə̇;per|, ;pipər|\ *n* [ISV *piperonyl* + *-ic*] **:** a crystalline acid $(CH_2O_2)C_6H_3COOH$ obtained by oxidation of piperonal

pip·er·oxan \,pipər+\ *n* -S [*piperidene* + *oxan*, a gas, CNO, fr. ¹*ox-* + *-ane*] **:** an adrenolytic drug $C_{14}H_{19}NO_2$ containing both a piperidine and a benzodioxan nucleus used in the form of its crystalline hydrochloride to detect the presence of epinephrine-producing tumors by the transient fall in blood pressure it produces

pipers news *n, chiefly Scot* **:** already familiar news

piper·y·lene \pīˈperə,lēn, pə̇ˈp-; ˈpipər-\ *n* -S [ISV *piperidine* + *-ylene*] **:** an oily diolefin hydrocarbon $CH_3CH{=}CHCH{=}CH_2$ isomeric with isoprene formed in the cracking of petroleum and also made synthetically (as by exhaustive methylation of piperidine); 1,3-pentadiene

¹**pipes** *pl of* PIPE, *pres 3d sing of* PIPE

²**pipes** \ˈpīps\ *n pl but sing or pl in constr* [fr. pl. of ¹*pipe*] **:** SCOURING RUSH

pipe–stap·ple \ˈpīp,stapəl\ *n* -S *Scot* **:** the stem of a tobacco pipe

pipestem \ˈ=,=\ *n* **1 :** something like the stem of a tobacco pipe; *specif* **:** a very thin arm or leg **2 :** any of several slender-stemmed plants: as **a :** FETTERBUSH **b** *also* **pipestem clematis :** a clematis (*Clematis lasiantha*) of California

pipe still *n* **:** a distillation apparatus composed of a series of pipes used esp. for petroleum oils and tar

pipestone \ˈ=,=\ *n* **:** a pink or mottled pink-and-white argillaceous stone carved by the Indians into tobacco pipes — compare CATLINITE

pipe stop *n* **:** an organ stop composed of flue pipes

pipe tap *n* **:** a tap for forming pipe threads

pipe thimble *n* **:** THIMBLE 2b

pipe thread *n* **:** a screw thread used on pipe and pipe fittings characterized by a somewhat fine pitch and usu. a tapering diameter

pipe tomahawk *n* **:** a tomahawk with a bowl in the head for use as a pipe (as in formal peace ceremonies) — compare CALUMET

pipe tongs *n* **:** a crude form of pipe wrench — compare CHAIN TONGS

pipe tree *n* **1 :** any of various shrubs having twigs formerly used for pipe stems: as **a :** LILAC **b :** ELDER **c :** MOCK ORANGE **2 :** CATALPA

¹**pi·pette** *also* **pi·pet** \(ˈ)pīˈpet *sometimes* pə̇ˈp-; *usu* -ed.+V\ *n* -S [F *pipette*, dim. of *pipe* — more at PIPE (cask)] **1 :** a small piece of apparatus with which fluids are transferred, measured, or absorbed (as in chemical operations) and which in the simplest form consists of a narrow glass tube into which the liquid is drawn up by suction and in which it is retained by closing the upper end — compare BURETTE, DROPPER 4a **2 :** a funnel-shaped arrangement inserted near the middle of a barometer with the small end down to prevent air bubbles from rising to the top

²**pipette** *also* **pipet** \"\ *vt* **pipetted; pipetted; pipetting; pipettes** *also* **pipets :** to transfer, draw off, measure, or apply with a pipette

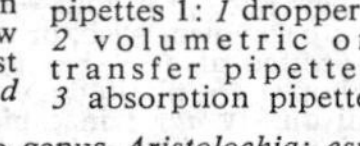
pipettes 1: *1* dropper, *2* volumetric or transfer pipette, *3* absorption pipette

pipe turner *n* **:** one of two or more workers who take sections of green pipe from the press, turn them socket end up, and put them on a truck for removal

pipe up *vi* **1 :** to begin to play (as on a pipe) or to sing or speak ⟨a few of us would like to *pipe up* . . . against this —C.E.Montague⟩ **2** *of the wind* **:** to increase in strength

pipe vine *n* **:** a climbing plant of the genus *Aristolochia*; *esp* **:** DUTCHMAN'S-PIPE

pipe–vine swallowtail *n* **:** an American butterfly (*Battus philenor*) having bluish green, pale-spotted wings and larvae that feed on the Dutchman's-pipe — called also *philenor butterfly*

pipe vise *n* **:** a vise shaped to hold pipe for threading, cutting, or reaming

pipewalker \ˈ=,==\ *n* **:** a watchman who patrols a pipeline

pipewood \ˈ=,=\ *n* **1 :** a white-flowered shrub (*Leucothoe populifolia*) of the southern U.S. from the wood of which pipe bowls are made **2 :** FETTERBUSH

pipework \ˈ=,=\ *n* **1 :** PIPE **2 :** the various sets of wooden and metal flue and reed pipe comprising the stops in a pipe organ

pipewort \ˈ=,=\ *n* **:** a plant of the genus *Eriocaulon*

pipe wrench *n* **:** a wrench for gripping and turning a pipe or other cylindrical surface usu. by use of two serrated jaws so designed as to grip the pipe when turning in one direction only — compare CHAIN TONGS, STILLSON WRENCH

pipe wrench

pipey *var of* PIPY

pip fruit *n* [⁴*pip*] *Austral* **:** POME FRUIT

pi·pi \ˈpēpē\ *n, pl* **pipi** *or* **pipis** [Maori] **1 :** a bivalve mollusk (*Mesodesma novae-zelandiae*) used as food in New Zealand **2 :** an edible Australian wedge shell (*Plebidonax deltoides*)

pipid \ˈpīpə̇d, ˈpip-\ *n* -S [NL *Pipidae*] **:** a toad of the family Pipidae

pip·i·dae \ˈpipə,dē\ *n pl, cap* [NL, fr. *Pipa*, type genus + *-idae*] **:** a small family of tropical toads completely lacking a tongue and comprising the Surinam toad and related forms

pipier *comparative of* PIPY

pipiest *superlative of* PIPY

pi·pi kau·la \,pēpēˈkau̇lə\ *n, pl* **pipi kaulas** [Hawaiian, fr. *pipi* beef (fr. E *beef*) + *kaula* rope] *Hawaii* **:** JERKED BEEF

pi·pil \pə̇ˈpē(ə)l\ *n, pl* **pipil** *or* **pipils** *usu cap* [Sp, of AmerInd origin] **1 a :** a Nahuatlan people or group of tribes in El Salvador, Guatemala, and Honduras **b :** a member of such people **2 :** the language of the Pipil people

pip·i·le \ˈpipə,lē\ *n, cap* [NL, fr. L *pipilare* to chirp, freq. of *pipare* — more at PIPE] **:** a genus of large crested So. American guans comprising the piping guans

pip·i·lo \ˈpipə,lō\ *n, cap* [NL, prob. fr. L *pipilare* to chirp] **:** a genus of American birds (family Fringillidae) of terrestrial habit — see TOWHEE

¹**pip·ing** \ˈpīpiŋ, -īpēŋ\ *n* -S [in sense 1, fr. ME, fr. gerund of *pipen* to pipe; in other senses, partly fr. ¹*pipe* + *-ing*; partly fr. gerund of ²*pipe* — more at PIPE] **1 a :** the music of a pipe **b :** a sound like that of a pipe ⟨the keen ~ of a field lark —Sidney Lanier⟩ **2 :** a quantity of pipe or system of pipes **3 :** a cutting of a jointed-stemmed or hollow-stemmed plant (as a carnation) **4 a** (1) **:** a narrow fold (as of bias-cut cloth) with or without an inserted cord that is stitched in seams or along edges as a trimming for clothing, slipcovers, curtains (2) **:** the trimming made in this fashion **b :** dough or decorative icing forced from a pastry tube **c :** a narrow piece of fabric or leather sewed in with the seam or edge of a shoe to give it finish **5 :** a pipe formed in iron or steel ingots in cooling **6 :** water erosion in a layer of subsoil or under or through a dam resulting in the formation of tunnels and caving

²**piping** \"\ *adj* [fr. pres. part. of ²*pipe*] **:** characterized by the music of the pipe rather than of the martial drum and fife **:** SOFT, TRANQUIL ⟨~ times of peace —Shak.⟩

³**piping** \"\ *adv* [ME, fr. ¹*piping*] **:** EXTREMELY, VERY — used in the phrase *piping hot*

piping crow *or* **piping crow–shrike** \ˈ=,=\ *n* **:** a black-and-white Australian magpie (*Gymnorhina tibicen*) that is the size of a small crow, is a good mimic, and is often kept in confinement

piping frog *n* **:** SPRING PEEPER

piping guan *n* **:** a guan of the genus *Pipile*

piping hare *n* **:** PIKA

pip·ing·ly *adv* **:** in a piping manner

pip·ing·ness *n* -ES **:** the quality or state of being piping

piping plover *n* **:** a small plover (*Charadrius melodus*) of eastern No. America that is smaller and paler than the semipalmated plover

piping rock *n* **:** a light olive gray that is paler than slate tan and paler and slightly redder than average covert gray — called also *gray stone, light grège*

pip·i·ri *also* **pip·pi·ree** \,pipəˈrē\ *or* **pit·ir·ri** \,pidəˈrē\ *n* -S [AmerSp *pipiri*, of imit. origin] **:** any of several West Indian flycatchers; *esp* **:** GRAY KINGBIRD

pipis *pl of* PIPI

pip·is·trelle *or* **pip·is·trel** \,pipə̇ˈstrel\ *n* -S [F *pipistrelle*, fr. It *pipistrello*, alter. of *vispistrello*, *vipistrello*, fr. L *vespertilion-*, *vespertilio* bat — more at VESPERTILIO] **:** a bat of the genus *Pipistrellus*; *esp* **:** a brown bat (*P. pipistrellus*) of Europe

pip·is·trel·lus \,pipə̇ˈstreləs\ *n, cap* [NL, fr. It *pipistrello*] **:** a nearly cosmopolitan genus of very small vespertilionid bats having a blunt tragus and 34 teeth

pip·it \ˈpipə̇t, *usu* -ə̇d.+V\ *n* -S [imit.] **:** any of various small singing birds of the family Motacillidae of nearly cosmopolitan range; *esp* **:** any of those belonging to the genus *Anthus*, resembling the true larks in habit, colors, and the long hind claw, and like the true larks singing on the wing — called also *titlark*; see MEADOW PIPIT, ROCK PIPIT, SPRAGUE'S PIPIT, TREE PIPIT

pip·kin \ˈpipkə̇n\ *n* -S [perh. fr. ¹*pipe* (cask) + *-kin*] **1 :** a small pot of earthenware or of metal usu. having a horizontal handle **2** *chiefly dial* **:** PIGGIN

pipped \ˈpipt\ *adj* [¹*pip* + *-ed*] **1 :** suffering from the pip **2** *slang* **:** INTOXICATED

pip·per \ˈpipə(r)\ *n* -S [²*pip* + *-er*] **:** the center or bead of a ring gunsight

pip·per·idge \ˈpipərij\ *var of* PEPPERIDGE

pip·pin \ˈpipə̇n\ *n* -S [ME *pepin*, *pipin*, fr. OF *pepin*] **1** *chiefly Brit* **:** ⁴PIP 1 **2 a :** a seedling apple or an apple from a seedling clone **b :** any of numerous apples that are typically of superior dessert quality and have usu. yellow or greenish yellow skins strongly flushed with red and lightly russeted — compare CODLING, COSTARD **3 :** a highly admired or very admirable person or thing

pipping *pres part of* PIP

pip–pip \(ˈ)pipˈpip\ *interj* [perh. imit. of a bicycle or automobile horn] *Brit* **:** so long **:** GOOD-BYE

pip·ple \ˈpipəl\ *vi* -ED/-ING/-S [perh. freq. of ²*pipe*] **:** to make the murmuring sound of a gentle wind or of rippling water

pip·py \ˈpipē\ *adj* -ER/-EST [⁴*pip* + *-y*] **:** full of pips

pip·ra \ˈpiprə\ *n* [NL, fr. Gk *pipra* woodpecker] **1** *cap* **:** a genus of birds (family Pipridae) containing the typical manakins **2** -S **:** MANAKIN

pip·ri·dae \ˈpiprə,dē\ *n pl, cap* [NL, fr. *Pipra*, type genus + *-idae*] **:** a family of birds (suborder Tyranni) consisting of the manakins and sometimes treated as a subfamily of the Cotingidae — **piprine** \ˈpi,prīn, ˈpī,p-\ *adj* — **piproid** \ˈpi,prȯid\ *adj*

pips *pl of* PIP, *pres 3d sing of* PIP

pip·sis·se·wa \pipˈsisəwə\ *n* -S [Cree *pipisisikweu*, lit., it (i.e., its juice) breaks it (i.e., a stone in the bladder) into small pieces] **:** an evergreen herb of the genus *Chimaphila*; *esp* **:** an herb (*C. umbellata*) whose astringent leaves have been used as a tonic and diuretic — called also *love-in-winter*

pip–squeak \ˈ=,=\ *n* [²*pip* + *squeak*] **1 :** a small or insignificant person **:** UPSTART **2 :** a small high-velocity shell used by the Germans in World War I

pip·ta·de·nia \,piptəˈdēnēə\ *n, cap* [NL, fr. Gk *piptein* to fall + NL *aden-* + *-ia*; fr. the deciduous antheral glands — more at FEATHER] **:** a large genus of tropical chiefly Brazilian shrubs and trees (family Leguminosae) with twice-pinnate leaves, small spicate flowers, and flat pods — see COHOBA

pip·tom·er·is \pipˈtämərə̇s\ [NL, fr. Gk *piptein* to fall + NL *-o-* + Gk *meris* part — more at MERIT] *syn of* JACKSONIA

pip·to·ste·gia root \,piptəˈstēj(ē)ə-\ *n* [NL *Piptostegia* genus of Convolvulaceae, fr. Gk *piptein* to fall + NL *-o-* + *steg-* + *-ia*] **:** a jalap from the root of a Brazilian bindweed (*Piptostegia pisonis*) — called also *Brazilian jalap*

pip·tu·rus \pipˈt(y)u̇rəs\ *n, cap* [NL, fr. Gk *piptein* to fall down + NL *-urus* — more at FEATHER] **:** a small genus of woody plants (family Urticaceae) of Australia and the Mascarene islands having alternate leaves, flowers in dense globular clusters, and a strong inner bark fiber — see QUEENSLAND GRASS-CLOTH PLANT

pipul \"\ *var of* PIPAL

1pi·pun·cu·lid \(ˈ)pī¦pəŋkyələ̇d\ *adj* [NL *Pipunculidae*] **:** of or relating to the Pipunculidae

2pipunculid \"\ *n* -s **:** a fly of the family Pipunculidae

pi·pun·cu·li·dae \ˌpī(ˌ)pən'kyüləˌdē, ˌpīˌpəŋ'k-, ˌpipən'k-\ *n pl, cap* [NL, fr. *Pipunculus*, type genus + *-idae*] **:** a family of two-winged flies (suborder Cyclorrhapha) including small flies having very large eyes and having larvae that are parasitic on other insects

pipy *also* **pip·ey** \'pīpē\ *adj* **pipier; pipiest** [¹*pipe* + *-y*] **1 :** containing tubular formations **2 :** having the hollow form of a pipe

pi·quance \'pēkən(t)s\ *n* -s **:** PIQUANCY

pi·quan·cy \-nsē\ *n* -ES **1 :** the quality or state of being piquant **:** PIQUANTNESS ⟨the sense that he was watched . . . added ~ to a journey so entirely sentimental —Thomas Hardy⟩ **2 :** something that is piquant; *esp* **:** a piquant dish ⟨restaurateurs . . . scouring Italy for *piquancies* to enhance their menus —S.J.Perelman⟩

pi·quant *also* **pi·quante** \'pēkənt, -ˌkänt, -ˌkant\ *adj* [*piquant* fr. MF, fr. pres. part. of *piquer* to prick, sting, nettle, pique; *piquante* fr. MF, fem. of *piquant* — more at PIKE] **1** *archaic* **:** disagreeably sharp **:** STINGING, PROVOCATIVE, CUTTING **2 :** agreeably stimulating to the palate **:** pleasantly tart, sharp, or biting **:** PUNGENT ⟨ham . . . curing in a ~ brine —*New Yorker*⟩ **3 :** arousing or having the power to arouse pleasant mental excitement **:** engagingly provocative ⟨the writing is never dull and often ~ —*Geog. Jour.*⟩ **:** agreeably challenging ⟨his comments are always ~ and sometimes blistering —*Times Lit. Supp.*⟩; *also* **:** having a lively arch charm ⟨she made a ~ pretty show with . . . her agreeable, slightly roguish face —Arnold Bennett⟩ **syn** see PUNGENT

piquant green *n* **:** a moderate yellow-green that is greener, lighter, and stronger than average moss green, yellower and deeper than average pea green, and yellower, darker, and slightly less strong than apple green (sense 1)

pi·quant·ly *adv* **:** in a piquant manner

pi·quant·ness *n* -ES **:** the quality or state of being piquant

piquant sauce *n* **:** a sauce with a sharp flavor (as from lemon juice, vinegar, capers, spices)

1pique \'pēk\ *n* -s [MF, fr. *piquer*] **1** *archaic* **:** mutual animosity **:** a state of strife **2 :** offense taken by one slighted or disdained **:** vexation or anger excited by a wound to one's vanity **:** a fit of resentment ⟨go off in a ~⟩ **syn** see OFFENSE

2pique \"\ *vb* -ED/-ING/-s [F *piquer* to prick, sting, nettle, pique — more at PIKE] *vt* **1 :** to arouse anger or resentment in **:** NETTLE, IRRITATE ⟨the Swiss will be *piqued* at the U.S. because of the higher tariff —*Wall Street Jour.*⟩; *specif* **:** to offend by slighting ⟨~ her by his apparent indifference⟩ **2 a :** to excite or arouse by a provocation, challenge, or rebuff ⟨a possible coincidence, which ~*s* one's curiosity —Johnson O'Connor⟩ **b :** to stimulate by wounding pride or inciting jealousy or rivalry ⟨~ him to violent efforts⟩ **3 :** to take pride in (oneself) **:** PLUME ⟨*piqued* herself upon her mastery of . . . philosophy —L.P.Smith⟩ ~ *vi* **:** to cause annoyance or irritation **syn** see PROVOKE

3pique \"\ *n* -s [F *pic*, fr. MF, prick, sting, game of piquet, fr. *piquer* to prick, sting — more at PIKE] **:** the making of 30 points in hand and play in piquet before the other player scores; *also* **:** the bonus of 30 points for this

4pique \"\ *vt* -ED/-ING/-s **:** to score a pique against in piquet ~ *vi* **:** to make a pique in piquet

5pique \'pē(ˌ)kā\ *n* -s [AmerSp, fr. Quechua *piki*] **1 :** CHIGGER **2 :** any of various ticks

6pi·qué *or* **pi·que** \(ˈ)pē¦kā, pə̇'kā\ *n* -s [F *piqué*, fr. past part. of *piquer* to prick, pierce, quilt — more at PIKE] **1 :** a durable clothing fabric of cotton, rayon, or silk woven orig. with crosswise ribs and now also with lengthwise ribs and figured effects obtained by the interlacing of a fine surface warp and a heavy back warp **2 :** tortoise shell or ivory inlaid with a design in gold or silver dots

7piqué \"\ *adj* [F, fr. past part. of *piquer*] **1 :** INLAID ⟨knife handles ~ with gold⟩ **2** *of a glove seam* **:** made by lapping one raw edge over another and stitching in place **3 :** SPICCATO **4** *ballet* **:** executed by stepping on the point of the supporting foot

8pique \'pēk\ *archaic var of* PEAK

pi·que·ria \pə̇'kirēə\ *n, cap* [NL, fr. Andrés *Piquer* †1772 Span. physician and author + NL *-ia*] **:** a small genus of tropical American plants that is closely related to and often included in *Stevia*

pi·que·ro \pə̇'ke(ˌ)rō, pə̇'k-\ *n* -s [AmerSp, fr. Sp, pikeman, fr. *pica* pike (fr. *picar* to prick, pierce, fr. — assumed — VL *piccare*) + *-ero* -er — more at PIKE] **:** any of several gannets of the western coast of America; *esp* **:** a booby of this region

1pi·quet *also* **pic·quet** \(ˈ)pē¦kā, pə̇'kā\ *n* -s [F, dim. of *pic* pique (at cards) — more at PIQUE] **:** a two-handed card game which is played with a piquet pack and in which points are scored for announcing some combinations of cards, for winning tricks, and for pique and repique

2piquet *var of* PICKET

piquet pack *n* [¹*piquet*] **:** a pack of 32 playing cards made by removing all cards below the sevens and used for many games

pi·quette \pē'ket, pə̇'k-\ *n* -s [F, fr. *piquer* to prick, sting, bite (the tongue) — more at PIKE] **:** a beverage made by steeping grape marc in water

pi·queur \-'kər(·)\ *n* -s [F, fr. *piquer* to prick, sting, goad + *-eur* -or] **1 :** an attendant directing the hounds in a hunt **2 :** a servant who runs before a carriage to clear the way

pi·quia \ˌpēkē¦ä\ *n* -s [Pg *piquiá*, fr. Tupi] **:** a tree of the genus *Caryocar*; *esp* **:** a So. American timber tree (*C. butyrosum*) bearing edible oily nuts much like typical souari nuts

pir \'pi(ə)r\ *n* -s [Hindi *pīr*, fr. Per] **:** a Muslim spiritual guide or saint in India or Pakistan

pi·ra·cy \'pīrəsē, -si\ *n* -ES [ML *piratia*, fr. LGk *peirateia*, fr. Gk *peiratēs* pirate + *-ia* -y — more at PIRATE] **1 :** robbery on the high seas **2 a** *common law* **:** an act of depredation with the intent of stealing committed on the high seas that would if committed on the land amount to a felony **:** such an act committed on unappropriated lands by a descent from the sea or using the sea as a basis of operations **b** *international law* (1) **:** an act or practice of violence or depredation that would be felonious if done ashore committed upon the high seas by one not acting under the authority of a politically organized community (2) **:** a similar act or practice committed upon unappropriated lands by a descent from the sea **3 :** an act resembling piracy; *esp* **:** an unauthorized appropriation and reproduction of another's production, invention, or conception esp. in infringement of a copyright **4 :** CAPTURE 3

pi·rae·us \(ˈ)pī¦rēəs\ *adj, usu cap* [fr. *Piraeus*, Greece] **:** of or from the city of Piraeus, Greece **:** of the kind or style prevalent in Piraeus

pi·ragua \pə̇'rägwə, -rag-\ *n* -s [Sp — more at PIROGUE] **1 :** a canoe made of a hollowed tree trunk **2 :** DUGOUT **3 :** a two-masted flat-bottomed boat undecked or decked only at the ends

pi·rai \pə̇'rī\ *n* -s [Pg *pirai, piray* & AmerSp *piray*, fr. Galibi & Guarani *pirai*] **:** CARIBE

pir·an·del·li·an \¦pirən¦delēən\ *adj, usu cap* [Luigi *Pirandello* †1936 Ital. novelist and dramatist + E *-ian*] **:** of, relating to, or befitting the writer Pirandello

pi·ran·ga \pə̇'raŋgə\ *n, cap* [NL] **:** a genus of tanagers including the scarlet, summer, and hepatic tanagers of No. America

pi·ra·nha *also* **pi·ra·ña** \pə̇'ranyə, -rän-\ *n* -s [*piranha* fr. Pg, fr. Tupi; *piraña* fr. AmerSp, fr. Pg] **:** CARIBE

pi·ra·ni gauge \pə̇'ränē-\ *n, usu cap P* [after Marcello St. *Pirani* b1880 Brit. physicist born in Germany] **:** a hot-wire manometer in which the cooling effect on the filament is deduced from its lowered resistance

pi·ra·ru·cu \pə̇¦rärə¦kü\ *n* -s [Pg *pirarucu, pirarucú*, fr. Tupi *pirá-urucú*, lit., red fish] **:** a large-scaled osteoglossid fish (*Arapaima gigas*) of the rivers of northern So. America that is held to attain a length of 15 feet and a weight of 500 pounds and is of great importance in the diet of the natives of the area

1pi·rate \'pīrə̇t, *usu* -ə̇d+V\ *n* -s *often attrib* [ME, fr. MF or L; MF, fr. L *pirata*, fr. Gk *peiratēs*, fr. *peiran* to attempt, make a try at — more at FEAR] **1 :** one who commits or practices piracy: as **a :** a robber on the high seas **b :** one noted for predatory practices ⟨financial ~*s*⟩ **c :** an infringer of the law of copyright **2 :** a ship used in piracy **3 :** a stream that has captured another

2pirate \"\ *vb* -ED/-ING/-s *vt* **1 :** to commit piracy upon **:** ROB **2 :** to take or appropriate by piracy: as **a :** to publish (as a book) without proper authorization esp. in infringement of copyright **b :** to take over and use (as a wavelength) in violation of exclusive assignment to another **c :** to lure (a worker) away from another employer by offers of betterment ~ *vi* **:** to commit or practice piracy

pirate bird *n* **:** JAEGER 3

pirate perch *n* **:** a small fish (*Aphredoderus sayanus*) of sluggish streams from New Jersey and Minnesota southward that is remarkable for having the vent in front of the pelvic fins and with the trout perches forms the order Salmopercae

pi·rat·i·cal \(ˈ)pī¦rad·ə̇kəl, pə̇'r-, -at|, |ēk-\ *also* **pi·rat·ic** \|ik, |ēk\ *adj* [*piratical* fr. MF *piratique* (fr. L *piraticus*) or L *piraticus* (fr. Gk *peiratikos*, fr. *peiratēs* pirate + *-ikos* -ic) + E *-al*; *piratic* fr. F *piratique* or L *piraticus* — more at PIRATE] **1 :** of, produced by, or being a pirate or piracy ⟨~ strongholds⟩ ⟨~ editions⟩ ⟨~ attackers⟩ ⟨~ enterprises⟩ **2 :** befitting or resembling a pirate ⟨a fierce ~ expression⟩ — **pi·rat·i·cal·ly** \|ə̇k(ə)lē, |ēk-, -li\ *adv*

pir·ca \'pirkə\ *n* -s [Sp, fr. Quechua *pirka*] **:** a crude dry masonry wall of the early Inca period

pi·ric·u·lar·ia \pə̇ˌrikyə'la(a)rēə, ˌpirəkyü'l-\ *n, cap* [NL, fr. L *pirum* pear + *-iculum*, dim. suffix + NL *-aria* — more at PEAR] **:** a form genus of imperfect fungi (family Moniliaceae) characterized by simple or slightly branched conidiophores producing terminal two-septate to many-septate solitary hyaline pear-shaped spores and including one form (*P. grisea*) that causes a leaf spot of various grasses

piriform *var of* PYRIFORM

pir·i·for·mis *or* **pyr·i·for·mis** \ˌpirə'fȯrmə̇s\ *n* -ES [*piriformis*, NL, alter. of *pyriformis*; *pyriformis*, NL, fr. ML *pyrum* pear (alter. of L *pirum*) + L *-iformis* -iform] **:** a muscle arising from the front of the sacrum, passing out of the pelvis through the greater sciatic foramen, and being inserted into the upper border of the great trochanter of the femur

pir·i·piri \ˌpirə'pirē\ *n* -s [Maori] **1 a :** a troublesome New Zealand weed (*Acaena sanguisorbae*) bearing burs covered with hooked bristles **b :** WHITE MAPAU **2** *also* **pirijiri :** a fragrant Asiatic and Australasian herb (*Haloragis micrantha*) of the family Haloragidaceae

pi·ri·gua \ˌpirərē¦gwä\ *n* -s [Pg *piririguá*, fr. Guarani] **:** a largely buff and brown So. American cuckoo (*Guira guira*) resembling the anis in habit

pirl \'pər(ə)l\ *vb* -ED/-ING/-s [origin unknown] **1** *archaic* **:** TWIST, TWINE **2** *chiefly Scot* **:** SPIN, REVOLVE

pir·lie \'pərlē\ *n* -s [prob. fr. *pirl* + *-ie*] **1** *Scot* **:** a small object; *specif* **:** the little finger **2** *Scot* **:** PIRLIE-PIG

pirlie-pig \'⸗⸗ˌ⸗\ *n, Scot* **:** a child's savings bank usu. made of crockery

pirn \'pərn, 'pirn\ *n* -s [ME *pirne*] **1 :** QUILL 1a(1) **2** *chiefly Scot* **:** any of various devices resembling a reel

piro \'pē(ˌ)rō\ *n, pl* **piro** *or* **piros** *usu cap* [Sp, of AmerInd origin] **1 a :** a Tanoan people of Pueblo Indians in central New Mexico and the state of Chihuahua, Mexico **b :** a member of such people **2 a :** an Arawakan people of eastern Peru **b :** a member of such people **c :** the language of such people

pi·ro·gen \pə̇'rōgən\ *or* **pi·ro·gi** \-gē\ *n pl* [Yiddish & Russ; Yiddish *pirogen*, pl. of *pirog* small filled pastry, fr. Russ; *pirogi* fr. Russ, pl. of *pirog* — more at PIROSHKI] **:** PIROSHKI

pi·rogue \'pēˌrōg, 'piˌr-, pə̇'r-, pē'r-, '⸗ˌrō\ *also* **pi·roque** \-ōk, -ō\ *n* -s [F, fr. Sp *piragua*, of Cariban origin; akin to Galibi *piraua* pirogue, Carib *piraguas*] **1 :** a dugout canoe **2 :** a boat like a canoe

pi·rol \'pēˌrōl, ⸗'⸗\ *n* -s [G, fr. MHG *piro*, of imit. origin] **:** GOLDEN ORIOLE

pirola *syn of* PYROLA

pirolaceae [NL, fr. *Pirola* (syn. of *Pyrola*) + *-aceae*] *syn of* PYROLACEAE

pi·root \pī'rüt\ *vi* -ED/-ING/-s [prob. alter. (influenced by *root*) of ²*pirouette*] **1** *South & Midland* **:** to go about idly or aimlessly — often used with *around* **2** *South & Midland* **:** to nose around **:** SNOOP ⟨went ~*ing* into a cave —J.F.Dobie⟩

piro·plasm \'pirəˌplazəm\ *or* **piro·plas·ma** \ˌpirə'plazmə\ *n, pl* **piroplasms** \'⸗⸗ˌplazəmz\ *or* **piroplas·ma·ta** \ˌ⸗⸗'plazməd·ə\ [NL *Piroplasma*] **:** a parasitic protozoan of the family Babesiidae — **piro·plas·mic** \¦⸗⸗¦plazmik\ *adj*

piro·plas·ma \ˌpirə'plazmə\ [NL, prob. fr. L *pirum* pear + NL *-o-* + *plasma* — more at PEAR] *syn of* BABESIA

1piro·plas·mid \¦pirə¦plazmə̇d\ *adj* [NL *Piroplasmidae* (syn. of *Babesiidae*), fr. *Piroplasma* + *-idae*] **:** of or relating to the Babesiidae

2piroplasmid \"\ *n* -s **:** PIROPLASM

piro·plas·mo·sis \ˌpirəˌplaz'mōsə̇s\ *n, pl* **piroplasmo·ses** \-ōˌsēz\ [NL, fr. *Piroplasma* + *-osis*] **:** infection with or disease caused by protozoans of the genus *Babesia* or the family Babesiidae including Texas fever and east coast fever of cattle, babesiasis of sheep, and malignant jaundice of the dog

piroque *var of* PIROGUE

pi·rosh·ki *also* **pi·roj·ki** \pə̇'rōshkē, -räsh-\ *n pl* [Yiddish & Russ; Yiddish *pirozshke* (sing.), fr. Russ *pirozhki*, pl. of *pirozhok* small pocket of pastry, dim. of *pirog* small filled pastry, prob. fr. *pir* banquet, feast; akin to Russ *pit'* to drink, OSlav *piti* — more at POTABLE] **:** small pastry turnovers stuffed with a savory filling

1pir·ou·ette \¦pirə¦wet, *usu* -ed·+V\ *n* -s [F, teetotum, pirouette, fr. MF *pirouet* teetotum, top; akin to F dial. (Béarn) *pire* peg] **1 :** a rapid whirling about of the body (as in a dance); *specif* **:** a full turn on the toe or ball of one foot in ballet **2 :** an advanced movement in horsemanship executed at a gallop in which a horse's shoulders describe a circle while his hind legs serve as a pivot

2pirouette \"\ *vi* -ED/-ING/-s [F *pirouetter*, fr. *pirouette*, n.] **1 :** to perform a pirouette **2 :** to turn about as if in a pirouette **:** turn about lightly and gracefully or within a narrow area ⟨vanes pirouetted in the wind —*Time*⟩ **syn** see TURN

pir·ou·ett·er \-ed·ə(r), -etə-\ *n* -s **:** one that pirouettes

pir·quet test *also* **pirquet reaction** \(ˈ)pir¦kā-\ *n, usu cap P* [after Baron Clemens von *Pirquet* †1929 Austrian pediatrician] **:** a tuberculin test made by applying a drop of tuberculin to a scarified spot on the skin

pir·rau·ra *or* **pir·rau·ru** \pə̇'raürə\ *n* -s [native name in Australia] **:** a legally designated sex mate other than husband or wife among some Australian aborigines; *also* **:** the relationship between such sex mates

pirs *pl of* PIR

pirs·son·ite \'pirsᵊnˌīt, 'pər-\ *n* -s [Louis V. *Pirsson* †1919 Am. mineralogist + *-ite*] **:** a mineral $Na_2Ca(CO_3)_2.2H_2O$ consisting of a hydrous calcium sodium carbonate and occurring in white or colorless orthorhombic crystals (hardness 3, sp. gr. 2.35)

pi·sa·ca *or* **pi·sa·cha** \pə̇'shächə\ *n* -s *usu cap* [Skt *piśāca*] **:** the Dard group of Indic languages

pis al·ler \¦pēzˌa¦lā, ¦pēˌza¦lā, pēˌza(ˌ)lā\ *n, pl* **pis allers** \-ā(z)\ [F, lit., to go worst] **:** a last resource or device for coping with a difficulty **:** EXPEDIENT, SHIFT ⟨Poor Laws were an unhappy *pis aller*, revealing the failure of society to deal . . . with its economic problems —R.M.MacIver⟩

1pi·san \'pēzᵊn\ *adj, usu cap* [*Pisa*, Italy + E *-an*] **1 :** of, relating to, or characteristic of Pisa **2 :** of, relating to, or characteristic of the people of Pisa

2pisan \"\ *n* -s *cap* **:** a native or inhabitant of Pisa

pi·sang \pə̇'säŋ\ *n* -s [Malay, banana, plantain] **:** PLANTAIN

pisang wax *n* **:** a wax obtained from the leaves of a plantain (*Musa paradisiaca*)

pi·sanite \pə̇'zäˌnīt, -zaˌn-\ *n* -s [G *pisanit*, fr. Félix *Pisani* †1920 French chemist and mineralogist + G *-it* -ite] **:** a mineral $(Fe,Cu)SO_4.7H_2O$ consisting of a hydrous iron copper sulfate isomorphous with melanterite and kirovite

pis·ant *var of* PISSANT

pi·as·ter \pə̇'sastə(r)\ *n, cap* [NL, fr. L *piscis* fish + NL *-aster* (star) — more at FISH] **:** a genus of large shallow-water typically 5-rayed starfishes (family Asteriidae) including the common purple or orange starfish (*P. ochraceus*) of the Pacific coast of No. America

pi·sau·ri·dae \pə̇'sȯrəˌdē\ *n pl, cap* [NL, fr. *Pisaura*, type genus (fr. L *Pisaurum* — Pesaro —, Italy) + *-idae*] **:** a family of hunting spiders that do not spin webs to catch their prey — compare LYCOSIDAE

pis·can \'piskən\ *adj* [L *piscis* fish + E *-an* — more at FISH] **:** of or relating to fishes

pis·ca·ry \'piskərē\ *n* -ES [in sense 1, fr. ME *piscarie*, fr. ML *piscaria*, fr. L, neut. pl. of *piscarius* of fish, of fishing, fr. *piscis* fish + *-arius* -ary; in sense 2, fr. ML *piscaria*, fr. L, fem. of *piscarius* — more at FISH] **1 :** FISHERY 4; *esp* **:** COMMON OF PISCARY **2 :** a fishing place

pis·cat·a·way \pə̇'skad·əˌwä\ *n, pl* **piscataway** *or* **piscataways** *usu cap* [fr. *Piscataway*, former Conoy Indian village in Prince George county, Maryland] **:** CONOY 1

pis·ca·tion \pə̇'skāshən\ *n* -s [LL *piscation-, piscatio*, fr. L *piscatus* (past part. of *piscari* to fish, fr. *piscis* fish) + *-ion-, -io* -ion — more at FISH] **:** FISHING

pis·ca·tor \pə̇'skād·ə(r), 'pi,sk-\ *n* -s [L, fr. *piscatus* + *-or*] **:** FISHERMAN, ANGLER

pis·ca·to·ri·al \¦piskə¦tōrēəl, -tȯr-\ *adj* [L *piscatorius* + E *-al*] **:** PISCATORY — **pis·ca·to·ri·al·ly** \-ēəlē, -li\ *adv*

pis·ca·to·ry \'piskəˌtōrē, -tȯr-, -ri\ *adj* [L *piscatorius*, fr. *piscatus* + *-orius* -ory] **1 :** of or relating to fishermen or fishing ⟨the ~ life⟩ **2 :** living by or given to fishing ⟨~ tribes⟩

pis·ces \'pī(ˌ)sēz, 'pī(ˌ)sēz *also* 'piˌskās *or* 'pē(ˌ)sēz\ *n pl* [in sense 1, fr. ME, fr. ML, fr. L, a constellation, fr. pl. of *piscis* fish; in sense 2, NL, fr. L, pl. of *piscis* — more at FISH] **1** *sing in constr, usu cap* **:** the 12th sign of the zodiac — see SIGN table, ZODIAC illustration **2** *cap, in some classifications* **:** a variously limited class of vertebrates comprising all the fishes and sometimes the cyclostomes and lancelets — compare CHOANICHTHYES, TELEOSTOMI

pisci- *comb form* [L, fr. *piscis*] **:** fish ⟨*pisci*fauna⟩ ⟨*pisci*culture⟩

pis·cic·o·la \pə̇'sikələ\ *n, cap* [NL, fr. *pisci-* + *-cola*] **:** a widely distributed genus of marine and freshwater leeches related to *Ichthyobdella* and parasitic on fishes or turtles

pis·ci·cul·tur·al \¦pisə¦kəlch(ə)rəl\ *adj* **:** of or relating to pisciculture — **pis·ci·cul·tur·al·ly** \-rəlē\ *adv*

pis·ci·cul·ture \'pisəˌkəlchə(r) *also* ˌ⸗⸗'⸗⸗\ *n* [prob. fr. F, fr. *pisci-* + *culture*] **:** fish culture

pis·ci·cul·tur·ist \¦⸗⸗¦kəlch(ə)rə̇st\ *n* -s **:** one who specializes in fish culture; *specif* **:** the superintendent of a state-operated fish hatchery

pis·cid·ia \pə̇'sidēə\ *n, cap* [NL, blend of *pisci-* and *-cidia* (fr. L *caedere* to kill); fr. the fact that leaves and bark of shrubs of this genus poison fish when thrown into the water — more at CONCISE] **:** a genus of shrubs or small trees (family Leguminosae) having pink or white and red flowers in panicles and indehiscent pods with black seeds — see JAMAICA DOGWOOD

pis·ci·fauna \¦pisə+\ *n* [NL, fr. *pisci-* + *fauna*] **:** the fishes of a given region

pis·ci·na \pə̇'s(h)ēnə, -sīnə\ *n, pl* **piscinas** \-nəz\ *or* **piscinae** \-shēˌnā, -sēˌnī, -sī(ˌ)nē\ [L, fr. *piscis* fish + *-ina* -ine — more at FISH] **1 :** an artificial reservoir or tank used by the ancient Romans esp. as a fishpond or swimming pool **2** [ML, fr. L] **:** a stone basin with a drain located near the altar of a church for disposing of water from liturgical ablutions — **pis·ci·nal** \-ēnᵊl, -īn-\ *adj*

1pis·cine \pə̇'sēn\ *n* -s [ME, fr. OF, fr. L & ML *piscina*] **:** PISCINA

2pis·cine \'piˌsīn, 'pīsēn, 'pīˌsīn\ *adj* [L *piscinus*, fr. *piscis* fish + *-inus* -ine] **:** of, relating to, or having the characteristics of fish

pis·cin·i·ty \pə̇'sinəd·ē\ *n* -ES **:** the quality or state of being a fish

pis·civ·o·rous \pə̇'siv(ə)rəs\ *adj* [*pisci-* + *-vorous*] **:** feeding on fishes

pis·co \'pi(ˌ)skō, 'pē(-\ *n* -s [Sp, fr. *Pisco*, Peru] **:** a So. American brandy that resembles French marc and is often used in cocktails

pisco sour *n* **:** a cocktail of Peruvian origin consisting of lime juice, pisco brandy, and sugar garnished with beaten egg white

pi·sé \(ˈ)pē¦zā\ *also* **pisé de terre** \(ˌ)⸗ˌ⸗də'te(ə)r\ *n, pl* **pisés** \-ā(z)\ *also* **pisés de terre** [*pisé* fr. F, fr. F dial. (Lyon), fr. MF, fr. past part. of *piser* to stomp, fr. (assumed) VL *pinsiare, pisiare*, alter. of L *pinsare, pisare* to beat, pound, crush; *pisé de terre* fr. F, lit., earth pisé; akin to L *pinsere* to pound, crush — more at PESTLE] **:** a building material consisting of stiff earth or clay rammed in between forms — compare ⁴COB, TAPIA

pis·gah sight \'pizgə\ *n, usu cap P* [fr. Mt. *Pisgah*, Palestine, from which Moses was allowed to see the Promised Land according to Deut 3:27] **:** a distant view (as of an unobtainable objective) ⟨only a *Pisgah sight* of the promised land of long-deferred discovery —I.B.Hart⟩

1pish \ps, psh; *often read as* 'pish\ *interj* [origin unknown] — used to express disdain or contempt

2pish \'pish\ *vb* -ED/-ING/-ES *vi* **:** to express disdain or contempt by or as if by saying *pish* ⟨~*ed* and pshawed a little at what had happened —Thomas Hughes⟩ ~ *vt* **:** to dismiss or reject by or as if by saying *pish*

pi·shogue *or* **pi·shoge** \pə̇'shōg\ *or* **pish·rogue** \(ˈ)pi¦shrōg\ *n* -s [IrGael *piseog*] **1** *Irish* **:** a wise saw or aphorism **2** *Irish* **a :** CHARM, INCANTATION, SPELL **b :** SORCERY, WITCHCRAFT

pish·pash \'pishˌpash, -ˌpäsh\ *n* -ES [origin unknown] *India* **:** a rice broth containing bits of meat

pish·posh \'pishˌpäsh\ *n* -ES [redupl. of ¹*pish*] **:** NONSENSE

1pi·sid·i·an \pə̇'sidēən, (ˈ)pī¦s-\ *adj, usu cap* [*Pisidia*, ancient country of southern Asia Minor + E *-an*] **1 :** of, relating to, or characteristic of ancient Pisidia **2 :** of, relating to, or characteristic of the people of Pisidia

2pisidian \"\ *n* -s *cap* **:** a native or inhabitant of Pisidia

pi·sid·i·um \-ēəm\ *n, cap* [NL, dim. of L *pisum* pea — more at PEA] **:** a genus of nearly cosmopolitan minute freshwater bivalves (family Sphaeriidae) usu. somewhat smaller than those of the genus *Sphaerium* and having the siphons united at their ends

1pi·si·form \'pīsəˌfȯrm, -īzə-\ *adj* [L *pisum* pea + E *-iform*] **:** resembling a pea in size or shape ⟨~ granules⟩

2pisiform \"\ *n* -s **:** a bone on the ulnar side of the carpus in most mammals and a few other vertebrates

pi·sis·tra·te·an \(ˌ)pīˌsistrə'tēən, ⸗'⸗⸗ˌ⸗⸗\ *adj, usu cap* [*Pisistratus* †527 B.C. tyrant of Athens + E *-an*] **:** of or relating to Pisistratus or esp. the critical revision of the Homeric poems attributed to him

pisk \'pisk\ *n* -s [origin unknown] **:** the common American nighthawk

pis·kun \'piskən\ *n* -s [Blackfoot] **:** a steep cliff sometimes with a corral or enclosure at the bottom that is used by American Indians for driving large numbers of buffalo to their slaughter

pis·ky \'piskē\ *dial Eng var of* PIXIE

pis·mire \'pisˌmī(ə)r, -izˌm-\ *n* -s [ME *pissemire*, fr. *pisse* piss + *mire* ant, of Scand origin; akin to OSw *myr, myra* ant, ON *maurr*; akin to MD *miere* ant, MLG *mīre*, Crimean Goth *miera*, L *formica*, Gk *myrmēx*, Av *maoiri-*; 1st constituent fr. the smell of anthills, due to the formic acid exuded by ants — more at PISS] **1 :** ANT **2 :** an insignificant or contemptible person ⟨what do you think I'd do with a young ~ like you —R.P.Warren⟩

pis·mo clam \'pizˌmō-\ *n, often cap P* [fr. *Pismo* Beach, Calif.] **:** a thick-shelled clam (*Tivela stultorum*) of the family Veneridae that occurs on the southwest coast of No. America and is used extensively for food

piso·lite \'pizəˌlīt, 'pī|, |sə-\ *n* -s [NL *pisolithus*, fr. Gk *pisos* pea + *-lithus* -lith] **:** a limestone composed of globular concretions about the size of a pea — compare OOLITE

piso·lith \-ˌlith\ *n* -s [ISV *piso-* (fr. Gk *pisos* pea) + *-lith*] **:** a pisiform concretion of larger size than an oolite

piso·lit·ic \¦⸗⸗¦lid·ik\ *adj* **:** of, relating to, or having the characteristics of pisolite

pi·so·ne \pə̇'sōnē\ *n, pl* **pisone** *or* **pisones** *usu cap* [Sp, of AmerInd origin] **1 :** an Indian people of northeastern Mexico perhaps related to the Janambre **2 :** a member of the Pisone people

pi·so·nia \pə̇'sōnēə, pī's-\ *n, cap* [NL, irreg. fr. Willem *Piso* †ab 1678 Dutch physician and traveler + NL *-ia*] **:** a genus of tropical often thorny trees, shrubs, and vines (family Nyctaginaceae) having small dioecious apetalous flowers and utricular fruits — see COCKSPUR 2b

pi·so·te \pə'sōd·ē\ *n* -s [AmerSp *pizote, pisote,* fr. Nahuatl *pitzotl*] : COATI

¹piss \'pis\ *vb* -ED/-ING/-ES [ME *pissen,* fr. OF *pissier,* fr. (assumed) VL *pissiare,* of imit. origin] *vi* : URINATE — usu. considered vulgar ~ *vt* **1** : to urinate in or on ⟨~ the bed⟩ — usu. considered vulgar **2** : to discharge as or as if urine ⟨~ blood⟩ — usu. considered vulgar

²piss \"\ *n* -ES [ME *pisse,* fr. *pissen,* v.] **1** : URINE — usu. considered vulgar **2** : an act of urinating — often used with *take;* usu. considered vulgar

pissant \'ˌ=ˌ=\ *n* [¹*piss* + *ant*] *chiefly dial* : ANT

piss away *vt, slang* : to let flow as if of no account : fritter away ⟨enough money to *piss away* from now until the day I die —Millard Lampell⟩

pissed \'pist\ *adj* **1** *slang* : ANGRY, DISGUSTED **2** *slang* : DRUNK

pissed off *adj, slang* : ANGRY, DISAPPOINTED, DISGUSTED ⟨a lot of guys . . . are *pissed off* at me 'cause I came in after them and made corporal —Norman Mailer⟩

pis·so·des \pə'sō(,)dēz\ *n, cap* [NL, fr. Gk *pissa* pitch + NL *-odes* — more at PITCH] : a holarctic genus of small weevils that feed on coniferous trees — see WHITE PINE WEEVIL

pis·soir \(')pi¦swär, (')pē¦s-\ *n* -s [F, fr. MF, fr. *pisser* to urinate, fr. OF *pissier* — more at PISS] : a public urinal usu. located on the street in some European countries and surrounded by a shield or screen

pisspoor \'ˌ=¦=\ *adj* [²*piss* + *poor*] *slang* : utterly inadequate or thoroughly unsatisfactory : DEPLORABLE, WRETCHED ⟨just plain ~, mean and shiftless —James Jones⟩ ⟨that's a ~ attitude —Joseph Landon⟩

pis·tache \pə'stash, (')pi¦s-\ *n* -s [F, fr. L *pistacium*] : PISTACHIO

pis·tach·io \pə'stashē,ō, -taash-, -taish- *also* -tăsh- *or* -(,)shō\ *n* -s [It *pistacchio,* fr. L *pistacium,* fr. Gk *pistakion* pistachio nut, dim. of *pistakē* pistachio tree, fr. Per *pistah*] **1 a** (1) : a small tree (*Pistacia vera*) of southern Europe and Asia Minor having leaves with 3 to 5 broad leaflets, greenish brown paniculate flowers, and a large fruit (2) : the edible green seed of the pistachio tree **b** : WITCH HAZEL 2a(1) **2** *or* **pistachio green** : a light yellowish green that is yellower and paler than apple green, deeper than ocean green, and yellower and duller than crayon green

pistachio nut *n* : the nut of the pistachio tree containing a single oblong greenish edible seed used esp. as a flavoring substance in cookery and confectionery

pis·ta·cia \pə'stashēə, -tăsh-\ *n* [NL, fr. Gk *pistakē* the pistachio tree] **1** *cap* : a small genus of trees (family Anacardiaceae) native to southern Europe, Asia, and No. America having simple or pinnate leaves, small dioecious apetalous flowers, and drupaceous fruits — see MASTIC TREE, PISTACHIO, TEREBINTH **2** -s : any tree of the genus *Pistacia*

pis·ta·cite \'pistə,sīt\ *n* -s [G *pistazit,* fr. L *pistacium* + G *-it* -ite] : EPIDOTE

pis·ta·reen \¦pistə¦rēn\ *n* -s [prob. modif. of Sp *peseta* — more at PESETA] : an old Spanish 2-real piece circulating in Spain, the West Indies, and the U. S. at the debased rate of ⅕ the piece of eight or 20 cents and in the U. S. after 1827 at 17 cents

piste \'pēst\ *n* -s [F, fr. MF, fr. OIt *pista,* fr. *pistare* to trample down — more at PISTON] **1** : a beaten track or trail made by an animal **2** : a hard packed ski trail or course

pis·tia \'pistēə\ *n* [NL, fr. Gk *pistos* liquid + NL *-ia*] **1** *cap* : a genus of tropical free-floating aquatic herbs (family Araceae) having tufted leaves and few-flowered spadices — see WATER LETTUCE **2** -s : any plant of the genus *Pistia*

pis·tic \'pistik\ *adj* [LL *pisticus,* fr. Gk *pistikos,* fr. *pistis* faith + *-ikos* -ic; akin to Gk *peithesthai* to believe, be persuaded, obey — more at BIDE] : of, relating to, or exhibiting faith

pis·til \'pistᵊl *sometimes* -stil\ *n* -s [NL *pistillum,* fr. L, pestle — more at PESTLE] : the ovule-bearing organ of a seed plant : the ovary with its appendages (as style and stigma) — compare GYNOECIUM; see FLOWER illustration

pistill- *comb form* [NL *pistillum*] : pistil ⟨*pistilline*⟩ ⟨*pistilloid*⟩

pis·til·late \'pistə,lāt, -ˌlət\ *adj* [*pistill-* + *-ate*] **1** : having or producing a pistil — see AMENT illustration **2** : having pistils but no stamens — compare STAMINATE

pis·til·line \-,līn, -lən\ *adj* [*pistill-* + *-ine*] : of, relating to, or consisting of a pistil

pis·til·lode \'pistə,lōd\ *also* **pis·til·lo·di·um** \ˌ==ˈlōdēəm\ *n* -s [NL *pistillodium,* fr. *pistill-* + Gk *-ōdēs* -ode + NL *-ium*] : a rudimentary pistil

pis·til·lo·dy \'pistə,lōdē\ *n* -ES [*pistill-* + *-ody*] : the metamorphosis of other organs into pistils

pis·til·loid \'pistə,lȯid\ *adj* [*pistill-* + *-oid*] : resembling or modified into a pistil ⟨~ sepals⟩

¹pis·tol \'pistᵊl\ *n* -s *often attrib* [MF *pistole,* fr. G, fr. MHG dial. (Silesia) *pischulle, pischol, pischczal,* fr. Czech *píšťal,* lit., pipe; akin to Russ *pischal* shawm, shepherd's pipes, harquebus, *pishchat'* to play the pipes, prob. all of imit. origin] **1** : a short firearm intended to be aimed and fired with one hand : REVOLVER — see AUTOMATIC PISTOL **2** : a handgun whose chamber is integral with the barrel — distinguished from *revolver;* see SINGLE-SHOT PISTOL

²pistol \"\ *vt* **pistoled** *or* **pistolled; pistoled** *or* **pistolled; pistoling** *or* **pistolling; pistols** : to shoot with a pistol

pistol carbine *n* : a pistol that has a removable butt piece and is therefore capable of being used as a pistol or as a carbine

pistol casebearer *n* : a casebearer that makes a curved case; *specif* : one that is the larva of a small No. American moth (*Coleophora malivorella*) and that feeds on the foliage of various fruit trees

pis·tole \pə'stōl\ *n* -s [MF, prob. back-formation fr. *pistolet*] **1** : an old gold 2-escudo piece of Spain **2** : any of several old gold coins of Europe having about the value of a pistole

pis·tol·eer \¦pistə¦li(ə)r\ *n* -s [¹*pistol* + *-eer*] : one who uses a pistol; *esp* : a soldier armed principally with a pistol

pistolet *n* -s [MF, perh. dim. of *pistole* pistol] *obs* : any of several gold coins of European countries; *esp* : PISTOLE

pistol grip *n* **1** : a grip of a shotgun or rifle shaped like a pistol stock **2** : a handle (as of a saw) shaped like a pistol stock

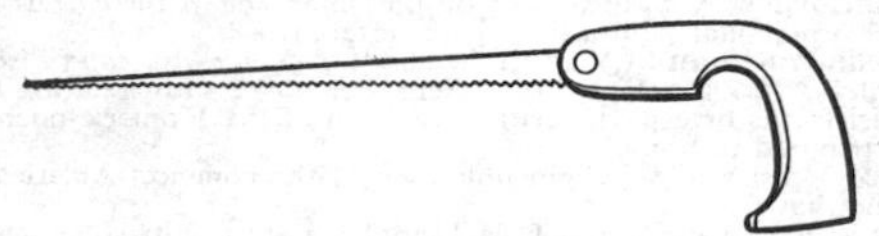

pistol grip of a keyhole saw

pis·tol·o·gy \pə'stäləjē\ *n* -ES [Gk *pistis* faith + E *-o-* + *-logy* — more at PISTIC] : a branch of theology dealing with faith

pistol prawn *or* **pistol shrimp** *n* : SNAPPING SHRIMP

pistol shot *n* **1** : the approximate distance a pistol will shoot or send a bullet or shot ⟨came within *pistol shot*⟩ **2** : one skilled in or accustomed to pistol shooting

pistol-whip \'ˌ=ˌ=ˌ=\ *vt* : to beat with a pistol; *specif* : to beat the head or face of with the side of a pistol

pis·ton \'pistən\ *n* -s [F, fr. MF, large pestle, fr. OIt *pistone,* fr. *pistare* to beat, pound, trample down (fr. ML *pistare,* fr. L *pistus,* past part. of *pinsere* to pound, crush) + *-one,* aug. suffix — more at PESTLE] **1** : a sliding piece moved by or moving against fluid pressure and usu. consisting of a short cylinder fitting within a cylindrical vessel along which it moves back and forth — compare CYLINDER 2b,2c, SLIDE VALVE **2 a** *or* **piston valve** : a sliding valve moving in a cylinder like an engine piston in a brass wind instrument and serving when depressed by a finger knob to add a crook to the tube and hence to lower its pitch **b** *or* **piston knob** : a push button on an organ console for bringing in a preselected registration

piston displacement *n* : the volume displaced by a piston in a cylinder (as in a pump or an engine) in a single stroke : the product of piston travel and cross-sectional area of the containing cylinder

piston drill *n* : a pneumatic percussion drilling machine in which the drill forms a continuation of the piston rod

piston engine *n* : an engine utilizing pistons working in cylinder and usu. involving reciprocating motion

pistonhead \'ˌ=ˌ=ˌ=\ *n* : the part of a piston that is made fast to the piston rod

pistonlike \'ˌ=ˌ=ˌ=\ *adj* : resembling a piston

pis·ton·phone \-,fōn\ *n* [*piston* + *-phone*] : an instrument for measuring acoustic intensity by the displacement of a piston resulting from the sound pressure upon it

piston pin *n* : WRIST PIN

piston pump *n* : a pump having a reciprocating piston operating in a cylinder so as to impart motion and pressure to the fluid by direct displacement

piston ring *n* : a metal ring for sealing the gap between a piston and the cylinder wall

piston rod *n* : a rod by which a piston is moved or by which it communicates motion

piston spring *n* : a spring for a piston ring

piston valve *n* **1** : a reciprocating valve consisting of a piston or connected pistons working in a cylindrical case provided with ports that are traversed by the valve **2** : PISTON 2a

pi·sum \'pīsəm, -īzəm\ *n, cap* [NL, fr. L, pea — more at PEA] : a small genus of Eurasian herbaceous vines (family Leguminosae) distinguished from *Lathyrus* by the enlarged summit of the style — see PEA

¹pit \'pit, *usu* -id·+V\ *n* -s [ME *pitt, pit,* fr. OE *pytt;* akin to OS *putti* well, OHG *pfuzzi, pfuzza* well, ON *pyttr* well, pit, pool, cesspool; all fr. a prehistoric WGmc-NGmc word prob. borrowed fr. L *puteus* well, pit; perh. akin to L *putare* to prune — more at PAVE] **1 a** : a hole, shaft, or cavity in the ground formed naturally (as by erosion) or artificially (as by digging): as (1) : a usu. open deep excavation or shaft that has been dug for taking a mineral deposit from the ground or for quarrying stone ⟨a gravel ~⟩ ⟨a coal ~⟩ (2) : a scooped-out place used for burning something (as charcoal, lime) (3) *dial chiefly Eng* : GRAVE ⟨thou hast kept me alive, that I should not go down to the ~ —Ps 30:3 (AV)⟩ (4) : a hole in the ground usu. covered over with something (as brushwood) and designed to serve as a trap into which wild animals may fall and so be captured (5) : a covered excavation (as in a field) used for storing produce (6) : PROPAGATING PIT (7) : an area dug out or sunk into the ground as a place of imprisonment (8) : an excavation (as beneath a furnace) for receiving cinders or ashes (9) : an area dug out as a shelter against gunfire **b** : an often sunken or depressed area designed for a particular use or purpose with reference to the surrounding or adjacent floor area: as (1) : an enclosure in which animals are kept or are made to fight each other as a sport ⟨a bear ~⟩ ⟨like a couple of gamecocks in a ~⟩ (2) *chiefly Brit* : the ground floor of a theater; *esp* : the part of this area at the rear (3) : ORCHESTRA PIT (4) : a usu. rectangular sunken area in a garage or service station designed to permit more convenient greasing of and repair work on the underside of a car — called also *grease pit* (5) : DROP PIT (6) : a sunken area in a foundry floor designed to catch cast metal (7) : a small area at one end of a bowling alley behind the pins that is designed to catch the pins when they are knocked down (8) : an area alongside an auto speedway used for refueling or repairing the cars (9) : an area in a securities or commodities exchange typically surrounded by a circle of steps in which members of one or the other branch of the exchange do the actual trading ⟨the wheat ~⟩ (10) : an area covered or filled with sawdust or similar soft material designed to cushion the impact of one (as a pole vaulter) landing on that spot after a leap (11) : an area in which gaming tables are placed in a casino **2** : an abyss conceived of as the abode of evil spirits and the damned : HELL ⟨a demon from the depths of the ~ —John Morley⟩ **3** : a hollow or indentation esp. in the surface of an animal body or plant body : a surface depression: as **a** : a natural hollow in the surface of the body; *esp* : a hollow below the lower end of the breastbone — usu. used in the phrase *pit of the stomach* **b** (1) : one of usu. several or many small more or less round indentations left as scars in the skin typically as a result of disease : POCKMARK (2) : a usu. developmental imperfection in the enamel of a tooth that takes the form of a small pointed depression **c** : one of the small depressions left in a surface (as of metal, stone) as a result of some eroding or corrosive agent dripping or spattering on it **d** : a minute depression in the secondary wall of a plant cell that is formed where secondary-wall material has not covered the primary wall and that has a function in the intercellular movement of water and dissolved material **e** : one of the small depressed lesions left in the surface of a plant by disease **4** : a plant disease that produces pits in the plants affected

²pit \"\ *vb* **pitted; pitted; pitting; pits** [ME *pitten,* fr. *pitt, pit,* n.] *vt* **1 a** : to put into or as if into a pit; *esp* : to store (as vegetables) in a pit **b** : to make pits in ⟨the field had been *pitted* by the explosions⟩; *esp* : to make small indentations (as pockmarks) in ⟨a face that had been *pitted* by smallpox⟩ ⟨packed sand that had been *pitted* by the heavy rain⟩ **2 a** : to set (as gamecocks) into or as if into a pit so as to fight ⟨*pitted* a pair of cocks against each other⟩ **b** : to set into opposition or rivalry : match against an opponent or competitor : OPPOSE ⟨*pitting* his courage and his will against terrific odds —E.O. Hauser⟩ ⟨we will be *pitted* against each other —T.B.Costain⟩ ⟨*pitting* one prizefighter against another⟩ ~ *vi* **1** : to yield to pressure (as of the finger) and temporarily retain the indentation so made ⟨tissue affected by edema will usually ~⟩ **2** : to form small indentations : become marked with pits ⟨a metal that *pitted* after contact with acid⟩

³pit \"\ *n* -s [D, fr. MD *pitte, pit* — more at PITH] : the stone of a drupaceous fruit (as a cherry) — compare ⁴PIP 1

⁴pit \"\ *vt* **pitted; pitted; pitting; pits** : to remove the pit from (a fruit)

⁵pit \"\ *chiefly Scot var of* PUT

pi·ta \'pēd·ə\ *n* -s [Sp & Pg] **1** : any of several fiber-yielding plants: as **a** : CENTURY PLANT **b** : YUCCA **c** : a Central American wild pineapple (*Ananas magdalenae*) **2 a** : the fiber of a pita **b** : any of several other fibers; *esp* : MAURITIUS HEMP

pit·a·hau·e·rat \,pid·ə'hau̇ə,rat\ *n, pl* **pitahauerat** *or* **pitahauerats** *usu cap* **1** : a people of the Pawnee confederacy **2** : a member of the Pitahauerat people

pit·a·haya \,pid·ə'hīə\ *or* **pi·taya** \pə'tīə\ *n* -s [Sp, fr. Taino *pitahaya*] **1** : any of several cacti (as *Lemaireocereus thurberi* or *Acanthocereus pentagonus*) of the southwestern U.S. and adjacent Mexico that have edible juicy fruits; *esp* : SAGUARO **2** : the highly colored fruit of a pitahaya that often is as large as a peach and has bright red juice

pi·tan·ga \pə'taŋgə\ *n* -s [Pg, fr. Tupi] : SURINAM CHERRY 2

pi·tan·gua \,pi,taŋ'gwä\ *n* -s [Pg *pitanguá,* fr. Tupi] : a large-billed flycatcher (*Megarhynchus pitangua*) of Central America and So. America

pi·tan·gus \pə'taŋgəs\ *n, cap* [NL, fr. Pg *pitanguá*] : a genus of tyrant flycatchers inhabiting chiefly the warmer parts of America

pit annulus *n* [¹*pit*] : the thicker outer rim of the membrane of some bordered pits

¹pit-a-pat \¦pid·ē¦pat, -it|, |i¦p- *sometimes* |ə¦p-; *usu* -ad·+V\ *or* **pit-pat** \'pit,p-\ *also* **pitty-pat** *like* PIT-A-PAT\ *or* **pitty-patty** \ˌ==¦pad·ē, -at|, |i\ *adv* (*or adj*) [imit.] **1** : with a succession of strong rapid beats (as of the heart) : PITTER-PATTER ⟨heart went *pit-a-pat*⟩ **2** : with a succession of light rapid pats (as of footfalls) ⟨came running *pit-a-pat* down the corridor in her bare feet⟩

²pit-a-pat \"\ *n* **1** : a pattering sound : PITTER-PATTER ⟨the *pit-a-pat* of rain on the roof⟩ **2** : an onset of palpitation (as from emotion) ⟨the *pit-a-pat* of two young hearts —John Dryden⟩

³pit-a-pat \"\ *vi* : to go pit-a-pat : PITTER-PATTER ⟨love *pit-a-patted* in their hearts —Donn Byrne⟩

pit aperture *n* [¹*pit*] : the opening from the lumen of a cell into a pit cavity in a plant

pi·ta·rah *also* **pat·ta·ra** \pə'tärə\ *n* -s [Hindi *piṭārā, peṭārā;* akin to Skt *piṭaka* pitarah] : a basket or box for carrying the clothing of a traveler by palanquin

pi·tau \'pē,tau̇\ *n* -s [Maori] : SILVER TREE FERN

pit band *n* : a theater or opera house orchestra ⟨the bright surface excitement of a Broadway *pit band* —*New Yorker*⟩

pitbird \'ˌ=ˌ=\ *n* [¹*pit* + *bird*] : REED WARBLER

pit border *n* [¹*pit*] : the extension of the secondary cell wall that forms a rim and overarches the pit cavity of a bordered pit

pit boss *n* **1** : a foreman in charge of workers in a given section of a coal mine or one in charge of all operations at a strip coal mine — compare SHIFT BOSS **2** : one that supervises the gaming tables in a casino during play

pit bull *or* **pit bullterrier** *n* : BULLTERRIER

pit·cair·nia \pit'ka(a)rnēə\ *n, cap* [NL, fr. William *Pitcairn* †1791 Eng. physician and botanist + NL *-ia*] : a large genus of tropical often epiphytic herbs (family Bromeliaceae) that have fleshy leaves with spiny margins and flowers with showy bracts

pit canal *n* [¹*pit*] : the passage in a bordered pit that is between the cell lumen and the pit chamber and that is esp. prominent when both secondary wall and pit border are thick

pit cavity *n* [¹*pit*] : the space within a plant cell pit

¹pitch \'pich\ *n* -ES [ME *pich,* fr. OE *pic,* fr. L *pic-, pix;* akin to Gk *pissa, pitta* pitch, OSlav *pĭkŭlŭ* pitch, L *opimus* fat, copious — more at FAT] **1** : any of various black or dark-colored viscous semisolid to solid substances obtained as residues in the distillation of tars or other organic materials: as **a** : a soft to hard and brittle substance that is obtained by distilling coal tar, contains principally aromatic resinous compounds together with aromatic and other hydrocarbons and their derivatives, and is used chiefly in waterproofing, impregnating, and binding **b** : a bright lustrous substance that is obtained by distilling wood tar, contains resin acids, and is used chiefly in plastics and insulating materials and in caulking seams **c** : a usu. soft substance that is obtained by distilling fats, fatty oils, or fatty acids (as from the manufacture of soap or candles), contains polymers and decomposition products, and is used chiefly in varnishes and paints and in floor coverings — called also *fatty acid pitch, stearin pitch* **2** : any of various bituminous substances ⟨mineral ~⟩ **3** : a resin that is obtained from various coniferous trees and is often of medicinal value ⟨pine ~⟩ **4** : any of various artificial mixtures (as of rosin with oils or waxes) resembling resinous or bituminous pitches; *specif* : a mixture of crude pitch, powdered resin, plaster of paris, and tallow used in metalcraft to form a base for supporting and fixing work while tooling or to furnish a supporting filling for a hollow object being worked on

²pitch \"\ *vt* -ED/-ING/-ES [ME *pichen,* fr. OE *pician,* fr. *pic,* n.] : to cover or smear with or as if with pitch : treat with pitch : apply pitch to

³pitch \"\ *vb* **pitched** *or archaic* **pight** \'pīt\ **pitched** *or archaic* **pight; pitching; pitches** [ME *picchen, pichen;* perh. akin to OE *picung* pricking — more at PICK] *vt* **1 a** *archaic* : to fix firmly in or on something : make secure ⟨built of the round sea pebbles ~*ed* in mortar —Joseph Jekyll⟩ **b** (1) : to erect (a tent) and fix firmly in place ⟨decided to ~ their tents there for the night⟩ (2) : to set up (a camp) by erecting tents ⟨moved the camp away from where it had been ~*ed*⟩ (3) : to set up (a wicket used in the game of cricket) by driving into the ground ⟨the wickets are ~*ed* opposite and parallel to each other⟩ **c** *archaic* : to spread out (as a net, a snare) and make secure ⟨~*es* toils to stop the flight —John Dryden⟩ **2** *archaic* **a** : to locate in or move into a particular place or position so as to cause to be situated securely or permanently ⟨the abrupt hill on which the town . . . is ~*ed* —William Black⟩ **b** : to turn (as the eyes, thoughts) toward something : DIRECT ⟨~*ing* her mind among the enjoyments of Corinth —Leigh Hunt⟩ **3** : THROW, FLING: as **a** : to take up (as hay) with a pitchfork and toss to a particular area ⟨watched the farmers ~*ing* hay⟩ **b** (1) : to bowl (a cricket ball) to a particular point (2) : to deliver (a baseball) to a batter ⟨~*ed* a fast ball to him and he struck out⟩ (3) : to toss (as coins) so as to cause to fall at or near a particular mark ⟨boys ~*ing* pennies⟩ ⟨liked to ~ horseshoes⟩ **c** : HURL ⟨~*ed* the spear over their heads⟩ **4 a** *obs* : to furnish with things that are stuck in or placed on ⟨~*ing* the top with multitude of stakes —Henry Holcroft⟩ **b** *archaic* : to set (as a road, path) with a layer of pebbles or stones **5 a** *chiefly Brit* : to set out or display (goods) for sale esp. in a market **b** : to sell, peddle, or advertise (goods) esp. in a high-pressure way ⟨~*ing* a new line of refrigerators⟩ **6** *obs* : to state or establish as definite ⟨first they ~ their conclusion, and then hunt about for premises —Joseph Hall⟩ **7 a** (1) : to cause to be at a particular level ⟨~*ed* their aspirations too high⟩ or of a particular overall quality ⟨~*ing* the conversation along idealistic lines⟩ (2) : to cause (as the voice) to have a particular highness or lowness of tone : give a particular musical pitch to ⟨~*ed* her voice too high⟩ (3) : to set in a particular musical key ⟨~*ed* the melody in the key of A⟩ **b** : to cause to be set at a particular angle ⟨~*ed* the roof too steep⟩ **8** *chiefly dial* : to put into the ground to grow : PLANT **9** : to cause to be loosened and lost ⟨the ship was in danger of ~*ing* her masts in the heavy sea⟩ **10** : PIT 2b **11 a** *chiefly Brit* : NARRATE, TELL ⟨~ a yarn that not even a child would have believed⟩ **b** : to utter, state, or deliver with a glibness typically marked by exaggeration, artificial fervor, insincerity, or deceptiveness ⟨was disgusted with the line she ~*ed*⟩ **12** : to start fermentation in (as wort) by adding some substance **13 a** : to lead (a card of a specified suit) in some games **b** : to establish (trump) by such leading **14** : to make a pitch shot with (a golf ball) **15 a** : to choose and put into a particular ball game as a usu. starting pitcher ⟨the manager had a hard time deciding which player to ~⟩ **b** : to play (a game of ball) in the position of pitcher ⟨~*ed* a perfect game⟩ ⟨~*ed* the first three innings⟩ **16** : to chip (a stone) so as to have straight lines and a flat surface : SQUARE **17** : ⁵FIT 2d(6) ~ *vi* **1 a** : to fall precipitately : fall headlong heavily : plunge headlong **b** (1) *of a ship* : to have the bow alternately plunge precipitately down and rise abruptly up ⟨~ and roll in a rough sea⟩ (2) *of an airplane* : to turn about a lateral axis so that the nose rises or falls in relation to the tail (3) *of a missile or spacecraft* : to turn about a lateral axis that is both perpendicular to the longitudinal axis and horizontal with respect to the earth **c** : to plunge forward with a movement suggestive of a pitching ship **d** : BUCK 1 **2 a** : ENCAMP ⟨~*ed* on the other side of the hill⟩ **b** (1) *archaic* : to settle down in a particular place or position ⟨the first settlers ~*ed* here —Jeremy Belknap⟩ (2) : to make a choice of something usu. in a rather casual way : fix on something — used with *on* or *upon* ⟨the place which he ~*ed* upon for his trading post —Washington Irving⟩ **3** : to incline forward and downward : SLOPE, DIP ⟨a vein of ore ~*ing* 36 degrees east⟩ **4 a** : to pitch something; *esp* : to pitch a baseball or softball ⟨a pitcher that really knows how to ~⟩ **b** : to play ball as a pitcher : have the position of pitcher ⟨~*ed* for 10 years before retiring⟩ **c** : to make a pitch shot in golf **5** *cricket, of a bowled ball* : to strike the ground before being played by a batsman ⟨the ball ~*ed* short of a length⟩ **6** : to exert oneself energetically against odds : fight courageously against difficulties and opposition ⟨no matter what happened, he stayed in there ~*ing*⟩ **syn** see PLUNGE, THROW — **pitch into 1** : to attack or assail with blows or words : BELABOR, SCOLD ⟨got mad and *pitched into* him with both fists⟩ ⟨said his mother would *pitch into* him when he got home⟩ **2** : to set to work on energetically ⟨decided to *pitch into* the job and get it over with⟩ — **pitch woo** : to make love : NECK

⁴pitch \"\ *n* -ES **1 a** (1) : the action of pitching (2) : a particular manner of pitching **b** *Brit* : a quantity of goods displayed for sale **2 a** : degree of slope : SLOPE: as (1) : the inclination of a roof as determined by the ratio of the height to the span (2) : the inclination of a flight of stairs as determined by the angle of the nosing line with the floor (3) : the angle of setting (as of a plowshare, a carpenter's plane iron, or a propeller blade) (4) : the angle that the cutting edge of a saw tooth makes with a line parallel to the points of the teeth (5) : the angle of a shotgun barrel from the vertical when the butt of the gun is at right angles to the vertical (6) : the angle at which finger holes are bored in a bowling ball (7) : the angle at which a heel is attached to the sole of a shoe (8) : the dip or inclination of a vein or bed of a mineral; *esp* : PLUNGE 4 **b** : the distance between two points of a mechanical part or between two such parts: as (1) : the distance between a point on a gear tooth or sprocket tooth and a corresponding point on the next tooth (2) : the distance between a point on one of the threads of a screw and a corresponding point on an adjacent thread (3) : the distance between a pair of paddles on a wheel (4) : the distance between a pair of rivet holes (5) : the distance between a pair of stays (as in a steam boiler) (6) **:** the distance between two

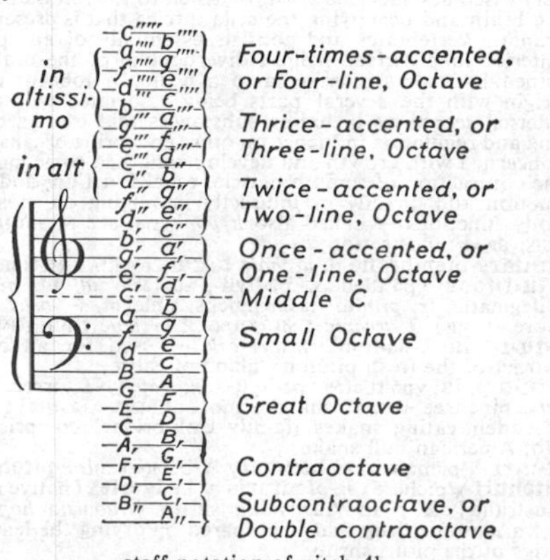

staff notation of pitch 4b

points on the circumference of an armature **c** (1) **:** the longitudinal distance between corresponding edges of successive perforations in motion-picture film (2) **:** the distance between successive grooves of a disc recording **d :** the distance advanced by a propeller in one revolution — called also *effective pitch* **e :** a unit of width of typewriter type based on the number of times a letter can be set in a linear inch ⟨elite is a 12-*pitch* type⟩ **f :** a unit of measure of carpet fineness based on the number of warp threads within a length of usu. 27 inches **g** (1) **:** the number of teeth (as of a gear) or of threads (as of a screw) per inch (2) **:** the number of grooves per inch in a disc recording **3 a** *archaic* **:** the highest point **:** SUMMIT ⟨driven headlong from the ~ of heaven —John Milton⟩ **:** the highest or most intense degree **:** ZENITH, ACME, TOP ⟨when the general hilarity was at its ~ —William Black⟩ ⟨singing at the ~ of their voices —J.H.Newman⟩ **b** *archaic* **:** ALTITUDE, ELEVATION ⟨just of his size, complexion, and ~ —Edmund Hickeringill⟩ ⟨flies at a much higher ~ —Henry Hallam⟩ **c** *archaic* **:** the tip of a piece of land (as a cape) extending into a body of water **4 a :** the relative level, intensity, or extent of some quality or state ⟨were at a high ~ of excitement⟩ **b** (1) **:** the highness or lowness of a musical tone dependent on the number of vibrations (as of the string of a musical instrument, the vocal cords) per second and the resultant corresponding number of sound waves reaching the ear per second in such a way that the greater the number of vibrations the higher the tone and the fewer the number of vibrations the lower the tone (2) **:** a tone produced by a particular number of vibrations per second and a corresponding number of sound waves per second and chosen as a standard (as in tuning musical instruments) — see ABSOLUTE PITCH, INTERNATIONAL PITCH, PHILHARMONIC PITCH **c** (1) **:** the

THE ABSOLUTE PITCHES OF THE PURE AND TEMPERED SCALES

NOTE	VIBRATIONS PER SECOND pure	tempered	NOTE	VIBRATIONS PER SECOND pure	tempered
c′	264	261.62	g′	396	391.99
d′	297	293.66	a′	440	440.00
e′	330	329.63	b′	495	493.88
f′	352	349.23	c″	528	523.25

difference in the relative vibration frequency of the human voice that contributes to the total meaning of ear-apprehended speech by being (as in Chinese) an integral part of a word and essential to the conveyance of its minimal meaning or by varying (as in English) according to the intended minimal meaning of a word with different meanings (2) **:** a definite relative pitch that is a significant phenomenon (as a phoneme) in speech — symbols 1 (highest), 2, 3, 4 (lowest) **5 :** a steep place **:** a steep ascent or descent **:** DECLIVITY **6 a :** a place where one stations oneself or where one settles down: as (1) *archaic* **:** a piece of ground selected for a place of residence **:** ABODE (2) *Brit* **:** the open-air stand of one who conducts business on the street ⟨a shoeblack, whose ~ is at the corner —*Punch*⟩ (3) **:** a place in a river chosen for angling (4) **:** the piece of ground assigned to a tributer in Cornwall **b** (1) *chiefly Brit* **:** a field used for playing some games (as soccer, cricket) (2) **:** the specially prepared part of a cricket field between the bowling creases **:** WICKET **7 :** LENGTH 10a **8 :** an all-fours game in which the first card led must be a trump; *esp* **:** AUCTION PITCH **9 a** *chiefly Brit* **:** CHAT **b** (1) **:** a typically high-pressure sales talk (2) **:** a commercial advertisement (3) **:** RECOMMENDATION, BOOST, PLUG **c :** a line of talk or way of speaking or writing marked by glibness and typically by exaggeration, artificial fervor, insincerity, or deceptiveness **10 a :** PITCH SHOT **b** (1) **:** the delivery of a baseball by a pitcher to a batter (2) **:** a baseball so thrown **c :** a pass in football

pitch accent *n* [¹*pitch*] **1 :** stress deriving from the relative acuteness of musical tones and tending to be accentuated by higher pitch **2 :** prominence given to a syllable or word by means of raised pitch or change of pitch

pit chamber *n* [¹*pit*] **:** the part of the pit cavity of a bordered pit enclosed by the overarching extension of the secondary cell wall

pitch-and-run shot \ˌ=ˌ=ˈ=-\ *or* **pitch-and-run** \ˈ=ˌ=ˈ=\ *n* [³*pitch*] **:** CHIP SHOT

pitch-and-toss \ˈ=ˌ=ˈ=\ *n* [³*pitch*] **:** a game in which the player who pitches coins nearest to a mark has first chance at tossing up all the coins played and winning those that fall heads up

pitch apple *n* [¹*pitch*] **:** a common tropical American tree (*Clusia rosea*) that has coarse evergreen leaves, solitary white or rose flowers, and a whitish resinous fruit and that when young often grows over other trees like a vine in such a way as to strangle them — called also *strangler fig*

pitch-black \ˈ=ˈ=\ *adj* [¹*pitch* + *black*, adj.] **:** of the color pitch black **:** extremely dark **:** intensely black ⟨a *pitch-black* night⟩ — **pitch-black·ness** *n*

pitch black *n* [¹*pitch* + *black*, n.] **1 :** a dark brown that is nearly black **2 :** a deep black

pitch·blende \ˈpich,blend\ *n* [part trans. of G *pechblende*, fr. *pech* pitch + *blende* — more at BLENDE] **:** a massive variety of uraninite occurring in metalliferous veins that ranges in color from brown to black and has a distinctive luster and that contains a slight amount of radium and is the principal ore mineral source of uranium

pitch bowl *n* **:** BULLET 3b

pitch box *n* **:** a shallow box of wood or metal used in metalcraft for holding pitch in order to form a bed for fixing or holding the work while tooling

pitch circle *n* [⁴*pitch*] **:** a pitch line in a circular gear that forms a circle concentric with the axis of the gear

pitch coal *n* [¹*pitch*] **:** a brittle lustrous bituminous coal or lignite

pitch cone *n* [⁴*pitch*] **:** a cone that constitutes the pitch surface of an ordinary bevel gear

pitch count *n* [⁴*pitch*] **:** a count of 4 points for an ace, 3 for a king, 2 for a queen, and 1 for a jack (as in the game of pitch)

pitch cylinder *n* [⁴*pitch*] **:** a cylinder that constitutes the pitch surface of a spur gear

pitch-dark \ˈ=ˈ=\ *adj* [¹*pitch*] **:** extremely dark **:** PITCH-BLACK — **pitch-dark·ness** \ˈ=ˈ==\ *n*

pitch diameter *n* [⁴*pitch*] **:** the diameter of the pitch circle of a wheel

pitched *past of* PITCH

pitched battle *n* [fr. past part. of ³*pitch*] **1 :** a battle in which the opposing forces have firm fixed positions that are clearly defined — distinguished from *skirmish* **2 :** an intensely fought battle in which the opposing forces are locked in close combat

pitched field *n*, *archaic* **:** PITCHED BATTLE

¹pitch·er \ˈpichə(r)\ *n* -s [ME *picher*, fr. OF *pichier*, fr. ML *bicarius* goblet, beaker — more at BEAKER] **1 a** (1) **:** a relatively large container for holding and pouring out liquids that is made typically of earthenware, glass, metal, or plastic and has a wide mouth with a broad lip or spout and a handle at one side or sometimes two ears (2) *chiefly Brit* **:** JUG 1b **b :** the contents of a pitcher **:** PITCHERFUL **c :** powdered pottery shards used in ceramics in bodies and glazes to improve properties — usu. used in pl. **2 :** ASCIDIUM; *esp* **:** a modified leaf of a pitcher plant in which the hollowed petiole and base of the blade form an elongated receptacle over which the outer part of the blade usu. projects like a lid

pitcher 1a(1)

²pitch·er \ˈ"\ *n* -s [³*pitch* + *-er*] **1 :** one that pitches: as **a :** the player that pitches in a game of baseball or softball — see BASEBALL illustration **b :** a worker that tosses bricks to a setter or loader **c :** a worker in a tan house who cleans out vats of used tanbark **2** *chiefly dial* **a :** one that loads cars underground in a coal mine **b :** one that attends to the laying down and taking up of temporary railways at the working faces **c :** one that picks over dumps for pieces of ore **3 :** a small object (as a marble, stone) used for tossing in some games **4 :** an iron golf club with a broad face lofted more than that of a mashie niblick — called also *number seven iron;* see IRON illustration

³pitcher \ˈ"\ *n* -s [²*pitch* + *-er*] **:** PARAFFINER

pitch·ered \-chə(r)d\ *adj* [¹*pitcher* + *-ed*] **1 :** having ascidia ⟨a ~ plant⟩ **2 :** developed into ascidia ⟨~ leaves⟩

pitch·er·ful \-chə(r),fu̇l\ *n*, *pl* **pitcher·fuls** *also* **pitchers·ful** \-chə(r),fu̇lz, -chə(r)z,fu̇l\ **:** the quantity held by a pitcher

pitcher house *n* [ME *picher hous*] *obs* **:** WINE CELLAR

pitcheri *var of* PITURI

pitcher molding *n* **:** the molding of clay ware in molds made of lightly fired clay

pitcher plant *n* **:** any of several plants esp. of the genera *Sarracenia*, *Nepenthes*, *Cephalotus*, and *Darlingtonia* with leaves which are either wholly or partly modified into forms resembling pitchers and in which insects are trapped and digested by the plant through liquids (as acid secretions or water prob. with the aid of proteolytic enzymes) contained by the leaves: as **a :** a bog herb (*Sarracenia purpurea*) of the northeastern U. S. with leaves modified into the form of broadly winged pitchers **b :** CALIFORNIA PITCHER PLANT **c :** AUSTRALIAN PITCHER PLANT

pitcher-plant family *n* **1 :** NEPENTHACEAE **2 :** SARRACENIACEAE

pitcher sage *n* **:** a Californian mint (*Sphacele calycina*) with pubescent or woolly herbage and large white flowers

pitcher's elbow *n* [²*pitcher*] **:** pain and disability associated with the tearing of tendons from their attachment on the epicondyle of the humerus often with involvement of tissues within and around the elbow joint

pitches *pl of* PITCH, *pres 3d sing of* PITCH

pitch-faced \ˈ=ˌ=\ *adj* [⁴*pitch*] **:** having a rough quarry finish along the vertical surface except for edges faced cleanly with a pitching chisel ⟨*pitch-faced* stonework⟩

pitch factor *n* [⁴*pitch*] **:** the ratio of the voltage induced in a short-pitch winding to the voltage that would be induced if the winding were full pitch

pitch-farthing *n* [³*pitch*] **:** CHUCK-FARTHING

pitch fir *n* [¹*pitch*] **:** PITCH PINE

¹pitch·fork \ˈpich,=\ *n* [ME *pychforke*, alter. (influenced by *pichen* to pitch, throw) of *pikforke*, fr. *pik* pick + *forke* — more at PITCH, PICK, FORK] **1 :** a usu. long-handled fork typically with two or three long somewhat curved prongs for pitching hay or straw or similar material **2 a :** the fruit of an herb of the genus *Bidens* **b pitchforks** *pl but sing or pl in constr* **:** BUR MARIGOLD

²pitchfork \ˈ"\ *vt* **1 :** to lift and toss with or as if with a pitchfork ⟨~*ed* the hay into the wagon⟩ **2 :** to thrust into something suddenly and unexpectedly or without preparation **:** throw into something precipitately and by surprise ⟨was ~*ed* into the job by destiny —G.W.Johnson⟩ ⟨their very success . . . ~*ed* them into the place of world leadership —*Times Lit. Supp.*⟩ ⟨is literally ~*ed* into astounding triumphs —Wolcott Gibbs⟩

pitchforks *adv* **:** very hard — usu. used in the phrase *rain pitchforks*

pitchhole \ˈ=ˌ=\ *n* [⁴*pitch* + *hole*] **:** a recess in a stone otherwise dressed true for setting

pitch hyperboloid *n* [⁴*pitch*] **:** a hyperboloid that constitutes the pitch surface of a skew bevel

pitchi \ˈpichē\ *n* -s [native name in Australia] **:** a large shallow elongated wooden receptacle much used by Australian aborigines as a container for food and drink

pitchier *comparative of* PITCHY

pitchiest *superlative of* PITCHY

pitch in *vi* **1 :** to set to work energetically **:** begin something energetically **:** pitch into something ⟨had a lot to do and decided to *pitch in*⟩ **2 :** to make a contribution toward commonly shared expenses **:** chip in ⟨had *pitched in* to rent a cottage —Martin Donohue⟩

pitch·i·ness \ˈpichēnəs, -chin-\ *n* -ES **:** the quality or state of being pitchy

pitching *n* -s [fr. gerund of ³*pitch*] **1 :** a stone facing on a slope of ground **2 :** a layer of coarse stone on a road

pitching chisel *or* **pitching tool** *n* **:** a chisel used for making an edge on the face of a stone

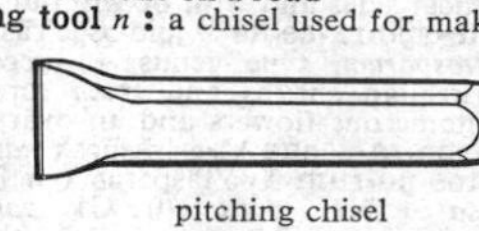
pitching chisel

pitching moment *n* [fr. pres. part. of ³*pitch*] **:** a moment tending to rotate an airplane or airfoil about its lateral axis

pitching niblick *n* **:** an iron golf club with a loft between those of a pitcher and a niblick — called also *number 8 iron;* see IRON illustration

pitching piece *n* **:** a beam supporting a staircase and located at the top of the stairs — opposed to *apron piece*

pitching yeast *n* **:** a yeast used in pitching (as wort)

pitch line *n* [⁴*pitch*] **1 :** the line on which the pitch of gear teeth or sprocket teeth is measured and which consists of an ideal line in a toothed gear or rack which bears such a relation to a corresponding line in another gear with which it works that the two lines will have a common velocity (as in rolling contact) **2 :** the line from which players lag in the game of marbles

¹pitch·man \ˈpichmən\ *n*, *pl* **pitchmen** [⁴*pitch* + *man*] **1 :** one who sells something **:** SALESMAN, VENDER; *esp* **:** one who vends gadgets or novelties or similar articles esp. on the streets or from a concession (as at a fair) ⟨demonstrated and hawked his product with the vigor of an oldtime ~ —*Time*⟩ **2 :** one that uses a fast line of talk to advertise and sell something or to cause something to be known and accepted ⟨frenetic commercials delivered by radio and television *pitchmen*⟩

²pitchman \ˈ"\ *n*, *pl* **pitchmen** [¹*pitch* + *man*] **:** an operator of a machine for grinding pitch for use with coke in the manufacture of carbon electrodes

pitch mining *n* [⁴*pitch*] **:** the mining of steeply inclined coal beds

pitch moth *n* [¹*pitch*] **:** any of several moths (as the sequoia pitch moth, the pitch twig moth) having larvae that bore into the wood of coniferous trees and so cause pitch to exude

pitch nodule maker *n* [¹*pitch*] **:** a pitch moth (*Petrova albicapitana*) whose larva is esp. destructive to lodgepole pine and jack pine in No. America

pitch ore *n* [¹*pitch*] **:** PITCHBLENDE

pitch out *vi* **:** to make a pitchout

pitchout \ˈ=ˌ=\ *n* [*pitch out*] **1 :** a pitch in the game of baseball that is deliberately wide of the plate so that the batter cannot hit it and that is usu. designed to enable the catcher to check or put out a base runner (as by breaking up a steal or preventing a squeeze play) **2 :** a lateral pass in the game of football made between two backs behind the scrimmage line

pitch peat *n* [¹*pitch*] **:** a black homogeneous peat with a waxy luster

pitch-penny \ˈ=,==\ *n* [³*pitch*] **:** PITCH-AND-TOSS

pitch pine *n* [¹*pitch*] **1 a :** any of several pines that yield pitch; *esp* **:** a 3-leaved pine (*Pinus rigida*) of eastern No. America closely related to the pond pine **b :** the wood of a pitch pine **2 :** a dark grayish green that is bluer, lighter, and stronger than average ivy, yellower and slightly lighter than Persian green, and yellower and lighter than hemlock green — called also *thyme* **3** *chiefly Midland* **:** KINDLING WOOD

pitch pipe *n* [⁴*pitch*] **:** a small reed pipe or flue pipe that is blown with the breath to produce one or more tones used for establishing the pitch in singing or in tuning an instrument

pitch pocket *n* [¹*pitch*] **:** a cavity in lumber that contains or has contained resin

pitch point *n* [⁴*pitch*] **:** the point of contact of the pitch lines of two gears or of a rack and pinion when in mesh

¹pitchpole *also* **pitchpoll** \ˈ=ˌ=\ *n* [³*pitch* + *poll* (head)] **:** SOMERSAULT

²pitchpole *also* **pitchpoll** *vb* -ED/-ING/-S *vi* **:** to turn end over end **:** SOMERSAULT ~ *vt* **:** to cause to turn end over end

pitch seam *or* **pitch streak** *n* [¹*pitch*] **:** a pitch-filled shake or check in lumber

pitch shot *n* [⁴*pitch*] **:** an approach stroke in golf in which the ball is lofted to the green with backspin so that the ball rolls very little after striking the green — compare CHIP SHOT

pitchstone \ˈ=ˌ=\ *n* [trans. of G *pechstein*, fr. *pech* pitch + *stein* stone] **:** a glassy rock that has a resinous luster and that contains more water than obsidian does

pitch surface *n* [⁴*pitch*] **:** the surface of either of two tangent imaginary friction wheels having the same axes and the same angular velocities as those of a pair of real gears in mesh

pitch tree *n* [¹*pitch*] **:** any of several resinous conifers: as **a :** KAURI PINE **b :** AMBOINA PINE **c :** NORWAY SPRUCE

pitch twig moth *n* [¹*pitch*] **:** a small largely reddish brown pitch moth (*Petrova comstockiana*) whose larvae attack various hard pines

pitch-up \ˈ=ˌ=\ *n* -s [fr. the verb *pitch up*] **:** the tendency of a climbing airplane esp. with swept-back wings to nose sharply upward beyond the control of the pilot

pitchuri *var of* PITURI

pitchwoman \ˈ=ˌ==\ *n*, *pl* **pitchwomen** [⁴*pitch* + *woman*] **:** a female pitchman

pitchy \ˈpichē, -chi\ *adj*, *usu* -ER/-EST [¹*pitch* + *-y*] **1 a :** full of pitch: as (1) **:** RESINOUS ⟨~ lumber⟩ (2) **:** coated, smeared, or sticky with pitch **:** TARRY ⟨a ~ road⟩ **b :** of, relating to, or having the qualities of pitch ⟨a ~ substance⟩ **2 :** as dark or as black as pitch **:** very dark **:** PITCH-BLACK ⟨went out into the ~ night⟩ — often used with *black* or *dark* ⟨the ~ black night⟩

pit coal *n* [¹*pit*] **:** coal mined from the earth **:** mineral coal — distinguished from *charcoal*

pit committee *n* **:** a joint committee of employer and workers dealing with the labor problems of a mine

pit disease *n* [¹*pit*] **:** an often fatal disease of oysters resulting from the presence of flagellates of the genus *Hexamita* in the blood stream and involving embolism and destruction of tissues

pit dwelling *n* **:** PIT HOUSE

pi·tei·ra \pəˈterə, -tārə\ *n* -s [Pg, fr. *pita* + *-eira* -ary (fr. L *-aria*)] **1 :** GIANT CABUYA **2 :** MAURITIUS HEMP

pit·e·ous \ˈpid·ēəs, -itē-\ *adj* [ME *piteus*, *piteous*, alter. (influenced by *pite* pity) of *pitous*, fr. OF *piteus*, fr. *pité* pity + *-eus* -ous — more at PITY] **1 a :** arousing or deserving pity or compassion ⟨had received ~ appeals for help —F. Tennyson Jesse⟩ **b** *archaic* **:** feeling pity or compassion **:** COMPASSIONATE, MERCIFUL **2** *archaic* **:** PALTRY, MEAN ⟨~ amends —John Milton⟩ — **pit·e·ous·ly** *adv* — **pit·e·ous·ness** *n* -ES

pitfall \ˈ=ˌ=\ *n* [ME, fr. *pit* + *fall*] **1 :** TRAP, SNARE; *specif* **:** a pit bridged by a cover of flimsy material or otherwise concealed or camouflaged and used to capture and hold animals or men falling into it **2 :** a hidden or not easily recognized danger, error, or source of injury or destruction into which one that is unsuspecting or incautious may fall ⟨the ~*s* of ignorance⟩

pit field *n* [¹*pit*] **:** an area in the wall of a plant cell in which one or more pits develop

pit game *n*, *pl* **pit game** *or* **pit games** [¹*pit*] **:** PIT GAME FOWL

pit game fowl *n* **:** a game fowl of the Modern Game class that is bred primarily for fighting and selected for vigor, muscularity, and aggressiveness — compare EXHIBITION GAME FOWL

¹pith \ˈpith, *dial* ˈpeth\ *n* -s [ME *pithe*, *pith*, fr. OE *pitha;* akin to MD & MLG *pit*, *pitte* pith, pit (of a fruit)] **1 a** (1) **:** a usu. continuous central strand of predominantly parenchymatous tissue that occurs in the stems of most vascular plants and some roots as part of the primary tissue system, is typically surrounded by vascular tissue, prob. functions chiefly in storage, and may disappear leaving a void in some plants (as many umbellifers) (2) **:** a slender soft core at the center of the heartwood of many logs consisting of the dried remains of the pith **b :** any of various loose spongy plant tissues that resemble true pith ⟨the white ~ lining the skin of an orange⟩ **c :** the soft or spongy interior of a part of the body: as (1) *archaic* **:** the spinal cord or bone marrow (2) **:** the medulla of a hair (3) **:** the spongy interior of a feather **2 a** (1) **:** the essential part of something **:** ESSENCE, CORE, MARROW ⟨individuality, which was the very ~ of liberty —H.J.Laski⟩ (2) **:** the very center **:** HEART ⟨people who live in the thick of politics and in the ~ of society —Francis Hackett⟩ **b :** substantial quality (as of meaning or content) **:** SOLIDITY, MEATINESS ⟨made a speech that lacked ~⟩ **3** *archaic* **:** VIGOR, ENERGY, STRENGTH ⟨took the ~ out of my legs —R.L.Stevenson⟩ **4 :** IMPORTANCE, WEIGHTINESS ⟨enterprises of great ~ and moment —Shak.⟩

²pith \ˈ"\ *vt* -ED/-ING/-S **1 a :** to kill (as cattle) by piercing or severing the spinal cord at or near the axis **b :** to destroy the spinal cord or entire central nervous system of (as a frog) usu. by passing a wire or needle up and down the vertebral canal **2 a :** to remove the pith from ⟨a plant stem that had been ~*ed*⟩ **b :** to draw out **:** SAP, EXTRACT ⟨could ~ so much of the vigor out of his body —C.E.Montague⟩

pithead \ˈ=ˌ=\ *n* **:** the top of a mining pit or coal shaft; *also* **:** the immediately adjacent ground and buildings

pit-headed \ˈ=ˌ==\ *adj* **:** having a pit on the surface of the head ⟨pit vipers are *pit-headed*⟩

pit-head frame \ˈ=ˌ=-\ *n* **:** HEADFRAME

pit·head·man \ˈ=ˌ=mən\ *n*, *pl* **pitheadmen 1 :** one that works about a pithead **2 :** one in charge of a pithead or pitheadmen

pithec- *or* **pitheco-** *comb form* [Gk *pithēk-*, *pithēko-*, fr. *pithēkos* — more at BEBUNG] **:** ape **:** monkey ⟨*pithec*anoid⟩ ⟨*pitheco*metric⟩

pi·the·can \pəˈthēkən, ˈpithək-\ *adj* [*pithec-* + *-an*] **:** of, relating to, or resembling apes, esp. the anthropoid apes

pith·e·can·thrope \ˌpithəˈkan,thrōp, ˈpithəkən-\ *n* -s [NL *pithecanthropus*] **:** PITHECANTHROPUS 2

pith·e·can·throp·ic \ˌpithə,kanˈthräpik\ *adj* [NL *pithecanthropus* + E *-ic*] **:** of, relating to, or resembling pithecanthropi

¹pith·e·can·thro·pid \ˌ=ˌ=ˈkan(t)thrəpəd; -,kanˈthrōp-, -räp-\ *adj* [NL *Pithecanthropidae*] **:** PITHECANTHROPIC

²pithecanthropid \ˈ"\ *n* -s **:** PITHECANTHROPUS 2

pith·e·can·throp·i·dae \ˌpithə,kanˈthräpə,dē\ *n pl*, *cap* [NL, fr. *Pithecanthropus*, type genus + *-idae*] **:** a formerly recognized family containing the genus *Pithecanthropus*

pith·e·can·thro·pine \ˌ=ˌ=ˈkan(t)thrə,pīn, -,kanˈthrōpən\ *n* -s [NL *pithecanthropus* + E *-ine*] **:** PITHECANTHROPUS 2 — **pithecanthropine** *adj*

¹pith·e·can·thro·poid \-ˈkan(t)thrə,pȯid\ *adj* [NL *pithecanthropus* + E *-oid*] **:** of, relating to, or resembling the pithecanthropi

²pithecanthropoid \ˈ"\ *n* -s **:** a pithecanthropoid mammal or fossil

pith·e·can·thro·pus \ˌpithəˈkan(t)thrəpəs, -,kanˈthrōp-\ *n* [NL, fr. *pithec-* + *-anthropus*] **1** *cap* **a :** a hypothetical group of extinct primates intermediate between man and the anthropoid apes **b :** a genus of extinct primitive men that includes two generally accepted species (*P. erectus* and *P. robustus*) known from skull and other bone fragments found in Javanese Pliocene gravels and sometimes the very similar Peking man and that comprises forms having a profile like that of an ape with very low forehead and undeveloped chin, a posture approaching that of modern man, and a brain of 900 to 1000 cubic centimeters which is larger than that of any known ape and smaller than that of any normal modern man — compare SINANTHROPUS **2** *pl* **pithecanthro·pi** \-ˌpī, -(ˌ)pē\ **:** an individual of the group or genus *Pithecanthropus*

pi·the·cia \pəˈthēsh(ē)ə\ *n, cap* [NL, fr. *pithec-* + *-ia*] **:** a genus of saki monkeys of northern So. America and the Amazon basin — **pi·the·cian** \-sh(ē)ən\ *adj or n*

pith·e·cism \ˈpithəˌsizəm\ *n* -s [ISV *pithec-* + *-ism*] **:** pithecoid characteristics present in man

¹pithe·coid \ˈpithəˌkȯid, pəˈthēˌk-\ *adj* [NL *Pithecia* + E *-oid*] **1 :** of or relating to *Pithecia* or closely related genera **2 a :** PITHECAN **b :** of, relating to, or resembling monkeys

²pithecoid \ˈ"\ *n* -s **:** a pithecoid individual

pith·e·coi·dea \ˌpithəˈkȯidēə\ *n pl, cap* [NL, fr. *pithec-* + *-oidea*] *in some classifications* **:** a suborder of Primates that is coordinate with Prosimii and Anthropoidea and includes the new-world monkeys and old-world monkeys

pith·e·co·lo·bi·um \ˌpithəkəˈlōbēəm\ *n, cap* [NL, fr. *pithec-* + Gk *lobion* small lobe, dim. of *lobos* lobe — more at SLEEP] **:** a large genus of tropical shrubs and trees (family Leguminosae) having bipinnate leaves and globose heads of flowers with many stamens and a twisted or coiled pod — see ALGARROBILLA, CAT'S-CLAW 1b, RAIN TREE, WILD TAMARIND

pith·e·co·log·i·cal \ˌpithəkəˈläjəkəl\ *adj* **:** of or relating to pithecology

pith·e·col·o·gy \ˌpithəˈkäləjē\ *n* -ES [*pithec-* + *-logy*] **:** the study of apes

pith·e·co·met·ric \ˌpithəkəˈme·trik\ *adj* [*pithec-* + *-metric*] **:** relating to measurements of the skeletons of apes

pith·e·co·mor·phic \-ˈmȯrfik\ *adj* [*pithec-* + *-morphic*] **:** resembling apes

pith·e·co·mor·phism \ˌ====ˈ=ˌfizəm\ *n* -s **:** structural resemblance to an ape

¹pi·the·cus \pəˈthēkəs; ˈpithək-,ˈpithēk-\ [NL, fr. Gk *pithēkos* monkey, ape — more at BEBUNG] *syn of* MACACA

²pithecus \ˈ"\ [NL, fr. Gk *pithēkos* ape, monkey] *syn of* PRESBYTIS

-pithecus \ˈ"\ *n comb form* [NL, fr. Gk *pithēkos*] **:** ape — in generic names ⟨*Sivapithecus*⟩

pithed *past of* PITH

pith fleck *or* **pith-ray fleck** \ˈ=,=-\ *n* **:** a minute spot in the wood of a tree that results from injury to the cambium by the boring of small dipterous larvae

pith·i·ly \ˈpithəlē, -li\ *adv* [ME, fr. *pithy* + *-ly*] **:** in a pithy manner ⟨impressed by the way in which they can summarize ~ great tracts of life —H.J.Laski⟩

pith·i·ness \-thēnəs, -thin-\ *n* -ES **1 :** the quality or state of being pithy **2 :** a disease of celery marked by the occurrence of soft spongy stalks and hearts

pithing *pres part of* PITH

pith knot *n* **:** a sound knot of timber with a pith hole not more than ¼ inch in diameter

pith·less \ˈpithləs\ *adj* **:** devoid of pith — **pith·less·ly** *adv*

pithole \ˈ=,=\ *n* [¹*pit* + *hole*] *dial chiefly Brit* **:** PIT, GRAVE

pi·thos \ˈpiˌthäs, ˈpī,-\ *n, pl* **pi·thoi** \-ˌthȯi\ [Gk — more at FISCAL] **:** a very large earthenware jar with a wide round mouth used throughout the ancient Greek world esp. for holding and storing large quantities of food (as grain) or liquids (as wine, oil) and sometimes for the burial of the dead

pit house *n* **1 :** a primitive habitation consisting of a pit dug in the earth and roofed over **2 :** a pit usu. with glass walls and roof for storing plants and for growing plants that prefer low temperatures

pith ray *n* **:** MEDULLARY RAY

pith rush *n* **:** STAFF RUSH

piths *pl of* PITH, *pres 3d sing of* PITH

pith tree *n* **:** AMBATCH

pithworm \ˈ=,=\ *n* **:** WIREWORM

pithy \ˈpithē, -thi, *dial* ˈpeth-\ *adj, usu* -ER/-EST [ME, fr. *pithe, pith* pith + *-y* — more at PITH] **1 a** (1) **:** of or resembling pith ⟨a ~ substance⟩ (2) **:** containing, filled with, or abounding in pith ⟨~ stems⟩ **b** *chiefly Scot* **:** STRONG, VIGOROUS **2 a :** containing much meaning and substance in a terse concentrated form **:** brief and to the point **:** full of significance **:** MEATY ⟨a ~ proverb⟩ ⟨a ~ summary⟩ ⟨wrote several ~ chapters⟩ **b :** marked by the use of pithy speech or writing ⟨a ~ speaker⟩ ⟨a ~ style⟩ **syn** see CONCISE

pithy gall *n* **:** a large rough furrowed oblong gall formed on blackberry canes by a small cynipid gall wasp (*Diastrophus turgidus*)

piti·able \ˈpid·ēəbəl, -itē-\ *adj* [ME *piteable*, fr. MF *piteable, pitiable*, fr. *pité, pitié* piety, pity + *-able* — more at PITY] **:** deserving, needing, or arousing pity **:** PITIFUL ⟨the ~ spectacle of a human being in distress —Lyman Bryson⟩ ⟨a ~ wretch⟩ ⟨a ~ attempt to be funny⟩ **syn** see CONTEMPTIBLE

piti·able·ness *n* -ES **:** the quality or state of being pitiable

piti·ably \-blē,-bli\ *adv* **:** in a pitiable manner ⟨struggle ~ for the preservation of an existence devoid of all warmth and light —M.R.Cohen⟩

pitied *past of* PITY

piti·er \ˈpid·ēə(r), -itē-\ *n* -s **:** one that pities

pities *pl of* PITY, *pres 3d sing of* PITY

piti·ful \ˈpid·iˌfəl, -it|, |əf-\ *adj, sometimes* **pitifuller**; *sometimes* **pitifullest** [ME *petefull*, fr. *pete, pite, pitie* pity + *-full, -ful* -ful — more at PITY] **1 a :** deserving or arousing pity **:** exciting or being such as to excite compassion ⟨one of those ~ refugees of which Europe was full —Upton Sinclair⟩ **b :** deserving or arousing contemptuous commiseration or pitying contempt **:** CONTEMPTIBLE ⟨the ~ wage scale —H.S. Truman⟩ **2** *archaic* **:** full of pity **:** COMPASSIONATE, MERCIFUL ⟨be ~ to my great woe —John Keats⟩

piti·ful·ly *adv* **:** in a pitiful manner

piti·ful·ness *n* -ES **:** the quality or state of being pitiful

piti·less \ˈpid·iˌləs, -it|, |ᵊl-\ *adj* [ME *piteeles*, fr. *pitee, pite* pity + *-les* -less] **1 a :** devoid of or unmoved by pity and compassion **:** showing no mercy **:** MERCILESS ⟨a ~ dictator⟩ **b** *archaic* **:** exciting no pity or compassion ⟨a corpse, dog-worried, ~ —J.S.Phillimore⟩ **2 :** grimly uncompromising ⟨a ~ acceptance of fact —H.G.Wells⟩ ⟨the almost ~ clarity of intelligence —P.E.More⟩

piti·less·ly *adv* **:** in a pitiless manner

piti·less·ness *n* -ES **:** the quality or state of being pitiless

pitirri *var of* PIPIRI

pit·less \ˈpitləs\ *adj* **:** having no pit

pitlike \ˈ=,=\ *adj* **:** resembling a pit

pit-making scale \ˈ=,==-\ *n* [¹*pit*] **:** PIT SCALE

pit·man \ˈpitmən\ *n* **1** *pl* **pitmen :** one who works in or near a pit: as **a :** a worker in a coal mine **b :** BOTTOM SAWYER **c :** a worker in a quarry **d :** one that greases or repairs or otherwise services the underside of cars and other vehicles in a garage **e :** one that stands in a pit under the track of an electric railway system using underground and overhead power supply and attaches and detaches the underground current collector or plow at changeover points **f :** one that lays mats or planks on soft ground as a foundation for construction machines and assists with the cleaning and operation of the machines — called also *matman* **g :** one that pulls hot metal tubes through the pit of an extrusion press and straightens them **2** *pl* **pitmans :** CONNECTING ROD

pitman chest *n* **:** a wind-chest used in many pipe organs that has esp. fast action and stop control

pit membrane *n* [¹*pit*] **:** a membrane of a plant pit that consists of primary wall and middle lamella and that closes the pit externally — called also *closing membrane*; compare TORUS

pitmirk \ˈ=,=\ *n* [¹*pit* + *mirk*] *Scot* **:** intense darkness

pi·tom·e·ter \pəˈtäməd·ə(r), pēˈt-\ *n* [*pitot* + *-meter*] **:** an instrument that consists essentially of two pitot tubes one of which is turned upstream and the other downstream and that is used to record autographically the velocity of a flowing liquid or gas

pi·ton \ˈpēˌtän, ˈpēˌtōⁿ, ˈpīˌt-, =ˈ=\ *n* -s [F, fr. MF, nail, screw eye] **1 :** a sharp peak of a mountain **2 :** a usu. iron spike, wedge, or peg that is driven into fissures or cracks (as of a rock or ice surface) so as to serve as a support (as for one climbing a mountain) and that often has an eye at one end through which safety ropes may be passed

pit orchestra *n* **:** PIT BAND

pitot-static tube \ˌpēˌtō|==-, pēˌtō|==-\ *n, often cap P* **:** a device that consists of a combination of a pitot tube and a static tube and that measures pressures in such a way that the relative speed of a fluid can be determined (as in an airspeed indicator) — called also *pitot tube*

1 2 3

pitot-static tube: *1* pitot opening, *2* static opening, *3* drain holes

pi·tot tube \(ˈ)pēˌtō-\ *also* **pitot** *n* -s *often cap P* [F (*tube de*) *Pitot*, after Henri *Pitot* †1771 French physicist and engineer] **1 :** a device that consists of a tube having a short right-angled bend which is placed vertically in a moving body of fluid with the mouth of the bent part directed upstream and is used with a manometer to measure the velocity of fluid flow **2 :** PITOT-STATIC TUBE

pit-pair \ˈ=,=\ *n* [¹*pit*] **:** two pits occurring opposite one another in the walls of adjacent cells of many higher vascular plants and acting together as a structural and functional unit

pit·pan \ˈpitˌpan\ *n* -s [Miskito *pitban* boat] **:** a long flat-bottomed canoe used esp. in Central America

pit-pat *var of* PIT-A-PAT

pit·pit \ˈpitˌpit\ *n* [imit.] **:** GUITGUIT

pit pony *n* [¹*pit*] *chiefly Brit* **:** a pony used for packing or haulage in a mine

pitprop \ˈ=,=\ *n* [¹*pit* + *prop*] **:** a usu. wooden upright used as a temporary support for a mine roof

pi·tri \ˈpi·trē\ *n, pl* **pitris** *or* **pitri** [Skt *pitṛ* father — more at FATHER] *Hinduism* **:** a deceased forefather viewed as semidivine

pit river indian *n, usu cap P&R&I* [fr. *Pit river*, Calif.] **:** ACHOMAWI

pit run *n* **:** BANK GRAVEL

pits *pl of* PIT, *pres 3d sing of* PIT

pit saw *n* **1 :** a long handsaw usu. with a handle at each end that is used chiefly for cutting a log lengthwise into planks and is worked by two men one of whom stands on or above the log and the other below it usu. in a pit **2** *or* **pit-saw file :** a single-cut file that is left uncut at the point and is used chiefly for sharpening pit saws

pit sawyer *n* **:** BOTTOM SAWYER

pit scale *n* **:** one of several scales of the genus *Asterolecanium* that cause serious injury to oaks

pit·ta \ˈpid·ə\ *n* [NL, fr. Telugu *piṭṭa* bird] **1** *cap* **:** a large genus (the type of the family Pittidae) of chiefly terrestrial nearly songless birds that are found principally in the southern part of Asia and in Australia and adjacent islands and that have short wings and tail, long legs, a stout bill, and brilliant plumage marked by sharply contrasting colors **2** -s **:** any bird of the genus *Pitta*

pit·tance \ˈpitᵊn(t)s\ *n* -s [ME *pitaunce*, fr. OF *pitance* piety, pity, allowance of food given a member of a religious house, fr. ML *pietantia, pitantia*, fr. *pietant-, pietans* (pres. part. of *pietari* to be pious, be charitable, fr. L *pietas* piety) + L *-ia* -y — more at PITY] **1 a** *archaic* **:** a gift or bequest made to a religious community (as to provide anniversary masses for a deceased person or to provide additional food or drink on festivals or similar occasions) **b :** a usu. small charitable gift (as of money, food, clothing) **:** ALMS **2 a :** a usu. small often barely sufficient portion, amount, or allowance ⟨had received a mere ~ of education⟩; *often* **:** a meager wage or remuneration ⟨lived in squalid, verminous slums, worked long hours for a ~ —W.S.Maugham⟩ **b :** a small special allowance (as of extra food or drink) apportioned out to the members of a religious community on festivals or similar occasions

pittara *var of* PITARAH

pitted *adj* [fr. past part. of ²*pit*] **:** marked with or having the form of a pit or pits ⟨the surface is very ~⟩

pit·ten \ˈpitᵊn\ *Scot past part of* PUT

¹pit·ter \ˈpid·ə(r), -itə-\ *vi* -ED/-ING/-S [imit.] **1 :** CHIRR, STRIDULATE ⟨~*ing* grasshoppers⟩ **2 :** PITTER-PATTER ⟨rain ~*ing* on a rooftop⟩

²pitter \ˈ"\ *n* -s [⁴*pit* + *-er*] **:** one that pits; *specif* **:** one that removes pits ⟨the cherry ~ and the sausage meat grinder are of interest merely as curios today —*Think*⟩

³pitter \ˈ"\ *n* -s [¹*pit* + *-er*] **:** one that takes care of gamecocks at a fight — compare HANDLER

¹pitter-patter \ˈpid·ə(r)ˌpad·ə(r), -itə . . . atə-\ *adv (or adj)* [imit.] **:** PIT-A-PAT ⟨her heart went *pitter-patter*⟩

²pitter-patter \ˈ"\ *n* **:** a pattering sound **:** PIT-A-PAT ⟨the *pitter-patter* of raindrops on a tin roof⟩

³pitter-patter \ˈ"\ *vi* **pitter-pattered**; **pitter-pattered**; **pitter-pattering**; **pitter-patters :** to go pitter-patter **:** PIT-A-PAT ⟨footsteps *pitter-pattered* down the hall⟩

pit·ti·cite \ˈpid·əˌsīt\ *n* -s [G *pittizit*, irreg. fr. Gk *pitta, pissa* pitch + G *-it* -ite — more at PITCH] **:** a brown massive mineral consisting of a hydrous ferric arsenate and sulfate

pit·ti·dae \ˈpid·əˌdē\ *n pl, cap* [NL, fr. *Pitta*, type genus + *-idae*] **:** a family of passerine birds comprising the pittas and related forms

pitting *n* -s [fr. gerund of ²*pit*] **1 :** the action or process of forming pits ⟨~ sometimes occurs on freshly painted surfaces⟩ **2 :** a particular arrangement of pits on a surface (as of wood) ⟨studied the ~ of each kind of timber⟩ **3 :** the action of putting gamecocks into a pit to fight; *also* **:** a division or round in a cockfight

pit·tite \ˈpid·ˌīt, -ī,tīt\ *n* -s *chiefly Brit* [¹*pit* + *-ite*] **:** one that frequents the pit of a theater

pit·to \ˈpid·(ˌ)ō\ *n* -s [native name in India] **:** GILLAR

pit tomb *or* **pit grave** *n* **:** a grave consisting of a deep pit with vertical sides and with or without a lateral niche

pit·to·spo·ra·ce·ae \ˌpid·əspəˈrāsēˌē\ *n pl, cap* [NL, fr. *Pittosporum*, type genus + *-aceae*] **:** a family of chiefly Australian shrubs and trees (order Rosales) with regular pentamerous flowers and an ovary with many ovules — **pit·to·spo·ra·ceous** \ˌ====ˈrāshəs\ *adj*

pit·tos·po·rum \pəˈtäspərəm\ *n* [Gk *pitto-* pitch (fr. *pitta, pissa*) + NL *-sporum* (fr. Gk *spora, sporos* seed) — more at PITCH, SPORE] **1** *cap* **:** a genus (the type of the family Pittosporaceae) of evergreen trees and shrubs of Asia, Africa, and Australasia that have often fragrant white or yellow flowers succeeded by berries with seeds embedded in a viscous substance — see LAUREL 4h, TARATA **2** -s **:** any tree or shrub of the genus *Pittosporum*

pitts·burgh *also* **pitts·burg** \ˈpitsˌbərg, -bōg, -bəig\ *adj, usu cap* [fr. *Pittsburgh*, Pa.] **:** of or from the city of Pittsburgh, Pa. ⟨*Pittsburgh* steel mills⟩ **:** of the kind or style prevalent in Pittsburgh

pitts·burgh·er *also* **pitts·burg·er** \-gə(r)\ *n* -s *cap* [*Pittsburgh*, Pa. + E *-er*] **:** a native or resident of Pittsburgh, Pa.

pittsburgh ivy *n, usu cap P* **:** an English ivy that has stiff stems and crowded leathery often ruffled leaves and that can be grown without support

pitty-pat *or* **pitty-patty** *var of* PIT-A-PAT

pi·tu·i·cyte \pəˈtüəˌsīt, pəˈtyü-\ *n* -s [NL *pituita* + E *-cyte*] **:** one of the pigmented more or less fusiform cells of the stalk and neural lobe of the pituitary gland that are usu. considered to be derived from neuroglial cells

pitu·i·ta \pəˈtüəd·ə, pəˈtyü-; ˌpitəˈwēd·ə, ˌpichəˈwīd·ə\ *n, pl* **pitu·i·tae** \-üəˌtē, -üəˌtī, -wēˌtī, -wīˌtē\ [NL, fr. L, phlegm, nasal mucus — more at PIP] **:** PITUITARY GLAND

¹pi·tu·i·tary \pəˈtüəˌterē, pəˈtyü-, -ri\ *adj* [L *pituitarius*, fr. *pituita* + *-arius* -ary] **1 a** *archaic* **:** MUCOUS **b :** of or relating to the pituitary gland **2 :** of, relating to, or resembling a type of physique that is marked by one or more symptom complexes (as acromegaly) and that is produced by secretory disturbances of the pituitary gland

²pituitary \ˈ"\ *n* -ES **1 :** PITUITARY GLAND **2 :** the cleaned, dried, and powdered posterior lobe of the pituitary gland of cattle that is used in the treatment of uterine atony and hemorrhage, shock, and intestinal paresis

pituitary basophilism *n* [²*pituitary* + *basophil* + *-ism*] **:** CUSHING'S DISEASE

pituitary fossa *n* **:** SELLA TURCICA

pituitary gland *also* **pituitary body** *n* [so called fr. the former belief that it secreted nasal mucus] **:** a small oval reddish gray very vascular endocrine organ attached to the infundibulum of the brain and occupying the sella turcica that is present in all craniate vertebrates and consists essentially of an epithelial anterior lobe derived from a diverticulum of the oral cavity joined by a pars intermedia to a posterior lobe of nervous origin with the several parts being associated with various internal secretions including substances that exert a controlling and regulating influence on other endocrine organs, others concerned with growth and development, and some modifying the contraction of smooth muscle, renal function, and reproduction and directly or indirectly impinging on most basic body functions — called also *hypophysis*; see NEUROHYPOPHYSIS; BRAIN illustration

pituitary membrane *n, archaic* **:** SCHNEIDERIAN MEMBRANE

pi·tu·i·tous \pəˈtüəd·əs, pəˈtyü-, -üətəs\ *adj* [L *pituitosus* phlegmatic, fr. *pituita* nasal mucus, phlegm + *-osus* -ous — more at PIP] **1** *archaic* **:** MUCOUS **2** *archaic* **:** PHLEGMATIC

Pi·tu·i·trin \-üəˌtrən\ *trademark* — used for an aqueous extract of the fresh pituitary gland of cattle

pi·tu·o·phis \pəˈtüəfəs, pəˈtyü-\ *n, cap* [NL, irreg. fr. Gk *pitys* pine tree + *ophis* snake — more at PINE, ANGUIS] **:** a genus of rodent-eating snakes (family Colubridae) comprising the No. American bull snakes

pit·u·ri \ˈpichərē\ *or* **bed·gery** \ˈbejərē\ *also* **pitch·eri** *or* **pitchuri** \ˈpichərē\ *n, pl* **pituris** *or* **bedgeries** [native name in Australia] **1 :** an Australian shrub (*Duboisia hopwoodii*) **2 :** a narcotic drug that is prepared by drying the leaves and twigs of the pituri shrub

pit viper *n* **:** any of various mostly New World highly specialized venomous snakes (as the rattlesnake, copperhead, water moccasin, fer-de-lance) that have a small depression on each side of the head between the eye and the nostril which is lined with sensory epithelium and innervated by branches of the trigeminal nerve, that have hollow perforated fangs usu. folded back in the upper part of the mouth but erected in striking, and that constitute the family Crotalidae

pitwood \ˈ=,=\ *n* **:** timber used chiefly for roof props in mines

pitwork \ˈ=,=\ *n* **:** pumping apparatus used in a mine shaft

pitwright \ˈ=,=\ *n* **:** one that does carpentry in and about a mine

¹pity \ˈpid·|ē, -it|, |i\ *n* -ES [ME *pite, pite*, fr. OF *pitez, pitié, pité*, fr. L *pietat-, pietas* piety, compassion, fr. *pie-* (fr. *pius* pious) + *-tat-, -tas* -ty — more at PIOUS] **1** *archaic* **:** MERCY, CLEMENCY ⟨saw that his judge was inclining to mercy, and he renewed his appeals for ~ —J.H.Shorthouse⟩ **2 a** (1) **:** sympathetic heartfelt sorrow for one that is suffering physically or mentally or that is otherwise distressed or unhappy (as through misfortune, difficulties) **:** COMPASSION, COMMISERATION ⟨felt the deepest ~ for the prisoners⟩ (2) **:** the capacity to feel such sorrow ⟨was habitually hardhearted and without ~⟩ **b :** a somewhat disdainful or contemptuous feeling of regret over the condition of one viewed by the speaker as in some way inferior or reprehensible ⟨leaves us less with a sense of repugnance . . . than with a sense of ~ for the man who could think of nothing better —T.S.Eliot⟩ **3 :** a cause of regret **:** a condition or circumstance that is to be regretted ⟨what a ~ that you didn't get here sooner⟩ ⟨it's a ~ that we can't be friends⟩ **syn** see SYMPATHY — **for pity's sake** — used typically to express surprise, indignation, annoyance, or entreaty ⟨*for pity's sake*, what are you doing here⟩ ⟨please don't fail me, *for pity's sake*⟩ — **have pity** *or* **take pity 1 :** to be merciful **:** show mercy ⟨*have pity* on us: for we have sinned —Bar 3: 2 (DV)⟩ **2 :** to become less severe **:** RELENT ⟨begged him not to be so harsh, but he *had no pity* upon them⟩

²pity \ˈ"\ *vb* -ED/-ING/-ES *vt* **1** *chiefly dial* **:** to cause to feel pity **:** move to pity ⟨it would ~ one's heart to observe the change —William Whiston⟩ **2 :** to feel pity for ⟨*pitied* them in their distress⟩ ⟨whom everybody *pities* because his daughter has disgraced him —Edmund Wilson⟩ ~ *vi* **:** to feel pity **:** have pity ⟨will not ~, nor spare, nor have mercy —Jer 13:14 (AV)⟩

pity·ing *adj* **:** expressing or feeling pity ⟨let him perish without a ~ thought of ours wasted upon him —Thomas De Quincey⟩ — **pity·ing·ly** *adv*

pit·y·lus \ˈpid·ələs\ *n, cap* [NL, fr. Gk *pitys* pine tree — more at PINE] **:** a genus of Central and So. American grosbeaks related to the cardinal bird but lacking a crest

pit·yo·cam·pa \ˌpid·ēōˈkampə\ *n* -s [L, fr. Gk *pityokampē*, fr. *pitys* pine tree + *-o-* + *kampē* caterpillar — more at -CAMPA] **:** the larva of a European processionary moth (*Cnethocampa pityocampa*) found on pine or fir trees

pit·y·ri·as·ic \ˌpid·əˌrīˈasik\ *adj* [ISV *pityrias-* (fr. NL *pityriasis*) + *-ic*] **:** of or affected with pityriasis

pit·y·ri·a·sis \ˌpid·əˈrīəsəs\ *n, pl* **pityria·ses** \-īəˌsēz\ [NL, fr. Gk, fr. *pityron* bran, scurf, dandruff + *-iasis*, n. suffix — more at -IASIS] **1 :** one of several skin diseases marked by the formation and desquamation of branny scales **2 :** a disease of domestic animals marked by dry epithelial scales or scurf due to alteration of the function of the sebaceous glands and possibly associated with digestive disorders

pit·y·ro·gram·ma \ˌpid·ərōˈgramə\ *n, cap* [NL, fr. Gk *pityron* bran + *gramma* letter — more at GRAM] **:** a small genus of terrestrial tropical ferns (family Polypodiaceae) that have fronds with a powdery yellowish or white undersurface and linear dorsal sori — see GOLD FERN, SILVER FERN

piu \ˈpyü, pēˈü\ *adv* [It *più*, fr. L *plus* — more at PLUS] **:** MORE — used to qualify another adverb or adjective that is used as a direction in music ⟨~ allegro⟩

piu·piu \ˈpēüˌpēü\ *n, pl* **piupiu** *or* **piupius** [Maori] **:** a short kilt made usu. of strips of flax and worn by Maoris for native dances and on ceremonial occasions

pi·u·ri *also* **pi·ou·ry** \pēˈ(y)ürē\ *n, pl* **piuris** *also* **pioury** [Hindi *piyūrī*; akin to Skt *pīta* yellow] **:** INDIAN YELLOW 1a

pi·ute \ˈpīˌ(y)üt, =ˈ=\ *usu cap, var of* PAIUTE

piute trout *n, usu cap P* **:** a brilliantly colored cutthroat trout native to a few small upland streams in eastern California near Lake Tahoe

pi·va \ˈpēvə\ *n, pl* **pivas** \-vəz\ *or* **pi·ve** \-(ˌ)vā\ [It, fr. (assumed) VL *pipa* pipe — more at PIPE] **1 :** an ancient Italian bagpipe or shawm **2 :** a 16th-century Italian dance form in quick triple meter

pi·val·ic acid \(ˈ)pīˌvalik-\ *n* [ISV *pinacolin* + *valeric* + *-ic*] **:** a crystalline acid $(CH_3)_3CCOOH$ isomeric with normal valeric acid and formed by oxidation of pinacolone; trimethylacetic acid

¹piv·ot \ˈpivət, *usu* -əd·+V\ *n* -s [F, fr. OF, fr. an assumed word akin to OProv *pua* tooth of a flax comb, fr. (assumed) VL *puga*, perh. fr. L *pungere* to prick — more at PUNGENT] **1 a :** a usu. short shaft or pin whose pointed end forms the fulcrum and center on which something turns about, oscillates, or balances: (1) **:** the pin of a hinge (2) **:** an axle on which a wheel turns (3) **:** the shaft on which the hands of a timepiece turn (4) **:** the pin on which a pointer (as of a compass) is balanced and turns **b** (1) **:** the pointed end of such a shaft or pin (2) **:** a real or apparent point or position on which something turns about, oscillates, or balances **c :** a usu. metallic pin holding an artificial crown to the root of a tooth **2 :** something that has an important role, position, or influence **:** something on which the activity, development, or course of something else depends or to which it is closely linked **:** a central or indispensable individual, element, or factor **:** something having a major or central role, function, or effect: as **a** (1) **:** the man or group of men around whom a body of troops wheels (as in changing front or direction or making a tactical maneuver) (2) **:** a key player or position (as on a football team) (3) **:** an individual on whom the condition or future of something depends ⟨elected a man that proved to be the ~ of the organization's success⟩ ⟨as if the ~ and pole of his life . . . was his mother —D.H.Lawrence⟩ **b :** an essential or vital component part (as of a piece of machinery) **c :** a central or crucial fact or condition about which a whole series of consequences revolves **:** central point **:** HEART, CRUX ⟨the ~ of the matter is whether they will or will not agree⟩ ⟨the ~ of the controversy —J.A. Todd⟩ **d :** a central point of attraction or interest ⟨public occasions when he himself is the ~ of attention —Stewart Cockburn⟩ **3 :** the action of turning about, oscillating, or balancing on or as if on a pivot: as **a :** the turn of the body from left to right on the backswing and from right to left on the downswing in hitting a golf ball **b :** the action in the game of basketball of stepping once or more than once in any direction with the same foot while keeping the other foot at its point of contact with the floor **c :** a dance step in which the dancer rotates on one foot and completes the step by shifting the weight to the other foot

²pivot \"\ *vb* -ED/-ING/-S [F *pivoter*, fr. *pivot*] *vi* **1 :** to turn about or oscillate or balance on or as if on a pivot ⟨the guns are mounted in such a way as to ~ easily⟩ ⟨the future ~*s* on what is done today⟩ **2 :** to change card partners at fixed intervals so as to have each player as a partner at some time during a partnership game **~** *vt* **1 :** to provide with, mount on, or attach by means of a pivot ⟨a ~*ed* mechanism⟩ **2 :** to cause to pivot ⟨~ himself sharply about on his heel⟩ ⟨~*ing* their life on some such particular motive —D.J.Unger⟩

³pivot \"\ *adj* [¹*pivot*] **1 :** turning on or as if on a pivot ⟨a ~ gun⟩ **:** equipped with a pivot ⟨~ gearing⟩ **2 :** PIVOTAL ⟨a ~ figure in the controversy⟩ ⟨a ~ man on a football team⟩

¹piv·ot·al \ˈpivəd·ᵊl, -ətᵊl\ *adj* [ISV ¹*pivot* + *-al*] **1 a :** of or relating to a pivot ⟨correct ~ dimensions⟩ **b :** constituting or functioning as a pivot ⟨a ~ shaft⟩ **2 :** that vitally affects the activity or development or course of something **:** central in importance, function, influence, or effect ⟨holds a ~ position⟩ ⟨one of the great ~ points of the war —S.L.A.Marshall⟩

²pivotal \"\ *n* -S **:** something that is pivotal

pivotal fault *n* **:** ROTARY FAULT

piv·ot·al·ly \-ᵊlē, -ᵊli\ *adv* **1 :** in a pivotal manner **:** as a pivot ⟨functioning ~⟩ **2 a :** by means of a pivot ⟨can be turned ~⟩ **b :** on a pivot ⟨is mounted ~⟩

pivot bearing *n* **:** STEP BEARING

pivot bridge *n* **:** a drawbridge in which one span turns about a central vertical axis

piv·ot·er \-d·ə(r), -tə-\ *n* -S [¹*pivot* + *-er*] **:** a worker who grinds pivots to the proper shape for timepiece balance staffs

pivot joint *n* **:** an anatomical articulation that consists of a bony pivot in a ring of bone and ligament (as that of the odontoid and atlas) and that permits rotatory movement only

pivot of maneuver : a part of an attacking force that attempts to immobilize an enemy while another part strikes a decisive blow

pivot pin *n* **1 :** KNUCKLE PIN **2 :** KINGBOLT

pivots *pl of* PIVOT, *pres 3d sing of* PIVOT

pivot stand *n* **:** a part of a gun mount which is secured to the platform and in which the pivot is enclosed — called also *pedestal*

pivot tooth *or* **pivot crown** *n* **:** an artificial crown attached to the root of a tooth by a pivot

¹pix *var of* PYX

²pix *pl of* PIC

¹pix·ie *or* **pixy** \ˈpiksē, -si\ *n, pl* **pixies** [origin unknown] **1 a :** FAIRY; *specif* **:** a cheerful sprite like an elf typically conceived of as playing mischievous tricks on householders or as dancing in the moonlight to the sound of crickets or frogs **b :** a playfully mischievous individual **:** PRANKSTER, RASCAL, ROGUE **2 :** a skullcap or a small hat with a pointed crown worn by women and girls

pixie 2

²pixie *or* **pixy** \"\ *adj* **:** playfully mischievous **:** given to or marked by pranks **:** PUCKISH, IMPISH, ROGUISH ⟨~ humor⟩ ⟨a ~ grin⟩ — **pixi·ness** \-nə̇s\ *n* -ES

³pixie *or* **pixy** *var of* PYXIE

pix·ie·ish *or* **pixy·ish** \-ēish, -i·ish\ *adj* [¹*pixie*, *pixy* + *-ish*] **:** PIXIE

pix·i·lat·ed *also* **pix·il·lat·ed** \ˈpiksə,lād·əd, -ātəd\ *adj* [¹*pixie* + *-lated* (as in the past part. of many verbs ending in *-late*, as *emulate*, *formulate*, etc.)] **1 a** (1) **:** mentally somewhat unbalanced **:** TOUCHED, DAFFY (2) **:** not altogether clear or coherent **:** BEWILDERED, CONFUSED ⟨have formed a rather ~ image of his country —Frederic Morton⟩ (3) **:** habitually in or seeming to be in a mild stupor or daze **:** BEMUSED ⟨has been ~ of late, never quite aware of what is going on⟩ (4) **:** under or seeming to be under a magic spell **:** ENCHANTED, BEWITCHED ⟨a countryside with an unreal ~ charm⟩ **b :** amusingly or fancifully unconventional **:** WHIMSICAL ⟨a ~ comedy⟩ **c :** playfully mischievous **:** PUCKISH, PRANKISH, PIXIE ⟨~ leprechauns⟩ ⟨~ humor⟩ **2 :** INTOXICATED, DRUNK ⟨pretty well ~ by the fourth drink⟩

pix·i·la·tion *also* **pix·il·la·tion** \,==ˈlāshən\ *n* -S **:** the quality or state of being pixilated

pixy stool *n* **1** *dial Eng* **:** TOADSTOOL **2** *dial Eng* **:** MUSHROOM

piyyut *or* **piyut** \pēˈyüt\ *n, pl* **piyyu·tim** *or* **piyu·tim** \(,)pē-yüˈtēm\ [LHeb *piyyūṭ* poem, poetry, fr. *piyyēṭ* to write poetry, fr. Gk *poiētēs* poet — more at POET] **:** a religious poem recited in the synagogue in addition to the traditional liturgy on Jewish festivals, special Sabbaths or ceremonial occasions

pize \ˈpīz\ *n* -S [origin unknown] *chiefly dial* **:** CURSE, MALEDICTION

piz·za \ˈpētsə\ *or* **pizza pie** *n* -S [It *pizza*, fr. (assumed) VL *picea* (perh. intended as trans. of MGk *pitta* cake, pie, fr. Gk, pitch), fr. L, fem. of *piceus* of pitch, fr. *pic-*, *pix* pitch + *-eus* -eous — more at PITCH] **:** a usu. large open pie made typically of thinly rolled bread dough spread with a spiced mixture (as of tomatoes, cheese, ground meat, garlic, oil) and baked

piz·ze·ria \,pētsəˈrēə *sometimes* ,pit-\ *n* -S [It, fr. *pizza* + *-eria* -ery] **:** an establishment (as a bakery, restaurant, shop) where pizzas are made and sold

¹piz·zi·ca·to \ˈpitsə̇ˈkäd·(,)ō, -sē;-, -kȧ|, |(,)tō\ *adv (or adj)* [It, past part. of *pizzicare* to pinch, pluck (strings), play pizzicato, fr. *pizzare* to sting, prick, pinch] **:** by means of plucking by the fingers instead of bowing **:** PLUCKED — used as a direction in music ⟨marked the opening part of the movement ~⟩ ⟨a brief section is played ~⟩ ⟨a series of ~ notes⟩

²pizzicato \"\ *n, pl* **pizzica·ti** \|d·(,)ē, |(,)tē\ *or* **pizzicatos :** a note or passage played by plucking strings

piz·zle \ˈpizəl\ *n* -S [prob. fr. Flem *pezel*; akin to LG *pesel*, *peisel* pizzle, MD *pese* sinew, bowstring, MLG *pēse* bowstring] **1 :** the penis of an animal (as a bull) **2 :** a whip made of a bull's pizzle

PJ *abbr* **1** police justice **2** presiding judge **3** probate judge

pj's \(ˈ)pē;jāz\ *n pl* [by abbr.] **:** PAJAMAS

pk *abbr* **1** pack **2** park **3** peak **4** peck

PK *abbr* psychokinesis

pK \(ˈ)pē;kā\ *symbol* the negative logarithm of the dissociation constant K or −log K that serves as a convenient measure of the strength of an acid ⟨K for acetic acid is 0.000018 or 1.8×10^{-5} from which *pK* is (5 − 0.25) or 4.75⟩ — compare PH

pkg *abbr* package

pkge *abbr* package

pkmr *abbr* packmaster

pkr *abbr* packer

pkt *abbr* **1** packet **2** pocket

pkwy *abbr* parkway

pky *abbr* pecky

pl *abbr* **1** pile **2** place **3** plain **4** plaster **5** plate **6** platoon **7** plural

PL *abbr* **1** partial loss **2** perception of light **3** phase line **4** poet laureate **5** private line **6** profit and loss **7** public law **8** public liability

plac- *or* **placo-** *comb form* [Gk *plak-*, *plako-* flat surface, tablet, fr. *plak-*, *plax* — more at PLEASE] **:** tablet **:** flat plate ⟨*plac*odont⟩ ⟨*placo*derm⟩

placa·bil·i·ty \,plakəˈbiləd·ē, -ətē, -i *also* ,plāk-\ *n* -ES [L *placabilitat-*, *placabilitas*, fr. *placabilis* + *-itat-*, *-itas* -ity] **:** the quality or state of being placable

placa·ble \ˈplakəbəl *also* ˈplāk-\ *adj* [ME, fr. L *placabilis*, fr. *placare* to soothe, placate + *-abilis* -able — more at PLEASE] **1 :** of a tolerant nature **:** easily soothed or satisfied **:** PEACEABLE, TRACTABLE ⟨indignities which might move even a ~ nature to fierce . . . resentment —T.B.Macaulay⟩ ⟨young people are almost always ~ —Samuel Butler †1902⟩ **2** *archaic* **:** characterized by serenity **:** PEACEFUL, QUIET ⟨the wind blew in momentary gusts, and then became more ~ —Nathaniel Hawthorne⟩ — **placa·bly** \-blē, -li\ *adv*

placa·ble·ness *n* -ES *archaic* **:** PLACABILITY

¹plac·ard \ˈpla,kärd, -kȧd, -,kə(r)d\ *n* -S [ME *placquart*, fr. MF, fr. *plaquier* to plate, plaster — more at PLAQUE] **1** *archaic* **:** a piece of armor plate (as a breastplate or backplate) ⟨pulled down his visor and clasped it to the ~ —Horace Smith⟩; *specif* **:** PLACCATE 1 **2 a** *obs* **:** an authorization or permit bearing an official seal **b** *archaic* **:** an official edict or proclamation **3 a :** a notice or announcement printed on one side of a sheet for posting in a public place **:** POSTER, SIGN ⟨every travel agent . . . has some sort of ~ in his window advertising one of the sightseeing tourist itineraries —Richard Joseph⟩ **b :** a small card or metal plaque ⟨a ~ on the door says "no admittance"⟩ ⟨leather belts with plain brass ~*s* or initialed —*New Yorker*⟩ ⟨a ~ on the fuselage lists performance data⟩

²placard \"\ *vt* -ED/-ING/-S **1 a :** to cover with or as if with posters ⟨~ a fence with advertisements⟩ ⟨ancestors whose portraits snootily ~ the . . . walls —Wyndham Lewis⟩ **b :** to post in a public place ⟨pictures of the occasion were . . . ~*ed* throughout eastern Europe —*Time*⟩ **2 :** to label or announce by or as if by posting **:** call attention to ⟨has never been my habit to ~ my movements like a court circular —John Buchan⟩ ⟨crimes ~*ed* by the evening papers —L.P.Smith⟩

pla·cate \ˈplā,kāt *also* ˈpla,- *sometimes* =ˈ= *or* plə'-, *usu* -kād-+V\ *vb* -ED/-ING/-S [L *placatus*, past part. of *placare* to placate — more at PLEASE] *vt* **:** to soothe or mollify esp. by making concessions **:** APPEASE ⟨the pressure . . . put on them to ~ public opinion —A.L.Funk⟩ **~** *vi* **:** to be conciliatory or help to reconcile differences ⟨flattering and *placating* and yet yielding no ground —F. Tennyson Jesse⟩ **syn** see PACIFY

pla·cat·er \-kād·ə(r)\ *n* -S [*placate* + *-er*] **:** one that placates; *esp* **:** MEDIATOR

pla·cat·ing·ly *adv* [fr. *placating*, gerund of *placate* + *-ly*] **:** in a placating manner

pla·ca·tion \plāˈkāshən, plaˈ-\ *n* -S [MF, fr. L *placation-*, *placatio*, fr. *placatus* (past part. of *placare* to placate) + *-ion-*, *-io* -ion — more at PLEASE] **:** an act of soothing or propitiating

pla·ca·tive \ˈplākəd·iv, ˈplak-\ *adj* [*placate* + *-ive*] **:** PLACATORY

pla·ca·to·ry \ˈplākə,tōrē, ˈplak-, -tȯr-, -ri\ *adj* [LL *placatorius*, fr. *placatus* + *-orius* -ory] **:** tending or intended to placate **:** CONCILIATORY

plac·cate \ˈplakət\ *n* -S [prob. alter. of *placard*] **1** *archaic* **:** an extra piece of armor worn over the lower part of the breast **2** *archaic* **:** a jacket or doublet lined with steel splints **:** BRIGANDINE

¹place \ˈplās\ *n* -S [ME, fr. MF, open space in a city, space, locality, fr. L *platea* broad street, fr. Gk *plateia* (*hodos*), fr. fem. of *platys* broad, flat; akin to Skt *pṛthu* broad, L *planta* sole of the foot] **1 a :** a way for admission or transit ⟨calling "~! ~!" to clear the way for their master —G.P.R. James⟩ ⟨~ is made for it on his class schedule —H.W.Dodds⟩ **b :** physical environment **:** SPACE ⟨all are strangers, rootless in ~ or time —T.H.White b.1915⟩ **c :** physical surroundings **:** ATMOSPHERE ⟨the feeling for ~ was in him like the feeling for a personality —R.L.Cook⟩ **2 a :** an indefinite region or expanse **:** AREA ⟨visit the far ~*s* of the earth⟩ ⟨small supplies of foreign ore . . . brought from ~*s* like No. Africa —Samuel Van Valkenburg & Ellsworth Huntington⟩ ⟨schools continued to spring up all over the ~ —Bernard Kalb⟩ **b** (1) **:** a building or locality used for a special purpose ⟨~ of amusement⟩ ⟨~ of worship⟩ ⟨a secondhand car ~ —Robert Westerby⟩; *specif* **:** eating place ⟨found a little Italian ~ with an eighty-five cent dinner —Mary McCarthy⟩ (2) *archaic* **:** an assembly point ⟨posted upon a parade, or ~ of arms —Daniel Defoe⟩ **c** *archaic* **:** the three-dimensional compass of a material object ⟨in the world I fill up a ~ which may be better supplied when I have made it empty —Shak.⟩ **d :** WHERE ⟨wished he could go some ~ and run a lunchroom —*Time*⟩ ⟨has no ~ to turn for allies —M.H.Rubin⟩ ⟨the magic rests, more than any ~ else, in a sense of ambiguity —M.F. Harrington⟩ **3 a :** a particular region or center of population ⟨Britain is an ideal ~ to tour by bus —Richard Joseph⟩ ⟨Denver, Salt Lake City, and hundreds of other ~*s*, large and small —*Motor Transportation in the West*⟩ **b :** an individual dwelling or estate **:** HOUSE, HOMESTEAD ⟨invited them to his ~ for the evening⟩ ⟨our twenty-eight-acre ~ on the edge of Baltimore —A.W.Turnbull⟩; *specif* **:** FARM ⟨a few ~*s* were . . . harrowing summer fallow —H.L.Davis⟩ **c :** a fortified military post ⟨to effect the release of . . . Americans held there, a group of American settlers in Texas attacked the ~ —E.C.Barker⟩ **d :** ¹SCENE 3 **4 a :** a particular portion of a surface **:** specific locality **:** SPOT ⟨worn ~ in a rug⟩ ⟨sore ~ on the back of the hand⟩ ⟨steep ~ in the road⟩ ⟨this is the right ~ —M.R.Werner⟩ **b** (1) **:** a passage in a piece of writing ⟨in ~*s* he might have been a little bolder in dealing with the . . . text —G.R.Crone⟩ (2) *obs* **:** a selected passage **:** TEXT ⟨comparing two ~*s* of Scripture —Thomas Fuller⟩ (3) **:** the point at which a reader left off ⟨dropped the book and lost her ~⟩ **c** *obs* **:** LOCUS CLASSICUS **5 a** (1) **:** relative position in the social scale **:** degree of prestige ⟨put the country people in their ~, and with a few tactful rebuffs . . . checked any undue familiarity —Lord Dunsany⟩ ⟨color drew a line around several million people who were thereby condemned to permanent inferiority of ~ —Oscar Handlin⟩ (2) **:** relative position of merit in any context **:** degree of importance ⟨the ~ of health in the life of the individual —Marie Theresa⟩ ⟨decisions which have brought our science and our engineering to their present ~ —H.S.Truman⟩ **b :** a step in a sequence ⟨in the first ~, the house . . . is haunted —Charles Lee⟩ ⟨from eleventh ~ . . . the city rose to seventh —*Amer. Guide Series: Md.*⟩ **c** (1) **:** one of the leading positions at the finish of a horse race — used of 1st or usu. 2d in the U.S. and of 1st, 2d, or 3d in England (2) **:** a leading position at the conclusion of any competition entitling the contestant to a prize or special recognition ⟨1st ~ in the dog show⟩ ⟨won a 2d ~ in the handcrafts division⟩ **6 a** (1) **:** a proper or designated niche ⟨the junior college has a ~ to fill in this emergency —L.L.Medsker⟩ ⟨scientific names are the surest way of indicating to biologists of various nations the ~*s* of insects . . . in the natural world —E.S. McCartney⟩ ⟨whenever an artist has a reasoned conception of any musical work as a unit . . . tempos naturally fall into ~ —Virgil Thomson⟩ (2) **:** a normal or suitable environment ⟨a frontier plantation . . . was no ~ to educate a boy —T.J. Wertenbaker⟩ ⟨turns to individual personality as the logical ~ to study cultural integration —H.J.Muller⟩ **b :** a fitting moment or appropriate point in a discussion ⟨this is not the ~ to discuss compensation —Robert Moses⟩ **c** *obs* **:** a reasonable basis **:** GROUND ⟨there is no ~ of doubting but that it was the very same —Henry Hammond⟩ **7 a** (1) **:** an available seat or accommodation ⟨~*s* were booked for him in the boat train —John Buchan⟩ ⟨has a 2-*place* sailplane⟩ ⟨Eton's 1100 nonscholarship ~*s* are booked solid until 1971 —*Newsweek*⟩; *esp* **:** a seat at a table ⟨a man drinking a glass of orange juice was sitting at the table . . . and two ~*s* farther along a second man was munching a piece of toast —Hamilton Basso⟩ (2) **:** PLACE SETTING ⟨seldom . . . sat down to a meal without laying one or two extra ~*s* for friends —David Garnett⟩ **b :** an empty or vacated position ⟨coffeehouses supplied in some measure the ~ of a journal —T.B.Macaulay⟩ ⟨lost his bike and had to get another in its ~⟩ **c :** a position dictated by circumstance ⟨put yourself in my ~⟩ ⟨in a tight ~ they still call on the North Wind —Alfred Duggan⟩ **8 :** the position of a figure in relation to others of a row or series; *esp* **:** the position of a digit within a numeral ⟨12 is a two ~ number⟩ ⟨in 316 the figure 1 is in the tens ~⟩ **9 a :** remunerative employment **:** JOB ⟨rather starve than take a ~ as a servant —Ellen Glasgow⟩ ⟨was offered a ~ on the *Times* to do political reporting —*Irish Digest*⟩; *esp* **:** public office ⟨no judge of a high court . . . views the function of his ~ so narrowly —B.N.Cardozo⟩ **b** (1) **:** a position of responsibility ⟨a policy imposed by a corrupt use of pension and ~ —J.H.Plumb⟩ (2) **:** a duty accompanying a position of responsibility ⟨it was not his ~ to make the final decision⟩ **c :** the prestige accorded to one in an influential position **:** RANK, STATUS ⟨would on no terms either collaborate with . . . or yield ~ to him —*Times Lit. Supp.*⟩ ⟨spent the remainder of her life . . . in an endless quest for preferment and ~ —*Time*⟩ **10 a :** a public square **:** PLAZA **b :** a short street or court; *often* **:** DEAD END — **in place 1** *obs* **:** on hand **:** PRESENT ⟨beholding worldly wights *in place*, leave off their work . . . to gaze on them —Edmund Spenser⟩ **2 :** in an original or proper place **:** in situ ⟨a piece of jawbone with the teeth *in place* —R.W. Murray⟩ ⟨kicked up his heels, a kind of shuffle dance *in place* —Eugene Walter⟩ **3 :** in a suitable environment **:** APPROPRIATE ⟨colonnaded mansions that would be more *in place* in Natchez —John Durant⟩ — **in place of** *prep* **:** as a substitute or replacement for **:** instead of ⟨*in place of* dues . . . is asked to make an annual contribution —E.B.Lyman⟩ ⟨a single executive *in place of* the former executive committee —Joseph Schafer⟩ — **out of place 1 :** out of harmony with the surroundings **:** MISPLACED, INCONGRUOUS ⟨a prizefighter feels somewhat *out of place* at a literary tea⟩ ⟨bathing suits look *out of place* in a hotel lobby⟩ **2 :** out of order **:** IMPROPER, INAPPROPRIATE ⟨the expression of his personal political convictions . . . is quite *out of place* and an unwarranted imposition on the reader —Hilary Corke⟩ — **place in the sun :** favorable position or status **:** ADVANTAGE, EMINENCE ⟨the laborer . . . toiling for a *place in the sun* —A.R.Williams⟩ ⟨Italian fiction has found its *place in the sun* —T.G.Bergin⟩ — **upon the place** *obs* **:** on the spot **:** IMMEDIATELY ⟨told him *upon the place*, I would serve his majesty —William Temple⟩

²place \"\ *vb* -ED/-ING/-S *vt* **1 :** to distribute in an orderly manner **:** ARRANGE, DISPOSE, STATION ⟨the furniture has been *placed* for a definite reason —Betty Fisk⟩ ⟨before the artist put any of the black in his picture . . . he *placed* all the principal branches —Ernest Knaufft⟩ ⟨five . . . strategically *placed* seaports —R.S.Thoman⟩ ⟨shows the emperor *placing* and giving orders to his artillery —Tom Wintringham⟩ **2 a :** to put into or as if into a particular position **:** cause to rest or lie **:** SET, FIX ⟨would ~ a finger on the list of figures she was tabulating —Jane Woodfin⟩ ⟨carbide . . . is finely ground and *placed* in electric cyanamide ovens —N.R.Heiden⟩ ⟨waste . . . talent and potential leadership by *placing* higher education beyond their reach —L.M.Chamberlain⟩ ⟨the growing railroad system *placed* increasing demands on iron and coal mines —R.H.Brown⟩ ⟨we have . . . been rather better *placed* than some to weigh the particular criticisms —Barbara Ward⟩ ⟨~ our faith in knowledge —H.I.Poleman⟩ **b :** to present for consideration — used with *before* ⟨the pending debate should be *placed* before a larger audience —Leo Cherne⟩ **c :** to put into a particular condition or state ⟨~ the company in a better financial position⟩ ⟨~ a performer under contract⟩ ⟨the airlines *placed* modern equipment into service —H.G.Armstrong⟩ **d :** to direct accurately to a desired area or previously determined spot ⟨disrupted the defenses with his uncanny ability to ~ the ball —A.J.Daley⟩ ⟨the bombs were *placed* directly upon the assigned target —Tex McCrary & D.E.Scherman⟩ **e :** to cause (the voice) to produce singing or speaking tones that are free and well resonated with reference to the adjustment of the vocal organs and resonance cavities **3 :** to appoint to a position ⟨was made lieutenant colonel and *placed* in command of a company —L.S.Mayo⟩ **4 a :** to find a place for: as (1) **:** to secure employment for ⟨~ the girl as a typist⟩ ⟨aims . . . to ~ all physically handicapped persons in remunerative positions —*Amer. Guide Series: Minn.*⟩ (2) **:** to find a residence for (a homeless child) ⟨boarding out with foster parents is the method to be given first consideration in *placing* a child —*Social Services in Brit.*⟩ **b** (1) **:** to find a publisher for (as a novel) ⟨the manuscript was . . . submitted to a literary agent in New York who was unable to ~ it —Haldeen Braddy⟩ (2) **:** to find a producer for (as a play) **5 a** (1) **:** to assign to a position in an order of progression **:** RANK ⟨of the factors of strategic intelligence . . . geography is often *placed* first —G.B. & Charlotte L. Dyer⟩ ⟨fails to sustain that mysterious quality of life which would ~ it among the real masterpieces of the novel —Carlos Lynes⟩ (2) **:** ESTIMATE ⟨the same area has iron ore reserves *placed* at 1.3 billion metric tons —*Americana Annual*⟩ **b** (1) **:** to assign to a chronological position ⟨the estimated time of burial was *placed* in the early Tintah stage —Meridel Le Sueur⟩ (2) **:** to assign to a category ⟨relatively profuse body hair clearly ~*s* the Caucasoids closest of all living races to the lower primates —Weston La Barre⟩ (3) **:** to recognize by identifying characteristics ⟨listening and *placing* the sounds that break the silence of a winter night —Rose Feld⟩; *specif* **:** to recall in context from a previous association ⟨the man looked familiar but he couldn't ~ him —Willard Robertson⟩ **c** (1) **:** to determine or announce the place of (contestants) in a race ⟨judges must occupy the judges' box . . . and their sole duty shall be to ~ the horses —Dan Parker⟩ (2) **:** to succeed in gaining a position for in a contest or competition ⟨*placed* two men on the . . . Olympic team —*Amer. Guide Series: Conn.*⟩ **6** *archaic* **:** ATTRIBUTE, ASCRIBE ⟨*placed* it all to judicious affection —Jane Austen⟩ **7 a :** to use (money) for the purchase or development of property for financial gain **:** INVEST ⟨~ a million dollars in bonds⟩ ⟨~ half of the capital of the firm in plane production⟩ **b** (1) **:** to give (an order for goods or services) to a supplier ⟨~ an order for a new generator⟩ ⟨~ an order to have the house painted⟩ (2) **:** to give an order for (a service) ⟨~ a telephone call⟩ ⟨~ a bet⟩ ⟨*placed* his insurance with another company⟩ **~** *vi* **1 :** to earn a top spot in a competition ⟨only the first three men or women to ~ in each event are honored —*Collier's Yr. Bk.*⟩ ⟨*placed* third in the bridge tournament⟩; *specif* **:** to come in second in a horse race ⟨bet on each horse to win, ~, or show⟩ **2 :** to propel an object accurately to a predetermined spot ⟨you cannot ~ to a yard by means of shoulder and arm energy alone —*Manchester Guardian Weekly*⟩ **syn** see SET

place·able \ˈplāsəbəl\ *adj* **:** capable of being placed

place bet *n* **1 :** a bet on a horse to finish no worse than second in a race **2 :** a bet that the shooter in a crap game will make his point or that a particular point will appear before a 7

pla·ce·bo *n* -S **1** \pläˈchā(,)bō\ [ME, fr. L, I shall please, 1st sing. fut. indic. of *placēre* to please; from the initial word of the first antiphon, Ps 114:9 (Vulgate) — more at PLEASE] **:** the vespers for the dead in the Roman Catholic Church **2** \pləˈsē(-\ [L, I shall please] **a :** an inert medicament or preparation given for its psychological effect esp. to satisfy the patient or to act as a control in an experimental series **b :** something tending to soothe or gratify ⟨the ~ of illusions —Martin Gumpert⟩

place brick *n* **:** a brick not fully burned — called also *sandal brick*; compare SAMEL

place card *n* **:** a card that marks a place reserved for occupancy ⟨airlines have in each seat pocket a *place card* to be left in the seat when leaving it temporarily⟩; *specif* **:** a small usu. decorated card inscribed with the name of a guest and set at the place he is to occupy at the dinner table

place hitter *n* **:** a baseball player who is able to hit a pitched ball to a chosen part of the playing field

placeholder \ˈ=,==\ *n* **:** a symbol in a mathematical or logical expression that may be replaced by the name of any element of a set — compare VARIABLE 2a

place isomerism *n* **:** POSITION ISOMERISM

¹place–kick \ˈ=,=\ *also* **placement kick** *n* **:** the kicking of a ball (as in football) placed or held in a stationary position on the ground — compare DROPKICK, PUNT

²place–kick \"\ *vt* **1 :** to kick (a ball) from a stationary position **2 :** to score by means of a place-kick ⟨*place-kicked* the extra point⟩ **~** *vi* **:** to make a place-kick ⟨ability to *place-kick* is a great asset to a fullback⟩

place·less \ˈplāslə̇s\ *adj* **:** lacking a fixed location — **place·less·ly** *adv*

placemaking \ˈ=,==\ *n* **:** the successive shifting of two bells in change ringing to make places

place·man \ˈplāsmən\ *n, pl* **placemen** *chiefly Brit* **:** a political appointee — often used disparagingly

place mat *n* **:** a small usu. rectangular table mat on which a place setting is laid

place·ment \ˈplāsmənt\ *n* -S [²*place* + *-ment*] **:** an act or instance of placing: as **a :** an orderly distribution or arrangement ⟨strategic ~ of artillery⟩ ⟨~ of lights for taking indoor portraits⟩ ⟨reasons for the ~ of material in a course —A.J. Flynn⟩ **b** (1) **:** the position of a ball set on the ground for a place-kick (2) **:** PLACE-KICK **c :** the accurate propulsion of a ball to a predetermined spot; *esp* **:** a tennis shot that is unreturnable by an opponent **d :** the art or practice of producing free and well-resonated voice tones ⟨the natural quality of a singing voice is enhanced by good ~⟩ **e :** the assignment of a student to a class or course on the basis of his ability or proficiency in the subject **f** (1) **:** the assignment of a worker to a suitable job ⟨service activities pay . . . dividends in better teacher ~ —R.H.Eckelberry⟩ (2) **:** the business of establishing contact between applicants and prospective employers

⟨~ is the province of the appointment bureau⟩ **g :** a transfer of custody (as of a minor or a defective) ⟨the effects of foster home ~ upon children's performances in intelligence tests —R.K.Merton⟩ ⟨to prevent the exploitation of a patient, the precise terms of each ~ are written out in detail —Ruth & Edward Brecher⟩ **h :** INVESTMENT ⟨foreign investors . . . have uniformly shown a preference for fixed-return ~s —R.E. Cameron⟩

placement test *n* **:** a test usu. given to a student entering an educational institution to determine his knowledge or proficiency in various subjects so that he may be assigned to appropriate courses or classes

place–money \ˈ⸗,⸗⸗\ *n* **:** money paid to those backing a horse to place in a race

place–name \ˈ⸗,⸗\ *n* **:** the name of a geographical locality (as of a city or town) ⟨little trace . . . of the Celts survived except in *place-names* —*Bavarian Palatinate*⟩

pla·cen·ta \plə'sentə\ *n, pl* **placentas** \-təz\ *also* **placen·tae** \-n,tē\ [NL, fr. L, flat cake, fr. Gk *plakount-, plakous,* fr. *plak-, plax* flat surface — more at PLEASE] **1 a :** the vascular organ in mammals except monotremes and marsupials that unites the fetus to the maternal uterus and intermediates the metabolic exchanges of the developing individual through a more or less intimate association of chorionic and usu. allantoic and of uterine mucosal tissues by which the fetal and maternal vascular systems are brought into intimate relation permitting exchange of materials by diffusion but without direct contact between fetal and maternal blood and which typically involves the interlocking of fingerlike or frondose vascular chorionic villi with corresponding modified areas of uterine mucosa — compare AFTERBIRTH **b :** any of various analogous organs in other animals (as some viviparous sharks and free-swimming tunicates) for the attachment of the young to the mother and its nourishment by her **2 :** a sporangium-bearing surface: as **a :** the part of the carpel of a seed plant bearing ovules — see PLACENTATION **b :** the point on a fern or fern ally leaf or sporophyll at which sporangia develop

¹pla·cen·tal \-tᵊl\ *adj* [NL *placentalis,* fr. *placenta* + L *-alis* -al] **1 :** of, relating to, having, or occurring by means of a placenta **2 :** of or relating to placental mammals

²placental \"\ *n* -s [NL *Placentalia*] **:** a placental mammal

placental barrier *n* **:** a semipermeable membrane made up of placental tissues and limiting the character and amount of material exchanged between mother and fetus

plac·en·ta·lia \,plasᵊn·'tālēə\ [NL, fr. *placenta* + *-alia*] *syn of* EUTHERIA

¹plac·en·ta·li·an \¦⸗⸗¦tālēən\ *adj* [NL *Placentalia* + E *-an*] **:** of or relating to the placental mammals

²placentalian \"\ *n* -s **:** PLACENTAL

placental sign *n* **:** a slight bloody discharge from the vagina coinciding with implantation of an embryo in the uterus

placenta pre·via \-ˈprēvēə\ *n, pl* **placentae previ·ae** \-vē,ē\ [NL, previous placenta] **:** an abnormal implantation of the placenta at or near the internal opening of the uterine cervix so that it tends to precede the child at birth usu. causing severe maternal hemorrhage

plac·en·tary \ˈplasᵊn,terē, plə'sentərē\ *adj* [NL *placentarius,* fr. *placenta* + L *-arius* -ary] **:** PLACENTAL

plac·en·tate \plə'sen,tāt\ *adj* [NL *placentatus,* fr. *placenta* + L *-atus* -ate] **:** having a placenta

plac·en·ta·tion \,plasᵊn·'tāshən\ *n* -s [NL *placenta* + E *-ation*] **1 a :** the development of the placenta and attachment of the fetus to the uterus during pregnancy **b :** the morphological type of a placenta ⟨discoidal ~⟩ **2 :** the arrangement or mode of attachment of the placentas and ovules in a plant ovary

plac·en·tif·er·ous \¦⸗⸗¦tif(ə)rəs\ *adj* [NL *placenta* + E *-iferous*] *archaic* **:** having a placenta

plac·en·ti·tis \,⸗⸗'tīd·əs\ *n, pl* **placentit·i·des** \-tid·ə,dēz\ [NL, fr. *placenta* + *-itis*] **:** inflammation of the placenta

plac·en·tog·ra·phy \-'tägrəfē\ *n* -ES [NL *placenta* + ISV *-o-* + *-graphy*] **:** roentgenographic visualization of the placenta after injection of an opaque medium

pla·cen·toid \plə'sen,tȯid\ *adj* [NL *placenta* + ISV *-oid*] **:** resembling a placenta

plac·en·to·ma \,plasᵊn·'tōmə\ *n, pl* **placentomas** \-məz\ *or* **placentoma·ta** \-məd·ə\ [NL, fr. *placenta* + *-oma*] **:** a tumor developed from retained placental remnants

plac·en·tome \ˈplasᵊn·,tōm\ *n* -s [NL *placenta* + E *-ome*] **:** the placenta and its adjuncts **:** the whole group of fetal and maternal tissues that are involved in placentation

¹plac·er \ˈplāsə(r)\ *n* -s [²*place* + *-er*] **:** one that places: as **a :** one that deposits or arranges ⟨bookbinder's ~⟩ ⟨enamel kiln ~⟩ **b :** one of the winners in a competition ⟨fifth ~ in the . . . Miss America competition —*Time*⟩

²plac·er \ˈplasə(r), -laas-\ *n* -s *often attrib* [Sp, fr. Catal, submarine plain, fr. *plaza* place, fr. L *platea* broad street — more at PLACE] **:** an alluvial, lacustrine, marine, eolian, or glacial deposit (as of sand or gravel) containing particles of gold or other valuable mineral — compare LODE

³placer \"\ *vb* -ED/-ING/-S *vt* **:** to extract (minerals) from sand or gravel by washing ~ *vi* **:** to work at placer mining

placer mining *n* **:** the process of extracting minerals from a placer esp. by washing, dredging, or hydraulic mining

places *pl of* PLACE, *pres 3d sing of* PLACE

place setting *n* **1 :** an arbitrary selection of dishes and flatware constituting a table service for one person **2 :** a basic purchasing unit of matched pieces usu. consisting of a dinner plate, salad or dessert plate, bread-and-butter plate, and cup and saucer in dinnerware and of a knife, fork, salad fork, soup spoon, teaspoon, and butter spreader in flatware

place setting 2 arranged on a place mat

pla·cet \ˈplāsət\ *n* -s [L, it pleases, 3d sing. pres. indic. of *placēre* to please — more at PLEASE] **:** an expression of approval or vote of assent; *specif* **:** EXEQUATUR 2

place theory *n* **:** a theory in physiology: the perception of pitch results from the ability of sounds of different pitch to stimulate different areas of the organ of Corti — compare TELEPHONE THEORY

plac·id \ˈplasəd, -laas-\ *adj* [L *placidus,* fr. *placēre* to please — more at PLEASE] **1 a :** marked by serenity **:** SMOOTH, TRANQUIL ⟨ribbon of sand . . . between the angry sea and the ~ bay —D.J.Lynde⟩ ⟨the ~ atmosphere of easy living —Louis Fischer⟩ **b :** free of interruption or disturbance **:** QUIET, UNEVENTFUL ⟨young men now arriving . . . at the age of forty have never known ~ times as adults —J.D.Hicks⟩ **2 a :** of a peaceable nature **:** MEEK, MILD ⟨a ~ lamb lying fast asleep —Elinor Wylie⟩ ⟨the relatively ~ crime of horse lifting —W.B.Bracke⟩ **b :** characterized by unruffled composure **:** CALM, PHLEGMATIC ⟨that ~ force . . . in many farmers —Guy McCrone⟩ ⟨so ~, so resigned that if the earth had opened at his feet he would have felt neither surprise nor fear —Herman Smith⟩; *specif* **:** COMPLACENT ⟨an air of ~ sufficiency which was the first hint . . . of the man's overweening, unmeasurable conceit —Joseph Conrad⟩ **syn** see CALM

pla·ci·da·men·te \plä,chēdə'mentē\ *adv* [It, fr. *placido* calm, quiet (fr. L *placidus*) + *-mente,* adv. suffix] **:** PLACIDLY, CALMLY — used as a direction in music

pla·cid·i·ty \plaˈsidəd-ē, plə'-, -ətē, -i\ *n* -ES [L *placiditas* fr. *placidus* placid + *-itat-, -itas* -ity] **:** the quality or state of being placid **:** COMPOSURE, SERENITY

plac·id·ly *adv* **:** in a placid manner **:** CALMLY, PHLEGMATICALLY, COMPLACENTLY

plac·id·ness *n* -ES [*placid* + *-ness*] *archaic* **:** PLACIDITY

placing–out \ˈ⸗⸗¦⸗\ *n* [*placing* (fr. gerund of ²*place*) + *out*] **:** a system of caring for dependent children by placing them in private families instead of putting them in institutions (as orphanages)

plac·it \ˈplasət\ *n* -s [ML *placitum*] *archaic* **:** DECREE, PETITION

plac·i·ta co·ro·nae \¦plasəd·əkəˈrō,nē\ *n pl* [ML] **:** PLEAS OF THE CROWN

plac·i·tum \ˈplasəd·əm\ *n, pl* **placi·ta** \-d·ə\ [ML, fr. L *placitum* opinion, decision, decree — more at PLEA] *archaic* **:** a judicial proceeding or decree

plack \ˈplak\ *n* -s [ME *plakke,* fr. MD *placke* a coin — more at PLAQUE] **1 :** a small billon coin of Scotland issued from James III to James VI; *also* **:** a corresponding unit of value ⟨half-*plack* coin⟩ **2** *archaic* **:** a paltry bit **:** TRIFLE

plack·et \ˈplakət, *usu* -əd·+V\ *n* -s [origin unknown] **1** *obs* **:** PUDENDUM **2 a** *or* **placket–hole :** a finished slit in a garment (as at the top of a skirt or petticoat making it easy to put on); *esp* **:** one giving access to an inner pocket **b** *archaic* **:** a pocket esp. in a woman's skirt ⟨in a ~ at her side is an old enameled watch —Leigh Hunt⟩ **c :** a finished opening usu. in a seam or bisecting an edge (as of a slipcover) assuring a snug fit when fastened **3** *archaic* **a :** PETTICOAT **b :** WOMAN ⟨was that brave heart made to pant for a ~ —John Fletcher⟩

plack·less \ˈplakləs\ *adj* [*plack* + *-less*] *chiefly Scot* **:** PENNILESS

placo- — see PLAC-

plac·ob·del·la \,pla,käb'delə\ *n, cap* [NL, fr. *plac-* + *-bdella*] **:** a common and widely distributed genus of freshwater leeches (family Glossiphoniidae) parasitic on aquatic vertebrates

plac·ode \ˈpla,kōd\ *n* -s [ISV *plac-* + *-ode*] **:** a platelike thickening of embryonic ectoderm from which a definitive structure develops ⟨ear ~⟩ ⟨olfactory ~⟩ — see LENS PLACODE

¹plac·o·derm \ˈplakə,dərm\ *adj* [*plac-* + Gk *derma* skin — more at DERM-] **1** *also* **plac·o·der·ma·tous** \¦⸗⸗¦dərməd·əs\ **:** having a cell wall of two or rarely more pieces and vertical pores in the wall — used of desmids of the family Desmidiaceae; distinguished from *saccoderm* **2** *or* **plac·o·der·mal** \¦⸗⸗¦dərməl\ [NL *Placodermi*] **:** of or relating to the Placodermi

²placoderm \"\ *n* -s [NL *Placodermi*] **:** a fish or fossil of the class Placodermi

plac·o·der·mi \,⸗⸗'dər,mī\ *n pl, cap* [NL, fr. *plac-* + Gk *derma* skin — more at DERM-] **:** a class of extinct fishes with an armor of large bony plates and primitive jaw structures that has been taken as equivalent to Antiarcha plus Arthrodira but is now usu. extended to include also the Acanthodii, Cycliae, and minor groups — compare CHONDRICHTHYES — **plac·o·der·moid** \¦⸗⸗¦dər,mȯid\ *adj*

¹plac·o·dont \ˈplakə,dänt\ *adj* [NL *Placodont-, Placodus* or *Placodontia*] **:** of or relating to the genus *Placodus* or suborder Placodontia

²placodont \"\ *n* -s **:** a reptile of the genus *Placodus* or suborder Placodontia

plac·o·don·tia \,⸗⸗'dänch(ē)ə\ *n pl, cap* [NL, fr. *Placodont-, Placodus,* genus of reptiles + *-ia*] **:** a suborder of Sauropterygia that is sometimes regarded as a separate order and that comprises armored Triassic reptiles resembling the turtles in many respects — see PLACODUS — **plac·o·don·tian** \¦⸗⸗¦dänch(ē)ən\ *adj*

plac·o·dus \ˈplakədəs\ *n, cap* [NL, fr. *plac-* + *-odus*] **:** a genus (the type of the family Placodontidae of the suborder Placodontia) comprising rather large extinct reptiles from the marine Trias of central Europe that have short broad bodies and broad flat molar teeth on the palate and dentary bones apparently adapted to crushing mollusks

plac·o·ga·noi·dei \,plakōgə'nōidē,ī\ [NL, fr. *plac-* + *Ganoidei*] *syn of* PLACODERMI

¹plac·oid \ˈpla,kȯid\ *adj* [*plac-* + *-oid*] **1 :** consisting of a basal plate of dentine of dermal origin embedded in the skin and bearing a projecting point or spine tipped with enamel — used of an elasmobranch fish scale; compare SHAGREEN **2** [NL *Placoidei*] **:** of or relating to the Placoidei

²placoid \"\ *n* -s [NL *Placoidei*] **:** a fish of the group Placoidei

pla·coi·dal \plaˈkȯidᵊl\ *or* **pla·coi·de·an** \-dēən\ *adj* [NL *Placoidei* + E *-al, -an*] **:** PLACOID 2

pla·coi·dei \-dē,ī\ *n pl, cap* [NL, fr. *plac-* + *-oidei*] *in former classifications* **:** a group of fishes with placoid scales equivalent or nearly so to Chondrichthyes and sometimes including the cyclostomes

placque *var of* PLAQUE

plac·u·la \ˈplakyələ\ *n, pl* **placulas** \-yələz\ *or* **placu·lae** \-yə,lē\ [NL, fr. *plac-* + L *-ula*] **:** the flattened blastula of urochordates or a similar oligochaete embryo

pla·cu·na \plaˈkyünə\ *n, cap* [NL, fr. Gk *plak-, plax* flat surface] **:** a genus of large flattened tropical bivalve mollusks (order Filibranchia) with extremely thin nearly transparent shells that is related to *Anomia* but sometimes made the type of a separate family — see WINDOWPANE OYSTER

plad·dy \ˈpladi\ *var of* PLAIDIE

pla·fond \plə'fän(d)\ *n* -s [F, fr. MF *platfonds,* fr. *plat* flat + *fonds* bottom, fr. L *fundus* — more at PLATE, BOTTOM] **1 :** a ceiling usu. of elaborate design formed by the underside of a floor **2 :** a French variant of auction bridge that is similar to contract bridge

pla·gal \ˈplāgəl\ *adj* [ML *plagalis,* fr. *plaga* plagal mode (prob. back-formation fr. *plagius* plagal, fr. MGk *plagios,* fr. Gk, oblique, sideways, crooked, fr. *plagos* side) + L *-alis* -al; akin to Gk *pelagos* surface of the sea, sea, L *plaga* covering, net, region — more at FLAKE] **1** *of an ecclesiastical mode or melody* **:** having the keynote on the 4th scale step — distinguished from *authentic* **2** *of a cadence* **:** having a concluding chord sequence consisting of the subdominant chord and its resolution to the tonic — see CADENCE illustration

plage \ˈpläzh\ *n* -s [F, beach, fr. It *piaggia,* fr. LL *plagia* beach, shore, fr. Gk *plagios* oblique, sideways — more at PLAGAL] **1 :** the beach of a seaside resort **2 :** a bright region on the sun seen in the light of calcium or hydrogen and often associated with sunspots — compare FLOCCULUS

plagi- *or* **plagio-** *comb form* [Gk, fr. *plagios* — more at PLAGAL] **:** oblique **:** aslant ⟨*Plagianthus*⟩ ⟨*plagiotropic*⟩

pla·gi·an·thus \,plājē'an(t)thəs\ *n, cap* [NL, fr. *plagi-* + *-anthus*] **:** a genus of Australasian shrubs and trees (family Malvaceae) having small flowers without bracteoles — see RIBBON TREE

pla·gia·rism \ˈplājə,rizəm *sometimes* -jēə,-\ *n* -s [*plagiary* + *-ism*] **1 :** an act or instance of plagiarizing ⟨virtually a free adaptation . . . and on the face of it a straight-out ~ —Antony Alpers⟩ **2 :** a plagiarized item ⟨his book is full of ~s⟩

pla·gia·rist \-rəst\ *n* -s [*plagiary* + *-ist*] **:** one who plagiarizes **:** one guilty of literary or artistic theft — **pla·gia·ris·tic** \¦⸗(⸗)⸗¦ristik, -tēk\ *adj*

pla·gia·rize \ˈ⸗(⸗)ə,rīz\ *vb* -ED/-ING/-S — *see -ize in Explan Notes* [*plagiary* + *-ize*] *vt* **:** to steal and pass off as one's own (the ideas or words of another) **:** use (a created production) without crediting the source ⟨a learned book of his . . . had been coolly *plagiarized* and issued in short version —*Times Lit. Supp.*⟩ ~ *vi* **:** to commit literary theft **:** present as new and original an idea or product derived from an existing source

pla·gia·ry \ˈplājē,erē, -jər-, -ri\ *n* -ES [L *plagiarius* kidnapper, plagiarist, fr. *plagium* hunting net (fr. *plaga* net) + *-arius* -ary — more at PLAGAL] **1** *obs* **:** KIDNAPPER **2** *archaic* **:** PLAGIARIST **3 :** PLAGIARISM ⟨not alone in his condemnation of literary imitation and ~ —N.F.Adkins⟩ ⟨famous *plagiaries* —*Univ. of Minn. Press Cat.*⟩

plagii *pl of* PLAGIUM

pla·gi·o·ceph·a·ly \,plājēō'sefəlē\ *n* -ES [*plagi-* + *-cephaly*] **:** a malformation of the head marked by obliquity of the main axis of the skull and usu. caused by closure of half of the coronal suture

pla·gi·o·chi·la \,plājēō'kīlə\ *n* [NL, fr. *plagi-* + Gk *cheilos* lip — more at GILL] **1** *cap* **:** a genus of mostly tropical leafy liverworts (family Jungermanniaceae) having succubous toothed or lobed leaves **2** -s **:** any liverwort of the genus *Plagiochila*

pla·gi·o·clase \ˈplājēə,klās\ *n* -s [ISV *plagi-* + *-clase;* orig. formed as G *plagioklas*] **:** a triclinic feldspar; *esp* **:** one of the calcium-sodium series comprising anorthite and albite and the intermediate bytownite, labradorite, andesine, and oligoclase — see MOONSTONE

pla·gi·o·cli·nal \¦plājēō¦klīnᵊl\ *adj* [*plagi-* + *-clinal*] **:** oblique to the general strike of rocks in the surrounding area

pla·gi·o·dont \ˈplājēə,dänt\ *adj* [ISV *plagi-* + *-odont*] **:** having the palatal teeth set obliquely or in two convergent series — used of a snake

pla·gi·o·graph \ˈplājēə,graf, -räf\ *n* [*plagi-* + *-graph*] **:** a pantograph that may be set at any angle to the drawing to be copied — called also *skew pantograph*

pla·gi·o·he·dral \,plājēō¦hēdrəl\ *or* **pla·gi·he·dral** \-jə¦-\ *adj* [*plagi-* + *-hedral*] **:** having an oblique spiral arrangement of faces **:** GYROIDAL ⟨~ quartz crystals⟩; *specif* **:** being a group of the isometric system characterized by 13 axes of symmetry but no center or planes

pla·gi·o·nite \ˈplājēə,nīt\ *n* -s [G *plagionit,* fr. Gk *plagion,* neut. of *plagios* oblique + G *-it* -ite — more at PLAGAL] **:** a mineral $Pb_5Sb_8S_{17}$ consisting of a lead antimony sulfide of a blackish lead-gray color and metallic luster (sp. gr. 5.4)

pla·gio·patagium \¦plājēō+\ *n, pl* **plagiopatagia** [NL, fr. *plagi-* + *patagium*] **:** an extensile membrane connecting the forelimb and hind limb (as of a bat or flying squirrel) and used when spread in flying or gliding

pla·gi·or·chi·idae \,plājēȯ(r)'kīə,dē\ *n pl, cap* [NL, fr. *Plagiorchis,* type genus + *-idae*] **:** a large family of digenetic trematodes that produce xiphidiocercaria — see PLAGIORCHIS

pla·gi·or·chis \,plājē'ȯrkəs\ *n, cap* [NL, fr. *plagi-* + Gk *orchis* testicle — more at ORCHIS] **:** a large genus (the type of the family Plagiorchiidae) of digenetic trematodes including parasites of the oviducts or intestine of various wild and domesticated birds and of the intestine of mammals

pla·gi·o·rhyn·chus \,plājēō'riŋkəs\ *n, cap* [NL, fr. *plagi-* + *-rhynchus*] **:** a genus of acanthocephalan worms parasitic in the intestine of domestic fowls and other birds

pla·gi·o·sto·ma·ta \,plājēō'stōməd·ə\ *also* **pla·gi·os·to·ma** \,plājē'ästəmə\ [NL, fr. *plagi-* + *-stomata, -stoma*] *syn of* PLAGIOSTOMI

pla·gi·o·stom·a·tous \¦plājēō¦stäməd·əs, -tōm-\ *or* **pla·gi·os·to·mous** \¦plājē¦ästəməs\ *adj* [*plagiostomatous* fr. NL *Plagiostomata* + E *-ous; plagiostomous* fr. NL *Plagiostomi* + E *-ous*] **:** PLAGIOSTOME

¹pla·gi·o·stome \ˈplājēə,stōm\ *adj* [NL *Plagiostomi*] **:** of or relating to the Plagiostomi

²plagiostome \"\ *n* -s **:** a fish of the group Plagiostomi

pla·gi·os·to·mi \,plājē'ästə,mī\ *n pl, cap* [NL, fr. *plagi-* + *-stomi*] *in some esp former classifications* **:** a group of fishes more or less exactly equivalent to Chondrichthyes or more restrictedly an order including the existing sharks and rays as distinguished from the chimaeras and the extinct primitive groups Pleuropterygii and Ichthyotomi — compare SELACHII

pla·gi·o·sto·mia \,plājēō'stōmēə\ [NL, fr. *Plagiostomi* + *-ia*] *syn of* PLAGIOSTOMI

pla·gi·o·trop·ic \¦plājēō·¦träpik\ *adj* [ISV *plagi-* + *-tropic;* orig. formed as G *plagiotropisch*] **:** having the longer axis inclined away from the vertical ⟨~ roots and lateral branches⟩ — compare ORTHOTROPIC — **pla·gi·o·trop·i·cal·ly** \-pək(ə)lē\ *adv*

pla·gi·ot·ro·pism \,plājē'ä·trə,pizəm\ *n* [ISV *plagi-* + *-tropism;* orig. formed as G *plagiotropismus*] **:** the quality or state of being or tending to be plagiotropic

pla·gi·ot·ro·pous \¦⸗⸗¦ä·trəpəs\ *adj* [ISV *plagi-* + *-tropous*] **:** PLAGIOTROPIC

pla·gi·ot·ro·py \,⸗⸗'ä·trəpē\ *n* -ES [ISV *plagi-* + *-tropy*] **:** PLAGIOTROPISM

pla·gi·um \ˈplājēəm\ *n, pl* **pla·gia** \-ēə\ [LL, prob. back-formation fr. L *plagiarius* kidnapper — more at PLAGIARY] *civil law* **:** KIDNAPPING

¹plague \ˈplāg *chiefly dial* ˈpleg\ *n* -s *often attrib* [ME *plage,* fr. MF, fr. LL *plaga,* fr. L, blow, wound, misfortune — more at PLAINT] **1 a :** a disastrous evil or affliction **:** CALAMITY, SCOURGE ⟨rebel regiments were a ~ upon the country, robbing, burning and committing every conceivable outrage —Kenneth Roberts⟩ ⟨the numbers racket and the dope ~ thrive —Herman Kogan⟩ — often used interjectionally to express annoyance or impatience ⟨a ~ o' both your houses —Shak.⟩ ⟨~ take it, what's keeping that boy⟩ **b :** a destructively numerous influx or multiplication of a noxious animal **:** INFESTATION ⟨~ of swarming locusts⟩ ⟨tremendous ~s of rats have devastated the rice fields —J.F.Embree & W.L. Thomas⟩ ⟨a ~ of leafworms destroyed a large part of the crops —*Amer. Guide Series: Texas*⟩ **2 a :** an epidemic disease causing a high rate of mortality **:** PESTILENCE ⟨a ~ of cholera⟩ ⟨the great ~ diseases . . . are rapidly approaching extinction —A.C.Morrison⟩ **b :** an acute contagious febrile disease caused by a bacterium (*Pasteurella pestis*), occurring in several forms, and usu. transmitted (as bubonic plague) from rats to man by the bite of infected fleas or directly (as pneumonic plague) from person to person — compare BLACK DEATH **3 a :** a cause of irritation or distress **:** NUISANCE, HARASSMENT ⟨having . . . been her husband's ~ because of the violence of her temper —W.B.Yeats⟩ ⟨wild dogs are a . . . ~ to squatters —Rachel Henning⟩ **b :** a sudden unwelcome increase or prevalence **:** OUTBREAK ⟨a ~ of broken dishes in the cafeteria —Stuart Chase⟩ ⟨a ~ of hot-dog stands and cheap amusements —*Amer. Guide Series: N.Y. City*⟩ ⟨a ~ of burglaries⟩

²plague \"\ *vt* -ED/-ING/-S **1 a :** to afflict with evil or calamity **:** SCOURGE, TORMENT ⟨mass poverty and unemployment continued to ~ the nation —F.L.Schuman⟩ **b :** to infect with a plague ⟨diseases that ~ mankind —*Wall Street Jour.*⟩ ⟨a disease that ~s watermelons —Jane Nickerson⟩ **2 a** (1) **:** to cause worry or distress to **:** TROUBLE, HARASS ⟨debts . . . *plagued* her after her husband's death —Ruth P. Randall⟩ ⟨back trouble . . . had been *plaguing* him increasingly in recent weeks —A.C.Spectorsky⟩ ⟨outmoded notions about race . . . still ~ this nation —Bradford Smith⟩ (2) **:** to slow up or put at a disadvantage **:** HAMPER, HANDICAP ⟨construction of the power plant . . . has been *plagued* by bad weather —*Annual Report of Ill. Power Co.*⟩ ⟨a series of injuries *plagued* the team⟩ ⟨the traffic detour . . . which has *plagued* motorists —*Springfield (Mass.) Daily News*⟩ **:** BURDEN ⟨the dance of today is *plagued* with exotic . . . mannerisms —John Martin⟩ **b :** to disturb or annoy persistently **:** BOTHER, NAG ⟨she talked, she wrote, she *plagued* him —Elizabeth Janeway⟩ ⟨something . . . every congressman is continually *plagued* to do by his constituents —*Christian Science Monitor*⟩ **syn** see WORRY

plagu·ed \ˈplegəd\ *adj* [fr. past part. of ²*plague*] *dial* **:** TROUBLESOME, IRRITATING

plague grasshopper *or* **plague locust** *n* **:** a grasshopper that may rapidly build up vast destructive swarms from a small localized population; *esp* **:** either of two Australian grasshoppers (*Chortoicetes terminifera* or *Austroicetes cruciata*)

plague·some \ˈplāgsəm\ *adj* [¹*plague* + *-some*] **1 :** TROUBLESOME **2 :** PESTILENTIAL

plague spot *n* **1 :** a hemorrhagic spot on the skin **2 :** a locality afflicted with a plague or regarded as a source of contamination

¹pla·guey *or* **plaguy** \ˈplāgē, -gi *chiefly dial* ˈpleg-\ *adj* [¹*plague* + *-y*] *chiefly dial* **1 :** of, relating to, or afflicted with a plague ⟨the ~ fever came aboard —*Ballad Book*⟩ **2 :** causing irritation or annoyance **:** TROUBLESOME ⟨a ~ newfangled safety rail —*Architect & Building News*⟩ ⟨no . . . ~ choice to be made —C.E.Montague⟩ — often used as an intensive ⟨no wonder the ~ fools can't talk English —J.C.Lincoln⟩

²plaguey *or* **plaguy** \"\ *adv* **:** to a troublesome extent **:** EXCESSIVELY ⟨it's so ~ cold —Max Peacock⟩

pla·gui·ly \-gəlē\ *adv* [¹*plaguey, plaguy* + *-ly*] *archaic* **:** ²PLAGUEY

plag·u·la \ˈplagyələ\ *n, pl* **plagu·lae** \-yə,lē\ [NL, prob. fr. L, curtain, dim. of *plaga* covering — more at PLAGAL] **:** a ventral sclerite in the pedicel of various spiders

plaice *also* **plaise** \ˈplās\ *n, pl* **plaice** *also* **plaise** [ME *plaice, plais,* fr. OF *plais, plaiz,* fr. LL *platensis,* prob. fr. Gk *platys* broad, flat — more at PLACE] **1 a :** a European flounder (*Pleuronectes platessa*) that grows to a weight of 8 or 10 pounds or more **b :** any of various American flatfishes; *esp* **:** SUMMER FLOUNDER **2** *dial Eng* **:** ¹FLUKE 2

¹plaid \ˈplad, -aa(ə)d\ *n* -s [ScGael *plaide*] **1 :** a rectangular length of tartan worn over the left shoulder by men and women as part of the Scottish national costume ⟨a ~ . . . which served him as a garment by day and a blanket by night —*Scots Mag.*⟩ **2 a :** a twilled woolen fabric with a tartan pattern used in making plaids **b :** a fabric with a woven or printed pattern of tartan or an imitation of tartan **3 a :** TARTAN 1 **b :** a woven or printed pattern of unevenly spaced stripes repeated in sequence and crossing each other at right angles ⟨the ~s of these shirts never saw the Scottish shore⟩

²plaid \"\ *adj* **:** having a multicolored cross-barred pattern ⟨~ vest⟩ ⟨~ blanket⟩

plaid·ed \-dəd\ *adj* [¹*plaid* + *-ed*] **1 :** wearing a plaid ⟨~ Highlander⟩ **2 :** PLAID

plaid·en \ˈplad³n\ *chiefly Scot var of* PLAIDING

plaid·ie \ˈpladi\ *n* -S [¹*plaid* + *-ie*] *Scot* **:** PLAID 1

plaid·ing \ˈpladiŋ\ *n* -S [¹*plaid* + *-ing*] **:** PLAID 2

plaid neuk *n, Scot* **:** a pocket formed by the sewed-up corner of a plaid

plai·do·yer \ˌpledwəˈyā\ *n* -S [F, fr. OF *plaidoyer* to plead, fr. *plaid* plea — more at PLEA] **:** an address, plea, or argument made esp. by an advocate in court

plaik \ˈplāk\ *var of* PLAYOCK

¹plain \ˈplān\ *vb* -ED/-ING/-S [ME *plainen, pleynen*, fr. MF *plaindre*, fr. L *plangere* to lament — more at PLAINT] *vi* **1** *archaic* **:** COMPLAIN; *specif* **:** to make a complaint against someone **2** *archaic* **:** to make a doleful sound **:** MOURN ⟨wind went . . . ~*ing* over the barren moor —Mary Linskill⟩ ~ *vt, archaic* **:** BEWAIL, BEMOAN

²plain \"\ *n* -S *archaic* **:** PLAINT

³plain \"\ *n* -S [ME *plain, pleyn*, fr. OF *plain*, fr. L *planum*, fr. neut. of *planus* level, flat] **1 a :** an extensive area of land having few inequalities of surface, being usu. fairly flat but sometimes having a considerable slope, and usu. being at low elevation though some (as the Great Plains of the U.S.) are as much as three or four thousand feet above sea level **:** a very widespread tract of level or rolling treeless country with a vegetation predominantly of short perennial grasses and annual forbs — often used in pl. ⟨from the ecological viewpoint there is no essential distinction between . . . prairie and ~*s* —F.E.Clements & V.E.Shelford⟩ **b :** a smooth flat or gently sloping part of an ocean floor ⟨the ~ of the ocean floor may be broken by long deep troughs —C.M. Nevin⟩ **c :** a broad unbroken expanse ⟨looking far over the mystic ~ of the waves —William Black⟩ ⟨a flat featureless snow ~ —G. de Q. Robin⟩ **2** *archaic* **a :** a field of battle **:** BATTLEGROUND ⟨lead forth my soldiers to the ~ —Shak.⟩ **b :** ⁴PLANE **3 :** something that is free from artifice, ornament, or extraneous matter ⟨nature and art, the ~ and the precious —J.H.Hagstrum⟩; *specif* **:** a usu. wool or cotton fabric of plain weave and solid color ⟨fine ~*s* . . . usually are finer yarn, higher thread-count cloths than print cloths —John Hoye⟩

⁴plain \"\ *adj* -ER/-EST [ME *plain, pleyn*, fr. MF *plain*, fr. L *planus* level, flat, plain — more at FLOOR] **1** *obs* **a :** FLAT ⟨his back is ~ to his tail —Edward Topsell⟩ **b :** PLANE **2 a** *archaic* **:** having an even surface **:** LEVEL, SMOOTH ⟨make the rougher places ~ —Catherine Winkworth⟩ **b** *of a merino sheep* **:** lacking folds or wrinkles ⟨a *plain*-bodied ewe⟩ **3 a :** lacking ornament **:** UNDECORATED ⟨a New England country church is traditionally a rather ~ building with a thin spire —Robert Holland⟩ **b** *heraldry* **:** not charged or engrailed **4 :** free of extraneous matter **:** PURE, UNADULTERATED ⟨takes his whiskey with ~ water⟩ ⟨the ~ colors . . . give such freshness to her work —*Yankee*⟩; *specif* **:** free of bubbles or other imperfections — used of glass **5 a** *archaic* **:** free of obstacles **:** OPEN ⟨give . . . battle in the ~ sea —John Speed⟩ **b :** free of impediments to view **:** UNOBSTRUCTED ⟨pastured out on the moors in ~ sight of us —Martha Kean⟩ **6 a** (1) **:** evident to the mind or senses **:** distinctly recognizable **:** OBVIOUS ⟨stared at him coldly, hatred and contempt very ~ in her face —Irwin Shaw⟩ ⟨the facts are undoubted; they are ~ matters of history —E.A.Freeman⟩ ⟨she's wild about him — it's as ~ as the nose on your face⟩ (2) **:** easily understood **:** CLEAR ⟨makes it . . . ~ that events develop quite independently of the people they affect —C.H.Rickword⟩ ⟨what, in ~ words, is the morality of culture —J.C.Powys⟩ **b :** characterized by candor **:** FRANK, BLUNT ⟨to be ~ with you, I will sing none —Izaak Walton⟩ ⟨an impressive honesty and a good deal of ~ speaking —Alan Bullock⟩ **c :** devoid of elaboration or subterfuge **:** BALD, UNDISGUISED ⟨made no attempt to harangue his listeners but stuck to the ~ facts⟩ ⟨~ anger seized me —Arthur Grimble⟩ **7 a :** belonging to the great majority of mankind **:** COMMON ⟨the ~ people everywhere . . . wish to live in peace with one another —F.D.Roosevelt⟩ **b** (1) **:** lacking special distinction **:** of a routine nature **:** ORDINARY ⟨writes not for musical specialists . . . but for the ~ operagoer —Ernest Newman⟩ ⟨~ common sense tells us that . . . gold and silver are practically useless except for what they will procure —W.P.Webb⟩ (2) **:** not being trump ⟨lost only one trick in each of the ~ suits —C.H.Goren⟩ **c :** characterized by lack of vanity or affectation ⟨just ~ folks — homespun, guileless and democratic —Thomas Pyles⟩ ⟨as ~ as an old shoe in dress, mannerisms, and the way he runs his business —*Time*⟩ **d :** avoiding waste or extravagance **:** FRUGAL ⟨every cent of tax money had to be put to some good ~ use —Dorothy C. Fisher⟩ **e :** of or relating to expressions used by the Quakers ⟨the use of *thee* and *thy* is characteristic of the ~ language⟩ **8 :** characterized by simplicity **:** UNCOMPLICATED: as **a** *of musical harmony* **:** using only essential chord tones ⟨the harmonic underpinning is a little ~ —Virgil Thomson⟩ **b :** devoid of strong seasoning or exotic ingredients ⟨~ home cooking⟩ **c** *of cloth* (1) **:** made in plain weave (2) **:** having no pattern **d** *of paper or board* (1) **:** made throughout of one grade of stock (2) **:** UNCOATED **9 a :** unremarkable either for physical beauty or ugliness **:** lacking allure **:** HOMELY ⟨a ~ woman with a face as hardy and simple and serviceable as the house —Rebecca West⟩ **b** *of livestock* **:** COARSE, INFERIOR ⟨a boar with a ~ head⟩

syn HOMELY, SIMPLE, UNPRETENTIOUS: PLAIN stresses lack of anything likely to attract attention — lack of ornament, complexity, extraneous matter, or strongly marked characteristics ⟨had no eccentricity even to take him out of the common run; he was just a good, dull, honest, *plain* man —W. S.Maugham⟩ ⟨a *plain* two-story frame house⟩ — and may suggest elegance ⟨his brown stockings . . . were of a fine texture; his shoes and buckles, too, though *plain*, were trim —Charles Dickens⟩ or frugality ⟨a *plain* skirt of serviceable gray flannel⟩ With reference to personal appearance it suggests lack of positive characteristics, contrasting with *beautiful* but implying no positive ugliness ⟨was not a *plain* woman, and she might have been very pretty still —Ellen Glasgow⟩ In reference to houses, furniture, food, and other elements of domesticity, HOMELY sometimes suggests *homey* and may indicate comfortable informality without ostentation ⟨his secluded wife ever smiling and cheerful, his little comfortable lodgings, snug meals, and *homely* evenings, had all the charms of novelty and secrecy —W.M.Thackeray⟩ It may connote warmth and simplicity ⟨a book-learned language, wholly remote from anything personal, native, or *homely* —Willa Cather⟩ With reference to appearance HOMELY in American but not usu. in British usage often falls between *plain* and *ugly* ⟨she was certainly not bad-looking now and she could never have been so *homely* as she imagined —Edmund Wilson⟩ SIMPLE may occasionally differ slightly from PLAIN in implying choice rather than compulsive circumstance ⟨what was then called the *simple* life . . . is recognizable as the austere luxury of a very cultivated poet —Agnes Repplier⟩ ⟨a monk of Lindisfarne, so *simple* and lowly in temper that he traveled on foot on his long mission journeys —J.R.Green⟩ UNPRETENTIOUS, stressing lack of vanity or affectation, may praise a person but depreciate a possession ⟨an *unpretentious* family doctor without the specialist's curt loftiness⟩ ⟨an *unpretentious* and battered old car⟩ **syn** see in addition EVIDENT, FRANK, LEVEL

⁵plain \"\ *vt* -ED/-ING/-S [ME *plainen*, fr. ⁴*plain*] **1** *obs* **:** PLANE ⟨the pavement thus laid is to be ~*ed* and polished —Philemon Holland⟩ **2** *of glass* **:** to free from bubbles or other imperfections **:** REFINE

⁶plain \"\ *adv* [⁴*plain*] **:** in a plain manner **:** without obscurity or ambiguity **:** CLEARLY, SIMPLY ⟨preached that it was just ~ wrong for some people, by tricks and wiles, to get a stranglehold on business —F.L.Allen⟩ ⟨the tiny snap as he closed the book came ~ to the colonel's ears —A.B.Mayse⟩

⁷plain \"\ *adv* [partly fr. ME *plein, playne* entire, complete, fr. MF *plein* full, fr. L *plenus*; partly fr. ⁶*plain* — more at FULL] *chiefly dial* **:** ENTIRELY, ABSOLUTELY ⟨the house was plumb ~ deserted, as anybody could see —Helen Eustis⟩

plain base *adj* [⁴*plain*] *of a bullet* **:** being without a gascheck

plain bob *n* **:** a method of ringing changes in which the treble alone has a plain hunt

plainchant \ˈ≈,≈\ *n* [F *plain-chant*, lit., plain song, trans. of ML *cantus planus*] **:** PLAINSONG

plain chart *n* **:** a nautical chart laid down on a Mercator projection

plain clothes *n* **:** unofficial clothes **:** the dress of an ordinary citizen ⟨man waiting for him was in *plain clothes* —Nancy Rutledge⟩ — opposed to *uniform*

plainclothes \ˈ≈¦≈\ *adj* [*plain clothes*] **:** not in uniform ⟨was directed to a ~ recruiting sergeant —Nigel Dennis⟩

plain·clothes·man \(ˈ)≈ˈ≈mən, -ˌman, -ˌmaa(ə)n\ *n, pl* **plainclothesmen :** a policeman who wears civilian clothes while on duty **:** DETECTIVE

plain component *or* **plain sequence** *n* **:** the sequence of letters in a substitution alphabet that identifies the plaintext letters — compare ALPHABET 1j

plain concrete *n* **:** concrete containing no steel reinforcing bars or wire or containing not more than two tenths of one percent of reinforcing

plain condensed milk *n* **:** EVAPORATED MILK — used esp. of the bulk commercial product as distinguished from the canned pasteurized consumer product

plain counterpoint *n* **:** STRICT COUNTERPOINT

plain dealing *adj* [⁶*plain*] **:** STRAIGHTFORWARD ⟨a *plain dealing* honest man —M.G.J. de Crèvecoeur⟩

plained *past of* PLAIN

¹plainer *comparative of* PLAIN

²plainer *n* [⁵*plain* + *-er*] *obs* **:** PLANER

plainest *superlative of* PLAIN

plain–hearted *adj* [⁴*plain* + *hearted*] **:** SINCERE, ARTLESS

plain hunt *n* [⁴*plain*] **:** a course followed by a single bell through a series of changes in change ringing in which the bell works from first or lead position to last place and back up again

plain hunting *n* **:** change ringing in which each bell has a plain hunt — see CHANGE RINGING illustration

plaining *n* -S [fr. gerund of ⁵*plain*] **:** FINING 1b

plain·ish \ˈplānish\ *adj* [⁴*plain* + *-ish*] **:** rather plain

plain jane *adj, usu cap J* [fr. the name *Jane*] **:** of the usual type **:** ORDINARY, UNREMARKABLE ⟨the *plain Jane* model . . . may be offered with optional trim —*Motor Life*⟩

plain knitting *n* **1 :** GARTER STITCH **2** *or* **plain knit :** STOCKINETTE STITCH

plain–laid \ˈ≈¦≈\ *adj, of a rope* **:** consisting of three, four, or six usu. left-handed strands twisted together in a direction opposite to that of the twist in the strands — compare CABLE-LAID

plain language *n* **:** language unconcealed by any cryptographic process

plain live axle *n* **:** an axle carrying both differential and road wheels

plain·ly *adv* [⁴*plain* + *-ly*] **:** in a plain manner: as **a :** with clarity of perception or comprehension **:** DISTINCTLY, CLEARLY **b :** in unmistakable terms **:** OBVIOUSLY **c :** with candor **:** FRANKLY **d :** SIMPLY, UNPRETENTIOUSLY

plain muscle *n* **:** SMOOTH MUSCLE

plain·ness \ˈplānnəs\ *n* -ES [ME *playnesse, pleynnesse*, partly fr. MF *plainesse, planece* flatness, fr. L *planities* flat surface, fr. *planus* flat, level; partly fr. ME *plain* + *-nesse* -ness — more at FLOOR] **:** the quality or state of being plain

plain of mars *usu cap P&M* [³*plain*] **:** an area in the center of the palm between Upper Mars and Lower Mars that when well developed or crossed with many lines is usu. held by palmists to indicate the presence of sudden temper

plain people *n, usu cap both Ps* [⁴*plain*] **:** members of any of various religious groups (as Mennonites, Dunkers, Amish, or Schwenkfelders) who wear plain clothes, adhere to old customs, and practice in general a simple way of life as a means of carrying out the biblical injunction not to be conformed to this world

¹plains *pres 3d sing of* PLAIN, *pl of* PLAIN

²plains \ˈplānz\ *adj, usu cap* [*Plains* (*Indian*)] **:** of or belonging to No. American Indians of the Great Plains or to their culture characterized by the horse, the tepee, geometric painting on tanned skin, and tailored garments decorated with beads and porcupine quills

plain sail *n* [⁴*plain*] **:** the ordinary working canvas of a sailing ship usu. including topgallant sails, royals, and a flying jib — see SAIL illustration

plain sailing *n* [alter. of *plane sailing*] **1 :** PLANE SAILING 1 **2 :** effortless progress over an unobstructed course **:** easy going

plain–saw \ˈ≈,≈\ *vt* [⁶*plain*] **:** TANGENT-SAW

plains cottonwood *or* **plains poplar** *n* [fr. the Great *Plains*] **:** a large poplar (*Populus sargentii*) chiefly of the Great Plains region of No. America having deeply furrowed gray bark and broadly oval leaves with coarse curved teeth and long points

plainscraft \ˈ≈,≈\ *n* [*plains* (pl. of ³*plain*) + *craft*] **:** knowledge of and skill in applying the lore of a plains environment

plains cree *n, usu cap P&C* **1 :** an Algonquian people formerly inhabiting the southwestern portion of the Cree territory — compare WOOD CREE **2 :** a member of the Plains Cree people

plain seam *n* [⁴*plain*] **:** a seam made with a single line of stitching inside the matched edges of two pieces of material

plain service *n* **:** a worship service unaccompanied with music

plains indian *n, usu cap P&I* [fr. the Great *Plains*, region of central No. America] **:** an Indian of the Algonquian, Athapaskan, Caddo, Kiowa, Siouan, or Uto-Aztecan nomadic peoples formerly inhabiting the Great Plains of central U.S. and Canada — called also *Buffalo Indian*

plains·man \ˈplānzmən\ *n, pl* **plainsmen** [Great *Plains* + *man*] **:** an inhabitant of the plains; *esp* **:** one skilled in plainscraft ⟨army scout and ~ —*Amer. Guide Series: Texas*⟩

plainsong \ˈ≈,≈\ *n* [trans. of ML *cantus planus*] **1 :** the ancient nonmetrical monophonic chant of the church service that is based on the ecclesiastical modes and is used today in some liturgical churches — called also *plainchant*; compare AMBROSIAN CHANT, CANTUS FIRMUS 1, GREGORIAN CHANT **2 a :** a chant melody used as a cantus firmus for contrapuntal treatment **b :** CANTUS FIRMUS 2 — compare PRICK SONG **3 :** a simple air or melody

plainspoken \ˈ≈¦≈≈\ *adj* [⁶*plain* + *spoken*] **:** characterized by candor **:** FRANK, STRAIGHTFORWARD — **plainspokenness** *n* -ES

plain·stanes \ˈplān,stānz\ *n pl* [⁴*plain* + pl. of *stane* stone] *Scot* **:** a flagstone sidewalk

plain stitch *n* [⁴*plain*] **:** KNIT STITCH

plain suit *n* [⁴*plain*] **:** a card suit that is not trump

plains vizcacha *n* [*plains* pl. of ³*plain*] **:** a large colonial vizcacha (*Lagostomus maximus*) of the grassy plains of southern So. America

plaint \ˈplānt\ *n* -S [ME, fr. MF, fr. L *planctus*, fr. *planctus*, past part. of *plangere* to strike, beat, beat one's breast, lament; akin to L *plaga* blow, Gk *plēgē* blow, *plēssein* to strike, OE *flōcan* to applaud, OHG *fluokhōn* to curse] **1 :** an audible expression of or as if of woe **:** LAMENTATION, WAIL ⟨a ~ over a lost doll⟩ ⟨did not squeal, as vulgar pigs do, but uttered a sweet little ~ —Raymond Weeks⟩ **2 a :** a critical protest **:** COMPLAINT ⟨their ~*s* to the papers gave a picture of suffering which impressed contemporary students of the social scene —Roy Lewis & Angus Maude⟩ **b :** a legal written complaint esp. in county-court practice in England

plaintext \ˈ≈,≈\ *n* **:** the plain-language form of an encrypted text or of its elements ⟨PA in the cipher represents TH in the ~⟩ — compare CIPHERTEXT, ³P 4

plaint·ful \ˈplāntfəl\ *adj* [*plaint* + *-ful*] **:** MOURNFUL

plain·tiff \ˈplāntəf\ *n* -S [ME *plaintif*, fr. MF, fr. *plaintif* lamenting, complaining — more at PLAINTIVE] **1 :** one who commences a personal action or lawsuit to obtain a remedy for an injury to his rights — opposed to *defendant*; compare PROSECUTOR **2 :** the complaining party in any litigation including demandant in real actions, the complainant in equity, and the libelant in divorce

plaintiff in error : a party who proceeds by writ of error or statutory substitute to obtain reversal of a judgment or order for errors of law appearing in the record

plain tire *n* [⁴*plain*] **:** BALD TIRE

plain·tive \ˈplāntiv, -tēv *also* -təv\ *adj* [ME *plaintif*, fr. MF, fr. *plaint* + *-if* -ive — more at PLAINT] **1** *archaic* **:** afflicted with grief or sadness **:** LAMENTING, PINING ⟨the aimless dead ~ for Earth —Rupert Brooke⟩ **2 :** expressive of suffering or woe **:** SORROWFUL, MELANCHOLY ⟨he sighed, his voice became ~ —Aldous Huxley⟩ ⟨~ songs . . . about green hills and pines in the night wind and lonesomeness and dying away from home —R.O.Bowen⟩ ⟨the clarinet sings, in its eerie ~ tone —Sara R. Watson⟩ — **plain·tive·ly** \-təvlē, -li\ *adv* — **plain·tive·ness** \-tivnəs, -tēv- *also* -təv-\ *n* -ES

plain turkey *n* [³*plain*] **:** the bustard (*Choriotis australis*) of Australia that is now becoming rare because of excessive hunting for sport and table

plain wanderer *n* **:** a small Australian bird (*Pedionomus torquatus*) similar to the button quails

plain weave *n* [⁴*plain*] **:** the simplest form of textile weave in which the weft yarns pass alternately over and under the warp yarns to form a checkerboard pattern

plain weave

plain work *n* **1 :** plain sewing **2 :** the surface produced on stone by chiseling off irregularities

plainwoven \ˈ≈¦≈≈\ *adj* **:** made in plain weave

¹plaise \ˈplāz\ *dial var of* PLEASE

²plaise *var of* PLAICE

plaister *var of* PLASTER

¹plait \ˈplāt, ˈplat, *usu* -d·+V\ *n* -S [ME *pleit, plait, plete*, fr. MF *pleit*, fr. (assumed) VL *plictus* fold, fr. (assumed) VL *plictus*, alter. (influenced by L *implictus, replictus*) of L *plicatus*, past part. of *plicare* to fold — more at PLY] **1 a :** a flat fold **:** PLEAT 1 **b :** one of the flattened folds on the inner wall of some gastropod shells **2 a :** a braid of hair, straw, or other material ⟨in an attractive ~ round her head —*Atlantic*⟩ ⟨wick . . . of cotton strands of good quality woven into a thin ~ —T.P.Hilditch⟩; *specif* **:** PIGTAIL ⟨used to have little bows on the ends of your ~*s* before you cut your hair —Dodie Smith⟩ **b :** braided fiber esp. for straw hats ⟨a roll of ~⟩ **3** *archaic* **:** a devious twist of character or conduct **:** QUIRK ⟨a simple heart . . . without ~*s* and folds —George Hakewill⟩

²plait \"\ *vt* -ED/-ING/-S [ME *pleiten, plaiten, pleten*, fr. *pleit, plait, plete* plait] **1 :** PLEAT 1 **2 a :** to interweave the strands or locks of **:** BRAID, INTERTWINE ⟨his hair was ~*ed* in a queue —Ethel Wilson⟩ ⟨flirting her white mane . . . to draw attention to the red ribbons it was ~*ed* with —George Orwell⟩ **b :** to make by plaiting ⟨~ a rug⟩ ⟨shoes often ~*ed* from thongs of hemp —Herbert Harris⟩ ⟨weaverbirds . . . ~*ed* their elaborate nests perfectly —E.A.Armstrong⟩ **3 :** to unite by or as if by interweaving ⟨~ . . . interrelated events into a clean-cut chronology —*Time*⟩ ⟨swallows . . . ~*ing* together the summer air all day —Kenneth Rexroth⟩

plait·ed \-d·əd\ *adj* [ME *pleited, plaited*, fr. past part. of *pleiten, plaiten* to plait] **1 a :** PLEATED **b :** BRAIDED, INTERWOVEN **c :** PLATED 4 **2** *obs* **:** having convolutions **:** INVOLVED, DEVIOUS ⟨time shall unfold what ~ cunning hides —Shak.⟩

plaited stitch *n* **:** an embroidery stitch having a braided appearance, usu. made in herringbone or basket-weave patterns

plait·er \-d·ə(r)\ *n* -S **1 :** one that plaits ⟨straw ~⟩ ⟨basket ~⟩ **2 :** PLEATER 3

plaiting *n* -S [fr. gerund of ²*plait*] **1 :** PLEATING 2 **2 :** the interlacing of three or more strands (as of hair or straw) **:** BRAIDING **3 :** the knitting together of two or more yarns usu. of different colors or fibers so that one appears on the face of a fabric and the other on the back

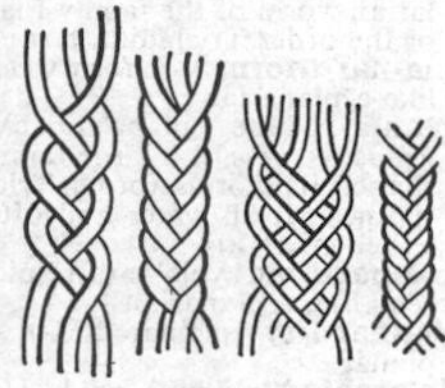
plaiting 2

pla·kat \pləˈkat, ˈplaˌkat\ *n* -S [Siamese, fighting fish] **:** BETTA

¹plan \ˈplan, -aa(ə)n\ *n* -S [F, plane, foundation, ground plan, partly fr. L *planum* level ground, fr. *planus* level, flat; partly fr. *planter* to plant, fix in place, fr. LL *plantare* — more at FLOOR, PLANT] **1 :** a drawing or diagram drawn on a plane: as **a :** a top view of a machine **b :** a representation of a horizontal section of a building — see GROUND PLAN **c :** a large-scale map of a small area **2 a :** one of numerous planes conceived as perpendicular to the line of vision and interposed between the eye and pictured objects **b :** one of several possible planes in a relief sculpture raising certain figures in the design above the ground **3 a :** a method of achieving something **:** a way of carrying out a design **:** DEVICE ⟨could not avoid suspecting that it was a ~ to obtain freedom in the evenings —Arnold Bennett⟩ **b :** a method of doing something **:** PROCEDURE, WAY ⟨the usual ~ is to bring with each course the implements considered correct for handling it —Agnes M. Miall⟩ **c :** a detailed and systematic formulation of a large-scale campaign or program of action ⟨drew up a secret ~ for the defense of the country⟩ ⟨the ~ called for the establishment of flexible four-year programs for the six basic industries —*Current Biog.*⟩ **d :** a proposed undertaking or goal **:** AIM, INTENTION ⟨had just entered college with the ~ of studying medicine —J.G.Cozzens⟩ **4 a :** an orderly arrangement of parts in terms of an overall design or objective ⟨the conventional ~ of state universities throughout the country —*Amer. Guide Series: Minn.*⟩ ⟨a ~ of life so delightfully simple —J.W.Krutch⟩ ⟨detailed to him the ~ of a very moral and aristocratical novel she was preparing —T.L.Peacock⟩ **b :** a schematic table or program of related parts or items ⟨drew up a ~ of study for himself⟩ ⟨the ~ of the graduation exercises⟩ **c :** a schedule or method of payment ⟨an easy-payment ~⟩ ⟨a pay-as-you-go ~⟩

syn PLAN, DESIGN, PLOT, SCHEME, and PROJECT can mean, in common, a proposed method of doing or making something or of achieving an end. PLAN implies mental formulation of a method, order, or form or a graphic representation of one, sometimes applying to an already achieved order ⟨her *plan* to try hitching rides in automobiles —Millen Brand⟩ ⟨drew *plans* for factory and home sites —*Amer. Guide Series: Md.*⟩ ⟨it imposes *plan* and meaning and order on its materials —W.V. O'Connor⟩ DESIGN adds to PLAN the idea of intention in the disposition of individual parts, often suggesting definiteness of pattern or a degree of order or harmony achieved ⟨a great man by accident rather than *design* —H.J.Laski⟩ ⟨a complex moral and philosophical *design* that lay behind the surface reality —J.W.Aldridge⟩ ⟨the *design* of constitutional governments —C.L.Jones⟩ PLOT connotes a laying out in or analyzing into distinguishable, proportioned, and comprehensible sections with attention to the proper relation of parts, applying now chiefly to the fundamental design of action or narrative in a literary or dramatic work or to a clandestine plan contrived by a group as for political revolution or assassination ⟨the fundamental elements of storytelling — suspense, pace, and clean-cut *plot* —*Current Biog.*⟩ ⟨a *plot* to overthrow the government⟩ SCHEME in the sense of a plan, design, or order, especially one revealed by analysis, suggests system and careful choice or ordering of detail ⟨the place of man in the *scheme* of things —E.D.Adrian⟩ ⟨the strong and the weak places in the general *scheme* of transportation by rail —O.S.Nock⟩ ⟨the rapid development of pension *schemes* —G.O.May⟩ ⟨the long-term *schemes* for building up India's economy —*Collier's Yr. Bk.*⟩ In more recently current use, it can apply to a plan motivated by craftiness or self-seeking ⟨a *scheme* to undermine public confidence in the administration⟩ ⟨a *scheme* to take over the control of a labor union⟩ PROJECT in current use is a neutral word designating any plan or prospective or actual undertaking or enterprise, often of considerable size ⟨his pet *project* of forming a citizens' committee⟩ ⟨the *project* consists of 80 farmsteads, each having a modern five-room house, a barn, and a poultry shed —*Amer. Guide Series: La.*⟩ ⟨a man of huge *projects* but small accomplishments⟩ In the verbal uses of the terms, PLAN, PLOT, and PROJECT signify to form or contrive a plan, plot, or project as distinguished by the noun meanings ⟨*planning* a dinner without taking into account the number of guests —M.R.Cohen⟩ ⟨*planned* my life from the outset largely and spaciously —Havelock Ellis⟩ ⟨a story thus *plotted* would choke on its own melodrama —Frederic Morton⟩ ⟨arguing whether the right to *plot* revolution is un-American —S.W. Chapman⟩ ⟨although his health was rapidly failing, he *pro-*

jected a new book —C.A.Dinsmore⟩ ⟨a group of New Haven citizens that *projected* a railway between New Haven and Hartford and obtained a charter for it —G.S.Bryan⟩ DESIGN signifies to formulate or achieve a design or intention ⟨*design* a new gown⟩ ⟨this book is *designed* to supply some of this information —R.M.Dawson⟩ SCHEME confines itself almost exclusively to the formulation of a scheme in the more current sense distinguished above, a clandestine, usu. self-seeking, planning or plotting ⟨open-air daylight creatures like us . . . called to plot and *scheme* and hide against the frozen silliness of the world —Eden Phillpotts⟩ ⟨*scheming* for a slice of official cake —S.H.Adams⟩ ⟨*scheming* to overthrow the party in power⟩

²plan \"\ *vb* **planned**; **planned**; **planning**; **plans** *vt* **1 :** to arrange the parts of **:** DESIGN ⟨*planned* the new school for beauty as well as utility⟩ ⟨*planned* the mural to blend with the architecture of the lobby⟩ ⟨*planned* his program for the next semester⟩ **2 :** to devise or project the realization or achievement of **:** prearrange the details of ⟨*planned* and organized extensive home-missionary programs —S.G.Hefelbower⟩ ⟨prepared to ~, instead of improvise, foreign policy —*Time*⟩ **3 :** to set down the features of in a plan **:** represent by a plan ⟨explored their houses, *planned* their cities —T.E.Lawrence⟩ **4 :** to have in mind **:** INTEND ⟨the many jewels she had accumulated and which she *planned* to leave them —R.B. Gehman⟩ ⟨~*s* a movie of the salvage operations —*Current Biog.*⟩ — sometimes used with *on* ⟨*planned* on seeing him later⟩ **5 :** to devise procedures or regulations for in accordance with a comprehensive plan for achieving a given objective (as in economic development or scientific research) ⟨*planning* a more balanced if less profitable economy with the resources available —David Mitrany⟩ ⟨proposed a central authority to ~ the state's future utilization of electric power on an overall basis —*Current Biog.*⟩ ~ *vi* **1 :** to make plans **:** DEVISE, CONTRIVE, SCHEME ⟨she must ~ — plot if she must —Pearl Buck⟩ **2 :** to set up economic or social controls or regulations ⟨found *planning* necessary during the war⟩ ⟨can be prepared to scrap the whole system of *planning* when the emergency passes —*New Republic*⟩ **syn** see ¹PLAN

¹plan- *or* **plano-** *comb form* [prob. fr. NL, fr. Gk, wandering, fr. *planos*; akin to Gk *planasthai* to wander — more at PLANET] **:** moving about **:** motile ⟨*plan*uria⟩ ⟨*plano*gamete⟩

²plan- *or* **plano-** *comb form* [L *planus* flat, level — more at FLOOR] **1 :** flat ⟨*plano*meter⟩ ⟨*plano*occipital⟩ **2 :** flatly ⟨*plano*rotund⟩ **3 :** flat and ⟨*plano*-concave⟩

plana *pl of* PLANUM

pla·naea \plə'nēə\ *n* -s [NL, fr. L *planus* flat — more at FLOOR] **:** a hypothetical organism in the form of a ciliated planula supposed to be a stage in the evolution of the higher animals

pla·nar \'plānə(r)\ *adj* [LL *planaris*, fr. L *planum* flat surface + *-aris* -ar — more at PLANE] **1 :** of or relating to a plane **:** lying in one plane **2 :** having a flat two-dimensional quality ⟨a picture based on ~ forms⟩

pla·nar·ia \plə'na(a)rēə\ *n* [NL, fr. fem. of LL *planarius* lying on a plane, fr. L *planum*] **1** *cap* **:** the type genus of Planariidae comprising 2-eyed planarian worms **2** -s **:** any worm of the genus *Planaria*; *broadly* **:** PLANARIAN

pla·nar·i·an \-ēən\ *n* -s [NL *Planariidae* + E *-an*] **:** a turbellarian worm of the family Planariidae; *broadly* **:** a turbellarian of the order Tricladida **:** TRICLAD

pla·nar·i·form \-rə,fȯrm\ *adj* [*planarian* + *-iform*] **:** shaped like a planarian

plan·a·ri·idae \,planə'rīə,dē\ *n pl, cap* [NL, fr. *Planaria*, type genus + *-idae*] **:** a large family of small soft-bodied usu. leaf-shaped flatworms (order Tricladida) that are almost all free-living in fresh water and often have well-developed eyespots — see PLANARIA

pla·nar·i·oid \plə'na(a)rē,ȯid\ *adj* [*planarian* + *-oid*] **:** resembling a planarian

pla·nar·i·ty \plə'narəd-ē\ *n* -ES **:** the quality or state of being planar

¹pla·nate \'plā,nāt\ *adj* [LL *planatus*, past part. of *planare* to flatten, level, fr. L *planus* flat — more at FLOOR] **:** FLATTENED, PLANE ⟨recognizes that there is a ~ bedrock surface beneath the gravels —K.M.Hussey⟩

²planate \"\ *vt* -ED/-ING/-S [back-formation fr. *planation*] **:** to erode to a plain **:** PLANE ⟨former low domes were *planated* by wave erosion —*Jour. of Geol.*⟩

pla·na·tion \plā'nāshən, plə'-\ *n* -s [⁴*plane* + *-ation*] **:** a process of erosion that produces flat surfaces: as **a :** lateral erosion by a meandering stream that widens its floodplain **b :** erosion by waves and currents that results in wave-cut platforms **c :** abrasive action of a glacier or of wind that planes or facets a previously rounded or irregular stone

planch \'planch\ *n* -ES [ME *plaunche* plank, fr. MF *planche*, fr. L *planca* — more at PLANK] **1** *dial Eng* **:** a plank floor **2 :** a flat plate (as of metal or baked clay)

plan·ché·ite \'plänchä,īt, ═'══\ *n* -s [F. *Planché*, proper name + F *-ite*] **:** a mineral $Cu_{15}Si_{12}O_{36}(OH)_8$(?) consisting of a blue fibrous copper silicate

plan·cher \'planchə(r)\ *n* -s [ME, fr. MF *plancher*, *planchier*, *plancier* plank floor or ceiling, fr. *planche* plank — more at PLANCH] **1** *obs* **:** a plank floor or platform **2 :** PLANCIER

plan·chet \'planchət\ *n* -s [*planch* + *-et*] **1 :** a piece of metal cut and prepared for striking as a coin **2 :** the piece of metal on which a coin has been struck

plan·chette \plan'shet\ *n* -s [F, lit., small board or plank, fr. *planche* plank + *-ette* — more at PLANCH] **1 :** a small usu. heart-shaped board supported on casters at two points and on a vertical pencil at a third that is believed to produce automatic writing when moved across a surface by the light pressure of the fingers of one or more persons **2 :** CIRCUMFERENTOR

planch·ing \'planchiŋ\ *n* -s [*planch* + *-ing*] *dial Eng* **:** a boarded floor **:** FLOORING

planching nail *or* **plensh·ing nail** \'plenchiŋ-\ *n* **:** a flooring nail

planch·ment \'planchmənt\ *n* -s [*planch* + *-ment*] **:** CEILING

plan·cier \plan'si(ə)r\ *n* -s [MF, plank floor or ceiling — more at PLANCHER] **:** the underside of a cornice **:** SOFFIT

planck constant \'pläŋk-\ *n*, *usu cap P* [after Max K. E. L. *Planck* †1947 Ger. physicist] **:** the constant *h* in the Planck radiation law now found also in numerous formulas concerned with quantized energy and having a probable value of 6.626×10^{-27} erg second (gCm^2sec^{-1})

planck distribution law *n*, *usu cap P* [after Max K. E. L. *Planck*] **:** PLANCK RADIATION LAW

planck·ian radiation \'plaŋkēən-\ *n*, *usu cap P* [Max K. E. L. *Planck* + E *-ian*] **:** BLACKBODY RADIATION

planck radiation law *n*, *usu cap P* [after Max K. E. L. *Planck*] **1 :** a law in physics: radiant energy arising from processes within atoms or molecules is emitted in finite quanta each of which is equal to the product of the radiation frequency by a universal constant *h* — see PLANCK CONSTANT **2 :** a law in physics: the energy density of radiation within a blackbody cavity at absolute temperature T in terms of the wavelength λ is given by

$$\Delta P\lambda=\frac{8\pi hc}{\lambda^5[\mathrm{EXP}\frac{hc}{K\lambda T}-1]}\Delta\lambda,$$

where ΔPλ is the energy density within a given small wavelength interval Δλ, *h* is the Planck constant, and *c* the speed of light, all quantities being in cgs units

planctonic *var of* PLANKTONIC

plan·dok \'plan,dӓk\ *n* -s [Malay *pĕlandok*] **:** CHEVROTAIN

¹plane \'plān\ *vb* -ED/-ING/-S [ME *planen*, fr. MF *planer*, fr. LL *planare* to make flat, level, fr. L *planus* flat, level — more at FLOOR] *vt* **1 :** to make smooth or even **:** LEVEL ⟨what student came but that you *planed* her path —Alfred Tennyson⟩ **2 :** to produce a plane surface on by the use of a planer **3 :** to remove by or as if by planing ⟨the mountainside had come away bodily, *planed* clean —Rudyard Kipling⟩ ~ *vi* **1 a :** to work with a plane **b :** to do the work of a plane **2 :** to extend in a smooth or level line without elevations or depressions ⟨mellow farmlands ~ to the water's edge —*Amer. Guide Series: Vt.*⟩ ⟨this sea that *planed* away in all directions —T.O.Heggen⟩

²plane \"\ *or* **plane tree** *n* -s [ME, fr. MF, fr. L *platanus*, fr. Gk *platanos*; akin to Gk *platys* broad — more at PLACE] **:** a tree of the genus *Platanus*

³plane \"\ *n* -s [ME, fr. MF, fr. LL *plana*, fr. *planare* to make

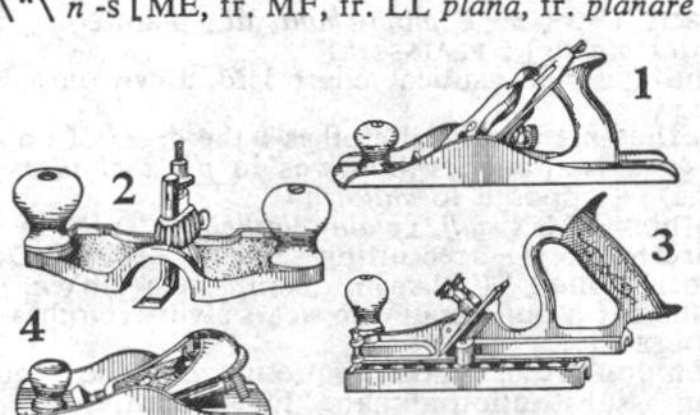

planes: *1* jack plane, *2* router plane, *3* tonguing and grooving plane, *4* block plane

level] **:** a tool for smoothing or shaping a surface of wood that consists of a smooth-soled stock as of wood or iron from the face of which projects slightly the steel cutting edge of a chisel set at an angle to the face with an aperture in the front for the escape of shavings — see BEADING PLANE, BENCH PLANE, BLOCK PLANE, BULLNOSED PLANE, CHAMFER PLANE, CIRCULAR PLANE, COMBINATION PLANE, DADO PLANE, DOVETAIL PLANE, FORE PLANE, JACK PLANE, JOINTER PLANE, MATCH PLANE, RABBET PLANE, ROUTER PLANE, SCRUB PLANE, SMOOTHING PLANE

⁴plane \"\ *n* -s [L *planum* level surface, fr. neut. of *planus* level, flat] **1 a** (1) **:** a surface such that the straight line that joins any two of its points lies wholly in that surface **:** a two-dimensional extent of zero curvature **:** a surface any intersection of which by a like surface is a straight line (2) **:** the graph of a linear equation in three dimensions **b** (1) **:** a flat or level material surface ⟨an inclined ~⟩ ⟨the faults have tilted a ~ to the west —*Jour. of Geol.*⟩ (2) **:** FACET ⟨the evening sunlight had begun to turn the smooth ~*s* of the prickly pears into trembling mirrors —Michael Swan⟩ **c :** an imaginary plane surface used to identify the position of a bodily organ or a part of the skull ⟨alveolocondylean ~⟩ **d :** SURFACE PLATE **e :** an inclined track (as in a coal mine) over which transportation of a string of cars or a train is effected by gravity or by external power (as by a stationary engine) **2 a :** a level of existence, consciousness, or development ⟨moved on a ~ of excited worldliness —H.S.Canby⟩ ⟨keep the conversation on an amicable ~ —P.G.Wodehouse⟩ ⟨on the intellectual ~⟩ ⟨on the religious ~⟩ **b :** any of the seven theosophical stages or states of manifestation of being **:** a sphere of existence in theosophy **c :** a stage in surgical anesthesia ⟨the patient can be brought into the second ~ of anesthesia in another location —*Jour. Amer. Med. Assoc.*⟩ **3 a :** one of the main supporting surfaces of an airplane ⟨a low-wing, all-metal single-*plane* craft —*Science News Letter*⟩ (*bi*plane) **b** [by shortening] **:** AIRPLANE ⟨jet ~⟩ ⟨transport ~ ⟩ **c :** DIVING PLANE

⁵plane \"\ *adj* [L *planus* flat, level — more at FLOOR] **1 :** having no elevations or depressions **:** forming part of a plane **:** FLAT, LEVEL ⟨a ~ surface⟩ **2 a :** of, relating to, or dealing with planes or two-dimensional figures only **b :** lying in a plane ⟨a ~ curve⟩ **syn** see LEVEL

⁶plane \"\ *vi* -ED/-ING/-S [F *planer*, fr. *plan* plane, fr. L *planum* level surface; fr. the level surface formed by the wings of a soaring bird] **1 a :** to soar on or as if on wings ⟨watching a gull ~ down in circles without moving a wing —G.W. Brace⟩ ⟨a great morpho butterfly leisurely *planing* along —H.M.Tomlinson⟩ **b** (1) *of a seaplane* **:** to move through the water at such a speed as to be supported by hydrodynamic and aerodynamic rather than by hydrostatic forces (2) *of a boat* **:** to skim across the surface of the water **:** lift partly out of the water while in motion ⟨these craft, when they reach a certain speed, ~ on the flat after sections of their hull —Peter Heaton⟩ **c :** to move downward as if on an inclined plane **:** GLIDE ⟨*planed* down toward it and in a few moments could make out that it was a ship —J.H.Marsh⟩ ⟨were pulling her stern first to keep her from diving and *planing* to the bottom —N.C. McDonald⟩ **2** [⁴*plane* (airplane)] **:** to travel by airplane ⟨had *planed*, trained and driven fifteen hundred miles —Paul Gallico⟩ **3** *of a submarine* **:** to move from one level to another ⟨ordered me to ~ upward two feet, to allow him to raise the periscope that much higher out of the water and thus see a little farther —E.L.Beach⟩

plane angle *n* **:** an angle formed by two intersecting lines each of which lies on a face of a dihedral angle and is perpendicular to the edge of the face

plane at infinity [⁴*plane*] **:** the aggregate of all points at infinity in projective geometry of three dimensions

plane bit *n* [³*plane*] **:** PLANE IRON

plane chart *n* [⁵*plane*] **:** a depiction of a small portion of the earth's surface as plane with meridians and parallels of latitude appearing as two systems of straight lines at right angles and all arc degrees as equal

plane curve *n* **:** a curve that lies wholly in a single plane

plane figure *n* **:** a geometrical configuration all of whose points lie in a plane

plane geometry *n* **:** a branch of elementary geometry that deals with plane figures

plane iron *n* [³*plane*] **:** the blade of a plane

planeload \'═,═\ *n* [⁴*plane*] **:** a load that fills an airplane **:** plane capacity

plane man *n* **:** DILLYMAN

plane-mile \'═,═\ *n* [⁴*plane* + *mile*] **:** a statistical unit denoting one mile traveled by one airplane

plane·ness \'plānnəs\ *n* -ES **:** the quality or state of being plane

plane of defilade [⁴*plane*] **:** a plane tangent to the mask and passing through the point from which protection (as from enemy fire or observation) is desired

plane of incidence : a plane containing an incident line (as a ray of light) and the normal to a surface (as of a mirror) at the point of incidence

plane of polarization : a plane in which the magnetic-vibration component of plane-polarized electromagnetic radiation lies

plane of projection : a plane that is intersected by imaginary lines drawn from the eye to every point on the object and that is therefore the plane on which the pictorial representation in perspective is formed

plane of sight : a vertical plane containing the line of sight of a gun

plane of site : a plane containing the line of site of a gun and a horizontal line perpendicular to it

plane of symmetry 1 : a plane through a crystal that divides the crystal into two parts that are mirror images of each other **2 :** a vertical fore-and-aft plane that divides an airplane into symmetrical halves

plane-parallel \'═¦══,═\ *adj* [⁵*plane*] **:** having two opposite faces plane and parallel ⟨a *plane-parallel* sheet of glass⟩

plane-polarized \'═¦══,═\ *adj* [⁴*plane*] *of a moving wave* **:** vibrating in a single plane ⟨a *plane-polarized* light wave⟩ ⟨a *plane-polarized* sound wave⟩

plan·er \'plānə(r)\ *n* -s [¹*plane* + *-er*] **:** one that planes: as **a :** a machine tool consisting essentially of a fixed bed, a reciprocating table to which the work is secured, and a device for holding the cutting tool stationary while each cut is taken and for moving the tool in position for the succeeding cut at the end of each cutting stroke, the power for moving the table being usu. transmitted to the table from the driving shaft through a train of gears — see CLOSED PLANER, CRANK PLANE, OPENSIDE PLANER, ROTARY PLANER, SHAPING PLANER **b :** a power tool for surfacing wood by means of a cutting tool that rotates across the width of the board that is fed under it **c :** a smooth-faced block of wood that is laid on the surface of type and tapped with a mallet to level the type or make a stone proof **d :** a grader with several blades to distribute and smooth earth or pavement material **e :** a worker who planes wood, stone, or metal

plan·era \'planərə\ *n, cap* [NL, after J. J. *Planer* †1789 Ger. botanist] **:** a genus of trees (family Ulmaceae) of southeastern U. S. resembling the hackberry but having an oval, ribbed, nutlike fruit — see PLANER TREE

planer center *n* **:** one of a pair of index centers bolted to the table of a planer and used to support work which is to be planed round or in which radial slots are to be cut

planer head *n* **:** a part of a planer that secures the cutting tool to the crossrail or housing and that contains the mechanism which feeds it toward the work

planer jack *n* **:** a jack used to level up the work to be machined on a planer

planer knife *n* **:** PLANE IRON

pla·ner tree \'plānə(r)-\ *n* [after J. J. *Planer* †1789 Ger. botanist] **:** a small-leaved No. American tree (*Planera aquatica*) bearing wingless fruit — called also *hornbeam, water elm*

¹pla·nes \'plā,nēz\ *n, cap* [NL, fr. Gk *planēt-*, *planēs* wanderer — more at PLANET] **:** a genus of small pelagic crabs with hairy legs

²planes *pres 3d sing of* PLANE, *pl of* PLANE

plane sailing *n* [⁵*plane*] **1 :** the navigation or conducting of a ship by neglecting the earth's curvature and considering the earth or a part of it as a plane **2 :** PLAIN SAILING 2

plane·shear \'plān,shi(ə)r\ *n* -s [alter. (influenced by *plane*, *sheer*) of *plancher*] **:** PLANK-SHEER

planes·man \'plānzmən\ *n, pl* **planesmen** [⁴*plane*] **:** one who operates the bow or stern diving planes on a submarine

plane surveying *n* [⁵*plane*] **:** ordinary field and topographical surveying in which the curvature of the earth is disregarded — compare GEODETIC SURVEYING

plane symmetry *n* [⁴*plane*] **:** symmetry with respect to a plane

¹plan·et \'planət, *usu* -əd.+V\ *n* -s [ME *planete*, fr. OF, fr. LL *planeta*, modif. (influenced by Gk *planētēs* wanderer) of Gk *planēt-*, *planēs*, lit., wanderer, fr. *planasthai* to wander; akin to ON *flana* to rush around, and prob. to L *planus* flat — more at FLOOR] **1 a :** a heavenly body seeming to have a motion of its own among the fixed stars ⟨therefore is the glorious ~ Sol in noble eminence enthroned —Shak.⟩ ⟨the moon, that ~ of love and death —Gilbert Highet⟩ **b** (1) **:** one of the bodies except a comet, meteor, or satellite that revolves around the sun in the solar system

TERRESTRIAL AND MAJOR PLANETS

SYMBOL	NAME	MEAN DISTANCE FROM THE SUN astronomical units	million miles	PERIOD IN DAYS OR YEARS	DIAMETER IN MILES
♃	Jupiter	5.20	483	12 years	86,800
♄	Saturn	9.54	886	29 years	71,500
♅	Uranus	19.18	1783	84 years	29,400
♆	Neptune	30.06	2794	165 years	28,000
⊕	Earth	1.00	93	365¼ days	7,913
♀	Venus	0.72	67	225 days	7,600
♂	Mars	1.52	142	687 days	4,200
♇	Pluto	39.52	3670	248 years	4,000?
☿	Mercury	0.39	36	88 days	2,900

(2) **:** a similar body that may possibly revolve around another star **c :** EARTH — usu. used with *the* ⟨one of these goals is a reasonable degree of communication spread out more evenly over the ~ —I.A.Richards⟩ **2 :** a heavenly body (as a star) held to influence the fate of human beings **3 :** a person or thing of great magnitude or brilliance **:** LUMINARY ⟨a major ~ who changed the whole direction of the scientific thought of his day⟩

²planet \"\ *or* **pla·ne·ta** \plə'nēd·ə\ *n* -s [ML *planeta*, perh. fr. Gk *planētēs* wanderer] **:** CHASUBLE

plane table *n* [⁴*plane*] **1 :** an instrument for plotting the lines of a survey directly from the observations and consisting essentially of a drawing board mounted on a tripod and fitted with a ruler that is pointed at the object observed usu. with the aid of a sighting device (as a telescope) — see ALIDADE **2 :** a large surface plate **3 :** an inclined plane used as a buddle

plane-table \'═,══\ *vb* [*plane table*] *vi* **:** to make use of a plane table ~ *vt* **:** to plot with a plane table

plan·et·al \'planəd·ᵊl\ *adj* [¹*planet* + *-al*] **:** PLANETARY

¹plan·e·tar·i·an \,planə'ta(a)rēən\ *adj* [fr. (assumed) LL *planetarius* + E *-an* — more at PLANETARY] **:** PLANETARY

²planetarian \"\ *n* -s **:** an inhabitant of a planet

plan·e·tar·i·ly \¦══'terəlē\ *adv* [¹*planetary* + *-ly*] **:** in the manner of or with reference to a planet ⟨will break through the tyranny of national boundaries and teach our children to think ~ —O.L.Reiser & Blodwen Davies⟩

plan·e·tar·i·um \,planə'ta(a)rēəm, -ter-, -tār-\ *n*, *pl* **planetariums** \-mz\ *or* **planetar·ia** \-ēə\ [*planet* + *-arium*] **1 a :** ORRERY 1 **b :** a model representing the solar system **2 a :** an optical device designed to project (as on a domed ceiling) various celestial images and effects (as the appearance of the nighttime sky) at a specific time and place **b :** a building or room housing such a device

¹plan·e·tary \'planə,terē, -ri\ *adj* [fr. (assumed) LL *planetarius* (whence LL *planetarius* astrologer), fr. *planeta* planet + L *-arius* -ary] **1 a :** of, relating to, or belonging to a planet ⟨~ orbit⟩ ⟨~ year⟩ **b :** caused or held to be caused by a planet ⟨a ~ plague —Shak.⟩ **c** (1) **:** ERRATIC, WANDERING ⟨a ~ vagabond⟩ (2) **:** having a motion like that of a planet **:** ORBITING **d :** IMMENSE ⟨it seemed not weeks, not even months or years, but a fantastic length of time, a ~ distance —Marcia Davenport⟩ **2 a :** of, relating to, or belonging to the earth **:** TERRESTRIAL ⟨~ rumblings and eructations —L.C.Eiseley⟩ **b :** GLOBAL, WORLDWIDE ⟨neither national nor continental but ~ —Lewis Mumford⟩ ⟨people had begun to think in ~ terms —Van Wyck Brooks⟩ **3 :** having or consisting of an epicyclic train of gear wheels ⟨~ drive⟩

²planetary \"\ *n* -ES **1 :** a planet or planetary body ⟨scanned the entire literary horizon for new *planetaries* —Carl Van Doren⟩ **2 :** PLANETARY NEBULA ⟨the observed speeds of expansion of the *planetaries* —R.H.Baker⟩

planetary configuration *n* **:** the apparent position of a planet in the sky in relation to its actual position in the solar system with reference to the earth and the sun

planetary electron *n* **:** an electron that moves about the atomic nucleus as part of an atom

planetary gear *or* **planetary gearing** *n* **:** PLANET DIFFERENTIAL

planetary hour *n* **:** HOUR 5

planetary house *or* **planetary mansion** *n* **:** ¹HOUSE 3b

planetary nebula *n* **:** a relatively small and generally ring-shaped nebula that is composed of gas expanding outward from a hot subluminous central star

planetary transmission *n* **:** a transmission or transmission system (as in an automobile) that uses a planet differential

planetary wind *n* **:** one of the major winds ⟨the trade winds, countertrades, and prevailing westerlies are *planetary winds*⟩

planet differential *or* **planet gear** *n* **:** an epicyclic train that has two contiguous and parallel main wheels usu. of equal diameter but of unequal number of teeth meshing with a single pinion

plan·e·tes·i·mal \,planə'tesəməl\ *n* -s [*planet* + *-esimal* (as in *infinitesimal*)] **:** one of numerous small solid heavenly bodies of undetermined characteristics that may have existed at an early stage of the development of the solar system

planetesimal hypothesis *n* **:** a hypothesis in astronomy: the planets have evolved by aggregation from planetesimals

plan·et·oid \'planə,tȯid\ *n* -s [¹*planet* + *-oid*] **1 :** a body resembling a planet **2 :** ASTEROID — **plan·et·oi·dal** \¦══'tȯidᵊl\ *adj*

plane tree *var of* PLANE

plane-tree family \'═,═-\ *n* [*plane tree*] **:** PLATANACEAE

plane-tree maple \'═,═-\ *n* [*plane tree*] **:** SYCAMORE 2

plane trigonometry *n* [⁵*plane*] **:** a branch of trigonometry that deals with plane triangles

planets *pl of* PLANET

planet-stricken \'═¦═,══\ *or* **planet-struck** \'═¦═,═\ *adj* **1 :** affected by the supposedly harmful influence of a planet **:** BLASTED **2 :** overcome by fear **:** PANIC-STRICKEN

planet wheel *n* [¹*planet*] **:** a gear wheel that revolves around the wheel with which it meshes in an epicyclic train — see SUN-AND-PLANET MOTION illustration

plane wave *n* [⁵*plane*] **:** a wave whose wave fronts are plane surfaces corresponding to parallel rays ⟨light waves from the distant stars are virtually *plane waves* when they strike a telescope lens⟩

planform \'═,═\ *n* [*plan* + *form*] **:** the contour of an airplane as viewed from above

plan·ful \'planfəl\ *adj* [¹*plan* + *-ful*] **1 :** full of plans **:** RE-

SOURCEFUL, SCHEMING ⟨a latter-day robber baron, ~, secretive, ruthless —Wolfgang Langewiesche⟩ **2 :** according to a plan ⟨persistent and ~ arousing of the mind —Hugo Münsterberg⟩ — **plan·ful·ly** \-fəlē\ *adv* — **plan·ful·ness** *n* -ES

plan·gen·cy \ˈplanjənsē\ *n* -ES [*plangent* + *-cy*] **:** the quality or state of being plangent **:** EXPRESSIVENESS ⟨there is about the spoken word a poignancy, a ~, directness and intimacy that is hard to match in print —Irwin Edman⟩

plan·gent \-jənt\ *adj* [L *plangent-, plangens,* pres. part. of *plangere* to strike, lament — more at PLAINT] **1 :** having a loud and reverberating sound **:** RESONANT ⟨let out a ~ roar —*New Yorker*⟩ ⟨~ organ music —J.L.Lowes⟩ **2 :** having an expressive esp. plaintive quality ⟨the long ~ ripple of the harp strings —Osbert Sitwell⟩ ⟨a strange, chanting cry, slow and ~ —C.G.D.Roberts⟩ — **plan·gent·ly** *adv*

plan·gi \ˈplanjē\ *n* -S [Malay *kain pĕlangi* bandanna cloth gaudily colored by tie dyeing, fr. *kain* cloth + *pĕlangi* striped in gay colors] **:** a technique of cloth decoration in which a woven fabric is bunched and bound before it is dyed — compare IKAT

plan·gor·ous \ˈplaŋgərəs\ *adj* [L *plangor* lamentation (fr. *plangere* to lament) + E *-ous* — more at PLAINT] **:** expressive of loud lamentation **:** WAILING

plani- *comb form* [L *planus* — more at FLOOR] **:** flat **:** level **:** plane ⟨*plani*form⟩ ⟨*plani*graphy⟩

-pla·nia \ˈplānēə\ *n comb form* -S [NL, fr. Gk, act of wandering, fr. *planos* wandering + *-ia* -y — more at PLAN-] **:** a wandering of (a specified substance) into a tract not its own ⟨meno*plania*⟩

plan·i·di·iform \ˌplanəˈdīəˌfȯrm\ *adj* [NL *planidium* + E *-iform*] **:** resembling a planidium

pla·nid·i·um \pləˈnidēəm\ *n, pl* **planid·ia** \-ēə\ [NL, fr. ¹*plan-* + *-idium,* dim. suffix, fr. Gk *-idion*] **:** a first-stage legless larva of various parasitic hymenopterous and dipterous insects

pla·ni·form \ˈplānəˌfȯrm, ˈplan-\ *adj* [ISV *plani-* + *-form*] **:** having or being a joint with nearly flat articular surfaces

pla·ni·gram \ˈplānəˌgram, ˈplan-\ *n* [*plani-* + *-gram*] **:** a roentgenogram made by planigraphy

pla·ni·graph \-ˌraf, -ˌräf\ *n* [*plani-* + *-graph*] **:** PLANIGRAM

pla·nig·ra·phy \pləˈnigrəfē\ *n* -ES [ISV *plani-* + *-graphy*] **:** a roentgenographic technique that makes on a film sharp images of structures in a predetermined plane and blurs images of other structures above and below

pla·ni·lla \pləˈnē(y)ə\ *n* -S [AmerSp, fr. dim. of Sp *plana* level ground, fr. fem. of *plano* level, flat, fr. L *planus* — more at FLOOR] **:** a level place used as a cleaning floor at a mine

pla·nim·e·ter \pləˈnimәd·ə(r)\ *n* [F *planimètre,* fr. *plani-* + *-mètre* -meter] **:** an instrument for measuring the area of any plane figure by passing a tracer around its boundary line

pla·ni·met·ric \ˌplānəˈme·trik, ˌplan-\ *adj* [*planimetry* + *-ic*] **1 :** of, relating to, or established by planimetry **2** *of a map* **:** having no indications of contour — **pla·ni·met·ri·cal·ly** \-rək(ə)lē\ *adv*

pla·nim·e·try \pləˈniməˌtrē\ *n* -ES [F *planimétrie,* fr. ML *planimetria,* fr. L *planus* flat + *-metria* -metry — more at FLOOR] **1 :** the measurement of plane surfaces — distinguished from *stereometry* **2 :** the natural and cultural features of terrain excluding relief as indicated on a map

planing machine *n* [fr. gerund of ¹*plane*] **:** a machine that planes: as **a :** PLANER **b :** a stationary machine for planing wood — compare BUZZ PLANER, CYLINDER PLANER **c :** a portable machine for planing a floor or deck **d :** a machine for planing stone slabs **e :** a rotary hand machine that fits over an engine steam chest and is used for planing the valve seat

planing mill *n* **:** a woodworking establishment in which wood is smoothed, cut, matched, and fitted

planing surface *n* [fr. gerund of ⁶*plane*] **:** a surface of a seaplane float or hull designed to receive dynamic lift from the free water surface upon which it moves

pla·ni·pen·nate \ˌplānəˈpeˌnāt\ *adj* [NL *Planipennia* + E *-ate*] **:** of or relating to the Planipennia

pla·ni·pen·nia \ˌ==ˈpenēə\ *n pl, cap* [NL, fr. *plani-* + L *penna* wing + NL *-ia* — more at PEN] **1** *in some classifications* **:** a suborder of Neuroptera that includes most of the typical neuropterans when Neuroptera is construed as including Megaloptera **2** *in some classifications* **:** an order or other group coextensive with Neuroptera

pla·ni·ros·tral \ˌplānəˈrästrəl\ *adj* [*plani-* + L *rostrum* beak + E *-al* — more at ROSTRUM] **:** having a broad flat beak

plan·ish \ˈplanish\ *vt* -ED/-ING/-ES [MF *planiss-,* stem of *planir,* fr. *plan* level, fr. L *planus* — more at FLOOR] **:** to make smooth or plane; *specif* **:** to condense, toughen, and polish by hammering lightly with or as if with a smooth-faced hammer

plan·ish·er \-shə(r)\ *n* -S **:** one that planishes; *specif* **:** a tool used for planishing

planishing hammer *n* [fr. gerund of *planish*] **:** a hammer with slightly convex faces that is used in sheet-metal work to smooth and shape surfaces

planishing hammer

plan·i·sphere \ˈplanəˌsfi(ə)r\ *n* [ML *planisphaerium,* fr. L *planus* flat, plane + *sphaera* sphere — more at FLOOR, SPHERE] **:** a representation of the circles of the sphere on a plane; *esp* **:** a polar projection of the celestial sphere and the stars on a plane with adjustable circles or other appendages for showing celestial phenomena (as the position of the heavens or the time of rising and setting of stars) for any given time — **plan·i·spher·ic** \ˌ==ˈsfirik, -fer-\ *adj*

planispiral *var of* PLANOSPIRAL

¹**plank** \ˈplaŋk, -aiŋk\ *n* -S [ME *plank, planke,* fr. ONF *planke,* fr. L *planca;* perh. akin to Gk *plak-, plax* flat surface, tablet — more at PLEASE] **1 a :** a heavy thick board that in technical specifications usu. has a thickness of 2 to 4 inches and a width of at least 8 inches — compare TIMBER **b** (1) **:** any of various objects made of a plank or planking (as a bench, table, or narrow footbridge) (2) **:** GANGPLANK ⟨was to lift ~ at four that afternoon —R.P.Warren⟩ **c :** PLANKING **d :** a heavy usu. oak board that is grooved to catch the drip and is used in cooking and serving food (as broiled meat or fish) **e :** a flat slab of some hard material ⟨asphalt ~⟩ ⟨concrete ~⟩ **2 :** something that supports ⟨the ~s of the peace system —Sigmund Neumann⟩ **3 a :** an article in the platform of a political party or group ⟨with temperance and opposition to slavery as the two specific ~s in its platform —*Amer. Guide Series: Maine*⟩ **b :** a principal item of a policy or program ⟨a cardinal ~ in Britain's patient Far Eastern policy —Benjamin Welles⟩

²**plank** \"\ *vt* -ED/-ING/-S [ME *planken,* fr. ¹*plank*] **1 :** to cover, floor, or lay with planks ⟨~*ed* the well over —Lucy M. Montgomery⟩ ⟨the ~*ed* streets fringing the mills and factories —*Amer. Guide Series: Wash.*⟩ ⟨no use ~*ing* a boat till you got her timbered out —G.W.Brace⟩ **2 :** to set down **:** DEPOSIT ⟨~*ed* himself in the chair⟩ ⟨~ the cash on the counter for a slice of sirloin —*Saturday Rev.*⟩ **3 :** to cook and serve on a plank usu. with an elaborate garnish (as of mashed potatoes or other vegetables) ⟨~*ed* shad⟩ ⟨~*ed* steak⟩ **4 :** to extend or place so as to resemble a plank ⟨hitched up his knee and ~*ed* a most unlovely boot firmly against the edge of the table —Ngaio Marsh⟩ ⟨turned around with his back ~*ed* against the wall —H.L.Davis⟩

plank buttress *n* [¹*plank*] **:** BUTTRESS ROOT

plank down *vb* [²*plank*] *vt* **1 :** to set down forcibly or with emphasis ⟨was herded into a corner and *planked down* among five other sufferers —Thomas Wood †1950⟩ ⟨delighted to slam us all in jail and *plank down* martial law —Laura Krey⟩ **2 :** to pay or put down (money) on the spot ⟨pulled out a silver dollar and *planked* it *down* for a year's subscription —A.W.Long⟩ ⟨*planked down* a fistful of money —*Irish Digest*⟩ ~ *vi* **:** to declare oneself forcibly or unmistakably ⟨*planked* squarely *down* on the side of the government —Mollie Panter-Downes⟩

plank·er \-kə(r)\ *n* -S [¹*plank* + *-er*] **:** FLOAT 5 d (1)

plank house *n* **:** a house built of planks; *esp* **:** one of the rather large usu. rectangular and elaborately constructed buildings prevailingly used by Indians but also by some Eskimos of the northwest coast of No. America and adjacent Siberia

planking *n* -S [fr. gerund of ²*plank*] **1 :** the act or process of covering or fitting out with planks **2** [¹*plank* + *-ing*] **a :** a quantity of planks **b :** a covering or flooring made of planks; *specif* **:** the outer and inner covering of the timbers of a wooden ship — see SHIP illustration

plank·less \-kləs\ *adj* **:** having no planks

plank owner *n* [¹*plank;* fr. the tradition that he becomes part owner of the ship] **:** a member of the first crew to serve on a newly commissioned ship

plank road *n* **:** a road built of planks laid crosswise on longitudinal timbers and widely used in the U. S. in the mid 19th century

plank root *n* **:** BUTTRESS ROOT

plank scraper *n* **1 :** FLOAT 5 d (1) **2 :** a V-shaped or trapezoid-shaped drag for the leveling of land for irrigation, for the construction of border levees, and for the cleaning out of lateral distributing ditches

plank-sheer \ˈ=,=\ *n* [alter. (influenced by *plank, sheer*) of *plancher*] **1 :** a heavy plank forming the outer edge of the deck of a vessel **2 :** the waterway (sense 2b) of a yacht

plank·ter \ˈplaŋktə(r)\ *n* -S [Gk *planktēr* wanderer, fr. *plang-,* stem of *plazesthai* to stray, wander — more at PLANKTON] **:** a planktonic organism

plank·tiv·o·rous \(ˌ)plaŋkˈtiv(ə)rəs\ *adj* [*plankton* + *-vorous*] **:** feeding on plankton

plank·tol·o·gy \plaŋkˈtäləjē\ *also* **plank·ton·ol·o·gy** \ˌplaŋktəˈnä-\ *n* -ES [*plankton* + *-logy*] **:** a branch of biology concerned with the study of plankton

plank·ton \ˈplaŋktən, -aiŋ-\ *n* -S [G, fr. Gk, neut. of *planktos* wandering, drifting, fr. *plang-,* stem of *plazesthai* to stray, drift, pass. of *plazein* to drive astray; akin to L *plangere* to strike — more at PLAINT] **:** the passively floating or weakly swimming animal and plant life of a body of water consisting chiefly of minute plants (as diatoms and blue-green algae) and of minute animals (as protozoans, entomostracans, and various larvae) but including also larger forms (as jellyfishes and salpae) that have only weak powers of locomotion — compare BENTHOS, NEKTON, TRIPTON — **plank·ton·ic** *also* **planc·ton·ic** \(ˈ)plaŋkˈtänik\ *adj*

plankton net *n* **:** a townet usu. made of fine-meshed silk bolting cloth that is used for the capture of plankton

plank·tont \ˈplaŋkˌtänt\ *n* -S [*plankton* + *-ont*] **:** PLANKTER

plank·ways \ˈplaŋˌkwāz\ *or* **plank·wise** \-wīz\ *adv* [¹*plank* + *-ways, -wise*] **:** in the direction of the length of timber **:** LENGTHWISE

plan·less \ˈplanləs\ *adj* **:** functioning or taking place without a plan or set goal ⟨a ~ course of study⟩ — **plan·less·ly** *adv*

plan·less·ness *n* -ES **:** the quality or state of being without plan **:** lack of system **:** DISORGANIZATION ⟨this ~, this indeterminate confusion of purpose —H.G.Wells⟩

planned *adj* [fr. past part. of ²*plan*] **1 :** INTENDED, PROJECTED ⟨his ~ trip abroad⟩ ⟨the ~ revision of the curriculum⟩ **2 a :** designed or carried out according to plan **:** ORDERLY ⟨a ~ highway system⟩ ⟨a ~ retreat⟩ ⟨~ migration on a vast scale —Stuart Chase⟩ **b :** not spontaneous **:** PREARRANGED ⟨a ~ demonstration⟩ ⟨a ~ outburst⟩ **3 :** subject to regulation and control in terms of a plan **:** ORGANIZED, SYSTEMATIZED ⟨all the signs are that the village of the next generation will be a ~ community —*Times Lit. Supp.*⟩

planned economy *n* **:** an economic system in which the elements of an economy (as labor, capital, and natural resources) are subject to government control and regulation designed to achieve the objectives of a comprehensive plan of economic development — compare FREE ECONOMY, FREE ENTERPRISE

Planned Parenthood *service mark* — used for research and dissemination of information on measures (as contraception or the treatment of infertility) designed to regulate the number and spacing of children in a family

plan·ner \ˈplanə(r), -aan-\ *n* -S **:** one who plans **:** DESIGNER, PROJECTOR; *specif* **:** one who supervises, participates in, or advocates social or economic planning ⟨a lawyer turned ~ who is active in New York housing and planning circles —Christopher Tunnard⟩

planning *n* -S [fr. gerund of ²*plan*] **:** the act or process of making or carrying out plans; *specif* **:** the establishment of goals, policies, and procedures for a social or economic unit ⟨city ~⟩ ⟨business ~⟩

planning board *n* **:** a body of citizens appointed to prepare or administer a plan (as for the growth and development of a city)

pla·no \ˈplā(ˌ)nō\ *adj* [²*plan-*] **:** having a flat surface ⟨true ~ lenses cannot produce prismatic effects —*Jour. Amer. Med. Assoc.*⟩

plano- — see PLAN-

plan·o·blast \ˈplanəˌblast\ *n* [¹*plan-* + *-blast*] **:** the medusa form of a hydroid — **plan·o·blas·tic** \ˌ==ˈblastik\ *adj*

¹**plan·occipital** \ˌplan+ˌ=ˈ===\ *adj* [²*plan-* + *occipital*] **:** having a flattened occiput

²**planoccipital** \"\ *n* **:** a person having a planoccipital skull

pla·no-concave \ˌplā(ˌ)nō+\ *adj* [²*plan-* + *concave*] **:** flat on one side and concave on the other — see LENS illustration

pla·no-convex \"+\ *adj* [²*plan-* + *convex*] **:** flat on one side and convex on the other — see LENS illustration

plan·o·ga·mete \ˈplanəgəˌmēt\ *n* [ISV ¹*plan-* + *gamete*] **:** a motile gamete; *esp* **:** one that is ciliated

plan·o·gam·ic \ˌplanəˈgamik\ *adj* [*planogamete* + *-ic*] **:** of or relating to a planogamete

¹**plan·o·graph** \ˈplānəˌgraf, -ˌräf\ *vt* -ED/-ING/-S [back-formation fr. *planography*] **:** to print by planography ⟨a ~*ed* pamphlet⟩

²**planograph** \"\ *n* [²*plan-* + *-graph*] **:** a print made by planography

pla·no·graph·ic \ˌ==ˈgrafik\ *adj* **:** produced by or used in planography ⟨~ printing⟩ ⟨printing from a ~ surface⟩

pla·nog·ra·phy \plāˈnägrəfē, plə-\ *n* -ES [²*plan-* + *-graphy*] **:** a process (as lithography or offset) for printing from a plane surface; *also* **:** matter printed by such process — compare INTAGLIO, LETTERPRESS, STENCIL

pla·nom·e·ter \pləˈnäməd·ə(r)\ *n* [²*plan-* + *-meter*] **:** a surface plate or other device for gauging a plane surface

pla·nom·e·try \-mə·trē\ *n* -ES [²*plan-* + *-metry*] **:** the art or process of producing or gauging a plane surface (as with a planometer)

pla·no·miller \ˈplānə+ˌ-\ *n* [²*plan-* + *miller*] **:** a milling machine resembling a planer

pla·no·milling machine \ˌplānō+ . . . -\ *n* **:** PLANOMILLER

pla·nont \ˈplaˌnänt\ *n* -S [¹*plan-* + *-ont*] **:** a motile organism (as the amoebula of various protozoans or the gamete of some phycomycetes)

¹**pla·nor·bid** \pləˈnȯrbəd\ *adj* [NL *Planorbidae*] **:** of or relating to the Planorbidae

²**planorbid** \"\ *n* -S **:** a snail of the family Planorbidae

pla·nor·bi·dae \-bəˌdē\ *n pl, cap* [NL *Planorbis,* type genus, + *-idae*] **:** a family of freshwater pulmonate snails having a single pair of tentacles with an eye at the base of each and gills as well as lungs and including numerous forms important as intermediate hosts of pathogenic trematode worms — see PLANORBIS

pla·nor·bis \-bəs\ *n, cap* [NL, fr. L *planus* flat + *orbis* ring, disk, orb — more at FLOOR] **:** a widely distributed genus (the type of the family Planorbidae) of snails with secondarily acquired gills, a fundamentally sinistral body, and a more or less discoidal and planospiral shell that may be either dextral or sinistral

plan·o·sol \ˈplanəˌsōl\ *n* -S [²*plan-* + L *solum* ground, soil — more at SOIL] **:** an intrazonal group of soils with strongly leached upper layer over a compacted clay or silt that is developed on smooth flat uplands in cool to warm humid to subhumid regions

pla·no·spiral \ˌplānō+\ *also* **pla·ni·spiral** \ˌplānə+\ *adj* [*planospiral* fr. ²*plan-* + *spiral; planispiral* fr. *plani-* + *spiral*] **:** having the shell coiled in one plane — used esp. of foraminifers and gastropod mollusks — **pla·no·spirally** \"+\ *adv*

plan·o·spore \ˈplanəˌspō(ə)r\ *n* [¹*plan-* + *spore*] **:** a motile spore **:** ZOOSPORE a

plan position indicator *n* **:** PPI

plans *pl of* PLAN, *pres 3d sing of* PLAN

Plan·sifter \ˈplanˌsiftə(r)\ *trademark* — used for any of several oscillating sifters arranged one above the other in a flour mill for separating and grading the stocks from the break rolls

¹**plant** \ˈplant, ˈplaa(ə)nt, ˈplaint, ˈplȧnt\ *vb* -ED/-ING/-S [ME *planten,* fr. OE *plantian,* fr. LL *plantare* to plant, fix in place, fr. L, to plant, fr. *planta* plant] *vt* **1 a :** to put in the ground and cover with soil so as to grow ⟨~ corn⟩ ⟨~ seeds⟩ **b :** to set in the ground for growth ⟨~ trees⟩ ⟨~ bushes⟩ **c :** to put plants to grow in **:** CULTIVATE ⟨cleans up and ~s the ground thus regained from the forest —J.G.Frazer⟩ ⟨the river overflowed the ~*ed* land —*Amer. Guide Series: Tenn.*⟩ **d :** IMPLANT ⟨the task of ~*ing* in the native-born generations a knowledge of the ancestral language —Oscar Handlin⟩ **2 a** (1) **:** to establish or institute in a particular place or region ⟨engaged in ~*ing* a colony of Germans in the valley —H.E. Scudder⟩ ⟨~*ed* the first church in that part of the colony —L. H.Beck⟩ (2) **:** to settle as a colonist ⟨~*ed* former soldiers in the border regions⟩ **b :** COLONIZE, POPULATE ⟨intending to return and ~ Delaware —John Winthrop⟩ **c :** to place (animals) in a particular locality so as to grow and multiply there ⟨underseas gardens in which the oysters are ~*ed,* cultivated, and harvested —*Amer. Guide Series: Conn.*⟩ ⟨~*ing* beavers for conservation purposes —Willis Peterson⟩ **d :** to stock with animals ⟨~*ed* his ranch with beef cattle⟩ ⟨~*ed* the stream with trout⟩ ⟨~*ed* the bay with clams⟩ **e :** INOCULATE 2 a (2) **3 a :** to place in or on the ground ⟨stakes were ~*ed* to determine the ice movement in the mountain region —G. de Q. Robin⟩ ⟨~*ed* a foot in a prairie-dog hole —F.B.Gipson⟩ **b :** to place firmly or forcibly ⟨came boiling out and ~*ed* herself in his path with her hands on her hips —Robert Murphy⟩ ⟨~*ed* a hard blow on his chin⟩ **c :** to set firmly in position **:** fix in place **:** ESTABLISH ⟨~*ed* obstruction buoys around a large coral head —K.M.Dodson⟩ ⟨remained ~*ed* in the rocker —J.C.Lincoln⟩ **4 a :** CONCEAL, HIDE ⟨the plunder was ~*ed* under the floor of a restaurant —*London Daily Chronicle*⟩ **b :** to conceal (something) temporarily where discovery may deceive or mislead ⟨~*ed* a gun in the butler's coat⟩ ⟨~*ed* gold nuggets in a worthless mine⟩ **c :** to covertly arrange publication or dissemination of ⟨politicians and officials exploit their intimacy with the press and ~ true or false stories with them —*Times Lit. Supp.*⟩ ⟨a report, undoubtedly ~*ed* by him, that he had gone to South America —Robert Shaplen⟩ **d :** to place or cause to be placed in a position under false colors ⟨~*ed* a spy on the committee's staff⟩ ⟨frequently the gang is not able to ~ a confederate inside the house —Richard Harrison⟩ **e :** to prepare beforehand **:** PREARRANGE ⟨carefully ~s the surprise word —*Britain Today*⟩ ⟨asked an obviously ~*ed* question⟩ **5 :** leave behind **:** ABANDON ⟨~*ed* his family and left them penniless⟩ **6 :** BURY, INTER ⟨these people believe in sealed copper coffins in vaults, and they are decidedly not ~*ed* but laid to rest —Mari Sandoz⟩ ⟨death lost some of its terrors when one could be ~*ed* neatly in a corner of one's own farm —Stuart Cloete⟩ ~ *vi* **1 :** to perform the act of planting ⟨this is perfect weather for ~*ing*⟩ **2 :** to become a plant **:** GROW

²**plant** \"\ *n* -S [ME *plante,* fr. OE, fr. L *planta,* prob. back-formation fr. (assumed) L *plantare* to tread the ground in planting, fr. L *planta* sole of the foot — more at PLACE] **1 a** (1) **:** a young tree, vine, shrub, or herb planted or suitable for planting **:** a vegetable, flower, fruit, or ornamental grown for or ready for transplanting ⟨cabbage ~s for sale⟩ ⟨thin the hill to four ~s⟩ — see HOUSEPLANT, POT PLANT, WILD FLOWER (2) *obs* **:** CUTTING, SLIP, SET **b** *archaic* **:** a sapling used as a cudgel or pole **c :** any of numerous organisms constituting the kingdom Plantae, being typically characterized by lack of locomotive movement or rapid motor response, by absence of obvious nervous or sensory organs though possessing irritability as indicated by specific response to stimuli, by possession of cell walls composed of cellulose, and by a nutritive system in which carbohydrates are formed photosynthetically through the action of chlorophyll and organic nutrients are not required, and exhibiting a strong tendency to alternation of a sexual with an asexual generation though one or the other may be greatly modified or almost wholly suppressed — see ALGA, FERN, FUNGUS, MOSS; ANIMAL, SAPROPHYTE **2 :** one thought to resemble a growing plant ⟨a sensitive ~ who must be shielded from shock⟩ **3 a :** the land, buildings, machinery, apparatus, and fixtures employed in carrying on a trade or a mechanical or other industrial business ⟨to meet the nation's telephone needs we again built a great deal of new physical ~ —C.F.Craig⟩ **b :** a factory or workshop for the manufacture of a particular product ⟨an automobile ~⟩ ⟨an ice-cream ~⟩ **c :** the total facilities available for production or service in a particular country or place ⟨a nation which both in present ~ and in natural resources is probably the richest in the world —*New Republic*⟩ ⟨not just the town's sewers but its streets, its schools — its whole ~ — had to be enlarged for the new arrivals —C.W.Thayer⟩ **d :** a piece of equipment or a set of machine parts functioning together for the performance of a particular operation ⟨a couple of experts armed with drills, an oxyacetylene ~, and other strange tools —F.W. Crofts⟩ **e** *chiefly Austral* **:** the equipment and personnel necessary for an enterprise (as stock raising or mining) ⟨such a ~ may consist of a head stockman, one or two other white men and up to twenty aboriginals —*Australian Veterinary Jour.*⟩ **f :** the physical equipment (as buildings or athletic fields) of an institution (as a college) ⟨several large bequests have enabled the school to expand its ~⟩ **4** [¹*plant*] **a :** stolen goods; *also* **:** a place for storing them **b** (1) **:** UNDERCOVER MAN ⟨joined the criminal ring as a ~⟩ (2) **:** fixed police surveillance ⟨to put a ~ on a suspect⟩ **c :** a swindling plot **:** a scheme to defraud **d** (1) **:** something deliberately placed so that its discovery may deceive or mislead ⟨left muddy footprints as a ~ to confuse the police⟩ (2) **:** something (as a news story or rumor) whose publication or dissemination is deliberately arranged by an individual or group for a particular purpose ⟨the story had all the earmarks of a propaganda ~⟩ **e** (1) **:** a seemingly casual statement or action deliberately inserted in a play to prepare the spectator for a later development or effect (2) **:** a person placed in an audience to take a seemingly spontaneous part in the proceedings **f :** a trap for wrongdoers ⟨the town has set up several ~s for traffic violators⟩ **5** [¹*plant*] **:** a way of standing **:** POSE ⟨took up a determined ~ in front of the door⟩ **6** [¹*plant*] **a :** a crop or growth of something planted ⟨the sugar beet is up to a good ~ once again —A.G.Street⟩ **b** (1) **:** the stocking of a place with animals (as fish or game) for conservation or sport ⟨the authorities made a small ~ of deer on the islands —C.C.Van Fleet⟩ (2) **:** an oyster that has been bedded as distinguished from one of natural growth, *also* **:** a young oyster suitable for transplanting

plan·ta \ˈplantə\ *n, pl* **plan·tae** \-nˌtē\ [NL, fr. L, sole of the foot — more at PLACE] **1 :** the back side of the shank of a bird's leg **2 a :** the flattened end of the proleg of a caterpillar **b :** a sclerite on the insect pretarsus

plant·able \ˈplantəbəl\ *adj* **:** capable of being planted ⟨~ trees⟩ ⟨~ fields⟩

plan·tad \ˈplanˌtad\ *adv* [L *planta* sole of the foot + E *-ad*] **:** toward the sole of the foot

plan·tae \ˈplanˌtē\ *n pl, cap* [NL, fr. L, pl. of *planta* plant] **:** the basic group of living things that comprises all the plants **:** PLANT KINGDOM — compare ANIMALIA, PROTISTA

plant·age \ˈplantij\ *n* -S [²*plant* + *-age*] *archaic* **:** VEGETATION

plan·tag·e·net \planˈtajənət\ *n* -S *cap* [*Plantagenet,* nickname of the family adopted as surname by Richard, Duke of York †1460] **:** a member of an English royal family founded by Geoffrey, Count of Anjou, through his marriage in 1128 with Matilda, daughter of Henry I of England, to which belonged the rulers of England from 1154 to 1485 — see ANGEVIN

plan·ta·gi·na·ce·ae \ˌplantəjəˈnāsēˌē\ *n pl, cap* [NL *Plantagin-, Plantago,* type genus + *-aceae*] **:** a family of dicotyledonous plants constituting the order Plantaginales and characterized by spicate or capitate tetramerous flowers with a membranous or scarious corolla and a fruit that is a pyxidium or an indehiscent nutlet — see PLANTAGO — **plan·ta·gi·na·ceous** \ˌ===ˈnāshəs\ *adj*

plan·ta·gi·na·les \ˌ===ˈnā(ˌ)lēz\ *n pl, cap* [NL *Plantagin-, Plantago* + *-ales*] **:** an order of plants coextensive with the family Plantaginaceae

plan·ta·go \plan'tā(ˌ)gō\ *n* [NL *Plantagin-, Plantago,* fr. L, plantain — more at PLANTAIN] **1** *cap* **:** a large genus (the type of the family Plantaginaceae) of acaulescent or short-stemmed chiefly dooryard or roadside weeds that have narrow or elliptic leaves and very small inconspicuous flowers in close-bracted spikes or heads — see [1]PLANTAIN, RIBGRASS **2** -s **:** any plant of the genus *Plantago*

plantago seed *n* **:** FLEASEED 1

[1]**plan·tain** \'plantᵊn, -ntən, *also* -n.ˌtān\ *n* -s [ME *plauntein, plantaine,* fr. OF *plantain, plantein,* fr. L *plantagin-, plantago,* fr. *planta* sole of the foot; fr. its broad leaves — more at PLACE] **:** a plant of the genus *Plantago* — see BROAD-LEAVED PLANTAIN, RUGEL'S PLANTAIN

[2]**plantain** \"\ *n* -s [MF *plantain,* fr. ML *plantanus,* alter. (influenced by L *planta* plant) of L *platanus* plane tree — more at PLANE] **:** [2]PLANE

[3]**plantain** \"\ *n* -s [Sp *plántano, plátano* plane tree, banana tree, fr. ML *plantanus* plane tree] **1 :** a banana plant (*Musa paradisiaca*) **2 :** the starchy fruit of the plantain that is a staple item of diet throughout the tropics when cooked and that is distinguished in appearance from the ordinary banana by its angular shape and yellowish green color

plantain

plantain eater *also* **plantain cutter** *n* [[3]*plantain*] **:** TOURACO

plantain family *n* [[1]*plantain*] **:** PLANTAGINACEAE

plantain lily *n* **:** a plant of the genus *Hosta* distinguished by plaited basal leaves and racemose white or violet flowers

plantain shoreweed *n* **:** SHOREWEED

plant·al \'plantᵊl\ *adj* [[2]*plant* + *-al*] **:** of or relating to plants **:** VEGETATIVE

plant anatomy *n* **:** ANATOMY 1 b

plant–animal \'=ˌ===\ *n* [NL *plantanimal,* trans. of Gk *zōophyton* zoophyte] **:** ZOOPHYTE

plan·tar \'plantə(r)\ *adj* [L *plantaris,* fr. *planta* sole of the foot + *-aris* -ar — more at PLACE] **:** of, relating to, or typical of the sole of the foot ⟨the ~ wart is in the skin rather than on it —H.K.Schwarzfeld⟩

plantar artery *n* **:** either of two branches into which the posterior tibial artery divides

plantar cushion *n* **:** a thick pad of fibrous tissue behind and under the navicular and coffin bones of the horse

plantar fascia *n* **:** a dense fibrous membrane of the sole of the foot that binds together the deeper structures

plan·tar·is \plan'ta(a)rəs\ *n, pl* **plantar·es** \-ˌrēz\ [NL, fr. L *plantaris* plantar] **:** a small muscle of the calf of the leg that arises from the lower end of the femur and the posterior ligament of the knee joint and is inserted with the tendon of Achilles by a very long slender tendon into the calcaneus

plantar ligament *n* **:** the superficial part of the inferior calcaneocuboid ligament in the sole of the foot

plantar nerve *n* **:** either of two nerves into which the tibial nerve divides

plantar reflex *n* **:** a reflex movement of flexing the foot and toes that after the first year is the normal response to tickling of the sole — compare BABINSKI REFLEX

plantar vein *n* **:** one of the veins that accompany the plantar arteries

plan·ta·tion \plan'tāshən, plaan-, plån-, *in southern US* " *or* -nt-'ā-\ *n* -s *often attrib* [L *plantation-, plantatio,* fr. *plantatus* (past. part. of *plantare* to plant) + *-ion-, -io* -ion] **1 a** *archaic* **:** the act or process of planting **b :** something that is planted ⟨plant the seeds of the harvest you want to reap in cleared, plowed soil and protect the ~ while it grows —Lincoln Steffens⟩ **2 a :** a usu. large group of plants under cultivation ⟨a ~ of nodding purple and ivory-colored lilacs —*New Yorker*⟩ **b :** GROVE ⟨screened from the converging roads by a ~ of copper beeches —Osbert Lancaster⟩ **c :** a cultivated oyster bed **3 a :** the settlement of people in a particular region **:** COLONIZATION ⟨forced ~s of English settlers —Seamus MacCall⟩ **b :** the founding or establishing of something **:** IMPLANTATION **4 a** *sometimes cap* **:** a settlement in a new country or region **:** COLONY ⟨a vessel from the overseas ~s —Leslie Thomas⟩ ⟨Rhode Island and Providence *Plantations*⟩ **b :** a minor division of local government in Maine **5 a :** a place that is planted **:** cultivated land ⟨the man creates the ~ by cutting down the trees of the forest, the woman turns the soil —J.G.Frazer⟩ **b :** a usu. large estate in a tropical or subtropical region that is generally cultivated by unskilled or semiskilled labor under central direction ⟨rich cotton land, cultivated in large ~s —*Amer. Guide Series: Ark.*⟩ **6 :** a moderate reddish brown that is lighter, stronger, and much yellower than roan and yellower, lighter, and stronger than mahogany

plantation rubber *n* **:** natural rubber grown esp. in the Malay Peninsula, Indonesia, and Ceylon chiefly from a Brazilian tree (*Hevea braziliensis*) imported into those areas

plantation walking horse *or* **plantation walker** *n, usu cap P & sometimes cap W&H* **:** TENNESSEE WALKING HORSE

plant band *n* **:** BAND 4 e

plant bed *n* **:** an area in which plants (as tomatoes or pansies) are grown usu. from seed until ready for transplanting to other locations

plant bug *n* **:** an insect of the hemipterous family Miridae including many that are destructive pests of plants — see TARNISHED PLANT BUG

plant cane *n* **:** a stalk of sugar cane of the first growth from the cutting — compare RATOON

plant collar *n* **:** a band of tar paper or similar material placed around the base of the stem of transplanted seedlings (as plants of the cabbage family) to protect them from injury by insects

plant cutter *n* **1 :** any of several birds of the family Phytotomidae **2 :** TOURACO

planté battery \plänᵗtā-\ *n, usu cap P* [after Gaston *Planté* †1889 French physicist] **:** a type of lead-acid storage battery

planted *past of* PLANT

plant·er \'plantə(r), -aan-, -ain-\ *n* -s [[1]*plant* + *-er*] **1 :** one that cultivates plants: as **a** (1) **:** FARMER (2) **:** one who owns or operates a plantation **b :** a planting machine **2 a :** one who settles or founds a place ⟨among the earliest ~s of York —W.M.Emery⟩; *esp* **:** one who helps to found a new colony or settles in it ⟨one of the ~s of Virginia⟩ **b :** one settled in Ireland on forfeited lands or in the holding of an evicted tenant **3 :** one who helps to establish a doctrine or institution ⟨one of the chief ~s of democracy in his country⟩ **4 :** a snag fixed at one end in a riverbed and standing almost rigidly — distinguished from *sawyer* **5** [[2]*plant* + *-er*] **:** an owner or operator of a fishing or shipping plant in Newfoundland **6 :** a container (as a box, pot, or hanging basket) in which plants are grown or placed for decorative purposes — compare CACHEPOT, DISH GARDEN

planter's punch *n* **:** a punch of rum, lime or lemon juice, sugar, water, and sometimes bitters, shaken with crushed ice and garnished with slices of fruit or mint

plant factor *n* **:** the ratio of the average power load of a plant to its rated capacity

plant food *n* **1 :** food materials used by plants **2 :** FERTILIZER

plant forcer *n* **:** HOT CAP

plant growth substance *n* **:** a growth regulator for plants

plant hopper *n* **:** an insect of the hemipterous families Membracidae, Fulgoridae, and various related groups

plant hormone *n* **1 :** a plant regulator (as indoleacetic acid or ethylene) produced by plants that usu. moves within the plant from the site of production to the site of action — called also *phytohormone* **2 :** a synthetic plant regulator

plant house *n* **:** a structure in which plants are kept or grown — compare CONSERVATORY, GREENHOUSE

plan·ti·gra·da \ˌplantə'grādə, plan'tigrədə\ *n pl, cap* [NL, fr. F *plantigrade*] *in former classifications* **:** a group consisting of the plantigrade carnivores

[1]**plan·ti·grade** \'plantəˌgrād\ *adj* [F, fr. L *planta* sole of the foot + F *-grade*] **:** walking on the sole with the heel touching the ground ⟨the bear and man are both ~ animals⟩ — opposed to *digitigrade*

[2]**plantigrade** \"\ *n* -s **:** a plantigrade animal

[1]**plant·ing** \'plantiŋ, -laan-, -lain-, -lån-, -tēŋ\ *n* -s [ME, fr. gerund of *planten* to plant] **1 :** the act or process of setting in the ground for cultivation **2 a :** PLANTATION 2 ⟨surrounded by many ~s of elm and maple —*Amer. Guide Series: Conn.*⟩ **b :** an area where plants are grown for commercial or decorative purposes **3 :** an act or instance of stocking or introducing animals (as fish, shellfish, or game) in a particular place **4 :** a process of introducing additional colors in woven fabrics (as rugs) by substituting one colored thread for another at intervals

[2]**planting** \"\ *adj* [[1]*planting*] **:** owning or operating a plantation ⟨the southern ~ aristocracy⟩

planting pit *n* [[1]*planting*] **:** a wooden or metal box sunk at the pit end of a pole-vault runway to prevent the vaulter's pole from slipping

planting stick *n* **:** DIBBLE

plant kingdom *n* **:** the one of the three basic groups of natural objects that comprises all living and extinct plants — compare ANIMAL KINGDOM, MINERAL KINGDOM

plant·less \'plantləs\ *adj* **:** having no plants ⟨a ~ desert⟩

plant·let \-lət\ *n* -s **:** a little plant

plant life *n* **1 :** FLORA, VEGETATION **2 :** the mode of life of plants

plantlike \'=ˌ=\ *adj, of an animal* **:** resembling a plant esp. in being fixed to a substrate and in exhibiting indeterminate growth ⟨certain ~ corals may continue to enlarge indefinitely⟩

plantlike flagellate *n* **:** any of various organisms constituting the subclass Phytomastigina, having many characteristics in common with typical algae, and being considered usu. as protozoans by protozoologists and as algae by algologists

plant·ling \'plantliŋ\ *n* -s [[2]*plant* + *-ling*] **:** PLANTLET

plant liqueur *n* **:** a liqueur made from plants, roots, herbs, and seeds first macerated in brandy and then distilled — compare FRUIT LIQUEUR

plant louse *n* **1 :** any of numerous small insects of the family Aphididae that live on plants and suck their juices; *broadly* **:** APHID **2 :** any of various small insects of similar habits; *esp* **:** JUMPING PLANT LOUSE

plan·toc·ra·cy \plan'täkrəsē\ *n* -ES [*planter* + *-o-* + *-cracy*] **1 :** government by planters **2 :** a ruling class made up of planters

plant out *vb* [[1]*plant*] *vt* **:** to transplant from a protected or enclosed place (as from a cold frame, pot, greenhouse) to the open ~ *vi* **:** to carry out a transplanting

plant patent *n* [[2]*plant*] **:** a patent granted to one who produces a new and distinctive plant by breeding or selection and propagates it asexually

plant pathologist *n* **:** a specialist in plant pathology

plant pathology *n* **:** a branch of botany that deals with the diseases of plants

plant physiologist *n* **:** a specialist in plant physiology

plant physiology *n* **:** a branch of botany that deals with plant functions

plant regulator *n* **:** a natural or synthetic organic substance (as an auxin or maleic hydrazide) other than a nutrient that acts in very small amounts to modify any physiological process in plants — compare PLANT HORMONE

plants *pres 3d sing of* PLANT, *pl of* PLANT

plants·man \'plantsmən\ *n, pl* **plantsmen 1 a :** one who raises or sells plants commercially **:** NURSERYMAN **b :** one who practices the science or art of raising plants **:** HORTICULTURIST **2 :** one who loves plants

plant sociology *n* **:** PHYTOSOCIOLOGY

plan·tu·la \'planchələ\ *n, pl* **plantu·lae** \-chəˌlē\ [NL, dim. of L *planta* sole of the foot — more at PLACE] **:** a small structure resembling a cushion found on the ventral surface of the tarsal segments of most insects — **plan·tu·lar** \-chələ(r)\ *adj*

plant·ule \'planˌchül\ *n* -s [NL *plantula,* dim. of L *planta* plant] **:** an embryo plant

plan·u·la \'planyələ\ *n, pl* **planu·lae** \-yəˌlē\ [NL, fem. dim. of L *planus* flat — more at FLOOR] **:** the very young free-swimming larva of a coelenterate that usu. has a flattened oval or oblong form and consists of an outer layer of ciliated ectoderm cells and an internal mass of endoderm cells — **plan·u·lar** \-yələ(r)\ *adj*

plan·u·loid \-yəˌlȯid\ *adj* [NL *planula* + E *-oid*] **:** resembling a planula

plan·u·loi·dea \ˌplanyə'lȯidēə\ [NL, fr. *planula* + *-oidea*] *syn of* MESOZOA

pla·num \'plānəm\ *n, pl* **pla·na** \-nə\ [L, neut. of *planus* flat — more at FLOOR] **:** a flat surface of bone esp. of the skull

plan view *n* **:** the appearance of an object as seen from above

planx·ty \'plaŋkstē\ *n* -ES [origin unknown] **1 :** an Irish melody for the harp written in triplets and slower than the jig **2 :** a dance to a planxty

plap·pert \'pläpə(r)t\ *n* -s [G, alter. of MHG *blaffert*] **:** BLAFFERT

[1]**plaque** *also* **placque** \'plak *chiefly Brit* 'plåk\ *n* -s [F, fr. MF, solid metal sheet, fr. *plaquier* to plate, fr. MD *placken* to piece, spot, patch, beat; akin to MD *placke* piece, spot, a coin, MHG *placke* spot, patch] **1 a :** an ornamental brooch; *esp* **:** the badge of an honorary order **b :** a flat thin piece (as of metal, clay, or ivory) used for decoration (as on a wall or in an article of furniture) ⟨a handsome ceramic ~ hung over the fireplace⟩ **c** (1) **:** an inscribed usu. metal tablet placed (as on a building or post) to identify a site or commemorate an individual or event ⟨roadside ~s mark historic battles and gallant deeds of bygone days —*Time*⟩ (2) **:** NAMEPLATE **d :** CHIP 5a **2 :** an abnormal patch or flattened area on some body part or surface: **a :** a localized patch of skin disease ⟨psoriatic ~⟩ **b :** a deposit of lipoid or fibrous matter in the wall of a blood vessel ⟨atheromatous ~s in the aorta⟩ **c :** a film of mucus harboring bacteria on a tooth **3 :** BLOOD PLATELET

[2]**pla·qué** \(')pla¦kā\ *adj* [F, fr. past part. of *plaquer* to plate, fr. MF *plaquier*] **:** EN PLACARD

pla·quette \(')pla¦ket\ *n* -s [F, fr. *plaque* + *-ette*] **1 :** a small plaque **2 :** a metal stamping die that is cut in relief and used to decorate the sides of leather bookbindings

[1]**plash** \'plash, -aa(ə)sh,-aish\ *n* -ES [ME *plasche,* fr. OE *plæsc;* akin to MD *plasch, plas* pool, plash; all prob. of imit. origin] **:** a shallow or marshy pool **:** PUDDLE ⟨the bird . . . bathed itself in some ~es nearby —Hugh McCrae⟩

[2]**plash** \"\ *vt* -ED/-ING/-ES [ME *plashen,* fr. MF *plaissier,* fr. OF, fr. *plais* hedge, twined fence, prob. fr. (assumed) VL *plaxus* entwined, alter. of L *plexus,* past part. of *plectere* to entwine, braid — more at PLY] *Brit* **:** PLEACH ⟨~ a hedge⟩

[3]**plash** \"\ *n* -ES [prob. imit.] **1 a :** a surface agitation of water with accompanying sound ⟨the measured ~ of oars —A.C.Benson⟩ ⟨the ceaseless ~ of the waves —William Black⟩ **b** (1) **:** a splashing movement of water ⟨~ of the fountains from the mouths of stone dolphins —Mark Schorer⟩ (2) **:** a movement or sound suggestive of the splashing of water ⟨the ~ of the paintbrush against the wall —Donald Windham⟩ ⟨the ~ of bare feet made him turn his head —Josephine Pinckney⟩ **c :** a dash or blotch esp. of color or light ⟨a few ~es of white in the breast of the duck —J.H.Robinson †1935⟩ ⟨effect of the wilder ~ of irresponsible prismatic impressions which vertigo had unloosed —Florence Gould⟩ **2** *dial chiefly Eng* **:** a heavy fall of rain

[4]**plash** \"\ *vb* -ED/-ING/-ES [perh. fr. D *plassen,* fr. MD, of imit. origin] *vt* **1 :** to break the surface of (water) so as to cause a surface agitation with an accompanying sound **:** SPLASH **2 :** DASH, SPATTER, SPECKLE ⟨no bird on dew-*plashed* wing —Walter de la Mare⟩ ~ *vi* **1 :** to dash or tumble about with a splashing or spattering sound — used esp. of water ⟨far below him ~*ed* the waters —H.W.Longfellow⟩ ⟨raindrops ~*ed* on the tile roof —Anne S. Mehdevi⟩ **2 :** to cause a splashing or spattering ⟨~*ing* of hooves in water —Robinson Jeffers⟩ ⟨could hear a slight ~*ing* as the bows of the lighter forged through the water —Miles Burton⟩

plash·ing·ly *adv* **:** with plashing movement or sound

[1]**plashy** \-shē, -shi\ *adj* -ER/-EST [[1]*plash* + *-y*] **:** abounding with pools or puddles ⟨down the steep, ~ path they poured —Rudyard Kipling⟩ **:** MARSHY ⟨~ brink of weedy lake —W.C. Bryant⟩ ⟨the heron fishes in his ~ pool —Walter de la Mare⟩

[2]**plashy** \"\ *adj* -ER/-EST [[3]*plash* + *-y*] **:** marked by plashes **:** SPLASHING, PLASHING ⟨a ~ tramp by the side of the bridge caught the sensitive ear —Washington Irving⟩

-pla·sia \'plāzh(ē)ə\ *or* **-pla·sy** \ˌplāsē, -lasē, pləsē\ *n comb form, pl* **-plasias** *or* **-plasies** [NL *-plasia,* fr. Gk *plasis* molding + NL *-ia* -y] **:** development **:** formation ⟨dys*plasia*⟩ ⟨homo*plasy*⟩ ⟨hetero*plasia*⟩

-pla·sis \ˌplāsəs\ *n comb form, pl* **-pla·ses** \-āˌsēz\ [NL, fr. Gk *plasis* molding, fr. *plassein* to mold] **:** molding ⟨ana*plasis*⟩ ⟨cata*plasis*⟩ ⟨para*plasis*⟩

plasm \'plazəm\ *n* -s [LL *plasma* form, mold] **:** PLASMA

plasm- *or* **plasmo-** *comb form* [F, fr. NL *plasma*] **1 :** plasma ⟨*plasm*apheresis⟩ ⟨*plasmo*dium⟩ **2 :** cytoplasm ⟨*plasmo*lysis⟩ ⟨*plasmo*gamy⟩ **3 :** protoplasm ⟨*plasmo*ptysis⟩

-plasm \ˌplazəm\ *or* **-plas·ma** \¦plazmə\ *n comb form* -s [G *-plasma,* fr. NL *plasma*] **:** formative or formed material (as of a cell or tissue) ⟨cyto*plasm*⟩ ⟨nucleo*plasm*⟩ ⟨karyo*plasma*⟩ ⟨meta*plasm*⟩

plas·ma \'plazmə\ *n* -s [G, fr. LL, form, mold, fr. Gk, fr. *plassein* to mold — more at PLASTER] **1 :** a faintly translucent cryptocrystalline variety of quartz of various shades of green **2** [NL, fr. LL, form, mold] **a :** the fluid part of blood, lymph, or milk that is distinguishable from suspended material (as fat globules or cells) and that in blood differs from serum essentially in containing the antecedent substance of fibrin in addition to the constituents of serum **b :** the juice that can be expressed from muscle **3** [NL] **:** PROTOPLASM **4 :** a mixture of starch and glycerol used as an ointment base **5 :** an ionized gas (as in the atmospheres of stars) containing about equal numbers of positive ions and electrons and differing from an ordinary gas in being a good conductor of electricity and in being affected by a magnetic field

plas·ma·blast \'plazməˌblast\ *n* -s [*plasma* + *-blast*] **:** a precursor of a plasma cell

plasma cell *n* **:** an antibody-secreting cell that develops from a lymphocyte with antigenic proteins on its surface

plas·ma·cyte \'plazməˌsīt\ *n* [ISV *plasma* + *-cyte*] **:** PLASMA CELL

plas·ma·cy·toid \¦==¦sīˌtȯid\ *adj* **:** resembling or derived from a plasma cell

plas·ma·gel \'plazmə+ˌ-\ *n* [*plasma* + *gel*] **:** gelated protoplasm; *esp* **:** the outer firm zone of a pseudopodium — compare PLASMASOL

plas·ma·gene \-ˌjēn\ *n* [ISV *plasma* + *-gene*] **:** a submicroscopic factor or determiner believed by some biologists to be present in the cytoplasm of cells and to influence physiological and hereditary phenomena of the cytoplasm much as genes are believed to do for the entire cell — compare PLASTOGENE — **plas·ma·gen·ic** \¦==¦jenik\ *adj*

plas·mal \'plazməl\ *n* -s [prob. back-formation fr. *plasmalogen*] **:** a substance consisting of one or more aldehydes of the type of those related to palmitic acid and stearic acid obtained in the form of an acetal (as by treatment of a plasmalogen with alkali)

plas·ma·lemma \¦plazmə+\ *n* [NL, fr. *plasma* + Gk *lemma* rind, husk — more at LEMMA] **:** the differentiated protoplasmic surface bounding a cell **:** PLASMA MEMBRANE

plas·mal·o·gen \plaz'maləjən, -ˌjen\ *n* -s [*plasm-* + *al*kali + connective *-o-* + *-gen*] **:** a phosphatide that is the precursor of plasmal in tissue

plasmal reaction *n* **:** a modified Feulgen reaction designed to detect aldehyde in tissue

plasma membrane *n* **1 :** an external semipermeable limiting layer of cell protoplasm that is commonly regarded as an oriented protein gel rich in lipoids and calcium and that is a major factor in regulating exchanges between the cell and its environment — called also *cell membrane, ectoplast;* see CELL WALL **2 :** a protoplasmic surface (as a tonoplast) regarded as similar in structure or function to the plasma membrane

plas·ma·pher·e·sis \ˌplazmə'ferəsəs\ *also* **plas·ma·phore·sis** \-ˌfə'rēsəs, -'fȯrəs-\ *n, pl* **plasmaphere·ses** \-ˌsēz\ [*plasmapheresis,* NL, fr. *plasm-* + Gk *aphairesis* action of taking off, removal; *plasmaphoresis,* NL, alter. (influenced by *-phoresis*) of *plasmapheresis* — more at APHAERESIS] **:** a process in which blood constituents and esp. red blood cells are separated from the plasma of an individual and returned to his circulatory system intact if he is a blood donor or minus various abnormal constituents (as sickle cells) if he is a patient

plas·ma·sol \'plazmə+ˌ-\ *n* [*plasma* + *sol*] **:** solated protoplasm; *esp* **:** the inner fluid zone of a pseudopodium or amoeboid cell — compare PLASMAGEL

plasmasome *var of* PLASMOSOME

plas·mat·ic \(')plaz¦mad·ik\ *adj* [*plasmatic* fr. Gk *plasmat-, plasma* + E *-ic*] **:** of, relating to, or occurring in plasma esp. of blood

plasmato- *comb form* [Gk *plasmat-, plasma*] **:** PLASM- ⟨*plasmato*parous⟩

plas·ma·top·a·rous \¦plazmə¦täpərəs\ *adj* [*plasmato-* + *-parous*] **:** discharging the protoplasmic contents of a conidium in an undivided mass that first becomes invested with a membrane or wall and then puts out a germ tube — used of various downy mildews

plas·ma·tor·rhex·is \ˌplazməd·ə'reksəs\ *n, pl* **plasmatorrhex·es** \-kˌsēz\ [NL, fr. *plasmato-* + *-rrhexis*] **:** the disruption of a cell by internal pressure due to swelling

-plas·mia \'plazmēə\ *n comb form* -s [NL, fr. *plasma* + *-ia*] **:** a (specified) condition of the blood plasm ⟨oligo*plasmia*⟩

plas·mic \'plazmik, -mēk\ *adj* [*plasm-* + *-ic*] **:** PROTOPLASMIC, PLASMATIC — **plas·mi·cal·ly** \-mək(ə)lē, -mēk-, -li\ *adv*

plas·min \'plazmən\ *n* -s [*plasm-* + *-in*] **:** a proteolytic enzyme that dissolves the fibrin of blood clots and that is formed by the activation of plasminogen (as by streptokinase) — called also *fibrinolysin*

plas·min·o·gen \plaz'minəjən, -ˌjen\ *n* -s [*plasmin* + connective *-o-* + *-gen*] **:** the precursor of plasmin found in blood plasma and serum — called also *profibrinolysin*

plasmo- — see PLASM-

Plas·mo·chin \'plazməkən\ *trademark* — used for pamaquine

plas·mo·cy·to·ma *or* **plas·ma·cy·to·ma** \ˌplazməsī'tōmə\ *n, pl* **plasmocyto·mas** \-məz\ *or* **plasmocytoma·ta** \-məd·ə\ [*plasmocytoma* fr. NL, alter. of *plasmacytoma; plasmacytoma* fr. NL, fr. ISV *plasmacyte* + NL *-oma*] **:** a myeloma composed of plasma cells

plasmod- *or* **plasmodi-** *or* **plasmodio-** *comb form* [NL *plasmodium*] **:** plasmodium ⟨*plasmodio*carp⟩ ⟨*plasmodi*trophoblast⟩ ⟨*plasmod*ic⟩

plas·mode \'plazˌmōd\ *n* -s [NL *plasmodium*] **:** PLASMODIUM 1a

plas·mo·des·ma \ˌplazmə'dezmə\ *also* **plas·mo·desm** \'==ˌdezəm\ *or* **plas·mo·des·mus** \ˌ==ˈdezməs\ *n, pl* **plasmodesma·ta** \ˌ==ˈməd·ə\ *or* **plasmodesmas** [*plasmodesma* fr. NL, fr. *plasm-* + Gk *desma* bond; *plasmodesm* ISV, fr. NL *plasmodesmus; plasmodesmus* fr. NL, fr. *plasm-* + Gk *desmos* band, bond — more at DESM-, DESMA] **:** a protoplasmic connection between cells **:** an intercellular bridge — called also *cell bridge* — **plas·mo·des·ma·tal** \¦==¦məd·ᵊl\ *or* **plas·mo·des·mal** \¦==¦=məl\ *or* **plas·mo·des·mic** \¦==¦=mik\ *adj*

plas·mo·di·al \(')plaz¦mōdēəl\ *also* **plas·mod·ic** \-¦mädik\ *or* **plas·mo·di·ate** \-¦mōdēt, -ˌāt\ *adj* [*plasmodial* ISV *plasmod-* + *-al; plasmodic* fr. *plasmod-* + *-ic; plasmodiate* fr. *plasmod-* + *-ate*] **:** of, relating to, or resembling a plasmodium

plas·mo·di·a·sis \ˌplazmə'dīəsəs\ *also* **plas·mo·di·o·sis** \(ˌ)plazˌmōdē'ōsəs\ *n, pl* **plasmodia·ses** \-əˌsēz\ *or* **plasmodio·ses** \-ōˌsēz\ [NL *Plasmodium* + *-iasis* or *-osis*] **:** MALARIA

plas·mo·di·cide \plaz'mōdəˌsīd\ *n* -s [*plasmod-* + *-cide*] **:** an agent used to kill malaria parasites

plas·mo·dieresis \¦plaz(ˌ)mō+\ *n, pl* **plasmodiereses** [NL, fr. *plasm-* + *dieresis* dividing, fr. Gk *diairesis* — more at DIAERESIS] **:** CYTOKINESIS 2

plas·mo·di·idae \ˌplazmə'dīəˌdē\ *n pl, cap* [NL, fr. *Plasmodium,* type genus + *-idae*] **:** a family of sporozoans (order Haemosporidia) that comprises the malaria parasites, is distinguished by alternation between the blood system of vertebrates and the digestive system of mosquitoes, and is usu. held to include a single genus (*Plasmodium*) — see LAVERANIA

plas·mo·di·o·carp \plaz'mōdēəˌkärp\ *n* -s [*plasmod-* + *-carp*] **:** a fructification in various slime molds that consists of an elongated sometimes branched reticulate body within which spores develop and is a modification of the plasmodium — compare AETHALIUM — **plas·mo·di·o·car·pous** \¦=¦===¦kär-pəs\ *adj*

plas·mo·di·oph·o·ra \ˌplaz(ˌ)mōdīˈäf(ə)rə\ *n, cap* [NL, fr. *plasmod-* + *-phora*] **:** the type genus of Plasmodiophoraceae comprising minute plant parasitic fungi that are sometimes included among the slime molds — see CLUBROOT

plas·mo·di·oph·o·ra·ce·ae \ˌ=(ˌ)==ˌäfəˈrāsēˌē\ *n pl, cap* [NL, fr. *Plasmodiophora*, type genus + *-aceae*] **:** a family of fungi (order Plasmodiophorales) having a multinuclear thallus and often causing hypertrophy in seed plants — see PLASMODIOPHORA — **plas·mo·di·oph·o·ra·ceous** \¦=(ˌ)==¦==¦=shəs\ *adj*

plas·mo·di·oph·o·ra·les \ˌ=(ˌ)==ˌäfəˈrā(ˌ)lēz\ *n pl, cap* [NL, fr. *Plasmodiophora* + *-ales*] **:** an order of fungi (subclass *Oomycetes*) having spores with unequal flagella

plas·mo·di·trophoblast \plaz¦mōdē+\ *n* [ISV *plasmod-* + *trophoblast*] **:** the syncytium of a chorion

plas·mo·di·um \plazˈmōdēəm\ *n* [NL, fr. *plasm-* + ISV *-ode* + NL *-ium*] **1** *pl* **plasmo·dia** \-dēə\ **a :** a motile multinucleate mass of protoplasm resulting from fusion of uninuclear amoeboid cells; *also* **:** an organism (as a particular stage of a slime mold) consisting of such a structure — compare COENOCYTE **b :** SYNCYTIUM 1 **2 a** *cap* **:** the type genus of Plasmodiidae including all the malaria parasites affecting man **b** *pl* **plasmodia :** an individual malaria parasite

plas·mod·ro·ma \plazˈmädrəmə\ *n pl, cap* [NL, fr. *plasm-* + *-droma* (fr. Gk *-dromos* -drome)] **:** a subphylum of Protozoa comprising the classes Mastigophora, Sarcodina, and Sporozoa and characterized by absence of cilia and possession of nuclei of one kind only — compare CILIOPHORA

plas·mog·a·my \plazˈmägəmē\ *n* -ES [ISV *plasm-* + *-gamy*] **:** fusion of protoplasts as distinguished from fusion of nuclei — compare KARYOGAMY

plas·mog·o·ny \-gənē, -ni\ *n* -ES [ISV *plasm-* + *-gony*] **1 :** ABIOGENESIS **2 :** PLASMOGAMY

plas·mol·y·sis \plazˈmäləsəs\ *n, pl* **plasmoly·ses** \-əˌsēz\ [NL, fr. *plasm-* + *-lysis*] **:** contraction or shrinking of the cytoplasm away from the wall of a living cell (as of a plant) due to loss of water by exosmosis

plas·mo·lyt·ic \¦plazmə¦lidik, -ēk\ *adj* [ISV *plasmolyt-* (fr. NL *plasmolysis*) + *-ic*] **:** of or relating to plasmolysis — **plas·mo·lyt·i·cal·ly** \-ək(ə)lē, -ēk-, -li\ *adv*

plas·mo·lyz·ability \ˌplazməˌlīzəˈbiləd·ē\ *n* **:** the capability of being plasmolyzed

plas·mo·lyz·able \¦=¦=ˈlīzəbəl\ *adj* **:** capable of being plasmolyzed

plas·mo·lyze \ˈ==ˌlīz\ *vb* -ED/-ING/-S *see -ize in Explan Notes* [NL *plasmolysis* + E *-ize*] *vt* **:** to subject to plasmolysis ~ *vi* **:** to undergo plasmolysis

plas·mon \ˈplazˌmän\ *also* **plas·mone** \-mōn\ *n* -S [G *plasmon*, fr. *plasma* — more at PLASMA] **:** the cytoplasm regarded as a system of hereditary determinants or agents comparable to the genomes — compare PLASMAGENE, PLASTOGENE

plas·mop·a·ra \plazˈmäpərə\ *n, cap* [NL, fr. *plasm-* + *-para* (fr. L *parere* to bring forth) — more at PARE] **:** a genus of downy mildews (family Peronosporaceae) having conidiophores that are blunt-tipped and branched at nearly right angles — see GRAPE MILDEW 2

plas·moph·a·gous \(ˈ)=¦mäfəgəs\ *adj* [*plasm-* + *-phagous*] **:** feeding on plasma — **plas·moph·a·gy** \=ˈ==jē\ *n* -ES

plas·mop·ty·sis \plazˈmäptəsəs\ *n, pl* **plasmopty·ses** \-əˌsēz\ [NL, fr. *plasm-* + *-ptysis*] **:** the bursting forth of protoplasm from a cell through rupture of the cell wall

plas·mo·quine \ˈplazməˌkwīn, -wēn, -ˌkwən\ *or* **plas·mo·quin** \-ˌkwən\ *n* -S [*plasm-* + *-quine* or *-quin* (fr. *quinine*)] **:** PAMAQUINE

plas·mo·some \ˈplazməˌsōm\ *or* **plas·mo·so·ma** \ˌ==ˈsōmə\ *or* **plas·ma·some** \ˈ==ˌsōm\ *n* -S [*plasmosome* fr. *plasm-* + *-some; plasmosoma* fr. NL, fr. *plasm-* + *-soma; plasmasome* fr. *plasma* + *-some*] **1 :** a true nucleolus **2 :** MICROSOME

plas·mot·o·my \plazˈmäd·əmē\ *n* -ES [ISV *plasm-* + *-tomy*; prob. orig. formed as G *plasmotomie*] **:** division of the plasmodium of a protozoan into two or more multinucleate parts

plasms *pl of* PLASM

-plasms *pl of* -PLASM

pla·some \ˈplāˌsōm, ˈplaˌ-\ *n* -S [G *plasom*, contr. of *plasmatosom*, fr. *plasmato-* + *-som* -some] **:** BIOPHORE

plast \ˈplast, -aa(ə)st, -aist\ *n* -S [*-plast*] **:** PLASTID

-plast \ˌplast, -aa(ə)st, -aist\ *n comb form* -S [MF *-plaste*, fr. LL *-plastus*, fr. Gk *-plastos*, fr. *plastos* formed, molded] **1 a :** thing made ⟨gypso*plast*⟩ ⟨melo*plast*⟩ **b :** plastic — esp. in names of groups of plastics ⟨pheno*plast*⟩ **2 a :** organized particle or granule **:** cell ⟨bio*plast*⟩ ⟨leuco*plast*⟩ **b :** formative cell **:** -BLAST ⟨odonto*plast*⟩

plas·tein \ˈplaˌstēn, -ˌstēən\ *n* -S [ISV *plast-* (fr. Gk *plastos* formed, molded) + *-ein* (as in *casein*); prob. orig. formed in G; fr. its tendency to pass over into hydrogel] **:** any of several substances resembling proteins precipitated by the action of proteolytic enzymes (as pepsin or papain) on the digestion products of protein

plas·te·line *or* **plas·ti·line** \ˈplastəˌlēn\ *also* **plas·ti·li·na** \ˌ==ˈlēnə\ *n* -S [fr. *Plastilina*, a trademark] **:** a nonhardening modeling clay made from clay mixed with oil or wax

¹plas·ter \ˈplastə(r), -laas-, -lais-, -läs-\ *also* **plais·ter** \ˈplās-\ *n* -S [ME *plaster, plastre*, fr. OE, fr. L *emplastrum*, fr. Gk *emplastron, emplastros*, fr. *emplastos* daubed on, plastered up, verbal of *emplassein* to plaster up, make stick, fr. *em-* ²*en-* + *plassein* to form, mold, plaster; akin to Gk *pelanos* round flat cake, L *planus* level, flat — more at FLOOR] **1 a :** an external application of a consistency harder than ointment that is prepared for use by spreading it on cloth (as gauze) or other material and that is adhesive at the ordinary temperature of the body; *also* **:** the application together with the material on which it is spread — see ADHESIVE PLASTER, MUSTARD PLASTER, POROUS PLASTER, STICKING PLASTER **b :** anything applied to heal or soothe **:** SALVE **2** [ME *plaster, plastre*, fr. MF *plastre*, fr. L *emplastrum*] **a :** a cementing material that is produced by expelling a gas or liquid from a natural material (as limestone or gypsum) and has cementing properties caused by reabsorption of the gas or liquid **b :** PLASTER OF PARIS **c :** a material that is applied in a plastic state (as by troweling) and hardens upon drying, that is used esp. for coating interior walls, ceilings, and partitions, and that is usu. made by mixing sand and water with gypsum plaster, quicklime, or hydrated lime to which hair or fiber may be added to act as a binder ⟨lime ~⟩ ⟨acoustical ~⟩ — see BOND PLASTER, CEMENT PLASTER, GAUGING PLASTER, KEENE'S CEMENT; compare BROWN COAT, FINISHING COAT, SCRATCH COAT; MORTAR, STUCCO **d :** LAND PLASTER **3 a :** a coating or surface of plaster (as on a wall or ceiling) esp. when hardened ⟨drive nails into the ~⟩ ⟨cracks in the ~⟩ **b :** PARGETING, PLASTERWORK **c :** a work of art made of plaster of paris

²plaster \"\ *also* **plaister** \"\ *vb* **plastered; plastered; plastering** \-t(ə)riŋ\ **plasters** [ME *plasteren*, partly fr. ¹*plaster* & partly fr. MF *plastrir*, fr. *plastre* plaster] *vt* **1 a :** to overlay or cover with plaster or a similar material ⟨~ a wall⟩ **b :** to smear or bedaub as if with plaster **:** COAT ⟨frequently fell and rose well ~*ed* with yellow clay —R.M.Lovett⟩ ⟨when the debris is solidly ~*ed* over with snow —V.A.Firsoff⟩ **2 a :** to apply a plaster to (as a wound or sprain) **b :** SOOTHE, ALLEVIATE, REMEDY **3 a :** to cover over or conceal as if with a coat of plaster ⟨has at bottom the feelings of a gentleman, but all these are so ~*ed* over with a stiff manner —H.J.Laski⟩ **:** repair or redecorate superficially as if by plastering ⟨the new owners doubled its size and ~*ed* it with the panels and doors of an ancient English manor house —Van Wyck Brooks⟩ **b :** to apply as a coating or incrustation ⟨typical of the veneer of antiquity which the sixteenth century loved to ~ over everything —R.A.Hall b.1911⟩ ⟨~*ed* with jewels or decked in uniform —*Saturday Rev.*⟩ **c :** to smooth down with or as if with a sticky or shiny substance ⟨wore his black hair ~*ed* down⟩ **4 :** to fasten or apply tightly to another surface ⟨~*ed* my ear again to the drawing-room window —Denton Welch⟩ ⟨rain sluicing down to ~ his ragged shirt to his body —Marcia Davenport⟩ **5 :** to treat with plaster of paris: as **a :** to fertilize (as land or a crop) with plaster of paris **b :** to add plaster of paris to grapes or new wine for the purpose of improving the color or keeping qualities of the wine **6 a :** to affix to or place upon esp. conspicuously or lavishly ⟨walls ~*ed* with show bills⟩ ⟨notices with which actresses ~ their books —G.B.Shaw⟩ ⟨portrait ~*ed* on a magazine cover⟩ ⟨the more chips you ~ on the table the more likely is the ball to stop in your number —John Irwin⟩ ⟨monotonous superlatives that were ~*ed* on movie previews —Edmund Wilson⟩ **b** (1) **:** to cause (an area) to be saturated with posters, placards, or advertising matter ⟨run off 500 placards and ~ the town with them —Joanna Spencer⟩ (2) **:** to cause to become known to many throughout a wide area ⟨having ~*ed* his nasty innuendoes around —Anthony West⟩ **7 :** to inflict heavy damage, injury, or casualties upon, esp. by a concentrated or unremitting attack **:** strike heavily and effectively ⟨warships ~*ing* the beach to clear the way for the invasion craft —C.D.Pearson⟩ ⟨plan was to ~ the positions on the forward hills —E.V.Westrate⟩ ⟨~*ed* his opponent for four rounds and then knocked him out⟩ ⟨~*ed* the opposing team⟩ ~ *vi* **:** to apply plaster

³plaster \"\ *adj* [¹*plaster*] **1** *also* **plaister** \"\ **:** made of plaster ⟨~ ornaments⟩ **2 :** SHAM ⟨elevate the patriot leaders into ~ models of inhuman perfection —H.B.Parkes⟩

plaster arch *n* **:** an untrimmed plaster opening in a building

plaster bandage *n* **:** gauze bandage impregnated with plaster of paris and used to form plaster casts

plaster base *n* **:** a material (as wood lath, metal lath, woven wire fabric, or plasterboard) on which plaster is to be applied

plasterbill \ˈ==ˌ=\ *n* [¹*plaster* + *bill*; so called fr. the conspicuous white markings on the head] **:** SURF SCOTER

plasterboard \ˈ==ˌ=\ *n* **:** a board used in large sheets as a backing (as for plaster or tile) or as a substitute for plaster in walls and consisting of several plies of pulpboard, paper, or felt usu. bonded to a hardened gypsum plaster core

plaster bond *n* **:** a bituminous coating applied to the inside surface of outside walls of buildings to exclude dampness

plaster cast *n* **1 :** a model in plaster of a person or thing **2 :** a rigid dressing made from gauze impregnated with plaster of paris and used for immobilizing injured parts of the body esp. to permit the healing of bone defects

plaster ceiling panel *n* **:** a section of a ceiling that is made to appear depressed or raised by furring on the joists before lathing is done

plaster clover *n* **:** WHITE SWEET CLOVER

plaster cove *n* **:** a cove usu. between a sidewall and ceiling that is made by nailing cove brackets against each stud and the corresponding ceiling joist and running continuous lath from sidewall to ceiling

plastered *adj, slang* **:** DRUNK, INTOXICATED

plas·ter·er \ˈ=st(ə)rə(r)\ *n* -S [ME, fr. *plasteren* to plaster + *-er*] **:** one that plasters: as **a :** one who applies plaster to cover surfaces (as walls or ceilings) or to fill in holes and rough places (as in walls, furniture, or castings) **b :** one who makes plaster casts **c :** one who molds and puts in place plaster panels and trim

plasterer's putty *n* **:** pure slaked lime made into a white paste and used in finishing plastered walls — see FINE STUFF

plaster grounds *n pl* **:** wood strips attached to a wall along the base and around windows, doors, or other openings to serve as guides for the plasterer and sometimes as nailing strips for the wood trim

plaster head *n* **:** a small strip of wood or metal used along projecting angles to protect the plaster

plaster hook *n* **:** FIRE HOOK 1

plas·ter·i·ness \-rēnəs\ *n* -ES **:** the quality or state of being plastery

plastering *n* -S [ME, fr. gerund of *plasteren* to plaster] **1 :** the act or process of applying a plaster (as to a wound) or a coating of plaster (as to a wall) **2 :** a coating of plaster or similar substance **3 :** DRUBBING ⟨gave the other side a ~ they wouldn't forget⟩

plaster key *n* **:** the portion of the plaster extending through the lath

plaster mold *n* **1 :** any of several imperfect fungi (as *Papulaspora byssina*) that invade cultivated mushroom beds and tend to form white or brown plastery patches on the surface **2 :** an injury to a mushroom bed caused by a plaster mold

plaster of paris *often cap 2d P* [ME; fr. its originating in Paris, France] **1 :** a fine white powder consisting essentially of the hemihydrate of calcium sulfate $CaSO_4.\frac{1}{2}H_2O$ or $2CaSO_4.H_2O$ that is made by calcining gypsum until it is partially dehydrated, that forms with water a paste which soon sets, and that is used chiefly for casts and molds, building materials (as plasters, tile, blocks, moldings, and stuccowork), and for surgical bandages — called also *calcined gypsum* **2 :** native gypsum

plasters *pl of* PLASTER, *pres 3d sing of* PLASTER

plaster saint *n* **:** one depicted or regarded as a person without human failings ⟨classed as nondelinquents, although they were no *plaster saints* —*Newsweek*⟩ ⟨author's knowledge of humanity runs too deep for him to paint a *plaster saint* —Gerald Walker⟩

plaster stone *n* **:** GYPSUM

plasterwork \ˈ==ˌ=\ *n* **:** plastering used to finish architectural constructions (as for the lining of rooms) — compare PARGETING

plas·tery \ˈplast(ə)rē, -laas-, -lais-, -läs-, -ri\ *adj* **:** resembling or having the properties or characteristics of plaster ⟨examples in which the paint assumes almost ~ texture —Stuart Preston⟩

¹plas·tic \ˈplastik, -laas-, -lais-, -tēk\ *adj* [L *plasticus*, fr. Gk *plastikos*, fr. *plastos* formed, molded (verbal of *plassein* to form, mold) + *-ikos* -ic — more at PLASTER] **1 a :** giving form **:** having power to form or create **:** CREATIVE, FORMATIVE ⟨the poor ~ power, such as it is, within me set to work —Charles Lamb⟩ ⟨in these ~ moments, everything is possible —Béla Menczer⟩ **b :** giving or able to give material or sensible form to conceptions of color, shape, tone, or movement arising from the subconscious ⟨~ sensibility —Herbert Read⟩ **2 a :** capable of being modeled or shaped **:** susceptible of modification or change ⟨~ clay⟩ ⟨the ~ quality of concrete before it hardens⟩ **b :** easily changed or modified **:** PLIANT, IMPRESSIONABLE ⟨strongest impressions are registered on the ~ and emerging personality —*Diseases of the Nervous System*⟩ ⟨~ affections of children —H.G.Wells⟩ **c :** characterized by mobility, pliancy, and flow or the simulation of these qualities ⟨~ dances⟩ ⟨~ and impressionistic style of modeling —*Encyc. Americana*⟩ ⟨peasant woman of superb and ~ proportions —Hervey Allen⟩ ⟨has the ~ face and the genuine warmth of personality which should make him a television natural —D.F.Schoenbrun⟩ **3 a** (1) **:** relating to, composed of, or producing three-dimensional forms or movement; *esp* **:** showing or producing a forceful effect of three-dimensional, cohesive form **:** SCULPTURAL ⟨~ aim in stonework —J.J. Sweeney⟩ (2) **:** having or producing the illusion of sculpture or relief ⟨a ~ figure in painting⟩ ⟨of the several ~ means, he used color most sparingly —Sheldon Cheney⟩ (3) **:** of, relating to, or employing plastique ⟨the ~ form and architectural construction of postwar ballets —Leonide Zarine⟩ **b :** characterized by concern with or emphasis upon form, solidity, and space as depicted esp. by means of lines, colors, or planes and esp. as differentiated from concern for illustrative content or decorative detail ⟨used color not only for decorative but for ~ purposes —David Sylvester⟩ ⟨~ isolation of the objects against a uniform ground —J.T.Soby & A.H.Barr b. 1902⟩ ⟨~ light brings out the three-dimensional qualities of set, scenery, or talent —Herbert True⟩ **c :** having or producing coherency, harmony, and vitality of form **:** ORGANIC ⟨revolutionary sense of the ~ whole —F.L. Wright⟩ **4 a :** capable of being deformed continuously and permanently in any direction without rupture under a stress exceeding the yield value ⟨the ~ yielding of rocks —C.M. Nevin⟩ ⟨slow movement of the ~ ice —V.C.Finch & G.T. Trewartha⟩ — distinguished from *elastic* **b :** of, relating to, or produced by plastic flow ⟨existence of a limiting stress below which no ~ strain occurs —R.S.T.Kingston & L.D. Armstrong⟩ **5** *biol* **a :** capable of variation and phylogenetic change **:** ADAPTABLE ⟨a ~ genus⟩ ⟨a ~ species⟩ **b :** capable of growth, repair, or differentiation ⟨a ~ tissue⟩ **6 :** of, relating to, involving, or by means of plastic surgery ⟨~ repair⟩ **7 :** of or relating to plastics **:** made of a plastic ⟨~ dishes⟩ ⟨~ rope⟩ ⟨~ manufacturing⟩

syn PLIABLE, PLIANT, DUCTILE, MALLEABLE, ADAPTABLE: PLASTIC may describe substances soft enough to mold and often liable to subsequent hardening and becoming fixed ⟨a *plastic* tar⟩ ⟨toys made of *plastic* substances⟩ ⟨when children are small we elders in charge are apt to suppose them altogether *plastic* —H.G.Wells⟩ PLIABLE suggests something easily bent, twisted, or manipulated ⟨*pliable* willow twigs⟩ ⟨I've always been a *pliable* sort of person, and I let the ladies guide me —Upton Sinclair⟩ ⟨a sturdier quality, which made her less *pliable* to the influence of other minds —Nathaniel Hawthorne⟩ PLIANT may stress flexibility to a slightly greater degree than PLIABLE but sometimes lacks the suggestions of submissiveness of the latter word ⟨a *pliant* rod⟩ ⟨in all these countries the Norse nature, supple and *pliant*, accepted the gifts of new experience, and in return imparted strength of purpose to peoples with whom the Norsemen mingled in marriage as well as war —H.O.Taylor⟩ DUCTILE describes what can be drawn out ⟨*ductile* copper wire⟩ or easily led or induced to flow ⟨a *ductile* liquid⟩ In ref. to persons it indicates complaisance or responsiveness to formative influences ⟨he is a big dimpled child with cream and rose complexion, self-willed yet *ductile*. He can be managed, if his petulance is understood —Francis Hackett⟩ MALLEABLE refers to what may be beaten into shape ⟨thin gold leaf is very *malleable*⟩ In ref. to persons it may indicate plasticity and may but does not necessarily suggest weakness and lack of independent will ⟨children, *malleable* as yet, innocent and unformed. He may impress their minds most dangerously —Elinor Wylie⟩ ⟨long enough for the Communist overseers to spot the more *malleable* individuals and concentrate on converting them into tools —Gladwin Hill⟩ ADAPTABLE, generally complimentary, applies to a thing, condition, or person that modifies readily to adjust to circumstances ⟨an *adaptable* appliance⟩ ⟨have proved themselves an uncommonly *adaptable* people —*Amer. Guide Series: Ariz.*⟩

²plastic \"\ *n* -S [LL *plasticus*, n., fr. L *plasticus*, adj., plastic] **1** *archaic* **:** MOLDER, SCULPTOR **2** [MF *plastique*, fr. *plastique*, adj., plastic, fr. L *plasticus*] **a :** the art of modeling or sculpturing figures — often used in pl. but sing. or pl. in constr. **b :** PLASTIQUE **3 a** (1) **:** a substance that at some stage in its manufacture or processing can be shaped by flow (as by application of heat or pressure) with or without fillers, plasticizers, reinforcing agents, or other compounding ingredients and that can retain the new solid often rigid shape under conditions of use (2) **:** any of a large group of materials of high molecular weight that usu. contain as the essential ingredient a synthetic or semisynthetic organic substance made by polymerization or condensation (as polystyrene or a phenol-formaldehyde resin) or derived from a natural material by chemical treatment (as nitrocellulose from cellulose), that are molded, cast, extruded, drawn, or laminated under various conditions (as by heat in the case of thermoplastic materials, by chemical condensation in the case of thermosetting materials or polyesters, or by casting during polymerization of monomers) into objects of all sizes and shapes including films and filaments — often used in pl. but sing. in constr.; compare ELASTOMER, RESIN 2, RUBBER 2a, SYNTHETIC RUBBER **b :** an article fabricated from a plastic **4 plastics** *pl but sing or pl in constr* **:** PLASTIC SURGERY

-plas·tic \¦plastik\ *adj comb form* [Gk *-plastikos*, fr. *-plastos* formed, molded, (fr. *plastos*, verbal of *plassein* to form) + *-ikos* -ic] **1 :** developing **:** forming **:** growing ⟨hetero*plastic*⟩ ⟨xylo*plastic*⟩ **2 :** of or relating to (something designated by a term ending in *-plasm, -plast*, or *-plasty*) ⟨rhino*plastic*⟩ ⟨proto*plastic*⟩

plas·ti·cal·ly \-tək(ə)lē, -tēk-, -li\ *also* **plas·tic·ly** \-kl-\ *adv* **1 :** in a plastic manner ⟨ice flowing ~ downward to form the body of a glacier⟩ **2 :** with respect to plastic qualities ⟨a picture considered ~⟩

plastic art *n* [trans. of F *art plastique*] **1 :** art in which modeling is used **2 :** an art (as painting or sculpture) in which substantial three-dimensional form or the effect of such form is achieved

plas·ti·cate \ˈplastəˌkāt\ *vt* -ED/-ING/-S [back-formation fr. *plasticator*] **:** to knead by means of a plasticator **:** MASTICATE

plas·ti·ca·tor \-ˌkād·ə(r)\ *n* -S [²*plastic* + *-ator*] **:** a machine for plasticizing rubber or mixing thermoplastic materials by means of a revolving screw

plastic binding *n* **:** mechanical binding in which the binding device is made of plastic

plastic cement *n* **:** a material in a plastic state used to seal narrow openings often reinforced with asbestos or other fibers

plastic cream *n* **:** cream that has been centrifuged at high speed causing it to form an oil-in-water emulsion

plastic deformation *or* **plastic flow** *n* **:** a permanent deformation or change in shape of a solid body without fracture under the action of a sustained force ⟨small changes in the density of crystals due to *plastic deformation* —Louise R. Smoluchowski⟩ ⟨*plastic flow* of crystalline rocks —*Jour. of Geol.*⟩

plastic foam *n* **:** EXPANDED PLASTIC

plas·ti·cim·e·ter \ˌplastəˈsimədə(r)\ *n* [*plasticity* + *-meter*] **:** a device for measuring plasticity (as of cement, lime pastes, mortars)

Plas·ti·cine \ˈplastəˌsēn, -aas-, -äs-\ *trademark* — used for a modeling paste

plas·ti·cism \-ˌsizəm\ *n* -S [²*plastic* + *-ism*] **:** the theory or practice of plastic art

plas·tic·i·ty \plaˈstisəd-ē, -sətē, -i\ *n* -ES **1 :** the quality or state of being plastic **:** capacity for being molded or altered ⟨the great adaptability and ~ of man —Curt Stern⟩ **2 :** the ability to retain a shape attained by pressure deformation; *specif* **:** the ability of particles to be displaced relatively to one another without at the same time being removed from their sphere of attraction — compare ELASTICITY **3 :** the capacity of organisms with the same genotype to vary in developmental pattern, in phenotype, or in behavior according to varying environmental conditions ⟨ants exhibit ~ in building habits —*Ecology*⟩

plasticity index *n* **:** difference in moisture content of soils between the liquid and plastic limits expressed in percentage

plas·ti·ci·za·tion \ˌplastəsəˈzāshən, -laas-,-lais-, -ˌsīˈz-\ *n* -S **:** the process of plasticizing or the state of being plasticized; *specif* **:** BREAKDOWN 6 b

plas·ti·cize \ˈ==ˌsīz\ *vt* -ED/-ING/-S *see -ize in Explan Notes* [²*plastic* + *-ize*] **:** to make plastic; *specif* **:** to break down (sense 3 b)

plas·ti·ciz·er \-zə(r)\ *n* -S **:** one that plasticizes; *specif* **:** a chemical substance added to natural and synthetic rubbers and resins to impart flexibility, workability, or distensibility — compare SOFTENER

plastic magnesia *n* **:** MAGNESIUM OXYCHLORIDE CEMENT

plastic operation *n* **:** an operation in plastic surgery

plastic patent *n* **:** a material resembling patent leather made usu. from vinyl resins

plastic plate *n* **:** a letterpress printing plate made from a molded plastic

plastics *pl of* PLASTIC

plastic sulfur *n* **:** sulfur in an amorphous form obtained usu. by pouring boiling sulfur into cold water and composed of molecules that are long chains of sulfur atoms

plastic surgeon *n* **:** a surgeon skilled in plastic surgery

plastic surgery *n* **:** the branch of surgery concerned with the repair or restoration of lost, injured, or deformed parts of the body chiefly by transfer of tissue

plas·tid \ˈplastəd\ *also* **plas·tide** \", -ˌstīd\ *n* -S [ISV, fr. Gk *plastides*, pl. of *plastis*, fem. of *plastēs* sculptor, molder, fr. *plastos* formed, molded; orig. formed as G *plastiden*, pl. — more at PLASTIC] **:** any of various small bodies of specialized protoplasm lying in the cytoplasm of cells (as those of plants and some protozoans), serving in many cases as organs or centers of special metabolic activities, and now generally regarded as persistent cell constituents multiplying by self-division — see CHLOROPLAST, CHROMOPLAST, LEUCOPLAST — **plas·tid·i·al** \(ˈ)pla¦stidēəl\ *adj*

plas·tid·i·um \plaˈstidēəm\ *n, pl* **plastid·ia** \-dēə\ [NL, fr. ISV *plastid*] **:** PLASTID

plas·ti·dome \ˈplastəˌdōm\ *n* -S [ISV *plastid* + *-ome*; orig. formed in F] **:** the plastids of a cell regarded as a functional unit

plas·ti·do·zoa \ˌplastədōˈzōə\ [NL, fr. ISV *plastid* + *-zoa*] *syn of* PROTOZOA
plas·tid·u·lar \(ˈ)plaˈstijələ(r)\ *adj* [ISV *plastidule* + *-ar*] **:** of or relating to a plastidule
plas·tid·ule \ˈplastəˌd(y)üll\ *n* -s [ISV *plastid* + *-ule;* orig. formed as G *plastidul*] **1 :** a hypothetical ultimate unit of protoplasm **:** ALTMANN'S GRANULES **2 :** a structural subunit of a plastid
-plasties *pl of* -PLASTY
plas·ti·fi·ca·tion \ˌplastəfəˈkāshən\ *n* -s [fr. *plastify*, after such pairs as E *identify: identification*] **:** PLASTICIZATION
plas·ti·fy \ˈplastəˌfī\ *vt* -ED/-ING/-ES [²*plastic* + *-fy*] **:** PLASTICIZE
plas·ti·gel \-ˌjel\ *n* [²*plastic* + *gel*] **:** a very viscous substance (as a paste resembling putty in consistency) obtained by adding a thickening agent to a plastisol
plastiline *also* **plastilina** *var of* PLASTELINE
plas·tin \ˈplastən\ *n* -s [ISV *plast-* (fr. Gk *plastos*) + *-in;* prob. orig. formed in G] **1 :** an acidophilic component of protoplasm more or less coextensive with the presumed highly polymerized protein framework of cytoplasm and nucleus **2 :** the substance of the true nucleolus
plas·ti·noid \ˈplastəˌnȯid\ *adj* [*plastin* + *-oid*] **:** resembling plastin
plas·tique \plaˈstēk\ *n* -s [F, lit., plastic, fr. MF — more at PLASTIC] **1 :** slow changes of position like moving sculpture without marked rhythm or dramatic theme in dancing **2 :** the technique of statuesque posing in dancing
plas·ti·sol \ˈplastəˌsȯl, -sōl\ *n* -s [²*plastic* + *-sol* (as in *hydrosol*)] **:** a relatively viscous dispersion of a powdered thermoplastic resin in a liquid plasticizer used chiefly in coatings, films, and molded products ⟨vinyl ~*s*⟩ — compare ORGANOSOL
plasto- *comb form* [Gk, fr. *plastos* formed, molded] **1 :** formation **:** development ⟨*plasto*chron⟩ ⟨*plasto*type⟩ **2 :** plasticity **:** plastic ⟨*plasto*meter⟩ ⟨*plasto*mer⟩ **3 :** cytoplasm ⟨*plasto*gamy⟩ ⟨*plasto*mere⟩ **4 :** plastid ⟨*plasto*gene⟩
plas·to·chron \ˈplastəˌkrän\ *n* -s [*plasto-* + Gk *chronos* time] **:** a unit of time corresponding to the interval between two successive similar, periodically repeated events (as the emergence of leaf primordia at any two successive nodes in a stem apex) — **plas·to·chron·ic** \ˌ==ˈkränik\ *adj*
plas·to·cyte \ˈ==ˌsīt\ *n* [*plasto-* + *-cyte*] **:** BLOOD PLATELET — **plas·to·cyt·ic** \ˌ==ˈsid·ik\ *adj*
plas·to·gam·ic \ˌ==ˈgamik\ *adj* **:** of or relating to plastogamy
plas·tog·a·my \plaˈstägəmē\ *n* -ES [ISV *plasto-* + *-gamy*] **:** PLASMOGAMY
plas·to·gene \ˈplastəˌjēn\ *n* [*plasto-* + *-gene*] **:** a submicroscopic factor or determiner reported to be present in the plastids in plant cells and to influence physiological and hereditary phenomena of the plastids — compare GENE, PLASMAGENE, PLASMON
plas·tome \ˈplaˌstōm\ *n* -s [by contr.] **:** PLASTIDOME
plas·to·mer \ˈplastəmə(r)\ *n* -s [*plasto-* + *-mer*] **:** a relatively tough usu. hard and rigid polymeric substance — compare ELASTOMER, ²PLASTIC 3
plas·to·mere \ˌmi(ə)r\ *n* -s [*plasto-* + *-mere*] **:** CHONDRIOMERE — compare CYTOMERE
plas·tom·e·ter \plaˈstäməd·ə(r), -mətə-\ *n* [*plasto-* + *-meter*] **:** an instrument for measuring plasticity or viscosity (as of rubber) — **plas·to·met·ric** \ˌplastōˈme·trik\ *adj* — **plas·tom·e·try** \plaˈstämə·trē, -ri\ *n* -ES
plas·to·some \ˈplastəˌsōm\ *n* -s [ISV *plasto-* + *-some*] **:** CHONDRIOSOME
plas·to·type \-ˌtīp\ *n* [*plasto-* + *type*] **:** an artificial specimen cast or molded directly from a type specimen (as of a fossil)
plas·tral \ˈplastrəl, -laas-\ *adj* [*plastron* + *-al*] **:** of or relating to a plastron
plas·tron \-trən\ *n* -s [MF, fr. OIt *piastrone*, aug. of *piastra* thin metal plate — more at PIASTER] **1 a :** a metal breastplate worn under the hauberk **b :** a quilted pad worn during fencing practice to protect the chest, waist, and side on which the weapon is held **2 a** (1) **:** the ventral part of the shell of a tortoise or turtle consisting typically of nine symmetrically placed bones overlaid by horny plates (2) **:** the ventral armor of other animals (as some extinct amphibians or glyptodonts) **b :** the modified posterior interambulacral area on the under side of a heart urchin **c :** the ventral plate of the cephalothorax of a spider — compare STERNUM **3 :** a separate or attached front for a garment usu. extending from neck to waist: **a :** a trimming like a bib for a woman's dress **b :** DICKEY 1 b **4 :** a thin film of air held by hydrofuge hairs of certain aquatic insects
plasts *pl of* PLAST
-plasts *pl of* -PLAST
-plasty \ˌplastē, -laas-, -lais-, -ti\ *n comb form* -ES [F *-plastie*, fr. Gk *-plastia* form, mold, fr. *-plastos* -plast + *-ia* -y] **:** plastic surgery ⟨dermato*plasty*⟩ ⟨auto*plasty*⟩ ⟨cine*plasty*⟩
-plasy — see -PLASIA
¹plat \ˈplat, *usu* -ad·+V\ *n* -s [OE *plaett;* akin to MD *plat* slap, ME *platten* to slap, MHG *platzen;* prob. all of imit. origin] *chiefly dial* **:** BUFFET, SLAP; *also* **:** a slapping sound
²plat \"\ *adj* [ME *plat, platte*, fr. MF *plat*, fr. OF — more at PLATE] **1** *obs* **:** FLAT, LEVEL **2** *chiefly dial* **:** PLAIN, STRAIGHTFORWARD
³plat \"\ *vt* **platted; platted; platting; plats** [ME *platten*, fr. *plat, platte*, adj., flat] *chiefly dial* **:** FLATTEN
⁴plat \"\ *n* -s [ME, fr. MF, fr. *plat*, adj., flat] **1** *archaic* **:** a flat surface or thing (as the flat of a sword, a flat piece of stone, the sole of the foot) **2** *archaic* **a :** PLACE, LOCALITY **b :** an expanse of open level land **:** PLATEAU, TABLELAND **3 a :** a platform, floor, or surface in or about a mine used esp. for loading and unloading ore
⁵plat \"\ *vt* **platted; platted; platting; plats** [ME *platen*, alter. (perh. influenced by ³*plat*) of *plaiten* to plait — more at PLAIT] **:** to form by braiding or interweaving **:** PLAIT
⁶plat \"\ *n* -s **:** platted work **:** BRAID, PLAIT
⁷plat \"\ *n* -s [ME *plaite*, fr. MF *plate*, fem. of *plat* something flat, fr. *plat*, adj. flat] **:** a small flat-bottomed, square-sterned rowboat
⁸plat \"\ *n* -s [prob. alter. (influenced by ⁴*plat*) of *plot* (ground)] **1 :** a small piece of ground **:** PLOT, QUADRAT **2 :** a plan, map, or chart ⟨started forth with a ~ of my destination that I made on a large sheet of notepaper —W.A. White⟩: as **a :** a precise and detailed plan showing the actual or proposed divisions, special features, or uses of a piece of land (as a town or town site or a real estate subdivision) **b :** an accurately scaled diagram showing boundaries and subdivisions of a piece of land together with data required for accurate identification of the various parts **3** *obs* **:** a plan, scheme, or outline (as of a course of action or a work of fiction or art) **:** ARRANGEMENT, DESIGN **4** *obs* **a :** a plan for securing adequate stipends from the endowments of the pre-Reformation church for the ministry of the Reformed Church of Scotland **b :** a commission in charge of such a plan
⁹plat \"\ *vt* **platted; platted; platting; plats 1 a** *obs* **:** to lay out **:** PLAN, ARRANGE **b :** to lay out a plan for the future development of (as a town or subdivision) usu. with a formally drafted plat ⟨San Francisco was *platted* as if it were a prairie town —*Time*⟩ **2 :** to make a plat of ⟨an entire project is laid out and *platted* —*Amer. Builder*⟩
¹⁰plat \ˈplä\ *n, pl* **plats** \-ä(z)\ [F, lit., plate, fr. *plat*, adj. flat] **:** a dish of food **:** food dressed for table
plat- — see PLATY-
plat *abbr* **1** platform **2** platoon
plat·a·can·tho·my·i·dae \ˌplad·əˌkan(t)thəˈmīəˌdē\ *n pl, cap* [NL, fr. *Platacanthomys*, type genus (fr. *platy-* + *acanth-* + *-mys*) + *-idae*] **:** a small family of myomorph rodents comprising the Asiatic spiny dormice and related forms
pla·tae·an \ˌplaˈtēən\ *adj, usu cap* [L *plataeeus* plataean (fr. *Plataeae* Plataea, fr. Gk *Plataiai*) + E *-an*] **:** of or relating to Plataea, a city of Boeotia in ancient Greece
plat·a·le·i·dae \ˌplad·əˈlēəˌdē\ *n pl, cap* [NL, fr. *Platalea*, type genus (fr. L *platalea* spoonbill) + *-idae;* akin to Gk *platys* flat, broad — more at PLACE] **:** a family of birds (order Ciconiiformes) that consists of the spoonbills and is often ranked as a subfamily of Threskiornithidae
plat·a·le·i·form \ˌ==ˈ==ˌfȯrm\ *adj* [NL *platalea* spoonbill + E *-iform*] **:** resembling a spoonbill **:** SPOON-BILLED
plat·an *or* **plat·ane** \ˈplatᵊn\ *n* -s [ME *platan*, fr. L *platanus*] **:** ²PLANE
plat·a·na·ce·ae \ˌplatᵊnˈāsēˌē\ *n pl, cap* [NL, fr. *Platanus*, type genus + *-aceae*] **:** a family of trees (order Rosales) coextensive with the genus *Platanus* — **plat·a·na·ceous** \ˌ==ˈāshəs\ *adj*
plat·a·nist \ˈplatᵊnəst\ *n* -s [NL *Platanista*] **:** an Indian susu
plat·a·nis·ta \ˌplatᵊnˈistə\ *n, cap* [NL, fr. L, a fish of the Ganges, fr. Gk *platanistēs;* akin to Gk *platē* oar, *platys* flat, broad] **:** the type genus of Platanistidae
plat·a·nis·ti·dae \-təˌdē\ *n pl, cap* [NL, fr. *Platanista*, type genus + *-idae*] **:** a family of toothed whales comprising the susu and related extinct forms
pla·tan·na \pləˈtanə\ *or* **plat·hand·er** \ˈplatˌhandə(r)\ *n* -s [Afrik *platanna*, prob. alter. of *plat-hander* one who is flat-handed, fr. D, fr. *plat* flat (fr. MD, fr. OF) + *hander* (fr. *hand*, fr. MD); akin to OHG *hant* hand — more at PLATE, HAND] **:** a frog (*Xenopus laevis*) of southern Africa that has strongly clawed feet
pla·ta·no \ˈplād·ə(ˌ)nō\ *n* -s [Sp *plátano* — more at PLANTAIN] **:** BANANA, PLANTAIN
plat·a·nus \ˈplad·ənəs\ *n* [NL, fr. L, plane tree — more at PLANE] **1** *cap* **:** a genus of trees (family Platanaceae) comprising the plane trees, being native in temperate regions, and having light brown often deciduous flaky bark, large palmately lobed leaves, and small monoecious flowers in globose heads — see LONDON PLANE, SYCAMORE 3a **2** -ES **:** any tree of the genus *Platanus*
platband \ˈ=ˌ=\ *n* [F *plate-bande*, lit., flat band, fr. MF, fr. *plate*, fem. of *plat* flat + *bande* band, strip — more at BAND] **1 a :** a horizontal band that is a member of a building and that takes the form of a lintel course, a flat arch, or one of a group of moldings **b :** ARCHITRAVE, EPISTYLE **c :** a list or fillet between the flutings of a column **2 :** a border of flowers or turf
platch \ˈplach\ *vb* -ED/-ING/-ES [prob. imit.] *Scot* **:** SPLASH, SMEAR
plat du jour \ˌplädəˈzhü(ə)r\ *n, pl* **plats du jour** \"\ [F, lit., dish of the day] **:** a dish that is emphasized as a feature of a restaurant bill of fare on a particular day
¹plate \ˈplāt, *usu* -ād·+V\ *n* -s [ME, fr. OF, fr. *plate*, fem. of *plat*, adj., flat, fr. (assumed) VL *plattus*, prob. fr. Gk *platys* flat, broad — more at PLACE] **1 a** (1) **:** a smooth usu. nearly flat and relatively thin piece of metal or other material **:** a substantial slice or lamina (2) **:** a perfectly flat sheet of material of uniform thickness throughout; *esp* **:** a sheet of rolled iron or steel usu. a quarter of an inch or more thick (3) **:** a flat circular piece usu. of metal that is either perforated or provided with bubble caps and that is set horizontally as one of a series at specified distances one above another esp. in a fractionating column or tower for effecting intimate contact between rising vapors and condensed liquid falling from plate to plate — called also *tray* **b** (1) **:** forged, rolled, or cast metal in sheets usu. thicker than ¼ inch (2) **:** a very thin layer of usu. precious metal deposited on a surface of base metal by plating (as electroplating) ⟨the ~ has worn off these spoons⟩ ⟨quadruple ~ silverware⟩ **c** (1) **:** one of the broad pieces of metal often on a backing (as of leather) that were used to reinforce and complete armor of linked mail (2) **:** one of the thin pieces making up plate armor; *also* **:** armor of such plates **:** PLATE ARMOR **d** (1) **:** a lamina or plaque that forms part of an animal body ⟨a carapace of bony ~*s*⟩; *esp* **:** an enlarged scale (as on the belly of a snake) (2) **:** the thin under portion of the forequarter of beef; *esp* **:** the back half of this cut as distinguished from the brisket — see BEEF illustration **e :** slaty rock or shale (as in a mine) **f** *chiefly Brit* **:** PLATE RAIL 1; *broadly* **:** any railroad rail **g :** a very light horseshoe without calks that is used esp. for racing **h** (1) **:** HOME PLATE (2) **:** a rectangular slab of whitened rubber 6 inches by 24 inches in size that is anchored flush with the ground at the spot where a softball or baseball pitcher must stand when delivering the ball to the batter — called also *box, pitcher's plate, rubber, slab;* see BASEBALL illustration **i :** the belly or the back of a violin **j :** a square or oblong piece of fur composed usu. of waste fur and small inferior pieces that are matched and sewn together and used for inexpensive garments or linings **2** [ME; partly fr. OF *plate* piece of silver, piece of metal; partly fr. OSp *plata* silver, money, metal plate, fr. (assumed) VL *plattus* flat] **a** (1) *obs* **:** a piece of money; *esp* **:** a coin of silver (2) **:** Spanish silver money (3) **:** a piece of plate money **b :** precious metal; *esp* **:** silver bullion ⟨the Spanish ~ ships⟩ ⟨melting coin into ~⟩ **c :** a heraldic roundel of silver **3** [ME, fr. MF, fr. fem. of OF *plat*, adj., flat] **a** (1) **:** domestic hollow ware (as dishes, flagons, cups) of gold or silver (2) **:** such vessels of base metals or of plated ware (3) *chiefly Brit* **:** SILVER 4 **b** (1) **:** a shallow usu. circular vessel (as of china, wood, or plastic) from which food is eaten (2) **:** an often larger vessel (as a platter or vegetable dish) from which food is served ⟨pass the meat ~⟩ ⟨a cake ~⟩ **c** (1) **:** an individual serving on a plate **:** PLATEFUL ⟨have a ~ of spaghetti⟩ (2) **:** a main course of a meal served in individual portions on the plate from which it is to be eaten ⟨the special ~ includes liver and onions, potatoes, with gravy, and green salad⟩ (3) **:** the food and service supplied to one person at a particular meal or social affair ⟨a fund-raising dinner at $100 a ~⟩ **d** (1) **:** a prize (as a cup or other piece of plate) given to the winner in an athletic or other contest (2) **:** a sports competition for a prize; *esp* **:** a horse race in which the contestants compete for a prize rather than for personally wagered stakes **e** (1) **:** a dish or pouch passed (as in a church) in taking collections (2) **:** a collection taken for a specific purpose or particular organization ⟨the ~ was a generous one⟩ **f** (1) **:** a flat glass dish used chiefly for culturing microorganisms; *esp* **:** PETRI DISH (2) **:** a film of more or less solid culture medium or a culture contained in such a dish **4 a :** a flat thin smooth piece (as of metal) on or from which something is or is to be embossed, molded, engraved, grained, deposited, or written ⟨a ~ for etching⟩ **b :** a surface from which printing is done: as (1) **:** a stereotype, electrotype, or plastic plate molded from a page of letterpress matter (2) **:** a metal or plastic sheet from which an inked image is transferred to a blanket (as in photo-offset) or direct to the paper (as in lithography) (3) **:** a flat and comparatively thin piece of copper or steel engraved in intaglio (as for banknotes or calling cards) — compare DIE 6h (4) **:** PHOTOENGRAVING **c :** a sheet of glass, metal, porcelain, or other material coated with a light-sensitive photographic emulsion; *usu* **:** DRY PLATE **d :** a copper plate coated with silver amalgam that is used in the amalgam process of extracting metals **e** (1) **:** the usu. flat or grid-formed anode of an electron tube at which electrons collect (2) **:** a metallic grid with its interstices filled with active material that forms one of the structural units of a storage cell or battery **5 :** a supporting or reinforcing element (as of a building): as **a** (1) **:** a horizontal timber laid on a wall or supported on posts or corbels to carry the trusses of a roof or the rafters directly (2) **:** either of the horizontal members at the top and bottom of a stud partition between which the studs are placed (3) **:** a supporting sill (as one over or under an opening) ⟨window ~*s*⟩ **b :** a heavy framed mine timber **c :** the part of an artificial set of teeth that fits to the mouth and holds the teeth in place; *broadly* **:** DENTURE **d :** a metal tab attached to the sole or heel of a shoe as a reinforcement intended esp. to minimize wear — compare CLEAT, HEEL PLATE, TOEPLATE **e :** the flat metal framework of a timepiece containing the bearing holes and jewels into which its wheel-pivots fit **f :** the metal structure that supports the strings of a piano **g :** a flat metal surface of or attached to a machine by which work is held fast (as for locating, indexing, leveling, turning, or machining) **h :** a thin flat narrow piece of metal (as stainless steel) that is used to repair bone defects or fractures **6 :** a relatively large illustration ⟨prepared the ~*s* on bristol board⟩; *esp* **:** a full-page illustration printed on different paper from accompanying text pages ⟨a book with color ~*s*⟩ **7** [by shortening] **a :** BOOKPLATE **b :** FASHION PLATE **c :** PLATE GLASS **8 :** a small cooking stove that is usu. heated with gas or electricity, has one or more heating units, and lacks an oven **:** HOT PLATE 2
²plate \"\ *vb* -ED/-ING/-S [ME *platen*, fr. *plate*, n.] *vt* **1 :** to cover or equip with plate or plates: as **a :** to overlay with metal plates ⟨the first ironclads were wooden ships *plated* with iron⟩; *esp* **:** to arm with armor plate **b :** to cover with an adherent layer (as of metal) mechanically, chemically, or electrically; *also* **:** to deposit (as a layer of metal) on the surface of something by such means **c :** to shoe (a horse) with plates **d :** to adorn or cover with metal plate ⟨~ a harness⟩ **e :** to fit with a specified kind of plate ⟨*plated* the books with her new bookplate⟩ **2 :** to form into or prepare as a plate: as **a :** to beat (as metal) into thin flat sheets **b** *printing* (1) **:** to make a plate from ⟨for long press runs type forms are often *plated* —R.R.Karch⟩ **:** make plates for ⟨~ a book⟩ (2) **:** to equip (as a printing press) with a plate or plates — sometimes used with *up* **c :** to impart a finish to (a sheet of paper) by subjecting to very high pressure between sheets of the material whose surface is to be duplicated **d :** to inoculate and culture (microorganisms) upon a plate; *also* **:** to distribute (an inoculum) upon a plate or plates for cultivation — often used with *out* **e :** to collect (a particular stamp) in all of the positions that were on the original sheet, identifying the positions by a philatelic study of matching characteristics (as perforations, plate numbers, printing defects) **3 a :** to fix or secure with a plate or plates **b :** to repair (as a fractured bone) with metal plates **4 a :** to knit or weave (fabric) with a face and back of different colors or fibers **b :** to spin (yarn) with a core and outside wrapping of different fibers ~ *vi* **:** to perform the action of plating or undergo the process of being plated ⟨a very pure silver that ~*s* out well⟩ ⟨learned to ~ expertly while still a boy⟩
plate-and-frame filter \ˌ==ˈ=-\ *n* **:** a filter press in which the spaces for the caked solid matter are formed by inserting hollow frames between each pair of plates instead of providing the plates with raised edges
plate armor *n* **1 :** body armor of plates of metal — see ARMOR illustration; compare MAIL 1 b **2 :** strong metal plate used esp. for protecting naval vessels or forts
¹pla·teau \(ˈ)plaˈtō *sometimes* pləˈt-\ *n, pl* **plateaus** *or* **plateaux** \-ōz\ [F, fr. MF, fr. *plat* flat — more at PLATE] **1 a** (1) **:** a flat and often galleried ornamental dish or salver (as for a tea service or condiments) (2) **:** an ornamental plaque (3) **:** a table top; *esp* **:** a removable and usu. decorated top (as of marble or inlay) (4) **:** an ornamental shelf (as in a whatnot) **b :** a woman's hat of a flat or plate-shaped style **2 a :** a usu. extensive land area having a relatively level surface raised sharply above adjacent land on at least one side and often dissected by canyons **:** TABLELAND ⟨the Columbia lava ~ in eastern Washington and Oregon⟩ ⟨the ~ region of central Bolivia⟩ — compare MESA **b :** a similar undersea feature **3 a :** a region of little or no change in the dependent variable of a graph; *esp* **:** a horizontal section of a learning curve indicating neither progress nor decline **b :** a relatively stable level, period, or condition; *esp* **:** one showing cessation or minimization of cyclical phenomena or of fluctuations up or down ⟨a price ~ interrupting an inflationary spiral⟩ ⟨output seems to have reached a ~⟩
²plateau \"\ *adj, usu cap* **1 :** ANASAZI **2 :** of or relating to the Indians of the No. American plateau area between the Cascade mountains and the Rocky mountains south of the great bend of the Fraser river or to their seminomadic food-gathering culture
³plateau \"\ *vi* -ED/-ING/-S **:** to reach a period or phase of stability **:** form a plateau **:** level off ⟨after initial logarithmic progress growth ~*ed* sharply⟩
plateau-basalt *n* **:** basalt extruded on continental areas that lacks olivine and may contain quartz
plateband \ˈ=ˌ=\ *n* [by alter.] **:** PLATBAND 1
plate battery *n* **:** B BATTERY
plate block *n* **:** a plate number block
plate bolt *n* **:** a bolt grommeted into the foundation of a building for securing a sill or plate
plate bone *n* **:** SCAPULA
plate budding *n* **:** plant budding in which a rectangular scion with bud is inserted under a longitudinal flap of bark on the stock in such a manner as to cover the exposed wood on the stock
plate bulb *n* **:** a steel or iron plate with a thickened edge of bulbous section
plate calender *or* **plate-glazing calender** *n* **:** PLATER
plate circuit *n* **:** an electric circuit including the plate and cathode of an electron tube
plate clutch *n* **:** DISK CLUTCH
plate column *n* **:** PLATE TOWER
plate count *n* **:** a determination of the degree of bacterial contamination of a sample (as of milk or semen) made by enumeration after a period of incubation of the colonies appearing in a plate that has been inoculated with a suitable dilution of the sample
plate culture *n* **:** a culture (as of bacteria) contained on a plate; *also* **:** the cultivation of such a culture
plate current *n* **:** a current flowing in the plate circuit of an electron tube that is equal to the electron flow from cathode to plate
plate cut *n* **:** a notch in the undersurface of a rafter at the point where it seats on the plate
plate cylinder *n* **:** the cylinder of a rotary printing press to which the printing plates are attached
plat·ed \ˈplād·əd, -lātəd\ *adj* [ME, fr. past part. of *platen* to plate — more at PLATE] **1 :** covered or furnished with plates or with metal (as for defense, ornament, or strength) **2 :** overlaid with a different and richer material (as gold or silver) ⟨~ forks⟩ ⟨~ ware⟩ **3 :** consisting of or made into thin sheets **4** *of yarn or knitted goods* **:** having a surface of one color or kind and a backing or core of another
plated leather *n* **:** leather that has been pressed under heat and heavy pressure to improve appearance and give polished surface; *also* **:** leather grained by embossing
plated lobster *n* **:** CRAYLET
plated parquet *n* **:** parquetry in which the inlays (as of selected hardwoods) are fixed on a framed deal backing
plate finish *n* **:** a finish that is applied to paper by plating; *also* **:** a similar finish that is applied by other means (as web glazing)
plate-finish \ˈ=ˌ==\ *vt* [fr. *plate finish*, n.] **:** PLATE 2c
plate·ful \ˈplātˌfu̇l\ *n, pl* **platefuls** *also* **platesful** \-tˌfu̇lz, -tsˌfu̇l\ **:** a quantity to fill a plate; *also* **:** a generous serving (as of food)
plate gear *n* **:** a gear having a solid web of material between the hub and rim
plate girder *or* **plate beam** *n* **:** a built-up girder resembling an I beam in cross section but having a rolled steel plate for a web and flanges that usu. consist of angles alone or angles and plates
plate glass *n* **:** flat glass of high quality formed by a process of continuous or semicontinuous rolling or sometimes by the rolling of metal cast on a table and then ground and polished so that the surfaces are plane and parallel
plate-glaze \ˈ=ˌ=\ *vt* **:** PLATE 2c
plateholder \ˈ=ˌ==\ *n* **1 :** one that holds plates; *esp* **:** one that places plates for molds **2 :** a flat lighttight container in which a light-sensitive photographic plate may be held in a camera and may be exposed by removal of a slide — see CAMERA illustration
plate horse *n* **:** PLATER 3
plate keel *n* **:** a ship's keel made of a flat plate or plates — compare BAR KEEL
platelayer \ˈ=ˌ=(=)\ *n* [¹*plate* + *layer*] *Brit* **:** a railroad laborer who lays and maintains rails **:** TRACKLAYER
plate·less \ˈplātləs\ *adj* **:** having or requiring no plate or plates ⟨~ printing⟩
plate·let \-lət\ *n* -s [ISV *plate* + *-let*] **:** a minute flattened body; *specif* **:** BLOOD PLATELET
plate letter *n* **:** a letter on a note or piece of paper money indicating the position the note had on the printing plate
platelike \ˈ=ˌ=\ *adj* **:** resembling a plate esp. in smooth flat form ⟨a ~ scale on the head of a lizard⟩
plat·el·min·thes \ˌplad·ˌelˈmin(t)thēz, -nˌthēz\ *syn of* PLATYHELMINTHES
plate lock *n* **1 :** a lock having the outer case of hard wood **2 :** a lock whose works are pivoted on a metal plate
plate·man \ˈplātmən\ *n, pl* **platemen 1 :** MIDDLER 3 **2 :** a worker at the breaker of a coal mine who picks rocks and oversize lumps from the coal before it is conveyed for further treatment or loading **3 :** AMALGAMATOR 2b

1plate mark *n* **1 :** HALLMARK **2 :** a depression of an etching or engraving made by the pressure of the edge of the plate upon the dampened paper while printing **3 :** an impression from a flat uninked plate to smooth a rough area prior to printing or to produce a blind panel

2plate mark *vt* [*1plate mark*] **:** to impress with a plate mark

plate meristem *n* **:** a meristem in which growth occurs chiefly through cell division in two planes resulting in a flat plate of tissue — compare MASS MERISTEM, RIB MERISTEM

plate metal *n* **:** refined iron run in molds and broken up for remelting or for use in a mix

plate mill *n* **:** a rolling mill for producing relatively thick flat metal products

plate modulation *n* **:** modulation in radio in which the modulating voltage is introduced into the plate circuit of the tube which provides the carrier

plate money *n* **:** money issued in Sweden in the 17th and 18th centuries consisting of large rectangular pieces of copper with values in daler denominations stamped in the corners and in the center

plat·en \ˈplatᵊn\ *n* -s *often attrib* [MF *plateine*, fr. *plate* thin plate, plaque (fr. OF, fr. fem. of *plat*, adj., flat) + *-ine* — more at PLATE] **1 a :** a flat plate (as of metal) usu. designed to press or to be pressed against by something: as (1) **:** a flat surface (as on a hand press or platen press) that presses the paper against the form (2) **:** the movable table of a planer or similar machine tool (3) **:** either of two plates of a testing machine that apply a load to a specimen under test (4) **:** a diaphragm or plate in a molding machine against which the flask is forced by pressure from below (5) **:** a sometimes heated flat surface against which materials are pressed for flattening, curing, or laminating (6) **:** a circular flanged rotating plate in a phonograph turntable upon which a record rests during reproduction **b :** a hard roll that serves as a backing against which the paper is pressed when the typebars of a typewriter strike to make an imprint **2** [by alter.] *obs* **:** PATEN 1

platen press *n* **:** a small printing press in which a platen presses the paper against a form secured to an opposed vertical flat bed — called also *job press;* compare CYLINDER PRESS, ROTARY PRESS

plate number *n* **1 :** a number that is the serial number of the plate from which a sheet of postage stamps is printed and that appears in the four margins of the printed sheet, at least once on each pane **2 :** a stamp or block of stamps with plate number attached

plate nut *n* **:** NUT PLATE

plate organ *n* **:** an insect sense organ covered by an integumentary plate

plat·e·o·sau·rus \ˌplad-ēəˈsȯrəs\ *n, cap* [NL, fr. Gk *platē* oar + NL *-saurus;* akin to Gk *platys* flat, broad — more at PLACE] **:** a genus of moderate-sized chiefly bipedal Triassic saurischian dinosaurs on the ancestral line of the Sauropoda

plate oven *n* **:** a double oven one part of which is used for heating split cylinders of sheet or cylinder glass before flattened into sheets and the other chamber for annealing the sheets

plate paper *n* **:** a soft paper with a smooth dull finish used for printing fine-line hand-engraved plates and woodcuts

plate press *n* **:** a press with a flat carriage and a roller used for printing from engraved steel or copper plates

plate printing *n* **:** printing from engraved steel or copper plates

plate proof *n* **:** a first or other proof taken from a plated letterpress printing surface

plat·er \ˈplād-ə(r), -lātə-\ *n* -s **1 :** one that plates: as **a** (1) **:** a worker that plates metal or metal objects with gold or silver (2) **:** one that applies a protective coating of nickel or similar substance to metal objects by means of an electrolytic bath — called also *bath plater, electroplater, vatman* (3) **:** one that coats plastic articles with metal plate (4) **:** a textile worker that plates fabric or yarn **b :** an operator of a machine for impressing the weave pattern of linen fabric onto paper **c :** a worker that presses hat brims by hand **2 :** a machine for plating paper — called also *plate calender* **3 a :** a horse that runs chiefly in purse races and esp. in claiming races **b :** an inferior racehorse

plate rail *n* **1** *chiefly Brit* **:** a primitive type of flat rail of cast iron with an upright ledge on the outer edge to keep wheels on the rail **2 :** a rail or narrow shelf along the upper part of a wall to hold plates or ornaments

plate rail 2

plate resistance *n* **:** the ratio of the potential difference between plate and cathode of a vacuum tube to the resulting current

plat·er·esque \ˌplad-əˈresk\ *also* **plat·e·res·co** \ˌ==ˈre(ˌ)skō\ *adj* [Sp *plateresco*, fr. *platero* silversmith (fr. *plata* silver) + *-esco* -esque — more at PLATE] **:** relating to or being a 16th century Spanish architectural style distinguished by a wealth and richness of ornamentation suggestive of silver plate

plater finish *n* **:** PLATE FINISH

plateroom \ˈ=ˌ=\ *n, Brit* **:** a room set aside for the storage of table and other plate

plates *pl of* PLATE, *pres 3d sing of* PLATE

platesful *pl of* PLATEFUL

plate ship *n* **:** TREASURE SHIP; *esp* **:** one of the Spanish treasure ships from America

plate system *n* **:** a system of quick freezing in which the freezing coils are placed in platelike arrangements

plate tower *n* **:** a tower or column provided with plates for use esp. in fractional distillation (as of petroleum distillates) — called also *plate column*

plate tracery *n* **:** decorative architectural tracery consisting of a series of patterns cut through a flat plate of stone

plate tumbler *n* **:** SLIDING TUMBLER

plate valve *n* **:** an automatic valve in which a lightweight thin disk, strip, or ribbon is constrained to move between the valve seat and valve cover according to variations in fluid pressure on its sides

plate vein *n, archaic* **:** the cephalic vein of a horse

plate voltage *or* **plate potential** *n* **:** the constant component of the potential difference between plate and cathode in an electron tube

plateway \ˈ=ˌ=\ *n* [*plate* + *way*] **:** a railway having plate rails

plate wheel *n* **:** a wheel the rim and hub of which are connected by a continuous plate of metal

platework \ˈ=ˌ=\ *n* **:** plated work

plat-eye \ˈ=ˌ=\ *n* [*plat* of unknown origin] **:** a ghost, spook, or evil spirit with fiery eyes

1plat·form \ˈplatˌfȯrm\ *n, often attrib* [MF *plate-forme*, lit., flat form, fr. *plate* (fem. of *plat* flat, fr. OF) + *forme* form, fr. OF — more at PLATE, FORM] **1 a :** a diagrammatic representation of something on the flat (as a ground plan or map) **b :** a plan of action or statement of policy **:** DESIGN, PATTERN, SCHEME: as (1) **:** a plan of ecclesiastical or religious policy or principles (2) **:** a declaration of the principles on which a group of persons or a party stand and on which they appeal for support; *esp* **:** a declaration of principles and policies of government adopted by a political party or an individual (as a candidate for political office) **2 :** a horizontal flat surface usu. higher than the adjoining area (as of floor or ground): as **a :** a permanent or temporary base for the mounting of guns **b** *obs* **:** a promenade on top of a building or wall **c** *also* **platform deck :** a light partial deck without sheer or crown on a ship **d** (1) **:** a natural or constructed terrace (2) **:** a small level space (as a ledge) on steep rocks (3) **:** a flat or nearly flat area of the earth's solid surface either above or below the surface of the sea that stands above adjacent areas on at least one side and is ordinarily smaller than a plateau — compare CONTINENTAL PLATEAU **e :** a raised flooring (as a stage or dais) in a building on which speakers, theatrical performers, or other persons show themselves to an audience **f :** an elevated ledge or shelf (as of a machine or freight station) used esp. for the reception or transfer of materials **g :** a raised area in either valve of some brachiopods to which the muscles attach **h** (1) *or* **platform sole :** a thick midsole of a shoe made of wood, cork, or other lightweight material and usu. covered with the same material as the upper — see SHOE illustration (2) *or* **platform shoe :** a shoe having a platform sole **3 a** *obs* **:** the site of or area occupied by something (as a building) **b** (1) **:** the grounds for or basis of something (as a decision, proposal, or action) (2) **:** a level of something (as conduct, discussion, or thought) **c** (1) **:** a place for public discussion (as of questions of public interest) **:** a lecture forum **:** LYCEUM ⟨during the ~ season⟩; *also* **:** public discussion of such matters (2) **:** public speaking ⟨a good ~ manner⟩

platform 2h(2)

2platform \"\ *vb* -ED/-ING/-S *vt* **1** *obs* **:** FORMULATE, OUTLINE **2 :** to furnish with a platform **3 :** to place on or as if on a platform ~ *vi* **:** to speak from or as if from a platform

plat·form·al·ly \-məlē\ *adv* **:** in the manner of a public speaker **:** ORATORICALLY

platform car *n* **:** FLATCAR

platformed *adj* **:** furnished with or formed as a platform **:** level on top

platform elevator *n* **:** ELEVATOR 1b

plat·form·er \ˈplatˌfȯrmə(r)\ *n* **1 :** a planner or deviser esp. of a political platform **2 :** a platform speaker

platform frame *n* **:** a light timber frame for buildings in which a platform is constructed at each floor and the studs for the next floor are erected on this platform usu. with an intervening soleplate — compare BALLOON FRAME

platform harvester *n* **:** a corn-harvesting machine having a sled platform or a wheel-mounted platform that carries knives to cut the cornstalks

Plat·form·ing \ˈplatˌfȯrmiŋ, -mēŋ\ *trademark* — used for a process for the reforming of gasoline with a supported catalyst containing some platinum that promotes dehydrogenation of naphthenes to aromatic hydrocarbons, isomerization and cracking of paraffin hydrocarbons, and desulfurization

plat·form·ism \ˌmizəm\ *n* -s **:** the making of political speeches or the exaggerated bombast characteristic of such speeches

plat·form·less \-mləs\ *adj* **:** lacking a platform

platform pipe *n* **:** an Amerindian tobacco pipe found in Hopewell sites that has a thin rectangular platform on the center of which the bowl rests

platform reef *n* **:** a flat tabula reef more extensive than a patch reef ⟨*platform reefs* are common off the coast of Australia⟩

platform road *n, Brit* **:** a station track for loading railroad trains

platform rocker *n* **:** a chair that is so sprung on a stable platform as to be capable of motion like that of a conventional rocking chair

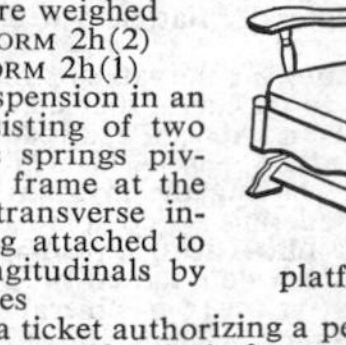

platform rocker

platform scale *or* **platform balance** *n* **:** a weighing machine with a flat platform on which objects are weighed

platform shoe *n* **:** PLATFORM 2h(2)

platform sole *n* **:** PLATFORM 2h(1)

platform spring *n* **:** a suspension in an automotive vehicle consisting of two longitudinal half-elliptic springs pivoted or shackled to the frame at the forward end and one transverse inverted half-elliptic spring attached to the rear of the two longitudinals by double shackles or crosses

platform ticket *n, Brit* **:** a ticket authorizing a person not himself traveling to go on the restricted platform at which trains arrive and depart (as to meet or speed a traveler)

platform truck *n* **:** a low-hung four-wheel hand truck without sides or a similar motorized vehicle for transporting heavy material

plathander *var of* PLATANNA

plat·hel·min·thes \ˌplatˌhelˈmin(t)thēz,-nˌthēz\ *syn of* PLATYHELMINTHES

plat·ic \ˈplad·ik\ *adj* [LL *platicus* broad, general, fr. Gk *platikos*, fr. *platos* breadth (fr. *platys* wide, broad, flat) + *-ikos* -ic; fr. the approximation being broad and not exact — more at PLACE] *of the conjunction of two astrologic planets* **:** falling within half the sum of the orbs but not within a single degree — compare PARTILE — **plat·ic·ly** *adv*

platier *comparative of* PLATY

platies *pl of* PLATY

platiest *superlative of* PLATY

pla·til·la \pləˈtilə\ *n* -s [Sp, dim. of *plata* silver, fr. OSp — more at PLATE] **:** a white linen fabric formerly made in Silesia

platin- *or* **platino-** *comb form* [NL *platinum*] **1 :** platinum ⟨*platino*type⟩ ⟨*platin*iridium⟩ **2 :** platinic acid ⟨*platin*ate⟩

1pla·ti·na \pləˈtēnə, ˈplatᵊnə\ *n* -s [Sp, platinum — more at PLATINUM] **:** PLATINUM; *esp* **:** crude native platinum

2platina \"\ *adj* **:** of the color platinum — used esp. of pale bluish gray furs ⟨a fascinating mink-tail print in brown or ~ tones —Lois Long⟩

platina fox *n* **:** a pale white-marked bluish gray fox that is a variety of the silver fox developed under domestication

1plat·i·nate \ˈplatᵊnˌāt\ *n* -s [*platin-* + *-ate*] **:** a salt of platinic acid

2platinate \"\ *vt* -ED/-ING/-S [*platin-* + *-ate*] **:** PLATINIZE

platina yellow *n* **:** GOLD PHEASANT

pla·tine \ˈplaˌtīn\ *adj, usu cap* [*Plate* river (Río de la Plata) in Argentina and Uruguay + E *-ine*] **:** bordering upon the River Plate or its chief tributaries ⟨the ~ portions of Argentina⟩

plating *n* -s [fr. gerund of *2plate*] **1 :** the art or process or an instance of covering something with a plate or plates and esp. with a superficial covering of metal **2 :** the formation of something (as metal) into plates **3 :** a surface made by plating: as **a :** a coating of metal plates; *esp* **:** defensive armor of metal (as steel) plates **b :** a thin coating of metal laid on another metal esp. for decorative effect **c :** the plates forming the hull, decks, and bulkheads of a ship — see SHIP illustration **d :** PLAITING 3

platini- *comb form* [NL *platinum*] **:** platinum ⟨*platini*chloride⟩ ⟨*platini*ferous⟩

pla·tin·ic \pləˈtinik, -nēk\ *adj* [ISV *platin-* + *-ic*] **:** of, relating to, or containing platinum — used esp. of compounds in which this element is tetravalent — compare PLATINOUS

platinic acid *n* **:** a weak acid $H_2Pt(OH)_6$ obtained as a yellowish white precipitate by hydrolysis of chloroplatinic acid; hexa-hydroxo-platinic acid

platinic chloride *n* **1 :** a reddish brown solid salt $PtCl_4$ obtained usu. by heating chloroplatinic acid with chlorine **2 :** CHLOROPLATINIC ACID — not used systematically

plat·i·ni·chloride \ˌplatᵊnə+\ *n* [*platini-* + *chloride*] **:** CHLOROPLATINATE

plat·in·iridium \ˌplatᵊn+\ *n* [*platin-* + *iridium*] **:** a mineral consisting of a natural alloy of iridium with platinum and other related metals occurring usu. in silver-white grains (hardness 6–7, sp. gr., 22.6–22.8)

platinite *var of* PLATYNITE

plat·i·nize \ˈplatᵊnˌīz\ *vt* -ED/-ING/-S [*platin-* + *-ize*] **:** to cover, treat, or combine with platinum or a compound of platinum: as **a :** to deposit platinum upon by simple immersion **b :** to coat with platinum black by electro-deposition or by chemical precipitation

platino- — see PLATIN-

plat·i·no·chloride \ˌplatᵊnō+\ *n* [*platin-* + *chloride*] **:** CHLOROPLATINITE

plat·i·no·cyanide \"+\ *n* [*platin-* + *cyanide*] **:** a fluorescent complex salt (as barium platinocyanide $Ba[Pt(CN)_4].4H_2O$) formed by the union of platinous cyanide with another cyanide; tetra-cyano-platinate (II) — called also *cyanoplatinite*

1plat·i·noid \ˈplatᵊnˌȯid\ *adj* [*platin-* + *-oid*] **:** resembling platinum

2platinoid *n* -s [ISV *platin-* + *-oid*] **1 :** an alloy chiefly of copper, nickel, and zinc used for forming electrical resistance coils and standards **2 :** a metal related to platinum

plat·i·no·type \ˈplatᵊnōˌtīp\ *n* [*platin-* + *type*] **:** a permanent photographic print having an image of platinum black obtained by the reduction of a platinum salt by a developer containing an iron salt (as ferrous oxalate) *also* **:** the process of making such a print

plat·i·nous \ˈplatᵊnəs\ *adj* [*platin-* + *-ous*] **:** of, relating to, or containing platinum — used esp. of compounds in which this element is bivalent — compare PLATINIC

1plat·i·num \ˈplat(ᵊ)nəm\ *n* -s [NL, fr. Sp *platina*, platinum, dim. of *plata* silver, fr. OSp — more at PLATE] **1 :** a very heavy precious metallic element that is typically grayish white, is noncorroding, ductile, and malleable, expands only slightly when heated and fuses with difficulty, has a relatively high electric resistance, and is chiefly bivalent and tetravalent, that occurs usu. native as grains and nuggets containing alloys (as with iridium, osmium, iron, copper) in alluvial deposits often associated with nickel sulfide and gold ores, and that is used chiefly in the form of alloys in special chemical ware and apparatus (as crucibles, dishes, foil, wire), in electrical and electronic devices, as a catalyst, in dental alloys, and in jewelry — symbol *Pt;* see ELEMENT table **2 :** a moderate gray that is lighter than median gray **3 :** a furbearer (as a fox or mink) of a light color phase that occurs esp. in ranch-bred animals

2platinum \"\ *adj* **1 :** of or relating to platinum **:** made of platinum (~ jewelry) **2 :** of the color platinum **3 :** belonging to the platinum color phase ⟨~ foxes⟩ **4 :** suggestive of the luxury value of platinum **:** COSTLY ⟨present-day ~ prices of basic needs⟩

platinum black *n* **:** a soft dull black powder of finely divided metallic platinum obtained by reduction and precipitation from solutions of its salts that is capable of occluding large volumes of hydrogen, oxygen, or other gases and that is used as a catalyst for hydrogenation or oxidation

platinum blonde *n* **1 :** a pale silvery blonde color that in human hair is usu. produced by bleach and a bluish rinse **2 :** a person whose hair is of the color platinum blonde

platinum metal *n* **:** any of the six precious metallic elements including platinum and elements resembling it in chemical and physical properties that belong to group VIII of the periodic table and are often subdivided into two triads one of which is composed of ruthenium, rhodium, and palladium whose specific gravities are about 12 and the other of which is composed of osmium, iridium, and platinum whose specific gravities are over 21

platinum paper *n* **:** photographic paper sensitized with a solution containing potassium chloroplatinite and ferric oxalate

platinum process *n* **:** the platinotype process

platinum sponge *n* **:** metallic platinum in a gray porous spongy form that is obtained by reducing ammonium chloroplatinate, that occludes large volumes of oxygen, hydrogen, and other gases, and that is used as a catalyst

plat·i·tude \ˈplad·əˌtüd, -atˌ, |ə-ˌtyüd\ *n* -s [F, fr. *plat* flat (fr. OF) + *-itude* (as in *altitude, rectitude*) — more at PLATE] **1 :** the quality or state of being dull or insipid **:** staleness of ideas or language **:** TRITENESS **2 :** a thought or remark that is flat, dull, trite, or weak **:** a dull, stale, or insipid truism **:** COMMONPLACE

plat·i·tu·di·nal \ˌ==ˈtüd(ᵊ)nəl, -ˈtyü-\ *adj* [fr. *platitude*, after such pairs as E *latitude: latitudinal*] **:** PLATITUDINOUS

1plat·i·tu·di·nar·i·an \ˌ==ˌtüdᵊnˈerēən, ˌ==ˌtyü-, -ᵊnˈa(a)r-, -ᵊnˈār-\ *n* -s [fr. *platitude*, after such pairs as E *latitude: latitudinarian*] **:** one given to platitudes

2platitudinarian \"\ *adj* **:** characterized by or addicted to platitudes

plat·i·tu·di·nize \ˌ==ˈ=dᵊnˌīz\ *vi* -ED/-ING/-S [*platitudinous* + *-ize*] **:** to utter platitudes **:** speak in platitudes — **plat·i·tu·di·niz·er** \-zə(r)\ *n* -s

plat·i·tu·di·nous \ˌ==ˈtüdᵊnəs, ˌ==ˈtyü-\ *adj* [fr. *platitude*, after such pairs as E *multitude: multitudinous*] **:** having the characteristics of a platitude **:** full of platitudes — **plat·i·tu·di·nous·ly** *adv*

pla·to·da \pləˈtōdə\ *or* **plat·o·dar·ia** \ˌplad·əˈda(a)rēə\ *or* **pla·to·des** \pləˈtō(ˌ)dēz\ [*platoda* fr. NL, fr. *platy-* + *-oda* -ode; *platodaria* fr. NL, fr. *platoda* + *-aria; platodes* fr. NL, fr. *platy-* + *-odes* -ode] *syn of* PLATYHELMINTHES

plat·ode \ˈplaˌtōd\ *n* -s [NL *Platoda*] **:** FLATWORM, PLATYHELMINTH

plat·oid \-ˌtȯid\ *adj* [*platy-* + *-oid*] **:** broad and flat; *esp* **:** resembling a flatworm

pla·to·nia \pləˈtōnēə\ *n, cap* [NL, fr. L *Platon, Plato* + NL *-ia*] **:** a small genus of So. American timber trees (family Guttiferae) with opposite pinnate veined leaves and showy usu. solitary terminal roseate flowers that are followed by globose edible single-seeded berries — see BACURY

pla·to·nian \pləˈtōnēən, plāˈ-, -nyən\ *adj, often cap* [L *Platon, Plato* (fr. Gk *Platōn*) + E *-ian*] **:** PLATONIC 1

1pla·ton·ic \pləˈtänik, plāˈ-, -nēk\ *adj* [L *platonicus*, fr. Gk *platōnikos* fr. *Platōn* Plato †347 B.C. Greek philosopher + *-ikos* -ic] **1** *usu cap* **:** of or relating to the philosopher Plato or Platonism; *specif* **:** being in accordance with or in the manner of Plato and his works **2 a** *often cap* (1) **:** constituting or relating to subsistent, transcendent, or eternal ideas (as Platonic forms) ⟨~ entities⟩ (2) **:** constituted by such ideas or forms ⟨a ~ heaven⟩ **b** *sometimes cap* (1) **:** involving, founded on, or being in harmony with platonic love ⟨a ~ relationship⟩ (2) **:** experiencing or professing platonic love **c** *sometimes cap* **:** of a theoretical, nominal, or academic nature **:** devoid of substantiality ⟨if the majority has only a ~ belief in it, the law will break down —Walter Lippmann⟩ ⟨purely ~ protestations⟩

2platonic \"\ *n* -s **1** *archaic, usu cap* **:** a follower of Plato **:** PLATONIST **2** *often cap* **:** emotion or behavior of a platonic lover — usu. used in pl.

pla·ton·i·cal \-nəkəl, -nēk-\ *archaic var of* PLATONIC

pla·ton·i·cal·ly \-nək(ə)lē, -nēk-, -li\ *adv, sometimes cap* **:** in a Platonic manner

platonic body *or* **platonic solid** *n* **:** any of the five regular geometrical solids comprising the simple tetrahedron, hexahedron, octahedron, dodecahedron, and icosahedron

pla·to·ni·cian \ˌplād·ōˈnishən\ *n* -s *usu cap* [F *platonicien*, fr. L *platonicus* platonic + F *-ien* -ian] **:** PLATONIST

platonic love *n, often cap P&L* **1 :** love conceived in the philosophy of Plato as an urge to union with the beautiful, ascending from passion for the individual to ecstasy in contemplation of the universal and ideal **2 :** a close relationship between two usu. opposite-sexed persons in which an element of sexual attraction or libidinal desire has been either so suppressed or so sublimated that it is generally believed to be absent

pla·to·nism \ˈplātᵊnˌizəm\ *n* -s [NL *platonismus*, fr. L *platon-, Platon, Plato* Plato †347 B.C. Greek philosopher (fr. Gk *Platōn*) + *-ismus* -ism] **1** *usu cap* **:** the philosophy of Plato stressing that ultimate reality consists of transcendent eternal universals which are the true objects of knowledge, that knowledge consists of reminiscence of these universals under the stimulus of sense perception, that objects of sense are not completely real but participate in the reality of the ideas, that man has a tripartite preexistent and immortal soul consisting of the appetitive functions, the spirited functions, and the intellect, and that the ideal state is aristocratic and made up of the three classes of artisans, soldiers, and philosopher-rulers — compare FORM, IDEALISM **2** *usu cap* **a :** the philosophic tradition established by Plato and extending through the Academy to the Alexandrian School and Plotinus — compare NEOPLATONISM **b :** any later revival of this tradition: as (1) **:** one during the Renaissance in Florence (2) **:** one in the 17th century in Cambridge University — compare CAMBRIDGE PLATONIST **c :** a particular formulation within the Platonic tradition **3** *sometimes cap* **a :** a tenet of Platonic philosophy **:** a platonic saying ⟨~s of poets⟩ **b :** any expression of idealism ⟨~ in the poetry of Shelley⟩ **4** *sometimes cap* **:** the doctrine or practice of platonic love **5** *sometimes cap* **:** a logical or mathematical theory incorporating within its language names for such abstract or higher level entities as classes — contrasted with *nominalism;* called also *terminological platonism*

pla·to·nist \-ᵊnəst\ *n* -s *usu cap* [ML *platonista*, fr. L *platon-, Platon, Plato* Plato †347 B.C. + *-ista* -ist] **:** a follower of Plato, his philosophy, or the Platonic tradition **:** an adherent or advocate of Platonism

pla·to·nis·tic \ˌplātᵊnˈistik, -tēk\ *adj* **1** *often cap* **a :** characteristic of or relating to Platonists or Platonism **b :** PLATONIC 1, 2a **2** *sometimes cap* **:** being in accordance with platonism; *specif* **:** including abstract entities

pla·to·nize \ˈplātᵊnˌīz\ *vb* -ED/-ING/-S *usu cap* [F *platoniser*, prob. fr. LGk *platōnizein*, fr. Gk *Platōn* Plato †347 B.C. + *-izein* -ize] *vi* **:** to adopt, imitate, or conform to Platonic opinions ~ *vt* **1 :** to explain in accordance with or adapt to Platonic doctrines **2 :** to render Platonic **:** IDEALIZE

¹pla·toon \plə'tün, pla'-\ *n* -s [F *peloton* platoon, ball — more at PELOTON] **1 a :** a small body of military personnel functioning as a unit: as (1) *archaic* **:** a body of men firing together (2) *archaic* **:** a small group drawn up in a hollow square to strengthen the angles of a formation (3) **:** a subdivision of a military unit (as a company) that normally consists of a headquarters unit and two or more squads or sections commanded by a lieutenant **b** *archaic* **:** a volley of shots **2 :** a group of persons sharing some common characteristic or activity ⟨a ~ of waiters⟩ ⟨a ~ of potential killers —Martin Levin⟩: as **a :** a squad of a police force working under a platoon system **b :** a squad of paid fire fighters on duty during a single shift **c :** a group (as of students) performing a particular activity at the same time **d :** a group of football players trained esp. for either offense or defense and intended to be sent into or withdrawn from the game as a body **3 :** a group of things of the same or similar kind existing together or viewed as a unit ⟨~s of empty bottles⟩

²platoon \"\ *vt* -ED/-ING/-S **:** to arrange in or divide into platoons ⟨the advantages from ~*ing* students in smaller schools⟩

platoon school *n* **:** a departmentalized school in which the pupils of each grade are organized into platoons that take turns in using the classrooms, shops, auditorium, gymnasium, and other physical resources of the school plant

platoon sergeant *n* **:** a noncommissioned army officer rating just below a master sergeant and above a staff sergeant

platoon system *n* **1 :** a system of assignment of divisions of the police of a large city to duty at stated times so that the city is equally policed at all hours **2 :** a system of football strategy in which defensive and offensive platoons are alternated in play

plats *pl of* PLAT, *pres 3d sing of* PLAT

plats du jour *pl of* PLAT DU JOUR

platt \'plat, 'plät\ *n* -s *usu cap* [G, by shortening] **:** PLATTDEUTSCH

platt·deutsch \'=,dȯich\ *n* -ES *cap* [G, fr. D *Platduitsch*, lit., Low German, fr. *plat* flat, level, low (fr. MD, fr. MF, flat) + *Duitsch* German, fr. MD *duutsch*, *dūtsch* — more at PLATE, DUTCH] **:** a colloquial language of northern Germany comprising a number of Low German dialects and of limited use as a literary language

platted *past of* PLAT

plat·te·land \'pläd·ə,länt\ *n, sometimes cap* [Afrik, fr. D, lit., flatland, fr. *platte, plat* flat, level, low + *land*, fr. MD; akin to OHG *lant* land — more at LAND] **:** the isolated rural sections of southern Africa **:** BACKVELD

¹plat·ter \'plad·ə(r), -atə-\ *n* -s [ME *plater*, fr. AF, fr. OF *plat* plate — more at PLATE] **1 :** a large shallow plate used esp. for serving meat **2 a** *or* **platter hat :** a woman's low-crowned hat that is distinctly flat in silhouette **b :** any of various broad flat objects ⟨the theater is . . . a cunningly contrived ~ of steel pipes and wooden planks —*New Yorker*⟩ **c :** a phonograph record or electrical transcription record **d :** HOME PLATE — **on a platter** *adv (or adj)* **:** without the least expenditure of effort **:** without difficulty **:** very easily ⟨can have the presidency *on a platter* —Jonathan Daniels⟩

platter 2a

²platter \"\ *n* -s [⁹*plat* + *-er*] **:** one that plats ⟨subdividers and ~s of land⟩

platter–faced \'==,=\ *adj* [¹*platter*] **:** having a broad flat face

¹**platting** *n* -s [fr. gerund of ⁵*plat*] **1 :** the action of one that plats some material **:** PLAITING **2 :** material that is plaited; *also* **:** plaited work (as of straw)

²**platting** *n* -s [fr. gerund of ⁹*plat*] **:** the action or process of mapping a surveyed area

platt·ner·ite \'platnə,rīt\ *n* -s [G *plattnerit*, fr. Karl Friedrich *Plattner* †1858 Ger. metallurgist + G *-it* -ite] **:** a mineral PbO_2 consisting of native lead dioxide usu. occurring in iron black masses of submetallic luster

platt·ner process \'pla|tnə(r)-, 'plä|\ *n, usu cap 1st P* [after Karl F. *Plattner* †1858 Ger. metallurgist] **:** a process for the extraction of gold (as from ores) by chlorination, solution, and precipitation

plat·ty \'plad·i, -ati\ *adj* [perh. fr. ⁸*plat* + *-y*] *dial Eng, of a crop* **:** spotty or uneven in growth

¹**platy** \'plād·ē, -ātē, -i\ *adj* -ER/-EST [¹*plate* + *-y*] **:** like a plate **:** consisting of plates or flaky layers — used chiefly of soil or mineral formations

²**platy** \'plad·ē, -atē, -i\ *n, pl* **platy** *or* **platys** *or* **platies** [fr. *platy-* (in NL *Platypoecilus*)] **:** a member of a genus (*Platypoecilus*) of small stockily built fishes that are native to southern Mexico, are highly favored for the tropical aquarium, and are notably variable in captivity ranging from the grayish or olive wild type stock through brilliant color variants and modified forms all of which are usu. regarded as varieties of a single species (*P. maculatus*)

platy- *also* **plat-** *comb form* [LL *plat-*, fr. Gk *plat-, platy-*, fr. *platys* — more at PLACE] **:** flat **:** broad ⟨platycnemic⟩ ⟨platoid⟩ ⟨platypoda⟩

platy·basic \¦plad·ē+\ *adj* [ISV *platy-* + *basic*] **:** relatively broad at the base ⟨a ~ skull⟩

platy·carya \¦==+\ *n, cap* [NL, fr. *platy-* + Gk *karya* nut tree — more at CARYA] **:** a small genus of Asiatic trees (family Juglandaceae) that have alternate pinnate leaves and small monoecious flowers in catkins which are followed by a small winged nut

platy·ce·lous *or* **platy·coe·lous** \¦plad·ē¦sēləs\ *also* **platyce·lian** *or* **platycoe·lian** \-lēən, -lyən\ *adj* [*platy-* + *-cele, -coele* + *-ous* or *-an*] *of a vertebra* **:** flat or concave ventrally and convex dorsally — compare OPISTHOCOELOUS

platy·cephalic \¦==+\ *also* **platy·cephalous** \¦==+\ *adj* [*platycephalic* fr. *platy-* + *-cephalic*; *platycephalous* ISV *platy-* + *-cephalous*] **:** having a head flat on top ⟨the chimpanzee is more ~ than . . . the gorilla —Arthur Keith⟩

platy·ce·phal·i·dae \,==sə'faləˌdē\ *n pl, cap* [NL, fr. *Platycephalus*, type genus + *-idae*] **:** a family of scorpaenid fishes comprising the flatheads

platy·ceph·a·lus \,=='sefələs\ *n, cap* [NL, fr. *platy-* + *-cephalus*] **:** the type genus of Platycephalidae

platy·ceph·a·ly \,=='sefəlē\ *also* **platy·ceph·a·lism** \-,lizəm\ *n, pl* **platycephalies** *also* **platycephalisms** [*platycephaly* ISV *platy-* + *cephal-* + *-y*; *platycephalism* fr. *platy-* + *cephal-* + *-ism*] **:** the condition of being platycephalic

platy·cer·cus \,=='sərkəs\ *n, cap* [NL, fr. Gk *platykerkos* flat-tailed, fr. *platy-* + *kerkos* tail] **:** a genus of chiefly Australian parrakeets comprising the rosella and related birds

platy·ce·ri·um \,=='sirēəm\ *n, cap* [NL, fr. *platy-* + Gk *kērion* honeycomb (fr. *kēros* wax) — more at CEREUS] **:** a genus of tropical Old World ferns (family Polypodiaceae) that are mostly epiphytic and have large flat lobed fronds often resembling the antlers of a stag — see STAGHORN FERN

plat·ycne·mia \,plad·ē(k)'nēmēə\ *n* -s [NL, fr. *platy-* + *-cnemia*] **:** the condition of being platycnemic

plat·ycne·mic \¦==¦nēmik\ *adj* [ISV *platy-* + *-cnemic*] *of a shinbone* **:** laterally flattened with a platycnemic index of 55 to 63

platycnemic index *n* **:** the ratio of the anteroposterior diameter of the shinbone to its lateral diameter multiplied by 100

plat·ycne·my \'==,nēmē\ *n* -ES [ISV, fr. NL *platycnemia*] **:** PLATYCNEMIA

platy·co·don \,plad·ē'kō,dän\ *n* [NL, fr. *platy-* + Gk *kōdōn* bell (fr. *koos* hollow, den); akin to Gk *koilos* hollow — more at CAVE] **1** *cap* **:** a genus of perennial herbs (family Campanulaceae) having large bell-shaped blue or white flowers with stamens that are much dilated at the base and a capsule that opens by apical valves — see BALLOONFLOWER **2** -s **:** any plant or flower of the genus *Platycodon*

platy·cra·nia \,=='krānēə\ *n* -s [NL, fr. *platy-* + *-crania*] **:** the condition of a skull caused by artificial flattening — **platy·cra·ni·al** \¦==¦nēəl\ *adj*

plat·yc·tene \¦plad·ik¦tēn\ *adj* [NL *Platyctenea*] **:** of or relating to the Platyctenea

plat·yc·te·nea \,=='tēnēə\ *n pl, cap* [NL, fr. *platy-* + Gk *kten-, kteis* comb — more at PECTINATE] **:** an order of ctenophores (class Tentaculata) in which the body is much flattened giving distinct dorsal and ventral surfaces — compare CTENOPLANA — **plat·yc·te·ne·an** \-nēən\ *adj or n*

platy·dactyl *also* **platy·dactyle** \¦plad·ē+\ *or* **platy·dacty·lous** \"+\ *adj* [*platydactyl* fr. *platy-* + *dactyl*; *platydactyle* fr. *platy-* + Gk *daktylos* finger, toe; *platydactylous* ISV *platy-* + *-dactylous*] **:** having flat digits — used esp. of lizards and frogs with flattened adhesive tips to the toes

platy·el·min·thes \-,el'min(t)thēz, -n,thēz\ *syn of* PLATYHELMINTHES

platy·fish \'plad·ē+,-\ *n* **:** PLATY

platy·gas·ter·i·dae \,==ga'sterə,dē\ *n pl, cap* [NL, fr. *Platygaster*, type genus (fr. *platy-* + *-gaster*) + *-idae*] **:** a family of serphoid wasps that are mostly parasites of gallflies

platy·hel·mia \-'helmēə\ [NL, fr. *platy-* + Gk *helmis* worm + NL *-ia*] *syn of* PLATYHELMINTHES

platy·helminth \¦==+\ *n, pl* **platyhelminths** *or* **platy·helminthes** [NL *Platyhelminthes*] **:** a worm of the phylum Platyhelminthes **:** FLATWORM

platy·helminthes \¦==+\ *n pl, cap* [NL, fr. *platy-* + Gk *helminth-, helmis* worm — more at HELMINTH-] **:** a phylum of soft-bodied bilaterally symmetrical usu. much flattened invertebrates comprising the planarians, flukes, tapeworms, and related worms and often also the nemerteans, having the body unsegmented or composed of a series of proglottides formed by strobilation, built up of ectoderm, endoderm, and mesoderm, and without body cavity, the space between the body wall and the various organs being filled with parenchyma, and distinguished by an excretory system made up of tubules that permeate the body and usu. communicate with the exterior and that end internally in flame cells — **platy·helminthic** *adj*

platy·hieric \¦==+\ *adj* [*platy-* + *-hieric*] **:** having a relatively wide sacrum with a sacral index of 106 or over — compare DOLICHOHIERIC, SUBPLATYHIERIC

platy·kur·tic \¦==¦kərd·ik\ *adj* [*platy-* + *kurt-* (fr. Gk *kyrtos* bulging, curved) + *-ic* — more at LEPTOKURTIC] **1** *of a frequency distribution curve* **:** being less peaked than the corresponding normal distribution curve **2 :** *of a frequency distribution* **:** being less concentrated about the mean than the corresponding normal distribution

platy·kurtosis \¦==+\ *n* [NL, fr. E *platykurtic* + NL *-osis*] **:** the condition of being platykurtic

platy·lep·a·did \,=='lepədəd, -,did\ *n* -s [NL *Platylepad-, Platylepas* + E *-id*] **:** a barnacle of the genus *Platylepas*

platy·lepas \¦==+\ *n, cap* [NL, fr. *platy-* + *Lepas*] **:** a genus of commensal barnacles common in warm seas where they live embedded in the skin of turtles, manatees, sea snakes, and fishes

platy·me·ria \,=='mirēə\ *n* -s [NL, fr. *platy-* + *mer-* + *-ia*] **:** the condition of being platymeric or of having platymeric femurs

platy·mer·ic \¦==¦merik\ *adj* [*platy-* + *mer-* + *-ic*] *of a thighbone* **:** laterally flattened with a platymeric index of 75 to 85

platymeric index *n* **:** the ratio of the anteroposterior diameter of the femur to its lateral diameter multiplied by 100

platy·my·ar·i·an \¦==,mī¦a(a)rēən\ *also* **platy·my·ar·i·al** \-rēəl\ *adj* [*platy-* + *my-* + *-aria* + *-an* or *-al*] *of nematode muscle cells* **:** having the myofibrils restricted to the region next the hypodermis — compare COELOMYARIAN

plat·y·nite *or* **plat·i·nite** \'plad·ə,nīt\ *n* -s [Sw *platynit*, fr. Gk *platynein* to widen, flatten (fr. *platys* broad, flat) + Sw *-it* -ite — more at PLACE] **:** a mineral $PbBi_2(Se,S)_3$ consisting of a lead and bismuth selenide and sulfide and occurring in thin iron-black metallic plates

platy·ope \'plad·ē,ōp\ *n* -s [back-formation fr. *platyopic*] **:** a platyopic individual

platy·o·pia \,plad·ē'ōpēə\ *n* -s [NL, fr. *platy-* + Gk *ōp-, ōps* face, eye + NL *-ia*] **:** broadness of face **:** the condition of being platyopic

platy·op·ic \¦==¦äpik, -¦ōp-\ *adj* [*platy-* + Gk *ōp-, ōps* face, eye + E *-ic* — more at EYE] **:** having a broad flat face

platy·pel·lic \¦==¦pelik\ *adj* [*platy-* + *-pellic*] **:** having a broad pelvis with a pelvic index of less than 90 — **platy·pel·ly** \'==,pelē\ *n* -ES

platy·pel·loid \¦==¦pe,lȯid\ *adj* [*platypellic* + *-oid*] *of a pelvis* **:** broad and flat **:** approaching a platypellic condition — compare GYNECOID

¹**platy·pez·id** \¦==¦pezəd\ *adj* [NL *Platypezidae*] **:** of or relating to the Platypezidae

²**platypezid** \"\ *n* -s [NL *Platypezidae*] **:** a fly of the family Platypezidae

platy·pez·i·dae \,=='pezə,dē\ *n pl, cap* [NL, fr. *Platypeza*, type genus (fr. *platy-* + Gk *peza* foot, lower part of a body) + *-idae*; akin to Skt *padya* of the foot, L *ped-, pes* foot — more at FOOT] **:** a small family of two-winged flies having larvae that breed in fungi and adults that often fly in swarms — see SMOKE FLY

pla·typ·o·da \plə'tipədə\ *n pl, cap* [NL, fr. *platy-* + *-poda*] **:** a division of Pectinibranchia comprising gastropod mollusks with the foot adapted for creeping — compare HETEROPODA — **pla·typ·o·dous** \-dəs\ *adj*

platy·po·dia \,=='pōdēə\ *n* -s [NL, fr. *platy-* + *-podia*] **:** FLAT-FOOTEDNESS

platy·pod·i·dae \,=='pädə,dē\ *n pl, cap* [NL, fr. *Platypod-, Platypus*, type genus (fr. Gk *platypod-, platypous* flat-footed) + *-idae*] **:** a family of ambrosia beetles occurring mainly in the tropics and subtropics

platy·poecilia \¦==+\ *or* **platy·poecilius** \"+\ [NL, fr. *platy-* + *Poecilia*, genus of fishes — more at POECILIIDAE] *syn of* PLATYPOECILUS

platy·poe·ci·lus \,=='pēsələs\ *n, cap* [NL, fr. *platy-* + Gk *poikilos* many-colored — more at PAINT] **:** a genus of topminnows (family Poeciliidae) comprising the platys

pla·typ·tera \plə'tiptərə\ *n pl, cap* [NL, fr. *platy-* + *-ptera*] *in former classifications* **:** an order of insects including the termites, bird lice, and other forms that are now divided among several orders

platy·pus \'plad·əpəs, -dē-, -,pu̇s\ *n* -ES [NL, fr. Gk *platypous* flat-footed, fr. *platy-* + *pous* foot — more at FOOT] **:** a small aquatic mammal (*Ornithorhynchus anatinus*) of the order Monotremata of southern and eastern Australia and Tasmania having a fleshy bill resembling that of a duck, dense blackish brown fur, 5-toed webbed feet, and a broad flattened tail, and being an expert swimmer and diver, inhabiting burrows near the water, feeding chiefly on aquatic mollusks, and unlike most mammals being oviparous, laying eggs about three fourths of an inch long — called also *duckbill, duckmole*

platy·pus·ary *also* **platy·pus·sa·ry** \-sərē\ *n* -ES [*platypus* + *-ary* (n. suffix)] **:** a place for care and exhibition of the platypus

platy·rhi·na \,plad·ē'rīnə\ *or* **platyrhi·ni** *or* **platyr·rhi·ni** \-ī,nī\ *syn of* PLATYRRHINA

platyrrhina \"\ *n pl, cap* [NL, fr. *platy-* + Gk *-rrhina*, neut. pl. of *-rrhin* -nosed, fr. *rhin-, rhis* nose — more at RHIN-] *in many classifications* **:** a division of Anthropoidea comprising the new-world monkeys all of which have a broad nasal septum, usu. 36 teeth, and often a prehensile tail — compare CATARRHINA, CEBIDAE

¹**plat·yr·rhine** \'plad·ə,rīn, -,rən\ *also* **plat·yr·rhin·i·an** \,==¦rinēən\ *or* **plat·y·rhine** *or* **plat·y·rhin·i·an** *n* -s [*platyrrhine, platyrhine* fr. *platyrrhine, platyrhine*, adj.; *platyrrhinian, platyrhinian* fr. F *platyrrhinien*, fr. Gk *platyrrhin-, platyrrhis* broadnosed (fr. *platy-* + *rhin-, rhis* nose) + F *-ien* -ian] **:** a platyrrhine individual

²**platyrrhine** \"\ *also* **platyrrhinian** \"\ *or* **platyrhine** *or* **platyrhinian** *adj* [*platyrrhine* fr. NL *Platyrrhina*; *platyrrhinian* fr. NL *Platyrrhina* + E *-an*; *platyrhine* fr. NL *Platyrhina*; *platyrhinian* fr. NL *Platyrhina* + E *-an*] **1 :** of or belonging to the Platyrrhina **2** [*platyrrhine, platyrhine* fr. *platy-* + *-rrhine* or *-rhine*; *platyrrhinian, platyrhinian* fr. *platyrrhinian, platyrhinian*, n.] **:** having a short broad nose with a high nasal index

plat·yr·rhin·ic \¦plad·ə¦rinik\ *adj* [¹*platyrrhine* + *-ic*] **:** PLATYRRHINE 2

platyr·rhi·ny \'==,rīnē\ *n* -ES [²*platyrrhine* + *-y*] **:** the condition of being platyrrhine **:** shortness and broadness of nose

platys *pl of* PLATY

pla·tys·ma \plə'tizmə\ *n, pl* **pla·tys·ma·ta** \-məd·ə\ *also* **platysmas** [NL, fr. Gk *platysma* flat piece, plate, fr. *platynein* to widen, flatten — more at PLATYNITE] **:** a broad thin layer of muscle on each side of the neck immediately under the superficial fascia that belongs to the group of facial muscles and is innervated by the facial nerve — **pla·tys·mal** \-zməl\ *adj*

¹**platy·so·mid** \¦plad·ē¦sōməd\ *adj* [NL *Platysomidae*] **:** of or relating to the Platysomidae

²**platysomid** \"\ *n* -s [NL *Platysomidae*] **:** a fish or fossil of the family Platysomidae

platy·som·i·dae \,=='sämə,dē, -sōm-\ *n pl, cap* [NL, fr. *Platysomus*, type genus (fr. Gk *platysōmos* broad-bodied, fr. *platy-* + *sōma* body) + *-idae* — more at -SOME] **:** a family of Carboniferous and Permian ganoid fishes (order Archistia) having a deep compressed body covered with rhombic scales joined by peg-and-socket joints

platy·spermic \¦==+\ *adj* [*platy-* + *-spermic*] *of a seed* **:** bilaterally symmetrical

platy·staph·y·line \¦==¦stafə,līn\ *adj* [*platy-* + *staphyl-* (fr. NL *staphylion*) + *-ine*] **:** having a broad flat palate

platy·ste·mon \,=='stēmən\ *n, cap* [NL, fr. *platy-* + Gk *stēmōn* warp, thread — more at STAMEN] **:** a genus of small annual herbs (family Papaveraceae) of the southwestern U.S. with linear leaves and creamy to pale yellow flowers

plat·ys·ten·ce·phal·ic \¦plad·ə¦stensə¦falik\ *adj* [Gk *platystatos* (superl. of *platys* broad) + E *encephalic* — more at PLACE] **:** having a dolichocephalic head with a wide pentagonal occiput and a prognathous jaw — **plat·ys·ten·ceph·a·ly** \,==,='sefəlē\ *n* -ES

platy·ster·ni·dae \,plad·ē'stərnə,dē\ *n pl, cap* [NL, fr. *Platysternon*, genus name of *Platysternon megacephalum* (fr. *platy-* + Gk *sternon* chest, breast) + *-idae* — more at STERNUM] **:** a family of Asiatic freshwater turtles (suborder Cryptodira) including a single species (*Platysternon megacephalum*) characterized by a relatively huge head with hooked mandibles and a very long tail

platy·stom·i·dae \,=='stämə,dē\ *n pl, cap* [NL, fr. *Platystomus*, type genus (fr. *platy-* + *-stomus*) + *-idae*] **:** a family of snout beetles with short beak, trapezoidal prothorax, and flexible palpi

¹**plaud** \'plȯd\ *n* -s [prob. back-formation fr. *plaudite*] *archaic* **:** PRAISE, APPLAUSE

²**plaud** \"\ *vt* -ED/-ING/-S [L *plaudere* to applaud] *archaic* **:** APPLAUD

¹**plau·dit** \'plȯdət, *usu* -əd·+V\ *n* -s [L *plaudite* applaud!, 2nd pers. pl. imper. of *plaudere* to applaud] **1 :** an act of applauding (as by clapping the hands) **:** a round of applause ⟨with the ~s of his audience still ringing in his ears —A.C. Cole⟩ **2 :** strong and openly expressed approval **:** enthusiastic approbation ⟨the book received the ~s of the critics⟩

²**plaudit** \"\ *vb* -ED/-ING/-S **:** APPLAUD

plau·di·te \'plȯdəd·ē\ *n* -s [L, applaud!] **1 :** an appeal for applause esp. by an ancient Roman actor **2** *obs* **:** PLAUDIT

plau·di·to·ry \'plȯdə,tōrē, -tȯr-, -ri\ *adj* [obs. E *plauditor* one who applauds (fr. E ²*plaudit* + *-or*) + E *-y*] **:** APPLAUSIVE, LAUDATORY

plau·si·bil·i·ty \,plȯzə'biləd·ē, -ətē, -i\ *n* -ES **1 :** the quality or state of being plausible **2 :** something plausible

¹**plau·si·ble** \'plȯzəbəl\ *adj, sometimes* -ER/-EST [L *plausibilis* deserving applause, pleasing, acceptable, fr. *plausus* (past part. of *plaudere* to applaud) + *-ibilis* -ible] **1** *obs* **a :** worthy of being applauded **b :** APPLAUSIVE, PLAUDITORY **:** expressing approval **2 :** obtaining approbation or favor **:** AGREEABLE, AFFABLE, POPULAR, SUITABLE ⟨a more ~ site for a house —E.B. White⟩ **3 a :** superficially fair, reasonable, or valuable **:** SPECIOUS ⟨a ~ pretext⟩ **b** *of a person* **:** apparently trustworthy or fair **:** superficially pleasing or persuasive **4 a :** superficially worthy of belief **:** CREDIBLE ⟨a ~ conclusion⟩ **b :** being such as may be accepted as real ⟨a jewel too big to be ~⟩ — **plau·si·ble·ness** *n* -ES

²**plausible** \"\ *n* -s **:** something (as a statement or an argument) that is plausible **:** PLAUSIBILITY

plau·si·bly \-blē, -li\ *adv* **:** in a plausible manner ⟨very ~ presented⟩ **:** so as to seem to accord with justice, propriety, or right ⟨delayed as long as they ~ could⟩

plau·sive \'plȯziv, -lȯs-\ *adj* [L *plausus* (past part. of *plaudere* to applaud) + E *-ive*] **1 :** manifesting praise or approval **:** APPLAUDING **2** *obs* **:** PLEASING, AGREEABLE **3** *archaic* **:** SPECIOUS

plaus·tral \'plȯstrəl\ *adj* [L *plaustrum* wagon + E *-al*; prob. akin to L *plaudere* to clap, beat, applaud] **:** of or relating to a wagon or cart

plaus·trum \-trəm\ *n, pl* **plaus·tra** \-trə\ *or* **plaustrums** [L] **:** an ancient Roman two-wheeled farm cart

plau·tine \'plȯ,tīn\ *adj, usu cap* [L *plautinus*, fr. *Plautus* †184 B.C. + L *-inus* -ine] **:** of, relating to, or in the style of the Roman comic dramatist Plautus who is noted for vivacious broad humor

¹**plau·tus** \'plȯd·əs\ *n, cap* [NL, fr. L, flat, flat-footed; akin to L *plaudere* to clap, applaud] **:** a genus of auks including the dovekie

²**plautus** \"\ [NL, fr. L, flat, flat-footed] *syn of* PINGUINUS

¹**play** \'plā\ *n -s often attrib* [ME *play, pley*, fr. OE *plega*; akin to OE *plegan* to play, MD *pleyen, playen* to frolic, play] **1 a :** an act of briskly handling, using, or plying a sword or other weapon or instrument ⟨a duelist famous for his brilliant ~⟩ ⟨indiscriminate gun ~ in the streets —Green Peyton⟩ **b** (1) *archaic* **:** a particular amusement **:** GAME, SPORT (2) **:** the conduct or carrying on of a game **:** the course of a game ⟨rain interfered with ~⟩ ⟨talking during ~ may be distracting⟩ (3) **:** a particular act, maneuver, or point in a game ⟨relied mostly on running ~s —G.S.Halas⟩ **:** manner or trick of playing ⟨his ~ is excellent⟩ **:** turn to play ⟨it's your ~⟩ (4) **:** the action between two downs in football (5) **:** the action in which cards are played after bidding in a card game **c** (1) *obs* **:** SEXUAL INTERCOURSE (2) **:** exchange of caresses in or as if in preparation for sexual intercourse **:** DALLIANCE ⟨sexual ~⟩ **d** (1) **:** recreational activity **:** FROLIC, SPORT; *esp* **:** the spontaneous or organized recreational activity of children ⟨in cooperative ~ children learn adjustments in a social group —Gertrude H. Hildreth⟩ (2) **:** JEST, FUN — usu. used in the phrase *in play* ⟨said it in ~, not in earnest⟩ (3) **:** the act or an instance of playing upon words or speech sounds esp. to achieve a humorous or rhetorical effect (as in punning) ⟨the title of this address is an obvious ~ upon the original meaning . . . of the term *philosophy* —C.W.Berenda⟩ ⟨take a familiar line of verse and turn it into a poem with an ironic ~ upon the original —Oscar Cargill⟩ — usu. used in the phrases *play of words* or *play on words* **e :** GAMBLING, GAMING ⟨lose a fortune in ~⟩ **1** *chiefly dial* (1) **:** HOLIDAY (2) **:** FAIR, WAKE **2 a** (1) **:** an act, way, method, or manner of proceeding **:** MANEUVER, MOVE ⟨the ~ was . . . to maintain the balance —S.H.Adams⟩ ⟨that was a ~ to get your fingerprints —Erle Stanley Gardner⟩ ⟨the ~ fell flat —*Atlantic*⟩ ⟨a very bad place for that kind of ~ —Raymond Chandler⟩ (2) **:** DEAL, VENTURE ⟨land available for any company . . . looking for a land ~ —*Edmonton (Alberta) Jour.*⟩ ⟨in this big oil ~, there are more than eighty drilling rigs —*Time*⟩ **b** (1) **:** OPERATION, EMPLOYMENT ⟨discouraged from the normal ~ of their talents —Gilbert Seldes⟩ ⟨his sense of humor was in ~ —R.M.Lovett⟩ ⟨other motives surely come into ~ —M.R.Cohen⟩ ⟨a program of reaction was put into full ~ —C.L.Jones⟩ ⟨he is above the ~ of party —Ernest Barker⟩ (2) **:** brisk, lively, or light activity involving change, variation, transition, or alternation **:** dynamic activity ⟨the ~ of a supremely fine and penetrating intelligence —F.R. Leavis⟩ ⟨accustomed to make their phrases a ~ of wit —George Meredith⟩ (3) **:** brisk, fitful, or light movement of something physical **:** movement marked by alternation or sudden transition ⟨the ~ of light and shadow on the dancing waves⟩ ⟨the gem presented a dazzling ~ of colors⟩ ⟨the ~ of a gusty wind —Amy Lowell⟩ ⟨~ of surf is most spectacular on stormy days —*Amer. Guide Series: Maine*⟩ (4) **:** free or unimpeded motion (as of a part of a machine) ⟨this type of universal joint permits shaft end ~ —Joseph Heitner⟩; *also* **:** the length or measure of such motion ⟨the cylinder has about an inch of ~⟩ (5) **:** scope or opportunity for action ⟨found ample ~ for this avocation in surrounding marshes —*Amer. Guide Series: La.*⟩ ⟨the position gave much ~ to his notable talents⟩ **c** (1) **:** temporary attention, interest, or patronage ⟨took the ~ away from puppets on television —Thomas Whiteside⟩ ⟨time was heavy on their hands and they were giving the . . . casino a great ~ —C.B.Davis⟩ (2) **:** emphasis or publicity esp. in public media of communica-

tion ⟨got very little ~ here the next day —E.J.Kahn⟩ ⟨official propaganda gives a heavy ~ to impressive statistics —*New Republic*⟩ ⟨wish the country received a better ~ in the American press —Hugh MacLennan⟩ (3) : a move or series of moves calculated to arouse affection, sympathy, or friendly feelings — usu. used with *make* ⟨quit making a ~ for him —James Jones⟩ ⟨made a big ~ for the girl —Will Herman⟩ ⟨since the ... audience has the votes, it is best to make your ~ for them —B.N.Cardozo⟩ **3 a** : the representation or exhibition of some action or story on the stage or in some other medium (as radio, television, or motion pictures) : the performance of a comedy, tragedy, or other dramatic piece ⟨going to the ~⟩ **b** : a dramatic composition : DRAMA **c** : PANTOMIME **4** : an act of playing a phonograph record through ⟨this needle should be good for hundreds of ~*s*⟩ **syn** see FUN, ²PLAY, ROOM — **in play 1** : so as to be engaged or occupied ⟨enabled him to escape by holding his attackers *in play*⟩ **2 a** : in such a condition or position as to be legitimately played : properly in the game : not dead ⟨the ball is *in play*⟩ **b** : still available for play — used of a card that has not yet been played — **out of play** : not in play : DEAD

²**play** \"\ *vb* -ED/-ING/-S [ME *playen, pleyen,* fr. OE *plegan*] *vi* **1 a** : to engage in recreational activity : amuse or divert oneself : FROLIC, SPORT ⟨children ~*ing* in the park⟩ **b** : to have sexual relations ⟨if he ~*s* with his wife in the evening there's another baby —Pramoedya Toer⟩; *esp* : to have promiscuous or illicit sexual relations — usu. used in the phrases *play around* or *play around with* ⟨you've got the wrong impression ... she doesn't ~ around —Calder Willingham⟩ ⟨girls who ~ around with men in uniform —Frederic Wakeman⟩ **c** (1) : to toy or move aimlessly to-and-fro ⟨hand was ~*ing* on the edge of the bed —Arnold Bennett⟩ — usu. used with *with* ⟨~*ed* disconsolately with her food —Louis Auchincloss⟩ ⟨~*ed* with his walking stick⟩ (2) : to deal or behave frivolously, mockingly, or playfully : MOCK, KID, JEST ⟨the sallies of those who ~*ed* at him in print —*Times Lit. Supp.*⟩ — usu. used with *with* ⟨don't ~ with me —Hartley Howard⟩ (3) : to deal in a light, speculative, or sportive manner : toy mentally ⟨they did not believe in ghosts, but ... they let their fancies ~ on the border line —Van Wyck Brooks⟩ — usu. used with *with* ⟨her mind ~*ed* with absurd fancies —Ellen Glasgow⟩ ⟨liked to ~ with ideas —Peggy Durdin⟩ ⟨rather ~*s* with the allegorical form —H.O.Taylor⟩ (4) : to make use of the double meaning of a word or of the similarity of sound of two words for stylistic or humorous effect — usu. used in the phrase *play on words* ⟨sometimes poets ~ on words in this fashion —E.S.McCartney⟩ **d** *Brit* : to be out of work or idle : take a holiday **2 a** (1) : to have an effect : OPERATE — used with *on* or *upon* ⟨the jungle scents ~*ed* upon my emotions —William Beebe⟩ ⟨see that direct heat does not ~ on dry enamel —*Gadgets Annual*⟩ (2) : to take advantage : make use — used with *on* or *upon* ⟨~*ing* ignobly upon selfish fears —V.L.Parrington⟩ ⟨~*ing* upon the divisive forces in the Western world —*N.Y. Times*⟩ (3) : to exert or seek to exert wiles or influence : PRACTICE — used with *on* or *upon* ⟨the enchantress ~*ing* upon him —George Meredith⟩ **b** (1) : to dart, spring, or fly to and fro : FLUTTER, FRISK ⟨watched the birds ~*ing* overhead⟩ ⟨dolphins ~*ing* about the ship⟩ (2) : to move, operate, or have effect in a lively or brisk and irregular, intermittent, or alternating manner ⟨had seen northern lights ~ across the autumnal skies —B.A.Williams⟩ ⟨a faint smile ~*ed* about her lips —Victoria Sackville-West⟩ ⟨muscles could be seen ~*ing* beneath his thin cotton shirt —Sherwood Anderson⟩ (3) *of a cockbird* : to exhibit itself (as in courtship display) **c** (1) : to move or function freely within prescribed limits : have free or full play ⟨a piston rod ~*s* within a cylinder⟩ (2) : to discharge, eject, or fire something or to become discharged, ejected, or fired repeatedly or so as to make a stream ⟨a stream of water ~*s* to keep the molten mass from congealing —*Monsanto Mag.*⟩ ⟨his cannon ~*ed* upon the besiegers from two sides⟩ **3 a** (1) : to perform on a musical instrument ⟨~ on a violin⟩ (2) : to sound in performance ⟨the organ is ~*ing*⟩ ⟨a chorale was ~*ing* on the phonograph —Glenn Scott⟩ (3) : to reproduce sound of recorded material ⟨records ~*ing* at rotational speeds of 33⅓ revolutions per minute⟩ **b** (1) : to act on a stage or in some other dramatic medium (as radio, motion pictures, or television) (2) : to be staged or presented : RUN ⟨what's ~*ing* at the picture shows —Shelby Foote⟩ (3) : to act so as to support or back up — used in the phrase *play up to* ⟨amusing to find how well they ~*ed* up to the theory of what an Oxford man ought to be —H.J.Laski⟩ ⟨amused him to ~ up to the popular idea of him —Gerald Bullett⟩ (4) : to make a strong effort or calculated move to gain favor, approval, or sympathy from or as if from a theater audience : make a play ⟨might ~ to popular prejudices to serve his political ends —V.L.Parrington⟩ ⟨sometimes inclined to ~ to their roadside audience —Norma Spring⟩ ⟨whenever he had an audience, he whined and ~*ed* for sympathy —D.H.Lawrence⟩ — often used in the phrase *play up to* ⟨when ... they weren't ~*ing* up to their public —Bennett Cerf⟩ ⟨now they would have to ~ up to this odd-looking, homely woman —Ida A. R. Wylie⟩ (5) : to lend itself to performance esp. theatrical ⟨the script reads well but ~*s* badly⟩ **4 a** : to engage or take part in a game ⟨~ at chess⟩ ⟨~*ed* in every major game this year⟩ **b** *archaic* : to exercise or fight with weapons esp. for amusement; *specif* : FENCE **c** : GAMBLE, GAME ⟨~*ed* for heavy stakes⟩ **d** (1) : to behave or conduct oneself in a specified way ⟨don't think I've ~*ed* quite fair —E.A.McCourt⟩ ⟨some cars ~ dirty —H.W.Young⟩ ⟨best to ~ safe⟩ (2) : to engage in a game of make-believe : assume a role in or as if in sport — used with *at* ⟨the commuter ~*ing* at country squire —Bergen Evans⟩ ⟨would ~ at being well-to-do local housewives —Grace Metalious⟩ (3) : to feign to be in a specified state or condition ⟨the ... fawn that she found in the woods, which ~*ed* dead —*Atlantic*⟩ ⟨don't ~ innocent⟩ (4) : to take part, engage, or collaborate in or assent to some activity ⟨took it for granted that he would ~ with the big industrialists —Alvin Johnson⟩ : COOPERATE ⟨no other nation can be sure ... whether we will simply refuse to ~ —Robert Lekachman⟩ — often used with *along* ⟨~*ed* along until he had enough evidence to hold all three —Morris Ploscowe⟩ ⟨willing to ~ along with him —Harvey Breit⟩ (5) : to function or operate so as to prove advantageous to or enhance the effectiveness of another — used with *into* ⟨the horizontal lines of the ... figure ~ into the central idea with splendid effect —Roger Fry⟩ ⟨easy thus to make one subject ~ into another —A.C.Benson⟩ esp. in the phrase *play into the hands of* ⟨decided on an unfortunate procedure that ~*ed* directly into the hands of the opposing party⟩ ~ *vt* **1 a** (1) : to engage in or occupy oneself with (a game or other amusement) ⟨~ baseball⟩ (2) : to engage in (some activity) as if in a game ⟨~ secret diplomacy and power politics —A.L.Guérard⟩ ⟨~ hooky⟩ (3) : to pursue a certain line of conduct toward : deal with, handle, or manage : TREAT ⟨deliberately ~*ing* the conversation as though this meal were like any other —Wirt Williams⟩ ⟨~*ed* him exactly the way I figured —J.M.Cain⟩ ⟨the law ~*s* the privilege differently —B.N.Meltzer⟩ — often used with impersonal *it* as object ⟨symptomatic ... of the desire to ~ it safe —Norman Cousins⟩ ⟨willing to ~ it on the level —Bill Hatch⟩ (4) : to set in opposition : PIT ⟨became adept at ~*ing* Japanese civilians against the military —E.T.Hall⟩ — usu. used with *off* ⟨able to ~ off one tribe against another —C.L.Jones⟩ (5) : to treat, use, or work upon (a person) for a certain end or as a member of a designated class : EXPLOIT, MANIPULATE — usu. used with *for* ⟨think you are only ~*ing* me for what you can get out of me —James Jones⟩ ⟨the king ... ~*ed* him for a sucker —DeLancey Ferguson⟩ **b** : to treat, practice, or deal with in a spirit of play : pretend to engage in : imitate in play ⟨children, who ~ life, discern its true law and relations more clearly than men —H.D.Thoreau⟩ ⟨the children were ~*ing* house⟩ ⟨~*ing* that they were cowboys and Indians⟩ ⟨let's ~ soldiers⟩ **c** (1) : to carry into execution ⟨~*ed* an important part in the affair⟩ ⟨~*ed* a strange and turbulent role —Carol L. Thompson⟩ (2) : to perform or execute for amusement or with a view to deceive or mock ⟨~*ing* their mischievous pranks at the maddest —J.G.Frazer⟩ ⟨~*ed* a trick on me⟩ (3) : to bring about (some devastating action or condition) : WREAK ⟨~ havoc⟩ **d** (1) : to assign an indicated degree of value, importance, or emphasis to — usu. used with *up* or *down* ⟨~*ing* down academic scholarship —H.W.Dodds⟩ ⟨the store also ~*s* up ... other makes —*Retailing Daily*⟩ ⟨trying to ~ herself down to me —Williams Forrest⟩ (2) : to give a certain emphasis to (a news story, feature, or other item) esp. by displaying more or less prominently ⟨the popular press ... ~*ed* this for all it was worth —C.H.Driver⟩ — usu. used with *up* or *down* ⟨interesting to see what items were ~*ed* up —Jacques Kayser⟩ ⟨urged to ~ down stories of crimes⟩ **2 a** (1) : to put on a performance of (a play) : perform as a spectacle ⟨~ an Elizabethan comedy⟩ (2) : to act in the character or part of : represent by acting ⟨a war story in which she ~*ed* a beautiful spy —*Current Biog.*⟩ (3) : to perform or be shown in ⟨has ~*ed* more than forty communities —R.W.Sarnoff⟩ : perform or be shown during or for the duration of ⟨~*ed* a tour in New England⟩ ⟨~*ed* a week in Boston⟩ **b** (1) : to perform or act the part of in real life : act or behave like or in the character of ⟨~ the fool⟩ ⟨~ truant⟩ ⟨do not expect boys of 15 to be ~*ing* the lover —H.E. Scudder⟩ (2) : to perform the part of (some disorganizing, disrupting, or ruinous agency) ⟨this ... routine of yours ~*s* hell with manifests and accounting —LaSelle Gilman⟩ ⟨brawled and generally ~*ed* the devil —Kenneth Roberts⟩ **3 a** (1) : to contend against in a game ⟨refused to ~ the challenger⟩ (2) : to use as a contestant in a game ⟨~*ed* his second team in the last quarter⟩ (3) : to fill (a certain position) on a team ⟨regularly ~*s* third base⟩ ⟨~*ed* quarterback⟩ **b** (1) : to risk at play : wager in a game : STAKE ⟨~*ed* his last few dollars⟩ (2) : to lose or squander in gambling — usu. used with *away* ⟨~*ed* away his inheritance⟩ (3) : to wager on ⟨~ the races⟩ ⟨~ the ponies⟩ (4) : to base a decision or action on : operate on the basis of ⟨~ a hunch⟩ ⟨~*ing* their luck instead of their skill —Nicholas Monsarrat⟩ **c** : to dispose (an implement of a game) purposefully and usu. irrevocably according to the conditions of the game: as (1) : to place (a card from one's hand) on the table usu. face-up and in one's turn esp. when another player has previously made a lead (2) : to move (a piece) in chess, checkers, backgammon, or a similar game (3) : to bet (a chip or a sum of money) in roulette or a similar game (4) : to strike (a bowled cricket ball) with the bat; *often* : to strike (a bowled cricket ball) defensively with no attempt to score **4 a** : to perform (music or a piece of music) on an instrument ⟨~ a waltz⟩ **b** : to perform music upon : cause to sound or give forth music ⟨~ the violin⟩ **c** : to attend with accompanying music in the performance of some action or movement ⟨would ~ them down the mountain, ~ them home —Stuart Cloete⟩ **d** (1) : to cause (as a radio or phonograph) to emit sounds (2) : to cause the recorded sounds of (as a record or a magnetic tape) to be reproduced **5** : to put in action or motion: as **a** : to wield or ply briskly, vigorously, or freely ⟨~*ing* knife and fork with gusto⟩ **b** : to discharge, fire, or set off with more or less repeated or continuous effect ⟨ ~ a rifle upon a fort⟩ ⟨~ a hose⟩ or to eject, throw, or force out in such a way ⟨~ a stream of water⟩ **c** : to cause to move, act, or operate briskly, lightly, and irregularly or intermittently ⟨~*ed* his flashlight along the line of feet —Frank Cameron⟩ **d** (1) : to allow (a hooked fish) to become exhausted by pulling against the line ⟨~*ed* the poor fish until it rolled, belly up, from exhaustion —Jim Rearden⟩ (2) : to deliberately keep in a state of suspense or uncertainty : play as though a fish on a line ⟨she ~*ed* him — sometimes delicately, sometimes with a less felicitous touch —Philip Guedalla⟩

syn PLAY, SPORT, DISPORT, FROLIC, ROLLICK, ROMP, and GAMBOL can mean, in common, to engage in an activity as a pleasure or amusement. PLAY, the most general, suggests an opposition to *work*; it implies activity, often strenuous, but emphasizes the absence of any aim other than amusement, diversion, or enjoyment ⟨children *playing* in the yard⟩ ⟨the hard-working business man often *plays* as hard as he works⟩ SPORT and DISPORT both imply a complete release from all seriousness, suggesting engagement in a pastime ⟨shall not *sport* with your impatience by reading what he says on that point —Jane Austen⟩ ⟨porters, messengers, and elevator boys, *sporting* wherever they are, with their sharp winks and sly smiles —Lin Yutang⟩ ⟨children *sporting* on the lawn⟩ ⟨good housewives *disporting* at a church picnic⟩ ⟨the sight of a tiny fish *disporting* himself with me in the tub —William Beebe⟩ FROLIC suggests generally more gaiety, levity, and spontaneousness than PLAY, applying often to the lighthearted activity of children at active play ⟨porpoises *frolicking* in the sea⟩ ⟨*frolicking* students⟩ ROLLICK adds the idea of exuberance or reveling, applying chiefly to youths or young adults ⟨a *rollicking* ship's crew⟩ ⟨a tavern full of *rollicking* revelers⟩ ROMP suggests a carefree boisterousness as of rough but happy children, usu. connoting running or racing in play ⟨a father *romping* in the living room with his small children⟩ ⟨young lions *romping* in the spring sunshine in their cages⟩ ⟨a buxom, attractive comedienne — *romps* rowdily through the sketches —*Newsweek*⟩ GAMBOL suggests the leaping and skipping of young lambs, connoting possibly more joy than FROLIC ⟨when whales *gambolled* in the bays —W.J. Dakin⟩ ⟨in the ecstasy of that thought they *gambolled* round and round, they hurled themselves into the air in great leaps of excitement —George Orwell⟩ The nouns PLAY, SPORT, DISPORT, FROLIC, ROMP and GAMBOL each signify the activity generally, or an instance of it, implicitly distinguished in the corresponding verb forms above

— **play ball 1** : to begin or resume playing a game — used as an official direction or signal (as by an umpire) **2** : COOPERATE ⟨you *play ball* with me and I'll *play ball* with you —E.C. Marston⟩ — **play both ends against the middle** : to play off opposing interests against each other to one's own ultimate profit — **play horse** : to play the fool ⟨don't *play horse* with me —Robert Murphy⟩ — **play old gooseberry** *dial chiefly Brit* : to play havoc — **play politics 1** : to act from considerations of partisan political advantage rather than principle or the general interest ⟨refused to *play politics* with foreign policy —A.E.Stevenson †1965⟩ **2** : to seek to gain one's ends by scheming or intrigue ⟨*play* office *politics*⟩ — **play possum 1** : to pretend to be asleep or dead ⟨after they've once drugged you, you *play possum* —Erle Stanley Gardner⟩ **2** : to feign ignorance — **play the field** : to have dates or romantic connections with more than one member of the opposite sex : avoid an exclusive or permanent attachment ⟨preferred *playing the field* to going steady —Geraldine Roberts⟩ — **play the game** : to act according to some code or set of standards : play fair or honorably ⟨wasn't *playing the game* in giving publicity to this confidential report —John Betjeman⟩ ⟨had not *played the game* in the past toward the fruit industry —*Farmer's Weekly (So. Africa)*⟩ — **play the market** : to speculate on the stock or produce exchanges — **play to the score** : to vary one's tactics (as in a card game) according to the state of the score — **play with oneself** : to engage in autoerotic activity; *specif* : MASTURBATE

playa \ˈplīə\ *n* -S [Sp, lit., beach, fr. ML *plagia* hillside, shoreline, prob. fr. Gk, sides, flanks, fr. neut. pl. of *plagios* oblique; akin to Gk *pelagos* sea — more at FLAKE] : the flat-floored bottom of an undrained desert basin that becomes at times a shallow lake which on evaporation may leave a deposit of salt or gypsum : SALT PAN

play·ability \ˌplāəˈbiləd·ē, -lətē, -i\ *n* : the quality or state of being playable

play·able \ˈplāəbəl\ *adj* : capable of or suitable for being played or played on ⟨harpsichord music is readily ~ —P.H. Lang⟩

playact \ˈ=,=\ *vb* [back-formation fr. *playacting*] *vi* **1 a** : to take part in theatrical performances esp. professionally : engage in playacting **b** : to pretend to be someone else (as children in play) : make believe ⟨children love to ~⟩ **2** : to engage in theatrical or insincere behavior : put on ⟨always felt she was ~*ing* —Eden Phillpotts⟩ ~ *vt* : to act out ⟨delighted to ~ the life of a policeman —*My Baby*⟩

playacting \ˈ=,==\ *n* [¹*play* + *acting*] : the act of one that playacts: as **a** : the activity or profession of an actor ⟨many people thought ~ was sinful —George Freedley & J.A.Reeves⟩ **b** : insincere or theatrical behavior : MAKE-BELIEVE, PRETENSE ⟨her coy clapping of her hands over mouth ... appears to have been ~ —E.D.Radin⟩

playactor \ˈ=,==\ *n* [¹*play* + *actor*] : ACTOR

playa lake *n* : a lake in an arid or semiarid region that evaporates during the drier months to leave a playa

play back *vi* : to use back play in cricket ~ *vt* : to run through (a disc or tape) recently recorded

playback \ˈ=,=\ *n* -S [*play back*] **1** : an act of reproducing a disc or tape sound recording often immediately after the recording process has been completed **2** *also* **playback machine** : a tape or disc sound reproducing device : TURNTABLE

playball \ˈ=,=\ *n* : a sponge or inflated ball that will bounce and is suitable for playing catch or other throwing and tossing games

playbill \ˈ=,=\ *n* : a bill advertising a play and usu. announcing the cast

Playbill *trademark* — used for a theater guide

playbook \ˈ=,=\ *n* : one or more plays in book form

playbox \ˈ=,=\ *n, chiefly Brit* : a box for a child's toys and personal belongings esp. at a boarding school

playboy \ˈ=,=\ *n* **1** *dial Brit* : a tricky untrustworthy person **2** : a typically young and wealthy man who lives a frivolous indolent life devoted chiefly to the pursuit of pleasure ⟨many simply became ~*s*, occasionally with diverting eccentricities —Christopher Rand⟩

playbroker \ˈ=,==\ *n* : an agent who acts as middleman between dramatists and managers or actors

play-by-play \ˌ==ˈ=\ *adj* **1** : being a running commentary on a sports event ⟨*play-by-play* descriptions ... of all games —*Amer. Guide Series: Mich.*⟩ **2** : circumstantially related : DETAILED ⟨this *play-by-play* account of the three men —J.W.Rogers⟩

playclothes \ˈ=,=\ *n pl* : comfortable, utilitarian, or informal clothing worn for leisure activities, sports, or play

playday \ˈ=,=\ *n* **1** : a day of play or diversion **2** : an informal athletic competition between teams composed of players from several participating schools

play debt *n, archaic* : a gambling debt

play doctor *or* **play fixer** *n* : a person who is called in to revise a play before its production

playdown \ˈ=,=\ *n* -S : one of a series of playoffs (as among the winning teams from different leagues or localities)

played \ˈplād\ *adj* [fr. *played out*, adj.] : PLAYED OUT

played out *adj* : worn out, finished, spent, or used up ⟨never seen a limper, dirtier, more *played out* deck of cards —Hamilton Basso⟩

play·er \ˈplāə(r), -le(ə)r, -leə\ *n* -S [ME *pleyer*, fr. OE *plegere*, fr. *plegan* to play + -*ere* -er — more at PLAY] **1** : one that plays: as **a** : a person who occupies himself for diversion : one who engages in recreational activity or amuses himself ⟨a ~ with illusion —L.A.Fiedler⟩ **b** (1) : a person who plays in or makes a practice of playing a usu. specified game (2) : a person who undertakes to play against all others in various games (as skat) **c** : a person who plays on a musical instrument **d** : a person who makes a profession of acting : ACTOR **e** *Brit* : a professional cricketer — compare GENTLEMAN 3d **f** : a mechanical device for automatically playing a musical instrument; *esp* : PIANO PLAYER **g** : RECORD PLAYER **2** : the ball to be played next in billiards, croquet, and similar games

player piano *n* : a piano that contains a mechanical piano player

playfair cipher *n, usu cap P* [after Lyon, Baron *Playfair* †1898 Brit. scientist & public official] : a cipher involving a digraphic substitution from a single alphabet square which begins with the letters of a keyword and continues with the remaining letters of the alphabet less J

K E Y W O
R D A B C
F G H I L
M N P Q S
T U V X Z

square for Playfair cipher

playfellow \ˈ=,=(,)=\ *n* : PLAYMATE

playfield \ˈ=,=\ *n* : a playground designed for outdoor athletics and games

play forward *vi* : to use forward play in cricket

play·ful \ˈplāfəl\ *adj* **1** : full of play : SPORTIVE ⟨a nice little, sleek ~ kitten —Bram Stoker⟩ **2** : indulging a sportive fancy : HUMOROUS, JOCULAR ⟨were discovering the charm of ~ satire —V.L.Parrington⟩ — **play·ful·ly** \-f(ə)lē, -li\ *adv* — **play·ful·ness** \-fəlnəs\ *n* -ES

playgirl \ˈ=,=\ *n* : a typically young woman who lives a frivolous indolent life devoted chiefly to pleasure ⟨a hard and handsome ~ —*Manchester Guardian Weekly*⟩

playgoer \ˈ=,=(ə)\ *n* : a person who frequently attends plays

playground \ˈ=,=\ *n* **1** : a piece of ground used for and usu. having special facilities for recreation esp. by children **2** : a locality suitable by nature or adaptation for vacation or holiday relaxation ⟨England's mountain ~ —L.D.Stamp⟩ **3** : the scene or arena of a specified activity ⟨the world of nature was chaotic — a ~ of supernatural forces —R.W. Southern⟩

playground ball *n* **1** : SOFTBALL **2** : an inflatable colored rubber ball (as of 5, 6, or 8 inches in diameter) used by children in simple games and for learning ball-handling skills

play gym *n* : GYM

playhouse \ˈ=,=\ *n* **1** : a building used for dramatic exhibitions : THEATER **2 a** : a small building, hut, or enclosed area made like one or more rooms of a house for children to play in and often built by children **b** : a toy house

playing *pres part of* PLAY

playing card *n* [*playing* fr. ME *playing, pleying*, fr. gerund of *playen, pleyen* to play — more at PLAY] **1** : a gaming implement made usu. of pasteboard in a standard size (as 2½″ or 2¼″ x 3½″ x .009″) as one of a set of 24 to 78 cards with identical backs, marked on its face to show its rank and suit, and used in playing any of numerous games **2** : a card of a pack in which the suits are marked with designating symbols (as of a spade, heart, diamond, and club) and ranks (as of the series A, K, Q, J, 10, 9, 8, 7, 6, 5, 4, 3, 2) **3** *pl* : a pack of playing cards

playing field *n* : a field for various games (as football, cricket, tennis); *esp* : the part of a field that is officially marked off for play

playing piece *n* : COUNTER 1b

playing trick *n* : a card or combination of cards that is expected to win a trick in bridge

playland \ˈ=,=\ *n* : PLAYGROUND ⟨the development of Alaska ... as a tourist and vacation ~ —*U.S. Code*⟩

play·less \ˈplāləs\ *adj* : devoid of play

play·let \-lət\ *n* -S [¹*play* + -*let*] : a short or slight play ⟨a tiny four-line ~ —F.M.Whiting⟩

playmaker \ˈ=,==\ *n* [¹*play* + *maker*] : a player who leads the scoring attack upon an opponent's goal (as in basketball or hockey)

playmate \ˈ=,=\ *n* : a companion in play

play money *n* : a metal or paper device made in obvious imitation of genuine coins or paper money chiefly for use in play by children

play·ock \ˈplāək\ *n* -S [ME (Sc) *playok*, prob. fr. ¹*play* + -*ok* (as in ME *bullok* bullock)] *Scot* : PLAYTHING

play off *vt* **1** : to complete the playing of (an interrupted or delayed contest) **2** : to break (a tie) by means of a play-off ~ *vi* : to participate in a play-off ⟨had to *play off* against last year's winner⟩

¹**play-off** \ˈ=,=\ *n* -S [fr. *play off*, v.] **1** : a final contest or series of contests to determine the winner among two or more contestants or teams that have tied **2** : a series of postseason contests to determine a championship

²**play-off** \ˈ=ˈ=\ *adj* : relating to a play-off

play on *vi* : to play a bowled ball onto one's wicket in cricket

play out *vt* **1 a** : to perform to the end ⟨*played out* ... the guilty role assigned to them —C.J.Rolo⟩ **b** : to bring to an end : use up : FINISH ⟨the pie's *played out* —W.M.Raine⟩ ⟨that graft's *played out* —S.H.Adams⟩ **2** : UNREEL, UNFOLD ⟨*played out* a length of line —Gordon Webber⟩ ~ *vi* **1** : to become spent or exhausted ⟨the twister raged along for about 400 feet before it *played out* —*Springfield (Mass.) Union*⟩ ⟨the pony ... *played out* twice —H.L.Davis⟩ **2** : to unreel or unfold to a considerable length ⟨the possibility of a snag when hose is *playing out* —W.Y.Kimball⟩

play-party \ˈ=,==\ *n* : a social gathering esp. of young people characteristic of the rural U.S. with entertainment consisting of dramatic games and swinging plays performed to the singing of ballads and clapping usu. without instrumental accompaniment

play·pen \'ˌ=,=\ *n* [¹*play* + *pen*] **:** a portable enclosure usu. consisting of a platform surrounded with a rail in which a baby or young child may safely play without direct supervision

playpen

play·pipe \'=,=\ *n* **:** a tapering metal pipe at the end of a fire hose for playing a stream of water

play–pretty \'=,==\ *n, chiefly Midland* **:** PLAYTHING, TOY

playreader \'=,==\ *n* **:** one who reads plays in manuscript and recommends their acceptance or rejection

playroom \'=,=\ *n* **1 :** a room fitted out or reserved for children to play in **2 :** RUMPUS ROOM

plays *pl of* PLAY, *pres 3d sing of* PLAY

play school *n* **1 :** KINDERGARTEN **2 :** a project in parent education enabling mothers to watch their children at play in a group and later discuss their observations with a teacher and other parents

playscript \'=,=\ *n* **:** a manuscript of a play

playshoe \'=,=\ *n* **:** a shoe designed for leisure wear

play·some \'plāsəm\ *adj* **:** PLAYFUL, WANTON, SPORTIVE — **play·some·ly** *adv* — **play·some·ness** *n* -ES

playsuit \'=,=\ *n* **:** a sports and play outfit made for women and children in one, two, or three pieces consisting usu. of a blouse and shorts and sometimes a matching skirt

play therapy *n* **:** psychotherapy in which a child is encouraged to reveal his feelings and conflicts in play rather than by verbalization ⟨emotional problems of the retarded child may yield to *play therapy* —Abraham Levinson⟩

plaything \'=,=\ *n* **1 :** TOY **2 :** someone or something that is played with ⟨a ~ of unscrupulous pressure groups —P.A. Sorokin⟩

playtime \'=,=\ *n* **1 :** a time for play or diversion **2 :** a time for the beginning of a stage performance

play up *vi, of a horse* **:** to resist control **:** fight the bit **:** REAR

play·ward \'plāwə(r)d\ *adj, archaic* **:** inclined to sport

playwright \'=,=\ *n* [¹*play* + *wright*] **1 :** a person who writes plays **2 :** a person who adapts material for stage, radio, television, or motion-picture production

playwrighting \'=,==\ *n* -S [by alter. (influence of *playwright*)] **:** PLAYWRITING

playwriting \'=,==\ *n* **:** the writing of plays **:** the activity or occupation of a playwright

play yard *n* **1 :** PLAYGROUND **2 :** PLAYPEN

plaza \'plazə, -lāzə, -läzə\ *n* -S [Sp, fr. (assumed) VL *plattea* broad street, plaza, fr. L *platea* street, courtyard — more at PLACE] **1 :** a public square in a city or town **:** an open square **:** MARKETPLACE **2 :** a broad paved open-air area used for the parking or servicing of motor vehicles or for the channeling of motor traffic **3 :** the section of a toll road at which the tollbooths are located — called also *toll plaza* **4 :** SHOPPING CENTER

pla·za de to·ros \,pläzədā'tōr(,)ōs\ *n, pl* **plazas de toros** \-zədā-\ [Sp, lit., plaza of bulls] **:** BULLRING

plaza gray *n* **:** SHELL GRAY

plbg *abbr* plumbing

plbr *abbr* plumber

¹**plea** \'plē\ *n* -S [ME *plaid, plait, plai, plee,* fr. OF *plaid, plait, plet* agreement, decision, decree, lawsuit, fr. ML & L; ML *placitum* court day, judicial proceeding, lawsuit, fr. L, something agreeable, opinion, decision, decree, fr. neut. of *placitus,* past part. of *placēre* to please, resolve, decide, decree — more at PLEASE] **1 a** *obs* **:** an action or cause in court **:** LAWSUIT **:** the presentation of a cause to the court — see COMMON PLEAS **b** *Scot* **:** CONTENTION, QUARRELING **2 :** an allegation made by a party in support of one's cause: as **a :** an allegation of fact — distinguished from *demurrer* **b** (1) **:** a defendant's answer to a plaintiff's declaration and demand in common-law practice (2) **:** an accused person's answer to a charge or indictment against him in criminal practice **c :** SPECIAL PLEA **d :** a plea of guilty to an indictment **3 :** something alleged or used to excuse or to justify **:** PRETEXT ⟨left the party early with the ~ of a headache⟩ **4** *obs* **:** something demanded **:** CLAIM ⟨none can drive him from the envious ~ of forfeiture —Shak.⟩ **5 :** an earnest entreaty **:** APPEAL, PETITION ⟨the powerful and compelling ~ for state's rights —Carol L. Thompson⟩ ⟨resisted ~*s* of many of his advisers —Herbert Feis⟩ **syn** see APOLOGY, PRAYER

²**plea** \"\ *vb* -ED/-ING/-S [ME *playen, pleyen,* fr. *plaid, plait, plai, plee,* n.] *chiefly Scot* **:** CONTEND, QUARREL

pleach \'plēch\ *vt* -ED/-ING/-ES [ME *plechen,* fr. ONF *plechier,* fr. L *plexus,* past part. of *plectere* to plait, weave — more at PLY] **1 a :** to cause to meet and intertwine to form a hedge **:** INTERLACE **b :** to renew by interweaving — usu. used of a hedge ⟨is now ~*ing* the hawthorn and wild plum —Elizabeth Berridge⟩ **2 :** to make into a braid **:** PLAIT — used of hair

pleached *adj* **1 :** twined together **:** INTERLACED **2 :** formed by the lacing of branches **:** fenced or covered over by intertwined boughs ⟨~ bower —Shak.⟩ ⟨away from the house to the ~ walk that led . . . down to the river —Louis Bromfield⟩

plead \'plēd\ *vb* **pleaded** \-dəd\ *or* **pled** \'pled\ **pleaded** *or* **pled; pleading; pleads** [ME *pleiden, plaiden, pleden,* fr. OF *pleidier, plaidier,* fr. ML *placitare,* fr. *placitum* plea — more at PLEA] *vi* **1 a** *obs* **:** to institute or prosecute an action in court **:** to go to law **:** LITIGATE **b** *obs* **:** to contend in debate or argument **:** WRANGLE **2 :** to make a plea or conduct pleadings in a cause or proceeding in a court **:** present an answer or pleading in defense or prosecution of an action **3 :** to argue for or against a claim **:** urge reasons for or against a thing **:** entreat or appeal earnestly **:** BEG, IMPLORE ⟨~*ed* for help —D.A.Stein⟩ ⟨he did not entreat or ~; he announced —Margaret Deland⟩ ~ *vt* **1 a** *obs* **:** to bring legal action against **b :** to urge or make a plea of (the law) in court **2 :** to discuss, defend, and attempt to maintain by arguments or reasons presented to a tribunal or person having authority to determine **:** argue at the bar **3 :** to allege or cite in or by way of a legal plea or defense **:** answer to a declaration, charge, or indictment **4 :** to allege in support or vindication **:** give as a plea in defense, apology, or excuse ⟨~*ed* ill health and private business as reasons for delaying —W.T.Utter⟩

plead·able \'plēdəbəl\ *adj* [ME *pledable,* fr. OF *pleidable, plaidable,* fr. *pleidier, plaidier* to plead — more at PLEAD] **:** able to be pleaded **:** capable of being lawfully maintained or of being alleged in defense, excuse, or vindication

plead·er \'plēdə(r)\ *n* -S [ME *pleder,* alter. of *plaidur, plaitour, pletour,* fr. OF *plaideor,* fr. *plaidier* to plead + *-eor* -*or* — more at PLEAD] **1 a :** one who conducts legal pleas esp. in court **:** ADVOCATE **b :** one who files a legal pleading **2 :** one who pleads **:** INTERCESSOR

¹**plead·ing** \'plēdiŋ, -dēŋ\ *n* -S [ME *pleiding, plaiding, pleding,* fr. gerund of *pleiden, plaiden, pleden* to plead] **1 a** *obs* **:** LITIGATION **b :** the acting as an advocate or pleader in a cause **c** (1) **:** the drawing of pleas or conducting of causes as an advocate (2) **:** the body of rules governing this **:** one of the successive statements now usu. written by which the plaintiff sets forth his cause and claim and the defendant his defense **:** the formal allegations and counter allegations made by plaintiff and defendant or by prosecutor and accused in an action or proceeding until issue is joined **2 :** the act or an instance of making a plea **3 :** a sincere entreaty or petition **:** ADVOCACY, INTERCESSION ⟨the special ~ of a friend —L.L. Biancolli⟩

²**pleading** \"\ *adj* [fr. pres. part. of *plead*] **:** IMPLORING, SUPPLIANT ⟨a ~ note in her voice⟩

plead·ing·ly *adv* **:** in a pleading manner

plea in abatement : a plea that postpones or defeats a cause of action not on the merits of the controversy but for some defect in or matter of form or procedure

plea in bar : a plea entered by the defendant that constitutes a bar to the plaintiff's action

plea in confession and avoidance : a plea admitting that the plaintiff once had a good cause of action as alleged but that it is barred by some subsequent or collateral matter pleaded in defense (as a repeal of the statute on which the cause of action is founded)

pleas·able \'plēzəbəl\ *adj* [ME *plesable,* fr. MF *plaisable,* fr. *plaisir* to please + *-able* — more at PLEASE] **:** capable of being pleased

pleas·ance \'plez°n(t)s\ *n* -S [ME *plesaunce,* fr. MF *plaisance* pleasure, fr. OF, fr. *plaisant*] **1 :** a feeling of pleasure **:** DELIGHT, GAIETY ⟨youth is full of ~; age is full of care —*Oxford Bk. of English Verse*⟩ **2** *obs* **:** a disposition to please **:** pleasing behavior **:** COURTESY **3 a :** PLEASANTNESS ⟨through the garden I was drawn — a realm of ~ —Alfred Tennyson⟩ **b :** a source of pleasure **:** DELIGHT ⟨the paintings . . ., to mention only the most famous of the ~*s* that have attracted many visitors to the house —S.N.Behrman⟩ **4 :** a pleasant place used for rest or recreation usu. consisting of a formal garden attached to a mansion or a small park ⟨tread green turf in a walled ~ —Phyllis & John Cradock⟩

pleas·ant \'plez°nt\ *adj, often* -ER/-EST [ME *plesaunt,* fr. MF *plaisant,* fr. pres. part. of *plaisir* to please — more at PLEASE] **1 :** agreeable to the senses **:** having a pleasing aspect **:** SATISFYING ⟨hills that make very ~ scenery —Jane Shellhase⟩ ⟨the changes make for a ~*er* life —C.B.Palmer b.1910⟩ **2 a :** divertingly gay and sprightly **:** MERRY ⟨there will be wit from one auctioneer, and ~ clowning from another —Cornelius Weygandt⟩ **b** *archaic* **:** causing diversion **:** LAUGHABLE **c :** merrily tipsy **:** hilariously drunk **3 :** having or characterized by good behavior and neat appearance **:** WELL-MANNERED ⟨a ~ scoundrel who certainly knew how to avoid risking his neck —H.J.Laski⟩ ⟨a very ~ person to live with —Mary Austin⟩

syn PLEASING, AGREEABLE, GRATEFUL, GRATIFYING, WELCOME: these adjectives agree in meaning very acceptable to or delighting the mind or senses. PLEASANT and PLEASING are often indistinguishable in having the basic meaning of the group, although usu. PLEASANT implies an objective quality while PLEASING suggests only the effect an object has upon one ⟨a *pleasant* riverside walk —S.P.B.Mais⟩ ⟨a bottle of . . . *pleasant* red or white wine —Harry Gilroy⟩ ⟨its streamlined shape is *pleasing* to the eye and appeals to the esthetic sense —H.G.Armstrong⟩ ⟨a *pleasing* group of white clapboard houses with small lawns —*Amer. Guide Series: Pa.*⟩ AGREEABLE implies a harmony with one's tastes or likings ⟨a small room . . . simple and *agreeable,* with whitewashed walls, rusty linen curtains at the windows, and a wide inviting wooden bed —Gordon Merrick⟩ ⟨a pretty face with its *agreeable* snub nose —Ethel Wilson⟩ GRATEFUL implies both pleasing and agreeable and stresses a satisfaction and esp. relief afforded the senses or mind ⟨the log fire was a *grateful* warmth against the lingering chill of April —Lucien Price⟩ ⟨the *grateful* smell of cooking pork grew every moment more perfect —Ethel Anderson⟩ ⟨placing every instrument in its most brilliant and *grateful* register —Virgil Thomson⟩ GRATIFYING applies chiefly to what affords mental pleasure by satisfying desires, hopes, or conscience ⟨the building is aesthetically *gratifying* —*Amer. Guide Series: La.*⟩ ⟨with *gratifying* rapidity this promise was fulfilled —Allan Nevins⟩ WELCOME even more than PLEASING stresses a pleasure or satisfaction given by the thing to which the word is applied, often suggesting a prior need or longing satisfied by the thing ⟨a screen playwright and craftsman of fresh-springing wit and *welcome* intelligence —Lee Rogow⟩ ⟨the sweet trill of a toad and the voice of the peeper are a *welcome* chorus —A.F.Gustafson⟩

pleas·ant·ly *adv* [ME *plesauntly,* fr. *plesaunt* + *-ly*] **:** in a pleasant manner ⟨live ~ together —Henry Adams⟩ ⟨skillfully and ~ written —H.E.Starr⟩

pleas·ant·ness *n* -ES **1 :** the quality or state of being pleasant **2 :** the elementary feeling that is aroused by agreeable stimuli

pleasantness–unpleasantness \'===;'====\ *n* **:** a continuum of states of feeling or of awareness of which pleasantness and unpleasantness are opposite poles esp. in respect to the motivation of behavior

pleas·ant·ry \'plez°ntrē, -ri\ *n* -ES [F *plaisanterie,* fr. MF, fr. *plaisant* + *-erie* -ery — more at PLEASANT] **1 :** an agreeable playfulness in conversation **:** good-humored banter **:** FACETIOUSNESS, JOCULARITY ⟨talked with fluency and spirit, and there was an archness and ~ in his manner —Jane Austen⟩ **2 :** a humorous act or speech **:** JEST, JOKE ⟨refused to be a party to the ~ —Ruth Park⟩ **3** *archaic* **:** PLEASANTNESS, PLEASURE ⟨engaged in other matters of business or ~ —Edmund Burke⟩

¹**please** \'plēz\ *vb* -ED/-ING/-S [ME *plesen, plaisen,* fr. MF *plaisir,* fr. L *placēre;* akin to OE *flōh* flat piece of stone, OHG *fluoh* cliff, ON *flō* layer, L *placare* to reconcile, placate, Gk *plak-, plax* flat surface, Lith *plakanas* flat, and perh. to OE *flōr* floor — more at FLOOR] *vi* **1 :** to afford or give pleasure, delight, or agreeable satisfaction **:** be agreeable ⟨the chief object of a play should be to ~ and entertain⟩ **2 :** to feel the desire or inclination **:** LIKE, WANT, WISH ⟨the fundamental American right to think as you ~ and say as you think —Archibald MacLeish⟩ ⟨an able man licensed by the times to do pretty much as he *pleased* —J.H.Hanford⟩ **3** *archaic* **:** to have the pleasure or kindness ⟨stranger, ~ to taste these bounties —John Milton⟩ ⟨will you ~ to enter the carriage —Charles Dickens⟩ ~ *vt* **1 :** to give pleasure to **:** make glad **:** GRATIFY ⟨*pleased* them by his hard work, his calm common sense —Beverly Smith⟩ **2 :** PLACATE, SATISFY; *specif* **:** to satisfy sexually **3 :** to be the will or pleasure of — used impersonally ⟨many boys, ~ God, will make the venture —J.H.Wilson⟩ ⟨may it ~ your Majesty⟩ **4** *archaic Scot* **:** to have or take pleasure in **:** LIKE **5 :** to satisfy (oneself) in respect to something **:** behave in a manner satisfactory to (oneself) **:** SUIT ⟨~ yourself as to whether you go⟩ ⟨*pleased* himself by administering justice impatiently —R.A.Billington⟩ ⟨finding that the sources themselves were far from uniform, I have sometimes *pleased* myself —McGeorge Bundy⟩

syn GRATIFY, DELIGHT, REJOICE, GLADDEN, EXHILARATE, TICKLE, TITILLATE, ARRIDE, REGALE: PLEASE indicates bringing happiness ranging from absence of discontent up to elation by something agreeing with one's wishes, tastes, or aspirations ⟨*pleased* by the suggestion⟩ ⟨a guest *pleased* by the reception given him⟩ ⟨*pleased* by his son's choice of profession⟩ GRATIFY may suggest stronger although perhaps less long-lived satisfaction at or as if at some particular action or occasion ⟨it *gratified* him to hear these gentlemen admire his fine stock —Willa Cather⟩ ⟨the notice . . . taken of her from the outset had *gratified* her —Robert Grant †1940⟩ ⟨wished to *gratify* his son by these eulogies —George Meredith⟩ DELIGHT applies to pleasing to the point of keenly felt and often vividly expressed intense transporting pleasure ⟨a dinner party satisfying the highest standard of hospitality, namely, that every guest be seated between persons certain to *delight* him and sure to kindle his affection —Alan Gregg⟩ ⟨the emergency ferry established there so *delighted* the handsome young actor that he spent the whole first day of the ferry service riding back and forth —*Amer. Guide Series: R.I.*⟩ REJOICE may suggest a joy marked by enthusiastic or festive happiness ⟨of even deeper happiness springing from the stirring of those faculties through which man *rejoices* in knowledge —H.O. Taylor⟩ GLADDEN suggests bringing happiness that encourages or alleviates grief, dubiousness, or gloom ⟨the comrades of the dead girl assemble in the temple on certain days to *gladden* her spirit with songs and dances —Lafcadio Hearn⟩ ⟨the springs which are under the earth and which break forth to refresh and *gladden* the life of flowers and the life of man —Laurence Binyon⟩ EXHILARATE indicates a raising to a high pitch of joy, happiness, triumph, or euphoria, with all gloom or worry dispelled ⟨realization affects people in one of two ways. It depresses them when they think how puny Man is against the Universe — or it *exhilarates* them when they consider his courage in attempting to conquer it —A.C.Clarke⟩ ⟨likely to brag a bit when *exhilarated* —S.H. Adams⟩ TICKLE may suggest a pleasurable physical sensation, one of tingling, thrilling, provoking laughs or chuckles or a comparable mental feeling ⟨the idea of himself as a parson *tickles* him: he looks down at the black sleeve on his arm, and then smiles slyly —G.B.Shaw⟩ ⟨so *tickled* he'd have wagged a tail if he'd had one —F.B.Gipson⟩ TITILLATE indicates pleasing and also interesting or intriguing ⟨*titillated* with something novel, flamboyant and sensational —C.E. Montague⟩ ⟨all this *titillates* our nerves: we think it exquisite, perfect —Irving Babbitt⟩ ARRIDE, now little used, may apply to what pleases, amuses, and calls forth laughter ⟨merry jests such as used to *arride* our ancestors —William Hardman⟩ REGALE suggests the large-scale entertainment or enjoyment of copious feasting ⟨farmers' wives *regale* the workers with brandied cakes and scuppernong grape pies —*Amer. Guide Series: N.C.*⟩

— **if you please :** if it is your pleasure, will, desire, or humor **:** if you like **:** if you wish — used to express courtesy, politeness, or emphasis ⟨unbridle him for a minute, *if you please* —Thomas De Quincey⟩ ⟨he was, *if you please,* a rascal⟩

²**please** \"\ *adv* **1** — used as a function word to express politeness or emphasis in a request ⟨any millionaires . . . will ~ skip the next few pages —Richard Joseph⟩ ⟨open the door, ~⟩ **2** — used as a function word to express polite affirmation ⟨would you like a martini? *Please*⟩

pleased \'plēzd\ *adj* [ME *plesed,* fr. past part. of *plesen* to please] **:** affected with or manifesting pleasure **:** CONTENTED, GRATIFIED ⟨expect your family to be ~ with your marriage —Mary Austin⟩ ⟨looking ~ —R.L.Stevenson⟩ — **pleased·ly** \-z(ə)dlē, -li\ *adv*

pleased·ness \-dnəs\ *n* -ES **:** the quality or state of being pleased

pleas·er \'plēzə(r)\ *n* -S **:** one that pleases ⟨remain the crowd ~ he had been in his last play —Leo Hughes⟩

¹**pleas·ing** \'plēziŋ, -zēŋ\ *n* -S [ME *plesing,* fr. gerund of *plesen* to please — more at PLEASE] **:** the act of one who pleases **:** the fact of being pleased **:** the giving of pleasure

²**pleasing** \"\ *adj* [ME *plesing,* fr. pres. part. of *plesen* to please] **:** giving pleasure **:** capable of being enjoyed **:** attractive to the senses **:** CHARMING, FAVORABLE, PALATABLE ⟨what I found most ~ . . . is the lake with the wildfowl flying over —S.P.B.Mais⟩ ⟨large rooms with ~ wood mantels and deep fireplaces —*Amer. Guide Series: Mich.*⟩ ⟨the ~ taste of homemade bread fresh from the oven⟩ **syn** see PLEASANT

pleas·ing·ly *adv* [ME *plesingly,* fr. *plesing* + *-ly*] **:** in a pleasing manner

pleas·ing·ness *n* -ES **:** the quality or state of being pleasing ⟨the liveliness and ~ of dark eyes —T.N.Carver⟩

pleas of the crown [trans. of ML *placita coronae*] **1 a** *Eng & Scots law* **:** the pleas or actions of which the crown formerly claimed exclusive jurisdiction as affecting the king's peace **b** *Scots law* **:** the judicial proceedings involving murder, rape, robbery, and willful fire-raising **2** *Eng law* **:** all criminal actions or proceedings

plea·sur·abil·i·ty \,plezh(ə)rə'biləd·ē\ *n* **:** the quality or state of being pleasurable

plea·sur·able *also* **plea·sure·able** \'plezh(ə)rəbəl, -lāzh-, -zhə(r)b-\ *adj* **1 :** capable of affording pleasure or satisfaction **:** GRATIFYING, PLEASANT ⟨full of happiness and of ~ excitement —Fred Whishaw⟩ ⟨good printing will make every book more ~ to read —Joseph Blumenthal⟩ **2** *obs* **:** seeking or loving pleasure ⟨you are very ~ —Ben Jonson⟩

plea·sur·able·ness *n* -ES **:** PLEASURABILITY

plea·sur·ably \-blē, -li\ *adv* **:** in a pleasurable manner

¹**plea·sure** \'plezhə(r), -lāzh-\ *n* -S *often attrib* [ME *plesure,* alter. (influenced by *-ure*) of *plesir, pleser,* fr. MF *plaisir,* fr. *plaisir* to please — more at PLEASE] **1 :** a particular desire or purpose **:** INCLINATION, WILL ⟨wait upon his ~ —Shak.⟩ ⟨it was his ~ . . . to take away the charters —Leslie Thomas⟩ **2 :** a state or condition of gratification of the senses or mind **:** an agreeable sensation or emotion **:** the excitement, relish, or happiness produced by expectation or enjoyment of something good, delightful, or satisfying ⟨the ~*s* which one can derive from the knowledge of literature —H.J.Fuller⟩ ⟨the ~ and pain of coming of age —Lee Rogow⟩ **3 a :** sensual gratification **b :** frivolous enjoyment or amusement **:** sensuous diversion ⟨he that loveth ~ shall be a poor man —Prov. 21:17 (AV)⟩ **4 :** a cause, source, or object of delight or joy ⟨vacations are supposed to be a ~ —Orville Prescott⟩ ⟨hill and valley making the town a ~ to see —Jane Shellhase⟩ **5 :** a quality which gives a feeling of pleasurability ⟨the ~ of tinkling ice in a tall glass⟩ **6 a :** a feeling of pleasantness accompanying release of tensions esp. from anticipatory states or instinctual needs **b :** PLEASANTNESS 2

syn PLEASURE, DELIGHT, JOY, DELECTATION, ENJOYMENT, and FRUITION all agree in signifying the agreeable emotion accompanying the possession, acquisition, or expectation of what is good or greatly desired. PLEASURE stresses the feeling of satisfaction or gratification, often suggesting an excitement or exaltation of the senses or mind ⟨a few beautiful things on which the eyes may dwell with *pleasure* day after day —Herbert Spencer⟩ ⟨the capacity for civilized enjoyment, for leisure and laughter, for *pleasure* in sunshine and philosophical discourse —Bertrand Russell⟩ ⟨contempt and admiration, queer sensations of disgust and *pleasure,* all mingled —John Galsworthy⟩ DELIGHT adds the idea of liveliness or obviousness in the satisfaction induced, often more unstable or less enduring than pleasure ⟨a kind of *delight* in being alive to greet the dawn —Louis Bromfield⟩ ⟨with what *delight* I find myself on this boat going home again —Katherine A. Porter⟩ ⟨my frenzy of *delight* at the possibilities of escape —Rudyard Kipling⟩ JOY can interchange with PLEASURE or DELIGHT but often implies a more deep-rooted rapturous emotion or intense happiness ⟨the thrill of *joy* that surged over him —O.E.Rölvaag⟩ ⟨the *joy,* severed from its spiritual sustenance, loses its high ecstasy —P.E.More⟩ DELECTATION suggests the reaction to pleasurable experience more or less consciously sought, received, or provided, connoting rather amusement or diversion than anything like deep-seated joy ⟨hardly ever wrote a letter that had not a smile or a laugh in it and for the *delectation* of the reader I will give a few examples of her manner —W.S.Maugham⟩ ⟨guards scatter perfume for the prisoners' *delectation* and musicians play concerts at unusual hours —C.W.Bird⟩ ⟨revived ancient, joyful customs for the *delectation* of islanders and visitors —Ernest Gruening⟩ ENJOYMENT like DELECTATION stresses the reaction to pleasurable experience but suggests a wider range of deeper pleasure from a mere transient though complete gratification to a deep-seated or long-lasting gratified happiness ⟨occasioned more amusement than *enjoyment* or a serious regard —H.V. Gregory⟩ ⟨the capacity for civilized *enjoyment,* for leisure and laughter, for pleasure in sunshine and philosophical discourse —Bertrand Russell⟩ ⟨the *enjoyment* of a full fruitful life⟩ FRUITION in an older sense now of rare occurrence signified pleasure in possession or enjoyment in attainment ⟨in love we must deserve nothing, or the fine bloom of *fruition* is gone —George Meredith⟩ ⟨no man has ever had the *fruition* of these marvels —John Buchan⟩

²**pleasure** \"\ *vb* **pleasured; pleasured; pleasuring** \-zh(ə)riŋ\ **pleasures** *vi* **1 :** to take pleasure **:** DELIGHT — often used with *in* ⟨get my fill of these here tropical fruits because I . . . do ~ in the flavor —C.W.Wilkinson⟩ **2 :** to seek pleasure **:** take a holiday or outing ⟨the streets are filled with plantation people . . . buying and selling and *pleasuring* around the hot catfish stands —C.B.Davis⟩ ~ *vt* **1 :** to give or afford pleasure to **:** GRATIFY, PLEASE ⟨I'll learn, just to ~ you —Elizabeth M. Roberts⟩ ⟨~*s* the actors somewhat more than it advances their education —*Newsweek*⟩ **2 :** to give sexual pleasure to

pleasureable *var of* PLEASURABLE

plea·sure·ful \-(r)fəl\ *adj* **:** full of pleasure **:** DELIGHTFUL, PLEASING ⟨language study afforded ~ relaxation —H.R. Warfel⟩

pleasure ground *n* **:** a ground laid out with ornamental features for pleasure ⟨build a vast *pleasure ground* and palace for himself —Clara E. Laughlin⟩

pleasure–house \'=,=\ *n* **:** a building used for pleasure and recreation

plea·sure·less \-(r)ləs\ *adj* **:** affording no pleasure ⟨the whole affair was ~ to her⟩

pleasuremonger \'==,==\ *n* **:** one whose only business is seeking pleasure

pleasure–pain \'=='=\ *n* [trans. of G *lust-unlust*] **:** PLEASANTNESS-UNPLEASANTNESS

pleasure principle *n* [trans. of G *lustprinzip*] **:** a tendency for man's behavior to be directed (as by the id) toward the immediate satisfaction of instinctual drives and immediate relief from pain or discomfort — compare REALITY PRINCIPLE

plea·sur·er \'plezh(ə)rə(r)\ *n* -S **:** one that gives or takes pleasure; *specif* **:** PLEASURE-SEEKER

pleasures *pl of* PLEASURE, *pres 3d sing of* PLEASURE

pleasure–seeker \'==,==\ *n* **:** one who looks for enjoyment

⟨an excuse for *pleasure-seekers* to see the sun rise —Linton Wells⟩

1pleasuring *n* -s [fr. gerund of *2pleasure*] **1 :** an act or instance of taking or giving pleasure ⟨changed from earning their living from farming . . . to the business of ~ —Mary H. Vorse⟩ **2 :** a pleasure trip : VACATION

2pleasuring *adj* [fr. pres. part. of *2pleasure*] **:** designed or used for pleasure ⟨taking their ease in great ~ grounds where the wilderness is preserved —R.M.Yoder⟩

pleas·ur·ist \'plezh(ə)rəst\ *n* -s **:** PLEASURE-SEEKER

1pleat \'plēt, *usu* -ēd.+V\ *vt* -ED/-ING/-S [ME *pleten* — more at PLAIT] **1 :** FOLD; *esp* **:** to form, crease, or arrange in pleats or folds similar to pleats ⟨~ a skirt⟩ ⟨~ a ruffle⟩ **2 :** PLAIT 2

2pleat \"\ *n* -s [ME *plete* — more at PLAIT] **1 a :** a creased or uncreased fold in cloth made by doubling material over on itself to form a section of three thicknesses, stitched, attached, or held along one side from which it hangs or flares free — see BOX PLEAT, INVERTED PLEAT, KICK PLEAT **b :** something resembling such a fold ⟨a ~ of skin⟩ ⟨a great flat acreage of sand, molded into endless neat ~*s* by the previous night's tides —Gerald Durrell⟩ **2 :** a double fold esp. in paper or leather (as in the accordion fold used typically on endpapers and in the pockets of books)

3pleat \"\ *adj* **:** PLEATED

pleated *adj* **1 a :** made with a pleat **b :** having pleats — often of a particular style ⟨knife-*pleated* skirt⟩ **2 :** resembling pleats ⟨pine and spruce trees drape a shaggy green shawl over the ~ terrain —R.L.Neuberger⟩

pleat·er \'plēd·ə(r)\ *n* -s **1 :** one that pleats or makes pleats in cloth, paper, or other material **2 :** one that presses or irons pleats **3 :** a textile worker who folds cloth after processing **4 :** TUCKER 1a(2)

pleater tape *n* **:** a wide stiff tape with a series of narrow slots used in pleating the tops of curtains

pleating *n* -s **1 :** the act or process of making a pleat **2 :** PLEAT; *collectively* **:** the pleats of a specific article (as a garment) **3 :** a style of pleat or arrangement of pleats ⟨sunburst ~⟩ ⟨accordion ~⟩

pleb \'pleb\ *n* -s [by shortening] **:** PLEBEIAN

plebe \'plēb\ *n* -s [F *plèbe*, fr. L *pleb-, plebs*] **1** *obs* **:** PLEBS **2** *also* **pleb :** a freshman esp. at a military or naval academy

1ple·be·ian *also* **ple·bi·an** \plə'bēən, plē'-\ *n* -s [L *plebeius* of the common people (fr. *plebes, plebs* common people) + E *-an*; akin to Gk *plēthos* throng, L *plenus* full — more at FULL] **1 :** a member of the Roman plebs **2 a :** one who is not of noble birth **b :** a member of the working class **:** one of the common people ⟨a simple ~ —C.H.Sykes⟩

2plebeian *also* **plebian** \"\ *adj* [L *plebeius* + E *-an*] **1 :** of or relating to the Roman plebs **2 a :** of or relating to the common people ⟨the old nobility . . . had swallowed its pride and married wholesale into ~ families —Nancy Mitford⟩ **b :** having characteristics attributed to the general populace **:** crude or coarse in manner or style **:** COMMONPLACE, EVERYDAY, HOMELY, UNDISTINGUISHED ⟨a wild ~ desire to slap the handsome girl's face —J.C.Powys⟩ ⟨his square ~ nose —G.M. Trevelyan⟩ — **ple·be·ian·ly** *adv*

ple·be·ian·ism *also* **ple·bi·an·ism** \-ə,nizəm\ *n* -s **:** plebeian character, manners, or style **:** CRUDENESS, VULGARITY ⟨a Greek philosopher in the midst of foreign ~ —*Irish Statesman*⟩ ⟨scorns no business for its ~ —Thomas Carlyle⟩

ple·be·ian·ize \-ə,nīz\ *vt* -ED/-ING/-S **:** to make plebeian, common, or vulgar

pleb·i·fi·ca·tion \,plebəfə'kāshən\ *n* -s [*plebs* + *-i-* + *-fication*] **:** the act of plebeianizing **:** the state of being plebeianized ⟨represents the ~ of the Romantic spirit —F.J.Mather⟩ ⟨begin with the attempt to popularize learning . . . but you will end in the ~ of knowledge —S.T.Coleridge⟩

ple·bis·ci·tary \plə'bisə,terē\ *also* **ple·bis·ci·tar·i·an** \=¦==-¦ta(a)rēən\ *adj* [*plebiscite* + *-ary* or *-arian* (fr. *-ary* + *-an*)] **:** of, relating to, based on, or of the nature of a plebiscite ⟨the ~ will of the whole people —Gordon Wright⟩

pleb·i·scite *also* **pleb·e·scite** \'plebə,sīt *also* -,sət *sometimes* 'plēbə,sīt *or* 'plebə,sēt; *usu* -d·+V\ *n* -s [in sense 1, fr. L *plebis scitum, plebiscitum*, fr. *plebis* (gen. of *plebs* common people) + *scitum* decree, fr. neut. of *scitus*, past part. of *sciscere* to try to find out, approve, decree, incho. of *scire* to know; in other senses, fr. F *plébiscite*, fr. L *plebiscitum* — more at PLEBEIAN, SCIENCE] **1 :** PLEBISCITUM 1 **2 :** a vote or decree of the people usu. by universal suffrage on some measure submitted to them by some person or body having the initiative — compare REFERENDUM **3 a :** a vote of the people usu. by universal adult suffrage of some specified district or region on the question put before them by a treaty of peace or by an international body as to choice of sovereignty **b :** the political machinery for expressing self-determination

pleb·i·sci·tum \,plebə'sīd·əm, ,plēb-\ *n, pl* **plebisci·ta** \-d·ə\ [L] **1 :** a vote or decree made by the ancient Roman comitia orig. binding only on the plebs **2 :** PLEBISCITE 2

plebs \'plebz\ *n, pl* **ple·bes** \'plē,bēz\ [L — more at PLEBEIAN] **1 :** the common people of ancient Rome consisting of a composite body of native or naturalized Romans of varying social origins — compare PATRICIAN **2 :** the general populace ⟨all this talk . . . was so much claptrap, inept fabrications to hoodwink the gullible ~ —F.S.Grafford⟩

ple·cop·tera \plə'käptərə\ *n pl, cap* [NL, fr. *pleco-* (fr. Gk *plekein* to plait, weave) + *-ptera* — more at PLY] **:** an order of insects constituted by the stone flies

1ple·cop·ter·an \-rən\ *n* -s [NL *Plecoptera* + E *-an*] **:** an insect of the order Plecoptera **:** STONE FLY

2plecopteran \"\ *adj* **:** of or relating to the Plecoptera

ple·cop·ter·id \-rəd\ *n* [NL *Plecoptera* + E *-id*] **:** PLECOPTERAN — **plecopterid** *adj*

plec·o·tine \'plekə,tīn\ *adj* [NL *Plecotus* + E *-ine*] **:** of or relating to the genus *Plecotus*

ple·co·tus \plə'kōd·əs\ *n, cap* [NL, fr. Gk *plekein* to twist, plait, weave + *ōt-, ous* ear — more at PLY, EAR] **:** a genus of bats (family Vespertilionidae) consisting of the common long-eared bat of Europe and Asia

plect- *or* **plecto-** *comb form* [Gk *plektos*, fr. *plekein*] **:** twisted ⟨*plect*enchyma⟩ ⟨*plecto*gnath⟩

plec·ta·nia \plek'tānēə\ *n, cap* [NL, fr. Gk *plektanē* wreath, coil (fr. *plekein* to plait) + NL *-ia*] **:** a genus of ascomycetous fungi with brightly colored, stalked, and often bristly apothecia that is often included in the closely related genus *Peziza*

plec·tas·ca·les \,plek,ta'skā,lēz\ *n pl, cap* [NL, fr. *plect-* + *asc-* + *-ales*] *in some classifications* **:** an order comprising ascomycetes in which the asci are not in a hymenial layer but are scattered throughout the tissue of perithecia or similar structures

plec·ten·chy·ma \plek'teŋkəmə\ *n* -s [NL, fr. *plect-* + *-enchyma*] **:** a parenchymatous tissue formed by massed and twisted filaments or tubular cells esp. in fungi and lichens — compare PROSENCHYMA, PSEUDOPARENCHYMA — **plec·ten·chym·a·tous** \¦plek,teŋ¦kimədəs\ *adj*

1plec·tog·nath \'plek,täg,nath\ *adj* [NL *Plectognathi*] **:** of or relating to the Plectognathi

2plectognath \"\ *n* -s **:** a fish of the order Plectognathi

plec·tog·na·thi \plek'tägnə,thī\ *n pl, cap* [NL, fr. *plect-* + *-gnathi*, pl. of *-gnathus*] **:** an order of bony fishes that generally have the maxillary bone united with the premaxillary, the posttemporal united with the skull, and the gill openings greatly reduced in size, have the ventral fins rudimentary or wanting and the body usu. covered with bony plates, spines, or small rough ossicles, and include the boxfishes, filefishes, globefishes, sunfishes, triggerfishes, and related forms — **plec·tog·nath·ic** \¦plek,täg¦nathik\ *adj* — **plec·tog·na·thous** \(')plek¦tägnəthəs\ *adj*

plec·to·my·ce·tes \,plektō,mī'sēd·ēz\ *also* **plec·to·my·ce·tae** \-d·ē\ *n pl, cap* [NL, fr. *plect-* + *-mycetes* or *-mycetae* (fr. Gk *mykēt-, mykēs* fungus, mushroom) — more at MYC-] *in some classifications* **:** a subclass of Ascomycetes coextensive with the order Plectascales — **plec·to·my·ce·tous** \¦==,=¦sēd-əs\ *adj*

plec·top·ter \plek'täptə(r)\ *n* -s [NL *Plectoptera*] **:** an insect of the order Plectoptera

plec·top·tera \plek'täptərə\ *n pl, cap* [NL, fr. *plect-* + *-ptera*] **:** an order of slender delicate insects that have membranous net-veined wings, that comprise the mayflies and related insects, and that were formerly included among the Neuroptera — see EPHEMERIDAE

1plec·top·ter·an \(')plek¦täptərən\ *or* **plec·top·ter·ous** \-rəs\ *adj* [NL *Plectoptera* + E *-an* or *-ous*] **:** of or relating to the Plectoptera

2plectopteran \"\ *n* -s **:** PLECTOPTER

1plec·to·spon·dyl \¦plektō¦spändəl\ *adj* [NL *Plectospondyli*] **:** of or relating to the Plectospondyli

2plectospondyl \"\ *n* -s **:** a fish of the order Plectospondyli

plec·to·spon·dy·li \,==¦spändə,lī\ *n pl, cap* [NL, fr. *plect-* + *-spondyli*] *in some classifications* **:** an order or other group comprising fishes with the anterior vertebrae modified and united and usu. being more or less coextensive with Ostariophysi — **plec·to·spon·dyl·ous** \¦==¦spändələs\ *adj*

plec·to·stele \'plektə,stēl *also* ,==¦stēlē\ *n* [*plect-* + *stele*] **:** an actinostele (as in a club moss) in which the xylem elements are arranged in usu. parallel plates

plec·tre \'plektə(r)\ *n* -s [F, fr. L *plectrum* — more at PLECTRUM] **:** PLECTRUM

plec·trid·i·al \(')plek¦tridēəl\ *adj* [NL *plectridium* + E *-al*] **:** having the form of a drumstick

plec·trid·i·um \plek'tridēəm\ *n, pl* **plectrid·ia** \-ēə\ [NL, fr. L *plectrum* + NL *-idium*] **:** a hammer-shaped or drumstick-shaped cell; *esp* **:** any of various rod-shaped bacteria formerly classed as a genus *Plectridium* in which one end becomes enlarged by the production of an endospore

plec·tron \'plek,trän\ *n* -s [Gk *plēktron*] **:** PLECTRUM 1

plec·trop·o·mus \plek'träpəməs\ *n, cap* [NL, fr. Gk *plēktron* + NL *-pomus* (fr. Gk *pōma* lid, cover); akin to Gk *pōy* herd, flock — more at FUR] **:** a genus comprising tropical Indo-Pacific percoid food fishes (as the coral cod of Australia) and others that are dangerously poisonous when eaten and being sometimes isolated in a separate family but usu. included among the Serranidae

plec·trum \'plektrəm\ *n, pl* **plec·tra** \-rə\ *or* **plectrums** [L, fr. Gk *plēktron* striking instrument, spur, fr. *plēk-* (stem of *plēssein* to strike) + *-tron*, suffix denoting an instrument — more at PLAINT] **1 :** a small thin piece of ivory, wood, metal, horn, quill, or other material used in playing on plucked stringed musical instruments (as the lyre, mandolin) **2** [NL, fr. L] **:** any of various anatomic parts that suggest a plectrum in form

plectra 1

pled *past of* PLEAD

1pledge \'plej\ *n* -s [ME *plegge*, fr. MF *plege*, fr. OF, fr. LL *plebium* security, fr. (assumed) LL *plebere* to pledge, prob. modif. (influenced by L *praebēre* to offer) of (assumed) OFrk *plegan* to be responsible for, guarantee; akin to OHG *pflegan* to take care of — more at PLIGHT, PREBEND] **1 a :** a person under early English law whose body is given as security for the performance of an obligation **:** HOSTAGE **b :** a chattel or object of personal property delivered by a debtor or obligor to a creditor or obligee to be kept by the latter until the debt or obligation is satisfied **:** an object given as security by pledge **c** (1) **:** a bailment of a chattel or object of personal property as security for the satisfaction of a debt or other obligation (2) **:** the contract, obligation, or form of property incidental to such a bailment **d :** an agreement involving the delivery as security but without transfer of title of objects capable of physical delivery as distinguished from a common-law mortgage which always involves a conditional transfer of title **e :** the transfer of a chose in action by delivery and transfer of title — compare MORTGAGE **2 :** the state of being held as a security or guaranty ⟨the camera spent three weeks in ~ at the shop —John Hersey⟩ **3 a :** something given or considered as a security for the performance of an act and usu. liable to forfeiture in case of nonperformance **b :** something in pawn ⟨kept the famous painting as a ~ that would be restored eventually to its original owner⟩ **4 :** something that is a token, sign, evidence, or earnest of something else ⟨the strong beat of his heart was a ~ of a vigorous life⟩ **5 :** a gage of battle ⟨threw his gauntlet as a sacred ~ —Edmund Spenser⟩ **6 :** a child that constitutes evidence of a bond between its parents **7 a :** an assurance of goodwill or favor given by drinking one's health **b :** the toasting of a person **8 a :** a promise or agreement by which one binds himself to do or forbear something ⟨in the typical Victorian romance a touch of the hand was a ~ of matrimony —M.D.Geismar⟩ **b :** a promise usu. in writing to refrain from using intoxicants or something considered harmful — usu. used with *the* ⟨takes a lifelong ~ to abstain from drinking whiskey —M.V.Reidy⟩ **9 a :** a promise to join a fraternity or secret society **b :** a person who has promised to join such a group but has not been initiated ⟨inculcating the doctrine of hospitality in all actives and ~*s* —J.E.Ivins⟩

syn EARNEST, TOKEN, PAWN, HOSTAGE: PLEDGE may apply to anything handed over as a security for fulfillment of a debt or promise or satisfaction of an obligation ⟨the pawnshop, where one waits nervously while the swarthy, shrewd-eyed attendant squints contemptuously at the *pledges* one offers —Donn Byrne⟩ ⟨property of the debtor in the creditor's possession was held as a valid *pledge* —*Harvard Law Rev.*⟩ EARNEST may designate a payment, usu. of money, serving to bind an agreement and indicate either the certainty or the likelihood of additional subsequent payments; in today's English it often indicates a reliable sign indicating a future course ⟨the boy or girl, man or woman, was hired and given the *earnest* . . . by the employer —F.D.Smith & Barbara Wilcox⟩ ⟨the gold on the surface was only an *earnest* of the gold veining the rocks beneath it —M.B.Eldershaw⟩ TOKEN may apply to any symbol or symbolizing action given as an indication of good faith, obligation, or indebtedness ⟨impossible to employ the Canadian Eskimos in the armed forces . . . (although a *token* group of four men from Aklavik has been officially enlisted) —Farley Mowat⟩ ⟨has not yet faced up to a service pay raise, though even a *token* raise could indicate to the regulars that they are held in some esteem —H. W.Baldwin⟩ PAWN indicates a person or thing given as a guaranty or security and eventually redeemable ⟨the folly of lending much money on such worthless *pawns*⟩ HOSTAGE usually refers to a person yielded into another's hands as a guaranty of the good intentions of the person or agency performing the yielding ⟨giving over their children as *hostages* to the invaders⟩

2pledge \"\ *vb* -ED/-ING/-S [ME *pleggen* to become surety for, fr. MF *plegier*, fr. OF, fr. *plege*, n.] *vt* **1 :** to give as a pledge **:** deposit (as a chattel) in pledge or pawn **:** make a pledge of **:** PAWN; *specif* **:** to assign as security for the repayment of a loan — compare COLLATERAL **2 :** to give assurance, promise, or evidence esp. of goodwill or favor by or in drinking to: **a** *obs* **:** to drink at the invitation of or in response to a toast proposed by **b :** to drink the health of **:** TOAST ⟨lifted his glass and *pledged* the beautiful girl⟩ **3 :** to bind by or as if by a pledge **:** PLIGHT ⟨*pledged* the signatory powers to meet the common danger —*Current Biog.*⟩ ⟨we mutually ~ to each other our lives, our fortunes, and our sacred honor —*U.S. Declaration of Independence*⟩ **4 a :** to assure or promise the performance of (as by a pledge) ⟨to ~ my vow, I give my hand —Shak.⟩ **b :** to promise seriously **:** UNDERTAKE ⟨I have *pledged* three stories —Malcolm Cowley⟩ **5 :** to cause (one) to make or sign a pledge ⟨was *pledged* to join a fraternity⟩ ~ *vi* **1 :** to give or make a pledge **:** become surety **2 :** to drink a pledge **syn** see PROMISE

pledg·ee \(')ple¦jē\ *n* -s **1 :** one to whom a pledge is given **2 :** one who holds property as a pledge

pledg·er \'plejə(r)\ *n* -s **:** one that pledges

pledges *pl of* PLEDGE, *pres 3d sing of* PLEDGE

pled·get \'plejət\ *n* -s [origin unknown] **1 :** a compress or small flat mass usu. of gauze or absorbent cotton that is laid over a wound or into a cavity to apply medication, exclude air, retain dressings, or absorb the matter discharged **2 :** a thread of oakum used in caulking a boat

pled·gor *or* **pled·geor** \(')ple¦jó(ə)r, 'plejə(r)\ *n* -s **:** PLEDGER

pleg·a·dis \'plegədəs\ *n, cap* [NL, fr. Gk *plēgad-, plēgas* scythe, sickle, fr. the stem of *plēssein* to strike — more at PLAINT] **:** a genus of birds (family Threskiornithidae) including the glossy ibis

ple·gia \'plēj(ē)ə\ *n* -s [*-plegia*] **:** PARALYSIS ⟨another type of ~⟩

-plegia \"\ *n comb form* -s [NL, fr. Gk *plēgē* blow, stroke (fr. the stem of *plēssein* to strike) + NL *-ia*] **:** paralysis of a specified nature ⟨para*plegia*⟩

-ple·gy \'plējē, -ji\ *n comb form* -ES [NL *-plegia*] **:** paralysis of a specified nature

ple·iad \'plēəd *also* 'plīəd\ *n* -s [F *Pléiade*, a group of 7 16th cent. Fr. poets, fr. MF, fr. *Pléiade*, a group of 7 tragic poets of ancient Alexandria, fr. Gk *Pleiades, Plēiades*, pl., fr. *Pleiades, Plēiades*, 7 stars in the constellation Taurus] **:** a group or cluster of illustrious or brilliant persons or things usu. seven in number ⟨educated a brilliant ~ of great masters of painting —*Encyc. Americana*⟩

ple·i·dae \'plēə,dē\ *n pl, cap* [NL, fr. *Plea*, type genus (fr. Gk *plein* to sail, float, swim) + *-idae* — more at FLOW] **:** a widely distributed family of small aquatic bugs

1plein air \'plān-\ *n* [F, lit., full air] **:** outdoor daylight ⟨to paint in *plein air*⟩ ⟨to render the high tonal values of the local *plein air*⟩

2plein air \"\ *adj* **1 :** relating to the method, action, or product of painting in outdoor daylight **2 :** of, relating to, or constituting a French art movement starting about 1865 which attempted to represent effects of outdoor light and air not observable in the studio

plein·air·ism \plā'na(a)(,)rizəm\ *or* **plein·air·isme** \plenerēs(mᵊ), -ēz(mᵊ), -s(mə), -z(mə)\ *n* -s [F *pleinairisme*, fr. *plein air* + *-isme* -ism] **:** the study, action, or product of plein air painting; *specif* **:** the plein air art movement in France

plein·air·ist \-,rəst\ *or* **plein·air·iste** \-ēst\ *n* -s [F *pleinairiste*, fr. *plein air* + *-iste* -ist] **:** an adherent or follower of a theory, method, or practice of plein air painting

plein jeu \'plaⁿ-\ *n, often cap P&J* [F, lit., full play] **:** a mixture stop in a pipe organ including the unison, octave, and fifth

pleio- *or* **pleo-** *or* **plio-** *comb form* [Gk *pleiōn, pleōn* — more at PLUS] **1 :** more ⟨*Pleio*cene⟩ ⟨*pleo*morphism⟩ ⟨*pleo*mastia⟩ ⟨*Plio*cene⟩ **2 :** Pliocene ⟨*Plio*hippus⟩ ⟨*Plio*pithecus⟩

plei·o·bar \'plīə,bär\ *n* [ISV *pleio-* + Gk *baros* weight — more at GRIEVE] **1 :** an area of high barometric pressure **2 :** an isobar of high pressure

plei·om·ery \plī'ämərē\ *n* -ES [ISV *pleio-* + *-mery*] **:** a state of having more than the normal number of floral leaves

pleiomorphic *var of* PLEOMORPHIC

plei·on \'plī,än\ *n* -s [NL, fr. Gk *pleiōn* more, greater — more at PLUS] **:** a region in meteorology of positive departure from the normal of an element (as pressure, temperature, rainfall) — **plei·o·ni·an** \(')plī¦ōnēən\ *adj*

plei·o·phyl·ly \'plīə,filē\ *n* -ES [ISV *pleio-* + *-phylly* (fr. *-phyll* + *-y*)] **:** an abnormal increase or excess in the number of leaves or leaflets

plei·o·taxy \'plīə,taksē\ *n* -ES [ISV *pleio-* + *-taxy*] **:** development of more than the normal number of parts (as bracts in a flower or inflorescence)

plei·o·trop·ic \¦plīə¦träpik\ *adj* [*pleio-* + *-tropic*] *of a gene* **:** producing more than one effect **:** having multiple phenotypic expressions ⟨a ~ gene that induces shortening of the ear and reduces general body size has been reported in the mouse⟩ — **plei·o·trop·i·cal·ly** \-pək(ə)lē\ *adv*

plei·ot·ro·pism \plī'ä·trə,pizəm\ *n* -s [*pleio-* + *-tropism*] **:** a condition produced by a pleiotropic gene

plei·ot·ro·py \-rəpē\ *n* -ES [ISV *pleio-* + *-tropy*] **:** the quality or state of being pleiotropic

pleis·to·cene \'plīstə,sēn\ *adj, usu cap* [ISV *pleisto-* (fr. Gk *pleistos* most) + *-cene*; akin to Gk *pleiōn* more — more at PLUS] **:** of, relating to, or constituting a subdivision of the Quaternary — see GEOLOGIC TIME table

plen *abbr* plenipotentiary

plena *pl of* PLENUM

ple·na·ri·ly \'plēnərəlē, 'plen-, plə'ner-\ *adv* **:** in a plenary manner ⟨an empire already beginning to enter the Commonwealth, and destined to enter it ~ —Ernest Barker⟩

ple·nar·ty \'plēnə(r)d·ē, 'plen-\ *n* -ES [ME *plenerte*, fr. MF *plenierté, plenerté*, fr. *plenier, plener* complete, full (fr. *plein, plen* full, fr. L *plenus*) + *-té* -ty — more at FULL] **:** the state of a benefice when occupied

ple·na·ry \'plēnərē, 'plen-, -ri\ *adj* [LL *plenarius*, fr. L *plenus* full + *-arius*, -ary — more at FULL] **1 :** complete in every respect **:** ABSOLUTE, PERFECT, UNQUALIFIED ⟨the ~ inspiration of the Bible —M.R.Cohen⟩ ⟨a ~ state of cleanliness —Arnold Bennett⟩ **2 :** fully attended or constituted **:** including all entitled to be present ⟨a ~ session of the legislature⟩ ⟨~ assembly⟩ **3 :** including all steps in due order **:** COMPLETE ⟨a ~ proceeding⟩ — opposed to *summary*

plenary council *n* [trans. of LL *concilium plenarium*] **:** an assembly of the ecclesiastical authorities of a country or larger territory

plenary indulgence *n* [trans. of ML *plenaria indulgentia*] *Roman Catholicism* **:** a remission of the entire temporal punishment due to sin

plenary inspiration *n* **:** divine inspiration covering all subjects dealt with — compare VERBAL INSPIRATION

ple·ne \'plēnē\ *adj* [L *plenus* full; trans. of LHeb *mālē*] **:** having the full orthographic or grammatical form given in Masoretic texts as corrections of the defective forms that appeared in ancient biblical texts ⟨~ spelling⟩ ⟨~ writings⟩ — compare KERE, KETHIB

ple·ne ad·mi·ni·stra·vit \'plēnēad,minə'strāvət\ [L] **:** he has fully administered — used at law referring to a plea in bar by an executor or administrator when sued by a creditor, heir, or legatee

ple·ni·lune \'plēnə,lün, 'plen-\ *n* -s [ME, fr. L *plenilunium*, fr. *plenus* full + *-i-* + *-lunium* (fr. *luna* moon) — more at FULL, LUNAR] **:** the time of full moon; *also* **:** a full moon

plen·i·po \'plenə,pō\ *n* -s [by shortening] **:** PLENIPOTENTIARY

ple·nip·o·tence \plə'nipəd·ən(t)s\ *n* -s **:** the quality or state of being invested with authority or power to transact business

ple·nip·o·tent \-nt\ *adj* [LL *plenipotent-, plenipotens*, fr. L *plenus* full + *-i-* + *potent-, potens* able, powerful — more at FULL, POTENT] **:** PLENIPOTENTIARY

plen·i·po·ten·tial \¦plenəpə¦tenchəl\ *adj* [LL *plenipotent-, plenipotens* + E *-ial*] **:** PLENIPOTENTIARY

1plen·i·po·ten·tia·ry \-chərē, -chē,erē, -ri\ *adj* [ML *plenipotentiarius*, adj. & n., fr. LL *plenipotent-, plenipotens* + *-i-* + L *-arius* -ary] **1 :** containing or conferring full power **:** invested with full power **:** ABSOLUTE, UNLIMITED ⟨countries with ~ parliaments —E.V.Rostow⟩ **2 :** of or relating to a plenipotentiary

2plenipotentiary \"\ *n* -ES [ML *plenipotentiarius*] **:** a person invested with full power to transact any business; *esp* **:** MINISTER PLENIPOTENTIARY

plen·ish \'plenish\ *vt* -ED/-ING/-ES [ME (Sc dial.) *plenyssen*, fr. MF *pleniss-*, stem of *plenir*, fr. OF, fr. *plein, plen* full, fr. L *plenus* — more at FULL] **1 a :** to fill up **b** *chiefly dial* **:** REPLENISH **2** *chiefly Brit* **:** to equip (a house or farm) with furnishings

plenishing *n* -s [fr. gerund of *plenish*] *chiefly Scot* **:** furniture, equipment, and stock esp. as needed to run a farm

ple·nist \'plēnəst\ *n* -s [L *plenus* full, complete + E *-ist*] **:** one who maintains that there are no vacuums in nature — compare VACUIST

plen·i·tude \'plenə,tüd, -ə,tyüd\ *or* **plent·i·tude** \-ntə-\ *n* -s [*plenitude* fr. ME, fr. MF or L; MF, fr. L *plenitudo*, fr. *plenus* full + *-i-* + *-tudo* -tude; *plentitude* alter. (influenced by *plenty*) of *plenitude* — more at FULL] **1 :** the quality or state of being full **:** absolute fullness **:** COMPLETENESS ⟨death . . . in the ~ of health, vigor, and aspirations —George Grote⟩ ⟨loves and sorrows that are great are destroyed by their own ~ —Oscar Wilde⟩ **2 :** a more than ample amount or number **:** great sufficiency **:** ABUNDANCE ⟨the ~ of plants around them —Napier Devitt⟩ ⟨sea gulls gorge themselves on a ~ of fish —Renate O'Connell⟩ ⟨her long skirts are voluminous and worn over a ~ of petticoats —Mabel S. Shelton⟩ ⟨exchange . . . their Old World stone cottages and thatched barns for a ~ of lumber —*Amer. Guide Series: Minn.*⟩ **3** *of a flower* **:** DOUBLENESS **4** *heraldry* **:** fullness of the moon

plen·i·tu·di·nous \¦plenə¦tüdᵊnəs, -ə¦tyü-\ *adj* [L *plenitudin-, plenitudo* plenitude + E *-ous*] **1 :** characterized by plenitude ⟨with manifold and ~ life —Robert Browning⟩ **2 :** PORTLY, STOUT — used humorously

plenshing nail *var of* PLANCHING NAIL

plen·te·ous \'plentēəs\ *adj* [ME *plentevous, plentious*, fr. OF *plentiveus, plentivous, plentious*, fr. *plentif* abundant (fr. *plenté* abundance, plenty + -if -ive) + -eus, -ous -ous — more at PLENTY] **1 :** bearing or yielding abundance **:** FRUITFUL, PRODUCTIVE — usu. used with *in* or *of* ⟨the seasons had been ~ in corn —George Eliot⟩ **2 :** constituting, characterized by, or existing in plenty ⟨gathered gold and silver, and ~ . . . goods —William Morris⟩ ⟨~ grace with thee is found —Charles Wesley⟩ **3** *obs* **:** giving liberally **:** BOUNTIFUL ⟨with ~ hand, bring clover grass —John Dryden⟩ **syn** see PLENTIFUL

plen·te·ous·ly *adv* [ME *plentivously, plentiously*, fr. *plentivous, plentious* + *-ly*] **:** in a plenteous manner ⟨he provided for her ~ while he lived —S.H.Adams⟩

plen·te·ous·ness *n* -ES [ME *plentivousnesse, plentiousnesse*, fr. *plentivous, plentious* + *-nesse* -ness] **:** the quality or state of being plenteous

plen·ti·ful \ˈplentəfəl, -tēf-\ *adj* **1 :** containing or yielding plenty **:** FRUITFUL, OPULENT ⟨a ~ land⟩ ⟨a ~ supper of roast and boiled beef and mutton —W.H.Hudson †1922⟩ **2 :** characterized by, constituting, or existing in plenty **:** NUMEROUS ⟨the deer are as ~ as the vast wilderness will support —S.H. Holbrook⟩ ⟨his religion . . . summoned him to serve the ~ reform movements of the day —V.L.Parrington⟩

syn PLENTEOUS, AMPLE, ABUNDANT, COPIOUS: these adjectives have the common meaning of more than adequate or sufficient yet not in excess. That is PLENTIFUL or PLENTEOUS of which there is a rich or full, usu. more than full, supply ⟨a *plentiful* supply of books⟩ ⟨butter is cheap when it is *plentiful*, and dear when it is scarce —G.B.Shaw⟩ ⟨aluminum, one of the world's most *plentiful* elements —*Amer. Guide Series: Pa.*⟩ ⟨a *plenteous* number of individual poems —*College English*⟩ ⟨a *plenteous* harvest —J.G.Frazer⟩ That is AMPLE which is generously sufficient to satisfy a particular requirement ⟨manufacturers had *ample* supplies on hand to meet the emergency —*Current Biog.*⟩ ⟨provide *ample* opportunity for fieldwork with Indian tribes —D.G.Mandelbaum⟩ ⟨*ample* proof of the power of words —*advt*⟩ ABUNDANT suggests a greater or richer supply than does PLENTIFUL ⟨her unselfish and *abundant* interests —Rex Ingamells⟩ ⟨the many small denominational colleges so *abundant* throughout the Middle West —G.P. Merrill⟩ COPIOUS, not quite interchangeable with PLENTIFUL, puts emphasis upon largeness of supply more than on fullness or richness ⟨his papers were *copious* and bizarre, and it took me nearly two hours to find the will —John Cheever⟩ ⟨his *copious* flaxen curls —Richard Garnett †1906⟩ ⟨washed down with *copious* drafts of beer —Green Peyton⟩

plen·ti·ful·ly \-f(ə)lē, -li\ *adv* **:** in more than adequate numbers or quantity **:** ABUNDANTLY

plen·ti·ful·ness *n* -ES **:** the quality or state of being plentiful

plentitude *var of* PLENITUDE

¹plen·ty \ˈplentē, -ti\ *n* -ES [ME *plente, plentee, plentie*, fr. OF *plenté*, fr. L *plenitat-, plenitas* fullness, abundance, fr. *plenus* full + *-itat-, -itas* -ity — more at FULL] **1 a :** a more than adequate number, quantity,or amount **:** a full supply **:** enough and to spare ⟨always gave them ~ of time —Seymour Blau⟩ ⟨cowboys on the range still do ~ of roping —S.E.Fletcher⟩ ⟨would have ~ of visitors —H.E.Scudder⟩ **b :** a large number or amount of something — used with *a* ⟨a ~ of things to be done —Verne Athanas⟩ ⟨what they asked for they got, and they asked for a ~ —*Amer. Mercury*⟩ **2 a :** an abundance esp. of material things that permit a satisfactory life **:** a condition or time of abundance ⟨the general feeling of ~ in this rich land —Pearl Buck⟩ ⟨a peace that seemed to bring ~ in its train —Stringfellow Barr⟩ **b plenties** *pl* **:** plentiful amounts esp. of things that constitute material comfort ⟨drink *plenties* of this milk too —J.L.Weldon⟩ **3 :** the quality or state of being copious **:** PLENTIFULNESS — often used with *in* ⟨down by the lake the daffodils were now in their ~ —Victoria Sackville-West⟩ ⟨will . . . gain pleasure and profit in ~ —H.M. Parshley⟩

²plenty \"\ *adj* [ME *plente*, fr. *plente*, n.] **1 :** ample in amount or supply **:** PLENTIFUL ⟨if reasons were as ~ as blackberries —Shak.⟩ ⟨bread is never too ~ in Indian households —Willa Cather⟩ **2 a** *chiefly dial* **:** existing in large quantity or number ⟨who has conies ~ to dispose of cheap —Jeremy Bentham⟩ **b :** AMPLE, MANY **:** more than enough ⟨he could get ~ men . . . to do his bidding —W.C.Tuttle⟩ ⟨there is ~ work to be done —*Time*⟩ ⟨you'll have ~ support from the other districts —Ralph Ellison⟩

³plenty \"\ *adv* **:** more than sufficiently **:** ABUNDANTLY, PLENTIFULLY ⟨they will talk ~, but not about themselves —J.L.Phelan⟩ ⟨her style is ~ vigorous enough —Florence Bullock⟩ ⟨the nights were ~ cold —F.B.Gipson⟩ ⟨a transatlantic holiday is ~ exciting —T.H.Fielding⟩

¹plenum \ˈplēnəm, -lēn-\ *n, pl* **plenums** \-mz\ *or* **plena** \-nə\ [NL, fr. L, neut. of *plenus* full — more at FULL] **1 a :** a space or all space every part of which is full of matter — opposed to *vacuum* **b** (1) **:** a condition in which the pressure of the air in an enclosed space is greater than that of the outside atmosphere (2) **:** an enclosed space in which such a condition exists; *esp* **:** a plenum chamber **2 a :** a general assembly of all members esp. of a legislative body **b :** the entire membership of a specific group **3 :** the quality or state of being full

²plenum \"\ *adj* **:** relating to or being a space in which a plenum exists ⟨a ~ chamber in a hot-air furnace⟩ ⟨the ~ system forces air into the room, causing a leakage outward although exhaust ducts may also be provided —V.M.Ehlers & E.W.Steel⟩

plenum ventilation *n* **:** a system of ventilation that applies the motive force at the inlets, drives the air through the rooms which become plenums, and avoids the incoming of cold drafts

pleo- — see PLEIO-

ple·o·chro·ic \ˌplēəˈkrōik\ *adj* [ISV *pleio-* + *-chroic*] **:** of, relating to, or having pleochroism

ple·och·ro·ism \plēˈäkrəˌwizəm\ *n* -S [ISV *pleochroic* + *-ism*] **:** the property possessed by a crystal of showing different colors when viewed by light that vibrates parallel to different axes — see DICHROISM, TRICHROISM

ple·och·ro·ous \-rəwəs\ *adj* [*pleio-* + *-chroous*] **:** PLEOCHROIC

ple·o·cy·to·sis \ˌplēōˌsīˈtōsə̇s\ *n, pl* **pleocyto·ses** \-ˈtōˌsēz\ [NL, fr. *pleio-* + *cyt-* + *-osis*] **:** an abnormal increase in the number of cells (as lymphocytes) in the cerebrospinal fluid

ple·o·dont \ˈplēəˌdänt\ *adj* [ISV *pleo-* (fr. Gk *pleos* full) + *-odont*; akin to Gk *plērēs* full — more at FULL] **:** having solid teeth ⟨~ reptiles⟩

ple·o·mas·tia \ˌplēəˈmastēə\ *n* -S [NL, fr. *pleio-* + *-mastia*] **:** a condition of having more than two mammary glands or nipples — **ple·o·mas·tic** \ˌ==ˈmastik\ *adj*

ple·o·ma·zia \ˌ==ˈmāz(h)ēə\ *n* -S [NL, fr. *pleio-* + *maz-* + *-ia*] **:** PLEOMASTIA

ple·o·me·tro·sis \ˌplēōmə·ˈtrōsə̇s\ *n, pl* **pleometro·ses** \-rōˌsēz\ [NL, fr. *pleio-* + Gk *mētēr* queen bee, mother + NL *-osis* — more at MOTHER] **:** the occurrence of several queens in a single nest of ants

ple·o·me·trot·ic \ˌ===ˈträd·ik\ *adj* [fr. NL *pleometrosis*, after such pairs as NL *narcosis*: E *narcotic*] **:** of, relating to, or characterized by pleometrosis

ple·o·morph \ˈplēəˌmȯrf\ *n* -S [back-formation fr. *pleomorphic*] **:** POLYMORPH 1, 2

ple·o·mor·phic \ˌ==ˈmȯrfik\ *also* **plei·o·mor·phic** \ˌplīə-\ *adj* [ISV *pleomorphism* + *-ic*] **:** of, relating to, or characterized by pleomorphism

ple·o·mor·phism \ˌ==ˈmȯ(r)ˌfizəm\ *n* -S [ISV *pleio-* + *-morphism*] **1 :** the occurrence of more than one distinct form in the life cycle of some plants (as the rusts) **2 :** POLYMORPHISM a

ple·o·mor·phous \ˌ==ˈmȯrfəs\ *adj* [ISV *pleomorphism* + *-ous*] **:** PLEOMORPHIC

ple·o·mor·phy \ˈ==ˌmȯrfē\ *n* -ES [*pleomorphous* + *-y*] **:** PLEOMORPHISM

ple·on \ˈplēˌän\ *n* -S [NL, fr. Gk *pleōn*, pres. part. of *plein* to sail; fr. the fact that it bears the swimming limbs — more at FLOW] **1 :** the abdomen of a crustacean **2 :** the telson of a king crab — **ple·o·nal** \-ēənᵊl\ *or* **ple·on·ic** \(ˈ)plēˈänik\ *adj*

ple·o·nasm \ˈplēəˌnazəm\ *n* -S [LL *pleonasmus*, fr. Gk *pleonasmos*, fr. *pleonazein* to be more, to be in excess, to be redundant, fr. *pleon*, neut. of *pleiōn, pleōn* more] **1 a :** iteration or repetition in speaking or in writing **:** the use of more words than those necessary to denote mere sense (as *the man he said, saw with his own eyes, true fact*); *esp* **:** the coincident use of a word and its substitute for the same grammatical function **:** REDUNDANCY, TAUTOLOGY **b :** an instance or example of such iteration **2 :** SUPERFLUITY ⟨a ~ or overflow of that great kindness —Samuel Purchos⟩

ple·o·naste \ˈplēəˌnast\ *n* -S [F, fr. Gk *pleonastos* abundant, fr. *pleonazein* to be more; fr. the many faces of the crystal] **:** CEYLONITE

ple·o·nas·tic \ˌplēəˈnastik\ *adj* [fr. *pleonasm*, after such pairs as E *spasm: spastic*] **:** of, relating to, or having the characteristics of pleonasm — **ple·o·nas·ti·cal·ly** \-tə̇k(ə)lē\ *adv*

pleonastic genitive *n* **:** DOUBLE POSSESSIVE

ple·o·nex·ia \ˌplēəˈneksēə\ *n* -S [Gk, fr. *pleonektein* to be greedy, to have or want more, fr. *pleon*, neut. of *pleiōn, pleōn* more + *echein* to have — more at PLEIO-, SCHEME] **:** AVARICE, COVETOUSNESS

ple·oph·a·gous \plēˈäfəgəs\ *adj* [*pleio-* + *-phagous*] **1 :** eating a variety of foods **2** *of a parasite* **:** not restricted to a single kind of host

ple·o·pod \ˈplēəˌpäd\ *n* -S [*pleio-* (fr. Gk *pleōn*, pres. part. of *plein* to sail) + *-pod*; fr. its being used for swimming — more at FLOW] **:** an abdominal limb of a crustacean

ple·op·o·dite \plēˈäpəˌdīt\ *n* -S [*pleopod* + *-ite*] **:** PLEOPOD

ple·o·sponge \ˈplēəˌspənj\ *n* [NL *Pleospongia*, fr. *pleio-* + *-spongia*] **:** any of various Lower and Middle Cambrian calcareous, cylindrical or cup-shaped, double-walled, porous fossils that may be the remains of sponges or primordial precursors of the true corals

ple·os·po·ra \plēˈäspərə\ *n, cap* [NL, fr. *pleio-* + *-spora*] **:** a genus of ascomycetous fungi (family Sphaeriaceae) having brown muriform ascospores in scattered or gregarious perithecia

ple·o·spo·ra·ce·ae \ˌplēəspəˈrāsēˌē\ *n pl, cap* [NL, fr. *Pleospora* + *-aceae*] **:** a family of ascomycetous fungi (order Sphaeriales) that is sometimes combined with Mycosphaerellaceae and that includes parasitic fungi which cause stem or leaf spot diseases or rots of economic plants

pler·er·gate \ˈpli'rərˌgāt\ *n* [Gk *plērēs* full + E *ergate* — more at FULL] **:** REPLETE

ple·ro·cer·coid \ˌplirəˈsərˌkȯid\ *n* -S [*plero-* (fr. Gk *plērēs* full) + *cerc-* + *-oid*] **:** the solid elongate infective larva of pseudophyllidean and some other tapeworms usu. occurring in the muscles of fishes — compare CYSTICERCUS, PROCERCOID

ple·ro·ma \pləˈrōmə\ *n, pl* **pleromas** *or* **pleromata** [LL, fullness, fr. Gk *plērōma* that which fills, fr. *plēroun* to make full, fr. *plērēs* full] **1 :** PLENITUDE: **a :** the fullness of divine excellencies and powers ⟨the ~ of the Godhead resides in Christ corporeally —Philip Schaff⟩ **b :** the fullness of being of the divine life held in Gnosticism to comprise the aeons as well as the uncreated monad or dyad from which they have proceeded **2** [NL, fr. LL, fullness] **:** PLEROME — **ple·ro·mat·ic** \ˌplirəˈmad·ik\ *adj*

pleroma violet *n* **:** a moderate purple that is bluer and duller than manganese violet or heliotrope (sense 4a) and bluer than average amethyst

ple·rome \ˈpliˌrōm\ *also* **ple·rom** \-irəm\ *n* -S [G *plerom*, fr. LL *pleroma*] **1 :** the central core of primary meristem of a plant or plant part that according to the histogen theory gives rise to the stele **2 :** the stelar region in a root tip

ple·roph·o·ry \pləˈräfərē\ *n* -ES [Gk *plērophoria*, fr. *plērophorein* to bring full measure, to fulfill, fr. *plērēs* full + *phorein*, freq. of *pherein* to carry — more at BEAR] *archaic* **:** complete assurance ⟨the ~ of faith —John Trapp⟩

ple·rot·ic water \pləˈräd·ik-\ *n* [*plerotic* fr. L *pleroticus* filling up, fr. Gk *plērōtikos*, fr. *plēroun* to make full + *-ikos* -ic] **:** GROUNDWATER

plesi- *or* **plesio-** *comb form* [NL *plesi-*, fr. Gk *plēsi-*, *plēsio-*, fr. *plēsios*, fr. *pelas* near — more at FELT] **:** close **:** near ⟨*plesio*morphous⟩ ⟨*plesio*saurus⟩

ple·si·an·thro·pus \ˌplēsēˈan(t)thrəpəs, -sēˌanˈthrōpəs\ *n, cap* [NL, fr. *plesi-* + *-anthropus*] **:** a genus of australopithecine apes with a distinctly humanlike skull — compare STERKFONTEIN APE-MAN

ple·si·o·bi·o·sis \ˌplēsēōˌbīˈōsə̇s\ *n, pl* **plesiobio·ses** \-ōˌsēz\ [NL, fr. *plesi-* + *-biosis*] **:** casual association of two or more colonies of social insects

ple·si·o·saur \ˈplēsēəˌsȯ(ə)r\ *n* -S [NL *Plesiosauria*] **:** a reptile or fossil of the suborder Plesiosauria

ple·si·o·sau·ria \ˌ===ˈsȯrēə\ *n pl, cap* [NL, fr. *plesi-* + *-sauria*] **1 :** a suborder of Sauropterygia comprising Mesozoic marine reptiles with dorsoventrally flattened bodies and limbs modified into paddles — compare PLESIOSAURUS **2** *in some classifications* **:** an order of Reptilia nearly coextensive with Sauropterygia — **ple·si·o·sau·ri·an** \ˌ===ˈsȯrēən\ *adj or n* — **ple·si·o·sau·roid** \-ōˌrȯid\ *adj*

ple·si·o·sau·rus \ˌ===ˈsȯrəs\ *n* [NL, fr. *plesi-* + *-saurus*] **1** *cap* **:** a genus of marine reptiles (suborder Plesiosauria) of the Mesozoic of Europe and No. America having a very long neck, a small head, and all four limbs developed as paddles for swimming **2** *pl* **plesiosau·ri** \-ōˌrī\ **:** any reptile of the genus *Plesiosaurus*

ple·sio·type \ˈplēsēəˌtīp\ *n* [*plesi-* + *type*] **1 :** a specimen that is both a homeotype and a hypotype **2 :** a specimen identified by other than the original author of a species

ples·site \ˈpleˌsīt\ *n* -S [G *plessit*, prob. fr. Gk *plēsi-* plesi- + G *-it* -ite] **:** a mineral consisting of an intimate intergrowth of kamacite and taenite in meteorites

ples·sor \ˈplesə(r)\ *n* -S [by alter.] **:** PLEXOR

ples·sy's green \(ˈ)pleˌsēz-\ *n, usu cap P* **:** a bluish green pigment consisting essentially of hydrated chromium phosphate $CrPO_4.nH_2O$

plet \ˈplet\ *dial var of* PLAT

pleth·o·don \ˈplethəˌdän\ *n* [NL *pleth-* (fr. Gk *plēthos* mass, magnitude, fr. *plēthein* to be full) + *-odon*] **1** *cap* **:** the type genus of Plethodontidae comprising New World terrestrial salamanders that lay large yolk-filled eggs and do not pass through an aquatic larval period — see RED-BACKED SALAMANDER **2** -S **:** a salamander of the genus *Plethodon*

¹pleth·o·dont \-nt\ *also* **pleth·o·don·tid** \ˌ==ˈdäntə̇d\ *adj* [NL *Plethodontidae*] **:** of or relating to the Plethodontidae

²plethodont \"\ *also* **plethodontid** \"\ *n* -S **:** a salamander of the family Plethodontidae

pleth·o·don·ti·dae \ˌ==ˈdäntəˌdē\ *n pl, cap* [NL, fr. *Plethodont-, Plethodon*, type genus + *-idae*] **:** a large family of small chiefly No. American terrestrial or freshwater salamanders that have neither lungs nor gills as adults — see PLETHODON

pleth·o·ra \ˈplethərə *sometimes* pləˈthōrə *or* -ˈthȯrə\ *n* -S [ML, fr. Gk *plēthōra* fullness, plethora, fr. *plēthein* to be full — more at FULL] **1 :** a bodily condition characterized by an excess of blood and marked by turgescence and a florid complexion **2 :** an often undesirable or hampering superfluity **:** EXCESS, PROFUSION ⟨a ~ of . . . attractions to look at —Janet Flanner⟩ ⟨to plow through a ~ of references —Dwight MacDonald⟩ ⟨the ~ of distracting activities —Virgil Thomson⟩ **3 :** a defect of wood resulting from excessive and uneven growth of the tissues

pleth·o·ric \ˈplethərik, pləˈthȯr-, -ˈthär-, -rēk\ *adj* [LL *plethoricus*, fr. Gk *plēthōrikos*, fr. *plēthōra* plethora + *-ikos* -ic] **1 :** marked by plethora ⟨a ~ condition⟩ **2 :** marked by excess or profusion ⟨that ~ opulence —*Asiatic Annual Register*⟩ ⟨~ volumes which slumber in decorous old libraries —J.H. Burton⟩

pleth·o·ry \ˈplethərē\ *n* -ES [fr. *plethoric*, after such pairs as E *allegoric: allegory*] *archaic* **:** PLETHORA ⟨the state of the nation is full even to ~ —Edmund Burke⟩

pleth·ron \ˈplethrən\ *n, pl* **pleth·ra** \-rə\ [Gk] **1 :** an ancient Greek unit of length equal to 100 Greek feet or 101.2 modern feet **2 :** a unit of area equal to one square plethron

ple·thys·mo·gram \pləˈthizməˌgram, -ism-\ *n* [ISV *plethysmo-* (fr. *plethysmograph*) + *-gram*] **:** a tracing made by a plethysmograph

ple·thys·mo·graph \-raf, -ráf\ *n* [ISV *plethysmo-* (fr. Gk *plēthysmos* multiplication, increase, fr. *plēthynein* to increase, fr. *plēthys, plēthos* mass, magnitude) + *-graph*; *orig.* formed as It *pletismografo*] **:** an instrument for determining and registering variations in the size of an organ or limb and in the amount of blood present or passing through it

ple·thys·mo·graph·ic \ˌ=ˌ==ˈgrafik\ *adj* **:** of, relating to, or made by means of the plethysmograph — **ple·thys·mo·graph·i·cal·ly** \-fə̇k(ə)lē\ *adv*

pleth·ys·mog·ra·phy \ˌplethəzˈmägrəfē, -thəs-\ *n* -ES **:** the use of the plethysmograph **:** examination by plethysmograph

ple·thys·mo·thal·lus \plə,thizməˈthaləs, -ism-\ *n* [NL, fr. Gk *plēthysmos* multiplication + NL *thallus*] **:** a dwarf filamentous thallus occurring in the life cycle of various brown algae and bearing at what appears to be a juvenile stage either unilocular or plurilocular sporangia

pleur- *or* **pleuri-** *or* **pleuro-** *comb form* [NL, fr. L, fr. Gk, side, rib, fr. *pleura*] **1 a :** pleura ⟨*pleur*ectomy⟩ ⟨*pleuri*septate⟩ ⟨*pleuro*genic⟩ **b :** pleura and ⟨*pleuro*pericarditis⟩ ⟨*pleuro*pedal⟩ **2 :** side **:** lateral ⟨*pleur*ite⟩ ⟨*pleuro*centrum⟩ **3 :** rib ⟨*pleur*al⟩

¹pleu·ra \ˈplu̇rə, ˈplürə\ *n, pl* **pleu·rae** \-ˌrē, -ˌrī\ *or* **pleuras** [ML, fr. Gk, side, rib — more at PLEURISY] **1 a :** either of a pair of two-walled sacs of serous membrane each lining one lateral half of the thorax, having an inner layer closely adherent to the corresponding lung, reflected at the root of the lung to form a parietal layer that adheres to the walls of the thorax, the pericardium, upper surface of the diaphragm, and adjacent parts, and containing a small amount of serous fluid that minimizes the friction of respiratory movements **b :** the membranous tissue making up the pleurae **2** [NL, fr. Gk] **:** a laterally located body part; *specif* **:** PLEURON

²pleura *pl of* PLEURON *or of* PLEURUM

-pleu·ra \ˈplu̇rə, ˈplürə\ *n comb form* -S [NL, fr. ML *pleura*] **:** lining **:** girdle ⟨endo*pleura*⟩ ⟨epi*pleura*⟩

pleu·ra·can·thea \ˌplu̇rəˈkan(t)thēə\ *or* **pleu·ra·can·thi·ni** \-rəˌkanˈthīˌnī\ *or* **pleu·rac·an·tho·dii** \ˌplu̇ˌrakənˈthōdēˌī\ [*pleurocanthea* fr. NL, fr. *pleur-* + *-acanthea* (fr. *-acanthus*); *pleuracanthini* fr. NL, fr. *pleur-* + *acanth-* + *-ini*; *pleuracanthodii*, fr. NL, fr. *pleur-* + *Acanthodii*] *syn of* ICHTHYOTOMI

pleu·ra·can·thus \ˌplu̇rəˈkan(t)thəs\ *n, cap* [NL, fr. *pleur-* + *-acanthus*] **:** a genus (the type of the family Pleuracanthidae) of Paleozoic sharks of the Carboniferous and Lower Permian of Europe and No. America having a subterminal mouth, long dorsal fin, and a strong serrated spine on the nape

¹pleu·ral \ˈplu̇rəl, ˈplür-\ *adj* [*pleur-* + *-al*] **1 :** of or relating to the pleura or the sides of the thorax **2 :** of or relating to a pleuron or pleurite

²pleural \"\ *n* -S [*pleur-* + *-al*] **1 :** a bony process in a turtle lying superficial to the ribs and uniting them and thereby forming most of the carapace **2 :** a rib or long ray of bone articulating with a vertebra and extending ventrally into the abdominal wall of a fish

pleural cavity *n* **1 :** the space between the two layers of pleura **2 :** the chest cavity

pleural effusion *n* **1 :** an exudation of fluid from the blood or lymph into a pleural cavity **2 :** an exudate in a pleural cavity

pleural ganglion *n* [ˈpleural] **:** either of a pair of ganglia in a mollusk that send nerves to the mantle and parts of the body wall behind the head and that often lie close to or are fused with the cerebral ganglia

pleural muscle *n* **:** any of several muscles that operate the insect wing

pleural sclerite *n* **:** any of several plates of the pleural area of the insect integument

pleur·ap·o·phys·i·al \ˌplu̇ˌrapəˈfizēəl\ *adj* [*pleurapophysis* + *-al*] **:** of, relating to, or having the characteristics of a pleurapophysis

pleur·apoph·y·sis \ˌplu̇rəˈpäfəsə̇s\ *n* [NL, fr. *pleur-* + *apophysis*] **:** a laterally or more or less ventrally directed process or appendage of a vertebra forming a rib or part corresponding to a rib **:** a rib that is a part of a vertebra

pleuri- — see PLEUR-

pleu·ric \ˈplu̇rik\ *adj* [F *pleurique*, fr. L *pleuricus* lateral, fr. Gk *pleurikos*, fr. *pleura* side, rib + *-ikos* -ic] **:** PLEURAL

pleu·ri·sy \ˈplu̇rəsē, ˈplür-, -si\ *n* -ES [ME *pleresie, pluresie*, fr. MF *pleuresie*, fr. ML *pleuresis*, alter. of LL *pleurisis*, alter. of L *pleuritis*, fr. Gk, fr. *pleura* side, rib + *-itis*; prob. akin to Gk *platys* flat, broad — more at PLACE] **1 :** inflammation of the pleura with or without effusion of an exudate into the pleural cavity — see DRY PLEURISY, WET PLEURISY **2** [influenced in meaning by L *plur-, plus* more — more at PLUS] *obs* **:** EXCESS, ABUNDANCE ⟨for goodness, growing to a ~, dies in his own too much —Shak.⟩

pleurisy root *n* **1 :** BUTTERFLY WEED **2 :** ASCLEPIAS 3a

pleu·rite \ˈplu̇ˌrīt\ *n* -S [*pleur-* + *-ite*] **1 :** any of various small sclerites in the pleural area of an arthropod; *sometimes* **:** PLEURON **2 :** the membranous part of the lateral abdominal wall of some insects

pleu·rit·ic \(ˈ)plüˈrid·ik, (ˈ)plu̇ˈ-, pləˈr-, -itˌ ēk\ *adj* [modif. (influenced by *pleurisy*) of MF *pleuretique* & ML *pleureticus*, fr. LL *pleuriticus*, fr. Gk *pleuritikos*, fr. *pleuritis* + *-ikos* -ic] **:** of, relating to, or suffering from pleurisy

pleu·ri·tis \plüˈrīd·ə̇s\ *n, pl* **pleurit·i·des** \-ˈrid·əˌdēz\ [L] **:** PLEURISY

pleuro- — see PLEUR-

pleu·ro·bra·chia \ˌplu̇rəˈbrākēə\ *n, cap* [NL, fr. *pleur-* + *brachia*] **:** a genus (the type of the family Pleurobrachiidae) of globose or ovoid relatively firm-bodied ctenophores

pleu·ro·branch \ˈplu̇rəˌbraŋk\ *also* **pleu·ro·bran·chia** \ˌ==ˈbraŋkēə\ *n, pl* **pleurobranchs** \-ks\ *also* **pleurobranchi·ae** \-kēˌē\ [*pleurobranch* ISV *pleur-* + *-branch*; *pleurobranchia* fr. NL, fr. *pleur-* + *-branchia*] **:** a gill of a crustacean arising from the side of the thorax — compare PODOBRANCH — **pleu·ro·bran·chi·al** \ˌ==ˈbraŋkēəl\ *or* **pleu·ro·bran·chi·ate** \-ēət, -ēˌāt\ *adj*

pleu·ro·bronchitis \ˌplu̇rō+\ *n* [NL, fr. *pleur-* + *bronchitis*] **:** combined pleurisy and bronchitis

pleu·ro·cap·sa \ˌplu̇rəˈkapsə\ *n, cap* [NL, fr. *pleur-* + L *capsa* chest, case — more at CASE] **:** a genus (the type of the family Pleurocapsaceae) of branching filamentous epiphytic blue-green algae reproducing by true endospores that is sometimes isolated in a separate order

pleu·ro·carp \ˈplu̇rəˌkärp\ *n* -S [ISV *pleur-* + *-carp*] **:** a pleurocarpous moss

pleu·ro·car·pi \ˌ==ˈkärˌpī\ *n pl, cap* [NL, fr. *pleur-* + *-carpi* (pl. of *-carpus*)] *in some classifications* **:** a group of mosses of the order Bryales comprising the pleurocarpous forms — compare ACROCARPI

pleu·ro·car·pous \ˌ==ˈkärpəs\ *also* **pleu·ro·car·pic** \-pik\ *adj* [*pleurocarpous* ISV *pleur-* + *-carpous*; *pleurocarpic* fr. *pleur-* + *-carpic*] *of a moss* **:** bearing the archegonia and antheridia on short lateral branches — compare ACROCARPOUS

pleu·ro·cen·tral \ˌplu̇rəˈsen·trəl\ *adj* [NL *pleurocentrum* + E *-al*] **:** of, relating to, or constituting a pleurocentrum

pleu·ro·centrum \"+\ *n* [NL, fr. *pleur-* + *centrum*] **:** one of a pair of dorsal and lateral elements of the centrum of the vertebra of a fish and of an extinct amphibian representing or formed from dorsal arcualia

pleu·roc·era \plu̇ˈräsərə\ *n, cap* [NL, fr. *pleur-* + *-cera*] **:** a large genus of American freshwater snails (suborder Taenioglossa) having the mantle edge entire and the copulatory organ not developed — compare THIARA — **pleu·roc·er·oid** \-səˌrȯid\ *adj*

pleu·ro·cerebral \ˌplu̇rō+\ *adj* [*pleur-* + *cerebral*] **:** connecting the pleural and cerebral ganglia of a mollusk

pleu·ro·coc·cus \ˌplu̇rəˈkäkəs\ *n* [NL, fr. *pleur-* + *-coccus*] *syn of* PROTOCOCCUS

pleu·ro·di·ra \ˌplu̇rəˈdīrə\ *n pl, cap* [NL, fr. *pleur-* + *-dira* (fr. Gk *derē, deirē* neck) — more at DER-] **:** an extensive group of freshwater turtles in which the neck cannot be retracted, but is bent laterally beneath the front of the carapace — compare MATAMATA — **pleu·ro·di·ran** \ˌ==ˈdīrən\ *adj or n* — **pleu·ro·dire** \ˈ==ˌdī(ə)r\ *adj or n*

pleu·ro·di·rous \ˌ==ˈdīrəs\ *adj* [NL *Pleurodira* + E *-ous*] **1** *of a turtle* **:** bending the neck laterally **2 :** of, relating to, or being a member of the group Pleurodira

pleu·ro·dis·cous \ˌplu̇rəˈdiskəs\ *adj* [*pleur-* + *disc-* + *-ous*] **:** laterally attached to a disk — used esp. of an appendage

¹pleu·ro·dont \ˈplu̇rəˌdänt\ *n* -S [*pleur-* + *-odont*] **:** a lizard having pleurodont teeth

²pleurodont \"\ *adj* [ISV *pleur-* + *-odont*] **1** *of teeth* **:** consolidated with the inner surface of the alveolar ridge without sockets — compare ACRODONT **2 :** having teeth that are pleurodont

pleu·ro·dyn·ia \ˌplu̇rəˈdinēə\ *n* -S [NL, fr. *pleur-* + *-odynia*] **1 :** a sharp pain in the side usu. located in the intercostal muscles and believed to arise from inflammation of fibrous tissue **2 :** EPIDEMIC PLEURODYNIA

pleu·ro·gen·ic \ˌplu̇rəˈjenik\ *or* **pleu·rog·e·nous** \(ˈ)plu̇ˈräjənəs\ *adj* [*pleur-* + *-genic* or *-genous*] **:** originating in the pleura

pleu·ro·loph·o·cer·cous \¦plu̇rə¦läfə¦sərkəs\ *adj* [*pleur-* + *loph-* + *cerc-* + *-ous*] **:** of, relating to, or being a small cercaria that has a long strong tail, a pair of fin folds, a protrusible oral sucker, and pigmented eye spots

pleu·ro·me·ia \plu̇'rōmēə\ *n, cap* [NL, fr. *pleur-* + ISV *-ome* + NL *-ia*] **:** a genus of Triassic fossil plants that is included in Lepidodendrales or isolated in a separate order, has characters in common with the genera *Sigillaria* and *Isoetes*, and is marked by an unbranched trunk arising from an enlarged lobulated root-bearing base terminating in a crown of long ligulate leaves, and bearing heterosporous cones at its apex

pleu·ron \'plu̇,rän\ *n, pl* **pleu·ra** \-ürə\ [NL, fr. Gk, rib, side; prob. akin to Gk *platys* flat, broad — more at PLACE] **1 :** a lateral part of a thoracic segment of an insect usu. consisting of an epimeron and an episternum **2 :** a lateral process of a somite of a crustacean between the tergum and sternum

¹pleu·ro·nec·tid \¦plu̇rə¦nektəd\ *adj* [NL *Pleuronectidae*] **:** of or relating to the Pleuronectidae

²pleuronectid \"\ *n* -s **:** a flatfish of the family Pleuronectidae

pleu·ro·nec·ti·dae \,==ˈnektə,dē\ *n pl, cap* [NL, fr. *Pleuronectes*, type genus (fr. *pleur-* + *-nectes*) + *-idae*] **:** a family of flatfishes (order Heterosomata) that have the eyes on the right side, the dorsal fin extending well forward on the head, and the mouth terminal — see FLOUNDER

pleu·ro·ne·ma \,plu̇rə'nēmə\ *n, cap* [NL, fr. *pleur-* + *-nema*] **:** a genus of holotrichous ciliates living in fresh and salt water and having an ovoid body with a folding undulating membrane — see HOLOTRICHA

pleu·ro·pedal \¦plu̇rə+, (ˈ)plu̇¦räpəd·ᵊl\ *adj* [*pleur-* + *pedal*] **:** connecting the pleural and pedal ganglia of a mollusk

pleu·ro·pericarditis \¦plu̇rō+\ *n* [NL, fr. *pleur-* + *pericarditis*] **:** inflammation of the pleura and the pericardium

pleu·ro·peritoneum *also* **pleu·ro·peritonaeum** \"+\ *n* [NL, fr. *pleur-* + *peritoneum, peritonaeum*] **:** the membrane lining the body cavity and covering the surface of the enclosed viscera of vertebrates that have no diaphragm — compare PERITONEUM

pleu·ro·pneumonia \"+\ *n* [NL, fr. *pleur-* + *pneumonia*] **1 :** inflammation of the pleura and lungs **:** pleurisy complicated by pneumonia; *specif* **:** a predominantly pulmonary form of shipping fever of horses **2 :** an acute febrile and often fatal inflammation of the lungs of cattle, sheep, and related animals resulting from infection by microorganisms of the family Mycoplasmataceae — see CONTAGIOUS BOVINE PLEUROPNEUMONIA

pleuropneumonia group *n* **:** a group of microorganisms coextensive with the family Mycoplasmataceae

pleuropneumonia-like organism \¦===¦=(=)=,=-\ *n* **:** a microorganism of the family Mycoplasmataceae

pleu·ro·po·di·al \¦plu̇rə¦pōdēəl\ *adj* [NL *pleuropodium* + E *-al*] **:** of or relating to a pleuropodium

pleu·ro·po·di·um \,==ˈpōdēəm\ *n* -s [NL, fr. *pleur-* + *-podium*] **1 :** either of a pair of glandular organs located on the first abdominal segment of an insect and believed to represent modified appendages **2 :** either of a pair of large fleshy lobes of the mantle of a sea hare

pleu·rop·ter·yg·i·an \plu̇¦räptə¦rijēən\ *adj* [NL *Pleuropterygii* + E *-an*] **:** of or relating to the subclass or order Pleuropterygii

pleu·rop·ter·yg·ii \=,==ˈrijē,ī\ *n pl, cap* [NL, fr. *pleur-* + *-pterygii*] **:** a subclass or order of small primitive Devonian elasmobranchs including the genus *Cladoselache* in which the paired fins are supported by unjointed parallel radial cartilages extending straight outward to the fin membrane and claspers are lacking

pleu·ro·sau·rus \,plu̇rə'sȯrəs\ *n, cap* [NL, fr. *pleur-* + *-saurus*] **:** a genus of slender serpentiform aquatic-limbed reptiles from the Upper Jurassic of Europe usu. regarded as eosuchians

pleu·ro·sig·ma \,plu̇rə'sigmə\ *n, cap* [NL, fr. *pleur-* + Gk *sigma*; fr. the shape of the diatoms] **:** a genus of diatoms of the family Naviculaceae

pleu·ros·te·al \plü'rästēəl\ *adj* [NL *pleurosteon* + E *-al*] **:** of or relating to a pleurosteon

pleu·ros·te·on \-ē,än\ *n* -s [NL, fr. *pleur-* + *-osteon*] **:** the anterolateral piece of the sternum of a young bird

pleu·ro·ster·ni·dae \,plu̇rə'stərnə,dē\ *n pl, cap* [NL, fr. *Pleurosternum*, type genus (fr. *pleur-* + *sternum*) + *-idae*] **:** a family of primitive fossil turtles that includes some of the earliest testudinates

pleu·ro·stig·ma \,plu̇rə'stigmə\ *n pl, cap* [NL, fr. *pleur-* + L *stigma*] *in some classifications* **:** a subclass of centipedes distinguished by paired tracheal spiracles in the sides of the segments — compare EPIMORPHA

pleu·ro·thot·o·nos \,plu̇rə'thätᵊnəs\ *n* -ES [NL, fr. Gk *pleurothen* from the side (fr. *pleura* side) + NL *tonus*] **:** a tonic spasm in which the body is curved laterally

pleu·rot·o·ma \plu̇'rädəmə\ [NL, fr. *pleur-* + *-toma*] *syn of* TURRIS

pleu·ro·to·mar·ia \,plu̇rəd·ə'ma(a)rēə\ *n, cap* [NL, fr. *pleur-* + *-toma* + *-aria*] **:** a large genus of nearly extinct two-gilled gastropods (suborder Rhipidoglossa) usu. having a trochiform nacreous shell with a broad sinus in the outer margin of the last whorl that extends back around the whorls as a raised band — **pleu·ro·to·mar·i·id** \¦===ˈma(a)rēəd\ *adj or n* — **pleu·ro·to·mar·i·oid** \-ē,ȯid\ *adj or n*

pleu·ro·trema·ta \,plu̇rə'tremәd·ə, -rēm-\ *n pl, cap* [NL, fr. *pleur-* + *-tremata*] **:** an order of Chondrichthyes comprising the sharks — compare HYPOTREMATA

pleu·ro·tus \plu̇'rōd·əs\ *n, cap* [NL, fr. *pleur-* + Gk *ōt-, ous* ear; fr. the shape of some members of the genus — more at EAR] **:** a genus of white-spored agarics having the pileus laterally sessile or with an eccentric stipe — see OLIVE TREE AGARIC, OYSTER MUSHROOM

pleu·ro·visceral \¦plu̇rō+\ *adj* [*pleur-* + *visceral*] **:** connecting the pleural and visceral ganglia of a mollusk

pleu·rum \'plu̇rəm\ *n, pl* **pleu·ra** \-rə\ [NL, by alter.] **:** PLEURON

pleus·ton \'plüstən\ *n* -s [ISV *pleus-* (fr. Gk *pleusis* sailing, fr. *plein* to sail) + *-ton* (as in *plankton*) — more at FLOW] **:** small but macroscopic floating organisms that form mats or layers on or near the surface of a body of water, that usu. include floatingalgae (as spirogyras), small floating spermatophytes (as the duckweeds), and associated small animals, and that usu. exclude anchored plants and larger floating spermatophytes (as the water hyacinth)—compare NEUSTON

pleus·ton·ic \(ˈ)plü¦stänik\ *adj* **:** of, relating to, or having the characteristics of pleuston

plew \'plü\ *n* -s [CanF *pelu*, adj., hairy, fr. F *pelu, poilu*, fr. *poil* hair, fr. OF *poil, peil*, fr. L *pilus* — more at ⁸PILE] *West & Canad* **:** a beaver skin

plex·i·form \'pleksə,fȯrm\ *adj* [NL *plexus* + E *-iform*] **:** of, relating to, or having the form or characteristics of a plexus ⟨the ~ layer of the retina⟩ ⟨~ synapse⟩ ⟨ships . . . pieced together on great ~ ways by giant cranes —*Life*⟩

Plex·i·glas \'pleksə,glas\ *trademark* — used for an acrylic resin or plastic

plex·im·e·ter \plek'simәd·ə(r)\ *n* [Gk *plēxis* stroke (fr. *plēssein* to strike) + E *-meter* — more at PLAINT] **:** a small hard flat plate (as of ivory) placed in contact with the body to receive the blow in mediate percussion — **plex·i·met·ric** \¦pleksə¦me·trik\ *adj* — **plex·im·e·try** \plek'simə·trē\ *n* -ES

plex·o·dont \'pleksə,dänt\ *adj* [L *plexus* network, twining, braid + E *-odont*] **:** of, relating to, or having molar teeth with complicated crown patterns and multiple roots

plex·or \'pleksə(r)\ *n* -s [NL, fr. Gk *plēxis* stroke + L *-or*] **:** a small hammer with a rubber head used in medical percussion — called also *plessor*

plexor

plex·ure \'plekshə(r)\ *n* -s [L *plexus* + E *-ure*] **1 :** the act or process of weaving together **2** [NL *plexus* + E *-ure*] **:** PLEXUS

plex·us \'pleksəs\ *n* -ES [NL, fr. L, network, twining, braid, fr. *plexus*, past part. of *plectere* to braid — more at PLY] **1 :** a network of anastomosing or interlacing blood vessels or nerves **2 :** an intricately interwoven combination of elements or parts in a cohering structure ⟨the ~ of the entire . . . system and its fifty departments —M.L.Bach⟩ ⟨in the ~ of financial affairs —Frank Norris⟩ ⟨a ~ of routes between western and eastern Europe —Derwent Whittlesey⟩

plf *or* **plff** *abbr* plaintiff

pli·a·bil·i·ty \,plīə'bilәd·ē, -lətē, -i\ *n* **:** the quality or state of being pliable **:** FLEXIBILITY, COMPLAISANCE ⟨the ~ of the metal⟩ ⟨with his usual ~, had yielded to their arguments —T.B. Macaulay⟩ ⟨their jocund ~, their readiness to lend themselves to improper uses —Norman Douglas⟩

pli·a·ble \'plīəbəl\ *adj* [ME *pliabylle*, fr. MF *pliable*, fr. *plier* to bend, ply + *-able* — more at PLY] **1 :** bending or creasing easily **:** FLEXIBLE, SUPPLE ⟨~ as a whip —Green Peyton⟩ ⟨~ . . . ash saplings —Ronald Duncan⟩ ⟨corduroy, as ~ as velvet —*advt*⟩ **2 :** yielding easily to the wishes or influence of others **:** COMPLAISANT, COMPLIANT ⟨a . . . self-controlled, ~ personality —Shepard Henkin⟩; *sometimes* **:** susceptible to corruption ⟨~ officials⟩ **3 :** adjustable to varying conditions **:** ADAPTABLE ⟨a culture more ~ and more ready to accept change —G.D.Taylor⟩ **syn** see PLASTIC

pli·a·ble·ness *n* -ES **:** PLIABILITY

pli·a·bly \-blē,-bli\ *adv* **:** in a pliable manner **:** DOCILELY

pli·an·cy \'plīənsē, -si\ *n* -ES [*pliant* + *-cy*] **:** the quality or state of being pliant **:** FLEXIBILITY, COMPLAISANCE ⟨for the good of his soul and the ~ of his mind —J.E.Gloag⟩ ⟨more quickness of observation and less ~ of temper than her sister —Jane Austen⟩

pli·ant \-nt\ *adj* [ME *pliaunt*, fr. MF *pliant*, pres. part. of *plier* to bend, ply] **1 :** yielding readily without breaking **:** bending or folding easily **:** FLEXIBLE, WORKABLE, LITHE ⟨modeled in the ~ material and then . . . hardened —Nathaniel Hawthorne⟩ ⟨a girl . . . with a slim, ~ figure —Inez Karma & Gilbert Millstein⟩ **2 :** easily influenced **:** YIELDING ⟨sees the . . . natives as a ~ mass —J.S.Redding⟩ ⟨had a ~ congressional majority —A.S.Link⟩ **3 :** SUITABLE, APT ⟨which I observing, took once a ~ hour —Shak.⟩ **4 :** lending itself to varied uses **:** ADAPTABLE ⟨a ~ style⟩ ⟨the clarinet . . . a very fluent and ~ instrument —Winthrop Sargeant⟩ **syn** see PLASTIC

pli·ant·ly *adv* **:** in a pliant manner

pliantness *n* -ES [ME *pliauntnes*, fr. *pliaunt* pliant + *-nes* -ness] **:** PLIANCY

pli·ca \'plīkə\ *n, pl* **pli·cae** \-ī,kē, -ī,sē\ [NL, fr. ML, fold, plait, musical ligature, fr. L *plicare* to fold — more at PLY] **1** *or* **plica po·lon·i·ca** \¦==pə'länəkə\ *pl* **plicae poloni·cae** \-nə,kē, -nə,sē\ [NL *plica polonica*, lit., Polish plait; fr. its frequent occurrence in Poland in the 17th century] **:** a state of the hair in which it becomes twisted, matted, and crusted, usu. as a result of neglect, filth, and infestation by vermin **2** [ML] **:** a fold or folded part: as **a :** a groove or fold of skin **b :** a longitudinal fold in a bryophyte leaf or a sporangium **3** [ML] **:** a ligature in medieval music

plica ala·ris \-ə'la(a)rəs\ *n, pl* **plicae ala·res** \-(,)rēz\ [NL, alar fold] **:** the fold of skin along the front of a bird's wing stretching from the shoulder to the wrist joint

plica cir·cu·la·ris \-,sərkyə'la(a)rəs\ *n, pl* **plicae circula·res** \-(,)rēz\ [NL, circular fold] **:** one of numerous permanent crescentic folds of mucous membrane found in the small intestine esp. in the lower part of the duodenum and the jejunum — called also *valvula connivens*

pli·cal \'plīkəl\ *adj* [*plica* + *-al*] **:** of, relating to, or having plicae

¹pli·cate \'plī,kāt\ *vt* -ED/-ING/-S [L *plicatus*, past part. of *plicare* to fold — more at PLY] **1 :** FOLD, PLEAT **2 :** to perform plication on

²pli·cate \", -kət\ *adj* [L *plicatus*, past part. of *plicare*] **1 :** folded lengthwise like a fan **:** PLAITED ⟨a ~ leaf⟩ — used esp. of vernation **2 :** FOLDED; *esp* **:** having the surface thrown up into or marked with parallel ridges (as the elytra of certain insects) — **pli·cate·ly** *adv* — **pli·cate·ness** *n* -ES

pli·cat·ed \-,kād·əd\ *adj* [fr. past part. of ¹*plicate*] **:** FOLDED, RIDGED ⟨the mouth is longitudinal with ~ lips, situated on the ventral surface —Laura Henry⟩

pli·ca·tile \'plīkəd·ᵊl, -,tīl, -,til\ *adj* [NL *plicatilis*, fr. *plicatus* (past part. of *plicare* to fold) + *-ilis* -ile] **:** capable of being folded; *specif* **:** folding lengthwise ⟨the ~ wings of certain insects⟩

pli·ca·tion \plī'kāshən\ *n* -s [ME *plicacioun*, prob. fr. (assumed) ML *plication-, plicatio*, fr. L *plicatus* (past part. of *plicare* to fold) + *-ion-, -io* -ion] **1 a :** the act or process of folding **b :** the quality or state of being folded **c :** FOLD **2 a :** the tightening of stretched or weakened bodily tissues or channels by folding the excess in tucks and suturing ⟨~ of the neck of the bladder⟩ **b :** the folding of one part on and the fastening of it to another (as areas of the bowel freed from adhesions and left without normal serosal covering) **3 a :** the action or process of the folding of geological strata **b :** a fold in a stratum

pli·cat·u·late \(ˈ)plī¦kachələt\ *adj* [²*plicate* + *-ule* + *-ate*] **:** minutely plicate

plica·ture \'plikə,chu̇(ə)r, -līk-, -,chər\ *n* -s [L *plicatura*, fr. *plicatus* (past part. of *plicare* to fold) + *-ura* -ure] **:** PLICATION

plié \(ˈ)plē¦ā\ *n* -s [F, fr. past part. of *plier* to bend, ply — more at PLY] **:** a bending of the knees by a ballet dancer with the back held straight

plied *adj* [fr. past part. of ¹*ply*] **:** composed of two or more strands ⟨~ yarn⟩ ⟨~ thread⟩ — compare PLY YARN

pli·ers *or* **ply·ers** \'plī(ə)rz, -īəz\ *n pl but sing or pl in constr* [¹*ply* + *-ers* (pl. of *-er*)] **:** a small pincers usu. with long roughened jaws for holding small objects or for bending and cutting wire — often used with *pair* ⟨a pair of ~s⟩

plies *pres 3d sing of* PLY, *pl of* PLY

¹plight \'plīt, *usu* -īd·+V\ *vt* -ED/-ING/-S [ME *plighten*, fr. OE *plihtan* to endanger, fr. *pliht* risk, danger; akin to OE *plēon* to expose to danger, MD *plien, plegen* to be responsible for, OHG *pflegan* to take care of] **:** to put or give in pledge **:** ENGAGE ⟨~ faith⟩ ⟨~ troth⟩ ⟨a ~*ed* bride⟩ ⟨he was half engaged . . . not absolutely ~*ed* —George Meredith⟩ **syn** see PROMISE

²plight \"\ *n* -s **:** a solemnly given pledge **:** ENGAGEMENT ⟨women . . . not famous for keeping their ~ —Sir Walter Scott⟩

³plight \"\ *n* -s [ME *plit*, fr. AF, fr. (assumed) VL *plictus* fold — more at PLAIT] **1 :** CONDITION, STATE; *esp* **:** bad state or condition **:** PREDICAMENT ⟨the ~ of the unemployed⟩ ⟨ruined landowners who do not dare to face their desperate ~ —Marc Slonim⟩ ⟨the ~ of the sensitive artist in a . . . standardized society —J.W.Aldridge⟩ **2 :** physical condition ⟨the horses are in fine ~⟩ ⟨lived . . . many years after in very good ~ —Thomas Gray⟩ **3** *archaic* **:** FOLD, PLAIT **4** *archaic* **:** ATTIRE, DRESS ⟨sit in silver ~ —John Keats⟩ **syn** see PREDICAMENT

⁴plight *vt* -ED/-ING/-S [ME *pliten*, fr. *plit*, n.] *obs* **:** PLAIT, FOLD

plim \"\ *vb* **plimmed; plimmed; plimming; plims** [perh. alter. of ²*plum*] *vi, dial chiefly Eng* **:** to increase in size **:** fill out **:** SWELL ⟨her bosom *plimmed* and fell —Thomas Hardy⟩ ~ *vt, dial chiefly Eng* **:** INFLATE, SWELL ⟨*plimming* her chest towards them —Joyce Cary⟩

plim·sol *also* **plim·sole** \'plim(p)səl, -m,sōl, -m,säl\ *or* **plim·sole** \-m(p)səl, -m,sōl\ *n* -s [prob. so called fr. a supposed resemblance between the upper edge of the mudguard and the Plimsoll mark on the side of a ship] *Brit* **:** a light shoe having a rubber sole and mudguard and a canvas top

plimsoll mark *also* **plimsoll line** *n, usu cap P* [after Samuel *Plimsoll* †1898 Eng. leader of shipping reform] **1 :** a circle intersected by a horizontal line that is marked amidships on the sides of a seagoing cargo ship to represent the summer load line and is accompanied by letters indicating the authority under which the ship is registered **:** the minimum summer freeboard mark — compare DRAFT MARK **2 a :** a set of load-line markings on a seagoing cargo ship including the Plimsoll mark and the graduated load lines beside it **b :** LOAD LINE 2

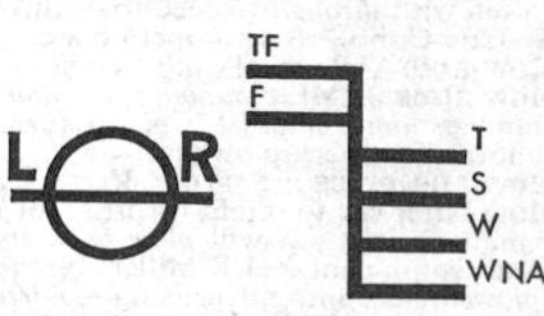

Plimsoll mark 2a: tropical freshwater mark, *TF;* freshwater mark, *F;* tropical load line, *T;* summer load line, *S;* winter load line, *W;* winter load line, North Atlantic, *WNA;* Lloyd's register of shipping, *LR*

¹plink \'pliŋk\ *vb* -ED/-ING/-S [imit.] *vi* **1 :** to make a tinkling sound **2 :** to shoot at random targets ⟨you'll probably do plenty of ~*ing* and informal target shooting —*Amer. Rifleman*⟩ ⟨people . . . who ~ with anything from a dime store bow and arrow to handmade equipment —*Sports Illustrated*⟩ ~ *vt* **1 :** to cause to make a tinkling sound ⟨~*ed* the little bell before him —Walter Goodman⟩ **2 :** to shoot at esp. in a casual manner ⟨like boys . . . ~*ing* cans from a riverbank —R.O.Bowen⟩

²plink \"\ *n* -s **:** a tinkling sound ⟨cricket chirp and ~ of samisens —Frederick Ebright⟩

plink·er \-kə(r)\ *n* -s **:** one who engages in plinking

plinth \'plin(t)th\ *n, pl* **plinths** \-n(t)s, -n(t)ths\ [L *plinthus*, fr. Gk *plinthos* plinth, brick; perh. akin to OE *flint* — more at FLINT] **1 a** (1) **:** a square vertically faced member immediately below the circular base of a column in classical architecture — see BASE illustration (2) **:** the lowest member of a pedestal **b :** the lowest member of a base **:** SUBBASE **c :** a block upon which the moldings of an architrave or trim are stopped at the bottom **2 a :** a square block serving as a base (as for a statue or vase) **b :** the squared base of something (as a vase or piece of furniture) **3 a** *or* **plinth course :** a course of stones forming a continuous foundation or base course (as of a rubble wall) **b :** a baseboard without a molded edge **4** *also* **plint** \-nt\ -s **:** a padded couch or low table used for massage or corrective physical exercises

plin·thi·form \'plin(t)thə,fȯrm\ *adj* [*plinth* + *-iform*] **:** shaped like a plinth

plio- — see PLEIO-

pli·o·cene \'plīə,sēn\ *adj, usu cap* [*pleio-* + *-cene*] **:** of or relating to a subdivision of the Tertiary — see GEOLOGIC TIME table

Plio·film \'plīə+,-\ *trademark* — used for a glossy moisture-proof membrane made of rubber hydrochloride and used chiefly for making raincoats, as packaging material, and as fruit wrapping

plio·hip·pus \,plīō'hipəs\ *n, cap* [NL, fr. *pleio-* + *-hippus*] **:** a genus of extinct one-toed horses from the No. American Pliocene having strongly hypsodont molar teeth

plio·pithe·cus \,plīōpə'thēkəs, -ō'pithəkəs\ *n, cap* [NL, fr. *pleio-* + *-pithecus*] **:** a genus of anthropoids found in the Upper Miocene and Lower Pliocene strata of Europe and possibly Asia having a very similar dentition to and commonly held to be ancestral to the gibbons

plio·saur \'plīə,sȯ(ə)r\ *n* -s [NL *Pliosaurus*] **:** a reptile of the genus *Pliosaurus* or the family Pliosauridae

plio·sau·ri·an \¦==¦sȯrēən\ *adj* [NL *Pliosaurus* + E *-an*] **:** of or relating to *Pliosaurus*

plio·sau·rus \,==ˈsȯrəs\ *n, cap* [NL, fr. *pleio-* + *-saurus*] **:** a genus (usu. the type of the family Pliosauridae) of extinct marine reptiles that is related to *Plesiosaurus* but distinguished by a much shorter neck and larger head

plio·thermic \¦plīō+\ *adj* [*pleio-* + *thermic*] **:** of or relating to a period in geological history of more than average warmth of climate

pli·o·tron \'plīə·,trän\ *n* -s [fr. *Pliotron*, a trademark] **:** a high vacuum tube containing a cathode, anode, and control grid that is used to control the flow of current in a single direction

plique–a–jour \¦plē(,)kä¦zhu̇(ə)r\ *n* -s [F] **:** a style of enameling in which more or less transparent enamels are fused into a pierced framework so that the light passes through the enamels and enhances their color producing an effect similar to that of stained glass

plis·kie *or* **plis·ky** \'pliski\ *n, pl* **pliskies** [origin unknown] *chiefly Scot* **:** PRACTICAL JOKE, TRICK

plis·sé *or* **plis·se** \(ˈ)plē¦sā, plə'sā\ *n* -s [F *plissé*, fr. *plissé*, past part. of *plisser* to pleat, fr. MF, fr. *pli* pleat, fold — more at PLY] **1 :** a textile finish that consists of forming permanently puckered designs by treating the cloth with a caustic soda solution which shrinks the treated sections and so causes the untreated parts to crinkle **2 :** a fabric usu. of cotton, rayon, or nylon that has been given a plissé finish

plmb *or* **plmg** *abbr* plumbing

pln *abbr* plain

ploat \'plōt\ *vt* -ED/-ING/-S [D *ploten* to pluck out (wool)] *chiefly Scot* **1 :** to pluck feathers from (a bird) ⟨~ your geese⟩ **2 :** CHEAT, FLEECE

plo·ce \'plō(,)sē\ *n* -s [LL, fr. Gk *plokē* complication, twisting, fr. *plekein* to plait — more at PLY] **:** emphatic repetition of a word with particular reference to its special significance (as in "a wife who was a wife indeed")

plo·ce·idae \plō'sēə,dē\ *n pl, cap* [NL, fr. *Ploceus*, type genus + *-idae*] **:** a large family of Old World passerine birds that are predominantly African, somewhat resemble finches, and comprise the weaverbirds — see PLOCEUS

plo·ce·iform \plō'sēə,fȯrm\ *adj* [NL *Ploceus* + E *-iform*] **:** resembling a weaverbird

plo·ceus \'plōsēəs, -ō,süs\ *n, cap* [NL, fr. Gk *plokeus* braider, plaiter, fr. *plekein* to plait] **:** a genus (the type of the family Ploceidae) comprising the baya and related Asiatic birds

¹plod \'pläd\ *vb* **plodded; plodded; plodding; plods** [imit.] *vi* **1 :** to walk heavily **:** move or travel slowly but steadily **:** TRUDGE ⟨cows . . . *plodding* past a gate to be milked —Andrew Buchanan⟩ ⟨wayfarers . . . ~ on for miles without speech —Thomas Hardy⟩ ⟨a caravan ~s across the sweeping sands —*Univ. of Ariz. Record*⟩ **2 :** to work laboriously, steadily, and monotonously **:** DRUDGE ⟨*plodded* straight ahead, doing over and over some appointed task —Sherwood Anderson⟩ ~ *vt* **1** *obs* **:** PLOT **2 :** to tread (as a path, a course) slowly or heavily ⟨the plowman homeward ~s his weary way —Thomas Gray⟩ ⟨*plodded* his way back —Herman Wouk⟩ **3 :** to pass (milled soap) through a plodder

²plod \"\ *n* -s **1 :** a plodding walk ⟨the fathers set off . . . by the usual way, a tedious ~ —G.W.Murray⟩ **2 :** the sound of a heavy tread (as that of a horse) **:** TRAMP ⟨the tired ~ of his step —Donn Byrne⟩

plod·der \-ädə(r)\ *n* -s **1 :** one that plods; *esp* **:** a person who proceeds or works slowly, steadily, and unimaginatively ⟨thick-witted, insensitive ~s . . . unable to follow the transcendental speculations of their opponents —C.W.Shumaker⟩ ⟨the ~s who do exactly what they're told —Ethelbert Robinson⟩ **2 :** a machine for making ribbons or chips of milled soap into cakes by means of a spiral screw that forces the soap into a compression chamber and through a die

plodding *adj* **1 :** marked by slowness and heaviness of movement ⟨a . . . ~ tale —Hollis Alpert⟩ ⟨~ in his speech —Richard Llewellyn⟩ **2 :** DULL, PEDESTRIAN ⟨the naturalistic writer's ~ accumulation of detail —C.J.Rolo⟩ — **plod·ding·ly** *adv* — **plod·ding·ness** *n* -ES

plodge \'pläj\ *vi* [prob. blend of ¹*plod* and *trudge*] *dial* **:** to wade or walk heavily

plo·dia \'plōdēə\ *n, cap* [NL] **:** a genus of phycitid moths that includes the Indian meal moth — compare PHYCITIDAE

ploi·ar·ia \plȯi'(y)a(a)rēə, plō'ya-\ *n, cap* [NL, prob. modif. of Gk *ploiarion* boat, dim. of *ploion* ship; akin to Gk *plein* to sail, float — more at FLOW] **:** the type genus of the family Ploiariidae comprising fragile-bodied bugs with elongated cylindrical heads, prominent eyes, raptorial forelimbs, and the remaining limbs greatly elongated and filamentous

¹ploi·ar·i·id \(ˈ)plȯi¦(y)a(a)rēəd, plō'ya-\ *adj* [NL *Ploiariidae*] **:** of or relating to the Ploiariidae

²ploiariid \"\ *n* -s [NL *Ploiariidae*] **:** a bug of the family Ploiariidae

ploi·a·ri·idae \,plȯi(y)ə'rīə,dē, ,plōyə-\ *n pl, cap* [NL, fr. *Ploiaria*, type genus + *-idae*] **:** a small cosmopolitan family of slender predaceous bugs related to the assassin bugs

-ploid \,plȯid\ *adj comb form* [ISV, fr. ²*diploid* & ¹*haploid*] **:** having or being a chromosome number that bears (such) a relationship to or is (so many) times the basic chromosome number characteristic of a given plant or animal group ⟨hetero*ploid*⟩ ⟨hexa*ploid*⟩ ⟨hepta*ploid*⟩ ⟨crossing 12-, 9-, and 8-*ploid* western blackberries —*Biol. Abstracts*⟩

ploi·dy \'plȯidē, -di\ *n* -ES [fr. such words as *diploidy, hexaploidy*] **:** degree of replication of chromosomes or genomes

ploi·ma \'plȯimə, -lōəmə\ *n pl, cap* [NL, fr. Gk *plōimos* fit for sailing; akin to Gk *plein* to sail, float] **:** a suborder of Monogononta or other large group of rotifers that are propelled by the ciliated disk only and that usu. have a forked and more or less retractile tail

1ploi·mate \-mət, -,māt\ *adj* [NL *Ploima* + E *-ate*] **:** of or relating to the Ploima

2ploimate \"\ *n* -s **:** a rotifer of the group Ploima

ploi·ter \'plȯitər\ *var of* PLOUTER

plom·bage \,pləm'bäzh\ *n* -s [F, plombage, action of filling a tooth, fr. *plomber* to fill a tooth, apply lead to, fr. OF *plomer* to apply lead to, fr. *plon* lead, fr. L *plumbum*) + *-age* — more at PLUMB] **:** sustained compression of the sides of a pulmonary cavity against each other to effect closure by pressure exerted by packing (as of paraffin or plastic sponge)

1plonk *var of* PLUNK

2plonk \'pläŋk\ *n* -s [perh. modif. of F *blanc* white (in *vin blanc* white wine) — more at BLANK] *Austral* **:** cheap or inferior wine

3plonk \"\ *n* -s [origin unknown] *slang* **:** a socially awkward, stodgy, or pompous person **:** BORE

ploo \'plü\ *dial Brit var of* PLOW

plook *var of* PLOUK

1plop \'pläp\ *vb* **plopped; plopped; plopping; plops** [imit.] *vi* **1 :** to fall, drop, or move suddenly with a sound like that of something dropping into water ⟨the first large drops . . . *plopping* loudly on the tar-paper roofs —Donald Windham⟩ ⟨terrapins sliding down the mud banks and *plopping* into the water —Gerald Durrell⟩ ⟨began to shake the branches . . . oranges *plopped* down —Evelyn Eaton⟩ **2 :** to allow the body to drop heavily ⟨she *plopped* into a chair⟩ ⟨weary troops . . . *plopped* down beside their infantry kits —W.R. Moore⟩ **~** *vt* **:** to put down, drop, or throw with a plop ⟨*plopped* the tray on the coffee table —Nancy Rutledge⟩ ⟨picked up the silvery wriggling fish . . . and *plopped* them into burlap bags —J.M.Brinnin⟩

2plop \"\ *n* -s **:** the sound made in plopping **:** a dull faintly explosive sound ⟨the soft ~ of a fish jumping —Shirley A. Grau⟩ ⟨the ~ of a toad on the stones —Josephine Johnson⟩ ⟨the ~ of the heavy ball against the leather of the mitt —Donald Windham⟩ — often used interjectionally

3plop \"\ *adv* **:** with a plop **:** PLUMP ⟨emptied its contents . . . ~, from a height on to my solar plexus —Aldous Huxley⟩ ⟨~ came the ball down to the corner of the green —Harry Vardon⟩

plosh \'pläsh\ *n* -ES [by alter.] **:** 3PLASH

plo·sion \'plōzhən\ *n* -s [fr. *explosion, implosion*] **:** EXPLOSION 2d

1plo·sive \'plōs|iv, |ēv *also* -ōz| *or* |əv\ *n* -s [fr. *2explosive, 2implosive*] **:** 2EXPLOSIVE 2

2plosive \"\ *adj* **:** of or relating to a plosive

1plot \'plät, *usu* -äd+V\ *n* -s [ME *plot, plotte* patch, spot, plot (of ground), fr. OE *plot* plot (of ground)] **1 a :** a small area of ground or of something on the ground; *esp* **:** such an area devoted to a particular purpose ⟨a little ~ of ground⟩ ⟨a garden ~⟩ ⟨vegetable ~*s*⟩ ⟨a setting of well-kept lawns and flower ~*s*⟩ **b :** a small portion of land in a cemetery usu. containing two or more graves ⟨buried in the family ~⟩ **c :** an area of land used for scientific study or experimentation **:** QUADRAT 2 ⟨an experimental ~⟩ ⟨stems were taken at random in . . . different parts of the ~*s* —*Jour. of Economic Entomology*⟩ ⟨proper selection of the sample or census ~ —L.W.Wing⟩ **d** (1) **:** a measured parcel of land ⟨divided the tract into ~*s*⟩ ⟨houses . . . erected on ~*s* ranging from a few to as many as 40 acres —*Amer. Guide Series: Fla.*⟩ (2) **:** an assemblage of adjacent parcels forming a single land unit ⟨concentrate the small . . . holdings into bigger ~*s* —H.R. Lieberman⟩ **2** *archaic* **:** a spot or patch (as on the skin) differing from the surrounding surface **3 :** a ground plan (as of a building or area) **:** PLAT **4 a :** the plan or pattern of events or the main story of a literary work (as a novel, play, short story, or poem) comprising the gradual unfolding of a causally connected series of motivated incidents **:** narrative structure ⟨complications of the ~⟩ ⟨a detective story with an ingenious ~⟩ ⟨a novel almost without ~⟩ **b** *obs* **:** 8PLAT 3 **5** [prob. back-formation fr. 1*complot*] **:** a secret plan contrived by one or more persons for accomplishing a usu. evil or unlawful end **:** CONSPIRACY, INTRIGUE ⟨a ~ to assassinate the king⟩ ⟨a ~ against the government⟩ **6 a :** a chart or map showing the movements or progress of a craft (as a ship, submarine, airplane) ⟨a ~ of the ship's course . . . should also be kept —*Manual of Seamanship*⟩ **b :** a location on a chart or map marked by the intersection of bearings or celestial lines of position **c :** a tactical, navigational, or control center aboard ship ⟨the gunnery liaison officer . . . feeding information to the fire control officer in ~ —*All Hands*⟩ **7 :** 1GRAPH 1

syn CONSPIRACY, CABAL, INTRIGUE, MACHINATION: PLOT suggests careful foresight in planning and a continuity or complexity of positive action by one or a number of persons of any sort ⟨the great Jesuit *plot* for the destruction of Protestant England and the invasion and conquest of the island by vast armies —S.M.Crothers⟩ CONSPIRACY differs from *plot* mainly in that it may indicate the persons involved ⟨Guy Fawkes was known as a member of the *conspiracy*⟩ It may suggest secrecy and unity within the band and carry a melodramatic effect. It may also suggest less positive action ⟨a *conspiracy* of silence⟩ or occas. philanthropic or benevolent aims. CABAL almost always endows the persons involved with a degree of eminence and is used mainly in matters political ⟨that moment at 1:20 in the morning of June, 1920, when a Senatorial *cabal*, the most venal since the days of President Grant, nominated Warren G. Harding for the Presidency —Irving Stone⟩ INTRIGUE suggests secret underhand maneuvering in an atmosphere of duplicity ⟨*intrigues* framed against the royal power and directed toward the disruption of the state —Hilaire Belloc⟩ ⟨the *intrigue* of special privilege in and upon the conquered countries —W.A.White⟩ ⟨the *intrigue* for place and the control of influence —J.H.Plumb⟩ MACHINATION suggests crafty maneuver, as though in an intrigue or plot ⟨the devilish *machinations* of an enchanter masquerading as a pious hermit —J.L.Lowes⟩ ⟨prevented authors and publishers from defeating the *machinations* of infringers —Margaret Nicholson⟩ **syn** see in addition PLAN

2plot \"\ *vb* **plotted; plotted; plotting; plots** *vt* **1 a :** to make a plot, map, or plan of **:** draw to scale **:** DELINEATE ⟨*plotting* this underground river —Martin Gardner⟩ **b :** to mark or note (as a site, position, or course) on or as if on a map or chart ⟨had *plotted* the reef on his chart⟩ ⟨~ . . . the exact position of the ship —Peter Heaton⟩ ⟨~ a course to that goal —*Time*⟩ ⟨~ the course of an airplane in flight from radar information⟩ **2 :** to measure out (land) in plots — usu. used with *out* ⟨new residential districts are all *plotted* out⟩ **3 a :** to locate and mark (a point) by means of coordinates **b :** to make (a curve) by marking out a number of plotted points ⟨*plotting* the thermal conductivity versus mean temperature —*Industrial Mineral Wool Products*⟩ **c :** to represent graphically (a mathematical equation) by means of a curve so constructed **4 :** to plan or contrive (as something evil or unlawful) esp. secretly ⟨*plotted* the murder of her husband⟩ **5 :** to invent or devise the plot of (a literary work) ⟨*plotted* his play carefully⟩ **~** *vi* **1 :** to scheme secretly and underhandedly **:** CONSPIRE ⟨~ for the coup d'etat —Geoffrey Bruun⟩ **2 :** to develop or outline a literary plot ⟨~*s* better than most novelists⟩ **syn** see 1PLAN

3plot \'plät\ *also* **plote** \-lōt\ *vt* **plotted; plotted; plotting; plots** *also* **plotes** [origin unknown] *chiefly Scot* **:** to subject to intense heat **:** SCALD, SCORCH

plo·tin·i·an \plō'tinēən\ *adj, usu cap* [*Plotinus* †A.D.270 Rom. Neoplatonic philosopher + E *-an*] **:** of or relating to Plotinus or Plotinism

plo·ti·nism \plō'tī,nizəm, 'plōt°n,i-\ *n* -s *usu cap* [*Plotinus* + E *-ism*] **:** the doctrines of the philosopher Plotinus — compare NEOPLATONISM

plo·ti·nist \-tīnəst, -t°nə-\ *n* -s *usu cap* [*Plotinus* + E *-ist*] **:** a follower of Plotinus

plot·less \'plätləs\ *adj* **:** lacking a plot ⟨a loosely constructed comparatively ~ novel⟩

plot·less·ness *n* -ES **:** the quality or state of being plotless

1plo·to·sid \plə'tōsəd\ *adj* [NL *Plotosidae*] **:** of or relating to the Plotosidae

2plotosid \"\ *n* -s [NL *Plotosidae*] **:** a catfish of the family Plotosidae

plo·to·si·dae \-sə,dē\ *n pl, cap* [NL, fr. *Plotosus*, type genus + *-idae*] **:** a family of chiefly tropical marine catfishes having an elongate eellike scaleless body and an arborescent movable organ of unknown function behind the vent

plo·to·sus \-səs\ *n, cap* [NL, prob fr. Gk *plōtos* floating, swimming + L *-osus* -ose; akin to Gk *plein* to sail, float — more at FLOW] **:** a genus (the type of the family Plotosidae) of marine catfishes

plots *pl of* PLOT, *pres 3d sing of* PLOT

plot's elm \'pläts-\ *or* **plot elm** *n* [prob. fr. the name *Plot*] **:** a European elm (*Ulmus plotii*) having an arching leader, pendulous branches, and subcordate bluntly serrate leaves

plot·tage \'pläd·ij\ *n* -s [1*plot* + *-age*] **1 :** the increment of value resulting from the combination of small tracts of land or lots into larger ones **2 :** the area included in a plot of land

plotted *past of* PLOT

1plot·ter \'pläd·ə(r), -ätə-\ *n* -s **:** one that plots: as **a :** a person who marks on a map or display board the positions of airplanes in flight **b :** a device for plotting; *specif* **:** a pencil holder in an instrument for plotting coordinates **c :** SCHEMER, CONSPIRATOR **d :** a contriver of a literary plot

2plot·ter \"\ *dial Eng var of* PLOUTER

plott hound \'plät-\ *n, usu cap P* [prob. after Jonathan *Plott* *fl* 1750 Am. dog breeder] **:** a large powerful usu. chiefly black hound of American origin used esp. in bear and boar hunting and believed to have resulted from crosses between German boarhounds, foxhounds, bloodhounds, and possibly other hound strains

plotting *pres part of* PLOT

plotting board *n* **:** a device for showing graphically the position of a stationary target or the periodic positions of a moving target with reference to the battery or batteries in artillery firing

plot·ty \'pläd·ē\ *adj* [1*plot* + *-y*] **:** of or relating to plot **:** marked by intricacy of plot or intrigue ⟨as long as a modern novel and ever so much more ~ —*Harper's*⟩

plo·tus \'plōd·əs\ [NL, fr. Gk *plōtos* floating, swimming] *syn of* ANHINGA

plouk \'plük\ *n* -s [ME *plowke*] *chiefly Scot* **:** a spot or blemish on the skin; *esp* **:** one caused by an infection **:** PIMPLE — **plouky** \-ki\ *adj*

plounce \'plaůn(t)s\ *vb* -ED/-ING/-S [prob. imit.] *vt, chiefly dial* **:** to plunge (a person) into water usu. as a punishment for being a scold **:** DUCK **~** *vi, dial* **:** to splash about **:** FLOUNDER

1plout \'plaůt\ *n* -s [prob. imit.] *chiefly Scot* **:** a sudden splash or sudden heavy rainfall

2plout \"\ *vi* -ED/-ING/-S *chiefly Scot* **:** to splash or fall with a splash

plou·ter \'plaůtər\ *vi* -ED/-ING/-S [prob. imit.] **1** *Scot* **:** to move about with splashing **:** WADE **2** *Scot* **:** POTTER

plov·div \'plȧv,dif, -lȯv-\ *adj, usu cap* [fr. *Plovdiv*, city in southern Bulgaria] **:** of or from the city of Plovdiv, Bulgaria **:** of the kind or style prevalent in Plovdiv

plover \'pləvə(r), -lōv-\ *n, pl* **plover** *or* **plovers** [ME, fr. MF *plover, plovier*, fr. (assumed) VL *pluviarius*, fr. L *pluvia* rain + *-arius* -ary — more at PLUVIAL] **1 :** any of numerous shore-inhabiting birds of the family Charadriidae that differ from the sandpipers in having a short, hard-tipped bill and usu. a stouter, more compact build, frequent plains, grassy uplands, and beaches, are mostly gregarious and migratory, and include several well-known small birds (as the ring plovers) and some larger forms (as black-bellied plover, golden plover, dotterel, lapwing) important as game birds **2 :** any of various birds related to the plover: as **a :** TURNSTONE **b :** any of various sandpipers; *esp* **:** UPLAND PLOVER — compare CRAB PLOVER, WRYBILL **3 :** BROCCOLI BROWN

plover page *or* **plover's page** *n, Scot* **:** a small sandpiper sometimes accompanying the larger plovers; *esp* **:** RED-BACKED SANDPIPER

plover quail *n* **:** PLAIN WANDERER

plovery \-ərē\ *adj* **:** abounding in plovers ⟨this ~ headland —W.B.Yeats⟩

1plow *or* **plough** \'plaů\ *n* -s [ME, plow, plowland, fr. OE *plōh* plowland; akin to MD *ploech* plow, OHG *pfluog*] **1 a** *archaic* **:** PLOWLAND 1 **b** *chiefly Brit* **:** plowed land **:** arable country ⟨eight acres of ~ —*Farmers Weekly (London)*⟩ ⟨was on ~ with the clay clinging to my shoes —Ralph Hammond Innes⟩ ⟨trotting across the ~ —Anthony Powell⟩ **2 :** an implement that is used to cut, lift, turn over, and partly pulverize the soil esp. in the preparation of a seedbed and that consists typically of a share for cutting, a moldboard for lifting and turning the soil usu. over a landside, a frog to which share, moldboard, and landside are attached, and a beam by which the implement is drawn — see DISC PLOW **3 :** any of various devices operating like a plow: as **a :** SNOWPLOW **b :** a ballast spreader **c :** an implement for unloading cars of earth or ballast **d :** a machine mounted on the side of a car body for ditching or grading at the side of the roadway **e :** a carpenter's plane for cutting a groove or rabbet **f :** a device for trimming the edges of books that consists of a knife resembling a chisel which is mounted on wood and slides between the runners of a lying press **g :** a device for making contact with the live wire or rail in a conduit **4** *plough, chiefly Brit* **:** 2FLUNK

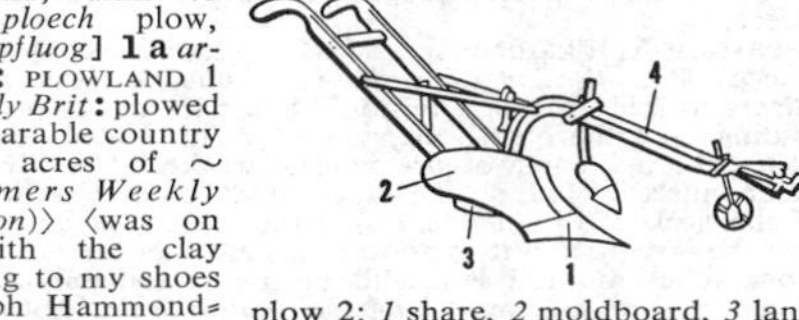

plow 2: *1* share, *2* moldboard, *3* landside, *4* beam

2plow *or* **plough** \"\ *vb* -ED/-ING/-S [ME *plowen, ploughen*, fr. *plow, plough*, n.] *vt* **1 a :** to turn up, break up, or trench (the soil) with a plow **:** till with or as with a plow ⟨~ a field⟩ **b :** to make (as a furrow) with a plow ⟨a brown furrow had been ~*ed* —*Atlantic*⟩ **2 a :** to cut into, tear up, or make furrows or ridges in (a surface) with or as if with a plow ⟨gophers that ~ and loosen the prairie soil —E.W.Teale⟩ ⟨~ the roads after a snowstorm⟩ — often used with *up* ⟨tanks . . . had ~*ed up* muddy roads —*N.Y.Times*⟩ **b :** to furrow (the face) deeply with wrinkles ⟨face . . . ~*ed* with labor and sorrow —Thomas Carlyle⟩ **c** *chiefly Midland* **:** CULTIVATE — used esp. of corn ⟨~*ing* corn all day . . . with his team and cultivator —Burl Ives⟩ **d :** IMPREGNATE 1 ⟨~ a woman⟩ ⟨he ~*ed* her, and she cropp'd —Shak.⟩ **3 :** to cleave the surface of or move through (water) ⟨ships ~*ing* the seven seas⟩ **4 :** to cut a groove or rabbet in (a piece of wood) with a carpenter's plow ⟨risers are cut to size but not ~*ed* —*Building, Estimating & Contracting*⟩ **5 :** to trim (as a book or paper) with a plow **6 :** to turn over (grain) so as to expose fresh surfaces to the air and equalize temperature in malting **7** *plough, chiefly Brit* **:** 1FLUNK **~** *vi* **1 a :** to use a plow **:** till with a plow ⟨the farmer ~*ed* all day⟩ **b :** to bear or admit of plowing ⟨the land ~*s* well now —Adrian Bell⟩ **2 a :** to move in a way resembling that of a plow cutting into or going through the soil ⟨the ship ~*ed* southward⟩ — used often with *through, along, into* ⟨we ~*ed* through the snow⟩ ⟨he ~*ed* through the crowds —S.H.Holbrook⟩ ⟨~*s* along at a ten-knot rate —William Beebe⟩ ⟨a truck ~*ed* into her parked car —*N.Y.Times*⟩ **b :** to proceed steadily and laboriously **:** PLOD ⟨kept ~*ing* ahead in spite of the difficulties⟩ — used often with *through* ⟨forced to ~ through a summer reading list —Jane Cobb⟩ **3 :** to operate a carpenter's plow

plow·able \'plaůəbəl\ *adj* **:** capable of being plowed

plow alms *n* [ME *ploualmes*, fr. *plou, plow, plough* plow, plowland + *almes* alms] **:** a penny formerly paid annually to the church for every plowland

plow and press *n* **:** 1PLOW 3f

plow back *vt* **:** to retain (profits) for reinvestment in a business ⟨management . . . will *plow back* its earnings into new plant and equipment —J.R.Miller⟩ ⟨requires that 10 percent be *plowed back* into advertising —*Fortune*⟩

plow beam *n* [ME *plowebeme*, fr. *plowe, plow, plough* plow + *beme, beem* beam] **:** 1BEAM 1d

plowboy *or* **ploughboy** \'=,=\ *n* **:** a boy who guides a horse in plowing **:** a country youth

plow drill *n* **:** a small usu. press drill that is attached behind a plow — compare 7DRILL 2, 2LISTER 2

plow·er *or* **plough·er** \'plaů(ə)r, -aůə\ *n* -s **:** one that plows **:** PLOWMAN

plowgang *or* **ploughgang** \'=,=\ *n* [1*plow* + *gang*, n.] **:** any of various old Scottish units of land area (as a unit equivalent to a bovate)

plowgate *or* **ploughgate** \'=,=\ *n* [1*plow* + *gate* (way)] **:** a unit of land area once used in Scotland and northern England prob. orig. equal to a plowland or carucate

plow–hand \'=,=\ *n* **:** a hired worker who operates a plow

plowhead *or* **ploughhead** \'=,=\ *n* [ME *ploghe hede*, fr. *ploghe, plow, plough* plow + *hede, heved, hed* head] **:** the clevis of a plow

plow·land *or* **plough·land** \'=,land\ *n* [ME *plowlond*, fr. *plow, plough* plow + *land, lond* land] **1 :** any of various old English units of land area **:** CARUCATE ⟨division of the arable land into units called ~*s*, each . . . composed of eight "oxgangs" —F.M. Stenton⟩ **2 a :** arable land ⟨a third of the ~ —*World Report*⟩ **b :** a plot of such land ⟨a green hillock at the edge of a ~ —John Drinkwater⟩

plow layer *n* **:** the upper layer of soil comprising that usu. turned in plowing

plowless farming *n* **:** the stirring of soil for crop production with an implement (as a duckfoot, blade, chisel) that does not invert the soil or bury the crop residues

plowline *or* **ploughline** \'=,=\ *n* **1 :** a rein to guide a plow horse **2 :** the level of the bottom of a plowed furrow

plow·man *or* **plough·man** \'=mən\ *n, pl* **plowmen** *or* **ploughmen** [ME, fr. *plow, plough* plow + *man*] **1 :** one that plows **:** HUSBANDMAN **2 :** a field laborer **:** COUNTRYMAN

plowman's–spikenard *n, pl* **plowman's–spikenards :** a European aromatic herb (*Inula squarrosa*) with rough leaves and corymbose yellow flower heads

plow monday *n, usu cap P&M* **:** the Monday after Epiphany once celebrated in many parts of England as the first day of plowing

plow out *vt* **1 a :** to bring to the surface by or as if by plowing **:** plow up **:** turn up **b :** to remove or eradicate with or as if with a plow **2 :** to excavate or hollow out by plowing or by a process suggestive of plowing ⟨deep gullies *plowed out* by the heavy rains⟩

plow packer *n* **:** a soil packer attached behind a plow

plow paddle *or* **plow pattle** *or* **plow pettle** *n* [*pattle, pettle* alter. of *paddle*] **:** PLOWSTAFF

plowpoint *or* **ploughpoint** \'=,=\ *n* **:** the point of a plowshare; *esp* **:** one that is detachable

plow press *n* **:** the press used with a bookbinder's plow

plow·right·ia \plaů'rīd·ēə\ [NL, fr. C. B. *Plowright*, 19th cent. Eng. mycologist + NL *-ia*] *syn of* DIBOTRYON

plows *pl of* PLOW, *pres 3d sing of* PLOW

plowshare *or* **ploughshare** \'=,=\ *n* -s [ME *plowghschare*, fr. *plowgh, plow, plough* plow + *schare, shaar* plowshare — more at SHARE] **:** the irregularly shaped part of a moldboard plow that cuts the furrow slice at the bottom and side, consists of a point which penetrates the soil first, a horizontal cutting edge, and a heel or outside corner, is usu. made of steel or chilled iron, and is either welded to or independent of the landside — compare BAR SHARE, SLIP SHARE, STONY SHARE

plowshare bone *n* **1 :** VOMER **2 :** PYGOSTYLE

plowshoe *or* **ploughshoe** \'=,=\ *n* **:** a casing or support for a plowshare

plow sole *or* **plow pan** *n* **:** a compacted layer of earth at the bottom of the furrow at the same depth — compare HARDPAN

plow spade *n* **:** PLOWSTAFF

plowstaff *or* **ploughstaff** \'=,=\ *n* [ME *ploustaf*, fr. *plou, plow, plough* plow + *staf* staff] **:** a spade or paddle for cleaning the plowshare

plow steel *n* [prob. so called fr. the use of strong wire rope in the formerly common procedure of plowing fields with a gang-plow pulled by a steam engine] **:** steel of high quality containing 0.5 to 0.95 percent carbon and used esp. for wire made into rope

plowter *var of* PLOUTER

plow truck *n* **:** a seat attachment on a pair of wheels that enables the plowman to ride

plow under *vt* **1 a :** to cover a green manure crop, crop residues, or barnyard manure by plowing **b :** to plow a field of a growing unharvested crop **2 :** to cause to disappear **:** BURY, OVERWHELM ⟨let us not *plow under* the family farmer —A.E. Stevenson b.1900⟩ ⟨talented students . . . were too often *plowed under* —E.A.Weeks⟩

plow up *vt* **1 :** to bring to the surface by or as if by plowing **:** turn, cast, or pull up with or as if with a plow ⟨had *plowed* quite a lot of arrowheads *up*⟩ ⟨*plow up* the beets —*Accent*⟩ ⟨by hard work had *plowed up* several nasty secrets⟩ **2 :** to break (ground) up by plowing

plow–up *or* **plough–up** \'=,=\ *n* -s [*plow up*] **:** the conversion of an area of virgin sod into cropland

plowwright *or* **ploughwright** \'=,=\ *n* [ME *plow wryhte*, fr. *plow, plough* plow + *wryhte, wrighte* wright] **:** one who makes or repairs plows

ploy \'plȯi\ *n* -s [prob. short for 2*employ*] **1** *chiefly Scot* **a :** PURSUIT, ACTIVITY; *esp* **:** one that involves enterprise or finesse ⟨entered with eagerness into the new ~ —S.R.Crockett⟩ ⟨cart ropes would not hold them back from such a ~ —Sir Walter Scott⟩ **b :** RAMBLE, ESCAPADE ⟨through lots of ~*s* together —Harry Lauder⟩ **2 :** a social amusement **:** FROLIC ⟨their ~ of that week happened to be rabbit-shooting with saloon pistols —*McClure's*⟩ ⟨it's a grand ~ for young folk —John Buchan⟩ **3 :** a tactic (as in games and social debate) intended to embarrass or frustrate one's opponent ⟨~*s* and gambits for use against such rivals as fishing companions, wine experts, and fellow club members —*New Yorker*⟩

pls *abbr* please

plstc *abbr* plastic

plstr *or* **plstrer** *abbr* plasterer

plt *abbr* **1** pilot **2** plate

pltf *abbr* plaintiff

pltg *abbr* plating

pltry *abbr* poultry

plu *abbr* plural

plu·chea \'plüshēə\ *n, cap* [NL, fr. N. A. *Pluche* †1761 Fr. naturalist] **:** a genus of herbs or subshrubs (family Compositae) of warm regions comprising the marsh fleabanes and having small corymbose heads of tubular flowers and often aromatic or fetid foliage

1pluck \'plək\ *vb* -ED/-ING/-S [ME *plucken*, fr. OE *pluccian*; akin to MD *plucken, plocken* to pluck, MHG *pflücken, pfocken*; all prob. fr. a prehistoric WGmc word borrowed fr. (assumed) VL *piluccare* to pick, clean — more at PLUSH] *vt* **1 :** to pull or pick off or out **:** gather by picking ⟨~ feathers from a fowl⟩ ⟨~ grapes⟩ **2 :** to remove something from by or as if picking or pulling off or out: as **a** (1) **:** to so remove a natural covering (as of feathers, hair, or wool) from the body of ⟨~ a chicken before cleaning⟩; *also* **:** to trim the hair of (a dog) with a stripping knife (2) **:** to free (a pelt) from guard hairs in processing (3) **:** to shape (an eyebrow) by pulling some of the hairs **b :** ROB, PLUNDER, FLEECE **3 a :** to move or separate forcibly (as by pulling, dragging, snatching) — used with adverbs expressive of direction (as *out, from, down, apart*) ⟨~*ed* the map down from the wall⟩ ⟨~*ing* the portiere aside⟩ ⟨~*ed* him back from danger⟩ **b** (1) **:** to tear down **:** DEMOLISH — usu. used with *down* ⟨the chapel was ~*ed* down by the inhabitants of the village⟩ (2) **:** to make humble **:** bring low — usu. used with *down* **c :** to tear to pieces **:** pull apart **:** DISSEVER, RIVE ⟨a violent wind ~*ed* the sails to bits⟩ **4 a :** to handle with a picking or pulling motion ⟨a sick child ~*ing* at the bedclothes⟩; *esp* **:** to pull sharply or with sudden force ⟨~*ed* the strings of his guitar⟩ **b :** to seize (as a person) by a part of the body or clothing ⟨~*ed* him by the sleeve to catch his attention⟩ **c :** to make (as a musical instrument) sound by plucking **5 a** *Brit* **:** to reject (as a candidate for a degree or position) for some deficiency or misdemeanor (as for failure to satisfactorily pass an examination) ⟨expected to be ~*ed* on his tripos⟩ **b :** to select (a military officer) for involuntary retirement ⟨~*ed* after 20 years of service and sent into involuntary retirement⟩ **c :** to remove (a person) from one situation in life and transfer him to another ⟨~*ed* from his prosaic routine by the draft⟩; *esp* **:** to draft from a position of lesser to one of greater responsibility ⟨the convention ~*ed* him from the pastorate to head the foreign mission board⟩ **6** *of a glacier* **:** to break loose and bear away (solid rock) in large masses — compare ABRADE **~** *vi* **1 a :** to pull **:** DRAG **b** *obs* **:** GRAB, STEAL **c :** PICK *vi* 5 ⟨a paper that ~*s* badly⟩ **2 :** to make a sharp pull or twitch : TUG — usu. used with *at* ⟨~*ing* at the folds of her skirt⟩

2pluck \"\ *n* -s [ME, fr. *plucken*, v.] **1 a** : an act of plucking or pulling; *esp* : a quick or sudden and forcible pull (as a twitch, tug, or jerk) **b** *obs* : SET-TO : BOUT, GO **2 a** : the heart, liver, lungs, and windpipe of a slaughtered animal esp. as an item of food **b** : the corresponding parts of a human cadaver **3** : something that is plucked or used in plucking ⟨spun out a small ~ of wool⟩ ⟨lost the ~ for his ukelele⟩ **4** : SPIRIT, COURAGE, RESOLUTION, NERVE **5** : the condition of being plucked; *esp*, *Brit* : failure in an examination **6** : DISTINCTNESS, SHARPNESS, BOLDNESS — used of a picture, drawing, or photograph **syn** see FORTITUDE

pluck–buffet \ˈplək,bəfət\ *n* [¹*pluck* + *buffet*, n.] : a former competition between archers in which the loser received a buffet

plucked \ˈpləkt\ *adj* [²*pluck* + *-ed*] *dial chiefly Eng* : having courage, spirit, or resolution ⟨what a good ~ one that boy of mine is —W.M.Thackeray⟩

plucked·ness \ˈplək(t)nəs, -kədn-\ *n* -ES : the condition of one that is plucked : BARENESS, NAKEDNESS

plucked wool *n* : wool plucked from the carcass of a sheep

pluck·er \ˈpləkə(r)\ *n* -s : one that plucks: as **a** : a person or machine that plucks poultry **b** : a person or machine that plucks furs

plück·er tube \ˈpli͡ikə(r)-, -lu̇\ *n, usu cap P* [after Julius *Plücker* †1868 Ger. mathematician and physicist] : a gas-filled discharge tube with a narrowly constricted straight portion in which the intensified luminosity adapts the tube to use in the spectroscopy of gases

pluck·i·ly \ˈpləkəlē, -li\ *adv* : in a plucky manner : with or so as to be expressive of pluck

pluck·i·ness \-kēnəs, -kin-\ *n* -ES : the quality or state of being plucky

plucking *pres part of* PLUCK

pluck·less \-kləs\ *adj* : lacking pluck : feeble in courage or moral stamina — **pluck·less·ness** *n* -ES

plucks *pres 3d sing of* PLUCK, *pl of* PLUCK

pluck up *vb* [ME *plucken up*, fr. *plucken* to pluck + *up*, adv.] *vt* **1** : to assume an appearance of : bring to the fore : SUMMON ⟨*plucked* his nerve *up* to demand an explanation⟩ **2** : to eradicate by or as if by tearing up by the roots ~ *vi* : to assume an appearance (as of valor) esp. in response to a particular stress

plucky \ˈpləkē, -ki\ *adj* -ER/-EST [²*pluck* + *-y*] **1** : having or marked by courage : COURAGEOUS, SPIRITED, BRAVE, RESOLUTE ⟨a ~ man⟩ ⟨a ~ stand against oppression⟩ **2** : clear in outline or detail : DISTINCT, SHARP — used esp. of a drawing or photograph **3** *of a stone or rock* : breaking with a conchoidal fracture under the hammer or chisel ⟨flint, obsidian, and some limestones are ~ rocks⟩

1pluff \ˈpləf\ *n* -s [E dial. *pluff*, v., to puff, fire a gun, of imit. origin] *Scot* : PUFF

2pluff \", ˈplüf\ *adj*, *dial* : soft and puffy

pluff·er \-fə(r)\ *n* -s [E dial. *pluff* to puff, fire a gun + E *-er*] *dial chiefly Brit* : POPGUN

pluffy \ˈpləfi\ *adj* [¹*pluff* + *-y*] *chiefly Scot* : puffy and fat

1plug \ˈpləg\ *n* -s *often attrib* [D, fr. MD *plugge* plug, peg; akin to MHG *pfloc* plug, peg] **1** : a piece of wood, metal, or other material used or serving to fill a hole: as **a** : STOPPER, STOPPLE, BUNG **b** : the plunger of a pump **c** : the piece in a cock that can be turned to regulate the flow of liquid or gas **d** : PLUG GAGE **e** : an obstructing mass of material in a bodily vessel or the opening of a skin lesion ⟨necrotic ~⟩ ⟨fibrinous ~⟩ **f** : a more or less columnar mass of intrusive igneous rock : the filling of the conduit leading to a volcanic vent; *also* : a body of rock salt of similar shape — compare BYSMALITH, ¹NECK 3b(2)c **g** : a filling for a hollow tooth **h** : a reference peg driven in flush with the surface of the ground **i** : a fusible boiler plug **j** : a piece of one kind of metal inserted in a hole in the center of a coin of another kind of metal **k** : a block of wood driven or inlaid in a wall to form a nailing surface **l** : the cylindrical piece in a pin-tumbler cylinder containing the keyhole and rotated by the key — see KEY PLUG **m** : a cylindrical piece of wood or metal placed in the tubular magazine of a repeating shotgun to reduce the ammunition capacity of the magazine **n** : a separate piece of leather inserted in the upper of a shoe esp. for contrast or ornament **o** : the rotating cone within the outer shell of a jordan **2** : a flat compressed cake of tobacco **3 a** (1) : BLOW, PUNCH (2) *slang* : BOXING, FISTICUFFS ⟨the noble art of ~⟩ **b** : SHOT ⟨took a ~ at the deer with his rifle⟩ **4** : a small core or segment that is removed from a larger object: as **a** : a piece cut from the center of a coin **b** : a core removed from something (as a watermelon or a bale of wool) as a representative sample on which to base an estimate of the quality of the whole **c** : a bit of material removed by a punch in forming a hole **5** : something inferior or defective of its kind: as **a** : an inferior and often aged or unsound horse ⟨a race for platers and ~s⟩; *also* : a quiet steady cold-blooded horse usu. of light or moderate weight ⟨stock includes three good farm ~s⟩ **b** (1) : a slow-selling book (2) **plugs** *pl* : REMAINDERS — **c** *slang* : an incompetent telegrapher **d** : a drudging student : GRIND **e** : a slow, stupid, or ineffective person ⟨a willing worker but a dull old ~⟩ **6 a** : FIREPLUG **b** : PLUG HAT **c** (1) : SPARK PLUG (2) : PLUG FUSE **7 a** : an artificial angling lure used primarily for casting, made of wood or plastic, and usu. rigged with one or more sets of gang hooks ⟨an underwater ~⟩ ⟨a subsurface ~⟩ **b** *Brit* : SQUID 3 **8** : any of various devices resembling or functioning like a plug: as **a** : either the tapered parts or the key of a plug and feather **b** : a piece of soft steel impressed by a punch to form a die **c** : a wedge or key used to secure a railroad rail in a chair **d** : an extension to replace the broken section of watch or clock arbor and or pivot, filtering over the arbor or into a hole drilled in the arbor **e** (1) : a male fitting used to make an electrical connection by insertion in a receptacle or body and having one or more contact-making parts or blades that serve to close a circuit or to attach a conductor or some other piece of electrical equipment to a circuit (2) : a device for connecting electric wires to a jack or fuseplug **9** : a piece of favorable publicity; *esp* : personal or product advertising incorporated in general matter ⟨gave the actor a ~ in her column⟩ ⟨some radio programs have become mere strings of ~s tacked together with music⟩

2plug \"\ *vb* **plugged; plugged; plugging; plugs** *vt* **1 a** : to stop, make tight, or secure (as an opening) by or as if by insertion of a plug ⟨*plugged* the leak with tar⟩ ⟨~ the bunghole tightly⟩ : close an opening in — often used with *up* ⟨grease *plugged* up the sink⟩ **b** : to fill a cavity in (a tooth) **c** : to close (a rivet) by hammering or pressing **2** : to remove a small core or segment from ⟨~ a watermelon to test its ripeness⟩ ⟨*plugging* cotton bales⟩ **3** *slang* **a** : to hit with a bullet : put a bullet into : SHOOT **b** : to strike with the fist : PUNCH **4** : to stop (an electric motor) reversing its direction of rotation **5 a** : to break off or proportion (a piece of stone) with a plug and feather — usu. used with *off* **b** : to remove a piece from the center of (a coin) and insert a piece of baser metal **c** : to alter (as a woodcut or die) by removing a portion and inserting a plug carved with the desired substitution **6** : to advertise or publicize insistently; *esp* : to publicize (a piece of music) by very frequent performances ~ *vi* **1** : to become stopped or occluded — usu. used with *up* ⟨the drain will ~ up if you let grease settle in it⟩ **2** : to work doggedly and persistently ⟨*plugged* away at his lessons⟩ **3** : to fire a shot or shots ⟨kept *plugging* away at the can⟩ **4** : ⁴ROOT; *also* : to advertise or publicize something insistently ⟨devoted much of his talk to *plugging* for the party candidate⟩

plug and feather *n* : a device for splitting stones consisting of two tapered pieces and a wedge-shaped key

plugboard \ˈ=,=\ *n* **1** : an electrical switchboard in which connections are made by means of plugs **2** : the part of a tabulating machine in which adjustments are made that determine the place at which a card is punched or stamped **3** : a panel in a computer or other electronic equipment having a multiplicity of female connectors into which male plugs are inserted to establish electrical control circuits

plug casing *n* : a casing for adapting a plug-fuse cutout base to a cartridge fuse

plug casting *n* : fishing by bait casting with a plug

plug center bit *n* : a center bit ending in a small cylinder instead of a point

plug cock *or* **plug bib** *n* **1** : a cock turned on or off by a plug **2** : a spigot that is merely driven into a barrel

plug drill *n* : a stonecutter's percussion drill

plug flow *n* : the slipping along of a material through a conduit without plastic shear ⟨thin clay extruded to form tile exhibits *plug flow*⟩

plug fuse *n* : an electric fuse that screws into a socket — compare CARTRIDGE FUSE

plug·ga·ble \ˈpləgəbəl\ *adj* : capable of or suitable for being plugged

plug gage *n* : a gage with an external measuring surface designed to check the contour or size of an opening

plugged \-gd\ *adj* **1** : furnished with a plug : BLOCKED, OBSTRUCTED ⟨suffering from a ~ sinus⟩ **2** *of a coin* : altered by the insertion of a plug of base metal

plug·ger \-gə(r)\ *n* -s : one that plugs: as **a** : a dental instrument used for driving and consolidating filling material in a tooth cavity **b** (1) : a steady, dogged, and usu. uninspired worker (2) : an enthusiastic supporter or encourager (as of a contestant) : ROOTER; *also* : one that gives insistent publicity (as to a person, product, or cause) **c** : a worker who fits plugs (as into barrels) **d** : JACKHAMMER **e** : a tool for removing plugs (as of turf)

plug·ger·man \-mən\ *n, pl* **pluggermen** : a miner who keeps ore moving through chutes as it is loaded into cars at a lower level

plugging *n* -s [fr. gerund of ²*plug*] **1** : the act of one that plugs; *also* : the act of stopping with a plug **2** : material used for a plug

plug·ging·ly *adv* [*plugging* (pres. part. of ²*plug*) + *-ly*] : so as to plug or form a plug

plug hat *n* : a man's stiff hat (as a bowler or a top hat) — **plug–hatted** \ˈ=ˌ==\ *adj*

plughole \ˈ=,=\ *n* : an opening in which a plug fits

plug in *vi* : to establish an electric circuit by inserting a plug ⟨outlets conveniently placed for *plugging in*⟩ ~ *vt* : to attach or connect (as a lamp, an electrical device) to a service outlet ⟨*plugged* the radio *in*⟩ ⟨wired and ready to be *plugged in*⟩

1plug–in \ˈ=,=\ *adj* [*plug in*] : designed to be plugged into an electrical circuit ⟨a *plug-in* broiler⟩

2plug–in \ˈ=,=\ *n* -s **1** : PLUG 8e(1) **2** : JACK 2*l*

plug key *n* : SWITCH PLUG

plug·less \ˈpləgləs\ *adj* : lacking a plug

pluglike \ˈ=,=\ *adj* : resembling or functioning like a plug

plug·man \ˈpləgmən\ *n, pl* **plugmen** **1** : the member of a gun crew (as in the U. S. Navy) whose duty is to open and close the breech plug or breechblock in firing **2** : a miner who attends pumps in a mine **3** : a plugger who fastens stoppers in bottoms of billet molds in which copper is to be cast

plugs *pl of* PLUG, *pres 3d sing of* PLUG

plug switch *n* : an electrical switch in which connection is made by means of a plug

plug tobacco *n* : tobacco in the form of plugs

plugtray \ˈ=,=\ *n* : TRAY 3

plug–ugly \ˈ=ˌ==\ *n* -ES *often attrib* **1** : a member of a gang of disorderly ruffians often active in political pressure and intimidation ⟨the *plug-uglies* took over the polls⟩ ⟨*plug-ugly* tactics⟩ **2** : a coarse uncouth fellow : TOUGH, ROUGHNECK

plug valve *n* : a valve or cock opened or closed by the turning of a usu. conical plug

plug weld *n* : a butt weld made in the opening of a slotted lap joint

1plum \ˈpləm\ *n* -s *often attrib* [ME *plum, plumme, plowme* plum, plum tree, fr. OE *plūme*; akin to OHG *pflūmo* plum tree; both fr. a prehistoric WGmc word borrowed fr. L *prunum* plum, fr. Gk *proumnon*] **1 a** : any of numerous trees and shrubs of the genus *Prunus* that have medium-sized globular to oval smooth-skinned fruits which are drupes enclosing a smooth elongated flattened seed and that include various improved forms cultivated for their fruits or for their ornamental flowers or foliage — compare CHERRY, PEACH; see DAMSON, GREENGAGE, PRUNE **b** : the fruit of a plum **c** : the streaked hard small-pored reddish brown wood of a plum tree esp. of the common European plum used to a limited extent for small cabinetwork and turnery **2 a** : any of various trees with edible fruits resembling plums: as (1) : a tree of the genus *Spondias* — see HOG PLUM (2) : PERSIMMON (3) : a tree of the genus *Flacourtia* — see GOVERNOR'S PLUM **b** : the fruit of such a tree **c** *chiefly New Eng* : any of various edible berries (as a partridgeberry, Juneberry, or huckleberry) **3 a** : a raisin when used in puddings or other dishes **b** : SUGARPLUM **4 a** *archaic* : the sum of £100,000 sterling ⟨worth half a ~ —Richard Steele⟩ **b** : something excellent or superior of its kind (as a choice passage in a book or an unusually good position) ⟨a fellowship that was the history department's ~⟩ — compare LEMON **c** : something desirable received or available as a recompense for service esp. through political patronage ⟨a senator with several ~s at his disposal⟩ **d** : an unexpected increment of property or money : WINDFALL — compare MELON **5** : a stone or mass of rock embedded in a matrix of a different kind (as a pebble in a conglomerate); *esp* : large stone added to concrete after mixing and placing but before hardening **6 a** : a variable color averaging a dark reddish purple that is bluer and duller than grape wine or royal purple (sense 1) and less strong and slightly darker than imperial **b** : a dark purple that is bluer, stronger, and slightly lighter than average prune, redder and duller than mulberry (sense 2a) and redder and less strong than mulberry purple

2plum \"\ *vi* **plummed; plummed; plumming; plums** [ME *plumen*] *dial chiefly Eng* : RISE, SWELL

3plum *var of* PLUMB

4plum \"\ *adj* **1** *dial Eng* : rounded out : PLUMP **2** *dial Eng, of a drink* : mild, smooth, and mellow

plu·ma \ˈplümə\ *n, pl* **plu·mae** \-(ˌ)mē, -ˌmī\ [NL, fr. L, small soft feather — more at FLEECE] : CONTOUR FEATHER

pluma \"\ *n* -s [AmerSp, fr. Sp, feather, fr. L, small soft feather] : any of several Caribbean sparid porgies (genus *Calamus*)

plu·ma·ceous \(ˈ)plüˈmāshəs\ *adj* [NL *plumaceus*, fr. *pluma* + L *-aceus* -aceous] : PENNACEOUS

plu·mach \(ˈ)plüˈmash\ *n* -s [ME *plumash*, fr. MF *plumache*, fr. *plume* feather] *archaic* : an ornamental plume (as on a helmet)

plu·mage \ˈplümij, -mēj\ *n* -s [ME, fr. MF, fr. OF, fr. *plume* feather (fr. L *pluma* small soft feather) + *-age*] **1** : the entire clothing of feathers of a bird — compare PELAGE **2** : a bunch or tuft of feathers used for ornament **3** : elaborate, showy, or ceremonial dress **4** : the suite of feathery fins of some aquarium fishes (as various goldfishes and the bettas)

plu·maged \-jd\ *adj* : having plumage — usu. used with a descriptively qualifying adverb ⟨brilliantly ~ parrots⟩ ⟨a fully ~ young bird⟩

plu·mas·sier \ˌplüməˈsi(ə)r; plüˈmasēˌā, -ēər\ *n* -s [MF, fr. *plumasse* large feather (fr. *plume* feather) + *-ier* -er] : one that prepares or deals in ornamental plumes or feathers

plu·mate \ˈplüˌmāt, -mət\ *adj* [NL *plumatus*, fr. L, covered with feathers, fr. *pluma* small soft feather + *-atus* -ate] : having a main shaft that bears many small hairs or filamentous parts — used of bodily hairs, antennae, or similar structures

plu·ma·tel·la \ˌplüməˈtelə\ *n* [NL, fr. L *plumatus* covered with feathers + NL *-ella*] **1** *cap* : a genus (the type of the family Plumatellidae) of freshwater phylactolaematous bryozoans having a chitinous ectocyst and forming branching colonies **2** -s : any bryozoan of the genus *Plumatella*

1plumb \ˈpləm\ *n* -s [ME *plom, plum, plumbe*, fr. (assumed) OF *plomb* lead, plummet (whence MF *plomb*), fr. OF *plon* lead, fr. L *plumbum*, of non-IE origin; akin to the source of Gk *molybos* lead, Basque *berun*] **1** : a little mass or weight of lead or other heavy material (as brass) attached to a line and used to indicate a vertical direction : PLUMMET, PLUMB BOB **2 a** : a lead or other weight: as (1) : a mariner's sounding lead (2) : a fishline sinker (3) : a sinker used to sound a stream or lake (4) : a clock weight **b** : a missile of lead — **out of plumb** *or* **off plumb** *adv* : out of the vertical : out of true

2plumb \"\ *also* **plum** \"\ *adv* [ME *plum, plom, plum, plumbe*, n.] **1** : straight down or occasionally up : VERTICALLY **2** : DIRECTLY, EXACTLY; *also* : IMMEDIATELY **3** *chiefly dial* : COMPLETELY, ABSOLUTELY, UTTERLY

3plumb \"\ *vb* -ED/-ING/-S [ME *plomben*, fr. *plom, plum, plumbe*, n.] *vt* **1** : to weight with lead **2 a** : to sound with a plumb; *also* : to measure the depth of (as water) by sounding **b** : to ascertain a quality (as depth, dimension, propriety) of : examine minutely and critically ⟨~ one's motives⟩ ⟨there were depths . . . beneath the story that he had never ~*ed* —Van Wyck Brooks⟩ **c** : to reach the nadir of ⟨~*ing* that abyss of misery⟩ **3 a** : to adjust or test by a plumb line : cause to be perpendicular ⟨~ a wall⟩ **b** : to be or make perpendicular to **4** : to seal with or as if with lead ⟨~ a joint⟩ ⟨luggage ~*ed* by the customs inspector⟩ **5** [back-formation fr. *plumber*] **a** : to supply with a system of plumbing ⟨~ a new house⟩ **b** : to work upon (something) as a plumber : install as part of a system of plumbing ⟨had a friend ~ his sink⟩ ~ *vi* **1** : to hang or fall vertically : be perpendicular ⟨the chimney ~*s* perfectly⟩ **2** [back-formation fr. *plumber*] : to work as a plumber : do plumbing

4plumb \"\ *also* **plum** \"\ *adj* [ME *plom*, fr. *plom, plum, plumbe*, n.] **1 a** : conforming to the direction of a line attached to a plumb ⟨the wall is ~⟩ **b** : perfectly true : level and smooth — used of a cricket wicket **2** : DOWNRIGHT, COMPLETE, ABSOLUTE **syn** see VERTICAL

5plumb \"\ *dial var of* PLUMP

6plumb \"\ *dial chiefly Eng var of* ²PLUM

plumb- *or* **plumbo-** *comb form* [L *plumb-*, fr. *plumbum*] : lead ⟨*plumb*ate⟩ ⟨*plumbo*jarosite⟩

plumb·able \ˈpləməbəl\ *adj* : capable of being plumbed

plum·ba·gin \ˌpləmˈbājən, -āgən; ˈplembəjən\ *n* -s [ISV *plumbag-* (fr. NL *Plumbago*) + *-in*] : a yellow crystalline phenolic compound $C_{11}H_8O_3$ having antibacterial and medicinal properties that occurs esp. in the roots of shrubs of the genus *Plumbago*; 5-hydroxy-2-methyl-1,4-naphthoquinone

plum·bag·i·na·ce·ae \ˌpləmˌbajəˈnāsēˌē\ *n pl, cap* [NL, fr. *Plumbagin-*, *Plumbago*, type genus + *-aceae*] : a family of plants (order Plumbaginales) that are widely distributed esp. in saline situations and have basal or alternate leaves, small clustered tubular flowers, and a fruit which is a utricle or an achene — see PLUMBAGO — **plum·bag·i·na·ceous** \ˌ===-ˈnāshəs\ *adj*

plum·bag·i·na·les \ˌ=ˌ=ˈnā(ˌ)lēz\ *n pl, cap* [NL, fr. *Plumbagin-*, *Plumbago* + *-ales*] : a small order of shrubby or herbaceous plants that is coextensive with the family Plumbaginaceae and is often included in the order Primulales

plum·bag·i·nous \ˌpləmˈbajənəs\ *adj* [L *plumbagin-*, *plumbago* galena + E *-ous*] : resembling graphite : consisting of or containing graphite

plum·ba·go \ˌpləmˈbā(ˌ)gō\ *n* [L, galena, leadwort, fr. *plumbum* lead] **1** -s : GRAPHITE **2** [NL *Plumbagin-*, *Plumbago*, fr. L *plumbagin-*, *plumbago*] **a** *cap* : a genus (the type of the family Plumbaginaceae) of herbs, shrubs, and woody climbers that are widely distributed in warm climates and have alternate sessile leaves and spicate blue, white, or rosy red flowers with a glandular calyx and a salver-shaped corolla **b** -s : any plant of this genus

plumbago blue *n* : a purplish gray that is bluer, lighter, and stronger than crane and bluer, lighter, and stronger than dove gray, zinc, or cinder gray

plumbago family *n* : PLUMBAGINACEAE

plumbago gray *n* : a pale purple to purplish gray that is bluer than heliotrope gray

plumbago slate *n* : a grayish purple that is redder and slightly darker than telegraph blue, bluer and darker than mauve gray, and bluer and paler than average rose mauve

plum·bane \ˈpləmˌbān\ *n* -s [*plumb-* + meth*ane*] **1** : a compound of lead and hydrogen; *esp* : the unstable tetrahydride PbH_4 **2** : a derivative of a plumbane

1plum·bate \ˈpləmˌbāt\ *n* -s [ISV *plumb*ic + *-ate*] : a salt (as calcium ortho-plumbate Ca_2PbO_4 or sodium hexa-hydroxo-plumbate $Na_2[Pb(OH)_6]$) formed by reaction of lead dioxide with basic oxides

2plumbate \"\ *adj* [*plumb-* + *-ate*] : of or relating to a middle American pottery with a lustrous metallic surface typically the color of lead but sometimes grayish green or orange

plumb bob *n* : the usu. conoidal and metal bob of a plumb line

plumb bond *n* : a masonry bond (as a clip bond or split bond) in which corresponding joints are precisely in line with one another; *also* : a masonry face exhibiting such a relation

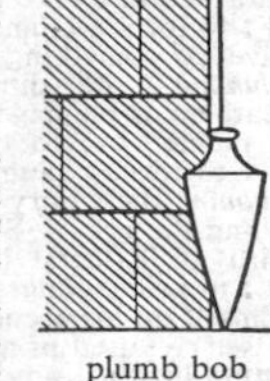

plumb bob

plumb cut *n* : a cut in a vertical plane; *esp* : the top cut face of a rafter that is designed to butt vertically against a ridgeboard — compare SEAT CUT

plumbed *past of* PLUMB

plum·be·ous \ˈpləmbēəs\ *adj* [L *plumbeus*, fr. *plumbum* lead + *-eus* -eous] **1** : consisting of or resembling lead : LEADEN **2 a** : having a dull gray color like that of lead **b** : of the color lead **3** *of a ceramic object* : finished or treated with a lead glaze

plumbeous gnatcatcher *n* : a bluish gray gnatcatcher (*Polioptila melanura melanura*) of the southwestern U. S. and adjacent Mexico distinguished by a jet black crown in the male

plumbeous vireo *n* : a dusky slaty gray vireo (*Vireo solitarius plumbeus*) of the Rocky mountain region

1plumb·er \ˈpləmə(r)\ *n* -s [ME *plummer, plumber*, fr. MF *plommier, plombier*, fr. L *plumbarius*, fr. *plumbarius*, adj., of or relating to lead, fr. *plumbum* lead + *-arius* -ary] **1** *obs* : a dealer or worker in lead **2** : one who installs, repairs, and maintains piping, fittings, and fixtures (as toilets, sinks, baths) that are involved in the distribution and use of water in a building (as for sanitary, industrial, or domestic purposes); *broadly* : one performing these services together with those of a gas fitter and steam fitter

2plumber \"\ *n* -s [³*plumb* + *-er*] : one who checks the vertical condition of structural components (as of a building)

plumb·er block \ˈpləmə(r)-\ *n* [earlier spelling of *plummer block*] : PLUMMER

plumber's friend *also* **plumber's helper** *n* : PLUNGER 2 e

plumber's furnace *n* : a portable heater for melting solder and lead

plumber's snake *n* : a long flexible rod or cable usu. of spring steel that is used to free clogged pipes

plumber's soil *n* : lampblack mixed with glue and water for use as a paint to prevent adhesion of solder

plumb·ery \ˈpləmərē\ *n* -ES [ME *plomerye*, fr. MF *plommerie* leadwork, fr. *plommier* dealer or worker in lead + *-ie* -y] **1** : a workshop (as in a medieval cathedral) for plumbing or leadwork **2** : the business or work of a plumber

plum·bic \ˈpləmbik\ *adj* [ISV *plumb-* + *-ic*] : of, relating to, or containing lead — used esp. of compounds in which this element is tetravalent; compare PLUMBOUS

plum·bif·er·ous \ˌpləmˈbif(ə)rəs\ *adj* [*plumb-* + *-iferous*] : containing lead

plumb·ing \ˈpləmiŋ, -mēŋ\ *n* -s [fr. gerund of ³*plumb*] **1 a** : the act of using a plumb, plummet, or plumb line **b** : a delving in or as if in examination or scrutiny ⟨lovely ~s of the psyche —F.R.Leavis⟩ **2 a** : the art or craft of working in lead **b** : a plumber's occupation or trade **3 a** : LEADWORK **b** (1) : plumber's work : the pipes, fixtures, and other apparatus concerned in the introduction, distribution, and disposal of water in a building (2) : TOILET 5 b — used with *the* **c** : a natural or artificial system of tubes, conduits, or channels

plumbing screw *n* : LEVELING SCREW

plum·bism \ˈpləmˌbizəm\ *n* -s [*plumb-* + *-ism*] : LEAD POISONING; *esp* : chronic lead poisoning

plum·bite \ˈpləmˌbīt\ *n* -s [ISV *plumb-* + *-ite*] : a salt formed in solution by reaction of lead monoxide with an alkali

plumb joint *n* [³*plumb* + *joint*] : a soldered lap joint in sheet-metal work

plum bladder *n* : PLUM POCKET

plumb·less \ˈpləmləs\ *adj* : impossible to plumb : FATHOMLESS

plumb level *n* : a level with a plumbing attachment (as a horizontal arm and a plumb line at right angles to the arm)

plumb line *n* **1 a** : a line or cord having at one end a plumb bob or other weight and used to determine verticality : PLUMMET **b** : PLUMB RULE **2 a** : a line directed to the center of gravity of the earth : a vertical line **b** *obs* : a line perpendicular to another **3** : SOUNDING LINE

plumb-line \ˈ=,=\ *vt* [*plumb line*] : to test the verticality or find the depth of by means of a plumb line; *broadly* : TEST, SCRUTINIZE

plum blotch *n* : a disease of plums caused by an imperfect fungus (*Phyllosticta congesta*) characterized by minute brown or gray angular leaf spots and irregular brown or gray blotches on the fruit

plumb·ly \ˈpləmlē, -li\ *adv* [⁴*plumb* + *-ly*] : straight downward

plumb·ness \-mnəs\ *n* -ES : the quality or state of being plumb or vertical

plumbo- — see PLUMB-

plum·bo·ferrite \ˌpləm(ˌ)bō+\ *n* -S [Sw *plumboferrit*, fr. *plumb-* + *ferr-* (fr. L *ferrum* iron) + *-it* -ite — more at FARRIER] : a mineral $PbFe_4O_7$ consisting of an oxide of lead and iron

plum·bog \ˈpləm,bäg\ *also* **plum·boy** \-bȯi\ *n* : DWARF RASPBERRY

plum·bo·gummite \ˌpləm(ˌ)bō+\ *n* -S [*plumb-* + *gumm-* (fr. L *gummi* gum) + *-ite* — more at GUM] **1** : a mineral $PbAl_3(PO_4)_2(OH)_5.H_2O$ consisting of a hydrous basic phosphate of lead and aluminum **2** : a group of isostructural minerals consisting of plumbogummite, gorceixite, goyazite, crandallite, deltaite, florencite, and dussertite and related to alunite and other sulfates isostructural with it

plum·bo·jarosite \"+\ *n* [*plumb-* + *jarosite*] : a mineral $PbFe_6(SO_4)_4(OH)_{12}$ consisting of a basic sulfate of iron and lead isostructural with jarosite

plum·bo·niobite \"+\ *n* [G *plumboniobit*, fr. *plumb-* + *niobit* niobite] : a niobite of complex composition resembling samarskite but containing lead and found in dark brown to black masses in pegmatite veins or massive slate

plum·bous \ˈpləmbəs\ *adj* [ISV *plumb-* + *-ous*] : of, relating to, or containing lead — used esp. of compounds in which this element is bivalent; compare PLUMBIC

plumb post *n* : one of the vertical members of a trestle bent — compare BATTER PILE

plumb rule *n* [ME *plomrewle*, fr. *plom, plum, plumbe*, n., plumb + *rewle, reule* rule] : a narrow board with a plumb line and bob used esp. by builders and carpenters

plumbs *pl of* PLUMB, *pres 3d sing of* PLUMB

plumb-stem bow *n* : a bow of a ship that is nearly perpendicular to the waterline

plum·bum \ˈpləmbəm\ *n* -S [L — more at PLUMB] : LEAD — symbol *Pb*

plum·cot \ˈpləm,kät, -,kət\ *n* -S [¹*plum* + *apricot*] : a hybrid between the plum and the apricot

plum curculio *n* : an American weevil (*Conotrachelus nenuphar*) that is very destructive to plums, cherries, nectarines, peaches, and other stone fruits and to apples, the adult feeding on the leaves of these trees and laying its eggs in crescent-shaped incisions made in the fruit and the larva migrating inward and feeding upon the pulp around the stone or core

plum duff *n* : a steamed or boiled plain flour pudding usu. containing raisins or currants

¹**plume** \ˈplüm\ *n* -S [ME, fr. MF, fr. L *pluma* small soft feather — more at FLEECE] **1** : a feather or feathers of a bird: as **a** : a large conspicuous or showy feather ⟨ostrich ~s⟩ **b** : a contour feather as distinguished from a down feather **c** : PLUMAGE 1 **d** : a cluster of distinctive feathers ⟨with a ~ of stiff white feathers projecting from the nape⟩ **2 a** : an ornament that consists of a feather, cluster of feathers, tuft of hair, or similar matter worn or displayed often as a symbol of position or rank ⟨wore a ~ of three ostrich feathers in her hair⟩ ⟨the horsehair ~ of an ancient helmet⟩ **b** : something that adorns or attracts attention like a plume : showy raiment and appurtenances : PLUMAGE 2 ⟨made fine with borrowed ~s⟩ **c** : a token of honor or prowess : a deserved prize, reward, or approval **3** : something that is felt to resemble a feather (as in shape, appearance, or lightness): as **a** (1) : a plumose appendage of a plant (as a pappus or the coma of a seed) (2) : PLUMULE 1 **b** : an elongated usu. open and mobile column or band (as of smoke, blowing sand or snow, or of cloud) **c** : a plumate part or structure on an animal; *esp* : a full bushy tail (as of a long-haired cat) **d** : a flaw in a gem (as an agate) **4** : PLUME MOTH

²**plume** \"\ *vb* -ED/-ING/-S [ME *plumen*, fr. MF *plumer* to pluck the feathers from (a bird), fr. OF, fr. *plume*, n.] *vi* **1** *obs*, *of a hawk* : to strip the prey of feathers **2** *obs* : to show self-satisfaction : take pride in oneself or one's accomplishments **3** : to form a plume : assume a plumose appearance; *esp* : to give off something in the form of a plume ⟨a cigarette still *pluming* in the ashtray⟩ ~ *vt* **1 a** : to provide (as a bird) with feathers or plumage : FEATHER **b** : to deck (as a helmet) with a plume **c** : to trick out (as a person) or array showily **d** : to form a plume of (as smoke) or in (as air) ⟨chimneys *pluming* the wintry sky⟩ ⟨an engine . . . *pluming* black smoke along the gray —William Sansom⟩ **2** *archaic* **a** : to strip (a bird) of feathers **b** : to rob or strip bare : DEPRIVE, DESPOIL **3** : to pride, congratulate, or take credit to (oneself) ⟨*plumed* himself on his accomplishment⟩ **4 a** : to dress the feathers of (itself) — used of a bird **b** : to preen and arrange (feathers)

plume bird *n* : any of various birds (as an egret or a bird of paradise) that are often hunted for their showy plumes

plumed \ˈplümd\ *adj* **1** *obs* : stripped of feathers : PLUCKED **2** : provided or adorned with or as if with a plume — often used in combination ⟨a white-*plumed* egret⟩

plumed partridge *n* : MOUNTAIN QUAIL

plumed thistle *n* : a thistle of the genus *Circium*

plume-footed \ˈ=,==\ *adj* : having the feet covered with feathers ⟨a *plume-footed* owl⟩

plume grass *n* **1** : a grass of the genus *Erianthus*; *esp* : RAVENNA GRASS **2** : an Australian grass of the genus *Dichelachne* with showy feathery flower panicles

plume hyacinth *n* : a large grape hyacinth (*Muscari comosum plumosum*) with a branched raceme of sterile flowers that have the petals very irregular, curled, and crisped forming tufts of narrow violet-blue segments

plume hydroid *n* : a hydrozoan of the family Plumulariidae

plume·less \ˈplümləs\ *adj* : lacking a plume : having no feathers

plumeless thistle *n* : a thistle of the genus *Carduus* — compare PLUMED THISTLE

plume·let \ˈplümlət\ *n* -S : a small tuft or plume

plumelike \ˈ=,=\ *adj* : resembling a plume usu. in form or texture

plume moss *n* : a branched feathery moss (*Hypnum crista-castrensis*) that commonly grows on decaying wood

plume moth *n* : any of numerous small slender moths constituting the family Pterophoridae and usu. having the wings deeply divided into two or more plumose lobes

plume-of-navarre \-nəˈvär\ *n* -S *often cap N* [prob. after Henry of *Navarre* (Henry IV) †1610 king of France] : WHITE-FRINGED ORCHIS

plume poppy *n* : any of several Asiatic herbs of the genus *Macleaya* (esp. *M. cordata*) widely cultivated for the showy plumy panicles of flowers

plum·er \ˈplümə(r)\ *n* -S : a person that hunts birds for their plumes

¹**plu·me·ria** \plüˈmirēə\ *n, cap* [NL, fr. *Plumerius* (latinized form of the name of Charles *Plumier*) + NL *-ia*] : a genus of tropical American shrubs or trees (family Apocynaceae) having thick fleshy branches and large highly fragrant, waxy-looking white, yellow, red, or pink flowers with a twisted corolla — see FRANGIPANI

²**plumeria** \"\ *n* -S [NL *Plumeria*] : FRANGIPANI

plume-royal \ˈ=ˈ==\ *n* -S : PURPLE-FRINGED ORCHID b

plum·ery \ˈplümərē\ *n* -ES [¹*plume* + *-ery*] : PLUMES, PLUMAGE

plumes *pl of* PLUME, *pres 3d sing of* PLUME

plu·met \ˈplümət, plüˈmet\ *n* -S [MF *plumete* small feather, fr. *plume* + *-ete* -et — more at PLUME] : a small tuft of feathers

plu·me·té \ˌplüməˈtā, ˈplüməd·ē\ *or* **plu·met·ty** \ˈplüməd·ē, (ˈ)plüˈmed·ē\ *adj* [ME *plumte*, fr. MF *plumeté* made so as to resemble a feather, prob. fr. *plumete* small feather] *heraldry* : divided into fusils marked in a manner supposed to represent feathers

plume thistle *n* : PLUMED THISTLE; *esp* : BULL THISTLE

plu·me·tis \ˌplüməˈtē\ *n, pl* **plumetis** \-ē(z)\ [F, fr. MF, hand embroidery, prob. fr. *plumete* small feather] : a fine lightweight dress fabric of cotton, wool, or rayon that is woven with raised dots or figures on a plain background producing a feathery or embroidered effect

plu·mette \(ˈ)plüˈmet\ *n* -S [¹*plume* + *-ette*] : PLUMET

plum family *n* **1** : ROSACEAE **2** : AMYGDALACEAE

plum fir *n* : a Chilean evergreen tree (*Podocarpus andina*) with an edible plumlike yellowish white fruit

plum-fruited yew \ˈ=,==-\ *n* : PLUM FIR

plum gouger *n* : a weevil (*Anthonomus scutellaris*) with a grub that feeds in and destroys plums, cherries, and sometimes other fruits

plum grape *n* : FOX GRAPE c

plu·mi·corn \ˈplüməˌkȯrn\ *n* -S [*plumi-* (fr. L *pluma* small soft feather) + *-corn* (fr. L *cornu* horn) — more at FLEECE, HORN] : one of the tufts of lengthened feathers on the head of various owls ⟨the earlike ~s of a great horned owl⟩

plu·mie·ra \plüˈmirə, ˌplüməˈirə\ *n* [NL, fr. Charles *Plumier* †1704 Fr. botanist] *syn of* PLUMERIA

plu·mie·ride \plüˈmiˌrīd, ˌplüməˈiˌr-, ˈplüməˌr-\ *n* -S [ISV *plumier-* (fr. NL *Plumiera*) + *-ide*] : a bitter crystalline glucoside $C_{21}H_{26}O_{12}$ found in trees of the genus *Plumeria*

plum·i·ness \ˈplümēnəs\ *n* -ES : the quality or state of being plumy

pluming *pres part of* PLUME

plu·mi·ped \ˈplüməˌped\ *also* **plu·mi·pede** \-ˌpēd\ *adj* [L *plumiped-, plumipes* having feathered feet (read by some editors at Catullus 58ª, 5 for the word which is now generally taken to be *plumipeda*), fr. *plumi-* (fr. *pluma* small soft feather) + *ped-, pes* foot — more at FOOT] **1** : having feet covered with feathers **2** : having winged feet

plum juniper *n* **1** : SYRIAN JUNIPER **2** : a Mediterranean juniper (*Juniperus Macrocarpa*) with a large berrylike glaucous blue fruit that turns brown after ripening

plum leafhopper *n* : a leafhopper (*Macropsis trimaculata*) that feeds on the foliage of various fruit trees and transmits the virus of peach yellows to peach trees

plum·less \ˈpləmləs\ *adj* : having or bearing no plums ⟨a ~ pudding⟩ ⟨barren ~ trees⟩

plumlike \ˈ=,=\ *adj* : resembling a plum, esp. a plum fruit

plummed *past of* PLUM

plum·mer \ˈpləmə(r)\ *also* **plummer block** *n* -S [prob. fr. the name *Plummer*] : a pillow block or bearing block

plummer-vinson syndrome \ˌpləmə(r)ˈvin(t)sən-\ *n, usu cap P&V* [after Henry S. *Plummer* †1937 and Porter P. *Vinson* b1890 Am. physicians] : a condition that is marked by difficulty in swallowing, atrophic changes in mouth, pharynx, and upper esophagus, and hypochromic anemia and is commonly considered to be due to a nutritional deficiency

¹**plum·met** \ˈpləmət, *usu* -əd+V\ *n* -S [ME *plomet*, fr. MF *plommet, plombet* ball of lead, fr. *plomb* lead + *-et* — more at PLUMB] **1 a** : SOUNDING LEAD **b** : PLUMB BOB; *also* : PLUMB LINE **c** *obs Scot* : a weighted knob on the pommel of a sword or dirk **d** *obs* : a leaden ball (as on the thong of a scourge) **e** : a weight for a clock **f** : a leaden weight on an angler's line **g** : a piece of lead formerly used for marking (as in ruling paper before writing) **h** : an ancient Egyptian amulet resembling a plumb bob **i** : a float that somewhat resembles a plumb bob in shape and is used to determine the specific gravity of a liquid **2** : something that weighs down or depresses

²**plummet** \"\ *vi* -ED/-ING/-S **1** : to fall perpendicularly ⟨the plane ~*ed* to earth⟩ **2** : to drop sharply and abruptly ⟨prices may ~ later⟩ ⟨blood pressure ~*ed* to 60/20⟩

plum·met·less \-mətləs\ *adj* : UNFATHOMABLE

plum·mi·ly \ˈpləmələ̄\ *adv* : in a plummy manner : so as to be plummy

plum·mi·ness \-mēnəs\ *n* -ES : the quality or state of being plummy

plum·ming \ˈpləmiŋ\ *n* -S [¹*plum* + *-ing*, n. suffix (action)] : degradation of a silver photographic image frequently manifested by a color change (as to purplish) occurring during drying esp. at elevated temperatures — called also *bronzing*

plum·my \ˈpləmē\ *adj* -ER/-EST [¹*plum* + *-y*] **1 a** : full of plums ⟨a rich ~ cake⟩ **b** : CHOICE, DESIRABLE, ADVANTAGEOUS ⟨got the *plummiest* appointment in the department⟩ **2 a** : resembling a plum or resembling that of a plum ⟨a dark ~ shade⟩ **b** : soft and full ⟨~ cheeks⟩ **c** *of the voice* : rich and mellow often to the point of affectation

plu·mose \ˈplüˌmōs\ *adj* [L *plumosus* downy, fr. *pluma* small soft feather + *-osus* -ose — more at FLEECE] **1** : having feathers or plumes : FEATHERED **2** : PLUMATE; *also* : having hairs or other parts plumate : FEATHERY, PLUMELIKE ⟨a ~ stigma⟩ — **plu·mose·ly** *adv* — **plu·mose·ness** *n* -ES — **plu·mos·i·ty** \plüˈmäsəd·ē\ *n*

¹**plump** \ˈpləmp\ *vb* -ED/-ING/-S [ME *plumpen*, of imit. origin] *vi* **1** : to drop, fall, sink, or come in contact with suddenly or heavily ⟨~*ed* to her knees in front of the fire⟩ ⟨~*ing* down with a sigh⟩ **2 a** *chiefly Brit* : to vote for only one candidate in an election in which one is entitled to vote for two or more **b** : to come out strongly in favor of something : support a point of view, aim, party, or person vigorously or as a partisan — used with *for* ⟨~*ed* for a third party ticket⟩ ⟨ready to ~ for any scheme that would improve the school system⟩ **3** : to come or go or arrive or depart suddenly, unexpectedly, or energetically ⟨~*ed* out of the house in a huff⟩ ⟨~*ed* down in this little town on a quiet Sunday⟩ ~ *vt* **1** : to drop, cast, plunge, or place all at once, suddenly and heavily, or with accurate firmness and an effect of determination ⟨~*ing* stones into the water⟩ ⟨washed and dressed the baby and ~*ed* him into his high chair⟩ **2** : to utter (as an opinion) suddenly or abruptly : blurt out **3** : to make favorable mention of : give support and favorable publicity to ⟨newspaper ads ~ the virtues of the Russian-built . . . car —*Newsweek*⟩

²**plump** \"\ *adv* **1** : with a sudden or heavy drop : suddenly and heavily ⟨fell ~ into the river⟩ **2** : straight down : VERTICALLY, PERPENDICULARLY; *also* : straight ahead : directly in front ⟨there was the deer ~ in our path⟩ **3** : without hesitation, circumlocution, or concealment : BLUNTLY, FLATLY, DIRECTLY, UNQUALIFIEDLY ⟨came out ~ for a lower tariff⟩

³**plump** \"\ *n* -S : an act of falling, plunging, or striking abruptly or heavily : a sudden plunge, heavy fall, or blow ⟨gave a ~ of his fist against the door⟩; *also* : the sound made by such an act ⟨fell into the brook with a ~⟩

⁴**plump** \"\ *adj* **1** : descending or facing directly **2** : done or made suddenly and without reservation : BLUNT, DIRECT, UNQUALIFIED **3** : paid at one time

⁵**plump** \", ˈplümp\ *n* -S [ME *plumpe*] **1** *chiefly dial* : CLUSTER, GROUP, CLUMP **2** : a flock of waterfowl ⟨a ~ of ducks⟩

⁶**plump** \ˈpləmp\ *adj* -ER/-EST [MD *plomp, plump* dull, blunt, stupid] **1 a** : having ample flesh : showing rounded, buxom, and usu. pleasing fullness ⟨a woman of medium height, a little ~ but not fat —Mary McCarthy⟩ ⟨the ~ figure and portly waist . . . of a genial and humorous man —J.R.Green⟩ **b** : marked by a full rounded form ⟨~ cushions with bright covers —Blanche E. Baughan⟩ ⟨secret thickets where the ~*est* beach plums ripen —Phyllis Duganne⟩ ⟨the wind . . . having driven ~ golden clouds across the sky —Rebecca West⟩ **2** : marked by amplitude, abundance, or richness ⟨what a ~ endowment to the . . . mouth of a prelate —John Milton⟩ ⟨the book is ~ with examples and citations —C.W.Collins⟩ **syn** see FAT

⁷**plump** \"\ *vb* -ED/-ING/-S *vt* : to cause to fill or swell out : FATTEN, DISTEND ~ *vi* : to fill or swell out : become fattened or distended

plum peach *n, chiefly Midland* : a clingstone peach

plump·en \ˈpləmpən\ *vb* -ED/-ING/-S [⁶*plump* + *-en*] : ⁷PLUMP

¹**plump·er** \-mpə(r)\ *n* -S [⁷*plump* + *-er*] **1** : one that swells out something; *esp* : something carried in the mouth to fill out the cheeks **2** : a solution used in tanning to remove acid from a hide and thus allow the tanning material to act quickly; *also* : a worker that applies this solution

²**plumper** \"\ *n* -S [¹*plump* + *-er*] **1 a** : an act or instance of falling suddenly or heavily (as from a horse) **b** *archaic* : a heavy blow **2** *chiefly Brit* : a vote given to one candidate only when the voter might vote for more than one for the same office (as for several candidates for a county council) **3** *dial* : a downright lie

plum pine *n* : BROWN PINE 2

¹**plumping** *adj* [fr. pres. part. of ¹*plump*] : very large : of exceptional size ⟨won by a ~ majority⟩

²**plumping** *n* -S [fr. gerund of ⁷*plump*] : a process of softening and swelling hide fibers by immersion in solution of acid or alkali

plump·ish \ˈpləmpish\ *adj* : somewhat plump : moderately stout ⟨~ women in tight shorts⟩

¹**plump·ly** *adv* [⁶*plump* + *-ly*] : in a plump way ⟨a ~ pretty matron⟩

²**plump·ly** *adv* [⁴*plump* + *-ly*] : in a wholehearted manner and without hesitation or circumlocution : firmly and directly ⟨came out ~ in support of the president's stand⟩

¹**plump·ness** *n* -ES [⁶*plump* + *-ness*] : the quality or state of being plump : fullness of form : CORPULENCE

²**plump·ness** *n* -ES [⁴*plump* + *-ness*] : freedom from hesitation or circumlocution in utterance : FORTHRIGHTNESS

plum pocket *n* **1** : a disease of plums caused by either of two fungi (*Taphrina pruni* and *T. communis*) and characterized by abortion of the stone leaving a cavity within the swollen distorted fruit — usu. used in pl. **2** : a fruit affected with plum pockets — called also *bladder plum*

¹**plumps** *pres 3d sing of* PLUMP, *pl of* PLUMP

²**plumps** \ˈpləmps\ *n pl but sing or pl in constr* [imit.] : a game of marbles in which the marble shot must hit the one shot at before striking the ground

plum pudding *n* **1 a** : a boiled or steamed pudding of flour or bread crumbs, raisins, currants, and other fruits, suet, eggs, and spices and other flavoring matters **b** : a pudding containing plums **2** : a muscular fibrous tissue that permeates the blubber of the tongue of some whales

plum-pudding \ˈ=ˈ==\ *adj* [*plum pudding*] : suggesting plum pudding esp. in the irregular jumbling or interlocking of diverse elements or parts ⟨*plum-pudding* mahoganies⟩

plum-pudding stone *n* : a conglomerate rock : PUDDING STONE

plum purple *n* **1** : PLUM 6a **2** : a dark violet that is redder and duller than Derby blue and less strong and slightly darker than blue plum — called also *cathedral, grape*

plumpy \ˈpləmpē\ *adj* -ER/-EST [⁶*plump* + *-y*] : PLUMP, CHUBBY

plums *pl of* PLUM, *pres 3d sing of* PLUM

plum scab *n* : PEACH SCAB

plum·stead peculiars \ˈpləmz,t|ed-, -,t|əd-, -m(,)st|\ *n pl, usu cap 1st P* [*Plumstead*, parish in Woolwich metropolitan borough, London, England] : PECULIAR PEOPLE 2

plum thrips *n* : PEAR THRIPS

plum tomato *n* **1** : any of several cherry tomatoes bearing red or yellow oblong fruits **2** : the fruit of a plum tomato used esp. for salads and preserves

plum tree *n* [ME *plumtre*, fr. OE *plūmtrēow*, fr. *plūme* plum + *trēow* tree] **1** : PLUM 1a **2** *slang* : a source of advantage (as political favors or appointments) ⟨never one to hesitate before shaking the *plum tree* for himself or his intimates⟩

plu·mu·la \ˈplümyələ\ *n, pl* **plumu·lae** \-ˌlē\ [NL] : PLUMULE

plu·mu·la·ceous \ˌplümyəˈlāshəs\ *adj* : relating to or like a plumule

plu·mu·lar \ˈplümyələ(r)\ *adj* : of or relating to a plumule

plu·mu·lar·ia \ˌplümyəˈla(a)rēə\ *n* [NL, fr. L *plumula* small soft feather + NL *-aria*] **1** *cap* : the type genus of Plumulariidae comprising hydrozoans with sessile zooids arranged on only one side of each branching plumose stem **2** -S : any hydrozoan of the genus *Plumularia* : PLUME HYDROID — **plu·mu·lar·i·an** \ˌ==ˈ=rēən\ *adj or n*

plu·mu·la·ri·idae \ˌplümyələˈrīəˌdē\ *n pl, cap* [NL, fr. *Plumularia*, type genus + *-idae*] : a large and widely distributed family of calyptoblastic hydrozoans — see PLUMULARIA

plu·mu·late \ˈplümyəˌlāt, -lət\ *adj* : finely plumose

plu·mule \ˈplü(ˌ)myül\ *n* -S [NL *plumula*, fr. L, small soft feather, dim. of *pluma* small soft feather — more at FLEECE] **1** : the primary bud of a plant embryo usu. situated at the apex of the hypocotyl and consisting of leaves and an epicotyl that elongates to extend the axis as a primary stem **2 a** : a down feather **b** : ANDROCONIUM

plu·mu·li·form \ˈplümyələˌfȯrm\ *adj* [NL *plumuliformis*, fr. L *plumula* small soft feather + *-iformis* -iform] : resembling a small downy feather

plu·mu·lose \ˈplümyəˌlōs\ *adj* [NL *plumulosus*, fr. *plumula* + L *-osus* -ose] : resembling or constituting a plumule

plum violet *n* : a dark red to purplish red — called also *canyon*

plum-web-spinning sawfly *n* : a sawfly (*Neurotoma inconspicua*) of the family Pamphiliidae with a larva that feeds on the foliage of plum and sand cherry

plum weevil *n* : PLUM CURCULIO

plum wine *n* : a dark reddish purple that is stronger and slightly redder and lighter than royal purple (sense 1), redder and paler than imperial, and redder, lighter, and stronger than average plum (sense 6a) or violet carmine

plumy \ˈplümē\ *adj* -ER/-EST [¹*plume* + *-y*] **1** : DOWNY **2** : covered or adorned with, abounding in, or resembling plumes : PLUMED, FEATHERY

plum-yew \ˈ=ˈ=\ *n* : any of several evergreen trees and shrubs (genus *Cephalotaxus*) of eastern Asia that are related to the yews, have large seeds enclosed in a fleshy envelope, and are sometimes cultivated as ornamentals

¹**plun·der** \ˈpləndə(r)\ *vb* **plundered**; **plundered**; **plundering** \-d(ə)riŋ\ **plunders** [G *plündern*, fr. MHG *plundern*, fr. *plunder, blunder* household goods, clothes, fr. MLG *plunder-*; akin to MD *plunder, plonder* household goods, clothes] *vt* **1 a** : to take the goods of by force (as in war) or wrongfully : PILLAGE, SPOIL, SACK ⟨laws about the ~*ing* of nonbelligerents⟩ **b** : to take or appropriate by force or wrongfully : STEAL, LOOT ⟨the raiders ~*ed* all the cattle⟩ **2** : to make extensive use of material from (an author or his work) without acknowledgment ⟨Shakespeare and his fellow-dramatists ~*ed* the Church legends —Henry Adams⟩ ~ *vi* : to commit robbery, spoliation, or looting **syn** see ROB

²**plunder** \"\ *n* -S **1** : an act of plundering (as in war) : PILLAGING; *also* : spoliation by extortion **2** : something that is taken by open force (as from an enemy) or by theft or fraud : PILLAGE, SPOIL, BOOTY, LOOT **3** *chiefly dial* **a** : personal property and effects : BAGGAGE; *also* : a freight shipment : FREIGHT **b** : goods and equipment used in an indicated situation or activity ⟨camping ~⟩; *esp* : household goods — called also *house plunder* **c** : trade goods : items for buying or selling **d** (1) : PROFIT, GAINS (2) : something garnered or collected ⟨a boyish ~ of nuts, grapes, and crab apples⟩ **e** : miscellaneous articles : JUNK

plun·der·able \-dərəbəl\ *adj* : capable of being plundered : worth plundering : subject to plunder

plun·der·age \-rij\ *n* -S **1** : an act or instance of plundering; *esp* : embezzlement of goods on shipboard **2** : property obtained by plunderage

plunderbund \ˈ=,=,=\ *n* [²*plunder* + *bund* (league)] : a league of commercial, political, or financial interests that exploits the public

plun·der·er \ˈplənd(ə)rə(r)\ *n* -S : one that plunders : PILLAGER

plun·der·less \-də(r)ləs\ *adj* : lacking plunder

plun·der·ous \-d(ə)rəs\ *adj* : given to or characterized by plundering

plunder room *n, chiefly Midland* : LUMBER ROOM

¹**plunge** \ˈplənj\ *vb* -ED/-ING/-S [ME *plungen, plongen*, fr. MF *plonger, plongier*, fr. (assumed) VL *plumbicare*, fr. L *plumbum* lead — more at PLUMB] *vt* **1 a** : to cause to penetrate or enter quickly and forcibly into some material medium : thrust or force into or in liquid, a penetrable substance, or a cavity : IMMERSE, SUBMERGE ⟨~ the body into water⟩ ⟨~ a dagger into the breast⟩ **b** *obs* : to baptize by immersion **c** : to sink (a potted plant) in the ground or in a bed of prepared material **2 a** : to cause to enter or force into some state or course of action usu. suddenly, unexpectedly, or violently and against opposition ⟨scoundrels that *plunged* the nation into needless war⟩ ⟨*plunging* himself into dissipation⟩ **b** *obs* : to harass or overwhelm esp. with difficulties **3 a** : to set (as the horizontal cross hair of a theodolite) in the direction of a grade in plunging a grade **b** : to turn over (as the telescope of a transit) on its horizontal transverse axis ~ *vi* **1** : to thrust or cast oneself into or as if into water : submerge oneself : dive or rush in : penetrate, sink, or enter suddenly or impetuously (as into a forest) **2 a** (1) : to pitch or throw oneself headlong or violently forward and downward (as of a horse or ship) (2) : to execute a football plunge **b** : to act with reckless haste : enter into some state or course of action usu. suddenly, unexpectedly, or unreasonably ⟨*plunged* into debt⟩ **c** : to bet or

gamble heavily and with seeming recklessness : risk large sums in hazardous enterprises **3 a :** to descend or dip suddenly ⟨the road *plunges* along the slope⟩ **b :** to incline downward — used esp. of a pipelike ore deposit, an anticline, or a syncline
syn PLUNGE, DIVE, and PITCH can mean in common to throw oneself or cause something to be thrown or thrust forward and downward with force into or as if into deep water. PLUNGE stresses the force of the movement forward and downward, often suggesting lack of intention and usu. implying a final total immersion ⟨to *plunge* bodily into the water after a forty-foot drop —C.S.Forester⟩ ⟨the schooner's bows rose dizzily to dip, then *plunge* —I.L.Idriess⟩ ⟨we are *plunged* once more into the war of nerves —*Times Lit. Supp.*⟩ ⟨horses *plunged* and tugged —Stephen Crane⟩ ⟨the singer drew breath and *plunged* into a new stanza —Florette Henri⟩ DIVE, usu. implying intention, suggests a certain skill in execution, less heaviness, and more grace ⟨an enormous water rat *dived* down from the bank —J.C.Powys⟩ ⟨the sun *dived* suddenly into the confusion of low, wooded islands along the western shore —Walter O'Meara⟩ ⟨she *dove* into the red pocketbook and, burrowing among the debris, came up at last with what she was after —Helen Howe⟩ ⟨*dive* a plane into the sea⟩ PITCH, in this comparison, usu. implies total absence of control ⟨*pitch* headlong over a cliff⟩ ⟨stumble and *pitch* forward on his face⟩ It can often apply to a plunging or tossing from side to side ⟨the ship began to *pitch* suddenly as the storm hit⟩ ⟨a horse *pitching* and plunging to dislodge a rider⟩
— **plunge a grade 1 :** to establish a grade between two points of known level by sighting a target set up at either point through a theodolite fixed at the other point, clamping the instrument, and then bringing the target into the fixed line of sight at any desired intermediate points on the grade — compare 2BONE 4 **2 :** to test (as a railroad embankment) as to its reliability or condition by prodding with a light pointed steel rod

2plunge \"\ *n* -s [ME, fr. *plungen, plongen,* v.] **1 :** a place for plunging or diving (as a swimming pool) **:** a deep place in water **:** a deep pool **2 :** a dive, leap, rush, or pitch into or as if into water **:** an act of pitching oneself headlong or violently forward and usu. downward ⟨take the water with a ~⟩: as **a :** a breaking of a wave **b :** a heavy fall (as of rain) **c :** a quick thrust into the line in a football game **d :** a brief swim **3 a** *chiefly dial* **:** involvement in a difficult or dangerous situation **:** STRAIT, DILEMMA **b :** an act or instance of engaging in heavy and reckless betting or hazardous speculation or expenditure **:** SPLURGE **4 :** the vertical angle between the lineation of a linear structural or textural fissure in rocks and a horizontal plane — used esp. of ore bodies, folds, or mineral orientations; compare 4PITCH 2a (8)

plunge basin *n* **:** a hollow excavated by falling water at the foot of a fall or cataract

plunge bath *n* **:** a bath in which the bather is immersed in or as if in a pool

plunge pool *n* **:** the water in a plunge basin; *also* **:** a small deep plunge basin

plung·er \-jə(r)\ *n* -s **1 :** a person that plunges: as **a :** DIVER **b :** a reckless gambler or speculator **c :** an operator of a pusher for moving iron and steel billets into and out of a furnace — called also *pusher* **d :** a worker who operates the guides on a rod-rolling mill **2 :** a device, piece of equipment, or apparatus that functions by plunging or is used in the plunging of something: as **a :** the rod carrying the valves in the inner assembly of an automobile tire valve unit **b** (1) **:** a sliding reciprocating piece driven by or against fluid pressure; *esp* **:** a long valveless piston used as a forcer in a force pump, as a ram in a hydraulic press, or in other similar situations (2) **:** a piece with a motion more or less like that of a ram or piston (as a device for firing the charge in a cartridge or a contact mine, the dasher of a churn, or the iron core of an electric sucking coil) **c :** a tank in which clay is worked with water to the proper consistence **:** BLUNGER **d :** the moving member that in molding ceramic or glassware by pressing forces clay or hot glass into shape **e :** a rubber suction cup attached to a wooden handle and used to free plumbing traps and waste outlets of minor obstructions

plunger 2e

plunger bucket *or* **plunger lift** *n* **:** a piston without a valve in a pump

plunger elevator *n* **:** HYDRAULIC ELEVATOR

plunge rod *n* **:** a leveling rod or a pointed steel rod used in plunging a grade

plunger piston *n* **:** PLUNGER 2b(1)

plunger pump *n* **:** FORCE PUMP

plunges *pres 3d sing of* PLUNGE, *pl of* PLUNGE

plunging *pres part of* PLUNGE

plunging fire *n* **:** direct fire from a superior elevation resulting in the projectiles striking the target (as ground) at a high angle

plung·ing·ly *adv* **:** in a plunging manner **:** with plunges or plunging

plunging rod *n* **:** PLUNGE ROD

1plunk \'pləŋk\ *also* **plonk** \'pläŋk, -ȯ-\ *vb* -ED/-ING/-S [imit.] *vt* **1 :** to pluck (as the string of a musical instrument) sharply so as to produce a quick, hollow, metallic, or harsh sound ⟨~*ing* the strings on a harp⟩; *also* **:** to play (a stringed instrument) in a plunking manner ⟨~*ed* the banjo⟩ **2 a :** to act on (as an object, a surface) so as to cause to give off a plunking sound; *also* **:** to move (as an object, a person) with a sudden or forceful movement usu. oriented to a particular place ⟨~*ed* herself into the chair⟩ ⟨~*ing* the books onto the table⟩ **b :** to strike (as a person) with the fist or a bullet ~ *vi* **1 :** to make a plunking sound ⟨frogs ~*ing* in the hollow⟩ **2 :** to drop or sink abruptly or heavily **:** PLUMP, DIVE ⟨~*ed* into the pool⟩ **3 :** to come out in favor of someone or something **:** SUPPORT — used with *for* ⟨the moderates finally ~*ed* for the party candidate⟩

2plunk \"\ *also* **plonk** \"\ *n* -s **1 a :** an act or instance of plunking **:** BLOW **b :** a sound of or as if of a musical instrument being plunked ⟨a ~ of hoofbeats⟩ **2** *slang* **:** DOLLAR ⟨paid 10 ~*s* for a ticket⟩

3plunk \"\ *also* **plonk** \"\ *adv* **1 :** with a plunking sound **:** PLUMP **2 :** PRECISELY, EXACTLY ⟨~ in the center —W.R. Kuhns⟩

plunk down *vi* **:** to drop abruptly **:** settle into position ⟨*plunked down* on the grass⟩ **~** *vt* **1 :** to put down usu. firmly or abruptly ⟨*plunked* his paper *down* on the table⟩ **:** settle (as oneself) into position ⟨*plunked* himself *down* on the bench⟩ **2 :** to pay out ⟨*plunked* $100 *down* for a suit⟩

plunk·er \-kə(r)\ *n* -s **:** one that plunks — see LURE illustration

plunky \-kē\ *adj* -ER/-EST **:** marked or marred by a plunking sound ⟨a ~ tune⟩

plun·ther \'plən(t)thə(r)\ *vi* -ED/-ING/-S [imit.] **:** PLOD, FLOUNDER

plup \'pləp\ *n* -s [imit.] **:** PLOP

1plu·per·fect \(ˈ)plü¦pərfə̇kt, -¦pəf-\ *adj* [modif. of LL *plusquamperfectus,* fr. L *plus* more + *quam* than + LL *perfectus* perfect (of a tense) — more at PLUS, QUANTITY, PERFECT] **1 :** PAST PERFECT **2 :** more than perfect or complete **:** SUPERLATIVE, UTTER — **plu·per·fect·ly** *adv* — **plu·per·fect·ness** *n*

2pluperfect \"\ *n* **1 :** the pluperfect tense of a language **2 :** a verb form in the pluperfect tense

1plu·ral \'plu̇rəl, 'plür-\ *adj* [ME *plurel, plural,* fr. MF & L; MF *plurel,* fr. L *pluralis,* fr. *plur-, plus* more + *-alis* -al] **1 :** belonging to a class of grammatical forms used to denote more than one ⟨~ noun⟩ ⟨~ pronoun⟩ ⟨~ endings⟩, used to agree with syntactically related forms denoting more than one ⟨~ verb⟩ ⟨~ adjective⟩, and used in languages (as ancient Greek) having a dual form to denote more than two — opposed to *singular* **2 :** relating to or consisting of or containing more than one ⟨~ citizenship⟩ ⟨~ winner⟩ or more than one kind or class ⟨~ population⟩ ⟨~ society⟩

2plural \"\ *n* -s [ME *plurel,* fr. *plurel, plural,* adj.] **:** the plural number or an inflectional form denoting it or a word in that form ⟨how such words form their ~*s*⟩

plural executive *n* **:** a group of officers or major officials (as a board of directors) or a committee that functions in making current decisions or in giving routine orders usu. the responsibility of an individual executive officer or official

plu·ral·ism \-rə,lizəm\ *n* -s **1 :** the quality or state of being plural ⟨ethical ~, which speculated on the variety of political systems that became possible once the moral value of group life was acknowledged —David Easton⟩ **2 a :** the holding by one person of two or more offices at once **b :** PLURALITY 2a **3 a :** a metaphysical theory that there are more than one or more than two kinds of ultimate reality — compare DUALISM, MONISM **b :** a metaphysical theory (as atomism or monadism) that reality is not an organic whole but is composed of a plurality of independent entities whether material or spiritual or both — contrasted with *monism* **4 a :** a state or condition of society in which members of diverse ethnic, racial, religious, or social groups maintain an autonomous participation in and development of their traditional culture or special interest within the confines of a common civilization **b :** a concept, doctrine, or policy proposing or advocating this state

plu·ral·ist \-ləst\ *n* **1 a :** a clergyman holding more than one benefice or living at a time **b :** a person holding two or more offices at once **2 :** one who holds a theory of pluralism or who advocates a state of pluralism

plu·ral·is·tic \¦=¦listik, -tēk\ *or* **plu·ral·ist** \'==ləst\ *adj* **:** of, relating to, or characterized by pluralism ⟨American culture is supremely *pluralist* in religion —Max Lerner⟩ — **plu·ral·is·ti·cal·ly** \¦=¦listək(ə)lē\ *adv*

pluralistic idealism *n* **:** a system of philosophical idealism emphasizing the multiplicity of selves and their individual experiences — contrasted with *monistic idealism;* compare LEIBNIZIANISM, PERSONALISM

plu·ral·i·ty \plü'ralәd·ē, plu̇'-, plə'-, -lətē, -i\ *n* -ES [ME *pluralite,* fr. MF *pluralité* large number, fr. LL *pluralitat-, pluralitas,* fr. L *pluralis* plural + *-itat-, -itas* -ity] **1 a :** the state of being plural ⟨~ of causes⟩ ⟨noun endings expressing ~⟩ **b :** the state of being numerous **c :** a large number or quantity **:** MULTITUDE **2 a :** the holding by one person of two or more benefices or livings at one time **b :** any of the benefices or livings so held **c :** the holding by one person of two or more offices or positions at one time **3 a :** a number greater than another number **b :** an excess of votes over those cast for an opposing candidate **c :** a number of votes cast for a candidate in a contest of more than two candidates that is greater than the number cast for any other candidate but not more than half the total votes cast — distinguished from *majority*

plu·ral·iza·tion \,plu̇rələ'zāshən, ,plür-, -,lī'-\ *n* -s [ISV *pluralize* + *-ation*] **:** the act of pluralizing

plu·ral·ize \'plu̇rə,līz, 'plür-\ *vb* -ED/-ING/-S *see -ize in Explan Notes* [ISV 1*plural* + *-ize*] *vt* **:** to make plural by using a plural form **:** attribute plurality to **~** *vi* **:** to take a plural **:** assume a plural form — **plu·ral·iz·er** \-zə(r)\ *n* -s

plu·ral·ly \-rəlē, -li\ *adv* [ME *pluraliche,* fr. *plurel, plural* plural + *-liche, -ly* -ly] **:** in a plural manner or in the plural form

plural marriage *n* **:** polygamous marriage esp. as once practiced by Mormons

plural vote *n* **:** the casting of more than one vote or the right of casting more than one vote or of voting in more than one constituency

plural wife *n* **:** a wife in a plural marriage; *esp* **:** a wife in unlawful polygamy who is not the lawful one

plu·rel \'plu̇rəl\ *n* -s [irreg. fr. 1*plural*] **:** a group or aggregate resulting from a process of categorizing or statistical analysis ⟨the age-classes of population . . . are purely nominal ~*s* with no tangible interaction —P.A.Sorokin⟩

pluri- *comb form* [L, fr. *plur-, plus* more — more at PLUS] **:** many **:** having or being more than one **:** MULTI- ⟨*pluri*axial⟩ ⟨*pluri*locular⟩

plu·ri·axial \¦plu̇rē+\ *adj* [*pluri-* + *axial*] **:** having more than one axis; *specif* **:** having flowers developed on secondary shoots — compare MONAXIAL

plu·ri·cellular \¦plu̇rə+\ *adj* [*pluri-* + *cellular*] **:** of, relating to, or involving several to many cells ⟨a tumor of ~ origin⟩

plu·ri·es \'plu̇rē,ēz\ *n, pl* **pluries** [ME, fr. LL, often, many times, fr. L *plur-, plus* more; fr. the use of the Latin word *pluries* in a writ of this kind] **:** any of one or more writs (as of fieri facias) issued after the first and alias writs have proved ineffectual

plu·ri·glandular \¦plu̇rə+\ *adj* [ISV *pluri-* + *glandular*] **:** of, relating to, affecting, or derived from more than one gland or kind of gland ⟨~ syndrome⟩ ⟨signs of ~ insufficiency —J.E. Kraus & W.A.D.Anderson⟩

plu·ri·lateral \"+\ *adj* [ISV *pluri-* + *lateral*] **:** MULTILATERAL

plu·ri·lingual \"+\ *adj* [*pluri-* + *lingual*] **:** MULTILINGUAL

plu·ri·loc·u·lar \¦plu̇rə¦läkyələ(r)\ *adj* [F *pluriloculaire,* fr. *pluri-* + *-loculaire* (fr. NL *loculus*)] **:** divided into chambers; *esp* **:** divided by longitudinal and transverse septa into many small chambers each producing a single diploid zoospore ⟨a ~ sporangium⟩

plu·ri·nominal \¦plu̇rə+\ *adj* [*pluri-* + *nominal*] **1 :** POLYNOMIAL **2 :** nominating or electing more than one representative ⟨~ district⟩

plu·rip·a·ra \plu̇'ripərə\ *n, pl* **pluripa·rae** \-pə,rē\ [NL, fr. *pluri-* + *-para*] **:** MULTIPARA

plu·ri·potent \¦plu̇rə+\ *adj* [*pluri-* + *potent*] *of embryonic tissue* **:** not fixed as to future developmental potentialities **:** PLASTIC

plu·ri·potentiality \"+\ *n* [*pluri-* + *potentiality*] **:** capacity to affect more than one organ or tissue

plu·ri·presence \"+\ *n* [*pluri-* + *presence*] **:** the theological notion of presence in more than one place at the same time ⟨~ of saints⟩

plu·ris pe·ti·tio \'plu̇rə̇spə̇'tishē,ō\ *n* [L, act of asking for more] *Scots law* **:** PLUS PETITIO

plu·ri·syllable \¦plu̇rə+\ *n* [*pluri-* + *syllable*] **:** a word of more than one syllable — compare POLYSYLLABIC

plu·ri·va·lent \¦plu̇rə¦vālənt, (ˈ)plü¦rivəl-\ *adj* [ISV *pluri-* + *valent*] **:** having several degrees of power or capability; *specif* **:** consisting of several associated homologous chromosomes ⟨~ chromatin rods⟩

plu·ri·valve \'plu̇rə,valv\ *adj* [prob. fr. (assumed) NL *plurivalvis,* fr. NL *pluri-* + *-valvis* (fr. *valva* valve)] **:** MULTIVALVE

plu·ri·verse \'plu̇rə,vərs\ *n* -s [*pluri-* + *-verse* (as in *universe*)] **:** the world as conceived according to a theory of pluralism — compare MULTIVERSE

plu·ri·vocalic \¦plu̇rə+\ *adj* [*pluri-* + *vocalic*] **:** having more than one vowel — compare UNIVOCALIC

plu·ri·vol·tine \¦plu̇rə¦vōl,tēn, -,tᵊn\ *adj* [*pluri-* + *-voltine* (as in *bivoltine*)] **:** having several generations a year — used esp. of a silkworm

plu·riv·o·rous \(ˈ)plü¦riv(ə)rəs\ *adj* [*pluri-* + *-vorous*] **:** living upon several hosts ⟨~ fungus⟩

1plus \'pləs\ *prep* [L *plur-, plus* more; akin to Gk *pleiōn, pleōn* more, L *plenus* full — more at FULL] **1 :** increased by **:** with the addition or increment of **:** with an addition ⟨four ~ five or mathematically expressed 4 + 5⟩ ⟨the debt ~ interest⟩ — compare MINUS **2 :** possessed of **:** having gained **:** WITH ⟨came home poorer and ~ a wife and three children⟩

2plus \"\ *n, pl* **plus·es** *also* **plus·ses** \-səz\ **1 :** PLUS SIGN **2 :** an added quantity **:** something additional or extra **3 :** a positive quantity **:** GAIN, ADVANTAGE ⟨the quiet operation of the system was an unexpected ~⟩ **4 :** SURPLUS

3plus \"\ *adj* **1 a :** requiring addition ⟨the ~ sign⟩ **b :** algebraically positive ⟨a ~ quantity⟩ **2 a :** having or receiving as an addition or gain — used predicatively ⟨he was ~ a useful nag on the deal⟩ **b :** having or being in addition to what is anticipated ⟨other ~ values were the excellent schools and good neighbors⟩ **3 a :** falling high in the range (as of quality or size) specified — usu. used postpositively ⟨a grade of C ~ in French⟩ ⟨a sheet of 12 ~ copper⟩ **b :** greater than that specified esp. in size ⟨a 100 ~ mesh⟩ ⟨a conglomerate of ~ one inch gravel⟩ **c :** possessing a specified quality to an exceptional or unanticipated degree ⟨a new higher waistline that is style ~⟩ ⟨his smile had charm ~⟩ **4 :** positively electrified **:** electrically positive **5 a :** reacting sexually to a morphologically indistinguishable but physiologically separable minus form — used of lower fungi in which maleness and femaleness are indeterminable as such; compare HETEROTHALLIC **b :** of, relating to, or exhibiting such a sexual character

4plus \"\ *vt* **plussed** \-st\ **plussed** \"\ **plus·sing** \-siŋ\ **plus·es** *also* **plusses** \-səz\ **:** to add something to **:** INCREASE ⟨hoping to ~ his sale⟩

plus fours *n pl* **:** knickerbockers for sports and country wear made four inches longer than ordinary knickerbockers for looseness and ease at the knees

plus fours

1plush \'pləsh\ *n* -ES [MF *peluche,* prob. fr. (assumed) MF *peluchier* to pick, pluck, clean, fr. OF, fr. (assumed) VL *piluccare* to pick, clean, irreg. fr. L *pilare* to remove the hair from, fr. *pilus* hair — more at PILE] **1 a :** a fabric that has an even pile longer and less dense than velvet pile, is made on a cotton ground with a pile of silk, mohair, rayon, or cotton, and is used esp. for upholstery **b plushes** *pl* **:** plush breeches such as are worn by some footmen **2 :** a natural substance (as grass) that is felt to resemble plush in softness or appearance

2plush \"\ *adj, sometimes* -ER/-EST **1 :** relating to, like, or made of plush **2 :** notably luxurious, expensive, or easy **:** highly superior of its kind ⟨a ~ job⟩ ⟨~ apartments⟩

plush copper *n* **:** CHALCOTRICHITE

plush head *n* **:** a curved head, top, or bottom of a piece of machinery that is convex on the outside

plushed \'pləsht\ *adj* **1 :** resembling plush **2 :** covered, dressed, or finished in plush

plush·i·ly \-shəlē\ *adv* **:** in a plushy manner **:** so as to resemble plush ⟨~ green lawns⟩

plushlike \'=,=\ *adj* **:** resembling plush esp. in having a soft piled surface

plush·ly *adv* **:** LUXURIOUSLY

plushy \'pləshē, -shi\ *adj* -ER/-EST **1 a :** having the texture or appearance of plush **:** soft and shaggy **b :** covered with plush **2 :** LUXURIOUS, RICH, SHOWY **:** PLUSH 2

plu·sia \'plüz(h)ēə\ *n* [NL, fr. Gk *plousios* rich; fr. the metallic markings on the wings; akin to Gk *ploutos* wealth] **1** *cap* **:** a large widely distributed genus (the type of the family Plusiidae) of moths that have a stout body, slender antennae, and the fore wings usu. with metallic markings **2** -s **:** any moth of *Plusia* or a closely related genus

1plu·si·id \'plüsēəd\ *adj* [NL *Plusiidae*] **:** of or relating to the Plusiidae

2plusiid \"\ *n* -s **:** a moth of the family Plusiidae

plu·si·idae \plü'sīə,dē\ *n pl, cap* [NL, fr. *Plusia,* type genus + *-idae*] **:** a family of moths that are closely related to and often included among the Noctuidae, have hairy eyes and larvae which move like spanworms, and include various economic pests — see PLUSIA

plus juncture *n* **:** OPEN JUNCTURE

plus lens *n* **:** CONVERGING LENS

plus pe·ti·tio \'pləspə̇'tishē,ō\ *n* [LL, fr. L *plus* more + *petitio* petition — more at PLUS] *Roman, civil, & Scots law* **:** a demanding by the plaintiff in his pleading of more than he proves either in amount or as to time or condition of performance

plus pressure *n* **:** pressure (as in a boiler) in excess of atmospheric pressure

plus·sage *also* **plus·age** \'pləsij\ *n* -s **:** an amount over and above another amount

plussed *past of* PLUS

plusses *pl of* PLUS, *pres 3d sing of* PLUS

plus sign *n* **1 :** a sign + denoting addition or a positive quantity — compare MINUS SIGN **2 :** an indication of desirable qualities **:** a favorable sign ⟨her neatness is a *plus sign*⟩

plussing *pres part of* PLUS

plus value *n* **:** a card or other value that is worth less than ½ probable trick but adds somewhat to the value of the hand in some methods of evaluating the strength of a hand in contract bridge

plut- *or* **pluto-** *comb form* [Gk *plout-, plouto-,* fr. *ploutos;* prob. akin to Gk *plein* to sail, float — more at FLOW] **:** wealth ⟨*plut*archy⟩ ⟨*pluto*mania⟩

plu·tarch \'plü,tärk, -tak\ *n* -s *sometimes cap* [after *Plutarch* †A.D.120? Greek biographer] **:** BIOGRAPHER

plu·tarch·an \-kən\ *or* **plu·tarch·ian** \(ˈ)plü¦tärkēən\ *adj, usu cap* [*Plutarch* + E *-an*] **1 :** of or relating to Plutarch, the Greek biographer **2 :** suggesting or typical of the distinguished men of whose lives Plutarch wrote ⟨a *Plutarchan* parallel⟩

plu·tar·chy \'plü,tärkē\ *n* -ES [*plut-* + *-archy*] **:** PLUTOCRACY

plute \'plüt\ *n* -s [by shortening & alter.] *slang* **:** PLUTOCRAT

plu·te·al \'plüd·ēəl\ *also* **plu·te·an** \-ən\ *adj* [*pluteus* + *-al* or *-an*] **:** of, relating to, or being a pluteus

plu·tel·la \plü'telə\ *n* [NL, perh. fr. Gk *ploutos* wealth + NL *-ella*] **1** *cap* **:** the type genus of Plutellidae **2** -s **:** any moth of the genus *Plutella; esp* **:** CABBAGE MOTH

1plu·tel·lid \-ləd\ *adj* [NL *Plutellidae*] **:** of or relating to the Plutellidae

2plutellid \"\ *n* -s [NL *Plutellidae*] **:** a moth of the family Plutellidae

plu·tel·li·dae \-lə,dē\ *n pl, cap* [NL, fr. *Plutella,* type genus + *-idae*] **:** a family of small often cryptically colored moths with narrow wings and with usu. green phytophagous larvae that include some economically important pests of cultivated plants — see PLUTELLA

plu·te·us \'plüd·ēəs\ *n, pl* **plu·tei** \-ē,ī\ *also* **pluteuses** [L] **1 a :** a low wall or parapet in ancient Roman architecture; *esp* **:** one used as a partition between the bases of columns **b :** an ancient Roman reading desk or storage place for manuscripts **2** [NL, fr. L] **:** the free-swimming bilaterally symmetrical larva of a sea urchin or ophiuran distinguished by several slender anteriorly projecting processes enclosing calcareous rods

plu·toc·ra·cy \plü'täkrəsē, -si\ *n* -ES [Gk *ploutokratia,* fr. *ploutos* wealth + *-kratia* -cracy] **1 :** government by the wealthy **:** the rule or dominion of wealth or of the rich **2 a :** a controlling or influential class of rich men **:** a body of plutocrats

plu·to·crat \'plüd·ə,krat, -ütə,- *usu* -ad·+V\ *n* -s [fr. *plutocracy,* after such pairs as E *aristocracy: aristocrat*] **:** a person with power or influence due to his wealth **:** a member of a plutocracy

plu·to·crat·ic \¦==¦krad·|ik, -at|, |ēk\ *also* **plu·to·crat·i·cal** \|ə̇kəl, |ēk-\ *adj* **:** of, relating to, or characteristic of plutocrats or plutocracy — **plu·to·crat·i·cal·ly** \|ə̇k(ə)lē, |ēk-, -li\ *adv*

plu·to·democracy \¦plüd·ō+\ *n* [*plut-* + *democracy*] **:** a democracy held to be controlled by people of wealth rather than by the common man ⟨attacks by Fascist dictators on western *plutodemocracies*⟩

plu·to·gogue \'plüd·ə,gäg *sometimes* -,gȯg\ *n* -s [*plut-* + *-gogue* (as in *demagogue*)] **:** a person who favors the wealthy or their interests or attempts to present them to the public in a favorable light — **plu·to·gogu·ery** \-,gäg(ə)rē, ,==ˈ=(=)= *sometimes* -gȯg-\ *n* -ES

plu·tol·a·try \plü'tälə·trē\ *n* -ES [*plut-* + *-latry*] **:** excessive devotion to wealth

plu·tol·o·gy \-ləjē\ *n* -ES [*plut-* + *-logy*] **:** the scientific study of wealth **:** theoretical economics

plu·to·ma·nia \,plüd·ə'mānēə\ *n* [NL, fr. *plut-* + LL *mania*] **:** excessive or abnormal desire for wealth; *also* **:** insanity marked by delusions of wealth

plu·to monkey \'plüd·(,)ō-\ *n, usu cap P* [after *Pluto,* Greek god of the subterranean world of the dead] **1 :** a long-tailed West African guenon monkey (*Cercopithecus leucampyx*) of a grizzled blackish color with a white frontal band **2 :** a red guenon (*Erythrocebas pyrrhonotus*) often kept as a pet in ancient Egypt and a favorite of present-day organ-grinders

plu·ton \'plü,tän\ *n* -s [prob. back-formation fr. *plutonic*] **:** a body of intrusive igneous rock of any size or shape; *esp* **:** one of large size that was originally deep-seated

plu·to·ni·an \plü'tōnēən, '====\ *adj* [L *plutonius* plutonian (fr. Gk *ploutōnios,* fr. *Ploutōn* Pluto, Greek god of the subterranean world of the dead) + E *-an*] **1** *sometimes cap* **a :** of or relating to the lower world **:** INFERNAL **b :** resembling the lower world **:** grim and gloomy **:** harsh and unpleasing ⟨a ~ darkness⟩ ⟨such ~ landscapes⟩ **2 :** PLUTONIC **1 3 :** of or relating to the planet Pluto

plu·ton·ic \(ˈ)plü¦tänik, -nēk\ *adj* [L *Pluton-, Pluto* Pluto (fr. Gk *Ploutōn*) + E *-ic*] **1 a :** relating to or being the theory of the plutonists **:** IGNEOUS **b :** originating or situated deep within the earth **2** *sometimes cap* **:** of or relating to the Greek god Pluto : PLUTONIAN 1

plutonic plug *n* **:** a plug composed of holocrystalline granular igneous rock (as granite or gabbro)

plutonic rock *n* **:** an igneous rock (as granite) of holocrystalline granular texture regarded as having solidified at considerable depth below the surface

plu·to·nism \ˈplüt°n,izəm\ *n* -s [*plutonium* + *-ism*] **:** poisoning from exposure to or absorption of radiations from plutonium

plu·to·nist \ˈplüt°nə̇st\ *n* -s [*plutonic* + *-ist*] **:** an adherent of the theory that the igneous rocks have solidified from magmas, some of them at great depth below the surface — opposed to *neptunist*

plu·to·nite \-°n,īt\ *n* -s [ISV *plutonic* + *-ite;* orig. formed as G *plutonit*] **:** a deep-seated rock

plu·to·ni·um \plüˈtōnēəm\ *n* -s [NL, fr. *Pluton-*, *Pluto* Pluto, most remote known planet in our solar system (fr. L *Pluton-*, *Pluto* Pluto, Greek god of the subterranean world of the dead) + *-ium*] **:** a radioactive metallic element of the actinide series that is similar chemically to uranium, that is usu. produced in nuclear reactors as the long-lived isotope of mass number 239 by spontaneous emission of an electron from neptunium obtained in turn from uranium 238, that is also found in minute quantities in pitchblende and other uranium-containing ores, that undergoes very slow disintegration with the emission of a helium nucleus to form uranium 235, and that is fissionable with slow neutrons to yield atomic energy for use in power plants or atom bombs — symbol *Pu;* see ELEMENT table, NEPTUNIUM SERIES

plu·to·nom·ic \ˌplüt°nˈämik\ *adj* [ISV *plutonomy* + *-ic*] **:** of or relating to political economy or economics

plu·ton·o·my \plüˈtänəmē\ *n* -ES [ISV *plut-* + *-nomy*] **:** POLITICAL ECONOMY : ECONOMICS

pluvi- *or* **pluvio-** *also* **pluvia-** *comb form* [ME *pluvy-*, fr. L *pluvi-*, fr. *pluvia*] **:** rain ⟨*pluvia*meter⟩ ⟨*pluvi*an⟩ ⟨*pluvio*graphy⟩

¹plu·vi·al \ˈplüvēəl\ *adj* [L *pluvialis*, fr. *pluvia* rain (fr. fem. of *pluvius* rainy, fr. *pluere* to rain) + *-alis* -al — more at FLOW] **1 :** of or relating to rain **:** characterized by abundant rain **2** *of a geologic change* **:** resulting from the action of rain or sometimes from the fluvial action of rainwater flowing in stream channels

²pluvial \"\ *n* -s [ML *pluviale* ecclesiastic's cope, fr. L, neut. of *pluvialis*, adj.] **1** *archaic* **:** an ecclesiastic's cope; *also* **:** a monarch's robe of state of similar design **2** [¹*pluvial*] **:** a prolonged period of wet climate in which the moisture relations of an affected area are profoundly altered (as by the formation of lakes or glaciers)

plu·vi·a·line \ˈplüvēə,līn\ *adj* [NL *Pluvialis* + E *-ine*] **:** of or relating to the plovers

plu·vi·a·lis \ˌplüvēˈāləs\ *n, cap* [NL, fr. L *pluvialis*, adj., pluvial] **:** a genus of Charadriidae including the golden plovers

plu·vi·an \ˈplüvēən\ *adj* [*pluvi-* + *-an*] **:** RAINY

plu·vi·o·graph \ˈplüvēə,graf, -rȧf\ *n* [ISV *pluvi-* + *-graph*] **:** a self-registering rain gauge

plu·vi·o·graph·ic \ˌ⸗⸗⸗ˈgrafik\ *also* **plu·vi·o·graph·i·cal** \-fə̇kəl\ *adj* [*pluviography* or *pluviograph* + *-ic* or *-ical*] **:** of or relating to pluviography or the pluviograph

plu·vi·og·ra·phy \ˌplüvēˈägrəfē\ *n* -ES [*pluvi-* + *-graphy*] **1 :** a branch of meteorology that deals with the automatic registration of precipitation (as of rain or snow) **2 :** graphic presentation of precipitation data

plu·vi·om·e·ter \ˌplüvēˈämədə(r)\ *also* **plu·vi·am·e·ter** \-ˈam-\ *n* [*pluviometer* prob. fr. F *pluviomètre*, fr. *pluvi-* + *-mètre* -meter; *pluviameter* alter. (influenced by L *pluvia* rain) of *pluviometer*] **:** RAIN GAGE

plu·vi·o·met·ric \ˌplüvēəˈme·trik\ *also* **plu·vi·o·met·ri·cal** \-rə̇kəl\ *adj* [ISV *pluvi-* + *-metric*, *-metrical*] **:** of, relating to, or used in the measurement of rainfall — **plu·vi·o·met·ri·cal·ly** \-rə̇k(ə)lē\ *adv*

plu·vi·om·e·try \ˌplüvēˈämə·trē\ *n* -ES [ISV *pluvi-* + *-metry*] **:** a branch of meteorology that deals with the measurement of rainfall

plu·vi·o·scope \ˈplüvēə,skōp\ *n* [ISV *pluvi-* + *-scope*] **:** RAIN GAGE

plu·vi·ose \ˈplüvē,ōs\ *adj* [L *pluviosus*] **:** marked by or regularly receiving heavy rainfall ⟨a ~ period⟩ ⟨~ areas⟩ — **plu·vi·os·i·ty** \ˌ⸗⸗ˈäsəd·ē\ *n* -ES

plu·vi·ous \ˈplüvēəs\ *adj* [ME *pluvyous*, fr. L *pluviosus*, fr. *pluvia* rain + *-osus* -ose] **:** of or relating to rain **:** RAINY, PLUVIOSE

¹ply \ˈplī\ *vb* **plied; plied; plying; plies** [ME *plien* to bend, fold, mold, fr. MF *plier* to bend, fold, fr. L *plicare* to fold; akin to OE *flohtenfōte* web-footed, OHG *flehtan* to braid, plait, ON *flētta* to braid, Goth *flahta* braid, L *plectere* to braid, plait, Gk *plekein* to plait, Skt *praśna* plaited basket] *vt* **1 a :** BEND, FOLD, MOLD **b :** to twist together (as two or more single yarns) **2** *obs* **:** to bend in will or sense **:** ADAPT ~ *vi* **1** *obs* **:** to be pliable **:** BEND; *also* **:** TWIST **2** *obs* **:** to be pliant **:** YIELD, COMPLY

²ply \"\ *n* -ES [ME (Sc) *ply* condition, fr. MF *pli* pleat, fold, fr. *plier*, v.] **1** *chiefly dial* **:** physical condition ⟨in good ~⟩ ⟨out of ~⟩ **2 :** FOLD, LAYER: **a :** one of the strands in a yarn composed of two or more strands **b :** one of several layers of cloth usu. sewn or laminated together ⟨a shirt collar that has three *plies* of cloth⟩ ⟨the body of a tire has several *plies* of rubberized fabric⟩ **c :** one of the interwoven webs in some fabrics and carpets **d :** one of the veneer sheets forming plywood **e :** a layer of a paper or paperboard composed of more than one web; *also* **:** a liner or filler of a pasteboard or combination board **f :** an arbitrary measure of thickness (as of paper) **3 a** *archaic* **:** BEND, CURVATURE ⟨the ~ of an animal's limb⟩ ⟨the ~ of the arm is the elbow⟩ **b :** a trend of mind or spirit **:** INCLINATION, BIAS

³ply \"\ *vb* **plied; plied; plying; plies** [ME *plien*, short for *applien* to apply] *vt* **1 a :** to use or wield diligently or vigorously and steadily **:** EXERT, EXERCISE ⟨~ an ax⟩ ⟨~ your wit⟩ ⟨go ~ thy needle; meddle not —Shak.⟩ **b :** to practice or perform diligently **:** apply oneself to ⟨~*ing* his trade⟩ **2 a :** to keep after **:** assail vigorously or continually **b :** to urge something importunately on **:** keep supplying ⟨~ her with questions⟩ ⟨*plied* the man with liquor⟩ **3 a** *obs* **:** to use (a tide or other natural aid) in working a ship **b :** to make a practice or business of rowing or sailing over or on ⟨the ferryboat *plies* the river⟩ ~ *vi* **1 a :** to employ oneself or work diligently or steadily **:** apply oneself **:** be in steady action ⟨those who ~ in freedom's cause⟩ ⟨oars ~*ing* strongly against the current⟩ **b** *Brit* **:** to wait regularly for business **:** have one's regular stand — used esp. of a porter, boatman, or other independent laborer ⟨a taxi driver ~*ing* for hire⟩ **2 a** *of a boat or its crew* **:** to work to windward **:** BEAT **b :** to direct one's course **:** STEER **c :** to go or travel more or less regularly between usu. specified points ⟨a steamer ~*ing* between opposite shores of the lake⟩ **syn** see HANDLE

plyboard \ˈ⸗,⸗\ *n* **1 :** PAPERBOARD **2 :** PLYWOOD

ply·er \ˈplī(ə)r, -īə\ *n* -s [¹*ply* + *-er*] **1 :** one that plies **2 plyers** *pl* **:** a balance of timbers in the form of a St. Andrew's cross used in raising and lowering a drawbridge

plyers *var of* PLIERS

ply·gain \ˈpli,gīn\ *n* -s [W, dawn, cockcrow, matins, plygain; akin to L *pullus* young fowl, young of an animal and to L *canere* to sing — more at FOAL, CHANT] **:** an old Welsh custom of carol or hymn singing at cockcrow on Christmas morning

plymetal \ˈ⸗,⸗⸗\ *n* **:** plywood sheathed on both sides with aluminum and used esp. in airplane construction

ply·mo·the·an \ˌpliməˈthēən\ *n* -s *cap* [irreg. fr. *Plymouth*, town in southeast Massachusetts + E *-an*] **:** a native or resident of Plymouth, Mass.

ply·mo·thi·an \"\ *n* -s *cap* [irreg. fr. *Plymouth*, city in southwest England + E *-an*] **:** a native or resident of Plymouth, England

¹plym·outh \ˈpliməth\ *adj, usu cap* [fr. *Plymouth*, England] **:** of or from the city of Plymouth, England **:** of the kind or style prevalent in Plymouth

²plymouth \"\ *n* -s *often cap* **:** FASHION GRAY

plymouth brother *n, pl* **plymouth brethren** *usu cap P&B* **:** a member of a religious body organized about 1830 at Plymouth, England, that takes the Bible as its sole guide, protests against sectarianism and rejects creeds and rituals, has no ordained ministry, organizes its meetings on a New Testament pattern, baptizes believers only, partakes of the Lord's Supper every Sunday, and emphasizes premillenialism

plymouth cloak *n, usu cap P* [fr. *Plymouth*, England; prob. fr. the idea that a returned traveler landing at Plymouth without money or adequate clothing could more easily provide himself with a staff to ward off possible beatings than with a cloak to cushion himself against them] *archaic* **:** STAFF, CUDGEL

plymouth porcelain *n, usu cap 1st P* **:** the first English commercial hard-paste porcelain made at Plymouth (1768–70) and continued at Bristol

plymouth rock *n, usu cap P&R* [fr. *Plymouth Rock*, the rock on which the Pilgrims are supposed to have landed in 1620 in Plymouth, Massachusetts] **1 :** an American breed of medium-sized single-combed dual-purpose domestic fowls that have long smooth yellow legs and occur in several color varieties (as white, barred, buff) **2 :** a bird of the Plymouth Rock breed

plywood \ˈ⸗,⸗\ *n* **:** a structural material consisting of sheets of wood glued or cemented together with the grains of adjacent layers arranged at right angles or at a wide angle and being made up (1) wholly of uniformly thin veneer sheets or (2) of usu. equal numbers of veneer sheets on either side of a thicker central layer — called also (1) *all-veneer plywood* (2) *lumber-core plywood;* compare LAMINATED WOOD

ply yarn *n* **:** yarn made by twisting together two or more strands that are often different in fiber and color

plzen *usu cap, var of* PILSEN

pm *abbr* **1** premium **2** premolar **3** pumice

PM \(ˈ)pēˈem\ *abbr or n* -s push money

PM *abbr* **1** past master **2** paymaster **3** peculiar meter **4** permanent magnet **5** *often not cap* per month **6** phase modulation **7** police magistrate **8** Pontifex Maximus **9** postmaster **10** *often not cap* [L *post meridiem*] afternoon **11** postmortem **12** prime minister **13** prize money **14** [L *pro mille*] per thousand **15** provost marshal **16** purchase money

Pm *symbol* promethium

PMG *abbr* **1** paymaster general **2** postmaster general **3** provost marshal general

PMH *abbr, often not cap* production per man-hour

pmk *abbr* postmark

PMO *abbr* principal medical officer

PMS *abbr* pregnant mare serum

pmt *abbr* payment

pn *abbr* **1** partition **2** position

PN *abbr* **1** *often not cap* please note **2** *often not cap* promissory note **3** psychoneurotic

PNA *abbr* pentose nucleic acid

-pnea *or* **-pnoea** \(p)(ˈ)nēə\ *n comb form* -s [NL, fr. Gk *-pnoia*, fr. *pnoia*, *pnoē* breathing, breath, fr. *pnein* to breathe] **:** breath **:** breathing ⟨hyper*pnea*⟩ ⟨poly*pnoea*⟩ ⟨oligo*pnea*⟩

pneu *abbr* pneumatic

pneum *abbr* pneumatic

pneum- *or* **pneumo-** *comb form* [NL, fr. Gk *pneum-*, fr. *pneuma*] **1 :** air **:** gas ⟨*pneumo*empyema⟩ ⟨*pneumo*pericardium⟩ **2 :** lung **:** pulmonary and ⟨*pneumo*gastric⟩ ⟨*pneum*ectomy⟩ **3 :** respiration ⟨*pneumo*gram⟩ **4 :** pneumonia **:** pneumonia and ⟨*pneumo*enteritis⟩ ⟨*pneumo*bacillus⟩ ⟨*pneumo*coccus⟩

pneu·ma \ˈn(y)ümə\ *n* -s [Gk, wind, air, breath, spirit] **1 a** (1) **:** an ethereal fiery stuff or universal spirit held by the ancient Stoics to be a cosmic principle (2) **:** the world soul or the spirit of God **b :** a life-giving principle in man; *specif* **:** the vital soul or spirit considered as a soul between body and spirit or as a spirit superior to both body and soul **2** [ML, fr. Gk, wind, breath] **a** (1) **:** a ligature in medieval music denoting a long florid phrase sung on one syllable or with no syllable (2) **:** a prolonged phrase sung in such manner **b :** NEUME 1

pneumat- *or* **pneumato-** *comb form* [LGk, fr. Gk, fr. *pneumat-*, *pneuma*] **1 :** spirit ⟨*pneumato*phobia⟩ ⟨*pneumato*graphy⟩ **2 :** air **:** vapor **:** gas ⟨*pneumato*lytic⟩ ⟨*pneumat*ize⟩ ⟨*pneumat*uria⟩ **3 :** respiration ⟨*pneumato*graph⟩ ⟨*pneumato*meter⟩ **4 :** pneumatic ⟨*pneumato*gram⟩

¹pneu·mat·ic \n(y)üˈmad·ik, -atik, -ēk *sometimes* nəˈm-\ *adj* [L *pneumaticus*, fr. Gk *pneumatikos*, fr. *pneumat-*, *pneuma* wind, air, breath, spirit (fr. *pnein* to breathe) + *-ikos* -ic; akin to OE *fnēosan* to sneeze — more at SNEEZE] **1 a :** of, relating to, or using air, wind, or other gas: (1) **:** moved or worked by air pressure either by a percussive action or by a rotary action ⟨~ chisel⟩ ⟨~ drill⟩ (2) **:** adapted for holding compressed air **:** inflated with air ⟨~ tire⟩ **b :** of or relating to pneumatics **2 :** of or relating to the pneuma; *esp* **:** SPIRITUAL **3 :** marked by or having cavities filled with air ⟨~ system of the pelican —E.A.Armstrong⟩ **4 :** having a well proportioned feminine figure; *esp* **:** having a full bust

²pneumatic \"\ *n* -s **1 :** a spiritual being; *specif* **:** one held by the Gnostics as belonging to the highest of the three classes into which mankind is divided **2 :** a pneumatic tire

pneumatic action *n* **:** an action employing compressed air and collapsible bellows for connecting and manipulating the movable parts of a pipe organ

pneu·mat·i·cal \-ad·ə̇kəl, -atə-, -ēk-\ *adj* [L *pneumaticus* + E *-al*] **:** PNEUMATIC

pneu·mat·i·cal·ly \-ə̇k(ə)lē, -ēk-, -li\ *adv* **:** in a pneumatic manner **:** by means of a pneumatic device

pneumatic caisson *n* **:** a caisson in which air pressure is used to keep out the water

pneumatic conveyor *or* **pneumatic elevator** *n* **:** CONVEYER 2 a (9)

pneumatic dispatch *n* **:** a system of tubes through which letters, packages, and related matter are sent by air pressure

pneumatic duct *n* **:** the duct that connects the air bladder with the alimentary canal in physostomous fishes

pneumatic gun *n* **:** a gun using compressed air or gas as the propulsive force usu. to throw dynamite or other high explosives

pneumatic hammer *n* **:** AIR HAMMER

pneu·ma·tic·i·ty \ˌn(y)üməˈtisəd·ē\ *n* -ES **:** the quality or state of being pneumatic; *specif* **:** a condition marked by the presence of air cavities

pneumatic physician *n* **:** a physician of an ancient Greek school of medical thought holding that health and disease depend on the proportions of the vital principle

pneumatic pile *n* **:** a tubular pile or large cylinder sunk by the atmospheric pressure exerted when the air is exhausted from a chamber at its lower end

pneumatic post *n* **:** the transmission of mail between post offices by pneumatic dispatch

pneumatic pump *n* **:** an air-exhausting pump **:** FORCE PUMP

pneu·mat·ics \n(y)üˈmad·iks, -atiks, -ēks *sometimes* nəˈm-\ *n pl but sing in constr* [*pneumat-* + *-ics*] **1 :** a branch of mechanics that deals with the mechanical properties of gases (as weight, pressure, elasticity) — compare AERODYNAMICS, AEROMECHANICS, AEROSTATICS **2** [NL *pneumatica*, fr. fem. of L *pneumaticus* pneumatic + E *-s*] **:** PNEUMATOLOGY

pneumatic syringe *n* **:** a stout tube closed at one end and provided with a piston for illustrating the phenomena of the compressibility of gases

pneumatic trough *n* **:** a trough that is filled with water or mercury for use in collecting gases

pneumatic tube *n* **:** a tube used in pneumatic dispatch

pneu·ma·tique \ˌn(y)üməˈtēk\ *n* -s [F, fr. *pneumatique*, adj., pneumatic, fr. L *pneumaticus*] **:** a letter or message transmitted by pneumatic dispatch

pneu·ma·tism \ˈn(y)ümə,tizəm\ *n* -s [*pneumat-* + *-ism*] **:** the manifestation of spiritual gifts; *specif* **:** observable phenomena and exterior signs frequently interpreted as indicating that one is possessed by the Holy Spirit

pneu·ma·ti·za·tion \ˌn(y)ümәd·əˈzāshən, -ətəˈz-, -ə,tīˈz-\ *n* -s [ISV *pneumatize* + *-ation*] **:** the presence or development of air-filled cavities in a bone

pneu·ma·tize \ˈ⸗⸗,tīz\ *vt* -ED/-ING/-S [*pneumat-* + *-ize*] **:** to make pneumatic; *esp* **:** to fill with air cavities

pneumatized *adj* **:** having air-filled cavities

pneumato- — see PNEUMAT-

pneu·ma·to·cele \ˈn(y)ümәd·ō,sēl\ *n* -s [MGk *pneumatokēlē*, a gaseous tumor, fr. Gk *pneumat-* + *kēlē* tumor] **:** a gas-filled cavity or sac occurring esp. in the lung

pneu·ma·to·cyst \-,sist\ *n* [*pneumat-* + *-cyst*] **1 :** the cavity of a pneumatophore **2 :** PNEUMATOPHORE 1

pneu·ma·tode \ˈn(y)ümə,tōd\ *n* -s [ISV *pneumat-* + *-ode*] **:** PNEUMATOPHORE

pneu·ma·to·gram \ˈn(y)ümәd·ō,gram\ *n* [ISV *pneumat-* + *-gram*] **1 :** PNEUMOGRAM **2 :** a message sent by pneumatic dispatch

pneu·ma·to·graph \-,graf\ *n* [ISV *pneumat-* + *-graph*] **:** PNEUMOGRAPH

pneu·ma·to·graph·ic \ˌ⸗⸗⸗ˈgrafik\ *adj* **1 :** of or relating to pneumatography **2 :** PNEUMOGRAPHIC

pneu·ma·tog·ra·phy \ˌn(y)üməˈtägrəfē, -fi\ *n* -ES [ISV *pneumat-* + *-graphy*] **1 :** writing held to be that of spirits and produced directly without a medium or material device **2 :** descriptive pneumatology

pneu·ma·to·logic \ˌn(y)ümәd·ō+\ *or* **pneu·ma·to·logical** \"+\ *adj* **:** of or relating to pneumatology

pneu·ma·tol·o·gist \ˌn(y)üməˈtäləjə̇st\ *n* -s **:** one trained or skilled in pneumatology; *specif* **:** one esp. prepared by training and experience to interpret the theological doctrine of the Holy Spirit

pneu·ma·tol·o·gy \-jē, -ji\ *n* -ES [NL *pneumatologia*, fr. *pneumat-* + *-logia* -logy] **1 a :** the doctrine or theory of spiritual beings (as the Holy Spirit and spirits between God and man) **b** (1) **:** the doctrine of spiritual phenomena (2) **:** magical or necromantic lore **2** *archaic* **:** a theory of the nature and functions of mind and soul **:** PSYCHOLOGY **3** *archaic* **:** the science of air or gases

pneu·ma·tol·y·sis \ˌ⸗⸗ˈtäləsə̇s\ *n* [NL, fr. *pneumat-* + *-lysis*] **:** the process by which pneumatolytic minerals are formed

pneu·ma·to·lyt·ic \ˌn(y)ümәd·ōˈlid·ik\ *adj* [ISV *pneumat-* + *-lytic*] **:** formed or forming by hot vapors or superheated liquids under pressure — used esp. of minerals and ores occurring in or near masses of igneous rock

pneu·ma·to·ma·chi·an \ˌ⸗⸗⸗ˈmākēən\ *n* -s *usu cap* [LGk *pneumatomachos* (fr. Gk *pneumat-* + *-machos* fighter — fr. *machesthai* to fight —) + E *-an*] **:** one who is hostile to or denies the divinity or personality of the Holy Spirit; *specif* **:** a member of a 4th century sect under the leadership of Macedonius, Bishop of Constantinople, holding the Holy Ghost to be a creature or created being

pneu·ma·tom·a·chist \ˌ⸗⸗ˈtäməkə̇st\ *n* -s *usu cap* [LGk *pneumatomachos* + E *-ist*] **:** PNEUMATOMACHIAN

pneu·ma·tom·a·chy \-kē\ *n* -ES *usu cap* [*pneumatomachist* + *-y*] **:** denial of the deity of the Holy Spirit

pneu·ma·tom·e·ter \ˌ⸗⸗ˈtämәd·ə(r)\ *n* [*pneumat-* + *-meter*] **1 :** an instrument for measuring the amount of force exerted by the lungs in respiration **2 :** SPIROMETER

pneu·ma·tom·e·try \-mə·trē\ *n* -ES [ISV *pneumat-* + *-metry*] **:** SPIROMETRY

pneu·ma·to·phore \ˈn(y)ümәd·ə,fō(ə)r, n(y)üˈmad·ə,-\ *n* -s [ISV *pneumat-* + *-phore*] **1 :** a muscular gas-containing sac that serves as a float on a siphonophore colony (as of members of the genus *Physalia*) **2 :** a submerged or exposed root often functioning as a respiratory organ of a swamp or marsh plant

pneu·ma·toph·o·rous \ˌn(y)üməˈtäf(ə)rəs\ *adj* **:** of, relating to, or having the characteristics of a pneumatophore

pneu·ma·toph·o·rus \-f(ə)rəs\ *n, cap* [NL, fr. *pneumat-* + *-phorus*] **:** a genus of small warm-water mackerels including the Pacific mackerel and the chub mackerel

pneu·ma·to·sis \ˌn(y)üməˈtōsə̇s\ *n, pl* **pneumato·ses** \-,sēz\ [NL, fr. Gk *pneumatōsis* inflation, fr. *pneumatoun* to inflate, turn into vapor (fr. *pneumat-*, *pneuma* wind, air, breath) + *-sis* — more at PNEUMATIC] **:** the presence of air or gas in abnormal places in the body

pneu·ma·tu·ria \ˌn(y)üməˈtu̇rēə, -əˈtyu̇-\ *n* -s [NL, fr. *pneumat-* + *-uria*] **:** passage of gas in the urine

pneume *var of* NEUME

pneu·mec·to·my \n(y)üˈmektəmē\ *n* -ES [ISV *pneum-* + *-ectomy*] **:** the surgical removal of lung tissue

pneumo- — see PNEUM-

pneu·mo·bacillus \ˌn(y)ümō+\ *n, pl* **pneumobacilli** [NL, fr. *pneum-* + *bacillus*] **:** a bacterium (*Klebsiella pneumoniae*) associated with pneumonia and other inflammations of the respiratory tract — called also *Friedländer's bacillus*

pneu·mo·branchia \ˌn(y)üməˈbraŋkēə\ *or* **pneu·mo·bran·chi·a·ta** \-,braŋkēˈäd·ə, -ād·ə\ *n pl, cap* [NL, fr. *pneum-* + *-branchia* or *branchiata*] *in former classifications* **:** a group of terrestrial snails (suborder Rhipidoglossa) comprising those (as members of the genus *Helicina*) in which the gills are replaced by a respiratory sac

pneu·mo·cele \ˈn(y)ümə,sēl\ *n* -s [ISV *pneum-* + *-cele*] **:** PNEUMATOCELE

pneu·mo·coc·cal \ˌ⸗⸗ˈkäkəl\ *also* **pneu·mo·coc·cic** \-ˈkäk(s)ik\ *adj* [NL *pneumococcus* + E *-al* or *-ic*] **:** of, caused by, or derived from pneumococci

pneu·mo·coc·ce·mia \ˌ⸗⸗,käkˈsēmēə, -äˈkēm-\ *n* -s [NL, fr. *pneumococcus* + *-emia*] **:** the presence of pneumococci in the circulating blood

pneu·mo·coc·cus \ˌ⸗⸗ˈkäkəs\ *n, pl* **pneumococ·ci** \-äˌkī, -ä(,)kē, -äk,sī, -äk(,)sē\ [NL, fr. *pneum-* + *-coccus*] **:** a bacterium (*Diplococcus pneumoniae*) that causes lobar pneumonia

pneu·mo·co·ni·o·sis *or* **pneu·mo·ko·ni·o·sis** \ˌ⸗mō,kōnēˈōsə̇s\ *also* **pneu·mo·no·co·ni·o·sis** *or* **pneu·mo·no·ko·ni·o·sis** \ˌ⸗mənō,k-\ *n, pl* **pneumoconio·ses** *or* **pneumokonio·ses** \-,sēz\ [*pneumoconiosis, pneumokoniosis* fr. NL, fr. *pneum-* + *-coniosis* (fr. ²*coni-* + *-osis*); *pneumonoconiosis, pneumonokoniosis* fr. NL, fr. *pneumon-* + *-coniosis* (fr. ²*coni-* + *-osis*)] **:** a disease of the lungs caused by the habitual inhalation of irritant mineral or metallic particles — compare ANTHRACOSIS, SILICOSIS

pneu·mo·dynamic \ˌn(y)ümō+\ *adj* [*pneum-* + *dynamic*] **:** acting by the force of gases in motion **:** PNEUMATIC

pneu·mo·encephalitis \ˌn(y)ümō+\ *n* [NL, fr. *pneum-* + *encephalitis*] **:** NEWCASTLE DISEASE

pneu·mo·encephalogram \"+\ *n* [*pneum-* + *encephalogram*] **:** a roentgenogram made by pneumoencephalography

pneu·mo·encephalograph \"+\ *n* [ISV *pneum-* + *encephalograph*] **:** PNEUMOENCEPHALOGRAM

pneu·mo·encephalographic \ˌ⸗⸗+\ *adj* **:** of or relating to pneumoencephalography — **pneu·mo·encephalographically** \"+\ *adv*

pneu·mo·encephalography \ˌ⸗⸗+\ *n* [ISV *pneum-* + *encephalography*] **:** roentgenography of the brain after the injection of air into the ventricles

pneu·mo·enteritis \ˌ⸗⸗+\ *n* [NL, fr. *pneum-* + *enteritis*] **:** pneumonia combined with enteritis

pneu·mo·gastric \"+\ *adj* [*pneum-* + *gastric*] **1 :** of or relating to the lungs and the stomach **2 :** VAGAL

pneumogastric nerve *also* **pneumogastric** *n* **:** VAGUS NERVE

pneu·mo·gram \ˈn(y)ümə,gram\ *n* [*pneum-* + *-gram*] **:** a record of respiratory movements obtained by pneumography

pneu·mo·graph \-,graf\ *n* [ISV *pneum-* + *-graph*] **:** an instrument for recording the thoracic movements or volume change during respiration

pneu·mo·graph·ic \ˌ⸗⸗ˈgrafik\ *adj* [ISV *pneum-* + *-graphic*] **:** of, relating to, or by means of pneumography — **pneu·mo·graph·i·cal·ly** \-fə̇k(ə)lē\ *adv*

pneu·mog·ra·phy \n(y)üˈmägrəfē\ *n* -ES [*pneum-* + *-graphy*] **1 :** a description of the lungs **2 :** roentgenography after the injection of air into a body cavity **3 :** the process of making a pneumogram

pneu·mo·hemothorax *also* **pneu·mo·haemothorax** \ˌn(y)ümō+\ *n* [NL, fr. *pneum-* + *hem-* + *thorax*] **:** accumulation of blood and gas in the pleural cavity

pneu·mo·hydrothorax \"+\ *n* [NL, fr. *pneum-* + *hydr-* + *thorax*] **:** HYDROPNEUMOTHORAX

pneu·mol·o·gy \n(y)üˈmäləjē\ *n* -ES [*pneum-* + *-logy*] **:** the scientific study of the respiratory organs

pneu·mol·y·sis \⸗ˈmäləsə̇s\ *n* [NL, fr. *pneum-* + *-lysis*] **:** PNEUMONOLYSIS

pneu·mo·mycosis \ˌn(y)ümō+\ *n* [NL, fr. *pneum-* + *mycosis*] **:** a fungus disease of the lung

pneumon- *or* **pneumono-** *comb form* [NL, fr. Gk, fr. *pneumōn*] **:** lung ⟨*pneumon*ectomy⟩ ⟨*pneumono*cele⟩

pneu·mo·nec·to·my \ˌn(y)üməˈnektəmē\ *n* -ES [ISV *pneumon-* + *-ectomy*] **:** excision of an entire lung or of one or more lobes of a lung — compare SEGMENTAL RESECTION

pneu·mo·nia \n(y)üˈmōnyə, nəˈm-, -ōnēə\ *n* -s [NL, fr. Gk *pneumonia,* fr. *pneumon-, pneumōn* lung, alter. (influenced by *pnein* to breathe) of *pleumōn* lung — more at SNEEZE, PULMONARY] **:** a disease of the lungs characterized by inflammation and consolidation followed by resolution and caused by microorganisms, viruses, chemical irritants, or foreign bodies — see BRONCHOPNEUMONIA, LOBAR PNEUMONIA, PRIMARY ATYPICAL PNEUMONIA

pneu·mon·ic \(ˈ)n(y)üˈmänik, nəˈm-\ *adj* [NL *pneumonicus,* fr. Gk *pneumonikos,* fr. *pneumon-* + *-ikos* -ic] **1 :** of or relating to the lungs **:** PULMONIC **2 :** of, relating to, or affected with pneumonia ⟨a ~ lung⟩ ⟨a ~ condition is also a frequent terminal state —K.F.Maxcy⟩

pneumonic plague *n* **:** plague of an extremely virulent form that involves chiefly the lungs and usu. is transmitted from person to person by droplet infection

pneu·mo·ni·tis \ˌn(y)ümə'nīdəs\ *n, pl* **pneumonit·i·des** \-ˈnidəˌdēz\ [NL, fr. *pneumon-* + *-itis*] **1 :** PNEUMONIA **2 :** a disease characterized by inflammation of the lungs esp. in patchy distribution

pneumonoconiosis *var of* PNEUMOCONIOSIS

pneu·mo·nog·ra·phy \ˌn(y)üməˈnägrəfē\ *n* -ES [*pneumon-* + *-graphy*] **:** X-ray photography of the lungs

pneumonokoniosis *var of* PNEUMOCONIOSIS

pneu·mo·nol·y·sis \ˌn(y)üməˈnäləsəs\ *n* [NL, fr. *pneumon-* + *-lysis*] **:** surgical freeing of the pleura so as to permit collapse of a lung involving (1) separation of the parietal pleura from the fascia of the chest wall or (2) separation of the visceral and parietal layers of pleura — called also (1) *external pneumonolysis,* (2) *internal pneumonolysis*

pneu·mo·noph·o·ra \ˌn(y)üməˈnäfərə\ *or* **pneumonophorae** \-əˌrē\ *n pl, cap* [NL, fr. *pneumon-* + *-phora* or *-phorae*] *in former classifications* **:** a division of Holothurioidea comprising forms with a respiratory tree — compare APNEUMONA

pneu·mo·no·ul·tra·mi·cro·scop·ic·sili·co·vol·ca·no·co·ni·o·sis \ˈn(y)ümə(ˌ)nō,əltrəˌmīkrəˈskäpik'silə(ˌ)kō,välˈkā-(ˌ)nō,kōnēˈōsəs\ *n* [NL, fr. *pneumon-* + ISV *ultramicroscopic* + NL *silic-* + *volcano* + *-coniosis* (fr. ²*coni-* + *-osis*)] **:** a pneumoconiosis caused by the inhalation of very fine silicate or quartz dust and occurring esp. in miners

pneu·mo·nys·sus \ˌn(y)üməˈnisəs\ *n, cap* [NL, prob. fr. *pneumon-* + Gk *hyssos* javelin; fr. the club-shaped peritreme] **:** a genus of mites (family Halarachnidae) that live in the air passages of mammals

pneu·mo·pericardium \ˈn(y)ümō+\ *n* [NL, fr. *pneum-* + *pericardium*] **:** accumulation of air or other gas in the pericardial sac

pneu·mo·peritoneum \"+\ *n* [NL, fr. *pneum-* + *peritoneum*] **1 :** a state in which air or other gas is present in the peritoneal cavity **2 :** the induction of pneumoperitoneum to alter pressure relations within the body cavity and relax a tuberculous lung

pneu·mo·peritonitis \"+\ *n* [NL, fr. *pneum-* + *peritonitis*] **:** peritonitis with the presence of gas in the peritoneal cavity

pneu·mo·stome \ˈn(y)ümə,stōm\ *n* -S [ISV *pneum-* + *-stome*] **:** the respiratory opening of a gastropod mollusk

pneu·mo·tachogram \ˈn(y)ümō+\ *n* [*pneum-* + *tachogram*] **:** a record of the velocity of the respiratory function obtained by use of a pneumotachograph

pneu·mo·tachograph \"+\ *n* [ISV *pneum-* + *tachograph*] **:** a device or apparatus for measuring the rate of the respiratory function

pneu·mo·taxic center \ˈn(y)ümə+...-\ *n* [*pneumotaxic* fr. *pneum-* + *taxic*] **:** a neural center in the upper part of the pons that provides inhibitory impulses on inspiration and thereby prevents overdistention of the lungs and helps to maintain alternately recurrent inspiration and expiration

pneu·mo·tectic \ˌ⸗⸗ˈtektik\ *adj* [*pneum-* + L *tectus* (past part. of *tegere* to enclose, cover) + E *-ic* — more at THATCH] **:** of, relating to, or constituting late magmatic stages of mineral deposition in which solutions and gases have a leading role

pneu·mo·thorax \ˈn(y)ümō+\ *n* [NL, fr. *pneum-* + *thorax*] **:** a state in which air or other gas is present in the pleural cavity and which occurs spontaneously as a result of disease or injury of lung tissue or puncture of the chest wall or is induced as a therapeutic measure to collapse the lung (as in tuberculosis)

pneu·mo·trop·ic \ˈn(y)üməˈträpik\ *adj* [*pneum-* + *-tropic*] **:** turning, directed toward, or having an affinity for lung tissues — used esp. of infective agents

pneu·mot·ro·pism \n(y)üˈmä·trə,pizəm\ *n* [*pneum-* + *-tropism*] **:** the quality or state of being pneumotropic

-pneus·ta \(p)ˈn(y)üstə\ *n pl comb form* [NL, fr. Gk *-pneustos* having (such) breath, fr. (assumed) Gk *pneustos* (verbal of Gk *pnein* to breathe) — more at SNEEZE] **:** animals having a (specified) mode of breathing — in higher taxa ⟨Enteropneusta⟩

PNG *abbr, often not cap* persona non grata

pnl *abbr* panel

-pnoea — see -PNEA

pnom·penh *or* **phnom penh** \pəˈnōmˈpen\ *adj, usu cap initial Ps* [fr. *Pnompenh, Phnom Penh,* city in Cambodia] **:** of or from Pnompenh, the capital of Cambodia **:** of the kind or style prevalent in Pnompenh

pnr *abbr* pioneer

pntd *abbr* painted

pntr *abbr* painter

pnxt *abbr* [L *pinxit*] he or she painted it

po *abbr* **1** poetry **2** point **3** pole

PO *abbr* **1** personnel officer **2** petty officer **3** pilot officer **4** postal order **5** post office **6** probation officer **7** putout

Po *symbol* polonium

poa \ˈpōə\ *n* [NL, fr. Gk, grass; akin to Gk *pidax* spring, Lith *pieva* meadow] **1** *cap* **:** a genus of grasses that are widely distributed in temperate and arctic regions and have open panicles with 2- to 6-flowered spikelets on which the upper scales exceed the empty ones — see KENTUCKY BLUEGRASS, WIRE GRASS **2** -S **:** any grass of the genus *Poa*

po·a·ce·ae \pōˈāsē,ē\ [NL, fr. *Poa* + *-aceae*] *syn of* GRAMINEAE

¹**poach** \ˈpōch\ *vt* -ED/-ING/-ES [ME *pochen,* fr. MF *pocher,* fr. OF *pochier,* lit., to put into a bag (the white of the egg being regarded as the bag in which the yolk is contained), fr. *poche* bag, pocket, of Gmc origin; akin to MD *poke* bag — more at POKE (bag)] **1 :** to cook in a liquid kept just below the boiling point ⟨trout *~ed* in bouillon⟩ **2 :** to cook (as an egg) in a poacher

²**poach** \"\ *vb* -ED/-ING/-ES [MF *pocher,* of Gmc origin; akin to MD *poken* to poke, stick — more at POKE (to prod)] *vt* **1** *dial chiefly Eng* **:** to push, shove, or thrust roughly or forcefully **:** POKE **2 :** to trample or cut up with hoofs **:** make soft or muddy **:** make mudholes in ⟨good for grass, too, to be trodden except they ~ it, where it's sodden —John Masefield⟩ **3 a :** to trespass on ⟨a field *~ed* too frequently by the amateur —*Times Lit. Supp.*⟩ — often used with *on* or *upon* ⟨what happens to a poet when he *~es* upon a novelist's preserves —Virginia Woolf⟩ **b :** to take (game or fish) by illegal methods **:** STEAL ⟨men were transported with the worst felons for *~ing* a few hares or pheasants —G.B.Shaw⟩ **4 :** POTCH **5 :** to wash free from acid, thoroughly mix, and make uniform by agitation in a boiling weakly alkaline solution followed by boiling water — used of cellulose nitrate pulp ~ *vi* **1** *dial chiefly Eng* **:** POKE **2 a :** to sink into mud or mire while walking **:** plod through mud or soft ground **:** plunge about **b :** to become soft or muddy and full of holes when trampled on ⟨swampy country that is inclined to ~ in the winter —W.G.Batt & A.V.Allo⟩ **3 :** to trespass for the purpose of stealing game **:** take game or fish illegally ⟨had taken to *~ing* as a means of supplying fresh meat for the table —H.D.Quillin⟩ **4 :** to play a ball in a racket game that should normally be played by one's partner

poached egg *n* [ME *poched egg*] **1 :** an egg dropped from its shell and cooked in simmering water for about five minutes — called also *dropped egg* **2 :** an egg cooked in a poacher

¹**poach·er** \ˈpōchə(r)\ *n* -S [²*poach* + *-er*] **1 a :** one that trespasses or steals ⟨catches the ~ on his preserve —*Time*⟩ **b :** one who kills or takes game or fish illegally ⟨~*s* of deer —William Faulkner⟩ **2 a :** BALDPATE 2 **b :** SEA POACHER **3 :** POTCHER **4** *or* **poacher tub :** a large tank with a rotating paddle wheel for poaching cellulose nitrate pulp

²**poacher** \"\ *n* -S [¹*poach* + *-er*] **1 :** a vessel fitted with a pan containing depressions or shallow cups in each of which an egg can be cooked over steam rising from boiling water in the bottom part **2 :** a shallow baking dish in which food (as fish) can be poached

poacher 1

poach·wood \ˈpōch,wu̇d\ *n* [perh. alter. of *campeachy wood*] **:** LOGWOOD 1a(1), 1a(2)

poachy \ˈpōchē, -chi\ *adj* -ER/-EST [²*poach* + *-y*] **:** easily cut up or made muddy by the feet of cattle **:** SODDEN, SWAMPY ⟨a ~ field⟩

po·a·les \pōˈā(ˌ)lēz\ [NL, fr. *Poa* + *-ales*] *syn of* GRAMINALES

po·a·nes \pōˈā(ˌ)nēz\ *n, cap* [NL] **:** a genus of skipper butterflies

POB *abbr* post-office box

pob·by \ˈpäbi\ *adj* -ER/-EST [origin unknown] *dial Brit* **:** puffed up **:** SWOLLEN

po·bla·ción \ˌpō,bläsēˈōn\ *n, pl* **poblacio·nes** \-ō(ˌ)nās\ [PhilSp, fr. Sp, population, town, fr. LL *population-, populatio* people — more at POPULATION] **:** a center of a municipality in the Philippines that is usu. the barrio that gives the municipality its name and is the seat of government

po' boy \ˈpō,⸗\ *also* **po' boy sandwich** *n* [alter. (in the attempt to represent southern U.S. pronunc.) of *poor boy, poor boy sandwich*] **:** POOR BOY

pobs \ˈpäbz\ *n pl* [prob. baby-talk alter. of *porridge*] *dial Eng* **:** PORRIDGE

POC *abbr, often not cap* port of call

po·can \ˈpōkən\ *or* **pocan bush** *n* [*pocan* modif. of *puccoon, pakon* (in some Algonquian language of Virginia) — more at POKE] **:** POKEWEED

po·chade \pōˈshäd\ *n* -S [F, fr. *pocher* to poach (an egg), sketch roughly + *-ade* — more at POACH] **:** a rough or quickly executed sketch or study

po·chard *also* **poa·chard** \ˈpōchə(r)d\ *n, pl* **pochards** *also* **pochard** [origin unknown] **:** any of numerous rather heavy-bodied diving ducks belonging chiefly to the genus *Aythya* and having large head and feet with legs placed far back under the body; *specif* **:** a common Old World duck (*A. ferina*) that greatly resembles the American redhead

po·ché \(ˈ)pōˈshā\ *n* -S [F, past part. of *pocher* to sketch roughly] **:** the black portion of an architectural plan representing solids (as walls and columns)

po·ched \-ād\ *adj* [*poché* + *-ed*] *of an architectural drawing* **:** having the parts representing solids filled in

pocher *var of* POTCHER

po·chette \pōˈshet\ *n* -S [F, dim. of *poche* pocket — more at POACH] **1 :** ³KIT **2 :** HANDBAG 2 **3 :** a small envelope of thin transparent paper for holding a stamp (as in an album)

po·chis·mo \pōˈchēz(ˌ)mō\ *n* -S [MexSp, fr. *poche, pocho* U.S. resident of Mexican origin (prob. fr. Sp *pocho* discolored) + Sp *-ismo* -ism] **1 :** a term of U.S. origin borrowed into Mexican Spanish and used along the border between the U.S. and Mexico esp. by U.S.-born Mexicans ⟨not a single ~ has added to the beauty of our Spanish language —F.G.Beraza⟩ **2 :** a vocabulary consisting of pochismos

po·choir \(ˈ)pōshˈwär\ *n* -S [F, stencil, stencil plate, fr. *pocher* to poach (an egg), sketch roughly, stencil — more at POACH] **:** a stencil process for making colored prints or adding color to a printed key illustration

po·cho·te \pəˈchōd·ē\ *n* -S [MexSp, fr. Nahuatl *pochotl*] **1 a :** any of several trees of the genus *Ceiba*; *esp* **:** CEIBA 2a **b :** a medium-sized tree (*Cochlospermum irtifolium*) having seeds covered with long cottony white hairs **2 :** the fiber of a pochote tree used as a stuffing esp. for mattresses

¹**pock** \ˈpäk\ *n* -S [ME *pokke,* fr. OE *pocc*; akin to MLG & MD *pocke* pock, G dial. *pfoche* pock, L *bucca* cheek, mouth] **1 a :** a pustule on the surface of the body in smallpox and other eruptive diseases; *also* **:** a spot like such a pustule **b :** HOLE ⟨guiding the car around another ~ in the road —Peter De Vries⟩ ⟨his eyes wide ~*s* of fear in a white face —Joseph Hilton⟩ **2** *chiefly dial* **:** POX

²**pock** \"\ *vt* -ED/-ING/-S **:** to mark with or as if with pocks **:** PIT ⟨the rains of twenty centuries had *~ed* that pure and haughty face —Compton Mackenzie⟩ ⟨the hull was *~ed* with dents —Frank Schreider⟩

³**pock** \"\ *chiefly dial var of* ¹POKE 1a(1)

pock–arred \ˈ⸗ˈärd, -ȧd\ *adj* [E dial. *pock-arr* pockmark (fr. ¹*pock* + *arr*) + *-ed*] *dial Brit* **:** POCKMARKED

¹**pock·et** \ˈpäkət, *usu* -əd·+V\ *n* -S [ME *poket,* fr. ONF *pokete,* dim. of *poke, poque* bag, of Gmc origin; akin to MD *poke* bag — more at POKE] **1 :** a coarse bag or sack; *esp* **:** one used in packing produce for market ⟨the packing of green beans and peas in orange ~*s* —W.J.C. van Rensburg⟩ ⟨rice ~*s*⟩ **2 a :** a small bag carried by a person **:** PURSE ⟨Lucy Locket lost her ~⟩ **b :** a small cloth bag sewed or inserted into a garment and left open at the top or side ⟨pants ~⟩ ⟨coat ~⟩ ⟨change ~⟩ **3 :** any of various units of weight; *esp* **:** an English unit for hops equal to 168 pounds **4 :** supply of money **:** MEANS ⟨ample choice of accommodations to fit all ~*s* —*Christian Science Monitor*⟩ ⟨the real gems I have seen were beyond my ~ —H.J.Laski⟩ **5 :** something that serves as a receptacle or container: as **a :** any of the bags at the corners or sides of a billiard table **b :** a superficial pouch in some animals (as the cheek pouch of the pocket gopher) **c** (1) **:** a receptacle usu. of strong paper and open at one end attached to the inside cover of a book (2) **:** ENVELOPE **d** (1) **:** the trap of a weir or pound net (2) **:** the cod of a seine **e :** a box (as in a sorting case) or space (as on a checkerboard) for holding classified or alphabetized items or counters **6 :** a small isolated area or group distinguished (as in substance, form, contents, or condition) from a larger area or group surrounding it ⟨~*s* of unemployment, scattered across the country —*U.S. News & World Report*⟩ ⟨~*s* here and there where the population has remained unchanged since remotest centuries —G.O.Williams⟩: as **a** (1) **:** a cavity found on or beneath the surface of the ground and containing a deposit (as of gold, oil, gas, or water) ⟨china clay and china stone found in great ~*s* on the surface of the granite masses —L.D. Stamp⟩ ⟨an oil ~ underlying the city —*Amer. Guide Series: Mich.*⟩ (2) **:** a small body of ore ⟨are not uniformly ore bearing, but rather punctuated with ~*s* and sheets of iron ore —*Amer. Guide Series: Minn.*⟩ **b :** a small abnormal enclosed formation in the body ⟨a ~ is formed with a center of degenerated and infected material —Morris Fishbein⟩ **c :** a battle area or a body of soldiers surrounded or nearly surrounded by enemy forces ⟨the woods might have been planned by a master strategist to hold ~*s* of resistance —*Infantry Jour.*⟩ **d :** AIR HOLE **7 :** a hollow place or cavity: as **a :** a mountain glen or hollow ⟨small villages resting solidly in the ~*s* of northern mountains —*Amer. Guide Series: N.J.*⟩ **b :** a socket into which something (as a post, stake, or bar) fits ⟨the bars slide into ~*s* in the interior of the reactor —Leon Svirsky⟩ **c :** a cavity in a casting or a high point in a pipeline where foreign substance (as dirt or air) can collect and possibly become detrimental to intended functioning **d :** a hole or recess in a building member (as a window frame or flue) ⟨a venetian blind ~⟩ ⟨a soot ~⟩ **e :** an interspace made by sewing a strip of canvas on a sail in which a batten or a light spar can be placed **f :** a space between two bowling pins **g :** a cavity made in a piece of meat by a deep cut or removal of a bone to permit the insertion of stuffing ⟨a ~ in a shoulder of veal⟩ ⟨a ~ roast⟩ **8 :** an enclosed place or area: as **a :** a bight on a lee shore ⟨a little ~ with a stone beach at the head of it —G.W.Brace⟩ **b :** BLIND ALLEY ⟨no ~*s* or dead ends in which pupils might be trapped —*Nat'l Fire Codes*⟩ **c :** the position of a contestant in a race hemmed in by others **9 a :** a temporary extension to a foundry flask **b :** a large core of a foundry mold enclosed on three sides by metal and well pierced — **in one's pocket 1 :** very close to one **2 :** in one's control or possession ⟨sure that local law enforcers were *in his pocket* —*Time*⟩ ⟨the museum job safely *in his pocket* —Jacob Hay⟩ — **in pocket** *adv* **1 :** provided with funds **2 :** in the position of having made a profit ⟨probably find himself *in pocket* in a good year —F.D.Smith & Barbara Wilcox⟩

²**pocket** \"\ *vb* -ED/-ING/-S *vt* **1 a :** to put away in or as if in one's pocket ⟨*~ed* his change⟩ ⟨*~ed* his tools⟩ ⟨*~ed* his winnings⟩ **b :** to appropriate to one's own use **:** STEAL ⟨*~ed* the money he collected for charity⟩ ⟨fail to ring up a sale, ~ the cash —H.N.Schisler⟩ **c :** to hold under one's personal control ⟨circumvented in his attempt to ~ the legislature —E. A.Weeks⟩ **d :** to veto (a bill) by retaining it unsigned until after a legislature has adjourned ⟨the president and some governors have the power to kill a bill by *~ing* it⟩ **2 :** to put up with **:** ACCEPT, SWALLOW ⟨if I calmly ~ the abuse, I am laughed at —Oliver Goldsmith⟩ ⟨cheerfully *~ed* a loss in some cases —Warner Olivier⟩ **3 :** to set aside **:** forget about **:** SUPPRESS ⟨had almost of necessity *~ed* his pride —A.J.Cronin⟩ ⟨~ his scruples⟩ **4 a :** to enclose in or as if in a pocket ⟨the ring of hills in which the town is *~ed* —*Amer. Guide Series: Pa.*⟩ ⟨it has walls . . . high rocky ones that ~ fern and orchis —D.C.Peattie⟩ **b :** to force into a pocket **:** prevent from running or moving freely **:** hem in ⟨~ a boat in such a manner that she cannot escape or get ahead —H.A.Calahan⟩ **c :** to drive (a ball) into a pocket of a pool table **5 :** to form into a pocket or pouch **:** collect (pus) in a pocket or pouch **6 :** to create or establish pockets in ⟨*~ed* the nation here and there with jobless —*Time*⟩ ⟨a *~ed* dress⟩ ~ *vi* **:** to form pockets ⟨an automatic press that performs shaping operations, such as bumping, heading, and *~ing* —*Dict. of Occupations*⟩

³**pocket** \"\ *adj* **1 a :** small or flat enough to be carried in the pocket ⟨a ~ dictionary⟩ ⟨a ~ flask⟩ **b :** reduced in size **:** smaller than others of its kind **:** MINIATURE ⟨the recent bloodless ~ civil war —Paul Hofmann⟩ **c :** CONDENSED ⟨a ~ drama⟩ ⟨a ~ lecture⟩ **2 :** of or relating to money **:** MONETARY ⟨our ~ interest has something to do with our attitude —*Textbooks in Education*⟩ **3 :** carried in or paid from one's own pocket **:** used for or consisting of small cash outlays ⟨an adequate sum for ~ expenses⟩ **4 :** ISOLATED ⟨modern art is not a ~ movement —Howard Devree⟩

pock·et·able \-əbəl\ *adj* **:** capable of being carried or put in a pocket ⟨the format of this series, the most ~ of them all —Arthur Hesilrige⟩ — **pock·et·able·ness** *n* -ES

pocket battleship *n* **:** a small battleship built so as to come within treaty limitations; *specif* **:** a German vessel of World War II having 10,000 tons displacement and carrying 11-inch and 6-inch guns

pocket beach *n* **:** a usu. small beach at the head of a bay or other inlet

pocket billiards *n pl but usu sing in constr* **:** POOL 2b

pocket bird *n* **:** SCARLET TANAGER

pocketbook \ˈ⸗⸗,⸗\ *n* **1** *usu* **pocket book :** a small book that can be carried in the pocket; *esp* **:** a paperback sold cheaply to reach a mass market ⟨the popular novelist would be satisfied with his income from serials and scenarios and *pocket books* —Randall Jarrell⟩ **2 a :** a pocket notebook ⟨made a series of notes in his ~ —Ngaio Marsh⟩ **b** (1) **:** a pocket-size flat or folding container for money and personal papers **:** WALLET (2) **:** PURSE **c :** HANDBAG 2 ⟨held ~*s* in their laps; one of the ~*s* was black, the other of some kind of alligator skin —Millen Brand⟩ **3 a :** financial resources **:** INCOME ⟨apartment-house or cottage rentals to meet the ~*s* of the white-collar workers —*Harper's*⟩ **b :** economic interests ⟨have no intention of voting against their own ~*s* or against the party of their forebears —Elmo Roper & Louis Harris⟩ **4** *also* **pocketbook clam** \ˈ⸗⸗,⸗-\ **:** a freshwater mussel (*Lampsilis ventricosus*) of the upper Mississippi drainage area that yields mother-of-pearl and is used in button making

pocket boom *n* **:** a storage boom for sorted logs

pocket borough *n* **1 :** a former English parliamentary constituency controlled by a single person or family — compare CLOSE BOROUGH, ROTTEN BOROUGH **2 :** a political unit controlled by a single person or group

pocket chronometer *n* **:** a pocket watch with a chronometer escapement or with an observatory rating

pocket conveyor *n* **:** a conveyor with pockets attached to an endless moving chain

pocket dry rot *n* **:** PECKINESS

pocketed bat *n* **:** a small brown free-tailed bat (*Tadarida femorosacca*) of California

pocket edition *n* **1 :** POCKETBOOK 1 **2 :** a miniature form of something ⟨this famous dwarf was, when young, a very perfect *pocket edition* of a man —*Atlantic*⟩

pock·et·ful \ˈpäkət,fu̇l\ *n, pl* **pocketfuls** *or* **pocketsful** \-t-,fu̇lz, -ts,fu̇l\ **:** as much or as many as the pocket will contain ⟨a ~ of money⟩ ⟨a ~ of cigars⟩

pocket gopher *n* **:** any of numerous No. American fossorial sciuromorph rodents (family Geomyidae) distinguished by fur-lined cheek pouches **:** GOPHER 2a

pocket–handkerchief \ˈ⸗⸗+\ *n* **1 :** a handkerchief carried in the pocket **2 :** something tiny ⟨established in a hut on a *pocket-handkerchief* of land —Fletcher Pratt⟩

pocket–hole \ˈ⸗⸗,⸗\ *n* **:** an opening in an article of clothing that gives access to a pocket

pock·et·ing \ˈpäkəd·iŋ, -ətiŋ, -ēŋ\ *n* -S [¹*pocket* + *-ing*] **:** any of various strong usu. cotton fabrics used for pockets esp. in suits and coats

pocket judgment *n* [so called fr. its summary enforcement] **:** STATUTE MERCHANT

pocketknife \ˈ⸗⸗,⸗\ *n, pl* **pocketknives :** a knife with a blade folding into the handle to fit it for being carried in the pocket

pock·et·less \ˈpäkətləs\ *adj* **:** having no pocket

pocket money *n* **:** money for small current personal expenses ⟨provided with weekly *pocket money* to assure a feeling of financial dignity —*Amer. Guide Series: Minn.*⟩ — called also *spending money*

pocket mouse *n, pl* **pocket mice :** any of various nocturnal burrowing rodents resembling mice and belonging to *Perognathus* and related genera (family Heteromyidae) that are found in arid parts of western No. America and have long hind legs and tail and fur-lined cheek pouches

pocket piece *n* **1 :** a coin or token kept in the pocket as a charm or good-luck piece ⟨the Scout Good Turn *pocket piece* —*Boy Scout Handbook*⟩ **2 :** a movable part in a window-frame pulley stile that gives access to the enclosed weight and sash cord

pocket pistol *n* **1 :** a small pistol **2 :** a pocket flask for liquor

pocket plum *n* **:** PLUM POCKET

pocket print *n* **:** a detachable core print left in the mold when a pattern is lifted

pocket rat *n* **:** any of various rodents with cheek pouches: as **a :** POCKET GOPHER **b :** POCKET MOUSE **c :** KANGAROO RAT

pocket rot *n* **:** a rot found esp. in timber that produces small pockets often filled with fungus threads, cellulose, or other substances, but eventually becoming empty cavities

pockets *pl of* POCKET, *pres 3d sing of* POCKET

pocket sheriff *n* **:** an English sheriff formerly appointed by the sole authority of the crown

pocket–size \ˈ⸗⸗ˈ⸗\ *or* **pocket–sized** \ˈ⸗⸗ˈ⸗\ *adj* **1 :** of a size convenient for the pocket ⟨a *pocket-size* book⟩ **2 :** small in scale **:** DIMINUTIVE ⟨a *pocket-size* country⟩

pocket veto *n* **:** an indirect veto of a legislative bill by an executive (as by the president or a state governor) through retention of the bill unsigned until after adjournment of the legislature

pock·ety \ˈpäkəd·ē, -ətē, -i\ *adj* [¹*pocket* + *-y*] **1 :** having an uneven distribution of ore — used of an ore deposit **2 :** forming, resembling, or having the characteristics of a pocket

pocking *pres part of* POCK

¹**pockmark** \ˈ⸗,⸗\ *n* [¹*pock* + *mark*] **:** a mark, pit, or depressed scar caused by smallpox

²**pockmark** \"\ *vt* **:** to cover with or as if with pockmarks **:** PIT, SCAR ⟨the mines that *~ed* the great coal and iron fields —Oscar Handlin⟩ ⟨the field was *~ed* with bomb craters —W. D.Edmonds⟩

pockmarked \ˈ⸗ˈ⸗\ *adj* **:** marked by or as if by smallpox

pock neuk *or* **pock nook** *n* [³*pock* + *neuk, nook*] **1** *chiefly Scot* **:** the bottom of a bag **2** *chiefly Scot* **:** financial resources **:** MEANS

pock pudding *n* [³*pock*] **1** *chiefly Scot* **:** BAG PUDDING **2** *chiefly Scot* **a :** a fat overfed person **b :** ENGLISHMAN — usu. used disparagingly

pocks *pl of* POCK, *pres 3d sing of* POCK

pock scab *n* [¹*pock*] *n* **:** POWDERY SCAB

pocky \ˈpäkē, -ki\ *adj* -ER/-EST [ME *pokky,* fr. *pokke* pock (mark) + *-y* — more at POCK] **1 :** covered with pocks; *specif* **:** SYPHILITIC **2 :** relating to or being a pock or the pox

po·co \ˈpō(ˌ)kō, ˈpȯ(-\ *adv* (*or adj*) [It, little, fr. L *paucus* — more at FEW] **:** in a slight degree **:** SOMEWHAT — used esp. as a direction in music ⟨~ allegro⟩

poco a poco \ˌ≈≈ä'≈(ˌ)≈\ *adv* [It] **:** little by little **:** GRADUALLY — used as a direction in music

po·co·cu·ran·te \ˌpōkōkyəˈrantē\ *adj* [It *poco curante* caring little, fr. *poco* little + *curante* caring (pres. part. of *curare* to care), fr. L *curant-, curans,* pres. part. of *curare* to take care of, heal — more at CURE] **:** not concerned **:** INDIFFERENT, NONCHALANT

po·co·cu·ran·tism \ˌ≈≈≈ˈran‚tizəm\ *also* **po·co·cu·ran·te·ism** \-ntē‚i-\ *n* -s **:** INDIFFERENCE, NONCHALANCE ⟨keep up their appearance of calm ~ —F.M.Ford⟩

po·co·sin *also* **po·co·son** *or* **po·co·sen** \pəˈkōsᵊn, ˈpōkəsən\ *n* -s [Delaware *pâkwesen,* fr. *pâkw-* shallow + *-sen* (suffix used to designate resting in place)] **:** SWAMP, MARSH; *esp* **:** an upland swamp on an interfluvial area of the coastal plain of the southeastern U.S.

¹pod \ˈpäd\ *n* -s [origin unknown] **1 :** a bit socket in a brace **2 :** a straight groove or channel in the barrel of a pod auger or similar tool

²pod \"\ *n* -s [prob. alter. (influenced by the *p* of *pea,* with which it is often associated) of ¹*cod*] **1 :** a dry dehiscent seed vessel or fruit that is either monocarpellary (as a legume, silique, or follicle) or composed of two or more carpels (as a capsule); *specif* **:** LEGUME **2 a :** BAG, POUCH, SAC; *esp* **:** a musk bag **b :** a protective envelope (as a cocoon) **c :** a grasshopper egg case **3 :** a number of animals (as seals or whales) closely clustered together **:** SCHOOL ⟨we lowered for a ~ of four or five whales —Herman Melville⟩ **4 :** POTBELLY 1a **5 a :** a roughly cylindrical ore body dwindling at each end like a cigar **b :** a similarly shaped mineral aggregate in schist or gneiss **6 :** a streamlined often detachable compartment slung under the wings or fuselage of an aircraft and used as a container (as for a jet engine, cargo, or weapons) ⟨jet ~⟩ ⟨rocket ~⟩ ⟨fuel ~⟩

³pod \"\ *vb* **podded; podded; podding; pods** *vi* **1 :** to assemble in pods **2 :** to produce pods ⟨rows of *podding* peas on hazel sticks —H.E.Bates⟩ ~ *vt* **:** to drive (seals) into pods

pod- *or* **podo-** *comb form* [Gk, fr. *pod-, pous* — more at FOOT] **1 :** foot ⟨*podology*⟩ ⟨*podoscaph*⟩ **2 :** hoof ⟨*pododerm*⟩ **3 :** peduncle **:** stalk ⟨*Podocarpus*⟩ ⟨*Podophthalmia*⟩

¹-pod \ˌpäd\ *n comb form* -s [Gk *-pod-, -pous,* fr. *-pod-, -pous,* adj. combining form, having (such or so many) feet, fr. *pod-, pous* foot] **:** one having (such or so many) feet ⟨*chenopod*⟩

²-pod \"\ *adj comb form* [Gk *-pod-, -pous*] **:** having (such or so many) feet ⟨*acanthopod*⟩

³-pod \"\ *also* **-pode** \ˌpōd\ *n comb form* -s [NL *podium* foot — more at PODIUM] **1 a :** footlike part ⟨*pseudopode*⟩ **b :** foot ⟨*nectopod*⟩ **2 :** -PODITE ⟨*endopod*⟩

POD *abbr* **1** pay on delivery **2** post office department

-po·da \pədə\ *n pl comb form* [NL, fr. Gk, neut. pl. of *-pod-, -pous* having (such or so many) feet] **:** ones having (such or so many) feet — in taxonomic names in zoology ⟨*Arthropoda*⟩ ⟨*Decapoda*⟩ ⟨*Heteropoda*⟩; compare -PUS

po·dag·ra \pəˈdagrə, ˈpädəg-\ *n* -s [ME, fr. L, fr. Gk, trap for the feet, foot disease of animals, gout, fr. *pod-* + *-agra*] **1 :** gout in the feet; *broadly* **:** GOUT **2 :** a painful condition of the big toe caused by gout — **po·dag·ral** \-grəl\ *adj* — **po·dag·ric** \-rik\ *adj* — **po·dag·rous** \-rəs\ *adj*

po·dal \ˈpōdᵊl\ *adj* [*pod-* + *-al*] **1 :** of or relating to a foot **2 :** being membranes attached to the neuropodia and notopodia of various polychaete worms

po·dal·ic \pōˈdalik\ *adj* [*pod-* + *-al* + *-ic*] **:** of, relating to, or by means of the feet ⟨used ~ version in the child's delivery⟩

po·da·li·ri·idae \ˌpōdᵊlə'rīə‚dē\ *n pl, cap* [NL, fr. *Podalirius,* type genus + *-idae*] **:** a family of large hairy long-tongued bees that are usu. solitary but include some which burrow in cliffs and form large communities

po·da·lir·i·us \ˌpōdᵊlˈirēəs\ *n, cap* [NL, after *Podalirius* (fr. L, fr. Gk *Podaleirios*), son of the legendary ancient Greek physician Asclepius] **:** the type genus of the family Podaliriidae

po·dar·gi·dae \pəˈdärjə‚dē\ *n pl, cap* [NL, fr. *Podargus,* type genus + *-idae*] **:** a family of Oriental and Australian birds (order Caprimulgiformes) comprising the frogmouths

po·dar·gus \-gəs\ *n, cap* [NL, fr. Gk *podargos* swift-footed, white-footed, fr. *pod-* + *argos* swift, white, shining — more at ARGENT] **:** the type genus of the family Podargidae

po·dar·thral \pəˈdärthrəl\ *adj* [NL *podarthrum* + E *-al*] **:** of or relating to the podarthrum

po·dar·thrum \-thrəm\ *n, pl* **podar·thra** \-rə\ [NL, fr. *pod-* + Gk *arthron* joint — more at ARTHR-] **:** the joint between the toes and the tarsometatarsus in a bird

po·da·tus \pəˈdād·əs\ *n, pl* **poda·ti** \-ād·‚ī\ [NL, fr. *pod-* + L *-atus* -ate] **:** PES

pod auger *n* [¹*pod*] **:** an auger having a pod

pod·axonia \ˌpäd+\ *n pl, cap* [NL, fr. *pod-* + *axonia*] *in some esp former classifications* **:** a group comprising the Brachiopoda, Bryozoa, and Gephyrea — **pod·ax·o·ni·al** \ˌpä‚dak¦sōnēəl\ *adj*

pod bit *n* [¹*pod*] **:** a bit having a pod

pod blight *n* [²*pod*] **:** a destructive disease of various legumes (as beans) caused by fungi of the genus *Diaporthe*

pod borer *n* [²*pod*] **:** an insect larva that bores into the pods of legumes — see BEAN-POD BORER

pod corn *n* [²*pod*] **:** an Indian corn (*Zea mays tunicata*) having each kernel enclosed in a chaffy shell similar to that of other cereals — called also *cow corn, husk corn*

podded *adj* [fr. past part. of ³*pod*] **1 :** having or producing pods — often used in combination ⟨long-*podded*⟩ **2 :** borne in a pod ⟨~ seeds⟩

podding *pres part of* POD

pod·dish \ˈpädish, -dēsh\ *n* -ES [alter. of *pottage*] *dial Eng* **:** PORRIDGE

¹pod·dy \ˈpädē, -di\ *adj* -ER/-EST [²*pod* + *-y*] *chiefly dial* **:** POTBELLIED

²poddy \"\ *n* -ES *chiefly Austral* **:** a domestic animal (as a calf, lamb, or foal) just taken from its mother

-pode — see -POD

po·de·on \ˈpōdē‚än, ˈpäd-\ *n, pl* **po·de·o·nes** \ˌ≈≈ˈō‚nēz\ [NL, fr. Gk *podeōn* ragged end (in an animal skin) where the feet or tail has been, mouth of a wineskin, fr. *pod-, pous* foot — more at FOOT] **:** the petiole of the abdomen of a hymenopteron

po·de·sta \ˌpōdəˈstä\ *n* -s [It *podestà, potestà,* lit., power, authority, fr. L *potestat-, potestas* — more at POTESTATE] **1 :** a chief magistrate with extensive powers elected in a medieval Italian town or republic **2 :** a subordinate judge or magistrate in some Italian towns **3 :** a chief executive of an Italian commune appointed by the central government in the Fascist regime

po·de·tial \pəˈdēshəl\ *adj* [*podetium* + *-al*] **:** of or relating to a podetium

po·de·ti·iform \-≈ˈshēə‚fȯrm\ *adj* [*podetium* + *-iform*] **:** like a podetium in form or appearance

po·de·tium \pōˈdēsh(ē)əm\ *n, pl* **pode·tia** \-)ə\ [NL, fr. *pod-* + *-etium* (origin unknown)] **1 :** a stalk on which the ascocarp is borne in various lichens (as of the genus *Cladonia*) **2 :** an organ or body resembling a stalk (as the seta of a moss)

po·dex \ˈpō‚deks\ *n, pl* **pod·i·ces** \ˈpädə‚sēz\ [L; akin to *pedere* to break wind — more at PETARD] **1 :** the anal region **:** RUMP **2** [NL, fr. L] **:** the pygidium of an insect

pod fern *n* [²*pod*] **1 :** FLOATING FERN **2 :** OREGON CLIFF BRAKE

podge \ˈpäj\ *n* -s [prob. alter. of *pudge*] **:** something podgy ⟨the baby a . . . flourishing ~ of flesh —W.M.Thackeray⟩

podg·er \-jə(r)\ *n* -s [origin unknown] **1 :** a small drift used to bring rivet holes into alignment **2 :** TOMMY

podg·i·ly \ˈpäjəlē, -li\ *adv* **:** in a podgy manner

podg·i·ness \-jēnəs, -jin-\ *n* -ES **:** the condition of being podgy

podgy \ˈpäjē, -ji\ *adj* -ER/-EST [*podge* + *-y*] **:** softly fat **:** PUDGY ⟨his pink, smooth, ~ face —Angus Wilson⟩

-po·dia \ˈpōdēə\ *n comb form* -s [NL, fr. Gk, fr. *pod-* + *-ia* -y] **:** condition of having (such) feet ⟨platy*podia*⟩

po·di·al \ˈpōdēəl\ *adj* [NL *podium* + E *-al*] **1 :** of or relating to a podium **2 :** of or relating to the pleural areas of an arthropod body segment in which the limbs are implanted

po·di·a·trist \pəˈdīə·trəst, pō'-\ *n* -s [*pod-* + *-iatrist*] **:** CHIROPODIST

po·di·a·try \-rē,-ri\ *n* -ES [*pod-* + *-iatry*] **:** CHIROPODY

pod·i·cal \ˈpädəkəl, -dēk-\ *adj* [L & NL *podic-, podex* + E *-al* — more at PODEX] **1 :** of or relating to the podex **2 :** being either of a pair of ventrolateral plates arising from the tenth abdominal segment and partially enclosing the anus of an orthopterous insect

pod·i·ceps \ˈpädə‚seps\ [NL, irreg. fr. L *podic-, podex* rump + *pes* foot — more at PODEX, FOOT] *syn of* COLYMBUS

pod·i·ci·ped·i·dae \ˌ≈≈səˈpedə‚dē\ *or* **pod·i·cip·i·dae** \ˌ≈≈ˈsipə‚dē\ [*Podicipedidae* fr. NL, fr. *Podiciped-, Podicipes* (syn. of *Colymbus*) (alter. of *Podiceps*) + *-idae; Podicipidae* fr. NL, fr. *Podicip-, Podiceps* + *-idae*] *syn of* COLYMBIDAE

po·dil·e·gous \pəˈdiləgəs\ *adj* [*pod-* + *-i-* + Gk *legein* to gather + E *-ous* — more at LEGEND] **:** gathering pollen by means of a pollen brush on the legs ⟨~ bees⟩ — compare GASTRILEGOUS

pod·ite \ˈpä‚dīt\ *n* -s [*-podite*] **:** a limb segment of an arthropod — **po·dit·ic** \pəˈdid·ik\ *adj*

-po·dite \pə‚dīt\ *n comb form* -s [ISV *pod-* + *-ite*] **:** segment of an appendage of an arthropod ⟨basi*podite*⟩ ⟨endo*podite*⟩ — **-po·dit·ic** \pə¦did·ik, -itik\ *adj comb form*

po·di·um \ˈpōdēəm\ *n, pl* **podiums** \-mz\ *or* **po·dia** \-ēə\ [L — more at PEW] **1 :** a low wall serving as a foundation, substructure, or terrace wall: as **a :** a dwarf wall around the arena of an ancient amphitheater serving as a base for the tiers of seats **b :** the masonry under the stylobate of a temple **2 a :** a balcony in an ancient Roman theater containing seats for the emperor and other spectators of high rank **b :** a raised platform or pedestal **:** DAIS ⟨the police direct traffic from round *podia* elevated six feet from the ground —*Saturday Rev.*⟩ ⟨there is one conductor who practically has the downbeat ready as he steps onto the ~ —Milton Cross⟩ **c :** LECTERN ⟨pounding the ~ and talking loudly —L.W.Youngdahl⟩ **3** [NL, fr. Gk *podion* small foot — more at PEW] **:** FOOT; *specif* **:** a tube foot of an echinoderm

-po·di·um \ˈpōdēəm\ *n comb form, pl* **-po·dia** \-ēə\ [NL, fr. L *podium*] **1 :** one having a (specified kind of) foot or part resembling a foot — in generic names ⟨Cheno*podium*⟩ ⟨Lyco*podium*⟩ **2 :** foot **:** footlike part ⟨pleuro*podium*⟩

pod·ler \ˈpädlər\ *also* **pod·ley** \-li\ *n, pl* **podlers** \-lərz\ *also* **podlies** \-liz\ *or* **po·dles** \-dᵊlz\ [prob. alter. of *podlok,* obs. var. of *pollack*] *chiefly Scot* **:** a young pollock

podlike \ˈ≈‚≈\ *adj* **:** resembling a pod

pod mahogany *n* **:** a medium to large-sized African tree (*Seymeria quanzensis*) having black seeds with a red cap — called also *mahogany bean, Rhodesian mahogany*

pod maize *n* **:** POD CORN

podo \ˈpä(ˌ)dō\ *n* -s [short for *podocarpus*] **1 :** any of several East African trees of the genus *Podocarpus* **2 :** the soft wood of a podo tree widely used for building, furniture, and crates

podo- — see POD-

podo·branch \ˈpädə‚braŋk\ *also* **podobran·chia** \ˌ≈≈ˈbraŋkēə\ *n, pl* **podobranchs** \-ks\ *also* **podobranchi·ae** \-kī‚ē\ [NL *podobranchia,* fr. *pod-* + *-branchia* (gill)] **:** a gill attached to the basal segment of a thoracic limb of a crustacean — compare ARTHROBRANCH, PLEUROBRANCH

podo·carp \ˈpädə‚kärp\ *n* -s [NL *Podocarpus*] **:** a plant of the genus *Podocarpus*

podo·car·pa·ce·ae \ˌ≈≈‚kärˈpāsē‚ē\ *n pl, cap* [NL, fr. *Podocarpus,* type genus + *-aceae*] *in some classifications* **:** a family of gymnosperms with simple persistent needlelike or scalelike leaves and 2-celled anthers — compare PODOCARPINEAE

podo·car·pic acid \ˌ≈≈¦kärpik-\ *n* [ISV *podocarp-* (fr. NL *Podocarpus*) + *-ic*] **:** a crystalline phenolic acid $C_{16}H_{20}$(OH) COOH that is derived from phenanthrene and related to the diterpenes and that is found esp. in resins from trees of the genus *Podocarpus*

podo·car·pin·e·ae \ˌ≈≈(ˌ)kärˈpinē‚ē\ *n pl, cap* [NL, fr. *Podocarpus* + *-ineae*] *in some classifications* **:** a section of the Taxaceae including *Podocarpus* and related genera — compare PODOCARPACEAE

podo·car·pus \ˌ≈≈ˈkärpəs\ *n* [NL, fr. *pod-* + *-carpus*] **1** *cap* **:** a genus of evergreen trees (family Taxaceae) widely distributed in the southern hemisphere and having a pulpy fruit with one hard seed — see BLACK PINE, KAHIKATEA, MIRO, PLUM FIR, YACCA **2** -ES **:** any tree of the genus *Podocarpus*

podo·derm \ˈpädə‚dərm\ *n* -s [*pod-* + *-derm*] **:** the dermal or growing part of the covering of the foot of a hoofed animal as distinguished from the epidermal or horny part

podo·dermatitis \¦pädō+\ *n* [NL, fr. *pod-* + *dermatitis*] **:** inflammation of the dermal tissue underlying the horny layers of a hoof: as **a :** FOOT ROT 2 **b :** LAMINITIS

po·dog·o·na \pəˈdägənə\ [NL, fr. *pod-* + *-gona* (fr. Gk *gonos* offspring, procreation, seed, genitals) — more at GON-] *syn of* RICINULEI

¹po·do·lian \pəˈdōlēən, -lyən\ *adj, usu cap* [*Podolia,* region in the southwestern Ukraine + E *-an*] **1 :** of, relating to, or characteristic of Podolia **2 :** of, relating to, or characteristic of the people of Podolia

²podolian \"\ *n* -s *cap* **:** a native or inhabitant of Podolia

po·do·lite \ˈpōdᵊl‚īt\ *n* -s [G *podolit,* fr. *Podolia* + G *-it* -ite] **:** CARBONATE-APATITE

po·dol·o·gy \pəˈdäləjē\ *n* -ES [*pod-* + *-logy*] **:** the scientific study of the morphology and physiology of the feet

pod·o·mere \ˈpädə‚mi(ə)r\ *n* -s [*pod-* + *-mere*] **:** a leg segment of an arthropod

po·doph·rya \pəˈdäfrēə\ *n, cap* [NL, fr. *pod-* + *-ophrya* (fr. Gk *ophryē, ophrys* crag, brow of a hill, eyebrow) — more at BROW] **:** a genus (the type of the family Podophryidae) of stalked subspherical naked suctorian protozoans common in fresh or salt water

pod·oph·thal·ma \ˌpä‚däfˈthalmə\ *or* **podophthalma·ta** \-məd·ə\ [*podophthalma,* NL, fr. *pod-* + *-ophthalma; podophthalmata,* NL, fr. *pod-* + *ophthalm-* + *-ata*] *syn of* PODOPHTHALMIA

pod·oph·thal·mia \-mēə\ *n pl, cap* [NL, fr. *pod-* + *-ophthalmia*] **1** *in some classifications* **:** a group comprising the stalk-eyed crustaceans **2** *in former classifications* **:** a division of Malacostraca comprising forms with the eyes supported on movable stalks and coextensive with the Phyllocarida, Euphausiacea, Mysidacea, Decapoda, and Stomatopoda — **pod·oph·thal·mi·an** \¦≈≈¦≈mēən\ *adj or n* — **pod·oph·thal·mic** \-mik\ *adj* — **pod·oph·thal·mous** \-məs\ *adj*

podophthalmite \¦päd+\ *n* [*pod-* + *ophthalmite*] **:** the distal segment of the eyestalk of a crustacean — **pod·ophthalmitic** \(¦)päd+\ *adj*

podo·phyl·lin \ˌpädəˈfilən\ *n* -s [ISV *podophyll-* (fr. NL *Podophyllum*) + *-in*] **:** a bitter light brown to greenish yellow resin that is irritating to the eye and other mucous membranes, that is obtained from podophyllum, and that is used as a cathartic, applied externally in solution in the treatment of venereal warts, and also used in cytological research for its property of inhibiting the division of malignant cells — called also *podophyllum resin*

podo·phyl·lo·tox·in \ˌ≈≈‚filəˈtäksən\ *n* [ISV *podophyllo-* (fr. NL *Podophyllum*) + *toxin*] **:** a crystalline polycyclic compound, $C_{22}H_{22}O_8$ constituting one of the active principles of the drugs podophyllum and podophyllin

podo·phyl·lous \¦pädə¦filəs\ *adj* [*pod-* + *-phyllous*] **:** of, relating to, or being the laminar dermal tissue underlying the horny layers of a hoof

podo·phyl·lum \ˌ≈≈ˈfiləm\ *n* [NL, fr. *pod-* + *-phyllum*] **1** *cap* **:** a small genus of herbs (family Berberidaceae) that have poisonous rootstocks, large palmate leaves, chiefly hexamerous flowers, and large fleshy sometimes edible berries — see MAYAPPLE **2** *pl* **podophyl·li** \-i‚lī\ *or* **podophyllums :** the rhizome and rootlet of the mayapple (*Podophyllum peltatum*) used as a cholagogue and cathartic; *also* **:** a similar product of an Indian herb (*P. emodi*) — called also *Indian podophyllum*

podophyllum resin *n* **:** PODOPHYLLIN

podos *pl of* PODO

podo·scaph \ˈpädə‚skaf\ *n* -s [*pod-* + Gk *skaphos* boat — more at SCAPH-] **:** one of a pair of canoe-shaped floats attached to the feet and used for walking on water with the aid of a paddle

podo·so·ma·ta \ˌ≈≈ˈsōməd·ə\ [NL, fr. *pod-* + *-somata*] *syn of* PYCNOGONIDA

podo·sphae·ra \-ˈsfirə\ *n, cap* [NL, fr. *pod-* + *-sphaera*] **:** a genus of powdery mildews (family Erysiphaceae) having perithecia with only a single ascus and rigid usu. dichotomously branched but sometimes simple appendages

podo·ste·ma·ce·ae \ˌ≈≈stəˈmāsē‚ē\ [NL, fr. *Podostemon* + *-aceae*] *syn of* PODOSTEMONACEAE

podo·ste·mad \ˌ≈≈ˈstē‚mad\ *n* -s [NL *Podostemon* + E *-ad*] **:** a podostemonaceous plant

podo·ste·mon \-‚mən\ *n* [NL, fr. *pod-* + Gk *stēmōn* thread-warp — more at STAMEN] **1** *cap* **:** a widely distributed genus (the type of the family Podostemonaceae) of rock-inhabiting submerged aquatic herbs having sessile involucrate flowers and poorly differentiated leaves — see RIVERWEED **2** -s **:** any plant of the genus *Podostemon*

podo·ste·mo·na·ce·ae \ˌ≈≈‚≈məˈnāsē‚ē\ *n pl, cap* [NL, fr. *Podostemon,* type genus + *-aceae*] **:** a family of aquatic fleshy herbs (order Podostemonales) with leaves and stems confluent that are natives of tropical regions, are often confined to submerged ledges or rocks of waterfalls, and have small perfect apetalous flowers

podo·ste·mo·na·ceous \¦≈≈¦≈¦nāshəs\ *or* **podo·ste·ma·ceous** \¦≈≈stə¦māshəs\ *adj* [NL *Podostemonaceae* or *Podostemaceae* + E *-ous*] **:** of or relating to the Podostemonaceae

podo·ste·mo·na·les \ˌ≈≈‚stēməˈnā(ˌ)lēz\ *n pl, cap* [NL, fr. *Podostemon* + *-ales*] **:** a small order of dicotyledonous aquatic plants that comprises solely the family Podostemonaceae and is often included in the order Rosales

podo·the·ca \ˌpädəˈthēkə\ *n, pl* **podothe·cae** \-ē‚sē\ [NL, fr. *pod-* + *-theca*] **:** the scaly covering of the foot of a bird or reptile — **podo·the·cal** \¦≈≈¦thēkəl\ *adj*

-po·dous \pədəs\ *adj comb form* [Gk *-pod-, -pous* having (such or so many) feet + E *-ous* — more at -POD] **:** having (such or so many) feet **:** -footed ⟨acantho*podous*⟩ ⟨hexa*podous*⟩

podo·za·mi·tes \ˌpädəzəˈmīd·(ˌ)ēz\ *n, cap* [NL, fr. *pod-* + *Zamia* + L *-ites* -ite] **:** a genus of fossil plants of the Mesozoic based upon the general resemblance of the leaflets to those of the cycads of the genus *Zamia*

pod pepper *n* **:** a pepper of the genus *Capsicum*

pod rot *also* **pod rot disease** *n* **:** a disease of cacao that produces lesions on the pods and that may be caused by either of two fungi (*Diplodia theobromae* or *Phytophthora faberi*)

pods *pl of* POD, *pres 3d sing of* POD

-pods *pl of* -POD

pod shrimp *n* **:** a crustacean (as of the genus *Estheria*) that has a bivalve shell

pod·snap·pery \(ˈ)päd¦snap(ə)rē\ *n* -ES *sometimes cap* [Mr. *Podsnap,* complacent Philistine in *Our Mutual Friend* (1864–5), by Charles Dickens †1870 Eng. novelist + E *-ery*] **:** an attitude toward life marked by complacency and a refusal to recognize unpleasant facts

pod spot *n* **:** a brownish spotting of bean pods caused by the anthracnose fungus

po·dunk \ˈpō‚dəŋk\ *n* -s *usu cap* [fr. *Podunk,* village near Worcester, Mass., or *Podunk,* locality in Conn.] **:** a small, unimportant, and isolated town

po·du·ra \pəˈd(y)u̇rə\ *n* [NL, fr. *pod-* + *-ura*] **1** *cap* **:** the type genus of Poduridae **2** -s **:** any insect of the genus *Podura* — **po·du·ran** \-rən\ *adj or n*

po·du·ri·dae \-rə‚dē\ *n pl, cap* [NL, fr. *Podura,* type genus + *-idae*] **:** a family of primitive insects (order Collembola) that lack a tracheal system and include the snow fleas and springtails

pod·zol *or* **podzol soil** *also* **pod·sol** *or* **podsol soil** \ˈpäd‚zäl(-), -‚säl(-), ≈ˈ≈(-)\ *n* -s [*podzol, podsol* fr. Russ *podzol,* fr. *zola* ashes; akin to OE *glōwan* to glow — more at GLOW] **:** any of a group of zonal soils that develop in a moist climate under coniferous or mixed forest or under heath vegetation and have an organic mat and a thin organic-mineral layer above a gray leached layer resting on a dark illuvial horizon enriched with amorphous clay — **pod·zol·ic** \(ˈ)≈¦≈ik\ *adj*

pod·zol·iza·tion *also* **pod·sol·iza·tion** \ˌ≈≈ə'zāshən\ *n* -s **:** an important process in the formation and modification of certain soils (as pedalfers) esp. in humid regions involving principally the leaching of the upper layers of soil and the accumulation of material in the lower layers with a resultant development of characteristic horizons; *specif* **:** the development of a podzol

pod·zol·ize *also* **pod·sol·ize** \ˈ≈≈‚īz\ *vb* -ED/-ING/-S *vt* **:** to convert into a podzol ~ *vi* **:** to undergo podzolization

poe *or* **poe·bird** \ˈpōē,-\ *n* -s [Tahitian *poe,* lit., pearl beads; fr. the two tufts of white on its throat] **:** TUI

POE *abbr* **1** port of embarkation **2** port of entry

poecil- *or* **poecilo-** *or* **poikil-** *or* **poikilo-** *comb form* [Gk *poikil-, poikilo-,* fr. *poikilos* — more at PAINT] **:** variegated **:** various ⟨*Poecil*ichthys⟩ ⟨*poecilo*gony⟩ ⟨*poikil*itic⟩ ⟨*poikilo*blast⟩

poe·cil·ich·thys \ˌpēsəˈlikthəs\ *n, cap* [NL, fr. *poecil-* + *-ichthys*] **:** a genus of No. American darters commonly found under large stones in swift streams

¹poe·cil·i·id \pēˈsilēəd\ *adj* [NL *Poeciliidae*] **:** of or relating to the Poeciliidae

²poeciliid \"\ *n* -s **:** a fish of the family Poeciliidae

poe·ci·li·idae \ˌpēsəˈlīə‚dē\ *n pl, cap* [NL, fr. *Poecilia,* type genus, fr. Gk *poikilia* condition of being marked with various colors, fr. *poikil-* poecil- + *-ia* -y) + *-idae*] **:** a large family of small New World viviparous fishes (order Microcyprini) comprising the topminnows and having the male anal fin modified as a copulatory organ — compare GUPPY, SWORDTAIL

poecilitic *var of* POIKILITIC

poe·ci·lo·cyt·ta·rous \¦pēsəlō¦sid·ərəs\ *adj* [*poecil-* + Gk *kyttaros* cell of a honeycomb + E *-ous*] **:** of, relating to, or being a type of nest of some social wasps (family Vespidae) in which the layers of brood comb are supported by the outer covering and a central support (as the limb of a tree) — compare PHRAGMOCYTTAROUS

poe·ci·log·o·ny \ˌpēsəˈlägənē\ *n* -ES [ISV *poecil-* + *-gony*] **:** a supposed method of development occurring in invertebrate animals where in the same species there are two kinds of young although the adults are exactly alike

po·em \ˈpōəm *also* -ō‚em *or* ÷-ōm\ *n* -s [MF *poeme,* fr. L *poema,* fr. Gk *poiēma, poēma,* fr. *poiein* to make, do, create, compose — more at POET] **1 :** a composition in verse ⟨wrote his account of the ball game in the form of a ~⟩ **2 :** a piece of poetry designed as a unit and communicating to the reader the sense of a complete experience ⟨a ~ is not a syllogism, and its essential unity and progression are psychological rather than logical —John Ciardi⟩ **3 :** a composition, creation, achievement, experience, or object likened to a poem (as in expressiveness, lyric beauty, or formal grace) ⟨a prose ~⟩ ⟨a symphonic ~⟩ ⟨the house we stayed in . . . was itself a ~ —H.J.Laski⟩

po·e·mat·ic \¦pōə¦mad·ik, -atik, -ēk\ *adj* [Gk *poiēmatikos,* fr. *poiēmat-, poiēma* + *-ikos* -ic] **:** POETIC

po·eph·a·ga \pōˈefəgə\ *n pl, cap* [NL, fr. Gk *poēphaga,* neut. pl. of *poēphagos* grass-eating, fr. *poa* grass + *-phagos* -phagous — more at POA] *in some esp former classifications* **:** a group including the kangaroos and related forms

po·eph·a·gous \(ˈ)≈¦≈≈gəs\ *adj* [Gk *poēphagos*] **1 :** HERBIVOROUS **2** [NL *Poephaga* + E *-ous*] **:** of or relating to the Poephaga

po·eph·a·gus \pōˈefəgəs\ *n, cap* [NL, fr. Gk *poēphagos* grass-eating] **:** a genus of mammals (family Bovidae) that comprises the Asiatic yak and is sometimes made a subgenus of *Bos*

poes *pl of* POE

po·e·sy *also* **po·e·sie** \ˈpōəzē, -sē, -i\ *n, pl* **poesies** [ME *poisie poesie,* fr. MF *poesie,* fr. L *poesis,* fr. Gk *poiēsis, poēsis* creation, making, poem, fr. *poiein* to make, do, create, compose + *-sis* — more at POET] **1 a :** a body of poems **:** the work produced by poets **:** POEM ⟨olden songs and *poesies* —John Keats⟩ **b :** poetic form or composition **:** POETRY ⟨there is only the one verbal art which is ~ —Herbert Read⟩ **c :** artificial, precious, or sentimentalized poetic writing ⟨the plush curtains of melodrama have been exchanged for the dainty chintzes of ~ —Michael Williams⟩ **2 :** POSY ⟨within the hoop of the betrothal or wedding ring it was customary to inscribe sentences or *poesies* —W.T. & Kate Pavitt⟩ **3 a :** poetic inspiration **:** creative or imaginative power ⟨the bold wings of ~ —William Wordsworth⟩ **b :** an imaginative, exalted, or idealized quality or spirit ⟨of love the ~, the passion —Robert Browning⟩

po·et \ˈpōə\|t, *in rapid speech sometimes* ˈpȯit; *usu* \|d·+V\ *n* -s [ME *poete, poete,* fr. OF *poete,* fr. L *poeta,* fr. Gk *poiētēs, poētēs* maker, composer, poet, fr. *poiein* to make, do, create, compose; akin to Skt *cinoti* he gathers, heaps up, piles in order, OSlav *činiti* to arrange; basic meaning: to pile up] **1 :** one who writes poetry **:** a maker of verses **2 :** a writer having great imaginative and expressive gifts and possessing a special sensitivity to language ⟨a ~ born, not made⟩ **3 :** a creative artist (as a composer or painter) whose work is marked by imagination, spontaneity, and lyricism ⟨a natural ~ with the camera —G.W.Stonier⟩ ⟨the first ~ of the piano in the history of music —*Time*⟩

po·et·as·ter \ˈpōə̇d‚astə(r), -ōə‚ta-, -aas- *sometimes* ‚ₛₛˈₛₛ\ *n* -s [NL, fr. L *poeta* + *-aster*] **:** a writer of worthless or inferior verses **:** a pretended poet **:** VERSIFIER ⟨indicative of the mistakes of ~*s* and would-be poets rather than of real poets —C.S. Kilby⟩

po·et·as·ter·ing \-t(ə)riŋ\ *n* -s **:** playing at poetry **:** dabbling in verse ⟨away with all ~ at dinner parties —W.M.Thackeray⟩

po·et·as·tery *or* **po·et·as·try** \-t(ə)rē\ *n* -ES **:** POETASTERING ⟨prevent young dramatists from wasting their budding talents on . . . pretentious ~ —Clare B. Luce⟩

po·e·taz narcissus \ˈpōə‚taz-\ *n* [NL *poetaz* (specific epithet of *Narcissus poetaz*), blend of *poeticus* (specific epithet of *N. poeticus*, fr. L, poetic) and *tazetta* (specific epithet of *N. tazetta*, fr. It *tazzetta* small basin, small cup, dim. of *tazza* basin, cup), the two species from which it is derived — more at POETIC, TAZZA] **:** any of various narcissus that are hybrids between the polyanthus narcissus and the poet's narcissus and have flowers four or more in a cluster and with a short crown that is not crisped

po·et·ess \ˈpōə̇d·ə̇s, -ōtə̇s\ *n* -ES [*poet* + *-ess*] **:** a female poet

po·et·ic \pōˈed·|ik, -et|, |ēk\ *adj* [MF *poetique*, fr. L *poeticus*, fr. Gk *poiētikos* capable of making, creative, poetic, fr. *poiētēs* maker, composer, poet + *-ikos* -ic — more at POET] **1 a :** of or relating to poets **:** appropriate to or characteristic of poets ⟨the personality truly and naturally ~ seems to be becoming rarer —Edmund Wilson⟩ ⟨had no ~ talents at all —*Times Lit. Supp.*⟩ ⟨a ~ face⟩ **b :** given to or occupied with poetry ⟨a ~ plowman⟩ ⟨a ~ family⟩ **2 a :** written in verse ⟨a ~ version of his earlier prose drama⟩ ⟨did a ~ paraphrase of the speech⟩ **b :** of, relating to, or suitable for poetry or poems ⟨a ~ renaissance⟩ ⟨his small ~ output⟩ ⟨a ~ subject⟩ **3 :** having or expressing the qualities of poetry ⟨~ movements of the whole body —G.B.Shaw⟩ ⟨this essentially ~ mode of thought — Kathleen Raine⟩ ⟨a darkly ~ architectural scene —Carlyle Burrows⟩ **4 :** stilted and artificial in diction or style ⟨the prose is ~ in the bad sense —M.D.Geismar⟩ ⟨uses the literary and always ~ phrase —*N.Y.Herald Tribune Bk. Rev.*⟩

po·et·i·cal \|ə̇kəl, |ēk-\ *adj* [ME, fr. L *poeticus* + ME *-al*] **1 :** POETIC **2 :** beyond or above the truth of history or nature **:** IDEALIZED ⟨the more ~ and elevated the ideas are which are clustered around marriage, the more probable it is that experience will produce disappointment —W.G.Sumner⟩

po·et·i·cal·i·ty \pō‚edə̇ˈkalə̇d·ē\ *n* -ES **:** poetic quality or expression ⟨the poem is a mere tumbled out spate . . . of *poeticalities* —F.R.Leavis⟩

po·et·i·cal·ly \pōˈed·|ə̇k(ə)lē, -et|, |ēk-, -li\ *adv* **:** in a poetic manner ⟨two themes which he strove to blend ~ rather than rationally —E.S.Bates⟩

po·et·i·cal·ness \-kəlnə̇s\ *n* -ES **:** poetic quality

po·et·i·cism \pōˈed·ə‚sizəm\ *n* -s [*poetic* + *-ism*] **:** an archaic, trite, or strained form of poetic expression ⟨the common stock of ~*s* that have fallen into public domain from the poetry of the past —John Ciardi⟩

po·et·i·cize \-‚sīz\ *vt* -ED/-ING/-s [*poetic* + *-ize*] **:** to put into poetry **:** give a poetic quality to ⟨not unaware of the life of today about her, but touching it only to ~ it —*N.Y. Herald Tribune Bk. Rev.*⟩

poetic justice *n* **:** an outcome of a fictitious or real situation in which vice is punished and virtue is rewarded usu. in a manner peculiarly or ironically appropriate to the particular situation

poetic license *n* **:** LICENSE 4

po·et·ics \pōˈed·|iks, -et|i, |ēks\ *also* **po·et·ic** \-k\ *n pl but usu sing in constr* [fr. *poetic*, adj., after L *poetica*, fr. Gk *poiētikē*, fr. fem. of *poiētikos*] **1 a :** a treatise on poetry or aesthetics ⟨the best attempt yet made to write a ~ of modern art —Joseph Frank⟩ **b :** poetic theory ⟨a fascinating and often valuable essay in ~ —*Times Lit. Supp.*⟩ **2 :** poetic practice ⟨exemplifies with peculiar force the general habit and tendency of Victorian *poetic* —F.R.Leavis⟩ **3 :** poetic feelings or utterances ⟨there was no discontent . . . no ~, no strong, balked emotion —*Bookman*⟩

po·et·i·cule \pōˈed·ə(‚)kyül\ *n* -s [*poet* + *-i-* + *-cule* (as in *animalcule*)] **:** POETASTER

po·et·ization \‚pōə̇d·əˈzāshən, -ōtəˈz-, -ə‚tīˈz-\ *n* -s **:** the act or an instance of poetizing

po·et·ize \ˈpōə̇d·‚īz, -ə‚tīz\ *vb* -ED/-ING/-s [MF *poetiser*, fr. *poete* poet + *-iser* -ize — more at POET] *vi* **:** to write poetry **:** write or speak poetically ⟨has *poetized* about what he has called reality and the imagination —R.H.Pearce⟩ ~ *vt* **:** POETICIZE ⟨to make anything significant one has to ~ it —Henry Miller⟩ — **po·et·iz·er** \-zə(r)\ *n* -s

poet laureate *n, pl* **poets laureate** *or* **poet laureates** [ME] **1 :** a poet honored (as by a university) for achievement in his art **2 :** a poet appointed for life by an English sovereign as a member of the royal household and formerly expected to compose poems for court and national occasions **3 :** one regarded by a country or region as its most eminent or representative poet

po·et·ling \ˈpōə̇tliŋ, -lēŋ\ *n* -s [*poet* + *-ling*] **:** an immature or petty poet **:** POETASTER ⟨the whine of our ~*s* —Sidney Alexander⟩

po·eto·mach·ia \pō‚ed·ōˈmakēə\ *n* -s [NL, fr. L *poeta* poet + NL *-o-* + Gk *-machia* -machy — more at POET] **:** a contest of poets; *specif* **:** a literary quarrel involving a number of Elizabethan dramatists

po·et·ress \ˈpōə̇·trə̇s, -ə̇t·r-\ *n* -ES [MF *poeteresse*, fem. of *poete* poet — more at POET] *archaic* **:** POETESS

po·et·ry \ˈpōə̇·trē, -ri, *also* -ə̇t·r-, *in rapid speech sometimes* ˈpȯi·t-\ *n* -ES [ME *poetrie*, fr. MF, fr. ML *poetria*, fr. L, poetess, fr. Gk *poiētria*, fr. *poiētēs* poet — more at POET] **1 a :** metrical writing **:** VERSE ⟨turns out 20 lines of ~ each day for the paper⟩ **b :** the productions of a poet **:** POEMS ⟨a collection of 16th century ~⟩ ⟨picked up a volume of ~⟩ **c poetries** *pl* **:** pieces of poetry **2 :** writing that formulates a concentrated imaginative awareness of experience in language chosen and arranged to create a specific emotional response through its meaning, sound, and rhythm **3 a :** a quality that stirs the imagination or gives a sense of heightened and more meaningful existence ⟨the ~ with which an American train is surrounded —Henri Peyre⟩ ⟨what are ceremonies but the manners and ~ of the state —*N.Y. Times Bk. Rev.*⟩ **b :** a quality of spontaneity and grace ⟨her dancing is pure ~⟩ ⟨has the technique and power of a great pianist, but his playing lacks ~⟩

poets *pl of* POET

poetsch process \ˈpech-\ *n, usu cap 1st P* [after F. H. *Poetsch*, 19th cent. Ger. mining engineer] **:** a method of excavating in which soft water-bearing formations are first artificially frozen and then mined while still solid

po·et·ship \ˈpōə̇t‚ship\ *n* [*poet* + *-ship*] **:** the state or function of a poet

poet's narcissus *also* **poet's daffodil** *n* **:** a narcissus (*Narcissus poeticus*) having fragrant, chiefly white, and usu. solitary flowers with a very shallow corona that is crisped and reddish on its edge

pog·a·mog·gan \‚pägəˈmägən\ *n* -s [of Algonquian origin;

pogamoggan of the Sioux

akin to Ojibwa *pägämägan* club, Cree *päkämâgan* hammer, lit., (something) used for striking] **:** a club used as a weapon or ceremonial object by various American Indian peoples and usu. consisting in the Great Lakes region of a flat curved club with a knobbed head and in the Plains region of a piece of stone fastened to the end of a slender stick covered with leather

po·gey bait *or* **po·gie bait** \ˈpōgē, -gi-\ *n* [*pogey*, *pogie* prob. alter. of *pogy*] *slang* **:** CANDY

pogge \ˈpäg\ *n* -s [origin unknown] **:** a sea poacher (*Agonus cataphractus*) of the north Atlantic

pog·gen·dorff illusion \ˈpägən‚dȯrf-\ *n, usu cap P* [after Johann C. *Poggendorff* †1877 Ger. physicist] **:** an apparent deflection of a straight line when it is interrupted by two lines parallel to each other

pog·gy \ˈpägē\ *n, pl* **poggies** *also* **poggy** [origin unknown] **:** a small whale

pogie *var of* POGY

pogies *pl of* POGY

pogon- *or* **pogono-** *comb form* [NL, fr. Gk *pōgōn-*, *pōgōno-*, fr. *pōgōn*] **:** beard **:** something resembling a beard **:** ⟨*Pogonia*⟩ ⟨*pogonotomy*⟩

-po·gon \ˈpō‚gän\ *n comb form* [NL, fr. Gk *pōgōn*, perh. fr. *pō-* (akin to Gk — Cyprian dial. — *pos* on, at) + *-gōn* (akin to Gk *genys* jaw) — more at POST-, CHIN] **:** beard — in generic names ⟨*Calopogon*⟩

po·go·na·tum \‚pōgəˈnād·əm, -ād·əm\ *n, cap* [NL, fr. *pogon-* + L *-atum* (neut. of *-atus* -ate)] **:** a genus of erect acrocarpous mosses (family Polytrichaceae) in which the leaves have ventral lamellae

po·go·nia \pəˈgōnyə, -nēə\ *n* [NL, fr. *pogon-* + *-ia*] **1** *cap* **:** a genus comprising terrestrial orchids of the north temperate zone that have a slender rootstock, one or few leaves, and a solitary terminal flower with a crested tip and being sometimes extended to include forms usu. placed in the genera *Isotria* and *Triphora* **2** -s **:** any orchid of *Pogonia* or a closely related genus

po·go·ni·on \-nēən\ *n* -s [NL, fr. Gk *pōgōnion* small beard, dim. of *pōgōn* beard — more at -POGON] **:** the most projecting median point on the anterior surface of the chin — see CRANIOMETRY illustration

pog·o·nip \ˈpägə‚nip\ *n* -s [Southern Paiute, fr. *pagina-* cloud, fog + *-pi*, n. suffix] **:** a dense winter fog containing frozen particles that is formed in deep mountain valleys of western U.S.

pogon iris \ˈpō‚gän-\ *n* [NL, subgenus of irises, fr. *pogon-* + *Iris*] **:** BEARDED IRIS

po·go·nol·o·gy \‚ₛₛˈnäləjē\ *n* -ES [NL *pogonologia*, fr. *pogon-* + L *-logia* -logy] **:** the study of or a treatise on beards

po·go·no·myr·mex \‚pōgənōˈmər‚meks\ *n, cap* [NL, fr. *pogon-* + Gk *myrmēx* ant — more at PISMIRE] **:** a widely distributed genus of harvester ants

po·go·no·mys \pəˈgōnə‚mis\ *n, cap* [NL, fr. *pogon-* + *-mys*] **:** a genus of prehensile-tailed rats of New Guinea

po·go·noph·o·ra \‚pōgəˈnäfərə\ *n pl, cap* [NL, irreg. fr. Gk *pōgōnophora*, neut. pl. of *pōgōnophoros* wearing a beard, fr. *pōgōno-* pogon- + *-phoros* -phorous] **:** a phylum or class of marine worms of uncertain systematic relationships that superficially resemble polychaetes but have a dorsal nervous system and obscure metamerism

po·go·not·o·my \‚pōgəˈnäd·əmē\ *n* -ES [*pogon-* + *-tomy*] **:** the cutting of a beard **:** SHAVING

po·go·not·ro·phy \‚ₛₛˈnä·trəfē\ *n* -ES [Gk *pōgōnotrophia*, fr. *pōgōno-* pogon- + *-trophia* -trophy] **:** beard growing

po·go stick \ˈpō‚gō-\ *n* [fr. *Pogo*, a trademark] **:** an upright pole with two foot rests and a strong spring at the bottom enabling the user to propel it along the ground by jumps

[1]**po·grom** \pəˈgrəm, (ˈ)pō¦grəm, ˈpōgrəm *sometimes* ˈpägrəm\ *n* -s [Yiddish, fr. Russ, lit., devastation, destruction, fr. *po-* like (fr. *po* on, at, according to) + *grom* thunder; akin to OE *of* of, from, off, and to OSlav *gromŭ* thunder, OE *grimm* grim — more at OF, GRIM] **:** an organized massacre and looting of helpless people usu. with the connivance of officials; *specif* **:** such a massacre of Jews

[2]**pogrom** \"\ *vt* -ED/-ING/-s **:** to massacre in a pogrom

po·grom·ist \-mə̇st\ *n* -s **:** one who organizes or takes part in a pogrom

po·gy *also* **po·gie** \ˈpōgē, -gi\ *n, pl* **pogies** [of Algonquian origin; akin to Abnaki *pôkagan* menhaden] **1 :** MENHADEN **2** *usu* **pogie a :** BLACK PERCH d **b :** a Pacific coast surf fish (*Holconotus rhodoterus*)

poh *a strong often trilled p-sound; often read as* ˈpō\ *interj* [origin unknown] — used to express contempt

po·ha \ˈpō(‚)hä\ *n* -s [Hawaiian *pohā*] *Hawaii* **:** cape gooseberry (*Physalis peruviana*)

po·hu·tu·ka·wa \pō‚hüd·əˈkäwə\ *n* -s [Maori] **1 :** a New Zealand tree (*Metrosideros tomentosa*) with crimson flowers and silvery leaves below **2 :** a New Zealand variety of the sweet potato

[1]**poi** \ˈpȯi, ˈpōē\ *adv* [It, fr. L *post* behind, after — more at POST-] **:** THEN, LATER, NEXT — used to qualify another word used as a direction in music ⟨adagio ~ allegro⟩

[2]**poi** \ˈpȯi, ˈpōē\ *n, pl* **poi** *or* **pois** [Hawaiian & Samoan] **1 :** a Hawaiian food made of taro root which is cooked and pounded and kneaded into a smooth pasty mass to which varying quantities of water are added, often allowed to ferment before being eaten, and traditionally eaten with the fingers **2 :** a Hawaiian or Samoan food made of mashed ripe bananas or pineapples to which coconut cream is usu. added

[3]**poi** \"\ *n, pl* **poi** *or* **pois** [Maori] **:** a small ball which is made typically of flax, grass, or rushes, to which a string of varying length is attached, and which is swung rhythmically by Maori performers in various dances and songs

poi·e·sis \pȯiˈēsə̇s\ *n, pl* **poie·ses** \-ē‚sēz\ [Gk *poiēsis* creation, making, poem — more at POESY] **:** the action or faculty of producing or doing something esp. creatively

-poi·e·sis \‚pȯiˈēsə̇s\ *n comb form, pl* **-poie·ses** \-ē‚sēz\ [NL, fr. Gk *poiēsis*] **:** production **:** formation ⟨hematopoiesis⟩ ⟨leukopoiesis⟩

poi·et·ic \(ˈ)pȯi¦ed·|ik, -et|, |ēk\ *adj* [Gk *poiētikos* capable of making, creative, poetic — more at POETIC] **:** of or relating to poiesis **:** CREATIVE ⟨a ~ shaper of his own destiny —C.P. Aiken⟩

-poi·et·ic \"\ *adj comb form* [Gk *poiētikos*] **:** productive **:** formative ⟨hematopoietic⟩

poi·gnance \ˈpȯin(y)ən(t)s\ *n* -s **:** POIGNANCY

poi·gnan·cy \-nsē, -si\ *n* -ES **1 :** the quality or state of being poignant ⟨acute sudden ~ of love —Havelock Ellis⟩ **2 :** an instance of poignancy ⟨experience filled with *poignancies*⟩

poi·gnant \-nt\ *adj* [ME *pugnaunt*, *poinaunt*, fr. MF *poignant*, pres. part. of *poindre* to prick, pierce, sting, fr. L *pungere* — more at PUNGENT] **1 a** *archaic* **:** sharp and piquant to the taste **b :** pungent and strongly pervasive in odor ⟨a ~ perfume, soft and languorous —Kenneth Roberts⟩ **2 a** (1) **:** painfully sharp with regard to the feelings **:** PIERCING, KEEN ⟨~ grief⟩ ⟨with a look of ~ regret on his face —Bram Stoker⟩ (2) **:** very moving **:** deeply affecting **:** TOUCHING ⟨the ~ spectacle of a little child without a home⟩ ⟨so many ~ memories —Havelock Ellis⟩ **b** (1) **:** STINGING, CUTTING ⟨his satire is particularly ~ —F.M.Godfrey⟩ ⟨~ sarcasm —Benjamin Disraeli⟩ (2) **:** INCISIVE, PENETRATING ⟨are revealed with ~ clarity —Joseph Frank⟩ (3) **:** making a strong impression **:** STRIKING ⟨a ~ paradox —J.T.Clark⟩ ⟨become both convincing and ~ to us —David Cecil⟩ **c :** URGENT, PRESSING, ACUTE ⟨the more ~ problems of human existence —M.R. Cohen⟩ **3** *obs* **:** having a physically sharp point **4 a :** keenly stimulating or pleasurable to the mind or feelings ⟨a more ~ felicity than he had yet experienced —Nathaniel Hawthorne⟩ ⟨ecstasy too ~ to endure —*Saturday Rev.*⟩ ⟨this kind of day . . . had a more ~ loveliness —Jan Struther⟩ **b :** deft and to the point ⟨her illustrations were apposite and ~ —Charles Lamb⟩ **:** APT, POINTED ⟨makes some brief but ~ observations —G.A.Panichas⟩ **syn** see MOVING, PUNGENT

poi·gnant·ly *adv* **:** in a poignant manner **:** with poignancy

poignard *var of* PONIARD

poikil- *or* **poikilo-** — see POECIL-

poi·ki·lit·ic \¦pȯikə¦lid·ik\ *or* **poe·ci·lit·ic** \¦pēsə¦-\ *adj* [*poecil-* + *-itic*] **:** of, relating to, or consisting of a structural pattern in igneous rocks in which a crystal of one mineral encloses smaller unoriented grains of another mineral so that a lustrous mottling effect is produced

poi·kilo·blast \pȯiˈkilə‚blast, ˈpȯikəlō‚b-\ *n* -s [ISV *poecil-* + *-blast*] **1 :** a nucleated poikilocyte **2 :** a large crystal of a metamorphic rock with a texture marked by the inclusion of small idioblasts — **poi·kilo·blas·tic** \¦ₛₛ¦blastik, ¦ₛₛₛ-\ *adj*

poi·kilo·cyte \ₛˈₛₛ‚sīt, ˈₛₛₛ-\ *n* -s [ISV *poecil-* + *-cyte*] **:** an abnormally formed red blood cell characteristic of various anemias

poi·kilo·cytosis \ₛ¦ₛₛ, ¦ₛₛₛ+\ *n, pl* **poikilocytoses** [NL, fr. ISV *poikilocyte* + NL *-osis*] **:** a condition marked by the presence of poikilocytes

poi·kil·osmotic \¦pȯikə̇l+\ *adj* [*poecil-* + *osmotic*] **:** lacking a bodily osmotic regulating mechanism and having body fluids with an osmotic pressure similar to that of the surrounding medium ⟨most lower marine invertebrates are ~⟩ — compare HOMOIOSMOTIC

poi·kilo·therm \pȯiˈkilə‚thərm, ˈpȯikəlō‚th-\ *n* -s [ISV *poecil-* + *-therm*; orig. formed in G] **:** an organism (as a frog) with a variable body temperature usu. slightly higher than the temperature of its environment **:** a cold-blooded organism

poi·kilo·ther·mic \ₛ¦ₛₛ¦thərmik, ¦ₛₛₛ-\ *also* **poi·kilo·ther·mal** \-məl\ *or* **poi·kilo·ther·mous** \-məs\ *adj* **:** of, relating to, or typical of a poikilotherm **:** COLD-BLOODED 2

poi·kilo·ther·mism \ₛ‚ₛₛˈthər‚mizəm, ˈₛₛₛ‚th-\ *n* -s **:** the state of being poikilothermic

poi·ki·lo·ther·my \-mē\ *n* -ES **:** POIKILOTHERMISM

poil \ˈpȯi(ə)l\ *n* -s [F, lit., hair, fr. L *pilus* — more at PILE] **:** a thread of raw silk used as a core for tinsel

poi·lu \(ˈ)pwä¦lü, *F* pwȧlü\ *n* -s [F, fr. *poilu* hairy, fr. MF, fr. *poil* hair] **:** a soldier in the French army; *esp* **:** a front-line French soldier in World War I

poi·men·ics \pȯiˈmeniks\ *n pl but usu sing in constr* [Gk *poimenikos* of a shepherd (fr. *poimen-*, *poimēn* shepherd, pastor + *-ikos* -ic) + E *-s*; akin to Gk *pōy* herd, flock — more at FUR] **:** the study or application of pastoral theology

poin·ci·ana \‚pȯin(t)sēˈanə, *esp in regions where it grows* ‚p(w)än-\ *n* [NL, fr. De *Poinci*, 17th cent. governor of part of the French West Indies + L *-ana*, fem. of *-anus* -an] **1** *cap* **:** a small genus of ornamental tropical trees or shrubs (family Leguminosae) that have bright orange or red flowers — see PRIDE OF BARBADOS **2** -s **:** any of various trees now or formerly included in the genus *Poinciana*; *esp* **:** ROYAL POINCIANA

poind \ˈpȯind, ˈpind\ *vt* -ED/-ING/-s [ME (Sc dial.) *punden*, *pynden*, fr. OE *pyndan* to dam up — more at PIND] *Scot* **:** to take forceful legal possession of esp. so as to sell under warrant

poinding *n* -s [ME *punding*, gerund of *punden* to poind] *Scots law* **:** a process by which a creditor seizes movable property so as to become vested with its title and the right of sale or appropriation in satisfaction of a debt

poin·set·tia \÷pȯinˈsed·|ə, |ēə, -set|\ *n* [NL, fr. Joel R. *Poinsett* †1851 Am. diplomat + NL *-ia*] **1 a** *cap, in some classifications* **:** a genus of chiefly tropical American herbs or woody plants (family Euphorbiaceae) with alternate leaves and cymose inconspicuous greenish flowers subtended by brightly colored involucral leaves that is now included as a section in the genus *Euphorbia* **b** -s **:** any plant of the genus *Euphorbia* that has flower clusters marked by showy involucral bracts; *esp* **:** a showy Mexican and So. American plant (*E. pulcherrima*) with tapering scarlet petallike leaves that surround small yellow flowers **2** -s **:** a strong to vivid red that is bluer and lighter than bright cherry red

[1]**point** \ˈpȯint *dial* ˈpīnt\ *n* -s [ME, partly fr. OF *point* prick, sting, small spot, dot, item, point in time or space, fr. L *punctum* small hole, spot, point in time or space, fr. neut. of *punctus*, past part. of *pungere* to prick, sting, pierce; partly fr. OF *pointe* sharp end, fr. (assumed) VL *puncta*, fr. L, fem. of *punctus*, past part. — more at PUNGENT] **1 a** (1) **:** one of the indivisible parts of an extended usu. abstract whole **:** an individual detail of a pair or group of details **:** ITEM, PARTICULAR ⟨said there were two ~*s* in the proposal that were important⟩ ⟨carefully considered each ~ of the argument⟩ ⟨said that in his new job he would have to watch a couple of ~*s*⟩ (2) **:** a distinguishing trait or feature **:** a differentiating detail **:** individualizing mark **:** CHARACTERISTIC ⟨was well aware of the teacher's good and bad ~*s*⟩ ⟨tact is one of her strong ~*s*⟩; *specif* **:** a feature of an animal's physical qualities or behavior esp. as figuring in evaluation of the animal's relative excellence of breed ⟨judges at a dog show carefully noting the ~*s* of each dog⟩ (3) **points** *pl* **:** the facial markings of a Siamese cat **:** MASK **b** (1) **:** the most important essential in some discussion or matter **:** the principal or central element **:** the precise part on which the rest turns or depends ⟨the ~ of his talk was that more effort was needed⟩ ⟨the ~ is they are doing as well as they can⟩ ⟨asked them not to digress and to keep to the ~⟩ ⟨became impatient with the witness and asked her to come to the ~⟩ (2) **:** the part of something spoken or written that gives it effectiveness or meaningfulness **:** the element on which applicability or cogency depends **:** the main idea or vital feature ⟨could not see the ~ of such a remark⟩ ⟨missed the whole ~ of the joke⟩ **c :** the quality of something spoken or written of being able to arouse interest and of being generally effective **:** pungent effectiveness arising esp. out of applicability **:** COGENCY, FORCE, PUNCH ⟨is a basically sound book but somehow lacks ~⟩ **2** *obs* **:** the state of being in a particular physical condition ⟨looked fairer and in better ~ than all the rest —John Evelyn⟩ **3 a** (1) **:** an end or object to be achieved **:** AIM, PURPOSE ⟨did not see what ~ there was in continuing the discussion⟩ (2) **:** something to be gained **:** BENEFIT, GOOD ⟨wondered whether there would be any ~ in seeing her⟩ **b :** something that one has proposed and is trying to get established or accepted **:** a particular line of argument **:** what one is driving at **:** THESIS, PROPOSITION ⟨said he was beginning to see her ~⟩ ⟨has unquestionably won his ~⟩ ⟨carried the ~ without difficulty and did as she wanted to⟩ ⟨made their ~ so that everyone was convinced⟩ **c** (1) **:** something that is the subject of discussion or attention ⟨asked what the ~ at issue was⟩ or concern ⟨with them the whole thing is a ~ of conscience⟩ **:** MATTER ⟨is a ~ of controversy⟩ ⟨a ~ of interest⟩ (2) **:** something (as a vital idea, an essential detail) that is important enough to require serious discussion or consideration ⟨told him that he had a ~ in what he said⟩ (3) **:** POINTER 8 **4 a** (1) **:** a particular narrowly limited part of a surface or of space that is singled out as occupying a usu. precisely indicated spot and that has usu. minimum extension or no relevant extension **:** a specific narrowly localized place having no relevant size or shape **:** a definite precisely indicated placement or position of something ⟨fire broke out at several ~*s* in the city⟩ ⟨walked to a ~ 50 yards north of the building⟩ ⟨struck the target at a ~ just left of center⟩ ⟨a satellite that was 200 miles from earth at its farthest ~⟩ (2) **:** a narrowly localized abstract spot used as a place of reference ⟨conceived of a line drawn from a ~ into infinity⟩ ⟨the shortest distance between any two ~*s* is a straight line⟩ (3) **:** a particular place (as a city, town, or region) **:** LOCALITY ⟨asked them what ~*s* they intended to visit⟩ ⟨stopped at a number of ~*s* along the way⟩ ⟨have come from distant ~*s*⟩ **b** (1) **:** a particular narrowly limited often critical interval of time singled out as occurring at a precisely indicated moment and having usu. minimum duration or no relevant duration **:** exact moment **:** precise instant **:** JUNCTURE ⟨at this ~ he was interrupted⟩ (2) **:** a time interval or set of circumstances occurring immediately or nearly immediately before something indicated **:** VERGE ⟨was on the ~ of refusing⟩ ⟨is at the very ~ of death⟩ ⟨found her on the ~ of hysterics⟩ **c** (1) **:** a particular narrowly limited step, stage, or degree in the condition or development of something that is typically singled out as critical or decisive or as otherwise highly significant or important ⟨had reached the ~ where nothing seemed to matter anymore⟩ ⟨arrived at the ~ of perfection⟩ ⟨a high ~ of civilization⟩ (2) **:** a definite measurable position in some kind of scale ⟨the ~ at which water begins to boil⟩ ⟨stock prices at their highest ~*s*⟩ **d** (1) **:** one of the undefined elements of a geometric system and esp. of a Euclidean geometric system; *also* **:** an element of an aggregate determined by an ordered set equal in number to the number of dimensions of the aggregate (2) **:** a real or complex number that is represented by a geometric point **5** *obs* **a :** CONCLUSION, TERMINATION **b :** DECISION, RESOLUTION **6 a :** the extreme terminal usu. sharp or narrowly rounded part of something (as a sword, arrow, awl, pin, hook, indicator) that is usu. formed by the gradual or abrupt decrease in width or

a b c
d
k e m
f
g h j

points 11: *a* dexter chief, *b* middle chief, *c* sinister chief, *d* honor, *e* fess, *f* nombril, *g* dexter base, *h* middle base, *j* sinister base, *k* dexter flank, *m* sinister flank thickness of the body which it terminates and that is typically used for piercing, pricking, indicating, or for some similar function : a usu. sharp, tapering, or otherwise narrowly converging end : TIP ⟨the sharp ~ of a needle⟩ ⟨forced the government on the people at the ~ of the sword⟩ ⟨both ~*s* of an anchor⟩ ⟨the ~ of a fishhook⟩ ⟨a weather vane with its ~ turned toward the north⟩ **b** : something with such a point: as (1) *obs* : a weapon used for stabbing or piercing (2) : an instrument used in etching and engraving (3) : a tool used in trimming and smoothing rough stone surfaces (4) : an instrument used to test the hardness of a mineral or gem **c** (1) : a piece of stone typically having a triangular shape and used chiefly by some prehistoric peoples as a tool or sometimes as a weapon (2) : an arrowhead without cutting edges : PILE (3) : GLAZIER'S POINT **d** (1) : a short steel pin placed in a printing press to perforate a sheet and so position it for register the next time it is run through the press — called also *press point* (2) : a piece of steel placed in the furniture of a printing form to mark a sheet at a certain place as a guide for folding (3) : a short sharp piece of serrated steel fastened to the furniture or a metal base in a printing form for slitting a sheet so that it can be registered on corresponding slits of a folding machine (4) : PIN 2 d **e** (1) : a device with a tapered point that controls the increase or decrease of stitches (as in machine-knitted fabrics) (2) : one of a series of needles in a lace machine used for controlling the size of the mesh **f** : a drive-pipe through which steam or water is introduced into frozen gravel to thaw it for mining or dredging **g** (1) : the contact or discharge extremity of an electric device (as a spark plug, contact break, lightning rod) (2) *chiefly Brit* : an electric outlet : SOCKET **7** : a projecting usu. tapering part of something: as **a** : a piece of land (as a promontory, cape) projecting into a body of water **b** : a sharp prominence ⟨beyond a ~ of rock⟩ : APEX, PEAK ⟨the towering ~*s* of a mountain range⟩ **c** : the shaped end of one of the pieces of a leaf spring **d** (1) : the tip of the chin (2) : the tip of the foot (3) : the tip of the tongue (4) : a tine of an antler (5) **points** *pl* : the extremities of an animal; *esp* : the legs, mane, and tail of a horse **e** (1) : POINT RAIL (2) : a railroad switch (3) : the tip of the angle between two rails in a railroad frog **f** : the head of the bow of a stringed instrument **8** : a short musical phrase: **a** *archaic* : a short phrase sounded as a signal (as in hunting, battle) **b** (1) : a phrase (as a fugue subject) in contrapuntal music (2) : the entry of such a phrase at one or the other part of a contrapuntal composition **9 a** (1) : a very small mark (as a dot, speck) on a surface : a tiny spot ⟨a blue background that was touched up with little ~*s* of gold⟩ (2) : something that in general size and appearance is suggestive of such a mark ⟨~*s* of light shone through the perforated paper⟩ ⟨the pupil of the eye was contracted to a minute ~⟩ **b** : a small mark used in writing or printing: as (1) : PUNCTUATION MARK; *esp* : PERIOD (2) : a simple or compound mark used as a supplementary mark (as for indicating vowels, differentiating letters similar in form, marking stress accent) in Semitic alphabets (3) : ¹DOT 2 e (4) : DECIMAL POINT (5) : one of the small raised impressions used in braille **c** : a note in medieval music : PUNCTUS **10 a** : a lace like a shoelace having aglet ends for tying parts of a garment or costume together and used esp. in the 16th and 17th centuries ⟨sleeves were joined to a bodice with ~*s*⟩ ⟨hose was tied to the doublet with ~*s*⟩ **b** : REEF POINT **c** : a short length of material (as silkworm gut, nylon) used in angling to attach an artificial fly to a leader **d** : a small piece of material (as gutta-percha, gold) used in dentistry as a temporary filling for teeth **11 a** : one of nine particular divisions of a heraldic shield or escutcheon that determine the position of a charge; *esp* : a horizontal segment located at the base of the field and bounded by two straight or concaved slanting lines that meet at or below the fess point **b** : one of the pendants of the label of a heraldic shield or escutcheon **12 a** (1) : one of the 32 precisely marked equidistant spots about the circumference of a compass card that indicate the direction in which the various parts of the horizon lie (2) : the difference of 11¼ degrees between two such successive points **b** : a part of the horizon indicated precisely or approximately by one of the points of a compass card **13** : a small detachment probing ahead of and scouting for an advance guard or following behind and protecting a rear guard **14 a** : LACE: as (1) : NEEDLEPOINT 1 (2) : BOBBIN LACE **b** *obs* : a piece of needlepoint used as a woman's head covering **c** (1) : a stitch used in the making of lace or in producing canvas work or sometimes in producing other similar work (2) : a line of fancy stitching on the back of a glove **d** : one of the stripes woven in the edge of a Hudson's Bay blanket to indicate the weight of the blanket **15** : one of 12 spaces marked off on each side of a backgammon board **16** : a unit of measurement (as of excellence, value, proficiency, extent): as **a** (1) : a unit of counting in the scoring of a game, contest, or other competition or match (2) : a unit used in evaluating the worth or strength of a hand in some card games (as bridge) **b** (1) : a unit of academic credit used in many educational institutions and granted in larger or smaller multiples according to the grade achieved in a course (2) : a unit of credit counting toward an individual's return from overseas military service or toward his release from military service and granted in larger or smaller multiples according to the length of service already done, the number of combat decorations awarded, or other qualifications **c** : a unit used in quoting prices of stocks, shares, and various commodities that is equivalent in the stock exchange of the U. S. to one dollar a share **d** : a unit that is used in Australia to measure the extent of rainfall and that is equivalent to ¹⁄₁₀₀ inch **e** : a unit that is used to measure the thickness of paper and paperboard and that is equivalent to ¹⁄₁₀₀₀ inch **f** : a unit that is used to measure the size of type used in printing and that is 0.013837 or approximately ¹⁄₇₂ inch — see TYPE illustration **g** : a unit used to measure the weight of diamonds that is equivalent to ¹⁄₁₀₀ carat **h** : a unit of value of coupons allotted for purchase of commodities in a rationing system **17** : the action of pointing: as **a** : the action of a hunting dog that scents or sees game and stiffens into an intently rigid attitude with head and gaze directed toward the game **b** : the action (as in some dance positions or movements) of extending one leg so that it supports no body weight and so that only the tips of the toes of the extended foot touch the floor **c** : a thrust or lunge made while fencing **18 a** : a particular position of a player in some games: as (1) : an off-side fielding position in cricket near the batsman and about in line with the popping crease — see CRICKET illustration (2) : the position to the right of the goal in lacrosse **b** : the player of a particular position in some games **19 a** : a run (as a cross-country run) made straight from one place to another **b** : the terminal place to which such a run is made **20** : one of the numbers 4, 5, 6, 8, 9, 10 that if thrown on the come-out in the game of craps gives the shooter the right to continue throwing until he wins by throwing the same number or loses by throwing a 7 — **at point 1** *obs* : in readiness ⟨let him keep *at point* a hundred knights —Shak.⟩ **2** *or* **at the point** *archaic* : on the verge : on the point : very near : just about — used with a following infinitive ⟨you are *at point* to lose your liberties —Shak.⟩ ⟨am *at the point* to die —Gen 25:32 (AV)⟩ — **in point 1** *heraldry* **a** : approaching at the tips so as to touch actually or nearly ⟨two or more piles *in point*⟩ **b** : ENTÉ EN POINT 1 **2** : RELEVANT, PERTINENT — used predicatively or postpositively ⟨mentioned a case *in point*⟩ — **in point of** *prep* : with regard to : in the matter of : with reference to ⟨*in point of* law⟩ ⟨*in point of* fact⟩ — **to point** *archaic* : in the smallest detail : fully and exactly ⟨all things thus happily performed *to point* —Robert Browning⟩ — **to the point** : RELEVANT, PERTINENT, APT ⟨made a suggestion that was altogether *to the point*⟩

²**point** \"\ *vb* -ED/-ING/-S [ME *pointen*, fr. MF *pointer*, partly fr. *pointe* point (sharp end), partly fr. *point* prick, small spot, dot — more at ¹POINT] *vt* **1 a** : to cause to have a sharp point : SHARPEN ⟨~*ing* a pencil with a knife⟩ **b** : to give added force, emphasis, or piquancy to : give more point to ⟨occasionally ~*ed* his remarks by slyly wagging his forefinger —G.B.Shaw⟩ — often used with *up* ⟨~*ed* up his narrative with effective use of dialect⟩ **2 a** (1) : to finish (as a wall) by filling the joints with cement, mortar, or other material (2) : to scratch out the old mortar from the joints of (as a wall) and fill in with new material — often used with *up* ⟨~*ed* up the brickwork⟩ **b** : to trim and smooth the surface of (stone) with a sharp tool — often used with *down* ⟨~*ing* down the block of granite⟩ **3 a** (1) : to mark the pauses or grammatical divisions in (something written or printed) : PUNCTUATE ⟨~*ing* the text of a speech⟩ (2) : to separate (a numerical figure) into groups by inserting a dot; *esp* : to separate (a decimal fraction) from a whole number by inserting a decimal point — usu. used with *off* ⟨~*ed* off the last two figures of 125⟩ **b** : to mark (as Hebrew words or words of other Semitic languages) with vowel points or other differentiating points **4 a** (1) : to indicate the position or direction of esp. by extending a finger toward the thing so indicated — usu. used with *out* ⟨~*ed* out the house where he used to live⟩ ⟨~*ing* out places of interest as they drove along⟩ (2) : to direct someone's attention to : call to someone's notice ⟨~*ed* out that several mistakes had been made⟩ ⟨~*ing* out the necessity of such a step⟩ ⟨let me ~ out that I knew nothing about the matter⟩ **b** *of a hunting dog* : to indicate the presence and place of (game) by stiffening into an intently rigid attitude with head and gaze directed toward the place so indicated ⟨a setter that ~*s* pheasant extraordinarily well⟩ **5 a** : to cause to be turned in a particular direction or toward a particular thing : DIRECT; *specif* : to cause the tip of (as a finger, stick, weapon, vehicle) to be extended, aimed, or turned in a particular direction or toward a particular thing ⟨~*ing* the gun at the target⟩ ⟨~*ed* the boat upstream⟩ **b** : to extend (a leg) in executing a point in dancing **6 a** : to taper and finish off the end of (a cable or rope) by interweaving the nettles **b** : to insert reef points through the eyelet holes of (a sail) **c** : to brace up sharp (the yards of a ship) **7** : to insert white hairs into (furs) to improve the appearance ⟨red fox dyed and ~*ed* to imitate silver fox⟩ **8** : to locate esp. in marble essential or selected points of (a piece of statuary) by drilling a hole to the proper depth at each point ⟨~*ing* a block of marble before beginning to cut a statue⟩ ~ *vi* **1 a** : to be of such a kind as to show or tend to show fairly convincingly the fact or probability of something specified : give or tend to give a fairly good indication of something specified — used with *to* or sometimes *toward* or *at* ⟨everything ~*s* to a bright future for them⟩ ⟨such symptoms ~ to a serious disorder⟩ **b** : to indicate the position or direction of something esp. by extending a finger toward the thing so indicated ⟨kept ~*ing* through the window⟩ — used with *at, to*, or *toward* before a specified object ⟨~*ed* at the map on the wall⟩ ⟨~*ed* to her brother and said he was the one⟩ **c** : to point game ⟨a dog that ~*s* well⟩ **2 a** : to lie extended, aimed, or turned in a particular direction or toward a particular thing ⟨a directional arrow that ~*ed* to the north⟩ ⟨the boat was ~*ing* upstream⟩ ⟨an indicator that ~*ed* toward an even number⟩ **b** : to execute a point in dancing **3** *of an abscess* : to come to a head **4** *of a ship* : to sail close to the wind — often used with *up* ⟨would ~ up better on the port tack —Nelson Hayes⟩ **5** *of a horse* : to rest a forefoot on the toe or hold a forefoot forward to remove the weight of the body from it **6** : to make special intensive preparations for meeting a particular sports opponent — used with *for* ⟨the team was ~*ing* for the game with the neighboring college⟩

point after touchdown : EXTRA POINT

point at infinity : an ideal mathematical point in projective geometry that preserves the magnitudes of all angles of a transformed plane

¹**point-blank** \'ˌ=ˈ=\ *n, pl* **point-blanks** [prob. fr. ²*point* + *blank* (bull's-eye)] **1 a** : the distance that a missile (as a bullet) flies along a nearly straight horizontal line from its starting point (as the barrel of a gun) before beginning to drop appreciably below that line **b** : the point at which a missile begins to drop appreciably below its initial nearly straight horizontal line of flight **2** : a shot aimed or fired straight at its target

²**point-blank** \"\ *adj* **1 a** (1) : marked by no appreciable drop below an initial nearly straight horizontal line of flight toward a target ⟨a projectile following a *point-blank* trajectory⟩ (2) : consisting of or lying within the distance within which something may be aimed or fired straight at a target without having to allow for appreciable drop in the line of flight of the missile shot or to be shot ⟨estimated the *point-blank* range of the gun⟩ ⟨there were lions at *point-blank* range —*Newsweek*⟩ **b** : aimed or fired straight at a target ⟨a *point-blank* shot⟩ **2** : that is direct, plain, and unequivocal : BLUNT ⟨a *point-blank* refusal⟩

³**point-blank** \"\ *adv* **1 a** (1) : with aim directed straight toward a target; *esp* : with aim so directed on a horizontal plane ⟨fired *point-blank* at the traitor —Desmond Ryan⟩ (2) : without dropping appreciably below an initial nearly horizontal line of flight toward a target ⟨an arrow whistling *point-blank* toward the bull's-eye⟩ **b** *archaic* (1) : in a straight direct line : DIRECTLY ⟨led him *point-blank* to the bed —M.L. Weems⟩ (2) : WHOLLY, ALTOGETHER ⟨so *point-blank* against the common sentiment —John Norris †1711⟩ **2** : in a direct, plain, and unequivocal manner : BLUNTLY ⟨asked her *point-blank* what she wanted⟩

point count *n* **1** : a method of evaluating the strength of a hand in the game of bridge by counting a set number of points for each high card held and often by adding points for long suits or short suits in the hand **2** : the value of a hand as evaluated by some method of point count

point d'an·gle·terre \ˌpwaⁿ,däⁿglə'te(ə)r\ *n, pl* **points d'angleterre** \"\ *usu cap A* [F, lit., lace from England] : a bobbin lace of Flemish origin made with applied bobbin or needlepoint designs

point d'ap·pui \ˌ=ˌda¦pwē\ *n, pl* **points d'appui** [F, lit., point of support] : FOUNDATION, BASE; *esp* : a base from which a military operation can be carried on

point de gaze \-də¦gäz, -gaz\ *n, pl* **points de gaze** [F, lit., lace of gauze] : a fine needlepoint lace of Belgian origin with a gauzy net ground ornamented with floral patterns

point d'es·pagne \-,de¦spanyə\ *n, pl* **points d'espagne** *usu cap E* [F, lit., lace from Spain] : a needlepoint lace of Spanish origin with usu. gold or silver threads or with heavy designs on a fine ground

point d'es·prit \-,de¦sprē\ *n, pl* **points d'esprit** [F, lit., lace of spirit] : a fine bobbinet with scattered woven dots used esp. for curtains, dresses, or trimmings

¹**point-device** \ˌpȯintdə¦vīs\ *adj, archaic* [ME *(at) point devis*, fr. *at* + *point* + *devis* fixed, set, fr. MF, fr. L *divisus*, past part. of *dividere* to divide — more at DIVIDE] : marked by punctilious often fussy attention to detail : METICULOUS ⟨*point-device* in its accouterments —J.L.Lowes⟩

²**point-device** \"\ *adv, archaic* : with punctilious often fussy attention to detail : METICULOUSLY ⟨was dressed *point-device* —Sir Walter Scott⟩

point d'hon·grie \ˌpwaⁿ,dōⁿ ¦grē\ *n, pl* **points d'hongrie** *usu cap H* [F, lit., lace from Hungary] : an embroidery of zigzag designs worked in bright graduated colors and formerly much used in canvas work esp. for upholstery and rugs

point duty *n, Brit* : the directing of traffic by a policeman stationed typically at an intersection — compare POINTSMAN

pointe \'pwaⁿt, 'pwant\ *n* -S [F, lit., point (sharp end) — more at POINT] **1** *ballet* : the extreme tip of the toe **2** *ballet* : a position of balance on the extreme tip of the toe

¹**point·ed** \'pȯintəd\ *adj* [ME, partly fr. *point* + *-ed*; partly fr. past part. of *pointen* to point — more at POINT] **1 a** : tapering to or ending in an esp. sharp point ⟨a ~ stick⟩ ⟨~ rocks jutting up from the surf⟩ **b** (1) *of an arch* : having a pointed crown ⟨Gothic architecture is characterized by the ~ arch⟩ (2) : marked by the use of the pointed arch ⟨~ architecture⟩ **2 a** : that is made so evident as to be quite conspicuous : made quite obvious ⟨her ~ lack of concern over what happened to him⟩ **b** : made quite unmistakable in meaning, reference, or application : clearly aimed or directed ⟨was disturbed by such ~ remarks⟩ ⟨a ~ allusion to what was going on⟩ **3 a** : PUNCTILIOUS, PRECISE, EXACT ⟨is described with ~ correctness —W.E.Gladstone⟩ **b** : keenly intent : CONCENTRATED, DETAILED ⟨would call for more ~ attention to the problems of colonial government —*Current Biog.*⟩ ⟨no guide to nature, humanity and much of history is more ~ than art —J.F.Dobie⟩ **4 a** : full of life and piquancy : LIVELY, ZESTFUL, STIMULATING, TANGY ⟨with just enough Irish malice to make the narrative ~ —H.J.Laski⟩ **b** : very much to the point : INCISIVE, TERSE : full of punch and effectiveness : EPIGRAMMATIC ⟨~ wit⟩ ⟨the writing is ~, vigorous —C.B.Hagan⟩ — **point·ed·ness** *n* -ES

²**pointed** *adj* [short for *appointed*, past part. of *appoint*] *obs* : SET, FIXED ⟨I'll not be tied to hours nor ~ times —Shak.⟩

point·ed·ly *adv* **1** : in a pointed manner : SIGNIFICANTLY: as **a** : in such a way as to make something clearly evident or conspicuous ⟨differing ~ therefore from the U. S. —Frank Gorrell⟩ **b** : in such a way as to make some meaning, reference, or application quite unmistakable ⟨have been so ~ uninterested —Claire Sterling⟩ ⟨~ ignored a question —Mary K. Hammond⟩ **c** : in a way that is incisive, terse, and very much to the point ⟨because it bears trenchantly and ~ on our life today —Leslie Rees⟩ ⟨discussed this situation more ~ —E.D. Canham⟩ **2** *dial* : by all means : very much : SURELY, CERTAINLY, INDEED ⟨I'm ~ shamed —Maristan Chapman⟩

point·er \'pȯintə(r)\ *n* -S [²*point* + *-er*] **1 a** : one that furnishes something with points: as (1) : one that points furs (2) : one that stitches points on gloves **b** : one that causes something to have a tapering end or sharp point: as (1) : one that sharpens pencils, drills, or similar objects (2) : one that tapers the teeth of combs or the ends of rods, springs, or similar objects **2** : one that indicates something : one that points out something: as **a** : a light tapered rod used typically by teachers or lecturers to call attention to details (as of material appearing on a blackboard) **b** : one of the hands of a clock or watch **c** : the indicator of a pair of scales or some similar indicator **d** : STATION POINTER **3** : a tool with a pointed end: as **a** : a bricklayer's tool used for clearing out old mortar in pointing **b** : a tool used in engraving, cutting, or boring **4** : one that points something in a particular direction; *specif* : one that raises a gun to a prescribed elevation in fixing it on a target — compare TRAINER **5 a** : a large strong slender smooth-haired gundog of Spanish origin that has usu. a white coat spotted here and there with brown or black patches, a long wide head with a marked depression between the prominent eyebrows and broad nose, soft long ears hanging close to the cheeks, and a moderately long tapered tail and that scents out and indicates the presence of game by stiffening into an intently rigid attitude with head and gaze directed toward the game and typically with the tail stretched out rigidly and with a forepaw raised and bent backward **b pointers** *pl* : MEN — distinguished from *setters* **6** : SNAKEPIECE **7** : POINT MAN **8** : a piece of information that is esp. helpful in learning to do or accomplish something : a useful suggestion or hint : TIP ⟨gave him some ~*s* on how to run the business⟩

pointes *pl of* POINTE

point-event \'==ˌ=ˌ=\ *n* : an event without extension in space or time

point·ful \'pȯintfəl\ *adj* : that is to the point : that has point : that has meaning, relevance, or force ⟨made a ~ remark⟩ — **point·ful·ly** \-fəlē\ *adv* — **point·ful·ness** \-fəlnəs\ *n* -ES

point function *n* : a variable (as the temperature of the air) each value of which is associated with and determined by the position of some point in space

pointier *comparative of* POINTY

pointiest *superlative of* POINTY

poin·til·lage \ˌpwaⁿtē¦(y)äzh, -ant-\ *n* -S [F, fr. *pointiller* + *-age*] : POINTILLISM

poin·til·lé \-(y)ā\ *adj* [F, fr. past part. of *pointiller* to mark with dots, stipple, fr. *point* dot — more at POINT] : decorated with closely spaced usu. gold dots made with a pointed tool ⟨a ~ leather book binding⟩

poin·til·lism *also* **poin·til·lisme** \'=tē,(y)izəm, -tᵊl,i-\ *n* -S [F *pointillisme*, fr. *pointiller* + *-isme* -ism] : the practice or technique of applying dots or tiny strokes of color elements to a surface so that when seen from a distance the dots or strokes blend luminously together

poin·til·list *also* **poin·til·liste** \-tē(y)əst, -tᵊlə-\ *n* -S [F *pointilliste*, fr. *pointiller* + *-iste* -ist] : one that uses pointillism

poin·til·lis·tic \¦=tē¦(y)istik, -tᵊl¦is-\ *adj* : of, relating to, or typical of pointillism or pointillists

pointing *n* -S [partly fr. ¹*point* + *-ing*; partly fr. gerund of ²*point*] **1 a** : punctuation marks **b** : vowel points or other differentiating marks used in some Semitic languages **c** : marks used in the texts of plainsong to indicate a division of verses corresponding to the musical division **2** : the material (as mortar) used in pointing something (as a brick wall) **3** : HEAD 20a **4** : a line of ornamental stitchwork (as on the back of a glove) **5** : a stride which is esp. characteristic of the Thoroughbred horse and in which extension is emphasized rather than flexion

point-instant \'=¦=ˌ=\ *n* -S : the smallest unit of space-time

point lace *n* : NEEDLEPOINT 1

point·less \'pȯintləs\ *adj* **1 a** : lacking a point : having a blunt end : UNPOINTED ⟨my pencils are all ~ —Charles Dickens⟩ **b** : lacking any scored points : SCORELESS ⟨the game ended in a ~ tie⟩ **2 a** : devoid of meaning, relevance, or purpose : SENSELESS ⟨a ~ remark⟩ ⟨a ~ life⟩ **b** : devoid of effectiveness, force, or punch : VAPID, FLAT, INSIPID ⟨~ attempts to be funny⟩ — **point·less·ly** *adv* — **point·less·ness** *n* -ES

point·let \'pȯintlət\ *n* -S [¹*point* + *-let*] : a very small point ⟨the ~ of a leaf⟩

point man *or* **point rider** *n* : one of the cowboys riding on each side of the front of a trail herd

point mutation *n* : GENE MUTATION

point of addition : a dot or similar mark used in medieval music to indicate an increase in the time value of a note

point of aim : an auxiliary mark or marker at which a target archer sights the arrow so as to achieve correct elevation

point of articulation : an immovable or relatively immovable part (as the upper teeth or lower lip) of the vocal tract that a more movable part (as the tongue) approaches or comes into contact with in an articulation

point of departure : a starting point esp. in a discussion ⟨chose conditions in the slums as a *point of departure*⟩

point of impact 1 : the point at which the projectile first strikes the ground or other material object **2** : the point at the center of the pattern of a shot charge fired from a shotgun

point of inflection : a point on a curve that separates an arc concave upward from one concave downward and vice versa

point of view 1 a (1) : a particular position (as in space, time, development) from which something is considered or evaluated : STANDPOINT, VIEWPOINT ⟨from the *point of view* of a child, many things in the adult world are mysterious⟩ (2) : a particular manner of considering or evaluating something ⟨has a very peculiar *point of view*⟩ **b** : a particular reasoned mental attitude toward or opinion about something ⟨asked him to indicate his *point of view*⟩ **2** : a particular indicated matter ⟨which from the *point of view* of climate and soils is best suited to agriculture —W.B.Fisher⟩

point plat \(')pwaⁿ ¦plä\ *n* [F, lit., flat lace] : FLAT POINT

point rail *n* : a tapering rail used in a railroad frog to permit switching

points *pl of* POINT, *pres 3d sing of* POINT

point-set \'=ˌ=\ *adj, of printing type* : cast with a width measurable in points — compare UNIT-SET

points·man \'pȯintsmən\ *n, pl* **pointsmen 1** *Brit* : a policeman stationed typically at an intersection to direct traffic — compare POINT DUTY **2** *Brit* : SWITCHMAN

point source *n* : a source of light or other radiation that is concentrated at a point

point system *n* **1** : a system of wage payment in which work is subdivided into units equivalent to the number of minutes that a task should take and the payment of the worker on the basis of the number of points of work accomplished in a given length of time — called also *Bedaux system* **2** : a system in which printing type and spacing materials are made in sizes that are exact multiples of the point

point-to-point \¦=='=\ *n* -S : a cross-country horse race from one specified point to another with each rider free to choose his own course : STEEPLECHASE

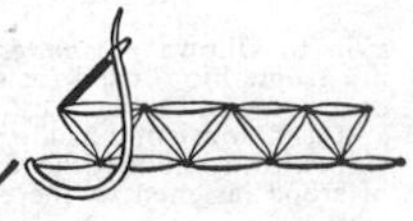

point turc

point turc *or* **point turque** \(')pwaⁿ ¦tərk\ *n, pl* **points turc** *or* **points turque** [F *point turc*, lit., Turkish lace] : an embroidery stitch done with very fine thread and a coarse needle which in passing through the fabric leaves a hole after the thread is drawn tight to resemble hemstitching and used esp. on curved lines (as in appliqué) where no thread can be drawn

pointy \'pȯintē\ *adj, usu* -ER/-EST [[1]*point* + *-y*] **1 :** coming to a rather sharp point **:** quite pointed ⟨a small, merry-looking man with a ~ nose —A.J.Liebling⟩ **2 :** having parts that stick out sharply here and there **:** marked by protruding points ⟨~ little firs —Jack Kerouac⟩

pois *pl of* POI

[1]**poise** \'pȯiz\ *vb* -ED/-ING/-S [ME *poisen* (also, to weigh), fr. MF *pois-*, stem of *peser*, fr. L *pensare* to weigh, ponder, consider — more at PENSIVE] *vt* **1** *archaic* **:** to weigh mentally **:** CONSIDER, PONDER, DELIBERATE ⟨would have seen him turn crimson in *poising* the question —A.W.Kinglake⟩ **2 :** BALANCE: **a** *archaic* **:** to bring into equilibrium with something else ⟨who ~*s* and proportions sea and land —William Cowper⟩ **b** *obs* **:** OFFSET, COUNTERBALANCE ⟨two contrary winds ~ each other —Henry Stubbe⟩ **c** (1) **:** to hold or carry in equilibrium **:** hold or carry steadily or evenly ⟨walked along gracefully with a water jar *poised* on her head⟩ ⟨*poised* a plate on the end of his finger⟩ **:** cause to be evenly or motionlessly supported or suspended ⟨for an instant the gull hung *poised* in the sky⟩ **:** hold supported or suspended without motion ⟨*poised* her fork and gave her guest a knowing look —Louis Bromfield⟩ ⟨masses of ice are *poised* at one moment and the next come crashing down —John Hunt & Edmund Hillary⟩ (2) **:** to keep (as something that is supported or suspended) in a steady position **:** keep from going one way or the other **:** STABILIZE ⟨the nonchalance with which the steersman *poised* the canoe —Ernest Beaglehole⟩ **d :** to hold or carry (as the head) in a particular way ⟨*poised* her head disdainfully —G.B. Shaw⟩ **3 :** to draw up into readiness **:** put into a position or attitude of readiness ⟨*poised* their armies for the battle⟩; *esp* **:** BRACE ⟨*poised* themselves for the ordeal awaiting them⟩ ~ *vi* **1 :** to become drawn up into readiness for something ⟨knew that they were *poising* for the encounter⟩ **2 :** HOVER ⟨the hawk *poised* momentarily and then struck⟩ **syn** see STABILIZE

[2]**poise** \"\ *n* -S [ME *poyse*, fr. MF *pois*, fr. L *pensum* weight, fr. neut. of *pensus*, past part. of *pendere* to weigh — more at PENDANT] **1 a** *obs* **:** HEAVINESS **b :** a definite mass (as a movable sliding block on a scale) used for its weight **2 a :** BALANCE, EQUILIBRIUM ⟨a watch spring in perfect ~⟩ ⟨a ~ between widely divergent impulses —F.R.Leavis⟩ **b** *archaic* **:** suspension of movement or activity ⟨the ~ of the flood tide . . . was only of brief duration —Frederick Leighton⟩ **3 a** (1) **:** easy composure of manner marked esp. by assurance and gracious dignity ⟨is a woman of ~ and charm⟩ **:** tranquil self-possession and self-confidence ⟨never lost his ~ under any circumstances⟩ ⟨have the ~ and security that goes with independence —W.F. McDermott⟩ ⟨are old enough to face them with a certain ~ —Bertrand Russell⟩ (2) **:** TRANQUILLITY, CALM, SERENITY ⟨without disturbing the ~ of a drawing room —Van Wyck Brooks⟩ ⟨is imperatively needed to give ~ to the nerves —Havelock Ellis⟩ ⟨known for his accomplishments, his ~ of mind, and his invariable courtesy —Edward Breck⟩ **b :** a particular way of carrying oneself **:** BEARING, CARRIAGE ⟨noted her very distinctive ~⟩ **syn** see BALANCE, TACT

[3]**poise** \'pwäz\ *n* -S [F, after Jean Louis Marie *Poiseuille* †1869 Fr. physician and anatomist] **:** a cgs absolute unit of viscosity that is equal to one dyne-second per square centimeter

poised *adj* [fr. past part. of [2]*poise*] **:** having poise: **a :** marked by balance or equilibrium ⟨as ~ as the flight of a gull —J.L. Lowes⟩ **b :** marked by easy composure of manner or bearing ⟨was perfectly ~ and sure of himself on all official occasions —E.H.Spicer⟩

pois·er \'pȯizə(r)\ *n* -S **1 :** one that poises; *specif* **:** one who balances the mass of a watch balance wheel about its staff **2 :** [3]HALTER

poi·seuille's law \(')pwä¦zə(r)z-, -zōz-\ *n, usu cap P* [after Jean L. M. *Poiseuille* †1869 French physician] **:** a statement in physics: the velocity of flow of a liquid through a capillary tube varies directly as the pressure and the fourth power of the diameter of the tube and inversely as the length of the tube and the coefficient of viscosity

pois green \'pwä-\ *n* [*pois* fr. F, pea, fr. L *pisum;* intended as part trans. of F *pois vert*, lit., green pea — more at PEA] **:** a grayish to moderate yellow green that is yellower and darker than mytho green and yellower and very slightly lighter than gage green

[1]**poi·son** \'pȯiz°n, *dial* 'pīz-\ *n* -S [ME *poisoun, poison*, fr. OF *poison* drink, philter, poisonous drink, poison, fr. L *potion-, potio* drink, fr. *potus* (past part. of *potare* to drink) + *-ion-, -io* -ion — more at POTABLE] **1 a :** a substance (as a drug) that in suitable quantities has properties harmful or fatal to an organism when it is brought into contact with or absorbed by the organism **:** a substance that through its chemical action usu. kills, injures, or impairs an organism ⟨strychnine, carbon monoxide, and other ~*s*⟩ — compare ECONOMIC POISON, PESTICIDE, TOXIN, VENOM **b** (1) **:** something destructive or harmful to the success, prosperity, or happiness of something else ⟨were generally considered boxoffice ~ —Edith Isaacs⟩ ⟨are plain political ~ —J.T.Norman⟩ (2) **:** something that undermines, interferes with, or blights the progress, activity, or welfare of something else ⟨her life was ruined by the ~ of lying gossip⟩ (3) **:** something that causes something else to become tainted, corrupted, rotten, or perverted ⟨the ~ of bad example⟩ **c** (1) **:** something obnoxious, disgusting, or nauseating ⟨most stage juveniles, especially in musicals, are pure ~ —John Mason Brown⟩ (2) **:** something totally at variance with one's tastes or inclinations **:** an object of aversion or abhorrence **:** something to be avoided ⟨diversions of that kind were pure ~ to him⟩ **2** *slang* **:** alcoholic drink; *esp* **:** strong liquor **3 :** a substance that inhibits the activity of another substance or the course of a reaction or process (as catalytic action, fluorescence, thermionic emission, nuclear fission) ⟨a catalyst ~⟩ ⟨fission ~*s*⟩ **4** *or* **poison circle** *or* **poison spot :** a game in which each player of a circle of players tries to force another into a designated central area so as to make him it

syn VENOM, VIRUS, TOXIN, BANE: POISON now refers to any matter that is lethal or very noxious (as strychnine, arsenic, carbon monoxide) or to anything thought of as having a similar effect ⟨a populace whose emotional life has been drugged by the sugared *poison* of pseudo art —Roger Fry⟩ ⟨the nineteenth century had brought this new *poison* of mystic tribalism into the common life of Europe —Stringfellow Barr⟩ VENOM may refer to a poison interjected with fierce malignant hostility ⟨the *venom* of the rattlesnake⟩ VIRUS may refer to a submicroscopic agency of infection working with insidious deadliness or deleteriousness ⟨the *virus* of infantile paralysis⟩ TOXIN, less used in figurative senses than others in this group, may refer to a destructive toxic substance generated within a plant or animal body ⟨the bacterial *toxins*, such as those of the organisms causing diphtheria, tetanus and botulism —W.A.Hagan⟩ BANE may apply to any cause of ruin, destruction, or great tribulation; in compounds it may designate poisonous substances and things ⟨the military mania which has been the *bane* of some countries⟩ ⟨ratsbane⟩

[2]**poison** \"\ *vb* **poisoned; poisoned; poisoning** \-z(°)niŋ\ **poisons** [ME *poisonen*, fr. *poisoun, poison*, n.] *vt* **1 a** (1) **:** to give poison to **:** kill or injure by means of poison ⟨was accused of ~*ing* her husband⟩ (2) **:** to put poison on or into ⟨~*ing* an arrow⟩ ⟨~*ed* the water⟩ (3) **:** to taint, infect, or impregnate with poison ⟨~*ed* the air with its fumes⟩ **b :** to produce an abnormal condition in through the action of a poison or toxic substance ⟨blood that has been ~*ed* by infection⟩ **2 a** (1) **:** to exert a baneful influence on **:** CORRUPT, VITIATE, PERVERT ⟨~*ing* minds with evil propaganda⟩ (2) **:** to cause to be unfavorably disposed toward a person ⟨malicious tales of that kind ~*ed* nearly everyone against him⟩ **b** (1) **:** to destroy, harm, or otherwise affect adversely as if by poison ⟨aching in mind and body, ~*ed* with fatigue —Felix Riesenberg⟩ (2) **:** to taint, infect, or impregnate as if with poison ⟨even such harmless pleasures were ~*ed* with suspicion —Virginia Woolf⟩ **c :** to make unfit (as for some indicated or implied use or purpose) through the addition or application of something ⟨~*ed* the soup with too much salt⟩ ⟨parts of it were so dry and ~*ed* with alkali dust that no life existed there —S.H.Adams⟩ **3 a :** to inhibit the activity of (as a catalyst) — compare PROMOTE **b :** to inhibit the course or occurrence of (as a reaction or phenomenon) ~ *vi* **:** to put poison into or on something ⟨was in the lower field next day, ~*ing* —G.S. Perry⟩

[3]**poison** \"\ *adj* [[1]*poison*] **1 :** POISONOUS ⟨a ~ plant⟩ ⟨a ~ drink⟩ **:** VENOMOUS ⟨talk about ~ tongues —Dan Wickenden⟩ **2 :** POISONED ⟨a ~ arrow⟩

[4]**poison** \"\ *adv, chiefly dial* **:** EXTREMELY, VERY ⟨was ~ pretty —Maristan Chapman⟩ ⟨felt ~ mean that week —Fitz Farrell⟩ ⟨is a ~ bad world —R.L.Stevenson⟩

poison arum *n* **:** a plant (*P. virginica*) of the genus *Peltandra*

poison ash *n* **1 :** POISON SUMAC **2 :** a torchwood (*Amyris balsamifera*) of the West Indies **3 :** FRINGE TREE

poison bean *n* **:** a shrub (*Daubentonia drummondii*) of the family Leguminosae that is found in the southern part of the U. S. and that bears poisonous seeds — called also *rattlebush* **2 :** a seed of the poison bean shrub

poisonberry \'==-— *see* BERRY\ *n* **:** any of several plants with small inedible or poisonous fruits: as **a :** a shrub of the genus *Cestrum* **b :** a West Indian shrub (*Bourreria succulenta*) of the family Boraginaceae with small flowers in corymbose cymes **c :** POISONBERRY TREE **d :** BITTERSWEET 2 a

poisonberry tree *n* **:** an Australian shrub (*Pittosporum phillyraeoides*) with bitter berries that are reputed poisonous and herbage that is used for fodder

poison black cherry *n* **:** the fruit of the belladonna

poison bulb *n* **:** a southern African blood lily (*Haemanthus toxicarius*) with a reputedly poisonous bulb

poison bush *n* **:** any of several poisonous or unwholesome Australian plants: **a :** a leguminous plant of *Gastrolobium* or the related genus *Gompholobium* with poisonous herbage **b :** a poisonous desert shrub (*Myoporum deserti*) **c :** POISON PEA; *esp* **:** DARLING PEA **d :** a tree (*Trema cannabina*) that is injurious to livestock because of the large amount of fiber it contains

poison camas *n* **:** a common perennial death camas (*Zigadenus nuttallii*); *broadly* **:** DEATH CAMAS

poison circle *n* **:** POISON 4

poison claw *n* **:** the maxilliped of a chilopod

poison creeper *n* **:** a poison ivy (*Rhus toxicodendron*)

poison cup *n* **:** DEATH CUP

poison darnel *n* **:** BEARDED DARNEL

poison dogwood *or* **poison elder** *n* **:** POISON SUMAC

poi·son·er \-z(°) nə(r)\ *n* -S [ME, fr. *poisonen* to poison + *-er*] **:** one that poisons

poison fish *n* **1 :** any of several fishes that have venomous spines **2 :** any of several fishes whose flesh contains poisonous alkaloids

poison flag *n* **:** any of several American irises (as *Iris versicolor*) with blue flowers

poison flour *n* **:** arsenic trioxide obtained by sublimation in a floury state

poison flower *n* **:** BITTERSWEET 2 a

poisonful *adj, obs* **:** POISONOUS

poison gas *n* **:** a poisonous gas or a liquid or solid giving off poisonous vapors designed (as in chemical warfare) to kill, injure, or disable by inhalation or contact

poison hemlock *n* **1** *or* **poison parsley :** a large branching biennial poisonous herb (*Conium maculatum*) native to Eurasia and Africa and adventive in No. America that has large decompound leaves with lanceolate pinnatifid leaflets, involucels of narrow bracts, and white flowers **2 :** any of several plants of the genus *Cicuta*

poi·son·ing \'pȯiz(°)niŋ, -nēŋ, *dial* 'pīz-\ *n* -S [ME *poysenynge*, fr. gerund of *poisonen* to poison — more at POISON] **:** the abnormal condition produced by a poison or toxic substance ⟨suffering from acute ~⟩

poison ivy *n* **1 :** any of several American plants of the genus *Rhus* of climbing, shrubby, or occas. arborescent habit that have ternate leaves, greenish flowers, and white berries and that produce an acutely irritating oil which causes a usu. intensely itchy skin rash when the herbage esp. if bruised is touched; *esp* **:** a climbing plant (*R. radicans*) that is esp. common in the eastern and central U.S. — see POISON OAK **2** *or* **poison laurel :** MOUNTAIN LAUREL 1

poison milkweed *n* **:** FLOWERING SPURGE

poison nut *n* **:** NUX VOMICA

poison oak *n* **:** any of several shrubby sumacs that are poison ivies: as **a :** POISON SUMAC **b :** a bushy poison ivy (*Rhus diversiloba*) of the Pacific coast **c :** a bushy poison ivy (*Rhus quercifolia*) of the southeastern U.S.

poi·son·ous \'pȯiz(°)nəs, *dial* 'pīz-\ *adj* **1 a :** that is poison or that has the qualities or effects of poison ⟨a ~ substance⟩ ⟨a stifling ~ atmosphere —Joseph Conrad⟩ **b** (1) **:** that contains or is mixed with or impregnated with poison ⟨a ~ liquid⟩ ⟨~ fumes⟩ (2) **:** that has been dipped into or touched or smeared with poison ⟨avoided the ~ tip of the arrow⟩ **2 a :** that destroys, harms, interferes with, or otherwise adversely affects in a manner suggestive of poison ⟨a double life that would be ~ to their continued happiness⟩ ⟨is ~ to any attempt at dispassionate thinking —*Saturday Rev.*⟩ **b :** that taints, corrupts, perverts, or prejudices esp. in an evil or insidious way ⟨the ~ effects of such deception⟩ ⟨secret spreading of ~ propaganda —F.D.Roosevelt⟩ **3 :** viciously spiteful **:** full of malice **:** VENOMOUS, MALIGNANT, MALEVOLENT ⟨~ slander⟩ ⟨gave her a ~ look⟩ ⟨the most ~ hostility —Dorothy C. Fisher⟩ ⟨wrote two ~ pamphlets which preserve the gossip and scandal of the day —R.W.Southern⟩ **4 :** altogether disagreeable ⟨was in a ~ temper —Ngaio Marsh⟩ **:** OBNOXIOUS, LOATHSOME, NAUSEATING ⟨thought the weather was positively ~⟩ ⟨such children in literature are often pretty ~ —Orville Prescott⟩ — **poi·son·ous·ly** *adv* — **poi·son·ous·ness** *n* -ES

poison out *vt* **:** to put poison into (a body of water) so as to destroy or stupefy fishes ⟨was *poisoned out* and all rough fishes were destroyed —*Report: W. Va. Conservation Commission*⟩

poison parsnip *n* **1 :** WILD PARSNIP **2 :** SPOTTED COWBANE

poison pea *n* **:** any of several plants of the genus *Swainsona* — compare DARLING PEA

poison-pen \¦==¦=\ *adj* **1 :** venomously written **:** written with malice and spite ⟨*poison-pen* brochures —J.R.Carlson⟩; *esp* **:** written usu. anonymously and with the intention of seriously harming or destroying another's reputation ⟨writing a *poison-pen* letter in disguised handwriting to the police —Georg Mann⟩ **2 :** marked by or given to poison-pen writing ⟨a *poison-pen* writer⟩

poison rye grass *n* **:** BEARDED DARNEL

poisons *pl of* POISON, *pres 3d sing of* POISON

poison sego *n* **:** DEATH CAMAS

poison spot *n* **:** POISON 4

poison sumac *n* **:** a smooth American swamp sumac (*Rhus vernix*) that has pinnate leaves and greenish flowers succeeded by greenish white berries and that produces an irritating oil like that of poison ivy and a lacquer resembling Japanese lacquer — called also *poison ash, poison dogwood*

poison tobacco *n* **:** HENBANE 1 a

poison tree *n* **1 :** BLIND-YOUR-EYES **2 :** POISON SUMAC **3 :** POISONWOOD 1

poison vetch *n* **:** any of several plants of the genus *Astragalus* that are poisonous to livestock — see LOCOWEED

poison vine *n* **:** POISON IVY

poisonweed \'==,=\ *n* **:** any of various plants of the western U. S. with a poisonous foliage: as **a :** any of several native or naturalized larkspurs **b :** any of several lupines — see LUPINOSIS

poisonwood \'==,=\ *n* **1 :** a caustic or poisonous tree (*Metopium toxiferum*) of the family Anacardiaceae occurring in Florida and the West Indies and having compound leaves, greenish paniculate flowers, and orange-yellow fruits **2 :** CRABWOOD **3 :** POISON SUMAC **4 :** MANCHINEEL

pois·son bleu \¦pwa,sō͞n¦blə(r·), -wä,s-, -lō\ *n* [F, lit., blue fish] **:** BLUE CAT

pois·son distribution \(')pwa¦sō͞n-, -wä¦\ *n, usu cap P* [after Siméon D. *Poisson* †1840 French mathematician and statistician] **:** a distribution in statistics that is a good approximation to the binomial distribution when the probability of success in a single trial is very small and the number of trials is very large

poisson's ratio *also* **poisson ratio** *n, usu cap P* [after S. *Poisson*] **:** the ratio of transverse to longitudinal strain in a material under tension

poi·trel \'pȯi·trəl\ *n* -S [MF *poitral*, fr. L *pectorale* breastplate, fr. neut. of *pectoralis* of the chest, pectoral — more at PECTORAL] **:** a medieval often richly decorated piece of armor used to protect the breast of a horse

poi·vrade \pwȧvrȧd\ *or* **poivrade sauce** *n* -S [F, fr. MF, fr. *poivre* pepper (fr. L *pipr-, piper*) + *-ade* — more at PEPPER] **:** a peppery sauce

poize *obs var of* POISE

po·joa·que \pō'(h)wȧkē\ *n, pl* **pojoaque** *or* **pojoaques** [Sp, of AmerInd origin] **1 :** a Tanoan people formerly found in New Mexico **2 :** a member of the Pojoaque people

po·kal \pō'käl\ *n* -S [G, fr. It *boccale* mug, jug, jar, fr. LL *baucalis* vessel for cooling wine or water, fr. Gk *baukalis*, prob. of non-IE origin] **:** a large usu. covered goblet typically made of glass or silver

[1]**poke** \'pōk\ *n* -S [ME, fr. ONF *poke, poque*, of Gmc origin; akin to OE *pocca, pohha* bag, pocket, MD *poke* bag, MHG *pfoch* pouch, purse, ON *poki* pouch, OE *pocc* pock — more at POCK] **1 a** (1) *chiefly South & Midland* **:** BAG, SACK ⟨take the boys a ~ of candy —H.D.Skidmore⟩ (2) **:** a pouch or purse for carrying nuggets of gold or gold dust ⟨threw their thick ~*s* of gold carelessly onto the counter —E.B.Lung⟩ (3) *slang* **:** WALLET **b** *chiefly dial* **:** POCKET **2** *slang* **:** an accumulated sum of money **:** WAD ⟨spent his ~ —Chesley Wilson⟩ ⟨struck it rich and kept his ~ —*Time*⟩ **3 a** (1) **:** a swelling (as a goiter) on the neck (2) **:** a swelling appearing on sheep and associated with liver fluke infestation **b :** a disease caused by liver fluke infestation

[2]**poke** \"\ *vb* -ED/-ING/-S [ME *poken;* akin to MD *poken* to poke, stick, MLG *pōken* to stick with a knife, and perh. to OIr *būalaim* I strike] *vt* **1** *archaic* **:** INCITE, ROUSE **2 a** (1) **:** to prod or jab with or as if with the end of one's finger or the end of a stick or with the end of some similar object ⟨*poked* him in the ribs and grinned broadly⟩ ⟨*poked* the burlap bag with a broom handle⟩ (2) **:** to set into movement or push or urge along by means of prodding or jabbing ⟨all he had ever done was ~ a team or explore the trail or push cattle along —A.B. Guthrie⟩ (3) **:** to stir up (as the coals of a fire) with or as if with a poker ⟨staring into the fireplace and occasionally *poking* the glowing embers⟩ **b** (1) **:** PIERCE, STAB ⟨a straw man that had been *poked* through with a pitchfork⟩ (2) **:** to produce by piercing, stabbing, or jabbing ⟨*poked* a hole in the drum⟩ **c** (1) **:** to strike with the fist **:** HIT, PUNCH, SOCK ⟨*poked* him in the nose⟩ (2) **:** to deliver (a blow) with the fist ⟨first *poked* a right to the chin and then a left to the body⟩ ⟨threatened to ~ him one⟩ **3 a** (1) **:** to move, thrust, or shove esp. with a quick action or with sudden force ⟨*poked* his head round the corner —Dorothy Sayers⟩ (2) **:** to cause to be directed in a particular direction or toward a particular thing by or as if by thrusting or shoving ⟨had *poked* the head of a boat into the mud —Frederick Way⟩ ⟨*poked* his finger at his client —Willa Cather⟩ **b :** to cause to stick out **:** cause to project ⟨kept *poking* her head in and out of the cab window —Louis Bromfield⟩ **c :** to thrust forward in such a way as to be intrusive **:** interpose or interject in a prying or otherwise meddlesome manner **:** push forward obtrusively ⟨asked him not to ~ his nose into other people's business⟩ ⟨*poking* their great stupid faces into everything —*Times Lit. Supp.*⟩ **4 :** to confine in some stodgy poky place ⟨didn't want to stay *poked* up in that town⟩ ~ *vi* **1 a :** to make a prodding, jabbing, or thrusting movement esp. repeatedly ⟨walked up and down and *poked* among the rocks —John Masefield⟩ **b :** to strike out at something with or as if with the fist ⟨kept *poking* at him but never hit him⟩ ⟨cranks who ~ at the schools —W.L.Miller⟩ **2 a :** to go investigating, looking about, or rummaging through something inquisitively without much order or system ⟨went into the attic where they *poked* about among old boxes and trunks —Louis Bromfield⟩ ⟨they went everywhere, they *poked* into everything —G.W. Johnson⟩ ⟨if he cared to ~ about in his unconscious —Clifton Fadiman⟩ **b :** to pry into something in an intrusive or otherwise meddlesome way ⟨is notoriously hostile to people who go *poking* into his private affairs —Irving Howe⟩ **3 a :** to live in or stay about a stodgy place **:** live in or hang about a place pokily ⟨doesn't want to ~ around in that town any longer⟩ **b :** to move or act with marked slowness **:** move or act in a largely ineffective, desultory, or aimless way **:** PUTTER, DAWDLE ⟨watched the traffic *poking* along the road⟩ ⟨just *poked* around at home and didn't accomplish much⟩ ⟨talked for a while and then *poked* off⟩ **4 a** (1) **:** to become stuck out **:** undergo thrusting out **:** PROTRUDE ⟨saw his head *poking* through the window⟩ (2) **:** to become extended or thrust forward ⟨saw to it that the railroad *poked* down closer to Texas —S.E.Fletcher⟩ ⟨into the jumbled wilderness . . . ~ the beginnings of a fabulous highway —R.L.Neuberger⟩ **b :** to come into sight or notice esp. with real or apparent suddenness **:** be visible or noticeable by being extended above, beyond, or out of something ⟨bell towers ~ above the trees —*Yale Rev.*⟩ — **poke fun at :** to make fun of in a usu. lightly bantering way and esp. slyly or indirectly **:** make an object of usu. light ridicule or mockery **:** KID ⟨*poke fun at* some of the stuffed shirts who have the largest incomes —Bruce Bliven b. 1889⟩

[3]**poke** \"\ *n* -S **1 a :** a quick thrust **:** JAB, DIG ⟨felt a ~ in the ribs⟩ **b :** a blow with the fist **:** PUNCH ⟨gave him a ~ on the nose⟩ **2 a** (1) **:** SLOWPOKE (2) **:** an annoyingly stupid individual **:** DUMBBELL **b :** COWBOY 3a **3 :** a poky place ⟨wondered how people put up with living in a little ~ like that —Mary Lavin⟩ **4 :** a device designed to keep an animal (as a cow, horse) from breaking through or jumping over fences and consisting typically of a collar from which a rod or pole hangs down at an angle so as to extend ahead of the animal **5 a :** a projecting brim on the front of a woman's bonnet **b :** POKE BONNET

poke 4

[4]**poke** \"\ *n* -S [modif. of *puccoon, pakon* (in some Algonquian language of Virginia) any of various plants used for staining and dyeing, fr. *pak* blood] **:** POKEWEED

[5]**poke** \"\ *n* -S [by shortening] **:** SHITEPOKE

pokeberry \'=-— *see* BERRY\ *n* [[4]*poke* + *berry*] **1 :** POKEWEED **2 :** one of the berries of the pokeweed

poke bonnet *n* [[3]*poke* (brim)] **:** a woman's bonnet with a projecting brim at the front

poke check *n* [[3]*poke*] **:** an act or instance of attempting to knock the puck away from an opponent in ice hockey by jabbing or thrusting at it with the stick

poke-easy \'=,==\ *n* -ES [[2]*poke*] *Midland* **:** one that moves about slowly and indolently and that is easy-going or lazy

poke-in \'=,=\ *n* -S [fr. *poke in*, v.] **:** STRANDER 2

poke bonnet

poke·lo·gan \'pōk,lōgən\ *or* **poke·lo·ken** \-ōkən\ *n* -S [of Algonquian origin; akin to Ojibwa *pokenogun* stopping place, Malecite *pecelāygan* stopping place, Natick *pohki* open, clear] *NewEng* **:** a usu. stagnant inlet or marshy place branching off from a stream or lake

poke milkweed *n* [[4]*poke*] **:** a milkweed (*Asclepias exaltata*) of the eastern U. S. with leaves resembling those of the pokeweed

poke pudding *n* [[1]*poke*] **:** POCK PUDDING

[1]**pok·er** \'pōkə(r)\ *n* -S [[2]*poke* + *-er*] **1 :** a rigid fairly heavy straight metal rod (as of iron, steel) that typically has one end fitted with or shaped into a handle and the other bent or hooked and that is usu. used for adjusting or stirring burning logs or coals (as in a fireplace) or similar burning material **2 :** a toothed rod attached to the bobbin rail of a spinning machine and used for giving an up-and-down movement to the bobbin rail

[2]**poker** \"\ *n* -S [prob. modif. of F *poque*, a card game somewhat similar to poker] **:** one of several card games (as draw poker, stud poker) in which a player bets that the value of the hand he holds is greater than the value of the hands held by the other players and in which each subsequent player must either equal or raise the bet already made or drop out of the game for

that deal and in which at the end of the betting the player

poker: hands in descending value: *1* royal flush, *2* straight flush, *3* four of a kind, *4* full house, *5* flush, *6* straight, *7* three of a kind, *8* two pairs, *9* one pair

holding the hand that has the highest value wins all that has been bet in that deal

poker dice *n pl* **1 :** dice usu. in sets of five with each one of the dice carrying on two or more of its faces the representation of a particular playing card (as the ace, king, queen, jack, ten, nine) instead of spots **2** *usu sing in constr* **:** one of several games which are played with poker dice or with regular dice and in which the object is to make and bet on winning combinations like those used in the game of poker

poker face *n* [²*poker*] **1 a** (1) **:** a face that does not reveal the feelings or thoughts of a person **:** a woodenly expressionless face **:** DEAD PAN ⟨conceals his emotions behind a *poker face* —P.G.Wodehouse⟩ (2) **:** a stolidly grave or solemn face ⟨they play their silly roles with *poker faces*⟩ **b :** one that has or that assumes a poker face ⟨asked why those *poker faces* had been invited to the party⟩ **2 :** stolid gravity or solemnity of manner ⟨wrote all this nonsense with a *poker face*⟩

poker–faced \ˈ⸗ˌ⸗⸗\ *adj* **1 a :** woodenly expressionless ⟨remained altogether *poker-faced* when he stepped before the judge⟩ **b :** stolidly grave or solemn ⟨described the escapade with *poker-faced* earnestness⟩ **2 :** marked by or showing a real or apparent lack of personal involvement or commitment **:** DETACHED, IMPERSONAL ⟨related every detail of the murder with *poker-faced* objectivity⟩

pok·er·ish \ˈpōk(ə)rish\ *adj* [fr. archaic E *poker* hobgoblin (prob. of Scand origin; akin to Norw *pokker* devil, ON *pūki*) + *-ish* — more at PUCK] *archaic* **:** that elicits a vague fear, dread, or awe **:** EERIE ⟨there is something ~ about a deserted dwelling, even in broad daylight —J.R.Lowell⟩

pokeroot \ˈ⸗ˌ⸗\ *n* [⁴*poke* + *root*] **:** POKEWEED

poker plant *n* [¹*poker*] **:** an herb (*Kniphofia uvaria*) that is found in the southern part of Africa and that has a spike of orange-red or scarlet flowers

poker spine *n* **:** a stiff spinal column resulting from rheumatoid arthritis

poker work *n* **:** PYROGRAPHY

pokes *pl of* POKE, *pres 3d sing of* POKE

poke salad *n* [⁴*poke*] *chiefly Midland* **:** the cooked young shoots of pokeweed

pokeweed \ˈ⸗ˌ⸗\ *n* [⁴*poke* + *weed*] **:** a tall coarse American perennial herb (*Phytolacca americana*) having young shoots that are edible, a thick fleshy poisonous root that yields emetic and purgative extracts, a smooth fairly succulent stem that ranges in color from green to purplish, large simple smooth leaves, small greenish white racemose flowers, and fleshy dark purple berries that contain poisonous seeds and yield emetic and purgative extracts and a crimson juice used in making an ink; *broadly* **:** a plant of the genus *Phytolacca*

pokeweed family *n* **:** PHYTOLACCACEAE

pokey *also* **poky** \ˈpōkē, -ki\ *n, pl* **pokeys** *also* **pokies** [alter. of earlier *pogie* workhouse, of unknown origin] *slang* **:** JAIL

pok·i·ly \ˈpōkəlē, -li\ *adv* **:** in a poky manner

pok·i·ness \-kēnəs, -kin-\ *n* -ES **:** the quality or state of being poky

poking *adj* [fr. pres. part. of ²*poke*] **:** PETTY, MEAN ⟨her face changed slowly from ~ suspicion to a brilliant . . . smile of welcome —Christopher Isherwood⟩

poking stick *n* **:** a small rod made of wood, bone, or metal and formerly used to stiffen the pleats of ruffs

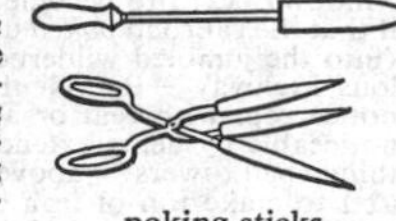

poking sticks

pok·kah boeng \ˈpäkəˌbüŋ\ *n* [Jav, lit., damaged top] **:** a disease of sugarcane caused by an ascomycetous fungus (*Gibberella frejikuroi*) and marked by chlorosis and splitting of the young leaves and by rotting of the growing point

po·ko·mam \ˌpōkōˈmäm\ *n, pl* **pokomam** *or* **pokomams** *usu cap* **1 a :** an Indian people of southeastern Guatemala **b :** a member of such people **2 :** a Mayan language of the Pokomam people

po·ko·mo \pəˈkō(ˌ)mō\ *n, pl* **pokomo** *or* **pokomos** *usu cap* **1 a :** a Bantu people of Kenya in Africa **b :** a member of such people **2 :** a Bantu language of the Pokomo people

po·kon·chi \pəˈkōnchē\ *n, pl* **pokonchi** *or* **pokonchis** *usu cap* **1 a :** an Indian people of north central Guatemala **b :** a member of such people **2 :** a Mayan language of the Pokonchi people

poku *var of* PUKU

poky *also* **pokey** \ˈpōkē, -ki\ *adj, usu* **pokier**; *usu* **pokiest** [²*poke* + *-y*] **1 a :** uncomfortably small or cramped and marked typically by lack of proper ventilation and lighting and by a generally unattractive appearance ⟨lived in a series of ~ houses, surrounded by a swarm of children —V.S. Pritchett⟩ ⟨~, hole-in-the-wall shops —Faubion Bowers⟩ ⟨inspected the cheerless, ~ rooms with their cheap furniture and threadbare carpets —Valentine Williams⟩ **b :** stagnating with general dullness and provincialism **:** STODGY, ONE-HORSE ⟨had no desire to remain in that ~ little town⟩ **2 a :** devoid of style, imagination, and taste **:** DOWDY ⟨was dressed in the *pokiest* way imaginable⟩ **b :** devoid of freshness, liveliness, or interest **:** UNSTIMULATING, DULL, DEAD ⟨is certainly a ~ place to go for a vacation⟩ ⟨has a ~ way of writing⟩ **3 a :** that is typical of a fuddy-duddy **:** prim and overly conservative **:** strait-laced and not up to date ⟨just a timid . . . ~ little creature worrying like a mole —Saul Bellow⟩ **b :** tediously concerned with what is obvious, trifling, or boring ⟨it feels merely ~ to say one thing more —William Empson⟩ **c :** not easily excited or aroused **:** ponderously phlegmatic ⟨is a ~ individual with little interest in the world about him⟩ **4 :** that moves or acts like a slowpoke **:** annoyingly slow **:** that pokes along ⟨infuriated with the ~ traffic⟩ ⟨is too ~ to get anything done efficiently⟩ ⟨asked her not to be so ~⟩

pol *abbr* **1** polar **2** polish; polished **3** political; politician; politics

POL *abbr* petroleum, oil, and lubricants

po·la·bi·an \pōˈläbēən\ *n* -s *usu cap* [*Polab* Polabian (of Slavic origin, akin to Pol *po* on and to Pol *Łaba* Elbe, river in Czechoslovakia and Germany) + *-an*] **1** *or* **po·lab** \pōˈläb\ **:** a member of a Slavic people formerly dwelling in the basin of the Elbe and on the Baltic coast of Germany **2 :** the extinct West Slavic language of the Polabians

po·la·bish \pōˈläbish\ *n* -ES *usu cap* [G *polabisch*, fr. *polabisch*, adj., being Polabian, fr. *polab-* Polabian (of Slavic origin; akin to Pol *po* on and to Pol *Łaba* Elbe) + *-isch* -ish (fr. OHG *-isc*)] **:** POLABIAN 2

¹**po·lac·ca** \pōˈlakə\ *n* -s [It, of unknown origin] **:** POLACRE

²**polacca** \"\ *n* -s [It, fr. fem. of *polacco* Polish, fr. Pol *Polak* Pole] **:** POLONAISE 2

¹**po·lack** *also* **po·lak** \ˈpōˌläk *sometimes* -lak\ *n* -s *usu cap* [Pol *Polak*] **1** *obs* **:** ⁶POLE 1 ⟨the Moscovites discomfited by the *Polacks* in the battle —Thomas North⟩ **2 :** a person of Polish birth or descent — usu. used disparagingly

²**polack** *also* **polak** \"\ *adj, usu cap* **:** POLISH — usu. used disparagingly

po·la·cre \pōˈläkə(r)\ *n* -s [F, modif. of It *polacca*] **:** a ship with two or three masts usu. chiefly in one piece and square or sometimes lateen sails used in the Mediterranean

po·lak \pōˈläk\ *n* -s [origin unknown] **:** BALSA

po·land \ˈpōlənd\ *adj, usu cap* [fr. *Poland*, country in central Europe] **:** of or from Poland **:** of the kind or style prevalent in Poland **:** POLISH

poland china *also* **poland** *n, usu cap P&C* [fr. *Poland*, country in central Europe + *China*, country in Asia] **1 :** an American breed of large compact white-marked black swine of the lard type **2** -s **:** an animal of the Poland China breed

po·land·er \ˈpōləndə(r)\ *n* -s *cap* [*Poland*, country in central Europe + E *-er*] **:** a native or inhabitant of Poland **:** POLE

pol·a·ni·sia \ˌpäləˈnizh(ē)ə, -isēə\ *n, cap* [NL, fr. *pol-* (fr. *poly-*) + ¹*anis-* + *-ia*; prob. fr. the large but varying number of stamens] **:** a genus of widely distributed herbs (family Capparidaceae) having palmate leaves and flowers with many stamens of unequal lengths — see CLAMMYWEED

¹**po·lar** \ˈpōlə(r)\ *adj* [NL *polaris*, fr. L *polus* pole + *-aris* -ar — more at POLE] **1 a :** of, relating to, or situated in the vicinity of one of the earth's two poles ⟨valley glaciers in both ~ and equatorial regions —Hugh Odishaw⟩ ⟨Antarctica is the only ~ continent —*Antarctica*⟩ **b** (1) **:** of, relating to, or suggesting the region around one of the earth's two poles ⟨~ weather⟩ ⟨~ waste⟩ ⟨~ night⟩ (2) **:** situated in, suitable for, coming from, or having the characteristics of the region around one of the earth's two poles ⟨~ air mass⟩ ⟨~ flying⟩ ⟨~ airplane⟩ ⟨~ sea⟩ **2 a :** of or relating to one or more physical poles (as of a sphere or magnet) ⟨~ magnetism⟩ **b :** having poles and as a result a property analogous to that of a magnet in that there is an associated directed line connecting the two poles at the ends of which line there are equal and opposite properties ⟨~ molecule⟩ **3 :** of, relating to, or like a polestar in serving as a guide ⟨~ principle⟩ ⟨this ~ idea provides the clue to both . . . systems —V.L.Parrington⟩ **4 :** diametrically opposite in nature, tendency, or action ⟨extreme and indefensible ~ positions —Hunter Mead⟩ ⟨for whom classicism and romanticism are not ~ but continuous —Harry Levin⟩ ⟨~ if not mutually hostile parties —Austin Warren⟩ **5 a :** ELECTROVALENT **b :** having a dipole ⟨~ compounds such as hydrogen chloride, ammonia, water⟩ ⟨alcohols and ketones are common ~ solvents⟩ **6 :** held to resemble a pole or axis around which all else revolves **:** PIVOTAL ⟨the ~ events of this informed study —Fraser Neiman⟩

²**polar** \"\ *n* -s **:** the secant of a conic through the points of tangency of the two tangents that can be drawn to the conic from an external point

polar air *n* **:** air that originates in a subpolar anticyclone and in regions somewhat south of those in which arctic air originates

polar axis *n* **1 :** the axis of rotation of an equatorial mounting that is set parallel to the earth's axis permitting a telescope to be turned in hour angle or right ascension **2 :** the reference line in polar coordinates from which the angle coordinate is measured

polar bands *n pl* **:** NOAH'S ARK 2

polar bear *n* **1 :** a large creamy white long-necked bear (*Thalarctos maritimus* or *Ursus maritimus*) inhabiting arctic regions of both hemispheres esp. along shores or among ice floes, having a long narrow skull and small molar teeth, and attaining a length of 9 feet and often a weight of 1000 pounds **2 :** a pale orange yellow to yellowish white — called also *Jersey cream*

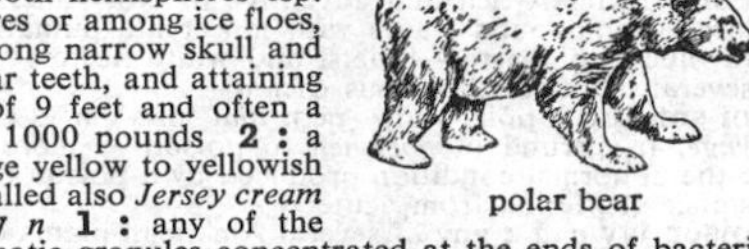

polar bear

polar body *n* **1 :** any of the metachromatic granules concentrated at the ends of bacteria (as the diphtheria bacillus *Corynebacterium diphtheriae*) **2 :** one of the minute bodies or cells that separate from the oocyte during maturation

polar cap *n* **:** a white spot at each pole of the planet Mars varying in size with the Martian seasons

polar capsule *n* **:** a specialized cell of a cnidosporidian spore that produces a coiled thread that presumably serves as a temporary attachment organelle when the spore ruptures

polar cattle *n pl* **:** MUSK-OXEN

polar circle *n* **:** one of the two parallels of latitude each at a distance from a pole of the earth equal to the obliquity of the ecliptic or about 23 degrees 27 minutes — compare ANTARCTIC CIRCLE, ARCTIC CIRCLE

polar code *n* **:** a telegraph message code obtained by polarity reversal of a direct current

polar coordinate *n* **:** either of two numbers that locate a point in a plane by its distance from a fixed point along a line to the point and the angle this line makes with a fixed line

polar coordinate paper *n* **:** graph paper laid out for plotting data in polar coordinates

polar coordinate system *n* **:** the series of points in a plane with each held to have a set of polar coordinates together with the reference elements and rules needed to locate each point by such a set of coordinates

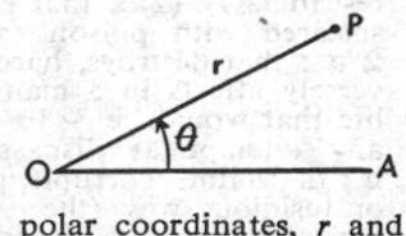

polar coordinates, *r* and *θ*; point, *P*; fixed point, *O*; distance from *O* to *P*, *r*; fixed line, *OA*; angle *AOP*, *θ*

polar curve *n* **:** a curve whose equation is in polar coordinates

polar distance *n* **:** the angular distance of any point on a sphere from one of its poles

polar equation *n* **:** an equation in polar coordinates

polar fox *n* **:** ARCTIC FOX

polar front *n* **:** the boundary between the cold air of a polar region and the warmer air of lower latitudes

polar graph *n* **:** a graph in polar coordinates

polar hare *n* **:** a large hare (*Lepus arcticus*) of arctic America related to the common European hares and almost completely white in winter

po·lar·ic \pōˈlarik\ *adj* **:** POLAR

po·lar·im·e·ter \ˌpōləˈrimədə(r)\ *n* [ISV *polar* + *-i-* + *-meter*] **1 :** an instrument for determining the amount of polarization of light or the proportion of polarized light in a partially polarized ray **2 :** a polariscope equipped with graduated circles for measuring the amount of rotation of the plane of polarization esp. by liquids — compare OPTICAL ROTATION

po·lar·i·met·ric \pōˌlarəˈme·trik\ *adj* [ISV *polarimetry* + *-ic*] **:** of or relating to polarimetry or the polarimeter ⟨~ equipment⟩

po·lar·im·e·try \ˌpōləˈrimə·trē\ *n* -ES [ISV *polar* + *-i-* + *-metry*] **:** the art or process of using the polarimeter (as in measuring the polarization of light)

po·lar·i·scope \pōˈlarəˌskōp, pəˈ- *also* -ler-\ *n* [ISV *polar* + *-i-* + *-scope*] **1 :** an instrument for studying the properties of or examining substances in polarized light consisting essentially of two Nicol prisms or other polarizing devices — compare ANALYZER, POLARIZER **2 :** POLARIMETER 2

po·lar·i·scop·ic \⸗ˌ⸗⸗ˈskäpik\ *adj* [ISV *polariscope* + *-ic*] **:** of, relating to, or obtained by the use of a polariscope ⟨~ observations⟩ — **po·lar·i·scop·i·cal·ly** \-pək(ə)lē\ *adv*

po·lar·i·ty \pōˈlarəd·ē, pəˈ-, -ətē, -i *also* -ler-\ *n* -ES [*polar* + *-ity*] **:** the quality or state of being polar: as **a :** the quality or condition inherent in a body that exhibits opposite properties or powers in opposite parts or directions or that exhibits contrasted properties or powers in contrasted parts or directions **:** the having of poles — compare MAGNET **b :** direction or attraction (as of inclination, feeling, or thought) toward a particular object **:** tendency or trend in a specific direction **c :** the particular either positive or negative state (as of a body) with reference to the two poles or to electrification **d** (1) **:** the observed axial differentiation of an organism or tissue into parts with distinctive properties or form (as head and tail or shoot and root) (2) **:** the underlying structural orientation held to account for orderly regeneration of lost parts of normal type in proper axial relation to the body as a whole (as in the growth of roots from the base of a cutting or the growth of a head at the anterior end of a planaria fragment) — compare GRADIENT CONCEPT **e** (1) **:** the principle, property, or condition of diametrical opposition (as in nature, tendency, or action) ⟨a cabinet system . . . produces a certain ~ in a nation —Ernest Barker⟩ ⟨the acute ~ between extreme passion and extreme control —Gilbert Highet⟩ (2) **:** an instance or case of such a relationship **:** something that is or is held to be diametrically opposite from something else **f** (1) **:** the relationship existing between two apparently opposed objects that nevertheless involve each other usu. by being dependent upon a mutual factor (as day and night or birth and death) — compare DIALECTIC 2b (2) **:** an instance or case of such a relationship

polarity cap *n* **:** an electric cap having knife-blade terminals so arranged that it can be inserted in its base or body in one way only

po·lar·iz·abil·i·ty \ˌpōləˌrīzəˈbilədˌē\ *n* **1 :** the quality or state of being polarizable **2 :** the electric dipole moment per unit electric intensity of a material or a molecule

po·lar·iz·able \ˈ⸗⸗ˌrīzəbəl, ˌ⸗⸗ˈ⸗⸗⸗\ *adj* [ISV *polarize* + *-able*] **:** capable of being polarized ⟨an ion that can be easily distorted is highly ~⟩

po·lar·iza·tion \ˌpōlərəˈzāshən, -ˌrīˈ-\ *n* -s [F *polarisation*, fr. *polariser* to polarize + *-ation*] **1 :** the action of polarizing or the state of being polarized: as **a** (1) **:** the action or process of affecting light or other transverse wave radiation so that the vibrations of the wave are confined to a single plane — called also *linear polarization, plane polarization* (2) **:** the action or process of affecting light or other transverse wave radiation so that the vibrations may be regarded as confined to two mutually perpendicular planes with the components having a particular relationship between their phases and amplitudes — called also *circular polarization, elliptical polarization* (3) **:** the state of radiation affected by either of these processes **b :** the deposition of gas on one or both electrodes of an electrolytic cell increasing the resistance and setting up a counter electromotive force ⟨so-called dry cells are notably subject to ~⟩ — called also *electrolytic polarization* **c :** an effect resulting from the slight shifting of the electrons in a dielectric when placed in an electric field; *specif* **:** the electric moment thus produced per unit volume of dielectric — called also *dielectric polarization* **d :** an effect occurring in atoms and molecules wherein a slight relative shift of electrons and nuclei is produced in an electric field **e :** MAGNETIZATION — called also *magnetic polarization* **2 a :** division (as of groups, ideologies, systems, or forces) into two opposites ⟨~ . . . made between writing journalistically and writing creatively —J.T.Farrell⟩ **b :** the concentration about opposing extremes of usu. conflicting groups or interests formerly ranged on a continuum ⟨~ of all sorts of antagonisms —Isaac Deutscher⟩ ⟨as a result of this ~ between right and left, the middle-of-the-road parties . . . have lost strength —Louis Wasserman⟩ **c :** the division (as of a society or force) into two elements concentrated about opposing extremes ⟨a ~ of society into two classes —Reinhard Bendix⟩ ⟨the ~ of power between two implacable enemies —M.B.Travis⟩ ⟨the ~ of European politics between two political extremes —Barbara Ward⟩

polarization figure *n* **:** INTERFERENCE FIGURE

po·lar·ize \ˈpōləˌrīz\ *vb* -ED/-ING/-s [F *polariser*, fr. NL *polaris* polar + F *-iser* -ize] *vt* **1 :** to cause (as light waves) to vibrate in a definite pattern **:** affect by polarization **2 :** to give polarity to **:** bring into a state of physical polarization **3 :** to direct or orient toward a specific polar point (as an object or principle) ⟨the whole society was *polarized* toward financial success —W.P.Webb⟩ ⟨when a young person . . . has his interest *polarized* and his life altered —John Mason Brown⟩ **4 :** to produce or bring about a polarization of **:** subject to or cause to exhibit polarization ⟨the campaign . . . tends to ~ people —R.M.Goldman⟩ ⟨a conflict . . . which ~*s* political life —L.S.Feuer⟩ ⟨this tactic . . . *polarized* the political elements into Right and Left camps —*Current History*⟩ **5 :** to serve as a focal point for the concentration of ⟨a bell tower which . . . ~*s* a deep local pride —K.R. Greenfield⟩ ⟨groups . . . have *polarized* what is most reactionary in our economic and social system —*New Republic*⟩ ~ *vi* **1 a :** to gather or become concentrated about opposing extremes ⟨political forces had *polarized* into right and left extremes —Andrew Roth⟩ **b :** to serve as a focal point about which such concentration may take place **2 :** to adhere to or become directed toward a specific polar object or principle ⟨some individuals ~ negatively by turning into cynical sensualists —P.A.Sorokin⟩

polarized–relay armature *n* **:** an armature in which the moving part is a permanent magnet

po·lar·iz·er \ˈpōləˌrīzə(r)\ *n* -s **:** one that polarizes; *specif* **:** the part of a polariscope receiving and polarizing the light — compare ANALYZER

polarizing angle *n* **:** the angle at which unpolarized light or other electromagnetic radiation must be incident upon a nonmetallic surface for the reflected radiation to acquire maximum plane polarization — called also *Brewster angle;* compare BREWSTER'S LAW

polarizing microscope *n* **:** a microscope equipped to produce polarized light for the examination of an object

polar lake *n* **:** a lake in which the surface temperature never exceeds 4°C

polar lights *n pl* **1 :** AURORA BOREALIS **2 :** AURORA AUSTRALIS

po·lar·ly *adv* **:** in a polar manner, direction, or degree ⟨atomic submarines moving ~⟩

polar maritime air *n* **:** air coming orig. from polar regions but having humidity and temperature properties modified by passing over relatively warm oceans

polar nucleus *n* **:** either of two nuclei that fuse in the center of the embryo sac of a seed plant to form the primary endosperm nucleus

po·lar·o·gram \pōˈlarəˌgram, ˈpōlərə,-\ *n* [ISV *polarization* + *-o-* + *-gram*] **:** the current-voltage diagram obtained during polarographic treatment of a solution

Po·lar·o·graph \-graf, -räf\ *trademark* — used for an instrument used in polarography

po·lar·o·graph·ic \⸗ˌ⸗⸗ˈgrafik, ˌ⸗⸗⸗ˈgrafik\ *adj* [*polarization* + *-o-* + *-graphic*] **:** of, relating to, or by means of polarography ⟨~ techniques⟩ ⟨~ waves⟩ — compare AMPEROMETRIC — **po·lar·o·graph·i·cal·ly** \-fək(ə)lē\ *adv*

po·lar·og·ra·phy \ˌpōləˈrägrəfē\ *n* -ES [ISV *polarization* + *-o-* + *-graphy*] **:** a method of qualitative or quantitative analysis used esp. in studying reversible oxidation-reduction phenomena that is based on current-voltage curves obtained during electrolysis of a test solution with a steadily increasing electromotive force between two mercury electrodes one of which is readily polarized and consists of a stream of fine mercury droplets whereas the other consists of a substantial pool of mercury into which the droplets fall

Po·lar·oid \ˈpōləˌrȯid\ *trademark* — used for a light-polarizing material comprising in one form oriented suspensions of dichroic particles in a light-transmitting medium and used esp. in eyeglasses and lamps to prevent glare and in various optical devices

po·lar·on \ˈpōləˌrän\ *n* -s [ISV *polar* + *-on*; prob. orig. formed in Russ] **:** a conducting electron in an ionic crystal together with the induced electric polarization of the surrounding lattice

polar ox *n* **:** MUSK-OX

polar plant *n* **:** COMPASS PLANT a

polar projection *n* **:** a cartographic projection of the sphere in which the point of sight is at the center and the plane of projection passes through one of the polar circles

polar ray *n* **:** an astral ray as contrasted with a spindle fiber

polars *pl of* POLAR

polar telescope *n* **:** a telescope that utilizes the polar axis for its tube and uses a mirror in front of the objective to direct the light into the tube

polar triangle *n* **:** a spherical triangle formed by the arcs of three great circles each of whose poles is the vertex of a given spherical triangle

polar valence *n* **1 :** ELECTROVALENCE **2 :** covalence characterized by unequal distribution of electrons between the atoms united

po·lar·ward \ˈpōlə(r)wə(r)d\ *adv (or adj)* **:** toward the polar regions

polar whale *n* **:** GREENLAND WHALE

po·la·touche \ˌpōlə'tüsh\ *n* -s [F, fr. Russ *poletusha*] **:** a small flying squirrel (*Sciuropterus volans*) native to northern Europe and Asia

pol·davy \päl'dāvē, pōl-\ *also* **pol·da·vis** \-vəs\ *n, pl* **pol·davies** *or* **poldavys** *also* **poldavis** [ME *poldavy*, prob. fr. *Pouldavid*, locality in Finistère department, northwest France] **:** a coarse canvas or sacking formerly used for sails esp. by the British

pol·der \'pōldə(r)\ *n* -s [D, fr. MD *polder, polre*] **:** a tract of low land reclaimed from the sea or other body of water (as by dikes or dams)

polderboy *or* **polderman** \'ˌ=ˌ=\ *n, pl* **polderboys** *or* **pol·dermen :** a workman engaged in making or maintaining a polder

¹pole \'pōl\ *n* -s [ME, fr. OE *pāl* pole, stake, fr. L *palus* stake; akin to L *pangere* to fasten — more at PACT] **1 a :** a long comparatively slender usu. cylindrical piece of wood or timber (as the stem of a small tree stripped of its branches) **b :** a similar typically cylindrical piece of metal or other substance **2 :** a pole of a specified nature and use: as **a :** an upright column to the top of which something is affixed or by which something is supported ⟨a birdhouse set on a ~⟩ ⟨telephone ~s⟩ ⟨a tent ~⟩ **b :** a long slender stick or staff manipulated by hand ⟨vault with a ~⟩ ⟨a boatman's ~⟩ **c :** one used as the handle of an implement ⟨the ~ of a harpoon⟩ **d :** an upright mast in a firehouse by which one may slide from one story to a lower story **e :** an upper part of the mast of a ship **f :** SKI POLE **g :** one of several distance markers placed ⅛ mile apart on the inner rail of a racetrack **h :** a shaft usu. of wood which extends from the front axle of a wagon between wheelhorses and by which the wagon is held back **:** TONGUE **i :** a short striped column used as a sign by tradesmen; *specif* **:** BARBER POLE **j :** a usu. horizontal bar or rod from which something may be hung ⟨a curtain ~⟩ **k :** TOTEM POLE **l :** FLAGPOLE **m :** a stick usu. of a specified length used for measuring **3 a :** a unit of length varying from one locality to another; *esp* **:** one measuring 16½ feet — compare PERCH, ROD **b :** a unit of area equal to a square rod or perch **:** one measuring 30¼ square yards ⟨plots of ground averaging about ten ~s each —John Galsworthy⟩ **4 :** the tail of various birds and animals; *esp* **:** the tail of an otter **5 :** the flowering stalk of a plant of the genus *Agave* (as the sisal) **6 :** a tree having a breast-high diameter of from 4 to 12 inches **7 :** the inside position on a racetrack **8** *usu cap* **:** QUTB — **under bare poles :** with furled sails ⟨how could she sail upwind *under bare poles* —S.H.Adams⟩

²pole \"\ *vb* -ED/-ING/-S *vt* **1 :** to furnish with poles for support ⟨peas were brushed . . . gourds *poled* —Nora Waln⟩ **2 :** to strike with a pole; *esp* **:** to hit or pierce with the end of a carriage pole **3 :** to act upon with a pole (as in stirring or pushing) **4 :** to impel or push (as a boat or raft) by means of a pole ⟨never ~ a boat from the bow —H.A.Calahan⟩ ⟨a canoe . . . *poled* by two men —*McClure's*⟩ **5 :** to convey (as hay or reeds) on poles ⟨~ hay into a barn⟩ **6 :** to hit (as a home run) with a free powerful swing of a baseball bat ⟨*poled* his twelfth home run in the sixth inning —*N.Y. Herald Tribune*⟩ **7 :** to subject (metal) to the operation of poling **8 :** to remove dew from (as grass on a putting green) with a long slender pole **9 :** ¹FOREPOLE ~ *vi* **1 :** to propel a boat with a pole ⟨*poled* up the sheltered creek —Cameron Hawley⟩ ⟨*poled* cautiously through the shallows —Francis Birtles⟩ **2** *Austral* **:** SPONGE, IMPOSE — usu. used with *on* **3 :** FLOWER — used of a plant of the genus *Agave* **4 :** to use one's ski poles to gain additional speed ⟨*poled* vigorously down the slope⟩

³pole \"\ *adj* **1 :** of or relating to a long slender cylindrical piece of wood or other pole **2 a :** made of poles ⟨~ bridge⟩ ⟨~ fence⟩ **b :** having a foundation made of piles or poles stuck into the ground ⟨~ barn⟩ ⟨~ cabin⟩ **3 :** attached to the end of a pole ⟨~ hook⟩ ⟨~ net⟩

⁴pole \"\ *n* -s [ME *pool*, fr. L *polus*, fr. Gk *polos* pivot, axis, pole; akin to Gk *kyklos* circle, wheel — more at WHEEL] **1 a :** either extremity of an axis of a sphere **b :** one of the two extremities of the earth's axis — called also *geographical pole*; see NORTH POLE, SOUTH POLE **2 :** something held to resemble a physical pole: as **a :** either of two opposites (as principles, ideas, or factors) forming part of the same system ⟨oscillations of the . . . national mind between the ~s of sentiment and intellect —René Wellek⟩ ⟨the major ~s of world power —*Atlantic*⟩ **b :** a point of guidance or attraction ⟨a ~ of attraction for all the peoples . . . under Communist oppression —*European Federation Now*⟩ ⟨the ~s around whom the discussion was supposed to revolve —D.W.Brogan⟩ ⟨the pivot and ~ of his life . . . was his mother —D.H. Lawrence⟩ **3** *archaic* **:** FIRMAMENT, HEAVENS, SKY ⟨when the night had veil'd the ~ —William Blake⟩ **4 a :** one of the two terminals of an electric cell, battery, or dynamo so related that if the two are connected by an external conductor an electric current will flow from the pole having the higher potential to the other — see NEGATIVE POLE, POSITIVE POLE **b :** one of two or more regions in a magnetized body at which the magnetic flux density is more or less concentrated — see NORTH POLE, SOUTH POLE **c :** a unit comprising the parts of a circuit breaker or switch that control one line of a circuit **5 a :** either of two morphologically or physiologically differentiated areas at opposite ends of an axis in an organism, organ, or cell — see ANIMAL POLE, VEGETAL POLE **b :** an eminence, region, or point on a cell where an axis ends (as at the origin of a nerve cell process or the base of a flagellum) **c :** either end of the spindle in mitosis **6 a :** the fixed point in a system of polar coordinates that serves as the origin **b :** one of the ends of the axis of a circle of a sphere **7 a :** the normal to a plane of a crystal erected through the origin of coordinates **b** (1) **:** the point on a unit sphere where a normal so erected intersects the sphere (2) **:** the projection usu. stereographic or gnomonic of such a point **8 :** the center of a reflecting or refracting surface that is bounded by a circle — **poles apart** *or* **poles asunder :** as far apart or as opposed as the poles of the earth **:** completely averse ⟨their characters . . . are *poles apart* —New Republic⟩ ⟨candidates . . . *poles apart* on international relations —*Christian Science Monitor*⟩ ⟨the leisured aristocratic class . . . *poles asunder* from the typical Pharisee —G.H.Box⟩

⁵pole \"\ *vt* -ED/-ING/-S **:** to determine or mark the terminal polarities of (as a generator or transformer)

⁶pole \"\ *n* -s *cap* [G, of Slavic origin; akin to Pol *Polak* Pole] **1 :** a native or inhabitant of Poland; *esp* **:** a member of the Slavic majority ethnic group of the Polish nation who is Polish-speaking and usu. Roman Catholic **2 :** a person of Polish descent **:** a descendant of natives of Poland ⟨the clannish barriers which now separate the *Pole*, the largest minority, from the Southerner and the Negro —A.G.Mezerik⟩

pole and satchel charge *n* **:** POLE CHARGE

¹pole·ax *or* **pole·axe** *or* **pol·lax** *or* **pol·laxe** \'pōˌlaks\ *n* [ME *polax, pollax*, fr. *pol, polle* head + *ax* — more at POLL] **1 a :** a battle-ax with a short handle and often a cutting edge or point opposite the blade **b :** one having a long handle and used as an ornamental weapon (as by members of a royal bodyguard) **2 :** a short ax with a strong hook at the top of the handle formerly used in naval warfare esp. by boarders **3 :** an ax made with a hammer face opposite the edge and used in slaughtering cattle

²poleax *or* **poleaxe** *or* **pollax** *or* **pollaxe** \"\ *vt* **:** to attack, strike, or fell with or as if with a poleax ⟨the oxen . . . were shot or ~*ed* —H.W.Nevinson⟩ ⟨the crowds . . . had already been ~*ed*, mentally and emotionally —Benedict Thielen⟩

pole bean *n* **:** any of various cultivated beans having long internodes and twining stems and forming elongated vines that are commonly trained to grow upright on poles or other supports — compare BUSH BEAN

pole blight *n* **:** a destructive disease of undetermined cause affecting white pines and characterized by shortening of the needle-bearing stems esp. in the upper crown, yellowing and shortening of the needles, abundant resin flow, and eventual death of the tree

pole boat *n* **:** a boat propelled by means of a pole

pole borer *n* **:** a cerambycid beetle (*Parandra brunnea*) having larvae that bore in shade trees and large poles (as telephone poles)

¹poleburn \'ˌ=ˌ=\ *n* [¹*pole* + *burn*, n.] **:** POLE ROT

²poleburn \"\ *vi* **:** to become affected with pole rot

pole–car \'ˌ=ˌ=\ *n* **:** a railroad car sometimes used in pole switching

pole·cat \'pōlˌkat, *usu* -ad.+V\ *n, pl* **polecats** *also* **polecat** *often attrib* [ME *polcat*, prob. fr. MF *poul, pol* cock + ME *cat*; prob. fr. its habit of feeding on poultry — more at PULLET] **1 a :** a European carnivorous mammal (*Mustela putorius* syn. *Putorius foetidus*) of which the ferret is considered a domesticated variety and which is about two feet long, dark brownish above with white markings on the head, and blackish below **b :** any of several closely related animals of eastern Europe and Asia **2 :** SKUNK; *esp* **:** one of the genus *Mephitis* **3** *Africa* **:** ZORIL **4 :** the common palm civet (*Paradoxurus hermaphroditus*) **5** *archaic* **:** a vile or contemptible person; *esp* **:** PROSTITUTE ⟨out of my door, you witch, you hag, . . . you ~ —Shak.⟩

polecat tree *or* **polecat wood** *n* **:** YELLOW BUCKTHORN

polecat weed *n* **:** SKUNK CABBAGE

pole cell *n* [⁴*pole* + *cell*] **:** a cleavage cell of the embryo of various insects and some other invertebrates regularly undergoing early chromatin diminution in somatic cells that retains the full chromatin complement and ultimately gives rise to the germ cells **:** one that enters the posterior extremity of the egg

pole chain *n* **1 :** GUNTER'S CHAIN **2 :** a chain joining the pole of a wagon to a horse's collar

pole charge *n* **:** a quantity of fused explosives fastened to the end of a pole and used in military attacks (as against pillboxes, dugouts, and cave positions)

pole–clipped \'ˌ=ˌ=\ *adj* **:** pruned or pollarded esp. with a pole type of pruner

pole–clipt *adj, obs* **:** POLE-CLIPPED ⟨thy *pole-clipt* vineyard —Shak.⟩

pole compass *n* **:** a compass raised (as on a pole) above the deck of an iron or steel ship to lessen the effect of the hull's magnetism

poled *past of* POLE

pole effect *n* **:** the minute change in wavelength and marked change in character of many spectral lines in light emanating from the central region of a metallic arc as compared with light originating near the electrodes

pole flounder *or* **pole fluke** *n* **:** WITCH FLOUNDER

pole·head \'pōlˌhed\ *n* [ME *polheved*, fr. *pol, polle* head + *heved* head — more at POLL, HEAD] *archaic* **:** TADPOLE

pole horse *n* **1 :** a horse harnessed beside the pole of a wagon; *specif* **:** a wheeler as distinguished from a leader **2 :** the horse having a starting position next to the inside rail in a harness race

poleis *pl of* POLIS

pole jack *n* **:** a jack used to pull out poles from their setting

pole jump *n* **:** POLE VAULT

pole lathe *n* **:** a primitive lathe in which the cord passing around the work to rotate it is fastened at its ends to the treadle and to an elastic pole above

pole·less \'pōlləs\ *adj* [¹*pole* & ⁴*pole*] **:** having no pole ⟨~ tent⟩ ⟨~ magnet⟩

pole·man \'pōlmən\ *n, pl* **polemen 1 :** one that uses a pole (as in surveying, lumbering, or fighting) **2 :** one that picks up the sound from a motion-picture stage by moving a microphone mounted on the end of an adjustable boom close to the speaking actors — called also *boom man*

pol·e·march \'päləˌmärk\ *n* -s [Gk *polemarchos*, fr. *polemos* war + *archos* ruler — more at ARCHI-] **:** a chieftain or military commander in ancient Greece; *esp* **:** the third archon in ancient Athens presiding at the court and having jurisdiction over the causes of the metics

pole mast *n* **:** a mast in one length or piece as distinguished from one made up of two pieces **:** a mast formed by a single spar

¹po·lem·ic \pə'lemik, pō'-, -mēk\ *n* -s [F *polémique*, fr. MF *polemique*, fr. *polemique*, adj.] **1 a :** a controversial discussion or argument **:** an aggressive attack on or the refutation of the opinions or principles of another ⟨the premises of our ~ against totalitarianism —J.M.Cameron⟩ ⟨dismiss these books as cold-war ~s —Karl Meyer⟩ ⟨repeating old and weary ~s —Irving Howe⟩ **b :** the art or practice of disputation or controversy ⟨neither descended to crude ~ —Richard Hoggart⟩ ⟨his active ~ against . . . liberals —A.C.McGiffert⟩ ⟨the style too frequently descends to the level of ~s —M.S.Handler⟩ — usu. used in pl. but usu. sing. in constr. ⟨the book . . . is a little masterpiece of ~s —Martin Gardner⟩ **2 :** one that controverts an opinion, doctrine, or system **:** an aggressive controversialist **:** DISPUTANT ⟨the sarcasms and invectives of the young ~ —T.B.Macaulay⟩ **3 polemics** *pl but usu sing in constr* **:** the branch of Christian theology devoted to the refutation of errors — compare APOLOGETICS, IRENICS

²polemic \"\ *adj* [F *polémique*, fr. MF *polemique*, fr. Gk *polemikos* of or relating to war, fr. *polemos* war + *-ikos* -ic; akin to OE *ealfelo* baleful, MHG *vālant* devil, ON *felmsfullr* frightened, Goth *usfilma* astonished, Gk *pelemizein* to shake, *pallein* to shake, brandish, hurl] **:** POLEMICAL ⟨written with a ~ purpose —A.C.McGiffert⟩ ⟨the militant and ~ position of the church in the empire —H.O.Taylor⟩ ⟨~ journalist⟩

po·lem·i·cal \-məkəl, -mēk-\ *adj* **1 :** of, relating to, or of the nature of a polemic or polemics **:** CONTROVERSIAL ⟨prefer their politics heated and ~ —Bernard Hollowood⟩ ⟨a regrettably ~ spirit in . . . the literature —Dexter Perkins⟩ **2 :** engaged in or addicted to polemics **:** DISPUTATIOUS ⟨~ and . . . not always fair to his opponents —K.S.Latourette⟩ ⟨~ writers⟩

po·lem·i·cal·ly \-mək(ə)lē\ *adv* **:** in a polemical manner **:** CONTROVERSIALLY ⟨criticism . . . too ~ stated —W.L.Miller⟩

po·lem·i·cist \-məsəst\ *n* -s **:** POLEMIST ⟨socialism's most suasive intellectual ~ —*Time*⟩

po·lem·i·cize \-məˌsīz\ *vi* -ED/-ING/-S **:** POLEMIZE ⟨*polemicized* both for and against communism —Ward Moore⟩

po·lem·ist \-məst *also* 'päləm-\ *n* -s [¹*polemic* + *-ist*] **:** one skilled in or given to polemics esp. as the advocate of a partisan cause ⟨the poet who is a ~ and pamphleteer —Louise Bogan⟩ ⟨preacher, teacher . . . and ~ for freedom —*Nation*⟩

pol·e·mize \'päləˌmīz\ *vi* -ED/-ING/-S [¹*polemic* + *-ize*] **:** to engage in controversy **:** dispute aggressively **:** indulge in polemics **:** argue or write polemically ⟨he did not ~ against the pleasures of the senses —S.L.Terrien⟩

pol·e·mo·ni·a·ce·ae \ˌpäləˌmōnē'āsēˌē\ *n pl, cap* [NL, fr. *Polemonium*, type genus + *-aceae*] **:** a widely distributed family of chiefly herbaceous plants (order Polemoniales) with often showy flowers that have a 3-loculate ovary and 5 stamens inserted on the corolla tube and alternating with its lobes — **pol·e·mo·ni·a·ceous** \ˌ=ˌ=ˌ=ˌ='āshəs\ *adj*

pol·e·mo·ni·a·les \ˌ=ˌ=ˌ=ˌ='ā(ˌ)lēz\ *n pl, cap* [NL, fr. *Polemonium* + *-ales*] **:** a large order of dicotyledonous herbs, shrubs, or trees having flowers with the stamens adnate to the corolla lobes and a single superior compound ovary

pol·e·mo·ni·um \ˌpälə'mōnēəm\ *n* [NL, fr. Gk *polemōnion*, a plant, perh. Greek valerian] **1** *cap* **:** a genus (the type of the family Polemoniaceae) of herbs having pinnate leaves and large cymose-paniculate flowers with herbaceous calyx, declinate stamens, and mucilaginous seeds — see GREEK VALERIAN **2** -s **:** any plant of the genus *Polemonium*

po·lem·o·scope \pō'leməˌskōp\ *n* [NL *polemoscopium*, fr. Gk *polemos* war + NL *-scopium* -scope; fr. its suggested use in war as a device for observing the enemy] **:** an opera or field glass with an oblique mirror arranged for seeing objects not directly before the eye

po·len·ske value \pō'len(t)skə-\ *also* **polenske number** *n, usu cap P* [after Eduard *Polenske*, 20th cent. Ger. chemist] **:** a value similar to a Reichert value that indicates the content in butter or other fat of the volatile water-insoluble acids (as capric acid and lauric acid)

po·len·ta \pō'lentə\ *n* -s [It, fr. L *pollenta* pearl barley — more at POLLEN] **:** mush orig. made of chestnut meal but now principally of cornmeal or sometimes of semolina or farina ⟨the popularity of ~ among Italian peasants⟩

pole of cold : a place where the winter cold is the most intense usu. located in the interior of a continent

pole of inaccessibility *often cap P&I* **:** the central point of a polar region most difficult of penetration

pole of the heavens : CELESTIAL POLE

pole piece *n* [¹*pole* + *piece*] **1 :** a stout harness strap connecting a horse's collar with the pole of a wagon **2 :** the ridgepole of a roof **3** [⁴*pole* + *piece*] **:** a piece of soft iron at a pole of an electromagnet usu. shaped to concentrate or direct the external flux in some desired path — see MAGNETO illustration

pole–pile \'ˌ=ˌ=\ *vt* **:** to stack (as lumber for drying) on end against a center pole

pole pitch *n* **:** the distance measured on the circumference of the armature from the center of one pole to the center of the next pole **:** 180 electrical degrees — compare COIL PITCH 2b(5)

pole plate *n* [¹*pole* + *plate*] **1 :** a horizontal timber resting on the tie beams of a roof rather than on the wall and supporting the ends of the rafters — compare PLATE 5a(1); see ROOF illustration **2** [⁴*pole* + *plate*] **:** a condensed platelike body developed at each pole of the spindle in various forms of mitosis esp. in protozoans

pole pruner *n* **:** a tool for pruning with the cutting parts on the end of a rod or pole 6 to 12 feet long

pol·er \'pōlə(r)\ *n* -s **:** one that poles: as **a :** POLE HORSE **b :** one that poles a boat (as a punt) **c :** a worker who performs the poling in a refining furnace **d :** a textile worker who puts yarn on poles for processing **e :** a worker who builds corduroy roads for skidding logs **f :** BOATMAN 1c

pole riding *n* **:** the action or an instance of reducing speed on a slope by weighting one's ski poles

pole rot *or* **pole sweat** *n* **:** a rotting that occurs while tobacco is on poles during curing — called also *poleburn*; compare HOUSEBURN

poles *pl of* POLE, *pres 3d sing of* POLE

polesaw \'ˌ=ˌ=\ *n* **:** a small curved saw blade mounted on a long handle and used for pruning branches beyond arm reach

polesaw

pole screen *n* **:** BANNER SCREEN

pole shoe *n* **:** an iron or steel plate sometimes attached to a field-magnet pole to support the field coil

po·le·sian \pō'lēzhən\ *n* -s *cap* [*Polesie*, district in southwest White Russia and northwest Ukraine, U.S.S.R. + E *-an*] **:** a member of a people inhabiting the eastern European district of Polesie and being dialectally Belorussian

poles·man \'pōlzmən\ *n, pl* **polesmen :** POLEMAN

¹polestack \'ˌ=ˌ=\ *vt* [¹*pole* + *stack*, v.] **:** POLE-PILE

²polestack \"\ *n* [¹*pole* + *stack*, n.] **:** a stack of hay hung on an upright pole or laid on poles for rapid curing

polestar \'ˌ=ˌ=\ *n* -s **1 :** the conspicuous star that at any period is nearest the north celestial pole — called also *North Star* **2 a :** a directing or controlling principle **:** GUIDE ⟨drove forward . . . into the new seas of political idealism trusting to the ~ of emancipated human nature —V.L.Parrington⟩ **b :** a center of attraction ⟨Indian liberty . . . provided a new ~ in political thinking —*Amer. Indian*⟩

pole step *n* **:** a lag screw usu. with an L-shaped end that when screwed into a telephone or electric light pole becomes a step for climbing

pole stock *n* **:** lumber used in making poles for vehicles and agricultural implements

pole strength *n* **:** a quantity corresponding to the amount of magnetic flux emanating from a given magnetic pole and expressed in terms of the unit magnetic pole

pole strip *n* **:** a template for spacing holes

pole switching *n* **:** switching by means of a pole extended from the side of a locomotive or a pole-car in front of a locomotive with the pole being used to push a car or cut of cars on a paralleling track to a designated classification track

pole tie *n* **:** SLABBED TIE

pole–timber \'ˌ=ˌ=ˌ=\ *adj* **:** having a minimum of 10 percent pole size or larger trees of which at least half are pole size ⟨*pole-timber* forest⟩ ⟨*pole-timber* stands⟩

pole trailer *n* **:** a dolly or rig to carry poles in tow behind a truck

pole transformer *n* **:** a distribution transformer designed for mounting on a pole or crossarm

pole trap *n* **1 :** a trap set on a pole **2 :** a trap arranged with a bent pole to swing the animal off the ground when the trap is sprung

pole trawl *or* **pole seine** *n* **:** a trawlnet having the mouth spread open with a pole or beam

pole vault *n* **:** a vault or vaulting with the aid of a pole; *specif* **:** a field event in athletics consisting of a vault for height over a crossbar

pole–vault \'ˌ=ˌ=\ *vi* [*pole vault*] **:** to attain a height by or as if by vaulting with the aid of a pole ⟨*pole-vaulted* 11 feet 4 inches⟩

pole–vaulter \'ˌ=ˌ=ˌ=\ *n* **:** an athlete who participates in the pole vault

pole vaulting *n* **:** the act or action of performing the pole vault

pole·ward \'pōlwə(r)d\ *also* **pole·wards** \-dz\ *adv (or adj)* **:** toward or in the direction of a pole of the earth ⟨Britain lay ~ of . . . its American colonies —R.H.Brown⟩ ⟨found in ~ areas⟩

polewood stage \'ˌ=ˌ=-\ *n* **:** a stage in the development of a forest when most of the trees are poles

po·ley \'pōlē\ *adj* [prob. irreg. fr. ⁴*poll* + *-y*] *Austral* **:** POLLED, HORNLESS ⟨a ~ cow⟩

po·leyn \'pōˌlān\ *n* -s [ME, fr. MF *polain*] **:** a piece of defensive armor usu. covering the knee

poli- *or* **polio-** *comb form* [NL, fr. Gk, gray, fr. *polios* — more at FALLOW] **1 :** of or relating to the gray matter of the brain or spinal cord ⟨*polio*myelitis⟩ **2 :** gray ⟨*Polianthes*⟩

po·li·a·nite \'pōlēəˌnīt\ *n* -s [G *polianit*, irreg. fr. Gk *polianesthai* to become white with foam (fr. *polios* gray) + G *-it* -ite] **:** pyrolusite in well-formed crystals

pol·i·an·thes \ˌpälē'an(t)ˌthēz\ *n, cap* [NL, fr. *poli-* + *-anthes*] **:** a small genus of Mexican tuberous herbs (family Amaryllidaceae) having tall stems and spikes of fragrant white flowers borne in pairs and with the tube of the perianth strongly curved

¹po·lice \pə'lēs, pō'-, *in rapid speech* 'plēs\ *n, pl* **police** *often attrib* [MF, conduct of public affairs, administration of government, fr. LL *politia*, fr. L, state, fr. Gk *politeia* citizenship, administration of government, state, fr. *politēs* citizen, fr. *polis* city; akin to Skt *pura* city and prob. to L *plenus* full — more at FULL] **1** *archaic* **:** social or group organization **:** CIVILIZATION ⟨insects whose faculties, ~, and sagacity have been . . . overrated —J.R.Johnson⟩ ⟨the age . . . was far less insecure in its condition of ~ —Thomas De Quincey⟩ **2** *archaic* **:** POLICY ⟨the ~ and interests of the Roman see —John Entick⟩ **3 a** (1) **:** the internal organization or regulation of a political unit (as a nation or state) **:** the control and regulation of such a unit through the exercise of governmental powers (2) **:** such control and regulation with respect to matters affecting the general comfort, health, morals, safety, or prosperity of the public **b :** the control and regulation of the affairs affecting the general order and welfare of a nonpolitical unit (as a camp) or area ⟨regulations regarding the ~ of this navigation —*Congress of Vienna 1815*⟩ ⟨the ~ of the boat is superior to the best regulated tavern —Anne Royall⟩ **c :** the organization or system of laws for effecting such control **4 a :** the department of government concerned primarily with the maintenance of public order, safety, and health and the enforcement of the laws and possessing executive, judicial, and legislative powers — see POLICE POWER **b :** the department of government having as its principal function the prevention, detection, and prosecution of public nuisances and crimes **5 a :** POLICE FORCE ⟨the metropolitan ~⟩ ⟨the ~ was there in force —Arthur Morrison⟩ ⟨the ~ and other local law enforcement bodies —Jack Lait & Lee Mortimer⟩ **b :** a member of a police force or constabulary **:** POLICEMAN — usu. used in pl. ⟨ask these two ~ all the questions —Thomas Sterling⟩ ⟨detectives, plainclothesmen and uniformed ~ —*N. Y. Herald Tribune*⟩ **6 a** (1) **:** an organization resembling the police force of a community **:** a group of persons officially entrusted with the duty of keeping order and enforcing regulations in a usu. specified area ⟨railway ~⟩ ⟨dock ~⟩ ⟨campus ~⟩ (2) **:** a member of such an organization — usu. used in pl. **b** (1) **:** a group of persons held to resemble such a police force in organization or function ⟨society . . . has its code and ~ as well as governments —W.M.Thackeray⟩ (2) **:** a member of such a group — usu. used in pl. ⟨members act as volunteer thought ~ —Paul Blanshard⟩ **7 :** the action or process of cleaning and putting in order (as a building or an area) ⟨the gun commander is responsible for the ∼ of his gun position⟩ **8 :** military personnel detailed to perform a usu. specified function — see KITCHEN POLICE

²police \"\ *vt* -ED/-ING/-S [in sense 1, fr. MF *policer*, fr. *police*, n.; in other senses, fr. ¹*police*] **1** *archaic* : to maintain law and order in (as a country) : GOVERN ⟨humane laws by which kingdoms are *policed* —John Donne⟩ **2 a :** to control, regulate, or keep in order by the use of police or a similar force or by means held to resemble the use of police ⟨a four-lane thoroughfare *policed* against speeding —*Amer. Guide Series: Texas*⟩ ⟨waters . . . *policed* by two sets of revenue officers —*Amer. Guide Series: Md.*⟩ ⟨the use of superstition for . . . *policing* the mob —Benjamin Farrington⟩ **b :** to guard or protect by means of police **3 :** to make clean and put in order (as a military camp) — often used with *up* **4 a :** to supervise the operation, execution, or administration of (as an agreement) to prevent or detect and prosecute violations of rules and regulations ⟨responsibility for *policing* the peace —Sumner Welles⟩ ⟨the role of government in *policing* welfare funds —Ed Marciniak⟩ ⟨use of an internal audit agency . . . to ∼ the financial and accounting activities —H.W.Bordner⟩ **b :** to exercise such a supervision over the policies and activities of ⟨a top-level committee to ∼ holders of government contracts —*New Republic*⟩ ⟨every industry has a moral obligation to ∼ itself —*Advertising & Selling*⟩ **5 :** to perform the functions (as regulation or protection) of a police force in or over ⟨state police charged with *policing* rural communities —*Amer. Guide Series: Mich.*⟩ ⟨ordered his 40,000-man army . . . to ∼ the land —*Current Biog.*⟩

police action *n* : a usu. localized military action undertaken by regular armed forces against persons held to be violators of the general international peace and order (as guerrillas, bandits, or aggressors) without a formal declaration of war ⟨the United Nations *police action* in Korea⟩ ⟨the war with Spain . . . was a relatively small *police action* —R.K.Burns⟩

police burgh *n* : a Scottish burgh having legally defined boundaries and possessing the privilege of having its own municipal council

police commissioner *n* **1 :** a member of a board of civilian officials legally charged with the making of policy for and the exercise of general supervisory powers over a police department **2 :** an appointed civilian official commissioned to regulate and control the appointment, duties, and discipline of the police and to act as the chief executive of the police department in a political unit (as a city)

police constable *n, Brit* : a policeman of the lowest rank

police court *n* : a court of record having jurisdiction over various minor offenses (as violations of motor vehicle laws or cases involving breach of the peace) corresponding to that of the justice of the peace under the common law and possessing power to bind over for trial in a superior court or for a grand jury persons accused of more serious offenses

police department *n* **1 :** a governmental department concerned with the administration of the police force ⟨an increased budget for the *police department*⟩ **2 :** POLICE FORCE ⟨call out the entire *police department*⟩

police dog *n* **1 :** a dog trained to assist police in their work esp. in tracking criminals **2 :** GERMAN SHEPHERD

po·lice·dom \pə'lēsdəm\ *n* -S : the total body of police : the police system

police force *n* : a professional body of trained officers and men entrusted by a government with the maintenance of public peace and order, the enforcement of laws, and the prevention and detection of crime

police inspector *n* : a superior officer of police usu. ranking next below a commissioner, superintendent, or chief

police jury *n* : the governing body of a Louisiana parish corresponding to a board of supervisors in the counties of other states

police justice *or* **police magistrate** *or* **police judge** *n* : a judge of a police court

po·lice·less \-sləs\ *adj* : lacking police

po·lice·man \pə'lēsmən, pō'-, *in rapid speech* 'plē-\ *n, pl* **policemen 1 a :** a member of a police force **b :** one held to resemble a member of a police force in acting to enforce rules or preserve order ⟨the priest as a moral ∼ in rural life —Paul Blanshard⟩ ⟨traditional ∼ over big business —T.R. Ybarra⟩ **2 :** an instrument (as a flat piece of rubber on the end of a glass rod) for removing solids from a beaker or other vessel

policeman fly *n* : any of several small Australian wasps that capture flies and store them in their burrows

po·lice·man·ship \-n,ship\ *n* : action or behavior held to characterize a policeman

police matron *n* : a woman in a municipal police department who has charge of women and children detained (as in a police station and jail)

police motu *n, usu cap P&M* : a pidgin language of the territory of Papua based on Motu

police offense *n* : a minor offense against order over which a police court may have final jurisdiction and which does not involve a right to jury trial

police office *n, chiefly Brit* : the headquarters of a municipal police department : POLICE STATION

police officer *n* : a member of a police force

police power *n* : the inherent power of a government to exercise reasonable control over persons and property within its jurisdiction in the interest of the general security, health, safety, morals, and welfare except where legally prohibited (as by constitutional provision)

police reporter *n* : a reporter assigned to cover crimes, arrests, and other police news

polices *pres 3d sing of* POLICE

police science *n* : the science dealing principally with the investigation and detection of crime — compare CRIMINOLOGY

police state *n* : a political unit (as a nation) characterized by repressive governmental control of political, economic, and social life usu. by an arbitrary exercise of power by the police and esp. secret police in place of the regular operation of the administrative and judicial organs of the government according to established legal processes : a totalitarian state — compare GARRISON STATE

police station *n* : the headquarters of the police for a particular locality : the place where the police assemble for orders and to which they take arrested persons

po·lice·woman \(ˌ)'≈,≈≈\ *n, pl* **policewomen :** a woman who is a member of the police : a woman doing police duty

policing *pres part of* POLICE

pol·i·cize \'pälə,sīz\ *vi* -ED/-ING/-S [¹*policy* + *-ize*] : to act in a politic, diplomatic, or crafty manner

pol·i·clinic \ˌpälə+\ *n* [G *poliklinik*, fr. Gk *polis* city + G *klinik* clinic, fr. F *clinique* — more at POLICE, CLINIC] **1 :** a clinic held formerly at private houses in a city or town for treatment of patients by advanced students under supervision of a professor who receives daily reports from the students **2 :** a dispensary or department of a hospital at which outpatients are treated — compare POLYCLINIC

¹pol·i·cy \'päləsē, -si\ *n* -ES *often attrib* [ME *policie*, fr. MF, fr. LL *politia* — more at POLICE] **1** *archaic* : the art or science of government : the conduct of public affairs **2** *archaic* : POLITY ⟨in well constituted *policies* provision is always made for the exercise of clemency —Joseph Gilbert⟩ **3** *archaic* : a wise scheme or device; *esp* : a cunning contrivance, stratagem, or trick **4 a :** prudence or wisdom in the management of public and private affairs : SAGACITY, SHREWDNESS, WISDOM, WIT ⟨decide upon . . . the ∼ or impolicy of these laws —R.B. Taney⟩ ⟨had I, with greater ∼, concealed my struggles —Jane Austen⟩ **b :** management, administration, or procedure based primarily on temporal or material interest : worldly wisdom : shrewdness based upon considerations of expediency : CRAFTINESS **5 a :** a definite course or method of action selected (as by a government, institution, group, or individual) from among alternatives and in the light of given conditions to guide and usu. determine present and future decisions **b** (1) **:** a specific decision or set of decisions designed to carry out such a chosen course of action (2) **:** such a specific decision or set of decisions together with the related actions designed to implement them **c :** a projected program consisting of desired objectives and the means to achieve them ⟨formulation of ∼⟩ **6** [ME (Sc) *polesy* (influenced in meaning by L *politus* polished, refined), fr. ME *policie* — more at POLITE] *obs Scot* **a :** the improvement of an estate, town, or building **b :** the improvements so made **c :** the improved grounds (as parkland) of an estate or country house in Scotland — usu. used in pl. ⟨house stands in about 20 acres of well-wooded *policies* —*advt*⟩ ⟨the *policies* of an old country house —John Buchan⟩

²policy \"\ *vt* -ED/-ING/-ES [MF *policier*, fr. *policie*, n.] *archaic* : to organize and regulate the internal order of : GOVERN

³policy \"\ *n* -ES *often attrib* [alter. (influenced by ¹*policy*) of earlier *police*, fr. MF, certificate, fr. OIt *polizza*, modif. of ML *apodixa* receipt, fr. MGk *apodeixis*, fr. Gk, proof, fr. *apodeiknynai* to point out, demonstrate + *-sis* — more at APODICTIC] **1 :** a certificate of insurance : a writing whereby a contract of insurance is made : the document containing the contract made by an insurance company with a person whose property or life is insured : an annuity contract or certificate of an insurance company — see BLANKET POLICY, FLOATER 8, FLOATING POLICY, LIMITED POLICY, OPEN POLICY, STANDARD POLICY, TIME POLICY, UNLIMITED POLICY, UNVALUED POLICY, VALUED POLICY, WAGER POLICY **2 a :** a daily lottery in which participants bet that certain numbers will be drawn from a lottery wheel **b :** NUMBER 11a

policyholder \'≈≈≈,≈≈\ *n* : one (as a person or firm) granted an insurance policy — used chiefly in life insurance

policy loan *n* : a loan granted by the insurer to the holder of a life insurance policy in an amount no greater than the cash value of the policy

policy proof of interest : a marine insurance policy provision whereby the underwriter agrees to dispense with all proof of insurable interest with the policy being stamped accordingly

policy science *n* : a social science dealing with the making and execution of policy (as in government or business)

policy slip *n* : a ticket showing the number a policy player has bet

policy wheel *n* : LOTTERY WHEEL

policy year *n* **1 :** a period comprising the 12 months extending usu. from noon of a given date to noon of the same date one year thereafter **2 :** a period of 24 months within which all the one-year policies written during the first 12 months thereof will have matured and the losses have become known — used in certain types of insurance accounting

pol·i·gar \'pälə,gär\ *n* -S *usu cap* [Marathi & Telugu; Marathi *pāḷegār*, fr. Telugu *pāḷegāḍu* or Kanarese *pāḷeyagāra*] : a subordinate feudal chief in the former Madras Presidency of India

po·li·gnac \ˌpōlēn'yak\ *n* -S [F, fr. Auguste Jules Armand Marie, Prince de *Polignac* †1847 Fr. ultraroyalist politician] **1 :** a card game in which a principal object is to avoid winning any jack in a trick **2 :** the jack of spades in polignac and other games

po·li·lla \pō'lē(y)ə\ *n* -S [AmerSp, fr. Sp, clothes moth] *West Indies* : POWDER-POST TERMITE

poling *n* -S [fr. gerund of ²*pole*] : a process used in refining some metals (as copper) that consists of the introduction of poles of green wood into the molten metal so as to generate gases that have a reducing action on oxides

poling board *n* : a vertical board used in the poling-board method to support the sides of an excavation

poling-board method \'≈≈,≈-\ *n* : a method of excavation (as of wells or trenches) by digging sections of from four to five feet each in depth with each section being sheathed with poling boards as it is finished

poling-boat \'≈≈,≈\ *n* : a usu. long narrow shallow draft boat with a flat bottom propelled with a pole

pol·i·ni·ces \ˌpälə'nī,sēz\ *n, cap* [NL, irreg. fr. L *Polynices*, legendary Theban warrior prince, fr. Gk *Polyneikēs*] : a genus of predacious marine snails (family Naticidae) having rather large globose shells and feeding chiefly on other mollusks (as clams) by drilling their way through the shell with their radula and extracting the soft parts within

po·lio \'pōlē,ō\ *n* -S *often attrib* [by shortening] : POLIOMYELITIS

polio- — see POLI-

po·lio·encephalitis \ˌpōlē(ˌ)ō+\ *n* [NL, fr. *poli-* + *encephalitis*] : inflammation of the gray matter of the brain

po·lio·encephalomyelitis \"+\ *n* [NL, fr. *poli-* + *encephal-* + *myelitis*] : inflammation of the gray matter of the brain and the spinal cord

po·lio·myelitic \"+\ *adj* [ISV *poliomyelitis* + *-ic*] : of, relating to, or affected with poliomyelitis

po·lio·myelitis \"+\ *n* [NL, fr. *poli-* + *myelitis*] : an acute infectious virus disease esp. of children that is characterized by fever, motor paralysis, and atrophy of skeletal muscles often with permanent disability and deformity and that results from inflammation and degeneration of the nerve cells in the anterior horns of the gray substance of the spinal cord — called also *acute anterior poliomyelitis, infantile paralysis*

po·lio·neuromere \"+\ *n* [*poli-* + *neuromere*] : a segment of gray matter of the spinal cord

pol·i·or·cet·ic \ˌpälē,ó(r)'sed·ik, -sēd-\ *adj* [Gk *poliorkētikos*, fr. *poliorkētēs* taker of cities (fr. *poliorkein* to besiege, fr. *polis* city + *herkos* fence, enclosure) + *-ikos* -ic — more at POLICE, EXORCISE] : of or relating to poliorcetics

pol·i·or·cet·ics \ˌ≈≈≈'sed·iks, -sēd-\ *n pl but usu sing in constr* [modif. (influenced by *-ics*) of Gk *poliorkētika*, fr. neut. pl. of *poliorkētikos*] : the art of conducting and resisting sieges

po·li·o·sis \ˌpōlē'ōsəs\ *n, pl* **polio·ses** \-ō,sēz\ [NL, fr. Gk *poliōsis* process of becoming gray, fr. *polios* gray + *-ōsis* -osis — more at FALLOW] : loss of color from the hair

polio vaccine *n* : a vaccine intended to confer immunity to poliomyelitis

¹po·lis \'pōləs\ *n, pl* **po·leis** \-ō,līs\ [Gk, city — more at POLICE] : a Greek city-state; *specif* : one in its ideal form as a community embodying the organization and fulfillment of man's social relations ⟨the ∼ is by nature prior to the household and to each of us —C.J.O'Neil⟩

²polis \"\ *Scot & Irish var of* POLICE

-po·lis \p(ə)ləs\ *n comb form* -ES [LL, fr. Gk, fr. *polis*] : city ⟨megal*opolis*⟩

¹pol·ish \'pälish, -lēsh, *esp in pres part* -ləsh\ *vb* -ED/-ING/-ES [ME *polisshen*, fr. OF *poliss-*, stem of *polir* to polish, fr. L *polire*; prob. akin to L *pellere* to drive, beat, push — more at FELT] *vt* **1 :** to make smooth and glossy by a mechanical process usu. by friction : give luster to : BURNISH ⟨glass . . . can be highly ∼*ed* and cut —G.S. & Helen McKearin⟩ ⟨cleanse and ∼ the teeth⟩ — sometimes used with *up* ⟨∼*ed* up the handle of the big front door —W.S.Gilbert⟩ **2 :** to smooth, soften, or refine in manners : free from social roughness, crudeness, or coarseness : imbue with refinement or culture : make elegant, cultured, or polite **3 :** to bring to a highly developed, finished, or refined state : remove technical imperfections or crudities from : improve in style : PERFECT ⟨readers who do not understand us should ∼ their wits —Stuart Chase⟩ ⟨∼*ed* himself into one of the nation's most adept . . . specialists —Oscar Fraley⟩ ⟨∼ our outdoor flag ceremonies —Elin Lindberg⟩ — often used with *up* ⟨∼ up his knowledge of . . . law —Beverly Smith⟩ **4** *archaic* : to transform or eliminate by polishing ⟨an overjudicious author . . . ∼*es* away the strength and energy of his thoughts —*Free-Thinker*⟩ ∼ *vi* : to become smooth : take on a gloss (as from or through friction) ⟨steel ∼*es* well⟩ — **polish apples** : APPLE-POLISH

²polish \"\ *n* -ES **1 :** a condition produced by or as if by polishing: **a :** a smooth glossy surface often produced by friction : GLOSS, LUSTER ⟨jade takes a high ∼⟩ ⟨a table with a high ∼⟩ **b :** an exterior quality characterized by refinement and culture : freedom from rudeness or coarseness ⟨the social class which is . . . still canine under its ∼ —George Meredith⟩ ⟨acquire a . . . university ∼ —Harvey Graham⟩ **c :** a state of high development or refinement : a high quality (as of construction, interpretation, or performance) usu. characterized by a freedom from technical imperfections or crudities ⟨a production more remarkable for high ∼ than warmth of poetic feeling —Richard Garnett †1906⟩ ⟨played . . . with the magnificent dash and ∼ of the true virtuoso —Winthrop Sargeant⟩ **2 :** the action or process of polishing ⟨∼ is the final act of the mollusk in the building of its shell —Joyce Allan⟩ **3 :** a preparation (as a liquid, cream, or wax) that is used to produce a gloss and often a color for the protection and decoration of a surface ⟨stove ∼⟩ ⟨shoe ∼⟩ ⟨furniture ∼⟩ **4 :** RICE POLISH

³pol·ish \'pōlish, -lēsh\ *adj, usu cap* [⁴*Pole* + *-ish*] **1 a :** of, relating to, or characteristic of Poland **b :** of, relating to, or characteristic of the Poles **2 :** of, relating to, or characteristic of the Polish language

⁴polish \"\ *n* **1** -ES *cap* : the Slavic language of the Poles **2 a** *usu cap* : a European breed of crested domestic fowls with small V-shaped combs **b** *pl* **polish**, *often cap* : a bird of this breed **3 a** *usu cap* : a breed of very small snow-white rabbits **b** *pl* **polish** *often cap* : a rabbit of this breed **4** -ES : a lace shoe being five inches or more from the heel seat to the top and having the upper higher at the back than at the front

pol·ish·able \'pälishəbəl\ *adj* : capable of being polished ⟨∼ and well-grained teak —J.H.Stocqueler⟩

¹polish-american \'≈≈'≈≈≈\ *n, cap P&A* : an American of Polish ancestry

²polish-american \"\ *adj, usu cap P&A* : of, relating to, or having the characteristics of a Polish-American

polish berry *n, usu cap P* : a scale (*Margarodes polonicus*) of north and central Europe whose body yields a red dye

polish carpet *or* **polish rug** *n, usu cap P* [³*polish*] **1 :** a Persian rug of the late 16th to 18th centuries having a silk pile and usu. interwoven gold and silver threads **2 :** a tapestry-woven rug in which some metal thread is used

polish checkers *or* **polish draughts** *n pl but sing in constr, usu cap P* : checkers played usu. on a special board of 100 squares in which the men can take opposing men by jumping backward as well as forward and kings can go any distance in one move

pol·ished \'pälisht, -lēsht\ *adj* [ME *polisshed*, fr. past part. of *polisshen* to polish] **1 a :** subjected to polishing : made smooth and glossy by a mechanical process and usu. by friction ⟨∼ plate glass⟩ ⟨∼ granite⟩ **b** (1) **:** naturally smooth and shining ⟨her ∼ cheekbones stood out with a porcelain firmness and finish —Elizabeth Pollet⟩ (2) **:** having a smooth and glossy surface produced by or as if by polishing ⟨trousers of well ∼ . . . homespun —John Buchan⟩ ⟨the young man's hair was ∼⟩ ⟨reflections . . . in that shining, ∼, shimmering expanse —Marjory S. Douglas⟩ **2 :** marked by cultivation and urbanity : characterized by elegance and refinement ⟨the growth of ∼ society —C.H.Grandgent⟩ ⟨the easy culture of a ∼ man of rank —J.A.Froude⟩ ⟨graces in the demeanor of a ∼ and noble person —R.W.Emerson⟩ **3 :** having, brought to, or characterized by a high degree of development, finish, or refinement : free from imperfections (as of interpretation, construction, or performance) ⟨highly ∼ piece of writing —B.C.L. Keelan⟩ ⟨∼ French⟩ ⟨his ∼, luminous, and animated eloquence —T.B.Macaulay⟩ ⟨the most ∼ actress whom this century has known —E.H.Collis⟩

polished rice *n* : white rice that is given a polish by rapidly revolving cylinders covered with pigskin

pol·ish·er \-shə(r)\ *n* -S : one that polishes: as **a :** a worker who polishes an article by hand or by machine to give it a clean smooth and usu. glossy finish **b :** a bookbinder's hand tool used hot to polish leathers, crush down leather grains, and eliminate blisters on cloth covers

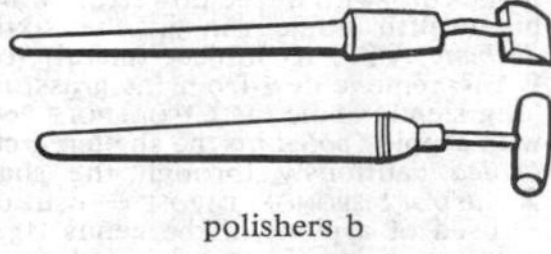

polishers b

polishing iron *n* : an iron burnisher; *esp* : a small smoothing iron used in laundries

polishing wheel *n* : a wheel consisting of layers of fabric impregnated with abrasive and adhesive for polishing

polish millet *n, usu cap P* : a crabgrass (*Digitaria sanguinalis*)

polish off *vt* : to finish off quickly or out of hand: as **a :** to knock out (as an opponent) ⟨handily *polished off* some of the best . . . middleweights —*Time*⟩ **b :** to dispose of summarily : finish off hastily : complete and dispense with ⟨*polished off* a volume in the evening —O.W.Holmes †1935⟩ ⟨the players *polished* this quintet *off* with a fierce brilliance⟩ **c :** to consume rapidly and completely ⟨*polished* the chicken *off* between them⟩

polish plait *n, usu cap 1st P* : PLICA 1

polish rabbit *n, usu cap P* : a rabbit of the Polish breed

polish sausage *n, usu cap P* : smoked link sausage made of coarsely ground pork and beef seasoned with garlic

polish swan *n, usu cap P* : a color phase of the mute swan having pale gray legs and feet

polish wheat *n, usu cap P* : a wheat (*Triticum polonicum*) or any of its varieties having large loose spikes with conspicuous papery glumes and very hard large long yellowish white kernels resembling those of durum wheat

po·lis·man \'pōləsmən\ *Scot & Irish var of* POLICEMAN

po·lis·soir \ˌpōlē'swär\ *n* -S [F, polishing implement, fr. MF, fr. *poliss-*, stem of *polir* to polish — more at POLISH] : a tool consisting of a flat wooden block with a long iron or steel handle and used in glass manufacturing for flattening out split cylinders of blown glass : an implement used for polishing or grinding

po·lis·tes \pō'li,stēz\ *n* [NL, fr. Gk *polistēs* founder of a city, fr. *polizein* to build a city, fr. *polis* city + *-izein* -ize — more at POLICE] **1** *cap* : an extensive genus of social wasps that have a spindle-shaped abdomen and wings which fold like a fan, are mostly black with yellow or brown markings, and make nests consisting of a single comb of papery material suspended by a peduncle and having no envelope **2** *pl* **polistes :** any wasp of the genus *Polistes*

polit *abbr* political

pol·i·tarch \'pälə,tärk\ *n* -S [Gk *politarchēs*, fr. *politēs* citizen + *-archēs* -arch] : a municipal magistrate in countries of the eastern Mediterranean under the Roman Empire ⟨the seven ∼*s* who ruled the city —*United Presbyterian Mag.*⟩

pol·it·bu·ro *also* **pol·i·tbu·reau** \'pälət,byü(ˌ)rō 'pōl- *also* pə'lit- *or* pə'lēt-\ *n* -S [*politburo* fr. Russ *politbyuro*, fr. *politicheskoe byuro* political bureau; *politbureau* part trans. of Russ *politbyuro*] **1 :** the principal policy-making and executive committee of a Communist party ⟨member of the Chinese ∼⟩ ⟨replacement of the Russian ∼ by a presidium⟩ — compare PRESIDIUM **2 :** an organized group held to resemble a Communist politburo in having a controlling position and absolute power

po·lite \pə'līt, pō'-, *usu* -īd+V\ *adj, often* -ER/-EST [ME *polyt*, fr. L *politus*, past part. of *polire* to smooth, polish — more at POLISH] **1** *obs* : POLISHED 1a ⟨edifices . . . made of the *politest* stone —William Whiston⟩ **2** *obs* : in good order : well kept : NEAT, TIDY **3 a :** of, belonging to, or having the characteristics of advanced culture : exhibiting polish, cultivation, elegance, and refinement : characterized by elevated and preferential usages ⟨Latin . . . became the vehicle of ∼ as well as official intercourse —H.O.Taylor⟩ ⟨part of a ∼ schooling —F.J. Mather⟩ ⟨∼ society⟩ ⟨∼ languages⟩ **b :** marked by refined cultured interests and pursuits esp. in arts and belles lettres and usu. not scientific, utilitarian, or controversial in character ⟨the Revolutionary upheaval produced no ∼ literature . . . comparable to its utilitarian prose —V.L.Parrington⟩ **4 a :** showing or characterized by correct social usage : marked by or exhibiting an appearance of consideration, tact, deference, courtesy, or grace resulting sometimes from sincere consideration of others and sometimes from mere regard for etiquette ⟨∼ answer⟩ ⟨∼ letter⟩ ⟨a man who thinks of living in the great world must be gallant, ∼, and attentive to please the women —Earl of Chesterfield⟩ **b :** marked by a lack of roughness or crudities : gentle or moderate in tone : designed not to offend ⟨things . . . ignored or minimized in ∼ history —G.G.Coulton⟩

syn see CIVIL

po·lite·ful \-ītfəl\ *adj* : full of politeness : very polite

pol·i·teia \ˌpälə'tīə\ *n* -S [Gk, constitution, citizenship, administration of government — more at POLICE] : CONSTITUTION; *specif* : the whole order of social and political relationships in a polis

po·lite·ly *adv* : in a polite manner: as **a** *obs* : SMOOTHLY ⟨no marble statue can be ∼ carved —John Milton⟩ **b** *obs* : in an elegant, polished, and cultured manner ⟨a niece whom he has ∼ educated in expensive finery —William Law⟩ **c :** in a courteous, socially correct, or refined manner : TACTFULLY ⟨∼ received by the dons and fellows —Romeyn Berry⟩ ⟨ruined or what we would now call ~ submarginal land —G.P.Musselman⟩

po·lite·ness *n* -ES **1** : the quality or state of being polite: as **a** *archaic* : mental polish : intellectual culture or refinement : elegance and good taste (as in a literary work) ⟨renowned for the ~ of the character and editions of what he has published —John Evelyn⟩ **b** : polished or refined manners : courteous or socially correct behavior ⟨~ mustn't be mistaken for civility —Richard Joseph⟩ ⟨the art of chill and consummate ~ —Arnold Bennett⟩ ⟨~ forbade they should contradict him —Samuel Lover⟩ **2** : a polite act or statement ⟨the old man, with many ~*es* . . . led him —*New Yorker*⟩ ⟨cutting ~*es* out of telegrams —Arnold Bennett⟩

pol·i·tes \ˈpälə,tēz\ *n, cap* [NL, prob. fr. Gk *politēs* citizen] : a widely distributed genus of skipper butterflies

pol·i·tesse \,pälə'tes\ *n* -S [F (influenced in meaning by F *poli* polished, polite, past part. of *polir* to polish), fr. MF, cleanness, neatness, fr. OIt *pulitezza*, fr. *pulito* clean, neat, polished (past part. of *pulire* to clean, polish), fr. L *politus* polished, past part. of *polire* to polish] : formal and cultivated politeness : DECOROUSNESS ⟨holding his temper on a rigid course with rules of ~ —*N.Y.Times*⟩ ⟨excel in hospitality, in ~, and . . . in kindness —*Harper's*⟩

po·li·tian \pō'lishən\ *n* -S [MF *policien*, fr. *policie* conduct of public affairs, administration of government + *-en* -an (fr. L *-anus*) — more at POLICY] *archaic* : POLITICIAN

¹pol·i·tic \ˈpälə,tik\ *adj* [ME *politik*, fr. MF *politique*, fr. L *politicus*, fr. Gk *politikos*, fr. *politēs* citizen + *-ikos* -ic — more at POLICE] **1** : POLITICAL ⟨their superiors in ~ and military virtues —Edmund Burke⟩ ⟨he with all his people made all but one ~ body —Philip Sidney⟩ — see BODY POLITIC **2** : characterized by shrewdness : skillfully contrived : EXPEDIENT, JUDICIOUS ⟨this land was famously enrich'd with ~ grave counsel —Shak.⟩ ⟨neither polite nor ~ to get into other people's quarrels —Ruth Park⟩ ⟨so long as it was ~ to profess loyalty —V.L.Parrington⟩ **3** : of, relating to, or having the nature of a constitutional as distinguished from a despotic government : CONSTITUTIONAL ⟨from . . . ~ government the inhabitants were brought under tyranny —Thomas Washington⟩ **4** : sagacious in devising or promoting a policy : skillful or ingenious in statecraft : prudent in management : characterized by political skill and ingenuity ⟨an astute and ~ statesman⟩ **5** : exercising, manifesting, or proceeding from craft : artful in address or procedure : shrewdly tactful : CUNNING, WORLDLY-WISE ⟨a ~ answer⟩ ⟨a ~ move⟩ ⟨a very ~ adversary⟩ **syn** see EXPEDIENT, SUAVE

²politic \"\ *n* -S **1** *archaic* : POLITICIAN ⟨amongst statesmen and ~*s* —Francis Bacon⟩ **2** *obs* : POLICY ⟨this did not suit with popish ~ —Richard Bentley †1742⟩ **3** *obs* : one that is indifferent toward religious matters : one concerned more with the affairs of the world than with religion ⟨worldlings and depraved ~*s* who are apt to condemn holy things —Francis Bacon⟩

¹po·lit·i·cal \pə'lid·ə̇kəl, pō'-, -it|, |ēk-, *in rapid speech* 'pli-\ *adj* [L *politicus* political + E *-al*] **1 a** : of or relating to government, a government, or the conduct of governmental affairs **b** : of or relating to matters of government as distinguished from matters of law ⟨~ sovereignty⟩ ⟨~ recognition of a new nation⟩ — compare LEGAL 3a **c** : engaged in civil as distinguished from military functions ⟨a ~ officer⟩ — see POLITICAL AGENT **d** : of, relating to, or concerned with the making as distinguished from the administration of governmental policy **2** *archaic* : POLITIC 2 ⟨whether it would be ~ to interfere —James Mill⟩ **3 a** : of, relating to, or concerned with politics **b** : of, relating to, or involved in party politics ⟨~ activity⟩ ⟨~ party⟩ — compare ADMINISTRATIVE, NONPARTISAN **4** : organized in governmental terms — see POLITICAL UNIT

²political \"\ *n* -S : one associated with politics; *esp* : POLITICAL PRISONER ⟨hundreds of ~*s* . . . who had escaped from a concentration camp —Anthony West⟩

political action *n* : action designed to attain a purpose by the use of political power or by activity in political channels; *specif* : such action by organized labor through recognized political means (as participation in party organization, in elections, and by lobbying) — contrasted with *direct action*

political agent *n* : an official appointed by the British government to act as resident adviser to the ruler of a protected state

political arithmetic *n* : a 17th and 18th century science dealing chiefly with the economic and demographic statistics of a political unit (as a nation or state)

political commissar *n* : COMMISSAR 1a

political crime *or* **political offense** *n* : a violation of the law or of the public peace for political rather than private reasons; *specif* : one directed against a particular government or political system ⟨*political offenses* . . . exclude any possibility of extradition —R.G.Neumann⟩

political economist *n* : a specialist in political economy

political economy *n* **1** : an 18th century branch of the art of government concerned with directing governmental policies toward the promotion of the wealth of the government and the community as a whole **2 a** : a 19th century social science comprising the modern science of economics but concerned principally with governmental as contrasted with commercial or personal economics **b** : a modern social science dealing with the interrelationship of political and economic processes

political executive *n* : the executive at the head of a government as contrasted with a chief of state

political geography *n* : a branch of geography that deals with human governments, the boundaries and subdivisions of political units (as nations or states), and the situations of cities — compare GEOPOLITICS

po·lit·i·cal·iza·tion \pə,lid·ə̇kələ'zāshən\ *n* -S : the action or process of politicalizing ⟨the total ~ of Russian arts and artists —*Saturday Rev.*⟩ ⟨the all-out ~ of economic life —J.H. Spigelman⟩

po·lit·i·cal·ize \pə'lid·ə̇kə,līz\ *vt* -ED/-ING/-S : to make political : imbue with politics ⟨the total state which seeks to ~ everything —*Saturday Rev.*⟩ ⟨combats the effort to ~ literature —C.I.Glicksberg⟩

political liberty *n* : the state or condition of those who are invested with the right effectually to share in framing and conducting the government under which they are politically organized — compare INDIVIDUAL LIBERTY

po·lit·i·cal·ly \pə'lid·ə̇|k(ə)lē, pō'-, -it|, |ēk-, -li, *in rapid speech* 'pli-\ *adv* **1** *archaic* : in a politic manner : POLITICLY ⟨~ pretended the utmost submission —Oliver Goldsmith⟩ **2** : in political terms : from a political point of view ⟨basic decisions . . . must be made by ~ accountable civilian officials —D.D. Eisenhower⟩ ⟨the ~ relevant aspects of cultures —Richard McKeon⟩ ⟨~ conscious people⟩

po·lit·i·cal·ness *n* -ES : the quality or state of being political

political party *n* : ¹PARTY 3b(1)

political prisoner *n* : a person in custody or imprisoned for a political offense

political process *n* : the process of the formulation and administration of public policy usu. by interaction between social groups and political institutions or between political leadership and public opinion

political rights *n pl* : the rights that involve participation in the establishment or administration of a government and are usu. held to entitle the adult citizen to exercise of the franchise, the holding of public office, and other political activities — compare CIVIL RIGHTS

political science *n* : a social science concerned chiefly with the description and analysis of political and esp. governmental institutions and processes and making use of factual material and methods selected from other social sciences (as sociology, psychology, economics, and history) : the study of the phenomena of politics : a science dealing with the political rather than the social, ethical, or economic relations of man : a field of inquiry devoted to an analysis of power in society — compare COMPARATIVE GOVERNMENT, CONSTITUTIONAL LAW, INTERNATIONAL RELATIONS, POLITICAL THEORY 2, POLITICS 8b, PUBLIC ADMINISTRATION

political scientist *n* : a specialist in political science

political theory *n* **1 a** : a theory having to do with the political relationships among men; *specif* : one concerned with the organization and basis of government ⟨*political theories* are generated by social frictions —A.S.Kaufman⟩ **b** : the general body of such theories ⟨a history of *political theory*⟩ **2** : a branch of political science concerned chiefly with the ideas of past and present political thinkers and the doctrines and proposals of political movements and groups ⟨discussion of the proper scope of governmental action . . . has usually been regarded as a proper part of *political theory* —F.W.Coker⟩

political unit *n* : a unit of territory defined by boundaries set by political authority and usu. having a separate political organization

political verse *n* : Byzantine or Modern Greek accentual verse; *esp* : verse of 15-syllabled iambic lines

po·lit·i·cas·ter \pə'lid·ə,kastə(r), ⸗,⸗⸗'⸗⸗\ *n* -S [prob. fr. ²*politic* + *-aster*] : an unstatesmanlike practitioner of politics : a petty or contemptible politician ⟨timorous, trimming ~*s*, all for the party without thought of the state —*N.Y.Times*⟩

po·li·ti·cian \,pälə'tishən\ *n* -S [¹*politic* + *-an*] **1** *obs* : a politic person; *esp* : a shrewd or crafty schemer **2** : one experienced in the art or science of government : one actively engaged in conducting the business of a government : one skilled or experienced in politics : STATESMAN ⟨a power ~⟩ ⟨the ~ and the civil servant work harmoniously together —Alexander Brady⟩ ⟨at once a barbarian potentate and an ambitious European ~ —J.A.Froude⟩ **3** : one addicted to or actively engaged in party politics: as **a** : one engaged in party politics as a profession or as a means of livelihood **b** : one primarily interested in political offices or profits derived from them as a source of private gain — often used disparagingly **c** : one motivated by narrow (as group, sectional, or personal) and usu. short-run interests as contrasted with the long-term welfare of the people as a whole — compare STATESMAN **4** *obs* : POLITIQUE

po·lit·i·cist \pə'lid·əsəst\ *n* -S [¹*politic* + *-ist*] : POLITICAL SCIENTIST

po·lit·i·cize \-d·ə,sīz\ *vb* -ED/-ING/-S [¹*politic* + *-ize*] *vi* : to discuss or discourse upon politics ~ *vt* : to give a political tone or character to : to bring within the realm of politics ⟨we want to moralize politics and not to ~ morals —K.R.Popper⟩ ⟨attempts to ~ the civil service⟩

pol·i·tick \ˈpälə,tik\ *vi* -ED/-ING/-S [prob. back-formation fr. *politics*] : to engage in political discussion or activity

pol·i·tick·er \-kə(r)\ *n* -S : one that politicks ⟨a big ~ for the governor's machine —John Beecher⟩

pol·i·tic·ly *adv* : in a politic manner : CRAFTILY, SHREWDLY ⟨purposely and ~ selected them as a foil to himself —E.S. Barrett⟩

pol·i·tic·ness *n* -ES : the quality or state of being politic

po·lit·i·co \pə'lid·ə,kō, pō'-, -itə,-\ *n, pl* **politicos** *also* **politicoes** [It *politico* or Sp *político*; It *politico* fr. *politico*, adj., political, fr. L *politicus*; Sp *político* fr. *político*, adj., political, fr. L *politicus* — more at POLITIC] : POLITICIAN 3 ⟨cringing ~*s* who bend to their influence —E.H.Wilson⟩ ⟨some sharp ~*s* . . . think the president won't run —*Wall Street Jour.*⟩ ⟨the support of veteran ~*s* throughout the state —W.V.Shannon⟩

politico- *comb form* [NL, fr. L *politicus* political] **1** : political and ⟨*politico*-diplomatic⟩ ⟨*politico*-military⟩ **2** : politics ⟨*politico*mania⟩ ⟨*politico*phobia⟩ **3** : political ⟨*politico*-pressure⟩ : politically ⟨*politico*-nationalist⟩ ⟨*politico*-orthodox⟩

pol·i·tics \ˈpälə,tiks\ *n pl but sing or pl in constr* [prob. modif. (influenced by *-ics*) of Gk *politika*, fr. neut. pl. of *politikos* political — more at POLITIC] **1 a** : the art or science of government : a science dealing with the regulation and control of men living in society : a science concerned with the organization, direction, and administration of political units (as nations or states) in both internal and external affairs : the art of adjusting and ordering relationships between individuals and groups in a political community **b** (1) : the art or science concerned with guiding or influencing governmental policy (2) : the art or science concerned with winning and holding control over a government (as by selection of governmental personnel) — compare PARTY POLITICS **2** : a branch of ethics concerned with the state or social organism as a whole rather than the individual person : a division of moral philosophy dealing with the ethical relations and duties of governments or other social organizations : public or social ethics **3** : political actions, practices, or policies ⟨protested against the ~ of the Vichy government —*Current Biog.*⟩ ⟨the same ~ were followed by his successors —*New Republic*⟩ ⟨it was not good ~ . . . to present this menacing figure as an incompetent fool —Gilbert Seldes⟩ **4 a** (1) : political affairs or business; *specif* : competition between competing interest groups or individuals for power and leadership (2) : activities concerned with governing or with influencing or winning and holding control of a government ⟨flinch at the thought of . . . participation in partisan ~ —John Lodge⟩ ⟨a university in which ~ had no place —Marjory S. Douglas⟩ ⟨trying to understand recent French ~ —Julian Towster⟩ (3) : activities concerned with achieving control, advancement, or some other goal in a nongovernmental group (as a club or office) **b** : political life esp. as a principal activity or profession ⟨~ is . . . the noblest career that a man can choose —J.L.McConaughy⟩ ⟨entered ~⟩ **c** : political activities characterized by artful and often dishonest practices esp. in securing the success of political parties or candidates ⟨dirty ward ~⟩ ⟨in the underworld of ~ —H.R.Penniman⟩ **5** : conduct of or policy in private affairs ⟨reading a lecture on . . . matrimonial ~ —Henry Fielding⟩ **6** : the political principles, convictions, opinions, or sympathies of a person ⟨his ~ was . . . reactionary enough —Lionel Trilling⟩ ⟨changed his ~ for advancement's sake —W.B.Yeats⟩ ⟨a woman's ~ are the man she loves —Owen Rhoscomyl⟩ **7** : the total complex of interacting and usu. conflicting relations between men living in society: **a** : the relations between men concerned with governing or with influencing or winning and holding control over a government **b** : the relations between leaders and nonleaders in any social grouping (as a political community, church, club, or trade union) **8 a** : POLITICAL SCIENCE **b** : the branch of political science dealing with the activities of political parties and pressure groups

pol·i·tique \,pälə'tēk\ *n* -S *usu cap* [F, fr. MF, fr. *politique*, adj., political, fr. L *politicus*] : one of a group of French moderates in the 16th century religious conflicts holding national unity of greater importance than the absolute predominance of a single sect and advocating religious toleration as the policy of the government

pol·i·ti·za·tion \,päləd·ə'zāshən\ *n* -S [irreg. fr. *politicize* + *-ation*] : the action or result of politicizing ⟨growing ~ and bureaucratization of the social structure —S.N.Eisenstadt⟩

pol·i·ture \ˈpälə,chů(ə)r\ *n* -S [It *pulitura*, fr. L *politura*, fr. *politus* polished (past part. of *polire* to polish) + *-ura* -ure — more at POLISH] *archaic* : ²POLISH 1 ⟨the beauty, ~, and hardness of shells —Emanuel Mendez da Costa⟩ ⟨men who wanted the ~ and the fineness of this age —John Johnson⟩

pol·i·ty \ˈpäləd·|ē, -ət|, |i\ *n* -ES [LL & L; LL *politia* conduct of public affairs, administration of government, fr. L, state — more at POLICE] **1** : political organization : civil order ⟨any form of ~ is more efficient than none —Walter Bagehot⟩ **2 a** : a specific form of political organization : a form of government ⟨a mixed ~⟩ ⟨an equalitarian ~⟩ **b** : an Aristotelian form of political organization in which the whole body of the people govern for the good of all and that constitutes a fusion of oligarchy and democracy **3** : the management of public or private affairs; *esp* : prudent, shrewd, or crafty administration ⟨I know little of stratagem and ~ —E.R.B.Lytton⟩ **4** : a politically organized unit (as a nation, state, or community) ⟨the humanistic spirit flourished . . . under various *polities* in Greece —Norman Foerster⟩ ⟨a dispute between the temporal and spiritual powers within the universal ~ —Renzo Sereno⟩ **5 a** : the form or constitution of a politically organized unit (as a nation or state) ⟨the character of the English ~ was gradually changing —T.B.Macaulay⟩ ⟨retains in some measure the traditional ~ of the states —*Indian White Paper*⟩ **b** : the form of government or organization of a religious denomination ⟨argued for a congregational ~ —J.C.Brauer⟩ ⟨wanted to change the ~ of the Anglican church —J.E.Neale⟩ **6** : POLICY ⟨stand up against flagrant wrongdoings . . . or against *polities* fatal to the nation —F.L.Paxson⟩

po·litz·er bag \pō'litsə(r)-\ *n, sometimes cap P* [after Adam *Politzer* †1920 Austrian otologist] : a soft rubber bulb used to inflate the middle ear by increasing air pressure in the nasopharynx

pol·je \ˈpōlye\ *n* -S [Serbo-Croatian, lit., field; akin to OSlav *polje* field — more at FLOOR] : an extensive depression having a flat floor and steep walls but no outflowing surface stream and found in a region having karst topography (as in parts of Yugoslavia)

polk *var of* POLK

¹pol·ka \ˈpōlkə *sometimes* ˈpōkə\ *n* -S *often attrib* [Czech, fr. Pol *Polka* Polish woman, fem. of *Polak* Pole] **1** : a vivacious couple dance of Bohemian origin with three steps and a hop in duple time **2** : a lively Bohemian dance tune in $\frac{2}{4}$ time

rhythm of a polka

²polka \"\ *also* **polk** \ˈpōlk\ *vi* -ED/-ING/-S [*polka* fr. ¹*polka*; *polk* irreg. fr. ¹*polka*] : to dance the polka

³polka \"\ *also* **polka jacket** *n* -S [¹*polka*] : a close-fitting often knitted jacket worn by women

polka dot \ˈpōkə- *also* ˈpōlkə-\ *n* [¹*polka* + *dot*, n.] : a dot of varying size usu. used in a pattern of one size dots evenly distributed in diamond outlines on a background of contrasting color esp. in textile design

polka-dot \ˈ⸗⸗,⸗\ *vt* [*polka dot*] : to spot with or as if with polka dots ⟨the tracks of mountain goats *polka-dotted* the dusty ridge —R.L.Neuberger⟩

polka mazurka *n* **1** : a modified polka using a mazurka step **2** : a dance tune in slow triple time accented on the last beat

¹poll \ˈpōl\ *n* -S *often attrib* [ME *pol, polle*, fr. MLG, head, top; prob. akin to L *bulla* bubble, LGk *bylla* stuffed things, Lith *bulis* buttocks] **1 a** : ¹HEAD 1 ⟨set his hat back on his ~ —Bryan MacMahon⟩ ⟨scratching his ~ —C.G.Glover⟩ **b** *obs* : ¹SKULL 1 **2 a** : a unit or an individual in a number ⟨a tax of forty pounds . . . per ~ to support the church —*Amer. Guide Series: Md.*⟩ **3 a** (1) : the hair-covered back and top of the human head ⟨all flaxen was his ~ —Shak.⟩ ⟨close-cropped ~*s* —T.B.Costain⟩ (2) : the region between the ears of some quadrupeds — see COW illustration **b** *obs* : CROWN 3a(1) **c** : ¹NAPE ⟨pierced his neck from throat to ~ —Thomas Hobbes⟩ **4** : the broad or flat end of a hammer or similar tool **5 a** (1) : the casting or recording of the votes of a body of persons : the voting at an election ⟨on the eve of the ~ —*Canadian Forum*⟩ (2) : a counting of votes cast (as in an election) **b** : the place where votes are cast or recorded — usu. used in pl. ⟨at the ~*s*, a voter . . . votes the ticket of his choice —F.A.Ogg & P.O.Ray⟩ ⟨as the voter leaves the ~*s*⟩ **c** : the period of time during which votes may be cast at an election ⟨the ~ at the . . . universities is restricted to five days —T.E.May⟩ **d** : the numerical result of the counting of votes cast : the total number of votes recorded ⟨a heavy ~⟩ ⟨elected to Congress at the head of the ~ —C.G.Bowers⟩ ⟨topped the popularity ~ —Myles McSweeney⟩ ⟨the ~ was low —*Blackwood's*⟩ **6** *obs* : a counting of heads : CENSUS **7** : POLL TAX ⟨an act for raising money by a ~ —*London Gazette*⟩ **8** : the crown of a hat or cap **9 a** : a questioning or canvassing of persons usu. selected at random or by quota from various groups for obtaining information or opinions esp. to be analyzed ⟨what a ~ gains in extensiveness it loses in intensiveness —L.W.Doob⟩ **b** : a record of the information obtained in such a poll ⟨his position has shifted in popularity ~*s* —John Mason Brown⟩

²poll \"\ *vb* -ED/-ING/-S [ME *pollen*, fr. *pol, polle*, n.] *vt* **1 a** : to cut off or cut short the hair or wool of : CLIP, CROP, SHEAR ⟨~ a man⟩ ⟨~ a man's head⟩ ⟨~ sheep⟩ **b** : to cut off or cut short (as hair or wool) **2** *archaic* : to plunder by or as if by excessive taxation : practice extortion on : DESPOIL, FLEECE, ROB ⟨the prince doth too much ~ his subjects with heavy tributes —George Wharton⟩ **3 a** : to cut off the head or top of (as a tree or plant); *specif* : POLLARD 1 **b** : to cut off or cut short the horns of (cattle) **4 a** : to receive and record the votes of ⟨the first . . . election to ~ the newly enfranchised women voters —Marion Wilhelm⟩ **b** (1) : to call on each member of (as a jury) to answer individually as to his concurrence in a verdict rendered (2) : to request each member of (as a delegation at a convention) to declare his vote individually **5** : to cut even without indentation — compare DEED POLL **6** *obs* : to count the heads of (as a group of persons) : ENUMERATE **7** : to receive (as votes) in or as if in an election ⟨his party . . . ~*ed* nearly twelve and a half million votes —Douglas Stuart⟩ ⟨~*ed* . . . 30 to 40 percent of the general election vote —V.O. Key⟩ **8** : to question or canvass in a poll ⟨70 percent of those ~*ed*⟩ ⟨~ attitudes on public issues⟩ ⟨~*ed* members of the delegation⟩ ~ *vi* : to cast one's vote at a poll : vote at an election ⟨a million Liberal voters ~*ed* for Conservative candidates —*Contemporary Rev.*⟩

³poll \"\ *adj* [prob. short for *polled*, past part. of ²*poll*] : polled rather than indented — used of a legal document; compare DEED POLL

⁴poll \"\ *n* -S [prob. fr. obs. E *poll*, adj., naturally hornless, short for E ¹*polled*] : a polled animal ⟨a Scotch ~⟩

⁵poll \ˈpäl, ˈpól\ *n* -S [fr. *Poll*, alter. of *Moll*, nickname for *Mary*] : POLL PARROT

⁶poll \ˈpäl\ *n* -S [Gk *polloi* many, pl. of *polys* much — more at POLY-] **1** : a group of students (as at Cambridge University) taking a pass degree rather than honors **2** *or* **poll degree** : a pass or ordinary degree (as at Cambridge) : a degree without honors

pol·lack *or* **pol·lock** \ˈpälək\ *n, pl* **pollack** *also* **pollacks** *or* **pollock** *also* **pollocks** [alter. of earlier *podlok*] : an important and highly esteemed marine food fish (*Pollachius virens*) of both coasts of the north Atlantic related to and resembling the cods but darker and more lustrous and with a longer lower jaw — called also *bluefish, coalfish, saithe*; see WALLEYE POLLACK

pol·lam \ˈpäləm\ *n* -S [Tamil *pāḷaiyam*, fr. Skt *pālayati* he guards; prob. akin to Skt *piparti* he brings over, rescues] : a district in India held in feudal tenure by a poligar

pol·lan *also* **pol·len** \ˈpälən\ *n, pl* **pollan** [origin unknown] : a whitefish (*Coregonus pollan*) of Irish lakes

¹pol·lard \ˈpälə(r)d\ *n* -S [ME, fr. *pol, polle* head + *-ard* — more at POLL] **1** : a clipped or base coin of foreign origin current in England in the late 13th century and equivalent to a penny — compare CROCARD **2** *obs* **a** : a stag that has cast its antlers **b** : a hornless animal (as a cow or sheep) **3 a** : a coarse bran obtained from wheat **b** : finely ground bran together with the scourings obtained from wheat during milling and used for livestock feed **4** : a tree that has been cut back to the trunk to promote the growth of a dense head of foliage

²pollard \"\ *adj* : having been pollarded : made into a pollard ⟨under the ~ lime trees —John Galsworthy⟩ ⟨a ~ oak⟩

³pollard \"\ *vt* -ED/-ING/-S **1** : to remove the crown of (a tree) : cut back or convert into a pollard ⟨~*ed* willows⟩ **2** : to cut or cause to become stunted in a manner suggesting a pollard

pollax *or* **pollaxe** *var of* POLEAX

poll–bill *n, obs* : a legislative bill providing for a poll tax ⟨levied . . . by a *poll-bill* and new assessments —David Hume †1776⟩

pollbook \ˈ⸗,⸗\ *n* **1** : an official register formerly used to record votes at an election **2** : an official register of electors entitled to vote at an election

poll clerk *n* : a clerk employed at an election esp. in recording votes

poll deed *n* : DEED POLL

¹polled \ˈpōld\ *adj* [ME, fr. past part. of *pollen* to poll, crop, shear — more at POLL] **1** *obs* : closely cropped or shaven ⟨~ heads⟩ **2** : having no horns : deprived of or having shed horns ⟨a ~ stag⟩ : naturally hornless ⟨~ cattle⟩ **3** : POLLARD ⟨~ trees⟩

²polled \ˌpōld\ *adj* [¹*poll* + *-ed*] : having a poll usu. of a specified kind — used chiefly in combination ⟨a red-*polled* girl⟩

polled angus *n, usu cap P&A* : ABERDEEN ANGUS

polled durham *or* **polled shorthorn** *n* **1** *usu cap P&D&S* : a hornless variety of the cattle breed Shorthorn **2** *often cap P&D&S* : an animal of the Polled Durham variety

polled·ness *n* -ES : the state of being hornless ⟨~ in cattle and sheep is usu. considered to be caused by a dominant but epistatic gene⟩

poll·ee \(ˈ)pō¦lē\ *n* -S : one who is questioned in a poll ⟨cited by 90 percent of the ~*s* —*N.Y. Times Bk. Rev.*⟩

¹pol·len \ˈpälən\ *n* -S *often attrib* [L *pollin-, pollen* fine flour, fine dust; akin to L *pollenta* pearl barley, *pulvis* dust, Gk *palē* fine meal, dust, *poltos* porridge, and prob. to Skt *palala* ground sesame seeds] **1** *obs* : fine flour or meal **2** [NL *pollin-, pollen,* fr. L] **a :** a mass of microspores in a seed plant appearing usu. as a fine dust made up of minute granular microspores typically formed in fours by reduction of a pollen mother cell with each grain consisting of a single cell that has a characteristically sculptured outer wall and gives rise on germination to a pollen tube through which its male generative element passes to the ovule for fertilization of the egg — compare TETRAD **b :** a dusty or pruinous bloom on the body of various insects

²pollen \"\ *vt* -ED/-ING/-S **:** to cover with pollen **:** POLLINATE

³pollen \"\ *var of* POLLAN

pollen analysis *n* **:** the identification and determination of frequency of pollen grains in peat bogs and other preservative situations as a means of dating fossil and other remains **:** the study of past vegetations and climates as indicated by the pollen content of the various layers of the earth's surface

pol·len·ate \'pälə,nāt, *usu* -ād·+V\ *vt* -ED/-ING/-S [by alter. (influenced by ¹*pollen*)] **:** POLLINATE 1

pol·len·ation \,pälə'nāshən\ *also* **pol·len·iza·tion** \,pälənə'zāshən\ *n* -s [*pollenation* alter. (influenced by ¹*pollen*) of *pollination; pollenization* fr. *pollenize* + *-ation*] **:** POLLINATION

pollen basket *n* **:** a smooth area on each hind tibia of a bee that is edged by a fringe of stiff hairs and serves to collect and transport pollen

pollen brush *n* **:** a scopa used in collecting pollen; *specif* **:** an arrangement of stiff hairs forming the margin of a pollen basket

pollen catarrh *or* **pollen fever** *n* **:** POLLINOSIS

pollen chamber *n* **:** a small chamber at the apex of the nucleus in some plants (as most gymnosperms) for the reception of the pollen

pollen count *n* **:** a count of the pollen content of the air useful in determining its infectivity in pollinosis

pollened *adj* [fr. past part. of ²*pollen*] **:** covered with or containing pollen

pollen grain *n* **:** one of the microsporic grains of which pollen is made up

pol·len·ize \'pälə,nīz\ *vt* -ED/-ING/-S [¹*pollen* + *-ize*] **:** POLLINATE ⟨bees *pollenized* the fruit trees —Betty MacDonald⟩

pol·len·iz·er \-zə(r)\ *n* -s **1 :** a plant that is a source of pollen ⟨there are wild apples that are effective ~*s*⟩; *esp* **:** a plant provided (as in an orchard) primarily to supply pollen to plants of another variety that are either deficient in pollen or self-sterile **2 :** POLLINATOR a

pollen–lethal \'⸗⸗'⸗⸗\ *n* -s **:** a lethal gene acting directly on the pollen grain that contains it

pollen mass *n* **:** POLLINIUM

pollen mother cell *n* **:** a cell that is derived from the hypodermis of the pollen sac and that gives rise by meiosis to four cells, each of which develops into a pollen grain

pol·le·noph·a·gous \,pälə'näfəgəs\ *adj* [¹*pollen* + *-o-* + *-phagous*] **:** feeding on pollen

pollenosis *var of* POLLINOSIS

pollen parent *n* **:** a male parent

pollen plate *n* **:** POLLEN BASKET

pollen profile *n* **:** the vertical distribution or stratification of buried or fossil pollen in any horizon or other layer of the earth's surface as an indicator of ancient vegetation

pollen sac *n* **:** one of the sacs in a seed plant that contain the pollen and that are initially four in number but are commonly reduced to two by disintegration of the intervening walls in the mature anther

pollen tube *n* **:** the tube that develops from the wall of a pollen grain and that in some forms (as the cycads) acts as a haustellate organ and in seed plants provides a passage through which the male nuclei reach the embryo sac to effect fertilization

poll·er \'pōlə(r)\ *n* -s **:** one that polls: as **a** *obs* **:** one that plunders or extorts esp. by the gathering of excessive taxes **b :** one that polls or lops trees **c :** POLLSTER ⟨answers . . . collected by the ~*s* —J.W.Albig⟩ ⟨sampling techniques . . . used in recent years by public opinion ~*s* —J.R.Miller⟩

po·lle·ra \pə'yerə\ *n* -s [AmerSp, fr. Sp, baby walker, chicken coop, fr. *pollo* chicken, fr. L *pullus* young fowl, young of an animal — more at FOAL] **:** a Latin-American fiesta costume usu. heavily embroidered and very full in the skirt

pollera

poll evil *n* **:** an inflammation identical with fistulous withers except in being located on the poll of a horse

pol·lex \'pä,leks\ *n, pl* **pol·li·ces** \-älə,sēz\ [NL *pollic-, pollex,* fr. L, thumb, big toe; akin to OSlav *palĭcĭ* thumb and prob. to L *pollēre* to be strong, be able] **1 :** the first digit of the forelimb **:** THUMB **2 :** the dactylopodite in the chela of a crustacean **3 :** a unit of length equal to one inch — used formerly in descriptions of invertebrate animals

pol·li·cal \'päləkəl\ *adj* [NL *pollic-, pollex* + E *-al*] **:** of or relating to a pollex

pol·lic·i·ta·tion \pə,lisə'tāshən\ *n* -s [L *pollicitation-, pollicitatio,* fr. *pollicitatus* (past part. of *pollicitari* to promise, fr. *pollicitus,* past part. of *pollicēri* to bid, offer, promise, fr. *pol-, por-* — akin to L *per* through — + *licēri* to bid) + *-ion-, -io* -ion; akin to L *licēre* to be permitted, be for sale — more at FARE, LICENSE] **1** *archaic* **:** the action or result of promising **:** PROMISE **2 a** *Roman law* **:** an offer unaccepted or informal promise not accepted by the promisee but made enforceable as to promise of dos by late legislation **b** *civil law* **:** a promise or proposal not accepted **:** an unaccepted offer

pollies *pl of* POLLY

pollin- *or* **pollini-** *comb form* [NL, fr. *pollin-, pollen* — more at POLLEN] **:** pollen ⟨*pollin*ic⟩ ⟨*pollini*ferous⟩

pol·li·nar·i·um \,pälə'na(a)rēəm\ *n, pl* **pollinar·ia** \-ēə\ [NL, fr. *pollin-* + *-arium*] **:** POLLINIUM

pol·li·nate \'pälə,nāt, *usu* -ād·+V\ *vt* -ED/-ING/-S [*pollin-* + *-ate,* v. suffix] **1 :** to apply pollen to the stigma of (a flower or plant) ⟨insects or wind ~ the majority of plants⟩ ⟨~ each flower by hand⟩ **2 :** to mark or smudge with or as if with pollen

pol·li·na·tion \,⸗⸗'nāshən\ *also* **pol·li·ni·za·tion** \,pälənə'zāshən\ *n* -s [ISV *pollin-* + *-ation* or *-ization*] **1 :** the act or process of pollinating **:** the transfer of pollen from a stamen to an ovule; *broadly* **:** fertilization of a flowering plant ⟨the complex ~ mechanisms of some orchids⟩ ⟨~ of fruit trees by insects⟩ **2 :** the state of being pollinated ⟨upon ~ the petals fall⟩

pol·li·na·tor \'pälə,nād·ə(r)\ *n* -s **:** one that pollinates: as **a :** an agent (as an insect) that pollinates flowers **b :** POLLENIZER 1

¹poll·ing \'pōliŋ, -lēŋ\ *n* -s [ME, action of cutting hair, fr. gerund of *pollen* to poll — more at POLL] **1 :** the action of one that polls; *specif* **:** the casting of ballots at an election ⟨the hours of ~ —H.R.Penniman⟩ **2 :** something that results from polling — usu. used in pl. ⟨the ~*s* of a beard⟩

²polling \"\ *adj* **1 :** of or relating to the registering or casting of votes (as at an election) ⟨~ day⟩ ⟨~ card⟩ **2 :** of or relating to the conduct of polls (as of public opinion) ⟨~ experts⟩ ⟨~ methods⟩

polling book *n* **:** POLLBOOK

polling booth *n* **:** a temporary structure in a polling place where the voting at an election is done

polling place *n* **:** the locality or the building where voters cast their ballots in an election

polling station *n, chiefly Brit* **:** POLLING PLACE

pol·lin·ic \pə'linik\ *also* **pol·lin·i·cal** \-nəkəl\ *adj* [*pollinic* ISV *pollin-* + *-ic; pollinical* fr. *pollinic* + *-al*] **:** of or relating to pollen

pol·li·nif·er·ous \,pälə'nif(ə)rəs\ *adj* [prob. fr. (assumed) NL *pollinifer* polliniferous (fr. NL *pollin-* + L *-fer* -ferous) + E *-ous*] **1 :** bearing or producing pollen **2 :** adapted for the purpose of carrying pollen

pol·li·nig·er·ous \-ij(ə)rəs\ *adj* [*pollin-* + *-gerous*] **:** POLLINIFEROUS

pol·lin·i·um \pə'linēəm\ *n, pl* **pollin·ia** \-ēə\ [NL, fr. *pollin-* + *-ium*] **:** the coherent mass of pollen grains that characterizes members of the Orchidaceae and Asclepiadaceae and often has a stalk bearing an adhesive disk that clings to visiting insects and facilitates withdrawal of the whole pollinium from its receptacle

pol·li·nize \'pälə,nīz\ *vt* -ED/-ING/-S [ISV *pollin-* + *-ize*] **:** POLLINATE 1

pol·li·niz·er \-zə(r)\ *n* -s **:** POLLENIZER

pol·li·no·di·um \,pälə'nōdēəm\ *n, pl* **pollino·dia** \-ēə\ [NL, fr. *pollin-* + *-odium* (irreg. fr. L *-oides* -oid)] **:** a hyphal branch that functions as an antheridium esp. in fungi of the class Phycomycetes

pol·li·nose \'pälə,nōs\ *adj* [NL *pollinosus,* fr. *pollin-* + L *-osus* -ose] *of an insect* **:** covered with pollen **:** PRUINOSE

pol·li·no·sis *or* **pol·le·no·sis** \,pälə'nōsəs\ *n, pl* **pollino·ses** *or* **polleno·ses** \-ō,sēz\ [*pollinosis* fr. NL, fr. *pollin-* + *-osis; pollenosis* alter. (influenced by *pollen*) of *pollinosis*] **:** an acute catarrhal disorder involving the mucous membranes of the eyes, nose, and respiratory tract often with asthmatic symptoms that recurs annually usu. in the spring or late summer and is caused by allergic sensitivity to pollens (as of ragweed, grasses, or trees) — called also *hay fever*

pol·li·wog *or* **pol·ly·wog** \'pälē,wäg, -wòg\ *n* -s [alter. of earlier *polwigge,* alter. of ME *polwygle,* prob. fr. *pol, polle* head + *wiglen, wigelen* to wiggle — more at POLL, WIGGLE] **1 :** TADPOLE **2 :** one who crosses the equator for the first time and undergoes an initiation (as by being tossed into seawater) by shellbacks

poll money *n, archaic* **:** POLL TAX

pollock *var of* POLLACK

pol·loi \pə'lȯi\ *n pl* [Gk, many, pl. of *polys* much — more at POLY-] **:** HOI POLLOI ⟨the ribald ~ . . . became derisively familiar —*Emporia (Kans.) Gazette*⟩

poll parrot *n* [⁵*poll* + *parrot,* n.] **:** a tame parrot

poll–parrot \'⸗,⸗⸗\ *vb* [*poll parrot*] *vt* **:** to speak, repeat, or imitate like a parrot ⟨*poll-parroting* nonsense —H.L.Mencken⟩ ~ *vi* **:** to chatter like a parrot

poll pick *n* **:** a single-pointed miner's pick having a short poll or striking head

polls *pl of* POLL, *pres 3d sing of* POLL

poll sickness *n* **:** POLL EVIL

poll·ster \'pōlztə(r), -lst-\ *n* -s **:** one that conducts or asks questions in a poll (as of public opinion) or that records or compiles data obtained by a poll

polltaker \'⸗,⸗⸗\ *n* **:** POLLSTER

poll tax *n* **:** a tax of a fixed rather than a graduated amount per head or person which is levied on adults and payment of which is often made a requirement for voting — compare HEAD TAX

pol·lu·cite \pə'lü,sīt, 'pälyə,-\ *n* -s [L *Polluc-, Pollux* Pollux + E *-ite* (after G *pollux* pollucite)] **:** a colorless transparent mineral $(Cs,Na)_2Al_2Si_4O_{12}.H_2O$ of the zeolite family consisting of hydrous cesium aluminum silicate and occurring massive or crystallizing in cubes

pol·lu·tant \pə'lüt^{ə}nt\ *n* -s **:** something that pollutes **:** a polluting substance, medium, or agent ⟨domestic wastes . . . are another chief source of ~*s* —*Pollution Problem*⟩ ⟨the great ~*s* are industrial plants and oil burners —*Automobilist*⟩

¹pol·lute \pə'lüt, *usu* -üd·+V\ *vt* -ED/-ING/-S [ME *polluten,* fr. L *pollutus,* past part. of *polluere,* fr. *pol-, por-* — akin to L *per* through — + *-luere* to soil, dirty; akin to L *lutum* mud, *lustrum* cave, bog, Gk *lyma* dirt, Alb (Tosk dial.) *lum* mud — more at FARE] **1 :** to render ceremonially or morally impure **:** impair the purity of **:** destroy or violate the sanctity of **:** CORRUPT, DEFILE, DESECRATE, PROFANE ⟨~ a temple⟩ ⟨~ a person's honor⟩ **2 :** to make physically impure or unclean **:** BEFOUL, DIRTY, TAINT ⟨~ a water supply by the introduction of sewage⟩ **syn** see CONTAMINATE

²pollute \"\ *adj* [ME *pollut, pollute,* fr. L *pollutus,* past part. of *polluere*] *archaic* **:** POLLUTED ⟨her naked shame ~ with sinful blame —John Milton⟩

pol·lut·ed \-üd·əd, -ütəd\ *adj* [ME, fr. past part. of *polluten* to pollute] **1 :** made unclean or impure **:** morally corrupt or defiled **:** physically tainted ⟨change . . . a pure stream into a ~ and poisoned ditch —O.W.Holmes †1935⟩ ⟨you . . . are ~ with your lusts —Shak.⟩ **2 :** very drunk ⟨so ~ she could hardly see —Trudi Stover⟩

pol·lut·er \-üd·ə(r)\ *n* -s **:** one that pollutes

pol·lu·tion \-üshən\ *n* -s [ME *pollucioun* emission of semen at other times than in coition, defilement, uncleanness, fr. MF & LL; MF *pollution,* fr. LL *pollution-, pollutio* defilement, uncleanness, fr. L *pollutus* (past part. of *polluere* to pollute) + *-ion-, -io* -ion] **1 :** emission of semen at other times than in coition **2 :** the action of polluting or the state of being polluted **:** DEFILEMENT, DESECRATION, IMPURITY, UNCLEANNESS ⟨streams subject to ~ by . . . mill wastes —C.R.Cox⟩ ⟨the dilution of atmospheric ~ —K.H.Jehm⟩ ⟨cleanse the king and the people from the ~ of any offenses —J.G.Frazer⟩ **3 :** crossbreeding when regarded as the source of degeneration of a stock

pol·lu·tion·al \-shən^{ə}l\ *adj* **:** of or relating to pollution ⟨~ material⟩ ⟨~ source⟩

pollux *n* -ES [G, fr. L *Polluc-, Pollux* Pollux, one of the Dioscuri (the other being L *Castor,* Gk *Kastōr*), twin heroes or demigods of Greek mythology, fr. Gk *Polydeukēs;* fr. its appearance with castorite (previously called *castor*)] *obs* **:** POLLUCITE

poll watcher *n* **:** a person assigned (as by a political party or candidate) to observe activities at a polling place to guard against illegal voting, fraudulent counting of ballots, and other violations of election laws

pol·ly \'pälē\ *n* -ES [fr. *Polly,* alter. of *Molly,* nickname for *Mary*] **:** POLL PARROT

pol·ly·an·na \,pälē'anə\ *n* -s *usu cap* [after *Pollyanna,* heroine of the novel *Pollyanna* (1913) by Eleanor Porter †1920 Am. fiction writer] **:** one having a disposition or nature characterized by irrepressible optimism and a tendency to find good in everything **:** an overly and often blindly optimistic person **:** an irritatingly cheerful person ⟨the facts on inflation are sugarcoated by the *Pollyannas* —*Atlantic*⟩ ⟨not such a *Pollyanna* as to deny the probability of recessions —*Dun's Rev.*⟩

pol·ly·an·na·ish \¦⸗⸗¦anə·ish\ *or* **pol·ly·an·nish** \-nish\ *adj, usu cap* **:** resembling or suggesting a Pollyanna esp. by having an optimistic nature characterized by a tendency to find good in everything ⟨its *Pollyannaish* outlook and blatant self-esteem —Arthur Knight⟩

pol·ly·an·na·ism \,⸗⸗'anə,izəm\ *also* **pol·ly·an·nism** \-a-,nizəm\ *n* -s *usu cap* **:** the overly optimistic and benevolently cheerful state of mind and point of view of a Pollyanna

polly–fox \'⸗⸗,⸗\ *vi* [origin unknown] *dial* **:** to sidestep an issue esp. by equivocation or evasion

polly mountain *n* [origin unknown] **:** BASIL BALM 2

pollywog *var of* POLLIWOG

po·lo \'pō(,)lō\ *n* -s *often attrib* [Balti, ball] **1 a :** a game of oriental origin played by teams of three or four players mounted on horseback and using mallets with long flexible handles to drive a wooden ball down the field and through goalposts **b :** any of several similar games (as one in which the players ride bicycles) **2 :** WATER POLO

polo coat *n* **:** a tailored overcoat for casual wear made of tan camel's hair cloth or other fabric in single-breasted or double-breasted style often with stitched edges and a half-belt

po·lo·crosse \'pōlō,krȯs\ *n* -s [*polo* + *lacrosse*] **:** a goal game combining elements of polo, lacrosse, and netball played by teams of six players mounted on horseback and using a sponge rubber ball and a stick with a head like that of a crosse and a handle and shaft like those of a polo stick

po·lo·cyte \'pōlə,sīt\ *n* -s [ISV ⁴*pole* + *-o-* + *-cyte*] **:** POLAR BODY 2

po·lo·ist \'pōlōəst\ *n* -s **:** a polo player

¹pol·o·naise \,pälə'nāz, ,pōl-\ *n* -s [F, fr. fem. of *polonais* Polish, fr. *Pologne* Poland, country in central Europe, fr. ML *Polonia*] **1 a :** an elaborate overdress that consists of a short-sleeved fitted waist and a draped cutaway overskirt **b** *Scot* **:** a tight-fitting jacket for boys **2 a :** a stately Polish processional dance fashionable in 19th century Europe **b :** the music for or suited to this dance in moderate ¾ time characterized typically by the rhythms of an eighth note and two sixteenths followed by either four eighths or a repetition of the rhythm of the first beat

rhythm of a polonaise

²polonaise \"\ *vi* -ED/-ING/-S **:** to dance a polonaise

³polonaise \¦⸗¦⸗\ *adj, usu cap* [F, fem. of *polonais* Polish] **:** made of or dressed with browned butter and bread crumbs ⟨sauce *Polonaise*⟩ ⟨cauliflower *Polonaise*⟩

pol·o·nay \,⸗⸗'nā\ *n* -s [prob. back-formation] *dial* **:** POLONAISE 1a

pol·o·nese \,⸗⸗'nēz, -ēs\ *n* -s *sometimes cap* [prob. modif. of F *polonaise*] **:** POLONAISE 1a

¹po·lo·ni·an \pə'lōnēən\ *adj, usu cap* [ML *Polonia* Poland + E *-an*] *archaic* **:** POLISH ⟨a *Polonian* Jew by birth —W.J. Mickle⟩

²polonian \"\ *n* -s *usu cap, archaic* **:** ⁶POLE 1 ⟨served against the Tartar and the *Polonian* —J.H.Burton⟩

³polonian \"\ *adj, usu cap* [*Polonius,* worldly-wise and long-winded old courtier in the tragedy *Hamlet* (about 1601) by William Shakespeare †1616 Eng. dramatist and poet + E *-an*] **:** resembling or held to resemble Polonius **:** having qualities or habits held to characterize Polonius

po·lo·nism \'pōlə,nizəm\ *n* -s *usu cap* [ISV *polon-* (fr. ML *Polonia* Poland) + *-ism*] **1 :** a quality or trait held to be distinctive of Poles or Polish culture **2 :** a characteristic feature of Polish occurring in another language or dialect

po·lo·nist \-nəst\ *n* -s *usu cap* [ML *Polonia* Poland + E *-ist*] **:** a specialist in the Polish language or Polish literature and culture

po·lo·ni·um \pə'lōnēəm\ *n* -s [NL, fr. ML *Polonia* Poland + NL *-ium;* fr. the fact that Marja Skłodowska Curie †1934 Fr. physical chemist, who together with her husband Pierre Curie †1906 Fr. chemist discovered polonium, was Polish by birth] **:** a radioactive metallic element that is similar chemically to tellurium and bismuth, that occurs in pitchblende and other uranium-containing ores, in radium-lead residues, and in old radon ampuls but can be produced in much larger quantities by bombarding bismuth with neutrons in nuclear reactors, and that emits a helium nucleus to form an isotope of lead — symbol *Po;* see ACTINIUM SERIES, THORIUM SERIES, URANIUM SERIES; ELEMENT table

po·lo·ni·za·tion \,pōlənə'zāshən\ *n* -s *often cap* **:** the act or process of polonizing or the state of being polonized ⟨resist the ~ of the Ukrainian upper classes —R. G. A. De Bray⟩

po·lo·nize \'pōlə,nīz\ *vt* -ED/-ING/-S *often cap* [ISV *polon-* (fr. ML *Polonia* Poland) + *-ize*] **1 :** to cause to acquire Polish customs or attitudes; *esp* **:** to force into conformity with Polish cultural patterns or governmental policies ⟨German cities assigned to Poland have been *polonized* —M.A.Pei⟩ ⟨the Polish clergy . . . use their influence to ~ the people —*Russian Poland*⟩ **2 :** to modify (a word or expression) to conform to characteristics distinctive of Polish ⟨difficult . . . to ~ English terms —B.W.A.Massey⟩

¹polony *adj, usu cap* [prob. fr. obs. E *Polony* Poland, fr. ML *Polonia*] *obs* **:** POLISH

²po·lo·ny \pə'lōnē\ *n* -ES *Scot* **:** POLONAISE 1b

³polony \"\ *n* -ES [alter. (influenced by ¹*polony*) of *Bologna* (in *bologna sausage*) — more at BOLOGNA] *Brit* **:** a dry partly cooked sausage made of various ingredients ⟨liver ~⟩ ⟨cervelat ~⟩

polo pony *also* **polo mount** *n* **:** a horse trained for use as a mount in playing polo and characterized primarily by endurance, speed, courage, and docility

pol·os \'pä,läs\ *n, pl* **po·loi** \-lȯi\ [Gk, polos, pivot, axis, pole — more at POLE] **:** a high crown or headdress of cylindrical shape, represented as worn by ancient Greek goddesses (as Demeter, Persephone, Hecate, and Aphrodite)

polo shirt *n* **:** a close-fitting pullover shirt for sportswear that is made of knitted cotton and has short or long sleeves and a turnover collar or a round banded neck — compare T-SHIRT

polo shirt

po·lov·tsi·an \pə'läftsēən, -ävt-; ÷-¦pälə¦vetsēən, ÷¦pōl-\ *n* -s *usu cap* [Russ *Polovtsy* (pl.) Cumans + E *-an*] **:** CUMAN

pol·ska \'pōlzkə, -lskə\ *n* -s [Sw, fr. *polsk* Polish, fr. Pol *polski*] **1 :** a Swedish folk dance derived from a Polish peasant dance **2 :** music for the polska in triple time and usu. in a minor key

pol·ster \'pōlztə(r), -lst-\ *n* -s [G, lit., cushion, fr. OHG *bolstar, polstar* bolster — more at BOLSTER] **:** CUSHION PLANT

¹polt \'pōlt\ *n* -s [origin unknown] *dial Eng* **:** a hard knock **:** BLOW, THUMP ⟨fetched me an awful ~ in the right side —*Blackwood's*⟩

²polt \"\ *vt* -ED/-ING/-S *dial Eng* **:** to knock or thump esp. with a stick or club

pol·ta·va \päl'tävə\ *adj, usu cap* [fr. *Poltava,* city in east central Ukraine, U.S.S.R.] **:** of or from the city of Poltava, U.S.S.R. **:** of the kind or style prevalent in Poltava

pol·ter·geist \'pōltə(r),gīst *sometimes* 'päl- *or* 'pȯl-\ *n* -s [G, fr. *poltern* to knock, rattle (fr. MHG *boldern, buldern*) + *geist* spirit, fr. OHG; akin to MLG *balderen* to make a noise — more at BOULDER, GHOST] **:** a noisy and usu. mischievous ghost **:** a spirit capable of making mysterious noises (as rappings)

¹poltfoot \'⸗,⸗\ *n, pl* **poltfeet** [prob. fr. ¹*polt* + *foot*] *archaic* **:** CLUBFOOT

²poltfoot \"\ *or* **poltfooted** \'⸗¦⸗⸗\ *adj* **:** having a clubfoot

pol·tin·nik \päl'tēnik\ *or* **pol·ti·na** \-ēnə\ *n* -s [*poltinnik* fr. Russ, half-ruble piece, fr. *poltina* half a ruble, fr. Old Russian *polŭtina,* prob. fr. *polŭ* half + *tina,* gen. of *tinŭ* ruble; *poltina* fr. Russ; prob. akin to L *duplus* double and to Gk *temnein* to cut — more at FOLD, TOME] **:** a Russian silver half-ruble or 50-kopeck piece

¹pol·troon \päl'trün\ *n* -s [MF *poultron,* fr. OIt *poltrone,* aug. of *poltro* colt, fr. (assumed) VL *pullitrus* (whence LL *polletrus*), irreg. fr. L *pullus* young of an animal — more at FOAL] **:** a spiritless coward **:** a mean-spirited wretch **:** CRAVEN, DASTARD ⟨lily-livered ~*s* lacking even the meager courage of a rabbit —P.G.Wodehouse⟩

²poltroon \"\ *adj* **:** characterized by complete cowardice **syn** see COWARDLY

pol·troon·ery \-n(ə)rē\ *n* -ES [MF *poltronnerie,* fr. *poltron, poultron* poltroon + *-erie* -ery] **:** behavior characteristic of a poltroon **:** want of spirit **:** mean pusillanimity **:** COWARDICE ⟨~ among politicians —G.W.Johnson⟩

pol·troon·ish \-nish\ *adj* **:** resembling a poltroon **:** COWARDLY ⟨a weak, almost ~ creature —*Quarterly Rev.*⟩ — **pol·troon·ish·ly** *adv*

pol·ver·ine \'pälvə,rēn\ *n* -s [It *polverino,* fr. *polvere* dust, fr. L *pulver-, pulvis* dust — more at POLLEN] **:** a potash or pearl ash from the Levant used in making fine glass

pol·warth *also* **pol·worth** \'pōlwə(r)th\ *n* [prob. fr. *Polwarth,* county in Victoria, southeast Australia] **1** *usu cap* **:** an Australian breed of rather large medium-wooled sheep developed from crosses of Merino and Lincoln sheep and noted for ability to withstand damp and cold **2** -s *often cap* **:** a sheep of the Polworth breed

poly \'pälē, -li\ *n* -s [by shortening] **:** a polymorphonuclear leukocyte

poly- *comb form* [ME, fr. L, fr. Gk, fr. *polys;* akin to L *plenus* full — more at FULL] **1 a :** many **:** several **:** diverse **:** much **:** MULTI-, PLURI- ⟨*poly*tonality⟩ ⟨*poly*centric⟩ ⟨*poly*cotyledon⟩ ⟨*poly*cross⟩ ⟨*poly*arthritis⟩ **b :** excessive **:** abnormal **:** HYPER- ⟨*poly*galactia⟩ ⟨*poly*chromia⟩ ⟨*poly*dactylous⟩ **2** *chem* **a :** containing more than one and esp. more than two or three units of (a specified substance) ⟨*poly*atomic⟩ ⟨*poly*sulfide⟩ — compare OLIG- **b :** ISOPOLY- ⟨*poly*molybdate⟩ **c :** polymerized **:** polymeric **:** polymer of (a specified monomer) ⟨*poly*ethylene⟩

poly *abbr* polytechnic

¹poly·acid \¦pälē+\ *n* [ISV *poly-* + *acid*] **1 :** an acid (as phosphoric acid) having more than one acid hydrogen atom **2 :** a complex acid of the group of isopoly or heteropoly acids

²polyacid \"\ *adj* **1 :** able to react with more than one molecule of a monoacid to form a salt — used esp. of bases **2 :** having more than one hydrogen atom replaceable by basic atoms or radicals — used of acids and acid salts

poly·acrylate \ˌpälē\ *n* [ISV *poly-* + *acrylate*] **:** a polymer of an acrylate **:** a salt or ester of polyacrylic acid

poly·acrylic acid \"+ . . . -\ *n* [*poly-* + *acrylic*] **:** a polymer of acrylic acid **:** a polycarboxylic acid $(-CH_2CH(COOH)-)_x$ formed by polymerization of an acrylic ester or acrylonitrile followed by hydrolysis

poly·acrylonitrile \ˌpälē+\ *n* [ISV *poly-* + *acrylonitrile*] **:** a solid polymer of acrylonitrile $(-CH_2CH(CN)-)_x$ that is soluble in dimethylformamide from which after appropriate blending it may be spun into textile filaments — compare ACRYLIC FIBER

poly·act \ˈpälē,akt\ *adj* [*poly-* + *-act*] **:** having many rays or radii — used esp. of a sponge spicule

poly·actinal *or* **poly·actine** \¦==+\ *adj* [*poly-* + *-actinal* or *-actine*] **:** POLYACT

¹poly·ad \ˈpälē,ad\ *n* -S [*poly-* + *-ad*] **1 :** a group consisting of several closely related parts or elements **2 :** a polyad atom, radical, or element

²polyad \"\ *adj* **1** *or* **poly·ad·ic** \¦==¦adik\ **:** of, relating to, or constituting a polyad **2** [*poly-* + *-ad*] **:** POLYVALENT

poly·adel·phia \ˌ==ə'delfēə\ *n pl, cap* [NL, fr. Gk, possession of many brothers, fr. *polyadelphos* with many brothers (fr. *poly-* + *adelphos* brother) + *-ia* -y] *in former classifications* **:** a class of plants having stamens united by the filaments into three or more fascicles

poly·adel·phous \¦==¦=fəs\ *adj* [NL *Polyadelphia* + E *-ous*] *of stamens* **:** united by the anthers into three or more groups — compare DIADELPHOUS, MONADELPHOUS

poly·allel \ˈpälē\ *adj* [*poly-* + *-allel* (as in *diallel*)] **:** DIALLEL

poly·alphabetic \"+\ *adj* [*poly-* + *alphabetic*] **:** using several substitution alphabets in turn — see MULTIPLE-ALPHABET CIPHER, PROGRESSIVE-ALPHABET CIPHER, VIGENÈRE CIPHER — **poly·alphabetically** \"+\ *adv*

poly·amide \"+\ *n* [ISV *poly-* + *amide*] **:** a compound characterized by more than one amide group; *esp* **:** a polymeric amide (as nylon or a polypeptide or a protein)

poly·amine \"+\ *n* [ISV *poly-* + *amine*] **:** a compound characterized by more than one amino group

poly·an·dria \ˌpälē'andrēə\ *n pl, cap* [NL, fr. *poly-* + *-andria*] *in former classifications* **:** a class of monoclinous plants including those with many hypogynous stamens

poly·an·dric \¦==¦=drik\ *adj* **:** relating to or characterized by polyandry

poly·an·drist \'==,=drəst, ,=='==\ *n* -S **:** one who practices polyandry **:** a polyandrous woman

poly·an·dri·um \ˌ=='=drēəm\ *also* **poly·an·dri·on** \-ē,än, -ēən\ *n* -S [LL, fr. Gk *polyandrion, polyandreion,* fr. *polyandrion* place where many people meet, fr. neut. of *polyandrios* of or connected with many men, fr. *poly-* + *andr-, anēr* man] **:** an ancient Greek burying ground esp. for men fallen in battle; *broadly* **:** CEMETERY

poly·an·drous \¦==¦=drəs\ *adj* [NL *Polyandria* + E *-ous*] **1 :** having many usu. free hypogynous stamens **2** [*polyandry* + *-ous*] **a :** practicing polyandry **b :** relating to or involving polyandry

poly·an·dry \'==,=drē\ *n* -ES [Gk *polyandria* condition of having many men, populousness, fr. *polyandros* having many men, having many husbands (fr. *poly-* + *andr-, anēr* man) + *-ia* -y — more at ANDR-] **1 a :** a marriage form in which one woman has two or more husbands at the same time — contrasted with *polygyny;* compare FRATERNAL POLYANDRY, MONANDRY, POLYGAMY **b :** the condition of having more than one male mate at one time **2 :** the state of being polyandrous

poly·an·gi·a·ce·ae \ˌpälē,anjē'āsē,ē\ *n pl, cap* [NL, fr. *Polyangium,* type genus + *-aceae*] **:** a family of myxobacteria living mostly in soils and on dung and having fruiting bodies in which the rod-shaped cells are enclosed in rounded cysts often brightly colored and covered by a membrane representing the remains of the vegetative slime

poly·an·gi·um \-'anjēəm\ *n, cap* [NL, fr. *poly-* + *-angium*] **:** the type genus of Polyangiaceae comprising myxobacteria with rounded usu. solitary unstalked fruiting bodies enclosed in a membrane

poly·an·tha \ˌpälē'an(t)thə\ *or* **polyantha rose** *n* -S [NL, fr. Gk *polyanthos* blooming, fr. *poly-* + *anthos* flower — more at ANTHOLOGY] **:** any of numerous dwarf hybrid bush roses derived chiefly from crosses of two species (*Rosa chinensis* and *R. multiflora*) and usu. treated in horticulture as a distinct species (*R. polyantha*) characterized by the free production of small and rarely fragrant flowers in large clusters — compare FLORIBUNDA

poly·an·thea \-'an(t)thēə, -,an'th-\ *n* -S [NL, fr. Gk, fem. of *polyanthēs* having many blossoms, fr. *poly-* + *anthos* flower] *archaic* **:** ANTHOLOGY

poly·an·thus \-'an(t)thəs\ *n, pl* **polyanthuses** \-n(t)thəsəz\ *or* **polyan·thi** \-n,thī\ [NL, fr. Gk *polyanthos* blooming] **1 :** any of various florists' primroses formerly supposed to have been derived from a species primula (*Primula elatior*) but now usu. considered a complex hybrid (*P. polyantha*) prob. derived from three primulas (*P. veris, P. elatior,* and *P. vulgaris*) **2** *or* **polyanthus narcissus :** a narcissus (*Narcissus tazetta*) having small umbeled white or yellow flowers with a spreading perianth and shallow crown and cultivated in several varieties

poly·arch \ˈpälē,ärk\ *adj* [ISV *poly-* + *-arch*] **:** having many protoxylem groups ⟨the ~ stele of a root⟩

poly·ar·chic \¦==¦ärkik\ *or* **poly·ar·chi·cal** \-rkəkəl\ *adj* **:** of or relating to a polyarchy ⟨tradition of ~ independence of the several ministers as department heads —C.J.Friedrich⟩

poly·ar·chism \'==,är,kizəm\ *n* -S **:** POLYARCHY

poly·ar·chy \-,kē\ *n* -ES [Gk *polyarchia,* fr. *polyarchos* ruling over many (fr. *poly-* + *archos* ruler) + *-ia* -y — more at ARCH-] **1 :** government by many persons **:** control of esp. political leaders by their followers — compare HIERARCHY **2 :** a group of many kingdoms ⟨filled Europe with a colorful ~ of innumerable tribes —D.C.Peattie⟩

poly·ar·gy·rite \ˌpälē'ärjə,rīt\ *n* -S [G *polyargyrit,* fr. *poly-* + *argyr-* + *-it* -ite] **:** a mineral $Ag_{24}Sb_2S_{15}$(?) consisting of a sulfide of antimony and silver occurring chiefly in indistinct cuboctahedrons

poly·arteritis \ˈpälē+\ *n* [NL, fr. *poly-* + *arteritis*] **:** PERIARTERITIS NODOSA

poly·arthritis \"+\ *n* [NL, fr. *poly-* + *arthritis*] **:** arthritis involving two or more joints

poly·articular \"+\ *adj* [ISV *poly-* + *articular*] **:** having or affecting many joints ⟨~ arthritis⟩

poly·atomic \"+\ *adj* [ISV *poly-* + *atomic*] **:** containing more than one or usu. more than two atoms ⟨~ molecules⟩

poly·autographic \"+\ *adj* [*polyautography* + *-ic*] *archaic* **:** done or produced by lithography ⟨~ albums⟩ ⟨~ printing⟩

poly·autography \"+\ *n* [*poly-* + *autography*] *archaic* **:** LITHOGRAPHY

¹poly·axon *also* **poly·axone** \"+\ *n* [*poly-* + *axon, axone*] **1 :** a nerve cell having several axons **2** [*poly-* + Gk *axōn* axle, axis — more at AXIS] **:** a polyaxon sponge spicule

²poly·axon *or* **poly·axonic** \ˌpälē+\ *adj* **:** having many axes ⟨~ spicules⟩

poly·basic \ˌpälē, -lə+\ *adj* [*poly-* + *basic*] **1 :** having more than one hydrogen atom replaceable by basic atoms or radicals — used of acids **2 :** containing more than one atom of a univalent metal or their equivalent — used of a salt **3 :** having more than one basic hydroxyl group **:** able to react with more than one molecule of a monoacid — used of bases and basic salts — **poly·basicity** \"+\ *n*

poly·ba·site \ˌpälē'bā,sīt, -lə'b-\ *n* -S [G *polybasit,* fr. *poly-* + *basi-* + *-it* -ite] **:** an iron-black metallic-looking ore $(Ag,Cu)_{16}Sb_2S_{11}$ of silver consisting essentially of silver, copper, sulfur, and antimony

poly·blast \'==,blast\ *n* [ISV *poly-* + *-blast*] **:** a wandering macrophage — **poly·blas·tic** \¦==¦blastik\ *adj*

poly·blend \ˈpälē, -lə+,-\ *n* [*poly-* + *blend*] **:** a colloidal mixture of one polymer with another (as of a vinyl resin with nitrile rubber)

po·lyb·o·rine \pə'libə,rīn\ *adj* [NL *Polyborus* + E *-ine*] **:** of or relating to the genus *Polyborus*

po·lyb·o·rus \-,rəs\ *n, cap* [NL, fr. Gk *polyboros* voracious, fr. *poly-* much (fr. *polys* much, many) + *-boros* devouring, gluttonous, fr. *bora* food, meat — more at POLY-, VORACIOUS] **:** a genus of long-winged hawks (family Falconidae) consisting of typical caracaras

pol·y·brid \(')pä¦librəd; 'pälēb-, -ləb-\ *n* -S [*poly-* + *hybrid*] **:** HETEROGEN

poly·butene \ˌpälē, -lə+\ *n* [*poly-* + *butene*] **:** POLYBUTYLENE

poly·butylene \"+\ *n* [*poly-* + *butylene*] **:** a polymer of one or more butylenes; *esp* **:** POLYISOBUTYLENE

poly·ca·on \ˌpälē'kā,än, -lə'k-\ *n, cap* [NL, perh. fr. *Polycaon,* in Greek legend ruler of ancient Messina] **:** a genus of beetles (family Bostrychidae) whose larvae bore into twigs and branches of various trees

poly·carboxylic \ˌpälē, -lə+\ *adj* [*poly-* + *carboxylic*] **:** containing more than one carboxyl group in the molecule

poly·carpellary \"+\ *adj* [*poly-* + *carpellary*] **:** consisting of several carpels — compare MONOCARPELLARY

poly·carpellate \"+\ *adj* [ISV *poly-* + *carpellate*] **:** having many carpels

poly·car·pic \ˌpälē¦kärpik, -lə¦k-\ *or* **poly·car·pous** \-rpəs\ *adj* [*polycarpic* prob. fr. NL *polycarpicus,* fr. *poly-* + *-carpicus* -carpic; *polycarpous* prob. fr. (assumed) NL *polycarpus,* fr. NL *poly-* + *-carpus* -carpous] **1 :** SYCHNOCARPOUS **2 :** having a gynoecium forming two or more distinct ovaries — **poly·car·py** \'==,=pē\ *n* -ES

poly·car·pon \ˌ=='=,pän\ *n, cap* [NL, fr. Gk *polykarpon,* a plant, fr. neut. of *polykarpos* fruitful, fr. *poly-* + *-karpos* fruit — more at HARVEST] **:** a small genus of herbs (family Caryophyllaceae) of temperate and warm regions having small white cymose flowers with 5-keeled sepals and 3 to 5 stamens

polycaryon *var of* POLYKARYON

polycaryotic *var of* POLYKARYOTIC

poly·cen·tric \ˌpälē¦sen·trik, -lə¦s-\ *adj* [*poly-* + *-centric*] **:** having many centers: as **a** *of chromosomes* **:** having several centromeres **b** *of cells* **:** having several centrosomes or division centers **c** *of organisms or groups* **:** having several centers of development or differentiation — compare MONOCENTRIC

poly·cen·trop·i·dae \ˌ==,sen·'träpə,dē\ *n pl, cap* [NL, fr. *Polycentropus,* type genus (prob. fr. *poly-* + *centr-* + *-pus*) + *-idae*] **:** a widely distributed family of caddis flies whose larvae are mostly carnivorous and usu. live in running water

poly·ceph·a·lous \¦==¦sefələs\ *also* **poly·ce·phal·ic** \-¸sə¦falik\ *adj* [*poly-* + *-cephalous* or *-cephalic*] *of a tapeworm larva* **:** having many scolices

poly·chae·ta \ˌ=='kēd·ə\ *n pl, cap* [NL, fr. Gk *polychaitēs* with much hair, fr. *poly-* much (fr. *polys* much, many) + *chaitē* long flowing hair — more at POLY- CHAETA] **:** a class of Annelida or in former classifications an order of Chaetopoda that comprises chiefly marine annelid worms usu. having paired setate appendages on most segments, a differentiated head with eyes, tactile processes and bristles, and chitinous jaws and being distinguished from the related oligochaete worms by possession of separate sexes and by a complex life history with a free-swimming trochophore larva — see ERRANTIA, SEDENTARIA

¹poly·chaete \'==,kēt\ *or* **poly·chae·tous** \¦==¦kēd·əs\ *adj* [*polychaete* fr. NL *Polychaeta; polychaetous* fr. NL *Polychaeta* + E *-ous*] **:** of or relating to the Polychaeta

²polychaete *also* **poly·chete** \'==,kēt\ *n* -S [NL *Polychaeta*] **:** an annelid worm of the class Polychaeta

poly·cha·sium \¦==¦kāzh(ē)əm\ *n, pl* **polycha·sia** \-(ē)ə\ [NL, fr. *poly-* + *-chasium* (as in *dichasium*)] **:** a cymose inflorescence in which each relative main axis produces more than two branches — compare DICHASIUM, MONOCHASIUM

poly·chloroprene \ˌpälē, -lə+\ *n* [*poly-* + *chloroprene*] **:** polymerized chloroprene — compare NEOPRENE

Poly Choke \'==+,-\ *trademark* — used for a device fitted to the muzzle of a shotgun that replaces the choke-bored section of the barrel with an adjustable mechanism which allows the firer to select the choke he needs

poly·choral \¦==+\ *adj* [*poly-* + *choral*] **:** ANTIPHONAL

poly·chord \'==+,-\ *adj* [Gk *polychordos,* fr. *poly-* + *-chordos* -chord] *archaic* **:** having many strings — used of a musical instrument

poly·chot·omous \ˌpälē¦käd·əməs, -lə¦k-\ *adj* [*poly-* + *-chotomous* (as in *dichotomous*)] **:** dividing or marked by division into many parts, branches, or classes; *esp* **:** dividing regularly and repeatedly into many divisions — compare DICHOTOMOUS — **poly·chot·o·my** \-mē\ *n* -ES

polychotomous key *n, biol* **:** a taxonomic key based on a choice between several alternative characters

poly·chrest \'==,krest\ *n* -S [ML *polychrestus,* fr. Gk *polychrēstos* useful for many purposes, fr. *poly-* + *chrēstos* useful — more at CHRESTOMATHY] **:** a drug or medicine of value as a remedy in several diseases — **poly·chres·tic** \¦==¦krestik\ *adj*

poly·chres·ty \'==,krestē\ *n* -ES [Gk *polychrēstia* great usefulness, fr. *polychrēstos* useful for many purposes + *-ia* -y] **:** a thing that has many uses; *specif* **:** POLYCHREST

poly·chro·ic \¦==¦krōik\ *adj* [ISV *poly-* + *-chroic*] **:** PLEOCHROIC

poly·chro·ism \'==(,)krō,izəm\ *n* -S [ISV *polychroic* + *-ism*] **:** PLEOCHROISM

poly·chro·ma·sia \ˌ==krō'māzh(ē)ə\ *n* -S [NL, fr. *poly-* + *-chromasia*] **:** the quality of being polychromatic; *specif* **:** POLYCHROMATOPHILIA

poly·chromate \ˌpälē, -lə+\ *n* [ISV *poly-* + *chrom-* + *-ate*] **:** a salt containing more than one or usu. more than two atoms of hexavalent chromium in the anion

poly·chromatic \"+\ *adj* [Gk *polychrōmatos* polychromatic (fr. *poly-* + *chrōmat-, chrōma* color, skin) + E *-ic* — more at CHROMATIC] **1 :** showing a variety or a change of colors **:** MULTICOLORED **2** [*poly-* + *chromatic*] *of a cell or tissue* **:** exhibiting polychromatophilia

poly·chromatophil *or* **poly·chromatophile** \ˌpälē, -lə+\ *n* -S [ISV, fr. NL *polychromatophilia*] **:** a young or degenerated red blood corpuscle staining with both acid and basic dyes

poly·chromatophilia \ˌpälē, -lə+\ *n* [NL, fr. *poly-* + *chromatophilia*] **:** the quality of being stainable with more than one type of stain; *esp* **:** stainable with both acid and basic dyes (as an abnormal red blood cell)

poly·chromatophilic *also* **poly·chromatophil** \ˌpälē, -lə+\ *adj* [*polychromatophilic* fr. NL *polychromatophilia* + E *-ic*; *polychromatophil* fr. *poly-* + *chromatophil*] **:** exhibiting polychromatophilia; *esp* **:** stainable with both acid and basic dyes ⟨~ erythroblasts⟩

¹poly·chrome \ˈpälē,krōm, -lə,k-\ *n* [G *polychrom,* fr. Gk *polychrōmos* of many colors, fr. *poly-* + *-chrōmos* colored, fr. *chrōma* color] **1 :** something of many colors **2 :** variegated coloring **3** *pharmacy* **:** ESCULIN

²polychrome \"\ *adj* **1 :** of, relating to, or made with several colors **:** decorated in various colors ⟨~ sculpture⟩ ⟨~ molding⟩ ⟨~ weaving⟩ **2 a :** of, relating to, or constituting a style of vase painting developed in Athens in the latter part of the 6th century B.C. using various colors (as black, white, red, and yellow) to paint decorative figures and other motifs on the outer surface of ware often prepared in advance with a coat of white slip — compare BLACK-FIGURE, RED-FIGURE **b :** of, relating to, or constituting a style of prehistoric vase painting distinguished by the application of two or more colors — compare MONOCHROME

³polychrome \"\ *vt* **:** to decorate or variegate in polychrome style ⟨a *polychromed* ceiling⟩

poly·chro·mia \ˌ=='krōmēə\ *n* -S [NL, fr. *poly-* + *-chromia*] *med* **:** excessive or abnormal pigmentation of the skin

poly·chro·mic \¦==¦==\ *adj* [*polychrome* + *-ic*] **:** POLYCHROMATIC 1

poly·chro·my \'==,=mē\ *n* -ES [F *polychromie,* fr. *polychrome,* n., (prob. fr. G *polychrom*) + *-ie* -y] **1 :** the art or practice of decorating (as sculpture or architectural ornaments) in combinations of several colors **2** ['*polychrome* + *-y*] **:** a polychrome surface or effect

poly·cir·rus \ˌpälē'sirəs, -lə's-\ *n, cap* [NL, fr. *poly-* + L *cirrus* curl, ringlet, bird's nest] **:** a genus (family Terebellidae) of soft-bodied polychaete worms — see BLOODWORM

¹poly·clad \'==,=\ *adj* [NL *Polycladida*] **:** of or relating to the Polycladida

²polyclad \"\ *n* -S [NL *Polycladida*] **:** a flatworm of the order Polycladida

poly·clad·i·da \ˌpälē'kladədə, -lə'k-\ *n pl, cap* [NL, fr. *Polycladus,* type genus (fr. Gk *polyklados* with many branches, fr. *poly-* + *klados* sprout, branch, twig) + NL *-ida* — more at GLADIATOR] **:** an order of Turbellaria comprising broad flattened often brightly colored marine flatworms in which the alimentary tract has many primary branches radiating from a central cavity, the ovaries and testes are numerous, and no vitellarium is developed

poly·clad·ine \¦==¦kla,dīn, -lā-, -,dᵊn\ *adj* [Gk *polyklados* + E *-ine*] **:** having several or many tines on the antlers

poly·clinic \ˌpälē, -lə+\ *n* [ISV *poly-* + *clinic*] **:** a clinic treating diseases of many sorts; *also* **:** a hospital for or an institution giving clinical instruction about all kinds of diseases — compare POLICLINIC

poly·component \"+\ *adj* [*poly-* + *component*] **:** MULTICOMPONENT

poly·condensation \"+\ *n* [ISV *poly-* + *condensation*] **:** a chemical condensation leading to the formation of a compound (as a polypeptide or a polyester) of high molecular weight — compare POLYMERIZATION

¹poly·conic \"+\ *adj* [*poly-* + *conic*] **:** relating to or based on many cones

²polyconic \"\ *n* **:** POLYCONIC PROJECTION

polyconic projection *n* **:** a map projection based on the development of a series of concentric cones placed over a sphere so that each cone is tangent to a different parallel with only that section of each unrolled cone that lies along a common central meridian and forms a strip on both sides of the line of tangency being utilized, all parallels being arcs of nonconcentric circles, and the meridians other than the central meridian being curved lines drawn through the true divisions of the parallels

poly·cot \ˈpälē,kät, -lə,k-\ *or* **poly·cot·yl** \-äd·ᵊl\ *n* -S [by shortening] **:** POLYCOTYLEDON

poly·cotyledon \ˌpälē, -lə+\ *n* [NL *polycotyledones,* pl., fr. *poly-* + *cotyledones,* pl. of *cotyledon*] **:** a plant (as the pine and other conifers) having more than two cotyledons

poly·cotyledonary \"+\ *adj* [*poly-* + *cotyledonary*] **:** having the placental villi in many definite groups

poly·cotyledonous \"+\ *adj* [NL *Polycotyledones* + E *-ous*] **:** having more than two cotyledons ⟨most gymnosperms are ~⟩

poly·cot·y·le·dony \¦==,käd·ᵊl¦ēdᵊnē\ *n* -ES [*polycotyledon* + *-y*] **:** abnormal increase in the number of cotyledons

poly·crase \'==,krās, -āz\ *n* -S [G *polykras,* fr. *poly-* + *-kras* (fr. Gk *krasis* mixing, combination) — more at KRASIS] **:** a mineral $(Y,Ca,Ce,U,Th)(Ti,Cb,Ta)_2O_6$ consisting of a columbate and titanate of the metals of the yttrium group that is isomorphous with euxenite (hardness 5–6, sp. gr. 5)

¹poly·cross \ˈpälē, -lə+,-\ *n* [*poly-* + *cross*] **:** a cross in which the female parent is known but the male may belong to any of several available strains and which is used in the production of new lines of some economic plants (as alfalfa)

²polycross \"\ *adj* **:** produced by a polycross ⟨~ seed⟩ **:** producing polycrosses ⟨~ nursery⟩

poly·crot·ic \ˌpälē¦kräd·ik, -lə¦k-\ *adj* [*poly-* + *-crotic*] *of the pulse* **:** having a complex or multiple beat and forming a curve with several secondary crests on a sphygmogram — compare DICROTIC, MONOCROTIC

poly·crystal \ˌpälē, -lə+,-\ *n* [*poly-* + *crystal*] **:** a polycrystalline body or object

poly·crystalline \"+\ *adj* [*poly-* + *crystalline*] **1 :** characterized by or consisting of crystals variously oriented **2 :** composed of more than one crystal ⟨a ~ metal⟩

¹po·lyc·te·nid \pə'liktənəd, ¦pälək¦tenəd\ *adj* [NL *Polyctenidae*] **:** of or relating to the Polyctenidae

²polyctenid \"\ *n* -S **:** a bug of the family Polyctenidae

pol·yc·ten·i·dae \ˌpälək'tenə,dē\ *n pl, cap* [NL, fr. *Polyctenes,* type genus (fr. *poly-* + Gk *-ktenēs* — fr. *kten-, kteis* comb) + *-idae* — more at PECTINATE] **:** a family of viviparous bugs of the order Hemiptera comprising the bat bugs

poly·cyclic \ˌpälē, -lə+\ *adj* [ISV *poly-* + *cyclic*] **:** having many cycles or rounds: as **a :** containing two or more usu. fused rings in the structure of the molecule (as in anthracene) — compare POLYNUCLEAR ⟨~ hydrocarbons⟩ **b :** of, relating to, or constituting a system of electric distribution in which currents of different voltages and frequencies are superposed on the same network **c (1) :** having many whorls or volutions **(2) :** having many cycles of tentacles **d :** POLYPHASIC

poly·cyesis \"+\ *n* [NL, fr. *poly-* + *cyesis*] **:** pregnancy with more than one fetus in the uterus

poly·cystic \"+\ *adj* [*poly-* + *cystic*] **:** having or involving more than one cyst ⟨~ kidney⟩ ⟨~ disease⟩

poly·cys·tis \ˌpälē'sistəs, -lə's-\ *n, cap* [NL, fr. *poly-* + *-cystis*] **:** a genus of free-floating colonial blue-green algae (family Chroococcaceae) often forming netted or irregular masses and frequently causing water bloom

poly·cyte \'==,sīt\ *n* [*poly-* + *-cyte*] **:** a blood granulocyte of normal size but more than usu. segmented nucleus that is present in various infections — compare MACROPOLYCYTE

poly·cy·the·mia *also* **poly·cy·thae·mia** \ˌ==,sī'thēmēə\ *n* -S [NL, fr. *poly-* + *-cyte* + *-emia*] **1 :** any condition marked by an abnormal increase in the number of circulating red blood cells **2** *or* **polycythemia ve·ra** \-'virə, -'verə\ **:** a disease characterized by increased concentration of hemoglobin and great absolute and relative increase in red cells accompanied by plethora, nosebleeds, and enlargement of the spleen — **poly·cy·the·mic** *also* **poly·cy·thae·mic** \¦==,=¦thēmik\ *adj*

¹poly·dac·tyl *also* **poly·dac·tyle** \¦==¦daktᵊl\ *adj* [Gk *polydaktylos* many-toed, fr. *poly-* + *daktylos* finger, toe] **:** having several or many digits; *esp* **:** having more than the normal number of toes or fingers ⟨~ strains of guinea pigs —*Genetics*⟩

²polydactyl \"\ *n* **:** one having more than the normal number of toes or fingers

poly·dac·tyl·ism \-ktə,lizəm\ *n* -S [ISV *polydactyl-* (fr. Gk *polydaktylos* many-toed) + *-ism*] **:** POLYDACTYLY

poly·dac·ty·lous \-ləs\ *adj* [*poly-* + *-dactylous*] **:** POLYDACTYL

poly·dac·ty·lus \ˌ=='=tələs\ *n, cap* [NL, fr. Gk *polydaktylos* many-toed] **:** a genus of fishes (family Polynemidae) found in warm seas

poly·dac·ty·ly \-lē\ *n* -ES [ISV *poly-* + *-dactyly*] **:** the condition of having more than the normal number of toes or fingers

poly·dae·mon·ism *also* **poly·de·mon·ism** \ˌpälē'dēmə,nizəm, -lə'd-\ *n* -S [*poly-* + *daemon, demon* + *-ism*] **:** belief in or worship of a multitude of demons or demoniacal powers — **poly·dae·mon·is·tic** *also* **poly·de·mon·is·tic** \'==,==¦istik\ *adj*

poly·dem·ic \ˌpälē¦demik, -lə¦d-\ *adj* [*poly-* + *endemic*] **:** native to or occurring in several regions

poly·dentate \ˌpälē, -lə+\ *adj* [*poly-* + *-dentate*] **:** attached to the central atom in a coordination complex by two or more bonds — used of ligands and chelating groups

poly·dimensional \"+\ *adj* [*poly-* + *dimensional*] **:** having many dimensions ⟨the ~ nature of documentary information —J.W.Perry⟩

poly·dip·sia *also* **poly·dyp·sia** \ˌpälē'dipsēə, -lə'd-\ *n* -S [NL, fr. *poly-* + *-dipsia,* fr. Gk *dipsa* thirst] **:** excessive or abnormal thirst — **poly·dip·sic** \¦==¦sik\ *adj*

poly·disk *or* **poly·disc** \'==,disk\ *adj* [*poly-* + *disk, disc*] *of a scyphistoma* **:** producing several ephyrae at one time — compare MONODISK

poly·disperse \¦==+\ *adj* [*poly-* + *disperse,* adj.] **:** characterized by particles of varying size in a dispersed phase

poly·dispersity \"+\ *n* **:** the state of being polydisperse ⟨opalescence is a mark of ~ —J.W.McBain⟩

po·lyd·o·mous \pə'lidəməs\ *adj* [*poly-* + Gk *domos* house + E *-ous* — more at TIMBER] **:** inhabiting several nests — used of ant colonies; compare MONODOMOUS

po·lyd·y·mite \pə'lidə,mīt\ *n* -S [G *polydymit,* fr. *poly-* + *dym-* (fr. Gk *didymos* twin) + *-it* -ite — more at -DYMUS] **:** a mineral Ni_3S_4 consisting of a nickel sulfide that is isomorphous with linnaeite, siegenite, carrollite, and violarite

polyecious *var of* POLYOICOUS

poly·ei·dic \ˌpälē¦īdik\ *adj* [*poly-* + *eid-* + *-ic*] **:** undergoing a series of conspicuous changes in form during development — used of insects exhibiting a marked metamorphosis — **poly·ei·dism** \-,dizəm\ *n* -S

poly·electrolyte \ˌpälē+\ *n* [*poly-* + *electrolyte*] **:** a substance of high molecular weight that is an electrolyte (as an ion-exchange resin, a protein, a nucleotide)

poly·embryonic *also* **poly·embryonate** *or* **poly·embryonal** \"+\ *adj* [*polyembryony* + *-ic* or *-ate* or *-al*] : consisting of or having several embryos : exhibiting polyembryony

poly·embryony \"+\ *n* [ISV *poly-* + *embryon-* + *-y*] : production of two or more embryos by an ovule or egg that is typical of many seed plants and that in some insects results in the production of hundreds of individuals from a single egg

poly·ene \'pälē,ēn\ *n* -s [ISV *poly-* + *-ene*] : an organic chemical compound containing many double bonds; *esp* : such a compound having the double bonds in a long aliphatic hydrocarbon chain (as in carotene or vitamin A) — **poly·enic** \¦==-¦ēnik, -¦en-\ *adj*

poly·energid \¦pälē+\ *adj* [ISV *poly-* + *energid;* orig. formed in G] : comprising several or many energids ⟨a coenocyte is ~⟩

poly·enzymatic \"+\ *adj* [*poly-* + *enzymatic*] : producing or containing several different enzymes

poly·ergus \,=='ərgəs\ *n* [NL, fr. Gk *polyergos* hardworking, fr. *poly-* much (fr. *polys* much, many) + *ergon* work — more at POLY-, WORK] **1** *cap* : a genus of ants containing the Amazon ants **2** -ES : any ant of the genus *Polyergus*

poly·ester \'==+,-\ *n* [ISV *poly-* + *ester*] **1** : a complex ester formed by polymerization or condensation (as of a polyhydric alcohol with a polybasic acid) for use chiefly in making fibers, resins, and plastics or as a plasticizer; *esp* : a linear polymer formed from a glycol and a dicarboxylic acid **2 a** : POLYESTER FIBER **b** : POLYESTER RESIN

polyester fiber *n* : a synthetic fiber consisting wholly or chiefly of a polyester; *esp* : a quick-drying resilient fiber made in filament and staple form from ethylene glycol and terephthalic acid or its dimethyl ester and often blended with other fibers (as wool or cotton)

poly·esterification \"+\ *n* [*polyester* + *-ification* (as in *esterification*)] : the formation of a polyester

polyester resin *or* **polyester plastic** *n* : any of various synthetic resins or plastics consisting of or made from polyesters: as **a** : ALKYD **b** : a resin that has the same chemical composition as the common polyester fiber but that is extruded as a film (as for use in packaging, as electrical insulation, or as a base for magnetic recording tapes) **c** : a thermosetting resin that is made from an unsaturated polyester (as one formed from a glycol and maleic acid or fumaric acid), cured by copolymerization (as with styrene), and often reinforced with fillers (as glass fibers) and that is used chiefly in impregnating and laminating and in making cast and molded products

poly·estrous *or* **poly·oestrous** \¦päle+\ *adj* [*poly-* + *estrous, oestrous*] : having more than one period of estrus in a year

poly·ethnic \"+\ *adj* [*poly-* + *ethnic*] : formed of or inhabited by many peoples ⟨~ areas⟩

poly·ethylene \"+\ *n* [*poly-* + *ethylene*] : a polymer of ethylene; *esp* : one of a group of partially crystalline lightweight thermoplastics $(-CH_2CH_2-)_x$ that have good resistance to chemicals, low moisture absorption and good insulating properties, that vary from soft to hard and from tough and flexible to rigid according to the conditions of manufacture (as at high, medium, or atmospheric pressure) and the type of catalyst, and that are used chiefly in the form of film (as in food packaging and garment bags), pipe and tubing, and molded products (as squeeze bottles and other containers) and as electrical insulation esp. in cables

polyethylene glycol *n* : a member of the series of water-soluble poly-ether glycols $HOCH_2CH_2(OCH_2CH_2)_nOH$ higher than diethylene glycol and triethylene glycol that vary from water-white liquids to waxy solids as the average molecular weight increases from 200 to 6000 or more, that are usu. obtained as mixtures by condensation of ethylene oxide with water or diethylene glycol, and that are used chiefly as lubricants (as in the rubber and textile industries), solvents, softeners, bases for pharmaceutical ointments and cosmetic creams, and in the form of their fatty acid esters as surface-active agents ⟨commercially available *polyethylene glycols* are designated by numbers that approximate their average molecular weights —Franklin Johnston⟩ — compare POLYGLYCOL

poly·foil \'pälē, -lə+,-\ *n* [*poly-* + *foil*] : MULTIFOIL

poly·functional \¦==+\ *adj* [*poly-* + *functional*] : having many functions ⟨~ acids⟩ — **poly·functionality** \"+\ *n*

po·lyg·a·la \pə'ligələ\ *n* [NL, fr. L, fr. Gk *polygalon* milkwort, fr. *poly-* much (fr. *polys* much, many) + *gala* milk — more at POLY-, GALAXY] **1** *cap* : a genus (type of the family Polygalaceae) of herbs and shrubs of temperate and warm regions having many-colored often showy flowers with the three sometimes crested petals united below into a tube and an irregular calyx with two petaloid sepals — see GAYWINGS, MILKWORT, SENEGA ROOT **2** -S : any plant of the genus *Polygala*

po·lyg·a·la·ce·ae \=,=='lāsē,ē\ *n pl, cap* [NL, fr. *Polygala*, type genus + *-aceae*] : a family (order Geraniales) of herbs, shrubs, or small trees widely distributed throughout both hemispheres and having irregular flowers with three to five petals, monadelphous stamens, and five sepals of which the two lateral are petaloid — **po·lyg·a·la·ceous** \=¦==¦lāshəs\ *adj*

poly·ga·lac·tia \,pälēgə'laksh(ē)ə, -äləg-, -ktēə\ *n* -S [NL, fr. *poly-* + *galact-* + *-ia*] : excessive milk secretion

poly·galac·tu·ro·nase \,pälē,ga,lak't(y)u̇rə,nās, -lə,g-, -‿gə'laktyər-, -āz\ *n* -S [*poly-* + *galacturonic* + *-ase*] : an enzyme that hydrolyzes the glycosidic linkages of polymerized galacturonic acids (as pectic acid) and that occurs esp. in microorganisms — compare PECTINASE

poly·gal·i·tol \,pälē'galə,tȯl, -älə'g-, -tōl\ *n* -S [NL *Polygala* + E *-itol*] : a crystalline anhydride $C_6H_{12}O_5$ of sorbitol found in species of milkwort (as *Polygala amara*); 1,5-anhydro-D-glucitol — called also *1,5-sorbitan*

poly·gam \'==,gam\ *n* -S [NL *Polygamia*] : a plant of the class Polygamia

poly·gamia \,=='gāmēə, -'gam-\ *n pl, cap* [NL, fr. Gk *polygamos* polygamous + NL *-ia*] *in former classifications* : a class of plants with both hermaphrodite and unisexual flowers on the same plant — **poly·gami·an** \¦==¦=mēən\ *adj*

poly·gam·ic \¦==¦gamik\ *also* **poly·gam·i·cal** \-məkəl\ *adj* [*polygamy* + *-ic* or *-ical*] : POLYGAMOUS — **poly·gam·i·cal·ly** \-mək(ə)lē\ *adv*

po·lyg·a·mist \pə'ligəməst\ *n* -S : one who practices polygamy — **po·lyg·a·mis·tic** \=¦==¦mistik\ *adj*

po·lyg·a·mize \='==,mīz\ *vi* -ED/-ING/-S *see -ize in Explan Notes* : to practice polygamy

po·lyg·a·mo·dioecious \pə¦ligə(,)mō+\ *adj* [*polygamous* + *dioecious*] : having some plants polygamous and some dioecious in the same species

po·lyg·a·mous \pə'ligəməs\ *adj* [Gk *polygamos*, fr. *poly-* + *-gamos* -gamous] **1** : of, relating to, characterized by, or involving polygamy : having a plurality of wives or husbands ⟨~ marriages⟩ **2** : bearing both hermaphrodite and unisexual flowers on the same plant **3** *zool* : having more than one mate at the same time — **po·lyg·a·mous·ly** *adv*

po·lyg·a·my \-mē,-mi\ *n* -ES [MF *polygamie*, fr. LL *polygamia*, fr. Gk, fr. *poly-* + *-gamia* (fr. *gamos* marriage + *-ia* -y) — more at BIGAMY] **1** : the state or fact of being polygamous; *specif* : a marriage form in which a spouse of either sex may possess a plurality of mates at the same time — used either inclusively of both polygyny and polyandry or exclusively of polygyny ⟨among the Batak of Palawan both ~ and polyandry exist⟩ ⟨the Mormons' former practice of ~⟩; compare BIGAMY, MONOGAMY **2** : possession of a plurality of benefices **3** : the condition of bearing both hermaphrodite and unisexual flowers on the same plant **4** *zool* : the condition of having more than one mate at one time

poly·gastric \¦pälē, -lə+\ *adj* [*poly-* + *gastric*] : having more than one digestive cavity ⟨a ~ protozoan⟩; *also* : having the stomach divided into several chambers — used of ruminants

[1]**poly·gene** \'==,jēn\ *or* **poly·ge·net·ic** \¦==‿jə¦ned·ik\ *adj* [ISV *poly-* + *-gene;* prob. orig. formed in G] *geol* : originating or developing in two or more ways or at two or more times (as a limestone partly clastic and partly biochemical or a volcano built up by a succession of eruptions)

[2]**polygene** \"\ *n* [ISV *poly-* + *gene*] : one of a group of nonallelic genes that collectively control the inheritance of a quantitative character or modify the expression of a qualitative character, that individually are of slight effect, and that prob. are not basically different from oligogenes, but produce their dissimilar effects through interaction of all the components of the genome — compare MULTIPLE FACTOR, QUANTITATIVE INHERITANCE

poly·genesic \¦==+\ *adj* [*poly-* + *genesic*] : of or relating to polygenism

poly·genesis \,==+\ *n* [NL, fr. *poly-* + *genesis*] **1** : polyphyletic origin — used esp. of infrahuman species; called also *polyphylesis;* compare POLYGENY **2** : POLYGENISM — **poly·genesist** \+'jenəsəst\ *n* -S

poly·genetic \¦pälē, -lə+\ *adj* [ISV *poly* + *genetic*] **1** : having many distinct sources : originating at various places or times **2** : of or relating to polygenesis : POLYPHYLETIC **3** *of a dye* : yielding more than one color or shade according to the mordant — **poly·genetically** \"+\ *adv*

poly·gen·ic \¦==¦jenik\ *adj* [ISV *poly-* + *-genic;* orig. formed as F *polygenique*] **1** : POLYGENE **2** : POLYGENETIC **3** [*poly-* + *genic*] : of, relating to, mediated by, or constituting polygenes

polygenic system *n* : a group of polygenes

po·lyg·e·nism \pə'lijə,nizəm\ *n* -S [ISV *polygeny* + *-ism*] : the doctrine or belief that existing human races have evolved from two or more distinct ancestral types — compare MONOGENISM

po·lyg·e·nist \-‿nəst\ *n* -S [ISV *polygeny* + *-ist*] : one who accepts the doctrine of polygenism

po·lyg·e·nis·tic \=¦==¦nistik\ *adj* : of or relating to polygenism

poly·genome hybrid *or* **poly·genomic hybrid** \¦pälē, -lə+. . .-\ *n* [*polygenome, polygenomic* fr. *poly-* + *genome, genomic*] : a hybrid individual that has more than two complete genomes which are derived from two or more dissimilar ancestors

po·lyg·e·nous \pə'lijənəs\ *adj* [*poly-* + *-genous*] : consisting of or containing many kinds or elements ⟨a ~ nation⟩

po·lyg·e·ny \-nē\ *n* -ES [*poly-* + *-geny*] **1** : the descent of man from two or more independent pairs of ancestors — compare MONOGENY **2** : POLYGENISM

poly·germ \'pälē, -lə+,-\ *n* [*poly-* + *germ*] : a cluster of germ cells or morulae in the polyembryonic development of some parasitic insects — **poly·germinal** \¦==+\ *adj*

poly·glandular \¦==+\ *adj* [ISV *poly-* + *glandular*] : of, relating to, or involving several glands ⟨a ~ endocrinopathy⟩

poly·glo·bu·lia \,==,glä'byülēə\ *n* -S [NL, fr. *poly-* + ISV *globulin* + NL *-ia*] : POLYCYTHEMIA

poly·glob·u·lism \-'gläbyə,lizəm\ *n* -S [NL *polyglobulia* + E *-ism*] : POLYCYTHEMIA

[1]**poly·glot** \'pälē,glät, -lə,g-, *usu* -gläd·+V\ *n* -S [Gk *polyglōttos, polyglōssos* speaking many languages, many-tongued, fr. *poly-* + *-glōttos -glōssos* tongued (fr. *glōtta, glōssa* tongue, language) — more at GLOSS] **1** : one who speaks or writes several languages **2** *usu cap* **a** : a book containing versions of the same text in several languages arranged for comparison usu. in parallel columns; *esp* : the Scriptures in several languages **b** : an edition of the Bible containing a monolingual text taken from a multilingual Bible **3** : a mixture or confusion of languages or nomenclatures ⟨a ~ of diagnostic labels and systems —G.N.Raines⟩

[2]**polyglot** \"\ *adj* **1 a** : speaking or writing several or many languages : MULTILINGUAL ⟨a ~ traveler⟩ **b** : composed of or belonging to numerous linguistic groups ⟨a ~ population⟩ ⟨a city of sharp extremes between the rich and transient and the mass of ~ poor —*Reporter*⟩ ⟨catering to the thousands of ~ seamen —*Amer. Guide Series: N.Y.City*⟩ **2** : containing matter in several languages ⟨a ~ sign⟩ ⟨a ~ dictionary⟩; *esp* : composed of correlative text in several languages often arranged in parallel columns ⟨a ~ Bible⟩ **3** : composed of elements from different languages ⟨verbose, erudite, and ~ slang —C.H.Sykes⟩ ⟨researchers themselves have inherited a curious ~ terminology —A.G.N.Flew⟩

poly·glot·ism *or* **poly·glot·tism** \-gläd·,izəm, -ä,tiz-\ *n* -S : the use of or ability to speak many languages : polyglot character

poly·glot·tal \¦==¦gläd·ᵊl, -ät|\ *or* **poly·glot·tic** \|ik, |ēk\ *or* **poly·glot·tous** \|əs\ *adj* [[1]*polyglot* + *-al* or *-ic* or *-ous*] : POLYGLOT — **poly·glot·tal·ly** \|ᵊlē, |ᵊli\ *adv*

poly·glycol \'pälē, -lə+\ *n* [*poly-* + *glycol*] : a polyethylene glycol or related compound of the ether-glycol type containing several ether linkages that yields one or more glycols on hydrolysis of these linkages

poly·gon \'pälē,gän, -lə,g- *sometimes* -‿gən\ *n* -S [LL *polygonum*, fr. Gk *polygōnon*, fr. neut. of *polygōnos* polygonal, fr. *poly-* + *-gōnos* (fr. *gōnia* angle, corner) — more at -GON] **1 a** : a closed figure consisting of straight lines joined end to end **b** : a closed figure on the surface of a sphere consisting of arcs of great circles joined end to end **2 a** : a polygonal or approximately polygonal object, area, or arrangement **b** : an often hexagonal block or arrangement of surficial material (as soil) forming part of a uniform pattern and often caused by alternate freezing and thawing of the crust — usu. used in pl. ⟨mud ~s⟩ ⟨stone ~s⟩ ⟨ice ~s⟩

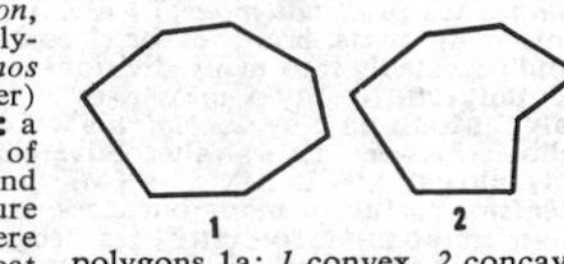

polygons 1a: *1* convex, *2* concave

po·lyg·o·na·ce·ae \pə,ligə'nāsē,ē\ *n pl, cap* [NL, fr. *Polygonum*, type genus + *-aceae*] : a family of herbs, shrubs, or trees (order Polygonales) chiefly of the north temperate zone having mostly entire leaves with stipules forming a sheath round the stem and flowers that are spicate and apetalous and including the buckwheats — **po·lyg·o·na·ceous** \=¦==¦nāshəs\ *adj*

po·lyg·o·nal \pə'ligənᵊl\ *adj* **1** : having many sides ⟨a ~ figure⟩ ⟨the ~ assault which the coordinated natural and social sciences could make upon the problems of society —J.R. Newman⟩ **2** : having a surface marked by a pattern of more or less polygonal blocks or spaces — see POLYGON 2 ⟨~ ground⟩ ⟨~ soil⟩ — **po·lyg·o·nal·ly** \-ᵊlē,-ᵊli\ *adv*

po·lyg·o·na·les \pə,ligə'nā(,)lēz\ *n pl, cap* [NL, fr. *Polygonum* + *-ales*] : an order of dicotyledonous plants coextensive with the family Polygonaceae

polygonal graph *n* : a statistical diagram composed of a circle and as many radii as there are elements to be compared

polygonal masonry *n* : masonry constructed of stones dressed with smooth faces that do not meet at right angles

polygonal number *n* : FIGURATE NUMBER

polygo·na·tion \,pälēgə'nāshən, -ləg-; pə,lig-\ *n* -S [ISV *polygon* + *-ation*] : the measurement of land by means of polygons — compare TRIANGULATION

poly·gon·a·tum \,pälē'gänəd·əm, -lə'g-\ *n* [NL, fr. L *polygonaton* sealwort, fr. Gk *polygonaton*, fr. neut. of *polygonatos* having many joints, fr. *poly-* + *gonat-, gony* knee] **1** *cap* : a genus of herbs (family Liliaceae) of the north temperate zone having erect or arching stems, entire leaves, axillary tubular flowers often in pairs, and globular black or blue berries **2** -S : any plant of the genus *Polygonatum*

po·lyg·o·nel·la \pə,ligə'nelə\ *n, cap* [NL, fr. *Polygonum* + *-ella*] : a small genus of heathlike herbs (family Polygonaceae) of eastern No. America with jointed stems, small narrow leaves, and small white or greenish apetalous flowers in panicled racemes — see JOINTWEED

poly·go·nia \,pälē'gōnēə, -lə'g-\ *n* [NL, fr. *poly-* + Gk *gōnia* angle] **1** *cap* : a genus of anglewing butterflies including many American insects (as the comma butterfly) and having wings that are mostly tawny brown or orange above with dark spots and border and mottled on the underside with grays and browns imitative of bark or dead leaves **2** -S : a butterfly of the genus *Polygonia*

poly·gon·ic \¦==¦gänik\ *or* **po·lyg·o·nous** \pə'ligənəs\ *adj* : POLYGONAL — **poly·gon·i·cal·ly** \¦pälē¦gänək(ə)lē, -lə¦g-\ *adv*

po·lyg·o·num \pə'ligənəm\ *n* [NL, fr. Gk *polygonon* knotgrass (*Polygonum aviculare*), fr. *poly-* + *-gonon* (fr. *gony* knee) — more at KNEE] **1** *cap* : a large widely distributed genus (the type of the family Polygonaceae) of herbs having prominent ocreae, thickened nodes, and flowers that are solitary and axillary or in spiked racemes — see KNOTGRASS, PERSICARIA **2** -S : any plant of the genus *Polygonum*

poly·gor·di·us \,pälē'gȯ(r)dēəs, -lə'g-\ *n, cap* [NL, prob. fr. *poly-* + *Gordius*, legendary founder of Phrygia — more at GORDIAN KNOT] : a genus (the type of the family Polygordiidae) comprising slender cylindrical many-segmented marine annelid worms belonging to the class Archiannelida and having the segmentation externally obscure and the sexes separate

[1]**poly·gram** \'==,gram\ *n* [Gk *polygrammos* marked with many lines, fr. *poly-* + *-grammos* (fr. *grammē* line, fr. *graphein* to write) — more at CARVE] : a figure determined by many lines

[2]**polygram** \"\ *n* [*poly-* (as in *polygraph*) + *-gram*] : a tracing made by a polygraph

poly·graph \-raf,-råf\ *n* [Gk *polygraphos* writing much, fr. *poly-* + *-graphos* (fr. *graphein* to write) — more at CARVE] **1** : a voluminous or versatile writer **2** : an instrument for recording tracings of several different pulsations simultaneously (as of the pulse, blood pressure, and respiration) — compare PATHOMETER **3** : LIE DETECTOR — see KEELER POLYGRAPH **4** : a cluster of two or more successive letters in cryptography

poly·graph·ic \¦==¦grafik\ *adj* **1 a** : VOLUMINOUS, VERSATILE ⟨a ~ writer⟩ **b** *of a book* (1) : dealing with a wide range of subjects ⟨a ~ treatise⟩ (2) : written by several authors or scribes ⟨a ~ manuscript⟩ **2** : proceeding (as in encipherment) by groups of two or more successive letters at a time ⟨~ substitution⟩ **3** : relating to, produced by, or employing a polygraph ⟨~ examination of the patient⟩ ⟨intelligence agency's ~ screening program —Dwight MacDonald⟩ — **poly·graph·i·cal·ly** \-fək(ə)lē\ *adv*

poly·graph·ist \'==,grafəst, -råf-; pə'ligrəf-\ *n* -S : one skilled in the use of a polygraph

po·lyg·ra·phy \pə'ligrəfē\ *n* -ES [NL *polygraphia*, fr. Gk, much writing, fr. *poly-* + *-graphia* -graphy] **1** *obs* : CRYPTOGRAPHY **2** : literary productiveness or versatility

poly·groove *or* **poly·grooved** \'pälē, -lə+\ *adj* [*poly-* + *groove* or *grooved*] : having many grooves ⟨a ~ rifle barrel⟩

poly·gyn·ia \,pälē'j|inēə, -lə'-, -'g|, |īn-\ *n pl, cap* [NL, fr. *poly-* + *-gynia*] *in former classifications* : a class of plants comprising those having flowers with more than 12 styles

po·lyg·y·nist \pə'lijənəst, -igə-\ *n* -S : one that practices or advocates polygyny

poly·gy·noe·cial \¦pälē|j|ə¦nēs(h)ēəl, -lə|, |g|, |i¦-, -shəl\ *adj* [*poly-* + NL *gynoecium* + E *-al*] : having or made up of several or many united gynoecia ⟨collective fruits are ~⟩

po·lyg·y·nous \pə'lijənəs, -igə-\ *also* **poly·gynic** \¦pälē¦j|inik, -lə¦-, -¦g|, |īn-\ *or* **poly·gyni·ous** \¦==¦=nēəs\ *adj* [*polygynous, polygynious* fr. *polygyny* + *-ous* or *-ious; polygynic* ISV *polygyny* + *-ic;* prob. orig. formed as F *polygynique*] **1** : relating to, practicing, or characterized by polygyny **2** : having many pistils **3** : of or relating to a species maintaining a number of fecundated females in its colony — used of social bees and ants

po·lyg·y·ny \pə'lijənē, -igə-\ *n* -ES [*poly-* + *-gyny*] **1** : a marriage form in which a man has two or more wives at the same time — contrasted with *polyandry;* compare POLYGAMY, SORORAL POLYGYNY **2** : the condition of having more than one female mate at one time **3** : POLYGAMY 3

poly·gyria \,pälē'jīrēə, -lə'j-, -jir-\ *n* -S [NL, fr. *poly-* + *gyr-* + *-ia*] : the condition of having an unusual number of cerebral convolutions

poly·halide \¦pälē, -lə +\ *n* [*poly-* + *halide*] : a halide containing more than one halogen atom in a molecule

poly·halite \,=='ha,līt, -'hā-\ *n* -S [G *polyhalit*, fr. *poly-* + *hal-* + *-it* -ite] : a mineral $K_2MgCa_2(SO_4)_4.2H_2O$ occurring usu. in fibrous masses of a brick-red color due to iron but consisting essentially of hydrous sulfate of calcium, magnesium, and potassium

[1]**poly·haploid** \¦pälē, -lə+\ *adj* [*poly-* + *haploid*] : of, relating to, or constituting the gametic chromosome number of a polyploid individual

[2]**polyhaploid** \"+\ *n* : a polyhaploid cell or individual

poly·haptenic \¦pälē, -lə+\ *adj* [*poly-* + *haptenic*] : containing more than one haptenic group

poly·harmony \"+\ *n* [*poly-* + *harmony*] : a harmonic structure that characteristically introduces two or more simultaneous musical harmonies or strata of harmony

poly·he·dral \¦pälē¦hēdrəl, -lə¦h- *sometimes chiefly Brit* -hed-\ *adj* [NL *polyhedron* + E *-al*] **1** : having the form of a polyhedron : having many faces ⟨a ~ solid⟩ **2** : relating to a polyhedron

polyhedral angle *n* : a portion of space partly enclosed by three or more planes whose intersections meet in a vertex

polyhedral disease *n* : POLYHEDROSIS

poly·he·dric \-drik\ *also* **poly·he·dri·cal** \-drəkəl\ *adj* [NL *polyhedron* + *-ic* or *-ical*] : POLYHEDRAL

poly·he·dron \¦==¦hē|drən *sometimes* |,drän *or chiefly Brit* -he|\ *n, pl* **polyhe·dra** \|‿drə\ *or* **polyhedrons** [NL, fr. Gk *polyedron*, neut. of *polyedros* with many seats (i.e., sides), fr. *poly-* + *hedra* seat, side — more at SIT] **1** : a figure or solid formed by plane faces **2** *also* **polyhedral body a** : one of the angular bodies often with hornlike appendages into which the zoospores of the water net and related algae develop and within which the vegetative coenobium develops **b** : one of the refractile many-sided bodies that are present in the terminal phases of an insect polyhedrosis and are regarded as products of tissue breakdown rather than as the infective agent of the disease

polyhedral angle at vertex *a* formed by lateral angles *b a c*, *c a d*, *d a e*, *e a f* and *f a b*

poly·he·dro·sis \,==‿hē'drōsəs\ *n, pl* **polyhedro·ses** \-ō,sēz\ [NL, fr. *polyhedron* + *-osis*] : any of several virus diseases of insect larvae characterized by dissolution of tissues and accumulation of polyhedral granules in the resultant fluid — called also *polyhedral disease;* compare SILKWORM JAUNDICE, WILT 2

poly·hi·dro·sis \¦pälē,hī¦drōsəs, -lə-, -‿hi¦-\ *also* **poly·idro·sis** \-ē,ī¦d-, -ēə¦d-\ *n, pl* **polyhidro·ses** *or* **polyidro·ses** \-ō,sēz\ [*polyhidrosis* fr. NL, fr. *poly-* + *hidrosis; polyidrosis* fr. NL, fr. *poly-* + *-idrosis*] : excessive secretion of perspiration

poly·his·tor \¦pälē¦histə(r), -lə¦h-\ *also* **poly·his·to·ri·an** \,==(,)hi'stōrēən\ *n* -S [*polyhistor* fr. Gk *polyistōr* very learned, fr. *poly-* very (fr. *polys* very, much, many) + *histōr* judge, learned, knowing; *polyhistorian* fr. *polyhistor* + *-an* — more at HISTORY] : POLYMATH

poly·his·tor·ic \¦==(,)hi¦stȯrik\ *adj* : POLYMATH

poly·his·to·ry \¦==¦hist(ə)rē\ *n* : POLYMATHY

poly·hybrid \¦pälē, -lə+\ *n* [ISV *poly-* + *hybrid*] : a hybrid whose parents differ in a number of characters : an individual or group heterozygous for more than one pair of genes — **poly·hybridism** \"+\ *n*

poly·hydramnios \"+\ *n* [NL, fr. *poly-* + *hydr-* + *amnios*] : HYDRAMNIOS

poly·hydric \"+\ *adj* [*poly-* + *-hydric*] **1** *archaic* : containing more than one atom of acid hydrogen **2** : POLYHYDROXY — used esp. of alcohols and phenols

poly·hydroxy \¦pälē, -lə+\ *adj* [*poly-* + *hydroxy*] : containing more than one hydroxyl group in the molecule : POLYHYDRIC

poly·ide·ic \¦pälē¦ī¦dēik\ *adj* [*poly-* + *idea* + *-ic*] : of, relating to, or characterized by polyideism

poly·ide·ism \,=='īdē,izəm\ *n* -S [*poly-* + *-idea* + *-ism*] : a state of absorption in a group of related ideas or memories — opposed to *monoideism*

poly·isobutylene \¦pälē+\ *n* [ISV *poly-* + *isobutylene*] : a polymer of isobutylene varying from a viscous oil to a sticky or rubbery solid; *esp* : an elastomer $(C_4H_8)_x$ that is formed at a low temperature (as −100°C) in the presence of a metal halide catalyst (as boron trifluoride) and that cannot be vulcanized unless a small amount of a proportion of isoprene or other diolefin has been incorporated with the isobutylene before polymerization — compare DIISOBUTYLENE, SYNTHETIC RUBBER

poly·isomere \"+\ *n* [*poly-* + *isomere*] : one of the simple repetitive segments characteristic of primitive organisms

poly·isomerism \"+\ *n* [*poly-* + *isomere* + *-ism*] : the tendency usu. regarded as primitive for an organism to be made up of a series of similar and equivalent parts — compare METAMERISM

poly·isoprene \"+\ *n* [*poly-* + *isoprene*] : a polymer of isoprene occurring naturally in a cis form as the rubber hydrocarbon and in the corresponding trans form as gutta and also produced synthetically in several forms

poly·isotopic \"+\ *adj* [*poly-* + *isotopic*] **:** of, relating to, or consisting of more than one isotope

poly·kar·yo·cyte \,päle'kareə,sīt, -lə'k-\ *n* -s [*poly-* + *kary-* + *-cyte*] **:** OSTEOCLAST — **poly·kar·yo·cyt·ic** \¦==¦===¦sid·ik\ *adj*

poly·karyon *also* **poly·caryon** \"+\ *n* [NL, fr. *poly-* + *karyon*] **:** a multinuclear cell or individual

poly·kary·ot·ic \+¦karē¦äd·ik\ *adj* [*poly-* + *kary-* + *-otic*] **:** having many nuclei or cells with many nuclei

poly·lem·ma \¦pälē¦lemə, -lə¦-\ *n* -s [*poly-* + *-lemma* (as in *dilemma*)] **:** an argument analogous to a dilemma in which many (as more than three) alternatives are presented in the major premise

poly·lingual \¦pälē, -lə+\ *adj* [*poly-* + *lingual*] **:** MULTILINGUAL ⟨~ area⟩ ⟨a ~ journal⟩

poly·literal \"+\ *adj* [*poly-* + *literal*] **1 :** POLYGRAPHIC ⟨~ transposition⟩ **2 :** representing each letter by a polygraph ⟨~ substitution⟩

poly·literally \"+\ *adv* **:** in a polyliteral manner **:** so as to be polyliteral

poly·lith \'==,lith\ *n* -s [*poly-* + *-lith*] **:** a megalithic structure (as a dolmen or stone circle) made of several or many stones — compare MONOLITH

poly·lith·ic \¦==¦lithik\ *adj* [*poly-* + *-lithic*] **:** composed of several or many stones or kinds of stone ⟨a ~ deposit⟩

poly·mas·tia \,=='mastēə\ *also* **poly·mas·ty** \'==,=tē\ *n, pl* **polymastias** *also* **polymasties** [NL, fr. *poly-* + *-mastia*] **:** the condition of having more than the normal number of breasts — **poly·mas·tic** \¦==¦=tik\ *adj*

poly·mas·ti·da \,=='mastədə\ *or* **poly·mas·ti·ga** \-təgə\ *or* **poly·mas·ti·go·da** \-,mastə'gōdə\ *or* **poly·mas·ti·go·ta** \-ōd·ə\ [NL, irreg. fr. *Polymastig-, Polymastix*] *syn of* POLYMASTIGINA

poly·mas·ti·gi·na \-,mastə'jīnə\ *n pl, cap* [NL, fr. *Polymastig-, Polymastix*, genus of flagellates (fr. *poly-* + Gk *mastig-, mastix* whip) + *-ina* — more at MASTIG-] **:** an order of small plastic usu. parasitic flagellates (subclass Zoomastigina) having several flagella and including various medically or economically important forms (as members of the genera *Costia, Chilomastix, Giardia, Hexamita*, and *Trichomonas*) — **poly·mas·ti·gine** \¦==¦mastə,jīn\ *adj*

1**poly·mas·ti·gote** \¦==¦mastə,gōt\ *adj* [alter. of earlier *polymastigate*, fr. *poly-* + *mastig-* + *-ate*] **1 :** having many flagella **2** [NL *Polymastigota*] **:** of or relating to the Polymastigina

2**polymastigote** \"\ *n* -s **:** a flagellate of the order Polymastigina

1**poly·math** \'==,math\ *n* -s [Gk *polymathēs* knowing much, fr. *poly-* + *-mathēs* (fr. *mathein, manthanein* to learn) — more at MATHEMATICAL] **:** one of encyclopedic learning ⟨such a survey requires a heroic ~ —Douglas Bush⟩ ⟨our most ambitious critics are ~*s* —R.G.Davis⟩ — called also *polyhistor*

2**polymath** \"\ *or* **poly·math·ic** \¦==¦mathik\ *adj* **:** learned in many fields — compare ERUDITE ⟨masters of the subtle schools are controversial, *polymath* —T.S.Eliot⟩ ⟨an original, vigorous, *polymathic* mind —B.R.Redman⟩

po·lym·a·thy \pə'liməthē\ *n* -ES [Gk *polymathia* much learning, fr. *polymathēs* knowing much + *-ia* -y] **:** the character or attainments of a polymath **:** encyclopedic learning ⟨scorn for mere ~ —G.W.Johnson⟩

poly·melia \,pälē'mēlēə, -lə'm-, -mel-, -lyə\ *also* **po·lym·e·ly** \pə'liməlē; 'pälē,mēlē, -älə,m-, -mel-\ *n, pl* **polymelias** *also* **polymelies** [NL *polymelia*, fr. *poly-* + *-melia*] **:** the condition of having more than the normal number of limbs

poly·menorrhea *also* **poly·menorrhoea** \¦pälē, -lə+\ *n* [NL, fr. *poly-* + *menorrhea*] **:** menstruation at abnormally frequent intervals — compare MENORRHAGIA

poly·mer \'päləmə(r), -lēm-\ *n* -s [ISV, back-formation fr. *polymeric;* prob. orig. formed in G] **:** a natural or synthetic chemical compound or mixture of compounds formed by polymerization and consisting essentially of repeating structural units; *esp* **:** HIGH POLYMER — compare COPOLYMER, DIMER, HOMOPOLYMER, ISOMER, MONOMER; MACROMOLECULE, PLASTIC, RESIN 2a, SYNTHETIC FIBER, SYNTHETIC RUBBER

po·lym·era \pə'limərə\ *n pl, cap* [NL, fr. *poly-* + *-mera*, neut. pl. of *-merus* -merous] *in some classifications* **:** a division of invertebrate animals having the body divided into numerous clearly defined segments

poly·me·ria \,=='mirēə, -,mə'rīə\ *n* -s [NL, fr. Gk *polymereia* condition of having many parts, fr. *polymerēs* having many parts + *-ia* -y] **:** the condition of having supernumerary parts or accessory organs

poly·mer·ic \¦==¦merik, -rēk\ *adj* [ISV *polymer-* (fr. Gk *polymerēs* having many parts, fr. *poly-* + *meros* part) + *-ic* — more at MERIT] **1 :** of, relating to, or consisting of a polymer **2 a :** of, relating to, involving, or being any of a group of nonallelic identical genes that collectively control various quantitative hereditary characters — compare MULTIPLE FACTOR, POLYGENE **b :** composed of several similar parts ⟨~ chromosomes⟩ **3 :** consisting of many segments ⟨a ~ annelid worm⟩ — **poly·mer·i·cal·ly** \-rək(ə)lē, -rēk-, -li\ *adv*

po·lym·er·ide \pə'limə,rīd, -,rəd\ *n* -s [ISV *polymeric* + *-ide*] *chiefly Brit* **:** POLYMER

po·lym·er·ism \pə'limə,rizəm; 'päləmə,rizəm, -lēm-\ *n* -s **:** the quality or state of being polymeric

po·lym·er·iz·able \pə'limə,rīzəbəl, =,=='===; 'päləm-, -lēm-, ,==='===\ *adj* **:** capable of polymerizing

po·lym·er·i·zate \pə'limərə,zāt; ,pälə'merə,zāt, -lē'm-\ *n* -s [ISV, prob. back-formation fr. *polymerization*] **:** a product of polymerization **:** POLYMER

po·lym·er·i·za·tion \pə,limərə'zāshən, ,päləm-, ,pälēm-, -,rī'z-\ *n* -s [ISV *polymer* + *-ization*] **1 a :** a chemical reaction in which two or more small molecules combine to form larger molecules that contain repeating structural units of the original molecules and that have the same percentage composition as the small molecules if the small ones were all of the same kind **:** the union of monomers to form polymers — see ADDITION POLYMERIZATION, CONDENSATION POLYMERIZATION, COPOLYMERIZATION; compare POLYCONDENSATION **b :** the state of being polymerized **2 :** ASSOCIATION 7 **3 :** reduplication of parts in the animal body

po·lym·er·ize \pə'limə,rīz, 'päləm-, 'pälēm-\ *vb* -ED/-ING/-S *see -ize in Explan Notes* [*polymer* + *-ize*] *vt* **:** to combine (small molecules) chemically into larger or esp. very large molecules **:** subject to polymerization ~ *vi* **:** to form larger molecules from small molecules **:** undergo polymerization

po·lym·er·iz·er \-zə(r)\ *n* -s **:** an operator of polymerization equipment

po·lym·er·ous \pə'limərəs\ *adj* [*poly-* + *-merous*] **1 :** having many parts or members in a whorl **2** [*polymer* + *-ous*] **:** POLYMERIC 1

polymer tempera *n* **:** an aqueous plastic-based paint used esp. in fine arts

po·lym·ery \pə'limərē, 'pälə,merē, 'pälē,-\ *n* -ES [ISV, fr. NL *polymeria*] **:** polymeric condition ⟨doubling of floral organs is a common manifestation of ~⟩

poly·me·ter \'pälē,mēd·ə(r), -lə,m-; pə'liməd·-\ *n* [ISV *poly-* + *-meter*] **:** any of various measuring instruments capable of indicating two or more quantities

poly·methine \¦pälē, -lə+\ *adj* [*poly-* + *methine*] **:** consisting of or containing a series of methylidyne groups ⟨~ chain⟩

polymethine dye *n* **:** any of a class of dyes (as cyanines or merocyanines) characterized by a resonance structure containing a conjugated chain of carbon atoms that is at least in part an open chain [as in $-CH(=CH-CH)_n=$] attached to two polar atoms (as two amino nitrogen atoms either one of which is considered to be positively charged) — see DYE table I

poly·methylene \"+\ *n* [ISV *poly-* + *methylene*] **1 :** a hydrocarbon constituted of methylene groups: as **a :** CYCLOPARAFFIN **b :** a polymer of high molecular weight that resembles polyethylene except for its entirely linear and unbranched structure and that is usu. made from diazomethane by loss of nitrogen **2 :** a bivalent radical $-(CH_2)_n-$ consisting of a series of methylene groups ⟨~ halides⟩

poly·methyl methacrylate \"+...-\ *n* [*polymethyl* fr. *poly-* + *methyl*] **:** a polymer of methyl methacrylate **:** METHYL METHACRYLATE 2

poly·metric \"+\ *adj* [*poly-* + *metric*] **:** relating to, exhibiting, involving, or employing a variety of meters

po·lym·e·try \pə'limə·trē\ *n* -ES [*polymetric* + *-y*] **:** the combination of different prosodic meters; *esp* **:** the use of different meters in different lines of the same poem or the same stanza

poly·microbic *or* **poly·microbial** \¦pälē, -lə+\ *adj* [*poly-* + *microbic* or *microbial*] **:** of, relating to, or caused by several types of microorganisms

poly·mig·nyte *or* **poly·mig·nite** \,pälē'mig,nīt, -ləm-\ *n* -s [Sw *polymignit*, fr. *poly-* + *mign-* (fr. Gk *mignynai* to mix) + *-it* -ite — more at MIX] **:** a mineral (Ca,Fe,Y,etc.,Zr,Th)$(Cb,Ti,Ta)O_4$ consisting of a niobate and titanate of the metals of the cerium group with iron and calcium

poly·mix·ia \-'miksēə\ *n, cap* [NL, fr. Gk, mixture of many components, fr. *poly-* + *mixis* act of mixing (fr. *mignynai* to mix) + *-ia* -y] **:** a genus of small deep-sea berycoid fishes coextensive with the family Polymixiidae and resembling the squirrelfishes but having smooth scales and a pair of barbels on the chin — **poly·mix·i·id** \¦==¦=sēəd\ *n or adj*

po·lym·nia \pə'limnēə\ *n, cap* [NL, prob. fr. L *Polymnia, Polyhymnia*, one of the Greek muses, fr. Gk] **:** a small genus of American and chiefly tropical herbs (family Compositae) having large lobed leaves and corymbose heads of discoid and radiate yellow or white flowers — see LEAFCUP

pol·ym·nite \'päləm,nīt, pə'lim-\ *n* -s [Gk *polymnios* full of moss (fr. *poly-* + *mnion* moss, seaweed) + E *-ite* — more at MNIUM] **:** a stone marked with dendrites and black lines so disposed as to suggest rivers and marshes

poly·molecular \¦pälē, -lə+\ *adj* [*poly-* + *molecular*] **1 :** consisting of many molecules esp. of different sizes ⟨high polymers are, in general, ~ —A.M.Sookne & Milton Harris⟩ **2 :** having a thickness of several molecules ⟨~ layers⟩ — compare MULTILAYER — **poly·molecularity** \"+\ *n*

poly·molybdate \"+\ *n* [*poly-* + *molybdate*] **:** any of various complex salts (as ammonium molybdate) regarded as derived from isopoly acids of molybdenum

1**poly·morph** \'pälē,mȯrf, -lə,m-\ *n* -s [ISV, fr. *polymorphous*] **1 :** a polymorphous organism; *also* **:** one of the several forms of such an organism **2 :** any of the crystalline forms of a polymorphous substance **3 :** a polymorphonuclear leukocyte

2**polymorph** \"\ *adj* **:** POLYMORPHIC

poly·mor·pha \,=='mȯrfə\ *n pl, cap* [NL, *poly-* + *-morpha*] *in some esp former classifications* **:** a suborder or other group of beetles including the Clavicornia and Serricornia

poly·mor·phe·an \¦==¦mȯrfēən, ¦==,=¦==\ *adj* [Gk *polymorphos* multiform + E *-an*] *archaic* **:** POLYMORPHIC

poly·mor·phic \¦==¦mȯrfik\ *adj* [Gk *polymorphos* multiform + E *-ic*] **1 :** POLYMORPHOUS b **2 :** having or occurring in several distinct forms **:** exhibiting polymorphism ⟨a ~ species⟩ ⟨man is both ~ and polytypic —*New Biology*⟩ — **poly·mor·phi·cal·ly** \-fək(ə)lē\ *adv*

poly·mor·phism \'==,mȯr,fizəm, ,=='===\ *n* -s [ISV *polymorphous* + *-ism*] **:** the quality or state of being polymorphous: as **a** (1) **:** capability of assuming different forms **:** capability of wide variation (2) **:** existence of a species in several forms independent of the variations of sex (as in various butterflies whose broods, appearing at different seasons, differ in size or color, or both, or in ants and termites, in which different castes exist) — compare DIMORPHISM, HETEROMORPHISM **b :** the property of crystallizing in two or more forms with distinct structures — compare ALLOTROPY

1**poly·mor·pho·nuclear** \¦pälē¦mȯrfə, -lə¦m- +\ *adj* [*polymorphous* + *nuclear*] **1** *of a leukocyte* **:** having the nucleus complexly lobed **2 :** being a neutrophil or other leukocyte of typical mature form with distinctly lobed nucleus

2**polymorphonuclear** \"\ *n* -s **:** a polymorphonuclear leukocyte

poly·mor·pho·nucleate \¦pälē¦mȯrfə, -lə¦m-+\ *adj* [1*polymorphonuclear* + *-ate*] **:** POLYMORPHONUCLEAR

poly·mor·phous \¦pälē¦mȯrfəs, -lə¦m-\ *adj* [Gk *polymorphos* multiform fr. *poly-* + *-morphos* -morphous] **:** having or assuming various forms, characters, styles, or functions ⟨a ~ god⟩: as **a :** POLYMORPHIC 2 **b :** crystallizing with two or more different structures — **poly·mor·phous·ly** *adv* — **poly·mor·phous·ness** *n* -ES

polymorphous–perverse \¦==¦===¦=, ¦==¦==¦=,=\ *adj* **:** relating to or exhibiting infantile sexual tendencies in which the genitals are not yet identified as the sole or principal sexual organs nor coitus as the goal of erotic activity and which are a basis for pregenital libidinal fixation

poly·mor·phy \'pälē,mȯrfē, -lə,m-\ *n* -ES [ISV *polymorph* + *-y*] **:** POLYMORPHISM

poly·my·ar·i·an \¦==,mī¦a(a)rēən\ *also* **poly·my·ar·i·al** \-ēəl\ *adj* [*poly-* + *-myaria* + *-an* or *-al*] **:** having many cells in each quadrant of a cross-section — used of the arrangement of muscle cells in a nematode worm

poly·my·ar·i·ty \,==,mī'arəd·ē\ *n* -ES [*polymyarian* + *-ity*] **:** the condition of being polymyarian

poly·my·odi \,pälē,mī'ō,dī, -lə,m-\ *n pl, cap* [NL, fr. *poly-* + *-myodi* (fr. Gk *myōdēs* muscular, fr. *mys* mouse, muscle) — more at MOUSE] *in former classifications* **:** a group of birds nearly equivalent to Passeres — **poly·my·odi·an** \¦==,=¦ōdēən\ *or* **poly·my·odous** \-dəs\ *adj*

poly·my·oid \¦==¦mī,ȯid\ *adj* [*poly-* + *my-* + *-oid*] **1 :** having many syringeal muscles **2** [NL *Polymyodi* + E *-oid*] **:** POLYMYODIAN

poly·myositis \¦pälē, -lə+\ *n* [NL, fr. *poly-* + *myositis*] **:** inflammation of several muscles at once

po·lym·y·thy \pə'limәthē; 'pälē,mithē, -lə,m-\ *n* -ES [NL *polymythia*, fr. Gk *polymythos* with many legends (fr. *poly-* + *mythos* myth) + NL *-ia* -y — more at MYTH] **:** the inclusion of many or several stories or plots in one narrative or dramatic work

poly·myx·in \,pälē'miksən, -lə,m-\ *n* -s [ISV, fr. NL *polymyxa* (specific epithet of *Bacillus polymyxa* — fr. *poly-* + *-myxa* —) + ISV *-in*] **:** any of several basic polypeptide toxic antibiotics that are obtained from strains of a soil bacterium (*Bacillus polymyxa*) and are active against gram-negative bacteria: as **a** *or* **polymyxin A :** one of three nephrotoxic antibiotics **b** *or* **polymyxin B :** the least toxic of the polymyxins used in the form of its sulfate chiefly in the treatment of some localized, gastrointestinal, or systemic infections

pol·y·nee \¦==¦nā\ *n* -s [Sw] **:** a tart made of rich cookie dough, filled with meringue to which ground almonds have been added, and topped with a cross made of two strips of the cookie dough

poly·nemid \,pälē'nēməd, -nem-\ *n* -s [NL *Polynemidae*] **:** a fish of the family Polynemidae

poly·nem·i·dae \-nemə,dē\ *n pl, cap* [NL, fr. *Polynemus*, type genus + *-idae*] **:** a family (usu. coextensive with a suborder Polynemoidea of Percomorphi) of fishes that resemble mullets but have the pectoral fin divided into two parts of which the upper is much like an ordinary fin and the lower is composed of several separate slender threadlike rays and abound on the sandy shores of warm seas, many of them being valued for food and some yielding isinglass

1**poly·ne·moid** \¦==¦nē,mȯid\ *adj* [NL *Polynemus* + E *-oid*] **:** resembling or related to the Polynemidae

2**polynemoid** \"\ *n* -s **:** a polynemoid fish

poly·ne·moi·dea \,== nə'mȯidēə\ *n pl, cap* [NL, fr. *Polynemus* + *-oidea*] **:** a suborder of Percomorphi coextensive with the family Polynemidae

poly·ne·mus \,pälē'nēməs, -lə'n-\ *n, cap* [NL, fr. *poly-* + Gk *nēma* thread — more at NEEDLE] **:** a genus (the type of the family Polynemidae) of fishes resembling mullets

poly·neph·ric \¦==¦nefrik\ *adj* [*poly-* + *-nephric*] *of an insect* **:** having many Malpighian tubules

1**poly·ne·sian** \¦pälə¦nēzhən, -ēsh-\ *adj, usu cap* [*Polynesia*, islands of the central Pacific ocean + E *-an*] **1 a :** of, relating to, or characteristic of Polynesia **b :** of, relating to, or characteristic of the Polynesians **2 :** of, relating to, or characteristic of the Polynesian languages **3 :** of, relating to, or being a biogeographic region or subregion of the Australian region that includes the smaller tropical Pacific islands

2**polynesian** \"\ *n* -s *cap* [*Polynesia* + E *-an*] **1 :** a member of any of the native peoples of Polynesia usu. classified as being a composite chiefly of the white, Mongoloid, and Melanesian races and described as having black wavy hair, black eyes, medium breadth of nose, medium prognathism, brown skin, tall stature, and large-boned build **2 :** a group of Austronesian languages spoken largely in Polynesia

polynesian chestnut *n, usu cap P* **1 :** a Polynesian tree (*Inocarpus edulis*) of the family Leguminosae **2 :** the edible kidney-shaped seed of the Polynesian chestnut

poly·neuritic \¦pälē, -lə+\ *adj* [NL *polyneuritis* + E *-ic*] **:** of, relating to, or marked by polyneuritis

poly·neuritis \"+\ *n* [NL, fr. *poly-* + *neuritis*] **:** neuritis of several peripheral nerves at the same time caused by alcoholism, metallic and other poisons, infectious disease, or vitamin deficiency (as of thiamine)

poly·neuropathy \"+\ *n* [*poly-* + *neuropathy*] **:** a disease of nerves; *esp* **:** a noninflammatory degenerative disease of nerves usu. caused by toxins (as of lead, alcohol)

1**pol·y·noid** \'pälə,nȯid, pə'linəwəd\ *adj* [NL *Polinoidae*] **:** of or relating to the Polynoidae

2**polynoid** \"\ *n* -s **:** a worm of the family Polynoidae **:** SCALE WORM

pol·y·noi·dae \,pälə'nȯi(,)dē, pə,linə'wī(,)dē\ *n pl, cap* [NL, fr. *Polynoe*, type genus (fr. Gk *Polynoē*, a sea nymph) + *-idae*] **:** a family of marine polychaete worms having the back covered with two rows of scales

1**poly·no·mi·al** \¦pälē¦nōmēəl, -lə¦n-\ *n* -s [*poly-* + *-nomial* (as in *binomial*)] **1 a :** a mathematical expression of two or more terms **b :** an algebraic function of one or more variables consisting of the sum of terms whose factors are constants or positive integral or zero powers of the variables — called also *integral rational function* **2 :** a technical name of a plant or animal consisting of a descriptive phrase of more than three words

2**polynomial** \"\ *adj* **1 :** having the character of a polynomial **2 :** consisting of many names or terms

poly·nuclear \¦pälē, -lə+\ *adj* [ISV *poly-* + *nuclear*] **:** containing more than one nucleus: **a :** POLYCYCLIC a **b :** containing more than one central atom or ion — used of coordination complexes **c :** POLYMORPHONUCLEAR

poly·nu·cle·o·sis \,==,n(y)üklē'ōsəs\ *n, pl* **polynucleo·ses** \-ō,sēz\ [NL, fr. ISV *polynucle-* (in *polynuclear*) + NL *-osis*] **:** the presence of an excess of polymorphonuclear leucocytes (as in the circulating blood)

poly·nucleotide \¦pälē, -lə+\ *n* [ISV *poly-* + *nucleotide*] **:** a nucleotide (as of a nucleic acid) consisting of many mononucleotides in combination

po·lyn·ya *also* **po·lyn·ia** \¦pälən¦yä\ *n* -s [Russ *polyn'ya*, fr. *polyĭ* open, hollow; akin to OSlav *polje* field — more at FLOOR] **:** an area of open water in sea ice — distinguished from *lead*

poly·odon \'pälēə,dän\ *n, cap* [NL, fr. *poly-* + *-odon*] **:** a genus (the type of the family Polyodontidae) of fishes containing the paddlefish — **poly·odont** \-nt\ *or* **poly·odon·toid** \¦===¦dän·,tȯid\ *adj or n*

poly·odon·tia \,pälēō'dänch(ē)ə\ *n* -s [NL, fr. *poly-* + *-odontia*] **:** the presence of more than the normal number of teeth

poly·odon·ti·dae \-ntə,dē\ *n pl, cap* [NL, fr. *Polyodont-, Polyodon*, type genus + *-idae*] **:** a family of fishes (order Chondrostei) comprising the genera *Polyodon* and *Psephurus*

polyoestrous *var of* POLYESTROUS

poly·oi·cism \,pälē'ȯi,sizəm, -ȯi,ki-\ *n* -s [ISV *polyoicous* + *-ism*] **:** the condition of being polyoicous

poly·oi·cous \¦==¦ȯikəs\ *or* **poly·oe·cious** \¦==¦ēshəs\ *also* **poly·ecious** \¦==¦ēshəs\ *adj* [*poly-* + Gk *oikia* house + E *-ous* — more at VICINITY] **:** having the archegonia and antheridia sometimes on the same plant and sometimes on different plants ⟨~ mosses⟩ ⟨~ liverworts⟩ — compare HETEROICOUS, PAROICOUS — **poly·oi·cous·ly** *or* **poly·oe·cious·ly** *adv* — **poly·oi·cous·ness** *or* **poly·oe·cious·ness** *n* -ES

poly·oi·cy \'==,ȯisē, -,ȯikē\ *n* -ES [ISV *polyoicous* + *-y*] **:** POLYOICISM

poly·ol \'==,ȯl, -,ōl\ *n* -s [ISV *poly-* + *-ol*] **:** a compound (as sorbitol or pentaerythritol) containing usu. several alcoholic hydroxyl groups **:** a polyhydric alcohol

poly·olefin \¦pälē+\ *n* [*poly-* + *olefin*] **1 :** an olefin containing many double bonds **2 :** a polymer of olefin (as polyethylene)

poly·on·y·mous \¦pälē¦änəməs\ *adj* [Gk *polyōnymos*, fr. *poly-* + *-ōnymos* (fr. *onoma* name) — more at NAME] **:** having many names **:** known by various names

poly·on·y·my \,=='änəmē\ *n* -ES [Gk *polyōnymia*, fr. *poly-* + *-ōnymia* (fr. *onoma* name + *-ia* -y)] **:** plurality of names **:** the use of various names for one thing

poly·opia \,pälē'ōpēə\ *n* -s [NL, fr. *poly-* + *-opia*] **:** perception of more than one image of a single object esp. with one eye **:** multiple vision **:** DIPLOPIA — **poly·opic** \¦==¦ōpik\ *adj*

poly·or·chi·dism \,=='ȯ(r)kə,dizəm\ *n* -s [ISV *poly-* + *-orchidism*] **:** a condition of having more than two testes

poly·organic \¦pälē+\ *adj* [*poly-* + *organic*] **:** having many organs

poly·os·tot·ic \¦pälē,ä¦städ·ik\ *adj* [ISV *poly-* + *-ost* + *-otic*] **:** involving or relating to many bones

poly·ovular \¦pälē+\ *adj* [*poly-* + *ovular*] **:** of, relating to, producing, or containing more than one ovum ⟨~ cycle⟩ ⟨~ follicle⟩

poly·ovulation \"+\ *n* [*poly-* + *ovulation*] **:** the production of several to many ova at a single ovulation ⟨~ appears to be a primitive mammalian characteristic⟩

poly·oxy·ethylene glycol \¦pälē,äksē + ...-\ *n* [*polyoxyethylene* fr. *poly-* + *oxy-* + *ethylene*] **:** POLYETHYLENE GLYCOL

poly·oxymethylene \¦pälē+\ *n* [*poly-* + *oxy-* + *methylene*] **:** a polymer or hydrated polymer of formaldehyde; *esp* **:** PARAFORMALDEHYDE

polyoxymethylene glycol *n* **:** a linear hydrated polymer $HO(CH_2O)_nH$ of formaldehyde — see PARAFORMALDEHYDE

pol·yp \'päləp\ *n* -s [MF *polype* octopus, nasal tumor, fr. L *polypus*, fr. Gk *polypous*, lit., many-footed, fr. *poly-* + *pous* foot — more at FOOT] **1 a** *also* **pol·ype** \"\ *archaic* **:** an animal (as an octopus, cuttlefish, or squid) having numerous feet or tentacles **b :** a typical coelenterate individual with a hollow tubular body having outer ectoderm separated from inner endoderm by mesogloea, terminating anteriorly in a central mouth surrounded by tentacles, and being posteriorly closed and attached to the substrate (as in *Hydra*) or more or less directly continuous with other individuals of a compound animal (as in *Obelia* or most corals) **:** ZOOID **2** [so called fr. the ramifications resembling the tentacles of an octopus] **a :** a projecting mass of swollen and hypertrophied mucous membrane (as in the nasal cavity) caused by chronic inflammation **b :** a pedunculated tumor (as of the lower intestine) that often undergoes malignant change

poly·parasitism \¦pälē, -lə+\ *n* [*poly-* + *parasitism*] **:** HYPERPARASITISM 2

pol·yp·ar·i·an \¦pälə¦pa(a)rēən\ *adj* [*polypary* + *-an*] **:** of or relating to a polypary

pol·yp·ar·i·um \,=='pa(a)rēəm\ *n, pl* **polypar·ia** \-ēə\ [NL, fr. ISV *polypary*] **:** POLYPARY

po·lyp·a·rous \pə'lipərəs\ *adj* [*poly-* + *-parous*] **:** POLYTOCOUS

pol·yp·ary \'pälə,perē\ *n* -ES [*polyp* + *-ary*] **:** the common investing structure or tissue in which the polyps of corals and other compound forms are embedded

pol·yp·ean \¦==¦pēən\ *adj* [*polyp* + *-an*] **:** relating to or like a polyp

pol·yp·ec·to·my \,=='pektəmē\ *n* -ES [*polyp* + *-ectomy*] **:** the surgical excision of a polyp

1**poly·ped** \'pälē,ped, -lə,p-\ *n* -s [*poly-* + *-ped*] **:** a polyped animal

2**polyped** \"\ *adj* **:** having many feet

poly·pe·da·tes \,== pə'dād·(,)ēz\ *n, cap* [NL, prob. irreg. fr. *poly-* + Gk *pēdētēs* leaper, dancer, fr. *pēdan* to leap, jump; akin to L *ped-, pes* foot — more at FOOT] **:** a genus (the type of the family Polypedatidae) of Old World tree frogs related to the Ranidae but distinguished by cylindrical transverse sacral processes

1**poly·pe·datid** \¦===¦dād·əd, -¦dad·əd\ *adj* [NL *Polypedatidae*] **:** of or relating to the Polypedatidae

2**polypedatid** \"\ *n* -s **:** a tree frog of the family Polypetadid

poly·pe·dat·i·dae \,==='dad·ə,dē\ *n pl, cap* [NL, fr. *Polypedates*, type genus + *-idae*] **:** a family of Old World tree frogs (suborder Diplasiocoela)

poly·peptide \¦pälē, -lə+\ *n* [ISV *poly-* + *peptide;* prob. orig.

formed as G *polypeptid*] **:** a polyamide that yields amino acids on hydrolysis but has a lower molecular weight than a protein and that is obtained by partial hydrolysis of proteins or by synthesis — compare PEPTIDE

poly·petal \"+\ *adj* [NL *polypetalus*] **:** POLYPETALOUS

poly·pet·a·lae \ˌ=='ped·ᵊlˌē\ [NL, fr. *poly-* + *-petalae*] *syn of* CHORIPETALAE

poly·petalous \¦==+\ *adj* [NL *polypetalus*, fr. *poly-* + *-petalus* -petalous] *of a flower or corolla* **:** consisting of or having petals that are not united **:** CHORIPETALOUS

poly·pet·aly \¦==¦ped·ᵊlē\ *n* -ES [*polypetal*ous + *-y*] **:** the condition of being polypetalous

po·lyph·a·ga \pə'lifəgə\ *n pl, cap* [NL, fr. Gk, neut. pl. of *polyphagos* eating too much] **:** a suborder of Coleoptera including all the beetles except the Adephaga

poly·phage \'pälēˌfāj, -ləˌf-\ *n* -S [L *polyphagus*, fr. Gk *polyphagos* eating too much] **:** one eating much or many kinds of food

poly·pha·gia \ˌ=='fāj(ē)ə\ *also* **po·lyph·a·gy** \pə'lifəjē\ *n, pl* **polyphagias** *or* **polyphagies** [Gk *polyphagia*, fr. *polyphagos* eating too much + *-ia* -y] **:** excessive appetite or voracious eating **:** BULIMIA — compare HYPERPHAGIA — **poly·pha·gian** \¦pälē¦fāj(ē)ən, -lə¦f-\ *adj or n*

poly·phag·ic \¦pälē¦fajik, -lə¦f-\ *adj* [L *polyphag*us glutton + E *-ic*] **:** POLYPHAGOUS

po·lyph·a·gism \pə'lifəˌjizəm\ *n* -S [L *poliphag*us + E *-ism*] **:** the habit of feeding on a variety of plants or animals **:** the condition of being polyphagous

po·lyph·a·gous \-fəgəs\ *adj* [Gk *polyphagos*, fr. *poly-* (fr. *polys* many, much) + *-phagos* -phagous — more at POLY-] **1 :** feeding on or utilizing many kinds of food; *specif* **:** feeding on various plants or animals ⟨~ insects⟩ — usu. used of an animal subsisting on a moderate variety of foods; distinguished from *omnivorous* and *pantophagous* **2 :** entering several host cells ⟨the ~ thallus of a parasitic fungus⟩ — compare MONOPHAGOUS

poly·pha·lan·gism \ˌpälēfə'lanˌjizəm, -fā'l-\ *n* -S [*poly-* + *phalange* + *-ism*] **:** the condition of having more than the normal number of phalanges in the fingers or toes

poly·pha·lan·gy \-njē\ *n* -ES [*poly-* + *phalange* + *-y*] **:** POLYDACTYLY

poly·pharmacal \¦pälē, -lə+\ *adj* [*polypharmacy* + *-al*] **:** of or relating to polypharmacy

poly·phar·ma·con \ˌ=='färməˌkän\ *n* [NL, fr. Gk *polypharmakon*, neut. of *polypharmakos* compounded of many drugs, fr. *poly-* + *-pharmakos*, fr. *pharmakon* drug — more at PHARMACY] **:** a remedy compounded of many ingredients

poly·pharmacy \¦==+\ *n* [*poly-* + *pharmacy*] **:** the practice of administering many different medicines esp. concurrently for the treatment of the same disease

poly·pharyngeal \¦pälē, -lə+\ *adj* [*poly-* + *pharyngeal*] *of a flatworm* **:** having several pharynges — **poly·pharyn·gy** \ˌ==fə'rinjē, -'farən-\ *n* -ES

poly·phasal \¦==+\ *adj* [*poly-* + *phasal*] **:** of or relating to a polyphase system **:** POLYPHASE

poly·phase \'==+ˌ-\ *adj* [ISV *poly-* + *-phase*] **:** having or producing two or more phases ⟨a ~ machine⟩ ⟨a ~ current⟩

polyphase induction motor *n* **:** an alternating-current motor having polyphase (as 3-phase) windings

poly·phas·er \"ə(r)\ *n* -S **:** a polyphase machine

poly·phasic \¦pälē, -lə+\ *adj* [*poly-* + *phasic*] *of an animal* **:** having several periods of activity interrupted by intervening periods of rest in each 24 hours **:** POLYCYCLIC ⟨an infant is essentially ~⟩ — compare MONOPHASIC

pol·y·pheme \'päləˌfēm\ *n* -S *usu cap* [F *Polyphème*, a Cyclops blinded by Ulysses in the epic poem *Odyssey* ascribed to *Homer*, traditional ancient Greek poet, fr. L *Polyphemus*, fr. Gk *Polyphēmos*] **:** GIANT, CYCLOPS — **pol·y·phe·mi·an** \¦==¦fēmēən\ *or* **pol·y·phe·mic** \-mik\ *or* **pol·y·phe·mous** \-məs\ *adj*

pol·y·phe·mus moth \¦==¦=məs-\ *n, often cap P* [*polyphemus* fr. NL (specific epithet of *Telea polyphemus*), fr. L *Polyphemus*, a Cyclops; fr. the eyelike spot on its hind wings] **:** a very large American silkworm moth (*Antheraea polyphemus*) of a yellowish or brownish color with a large eyelike spot in each hind wing and a larva that is very large and bright green with silvery tubercles and with oblique white stripes on the sides and that feeds on the oak, chestnut, willow, cherry, apple, and other trees

poly·phenol \¦pälē, -lə+\ *n* [ISV *poly-* + *phenol*] **:** a polyhydroxy phenol — **poly·phenolic** \"+\ *adj*

poly·phenolase \¦pälē, -lə+\ *n* -S [*polyphenol* + *-ase*] **:** POLYPHENOL OXIDASE

polyphenol oxidase *n* **:** any of several copper-containing enzymes (as laccase) that catalyze the oxidation esp. of diphenols and polyphenols to quinones — compare PHENOL OXIDASE, TYROSINASE

poly·phloes·boe·an \¦pälē¦fles¦bēən, ¦pälə¦-, -sˌbēən\ *or* **poly·phlois·boi·an** \-¦flȯis¦bȯiən\ *or* **polu·phlois·boi·an** \¦päl(y)ə¦-\ *adj* [Gk *polyphloisbos* (fr. *poly-* + *phloisbos* confused roaring noise) + E *-an;* perh. akin to Gk *aphloismos* foaming of the mouth, *phlidan* to be too moist, become soft — more at BLOAT] **:** loud-roaring ⟨the ~ sea⟩

poly·phone \'==ˌfōn\ *n* [*poly-* + *-phone*] **1 :** a music box that by means of perforated disks can play a number of tunes **2 :** a symbol or group of symbols having more than one phonetic value (as *ea* in English, which represents \ā\ in *break* and \ē\ in *freak*)

poly·phonemic \¦pälē, -lə+\ *adj* [*poly-* + *phonemic*] **:** constituting, consisting of, or standing for more than one phoneme

poly·phon·ic \¦==¦fänik\ *or* **po·lyph·o·nous** \pə'lifənəs\ *adj* [Gk *polyphōn*os having many tones (fr. *poly-* + *-phōnos*—fr. *phōnē* sound—) + E *-ic* or *-ous* — more at BAN] **1 a :** consisting of or relating to two or more distinct melodies combined into a unified musical composition **:** CONTRAPUNTAL ⟨~ traditions of the baroque —P.H.Lang⟩ — compare MONOPHONIC **b** *of a musical instrument* **:** capable of giving more than one tone at a time **2 :** having or consisting of many sounds or voices ⟨morning's ~ sounds⟩ **3** *phonetics* **:** being a polyphone — **poly·phon·i·cal·ly** *or* **po·lyph·o·nous·ly** *adv*

polyphonic prose *n* **:** a freely rhythmical prose employing characteristic devices of verse (as alliteration, assonance, rhyme) except strict meter

po·lyph·o·nist \pə'lifənəst\ *n* -S [*polyphony* + *-ist*] **:** one skilled in polyphony **:** CONTRAPUNTIST

po·lyph·o·ny \-nē\ *n* -ES [Gk *polyphōnia* variety of tones, fr. *polyphōnos* having many tones + *-ia* -y] **1 :** musical composition in simultaneous and harmonizing but melodically independent and individual parts or voices **:** COUNTERPOINT — compare HOMOPHONY **2 :** multiplicity of sounds (as in reverberations of an echo) **3 a :** representation by polyphones **b :** the fact of being a polyphone

poly·phosphate \¦pälē, -lə+\ *n* [*poly-* + *phosphate*] **:** a salt or ester of a polyphosphoric acid — see SODIUM TRIPOLYPHOSPHATE

poly·phosphoric acid \"+ . . . -\ *n* [*polyphosphoric* fr. *poly-* + *phosphoric*] **:** any of a series of condensed phosphoric acids (as pyrophosphoric acid) containing more than one atom of phosphorus

poly·phy·le·sis \ˌ==ˌfī'lēsəs\ *n, pl* **polyphyle·ses** \-ēˌsēz\ [NL, fr. ISV *polyphyletic*, after such pairs as ISV *genetic:* NL *genesis*] **:** POLYGENESIS

poly·phy·let·ic \¦==¦fī¦led·ik\ *adj* [ISV *polyphyl-* (fr. Gk *polyphylos* of many tribes, fr. *poly-* + *phylē* tribe, race) + *-etic;* orig. formed as G *polyphyletisch* — more at PHYL-] **:** of or relating to more than one stock **:** derived (as by convergence) from more than one ancestral line — opposed to *monophyletic* — **poly·phy·let·i·cal·ly** \-d·ək(ə)lē\ *adv* — **poly·phy·let·i·cism** \ˌ==ˌ='led·əˌsizəm\ *n* -S

polyphyletic theory *n* **:** a theory in physiology: the several cellular elements of the blood originate in two or more distinct stem cells — compare MONOPHYLETIC THEORY

poly·phyle·tism \ˌ=='fīləˌtizəm, -'fil-\ *n* -S [ISV *polyphylet-* (fr. *polyphyletic theory*) + *-ism*] **:** adherence to the polyphyletic theory — **poly·phyle·tist** \-ˌtəst\ *n* -S

poly·phyle·ty \-ləd·ē\ *n* -ES [*polyphylet*ic + *-y*] **:** POLYPHYLESIS

poly·phyl·la \ˌpälē'filə, -älə'f-\ *n, cap* [NL, fr. Gk *polyphyllos* with many leaves, fr. *poly-* + *phyllon* leaf — more at BLADE] **:** a holarctic genus of large brown beetles (family Melolonthidae) — see JUNE BEETLE

poly·phylogeny \¦==+\ *n* [*poly-* + *phylogeny*] **:** development of a group through combination and evolution of qualities derived from more than one ancestral group **:** POLYGENESIS

poly·phy·ly \'==ˌfīlē\ *n* -ES [ISV *polyphyl-* (fr. Gk *polyphylos* of many tribes) + *-y*] **:** POLYPHYLESIS

[1]**poly·phy·odont** \¦==¦fīəˌdänt\ *adj* [Gk *polyphyēs* manifold (fr. *poly-* + *-phyēs*, fr. *phyein* to bring forth, produce) + *odont-, odous* tooth — more at BE, TOOTH] **:** having several or many sets of teeth in succession ⟨sharks and some teleost fishes are ~⟩ — distinguished from *diphyodont* and *monophyodont* — **poly·phy·odonty** \-tē\ *n* -ES

[2]**polyphyodont** \"\ *n* -S **:** a polyphyodont animal

[1]**polypi** *pl of* POLYPUS

[2]**poly·pi** \'päləˌpī, -əˌpē\ *n pl, cap* [NL, fr. L, pl. of *polypus*] *in former classifications* **:** a class of invertebrates more or less corresponding to Anthozoa

pol·yp·ide \'päləˌpīd\ *n* -S [*polyp-* + *-ide* (alter. of *-id*)] **:** one of the individual zooids of a bryozoan colony **:** POLYP

po·lypi·dom \pə'lipədəm, -ˌdäm\ *n* -S [*polyp* + *-i-* + Gk *domos* house — more at TIMBER] *archaic* **:** POLYPARY

pol·yp·if·er·ous \¦pälə¦pif(ə)rəs\ *or* **pol·yp·ig·er·ous** \-ij(ə)rəs\ *adj* [*polyp* + *-iferous* or *-gerous*] **:** bearing polyps

pol·yp·ite \'päləˌpīt\ *n* -S [*polyp* + *-ite*] **1 :** one of the zooids of a coral, hydroid, or siphonophore **2 :** a feeding zooid or hydranth distinguished from a dactylozooid or other modified or degenerate zooid

poly·pla·coph·o·ra \ˌpälēˌpla'käfərə, -äləˌp-\ *n pl, cap* [NL, fr. *poly-* + *plac-* + *-phora*] **:** an order of Amphineura comprising the chitons all of which have the foot occupying the whole ventral surface of the body and the shell composed of eight calcified dorsal plates — **poly·pla·coph·o·ran** \¦==ˌ=-¦=fərən\ *adj or n* — **poly·plac·o·phore** \ˌ=='plakəˌfō(ə)r\ *n* -S — **poly·pla·coph·o·rous** \¦==¦pla¦käfərəs\ *adj*

poly·plastic \¦pälē, -lə+\ *adj* [*poly-* + *plastic*] **:** assuming or able to assume many forms

poly·plec·tron \ˌ=='plektrən, -ˌträn\ *n, cap* [NL, fr. *poly-* + *plectron*] **:** a genus of large showy Asiatic pheasants consisting of the peacock pheasants

[1]**poly·ploid** \'päləˌplȯid\ *adj* [ISV *poly-* + *ploid*] **:** having or being a chromosome number that is a multiple greater than two of the monoploid number ⟨a ~ cell⟩ — compare ALLOPOLYPLOID, DIPLOID, HAPLOID, HEXAPLOID — **poly·ploi·dic** \¦==-¦plȯidik\ *adj*

[2]**polyploid** \"\ *n* -S **:** a polyploid individual

polyploid complex *n* **:** a complex group of interrelated hybrids produced by the intercrossing of related autopolyploids and allopolyploids that is in some respects comparable to a taxonomic genus — compare POLYPLOID SERIES

poly·ploid·iza·tion \ˌ==ˌplȯidə'zāshən\ *n* -S [*polyploidize* + *-ation*] **:** the act or process of polyploidizing

poly·ploid·ize \'==ˌplȯiˌdīz\ *vb* -ED/-ING/-S [*polyploid* + *-ize*] *vt* **:** to cause to become polyploid ⟨~ a plant⟩ ~ *vi* **:** to induce polyploidy ⟨a *polyploidizing* agent⟩

poly·ploid·ogen \ˌ=='plȯidəjən, -ˌjen\ *n* -S [*polyploid* + *-o-* + *-gen*] **:** a chemical substance that is capable of inducing polyploidy in cells

poly·ploid·ogen·ic \¦==¦==¦jenik\ *adj* [*polyploidogen* + *-ic*] **:** constituting or having the capacity to induce polyploidy in the cell

polyploid series *n* **:** a group of related forms or species having chromosome sets that are different multiples of the same monoploid set — compare POLYPLOID COMPLEX

poly·ploi·dy \'==ˌplȯidē\ *n* -ES [ISV *polyploid* + *-y*] **:** the condition of being polyploid

pol·yp·nea *or* **pol·yp·noea** \¦päləp¦nēə\ *n* -S [NL, fr. *poly-* + *-pnea, -pnoea*] **:** rapid or panting respiration — **pol·yp·ne·ic** *or* **pol·yp·noe·ic** \¦==¦nēik\ *adj*

pol·yp·neus·tic \¦päləp¦n(y)üstik\ *adj* [*poly-* + Gk *pneustikos* of breathing, fr. (assumed) Gk *pneustos* (verbal of Gk *pnein* to breathe) + Gk *-ikos* -ic — more at PNEUMATIC] *of an insect* **:** having at least three pairs of functional spiracles

[1]**poly·pod** \'pälēˌpäd, -ləˌp-\ *n* [ME *pollypod*, prob. fr. MF *polipode*, fr. L *polypodium* polypody] **:** [1]POLYPODY

[2]**polypod** \"\ *adj* [Gk *polypod-, polypous* — more at POLYP] **1 :** having many feet or legs **2** [NL *polypoda*] **:** having abdominal limbs ⟨~ insect larvae⟩

[3]**polypod** \"\ *n* [NL *polypoda*] **:** a polypod animal (as an insect larva)

po·lyp·o·da \pə'lipədə\ *n, pl* **polypo·dae** \-ˌdē, -ˌdī\ [NL, modif. of Gk *polypod-, polypous*] **:** an insect larva having abdominal legs

poly·po·dia \ˌpälē'pōdēə, -lə'p-\ *n* -S [NL, fr. *poly-* + *-podia*] **:** a condition of having more than the normal number of feet

poly·po·di·a·ce·ae \ˌ==ˌ=='āsēˌē\ *n pl, cap* [NL, fr. *Polypodium*, type genus + *-aceae*] **:** a large family of ferns (order Filicales) having erect or creeping rootstocks with scattered or clustered fronds and the fertile bearing annulate stalked sporangia disposed in sori — **poly·po·di·a·ceous** \¦==ˌ==-¦āshəs\ *adj*

poly·po·di·um \ˌ=='pōdēəm\ *n, cap* [NL, fr. L, polypody, fr. Gk *polypodion*, fr. *polypodion*, dim. of *polypod-, polypous* many-footed] **:** a genus (the type of the family Polypodiaceae) of ferns containing the polypodies and distinguished by the roundish naked sori

po·lyp·o·dous \pə'lipədəs\ *adj* [*poly-* + *-podous*] **:** POLYPOD

[1]**poly·po·dy** \'pälēˌpōdē, -ləˌp-\ *n* -ES [ME *polypodie*, fr. L *polipodium*] **:** a fern of the genus *Polypodium*; *esp* **:** a fern (*P. vulgare*) found throughout No. America and most of Europe and Asia that has creeping rootstocks and pinnatifid fronds with entire segments

[2]**polypody** \"\ *n* -ES [F *polypodie*, fr. Gk *polypodia*, fr. *polypod-, polypous* many-footed] **:** a condition of having many legs — used esp. of an insect embryo or larva

polypody family *n* **:** POLYPODIACEAE

pol·yp·oid \'päləˌpȯid\ *or* **pol·yp·oi·dal** \¦==¦pȯidᵊl\ *adj* [*polypoid* fr. ISV *polyp* + *-oid; polypoidal* fr. *polyp* + *-oid* + *-al*] **1 :** resembling a polyp **2 :** marked by the formation of lesions suggesting polyps ⟨~ degeneration⟩ ⟨~ carcinoma⟩

po·lyp·o·ra·ce·ae \pəˌlipə'rāsēˌē; ˌpälēp-, ˌpäləp-\ *n pl, cap* [NL, fr. *Polyporus*, type genus + *-aceae*] **:** a family of pore-bearing fungi (order Polyporales) having a soft texture when young, but commonly becoming firm, corky, or woody with age and often forming shelflike growths on trees — compare BOLETACEAE, BRACKET FUNGUS, FOMES — **po·lyp·o·ra·ceous** \pə¦lipə¦rāshəs; ¦pälēp-, ¦päləp-\ *adj*

po·lyp·o·ra·les \pəˌlipə'rā(ˌ)lēz; ˌpälēp-, ˌpäləp-\ *n pl, cap* [NL, fr. *Polyporus* + *-ales*] **:** an order of basidiomycetous fungi (subclass Homobasidiomycetes) that is often included in Agaricales and that includes chiefly saprophytic fungi (as of wood) typically with shelflike or resupinate fruiting bodies which have a smooth or wrinkled often porose hymenium — compare CLAVARIACEAE, HYDNACEAE, POLYPORACEAE

poly·pore \'pälēˌpō(ə)r, -ləˌp-\ *n* [NL *Polyporus*] **:** PORE FUNGUS

po·lyp·o·rite \pə'lipəˌrīt\ *n* -S [NL *Polyporus* + E *-ite*] **:** a fossil fungus of the genus *Polyporus; also* **:** any similar or related form

po·lyp·o·roid \pə'lipəˌrȯid\ *adj* [NL *Polyporus* + E *-oid*] **:** relating to or resembling a pore fungus esp. of the genus *Polyporus*

po·lyp·o·rus \pə'lipərəs\ *n, cap* [NL, fr. Gk *polyporos* with many passages, fr. *poly-* + *poros* passage, pore — more at FARE] **:** a genus (the type of the family Polyporaceae) of fungi having stipitate or sessile fruiting bodies and including important pathogens of various trees (as birches and conifers)

pol·yp·ose \'päləˌpōs\ *adj* [*polyp* + *-ose*] **:** POLYPOUS

pol·yp·o·sis \ˌpälə'pōsəs\ *n, pl* **polypo·ses** \-ōˌsēz\ [NL, fr. *polypus* + *-osis*] **:** a condition characterized by the presence of numerous polyps ⟨~ of the colon⟩ ⟨multiple ~⟩

pol·yp·ous \'päləpəs\ *adj* [*polyp* + *-ous*] **:** relating to, of the nature of, or like a polyp

poly·pragmatic *also* **poly·pragmatical** \¦pälē, -lə+\ *adj* [LGk *polypragmat*os (fr. Gk *polypragmatein* to be busy with many things, to be meddlesome, fr. *poly-* + *pragmat-, pragma* deed, affair) + E *-ic* or *-ical* — more at PRAGMATIC] **:** concerned with things not one's own affair **:** MEDDLESOME

poly·pragmatism \ˌ==+\ *n* [*polypragmat*ic + *-ism*] **:** MEDDLESOMENESS ⟨a critique of poetical ~ —George Saintsbury⟩

poly·pragmatist \"+\ *n* [*polypragmat*ic + *-ist*] **:** BUSYBODY

poly·propylene \¦pälē, -lə+\ *n* [*poly-* + *propylene*] **:** a polymer of propylene; *esp* **:** a substance resembling polyethylene or polyisobutylene used chiefly in making fibers, films, and molded and extruded products

[1]**poly·protodont** \"+\ *adj* [NL *Polyprotodontia*] **:** of or relating to the Polyprotodontia

[2]**polyprotodont** \"\ *n* -S **:** a marsupial of the suborder Polyprotodontia

poly·pro·to·don·tia \ˌ==ˌprōd·ə'dänch(ē)ə\ *n pl, cap* [NL, fr. *poly-* + *prot-* + *-odontia*] *in some classifications* **:** a suborder of marsupials including the dasyures, Tasmanian wolves, opossums, bandicoots, and other largely or entirely carnivorous or insectivorous forms having specialized canines and four or five upper incisors and two or three lower incisors on each side — compare DIDACTYLA, DIPROTODONTIA

polyps *pl of* POLYP

poly·psychic *also* **poly·psychical** \¦pälē, -lə+\ *adj* [ISV *poly-* + *psyche* + *-ic* or *-ical*] **:** having many souls or modes of intelligence

poly·psychism \ˌ==+\ *n* [ISV *poly-* + *psyche* + *-ism*] **:** belief in many souls in one person

[1]**po·lyp·ter·id** \pə'liptərəd\ *adj* [NL *Polypteridae*] **:** of or relating to the Polypteridae

[2]**polypterid** \"\ *n* -S **:** a fish of the family Polypteridae

pol·yp·ter·i·dae \ˌpäləp'terəˌdē\ *n pl, cap* [NL, fr. *Polypterus*, type genus + *-idae*] **:** a family of primitive African fishes (order Cladistia) containing the recent genus *Polypterus* and known from fossil remains since the Upper Eocene

po·lyp·ter·is \pə'liptərəs\ [NL, fr. *poly-* + *-pteris*] *syn of* GAILLARDIA

[1]**po·lyp·ter·oid** \-ˌrȯid\ *adj* [NL *Polypterus* + E *-oid*] **:** like or related to the family Polypteridae ⟨a ~ fish⟩

[2]**polypteroid** \"\ *n* -S **:** a polypteroid fish

po·lyp·ter·us \pə'liptərəs\ *n, cap* [NL, fr. Gk *polypteros* many-winged, fr. *poly-* + *-pteros* -winged (fr. *pteron* wing, feather — more at FEATHER] **:** the type genus of Polypteridae that comprises primitive fishes of the larger rivers of tropical Africa having an elongate body covered with rhombic enameled scales, a dorsal fin reduced to a series of finlets, pectoral fins taking the form of a rounded lobe supported on a short arm, and an air bladder functioning as an accessory breathing organ — see BICHIR, ERPETOICHTHYS

pol·yp·to·ton \ˌpäləp'tōˌtän\ *n, pl* **polypto·ta** \-ōd·ə\ [LL, fr. Gk *polyptōton*, neut. of *polyptōtos* using many cases of the same word, fr. *poly-* + *-ptōtos* (fr. *piptein* to fall, influenced in meaning by Gk *ptōsis* case) — more at SYMPTOM] **:** the rhetorical repetition of a word in a different case, inflection, or voice in the same sentence (as in Tennyson's "my own heart's heart, and ownest own, farewell")

po·lyp·tych \'päləpˌtik, pə'lipt-\ *n* -S [Gk *polyptychos* with many folds, folded many times, fr. *poly-* + *-ptychos* (akin to Gk *ptychē* fold, layer)] **:** an arrangement of four or more panels (as of a painting) usu. hinged and folding together ⟨an altarpiece in the form of a ~⟩ — compare DIPTYCH, TRIPTYCH

poly·pus \'päləpəs, -lēp-\ *n* [L — more at POLYP] **1** *pl* **poly·pi** \-ˌpī, -ˌpē\ *or* **polypuses :** POLYP 2 **2** *cap* [NL, fr. L, polyp] **:** a genus of octopuses

poly·rhythm \¦pälē, -lə+\ *n* [*poly-* + *rhythm*] **:** the simultaneous combination of contrasting rhythms in a musical composition

poly·rhythmic \"+\ *adj* [ISV *poly-* + *rhythmic*] **1 :** having many rhythms; *specif* **:** having many usu. varied rhythmic feet to the line ⟨~ verse⟩ **2 :** having two or more rhythms proceeding simultaneously in different musical parts

polys *pl of* POLY

poly·saccharide \"+\ *n* [ISV *poly-* + *saccharide*] **:** a carbohydrate decomposable by hydrolysis into two or more molecules of monosaccharides (as glucose) or their derivatives; *esp* **:** one of the more complex carbohydrates $(C_6H_{10}O_5)_x$ (as starch or cellulose) — compare OLIGOSACCHARIDE

poly·saccharose \"+\ *n* [*poly-* + *saccharose*] **:** POLYSACCHARIDE

poly·saprobe \"+\ *n* [ISV *poly-* + *saprobe*] **:** a polysaprobic individual

poly·saprobic \"+\ *adj* [ISV *poly-* + *saprobic*] **:** living in a medium that is rich in decomposable organic matter and nearly free from dissolved oxygen ⟨~ sewage organisms⟩

poly·schematic \"+\ *adj* [LGk *polyschēmat*os (fr. Gk *poly-* + *schēmat-, schēma* form, shape, scheme) + E *-ic*] **:** POLYSCHEMATIST

poly·schematist \"+\ *or* **poly·sche·ma·tis·tic** \"+¦skēmə¦tistik\ *adj* [*polyschematist* fr. Gk *polyschēmatistos* multiform, composed of various metres, fr. *poly-* + *-schēmatistos* (fr. *schēmatizein* to take shape, give form — fr. *schēmat-, schēma* form, shape — + *-izein* -ize); *polyschematistic* fr. *polyschematist* (taken as a noun) + *-ic* — more at SCHEME] **:** capable of assuming many different metrical forms — used esp. of classical meters in which variations or substitutions without regard for temporal equivalence were allowed

polyschematist dimeter *n* **:** a classical prosodic unit of eight syllables whose first four, middle four, or last four syllables form a choriambus with the other syllables being indeterminate as to quantity and which is considered by many to be the basic figure of all rhythms of the aeolic class

poly·scope \'pälēˌskōp, -ləˌs-\ *n* [*poly-* + *-scope*] **:** DIAPHANOSCOPE — **poly·scop·ic** \¦==¦skäpik\ *adj*

poly·se·mant \ˌ=='sēmənt\ *n* -S [LGk *polysēmantos* with many meanings, fr. Gk *poly-* + *sēmantos*, verbal of *sēmainein* to mean, mark, signal, fr. *sēma* sign — more at SEMANTICS] **:** a word having more than one meaning — **poly·semantic** \¦==+\ *adj*

po·ly·se·mous \¦pälē¦sēməs, -lə'-; pə'lisəm-\ *adj* [LL *polysemus*, fr. Gk *polysēmos* with many meanings, fr. *poly-* + *sēma* sign] **:** having many meanings ⟨explains that his poem is ~ —C.S.Singleton⟩ ⟨excited by the difficult, the ambiguous, the ~ —R.G.Davis⟩

po·ly·se·my \'pälēˌsēmē, -ləˌ-; pə'lisəm-\ *n* -ES [NL *polysemia*, fr. LL *polysemus* polysemous + L *-ia* -y] **:** multiplicity of meaning ⟨English is less exposed to ~ than French —Stephen Ullmann⟩

poly·sepalous \¦pälē, -lə+\ *adj* [*poly-* + *-sepalous*] **:** having separate sepals

poly·serositis \"+\ *n* [NL, fr. *poly-* + *serositis*] **:** inflammation of several serous membranes (as the pleura, pericardium, and peritoneum) at the same time

poly·si·pho·nia \ˌ==ˌsī'fōnēə\ *n, cap* [NL, fr. *poly-* + *siphon-* + *-ia*] **:** a large genus of red algae (family Rhodomelaceae) having usu. a filamentous much-branched thallus variable in shape and size but in cross section showing a single axial cell surrounded by a sheath of tubular cells at least in the axis and main branches

poly·si·phon·ic \¦==¦sī¦fänik\ *adj* [*poly-* + *siphon-* + *-ic*] **:** consisting of several tubes or rows of cells ⟨the ~ thallus of many red or brown algae⟩ — compare MONOSIPHONIC

poly·somatic \¦==+\ *adj* [*polysomaty* + *-ic*] **:** of, relating to, or exhibiting polysomaty

poly·so·ma·ty \ˌ=='sōməd·ē\ *n* -ES [ISV *poly-* + *somat-* + *-y;* orig. formed as G *polysomatie*] **:** the replication in somatic cells of the chromosome number through division of chromosomes without subsequent nuclear division

[1]**poly·so·mic** \¦==¦sōmik\ *adj* [ISV *poly-* + *-somic*] **:** having one or a few chromosomes present in greater or smaller number than the remaining chromosomes

[2]**polysomic** \"\ *n* -S **:** a polysomic individual

poly·so·my \'pälēˌsōmē, -ləˌs-\ *n* -ES [ISV *polysom*ic + *-y*] **:** the condition of being polysomic

poly·speed \'pälē, -lə+ˌ-\ *adj* [*poly-* + *speed*] **:** capable of several speeds ⟨~ motor⟩

poly·sper·mic \¦==¦spərmik\ *adj* [*poly-* + *-spermic*] **:** of or relating to polyspermy ⟨~ fertilization⟩

poly·sper·my \'==ˌ=mē\ *n* -ES [ISV *poly-* + *-spermy*] **:** the entrance of several spermatozoa into one egg — compare MONOSPERMY

poly·spondyli \¦pälē, -lə+\ [NL, fr. *poly-* + *-spondyli*] *syn of* HOLOCEPHALI

poly·spon·dyl·ic \¦==¦spän¦dilik\ *adj* [*poly-* + *spondylic*] **:** of, relating to, or having a vertebral column (as in the chimaeroid fishes) in which the calcified portion has the form of numerous slender rings surrounding the notochord — **poly·spon·dy·lous** \-ndələs\ *adj* — **poly·spon·dy·ly** \-lē\ *n* -ES

po·lys·po·ra \pə'lispərə\ *n, cap* [NL, *poly-* + *-spora*] **:** a genus of imperfect fungi (family Melanconiaceae) forming minute acervuli directly over the stomata with hyaline nonseptate conidia of varying shape — see BROWNING 3a

poly·sporangium \¦pälē, -lə+\ *n* [NL, fr. *poly-* + *sporangium*] **:** a sporangium containing many spores

poly·spore \'==,spō(ə)r\ *n* [ISV *poly-* + *spore;* prob. orig. formed in F] **:** one of a group of 12 to 16 spores produced instead of a tetraspore by various red algae

poly·spored \-ō(ə)rd\ *adj* [*poly-* + *spore* + *-ed*] **:** having many spores

poly·spor·ic \¦==¦spōrik\ *or* **poly·spor·ous** \-rəs, pə'lispərəs\ *adj* [*poly-* + *-sporic, -sporous*] **:** POLYSPORED

poly·stachy·ous \¦pälē¦stakēəs, -tāk-\ *adj* [*poly-* + *stachy-* (fr. Gk *stachys* ear of grain) + *-ous* — more at STING] **:** having many spikes ⟨~ grasses⟩

poly·stele \'==,stēl *also* ¦==¦stēlē\ *n* [*poly-* + *stele*] **:** a stele that consists of a number of like vascular units dispersed in parenchymatous tissue (as in a fern or monocotyledon) — see MERISTELE — **poly·ste·lic** \¦==¦stēlik\ *adj* — **poly·ste·ly** \'==,stēlē\ *n* -ES

poly·stemo·nous \¦==¦stēmənəs, -tem-\ *adj* [prob. fr. (assumed) NL *polystemonus,* fr. NL *poly-* + (assumed) NL *-stemonus* -stemonous] **:** POLYANDROUS 1

po·lys·ti·choid \pə'listə,kȯid\ *adj* [NL *Polystichum* + E *-oid*] **:** resembling a fern of the genus *Polystichum*

po·lys·ti·chous \-kəs\ *adj* [Gk *polystichos,* fr. *poly-* + *stichos* row, line — more at DISTICH] **:** arranged in several rows ⟨the ~ spike of maize —P.C.Mangelsdorf⟩ — compare DISTICHOUS

po·lys·ti·chum \-kəm\ *n, cap* [NL, fr. Gk *polystichon,* neut. of *polystichos* of many rows, of many lines] **:** a genus of chiefly northern ferns (family Polypodiaceae) having lanceolate pinnate or bipinnate often evergreen fronds with the veins free and the indusia lacking sinuses and centrally peltate — see CHRISTMAS FERN, HOLLY FERN

poly·stic·tus \,pälē'stiktəs, -lə's-\ *n, cap* [NL, fr. Gk *polystiktos* much-spotted, fr. *poly-* much (fr. *polys* much, many) + *stiktos* spotted, pricked, verbal of *stizein* to prick — more at POLY-, STICK] *in some classifications* **:** a large genus of pore fungi (family Polyporaceae) having leathery often showy annual sporophores, growing on and causing decay of wood (as timbers or wounds of trees), and being now divided among several distinct genera

po·lys·to·ma \pə'listəmə\ *n, cap* [NL, fr. Gk *polystomos* many mouthed, fr. *poly-* + *-stomos* -stomous] **:** a genus (the type of the family Polystomatidae) of monogenetic trematode worms including several species that occur in the urinary bladder of batrachians

po·lys·to·mat·i·dae \=,=='mad·ə,dē; ,pälēstō'm-, -lə̇s-\ *n pl, cap* [NL, fr. *Polystomat-, Polystoma* + *-idae*] **:** a family comprising monogenetic trematode worms with a group of strong suckers and usu. a pair of chitinous hooks at the posterior end

poly·stomatous \¦pälē, -lə+\ *adj* [*poly-* + *-stomatous*] **:** having many mouths, openings, or suckers

[1]**poly·stome** \'==,stōm\ *n* -S [F, fr. Gk *polystomos* many-mouthed] **:** a polystomatous individual (as a monogenetic trematode worm)

[2]**polystome** \"\ *adj* **:** POLYSTOMATOUS

poly·sto·mea \,pälē'stōmēə, -lə's-\ [NL, fr. Gk *polystomos* many-mouthed] *syn of* MONOGENEA

poly·sto·mi·dae \-mə,dē\ [NL, fr. *Polystoma* + *-idae*] *syn of* POLYSTOMATIDAE

[1]**poly·style** \'==+,-\ *also* **poly·stylar** \¦==+\ *adj* [*polystyle* fr. Gk *polystylos,* fr. *poly-* + *stylos* pillar; *polystylar* fr. Gk *polystylos* + E *-ar* — more at STEER] **:** having or supported by many columns ⟨a ~ court⟩

[2]**polystyle** \"\ *n* **:** a polystyle hall or edifice

poly·styrene \¦pälē, -lə+\ *n* [*poly-* + *styrene*] **:** a polymer of styrene; *esp* **:** a rigid transparent thermoplastic characterized by good physical and electrical insulating properties, low moisture absorption, and yellowing in sunlight and used either unmodified or sometimes modified (as for improving impact strength or heat resistance) chiefly in making containers and other molded products (as for radios, electrical apparatus, refrigerators) and sheet materials — compare STYRENE PLASTIC

poly·sulfide \"+\ *n* [ISV *poly-* + *sulfide*] **:** a sulfide containing two or more atoms of sulfur in the molecule

polysulfide rubber *n* **:** any of various synthetic rubbers made by the reaction of a sodium polysulfide with an organic dichloride (as ethylene dichloride or a dichloro derivative of ethyl formal), characterized in general by good resistance to oxygen, light, oils, and solvents, impermeability to gases, and poor tensile strength and abrasion resistance, and used chiefly in mechanical rubber goods, in adhesives, binders, and sealing compositions, and in coatings (as for textiles)

poly·sulfuration \"+\ *n* [*poly-* + *sulfuration*] **:** formation of polysulfides

poly·syllabic *also* **poly·syllabical** \¦pälē, -lə+\ *adj* [ML *polysyllabus* polysyllabic (fr. Gk *polysyllabos,* fr. *poly-* + *syllabē* syllable) + E *-ic* or *-ical* — more at SYLLABLE] **1 :** having three or usu. four or more syllables ⟨penchant for ~ words —Campbell Dixon⟩ ⟨~ stem⟩ — compare PLURISYLLABLE **2 :** having or characterized by polysyllabic words ⟨a ~ statement of the obvious —A.C.Spaulding⟩ — **poly·syllabically** \"+\ *adv*

poly·syl·la·bism \,=='silə,bizəm\ *n* -S [ML *polysyllabus* + E *-ism*] **1 :** the use of polysyllables **2 :** a polysyllabic word

[1]**poly·syllable** \¦==+\ *n* [modif. (influenced by *syllable*) of ML *polysyllaba* word of many syllables, fem. of *polysyllabus*] **:** a polysyllabic word

[2]**polysyllable** \"\ *adj* **:** POLYSYLLABIC

poly·syllogism \¦pälē, -lə+\ *n* [*poly-* + *syllogism*] **:** a systematic series of syllogisms

poly·syllogistic \"+\ *adj* [*polysyllogism* + *-istic*] **:** of, relating to, or constituting a polysyllogism

poly·symmetrical \"+\ *adj* [*poly-* + *symmetrical*] **:** divisible into like parts by more than one axial plane **:** ACTINOMORPHIC — used esp. of a flower — **poly·symmetrically** \"\ *adv*

poly·syn·det·ic \,==sən¦ded·ik, -¦sin,de-\ *adj* [NL *polysyndeton* + E *-ic*] **:** characterized by polysyndeton — **poly·syn·det·i·cal·ly** \-d·ə̇k(ə)lē\ *adv*

poly·syn·de·ton \,=='sində,tän, -tən\ *n, pl* **polysyndetons** \-,tänz, -tənz\ *or* **polysynde·ta** \-tə\ [NL, fr. LGk, neut. of *polysyndetos* using many conjunctions, connected, fr. Gk *poly-* + *syndetos* bound together — more at ASYNDETON] **:** repetition of conjunctions in close succession (as in *we have ships and men and money and stores*) — opposed to *asyndeton*

poly·synthesis \¦pälē, -lə+\ *n* [NL, *poly-* + *synthesis*] **:** the synthesis of several elements; *specif* **:** POLYSYNTHESISM

poly·syn·the·sism \,==+\ *n* -S [*polysynthesis* + *-ism*] **:** the uniting of many parts into one **:** a high degree of synthesis; *specif* **:** a grammatical practice of some languages (as American Indian) of combining word elements into a single word that is equivalent to a sentence in other languages

poly·synthetic *also* **poly·synthetical** \¦==+\ *adj* [LGk *polysynthetos* much compounded (fr. Gk *poly-* much — fr. *polys* much, many — + *synthetos* compounded, put together, fr. *syntithenai* to put together) + E *-ic* or *-ical* — more at POLY-, SYNTHESIS] **:** characterized by polysynthesism — **poly·synthetically** \"+\ *adv*

poly·syn·the·tism \,==+'sin(t)thə,tizəm\ *n* -S [*polysynthetic* + *-ism*] **:** POLYSYNTHESISM

[1]**poly·technic** *also* **poly·technical** \"+\ *adj* [*polytechnic* fr. F *polytechnique,* fr. Gk *polytechnos* skilled in many arts (fr. *poly-* + *technē* art, skill) + F *-ique* -ic; *polytechnical* fr. ²*polytechnic* + *-al* — more at TECHNICAL] **:** of, relating to, or devoted to instruction in many technical arts or applied sciences ⟨a ~ institute⟩ ⟨~ research⟩

[2]**polytechnic** \"\ *n* **:** a polytechnic school

poly·technician \¦==+\ *n* [F *polytechnicien,* fr. *polytechnique* + *-ien* -ian] **:** a student or graduate of a polytechnic school esp. in France

poly·tech·ni·za·tion \,==,teknə̇'zāshən\ *n* -S [*poly-* + *-techny* + *-ization*] **:** practical application of scientific principles throughout a national economy

poly·tene \'==,tēn\ *adj* [ISV *poly-* + *-tene* (fr. L *taenia* band) — more at TAENIA] **:** relating to, being, or having chromosomes each of which consists of many strands with the corresponding chromomeres in contact — see SALIVARY CHROMOSOME — **poly·tenic** \¦==¦tēnik, -ten-\ *adj* — **poly·te·ny** \'==,tēnē\ *n* -ES

poly·terpene \¦pälē, -lə+\ *n* [ISV *poly-* + *terpene*] **:** a natural or synthetic polymer $(C_5H_8)_x$ of a terpene hydrocarbon: as **a :** RUBBER HYDROCARBON **b :** a thermoplastic resin or viscous liquid obtained by polymerization of turpentine or a nopinene fraction by means of a catalyst (as aluminum chloride) and used chiefly in adhesives and rubber goods

poly·tetrafluoroethylene \"+\ *n* [*poly-* + *tetrafluoroethylene*] **:** a polymer of tetrafluoroethylene; *esp* **:** a tough resin characterized by good resistance to chemicals, heat, and weathering and good electrical insulating properties and used chiefly in making molded products (as gaskets), in electrical insulation, and in coatings

[1]**poly·tha·la·mia** \,==thə'lāmēə\ [NL, fr. *poly-* + Gk *thalamos* chamber + NL *-ia* — more at THALAMUS] *syn of* TETRABRANCHIA

[2]**polythalamia** \"\ *n pl, cap* [NL, fr. *poly-* + Gk *thalamos* + NL *-ia*] **:** a division of Foraminifera including those having a many-chambered shell or sometimes including all the Foraminifera — **poly·tha·la·mi·an** \¦===¦=mēən\ *adj* — **poly·tha·lam·ic** \¦==='lamik\ *adj*

poly·thal·a·mous \¦==¦thaləməs\ *adj* [*poly-* + *thalam-* (fr. Gk *thalamos* chamber), + *-ous*] **:** many-chambered; *also* **:** forming or characterized by many-chambered tests or cysts ⟨~ foraminiferans⟩ ⟨~ gall insects⟩

poly·the·ism \'pälē(,)thē,izəm, -lə̇(-\ *n* [F *polythéisme,* fr. LGk *polytheos* believing in many gods (fr. Gk, of many gods, fr. *poly-* + *theos* god) + F *-isme* -ism — more at THE-] **:** the belief in or worship of a plurality of gods ⟨ancient ~s of Babylon and Egypt —*Brit. Bk. News*⟩

poly·the·ist \-,thēə̇st\ *n* **:** one who believes in or worships a plurality of gods

poly·the·is·tic \¦==(,)thē¦istik\ *also* **poly·the·is·ti·cal** \-stə̇kəl, -stēk-\ *adj* [*polytheist* + *-ic* or *-ical*] **:** of, relating to, or characterized by polytheism **:** believing in or worshiping a plurality of gods — **poly·the·is·ti·cal·ly** \-stə̇k(ə)lē, -stēk-, -li\ *adv*

poly·the·lia \,=='thēlēə\ *n* -S [NL, fr. *poly-* + *thel-* (fr. Gk *thēlē* nipple) + *-ia* — more at FEMININE] **:** a condition of having more than the normal number of nipples

poly·thene \'==,thēn\ *n* -S [contr. of *polyethylene*] **:** polyethylene used as a plastic

poly·thionic acid \¦pälē, -lə+. . .-\ *n* [ISV *poly-* + *thionic*] **:** a thionic acid containing more than two sulfur atoms in the molecule

po·lyt·o·cous \pə'lid·əkəs\ *adj* [Gk *polytokos,* fr. *poly-* + *tokos* offspring, fr. *tiktein* to bear, beget — more at THANE] **:** producing many eggs or young at one time ⟨~ mammals⟩ — compare MONOTOCOUS

poly·to·ma \,pälē'tōmə, -lə̇'t-\ *n, cap* [NL, fr. *poly-* + *-toma* (fr. Gk *temnein* to cut) — more at TOME] **:** a common genus of colorless saprozoic plantlike flagellates (order Phytomonadina) having paired anterior flagella, lacking chromatophores, and being widely distributed in stagnant freshwater

po·lyt·o·mous \pə'lid·əməs\ *adj* [*poly-* + *-tomous* (as in *dichotomous*)] **1 :** divided into more than two secondary parts or branches — compare DICHOTOMOUS **2 :** PINNATIFID

po·lyt·o·my \-mē\ *n* -ES [ISV *poly-* + *-tomy*] **1 :** polytomous character or condition ⟨a typical ~ consists of a whorl of three to six branches surrounding an open axil —*Bryologist*⟩ **2 :** division into more members or classes than three — compare TRICHOTOMY

poly·tonal \¦pälē, -lə+\ *adj* [*poly-* + *tonal*] **:** relating to or characterized by polytonality ⟨exciting rhythms and ~ harmonies —*Time*⟩ — **poly·tonally** \"+\ *adv*

poly·ton·al·ism \¦==¦tōnᵊl,izəm\ *n* -S [*polytonal* + *-ism*] **:** the practice or theory of using polytonal combinations in musical composition

poly·ton·al·ist \-ᵊlə̇st\ *n* [*polytonal* + *-ist*] **:** one skilled in polytonality

poly·tonality \¦==+\ *n* [*polytonal* + *-ity*] **:** the simultaneous use of two or more musical keys or tonalities; *also* **:** the effect of such a combination

poly·tone \'==+,-\ *n* [*poly-* + *tone*] **:** utterance characterized by varied tone or pitch — compare MONOTONE

poly·tonic \¦==+\ *adj* [*poly-* + *tonic*] **:** having several pitch tones ⟨~ languages⟩

poly·topic \"+\ *adj* [ISV *poly-* + *top-* + *-ic*] *of a kind of organism* **:** occurring or originating in two or more disjunct areas ⟨~ species⟩ — **poly·topically** \"+\ *adv*

poly·to·pism \'==,tō,pizəm, pə'lid·ə,p-\ *n* -S [*poly-* + *top-* + *-ism*] **:** independent origin of a systematic group at more than one place presumably by identical change in scattered individuals of its precursor — compare MONOTOPISM

poly·to·py \-,pē\ *n* -ES [*polytopic* + *-y*] **:** the condition of a group that is polytopic **:** POLYTOPISM

po·lyt·ri·cha·ce·ae \pə,li·trə'kāsē,ē\ *n pl, cap* [NL, fr. *Polytrichum,* type genus + *-aceae*] **:** a family of usu. large acrocarpous mosses (order Polytrichales) that have simple or branching erect shoots growing from an underground stem, leaves with the costae bearing longitudinal lamellae of variable structure, antheridia borne in conspicious saucer-shaped terminal rosettes, and capsules which are characteristically angular in cross section with a peristome several cells thick — see POGONATUM, POLYTRICHUM — **po·lyt·ri·cha·ceous** \=¦==¦kāshəs\ *adj*

po·lyt·ri·cha·les \=,=='kā(,)lēz\ *n pl, cap* [NL, fr. *Polytrichum* + *-ales*] **:** an order of Musci that is coextensive with the family Polytrichaceae or sometimes includes this together with the genus *Dawsonia* — see DAWSONIALES

poly·trich·i·dae \,pälē'trikə,dē, -lə̇-'t-\ *n pl, cap* [NL, fr. *Polytrichum* + *-idae*] **:** a small subclass of mosses comprising the orders Polytrichales and Dawsoniales

po·lyt·ri·chous \pə'li·trəkəs\ *adj* [Gk *polytrichos* very hairy, fr. *poly-* very, much (fr. *polys* much, many) + *-trichos* -trichous] **:** thickly covered with hairs or cilia

po·lyt·ri·chum \-kəm\ *n, cap* [NL, fr. L *polytrichon* golden-hair, fr. Gk, maidenhair, fr. neut. of *polytrichos* very hairy] **:** a large genus (the type of the family Polytrichaceae) of mosses chiefly of temperate and arctic regions — see HAIRCAP MOSS

poly·troch \'pälē,träk, -lə̇,t-\ *or* **po·lyt·ro·chal** \pə'li·trəkəl\ *or* **po·lyt·ro·chous** \-kəs\ *adj* [*polytroch* fr. NL *polytrochus,* fr. *poly-* + *-trochus* having (such) a ciliated band; *polytrochal* fr. NL *polytrochus* + E *-al; polytrochous* fr. NL *polytrochus* — more at -TROCHA] **:** having many circles of cilia ⟨~ larvae⟩

poly·troph·ic \¦pälē¦träfik, -lə̇¦t-\ *adj* [*poly-* + *-trophic*] **1 :** deriving nourishment from more than one organic substance ⟨~ pathogenic bacteria⟩ **2 :** producing nutritive cells one of which is attached to each developing egg in the ovary — used of an insect or the ovary of an insect; compare ACROTROPHIC, PANOISTIC

poly·trop·ic \-äpik\ *adj* [*poly-* + *-tropic*] **:** visiting many kinds of flowers for nectar — used of an insect ⟨~ bees⟩; compare MONOTROPIC, OLIGOTROPIC

poly·type \'==,tīp\ *n* [*poly-* + *type*] **:** one of several polymorphic crystal structures **:** POLYMORPH

poly·typ·ic \¦==¦tipik\ *adj* [*poly-* + *type* + *-ic* or *-ical*] **1** *also* **poly·typ·i·cal** \-pə̇kəl\ **:** represented by several or many types or subdivisions ⟨~ species⟩ — opposed to *monotypic* **2 :** of, relating to, or being a polytype ⟨~ crystal⟩ — **poly·typ·i·cism** \,==¦==pə,sizəm\ *n* -S

poly·urethane *or* **poly·urethan** \¦pälē, -lə+\ *n* [ISV *poly-* + *urethane, urethan*] **:** any of various polymers that contain —NHCOO— linkages of the type found in carbamic esters, that are obtained by reaction of a di- or tri-isocyanate ester usu. with a polyester or a glycol (as a polyglycol), and that are used chiefly in making flexible and rigid foams, elastomers, and resins for coatings and adhesives

poly·uria \,pälē'yu̇rēə, -lə̇'y-\ *n* -S [NL, fr. *poly-* + *-uria*] **:** excessive secretion of urine in physiologic or pathologic conditions

poly·uronic acid \¦pälē, -lə+. . .-\ *n* [*polyuronic* fr. *poly-* + *uronic* (in *uronic acid*)] **:** a polymer of a uronic acid ⟨alginic acid is a *polyuronic acid*⟩

poly·uro·nide \,=='yu̇rə,nīd, -,nə̇d\ *n* -S [ISV *polyuronic* (in *polyuronic acid*) + *-ide*] **:** a polymeric substance consisting of uronic acid units with glycosidic linkages often in combination with monosaccharides and occurring widely in plants (as in gums and pectic substances) and in soils ⟨the ~ hemicelluloses are cell wall components widely distributed in the plant world —J.F.Bonner⟩

poly·valence *or* **poly·valency** \¦pälē, -lə+\ *n* [*polyvalence* ISV, fr. *polyvalent,* after such pairs as E *absent: absence; polyvalency* fr. *polyvalent* + *-cy*] **:** the state of being polyvalent

[1]**poly·valent** \"+\ *adj* [ISV *poly-* + *valent*] **:** having multiple valence: as **a** (1) **:** having a valence or oxidation state greater usu. than two ⟨~ ions⟩ (2) **:** having variable valence or oxidation state ⟨nitrogen is ~, exhibiting oxidation states of from −3 to +5 in compounds⟩ **b** (1) **:** capable of interacting with or counteracting more than one toxin, antigen, or kind of microorganism ⟨a ~ vaccine⟩ ⟨~ antivenin⟩ (2) **:** effective against or sensitive toward more than one exciting agent ⟨~ immunity⟩ ⟨~ sensitivity⟩ **c :** MULTIVALENT 2

[2]**polyvalent** \"\ *n* -S **:** a multivalent chromosome group

[1]**poly·vinyl** \¦pälē, -lə+\ *n* [ISV *poly-* + *vinyl*] **:** a polymerized vinyl compound, vinyl resin, or vinyl plastic

[2]**polyvinyl** \"\ *adj* **:** relating to or being a polymerized vinyl compound

polyvinyl acetal *n* **:** any of a group of thermoplastic resins made by condensing polyvinyl alcohol with an aldehyde and used chiefly in the form of sheets and films, molded products, coatings, and adhesives; *esp* **:** the resin made from acetaldehyde

polyvinyl acetate *n* **:** a polymer of vinyl acetate; *esp* **:** a thermoplastic material $[-CH_2CH(OOCCH_3)-]_x$ obtained usu. in the form of a colorless to straw-colored stable solid resin or a milk-white emulsion in water and used chiefly in adhesives, textile finishes, water-base emulsion paints, and other coatings and in making polyvinyl alcohol and polyvinyl acetals

polyvinyl alcohol *n* **:** a polymer of vinyl alcohol; *esp* **:** a thermoplastic resin that is soluble or swells in water, that if obtained by complete hydrolysis of polyvinyl acetate has the formula $[-CH_2CH(OH)-]_x$ or if by partial hydrolysis contains some acetate groups, and that is used chiefly as emulsifiers, adhesives, and films resistant to solvents and abrasion, and in making molded and extruded products and polyvinyl acetals

polyvinyl butyral *n* **:** a tough flexible transparent moisture-resistant polyvinyl acetal resin made from polyvinyl alcohol and butyraldehyde and used chiefly as the interlayer in safety glass and other laminated products and as a coating for textiles

polyvinyl chloride *n* **:** a polymer of vinyl chloride; *esp* **:** a thermoplastic resin $(-CH_2CHCl-)_x$ that is characterized by chemical inertness, resistance to weathering, electrical resistivity, and rigidity unless it is plasticized and that is used chiefly for electrical insulation, coated fabrics, films, sheets, and pipes

polyvinyl formal *n* **:** a polyvinyl acetal resin made from polyvinyl alcohol and formaldehyde and used chiefly in insulating enamels and other coatings

poly·vinylidene \¦pälē, -lə+\ *adj* [*poly-* + *vinylidene*] **:** relating to or being a polymerized vinylidene compound

polyvinylidene chloride *n* **:** a polymer of vinylidene chloride: as **a :** an insoluble crystalline thermoplastic homopolymer $(-CH_2CCl_2-)_x$ **b :** SARAN

poly·vi·nyl·pyrrolidone \¦==¦==+\ *n* [*poly-* + *vinyl* + *pyrrolidone*] **:** a water-soluble chemically inert solid polymer $(-CH_2CHC_4H_6NO-)_n$ made by polymerizing of *N*-vinyl-pyrrolidone and used chiefly in medicine as a vehicle for drugs (as iodine) and esp. formerly as a plasma expander

polyvinyl resin *n* **:** VINYL RESIN

poly·vol·tine \¦pälē¦vōl,tēn, -lə̇¦v-, -,tᵊn\ *adj* [*poly-* + *-voltine* (as in *bivoltine*)] **:** MULTIVOLTINE

[1]**po·lyx·e·nid** \pə'liksənə̇d; ¦päl|ək¦senə̇d\ *adj* [NL *Polyxenidae*] **:** of or relating to the Polyxenidae

[2]**polyxenid** \"\ *n* -S **:** a millipede of the family Polyxenidae

pol·yx·en·i·dae \,päl|ək'senə,dē\ *n pl, cap* [NL, fr. *Polyxenus,* type genus + *-idae*] **:** a cosmopolitan family of small pselaphognathous millipedes having 10 body rings, 13 pairs of legs, and very small eyes

po·lyx·e·nus \pə'liksənəs\ *n, cap* [NL, fr. *poly-* + Gk *xenos* guest, host] **:** a cosmopolitan genus (the type of the family Polyxenidae) of millipedes

[1]**poly·zoa** \,pälē'zōə, -lə̇'z-\ [NL, fr. *poly-* + *-zoa*] *syn of* BRYOZOA

[2]**polyzoa** \"\ [NL, fr. *poly-* + *-zoa*] *syn of* ²CESTODA

poly·zo·al \¦==¦zōəl\ *adj* [NL *Polyzoa* + E *-al*] **1 :** BRYOZOAN **2 :** CESTODE

poly·zo·an \-ōən\ *adj or n* [NL *Polyzoa* + E *-an*] **1 :** BRYOZOAN **2 :** CESTODE

poly·zo·ar·i·al \¦==¦zō¦a(a)rēəl\ *adj* [NL *polyzoarium* + E *-al*] **:** of or relating to a polyzoarium

poly·zo·ar·i·um \,=='=rēəm\ *also* **poly·zo·a·ry** \,==¦zōərē\ *n, pl* **polyzoar·ia** \,==='=rēə\ *also* **polyzoaries** \,==='zōərēz\ [*polyzoarium* fr. NL, fr. *Polyzoa* + *-arium; polyzoary* fr. NL *Polyzoa* + E *-ary*] **:** a bryozoan colony or the supporting skeleton of such a colony

poly·zo·ic \¦==¦zōik\ *adj* [*poly-* + *-zoic*] **1 :** composed of many zooids; *esp* **:** POLYZOOTIC **2 :** producing many sporozoites **3 :** containing many kinds of animals or many animals — used of habitats

[1]**poly·zo·oid** \-ō,ȯid\ *adj* [NL *Polyzoa* + E *-oid*] **:** resembling a polyzooid

[2]**polyzooid** \"\ *n* **:** POLYPIDE

poly·zo·on \,=='zō,än\ *n, pl* **poly·zoa** \-ōə\ *or* **polyzoons** [NL, fr. *poly-* + *-zoon*] **:** POLYPIDE

poly·zo·ot·ic \¦==,zə¦wäd·ik, -zō¦ä-\ *adj* [*poly-* + *zo-* + *-otic*] **:** made up of numerous zooids; *specif* **:** consisting of a linear series of similar segments ⟨~ tapeworms⟩ — distinguished from *monozootic*

[1]**pom** \'päm\ *n* -S [by shortening] **1 :** POMPON **2 :** POMERANIAN

[2]**pom** \"\ *n* -S [imit.] **:** BANG ⟨the dull ~ of a distant cannon⟩ — often used interjectionally

[3]**pom** \"\ *vi* **pommed; pommed; pomming; poms** [imit.] **:** to sound with the characteristic noise of a small caliber automatic or semiautomatic cannon ⟨the guns *pommed* loudly and the charges . . . arced up and out —Wirt Williams⟩

pom·ace *or* **pum·ace** \'pəməs\ *n* -S [prob. fr. ML *pomacium* cider, fr. LL *pomum* apple, fr. L, fruit] **1 :** the substance of apples or a similar fruit crushed by grinding (as in making cider) or the residue of grape skins, seeds, and stems remaining after pressing of wine grapes **2 :** the substance of anything (as fish or castor bean) mashed or crushed to a pulpy mass

po·ma·ce·ae \pō'māsē,ē\ [NL, fr. LL *pomus* apple tree (fr. L, fruit tree, fr. *pomum* fruit) + NL *-aceae*] *syn of* MALACEAE

pomace fly *n* **:** FRUIT FLY

[1]**po·ma·cen·trid** \¦pōmə¦sen·trə̇d\ *adj* [NL *Pomacentridae*] **:** of or relating to the Pomacentridae

[2]**pomacentrid** \"\ *n* -S **:** a fish of the family Pomacentridae

po·ma·cen·tri·dae \,=='sen·trə,dē\ *n pl, cap* [NL, fr. *Pomacentrus,* type genus (fr. Gk *pōmat-, pōma* lid, cover + *kentron* sharp point) + *-idae;* akin to Skr *pāti* he protects — more at FUR, CENTER] **:** a family of small usu. brightly colored marine percoid fishes having only two spines in the anal fin and comprising the damselfishes of tropical coral reefs — **po·ma·cen·troid** \¦==¦sen,trȯid\ *adj or n*

po·ma·cen·trus \,=='sen·trəs\ *n, cap* [NL — more at POMACENTRIDAE] **:** the type genus of the family Pomacentridae

po·ma·ceous \pō'māshəs\ *adj* [NL *pomaceus,* fr. LL *pomum* apple (fr. L *pomum* fruit) + L *-aceus* -aceous] **1 :** of or relating to apples **:** like or typical of an apple ⟨~ harvest⟩ ⟨~ shape⟩ **2** [NL *Pomaceae* + E *-ous*] **a :** belonging to the Malaceae **b :** having the nature or appearance of a pome

[1]**po·ma·das·id** \¦pōmə¦dasə̇d, pō'madəs-\ *adj* [NL *Pomadasidae*] **:** of or relating to the Pomadasidae

[2]**pomadasid** \"\ *n* -S **:** a fish of the family Pomadasidae

po·ma·das·i·dae \,pōmə'dasə,dē\ *n pl, cap* [NL, irreg. fr. *Pomadasys,* type genus + *-idae*] **:** a family of percoid fishes comprising the grunts

po·ma·da·sy·i·dae \,==,də'sīə,dē\ [NL, fr. *Pomadasys,* type genus + *-idae*] *syn of* POMADASIDAE

po·ma·das·ys \,=='dasə̇s\ *n, cap* [NL, fr. Gk *pōmat-, pōma* lid + *dasys* shaggy, thick with hair — more at POMACENTRIDAE, DENSE] **:** the type genus of the family Pomadasidae

¹po·made \pə'mād, pō'm-, -mäd\ *n* -s [MF *pommade,* fr. It *pomata,* fr. *pomo* apple (fr. LL *pomum,* fr. L, fruit) + *-ata* -ade; fr. the original use of apples as an ingredient] **1 :** a cosmetic ointment made formerly from apples, lard or other grease, and spices or perfumes **:** a perfumed ointment **:** POMATUM; *esp* **:** a fragrant usu. medicated unguent for the hair or scalp **2 :** any of various soft greasy perfumed substances (as the perfumed fat obtained in the enfleurage process)

²pomade \"\ *vt* -ED/-ING/-S **:** to apply pomade to **:** dress with pomade

po·ma·der·ris \,pōmə'derəs\ *n, cap* [NL, fr. Gk *pōmat-, pōma* lid, cover + *derris* skin, leather covering, fr. *derein* to skin — more at POMACENTRIDAE, DERM-] **:** a genus of hoary pubescent Australasian shrubs (family Rhamnaceae) having alternate leaves and cymose white or yellowish flowers with the ovary partly adnate to the calyx

po·man·der \(')pō¦mandə(r)\ *n* -s [ME, modif. of MF *pome d'ambre, pomme d'embre,* fr. ML *pomum de ambra,* lit., apple or ball of amber] **1 a :** a mixture of perfumed or aromatic substances usu. made in a ball and enclosed in a perforated bag or box and formerly carried on the person as a guard against infection **b :** a box or a hollow fruit-shaped ball containing such a mixture **2 :** something resembling or suggesting a pomander (as in shape or scent); *esp* **:** a clove-studded orange or apple hung in a clothes closet

pomander 1b

po·ma·rine \'pōmə,rīn, -,rən\ *adj* [F *pomarin,* fr. Gk *pōmat-, pōma* lid + *rhin-, rhis* nose — more at POMACENTRIDAE, RHIN-] **:** having the nostrils somewhat roofed over by the horny plate forming the ridge of the bill

pomarine jaeger *n* **:** a jaeger (*Stercorarius pomarius*) larger and darker than the parasitic jaeger having somewhat elongated but obtuse middle tail feathers

po·mar·ro·sa \,pōmə'rōsə\ *n* -s [Sp, fr. *poma* apple (fr. — assumed — VL) + *rosa* rose-colored, fr. *rosa* rose, fr. L — more at POME] **1** *West Indies* **:** MALAY APPLE **2** *West Indies* **:** ROSE APPLE

po·mat·i·op·sis \pō,mad·ē'äpsəs\ *n, cap* [NL, fr. Gk *pōmatias,* a snail with a shell furnished with a lid (fr. *pōmat-, pōma* lid) + NL *-opsis* — more at POMACENTRIDAE] **:** an American genus comprising amphibious pulmonate snails that include intermediate hosts of the lung fluke (*Paragonimus westermanii*) and other trematodes and being placed in the family Bulimidae or made the type of a separate family

po·ma·to \pə'mād·(,)ō, -mäd·-\ *n* -ES [blend of *potato* and *tomato*] **:** a plant chimera produced by grafting tomato scions on potato plants — called also *potomato, topato*

¹po·mat·o·mid \pə'mad·əməd\ *adj* [NL *Pomatomidae*] **:** of or relating to the Pomatomidae

²pomatomid \"\ *n* -s **:** a fish of the family Pomatomidae

po·ma·tom·i·dae \,pōmə'tämə,dē\ *n pl, cap* [NL, fr. Gk *Pomatomus,* type genus + *-idae*] **:** a family of percoid fishes consisting of the genus *Pomatomus* and containing solely the nearly cosmopolitan bluefish

po·mat·o·mus \pə'mad·əməs\ *n, cap* [NL, fr. Gk *pōmat-, pōma* lid + *-tomos* cutting, fr. *temnein* to cut; fr. the cut appearance of the opercle — more at TOME] **:** a genus of fishes coextensive with the family Pomatomidae

po·mat·o·rhine \pə'mad·ə,rīn, -,rən\ *adj* [NL *pomatorhinus* fr. Gk *pōmat-, pōma* lid + *rhin-, rhis* nose — more at POMACENTRIDAE, RHIN-] **:** POMARINE

po·ma·tum \pə'mād·əm, pō'm-, -mäd·-\ *n* -s [NL, fr. LL *pomum* apple, fr. L, fruit] **:** OINTMENT; *esp* **:** a perfumed unguent for the hair or scalp

po·ma·tumed \-md\ *adj* [NL *pomatum* + E *-ed*] **:** POMADED

¹pome \'pōm\ *n* -s [ME, fr. MF *pomme,* pome, apple, ball, fr. OF *pome,* fr. (assumed) VL *poma* apple, fr. LL *pomum,* fr. L, fruit] **1 :** a fleshy accessory fruit (as of an apple) consisting of a central core with usu. five seeds enclosed within a bony or papery capsule made up of fused carpels and of an outer thickened fleshy layer made up of the much enlarged receptacle — see FRUIT illustration **2 :** a metal ball or globe

²pome \"\ *vi* -ED/-ING/-S [F *pommer,* fr. *pomme* — more at ¹POME] *obs, of a cabbage or lettuce* **:** to form a head or heart

pome-citron \'≈¦≈≈\ *n* [*pome* + *citron*] *archaic* **:** CITRON

pome fruit *n* **:** POME 1; *also* **:** a plant that bears pomes **:** a tree or shrub of the family Malvaceae

pome·gran·ate \'päm(ə),granət *also* 'pəm,g- *or* ,≈≈'≈≈ *or* (,)≈-'≈≈; *usu* -əd·+V\ *n* -s *often attrib* [ME *poumgarnet, pomegranard,* fr. MF *pomme grenate,* fr. OF *pome grenate,* fr. *pome* apple, fruit + *grenate* seedy, fr. L, fem. of *granatus* — more at POME, GRENADE] **1 a :** the several-celled angular berry of a tropical African and Asiatic tree (*Punica granatum*) that is about the size of an orange, contains many seeds in a crimson acid pulp which is eaten raw or made into a beverage, and has a thick astringent rind used esp. formerly in medicine and tanning and together with the flowers of the tree as the source of a red dye **b :** the tree that bears pomegranates **2** *Austral* **:** NATIVE POMEGRANATE **3 :** CANADA PLUM **4 :** a dark red that is yellower and slightly darker and less strong than cranberry and yellower, lighter, and stronger than average garnet or average wine

pomegranate melon *n* **1 :** DUDAIM MELON **2 :** MANGO MELON

pomegranate purple *n* **:** a moderate red to purplish red that is very slightly redder and stronger than madder carmine

¹pomeis *pl of* POMME

²pomeis *var of* POMME

pom·e·lo \'päma,lō, 'pəm-\ *also* **pum·me·lo** *or* **pum·e·lo** \'pəm-\ *n* -s [alter. of *pompelmous*] **1 :** SHADDOCK **2 :** GRAPEFRUIT

¹pom·er·a·nian \,pämə¦rānēən, -nyən\ *adj, usu cap* [*Pomerania,* historical region in northern Europe + E *-an*] **:** of or relating to the region Pomerania in northern Europe bordering on the Baltic sea and lying from the west of Rügen Island to the Vistula river

²pomeranian \"\ *n* **1** -s *cap* **:** an inhabitant or native of the Baltic littoral or of the seacoast provinces on the Baltic known as Pomerania **2 a** *usu cap* **:** a breed of very small compact short-coupled long-haired dogs of the Spitz type **b** -s *often cap* **:** a dog of this breed

po·mer·id·i·an \,pōmə¦ridēən\ *adj* [L *pomeridianus* postmeridian, alter. of *postmeridianus* — more at POSTMERIDIAN] **:** blossoming after noon

po·me·ri·um *also* **po·moe·ri·um** \pō'mirēəm\ *n, pl* **pome·ria** *also* **pomoe·ria** \-rēə\ [L *pomerium, pomoerium,* fr. *post* behind + *moerus, murus* wall — more at POST-, MUNITION] **:** a narrow strip of land marked off around an ancient Roman town or city and held sacred

pometté *var of* POMMETTÉE

pomewater \'≈,≈≈\ *n* [ME, fr. ¹*pome* + *water*] *dial chiefly Brit* **:** a large sweet apple

¹pom·fret \'pämfrət, 'pəm-\ *n* -s [alter. of earlier *pamflet,* prob. fr. F *pample,* fr. Pg *pampo*] **1 :** a deep-bodied sooty-black pelagic spiny-finned fish (*Brama raii*) of the north Atlantic and North Pacific oceans that is valued for food; *also* **:** any of several closely related fishes **2 :** any of several food fishes of the family Stromateidae; *esp* **:** an East Indian fish (*Stromateoides argenteus*) resembling the common harvest fish

²pomfret \"\ *also* **pomfret cake** *n* -s [fr. *Pomfret* (now *Pontefract*), municipal borough of Yorkshire, England] *dial Brit* **:** a small black flat confection (as of licorice)

pomi- *comb form* [LL *pomum,* fr. L, fruit] **:** apple ⟨*pomi*form⟩ ⟨*pomi*vorous⟩

po·mif·er·ous \(')pō¦mif(ə)rəs\ *adj* [L *pomifer* fruitbearing, fr. *pomum* + *-fer* -ferous] **:** bearing pomes

po·mi·form \'pōmə,fȯrm\ *adj* [ISV *pomi-* + *-form*] **:** shaped like an apple

poming *pres part of* POME

pomme \'päm, -ə-, -ȯ-, -ō-\ *also* **po·meis** \'pōməs\ *n, pl* **pomeis** [*pomme* fr. F, apple, fr. MF; *pomeis* fr. *pomeis,* pl. of (assumed) after *pomey,* alter. of *pomme* — more at POME] *heraldry* **:** a roundel vert

pomme blanche \(')≈¦bläⁿsh\ *n* [F, white apple] **:** BREADROOT 1

pommed *past of* POM

pomme de prairie \¦≈də¦≈≈\ *n* [F, prairie apple] **:** BREADROOT 1

pom·mée \(')pä¦mā, ¦pə-, (')pō¦-, (')pȯ¦-, '≈mē\ *adj* [F *pommée,* fr. MF *pomme* apple, ball + *-ée* -ed — more at POME] *of a cross* **:** having the end of each arm terminating in a ball or disk — called also *bourdonnée, pommelée, pommettée;* see CAPUCHIN CROSS; CROSS illustration

¹pom·mel \'pəməl, 'päm-\ *also* **pum·mel** \'pəm-\ *n* -s [ME *pomel,* fr. MF, fr. (assumed) VL *pomellum* ball, knob, dim of LL *pomum* apple, fr. L, fruit] **1 :** a usu. ornamental terminal knob: as **a :** the knob on the hilt of a sword or saber **b :** the protuberance at the front and top of a saddlebow — compare CANTLE **c :** FINIAL **2 :** a long-handled bat used in knur and spell **3 :** either of a pair of removable handles used on the back of a gymnastics horse **4 :** the plunger of a machine for extruding plastics

²pom·mel \'pəməl\ *vt* **pommeled** *or* **pommelled; pommeled** *or* **pommelled; pommeling** *or* **pommelling** \-m(ə)liŋ\

pommels [¹*pommel*] **:** PUMMEL

³pom·mel \'pəməl, 'päm-\ *n* -s [F *paumelle,* fr. *paume* palm of the hand — more at PALM] **:** a tool used for softening and raising the grain of or producing a velvety appearance on fancy leathers

pom·meled \-ld\ *adj* [¹*pommel* + *-ed*] **:** provided with a pommel

pom·me·lée *or* **pom·mel·lé** \¦pämə¦lā, ¦pəm-, ¦pȯm-, ¦pōm-, '≈≈¦lē\ *or* **pom·mel·ly** \'≈≈¦lē\ *adj* [MF *pomel* + *-é, -ée* -ed] **:** POMMÉE

pom·mel·er \'pəm(ə)lə(r)\ *n* -s **:** one that pommels

pom·me·lion \pə'mēlyən\ *n* -s [¹*pommel*] *archaic* **:** CASCABEL 1

pom·mer \'pȯmə(r)\ *n* -s [G, fr. MHG *bumhart,* fr. It *bombarda* — more at BOMBARDE] **:** BOMBARDON

pommetée *var of* POMMETTÉE

pom·met·tée *or* **pom·met·ty** \'pämad·ē\ *also* **po·met·té** *or* **pom·me·tée** \¦pämə¦tā, ¦pəm-, ¦pȯm-, ¦pōm-, '≈məd·ē\ *adj* [F *pommette* little knob (dim. of *pomme* apple, ball) + *-é, -ée* -ed] **1 :** POMMÉE **2 :** adorned with small balls or circles at the angles of the terminations of the arms — used of a cross clechée or urdée

pomming *pres part of* POM

¹pom·my *or* **pom·mie** \'pəmi\ *dial Eng var of* POMACE

²pom·my \'pämē\ *n* -ES *sometimes cap* [origin unknown] *slang Austral* **:** an English immigrant; *esp* **:** one recently arrived — usu. used disparagingly

po·mo \'pō(,)mō\ *n, pl* **pomo** *or* **pomos** *usu cap* **1 a :** an Indian people of the Russian river valley and adjacent coast in northern California **b :** a member of such people **2 :** a Kulanapan language of the Pomo people **3 :** KULANAPAN

pomoerium *var of* POMERIUM

po·mol·o·bus \pə'mäləbəs\ *n, cap* [NL, prob. irreg. fr. Gk *pōmat-, pōma* lid + NL *-lobus* — more at POMACENTRIDAE] **:** a genus of small fishes (family Clupeidae) including the common alewife and the skipjack (*Pomolobus chrysochloris*)

po·mo·log·i·cal \,pōmə¦läjəkəl, -jēk-\ *adj* **:** of or relating to pomology — **po·mo·log·i·cal·ly** \-jək(ə)lē, -jēk-, -li\ *adv*

po·mol·o·gist \pō'mäləjəst, pō'-\ *n* -s **:** a horticulturist who specializes in pomology

po·mol·o·gy \-jē,-ji\ *n* -ES [NL *pomologia,* fr. L *pomum* fruit + *-logia* -logy] **1 :** the science of the cultivation of fruits; *also* **:** a treatise on such a science **2 :** the science or practice of growing, storing, processing, and marketing fruits

po·mox·is \pə'mäksəs\ *n, cap* [NL, fr. Gk *pōmat-, pōma* lid + *oxys* sharp — more at POMACENTRIDAE, OXY-] **:** a genus of sunfishes (family Centrarchidae) including the No. American black and white crappies

¹pomp \'pämp\ *n* -s [ME, fr. MF *pompe,* fr. L *pompa* procession, pomp, fr. Gk *pompē,* fr. *pempein* to send, send off, escort] **1 :** a show of magnificence **:** brilliant display **:** SPLENDOR ⟨the ~ and vanity of an imperial court⟩ **2 :** a ceremonial or festal procession, pageant, or parade **3 a :** ostentatious display **:** VAINGLORY ⟨the devil and all his ~*s*⟩ **b :** a flashy, ostentatious, or tawdry gesture, action, or flourish **syn** see DISPLAY

²pomp \"\ *vi* -ED/-ING/-S **:** to be pompous or act in a pompous manner

³pomp \"\ *n* -s [by shortening] **:** POMPADOUR 1

pomp *abbr* pomposo

pom·pa·dour \'pämpə,dō(ə)r, -dȯ(ə)r, -dōə, -ȯ(ə) *sometimes* -dü(ə)r *or* -üə\ *n* -s [after Jeanne Antoinette Poisson, Marquise de *Pompadour* †1764 mistress of King Louis XV of France] **1 a** (1) **:** a woman's style of hairdressing in which the hair is brushed into a loose full roll around the face and is often supported by a rat (2) **:** a man's style of hairdressing in which the hair is combed back so as to stand erect **b :** hair dressed in a pompadour **2 a :** a pink or crimson fabric for clothing **b :** a textile design of small printed or woven floral effects esp. in crimson, pink, or blue on silk or cotton fabrics **3 :** a South American chatterer (*Xipholena punicea*) of brilliant reddish purple color with white wings **4** *or* **pompadour green :** a moderate blue that is greener and duller than average copen or Dresden blue, redder, stronger, and slightly lighter than azurite blue, and greener and paler than bluebird

pompadour 1a(1)

pom·pa·doured \-d\ *adj* [*pompadour* + *-ed*] **:** arranged in a pompadour ⟨~ hair⟩

pom·pa·no *also* **pam·pa·no** \'pämpə,nō, 'pəm-\ *n, pl* **pompano** *or* **pompanos** [Sp *pámpano* vine tendril, a kind of fish, fr. L *pampinus* vine tendril] **1 a :** a marine carangid fish (*Trachinotus carolinus*) of the southern Atlantic and Gulf coasts of No. America that is an excellent food fish, reaches a length of 18 inches, has a deep thin body, is toothless when adult, and is covered with small scales with a blue, silver, or golden luster **b :** any of various other carangid fishes: as (1) **:** ROUND POMPANO (2) **:** a large bluish and silvery food and sport fish (*Hynnis cubensis*) of the Caribbean area (3) **:** LONGFIN POMPANO (4) **:** ³PERMIT **1 2 :** a small bluish or greenish butterfish (*Palometa simillima*) of the Pacific coast that is an excellent food fish

pompano clam *also* **pompano shell** *n* **:** a bivalve of the genus *Donax* **:** COQUINA

pompatic *also* **pompatical** *adj* [LL *pompaticus* showy, splendid, fr. *pompatus* (past part. of *pompare* to perform with pomp, fr. L *pompa* pomp) + L *-icus* -ic] *obs* **:** POMPOUS

¹pom·pe·ian *also* **pom·pei·ian** \(')päm¦pā(y)ən, -m¦pē(-\ *adj, usu cap* [L *pompeianus,* fr. *Pompeii,* ancient city in southern Italy + *-anus* -an] **1 :** of or relating to the ancient city Pompeii **2 :** of, relating to, or characteristic of the art and culture of Pompeii

²pompeian *also* **pompeiian** \"\ *n* -s *cap* [L *pompeianus,* fr. *pompeianus,* adj.] **:** a native or inhabitant of Pompeii

pompeian blue *n, often cap P* **:** a bluish gray to grayish blue

pompeian red *n, often cap P* **:** a grayish red that is yellower and paler than bois de rose, yellower, lighter, and stronger than blush rose or livid brown, and yellower and stronger than appleblossom — called also *dragon's blood*

pompeian yellow *n, often cap P* **:** a moderate orange yellow that is redder and less strong than yellow ocher and duller than deep chrome yellow

pom·peii \(')päm¦pā *sometimes* päm'pā,ē, *chiefly Brit* 'pämpi,ī *or* päm'pē,ī\ *n, often cap* [fr. *Pompeii,* ancient city in southern Italy] **:** a moderate to deep reddish brown — called also *burnt rose*

pom·pel·mous *also* **pom·pel·moose** \'pämpəl,müs\ *n, pl* **pompelmouses** *or* **pompelmooses** [D *pompelmoes*] **:** SHADDOCK

pom·pho·lyx \'päm(p)fə,liks\ *n* -ES [NL *pompholyg-, pompholyx,* fr. Gk, bubble] **1** *or* **pom·pho·lix** \"\ **:** impure zinc oxide produced by burning zinc or roasting its ores **:** FLOWERS OF ZINC **2 :** a skin disease marked by an eruption of vesicles esp. on the palms and soles

pom·pho·poea \,päm(p)fə'pēə\ *n, cap* [NL, fr. Gk *pomphos* blister + *-poia,* fem. of *-poios* (fr. *poiein* to make, produce) — more at PEMPHIGUS, POET] **:** a genus of blister beetles including some with adults that feed on foliage and blossoms of many fruit and ornamental trees — see SAY BLISTER BEETLE

pom·pier *in sense 1* ¦pämpē¦ā, (')pämp¦yā, *in sense 2* (')pämp¦pi(ə)r *or like sense 1*\ *adj* [F, fr. *pompier* pump maker, fireman, fr. *pompe* pump (fr. It *pompa,* perh. fr. Sp *bomba*) + *-ier* -er; fr. the alleged resemblance of armed heroes in academic mythological paintings to firemen — more at PUMP] **1 :** tritely or insipidly academic ⟨~ art⟩ **:** marked by pretentious and stereotypical themes or treatment ⟨a ~ stage setting⟩ **2** [F, fireman] **:** of or relating to the personal equipment of a fire-fighting crew ⟨~ hatchet⟩

pompier ladder *also* **pompier** *n* -s **:** a fireman's scaling ladder consisting of a pole with crossbars for rungs and a hook at one end

¹pom·pi·lid \'pämpələd\ *or* **pom·pi·loid** \-,lȯid\ *adj* [*pompilid* fr. NL *Pompilidae; pompiloid* fr. NL *Pompilus* + E *-oid*] **:** of or relating to the Pompilidae

²pompilid \"\ *n* -s **:** a wasp of the family Pompilidae

pom·pil·i·dae \päm'pilə,dē\ *n pl, cap* [NL, fr. *Pompilus,* type genus + *-idae*] **:** a large family of slender usu. black fossorial short-petioled wasps with oval abdomen and strong spinose legs of which most (as the tarantula killer) burrow in the ground and provision their nests with spiders

pom·pi·lus \'pämpələs\ *n, cap* [NL, fr. Gk *pompilos,* a fish that follows ships, fr. *pempein* to send, send off, escort] **:** the type genus of the family Pompilidae

pomping *pres part of* POMP

pom·pi·on \'pämpēən\ *n* -s [modif. of MF *pompon* — more at PUMPKIN] **1** *chiefly dial* **:** PUMPKIN **2** *obs* **:** a corpulent oaf

pompion berry *n* **:** HACKBERRY

pomp·less \'pämpləs\ *adj* **:** lacking pomp **:** DRAB, COMMONPLACE

pom-pom \'päm,päm\ *n* -s [imit.] **1 a :** a fully automatic carriage-mounted 37 millimeter gun firing explosive shells and used by both sides during the Boer War **b :** a usu. fully automatic gun of 20 to 40 millimeters usu. firing explosive shells and mounted on ships in pairs, fours, or eights — called also *Chicago piano* **2** [by alteration] **:** POMPON

pom-pom girl *n* **:** PICKUP, PROSTITUTE

pom-pom-pull·away \,päm,päm'pülə,wā\ *n* **:** a form of tag in which the players make a dash for a goal at the signal "pom-pom-pullaway"

¹pom·pon \'päm,pän\ *n* -s [F, fr. MF *pompe* tuft of ribbons, perh. fr. *pompe* pomp] **1 :** an ornamental ball or tuft (as of yarn, feathers, leather, paper) used on clothing esp. of women and children and on caps and fancy dress costumes **2 a :** any of various hardy garden chrysanthemums with flower heads resembling a pompon **b :** a dwarf cabbage rose (*Rosa centifolia pomponia*) with small bright red flowers **c :** any of various dahlias with flower heads usu. not more than two inches in diameter — compare BALL DAHLIA

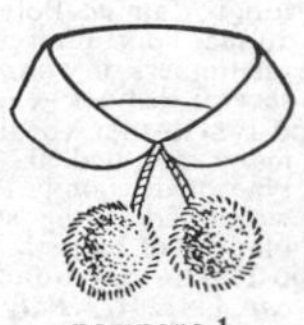
pompons 1

²pompon \"\ *or* **pom·poon** \päm'pün\ *n* -s [AmerSp *pompón*] **:** a dusky gray food fish (*Anisotremus surinamensis*) related to the porkfish and found from Louisiana and Florida southward — called also *black margate*

pom·pos·i·ty \päm'päsəd·ē, -ətē, -i\ *n* -ES [LL *pompositat-, pompositas,* fr. *pomposus* pompous + *-itat-, -itas* -ity — more at POMPOUS] **1 :** pompous demeanor, speech, or action **:** POMPOUSNESS **2 :** a pompous gesture, habit, or action

pom·po·so \päm'pō(,)sō\ *adv (or adj)* [It, fr. LL *pomposus*] **:** POMPOUSLY, IMPOSINGLY — used as a direction in music

pomp·ous \'pämpəs\ *adj* [ME, fr. MF *pompeux,* fr. LL *pomposus,* fr. L *pompa* pomp + *-osus* -ous] **1 :** of, relating to, or suggestive of pomp **:** ornately showy and pretentiously dignified **:** overly magnificent ⟨~ Roman colonnades⟩ **2 :** SELF-IMPORTANT ⟨a ~ policeman⟩ **3 :** too elevated and dignified for the subject matter ⟨~ language⟩ **:** excessively ornate ⟨~ figures of speech⟩

pomp·ous·ly *adv* **:** in a pompous manner

pomp·ous·ness *n* -ES [ME *pompousnesse,* fr. *pompous* + *-nesse* -ness] **:** the quality or state of being pompous

pomps *pl of* POMP, *pres 3d sing of* POMP

poms *pl of* POM, *pres 3d sing of* POM

pom·ster \'pämztə(r), -m(p)st-\ *vi* -ED/-ING/-S [prob. of Corn origin] *dial Eng* **:** to treat illness without having sufficient knowledge or skill in medicine

pon \(¦)pän, (¦)pən\ *prep* [by shortening] **:** UPON

pon *abbr* pontoon

pona·pe·an \,pōnə'pāən, ,pän-\ *n* -s *cap* [fr. *Ponape,* one of the Caroline islands + E *-an*] **1 :** a Micronesian of the island of Ponape in the Caroline islands **2 :** the Austronesian language spoken on Ponape

pon·ca *or* **pon·ka** \'päŋkə\ *n, pl* **ponca** *or* **poncas** *or* **ponka** *or* **ponkas** *usu cap* **1 a :** a Siouan people of the Missouri river valley in northeastern Nebraska **b :** a member of such people **2 :** a dialect of Dhegiha spoken by the Ponca people

ponce \'pän(t)s\ *n* -s [origin unknown] *slang Brit* **:** PIMP

pon·ceau \(')pän¦sō\ *n* -s [F, fr. OF *pouncel* red poppy, prob. fr. dim. of *paon* peacock, fr. L *pavon-, pavo* — more at PAVO] **1 :** a strong red to reddish orange — called also *coquelicot, granat* **2 :** a small bridge or culvert **3** *usu cap* **:** any of several azo dyes giving red colors: as **a** *or* **ponceau R :** an acid monoazo dye that dyes wool scarlet red and is used also in making organic pigments — see DYE table I (under *Acid Red 26*) **b** *or* **ponceau 3RB :** an acid disazo dye that dyes wool bluish scarlet and is used also as a biological stain for cytoplasm — called also *Biebrich scarlet;* see DYE table I (under *Acid Red 66*)

ponce·let \'pän(t)slət\ *n* -s [after Jean Victor *Poncelet* †1867 Fr. engineer] **:** a unit of power in physics equal to the amount of power obtained from an output of 100 kilogram-meters per second

poncelet wheel *n, usu cap P* [after Jean Victor *Poncelet*] **:** an undershot waterwheel that is suitable for falls of less than six feet

pon·cho \'pän(,)chō\ *n* -s [AmerSp, fr. Araucanian *pontho* woolen fabric] **1 :** a cloak resembling a blanket with a slit in the middle for the head worn chiefly by Spanish Americans **2 :** a garment made like a poncho and usu. of rubber, waterproofed cloth, or plastic for wear chiefly as a raincoat

pon·choed \-ōd\ *adj* **:** wearing a poncho

pon·ci·rus \pän'sīrəs\ *n, cap* [NL, fr. F *poncire,* prob. fr. L *pomum* fruit + *citreum* citron, fr. *citrus* citron tree — more at CITRON] **:** a genus of low thorny Chinese trees (family Rutaceae) that have trifoliate deciduous leaves and are sometimes included in the genus *Citrus* — compare CITRANGE, TRIFOLIATE ORANGE

poncho 2

¹pond \'pänd\ *n* -s *often attrib* [ME *ponde,* alter. of *pounde, poonde* enclosure — more at POUND] **1** *Brit* **:** a body of water artificially confined **2 :** a body of water usu. smaller than a lake and larger than a pool either naturally or artificially confined **3 :** POOL

²pond \"\ *vb* -ED/-ING/-S *vt* **1 :** to cause (as a stream) to form a pond **:** IMPOUND — *usu* used with *up* **2 :** to cover (concrete) with a pool of water for the purpose of curing **~** *vi* **:** to form a pond or pool

³pond \"\ *n* -s [D, pound; akin to E *pound*] **:** a gold coin of the former South African Republic equivalent to the English sovereign and struck 1892 to 1902

pond·age \'pändij, -dēj\ *n* -s [²*pond* + *-age*] **:** the storage capacity of a pond or reservoir

pond apple *n* **1 :** a small evergreen tree (*Annona glabra*) of southern Florida and tropical America **2 :** the edible ovoid brownish yellow fruit of the pond apple

pondbush \'≈,≈\ *n* **:** POND SPICE

pond cypress *also* **pond bald cypress** *n* **:** a bald cypress (*Taxodium ascendens*) of the southeastern U. S. differing from the closely related common bald cypress (*T. distichum*) only in being of smaller size and in having subulate leaves and erect branchlets

pond dogwood *n* **:** BUTTONBUSH

pond duck *n* **:** a wild duck: as **a :** HOODED MERGANSER **b :** MALLARD

pond·ed \'pändəd\ *adj* [¹*pond* + *-ed*] **:** covered with ponds ⟨a ~ area⟩ **:** provided with a pond ⟨~ game preserves⟩

1pon·der \'pändə(r)\ *vb* **pondered; pondered; pondering** \-d(ə)riŋ\ **ponders** [ME *ponderen, pondren*, fr. MF *ponderer*, fr. L *ponderare* to weigh, ponder, fr. *ponder-, pondus* weight — more at PENDANT] *vt* **1 :** to weigh in the mind **:** EVALUATE, APPRAISE ⟨~*ed* the child, and the life she had thus far lived —Elizabeth M. Roberts⟩ **2 :** to deliberate over **:** think out ⟨~ the shape and size of a new product⟩ **3 :** to think about **:** muse over ⟨~ the events of history⟩ **~** *vi* **:** to think or consider esp. quietly, soberly, and deeply — often used with *on* or *over* ⟨~ over a moral issue⟩

syn PONDER, MEDITATE, MUSE, and RUMINATE can mean to consider something attentively or with more or less deliberation. PONDER can suggest a careful weighing and balancing of considerations bearing on a matter, or a mere deliberative even though inconclusive thinking about something ⟨United States customs officials *pondered* whether to admit as art and as sculpture a work by the Rumanian modernist —Thomas Munro⟩ ⟨I shall *ponder* the matter carefully, my friends, and with the help of prayer, I may yet arrive at some solution of our difficulties —Elinor Wylie⟩ ⟨they demand a good deal of careful *pondering* and the recollection of pertinent facts —J.H. Robinson †1936⟩ ⟨*pondered* over God's greatness and incomprehensibility —H.O.Taylor⟩ MEDITATE suggests more a directing or focusing of one's thoughts in an effort to comprehend something, or it can suggest merely deep consideration, often with a purpose or plan in mind to be settled ⟨the young priest blotted himself out of his own consciousness and *meditated* upon the anguish of his Lord —Willa Cather⟩ ⟨*meditated* with concentrated attention on the problem of flight —Havelock Ellis⟩ ⟨what she *meditated* doing on England's behalf —C.S.Forester⟩ MUSE can come close to MEDITATE but more often suggests a mere more or less focused daydreaming as in remembrance ⟨he sat immovably, like one that *mused* on some great purpose—Thomas De Quincey⟩ ⟨he *mused* wretchedly, as he walked homeward, what might she not do? —William McFee⟩ ⟨still a pleasant mystery; enough to *muse* over on a dull afternoon —Elmer Davis⟩ ⟨not so much in order to read it as to *muse* with kindly condescension over this token of bygone fashion —Virginia Woolf⟩ RUMINATE usu. implies a going over the same matter again and again, suggesting less than the other terms a deliberative weighing or a focusing or absorption ⟨I sit at home and *ruminate* on the qualities of certain little books like this one —L.P.Smith⟩ ⟨forty years of *ruminating* on life —Waldemar Kaempffert⟩ ⟨the characters of the new friends he made interested him tremendously, and he could *ruminate* upon them when alone —Osbert Sitwell⟩ ⟨to teach philosophy, write, and *ruminate* beneath elms —Whitney Balliett⟩

2ponder \"\ *n* -S **:** an act of pondering or reflecting **:** REVERIE

pon·der·ability \,pänd(ə)rə'bilәd·ē, -ətē, -i\ *n* **:** the quality or state of being ponderable

1pon·der·able \'=d(ə)rəbəl\ *adj* [LL *ponderabilis*, fr. L *ponderare* to ponder + *-abilis* -able] **:** capable of being weighed, examined, evaluated, or considered for appraising **:** having weight ⟨something ~ from the outer world — something of which we can say that its weight is so and so —James Jeans⟩ **syn** see PERCEPTIBLE

2ponderable \"\ *n* -S **1 :** something that can be pondered **2 :** something morally or intellectually weighty — compare IMPONDERABLE

pon·der·ably \-blē, -li\ *adv* [1*ponderable* + *-ly*] **1 :** WEIGHTILY **2 :** CONSIDERABLY

pon·der·al \'pändərəl\ *adj* [L *ponder-, pondus* weight + E *-al*] **:** of or relating to weight **:** estimated in terms of weight

ponderal index *n, anthrop* **:** a measure of relative body mass expressed as the ratio of the cube root of body weight to stature multiplied by 100

pon·der·ance \'pänd(ə)rən(t)s\ *or* **pon·der·an·cy** \-nsē, -si\ *n, pl* **ponderances** *or* **ponderancies** [L *ponderare* to weigh + E *-ance, -ancy*] **1 :** WEIGHT **2 :** GRAVITY, CONSEQUENCE

1pon·der·ate \'pändə,rāt\ *vt* -ED/-ING/-S [L *ponderatus*, past part. of *ponderare* to weigh — more at PONDER] **:** to weigh down **:** give substance to

2pon·der·ate \'pänd(ə)rət\ *adj* [L *ponderatus*, past part. of *ponderare* to ponder] **:** DELIBERATE ⟨~ consideration⟩

pon·der·a·tion \,pändə'rāshən\ *n* -S [L *ponderation-, ponderatio*, fr. *ponderatus* + *-ion-, -io* -ion] **:** an act or the action of pondering

pondered *past of* PONDER

pon·der·er \'pänd(ə)rə(r)\ *n* -S **:** one that ponders

pondering *adj* [fr. pres. part. of 1*ponder*] **:** THOUGHTFUL, MEDITATIVE ⟨a ~ demeanor⟩

pon·der·ing·ly *adv* **:** in a pondering manner ⟨examine objects ~⟩

pon·der·ment \'pändə(r)mənt\ *n* -S **:** the action of pondering **:** deep thought ⟨twitching a facial muscle now and then to show ~ —Nigel Dennis⟩

pon·dero·motive \¦pändərō+\ *adj* [L *ponder-, pondus* weight + E *-o-* + *motive* — more at PENDANT] **:** tending to produce movement of a body — used of mechanical forces of interaction between electric currents and magnetic fields; compare ELECTROMOTIVE FORCE, MAGNETOMOTIVE FORCE

pon·der·o·sa pine \,pändə'rōsə-\ *n* [NL *Pinus ponderosa*, lit., heavy pine] **1 :** a common and widely distributed timber tree (*Pinus ponderosa*) of western No. America often reaching a height of 100 feet and having dark green leaves in bundles of 2 to 5 and 4 to 7 inches long, tawny yellowish bark, and strong reddish wood — called also *bull pine, western white pine, western yellow pine* **2 :** the wood of a ponderosa pine tree

pon·der·os·i·ty \,pändə'räsəd·ē, -ətē, -i\ *n* -ES [ML *ponderositat-, ponderositas*, fr. L *ponderosus* + *-itat-, -itas* -ity] **:** the quality or state of being ponderous

pon·der·ous \'pänd(ə)rəs\ *adj* [ME, fr. MF *pondereux*, fr. L *ponderosus*, fr. *ponder-, pondus* weight + *-osus* -ous — more at PENDANT] **1 :** of very great weight ⟨a ~ stone⟩ **:** extremely or oppressively heavy ⟨a ~ burden⟩ **2 :** unwieldy or clumsy because of weight and size ⟨a ~ weapon⟩ ⟨~ furniture⟩ **3 :** oppressively or unpleasantly dull ⟨a ~ book⟩ **:** UNINSPIRED, PEDESTRIAN ⟨~ comment⟩ **4 :** slow and laborious ⟨a ~ yawn⟩ **syn** see HEAVY

ponderous borer *n* **:** a borer that is the larva of a cerambycid beetle (*Ergates spiculatus*) and is destructive to felled coniferous trees in the western U.S.

pon·der·ous·ly *adv* [ME, fr. *ponderous* + *-ly*] **:** in a ponderous manner ⟨move ~⟩ ⟨staid presentations of French classics put on with ~ realistic stage sets —Guy Dumur⟩

pon·der·ous·ness *n* -ES **:** the quality or state of being ponderous

ponderous spar *n, obs* **:** BARITE

ponders *pres 3d sing of* PONDER, *pl of* PONDER

pondfish \'=,=\ *n* [1*pond* + *fish*] **:** any of many small American freshwater sunfishes (family Centrarchidae)

pondgrass \'=,=\ *n* **:** a submerged aquatic herb (*Potamogeton pectinatus*) common in Europe and No. America with fine threadlike leaves, spikes of greenish flowers, and small hard bony fruits

pond hen *n* **:** a common coot (*Fulica americana*) of No. America

pon·di·cher·ry eagle \¦pändə¦cherē-, -¦sherē-\ *n, usu cap P* [fr. *Pondicherry*, settlement of former French India] **:** BRAHMINY KITE

pondicherry vulture *n, usu cap P* **:** a very large black vulture (*Torgos calvus*) of India and Burma

ponding *pres part of* POND

pond·let \'pändlət\ *n* -S [1*pond* + *-let*] **:** a small pond

pond lily *n* **:** WATER LILY

pond·man \'=mən\ *n, pl* **pondmen** [1*pond* + *man*] **:** a sawmill worker who attends to the storage of logs in a pond, selects those to be sawed, and drives them with a pike pole to the log chute

pon·do \'pän(,)dō\ *n, pl* **pondo** *or* **pondos** *usu cap* **1 :** a Bantu-speaking people of Pondoland in eastern Cape Province, So. Africa — called also *Mpondo* **2 :** a member of the Pondo people

pon·dok·kie \'pän,däkē\ *n* -S [Afrik, dim. of *pondok*, fr. Malay *pondók* hut, leaf shelter] *Africa* **:** a crude hut **:** HOVEL

pon·do·sa pine \pän'dōsə-\ *n* [by contr.] **:** PONDEROSA PINE

pond pine *n* [1*pond*] **1 :** a pine (*Pinus serotina*) of the sandy swamps of the southern U. S. having leaves in bundles of three and short oblong cones **2 :** the soft brittle coarse-grained wood of the pond pine tree

ponds *pl of* POND, *pres 3d sing of* POND

pond scum *n* **1 :** any free-floating filamentous alga of the family Zygnemataceae; *esp* **:** SPIROGYRA **2 :** the mass of tangled filaments formed by any pond scum on stagnant or quiet waters

pond-scum parasite *n* [*pond scum*] **:** a fungus of the order Chytridiales

pondside \'=,=\ *n* [1*pond* + *side*] **:** a piece of land beside a pond

pond skater *n* **:** WATER STRIDER 1

pond snail *n* **:** a pond-dwelling snail esp. of the genus *Physa* often used as an aquarium scavenger

pond spice *n* **:** an American spicy shrub (*Litsea aestivalis*) growing in ponds and swamps from Virginia to Florida and having small oval leaves and axillary umbels of small yellow flowers

pond thatch *or* **pond top** *or* **pond top palmetto** *n* **:** CABBAGE PALMETTO

pondweed \'=,=\ *n* [1*pond* + *weed*] **1 :** any of several aquatic plants of *Potamogeton* or a closely related genus **2 :** HORNED PONDWEED

pondweed family *n* **:** POTAMOGETONACEAE

pondy \'pändē\ *adj* -ER/-EST [1*pond* + *-y*] **1 :** having many ponds ⟨~ land⟩ **2 :** MARSHY

1pone \'pōn\ *n* -S [of Algonquian origin; akin to Delaware *äpân* baked, Passamaquoddy *äbân*] **1** *South & Midland* **:** a cake of stiff cornmeal batter shaped into an oval in the palms and baked, fried, or boiled **2** *also* **pone bread** *South & Midland* **:** corn bread in the form of pones **3** *South & Midland* **:** a pudding of grated sweet potato, milk, sugar, butter, and spices baked and served as dessert

2pone \'pō(,)nē, 'pōn\ *n* -S [L, imper. sing. of *ponere* to place — more at POSITION] **1 :** the player usu. on the dealer's right who cuts the cards in a card game **2 :** the dealer's opponent in a two-handed card game

3pone \'pōn\ *n* -S [perh. fr. 1*pone*] *South* **:** LUMP, SWELLING ⟨raised a ~ on his head⟩

ponent *adj* [It *ponente* west, fr. ML *ponent-, ponens*, fr. L, setting, pres. part. of *ponere* to place, set — more at POSITION] *obs* **:** WESTERN, OCCIDENTAL

po·ne·ra \pə'nirə\ *n, cap* [NL, fr. Gk *ponēra*, fem. of *ponēros* wretched, wicked, good-for-nothing, fr. *ponos* toil, trouble, fr. *penesthai* to toil, be in need] **:** a cosmopolitan genus of stinging ants having an elongate abdomen supported on a petiole of one segment but with a constriction between the first and second abdominal segments

po·ne·ra·moe·ba \pə,nirə'mēbə\ [NL, fr. Gk *ponēros* wicked, good-for-nothing + NL *Amoeba*] *syn of* ENTAMOEBA

1po·ner·ine \'pōnə,rīn, -,rən\ *adj* [NL *Ponera* + E *-ine*] **:** of or related to the genus *Ponera* ⟨~ ants⟩ ⟨~ genera⟩

2ponerine \"\ *n* -S **:** any of various ants of *Ponera* and closely related genera that are usu. considered to constitute a subfamily of Formicidae

pon·er·ol·o·gy \,pänə'räləjē\ *n* -ES [Gk *ponēros* wicked + E *-logy*] **:** a branch of theology dealing with the doctrine of evil — compare HAMARTIOLOGY

poney *var of* PONY

1pong \'päŋ, 'pòŋ\ *n* -S [imit.] **:** a hollow ringing sound

2pong \"\ *vi* -ED/-ING/-S **:** to make a hollow ringing sound

3pong \'päŋ\ *vi* -ED/-ING/-S [origin unknown] *chiefly Brit* **:** to improvise on the stage (as in order to cover up a fluff)

ponga \'päŋ(g)ə, 'pəŋ-\ *n* -S [Maori] **:** a tree fern (*Cyathea dealbata*) of New Zealand

pon·gee \(')pän¦jē\ *n* -S [Chin (Pek) *pen3 chi1*, fr. *pen3* own + *chi1* loom] **1 :** a thin soft clothing and curtain fabric of Chinese origin woven from uneven threads of raw silk and possessing a characteristic ecru or tan color; *also* **:** an imitation of this fabric in cotton or rayon **2 :** a light yellowish brown that is redder, lighter, and stronger than khaki and yellower and paler than cinnamon

1pon·gid \'pänjəd\ *adj* [NL *Pongidae*] **:** of or relating to the Pongidae

2pongid \"\ *n* -S **:** an anthropoid ape of the family Pongidae

pon·gi·dae \-jə,dē\ *n pl, cap* [NL *Pongo*, type genus + *-idae*] **:** a family of primates consisting of the anthropoid apes and including the gorillas, chimpanzees, orangutans, and gibbons

1pon·go \'päŋ(,)gō\ *n* [NL, fr. Kongo *mpongi, mpungu*] **1** *cap* **:** a genus of anthropoid apes comprising the orangutans **2** -S **:** an anthropoid ape; *esp* **:** ORANGUTAN

2pongo \"\ *n* -S [AmerSp, fr. Quechua *puncu* door] **:** a canyon or gorge in So. America esp. cutting through a ridge or mountain range

pon·gol \'päŋ,gäl\ *n* -S *cap* [Tamil *poṅkal* boiling, a preparation of boiled rice; fr. the rice's being offered at the festival] **:** the great Tamil New Year's festival of southern India beginning the month Magh

pon·gyi *also* **phon·gyi** *or* **poon·ghie** \(')pōn¦jē, (')pün-\ *n* -S [Burmese *phungyī*, fr. *phun* glory + *gyī* great] **:** a Buddhist priest of Burma

pon·haws *or* **pon·hoss** *also* **pon·hass** *or* **pon·haus** *or* **pon·hos** \'pän,hòs, 'pən-, -òz\ *n* -ES [PaG *pannhas*, fr. G dial., dish of leftovers, lit., pan hare, fr. G dial. *panne* pan + *has* hare, fr. OHG *haso*; akin to OHG *pfanna* pan — more at PAN, HARE] *Midland* **:** SCRAPPLE

1pon·iard \'pänyə(r)d\ *or* **poi·gnard** \'pòinyə(r)d, 'pwän-\ *n* -S [MF *poignard*, fr. *poing* fist, fr. L *pugnus* — more at PUNGENT] **:** a dagger with a usu. slender triangular or square blade

2poniard \"\ *vt* -ED/-ING/-S **:** to pierce or kill with a poniard

ponied *past of* PONY

ponies *pl of* PONY, *pres 3d sing of* PONY

ponka *usu cap, var of* PONCA

po·nor \'pō,nò(ə)r\ *n* -S [Serbo-Croatian] **:** a steep-sided sinkhole

pons \'pänz\ *or* **pons va·ro·lii** \-və'rōlē,ī\ *n, pl* **pon·tes** \'pän·(,)tēz\ *or* **pontes varolii** *usu cap V* [*pons*, NL, fr. L, bridge; *pons varolii*, NL, lit., bridge of Varoli, after Costanzo *Varoli* †1575 Ital. surgeon and anatomist — more at FIND] **:** a broad mass of chiefly transverse nerve fibers conspicuous on the ventral surface of the brain of man and lower mammals at the anterior end of the medulla oblongata, extending up in a robust cord on either side to form the middle cerebellar peduncle, and enclosing irregular masses of gray matter which serve as important relay stations in the path from the cerebral cortex to the opposite side of the cerebellum — see BRAIN illustration

pons asi·no·rum \-,asᵊn'ōrəm\ *n* -S [NL, asses' bridge] **1 a :** ASSES' BRIDGE **b :** a critical test of ability imposed upon the inexperienced or ignorant ⟨those who have passed the *pons asinorum* in the inner life —George Santayana⟩ **2 :** a geometrical figure attributed to Petrus Tartaretus (fl. 1480) used to show the various relations of the middle terms of syllogisms

pont \'pänt\ *n* -S [D, fr. L *ponto* punt, pontoon — more at PONTOON] *Africa* **:** FERRYBOAT

pont *abbr* **1** *often cap* [L *pontifex*] bishop **2** pontoon

pon·tage \'päntij\ *n* -S [ME *pountage*, fr. MF *pontage*, fr. ML *pontaticum*, fr. L *pont-, pons* bridge + *-aticum* -age — more at FIND] **:** a duty or tax paid in lieu of personal service for the building and repairing of bridges; *also* **:** a toll for the use of a bridge devoted to its maintenance

pon·tal \'päntᵊl\ *adj* [L *pont-, pons* + E *-al*] **:** of or relating to a bridge

pon·ta·nia \pän·'tānēə, -nyə\ *n, cap* [NL, prob. fr. the proper name *Pontano* + NL *-ia*] **:** a widely distributed genus of sawflies including many that are gall makers on willow and poplar

ponte *or* **pontee** *var of* PUNTY

pon·te·de·ria \,päntə'dirēə\ *n, cap* [NL, fr. Giulio *Pontedera* †1757 Ital. botanist + NL *-ia*] **:** a genus (the type of the family Pontederiaceae) of American aquatic plants having leaves with long sheathing petioles and flowers in a dense spike — see PICKERELWEED

pon·te·de·ri·a·ce·ae \,==,dirē'āsē,ē\ *n pl, cap* [NL, fr. *Pontederia*, type genus + *-aceae*] **:** a family of monocotyledonous aquatic or bog plants (order Xyridales) having perfect more or less irregular flowers subtended by spathes resembling leaves — **pon·te·de·ri·a·ceous** \¦==¦==¦āshəs\ *adj*

pon·ti·a·nak *also* **pon·ti·a·nac** \,päntē'änək, *attrib* ¦==¦==\ *n* -S [fr. *Pontianak*, Borneo, Indonesia] **1** *also* **pontianak resin :** a hard semifossil Manila copal gathered in Borneo from wounds of trees of the genus *Agathis* and used in varnishes **2** *also* **pontianak gum :** JELUTONG

1pon·tic \'päntik\ *adj* [L *ponticus*, fr. Gk *pontikos*, fr. *Pontos* the Black sea, Pontus (country in northeast Asia Minor) + *-ikos* -ic] **1** *usu cap* **:** of or relating to Pontus or the Black sea **2** [so called fr. the quality of certain Pontic fruits] *obs* **:** SOUR, ASTRINGENT **3** [Gk *pontos* sea + E *-ic* — more at FIND] **:** of or relating to sediments deposited in comparatively deep and stagnant water

2pontic \"\ *n* -S [fr. L *pont-, pons* bridge + E *-ic* — more at FIND] **:** an artificial tooth on a dental bridge.

pon·ti·cel·lo \,päntə'che(,)lō\ *n* -S [It, dim. of *ponte* bridge, fr. L *pont-, pons*] **1 :** the bridge of a bowed stringed musical instrument **2 :** a change in register in the voice (as of a boy at puberty) **:** BREAK

pon·tic·u·lus \pän·'tikyələs\ *n, pl* **ponticu·li** \-ə,lī\ [NL, fr. L, dim. of *pont-, pons* bridge — more at FIND] **1 :** a slight ridge **2 :** a bridge of transverse nerve fibers between the pyramids of the medulla and the pons — called also *propons*

pon·ti·fex \'päntə,feks\ *n, pl* **pon·tif·i·ces** \pän·'tifə,sēz\ [L — more at PONTIFF] **1 :** a member of the council of 9 or later 15 or 16 priests forming the most important part of the Roman religious body **2 :** HIGH PRIEST **3 :** POPE

pon·tiff \'päntəf\ *n* -S [F *pontif*, fr. L *pontific-, pontifex*, lit., bridgemaker, fr. *pont-, pons* bridge + *-fic-, -fex* (fr. *facere* to make, do) — more at FIND, DO] **1 :** PONTIFEX **2 :** BISHOP; *specif* **:** POPE **3 :** a high priest or chief religious figure ⟨Zoroastrian ~*s* and teachers⟩ **4** *or* **pontiff purple :** a deep purple that is bluer than hyacinth violet, bluer and darker than petunia violet, and bluer, lighter, and stronger than imperial purple (sense 2)

pontific *adj* [*pontiff* + *-ic*] *obs* **:** PONTIFICAL

1pon·tif·i·cal \(')pän·¦tifəkəl, -fēk-\ *adj* [L *pontificalis*, fr. *pontific-, pontifex* pontifex + *-alis* -al] **1 a :** of or relating to a pontiff, bishop, or prelate **:** EPISCOPAL ⟨~ authority⟩ **b :** celebrated by a bishop ⟨~ mass⟩ **2 :** of or relating to a pontifex or high priest **3 :** excessively often pretentiously dignified or authoritative **:** POMPOUS, DOGMATIC ⟨a ~ professor⟩ ⟨~ statements⟩ ⟨pseudo-scientific gobbledygook and ~ hooey —*Newsweek*⟩ **4** *obs* **:** of or relating to a bridge or bridge building — **pon·tif·i·cal·ly** \-k(ə)lē, -li\ *adv*

2pontifical \"\ *n* -S **1** [ML *pontificalia*] **:** episcopal attire; *specif* **:** the insignia of the episcopal order worn by a prelate when celebrating pontifically and including buskins, sandals, gloves, dalmatic, tunicle, ring, pectoral cross, and miter — usu. used in pl. **2** [ML *pontificale*, fr. neut. of L *pontificalis* of a pontiff] **:** a book containing the forms for sacraments and rites performed by a bishop

pon·tif·i·ca·lia \(,)pän·,tifə'kālēə, -lyə\ *n pl* [ML, fr. neut. pl. of L *pontificalis* of a pontiff] **:** PONTIFICALS

pon·tif·i·cal·i·bus \-'kaləbəs\ *n pl* [fr. the ML phrase *in pontificalibus* in pontificals] **:** the attire or vestments of one's office ⟨the bishop received him in ~⟩ ⟨stately and splendid in the full glory of his ~⟩

pontifical indiction *n* **:** ROMAN INDICTION

pon·tif·i·cal·i·ty \(,)pän·,tifə'kaləd·ē, -ətē, -i\ *n* -ES [MF *pontificalité*, fr. *pontifical* (fr. L *pontificalis*) + *-ité* -ity] **1 a :** the state, office, dignity, or rule of a pontiff **b** (1) **:** POPE (2) **:** PAPACY **2 :** extreme or exaggerated dignity **:** POMPOUSNESS ⟨the ~ of a second-rate diplomat⟩

pontifical mass *n, often cap P&M* **:** a solemn mass celebrated by a bishop or by one of the higher ecclesiastical prelates

pontifical ring *n* **:** a ring worn by Roman Catholic prelates and others symbolic of their spiritual marriage with the church

1pon·tif·i·cate \pän·'tifəkət, -fə,kāt, *usu* -d·+V\ *n* -S [L *pontificatus*, fr. *pontific-, pontifex* pontiff + *-atus* -ate — more at PONTIFF] **:** the state, office, or term of office of a pontiff

2pon·tif·i·cate \-ə,kāt, *usu* -ād·+V\ *vb* -ED/-ING/-S [ML *pontificatus*, past part. of *pontificare* to act as pontiff, fr. L *pontific-, pontifex*] *vi* **1 :** to officiate as a pontiff esp. at mass **2 :** to deliver oracular utterances or dogmatic opinions ⟨a columnist who ~*s*⟩ ⟨too often *pontificated* on matters outside their field⟩ **3 :** to comport oneself with excessive dignity or pomposity **:** assume exaggerated authority or oracularity **~** *vt* **:** to state in a dogmatic or pompous manner ⟨editors . . . ~ that it is only a memory —A.G.Mezerik⟩

pon·tif·i·ca·tion \(,)=,=='kāshən\ *n* -S [2*pontificate* + *-ion*] **:** dogmatic or oracular pronouncement ⟨pundits delivered themselves of weighty ~*s*⟩

pon·tif·i·ca·tor \='==,kād·ə(r), -ātə-\ *n* -S [2*pontificate* + *-or*] **:** one that pontificates

pontifices *pl of* PONTIFEX

pontificial *adj* [L *pontificius* of a pontiff (fr. *pontific-, pontifex*) + E *-al*] *obs* **:** PONTIFICAL

pon·til \'päntᵊl\ *n* -S [F, perh. fr. It *puntello*, dim. of *punto* point, fr. L *punctum* — more at POINT] **:** PUNTY

pon·tile \'pän·,tīl, -ntᵊl\ *also* **pon·til** \-ntᵊl\ *adj* [LL *pontilis* of a bridge, fr. L *pont-, pons* bridge + *-ilis* -ile — more at FIND] **:** PONTINE

pontil mark *n* **:** BULL'S-EYE 4a

1pon·tine \'pän·,tīn, -tēn\ *adj, usu cap* [L *pomptinus, pontinus*, fr. *Pomptinus*, name of a local tribe] **:** of or relating to a marshy area between Rome and Naples now largely reclaimed

2pontine \"\ *adj* [NL *pont-, pons* + ISV *-ine*] **1 :** of or relating to the pons **2** [L *pont-, pons* bridge + E *-ine*] **:** appropriate for a bridge ⟨~ sites⟩

3pontine \"\ *adj, usu cap* [*Pontus*, ancient country in northeast Asia Minor + E *-ine*] **:** of or relating to the Black sea areas once part of the pre-Christian kingdom of Pontus

pontine flexure *n* [2*pontine*] **:** a flexure of the embryonic hindbrain that serves to delimit the developing cerebellum and medulla oblongata

pon·tive \'päntiv\ *adj* [NL *pont-, pons* + E *-ive*] **:** lying near or adjacent to the pons

pont l'é·vêque \¦pōⁿlə¦vek, -lā¦-\ *n* -S *usu cap P&E* [fr. *Pont l'Évêque*, town in northwest France] **:** a firm cheese with soft center and mild flavor that is made of whole milk often with added cream and artificially colored yellow

ponto *var of* PUNTO

Pon·to·caine \'päntə,kān\ *trademark* — used for tetracaine

pon·to·caspian \¦pän·(,)tō+\ *adj, usu cap* [L *Pontus* the Black sea + *-o-* + E *Caspian*] **:** of or relating to the region about the Black and Caspian seas

pon·to·cerebellar \"+\ *adj* [NL *pont-, pons* + *-o-* + ISV *cerebellar*] **:** of or relating to the pons and the cerebellum

pon·ton \'päntᵊn, -ntən *or like* PONTOON\ *n* -S *often attrib* [F — more at PONTOON] **:** PONTOON ⟨the landing wharf of rusty ~*s* —John Dos Passos⟩ ⟨~ barges⟩ ⟨a ~ battalion⟩

pon·ton·eer \¦päntᵊn¦i(ə)r, -tə¦ni-, -iə\ *n* -S [*ponton* + *-eer*] **:** PONTONIER

pon·ton·ier \"\ *n* -S [F *pontonnier*, fr. *ponton* + *-ier* -er] **:** an individual engaged in constructing a pontoon bridge or assigned to a military unit organized for that purpose

1pon·toon \pän·'tün\ *n* -S *often attrib* [F *ponton* floating bridge, punt, fr. L *ponton-, ponto*, fr. *pont-, pons* bridge — more at FIND] **1 :** a flat-bottomed boat; *esp* **:** a low flat vessel resembling a barge, bearing cranes, capstans, and other machinery, and used in careening ships, raising weights, drawing piles, and in other similar operations **2 :** a wooden flat-bottomed boat or other usu. portable float (as a metallic cylinder or frame covered with waterproof material) used esp. by an army in making temporary bridges **3 :** a float of an airplane

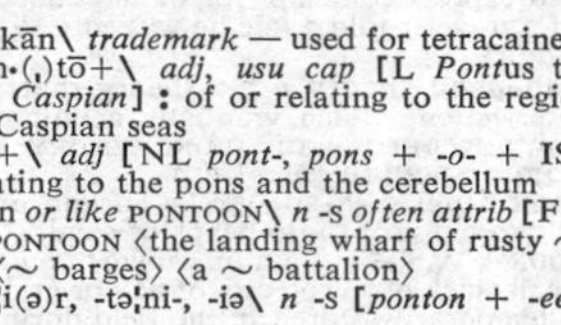

pontoons 2 supporting a bridge

2pontoon \"\ *vt* -ED/-ING/-S **:** to bridge or cross by a pontoon bridge or with pontoons — **pon·toon·er** \-nə(r)\ *n* -S

3pontoon \"\ *n* -S [prob. alter. of *vingt-et-un*] *Brit* **:** TWENTY-ONE

pontoon bridge *or* **ponton bridge** *n* **:** a bridge whose deck is supported on pontoons

ponts *pl of* PONT

ponty *var of* PUNTY

pon·ty·pool \¦päntē¦pül\ *adj, usu cap* [fr. *Pontypool*, urban district in Monmouthshire, England] **:** of, relating to, or being japanned metalware (as trays, salvers, boxes) decorated with floral and landscape designs against red, black, or other colorful backgrounds and produced in England esp. during the 18th and 19th centuries

[1]**po·ny** *also* **po·ney** \'pōnē, -ni\ *n, pl* **ponies** *also* **poneys** [earlier *powny, powney*, prob. fr. obs. F *poulenet*, dim. of *poulain*, fr. ML *pullanus*, fr. L *pullus* young of an animal, foal — more at FOAL] **1 a :** a small horse; *esp* **:** a horse of any of several breeds of very small stocky animals noted for their gentleness and endurance (as the horses of Iceland and the Shetland islands) and usu. restricted to those not over 14 or sometimes 14¼ hands in height except for the horses used in polo which may measure up to 15 hands **b :** a bronco, mustang, or other similar horse of the western U. S. **c :** RACEHORSE — usu. used in pl. ⟨bet on the *ponies*⟩ **d** *or* **pony skin :** the skin of a pony used as fur ⟨a ~ coat⟩ **2 :** something smaller than standard: as **a :** a small liqueur or beer glass or the amount it can hold **b :** a diminutive dancer in a chorus line **3** *Brit* **:** the amount of 25 pounds **4 :** a literal often interlinear translation of a foreign language text; *esp* **:** one used illegitimately by students in preparing or reciting lessons

[2]**pony** \"\ *vb* -ED/-ING/-ES *vt* **1 :** to pay (money) esp. in settlement of an account — used with *up* ⟨had to *pony up* added fares before boarding their planes —*Newsweek*⟩ **2 :** to translate with the aid of a pony **3 :** to limber up (a racehorse) by galloping on a lead line or sending out with a stable pony ~ *vi* **:** to pay up — used with *up*

[3]**pony** \"\ *adj* **1 :** of a size smaller than usual ⟨a ~ glass of beer⟩ ⟨a ~ glass⟩ ⟨a ~ insulator⟩ **2 :** limited to a brief daily account of only the most important news sent by telegraph, telephone, or mail (as that subscribed to by many small local papers or radio stations) ⟨a ~ report⟩ ⟨a ~ service⟩

pony backfield *n* **:** a backfield in football composed of players who are small and fast

pony cart *n* **:** DONKEY CART

pony engine *n* **:** a small switching locomotive

pony express *n* **:** a rapid postal and express system operating by relays of ponies

pony grass *n* **:** a perennial grass (*Calamagrostis neglecta*) of the north temperate zone forming valuable forage in the Rocky mountains

pony league *n, often cap P&L* **:** a commercially sponsored baseball league made up of teams whose players are boys from 13 to 15 years old — compare LITTLE LEAGUE

pony mixer *n* **:** a machine with rotating agitators and rotating can for mixing pastes (as for paints, printing ink, pharmaceutical ointments)

pony rougher *n* **:** STRANDER 2

pony support *n* **:** a portable standard of adjustable height used as a support (as for a pipe)

ponytail \'==,=\ *n* **:** a style of hairdressing in which the hair is arranged to resemble the tail of a horse or pony

ponytail

pony truck *n* **:** a two-wheeled swivel truck used under the front end of a locomotive

pony truss *n* **:** a truss (as in bridge building) so low that overhead bracing cannot be used

poo \'pü\ *dial var of* PULL

POO *abbr* post office order

[1]**pooch** \'püch\ *chiefly dial var of* POUCH

[2]**pooch** \"\ *also* **pooched** \-cht\ *adj* [*pooch*, short for *pooched*, fr. past part. of [1]*pooch*] *dial* **:** protruding abnormally **:** DISTENDED

[3]**pooch** \"\ *n* -ES [origin unknown] *slang* **:** DOG

pood *or* **poud** *or* **pud** \'püd, -üt\ *n* -S [Russ *pud*, fr. ON *pund* pound — more at POUND] **:** a Russian unit of weight equal to about 36.11 pounds

[1]**poo·dle** \'püdᵊl\ *n* [G *pudel*, short for *pudelhund*, fr. *pudeln* to splash (fr. *pudel* puddle, fr. LG) + *hund* dog — more at PUDDLE] **1 a** *usu cap* **:** an old breed of active intelligent heavy-coated solid-colored dogs of uncertain origin but possibly derived from some type of European retriever or spaniel that are often kept as pets but also make superior gun dogs and retrievers and are readily trained as performers and that occur in toy, miniature or standard, and large varieties differing only in size and weight **b** -S *sometimes cap* **:** a dog of the Poodle breed **2** -S **:** a woolen fabric having a surface texture like a poodle's coat

[2]**poodle** \"\ *vt* **poodled; poodled; poodling** \-d(ᵊ)liŋ\ **poodles :** to clip the hair of in a short curly style

poodle dog *n* **:** POODLE; *esp* **:** any small pet dog that follows its master around

poo·er \'püər\ *chiefly Scot var of* POWER

poof \'püf\ *interj* [imit.] — used to express contempt, disdain, or disapproval

poogye *var of* PUNGI

pooh \'pü, 'pü\ *or* **pooh-pooh** \¦pü¦pü\ *n* -S [origin unknown] **:** an expression of contempt, disapproval, or impatience ⟨quietly anticipates the skeptic's every ~ —*New Yorker*⟩ ⟨a few ~*s* and a tush about cover that —P.G.Wodehouse⟩ — often used interjectionally

pooh-bah *also* **poo-bah** \'pü¦bä\ *n* -S *often cap P&B* [*Pooh-Bah*, name of character in Gilbert and Sullivan's opera *The Mikado* (1885) bearing the title Lord-High-Everything-Else] **1 :** one holding many public or private offices ⟨the municipal treasurer . . . is usu. assigned additional duties and often becomes a veritable village *poo-bah* —J.R.Hayden⟩ **2 a :** one in high position **b :** one who gives the impression of being a person of importance

pooh-pooh \¦pü¦pü\ *also* **pooh** \'pü\ *vb* -ED/-ING/-S [[1]*pooh*] *vi* **:** to express contempt or impatience esp. by saying *pooh* ~ *vt* **:** to express contempt for or impatience with **:** make light of ⟨if a traveler told a tale he was sure to *pooh-pooh* it —Virginia Woolf⟩

pooh-pooh theory *n* **:** a theory that language originated in interjections which gradually acquired meaning — compare BOWWOW THEORY, DINGDONG THEORY

pooja *or* **poojah** *var of* PUJA

[1]**pook** \'pük\ *vt* -ED/-ING/-S [origin unknown] *dial Eng* **:** to pile (a cut crop) into heaps or small stacks

[2]**pook** \"\ *n* -S [origin unknown] *dial chiefly Eng* **:** a heap or small stack of a crop esp. of hay or grain that has been cut and is temporarily stored in the field during one stage of harvesting

[3]**pook** \"\ *vt* [origin unknown] *chiefly Scot* **:** to pluck or pull at

poo·ka *also* **phoo·ka** \'pükə\ *n* -S [IrGael *pūca*, perh. fr. OE, puck] **:** a mischievous or malignant goblin or specter held in Irish folklore to appear in the form of a horse and to haunt bogs and marshes

poo·kawn *or* **poo·kaun** \pü'kȯn\ *n* -S [IrGael *pūcān*] *Irish* **:** a small fishing boat usu. with one mast, equipped with oars as well as sails, and often lateen-rigged

pookoo *var of* PUKU

[1]**pool** \'pül\ *n* -S [ME, fr. OE *pōl*; akin to MLG *pōl* pool, OHG *pfuol*] **1 a** (1) **:** a small and rather deep body of fresh water (as one fed by a spring) (2) **:** a quiet place in a stream (3) **:** a reservoir for water (4) **:** a body of water forming above a dam or the closed gates of a lock (5) **:** TIDE POOL **b :** something held to resemble a pool (as in form, depth, quiet) ⟨a ~ of silence enveloped them —Louis Bromfield⟩ ⟨rests quietly in the deep ~ of memory —William Beebe⟩ ⟨sunlight lay . . . in fresh ~*s* of cool light —Gordon Merrick⟩ ⟨his eyes are deep ~*s* of self-confession —Howard Taubman⟩ **2 :** a small body of standing or stagnant water or other liquid **:** PUDDLE ⟨saw the small ~ of blood⟩ **3 :** a continuous area of porous sedimentary rock which yields petroleum or gas on drilling **4 a :** SWIMMING POOL **b :** WADING POOL

[2]**pool** \"\ *vb* -ED/-ING/-S *vi* **1 :** to form a pool ⟨swift-flowing water that ~*ed* and snaked down between the rocks and ice —*Atlantic*⟩ ⟨now the drops run and ~ together —V.S. Pritchett⟩ **2** *of blood* **:** to accumulate or become static (as in the veins and capillaries of a body part or organ) ⟨become tourniquets, preventing the blood from ~*ing* —*Time*⟩ ~ *vt* **1 a :** to cut (a hole) to insert a wedge for splitting (as in mining or quarrying) **b :** to undercut or undermine (as coal) esp. in excavating **2 :** to form pools in ⟨was deeply rutted and ~*ed* with rain —Evan Coombes⟩ **3 :** to cause (blood) to pool usu. as a result of defective circulation

[3]**pool** \"\ *n* -S [F *poule* stakes in a card game, lit., hen — more at PULLET] **1 a** (1) **:** an aggregate stake to which each player of a game has contributed (2) **:** an old game of cards in which there is a pool ⟨sat down with her female friends to a ~ of cards and a dish of coffee —W.M.Thackeray⟩; *also* **:** a party of players for such a game **b :** all the money bet by a number of persons on the result of a particular event with the aggregate to be paid to the winner or divided among several winners according to conditions established in advance **2 a :** a game played on an English billiard table in which each of the players stakes a certain sum with the winner taking all; *also* **:** a game at a public billiard room **b :** any of various games of billiards played on a pool table having six pockets with usu. 15 object balls that may be numbered or plain and a cue ball — see CONTINUOUS POOL, FIFTEEN BALL, SNOOKER; compare CAROM BILLIARDS **3 a :** any aggregation of the interests or property of different persons made to further a joint undertaking or end by subjecting them to the same control and a common liability: as (1) **:** a common fund or combination of interests for the common adventure in buying or selling; *esp* **:** one for speculating in or manipulating the market price of securities, grain, or other commodities (2) **:** a combination between competing business houses or corporations for the control of traffic by removing competition **b :** the persons who so combine their interests or property — see TRUST **4 :** a fencing contest in which each member of a team successively engages each member of another team **5 :** a readily available supply: as **a** (1) **:** the whole quantity of material or of a particular substance present in the body and freely available for function or the satisfying of metabolic demands of the cells (as of blood in the capillaries or of neurons available to complete various neural circuits) ⟨the circulating metabolic ~⟩ ⟨the acetate ~⟩ (2) **:** a body product (as blood or one of its derivatives) collected from many donors and stored for later use (as for transfusions or a source of antibodies) **b** (1) **:** an aggregation usu. made by a group and used mutually for the benefit of all ⟨a ~ of ideas contributed by a wide range of experienced teachers —*Geog. Jour.*⟩ (2) **:** a group of separately owned objects used cooperatively for the benefit of all concerned; *esp* **:** CAR POOL **c** (1) **:** the total manpower available in an area ⟨armies . . . can be readily reinforced in case of emergency from the reserve ~ —Joseph Rosenfarb⟩ (2) **:** a group of employees held in readiness by an employer for assignment as needed ⟨a stenographic ~⟩ (3) **:** a skilled trained group esp. in a specialized field capable of being utilized ⟨a ~ of brilliant scientists who accelerate the development of atomic power —T.E.Murray⟩ ⟨a ~ of trained actors and directors who will impose less limitation on the playwright —Henry Hewes⟩ **d :** the total amount often of a strategic material or resource that is for use or in reserve ⟨new oil discoveries are wanted to replenish the ~⟩ ⟨the government with unlimited access to the paper ~ —Lucien Price⟩ ⟨its enormous ~ of patents —*New Republic*⟩ **6 :** an installation which maintains and administers a supply of something; *esp* **:** MOTOR POOL

[4]**pool** \"\ *vb* -ED/-ING/-S *vt* **:** to put together in a pool **:** contribute to a common fund or effort often on the basis of a mutual division of profits or losses or an equal share of benefits **:** make a common interest of ⟨would ~ their money now and . . . put a real show on the road —F.B.Gipson⟩ ⟨special consultants have ~*ed* their talents and knowledge —L.R.Sander⟩ ⟨teachers . . . had again ~*ed* their experiences —Lucy S. Mitchell⟩ ~ *vi* **:** to organize a pool **:** combine with others in a pool

[5]**pool** \"\ *n* -S [Russ *pul* — more at PUL] **:** PUL 1

pool bottle *n* **:** a leather bottle from which small numbered balls are distributed to the players in some games of pool (as to determine the order of playing)

pool hole *n* [[2]*pool*] *mining* **:** a hole cut in pooling

poo·li \'pülē\ *n* -S [Mende *puli*, a species of *Bauhinia*] **1 :** a tropical African timber tree (*Cordia platythyrsa*) **2 :** the moderately soft wood of the pooli

poolroom \'=,=\ *n* [[3]*pool* + *room*] **1 :** a room in which bookmaking is carried on **2 :** a usu. public room or establishment equipped for the playing of pool and other games

poolroot \'=,=\ *n* [[1]*pool* + *root*] **:** a common perennial herb (*Eupatorium aromaticum*) of the eastern U.S. with opposite leaves and loose clusters of heads of white tubular flowers

pools *pl of* POOL, *pres 3d sing of* POOL

pool selling *n* [[3]*pool*] **:** the selling or distribution of chances in a betting pool

poolside \'=,=\ *n* [[1]*pool* + *side*] **:** the area surrounding a swimming pool

pool table *n* [[3]*pool*] **:** a pocketed billiard table on which pool is played — compare BILLIARD TABLE

pool train *n* [[3]*pool*] **:** a train operated by either of two or more railroads connecting the same points on which tickets of other participating railroads are accepted with revenues divided as specified in the pool agreement

poolwort \'=,=\ *n* -S [[1]*pool* + *wort*] **1 :** POOLROOT **2 :** WHITE SNAKEROOT

pooly \'pülē\ *adj* -ER/-EST [[1]*pool* + *-y*] **:** resembling a pool **:** having many pools **:** SWAMPY

[1]**poon** \'pün\ *or* **poon tree** *n* [Malayalam *punna*] **1 :** any of several trees (genus *Calophyllum*) of the East Indies and the Pacific islands; *esp* **:** MASTWOOD **2 :** the hard light wood of poon used esp. for masts and spars

[2]**poon** \'pün\ *chiefly Scot var of* POUND

[1]**poo·na** \'pünə\ *adj, usu cap* [fr. *Poona*, city in western India] **:** of or from the city of Poona, India **:** of the kind or style prevalent in Poona

[2]**poona** \"\ *n* -S [fr. Poona, India, where it originated] **:** BADMINTON

poo·nac \'pü,nak\ *n* -S [Sinhalese *punakku*, fr. Skt *piṇyāka*] **:** COCONUT CAKE

poona pea *n* [origin unknown] **:** PIGEON PEA

poonghie *var of* PONGYI

poon·tang \'pün.,taŋ\ *n* -S [F *putain* prostitute, fr. OF *pute* girl, fr. (assumed) VL *putto, putta* child, fr. L *putus*; akin to L *puer* boy, child, Skt *putra* child, son — more at FEW] *slang* **:** SEXUAL INTERCOURSE

[1]**poop** \'püp\ *vb* -ED/-ING/-S [ME *poupen*, of imit. origin] *vi* **1 a :** to make a short jarring sound **:** toot a horn; *also* **:** GULP **b** (1) **:** to shoot a gun (2) **:** to make loud bangings (as a gun) **2 :** to emit intestinal gas — usu. considered vulgar ~ *vt* **:** to cause to discharge **:** FIRE ⟨we ~*ed* off a salvo in the direction of the sound —S.H.Baker⟩

[2]**poop** \"\ *n* -S **1 :** a short jarring sound **:** GULP, TOOT **2 a :** an act of defecation — usu. used with *take*; usu. considered vulgar **b :** intestinal gas expelled through the anus — usu. considered vulgar

[3]**poop** \"\ *n* -S [MF *poupe*, fr. L *puppis*] **1** *obs* **:** the afterpart of a ship **:** STERN **2 a :** an enclosed superstructure at the afterpart of a ship above the main deck often in ships of the 16th and 17th centuries raised to a great height **b :** POOP DECK

[4]**poop** \"\ *vt* -ED/-ING/-S **1 :** to break over the poop or stern of ⟨the huge seas are beginning to ~ her very badly —Raymond McFarland⟩ **2 :** to ship (a sea or wave) over the stern ⟨outside in the ocean there is serious danger in ~*ing* a following wave —H.A.Calahan⟩

[5]**poop** *vt* -ED/-ING/-S [origin unknown] *obs* **:** to practice deceit upon **:** CHEAT, COZEN

[6]**poop** \'püp\ *n* -S [short for *nincompoop*] **:** a foolish or useless person ⟨regarded by many as a pompous old ~ —H.A.Smith⟩

[7]**poop** \"\ *vb* -ED/-ING/-S [origin unknown] *vt, slang* **:** to put out of breath or wind thoroughly; *also* **:** to wear out **:** EXHAUST ⟨those last eight miles just ~*ed* everybody —*Infantry Jour.*⟩ ⟨found himself completely ~*ed*⟩ ~ *vi* **:** to become exhausted **:** cease completely — often used with *out* ⟨this ivy was green at a time when other ivies had ~*ed* out —*New Yorker*⟩

[8]**poop** \"\ *n* -S [origin unknown] *slang* **:** official or unofficial information ⟨gave us all the ~ he had gathered from his usual reliable sources⟩

poop cabin *n* [[3]*poop*] **:** a ship's cabin whose roof is the poop deck

poop deck *n* **:** a partial usu. weather deck above the main deck in the afterpart of a ship

poop royal *n* **:** the highest and aftermost deck over the poop in large old-time ships

[1]**poor** \'pu̇(ə)r, -u̇ə, *esp South, NE, & Brit* 'pōə *or* 'pō(ə)r *or* 'pȯ(ə) *or* 'pȯ(ə)r\ *adj* -ER/-EST [ME, *povere, poure, pore*, fr. OF *povre, poure*, fr. L *pauper*; akin to L *paucus* little and to L *parere* to bring forth, *parare* to acquire — more at FEW, PARE] **1 a :** lacking material possessions **:** existing without the luxuries and often the necessities of life **:** having little money ⟨they were so ~ that they couldn't afford things —Mary Austin⟩ ⟨homes of ~*er* folk have their gardens —D.C.Buchanan⟩ **b :** of, relating to, or characterized by poverty **2 a :** wanting in amount or capacity **:** less than adequate **:** DEFICIENT, MEAGER, SCANTY ⟨they gripe . . . loudly in winters of ~ snow —R.S.Monahan⟩ ⟨was largely responsible for the ~ attendance —R.W.Southern⟩ ⟨disappointed in the ~ crop⟩ **b :** small in worth ⟨one ~ pennyworth of sugar candy —Shak.⟩ **c** *of lime* **:** LEAN 3c **3 :** worthy of being pitied **:** being in a position to excite compassionate regard ⟨the ~ guard had started to cry out —S.H.Holbrook⟩ ⟨the ~ things all got colds —Charlton Laird⟩ **4 a :** inferior in quality **:** having little distinction, value, or worth ⟨inscription painted in ~ Latin on a nearby wall —C.A.Robinson⟩ ⟨displayed very ~ sportsmanship⟩ **b :** of lowly disposition **:** HUMBLE, UNPRETENTIOUS ⟨if it would be prudent to interrupt . . . on his ~ trivial account —Thomas Hardy⟩ **c :** mentally or ethically inferior **:** mean or small of spirit ⟨neighbors seemed to him ~ fellows with too little spirit to be free men —V.L.Parrington⟩ ⟨they are base, ~, contemptible fellows —Robert Burton⟩ **d :** having little significance **:** TRIVIAL ⟨each one of those great sciences was in its dim and ~ beginning —F.W.H.Myers⟩ **5 a :** being in an emaciated condition **:** LEAN, SCRAWNY ⟨in first-class breeding condition, neither too fat nor in any way ~ —Henry Wynmalen⟩ **b** *chiefly dial* **:** lacking necessary strength **:** not in good condition **:** FEEBLE, THIN ⟨looked ~ after the hard winter⟩ **6 :** characterized by unproductiveness **:** BARREN — used of land ⟨only in the remote and ~*est* sections . . . is the dull and drudging farmwife of thirty years ago met today —*Amer. Guide Series: Minn.*⟩ **7 :** fairly unsatisfactory **:** INDIFFERENT, UNFAVORABLE ⟨the condescending . . . tone which betrays a ~ opinion of the reader —John Farrelly⟩ ⟨the business of a printer being generally thought a ~ one —Benjamin Franklin⟩ **8 :** characterized by inefficiency or failure to meet a standard ⟨drawbacks in operational use because of ~ precision —J.P.Baxter b.1893⟩

syn POOR, INDIGENT, NEEDY, DESTITUTE, PENNILESS, IMPECUNIOUS, POVERTY-STRICKEN, and NECESSITOUS agree in signifying having barely enough money or possessions to support life or having less money or fewer possessions than are essential. POOR is the most general, applying to both those in want and those who commonly must live below a comfortable standard of living ⟨a pretty child bought from miserably *poor* parents under a contract —Lafcadio Hearn⟩ ⟨a man may be too *poor* to maintain a wife —Edward Westermarck⟩ ⟨the resulting waste of resources can make a *poor* people in a barren land —H.W.Odum⟩ ⟨*as poor* as church mice⟩ INDIGENT and NEEDY, the first more literary than the second, both imply pressing or urgent want ⟨the depression had left a number of them *indigent*, without state or federal relief —Green Peyton⟩ ⟨the skyrocketing costs put a rapidly increasing number of people in the medically *indigent* class —J.H.Means⟩ ⟨*needy* children in migrant farm worker families —*Current Biog.*⟩ ⟨to aid *needy* and deserving students —*Official Register of Harvard Univ.*⟩ DESTITUTE implies dire and dangerous need, suggesting the calamitous and wretched ⟨left *destitute* to face the prospect of a bleak and impoverished old age —John Galsworthy⟩ ⟨soldiers who by death or illness had left their wives and children *destitute* —A.V.D.Honeyman⟩ PENNILESS and IMPECUNIOUS can be equivalent in indicating the lack of money or resources on which to live or live decently and in not carrying the immediate connotations of calamitousness or wretchedness as does *destitute*. IMPECUNIOUS differs from PENNILESS in often suggesting a habitual or chronic condition ⟨this very beautiful English girl was a *penniless* governess, left stranded in Germany by an employer —Margaret Deland⟩ ⟨remembered by his associates as the bright but *penniless* youth whose climb to fame rivaled the most incredible of the Alger stories —*Amer. Guide Series: Minn.*⟩ ⟨the *impecunious* artists and writers of New York —Jerome Mellquist⟩ ⟨my greatest treat as a small and *impecunious* Scots boy was to visit friends of my mother who were "big people" —Aylmer Vallance⟩ POVERTY-STRICKEN signifies indigent or destitute but stresses more the suffering or strain attendant upon dire poverty ⟨the bulk of the pioneers was formed by *poverty-stricken* people who migrated from densely populated areas —J.F.Embree & W.L.Thomas⟩ ⟨a *poverty-stricken* primary school —H.R.Warfel⟩ NECESSITOUS, less common than the preceding words, is equivalent to *needy*, sometimes connoting insistent demands for relief ⟨fifty *necessitous* persons are being assisted at a total annual cost of over £1,500 —*Veterinary Record*⟩ ⟨in no sense of the word were they *necessitous* or poor —Jane Austen⟩ ⟨a greedy and *necessitous* public —Edmund Burke⟩

[2]**poor** \"\ *n, pl* **poor :** one that is poor — usu. used collectively ⟨for you always have the ~ with you —Mt 26:11 (RSV)⟩ ⟨respected by both rich and ~⟩

[3]**poor** \'püər\ *chiefly dial var of* POWER

[4]**poor** \'pu̇(ə)r\ *or* **poor cod** *n* -S [*poor*, short for *poor cod*, fr. [1]*poor* + *cod*] **:** a small European codfish (*Gadus minutus*) considered of little worth

poor box *n* [[2]*poor*] **:** a box for alms for the poor; *esp* **:** one placed near the door of a church

poor boy *n* [[1]*poor*] **:** a sandwich made of a loaf of French bread split lengthwise, buttered, and filled with one or more meats — compare GRINDER

poor clare *n, usu cap P&C* **:** a nun of an order founded early in the 13th century at Assisi by St. Clare under the direction of St. Francis

poor convict's oath *n* **:** an oath required of a prisoner unable to pay his fine that entitles him to a release on certain conditions

poor debtor *n* **:** a debtor who has no property or not more than a certain small amount of property subject to execution or who has delivered up his property for the benefit of his creditors in the manner prescribed by law

poor-debtor law *n* [*poor debtor*] **:** a law providing relief for debtors usu. by affording them time to pay their just debts by installments, or by freeing them from arrest or imprisonment on their delivering all their property not exempt from creditors to a trustee or other public officer for the benefit of the creditors, or on their taking an oath that they have property within the amount exempted from the claims of creditors

poor debtor's oath *n* **:** the oath to the facts bringing a person within the purview of a poor-debtor law and required to obtain the benefit of that law

poore *obs var of* POOR

poorer *comparative of* POOR

poorest *superlative of* POOR

poor farm *n* [[2]*poor*] **:** a farm maintained at public expense for the support and employment of needy or dependent persons

poorhouse \'=,=\ *n* [[2]*poor* + *house*] **:** a place maintained at public expense to house needy or dependent persons

poor·ish \'pu̇rish\ *adj* [[1]*poor* + *-ish*] **:** rather poor ⟨the piano reproduction is ~ by contemporary standards —Norman Cousins⟩ ⟨brought within the means of ~ educated people the pleasures of culture and of companionship —*Australasian*⟩

poor joe *n* [modif. of Gullah *pojo* heron] **:** GREAT BLUE HERON

poor john *n, often cap P&J* [[1]*poor*] **1** *archaic* **:** small cod or hake dried and salted **2** *archaic* **:** plain coarse food

poor-land-weed \'=,=,=\ *n* **:** BUTTONWEED 1

poor law *n* [[2]*poor*] **:** a law providing for or regulating the public relief or support of the poor

[1]**poor·ly** \'pu̇(ə)rlē, 'pu̇əlē, -li, *esp in southern US, NE, & Brit* 'pō(ə)r- *or* 'pōəl- *or* 'pȯ(ə)r- *or* 'pȯ(ə)l-\ *adv* [ME *pourely*, fr. *poure* poor + *-ly*] **:** in a poor manner or condition: as **a :** very inadequately **:** in an inferior or imperfect way **:** INEFFECTIVELY, INSUFFICIENTLY, UNDESIRABLY ⟨millions of students can write ~ without knowing any grammar at all —James Binney⟩ ⟨a pioneer college with few buildings, ~

equipped —A.B.Noble⟩ **b** : in actual want ⟨would live as ~ now as he did more than a hundred years ago — Philip Toynbee⟩ **c** *obs* : without generosity : SHABBILY ⟨a man who ~ left me —Richard Steele⟩ **d** *archaic* : without spirit or courage : ABJECTLY ⟨to set free the minds . . . from longing to return ~ under that captivity of kings —John Milton⟩

²poorly \"\ *adj* : somewhat ill : not in good health : INDISPOSED ⟨had been ~ lately⟩ ⟨she was ~ with the slow fever —Conrad Richter⟩

poor man's cabbage *n* : a winter cress (*Barbarea verna*)

poor man's mustard *n* : GARLIC MUSTARD

poor man's orchid *n* : BUTTERFLY FLOWER

poor man's pepper *n* **1** : PEPPERGRASS 1; *esp* : BIRD'S-PEPPER **2** : a stonecrop (*Sedum acre*)

poor man's shilling *n, pl* **poor man's shillings** : HONESTY 3

poor man's soap *n* [so called because it will make a lather with water] : HARDHACK 1

poor man's weatherglass *n* [so called because it opens its blossoms only in fair weather] : SCARLET PIMPERNEL

poormaster \ˈ⸗,⸗⸗\ *n* [²*poor* + *master*] : a supervisor of the relief of the poor

poor mouth *n, Midland* : a profession or protestation of poverty — often used with *make* ⟨when you ask him for a donation he makes a *poor mouth*⟩

poor·ness *n* -ES [ME *pourenesse*, fr. *poure* poor + *-nesse* -ness] : the quality or state of being poor

poor pine *n* [¹*poor*] : any of several pines of the southern U.S. growing in poor soil: as **a** : SPRUCE PINE 1a **b** : SHORTLEAF PINE 1

poor preacher *or* **poor priest** *n* : one of an English order of itinerant preachers founded by John Wycliffe and composed of followers who went out two by two practicing apostolic poverty and pledged but not by permanent vows to bring the Gospel to the people

poor pussy *n* : a game in which one player who represents the pussy kneels successively before the others who must refrain from laughing as they stroke his head and address him as "poor pussy"

poor rate *n* [²*poor*] : an assessment levied for the relief of the poor

poor relation *n* [¹*poor*] : one that is regarded as holding a subordinate or inferior position ⟨modern dance . . . is the *poor relation* among the theater arts —E.R.Bentley⟩ ⟨the humanities have become *poor relations* — *Report: (Canadian) Royal Commission on Nat'l Development*⟩

poor relief *n* [²*poor*] : relief or assistance usu. administered by local officials with funds from the local treasury for the aid of the needy in a community

poor robin's plantain *n, usu cap P&R* [¹*poor*] **1** : ROBIN'S PLANTAIN **2** : RATTLESNAKE WEED 1

poor soldier *n* : FRIARBIRD 1

poor-spirited \ˈ⸗ˈ⸗⸗⸗\ *adj* : having or showing a mean spirit : COWARDLY, BASE — **poor-spirited·ly** *adv* — **poor-spirited·ness** *n* -ES

poort \ˈpō(ə)rt, ˈpu̇(ə)-\ *n* -S [Afrik, fr. D, gate, gateway, fr. L *porta* — more at PORT] *southern Africa* : a pass between or across mountains

poor·tith \ˈpōr,tith\ *n* -S [OF *poverteit, povretet, poverté*, fr. L *paupertat-, paupertas* poverty — more at POVERTY] *chiefly Scot* : POVERTY

poor white *n* [¹*poor*] : a member of an inferior or underprivileged white social group — often taken to be offensive ⟨if these bad farming practices persisted . . . some settlers were in danger of becoming *poor whites* — *Farmer's Weekly (So. Africa)*⟩

poorwill \ˈpu̇(ə)r,wil\ *n* -S [imit.] : a bird of the western U.S. and Mexico (*Phalaenoptilus nuttallii*) that is similar to the whippoorwill but smaller and that has a note of two syllables only

¹poot \ˈpüt\ *dial Brit var of* POULT

²poot \"\ *interj* [origin unknown] — used to express disgust

¹pop \ˈpäp\ *vb* **popped; popped; popping; pops** [ME *poppen*, of imit. origin] *vt* **1 a** : to strike or knock sharply : HIT ⟨*popped* him on the jaw and knocked him cold⟩ **b** : ASSAULT, ATTACK **c** : BREAK **2** : to push, put, or thrust suddenly ⟨*popping* questions to his class⟩ ⟨*popping* the berry into her mouth —Virginia Woolf⟩ ⟨couldn't go out without *popping* my head round the door —Fred Majdalany⟩ **3** : to cause to explode or burst open ⟨the corn is *popped* —Jane Nickerson⟩ ⟨*popped* his gum twice —Jean Stafford⟩ **4** : to fire at : SHOOT ⟨went into the woods hoping to ~ a rabbit or two⟩ **5** *Brit* : HOCK, PAWN ~ *vi* **1 a** : to go, come, enter, or issue forth quickly or suddenly : occur or appear unexpectedly ⟨*popped* around the corner of the house and confronted me —C.B. Kelland⟩ ⟨*popped* into his head out of the blue —John Kobler⟩ **b** : to move with agility : DART, JUMP ⟨the private looked up startled, then *popped* to . . . attention —James Jones⟩ **2** : to make or burst with a sharp sound : EXPLODE **3** : to protrude from the sockets ⟨eyes *popping* with amazement⟩ ⟨eyes were on the point of *popping* out of his head —T.B.Costain⟩ **4** : to shoot with a firearm ⟨~ at a target⟩ ⟨~ at a bird⟩ **5** : to form blisters : BLOW — used esp. of lime and mortar **6 a** : to hit a short high fly in baseball that is easily caught ⟨*popped* to left field⟩ — often used with *up* or *out* **b** *cricket, of a bowled ball* : to rise sharply and travel through the air erratically after pitching — often used with *up* **7** : BACKFIRE 2 — **pop the question** : to propose marriage

²pop \"\ *n* -S [ME, fr. *poppen* to pop] **1 a** *dial chiefly Eng* : BLOW, KNOCK, STROKE **b** : POP FLY **2 a** : a small sharp quick explosive sound ⟨the faint ~ of buttons being undone —Gordon Merrick⟩ ⟨the cork flew off with a ~⟩ **b** : the time taken by the sound of a pop : INSTANT **3 a** (1) : a shot from a gun ⟨when he took a ~ at you, he was playing for keeps with your life —Theodore Draper⟩ (2) : GUN ⟨the lad got the pistol . . . and the old man fearing he might do other mischief took the ~ away from him —D.D.Martin⟩ **b** : ATTEMPT, CRACK, EFFORT, GO, TRY ⟨about to take another ~ at matrimony —P.G.Wodehouse⟩ **4** : a mark or spot made by a quick stroke : DOT **5** [so called fr. the sound made by breaking the inflated calyx] **a** : any of several West Indian plants of the genus *Physalis* **b** : the inflated calyx of a pop plant **6** [so called from the sound made by drawing the cork of the container] : a flavored carbonated beverage (as orange soda, root beer) : SODA POP ⟨picnics were held with free ~ and hamburgers —D.L.Cohn⟩ **7 a** *dial Eng* : REDWING **b** *Louisiana* : PAINTED BUNTING **8** : a small boss with an inserted setscrew

³pop \"\ *adv* : like or with a pop : SUDDENLY ⟨I don't know why suddenly everything should go ~⟩ — often used interjectionally

⁴pop \"\ *n* -S [by shortening] : POPPET

⁵pop \"\ *n* -S [short for *poppa*] : FATHER — not often in formal use

⁶pop \"\ *n* -S [by shortening fr. *popular*] **1 pops** *pl but usu sing in constr* : a popular orchestra or concert ⟨went to hear the Boston *Pops*⟩ **2** : a popular tune or recording

⁷pop \"\ *also* **pops** \ˈpäps\ *adj* : characterized by a popular tune or a mixture of popular and classical music calculated to appeal to the people in general ⟨become a singer of ~ tunes —Morroe Berger⟩

pop *abbr* **1** popular; popularly **2** population

POP *abbr* printing-out paper

pop·a·dam *or* **pop·a·dum** \ˈpäpədəm\ *n* -S [Tamil-Malayalam *pappaṭam*] : an Indian cake often eaten with curry and made of a thin strip or a ball of gluten flour or cornmeal fried in oil or other fat

pop ash *n* [¹*pop*] : a water ash (*Fraxinus caroliniana*)

popcorn \ˈ⸗,⸗\ *n* [contraction of *popped corn*, fr. *popped* (past part. of ¹*pop*) + *corn*] **1 a** : a variety (*Zea mays everta*) of Indian corn having small ears and small pointed or rounded kernels with very hard corneous endosperm that on exposure to dry heat are popped or everted by the explosion of the contained moisture and form a white starchy mass many times the size of the original kernel **b** : the corn when popped **2** : a light yellow that is greener and slightly lighter than average maize and duller than chrome lemon **3** *also* **popcorn stitch** : a crochet stitch forming raised balls resembling popcorn

popcorn flower *n* : a plant of the genus *Plagiobothrys* (family Boraginaceae) usu. having crowded white flowers on a one-sided curved spike

popdock \ˈ⸗,⸗\ *n* [¹*pop* + *dock*] : FOXGLOVE

pope \ˈpōp\ *n* -S [ME, fr. OE *pāpa*, fr. LL *papa*, fr. Gk *pappas, papas*, title of bishops, lit., papa — more at PAPA] **1 a** *often cap* : the bishop of Rome as head of the Roman Catholic Church **b** : the Eastern Orthodox or Coptic patriarch of Alexandria **c** : an Eastern Orthodox priest **2** : a spiritual head of any of various non-Christian religions ⟨the Taoist ~⟩ ⟨the Caodaist ~⟩ **3** : one held to resemble a pope usu. in authority or position ⟨schoolmasters, professors . . . ~*s* of knowledge — Holbrook Jackson⟩ **4** : ¹RUFF 1 **5** : any of various birds: as **a** *dial Eng* : PUFFIN **b** *dial Eng* : BULLFINCH **c** *dial Eng* : RED-BACKED SHRIKE

pope day *n, usu cap P&D* [so called fr. the fact that the Gunpowder Plot was popularly regarded as inspired by the Pope] : GUY FAWKES DAY

pope·dom \ˈpōpdəm\ *n* -S [ME, fr. OE *pāpdōm*, fr. *pāpa* pope + *-dōm* -dom] **1** : the office or tenure of a pope : PAPACY ⟨during the ~ of Vigilius⟩ **2** : a rank or office of supreme religious authority ⟨the Caodaist ~⟩

pope·hood \ˈpōp,hu̇d\ *n* [ME *popehode*, fr. OE *pāpanhād*, fr. *pāpa* pope + *-hād* -hood] : the office or tenure of pope

pope·ism \ˈpō,pizəm\ *n* -S [*pope* + *-ism*] : POPERY

pope joan *n, usu cap P&J* [fr. *Pope Joan*, fictitious female pope] : a card game resembling Michigan and fan-tan; *also* : the nine of diamonds in this game

pop·e·line \ˌpäpəˈlēn\ *n* -S [F, fr. E *poplin*] : a clothing fabric that has a silk or rayon warp and a wool filling and resembles poplin or rep

pope·ling \ˈpōpliŋ\ *n* -S [*pope* + *-ling*] **1** *obs* : PAPIST **2** : a petty or deputy pope

pope·ly *adj* -ER/-EST [*pope* + *-ly*] : characteristic of a pope : PAPAL

pope night *n, usu cap P&N* : the night of Pope Day

pop·ery \ˈpōp(ə)rē\ *n* -ES *sometimes cap* [*pope* + *-ery*] : ROMAN CATHOLICISM; *esp* : its government and forms of worship — usu. used disparagingly

pope's-eye \ˈ⸗ˌ⸗\ *n, pl* **pope's-eyes** : the lymphatic gland in the thigh of an ox or sheep

pope's head *n* : a long-handled brush usu. used for dusting ceilings or washing windows

pope·ship \ˈpōp,ship\ *n* [ME, fr. *pope* + *-ship*] : POPEDOM

pope's nose *n* : the part of a bird that corresponds to the tail of a mammal and forms a broad flattened lobe bearing the tail feathers and usu. a dorsal uropygial gland — called also *parson's nose*

pop·ess \ˈpōpə̇s\ *n* -ES [*pope* + *-ess*] : a female pope

pop·eye \ˈpä,pī\ *n* [prob. back-formation fr. *popeyed*] **1** : a staring bulging eye **2 a** : an exophthalmic condition of fishes due to infestation of the eye by larval trematode worms **b** : a fish affected with this condition

pop·eyed \-īd\ *adj* [¹*pop* + *eyed*] : having eyes that bulge (as from disease, excitement) ⟨the galleries ~ with amazement —*Time*⟩ ⟨the wombat's charming but ~ offspring peer out from this pouch —Barrett McGurn⟩

pop fly *n* [¹*pop*] : a fly ball hit without much force and usu. caught easily by an infielder

pop foul *n* : a pop fly hit into foul territory in baseball

pop goes the weasel [¹*pop*] : an English country longways in which each dancer in turn is popped under the arms of a couple with hands joined; *also* : an American square dance derived from this

popgun \ˈ⸗,⸗\ *n* [²*pop*] **1** : a child's toy gun consisting of a tube and rammer for shooting ammunition (as pellets, corks) by compression of air **2** : any firearm regarded as ridiculously inadequate

pophole \ˈ⸗,⸗\ *n* [¹*pop*] : a small opening through which an animal may pass (as from a coop to an outdoor run)

pop·i·an *also* **pop·e·an** \ˈpōpēən\ *adj, usu cap* [Alexander *Pope* †1744 Eng. poet + *-ian, -an*] : of, relating to, or resembling Alexander Pope or his poetry ⟨the fashionable *Popian* couplet —George Saintsbury⟩

po·pil·lia \pəˈpilēə\ *n, cap* [NL, fr. L *Popillia* Roman gentile name] : a genus of beetles of the family Scarabaeidae — see JAPANESE BEETLE

pop·i·nac *also* **pop·i·nack** \ˈpäpə,nak\ *n* -S [modif. of *opopanax*] : HUISACHE

pop·in·jay \ˈpäpən,jā\ *n* [ME *papejay, papengay*, fr. MF *papegai, papejai*, fr. Ar *babghā'*] **1** *obs* : PARROT **2** *heraldry* : a parrot or parakeet usu. depicted in green with red legs and beak **3** : one thought to resemble a parrot or parakeet (as because of excessive ostentation in clothes, senseless volubility, or vain posturing) ⟨had been stricken too sorely by the bitter struggle to be caught by military ~*s*—V.L.Parrington⟩ ⟨a curse on the tanner's grandson and his French ~*s* — Charles Kingsley⟩ **4** *dial Eng* : GREEN WOODPECKER

popinjay green *n* : PARROT GREEN

pop·ish \ˈpōpish\ *adj, sometimes cap* [*pope* + *-ish*] : Roman Catholic — often used disparagingly

pop·ish·ly *adv* : in a popish manner

¹pop·lar \ˈpäplə(r)\ *n* -S [ME *poplere*, fr. MF *pouplier*, fr. *pouple, peuple* poplar, fr. L *populus*] **1 a** : a tree of the genus *Populus* — see TREE illustration **b** : the soft light-colored nondurable wood of a poplar; *esp* : the wood of the aspen used for paper pulp **2** : TULIP TREE 1

²poplar \"\ *adj* **1** : of or relating to the tulip tree or the poplar **2** : made of the wood of the tulip tree or of poplar

poplar and willow borer *n* : a grub that is the larva of a European weevil (*Sternochetus lapathi*) now established in many parts of the U.S. and that bores in stems esp. of various poplars and willows

poplar birch \ˈ⸗⸗-\ *also* **poplar-leaved birch** \ˈ⸗⸗,⸗-\ *n* : any of several white birches with leaves resembling those of the poplar; *esp* : AMERICAN GRAY BIRCH

poplar borer *n* : a longicorn beetle (*Saperda calcarata*) whose larva bores in and destroys various poplars

poplar box *n* : an Australian gum tree (*Eucalyptus polyanthemos*) with ashy gray bark, nearly round long-stalked leaves, and small umbellate flowers

poplar canker *n* : a branch or trunk canker of poplars esp. damaging to the Lombardy poplar and caused by a fungus (*Dothichiza populea*)

pop·lared \ˈpäplə(r)d\ *adj* [¹*poplar* + *-ed*] : planted with or abounding in poplars

poplar goat moth *n* : a large gray and black carpenter moth (*Acossus centerensis*) whose larva bores in poplar trees

poplar hawk moth *n* : a large European sphingid moth (*Smerinthus populi*) the larva of which feeds on the foliage of poplar

pop·lar·ism \ˈpäplə,rizəm\ *n* -S *usu cap* [*Poplar*, metropolitan borough of east London + E *-ism*] : a municipal policy of providing poor relief and esp. unemployment compensation in amounts held to be extravagant and productive of unjustly high taxes

poplar leaf fig *n* : a large West Indian fig (*Ficus laevigata*) having a small red fruit

poplar tentmaker *n* : a caterpillar that is the larva of a notodontid moth (*Ichthyura inclusa*) and that feeds on poplar foliage

poplar vagabond aphid *n* : an aphid (*Mordwilkoja vagabundus*) that infests poplars in the U. S. and Canada and causes galls on the twigs

poplar worm *n* : the larva of any of various lepidopterans injurious to poplar trees; *esp* : the larva of a dagger moth (*Acronicta lepusculina*) that feeds on the cottonwood

pople *var of* POPPLE

pop·lin \ˈpäplən\ *n* -S [F *papeline*, perh. fr. *Poperinge*, Flemish textile city] : a strong plainwoven fabric characterized by fine crosswise ribs that is made of various fibers singly or in combination and is used esp. for clothing and curtains

pop·lit·e·al *also* **pop·li·tae·al** \(ˈ)päpˈlid·ēəl, -itē-, ˌpäpləˈtē-\ *adj* [fr. NL *popliteus* of the ham + E *-al* — more at POPLITEUS] : of or relating to the back part of the leg behind the knee joint

popliteal artery *n* : the continuation of the femoral artery that after passing through the thigh crosses the popliteal space and soon divides into the anterior and posterior tibial arteries

popliteal muscle *n* : POPLITEUS

popliteal nerve *n* : either of two branches into which the sciatic nerve divides usu. in the lower part of the thigh with the larger branch passing through the popliteal space and continuing downward as the tibial nerve and the smaller branch forming the peroneal nerve

popliteal notch *n* : a depression on the back of the head of the tibia between the tuberosities

popliteal space *n* : a lozenge-shaped space at the back of the knee joint

popliteal vein *n* : a vein formed by the union of the tibial veins and ascending through the popliteal space to the thigh where it becomes the femoral vein

pop·lit·e·us \päpˈlid·ēəs, -itēəs, ˌpäpləˈtēəs\ *n, pl* **poplit·ei** \-ē,ī\ [NL, fr. *popliteus* of the ham, fr. L *poplit-, poples* ham of the knee] : a flat muscle extending from the outer condyle of the femur to the tibia and forming part of the floor of the popliteal space

pop·o·crat \ˈpäpə,krat\ *n* -S *usu cap* [*populist* + *democrat*] : a Democrat supporting Populist policies in the last decade of the 19th century — usu. used disparagingly

pop off *vi* [¹*pop*] **1 a** : to leave suddenly ⟨*popped off* to town without telling anyone⟩ **b** : to die unexpectedly ⟨*popped off* at the age of forty⟩ **2** : to talk without thinking often loudly or angrily ⟨*popping off* about taxes⟩

pop-off \ˈ⸗,⸗\ *n* -S [¹*pop* + *off*] **1** : one who talks loosely or loudly ⟨is glib, volcanic . . . a *pop-off* —*Kiplinger Washington Letter*⟩ **2** *ceramics* : a small bit of defective enamel that loosens during drying or firing

po·poi \ˈpō,pȯi\ *n* -S [Marquesan] : a food of the Marquesas islands similar to Hawaiian poi but commonly made of both fresh and preserved cooked and pounded breadfruit

po·po·lo·ca \ˌpōpəˈlōkə\ *or* **po·po·lo·co** \-lō(,)kō\ *n, pl* **popoloca** *or* **popolocas** *or* **popoloco** *or* **popolocos** *usu cap* [MexSp, fr. Nahuatl *popoloca*] **1 a** (1) : a Popolocan people of southern Pueblo, Mexico (2) : a member of such people **b** : the language of such people **2** : CHOCHO **3** : POPOLUCA **4** : XINCA

po·po·lo·can \-lōkən\ *n* -S *usu cap* [*Popoloca* + *-an*] : a language family of the states of Oaxaca and Pueblo in Mexico comprising Popoloca and Chocho

po·po·lu·ca \ˌpōpəˈlükə\ *n, pl* **popoluca** *or* **popolucas** *usu cap* [MexSp, alter. of *popoloca*] **1 a** : a Zoquean people of southern Vera Cruz, Mexico **b** : a member of such people **2** : the language of the Popoluca people

po·po·ti·llo \ˌpōpəˈtē(,)(y)ō\ *n* -S [MexSp, a gnetaceous plant, fr. Nahuatl *popotl* broom] : MORMON TEA

popover \ˈ⸗,⸗⸗\ *n* -S [¹*pop* + *over*] : a quick bread made from a thin batter of eggs, milk, and flour and subjected in the first stage of baking to such heat that steam expands it into a hollow shell

po·po·vets \pəˈpȯvəts\ *n, pl* **po·pov·tsy** \-ȯftsē\ *usu cap* [Russ, fr. *popov-* (pl. stem of *pop* priest) + *-ets* agent suffix — more at BEZPOPOVETS] : a member of one of the major groups of the Raskolnik in Russia which maintains the hierarchical structure of episcopate and priesthood and is thereby distinguished from the priestless branch of the Bezpopovtsy — compare BEZPOPOVETS

pop·pa \ˈpäpə\ *n* -S [by alter.] : PAPA

pop·pa·ble \ˈpäpəbəl\ *adj* [¹*pop* + *able*] : capable of being popped ⟨~ corn⟩

pop-paw \ˈpäp,pȯ\ *dial var of* PAPAW

pop·pe·an \ˈpäpēən\ *adj* [irreg. fr. *poppy* + *-an*] : of or relating to the juice of the poppy

popped *past of* POP

pop·per \ˈpäpə(r)\ *n* -S [¹*pop* + *-er*] **1** : one that pops (as a firearm) **2 a** : a utensil for popping corn **b** : a corn variety suitable for popping **3** : ²POP 5a **4** : CRACKER 2b

pop·pet \ˈpäpət, *usu* -əd·+V\ *n* -S [ME *popet* — more at PUPPET] **1** *chiefly Brit* : LITTLE ONE, DEAR **2 a** *Midland* : DOLL **b** *obs* : MARIONETTE **3 a** : an upright support or guide of a machine that is fastened at the bottom only (as a lathe poppethead) **b** *or* **poppet valve** : LIFT VALVE **4 a** : one of the timber supports at the forward and after ends of a ship that form part of the launching cradle **b** : any of the small pieces of wood on a boat's gunwale supporting or forming the oarlocks

poppethead \ˈ⸗⸗,⸗\ *n* [*poppet* + *head*] **1** : a lathe tailstock or sometimes headstock **2** *Brit* : the headframe of a mining shaft

pop·pied \ˈpäpēd\ *adj* [*poppy* + *-ed*] **1** : growing or overgrown with poppies **2** : drugging or sleep-inducing like poppy juice : characterized by somnolence : DROWSY, INDOLENT ⟨fleeting ~ afternoons —Elizabeth Lomax⟩

popping *adj* [fr. pres. part. of ¹*pop*] **1** : protruding or seeming to protrude : BULGING ⟨before the ~ eyes of the men at the ship's rail —T.W.Wall⟩ **2** : INTERMITTENT, OCCASIONAL, SPORADIC ⟨the patrol was pinned down by ~ fire from a small clump of woods⟩ **3** : full of action : LIVELY : able to pop

popping crease *n* [fr. gerund of ¹*pop*] *cricket* : a line 4 feet in front of and parallel with either bowling crease that marks the forward limit of the batsman's ground

¹pop·ple *also* **po·ple** \ˈpäpəl\ *n* -S [ME *popul, popil*, fr. OE *popul*, fr. L *populus*] *chiefly dial* : POPLAR 1 ⟨the country is big, wide, open with . . . clumps of ~ —W.F.Brown b. 1903⟩

²popple *also* **pople** \"\ *vi* -ED/-ING/-S [ME *poplen*, prob. of imit. origin] **1** : to heave or toss about ⟨small trembling waves *poppled* and frothed in midstream —R.F.Burton⟩ **2** : to bob about on or as if on agitated waters

³popple *also* **pople** \"\ *n* -S **1** : a heaving of water (as from boiling or from the wind) ⟨no sound but the ~ of water against the bow —Joyce Cary⟩ **2** : a choppy sea

⁴popple \"\ *dial Brit var of* POPPY

pop·ply \ˈpäp(ə)lē\ *adj* -ER/-EST [³*popple* + *-y*] : CHOPPY

pop·py \ˈpäpē, -pi\ *n* -ES [ME *popi*, fr. OE *popig, popæg*, modif. of (assumed) VL *papavum* (whence OF *pavo*), alter. of L *papaver*; perh. akin to L *papula* papule] **1** : any of numerous annual, biennial, and perennial herbs or rarely subshrubs of *Papaver* or sometimes of closely related genera having showy flowers usu. of white or shades of red or yellow and including many that are cultivated as ornamentals of which the annuals are derived chiefly from the opium and corn poppies and the perennials from the Oriental poppy, alpine poppy, and Iceland poppy — see CAPSULE illustration **2 a** : an extract from the poppy used in medicines **b** : something possessing the narcotic qualities of the poppy **3** *or* **poppy red** : a strong reddish orange that is redder and lighter than paprika and redder and deeper than fire red, scarlet vermilion, or average coral red **4** : POPPYHEAD

poppy

poppy anemone *also* **poppy anemony** *n* : a perennial tuberous European herb (*Anemone coronaria*) widely cultivated for its red, blue, or white scapose flowers

poppy ash *n* : a water ash (*Fraxinus caroliniana*)

poppy bee *n* : a leaf-cutting bee (*Osmia papaveris*) which lines its cells with pieces of poppy petals

pop·py·cock \ˈpäpē,käk, -pi,-\ *n* -S [D dial. *pappekak*, lit., soft dung, fr. D *pap* pap + *kak* dung, fr. *kakken* to void excrement, fr. L *cacare* — more at CACK] : empty talk : foolish nonsense : BOSH

poppy day *n, usu cap P&D* : a day on which contributions for war veterans are solicited and artificial red poppies are given to the contributors

poppy family *n* : PAPAVERACEAE

poppyfish \ˈ⸗⸗,⸗\ *n* : HARVEST FISH a

poppyhead \ˈ⸗⸗,⸗\ *n* : a raised ornament often in the form of a finial generally used on the tops of the upright ends or elbows terminating seats in Gothic churches

poppy mallow *n* : a plant of the genus *Callirrhoë*; *esp* : a showy often cultivated plant (*C. involucrata*) with palmately or pedately cleft leaves and red flowers borne throughout the summer

poppy seed *n* : the seed of the poppy and esp. of the opium poppy used as a food (as in bakery products) and as the chief source of poppy-seed oil — compare ⁶MAW

poppy-seed oil *also* **poppy oil** *n* : a pale to reddish drying oil obtained from the seeds esp. of the opium poppy and used chiefly as a food, in artist's colors, and in soap

poppyhead

poppy show *n* [alter. of *puppet show*] *chiefly dial* : PUPPET SHOW

poppywort \'==,=\ *n* [*poppy* + *wort*] **:** a plant of the family Papaveraceae

popquiz *n* [²*pop*] **:** a quiz given without previous announcement or opportunity for preparation

¹**pops** *pl of* POP, *pres 3d sing of* POP

²**pops** *var of* POP

popshop \'=,=\ *n* [¹*pop* + *shop*] *Brit* **:** PAWNSHOP

Pop·si·cle \'päpsəkəl, -sēk-\ *trademark* — used for a confection made of water, flavoring, and coloring frozen on a stick without stirring

popskull \'=,=\ *n* [¹*pop* + *skull*] *chiefly Midland* **:** inferior or cheap whiskey

pop·sy \'päpsē\ *n* -ES [⁴*pop* + -*sy*] **:** GIRL, GIRL FRIEND, SWEETHEART

pop–the–whip \'==ˈ=\ *n* [¹*pop*] **:** CRACK-THE-WHIP

pop·u·lace \'päpyələs, *chiefly in southern U S* -pəl-\ *n* -S [MF, fr. It *popolaccio* rabble, pejorative of *popolo* the people (fr. L *populus*)] **1 :** the common people **:** the rank and file without wealth or position ⟨"the quality" . . . had to rub shoulders with the general ~ —W.S.Clark⟩ **2 :** the total number of people or inhabitants ⟨the ~ insists that this is the most beautiful town —Phil Stong⟩

pop·u·la·cy \-sē\ *n* -ES [alter. (influenced by *aristocracy*) of *populace*] *archaic* **:** POPULACE

¹**pop·u·lar** \-lə(r)\ *adj* [L *popularis* of the people, fr. *populus* the people (prob. of Etruscan origin) + -*aris* -ar] **1 :** relevant to any of the people ⟨~ action at law⟩ **2 a :** of or relating to the general public **:** constituted or carried on by the people ⟨its few noble horsemen . . . even in those days did not like ~ rebellions —Tom Wintringham⟩ ⟨in times of ~ panic . . . freedom of speech becomes important —Zechariah Chafee⟩ **b** (1) **:** of, relating to, or by the people (as of a nation or state) as a whole as distinguished from a specific class or group ⟨choosing the president by ~ suffrage rather than by majority vote of the assembly —*Current Biog.*⟩ ⟨~ government⟩ (2) **:** of, favoring, or involving participation by the common people as distinguished from a specific class or group ⟨the ~ party in provincial elections⟩ ⟨a truly ~ revolution⟩ (3) **:** based upon or alleged to be based upon the will of the people **:** involving or held to involve participation by all or the great majority of the people ⟨the Roman constitution . . . was ~ in form —J.A.Froude⟩ ⟨communist ~ democracies⟩ (4) **:** representing and usu. chosen by vote of the common people as distinguished from a specific class or group ⟨the House of Commons, not the House of Lords, is the ~ branch of the British parliament⟩ ⟨electing truly ~ representatives —*Hindustan Times*⟩ ⟨a ~ assembly⟩ **3 a** *obs* **:** being of low birth **:** PLEBEIAN **b** *archaic* **:** having low tastes **4 a :** adapted to or indicative of the understanding and taste of the majority **:** easy to comprehend **:** not abstruse, complicated, or profound **:** requiring no specialized knowledge or training to appreciate ⟨publishes excellent ~ and technical bulletins —*Amer. Guide Series: N.Y.City*⟩ ⟨drama . . . took on a more ~ form, being frequently enacted outside the churches —O.Elfrida Saunders⟩ ⟨the difficulty of writing ~ science —T.H.Savory⟩ **b :** suited to the financial means of the majority of people **:** moderate in cost **:** INEXPENSIVE ⟨there was room for a weekly journal at a ~ price —John Buchan⟩ ⟨charcoal, a ~ fuel for cooking —*Amer. Guide Series: Fla.*⟩ **5 :** marked by attempts to gain general goodwill or to curry favor at large ⟨the hypocritical ~ first acts of the usurper⟩ **6** *obs* **:** thickly inhabited **:** CROWDED, POPULOUS **7 a :** having wide or general currency esp. among the rank and file **:** PREVALENT, WIDESPREAD **:** frequently encountered or widely accepted ⟨a ~ instead of an accurate and legal conception —O.W.Holmes †1935⟩ ⟨the use of . . . homespun medicines declines, but some of the more ~ are still used —*Amer. Guide Series: Ark.*⟩ ⟨the ~ conviction that there is a poetic vision of things —Samuel Alexander⟩ **b :** well liked or admired by a particular group or circle ⟨campsites . . . are ~ with deer hunters and trout fishermen —*Amer. Guide Series: Nev.*⟩ **8 :** commonly liked or found pleasant or praiseworthy **:** APPROVED **:** given general praise, enthusiasm, liking, or support ⟨the lucidity and brevity that make a first-class ~ orator —*Times Lit. Supp.*⟩ ⟨book hotel reservations well in advance at all the most ~ places —Richard Joseph⟩ ⟨triumphantly ~ without the slightest effort on his own part —Elinor Wylie⟩ **9 :** originating among or composed or transmitted by the people, esp. by the unlettered ⟨in all times and places, there have been ~ arts of song, dance, storytelling —John Dewey⟩ **syn** see COMMON

²**popular** \"\ *n* -S *archaic* **:** ⁶POP 1

popular action *n* **:** an action to recover a penalty given by a statute to anyone who sues for it — compare QUI TAM

popular etymology *n* **:** FOLK ETYMOLOGY

popular front *n, often cap P&F* **:** a working coalition of leftist and sometimes middle-of-the-road political parties against a common opponent (as fascism); *specif* **:** one sponsored and dominated by Communists as a device for gaining power ⟨ally Laborites with Communists in a *Popular Front* —*Time*⟩ ⟨official opposition to a *Popular Front* —*Manchester Guardian Weekly*⟩ ⟨Chile was ruled by a *popular front* government —W.L.Schurz⟩

pop·u·lar·i·ty \,==ˈlarəd·ē, -rətē, -i *also* -ler-\ *n* -ES [¹*popular* + -*ity*] **1** *obs* **:** democracy as a principle or a form of government **2** [L *popularitat-, popularitas*, fr. *popularis* popular + -*itat-, -itas* -ity] **:** the act or means of currying favor with the populace ⟨the fixed professional ~ of a hotelkeeper's wife —*Saturday Rev.*⟩ **3 :** the quality or state of being popular **:** the manifest approval or esteem of many persons or of people in general ⟨his gift of friendship and charm soon won him . . . affection and ~ —F.J.Mather⟩ **4** [obs. F *popularité*, fr. LL *popularitat-, popularitas*, fr. L *popularis* of the people + -*itat-, -itas* -ity — more at POPULAR] *archaic* **:** POPULACE

pop·u·lar·iza·tion \,==lərəˈzāshən, -,rī'-\ *n* -S **1 :** an act of popularizing or the state of being popularized ⟨with the ~ of the buggy . . . a demand rose for light harness —V.S.Clark⟩ **2 :** something that is popularized; *esp* **:** a publication in terms comprehensible to the average man ⟨divides the true folk tale from the ~ and that in turn from the work of art —*Yale Rev.*⟩

pop·u·lar·ize \'==lə,rīz\ *vb* -ED/-ING/-S *see* -*ize in Explan Notes* [¹*popular* + -*ize*] *vi* **:** to cater to popular taste ⟨insisted on a high scholastic standard; he would not ~⟩ ~ *vt* **:** to make popular: as **a :** to gain approval for **:** cause to be liked or esteemed ⟨done everything to ~ an art gallery —R.M. Yoder⟩ ⟨*popularized* literacy throughout . . . Latin America —Jerome Ellison⟩ ⟨credited with having *popularized* the island as a resort for artists —*Amer. Guide Series: Maine*⟩ **b :** to present (as a subject) in a form intelligible or interesting to those not specialists or trained thinkers ⟨synthesized a great deal of scholarship, *popularizing* . . . its results —S.C.Chew⟩ — **pop·u·lar·iz·er** \-zə(r)\ *n* -S

pop·u·lar·ly *adv* **:** in a popular manner ⟨science cannot be at once accurately and ~ reported —F.L.Mott⟩

popular song *n* **:** a song of wide appeal that is easily performed and memorized and usu. has a relatively brief vogue — compare FOLK SONG

popular sovereignty *n* **1 :** a doctrine in political theory that sovereignty is vested in the people as a whole rather than in a particular individual or group (as a ruling dynasty) and as a result that government is created by and subject to the will of the people ⟨establish the doctrine of *popular sovereignty* as the foundation of modern Europe — *Times Lit. Supp.*⟩ — compare LIMITED 2, MAJORITY RULE, SOCIAL CONTRACT **2 a :** a principal doctrine of the pre-Civil War controversy over slavery specifying that the people of a territory like the people of a state should be free to regulate their domestic concerns without Congressional interference; *specif* **:** the doctrine asserting the right of the people living in a newly organized territory to decide by vote of their territorial legislature whether or not slavery would be permitted in the territory

pop·u·late \'==,lāt, *usu* -ād·+V\ *vb* -ED/-ING/-S [ML *populatus*, past part. of *populare* to people, fr. L *populus* people — more at POPULAR] *vt* **1 :** to have a place in **:** make up the population of **:** INHABIT, OCCUPY ⟨the galaxies *populating* the space of the universe —George Gamow⟩ ⟨characters created . . . to ~ his novel —John McCarten⟩ **2 :** to furnish or provide with inhabitants **:** PEOPLE ⟨the large rooms seemed well *populated* —E.C.Marston⟩ ⟨very heavily *populated* with all forms of wildlife —J.B.Robson⟩ ~ *vi* **:** to become populous **:** PROPAGATE

pop·u·la·tion \,==ˈlāshən\ *n* -S [LL *population-, populatio*, fr. L *populus* people + -*ation-, -atio*, -ation] **1 a :** the whole number of people or inhabitants occupying a specific geographical locality (as an institution, a country, a world) ⟨when in operation, the building will have a daily ~ of 35,000 —*Pencil Points*⟩ ⟨the entire adult male ~ of the island except for two old men —Thor Heyerdahl⟩ **b :** the total number or amount of things esp. within a given area ⟨the tractor ~ of American farms increased —*Reporter*⟩ ⟨an enormous ~ of china, ivory, and bronze figures —Osbert Lancaster⟩ **2 :** the act or process of populating ⟨encourage ~ of colonies⟩ **3 a :** a body of persons having some quality or characteristic in common and usu. thought of as occupying a particular area ⟨a floating ~ of drifters and rogues⟩ ⟨a healthy rural ~⟩ **b** (1) **:** the organisms inhabiting a particular area or biotope ⟨an interesting xerophilic ~⟩ ⟨the Southern states have shown an average increase . . . in their beef ~s —*N.Y.Times*⟩ (2) **:** a group of interbreeding biotypes that represents the level of organization at which speciation begins — compare RACIATION **4** *math* **:** a group of individual persons, objects, or items from which samples are taken for measurement statistically — **pop·u·la·tion·al** \,==ˈlāshənᵊl, -shnəl\ *adj*

population dynamics *n pl but sing or pl in constr* **1 :** a branch of knowledge concerned with the sizes of populations and the factors involved in their maintenance, decline, or expansion **2 :** the sequence of population changes characteristic of a particular organism

pop·u·la·tion·ist \,==ˈlāsh(ə)nəst\ *n* -S [*population* + -*ist*] **1 :** an advocate of population control (as Malthusianism) **2 :** DEMOGRAPHER

population pressure *n* **:** the sum of the factors (as increase in numbers or excessive food consumption) within a population that reduce the ability of an environment to support the population and that therefore tend to result in migration and expansion of range or in extinction or decline of the population

pop·u·lin \'päpyələn\ *n* -S [F *populine*, fr. L *populus* poplar + F -*ine* -in] **:** a sweet crystalline glucoside $C_{20}H_{22}O_8$ found in aspen bark and leaves and poplar buds; benzoyl-salicin

pop·u·lism \'==,lizəm\ *n* -S *usu cap* [*populist* + -*ism*] **:** the political and economic doctrines advocated by the Populists

¹**pop·u·list** \-ləst\ *n* -S *usu cap* [L *populus* the people + E -*ist*] **1 :** a member of a U.S. political party formed in 1891 and active esp. in the presidential campaign of 1892 primarily to represent agrarian interests and to advocate the free coinage of silver and government control of monopolies **2 :** a member of a political party purporting to represent the rank and file of the people

²**populist** \"\ *also* **pop·u·lis·tic** \;==ˈlistik, -tēk\ *adj, often cap* [¹*populist*] **:** of, relating to, or advocating Populism ⟨bitter attacks upon the Court were splashed in the *Populist* press —A.F.Westin⟩

pop·u·los·i·ty \,==ˈläsəd·ē\ *n* -ES [L *populos*us + E -*ity*] *archaic* **:** POPULOUSNESS

pop·u·lous \'==ləs\ *adj* [L *populosus*, fr. *populus* people + -*osus* -ous — more at POPULAR] **1 :** having a large population **:** densely populated **:** thickly settled ⟨this new and ~ community —Willa Cather⟩ ⟨one of the most prosperous and ~ areas of its size in the U. S. —R.F.Weld⟩ **2 a :** large in numbers **:** NUMEROUS ⟨the Navajos would be as ~ as we are now —Henry Miller⟩ **b :** filled to capacity **:** CROWDED ⟨these narrow streets were ~ with students —A.T.Quiller-Couch⟩ ⟨a large and ~ ship —Herman Melville⟩ **3 :** of or relating to the people **:** POPULAR — **pop·u·lous·ly** *adv*

pop·u·lous·ness *n* -ES **:** the quality or state of being populous

pop·u·lus \'==ləs\ *n, cap* [NL, fr. L, poplar] **:** a genus of trees (family Salicaceae) that is native to the northern hemisphere, that has resinous buds, numerous stamens, incised bracts, and elongated stigmas, and that is well known in cultivation — see POPLAR; compare SALIX

¹**pop–up** \'=,=\ *n* -S [¹*pop* + *up*] **:** one that pops up: as **a :** POP FLY **b :** a slow high shot in a racket game usu. near the net

²**pop–up** \"\ *adj* **:** of, relating to, or having a device that pops up ⟨a *pop-up* toaster⟩ ⟨a *pop-up* valve⟩

pop valve *n* [¹*pop*] **:** a safety valve designed to open when the pressure of a fluid exceeds the force exerted by the spring that normally keeps the valve closed

popweed \'=,=\ *n* [¹*pop* + *weed*] **1 :** a common bladderwort (*Utricularia vulgaris*) of Europe **2 :** BLADDER WRACK

por *abbr* **1** portion **2** portrait

POR *abbr, often not cap* **1** payable on receipt **2** pay on return

-po·ra \,pərə, 'pōrə\ *n comb form* [NL, fr. L *porus* bodily passage, pore — more at PORE] **:** one or ones having (such) a passage or pore or (such or so many) passages or pores — chiefly in generic names ⟨*Heliopora*⟩ ⟨*Millepora*⟩

por·al \'pōrəl, 'pȯr-\ *adj* [*pore* + -*al*] **:** of or relating to the body pores

por·bea·gle \'pȯ(r),bēgəl\ *or* **porbeagle shark** \"-\ *also* **pro·bea·gle** \'prō,bēgəl\ *n* -S [Corn *porgh-bugel*] **:** a voracious viviparous shark (*Lamna nasus*, syn. *L. cornubica*) of the north Atlantic and Pacific oceans having a pointed nose and a crescent-shaped tail and reaching a length of about eight feet

porc *abbr* porcelain

por·cate \'pȯr,kāt\ *or* **por·cat·ed** \-ād·əd\ *adj* [L *porca* drainage ditch + E -*ate* — more at FURROW] **:** having furrows broader than intervening ridges

por·ce·lain \'pōrs(ə)lən, -ōrs-, -ōəs-, -ȯ(ə)s- *sometimes* -sə-,lān\ *n* -S *often attrib* [MF *porcelaine* cowrie shell, porcelain (fr. the resemblance of its finish to the surface of the shell), fr. It *porcellana*, fr. *porcello* little pig, vulva (fr. L *porcellus*, dim. of *porcus* pig, vulva) + -*ana* -an; fr. the resemblance of the shell to the female pudenda — more at FARROW] **1 a :** a hard, fine-grained, nonporous, sonorous, and usu. translucent and white ceramic ware that has a hard paste body, is fired at a high temperature, and is used esp. for table and ornamental wares, industrial and chemical wares, and esp. formerly for dentures — compare ¹CHINA, EARTHENWARE, POTTERY, STONEWARE **b :** SOFT PASTE 2 **2 :** an article of porcelain

porcelain ampelopsis *also* **porcelain vine** *n* **:** a woody vine (*Ampelopsis brevipedunculata*) of eastern Asia with blue or lilac berries that suggest porcelain

porcelain blue *n* **:** a grayish blue that is greener and paler than electric or copenhagen and greener, lighter, and stronger than Gobelin

porcelain cement *n* **:** a substance (as equal parts of gutta-percha and shellac mixed at a gentle heat) for causing porcelain to adhere to porcelain when applied at elevated temperatures

porcelain clay *n* **:** KAOLIN

porcelain crab *n* **:** any of several anomuran crabs of the family Porcellanidae having a smooth porcelaneous carapace

por·ce·lained \-nd\ *adj* [*porcelain* + -*ed*] **:** coated with or resembling porcelain

porcelain enamel *n* **:** VITREOUS ENAMEL

porcelain green *n* **:** a moderate bluish green that is greener and paler than sea blue and greener and duller than Bremen blue

por·ce·lain·ite \-lə,nīt\ *n* -S [*porcelain* + -*ite*] **:** baked clay or shale found in burned-out coal mines

por·ce·lain·iza·tion \,pōrs(ə)lənəˈzāshən, -sə,lān-, -,nī'z-\ *n* -S **:** the act or process of porcelainizing

por·ce·lain·ize \'=s(ə)lə,nīz\ *vt* -ED/-ING/-S [*porcelain* + -*ize*] **:** to convert into porcelain or something resembling it; *esp* **:** to fire a vitreous coating on (steel or other metal)

porcelain jasper *n* **:** porcellanite resembling jasper

por·ce·lain·ous \'=s(ə)lənəs, -sə,lān-\ *adj* [*porcelain* + -*ous*] **:** PORCELANEOUS

porcelain paper *n* **:** a heavy transparent paper used in novelties and greeting cards

porcelain stone *n* **:** CHINA STONE 1

por·ce·la·neous *or* **por·cel·la·neous** \;=səˈlānēəs\ *adj* [It *porcellana* porcelain + E -*eous*] **:** of, relating to, or resembling porcelain ⟨~ shells⟩ ⟨~ glass⟩

por·ce·lan·ic *or* **por·cel·lan·ic** \-ˈlanik\ *adj* [It *porcellana* + E -*ic*] *of rock* **:** resembling porcelain

por·ce·la·nous *or* **por·cel·la·nous** \'=sələnəs, ;=sə;lānəs, (ˈ)=;selən-\ *adj* [It *porcellana* + E -*ous*] **:** PORCELANEOUS

por·ce·lit·er \'==,līd·ə(r)\ *n* -S [*porcelain* + -*ite* (commercial product) + -*er*] **:** a worker who bakes vitreous enamel on castings

por·cel·lana \,==ˈlanə, -ˈlā-, -ˈlä-\ *n, cap* [NL, fr. It, porcelain — more at PORCELAIN] **:** a cosmopolitan genus of littoral porcelain crabs that is the type of the family Porcellanidae — **por·cel·la·ni·an** \;==ˈnēən\ *adj or n*

¹**por·cel·la·nid** \,==;==nəd\ *adj* [NL *Porcellanidae*] **:** of or relating to the Porcellanidae

²**porcellanid** \"\ *n* -S **:** a crustacean of the family Porcellanidae

por·cel·la·ni·dae \,==ˈnə,dē\ *n pl, cap* [NL, fr. *Porcellana*, type genus + -*idae*] **:** a large family of anomuran crustaceans that resemble the true crabs and comprise the porcelain crabs and related forms

por·cel·la·nite \'=s(ə)lə,nīt\ *n* -S [G *porzellanit*, fr. *porzellan* porcelain (fr. It *porcellana*) + -*it* -ite] **:** a hard dense siliceous rock having the appearance of unglazed porcelain on fresh fractures

por·cel·lio \pȯrˈselē,ō\ *n, cap* [NL *Porcellion-, Porcellio*, fr. L, wood louse, sow bug, fr. *porcellus* little pig, dim. of *porcus* pig — more at FARROW] **:** an Old World genus of terrestrial isopods that is the type of the family Porcellionidae and includes one form (*P. scaber*) which has been introduced into the U. S.

por·cel·li·on·i·dae \,=,==ˈänə,dē\ *n pl, cap* [NL *Porcellion-, Porcellio*, type genus + -*idae*] **:** a large and widely distributed family of terrestrial isopods with 2-jointed antennae

porch \'pō(ə)rch, -ȯ(ə)rch, -ōəch, -ȯ(ə)ch\ *n* -ES [ME *porche*, fr. OF, fr. L *porticus* portico, colonnade, fr. *porta* gate, entrance — more at FORD] **1 :** a covered entrance to a building usu. with a separate roof and often large enough to serve as an outdoor seating or walking space **:** VERANDA **2** *obs* **:** a covered walk **:** COLONNADE, PORTICO **3** *dial Eng* **a :** SIDE CHAPEL **b :** TRANSEPT **4 :** a place for waiting before entering **:** ENTRANCE, PASSAGE **syn** see BALCONY

porch box *n* **1 :** a box containing soil for growing flowers or ornamental plants on a porch — compare WINDOW BOX **2 :** an insulated box in which bottled milk is left in house delivery

porch climber *n* **:** CAT BURGLAR, SECOND-STORY MAN

porched \-cht\ *adj* [*porch* + -*ed*] **:** having a porch

por·cine \'pȯr,sīn, -,sēn, -sᵊn\ *adj* [L *porcinus* swinish, fr. *porcus* pig + -*inus* -ine — more at FARROW] **:** of, relating to, or suggesting swine ⟨a surly and ~ sprat of a man —T.B. Costain⟩ ⟨comparison between human and ~ pleasures —Lucius Garvin⟩ ⟨~ brucellosis⟩

por·cine·ly *adv* **:** SWINISHLY ⟨imperially and ~ filling his clothes and the great leather couch —R.P.Warren⟩

¹**por·cu·pine** \'pȯrkyə,pīn, *chiefly dial* -kə,p- *or* -kē,p-\ *n* -S *often attrib* [ME *porke despyne, porkepin*, fr. MF *porc espin*, fr. OIt *porcospino*, fr. L *porcus* pig + *spina* thorn, prickle — more at SPINE] **1 a :** any of various relatively large hystricomorph rodents having stiff sharp erectile bristles mingled with the hair of the pelage and constituting the Old World terrestrial family Hystricidae and the New World arboreal family Erethizontidae — see BRUSH-TAILED PORCUPINE, CANADA PORCUPINE, LONG-TAILED PORCUPINE **b :** ECHIDNA 1 **2 a** *or* **porcupine beater** *or* **porcupine roller :** any of various rollers or cylinders covered with wire pins, card clothing, or beater blades and used for fiber preparation or spinning processes **b :** any of various other toothed mechanical devices **3 :** HEDGEHOG 4b

porcupine

²**porcupine** \"\ *vt* -ED/-ING/-S **1 :** to cause to bristle **2 :** to prick with or as if with porcupine quills

porcupine anteater *n* **:** ECHIDNA 1

porcupine boiler *n* **:** a boiler with a central drum and radiating tubes

porcupine crab *n* **:** a spiny anomuran crustacean (*Lithodes hystrix*) of the coast of Japan that resembles a crab

porcupine fish *n* **:** any of various fishes of the family Diodontidae and esp. of the genus *Diodon* that are widespread in tropical seas and have flesh which is usu. regarded as inedible or poisonous

porcupine grass *n* **1 :** a tall stout grass (*Stipa spartea*) of the western U.S. that has grains with long hygroscopic awns which by their twisting and untwisting often penetrate the wool and even the flesh of sheep and that affords good forage and hay **2 :** SPINIFEX 2

porcupine rat *n* **:** SPINY RAT 1

porcupine wood *n* [so called fr. the resemblance of its markings to porcupine quills] **:** the outer wood of the coconut palm

por·cu·pin·ish \-nish\ *adj* **:** resembling a porcupine or the spines of one **:** DEFENSIVE, PRICKLY

¹**pore** \'pō(ə)r, -ȯ(ə)r, -ōə, -ȯ(ə)\ *vb* -ED/-ING/-S [ME *pouren, puren*] *vi* **1 :** to gaze intently or fixedly **:** look searchingly **:** STARE ⟨*pored* . . . on her lovely and large brown eyes —Edmund Wilson⟩ ⟨those who ~ over the microscope —R.W. Morin⟩ **2 :** to devote oneself to attentive reading **:** be deep in study — used chiefly with *over* ⟨*pored* over every single page of that thick novel —H.W.Carter⟩ **3 :** to reflect or meditate steadily **:** PONDER — used with *on* or *upon* ⟨began to ~ upon religious problems —Cecil Sprigge⟩ **4** *archaic* **:** to peer nearsightedly ~ *vt* **:** to bring to some state by poring ⟨*pored* himself blind⟩ ⟨*pored* her eyes out over his letters⟩

²**pore** \"\ *n* -S [ME *poore, pore*, fr. MF *pore*, fr. L *porus*, fr. Gk *poros* passage, pore — more at FARE] **1 a :** a minute opening esp. in an animal or plant by which matter passes through a membrane **b :** the cross section of a vessel element or tracheid often including both lumen and wall **c :** GERM PORE **2 a :** a small interstice (as in stone) admitting absorption or passage of liquid **b :** such interstices indicating density ⟨a mineral's fine ~s⟩ **3 :** one of countless minute darkish dots mottling the sun

-pore \,pō(ə)r, -ȯ(ə)r, -ōə, -ȯ(ə)\ *n comb form* -S [L *porus* — more at PORE] **:** opening ⟨*atriopore*⟩ ⟨*blastopore*⟩

pore canal *n* [²*pore*] **:** any of the fine cylindrical channels traversing the cuticle of an insect and often containing a process of an epidermal cell

pored \-ō(ə)rd, -ȯ(ə)rd, -ōəd, -ȯ(ə)d\ *adj* [²*pore* + -*ed*] **:** having pores

pore fungus *or* **pore mushroom** *n* [²*pore*] **:** a fungus of the family Boletaceae or Polyporaceae distinguished by having the spore-bearing surface within tubes or pores — called also *polypore*

po·rel·la \pəˈrelə\ *n, cap* [NL, fr. L *porus* pore + -*ella*] **:** a genus of leafy liverworts (family Jungermanniaceae) having distinct and entire underleaves and lingulate to oblong lobules and sometimes placed in a separate family because of the characteristic incomplete dehiscence of the capsule

pore multiple *n* [²*pore*] **:** a radial row of two or more plant pores flattened at their points of contact so as to suggest several divisions of a single pore

pore–plate \'=,=\ *n* [²*pore*] **:** an olfactory sense organ of an insect

por·er \-ōrə(r), -ȯrə(r)\ *n* -S [¹*pore* + -*er*] **:** one that pores ⟨the author . . . is no mere ~ over maps —H.J.Rose⟩

porge \'pȯrj\ *vt* -ED/-ING/-S [Judeo-Spanish *porgar*, fr. Sp *purgar* to purge, fr. L *purgare* — more at PURGE] **:** to make (a slaughtered animal) ceremonially clean by removal of the forbidden fat, veins, and sinews according to Jewish ritual

porg·er \-jər\ *n* -S **:** one that porges

por·gy *also* **por·gee** \'pȯrgē, 'pȯ(ə)g- *sometimes* 'pōg-\ *n, pl* **porgies** *also* **porgy** *or* **porgees** *or* **porgee** [alter. of *pargo*] **1 a :** a sparid food fish (*Pagrus pagrus*) that inhabits the Mediterranean and the Atlantic coasts of Europe and America, has a compressed oblong body and strong teeth in both jaws, and is crimson with blue spots — called also *red porgy* **b :** any of various other fishes of the family Sparidae (as a scup or pinfish) — see GRASS PORGY, JOLTHEAD PORGY **2 :** any of various teleost fishes of families other than Sparidae: as **a :** MARGATE **b :** any of several surf fishes **c :** MENHADEN

pori *pl of* PORUS

po·ria \'pōrēə\ *n, cap* [NL, fr. L *porus* pore + NL -*ia*] **:** a genus of pore fungi (family Polyporaceae) having sporophores that are flat or that resemble a crust — see TUCKAHOE

po·ri·ci·dal \;pōrəˈsīdᵊl\ *adj* [ISV *pori-* (fr. L *porus* pore) + -*cid-* (fr. L *caedere* to cut) + -*al* — more at CONCISE] **:** dehiscing through pores — see FRUIT illustration

po·rif·era \pəˈrif(ə)rə, pōˈr-\ *n pl, cap* [NL, fr. L *porus* pore + -*i-* + -*fera*, neut. pl. of -*fer* -ferous] **:** a phylum of primitive invertebrate animals comprising the sponges and having a cellular grade of construction without true tissue or organ formation but with the body permeated by canals and chambers through which a current of water flows and passes in its course through one or more cavities lined with choanocytes — **po·rif·er·al** \-rəl\ *adj* — **po·rif·er·an** \-rən\ *adj or n*

po·rif·er·ous \-rəs\ *adj* [L *porus* pore + E *-iferous*] **1** : provided with pores **2** [NL *Porifera* + E *-ous*] : of or relating to the Porifera

po·ri·form \'pōrə,fȯrm\ *adj* [L *porus* pore + E *-iform*] : resembling a pore

po·ri·na \pə'rīnə, -rēnə\ *or* **porina grub** *n* -S [NL] : a subterranean caterpillar destructive to turf in New Zealand

poriness *n* -ES [*pory* + *-ness*] *obs* : POROSITY

1poring *adj* [fr. pres. part. of *1pore*] : PEERING

2poring *n* -S [ME *pouring*, fr. gerund of *pouren* to pore] : an act of peering or gazing intently

po·ri·on \'pōrē,än\ *n, pl* **po·ria** \-ēə\ *or* **porions** [NL, fr. Gk *poros* passage + *-ion*, dim. suffix — more at FARE] : the midpoint on the upper margin of the external auditory meatus

po·ri·tes \pə'rīd·(,)ēz\ *n, cap* [NL, fr. L *porus* pore + NL *-ites*] : a genus (the type of the family Poritidae) comprising important reef-building corals with 12-rayed calyculi and a very dense skeleton that is branched or massive and globular

1po·ri·toid \pə'rīd·,ȯid, -rid·-\ *adj* [NL *Poritidae* family of corals (fr. *Porites*, type genus + *-idae*) + E *-oid*] : like or related to the family Poritidae

2poritoid \"\ *n* -S : a poritoid coral

pork \'pō(ə)rk, -ȯ(ə)rk, -ōək, -ȯ(ə)k\ *n* -S *often attrib* [ME *pork, porke*, fr. OF *porc* pig, hog, fr. L *porcus* — more at FARROW] **1** : the fresh or salted flesh of swine when dressed for food **2** *archaic* : HOG, SWINE **3** : money grants, public works, or government jobs used by politicians as patronage with more regard to political advantage than to the public good ⟨talk about economy out of one side of their mouths while voting for ~ out of the other —*Newsweek*⟩

pork barrel *n* : a government project or appropriation yielding rich patronage benefits ⟨it would create an enormous *pork barrel* which, under a politically minded secretary of agriculture, would have incalculable political potency —Raymond Moley⟩

pork–barreling \'=,===\ *n* -S : the promotion of political pork barrels ⟨keeps his hold on his constituents through unashamed *pork-barreling*, busying himself getting federal money for bridges, roads, buildings, and military installations —*Newsweek*⟩

pork·bur·ger \'=,bərgər\ *n* -S [*pork* + *-burger*] **1 a** : ground pork **b** : a cooked patty of ground pork **2** : a sandwich consisting of a patty of porkburger in a split round bun

cuts of pork: *1* hind foot, *2* ham, *3* fatback, *4* loin, *5* side, *6* Boston butt, *7* picnic ham, *8* jowl, *9* forefoot

pork butcher *n* **1** : one that butchers hogs **2** : a dealer in pork and pork products

pork·chop·per \'=,chäpə(r)\ *n* [*pork chops*, labor-union slang for economic benefits + *-er*] : a labor-union officer regarded by fellow unionists as motivated chiefly by self-interest

pork·er \-kə(r)\ *n* -S [*pork* + *-er*] : HOG; *esp* : a young pig fattened for table use as fresh pork — compare BACON HOG

pork·et \-kət\ *n* -S [ONF, dim. of OF *porc* pig — more at PORK] : a young pig : PORKER

porkfish \'=,=\ *n, pl* **porkfish** *or* **porkfishes** [*pork* + *fish*] : a black yellow-striped grunt (*Anisotremus virginicus*) of the western Atlantic from Florida to Brazil

pork·ish \-kish\ *adj* : SWINISH

pork·ling \-kliŋ\ *n* -S : a young pig : PIGLET

pork measles *n pl but sing or pl in constr* : infestation of muscles and esp. those of swine with cysticerci of the pork tapeworm

porkpie \'=;=\ *or* **porkpie hat** *n* [so called from its resemblance in shape to a pork pie] : a felt, straw, or cloth hat for informal wear having a low telescoped crown, flat top, and brim turned up all around or up in back and down in front

pork tapeworm *n* : an armed tapeworm (*Taenia solium*) that infests the human intestine as an adult, has a cysticercal larva that typically develops in swine, and is contracted by man through ingestion of the larva in raw or imperfectly cooked pork

porkpie

1porky \'pōrkē, -ȯrk-, -ōək-, -ȯ(ə)k-, -ki\ *adj* -ER/-EST : of or relating to pork; *esp* : FAT, GREASY

2por·ky \'pȯrkē, 'pō(ə)k-, -ki\ *n* -ES [*porcupine* + *-y*] : PORCUPINE

por·noc·ra·cy \pȯ(r)'näkrəsē\ *n* -ES [Gk *pornē* harlot + *-cracy* — more at PORNOGRAPHY] : government by harlots

por·no·crat \'pȯ(r)nə,krat\ *n* -S [fr. *pornocracy*, after such pairs as E *democracy: democrat*] : a member of a pornocracy

por·no·graph \'pȯ(r)nə,graf, -rȧf\ *n* [F *pornographe*, fr. Gk *pornographos* writing of harlots — more at PORNOGRAPHY] **1** : PORNOGRAPHER **2** [Gk *pornē* + E *-graph*] : a pornographic picture or writing

por·nog·ra·pher \pȯ(r)'nägrəfə(r)\ *n* -S [Gk *pornographus* + E *-er*] : one that produces pornography

por·no·graph·ic \,pȯ(r)nə¦grafik, -fēk\ *adj* [*pornography* + *-ic*] : of or relating to licentious art or literature : pandering to base appetite or desire : descriptive or suggestive of lewdness : OBSCENE ⟨only the prurient could consider the sequence ~ —A.L.Mayer⟩ ⟨merely gross, a scatological rather than a ~ impropriety —Aldous Huxley⟩ — **por·no·graph·i·cal·ly** \-fək(ə)lē, -fēk-, -li\ *adv*

por·nog·ra·phy \pȯ(r)'nägrəfē, -fi\ *n* -ES [Gk *pornographos* writing of harlots (fr. *pornē* harlot + *-graphos* writing) + E *-y* — more at PAIR, -GRAPH] **1** : a description of prostitutes or prostitution **2** : a depiction (as in writing or painting) of licentiousness or lewdness : a portrayal of erotic behavior designed to cause sexual excitement — compare EROTICA

poro- *comb form* [Gk *poros* pore] : pore ⟨*porogamy*⟩

po·ro·ceph·a·li·a·sis \,pōrō,sefə'līəsəs\ *n, pl* **porocephaliases** [NL, fr. *Porocephalus* + *-iasis*] : infestation with or disease caused by a linguatulid worm of the family Porocephalidae

po·ro·ce·phal·i·da \-sə'faləda\ *n pl, cap* [NL, fr. *Porocephalus* + *-ida*] : an order of tongue worms that have the female genital pore posterior and include all the tongue worms that parasitize mammals and some parasites of reptiles — compare LINGUATULA, POROCEPHALIDAE

po·ro·ce·phal·i·dae \-,dē\ *n pl, cap* [NL, fr. *Porocephalus*, type genus + *-idae*] : a family of tongue worms (order Porocephalida) having cylindrical bodies and occurring as adults in the lungs of reptiles and as young in various vertebrates including man

po·ro·ceph·a·lus \-'sefələs\ *n, cap* [NL, fr. *poro-* + *-cephalus*] : the type genus of Porocephalidae

po·ro·ches \pä'rō,kes\ *n* -ES [Yiddish *proykhes*, fr. Heb *pārokheth*] : PAROCHETH

po·ro·cyte \'pōrə,sīt\ *n* -S [*poro-* + *-cyte*] : one of the large tubular cells that constitute the wall of the incurrent canals in some sponges

po·ro·gam·ic \,pōrō¦gamik\ *or* **po·rog·a·mous** \(')pōr¦ägəməs\ *adj* [*poro-* + *-gamic, -gamous*] : of, relating to, or marked by porogamy

po·rog·a·my \pō'rägəmē\ *n* -ES [ISV *poro-* + *-gamy*; prob. orig. formed in G] : entrance of the pollen tube in a seed plant through the micropyle — compare CHALAZOGAMY

po·ro·kai·whir·ia \,pōrō,kī'(h)wirēə\ *n* -S [Maori *porokaiwhiri*] : a small or shrubby New Zealand tree (*Hedycarya arborea*) of the family Monimiaceae with opposite short-petioled leaves and inconspicuous flowers in axillary panicles followed by bright red drupes

po·rom·e·ter \pə'rämәd·ə(r)\ *n* [*poro-* + *-meter*] : an instrument for measuring the area of the stomatal openings of a leaf by the amount of a gas passing through a given area of it

po·ro·plastic \,pōrō+\ *adj* [*porous* + *-o-* + *plastic*] : both porous and plastic — used of a special felt for splints, jackets, or comparable objects

po·ro·po·ro \'pōrō,pōr(,)ō\ *n* -S [Maori] *NewZeal* : KANGAROO APPLE

po·ro·ro·ca \,pu̇rə'rōkə, ,pōr-\ *n* -S [Pg, fr. Guarani] : a tidal bore esp. at the mouth of the Amazon

po·ros \'pō,räs\ *n* -ES [Gk *pōros* poros, chalkstone, bladder stone] : a coarse limestone found in the Peloponnesus and extensively used as a building material by the ancient Greeks

po·ro·scope \'pōrə,skōp\ *n* [*poro-* + *-scope*] : an instrument for testing porosity

po·ro·scop·ic \,pōrə¦skäpik\ *adj* [ISV *poroscopy* + *-ic*] : of or relating to poroscopy

po·ros·co·py \pə'räskəpē\ *n* -ES [ISV *poro-* + *-scopy*] : examination of impressions left by the sweat pores of fingers to check or support fingerprint evidence

po·rose \'pō,rōs, 'pȯ,rōs\ *adj* [ML *porosus*, fr. L *porus* pore + *-osus* -ose] : POROUS; *specif* : divided into or so convoluted as to form a continuous series of pores ⟨a ~ hymenium⟩

po·ro·sim·e·ter \,pōrō'simәd·ə(r)\ *n* [*porosity* + *-meter*] : an instrument for measuring porosity

po·ro·sis \pə'rōsəs\ *n, pl* **poro·ses** \-ō,sēz\ *or* **porosises** [NL, fr. L *porus* pore + NL *-osis*] : a condition (as of a bone) characterized by porosity; *specif* : rarefaction (as of bone) with increased translucency to X rays

po·ros·i·ty \pə'räsəd·ē, pō'-, pȯ'-, -sətē, -i\ *n* -ES [ML *porositat-, porositas*, fr. *porosus* porous + L *-itat-, -itas* -ity] **1** : the quality or state of being porous ⟨led to ~ and cracking in the weld zone —*Steel*⟩; *specif* : the ratio of the volume of interstices of a material to the volume of its mass ⟨the thimble has been made in two *porosities* —*Jour. of Research*⟩ **2** : something that is porous : a porous part or area

1po·rot·ic \pə'räd·ik\ *n* -S [NL *poroticus* forming callus, fr. (assumed) Gk *pōrōtos* (verbal of Gk *pōroun* to harden, form callus, fr. *pōros* poros, chalkstone) + L *-icus* -ic] : a medicine favoring the formation of callus

2porotic \"\ *adj* [L *porus* pore + E *-otic*] : exhibiting or marked by porous structure or osteoporosis ⟨~ bone⟩ ⟨~ alteration of teeth⟩

po·rous \'pōrəs, 'pȯr-\ *adj* [ME, fr. ML *porosus*, fr. L *porus* pore + *-osus* -ous] **1 a** : full of pores : capable of absorbing moisture : permeable by liquids **b** : possessing vessels or pores — compare DIFFUSE-POROUS, RING-POROUS **2** : full of holes : INSUBSTANTIAL ⟨implications of such judgments are much too far-reaching to be attained by so ~ a procedure —T.A.Sebeok⟩ ⟨the largely unfenced international boundary . . . inevitably has been very ~ —Gladwin Hill⟩ — **po·rous·ly** *adv* — **po·rous·ness** *n* -ES

porous cell *or* **porous cup** *n* : a cylindrical vessel of porous earthenware used in an electrical cell to keep two liquids from mixing freely

porous plaster *n* : a commercial medicated plaster spread on perforated cloth

por·pen·tine \'pȯ(r)pən·,tīn\ *n* -S [by alter.] *obs* : PORCUPINE

por·phin \'pȯrfən\ *also* **por·phine** \", -,fēn\ *n* -S [*porphyrin*] : a deep purple crystalline compound $C_{20}H_{14}N_4$ that is made synthetically from pyrrole and formaldehyde, contains four pyrrole rings joined by methenyl groups so as to give a heterocyclic arrangement, and forms the essential skeletal structure of the porphyrins, heme, and chlorophyll — compare STRUCTURAL FORMULA

porphin

porphobilinogen *n* -S [prob. fr. *porphyrin* + *-o-* + *bili-* + *-in* + *-o-* + *gen*] : a dicarboxylic acid $H_2NCH_2(C_4H_2N)(CH_2COOH)CH_2CH_2COOH$ that is derived from pyrrole and formed from two molecules of delta-amino-levulinic acid, that is found in the urine in acute porphyria, and that on condensation of four molecules yields uroporphyrin and other porphyrins

por·phy·ra \'pȯ(r)fərə\ *n, cap* [NL, fr. Gk, purple fish, purple] : a genus of red algae (family Bangiaceae) with thin gelatinous red or purple fronds furnishing the edible red laver

por·phy·ra·ce·ae \,==ˈrāsē,ē\ [NL, fr. *Porphyra*, + *-aceae*] *syn of* BANGIACEAE

por·phyr·a·tin \pȯ(r)'firətən\ *n* -S [*porphyrin* + *hematin*] : any of the complex compounds (as hematin) of porphyrins with metals

por·phyr·ia \pȯ(r)'firēə, -fīr-\ *n* -S [NL, fr. ISV *porphyrin* + NL *-ia*] : a pathological state in man and some lower animals that is often due to genetic factors, is characterized by abnormalities of porphyrin metabolism, and results in the excretion of large quantities of porphyrins in the urine and in extreme sensitivity to light

1por·phyr·i·an \(')pȯ(r)¦firēən\ *also* **por·phyre·an** \", pȯ(r)fə¦rē-\ *adj, usu cap* [*Porphyry* 3d cent. A.D. Greek philosopher + E *-an*] : of or relating to the Neoplatonist Porphyry or his writings or doctrines — compare TREE OF PORPHYRY

2porphyrian \"\ *also* **por·phyr·i·an·ist** \-əst\ *n* -S *usu cap* : an adherent of Porphyry or of his doctrines

porphyrian tree *n, usu cap P* : TREE OF PORPHYRY

por·phy·rin \'pȯ(r)fərən\ *n* -S [Gk *porphyra* purple + ISV *-in*] : any of a group of reddish brown to purplish black metal-free usu. octa-substituted derivatives of porphin (as protoporphyrin or coproporphyrin) that emit an intense red fluorescence in ultraviolet light and are photosensitizing agents, that are components often in combination with proteins of most respiratory pigments of plants and animals and some enzymes (as cytochrome oxidase, catalase, and peroxidase), that are found in oil, shale, petroleum, asphalts, and coal, and that are obtained esp. from chlorophyll or from hemoglobin

porphyrine *n* -S [Gk *porphyra* purple + ISV *-ine*] : an alkaloid $C_{21}H_{25}N_3O_2$ obtained as a bitter amorphous powder from Australian fever bark

por·phy·rin·uria \,==rə'n(y)u̇rēə\ *n* -S [NL, fr. ISV *porphyrin* + NL *-uria*] : the presence of porphyrin in the urine

por·phyr·io \pȯ(r)'firē,ō\ *n* [NL, fr. L *porphyrion-, porphyrio* water hen, fr. Gk *porphyriōn*, fr. *porphyra* purple] **1** *cap* : a genus of birds (family Rallidae) consisting of the Old World purple gallinules **2** -S : any bird of the genus *Porphyrio*

por·phy·rite \'pȯ(r)fə,rīt\ *n* -S [L *porphyrites* purple colored stone, porphyry, fr. Gk *porphyritēs (lithos)*, fr. *porphyra* purple + *-itēs*, adj. suffix] **1** : an Egyptian red porphyry **2** : a quartz-free porphyry whose feldspar is plagioclase

por·phy·rit·ic \,==¦rid·ik\ *adj* [ML *porphyriticus*, fr. Gk *porphyritikos*, fr. *porphyritēs (lithos)* porphyry + *-ikos* -ic] **1** : of or relating to porphyry ⟨a ~ column⟩ **2** : having distinct crystals (as of feldspar, quartz, or augite) in a relatively fine-grained base that is often aphanitic, cryptocrystalline, or glassy — compare GROUNDMASS, PHENOCRYST — **por·phy·rit·i·cal·ly** \-d·ək(ə)lē\ *adv*

por·phyro·blast \pȯ(r)'firə,blast, 'pȯ(r)fərō,b-\ *n* [Gk *porphyra* purple + ISV *-blast*] : METACRYST — **por·phyro·blas·tic** \¦==¦blastik, ¦===¦-\ *adj*

por·phyro·gene \=ˈ==,jēn, '===,-\ *n* -S [by shortening & alter.] : PORPHYROGENITE

por·phy·rog·e·nite \,pȯ(r)fə'räjə,nīt, -fərō'je,n-\ *or* **por·phy·ro·gen·i·tus** \-fərō'jenəd·əs\ *n, pl* **porphyrogenites** \-,nīts\ *or* **porphyrogeni·ti** \-,nə,tī\ [ML *porphyrogenitus*, fr. MGk *porphyrogennētos*, fr. Gk *porphyra* purple + *gennētos* born, fr. *gennan* to bear; akin to Gk *gignesthai* to be born — more at KIN] : a son born after the accession of his father to the throne : one born in the purple

por·phy·roid \'pȯ(r)fə,rȯid\ *n* -S [*porphyry* + *-oid*] : a more or less schistose metamorphic igneous or sedimentary rock with porphyritic texture

por·phy·rop·sin \,pȯ(r)fə'räpsən\ *n* -S [Gk *porphyra* purple + E *-opsin*] : a purple pigment in the retinal rods of freshwater fishes that resembles rhodopsin both biologically and chemically and differs structurally only in having an additional double bond in the molecule and that is bleached by light to opsin and the retinene related to vitamin A_2 and is regenerated in the dark

por·phy·rous \'pȯ(r)fərəs\ *adj* [Gk *-porphyros* having a purple color, fr. *porphyra* purple] : PURPLE

por·phyr·oxine \¦pȯ(r)fə¦rä+,-\ *n* [Gk *porphyra* purple + E *oxine*] : a crystalline opium alkaloid $C_{19}H_{23}NO_4$ whose solutions in dilute acid turn red on exposure to air

por·phyr·u·la \pȯ(r)'fir(y)ələ\ *n, cap* [NL, fr. Gk *porphyra* purple + NL *-ula*] : a genus of birds (family Rallidae) including the African and American purple gallinules

por·phy·ry \'pȯ(r)fərē, -ri\ *n* -ES [ME *porfurie*, fr. (assumed) AF *porfirie*, fr. ML *porphyrium*, alter. of L *porphyrites* — more at PORPHYRITE] **1 a** : an Egyptian rock consisting of feldspar crystals embedded in a compact dark red or purple groundmass much used by the ancient Romans — compare PORPHYRITE **b** : any igneous rock of porphyritic texture regardless of its mineral composition **c** : an igneous rock containing two generations of the same mineral with the minerals of one generation usu. distinctly larger than those of the other **d** : any of various igneous rocks without porphyritic texture that occur in connection with ores **2** *obs* : a porphyry slab; *esp* : one used for triturating drugs **3** *West* : PORPHYRY COPPER — usu. used in pl.

porphyry copper *n, West* : a large low-grade disseminated copper deposit

porphyry shell *n* : an olive shell (*Oliva porphyria*) having a dark-red or brown polished surface with light spots

por·pi·ta \'pȯ(r)pəd·ə\ *n, cap* [NL, fr. Gk *porpē* brooch; prob. akin to Gk *peirein* to pierce, *peran* to pass through — more at FARE] : a genus of small bright-colored siphonophores that float in the warmer parts of the ocean and have a large feeding zooid and a float in the center surrounded by smaller nutritive and reproductive zooids and by slender dactylozooids near the margin — **por·pi·toid** \-)pə,tȯid\ *adj or n*

1por·poise \'pȯrpəs, -ōəp-\ *n* -S [ME *porpeys, porpoys*, fr. MF *porpeis, porpois*, fr. ML *porcopiscus*, fr. L *porcus* pig + *piscis* fish — more at FARROW, FISH] **1** : any of various small gregarious toothed whales of the genus *Phocaena* having a blunt rounded snout that does not form a projecting beak; *esp* : a common toothed whale (*P. phocaena*) of the north Atlantic and Pacific that is 5 to 8 feet long and usu. blackish above and whitish below — called also *harbor porpoise*; compare DOLPHIN 1a **2** : any of various small toothed cetaceans; *esp* : any such cetacean with a short beak (as a member of the genus *Cephalorhynchus* of the southern hemisphere) **3** : any of several dolphins (as the common dolphin or the bottle-nosed dolphins) **4** : a synchronized swimming stunt consisting of a headfirst surface dive executed in either pike or tuck position to a point of complete vertical submergence

2porpoise \"\ *vi* -ED/-ING/-S **1** : to leap or plunge like a porpoise ⟨penguins *porpoised* away on all sides —*Nat'l Geographic*⟩ **2** *of an underwater craft or object* : to break the surface of the water : BROACH **3** *of an airplane or surface craft* : to slap the surface : SKIP

porpoise oil *n* : a pale yellow fatty oil obtained from the body, head, or jaw of a porpoise and used esp. as a fine lubricant — compare DOLPHIN OIL

porpoise whale *n* : a New Zealand ziphioid whale (*Berardius arnuxi*)

por·po·rate \'pȯ(r)pərət\ *adj* [It *porporato*, fr. L *purpuratus*, fr. *purpura* purple + *-atus* -ate — more at PURPLE] : clad in purple

por·ra·ceous \(')pȯ¦rāshəs, pə'r-\ *adj* [L *porraceus*, fr. *porrum* leek + *-aceus* -aceous; akin to Gk *prason* leek] : having the clear light green color of leek leaves

1por·rect \pə'rekt, pȯ'r-\ *vt* -ED/-ING/-S [ME *porrecten*, fr. L *porrectus*, past part. of *porrigere* to stretch out, extend, fr. *por-* (akin to L *per* through) + *regere* to direct — more at FARE, RIGHT] **1** *archaic* : to put forward : stretch out : EXTEND **2** : PRESENT, TENDER **3** *admiralty law* : to produce for examination (as a bill of costs) — **por·rec·tion** \-kshən\ *n* -S

2porrect \"\ *adj* [L *porrectus*] : extended forward : stretched out

por·ret \'pȯrət\ *n* -S [ME *poret*, fr. OF, fr. L *porrum* leek + OF *-et* — more at PORRACEOUS] **1** *chiefly dial* : LEEK, SCALLION **2** *chiefly dial* : a small onion **3** : LEEK 2b

por·ridge \'pȯrij, 'pär-, -rēj\ *n* -S [alter. (prob. influenced by ME *porray*, a kind of pottage, fr. MF *poree*, fr. ML *porrata*, fr. L *porrum* leek + LL *-ata* -ade) of *pottage*] **1** : a soup of meat and vegetables often thickened with barley or other cereal **2** : a soft food made by boiling meal of grains or legumes in milk or water until thick ⟨oatmeal ~⟩ ⟨bean ~⟩ **3** : HODGEPODGE ⟨contemporary playwrights . . . produce only the thinnest ~ when they turn to undramatic prose —John Mason Brown⟩

por·ridgy \-jē,-ji\ *adj* : of, relating to, or resembling porridge ⟨a ~ modern wallpaper —Jan Struther⟩

por·rin·ger \-rənjə(r)\ *n* -S [alter. of *pottinger*] **1** : a dish for porridge or similar food; *esp* : a low one-handled usu. metal bowl or cup from which children eat or are fed ⟨a silver ~⟩ **2** : a hat or cap that resembles a porringer

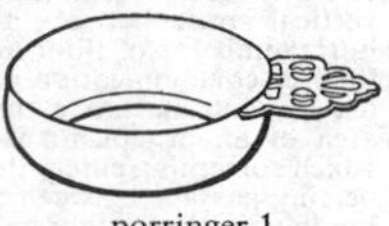

porringer 1

por·ritch \-rich\ *chiefly Scot var of* PORRIDGE

por·ro prism \'pȯ(,)rō-\ *n, usu cap 1st P* [after Ignazio *Porro* †1875 Ital. engineer] : an optical device that inverts and reverses right and left an image viewed through it, that consists usu. of a pair of isosceles right-angled prisms so arranged that a beam of light entering the hypotenuse face of one is totally reflected twice before emerging at the same face and entering the second prism at its hypotenuse face and being again doubly reflected, and that makes possible a shortening of the physical length of the instrument in which it is used — see PRISM BINOCULAR

1port \'pō(ə)r\|t, -ȯ(ə)r\|, -ōə\|, -ȯ(ə)\|, *usu* \|d· +V\ *n* -S [ME, partly fr. OE (fr. L *portus* passage, house door, port); partly fr. OF, fr. L *portus* — more at FORD] **1 a** : a place where ships may ride secure from storms : HARBOR, HAVEN ⟨wonder if so small a barque can . . . make the ~ —E.J.Schoettle⟩ **b** (1) : REFUGE (2) : DESTINATION, GOAL **2 a** : a harbor town or city where ships may take on or discharge cargo : the starting point or the destination of a voyage : a place to or from which goods may be shipped **b** : the entire geographical harbor area of a place ⟨the ~ of San Francisco⟩ **c** : AIRPORT ⟨the ~ is free of obstructions — no mountains or tall buildings impede an approach or takeoff —Cornelius Ryan⟩ **3** : PORT OF ENTRY **syn** see HARBOR

2port \"\ *vt* -ED/-ING/-S **1** *obs* : to make port at **2** *obs* : to bring to port

3port \"\ *n* -S [ME *port, porte*, fr. MF *porte* gate, door, fr. L *porta* passage, gate; akin to L *portus* passage, port — more at FORD] **1** *chiefly Scot* : GATE, PORTAL; *esp* : a city gate **2** *chiefly Scot* : a market for hiring of laborers usu. held near the gate of a town **3** : an opening or passageway between two woods or stones or between a wood and the jack in lawn bowling or curling **4** : an upward curve or tongue groove in the mouthpiece of some bits to put pressure on the sensitive bars of a horse's mouth **5 a** : an opening for intake or exhaust of air, gas, steam, water, or other fluid esp. in a valve seat or valve face **b** : the area of opening in a cylinder face of a passageway for the working fluid in an engine **c** : any such passageway connecting the cylinder with the cylinder face or the latter with the exhaust **6 a** : an opening in a ship's side to admit light or air or to load cargo : PORTHOLE **b** *archaic* : the shutter or cover for a porthole **7 a** : an opening in the receiver of a firearm through which empty shells are ejected **b** : an opening in some repeating firearms through which cartridges are loaded into the magazine **8** : a hole or slit in an armored vehicle or fortification through which guns may be fired

4port \"\ *n* -S [ME, fr. MF, fr. *porter* to carry, bear] **1** : the manner in which one bears himself : BEARING, DEMEANOR, MIEN ⟨pride in their ~, defiance in their eye, I see the lords of humankind pass by —Oliver Goldsmith⟩ **2** *archaic* : manner or style of living : DIGNITY, STATE **3** *obs* : the action of carrying mail or the fee for it : POSTAGE **4** : the position in which a military weapon is carried when ported

5port \"\ *vb* -ED/-ING/-S [MF *porter* to carry, fr. L *portare* — more at FARE] *vt, obs* : CARRY, TRANSPORT ~ *vi, of a horse* : to paw the bedding and strike the floor with the forefeet — often used with *back*

6port \"\ *n* -S [prob. fr. ¹*port* or ³*port* (porthole)] : the left side of a ship or airplane looking forward : LARBOARD — opposed to *starboard*

7port \"\ *vt* -ED/-ING/-S : to turn or put (a helm or rudder) to the left

8port \"\ *adj* : of, relating to, or situated to port

9port \"\ *n* -S [fr. *Oporto, O Porto* (now Porto), city in Portugal] **1** : a fortified sweet wine of rich taste and aroma from the valley of the Douro, Portugal — see RUBY PORT, TAWNY PORT, VINTAGE PORT, WHITE PORT **2** : any of numerous wines originating in various parts of the world and resembling the port of Portugal in varying degrees ⟨California ~⟩ **3** : a very dark red that is slightly bluer than mulberry fruit

10port \"\ *n* -S [ScGael] *chiefly Scot* : a tune or air esp. on a bagpipe

11port \"\ *n* -S [by shortening] *Austral* : PORTMANTEAU

port *abbr* **1** portable **2** portfolio **3** portrait

por·ta \'pōrd·ə\ *n, pl* **por·tae** \-d·,ē, -d·,ī\ [NL, fr. L, gate — more at FORD] : HILUM 2a; *specif* : the transverse fissure of the liver — called also *porta hepatis*

por·ta·bil·i·ty \,pōr|d·ə'biləd·ē, ,pȯ(r)|, ,pōə|, |tə-, -lətē, -i\ *n* -ES : the quality or state of being portable

1por·ta·ble \'==bəl\ *adj* [ME, fr. MF, fr. LL *portabilis*, fr. L *portare* to carry + *-abilis* -able — more at FARE] **1** : capable of being carried : easily or conveniently transported ⟨light or manageable enough to be readily moved ⟨a ~ grill⟩ ⟨a ~ power drill⟩ **2** *obs* **a** : BEARABLE, SUPPORTABLE **b** : NAVIGABLE — **por·ta·bly** \-blē,-bli\ *adv*

2portable \"\ *n* -S : something portable: as **a** : a portable schoolhouse or other building **b** : a portable typewriter **c** : a portable radio or television set

por·ta·ble·ness *n* -ES : PORTABILITY

por·ta·caval \;pōrd·ə+\ *also* **por·to·caval** \-rd·(,)ō+\ *adj* [²*portal* + *caval*] : extending from the portal vein to the vena cava

portacaval shunt *n* : a surgical shunt by which the portal vein is made to empty into the caval vein in order to bypass a damaged liver

portable b

por·ta cipher \'pōrd·ə-\ *n, usu cap P* [after Giambattista della *Porta* †1615 Ital. physicist] : polyalphabetic substitution with reciprocal alphabets formed by sliding the second half of a normal alphabetic sequence against the first half

1por·tage \'pōr|d·ij, 'pȯr|, 'pōə|, 'pȯ(ə)|, |t|, |ēj; *also* (')=;täzh, -täzh\ *n* -S [ME, fr. MF, fr. *porter* to carry + *-age* — more at PORT] **1** : the labor of carrying or transporting ⟨force the proud young men, who ought to be warriors, to do ~, always considered woman's work —H.R.Collins⟩ **2 a** *obs* : a ship's burden : TONNAGE **b** *obs* : CARGO, FREIGHT **c** *archaic* : the cost of carriage : PORTERAGE 2 **3 a** *obs* : cargo carried for a sailor joining in a common adventure in lieu of all or part of his wages **b** *obs* : the space allotted for such cargo **c** *archaic* : a sailor's wages **4 a** : the carrying of boats or goods overland from one river or lake to another or around a rapids ⟨had to be carried over a canoe route 800 miles long with some 40 or more ~s —J.D.Leechman⟩ — called also *haulover* **b** : the route followed in making such a transfer ⟨a modest military post was established to protect the ~ —*Amer. Guide Series: La.*⟩

2portage \"\ *vb* -ED/-ING/-S *vt* : to make a portage with : CARRY, PACK ⟨where the falls were too angry we *portaged* our gear —Farley Mowat⟩ ~ *vi* : to make a portage ⟨we *portaged* six times —*Alaska Sportsman*⟩

por·ta·gue \'pōrd·ə,gyü\ *n* -S [irreg. fr. *portuguese*] : a Portuguese gold coin of the 16th century

por·tail \(')pōr¦tā(ə)l\ *n* -S [F, fr. MF *portal*] : PORTAL 2 a

1por·tal \'pōr|d·ᵊl, 'pȯr|, 'pōə|, 'pȯ(ə)|, |tᵊl\ *n* -S [ME, fr. MF, fr. ML *portale* city gate, porch, fr. neut. of *portalis* of a gate, fr. L *porta* gate + *-alis* -al — more at FORD] **1** : DOOR, GATE, ENTRANCE; *esp* : a grand or imposing one **2 a** : the whole architectural composition surrounding and including the doorways and porches of a church ⟨the church door ... is set in a remarkable ~ —M.C.A.Henniker⟩ **b** : a large roofed opening in a Spanish-American building : PORCH **c** : the corner of a room separated by wainscoting to form a short passage to another room **3 a** : the space between the first two principal trusses at each end of a trussed bridge **b** : any vertical space between two uprights included between two horizontals (as of floor and ceiling) which must be kept open for free communication in a building of skeleton construction **c** : the entrance to a tunnel **4** : a communicating part or area of an organism: as **a** : PORTAL VEIN **b** : the point at which something enters the body ⟨~s of infection⟩ **c** : the connecting passage between foregut and midgut and midgut and hindgut in the vertebrate embryo

2portal \"\ *adj* [NL *porta* + E *-al*] **1** : of or relating to the transverse fissure on the underside of the liver where most of the vessels enter **2** : of, relating to, carried out by, or being any large vein that collects blood from one part of the body and distributes it in another part through a capillary network — see PORTAL VEIN, RENAL PORTAL VEIN

por·taled *or* **por·talled** \-ᵊld\ *adj* [¹*portal* + *-ed*] : having a portal

portal hypertension *n* [²*portal*] : hypertension produced by the pressure from accumulated blood in the portal system usu. associated with cirrhotic changes in the liver and accompanied by the formation of hemorrhagic varices in the esophagus

portal system *n* : a system of veins that begins and ends in capillaries — compare PORTAL, PORTAL VEIN

portal-to-portal \;==;==\ *also* **portal** *adj* [¹*portal*] : of or relating to the time spent by a workman in traveling from the entrance to his employer's property to his actual working place (as in a mine) and in returning after the work shift ⟨the basic work day was materially shortened by payment for travel time under the *portal-to-portal* principle —G.W. Stocking⟩

portal vein *n* [²*portal*] : a large vein formed by fusion of other veins that terminates in a capillary network and delivers blood to some area other than the heart; *specif* : a vein carrying blood from the digestive organs and spleen to the liver where the nutrients such blood carries are altered by liver cells before passing into the systemic circulation — called also *hepatic portal vein;* see RENAL PORTAL VEIN

por·ta·men·to \,pōrd·ə'men(,)tō\ *n, pl* **porta·men·ti** \-n(,)tē\ [It, lit., act of carrying, fr. *portare* to carry (fr. L) + *-mento* -ment — more at FARE] **1** : a continuous glide effected by the voice, a trombone, or a bowed stringed musical instrument in passing from one tone to another **2** : PORTATO

por·tance \'pōrtᵊn(t)s\ *n* -S [MF, fr. *porter* to carry + *-ance* — more at PORT] *archaic* : BEARING, CARRIAGE, DEMEANOR

port arms *n* [fr. the imper. phrase *port, arms*] : a position in the manual of arms in which the rifle is held diagonally in front of the body so that the barrel is at the left shoulder — often used as a command

port ar·thur \(')pōrd·¦ärthər\ *adj, usu cap P&A* [fr. *Port Arthur*, city in Manchuria] : of or from the city of Port Arthur, now forming part of Port Arthur-Dairen, Manchuria : of the kind or style prevalent in Port Arthur

port arms

por·ta·tile \'pōrd·ə,tīl\ *adj* [ML *portatilis*, fr. L *portatus* (past. part. of *portare* to carry) + *-ilis* -ile — more at FARE] : PORTABLE — used of an altar

por·ta·tive \'pōrd·əd·iv\ *adj* [ME *portatif*, fr. MF, fr. L *portatus* + *-if* -ive] : PORTABLE ⟨the ~ harp and chime —Virgil Thomson⟩

portative organ *n* : a small portable pipe organ formerly used in processions

por·ta·to \pōr'täd·(,)ō\ *n* -S [It, fr. *portato* (past part. of *portare* to carry), fr. L *portatus* — more at PORTATILE] : semidetached phrasing in musical performance

port-au-prince \,pōrd·(,)ō¦prin(t)s, -¦praⁿs\ *adj, usu cap both Ps* [fr. *Port-au-Prince*, capital of Haiti] : of or from Port-au-Prince, the capital of Haiti : of the kind or style prevalent in Port-au-Prince

port authority *n* [¹*port*] : a governmental commission empowered to manage or construct port facilities

port bow *n* [⁸*port*] : the port surface of a ship's hull that curves inward to the stem — distinguished from *starboard bow*

port captain *n* [¹*port*] : an official of a steamship line responsible for its ships during their stay in port

port charge *n* : a fixed charge (as wharfage, towage, pilotage) against a ship or its cargo in port

port·crayon \(')pōrt+\ *n* [F *porte-crayon*, fr. *porter* to carry + *crayon* — more at PORT] *archaic* : a metal holder for a drawing or writing crayon

1port·cul·lis \pōrt'kələs\ *n* -ES [ME *portculis, port colice*, fr. MF *porte coleice*, fr. OF — more at COULISSE] **1** : a large grating of iron bars or heavy timbers suspended by chains over the gateway of a fortified place and lowered between grooves to prevent passage **2** : a portcullis or a lattice used as a heraldic charge **3** : a silver halfpenny issued by Elizabeth I in 1599 having a portcullis on the obverse

portcullis 1

2portcullis \"\ *vt* -ED/-ING/-ES : to furnish or close with or as if with a portcullis : BAR, SHUT

portcullis money *n* : English silver coins (crowns, half crowns, shillings, sixpence) of the reign of Elizabeth I struck for the East India Company and having a figure of a portcullis on the reverse

port de bras \;pōrdə¦brä\ *n* [F, lit., carriage of the arm] : the practice and technique of arm movement in ballet

port differential *n* [¹*port*] : a differential between the freight rate from an inland point to a port and that to another port established as a basing point

port du sa·lut \;pōrdəsə¦lü, -,sa¦-\ *n, usu cap P&S* [F *port-salut*, fr. *Port du Salut*, Trappist abbey in northwest France] : TRAPPIST CHEESE

porte co·chere \;pōrtkō¦she(ə)r\ *n* -S [F *porte cochère*, lit. coach door] **1** *archaic* : a passageway through a building or screen-wall designed to let vehicles pass from the street to an interior courtyard **2** : CARRIAGE PORCH

port·ed \'pōrd·əd\ *adj* [³*port* + *-ed*] **1 a** : provided with a port **b** : shut in or closed by a gate **2** [fr. past part. of ⁵*port*] : held in the position of port — ⟨standing with rifles ~⟩

porte·feuille \;pōrd·ə;fər(·)\ *n* -S [F, fr. *porter* to carry + *feuille* leaf, sheet — more at PORT, FOIL] *archaic* : PORTFOLIO

port eg·mont hen \-'eg,mänt-\ *n, usu cap P&E* [fr. *Port Egmont*, Falkland islands] : a large skua (*Catharacta skua antarctica*) of the southern hemisphere

port eliz·a·beth \,pōrd·ᵊl¦iz(ə)bəth\ *adj, usu cap P&E* [fr. *Port Elizabeth*, city in southern Union of So. Africa] : of or from the city of Port Elizabeth, Union of So. Africa : of the kind or style prevalent in Port Elizabeth

porte-monnaie \'pōrt,mənē, =¦==; ¦pōrt_mo¦nā\ *n* -S [F, fr. *porter* to carry + *monnaie* coined money, fr. MF *moneie* — more at PORT, MONEY] : a small pocketbook or purse

por·tend \(')pȯr¦tend, (')pȯ(ə)¦t- *also* (')pōr¦t- *or* (')pōə¦t-\ *vt* -ED/-ING/-S [ME *portenden*, fr. L *portendere* to foretell, predict, fr. *por-* (akin to L *per* through) + *tendere* to stretch — more at FARE, TEND] **1** : to give an omen or anticipatory sign of : BODE, PRESAGE ⟨~ at least the beginnings of tax relief for small business —*Nation's Business*⟩ ⟨that the appearance of the black pig ~s serious trouble in Ireland is generally believed —*Irish Digest*⟩ **2** : FORECAST, PREDICT ⟨where this process will stop no one can ~ —D.M.Friedenberg⟩ **3** : INDICATE, MEAN, SIGNIFY ⟨perhaps the present concern with the values of liberal arts education ... ~s an intellectual anemia —Ann Spinney⟩ **4** [F *pourtendre*, fr. MF *portendre*, modif. of L *protendere*, fr. *pro* forth, before + *tendere* to stretch — more at FOR] *obs* : to stretch out before : EXTEND **syn** see FORETELL

por·tent \'=,tent *sometimes* =¦=\ *n* -S [L *portentum*, fr. neut. of *portentus*, past part. of *portendere* to portend] **1** : something that foreshadows a coming event : OMEN, SIGN ⟨it is only natural that ~s should play a large part in the activities of crabbers, oystermen, and fishermen —*Amer. Guide Series: Md.*⟩ ⟨a hopeful ~ of the scope of discussion that may be expected to develop —Vera M. Dean⟩ **2** : prophetic indication, meaning, or significance ⟨something not yet clearly to be seen, but at least of hopeful ~ in the changing world —Martin Flavin⟩ **3** : MARVEL, PRODIGY, WONDER ⟨the old maps ... and their ~s and monsters of the deep —Van Wyck Brooks⟩

portentive *adj* [L *portentus* + E *-ive*] *obs* : PORTENTOUS

por·ten·tous \(')=¦tentəs, *sometimes* ÷ -nchəs\ *adj* [L *portentosus*, fr. *portentum* portent + *-osus* -ous] **1** : of, relating to, or constituting a portent : pregnant with consequence or possibility ⟨the events under discussion are ~ —Philip Hamburger⟩ **2** : eliciting amazement or wonder : MARVELOUS, MONSTROUS, PRODIGIOUS ⟨the extraordinary old man gave him a second ~ wink —J.C.Powys⟩ **3** : exhibiting gravity or ponderousness : self-consciously weighty : INFLATED, POMPOUS ⟨a voice that manages to be both cozy and ~ —Gilbert Seldes⟩ ⟨regarded all these things with a ~ solemnity —H.G. Wells⟩ ⟨the style is so ~ that one expects up to the last paragraph that something of moment is about to be revealed —Dachine Rainer⟩ **syn** see OMINOUS

por·ten·tous·ly *adv* : in a portentous manner ⟨~, ... the panting engines began to roll slowly toward each other —*Time*⟩

por·ten·tous·ness *n* -ES : the quality or state of being portentous

por·te·ous roll \'pōrtēəs-\ *or* **porteous** *n* -ES [ME *porthors, portous, portes*, portable breviary, manual, fr. OF *portehors*, fr. *porter* to carry + *hors* out, fr. L *foris;* akin to L *fores* door — more at PORT, DOOR] *Scots law* : a roll of offenders formerly prepared by the justice clerk

1por·ter \'pōr|d·ər, 'pȯr|d·ər, 'pōə|d·ər, 'pȯ(ə)|d·ə(r, |tə-\ *n* -S [ME, fr. OF *portier*, fr. LL *portarius*, fr. L *porta* gate + *-arius* -ary — more at FORD] **1** *chiefly Brit* : a person stationed at a door or gate to admit or assist those entering ⟨at the entrance to the office block was a ~ in a blue uniform —F.W.Crofts⟩ **2** : DOORKEEPER 2

2porter \"\ *n* -S [ME *portour*, fr. MF *porteour*, fr. LL *portator*, fr. L *portatus* (past part. of *portare* to carry) + *-or* — more at FARE] **1** : one who carries burdens: as **a** : one who is employed to carry baggage for patrons at a hotel or transportation terminal **b** : a handler of cargo **c** *archaic* : one that conveys or carries something (as news or disease) **2** : a parlor-car or sleeping-car attendant who waits on passengers and makes up berths **3** [short for *porter's beer;* fr. its originally having been made for porters] : a weak stout that is rich in saccharine matter and contains about four percent of alcohol **4 a** *archaic* : any of various mechanical devices (as a lever or a wheeled carriage) for lifting, supporting, or moving **b** : a bar of iron or steel at the end of which a forging is made **5** *Scot* : ²BEER **6** : one who does routine cleaning of the premises, furniture, and equipment of a store, bank, school, or office building or cleans the working areas in a mill or factory **7** : BULL COOK

3porter \"\ *vb* -ED/-ING/-S *vt* : to transport or carry as or by a porter ~ *vi* : to act as a porter

por·ter·age \-ərij\ *n* -S [²*porter* + *-age*] **1** : the occupation or work of a porter : the carrying of things by human labor **2** : the charge for transportation by porter

porteress *var of* PORTRESS

porterhouse \'==,=\ *n* [²*porter* + *house*] **1** *archaic* : a house where porter and other malt liquors are sold **2** *also* **porterhouse steak** : a large steak cut from the thick end of the short loin and containing a T-shaped bone and a large piece of tenderloin — compare T-BONE; see BEEF illustration

porterly *adj* [²*porter* + *-ly*] *obs* : of, relating to, or resembling a porter : RUDE, VULGAR

porter's chair *n* [¹*porter*] : a chair with its back rising to form a hood and its sides enclosed against drafts

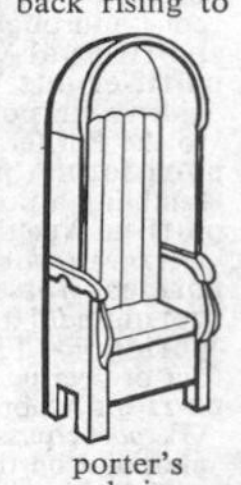
porter's chair

portesse *n* -S [alter. of ME *portes* — more at PORTEOUS ROLL] *obs* : BREVIARY 2a

portfire \'=,=\ *n* [part trans. of F *porte-feu* fr. *porter* to carry + *feu* fire — more at PORT] : a fuze or match for firing guns or fireworks: as **a** : a paper case filled with a composition of niter, sulfur, and mealed powder **b** : a slow-burning fuze (as a billet of wood impregnated with potassium nitrate) or an incendiary cord or tube for igniting fuzes of blasting charges

port·fo·lio \pōrt'fōlē,ō, pȯrt-, pōət-, pȯ(ə)t-, -fōl(,)yō\ *n* [alter. of earlier *porto folio*, modif. of It *portafoglio*, fr. *portare* to carry + *foglio* leaf, sheet, fr. L *folium* leaf — more at PORTAMENTO, BLADE] **1** : a flat portable case (as a briefcase, a large heavy envelope, or a loose-leaf binder) for carrying papers or drawings **2** [so called fr. the use of such a case to carry documents of state] : the office and functions of a minister of state or member of a cabinet ⟨received the ~ of war⟩ **3** : the securities held by an investor or the commercial paper held by a bank or other financial house ⟨expanded the mortgage ~⟩

portfolio investment *n* : investment by purchase of securities — contrasted with *direct investment*

portgrave *or* **portgreve** *var of* PORTREEVE

por·thet·ria \pȯ(r)'thetrēə\ *n, cap* [NL, fr. Gk *porthein* to destroy, ravage + *-tria*, fem. agent suffix; akin to Gk *perthein* to destroy, ravage — more at BOARD] : a genus of Lymantriidae including the gypsy moth

por·theus \'pōrthēəs, -,th(y)üs\ *n, cap* [NL, fr. Gk *porthein* + *-eus*, agent suffix] : a genus of extinct Cretaceous isospondylous fishes notable for their great size and strong teeth

porthole \'=,=\ *n* [³*port* + *hole*] **1** : an opening (as a window) in the side of a ship or airplane **2** : an embrasure or loophole through which to shoot **3** : ³PORT 5

por·tia tree \'pōrshə-\ *n, sometimes cap P* [Tamil *puraśu*] : a tropical tree (*Thespesia populnea*) that is closely related to the majaguas, has rounded cordate leaves and showy yellow and purple flowers, yields a valuable pinkish to dark red close-textured wood resistant to warping and an oil from its seeds, and is sometimes cultivated as an ornamental — called also *bendy tree, seaside mahoe, tulip tree*

por·ti·co \'pōrd|ə,kō, 'pȯr|, 'pōə|, 'pȯ|, |t|, |ē,-\ *n, pl* **porticoes** *or* **porticos** [It, fr. L *porticus* — more at PORCH] : a colonnade or covered ambulatory esp. in classical architecture and usu. at the entrance of a building **syn** see BALCONY

por·ti·coed \-ōd\ *adj* [*portico* + *-ed*] : having a portico

por·ti·cus \-,kəs\ *n* -ES [L] *archaic* : PORTICO

por·tiere \;pōr|d·ē;e(ə)r, (')pōr|;ti(ə)r, 'pōr|d·ēər, (')pōr|-;tye(ə)r, -pȯr|, -pōə|, -pȯ(ə)|, -eə,-iə,-ēə\ *n* -S [F *portière*, fr. fem. of OF *portier* doorkeeper — more at PORTER] : a curtain hanging across a doorway

por·ti·fo·ri·um \,pōrd·ə'fōrēəm\ *n, pl* **portiforiums** \-ēəmz\ *or* **portifo·ria** \-ēə\ [ML, fr. L *portare* to carry + *foris* out; akin to L *fores* door — more at FARE, DOOR] : BREVIARY 2a

porting *n* -S [³*port* + *-ing*] : the provision or arrangement of intake or exhaust openings or other ports on an engine

por·tio \'pōrshē,ō, -rd·ē-\ *n, pl* **porti·o·nes** \,pōrshē'ō(,)nēz, ,pōrd·ē'ō,nās\ [NL *portion-, portio*, fr. L, portion] : PART, SEGMENT, DIVISION ⟨the visible ~ of the cervix⟩

1por·tion \'pōrshən, -ȯr-, -ōə-, -ȯ(ə)-\ *n* -S [ME, fr. OF, fr. L *portion-, portio;* akin to L *part-, pars* part] **1** : an individual's part or share of something: as **a** : a share of an estate received by gift or inheritance ⟨Father, give me the ~ of goods that falleth to me —Lk 15: 12 (AV)⟩ **b** : DOWER 2a **c** : enough food to serve one person at one meal or enough of one kind for a helping ⟨individual ~s of meat were precisely weighed out in the restaurant kitchen⟩ **2** : the share of an individual or group in human fortune or destiny : LOT, FATE ⟨the preacher had told him hell would be his ~ —J.L.Lowes⟩ **3 a** : a part of a whole ⟨~s of this park are particularly well-adapted for picnic and camping purposes —*Amer. Guide Series: Md.*⟩ **b** : a limited amount or quantity ⟨the major ~ of our fears would be at an end —J.C.Fitzmaurice⟩ **4** : the weekly selection of the Pentateuch read in a synagogue — compare PARASHAH **syn** see FATE, PART

2portion \"\ *vt* **portioned**; **portioned**; **portioning** \-sh(ə)niŋ\ **portions** [ME *portionen*, fr. MF *portionner*, fr. OF *portion* share, portion] **1** : to divide into portions : distribute in shares **2** : to allot or give to as a portion : DOWER, ENDOW **syn** see APPORTION

portional *adj* [ME, fr. LL *portionalis* partial, fr. L *portion-, portio* portion + *-alis* -al] **1** *obs* : PARTIAL **2** [¹*portion* + *-al*] *obs* : of, relating to, or constituting a portion or dowry

por·tion·er \-sh(ə)nə(r)\ *n* -S [partly fr. ²*portion* + *-er*, partly fr. ¹*portion* + *-er*] : one that portions or has a portion: as **a** *Scots law* : the owner of a portion of a decedent's estate : a small laird — see HEIR PORTIONER **b** : PORTIONIST 2

por·tion·ist \-sh(ə)nəst\ *n* -S [ML *portionista*, fr. L *portion-, portio* portion + *-ista* -ist] **1** : POSTMASTER 3 **2** : an incumbent of a benefice shared by two or more clergymen

por·tion·less \-shənləs\ *adj* : having no portion; *esp* : having no dowry or inheritance

portion natural *n* [¹*portion* + *natural*, adj.] *Scots law* : a child's legitim

port jack·son fig \-'jaksən-\ *n, usu cap P&J* [fr. *Port Jackson*, New So. Wales, Australia] : an Australian fig (*Ficus rubiginosa*) resembling the banyan, sometimes planted for ornament, and introduced into southern Africa for brushwood

port jackson pine *n, usu cap P&J* : an Australian cypress pine (*Callitris cupressiformis*) having globular cones with scales much dilated upward

port jackson shark *n, usu cap P&J* : a shark of the genus *Heterodontus; esp* : a small harmless shark (*H. japonicus*) of Australasian coastal waters that is brown to reddish brown and feeds chiefly on mollusks

port·land \'pōrtlənd, -ȯrt-, -ōət-, -ȯ(ə)t-\ *adj, usu cap* **1** [fr. *Portland*, city in southwest Maine] : of or from the city of Portland, Maine ⟨*Portland* harbor⟩ : of the kind or style prevalent in Portland, Maine **2** [fr. *Portland*, city in northwest Oregon] : of or from the city of Portland, Oreg. : of the kind or style prevalent in Portland, Oreg.

portland arrowroot *or* **portland sago** \"-\ *n, usu cap P* [fr. Isle of *Portland*, peninsula in southern England] **1** : arum from the cuckoopint **2** : CUCKOOPINT

portland blast-furnace slag cement *n* [*portland cement*] : a cement produced by intimately intergrinding a mixture of portland cement clinker and granulated blast-furnace slag in widely varying proportions

portland cement *n* [fr. Isle of *Portland;* fr. its resemblance to Portland stone] : a hydraulic cement made by finely pulverizing the clinker produced by calcining to incipient fusion a mixture of argillaceous and calcareous materials — see ALUMINA CEMENT; compare AIR ENTRAINMENT, NATURAL CEMENT, PORTLAND BLAST-FURNACE SLAG CEMENT

port·land·er \'=ləndə(r)\ *n* -S *cap* [*Portland* + *-er*] : a native or resident of Portland, Oreg. or Portland, Me.

port·land·ite \-,dīt\ *n* -S [*portland* (*cement*) + *-ite*] : CALCIUM HYDROXIDE

portland-pozzolan cement \;==;===-\ *n* [*portland cement* + *pozzolana*] : a portland cement to which pozzolana is added during the grinding of the cement clinker

portland stone *n* [fr. Isle of *Portland*, peninsula in southern England, its locality] **1** *usu cap P* : a yellowish white oolitic building limestone **2** *usu cap P* [fr. *Portland*, town in southern Connecticut, its locality] : a purplish brown sandstone **3** *often cap P* : LIGHT STONE

portland tern *n* : ARCTIC TERN

port·last \'pōrt,last\ *n* -S [origin unknown] : the upper edge of a gunwale : a bulwark rail — called also *portoise*

portledge *n* [alter. (perh. influenced by *privilege*) of *portage*] *obs* : PORTAGE 3

port·let \'=lət\ *n* -S [¹*port* + *-let*] : a small harbor

portlight \'=,=\ *n* [³*port* + *light*] **1** : the glass pane in a ship's porthole **2 :** a glass-paned porthole that admits light but cannot be opened **:** DEADLIGHT

port·li·ness \'pōrtlēnəs, -ȯrt-, -ōət-, -ȯ(ə)t-, -lin-\ *n* -ES **:** the quality or state of being portly

port·ly \-lē,-li\ *adj* [⁴*port* + -*ly*] **1** *chiefly dial* **:** DIGNIFIED, STATELY **2 :** heavy or rotund of body **:** CORPULENT, STOUT ⟨the plump figure and ~ waist were those of a genial and humorous man —J.R.Green⟩ ⟨their history has been padded out in ~ volumes —Edward Clodd⟩ **syn** see FAT

port mac·quar·ie pine \'=mə'kwȯrē-\ *n, usu cap 1st P&M* [fr. *Port Macquarie*, New So. Wales, Australia] **:** an Australian sandarac tree (*Callitris macleayana*)

port·man \'=mən\ *n, pl* **portmen** [ME, fr. OE, fr. ¹*port* + *man*] **:** an inhabitant or burgess of a port

¹**port·man·teau** \pōrt'mant(,)ō, pȯrt-, pōət-,pȯt-, -maan-, -n,tō\ *n, pl* **portmanteaus** *or* **portmanteaux** \-ōz\ [MF *portemanteau*, fr. *porter* to carry + *manteau* mantle, fr. L *mantellum* — more at PORT] **:** TRAVELING BAG; *esp* **:** a large bag of the gladstone type

²**portmanteau** \=ˈ=(,)=, '=,=,=\ *adj* **:** combining more than one use or quality ⟨a ~ signature which covers a husband-and-wife collaboration —George Milburn⟩ ⟨its central character is a ~ figure whose traits are derived from several mythical heroes —D.G.Hoffman⟩

portmanteau word *also* **portmanteau** *n* **1 :** ³BLEND d **2 :** COUNTERWORD

port·man·tle \'pōrt,mant°l, =ˈ=\ *n* [part trans. of F *portmanteau*] *archaic* **:** PORTMANTEAU

port·man·tol·o·gism \,pōrt,man·'tälə,jizəm, -,mən-·\ *n* -S [*portmanteau* (*word*) + *log-* + *-ism*] **:** ³BLEND d

portmantua *n, obs* [by alter.] **:** PORTMANTEAU

port mark *n* [¹*port*] **:** a mark showing the final destination of a shipping package

portmote *or* **portmoot** \'=,=\ *n* [*portmote* fr. ML *portimotus*, fr. OE *port* + *gemōt* gemot; *portmoot* fr. *port* + *moot*] **:** the court of an English borough or seaport; *also* **:** a town administrative assembly

pôrto *adj, usu cap* [Pg] **:** OPORTO

pôr·to ale·gre \'pōrd·ōə'legrə\ *adj, usu cap P&A* [fr. *Pôrto Alegre*, seaport city of southern Brazil] **:** of or from the city of Pôrto Alegre, Brazil **:** of the kind or style prevalent in Pôrto Alegre

portocaval *var of* PORTACAVAL

port of call ['*port*] **1 :** an intermediate port where ships customarily stop for supplies, repairs, or transshipment of cargo **2 :** a stop included on an itinerary; *esp* **:** a place habitually visited

port of discharge : a port where a ship voluntarily and without cause of necessity breaks bulk and discharges part or all of its cargo

port of entry 1 : a place where foreign goods may be cleared through a customhouse **2 :** a place where an alien may be permitted to enter a country

port-of-spain \'==ˈ=\ *adj, usu cap P&S* [fr. *Port of Spain*, seaport in northwest Trinidad] **:** of or from the city of Port of Spain, Trinidad **:** of the kind or style prevalent in Port of Spain

por·toise \'pōrd·əs, -əz\ *n* -S [origin unknown] **:** PORTLAST

por·to·lan \'pōrd·°lən\ *or* **por·tu·lan** \", -rchəl-\ *n* -S [It *portolano*] **:** PORTOLANO

por·to·la·no \,pōrd·°l'ä(,)nō\ *n, pl* **portolanos** \-ōz\ *or* **portola·ni** \-nē\ [It, harbor official, pilot, navigation manual, fr. ML *portulanus*, harbor official, fr. L *portus* port] **:** a medieval navigation manual illustrated with charts

por·to-no·vo \'pōrd·ō'nō(,)vō\ *adj, usu cap P&N* [fr. *Porto-Novo*, seaport town in Dahomey] **:** of or relating to Porto-Novo, the capital of Dahomey **:** of the kind or style prevalent in Porto-Novo

port or·ford cedar \-'ȯ(r)fə(r)d-\ *n, usu cap P&O* [fr. *Port Orford*, Curry co., Oregon] **1 :** a large evergreen timber tree (*Chamaecyparis lawsoniana*) of western No. America occas. with a trunk diameter of 12 feet and often 200 feet high **2 :** the light pale yellow to brown decay-resistant lumber of Port Orford cedar

porto rican *usu cap P&R, var of* PUERTO RICAN

¹**por·trait** \'pōr·trə\|t, 'pȯr-, 'pōə-, 'pȯ(ə)-, -,trā|, *usu* |d.+V\ *vt* -ED/-ING/-S [prob. fr. obs. *portrait* portrayed, fr. ME, fr. MF, past part. of *pourtraire* to portray — more at PORTRAY] *archaic* **:** PORTRAY

²**portrait** *n* -S [MF, fr. past part. of *portraire* to portray] **1 :** PICTURE; *esp* **:** a painting, drawing, or other pictorial representation of a person usu. showing his face ⟨the best-known photographic ~*s* of internationally important personages —*Current Biog.*⟩ **2 :** a sculptured figure **:** BUST, STATUE ⟨has modeled some notable ~*s* of women —*Current Biog.*⟩ **3 :** a visible representation or likeness **:** IMAGE, SIMILITUDE ⟨seemed a veritable ~ of his father⟩ **4 :** a graphic portrayal in words **:** a verbal description ⟨such ~*s* reveal as clearly as the longer poems his weight of intellect —*Ency. Americana*⟩ ⟨show that in the final analysis the primary purpose of fiction is not education, not history, not even a ~ of truth, but the entertainment of the reader —F.O.Baker⟩

portrait attachment *n* **:** an attachment lens used on a fixed-focus camera for photographing near objects

portrait bust *n* **:** a bust representing the actual features of an individual

por·trait·ist \|d·əst, |tə-\ *n* -S [²*portrait* + *-ist*] **:** a maker of portraits (as in painting, photography, or sculpture)

portrait lens *n* **:** a compound photographic lens with a relatively high aperture and usu. a means for softening definition esp. in taking portraits

¹**por·trai·ture** \-·,trə,chů(ə)r, -,chər, -·trə-,tyů(ə)r, -·trə,tů(ə)r, -ùə, -chə\ *n* -S [ME *portreitoure*, fr. MF *portraiture*, fr. *portrait* + *-ure*] **1 :** the making of portraits by painting, drawing, photography, or otherwise **:** PORTRAYAL **2 a :** a portrait in graphic art **b :** a sculptured portrait **3 :** depiction in words **:** verbal description ⟨faithfulness in the . . . ~ depends upon the individual writer's art —Wilfred Partington⟩ **4** *obs* **:** APPEARANCE, FORM, SHAPE

²**portraiture** \"\ *vt* -ED/-ING/-S *archaic* **:** PORTRAY

¹**por·tray** \(')pōr·trā, (')pȯr·,-, (')pōə·;-, (')pȯ(ə)·;- *also* pə(r)·'t-\ *vt* -ED/-ING/-S [ME *portraien*, fr. MF *portraire*, fr. L *protrahere* to draw forth, to reveal, expose, fr. *pro* forth, before + *trahere* to draw — more at FOR, DRAW] **1 :** to represent by drawing, painting, engraving **:** make a picture or image of **:** DELINEATE, DEPICT ⟨~*s* with sure but sparing brush strokes an unforgettable face⟩ **2 a :** to describe in words **:** present a verbal picture of ⟨a novelist who ~*s* life the way most of us see it —Bernice Matlowsky⟩ **b :** to play the role of **:** represent dramatically **:** ENACT ⟨a star who unquestionably conveyed to audiences the very essence of the character he was ~*ing* —J.F. Wharton⟩ **syn** see REPRESENT

²**portray** \", =ˈ=\ *n* -S *archaic* **:** PORTRAYAL, PORTRAIT

por·tray·al \-'trā(ə)l *sometimes* 'pōr,-,, 'pȯr-,-, 'pōə-,-, 'pȯ(ə)-,-\ *n* -S ['*portray* + *-al*] **1 :** the act or process of portraying **:** DESCRIPTION, REPRESENTATION **2 :** PORTRAIT

por·tray·er \(')=·'trāə(r), -re(ə)r, -reə\ *n* -S [ME, fr. *portraien* to portray + *-er*] **:** one that portrays

por·tray·ment \-rāmənt\ *n* -S ['*portray* + *-ment*] **:** PORTRAYAL

port·reeve \'pōrt·,rēv\ *or* **port·grave** \-t,grāv\ *or* **port·greve** \-t,grēv\ *n* -S [*portreeve* fr. ME *portereve, portreve*, fr. OE *portgerēfa*, fr. *port* + *gerēfa* reeve; *portgreve*, ME, alter. (influenced by OE *portgerēfa*) of *portreve*; *portgrave*, alter. (influenced by MD *portgrave* portreeve) of *portgreve*] **1 :** a bailiff or mayor charged with keeping the peace and with other duties in a port or market borough of early England **2 :** the chief officer of a seaport town

por·tress \'pōr·trəs\ *also* **por·ter·ess** \-ōrd·ərəs, -ōr·trəs\ *n* -ES [ME *porteresse*, fr. *porter* + *-esse* -ess] **:** a female porter: as **a :** a doorkeeper in a convent or apartment house **b :** CHARWOMAN

port risk insurance *n* [¹*port*] **:** marine insurance covering a ship while in port

port roy·al·ist \'pōrt·'rȯiələst\ *n, usu cap P&R* [F *port-royaliste*, fr. *Port-Royal*, name of a convent near Versailles, France + *-iste* -ist] **:** a member or adherent of a 17th century French Jansenist lay community distinguished as logicians and educators

ports *pl of* PORT, *pres 3d sing of* PORT

port said \(')=·ˈsīd *also* ˈ=sä;ēd *sometimes* (')=ˈsād\ *adj, usu cap P&S* [fr. *Port Said*, seaport city in northeast Egypt] **:** of or from the city of Port Said, Egypt **:** of the kind or style prevalent in Port Said

port sa·lut \'pōrsə'lü, -,sa'-\ *n, usu cap P&S* [F *port-salut*, fr. *Port du Salut*, Trappist abbey in northwest France] **:** TRAPPIST CHEESE

portside \'=,=\ *adj* [⁸*port* + *side*] **:** LEFT, LEFTIST ⟨the same ~ political tack —*Newsweek*⟩

port·sid·er \"ə(r)\ *n* [⁸*port* + *side* + *-er*] **:** SOUTHPAW

ports·man \'pōrtsmən\ *n, pl* **portsmen** [Cinque *Ports*, group of seaport towns in southeast England + E *man*] **:** an inhabitant or citizen of one of the English Cinque Ports

ports·mouth \'pōrtsməth, -ȯrt-, -ōət-, -ȯ(ə)t-\ *adj, usu cap* [fr. *Portsmouth*, seaport and county borough in southern England] **:** of or from the county borough of Portsmouth, England **:** of the kind or style prevalent in Portsmouth

port speed *n* [¹*port*] **:** the speed with which a ship's cargo is handled

port tack *n* [⁸*port*] **:** the tack on which the wind comes from a sailing ship's port side

por·tu·gais \'pōrchə'gā\ *n* -ES [F, Portuguese, fr. Pg *português*] **:** BLACK ANGELFISH

por·tu·gal \'pōr|chəgəl, 'pȯr|, 'pōə|, 'pȯ(ə)|, -chēg-\ *adj, usu cap* [fr. *Portugal*, country in southwest Europe] **:** of or from Portugal **:** of the kind or style prevalent in Portugal **:** PORTUGUESE

portugal laurel *n, usu cap P* **:** a European evergreen shrub (*Prunus lusitanica*) with handsome foliage and white flowers

por·tu·gee \'pōrd·ə,gē, -d·ē,gē\ *n, usu cap* [back-formation fr. ²*Portuguese*, pl.] *substand* **:** PORTUGUESE

¹**por·tu·guese** \'pōr|chə'gēz, 'pȯr|, 'pōə|, 'pȯ|\ *adj, usu cap* [Pg *português*, fr. *Portugal* + *-ēz* -ese] **1 a :** of, relating to, or characteristic of Portugal **b :** of, relating to, or characteristic of the people of Portugal **2 :** of, relating to, or characteristic of the Portuguese language

²**portuguese** \"\ *n, pl* **portuguese** *cap* **1 a :** a native or inhabitant of Portugal **b :** a person of Portuguese descent **2 :** the Romance language of Portugal and Brazil

portuguese bowline *n, usu cap P* **:** a bowline knot having a large double bight producing two loops often used for hoisting a person as if in a chair seat by running one loop under the arms — called also *French bowline*

Portuguese bowline

portuguese cypress *or* **portuguese cedar** *n, usu cap P* **:** an ornamental Mexican evergreen tree (*Cupressus lusitanica*) long considered a native of southeastern Europe and the Azores and having pendulous branches and appressed acute leaves

portuguese man-of-war *n, usu cap P* **:** any of several large brilliantly colored chiefly tropical siphonophores (genus *Physalia*) that float on the surface of the sea by means of a large bladderlike pneumatophore with a crest like a sail on its upper side and with a cluster of zooids at one side of the lower surface equipped with numerous powerful nematocysts capable of causing serious injury to man and including very long tentacular dactylozooids and much shorter gastrozooids and gonozooids

portuguese man-of-war fish *n, usu cap P* **:** MAN-OF-WAR FISH

portuguese red *n, often cap P* **:** CARTHAMUS RED

por·tu·laca \,pōrchə'lakə *sometimes* -rd·°l'a-\ *n* [NL, fr. L, purslane, fr. *portula*, dim. of *porta* gate; fr. the lid of its capsule that opens like a gate — more at FORD] **1** *cap* **:** a genus of mainly tropical succulent herbs (family Portulacaceae) having usu. yellow, pink, red, white, or purple ephemeral flowers with 4 to 6 petals and a partly inferior one-celled ovary — see PURSLANE **2** -S **:** any plant of the genus *Portulaca*; *esp* **:** a plant (*P. grandiflora*) widely cultivated for its showy flowers

por·tu·la·ca·ce·ae \,==,lə'kāsē,ē\ *n pl, cap* [NL *Portulaca*, type genus + *-aceae*] **:** a family of usu. succulent herbs (order Caryophyllales) having perfect regular flowers with two sepals and 4 to 5 hypogynous petals and a capsular often circumscissile fruit — **por·tu·la·ca·ceous** \'===ˈkāshəs\ *adj*

por·tu·la·car·ia \,==='ka(a)rēə\ *n, cap* [NL, fr. L *portulaca* purslane + *-aria* -ary] **:** a genus of southern African shrubs (family Portulacaceae) with opposite obovate fleshy leaves and small pink flowers clustered in the upper leaf axils

portulan *var of* PORTOLAN

¹**por·tu·nid** \pȯr'tünəd, -r-'tyü-\ *adj* [NL *Portunidae*] **:** of or relating to the Portunidae

²**portunid** \"\ *n* -S **:** a crab of the family Portunidae

por·tu·ni·dae \=ˈ=nə,dē\ *n pl, cap* [NL *Portunus*, type genus + *-idae*] **:** a family of crabs (superfamily Brachyrhyncha) consisting of the swimming crabs and having a subquadrate carapace and the last pair of legs usu. with the terminal joint flattened like a paddle

por·tu·nus \-nəs\ *n, cap* [NL, fr. L, god of harbors] **:** the type genus of the family Portunidae comprising the English lady crab and related forms

port warden *n* [¹*port*] **1** *Brit* **:** an inspector of cargo and stowage **2 :** an administrative officer in charge of the channels, facilities, and traffic of a port **:** HARBOR MASTER

port watch *n* [⁸*port*] **:** the half of a ship's company that alternates with the starboard watch in working the ship in successive daily duty periods

port-wine stain *or* **port-wine mark** \=ˈ=-\ *n* [⁹*port*] **:** a reddish purple superficial hemangioma of the skin commonly occurring as a birthmark; *sometimes* **:** a flat vascular nevus

¹**porty** \'pōrd·ē\ *adj* [⁹*port* + *-y*] **:** of or relating to port wine or suggestive of port drinkers

²**por·ty** \"\ *n* -ES [F *portée*, fr. fem. of past part. of *porter* to carry — more at PORT] **:** a large core print

por·ule \'pōr(,)yül, -r(,)ül\ *n* -S [²*pore* + *-ule*] **:** a small pore — **por·u·lose** \-(y)ə,lōs\ *adj* — **por·u·lous** \-ləs\ *adj*

po·rus \'pōrəs\ *n, pl* **po·ri** \-r,ī\ *or* **poruses** [NL, fr. L, pore] **:** a bodily pore or pit; *esp* **:** one of the pits on the body of an insect connected with the sense organs — compare TRICHOPORE

por·wi·gle \'pȯr,wigəl\ *n* -S [alter. of ME *polwygle* — more at POLLIWOG] **:** TADPOLE

pory \'pōrē\ *adj* [²*pore* + *-y*] *archaic* **:** POROUS

por·za·na \pȯ(r)'zānə, -zänə\ *n, cap* [NL, fr. It, crake] **:** a genus of small short-billed rails including the sora

pos *abbr* **1** position **2** positive **3** possession **4** possessive

po·sa·da \pō'sädə, pə'-\ *n* -S [Sp, fr. fem. of *posado* (past part. of *posar* to put up for the night, lodge), fr. LL *pausatus*, past part. of *pausare* to halt, stop, rest — more at PAUSE] **:** an inn in Spanish-speaking countries

po·sau·ne \pō'zaùnə\ *n, pl* **posau·nen** \-nən\ [G, fr. MHG *busīne, busūne* trumpet, fr. OF *buisine, busine*, fr. L *bucina*, prob. fr. *bu-* (fr. *bos* head of cattle) + *-cina* (fr. *canere* to sing) — more at COW, CHANT] **1 :** TROMBONE **2 :** a reed stop in a pipe organ imitating the trombone tone

POSB *abbr* post office savings bank

¹**pose** \'pōz\ *vb* -ED/-ING/-S [ME *posen*, fr. MF *poser*, fr. (assumed) VL (Gaul) *pausare* (influenced in meaning by L *pos-*, perfect stem of *ponere* to put, place), fr. LL, to stop, rest — more at POSITION, PAUSE] *vt* **1 a :** to put or set in place or in a given position ⟨*posed* his spectacles, and read the obituary —Arnold Bennett⟩ ⟨this hat features an elongated . . . brim *posed* midway down on the forehead —*Women's Wear Daily*⟩ **b :** to place (as a model or sitter) in a studied attitude with attention to posture and ensemble ⟨great photographers have *posed* her —Joseph Bryan⟩ **2 a :** to put or set forth **:** PRESENT, OFFER ⟨a number of the points . . . were *posed* in an unsatisfactory way —*N. Y. Times*⟩ ⟨*posed* a resistance to the . . . concept —Roger Burlingame⟩ ⟨*posed* the greatest threat of dismemberment —E.S.Morgan⟩ **b :** PROPOUND ⟨*posing* so many puzzles —*Irish Digest*⟩ ⟨~ exactly the same issue —S.L. Payne⟩ ⟨questions which can be *posed* by the students themselves —*Bard College Bull.*⟩ ~ *vi* **1 :** to place oneself in a given posture or attitude usu. for artistic purposes ⟨~ for a photographer⟩ ⟨~ for a picture⟩ ⟨the birds were quiet and *posed* beautifully —C.L.Barrett⟩ **2 :** to assume a given attitude or character usu. with a view to deceive or impress **:** strike an attitude **:** ATTITUDINIZE ⟨*posed* in public speeches as a man of the people —G.A.Craig⟩ ⟨good poetry does not ~ —C.S.Kilby⟩

²**pose** \"\ *n* -S [F, fr. *poser*] **1 :** a fixed or sustained posture of the body or of a part of the body ⟨the free ~ of the girl —Winston Churchill⟩; *esp* **:** one assumed for artistic effect ⟨a set of about three short ~*s* culminating in a grand tableau —Faubion Bowers⟩ or affectation ⟨his every movement is a ~⟩ **2 a :** a mental posture **:** frame of mind ⟨the ~ of the book is one of critical detachment —A.M.Schlesinger b. 1917⟩ **b :** an attitude that is affected **:** an attitude assumed for effect **:** PRETENSE ⟨his directness was a ~, his professional ~ —Louis Auchincloss⟩ ⟨his deprecation of the human strikes us a kind of ~ —L.A.Fiedler⟩ **c :** POSING, ATTITUDINIZING ⟨an age of ~⟩ ⟨an everyday touch and a minimum of ~ —Jack Gould⟩

³**pose** \"\ *n* -S [ME *pos*, perh. of Scand origin; akin to ON *posi* pouch, purse; akin to OE *posa, pusa* bag, OHG *pfoso* pouch, and perh. to OE *pocca, pohha* bag — more at POKE] *chiefly Scot* **:** a secret treasure **:** HOARD

⁴**pose** \"\ *vt* -ED/-ING/-S [short for earlier *appose*, fr. ME *apposen*, alter. of *opposen* to oppose — more at OPPOSE] **1** *obs* **:** QUESTION **2 :** to puzzle by or as if by questioning **:** put in a quandary **:** BAFFLE, NONPLUS ⟨determined not to be *posed* —Lucy M. Montgomery⟩

¹**pos·er** \'pōzə(r)\ *n* -S [short for earlier *apposer*, fr. obs. *appose* + *-er*] **1** *archaic* **:** a person who questions; *specif* **:** EXAMINER **2 :** a puzzling or baffling question or problem **:** PUZZLE ⟨sets some ~*s* for the literary critics to answer —*Times Lit. Supp.*⟩

²**poser** \"\ *n* -S [¹*pose* + *-er*] **:** a person who poses or attitudinizes

po·seur *R* (')pō'zər, + V -'zər·; *-R* -'zə, + *suffixal vowel* -'zər· *also* -'zər, + *vowel in a word following without pause* -'zər· *or* -'zə *also* -'zər\ *n* -S [F, fr. *poser* to pose + *-eur* -or — more at POSE] **:** a person who habitually pretends to be what he is not **:** one who is affected or insincere in his bearing and actions ⟨whom he regards as ~*s* and cultural fakers —Hunter Mead⟩

po·seuse \(')pō'zə(r)z, -zəz, -zəiz\ *n* -S [F, fem. of *poseur*] **:** a female poseur

¹**posh** \'päsh\ *n* -ES [imit. of the sound made by walking through slush] *archaic* **:** a slushy mass (as of mud or broken ice) ⟨~ and ice in the river —Walt Whitman⟩

²**posh** \"\ *adj* [origin unknown] **1 :** smart or spruce in appearance **2 :** elegant or luxurious in an extreme degree ⟨a ~ finishing school⟩

³**posh** *interj* — used to express disdain or contempt

poshteen *var of* POSTEEN

po·sied \'pōzēd, -zid\ *adj* [*posy* + *-ed*] **1 :** inscribed with a posy or motto **2 :** provided with posies **:** FLOWERY

posies *pl of* POSY

posing *pres part of* POSE

pos·ing·ly *adv* **:** in a posed manner

¹**pos·it** \'päzət, *usu* -əd·+V\ *vt* -ED/-ING/-S [L *positus*, past part. of *ponere* to place, put, lay down — more at POSITION] **1 :** to dispose or set firmly **:** place in relation to other objects **:** FIX ⟨his glance stayed ~*ed* on the spot —Hugh McCrae⟩ ⟨the problem so ~*ed* in a philosophical context —Bernard Smith⟩ **2 :** to postulate often in the absence of supporting evidence **:** take as actual **:** assume or affirm the existence of ⟨if she needs salvation, she will ~ a savior —George Santayana⟩ ⟨every code of law ~*s* a lawgiver —A.L.Guérard⟩ **syn** see PRESUPPOSE

²**posit** \"\ *n* -S **:** something that is posited; *specif* **:** an event or an assumption for which there is insufficient inductive evidence

¹**po·si·tion** \pə'zishən, pō'-\ *n* -S [MF, fr. L *position-, positio*, fr. *positus* (past part. of *ponere* to put, place, fr. — assumed — OL *posinere*, fr. *po-* away + *sinere* to lay, let, leave) + *-io*, *-ion*; akin to L *post* after — more at POST-, SITE] **1 :** an act of placing or arranging: as **a :** an act of laying down or stating a proposition or thesis **:** AFFIRMATION **b :** an arranging in order (as of military forces or chess pieces) **2 a :** a proposition or thesis laid down **:** ASSERTION, STATEMENT ⟨the proper response to the ~ that atomic secrets merit unique protection is not a denial but a series of questions —J.G.Palfrey⟩ **b :** the ground or point of view adopted with reference to a particular subject **:** mental attitude **:** way of thinking about or viewing something ⟨took a radical ~ on the zoning issue⟩ ⟨took the ~ that the law must be enforced at all costs⟩ **c :** a market commitment (as in securities or commodities) ⟨had heavy ~ in steels⟩; *also* **:** the inventory of a market trader (as a security dealer) **3 :** the point or area in space actually occupied by a physical object or into which it is placed: as **a :** proper or natural location in relation to other items ⟨the ~ of the heart⟩ ⟨put the lever in operating ~⟩ **:** STAND ⟨took their ~ at the end of the line⟩ **b :** an area or locality occupied by combat units esp. in a defensive operation **:** a location (as of a battery) from which weapons are fired **c :** geographical location ⟨radioed the control tower for his ~⟩ **4 :** arrangement or ordering of parts or aspects in relation to one another or to an external source of orientation: as **a** (1) **:** bodily posture ⟨crouched in a cramped ~⟩ ⟨proper ~ is of the utmost importance in showing livestock⟩ (2) **:** any of the postures of the feet and arms on which all steps and movements of classical ballet are based ⟨the five ~*s* of the feet⟩ (3) **:** an arrangement of the parts of the body considered particularly desirable for some medical or surgical procedure ⟨knee-chest ~⟩ ⟨obstetrical ~⟩ **b :** any of the arrangements of surfaces with the vertical in which the movement of a timepiece is adjusted to run **c** (1) **:** the disposition of the notes or tones of a chord with reference to the lowest voice part, the uppermost voice part, or their nearness to each other in pitch ⟨open or close ~⟩ (2) **:** one of the points on the fingerboard of a stringed instrument where the strings are stopped by the fingers to produce various pitches (3) **:** one of the seven definite degrees of extension of the trombone slide **5 :** relative place, situation, or standing ⟨man's ~ in nature⟩ ⟨the economic ~ of the city⟩: as **a :** social or official rank or status ⟨a humble man satisfied with his ~⟩; *esp* **:** elevated standing ⟨a man of ~⟩ **b** (1) **:** OFFICE, EMPLOYMENT, VOCATION ⟨took a ~ in the department of state⟩ — often used to distinguish a superior or intellectual occupation from a job of labor (2) **:** the group of tasks and responsibilities making up the duties of an employee ⟨the ~ can best be filled by a college-trained man⟩ ⟨this ~ involves both bookkeeping and typing⟩ **c :** a spot, situation, or condition that conveys some advantage (as against another) ⟨maneuvering for ~⟩ **6 :** the condition in Greek or Latin prosody of having a short vowel followed by two consonants or a double consonant (as *x* or *z*) making its syllable long ⟨in *vŏlvŭnt* the syllables are long by ~⟩

²**position** \"\ *vb* **positioned; positioned; positioning** \-sh(ə)niŋ\ **positions** *vt* **:** to put in a or the proper position **:** PLACE, SITUATE ⟨~*ed* themselves to act at once⟩ ~ *vi* **:** to assume or maintain a position

po·si·tion·al \-shən°l, -shnəl\ *adj* **1 :** of, relating to, or fixed by position **2 :** relatively immobile **:** involving little movement ⟨~ warfare⟩ **3 :** dependent on position or environment or context ⟨the front-articulated \k\ in \kē\ *key* and the back-articulated \k\ in \kül\ *cool* are ~ variants⟩

position analysis *n* **:** JOB ANALYSIS

position angle *n* **:** an angle on the celestial sphere denoting the orientation of one object or celestial body with respect to another (as the orientation of the line joining the components of a double star usu. measured from north through east up to 360 degrees, or the orientation of the axis of the sun, moon, planet, satellite, or star with respect to the north direction in the sky)

position artillery *n* **:** heavy artillery chiefly of fieldworks

position buoy *n* **:** FOG BUOY 2

position effect *n* **:** the part of the effect of a gene that is due to its interaction with adjacent genes and is subject to modification when the spatial relationships of the gene change (as by translocation or inversion)

po·si·tion·er \-sh(ə)nə(r)\ *n* -S **:** one that positions; *esp* **:** a mechanical device for placing or holding a body in position during an operation (as welding or drilling)

position finder *n* **:** a gunnery instrument for finding by triangulation the exact position and range of a ship or target

positioning *n* -S [fr. *positioning*, pres. part. of ²*position*] **:** a placing or arranging in position **:** POISING, POSING ⟨proper ~ of the masses is essential to a balanced composition⟩

position in readiness : location and condition in which troops are held prepared for prompt action as soon as the enemy's course of action is known

position isomerism *n* **:** isomerism in which a substituting atom or group occupies different positions

po·si·tion·less \pə'zishənləs, pō'-\ *adj* **:** lacking a position

position light *n* **:** any of the lights mounted on a night-flying airplane to serve as a warning to other airplanes (as a red light on the port side, a green light on the starboard side, and a white light aft)

position light signal *n* **:** a fixed railroad signal that gives its indications by varying the positions of two or more lights

position line *n* **:** LINE OF POSITION

position micrometer *n* **:** a filar-micrometer attachment for the equatorial telescope to measure position angles and angular separations (as of double stars)

positions *pl of* POSITION, *pres 3d sing of* POSITION

position target *n* **:** a railroad day signal that indicates by its position whether the accompanying switch is open or closed

position vector *n* **:** the vector of a point drawn from an origin to the point

pos·i·ti·val \ˌpäzəˈtīvəl\ *adj* [1*positive* + *-al*] **:** REAL, OBJECTIVE — opposed to *ideal*

1**pos·i·tive** \'päzəd·iv, -z(ə)tiv\ *adj, sometimes* -ER/-EST [ME, fr. OF *positif*, fr. L *positivus*, fr. *positus* (past part. of *ponere* to put, place, lay down) + *-ivus* -ive — more at POSITION] **1 a :** arbitrarily or formally laid down or imposed **:** prescribed by express enactment ⟨~ laws⟩ ⟨the formal and ~ rather than natural manners of the royal court⟩ **b :** expressed clearly, certainly, or peremptorily with no doubt, reservation, or unclarity ⟨never use them. That is ~ enough —A.T.Quiller-Couch⟩ **c** (1) **:** fully assured in opinion or utterance ⟨he is ~ that he is right⟩ (2) **:** SELF-ASSURED, DOGMATIC ⟨a very ~ man⟩ **2 a :** belonging to or constituting the degree of comparison that is expressed in English by the unmodified and uninflected form of an adjective (as *young*) or adverb (as *rapidly*) and that does not denote an increase or any specified level of the quality, quantity, or relation expressed by the adjective or adverb ⟨the ~ degree⟩ ⟨the ~ form *narrow*⟩ — compare COMPARATIVE 1, COMPARISON 3, SUPERLATIVE 1 **b** (1) **:** independent of changing circumstances or relations **:** not subject to comparison **:** free from conditions ⟨a ~ concept of nature⟩ — often distinguished from *comparative* and *relative* (2) **:** being or relating to a motion or device that is definite, unyielding, constant, or certain in its action ⟨a ~ system of levers⟩ **c :** unquestionably being the thing named **:** absolutely such ⟨~ proof⟩ **:** SHEER, UTTER — often used as an intensifier ⟨a ~ shame⟩; compare ABSOLUTE, DOWNRIGHT **3 a :** concerned with facts and matters of practical experience rather than theory or speculation ⟨~ philosophies⟩ **b :** actual or real as distinguished from fictitious ⟨a ~ phenomenon⟩ ⟨~ social tensions⟩ **c :** characterized by the performance of an active and direct role in the economic and social life of a political unit by directly undertaking functions and services (as the regulation of business and labor, establishment of agricultural price supports, provision of social security, and the conservation of natural resources) as contrasted with a restriction to the more limited functions of keeping peace and order ⟨~ government⟩ **4 a :** having or expressing condition, existence, character, or other quality actually present in a real manner or to an absolutely measurable degree as distinguished from merely lacking or failing to express an opposed quality **:** CONCRETE, GENUINE ⟨a slight ~ change in temperature over the centuries⟩ ⟨a ~ definition⟩ ⟨the people should have a more ~ voice in government⟩: as (1) **:** logically affirmative **:** capable of being constructively applied ⟨~ proposals for the betterment of society⟩ (2) **:** subject to scientific verification **:** EMPIRICAL — distinguished from *speculative* (3) **:** having rendition of light and shade similar in tone to the tones of the original subject — used esp. in photography ⟨a ~ image⟩ (4) **:** having properties required to produce a positive image ⟨a ~ film⟩ **b :** numerically greater than zero **:** not negative **:** PLUS — used of real quantities ⟨~ integers⟩ ⟨a ~ correlation⟩ **c :** reckoned, proceeding, or acting in a direction arbitrarily or customarily taken as that of increase, progressive motion, or superiority **:** opposed in character or effect to anything construed as negative ⟨the rotation of the earth is usu. taken as ~⟩ ⟨we are making some ~ progress⟩: as (1) **:** relating to, composed of, or charged with positive electricity (2) **:** losing electrons **:** ELECTROPOSITIVE 2a **:** BASIC 3a (3) **:** transmitting an ordinary ray with greater speed than an extraordinary — used esp. of a uniaxial doubly refracting crystal (as of ice or quartz) (4) **:** DEXTROROTATORY (5) **:** seeking the north — used of a magnetic pole (6) **:** oriented, directed, or moving toward a source of stimulation or characterized by such orientation, direction, or movement ⟨~ phototaxis⟩ ⟨a ~ response to light⟩ (7) **:** of, relating to, or constituting a method of steering or turning a vehicle in which the steering wheels move so that they describe concentric arcs in making a turn to ensure freedom from sideslip or harmful resistance (8) **:** characterized by or relating to upward movement or greater than average density or magnetic properties of the earth's crust ⟨~ gravity anomaly⟩ **d :** falling on a given side of a line or plane — used esp. in mathematics **5 a :** marked by acceptance or approval **:** indicating agreement or affirmation ⟨a strongly ~ response from the audience⟩ **b :** affirming the presence of that sought or suspected to be present ⟨a ~ test for blood⟩ ⟨a ~ case history⟩ **6 :** being or relating to a device giving a to-and-fro motion ⟨a ~ dobby⟩ ⟨a ~ tappet⟩ **syn** see SURE

2**positive** \"\ *n* -S **:** something that is positive: as **a** *obs* **:** POSITIVE LAW **b :** the positive degree of comparison in a language **:** a positive form of an adjective or adverb **c :** something of which an affirmation can be made **:** a real thing **:** REALITY **d** (1) **:** POSITIVE ORGAN (2) **:** POSITIVE PLATE (3) **:** POSITIVE POLE **e :** a positive photograph or a print from a negative (as on printing paper or film)

positive acceleration *n* **:** headward acceleration

positive afterimage *n* **:** a visual afterimage that retains the same light, dark, and color relationships as those appearing in the original image — opposed to *negative afterimage*

positive birefringence *n* **:** birefringence of a medium (as quartz) that transmits the ordinary rays with greater speed than the extraordinary

positive block *n* **:** a block in which only one railroad train is allowed to be at one time — compare BLOCK SYSTEM

positive buoyancy *n* **:** a condition of weight and mass relationships of a ship (as a submarine) in which it will float unless mechanical devices (as diving planes) are employed or unless additional weight is taken on

positive clutch *n* **:** CLAW CLUTCH

positive column *n* **:** the region in an electric discharge that extends from the anode to the Faraday dark space

positive easement *or* **positive servitude** *n* **:** an easement entitling its holder to do something affecting the land of another in such a way that the holder would be guilty of trespass or nuisance were it not for the easement — compare NEGATIVE EASEMENT

positive electricity *n* **:** electricity of which the elementary unit is the proton

positive electron *n* **:** POSITRON

positive feedback *n* **:** a feedback of such polarity and phase as to increase the net gain of an amplifier

positive form *n* **:** either of a pair of congruent crystal forms that together correspond to a single form in a class of higher symmetry

positive fraud *n* **:** FRAUD 1a(1)

positive G *n* **:** the G force exerted on the human body in a headward direction during acceleration

positive law *n* **1 :** the aggregate of legal precepts established or recognized by the authority of the state as contrasted with natural law or a body of ideal precepts **2 :** religious laws revealed by God (as the early Jewish law)

positive lens *n* **:** a lens that is thickest at its center and thinner toward its outer portions thus causing light which passes through it to converge **:** CONVERGING LENS

positive light modulation *or* **positive transmission** *n* **:** a system of television in which an increase in the brightness of the picture corresponds to an increase in the signal strength

pos·i·tive·ly \'päzəd·əvlē, -z(ə)tə-, *in sense 2 often* ˌ=(=)'tiv-\ *adv* **1 :** in a positive manner **:** so as to be positive **2 :** EXTREMELY, OBVIOUSLY, NOTABLY, CERTAINLY — used chiefly to intensify a statement ⟨~ the best cake I ever ate⟩ ⟨~ shabby⟩ ⟨~ true⟩

positive misprision *n* **:** a misprision resulting from the commission of an act that ought not to have been committed — distinguished from *negative misprision*

positive motion *n* **:** motion that is transferred (as by gears, cranks, or belts) without slippage — compare FRICTION DRIVE

pos·i·tive·ness \'=(=)tivnəs\ *n* -ES **:** the quality or state of being positive; *esp* **:** dogmatic assertiveness

positive optical activity *n* **:** the optical activity of a dextrorotating medium

positive organ *n* **1** *obs* **:** a stationary as distinguished from a portative organ; *also* **:** CHAMBER ORGAN **2 :** a division of an organ used primarily for tonal contrast or supplement to the great organ; *sometimes* **:** CHOIR ORGAN

positive philosophy *n* **:** POSITIVISM 1

positive plate *n* **:** the electrode of a voltaic cell or storage cell that is at the higher potential when the circuit is open

positive pole *n* **1 :** the terminal of a voltaic cell or storage cell that is connected to the positive plate **2 :** the north-seeking pole of a magnet

positive potential *n* **:** an electric potential higher than that of the earth or of other conductor taken as an arbitrary zero of potential

positive pressure *n* **:** pressure of a gas in excess of atmospheric pressure or of an arbitrary standard ⟨inspiratory positive pressures of 5 to 15 cm H_2O were employed —*Jour. Amer. Med. Assoc.*⟩

positiver *comparative of* POSITIVE

positive ray *n* **:** a stream of positively charged ions moving toward the cathode in a discharge tube

positive religion *n* **:** a religion that has a definite historic founder

positive skewness *n* **:** statistical skewness in which a distribution is skewed toward the positive side of the mean

positivest *superlative of* POSITIVE

positive stability *n* **:** the tendency of a ship to return to previous position when inclined

positive temperature coefficient *n* **:** a larger than 1 ratio of a quantity (as resistance or length) at a higher temperature to the corresponding value of the quantity at a lower temperature

positive theology *n* **1 :** theological doctrine that describes the divine nature according to positive categories **2 :** a theology that instead of beginning with the philosophy of religion takes as its content the gospel as given by biblical theology and presents it directly in systematic form

positive valence *n* **1 :** the valence of a positively charged ion **2 :** the number of electrons an atom can give up ⟨sodium has a *positive valence* of 1⟩

pos·i·tiv·ism \'päzəd·iˌvizəm, -z(ə)tiˌ-\ *n* -S [F *positivisme*, fr. *positif* positive + *-isme* -ism — more at POSITIVE] **1 a :** a system of philosophy holding that theology and metaphysics belong to earlier or imperfect modes of knowledge whereas positive knowledge is based on natural phenomena and their spatiotemporal properties and invariant relations or upon facts as elaborated and verified by the methods of the empirical sciences — compare THERAPEUTIC POSITIVISM **b :** LOGICAL POSITIVISM **2 :** the quality or state of being positive **:** DOGMATISM, CONFIDENCE, CERTAINTY ⟨exhibiting an undue ~⟩ **3 a :** the Lombrosian school of criminology or its theories **b :** the theory or doctrine that society is susceptible of analysis in purely objective mechanistic terms and that social values and normative standards are mere epiphenomena **4 :** a theory that law is restricted to the man-made statute law without ethical or ideological content as distinguished from natural law or moral law

1**pos·i·tiv·ist** \-ˌvəst\ *n* -S [F *positiviste*, fr. *positif* + *-iste* -ist] **:** a subscriber to or adherent of positivism

2**positivist** \"\ *adj* **:** being a positivist **:** exhibiting, relating to, or characteristic of any form of positivism ⟨the spiritual barrenness of a ~ conception of reality —*Times Lit. Supp.*⟩

pos·i·tiv·is·tic \ˌ=(=)=ˈvistik, -tēk\ *adj* **:** of or relating to positivism or positivists **:** like or tending to positivism ⟨~ knowledge was concerned with merely physical utilities —John Dewey⟩ — **pos·i·tiv·is·ti·cal·ly** *adv* \-tək(ə)lē, -tēk-, -li\

pos·i·tiv·i·ty \ˌ=(=)'tivəd·ē, -ətē, -i\ *n* -ES [1*positive* + *-ity*] **:** something that is positive **:** the quality or state of being positive **:** POSITIVENESS

pos·i·ton \'päzəˌtän\ *n* -S [*positive* + *-on*] **:** POSITRON

pos·i·tor \'päzəd·ə(r)\ *n* -S **:** one that posits; *esp* **:** the person making a statement or providing a segment of information — compare PROBAND

pos·i·tri·no \ˌpäzə·'trē(ˌ)nō\ *n* -S [*positron* + *-ino* (as in *neutrino*)] **:** a hypothetical atomic particle similar to the neutrino and having an immeasurably small mass and a positive charge

pos·i·tron \'päzə·ˌträn\ *n* -S [blend fr. *positive electron*] **:** a positively charged particle having the same mass and magnitude of charge as the electron — called also *positive electron*

pos·i·tro·ni·um \ˌpäzə·'trōnēəm\ *n* -S [NL, fr. ISV *positron* + NL *-ium*] **:** a short-lived system suggestive of an atom and analogous to the hydrogen atom consisting of a positron and an electron bound together

posits *pres 3d sing of* POSIT, *pl of* POSIT

pos·i·tum \'päzəd·əm\ *n* -S [L, neut. of *positus*, past part. of *ponere* to place, put, lay down — more at POSITION] **:** something that is posited or laid down

pos·i·ture \'päzəchə(r)\ *n* -S [L *positura* — more at POSTURE] **1** *obs* **:** PLACING, SITUATION, LOCALITY **2 a :** POSTURE **b :** CONFIGURATION

posn *abbr* position

1**pos·na·nian** \(')päzˈnānēən, -nyən\ *adj, usu cap* [*Poznań*, province and city in Poland + E *-ian*] **:** of or relating to the Polish province of Poznan or the city of Posen

2**posnanian** \"\ *n* -S *cap* **1 :** a native or resident of Poznan or Posen **2 :** the dialect of Poznan upon which standard Polish is based

po·sol \pō'sōl\ *also* **po·so·le** *or* **po·zo·le** \-ō(ˌ)lā\ *n* -S [AmerSp *posol*, *pozol*, *posole*, *pozole*, fr. Nahuatl *pozolli*, lit., foamy, fr. *pozol* foam] **1 :** a thick chiefly Spanish-American soup made of pork, corn, garlic, and chili **2 :** a Spanish-American drink made of cornmeal, water, and sugar ⟨began arriving with food, . . . *posole* and fruit —Oliver LaFarge⟩

poso·logic \ˌpäsəˈläjik\ *also* **poso·log·i·cal** \-jəkəl\ *adj* **:** of or relating to posology

po·sol·o·gy \pə'säləjē\ *n* -ES [F *posologie*, fr. Gk *posos* how much + F *-logie* -logy; akin to L *quotus* how many — more at QUOTE] **:** a branch of medical science concerned with dosage

pos·po·li·te \pò'spòlyētə\ *n* -S [Pol, *pospolite* (*ruszenie*) general levy, fr. *pospolite* (neut. of *pospolity* general) + *ruszenie* movement, levy] **:** a former Polish militia in Poland consisting of the gentry called out in case of invasion

poss \'päs\ *vb* [ME *possen*, prob. fr. MF *pousser* — more at PUSH] *dial* **:** THRUST, PUSH, POUND

poss *abbr* **1** possession **2** possessive **3** possible; possibly

pos·se \'päsē\ *n* -S [ML *posse* (*comitatus*), fr. *posse* power (fr. L, to be able, have power) + *comitatūs*, gen. of *comitatus* county — more at POTENT] **1 :** POSSE COMITATUS **2 a :** a force with legal authority **:** a detachment or body (as of police) often assigned to or brought together because of a particular emergency **b :** a crowd or throng usu. sharing some common interest **3 :** POSSIBILITY, POTENTIALITY — see IN POSSE

posse comitatus *n* [ML] **:** the power of a county: **a :** the entire body of the inhabitants who may be summoned by the sheriff to assist in preserving the public peace (as in a riot) or in executing a legal precept that is forcibly opposed including under the common law every male inhabitant who is above 15 years of age and not infirm **b :** a body of persons so summoned

pos·se·man \'päsēmən\ *n, pl* **possemen :** a member of a posse ⟨are without authority to . . . contract for the services of *possemen* —*U. S. Daily*⟩

pos·sen·trie \'päsᵊn·trē\ *n* -S [D, modif. of E *poison tree*] **:** SANDBOX TREE

pos·sess \pə|'zes, pō|, |'ses\ *vt* -ED/-ING/-ES [ME *possessen*, fr. MF *possesser*, fr. L *possessus*, past part. of *possidēre* to own, possess (fr. *potis* able, possible + *-sidēre*, fr. *sedēre* to sit) & *possidĕre* to take possession of, fr. *potis* + *sidere* to sit down, fr. the stem of *sedēre* to sit — more at POTENT, SIT] **1 a** *obs* **:** INSTALL, INSTATE **:** ESTABLISH **b :** to make (as a person) the owner or holder (as of property, power, or knowledge) **:** FURNISH — used with *of* or *with* ⟨I will ~ you of that ship and treasure —Shak.⟩ **c :** to be in possession of (something) **:** HAVE ⟨~*ed* of riches⟩ ⟨~*ed* of a strong back⟩ **2** *obs* **:** to be located or situated at **:** OCCUPY, INHABIT **3 a :** to have and hold as property **:** have a just right to **:** be master of **:** OWN ⟨~*ing* lands and money⟩ **b :** to have as a property, adjunct, attribute, or other collateral quality ⟨~*es* great patience⟩ ⟨~*ing* the respect of his fellows⟩ **c :** to have knowledge of or skill in ⟨~*ing* several languages besides his native tongue⟩ **4 a :** to take into one's possession **:** seize or gain control of **:** make one's own ⟨this the regal seat: ~ it, York —Shak.⟩ **b :** to enter into and influence powerfully or control **:** DOMINATE ⟨~*ed* of a demon⟩ ⟨what could have ~*ed* him to act so⟩ ⟨a man ~*ed* with rage⟩ **c :** to bring or cause to fall under the influence, possession, or control of some emotional or intellectual reaction ⟨periodically ~*ed* with a melancholy reserve⟩ **d :** to maintain or keep in a usu. specified condition (as of control or tranquillity) ⟨~*ing* himself firmly in the face of provocation⟩ ⟨the need to ~ one's soul in patience⟩ **e** *archaic* (1) **:** PERSUADE, INFLUENCE, CONVINCE (2) **:** to impart information to **:** INSTRUCT, ACQUAINT **f :** to copulate with **5** *obs* **:** to occupy or engross the thoughts of **syn** see HAVE

pos·sess·able *also* **pos·sess·ible** \-səbəl\ *adj* **:** capable of being held as or converted into a possession

pos·sessed \-st\ *adj* [fr. past part. of *possess*] **1** *obs* **:** held as a possession **2 a :** influenced or controlled by something (as an evil spirit or a passion) ⟨these ~ fools⟩; *often* **:** MAD, CRAZED **b :** urgently desirous to do or have something **3 :** SELF-POSSESSED, COOL, CALM **4 :** used in a construction to indicate what is possessed ⟨*dog* in the phrase "Bill's dog" is a ~ noun⟩ — usu. used of a form different from that used in other constructions (as in Hebrew and several Amerindian languages) — **pos·sessed·ly** \-sədlē, -stlē, -li\ *adv* — **pos·sessed·ness** \-sədnəs, -stnəs\ *n* -ES

pos·sess·ing·ly *adv* **:** so as to possess **:** in a possessing manner **:** CAPTIVATINGLY

pos·ses·sion \pə'zeshən, '-sesh-, pō-\ *n* -S [ME *possessioun*, fr. MF *possession*, fr. L *possession-*, *possessio*, fr. *possessus* (past part. of *possidēre* to own, possess & *possidĕre* to take possession of) + *-ion-*, *-io* -ion — more at POSSESS] **1 a :** the act or condition of having in or taking into one's control or holding at one's disposal ⟨the enemy's ~ of the town⟩ ⟨have several old manuscripts in my ~⟩ **b :** actual physical control or occupancy of property by one who holds for himself and not as a servant of another without regard to his ownership and who has legal rights to assert interests in the property against all others having no better right than himself ⟨the locker shall remain in the student's ~ throughout the course⟩ — distinguished from *custody;* compare DETENTION 3 **c :** COPULATION **d :** control of the playing piece (as a ball or puck) in football, basketball, ice hockey, or other game **:** the right of a team to put such piece in play ⟨the home team took ~ on its own one yard line⟩ **2 :** something owned, occupied, or controlled **:** a thing possessed ⟨his own ~ for which he owes nothing to any man⟩: as **a possessions** *pl* **:** the aggregate of things owned **:** WEALTH **b** (1) **:** a piece of land (2) *Scot* **:** a small farmhold **c :** a territory subject to a ruler or government ⟨domestic and foreign ~*s* of the Crown⟩ **d :** an area subject to a government but not fully integrated into the nation to which the government belongs ⟨colonial and territorial ~*s*⟩ ⟨by judicial decision Puerto Rico was declared "to be appurtenant to" the U. S., albeit not a part of it — a mere ~ —Antonio Fernós-Isern⟩ **3 :** the condition or fact of being possessed by something ⟨the town's ~ by the enemy⟩: as **a :** the condition of being dominated by something (as an extraneous personality, demon, passion, idea, or purpose) ⟨there were tales of bewitchings and ~*s*⟩ **b :** a psychological state in which an individual's normal personality is replaced by another **c :** the fact or condition of being self-controlled ⟨his ~ in the emergency was absolute⟩ **4 :** an Aristotelian category having the form of a permanent disposition or state

pos·ses·sion·al \-shənᵊl, -shnəl\ *adj* **:** of or constituting possession **:** having property — **pos·ses·sion·al·ly** \-ᵊl|ē, -əl|, |i\ *adv*

pos·ses·sion·al·ism \-ᵊlˌizəm, -əˌli-\ *n* -S **:** the principle or practice of private ownership of property

pos·ses·sion·ary \-shəˌnerē\ *adj* **:** of or relating to possession **:** arising from possession

pos·ses·sion·ate \-shənət\ *adj* [ME, fr. ML *possessionatus* fr. L *possession-*, *possessio* possession + *-atus* -ate] **:** having possessions or endowments

pos·ses·sioned \-shənd\ *adj* **:** having possessions

pos·ses·sion·er \-sh(ə)nə(r)\ *n* -S [ME *possessiouner*, fr. *possessioun* possession + *-er* — more at POSSESSION] **1 a** *obs* **:** a property holder **b** *archaic* **:** a member of a religious order holding endowments (as of lands or buildings) — often taken as offensive **2 :** one appointed to renew boundary landmarks in the southern U. S.

pos·ses·sion·ist \-sh(ə)nəst\ *n* -S **:** a believer in possession by spirits

pos·ses·sion·less \'-shənləs\ *adj* **:** lacking possessions — **pos·ses·sion·less·ness** *n* -ES

1**pos·ses·sive** \pə|'zesiv, pō|, |'ses-|, -ēv\ *adj* [MF *possessif*, fr. L *possessivus*, fr. *possessus* (past part. of *possidēre* to own, possess) + *-ivus* -ive — more at POSSESS] **1 a :** of, relating to, or constituting a grammatical case that denotes ownership or a relation felt to be analogous to ownership ⟨in "John's hat" the word *John's* is in the ~ case⟩ — compare GENITIVE **b :** of, relating to, or constituting a word or word group that denotes ownership or a relation felt to be analogous to ownership **c :** of or relating to the possessive case ⟨a ~ construction⟩ **2 :** of or tending to possession **:** manifesting possession or the desire to possess or hold as one's own **:** POSSESSORY ⟨the ~ instinct⟩ ⟨a ~ nature⟩ **3** *of a compound word* **:** belonging to the bahuvrihi class — **pos·ses·sive·ly** \-səvlē, -sēv-, -li\ *adv* — **pos·ses·sive·ness** *n* -ES

2**possessive** \"\ *n* -S **1 :** the possessive case **2 :** a possessive word or word group

possessive adjective *n* **:** a pronominal adjective expressing possession (as *my* in *my hat*, *his* in *his answer*)

possessive pronoun *n* **:** a pronoun that derives from a personal pronoun and denotes possession and other analogous relations (as *his* in "his is better than John's")

pos·ses·sor \pə'zesə(r), -'ses-, pō'-\ *n* -S [ME *possessour*, fr. MF *possesseur*, fr. L *possessor*, fr. *possessus* + *-or*] **1 :** one that possesses **:** one that occupies, holds, owns, or controls **2 :** one that holds property without title — called also *naked possessor;* contrasted with *owner* **3** *usu cap* **:** JOSEPHITE

possessoress *n* -ES *obs* **:** a female possessor

pos·ses·so·ri·ness \pə'zesərēnəs, pō'-, -'ses-\ *n* -ES **:** the quality or state of being possessory

pos·ses·sor·ship \='==ˌship\ *n* **:** the condition of a possessor

pos·ses·so·ry \pə'zesərē, pō'-, -'ses-, -ri\ *adj* [LL *possessorius*, fr. *possessus* (past part. of *possidēre* to possess) + *-orius* -ory — more at POSSESS] **1 a :** of or relating to possession or a possessor **:** constituting or having the nature of possession **b :** arising out of, affecting, relating to, or confirming possession ⟨a ~ interest⟩ ⟨a ~ action at law⟩ **2 :** having or holding possession ⟨a ~ lord⟩ **3 :** characteristic of a possessor **:** POSSESSIVE ⟨a ~ spirit⟩

possessory action *n* **:** an action at law founded on a right of possession and brought to recover or obtain possession as: **a** (1) **:** a real action formerly used under Old English law to regain possession of a freehold (2) **:** an action founded on mere possession and sometimes used to try title indirectly **b :** a suit under admiralty law to recover possession of a ship under claim of title **c** (1) **:** an action under Scots law to vindicate and recover possession of goods heritable or movable (2) **:** an action in Louisiana to be secured in possession or restored to the possession of an immovable

1**pos·set** \'päsət, *usu* -əd·+V\ *n* -S [ME *poshet*, *poshoote*, *possot*] **:** a hot drink consisting essentially of sweetened and spiced milk curdled with ale or wine, and sometimes thickened with bread ⟨egg ~⟩ ⟨sack ~⟩

2**posset** \"\ *vt* -ED/-ING/-S **1 :** to cause to curdle or coagulate **2 :** to pamper with delicacies ⟨cosseted and ~*ed* and prayed over — O.W.Holmes †1894⟩

posset cup *n* : a 2-handled usu. covered and spouted vessel used esp. in the 17th and 18th centuries for possets and invalid feeding

posset cup

posset pot *n* **1** : a two-handled usu. vessel used for making posset **2** : POSSET CUP
pos·si·bi·le \pə'sibə,lē\ *n, pl* **pos·si·bil·ia** \,päsə'bilēə\ [NL, fr. L, neut. of *possibilis* possible — more at POSSIBLE] : something that is possible or conceivable without contradiction or that may or might be the case
pos·si·bi·lism \'päsəbə,lizəm, pə'sibə,l-\ *n* -S [F *possibilisme*, fr. L *possibilis* + F *-isme* -ism] : the beliefs or practices of a possibilist
pos·si·bi·list \-,ləst\ *n* -S *often attrib* [F *possibiliste*, fr. L *possibilis* + F *-iste* -ist] : a member of a political party that attempts (as in the way of reform) only what is regarded as immediately possible or practicable: as **a** : one of a party of Republicans in Spain **b** : one of a party of Socialists in France
pos·si·bil·i·tate \,päsə'bilə,tāt\ *vt* -ED/-ING/-S [*possibility* + *-ate*] : to make possible
pos·si·bil·i·ty \-ləd·ē, -ətē, -i\ *n* -ES [ME *possibilite*, fr. MF *possibilité*, fr. L *possibilitat-, possibilitas*, fr. *possibilis* possible + *-itat-, -itas* -ity] **1** : the character, condition, or fact of being possible whether theoretically, in general, or under a specified set of conditions ⟨the ~ of miracles⟩ ⟨the constant ~ of failure⟩ **2** : something that is possible : CONTINGENCY ⟨within the range of ~⟩ : a particular thing that may take place, eventuate, or be manipulated to some end ⟨but one ~ remains⟩ **3** *archaic* : one's utmost power, capacity, or ability esp. as determined by circumstances ⟨to the ~ of thy soldiership —Shak.⟩ **4** *obs* : pecuniary means or pecuniary prospects — usu. used in pl. **5 possibilities** *pl* : potential or prospective value : possible uses, achievements, or other desired qualities ⟨a man of undetermined *possibilities*⟩
possibility of reverter : a future interest in property left to a transferor or his successor in interest that is subject to a condition precedent
1pos·si·ble \'päsəbəl\ *adj, sometimes* -ER/-EST [ME, fr. MF, fr. L *possibilis*, fr. *posse* to be able + *-ibilis* -ible — more at POTENT] **1 a** : falling or lying within the powers (as of performance, attainment, or conception) of an agent or activity expressed or implied : being within or up to the limits of one's ability or capacity as determined by nature, authority, circumstances, or other controlling factor ⟨a ~ but difficult task⟩ — compare ACTUAL **b** : falling within the bounds of what may be done, occur, be conceived, or be attained within the framework of nature, custom, or manners ⟨a cure is still ~⟩ ⟨not ~ to see the patient⟩ **c** : being such to the utmost degree ⟨as coarse as it was ~ to be⟩ ⟨the largest number ~⟩ **2** *obs* : ABLE **3 a** : that may or may not occur : that may chance : dependent on contingency : neither probable nor impossible ⟨put by for ~ emergencies⟩ ⟨it is ~ that she will come⟩ **b** : LIKELY, PROBABLE — usu. used with an adverb expressing doubt ⟨scarcely ~⟩ ⟨barely ~ that it will rain⟩ **4** : having an indicated potential by nature or circumstances : able or fitted to become, be used, or otherwise serve ⟨every native-born American is a ~ president⟩ ⟨a ~ site for a capitol⟩ **5** : capable of being surmounted, traversed, or dealt with; *esp* : neither unacceptable nor intolerable ⟨the new neighbors were ~⟩ — often used with an adverb expressing doubt ⟨scraped together a just ~ meal⟩
syn PRACTICABLE, FEASIBLE: POSSIBLE is used to dispel doubt that something may or does occur or exist or may come to exist ⟨the regime of religious toleration has become *possible* only because we have lost the primal intensity of religious conviction —M.R.Cohen⟩ ⟨although he still asserts that community of goods would be the ideal institution, he reluctantly abandons it as a basis for a *possible* state —G.L.Dickinson⟩ PRACTICABLE refers to what may be readily effected, executed, practiced, used, or put into operation ⟨trial by jury — an institution in which . . . we have the very abstract and essence of all *practicable* democratic government —W.H.Mallock⟩ ⟨the only *practicable* tactics to be pursued were those of the routine police procedure —W.H.Wright⟩ FEASIBLE may designate what is likely to work out or be put into effect successfully or what in a difficult situation seems the expedient least liable to fail ⟨cheap iron and steel made it *feasible* to equip larger armies and navies than ever before —Lewis Mumford⟩ ⟨only the most simple types of utilization are *feasible* —Samuel Van Valkenburg & Ellsworth Huntington⟩ **syn** see in addition PROBABLE
2possible \"\ *adv, archaic* : POSSIBLY
3possible \"\ *n* -S **1 a** : POSSIBILITY, POTENTIALITY — usu. used in pl. ⟨all the infinite number of ~*s* —Jonathan Edwards⟩ **b** : all that can be done : BEST ⟨had done my ~ . . . to gratify you —Robert Southey⟩ **2 possibles** *pl* : necessary things (as supplies, equipment, money) ⟨the hunters departed, each to look after his traps and ~*s* —Mayne Reid⟩ **3** : the highest attainable score for a number of rounds fired in target shooting; *broadly* : the highest attainable score in a competition
pos·si·ble·ness *n* -ES : the quality or state of being possible : POSSIBILITY ⟨the ~ of such a feat⟩
pos·si·bly \'päsəblē, -li\ *adv* [ME, fr. *possible* + *-ly*] **1** : in a possible manner : by possible means : by any possibility ⟨not ~ true⟩ ⟨could you ~ agree⟩ **2** : by merest chance : MAYBE, PERHAPS ⟨~ he will recover⟩
pos·sie *also* **pos·sy** \'päsi\ *n, pl* **possies** [alter. of *position*] *Austral* : POSITION, PLACE
possn *abbr* possession
1pos·sum \'päsəm\ *n* -S [by shortening] : OPOSSUM
2possum \"\ *vb* -ED/-ING/-S *vi* **1** : to play possum **2** : to hunt the opossum ~ *vt* : FEIGN, PRETEND ⟨~*ing* surprise⟩
possum belly *n, slang* : a storage space beneath the flooring of a vehicle
possum fruit *also* **possum apple** *n* : PERSIMMON
possum grape *n* **1 a** : CHICKEN GRAPE **b** : a wild grape (*Vitis baileyana*) of the southeastern U.S. resembling the chicken grape but having angled branchlets and leaves with lower surfaces permanently pilose **2** : CISSUS 2
possum haw *n* **1** : BEARBERRY 3 **2** : a withe rod (*Viburnum nudum*)
possum oak *n* : a tall water oak (*Quercus nigra*) of the southeastern U.S. that is often cultivated as a shade tree
possum-trot plan \'==,=-\ *n* : a plan of a house in two parts

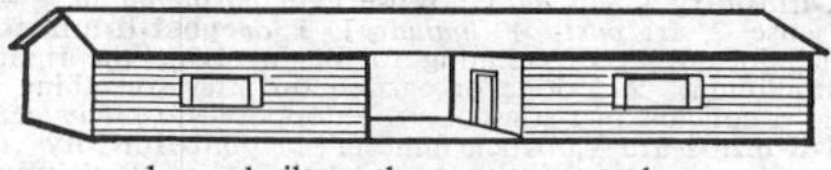

house built on the possum-trot plan

with a breezeway between — compare DOGTROT 2
possumwood \'==,=\ *n* **1** : PERSIMMON **2** : the light soft wood of the sandbox tree **3** : OPOSSUM WOOD
1post \'pōst\ *n* -S [ME, fr. OE; akin to OFris, MD, & MLG *post*, OHG *pfosto*; all fr. a prehistoric WGmc word borrowed fr. L *postis*; akin to OE *fierst, first* ridgepole, MLG *verst*, OHG *first* ridgepole, Gk *pastas* porch, colonnade, Skt *pṛṣṭha* back, roof, top; all fr. a prehistoric IE compound whose 1st constituent is akin to Skt *pra-* before, forward, and whose 2d constituent is akin to L *stare* to stand — more at FOR, STAND] **1** : a piece of timber or other solid substance (as metal) fixed or intended to be fixed firmly in an upright position esp. as a stay or support : PILLAR, PROP: as **a** : a square timber set on end to support a structural member (as a wall or girder) esp. at a corner of a building : UPRIGHT, COLUMN **b** : one of the pillars supporting an arch or lintel : DOORJAMB, GATEPOST **c** : one of the stakes of a fence or railing : PICKET **d** : STERNPOST **e** : one of the main upright timbers of a framed set in mining : STUDDLE **f** : the pin of a pinlock **g** : BINDING POST 1 **h** : BINDING POST 2 **2** : a pole or stake set up to mark or indicate: as **a** : a boundary marker **b** : a stand for the display of public notices **c** : a pole marking the starting point or the finishing point in horse racing ⟨starting ~⟩ ⟨winning ~⟩ **3** : an upright metal blade forming the front sight of a firearm
2post \"\ *vt* -ED/-ING/-S **1** : to affix (as a paper or bill) to a post, wall, or other usual place for public notices : PLACARD ⟨~ the notice on the bulletin board⟩ ⟨signs are ~*ed* throughout the state⟩ **2 a** : to publish, announce, or advertise by or as if by the use of a placard ⟨the students' grades are ~*ed*⟩ ⟨the yardmaster . . . ~*s* the track number —*Monsanto Mag.*⟩ ⟨the ~*ed* price for . . . crude oil —*N.Y.Times*⟩ **b** : to denounce (as a person or institution) by public notice ⟨~*ed* the theater as unfair —Upton Sinclair⟩ ⟨harry and ~ a man for his losings —Rudyard Kipling⟩ **c** : to enter (a name) on a public listing ⟨nurses ~*ed* for night duty⟩ ⟨~*ed* missing in the flood —John Blight⟩ **d** : to forbid (property) to trespassers under penalty of legal prosecution by notices placed along the boundaries ⟨~ a brook⟩ ⟨wandering around ~*ed* property —Ronald Sercombe⟩ **e** : to gain recognition for (a score or performance) ⟨~*ed* a 69 to take the first-round lead⟩ ⟨~*ed* an average of 177.34 miles per hour⟩
3post \"\ *adj* : of or relating to the start or to the post at the starting point of a horse or dog race ⟨~ position⟩ ⟨~ time⟩
4post \"\ *n* -S [MF *poste* relay station, man stationed at a relay station, post, fr. OIt *posta* place assigned to a horse in a stable, relay station, fr. *posta*, fem. of *posto* (past part. of *porre* to put), fr. L *positus*, past part. of *ponere* to put, place — more at POSITION] **1 a** *obs* (1) : one of the men stationed or appointed in a series of places along a through road to go each from his station to the next with the state packet of dispatches and letters (2) : one so stationed or appointed to carry letters generally (3) : one appointed to furnish a change of horses to through messengers carrying such matter **b** : a special carrier of messages or letters : COURIER; *esp* : one following a fixed route **c** *chiefly Scot* : a postal carrier : POSTMAN **d** : a vehicle or ship used to carry the mails **2** *archaic* **a** : one of a series of stations for keeping horses for relays **b** : the distance between any two such consecutive stations : STAGE **3** *chiefly Brit* **a** : a nation's organization or system for handling the transmission of letters and other matter : MAIL 3a ⟨a letter delayed in the ~⟩ ⟨exchange of books by ~ —Thomas Joy⟩ **b** : the matter sent or received : MAIL 3b ⟨delivered his ~ to a house and moved on —Cyril Cusack⟩ **c** (1) : a single dispatch of mail ⟨catch the last ~ with it —Arnold Bennett⟩ (2) : the matter received in the mail at one time or by one person : MAIL 2b ⟨the ~ came with tea —Cecil Beaton⟩ **d** : POST OFFICE **e** : POSTBOX **f** : POSTAGE 3 **4** : GENERAL POST 1 **5** : the act of posting in horseback riding ⟨the rhythm of a ~ is not difficult once it has been achieved⟩
5post \"\ *vb* -ED/-ING/-S *vi* **1 a** : to travel with post-horses ⟨~*ing* in private carriages . . . the most comfortable and convenient method of traveling —Hugh McCausland⟩ **b** : to ride or travel with haste : HURRY ⟨off he ~*ed* to Louisville —S.H. Adams⟩ **2** : to rise forward and upward from a riding saddle when one diagonal pair of the horse's legs is off the ground and to return to the saddle when the opposite diagonal pair is off the ground supporting one's weight primarily by the knees and thighs **3** : to dispatch mail ⟨not only shopped early but ~*ed* early —Rose Macaulay⟩ ~ *vt* **1 a** *archaic* : to dispatch (a person) in haste **b** *obs* : to convey speedily **c** *obs* : to dispatch by a post or messenger **2** : MAIL ⟨stroll down the street to ~ a letter —Elspeth Huxley⟩ **3 a** : to transfer or carry (an entry or item) from a book of original entry to the proper account in a ledger : transfer (an entry or item) from one record to another **b** (1) : to complete (a ledger) by the transfer and proper entry of all items from antecedent books — used usu. with *up* ⟨~ up the general ledger⟩ (2) : to make transfer entries in (all books) to complete the record ⟨~ up the books for the month⟩ **4** : to make (a person) familiar with a subject : INFORM ⟨is better ~*ed* than . . . his audience —A.T.Weaver⟩ ⟨keep them ~*ed* as to what is going on —Shipley Thomas⟩ — used sometimes with *up* ⟨shows himself thoroughly ~*ed up* —*Times Lit. Supp.*⟩
6post \"\ *adv* [4*post* (as in the phrase *to ride in post*)] : with post-horses : like a courier : at full speed : EXPRESS ⟨journeying ~⟩ ⟨ride ~⟩
7post \"\ *n* -S [MF *poste*, fr. OIt *posto*, fr. past part. of *porre* to put — more at 4POST] **1 a** : the place at which a soldier is stationed; *esp* : the fixed locality or stretch of ground guarded and patrolled by a sentry or outpost ⟨walking his ~ as ordered⟩ **b** : the prescribed place (as for an officer or for the colors) in a formation of troops **c** : the place at which a body of troops is stationed : CAMP, FORT ⟨every noncoms' club on the ~ —James Jones⟩ **d** (1) : a local subdivision of a veterans' organization (as the American Legion) (2) : a unit of five or more explorers (as of the Boy Scouts of America) corresponding to a boy scout troop **e** : one of two bugle calls sounded at tattoo (as in the British Army) ⟨last ~⟩ **2 a** : a station or position esp. to which a person is assigned ⟨~ of duty⟩ ⟨~ of danger⟩ ⟨we took ~ close to the . . . fence —S.P.B.Mais⟩ ⟨heroes still at their ~*s* —Wynford Vaughan-Thomas⟩ **b** : shooting position (as in field archery or skeet) **c** : a position taken by a player in basketball as a focal point of offensive attack **3** : an office or position to which a person is appointed ⟨a good ~ in the public service⟩ ⟨held various ~*s* —*Lamp*⟩ ⟨teaching ~*s* in our colleges —E.J.Simmons⟩ **4 a** : TRADING POST, SETTLEMENT ⟨sent medical supplies to the outlying ~⟩ **b** : a station on the floor of a stock exchange at which trade in a particular issue or group of issues is carried on
8post \"\ *vt* -ED/-ING/-S **1 a** : to station in a given place ⟨window where she had ~*ed* herself for observation —Owen Wister⟩ ⟨repair ships . . . are ~*ed* along the route —Robert Pocock⟩ **b** : to assign (a sentry) to a post ⟨~*ed* picket sentries —Charles Beadle⟩ **c** : to carry (the national flag) ceremoniously to a designated position ⟨~*ing* the colors⟩ **d** : to place (a chessman) on a square for continued occupancy ⟨the bishop and queen are badly ~*ed* —*New Complete Hoyle*⟩ **2** *chiefly Brit* : to assign to a unit or location (as in the military or civil service) ⟨~*ed* to a regiment —Earle Birney⟩ ⟨~*ed* to his home district —*Scots Mag.*⟩ **3 a** : to lay down (as money or a deposit) : put up (a stake) **b** : to furnish (as bond) to the proper authority ⟨~*ed* bail for the suspect⟩ ⟨~ the collateral required⟩
9post \"\ *n* -S [origin unknown] **1** : a pile of wet sheets of handmade paper interleaved with felt in papermaking **2** : a charge of ore for a smelting furnace
10post \"\ *adv* [L — more at POST-] : lying behind : posterior in position ⟨~ diaphragmatic organs⟩
11post \"\ *n* -S [by shortening] *slang* : POSTMORTEM ⟨a report on the ~⟩
12post \"\ *vt* -ED/-ING/-S *slang* : to conduct a postmortem on (a body) ⟨the corpse has been ~*ed*⟩
post- *prefix* [ME, fr. L, fr. *post* (adv. & prep.); akin to Gk (Arcadian & Cyprian dial.) *pos* toward, on, at, Skt *paśca* behind, after, later, OE *of* of, from, off — more at OF] **1 a** : after : subsequent : later ⟨*post*date⟩ ⟨*post*entry⟩ ⟨*post*nati⟩ **b** : behind ⟨*post*fix⟩ : posterior ⟨*post*abdomen⟩ : following after ⟨*post*consonantal⟩ **2 a** : subsequent to : later than ⟨*post*adolescence⟩ ⟨*post*classical⟩ ⟨*post*operative⟩ ⟨*post*war⟩ **b** : behind : posterior to ⟨*post*antennal⟩ ⟨*post*cardinal⟩ ⟨*post*ocular⟩
post *abbr* postal
post·abdomen \(ˌ)pōst+\ *n* [NL, fr. *post-* + *abdomen*] **1** : a posterior differentiated part of the abdomen; *specif* : the slender posterior sting-bearing portion of the abdomen of a scorpion **2** : a posterior part of the body beyond the abdomen proper — **post·abdominal** \ˌ=+\ *adj*
post·absorptive \ˌ=+\ *adj* [*post-* + *absorptive*] : following or typical of the period following absorption of nutrients from the alimentary canal ⟨~ blood sugar level⟩ ⟨the ~ state⟩
post·age \'pōstij, -tēj\ *n* -S [4*post* + *-age*] **1** *obs* : conveyance or dispatch of mail by post **2** *archaic* : a postal service **3** : the fee for postal service ⟨the rate of ~ charged on the parcel —*U.S. Official Postal Guide*⟩ **4** : adhesive stamps or printed indicia representing postal fees ⟨covers must bear ~ at the first-class rate —*Stamps*⟩
postage currency *n* : a fractional paper currency bearing the facsimiles of postage stamps; *esp* : one issued by the U.S. between August 1862 and May 1863
postage-due stamp \ˌ==ˌ=-\ *n* : a stamp placed by a post office on an article of mail (as on a business reply card or envelope) to indicate an amount of postage or a special service fee to be paid before the article may be received by the addressee
postage impression *or* **postage-paid impression** \ˌ==ˌ=-\ *n* : METER IMPRESSION
postage meter *or* **postal meter** *n* : a machine that prints postal indicia on pieces of mail, records the amount of postage given in the indicia, and subtracts it from a total amount which has been paid at a post office and for which the machine has been set; *also* : a machine that so marks mail on deposit of a coin in a slot
postage paper *n* : POSTAL PAPER
postage stamp *n* : an adhesive stamp or an imprinted stamp on a piece of postal stationery issued by a postal service for use on mail matter as evidence of prepayment of postage
1post·al \'pōstəl\ *adj* [F, fr. *poste* post, mail + *-al* — more at POST (mail)] **1** : of or relating to the posts or mails or to the post office ⟨~ service⟩ ⟨~ career⟩ ⟨~ inspector⟩ ⟨a ~ agreement between governments⟩ **2** : of or relating to a system of carrying goods or passengers on a railroad for a uniform rate irrespective of distance ⟨the ~ principle⟩ ⟨the ~ tariff⟩ **3** : conducted by mail ⟨~ chess⟩ ⟨~ tuition⟩
2postal \"\ *n* -S : POSTAL CARD ⟨drop a ~ to the editor —*Congressional Record*⟩
postal bus *n* : HIGHWAY POST OFFICE
postal car *n* : RAILWAY MAIL CAR
postal card *n* : POSTCARD
postal clerk *n* : a clerk in a post office; *specif* : one assigned to sort and distribute mail in railway post offices
postal course *n, Brit* : a course of study conducted by mail — compare CORRESPONDENCE SCHOOL
postal currency *n* : POSTAGE CURRENCY
postal delivery zone *or* **postal zone** *n* : ZONE 5c
postal fiscal stamp *n* : a stamp issued as a revenue stamp but used as a postage stamp
post·al·ly \'pōstəlē, -li\ *adv* [1*postal* + *-ly*] **1** : in a postal manner : for postal purposes ⟨a ~ used stamp⟩ **2** : by or on postage stamps ⟨a ~ commemorated anniversary⟩
postal match *n* : a rifle or pistol match in which the winner is determined by comparison of targets mailed to judges for scoring
postal money order *n* : MONEY ORDER
postal note *n* : POSTAL ORDER
postal order *n, Brit* : a postal money order that is issued in fixed denominations, is payable to a particular person and at a particular office, and may be crossed for payment through a bank
postal paper *n* **1** : postage stamps ⟨the *postal paper* of . . . the United States and its possessions —K.B.Stiles⟩ **2** : POSTAL STATIONERY ⟨pioneer in issuing airmail *postal paper* —K.B. Stiles⟩
postal savings bank *n* : a savings bank conducted by a government through the local post offices
postal stationery *n* : government-issued stationery (as letter sheets, envelopes, postcards) bearing imprinted stamps
postal storage car *n* : a railroad car for transporting mail that lacks facilities for sorting or distribution en route — compare RAILWAY MAIL CAR
postal tax stamp *n* : a government stamp required on mail not for postage but for some public fund (as for a public health project)
postal union *n* : an international agreement to observe uniform regulations governing international mail
pos·ta·ment \'pōstəmənt\ *n* -S [G, fr. (assumed) obs. It *postamento*, fr. *postare* to place, put (fr. *posto*, past part. of *porre* to put) + *-mento* -ment (fr. L *-mentum*) — more at POST] **1 a** : PEDESTAL, BASE **b** : STEREOBATE **2** : a frame, mount, or molding for a work in relief
post-and-lintel \ˌ==ˈ=\ *adj* : of or relating to a system of architectural construction based on vertical supports and horizontal beams as distinguished from systems based on arches or vaults
post and pair *n* [*post* prob. fr. It *posta* stake, wager, fr. fem. of *posto*, past part. of *porre* to put — more at POST] : a card game popular in 16th and 17th century England that was played with hands of three cards
post-and-stall \ˌ==ˈ=\ *adj* [1*post*] : BORD-AND-PILLAR
post·anoxic \(ˌ)=+\ *adj* [*post-* + *anoxic*] : following a period of anoxia ⟨~ respiratory rhythms⟩ ⟨a ~ hyperpnea, greater than that attained during hypoxia —T.G.Bernthal⟩
post·antennal \(ˈ)=+\ *adj* [*post-* + *antennal*] : located behind the antennae of an insect ⟨~ appendage⟩ ⟨~ organ⟩ ⟨the ~ third brain segment of an insect⟩
post·arteriolar \ˌ=+\ *adj* [*post-* + *arteriolar*] : following after the arterioles : CAPILLARY ⟨~ bed⟩
post·atomic \"+\ *adj* [*post-* + *atomic*] **1** : subsequent to the release of atomic energy **2** : subsequent to the explosion of the first atomic bomb ⟨the ~ world⟩ ⟨the ~ age⟩
post·audit \(ˈ)=+\ *n* [*post-* + *audit*] : an audit made subsequent to the final settlement of a transaction — contrasted with *preaudit*
post·axial \"+\ *adj* [*post-* + *axial*] : located behind the axis of the body; *esp* : of or relating to the posterior side of the axis of a vertebrate limb (the ulnar side of the forelimb or fibular side of the hind limb) — **post·axially** \"+\ *adv*
postbag \'=,=\ *n* [4*post* + *bag*] **1** *chiefly Brit* : MAILBAG **2** *chiefly Brit* : a single batch of letters or other mail : MAIL 2 b ⟨could infer this merely from my own ~ —George Orwell⟩
post·bellum \(ˈ)pōs(t)ˈbeləm\ *adj* [L *post bellum* after the war] : existing after the war : of, relating to, or characteristic of the period following a war and esp. following the American Civil War ⟨the ~ generation⟩ ⟨the ~ South⟩ ⟨his ~ insistence on racial equality —*Va. Quarterly Rev.*⟩
post binder *n* [1*post*] : a loose-leaf binder having metal posts designed to pass through holes punched in the sheets

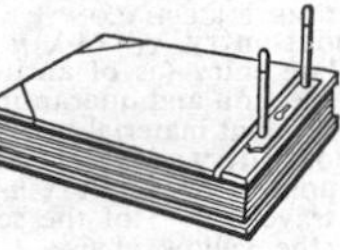

post binder

postbox \'=,=\ *n* [4*post* + *box*] : MAILBOX; *esp* : a public mailbox
postboy \'=,=\ *n* [4*post* + *boy*] **1** : POSTRIDER **2** : POSTILION
post·brachium \(ˈ)=+\ *n* [NL, fr. *post-* + *brachium*] : the brachium of the inferior colliculus
post·branchial body \(ˈ)=+-\ *n* [*post-* + *branchial*] : an outpocketing from the fourth visceral pouch of a vertebrate embryo that is believed to be a vestigial fifth pouch and that gives rise to all or part of the parathyroids
post·breeding \"+\ *adj* [*post-* + *breeding*] : following a period of physiological fitness for reproduction ⟨~ regressive changes⟩ — see 2COLLAPSE 5
post·canonical \ˌ=+\ *adj* [*post-* + *canonical*] : written subsequent to writings included in a canon esp. of Scripture
post captain *n* [7*post*] : a naval officer holding a captain's commission as distinguished from one bearing the courtesy title of captain
1postcard \'=,=\ *n* [4*post* + *card*] : a card for bearing a message through the mail without an envelope: **a** (1) : a card to which an adhesive stamp must be affixed (2) : such a card having a decoration (as a picture) on one side **b** : a card bearing a government-imprinted stamp or official reply-paid indicia
2postcard \"\ *vt* **1** : to relate by postcard ⟨~*s* that all is well⟩ **2** : to communicate with by postcard ⟨~ us today⟩
post·cardinal \(ˈ)=+\ *adj* [*post-* + *cardinal*] : lying behind or caudal to the heart; *esp* : of, relating to, or being a vein on either side in mammalian and other embryos and in some fishes that drains the mesonephros and the portion of the trunk caudal to the heart
post·cava \"+\ *n* [NL, fr. *post-* + *cava*] : the inferior vena cava of vertebrates higher than fishes — **post·caval** \"+\ *adj*
post cedar *n* [1*post*] **1** : SOUTHERN WHITE CEDAR **2** : INCENSE CEDAR
post·ce·nal *or* **post·coe·nal** \(ˈ)pōs(t)ˈsēnəl\ *adj* [*post-* + L *cena* dinner + E *-al* — more at CÉNACLE] : occurring after dinner : POSTPRANDIAL
post·central \(ˈ)=+\ *adj* [*post-* + *central*] : located behind a center or central structure; *esp* : located behind the central sulcus of the cerebral cortex ⟨the ~ gyrus⟩ ⟨the ~ sulcus⟩
post·centrum \"+\ *n* [NL, fr. *post-* + *centrum*] : a distinct posterior part of the centrum of a vertebra in some fishes formed by coossification of the interventral and interdorsal arcualia — opposed to *precentrum*
post chaise *n* [4*post*] : a carriage for traveling post usu. having a closed body on four wheels and seating two to four persons
post chariot *n* : a carriage for traveling post; *specif* : a kind of light four-wheeled carriage with a driver's seat in front
post·cholecystectomy syndrome \(ˈ)=+-\ *n* [*post-* + *cholecystectomy*] : BILIARY DYSKINESIA
post·ci·bal \(ˈ)pōs(t)ˈsībəl\ *adj* [*post-* + LL *cibalis* of food,

fr. L *cibus* food + *-alis* -al — more at CIBARIAL] **:** occurring after a meal

post·classic \(ˈ)=+\ *or* **post·classical** \"+\ *adj* [*post-* + *classic, classical*] **:** of or relating to a period (as in art or literature) subsequent to one regarded as classical ⟨the sonata form is a concept created by the ~ nineteenth century —P.H. Lang⟩ — **post·classicism** \"+\ *n*

post·climax \(ˈ)=+\ *n* [*post-* + *climax*] **:** a relatively stable ecological community requiring a greater amount of available moisture than that generally available to a climax and occurring typically where locally abundant soil moisture compensates for a generally deficient precipitation ⟨a forest ~ on a moist northward-facing slope within a grassland climax⟩ — compare PRECLIMAX

post·clypeus \"+\ *n* [NL, fr. *post-* + *clypeus*] **:** the upper or proximal portion of the clypeus in some insects — compare ANTECLYPEUS

post coach *n* [[4]*post*] **:** STAGECOACH; *specif* **:** one used for carrying the mails

post·coital \(ˈ)=+\ *adj* [*post-* + *coital*] **:** occurring or existing after coitus

post·colonial \ˌ=+\ *adj* [*post-* + *colonial*] **:** having the characteristics of the American colonial style of architecture but executed in the period following the revolution

post·commissural \(ˈ)=+\ *adj* [*postcommissure* + *-al*] **:** of, relating to, or transmitted by the postcommissures of the brain

post·commissure \"+\ *n* [*post-* + *commissure*] **:** one of the bands of white matter that bound the third ventricle of the brain posteriorly

post–common \(ˈ)=+\ *n* [ME *post-comoun*, fr. ML *post-communio*] **:** POST-COMMUNION

post–communion \ˌ=+\ *n, often cap P&C* [ML *postcommunio*, fr. L *post-* + LL *communio* communion — more at COMMUNION] **:** the portion of a Christian communion service that follows the communicating of the congregation

post·consonantal \(ˌ)=+\ *adj* [*post-* + *consonantal*] **:** immediately following a consonant

post·cornu \(ˈ)=+\ *n* [NL, fr. *post-* + L *cornu* horn, something shaped like a horn — more at HORN] **:** a posterior horn of the lateral ventricle

post·cranial \(ˈ)=+\ *adj* [*post-* + *cranial*] **:** lying behind the head **:** of the trunk and limbs ⟨bones of the ~ skeleton⟩

post croaker *n* [[1]*post*] **:** SPOT 7

post·dam \(ˈ)=+\ *n* [*post-* + *dam*] **:** a posterior extension of a full denture to accomplish a complete seal between denture and tissues

[1]**post·date** \(ˈ)=+\ *n* [*post-* + *date* (n.)] **:** a subsequent date; *esp* **:** a date assigned to an event or affixed to a document that is later than its actual date ⟨a ~ on a bill of exchange⟩

[2]**postdate** \"\ *vt* [*post-* + *date* (v.)] **1 a :** to date (a document) as of a time subsequent to that of execution ⟨~ a check⟩ **b :** to assign (an event) to a date subsequent to that of actual occurrence ⟨*postdated* her birth⟩ **2 :** to follow (something) in time ⟨the words ~ the rest of the inscription —R.S. Rogers⟩

[1]**post·dental** \(ˈ)=+\ *adj* [ISV *post-* + *dental*] *of a consonant* **:** produced with the point of the tongue at the backs of the upper front teeth

[2]**postdental** \"\ *n* **:** a postdental consonant

post·depositional \(ˌ)=+\ *adj* [*post-* + *depositional*] **:** occurring or produced after deposition of the sediments involved — used of a geological change or formation

[1]**post·diluvian** \ˌ=+\ *also* **post·diluvial** \"+\ *adj* [*post-* + *diluvian* or *diluvial*] **:** of or relating to the period after the flood described in the Bible ⟨~ man⟩

[2]**post·diluvian** \(ˌ)=+\ *n* -S **:** one living after the flood described in the Bible

post·disseisin *or* **post·disseizin** \ˌ=+\ *n* [AF *postdisseisine*, fr. *post-* + *disseisine* disseisin — more at DISSEISIN] **:** a second disseisin by the same disseisor from lands recovered by the assize of novel disseisin; *also* **:** the writ that lay for it

post·doctoral \(ˈ)=+\ *also* **post·doctorate** \"+\ *adj* [*post-* + *doctoral* or *doctorate*] **:** relating to, awarded for, or engaged in advanced academic or professional work after the attainment of a doctor's degree ⟨~ training program⟩ ⟨~ student⟩ ⟨~ studies⟩

post·ea \ˈpōstēə\ *n* -S [L, afterward, fr. *post* after + *ea*, prob. abl. of *ea*, fem. of *is* this, that, he — more at POST-, ITERATE] **:** the entry made by the trial judge after a verdict reciting that issue was joined and summarizing the proceedings

po·steen \pōˈstēn\ *or* **po·shteen** \-ˈs(h)tēn\ *or* **po·stin** \-ˈstēn\ *n* -S [Per *pōstīn* of leather, fr. *pōst* skin, fr. MPer] **:** an Afghan pelisse made of leather with the fleece on

post·embryonic \(ˌ)=+\ *also* **post·embryonal** \(ˈ)=+\ *adj* [*post-* + *embryonic* or *embryonal*] **:** succeeding the embryonic stage

post·emergence \ˌ=+\ *adj* [*post-* + *emergence*] **:** used or occurring in the stage between the emergence of a seedling and the maturity of a crop plant ⟨~ herbicides⟩ ⟨~ development⟩

post·encephalitic \(ˌ)=+\ *adj* [*post-* + *encephalitic*] **:** developing after and presumably as a result of encephalitis ⟨~ parkinsonism⟩

post·encephalitis \ˌ=+\ *n* [NL, fr. *post-* + *encephalitis*] **:** symptoms or residual abnormality remaining after recovery from epidemic encephalitis

post·encephalon \"+\ *n* [NL, fr. *post-* + *encephalon*] **:** METENCEPHALON

post·entry \(ˈ)=+\ *n* [*post-* + *entry*] **1 :** a subsequent or late entry (as of an item missed in an account) **2 :** the inspection and quarantine detention period following admission of plant material at a port of entry

post entry *n* [[3]*post*] **:** a last minute entry in a race or competition

[1]**post·er** \ˈpōstə(r)\ *n* -S [[5]*post* + *-er*] **1 a** *archaic* **:** a swift traveler ⟨~*s* of the sea and land —Shak.⟩ **b :** POST-HORSE ⟨the yellow chaise . . . and . . . four ~*s* —Charles Lever⟩ **2 :** one that mails a letter **3 a :** one that posts bookkeeping entries **b :** POSTING CLERK

[2]**poster** \"\ *n* -S *often attrib* [[2]*post* + *-er*] **1 :** a bill or placard intended to be posted in a public place; *specif* **:** one that is decorative or pictorial **2 :** POSTER STAMP

[3]**poster** *vt* -ED/-ING/-S **:** to affix (posters) to ⟨~*ed* the wall⟩

poster color *n* **:** a paint with a gum or glue-size binder sold usu. in jars — compare [4]DISTEMPER

poste res·tante \ˌpō,steˈstänt\ *n* [F, lit., remaining (staying) mail] **:** GENERAL DELIVERY

pos·te·ri·ad \päˈstirē,ad\ *adv* [*posterior* + *-ad*] **:** POSTERIORLY

[1]**pos·te·ri·or** \(ˈ)pō,stirē ə(r), (ˈ)pä¦-, -¦stēr-\ *adj* [L, compar. of *posterus* next, following, coming after, fr. *post* after — more at POST-] **1 a :** after in time **:** SUBSEQUENT **b :** logically consequent **2 a :** situated toward the back **:** after in place — opposed to *anterior* **b :** ADAXIAL — compare ANTERIOR **c** (1) **:** situated at or toward the hinder end of the body **:** CAUDAL (2) **:** DORSAL — used of human anatomy in which the upright posture makes dorsal and caudal identical — **pos·te·rior·ly** *adv*

[2]**posterior** \"\ *n* -S **1 posteriors** *pl, archaic* **:** DESCENDANTS ⟨neither he, nor his ~*s* from generation to generation, shall sit upon it —Sir Walter Scott⟩ **2 :** a posterior thing or part; as **a :** the rear end of a quadruped **b :** BUTTOCKS ⟨smacked him on his ~ and sent him out to play⟩ — often used in pl. ⟨when she laughed, which was often, her ~*s* gave a just-perceptible upward leap —Robertson Davies⟩

posterior femoral cutaneous nerve *n* **:** a nerve arising from the sacral plexus of each side leaving the pelvis in company with the sciatic nerve through the greater sciatic foramen to be distributed to the skin of the perineum and of the back of the thigh and leg

posterior foramen *n* **:** the opening in an insect's head leading to the thoracic cavity

posterior horn *n* **1 :** a dorsal column of gray matter in the spinal cord **2 :** the part of a lateral ventricle of the brain that extends inward and backward

pos·te·ri·or·ic \(ˌ)=¦=¦örik\ *adj* [(*a*) *posteriori* + *-ic*] **:** A POSTERIORI — **pos·te·ri·or·i·cal·ly** \-rək(ə)lē\ *adv*

pos·te·ri·or·i·ty \(ˌ)=,==ˈörəd·ē, -ˈär-\ *n* -ES [ME *posteriorite*, fr. ML *posterioritas*, fr. L *posterior* + *-itas* -ity] **1 :** the quality or state of being later or subsequent — opposed to *priority* **2** *obs* **:** INFERIORITY

posteriormost \=ˈ===,=\ *adj* [[1]*posterior* + *most*] **:** farthest back in time, order, or position

posterior naris *n* **:** the opening or one of the paired openings between the nasal cavity and the pharynx or mouth

posterior nasal spine *n* **:** the nasal spine that is formed by the union of processes of the two palatine bones and projects between the posterior nares

posterior paralysis *n* **:** progressive weakness and loss of function accompanied by modification of joints and bones of the hindquarters of young pigs receiving inadequate vitamin D and calcium

post·er·ist \ˈpōstərəst\ *n* -S [[2]*poster* + *-ist*] **:** one who designs or makes posters

pos·ter·i·ty \päˈsterəd·ē, -rətē, -i\ *n* -ES [ME *posterite*, fr. MF *posterité*, fr. L *posteritat-*, *posteritas*, fr. *posterus* coming after + *-itat-*, *-itas* -ity — more at POSTERIOR] **1 :** the offspring of one progenitor to the furthest generation **:** DESCENDANTS ⟨secure the blessings of liberty to ourselves and our ~ —*U.S. Constitution*⟩ **2 :** all succeeding generations **:** future time ⟨for the benefit of ~⟩ ⟨transmit to ~⟩ ⟨do the best we can . . . leaving ~ free to do better —G.B.Shaw⟩

[1]**pos·tern** \ˈpōstə(r)n, ˈpäs-\ *n* -S [ME *posterne*, fr. OF, alter. of *posterle*, fr. LL *posterula* little secret door, dim. of *postera* back door, fr. fem. of L *posterus* coming after — more at POSTERIOR] **1 a :** a back door or gate **:** a private or side entrance or way **b :** an obscure or disreputable way of entrance or escape **2 :** a subterraneous passage between the ditch and the interior of either the main works or outworks of a fortification

[2]**postern** \"\ *adj* **:** situated at the back, rear, or side **:** PRIVATE ⟨the ~ gate of the abbey⟩ ⟨a ~ door⟩

postero- *comb form* [L *posterus* coming after — more at POSTERIOR] **1 :** posterior and ⟨*postero*anterior⟩ ⟨*postero*-lateral⟩ **2 :** at the back part of ⟨*postero*dorsal⟩

pos·tero·dorsad \ˌpästərō+\ *adv* [*postero-* + *dorsad*] **:** POSTERODORSALLY

pos·tero·dorsal \" +\ *adj* [*postero-* + *dorsal*] **:** of or relating to the posterior part of the back — **postero·dorsally** \"+\ *adv*

pos·tero·external \"+\ *adj* [*postero-* + *external*] **:** posterior and external in location or direction

pos·tero·internal \"+\ *adj* [*postero-* + *internal*] **:** posterior and internal in position or direction

pos·tero·lateral \"+\ *adj* [*postero-* + *lateral*] **:** posterior and lateral in position or direction

pos·tero·median \"+\ *adj* [*postero-* + *median*] **:** located on or near the dorsal midline of the body or a body part

[1]**pos·tero·temporal** \"+\ *adj* [*postero-* + *temporal*] **:** of or relating to the supraclavicle of a fish

[2]**posterotemporal** \"\ *n* **:** the supraclavicle of a fish

pos·tero·ventrad \"+\ *adv* [*postero-* + *ventrad*] **:** in a posterior and ventral direction **:** at once posteriorly and ventrally

pos·tero·ventral \"+\ *adj* [*postero-* + *ventral*] **:** situated posteriorly and ventrally

poster paint *n* [[2]*poster*] **:** POSTER COLOR

poster panel *n* **:** an outdoor structure having a standardized size surface on which advertising posters may be posted

posters *pl of* POSTER, *pres 3d sing of* POSTER

poster stamp *or* **poster seal** *n* **:** a charity seal made in extra large size

post·ery \ˈpōstərē\ *adj* [[2]*poster* + *-y*] **:** resembling a poster in pictorial effect ⟨an irregular solid background with altogether pleasing and ~ results —*Printer's Ink*⟩

post exchange *n* [[7]*post*] **:** a shop at a military installation at which merchandise and services are sold to military personnel and authorized civilians

post·exilic \ˌ=+\ *also* **post·exilian** \"+\ *adj* [*post-* + *exilic* or *exilian*] **:** existing or happening after the Exile or the Babylonian Captivity of the Jews esp. during the period of 538 B.C. to A.D. 1 ⟨~ Judaism⟩ ⟨~ Hebrew⟩

post·exist \ˌ=+\ *vi* [*post-* + *exist*] **:** to exist after death — **post·existence** \"+\ *n*

post·face \ˈpōs(t)fəs\ *n* [F, fr. *post-* + *-face* (as in *préface* preface) — more at PREFACE] **:** a brief article or note (as of explanation) placed at the end of a publication

postfact *n* [L *postfactum*, neut. of *postfactus* done afterwards, fr. *post-* + *factus*, past part. of *facere* to do — more at DO] *obs* **:** a subsequent deed or occurrence

post–factum \(ˈ)=+\ *adj* [L *post factum* after the fact] **:** occurring after the fact **:** ex post facto **:** RETROSPECTIVE ⟨*post-factum* discussions of decisions —*America*⟩

post–fine \ˈ=,=\ *n* [*post-* + *fine*] **:** money paid in early English law for license to levy a fine — called also *King's silver*

[1]**post·fix** \ˈ=,=\ *n* -ES [*post-* + *-fix* (as in *prefix*)] **:** a letter, syllable, or word added to the end of another word **:** SUFFIX

[2]**postfix** \(ˈ)=¦=\ *vt* **:** to affix at the end; *specif* **:** to add (a letter or syllable) to the end of a word

post flag *n* [[7]*post*] **:** the national flag measuring 19 feet fly by 10 feet hoist ordinarily used at a military post (as of the U.S. Army)

post·form \(ˈ)=+\ *vt* [*post-* + *form*] **:** to shape subsequently (as a sheet material after laminating)

post–free \(ˈ)=¦=\ *adj* [[4]*post* + *free*] *chiefly Brit* **:** POSTPAID

[1]**post·frontal** \"+\ *adj* [*post-* + *frontal*] **:** situated behind the frontal bone or frontal region of the skull or in reptiles the frontal shield; *specif* **:** indicating a bone behind and above the orbit of which it commonly forms part of the border that is present in many vertebrates and corresponds to the postorbital process of the frontal bone of various birds and mammals

[2]**postfrontal** \"\ *n* **:** a postfrontal part (as a bone or scale); *specif* **:** the sphenotic bone of a fish

post·furca \"+\ *n* [NL, fr. *post-* + *furca*] **:** the posterior one of the forked internal thoracic processes of the sternum of an insect — **post·furcal** \"+\ *adj*

post·ganglionary \(ˈ)=+\ *adj* [*post-* + *ganglionary*] **:** occurring beyond, behind, or distal to a ganglion

post·ganglionic \(ˌ)=+\ *adj* [*post-* + *ganglionic*] **:** lying behind, beyond, or distal to a ganglion — used of the axons of neurons whose cell bodies lie within an autonomic ganglion; compare PREGANGLIONIC

post·gena \(ˈ)=+\ *n* [NL, fr. L *post-* + *gena*] **:** the lateral part of the area of the insect cranium between the occipital and postoccipital sutures

post·glacial \(ˈ)=+\ *adj* [ISV *post-* + *glacial*] **:** occurring after a period of glaciation (as the Pleistocene)

[1]**post·glenoid** \(ˈ)=+\ *also* **post·glenoidal** \ˌ=+\ *adj* [*post-* + *glenoid, glenoidal*] **:** situated behind the glenoid fossa

[2]**postglenoid** \"\ *n* -S **:** a flattened expansion of the squamosal part of the temporal bone lying posterior to the glenoid fossa

post·gnathal \(ˈ)=+\ *adj* [*post-* + *gnathal*] **:** situated behind the gnathal region of an insect's head

post·grad \(ˈ)=+\ *n* [by shortening] *slang* **:** POSTGRADUATE

[1]**post·graduate** \(ˈ)=+\ *adj* [*post-* + *graduate*] **1 :** GRADUATE 1b **2 :** of, relating to, or engaged in study following graduation from high school usu. concentrating on preparation for college entrance

[2]**postgraduate** \"\ *n* **:** a student continuing his education after graduation from high school or college

[1]**posthaste** \(ˈ)=¦=\ *n* [[4]*post* (courier) + *haste*] *archaic* **:** speed in traveling (as of a post or courier) **:** great haste — used chiefly in the phrase *in posthaste*

[2]**posthaste** \"\ *adv* **:** with great speed **:** in great haste **:** by the fastest possible means ⟨riding ~⟩ ⟨sent ~ for his lawyer⟩

[3]**posthaste** \"\ *adj, obs* **:** SPEEDY, IMMEDIATE ⟨requires your haste, ~ appearance —Shak.⟩

post·heating \(ˈ)=+\ *n* [*post-* + *heating*] **:** the process of heating a metal after welding in order to decrease the rate of cooling to room temperature

pos·thi·tis \(ˌ)päsˈthīd·əs\ *n, pl* **pos·thit·i·des** \-thid·ə,dēz\ [NL, fr. Gk *posthē* penis, foreskin + NL *-itis* — more at PENIS] **:** inflammation of the prepuce

post hoc \(ˈ)pōstˈhäk\ *adv* [L; fr. the use of the proposition *post hoc, ergo propter hoc* meaning "after this, therefore because of this" as an example of the fallacy of arguing from mere temporal sequence to cause and effect relationship] **:** after this — compare PROPTER HOC

posthole \ˈ=,=\ *n* [[1]*post* + *hole*] **1 :** a hole sunk in the ground to hold a fence post **2 :** a shallow oil well

post–hole digger *n* **:** a tool for digging postholes; *esp* **:** one operated from the power takeoff on a tractor

post horn *n* [[4]*post*] **:** a simple straight or coiled brass or copper wind instrument with cupped mouthpiece used esp. by postilions of the 18th and 19th centuries

post horn

post–horse \ˈ=,=\ *n* [[4]*post*] **:** a horse for use by postriders or in riding post

posthouse \ˈ=,=\ *n* [[4]*post* + *house*] **1 :** a house or inn for exchanging post-horses and accommodating postriders **2** *archaic* **:** POST OFFICE

post·hu·ma \ˈpäschəmə, päˈst(y)əmə\ *n pl* [L *postuma, posthuma*, neut. pl. of *postumus, posthumus*] **:** posthumous writings

posthume *adj* [MF *postume, posthume*, fr. L *postumus, posthumus*] *obs* **:** POSTHUMOUS

post·hu·mous \ˈpäschəməs, päˈst(y)üməs *sometimes* (ˈ)pō-\ *adj* [L *posthumus*, by folk etymology (influence of *humus* earth) fr. *postumus*, superl. of *posterus* coming after — more at HUMBLE, POSTERIOR] **1 :** born after the death of the father ⟨a ~ son⟩ **2 :** published after the death of the author ⟨a ~ volume of poems⟩ **3 :** following or occurring after one's death ⟨~ fame⟩ ⟨~ vindication⟩ — **post·hu·mous·ly** *adv* — **post·hu·mous·ness** *n* -ES

post·hypnotic \(ˌ)=+\ *adj* [ISV *post-* + *hypnotic*] **:** of, relating to, or characteristic of the period following a hypnotic trance during which the subject will still carry out suggestions made by the operator during the trance state ⟨~ suggestion⟩ — **post·hypnotically** \"+\ *adv*

post·hypophysis \ˌ=+\ *n* [NL, fr. *post-* + *hypophysis*] **:** the posterior lobe of the pituitary body

pos·ti·cal \ˈpästəkəl\ *also* **pos·tic** \-tik\ *adj* [L *posticus*, adj., that is behind, fr. *post* after, behind + *-icus* -ic, -ical — more at POST-] **:** POSTERIOR — **pos·ti·cal·ly** \-tək(ə)lē\ *adv*

pos·tiche \päˈstēsh, pó'-, ˈ=,=\ *n* -S [F, fr. Sp *postizo*, fr. *postizo* false, artificial, short for *apostizo*, fr. LL *appositicius* added, fr. L *appositus* (past part. of *apponere* to place near, apply to, add) + *-icius* -itious — more at APPOSITE] **:** false hair: as **a :** SWITCH **b :** TOUPEE

pos·ti·cous \päˈstīkəs\ *adj* [L *posticus*, fr. *post* behind, after + *-icus* -ic — more at POST-] **1 :** POSTERIOR **2 :** situated on the outer side of a filament — used of an extrorse anther

post·ictal \(ˈ)=+\ *adj* [*post-* + *ictal*] **:** following a sudden attack (as of epilepsy) ⟨~ drowsiness⟩

pos·ti·cum \päˈstīkəm\ *n, pl* **posti·ca** \-kə\ [L, rear of a building, back door, fr. neut. of *posticus* back, posterior — more at POST] **:** a portico behind an ancient Greek or Roman temple

post·ie \ˈpōsti\ *n* -S [[4]*post* + *-ie*] *Scot* **:** POSTMAN

[1]**pos·til** \ˈpästəl\ *n* -S [ME *postille*, fr. MF, fr. ML *postilla*, prob. fr. *post illa* (*verba textus*) after those words of the text, fr. L *post* after + *illa*, neut. acc. pl. of *ille* that — more at POST-, ALARM] **1 a :** a marginal note **:** COMMENT; *specif* **:** an explanatory marginal note in the Bible **b postils** *pl, obs* **:** COMMENTARY **2 a** *obs* **:** a short homily on a Scriptural passage; *esp* **:** one on the Gospel or Epistle for the day **b :** a collection of such homilies

[2]**postil** \"\ *vt* **postiled** *or* **postilled**; **postiled** *or* **postilled**; **postiling** *or* **postilling**; **postils** [ME *postilen*, fr. MF *postiller*, fr. ML *postillare*, fr. *postilla*] *archaic* **:** to write marginal comments in (a text) **:** ANNOTATE, GLOSS

pos·til·ion *or* **pos·til·lion** \pōˈstilyən, pəˈ-\ *n* -S [MF *postillon*, fr. It *postiglione*, fr. *posta* post — more at POST (mail)] **1** *obs* **:** POSTRIDER, POSTBOY, COURIER **2 :** one who rides as a guide on the near horse of a pair or of one of the pairs attached to a coach or post chaise esp. without a coachman **3 :** a woman's hat with a high narrow crown and a narrow rolled brim

postilion 3

post·impressionism \ˌ=+\ *n, usu cap* [F *postimpressionisme*, fr. *post-* + *impressionisme* impressionism — more at IMPRESSIONISM] **:** a chiefly French movement comprising artists of disparate styles (as Cézanne, Van Gogh, and Gaugin) that followed impressionism about 1880 and stressed picture composition or expressionism over naturalistic representation

post·impressionist \"+\ *n* [F *postimpressioniste*, fr. *post-* + *impressioniste* impressionist — more at IMPRESSIONIST] **:** an adherent or follower of Postimpressionism

post·impressionistic \"+\ *adj* **:** of, relating to, or resembling Postimpressionism — **post·impressionistically** \"+\ *adv*

postin *var of* POSTEEN

[1]**posting** *adj, archaic* [fr. pres. part. of [5]*post*] **:** SPEEDY, FLEETING

[2]**posting** *n* -S [fr. gerund of [5]*post*] **1 a :** the act of transferring an entry or item from a book of original entry to the proper account in a ledger **b :** the record in a ledger account resulting from the transfer of an entry or item from a book of original entry ⟨the debit ~ was made in the cash account⟩ **2 :** MAILING ⟨holiday ~*s*⟩

[3]**posting** *n* -S [fr. gerund of [8]*post*] **:** appointment to a post or command ⟨my next ~ had been announced —*Atlantic*⟩

posting box *n, Brit* **:** a public mailbox

posting clerk *n* **:** one who records details of business transactions and posts entries to the proper records

posting machine *n* **:** a business machine esp. designed for the posting of ledgers and other business history records or the performing of similar operations (as the recording and totaling of running bank deposits and withdrawals)

post·juvenal \(ˈ)=+\ *adj* [*post-* + *juvenal*] **:** following or terminating the juvenal stage of a bird's life history — compare JUVENAL PLUMAGE, [2]JUVENILE 2b

post–kantian \"+\ *adj, usu cap K* [*post-* + *Kantian*] **:** following after Kant; *specif* **:** of or relating to the school of idealists (as Fichte, Schelling, and Hegel) who followed Kant and developed some of his ideas

post·larva \"+\ *n* [NL, fr. *post-* + *larva*] **:** an immature fish after complete absorption of the yolk sac but before it has attained the appearance of a miniature adult **:** an advanced fry — **post–larval** \"+\ *adj*

post·liminary \"+\ *adj* [in sense 1, fr. *postliminium* + *-ary*; in sense 2, fr. *post-* + *liminary*] **1** *or* **post·li·min·i·ary** \ˌ=ləˈminē,erē\ **:** of, relating to, or involving the right of postliminium **2 :** done or carried on after something else or as a conclusion **:** SUBSEQUENT — opposed to *preliminary*

post·li·min·i·um \ˌpōs(t)ləˈminēəm\ *or* **post·lim·i·ny** \(ˈ)=ˈlimənē\ *n, pl* **postlimin·ia** \ˌ=ləˈminēə\ *or* **postliminies** [L *postliminium*, fr. *post-* + *limin-*, *limen* threshold — more at LIMB] **1 :** a Roman legal doctrine whereby those captured by an enemy are regarded as having died freemen before capture to protect those claiming under them and whereby upon their return to the jurisdiction of Rome the captives regain their suspended property and civil rights **2 :** the right or rule of international law under which when persons or things taken by an enemy in war come again under the control of their own state they as a general rule regain the rights belonging or relating to them before capture

post locust *n* [[1]*post*] **:** LOCUST 3a(2)

post·lude \ˈpōst,lüd, -ō,sl-\ *n* -S [*post-* + *-lude* (as in *prelude*)] **1 :** a closing piece of music or the closing section of a piece; *esp* **:** an organ voluntary at the end of a church service **2 :** a closing phase (as of an historical epoch or literary work) **:** EPILOGUE

post·lu·di·um \(ˈ)=ˈlüdēəm\ *n* -S [NL, fr. *post-* + *-ludium*, (as in ML *praeludium* prelude) — more at PRELUDE] **:** POSTLUDE 1

[1]**post·man** \ˈpōs(t)mən, -,man, -aa(ə)n\ *n, pl* **postmen** [[4]*post* + *man*] **:** MAIL CARRIER

[2]**postman** \"\ *n, pl* **postmen** [[1]*post* + *man*; fr. the fact that his place in the court was beside the post used as a measure of length in excise cases] **:** a junior barrister in the former English Court of Exchequer having precedence in motion except in Crown business — compare TUBMAN 1

postman's knock *n* **:** a British game similar to post office

[1]**postmark** \ˈ=,=\ *n* [[4]*post* + *mark*] **:** an official postal marking on a piece of mail; *specif* **:** a mark showing the name of the post office and the date and sometimes the hour of

mailing and often serving as the actual and only cancellation

²postmark \"\ *vt* **:** to put a postmark on ⟨~ a letter⟩

postmark ad *or* **postmark advertisement** *n* **:** CACHET 4b

post·master \'ˌ,ˌ=\ *n* [⁴*post* + *master*] **1 a :** an official in charge of posts or couriers **b :** a local official charged with carrying the mails from his station to the next **c :** a local official in charge of receiving and distributing the mail **d :** one who has charge of a post office **2 a :** one who has charge of a station for accommodation of travelers **b :** one who supplies post-horses **3 :** a holder of a scholarship (as at Merton College, Oxford) orig. entitling the recipient to an allowance of food

postmaster general *n, pl* **postmasters general** *also* **postmaster generals :** an official in charge of a national post office department

post·mas·ter·ship \-,ship\ *n* **:** the office of postmaster

postmaster's stamp *or* **postmaster stamp** *n* **:** a provisional postage stamp issued by a postmaster in the U.S. from 1845 to 1847 or Bermuda from 1848 to about 1856 to pay for government postal service for which government stamps had not yet been issued — compare CARRIER'S STAMP

post·maturation \(ˈ)ˌ+\ *n* [*post-* + *maturation*] **:** changes that may occur in a fruit when it ripens on the plant

post·maturity \ˌ+\ *n* [*post-* + *maturity*] **:** the quality or state of being past the period of maturity ⟨~ of a fetus⟩

post·media \(ˈ)ˌ+\ *n* [NL, fr. *post-* + *media*] **:** a postmedian vein

post·median \(ˈ)ˌ+\ *also* **post·medial** \"+\ *adj* [*post-* + *median* or *medial*] **1 :** located behind the middle (as of the body) **2 :** of or relating to a vein of the wing of an insect that is now regarded as a branch of the cubitus

post·menopausal \(ˈ)ˌ+\ *adj* [*post-* + *menopausal*] **1 :** having undergone menopause ⟨~ women⟩ **2 :** occurring after menopause ⟨~ vaginitis⟩

post·menopause \(ˈ)ˌ+\ *n* [*post-* + *menopause*] **:** a period of life after cessation of the menses

post·mentum \(ˈ)ˌ+\ *n* [NL, fr. *post-* + *mentum*] **:** the part of the insect labium that is attached to the cranium

post·meridian \ˌ+\ *adj* [L *postmeridianus*, fr. *post-* + *meridianus* meridian — more at MERIDIAN] **:** occurring after noon **:** of or relating to the afternoon ⟨the ~ hours of the day⟩

post me·rid·i·em \ˌməˈridēəm, -ē,em\ *adj* [L, after noon] **:** being after noon — abbr. *p.m., P.M.*

post-mill \'ˌ,ˌ\ *n* [¹*post*] **:** a windmill supported by a single sturdy post about which it revolves to face the wind

¹post·millenarian \(ˈ)ˌ+\ *n* [*post-* + *millenarian*] **:** one who holds the doctrine of postmillennialism

²postmillenarian \"\ *adj* **:** of or relating to the postmillenarians or postmillennialism

post·millenarianism \"+\ *n* **:** POSTMILLENNIALISM

post·millennial \ˌ+\ *also* **post·millennian** \"+\ *adj* [*post-* + *millennial* or *millennian*] **1 :** coming after or relating to the period after the millennium **2 :** espousing the doctrine of postmillennialism

post·millennialism \ˌ+\ *n* **:** a theological doctrine that the second coming of Christ will be after the millennium which is to come as the result of the Christianization of the world without miraculous intervention — opposed to *premillennialism*; compare AMILLENNIALISM

post·millennialist \"+\ *n* **:** an adherent of postmillennialism

post·mineral \(ˈ)ˌ+\ *adj* [*post-* + *mineral*] **:** originating later than associated mineral deposits ⟨a ~ dike⟩

postmistress \'ˌ,ˌ=\ *n* [⁴*post* + *mistress*] **:** a female postmaster

post·mortal \(ˈ)ˌ+\ *adj* [*post-* + *mortal*] **:** occurring after death ⟨~ wounds⟩ ⟨~ decomposition⟩ — **post·mortally** \"+\ *adv*

post-mor·tem \(ˈ)pōs(t)ˈmȯrtəm\ *adv* [L *post mortem*] **:** after death ⟨seven cases examined *post-mortem*⟩

¹postmortem \"\ *adj* [L *post mortem*] **1 a :** of or relating to the period after death ⟨~ changes⟩ **b :** following the event ⟨~ analysis of a bridge hand⟩ **2 :** of, relating to, or used in a postmortem examination ⟨a ~ table⟩

²postmortem \"\ *n* -s **1 :** POSTMORTEM EXAMINATION **2 :** an examination or analysis after the event ⟨a ~ on the election⟩ ⟨held a ~ on their bidding tactics⟩

³postmortem \"\ *vb* -ED/-ING/-S [²*postmortem*] *vt* **:** to perform a postmortem on ~ *vi* **:** to make a postmortem

postmortem dividend *n* **:** a dividend paid after an insured person's death representing his share in surplus for the current year

postmortem examination *n* **:** an examination of the body after death usu. with such dissection as will expose the vital organs for determining the cause of death or the character and extent of changes produced by disease **:** AUTOPSY

post·naris \(ˈ)ˌ+\ *n* [NL, fr. *post-* + L *naris* nostril — more at NOSE] **:** one of the posterior nares

¹post·nasal \(ˈ)ˌ+\ *adj* [*post-* + *nasal*] **:** lying or occurring posterior to the nose ⟨a ~ scale⟩

²postnasal \"\ *n* **:** a postnasal part; *specif* **:** a scale or either of a pair of scales lying behind the nasal of most lizards

postnasal drip *n* **:** flow of mucous secretion from the posterior part of the nasal cavity onto the wall of the pharynx occurring usu. as a chronic accompaniment of an allergic state (as hay fever)

post·natal \"+\ *adj* [ISV *post-* + *natal*] **:** occurring after birth ⟨~ development⟩; *specif* **:** of or relating to an infant immediately after birth ⟨~ care⟩ — compare NEONATAL — **post·natally** \"+\ *adv*

post·nate \ˈpōs(t)ˌnāt\ *adj* [ML *postnatus* born after, fr. *post-* + *natus* born — more at NATION] *archaic* **:** arising or developing later **:** SUBSEQUENT

post·na·tus \(ˈ)pōs(t)ˈnād·əs\ *n, pl* **postna·ti** \-ā,tī\ [ML] **:** a person born after an event esp. with reference to the existence of political rights (as a person born in one of the 13 American colonies after the Declaration of Independence) — usu. used in pl. ⟨of the slaves only the *postnati* were freed⟩; opposed to *antenatus*

post-nicene \(ˈ)ˌ+\ *adj, cap N* [*post-* + *Nicene*] **:** of or relating to times subsequent to the Council of Nicaea esp. within the patristic period

post note *n* [⁴*post*] **:** a bank note payable to order at a specified future time as distinguished from one payable to bearer on demand; *specif* **:** one issued as a circulating medium by banks and financial institutions before the American Civil War

post·notum \(ˈ)ˌ+\ *n* [NL, fr. *post-* + *notum*] **:** a small dorsal sclerite on the insect thorax posterior to the notum — called also *postscutellum*

post·nuptial \(ˈ)ˌ+\ *adj* [*post-* + *nuptial*] **:** made or happening after marriage or mating ⟨~ journey⟩ — **post·nuptially** \"+\ *adv*

postnuptial settlement *also* **postnuptial agreement** *or* **postnuptial contract** *n* **:** a legal settlement after marriage of property by one spouse upon the other often but not necessarily in contemplation of separation or divorce

post oak *n* [¹*post*] **:** any of several American oaks with tough moisture-resistant woods used esp. for fence posts; *esp* **:** a medium-sized oak (*Quercus stellata*) of the eastern and central U.S. that has a scaly fissured reddish brown bark, dark green lyrate pinnatifid leaves, and moderately large obtusely ovoid acorns — called also *box white oak, brash oak, iron oak*

post-oak grape *n* **1 :** a tall growing grape of the southern and central U.S. that is usu. considered a variety (*Vitis labrusca lincecumii*) of the common American fox grape **2 :** the large edible purplish black slightly bloomy fruit of the post-oak grape

¹post-obit \(ˈ)ˌ+\ *adj* [L *post obitum* after death] **:** occurring or taking effect after death ⟨*post-obit* liquidation⟩ ⟨a *post-obit* gift⟩

²post-obit \"\ *n* **:** POST-OBIT BOND

post-obit bond *n* **:** a bond payable after a person's death; *esp* **:** one made by a reversioner to secure payment of a loan with a bonus and interest and to be paid out of his reversion on its vesting in him

post·obituary \ˌ+\ *adj* [*post-* + *obituary*] **:** POST-OBIT

post·occipital suture \ˌ+-\ *n* **:** a posterior groove on the cranium of an insect having tentorial pits at each end and forming internally a ridge on which dorsal neck and prothoracic muscles find their attachment

post·occiput \(ˈ)ˌ+\ *n* [*post-* + *occiput*] **:** the posterior rim of the insect cranium

¹post·ocular \(ˈ)ˌ+\ *adj* [ISV *post-* + *ocular*] **:** located behind the eye — used esp. of one or more scales in a snake or lizard

²postocular \"\ *n* **:** a part (as a shield or scale) that is postocular

post office *n* [⁴*post* + *office*] **1 a :** a government department charged with regulating and handling the transmission of mail in a country ⟨in the U. S. the *post office* is an executive department and its chief official, the postmaster general, is a member of the president's cabinet⟩ **b :** a section of a post office department handling the mail for a particular place (as a city or town) ⟨a list of the *post offices* of Canada⟩ **c** (1) **:** a building or a section of a building housing facilities and staff for carrying out all or some of the functions of a post-office department (2) **:** a railway car or train or a bus or truck fitted for the sorting of mail in transit **d :** a place where mail is handled for dispatch and delivery ⟨a camp *post office*⟩ ⟨a university *post office*⟩ **2 :** a game in which a player acting as postmaster or postmistress may exact a kiss from one of the opposite sex as payment for the pretended delivery of a letter

post-office *adj* **:** of, relating to, or issued or conducted by the government through the post office ⟨a *post-office* annuity⟩ ⟨a *post-office* savings bank⟩

post-office address *n* **:** an address for mail

post-office box *n* **:** a rented compartment in a post office for the keeping of mail that is not to be delivered but is to be called for by the renter — see CALL BOX 1, LOCKBOX

post-office car *n* **:** RAILWAY MAIL CAR

post-office order *n, Brit* **:** a money order issued by a post office but not bearing the name of the payee which is given on an accompanying letter of advice

post-office red *n* **:** a deep reddish orange to dark reddish brown

post·operative \(ˈ)ˌ+\ *adj* [ISV *post-* + *operative*] **:** following a surgical operation ⟨~ care⟩ ⟨~ complications⟩ — **post·operatively** \"+\ *adv*

post·oral \(ˈ)ˌ+\ *adj* [*post-* + *oral*] **:** situated behind the mouth

¹post·orbital \(ˈ)ˌ+\ *adj* [*post-* + *orbital*] **:** situated behind the orbit ⟨the ~ scales of some fishes and reptiles⟩ **: a :** being a downwardly directed process of the frontal bone of many mammals and birds that forms part of the outer or posterior border of the orbit and in some lower vertebrates is borne on or represented by the postfrontal bone **b :** being a bone behind and below the postfrontal in many reptiles that forms part of the boundary of the orbit

²postorbital \"\ *n* **:** a postorbital part (as a bone or scale)

post·or·bi·to·squamosal arch \ˌȯ(r)bə,tō+ . . . -\ *n* [²*postorbital* + *-o-* + *squamosal*] **:** a bony arch made up of fused portions of the postorbital and squamosal bones that separates the two temporal openings in a diapsid reptile

post·otic \(ˈ)ˌ+\ *adj* [*post-* + *otic*] **:** posterior to the otic vesicle

postpaid \(ˈ)ˌˈ\ *adj* [⁴*post* + *paid*] **:** having postage paid by the sender and not chargeable to the receiver

¹post·palatal \"+\ *adj* [ISV *post-* + *palatal*] **1 :** POSTPALATINE **2 a :** articulated against the rear third or the rear half of the hard palate **b :** articulated against the rear half of the palate as a whole **:** articulated against the soft palate or velum **:** VELAR

²postpalatal \"\ *n* **:** a postpalatal part or sound

¹post·palatine \"+\ *adj* [*post-* + *palatine*] **:** located behind the palate or palatine bones; *specif* **:** of, relating to, or constituting a pair of bones now believed to be the pterygoids that are found on the skulls of some reptiles (as crocodiles)

²postpalatine \"\ *n* **:** a postpalatine part

post·paleolithic \(ˈ)ˌ+\ *adj, usu cap 2nd P* [*post-* + *paleolithic*] **:** of, relating to, or constituting the period following the Paleolithic or initiating the Neolithic

¹post·parietal \ˌ+\ *adj* [*post-* + *parietal*] **:** located behind parietal elements

²postparietal \"\ *n* **:** a postparietal part (as a scale)

post·par·tum \(ˈ)pōsˈpärd·əm\ *or* **post·par·tal** \-d·ᵊl\ *adj* [*postpartum* fr. L *post partum* after birth; *postpartal* fr. L *post partum* + E *-al*] **:** following parturition ⟨~ care⟩ ⟨*postpartal* examination⟩ ⟨the ~ period of 40 days —O.G.Simmons⟩

post·petiole \(ˈ)ˌ+\ *n* [*post-* + *petiole*] **:** the second segment of the pedicel of some ants

post·phragma \(ˈ)ˌ+\ *n* [NL, fr. *post-* + *phragma*] **:** the phragma of the postnotum of an insect

post·pituitary \ˌ+\ *adj* [*post-* + *pituitary*] **1 :** situated behind the pituitary body or the sella turcica **2 :** arising in or derived from the posterior lobe of the pituitary body

post·pon·able \(ˈ)pōs(t)ˈpōnəbəl, ˌpəs(t)ˈp-\ *adj* **:** capable of being postponed

post·pone \(ˈ)pōs(t)ˈpōn, ˌpəs(t)ˈ-\ *vt* -ED/-ING/-S [L *postponere* to put after, neglect, postpone, fr. *post-* + *ponere* to place, put — more at POSITION] **1 :** to hold back to a later time **:** DEFER, DELAY ⟨~ payments for a year⟩ ⟨~ further discussion of the matter⟩ ⟨the meeting is *postponed* until next week⟩ ⟨*postponed* doing her housework for a few hours⟩ **2 a :** to place after **:** put nearer the end ⟨*postponing* the verb in German⟩ — used esp. of words and particles **b :** to place after in order of precedence, preference, or importance **:** SUBORDINATE ⟨English law in its canons of inheritance *postponed* the daughter to the son —Frederick Pollock & F.W.Maitland⟩ ⟨wish you never to ~ your business to literary trifling —G.B.Shaw⟩ **syn** see DEFER

post·pone·ment \-mənt\ *n* -s **:** the act of postponing or the condition of being postponed **:** DEFERMENT, DELAY ⟨ordered a 30-day ~⟩ ⟨the temporary ~ of inflation —Clark Kerr⟩

post·pose \(ˈ)pōs(t)ˈpōz\ *vt* [MF *postposer*, modif. (influenced by *poser* to put, place) of L *postponere* (perfect stem *postpos-*)] **1** *obs* **:** POSTPONE 2a,b **2 :** to place (as a particle) after a grammatically related word ⟨the articles . . . are *postposed* in Scandinavian and Rumanian —M.H.Swadesh⟩

post·position \ˌ+\ *n* [F, fr. *postposer* + *-ition* (as in *position*)] **1 :** the postposing of a grammatical element **2 :** a postposed word or particle; *esp* **:** a word or suffix (as *-ward* in *cityward*) having the function of a preposition — **post·positional** \"+\ *adj* — **post·positionally** \"+\ *adv*

¹post·positive \(ˈ)ˌ+\ *adj* [LL *postpositivus*, fr. L *postpositus* (past part. of *postponere* to put after, neglect, postpone) + *-ivus* -ive — more at POSTPONE] **:** placed after another word **:** characterized by postposition — **post·positively** \"+\ *adv*

²postpositive \"\ *n* -s **:** a postpositive particle or word

post·prandial \(ˈ)ˌ+\ *adj* [*post-* + *prandial*] **:** of, relating to, or occurring in the period after a meal esp. dinner ⟨~ speeches⟩ ⟨~ nap⟩ ⟨~ air of well-being —Brendan Gill⟩ ⟨an abnormal ~ blood sugar level —*Jour. Amer. Med. Assoc.*⟩ — **post·prandially** \"+\ *adv*

post·predicament \ˌ+\ *n* [ML *postpraedicamentum*, fr. L *post-* + LL *praedicamentum* predicament — more at PREDICAMENT] **:** any one of the five supplementary categories of opposition, priority, simultaneity, movement, and possession treated in the probably spurious chapters 10 to 15 of Aristotle's *Categories* — compare CATEGORY 1a

post·primary \(ˈ)ˌ+\ *adj* [*post-* + *primary*] *chiefly Brit* **:** subsequent to primary ⟨~ education⟩ ⟨~ schools⟩

post·pubertal \"+\ *adj* [*post-* + *pubertal*] **:** occurring after puberty

post·pubic \(ˈ)ˌ+\ *adj* [NL *postpubis* + E *-ic*] **:** of or relating to the postpubis

post·pubis \"+\ *n* [NL, fr. *post-* + *pubis*] **:** the part of the pubic bone in birds and some reptiles that lies behind the acetabulum, in birds represents the true pubis, and in reptiles is a distinct process

post·pyramidal \ˌ+\ *adj* [*post-* + *pyramidal*] **:** lying behind the pyramids of the medulla oblongata ⟨the ~ nucleus⟩

post race *n* [¹*post*] **:** a horse or dog race in which each subscriber declares at the usual time before a race the animal he will run

post·record \ˌ+\ *vt* [*post-* + *record*] **:** to record (voice or sound effects) after the corresponding scene has been photographed in making movies

post·reduction \"+\ *n* [*post-* + *reduction*] **:** the reduction of chromosomes in the second meiotic division

post rem \(ˈ)pōˈstrem\ *or* **post res** \-rās\ *adv* [*post rem* fr. L, after the thing; *post res* fr. L, after the things] **:** logically subsequent to the existence of particulars — compare AVICENNISM

pos·tre·mo·geniture \päˈstrēmō+\ *n* [L *postremus* last (superl. of *posterus* coming after) + E *-o-* + *geniture* — more at POSTERIOR] **:** ULTIMOGENITURE

postrider \'ˌ,ˌ=\ *n* [⁴*post* + *rider*] **:** a courier or mail carrier using post-horses

post-ripeness \(ˈ)ˌ+\ *n* [*post-* + *ripeness*] **:** the condition of a fruit that has undergone changes following ripening

post road *n* [⁴*post*] **1 :** a road used for the conveyance of mail: as **a :** one having a series of posthouses or stations **b :** one designated to be used by official carriers of mail **2 :** a road, airway, waterway, or railway over which mail is carried during the time in transit **3 :** a city letter-carrier route

pos·trorse \ˈpō,strȯrs, ˈpä-\ *adj* [*post-* + *-rorse* (as in *antrorse*)] **:** RETRORSE — opposed to *antrorse*

post route *n* [⁴*post*] **:** a route prescribed for a mail carrier to take in his regular delivery trips

post-runner \'ˌ,ˌ=\ *n* [⁴*post*] **1 :** one who carries the post on foot **2 :** a speedy messenger **:** COURIER

posts *pl of* POST, *pres 3d sing of* POST

post·scapula \(ˈ)ˌ+\ *n* [NL, fr. *post-* + *scapula*] **:** the infraspinous part of the scapula — **post·scapular** \"+\ *adj*

post·score \(ˈ)ˌ+\ *vt* [*post-* + *score*] **:** POSTRECORD

post·script \ˈpōs(t),skript\ *n* [NL *postscriptum*, fr. L, neut. of *postscriptus*, past part. of *postscribere* to write after, fr. *post-* + *scribere* to write — more at SCRIBE] **:** a note or series of notes appended to a completed composition (as a letter, article, or book) usu. giving an afterthought or additional information ⟨added a ~ to the . . . manuscript —R.H.Gabriel⟩ ⟨included in the autobiography as a sort of ~ —*Harper's*⟩ — abbr. *PS, ps*

post·scrip·tum \(ˈ)pōs(t)ˈskriptəm\ *n, pl* **postscrip·ta** \-ptə\ [NL] **:** POSTSCRIPT

post·scutellar \ˌ+\ *adj* [NL *postscutellum* + E *-ar*] **:** of or relating to the postnotum

post·scutellum \"+\ *also* **post·scutum** \"+\ *n* [NL, fr. *post-* + *scutellum*] **:** POSTNOTUM

post·sphenoid \(ˈ)ˌ+\ *n* [*post-* + *sphenoid*] **:** the posterior portion of the sphenoid bone developed in five separate parts consisting of a central basisphenoid, the two alisphenoids, and the two medial pterygoid laminae

post·spinal \"+\ *adj* [*post-* + *spinal*] **:** that follows spinal anesthesia ⟨a ~ headache⟩

post·synaptic \ˌ+\ *adj* [*post-* + *synaptic*] **:** following synapsis **:** belonging to the kind that exists after synaptic alteration ⟨a ~ chromosome⟩

post·synchronization \(ˈ)ˌ+\ *n* [ISV *postsynchronize* + *-ation*] **:** the act or process of postsynchronizing

post·synchronize \(ˈ)ˌ+\ *vt* [ISV *post-* + *synchronize*] **:** to add (speech or sound effects) in synchronism with the action after a scene has been photographed in making movies

¹post·synsacral \(ˈ)ˌ+\ *adj* [*post-* + NL *synsacrum* + E *-al*] **:** situated behind the synsacrum

²postsynsacral \"\ *n* -s **:** a caudal vertebra in birds

post·systolic \ˌ+\ *adj* [*post-* + *systolic*] **:** following the systole of the heart ⟨a ~ murmur⟩

post·temporal \(ˈ)ˌ+\ *n* [*post-* + *temporal*] **:** a bone connecting the back part of the skull and the dorsal part of the pectoral arch in most teleost fishes

post·tension \"+\ *vt* [*post-* + *tension*] **:** to apply tension to (reinforcing steel) after concrete has set

post·tibia \"+\ *n* [NL, fr. *post-* + *tibia*] **:** the tibia of a hind leg of an insect

post·tonic \"+\ *adj* [*post-* + *tonic*] **1** *of a sound* **:** immediately following or constituting one of a succession of consonants immediately following a vowel having stress **2** *of a syllable* **:** immediately following a syllable having stress

post town *n* [⁴*post*] **1 :** a town having the chief post office of a local area **2** *Brit* **:** a town having a post office which is the distribution point for mail to the smaller local post offices in a given area and whose name must be part of the address on mail to any place within that area

post trader *n* [⁷*post*] **:** one of the sutlers appointed by the secretary of war for each post in the U. S. military service

post·traumatic \ˌ+\ *adj* [ISV *post-* + *traumatic*] **:** following or resulting from trauma ⟨~ epilepsy⟩

¹post·tympanic \ˌ+\ *adj* [*post-* + *tympanic*] **:** situated behind the tympanic bone or external auditory meatus

²posttympanic \"\ *n* **:** a posttympanic part; *specif* **:** a posttympanic ossicle present in some mammals

pos·tu·lan·cy \ˈpäschələnsē, -si\ *also* **pos·tu·lance** \-lən(t)s\ *n, pl* **postulancies** *also* **postulances 1 :** the quality or state of being a postulant esp. in a religious order **2 :** the period during which a person remains a postulant

pos·tu·lant \-lənt\ *n* -s [F, fr. ML *postulant-, postulans*, pres. part. of *postulare*] **1 :** a candidate for admission to a religious order in the stage preliminary to the novitiate **2 :** a person on probation before being admitted as a candidate for ordination in the Protestant Episcopal Church **syn** see NOVICE

postulata *pl of* POSTULATUM

¹pos·tu·late \ˈpäschə,lāt, *usu* -ād·+V\ *vt* -ED/-ING/-S [ML *postulatus*, past part. of *postulare*, fr. L, to ask for, demand, request, fr. (assumed) *posctus*, past part. of *poscere* to ask for urgently, beg, demand; akin to OHG *forsca* question, OIr *arco* I request, Skt *prcchā* question, inquiry, L *prex* prayer, request — more at PRAYER] **1 :** to request (a higher ecclesiastical authority) to sanction the promotion of a person who is canonically disqualified **:** nominate (a person) subject to the sanction of a higher authority **2** [L *postulatus*, past part. of *postulare*] **:** DEMAND, CLAIM ⟨*postulated* . . . supremacy over this nation —William Tooke⟩ **3 :** to assume or claim as true, existent, or necessary ⟨~*s* that energy is expended within the plant —P.R.White⟩ **:** depend upon or start from the postulate of ⟨~*s* complete lack of respect for the . . . people —G.W.Johnson⟩ **4 :** to assume as a postulate or axiom (as in logic or mathematics) **syn** see PRESUPPOSE

²postulate \-lət, -,lāt, *usu* -d·+V\ *n* -s [in sense 1, fr. L *postulatum*, fr. neut. of *postulatus*, past part. of *postulare;* in other senses, fr. ML *postulatum*, fr. L] **1** *archaic* **:** DEMAND, STIPULATION **2 :** a proposition advanced with the claim that it be taken for granted or as axiomatic **:** an essential presupposition, condition, or premise (as for a train of reasoning, a philosophic system, or a school of thought) **:** an underlying hypothesis or assumption ⟨both science and religion have their ~*s*⟩ ⟨life is built upon certain ~*s* —Bertrand Russell⟩ ⟨these ~*s* of present-day income accounting —*Harvard Law Rev.*⟩ **3 :** a statement (as in logic or mathematics) that is assumed and therefore requires no proof of its validity **:** AXIOM ⟨the parallel ~⟩

pos·tu·la·tion \ˌˈlāshən\ *n* -s [ME *postulacion*, fr. MF *postulation*, fr. ML *postulation-, postulatio*, fr. L, demand, request, fr. *postulatus* + *-ion-, -io* -ion] **1 a :** an act of postulating ⟨the ~ of surviving spirits might look plausible —A.G.N.Flew⟩ **b :** POSTULATE, ASSUMPTION ⟨admit as a ~⟩ **2 :** a formal petition of a plaintiff in Roman law to the praetor for leave to prosecute an action or to make an accusation

pos·tu·la·tion·al \ˌˈlāshənᵊl, -shnəl\ *adj* **:** of, relating to, or involving the use of postulates ⟨science is a ~ system —C.I.Glicksberg⟩; *specif* **:** depending on a set of mathematical postulates ⟨the ~ method was applied to geometry —S.S.Stevens⟩ — **pos·tu·la·tion·al·ly** \-ᵊlē, -əl\|, \|i\ *adv*

postulational system *n* **:** AXIOM SYSTEM

pos·tu·la·tor \ˈpäschə,lād·ə(r), -ātə-\ *n* -s [ML, fr. L, claimant, plaintiff, fr. *postulatus*] **:** the official who presents a plea for beatification or canonization in the Roman Catholic Church — compare DEVIL'S ADVOCATE

pos·tu·la·to·ry \ˈ=ˌlə,tōrē, -tȯr-, -ri\ *adj* [ML *postulatorius*, fr. L, petitionary, fr. *postulatus* (past part. of *postulare* to postulate) + *-orius* -ory — more at POSTULATE] **:** involving assumptions **:** HYPOTHETICAL

pos·tu·la·tum \ˌpäschəˈlād·əm\ *n, pl* **postula·ta** \-ād·ə\ [ML & L — more at POSTULATE] **:** POSTULATE

pos·tur·al \ˈpäschərəl\ *adj* **:** of, relating to, or involving posture ⟨~ tension⟩ ⟨~ albuminuria⟩ ⟨~ exercises⟩

¹pos·ture \ˈpäschə(r)\ *n* -s [F, fr. It *postura*, fr. L *positura*, position, fr. *positus* (past part. of *ponere* to place, put) + *-ura* -ure — more at POSITION] **1 :** relative arrangement of the different parts esp. of the body : the characteristic position or bearing of the body or that assumed for a special purpose ⟨exercises for good ~⟩ ⟨a sitting ~⟩ ⟨~ at the table⟩; *specif* : the pose of a model or artistic figure ⟨draws her in three ~s⟩ **2** : relative place or position : SITUATION ⟨the ~ of the earth to the sun⟩ ⟨forced the English phrases into makeshift ~s —W.K.Wimsatt⟩ **3** : state or condition at a given time; *esp* : situation relative to the attitude of persons or the disposition of things involved ⟨survey the ~ of affairs —John Buchan⟩ ⟨put the country in a ~ of defense⟩ **4** : frame of mind : ATTITUDE ⟨a ~ of moral superiority —R.L. Strout⟩ **syn** see STATE

²posture \"\ *vb* -ED/-ING/-S *vt* **1** : to put into or make assume a given posture : POSE ⟨a ballet mistress *posturing* her dancers⟩ ⟨figures . . . *postured*, as in sculpture —Sheldon Cheney⟩ **2** *obs* : to put in place : SET ~ *vi* **1** : to assume a particular physical posture or series of postures; *esp* : to strike a pose for effect ⟨a young woman *postured* in leg-revealing shorts —*Time*⟩ **2** : to assume an artificial or pretended attitude : POSE, ATTITUDINIZE ⟨*posturing* as the friend of the oppressed⟩ ⟨you've *postured* . . . till everyone's sick of you —Stephen McKenna⟩

pos·tur·er \-chərə(r)\ *n* -S : one that postures: as **a** : CONTORTIONIST ⟨circus freaks and ~s⟩ **b** : POSEUR ⟨an incorrigible ~⟩

posturing *n* -S [fr. gerund of ²*posture*] : ceremonial pantomiming in China accompanied by music and formerly performed in a ritual manner at state sacrifices

post·velar \(ˈ)⸗+\ *adj* [*post-* + *velar*] : articulated against the rear half of the velum or soft palate

¹post·verbal \(ˈ)⸗+\ *adj* [*post-* + *verbal*] : formed after or from a verb

²postverbal \"\ *n* : a noun formed from a verb ⟨names of male occupations . . . from ~s —Yakov Malkiel⟩

post·vocalic \ˌ⸗+\ *adj* [ISV *post-* + *vocalic*] : immediately following a vowel

post·war \(ˈ)⸗+\ *adj* [*post-* + *war*] : occurring after a war ⟨the ~ revival of the theater⟩ : of or relating to the period after a war ⟨~ inflation⟩ ⟨the ~ scene⟩

postwoman \ˈ⸗,⸗⸗\ *n, pl* **postwomen** [⁴*post* + *woman*] : a woman mail carrier

post·zygapophysis \(ˌ)⸗+\ *n* [NL, fr. *post-* + *zygapophysis*] : a posterior or inferior zygapophysis

posy \ˈpōzē, -zi\ *n* -ES [alter. of *poesy*] **1** : a brief sentiment, motto, or legend often in verse (as an inscription on a ring) ⟨~ at the beginning of his book . . . Commend it or Amend it —John Hoskins⟩ ⟨is this the prologue or the ~ of a ring? —Shak.⟩ **2** : BOUQUET, NOSEGAY, FLOWER ⟨a tight ~ of wild flowers —V.V.Nabokov⟩ **3** : ANTHOLOGY ⟨a ~ of funny stories —Edmund Gosse⟩

posy pea *n, dial* : SWEET PEA

¹pot \ˈpät, *usu* -äd.+V\ *n* -S [ME *pot, pott*, fr. OE *pott;* akin to OFris *pott* pot, MD *pot*, MLG *pot, put*, and perh. to OE *-pūte*, a fish with a large head — more at POUT] **1 a** : a usu. rounded metal or earthen container of varying size used chiefly for domestic purposes: as (1) : a container used for boiling or cooking — compare KETTLE (2) : a container for a beverage (3) : CHAMBER POT **b** : such a container with its contents ⟨give her a ~ and a cake —Daniel Defoe⟩ ⟨~ of tea⟩ **c** *archaic* : any of several quantities or measures ⟨a ~ of sugar weighs about 70 pounds —*Annual Register*⟩ **2 a** *chiefly Scot* : a pit or depression in the ground or in the bed of a stream **b** *archaic* : the abyss of hell **3 a** *dial Eng* : a basket or box used chiefly like one of a pair of panniers **b** : an enclosed framework of wire, wood, or wicker for catching fish, eels, or lobsters — compare POUND NET **4 a** : CRUCIBLE 1 **b** : a large round metal receptacle used as part of a still **c** : a valve chamber in a compound-pressure steam pump **d** : an electrolytic cell used in recovering some metals (as aluminum) from a fused electrolyte **5** : a leather or steel protective cap or helmet worn chiefly in the 17th century **6 a** (1) : a large amount (as of money) ⟨inherited ~ of money⟩ ⟨has ~s of wealth⟩ (2) : the total prize or aggregate of bets to be won at the outcome of a particular event or contest (3) : a common resource or fund that may be created or drawn upon by a number of individuals or groups ⟨all the assets and production go into a common ~ on which they live —R.R.Nathan⟩ **b** (1) : the total of the bets made in poker or other card games on the outcome of any one deal and usu. accumulated in a pile in the center of the table : POOL (2) : a period or interval including the deal, betting, showdown, and determination of the winner in poker : one complete unit or round of play in a poker game **7** *slang Brit* : FAVORITE **8** : a paper case holding the garniture at the head of a fireworks rocket **9** [by shortening] : POTSHOT **10** [by shortening] *slang* : POTBELLY **11** : an important or prominent person ⟨they're sure to have some big ~ . . . who knows all about the house —J.D. Beresford⟩ **12** : RUIN, DETERIORATION ⟨business had gone to ~ —Alan Hynd⟩ **13** *slang* : an electronic volume control or fading device **14** [²*pot*] : a shot in which a billiard ball is potted **15** *slang* : MARIJUANA

²pot \"\ *vb* **potted; potted; potting; pots** *vt* **1** *slang Brit* : FOOL, DECEIVE, OUTWIT ⟨it is no hard matter to puzzle and to ~ you with authority —Richard Montagu⟩ **2** : to place or pack in a pot: **a** : to put up in a pot or sealed jar : CAN, PRESERVE **b** : to place (as a seedling or bulb) in an earth-filled pot for cultivation — often used with *up* **3** *Brit* : to pocket (an object ball) in a game of billiards or pool **4 a** : to shoot or kill (game) for food rather than as a sport **b** : POTSHOT ⟨it was nice, he thought, not to have to . . . sleep like a cat lest one be *potted* like a sitting rabbit —P.E.Lehman⟩ **5** : to make or shape (earthenware) as a potter ⟨a round bowl has an alternating panel design . . . and is well *potted* —W.E.Cox⟩ **6** : to treat (sodium nitrate) in a pot with sulfuric acid to form nitric acid **7** : to make superficially attractive by eliminating or oversimplifying difficult matters and emphasizing the exciting and attractive : GLAMORIZE ⟨a democracy, sometimes called educated, that prefers its information *potted*, pictorial, and spiced with sensation —Wilson Harris⟩ ~ *vi* **1** *obs* : to drink an intoxicating beverage from a pot **2** : to take a potshot : SHOOT ⟨we . . . *potted* at alligators in the reeds —Howard Clewes⟩

pot *abbr* **1** potential **2** potion **3** pottery

po·ta·bil·i·ty \ˌpōd·əˈbiləd·ē\ *n* : the quality or state of being potable

¹po·ta·ble \ˈpōd·əbəl, -ōtəb-\ *adj* [LL *potabilis*, fr. L *potare* to drink + *-abilis* -able; akin to L *bibere* to drink, Gk *pinein*, OSlav *piti* to drink, Skt *pāti, pibati* he drinks] : suitable, safe, or prepared for drinking ⟨the treatment of water supplies to make them safely ~ —A.C.Morrison⟩ — **po·ta·ble·ness** *n* -ES

²potable \"\ *n* -S : a liquid suitable for drinking : BEVERAGE, DRINKABLE

po·tage \pōˈtäzh\ *n* -S [MF, thick soup, pottage, fr. OF, pottage, fr. *pot* (of Gmc origin; akin to MD *pot*) + *-age* — more at POT] : a thick soup — compare POTTAGE

pot·a·ger \ˈpäd·ijə(r)\ *n* -S [F, fr. MF *potagier* cook that makes thick soup or pottage, fr. *potage* + *-ier* -er] : a cook whose specialties are soup, broth, and bouillon

po·tag·er·ie *or* **po·tag·ery** \pōˈtajərē\ *n, pl* **potageries** [obs. F *potagerie*, fr. MF, fr. *potage* + *-erie* -ery] : garden vegetables and herbs

pot ale *n* : the residue of fermented wort left in a still after whiskey or alcohol has been distilled off and used for feeding swine

potam- *or* **potamo-** *comb form* [L *potamo-*, fr. Gk *potam-*, *potamo-*, fr. *potamos*; akin to Gk *piptein* to fall — more at FEATHER] **1** : river ⟨*potamic*⟩ ⟨*potamo*dromous⟩ **2** : electric current ⟨*potamo*meter⟩

pot·a·man·thi·dae \ˌpäd·əˈman(t)thəˌdē\ *n pl, cap* [NL, fr. *Potamanthus*, type genus (fr. *potam-* + *-anthus*) + *-idae*] : a small widely distributed family of mayflies

po·tam·ic \pəˈtamik\ *adj* [*potam-* + *-ic*] : of or relating to rivers or the navigation of rivers

pot·a·mo·benthos \ˌpad·əmō+\ *n* [*potam-* + *benthos*] : benthonic organisms of a river

pot·a·mo·bi·us \ˌpäd·əˈmōbēəs\ [NL, fr. *potam-* + *-bius*] *syn of* ASTACUS

pot·a·mo·choe·rus \ˌpad·əmōˈkērəs\ [NL, fr. *potam-* + *-choerus*] *syn of* KOIROPOTAMUS

pot·a·mod·ro·mous \ˌpäd·əˈmädrəməs\ *adj* [*potam-* + *-dromous*] *of a fish* : migratory in fresh water

pot·a·mog·a·le \ˌpäd·əˈmägəlē\ *n, cap* [NL, fr. *potam-* + Gk *galē* weasel — more at GALEA] : a genus (the type of a family Potamogalidae) of West African aquatic insectivores that contains the otter shrew — **pot·a·mog·a·lid** \ˌ⸗⸗ˈmägələd\ *adj*

pot·a·mo·ge·ton \ˌpäd·əmōˈjēˌtän\ *n* [NL, fr. L, pondweed, fr. Gk *potamogeitōn*, fr. *potamos* river + *geitōn* neighbor] **1** *cap* : a large genus of aquatic herbs (family Potamogetonaceae) that are found in quiet waters throughout temperate regions and have spicate flowers with a four-parted perianth and usu. floating leaves — see PONDGRASS, PONDWEED **2** -S : any plant of the genus *Potamogeton*

pot·a·mo·ge·to·na·ce·ae \ˌ⸗⸗⸗ˌjēd·əˈnāsēˌē\ *n pl, cap* [NL, fr. *Potamogeton*, type genus + *-aceae*] : a family of aquatic herbs (order Naiadales) having floating or submerged leaves, simple flowers without a perianth, and a fruit like a nut or a drupe — **pot·a·mo·ge·to·na·ceous** \ˌ⸗⸗⸗ˌ⸗⸗ˈnāshəs\ *adj*

pot·a·mog·ra·pher \ˌpäd·əˈmägrəfə(r)\ *n* -S : a specialist in potamography

pot·a·mo·graph·ic \ˌpäd·əməˈgrafik\ *adj* [ISV *potamography* + *-ic*] : of or relating to potamography

pot·a·mog·ra·phy \ˌpäd·əˈmägrəfē\ *n* -ES [ISV *potam-* + *-graphy*] : the description of rivers

pot·a·mo·log·i·cal \ˌpäd·əˈmäləjəkəl\ *adj* : of or relating to potamology

pot·a·mol·o·gist \ˌpäd·əˈmäləjəst\ *n* -S : a specialist in potamology

pot·a·mol·o·gy \-jē\ *n* -ES [ISV *potam-* + *-logy*] : the study of rivers

pot·a·mom·e·ter \ˌpäd·əˈmäməd·ə(r)\ *n* [*potam-* + *-meter*] : CURRENT METER

pot·a·mon·i·dae \ˌpäd·əˈmänəˌdē\ *n pl, cap* [NL, fr. *Potamon*, type genus (fr. Gk *potamos* river) + *-idae*] : a family of freshwater crabs (superfamily Brachyrhyncha) whose young undergo metamorphosis in the egg and hatch as miniature adults — see RIVER CRAB

pot·a·mo·plankton \ˈpäd·əmō+\ *n* [ISV *potam-* + *plankton*] : plankton of rivers

pot arch *n* : a kiln used in preheating clay pots before they are placed in the furnace for hardening

po·tar·ite \pəˈtäˌrīt\ *n* -S [*Potaro*, river in British Guiana + E *-ite*] : a mineral PdHg consisting of a natural alloy compound of palladium and mercury

¹pot·ash \ˈpäd·ˌash, -äˌta-, -aash, -aish\ *n* [sing. of *pot ashes* (fr. ¹*pot* + *ashes*, pl. of *ash*), trans. of obs. D *potaschen*, pl. (whence obs. D *potasch*, sing., now D *potas*)] **1 a** : POTASSIUM CARBONATE; *esp* : that obtained in colored impure form by leaching wood ashes, evaporating the lye usu. in an iron pot, and calcining the residue — compare PEARL ASH **b** : POTASSIUM HYDROXIDE **2 a** : potassium oxide K_2O in combined form as determined by analysis (as of fertilizers) ⟨soluble ~⟩ **b** : POTASSIUM — not used systematically ⟨~ salts⟩ ⟨sulfate of ~⟩ **3** : any of several potassium salts (as potassium chloride or potassium sulfate) often occurring naturally and used esp. in agriculture and industry ⟨~ deposits⟩ ⟨~ fertilizers⟩

²potash \"\ *vt* : to treat with potash; *specif* : to case harden with potassium ferrocyanide

potash alum *n* : ALUM 1a

potash bulb *n* : an arrangement of glass bulbs designed to hold a solution of potassium hydroxide and used for absorbing carbon dioxide in chemical analysis — often used in pl.

potash hunger *n* : a potash deficiency disease of plants marked by retarded or dwarfed growth of storage organs or of terminal shoots in woody plants and by whitish or brownish spots on the leaves followed by general blighting and death of the plant

potash soap *n* : a soft soap made with potash

po·tas·sa \pəˈtasə\ *n* -S [NL, fr. E ¹*potash*] : POTASH

pot·as·sam·ide \ˌpäd·əˈsaˌmīd, pəˈtasəˌ-, -ˌməd\ *n* [*potassium* + *amide*] : POTASSIUM AMIDE

po·tas·sic \pəˈtasik\ *adj* [NL *potassicus*, fr. *potassa* + L *-icus* -ic] : of, relating to, or containing potassium

pot·as·sif·er·ous \ˌpäd·əˈsif(ə)rəs\ *adj* [*potassium* + *-ferous*] : containing potash or other compounds of potassium ⟨~ salts⟩

po·tas·si·um \pəˈtasēəm, pō-, -aas- *sometimes* -syəm\ *n* -S [NL, fr. *potassa* + *-ium*] : a silver-white soft light low-melting univalent metallic element of the alkali metal group that is more reactive than sodium, oxidizing rapidly in air and reacting violently with water with the evolution of hydrogen which takes fire, that occurs abundantly in nature in combined form in minerals (as sylvite, langbeinite, and many silicates), in seawater and brines, and in plants and animals, that is prepared in the metallic state from several of its compounds by electrolysis or by reduction (as with sodium vapor) and must be preserved under kerosine or other inert hydrocarbon liquid, and that is used chiefly as a reducing agent and in synthesis — symbol *K*; see ELEMENT table

potassium acid oxalate *or* **potassium binoxalate** *n* : POTASSIUM OXALATE b

potassium acid tartrate *or* **potassium bitartrate** *n* : CREAM OF TARTAR

potassium alum *n* : ALUM 1a

potassium amide *n* : a crystalline compound KNH_2 obtained by heating potassium in ammonia

potassium arsenite *n* : a poisonous salt made by boiling arsenic trioxide with potassium bicarbonate solution and used chiefly in medicine — see FOWLER'S SOLUTION

potassium bicarbonate *or* **potassium acid carbonate** *n* : a crystalline salt $KHCO_3$ that gives a weakly alkaline reaction in aqueous solution and that is made by passing carbon dioxide into a solution of potassium carbonate; potassium hydrogen carbonate

potassium bisulfate *or* **potassium acid sulfate** *n* : a crystalline salt $KHSO_4$ that gives an acid reaction in solution, that is made by treating potassium sulfate with sulfuric acid, and that is used chiefly in making cream of tartar and as a flux; potassium hydrogen sulfate

potassium bromate *n* : a crystalline salt $KBrO_3$ used chiefly as an oxidizing agent and in improving the baking properties of flour

potassium bromide *n* : a crystalline salt KBr having a biting saline taste that is used chiefly in medicine as a sedative, in photography for making gelatin-silver bromide emulsions and as a restrainer in developing, and in engraving and lithography

potassium carbonate *n* : either of two potassium salts of carbonic acid: **a** : the deliquescent crystalline normal salt K_2CO_3 that gives a strongly alkaline reaction in aqueous solution, that was obtained orig. from wood ashes but is now made usu. from potassium chloride (as by electrolysis to potassium hydroxide followed by carbonation), and that is used chiefly in making hard glass, soft soap, and in other ways similarly to sodium carbonate — see POTASH 1a **b** : POTASSIUM BICARBONATE

potassium chlorate *n* : a crystalline salt $KClO_3$ with a cooling saline taste that is made by electrolysis of potassium chloride or by reaction of potassium chloride with another chlorate (as sodium chlorate) and that is used chiefly as an oxidizing agent in matches, fireworks, and explosives

potassium chloride *n* : a crystalline salt KCl occurring as the mineral sylvite in carnallite and in natural waters and used chiefly as a fertilizer and in making other potassium compounds

potassium chromate *n* : a yellow crystalline salt K_2CrO_4 having uses similar to those of sodium chromate

potassium cobaltinitrite *n* : a yellow crystalline salt $K_3Co(NO_2)_6$ used as a pigment and as an insoluble salt of potassium in analysis; potassium hexa-nitro-cobalt-ate(III) — see COBALT YELLOW

potassium cyanate *n* : a crystalline salt KOCN made by oxidizing potassium cyanide or by heating a mixture of potassium carbonate and urea and used chiefly to kill crabgrass on lawns

potassium cyanide *n* : an exceedingly poisonous deliquescent crystalline salt KCN made usu. by heating potassium carbonate and carbon with ammonia and used chiefly in electroplating and in the cyanide process

potassium dichromate *or* **potassium bichromate** *n* : a bitter poisonous orange-red crystalline salt $K_2Cr_2O_7$ used chiefly in sensitizing gelatin in photography, in textile and leather finishes, and as an oxidizing agent (as in safety matches and fireworks)

potassium ferricyanide *n* : a red crystalline salt $K_3Fe(CN)_6$ made by oxidizing potassium ferrocyanide with chlorine and used chiefly as a photographic bleach and in coating blueprint paper — called also *red prussiate of potash*

potassium ferrocyanide *n* : a tough yellow crystalline salt $K_4Fe(CN)_6$ made from the cyanogen compounds obtained as by-products in the carbonization of coal or directly by reaction of potassium cyanide with ferrous salts and used chiefly in making iron blue pigments — called also *yellow prussiate of potash*

potassium fluoride *n* : any of several salts made usu. by reaction of hydrofluoric acid with potassium carbonate: as **a** : the hygroscopic crystalline normal salt KF used chiefly as a solder flux and as a fluorinating agent in organic synthesis **b** *or* **potassium bifluoride** : the poisonous corrosive crystalline acid fluoride KHF_2 used chiefly as an electrolyte in the manufacture of fluorine and as a solder flux : potassium hydrogen fluoride

potassium hydrate *n* : POTASSIUM HYDROXIDE — not used systematically

potassium hydroxide *n* : a brittle white deliquescent solid KOH that dissolves with much heat in less than its weight of water to form a strongly alkaline and caustic solution, that is made usu. by electrolysis of a solution of potassium chloride, and that is used chiefly in making soap, in bleaching and mercerizing, and as a reagent in chemistry — called also *caustic potash*

potassium hypochlorite *n* : an unstable salt KOCl known chiefly in aqueous solution — see JAVELLE WATER a

potassium iodide *n* : a crystalline salt KI that is very soluble in water and is used chiefly in making photographic emulsions, in organic synthesis, in medicine (as in Lugol's solution), and in iodized table salt

potassium manganate *n* : an unstable green salt K_2MnO_4 readily converted into potassium permanganate

potassium mercuric iodide *n* : a poisonous yellow deliquescent crystalline complex salt K_2HgI_4 used as a disinfectant and as a chemical reagent; potassium tetra-iodomercurate(II) — see NESSLER'S REAGENT

potassium nitrate *n* : a soluble crystalline salt KNO_3 with a cooling saline taste that occurs as a product of nitrification in most arable soils esp. in hot dry countries where it is extracted by leaching but that is usu. made by reaction of potassium chloride and sodium nitrate, that decomposes on strong heating into potassium nitrite KNO_2 and oxygen, and that is used chiefly in making black powder, matches, and fireworks and in curing meat — called also *niter, saltpeter*

potassium oxalate *n* : any of three crystalline oxalates of potassium: **a** : the normal efflorescent soluble salt $K_2C_2O_4.H_2O$ used chiefly in preventing the clotting of blood (as in blood tests) and formerly in photography **b** : a bitter poisonous acid salt $KHC_2O_4.H_2O$ found esp. in oxalis and rhubarb and used chiefly in removing ink stains and scouring metals; potassium hydrogen oxalate — called also *potassium acid oxalate, salt of sorrel* **c** : POTASSIUM TETROXALATE

potassium oxide *n* : an oxide of potassium; *esp* : the deliquescent monoxide K_2O

potassium perchlorate *n* : a crystalline salt $KClO_4$ used chiefly in explosives and fireworks

potassium permanganate *n* : a salt $KMnO_4$ that crystallizes in dark purple prisms having a blue metallic luster and dissolves in water with a purple-red color, that is made usu. by reaction of manganese dioxide and potassium hydroxide and oxidation of the manganate formed, and that is used chiefly as an oxidizing and bleaching agent and as a disinfectant

potassium persulfate *n* : a crystalline salt $K_2S_2O_8$ used chiefly in oxidizing and bleaching and as a promoter of polymerizations (as in the manufacture of GR-S rubber)

potassium phosphate *n* **1** : one of the three orthophosphates of potassium analogous to the simple sodium orthophosphates **2** : a phosphate of potassium (as tetra-potassium pyrophosphate $K_4P_2O_7$) other than an orthophosphate

potassium sodium tartrate *n* : ROCHELLE SALT

potassium sulfate *n* : either of two crystalline sulfates of potassium: **a** : the normal salt K_2SO_4 occurring naturally esp. in complex sulfates (as langbeinite, polyhalite) and used chiefly as a fertilizer and in the manufacture of alums and other chemicals and of gypsum wallboard to accelerate the setting time **b** : POTASSIUM BISULFATE

potassium tetroxalate *n* : a relatively insoluble crystalline complex acid salt $KHC_2O_4.H_2C_2O_4.2H_2O$ used chiefly in removing rust marks and as a reference standard in analyzing bases and permanganates

potassium thiocyanate *n* : a hygroscopic crystalline salt KSCN having uses similar to those of sodium thiocyanate

po·ta·tion \pōˈtāshən\ *n* -S [ME *potacioun*, fr. MF *potation*, fr. L *potation-, potatio* act of drinking, fr. *potatus* (past part. of *potare* to drink) + *-ion-, -io* -ion — more at POTABLE] **1 a** : a usu. alcoholic drink or brew ⟨the root . . . whence their favorite ~ is extracted —James Cook⟩ **2 a** : the act of drinking ⟨you did rather abstain from ~ —Sir Walter Scott⟩ **b** : DRAFT 4a ⟨under the stimulus of several ~s —S.H.Adams⟩ **c** : indulgence in drinking alcoholic beverages ⟨men who were . . . the worse for ~ —Frederick Marryat⟩ ⟨the arrival of planes . . . occasioned like gourmandising and ~ —*Time*⟩

po·ta·to \pəˈtād·(ˌ)ō, -ā(ˌ)tō, -ād·ə, -ātə *sometimes* pəd·ˈād·-\ *n* -ES *often attrib* [Sp *patata*, fr. Taino *batata*] **1** : SWEET POTATO **2 a** (1) : an erect herb (*Solanum tuberosum*) that has compound pinnate leaves, white, yellow, blue, or purple flowers, and green, yellowish, or purplish berries, is native to the highlands of So. and Central America, and is widely cultivated esp. in the temperate regions as a garden vegetable (2) : the edible starchy tuber that is an enlargement of an underground stem of this plant — called also *Irish potato, white potato* **b** : any of several other plants of the genus *Solanum* (as Uruguay potato)

potato alcohol *n* : alcohol distilled from a potato mash

potato aphid *n* : a common aphid (*Macrosiphum euphorbiae*) that occurs on the potato and many other plants as well as on some orchard trees and that usu. overwinters on rosebushes

potato apple *n* : the berry of the potato

potato ball *n* **1 a** : a small ball cut from a potato with a special scoop **b** : a potato croquette **2** : POTATO APPLE

potato bean *n* **1** : YAM BEAN **2** : GROUNDNUT 2 a

potato beetle *or* **potato bug** *n* : an insect that attacks potato plants; *esp* : COLORADO POTATO BEETLE

potato blight *or* **potato disease** *also* **potato mildew** *or* **potato mold** *or* **potato murrain** *n* : a blight or decay that attacks the potato — compare EARLY BLIGHT, LATE BLIGHT

potato cake *n* : cold mashed potato shaped into a circular flattened cake, often rolled in flour, and fried

potato canker *n* **1** : POTATO WART **2** : a powdery scab in which there is destruction of the flesh of the tuber that leaves hollowed out eroded areas which are larger than the usual spots

potato chip *n* : a thin slice of raw white potato fried crisp in deep fat

potato crisp *n, chiefly Brit* : POTATO CHIP

potato-digger \ˈ⸗ˌ⸗⸗ˌ⸗⸗\ *n* : a machine or implement for digging potatoes

potato family *n* : SOLANACEAE

potato fern *n* **1** : a fern (*Marattia fraxinea*) of New Zealand that has a large edible starchy rootstock **2** : a fern (*Dryopteris cordifolia*) of Australia that has small ovoid tubers which are edible

potato flea beetle *n* : a small oval shining black flea beetle (*Epitrix cucumeris*) that injures the leaves of various plants

potato flour *or* **potato starch** *n* : a flour that is prepared from potatoes which are ground to pulp and washed free of fiber

potato fork *n* : a hand fork with several curved tines used for digging potatoes

potato fungus *n* : a fungus causing late blight

potato grub *n* : a larva of a potato moth

potato hook *n* : a hand tool with long hooked tines used for digging potatoes and other tuber crops

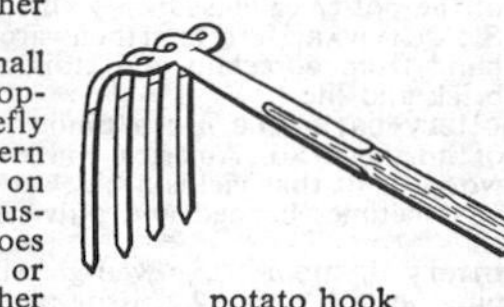
potato hook

potato leafhopper *n* : a small green white-spotted leafhopper (*Empoasca fabae*) chiefly of the eastern and southern U. S. that is a serious pest on many cultivated plants causing hopperburn on potatoes and browning, yellowing, or stunting of various other plants (as beans, dahlias, or alfalfa) — called also *apple and potato leafhopper;* compare APPLE LEAFHOPPER

potato–leaved tomato \ˌ=ˈ==ˌ=-\ *n* : a tomato (*Lycopersicon esculentum grandifolium*) having large leaves with few entire-margined primary leaflets and few or no secondary leaflets

potato masher *n* **1** : any of several kitchen utensils for mashing cooked potatoes **2** : a grenade having a wooden handle by which it is thrown

potato mosaic *n* : any of various virus diseases of the potato characterized chiefly by more or less mottling of the foliage — compare AUCUBA MOSAIC, CALICO, CRINKLE, CURLY DWARF, RUGOSE MOSAIC

potato moth *or* **potato tuber moth** *n* : a grayish brown gelechiid moth (*Phthorimaea operculella*) whose larva is the potato tuberworm

potato mottle *or* **potato virus X** *or* **potato X virus** *n* : LATENT VIRUS DISEASE

potato onion *n* : MULTIPLIER ONION

potato psyllid *n* : a hemipterous insect (*Paratrioza cockerelli*) that feeds on potato and tomato plants and causes psyllid yellows

potato race *n* : a race in which each runner attempts to retrieve a series of potatoes or other small objects one at a time

potato ring *n* : a ring or hoop of ceramic or metalware used in Ireland in the 18th century as a stand for a bowl or similar article : DISH RING

potato root eelworm *also* **potato root nematode** *n* : GOLDEN NEMATODE

potato rot nematode *n* : a plant-parasitic nematode (*Ditylenchus destructor*) that attacks roots and tubers (as of potato or sugar beet) causing dry rugose lesions highly susceptible to secondary invasion by fungi and that has long been a serious pest of potatoes in northern Europe and is now known also from widely separated points in No. America

po·ta·to·ry \ˈpōd·əˌtōrē\ *adj* [LL *potatorius*, fr. L *potatus* (past part. of *potare* to drink) + *-orius* -ory — more at POTABLE] : of, relating to, or given to drinking

potato scab *n* : any of various diseases of the potato characterized by crusty rough spots or scabs on the tubers; *specif* : a disease that is characterized by lesions of brownish corky tissue, is caused by an actinomycete (*Streptomyces scabies*), and is esp. damaging in alkaline soils — called also *corky scab;* compare POWDERY SCAB

potato set *n* : a potato tuber or part of a tuber that has at least one eye and is used for planting

potato–sick \ˌ=ˈ==ˌ=\ *adj, of land* : exhausted by successive crops of potatoes

potato slump *n* : the dregs or residue from the alcoholic distillation of fermented potatoes

potato stalk borer *n* : a larva of a potato weevil

potato tree *n* : any of several arborescent or nearly arborescent plants of the genus *Solanum* (as the Brazilian *S. macranthum* and the Chilean *S. crispum*) none of which are true potatoes

potato tuberworm *n* : a small pale brown-headed caterpillar that is the larva of the potato moth and that mines in the leaves and bores in the stems of potato, tobacco, and related plants and commonly overwinters in potato tubers — called also *splitworm*

potato vine *n* : POTATO 2 a (1)

potato wart *n* : a fungous disease of potato tubers caused by a pond scum parasite (*Synchytrium endobioticum*) and characterized by dark warty spongy excrescences that are yellow or light brown when young and that originate in the eyes of the tuber

potato weevil *n* : an American weevil (*Trichobaris trinotata*) whose larva lives in the stalks of potato plants

potato whiskey *n* : whiskey distilled from potatoes

potato wilt *n* : a wilt of potatoes; *esp* : one caused by fungi (as *Fusarium oxysporum* or *Verticillium alboatrum*)

potato worm *n* : a large green white-striped caterpillar that is the larva of a hawkmoth (*Protoparce quinquemaculata*)

pot–au–feu \ˌpōd·ōˈfə̄\ *n, pl* **pot–au–feu** [F, lit., pot on the fire] : a French dish consisting of a thick soup of meat and many vegetables

pot·a·wat·o·mi *also* **pot·a·wat·a·mi** *or* **pot·ta·wat·to·mi** *or* **pot·ta·wat·ta·mi** \ˌpäd·əˈwädəmē\ *n, pl* **potawatomi** *or* **potawatomis** *usu cap* **1 a** : an Indian people of the lower peninsula of Michigan and adjoining states **b** : a member of such people **2** : the Algonquian language of the Potawatomi people

potbank \ˈ=ˌ=\ *n* [¹*pot* + *bank* (bench)] *dial chiefly Eng* : a place where pottery is made

pot barley *n* : HULLED BARLEY

potbellied \ˈ=ˌ==\ *adj* [*pot* + *bellied*] : having a potbelly or a bulging part suggestive of a potbelly ⟨a ~ man⟩ ⟨a ~ stove⟩

potbelly \ˈ=ˌ==\ *n* [¹*pot* + *belly*] **1 a** : an enlarged, swollen, or protruding belly or stomach **b** : a condition characterized by a potbelly and among children or animals symptomatic of disease or improper diet **2** : a person having a protuberant belly **3** : a stove with a rounded or bulging body

potboil \ˈ=ˌ=\ *vi* [¹*pot* + *boil*] : to produce potboilers ⟨the man who has to ~ for a living seldom accomplishes anything of an exceptional character —*Reynold's Newspaper*⟩ ⟨was a financial failure and . . . must go back once more to ~*ing* —H.D.Piper⟩

potboiler \ˈ=ˌ==\ *n* [¹*pot* + *boiler*] **1** *archaic* : POTWALLOPER **2** : a usu. inferior work of art or literature produced chiefly for monetary return ⟨published many popular historical ~*s* . . . out of which he makes a great deal of money —Harold Strauss⟩ **3** : one that produces a potboiler ⟨several ~*s* have since helped themselves to this material —*Saturday Rev.*⟩

potbelly 3

pot bottom *n* : a boulder or concretion in a roof slate that is rounded like the bottom of a pot

pot–bound \ˈ=ˌ=\ *adj, of a potted plant* : having roots so densely matted as to allow little or no space for further growth

potboy \ˈ=ˌ=\ *n* : a boy who carries pots of ale, beer, and other drink in a public house or tavern

pot burner *n* : an oil burner in which the oil is vaporized by air entering through a perforated shell that surrounds the pot containing the oil

¹**potch** \ˈpäch\ *dial Brit var of* POACH

²**potch** \"\ *vt* -ED/-ING/-ES [alter. of ²*poach*] : to bleach (pulp) in a potcher

pot cheese *n* **1** : COTTAGE CHEESE **2** : COOK CHEESE

potch·er *also* **poch·er** \ˈpächə(r)\ *n* -s [alter. of ¹*poacher*] : an engine of the hollander type but without a bedplate used for breaking up paper stock, washing, and bleaching

potch·er·man \-(r)mən\ *n, pl* **potchermen** : a man who operates a potcher

pot–clay \ˈ=ˌ=\ *n* : a fireclay suitable for the manufacture of the melting pots used in glassmaking

pot–color \ˈ=ˌ==\ *vt* : to color (molten glass) in a glass pot

pot–companion \ˈ=ˌ=ˌ==\ *n, archaic* : a drinking companion

pot culture *n* : the growing of plants in flower pots

¹**pote** \ˈpōt\ *vt* -ED/-ING/-S [ME *poten*, fr. OE *potian* — more at PUT] **1** *dial Eng* : PUSH, SHOVE, NUDGE **2** *dial Eng* : KICK, POKE

²**pote** \"\ *n* -s *dial Eng* : THRUST, KICK

pot earth *n* : POTTER'S CLAY

pot·e·cary \ˈpätəˌkarī\ *n* -ES [ME *potecarie*, short for *apotecarie* — more at APOTHECARY] *dial chiefly Eng* : APOTHECARY

po·teen \pəˈtēn, pōˈ-\ *also* **po·theen** \-ˈthēn\ *or* **pot·teen** \päˈtēn\ *n* -s [IrGael *poitín* small pot, whiskey made in a private still, fr. *pota* pot (fr. E ¹*pot*) + *-ín* -een] : illicitly distilled whiskey of Ireland made variously from barley, potatoes, or sugar and molasses

pot egg *n, Brit* : a dummy nest egg for a fowl

po·tem·kin village \pəˈtem(p)kən-\ *n, usu cap P* [after Grigori A. *Potemkin* †1791 Russ. statesman; fr. the story that Potemkin once had impressive fake villages built along a route that Catherine the Great was to travel] : an imposing or pretentious facade or display designed to obscure or shield an unimposing or undesirable fact or condition : FALSE FRONT ⟨the visitors are shown no *Potemkin villages* but allowed to see things as they are⟩

¹**po·tence** \ˈpōtᵊn(t)s\ *n* -s [ME, fr. MF, fr. L *potentia* potency, power] **1** : POTENCY **2** : the integrated dominance effect of a group of polygenes

²**potence** \"\ *n* -s [ME, fr. MF, crutch, gibbet, fr. L *potentia* potency, power] **1** : CROSS, GIBBET **2 a** : the stud of a watch in which the bearing for the lower pivot of the verge is made **b** : a supporting bracket used in watchwork **3** : a military formation in which a part of a line is thrown forward or backward at an angle to the main line

³**potence** \" *also* **po·ten·cee** \-nsē\ *adj* [MF *potencee*, fr. *potence* crutch, gibbet] : ²POTENT

po·ten·cy \ˈpōtᵊnsē, -si\ *n* -ES [L *potentia* potency, power, fr. *potent-*, *potens* potent, powerful + *-ia* -y] **1** : the quality or state of being potent: **a** : FORCE, POWER, AUTHORITY ⟨if land armies ever lose their ~ —Green Peyton⟩ ⟨a place of ~ and sway o' the state —Shak.⟩ ⟨massed activity has a ~ which individual effort can no longer claim —John Dewey⟩ **b** (1) : the ability or capacity to achieve a result or effect : EFFECTIVENESS ⟨the ~ of prominence for good or ill is not to be denied —F. L.Mott⟩ ⟨the ~ of religious faith to deal with fear, anxiety, and tension —*Saturday Rev.*⟩ (2) : the ability or capacity to influence or affect thought or feeling ⟨these lines . . . have, in addition, a very remarkable ~ of suggestion —F.R.Leavis⟩ ⟨must not doubt the ~ of our ideas —C.M.Fuess⟩ ⟨the charm and emotional ~ of the music —Edward Sackville-West & Desmond Shawe-Taylor⟩ **c** (1) : chemical or medicinal strength or efficacy ⟨the ~ of the drink⟩ ⟨the ~ of the drug⟩ ⟨the material had lost its ~ by being exposed to light —*Current Biog.*⟩ (2) : physical or phenomenal intensity or force ⟨figured out that less than 100 H-bombs of 1954 ~ could lay down a saturation pattern of poisonous fallout —*New Republic*⟩ **d** : the ability to copulate — usu. used of the male **2 a** : POTENTIALITY 1 ⟨clung to our atoms as the inmost nucleus of matter and as containing the promise and ~ of life and mind —W.L.Sullivan⟩ ⟨submitted . . . only to the finest human *potencies*, which is to say, to the potentiality of being human —*New Republic*⟩ **b** : the capacity for acting or being acted upon and hence for undergoing change ⟨a ball has a ~ for being thrown⟩ ⟨a teacher is necessary to lead the student to an actual knowledge of what he knew only in ~ —Henri DuLac⟩ **c** : initial total inherent capacity for development of a particular kind prior to the establishment of limiting controls — compare COMPETENCE **3 a** : one that has power or authority ⟨it is his ~'s wish —Rafael Sabatini⟩ **b** : a supernatural or demonic power; *specif* : a minor often local god ⟨pray to the *potencies* of rebirth and resurrection in nature and human love —Hans Meyerhoff⟩

¹**po·tent** \ˈpōtᵊnt\ *n* -s [ME, crutch, support, modif. of MF *potence* crutch, gibbet] **1** *archaic* : SUPPORT, STAY **2** : a heraldic fur consisting of rows of interlocking upright and inverted short-stemmed T-shaped panes alternately argent and azure unless other tinctures are specified and so placed one beneath another that each pane stands head to head or foot to foot with one of the other tinctures

²**potent** \"\ *adj* [obs. E *potent*, n., crutch, fr. ME, crutch, support] *of a heraldic cross* : having flat bars across the ends of the arms — see CROSS illustration

potent 2

³**potent** \"\ *adj* [ME (Sc), fr. L *potent-*, *potens* (used as pres. part. of *posse* to be able, fr. *potis esse*, fr. *potis* able, capable + *esse* to be), pres. part. of (assumed) OL *potēre* to be powerful, be able, fr. L *potis* able, capable; akin to Goth *brūthfaths* bridegroom, Gk *posis* husband, Skt *pati* master] **1** : having or wielding strength, force, or authority : POWERFUL, STRONG ⟨increasing the capabilities of the ground soldier by providing him with increasingly ~ weapons —W.P.Corderman⟩ ⟨mixing the players of the first two teams would produce a ~ offensive —Eddie Beachler⟩ ⟨received the ~ machine endorsement as candidate for secretary of state —Blanton Fortson⟩ **2 a** : having or wielding influence : possessing the capacity to mold or alter thought or feeling : COGENT, AFFECTIVE ⟨a numerically inferior but intellectually ~ group —K.S.Davis⟩ ⟨still more ~ arguments for ending the struggle were found in the suffering caused by the . . . famine —W.C.Ford⟩ ⟨music is perhaps the most ~ agent for . . . inducing men to forget their differences —Jane Addams⟩ **b** : producing or capable of producing an effect or result : PREGNANT, INSTRUMENTAL, CAUSAL ⟨deals with what he looks upon as a ~ factor in delinquency —Winfred Overholser⟩ ⟨the most ~ and characteristic phase of the whole industrial revolution, the connection of iron with coal —G.M.Trevelyan⟩ **3 a** : chemically or medicinally effective : EFFICACIOUS ⟨nearly doubled the period during which the vaccine could be kept ~ —V.G.Heiser⟩ **b** : rich in a characteristic ingredient : STRONG ⟨~ tea⟩ ⟨a ~ drink⟩ **4** : able to copulate — usu. used of the male

⁴**potent** *n* **1** *obs* : one having power or authority : POTENTATE **2** *obs* : a formal military order : WARRANT

po·ten·tate \ˈpōtᵊnˌtāt, *usu* -ād·+V\ *n* -s [ME *potentat*, fr. LL *potentatus*, fr. L, power, fr. *potent-*, *potens* potent, powerful + *-atus* -ate] **1** : one who possesses great power or sway : RULER, PRINCE, DICTATOR ⟨was not an oriental ~, but a modern, liberal, constitutional monarch —*Time*⟩ ⟨these great ~*s* of Paris fashion —E.O.Hauser⟩ ⟨son of a mighty film ~ —Bennett Cerf⟩ **2** *archaic* : a powerful nation, city, or company **3** : the chief officer of a secret fraternal order

¹**potent–counterpotent** \ˌ==ˌ=ˈ==ˌ=\ *adj* : ²POTENT

²**potent–counterpotent** \"\ *n* **1** : ¹POTENT 2 **2** : COUNTERPOTENT

po·ten·tia \pəˈtenchēə\ *n* -s [LL, fr. L, potency, power — more at POTENCY] : DYNAMIS

¹**po·ten·tial** \pəˈtenchəl, pōˈ-\ *adj* [ME *potencial*, fr. LL *potentialis* potential, powerful, fr. LL *potentia* dynamis, state of that which is not yet fully realized & L *potentia* potency, power + L *-alis* -al] **1 a** : existing in possibility : having the capacity or a strong possibility for development into a state of actuality ⟨field studies of existing and ~ book markets —*Collier's Yr. Bk.*⟩ ⟨the detection of incipient or ~ disease of the nervous system —H.G.Armstrong⟩ ⟨too small to provide . . . for the ~ needs for reconstruction and development that will emerge in the postwar years —L.G.Melville⟩ ⟨~ leader⟩ ⟨~ profit⟩ ⟨~ use⟩ — compare ACTUAL **b** : having the capacity for acting or being acted upon and hence for undergoing change — compare POTENCY **2** *archaic* : ²POTENT **3** : expressing possibility ⟨~ subjunctive⟩; *specif* : of, relating to, or constituting a verb phrase expressing possibility, liberty, or power by the use of an auxiliary (as *may, can*) with the infinitive of the verb (as in "it may rain", "he can write") **syn** see LATENT

²**potential** \"\ *n* -s **1** : something that exists in a state of potency or possibility for changing or developing into a state of actuality ⟨industrial location in new areas will make use of labor and other ~*s* which might otherwise remain untapped —*New Republic*⟩ ⟨a sound source with an unplumbed ~ for novelty and expression —*Time*⟩ ⟨in joining together at fertilization, germ cells add to the total gene ~ of an organism by the fusion of two heredities —Weston LaBarre⟩ ⟨growth ~⟩ ⟨human ~⟩ ⟨industrial ~⟩ ⟨leadership ~⟩ ⟨military ~⟩ **2** : any of various functions (as a scalar function so related to the vector that the vector is its gradient) from which the intensity or the velocity at any point in a field may be calculated; *specif* : ELECTRIC POTENTIAL

potential barrier *n* : a region in which particles (as alpha particles, photoelectrons, or thermions) are decelerated or stopped by a repulsive force

potential cautery *n* : an agent (as a caustic or escharotic) used to destroy tissue by chemical action — compare ACTUAL CAUTERY

potential coil *or* **potential winding** *n* : a coil or winding connected in shunt across a circuit (as in a wattmeter)

potential difference *n* : the difference in electric potential between two points that represents the work involved or the energy released in the transfer of a unit quantity of electricity from one point to the other

potential divider *n* : VOLTAGE DIVIDER

potential energy *n* : the energy of a particle or body dependent upon its position

potential gradient *n* : the vector that represents the rate at which a potential changes with position in a specified direction; *specif* : the rate of change with height of the atmospheric electric potential

potential head *n* : ELEVATION HEAD

po·ten·ti·al·i·ty \pəˌtenchēˈalədē, pōˌ-, -ətē, -i *also* (ˌ)pōˌtenˈcha- *or* pəˌtenˈcha-\ *n* -ES [ML *potentialitat-*, *potentialitas*, fr. LL *potentialis* potential, powerful + L *-itat-*, *-itas* -ity] **1** : the capacity or possibility for changing or developing into a state of actuality ⟨the magnificent richness of human ~ and the paltriness of human achievement —Paul Pickrel⟩ ⟨economic ~⟩ ⟨growth ~⟩ ⟨propaganda ~⟩ ⟨war ~⟩ **2** : POTENTIAL 1 ⟨present at birth as *potentialities* which later grow and develop —Abram Kardiner⟩ ⟨possible risks which have been seized upon as actualities when they have been merely *potentialities* —T.S.Eliot⟩ **3** *archaic* : the quality or state of being potent ⟨I have the power, the ~ of walking —S.T. Coleridge⟩

po·ten·tial·ize \pəˈtenchəˌlīz, pōˈ-\ *vt* -ED/-ING/-S : to make potential

po·ten·tial·ly \-chəlē, -li\ *adv* [ME *potencially*, fr. *potencial* potential + *-ly*] **1** : in a potential or possible state or condition : with a possibility or capacity for becoming actual ⟨consider the contribution made by science both actually and still more ~ to agriculture —John Dewey⟩ ⟨~ as revolutionary . . . as the discovery of the atomic bomb —Vera M. Dean⟩ ⟨~ capable⟩ ⟨introducing ~ dangerous innovations⟩ ⟨~ most productive⟩ ⟨~ useful⟩ **2** *archaic* : in a powerful or authoritative manner

po·ten·tial·ness *n* -ES : POTENTIALITY

potential temperature *n* : the temperature that a sample of air attains if reduced to a pressure of 1000 millibars without receiving or losing heat to the environment

potential well *or* **potential hole** *n* : a sharply defined region of minimum potential in a field of force — compare POTENTIAL BARRIER

po·ten·ti·ate \pəˈtenchēˌāt\ *vb* -ED/-ING/-S [L *potentia* potency, power + E *-ate*; intended as trans. of G *potenzieren*] *vt* : to make potent or more effective ⟨a poet's work may be *potentiated* by his experience of war and of suffering —*N.Y. Herald Tribune Bk. Rev.*⟩: as **a** : to make (as a drug) more physiologically active **b** : to cause an increase in (physiological activity or effect usu. of a drug) ⟨the effects of morphine on the stomach are *potentiated* by cholinergic drugs —B.P. Babkin & M.H.F.Friedman⟩ ~ *vi* : to make something potent or more effective

po·ten·ti·a·tion \=ˌ=ˌ=ˈāshən\ *n* -s : the act or process of potentiating

po·ten·ti·a·tor \=ˈ==ˌād·ə(r)\ *n* -s : one that potentiates; *esp* : a chemical agent or drug that potentiates

po·ten·til·la \ˌpōtᵊnˈtilə\ *n* [NL, fr. ML, garden valerian, fr. L *potent-*, *potens* potent, powerful + ML *-illa* — more at POTENT] **1** *cap* : a large genus of herbs and shrubs (family Rosaceae) that are abundant in temperate regions, have alternate pinnate or palmate leaves, yellow, purple, or white flowers with a persistent bracted calyx and five petals, and a fruit consisting of many small achenes heaped on a dry receptacle, and include several which are cultivated as ornamentals — see CINQUEFOIL **2** -s : any plant of the genus *Potentilla*

po·ten·ti·om·e·ter \pəˌtenchēˈäməd·ə(r)\ *n* [ISV ²*potential* + *-o-* + *-meter*] **1** : an instrument for the precise measurement of electromotive forces by which a part of the voltage to be measured is balanced against that of a known electromotive force and computed therefrom by the law of fall of potential **2** : VOLTAGE DIVIDER

po·ten·ti·o·met·ric \pəˌtenchēəˈme·trik\ *adj* [*potentiometer* + *-ic*] : of, relating to, or by means of a potentiometer — **po·ten·ti·o·met·ri·cal·ly** \-rək(ə)lē\ *adv*

po·ten·ti·om·e·try \pəˌtenchēˈämə·trē\ *n* -ES [ISV ²*potential* + *-o-* + *-metry*] : the measurement of electromotive forces by means of a potentiometer; *also* : the use or application of such measurement

po·tent·ize \ˈpōtᵊnˌtīz\ *vt* -ED/-ING/-S : to make potent or effective

po·tent·ly *adv* : in a potent manner

po·tent·ness *n* -ES : the quality or state of being potent

potents *pl of* POTENT

po·te·ri·um \pōˈtirēəm\ *n, cap* [NL, fr. Gk *potērion* drinking cup (or, a plant, prob. goat's thorn); akin to Gk *pinein* to drink — more at POTABLE] : a small genus of thorny shrubs or herbs (family Rosaceae) with pinnate leaves and greenish flowers — see SALAD BURNET

potes *pres 3d sing of* POTE, *pl of* POTE

po·tes·tal \pōˈtestᵊl\ *adj* [*potestas* + *-al*] : of or relating to potestas

po·tes·tas \-eˌstäs, -tas\ *n, pl* **potesta·tes** \ˌpōˌteˈstäˌtās, ˌpäd·əˈstäd·(ˌ)ēz\ [L *potestat-*, *potestas* power, irreg. fr. *potis* able, capable + *-tat-*, *-tas* -ty — more at POTENT] : the legal authority of a Roman citizen over his descendants and others in his household — compare PATRIA POTESTAS

potestas ab·sti·nen·di \-ˌäbztəˈnen(ˌ)dē, -ˌäpst-; -ˌabztəˈnen(ˌ)dē, -ˌdī\ *n* [L, power of refusing] : the right granted by the praetorian law of ancient Rome to a necessary family heir to decline the inheritance; *also* : the power to exercise this right — called also *beneficium abstinendi*

potestate *n* -s [ME *potestat*, fr. L *potestat-*, *potestas*, lit., power] *obs* : one having power or authority

potestative *adj* [LL *potestativus*, fr. L *potestat-*, *potestas* power + *-ivus* -ive] *obs* : having power or authority : POTENT

po·tes·ta·tive condition \ˈpōd·əˌstād·iv-\ *n* : a condition or term of a legal agreement that is completely within the power and control of one of the parties and that makes the agreement unenforceable for lack of mutuality of obligation

pot–eye \ˈ=ˌ=\ *n* : a ringlike device by which cloth or other textile material is guided during processing

pot·ful \ˈpätˌfu̇l\ *n* -s [ME, fr. ¹*pot* + *-ful*] : the quantity held by a pot

pot furnace *n* **1** : a furnace containing several pots or crucibles in which different small batches of glass may be melted **2** : a metallurgical furnace in which the charge is contained in a pot

potgun \ˈ=ˌ=\ *n* **1 a** *archaic* : POPGUN **b** *obs* : PISTOL **2** *obs* : a loud or boastful talker

pothanger \ˈ=ˌ==\ *n* : a rack, bar, or other device for hanging a pothook or a pot over a fire usu. in a fireplace

pot hat *n* : a hat with a stiff crown; *esp* : DERBY

pothead \ˈ=ˌ=\ *n* **1** : BLACKFISH 2 **2** : a form of terminal hermetically sealed to the sheath of an electric cable for making a moistureproof connection between the wires within the cable and those outside

poth·e·cary \ˈpäthəˌkerē\ *n* -ES [alter. of *potecary*] *chiefly dial* : APOTHECARY

potheen *var of* POTEEN

¹**poth·er** \ˈpäthə(r)\ *n* -s [origin unknown] **1 a** : a noisy disturbance : BUSTLE, COMMOTION ⟨the ~ of city traffic⟩ **b** : a vocal stir or controversy over a trivial or minor matter : FUSS ⟨the lack of storage facilities about which so much ~ was emitted during the campaign —Raymond Moley⟩ ⟨this ~ over a small point —B.T.Ellis⟩ ⟨the great ~ raised by civil service reform back in the 1880's —W.G.Carleton⟩ **2** : a choking cloud or condition of dust or smoke ⟨rushed off in a terrific haste and ~ of dust —Arnold Bennett⟩ **3** : a state of agitating worry or concern : TURMOIL, STEW **syn** see STIR

²**pother** \"\ *vb* -ED/-ING/-S *vt* **:** to trouble or disturb esp. about a trivial or minor matter **:** PERPLEX, VEX ⟨~*s* himself over unnecessary detail⟩ ~ *vi* **:** to trouble or concern oneself esp. with a trivial or minor matter **:** FUSS, WORRY, PUZZLE ⟨~*ed* all evening over the bus schedule⟩
potherb \ˈ=,=\ *n* **1 :** an herb that is boiled for use as a vegetable; *esp* **:** wild greens gathered for food **2 :** a cultivated herb (as mint) used to season food
poth·er·ment \ˈpäthə(r)mənt\ *n* -S *dial* **:** BOTHERMENT
potholder \ˈ=,==\ *n* **:** a usu. cloth pad for protecting the hands against hot cooking utensils
pothole \ˈ=,=\ *n* **1 a :** a circular hole formed in the rocky bed of a river or stream by the grinding action of stones or gravel whirled round by the water — called also *kettle* **b :** a pot-shaped hole in the surface of a pavement **c :** a circumscribed body of water frequented by wildfowl **2 :** a deep cave opening upward to the surface
pot·hol·er \ˈpät,hōlə(r)\ *n* **:** SPELUNKER
pothook \ˈ=,=\ *n* [ME *pothoke*, fr. ¹*pot* + *hoke*, *hok*, *hook* hook] **1 :** a hook in the form of a long or short S for hanging pots over an open fire from a crane or a bar in the throat of a chimney — called also *hake* **2 :** an iron collar worn as punishment esp. by a captured runaway slave — usu. used in pl. **3 a** (1) **:** a written letter or character resembling a pothook in shape and used in teaching writing — see HANGER 4 (2) **:** writing marked by letters so formed ⟨it is impossible to decipher her ~*s*⟩ **b** *slang* **:** a nine of any suit in a pack of playing cards

pot-hooks 1

¹**po·thos** \ˈpō,thäs\ [NL, fr. Sinhalese *pōtā* ivy= arum] *syn of* SCINDAPSUS
²**pothos** \"\ *n*, *pl* **pothos** *also* **pothoses :** IVY= ARUM
pothouse \ˈ=,=\ *n* **:** ALEHOUSE, TAVERN 1b
pothunter \ˈ=,==\ *n* **1 :** a hunter who shoots chiefly to fill his bag without regard for the rules or spirit of sport **2 :** one who contests or competes merely to win prizes **3 :** a nonprofessional archaeologist who collects archaeological objects chiefly for his own pleasure or profit; *esp* **:** one who collects such objects without maintaining an adequate record or injures or destroys an archaeological site
pot-hunting \ˈ=,==\ *n* **1 :** the act of hunting chiefly to bag game without regard for the rules or spirit of sport **2 :** the act of contesting or competing chiefly for the prize or winnings **3 :** the act of hunting for archaeological findings in an amateur manner
po·tiche \pōˈtēsh\ *n* -S [F, fr. *pot* — more at POTAGE] **:** a vase having a separate cover, a body usu. rounded or polygonal with nearly vertical sides, a rounded shoulder, and a tapered neck
po·ti·cho·ma·nia \,pōd·əshōˈmānēə\ *also* **po·ti·chi·ma·nie** \-shēˈmānē\ *n* -S [*potichomania* part trans. of F *potichomanie*, fr. *potiche* + *-o-* + *manie* mania, fr. LL *mania; potichimanie* alter. (influenced by *-i-*) of F *potichomanie*] **:** the art or process of imitating painted porcelain ware
¹**po·tion** \ˈpōshən\ *n* -S [ME *pocioun*, fr. MF *potion*, fr. L *potion-*, *potio* potion, drink, fr. *potus* (past part. of *potare* to drink) + *-ion-*, *-io* -ion — more at POTABLE] **:** a liquid mixture or dose of a medicine or drug ⟨physician . . . daily prepares a nourishing ~ —*Springfield (Mass.) Union*⟩ ⟨gave him love ~*s* to increase his ardor —Willa Cather⟩ ⟨sleeping ~⟩
²**potion** \"\ *vt* -ED/-ING/-S *archaic* **:** to administer a potion to **:** DOSE, DRUG
pot kiln *n* **1 :** a small limekiln **2 :** a kiln for firing clay pots
¹**pot·latch** *also* **pot·lach** \ˈpät,lach\ *n* -ES [Chinook Jargon, fr. Nootka *patshatl* giving, gift] **1 :** a ceremonial feast or festival of the Indians of the northwest coast given for the display of wealth to validate or advance individual tribal position or social status and marked by the host's lavish destruction of personal property and an ostentatious distribution of gifts that entails elaborate reciprocation **2** *Northwest* **:** a social event or celebration **:** PARTY, GET-TOGETHER
²**potlatch** \"\ *vt* **1 :** to hold or give a potlatch for (as a tribe or group) ⟨a clan . . . being ~*ed* by a neighboring clan —F.C. Hibben⟩ **2 :** to give (as a gift) esp. with the expectancy of reciprocation ⟨told her to make a start by getting friendly with her . . . uncle, even if she has to ~ a little stuff to him off the shelves —N.C.McDonald⟩ ~ *vi* **:** to hold or give a potlatch
pot layering *n* **:** air layering in which the rooting medium is held in a small pot
pot lead *n* [trans. of D *potlood*] **:** graphite esp. as used on the bottoms of racing boats
pot-lead \ˈ=,=\ *vt* [*pot lead*] **:** to coat (as the hull of a racing boat) with pot lead
potleg \ˈ=,=\ *n* **:** broken pieces of cast iron used as shot
pot·lick·er *also* **pot·lik·ker** \ˈpät,likə(r)\ *n* -S [¹*pot* + *licker*] *dial* **:** a mongrel dog; *esp* **:** STRAY
potlid \ˈ=,=\ *n* [ME *potlede*, fr. ¹*pot* + *lede*, *lid* lid] **1 :** the lid or cover of a pot **2** *or* **pat·lid** \ˈpat,lid\ **:** a curling stone that comes to rest on the tee
pot·lik·ker *or* **pot·lick·er** \ˈpät,likə(r)\ *South & Midland var of* POT LIQUOR
pot limit *n* **:** a betting limit imposed in a poker game whereby no raise may be greater than the amount in the pot at the time the raise is made
potline \ˈ=,=\ *n* **:** a row of electrolytic cells used in the production of aluminum
pot liquor *n* **:** the liquid left in a pot after cooking meat, vegetables, or greens
potluck \ˈ=ˈ=\ *n* **1 :** the regular fare or meal available to a guest for whom no special preparations have been made ⟨tied their horses to the corral gate and came in to take ~ with us —Burges Johnson⟩ **2 :** the luck or chance of succeeding events or possibilities ⟨I should relish every hour and what it brought me, the ~ of the day —R.W.Emerson⟩ ⟨will resign and try ~ among the bigger banks —Brendan Gill⟩ ⟨season-ticket holders buy out 85% of the house in advance and take ~ —*Time*⟩
potluck supper *or* **potluck dinner** *n* **:** COVERED-DISH SUPPER
pot·man \ˈpätmən\ *n*, *pl* **potmen 1 a :** a servingman employed in a public house — compare POTBOY **b :** a worker employed by a hotel or restaurant to wash pots and pans by hand **2 :** a worker who reduces aluminum in a battery of reduction pots by an electrolytic process **3 :** a chemical worker who dehydrates concentrated caustic solutions by boiling off excess water in cast-iron pots
pot marigold *n* **:** a common European annual garden plant (*Calendula officinalis*) widely grown for ornament — called also *Scotch marigold*
pot marjoram *n* **:** WILD MARJORAM
pot metal *n* **1 a :** an alloy of copper and lead used esp. for making large vessels **b :** a cast iron used for making pots and other hollow ware **2 a :** glass that is melted in a pot **b :** stained glass whose colors are incorporated with melted glass in the pot
pot of gold : a large sum of money often obtained quickly or fabulously **:** BONANZA; *also* **:** the opportunity or prospect of making a large sum of money ⟨the *pot of gold* was seen in real estate, trade, timber, and commerce —*Amer. Guide Series: Wash.*⟩
po·to·ma·nia \,pōd·əˈmānēə\ *n* [NL, fr. Gk *poton* drink + LL *mania*; akin to Gk *pinein* to drink — more at POTABLE] **:** DIPSOMANIA
po·to·ma·to \,pōd·əˈmād·(,)ō\ *n* -ES [blend of *potato* and *tomato*] **:** POMATO
po·tom·e·ter \pōˈtäməd·ə(r)\ *n* [Gk *poton* drink + E *-meter*] **:** an apparatus for measuring the rate of transpiration in a plant by determining the amount of water absorbed
pot on *vt* **:** to transplant (as a potted plant) to a larger pot
po·too \pōˈtü\ *n* -S [imit.] **:** a large goatsucker (*Nyctibius griseus*) of So. America and the West Indies
po·to·roo \,pōd·əˈrü\ *n* -S [native name in New South Wales, southeast Australia] **:** RAT KANGAROO
po·to·ro·us \,päd·əˈrōəs\ *n*, *cap* [NL, fr. *potoroo* (native name in New South Wales)] **:** a genus of marsupial mammals comprising the common Australian rat kangaroos
pot oven *n* **:** an oven consisting of a heated iron plate covered by a pot
potpie \ˈ=ˈ=\ *n* **1 :** meat and vegetables covered with pastry and boiled or baked in a pot **2 :** DEEP-DISH PIE
pot plant *n* **:** a potted plant or one suitable for growing in a pot
pot·pour·ri \ˌpōpəˈrē *sometimes* pätˈpu̇rē\ *n* -S [F *pot pourri* (trans. of Sp *olla podrida*), fr. *pot* + *pourri* rotten, past part. of *pourrir* to rot, fr. L *putrescere* — more at POTAGE, PUTRESCENT] **1 :** OLLA PODRIDA 1 **2 :** a jar of flower petals mixed with spices and used for scent or perfume **3 a :** a series of melodies arranged or played in succession **:** MEDLEY ⟨a ~ of songs, sketches, parodies, and ballets —Hollis Alpert⟩ ⟨~ of familiar American cowboy tunes —Winthrop Sargeant⟩ **b :** a group or collection of miscellaneous literary productions ⟨a ~ of stories, sketches, poetry, and drama —H.M.Gloster⟩ **c :** a general mixture of often disparate or unrelated materials or subject matter ⟨a ~ of ancient history, Asiatic lore, current power politics, violent adventure —Linton Wells⟩ ⟨the ~ of dreams, barbarities, intrigues, wars and personalities that went into the . . . new empire —H.C.Wolfe⟩ ⟨a ~ of miscellaneous observations and reflections on his travels —Barrington Moore⟩
pot·rack \ˈpäˈtrak\ *vi* [imit.] **:** to make the natural high shrill noise of a guinea fowl
po·tre·ro \pəˈtre(,)rō\ *n* -S [Sp, colt pasture, fr. *potro* colt, fr. (assumed) VL *pullitrus* — more at POLTROON] *chiefly Southwest* **:** a meadow or pasture esp. on a ranch
po·tro \ˈpō·(,)trō\ *n* -S [Sp, colt] *Southwest* **:** COLT; *also* **:** an untamed bucking horse
pot roast *n* [¹*pot* + *roast*, n.] **:** a piece of tough beef or other meat cooked by braising usu. on top of the stove — see BEEF illustration
pot-roast \ˈ=,=\ *vt* [*pot roast*] **:** to roast in a pot usu. on top of a stove
pot-rustler \ˈ=,=(=)=\ *n* **:** a ranch or camp cook
pots *pl of* POT, *pres 3d sing of* POT
pots·dam \ˈpäts,dam, -aam\ *adj*, *usu cap* [fr. *Potsdam*, city in eastern Germany] **:** of or from the city of Potsdam, Germany **:** of the kind or style prevalent in Potsdam
pot seine *n* **:** POUND NET
pot·sherd \ˈpät,shərd, -shəd, -shəid\ *n* -S [ME *pot-schoord*, fr. ¹*pot* + *schoord*, *shard*, *sherd* shard] **:** a piece of a broken earthen pot **:** a pottery fragment ⟨~*s* unearthed at an excavation⟩
pot-shoot \ˈ=,=\ *vi* **:** POTSHOT ⟨there was considerable *pot= shooting* back and forth —S.L.A.Marshall⟩ — **pot-shooter** \ˈ=,==\ *n*
¹**potshot** \ˈ=,=\ *n* [¹*pot* + *shot*, n.; fr. the idea that casual shooting is unsportsmanlike and hence characteristic of a hunter whose only object is to kill game for the cooking pot] **1 :** a shot taken in a random, casual, or sporadic manner ⟨taking ~*s* at passing rabbits —Green Peyton⟩ ⟨scattered in tall grass . . . and popped up occasionally for a ~ —Walter Karig⟩ **2 :** a critical remark or comment made in a random or sporadic manner ⟨taking clerical ~*s* at those who hold opposing views —Riley Hughes⟩ ⟨had taken a ~ at the other's way of putting the truth —J.H.Randall⟩ ⟨subjects which require serious discussion, not verbal ~*s* —C.H.Page⟩
²**potshot** \"\ *vb* **potshot** *also* **potshotted; potshot** *also* **potshotted; potshotting; potshots** *vt* **:** to attack or shoot with a potshot ⟨skirmishing and *potshotting* each other —Ray Josephs⟩ ⟨pausing periodically to ~ people who think high= flown language is better —*Time*⟩ ~ *vi* **:** to take a potshot ⟨they ~ at the carabinieri —Janet Flanner⟩ ⟨*potshotting* from 1000 yards —Georg Meyers⟩ ⟨*potshotting* at the administrative departments —*Atlantic*⟩
pot signal *n* **:** a small revolving fixed signal used in railroading as a substitute for a dwarf signal
pot sleeper *n*, *Brit* **:** a convex cast-iron or steel disk with a clamp on top that is used to fasten railroad rails in places where wooden ties are impractical
pot spinning *n* **:** a process in rayon manufacture in which the coagulated filament is fed into a revolving pot and by centrifugal force deposited on the inside in the form of a cake
pot steel *n* **:** a cast or crucible steel
potstick \ˈ=,=\ *n* [ME *potsticke*, fr. ¹*pot* + *sticke* stick] *chiefly dial* **:** a stick for stirring the contents of a pot
pot still *n* **:** a still used esp. in the distillation of Irish grain whiskey and Scotch malt whiskey in which the heat of the fire is applied directly to the pot containing the mash
potstone \ˈ=,=\ *n* [trans. of NL *lapis ollaris*] **1 :** a more or less impure steatite used esp. in prehistoric times to make cooking vessels **2** [¹*pot* + *stone*] **:** POT BOTTOM
pot·sy \ˈpätsē\ *n* -ES [origin unknown] **:** HOPSCOTCH; *also* **:** the object thrown in this game
pot·tage \ˈpäd·|ij, -ät|, |ēj\ *n* -S [ME *potage*, fr. OF — more at POTAGE] **1 :** vegetables or vegetables and meat cooked to softness and seasoned **2 :** MESS OF POTTAGE **3 :** POTAGE **4** *archaic* **:** OATMEAL
pot·tah \ˈpäd·ə\ *n* -S [Hindi *paṭṭā*, fr. Skt *paṭṭaka*, fr. *paṭṭa* copper plate for grants] **:** a certificate of tenure **:** TITLE DEED **:** LEASE
pottawattomi *or* **pottawattami** *usu cap*, *var of* POTAWATOMI
potted *adj* **1 :** preserved in a closed pot, jar, or can **2 :** planted or grown in a pot **3 :** made easily comprehensible or superficially attractive by abridgment or glamorization **:** CANNED ⟨emitted the ~ history . . . — dates, regicides, amours, assassinations at a mile a minute —Frank Clune⟩ ⟨real scholarship and serious criticism in contradistinction to ~ "culture" —*Times Lit. Supp.*⟩ ⟨versions ~ for radio —*Times Lit. Supp.*⟩ ⟨~ pocket-book format —*Brit. Book News*⟩ **4** *slang* **:** DRUNK
potteen *var of* POTEEN
¹**pot·ter** \ˈpäd·ə(r), -ätə-\ *n* -S [ME *pottere*, fr. OE, fr. *pott* pot + *-ere* -er] **:** one that makes pottery ⟨for I remember stopping by the way to watch a ~ thumping his wet clay —Edward FitzGerald⟩
²**potter** \"\ *vb* -ED/-ING/-S [prob. freq. of ¹*pote*] *vi* **1** *dial chiefly Brit* **:** to poke or prod lightly and repeatedly **2 :** PUTTER ⟨bad weather finds him ~*ing* around, nailing new lobster pots, painting, repairing his gear —A.J.Cronin⟩ ⟨~*ed* around with it for a while and then gave up —*New Yorker*⟩ ⟨~*ing* about in a canoe on summer afternoons —Richard Aldington⟩ ⟨the trolley ~*ed* through that part of town in a desultory, neighborly way —*New Yorker*⟩ ⟨~*ing* among the ruins of the old casino —Alan Moorehead⟩ **3** *of a dog* **:** to quest indecisively ~ *vt* **1** *dial Eng* **:** BOTHER, IRRITATE, ANNOY **2 :** to waste by idling or trifling — often used with *away*
³**potter** \"\ *n* -S [²*pot* + *-er*] **:** POTHUNTER 1
⁴**potter** \"\ *n* -S [prob. fr. ¹*pot* + *-er*] **:** RED-BELLIED TERRAPIN
potter bee *n* **:** any of various bees (as of the genera *Anthidium* and *Megachile*) that construct nests of mud or pebbles cemented together and commonly attached to a plant stem — compare POTTER WASP
pot·ter·er \ˈpäd·ərə(r)\ *n* -S **1 :** one that acts or moves in an unsystematic or ineffective manner **2 :** a hunting dog that potters
pot·ter·ing·ly *adv* **:** in a pottering manner
potter's clay *n* **:** a clay used or suitable for use by potters
potter's field *n* [so called fr. the mention in Mt 27:7 of the purchase of a potter's field for use as a graveyard] **:** a public burial place (as in a city) for paupers, unknown persons, and criminals
potter's flint *n* **:** silica in the form of powdered quartz orig. made by pulverizing flint pebbles
potter's wheel *n* **:** a usu. horizontal disk revolving on a vertical spindle and carrying the clay in the operation of throwing

potter's wheel

potter wasp *n* **:** any of various solitary wasps usu. of the genus *Eumenes* that construct vase-shaped cells of sand and mud for their young — compare MASON WASP, POTTER BEE
pot·tery \ˈpäd·ərē, -ätə-, -ä·trē, -ri\ *n* -ES [MF *poterie*, fr. OF, fr. *potier* potter (fr. *pot* + *-ier* -er) + *-ie* -y — more at POTAGE] **1 :** a place where clayware is made and fired **2 a :** the art or craft of the potter ⟨a class in ~⟩ **b :** the manufacture of clayware **3 :** CLAYWARE; *esp* **:** earthenware as distinguished on the one hand from porcelain and stoneware and on the other from brick and tile
pottery-bark tree *n* **:** a timber tree (*Licania heteromorpha*) of northern So. America characterized by exceedingly hard wood, fruit that yields a black dye, and a siliceous bark that is sometimes burned and pulverized for mixing with pottery clay
pottery tissue *n* **:** **1** a well-glazed tissue paper used for wrapping pottery ware **2 :** tissue paper used for putting transfers on pottery ware
pottery tree *n* **:** a Brazilian tree (*Moquilea tomentosa*) of the family Rosaceae having a bark that is burned and pulverized for mixing with pottery clay
pottery ware *n* **:** POTTERY 3
pot·ti·a·ce·ae \,päd·ēˈāsē,ē\ *n pl*, *cap* [NL, fr. *Pottia*, type genus (fr. J.F.*Pott* †1805 Ger. botanist + NL *-ia*) + *-aceae*] **:** a family of acrocarpous usu. low-growing mosses (order Pottiales) whose peristome when present has 16 entire or divided and often twisted teeth
pot·ti·a·les \-ā(,)lēz\ *n pl*, *cap* [NL, fr. *Pottia* + *-ales*] **:** an order of Musci comprising mosses that have gametophores with many-ranked leaves having a distinct midrib and a usu. acrocarpous sporophyte with a capsule having either a simple 16-toothed peristome or none
potting *n* -S **1 :** the act of one that pots: as **a** *archaic* **:** the act of drinking alcoholic beverages **b :** the making of pottery **c :** CANNING **d :** the act of planting or transplanting in a pot **2 :** the process of supplying nitrous fumes in sulfuric acid manufacture by action of sulfuric acid on a nitrate in iron pots **3 :** a wet-finishing process for giving woolens a glossy surface and a soft hand
pot·tin·gar \ˈpätiŋgər\ *n* -S [ME (Sc), alter. of ME *potecarie* — more at POTECARY] *chiefly Scot* **:** APOTHECARY
potting compound *n* **:** a protective insulating and sealing plastic used to embed electric coils in a container
¹**pot·tin·ger** \ˈpäd·ənjə(r)\ *n* -S [ME *potinger*, alter. of *poteger*, fr. AF *potageer*, fr. MF *potager*, adj., of or relating to pottage, fr. *potage* pottage — more at POTAGE] *chiefly dial* **:** PORRINGER
²**pottinger** \"\ *n* -S [alter. of ME *potagere*, fr. MF *potagier* — more at POTAGER] **1** *archaic* **:** a maker of pottage **:** COOK **2** [influenced in meaning by *pottingar*] *archaic* **:** APOTHECARY
pot·tle \ˈpäd·ᵊl\ *n* -S [ME *potel*, fr. OF, fr. *pot* + *-el*] **1 :** a liquid or dry measure equal to a half gallon **2 a :** a container holding about one pottle **b :** a pottle of wine or liquor **3 :** a vessel or small basket for holding fruit
pottle pot *n* [ME *potel pot*, fr. *potel* pottle + ¹*pot*] **:** a pot or tankard holding two quarts
pot·to \ˈpäd·(,)ō\ *n* -S [of Niger-Congo origin; akin to Wolof *pata* tailless monkey of average size with black hair and red breast, Twi *aˈpɔ̃sɔ́w³* fierce animal resembling a monkey] **1 :** any of several African lorisid lemurs (genera *Arctocebus* and *Perodicticus*); *esp* **:** a West African lemur (*Perodicticus potto*) that resembles the slow loris in its nocturnal, arboreal, and slow-moving habits, is reddish gray in color, and has an index finger and tail that are vestigial **2 :** KINKAJOU
pott's disease \ˈpäts-\ *n*, *usu cap P* [after Percivall *Pott* †1788 Eng. surgeon] **:** tuberculosis of the spine with destruction of bone resulting in curvature of the spine and occas. in paralysis of the lower extremities
pott's fracture *n*, *usu cap P* **:** a fracture of the lower part of the fibula accompanied with injury to the tibial articulation so that the foot is dislocated outward
¹**pot·ty** \ˈpäti\ *adj* [prob. fr. ¹*pot* + *-y*, adj. suffix] **1** *Brit* **:** of minor importance **:** TRIVIAL, INSIGNIFICANT ⟨just one of those ~ little country affairs —P.G.Wodehouse⟩ **2** *slang chiefly Brit* **:** slightly crazy **:** FOOLISH ⟨gone ~ on the subject —Allan Sangster⟩ ⟨driving him ~ with her demands —C.D. Lewis⟩ **3 :** haughty or supercilious in bearing or speech **:** SNOBBISH ⟨our petty rights here, our ~ dignity there —John Galsworthy⟩ ⟨a futile, ~, upper-class gentleman —Brooks Atkinson⟩ ⟨the ~, pseudocultivated tones of some . . . clubwoman —Austin Warren⟩
²**pot·ty** \ˈpäd·ē\ *n* -ES [¹*pot* + *-y*, n. suffix] **:** a small child's pot for voiding or defecation
potty-chair \ˈ==,=\ *n* **:** a child's chair having an open seat under which a pot or other receptacle is placed for toilet training

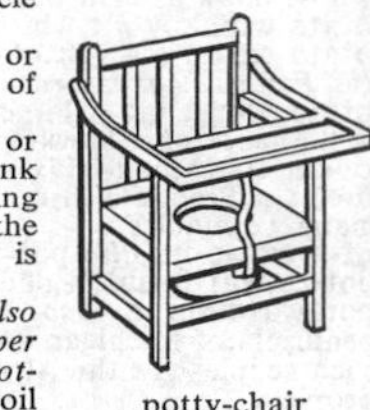
potty-chair

pot-valiant \ˈ=ˈ==\ *adj* **:** bold or courageous under the influence of alcoholic drink
pot-valor \ˈ=ˈ==\ *n* **:** boldness or courage resulting from alcoholic drink
pot valve *n* **:** a safety valve resembling an inverted pot with a recess in the crown in which the valve lever is fulcrumed
pot·wal·lop·er \ˈpä,twäləpə(r)\ *also* **pot·wal·ler** \-lə(r)\ *n* [*potwalloper* alter. (influenced by *wallop*) of *potwaller*, fr. ¹*pot* + obs. E *wall* to boil (fr. ME *wallen*, fr. OE *weallan*) + E *-er* — more at WELL] **:** a voter living in an English borough before the Reform Act of 1832 and qualifying for suffrage as a householder by the boiling of his own pot at his own fireplace
pot-walloping \ˈ=ˈ===\ *adj* [¹*pot* + *walloping*, pres. part. of *wallop* (to boil)] *Brit* **:** qualifying for suffrage by maintaining an independent household **:** being a potwalloper **:** consisting of potwallopers ⟨*pot-walloping* constituents⟩ ⟨*pot-walloping* vote⟩ ⟨*pot-walloping* borough⟩
potware \ˈ=,=\ *n* **:** POTTERY 3
pot wheel *n* **:** NORIA
potwork \ˈ=,=\ *n* **:** POTTERY
pou \ˈpü\ *chiefly Scot var of* PULL
¹**pouch** \ˈpau̇ch\ *n* -ES [ME *pouche*, fr. MF *pouche*, *poche*, of Gmc origin; akin to MD *poke* bag — more at POKE] **1 a** *archaic* **:** a small drawstring bag for carrying money **:** PURSE, POKE ⟨tester I'll have in ~ when thou shalt lack —Shak.⟩ **b :** a woman's handbag with soft sides and rounded shape usu. mounted on a frame or closed with a zipper or drawstring — compare ENVELOPE 4 **2 a :** a sack or satchel of small or moderate size for storing or transporting goods ⟨bullet ~⟩ ⟨tobacco ~⟩; *specif* **:** a bag with a locking device for the transmission of first class mail or diplomatic dispatches **b** *chiefly Scot* **:** POCKET **c :** PACKET ⟨hermetically sealed ~*es* . . . for use on such products as dry soups —N.A.Cooke⟩ **3 :** an anatomical structure felt to resemble a pouch: as **a** (1) **:** BAG 3a(4) (2) **:** CORPORATION 6 (3) **:** a fluid-filled cyst or sac **b :** MARSUPIUM 1a, 1b **c :** CHEEK POUCH **d :** the large gular space at the base of the lower mandible of a pelican **e :** a saccular plant part (as a silique or utricle)
²**pouch** \"\ *vb* -ED/-ING/-ES *vt* **1 :** to put into or as if into a pouch **:** POCKET ⟨sold justice and ~*ed* the price of every pardon —Francis Hackett⟩; *specif* **:** to put (as mail or dispatches) into locked bags ⟨the Baltimore mail was sorted . . . and ~*ed* by 4:20 A.M. —*Sat. Eve. Post*⟩ ⟨government of a twentieth-century diplomat ~*es* to him . . . a truly generous quantity of informative material —R.S.Simpson⟩ **2 a** *archaic* **:** SWALLOW ⟨allowing the fish . . . to ~ the bait —Thomas Best⟩ **b :** to store or carry in a pouch in the mouth ⟨squirrels ~*ing* acorns⟩ **3 :** to make puffy or protuberant ⟨ill health had . . . ~*ed* the loose flesh under his eyes —Ellen Glasgow⟩ ⟨up comes the great bill, ~*ed* with fish —A.J.Cronin⟩ ~ *vi* **1 :** to form a pouch **:** puff out **:** PROTRUDE ⟨snow-white hair and a ~*ing* bosom —Marguerite Steen⟩ **2 :** to transmit mail or dispatches to a destination in a locked bag
³**pouch** \ˈpōch\ *dial Eng var of* POACH
pouch bone *n* **:** MARSUPIAL BONE
pouched \ˈpau̇cht\ *adj* **:** having or forming a pouch ⟨~ mammal⟩ ⟨the ~ sagging flesh of his face —Moray Firth⟩
pouched dog *n* **:** TASMANIAN WOLF
pouched frog *or* **pouched toad** *n* **:** MARSUPIAL FROG
pouched marmot *n* **:** GROUND SQUIRREL 1c
pouched mole *n* **:** MARSUPIAL MOLE
pouched mouse *n* **1 a :** POCKET MOUSE **b :** POUCHED RAT c **2 :** any of numerous marsupial mice of *Phascogale* or related genera

pouched rat *n* **:** any of several African murid rodents with cheek pouches: as **a** *or* **pouched gopher :** POCKET GOPHER **b :** KANGAROO RAT **c :** an African rodent of *Cricetomys* or the related genus *Sarcostomus* **d :** a spiny pocket mouse (*Heteromys melanoleucus*)

pouched stork *n* **:** ADJUTANT BIRD

pouch·less \'pau̇chləs\ *adj* **:** having no pouch; *specif* **:** having no marsupium ⟨~ mammals⟩

pouch of doug·las \-'dəgləs\ *usu cap D* [after James *Douglas* †1742 Scot. anatomist] **:** a deep peritoneal recess between the uterus and the upper vaginal wall anteriorly and the rectum posteriorly

pouch of rathke *usu cap R* **:** RATHKE'S POUCH

pouch table *n* **:** BAG TABLE

pouchy \'pau̇chē\ *adj* -ER/-EST **:** having, tending to have, or resembling a pouch **:** POUCHED, PUFFY ⟨~ handbag⟩ ⟨the skin . . . is soft and a little ~ from fatigue —Walter Bernstein⟩

poud *var of* POOD

pou·dre B \¦püdə(r)¦bē, ¦püdrə¦bē\ *n* [F, fr. *poudre* powder + *B*, initial letter of the surname of Georges Ernest Jean Marie *Boulanger* †1891 Fr. general — more at POWDER] **:** a smokeless French rifle powder consisting essentially of about two thirds guncotton and one third pyroxylin

poudre blue \¦püdə(r)-\ *n* [alter. (influenced by F *poudre*) of *powder blue*] **:** POWDER BLUE 2a

pou·dre de riz \¦püdrədə¦rē\ *n* [F] **:** RICE POWDER

pou·drette \(')pü¦dret\ *n* -S [F, fr. *poudre* + *-ette*] **:** dried deodorized night soil mixed with various substances (as charcoal and gypsum) and used as a fertilizer

pou·dreuse \(')pü¦drərz, -drəz\ *n* -S [F, fr. *poudre* powder] **:** a small dressing table with a mirror that usu. folds down into the top

pouf *also* **pouff** *or* **pouffe** \'püf\ *n* -S [F *pouf*, of imit. origin] **:** something that is inflated or insubstantial: as **a :** PUFF 3b(3) **b :** a bouffant or fluffy part of a garment or clothing accessory ⟨a taffeta ~ tacked on the back of a tight skirt —*Harper's Bazaar*⟩ ⟨an ivory velours . . . trimmed with a ~ of fine black plumes —*Hats*⟩ **c** (1) **:** a plumply upholstered usu. circular backless couch or hassock **:** OTTOMAN (2) **:** PUFF 3b(4) **d :** an evanescent whiff (as of smoke) often accompanied by a muffled report ⟨with a little ~, the lights went out —Anne S. Mehdevi⟩ — often used interjectionally to express extreme transience or suddenness of disappearance ⟨if you offer less, ~, he is gone —H.O.Storm⟩

poufed *or* **pouffed** \-ft\ *adj* [*pouf* + *-ed*] **:** PUFFED 1a(2), BLOUSED 3

poul *n* -S [Per *pūl*] **:** PUL

pou·laine \(')pü¦lān\ *n* -S [MF, fr. fem. of *poulain* Polish] **1 :** the long pointed toe of a crakow **:** PIKE **2 :** CRAKOW

pou·larde *also* **pou·lard** \(')pü¦lärd\ *n* -S [F *poularde*, fr. MF *pollarde*, fr. *polle*, *poule* hen — more at PULLET] **:** a pullet that has been sterilized by removing either the ovaries or a part of the oviduct usu. to produce fattening — compare CAPON

pou·lard·ize \-ˌdīz\ *vt* -ED/-ING/-S [*poularde* or *poulard* + *-ize*] **:** to make a poularde of (a pullet)

poulard wheat \"-\ *n* [part trans. of F *blé poulard*, fr. *blé* wheat + *poulard*, prob. fr. *poularde*] **:** a wheat (*Triticum turgidum*) little grown in the U. S. having 4-sided compact awned spikes that tend to branch in some varieties, rather short thick humped yellowish to red kernels, and long thick pithy or solid stems, and used chiefly for stock feed — called also *cone wheat, English wheat, rivet wheat*

pouldron *var of* PAULDRON

poule \'pül\ *n* -S [F, lit., chicken, hen] **:** PROSTITUTE

pou·lette \(')pü¦let\ *or* **poulette sauce** *n* -S [F *poulette* (esp. in the expression *sauce poulette* poulette sauce), lit., chick, fr. OF *polete*, fr. *pole*, *poule* hen + *-ete* -ette] **:** velouté with added egg yolk

poulp *or* **poulpe** \'pülp\ *n* -S [F *poulpe*, fr. L *polypus* — more at POLYP] **:** OCTOPUS

poul·sen arc \'pau̇lzən-, -lsən-\ *n*, *usu cap P* [after Valdemar *Poulsen* †1942 Dan. electrical engineer] *physics* **:** a direct-current arc formerly used for producing undamped high-frequency oscillations

poult \'pōlt\ *n* -S [ME *pulte* young fowl, alter. of *polet* young chicken, young fowl — more at PULLET] **1 a :** a young turkey esp. in its early weeks **b :** a young chicken, pheasant, grouse, or other fowl **2** *chiefly Scot* **a :** CHILD **b :** one that behaves like a child

poult-de-soie \¦püdə¦swä; ¦püd¦swä, (')püt¦s-\ *also* **poult** \'pü(lt)\ *n* -S [F *pou-de-soie*, *poult-de-soie*] **:** a plainwoven usu. solid color silk fabric with fine full ribs used for women's clothing

poulter *n* -S [ME *pulter*, fr. MF *pouletier*, fr. OF, fr. *polet*, *poulet* young chicken, young fowl + *-ier* -er — more at PULLET] *obs* **:** POULTERER

poul·ter·er \'pōltərə(r)\ *n* -S [*poulter* + *-er*] **:** one that deals in poultry

poul·ter's measure \'pōltə(r)z-\ *n* [so called fr. the former practice of occasionally giving one or two extra when counting eggs by dozens] **:** a meter in which lines of 12 and 14 syllables alternate

1**poul·tice** \'pōltəs\ *n* -S [alter. of earlier *pultes*, fr. ML, pap, fr. L, pl. of *pult-*, *puls* porridge made of meal and pulse — more at PULSE] **:** a soft mass (as of bread, bran, or medicated clay) usu. heated and spread on cloth for application to sores, inflamed areas, or other lesions, to supply moist warmth, relieve pain, or act as a counterirritant or antiseptic — called also *cataplasm*; compare PLASTER

2**poultice** \"\ *vt* -ED/-ING/-S **1 :** to apply a poultice to **:** dress with a poultice **2 :** to apply a mudcap to (as an explosive or a rock surface) preparatory to surface blasting

poul·try \'pōl·trē, -ri\ *n* -ES *often attrib* [ME *pultrie*, fr. MF *pouleterie*, fr. OF, fr. *pouletier* + *-ie* -y] **:** domesticated birds that serve as a source of eggs or meat and that include among commercially important kinds chickens, turkeys, ducks, and geese and among kinds chiefly of local interest guinea fowl, peafowl, pigeons, pheasants, and others

poultry bug *n* **:** a cimicid bug (*Haematosiphon inodorus*) that is an ectoparasite on poultry and occas. on man in the southern U. S. and Mexico

poultry flea *n* **:** a flea (*Ceratophyllus gallinae*) that attacks poultry

poul·try·less \-ləs\ *adj* **:** having no poultry

poultry louse *n* **:** any of several biting lice (genus *Menopon*) that attack poultry; *esp* **:** SHAFT LOUSE

poul·try·man \-mən\ *n*, *pl* **poultrymen 1 a :** one that raises domestic fowls esp. on a commercial scale for the production of eggs and meat **b :** a dealer in poultry or poultry products **2 :** one employed by a hotel or restaurant to pick, clean, and cut fowls

poultry mite *n* **:** CHICKEN MITE

poultry pin *n* **:** SKEWER 1

poultry tick *n* **1 :** CHICKEN TICK **2 :** CHICKEN MITE

poultry wire *n* **:** CHICKEN WIRE

pou·na·mu \pō'nä(ˌ)mü\ *n* -S [Maori] **1 :** NEPHRITE **2 :** a Maori weapon or implement made of nephrite

1**pounce** \'pau̇n(t)s\ *vt* -ED/-ING/-S [ME *pounsen*, alter. of *pounsonen*, fr. MF *poinçonner* to stamp, fr. *poinçon* pointed tool — more at PUNCHEON] **1** *archaic* **:** to ornament with perforations ⟨a mantle of cloth of silver, *pounced* with his cipher, lined with blue velvet —W.H.Ainsworth⟩ **2 :** to ornament (metal) by hammering on the reverse side (as in repoussé work) **:** EMBOSS **3** *obs* **a :** to perforate with a pointed instrument **:** PRICK, PIERCE **b :** TATTOO

2**pounce** \"\ *n* -S [ME, talon, sting, prob. by shortening & alter. fr. *punson* pointed tool, dagger — more at PUNCHEON] **1 a :** the claw of a bird of prey **:** TALON ⟨from her griping ~ the greedy prey doth rive —Edmund Spenser⟩ **b :** something capable of inflicting injury ⟨always ready with a ripping verbal ~ —Carlos Baker⟩ **2** *now dial* **:** PUNCH, POKE ⟨gave his bedfellow a ~ with his foot to waken him —S.R.Crockett⟩

3**pounce** \"\ *vb* -ED/-ING/-S *vt* **:** to seize with or as if with the talons ⟨cannot ~ the quarry on the ground —Gilbert White⟩ ~ *vi* **1 a :** to make an abrupt assault ⟨were suddenly *pounced* upon by a dozen or more ruffians with clubs —H.A.Chippendale⟩ **b :** to seize upon and make capital of something (as another's blunder or ineptitude) ⟨*pouncing* on the effect of the particular moment . . . the flicker of transient light —Eric Newton⟩ ⟨~*s* ferociously on a trivial error of fact —C.W. Shumaker⟩ **2 :** to spring suddenly or make a sudden grab ⟨ready to ~ at the phone when it rings⟩ ⟨~*s* on his riding boots . . . and begins pulling them on —G.B.Shaw⟩

4**pounce** \"\ *n* -S [3*pounce*] **1 :** the act of one that pounces ⟨the ~ and sparkle of the . . . wave —*Times Lit. Supp.*⟩ **2 :** a card game for from 3 to 12 players in which each person plays his own game of Canfield but may build on any of the aces in the center of the table and which is won by the one who gets rid of his stock first

5**pounce** \"\ *vt* -ED/-ING/-S [MF *poncer* to polish with pumice, fr. *ponce* pumice] **1 :** to put a smooth finish on (a hat) by rubbing with an abrasive ⟨felt bodies are *pounced* both inside and out —*Evolution of Hats*⟩ **2** *archaic* **:** to scatter with small particles **:** SPRINKLE, FLECK ⟨your azure robe . . . *pounced* with stars —Robert Herrick †1674⟩; *specif* **:** to dust (as paper or parchment) with a resinous powder to prevent ink or colors from spreading **3 a :** to transfer (a design) by applying powder through a perforated outline or stencil **b :** to force (powder) through the perforations of an outline or stencil

6**pounce** \"\ *n* -S [F *ponce* pumice, fr. LL *pomic-*, *pomex*, fr. L *pumic-*, *pumex* — more at FOAM] **1 :** a fine powder (as of sandarac with pumice or cuttlefish bone) formerly used to prevent ink from spreading on unsized paper or over an erasure and also to prepare parchment to take writing **2** [F *ponce* pounce bag, fr. (assumed) MF *ponce*, fr. MF *ponce* pumice] **a :** a fine powder (as pulverized chalk or charcoal) for use with a perforated pattern in transferring a design **b :** a perforated pattern **c** *or* **pounce bag :** a small cloth bag filled with powder for pouncing

pounce box *n* **:** a box with a perforated lid for holding and sprinkling pounce

pounce paper *n* **:** an abrasive paper that is used in pouncing hats

pounc·er \-n(t)sə(r)\ *n* -S **:** one that pounces; *specif* **:** a worker who pounces felt hats

pouncet-box \'pau̇n(t)sət-\ *n* [*pouncet-* prob. fr. (assumed) MF *poncette* small pounce bag (whence F *poncette*), fr. (assumed) MF *ponce* pounce bag (whence F *ponce*) + MF *-ette*] **1** *archaic* **:** POMANDER 1b **2** *archaic* **:** POUNCE BOX

pounce tree *n* **:** SANDARAC TREE 1

pouncing *n* -S [fr. gerund of 3*pounce*] **1 :** 4POUNCE 1 **2** [fr. gerund of 5*pounce*] **:** the process of putting a smooth finish on a felt hat

pouncy \'pau̇n(t)sē\ *adj* -ER/-EST [3*pounce* + *-y*] **1 :** PUNCHY **2 :** having a tendency toward abrupt assault

1**pound** \'pau̇nd\ *n*, *pl* **pounds** \-n(d)z\ *also* **pound** *often attrib* [ME, fr. OE *pund*; akin to OHG *phunt* pound, ON & Goth *pund*; all fr. a prehistoric Gmc word borrowed fr. L *pondo* pound; akin to L *pondus* weight — more at PENDANT] **1 :** any of various units of mass and weight: as **a :** a unit equal to 12 troy ounces or 5760 grains or 0.3732417216 kilogram formerly used in weighing gold, silver, and a few other costly materials — called also *troy pound* **b :** a unit now in general use among English-speaking peoples equal to 16 avoirdupois ounces or 7000 grains or 0.45359237 kilogram ⟨a 7-*pound* roast⟩ — called also *avoirdupois pound; see* MEASURE table **2 a** *or* **pound sterling :** the basic monetary unit of the United Kingdom — see MONEY table **b** *or* **pound scots** *usu cap S* **:** a monetary unit of Scotland before union with England, similar to the English pound but by the time of union much debased in value **c :** any of a number of basic monetary units of other countries (as Ireland, Egypt, Lebanon, Syria, Cyprus, Sudan) — see MONEY table **d :** a note representing one pound **e :** a gold coin worth or representing one pound unit (as a Syrian gold pound) — see SOVEREIGN **f :** LIRA — **pound of flesh :** something which is justly due but which if given inflicts great injury on the giver ⟨the *pound of flesh* which I demand of him is dearly bought, 'tis mine, and I will have it —Shak.⟩ ⟨loan sharks exacting their *pound of flesh*⟩

2**pound** \"\ *vt* -ED/-ING/-S *Brit* **:** to ascertain the variation from standard of (coins) by weighing together the number that should weigh one or more pounds

3**pound** \"\ *vb* -ED/-ING/-S [alter. of ME *pounen*, fr. OE *pūnian*; prob. akin to D *puin* rubbish, rubble] *vt* **1 :** to grind with or as if with a mortar and pestle **:** PULVERIZE, CRUSH ⟨a prescription was being ~*ed* up in a mortar —William Beebe⟩ ⟨he was being ~*ed* between . . . loyalty and the howling respectability of the great world —Donald Davidson⟩ **2 a :** to strike with or as if with heavy blows **:** BEAT, HAMMER ⟨~ nails into a board⟩ ⟨~ a typewriter⟩ ⟨breakers ~ the beach⟩ ⟨peaks rose darkly, ~*ing* his senses —Florette Henri⟩ ⟨surface vessels continued to ~ enemy coastal targets —*N. Y. Times*⟩ **b :** to produce by means of repeated vigorous strokes — usu. used with *out* ⟨~ out a tune on the piano⟩ ⟨~ out a story on the typewriter⟩ **c :** to compel assimilation of by insistent repetition ⟨day after day the facts were ~*ed* home to them —Ivy B. Priest⟩ — often used with *in* or *into* ⟨~ Latin into the head of a youngster —C.M.Fuess⟩ **3 a :** to traverse or proceed along heavily or persistently **:** LUMBER, TRAMP ⟨world's heaviest aircraft, ~*ed* and blasted her way down the runway —Lou Stoumen⟩ ⟨~*ed* the pavements trying to find work —Frank O'Leary⟩ **b :** to compress by constant trampling ⟨streets . . . of reddish, clayey earth, ~*ed* to rocklike hardness by countless human feet —Tom Marvel⟩ ~ *vi* **1 a :** to strike repeated blows **:** beat or knock heavily **:** THUMP ⟨talking politely at the conference table instead of ~*ing* on it —*Newsweek*⟩ ⟨their hearts ~, and pulse rate may climb to 160 beats a minute —J.D.Ratcliff⟩ ⟨~*s* doggedly . . . at the central theme —Roger Shattuck⟩; *specif* **:** to slap the water violently and repeatedly — used of a ship ⟨if you spread the ballast out . . . she will be less likely to ~ when punching into a hard sea —Peter Heaton⟩ **b :** to keep up a battering assault ⟨these thoughts ~*ed* and hammered in her indignant consciousness —J.C.Powys⟩ ⟨all day long the sun ~*ed* down through the breathless air —T.O.Heggen⟩ ⟨the mother ~*s* at him for his drinking —Arna W. Bontemps⟩ — often used with *away* ⟨the two fleets ~*ed* away at each other until nightfall —*Amer. Guide Series: Vt.*⟩ **2 a :** to move heavily or fast usu. with an accompanying repetitive sound of impact **:** THUNDER, PELT ⟨on its rocky shore a heavy surf ~*s* ceaselessly —*Amer. Guide Series: Maine*⟩ ⟨a fast rider was ~*ing* down the road —J.D. Horan⟩ ⟨a low-flying Lancaster was ~*ing* home heavily, steadily —Earle Birney⟩ **b :** to work hard or hard and continuously — used with *away* ⟨kept ~*ing* away at his job⟩ **c :** to make a thumping noise ⟨the engine was ~*ing*⟩ **syn** see BEAT — **pound one's ear :** SLEEP ⟨each trucker driving four hours, then *pounding his ear* in the vehicle's sleeper berth while his partner drove —A.L.Davis⟩

4**pound** \"\ *n* -S **:** an act of pounding **:** BLOW, THUD ⟨destroys with heavy ~*s* his little caricature —Louis Auchincloss⟩ ⟨the ~ of feet in the passageway⟩

5**pound** \"\ *n* -S [ME, enclosure, pound, fr. OE *pund-*] **1 a :** a public enclosure for strays or unlicensed animals **:** PINFOLD ⟨dog ~⟩ **b** *dial* **:** a pen or enclosure for domestic animals (as cattle or sheep) **:** BARNYARD, CORRAL **c :** an enclosure for trapping wild animals ⟨an old buffalo ~, built of logs —*Amer. Antiquity*⟩ **d :** a depot for holding personal property until redeemed by the owner ⟨tow services and ~*s* for cars tagged for obstructing traffic —J.C.Ingraham⟩ **2 :** a place or condition of confinement ⟨find his honor in a ~, hemmed by a triple circle round —Jonathan Swift⟩ ⟨buckled straps . . . held the sleeves in ~ —P.A.Rollins⟩ **3** *dial Eng* **:** POND **4 a** (1) **:** a confine in which fish are caught or kept; *specif* **:** the inner compartment of a fish trap or pound net which retains the fish (2) **:** POUND NET **b** (1) **:** a tank full of water in which live lobsters are kept (2) **:** an establishment selling live lobsters

6**pound** \"\ *vt* -ED/-ING/-S [ME *pownen*, fr. *pound*, n., enclosure, pound] **1** *archaic* **:** to confine in or as if in an enclosure **:** PEN **2** *archaic* **:** to dam up (water) **:** IMPOUND

pound·able \-ndəbəl\ *adj* [6*pound* + *-able*] *obs* **:** subject to impoundment — used of livestock

1**pound·age** \-ndij, -ndēj\ *n* -S [ME, fr. 1*pound* + *-age*] **1 a :** a tax levied in pounds sterling ⟨payment of a ~ on profits —A.R.Wagner⟩; *specif* **:** a subsidy of twelve pence per pound on exports and imports formerly granted to the crown **b :** an agent's fee **:** COMMISSION ⟨no ~ was charged for the orders —*Manchester Guardian Weekly*⟩ **2 a :** a charge per pound of weight ⟨letters forwarded on a ~ basis —*Westminster Gazette*⟩ **b :** weight in pounds ⟨most of this ~ was around his middle —Herbert Asbury⟩; *specif* **:** the number of pounds of salt in a gallon or a cubic foot of brine

2**poundage** \"\ *n* -S [6*pound* + *-age*] **1 :** the act of impounding or the state of being impounded ⟨~ of cattle⟩ ⟨knows . . . the ~ of every well's water —Lawrence Durrell⟩ **2 :** a fee charged for the release of an impounded animal

pound·al \-ndᵊl\ *n* -S [1*pound* + *-al* (as in *quintal*)] **:** the unit of force in the fps system equal to the force that would give a free mass of one pound an acceleration of one foot per second per second — compare DYNE

pound brush *n* **:** a housepainter's brush of any of the largest sizes

pound cake *n* [so called fr. the original method of measuring the principal ingredients in pounds] **:** a rich butter cake made with many eggs and a large amount of shortening in proportion to the amount of flour used

pound degree *n* **:** BRITISH THERMAL UNIT

1**pound·er** \'pau̇ndə(r)\ *n* -S [3*pound* + *-er*] **:** one that crushes or hammers

2**pounder** \"\ *n* -S [6*pound* + *-er*] *archaic* **:** POUNDMASTER

3**pounder** \"\ *n* -S [1*pound* + *-er*] **1 a :** one that weighs a usu. specified number of pounds ⟨making the ~*s* rise to the May fly —Alasdair Carmichael⟩ ⟨a helmet which protects a 200-*pounder* surely will protect a smaller man —R.M.Yoder⟩ **b :** a gun throwing a projectile of a specified weight ⟨as many as 100 guns, mostly 25-*pounders* —*Time*⟩ **2 :** something (as a bank note or a jewel) having the value of a specified number of pounds sterling ⟨the note was a ten-*pounder*⟩

pound-foolish \'=¦==\ *adj* **:** imprudent in dealing with large sums or matters — used chiefly in the phrase *penny-wise and pound-foolish*

pound-foot \'=¦=\ *n*, *pl* **pound-feet :** FOOT-POUND 2

1**pounding** *n* -S [fr. gerund of 3*pound*] **1 :** the act or process of pulverizing or compacting **:** CRUSHING **2 a :** an act or instance of striking with or as if with heavy blows **:** BEATING, HAMMERING ⟨the ~ of his gavel —Marya Mannes⟩ ⟨withstand the ~ of heavy artillery —*N. Y. Times*⟩ **b :** the action of proceeding (as by walking, riding) fast or heavily or of moving with a succession of bumps or the repetitive sound produced by such movement **:** THUDDING, THUNDERING ⟨the ~ of horses' hoofs —S.H.Holbrook⟩ ⟨~ of the waves —Joyce Cary⟩

2**pounding** \"\ *n* -S [1*pound* + *-ing*; fr. the custom of giving a pound of sugar or some other edible commodity] *South & Midland* **:** DONATION PARTY

poundkeeper \'=ˌ==\ *n* **:** POUNDMASTER

pound-lock \'=ˌ=\ *n* [5*pound* + *lock*] **:** a lock designed to impound the water of a river

poundmaster \'=ˌ==\ *n* **:** the keeper of a pound ⟨when he was ~ he tried all afternoon to lasso a dog —John Steinbeck⟩

pound mile *n* **:** the transport of one pound of mail or express for one mile

pound net *n* **:** a fish trap consisting of a long wing of net

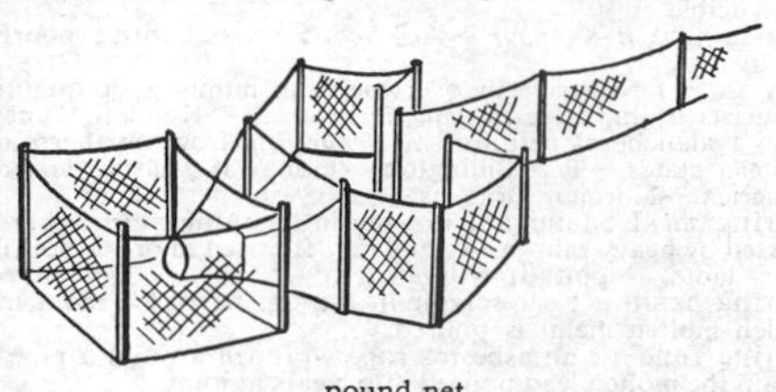

pound net

directing the fishes into the heart and on through a check valve into an inner enclosure which usu. has a closed bottom of net or wire mesh, can sometimes be raised to gather the fishes, or in other variations is equipped with spillers in which the catch is hauled to the surface — compare LEADER 1i(1), POT 3b, SEINE

pound netter *n* **:** one that fishes with a pound net

pound party *n*, *chiefly South & Midland* **:** DONATION PARTY

pound scots *n*, *usu cap S* **:** 1POUND 2b

pound sterling *n* **:** 1POUND 2a

pou·part's ligament \(')pü¦pärz-\ *n*, *usu cap P* [after François *Poupart* †1709 Fr. physician] **:** the thickened lower border of the aponeurosis of the external oblique muscle of the abdomen extending from the anterior superior spine of the ilium to the pubic tubercle continuous below with the fascia lata, and forming the external pillar of the external abdominal ring and a part of the anterior boundary of the femoral ring — called also *inguinal ligament*

1**pour** \'pō(ə)r, 'pȯ(ə)r, -ōə, -ȯ(ə) *sometimes* 'pu̇(ə)r *or* -u̇ə\ *vb* -ED/-ING/-S [ME *pouren*] *vt* **1 a** (1) **:** to cause or allow to flow **:** emit in a steady stream **:** DIFFUSE, DISCHARGE ⟨~*ed* out torrents of water —J.G.Vaeth⟩ ⟨~ grain into an elevator⟩ ⟨ranges . . . ~ rivers down to the coast —M.B.Eldershaw⟩ ⟨summer ~*s* warm sunlight . . . into the valleys —*Amer. Guide Series: Va.*⟩ (2) **:** to dispense from a container ⟨~ a drink⟩ ⟨~ tea⟩ **b :** to supply copiously **:** convey as if through a sluice **:** CHANNEL, SPOUT ⟨~ men and money into the Netherlands —Stringfellow Barr⟩ ⟨~ out a torrent of words⟩ ⟨~*ed* ridicule on the elaborate . . . analysis —Richard Hartshorne b. 1899⟩ ⟨armies . . . that the Germans ~*ed* across Europe —Tom Wintringham⟩ ⟨sweet-tempered . . . pastors ~*ed* forth comfort and learning —Sinclair Lewis⟩ ⟨trying to ~ sympathy all over the poor man —D.B.Chidsey⟩; *specif* **:** to send in a concentrated volley ⟨~*ed* 30 bullets into his plane —Ed Cunningham⟩ **c :** to produce in abundance — used with *forth* or *out* ⟨travel-books . . . that our presses ~ forth in floods —Louise Pound⟩ ⟨keep ~*ing* out millions of cars, trucks and buses every year —*Motor Transportation in the West*⟩ **d :** to apply in liberal amounts (as for coercion or to supply motive power) ⟨~*ed* the whip into the mules —Andy Adams⟩ ⟨~*ed* on the steam⟩ ⟨began to ~ heat on the business office —*Human Organization*⟩ ⟨~*ed* in every ounce of power but couldn't make it⟩ **2 a :** to expend wholly ⟨those who most long for peace now ~ their lives on war —Muriel Rukeyser⟩ **b :** to give full expression to or a detailed account of **:** SPILL, VENT ⟨before our Father's throne, we ~ our ardent prayers —John Fawcett⟩ ⟨thrasher from cactus and mesquite ~*s* forth his song —D.C.Peattie⟩ ⟨~*s* out her troubles to them —Bosley Crowther⟩ ⟨~*ing* out his feelings in his poetry —Ruth R. Chapman⟩ **3 a :** to cause to flow or to pass as if flowing into a mold ⟨~ steel⟩ ⟨~ agar⟩ ⟨~ concrete⟩ ⟨nine sergeants were ~*ed* into plain clothes and set up in an office at Old Scotland Yard —J.D.Carr⟩ ⟨~*ed* the barefooted doctor into the coach, gave him a quart of whiskey to work on, and pulled out —F.B.Gipson⟩ **b :** to form by running plastic mixes of concrete into place in forms ⟨~ a foundation wall⟩ ~ *vi* **1 a** (1) **:** to move with a continuous flow **:** issue or glide incessantly **:** GUSH, RUN ⟨creeks ~*ing* down from the uplands —Nan McDonald⟩ ⟨wind ~*s* over the mountains —C.P. Aiken⟩ ⟨smoke . . . ~*ed* up from the blazing houses —Kenneth Roberts⟩ ⟨line ~*s* off your reel —C.C.Van Fleet⟩ (2) **:** to rain heavily **:** TEEM ⟨it was raining — but not ~*ing* —Robbie Barcroft⟩ **b :** to progress or be channeled continuously **:** move in a body **:** STREAM, SWARM ⟨Marines ~*ed* ashore and secured the beachhead —H.L.Merillat⟩ ⟨the promenading public still slowly ~*ed* up and down Fifth Avenue —Edith Wharton⟩ ⟨all this lore ~*ed* into a big filing cabinet —H.W. Thompson⟩ ⟨traffic ~*ed* over the new highway —G.R. Stewart⟩ ⟨our own stuff was ~*ing* back on them —Fred Majdalany⟩ ⟨from your farms today food ~*s* . . . to every corner of the country —A.E.Stevenson †1965⟩ **c :** to emanate in a flood ⟨a spate of English grammars began to ~ off the presses —N.C.Stageberg⟩ ⟨personality ~*s* out of him —Victor Thompson⟩ ⟨calypsos ~*ing* out of . . . jukeboxes —Paul Hofmann⟩ **d :** to preside at a tea table ⟨she was asked to ~ at a little reception for the performers after the concert⟩ **2 :** to find an outlet **:** be given full expression ⟨channels . . . through which those emotions might ~ —Oscar Handlin⟩

syn POUR, STREAM, GUSH, and SLUICE can mean, in common, to send forth liquid, or something suggesting liquid, copiously. POUR stresses the abundance of the issuing or sending forth, usu. implying emission in a continuous stream ⟨the torrential rain *poured* down for days⟩ ⟨to *pour* tributes on his head⟩ ⟨mail *poured* in in answer to the advertisement⟩ ⟨the crowd *poured* out of the front doors⟩ STREAM suggests a flow limited by issuance through a channel or from an opening ⟨tears *streamed* from her eyes⟩ ⟨light *streamed* through the window⟩ ⟨the rain *streamed* down the bank in small rivulets⟩ GUSH stresses a suddenness and copiousness of the pouring forth as of something released from a close confinement ⟨blood *gushed* from the wound⟩ ⟨the spring *gushed* forth⟩ ⟨words *gushed* from her in gratitude⟩ SLUICE in this comparison always implies a confining flume or a channeled abundance of liquid ⟨the rain fell with a frightening violence, . . . turning the opposite wall of the canyon into a *sluicing* cascade of muddy water —B.A.Williams⟩ ⟨the Connecticut, *sluicing* down between the Green and White mountains —R.W.Howard⟩ ⟨thrust her hands into the stream, then raised them, dripping, to *sluice* her face —Rebecca West⟩

— pour it on 1 : to exert maximum force or energy **:** move or cause to move at top speed or intensity ⟨didn't run at top speed for much more than a furlong, but when he did he must have *poured it on* —G.F.T.Ryall⟩ ⟨allied bombers . . . began really to *pour it on* —Alfred Friendly⟩ ⟨companies . . . taking it relatively easy on production may now be tempted to *pour it on* —J.D.Williams⟩ **2 :** to give unstinted expression to an idea or attitude ⟨gave them a ten-minute talk in which he "really *poured it on*" —*N. Y. Herald Tribune*⟩

²pour \"\ *n* -s **1 :** the action of pouring **:** FLOOD, STREAM ⟨seals . . . carved sheer as cameos in the moon's full ~ —E.W. Barker⟩ ⟨a great ~ of contemptuous invective —*Times Lit. Supp.*⟩; *esp* **:** a heavy fall of rain **2 a :** the action of running a plastic material into a mold or form ⟨carpenters were stripping and placing forms for the next ~ —*New Era in Concrete*⟩ **b :** the amount placed in a mold or form at one time ⟨some mechanics use two ~*s* of lead to fill the joint completely —*Building, Estimating & Contracting*⟩ **3 a :** the principal opening by which molten metal enters a mold **b :** the superfluous metal adhering to the casting and resulting from the head metal in such an opening — called also *pourpiece*

pour·abil·i·ty \ˌpōrəˈbilədē, ˌpȯr- *sometimes* ˌpu̇r-\ *n* -ES **:** adaptability to being poured ⟨the poor ~ of the material —*Modern Plastics Catalog*⟩

pour·able \ˈ==bəl\ *adj* **:** capable of being poured

pour batter *n* **:** batter of such consistency as to pour from a bowl or pitcher usu. made in a proportion of equal parts of flour and liquid — compare DROP BATTER

pour·boire \(ˈ)pu̇rbˌwär\ *n* -S [F, fr. *pour boire* for drinking, in order to drink, fr. *pour* for, in order to + *boire* to drink, fr. L *bibere* — more at PURCHASE, POTABLE] **:** TIP, GRATUITY

pourcontrell *n* -S [origin unknown] *obs* **:** OCTOPUS

poured *past of* POUR

pour·er \ˈpōrə(r), ˈpȯr- *sometimes* ˈpu̇r-\ *n* -S **:** one that pours; *specif* **:** a foundry worker who pours molten metal from a ladle or crucible

pour·ie \-ri\ *n* -S [¹*pour* + *-ie*] *Scot* **:** a vessel with a pouring spout

pour in *vi* **:** to arrive in overwhelming numbers or quantity ⟨tourists fly in, drive in, *pour in* by train —Kenneth Tynan⟩ ⟨the avalanche of petitions . . . *poured in* from northern and eastern states —R.A.Billington⟩ ⟨money is *pouring in* from America —Norman Douglas⟩

pouring *adj* **1 :** falling or flowing in quantities; *esp* **:** characterized by heavy rain ⟨a ~ wet day⟩ **2 :** used in or for pouring ⟨a ~ ladle⟩ — **pour·ing·ly** *adv*

pouring basin *n* **:** a reservoir in the top part of a mold into which molten metal is poured

pouring rope *n* **:** an asbestos rope wrapped around a pipe to retain the molten lead poured into a calked joint

pour·par·ler \ˌpu̇rˌpärˈlā, ==ˈ=\ *n* -S [F, fr. MF, fr. *pourparler*, v., to discuss with a view to reaching an agreement, fr. OF, fr. *pour* for, before + *parler* to speak — more at PURCHASE, PARLEY] **:** a preliminary discussion esp. in advance of the formulation of a treaty ⟨was holding full-dress ~*s* in London —James Dugan⟩

pourparty *var of* PURPARTY

pourpiece \ˈ=,=\ *n* **:** POUR 3b

pour plate *n* **:** a plate prepared by mixing the inoculum with the cooled but still fluid medium before pouring the latter into the petri dish

¹pour·point \ˈpu̇r,pȯint, -rp,want\ *n* -S [ME *purpoynt*, fr. MF *pourpoint*, fr. OF *porpoint*, fr. *porpoint*, adj., quilted, embroidered, alter. (influenced by OF *pour* for) of (assumed) VL *perpunctus*, past part. of (assumed) VL *perpungere* to perforate, fr. L *per* through + *pungere* to prick, sting, pierce — more at FARE, PURCHASE, PUNGENT] **:** a padded and quilted doublet ⟨his coat of mail . . . and the coarse linen ~ that had been worn with it —T.B.Costain⟩ — compare GAMBESON

²pourpoint \"\ *vt* -ED/-ING/-S **:** QUILT

pour point *pronunc at* ¹POUR + ˌpȯint\ *n* **:** the lowest temperature at which a substance (as a lubricating oil) flows under specified conditions

pourpresture *var of* PURPRESTURE

pours *pres 3d sing of* POUR, *pl of* POUR

pour test *n* **:** a test to determine the pour point by chilling a sample — compare COLD TEST

pourtray *archaic var of* PORTRAY

pourveyance *var of* PURVEYANCE

pousse-café \ˌpüskəˈfā, -ü,skaˈ-\ *n* [F, lit., coffee pusher, fr. *pousser* to push + *café* coffee, fr. Turk *kahve* — more at PUSH, COFFEE] **1 :** an after-dinner drink consisting of several liqueurs of different colors and specific gravities poured so as to remain in separate layers **2 :** a small drink of brandy or a liqueur taken with black coffee following a dinner

pous·sette \(ˈ)püˈset\ *vi* -ED/-ING/-S [F, pushpin (game), baby carriage, fr. *pousser* to push + *-ette*] **:** to swing in a semicircle hands joined with one's partner, in or as if in a country-dance

pous·sin \(ˈ)püˈsaⁿ\ *n* -S [F, fr. LL *pullicenus* young table fowl, dim. of L *pullus* young bird, young of an animal — more at FOAL] **:** a young chicken of about one pound weight for table use **:** a small broiler

pou sto \ˈpüˈstō, *chiefly Brit* ˈpau̇ˈ-\ *n* [Gk *pou stō* where I may stand; fr. a statement attributed (in various forms) to Archimedes, "Give me a place to stand (lit., where I may stand) and I will move the earth"] **:** a standing place or vantage point **:** BASE, BASIS

¹pout \ˈpau̇t, *usu* -au̇d.+V\ *n, pl* **pout** *or* **pouts** [prob. fr. (assumed) ME *poute*, a fish with a large head, fr. OE *-pūte*; akin to ME *pouten* to pout, MD *puut* frog, Norw *pute* cushion, Skt *budbuda* bubble; basic meaning: swelling] **1 :** BIB 2 **2 :** BULLHEAD 1b **3 :** EELPOUT

²pout \"\ *vb* -ED/-ING/-S [ME *pouten*] *vi* **1 a :** to show displeasure by thrusting out the lips or wearing a sullen expression ⟨~*ed* and seemed about to cry⟩ **b :** SULK ⟨the minority leader . . . held aloof, almost ~*ing*, from the fight —*New Republic*⟩ **2 a :** to swell out **:** PROTRUDE ⟨his mouth . . . ~*ed* in a way that suggested petulance and undisciplined sensuality —John Wain⟩ **b :** to jut out or become distended ⟨on a cut surface the ends of the cords ~ —J.P.Greenhill⟩ ⟨the paper ~*ed* up in vigorous flame —Shea Murphy⟩ **~** *vt* **1 a :** to push out or swell out **:** PROTRUDE ⟨~*ed* her lips for a kiss —Maurice Hewlett⟩ **b :** to fluff out or up ⟨the falcon was . . . twice his size with ~*ed* feathers —Theodora Keogh⟩ **2 :** to say with a pout ("My feet are killing me," she ~*ed* —*N. Y. Herald Tribune*⟩

³pout \"\ *n* -S **1 :** a protrusion of the lips expressive of displeasure **2 pouts** *pl* **:** a fit of pique ⟨had the ~*s*⟩

¹pout·er \ˈpau̇də(r), -au̇tə-\ *n* -S [²*pout* + *-er*] **1 :** one that pouts **2 :** a domestic pigeon of a breed that is characterized by long legs, slender body, erect carriage, and a remarkably distensible crop which they have a habit of dilating, and that occurs in several varieties sometimes regarded as separate breeds ⟨the ~ . . . expands its throat, almost hiding the rest of its body behind the great balloon —*All-Pets Mag.*⟩

²pou·ter \ˈpōtər, ˈpau̇t-, ˈpüt-\ *vb* -ED/-ING/-S [prob. by alter.] *chiefly Scot* **:** POTTER

pou·te·ria \pau̇ˈtirēə, püˈt-\ *n, cap* [NL] **:** a large genus of chiefly tropical American timber trees (family Sapotaceae) with flower clusters borne in the leaf axils and usu. edible fruit

pout·ing·ly *adv* **:** in a pouting manner

pouty \ˈpau̇dē\ *adj* -ER/-EST **1 :** looking or tending to look petulant **:** SULKY ⟨had a ~ look on his face⟩ **2 :** tending to protrude ⟨the mucous membrane . . . is ~ —*Western Osteopath*⟩

poverish *vt* -ED/-ING/-ES [ME *povereshen*, alter. of MF *empovriss-*, stem of *empovrir* — more at IMPOVERISH] *archaic* **:** IMPOVERISH

pov·er·ty \ˈpävə(r)d·ē, -)t|, |i\ *n* -ES [ME *poverte*, fr. OF *poverté*, fr. L *paupertat-, paupertas*, fr. *pauper* poor + *-tat-, -tas* -ty — more at POOR] **1 a :** lack or relative lack of money or material possessions **:** PRIVATION, WANT ⟨transition from a life of almost the greatest pomp and circumstance . . . to one just, but only just, above the line of genteel ~ —Geoffrey Gorer⟩ ⟨in ~, morality and even a touch of happiness was possible, never in destitution —R.A.Schermerhorn⟩ ⟨had roamed the picturesque poor quarters . . . but this ugly, barren ~ on the Spanish land was his first view of some men's helpless fate —Janet Flanner⟩ **b :** renunciation as a member of a religious order of the right as an individual to own, to receive by inheritance or gift, or to dispose of property **2 a :** meagerness of supply **:** SCARCITY, DEARTH ⟨biographer . . . is necessarily embarrassed by the ~ of personal information preserved —John Loftis⟩ ⟨the cold thin atmosphere of his work was due . . . to a ~ of ideas and sensuous imagery —V.L. Parrington⟩ **b :** poorness in kind or quality **:** INFERIORITY ⟨cannot hide ~ of form under an opulent mask of orchestral color —Hunter Mead⟩ **c :** lack of desirable elements or attributes **:** DEFICIENCY ⟨the . . . ~ of North and Northeastern Africa in river-producing power —Samuel Haughton⟩ ⟨suffered . . . from a certain ~ in our English critical vocabulary —Irving Babbitt⟩ ⟨slums cause spiritual ~ in many lives —J.T.Fanell⟩ **3 a :** debility due to malnutrition **:** FEEBLENESS, EMACIATION ⟨produce insufficient fodder . . . and one or two ranches suffered quite heavy losses from ~ —*Report: Northern Rhodesia Veterinary Dept.*⟩ **b :** lack of fertility ⟨~ of the soil⟩

poverty grass *n* **1 :** any of several slender grasses: as **a :** an erect American grass (*Aristida dichotoma*) with dichotomously branched culms found in dry sandy soil **b :** an oat grass (*Danthonia spicata*) **2 :** BEACH HEATHER **3 :** BROOM CROWBERRY **4 :** RABBIT-FOOT CLOVER

poverty pine *n* **:** JERSEY PINE

poverty plant *n* **:** BEACH HEATHER

poverty poker *n* **:** any form of poker played with the agreement that when a player has lost a specified amount he may continue to play without increasing his loss

poverty-stricken \ˈ===,==\ *adj* **:** afflicted by or exhibiting poverty ⟨a *poverty-stricken* immigrant in a cold-water flat⟩ ⟨the modern notion of the Elizabethan stage as a bare and *poverty-stricken* affair, "with no scenery" —Leslie Hotson⟩ ⟨beasts . . . *poverty-stricken* to the point of death —F.D. Davison⟩ **syn** see POOR

povertyweed \ˈ===,=\ *n* **:** any of various weedy plants growing esp. on poor soils: as **a :** COWWHEAT **b :** SPURRY **c :** a troublesome aromatic weed (*Iva axillaris*) found esp. in alkali regions of the western U. S. **d :** PEARLY EVERLASTING **e :** BUTTONWEED 1 **f :** any of several annual herbs of the genus *Monolepis*, family Chenopodiaceae; *esp* **:** a weed (*M. nuttalliana*) of the western U. S. with fleshy stems, slender-petioled narrow leaves, and small flowers in clusters in the upper axils

po·vi·done \ˈpōvə,dōn\ *n* -S [*polyvinylpyrrolidone*] **:** POLYVINYLPYRROLIDONE

po·vin·dah \pōˈvində\ *n* -S *usu cap* [Pashto] **:** one of a caste or class of soldier merchants trading between northern India and central Asia

¹pow \ˈpō, ˈpau̇\ *n* -S [alter. of ¹*poll*] *dial* **:** HEAD, POLL ⟨blessings on your frosty ~ —Robert Burns⟩

²pow \ˈpau̇\ *n* -S [imit.] **:** a sound of a blow or explosion ⟨the ~ of an ax on a tree⟩ ⟨heard the ~ of a blowout —*Ethyl News*⟩ — often used interjectionally

POW *abbr or n* -S prisoner of war

pow·an \ˈpōən\ *n, pl* **powan** *or* **powans** [origin unknown] **:** a whitefish (*Coregonus clupeoides*) of Loch Lomond and Lock Eck in Scotland

¹pow·der \ˈpau̇də(r)\ *n* -S *often attrib* [ME *poudre*, fr. OF, fr. L *pulver-, pulvis* dust — more at POLLEN] **1 :** a substance composed of fine particles: as **a :** dry pulverized earth or disintegrated matter **:** DUST **b :** the spores of lycopodium — see LYCOPODIUM POWDER **c** *or* **powder snow :** fine dry light snow ⟨five inches new ~; skiing excellent⟩ — compare CORN SNOW **2 :** a powdered preparation **:** a product in the form of discrete usu. fine particles ⟨metal ~*s*⟩: as **a :** a medicine or medicated preparation in powdered form ⟨antiseptic ~⟩ ⟨digestive ~⟩ ⟨~*s* . . . prepared extemporaneously by the pharmacist —E.F.Cook & E.W.Martin⟩ **b :** a finely ground or dehydrated condiment or food ⟨curry ~⟩ ⟨ice cream ~⟩ **c :** a usu. perfumed cosmetic esp. for the skin or hair **3 a :** any of various solid explosives used chiefly in gunnery and blasting: as (1) **:** GUNPOWDER (2) **:** BLACK POWDER (3) **:** SMOKELESS POWDER (4) **:** DYNAMITE **b :** impetus or explosive force ⟨the postponement seemed to add ~ to the . . . issue —*Newsweek*⟩

²powder \"\ *vb* **powdered; powdered; powdering** \-d(ə)riŋ\ **powders** [ME *poudren*, fr. OF *poudrer* to cover with dust, fr. *poudre*, n.] *vt* **1 a :** to cover with or as if with powder **:** DUST ⟨a friar . . . stood at the door, his habit and beard ~*ed* with snow —Robert Brennan⟩ ⟨mildew . . . ~*s* it as white as a clown —Andrew Young⟩ **b :** to apply a cosmetic powder to ⟨pulled out her compact and ~*ed* her nose⟩ ⟨their heads ~*ed* with gold —Effie Gray⟩ **2 :** SCATTER, BESTREW ⟨nose ~*ed* with golden freckles —Ellen Glasgow⟩ ⟨white chiffon ~*ed* with minute gold beads —*Country Life*⟩; *specif* **:** to sow with small heraldic charges ⟨~ their red mantlings with gold billets —W.H. St. John Hope⟩ — compare SEMÉ **3** *archaic* **:** to sprinkle with a condiment ⟨give you leave to ~ and eat me too —Shak.⟩; *specif* **:** to preserve by salting **4 a :** to reduce to powder by grinding **:** COMMINUTE, PULVERIZE, TRITURATE **b :** to convert into powder by means other than grinding **~** *vi* **1 a :** to be reduced to powder **:** become pulverized **:** crumble into dust ⟨two skeletons . . . ~*ed* upon exposure, and could not be measured —C.S.Coon⟩; *specif* **:** CHALK ⟨using too thin varnish in printer's ink causes it to ~⟩ **b :** to shed powder ⟨the bulrushes . . . were ripe and ~*ing* —Rumer Godden⟩ **2 :** to apply or use cosmetic powder ⟨girls not old enough to paint and ~⟩ ⟨actors ~ with the left hand for luck⟩ **3** *slang* **:** to go away in a hurry **:** DECAMP, ESCAPE ⟨instead of ~*ing* out of town right away, I buy some new clothes —H.L. Dutkin⟩

³powder \"\ *n* -S [origin unknown] *chiefly dial* **:** a sudden impetuous rush or irrational hurry — often used in *in* or *with* ⟨a knocking at the gate, laid on in haste with such a ~ —Samuel Butler †1680⟩

⁴powder \"\ *vi* -ED/-ING/-S *chiefly dial* **:** to rush or hurry esp. impetuously ⟨gallops up to us, the groom ~*ing* afterward —W.M.Thackeray⟩

powder bag *n* **:** a fabric container for the propelling charge in separate-loading or semifixed ammunition

powder barrel *n* **:** a barrel usu. of 100-pound capacity for storing or transporting powder

powder base *n* **:** a cosmetic cream or other foundation for use under face powder

powder blue *n* **1 :** a pigment consisting of powdered smalt **2 a** *or* **powdered blue :** a variable color averaging a pale blue that is greener and paler than Sistine, greener, lighter, and stronger than average cadet gray or old blue, and greener and duller than blue flower — called also *poudre blue* **b :** the color smalt

powder charge *n* **:** the charge of powder for propelling a projectile

powder coupling *n* **:** a coupling in which the power-transmitting fluid is finely divided steel

powder down *n* **:** modified down feathers in some birds (as herons, parrots, tinamous, frogmouths) that grow continuously and disintegrate at the ends

pow·dered \ˈpau̇də(r)d\ *adj* [ME *poudred*, fr. past part. of *poudren* to powder] **1** *now dial Brit* **a :** SPICED, SEASONED **b :** PICKLED, PRESERVED **2 :** patterned or strewn with small objects ⟨the vast . . . sky, ~ with innumerable stars —W.H. Hudson †1922⟩ ⟨bindings ~ with monograms and fleurs-de-lis —Edith Diehl⟩ **3 :** reduced to a powder **:** PULVERIZED ⟨~ chalk⟩ ⟨~ coal⟩ **4** *obs* **:** subjected to sweating in a powdering tub **5 :** dressed or treated with powder ⟨the ~ coiffures of the French court —Lois Long⟩ ⟨~, weighted silks —*Atlantic*⟩

powdered milk *n* **:** DRIED MILK

powdered sugar *n* **:** sugar derived from granulated sugar by grinding to several grades of fineness with flour added to prevent caking — compare CONFECTIONERS' SUGAR

pow·der·er \-dərə(r)\ *n* -S **:** one that powders; *specif* **:** a worker who rubs powder onto a hat before it is lured

powder flag *n* **:** a red flag hoisted by a ship loading or discharging explosives or flammable fuel in bulk

powder hole *n* **:** DRY HOLE 2

powder horn *n* **1 :** a flask for carrying gunpowder; *esp* **:** one made of the horn of an ox or cow **2 :** a plant of the genus *Cerastium*

powder horn *1*

powdering *n* -S [ME *poudringe*, fr. gerund of *poudren* to powder] **1 :** the act or an instance of applying a powder ⟨the ~ of a wig⟩ **2 :** ornamentation with a multitude of small objects ⟨wore his mother's arms but . . . added a ~ of golden fleurs-de-lis on the silver border —H.S.London⟩ **3 :** a powdery deposit ⟨snow ~*s* in the valleys —R.S.G.Hall⟩

powdering tub *n* **1** *archaic* **:** a tub for salting meat **2** *obs* **:** a sweating tub for the cure of venereal disease ⟨to the spital go, and from the *powd'ring tub* of infamy fetch forth the lazar kite —Shak.⟩

powder keg *n* **1 :** a small usu. metal cask for holding gunpowder or blasting powder **2 :** something liable to explode ⟨merchant seamen see a tanker as a potential *powder keg*⟩ ⟨politicos . . . sitting uneasily on the *powder keg* of Arabian Nationalism —*Saturday Rev.*⟩

pow·der·man \-də(r),man, -ˌmən\ *n, pl* **powdermen 1 :** one who works with explosives: as **a :** one whose work is blasting with powder **b :** one in charge of the storage and issuance of explosives at a mine **c :** one who screens and melts trinitrotoluene and fills projectile cases **2 :** a worker who blends and heats the powders from which plastics are molded

powder metallurgy *n* **:** the production of metal powders and their utilization in the production of shaped parts

powder method *n* **:** DEBYE-SCHERRER METHOD

powder monkey *n* **1 :** one who transports powder from the magazine to the guns esp. on shipboard ⟨*powder monkeys* skidded over the wet decks, their deadly burdens cradled in their desperate arms —Frank Yerby⟩ ⟨was made *powder monkey* for the artillery squad who fired the cannon at sundown —F.B.Gipson⟩ **2 :** one who carries or has charge of powder or other explosives in mining or blasting operations

powder of al·ga·roth \-ˈalgə,rȯth, -rath\ *usu cap A* [part trans. of F *poudre d'algaroth*, fr. *poudre* powder + *d'* of + *algaroth* powder of algaroth, fr. It *algarotto*, fr. Vittorio *Algarotto* †1604 Ital. physician] **:** a white powder of variable composition consisting principally of antimony oxychloride formed by the action of much water on antimony trichloride and used chiefly in the preparation of tartar emetic and formerly in medicine

powder paint *n* **:** a paint packaged as a powder having a binder (as casein, glue, cement) for use in water solution

powder pattern *n* **:** a pattern of lines or arcs recorded on photographic film by the Debye-Scherrer method

powder photograph *n* **:** the photographic record made by the Debye-Scherrer method

powder post *n* **:** a defective powdery condition of wood caused chiefly by powder-post beetles — **powder-posted** \ˈ==,pōstəd\ *adj*

powder-post beetle *also* **powder-post borer** *n* **:** any of several beetles (family Lyctidae) having larvae that feed in very dry wood or lumber and reduce the interior to powder — compare ANOBIUM, FURNITURE BEETLE

powder-post termite *n* **:** a dry-wood termite (*Cryptotermes brevis*) that is widely distributed in warm regions and is extremely destructive of seasoned wood

powder puff *n* **1 :** a small fluffy pad or other device for applying cosmetic powder **2** *or* **powder puff cactus :** a globose cactus (*Mammillaria bocasana*) with yellowish white flowers and radial spines represented by long white silky hairs

powder ring *n* **:** a fabric ring containing an increment of the propelling charge for a weapon (as a mortar)

powder room *n* **1 a :** a rest room for women **b :** a small usu. prettified first floor lavatory and dressing room in a home provided esp. for the convenience of women guests **2 :** BATHROOM

powder rose *n* **:** a grayish yellowish pink that is redder and deeper than iris mauve

powders *pl of* POWDER, *pres 3d sing of* POWDER

powder snow *n* **:** POWDER 1c

powder table *n* **:** POUDREUSE

powder train *n* **:** an element used in some fuses to obtain time action

pow·dery \ˈpau̇dərē, -ri\ *adj* [ME *powdry*, fr. *powdre, poudre* powder + *-y*] **1 a :** resembling or consisting of powder ⟨~ dust⟩ ⟨~ snow⟩ **b :** easily reduced to powder **:** CRUMBLING, FRIABLE ⟨the trail continued under the brown and ~ carpet —R.T.Bird⟩ **2 :** covered with or as if with powder **:** DUSTY, CHALKY ⟨the ~ gray of a frightened native —Marguerite Steen⟩ ⟨Pierrot . . . sad, ~, languishing —Sheldon Cheney⟩ ⟨the frescoes are ~ —Aline B. Saarinen⟩

powdery mildew *n* **1 :** a perfect fungus of the family Erysiphaceae or an imperfect fungus of the genus *Oidium* distinguished by the abundant powdery conidia produced on the host **2 :** a plant disease caused by a powdery mildew — compare DOWNY MILDEW

powdery scab *n* **:** a disease of potato tubers caused by a fungus (*Spongospora subterranea*) and characterized by nodular discolored lesions which at maturity burst to expose a powdery mass of spores in circular pits surrounded by the lighter colored frayed remnants of the skin of the tuber — called also *pock scab*

pow·ell·ite \ˈpau̇ə,līt\ *n* -S [John W. *Powell* †1902 Am. geologist + E *-ite*] **:** a mineral $CaMoO_4$ consisting of a calcium molybdate occurring in small yellow tetragonal pyramidal crystals isomorphous with scheelite

¹pow·er \ˈpau̇(ə)r, -au̇ə, *esp in Southern US* -au̇wə(r\ *n* -S *often attrib* [ME, fr. OF *poer, poeir*, fr. *poer, poeir*, v., to be able, fr. (assumed) OL *potēre* — more at POTENT] **1 a :** a position of ascendancy **:** ability to compel obedience **:** CONTROL, DOMINION ⟨party in ~⟩ ⟨there are no . . . assignable boundaries to sovereign ~ —J.H.Hallowell⟩ ⟨bidding for personal ~ and aiming to make himself absolute dictator —A.P.Ryan⟩ ⟨knowledge meant ~ over nature —W.A.Kaufmann⟩ **b** (1) **:** a military force or its equipment ⟨mechanized, motorized, horse and foot units . . . make the enemy a formidable ~ —Shipley Thomas⟩ ⟨sea-borne air ~ successfully challenged land-based planes —*Atlantic*⟩ (2) **:** ability to wage war ⟨his military ~ absolutely crushed —Oscar Handlin⟩ **c** *chiefly dial* **:** a large number or quantity **:** MULTITUDE, ABUNDANCE, HEAP ⟨there had been such a ~ of elderberries the year before —Mary Webb⟩ ⟨contains a ~ of fine Arizona scenery —*Newsweek*⟩ **2 a** (1) **:** capability of acting or of producing an effect ⟨purchasing ~⟩ ⟨countries behind the Iron Curtain would make the same choice if they had the ~ —A.J.Toynbee⟩ ⟨the urbane ~ of reason, and the persuasive influence of just consideration —Gilbert Parker⟩ ⟨learned more about the ~ and the beauty of clear design by reading . . . sonnets —Janna Burgess⟩ (2) **:** a mental or physical ability or aptitude **:** FACULTY, TALENT ⟨their visual sense was far more highly developed than their ~ of smell —W.E.Swinton⟩ ⟨a man who has learned the technique of scientific investigation has added a new ~ to his mind —Benjamin Farrington⟩ ⟨showed his ~ as a playwright —A.H.Quinn⟩ — often used in pl. ⟨a man of fine mental ~*s* —C.B.Fisher⟩ ⟨test your ~*s* of observation —Richard Harrison⟩ ⟨loath to believe that a bird so small . . . could possess such vocal ~*s* —John Burroughs⟩ (3) **:** performance measured without consideration of the element of speed **b :** political sway **:** social sway **:** INFLUENCE, PRESTIGE ⟨when the Democratic party regained ~ in the state, he was reappointed surrogate —H.W.H.Knott⟩ ⟨a man of ~ with the Sioux, rescued the three captives —I.B.Richman⟩ **3 a** (1) **:** a delegated right or privilege **:** PREROGATIVE ⟨invaded his ∼*s* as commander-in-chief —Isabel Whittier⟩ ⟨not necessary for Congress to trace back every one of its ∼*s* to some single grant of authority —F.A.Ogg & P.O.Ray⟩ (2) **:** delegated authority ⟨an emissary with ∼ to negotiate⟩ **b :** a document conferring legal authority ⟨not until the end of September did the British representative . . . show satisfactory ∼*s* to treat with the thirteen United States of America —W.C. Ford⟩ **c :** legal authority ⟨the ∼ to bestow degrees was granted by the legislature in 1820 —*Amer. Guide Series: Maine*⟩ ⟨argument began over the nature of the proposed pact and whether it would deprive Congress of the ∼ to declare war —L.B.Burbank⟩; *specif* **:** the ability to change legal relations — compare COLLATERAL POWER, GENERAL POWER OF APPOINTMENT, POWER APPENDANT, POWER COUPLED WITH AN INTEREST, POWER IN GROSS, POWER OF APPOINTMENT, POWER OF ATTORNEY, SPECIAL POWER **4 :** one that has influence or authority ⟨was a ∼ in ecclesiastical councils —H.E.Starr⟩ ⟨the organs of justice . . . are the chief ∼ in the state —Jacques Maritain⟩ ⟨I wish the ∼*s* that be would send me out there —Rose Macaulay⟩ ⟨preferred in politics to be the ∼ behind the throne —Louis Bromfield⟩; *specif* **:** a sovereign state ⟨the brutal and unprovoked assault . . . has caused reassessment of the foreign policies of the western ∼*s* —*Army-Navy-Air Force Jour.*⟩ **5 a powers** *pl, often cap* [ME *poweris* (pl.), trans. of LL *potestates*, trans. of Gk *exousiai*] **:** the sixth order in the celestial hierarchy ⟨the ∼*s* and Thrones above —John Keble⟩ **b :** a supernatural being or occult force or the ability to control them ⟨the sky . . . is the male ∼ —J.G.Frazer⟩ ⟨a good ∼ called God —*Time*⟩ ⟨shamanistic ∼*s* . . . were associated with animal or abstract beings —M.J.Herskovits⟩ **c** *dial* **:** the religious fervor of a revivalist — used with *the* ⟨almost got the ∼ with the rest of them if for no other reason than the coffee and sandwiches —H.A.Chippendale⟩ **6 a :** physical might or resources **:** STRENGTH, SOLIDITY ⟨punishment calls for clear predominance of ∼ —H.D.Gideonse⟩ ⟨the dancer is . . . using only a portion of his ∼ —Reginald & Gladys Laubin⟩ ⟨a great flood moving with majesty and ∼ —Willa Cather⟩ ⟨the building has unusual ∼ —*Amer. Guide Series: N.Y. City*⟩ **b :** mental or moral efficacy **:** VIGOR, INTENSITY ⟨laid down with great ∼ and insight a spiritual philosophy —W.R.Inge⟩ ⟨the ∼ of his curiosity surprised him —Morley Callaghan⟩ ⟨it is fine, sturdy stuff and more ∼ to him —G.N.Shuster⟩ **c :** political or national might ⟨present-day tendency . . . to speak of the state almost exclusively in terms of ∼ —*Amer. Polit. Sci. Rev.*⟩ **7 a :** the number of times as indicated by an exponent a number occurs as a factor in a product; *also* **:** the product itself **b :** the property that a mathematical aggregate has in common with all equivalent aggregates **:** the cardinal number that two or more aggregates share **8 a :** an inherent property or effect ⟨they are . . . ∼*s* of material substances —Grace De Laguna⟩ ⟨adrenalin . . . has the ∼ of constricting the blood vessels —Morris Fishbein⟩ **b** (1) **:** the phonetic value of a letter ⟨the ∼ of K was usually written by C —Stanley Wemyss⟩ (2) **:** the meaning of a word or phrase **9 a** *archaic* **:** SIMPLE MACHINE **b** (1) **:** a source or means of supplying energy ⟨muscle ∼⟩ ⟨tractor ∼⟩ ⟨wind ∼⟩ ⟨atomic ∼⟩ ⟨using horses and mules for ∼ —C.B.Bender⟩; *esp* **:** ELECTRICITY ⟨the shortage of ∼ dims the streets —Wyndham Lewis⟩ (2) **:** energy supplied from such sources **:** MOTIVE POWER ⟨gathered their herds and started them on their own ∼ in charge of cowboys —W.P.Webb⟩ ⟨ships . . . arrive, dock, and depart under their own ∼ —*Amer. Guide Series: N.C.*⟩ **c :** the time rate at which work is done or energy emitted or transferred ⟨mechanical ∼ of the internal combustion engine —A.C.Morrison⟩ — usu. expressed in horsepower or watts **10 a :** MAGNIFICATION 1 b **b :** the reciprocal of the focal length of a lens

syn CONTROL, AUTHORITY, JURISDICTION, COMMAND, DOMINION, SWAY: POWER indicates possession of the ability to wield coercive force, permissive authority, or substantial influence ⟨the Governor's position is no longer one merely of dignity and honor, but of constantly increasing *power* —*Amer. Guide Series: Mass.*⟩ ⟨the trustees have *power* to appoint and displace professors, tutors, and other officers —John Marshall⟩ or to make effective use of one's capacities ⟨the Senate had been voting according to direction for so long that they seemed to have lost the *power* of independent decisions —Robert Graves⟩ CONTROL emphasizes the power of direction or restraint ⟨his nervous exasperation had grown so much that now very often he used to lose *control* of his voice —Joseph Conrad⟩ ⟨he is likely to be the most hated man, because he exercises the greatest *control* —Abram Kardiner⟩ ⟨all such laws shall be subject to the revision and *control* of the Congress —*U. S. Constitution*⟩ AUTHORITY usu. implies the granting of power for a specific purpose and within a carefully delineated frame of reference ⟨by *authority* we mean the established right, within any social order, to determine policies, to pronounce judgments on relevant issues, and to settle controversies, or, more broadly, to act as leader or guide to other men —R.M.MacIver⟩ but may also refer to influence derived from public sanction ⟨some of the new philosophies undermine the *authority* of science, as some of the older systems undermined the *authority* of religion —W.R.Inge⟩ JURISDICTION usu. applies to official power and responsibility formally determined and demarcated ⟨in all cases affecting ambassadors, other public ministers, and consuls, and those in which a State shall be a party, the Supreme Court shall have original jurisdiction —*U. S. Constitution*⟩ ⟨there can be no doubt as to the *jurisdiction* of this court to revise the judgment of the Circuit Court, and to reverse it for any error apparent on the record —R.B.Taney⟩ ⟨many of the smaller squires and most of the larger ones had the right to private *jurisdiction;* the number of nobles with the right to put a man to death upon their own estates was appreciable —Hilaire Belloc⟩ COMMAND stresses the power to make arbitrary decisions and to compel obedience ⟨in war the president assumes *command* of the army and navy⟩ ⟨he had no *command* among the men, and people did what they pleased with him —R.L.Stevenson⟩ or it may imply self-mastery or mastery over one's resources ⟨the author's *command* of his material is admirable, and his presentation masterly —H.O.Taylor⟩ DOMINION indicates ultimate sovereignty or supreme authority ⟨neither the English nor colonial Governments claimed or exercised any *dominion* over the tribe or nation by whom it was occupied, nor claimed the right to the possession of the territory, until the tribe or nation consented to cede it —R.B.Taney⟩ ⟨the four wars between England and France for *dominion* in North America —*Amer. Guide Series: N.C.*⟩ SWAY, somewhat rhetorical in effect, indicates a sweeping extent over which dominant power or dominion is exercised ⟨it was as a successful warlord that the dictator Julius Caesar, after the defeat of Pompey at Pharsalia in 48 B.C., had brought the whole Roman world under the *sway* of one supreme military commander —P.N.Ure⟩ ⟨in 1673 the Dutch recaptured the Colony, but in 1674 it was restored by treaty to the English, who promptly resumed their *sway* —*Amer. Guide Series: N.Y.*⟩ ⟨no government, whatever its nature or form, can hold absolute *sway* in the multitudinous ramifications of human activity —*Encyc. Americana*⟩

syn POWER, FORCE, ENERGY, STRENGTH, MIGHT, PUISSANCE, ARM can signify the ability to exert effort for a purpose. POWER signifies ability, latent, exerted, physical, mental or spiritual, to act, be acted upon, effect or be effected, sometimes designating the thing having this ability ⟨*power*, which is any and every capacity to produce results —*Amer. Polit. Sci. Rev.*⟩ ⟨the immense property value of the slaves and the *power* of the owners to control all the political agencies of the government —W.C.Ford⟩ ⟨the *power* of the bridge to withstand great weights⟩ ⟨the precious *power* to lift the minds and hearts of children —R.H.Wittcoff⟩ ⟨the *power* to understand and be affected by music⟩ ⟨who was a *power* in marine and financial circles in New York —H.W.H.Knott⟩ FORCE stresses the actual exercise of power, often applying to something which exercises its power efficaciously ⟨to charge against a door with enough *force* to break it down⟩ ⟨a society crowded by almost every other *force* toward like-mindedness and conformity —Oscar Handlin⟩ ⟨a powerful political *force*⟩ ⟨a police *force*⟩ ENERGY contrasts with latent power, denoting the power expended or capable of being transformed into work; in common use it implies stored-up power; in the physical sciences it is conceived of as one of two possible aspects of matter (the other being mass) and signifying, roughly, the capacity for work, realized or potential ⟨how the immense *energy* of volcanoes might be harnessed for man's use —Howel Williams⟩ ⟨measuring the physical output may furnish some rough estimate of the *energy* given out by the worker —J.A. Hobson⟩ ⟨*energy* for sudden action, rapidity of decision, mystical fusion of reason and passion, which characterizes men created to act —William Troy⟩ ⟨the electrical *energy* expended in the circuit is derived from the chemical *energy* of the freshly compounded battery —K.K.Darrow⟩ ⟨*energy* and mass are two aspects of the same entity, and when the energy departs the corresponding amount of mass also departs —A. S.Eddington⟩ STRENGTH applies to the power residing in a thing as a result of qualities or properties (as health or soundness in bodily condition, or numbers or great equipment in military organization) that enable it to exert force or manifest great energy as in resistance, attack, or endurance ⟨a man of great *strength*⟩ ⟨a wall of great *strength*⟩ ⟨a political party of great *strength*⟩ ⟨a military force of great *strength*⟩ MIGHT, somewhat literary, suggests great or superhuman power or force ⟨sportsmen have risen in their articulate *might* and blasted the proposals out of legislative halls —*Amer. Guide Series: Mich.*⟩ ⟨the most savage winter in the memory of the Colonies hurled its icy *might* against the Americans at Valley Forge —F.V.W.Mason⟩ although in certain current fixed constructions it still retains its older sense of strength or force ⟨they reserve to themselves the right to curse the city's shortcomings with *might* and main —*Amer. Guide Series: Md.*⟩ ⟨Washington remonstrated with all his *might* —H.E.Scudder⟩ PUISSANCE, rhetorical and literary, is similar to MIGHT but suggests a display of power ⟨the sapience and *puissance* of the American businessman in general and the American financier in particular —G.W.Johnson⟩ ⟨their legs had lost almost all *puissance;* for minutes they would stand virtually in place, unable to coordinate their thighs and feet to move forward —Norman Mailer⟩ ARM in this connection is the figurative extension of *arm*, the human limb, and signifies operative and effective power or that in which such power resides; or it can, in related but specialized use, signify a branch of the service ⟨the strong *arm* of the law⟩ ⟨the military was a fairly good *arm* of the American people —T.D.Clark⟩ ⟨until all *arms* of the international fighting services are up to strength —A.P.Ryan⟩

[2]**power** *vb* -ED/-ING/-S *vt* **1 :** to give strength to **:** make powerful ⟨warships . . . other craft, ∼*ed* by 80,000,000 horsepower —*Time*⟩ **2 a :** to supply with or propel by means of motive power ⟨tankers . . . fetch the fuel that ∼*s* trains and trucks —Andrew Boyd⟩ ⟨are you waiting for me to ∼ you out the door —F.W.Booth⟩; *esp* **:** to furnish with electricity ⟨tiny atomic batteries designed to ∼ the electronic brains in guided missiles —*Newsweek*⟩ **b :** to give impetus to ⟨decision to revenge . . . his wife, is ∼*ed* by a quiet, controlled anger —*Atlantic*⟩ ∼ *vi* **:** to move under power ⟨we ∼*ed* cautiously into a fog —Thomas Morgan⟩

powerable *adj* [[1]*power* + *-able*] *obs* **:** POWERFUL

power amplifier *n* **:** an amplifier that can produce relatively large power output usu. greater than one watt

power appendant *or* **power appurtenant**, *n* **:** a power coupled with an interest that the donee can exercise only out of an estate held by him (as a grant by the holder of a life estate of a lease) — distinguished from *power in gross*

powerboat \'==¦=\ *n* **:** a motorboat esp. of substantial engine power

power brake *n* **:** automotive brake with engine power used to amplify the torque applied at the pedal by the driver

power car *n* **1 a :** a railroad car equipped with machinery for supplying heat and electricity to a train **b :** a railroad car having controls for operation alone or with other cars as a train **2 :** a usu. faired in structure supported from or suspended beneath the hull of an airship and carrying the engine or engines used for propulsion

power coupled with an interest : a power accompanying an interest of the donee in the property to which the power relates — distinguished from *collateral power*

power dive *n* [[1]*power* + *dive*, n.] **:** a steep dive of or as if of an airplane accelerated by the power of the engine ⟨made a succession of *power dives* upon the enemy ships —*Manchester Guardian Weekly*⟩ ⟨watched a falcon rise . . . then plummet downward in a magnificent *power dive* —H.M.Robinson⟩

power-dive \¦==¦=\ *vb* [*power dive*] *vi* **:** to dive steeply with the added impetus of motive power ⟨*power-dived* from 20,000 feet⟩ ∼ *vt* **:** to cause to go into a power dive ⟨practically *power-dived* this old crate into the Mediterranean to get away —Lowell Bennett⟩

power duster *n* **:** a motor-driven agricultural machine for spreading insecticidal dusts

powered \¦paù(ə)rd, -aùəd, -aùwəd\ *adj* **:** having, producing, or propelled by means of power ⟨∼ aircraft⟩ ⟨∼ flight⟩ ⟨great ∼ engines⟩ — often used in combination ⟨kerosine-*powered* jet-propulsion engines⟩

power factor *n* **:** the ratio of the mean actual power in an alternating-current circuit measured in watts to the apparent power measured in volt-amperes, being equal to the cosine of the phase difference between electromotive force and current

[1]**pow·er·ful** \'paù(ə)rfəl, -aùəf-,-aùwəf-, *-R chiefly substand* -aùf-\ *adj* [ME *powerfull*, fr. [1]*power* + *-full*, *-ful* -ful] **1 a :** having great force or potency **:** STRONG, COMPELLING ⟨∼ state⟩ ⟨∼ leader⟩ ⟨∼ physique⟩ ⟨∼ solvent⟩ ⟨images that are always ∼, imaginative, and solid —Whitney Balliett⟩ ⟨the . . . ∼ immediacy of hunger —Lionel Trilling⟩ ⟨a ∼ influence for good —C.C.Walcutt⟩ **b :** having great prestige or effect **:** INFLUENTIAL, STIMULATING ⟨∼ clique⟩ ⟨∼ journal⟩ ⟨the ∼ Senate Foreign Relations Committee —Vera M. Dean⟩ ⟨love of the outdoors was a ∼ factor in his decision to take up farming⟩ ⟨music is ∼ in the building up of . . . expansiveness of personality —H.A.Overstreet⟩ **2 :** endowed with talent or ability **:** CAPABLE ⟨here is one of our most ∼ performers refusing to show his power —E.R.Bentley⟩ **3** *chiefly dial* **:** great in amount or extent **:** BIG, CONSIDERABLE ⟨think if they raise 75 or a hundred bu. of wheat they have a ∼ crop —A.E.Fife⟩ — **pow·er·ful·ly** \-f(ə)lē, -li\ *adv*

[2]**powerful** \"\ *adv, chiefly dial* **:** to a great degree or extent **:** VERY ⟨was ∼ glad to see me —Mark Twain⟩ ⟨it was ∼ dark going down through the holler —H.E.Giles⟩

pow·er·ful·ness \-fəlnəs\ *n* -ES *archaic* **:** POWER

power gas *n* **:** a cheap gas (as Mond gas) made for producing power esp. for driving gas engines

power grid *n* **:** a network of electrical transmission lines connecting a multiplicity of generating stations to loads over a wide area

powerhouse \'==,=\ *n* **1 a :** a building in which mechanical, electrical, or other power is generated; *specif* **:** an electric utility generating station **b :** a source of influence or inspiration ⟨protegés of party ∼*s* —*New Republic*⟩ ⟨the meeting for worship is . . . the ∼ of everything Quakerism has accomplished —W.W.Comfort⟩ **2 :** one having or wielding great power: as **a :** an individual of unusual physical or mental capacity ⟨a ∼ with sandpaper lungs, stomped his foot and opened his mouth —Truman Capote⟩ ⟨a ∼ of a woman teacher —*Time*⟩ ⟨no other . . . trout can boast of greater fighting qualities; he is a ∼ —Alexander MacDonald⟩ **b :** an effective well-coordinated group ⟨the combo is a real ∼ . . . with the authentic feeling for the music —*Christian Science Monitor*⟩; *specif* **:** an athletic team characterized by strong aggressive play ⟨two perennial ∼*s*, Notre Dame and Army —*Americana Annual*⟩ **c :** a very strong hand held by one player in a card game **d :** a group or list of influential people ⟨has lined up a ∼ to officiate at its Fiction Writers Conference —Bennett Cerf⟩

power in gross : collateral power exercisable by the donee only in the creation of such estates as will not attach to that which he himself holds or be satisfied out of his own interest — distinguished from *power appendant*

power landing *n* **:** an airplane landing in which the power is not cut until contact has been made with the landing surface

pow·er·less \-aù(ə)rləs, -aùəl-,-aùwəl-\ *adj* **1 :** devoid of strength or resources **:** HELPLESS, IMPOTENT ⟨∼ in the hands of her remorseless . . . enemy —W.M.Thackeray⟩ **2 :** lacking the authority or capacity to act **:** UNABLE — used with following infinitive ⟨arguing that he was ∼ to do away with the odious institution —Lytton Strachey⟩ ⟨became entangled in the marsh . . . and was ∼ to make the attack —*Amer. Guide Series: La.*⟩ — **pow·er·less·ly** *adv*

pow·er·less·ness *n* -ES **:** the quality or state of being powerless **:** IMPOTENCE

power load *n* **:** the part of the output of an electric power plant used for the operation of motors or heating devices

power loading *n* **:** the weight per horsepower of an airplane usu. computed on the basis of full load and of power in air of standard density

pow·er·man \-aù(ə)rmən, -aùəm-,-aùwəm-, -ˌman, -ˌmaa(ə)n\ *n, pl* **powermen :** a specialist in the installation, operation, and maintenance of generating equipment for electric power

power mower *n* **:** a motor-driven lawn mower

power net *n* **:** a usu. nylon knitted elastic fabric used for corsets and girdles

power of appointment : a legal authority granted under a deed or will authorizing the donee to dispose of an estate in a specified manner for his own benefit or the benefit of others

power of attorney : a legal instrument authorizing one to act as the attorney or agent of the grantor either generally for the management of a specified business or enterprise or more often specifically for the accomplishment of a particular transaction — called also *letter of attorney*

power of termination : the right of a grantor or his successors in interest to enter upon an estate granted upon a condition after breach of the condition in order to terminate the granted estate and revest it in the grantor or his successors

power-operate \¦==¦=(=),=\ *vt* **:** to operate (as a tool, machine, device) by mechanical power

power pack *n* **1 :** a unit consisting typically of transformer, rectifier, and filter for obtaining a moderate steady direct current from an alternating-current service ⟨*power pack* for a camera flash⟩ ⟨*power pack* for a capacitor⟩ ⟨*power packs* for guided missiles⟩ **2** *or* **power package :** an airplane engine with cowling and accessories designed for installation or removal as a unit — compare POWER UNIT

power plant *n* **1 :** POWERHOUSE 1 a **2 :** an engine and related parts (as carburetion system, ignition apparatus, transmission) supplying the motive power of a self-propelled vehicle ⟨an aeroplane can be considered as being divided into two main parts, the *power plant* and the airframe —*Manual of Seamanship*⟩ ⟨a 90- or 99-inch wheelbase car . . . tough enough to take any *power plant* up to 450 horsepower —Les Nehamkin⟩

power play *n* **1 :** an offensive play (as in football or hockey) in which mass interference is provided at a particular point or in a particular zone **2 :** a military, diplomatic, or political action or maneuver resembling a power play in sports ⟨worked a successful *power play* . . . by sending in elements of three divisions from the northeast and elements of a fourth division from the east —*N.Y. Times*⟩

power-political \¦===¦===\ *adj* [fr. *power politics*, after E *politics: political*] **:** of, relating to, or having the characteristics of power politics ⟨economic policy as *power-political* weapon —Andreas Dorpalen⟩ ⟨*power-political* maneuvers by great powers —J. S. Roucek⟩

power politician *n* [fr. *power politics*, after E *politics: politician*] **:** one that believes in, advocates, or practices power politics

power politics *n pl but sing or pl in constr* [trans. of G *machtpolitik*] **:** politics based primarily on the use of power as a coercive force rather than upon ethical precepts ⟨less savory incidents of church *power politics* —W.H.Chamberlin⟩; *esp* **:** international politics characterized by attempts to advance national interests (as the achievement and maintenance of security) or to obtain concessions from rivals through coercion on the basis of military and economic strength ⟨a statesman conversant with the facts of *power politics* —E.M.Earle⟩ ⟨eliminate *power politics* and replace them with a kind of mystical international cooperation —G.L.Kirk⟩ ⟨give up our *power politics* . . . and turn instead to treaty rights and principle and law —T.K.Finletter⟩ — compare BALANCE OF POWER, MACHTPOLITIK, REALPOLITIK

powers *pl of* POWER, *pres 3d sing of* POWER

power shovel *n* **:** a power-operated shovel consisting of a boom or crane that supports a dipper handle with a dipper at the end of it and used principally for excavation and removal of debris

power stall *n* **:** an airplane stall with the power on usu. occurring in a pull-up or in an attempt to climb too rapidly

power-stall landing *n* **:** a landing made with the airplane in the normal landing attitude, with power on, at an airspeed just sufficient to maintain the lifting power of the wings

power station *n* **:** POWERHOUSE 1 a

power steering *n* **:** automotive steering with engine power used to amplify the torque applied at the steering wheel by the driver

power stroke *n* **:** the stroke in the cycle of an internal-combustion engine during which the piston is propelled by the pressure of the expanding steam or gases

power supply *n* **:** a device providing power to electronic equipment and sometimes designated *A*, *B*, or *C* according to its function of heating vacuum tube cathodes, causing a flow of electron current in plate circuits, or applying a direct voltage in grid circuits

power take-off *n* **:** a supplementary mechanism on a truck or tractor enabling the engine power to be used to operate nonautomotive apparatus (as winches, pumps, saws, cement mixers)

power test *n* **:** a psychological test of knowledge or skill in which the time taken to complete the test is not considered **:** test of ability apart from speed

power train *n* **1 :** the intervening mechanism (as drive shaft, coupling, clutch, transmission, differential) of a vehicle between engine and propeller or driven axle **2 :** a rail unit comprising a locomotive and power-generating equipment on cars for use at army stations or in a community emergency

power tube *n* **:** a vacuum tube of large output suitable for use as a generator of alternating current or as a power amplifier

power unit *n* **:** an engine usu. of the internal-combustion type mounted with accessories for use in portable operation of mechanical equipment — compare POWER PACK 2

pow·ha·tan \¦paùə¦tan, paù'hatᵊn\ *n, pl* **powhatan** *or* **powhatans** *usu cap* **1 a :** an Algonkian people of eastern Virginia **b :** a member of such people **2 :** an Algonkian language of the Powhatan people

pow·itch \'paùich\ *n, pl* **powitch** [Chinook Jargon, fr. Chinook *-páuč*] **:** OREGON CRAB APPLE

pow·nie \'pōni\ *Scot var of* PONY

powre *obs var of* POUR

pows *pl of* POW

pow·sow·dy \'pō,sōdi, 'paù,saùdi, ='==\ *n* -ES [origin unknown] *dial Brit* **:** any of various dishes ranging from sheep's head broth to an ale posset and including often incongruous mixtures

pow·ther \'püthər\ *Scot var of* POWDER

[1]**pow·wow** \'paù,waù\ *n* -S [of Algonquian origin; akin to Natick *pauwau* conjurer, he uses divination, Narraganset *powwaw*] **1 a :** a No. American Indian conjurer or medicine man **b** (1) **:** healing by incantation or magic among the Pennsylvania Dutch (2) *or* **powwow doctor :** a practitioner of this art ⟨the richest ∼ in York . . . is said to receive as much as $50 for a treatment —*Nation*⟩ **2 a :** a No. American Indian ceremony (as for the cure of disease, success in hunting, victory in war) often accompanied by great noise, feasting, and dancing **b** (1) **:** a tribal council (2) **:** a conference with an Indian leader or group ⟨held a ∼ with the head medicine man —F.B.Gipson⟩ **3 a :** a social gathering or celebration; *esp* **:** a noisy one **:** FROLIC ⟨then came the ∼, with the Old Man the guest of honor —H.A.Chippendale⟩ **b :** a meeting or conference for discussion **:** SESSION ⟨brought together in a two-day ∼ businessmen . . . scholars, journalists, and government officials —F.L.Allen⟩ ⟨official small fry . . . that modestly take up wall space at international ∼*s* —Janet Flanner⟩; *esp* **:** a meeting to discuss political strategy ⟨indicated here at a . . . Democratic ∼ that any party presidential campaign will lean heavily on the administration foreign policy record —*Christian Science Monitor*⟩ **c :** an informal conversation or interview ⟨in Rome the year before . . . had a fine ∼ with the Pope —Bruce Marshall⟩; *esp* **:** a deliberative huddle ⟨the . . . group, which held frequent little ∼*s*, often gained time for further deliberations by bidding in smaller jumps —S.G.Thompson⟩

²powwow \ˈ", ˌ=ˈ=\ *vb* -ED/-ING/-S *vi* **1 :** to hold or take part in a ceremonial or conjuring session; *esp* **:** to practice healing by incantation or magic **2 :** to have a meeting or take part in a discussion ⟨invited them to stack their arms in the yard, and come inside the shack and ~ —W.A.Fraser⟩ ~ *vt* **:** to subject to treatment by incantation or magic ⟨had one of his eyes ~*ed*⟩

¹pox \ˈpäks\ *n, pl* **pox** *or* **poxes** [alter. of *pocks*, pl. of ¹*pock*] **1 a :** any of various virus diseases characterized by pustules or eruptions — usu. used in combination ⟨chicken *pox*⟩ ⟨cow*pox*⟩ ⟨fowl *pox*⟩ **b** *archaic* **:** SMALLPOX **c :** SYPHILIS — not often in formal use ⟨most of them had a dose of clap or ~ and some had a double dose —Bruce Siberts⟩ **2 :** an afflictive rash **:** repellent cluster **:** PLAGUE ⟨a ~ of garish neon lights —Robert Cahn⟩ ⟨a ~ of jeering urchins —*New Yorker*⟩ ⟨the world . . . is covered by a ~ of danger spots —*N.Y.Times*⟩ — often used interjectionally ⟨a ~ on the girl —Virginia Woolf⟩ **3 a :** a disease of sweet potatoes caused by actinomycetes of the genus *Streptomyces* and characterized by pitted lesions on the roots or tubers — called also SOIL ROT **b :** STORAGE SPOT

²pox \ˈ"\ *vt* -ED/-ING/-ES *archaic* **:** to infect with a pox and esp. with syphilis

poxy \ˈpäksē\ *adj* -ER/-EST **:** afflicted with or as if with a pox

poyn·ting's theorem \ˈpȯintiŋz-\ *n, usu cap P* [after John H. *Poynting* †1914 Eng. physicist, its originator] **:** a statement in electromagnetic theory: the transfer of energy by an electromagnetic wave is at right angles to both electric and magnetic components of the wave vibration and its rate is proportional to the vector product of their amplitudes

poy·ou \ˈpȯi(ˌ)(y)ü\ *n* -S [Guarani *tatu-pó-yu*, lit., armadillo with a yellow hand, fr. *tatu* armadillo + *pó* hand + *yu* yellow] **:** PELUDO

poz·nan \ˈpōzˌnan, -ˌnän, -ˌnən; ˈpäzˌnan, -ˌnən; ˈpȯzˌnän, -ˌän\ *adj, usu cap* [fr. *Poznán*, city in west central Poland] **:** of or from the city of Poznan, Poland **:** of the kind or style prevalent in Poznan

pozole *var of* POSOL

poz·zo·la·na \ˌpätsəˈlänə\ *or* **poz·zo·lan** \ˈpätsələn\ *also* **poz·zu·o·la·na** \ˌpütsəwəˈlänə\ *or* **puz·zo·lan** \ˈpütsələn\ *or* **puz·zo·la·na** \ˌpütsəˈlänə\ *n* -S [It *pozzolana* fr. ML *putheolana*, fr. L *puteolana*, fem. of *puteolanus*, adj., of or belonging to Puteoli, fr. *Puteoli* (now *Pozzuoli*), seaport in southern Italy + L *-anus* -an] **1 :** an aggregate material (as volcanic ash, tuff) used by the ancient Romans as an ingredient of mortar **2 :** any pulverulent siliceous or siliceous and aluminous substance that reacts chemically with slaked lime at ordinary temperature and in the presence of moisture to form a cementitious compound **3 :** a mortar or hydraulic cement consisting essentially of pozzolana and slaked lime — compare PORTLAND-POZZOLAN CEMENT

poz·zo·la·nic \ˌpätsəˈlänik\ *also* **puz·zo·la·nic** \ˌpüt-\ *or* **poz·zu·o·la·nic** \ˌpätsəwəˈl-\ *adj* **:** of, relating to, or having the properties of a pozzolana

pp *abbr* **1** pages **2** [L *papa*] pope **3** [L *patres*] fathers **4** pianissimo

PP *abbr* **1** parcel post **2** parish priest **3** part paid **4** parts per **5** past participle **6** peak to peak **7** pellagra preventive **8** *often not cap* [L *per procurationem*] by proxy or by the agency of **9** personal property **10** picked ports **11** [It *più piano*] more softly **12** postpaid **13** pounds pressure **14** power plant **15** prepaid **16** privately printed **17** [L *punctum proximum*] near point

PPA *abbr, often not cap* per power of attorney

p paper *n, usu cap 1st P* **:** perfect paper — compare M PAPER, N PAPER

PPC *abbr* **1** [Fr *pour prendre congé*] to take leave **2** *often not cap* picture postcard

ppd *abbr* **1** postpaid **2** prepaid

PPD *abbr* purified protein derivative

pp factor \ˈpēˈpē-\ *n, usu cap both Ps* [*pellagra-preventive factor*] **:** PELLAGRA-PREVENTIVE FACTOR

pph *abbr* pamphlet

PPI \ˌpē(ˌ)pēˈī\ *n* -S [*plan position indicator*] **:** a radarscope on which spots of light representing reflections of radar waves indicate the range and bearing of objects such as airplanes, ships, buildings, cliffs, and mountains

PPI *abbr, often not cap* **1** parcel post insured **2** policy proof of interest

ppl *abbr* participle

PPM *abbr, often not cap* parts per million

ppn *abbr* precipitation

ppp *abbr* pianissimo, double pianissimo

PPS *abbr* **1** parliamentary private secretary **2** [L *post postscriptum*] additional postscript **3** pulses per second

ppt *abbr* precipitate

pptn *abbr* precipitation

PQ *abbr* **1** personality quotient **2** previous question

pr *abbr* **1** pair **2** pounder **3** power **4** prayer **5** preferred **6** presbyopia **7** present **8** price **9** priest **10** primitive **11** prince **12** printed; printer **13** prior **14** private **15** pronoun **16** pronounced **17** pronunciation **18** prose **19** proved

PR *abbr* **1** parliamentary report **2** payroll **3** pitch ratio **4** [L *populus Romanus*] Roman people **5** press release **6** prize ring **7** proportional representation **8** [L *pro rata*] in proportion **9** public relations **10** [L *punctum remotum*] far point

Pr *symbol* **1** praseodymium **2** propyl

praam *var of* PRAM

prab·ble \ˈprabəl\ *n* -S [alter. of ²*brabble*] *chiefly dial* **:** QUARREL, SQUABBLE — often used in the phrase *pribbles and prabbles*

pra·bhu \ˈprə(ˌ)bü\ *n* -S [Skt, lit., excelling, mighty, fr. *prabhavati* he surpasses, is powerful, fr. *pra-* before + *bhavati* he becomes, is — more at FOR, BE] **1** *India* **:** LORD, CHIEF **2** *India* **:** a member of the writer caste in western India

¹prac·tic \ˈpraktik\ *adj* [ME *practik*, fr. MF *practique, pratique*, fr. LL *practicus* — more at PRACTICAL] **1 :** PRACTICAL **2** *obs* **:** PRACTICED, EXPERIENCED, SKILLED; *also* **:** CUNNING

²practic \ˈ"\ *n* -S [ME *practik*, fr. MF *practique, pratique*, fr. LL *practice*, fr. Gk *praktikē*, fr. fem. of *praktikos* practical — more at PRACTICAL] **1 :** PRACTICE **2** *also* **prac·tick** \ˈ"\ *Scots law* **:** the ancient reported decision of the Court of Session used to show the customary practices and law — usu. used in pl.

prac·ti·ca·bil·i·ty \ˌpraktəkəˈbiləd-ē, -tēk- -lətē, -i\ *n* **1 :** the quality or state of being practicable **2 :** something that is practicable

prac·ti·ca·ble \ˈpraktəkəbəl, -tēk-\ *adj* [modif. (influenced by *practic*) of F *praticable*, fr. MF, fr. *pratiquer* to practice (fr. *pratique* practice) + *-able* — more at PRACTIC] **1 :** possible to practice or perform **:** capable of being put into practice, done, or accomplished **:** FEASIBLE ⟨a ~ method⟩ ⟨a ~ aim⟩ **2 a :** capable of being used **:** USABLE ⟨a ~ weapon⟩ **b** *of a theatrical property* **:** that may be used as real ⟨a ~ door at the back of the stage⟩ **syn** see POSSIBLE

prac·ti·ca·ble·ness *n* -ES **:** PRACTICABILITY 1

prac·ti·ca·bly \-blē, -li\ *adv* **:** in a practicable manner **:** so as to be practicable

¹prac·ti·cal \ˈpraktəkəl, -tēk-\ *adj, sometimes* -ER/-EST [LL *practicus* practical (fr. Gk *praktikos*, fr. *praktos*, verbal of *prassein, prattein* to pass through or over, experience, transact, negotiate, practice) + *-ikos* -ic) + E *-al*; akin to Gk *peran* to pass through — more at FARE] **1 a :** actually or actively engaged in some course of action or occupation ⟨a ~ man but no theorist⟩ **b :** pursuing an occupation as a means of livelihood rather than as an avocation or sideline ⟨the conflicting views of ~ farmers and country gentlemen⟩ **2 a :** of, relating to, or consisting or manifested in practice or action — compare IDEAL, SPECULATIVE, THEORETICAL ⟨a ~ matter⟩ ⟨~ questions⟩ **b :** being such in practice, conduct, effect, or essential character **:** VIRTUAL ⟨our ~ freedom is better than your nominal liberty⟩ **3 :** available, usable, or valuable in practice or action **:** capable of being turned to use or account **:** USEFUL ⟨a ~ acquaintance with a language⟩ ⟨~ economy⟩ **4 a :** given or disposed to action as opposed to speculation or abstraction **b :** skillful or experienced from practice **:** evincing practice or skill **:** capable of applying knowledge to some useful end ⟨a ~ mind⟩ **c** (1) **:** qualified by practice or practical training but lacking the highest professional training ⟨the duties of ~ and graduate nurses⟩ (2) **:** designed to supplement theoretical training by experience ⟨~ work in the field or laboratory⟩ (3) *chiefly Brit* **:** concerned with or used in connection with practical training ⟨a ~ room⟩ ⟨~ examinations⟩ **5 :** aware of and willing to overlook or participate in chicaneries or irregularities **:** UNSCRUPULOUS ⟨a ~ politician who knew which side his bread was buttered on⟩ **6 :** PRACTICABLE 2b **7 :** PRACTICING ⟨a ~ Catholic⟩

²practical \ˈ"\ *n* -S **:** an examination requiring demonstration of some practical skill

practical art *n* **:** an art (as of handicraft) that serves ordinary or material needs — compare FINE ART, LIBERAL ARTS

practical astronomy *n* **:** a branch of astronomy dealing with the making of observations of the celestial bodies for navigation and other position-finding purposes on the earth — compare NAUTICAL ASTRONOMY

prac·ti·cal·ism \-kəˌlizəm\ *n* -S **:** devotion to practical matters

prac·ti·cal·ist \-ˌləst\ *n* -S **:** an advocate or adherent of what is practical

prac·ti·cal·i·ty \ˌpraktəˈkaləd-ē, -lətē, -i\ *n* -ES **1 :** the quality or state of being practical **2 :** a practical matter or an instance of being practical

prac·ti·cal·ize \ˈpraktəkəˌlīz\ *vt* -ED/-ING/-S **:** to make practical

practical joke *n* **:** a joke whose humor stems from the tricking or abuse of an individual placed somehow at a disadvantage

practical joker *n* **:** a person addicted to the perpetration of practical jokes

practical judgment *n* **:** a judgment as to action or fitness **:** a judgment of the practical reason **:** an ethical judgment

prac·ti·cal·ly \ˈpraktək(ə)lē, -tēk-, -li, *dial & rapid speech* ˈprakl-\ *adv* **1 :** not theoretically **:** REALLY ⟨~ worthless⟩ **2 :** by means of practice **:** by experience or experiment ⟨~ acquainted with a subject⟩ **3 a :** in actual practice or use **:** to all practical purposes though not entirely or absolutely **:** VIRTUALLY ⟨a ~ inert solution⟩ ⟨~ inexhaustible resources⟩ ⟨a ~ perfect fit⟩ **b :** NEARLY, ALMOST ⟨it rained ~ all night⟩ ⟨the bottle is ~ full⟩

practical music *n* **:** APPLIED MUSIC

prac·ti·cal·ness *n* -ES **:** PRACTICALITY 1

practical nurse *n* **:** a nurse that cares for the sick professionally without having the training or experience required of a registered nurse; *esp* **:** a person who has undergone training and obtained a license from a state or other legal authority qualifying her to provide routine care to the sick

practical politics *n pl but sing or pl in constr* **1 :** matter for concrete action as distinguished from theoretical discussion **2 :** political intrigue, scheming, or action involving dishonorable or dishonest dealings

practical reason *n* **1 :** reason concerned with the practical accomplishment of chosen ends — contrasted with *theoretical reason* **2** *Kantianism* **:** the action or office of reason in matters of the will; *specif* **:** the determination of the grounds or universal laws of voluntary action by reason

practical theology *n* **:** the branches of theological study that deal with the institutional activities of religion covering esp. homiletics, pastoral theology, church polity, science of church administration, and liturgics

practical unit *n* **:** any of various electric and magnetic units selected for convenience as to size for use in actual practical measurements

prac·ti·cant \ˈpraktəkənt\ *n* -S [ML *practicant-, practicans*, pres. part. of *practicare* to practice medicine, fr. *practice* practice — more at PRACTIC] **:** PRACTITIONER

¹prac·tice *or* **prac·tise** \ˈpraktəs\ *vb* -ED/-ING/-S [ME *practisen*, fr. MF *practiser, pratiser*, fr. *practique, pratique* practice + *-iser* -ize — more at PRACTIC] *vt* **1** *obs* **a :** to make use of **:** USE, EMPLOY **b :** FREQUENT, HAUNT **2 a :** to exercise oneself in for instruction or improvement or for the acquisition of discipline, proficiency, or dexterity ⟨*practiced* the piano every day⟩ **b :** to exercise (another) in something for similar purposes **:** TRAIN, DRILL ⟨*practicing* the children in penmanship⟩ **3 a** *archaic* **:** to carry on or engage in (an activity or process) **b** *obs* (1) **:** to work out (as a sum) (2) **:** to act in (a play) **c :** to do or perform often, customarily, or habitually **:** make a practice of **:** engage regularly in ⟨~ politeness and grace⟩ **4 a** *obs* **:** to put (as a law) into effect **b :** to give practical expression to **:** act in a manner consonant with ⟨a man who ~*s* the religion that he preaches⟩ **c :** to follow (as an art, profession, or trade) as a way of life **:** be professionally engaged in ⟨*practiced* medicine for 40 years⟩ **5** *obs* **a :** to bring about **:** be responsible for **:** cause to take place **b :** to scheme to bring about **:** PLAN, PLOT **c :** to make an effort (as to do or cause something) **:** TRY **6** *archaic* **:** CONSTRUCT ~ *vi* **1 :** ACT, OPERATE, PROCEED **2 :** to perform an act often or customarily in order to acquire proficiency or skill ⟨~ with the broadsword⟩ ⟨~ on the piano⟩ **3 :** to exercise or pursue an employment or profession (as medicine or law) actively **4** *archaic* **a :** to plan or scheme esp. for a bad purpose **:** use or try artifices or stratagems **:** PLOT, INTRIGUE ⟨he will ~ against thee by poison —Shak.⟩ **b :** to deal or treat with someone esp. for the purpose of influencing or winning over **:** NEGOTIATE **5 :** to do something habitually ⟨*practicing* is better than preaching⟩

syn PRACTICE, EXERCISE, and DRILL can mean in common to perform or cause to perform an act or series of acts repeatedly, esp. for the purpose of attaining dexterity. PRACTICE stresses doing, esp. habitually, regularly, or over and over, commonly for the attainment of skill ⟨*practice* good deeds⟩ ⟨*practicing* horrible customs —*Sociology & Social Research*⟩ ⟨*practice* scales on the piano⟩ ⟨*practice* golf strokes⟩ EXERCISE stresses a keeping in action or use and usu. presupposes a power which can be developed or strengthened by activity or manifest in practice ⟨*exercise* responsibility for the public safety while driving⟩ ⟨the reader is being asked to *exercise* taste —William Empson⟩ ⟨the power now contested was *exercised* by the first Congress —John Marshall⟩ It commonly also signifies practice of physical movement of some kind specifically for the attainment of health or physical vigor ⟨*exercise* each morning by walking to work⟩ DRILL connotes an intention of fixing physical or mental habits by repetition as of group movements in unison or grammatical rules ⟨*drill* a class in the fundamentals of table manners⟩ ⟨*drill* a group of army recruits in the manual of arms⟩ The distinctions between the nouns PRACTICE, EXERCISE, and DRILL may be derived from the distinctions between the corresponding verb uses ⟨the *practice* of witchcraft⟩ ⟨the *exercise* of reason⟩ ⟨an *exercise* for developing the shoulders⟩ ⟨*drill* in the manual of arms⟩ ⟨a *drill* in grammatical rules⟩

²practice *also* **practise** \ˈ"\ *n* -S **1 a** *obs* (1) **:** performance or operation of something **:** EXECUTION (2) **:** a mode of acting or proceeding **b :** actual performance or application of knowledge as distinguished from mere possession of knowledge **:** performance or application habitually engaged in; *usu* **:** repeated or customary action **:** USAGE ⟨the ~ of rising early or working hard⟩ **c** (1) **:** the usual mode or method of doing something ⟨the ~ is to use a local anesthetic⟩ (2) **practices** *pl* **:** habitual conduct that is socially, ethically, or otherwise unacceptable ⟨the unwholesome ~*s* of folk medicine⟩ ⟨departing these evil ~*s*⟩ **2 a** (1) *obs* **:** skillful or artful management **:** dexterity in contrivance or the use of means (2) **:** treacherous contriving; *also* **:** SCHEME, PLOT **b** *archaic* (1) **:** NEGOTIATION (2) **:** INTRIGUE **c** *archaic* **:** the act of using artifice or influence upon **:** imposing or working upon **3 a :** systematic exercise for instruction or discipline ⟨troops called out for ~⟩ ⟨~ makes perfect⟩ ⟨daily piano ~⟩ **b** *archaic* (1) **:** a practical treatise (2) **:** practical proficiency or skill acquired by systematic action or exercise ⟨this disease is beyond my ~ —Shak.⟩ **4 a :** the exercise of a profession or occupation ⟨the ~ of law⟩ **b :** professional business or work esp. as an incorporeal property ⟨a lucrative ~⟩ ⟨sold his ~⟩ **5 :** the form, manner, and order of conducting and carrying on suits and prosecutions through their various stages according to law **syn** see HABIT — **in practice** *adv* **1 a :** in actual or accepted usage **:** as a fact **b** *obs* **:** in customary or present use **:** in vogue **2 :** in such a condition as a result of practice as to be able to perform in an effective or superior manner ⟨athletes must keep *in practice*⟩ — **out of practice** *adv* **:** in such a condition as a result of lack of practice as to be unable to perform in an effective or superior way ⟨*out of practice* on the piano⟩

practice curve *n* **:** a graphic representation of change in performance as a function of practice

practiced *or* **practised** *adj* **1 :** EXPERIENCED, EXPERT, SKILLED ⟨a ~ marksman⟩ ⟨a ~ palate⟩ **2 :** tried or done habitually in order to acquire proficiency **:** learned by practice ⟨a ~ skill⟩ ⟨sat with ~ poise⟩ **3** *archaic* **:** used or frequented habitually

prac·ticed·ness *n* -ES **:** the quality or state of being practiced

prac·tic·er *or* **prac·tis·er** \-sə(r)\ *n* -S [ME *practisour*, fr. *practisen* + *-our* -or] **:** one that practices: as **a :** one that exercises a profession **:** PRACTITIONER **b :** a habitual performer of a particular act ⟨man as a maker and ~ of culture —T.D.McCown⟩; *esp* **:** an adherent of a faith or code of behavior ⟨a ~ of yogi⟩ **c :** SCHEMER, PLOTTER

practice school *n* **:** a demonstration school

practice teacher *n* **:** one doing practice teaching **:** STUDENT TEACHER

practice teaching *n* **:** teaching by a student preparing for a teaching career for the purpose of practicing educational skills and methods under the supervision of an experienced teacher

prac·ti·cian \prakˈtishən\ *n* -S [alter. (influenced by *practic*) of ME (Sc dial.) *praticiane*, fr. MF *praticien*, fr. *pratique* practice + *-ien* -ian — more at PRACTIC] **:** one acquainted or skilled by practice **:** a practiced or practical person; *also* **:** PRACTITIONER

prac·tic·ing *or* **prac·tis·ing** \ˈpraktəsiŋ, -sēŋ\ *adj* [ME *practesynge*, fr. pres. part. of *practisen* to practice — more at PRACTICE] **:** actively engaged in an indicated career or way of life ⟨a ~ physician⟩ ⟨~ Catholics⟩

practick *var of* PRACTIC

practics *pl of* PRACTIC

prac·ti·cum \ˈpraktəkəm, -tēk-\ *n* -S [G *praktikum*, fr. LL, neut. of *practicus* practical — more at PRACTICAL] **:** a unit of work done by an advanced university student that involves practical application of previously studied theory and the collection of data for future theoretical interpretation (as in practice teaching)

practise *var of* PRACTICE

prac·ti·tion·er \prakˈtish(ə)nə(r)\ *n* -S [*practition-* (alter. of *practician*) + *-er*] **1 :** one that exercises an art, science, or profession (as law, medicine, or engineering) — see GENERAL PRACTITIONER **2 :** one that does something or follows some course or regimen habitually or customarily **3** *obs* **:** one that practices something (as an art or a profession) to acquire or maintain proficiency **:** a learner or novice **4 :** one who engages in the public practice of Christian Science healing and applies it to human ills and problems

prad \ˈprad\ *n* -S [modif. of D *paard*, fr. MD *pert, paert, part*, fr. LL *paraveredus* post horse for secondary roads — more at PALFREY] *chiefly Austral* **:** HORSE

prae·ci·pe *or* **pre·ci·pe** \ˈprēsəˌpē, ˈpres-\ *n* -S [ME *precipe*, fr. ML, fr. L *praecipe*, imper. of *praecipere* to take beforehand, to give rules or precepts, admonish, enjoin — more at PRECEPT] **1 :** any of various legal writs commanding a person to do something or to appear and show cause why he should not **2 :** a written order addressed to the clerk or prothonotary of a court requesting the issuance of a specified writ and containing the pertinent information therefor

praecipe in cap·i·te \-inˈkapəˌtē\ *n* [NL] **:** a writ of right issuing from a Chancery Court in aid of a disseized tenant of land in chief holding immediately of the crown — compare PRAECIPE 1

prae·cip·u·um \prēˈsipyəwəm\ *n, pl* **praecip·ua** \-yəwə\ [L, fr. neut. of *praecipuus* taken beforehand, fr. *praecipere* to take beforehand — more at PRECEPT] **1** *Roman law* **:** a portion received from an inheritance before general distribution **2** *Scots law* **:** an additional share or bonus (as received by the eldest of several female heirs portioners)

prae·co·ces *or* **pre·co·ces** \ˈprekəˌsēz\ *n pl, often cap* [NL, fr. L *praecoces*, masc. & fem. pl. of L *praecoc-, praecox* ripe before its time, premature — more at PRECOCIOUS] **:** precocial birds

prae·cog·ni·tum \prēˈkägnəd-əm\ *n, pl* **praecogni·ta** \-d-ə\ [L, neut. of *praecognitus*, past part. of *praecognoscere* to foreknow — more at PRECOGNITION] **:** something known or that should be known in order to understand something else

prae·di·al *or* **pre·di·al** \ˈprēdēəl\ *adj* [ML *praedialis*, fr. L *praedium* + *-alis* -al] **1 :** being or made up of land or immovable property or the profits therefrom **:** LANDED — used chiefly with reference to the Roman and civil law systems and practically equivalent to the *real* of English law **2 :** of, relating to, or arising from land or landed property **:** attached to land ⟨~ slaves⟩ ⟨a ~ relationship⟩

praedial larceny *n* **:** theft of growing crops

praedial servitude *n, Roman & civil law* **:** a service, burden, or charge granted for the benefit of a tract of land affecting and exercised against another tract and resembling the easement at common law against a servient tenement in favor of a dominant tenement

praedial tithe *n* **:** a tithe payable out of farm produce or the products of the soil (as grain or firewood)

prae·di·um \ˈprēdēəm\ *n, pl* **prae·dia** \-dēə\ [L, fr. *praed-, praes* surety, bondsman — more at PREST] **:** landed property **:** a tenement of land — see PRAEDIUM RUSTICUM, PRAEDIUM URBANUM

praedium dom·i·nans \-ˈdäməˌnanz\ *n* [L, dominant praedium] **:** a dominant tenement, estate, or tract of land having the benefit of an easement or servitude exercisable against and affecting another tenement or tract

praedium rus·ti·ca·num \-ˌrəstəˈkānəm\ *n* [L, country praedium] *Roman, civil, & Scots law* **:** land upon which no building stands whether in town or country

praedium rus·ti·cum \-ˈrəstəkəm\ *n* [L, rustic praedium] *Roman & civil law* **:** land adapted to and used for agricultural or pastoral purposes — compare PRAEDIUM URBANUM

praedium ser·vi·ens \-ˈsərvēˌenz\ *n* [L, servient praedium] **:** the servient tenement, estate, or tract of land against which another dominant tenement, estate, or tract enjoys or exercises an easement or servitude

praedium ur·ba·num \-ˌərˈbānəm\ *n, pl* **praedia urba·na** \-nə\ [L, town praedium] *Roman, civil, & Scots law* **:** land, whether in town or country, upon which a house or other building stands and the land immediately adjacent thereto used for purposes incidental to the enjoyment of the buildings

praefect *var of* PREFECT

praejudiciary *var of* PREJUDICIARY

praelect *var of* PRELECT

prae·lec·tor *also* **pre·lec·tor** \prēˈlektə(r)\ *n* -S [NL, fr. LL *praelector* one that reads aloud and expounds upon an author, fr. L *praelectus* (past part. of *praelegere* to read aloud and expound) + *-or* — more at PRELECT] **1 :** a reader, lecturer, or professor in a college or university **2 :** a college officer (as in Cambridge University) in charge of presenting members of the college to the university for matriculation and graduation

prae·lu·di·um *or* **pre·lu·di·um** \prēˈlüdēəm\ *n, pl* **prae·lu·dia** *or* **pre·lu·dia** \-dēə\ [ML — more at PRELUDE] **:** PRELUDE

praemium *obs var of* PREMIUM

¹prae·mu·ni·re *or* **pre·mu·ni·re** \ˌprēmyəˈnīrē\ *n* -S [ME *praemunire* (*facias*), fr. ML, that you cause to warn (prominent words in the writ), fr. *praemunire* to warn (influenced in meaning by L *praemonēre* to forewarn) (fr. L, to fortify, fr. *prae-* pre- + *munire* to fortify) + *facias* that you cause — more at PREMONITION, MUNITION] **:** a legal writ charging an offense of procuring translations, processes, excommunications, bulls, or other actions or benefits from the pope against the king, his crown, and realm

²praemunire \ˈ"\ *vt* -ED/-ING/-S *archaic* **:** to prosecute for or convict of praemunire

¹prae·nes·tine \prēˈnestən\ *adj, usu cap* [L *Praenestinus*, fr. *Praeneste*, ancient city in Latium, Italy + L *-inus* -ine] **:** relating to or characteristic of the city of Praeneste ⟨the engraved cylindrical *Praenestine* cists⟩

²praenestine \ˈ"\ *n* -S *usu cap* **:** a language closely related to or a dialect of Latin known from a small body of inscriptions from as early as the 6th century B.C.

prae·no·men *or* **pre·no·men** \(ˈ)prēˈnōmən\ *n, pl* **praenomens** \-nz\ *or* **praenom·i·na** \-ˈnämənə, -ˈnōm-\ *or* **prenomens** *or* **prenomina** [L, *praenomen*, fr. *prae-* pre- + *nomen* name — more at NAME] **1 :** the first name of a person;

esp **:** the first of the usual three names of an ancient Roman by which he was distinguished from others of the same family ⟨in the name Marcus Tullius Cicero, Marcus is the ~⟩ — compare AGNOMEN, COGNOMEN, NOMEN **2 :** the first independent element of a name (as of a place or a biological species) ⟨in the binomial *Cynomys ludovicianus, Cynomys* is both generic name and ~⟩

praepositor *var of* PREPOSITOR

prae·pos·tor *or* **pre·pos·tor** \prē'pästə(r)\ *also* **prae·pos·i·tor** *or* **pre·pos·i·tor** \-äzət-\ *n* -s [ML *praepositor, praepostor,* fr. L *praepositus, praepostus* (past part. of *praeponere* to put in front, put in charge of) + *-or* — more at PREPOSITION] **:** a monitor at an English public school

praeses *var of* PRESES

praesidium *var of* PRESIDIUM

prae·tax·a·tion *or* **pre·tax·a·tion** \,prē,tak'sāshən\ *n* [ML *praetaxatus* (past part. of *praetaxare* to reckon beforehand, fr. *prae-* pre- + *taxare* to estimate, reckon) + E *-ion* — more at TAX] **:** the act or privilege of voting before others esp. as exercised by a small powerful group in selecting a monarch

praeter- — see PRETER-

prae·tex·ta *also* **pre·tex·ta** \prē'tekstə\ *n, pl* **praetex·tae** \-k,stē\ [L (toga) *praetexta,* lit., bordered toga, fr. *toga* + *praetexta,* fem. of *praetextus* bordered, fr. past part. of *praetexere* to weave in front, fringe, border — more at PRETEXT] **:** a white robe with a purple border orig. worn by an ancient Roman magistrate or priest and later by a Roman boy before he assumed the toga virilis or until about the end of his 14th year and by a girl until marriage

prae·tor *also* **pre·tor** \'prēd·ə(r), -ētə-\ *n* -s [ME *pretor,* fr. L *praetor,* prob. fr. *praeitus* (past part. of *praeire* to go ahead, lead the way, fr. *prae-* pre- + *ire* to go) + *-or* — more at ISSUE] **:** an ancient Roman magistrate ranking below a consul

prae·to·ri·al *also* **pre·to·ri·al** \prē'tōrēəl, prə'-, -tȯr-\ *adj* [L *praetorius* of a praetor + E *-al*] **:** PRAETORIAN

¹prae·to·ri·an *also* **pre·to·ri·an** \-rēən\ *adj* [L & LL *praetorianus,* fr. L *praetorius* of a praetor (fr. *praetor*) + *-anus* -an] **1 a :** of or relating to a Roman praetor **:** exercised by a praetor **b :** of, relating to, or created by the praetor's equitable power **2** *usu cap* **:** of, relating to, or constituting the bodyguard of a Roman emperor **3 :** resembling or characteristic of the Praetorian soldiers esp. in respect to corruption or political venality

²praetorian *also* **pretorian** \"\ *n* -s **1 :** a person (as an ex-praetor) of praetorian rank **2** *usu cap* **:** a soldier of the Praetorian Guard **3 :** a defender of an established order **:** CONSERVATIVE

praetorian cohort *n* **1 :** a picked body of troops that formed the guard of a praetor, or of a general in command of an army under the Roman republic **2** *usu cap P* **:** a cohort of the Praetorian Guard

praetorian guard *n, usu cap P&G* **:** a member of the bodyguard of the emperor of ancient Rome instituted by Augustus and consisting at first of 9 and later of 10 cohorts and coming to have great power in the making and unmaking of emperors until suppressed by Constantine in A.D. 312

prae·to·ri·an·ism \=ˈ=rēə,nizəm\ *n* -s **:** a corrupt military despotism

praetorian law *n* [trans. of L *jus praetorium*] *Roman law* **:** a system of equity developed by the praetors after their acquisition about 149 B.C. of criminal jurisdiction providing for their right to allow an action not provided for by law, their right to disallow an action that would strictly lie by the jus civile, and their right to allow an equitable defense where no defense was provided by law

prae·to·ri·um *also* **pre·to·ri·um** \prē'tōrēəm\ *n* -s [L *praetorium,* fr. neut. of *praetorius* of a praetor — more at PRAETORIAN] **1 a :** an ancient Roman general's tent in a camp **b :** a council of war held in such a tent **2 a :** the official residence of an ancient Roman governor **b :** a splendid countryseat or a palatial residence esp. in ancient Rome

prae·tor·ship *also* **pre·tor·ship** \'prēd·ə(r),ship\ *n* **:** the office or period of office of a praetor

¹prag·mat·ic \prag'mad·|ik, praig-, -mat|, |ēk\ *n* -s [in sense 1, fr. LL *pragmatica (sanctio),* fr. L *pragmatica* (fem. of *pragmaticus,* adj.) + *sanctio* decree; in sense 2, fr. L *pragmaticus,* fr. *pragmaticus,* adj.; in sense 3, fr. ²*pragmatic*] **1 :** PRAGMATIC SANCTION **2** *obs* **:** one skilled in affairs or business **3 :** an officiously busy person **:** MEDDLER, BUSYBODY

²pragmatic \(')=¦==\ *adj* [L *pragmaticus* skilled in law or business, fr. Gk *pragmatikos,* fr. *pragmat-, pragma* deed, affair (fr. *prassein, prattein* to pass through, experience, practice) + *-ikos* -ic — more at PRACTICAL] **1 :** of or relating to the affairs of a community or state — compare PRAGMATIC SANCTION **2 :** active in affairs **:** BUSY; *often* **:** OFFICIOUS, MEDDLING **3 :** stiff in one's opinion **:** CONCEITED, OPINIONATED, DOGMATIC **4 :** PRACTICAL, MATTER-OF-FACT **5 :** dealing with events in such a manner as to show their interconnection **6 a** *Kantianism* **:** prescribing the means necessary to the attainment of happiness **b :** of or relating to philosophic pragmatism; *esp* **:** of or relating to the philosophic pragmatism of Peirce, James, and Dewey

prag·mat·i·ca \prag'mad·əkə\ *n, pl* **pragmati·cae** \-d·ə,sē\ *or* **pragmaticas** [Sp *pragmática,* fr. LL *pragmatica (sanctio)*] **:** PRAGMATIC SANCTION

prag·mat·i·cal \(')prag¦mad·|əkəl, -raig-, -at|, |ēk-\ *adj* [L *pragmaticus* + E *-al*] **1** *archaic* **:** PRAGMATIC 1 **2 :** of, relating to, or concerned with the practice or the practical side of anything **:** PRACTICAL, MATTER-OF-FACT **3** *obs* **:** of, relating to, or experienced in business or affairs **:** ACTIVE, BUSINESSLIKE, ENERGETIC, SKILLED **4 :** objectionably busy **:** FORWARD, OFFICIOUS, MEDDLESOME; *also* **:** CONCEITED, DOGMATIC **5 :** PRAGMATIC 6 b

prag·mat·i·cal·i·ty \prag,mad·ə'kaləd·ē\ *n* -ES **:** the quality or state of being pragmatical

prag·mat·i·cal·ly \(')prag¦mad·|ək(ə)lē, -raig-, -at|, |ēk-, -li\ *adv* **:** so as to be pragmatic or pragmatical **:** in a pragmatic or pragmatical manner

prag·mat·i·cal·ness *n* -ES **:** the quality or state of being pragmatic

pragmatic anthropology *n, Kantianism* **:** practical ethics

prag·mat·i·cism \prag'mad·ə,sizəm\ *n* -s **1 :** PRAGMATICALNESS **2 :** the philosophic doctrine of C.S.Peirce

prag·mat·i·cist \-.səst\ *n* -s **:** an advocate of pragmaticism

pragmatic maxim *n* **:** a statement of principle in the pragmaticism of Charles S. Peirce: in order to ascertain the meaning of an intellectual conception one should consider what practical consequences might conceivably result by necessity from the truth of that conception and the sum of these consequences will constitute the entire meaning of the conception

prag·mat·ics \prag'mad·iks\ *n pl but sing or pl in constr* **:** a branch of semiotic that deals with the relation between signs or linguistic expressions and their users — distinguished from *semantics* and *syntactics*

pragmatic sanction *n* [trans. of LL *pragmatica sanctio*] **1 :** an imperial constitution or decree answering a request or petition of a college, municipality, or other public body of the Byzantine Empire concerning its public affairs **2 :** a solemn decree issued by the head of a state on a weighty matter and having the force of a fundamental law

prag·ma·tism \'pragmə,tizəm, 'praig-\ *n* -s [²*pragmatic* + *-ism*] **1 :** pedantic assertiveness **:** DOGMATISM, OFFICIOUSNESS **2 :** practical treatment of things **:** MATTER-OF-FACTNESS **3 :** the pragmatic or philosophical method in the treatment of history or literature **4 a :** emphasis in philosophical thought on the application of ideas or the practical bearings of conceptions and beliefs **b :** an American movement in philosophy founded by Peirce and James and marked by the doctrines that the meaning of conceptions is to be sought in their practical bearings, that the function of thought is as a guide to action, and that the truth is preeminently to be tested by the practical consequences of belief

¹prag·ma·tist \-məd·əst, -mətəst\ *n* -s [²*pragmatic* + *-ist*] **:** one who is pragmatic: as **a :** BUSYBODY **b :** an adherent of pragmatism

²pragmatist \"\ *adj* **:** PRAGMATISTIC

prag·ma·tis·tic \¦==¦tistik\ *adj* **:** of, relating to, or constituting pragmatism

prag·ma·tize \'==,tīz\ *vt* -ED/-ING/-S [Gk *pragmat-, pragma* deed, affair + E *-ize*] **:** to consider, represent, or embody (something unreal) as fact **:** MATERIALIZE, RATIONALIZE —

prag·ma·tiz·er \-zə(r)\ *n* -s

prague \'präg *sometimes* 'prāg\ *adj, usu cap* [fr. *Prague,* Czechoslovakia] **:** of or from Prague, the capital of Czechoslovakia **:** of the kind or style prevalent in Prague

¹pragu·i·an \-gēən\ *adj, usu cap* [*Prague,* Czechoslovakia, the focal point of the *Cercle Linguistique de Prague* (Prague Linguistic Circle) + E *-ian*] **:** of or relating to a group of linguists and literary scholars noted for important advances in theory and procedure esp. in phonemics and textual analysis made between World War I and World War II

²praguian \"\ *n* -s *usu cap* **:** a member or adherent of the Praguian group of linguists and literary scholars

prahu *var of* PRAU

prai·ri·al \'prerēəl\ *adj* [F, fr. *prairie* + *-al*] **:** of or relating to prairies or to prairie land

prai·rie \'prerē, -ri *also* 'pra(a)r- *or* 'prār-, *chiefly substand* pə'r-\ *n* -s *often attrib* [F, fr. OF *praerie,* fr. (assumed) VL *prataria,* fr. L *pratum* meadow + *-aria* -ary; akin to L *pravus* crooked, wrong, bad, MIr *ráth, ráith* earthworks, fortification MW bed*rawt* grave mound] **1 :** a meadow or tract of grassland: as **a :** an extensive tract of level or rolling land in the Mississippi valley characterized in general by a deep fertile soil and except where cultivated by a covering of tall coarse grasses mostly without trees — compare PAMPA, PLAIN, SAVANNA, STEPPE **b :** one of the plateaus into which the prairies proper merge on the west and whose treeless state is due to dryness **c :** a low sandy wet and often water-covered grass-grown tract in the Florida pinewoods **2 :** a light yellowish brown that is stronger and slightly redder and lighter than khaki, darker and slightly yellower than walnut brown, and slightly darker than manila

prairie acacia *n* **:** a low thornless No. American shrub (*Acacia angustissima*) with feathery leaves and globose heads of yellow flowers

prairie alligator *n, chiefly Midland* **:** STICK INSECT

prairie anemone *n* **:** a pasqueflower (*Pulsatilla ludoviciana*)

prairie ant *n* **:** any of several ants inhabiting prairies; *esp* **:** a common ant (*Pogonomyrmex occidentalis*) of the central plains of the U.S.

prairie antelope *n* **:** PRONGHORN

prairie apple *n* **1 :** BREADROOT 1 **2 :** an earth plum of the genus *Geoprumnon*

prairie aster *n* **:** a violet-flowered perennial aster (*Aster turbinellus*) of the central U.S. having solitary heads

prairie bass *n* **:** BOWFIN

prairie bean *n* **1 :** METCALFE BEAN **2 :** BUSH PEA

prairie beardgrass *n* **:** a bunchgrass (*Andropogon scoparius*)

prairie berry *n* **:** TROMPILLO

prairie bird *n* **:** any of several birds that frequent open grasslands (as the horned lark or the prairie chicken)

prairie bird's-foot trefoil *n* **:** an annual No. American herb (*Lotus americanus*) with red or rose-colored flowers

prairie bitters *n pl but sing or pl in constr* **:** a drink of buffalo gall in water used in folk medicine

prairie brant *n* **:** WHITE-FRONTED GOOSE

prairie breaker *n* **:** a plow with a long low moldboard that is designed to cut a wide shallow furrow (as in virgin sod) and turn the slice completely over

prairie brown *n* **:** a brownish orange that is less strong and slightly yellower and lighter than spice and slightly redder and darker than Windsor tan, Titian, amber brown, or gold pheasant

prairie button snakeroot *n* **:** KANSAS GAY-FEATHER

prairie chicken *or* **prairie fowl** *or* **prairie grouse** *n* **1 a :** a grouse (*Tympanuchus cupido pinnatus*) of the Mississippi valley from Manitoba to Texas having the upper part streaked and spotted with rufous and black and the underparts white evenly barred with blackish and on each side of the neck a patch of bare inflatable skin — called also *greater prairie chicken* **b :** a smaller similar bird (*T. pallidicinctus*) of western Texas — called also *lesser prairie chicken;* compare HEATH HEN **2 :** SHARP-TAILED GROUSE

prairie clover *n* **:** a plant of the genus *Petalostemon*

prairie cock *n* **:** a male prairie chicken

prairie coneflower *n* **:** a plant of the genus *Ratibida; esp* **:** a rough perennial herb (*R. columnifera* or *Lepachys columnifera* or *Obelisteca columnifera*) with a yellow head of few rays but an elongated disk of tubular flowers

prairie cordgrass *n* **:** a cordgrass (*Spartina pectinata*) of No. America having leaves with scarious margins and glumes with long awns

prairie crab *or* **prairie crab apple** *n* **:** IOWA CRAB

prairie crocus *n, chiefly Midland* **:** PASQUEFLOWER

prai·ried \'prerēd\ *adj* **:** having prairies

prairie dock *n* **1 :** a tall weedy compass plant (*Silphium terebinthinaceum*) with broad heads of yellow ray flowers **2 :** AMERICAN FEVERFEW

prairie dog *also* **prairie marmot** *n* **:** a colonial American burrowing rodent (genus *Cynomys*) related to the ground squirrels and marmots; *esp* **:** a stocky gregarious rodent (*C. ludovicianus*) of the plains of western No. America from Montana to northern Mexico that is plain grayish or reddish buff with a black tip to the tail — see PRAIRIE DOG TOWN

prairie dog

prairie dog town *n* **:** a group of associated burrows of the prairie dog often opening from a common mound or hillock

prairie-dog weed *n* **:** FETID MARIGOLD

prairie dropseed *n* **:** a grass (*Sporobolus heterolepis*) chiefly of the prairies of No. America having ovoid panicles, very long narrow leaves, and the second glume of each spikelet with a carinate tip

prairie falcon *n* **:** a falcon (*Falco mexicanus*) that resembles the Old World lanner and is about 18 inches long, pale grayish brown above, and white streaked with brown below

prairie false boneset *n* **:** a perennial herb (*Kuhnia glutinosa*) having oblong or lanceolate 3-ribbed leaves that are densely puberulent beneath

prairie fire *n* **1 :** INDIAN PAINTBRUSH 1 **2 :** a fire in open grassland

prairie flax *n* **:** a western No. American perennial flax (*Linum lewisii*) having blue flowers in a few-flowered inflorescence

prairie fox *n* **:** KIT FOX

prairie goose *n* **:** HUTCHINS'S GOOSE

prairie gourd *n* **:** a perennial gourd (*Cucurbita foetidissima*) of dry parts of the central and southwestern U.S. and Mexico that has a thick fusiform taproot, ovate to slightly lobed leaves, and a small hard smooth bitter green-and-orange fruit

prairie grain wireworm *n* **:** a wireworm that is the larva of an elaterid beetle (*Ctenicera destructor*) and that is often highly destructive to sprouting grains, esp. wheat

prairie grass *n* **1 :** any of several grasses found on the prairies of the U.S. (as *Sporobolus Cryptandrus* and *Sphenopholis obtusata*) **2** *Austral* **:** RESCUE GRASS

prairie grub *n* **:** HOP TREE

prairie hare *n* **:** WHITE-TAILED JACKRABBIT

prairie hay *n* **:** hay made from native prairie grass

prairie hen *n* **1 :** PRAIRIE CHICKEN **2 :** CLAPPER RAIL

prairie horned lark *n* **:** a horned lark (*Otocoris alpestris praticola*) of east-central No. America with a pale yellow or whitish throat and white patches over and behind the eyes

prairie indigo *n* **:** a stocky glaucous white-flowered false indigo (*Baptisia leucantha*) of the Mississippi drainage

prairie june grass *n, usu cap J* **:** JUNE GRASS 2

prairie lily *n* **1 :** WESTERN RED LILY **2 :** a rough-hairy perennial herb (*Nuttallia decapetala*) with a solitary yellowish white flower **3 :** EVENING STAR 2

prairie lotus *or* **prairie trefoil** *n* **:** PRAIRIE BIRD'S-FOOT TREFOIL

prairie mallow *n* **:** MOSS ROSE 1 b

prairie mimosa *n* **:** a glabrous perennial herb (*Desmanthus illinoensis*) of the prairies of No. America with fruits in dense globose heads

prairie mole *n* **:** a large mole (*Scalopus aquaticus machrinus*) of the north-central U.S.

prairie orchid *n* **:** a fringed orchis (*Habenaria leucophaea*) of boggy or wet lands chiefly of the north-central U.S. that bears lax racemes of very fragrant creamy or greenish white flowers

prairie owl *n* **1 :** BURROWING OWL **2 :** SHORT-EARED OWL

prairie oyster *n* **1 :** a raw egg or egg yolk taken whole with seasoning, vinegar, and sometimes brandy esp. as a pick-me-up **2** *chiefly dial* **:** a testis of a bull calf used as food — compare MOUNTAIN OYSTER

prairie peppergrass *n* **:** a weedy No. American peppergrass (*Lepidium densiflorum*) chiefly of the central and western U.S.

prairie phlox *n* **:** a No. American perennial herb (*Phlox pilosa*) with ciliate lanceolate leaves and a terminal corymb of pink, purple, or white flowers

prairie pigeon *n* **1 :** UPLAND PLOVER **2 :** GOLDEN PLOVER **3 :** PECTORAL SANDPIPER

prairie pine *n* **:** a gayfeather (*Liatris spicata*)

prairie pink *n* **:** SKELETON WEED 2 a

prairie plover *n* **1 :** UPLAND PLOVER **2 :** GOLDEN PLOVER **3 :** MOUNTAIN PLOVER

prairie plum *n* **:** CHICKASAW PLUM

prairie pointer *n* **:** SHOOTING STAR 2

prairie potato *or* **prairie turnip** *n* **:** BREADROOT 1

prairie ragweed *n* **:** BURWEED MARSH ELDER

prairie rattlesnake *or* **prairie rattler** *n* **:** any of several moderate-sized rattlesnakes that are varieties of a species (*Crotalus viridis*) and are widely distributed esp. between the Mississippi river and the Rocky mountains

prairie rocket *n* **1 :** any of several western American cruciferous herbs of the genus *Cheiranthus* having large yellow flowers **2 :** any of several plants of the genus *Erysimum*

prairie rose *n* **:** a climbing rose (*Rosa setigera*) chiefly of the central U.S. having usu. trifoliolate leaves and large pink flowers that fade to white

prairies *pl of* PRAIRIE

prairie sabbatia *n* **:** a prairie herb (*Sabbatia campestris*) with ovate-lanceolate leaves and solitary lilac-colored flowers

prairie sage *n* **:** a perennial cottony-white herb (*Artemisia gnaphalodes*) with numerous small paniculate heads of yellowish flowers

prairie sagewort *n* **:** a wormwood (*Artemisia frigida*) that is a silky-leaved aromatic subshrub of dry northerly parts of the northern hemisphere

prairie schooner *or* **prairie wagon** *n* **:** a broad-wheeled covered wagon made smaller than a Conestoga wagon with a body having less upward curve toward the ends and used by pioneers in cross-country travel

prairie schooner

prairie senna *n* **:** SENSITIVE PEA

prairie smoke *n* **1 :** a No. American perennial herb (*Geum triflorum*) with basal pinnate leaves, purple flowers, and plume-tipped fruit **2 :** PASQUEFLOWER

prairie soil *n* **:** a zonal group of soils developed in a temperate relatively humid climate under tall grass and characterized by a dark brown or grayish brown surface horizon that grades through brown soil to the lighter colored parent material at two to five feet

prairie spurge *n* **:** a wiry weedy annual spurge (*Chamaesyce nuttallii*) of the central and southwestern U.S. with bright green foliage and greenish white axillary solitary flowers

prairie squirrel *n* **:** any of various ground squirrels (as *Citellus franklini, C. tridecemlineatus,* and *C. richardsoni*) of the prairies of western No. America

prairie star *n* **:** WOODLAND STAR

prairie sunflower *n* **1 :** an annual sunflower (*Helianthus petiolaris*) with rather slender usu. branching stems that is common in the central U.S. **2 :** SHOWY SUNFLOWER

prairie titlark *n* **:** a common and widely distributed pipit (*Anthus spinoletta rubescens*) of No. America

prairie vetchling *n* **:** an everlasting pea (*Lathyrus decaphyllus*) of the central U.S. with erect leaflets, angled stems, and showy purple flowers

prairie violet *n* **:** a stemless violet (*Viola pedatifida*) of central No. America with palmately divided leaves and violet-colored flowers

prairie wake-robin *n* **:** a perennial trillium (*Trillium recurvatum*) of the central U.S. with a dark purple sessile flower

prairie warbler *n* **:** a small warbler (*Dendroica discolor*) of eastern No. America that has the back olive green spotted with rufous, the underparts yellow, and the sides of the head and body streaked with black

prairieweed \'==,=\ *n* **:** a shrubby cinquefoil (*Potentilla fruticosa*) that is sometimes a pernicious weed esp. on wet limy soil

prairie white-fringed orchid *n* **:** PRAIRIE ORCHID

prairie willow *n* **:** a slender shrubby but highly variable willow (*Salix humilis*) of dry lands and barrens of No. America having elliptical leaves with toothed or crinkled margins

prairie wolf *n* **:** COYOTE

prairie wool *n* **:** native prairie herbage cured and dried in nature

prai·ril·lon \prā'rilyən, pre'rilən\ *n* -s [AmerF, dim. of F *prairie* — more at PRAIRIE] **:** a small prairie

prais·able \'prāzəbəl\ *adj* [ME *preisable,* fr. *preisen* to praise + *-able*] **:** PRAISEWORTHY — **prais·able·ness** *n* -ES — **prais·ably** \-blē\ *adv*

¹praise \'prāz\ *vb* -ED/-ING/-S [ME *preisen, praisen,* fr. MF *preisier* to prize, value, praise, fr. LL *pretiare* (often spelled *preciare* in later MSS) to value, prize, fr. L *pretium* price, value — more at PRICE] *vt* **1 a :** to express approbation of **:** EXTOL, COMMEND, APPLAUD ⟨*praised* beyond his merits⟩ **b :** to glorify (a god or a saint) by homage and ascription of perfections esp. in song **:** LAUD, MAGNIFY ⟨~ him . . . all his host —Ps 148:2 (RSV)⟩ **2 a** *archaic* **:** to determine the worth of **:** APPRAISE **b** *obs* **:** to hold in esteem **:** VALUE, PRIZE **3** *obs* **:** to win or gain praise or commendation for **~** *vi* **:** to express praise **:** make laudatory comments

²praise \"\ *n* -s [ME *preyse,* fr. *preisen, praisen,* v.] **1 a :** an act of praising **:** the quality or state of being praised **:** commendation for worth or excellence **:** approval expressed **:** honor rendered because of excellence or worth **:** LAUDATION **b :** the act of glorifying or extolling God or a god **:** WORSHIP; *esp* **:** worship by song as distinguished from prayer and other acts ⟨a service of ~⟩ **2** *archaic* **:** an object, subject, ground, or reason of praise ⟨he is your ~; he is your God —Deut 10:21 (RSV)⟩

praise·ful \-zfəl\ *adj* [ME *preiseful, praiseful,* fr. *preisen, praisen* + *-ful*] **1** *archaic* **:** meriting praise **:** LAUDABLE **2 :** full of, abounding in, or giving praise **:** LAUDATORY — **praise·ful·ly** \-fəlē, -li\ *adv* — **praise·ful·ness** *n* -ES

praise house *n* **:** a small meetinghouse usu. in the southeastern U.S. where religious services consisting mainly of song are held mostly during week-nights as a supplement to Sunday church services

praise·less \-zləs\ *adj* **:** receiving or meriting no praise

praise meeting *n* **:** a religious service mainly of song and often of a joyous informal nature

prais·er \-zə(r)\ *n* -s [ME *preiser, praiser,* fr. *preisen, praisen* to praise + *-er*] **:** one that praises: as **a** *obs* **:** APPRAISER **b :** LAUDER, EULOGIST **c :** WORSHIPER

praise·worth·i·ly \'prāz,wərthəlē\ *adv* **:** in a praiseworthy manner **:** so as to be praiseworthy or to have a praiseworthy result

praise·worth·i·ness \-thēnəs\ *n* -ES **:** the quality or state of being praiseworthy

praiseworthy \'=,==\ *adj* [²*praise* + *worthy*] **:** deserving of praise **:** CREDITABLE, LAUDABLE, WORTHY

prais·ing·ly *adv* **:** in a praising manner **:** with praise

praiss \'prēs\ *n* -ES [F, prob. fr. *presser* to press — more at PRESS] **:** a fluid extract of tobacco **:** the juice of tobacco **:** TOBACCO WATER

praj·na \'prəjnə\ *n* -S [Skt *prajñā*, fr. *prajānāti* he knows, fr. *pra-* before, forward + *jānāti* he knows — more at KNOW] **:** transcendental wisdom or supreme knowledge in Buddhism gained through intuitive insight

pra·ka·ra·na \prə'karənə\ *n* -S [Skt, production, creation, discussion, topic, prakarana, fr. *prakaroti* he makes, produces, accomplishes] **:** a drama of India involving fictional situations from ordinary life

pra·krit \'prä,krit\ *n* -S *cap* [Skt *prākṛta*, fr. *prākṛta*, natural, usual, vulgar, fr. *prakṛti* original form, nature, fr. *prakaroti* he produces, fr. *pra-* before, forward + *karoti* he does, makes — more at FOR, KARMA] **1 :** any or all of the ancient Indic languages or dialects other than Sanskrit including Magadhi, Maharashtri, Sauraseni, Ardhamagadhi **2 :** any of the modern Indic languages

prak·ri·ti \'prəkrəd·ē\ *n* -S [Skt *prakṛti*] **1 :** unmanifested cosmic energy or potential matter that in Sankhya philosophy is constituted of the three gunas and that in contact with purusha produces a disequilibrium among the gunas which in turn results in the production of the manifested world **2 :** the phenomenal world **:** MATTER, NATURE

pra·krit·ic \prə'krid·ik\ *adj* **1** *usu cap* **:** relating to, from, or resembling Prakrit **2** *sometimes cap* **:** VERNACULAR, DIALECTIC

pral·a·ya \'prələyə\ *n* -S *usu cap* [Skt, lit., end, destruction] **:** a period of dissolution or destruction of the manifested universe at the end of a kalpa according to Hindu philosophy **:** the end of the world

pra·line \'prä,lēn, 'prā,- *also* 'prā,- *or* 'prō,- *or* ='=\ *n* -S [F, after Field Marshal César de Choiseul, Count Plessis-*Praslin* †1675 Fr. soldier whose cook invented the confection] **1 :** a confection of nut kernels: **a :** almonds roasted in boiling sugar until brown and crisp and sometimes pulverized or made into a paste **b :** a round patty of creamy brown sugar containing pecan meats **2 :** DARK BEAVER

prall·tril·ler \'präl-,trilə(r)\ *n* -S [G, fr. *prallen* to rebound (alter. — influenced by MHG *pralte*, past, & *gepralt*, past part. — of MHG *prellen*) + *triller* trill, fr. It *trillo*; akin to LG *prall* full, tight, OFris *pralling* testicle — more at TRILL] **:** a melodic musical grace made by a quick alternation of a principal tone with an upper auxiliary tone — called also *inverted mordent*

pralltriller: *1* as written, *2* as performed

¹pram *also* **praam** \'prăm\ *n* -S [D *praam*, fr. MD *praem*; akin to MLG *prām* pram] **:** a small lightweight nearly flat-bottomed boat that has very broad transom and usu. squared-off bow, is of lapstrake construction or now often of molded plywood or plastic, is designed for use with oars, sail, or outboard motor, and is of Scandinavian origin though now widely used as a tender for larger boats

²pram \'pram\ *n* -S *often attrib* [by shortening & alter. fr. *perambulator*] **1** *chiefly Brit* **:** PERAMBULATOR **:** BABY CARRIAGE **2** *chiefly Brit* **:** a milkman's handcart

³pram \"\ *vt* **prammed; prammed; pramming; prams** *chiefly Brit* **:** to air or take about (as a child) in or as if in a baby carriage

pram·ni·an \'pramnēən\ *adj, usu cap* [L *Pramnius* Pramnian (fr. Gk *Pramnios*) + E *-an*] **:** being a strong ancient Greek wine

pra·na \'pränə\ *n* -S [Skt *prāṇa*, lit., breath, fr. *pra-* before, forward + *aniti* he breathes — more at FOR, ANIMATE] **:** a life breath or vital principle in Vedic and later Hindu religion **:** any of the three or more vital currents **:** the principle of life moving in the human body

¹prance \'pran(t)s, -raa(ə)n-, -rain-, -răn-\ *vb* -ED/-ING/-S [ME *prauncen*] *vi* **1** *of a quadruped* **:** to spring or bound from the hind legs or move by so doing — used esp. of a mettlesome horse **2 :** to ride or drive a prancing horse **:** cause one's horse to prance while riding or driving often to attract attention or as an expression of exuberant feelings **3 a :** to walk or progress with ostentation or parade **:** SWAGGER ⟨*pranced* out of the room in a dudgeon⟩ **b :** DANCE, CAPER **~** *vt* **:** to cause (a horse) to prance

²prance \"\ *n* -S **:** an act or instance of prancing: as **a :** a prancing movement; *esp* **:** a sharp forward raising of alternate knees with well-extended toes in dancing **b :** SWAGGER

prance·ful \-sfəl\ *adj* **:** SPIRITED, DASHING

pranc·er \-sə(r)\ *n* -S **:** one that prances: as **a :** HORSE; *esp* **:** a mettlesome or fiery horse **b :** a rider of a spirited horse **c :** DANCER, CAPERER

pranc·ing·ly *adv* **:** in a prancing manner

prancy \-sē\ *adj* -ER/-EST **:** characterized by prancing **:** inclined to prance

pran·di·al \'prandēəl\ *adj* [L *prandium* late breakfast, luncheon (perh. fr. *pram-* early + *-dium*, fr. the stem of *edere* to eat) + E *-al*; akin to Goth *fruma* first — more at FOREMOST, EAT] **:** of or relating to a meal (as dinner) — usu. used in combination ⟨*preprandial* potations⟩ ⟨*postprandial* oratory⟩

pran·di·al·ly \-lē\ *adv* **:** at or over a meal

prandtl number \'prănt^əl\ *n, usu cap P* [after Ludwig *Prandtl* †1953 Ger. physicist; trans. of G *Prandtlsche zahl*] **:** the ratio of the product of the coefficient of viscosity and the specific heat at constant pressure to the thermal conductivity in fluid flow used esp. in the study of heat transfer in mechanical devices

¹prang \'praŋ\ *vb* -ED/-ING/-S [imit.] *vt* **1** *slang chiefly Brit* **:** to damage or destroy by aerial bombing ⟨~*ing* shore installations⟩ **2** *slang chiefly Brit* **:** to cause (an airplane) to crash **3** *slang chiefly Brit* **:** to bump into **:** STRIKE, HIT ⟨~*ed* the other car⟩ ⟨~*ed* his sister with a stick⟩ **~** *vi, slang chiefly Brit* **:** to perform an action of pranging; *esp* **:** to crash an airplane

²prang \"\ *n* -S *slang chiefly Brit* **:** CRASH

¹prank \'praŋk, -ai-\ *vt* -ED/-ING/-S [ME *pranken*] *obs* **:** to make pleats in **:** FOLD

²prank \"\ *vi* -ED/-ING/-S [origin unknown] **1** *dial chiefly Eng* **:** PRANCE **2** *obs* **:** to play tricks maliciously or in the performance of magic **3 :** to play pranks **:** cut up **:** FROLIC

³prank \"\ *n* -S **:** TRICK: **a** *obs* **:** a malicious or harmful act **b** *archaic* **:** a spell or act of magic or conjuring **:** a bit of sleight of hand **c :** a gay or sportive action **:** a ludicrous or mildly mischievous act **:** FROLIC, CAPER, PRACTICAL JOKE ⟨sent the child's painting to the academy as a ~⟩

⁴prank \"\ *vb* -ED/-ING/-S [prob. fr. D *pronken* to strut, show off, get dressed up, fr. MD; akin to MLG *prunken* to strut, show off, MHG *gebrunkel* glitter of metal] *vt* **1 :** to adorn in a gay or showy manner **:** dress or equip ostentatiously ⟨~*ed* herself out in her best⟩ **2 :** ADORN, DECK, SPANGLE ⟨flowers ~*ing* the meadow⟩ — often used with *with* ⟨a book ~*ed* with pretty fancies⟩ **~** *vi* **:** to make ostentatious show

prank·er \-kə(r)\ *n* -S [²prank + *-er*] **1** *archaic* **:** PRANCER **2 :** PRANKSTER

prank·ful \-kfəl\ *adj* [³prank + *-ful*] **:** full of or given to pranks **:** MISCHIEVOUS

prank·i·ness \-kēnəs\ *n* -ES **:** the quality or state of being pranky

prank·ing·ly *adv* **:** in a pranking manner **:** SHOWILY, OSTENTATIOUSLY

prank·ish \-kish\ *adj* [³prank + *-ish*] **1 :** full of pranks **:** FROLICSOME ⟨a ~ boy⟩ **2 :** being or having the nature of a prank ⟨a ~ trick⟩ — **prank·ish·ly** *adv* — **prank·ish·ness** *n* -ES

pran·kle \-kəl\ *vi* [freq. of ²prank] *archaic* **:** to prance or caper lightly

prank·some \-ksəm\ *adj* [³prank + *-some*] **:** PRANKISH 1

prank·ster \-kstə(r)\ *n* -S [³prank + *-ster*] **:** a player of pranks; *often* **:** a somewhat malicious but not vicious trickster or practical joker ⟨~*s* deflated the tires of his car —*Life*⟩ ⟨one ~ took the police cruiser and parked it around the block⟩

pranky \-kē\ *adj* -ER/-EST [³prank + *-y*] **:** given to playing pranks **:** characterized by pranks

prao *var of* PRAU

prase \'prāz\ *n* -S [F, fr. L *prasius*, fr. Gk *prasios*, fr. *prasios*, adj., leek green, fr. *prason* leek — more at PORRACEOUS] **:** a variety of chalcedony that is translucent and leek green

pra·seo·didymium \,prāzē(,)ō+\ *n* -S [NL, irreg. fr. Gk *prasios, praseios* leek green + NL *didymium*] **:** PRASEODYMIUM

pra·seo·dym·i·um \-'dimēəm\ *n* -S [NL, alter. of *praseodidymium*] **:** a yellowish white trivalent metallic element of the rare-earth group that occurs usu. with cerium, lanthanum, and neodymium, that forms green salts, and that is used chiefly in the form of its salts in coloring glass greenish yellow — symbol *Pr*; see DIDYMIUM; ELEMENT table

pra·sine \'prā,zēn, -,z^ən, -,zīn\ *adj* [L *prasinus*, fr. Gk *prasinos*, fr. *prason* leek] **1 :** having the green color of a leek **2** *or* **pra·si·nous** \-āz^ənəs\ **:** of the color leek

pras·oid \'prā,zȯid\ *adj* [ISV *prase* + *-oid*] **:** resembling prase ⟨a ~ mineral⟩

¹prat \'prat\ *n* -S [ME *pret, pratte*, fr. OE *prætt* — more at PRETTY] *chiefly Scot* **:** TRICK; *esp* **:** one that is low or mean

²prat \"\ *n* -S [origin unknown] **:** BUTTOCKS — sometimes considered vulgar

³prat \"\ *vt* **pratted; pratted; pratting; prats :** to nudge or push (as a person) with the buttocks — sometimes considered vulgar ⟨*pratted* him away from the ticket window⟩

pra·tal \'prād·^əl\ *adj* [LL *pratalis*, fr. L *pratum* meadow + *-alis* -al — more at PRAIRIE] **:** of, relating to, or growing or living in meadows

¹prate \'prāt, *usu* -ād·+V\ *vb* -ED/-ING/-S [ME *praten*, fr. MD; akin to MD & MLG *pratten* to pout, and perh. to Russ *bredit'* to talk nonsense, obs. Pol *brzedzić* to gossip] *vi* **1 a :** to talk at length and to little purpose **:** be loquacious **:** chatter foolishly and without real understanding ⟨*prating* of responsibility⟩ ⟨*prated* on about his wealth⟩ **b :** to speak boastingly or maliciously **2** *of an animal* **:** to make a characteristic repetitive sound ⟨the *prating* of passenger pigeons⟩ **~** *vt* **:** to utter foolishly **:** BABBLE ⟨what nonsense would the fool, thy master, ~ —John Dryden⟩

²prate \"\ *n* -S **:** an act of prating **:** trifling talk **:** unmeaning or idle loquacity **:** CHATTER

prat·er \'prād·ə(r), -ātə-\ *n* -S [ME, fr. *praten* + *-er*] **:** one that prates

prat·fall *also* **pratt·fall** \'prat,=\ *n* [²prat + *fall*] **1 :** a fall on the buttocks ⟨burlesque often relies on ~*s* for its humor⟩ **2 :** a humiliating mishap or blunder

pra·tie \'prād·ē\ *n* -S [by alter.] *dial* **:** POTATO

pra·ti·mok·sha \,prəd·ē'mōkshə\ *or* **pa·ti·mok·kha** \,pəd·ē'mōkə\ *n* -S [Pali & Skt; Pali *patimokkha*, fr. Skt *pratimokṣa*, lit., liberation, deliverance, fr. *prati* toward, near + *mokṣa* liberation] **:** Buddhist rules of monastic discipline

pra·tin·co·la \prə'tiŋkələ\ [NL, fr. L *pratum* meadow + *incola* inhabitant, fr. *in-* ²in- + *-cola* (fr. *colere* to cultivate, dwell) — more at PRAIRIE, WHEEL] *syn of* SAXICOLA

prat·in·cole \'prat^ən,kōl, -ad·iŋ,k-\ *n* -S [NL *Pratincola*] **:** a limicoline bird of the genus *Glareola*; *esp* **:** a common bird (*G. pratincola*) of parts of Europe, Asia, and Africa, having the upper parts light brown, the throat buff bordered by a black line, the breast brownish, and the abdomen white

pra·tin·co·line \prə'tiŋkə,līn\ *n* -S [NL *Pratincola* + E *-ine*] **:** PRATINCOLE

pra·tin·co·lous \-ləs\ *adj* [L *pratum* meadow + *incola* inhabitant + E *-ous*] **:** living in meadows or low grassy situations ⟨~ ants⟩

prating *n* -S [ME, fr. gerund of *praten* to prate — more at PRATE] **1 :** foolish chatter **:** platitudinous discourse **:** evil speaking **2 :** recurrent chattering natural sound of an animal (as a pullet coming into lay)

prat·ing·ly *adv* **:** in a prating manner

pra·tique \pra'tēk, prə'tēk, 'prad·,ēk\ *n* -S [F *pratique* practice, intercourse, pratique — more at PRACTIC] **:** permission to hold intercourse given to a ship after compliance with quarantine regulations or on presenting a clean bill of health

pra·tol \'prā,tōl, -tȯl\ *n* -S [NL *pratense* (specific epithet of *Trifolium pratense*, fr. L, neut. of *pratensis* growing in meadows, fr. *pratum* meadow + *-ensis* -ese) + E *-ol* — more at PRAIRIE] **:** a crystalline phenolic flavone derivative $HOC_{15}H_8O_2OCH_3$ found in clover

¹prat·tle \'prad·^əl, -at^əl\ *vb* **prattled; prattled; prattling** \-d·^əliŋ, -t(^ə)liŋ\ **prattles** [LG *pratelen*, fr. MLG *prätelen*; akin to MD *praten* to prate — more at PRATE] *vi* **1 :** to talk or say much and idly **:** PRATE **2 :** to utter meaningless sounds that are suggestive of the chatter of children ⟨water *prattling* over rocks⟩ **~** *vt* **:** to say lightly and artlessly **:** BABBLE ⟨*prattled* his secret to unfriendly ears⟩

²prattle \"\ *n* -S **1 :** trifling or empty talk or chatter **:** trivial loquacity **:** PRATE, BABBLE **2 :** a sound (as of a brook) that is meaningless and repetitive like the chatter of children

prat·tle·ment \-mənt\ *n* -S [¹prattle + *-ment*] **:** PRATTLE

prat·tler \'pradlə(r), -ad·^əl-, -at^əl-\ *n* -S **:** one that prattles; *esp* **:** a child too young to have acquired complete speech control and full vocabulary

prat·tling·ly *adv* **:** in a prattling manner **:** with prattle

pratt truss \'prat-\ *n, usu cap P* [fr. the name *Pratt*] **:** a truss having vertical members between the upper and lower members and diagonal members sloping toward the center

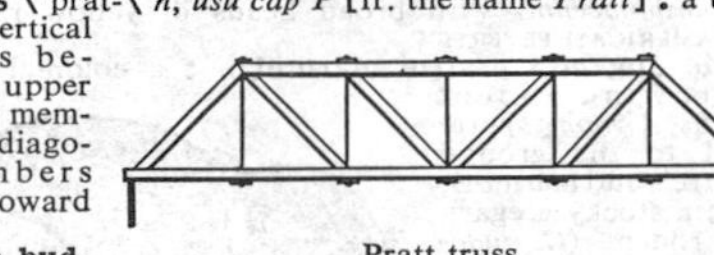

Pratt truss

pra·tye·ka bud·dha \prə·¦tyākə+\ *n, usu cap P&B* [Skt *pratyekabuddha*, fr. *pratyeka* single (fr. *praty-* — fr. *prati* toward, against — + *eka* alone) + *buddha* — more at BUDDHA] **:** one who having attained enlightenment enters Nirvana without turning back to teach others

pra·ty·len·chus \,prād·^əl'eŋkəs, ,prad-\ *n, cap* [NL, blend of L *pratum* meadow and NL *Tylenchus* — more at PRAIRIE] **:** a genus of plant-parasitic nematodes (family Tylenchidae) associated with root rots of various economically important plants — compare MEADOW NEMATODE

prau \'praů\ *or* **pra·hu** \", 'prä(,)hü\ *or* **prao** \'praů\ *or* **proa** \'prōə\ *also* **prow** *or* **praw** \'praů\ *n* -S [Malay *pĕrahu*, prob. fr. Marathi *paḍāv*] **:** one of several usu. undecked Indonesian boats propelled by sails, oars, or paddles; *esp* **:** a swift light sailing craft about 30 feet long and 4 feet wide which has an upcurved sharply stem and stern so that sailing in either direction is possible, which has a curved windward side and a straight leeward side with a small canoe or other outrigger attached, and which has a large triangular sail attached to a long yard and hung obliquely from a short mast

prav·i·ty \'pravəd·ē\ *n* -ES [L *pravitas* crookedness, depravity, fr. *pravus* crooked, wrong, bad + *-itas* -ity — more at PRAIRIE] **1** *archaic* **:** DEPRAVITY, WICKEDNESS **2** *archaic* **:** BADNESS, FOULNESS; *esp* **:** physical corruption

¹prawn \'prȯn, -rän\ *n* -S [ME *prayne, prane*] **1 a :** any of numerous decapod crustaceans that have slender legs, long antennae, a large strong compressed abdomen, and a prominent serrated rostrum, are widely distributed in fresh and salt waters in warm and temperate regions and highly esteemed as food, and vary in size from an inch or so to the size of a lobster **b :** any of various other crustaceans: as (1) **:** NORWAY LOBSTER (2) **:** SHRIMP **2** *or* **prawn pink :** CREVETTE

²prawn \"\ *vi* -ED/-ING/-S **1 :** to fish for prawns **2 :** to fish using prawns for bait — **prawn·er** \-nə(r)\ *n* -S

prawn killer *n* **:** SQUILLA

prawny \-nē\ *adj* **:** of, relating to, or like prawns

prax·e·an \'praksēən\ *also* **prax·e·an·ist** \-nəst\ *n* -S *usu cap* [*Praxeas*, 2d cent. A.D. Asia Minor heretic + E *-an* or *-ist*] **:** a follower of Praxeas who was a leader of the modalistic Monarchians; *specif* **:** a modalistic Monarchian

prax·e·o·log·i·cal \¦praksēə¦läjəkəl\ *adj* **:** of or relating to praxeology

prax·e·ol·o·gy *also* **prax·i·ol·o·gy** \,praksē'äləjē\ *n* -ES [*praxeology* alter. of *praxiology*; *praxiology* fr. *praxis* + *-o-* + *-logy*] **:** the study of human action and conduct

-prax·ia \'praksēə\ *n comb form* -S [NL, fr. Gk *praxis* action + NL *-ia*] **:** performance of movements ⟨echo*praxia*⟩ ⟨para*praxia*⟩

prax·is \'praksəs\ *n, pl* **prax·es** \-k,sēz\ [ML, fr. Gk, doing, action, fr. the stem of *prassein, prattein* to pass through, experience, practice + *-sis* — more at PRACTICAL] **1 :** ACTION, PRACTICE: as **a :** exercise or practicing of an art, science, or skill **b :** usual or conventional conduct **:** HABIT, CUSTOM

-prax·is \'praksəs\ *n comb form, pl* **-prax·is·es** \-ksəsəz\ *also* **-prax·es** \-k,sēz\ [NL, fr. Gk *praxis* doing, action] **:** therapeutic treatment usu. by a (specified) system or agency ⟨chiro*praxis*⟩ ⟨radio*praxis*⟩

prax·it·e·le·an \(¦)prak¦sid·^əl¦ēən\ *adj, usu cap* [*Praxiteles*, 4th cent. B.C. Greek sculptor + E *-an*] **:** of, relating to, or having the characteristics of Praxiteles or his sculpture

pray \'prā\ *vb* -ED/-ING/-S [ME *preyen, prayen*, fr. OF *preier*, fr. L *precari*, fr. *prec-, prex* request, entreaty, prayer; akin to OE *gefrǣge* hearsay, report, *fricgan, frignan, frīnan* to ask, inquire, OHG *frāga* question, *frāgēn* to ask, ON *frētt* question, *fregna* to inquire, find out, Goth *fraihnan* to find out by inquiry, Toch A *prak-* to ask, Skt *prāś* interrogation, *prcchati* he asks] *vt* **1 :** ENTREAT, IMPLORE: as **a :** to make supplication to (a god) **b** (1) **:** to ask (someone) to do something usu. humbly or as an inferior to a superior **:** CRAVE ⟨~*ed* the king to give them land⟩ — often used as a function word in introducing a question, request, or plea ⟨~ tell me the time⟩ ⟨~ let us hurry⟩; compare PLEASE (2) **:** to ask earnestly for (something) **:** supplicate for **:** BEG ⟨I know not how to ~ your patience —Shak.⟩ **c :** to ask (someone) for or on behalf of another ⟨we ~ you . . . be ye reconciled to God —2 Cor 5:20 (AV)⟩ **2** *obs* **:** to ask or entreat to come **:** INVITE **3 a :** to accomplish, put, or bring, by praying ⟨~ a soul out of purgatory⟩ **b :** to overcome (someone) by prayer — used with *down* or *out* ⟨he ~*ed* down his rival⟩ **~** *vi* **:** to make request with earnestness or zeal esp. for something desired **:** make entreaty or supplication **:** offer prayer to a divine being; *specif* **:** to address a god with adoration, confession, supplication, or thanksgiving — **pray in aid** *or* **pray aid :** to claim or call in aid (as when under English law calls are made upon another for assistance in proving one's title or right) — see AID 4 — **pray over :** to send up a prayer for **:** supplicate concerning; *often* **:** to publicly or ostentatiously offer prayer concerning the evil ways of ⟨*prayed over* by the elders of the church⟩

praya \'prīə\ *n* -S [Pg *praia*, fr. ML *plagia* hillside, shoreline — more at PLAYA] **:** BEACH, STRAND **:** WATERFRONT

¹prayer \'pra(a)(ə)r, 'pre|, |ə\ *n* -S *often attrib* [ME *preyere, prayere*, fr. OF *preiere*, fr. L, fem. of *precarius* obtained by entreaty or prayer, fr. L *prec-, prex* request, entreaty, prayer + *-arius* -ary — more at PRAY] **1 a :** a solemn and humble approach to Divinity in word or thought usu. involving beseeching, petition, confession, praise, or thanksgiving ⟨devoted a moment to silent ~ before beginning his task⟩ **b :** an earnest request to someone for something: as (1) **:** the part of a petition or memorial (as to a legislature) that specifies the thing desired (2) **:** the part of a bill in equity or other pleading that specifies the relief sought (3) **:** a request (as by a charge to a jury) for action by the court (4) **:** a formal motion in the British Parliament to invalidate a ministerial order or regulation **c prayers** *pl* **:** earnest good wishes ⟨whatever you decide you have my ~*s*⟩ **2 :** the act or practice of praying **:** the addressing of words or thought to Divinity in petition, confession, praise, or thanksgiving ⟨public ~ was then an accepted custom⟩ ⟨friends and neighbors gathered in ~ for the dead⟩ **3 :** a religious service consisting chiefly of prayers — often used in pl. ⟨had regular family ~*s*⟩ **4 :** a set form of words used in praying **:** a formula of supplication, confession, praise, or thanksgiving addressed to God or an object of worship ⟨a book of ~*s* for different occasions⟩ **5 :** something prayed for **:** a subject of prayer ⟨God granted their ~⟩ **6 :** a slight or minimal chance (as to succeed or survive) ⟨a second-rate maritime power without a ~ of meeting military shipping needs —*N.Y. Times*⟩ ⟨hadn't a ~ to recover⟩

syn PRAYER, SUIT, PLEA, PETITION, APPEAL signify, in common, an earnest, usu. formal, request for something. PRAYER implies that the request is made to one in authority or power and usu. suggests humility and fervor ⟨a very long distance between what the Department of Justice asks for in its *prayer* for relief and what the courts will grant in the form of a remedy —E.S.Mason⟩ ⟨to all my tearful *prayers* —W.S.Gilbert⟩ SUIT implies a deferential and formal petition as to a court or legislative body, although the term is not common today except in legal use or in application to the addresses of a suitor to his loved one ⟨*suits* for violation of contracts are allowed against a union's funds —Philip Taft⟩ ⟨a *suit* in which the college trustees sought to defend their rights against the new political forces —A.C.Cole⟩ ⟨she returned his love, spurning the *suit* of . . . —*Amer. Guide Series: N.C.*⟩ PLEA usu. implies argument and urgent entreaty of which self-justification, a desire for vindication or support, or partisanship is often the motive ⟨his fiancée jilted him on the *plea* that he cared more for the house than for her —*Amer. Guide Series: Md.*⟩ ⟨a *plea* for postwar preparedness —*Current Biog.*⟩ ⟨a *plea* for international peace —Merle Curti⟩ PETITION implies a formal and specific request, often in writing, presented to a person or body that has power to grant it and usu. implying no humility or use of entreaty but rather the exercise of a right ⟨students who have exceeded the maximum number of absences will have a right to *petition* the Committee on Attendance for reinstatement —*Loyola Univ. Bull.*⟩ ⟨the *petition* must be addressed to the Commissioner of Patents . . . and must be signed by the inventor —*General Information Concerning Patents*⟩ ⟨divorce *petitions* —Robert Reid⟩ APPEAL implies the call for attention to and favorable consideration of one's plea, often suggesting an insistence, as in a legal appeal from an inferior to a superior court, or a plea to the emotions ⟨the *appeal* of the abandoned child —Joseph Conrad⟩ ⟨the *appeal* to sex —C.W.Cunnington⟩ ⟨make an *appeal* from the decision of the county court⟩

²pray·er \'prāə(r), -re(ə)r, -reə\ *n* -S [ME *preyere, prayere*, fr. *preyen, prayen* to pray + *-ere* -er — more at PRAY] **:** one that prays **:** SUPPLICANT

prayer bead *n* **1 prayer beads** *pl* **:** a string of beads by which prayers are counted; *specif* **:** ROSARY **2 :** JOB'S TEARS

prayer bones *n pl* **:** KNEES

prayer book *n* **1 :** a book containing prayers and often forms of worship and used in religious services or in private devotions **2** *slang* **:** a narrow piece of holystone used in the hand to scrub crevices in the deck of a ship

prayer desk *n* **:** PRIE-DIEU

prayer·ful \'pra(ə)rfəl, -re|, |əf-\ *adj* **1 a :** given to prayer **:** DEVOUT **b :** characterized by or indicative of prayer **:** DEVOTIONAL **2 :** carefully thorough **:** EARNEST — **prayer·ful·ly** \-fəlē, -li\ *adv* — **prayer·ful·ness** \-lnəs\ *n* -ES

prayerhouse \'=,=\ *n* **:** a chapel or other place where services of prayer and worship are held

prayer in aid : AID PRAYER

prayer·less \-a(ə)rləs, -e|, |əl-\ *adj* **:** using no prayer ⟨a ~ meeting⟩ — **prayer·less·ly** *adv* — **prayer·less·ness** *n* -ES

prayer life *n* **:** an individual's private practice of prayer ⟨the *prayer life* of Jesus⟩

prayerlike \'=,=\ *adj* **:** having the impact or form of prayer

prayer meeting *or* **prayer service** *n* **:** a meeting or gathering for prayer to God; *esp* **:** a Protestant Christian service of worship usu. held regularly on a week night and frequently highlighted by evangelistic or revivalistic preaching

prayer plant *n* **:** a maranta (*Maranta leuconeura kerchoviana*) that is native to Brazil but widely used as an ornamental foliage plant and that has large leaves with red spotting beneath and white purple-striped flowers

prayer rug *or* **prayer carpet** *or* **prayer mat** *n* **:** a small Oriental rug used by Muslims to kneel on when praying and characteristically showing the design of a mihrab

prayers *pl of* PRAYER

prayer scarf *or* **prayer shawl** *also* **prayer cloak** *n* **:** TALLITH

prayer stick *or* **prayer feather** *or* **prayer plume** *n* **:** a feather-decorated stick used by Indians of the southwestern U.S. to convey symbolically a ceremonial offering and a supplicatory prayer

prayer stool *n* **:** a stool to kneel on when praying

prayer tower *n* **:** MINARET

prayer wheel *n* **:** a cylinder of wood or metal revolving on an axis and containing written prayers that are considered efficacious by Tibetan Buddhists

prayerwise \'=,=\ *adv* **:** in the manner of or by way of prayer

¹praying *n* -S [ME *preying, praying*, fr. gerund of *preyen, prayen* to pray — more at PRAY] **:** the act, an instance, or the custom of making prayer

²praying *adj* [ME *preying, praying*, fr. pres. part. of *preyen*,

prayen] **:** habituated or devoted to prayer **:** accustomed to pray ⟨a ~ man⟩ — **pray·ing·ly** *adv*
praying indian *n, usu cap P&I* **:** a member of an indigenous No. American people converted to Christianity by English colonial settlers
praying mantis *also* **praying mantid** *n* [so called fr. the posture of such insects, with the forelimbs extended as though in prayer] **:** MANTIS; *esp* **:** the common mantis (*Mantis religiosa*)
praying shawl *also* **praying scarf** *n* **:** TALLITH
prays *pres 3d sing of* PRAY
prchst *abbr* parachutist
prcht *abbr* parachute
pre- *prefix* [ME, fr. OF & L; OF, fr. L *prae-*, fr. *prae* — more at FOR] **1 a** (1) **:** earlier than **:** prior to **:** before ⟨*pre*departure⟩ ⟨*pre*historic⟩ ⟨*pre*-Slavic⟩ ⟨*pre*-Victorian⟩ (2) **:** preparatory or prerequisite to ⟨*pre*medical⟩ ⟨*pre*professional⟩ (3) **:** in a formative, incipient, or preliminary stage ⟨*pre*cartilage⟩ **b :** in advance **:** beforehand ⟨*pre*cut⟩ ⟨*pre*judge⟩ ⟨*pre*plan⟩ **2 a :** in front of **:** before ⟨*pre*anal⟩ ⟨*pre*axial⟩ ⟨*pre*molar⟩ **b :** at the front **:** anterior **:** constituting a front part ⟨*pre*abdomen⟩ ⟨*pre*sternum⟩ **3 a :** exceedingly ⟨*pre*noble⟩ ⟨*pre*adore⟩ **b** *petrography* **:** predominating in a ratio greater than 5:3 ⟨*pre*alkalic⟩ ⟨*pre*calcic⟩ ⟨*pre*chloric⟩
pre·abdomen \(ˌ)prē+\ *n* [*pre-* + *abdomen*] **:** the enlarged anterior portion of the abdomen of a scorpion
pre·acanthella \ˌprē+\ *n* [NL, fr. *pre-* + *acanthella*] **:** ACANTHELLA
¹**preach** \ˈprēch\ *vb* -ED/-ING/-ES [ME *prechen*, fr. OF *preechier, prechier, precher*, fr. LL *praedicare*, fr. L, to proclaim publicly, praise, fr. *prae-* pre- + *dicare* to proclaim, dedicate — more at DICTION] *vi* **1 :** to proclaim the gospel **:** discourse publicly on a religious subject or from a text of Scripture **:** deliver a sermon ⟨~*ed* on grace to a large congregation⟩ **2 :** to urge acceptance or abandonment of an idea or course of action ⟨~*ed* against speculation and in favor of honest investment — Arthur Pound⟩; *specif* **:** to exhort in an officious or tiresome manner ⟨kept ~*ing* at his students about studying⟩ **~** *vt* **1 :** to set forth in a sermon or a formal religious address ⟨the minister's duty to ~ the Word of God⟩ ⟨~ the gospel⟩ **2 :** to advocate earnestly (as by public speaking or writing) ⟨~ the doctrine of states' rights⟩ **:** INCULCATE ⟨puppet shows that ~ safety —*Lamp*⟩ **3 :** to utter publicly (as a sermon) **:** DELIVER ⟨~*ed* a homily on forgiveness⟩ **4 :** to bring, put, or affect by preaching ⟨~*ed* the . . . church out of debt —*Amer. Guide Series: Va.*⟩
²**preach** \"\ *n* -ES **:** EXHORTATION
preach·able \-chəbəl\ *adj* **:** suitable for preaching from or about
preach·er \-chə(r)\ *n* -S [ME *prechour*, fr. OF *preecheur, precheur*, fr. *preechier, prechier* to preach + *-eur* -or — more at PREACH] **1 :** one that preaches: **a :** one who discourses publicly on religious subjects **:** one whose function is to preach sermons **:** MINISTER **b :** one who inculcates or exhorts something earnestly or officiously ⟨the ~ of a nobler creed of morals —John Buchan⟩ ⟨a ~ of class hatred⟩ **2 :** DOMINICAN
preacher bird *also* **preacher** *n* **:** RED-EYED VIREO
preach·er·less \-chə(r)ləs\ *adj* **:** having no preacher
preach·er·ly \-lē\ *adj* **:** of or befitting a preacher ⟨a ~ attitude⟩
preach·er·ship \-chə(r)ˌship\ *n* **:** the office of preacher ⟨appointed to a university ~⟩
preach·ifi·ca·tion \ˌprēchəfəˈkāshən\ *n* -S [fr. *preachify*, after such pairs as E *edify: edification*] **:** an act or product of preachifying
preach·ify \ˈprēchəˌfī\ *vi* -ED/-ING/-ES [¹*preach* + *-ify*] **:** to preach ineptly or tediously
preach·i·ly \-chəlē\ *or* **preach·ing·ly** *adv* **:** in a manner suiting a sermon or preachment
preach·i·ness \-chēnəs\ *n* -ES **:** the quality or state of being preachy
preaching *n* -S [ME *preching*, fr. gerund of *prechen* to preach — more at PREACH] **1 :** the act, practice, or art of delivering a sermon or exhortation **2 :** SERMON, PREACHMENT **3 :** a public religious service emphasizing a sermon
preaching cross *n* **:** a cross sometimes surmounting a pulpit erected outdoors at a preaching place
preach·ment \ˈprēchmənt\ *n* -S [ME *prechement*, fr. MF, fr. *precher* to preach + *-ment* — more at PREACH] **1 :** the act or practice of preaching ⟨convert men to an obedience of law by ~ and moral suasion —Glenn Hegley⟩ **2 :** an instance of preaching **:** SERMON, EXHORTATION; *specif* **:** a tedious or unwelcome exhortation or discourse ⟨twist the facts into a crusade or a ~ —*Current Biog.*⟩
preachy \-chē\ *adj* -ER/-EST **:** given to preaching or having a preaching style **:** marked by obvious moralizing **:** DIDACTIC ⟨have been ~ in tone and have urged Soviet people to live according to the precepts of Marxism-Leninism —F.C. Barghoorn⟩
¹**pre·adamite** \prē+\ *n* [NL *praeadamita*, fr. L *prae-* pre- + *Adam* (the first man in the Bible) + L *-ita* -ite] **1 :** an inhabitant of the earth before Adam **2 :** one who holds that men existed before Adam; *specif* **:** a follower of the doctrine of Isaac La Peyrère that only the Jews are descendants of Adam and that the Gentiles descend from men who lived before Adam
²**pre·adamite** \(ˌ)prē+\ *also* **pre·adamic** \ˌprē+\ *or* **pre·adamical** \(ˌ)prēˌadəˈmidəkəl\ *adj* **:** existing before Adam **:** of a time prior to that of Adam
pre·adamitism \prē+\ *n* **:** belief in the existence of preadamites
pre·adapt \ˌprē+\ *vt* [*pre-* + *adapt*] **:** to endow with preadaptation
pre·adaptation \(ˌ)prē+\ *n* [*pre-* + *adaptation*] **1 :** adaptation prior in time to some specified change or condition **2 a :** the possession by a group or an organism of characters that are not adapted to the ancestral environment but that favor survival in some other environment **b :** a preadaptive character
pre·adaptive \ˌprē+\ *adj* **:** of, relating to, or characterized by preadaptation
pre·admission \ˌprē+\ *n* [*pre-* + *admission*] **:** admission (as of steam or a combustible mixture) to an engine cylinder before the back stroke is completed with intent to increase the cushioning
pre·adolescence \(ˌ)prē\ *n* [*pre-* + *adolescence*] **:** the period of human development just preceding adolescence; *specif* **:** the period between the approximate ages of 9 and 12
¹**pre·adolescent** \"+\ *adj* [*pre-* + *adolescent*] **1 :** of, characteristic of, or occurring during preadolescence ⟨the ~ years⟩ ⟨~ changes⟩ ⟨~ problems⟩ **2 :** that is in the stage of preadolescence ⟨a ~ girl⟩
²**pre·adolescent** \"\ *n* **:** a preadolescent child
pre·adult \ˌprē+\ *adj* [*pre-* + *adult*] **:** preceding adulthood
pre·agonal \(ˈ)prē+\ *adj* [*pre-* + *agonal*] **:** immediately preceding the death agony
¹**pre·am·ble** \ˈprēˌambəl, -ˌaam-, ˌ=ˈ==\ *n* -S [ME, fr. MF *preambule*, fr. ML *praeambulum*, fr. LL, neut. of *praeambulus* walking in front, fr. L *prae-* pre- + *-ambulus* (fr. *ambulare* to walk) — more at AMBLE] **1 :** an introductory part (as to a book, document) **:** INTRODUCTION, PREFACE; *specif* **:** the introductory part of a statute, ordinance, or regulation that states the reasons and intent of the law or regulation or is used for other explanatory purposes (as to recite facts knowledge of which is necessary to an understanding of the law or to define or limit the meanings of words used in the law) — compare PURVIEW **2 :** an introductory fact or circumstance **:** PRELIMINARY; *esp* **:** one that gives indication of what is to follow
²**preamble** \"\ *vi* -ED/-ING/-S **:** to make a preamble
pre·am·bu·lar \(ˈ)=ˈ=byələ(r)\ *or* **pre·am·bu·lary** \-ˌlerē\ *or* **pre·am·bu·la·to·ry** \-ləˌtōrē\ *adj* [ML *praeambulum* + E *-ar* or *-ary* or *-atory*] **:** of, relating to, or of the character of a preamble **:** INTRODUCTORY, PRELIMINARY
pre·am·bu·late \=ˈ=byəˌlāt\ *vi* -ED/-ING/-S [ML *praeambulum* + E *-ate*] **:** to make a preamble — **pre·am·bu·la·tion** \(ˌ)=ˌ==ˈlāshən\ *n*
pre·amp \ˈprēˌamp, ˌ=ˈ=\ *n* [by shortening] **:** PREAMPLIFIER
pre·amplifier \(ˈ)prē+\ *n* [*pre-* + *amplifier*] **:** an amplifier designed to amplify extremely weak signals obtained from a microphone, phonograph pickup, or television camera before the signals are fed to additional amplifier circuits
¹**pre·anal** \"+\ *adj* [*pre-* + *anal*] **:** situated in front of the anus ⟨a ~ gland⟩
²**preanal** \"\ *n* **:** a preanal part (as a scale or plate)
¹**pre·anesthetic** \(ˌ)prē+\ *adj* [*pre-* + *anesthetic*] **:** used before administration of an anesthetic ⟨~ medication⟩ ⟨~ agent⟩
²**preanesthetic** \"\ *n* **:** a substance used to induce an initial light state of anesthesia
pre·animism \ˌprē+\ *n* [*pre-* + *animism*] **:** a theory that preceding animism there was a definite concept of the supernatural among primitive people; *specif* **:** ANIMATISM
pre·apprehension \(ˌ)prē+\ *n* [*pre-* + *apprehension*] **1 :** an apprehension or opinion formed before examination or knowledge **:** a preconceived notion **2 :** a fear of some evil that may come about **:** FOREBODING
pre·arrange \ˌprē+\ *vt* [*pre-* + *arrange*] **:** to arrange beforehand — **pre·arrangement** \"+\ *n*
pre·aspirated \(ˈ)prē+\ *adj* [*pre-* + *aspirated*] **:** having at the onset of articulation some degree of \h\ ⟨a ~ stop consonant⟩
pre·aspiration \(ˌ)prē+\ *n* [*pre-* + *aspiration*] **:** the addition of a preaspirated sound
pre·assembled \ˌprē+\ *adj* [*pre-* + *assembled*] **:** assembled beforehand
pre·assigned \"+\ *adj* [*pre-* + *assigned*] **:** assigned beforehand
pre·atomic \ˌprē+\ *adj* [*pre-* + *atomic*] **:** of or relating to a time before the use of the atom bomb and atomic energy ⟨the ~ age⟩ ⟨~ weapons⟩
pre·audience \(ˈ)prē+\ *n* [*pre-* + *audience*] **:** the right to be heard before another is heard; *specif* **:** precedence at the bar among barristers and law officers
pre·audit \"\ *n* [*pre-* + *audit*] **:** an audit made prior to the final settlement of a transaction — contrasted with *postaudit*
pre·axiad \(ˈ)prēˈakséˌad\ *adv* [*pre-* + *axi-* + *-ad*] **:** PREAXIALLY
pre·axial \(ˈ)prē+\ *adj* [*pre-* + *axial*] **:** situated in front of the axis of the body
pre·axially \"+\ *adv* **:** in a preaxial direction
preb *abbr* prebend; prebendary
pre·bait \ˈprē+ˌ-\ *vt* [*pre-* + *bait*] **:** to attract (rodents or other animals) to a feeding site with food esp. as a preliminary to a control campaign using poisoned baits
pre·bath \"+ˌ-\ *n* [*pre-* + *bath*] **:** a fluid (as a hardening solution or wetting agent) in which exposed photographic materials are immersed before development
preb·end \ˈprebənd\ *n* -S [ME *prebende*, fr. MF, fr. ML *praebenda*, fr. LL, subsistence allowance granted by the state, fr. L, fem. of *praebendus*, gerundive of *praebēre* to hold forth, offer, supply, contr. of *praehibēre*, fr. *prae-* pre- + *-hibēre* (fr. *habēre* to hold, have) — more at GIVE] **1 :** the stipend or maintenance granted out of the estate of a cathedral or collegiate church to a canon or member of a chapter thereof **2 a :** the land or tithe from which a prebend comes **b :** the holding of such land or tithe as a benefice **3 :** PREBENDARY
preben·dal \prəˈbendᵊl, ˈprebən-\ *adj* **:** of, relating to, or being a prebend or prebendary **:** holding a prebend
prebendal stall *n* **1 :** a prebendary's stall in a cathedral **2 :** a prebendary's benefice
preb·en·dary \ˈprebənˌderē\ *n* -ES [ML *praebendarius*, fr. *praebenda* prebend + L *-arius* -ary] **1 a :** a member of a cathedral or collegiate church chapter receiving a prebend in consideration for his officiating at stated times in the church **b :** an honorary canon in the Church of England with the title but not the emoluments of a prebend **2** *obs* **:** a prebendary's benefice or office **:** PREBEND
¹**pre·bind** \"+ˌ-\ *vt* [*pre-* + *bind*] **:** to bind (a book) in durable materials esp. for circulating library use; *often* **:** to give (a book) a durable original binding — compare REBIND
²**pre·bind** *or* **pre·bound** \"+ˌ-\ *n* **:** a prebound book
prebloom spray \ˈprēˌ=-\ *n* [*prebloom* fr. *pre-* + *bloom*] **:** a pesticidal spray applied to orchard trees between the time the buds show first color and the full opening of blossoms
pre·board \"+ˌ-\ *vt* [*pre-* + *board*] **:** to place (a stocking or garment) on a board before scouring and dyeing
pre·break \"+ˌ-\ *vt* [*pre-* + *break*] **:** to bend (paperboard) in score lines to aid in forming into final shape
pre·bronchial \(ˈ)prē+\ *adj* [*pre-* + *bronchial*] **:** situated in front of the bronchus; *esp* **:** being an air sac on each side of the esophagus of a bird
prec *abbr* preceding
¹**pre·cambrian** \(ˈ)prē+\ *adj, usu cap* [*pre-* + *Cambrian*] **:** prior to the Cambrian **:** of or relating to all of geological history prior to the Cambrian — see GEOLOGIC TIME table
²**precambrian** \"\ *n, usu cap* **:** the Precambrian era or system of rocks
precambrian shield *n, usu cap P* **:** the nuclear area of Precambrian rocks present in each of the continents
¹**pre·cancel** \(ˈ)prē+\ *vt* [*pre-* + *cancel*] **1 :** to cancel (an adhesive or imprinted postage stamp) in advance of use usu. with printed horizontal bars and the name of the city or city and state of the user for use by special permit on certain classes of mail sent in large quantities **2 :** to precancel the imprinted stamp on (a stamped envelope or postcard) — **pre·cancellation** \(ˌ)prē+\ *n*
²**precancel** \"\ *n* **:** a precanceled stamp
pre·can·cer·osis \(ˌ)prēˌkan(t)səˈrōsəs\ *n, pl* **precancero·ses** \-ōˌsēz\ [NL, fr. ISV *precancerous* + NL *-osis*] **:** a condition marked by the presence of one or more precancerous lesions
pre·cancerous \(ˈ)prē+\ *adj* [ISV *pre-* + *cancerous*] **:** that may become cancerous ⟨a ~ lesion⟩ **:** tending to become malignant ⟨all intestinal polyps are ~ —E.R.Fisher & R.B. Turnbull⟩
pre·capitalist *or* **pre·capitalistic** \"+\ *adj* [*pre-* + *capitalist* or *capitalistic*] **:** characterized by independent individual production and direct marketing
pre·car·i·al \prēˈka(a)rēəl, -ker-, -kār-\ *adj* **:** of, relating to, or being a precarium ⟨~ transactions⟩ ⟨~ tenure⟩
pre·car·i·ous \-rēəs\ *adj* [L *precarius* obtained by entreaty or prayer, obtained by mere favor, doubtful, uncertain — more at PRAYER] **1** *archaic* **:** depending on the will or pleasure of another **:** held on sufferance **:** liable to be changed or lost at the pleasure of another **2 :** dependent upon uncertain premises **:** DUBIOUS **3** *obs* **:** IMPORTUNATE, BEGGING **4 a :** dependent on chance circumstances, unknown conditions, or uncertain developments **:** UNCERTAIN ⟨unfavorable weather . . . and too great dependence on a single ~ crop do not bring disaster as they once did —Samuel Van Valkenburg & Ellsworth Huntington⟩ **b :** characterized by a lack of security or stability that threatens with danger ⟨the ~ safety of an ice floe —G. de Q. Robin⟩ ⟨faced trouble inside his ~ four-party coalition government —*Time*⟩ **5 :** PRECARIAL **syn** see DANGEROUS
pre·car·i·ous·ly *adv* **:** in a precarious manner ⟨perched ~ on a narrow board, sixty feet above the floor —Robert Berkelman⟩
pre·car·i·ous·ness *n* -ES **:** the quality or state of being precarious
pre·car·i·um \-rēəm\ *n, pl* **precar·ia** \-rēə\ [L, fr. neut. of *precarius*] **1** *Roman, civil, & Scots law* **a :** something granted or lent to be returned or redelivered at the will of the grantor **b :** a contract making a loan or grant upon such terms or the tenure by which it is held **:** a tenancy at will **2** *medieval European feudal law* **:** any of various estates or tenures that grew out of the original precarium characterized by more or less uncertainty or limitation of the duration and arduousness of the conditions of tenure — compare BENEFICE
pre·cartilage \(ˈ)prē+\ *n* [*pre-* + *cartilage*] **:** embryonic tissue from which cartilage is formed — **pre·cartilaginous** \(ˌ)prē+\ *adj*
pre·cast \ˈprē+ˌ-\ *vt* [*pre-* + *cast*] **:** to cast and finish (as concrete slabs, piles) before placing in position
¹**prec·a·tive** \ˈprekədiv\ *adj* [LL *precativus*, fr. L *precatus* (past part. of *precari* to entreat, pray) + *-ivus* -ive — more at PRAY] **1 :** PRECATORY, BESEECHING ⟨a ~ utterance⟩ **2 :** of, relating to, or constituting a verb form expressing a wish or request
²**precative** \"\ *n* -S **:** a precative verb form
prec·a·to·ry \-kəˌtōrē\ *adj* [LL *precatorius*, fr. L *precatus* + *-orius* -ory] **:** of, relating to, or expressive of entreaty **:** SUPPLICATORY
precatory trust *n* **:** a trust created by precatory words construed as mandatory
precatory words *n pl* **:** words of recommendation, request, entreaty, wish, or expectation employed in legal instruments (as wills) and often resulting in no effective gift or rights being created
¹**pre·cau·tion** \prēˈkȯshən, prəˈk-\ *n* [F *précaution*, fr. LL *praecaution-, praecautio*, fr. L *praecautus* (past part. of *praecavēre* to guard against, fr. *prae-* pre- + *cavēre* to be on one's guard) + *-ion-, -io* -ion — more at SHOW] **1 :** previous caution or care **:** caution employed foresightedly ⟨warned of the need for ~⟩ **2 :** a measure taken beforehand to ward off evil or secure good or success **:** an act of foresight **:** a precautionary act ⟨take ~*s* against accident⟩
²**precaution** \"\ *vt* **:** to put (a person) on guard **:** FOREWARN
pre·cau·tion·ary \-ˌnerē, -ri\ *also* **pre·cau·tion·al** \-ˌnᵊl\ *adj* **:** of, relating to, or having the character of a precaution **:** advising, suggesting, or using caution beforehand ⟨~ measures against epidemic⟩ ⟨helped avert panic by ~ advice⟩
pre·cau·tious \-shəs\ *adj* **:** using precaution **:** PRECAUTIONARY — **pre·cau·tious·ly** *adv* — **pre·cau·tious·ness** *n*
pre·cava \(ˈ)prē+\ *n, pl* **precavae** [NL, fr. *pre-* + *cava*] **1 :** SUPERIOR VENA CAVA **2 :** either of a pair of veins in a squid that passes through the kidney and enters the branchial heart of the same side of the body — **pre·caval** \"+\ *adj*
precaval sinus *n* **:** DUCT OF CUVIER
pre·ced·able \prēˈsēdəbəl, prəˈs-\ *adj* **:** that can be preceded
¹**pre·cede** \-ēd\ *vb* -ED/-ING/-S [ME *preceden*, fr. MF *preceder*, fr. L *praecedere*, fr. *prae-* pre- + *cedere* to go — more at CEDE] *vt* **1** *obs* **:** to go before in quality or degree **:** EXCEED, SURPASS **2 :** to go before in rank, dignity, or importance **:** take precedence of ⟨countries that ~ ours in per capita contributions⟩ **3 :** to be, go, or come before in arrangement or sequence **:** be, go, or move before or in front of ⟨solidly constructed mansion *preceded* by a large oval lawn —E.E.Cummings⟩ **4 :** to go before in order of time **:** be earlier than **:** occur before with relation to something ⟨military penetration *preceded* settlement —*Amer. Guide Series: Minn.*⟩ **5 :** to cause to be preceded **:** PREFACE, INTRODUCE — used with *by* or *with* before the instrumental object ⟨~ his address with a welcome to the visitors⟩ **6 :** to rise earlier than and move in front of (another star) in the apparent rotation of the heavens **~** *vi* **:** to go or come before **:** have precedence ⟨the statistics for the year that *preceded*⟩
²**precede** \"\ *n* -S **:** a brief item placed before a newspaper story to give its latest development
prece·dence \÷ˈpresədən(t)s, prēˈsēdᵊn(t)s, prəˈs- *also* ÷ˈpresedᵊn- *sometimes* ÷ˈprestən-\ *n* -S **1 a** *obs* **:** ANTECEDENT **b :** the fact of preceding in time **:** the earlier place or occurrence **2 :** the right or privilege of preceding others ⟨dealt cards for ~ —Evelyn Waugh⟩; *specif* **:** the right to superior honor on a ceremonial or formal social occasion ⟨ladies always have the ~ of gentlemen —Noreen Routledge⟩ **3 :** the order of preference (as in seats of honor or initiative of departure) observed usu. according to rank on ceremonial or formal social occasions ⟨seated the officials and diplomats according to ~⟩ **4 :** consideration before others **:** priority of importance **:** PREFERENCE ⟨weapons must . . . take ~ of exports —Vera M. Dean⟩ ⟨a motion to adjourn has ~ over all others⟩
prece·den·cy \-nsē\ *n* -ES **:** PRECEDENCE
¹**prece·dent** \(ˈ)prēˈsēdᵊnt, prəˈs-, *or like* ²PRECEDENT\ *adj* [ME, fr. MF, fr. L *praecedent-, praecedens*, pres. part. of *praecedere* to precede — more at PRECEDE] **1 :** going before in time **:** ANTERIOR, PRECEDING, ANTECEDENT ⟨a series of ~ causes going back to infinity —C.H.Whiteley⟩ **2 :** going before in order or arrangement ⟨a ~ theorem⟩
²**prec·e·dent** \ˈpresədənt *also* -ədᵊnt *or* -estənt *sometimes* -rēs- *or* -rez(ə)d- *or* -əˌdent\ *n* -S [ME, fr. MF, fr. *precedent*, adj.] **1 a :** something that precedes; *esp* **:** an earlier occurrence of a similar character ⟨~*s* would seem to show that the reduction of armaments is conducive to war —F.A.Voigt⟩ **b :** a rough draft of a writing **:** ORIGINAL **c :** TOKEN, SIGN **2 a** (1) **:** something done or said that may serve as an example or rule to authorize or justify a subsequent act of the same or an analogous kind **:** an authoritative example ⟨took the exploits of the American colonists as a ~ for subversive activity⟩ (2) **:** the norm for subsequent practice set by such a precedent ⟨the founder also set the ~ of only paying himself a salary —*Current Biog.*⟩ (3) **:** prevailing custom established by long practice **:** CONVENTION ⟨followed historical ~ in organizing the town⟩ ⟨broke ~ when they elected a woman⟩ **b :** a judicial decision, a form of proceeding, or course of action that serves as a rule for future determinations in similar or analogous cases **:** an authority to be followed in courts of justice — compare DICTUM **3 a :** a person or thing serving as a model **b** *obs* **:** SPECIMEN, INSTANCE
³**prec·e·dent** \-ent *also* -ənt *or* -ᵊnt\ *vt* -ED/-ING/-S **:** to furnish with or support or justify by a precedent
precedent condition *n* **:** CONDITION PRECEDENT
prec·e·den·tial \ˌpresəˈdenchəl *sometimes* -rēsə- *or* -rezə-\ *adj* [²*precedent* + *-ial*] **1 :** having the character of or constituting a precedent **:** having force as an example for imitation ⟨~ acts⟩ ⟨a ~ case⟩ **2 :** having precedence **:** PRELIMINARY, ANTECEDENT
prec·e·dent·less *pronunc at* ²PRECEDENT + ləs\ *adj* **:** having no precedent
prece·dent·ly *pronunc at* ¹PRECEDENT + lē *or* li\ *adv* [¹*precedent* + *-ly*] **:** BEFOREHAND
preceding \(ˈ)=ˈ==\ *adj* [fr. pres. part. of *precede*] **1 :** that precedes **:** going before (as in order, rank, time, or place) ⟨had not eaten since the ~ day⟩ ⟨already stated in the ~ paragraph⟩ **2 :** west of or moving in the direction toward which stars appear to travel by diurnal motion — compare FOLLOWING
precel *vi* **precelled; precelled; precelling; precels** [ME *precellen*, fr. L *praecellere*, fr. *prae-* pre- + *-cellere* to rise, project — more at EXCEL] *obs* **:** SURPASS, EXCEL
precellence *or* **precellency** *n* [*precellence* fr. ME, fr. LL *praecellentia*, fr. L *praecellent-, praecellens* (pres. part. of *praecellere*) + *-ia* -y; *precellency* fr. LL *praecellentia*] *obs* **:** EXCELLENCE, PREEMINENCE
pre·censor \(ˈ)prē+\ *vt* [*pre-* + *censor*] **:** to censor (a publication or film) before its release to the public ⟨only half a dozen states ~ movies —*Scientific Monthly*⟩
pre·cent \prēˈsent, prəˈs-\ *vb* -ED/-ING/-S [L *praecentare*, fr. *praecentus*, past part. of *praecinere*] *vi* **:** to act as precentor **:** lead a choir or congregation in singing **~** *vt* **:** to lead in singing (as a psalm)
pre·cen·tor \-ntə(r)\ *n* -S [LL *praecentor* leader of music, fr. L *praecentus* (past part. of *praecinere* to sing or play before — an audience —, fr. *prae-* pre- + *-cinere*, fr. *canere* to sing) + *-or* — more at CHANT] **1 :** a leader of the choir in a cathedral, collegiate, or monastic church **2 :** an official in a cathedral church ranking in cathedrals of the Old Foundation next to the dean and charged with various administrative duties; *esp* **:** one responsible for directing the arrangements for divine service **3 :** the leader of congregational singing in a church having no choir and often no instrumental accompaniment **4 :** CANTOR 2
pre·cen·to·ri·al \ˌprēˌsenˌtōrēəl\ *adj* **:** of or relating to a precentor
pre·cen·tor·ship \prēˈsentə(r)ˌship, prəˈs-\ *n* **:** the office, function, or term of a precentor
pre·central \(ˈ)prē+\ *adj* [*pre-* + *central*] **1 :** situated in front of the central sulcus of the brain ⟨the ~ sulcus⟩ **2 :** of or relating to a precentrum
pre·centrum \"+\ *n* [NL, fr. *pre-* + *centrum*] **1 :** a distinct anterior portion of the centrum of a vertebra commonly bearing the neural and hemal arches in a fish that has vertebra with postcentra **2 :** one of an alternate series of vertebral centra occurring in some fishes and having both hemal and neural arches
pre·cept \ˈprēˌsept\ *n* -S [ME, fr. L *praeceptum*, fr. neut. of *praeceptus*, past part. of *praecipere* to take beforehand, give rules or precepts, admonish, instruct, fr. *prae-* pre- + *-cipere* (fr. *capere* to take, seize) — more at HEAVE] **1 :** a command or principle intended as a general rule of action ⟨the dominance of his party was the most important ~ of his life —Carol L. Thompson⟩: as **a :** a commandment enjoined respecting moral conduct ⟨observe the sixth commandment not as a ~ of divine law but as a counsel of profitable prudence —W.L. Sullivan⟩ **b :** a working rule respecting the technique of an art or science ⟨by ~ and example was largely instrumental in

rescuing English poetry —Gerald Bullett〉 **2 :** a written order or mandate issued by legally constituted authority to a person commanding or authorizing him to do something: as **a :** an order, warrant, or writ issued pursuant to law to an administrative officer; *usu* **:** a command in the nature of civil or criminal process **b :** the direction or command of a feudal superior to an agent or official to admit a tenant to occupancy 〈the ~ of sasine in Scots law〉 **c** *Brit* **:** an order requiring payment or collection of a local tax **syn** see LAW

pre·cept·ee \ˌprēˌsepˈtē; prēˈ≈,≈, prəˈ-\ *n* -s [*preceptor* + *-ee*] **:** one that works for and studies under a preceptor in order to obtain practical professional experience and training 〈a ~ in urology〉 — compare INTERN

preceptial *adj* [*precept* + *-ial*] *obs* **:** PRECEPTIVE

pre·cep·tion \prēˈsepshən, prəˈs-\ *n* -s [L *praeception-, praeceptio,* fr. *praeceptus* (past part. of *praecipere* to take beforehand) + *-ion-, -io* -ion — more at PRECEPT] *Roman law* **:** the taking before general distribution of an estate of something as a legacy under an option to select granted by the will to the legatee

pre·cept·ist \ˈprēˌseptəst\ *n* -s [*precept* + *-ist*] **:** a maker of or believer in precepts **:** DOGMATIST

pre·cep·tive \prēˈseptiv, prəˈs-, -tēv\ *adj* [ME, fr. MF *preceptif,* fr. L *praeceptivus,* fr. *praeceptus* (past part. of *praecipere* to take beforehand, give rules or precepts to, instruct) + *-ivus* -ive — more at PRECEPT] **:** giving precepts **:** having the character of a precept **:** MANDATORY, DIDACTIC 〈the ~ parts of the Bible〉 〈~ grammar〉 — **pre·cep·tive·ly** \-təvlē, -li\ *adv*

precept of cla·re con·stat \-ˌklā(ə)rēˈkänzˌtat\ [*clare constat* fr. L, it is clearly established] *Scots law* **:** a deed in which a superior recognizes the title of the heir of a deceased vassal or tenant to enter upon the superior's land — compare WRIT OF CLARE CONSTAT

pre·cep·tor \prēˈseptə(r), prəˈs-, ˈprēˌs-\ *n* -s [ME *preceptur,* fr. L *praeceptor* teacher, instructor, fr. *praeceptus* (past part. of *praecipere*) + *-or*] **1 a :** TEACHER, TUTOR **b :** the headmaster or principal of a school **2** [ML *praeceptor,* fr. L] **:** the head of a preceptory of Knights Templars **3 a :** a practicing physician who takes an undergraduate medical student as a resident student and gives him personal training in the practice of medicine **b :** a specialist in a branch of medicine or surgery who takes a young physician as a resident student and gives him personal training in his specialty 〈a ~ in obstetrics and gynecology〉

¹pre·cep·to·ri·al \ˌprēˌsepˈtōrēəl\ *adj* [*preceptor* + *-ial*] **1 :** of or relating to a preceptor 〈~ duties〉 **2 :** making use of preceptors 〈~ system〉

²preceptorial \"\ *n* -s **:** a class or course given at some colleges and universities for advanced students and emphasizing independent reading, informal discussion in small groups, and individual conferences with a teacher

pre·cep·tor·ship \prēˈseptə(r)ˌship, prəˈs-, ˈprēˌs-\ *n* **1 :** the position of a preceptor **2 :** the state of being a preceptee **:** a period of training under a preceptor

pre·cep·to·ry \-t(ə)rē\ *n* -ES [ML *praeceptoria,* fr. *praeceptor* preceptor (among the Knights Templars) + L *-ia* -y — more at PRECEPTOR] **1 a :** a subordinate house or community of the Knights Templars established on one of the provincial estates of the order; *broadly* **:** COMMANDERY 2a(1) **b :** COMMANDERY 3 **2 a :** the manor or estate supporting a preceptory **b :** the buildings housing a preceptory

pre·cep·tress \-ptrəs\ *n* -ES [*preceptor* + *-ess*] **:** a female preceptor

pre·ceramic \ˌprē+\ *adj* [*pre-* + *ceramic*] **:** of or relating to an age or culture prior to the period when pottery making appears 〈~ epoch〉 〈~ archaeological site〉

pre·ces \ˈprēˌsēz\ *n pl* [L, prayers, pl. of *prec-, prex* prayer — more at PRAY] **:** short petitions said in liturgical worship in alternation by the minister and congregation

pre·cess \prēˈses, prəˈs-\ *vi* -ED/-ING/-ES [back-formation fr. *precession*] **:** to progress with a movement of precession 〈will cause the axis to ~ about the tangent —*Nature*〉

pre·ces·sion \-eshən\ *n* -s [NL *praecession-, praecessio,* fr. ML, action of preceding, fr. L *praecessus* (past part. of *praecedere* to precede) + *-ion-, -io* -ion — more at PRECEDE] **:** a comparatively slow gyration of the rotation axis of a spinning body (as a top) about another line intersecting it so as to describe a cone caused by the application of a torque tending to change the direction of the rotation axis and being a motion continuously at right angles to the plane of the torque producing it

pre·ces·sion·al \-shənᵊl, -shnəl\ *adj* **:** of or relating to precession 〈~ movement〉

precession of the equinoxes [trans. of NL *praecessio aequinoctiorum*] **:** a slow westward motion of the equinoctial points along the ecliptic caused by the action of sun and moon upon the protuberant matter about the earth's equator in connection with its diurnal rotation

pre–chellean \(ˈ)prē+\ *adj, usu cap C* [*pre-* + *Chellean*] **:** of, relating to, or constituting a Lower Pleistocene culture preceding the Abbevillian and characterized by crudely flaked stone hand axes and rostrocarinates

pre·chelonian \ˌprē+\ *n* [*pre-* + *chelonian*] **:** an actual or hypothetical primitive reptile considered to be ancestral to modern turtles

pre·chlorination \(ˌ)prē+\ *n* [*pre-* + *chlorination*] **:** chlorination of water before filtration

pre·chordal \(ˈ)prē+\ *adj* [*pre-* + *chordal*] **:** anterior to the notochord — used esp. of the trabeculae of an embryonic cranium

pre–christian \"+\ *adj, usu cap C* [*pre-* + *Christian*] **1 :** of or being a time before the beginning of the Christian era 〈the *pre-Christian* centuries〉 **2 :** of or being a time before the introduction or prevalence of Christianity in a locality

pre·chrome \"+\ *adj* [*pre-* + *chrome*] **:** CHROME-MORDANT

pre·ci·bal \(ˈ)prēˈsībəl\ *adj* [*pre-* + LL *cibalis* of food, fr. L *cibus* food + *-alis* -al — more at CIBARIAL] **:** occurring before meals

pré·cieuse \(ˈ)prāsˈyə(r)z, ˌprāsē(y)|, |əz\ *n, pl* **précieuses** \"\ [F, fr. *précieuse,* adj.] **:** an affected woman of polite society; *esp* **:** one of the literary women of the French salons of the 17th century

¹pré·cieux \|ə, |ər(·), |ə\ *or* **pré·cieuse** \|ə(r)z, |əz\ *adj* [F *précieux,* masc., lit., precious (fr. OF *precios, precieus*), *précieuse,* fem. of *précieux* — more at PRECIOUS] **:** extremely or excessively refined **:** AFFECTED 〈still a dandy, ~ to his slim finger tips —John Gunther〉

²précieux \"\ *n, pl* **précieux** \"(z)\ [F, fr. *précieux,* adj.] **:** a man marked by preciosity

pre·cinct \ˈprēˌsiŋ(k)t, *chiefly archaic* ≈ˈ≈\ *n* -s [ME *precincte,* fr. ML *praecinctum,* fr. L, neut. of *praecinctus,* past part. of *praecingere* to gird about, encircle, fr. *prae-* pre- + *cingere* to gird — more at CINCTURE] **1 :** a part of a territory (as a city) having definite bounds or functions and often established for administrative purposes **:** DISTRICT 〈a school ~〉 〈a bold municipal experiment in planning a whole business ~ of offices and shops —Lewis Mumford〉: as **a :** SOCIETY 3b(1) **b :** one in colonial Massachusetts having a political status and powers partially separate from its parent town and usu. being eventually incorporated as a separate town **c :** a subdivision of a county, town, city, or ward for election purposes — called also *election district* **d :** a division of a city for police control **2 a :** an enclosure bounded by the walls or other limits of a building or place or by an imaginary line around it 〈the ~ of the fortification —J.A.Davison〉 〈demand . . . for the admission of females to the club ~*s* —F.L.Allen〉 **b :** a sphere of thought, action, or influence **:** DOMAIN 〈an attitude common in the ~*s* of industry〉 **c :** a space within the grith of a house or borough where one is exempt from arrest in the customary law of the Anglo-Saxons and some other Teutons **3 :** the region immediately surrounding a place **:** ENVIRONS — usu. used in pl. 〈the ~*s* of the inn —Thomas Hardy〉 **4 :** a surrounding or enclosing line or surface **:** BOUND — usu. used in pl. 〈a ruined tower within the ~*s* of the squire's grounds —T.L.Peacock〉

precinct captain *also* **precinct leader** *n* **:** the party leader of an election precinct — compare COMMITTEEMAN

pre·ci·os·i·ty \ˌpreshēˈäsəd·ē, -sətē, -i *sometimes* -esē-\ *n* -ES [ME *preciousite, preciosite* preciousness, fr. MF *precieusité, preciosité,* fr. L *pretiositat-, pretiositas,* fr. *pretiosus* + *-itat-, -itas* -ity] **1** *archaic* **:** something precious **2** [F *préciosité,* fr. MF *precieusité, preciosité* preciousness] **a :** fastidious or excessive refinement (as in language) 〈he had the fastidiousness, the ~, the love of archaisms, of your true decadent —R.L.Douglas〉; *specif* **:** the affected purism and sententiousness characteristic of the French précieuses of the 17th century **b :** an instance of preciosity 〈uttering obtuse and outmoded *preciosities*〉

¹pre·cious \ˈpreshəs\ *adj* [ME, fr. OF *precios, precieus,* fr. L *pretiosus,* fr. *pretium* price, value + *-osus* -ous — more at PRICE] **1 :** of great value or high price: as **a :** of such extreme value that a suitable price is hard to estimate **:** PRICELESS, INVALUABLE **b** *of a gemstone* **:** of highest value commercially because of its beauty, rarity, or hardness **2 :** of great nonmaterial value **:** very highly esteemed or cherished **:** DEAR 〈we went up the wrong valley and lost several ~ days —Heinrich Harrer〉 〈a very useful report, with the ~ qualities of objectivity, balance and good humor —*advt*〉 **3 a :** PARTICULAR, FASTIDIOUS **b :** OVERNICE, OVERREFINED 〈divorced from the social instinct, thought . . . tends to become finicky and ~ —Bertrand Russell〉 **c :** AFFECTED, POSING, HYPOCRITICAL 〈have made culture appear to be a power in whose service people could grow dry, intolerant, and ~ —Katharine F. Gerould〉 **4 a :** FINE, GREAT — used as an intensive 〈opened the territory to some ~ scoundrels —*Amer. Guide Series: Oregon*〉 **b :** WORTHLESS — used ironically 〈nobody would care if he went to his ~ Rome and stayed there —L. C. Douglas〉 **syn** see COSTLY

²precious \"\ *adv* **:** EXTREMELY, VERY 〈no equipment and ~ few drugs —Nevil Shute〉 〈she actually has ~ little to say about what roles she is going to play —Robert Trumbull〉

precious coral *n* **:** RED CORAL

pre·cious·ly *adv* [ME, fr. *precious* + *-ly*] **1 :** in a precious manner **2 :** PRECIOUS

precious metal *n* **:** any of the less common and highly valuable metals (as gold, silver, and the platinum metals) — compare NOBLE METAL

pre·cious·ness *n* -ES [ME *preciousnesse,* fr. *precious* + *-nesse* -ness] **:** the quality or state of being precious

precious stone *n* **:** GEMSTONE

¹precipe *n* -s [irreg. fr. L *praecipit-, praeceps,* fr. neut. of *praecipit-, praeceps* headlong] *obs* **:** PRECIPICE

²precipe *var of* PRAECIPE

prec·i·pice \ˈpresəpəs\ *n* -s [MF, fr. L *praecipitium,* fr. *praecipit-, praeceps* headlong, fr. *prae-* pre- + *-cipit-, -ceps* (fr. *caput* head) — more at HEAD] **1** *obs* **:** a sudden or headlong fall **2 :** a very steep, perpendicular, or overhanging place (as the face of a cliff) **:** an abrupt declivity **:** a sheer cliff **3 :** a hazardous situation **:** the brink of disaster

pre·cip·i·ta·bil·i·ty \prēˌsipəd·əˈbiləd·ē, prəˌs-\ *n* **:** the quality or state of being precipitable

pre·cip·i·ta·ble \≈ˈ≈pəd·əbəl\ *adj* [ˈ*precipitate* + *-able*] **:** capable of being precipitated

pre·cip·i·tance \-d·ən(t)s, tən-\ *n* -s **:** PRECIPITANCY

pre·cip·i·tan·cy \-nsē, -nsi\ *n* -ES **:** precipitant motion or action **:** headlong haste 〈ran from the room with startling ~〉 〈effected the changes with a ~ that stirred up resistance〉

¹pre·cip·i·tant \-nt\ *adj* [F *précipitant,* fr. L *praecipitant-, praecipitans,* pres. part. of *praecipitare*] **:** PRECIPITATE 〈steer a middle course between chronic indecision and ~ judgment —A.S.Eddington〉 — **pre·cip·i·tant·ly** *adv* — **pre·cip·i·tant·ness** *n* -ES

²precipitant \"\ *n* -s **:** something causing precipitation; *specif* **:** an agent that causes the formation of a precipitate

¹pre·cip·i·tate \prēˈsipəˌtāt, prəˈs-, *usu* -ād·+V\ *vb* -ED/-ING/-s [L *praecipitatus,* past part. of *praecipitare,* fr. *praecipit-, praeceps* headlong — more at PRECIPICE] *vt* **1 a :** to throw violently (as upon an object of attack) **:** HURL 〈in dismay he ~*s* himself once more upon his task —Eric Blom〉 **b :** to throw down 〈the Congo ~*s* itself between the mountains, forming some thirty-two separate rapids and cataracts —Tom Marvel〉 〈*precipitated* himself into skepticism —Kingsley Price〉 **2 a :** to cause to move or act very rapidly **:** urge or press on with eager haste or violence 〈the completion of the railroad . . . *precipitated* the extinction of water-borne commerce —*Amer. Guide Series: Maine*〉 **b :** to cause to happen or come to a crisis suddenly, unexpectedly, or too soon **:** bring on quickly or abruptly 〈that the sudden withdrawal of alcohol from a chronic alcoholic may ~ a delirium —*Ency. Americana*〉 〈the power of dissolving Congress and *precipitating* a national election —A.N.Holcombe〉 **3 a** (1) **:** to cause to separate as a precipitate 〈water ~*s* camphor from its alcoholic solution〉 (2) **:** to cause (vapor) to condense and fall or deposit 〈an ice-filled glass ~*s* moisture from the air〉 **b :** to give distinct or substantial form to **:** body forth 〈ward membership . . . may easily ~ itself into many visible forms of behavior —Edward Sapir〉 ~ *vi* **1 a :** to fall headlong **b :** to descend steeply **c :** to fall or come suddenly into some condition (as ruin) 〈Fascism *precipitated* toward its agony —Cecil Sprigge〉 **2 :** to move or act precipitately **3 :** to become separate or distinct **:** take material or observable form 〈this desire or tendency ~*s* into observable motion whenever counteracting causes are removed —Arthur Pap〉: as **a :** to separate from a solution as a precipitate **b :** to condense from a vapor and fall as rain or snow **syn** see SPEED

²pre·cip·i·tate \-pəd·ə̇|t, -pətə|, -pəˌtā|, *usu* |d·+V\ *n* -s [NL *praecipitatum,* fr. L, neut. of *praecipitatus,* past part. of *praecipitare*] **1 :** a substance separated from a solution in a concrete state as a result of a chemical or physical change (as by the action of a reagent or of cold); *esp* **:** an insoluble amorphous or crystalline solid that may fall to the bottom, may be diffused through the solution, or may float at or near the top and that can often be separated from the liquid by filtration **2 :** a product, result, or outcome of some process or action 〈inductive generalizations . . . are the ~ of past experience —H.N.Lee〉

³precipitate \"\ *adj* [L *praecipitatus,* past part. of *praecipitare*] **1 :** exhibiting a lack of due deliberation or care **:** acting with, done, or caused by unwise haste **:** RASH, PREMATURE 〈Brazil was prompt, but not ~, in accommodating itself to the change —Walter Karig〉 〈she was resolved to lose nothing by neglect or delay, but she also meant to do nothing ~ —H.G. Wells〉 **2 a :** falling, flowing, or rushing with steep descent **b :** very steep **:** PRECIPITOUS 〈bare ~ cliffs —*Amer. Guide Series: Vt.*〉 **3 :** marked by extreme or excessive speed or haste **:** violently rapid 〈an army in ~ flight〉 〈born . . . by ~ delivery in a physician's office —*Jour. Amer. Med. Assoc.*〉 **:** SUDDEN, ABRUPT 〈hoping that her departure would not seem indecently ~ —Victoria Sackville-West〉

syn HEADLONG, IMPETUOUS, HASTY, ABRUPT, SUDDEN: PRECIPITATE applies to what is done hurriedly or rashly without expected expenditure of time and may suggest lack of due consideration 〈we'll load up the equipment and pull out in the morning — why be so *precipitate* —P.B.Kyne〉 〈a *precipitate* attack was launched —S.M.Wilson〉 HEADLONG indicates tearing rush with rash lack of observation and forethought 〈thousands and thousands of Belgians, pursuing with incredible speed and fury the Roman cavalry which soon turned in *headlong* flight —A.C.Whitehead〉 〈a *headlong* leap into unconsidered undertakings —S.L.A.Marshall〉 IMPETUOUS may apply to hasty forcible impulsiveness or impatience that precludes thoughtful prudence 〈the *impetuous* Spaniard rushed eagerly into the water up to his armpits and drank greedily —*Amer. Guide Series: Calif.*〉 〈*impetuous* rhetoric sweeps the author on to absurd generalizations —*Reporter*〉 HASTY, in addition to stressing the notion of hurry, may suggest carelessness, thoughtlessness, or anger 〈*hasty* makeshifts take the place of planning, and temporary adaptations become fixed as permanent maladjustments —Arthur Geddes〉 〈faithful observation accompanied by reasonable inference, as opposed to the careless use of the senses and the *hasty* guessing that characterize most people —Norman Foerster〉 ABRUPT applies to that which is done with sudden sharpness breaking away from a previous course or performed without warning or intimation 〈the frequent *abrupt* about-face maneuvers performed by Soviet propagandists —T.P.Whitney〉 〈the reasoning that leads to this conclusion should be less *abrupt.* Jumping to conclusions is not permissible even among philosophers —O. S.J.Gogarty〉 SUDDEN may heighten the notions of unexpectedness and haste without necessarily implying a break from a previous course 〈the car came to a stop, so *sudden* that it pitched both Clara and Hugh out of their seats —Sherwood Anderson〉 〈after the southern attack on Fort Sumter, there was a *sudden* and remarkable transformation of feeling in the North —W.A.Swanberg〉 〈the *sudden* rush of a fresh, strong, exhilarating, and unpredictable wind —B.R.Redman〉

precipitated chalk *n* **:** precipitated calcium carbonate

precipitated sulfur *n* **:** sulfur obtained as a pale yellowish or grayish amorphous or microcrystalline powder by precipitation (as from the reaction of a polysulfide with an acid) and used chiefly in treating skin diseases

pre·cip·i·tate·ly *adv* **:** in a precipitate manner **:** HEADLONG, HASTILY, RASHLY 〈a visitor arrived unexpectedly and we all fled ~ —Henry Miller〉 〈in no danger . . . of plunging ~ into marriage —Ellen Glasgow〉

pre·cip·i·tate·ness *n* -ES **:** the quality or state of being precipitate **:** PRECIPITANCY

pre·cip·i·ta·tion \(ˌ)prēˌsipəˈtāshən, prəˌs-\ *n* -s [MF or L; MF, fr. L *praecipitation-, praecipitatio,* fr. *praecipitatus* + *-ion-, -io* -ion] **1 :** the quality or state of being precipitate **:** PRECIPITANCY, HASTE 〈had acted with some ~ and had probably started out upon a wild-goose chase —Dorothy Sayers〉 **2 a :** an act, process, or instance of precipitating 〈a ~ of this issue . . . at the present time —A.H.Vandenberg〉: as (1) **:** the process of forming a precipitate from a solution — compare COAGULATION 1b, FLOCCULATION 1 (2) **:** the process of precipitating or removing solid or liquid particles from a smoke or gas by electrical means **:** ELECTROSTATIC PRECIPITATION **b :** a deposit on the earth of hail, mist, rain, sleet, or snow; *also* **:** the quantity of water deposited **3 :** something precipitated; *specif* **:** PRECIPITATE 1

precipitation hardening *n* **:** the process of hardening an alloy by a heat treatment or aging method that causes a constituent to precipitate from solid solution

precipitation heat treatment *n* **:** a treatment involving the heating or aging of an alloy at elevated temperature to cause a constituent to precipitate from solid solution

precipitation number *n* **:** an index of the proportional amount of solid matter precipitated from oil under test

precipitation static *n* **:** static produced in airborne radio equipment by the striking of rain, snow, hail, dust particles or other particles in the atmosphere on the antenna and surfaces of an airplane

pre·cip·i·ta·tive \≈ˈ≈≈ˌtād·iv, -ˌtəd-\ *adj* **:** tending to or inducing precipitation

pre·cip·i·ta·tor \-ˌtād·ə(r), -ātə-\ *n* -s **:** one that precipitates: as **a** (1) **:** a person who precipitates some act or event **:** HASTENER (2) **:** an operator of a precipitating machine (3) **:** a worker who precipitates silver or gold from cyanide solution in zinc boxes or with zinc dust **b** (1) **:** an apparatus for causing precipitation (2) **:** an apparatus used in electrostatic precipitation that contains the collecting and discharge electrodes and may be characterized by a series of parallel pipes or plates through or between which the gas passes — called also *electrical precipitator, electrostatic precipitator*

pre·cip·i·tin \≈ˈsipəd·ən\ *n* -s [ISV *precipitate* + *-in*] **:** an antibody that forms an insoluble precipitate when it unites with its antigen — compare AGGLUTININ

pre·cip·i·tin·o·gen \≈ˌ≈≈ˈtinəjən, -ˌjen\ *n* -s [*precipitin* + *-o-* + *-gen*] **:** an antigen that stimulates the production of a specific precipitin — **pre·cip·i·tin·o·gen·ic** \≈ˌ≈≈ˌ≈≈ˈjenik\ *adj*

precipitin reaction *n* **:** the specific reaction of a precipitin with its antigen to give an insoluble precipitate

precipitin test *n* **:** a serologic test using a precipitin reaction to detect the presence of a specific antigen; *specif* **:** a criminological test determining the human or other source of a blood stain 〈show by a *precipitin test* that this is dog blood —Erle Stanley Gardner〉

precipitious *adj* [L *percipitium* + E *-ous*] **:** PRECIPITOUS

pre·cip·i·tous \prēˈsipəd·əs, prəˈs-, -pətəs\ *adj* [F *précipiteux,* fr. MF *precipiteux,* fr. L *praecipitium* precipice + MF *-eux* -ous — more at PRECIPICE] **1 :** marked by great rapidity, haste, or lack of caution **:** PRECIPITATE, HASTY, SUDDEN, RASH 〈psychoses . . . shorter, more fleeting and more ~ in onset —I.I.Weiss〉 **2 a :** having the character of a precipice **:** very steep, perpendicular, or overhanging in rise or fall 〈a ~ slope〉 〈a ~ bluff〉 **b :** having very steep, perpendicular, or overhanging sides **:** containing precipices 〈~ mountains〉 〈a ~ gorge〉 **c :** having a very steep ascent 〈~ stairs〉 〈a ~ street〉 **syn** see STEEP

pre·cip·i·tous·ly *adv* **:** in a precipitous manner **:** ABRUPTLY, SUDDENLY 〈mountains rising ~ from the shore〉 〈~ increase the birthrate〉

pre·cip·i·tous·ness *n* -ES **:** the quality or state of being precipitous

Pre·cip·i·tron \prēˈsipəˌträn, prəˈs-\ *trademark* — used for an electrostatic air-cleaning apparatus that ionizes floating particles of dust, pollen, fumes, and smoke and then precipitates the particles on charged collecting elements usu. in the form of plates

¹pré·cis \(ˈ)prāˌsē; ˈprāsē, -si\ *n, pl* **précis** \-ēz\ [F, fr. *précis* precise] **1 :** a concise epitome or abstract (as of a book or a case) **:** a brief summary of essential points, statements, or facts 〈a ~ of French history〉 **2 :** the act or practice of writing such statements **syn** see COMPENDIUM

²pre·cis \ˈprēsəs\ *n, cap* [NL] **:** a widely distributed genus of chiefly tropical nymphalid butterflies that includes the buckeye of No. and So. America

¹pre·cise \prēˈsīs, prəˈs-\ *adj, sometimes* -ER/-EST [MF *precis,* fr. L *praecisus,* past part. of *praecidere* to cut off, shorten, fr. *prae-* pre- + *-cidere* (fr. *caedere* to cut) — more at CONCISE] **1 a** (1) **:** characterized by a definite often terse statement or specific meaning **:** devoid of anything vague, equivocal, or uncertain 〈this is no time for generalities and I will venture to be ~ —Sir Winston Churchill〉 〈find a more ~ term than *good* to describe the work〉 (2) **:** measured or measuring in mathematically often minutely exact units 〈the ~ velocity of the satellite〉 〈~ figures recording the racer's time to the hundredth of a second〉 〈the ~ techniques of microchemistry〉 〈a ~ balance〉 (3) **:** having distinct often close limits **:** exactly delimited 〈energy . . . released in ~ channels, as when a current causes the glow in a bulb —E.A.Armstrong〉 〈determine the ~ meaning of the term〉 〈standardization through ~ control of processing〉 (4) **:** exact to a point **:** being without deviation **:** ABSOLUTE 〈hit the mark with ~ accuracy〉 〈that totalitarianism is the ~ opposite of anarchy〉 **b :** developed or indicated in specific or minute detail 〈working out the ~ relationship of the languages —Edward Sapir〉 **2 :** conforming strictly to an exact pattern or standard **:** shaped, arranged, or performed with minute conformity to a pattern 〈flying a beautiful, tight, ~ formation —Walter Bernstein〉 **:** rigorous in observing a rule, code, or convention **:** SCRUPULOUS, FASTIDIOUS 〈a ~, magisterial person . . . incapable of letting the most trivial mistake go uncorrected —Gerald Bullett〉; *specif* **:** PURITANICAL **3 :** distinguished from every other **:** VERY 〈the ~ task for which he was born —L.P.Smith〉 〈arrived just at that ~ moment〉 **4 :** sharply distinct in appearance or sound 〈the ~ images in the camera finder〉 〈speaks . . . with a ~ British accent —*Current Biog.*〉 **syn** see CORRECT

²precise \"\ *vt* -ED/-ING/-s **:** to make precise **:** state, define, or determine exactly or strictly **:** PARTICULARIZE

pre·cise·ly *adv* **:** in a precise manner **:** EXACTLY, EXPRESSLY, DEFINITELY, PUNCTILIOUSLY 〈measure off ~ three yards〉 〈trails off into rhetoric ~ where he should be both specific and firm —Howard M. Jones〉 〈an outcome ~ opposite to his expectation〉

pre·cise·ness *n* -ES **:** the quality or state of being precise (as in speech or conduct)

pre·ci·sian \-ˈsizən\ *n* -s [ˈ*precise* + *-ian*] **1 :** a person who stresses or practices scrupulous adherence to a strict standard of religious observance or morality; *specif* **:** PURITAN 1 **2 :** PRECISIONIST

pre·ci·sian·ism \-ˌnizəm\ *n* -s **:** the quality or state of being a precisian **:** the practice of a precisian; *specif* **:** PURITANISM

¹pre·ci·sion \prēˈsizhən, prəˈs-\ *n* -s [in sense 1, fr. L *praecision-, praecisio* act of cutting off, fr. *praecisus* (past part. of *praecidere* to cut off) + *-ion-, -io* -ion; in other senses, fr. F *précision,* fr. L *praecision-, praecisio* act of cutting off — more at PRECISE] **1** *obs* **:** PRESCINDING, ABSTRACTION **2 a :** the quality or state of being precise **:** exact limitation **:** EXACTNESS,

DEFINITENESS ⟨defining words with utmost care, they fashioned their statements of doctrine with meticulous ~ —C.A.Dinsmore⟩ ⟨drove . . . emperors with the ~ of an automaton —Norman Douglas⟩; *esp* **:** the degree of refinement with which an operation is performed or a measurement stated ⟨the number, 2.42, shows a higher ~ than 2.4, but it is not necessarily any more accurate —*Amer. Society of Civil Engineers*⟩ — contrasted with *accuracy* **b** (1) **:** the degree of agreement of repeated measurements of a quantity (2) **:** the deviation of a set of estimates from their mean **3 :** an instance of precision **:** NICETY ⟨suspicion of the ~s of language —F.S.C.Northrop⟩
²precision \"\ *adj* **:** marked by precision of execution or measurement ⟨a ~ landing⟩ ⟨a troop of ~ dancers⟩: as **a :** adapted for extremely fine or accurate measurement, observation, or operation ⟨a ~ level . . . will detect a variation of as little as .0025″ per foot —*Metals & Alloys*⟩ ⟨~ cartography⟩ **b :** held to low tolerance in manufacture or finishing ⟨a ~ gear⟩ ⟨a ~ finish⟩ ⟨~ parts⟩
precision block *n* **:** GAGE BLOCK
precision bombing *n* **:** the dropping of aerial bombs by means of a bombsight upon a narrowly defined target (as a ship or factory) esp. so as not to straddle or overspread — compare AREA BOMBING, PINPOINT, SATURATE
pre·ci·sion·ist \-zh(ə)nəst\ *n* -s **:** one who professes, practices, or lays great stress upon precision (as in language or ritual) **:** PURIST
pre·ci·sive \-ˈsīsiv, -īziv\ *adj* [in sense 1, fr. L *praecisus* + E *-ive;* in sense 2, fr. ¹*precision* + *-ive*] **1 :** cutting off, separating, or defining one thing or person from all others ⟨~ censure⟩ ⟨~ abstraction⟩ **2 :** having or marked by precision or exactness
preclassic *or* **preclassical** \(ˈ)prē+\ *adj* [*pre-* + *classic, classical*] **1 :** of or relating to a time before the classical period (as of an art) **2 :** of or being a European court dance of the 15th and 16th centuries
pre·climax \"+\ *n* [*pre-* + *climax*] **:** a relatively stable ecological community requiring a lesser amount of available moisture than that generally available to the climax and occurring typically where local soil conditions partially nullify a generally adequate precipitation ⟨a grassland ~ within a forest climax⟩ — compare POSTCLIMAX
pre·clinical \"+\ *adj* [*pre-* + *clinical*] **1 :** of or relating to the period preceding clinical manifestations ⟨the ~ stage of a disease of slow onset⟩ **2 :** of or relating to the period preceding the clinical study of medicine ⟨the ~ years⟩; *specif* **:** of or relating to the first two years of the prescribed medical course devoted to the study of basic sciences (as anatomy, physiology, pathology) ⟨~ studies⟩ **3 :** of, relating to, or being a science basic to medicine ⟨research in the ~ sciences⟩
pre·clud·able \prēˈklüdəbəl, prəˈk-\ *adj* **:** capable of being precluded
pre·clude \-üd\ *vt* -ED/-ING/-S [L *praecludere*, fr. *prae-* pre- + *-cludere* (fr. *claudere* to close) — more at CLOSE] **1** *archaic* **:** to put a barrier before **:** shut up **:** HINDER, STOP, IMPEDE, CLOSE **2 :** to shut out or obviate by anticipation **:** prevent or hinder by necessary consequence or implication **:** deter action of, access to, or enjoyment of **:** make ineffectual ⟨the adoption of one choice often necessarily ~s the use of another —C.I. Glicksberg⟩ ⟨engagements . . . ~ the principal from extending this trip —D.L.Gales⟩ **syn** see PREVENT
pre·clu·sion \-üzhən\ *n* -s [L *praeclusion-, praeclusio*, fr. *praeclusus* (past part. of *praecludere*) + *-ion-, -io* -ion] **:** an act of precluding or state of being precluded **:** a shutting out **:** prevention by anticipation
pre·clu·sive \-üsiv *also* -üz\ *adj* [L *praeclusus* + E *-ive*] **:** shutting out **:** precluding or tending to preclude **:** PREVENTIVE ⟨~ buying — purchasing vital materials to keep them from going to the Axis —Robert Reuben⟩ — **pre·clu·sive·ly** \|əvlē\ *adv*
pre·coagulation \ˌprē+\ *n* [*pre-* + *coagulation*] **:** chemical treatment with a coagulant before filtration
precoces *var of* PRAECOCES
pre·co·cial \prēˈkōshəl, prəˈk-\ *adj* [NL *precoces* + E *-ial*] *of a newly born or hatched individual* **:** capable of a high degree of independent activity from birth ⟨the chicks of gallinaceous birds are ~⟩ — compare ALTRICIAL
pre·co·cious \-shəs\ *adj* [L *praecoc-, praecox* early ripening, premature, precocious (fr. *prae-* + *-coc-, -cox*, fr. *coquere* to cook, ripen) + E *-ious* — more at COOK] **:** exceptionally early in development: **a :** flowering, fruiting, or developing before the usual time **:** early or prematurely ripe or developed — used of a plant or its organs **b :** manifesting at an early age some of the mental or physical characteristics usu. associated with maturity ⟨a ~ child⟩ ⟨a ~ genius⟩ **c :** characterizing, done, or made by a precocious individual ⟨a ~ achievement⟩ ⟨at the ~ age of 25 he had written a masterpiece⟩ **d :** appropriate to a period later than that of actual occurrence ⟨a ~ culture⟩ ⟨a ~ heat wave⟩ — **pre·co·cious·ly** *adv* — **pre·co·cious·ness** *n* -ES
pre·coc·i·ty \-ˈkäsəd·ē, -ətē, -i\ *n* -ES [L *praecoc-, praecox* + E *-ity*] **:** the quality or state of being precocious: as **a :** early flowering or early ripening **b :** exceptionally early or premature development; *esp* **:** early development of the mental powers **:** FORWARDNESS **c :** early sexual maturity of poultry resulting in initiation of egg laying at an early age
precocity theory *n* **:** a theory in biology: early condensation of the chromosomes induces a characteristic prophase pairing that is the fundamental factor distinguishing meiosis from mitosis
pre·cogitate \(ˈ)prē, prə+\ *vt* -ED/-ING/-S [L *praecogitatus*, past part. of *praecogitare*, fr. *prae-* pre- + *cogitare* to think — more at COGITATE] **:** PREMEDITATE — **pre·cogitation** \(ˌ)prē, prə+\ *n* -s
pre·cognition \ˌprē+\ *n* [LL *praecognition-, praecognitio*, fr. L *praecognitus* (past part. of *praecognoscere* to foreknow, fr. *prae-* pre- + *cognoscere* to know) + *-ion, -io*, -ion — more at COGNITION] **1 :** previous cognition **:** FOREKNOWLEDGE; *specif* **:** clairvoyance relating to a future or not yet experienced event or state **2** *Scots law* **a :** an ex parte preliminary examination (as in a criminal case) **b :** the evidence taken in such an examination
pre·cognitive \(ˈ)prē+\ *adj* **:** giving precognition ⟨a ~ dream⟩
pre·cognize \(ˌ)prē+\ *vt* [*pre-* + *cognize*] **:** to know beforehand
pre·cognosce \(ˌ)prē+\ *vt* -ED/-ING/-S [L *praecognoscere* to foreknow] *Scots law* **:** to examine in the proceeding of precognition
pre·columbian \ˌprē+\ *adj, usu cap C* [*pre-* + *Columbian*] **:** preceding or belonging to the time before the discovery of America by Columbus ⟨*pre-Columbian* times⟩ ⟨an exhibition of *pre-Columbian* art⟩
precombustion chamber \ˌ==ˌ==-\ *n* [*pre-* + *combustion*] **:** an auxiliary space in which combustible gases are ignited and combustion started ahead of the main combustion chamber of a jet or gas engine
precombustion engine *n* **:** a mixed cycle internal combustion engine with a small uncooled precombustion chamber in which a portion of the mixture is ignited and in turn ignites the cylinder charge
pre·commissure \(ˈ)prē+\ *n* [*pre-* + *commissure*] **:** the anterior commissure of the brain
pre·compose \ˌprē+\ *vt* [*pre-* + *compose*] **:** to compose beforehand
pre·conceive \"+\ *vt* [*pre-* + *conceive*] **:** to form an opinion of beforehand **:** form a previous notion or idea of; *esp* **:** to form (as an opinion) without adequate evidence or through prejudice ⟨held to his *preconceived* opinion despite the new evidence⟩
pre·concept \(ˈ)prē+\ *n* [*pre-* + *concept*] **:** a rudimentary idea intermediate between an ordinary recept and a fully developed concept
pre·conception \ˌprē+\ *n* [*pre-* + *conception*] **:** an act or an instance of preconceiving **:** a conception or opinion previously formed **:** PREJUDICE, PREPOSSESSION
pre·conceptual \"+\ *adj* **:** of, relating to, or marked by a preconception
pre·concert \"+\ *vt* [*pre-* + *concert*] **:** to arrange beforehand **:** settle by prior agreement
preconcerted *adj* **:** previously arranged — **pre·con·cert·ed·ly** *adv* — **pre·con·cert·ed·ness** *n* -ES

pre·condemn \ˌprē+\ *vt* [*pre-* + *condemn*] **:** to condemn before trial or without due consideration **:** PREJUDGE
¹pre·condition \"+\ *n* [*pre-* + *condition* (n.)] **:** something that must exist before something else can come about **:** CONDITION, PREREQUISITE, QUALIFICATION ⟨prepared to negotiate . . . without any ~s —*N.Y. Times*⟩ ⟨the indispensable ~ of success, the support of a united party —M.W.Straight⟩
²precondition \"\ *vt* [*pre-* + *condition* (v.)] **1 :** to put (a thing) in proper or desired condition in advance or in preparation for some intended treatment or processing ⟨~ the surface of the mineral to be separated —*Science*⟩ **2 :** to put (a person) in preparation for some argumentative presentation or some mental test or shock ⟨merchandisers were seeking ways to ~ the customer to buy their product —Vance Packard⟩
preco·ni·za·tion \ˌprekənəˈzāshən, ˌprēk-, -ˌnīˈz-\ *n* -s [ML *praeconization-, praeconizatio*, fr. *praeconizatus* (past part. of *praeconizare*) + L *-ion-, -io* -ion] **:** the act or process of preconizing (as a bishop)
preco·nize \ˈ==ˌnīz\ *vt* -ED/-ING/-S [ML *praeconizare*, fr. L *praecon-, praeco* herald, crier (prob. fr. *praedicare* to proclaim publicly) + LL *-izare* -ize — more at PREACH] **1 :** to announce or commend publicly **2 :** to summon publicly or by name **3** *Roman Catholicism* **:** to approve (a high ecclesiastical appointment) publicly by papal proclamation in consistory
pre·conquest \(ˈ)prē+\ *adj* [*pre-* + *conquest*] **:** of or relating to times before the conquest of a country or people ⟨~ Normandy⟩ ⟨~ sculptured stones —F.M.Stenton⟩
¹pre·conscious \"+\ *adj* [*pre-* + *conscious*] **1 :** not present in consciousness but capable of being recalled without encountering any inner resistance or repression — compare CENSORSHIP **2 :** preceding the development of self-consciousness or awareness — **pre·consciously** \"+\ *adv*
²preconscious \"\ *n* **:** the preconscious part of mental life or psychic content in psychoanalysis
pre·consonantal \(ˌ)prē+\ *adj* [*pre-* + *consonantal*] **:** immediately preceding a consonant
pre·contact \(ˈ)prē+\ *adj* [*pre-* + *contact*] **:** of or relating to the period before contact of a primitive people with a more advanced culture
¹pre·contract \"+\ *n* [ME *precontracte*, fr. *pre-* + *contracte, contract* contract — more at CONTRACT] **:** a contract preceding another; *esp* **:** an informal agreement of marriage made per verba de praesenti and formerly disabling one from entering into a similar contract with another person
²pre·contract \(ˌ)prē+\ *vt* [*pre-* + *contract* (v.)] **:** to contract, engage, or stipulate by precontract
pre·cook \(ˈ)prē+\ *vt* [*pre-* + *cook*] **:** to cook (food) partially or entirely before final cooking or reheating ⟨~ cereal before packaging⟩ ⟨~ meat before reheating for a meal⟩
pre·cool \"+\ *vt* [*pre-* + *cool*] **:** to cool (as fresh fruit, vegetables, or meat) artificially to refrigeration temperature before shipment
pre·cooler \(ˈ)prē+\ *n* **:** a device (as a heat exchanger) for cooling a fluid or gas before it is used (as by a mechanical device)
pre·coracoid \"+\ *n* [*pre-* + *coracoid*] **1 :** an anterior and ventral bony or cartilaginous element of the shoulder girdle in front of the coracoid proper that occurs in many amphibians and reptiles and is often represented in the latter by a process of the coracoid **2 :** MESOCORACOID
pre·cordial \"+\ *adj* [prob. fr. MF, fr. *pre-* + *cordial*, fr. ML *cordialis* — more at CORDIAL] **:** situated or occurring in front of the heart **:** involving the precordium
precordial region *n* **:** PRECORDIUM
pre·cor·di·um \prēˈkȯ(r)dēəm\ *n, pl* **precor·dia** \-ēə\ [NL, fr. *pre-* + L *cord-, cor* heart + NL *-ium* — more at HEART] **:** the part of the ventral surface of the body overlying the heart and stomach and comprising the epigastrium and the lower median part of the thorax
pre·cornu \(ˈ)prē+\ *n* [NL, fr. *pre-* + *cornu*] **:** the anterior cornu of a lateral ventricle
pre–cortesian \ˌprēˌkȯ(r)ˈtēzēən, -tēzhən\ *adj, usu cap C* [*pre-* + Hernán *Cortés* (Cortez) †1547 Span. conqueror of Mexico + E *-ian*] **:** of or relating to the period before the conquest of Mexico by Cortez
pre·costa \(ˈ)prē+\ *n* [NL, fr. *pre-* + *costa*] **:** a small vein anterior to the costa in the wings of a primitive insect — **pre·costal** \"+\ *adj*
pre–crag \ˈprē+ˌ-\ *adj, usu cap C* [*pre-* + *crag* (sedimentary rock)] **:** of or relating to a hypothetical preglacial stage of Lower Paleolithic culture ⟨*pre-Crag* flints⟩
pre·critical \(ˈ)prē+\ *adj* [*pre-* + *critical*] **1 :** that is prior to the development of critical capacity ⟨in ~ cultures, myths of magic . . . tend to prevail —*Amer. Anthropologist*⟩ **2 :** being prior to the publication of Immanuel Kant's *Critique of Pure Reason*
pre·crural \"+\ *adj* [*pre-* + *crural*] **:** situated in front of the leg or thigh
pre·cuneus \"+\ *n* [NL, fr. *pre-* + *cuneus*] **:** a somewhat rectangular gyrus bounding the mesial aspect of the parietal lobe of the cerebrum and lying immediately in front of the cuneus
pre·current \"+\ *adj* [L *praecurrent-, praecurrens*, pres. part. of *praecurrere*] **:** occurring beforehand **:** ANTICIPATORY
precurse *n* -s [L *praecursus*, past part. of *praecurrere* to run before, precede, fr. *prae-* pre- + *currere* to run — more at CURRENT] *obs* **:** something that presages a future event
pre·cur·sive \prēˈkərsiv, prəˈk-\ *adj* **:** PRECURSORY, PROGNOSTICATIVE
pre·cur·sor \=ˈkərsər, -ˈkəsə(r, -ˈkəisə(r, ˈprē,==\ *n* -s [L *praecursor*, fr. *praecursus* + *-or*] **1 a :** one that precedes and indicates the approach of another ⟨headaches . . . were the ~s of breakdown and helpless invalidism —V.S.Pritchett⟩ **b :** one that precedes another in an office or process **:** PREDECESSOR, FORERUNNER ⟨Greek mathematics was the ~ to modern mathematics —Harry Lass⟩ **2 :** a substance from which another substance is formed esp. by natural processes ⟨ethyl alcohol is the ~ of acetic acid in the formation of vinegar⟩ — compare PROVITAMIN, ZYMOGEN
pre·cur·so·ry \-sərē, -ri\ *adj* [L *praecursorius*, fr. *praecursus* + *-orius* -ory] **:** having the character of a precursor **:** PRECEDING, PRELIMINARY, PREMONITORY ⟨~ symptoms of a fever⟩
pre·cut \ˈprē+ˌ-\ *vt* [*pre-* + *cut*] **1 :** to cut to proper dimensions (the parts of a house) **2 :** to cut the parts of (a house) for prefabrication assembly
pre·cyst \ˈprē+ˌ-\ *n* [*pre-* + *cyst*] **:** a differentiated phase in many protozoans that lays down the resting cyst and is characterized by structural simplification and modified metabolic activities involving the increase of storage products and the termination of active feeding — **pre·cystic** \(ˈ)prē+\ *adj*
pred *abbr* predicate; predicative
pre·da·cious *or* **pre·da·ceous** \prēˈdāshəs, prəˈd-\ *adj* [*predacious*, fr. L *praedari* to plunder, prey upon + E *-acious* (as in *rapacious*); *predaceous*, alter. (influenced by E *-aceous*) of *predacious* — more at PREY] **1** *usu predaceous* **:** preying on other animals **:** exhibiting or relating to predatism **:** PREDATORY ⟨a ~ kind of animal — the early geological gangster —W.E.Swinton⟩ **2 :** marked by rapacity **:** tending to devour or despoil — **pre·da·cious·ness** *n* -ES
pre·dac·i·ty \-dasəd·ē\ *n* -ES [fr. *predacious*, after such pairs as E *rapacious: rapacity*] **:** the quality or state of being predacious ⟨a boy . . . with plenty of drive and ~ —Max Lerner⟩
¹pre–darwinian \ˌprē+\ *adj, usu cap D* [*pre-* + *darwinian*] **:** of or relating to the period or to the beliefs prevalent before enunciation of the Darwinian theory
²pre–darwinian \"\ *n, usu cap D* **:** a holder of pre-Darwinian beliefs
pre·darwinianism \"+\ *n, usu cap D* **:** the beliefs of the pre-Darwinians
¹pre·date \ˈprē+ˌ-\ *vt* [*pre-* + *date*] **1 :** ANTEDATE 1 **2 :** to precede in date **:** be earlier in time than
²pre·date \"+,-\ *n* **:** an edition of a newspaper carrying a dateline later than the date of issue ⟨Sunday ~s of metropolitan newspapers are sent to many small towns⟩
pre·da·tion \prēˈdāshən, prəˈd-\ *n* -s [L *praedation-, praedatio*, fr. *praedatus*, (past part. of *praedari* to plunder) + *-ion-, -io* -ion — more at PREY] **1 :** the act of preying or plundering **:** DEPREDATION, DESPOILMENT, RAPACITY ⟨the enlightened monarchs . . . were not averse to an occasional war of ~ —Morris Watnick⟩ **2 :** a mode of life in which food is primarily obtained by killing and consuming animals ⟨~ reduces the size of the prey population, which responds by more rapid growth —*Scientific Monthly*⟩ — compare MUTUALISM, PARASITISM
predation pressure *n* **:** the effects of predation on a natural community esp. with respect to the survival of species preyed upon
pred·a·tism \ˈpredəˌtizəm\ *n* -s [*preda*tory + *-ism*] **:** the habit or practice of living by predation or as a predator — used chiefly of wild animals; compare COMMENSALISM, PARASITISM
pred·a·tive \-dəd·iv\ *adj* [L *praedatus* + E *-ive*] **:** PREDATORY
pred·a·tor \ˈpredəd·ə(r), -edətə- *also* -edəˌtō(ə)r *or* -ō(ə)\ *n* -s [L *praedator* plunderer, hunter, fr. *praedatus* (past part. of *praedari* to plunder, prey on) + *-or* — more at PREY] **1 :** one that preys, destroys, or devours ⟨of all the man-made agents of destruction, . . . the motorcar is the most voracious ~ —Eugene Kinkead⟩ **2 :** an animal that depends on predation for its food: **a :** CARNIVORE; *esp* **:** an animal that preys on one or more other animals that man wishes to preserve for his own use **b :** INSECTIVORE **3** *law* **:** an animal or bird not regarded as game and not protected by game laws
pred·a·to·ri·al \ˌpredəˈtōrēəl, -tȯr-\ *adj* [L *praedatorius* predatory + E *-al*] **:** PREDATORY
pred·a·to·ri·ly \ˌ==ˈ==rəlē, -li\ *adv* **:** in a predatory manner
pred·a·to·ri·ness \-rēnəs, -rin-\ *n* -ES **:** the quality or state of being predatory
pred·a·to·ry \ˈpredəˌtōrē, -tȯr-, -ri\ *adj* [L *praedatorius*, fr. *praedatus* (past part. of *praedari* to plunder, prey) + *-orius* -ory — more at PREY] **1 a :** of, relating to, or practicing plunder, pillage, or rapine **:** using violence or robbery for aggrandizement ⟨seven years of ~ warfare —*Amer. Guide Series: N.Y.*⟩ ⟨a ~ class of capitalists —J.D.Hart⟩ **b :** disposed or showing a disposition to injure or exploit others for one's own gain ⟨the girl was small, too small, with severe elegance and with a ~ face —D.C.Loughlin⟩ **2** *obs* **:** DESTRUCTIVE, HARMFUL, INJURIOUS **3 :** living by predation **:** PREDACIOUS; *also* **:** adapted to predation
pre·dawn \ˈprē+ˌ-\ *adj* [*pre-* + *dawn*] **:** of or relating to the time just before dawn
prede *vb* -ED/-ING/-S [L *praeda* booty, plunder — more at PREY] *obs* **:** PLUNDER
¹pre·decease \ˌprē+\ *vb* [*pre-* + *decease*] *vt* **:** to die before (another person) ~ *vi* **:** to die first
²predecease \"\ *n* [*pre-* + *decease*] **:** prior decease
prede·ces·sor \ˈpredəˌsesə(r) *also* ˈprēd- *or* -edē,- *or* -edi,- *or* -se,sȯ(ə)r *or* -ō(ə) *or* ˌ==ˈ=(ˌ)=\ *n* -s [ME *predecessour*, fr. MF *predecesseur*, fr. LL *praedecessor*, fr. L *prae-* pre- + *decessor* retiring governor, fr. *decessus* (past part. of *decedere* to depart, retire from office) + *-or* — more at DECEASE] **1 a :** one that precedes; *esp* **:** a person who has previously occupied a position or office to which another has succeeded ⟨dwell with satisfaction upon the poet's difference from his ~s —T.S. Eliot⟩ ⟨was my ~ in title to the house⟩ **b :** something that has been followed or displaced by another ⟨sun-dried bricks, the ~s of burnt brick —Fiske Kimball⟩ ⟨the edifice follows the general style and proportions of its ~ —*Amer. Guide Series: Vt.*⟩ **2** *archaic* **:** ANCESTOR
pre·decide \ˌprē+\ *vt* [*pre-* + *decide*] **:** to decide in advance ⟨the fiscal monster which ~s everything —*Life*⟩
pre·declare \"+\ *vt* [*pre-* + *declare*] *archaic* **:** to declare beforehand
pre·define \"+\ *vt* [*pre-* + *define*] **:** to define or determine in advance — **pre·definition** \(ˌ)prē+\ *n*
pre·delinquent \ˌprē+\ *adj* [*pre-* + *delinquent*] **:** behaving so as to suggest future delinquency **:** developing or tending toward delinquency
pre·del·la \prəˈdelə\ *n, pl* **predel·le** \-elē, -e(ˌ)lā\ [It, stool, prayer stool, step of an altar, prob. fr. OHG *bret* board; akin to OE *bord* board] **1 a :** a step or platform on which an altar is placed — called also *footpace* **b :** a painting or sculpture on the face of a predella **2 a :** SUPERALTAR **b :** GRADINE, RETABLE **c :** a painting or sculpture along the front of a superaltar or forming a border or frame at the foot of an altarpiece **3 :** a secondary painting constituting a border or other appendage to a principal one
pre·dental \(ˈ)prē+\ *adj* [*pre-* + *dental*] **:** preliminary to or preparing for a course in dentistry
pre·dentary \"+\ *adj* [*pre-* + *dentary*] **:** of, relating to, or being a bone in the lower jaw of some dinosaurs that is situated in front of the dentary bones
pre·den·ta·ta \ˌprēˌdenˈtädə, -tād·ə\ [NL, fr. L *prae-* pre- + *dentata*, neut. pl. of *dentatus* toothed — more at DENTATE] *syn of* ORNITHISCHIA
pre·dentin \(ˈ)prē+\ *n* [*pre-* + *dentin*] **:** immature uncalcified dentin consisting chiefly of fibrils
pre·depression \ˌprē+\ *adj* [*pre-* + *depression*] **:** of or relating to the economic situation existing before a business depression ⟨very oppressive ~ salary contracts —*Harper's*⟩
pre·design \"+\ *vt* [*pre-* + *design*] *archaic* **:** to design or plan beforehand
pre·designate \(ˈ)prē+\ *vt* [*pre-* + *designate*] **1 :** to designate beforehand ⟨subjects were . . . to respond whenever any one of a set of eight *predesignated* letters appeared —*Biol. Abstracts*⟩ **2 :** to specify (the expected character of a sample) in advance of or independently of examination of the sample in order to avoid fallacious inference — **pre·designation** \(ˌ)prē+\ *n*
¹pre·des·ti·nar·i·an \(ˌ)prēˌdestəˈna(a)rēən\ *adj* [*predestina*tion + *-arian* (as in *trinitarian*, adj.)] **:** of or relating to predestination **:** holding the doctrine of predestination
²predestinarian \"\ *n* -s [*predestination* + *-arian*] **1 :** a believer in esp. theological predestination ⟨the nature of man is a subject for quarrels between . . . free-willers and ~s —J.R.Chamberlain⟩ **2 :** FATALIST
pre·des·ti·nar·i·an·ism \(ˌ)=ˌ==ˈ===ˌnizəm\ *n* -s [²*predestinarian* + *-ism*] **:** the system or doctrine of the predestinarians
¹pre·des·ti·nate \prēˈdestənət, -ˌnāt\ *adj* [ME, fr. L *praedestinatus*, past part. of *praedestinare* to determine beforehand, — more at PREDESTINE] **1 :** foreordained by God's decree or eternal purpose **2 :** destined, fated, or determined beforehand ⟨there is a sense of ~ inevitability about its passage . . . with its sixteen silvered cars —W.D.Edmonds⟩
²predestinate \"\ *n* -s **:** a person predestinated to eternal life
³pre·des·ti·nate \-ˌnāt\ *vt* [ME *predestinaten*, fr. L *praedestinatus*, past part. of *praedestinare*] **1 :** to foreordain to an earthly or eternal lot or destiny (as salvation or damnation) by divine purpose or decree ⟨for whom he did foreknow, he also did ~ to be conformed to the image of his Son —Rom 8:29 (AV)⟩ **2** *archaic* **:** to choose, fix, or settle beforehand **:** PREDETERMINE
pre·des·ti·na·tion \(ˌ)=ˌ==ˈnāshən\ *n* [ME *predestinacion*, fr. LL *praedestination-, praedestinatio*, fr. L *praedestinatus* (past part. of *praedestinare* to predestine) + *-ion-, -io* -ion] **1 :** the act of predestinating or the state of being predestinated **:** FATE, FOREORDINATION, DESTINY ⟨the freshman comes with a kind of fatal ~ —Irwin Edman⟩ **2 :** the theological doctrine that all events throughout eternity have been foreordained by divine decree or purpose; *esp* **:** the foreordination by God of each individual's ultimate destiny particularly to eternal life ⟨Calvin's doctrine of ~ includes the decree of reprobation, which Lutheran confessions exclude⟩ — see ELECTION 1 d
pre·des·ti·na·tion·al \(ˌ)=ˌ==ˈnāshənᵊl, -shnəl\ *adj* **:** of or relating to predestination
pre·des·ti·na·tion·ist \(ˌ)=ˌ==ˈnāsh(ə)nəst\ *n* -s [*predestination* + *-ist*] **:** PREDESTINARIAN
pre·des·ti·na·tor \=ˈ==ˌnād·ə(r)\ *n* -s [*predestinate* + *-or*] **1 :** one that predestinates **2** *archaic* **:** PREDESTINARIAN
pre·destine \(ˈ)prē+\ *vt* [ME *predestinen*, fr. MF or L; MF *predestiner*, fr. L *praedestinare* to determine beforehand, fr. *prae-* pre- + *destinare* to determine — more at DESTINE] **:** to destine, decree, determine, appoint, or settle beforehand **:** foreordain esp. by divine decree or eternal purpose ⟨advocates of the doctrine of double predestination maintain that God ~s some to eternal life and others to eternal death⟩
pre·destiny \"+\ *n* [*pre-* + *destiny*] **:** PREDESTINATION, FATE
pre·determinate \"+\ *adj* [LL *praedeterminatus*, fr. past part. of *praedeterminare* to predetermine] **:** PREDETERMINED

pre·determination \"+\ *n* [partly fr. *predetermine* + *-ation*, partly fr. *pre-* + *determination*] **:** the act of predetermining or the state of being predetermined: as **a** *archaic* **:** a decision made beforehand esp. without due consideration **b :** the ordaining of events beforehand **c :** PREDESTINATION ⟨the ~ of God's will⟩ **d :** a previous mental determination **:** a purpose formed beforehand **e :** a fixing or settling in advance ⟨this is not an insinuation that there was any ~ of such a sequence of developmental steps leading to ourselves —A.L. Kroeber⟩ **f :** the calculation or discovery of something beforehand ⟨~ of the cost of construction⟩

pre·determine \"+\ *vb* [LL *praedeterminare*, fr. L *prae-* pre- + *determinare* determine] *vt* **1 a :** FOREORDAIN, PREDESTINE **b :** to determine beforehand **:** settle in advance ⟨it is impossible to ~ the specific problems that he will meet —W.J.Reilly⟩ **2 :** to impose a direction or tendency on beforehand **~** *vi* **:** to determine or resolve beforehand

predetermined cost *n* **:** a cost estimated or computed in advance of production to which it applies — see STANDARD COST; compare ACTUAL COST, HISTORICAL COST

pre·determinedly \¦prē+\ *adv* [*predetermined* (past part. of *predetermine*) + *-ly*] **:** in a predetermined manner

pre·determinism \"+\ *n* [*predetermine* + *-ism*] **:** the view that the development of the individual is predetermined by heredity

predial *var of* PRAEDIAL

pre·diastolic \(¦)prē+\ *adj* [*pre-* + *diastolic*] **:** occurring or audible before the diastole of the heart ⟨a ~ murmur⟩

[1]**pred·i·ca·ble** \'predəkəbəl, -dēk-\ *n* -s [ML *praedicabile*, fr. neut. of *praedicabilis* capable of being predicated, fr. LL *praedicare* to predicate + L *-abilis* -able] **:** something that may be predicated **:** a general attribute of a class; *esp* **:** one of the five most general kinds of attribution in traditional logic that include genus, species, difference, property, and accident

[2]**predicable** \"\ *adj* [ML *praedicabilis*] **:** capable of being predicated or asserted

pre·dic·a·ment \prē'dikəmənt, prə̇'d-, *in sense 1 usu* 'predək- *or* 'predēk-\ *n* -s [ME, fr. LL *praedicamentum*, fr. *praedicare* to predicate + L *-mentum* -ment; trans. of Gk *katēgoria* category] **1 :** the character, status, or classification assigned by a predication; *specif* **:** CATEGORY 1 **2** *archaic* **:** CONDITION, STATE **3 :** a difficult, perplexing, or trying situation **:** a position imposing a hard or unwelcome choice ⟨everywhere he could observe, in new shapes and sizes, the old ~*s* and follies of men —E.B.White⟩ **4 :** a near near-fall in wrestling that scores one point for the aggressor

syn DILEMMA, QUANDARY, PLIGHT, SCRAPE, FIX, JAM, PICKLE: PREDICAMENT suggests a difficult situation bringing perplexity about best procedure for extrication, sometimes with lack of freedom to do what one would prefer ⟨the *predicament* of our contemporary English drama, forced to deal almost exclusively with cases of sexual attraction, and yet forbidden to exhibit the incidents of that attraction or even to discuss its nature —G.B.Shaw⟩ ⟨in the *predicament* with which our civilization now finds itself confronted — the problem, namely, how to find healthy, happy leisure for all the working millions who are now being liberated by machines from their day-long toils —L.P.Smith⟩ DILEMMA may apply to a predicament extending a choice between equally unpleasant or unsatisfactory alternatives ⟨a *dilemma* arose, when the weary emigrants came to a point where the stream forked, and no one knew which fork to follow —G.R.Stewart⟩ ⟨his *dilemma* is that he can neither use his terms with the simple directness of the natural scientist pointing to physical factors, nor with the assurance of a philosopher who has some source for their meaning in the system from which he begins his deduction —R.M.Weaver⟩ QUANDARY may focus attention on puzzlement and perplexity without clear analysis between possible choices ⟨he was in a greater *quandary* than ever. Lord, Lord, he thought, what had he got into? —Theodore Dreiser⟩ PLIGHT may refer to any unfortunate, trying, or unhappy situation ⟨why then discharge the men from the electric plant and then try to support them anyway, seeing that they are not likely to get other employment, or, if they do, will displace others who would be in a similar *plight* —M.R.Cohen⟩ ⟨the *plight* of the ten million forgotten men and women living at or below the destitution level —R.H.S.Crossman⟩ SCRAPE may refer to a situation, often one in which one has involved oneself carelessly or rashly, from which he becomes disentangled with difficulty or loss, esp. one impairing his reputation ⟨other young clergymen, much greater fools in many respects than he, would not have got into these *scrapes*. He seemed to have developed an aptitude for mischief —Samuel Butler †1902⟩ ⟨he escapes from trouble only to become idiotically conceited; and in the grip of conceit he plunges dementedly into a more ghastly *scrape* than the last —F.A.Swinnerton⟩ FIX and JAM, informal words, stress involvement and entanglement from which extrication is difficult ⟨I am . . . self-employed, and when you are in that *fix* you cannot tell when you are on vacation and when you are working —Frank Sullivan⟩ ⟨they get sick and it puts them in a *jam* and they end up under a pile of bills —Hamilton Basso⟩ PICKLE, now rather dated, may refer to any particularly embarrassing or sorry situation ⟨I worked hard enough to earn my passage and my victuals. But when I was left ashore in Melbourne I was in a pretty *pickle* —G.B. Shaw⟩ **syn** see in addition CLASS

pred·i·ca·men·tal \¦predəkə¦mentᵊl, -dēk- *sometimes* prē¦dik- *or* prə̇¦d-\ *adj* **:** of or relating to a predicament (sense 1)

[1]**pred·i·cant** \'predəkənt, -dēk-\ *n* -s [MF, fr. LL *praedicant-*, *praedicans*, pres. part. of *praedicare* to preach — more at PREACH] **1 :** PREACHER; *specif* **:** a preaching friar **:** DOMINICAN **2** [modif. of D *predikant*] **:** PREDIKANT

[2]**predicant** \"\ *adj* [LL *praedicant-*, *praedicans*, pres. part. of *praedicare* to preach] **:** devoted to preaching ⟨the Dominicans are a ~ order⟩

[1]**pred·i·cate** \'predəkə̇t, -dēk- *sometimes* -də,kā|; *usu* |d·+V\ *n* -s [LL *praedicatum*, fr. neut. of *praedicatus*, past part. of *praedicare* to predicate, preach, fr. L, to proclaim publicly, assert — more at PREACH] **1 a :** something that is affirmed or denied of the subject in a proposition in logic ⟨in "paper is white", whiteness is the ~⟩ **b :** a term designating a property or relation **:** a propositional function of one or more arguments **2 :** the part of a sentence or clause that expresses what is said of the subject and that usu. consists of a verb with or without objects, complements, or adverbial modifiers **3 :** a title asserting something ⟨"mother of God" is a ~ of Mary⟩

[2]**pred·i·cate** \-də,kāt, *usu* -ād·+V\ *vb* -ED/-ING/-S [LL *praedicatus*, past part. of *praedicare* to assert, predicate, preach, fr. L, to proclaim publicly, assert — more at PREACH] *vt* **1 a :** AFFIRM, DECLARE, PROCLAIM **b** *archaic* **:** PREACH **c** *obs* **:** COMMEND, PRAISE **2 a :** to assert or affirm as a quality, attribute, or property — used with following *of* ⟨~*s* intelligence of man⟩ **b** *logic* **:** to affirm of the subject of a proposition **:** make (a term) the predicate in a proposition **3 :** FOUND, BASE ⟨any code of ethics must be *predicated* upon the basic principles of truth and honesty —H.A.Wagner⟩ **4** [by alter.] *archaic* **:** PREDICT **5 :** to convey an implication of ⟨~*s* the arrival of a revolutionary situation —George Soule⟩ **~** *vi* **:** to assert something about another thing **:** AFFIRM, DECLARE **syn** see ASSERT

[3]**pred·i·cate** *pronunc at* [1]PREDICATE\ *adj* **:** belonging to the predicate; *specif* **:** completing the meaning of a copula or link verb ⟨~ noun⟩ ⟨~ adjective⟩

predicate calculus *n* [trans. of G *prädikatenkalkül*] **:** FUNCTIONAL CALCULUS

predicate nominative *n* **:** a predicate noun or pronoun in the nominative or common case completing the meaning of a link verb (as *consul* in "Caesar consul erat" or "Caesar was consul")

predicate term *n* [[1]*predicate*] **:** PREDICATE 1 a

predicate variable *n*, *logic* **:** a variable for which a predicate may be substituted

pred·i·ca·tion \,predə'kāshən\ *n* -s [ME *predicacion*, fr. OF *predication*, fr. L *praedication-*, *praedicatio*, act of proclaiming, fr. *praedicatus* (past part. of *praedicare* to proclaim) + *-ion-*, *-io* -ion — more at PREACH] **1** *archaic* **a :** an act of proclaiming or preaching **b :** SERMON **2 :** an act or instance of predicating **:** AFFIRMATION, ASSERTION: as **a :** the expression of action, state, or quality by a grammatical predicate **b** *logic* **:** the affirming something of another thing; *esp* **:** the attachment of a predicate to a subject, ascription of a property to an individual, or assignment of something to a class — see ESSENTIAL PREDICATION; compare SUBJECTION

pred·i·ca·tional \¦==¦kāshənᵊl, -shnəl\ *adj* [*predication* + *-al*] **:** of, relating to, or forming a predication or a predicate

pred·i·ca·tive \'predə,kād·|iv, -āt|, |ēv, *chiefly Brit* pri'dikətiv\ *adj* [LL *praedicativus*, fr. *praedicatus* (past part. of *praedicare* to assert, predicate) + L *-ivus* -ive] **:** expressing affirmation or predication **:** DECLARATORY; *esp* **:** constituting a predicate or part of one — **pred·i·ca·tive·ly** \-ə̇vlē, -li\ *adv*

pred·i·ca·tor \'predə,kād·ə(r), -atə-\ *n* -s [MF *predicatour*, fr. LL *praedicator*, fr. L, proclaimer, fr. *praedicatus* (past part. of *praedicare* to proclaim) + *-or* — more at PREACH] **1 :** one that predicates **2** *archaic* **:** PREACHER; *esp* **:** a preaching friar

pred·i·ca·to·ry \'predəkə,tōrē\ *adj* [LL *praedicatorius*, fr. *praedicatus* (past part. of *praedicare* to preach + L *-orius* -ory] **:** of or relating to preaching

pre·dict \prē'dikt, prə̇'d-\ *vb* -ED/-ING/-S [L *praedictus*, past part. of *praedicere* to predict, fr. *prae-* pre- + *dicere* to say — more at DICTION] *vt* **:** to declare in advance **:** PROPHESY ⟨the katydids ~ frost in six more weeks —Corey Ford⟩ **~** *vi* **:** to make a prediction **:** PROPHESY **syn** see FORETELL

pre·dict·abil·i·ty \=,=əbīləd·ē, -lətē, -i\ *n* **:** the quality or state of being predictable

pre·dict·a·ble \='==bəl\ *adj* [*predict* + *-able*] **:** capable of being foretold ⟨are clearly drifting into ~ chaos and critical dilution of standards —H.D.Gideonse⟩ — **pre·dict·a·bly** \-blē,-bli\ *adv*

predicted firing *n* [fr. past part. of *predict*] **:** the firing at a point at which a moving target will arrive at the same time as the projectile according to predictions based on observations — compare [2]LEAD 3 g

pre·dic·tion \prē'dikshən, prə̇'d-\ *n* -s [L *praediction-*, *praedictio*, fr. *praedictus* (past part. of *praedicere* to predict) + *-ion-*, *-io* -ion] **1 a :** an act of predicting **b :** something that is predicted **:** FORECAST, PROPHECY **2** *obs* **:** PORTENT **3 :** an inference regarding a future event based on probability theory

pre·dic·tive \-ktiv\ *adj* [LL *praedictivus*, fr. L *praedictus* + *-ivus* -ive] **:** of, relating to, or usable or valuable for prediction — **pre·dic·tive·ly** \-tə̇vlē\ *adv*

pre·dic·tor \-ktə(r)\ *n* -s [ML *praedictor*, fr. L *praedictus* + *-or*] **1 :** one that predicts ⟨every hillside and prairie mile and desert ridge is a mirror of the past and a ~ of the future —R. W.Howard⟩ **2 :** a mechanism for controlling antiaircraft fire by calculating the precise position of an aircraft on arrival of a shell

pre·dic·to·ry \-ktərē\ *adj* [*predict* + *-ory*] *archaic* **:** PREDICTIVE, PROPHETIC

pre·digest \(¦)prē+\ *vt* [*pre-* + *digest*] **1 :** to subject to predigestion **:** digest beforehand **2 :** to simplify for easy use ⟨want our great works even more thoroughly ~*ed* in the form of textbooks, condensations, summaries, and the like —Crane Brinton⟩

pre·digestion \¦prē+\ *n* [*pre-* + *digestion*] **1** *obs* **:** premature or too rapid digestion **2 :** artificial partial digestion of food (as by enzymatic action) for use in illness or impaired digestion

pre·di·kant \¦prādē¦känt\ *n* -s [D, fr. MF *predicant* — more at PREDICANT] **:** PREACHER; *specif* **:** a minister of the Dutch Reformed Church

predi·lect \¦predᵊl¦ekt, -rēd-, -ē,dī,le-\ *or* **predi·lect·ed** \-tə̇d\ *adj* [*predilect* fr. ML *praedilectus*, past part. of *praediligere; predilected* fr. *predilect* + *-ed*] **:** PREFERRED, CHOSEN ⟨not the most obstinately ~ optimism can blind us to the growing canker —H.B.Alexander⟩

predi·lec·tion \¦predᵊl¦ekshən, -də¦le- *also* -rēdᵊl- *sometimes* -rē,dī¦le-\ *n* -s [F *prédilection*, fr. ML *praedilectus*, (past part. of *praediligere* to prefer, love more, fr. L *prae-* pre- + *diligere* to love) + F *-ion* — more at DILIGENT] **:** a favorable prepossession **:** INCLINATION, LIKING, PREFERENCE ⟨a ~ for straight bourbon —C.V.Little⟩

syn PARTIALITY, PREPOSSESSION, PREJUDICE, BIAS: PREDILECTION indicates a previous liking or temperamental predisposition ⟨one or two authors of fiction for whom I have a *predilection* and whose works I look out for —A.C.Benson⟩ ⟨the person with a *predilection* for history may think of such treasured shrines as Independence Hall, Valley Forge Park, and the Gettysburg Battlefields —*Amer. Guide Series: Pa.*⟩ PARTIALITY indicates a disposition to favor a person or thing, sometimes unfairly or with partisanship or undue fondness ⟨fond *partiality* for their own daughters' performance, and total indifference to any other person's —Jane Austen⟩ ⟨sometimes newcomers to the fleet were a bit annoyed over the skipper's *partiality* toward this absentminded youth —L.C. Douglas⟩ PREPOSSESSION implies a fixed idea or notion, esp. a value judgment, that dominates and is likely to preclude objective judgment of something seeming counter to it ⟨we have not only to realise how our own *prepossessions* and the metaphysical figments of our own creation have obscured the simple realities of religion and science alike —Havelock Ellis⟩ PREJUDICE indicates a preconceived notion, a judgment before evidence is available, or an unreasoned prepossession, often an unfavorable one marked by suspicion, dislike, or antipathy ⟨but she had *prejudices* on the side of ancestry; she had a value for rank and consequence, which blinded her a little to the faults of those who possessed them —Jane Austen⟩ ⟨every one I knew well in Sligo despised Nationalists and Catholics, but all disliked England with a *prejudice* that had come down perhaps from the days of the Irish Parliament —W.B.Yeats⟩ BIAS may indicate an imbalance or distortion in judgment with a resulting unreasoned and unfair inclination for or against a person or thing ⟨we can discover some of our own peculiarities, our own particular slant or *bias* —A.J.Toynbee⟩ ⟨the personal *bias* of the brilliant founder of psychoanalysis has given the Freudian psychology more than one twist —Edward Sapir⟩

pre·diluvian \¦prē+\ *adj* [*pre-* + L *diluvium* flood + E *-an* — more at DELUGE] **:** ANTEDILUVIAN 1

preding *pres part of* PREDE

pre·dispose \¦prē+\ *vb* [*pre-* + *dispose*] *vt* **:** to dispose in advance **:** make susceptible **:** INCLINE ⟨there was little about this baby-faced young man to ~ people in his favor —Thomas Mann⟩ ⟨~ the miner to rheumatism —Lewis Mumford⟩ **~** *vi* **:** to bring about susceptibility ⟨exposure to cold and dampness . . . ~ to infection —H.J.Morgan⟩

predisposed *adj* [fr. past part. of *predispose*] **1 :** having a predisposition **:** INCLINED, SUSCEPTIBLE, TENDING **2 :** arranged or settled in advance ⟨took up his ~ place in society⟩

pre·disposition \(¦)prē+\ *n* [*pre-* + *disposition*] **:** a condition of being predisposed **:** INCLINATION, TENDENCY ⟨habits and ~*s* requisite to . . . painstaking work on one manuscript —Harry Bober⟩ ⟨there is less ~ to attend college in the face of discouraging odds in some homes than in others —B.G. Gallagher⟩ ⟨a certain degree of hereditary ~ to cancer is apparent in man —G.E.Wakerlin⟩

predivine *vb* [L *praedivinare*, fr. *prae-* pre- + *divinare* to divine] *obs* **:** to divine beforehand

pred·most race \pər'zhed,mōst-\ *n*, *usu cap P* [fr. *Předmost*, village in central Czechoslovakia] **:** BRÜNN RACE

pred·nis·o·lone \pred'nisə,lōn\ *n* -s [*prednis-* (as in *prednisone*) + *-ol* + *-one* (as in *prednisone*)] **:** a glucocorticoid $C_{21}H_{28}O_5$ that is a dehydrogenated analogue of hydrocortisone, is similar in biological action to prednisone, and is often used in the form of an ester or a methyl derivative

pred·ni·sone \'prednə,sōn\ *n* -s [prob. fr. *pre*gnane + *-diene* + cort*isone*] **:** a crystalline or amorphous glucocorticoid drug $C_{21}H_{26}O_5$ that is a dehydrogenated analogue of cortisone, is more active biologically than cortisone, and is used similarly

pre·dom·i·nance \prē'dämənən(t)s, prə̇'d-\ *n* [F *prédominance*, fr. MF *predominer* to predominate + *-ance*] **1 a :** the quality or state of being predominant **:** controlling influence **:** ASCENDANCY ⟨her great tradition of continued ~ and uninterrupted empire —Hilaire Belloc⟩ **b :** numerical superiority **:** MAJORITY, PREVALENCE ⟨a ~ of water colors marked the exhibition⟩ **2 :** the power or influence over human affairs assigned in astrology to heavenly bodies

pre·dom·i·nan·cy \-nənsē, -si\ *n* -ES [[1]*predominant* + *-cy*] **:** PREDOMINANCE

[1]**pre·dom·i·nant** \-nənt\ *adj* [MF *predominant*, fr. ML *praedominant-*, *praedominans*, pres. part. of *praedominari* to predominate, fr. L *prae-* pre- + *dominari* to rule, govern — more at DOMINATE] **:** holding an ascendancy **:** having superior strength, influence, authority, or position **:** CONTROLLING, DOMINATING, PREVAILING ⟨the town and the school district were the ~ governmental units —Margie Malmberg⟩ ⟨could yield to the pressure of a ~ self-interest —J.L.Motley⟩ **syn** see DOMINANT

[2]**predominant** \"\ *n* **1 :** one that predominates **2 :** an organism occupying a position of marked importance in an ecological community without being a true dominant; *esp* **:** a vertebrate holding a conspicuous position in a predominantly plant community ⟨the buffalo constituted a true ~ on the western grass lands⟩

pre·dom·i·nant·ly *adv* **:** in a predominant manner

[1]**pre·dom·i·nate** \-mənə̇t\ *adj* [alter. (influenced by *moderate*, adj.) of *predominant*] **:** PREDOMINANT ⟨the ~ gonadal sex in cases of true hermaphroditism —*Jour. Amer. Med. Assoc.*⟩ — **pre·dom·i·nate·ly** *adv*

[2]**pre·dom·i·nate** \prē'dämə,nāt, prə̇'d-, *usu* -ād·+V\ *vb* [ML *praedominatus*, past part. of *praedominari* to predominate — more at PREDOMINANT] *vi* **1** *obs* **:** to have determining astrological influence **2 a :** to exert controlling power or influence **:** exercise superiority (as in strength or authority) **:** GOVERN, PREVAIL, RULE ⟨moral and humane tendencies . . . normally ~ over the sadistic strain in human nature —Alfred Cobban⟩ **b :** to hold advantage in numbers or quantity **:** PREPONDERATE ⟨sagebrush is the *predominating* growth —G.R.Stewart⟩ **~** *vt* **:** to exert control over **:** DOMINATE, GOVERN, RULE ⟨his smile *predominated* his features —Alvin Redman⟩ ⟨hardwoods . . . ~ the forest lands there —*Subscription Books Bull.*⟩

pre·dom·i·nat·ing·ly \='==,===, =,=='===\ *adv* [*predominating* (pres. part. of *predominate*) + *-ly*] **:** PREDOMINANTLY

pre·dom·i·na·tion \=,=='nāshən\ *n* [*predomine* + *-ation*] **:** PREDOMINANCE

predomine *vb* [MF *predominer*, fr. ML *praedominari*] *obs* **:** PREDOMINATE

pre·doom \(')prē+\ *vt* [*pre-* + *doom*] **1** *archaic* **:** to doom or condemn beforehand **2** *archaic* **:** to condemn to (a penalty) in advance

pre–dravidian \¦prē+\ *n*, *usu cap D* [*pre-* + *Dravidian*] **:** a member of an ethnic group chiefly in India believed by some anthropologists to be a blend of Negrito and proto-Australoid or Veddoid

pre·dreadnought \'prē+¦-\ *n* [*pre-* + *dreadnought*] **:** the heaviest battleship carrying mixed-caliber batteries and preceding development of the dreadnought

pre·dynastic \¦prē+\ *adj* [*pre-* + *dynastic*] **:** of or relating to a time before dynasties, esp. before the ancient Egyptian dynasties ruling from about 3400 B.C.

pree \'prē\ *vt* **preed**; **preed**; **preeing**; **prees** [short fr. *preve*, to test, prove, fr. ME *proeven*, *preven* fr. OF *preuv-*, pres. stem of *prover* to test, prove — more at PROVE] *Scot* **:** to taste tentatively **:** SAMPLE — **pree the mouth of** *Scot* **:** KISS

pre·echo \(')prē+\ *n* [*pre-* + *echo*] **:** an echo in a sound recording (as a phonograph record) that is mechanically induced by a manufacturing fault and is heard before the sound causing it when the recording is played

pre·eclampsia \¦=+\ *n* [NL, fr. *pre-* + *eclampsia*] **:** a toxic condition developing in late pregnancy characterized by a sudden rise in blood pressure, excessive gain in weight, generalized edema, albuminuria, severe headache, and visual disturbances — **pre·eclamptic** \"+\ *adj*

preef \'prēf\ *chiefly Scot var of* PROOF

[1]**pre·election** \¦prē+\ *n* [*pre-* + *election*] **1 a** *obs* **:** PREFERENCE **b :** PREDESTINATION **2** *archaic* **:** election in advance

[2]**preelection** \"\ *adj* [*pre-* + *election*] **:** preceding an election ⟨a ~ campaign leaflet —*New Yorker*⟩ ⟨~ meeting⟩ ⟨~ pledge⟩

pre·electric \"+\ *or* **pre·electrical** \"+\ *adj* [*pre-* + *electric* or *electrical*] **:** preceding general use of electricity

preem \'prēm\ *n* -s [by shortening & alter.] *slang* **:** PREMIERE 1

pre·emergence \¦prē+\ *adj* [*pre-* + *emergence*] **:** used or occurring before emergence of seedlings aboveground ⟨dramatic success has been achieved with ~ herbicides —*Chem. & Engineering News*⟩ ⟨no ~ injury occurred in the field —*Experiment Station Record*⟩

preemie *var of* PREMIE

pre·em·i·nence \prē'emənən(t)s\ *n* [ME, fr. LL *praeeminentia*, fr. *praeeminent-*, *praeeminens* preeminent + L *-ia* -y] **1 :** the quality or state of being preeminent **:** superiority in rank, position, or influence **:** surpassing excellence **:** dominant authority ⟨more important than any legal sanction was . . . the personal ~ he had won —John Buchan⟩ ⟨corn moved forward . . . in the race with soybeans for ~ as a chemurgic crop —*Collier's Yr. Bk.*⟩ **2** *archaic* **:** a particular distinction or honor or an outstanding quality

pre·em·i·nen·cy \-nənsē\ *n* [LL *praeeminentia*] *archaic* **:** PREEMINENCE

pre·em·i·nent \-nənt\ *adj* [LL *praeeminent-*, *praeeminens*, fr. L, pres. part. of *praeeminere* to be outstanding, excel, fr. *prae-* pre- + *eminere* to stand out — more at EMINENT] **:** having paramount rank, dignity, or importance **:** FIRST, OUTSTANDING, SUPREME ⟨was able to achieve to a ~ degree the combination of two great gifts —M.R.Cohen⟩ ⟨the ~ classic in its category —R.L.Taylor⟩ ⟨the cuisine is . . . ~ for its seafood —E.A. Weeks⟩ — **pre·em·i·nent·ly** *adv*

pre·emphasis \(')prē+\ *n* [*pre-* + *emphasis*] **:** the intentional alteration of the relative strengths of signals at different frequencies (as in radio and in disc recording) to reduce adverse effects (as noise) in the following parts of the system

pre·empt \prē'em(p)t\ *vb* -ED/-ING/-S [back-formation fr. *preemption*] *vt* **1 :** to settle upon (public land) with a right of preemption **:** take by preemption **2 :** to seize upon to the exclusion of others **:** take for oneself **:** APPROPRIATE ⟨prose has ~*ed* a lion's share of the territory once held . . . by poetry —J.L.Lowes⟩ ⟨as the immigrants ~*ed* the central areas of the cities, the older stock moved out toward the . . . suburbs —Oscar Handlin⟩ **~** *vi* **:** to make a preemptive bid in bridge **syn** see APPROPRIATE

pre·emp·tion \-'em(p)shən\ *n* -s [ML *praeemptus* (past part. of *praeemere* to buy beforehand, fr. L *prae-* pre- + *emere* to take, buy) + E *-ion* — more at REDEEM] **1 :** the act or right of purchasing before others: as **a :** the privilege or prerogative formerly enjoyed by the king of buying provisions at an appraised valuation for his household in preference to others **b :** the prior right belonging among some primitive peoples to persons standing in various family, tribal, or neighborhood relations to purchase property sold or proposed to be sold to a stranger at the price offered by the stranger **c :** the right of a belligerent to seize and purchase at an appraised price other contraband of war than absolute contraband belonging to a neutral and en route to an enemy in its own territory or on the high seas or in unappropriated territory **d :** a preemption right or a piece of land occupied under one **2 :** a prior seizure or appropriation **:** a taking possession before others ⟨raises the question of federal ~ of the security field —*Report: Amer. Civil Liberties Union*⟩ ⟨the agency's ~ of all . . . power and responsibility —A.G.Harper⟩

pre·emp·tion·er \-sh(ə)nə(r)\ *n* -s [*preemption* + *-er*] **:** the holder of a preemption right; *also* **:** PREEMPTOR

preemption right *n* **:** a right of preemption; *specif* **:** a right given by public land laws whereby a citizen may claim and buy under stated conditions a portion not exceeding 160 acres of public land

pre·emp·tive \-m(p)tiv, -tēv *also* -təv\ *adj* [ML *praeemptus* + E *-ive*] **1 :** of or relating to preemption **:** having power to preempt **:** PREEMPTING **2 :** of, relating to, or constituting a bid in bridge that is higher than necessary and is designed to shut out shifts by the partner or bids by the opponents — **pre·emp·tive·ly** \-tə̇vlē, -li\ *adv*

preemptive right *n* **:** the right of existing shareholders to purchase additional stock offered for sale for cash prior to its being offered for sale to others

pre·emp·tor \prē'em(p)tə(r) *also* -,tȯ(ə)r *or* -ȯ(ə)\ *n* -s [ML *praeemptus* + E *-or*] **:** one that preempts; *specif* **:** one that preempts land

pre·emp·to·ry \-m(p)t(ə)rē, -ri\ *adj* [ML *praeemptus* + E *-ory*] **:** of or relating to preemption

preems *pl of* PREEM

[1]**preen** \'prēn\ *n* -s [ME *prene*, fr. OE *prēon;* akin to MD *priem* bodkin, MLG *prēn*, *prīm* pin, awl, MHG *pfrieme* awl] **1** *dial chiefly Brit* **a :** a metal pin ⟨needles and ~*s*⟩ **b :** BROOCH **2** *dial chiefly Brit* **:** something of trifling value ⟨he never cared a ~ for her —G.O.Brown⟩

[2]**preen** \"\ *vt* -ED/-ING/-S [ME *prenen*, fr. *prene*] *chiefly Scot* : [2]PIN

[3]**preen** \"\ *vb* -ED/-ING/-S [ME *preinen*, alter. (influenced by ME *prenen*) of *proinen, prunen*] *vt* **1** : to trim or dress with or as if with the beak or the tongue ⟨pigeons ~*ed* themselves and cooed softly —D.H.Lawrence⟩ ⟨a cat ~*s* its fur⟩ **2** : to dress or smooth (oneself) up : arrange (the clothing or hair) fastidiously ⟨he ~*ed* back his hair, which lay slick and thin on his head —D.C.Loughlin⟩ **3** : to pride or congratulate (oneself) for achievement ⟨~*ed* himself on having put across another sharp deal —David Walden⟩ ⟨~*ed* himself upon his sapience —Amy Lowell⟩ ~ *vi* **1** : to make sleek : DRESS, TRIM **2** : GLOAT, SWELL ⟨~*ed* as he addressed the convention opening —*Newsweek*⟩ ⟨she ~*ed*, approving her adolescence —Virginia Woolf⟩

pre·engage \ˌprē+\ *vb* [*pre-* + *engage*] *vt* : to engage beforehand: as **a** : to bind by a prior obligation or pledge esp. of marriage **b** : to win over or obtain beforehand : PREPOSSESS **c** : PREOCCUPY ~ *vi* : to bind or pledge oneself beforehand

pre·engagement \"+\ *n* [partly fr. *pre-* + *engagement*, partly fr. *preengage* + *-ment*] **1** : the act of preengaging or the state of being preengaged : a prior engagement or obligation; *esp* : a previous engagement to marry **2** : PREOCCUPATION

pre·engineering \(ˌ)ē+\ *adj* [*pre-* + *engineering*] : preliminary to or preparing for an engineering course

preen gland *n* [[3]*preen*] : UROPYGIAL GLAND

pre·equalization \(ˌ)prē+\ *n* [*pre-* + *equalization*] : PRE-EMPHASIS

pre·erythrocytic \ˌprē+\ *adj* [*pre-* + *erythrocytic*] : of, relating to, or being exoerythrocytic stages of a malaria parasite that occur before the red blood cells are invaded

prees *pres 3d sing of* PREE

pre·essential \ˌprē+\ *n* [*pre-* + *essential*] : a prerequisite essential

pre·establish \"+\ *vt* [*pre-* + *establish*] : to establish beforehand

preestablished harmony *n* [fr. past part. of *preestablish*] : a harmony declared by the philosopher Leibniz to be established eternally in advance between all monads but esp. between mind and matter

pre·examination \ˌprē+\ *n* [*pre-* + *examination*] : examination in advance or previously

pre·exile \(ˈ)prē+\ *adj* [*pre-* + *exile*] : PREEXILIAN

pre·exilian \ˌprē+\ *or* **pre·exilic** \"+\ *adj* [*preexilian* fr. *pre-* + L *exilium* + E *-an*; *preexilic* fr. *pre-* + *exile* + *-ic*] : previous to the exile of the Jews to Babylon in about 600 B.C.

pre·exist \"+\ *vb* [*pre-* + *exist*] *vi* : to exist earlier ~ *vt* : to exist before (something) ⟨monuments that ~ written history⟩

pre·existence \"+\ *n* [*pre-* + *existence*] **1** : existence in a former state or previous to something else; *specif* : existence of the soul before its union with the body — compare TRANSMIGRATION **2 a** : existence of Jesus Christ's human soul prior to his physical conception **b** : existence of the Messiah before his first advent **c** : eternal existence of the second person of the Trinity **d** : eternal existence in God of Christ as a rational principle of self-revelation in the cosmos **e** : ideal existence of Christ in the mind and eternal purpose of God

pre·existent \"+\ *adj* [*pre-* + *existent*] : existing previously : existing before something

pre·ex·ist·ent·ism \"+ˌizəm\ *n* [*preexistent* + *-ism*] : a theory that the life of the soul antedates that of the body

pre·expose \ˌprē+\ *vt* [*pre-* + *expose*] : to expose in advance or prematurely

pre·exposure \"+\ *n* [*pre-* + *exposure*] : a preliminary exposure; *specif* : a slight uniform exposure given to a sensitive photographic film or plate prior to the main exposure usu. to increase its sensitivity

preeze \ˈprēz\ *chiefly Scot var of* PRESS

pref *abbr* **1** preface **2** prefatory **3** prefect; prefecture **4** preference **5** preferred **6** prefix

[1]**pre·fab** \(ˈ)prē¦fab\ *adj* [by shortening] : PREFABRICATED

[2]**prefab** \"\ *n* -S : a prefabricated house or structure

pre·fabricate \(ˈ)prē+\ *vt* [*pre-* + *fabricate*] **1** : to fabricate all or most of the parts of (as a house) at a factory so that construction consists mainly of assembling and uniting standardized parts **2** : to produce synthetically or artificially : develop in a superficially plausible or stereotyped manner ⟨the novel's circumstances and characterizations have been tailor-made to fit a *prefabricated* scheme which is essentially false and gratuitous —Jerome Stone⟩ — **pre·fabrication** \(ˌ)prē+\ *n*

pre·fabricator \(ˈ)=+\ *n* [*prefabricate* + *-or*] : one that prefabricates; *esp* : a maker of prefabricated houses

[1]**pref·ace** \ˈprefəs\ *n* -S [ME, fr. MF, fr. ML *prefatia*, alter. of L *praefation-, praefatio* preliminary remarks, fr. *praefatus* (past part. of *praefari* to say beforehand, fr. *prae-* pre- + *fari* to say, speak) + *-ion-, -io* -ion — more at BAN] **1** *often cap* : a eucharistic prayer of thanksgiving common to most Christian liturgies forming in the Roman rite an introduction to the canon **2** : the introductory remarks of a speaker or the author's introduction to a book usu. explaining the object and scope of what follows : FOREWORD, PROLOGUE **3** : a brief paraphrase or comment formerly made upon a psalm before the singing of it in a Scottish church **4** : an approach to something : PRELIMINARY ⟨our defeat and dismay may be the ~ to our successors' victory —T.S.Eliot⟩

[2]**preface** \"\ *vb* -ED/-ING/-S *vi* **1** : to make introductory remarks or write a preface **2** *archaic* : to give a commentary upon a psalm about to be sung in a Scottish church ~ *vt* **1** : to say or write as preface ⟨a note *prefaced* to the score —Edward Sackville-West & Desmond Shawe-Taylor⟩ **2** : to usher in : PRECEDE, HERALD ⟨her cousin *prefaced* his speech with a solemn bow —Jane Austen⟩ ⟨whether the coming years will ~ a durable peace or another disastrous war —J.F.Dulles⟩ **3** : to introduce by or begin with a preface : furnish with a preface ⟨~*s* it with a reasoned and sagacious introduction —Anthony Powell⟩ **4** : to stand in front of : FRONT ⟨shows the entrance . . . *prefaced* by an open octagonal porch —John Summerson⟩ **5** : to go before as a preface : be a preface to ⟨its hardships and frustrations *prefaced* those of subsequent parties traveling in the same direction —T.D.Clark⟩ **6** *archaic* : to paraphrase or comment on (a psalm) in a Scottish church

pref·ac·er \-sə(r)\ *n* -S [*preface* + *-er*] : the maker or writer of a preface

pre·fashion \(ˈ)prē+\ *vt* [*pre-* + *fashion*] : to fashion beforehand

pre·fa·tial *or* **pre·fa·cial** \prēˈfāshəl, (ˈ)preˈf-\ *adj* [ML *prefatia* preface + E *-al*] : PREFATORY

pref·a·to·ri·al \ˌprefəˈtōrēəl, -tȯr-\ *adj* [*prefatory* + *-al*] : PREFATORY — **pref·a·to·ri·al·ly** \-rēəlē, -li\ *adv*

pref·a·to·ri·ly \ˌ==ˈ=rəlē, -li\ *adv* [*prefatory* + *-ly*] : in a prefatory manner : as a preface

pref·a·to·ry \ˈprefəˌtōrē, -tȯr-, -ri\ *adj* [L *praefatus* (past part. of *praefari* to say beforehand) + E *-ory* — more at PREFACE] **1** : of, relating to, or constituting a preface : INTRODUCTORY, PRELIMINARY ⟨~ statement⟩ **2** : located in front ⟨a broad ~ arch to the main apse —A.W.Clapham⟩

pre·fect *also* **prae·fect** \ˈprēˌfekt\ *n* -S [ME, fr. MF, fr. L *praefectus*, fr. past part. of *praeficere* to place at the head of, fr. *prae-* pre- + *facere* to make — more at DO] **1** : any of various high officials or magistrates of differing functions and ranks placed at the head of particular commands, charges, or departments in ancient Rome **2** : a chief officer or chief magistrate : PRESIDENT ⟨~ of Paris police⟩ ⟨the ~ of one of the congregations of cardinals⟩ ⟨~ of the ladies' sodality⟩ **3** : a student monitor or praepostor in English public or secondary schools and some American private schools

prefect apostolic *n, pl* **prefects apostolic** [NL *praefectus apostolicus*] : the supervising head of a prefecture apostolic

pre·fec·to·ral \(ˈ)prē¦fekt(ə)rəl\ *adj* [F *préfectoral*, fr. L *praefectus* prefect + F *-oral* (as in *électoral*)] : PREFECTORIAL

pre·fec·to·ri·al \ˌprēˌfekˈtōrēəl, -tȯr-\ *adj* [LL *praefectorius* (fr. L *praefectus* prefect + *-orius* -ory) + E *-al*] : of or relating to a prefect — **pre·fec·to·ri·al·ly** \-rēəlē, -li\ *adv*

prefect's court *n* : a court having probate jurisdiction in New Mexico

pre·fec·tur·al \(ˈ)prē¦fekchərəl\ *adj* [*prefecture* + *-al*] : of or relating to a prefecture

pre·fec·ture \ˈ=ˌ=chə(r)\ *n* -S [L *praefectura*, fr. *praefectus* prefect + *-ura* -ure] **1** : the office, position, jurisdiction, or term of office of a prefect : PRESIDENCY, SUPERINTENDENCY **2** : the official residence of a prefect **3** : the district governed by a prefect (as in the Roman Empire, in France, or in Japan)

prefecture apostolic *n, pl* **prefectures apostolic** [NL *praefectura apostolica*] *Roman Catholicism* : a district of a missionary territory in its initial stage of ecclesiastical organization

pre·fecundation \(ˌ)prē+\ *n* [*pre-* + *fecundation*] : the changes or conditions preceding fecundation esp. in the female generative organs — **pre·fecundatory** \ˌ=+\ *adj*

pre·fer \R prēˈfər, prə̇ˈ-, + *vowel* -fər-; *-R* -fə̄, + *suffixal vowel* -fər- *also* -fə̄r, + *vowel in a following word* -fər- *or* -fə̄ *also* -fə̄r\ *vt* **preferred**; **preferred**; **preferring**; **prefers** [ME *preferren*, fr. MF *preferer*, fr. L *praeferre* to bear before, put before, prefer, fr. *prae-* pre- + *ferre* to bear, carry — more at BEAR] **1 a** *archaic* : to promote or advance to a rank or position ⟨has *preferred* me to the valuable rectory of this parish —Jane Austen⟩ **b** *archaic* : to move ahead or set forward **c** *obs* : to help bring about (a result) **2** : to have a preference for : CHOOSE : like better : value more highly ⟨*preferred* to live abroad —Edward Shils⟩ ⟨the rye grasses ~ cool and moist conditions —*Farmer's Weekly (So. Africa)*⟩ ⟨that peculiar taint of barbarism which makes men ~ occasional disobedience to systematic liberty —H.T.Buckle⟩ ⟨*preferred* that excellence should thrive rather than be obscured by a many-voiced mediocrity⟩ **3** : to give (a creditor) priority : pay (a creditor) before or rather than another **4** *archaic* : to put or set forward or before someone : OFFER, PRESENT, RECOMMEND, INTRODUCE **5** : to bring or lay (as a charge, complaint, or indictment) against a person ⟨*preferred* charges against him⟩ **6** : to bring forward or lay before one for consideration, decision, or action : PROPOSE ⟨the young man seems to be *preferring* some request which the elder one is indisposed to grant —Ambrose Bierce⟩ **7** : to show preference for (one of two or more card suits bid by one's partner) **syn** see OFFER

pref·er·a·bil·i·ty \ˌpref(ə)rəˈbiləd·ē, -lətē, -i\ *n* [*preferable* + *-ity*] : PREFERABLENESS

pref·er·a·ble \ˈpref(ə)rəbəl *also* -fərb- *sometimes* prēˈfər- *or* prə̇ˈf-\ *adj* [F *préférable*, fr. *préférer* to prefer (fr. MF *preferer*) + *-able*] **1** : worthy to be preferred : having greater value or desirability **2** *obs* : exercising preference : PREFERENTIAL — **pref·er·a·bly** \-blē, -bli\ *adv*

pref·er·a·ble·ness \-bəlnə̇s\ *n* -ES : the quality or state of being preferable

pref·er·ence \ˈprefər(ə)n(t)s, -frən-\ *n* -S [F *préférence*, fr. ML *praeferentia*, fr. L *praeferent-, praeferens* (pres. part. of *praeferre* to prefer) + *-ia* -y] **1** *archaic* : PREFERABLENESS, SUPERIORITY **2 a** : the act of preferring or the state of being preferred : choice or estimation above another : higher valuation or desirability ⟨the passionate sincerity of artists and other intellectuals may still be warped by wishful ~*s* —H.J.Muller⟩ **b** : the power or opportunity of choosing ⟨gave him his ~⟩ **3** : PREFERMENT, PROMOTION ⟨the navy . . . passed him over in ~ —Taliaferro Boatwright⟩ **4 a** : the legal right to prior payment of a debt (as the expense of administration of an insolvent estate) **b** : the payment without legal justification of a debt either in full or to an extent injuring other creditors entitled to be treated on a basis of equality (as under bankruptcy or insolvency laws) **c** : DISCRIMINATION 4b **5** : someone or something that is preferred : an object of choice : FAVORITE ⟨which is your ~⟩ **6 a** : the practice of giving one or more countries legal advantages over others in international trade esp. by reduced tariffs — compare IMPERIAL PREFERENCE **b** : an advantage given one customer above others **7** : the right given by a corporation's charter to one or more classes of stocks to receive a dividend before dividends may be paid on junior shares **8 a** : a three-handed form of vint **b** : the act of bidding in bridge so as to show superior support for one of two or more suits bid by one's partner by a bid in the partner's first suit or by passing his second or third suit **syn** see CHOICE

preference stock *n, Brit* : PREFERRED STOCK

pref·er·en·dum \ˌprefəˈrendəm\ *n, pl* **preferen·da** \-də\ [NL, fr. L, neut. of gerundive of *praeferre* to prefer] : the range of a gradient item (as light, temperature, or moisture) that seems to be positively attractive to a motile organism when a selection is available

pref·er·ent \ˈpref(ə)rənt\ *adj* [L *praeferent-, praeferens*, pres. part. of *praeferre* to prefer] : exhibiting or enjoying preference

pref·er·en·tial \ˌprefəˈrenchəl\ *adj* [ML *praeferentia* preference + E *-al*] **1** : of, relating to, or showing preference : offering or constituting an advantage ⟨~ treatment⟩ **2** : of, relating to, employing, or creating a preference in trade relations ⟨a ~ rate⟩ — **pref·er·en·tial·ly** \-chəlē, -li\ *adv*

preferential ballot *n* : a ballot listing several candidates for an office and used in preferential voting

preferential hiring *n* : a policy agreed to by an employer to hire qualified union members if they are available with the understanding that nonunion workers may be hired without being required to join the union when the union cannot supply men

pref·er·en·tial·ism \-əˌlizəm\ *n* -S [*preferential* + *-ism*] : the policy or practice of granting preferences in international trade

pref·er·en·tial·ist \-ləst\ *n* -S [*preferential* + *-ist*] : an adherent of preferentialism

preferential mating *n* : mating with a relative with whom marriage is enjoined under tribal rules — compare LEVIRATE, SORORATE

preferential primary *n* : PRESIDENTIAL PRIMARY

preferential shop *n* : a shop in which under a labor contract the management gives preference to members of the union chiefly in hiring, layoffs, and dismissals and often also in promotions and work shifts, but is free to hire outside the union membership when the union is unable to supply workers

preferential tariff *n* : a tariff schedule under which one or more nations are given lower rates or other advantages over others

preferential voting *also* **preferential system** *n* : a system of voting whereby the voter indicates his order of preference for each of the candidates listed on the ballot for a specified office so that if no candidate receives a majority of first preferences the first and second preferences and if necessary third and other preferences may be counted together until one candidate obtains a majority — called also *alternative vote*; compare HARE SYSTEM, PROPORTIONAL REPRESENTATION

pre·fer·ment \prēˈfərmənt, prə̇-, -fə̄m-, *sometimes* ˈprefə(r)m-\ *n* -S [ME *preferrement*, fr. *preferren* to prefer + *-ment*] **1 a** : advancement or promotion in dignity, office, or station ⟨he could see lesser musicians receiving ~, and it galled him —Howard Taubman⟩ **b** : a position or office of honor or profit **2** *obs* : an act of preference or choice **3** : priority or seniority in right esp. to receive payment or to purchase property on equal terms with others **4** : the act of making, bringing, or laying ⟨feared that ~ of charges would quickly follow discovery⟩

[1]**preferred** *past of* PREFER

[2]**preferred** *n* -S [by shortening] : PREFERRED STOCK

preferred creditor *n* [[1]*preferred*] : a creditor whose claim takes legal precedence over other claims

preferred lie *n* : an improved lie to which a golf ball may sometimes be moved in play without penalty

preferred stock *n* **1** : stock assured by a corporation's charter of dividends before any are paid on the common and usu. also having preference in distribution of assets **2** *Brit* : common stock that takes a specified dividend ahead of a deferred common

pre·fer·rer \prēˈfərə(r), prə̇ˈ- *also* -ˈfə̄rə(r\ *n* -S [*prefer* + *-er*] : one that prefers: as **a** : PROMOTER, PATRON **b** : one that presents or submits something

preferring *pres part of* PREFER

prefers *pres 3d sing of* PREFER

pre·fig·u·rate \prēˈfigyəˌrāt\ *vt* [LL *praefiguratus*, past part. of *praefigurare* to prefigure] : PREFIGURE

pre·figuration \(ˌ)prē+\ *n* [LL *praefiguration-, praefiguratio*, fr. *praefiguratus* + L *-ion-, -io* -ion] **1** : the act of prefiguring or the state of being prefigured **2** : something that prefigures : an antecedent image or representation : FORECAST, FORESHADOWING, PROTOTYPE ⟨by that trick of lighting a ~ of age fell across her —Ngaio Marsh⟩

pre·figurative \(ˈ)prē+\ *adj* [ML *praefigurativus*, fr. LL *praefiguratus* + L *-ivus* -ive] : of, relating to, or showing by prefiguration : FORESHOWING, PREFIGURING — **pre·figuratively** \"+\ *adv* — **pre·figurativeness** \"+\ *n*

pre·figure \(ˈ)prē+\ *vt* [ME *prefiguren*, fr. LL *praefigurare*, fr. L *prae-* pre- + *figurare* to shape, picture — more at FIGURE] **1** : to show, suggest, or announce beforehand : offer or constitute an antecedent type, image, or likeness of : represent in advance ⟨children who supply us with the images by which we ~ the angelic choirs —Mary Austin⟩ **2** : to picture or imagine beforehand : FORESEE, PREDICT ⟨few writers care to ~ the future, even for so short a span —*Times Lit. Supp.*⟩

pre·fig·ure·ment \-mənt\ *n* -S [*prefigure* + *-ment*] : an image or likeness conceived or presented beforehand : a representation, embodiment, or typification in advance ⟨a ~ of 20th century dictatorships —Geoffrey Bruun⟩

pre·filter \(ˈ)prē+\ *n* [*pre-* + *filter*] : a preliminary filter

prefine *vt* [L *praefinire*, fr. *prae-* pre- + *finire* to limit — more at DEFINE] *obs* : to limit, determine, or define beforehand

pre·finish \(ˈ)prē+\ *vt* : to finish beforehand

[1]**pre·fix** \ˈprēˌfiks, prēˈf-, prə̇ˈf-\ *vt* [ME *prefixen*, fr. MF *prefixer*, fr. *pre-* + *fixer* to fix, fr. *fix* fixed, fr. L *fixus*, past part. of *figere* to fix, fasten — more at DIKE] **1** *archaic* : to fix or appoint beforehand : establish (as a boundary, a decision, or a goal) in advance **2** [partly fr. [2]*prefix*] : to place in front : add as a prefix ⟨it was flattering to a young man to be able to ~ the title of professor to his name —A.W.Long⟩

[2]**pre·fix** \ˈprēˌfiks\ *n* -ES [NL *praefixum*, fr. L, neut. of past part. of *praefigere* to fasten before, fr. *prae-* pre- + *figere*] **1** : a sound or sequence of sounds or in writing a letter or sequence of letters occurring as a bound form attached to the beginning of a word, base, or phrase and serving to produce a derivative word or an inflectional form — compare AFFIX, INFIX, SUFFIX **2** : a title used before a person's name **3** : the quantifier or group of quantifiers preceding the matrix of a formula esp. in prenex normal form

pre·fix·al \ˈprēˌfiksəl, =ˈ==\ *adj* [[2]*prefix* + *-al*] : of, relating to, or constituting a prefix : PREFIXED — **pre·fix·al·ly** \-səlē, -li\ *adv*

[1]**pre·fix·a·tion** \ˌprēˌfikˈsāshən\ *n* -S [[1]*prefix* + *-ation*] : formation or inflection by means of prefixes

[2]**prefixation** \ˌprē+\ *n* [*pre-* + *fixation*] : development or treatment prior to photographic fixation

prefixed *adj* [fr. past part. of [1]*prefix*] **1** *archaic* : settled beforehand : PREDETERMINED **2** : attached as a prefix — **prefixed·ly** \(ˈ)prēˈfiksədlē, -kstlē, -li\ *adv*

pre·fix·ion \prēˈfikshən\ *n* -S [MF *prefixion*, fr. *prefixer* to prefix + *-ion*] **1** *obs* : a fixing or appointing beforehand : PREAPPOINTMENT **2** : the placing of a word or particle before and usu. in combination with a word

pre·fixture \(ˈ)prē+\ *n* [[1]*prefix* + *-ture* (as in *fixture*)] **1** : an act of prefixing **2** : PREFIX

pre·flight \(ˈ)prē+\ *adj* [*pre-* + *flight*] : preparing for or preliminary to flight esp. of an airplane

pre·flood \"+\ *adj* [*pre-* + *flood*] : of, relating to, or remaining from a time before a flood

pre·focus \"+\ *vt* [*pre-* + *focus*] : to focus beforehand (as automotive headlights before installation)

[1]**pre·form** \"+\ *vt* [L *praeformare*, fr. *prae-* pre- + *formare* to form] **1** : to form beforehand : shape previously ⟨their natures and ~*ed* faculties —Shak.⟩ **2** : to fix or determine the form of beforehand : PREDETERMINE **3** : to bring to approximate preliminary shape and size (as a gemstone before final cutting and polishing)

[2]**preform** \"\ *n* : any of various objects of manufacture or handicraft after preliminary shaping: as **a** : a roughed-out gemstone **b** : BISCUIT 6a **c** : a tablet or roughly shaped unit of plastic molding composition that facilitates handling and weighing

pre·formant \(ˈ)prē+\ *n* [*pre-* + *formant*] : PREFORMATIVE

pre·formation \(ˌ)prē+\ *n* [*pre-* + *formation*] **1** : the act or an instance of forming beforehand : previous formation **2** : a now discredited theory in biology that every germ cell contains the organism of its kind fully formed and complete in all its parts and that development consists merely in increase in size from microscopic proportions to those of the adult — compare ENCASEMENT 1b

pre·for·ma·tion·ism \-shəˌnizəm\ *also* **pre·form·ism** \(ˈ)prē¦fȯ(r)ˌmizəm\ *n* -S [*preformationism* fr. *preformation* + *-ism*; *preformism* fr. [1]*preform* + *-ism*] : PREFORMATION 2

pre·for·ma·tion·ist \-_nəst\ *also* **pre·form·ist** \-_məst\ *n* -S : an adherent of preformationism

[1]**pre·formative** \(ˈ)prē+\ *adj* [L *praeformatus* (past part. of *praeformare* to preform) + E *-ive*] **1** : PREFORMING **2** [*pre-* + *formative*, adj.] : being a prefix ⟨a ~ affix⟩ : characterized by the use of preformatives ⟨the ~ conjugation⟩

[2]**preformative** \"\ *n* [*pre-* + *formative*, n.] : PREFIX 1 — used esp. in Semitic grammar; contrasted with *afformative*

preformed wire rope *n* [fr. past part. of [1]*preform*] : a wire rope of which each wire and strand has been given in advance the helical shape it will have in the rope with resultant increased safety

pre·former \(ˈ)prē+\ *n* -S [[1]*preform* + *-er*] : one that preforms

pre·for·mis·tic \(ˌ)prēˌfȯ(r)ˈmistik\ *adj* [*preformist* + *-ic*] : of, relating to, or in accord with the theory of preformation or its supporters

[1]**pre·frontal** \(ˈ)prē+\ *adj* [*pre-* + *frontal*] : anterior to a frontal structure ⟨a ~ bone⟩ ⟨~ convolution⟩: **a** : of or relating to a bone anterior and lateral to the frontal bone of some vertebrates ⟨the ~ ectethmoid of a teleost fish⟩ **b** : of, relating to, or being a plate or scale in the center or on each side of the head of some reptiles and fishes in front of the frontal scale **c** : of, relating to, or constituting the anterior part of the frontal lobe of the brain bounded posteriorly by the ascending frontal convolution

[2]**prefrontal** \"\ *n* : a prefrontal part (as a scale or bone)

prefrontal lobe *n* : the anterior part of the frontal lobe made up chiefly of association areas and mediating various inhibitory controls — compare LOBOTOMY

prefrontal lobotomy *also* **prefrontal leucotomy** *n* : lobotomy in which the frontal lobe of the brain is reached through holes drilled in the skull

pre·ful·gence \prēˈfəljən(t)s\ *or* **pre·ful·gen·cy** \-nsē, -si\ *n* [*prefulgence* fr. *prefulgent*, after such pairs as E *benevolent*: *benevolence*; *prefulgency* fr. *prefulgent*, after such pairs as *efficient*: *efficiency*] : the quality or state of being prefulgent

pre·ful·gent \-nt\ *adj* [L *praefulgent-, praefulgens*, fr. pres. part. of *praefulgēre*, to shine forth, fr. *prae-* pre- + *fulgēre* to shine — more at FULGENT] : surpassingly fulgent : shining most brightly

pre·game \(ˈ)prē+\ *adj* [*pre-* + *game*] : preparatory to or preceding a game ⟨~ warm-up⟩ ⟨showered with gifts in a ~ ceremony⟩

pre·ganglionic \(ˌ)prē+\ *also* **pre·gangliar** \(ˈ)prē+\ *adj* [*preganglionic* fr. *pre-* + *ganglion* + *-ic*; *pregangliar* fr. *pre-* + *ganglion* + *-ar*] : anterior or proximal to a ganglion; *specif* : being, affecting, involving, or relating to a usu. medullated efferent nerve fiber arising from a cell body in the central nervous system and terminating in an autonomic ganglion — compare POSTGANGLIONIC

pre·genial \(ˈ)prē+\ *adj* [*pre-* + Gk *geneion* chin + E *-al* — more at GENIAL] : located in front of the chin; *esp* : of, relating to, or being the anterior scales of the chin in reptiles

pre·geniculate \ˌ=+\ *adj* [*pre-* + *geniculate*] : of, relating to, or arising from a lateral geniculate body

pre·genital \(ˈ)=+\ *adj* [*pre-* + *genital*] : of, relating to, or characteristic of the oral, anal, urethral, and phallic phases of psychosexual development — compare POLYMORPHOUS-PERVERSE

pre·geological \(ˌ)prē+\ *adj* [*pre-* + *geological*] : antedating reliable geological data or responsible theory

pre·gestational \(ˌ)prē+\ *or* **pre·gestation** \ˌ=+\ *adj* [*pre-* + *gestational* or *gestation*] : taking place before the commencement of pregnancy ⟨~ flushing of ewes⟩

pre·ghie·ra \prāgˈyerə\ *n* -S [It *preghiera* prayer, fr. Prov *pregueira*, fr. ML *precaria* — more at PRAYER] : PRAYER; *specif* : a short instrumental musical composition in devotional mood

pre·glacial \(ˈ)prē+\ *adj* [*pre-* + *glacial*] : prior to a period of glaciation; *specif* : prior to the Pleistocene

preg·na·ble \'pregnəbəl\ *adj* [alter. (influenced by *pregnant*) of earlier *preignable*, alter. (influenced by such words as *reign*, *deign*, with silent *g*) of ME *prenable*, fr. MF — more at IMPREGNABLE] **1 :** vulnerable to capture **:** EXPUGNABLE ⟨a ~ fort⟩ **2** [*pregnate* + *-able*] **:** capable of being impregnated ⟨a ~ cat⟩

preg·nance \-nən(t)s\ *n* -s [fr. *pregnant*, after such pairs as E *benevolent: benevolence*] **:** PREGNANCY

preg·nan·cy \-nənsē, -si\ *n* -ES [*pregnant* + *-cy*] **1 a :** the condition of being pregnant **:** the state of being with young **:** GESTATION **b :** FERTILITY, FRUITFULNESS ⟨~ of the soil⟩ **2 a :** fertility or inventiveness of mind ⟨there was a depth and ~ in the Greek imagination —P.E.More⟩ **b :** significant quality **:** MEANINGFULNESS ⟨the traditional ~ of all great art —C.E.Montague⟩ ⟨phrases of homely vigor or happy ~ —J.L. Lowes⟩ **3** *obs* **:** promising quality **:** appearance of future usefulness or success **4 :** latent potentiality **:** richness in possible consequence or significance

pregnancy disease *n* **:** a disease of pregnant ewes that is due to carbohydrate deficiency, is marked by dullness, staggering, and collapse, and is esp. frequent in ewes carrying twins or triplets — compare KETOSIS

pregnancy test *n* **:** a physiological test to determine the existence of pregnancy in an individual (as the bitterling or Friedman test)

preg·nane \'preg,nān\ *n* -s [ISV *pregnant* + *-ane;* fr. the occurrence of its derivatives in pregnancy urine] **:** a crystalline saturated steroid hydrocarbon $C_{21}H_{36}$ that is related to cholane and is the parent compound of the corticoid and progestational hormones; 17-ethyl-androstane

pregnanediol \'=,='=,=\ *n* -s [ISV *pregnane* + *-diol*] **:** a crystalline biologically inactive dihydroxy derivative $C_{21}H_{34}(OH)_2$ of pregnane that is formed by reduction of progesterone and is found esp. in pregnancy urine in the form of its glucuronide

[1]**preg·nant** \'pregnənt\ *adj* [ME *preignant*, fr. MF, fr. pres. part. of *preindre* to press, fr. OF *priembre*, fr. L *premere* — more at PRESS] *archaic* **:** COGENT, CONVINCING, FORCIBLE, PRESSING ⟨a ~ example⟩

[2]**pregnant** \"\ *adj* [ME, fr. L *praegnant-*, *praegnans*, alter. (influenced by *-ant-*, *-ans* -ant) of earlier *praegnat-*, *praegnas*, fr. *prae-* pre- + *gnat-* (fr. root of *nasci* to be born) — more at NATION] **1 a :** containing unborn young within the body **:** preparing to bring forth **:** GRAVID, GESTATING **b :** of or relating to pregnancy ⟨~ urine⟩ **c :** being about to produce or realize **:** containing as implicit **:** capable of producing ⟨the ideals with which the modern world is ~ —Walter Lippmann⟩ **2 a :** abounding in fancy, wit, or resource of mind **:** FERTILE, GERMINAL, INVENTIVE ⟨all this has been said . . . by great and ~ artists —*Times Lit. Supp.*⟩ **b** *obs* **:** full of promise **:** quick of apprehension **3 :** rich in significance or implication **:** heavy with suggestion or import **:** having possibilities of development or consequence **:** MEANINGFUL, WEIGHTY ⟨the journal brimmed over with his thoughts, many of them thin, diffuse, abstract, others nutty and ~ —Van Wyck Brooks⟩ **4 :** containing the germ or shape of future events **:** bearing latent potentialities, results, or issues ⟨the 1930s were ~ years —Gordon Bell⟩ **5** *obs* **:** OPEN, READY, RECEPTIVE ⟨my matter hath no voice, lady, but to your own most ~ and vouchsafed ear —Shak.⟩ **6 :** exhibiting fertility **:** TEEMING ⟨all nature seemed ~ with life —L.F. Herreshoff⟩ **syn** see EXPRESSIVE

preg·nant·ly *adv* **:** in a pregnant manner

preg·nate \'preg,nāt\ *vb* -ED/-ING/-S [LL *praegnatus*, past part. of *praegnare* to be pregnant, back-formation fr. L *praegnans* pregnant] *vi*, *obs* **:** to become fertile ~ *vt* [by shortening] **:** IMPREGNATE

preg·nene \'preg,nēn\ *n* -s [ISV *pregnane* + *-ene*] **:** an unsaturated derivative $C_{21}H_{34}$ of pregnane containing one double bond in the molecule

preg·nen·in·o·lone \,preg,nē'ninᵊl,ōn\ *n* -s [ISV *pregnene* + *-in* + *-ol* + *-one*] **:** ETHISTERONE

preg·nen·o·lone \preg'nēnᵊl,ōn\ *n* -s [ISV *pregnene* + *-ol* + *-one*] **:** a crystalline unsaturated hydroxy steroid ketone $C_{21}H_{32}O_2$ formed by the oxidation of cholesterol (as in living cells), stigmasterol, diosgenin, or other steroids and yielding progesterone on dehydrogenation; 3-hydroxy-5-pregnen-20-one

pre·gummed paper \(')prē+-\ *n* [*pre-* + *gummed*] **:** postage-stamp paper that is gummed before being printed

pregustation *n* [L *praegustatus* (past part. of *praegustare* to taste beforehand, fr. *prae-* pre- + *gustare* to taste) + E *-ion* — more at CHOOSE] *obs* **:** a tasting in advance **:** FORETASTE

pre·hallux \(')prē+\ *n* [NL, fr. *pre-* + *hallux*] **:** a rudimentary extra toe or a process that appears as a rudiment of a toe on the preaxial side of the hallux (as of a frog) — called also *calcar*

pre·halter \(')prē+\ *n*, *pl* **pre·halteres** \¦=+\ [NL, fr. *pre-* + *halter*] **:** the squama of a dipterous insect

pre·haps \prē'haps, prə'-\ *dial var of* PERHAPS

pre·harvest \(')prē+\ *adj* [*pre-* + *harvest*] **:** occurring or used shortly before the time for harvesting ⟨a ~ drop of fruit⟩

preharvest spray *n* **:** a hormone spray used to prevent preharvest drop of tree fruits (as apples)

pre·hearing \(')prē+\ *adj* [*pre-* + *hearing*] **:** preliminary to a hearing

pre·heat \"+\ *vt* [*pre-* + *heat*] **:** to heat beforehand: as **a :** to heat (an oven) to a designated temperature before placing food therein **b :** to heat (an engine) to an operating temperature before operation **c :** to heat (metal) prior to a thermal or mechanical treatment

pre·heater \"+\ *n* [*preheat* + *-er*] **:** any of various devices for preliminary heating: as **a :** a heat exchanger used in brewing and distilling **b :** any of various devices for using waste heat for preliminary heating in petroleum refining processes

pre–hellenic \¦prē+\ *adj*, *usu cap H* [*pre-* + *hellenic*] **:** of, relating to, or characteristic of the phases and periods of civilization in Greek lands before the rise of the Hellenic or classical Greek culture — compare AEGEAN, CYCLADIC, HELLADIC, MINOAN, MYCENAEAN

pre·hend \prē'hend\ *vt* -ED/-ING/-S [L *prehendere* — more at PREHENSILE] **1 :** SEIZE **2 :** APPREHEND

pre·hen·si·ble \prē'hen(t)səbəl\ *adj* [L *prehensus* (past part. of *prehendere*) + E *-ible*] **:** capable of being seized

pre·hen·sile \prē'hen(t)səl\ *adj* [F *préhensile*, fr. L *prehensus* (past part. of *prehendere* to grasp, seize, fr. *pre-* — fr. *prae-* pre- — + *-hendere* — akin to ON *geta* to get) + F *-ile* — more at GET] **1 :** adapted for seizing or grasping esp. by wrapping around ⟨the ~ tail of a monkey⟩ ⟨a ~ upper lip . . . used to pluck foliage —Grace H. Glueck⟩ **2 a :** gifted with mental grasp or moral or aesthetic insight or perception ⟨our poets — those gifted strangely ~ men —A.T.Quiller-Couch⟩ **b :** showing cupidity **:** AVARICIOUS, GREEDY ⟨increased the staff of his ~ employees —J.B.Cabell & A.J.Hanna⟩ — **pre·hen·sil·i·ty** \,prē(,)hen'silәd·ē\ *n* -ES

pre·hen·sion \prē'henchən\ *n* -s [L *prehension-*, *prehensio*, fr. *prehensus* + *-ion-*, *-io* -ion] **1 :** the act of taking hold, seizing, or grasping (as with the hand); *specif* **:** the conveyance of food or drink into the mouth **2 a :** mental apprehension **b :** an apprehension that may or may not be cognitive

pre·hen·sive \-n(t)siv, -sēv *also* -səv\ *adj* [L *prehensus* + E *-ive*] **1 :** PREHENSILE **2 :** of or relating to prehension

pre·hen·so·ri·al \¦prē(,)hen¦sōrēəl, -sȯr-\ *adj* [NL *prehensorium* organ adapted for grasping (fr. L *prehensus* + *-orium*) + E *-al*] **:** PREHENSILE

prehensorial foot *n* **:** TOXICOGNATH

pre·hepatic \¦prē+\ *adj* [*pre-* + *hepatic*] **:** anterior to or in front of the liver

pre·he·pat·i·cus \,prēhə'pad·əkəs\ *n* -ES [NL, fr. L *prae-* pre- + Gk *hēpat-*, *hēpar* liver, + L *-icus* -ic — more at HEPATIC] **:** the embryonic connective and vascular tissues from which the interstitial part of the liver is developed

pre–hispanic \¦prē+\ *adj*, *usu cap H* [*pre-* + *hispanic*] **:** of or relating to cultures prior to Spanish conquests in the western hemisphere

pre·historian \"+\ *n* [*prehistory* + *-an*] **:** an archaeologist who specializes in prehistoric man and his culture

pre·his·tor·ic \¦prē(h)i¦stȯrik, -tär-, -rēk\ *or* **pre·his·tor·i·cal** \-rəkəl, -rēk-\ *adj* [*pre-* + *historic*, *historical*] **:** of, relating to, or existing in times antedating written history — **pre·his·tor·i·cal·ly** \-rək(ə)lē, -rēk-, -li\ *adv*

prehistoric archaeology *n* **:** the study of prehistoric human evidences (as artifacts and fossilized human remains)

pre·history \(')prē+\ *n* [*pre-* + *history*] **1 :** the study of prehistoric man ⟨many different sciences, notably geology, paleontology, archaeology, comparative anatomy, and even psychology, have combined to give us that body of knowledge which we call ~ —R.W.Murray⟩ **2 :** a history of the antecedents of an event or situation ⟨the ~ of existing racial tensions must be considered⟩

prehn·ite \'prā,nīt, 'pre,-\ *n* -s [G *prehnit*, fr. Col. Van *Prehn* 18th cent. Dutch officer who brought it from the Cape of Good Hope + G *-it* [1]-ite] **:** a pale green mineral $Ca_2Al_2Si_3O_{10}(OH)_2$ that occurs in crystalline aggregates having a botryoidal or mamillary structure but only rarely in distinct crystals and that is a basic calcium aluminum silicate (hardness 6–6.5, sp. gr. 2.80–2.95)

prehn·i·tene \-,nə,tēn\ *n* -s [ISV *prehnitic* (*acid*) + *-ene*] **:** a liquid aromatic hydrocarbon $C_6H_2(CH_3)_4$ prepared with other hydrocarbons by methylation of mesitylene or pseudocumene by means of the Friedel-Crafts reaction; 1,2,3,4-tetramethyl-benzene

prehn·it·ic acid \(')prā¦nid·ik-, (')pre¦-\ *n* [ISV *prehnite* + *-ic;* prob. fr. the resemblance of the crystals to the mammillae on prehnite] **:** either of two isomeric acids derived from benzene: **a :** MELLOPHANIC ACID b **b :** a crystalline acid $C_6H_2(COOH)_4$ formed esp. by oxidation of prehnitene; 1,2,3,4-benzene-tetracarboxylic acid

pre·holiday \(')prē+\ *adj* [*pre-* + *holiday*] **:** preceding a holiday

pre–homeric \¦prē+\ *adj*, *usu cap H* [*pre-* + *homeric*] **:** antedating the Greek poet Homer or the Homeric writings

[1]**pre·hominid** \(')prē+\ *adj* [NL *Prehominidae*] **:** of or relating to the Prehominidae

[2]**prehominid** \"\ *n* -s **:** one of the Prehominidae

pre·hominidae \¦prē+\ *n pl*, *cap* [NL, fr. *pre-* + *homin-*, *homo* + *-idae*] **:** the extinct manlike primates when regarded (as by some anthropologists) as constituting a family

[1]**pre·human** \(')prē+\ *adj* [*pre-* + *human*] **1 :** antedating the appearance of human beings **2 :** being or relating to an animal in some respects like an ape but regarded as an ancestor of human beings

[2]**prehuman** \"\ *n* **:** a prehuman animal

pre·hydration \¦prē+\ *n* [*pre-* + *hydration*] **:** preliminary hydration

pre·hypophysis \"+\ *n* [NL, fr. *pre-* + *hypophysis*] **:** the anterior lobe of the pituitary body

prei·gnac \pren'yak\ *n* -s *often cap* [fr. *Preignac*, commune of Gironde dept., southwest France] **:** any of several aromatic fruity French red or white still wines

pre·ignition \¦prē+\ *n* [*pre-* + *ignition*] **:** ignition in an internal-combustion engine occurring while the inlet valve is open or before compression is completed — compare AUTOIGNITION

pre·imaginal \"+\ *adj* [*pre-* + *imaginal*] **:** of, relating to, occurring in, or constituting a stage in insect development that immediately precedes the imago

pre·imagine \"+\ *vt* [*pre-* + *imagine*] **:** to imagine in advance **:** PRECONCEIVE

pre–inca \(')prē¦iŋkə\ *adj*, *usu cap I* [*pre-* + *inca*] **:** of or relating to the pre-Incans or their culture ⟨*pre-Inca* pottery⟩

pre–incan \-kən\ *n*, *usu cap I* [*pre-inca* + *-an*] **:** a native of Bolivia, Ecuador, or Peru of the prehistoric period preceding the rise of the Inca Empire

pre·incarnate \¦prē+\ *adj* [*pre-* + *incarnate*] **:** of, relating to, or having existence before incarnation — used esp. of the second person of the Trinity

pre·inclined \"+\ *adj* [*pre-* + *inclined*] **:** prepared in advance **:** READY ⟨~ to accept his apology⟩

pre·indicate \(')prē+\ *vt* [*pre-* + *indicate*] **:** to point out in advance **:** PRESAGE, PROGNOSTICATE, FORESHOW

pre·induction \¦prē+\ *adj* [*pre-* + *induction*] **:** occurring or available prior to induction into military service ⟨~ tests⟩ ⟨~ training⟩

pre·industrial \"+\ *adj* [*pre-* + *industrial*] **:** not based on or characterized by a preponderance of industry ⟨a ~ stage of social organization⟩ ⟨~ areas⟩

pre·infection \"+\ *n* [*pre-* + *infection*] **:** an infection that is established in the body but not yet clinically manifested

pre·infective \"+\ *adj* [*pre-* + *infective*] **:** insufficiently mature to produce infection — used esp. of helminth larvae

pre·inform \"+\ *vt* [*pre-* + *inform*] **:** to provide with advance information ⟨~*ed* that his wife would be there⟩

pre·install \"+\ *vt* [*pre-* + *install*] **:** to install (as passages for wiring or pipes) in a building during construction to provide for future changes and adaptations

pre·insula \(')prē+\ *n* [NL, fr. *pre-* + *insula*] **:** the anterior part of the cerebral island of Reil

pre·intone \¦prē+\ *vt* [*pre-* + *intone*] **:** to intone beforehand in a low voice

pre·invasion \"+\ *adj* [*pre-* + *invasion*] **:** taking place in the period immediately preceding a military invasion ⟨~ diplomacy⟩

pre·invasive \"+\ *adj* [*pre-* + *invasive*] **:** not yet become invasive — used of malignant cells or lesions remaining in their original focus

pre·inventory \(')prē+\ *adj* [*pre-* + *inventory*] **:** occurring or available immediately before the taking of an inventory ⟨~ sales⟩ ⟨an excellent ~ bargain⟩

pre–islamic \¦prē+\ *adj*, *usu cap I* [*pre-* + *islamic*] **:** existing prior to the development and acceptance of the Muslim religion ⟨*pre-Islamic* Arabs⟩ ⟨*pre-Islamic* cultures of Asia Minor⟩

[1]**pre·ja·cent** \prē'jāsᵊnt\ *adj* [MF, fr. L *praejacent-*, *praejacens*, pres. part. of *praejacēre* to lie before, fr. *prae-* pre- + *jacēre* to lie — more at ADJACENT] **1** *obs* **:** PREEXISTING **2 :** being an antecedent proposition in logic from which another is developed

[2]**prejacent** \"\ *n* -s **:** a prejacent proposition in logic

pre·je·val·sky's horse \,prejə'välzkēz-, -lskēz-\ *usu cap P* [by alter.] *var of* PRZHEVALSKI'S HORSE

pre·job \(')prē+\ *adj* [*pre-* + *job*] **:** occurring before employment ⟨~ training⟩

pre·judge \(')prē¦jəj\ *vt* [MF *prejuger*, fr. L *praejudicare*, fr. *prae-* pre- + *judicare* to judge — more at JUDGE] **1 :** to judge before hearing or before full and sufficient examination **:** decide or sentence by anticipation **:** pass judgment on beforehand **2** *obs* **:** to anticipate the judgment of (another)

pre·judg·er \-jəjə(r)\ *n* -s **:** one who passes judgment beforehand

pre·judg·ment \-jəjmənt\ *n* [F *préjugement*, fr. MF *prejuger* + *-ment*] **:** an act or instance of prejudging **:** decision without adequate examination **:** PREJUDICE

pre·ju·di·cal \prē'jüdəkəl\ *adj* [by alter.] **:** PREJUDICIAL

[1]**prejudicate** *vb* -ED/-ING/-S [L *praejudicatus*, past part. of *praejudicare* to prejudge] *vt* **1** *obs* **:** to affect in a prejudicial manner **2** *obs* **:** PREJUDGE ~ *vi*, *obs* **:** to form a judgment prematurely or on the basis of incomplete or imperfect evidence

[2]**prejudicate** *adj* [L *praejudicatus* prejudged, fr. past part. of *praejudicare*] **1** *obs* **:** decided beforehand **2** *obs* **:** PRECONCEIVED **3** *obs* **:** BIASED; PREJUDICED — **prejudicately** *adv*, *obs*

pre·ju·di·ca·tion \prē,jüdə'kāshən\ *n* -s [L *praejudicatus* (past part. of *praejudicare*) + E *-ion*] **1 :** an act of prejudging **:** opinion formed in advance of or without adequate examination of evidence **2 a :** a preliminary inquiry and determination of issues not directly involved in the merits of an action under Roman law **b :** a previous decision of a point at law **:** PRECEDENT

prejudicative *adj* [L *praejudicatus* + E *-ive*] *obs* **:** PREJUDGING

[1]**prej·u·dice** \'prejədəs\ *n* -s [ME, fr. OF, fr. L *praejudicium* previous judgment, precedent, detriment, fr. *prae-* pre- + *judicium* judgment, fr. *judic-*, *judex* judge — more at JUDGE] **1 a :** injury or damage due to some judgment or action of another (as in disregard of a person's right) **:** resulting detriment — now used chiefly in phrases ⟨in the ~ of⟩ ⟨to the ~ of his own interests⟩; compare WITHOUT PREJUDICE, WITH PREJUDICE **b** *obs* **:** injury in general **:** DETRIMENT, HURT **2 a** (1) **:** preconceived judgment or opinion **:** leaning toward one side of a question from other considerations than those belonging to it **:** unreasonable predilection for or objection against something (2) **:** an opinion or leaning adverse to anything without just grounds or before sufficient knowledge **b :** an instance of such judgment or opinion **:** an unreasonable predilection, inclination, or objection **c :** an irrational attitude of hostility directed against an individual, a group, a race, or their supposed characteristics — compare *discrimination* **3** *obs* **a :** an opinion or judgment formed beforehand or without due examination **:** PREJUDGMENT **b :** PROGNOSTICATION **c :** EXPECTATION, ANTICIPATION **syn** see PREDILECTION

[2]**prejudice** \"\ *vt* -ED/-ING/-S [ME *prejudisen*, fr. MF *prejudicier*, fr. OF *prejudice* prejudice] **1 :** to injure or damage by some judgment or action usu. at law; *broadly* **:** to cause injury to **:** HURT, DAMAGE, IMPAIR ⟨~ a good cause⟩ **2 :** to cause to have prejudice **:** prepossess with opinions formed without due knowledge or examination **:** bias the mind of **:** give an unreasonable bent to ⟨~ a critic⟩ — not often used of favorable prejudice ⟨if anything could ~ me in her favor⟩ **3** *obs* **:** to judge beforehand usu. unfavorably **:** PREJUDGE

prej·u·diced \-st\ *adj* [fr. past part. of *prejudice*] **:** having a prejudice, prepossession, or bias for or against — **prej·u·diced·ly** *adv*

prej·u·dice·less \-sləs\ *adj* **:** free from prejudice **:** not prejudiced

prejudiciable *adj* [ME, fr. MF, fr. *prejudicier* to prejudice + *-able*] *obs* **:** PREJUDICIAL 1

prej·u·di·cial \¦prejə¦dishəl\ *adj* [ME, fr. ML *praejudicialis*, fr. L *praejudicium* prejudice + *-alis* -al] **1 :** tending to injure or impair **:** HURTFUL, DAMAGING, DETRIMENTAL ⟨too high a temperature is ~ to the soap —T.P.Hilditch⟩ **2** *obs* **:** being or taking the form of prejudice **:** biased, possessed, or blinded by prejudices **3 :** leading to premature judgment or unwarranted opinion — **prej·u·di·cial·ly** \-shəlē, -li\ *adv* — **prej·u·di·cial·ness** *n* -ES

pre–judicial \¦prē+\ *adj* [LL *praejudicialis* of a preceding judgment, fr. L *praejudicium* preceding judgment + *-alis* -al — more at PREJUDICE] **:** coming or decided prior to the hearing before the judex under Roman law

pre·judiciary *or* **prae·judiciary** \"+\ *adj* [L *praejudicium* prejudice + E *-ary*] **:** PREJUDICIAL

prej·u·di·cious \¦prejə¦dishəs\ *adj* [L *praejudicium* + E *-ous*] **:** PREJUDICIAL 1 — **prej·u·di·cious·ly** *adv*

preke *n* -s [origin unknown] *obs* **:** OCTOPUS

pre·kindergarten \(')prē+\ *adj* [*pre-* + *kindergarten*] **1 :** designed for or characteristic of children too young for kindergarten ⟨~ problems⟩ ⟨~ training⟩ **2 :** very young, elementary, or immature ⟨~ children⟩ ⟨~ politics⟩

pre·know \"+\ *vt* [*pre-* + *know*] **:** to know beforehand **:** FOREKNOW — **pre·knowledge** \"+\ *n*

pre·labial \"+\ *adj* [*pre-* + L *labium* lip (or NL *labium*) + E *-al*] **1 :** situated before the lips or a labium **2** [NL *prelabium* + E *-al*] **:** of or relating to a prelabium

pre·labium \"+\ *n* [NL, fr. *pre-* + *labium*] **:** the movable distal part of the insect labium

pre·lacteal \"+\ *adj* [*pre-* + *lacteal*] **1 :** preceding the milk teeth — used of early rudimentary teeth of marsupials **2 a** *of an infant food* **:** taken before milk **b** *of infant feeding* **:** preceding the taking of milk

prel·a·cy \'preləsē, -si\ *n* -ES [ME *prelacie*, fr. AF, fr. ML *praelatia* fr. *praelatus* prelate + L *-ia* -y] **1 :** the office or dignity of a prelate **:** a benefice held by a prelate **2 :** the whole body of ecclesiastical dignitaries **:** PRELATES **3 :** church government by prelates **:** EPISCOPACY

pre·lap·sar·i·an \¦prē,lap¦sa(a)rēən\ *adj* [*pre-* + L *lapsus* fall + E *-arian* (as in *infralapsarian*) — more at LAPSE] **:** characteristic of or belonging to the time or state before the fall of man

pre·larva \(')prē+\ *n* [*pre-* + *larva*] **:** a newly-hatched and very immature larva usu. differing markedly from the typical larva of its kind

prel·ate \'prelət, *usu* -əd·+V\ *n* -s [ME *prelat*, fr. OF, fr. ML *praelatus*, fr. L (suppletive past part. of *praeferre* to prefer), fr. *prae-* pre- + *latus*, suppletive past part. of *ferre* to bear — more at TOLERATE] **1 a :** an ecclesiastic of superior rank and authority **:** a dignitary of a church **b :** a member of an episcopate **c** *obs* **:** a chief priest (as of the Jews or druids) **d :** the chaplain of a fraternal society or other order **2** *obs* **:** a person in authority **:** SUPERIOR, CHIEF, LEADER **3 :** a moderate violet that is deeper and slightly bluer than Parma violet (sense 2a) and bluer than Roman purple

prel·ate·ship \-tship\ *n* [*prelate* + *-ship*] **:** the office or status of a prelate — sometimes used as a form of address

prel·at·ess \-ləd·əs\ *n* -ES [*prelate* + *-ess*] **1 :** a female prelate (as an abbess) **2 :** the wife of a prelate

pre·la·tial \prē'lāshəl\ *adj* [ML *praelatia* prelacy + E *-al*] **:** PRELATIC

pre·lat·ic \-lad·ik\ *or* **pre·lat·i·cal** \-d·əkəl\ *adj* [*prelate* + *-ic*, *-ical*] **1** *usu prelatic* **:** of, relating to, constituting, or resembling a prelate or prelacy **2** *usu prelatical* **:** adhering to prelacy **:** EPISCOPAL — often used disparagingly — **pre·lat·i·cal·ly** \-d·ək(ə)lē\ *adv*

pre·la·tion \prē'lāshən\ *n* -s [ME, fr. MF, fr. L *praelation-*, *praelatio*, fr. *praelatus* (suppletive past part. of *praeferre* to prefer) + *-ion-*, *-io* -ion — more at PRELATE] **:** an act of preferring or the condition of being preferred **:** PREFERMENT, PROMOTION

prelatish *adj* [*prelate* + *-ish*] **:** PRELATIC

prelatism *n* -s [*prelate* + *-ism*] *obs* **:** episcopacy or adherence to it — usu. used disparagingly ⟨the councils . . . were foully corrupted with ungodly ~ —John Milton⟩

prel·a·tist \'preləd·əst\ *n* -s [*prelate* + *-ist*] **:** one who supports or advocates prelacy; *esp* **:** HIGH CHURCHMAN — usu. used disparagingly

prel·a·tize \-lə,tīz\ *vb* -ED/-ING/-S [*prelate* + *-ize*] *vt* **:** to make prelatical **:** bring under prelatical influence ~ *vi* **:** to be or become prelatical

prel·at·ry \-lətrē\ *n* -s [*prelate* + *-ry*] **:** PRELACY

prel·a·ture \-lə,chu̇(ə)r\ *n* -s [F *prélature*, fr. ML *praelatura*, fr. *praelatus* prelate + L *-ura* -ure] **1 a :** the status or dignity of a prelate **:** PRELACY 1 **b :** an order of prelates **2 :** a prelatic benefice or bishopric

prelaty *n* -ES [ML *praelatia* — more at PRELACY] *obs* **:** PRELACY

pre·law \(')prē+\ *adj* [*pre-* + *law*] **:** occurring before the commencement of studies in law **:** forming a foundation for legal studies ⟨~ studies⟩; *also* **:** taking or studying a prelaw course ⟨~ and predental students⟩

prêle \'prel\ *n* -s [F, alter. (resulting fr. incorrect division of *l'aprêle*) of (assumed) earlier *aprêle*, fr. OF *asprele*, fr. (assumed) VL *asperella* (whence It *asprella*, *sprella*), fr. L *asper* rough + *-ella*] **:** HORSETAIL, SCOURING RUSH

pre·lect *also* **prae·lect** \prē'lekt\ *vi* -ED/-ING/-S [L *praelectus*, past part. of *praelegere* to read aloud and expound — more at PRAELECTOR] **:** to discourse publicly **:** LECTURE ⟨would ~ over some thriving plant —R.L.Stevenson⟩

pre·lec·tion *or* **prae·lec·tion** \-kshən\ *n* -s [L *praelection-*, *praelectio*, fr. *praelectus* + *-ion-*, *-io* -ion] **1 :** a lecture or discourse read or delivered in public (as to students) **2** [L *prae-* pre- + *lection-*, *lectio* act of reading — more at LECTION] **:** a previous reading **:** a reading beforehand

prelector *var of* PRAELECTOR

pre·legacy \(')prē+\ *n* [*pre-* + *legacy*] **:** a legacy under Roman or civil law payable before the testator's estate is distributed to heirs and general legatees

pre·legal \"+\ *adj* [*pre-* + *legal*] **:** PRELAW

pre·leukemic \¦prē+\ *adj* [*pre-* + *leukemic*] **:** occurring before the development of overt leukemia ⟨a ~ latent phase⟩

pre·li·ba·tion \,prēlī'bāshən\ *n* [L *praelibation-*, *praelibatio*, fr. *praelibatus* (past part. of *praelibare* to taste beforehand, fr. *prae-* pre- + *libare* to pour as an offering, to taste) + *-ion-*, *-io* -ion — more at LIBATION] **1 :** FORETASTE **2 :** a preliminary offering or an offering of first fruits

pre·liberation \¦prē+\ *adj* [*pre-* + *liberation*] **:** existing before a liberation ⟨~ patriots⟩

pre·license \(')prē+\ *adj* [*pre-* + *license*] **:** occurring prior to or leading to the issuance of a license ⟨~ training⟩

[1]**pre·life** \'prē,līf\ *n* [*pre-* + *life*] **:** a life conceived as lived before one's present earthly life — compare AFTERLIFE

[2]**prelife** \"\ *adj* [*pre-* + *life*] **:** of, relating to, or occurring during the time preceding the first appearance of life on earth

pre·lim \'prē,lim, prə'lim\ *n or adj* [by shortening] *slang* **:** PRELIMINARY

pre·lim·i·nar·i·ly \prə¦limə¦nerəlē\ *adv* **:** in a preliminary manner **:** as a preliminary ⟨~ to this decision⟩

[1]**pre·lim·i·nary** \prəˈliməˌnerē, prēˈ-, -ri\ *n* -ES [F *préliminaires*, pl., fr. ML *praeliminaris*, adj.] **:** something that precedes a main discourse, work, design, or business **:** something introductory or preparatory (as a preparatory step or measure): as **a :** a preliminary scholastic examination (as of a candidate for a higher degree) **b :** a contest designed to eliminate the less qualified competitors (as in a sport) prior to a decisive contest **c preliminaries** *pl, Brit* **:** FRONT MATTER **d :** a minor match or contest that precedes the main event (as of a boxing card)

[2]**preliminary** \"\ *adj* [F *préliminaire*, fr. ML *praeliminaris*, fr. L *prae-* pre- + *limin-, limen* threshold + *-aris* -ar — more at limb] **1 :** preceding the main discourse or business **:** INTRODUCTORY, PREVIOUS ⟨~ articles to a treaty⟩ **2 :** lying before **:** leading to **:** being at the threshold of ⟨hills that are ~ to the mountains —John Burroughs⟩

[3]**preliminary** \"\ *adv* **:** as a preliminary

pre·limit \(ˈ)prē+\ *vt* -ED/-ING/-S [*pre-* + *limit*] **:** to keep within prescribed bounds **:** set the bounds of in advance ⟨the council strictly ~*ed* the scope of the committee's function⟩

pre·lingual \"+\ *adj* [*pre-* + *lingual*] **:** previous to the use, acquisition, or development of language ⟨an infant in the ~ stage⟩

pre·linguistic \¦prē+\ *adj* [*pre-* + *linguistic*] **:** PRELINGUAL

pre–linnaean \¦prē+\ *adj, sometimes cap L* [*pre-* + *linnaean*] **:** of, relating to, or dating from the period prior to the adoption of binomial nomenclature by Linnaeus

pre·literacy \(ˈ)prē+\ *n* [*pre-* + *literacy*] **:** the period in the life of a society or culture antedating the use of writing or the keeping of written records

pre·literary \"+\ *adj* **1** [*pre-* + L *litterae, literae* writing + E *-ary* — more at LETTER] **:** PRELITERATE **2** [*pre-* + *literary*] **:** preceding the development of a written literature

[1]**pre·literate** \"+\ *adj* [*pre-* + *literate*] **1 :** antedating the use of writing ⟨ancient ~ cultures⟩ **2 a :** not yet having attained a level of cultural development employing a written language **b :** lacking the use of writing **:** NONLITERATE ⟨~ people now living⟩

[2]**preliterate** \"\ *n* **:** a preliterate person

pre·lith·ic \prēˈlithik\ *adj* [*pre-* + *-lithic*] **:** not yet having advanced to the use of stone implements — used of largely hypothetical stages of human culture or evolution

pre·localization \¦prē+\ *n* [*pre-* + *localization*] **:** segregation in the egg or by early cleavage divisions of material destined to form particular tissues or organs

pre·logging \(ˈ)prē+\ *n* [*pre-* + *logging*] **:** the harvesting prior to a major logging operation of those trees that would otherwise be lost or damaged during that operation

pre·logical *also* **pre·logic** \"+\ *adj* [*prelogical* fr. *pre-* + *logical; prelogic* fr. *pre-* + L *logicus* logical, fr. Gk *logikos* — more at LOGICAL] **:** not yet logical **:** belonging to or characterized by a supposed primitive mode of thought with no regard for logical consistency — **pre·logicality** \¦prē+\ *n* — **pre·logical·ly** *adv*

pre·loral *or* **pre·loreal** \(ˈ)prē+\ *adj* [*pre-* + *loral, loreal*] **:** situated in front of the lores

[1]**prel·ude** \ˈprelˌyüd, ˈpräl‚üd, ˈpreˌlüd, ˈprālˌyüd, ˈprēˌlüd; *the first pronunciation is heard more often for nonmusical than for musical senses, the ā pronunciations vice versa; the ē pronunciation is rarely heard for musical senses*\ *n* -S [MF *prelude*, fr. ML *praeludium*, fr. L *praeludere* to prelude] **:** an introductory performance, action, event, or other matter, preceding and preparing for a principal or a more important matter **:** a preliminary part **:** INTRODUCTION, PREFACE: as **a :** a musical section or movement introducing the theme or chief subject (as of a fugue, suite) or serving as an introduction to an opera or oratorio **b :** an opening voluntary (as in a church service) **c :** a separate concert piece usu. for piano or orchestra and usu. based entirely on a short motive

[2]**prelude** \"\ *vb* -ED/-ING/-S [L *praeludere* to play beforehand, to prelude, preface, fr. *prae-* pre- + *ludere* to play — more at LUDICROUS] *vi* **:** to give or serve as a prelude **:** furnish an introduction **:** be introductory; *esp* **:** to play a musical introduction ~ *vt* **1 :** to serve as prelude to **:** precede as introductory **:** FORESHADOW **2 :** to play as a prelude **:** play or perform a prelude to

prel·ud·er \-də(r)\ *n* -S **1 :** one that preludes **2 :** something that constitutes a prelude

pre·lu·di·al \prēˈlüdēəl\ *adj* [ML *praeludium* prelude + E *-al*] **:** relating to or having the form or position of a prelude **:** INTRODUCTORY

pre·lu·dio \prāˈlüdyō\ *n, pl* **prelu·di** \-dē\ [It, lit., prelude, fr. ML *praeludium*] **:** a musical prelude

pre·lu·di·ous \prēˈlüdēəs\ *adj* [ML *praeludium* + E *-ous*] **:** PRELUDIAL — **pre·lu·di·ous·ly** *adv*

preludium *var of* PRAELUDIUM

prel·u·dize *pronunc at* [1]PRELUDE + ˌīz\ *vi* -ED/-ING/-S [[1]*prelude* + *-ize*] **:** to play or compose a prelude

pre·lumbar \(ˈ)prē+\ *adj* [*pre-* + *lumbar*] **:** lying or occurring in front of the lumbar vertebrae or region

pre·lu·sion \prēˈlüzhən\ *n* -S [L *praelusion-, praelusio*, fr. *praelusus* (past part. of *praeludere* to prelude) + *-ion-, -io* -ion] **:** something going before **:** PRELUDE, INTRODUCTION

pre·lu·sive \-üsiv\ *or* **pre·lu·so·ry** \-üsərē\ *adj* [L *praelusus* (past part. of *praeludere* to prelude) + E *-ive, -ory*] **:** constituting or having the form of a prelude **:** INTRODUCTORY **:** indicating that something is to follow ⟨a ~ warning⟩ — **pre·lu·sive·ly** \-səvlē\ *or* **pre·lu·so·ri·ly** \-sərəlē\ *adv*

prem *abbr* **1** premier **2** premium

pre·makeready \(ˈ)prē+\ *n* [*pre-* + *makeready*] **:** work constituting makeready (as underlaying low cuts) done to a printing surface before it is placed on the press

pre·malignant \¦=+\ *adj* [*pre-* + *malignant*] **:** PRECANCEROUS

pre·man \(ˈ)prēˌman, -aa(ə)n\ *n, pl* **premen** [*pre-* + *man*] **:** a hypothetical ancient primate constituting the immediate ancestor of man **:** PREHOMINID

pre·mandibular \¦prē+\ *adj* [*pre-* + *mandibular*] **:** situated in front of a mandible **:** PREDENTARY

pre·marital \(ˈ)=+\ *adj* [*pre-* + *marital*] **:** existing or occurring before marriage ⟨~ illusions⟩ ⟨~ experimentation⟩

pre–marxian \(ˈ)=+\ *or* **pre–marxist** \"+\ *adj, usu cap M* [*pre-* + *Marxian, Marxist*] **:** existing before Karl Marx or his socialistic doctrines ⟨*pre-Marxian* socialists⟩

pre·mastery \(ˈ)prē+\ *n* [*pre-* + *mastery*] **:** attainment of a skill or technique in advance of need

pre·matrimonial \(¦)=+\ *adj* [*pre-* + *matrimonial*] **:** occurring before marriage

pre·maturation \"+\ *n* [*pre-* + *maturation*] **:** unusually or abnormally early attainment of maturity

[1]**pre·mature** \¦prē *chiefly Brit* ¦pre+\ *adj* [L *praematurus* very early, too early, untimely, fr. *prae-* pre- + *maturus* ripe, mature] **1** *obs* **:** mature or ripe before the proper or usual time **2 a :** happening, arriving, existing, or performed before the proper or usual time **:** adopted, arriving, or received too soon **:** too early **:** UNTIMELY ⟨a ~ fall of snow⟩ ⟨~ reports⟩ **b** (1) *of a human infant* **:** born after a gestation period of less than 37 weeks or sometimes with a birth weight between two and five and one half pounds irrespective of the length of gestation (2) **:** of, relating to, or for the use of a premature infant ⟨~ diets⟩

[2]**premature** \"\ *n* -S **:** something that comes, happens, or occurs before the expected time: as **a :** an infant prematurely born **b :** a shell that bursts before the desired time

[3]**premature** \"\ *vi* **:** to explode prematurely — used esp. of a bomb or torpedo

premature delivery *or* **premature labor** *n* **:** expulsion of the human fetus after the 28th week of gestation but before the normal time

pre·ma·ture·ly *adv* **:** in a premature manner **:** before the proper time **:** too soon

pre·ma·ture·ness *n* -ES **:** the quality or state of being premature **:** PREMATURITY

pre·maturity \¦prē *chiefly Brit* ¦pre+\ *n* [partly fr. F *prématurité* (fr. *pré-* pre- + *maturité* maturity, fr. L *maturitat-, maturitas*), partly fr. *premature* + *-ity*] **:** the quality or state of being premature: as **a :** early ripeness or flowering of a plant **b :** early maturity or development **:** PRECOCITY **c :** untimely maturity **:** undue earliness or haste **:** HASTINESS **d :** the condition of an infant born viable but before its proper time

pre·maxilla \¦prē+\ *n* [NL, fr. *pre-* + *maxilla*] **:** either member of a pair of bones of the upper jaw of vertebrates situated between and in front of the maxillae that in man form the median anterior part of the superior maxillary bones but in most other mammals are distinct and bear the incisor teeth and in birds coalesce to form the principal part of the upper mandible — see FISH illustration

[1]**pre·maxillary** \(¦)prē+\ *adj* [ISV *pre-* + *maxillary*] **1 :** situated in front of the maxillary bones **2 :** constituting or relating to the premaxillae

[2]**premaxillary** \"\ *n* [[1]*premaxillary*] **:** PREMAXILLA

[1]**pre·med** \(ˈ)prē¦med\ *adj* [by shortening] **:** PREMEDICAL

[2]**premed** \"\ *or* **pre·medic** \(ˈ)prē+\ *n* -S [short for *premedical*] **:** a premedical student or course of study

pre·media \(ˈ)prē+\ *n* [NL, fr. *pre-* + *media*] **:** a premedian vein (as in the wing of an insect)

[1]**pre·median** \"+\ *or* **pre·medial** \"+\ *adj* [*pre-* + *median, medial*] **1 :** lying in front of the middle of the body **2** [*premedia* + *-an, -al*] **:** of, relating to, or being a vein of the wing of an insect now usu. regarded as a part of the media

[2]**premedian** \"\ *or* **premedial** \"\ *n* **:** a premedian vein

pre·medical \(ˈ)prē+\ *adj* [*pre-* + *medical*] **:** preceding and preparing for the professional study of medicine ⟨the ~ course in a university⟩ ⟨a ~ student⟩

pre·medicate \"+\ *vt* [*pre-* + *medicate*] **:** to administer premedication to **:** treat by premedication

pre·medication \(¦)prē+\ *n* **:** preliminary medication (as the giving of a quieting drug before an operation or before the induction of anesthesia)

pre·medieval \"+\ *adj* [*pre-* + *medieval*] **:** preceding the Middle Ages ⟨is almost an allegory of ~ times —*Literary Digest*⟩

[1]**pre·meditate** \(ˈ)prē+\ *vb* [L *praemeditatus*, past part. of *praemeditari* to premeditate, fr. *prae-* pre- + *meditari* to meditate] *vt* **:** to think on and revolve in the mind beforehand **:** contrive and design previously **:** con over in advance ⟨with words *premeditated* thus he said —John Dryden⟩ ⟨carefully *premeditating* each step of his plan⟩ ~ *vi* **:** to think, consider, or deliberate beforehand

[2]**premeditate** *obs var of* PREMEDITATED

premeditated *adj* [fr. past part. of [1]*premeditate*] **:** characterized by fully conscious willful intent and a measure of forethought and planning **syn** see DELIBERATE

pre·med·i·tat·ed·ly *adv* **:** in a premeditated manner **:** with premeditation

pre·med·i·tat·ed·ness *n* -ES **:** the quality or state of being premeditated

pre·med·i·tate·ly \(ˈ)=¦medəˌtātlē\ *archaic var of* PREMEDITATEDLY

pre·med·i·tat·ing·ly *adv* [*premeditating* (pres. part. of [1]*premeditate*) + *-ly*] **:** in the manner of one premeditating ⟨dwelt ~ on the possibility of violent action⟩

pre·meditation \(¦)prē+\ *n* [ME *premeditacion*, fr. L *praemeditation-, praemeditatio*, fr. *praemeditatus* (past part. of *praemeditari* to premeditate) + *-ion-, -io* -ion] **:** an act or instance of meditating beforehand: as **a :** previous deliberation as to action **:** planning and contriving **:** FORETHOUGHT **b :** consideration or planning of an act beforehand that shows intent to commit that act ⟨purchase of poison before a murder may evidence ~⟩

pre·meditative \(ˈ)=+\ *adj* [*premeditate* + *-ive*] **:** given to or characterized by premeditation

pre·meditator \(ˈ)prē+\ *n* [*premeditate* + *-or*] **:** one that premeditates

pre·melting \"+\ *n* [*pre-* + *melting*] **:** partial melting below the melting point

pre·menarche \¦prē+\ *n* [*pre-* + *menarche*] **:** the period in the life of a girl preceding the establishment of menstruation — **pre·menarcheal** \"+\ *adj*

pre·mendelian \¦prē+\ *adj, usu cap M* [*pre-* + *mendelian*] **:** preceding the knowledge or acceptance of Mendel's laws ⟨*pre-Mendelian* concepts of genetics⟩

pre·menopausal \(¦)prē+\ *adj* [*premenopause* + *-al*] **:** of, relating to, or being in the period just preceding menopause ⟨~ women⟩

pre·menopause \(ˈ)prē+\ *n* [*pre-* + *menopause*] **:** the period or physiological state that immediately precedes the menopause

pre·menstrual \"+\ *adj* [*pre-* + *menstrual*] **:** of or relating to the period just preceding menstruation ⟨~ changes in the uterus⟩ — **pre·men·stru·al·ly** \-əlē, -li\ *adv*

pre·menstruum \(ˈ)=+\ *n* [NL, fr. *pre-* + ML *menstruum* menses — more at MENSTRUUM] **:** the period or physiological state that immediately precedes menstruation

pre·mentioned \"+\ *adj* [*pre-* + *mentioned*, past part. of [2]*mention*] **:** mentioned previously

pre·men·tum \prēˈmentəm\ *n* [NL, fr. *pre-* + *mentum*] **:** the part of the insect labium lying in front of the mentum and bearing a pair of lobes

pre·meridian \¦prē+\ *adj* [*pre-* + *meridian*] **:** happening or being before noon

pre–messianic \(¦)=+\ *adj, often cap M* [*pre-* + *messianic*] **:** existing or occurring before the appearance of a messiah

pre·metallic \¦prē+\ *adj* [*pre-* + *metallic*] **:** previous to the knowledge of the use of metals

pre·metallized \(ˈ)=+\ *adj, of a dye* **:** combined with chromium or other metal before addition to the dye bath

pre·metaphase \(ˈ)prē+\ *n* [*pre-* + *metaphase*] **:** PROMETAPHASE

premia *pl of* PREMIUM

pre·mi·ate \ˈprēmēˌāt\ *vt* -ED/-ING/-S [ML *praemiatus*, past part. of *praemiare* to reward, fr. L *praemium* reward — more at PREMIUM] **:** to give a prize or premium to or for

pre·mie *or* **pree·mie** \ˈprēmē\ *n* -S [by shortening and alter. fr. [2]*premature*] **:** a premature infant

[1]**pre·mier** \(ˈ)prē¦mi(ə)r, -miə, prəˈm- *sometimes* ˈpri‚m- *or* (ˈ)pre¦m- *or* (ˈ)pra¦m-; ˈprēmēə(r) *also* ˈprem- *or* ˈprim- *sometimes* ˈpräm-; *also* prəmˈyi(ə)r *or* -yiə *or* (ˈ)prē¦my-, *or* ˈprim‚y- *sometimes* (ˈ)prem¦y-; *also* (ˈ)prem¦ye(ə)r *or* -yeə *sometimes* prəmˈy- *or* ˈprim‚y-; *sometimes* ¦premē¦e(ə)r *or* -¦eə *or* ˈprēm- *or* ˈprim-; *sometimes* ˈpremyə(r) *or* ˈprēm- *or* ˈprim-; *sometimes* (ˈ)pre¦me(ə)r *or* -meə *or* (ˈ)prē¦m-\ *adj* [ME *primier*, fr. MF *premier* first, chief, fr. L *primarius* of the first rank, principal — more at PRIMARY] **1 :** first in position, rank, or importance **:** CHIEF, PRINCIPAL, LEADING ⟨the ~ place⟩ ⟨a ~ angling fish —J.L.B.Smith⟩ **2 :** first in time **:** most ancient **:** EARLIEST ⟨a ~ peer is one bearing the oldest title of his degree⟩

[2]**premier** \"\ *n* -S [F, fr. *premier*, first, chief, fr. MF] **1 :** PRIME MINISTER ⟨the French ~⟩ ⟨the ~ of Western Australia⟩ ⟨the ~*s* of the Canadian provinces⟩ **2** *often cap* [fr. the *Premier* diamond mine, near Pretoria, south central Transvaal] **:** a diamond characterized by white color inclined toward bluish in sunlight but yellowish in artificial light **3 :** PREMIER DANSEUR

premier danseur *n* [F, lit., first dancer] **:** the principal male dancer in a ballet company

[1]**pre·miere** \(ˈ)prim¦ye(ə)r, -yeə, prəmˈy-, (ˈ)prem¦y-, (ˈ)prēm-y- *sometimes* (ˈ)präm¦y-; (ˈ)prē¦mi(ə)r, -miə, prəˈm- *sometimes* (ˈ)pre¦m-; *also* ¦primē¦e(ə)r *or* -¦eə *or* ¦prem- *sometimes* ˈpremēə(r) *or* ˈprēm- *or* ˈprim-; *sometimes* (ˈ)prēm¦ye(ə)r *or* yeə *or* (ˈ)prim¦y- *or* ˈprimy-; *sometimes* (ˈ)pre¦me(ə)r *or* -meə *or* ˈpremyə(r)\ *n* -S [F *première*, fr. *première*, fem. of *premier* first, chief] **1 :** a first performance or exhibition (as of a play) **:** FIRST NIGHT **2 :** the leading lady of a group: as **a :** the chief actress of a theatrical cast **b :** PREMIERE DANSEUSE

[2]**premiere** \", *but* -meə(r) *is more frequent than for the noun*\ *adj* [alter. (influenced by [1]*premiere*) of [1]*premier*] **:** FIRST, OUTSTANDING, CHIEF ⟨a ~ performance⟩ ⟨the ~ dance of the program⟩

[3]**premiere** *or* **premier** \"\ *vb* **premiered; premiered; premiering; premieres** *or* **premiers** [[1]*premiere*] *vt* **:** to give a first public performance or showing of ~ *vi* **1 :** to have a first public performance or showing **2 :** to appear for the first time as a star or featured performer (as in a play)

premiere danseuse *n* [F *première danseuse*, lit., first female dancer] **:** the principal female dancer in a ballet company

pre·mier·ship *pronunc at* PREMIER +ˌship\ *n* [[1]*premier* + *-ship*] **:** the position or office of a premier

pre·military \(ˈ)prē+\ *adj* [*pre-* + *military*] **:** preceding military service or activity

pre·milk \(ˈ)=+\ *adj* [*pre-* + *milk*] **:** previous to the appearance of milk — used chiefly of a stage of seed development ⟨seeds collected in ~ . . . stages —*Experiment Station Record*⟩

[1]**pre·millenarian** \(¦)=+\ *adj* [*pre-* + *millenarian*] **:** of, relating to, or constituting the doctrine of premillennialism

[2]**premillenarian** \"\ *n* **:** one that holds the doctrine of premillennialism

pre·millenarianism \"+\ *n* [[1]*premillenarian* + *-ism*] **:** PREMILLENNIALISM

pre·millennial \¦prē+\ *adj* [*pre-* + *millennium* + *-al*] **:** coming before a millennium **:** previous to the millennium ⟨an expectation that Christ's Second Advent will be ~⟩ — **pre·millennially** \"+\ *adv*

pre·millennialism \"+\ *n* [*premillennial* + *-ism*] **:** the doctrine that the second coming of Christ precedes and ushers in the millennium — opposed to *postmillennialism*

pre·millennialist \"+\ *n* [*premillennial* + *-ist*] **:** PREMILLENARIAN

pre·mil·len·ni·al·ize \-əˌlīz\ *vi* -ED/-ING/-S [*premillennial* + *-ize*] **:** to preach premillennialism

pre·millennian \"+\ *adj* [*pre-* + *millennium* + *-an*] **:** PREMILLENNIAL

pre·mineral \(ˈ)=+\ *adj* [*pre-* + *mineral*] **:** of earlier origin than associated mineral deposits ⟨a ~ fault⟩

premio *n* [It, reward, prize, insurance premium, fr. L *praemium* profit, reward — more at PREMIUM] *obs* **:** PREMIUM

pre·mis·al \prēˈmīzəl\ *n* -S [[2]*premise* + *-al*] **:** the act or an instance of making or stating a premise

[1]**prem·ise** *also* **prem·iss** \ˈpreməs\ *n, pl* **premises** *also* **premisses** [in sense 1, fr. ME *premisse*, fr. MF, fr. ML *praemissa*, fr. L, fem. of *praemissus*, past part. of *praemittere* to place ahead, send ahead, fr. *prae-* pre- + *mittere* to send; in other senses, fr. ME *premisses*, fr. ML *praemissa*, fr. L, neut. pl. of *praemissus* — more at SMITE] **1 :** a proposition antecedently supposed or proved **:** a basis of argument: as **a :** a proposition in logic stated or assumed as leading to a conclusion **:** either of the first two propositions of a syllogism from which the conclusion is drawn **b :** something assumed or taken for granted **:** PRESUPPOSITION; *esp* **:** something implied as a condition **:** condition stated beforehand **:** STIPULATION ⟨the ~*s* observed, thy will by my performance shall be served —Shak.⟩ **2 premises** *pl* **:** matters previously stated or set forth: as **a :** the part of a deed preceding the habendum, being formerly the first of eight parts making up an old-style deed and serving to state the names and addresses of the parties and to make the recitals necessary to explain the transaction (as the consideration, the capacity of the parties to act, and the identity of the land to be conveyed) **b :** the part of a bill in equity that sets forth the causes of complaint, the parties against whom redress is sought, and other pertinent explanatory matter **3 premises** *pl* **a** *archaic* **:** property that is conveyed by bequest or deed **b :** a specified piece or tract of land with the structures on it **c :** a building, buildings, or part of a building covered by or within the stated terms of a policy (as of fire insurance) **d :** the place of business of an enterprise or institution **4** *obs* **:** an antecedent happening or circumstance — usu. used in pl.

[2]**premise** \", prēˈmīz\ *vb* -ED/-ING/-S [partly fr. [1]*premise*, partly fr. MF *premis, premise*, past part. of *premetre* to place ahead, fr. L *praemittere* — more at [1]PREMISE] *vt* **1 a :** to set forth beforehand or as introductory to a main subject **:** offer previously as something to explain or aid in understanding what follows (as a premise or first proposition on which rest subsequent reasonings) ⟨I ~ these particulars that the reader may know that I enter upon it as a very ungrateful task —Joseph Addison⟩ **b :** to presuppose or imply as preexistent **:** postulate as a condition precedent **2** *archaic* **:** to use, send, or do in advance or as an initial step **:** put before something else; *esp* **:** to do or use in the initial phase of a medical or surgical treatment **3 :** to introduce by or with some pertinent thing ⟨let me ~ my argument with a bit of history⟩ ~ *vi* **:** to make a premise **:** set something forth as a premise **syn** see PRESUPPOSE

pre·mit \prēˈmit\ *vt* **premitted; premitted; premitting; premits** [L *praemittere* to place ahead] *archaic* **:** PREMISE

[1]**pre·mi·um** \ˈprēmēəm, *esp Brit* -myəm\ *n, pl* **premiums** \-mz\ *also* **pre·mia** \-mēə, -myə\ [L *praemium* booty, profit, reward, fr. *prae-* pre- + *-emium* (fr. *emere* to take, buy) — more at REDEEM] **1 a :** a reward or recompense for a particular act **:** a prize to be won for superior performance or successful competition **:** AWARD ⟨a ~ for the best yearling steer exhibited⟩ ⟨encouraging children with ~*s* for good conduct⟩ **b :** something paid over and above a fixed wage, price, or other remuneration **:** BONUS ⟨immediately after the war a new car could only be obtained by paying a considerable ~⟩ ⟨with incentive pay and other ~*s* his income was nearly double the basic wage⟩ ⟨a third shift ~⟩ **c** (1) **:** something offered or given for the loan of money usu. apart from or in addition to interest ⟨had to pay a ~ to get his mortgage⟩ (2) **:** a sum in advance of or in addition to the nominal value of something; *esp* **:** such a sum added to the face or par value of a mortgage or security usu. as a condition of redeeming it at a particular time or under specified circumstances ⟨bonds callable at a ~ of six percent⟩ **d :** something (as an article of merchandise) given without charge or at less than usual price with the purchase of a product or service **e :** BONUS 4 **2 a :** the consideration paid in money or otherwise for a contract of insurance in the form of an initiation fee, an admission fee, an assessment, or a stipulated single or periodic payment according to the nature of the insurance — see EARNED PREMIUM, GROSS PREMIUM, LEVEL PREMIUM, MINIMUM PREMIUM, NATURAL PREMIUM, NET PREMIUM, SINGLE PREMIUM, UNEARNED PREMIUM **b :** a payment made for instruction (as under an apprentice system) in a trade or profession **3 :** a high value or a value in excess of that normally or usu. expected ⟨put a ~ on accuracy⟩ ⟨gold coin had a considerable ~ over paper money⟩ ⟨selling at a ~⟩ ⟨found housing at a ~⟩ ⟨a ~ on honesty in government⟩

[2]**premium** \"\ *adj* **1 :** of exceptional quality or ability ⟨a ~ student⟩ ⟨~ products⟩ **2 :** commanding a higher than usual price esp. because of superior quality ⟨~ gasolines⟩

premium loan *n* **:** a loan made in the amount of and for the purpose of paying a premium due upon a life insurance policy and constituting a lien against the policy

premium note *n* **:** a note given by the insured in payment of all or a portion of the premium on an insurance policy

premium system *n* **:** a system for paying workmen in which the workman's hourly rate is guaranteed and a premium (as a percentage of the hourly wage) is paid for doing the work in less than the standard time specified

[1]**pre·mix** \(ˈ)prē+\ *vt* [*pre-* + *mix*] **:** to mix before use ⟨possible to ~ the ore at the shipping point, thus saving time at the iron works —*Amer. Guide Series: Mich.*⟩

[2]**pre·mix** \ˈ=,=\ *n* **:** a mixture of ingredients (as the dry materials for a cake batter or high protein supplements for an animal ration) designed to be mixed with other ingredients (as the liquid materials for a cake batter or high carbohydrate parts of an animal ration) before use

pre·modern \(ˈ)prē+\ *adj* [*pre-* + *modern*] **:** antedating the modern **:** not of the current kind, form, or style

[1]**pre·molar** \"+\ *adj* [*pre-* + *molar*] **:** situated in front of or preceding the molar teeth; *usu* **:** being or relating to those teeth of a mammal in front of the true molars and behind the canines when the latter are present

[2]**premolar** \"\ *n* **1 :** a premolar tooth that is in man one of two in each side of each jaw — called also *bicuspid* **2 :** a milk tooth that occupies the position later taken by a premolar tooth of the permanent dentition

pre·monish \(ˈ)prē+\ *vb* -ED/-ING/-ES [*pre-* + *monish*] *vt* **:** to admonish beforehand **:** give previous warning to ~ *vi* **:** to give warning in advance — **pre·mon·ish·ment** \-mənt\ *n* -S

pre·mo·ni·tion \ˌprēməˈnishən, ˌprem-\ *n* -S [MF, fr. LL *praemonition-, praemonitio*, fr. L *praemonitus* (past part. of *praemonēre* to warn in advance, fr. *prae-* pre- + *monēre* to warn) + *-ion-, -io* -ion — more at MIND] **1 :** previous warning, notice, or information **:** FOREWARNING ⟨falling leaves gave a ~ of coming winter⟩ **2 :** anticipation of an event without conscious reason **:** PRESENTIMENT ⟨felt a ~ of danger⟩

pre·mon·i·tor \prēˈmänəd·ə(r)\ *n* [L *praemonitor*, fr. *praemonitus* + *-or*] : one that premonishes

pre·mon·i·to·ri·ly \≠ˌmänəˌtōrəlē, -tȯr-, -lē\ *adv* : in a premonitory manner

pre·mon·i·to·ry \≠ˈ≠≠ˌtōrē, -tȯr-, -ri\ *also* **pre·mon·i·tary** \-ˌterē, -ri\ *adj* [LL *praemonitorius*, fr. L *praemonitus* + *-orius* -ory] : giving previous warning or notice ⟨~ symptoms of disease⟩

premonstrate *vt* [L *praemonstratus*, past part. of *praemonstrare* to show beforehand, fr. *prae-* pre- + *monstrare* to show — more at MUSTER] *obs* : to show or represent beforehand

¹**pre·mon·stra·ten·sian** \(ˌ)prēˌmän(t)strəˈtenchən\ *n* -s *usu cap* [ML *praemonstratensis*, fr. *praemonstratensis* of Prémontré (fr. *Praemonstratus* Prémontré, abbey in northern France + L *-ensis* -ese) + E *-an*] : a member of an order of regular canons founded by St. Norbert at Prémontré near Laon, France, in 1119

²**premonstratensian** \"\ *adj, usu cap* : of or relating to the Premonstratensians

pre·mon·stra·tion \ˌprēˌmänˈstrāshən\ *n* -s [LL *praemonstration-*, *praemonstratio*, fr. L *praemonstratus* (past part. of *praemonstrare* to show beforehand) + *-ion-*, *-io* -ion — more at PREMONSTRATE] *obs* : a showing forth in advance

pre·moral \(ˈ)prē+\ *adj* [*pre-* + *moral*] : existing or like that existing before the development of a moral code in society

pre·morse \prēˈmȯrs\ *adj* [L *praemorsus*, fr. past part. of *praemordēre* to bite off in front, fr. *prae-* pre- + *mordēre* to bite — more at SMART] : bitten off : terminated abruptly or as if bitten off : irregularly truncate ⟨a ~ root⟩

pre·mortal \(ˈ)prē+\ *adj* [*pre-* + *mortal*] **1** : existing prior to the presumed assumption of mortality by man **2** [*premortem* + *-al*] : existing or taking place immediately before death ⟨~ injuries⟩

pre·mortem \(ˈ)prēˈmȯrtəm\ *adj* [L *prae mortem* before death] : PREMORTAL 2

pre·mortuary \(ˈ)prē+\ *adj* [*pre-* + *mortuary*] : occurring or relating to what occurs before a funeral; *also* : prepared in advance for or as if for a funeral ⟨a ~ tribute⟩

pre·mo·tion \prēˈmōshən\ *n* [ML *praemotion-*, *praemotio*, fr. LL *praemotus* (past part. of *praemovēre* to move beforehand, fr. L *prae-* pre- + *movēre* to move) + L *-ion-*, *-io* -ion] : movement or excitation to action beforehand; *specif* : the inspiration or determination (as by divine power) of an action beforehand

pre·move \-ˈmüv\ *vt* [LL *praemovēre* to move beforehand] : to move or excite to action beforehand; *specif* : to determine (as by divine inspiration) the action of beforehand — **pre·move·ment** \-mənt\ *n*

pre–muhammadan \ˌ≠+\ *adj, usu cap M* [*pre-* + *muhammadan*] : PRE-ISLAMIC

pre·mundane \(ˌ)prē+\ *adj* [*pre-* + *mundane*] : existing before the creation of the world

pre·mune \prēˈmyün\ *adj* [back-formation fr. *premunition*] : exhibiting premunition

premunire *var of* PRAEMUNIRE

premunite *vt* [L *praemunitus*, past part. of *praemunire* to fortify in front or beforehand] *obs* : to fortify in front or beforehand

pre·mu·ni·tion \ˌprēmyəˈnishən\ *also* **pre·mu·ni·ty** \prēˈmyünəd·ē\ *n, pl* **premunitions** *also* **premunities** [*premunition* fr. L *praemunition-*, *praemunitio* fortification in advance, fr. *praemunitus* (past part. of *praemunire* to fortify in front or beforehand, fr. *prae-* pre- + *munire* to fortify) + *-ion-*, *-io* -ion; *premunity* fr. *premune* + *-ity* — more at MUNITION] **1** *archaic* : PREMONITION **2 a** *archaic* : an advance provision of protection (as against military attack) **b** : resistance to a disease due to the existence of its causative agent in a state of physiological equilibrium in the host **c** : immunity to a particular infection due to the previous presence of the causative agent in the host

pre·mu·ni·to·ry \prēˈmyünəˌtōrē\ *adj* [L *praemunitus* (past part. of *praemunire*) + E *-ory*] : relating to or involving a praemunire

pre·mu·nize \ˈprēmyəˌnīz\ *vt* -ED/-ING/-S [*premune* + *-ize*] : to induce premunition in

pre–mycenaean \(ˌ)prē+\ *adj, usu cap M* [*pre-* + *mycenaean*] : of or relating to a civilization in Greek lands earlier than the period to which characteristic Mycenaean objects belong

pre·myelocyte \(ˈ)≠+\ *n* [*pre-* + *myelocyte*] : a partially differentiated granulocyte in bone marrow having the characteristic granulations but lacking the specific staining reactions of a mature granulocyte of the blood

pre·name \ˈ≠,≠\ *n* [*pre-* + *name*] : FORENAME

pre·nan·thes \prēˈnanˌthēz\ *n, cap* [NL, fr. Gk *prēnēs* prone (akin to *pro* before, forward) + NL *-anthes* — more at FOR] : a genus of No. American and Asiatic perennial herbs (family Compositae) with lobed or pinnatifid leaves and small heads of drooping ligulate flowers — see RATTLESNAKE ROOT

pre·narial \(ˈ)prē+\ *adj* [*pre-* + *narial*] : relating to or situated in front of the nostrils

pre·naris \(ˈ)prē+\ *n, pl* **prenares** [NL, fr. *pre-* + *naris*] : either of the anterior nares

¹**pre·nasal** \"+\ *adj* [*pre-* + *nasal*] : situated in front of the nasal bones, nose, or nostrils

²**prenasal** \"\ *n* : a prenasal part (as a scale); *esp* : a bone or cartilage in the snout of various animals (as swine)

pre·nasalization \(ˌ)≠+\ *n* [*pre-* + *nasalization*] : pronunciation of a stop sound with a brief interval of nasalization that is not ascribable to a preceding segment of speech

pre·nasalized \(ˈ)≠+\ *adj* [*pre-* + *nasalized*] : marked by prenasalization

pre·natal \(ˈ)≠+\ *adj* [*pre-* + *natal*] : occurring, existing, or taking place before birth : ANTENATAL ⟨~ care⟩ ⟨the ~ period⟩ — **pre·natally** \"+\ *adv*

pre·na·tal·ist \-ᵊləst\ *n* -s : a believer in the prenatal divinity of Jesus

pren·der *also* **pren·dre** \ˈprendə(r)\ *n* -s [MF *prendre* to take, fr. L *prehendere*, *prendere* to seize, grasp — more at PREHENSILE] : the power or right under the law of taking a thing without its being offered

pre·neural \(ˈ)prē+\ *adj* [*pre-* + *neural* (*plate*)] : situated in front of or anterior to the neural plate — used esp. of a bone forming part of the carapace of a turtle

pre–newtonian \ˌprē+\ *adj, usu cap N* [*pre-* + *newtonian*] : existing prior to the development of Newtonian philosophy or physics

pre·nex normal form \ˈprēˌneks-\ *n* [LL *praenexus* tied up or bound in front, fr. L *prae-* pre- + *nexus*, past part. of *nectere* to tie, bind — more at ANNEX] : a normal form of an expression in the functional calculus in which all the quantifiers are grouped without negations or other connectives before the matrix so that the scope of each quantifier extends to the end of the formula

pre–noachian \ˌprē+\ *adj, usu cap N* [*pre-* + *noachian*] : existing before the Noachian deluge

pre·noble \(ˈ)prē+\ *adj* [*pre-* + *noble*] : eminently noble

pre·nodal \"+\ *adj* [*pre-* + *nodus* + *-al*] : situated between the nodus and the base of the wing of an insect

pre·nol·epis \prēˈnäləpəs\ *n, cap* [NL, fr. Gk *prēnēs* prone + NL *-lepis* — more at PRENANTHES] : a large and widely distributed genus of ants

prenomen *var of* PRAENOMEN

¹**pre·nom·i·nal** \prēˈnämənᵊl\ *adj* [L *praenomin-*, *praenomen* + E *-al*] : of, relating to, or constituting a praenomen

²**pre·nominal** \(ˈ)prē+\ *adj* [*pre-* + L *nomin-* *nomen* name, noun + E *-al* — more at NAME] : placed or coming before a noun ⟨the ~ form of a possessive pronoun⟩

¹**prenominate** *adj* [LL *praenominatus*, past part. of *praenominare* to name before, fr. *prae-* pre- + *nominare* to name — more at NOMINATE] *obs* : previously mentioned

²**prenominate** *vt* [LL *praenominatus*, past part. of *praenominare*] *obs* : to mention previously — **prenomination** *n, obs*

pre–norman \(ˈ)prē+\ *adj, usu cap N* [*pre-* + *norman*] : of, relating to, or occurring in England prior to the Norman conquest

pre·notice \"+\ *n* [*pre-* + *notice*] : notice or warning given or received in advance

pre·notification \(ˌ)≠+\ *n* [*pre-* + *notification*] : PRENOTICE

pre·notify \(ˈ)≠+\ *vt* [*pre-* + *notify*] : to give prenotice to : warn or notify in advance

pre·notion \"+\ *n* [L *praenotion-*, *praenotio* previous notion, preconception, fr. *prae-* pre- + *notion-*, *notio* idea, conception — more at NOTION] **1** : PRESENTIMENT, PREMONITION, FOREKNOWLEDGE **2** : a preconceived idea formed without actual experience

prent \ˈprent\ *dial Brit var of* PRINT

¹**pren·tice** \ˈprentə̇s\ *n* -s [ME *prentis*, short for *apprentis* — more at APPRENTICE] **1** : APPRENTICE 1, LEARNER **2** *or* **prentice of law** *obs* : APPRENTICE 2 a

²**prentice** \"\ *adj* **1** : of, relating to, or characteristic of an apprentice ⟨~ work⟩ ⟨~ training⟩ **2** : not fully skilled : incompletely trained : INEXPERIENCED ⟨tried his ~ hand at modern drama⟩; *also* : crude and imperfect : lacking in finish or polish ⟨a ~ effort⟩ ⟨~ touches that marred the concept⟩

³**prentice** \"\ *vt* -ED/-ING/-S : APPRENTICE

pre·nuptial \(ˈ)prē+\ *adj* [*pre-* + *nuptial*] : ANTENUPTIAL

pre·occasioned \ˌ≠+\ *adj* [*pre-* + *occasioned*, past part. of ²*occasion*] : caused by some previous happening ⟨anger ~ by his neglect⟩

pre·occipital \"+\ *adj* [*pre-* + *occipital*] : situated in front of the occiput or an occipital part (as the occipital lobe of the brain) ⟨~ lesions⟩

pre·occupancy \(ˈ)≠+\ *n* [*pre-* + *occupancy*] **1** : an act or the right of taking possession before another : PREOCCUPATION ⟨the ~ of wild land⟩ **2** [*preoccupy* + *-ancy*] : the condition of being completely busied or preoccupied

¹**pre·occupant** \(ˈ)≠+\ *adj* [L *praeoccupant-*, *praeoccupans*, pres. part. of *praeoccupare* to occupy in advance] : occupying in advance

²**preoccupant** \"\ *n* [*pre-* + *occupant*] : one that occupies something (as a piece of land) ahead of others : a prior occupant

preoccupate *vt* -ED/-ING/-S [L *praeoccupatus*, past part. of *praeoccupare* to seize beforehand, anticipate] **1** *obs* **a** : to take before : ANTICIPATE **b** : SURPRISE, FORESTALL **2** *obs* : PREPOSSESS, PREJUDICE

pre·occupation \(ˌ)≠+\ *n* [L *praeoccupation-*, *praeoccupatio* act of seizing beforehand, fr. *praeoccupatus* (past part. of *praeoccupare* to seize beforehand, fr. *prae-* pre- + *occupare* to seize, occupy) + *-ion-*, *-io* -ion — more at OCCUPY] **1 a** : an act of preoccupying or the condition of being preoccupied : PREPOSSESSION **b** : extreme or excessive concern with something : complete engrossment of the mind or interests ⟨his ~ with business left little time for his family⟩ **c** : something that causes preoccupation or engages the attention ⟨the ~s of daily life⟩ **2** *obs* : PROLEPSIS 2b

pre·occupied \(ˈ)≠+\ *adj* [fr. past part. of *preoccupy*] **1 a** : lost in thought : ENGROSSED, ABSORBED **b** : already occupied : FILLED **2** : previously applied to some other group and therefore unavailable according to the rules of nomenclature for use in a new sense — used of a biological generic or specific name

pre·oc·cu·pied·ly \-pī(ə)dlē, -li\ *adv* : in a preoccupied manner

pre·occupy \(ˈ)≠+\ *vt* [*pre-* + *occupy*] **1** : to engage, occupy, or engross the interest or attention of beforehand or preferentially : PREENGAGE, PREPOSSESS **2** : to occupy or take possession of before another ⟨~ a country not before held⟩ **3** : to fill beforehand : occupy in advance of

¹**pre·ocular** \(ˈ)≠+\ *adj* [*pre-* + L *oculus* eye + E *-ar* — more at EYE] : situated in front of the eye ⟨an insect with the antennae ~ in position⟩

²**preocular** \"\ *n* : a preocular part ⟨~s and other scales of a snake⟩

pre·oedipal \(ˈ)≠+\ *adj* [*pre-* + *oedipal*] : antedating the occurrence of oedipal conflict

pre·operative \"+\ *adj* [*pre-* + *operative*] : occurring during the period preceding a surgical operation — **pre·operatively** \"+\ *adv*

pre·opercle \(ˌ)prē+\ *also* **pre·operculum** \ˌ≠+\ *n, pl* **preopercles** *also* **preopercula** [NL *preoperculum*, fr. *pre-* + *operculum*] : a flat membrane bone in the gill cover of most fishes lying immediately in front of the opercle

pre·opercular \ˌ≠+\ *adj* [NL *preoperculum* + E *-ar*] : being or relating to a preopercle

pre·opinion \"+\ *n* [*pre-* + *opinion*] : an opinion previously formed : PRECONCEPTION, PREJUDICE

pre·optic \(ˈ)≠+\ *adj* [*pre-* + *optic*] : situated in front of an optic part or region ⟨~ tracts in the brain⟩

pre·option \(ˈ)≠+\ *n* [*pre-* + *option*] : the right or privilege of making a selection (as from available goods) before others ⟨the king having always the ~ of the spoils of war⟩

pre·oral \(ˈ)≠+\ *adj* [*pre-* + *oral*] : situated in front of or anterior to the mouth — **pre·orally** \"+\ *adv*

¹**pre·orbital** \(ˈ)≠+\ *adj* [*pre-* + *orbit* + *-al*] **1** : situated in front of the orbit ⟨the ~ membrane bone of bony fishes⟩ **2** : occurring before going into or being in orbit

²**preorbital** \"\ *n* : a preorbital part; *esp* : a large membrane bone that is situated just in front of the orbit in many teleost fishes

pre·ordain \ˌ≠+\ *vt* [*pre-* + *ordain*] : to decree or ordain in advance : order or assure the occurrence of beforehand : FOREORDAIN

pre·ordainment \ˌ≠+\ *n* -s [*preordain* + *-ment*] : the quality or state of being preordained

pre·order \(ˈ)≠+\ *vt* [*pre-* + *order*] **1** : to plan out in order or arrange beforehand : FOREORDAIN **2** : to give an order for in advance ⟨it is wise to ~ very special dishes when making your reservation⟩

preordinance *n* [ME, fr. *pre-* + *ordinance*] *obs* : antecedent decree

pre·ordination \(ˌ)≠+\ *n* [LL *praeordination-*, *praeordinatio*, fr. *praeordinatus* (past part. of *praeordinare* to preordain, fr. L *prae-* pre- + *ordinare* to order, ordain) + *-ion-*, *-io* -ion — more at ORDAIN] : the action or an act or instance of preordaining or foreordaining

pre·organic \(ˌ)≠+\ *adj* [*pre-* + *organic*] : formed or occurring before the beginning of life ⟨~ evolution⟩

pre·original \ˌ≠+\ *adj* [*pre-* + *original*] : occurring in or dating from a period preceding the accepted period of origin of something ⟨the curious ~ form of the [work], an unfinished but printed version —*Modern Language Notes*⟩ — **pre·originally** \"+\ *adv*

pre·outfit \(ˈ)≠+\ *vt* [*pre-* + *outfit*] : to outfit in advance ⟨~ a party for mountain climbing⟩

pre·ovu·la·to·ry \(ˈ)prēˌävyələˌtōrē\ *adj* [*pre-* + *ovulate* + *-ory*] : occurring in or having the form typical of the period immediately preceding ovulation ⟨the ~ phase of the cycle⟩ ⟨~ endocrine relations⟩

pre·oxygenation \(ˌ)prē+\ *n* [*pre-* + *oxygenation*] : inhalation of large quantities of essentially pure oxygen usu. as a prelude to some activity (as high-level flight) in which it is desirable to minimize nitrogen and maximize oxygen in the blood and tissues

¹**prep** \ˈprep\ *n* -s [short for *preparation*] **1** *Brit* **a** : preparation of study assignments : HOMEWORK ⟨I may stay for three≠quarters of an hour, and then I must go and do my ~ —Archibald Marshall⟩ **b** : a specific time or place set aside for study ⟨supposed to superintend tea and evening ~ —H.G. Wells⟩ ⟨collected their books and went into ~ —Hugh MacLennan⟩ **2** [short for ¹*preparatory*] **a** : PREPARATORY SCHOOL **b** : a preparatory school student **3** : the act or an instance of preparing a patient for a surgical operation ⟨the floor nurse had three ~s to do⟩ **4** *horse racing* : a trial run

²**prep** \"\ *vb* **prepped**; **prepped**; **prepping**; **preps** *vi* **1** : to attend preparatory school ⟨the place where he *prepped* for college⟩ **2** : to engage in preparatory study or training ⟨entered medical school to ~ for the study of psychiatry —Gilbert McKean⟩ ⟨*prepped* for his new post abroad⟩ ~ *vt* **1** : to prepare for an examination, assignment, or course of study ⟨youths of higher mental caliber but not as well *prepped* —*Newsweek*⟩ **2** : to prepare for a surgical operation ⟨an orderly came in to ~ him for the appendectomy⟩

prep *abbr* **1** preparation; preparatory; prepare **2** preposition

¹**pre·pack** \(ˈ)≠+\ *or* **pre·package** \(ˈ)≠+\ *vt* [*pre-* + *pack*, v. *or package*, v.] : to enclose in a prepack

²**prepack** \"\ *or* **prepackage** \"\ *n* : a usu. transparent package (as of food or a manufactured article) prepared or wrapped beforehand for the individual consumer by a manufacturer, distributor, or retailer

pre·paid expense \(ˈ)≠ˌ≠-\ *n* : DEFERRED CHARGE

prepaid station *n* : a railroad station to which freight cannot be shipped C.O.D. — contrasted with *open station*

pre·palatal \(ˈ)prē+\ *adj* [ISV *pre-* + *palatal*] : articulated against the front third or half of the hard palate or against the front third of the palate as a whole

pre·par·able \prēˈpa(a)rəbəl, -ˈper-, ˈprep(ə)rə-\ *adj* : capable of being prepared

prep·a·rate \ˈprepərət\ *adj* [ME *preparat*, fr. L *praeparatus*, past part. of *praeparare* to prepare] : PREPARED, READY ⟨the dark entrails of the ~ earth —S.V.Benét⟩

pré·pa·ra·teur \ˌprepərəˈtər(·)\ *n* -s [F, lit., one that prepares, fr. LL *praeparator*, fr. L *praeparatus* (past part. of *praeparare* to prepare) + *-or*] : a laboratory assistant ⟨turned the cucumber over to my ~ and began on my fish —William Beebe⟩

prep·a·ra·tion \ˌprepəˈrāshən\ *n* -s [ME *preparacion*, fr. MF *preparation*, fr. L *praeparation-*, *praeparatio*, fr. *praeparatus* (past part. of *praeparare* to prepare) + *-ion-*, *-io* -ion] **1 a** : the action or process of making something ready for use or service ⟨began ~ of the land for sowing⟩ ⟨finished the ~ of the manuscript for the printer⟩ **b** : the action or process of putting something together : COMPOUNDING ⟨skilled in the ~ of home remedies⟩ ⟨spent several years in the ~ of his masterpiece⟩ ⟨has made the ~ of meals easier⟩ **c** : the action or process of getting ready for some occasion, test, or duty : TRAINING ⟨exercised regularly in ~ for the fight⟩ ⟨a period of observation in ~ for assuming the post —*Current Biog.*⟩ **2** : a state of being prepared : FITNESS, PREPAREDNESS, READINESS ⟨the car was in excellent ~ for the trip⟩ **3 a** : ritual acts and observances preceding the Jewish Sabbath or other festival ⟨it was the day of ~ for the Passover —Jn 19:14 (RSV)⟩ **b** : liturgical prayers or private devotions said by one preparing for a sacrament (as the celebration of the Eucharist) or in advance of communicating; *also* : the first part of the Communion service **4 a** : a preliminary measure or plan : an action taken to expedite or prepare the way for something — usu. used in pl. ⟨~s for new elections were started at once —*Americana Annual*⟩ **b** : the anticipation of a dissonant tone as a consonance in the preceding chord; *also* : the tone so sounded — see SUSPENSION illustration **c** (1) : work done by a teacher or student in preparing for a class; *specif* : a unit of time regularly devoted by a teacher to preparing for a class ⟨prefer teaching five sections, with three or four ~s —H.R.Douglass⟩ (2) *Brit* : PREP **d** : heavy fire delivered before an attack to disrupt the enemy's defenses and communications ⟨artillery ~⟩ **e** : a series of processes (as cataloging, shelflisting, marking) that a book is put through before it reaches the library shelves **5** : something that is prepared : something made, equipped, or compounded for a specific purpose ⟨caffeine is one of the more common ingredients found in pharmaceutical ~s —*Jour. Amer. Pharmaceutical Assoc.*⟩ ⟨a widely sold ~ for colds⟩

preparation hymn *n* : a hymn preceding the sermon in an order of service used by Free Churches

prep·a·ra·tion·ist \-sh(ə)nəst\ *n* -s : one who believes in preparedness esp. for war

¹**pre·par·a·tive** \prēˈpa(a)rəd·iv, -ˈper-, -rətiv\ *n* -s [ME *preparatif*, fr. MF, fr. L *praeparatus* (past part. of *praeparare* to prepare) + MF *-if* -ive (n. suffix)] **1 a** : something that prepares the way for or serves as a preliminary to something else : PREPARATION ⟨the best ~ in the world . . . for thoughtless, unburdened sleep —H.R.Steeves⟩ **b** *archaic* : something administered to a person to prepare him for a particular medication or course of treatment **2** : a military or naval signal to make ready

²**preparative** \"\ *adj* [MF *preparatif*, fr. ML *praeparativus*, fr. L *praeparatus* (past part. of *praeparare* to prepare) + *-ivus* -ive (adj. suffix)] : PREPARATORY

³**preparative** \"\ *adv* : PREPARATIVELY

pre·par·a·tive·ly \-əvlē\ *adv* : by way of preparation

pre·par·a·tor \prēˈparəd·ə(r), ˈprepəˌrād-\ *n* -s [LL *praeparator* one that prepares] : one who prepares something; *specif* : one who prepares specimens for scientific use or museum display

pre·par·a·to·ri·ly \prēˈparəˌtōrəlē, prəˈ-, -tȯr-, -li *also* -ˈper- *or* ˈprep(ə)rəˌt- *sometimes by* r-*dissimilation* ÷ˈprepəˌt-\ *adv* : in a preparatory manner : by way of preparation

¹**pre·par·a·to·ry** \prēˈparəˌtōrē, prəˈ-, -tȯr-, -ri *also* -ˈper- *or* ˈprep(ə)rəˌt- *sometimes by* r-*dissimilation* ÷ˈprepəˌt-\ *adj* [ME, fr. LL *praeparatorius*, fr. L *praeparatus* (past part. of *praeparare* to prepare) + *-orius* -ory] : preparing or serving to prepare for something : INTRODUCTORY, PRELIMINARY ⟨~ education⟩ ⟨~ training⟩

²**preparatory** \"\ *n* -ES : PREPARATIVE

³**preparatory** \"\ *adv* : PREPARATORILY ⟨found the veteran cleaning out his desk ~ to departure —S.H.Adams⟩

preparatory school *n* **1** : a usu. private school preparing students primarily for college **2** *Brit* : a private elementary school preparing students primarily for public schools

preparatory seminary *n* : a Roman Catholic school for young men intending to enter the priesthood that corresponds to a high school and junior college and has a course of study emphasizing philosophy during the last two years — called also *junior seminary, minor seminary*

pre·pare \prēˈpa(a)(ə)r, prəˈ-, -pe(ə)r, -pa(a)ə, -peə\ *vb* -ED/-ING/-S [ME *preparen*, fr. MF *preparer*, fr. L *praeparare*, fr. *prae-* pre- + *parare* to prepare, procure — more at PARE] *vt* **1 a** : to make ready beforehand for some purpose : put into condition for a particular use, application, or disposition ⟨telling him to cut the weeds and to ~ ground for winter crops —Elizabeth M. Roberts⟩ ⟨*prepared* the guest room for their visitor⟩ ⟨*prepared* the patient for the operation⟩ **b** : to make ready for eating ⟨would rather starve to death than eat food *prepared* over such fires —J.G.Frazer⟩ **c** : to put into a suitable state of mind for something ⟨*prepared* her gradually for the shocking news⟩ ⟨*prepared* the people for a long struggle⟩ **d** : to equip with necessary knowledge and skill (as for a specific profession, occupation, or test) : EDUCATE, TRAIN ⟨*prepared* himself for the legal profession —*Current Biog.*⟩ ⟨*preparing* pupils for college entrance examinations —D.E. Smith⟩ **2 a** : to get ready beforehand : procure as suitable or necessary : PROVIDE ⟨given the job of *preparing* the equipment for the trip⟩ **b** : to work out beforehand : plan the details of : get ready ⟨*prepared* his strategy for the coming campaign⟩ **3** : to become proficient in beforehand : study or work on for a particular purpose or occasion ⟨*prepared* his assignment for the next day⟩ ⟨the players *prepared* their parts —Malcolm Muggeridge⟩ **4 a** : to put together : COMPOUND ⟨*prepared* a vaccine from live virus⟩ ⟨*prepared* the doctor's prescription⟩ **b** : MAKE, PRODUCE ⟨unsuccessful in his attempts to ~ the metal by electrolysis —*Encyc. Americana*⟩ **c** : to put into written form : draw up ⟨*prepared* and issued a vigorous manifesto —*Britain Today*⟩ ⟨directed the commission to ~ proposals for the regulation, limitation, and balanced reduction of all armed forces —*Americana Annual*⟩ **5 a** : to anticipate and modify (as a dissonance or its effect) by sounding the dissonant tone in the preceding consonant musical chord **b** : to lead up to (as a tone or an ornament) by a prefatory tone ⟨a *prepared* trill⟩ **6** : to lead up to ⟨the age of peace and prosperity that *prepared* the war —F.R.Leavis⟩ ~ *vi* **1 a** : to make oneself ready : get ready ⟨he *prepared* for teaching⟩ **b** : to arrange things in readiness : make ready ⟨the nation *prepared* for war⟩ **2** *archaic* : to get ready for a journey or expedition ⟨are actually preparing for England —Robert Bage⟩

syn FIT, QUALIFY, CONDITION, READY: PREPARE is a rather general term indicating a process, purposive, considered, and involving various steps whereby something is made ready ⟨*prepare* a large meal⟩ ⟨*prepare* the ground for spring crops⟩ ⟨*prepare* a patient for an operation⟩ ⟨*prepare* oneself for the ministry⟩ ⟨*preparing* a speech on the subject⟩ ⟨I had intended, when the time came, to *prepare* a second edition of this book —T.S.Eliot⟩ FIT may indicate equipping and repairing; it may apply to the process of training and gradually remedying deficiencies and acquiring skills, crafts, accomplishments, attitudes for some specific activity or situation ⟨about 60 destroyers *fitted* with echo-ranging gear —J.P.Baxter b. 1893⟩ ⟨I had *fitted* myself to do everything, from sweeping out to writing the editorials and keeping the bank account —W.A.White⟩

⟨the soldier's efforts to *fit* himself into the new world made possible by his sweat and blood —Dixon Wecter⟩ ⟨parents whose duty it is to *fit* children for carrying on life —Herbert Spencer⟩ QUALIFY may imply formal fulfillment of requirements or definite experience or accomplishment demonstrating fitness ⟨a *qualified* accountant⟩ ⟨*qualified* to practice medicine⟩ ⟨combined with a subsequent three years of seminary training, it *qualifies* graduates to enter into the ministry of the church —*Amer. Guide Series: Mich.*⟩ ⟨teams winning in the *qualifying* rounds⟩ CONDITION may indicate the steady, cumulative course or process of bringing into a certain condition, often a careful procedure for achieving a certain desired condition ⟨compulsory education, the press, the cinema, and the wireless are weapons possibly even stronger than the atom bomb, and the art of using them for the *conditioning* of men's minds and characters is much enhanced by modern developments in psychology and sociology —Walter Moberly⟩ ⟨these early circumstances and experiences profoundly *conditioned* him —Carl Van Doren⟩ ⟨the religious emotion to which I had been *conditioned* in my childhood —R.M.Lovett⟩ READY may apply to quick preliminary equipping, ordering, and preparing immediately before entering into some activity or function ⟨the whole town took part in helping to *ready* the outdoor theater —Marguerite Johnson⟩ ⟨under this great silvery dome they were *readying* the 200-inch eye for its night's vigil on the universe —G.W.Gray b. 1886⟩ ⟨the expedition *readied* itself during the summer at the little Dutch town of Helvoet Sluys —Oscar Handlin⟩

— prepare the way : to clear the way ⟨the orator *prepared the way* for his proposal —R.M.Weaver⟩ ⟨management has to take the time and effort needed to *prepare the way* —Bruce Payne⟩

prepared *adj* **1 :** made ready, fit, or suitable beforehand **:** READY, EQUIPPED **2 :** subjected to a special process or treatment ⟨~ ergot⟩ **— pre·pared·ly** \-r(ə)dlē, -li\ *adv*

prepared bid *n* **:** an opening bid in contract bridge that promises ability to rebid safely if one's partner responds with a suit-bid — compare ANTICIPATION 6

prepared chalk *n* **:** native calcium carbonate ground to a fine powder and freed of most of its impurities by elutriation — called also *drop chalk*

pre·pared·ness \-r(ə)dnəs\ *n* -ES **:** the state of being prepared **:** READINESS; *specif* **:** a state of adequate preparation in case of war

prepared opium *n* **:** raw opium that has been treated to render it fit for smoking and that contains about eight percent of morphine — called also *chandu, smoking opium*

prepared roofing *n* **:** roofing consisting of asbestos felt or rag felt saturated with asphalt and assembled with asphalt cement — called also *roll roofing*

prepared sizes *n pl* **:** the four largest sorted sizes of anthracite coal ⟨broken, egg, stove, and chestnut are *prepared sizes*⟩ — compare STEAM SIZES

pre·parental \ˌprē+\ *adj* [*pre-* + *parental*] **:** preceding parenthood ⟨~ teaching of prospective mothers and fathers⟩

pre·par·er \prēˈpa(a)rə(r), -ˈper-\ *n* -S **:** one that prepares; *esp* **:** a worker who performs the preliminary or initial steps of a manufacturing process

pre·parietal \ˌprē+\ *adj* [*pre-* + *parietal*] **1 :** situated in front of parietal structures ⟨a ~ scale in front of the parietal plate in snakes⟩ **2 :** of, relating to, or constituting the anterior part of the parietal convolutions of the brain

pre·par·tum \(ˈ)prēˈpärd·əm\ *also* **pre·par·tal** \-d·ᵊl\ *adj* [*prepartum* fr. *pre-* + *-partum* (as in *postpartum*); *prepartal* fr. *prepartum* + *-al*] **:** ANTEPARTUM

pre·patellar \ˌprē+\ *adj* [*pre-* + *patellar*] **1 :** situated in front of the patella **2 :** of, relating to, or constituting a synovial bursa between the patella and the skin — compare HOUSEMAID'S KNEE

pre·patent \(ˈ)ₑ+\ *adj* [*pre-* + *patent*] **:** existing in an unobserved state **:** LATENT

prepatent period *n* **:** the period between infection with a parasite and the demonstration of the parasite in the body esp. as determined by the recovery of an infective form (as oocysts or eggs) from the feces

pre·pausal \(ˈ)prē+\ *adj* [*pre-* + *pausal*] **:** preceding a pause

pre·pay \(ˈ)prē+\ *vt* [*pre-* + *pay*] **:** to pay in advance ⟨~ freight charges⟩ ⟨~ the interest on the loan⟩

pre·payment \"+\ *n* [*pre-* + *payment*] **:** payment in advance

prepay station *n* **:** PREPAID STATION

prepd *abbr* prepared

pre·pectus \(ˈ)ₑ+\ *n* [NL, fr. *pre-* + *pectus*] **:** the anterior marginal sclerite of the episternum of an insect; *esp* **:** such a sclerite of the mesepisternum of some hymenopterons

pre·pend \prēˈpend\ *vt* -ED/-ING/-S [*pre-* + *-pend* (as in *perpend*)] **:** CONSIDER, PREMEDITATE ⟨make jokes with malice ~*ed* —Charles Lamb⟩

pre·penial \(ˈ)prē+\ *adj* [*pre-* + *penial*] **:** lying in front of the penis ⟨the ~ scrotum of a marsupial⟩

pre·pense \(ˈ)prēˈpen(t)s\ *adj* [short for obs. E *prepensed*, alter. (influenced by E *pre-*) of obs. E *purpensed*, fr. ME, past part. of *purpensen* to premeditate, fr. MF *pourpenser* to plan, resolve, fr. OF, fr. *pour* for + *penser* to think — more at PURCHASE, PENSIVE] **:** deliberated, contrived, or planned beforehand **:** AFORETHOUGHT, PRECONCEIVED, PREMEDITATED — usu. used postpositively ⟨malice ~⟩

pre·pense·ly *adv* **:** with premeditation **:** DELIBERATELY

pre·perceive \ˌprē+\ *vt* [*pre-* + *perceive*] **:** to have an anticipation of or be in a state of readiness for (a perception)

pre·perception \"+\ *n* [*pre-* + *perception*] **:** readiness for or anticipation of a perception **— pre·perceptive** \"+\ *adj*

prepg *abbr* preparing

pre·phenic acid \(ˈ)prē+-\ *n* [*prephenic* fr. *pre-* + *phen-* + *-ic*] **:** a quinonoid dicarboxylic acid $HOC_6H_5(COOH)CH_2COCOOH$ formed as an intermediate in the biosynthesis of aromatic amino acids from shikimic acid

pre·phragma \(ˈ)prē+\ *n* [NL, fr. *pre-* + *phragma*] **:** the anterior phragma of the notum of an insect

pre·pink spray \(ˈ)ₑ¦ₑ-\ *n* [*prepink* fr. *pre-* + *pink*] **:** a spray applied esp. to apple trees after the leaves and buds show but before pinkish color is apparent — compare PINK SPRAY

pre·placement \(ˈ)ₑ+\ *adj* [*pre-* + *placement*] **:** occurring before employment or assignment to a job ⟨~ examination⟩

pre·placental \ˌₑ+\ *adj* [*pre-* + *placental*] **:** existing or arising before the formation of a placenta

pre·plan \(ˈ)ₑ+\ *vb* [*pre-* + *plan*] *vt* **:** to plan in advance ⟨the service could not have been premeditated or *preplanned*, since no imagination could have foreseen its need —T.O. Beachcroft⟩ ~ *vi* **:** to make plans beforehand ⟨the damage-control officer must ~ —L.J.Levert⟩

prepn *abbr* preparation

pre·pol·lent \(ˈ)prēˈpälənt\ *adj* [L *praepollent-, praepollens*, pres. part. of *praepollēre* to surpass in power, fr. *prae-* pre- + *pollēre* to be strong, be able — more at POLLEX] **:** superior in influence or power **:** PREDOMINANT

pre·pollex \(ˈ)ₑ+\ *n* [NL, fr. *pre-* + *pollex*] **:** an extra digit or rudiment of a digit on the preaxial side of a thumb

pre·pon·der \prēˈpändə(r)\ *vi* -ED/-ING/-S [L *praeponderare*] **:** PREPONDERATE

pre·pon·der·ance \-d(ə)rən(t)s\ *n* -S [fr. *preponderant*, after such pairs as E *abundant: abundance*] **1 :** a superiority in weight; *specif* **:** the excess of weight of the part of a cannon behind the axis of the trunnions over that in front **2 :** a superiority in power, influence, importance, or strength ⟨this overwhelming ~ of American power and wealth —Barbara Ward⟩ ⟨the immense ~ of good over evil —C.W.Eliot⟩ ⟨the ~ of the evidence⟩ **3 a :** a superiority or excess in number or quantity ⟨give numerical ~ in the lower house to the uplands of the state —U.B.Phillips⟩ ⟨the ~ of small farms was also advantageous to the slave —*Amer. Guide Series: Tenn.*⟩ **b :** MAJORITY ⟨the great ~ of the animals on the road are mules —Christopher Rand⟩

pre·pon·der·an·cy \-nsē, -si\ *n* -ES [*preponderant* + *-cy*] **:** the quality or state of being preponderant **:** superior weight, influence, importance, or power **:** DOMINANCE

pre·pon·der·ant \-nt\ *adj* [L *praeponderant-, praeponderans*, pres. part. of *praeponderare* to preponderate] **1 :** having superior weight, force, or influence **:** PREDOMINANT, PREPONDERATING ⟨the ~ tone of the residential sections . . . is that of the middle-income group —*Amer. Guide Series: N.C.*⟩ **2 :** having greater prevalence ⟨always ~ in numbers, and often in influence and power —H.O.Taylor⟩ **syn** see DOMINANT

pre·pon·der·ant·ly *adv* **:** in a preponderant manner or to a preponderant extent **:** PREDOMINANTLY

[1]**pre·pon·der·ate** \-ˌrāt, *usu* -ād·+V\ *vb* -ED/-ING/-S [L *praeponderatus*, past part. of *praeponderare* to exceed in weight or influence, preponderate, fr. *prae-* pre- + *ponderare* to weigh, fr. *ponder-, pondus* weight — more at PENDANT] *vt* **1** *archaic* **:** OUTWEIGH **2** *archaic* **:** to weigh down **:** INCLINE ~ *vi* **1 a :** to exceed in weight **:** turn the scale ⟨when surplus energy has accumulated in such bulk as to ~ over productive energy —Brooks Adams⟩ **b :** to descend or incline downward **:** become weighed down **2 :** to exceed in influence, power, or importance **:** PREDOMINATE ⟨state ownership will inevitably ~ in the heavy industries —Owen & Eleanor Lattimore⟩ **3 :** to exceed in numbers **:** form a majority ⟨it is the first glory of this volume that such poems ~ in it —*Times Lit. Supp.*⟩

[2]**preponderate** \-rət\ *adj* [L *praeponderatus*, past part. of *praeponderare*] **:** PREPONDERANT **— pre·pon·der·ate·ly** *adv*

preponderating *adj* **:** PREPONDERANT ⟨governments are not in general fully conscious of the ~ importance of science —*Endeavour*⟩ **syn** see DOMINANT

pre·pon·der·at·ing·ly *adv* **:** PREPONDERANTLY

pre·pon·der·a·tion \prēˌpändəˈrāshən\ *n* -S [LL *praeponderation-, praeponderatio*, fr. L *praeponderatus* (past part. of *praeponderare*) + *-ion-, -io* -ion] **1 :** PREPONDERANCE **2** *archaic* **:** the addition of weight to one side of a balance

pre·pon·der·ous \ₑˈₑd(ə)rəs\ *adj* [*pre-* + *ponderous*] **:** PREPONDERANT **— pre·pon·der·ous·ly** *adv*

pre·pontine \(ˈ)prē+\ *adj* [*pre-* + *pontine*] **:** in front of the pons

pre·pose \(ˈ)prēˈpōz\ *vt* -ED/-ING/-S [F *préposer*, fr. MF *preposer* to put in front, prefer, put in charge of, modif. (influenced by *poser* to put, place) of L *praeponere* (perfect stem *praepos-*) — more at POSE] **:** to place before or in front of something **:** PREFIX; *specif* **:** to place (as a particle) before a grammatically connected word ⟨the articles are *preposed* in most languages —M.H.Swadesh⟩

prep·o·si·tion \ˌprepəˈzishən\ *n* -S [ME *preposicioun*, fr. L *praepositionem, praepositio* (trans. of Gk *prothesis*), fr. *praepositus* (past part. of *praeponere* to put in front, put in charge of, fr. *prae-* pre- + *ponere* to put, place) + *-ion-, -io* -ion — more at POSITION] **1 :** a linguistic form that combines with a noun, pronoun, or noun equivalent to form a phrase that typically has an adverbial, adjectival, or substantival relation to some other word (as *of* in "they are proud of him", *with* in "the man with a red face", or *outside* in "it came from outside the house") **2** [influenced in meaning by *pre-* & *position*] **:** the act of placing before or the state of being placed before **:** position before

prep·o·si·tion·al \ˌₑₑˈzishənᵊl, -shnəl\ *adj* [ISV *preposition* + *-al*] **:** of, relating to, or formed with a preposition ⟨~ phrases⟩ **— prep·o·si·tion·al·ly** \-ᵊlē, -əlē, -li\ *adv*

prepositive *adj* [LL *praepositivus*, fr. L *praepositus* (past part. of *praeponere* to put in front + *-ivus* -ive] **:** put before **:** PREFIXED ⟨~ particles in Mongolian⟩ **— prepositively** *adv*

pre·pos·i·tor *or* **prae·pos·i·tor** \prēˈpäzəˌtȯ(ə)r\ *n* -S [ML, fr. L *praepositus* (past part. of *praeponere*) + *-or*] **:** the principal who appoints an institor under Roman or Scots law

pre·pos·i·ture *also* **prae·pos·i·ture** \-əchə(r)\ *n* -S [ME *preposture*, fr. ML *praepositura*, fr. LL, position of authority, fr. L *praepositus* director, chief, man in charge + *-ura* -ure] **:** the office or dignity of a provost of a priory or collegiate church **:** PROVOSTRY

pre·pos·i·tus *also* **prae·pos·i·tus** \prēˈpäzəd·əs\ *n, pl* **pre·posi·ti** *also* **praeposi·ti** \-ˌtī\ [ML, abbot, prior, provost, fr. L *praepositus* director, chief, man in charge, fr. *praepositus*, past part. of *praeponere* to put in front, put in charge of — more at PREPOSITION] **1 a :** ABBOT **b :** PRIOR 1a **2 :** the head of a cathedral or collegiate chapter **:** PROVOST

pre·possess \ˌprē+\ *vt* [*pre-* + *possess*] **1** *obs* **:** to take previous possession of **2 :** to influence or affect strongly beforehand **:** cause to be preoccupied with an idea, belief, or attitude ⟨was ~*ed* with the notion of his own superiority⟩ **3 a :** to influence beforehand for or against someone or something **:** PREJUDICE ⟨in spite of that sliding eye, which often ~*ed* one to doubt . . . he did seem to be telling the truth —C.D. Lewis⟩ **b :** to induce to a favorable opinion beforehand ⟨was not ~*ed* by his appearance —Agatha Christie⟩

prepossessing *adj* **1** *archaic* **:** creating prejudice ⟨this awkward ~ visage of mine —Oliver Goldsmith⟩ **2 :** tending to please or arouse confidence **:** creating a favorable impression **:** ATTRACTIVE ⟨strong and vigorous, and of ~ appearance —E.G.Nash⟩ ⟨a ~ and engaging book —John Berryman⟩ **— pre·pos·sess·ing·ly** *adv* **— pre·pos·sess·ing·ness** *n* -ES

pre·possession \ˌprē+\ *n* [*pre-* + *possession*] **1** *archaic* **:** prior occupancy or possession **2 :** an attitude, belief, or impression formed beforehand **:** a preconceived opinion **:** BIAS, PREJUDICE ⟨his moral ~*s* held his sensibility in check —C.I. Glicksberg⟩ ⟨had repeatedly to amend their ~*s* and especially their assumptions about the country —Bernard De Voto⟩ **3 :** a concentration on one idea or object to the exclusion of others **:** PREOCCUPATION ⟨an amazing ~ with financial concerns —T.A.Sherman⟩ **syn** see PREDILECTION

pre·pos·ter·ous \prēˈpäst(ə)rəs, prəˈ-\ *adj* [L *praeposterus*, lit., reversed, fr. *prae-* pre- + *posterus* next, following — more at POSTERIOR] **1 a :** contrary to nature, reason, or common sense **:** ABSURD, NONSENSICAL ⟨so many seemingly incredible and ~ things were true nevertheless —Ellen Glasgow⟩ **b :** ridiculous in appearance or manner **:** GROTESQUE ⟨false nose and ~ spectacles —Eric Keown⟩ ⟨uses its ~ Elizabethan collar as a storehouse for food —Bill Beatty⟩ **2 :** having or placing something first that should be last ⟨an infuriating book . . . a ~ one in inverting with absolute conviction a comfortable and rarely questioned order of values —*Times Lit. Supp.*⟩ **syn** see FOOLISH

pre·pos·ter·ous·ly *adv* **1 :** NONSENSICALLY, ABSURDLY ⟨a poor but almost ~ happy government clerk —*Time*⟩ **2 :** in an inverted or unnatural order or position **:** with the hind part foremost ⟨tumbled to earth and stayed a mighty while ~ —George Chapman⟩

—pre·pos·ter·ous·ness *n* -ES **:** the quality or state of being preposterous **:** ABSURDITY

prepostor *or* **prepositor** *var of* PRAEPOSTOR

pre·po·tence \prēˈpōtᵊn(t)s\ *n* [F *prépotence*, fr. L *praepotentia*] **:** PREPOTENCY

pre·po·ten·cy \-nsē, -si\ *n* [L *praepotentia*, fr. *praepotent-, praepotens* + *-ia* -y] **1 :** the quality or state of being prepotent **:** PREDOMINANCE ⟨not a policy of self-defence but of ~ and imperialism —*Times Lit. Supp.*⟩ **2 :** the ability of one individual or strain to transmit its characters to offspring to a greater extent than the other parent individual or strain because of an accumulation of homozygous dominant genes

pre·po·tent \-tᵊnt\ *adj* [ME, fr. L *praepotent-, praepotens*, pres. part. of *praeposse* to be more powerful, fr. *prae-* pre- + *posse* to be able — more at POTENT] **1 a :** having exceptional power, authority, or influence **:** PREEMINENT ⟨had long been ~ as an influence in taste and practice —F.R.Leavis⟩ **b :** exceeding others in power **:** SUPERIOR ⟨the soul may be seen as ~ over mere things —Weston La Barre⟩ **2 :** exhibiting genetic prepotency **:** DOMINANT **3 :** having priority over other response tendencies esp. by virtue of maturational primacy, recentness of emission or evocation, repetition with positive reinforcement, or greater motivational charge ⟨the ~ response is that with the greatest immediately effective habit strength⟩ **— pre·po·tent·ly** *adv*

prepped *past of* PREP

prepping *pres part of* PREP

pre·prandial \(ˈ)prē+\ *adj* [*pre-* + *prandial*] **:** of, relating to, or suitable for the time immediately before dinner ⟨a ~ drink⟩

pre·preference \"+\ *adj* [*pre-* + *preference*] *Brit* **:** having priority over preference shares or bonds either as to payment of interest or dividends or as to security for repayment of principal

[1]**pre·print** \(ˈ)ₑ+\ *n* [*pre-* + *print*, n.] **1 :** a printing issued in advance of book or periodical publication; *esp* **:** a portion of a larger work (as a chapter of a book or an article in a magazine) issued before publication of the whole ⟨~*s* of a review⟩ ⟨~*s* of an advertisement⟩ — compare FASCICLE, INSTALLMENT **2 :** a printing of a speech, lecture, or paper issued before its formal delivery

[2]**preprint** \"\ *vt* [*pre-* + *print*, v.] **:** to print and issue in advance of publication or delivery

pre·professional \ˌₑ+\ *adj* [*pre-* + *professional*] **:** of or relating to the period preceding specific study for or practice of a profession ⟨~ education⟩ ⟨~ interests⟩

pre·prophetic \"+\ *adj* [*pre-* + *prophetic*] **:** constituting or relating to the period preceding the writings of the Hebrew prophets ⟨~ religious observances⟩

preps *pl of* PREP, *pres 3d sing of* PREP

prep school *n* [by shortening] **:** PREPARATORY SCHOOL

pre·psychotic \ˌprē+\ *adj* [*pre-* + *psychotic*] **:** preceding or predisposing to psychosis **:** possessing recognizable features prognostic of psychosis ⟨~ behavior⟩ ⟨~ personality⟩

pre·pub \(ˈ)prēˈpəb\ *n* -S [by shortening] **:** PREPUBLICATION

pre·pubertal \(ˈ)prē+\ *or* **pre·puberal** \"+\ *adj* [*prepubertal* fr. *pre-* + *puberty* + *-al*; *prepuberal* fr. *pre-* + *puberal*] **:** of or relating to prepuberty **— pre·pu·ber·tal·ly** \-əlē\ *or* **pre·pu·ber·al·ly** \-əlē\ *adv*

pre·puberty \(ˈ)prē+\ *n* [*pre-* + *puberty*] **:** the period esp. in the life of a human being immediately preceding puberty; *broadly* **:** the period between infancy and the beginning of puberty in man or other higher vertebrates

pre·pubescence \ˌₑ+\ *n* [*pre-* + *pubescence*] **:** PREPUBERTY

pre·pubescent \"+\ *adj* [*pre-* + *pubescent*] **:** PREPUBERAL

pre·pubic \(ˈ)ₑ+\ *also* **pre·pubian** \"+\ *adj* [*prepubic* fr. *pre-* + *pubic*; *prepubian* ISV *pre-* + *pub-* (fr. NL *pubis*) + *-an*] **1 :** in front of the pubis **2** [*prepubis* + *-ic* or *-an*] **:** relating to or constituting the prepubis

pre·pubis \(ˈ)ₑ+\ *n* [NL, fr. *pre-* + *pubis*] **:** the part of the pubis of a reptile or bird that lies in front of the acetabulum, is best developed in ornithischian dinosaurs in which it is regarded as the homologue of the true pubis of other reptiles and higher groups, and in birds is derived largely from the ilium **2 a :** EPIPUBIS **b :** an epipubic bone

pre·publication \(ˌ)ₑ+\ *n* [*pre-* + *publication*] **:** a copy of a book or other printed work issued in advance of publication

pre·publish \(ˈ)ₑ+\ *vt* [*pre-* + *publish*] **:** to issue in advance of publication

pre·puce \ˈprēˌpyüs\ *n* -S [ME, fr. MF, fr. L *praeputium*, fr. *prae-* pre- + *-putium* (akin to Belorussian *potka* penis); prob. akin to Skt *pusyati* he thrives, flourishes — more at FOG] **:** FORESKIN; *also* **:** a similar fold investing the clitoris

pre·pueblo \(ˈ)ₑ+\ *or* **pre·puebloan** \"+\ *adj, usu cap 2d P* [*pre-* + *pueblo* or *puebloan*] **:** of or belonging to a prehistoric culture in southwestern U.S. and the adjacent part of Mexico immediately preceding the Pueblo — compare BASKET MAKER, HOHOKAM

pre·pupa \(ˈ)ₑ+\ *n* [NL, fr. *pre-* + *pupa*] **1 :** a stage in the development of many holometabolic insects immediately preceding the change to a pupa and usu. marked by cessation of feeding **2 :** an insect in the prepupal stage **— pre·pupal** \"+\ *adj*

pre·pu·tial *also* **pre·pu·cial** \(ˈ)prēˈpyüshəl\ *adj* [*preputial* fr. L *praeputium* + E *-al*; *prepucial* alter. (influenced by *prepuce*) of *preputial*] **:** of, relating to, or constituting a prepuce

pre·pu·ti·um \prēˈpyüsh(ē)əm\ *n, pl* **prepu·tia** \-)ə\ [L *praeputium*] **:** PREPUCE

pre·pyloric \ˌprē+\ *adj* [*pre-* + *pyloric*] **:** situated in front of the pylorus

[1]**pre-raphaelite** \(ˈ)prē+\ *n, usu cap P&R* [*pre-* + *Raphael* †1520 Ital. painter + E *-ite*] **1 a :** a member of a brotherhood of artists formed in England in 1848 and dedicated to restoring in painting and propagating in criticism the artistic principles and practices (as fidelity to nature, sincerity, and delicacy of finish) regarded as characteristic of Italian art before Raphael **b :** an artist or writer influenced by the ideas or work of members of the Pre-Raphaelite brotherhood **2 :** a modern artist dedicated to restoring early Renaissance ideals or methods **3 :** an Italian painter active before the time of Raphael's fame and influence; *esp* **:** one active in the earlier part of the 14th century

[2]**pre-raphaelite** \"\ *adj, usu cap P&R* **:** of or relating to Pre-Raphaelitism or Pre-Raphaelites

pre-raphaelitism *also* **pre-raphaelism** \"+\ *n, usu cap P&R* [*pre-raphaelitism* fr. [1]*pre-raphaelite* + *-ism*; *pre-raphaelism* fr. *pre-* + *Raphael* + E *-ism*] **:** the principles, practice, or style of Pre-Raphaelites

pre·rational \(ˈ)prē+\ *adj* [*pre-* + *rational*] **:** preceding the development of intelligence ⟨~ instincts⟩

pre·record \ˌprē+\ *vt* [*pre-* + *record*] **:** PRESCORE

prerecorded tape *n* [*prerecorded* fr. past part. of *prerecord*] **:** magnetic tape on which sound has been recorded before the tape is offered for sale

pre·reduction \ˌprē+\ *n* [*pre-* + *reduction*] **:** reduction of chromosomes in the first meiotic division

pre·release \"+\ *n* [*pre-* + *release*] **:** a release in advance of the usual or expected time: as **a :** a showing of a movie before the date set for its release **b :** an opening to the exhaust in a steam engine before the end of a stroke in order to minimize back pressure

prerequire \"+\ *vt* [*pre-* + *require*] *archaic* **:** to require beforehand

[1]**pre·requisite** \(ˈ)prē+\ *n* [*pre-* + *requisite*, n.] **1 :** something that is required beforehand **:** something that is necessary to an end or to the carrying out of a function ⟨payment of the tax as a ~ for voting —*Amer. Guide Series: Ark.*⟩ ⟨the days before there were anesthetics, when speed was one of the ~*s* of a surgeon —O.S.J.Gogarty⟩ **2 a :** an educational requirement that a student must satisfy before he is permitted to do advanced work ⟨a bachelor's degree is a ~ for graduate work⟩ **b :** a course that a student must complete as a sensible or arbitrary requirement for another course ⟨freshman composition is a ~ for advanced composition⟩

[2]**prerequisite** \"\ *adj* [*pre-* + *requisite*, adj.] **:** required beforehand **:** necessary as a preliminary condition

pre·resolve \ˌprē+\ *vi* [*pre-* + *resolve*] *archaic* **:** to make up one's mind beforehand

pre·revolutionary \(ˌ)prē+\ *adj* [*pre-* + *revolutionary*] **:** of or belonging to a time before a revolution; *specif* **:** of or belonging to the time before the American Revolution

pre·ripen \(ˈ)prē+\ *vt* [*pre-* + *ripen*] **:** to ripen (fruit) artificially in order to facilitate its safe shipment

pre·rog·a·ti·val \prēˌrägəˈtīvəl\ *adj* **:** of or relating to a prerogative

[1]**pre·rog·a·tive** \prēˈrägəd·iv, prəˈ-, -ətiv, *by r-dissimilation* ₌pəˈ-\ *n* -S [ME, fr. MF & L; MF *prerogative*, fr. L *praerogativa* preference, privilege, Roman century chosen by lot to be the first to vote in the comitia, fr. fem. of *praerogativus* that votes first, that is first asked to express an opinion, fr. *praerogatus* (past part. of *praerogare* to ask before another, fr. *prae-* pre- + *rogare* to ask) + *-ivus* -ive — more at RIGHT] **1 a** (1) **:** a right attached to an office or rank to exercise a special privilege or function; *specif* **:** an official and hereditary right (as of a royal sovereign) that may be asserted without question and for which there is in theory no responsibility or accountability as to the fact and manner of its exercise though in practice it is usu. limited by the power of public opinion or by statute and is generally (as in England) exercised on the advice of ministers who are responsible to a legislative body (2) **:** a sovereign right inhering in a state or in the head of a state ⟨the ~ of the president to commute punishments and grant reprieves or pardons⟩ **b :** a special right or privilege belonging to a person, group, or class of individuals ⟨cruelty remains the special ~ of men —Christine Weston⟩ ⟨in his youth, to sit thus was the ~ of the gentry —Oscar Handlin⟩ **c :** a privilege, advantage, or precedence attaching to one who holds an office **2 a :** a special quality that gives superiority **:** a distinctive excellence ⟨the lively nature and gay wit which were the family ~ —*Modern Philology*⟩ **b** *obs* **:** PRECEDENCE, PREEMINENCE ⟨give me leave to have ~ —Shak.⟩ **3 :** a right of voting first **syn** see RIGHT

[2]**prerogative** \"\ *adj* [ME (Sc), fr. ML *praerogativus*, fr. L, that votes first] **1 :** of, relating to, or deriving from a prerogative **:** existing or exercised by special right or privilege **:** PRIVILEGED ⟨~ power⟩ ⟨~ right⟩ **2 :** privileged to vote first ⟨~ century of Roman citizens⟩ **3 :** of or relating to a prerogative court ⟨~ records⟩ ⟨~ procedure⟩

prerogative court *n* **1 :** an ecclesiastical court formerly exercising probate jurisdiction with respect to wills and estates of decedents **2 :** a court formerly appointed by the royal governor of an American colony **3 :** ORPHANS' COURT

pre·rog·a·tived \-vd\ *adj* **:** endowed with a prerogative **:** PRIVILEGED ⟨tis the plague of great ones; ~ are they less than the base —*Shak.*⟩

prerogative instance *n* **:** a crucial instance in induction **:** an instance of first importance

prerogative writ *n* **:** any of various writs of procedendo, certiorari, mandamus, prohibition, quo warranto, and habeas corpus issued orig. in England by the exercise of the royal prerogative and now in the discretion of the courts and directed usu. to the parties whose action is to be controlled and not to the sheriff — called also *extraordinary writ*

pre·rolandic \¦prē+\ *adj* [*pre-* + *rolandic*] **:** PRECENTRAL 1

prerotation device \"+-\ *n* [*prerotation* fr. *pre-* + *rotation*] **:** a device for setting the landing wheels of an airplane in rotation prior to the initial contact with the ground in landing in order to reduce landing shock and damage to tires

pre·rupt \prē'rəpt\ *adj* [L *praeruptus*, past part. of *praerumpere* to break off in front, fr. *prae-* pre- + *rumpere* to break — more at REAVE] **1 :** broken off abruptly **:** PRECIPITOUS, STEEP **2 :** lacking an introduction **:** ABRUPT

pres *abbr* **1** present **2** presentation **3** presidency; president; presidential **4** pressure **5** presumptive

pre·sa \'prāsə\ *n, pl* **pre·se** \-sā\ [It, lit., action of taking, seizure, fr. fem. of *preso* (past part. of *prendere* to take, seize), fr. L *prehensus*, past part. of *prehendere* to grasp, seize — more at PREHENSILE] **:** a mark or cue (as :S: or ※) indicating the point of entry of the successive voice parts of a canon

pre·sacral \(ˈ)prē+\ *adj* [*pre-* + *sacral*] **:** effected by way of the anterior aspect of the sacrum ⟨~ nerve block⟩

¹pres·age \'presij, -sēj\ *n* -s [ME, fr. L *praesagium*, fr. *praesagire* to have a presentiment of, fr. *prae-* pre- + *sagire* to perceive keenly — more at SEEK] **1 :** something that foreshadows or portends a future event **:** a warning or indication of something about to happen **:** OMEN, PROGNOSTIC ⟨the coming of the swallow is a true ~ of the spring —John Worlidge⟩ ⟨sees a lunar rainbow . . . as a ~ of good fortune —Van Wyck Brooks⟩ **2 :** an intuition or feeling of what is going to happen in the future **:** FOREBODING, PRESENTIMENT ⟨feel in his nerves the ~ of a storm —Charlton Ogburn⟩ ⟨artists whom the ~ of an early death stimulates —Roger Fry⟩ **3** *archaic* **:** an utterance foretelling something future **:** PREDICTION, PROGNOSTICATION ⟨expected as ill a ~ . . . from those fortune tellers —Edward Hyde⟩ **4 :** foreknowledge of the future **:** PRESCIENCE ⟨if there be aught of ~ in the mind —John Milton⟩ **5 :** AUGURY 3 ⟨hand . . . raised in ~ of volunteered information —*New Yorker*⟩ ⟨a firm steel bridge as ~ of what is ahead —William Sansom⟩ ⟨birds of evil ~ —Edmund Burke⟩

²pres·age \", prē'sāj, prə'-\ *vb* -ED/-ING/-S [MF *presager*, fr. *presage* omen, fr. L *praesagium*] *vt* **1 a :** to give an omen or warning of **:** signify beforehand by supernatural means **:** FORESHADOW, PORTEND ⟨evil luck was *presaged* . . . by a dog crossing the hunter's path —*Amer. Guide Series: Ind.*⟩ ⟨sensation of creeping uneasiness which *presaged* some kind of trouble —Marcia Davenport⟩ ⟨fiery meteors may ~ death and destruction —Christopher Marlowe⟩ **b :** to point to or indicate in advance **:** give prior indication of by natural means **:** provide a symptom of **:** PREINDICATE ⟨dropsy . . . almost invariably ~*s* cardiac failure —F.A.Faught⟩ ⟨Democratic gains aren't significant enough to ~ drastic legislative changes —*Wall Street Jour.*⟩ **2 :** to indicate or calculate in advance **:** FORECAST, FORETELL, PREDICT ⟨lands he could measure, terms and tides ~ —Oliver Goldsmith⟩ **3 :** to have a presentiment or prevision of **:** feel beforehand **:** FOREBODE 2 ⟨from the preliminaries . . . he was only able to ~ danger and disaster —A.W. Tourgee⟩ ~ *vi* **1** *obs* **:** to have a presentiment or foreknowledge **2 :** to make or utter a prediction ⟨prophecy would fain ~ auspiciously —J.B.Mozley⟩ — sometimes used with *of* ⟨by certain signs we may ~ of heats and rains —John Dryden⟩ **syn** see FORETELL

pres·age·ful \'presijfəl\ *adj* **:** full of presage or presages **:** FOREBODING, FOREKNOWING, OMINOUS, PROPHETIC ⟨a ~ mood⟩ ⟨~ victory⟩ ⟨that . . . ~ gloom of yours —Alfred Tennyson⟩

presagement *n* -s *obs* **:** the action of one that presages **:** a result of presaging **:** FOREBODING, OMEN, PRESENTIMENT, PORTENT ⟨whether he had any ominous ~ before his end —Henry Wotton⟩

presager *n* -s *obs* **:** one that presages ⟨unusual signs, ~*s* of strange terrors to the world —*Shak.*⟩

presaging *adj* **:** characterized by presage ⟨~ tokens of success —Daniel Defoe⟩ ⟨a ~ intelligence⟩

pres·ag·ing·ly *adv* **:** in a manner full of presages or characterized by presage

presagious *adj* [MF *presagieux*, fr. *presage* omen + *-ieux* -ious] *obs* **:** of the nature of a presage **:** full of presages ⟨~ dreams —James Heath⟩

pre·sanctified \(ˈ)prē+\ *adj* [*pre-* + *sanctified*; trans. of ML *praesanctificatus*, trans. of MGk *proēgiasmenos*] **:** consecrated at a previous service — used of Eucharistic elements ⟨a ~ Host⟩ ⟨liturgy of the ~⟩

presby- or **presbyo-** *comb form* [NL, fr. Gk *presby-* older, fr. *presbys* old man — more at PRIEST] **:** old age ⟨*presbyopia*⟩ ⟨*presbyophrenia*⟩

pres·by·cu·sis \ˌprezbə'kyüsəs, -esb-\ or **pres·by·a·cu·sia** \-bēə'kyüzh(ē)ə\ *also* **pres·by·a·cou·sia** \-'küzh-\ *n, pl* **presbycu·ses** \-ü,sēz\ or **presbyacusias** *also* **presbyacousias** [*presbycusis* fr. *presby-* + *-cusis* (fr. Gk *akousis* hearing); *presbyacusia*, *presbyacousia* fr. NL, fr. *presby-* + *-acousia* — more at -ACOUSIA] **:** a condition of hearing less acutely that occurs in old age

pres·by·ope \'prezbē,ōp, -esb-\ *n* -s [prob. fr. F, fr. *presby-* + *-ope*] **:** one that has presbyopia **:** a farsighted person

pres·by·o·phre·nia \ˌprezbēə'frēnēə, -esb-\ *n* -s [NL, fr. *presby-* + *-phrenia*] **:** a form of senile dementia occurring chiefly in women and characterized by loss of memory often to the point of disorientation with preservation of mobility, loquacity, good spirits, and considerable mental alertness — **pres·by·o·phren·ic** \¦==¦frenik\ *adj*

pres·by·o·pia \ˌprezbē'ōpēə, -esb-\ *n* -s [NL, fr. *presby-* + *-opia*] **:** a condition of defective elasticity of the crystalline lens of the eye usu. in old age resulting in difficulty of accommodation and inability to attain a sharp focus for near vision — compare HYPEROPIA

¹pres·by·op·ic \¦==¦äpik\ *adj* [*presbyopia* + *-ic*] **:** affected by presbyopia **:** FARSIGHTED

²presbyopic \"\ *n* -s **:** a presbyopic person

pres·by·ter \'prezbəd·ə(r), -esb-, -ətə-\ *n* -s [LL, presbyter, elder, fr. Gk *presbyteros* — more at PRIEST] **1 :** an official in the early Christian church vested with the task of providing leadership as an overseer usu. over a local congregation **2 :** a clergyman ranking immediately below a bishop in the more liturgical churches that have episcopal polities (as the Eastern Orthodox Church and the Anglican Church) **:** PRIEST 1a(1) ⟨bishops, ~*s* and deacons consecrated or ordained in the Church of South India —*Brit. Book News*⟩ **3 :** an elder in a Presbyterian church **4** *usu cap, archaic* **:** PRESBYTERIAN

pres·byt·er·al \(ˈ)prez¦bidərəl, -es¦-\ *adj* [ML *presbyteralis* of a priest, fr. LL, of a presbyter, fr. *presbyter* + L *-alis* -al] **:** PRESBYTERIAL

pres·byt·er·ate \=¦==rət, -,rāt\ *n* -s [LL *presbyteratus* office of a presbyter, fr. *presbyter* + L *-atus* -ate] **1 :** a body of presbyters or elders **:** PRESBYTERY 2 **2 :** the office or position of a presbyter or elder

pres·by·tère \ˌprezbə'te(ə)r\ *n* -s [F, fr. MF *presbitaire* presbytère, group of priests serving a particular church, fr. ML *presbyterium* group of priests, priesthood, fr. LL, group of presbyters, office of a presbyter, presbytery (part of a church where the clergy sit) — more at PRESBYTERY] **:** the residence of a Roman Catholic parish priest

pres·by·ter·ess \'prezbəd·ərəs\ *n* -ES [part trans. of ML *presbyterissa*, fr. *presbyter* priest (fr. LL, presbyter, elder) + LL *-issa* -ess] **1 a :** the wife of a presbyter or priest in one of the early medieval churches; *esp* **:** one coming under the operation of the rule requiring the continence of clergymen **b :** a priest's concubine **2 :** a woman serving as a presbyter or elder in one of the early medieval churches **:** one of a body of aged widows dedicated to the service of the church and constituting an ecclesiastical order **3 :** the wife of a priest of the Eastern Orthodox Church

¹pres·by·te·ri·al \¦prezbə¦tirēəl, -esb-, -tēr-\ *adj* [*presbytery* + *-al*] **1** *usu cap, archaic* **:** PRESBYTERIAN **2 2 :** of or relating to a presbyter or a body of presbyters ⟨a ~ title⟩ **3 :** of, relating to, or based upon a local presbytery ⟨substitute a ~ . . . polity for episcopacy —W.E.Garrison⟩ **4** *usu cap* [*²presbyterial*] **:** of or relating to a Presbyterial ⟨*Presbyterial* officers⟩ ⟨*Presbyterial* meeting⟩

²presbyterial \"\ *n* -s *usu cap* **:** an organization of Presbyterian women associated with a presbytery — compare SYNODICAL

pres·by·te·ri·al·ly \-rēəlē, -li\ *adv* **:** by a presbytery **:** in a presbyterial manner

¹pres·by·te·ri·an \-rēən\ *adj* [*presbytery* + *-an*] **1** *often cap* **:** having or characterized by a graded system of representative ecclesiastical bodies (as presbyteries, sessions, and a general assembly) exercising legislative and judicial powers ⟨in local affairs the churches are ~ in government —F.S.Mead⟩ — compare CONGREGATIONAL 2, EPISCOPAL 2a **2** *usu cap* **a :** of, relating to, or constituting a Protestant Christian church that is presbyterian in government and traditionally Calvinistic in doctrine ⟨a *Presbyterian* minister⟩ ⟨the *Presbyterian* Church of Canada⟩ — compare REFORMED **b :** characterizing or held to characterize a member of such a church ⟨a *Presbyterian* conscience⟩ ⟨a thorough-going *Presbyterian* distaste for bishops —E.R.R.Green⟩

²presbyterian \"\ *n* -s *usu cap* **:** a member of a Presbyterian church **:** a supporter of Presbyterianism

pres·by·te·ri·an·ism \ˌ==¦tirēə,nizəm, -tēr-\ *n* -s **1** *usu cap* **a :** the presbyterian form of church government ⟨~ declared to be the only lawful government —A.C.McGiffert⟩ **b :** belief in or adherence to such church government **2** *cap* **:** the faith and polity of the Presbyterian Church; *esp* **:** the principles of Presbyterians including the right of all members of the church to share in its government exercised through elders chosen or approved by them, the recognition of only one order in the Christian ministry with all members equal and exercising all ministerial functions, and the unity of the whole church expressed in a graded system of church courts composed of ministers and elders **3** *usu cap* **:** the whole body of Presbyterian churches

pres·by·te·ri·an·ize \-,nīz\ *vt* -ED/-ING/-S *often cap* **:** to make presbyterian ⟨resolved to *Presbyterianize* the university —G.C.Brodrick⟩

pres·by·te·ri·an·ly *adv, usu cap* **:** in a Presbyterian manner or direction ⟨a *Presbyterianly* inclined church⟩

pres·by·ter·ism \'prezbəd·ə,rizəm\ *n* -s *usu cap* [*presbyter* + *-ism*] *archaic* **:** PRESBYTERIANISM

pres·by·ter·i·um \ˌprezbə'tirēəm\ *n* -s [LL] **1 :** PRESBYTERY 1 **2 :** PRESBYTERY 6

pres·by·ter·ship \'prezbəd·ə(r),ship\ *n* [*presbyter* + *-ship*] **:** PRESBYTERATE 2

pres·by·tery \'prezbə,terē, -resb-, -ri\ *n* -ES [ME *presbytory*, fr. LL *presbyterium* group of presbyters, office of a presbyter, presbytery (part of a church where the clergy sit), fr. Gk *presbyterion* group of presbyters, office of a presbyter, fr. *presbyteros* presbyter, elder — more at PRIEST] **1 a :** the division in an ancient church lying east of the sanctuary and containing the seats of the bishop and clergy **b :** the part of a church (as the choir or sanctuary or both) reserved for the officiating clergy **2 :** a ruling body in Presbyterian churches consisting of all the ministers of and one or more representative elders from each of the congregations within a specific district, having legislative and judicial powers, and ranking in authority above the session but below the synod — compare CLASSIS, COLLOQUY 2, CONSISTORY 2 d **3 :** the district within which the congregations under the authority of a presbytery are situated **:** the jurisdiction of a presbytery **4 :** the Presbyterian polity — compare EPISCOPACY 1, INDEPENDENCY **5** *obs* **:** PRESBYTERATE 2 **6 :** a body of presbyters in an early Christian church **7 :** the house of a presbyter; *specif* **:** PRESBYTÈRE

pres·byt·ic \(ˈ)prez¦bid·ik\ *adj* [ISV *presbyt-* (fr. NL *presbytia* presbyopia, fr. Gk *presbytēs* old man + NL *-ia*) + *-ic*] **:** FARSIGHTED ⟨~ eyes⟩

pres·by·tis \prez'bīd·əs\ *n, cap* [NL, fr. Gk, old woman, fem. of *presbytēs* old man, fr. *presbys* old man — more at PRIEST] **:** a genus of old-world monkeys consisting of the langurs

pre·scap·u·la \prē'skapyələ\ *n* [NL, fr. *pre-* + L *scapula*] **:** the supraspinous part of the scapula

pre·scapular \(ˈ)prē+\ *adj* [*pre-* + *scapular*] **1 :** situated anterior to the scapula **2** [*prescapula* + *-ar*] **:** of, relating to, or being the prescapula

¹pre·school \(ˈ)prē+\ *adj* [*pre-* + *school*, n.] **:** of, relating to, or constituting the period in a child's life from infancy to the age of five or six ordinarily preceding attendance at elementary school but often occupied by attendance at nursery school or kindergarten

²preschool \'prē+,-\ *n* **:** NURSERY SCHOOL, KINDERGARTEN

pre·school·er \'prē,skülə(r)\ *n* -s [*preschool* + *-er*] **:** a child who is not old enough to attend elementary school **:** a pupil in a kindergarten or nursery school **:** KINDERGARTNER 1

pre·science \'prē|sh(ē)ən(t)s, 'pre|, |s(ē)-\ *n* -s [ME, fr. LL *praescientia*, fr. L *praescient-*, *praesciens* + *-ia* -y] **1 :** foreknowledge of events: **a :** omniscience with regard to the future usu. held to be a divine attribute ⟨belief in the absolute ~ . . . of God —Frank Thilly⟩ ⟨God's certain ~ of the volitions of moral agents —Jonathan Edwards⟩ **b :** the human faculty or quality of being able to anticipate the occurrence or nature of future events **:** FORESIGHT ⟨the acute phatic ~ of a mother when her child is concerned —Weston La Barre⟩ ⟨country people seem to have a greater ~ of snow —Adrian Bell⟩ ⟨foresaw the great dangers . . . with far more ~ than most well-informed people —Sir Winston Churchill⟩ **2 :** an instance of foreknowledge or foresight ⟨~*s* like these do come to us sometimes —Kenneth Roberts⟩

pre·scient \-nt\ *adj* [L *praescient-*, *praesciens*, pres. part. of *praescire* to know beforehand, fr. *prae-* pre- + *scire* to know — more at SCIENCE] **:** having or marked by prescience **:** having foreknowledge **:** characterized by foresight ⟨~ of what he was later to fulfill —H.O.Taylor⟩ ⟨some extraordinarily ~ memoranda on the probable course of postwar relationships —R.H.Rovere⟩

pre·scientific \(ˌ)prē+\ *adj* [*pre-* + *scientific*] **1 :** preceding the development or the acquisition of scientific knowledge ⟨terms familiar to the ~ era —J.C.Swaim⟩ ⟨a ~ stage of cultural development⟩ **2 :** of, belonging to, or having the characteristics of a period before the rise of modern science or a state prior to the application of scientific method ⟨~ man assumed the prevalence of a divine law —James Ward⟩ ⟨a primitive ~ view⟩ ⟨the thesis . . . that native culture is ~ —David Bidney⟩

pre·scient·ly *adv* **:** with prescience or foresight ⟨more ~ than those in organization they grasped the antithesis —W.H. Whyte⟩

pre·scind \prē'sind\ *vb* -ED/-ING/-S [L *praescindere* to cut off in front, fr. *prae-* pre- + *scindere* to cut, split — more at SHED] *vt* **1** *archaic* **:** to cut short, off, or away **:** SEVER ⟨the brevity of his reign ~*ed* many . . . hopes of his good government —Richard Brathwaite⟩ **2 :** to abstract by an act of attention **:** detach for purposes of thought **:** separate in consideration — used with *from* ⟨its momentousness . . . ~*ed* their minds from the goat —Malcolm Lowry⟩ ⟨I cannot ~ . . . the existence of a sensible thing from being perceived —George Berkeley⟩ ~ *vi* **:** to abstract or detach oneself — used with *from* ⟨we have ~*ed* from all these concrete characteristics —Peter Dunne⟩ ⟨if we ~ entirely from any audience consideration —*Quarterly Jour. of Speech*⟩ **syn** see DETACH

prescious *adj* [L *praescius*, fr. *praescire* to know beforehand + *-ius* -ious] *obs* **:** PRESCIENT

pre·score \(ˈ)prē+\ *vt* [*pre-* + *score*] **:** to record (as dialogue, music, or sound effects) in advance for use when the corresponding scenes are photographed in making movies

pres·cott scale \'preskət-\ *n, usu cap P* [prob. fr. the name *Prescott*] **:** a scale (*Matsucoccus vexillorum*) that attacks pines in the western U.S.

pre·scribe \prē'skrīb, prə'-\ *vb* -ED/-ING/-S [ME *prescriben* to hold or possess by right of prescription, fr. ML *prescribere* to claim by right of prescription, fr. L *praescribere* to write at the beginning, order, direct, prescribe, fr. *prae-* pre- + *scribere* to write; in several senses directly fr. L *praescribere* — more at SCRIBE] *vi* **1 :** to claim a title to something by right of prescription **:** assert a prescriptive right or claim **2 :** to lay down a rule **:** give directions **:** DICTATE, DIRECT **3 a :** to write or give medical prescriptions ⟨~ for a patient⟩ **b :** to give advice in the manner of a doctor giving a medical prescription **4 :** to become by prescription invalid or unenforceable ⟨various rights ~ in twenty years⟩ ~ *vt* **1 a :** to lay down authoritatively as a guide, direction, or rule of action **:** impose as a peremptory order **:** DICTATE, DIRECT, ORDAIN ⟨the code of behavior which the culture ~*s* for child training —Franz Alexander⟩ ⟨legislatures may ~ qualifications . . . for admission to the bar —H.S.Drinker⟩ ⟨right convention ~*s* that such meetings open with prayer —D.L. Cohn⟩ **b :** to specify with authority ⟨the fixed routine of *prescribed* duties —Oscar Wilde⟩ ⟨purchased by the department at *prescribed* prices —*Farmer's Weekly (So. Africa)*⟩ **c :** to require (as a person) to follow a direction or rule of action ⟨*prescribed* to take the following oath —C.W.Ferguson⟩ **2** *obs* **:** to describe in advance **:** foretell or make a prophecy of in writing **3 :** to direct, designate, or order the use of as a remedy ⟨the doctor *prescribed* quinine⟩ ⟨we ~ a certain amount of art for ourselves as a kind of corrective —Louis Kronenberger⟩ **4 :** to keep within limits or bounds **:** CONFINE, RESTRAIN ⟨*prescribed* to one poor solitary place — Michael Drayton⟩

syn ASSIGN, DEFINE: PRESCRIBE indicates authoritative dictating or commanding, with explicit clear direction ⟨a doctor *prescribing* medicine for a patient⟩ ⟨payment of the tax as a prerequisite for voting was *prescribed* by a constitutional amendment —*Amer. Guide Series: Ark.*⟩ ⟨the power to *prescribe* rules of conduct was delegated to the President —C.J.Friedrich⟩ ASSIGN may imply arbitrary or chance allotment, designation, or determination for the sake of some such end as harmonious operation, smooth routine, or proper or practical functioning or procedure ⟨*assign* an officer to a military unit⟩ ⟨*assigned* to the night shift⟩ ⟨the clause, *assigning* original jurisdiction to the supreme court —John Marshall⟩ DEFINE may indicate an exact delineation or demarcation to prevent confusion or conflict ⟨*defining* the jurisdiction of various courts⟩ ⟨*defined* still more clearly the extent to which the nations of this continent are willing to combine their military power to defend any American republic from an aggressor —S.G.Inman⟩ ⟨obscure symbolisms which *define* the relation of various age groups to each other —Edward Sapir⟩ **syn** see in addition DICTATE

pre·scrib·er \-bə(r)\ *n* -s **:** one that prescribes ⟨the ~ should specify the drug strength of a potent agent —W.H.Blome & C.H.Stocking⟩

¹pre·script \'prē,skript, =ˈ=\ *adj* [ME *prescripte*, fr. L *praescriptus*, past part. of *praescribere* to prescribe] **:** prescribed as a rule **:** ordained or appointed by authority ⟨a ~ form of words —Jeremy Taylor⟩

²prescript \"=,=\ *n* -s [L *praescriptum*, fr. neut. of *praescriptus*, past part. of *praescribere*] **1 :** something prescribed as a rule **:** COMMAND, DIRECTION, INSTRUCTION, LAW, ORDINANCE, PRECEPT, REGULATION ⟨the constitution of the church . . . set down by divine ~ —John Milton⟩ ⟨according to the ~*s* of existing law —J.W.Burgess⟩ **2** *archaic* **:** a medical prescription ⟨your ~ is compounded of . . . delicate simples —Samuel Harsnett⟩

pre·scrip·ti·ble \prē'skriptəbəl\ *adj* [MF *prescriptible*, fr. ML *prescriptibilis*, fr. *prescriptus* (past part. of *prescribere* to claim by right of prescription) + L *-ibilis* -able] **:** depending on or derived from prescription **:** proper to be prescribed **:** subject to prescription

pre·scrip·tion \prē'skripshən, prə'-\ *n* -s *often attrib* [ME *prescripcion*, fr. MF *prescription*, fr. LL *praescription-*, *praescriptio* prescription (sense 2a), fr. L, prefatory writing, order, rule, fr. *praescriptus* (past part. of *praescribere* to write at the beginning, order, direct, prescribe) + *-ion-*, *-io* -ion; in several senses directly fr. L *praescription-*, *praescriptio*] **1 a** (1) **:** the establishment of a claim of title to something under common law orig. by virtue of immemorial use and enjoyment or usu. in modern times by use and enjoyment for a period fixed by statute (as 20 years) ⟨a municipal corporation can be brought into existence by ~ —J.E.Pate⟩ ⟨gaining a right by ~ —O.W.Holmes †1935⟩ (2) **:** the acquisition under common law of incorporeal interests in land (as easements) by such a process as distinguished from acquisition of title by adverse possession ⟨~ is based upon the legal fiction that possession was originally acquired under a grant⟩ **b :** the right or title acquired under common law by possession had during the time and in the manner fixed by law **2 a :** the operation of the Roman law whereby rights might be acquired or extinguished by limitation of the time within which the owner might have his remedy under the praetorian law — distinguished from *usucapion* **b :** the operation of the civil law whereby rights might be established by long exercise of their corresponding powers or extinguished by prolonged failure to exercise such powers **:** a civil law process in which the usucapion and prescription of Roman law are merged **3 :** the action of prescribing **:** the process of making claim to something (as a title) by long use and enjoyment **4 :** the action of prescribing **:** the process of laying down authoritative rules or directions ⟨~ of the duty of an individual towards others —R.M.MacIver⟩ ⟨the issue of . . . ~ or free choice in education —Sidney Hook⟩ **5 a** (1) **:** a written direction for the preparation, compounding, and administration of a medicine (2) **:** a prescribed remedy **b :** a written formula for the grinding of corrective lenses for eyeglasses **c :** a written direction for the application of physical therapy measures (as directed exercise or electrotherapy) in cases of injury or disability **d :** something resembling or held to resemble such a medical direction ⟨step-by-step ~*s* for improving executive performance —*Dun's Rev.*⟩ ⟨a useful ~ for depression unemployment —L.G.Reynolds⟩ ⟨a ~ of spiritual aspirin doled out to a nervous reader —Ben Bradford⟩ **6 a :** custom of ancient or long continued character usu. having an authoritative status ⟨morals . . . were by ~ singularly unconstrained —E.J.Simmons⟩ ⟨they had no religious reverence for ~ —T.B.Macaulay⟩ **b :** claim founded upon ancient custom or long continued use **7** *obs* **:** the action of laying down boundaries, limits, or restrictions **:** CIRCUMSCRIPTION, LIMITATION **8 :** something prescribed; *specif* **:** PRESCRIPT 1 ⟨peremptory ~*s* as to the only correct use of language —E.W.Hall⟩ ⟨one year of English is a practically universal ~ —H.N.Fairchild⟩ **9 :** a plea or clause placed at the beginning of the formula in an action under Roman law and limiting the scope of the claim or the remedy (as to a certain time)

prescription drug *n* **:** a drug that can be bought only as prescribed by a physician — compare OVER-THE-COUNTER 2

pre·scrip·tion·ist \-shənəst\ *n* -s **:** a writer or compounder of prescriptions

pre·scrip·tive \prē'skriptiv, prə'-, -tēv *also* -təv\ *adj* [in sense 1, prob. fr. *²prescript* + *-ive*; in other senses, fr. *prescription*, after such pairs as E *description*: *descriptive*] **1 :** serving to prescribe **:** laying down rules or directions **:** giving precise instructions ⟨direct primary legislation is largely permissive rather than ~ —V.O.Key⟩ ⟨traditional grammarians gave ~ rules of usage —A.S.Hornby⟩ **2 :** acquired by, founded upon, or determined by prescription **:** established in or as if in law by immemorial use and enjoyment ⟨the ~ rights and privileges of the nobles —*Indian White Paper*⟩ ⟨our constitution is a ~ constitution —Edmund Burke⟩ ⟨members of the upper chamber by ~ right⟩ **3 :** arising from or recognized by long-standing custom **:** established by tradition or usage **:** CUSTOMARY ⟨his ~ corner at the winter's fireside —Nathaniel Hawthorne⟩ ⟨compliments to which there is no stated and ~ answer —Samuel Johnson⟩ — **pre·scrip·tive·ly** \-təvlē\ *adv*

pre·scrip·tiv·ist \-təvəst\ *n* -s [*prescriptive* + *-ist*] **:** one who advocates prescriptive principles esp. in grammar ⟨learned to distrust . . . ~*s* —E.P.Hamp⟩

prescrive *vb* -ED/-ING/-S [ME (Sc) *prescriven* to become by prescription invalid or unenforceable, fr. MF *prescrire* to direct, prescribe, invalidate, annul (3d pers. pl. pres. indic. *prescrivent*), fr. ML *prescribere* to claim by right of prescription & L *praescribere* to write at the beginning, order, direct, prescribe — more at PRESCRIBE] *obs Scot* **:** PRESCRIBE

pre·scu·tal \(ˈ)prē¦skyüd·ᵊl\ *adj* [*prescutum* + *-al*] **:** of or relating to the prescutum

prescutal ridge *n* **:** an inner ridge corresponding to the outer prescutal suture on the thorax of an insect

prescutal suture *n* **:** a transverse groove on the mesonotum and metanotum of most insects separating the prescutum and scutum and forming the prescutal ridge on the inner surface

pre·scutellar \¦prē+\ *adj* [*pre-* + *scutellar*] **:** of, relating to, or situated on the area in front of the scutellum of insects

pre·scutum \(ˈ)prē+\ *n, pl* **prescuta** [NL, fr. *pre-* + *scutum*] **:** the anterior piece of the dorsal part or tergum of a thoracic segment of an insect

presdl *abbr* presidential

prese *pl of* PRESA

¹**pre·season** *or* **pre·seasonal** \(ˈ)prē+\ *adj* [*preseason* fr. *pre-* + *season*, n.; *preseasonal* fr. *pre-* + *seasonal*] **:** of, relating to, or during the time preceding a season ⟨~ football practice⟩ ⟨*preseasonal* treatment of hayfever⟩

²**pre·season** \ˈprē+,-\ *n* [*pre-* + *season*, n.] **:** a period of time immediately preceding a season ⟨the quietness of a summer resort during the ~⟩

pre·select \¦prē+\ *vt* [*pre-* + *select*] **:** to select beforehand ⟨a ~*ed* slate of candidates⟩ ⟨sets off . . . a flashing light when a ~*ed* speed is exceeded —*Motor Life*⟩

pre·selection \"+\ *n* [*preselect* + *-ion*] **:** selection in advance ⟨~ of the variables to be correlated —R.B.Cattell⟩

pre·se·lec·tor \ˌprēsə̇ˈlektə(r)\ *n* [*preselect* + *-or*] **:** the part of a radio receiver and esp. a superheterodyne receiver in which the incoming signal receives its first filtering

pre·sell \(ˈ)prē+\ *vt* [*pre-* + *sell*] **:** to precondition (as merchandise or customers) by advertising and devices of salesmanship for a subsequent purchase

pres·ence \ˈprezᵊn(t)s\ *n* -s [ME, fr. MF, fr. L *praesentia*, fr. *praesent-, praesens* present + *-ia* -y — more at PRESENT] **1 a :** the fact or condition of being present **:** the state of being in one place and not elsewhere **:** the condition of being within sight or call, at hand, or in a place being thought of **:** the fact of being in company, attendance, or association **:** the state of being in front of or in the same place as someone or something ⟨the ~ of free nitrogen bubbles in the body tissues —H.G.Armstrong⟩ ⟨hidden in the jungle, their ~ undiscovered —Joseph Millard⟩ ⟨the indwelling ~ of the Divine Spirit in the human soul —W.R.Inge⟩ ⟨the effective ~ of Britain on the European political scene —Percy Winner⟩ **b :** the manner in which Christ is held in some branches of the Christian church to be present in the Eucharist — compare REAL PRESENCE **2 a :** the part of space within one's ken, call, or influence **:** the vicinity of or the area immediately near one **:** the place in front of or around a person ⟨he came into the ~ of the king⟩ ⟨in her ~ he could scarcely speak⟩ ⟨removed his hat in the ~ of ladies⟩ **b :** the vicinity of one of superior or exalted rank ⟨survey the secretary's humor before entering the ~ —R.H.Ferrell⟩; *specif* **:** the area proximate to a royal personage **c** *obs* **:** PRESENCE CHAMBER ⟨two great cardinals wait in the ~ —Shak.⟩ **3** *archaic* **:** a number of persons assembled **:** ASSEMBLY, COMPANY ⟨here is like to be a good ~ of worthies —Shak.⟩ ⟨the ~ was so numerous that little could be caught of what they said —Thomas Jefferson⟩ **4 :** the consecrated elements of the Eucharist held in some branches of the Christian church to be identical with the body and blood of Christ **5 :** one that is present: as **a :** the actual person or thing having the specified status of being present — used with possessive ⟨your royal ~*s* be rul'd by me —Shak.⟩ ⟨a fiery column charioting his Godlike ~ —John Milton⟩ **b :** a person present in the flesh; *specif* **:** one having a dignified, noble, or impressive appearance **c :** something present of a visible or concrete nature ⟨the impersonal radar reports simply a ~ —*Lamp*⟩ **d :** one having existence or influence in the present ⟨these rocks are not dead masses but ~*s* imbued with an . . . ancient life that still continues —*Times Lit. Supp.*⟩ **e :** one that is present (as in a particular area or medium) and that usu. exerts influence or holds an important position thereby ⟨not . . . as an actor on the stage but rather as a ~ behind the scenes —*Times Lit. Supp.*⟩ ⟨introduced himself in the later books as a kind of ~ —John Arthos⟩ **6 a :** the bearing, carriage, mien, or air of a person **:** personal appearance ⟨a man of heavy, uninspiring ~ but considerable eloquence —Cicely V. Wedgwood⟩; *esp* **:** fine, stately, or distinguished bearing ⟨her carriage is superb and she has ~ —John Martin⟩ ⟨a small birdlike person, of no ~ —Rose Macaulay⟩ **b :** a quality of poise and effectiveness and ease of performance that enables a performer to achieve a close and sympathetic relationship with his audience ⟨the American singer must acquire . . . the sense of ~ on a stage —Rudolf Bing⟩ ⟨that sense of a measured and boundless ~ that fine acting must afford —*New Republic*⟩ **7 :** something (as a spirit, being, or influence) felt or believed to be present ⟨an intangible, mysterious ~ seemed to be creeping closer . . . upon them —O.E.Rölvaag⟩; *esp* **:** one having a divine or spiritual nature ⟨before creation a ~ existed —Witter Bynner⟩ ⟨she could have imagined a seraphic ~ in the room —George Meredith⟩ **8 :** a quality in sound reproduction that gives a listener the illusion of being in the same room as the original source of sound rather than in the room with the sound-reproducing system ⟨music with concert-hall ~ recorded on professional equipment —*advt*⟩ **9 :** the degree of occurrence of a specific unit (as a biological species or chemical element) ⟨carbon showed a ~ of 40 percent in the samples tested⟩

presence chamber *n* **:** the room where a great personage (as a monarch) receives company or those entitled to come into his presence

presence of mind [trans. of L *praesentia animi*] **:** self-control so maintained in an emergency, in danger, or in an embarrassing situation that one can say or do the right thing **:** unshaken calmness and readiness of thought

pre·senile \(ˈ)prē+\ *adj* [ISV *pre-* + *senile*] **1 :** of, relating to, or constituting the period immediately preceding the development of senility in an organism or person ⟨the ~ period of life⟩ ⟨the ~ decline of vital powers⟩ **2 :** prematurely displaying symptoms of senile psychosis

pre·se·nil·i·ty \ˌprēsə̇ˈniləd·ē\ *n* [*presenile* + *-ity*] **1 :** premature senility **2 :** the period of life immediately preceding senility

pre·sensation \¦prē+\ *n* [*pre-* + *sensation*] **:** a perception or feeling of something before it appears, develops, or exists **:** ANTICIPATION, FOREBODING, PRESENTIMENT

pre·sen·sion \prēˈsenchən\ *n* -s [L *praesension-, praesensio*, fr. *praesensus* (past part. of *praesentire* to perceive beforehand) + *-ion-, -io* -ion — more at PRESENTIENT] *archaic* **:** PRESENSATION ⟨appeared to have a very decided ~ of his untimely death —E.A.Seymour⟩

¹**pres·ent** \ˈprezᵊnt\ *n* -s [ME, fr. OF, fr. *presenter* to present] **1 :** something presented or given **:** DONATION, GIFT ⟨Christmas ~*s*⟩ ⟨brought home ~*s* for the children⟩ **2 :** PRESENTATION 1 ⟨made her a ~ of a diamond necklace⟩

²**pre·sent** \prēˈzent, prə̇ˈ-\ *vb* -ED/-ING/-s [ME *presenten*, fr. OF *presenter*, fr. L *praesentare*, fr. *praesent-, praesens*, pres. part. of *praeesse*] *vt* **1 a :** to bring or introduce into the presence of someone (as a superior) **:** to introduce for acquaintance ⟨the ambassador was ~*ed* to the president⟩ ⟨the small boy ~*ed* himself before his father⟩ ⟨offered to ~ his friend to the attractive young lady⟩ **b :** to dedicate by bringing before or into the presence of God ⟨~*ed* Christ in the temple⟩ **c :** to introduce formally at court esp. to the sovereign **d :** to bring (a candidate) before university authorities for examination or for conferral of a degree **e :** to bring (as an entertainer) before the public **2 :** to make a present or donation to **:** furnish or provide (as a person) with something by way of a present or gift **3 a :** to lay or put before a person for acceptance **:** offer as a gift **:** give or bestow formally **b :** to offer or convey by way of message, greeting, or compliment **c :** to hand or pass over usu. in a ceremonious way **:** deliver formally for acceptance **4 a :** to lay (as a charge) before a court as an object of inquiry **:** give notice officially of (as a crime or offense) **:** find or represent judicially ⟨the grand jury ~*ed* many offenses⟩ **b** (1) **:** to bring a formal public charge against **:** charge formally **:** ACCUSE (2) **:** to bring an indictment or presentment against **5 :** to nominate (a clergyman) to a benefice **6** *archaic* **:** to represent (a character) on the stage **:** act the part of **:** PERFORM, PERSONATE **7** *obs* **:** to make an open offer of (as battle) **8 :** to aim, point, or direct so as to face something or in a particular direction **9 :** MANIFEST ⟨patients who ~ symptoms of malaria⟩ ~ *vi* **1 :** to make a presentation of a clergyman to the ordinary for institution to an ecclesiastical office **2 :** to present a weapon (as a rifle) **3** *obs* **:** to blow favorably — used of the wind **4 a :** to become directed toward the opening of the uterus — used esp. of parts of a fetus ⟨premature babies which ~ by breech —*Yr. Bk. of Obstetrics & Gynecology*⟩ **b :** to become manifest ⟨gonorrhea in heterosexual men typically ~*s* as an anterior urethritis with a spontaneous purulent urethral exudate and dysuria —A.W. Karchmer⟩ **5 :** to come forward as a patient **syn** see OFFER

³**present** \"\ *n* -s **1 :** the position of a firearm ready to be fired or of a lance or similar weapon ready to be used in attack ⟨bring the rifle down to the ~⟩ **2 :** the position of present arms ⟨soldiers standing at ~⟩

⁴**pres·ent** \ˈprezᵊnt\ *adj* [ME, fr. OF, fr. L *praesent-, praesens*, pres. part. of *praeesse* to be before one, be at hand, fr. *prae-* pre- + *esse* to be — more at IS] **1 :** now existing or in progress **:** begun but not ended **:** now being in view, being dealt with, or being under consideration **:** being at this time **:** not past or future **:** CONTEMPORARY ⟨to understand the ~ institutions we must . . . comprehend something of their history —J.B. Conant⟩ ⟨12 pioneer papers have survived to the ~ day —*Amer. Guide Series: Minn.*⟩ ⟨in 1909 the . . . house again burned and the ~ hostelry of the same name was built —*Amer. Guide Series: N.H.*⟩ **2 a :** being in one place and not elsewhere **:** being within reach, sight, or call or within contemplated limits **:** being in view or at hand **:** being before, beside, with, or in the same place as someone or something ⟨both men were ~ at the meeting⟩ ⟨~ company excepted⟩ — used interjectionally to indicate one's presence esp. in answer to a roll call **b :** existing in something (as a class or case) mentioned or under consideration ⟨in the Hemiptera . . . wings may be ~ or absent —T.H.Huxley⟩ **3 :** constituting the one actually involved, at hand, or being considered ⟨the ~ writer⟩ ⟨the ~ volume⟩ **4 :** of, relating to, or constituting a verb tense that is expressive of present time or the time of speaking **5 :** existing at or belonging to the time under consideration **:** contemporaneous with a specified past time ⟨there existed in preconquest England a church . . . united to the see of Rome by ancient tradition and ~ reverence —F.M.Stenton⟩ **6** *obs* **a :** having one's mind or thoughts directed toward a matter at hand **:** intent upon something **:** ATTENTIVE **b :** having self-possession **:** COLLECTED **7** *archaic* **:** immediately accessible or available (as in providing assistance) **:** ready at hand ⟨this sum . . . was a large and ~ resource —James Mill⟩ **8** *archaic* **:** immediately operative or effective **:** IMMEDIATE, INSTANT ⟨the queen . . . demanded the ~ payment of some arrears —Thomas Fuller⟩ ⟨an ambassador . . . desires a ~ audience —Philip Massinger⟩

⁵**present** \"\ *n* -s [ME, fr. OF, fr. L *praesent-, praesens*, fr. *praesent-, praesens*, pres. part. of *praeesse*] **1 a** *obs* **:** present occasion or affair **:** business or action in hand **b presents** *pl* **:** the present words or statements **:** the present legal instrument (as a deed of conveyance, lease, or power of attorney) or other writing **:** the document in which these words are used ⟨know all men by these ~⟩ **2 a :** the present tense of a language **b :** a verb form in the present tense **3 :** the present time **:** the time being or contemplated ⟨another of those periods, much like the ~ —Ruth Moore⟩ ⟨from 1700 to the ~ —*Bull. of Bates Coll.*⟩ — compare FUTURE 1, PAST — **at present** *adv* **:** at the present time **:** just now ⟨the materials *at present* within my command —Mary W. Shelley⟩ ⟨*at present* he regrets what he has done —Jane Austen⟩ — **at this present** *adv, archaic* **:** at the present time ⟨nations which *at this present* are in high repute —Marchamont Needham⟩ — **for the present** *adv* **:** for the time being **:** TEMPORARILY ⟨leave it at that *for the present* —Virgil Thomson⟩ ⟨*for the present* men are expendable, tanks aren't —Fred Majdalany⟩ — **in present** *adv, obs* **:** at the present time ⟨man's joy and pleasure rather hereafter than *in present* is —George Herbert⟩

pre·sent·abil·i·ty \prēˌzentəˈbiləd·ē\ *n* **:** the quality or state of being presentable ⟨candidates screened for ~ on television⟩

pre·sent·able \prēˈzentəbəl, prə̇ˈ-\ *adj* [²*present* + *-able*] **1 :** appropriate for or liable to legal presentment ⟨~ offenses⟩ ⟨a ~ offender⟩ **2 :** capable or admitting of being presented (as to a person or the mind) **:** suitable to be offered, set forth, or brought forward **:** appropriate for presentation ⟨emotions ~ only in music⟩ **3** *archaic* **:** admitting of the presentation of a clergyman — used of an ecclesiastical benefice **4 :** having a bearing or appearance that will satisfy or give pleasure to others **:** in condition to be seen or inspected esp. by the critical **:** suitable (as in attire or behavior) for presentation into society or company **:** fit to be seen ⟨dinner . . . at a ~ restaurant —*N.Y. Times*⟩ ⟨an adequate number of ~ domestic servants —Roy Lewis & Angus Maude⟩ ⟨give me a minute to make myself ~ —Kenneth Roberts⟩

pre·sent·ably \-blē\ *adv* **:** in a presentable manner

present arms *n* [fr. the imper. phrase *present arms*] **:** a position in the manual of arms in which the rifle is held perpendicularly in front of the center of the body ⟨*present arms* is analogous to a salute⟩ — often used as a command

present arms

pre·sen·ta·tion \ˌprēˌzenˈtāshən, ˌprezᵊn-, ˌprēzᵊn-\ *n* -s *often attrib* [ME *presentacioun*, fr. MF *presentation*, fr. LL *praesentation-, praesentatio*, fr. L *praesentatus* (past part. of *praesentare* to present) + *-ion-, -io* -ion — more at PRESENT] **1 :** the act of presenting: as **a** (1) **:** the act, power, or privilege esp. of a patron of applying usu. by deed to the bishop or ordinary for the institution of one nominated to a benefice (2) **:** the appointment to a benefice through being so presented — compare COLLATION, NOMINATION **b :** the nomination by one ecclesiastical authority (as a vestry) of a candidate to be appointed by another (as a bishop) **c** *often cap* **:** the act of formally presenting a person before God as a ceremonial religious act ⟨the ~ of Christ in the temple⟩ **d :** the act of presenting usu. in a formal manner for acceptance **:** BESTOWAL, DELIVERY ⟨the ~ of an honors thesis —*Official Register of Harvard Univ.*⟩ ⟨~ of the colors⟩ **e :** the act of setting forth for the notice or attention of the mind **:** STATEMENT ⟨the ~ of information . . . by the executive to Congress —Vera M. Dean⟩ ⟨the military officer must learn to make staff ~*s* —Dallas Albritton⟩ ⟨limited most novelists to the ~ . . . of the life they know best —F.B.Millett⟩ **f :** the act of presenting to sight or view **:** pictorial, theatrical, or symbolic representation **:** DISPLAY, EXHIBITION, SHOW ⟨news happenings which . . . lend themselves to visual ~ —*Current Biog.*⟩ ⟨~ of a ballet⟩ **g :** the act of formally presenting a candidate (as for examination or for conferral of a degree) **h :** the formal or ceremonious introduction of a person (as to an assembly or at a royal court) ⟨~ of a nationally recognized speaker to the . . . student body —*Bull. of Meharry Med. Coll.*⟩ ⟨induce . . . one of the great ladies of the court to act as sponsor at her ~ —R.D.Benn⟩ **2 :** someone or something presented: as **a :** a symbol or image that represents something ⟨~ on a radar screen⟩ **b :** something offered or given **:** DONATION, GIFT, PRESENT ⟨make this scholarship an annual ~ —*Springfield (Mass.) Union*⟩ **c :** one set forth, represented, or delineated for the attention of the mind ⟨the author of a more formal ~ —Arthur Knight⟩ **3 :** the position in which the fetus lies in the uterus in labor with respect to the mouth of the uterus ⟨face ~⟩ ⟨breech ~⟩ **4 :** a datum of perception or sense appearance; *specif* **:** the element in the cognition of an object which is given by direct awareness as distinguished from that which is added by association or thinking ⟨a visual ~ of a baseball . . . is spatially bidimensional —Nelson Goodman⟩ **5 :** appearance in conscious experience either as a sensory product or as a memory image **6** *usu cap* **a :** CANDLEMAS 1 **b :** a church feast celebrating the presentation of the Virgin Mary in the temple observed in both Eastern Orthodox and Roman Catholic churches on November 21 **7 :** the method by which radio, navigation, or radar information is given to the operator (as the pilot of an airplane)

pre·sen·ta·tion·al \¦=(ˌ)=¦tāshənᵊl, -shnəl\ *adj* **1 :** of or relating to a presentation, presentations, or presentationism in philosophy or psychology **2 :** of, characterized by, or belonging to a style of theatrical production designed to present a story in theatrical forms ⟨the ~ theater⟩ ⟨~ method⟩ **3 :** NOTIONAL 4 b (1)

presentation copy *n* **:** a copy of a book or a similar publication inscribed by the author and used as a presentation

pre·sen·ta·tion·ism \ˌ=(ˌ)=ˈtāshəˌnizəm\ *n* -s **:** MONISM 1 b — compare REPRESENTATIONISM

presentation piece *n* **:** a coin or medal struck for use as a gift or prize

presentation time *n* **:** the minimum time of application of a given stimulus required to effect a response — compare ACTION TIME, REACTION TIME

pre·sen·ta·tive \prēˈzentəd·|iv, prə̇ˈ-, -ət| *also* |əv\ *adj* [²*present* + *-ative*] **1 :** subject to ecclesiastical presentation **:** carrying with it the right of presentation ⟨a ~ benefice⟩ **2 :** of the nature of a philosophical or psychological presentation **a :** known or capable of being known directly rather than through cogitation ⟨the ~ elements in a cognition⟩ **b :** having the power or function of apprehending directly **:** INTUITIVE, PERCEPTIVE ⟨a ~ faculty⟩ **c :** of, relating to, derived from, or concerned with one or more presentations ⟨~ theories⟩ **3 :** NONREPRESENTATIONAL

present-day \¦=¦=\ *adj* [fr. the phrase *present day*] **:** now existing or occurring **:** CURRENT ⟨*present-day* local government is mainly concerned with . . . public services —W.E.Jackson⟩ ⟨their survival among millions of *present-day* peoples —J.H. Steward⟩ ⟨the *present-day* remains of . . . irrigation canals —R.W.Murray⟩

presented *past of* PRESENT

pres·en·tee \ˌprezᵊn¦tē\ *n* -s [ME, fr. MF *presenté*, fr. *presenté*, past part. of *presenter* to present] **1 :** one that is presented; *esp* **:** a clergyman presented to a benefice ⟨rob the ~*s* of . . . their tithes —G.G.Coulton⟩ **2 :** one to whom something is presented ⟨believing ~*s* in return supplied him with small sums of money —Thomas Campbell⟩

pre·sentence \(ˈ)prē+\ *adj* [*pre-* + *sentence*, n.] **:** of, based upon, or constituting an investigation into the character and background of a convicted offender as a means of collecting information useful to the sentencing judge ⟨the ~ reports of probation officers may help determine a fair and proper sentence⟩

pre·sent·er *also* **pre·sen·tor** \prēˈzentə(r), prə̇ˈ-\ *n* -s [*presenter* fr. ²*present* + *-er*; *presentor* fr. earlier *presentour*, fr. MF, fr. *presenter* to present + *-our*, *-eur* -or — more at PRESENT] **:** one that presents ⟨the best ~ for all sales ideas —D.H. McCollum⟩ ⟨the ~ merely introduced the characters —Muriel C. Bradbrook⟩ ⟨the ~ of a bank draft⟩

pre·sen·tial \prēˈzenchəl\ *adj* [LL *praesentialis*, fr. L *praesentia* presence + *-alis* -al — more at PRESENCE] **1 :** of, relating to, or constituting the present **:** IMMEDIATE **2 :** of, relating to, or formed from the present stem of a verb

pre·sen·ti·al·i·ty \prēˌzencheˈaləd·ē\ *n* -ES [ML *praesentialitat-, praesentialitas*, fr. LL *praesentialis* + L *-tat-, -tas* -ty] *archaic* **:** the quality or state of being present (as in time or place)

presentially *adv, obs* **:** in a presential manner ⟨exhibits the sacrifice . . . actually and ~ in heaven —Jeremy Taylor⟩

presentiate *vt* -ED/-ING/-s [L *praesentia* presence + E *-ate* (v. suffix)] *obs* **:** to make present (as in time or space) ⟨that place where thou art pleased to ~ thyself —Henry Hammond⟩

pre·sen·tient \prēˈsenchənt\ *adj* [L *praesentient-, praesentiens*, pres. part. of *praesentire* to perceive beforehand, fr. *prae-* pre- + *sentire* to feel — more at SENSE] **:** apprehensive in advance **:** having a presentiment **:** feeling or perceiving beforehand — usu. used with *of* ⟨ravenous fowls . . . ~ of their food —Robert Southey⟩

pre·sen·ti·ment \prēˈzentəmənt, prə̇ˈ-\ *n* -s [obs. F *presentiment* (now *pressentiment*), fr. MF *presentiment, pressentiment*, fr. *presentir* to have a presentiment of (fr. L *praesentire* to perceive beforehand) + *-ment*] **1 a :** an impression, conviction, or feeling that something will or is about to happen **:** a vague expectation of a future event that seems to be a direct perception although it has no basis in fact ⟨I've a strong ~ it'll prove a success —J.C.Powys⟩ ⟨the almost total lack of ~ of the new forces about to be released —S.T.Possony⟩ **b :** an antecedent impression or conviction of something unpleasant, distressing, or calamitous about to happen **:** an anticipatory fear **:** FOREBODING, PREMONITION ⟨a thousand ~*s* of evil to her beloved —Jane Austen⟩ **2 :** an opinion or conception formed prior to actual knowledge of something **:** PREJUDGMENT ⟨reason has a ~ of objects which possess a great interest for it —Friedrich Max Müller⟩ **syn** see APPREHENSION

presenting *pres part of* PRESENT

pres·en·tist \ˈprezᵊntə̇st\ *n* -s [⁴*present* + *-ist*] **:** one who holds that biblical prophecy esp. of the Apocalypse is now in course of fulfillment — compare PRETERIST, FUTURIST

pres·ent·ly *adv* [ME, fr. ⁴*present* + *-ly*] **1 a** *archaic* **:** without delay or hesitation **:** FORTHWITH, IMMEDIATELY ⟨and ~ the fig-tree withered away —Mt 21:19 (AV)⟩ **b :** after a little while **:** before long **:** after a short time **:** BY AND BY 2, SHORTLY, SOON ⟨a long-suffering type but ~ even he becomes fed up —John McCarten⟩ ⟨leaving the older section, we ~ reached the newest development —Joseph Wechsberg⟩ ⟨I'll be there ~⟩ **2 a :** at the present time **:** at present **:** at this time **:** NOW ⟨fix it with the tools ~ at hand —T.W.Arnold⟩ ⟨the dangerous situation in which this nation ~ finds itself —Adrienne Koch⟩ ⟨expenses . . . in these categories ~ cannot be deducted —*U. S. Code*⟩ **b :** at the time indicated or referred to **:** at that time ⟨towns where, ~, the courthouses . . . were of brick —*Amer. Guide Series: Tenn.*⟩ **3** *obs* **:** IMMEDIATELY 1 ⟨~ without the chapel is the burse —Peter Heylin⟩ **4 :** by way of immediate consequence or necessity **:** as a direct result **:** by direct inference **:** CONSEQUENTLY, DIRECTLY, NECESSARILY ⟨we do not infer, nor doth it ~ follow, that the present reading is corrupt —Brian Walton⟩

pre·sent·ment \prēˈzentmənt, prə̇ˈ-\ *n* -s [ME *presentement*, fr. MF, fr. OF, fr. *presenter* to present + *-ment* — more at PRESENT] **1** *archaic* **:** the act of presenting a clergyman to a benefice **2 :** the act of presenting to an authority a formal statement of a matter to be dealt with: **a :** the notice taken or statement made by a grand jury of any offense or unlawful state of affairs from their own knowledge or observation without any bill of indictment laid before them ⟨grand jury has just returned a ~ on the subject of lawlessness —*Commonweal*⟩ ⟨special grand jury . . . returned a ~ —*N. Y. Herald Tribune*⟩ **b :** a similar statement formerly made by a magistrate or constable **c :** a formal complaint made by the authorities of a parish to the bishop or archdeacon at his visitation **3 a :** representation in art of an object (as by a picture, image, or graphic description) **:** DELINEATION ⟨the actuality of ~ for which he is noted⟩ **b :** something that makes this representation (as a portrait or likeness) ⟨a curious ~ of the Trinity occurs several times in church windows —O. Elfrida Saunders⟩ **4 :** a theatrical or dramatic representation (as the performance of a play) **5 :** PRESENTATION 1d ⟨settle matters about the ~ of the petition —Edmund Burke⟩; *specif* **:** the act of producing and offering at the proper time and place a document (as a matured note, bill of exchange, or check) requiring to be accepted or paid by another **6 a :** the act of presenting to view, perception, notice, or consciousness **:** DESCRIPTION, STATEMENT, SUGGESTION **b :** something that is set forth, presented, or exhibited **7 :** the appearance, aspect, form, or mode in which something is presented **8 a :** the appearing of something before the mind **:** PRESENTATION 5 **b :** the content of a perception or a thought as it stands before the mind

presentment of englishry *usu cap E* **:** the presentation of proof that a slain person was of English rather than Norman birth as an excuse for not paying a fine levied by the Norman kings of England upon local governmental units for the murder of a Norman

present money *n* [⁴*present*] *obs* **:** READY MONEY ⟨the temptation of a pistole *present money* never faileth —George Berkeley⟩

pres·ent·ness *n* -ES **:** the quality or state of being present ⟨a study of the pastness of the present and . . . of the ~ of the past —R.E.Spiller⟩

presentor *var of* PRESENTER
present participle *n* **:** a participle that typically expresses present action in relation to the time expressed by the finite verb in its clause and that in English is traditionally one of the principal parts of the verb, is formed with the suffix *-ing*, and is used in the formation of the progressive tenses
¹present perfect *adj* [⁴*present* + *perfect*, adj.] **:** of, relating to, or constituting a verb tense that is traditionally formed in English with *have* and that expresses action or state completed at the time of speaking
²present perfect *n* **1 :** the present perfect tense of a language **2 :** a verb form in the present perfect tense
presents *pl of* PRESENT, *pres 3d sing of* PRESENT
present tense *n* [ME *present tens*] **:** the tense of a verb that expresses action or state in the present time and is used of what occurs or is true at the time of speaking (as in "I am in a hurry" or "he is singing") and of what is habitual or characteristic (as in "he pays his debts" or "he dresses well") or is always or necessarily true (as in "the sun shines by day" or "a straight line is the shortest distance"), that is sometimes used to refer to action in the past (as in the historical present), and that is sometimes used for future events (as in "Christmas falls on Friday next year")
present value *also* **present worth** *n* **:** the principal of a sum of money payable at a future date that drawing interest at a given rate will amount to the given sum at the date on which this sum is to be paid ⟨at 6% interest the *present value* of $106 due one year hence is $100⟩ — compare ARITHMETICAL DISCOUNT
pre·serv·able \prē'zərvəbəl, prə'-\ *adj* **:** capable of being preserved
pre·serv·al \-vəl\ *n* -s **:** PRESERVATION ⟨~ and removal of . . . mineral beds —A.M.Bateman⟩
pres·er·va·tion \,prezə(r)'vāshən\ *n* -s [ME, fr. MF, fr. ML *praeservation-*, *praeservatio*, fr. *praeservatus* (past part. of *praeservare* to preserve) + L *-ion-*, *-io* -ion] **:** the act of preserving or the state of being preserved ⟨fostered the ~ of local speechways —Hans Kurath⟩ ⟨essential to the ~ of my regard —Jane Austen⟩ ⟨in a good state of ~ —*Amer. Guide Series: Texas*⟩
pres·er·va·tion·ist \-sh(ə)nəst\ *n* -s **:** one that advocates the preservation of a species (as of wildlife) from extinction
¹pre·serv·a·tive \prē'zərvəd·|iv, prə'-, -zōv-, -zəiv-, -vət| *also* |əv\ *adj* [ME, fr. ML *praeservativus*, fr. *praeservatus* (past part. of *praeservare* to preserve) + L *-ivus* -ive] **:** having the power of preserving **:** tending to preserve ⟨bound together for ~ purposes —*Springfield (Mass.) Union*⟩ ⟨need for ~ action —A.N.Whitehead⟩
²preservative \"\ *n* -s [ME, fr. *preservative*, adj.] **:** something that preserves or has the power of preserving: as **a** *archaic* **:** a medicine designed to preserve one's health by preventing or providing a protection from disease **:** a safeguard against poison or infection ⟨hope his restoratives and his ~*s* will . . . be effectual —Samuel Johnson⟩ **b :** a preservative quality, principle, or factor ⟨accounts federalism the ~ of the American system —G.W.Johnson⟩ ⟨their pleasantest ~ from want —Jane Austen⟩ ⟨public life seems to be a good ~ . . . for congressmen —Elmer Davis⟩ **c :** a substance added to chemicals, natural products, fabrics, or food products to preserve them against decay, discoloration, or spoilage under conditions of storage or nonchemical use ⟨salt, sugar, and spice are common food ~*s*⟩ **d :** a substance impregnated into or covering wood to prevent attack by insects and other organisms **e :** a chemical (as sodium sulfite) for retarding oxidation of photographic solutions
preservative medium *n* **:** MEDIUM 8b
pre·serv·a·tize \-və,tīz\ *vt* -ED/-ING/-S [²*preservative* + *-ize*] **:** to treat (as food) with a preservative ⟨*preservatized* butter⟩
preservatory *n* -ES [ML *praeservatus* (past part. of *praeservare* to preserve) + E *-ory*] *obs* **:** a charitable house of refuge for unemployed, deserted, or destitute women and girls
¹pre·serve \prē'zərv, prə'-, -zōv, -zəiv\ *vb* -ED/-ING/-S [ME *preserven*, fr. MF *preserver*, fr. ML *praeservare*, fr. LL, to observe, fr. L *prae-* pre- + *servare* to keep, guard — more at CONSERVE] *vt* **1 :** to keep safe from injury, harm, or destruction **:** guard or defend from evil **:** PROTECT, SAVE ⟨thornbushes . . . are *preserved* by superstition —O.S.J.Gogarty⟩ ⟨their knowledge of the Marxist conspiracy should be put to use to ~ the republic —Howard Rushmore⟩ **2 a :** to keep alive, intact, in existence, or from decay ⟨~ an old house⟩ ⟨the right of trial by jury shall be *preserved* —*U. S. Constitution*⟩ ⟨among the deeds *preserved* in the courthouse —*Amer. Guide Series: Pa.*⟩ **b :** to retain in one's possession ⟨~ my shaky dignity —Reginald Kell⟩ ⟨*preserved* their detachment —Dexter Perkins⟩ **c :** MAINTAIN ⟨~ a correspondence⟩ **3 a :** to keep or save from decomposition (as by refrigeration, curing, or treating with a preservative) ⟨~ specimens or skins to be stuffed⟩ ⟨~ milk indefinitely⟩ **b :** to can, pickle, or similarly prepare (as fruits or vegetables) for future use ⟨~ peaches⟩ **4 :** to keep up and reserve for personal or special use ⟨~ game or fish by raising and protecting it⟩ ⟨~ a stream or field⟩ ~ *vi* **1 :** to remain fresh or in its original state **:** KEEP **2 :** to make preserves **3 :** to raise and protect game for purposes of sport **4 :** to endure or stand the process of preservation (as by canning or pickling) ⟨duck eggs do not ~ satisfactorily —F.D. Smith & Barbara Wilcox⟩
²preserve \"\ *n* -s **1 :** something that preserves or is designed to preserve; *specif* **:** GOGGLE 2 **2 a :** fruit canned or made into jams or jellies ⟨black-currant ~⟩ — often used in pl. **b :** fruit cooked whole or in large pieces with sugar so as to keep its shape ⟨quince ~⟩ — often used in pl. ⟨strawberry ~*s*⟩ **3 :** an area (as a tract of land or body of water) restricted for the protection and preservation of animals, trees, or other natural resources ⟨our Adirondack mountains with their enormous forest ~ —Averell Harriman⟩ ⟨a wildlife ~⟩; *esp* **:** one used primarily for regulated hunting or fishing **:** RESERVE ⟨a state game ~⟩ — compare SANCTUARY 4 **4 :** something (as a place, occupation, or sphere of activity) that is sacred to or reserved exclusively for certain persons ⟨regarded the diplomatic service as a ~ for their younger sons —G.B.Shaw⟩ ⟨translation . . . has been the ~ of scholarly jargonists —Dudley Fitts⟩ ⟨recognizing . . . the Baltic states as a Soviet ~ —*Times Lit. Supp.*⟩
pre·serv·er \-və(r)\ *n* -s **:** one that preserves (as from destruction, injury, or decay) ⟨God the creator and ~ of all mankind —*Bk. of Com. Prayer*⟩ ⟨game ~⟩ ⟨steel ~⟩
pre·serv·er·ess \-vərəs\ *n* -ES *archaic* **:** a female preserver
pre·service \(')prē+\ *adj* [*pre-* + *service*, n.] **:** of, relating to, or taking place during a period of time preceding active service (as in a profession or the armed forces) ⟨protect the veteran's right to reemployment in his ~ job —H.S.Truman⟩ — compare IN-SERVICE
preserving melon *n* **:** CITRON
pre·ses \'prē,sēz\ *n*, *pl* **preses** [L *praesid-*, *praeses* guard, president, ruler, fr. *praesidēre* to guard, preside over] *chiefly Scot* **:** the president or presiding officer (as of a meeting or group) **:** CHAIRMAN
pre·session \(')prē+\ *adj* [*pre-* + *session*] **:** occurring before a session (as of a legislative body) ⟨a ~ caucus⟩
pre·set \"+\ *vt* [*pre-* + *set*] **:** to set beforehand ⟨a new control device that is ~ to shift the dial and change the volume at the desired time —*Time*⟩
pre·sexual \"+\ *adj* [*pre-* + *sexual*] **:** preceding sexual development or maturity
pre·shrink \"+\ *vt* [*pre-* + *shrink*] **:** to subject (as yarn or fabric) to shrinking during manufacture
pre·shrunk \"+\ *adj* [*pre-* + *shrunk*] **:** of, relating to, or constituting a fabric subjected to a shrinking process during manufacture to reduce later shrinking (as from laundering)
pre·side \prē'zīd, prə'-\ *vb* -ED/-ING/-S [L *praesidēre* to guard, preside over, fr. *prae-* pre- + *sedēre* to sit — more at SIT] *vi* **1 a :** to occupy the place of authority (as in an assembly) **:** act as president, chairman, or moderator (as of a group or meeting) **:** direct, control, or regulate proceedings as chief officer ⟨the mayor ~*s* in council meetings —F.A.Ogg & P.O. Ray⟩ ⟨the chief justice ~*s* over the supreme court⟩ ⟨~ at a public meeting⟩ **b :** to occupy a similar position or perform similar duties ⟨~ over a funeral service⟩ ⟨~ over a literary salon⟩ ⟨~ at tea⟩ **2 :** to exercise superintendence, guidance, direction, or control ⟨called to ~ over her son's bereft family —R.K.Leavitt⟩ ⟨*presided* over one of the . . . forges in the blacksmith shop —Ben Riker⟩ ⟨~ over a radio program⟩ **3 :** to occupy the most conspicuous position **:** sit or reign supreme ⟨gently rugged country *presided* over by . . . mountains —R.W.Hatch⟩ ⟨an 18th century tallboy in . . . the hall where it ~*s* in silent majesty —H.J.Laski⟩ **4 :** to occupy the position of chief or featured instrumental performer orig. as director of a group of musicians — used with *at* ⟨~ at the organ⟩ ~ *vt* **:** to exercise control or superintendence over **:** DIRECT, RULE ⟨those that were to ~ the naval affairs —Thomas Manley⟩
pres·i·dence \'prez(ə)dən(t)s\ *n* -s [MF, office of president, fr. ML *praesidentia*] **1 :** the action or fact of presiding **:** DIRECTION, SUPERINTENDENCE ⟨by the ~ and guidance of an unseen governing power —William Wollaston⟩ **2 :** PRESIDENCY 1a ⟨preserve both the senate and the ~ —P.G.Hamerton⟩
pres·i·den·cy \'prez(ə)dənsē, -si *also* -zəd³ns- *or* -zə,den(t)s-\ *n* -ES [ML *praesidentia*, fr. L *praesident-*, *praesidens* president, ruler + *-ia* -y] **1 a :** the office of president ⟨elected to the ~ of . . . the hotel corporation —*Current Biog.*⟩ ⟨assumed the ~ of the university⟩ **b** *sometimes cap* (1) **:** the office of president of the U. S. ⟨the ~ . . . is preeminently a place of moral leadership —F.D.Roosevelt⟩ ⟨an avowed candidate for the ~ —*Nation*⟩ (2) **:** the American governmental institution comprising the office of president and the various administrative and policy-making agencies directly associated with the president of the U. S. ⟨the ~ . . . was proliferating into countless people, councils, and commissions —Douglass Cater⟩ **2 :** the term during which a president holds office ⟨the third year of his ~⟩ **3 :** the action or function of one that presides **:** SUPERINTENDENCE ⟨such a body . . . met by his advice and under his ~ —F.M.Stenton⟩ ⟨the ~ and guidance of some superior agent —John Ray⟩ **4 :** one of three great divisions (Madras, Bombay, and Bengal) of British India orig. forming a district under a president of the East India Company and later a province under the administration of a governor **5 :** a council of three in the Mormon Church consisting of a president and two counselors and having jurisdiction in spiritual or temporal matters throughout the church or a stake or within a smaller unit (as a quorum) — compare FIRST PRESIDENCY **6 :** one of the four or five former divisions of the British colony of the Leeward Islands ⟨by the Leeward Islands Act, 1956 . . . each of the 4 *presidencies* became a colony —*Statesman's Yr. Bk.*⟩
¹pres·i·dent \-nt\ *n* -s [ME, fr. MF, fr. L *praesident-*, *praesidens* president, ruler, fr. *praesident-*, *praesidens*, pres. part. of *praesidēre* to guard, preside over] **1 :** an official chosen to preside over a meeting or assembly ⟨~ of a ball⟩ ⟨~ of a bullfight⟩ ⟨~ of the teachers' conference⟩ **2 :** an appointed governor of a subordinate political unit (as a province, colony, or city) **3 :** the chief officer of a corporation, company, institution, society, or similar organization usu. entrusted with the direction and administration of its policies ⟨colleges and universities are usu. headed by a ~ —Kenneth Holland⟩ ⟨chosen ~ of the Turkish Historical Society —*Current Biog.*⟩ ⟨~ of the nation's largest steel company⟩ **4 a :** the presiding officer of a governmental body (as an advisory council, administrative board, or legislative assembly) ⟨the constitution . . . makes the vice-president of the U. S. ~ of the senate —F.A.Ogg & P.O.Ray⟩ ⟨~ of the U. N. general assembly⟩ — compare LORD PRESIDENT OF THE COUNCIL **b :** the presiding judge or justice of a court of law ⟨~ of the Court of Session in Scotland⟩ ⟨~ of the Probate, Divorce and Admiralty Division of the Supreme Court of Judicature⟩ ⟨joint ~*s* of the shire court —F.M.Stenton⟩ **c :** the elected governor usu. serving as head of an executive council in several of the original 13 states of the U. S. during their existence as British colonies and also during the late 18th century after the Revolution ⟨~ of Pennsylvania⟩ ⟨in 1608 . . . made ~ of Virginia —*Brit. Book News*⟩ **5** *obs* **:** a presiding deity, patron, or genius **:** GUARDIAN ⟨great ~ of fire —George Chapman⟩ **6 a :** an elected official serving as both chief of state and chief political executive in a republic having a presidential government ⟨the executive power shall be vested in a ~ of the United States —*U. S. Constitution*⟩ **b :** an elected official having the position of chief of state but usu. only minimal political powers in a republic having a parliamentary government ⟨Israel's ~ . . . is not head of the executive and his actual powers are very limited —Misha Louvish⟩ ⟨the ~ of France under the Third Republic resembled a constitutional monarch⟩ **7 :** a church leader of the Mormon Church who with two counselors forms the first presidency or the presidency of a stake or smaller unit **8** *Brit* **:** the captain of a racing crew
²president \"\ *adj* [ME, fr. L *praesident-*, *praesidens*, pres. part. of *praesidēre*] *archaic* **:** occupying the first rank or chief place **:** PRESIDING ⟨residence of the ~ priest of the province —Z.M.Pike⟩
pres·i·den·te \,prezə'dentē\ *n* -s [AmerSp, fr. Sp, president, fr. L *praesident-*, *praesidens* president, ruler] **:** a cocktail consisting of rum, curaçao, dry vermouth, and grenadine shaken or stirred with cracked ice
pres·i·dent·ess \'prez(ə)dəntəs\ *n* -ES **1 :** a female president **:** a woman that presides ⟨formed a tea society with the parson's wife for ~ —J.F.Cooper⟩ **2 :** the wife of a president
president general *n* **:** the chief presiding officer in an organized system (as a religious or fraternal order or a federation of states or provinces) usu. having subordinate officers of presidential rank or title ⟨*president general* of the Daughters of the American Revolution⟩ ⟨proposed a *president general* for the North American colonies⟩
pres·i·den·tial \¦prezə¦denchəl *sometimes* (')prez¦-\ *adj* [ML *praesidentialis*, fr. *praesidentia* presidency + L *-alis* -al — more at PRESIDENCY] **1 a :** of, relating to, or exercised by a president ⟨a man of ~ stature —*N. Y. Times*⟩ ⟨~ patronage⟩ ⟨~ aide⟩ ⟨~ policy⟩ **b :** of or relating to the election of a president ⟨~ campaign⟩ ⟨~ convention⟩ **c :** performing functions delegated by or under the authority of a president ⟨~ agent⟩ ⟨~ commission⟩ **2** *obs* **:** having the function of presiding or watching over ⟨govern them . . . by a ~ angel —Robert Gell⟩ **3 :** of, based upon, or having the characteristics of presidential government ⟨~ system⟩ ⟨~ republic⟩
presidential government *n* **:** a system of government in which the position and powers of both chief of state and chief political executive are concentrated in a president who is chosen independently of the legislature for a fixed term and who in position, duties, and powers is constitutionally independent of the legislature — compare PARLIAMENTARY GOVERNMENT
pres·i·den·tial·ly \-chəlē\ *adv* **1 :** in the character or person of a president ⟨each of the great powers will be represented ~ —*London Daily News*⟩ **2 :** so far as concerns the president or the presidency of the U. S. ⟨states voting Republican ~ —V.O.Key⟩
presidential primary *also* **presidential preference primary** *n* **:** a primary in which the voters indicate preferences for nominees for president of the U. S. directly by vote or indirectly through the choice of delegates to the presidential nominating convention — called also *preferential primary*
presidential year *n* **:** a year in which a presidential election is held
president pro tempore *n*, *pl* **presidents pro tempore :** a member of the U. S. senate and usu. a leader of the majority party who is chosen to serve as presiding officer of the senate in the absence of the vice-president; *also* **:** a similar officer in another legislative body ⟨*president pro tempore* of the state senate⟩ ⟨*president pro tempore* of the provincial congress⟩
presidents' day *n*, *usu cap P&D* **:** WASHINGTON'S BIRTHDAY 2
pres·i·dent·ship \'prez(ə)dənt,ship\ *n* **1 :** the office of president ⟨contests for the ~*s* and chairmanships of civic bodies —*Hindustan Times*⟩ ⟨accepted the ~ of the . . . association —*Modern Language Teaching*⟩ **2 :** the period of incumbency of a president ⟨the 17th year of his ~ —Cotton Mather⟩
pre·sid·er \prē'zīdə(r), prə'-\ *n* -s **:** one that presides
presides *pres 3d sing of* PRESIDE
pre·sid·i·al \prə'sidēəl\ *adj* [LL *praesidialis* of a garrison, fr. L *praesidium* defense, garrison, fortification (fr. *praesid-*, *praeses* guard, president, ruler, fr. *praesidēre* to guard, preside over) + *-alis* -al — more at PRESIDE] **1 :** of, having, or constituting a garrison ⟨three ~ castles in this city —James Howell⟩ **2** [influenced in meaning by LL *praesidalis* of a provincial governor, fr. L *praesid-*, *praeses* guard, president, ruler + *-alis* -al] **a :** PRESIDENTIAL 1 ⟨~ power⟩ ⟨~ cabinet⟩ **b :** PRESIDENTIAL 2 ⟨judgment holds in me a ~ seat —Charles Cotton⟩ **3** [F *présidial* being a presidial court, fr. MF *presidial*, alter. (influenced by LL *praesidialis* of a garrison) of *presidal*, fr. LL *praesidalis* of a provincial governor] **:** of or relating to a province **:** PROVINCIAL ⟨~ seat of justice⟩ — see PRESIDIAL COURT
presidial court *or* **presidial** *n* [*presidial court* part trans. of F *cour présidial*, fr. MF *cour presidial*, alter. (influenced by LL *praesidialis* of a garrison) of *cour presidal*, fr. *cour* court + *presidal* being a presidial court, fr. LL *praesidalis* of a provincial governor; *presidial* fr. F *présidial*, fr. *présidial*, adj. (in the term *cour présidial*)] **:** a court of justice under the ancien régime in French cities without a parliament
pre·sid·i·ary \-dē,erē\ *adj* [L *praesidiarius*, fr. *praesidium* defense, garrison, fortification + *-arius* -ary] **:** PRESIDIAL 1 ⟨~ cohorts were stationed at every threatened point —Charles Merivale⟩
presiding *pres part of* PRESIDE
presiding bishop *n* **1 :** the president of the executive council of the Protestant Episcopal Church who is elected by the general convention **2 :** the chief member of the presiding bishopric of the Mormon Church
presiding bishopric *n* **:** the chief office of the Aaronic priesthood in the Mormon Church filled by three persons and supervised by the first presidency
presiding elder *n* **:** DISTRICT SUPERINTENDENT
pre·sidio \prə'sidē,ō, -sēd-\ *n* -s [Sp, fr. L *praesidium* defense, garrison, fortification] **:** a garrisoned place; *specif* **:** a military post or fortified settlement in areas currently or orig. under Spanish control ⟨one of the first settlements in Texas not established as a ~ —*Amer. Guide Series: Texas*⟩ ⟨a sleepy Mexican ~ with fortifications rusting —C.C.Dobie⟩
pre·sid·i·um \prē'sidēəm, prə'-, -'zi-\ *also* **prae·sid·i·um** \", prī-\ *n*, *pl* **presid·ia** \-dēə\ *or* **presidiums** [Russ *prezidium*, fr. L *praesidium* defense, garrison, fortification] **1 :** a permanent executive committee selected in Communist countries from a larger body in theory to act for the larger body when in recess but usu. regarded as exercising full powers for and in the name of the parent body ⟨the ~ . . . in practice is the effective working part of the Supreme Soviet —J.A. Corry⟩ ⟨the ~ of the central committee . . . replaced the politburo —Julian Towster⟩ ⟨the ~ of the Yugoslav parliament —M.S.Handler⟩ — compare POLITBURO 1 **2 :** a presiding or executive committee in a nongovernmental organization ⟨elected to the three-man ~ of the . . . orchestra association —*Springfield (Mass.) Union*⟩
pre·sign \prē+\ *vt* -ED/-ING/-S [*pre-* + *sign*] *archaic* **:** PRESIGNIFY ⟨agents of destruction . . . ~ regeneration —P.J.Bailey⟩
pre·sig·ni·fi·ca·tion \,prē,signəfə'kāshən\ *n* [LL *praesignification-*, *praesignificatio*, fr. L *praesignificatus* (past part. of *praesignificare*) + *-ion-*, *-io* -ion] *archaic* **:** PRESAGE ⟨the broad arrow, the mysterious ~ of mischief —J.P.Kennedy †1870⟩
pre·sig·ni·fy \prē'signə,fī\ *vt* -ED/-ING/-ES [L *praesignificare*, fr. *prae-* pre- + *significare* to signify] **:** to intimate or signify beforehand **:** PRESAGE ⟨a long cloud . . . *presignified* a violent storm —Richard Chandler⟩
pre·simian \(')prē+\ *adj* [*pre-* + *simian*] **:** existing or happening before the existence of anthropoid apes
¹pre-socratic \¦prē+\ *adj*, *sometimes cap P & usu cap S* [*pre-* + *socratic*] **:** of or relating to Greek philosophy or philosophers before Socrates; *esp* **:** of or relating to the members or the ideas of the Ionian, Pythagorean, and Eleatic schools, the school of the atomists, and sometimes the Sophists ⟨*pre-Socratic* thought⟩
²pre-socratic \"\ *n* -s *sometimes cap P & usu cap S* **:** a pre-Socratic philosopher ⟨a fundamental doctrine on which the *pre-Socratics* had been agreed —Friedrich Solmsen⟩
pre·so·ma \prē'sōmə\ *n* -s [NL, fr. *pre-* + *-soma*] **:** the anterior part of the body in an invertebrate in which a clearly defined head is lacking
pre·somite \(')prē+\ *adj* [*pre-* + *somite*] **:** occurring before the formation of somites ⟨~ period of the chick embryo⟩ **:** not yet divided into somites ⟨a ~ human embryo⟩
¹pre·sphenoid \"+\ *n* [*pre-* + *sphenoid*] **:** a presphenoid bone or cartilage usu. united with the basisphenoid in the adult and in man forming the anterior part of the body of the sphenoid
²presphenoid \"\ *also* **pre·sphenoidal** \¦prē+\ *adj* [*presphenoid* fr. ¹*presphenoid*; *presphenoidal* fr. ¹*presphenoid* + *-al*] **:** indicating or relating to a median part of the vertebrate skull anterior to the basisphenoid
pre·sphygmic \(')prē+\ *adj* [ISV *pre-* + *sphygmic*] **:** occurring before the pulse beat ⟨a ~ arterial thrill⟩
pre·spi·nous \prē'spīnəs\ *adj* [*pre-* + *spine* + *-ous*] **:** PRESCAPULAR 2
pre·spiracular \¦prē+\ *adj* [*pre-* + *spiracular*] **:** anterior to the spiracle
¹press \'pres\ *n* -ES *often attrib* [ME *presse*, *prees*, fr. OF *presse*, fr. *presser* to press — more at ²PRESS] **1 a :** a crowd of people or a crowded condition **:** MULTITUDE, THRONG ⟨there was . . . a ~ of people trying to force their way past the powerful yeomen ushers —Leslie Hotson⟩ ⟨perched on the folded-down top of a convertible, to roll down the boardwalk with a ~ of people following her car —Pete Martin⟩ **b** *archaic* **:** the crush or melee of cavalry or foot soldiers in battle **c :** a thronging or crowding forward or together ⟨had difficulty keeping his feet in the ~ and surge of the mob⟩ ⟨had been pushed out of their home territories by the ~ of white settlement —*Amer. Guide Series: Ind.*⟩ **2 a :** an apparatus or machine by which a substance is cut or shaped (as by pressing, drawing, or stamping), by which an impression of a body is taken, by which a material is compressed or packed, by which pressure is applied to a body, by which liquid is expressed, or by which a cutting tool (as a drill) is fed into the work by applied pressure — compare CHEESE PRESS, DRILL PRESS, FORMING PRESS, HYDRAULIC PRESS, PUNCH PRESS **b :** a building containing presses or a business using presses **c :** a medieval apparatus in which an accused person refusing to plead was crushed until he yielded or died **3 :** CLOSET, CUPBOARD — compare CLOTHESPRESS **4** [²*press*] **:** the act of pressing or pushing something **:** PRESSURE ⟨a ~ of a button⟩ ⟨a ~ of the hand⟩ ⟨finishes with a light ~ of the earth over the newly planted seed⟩ ⟨could no longer stand against the steady ~ of the Roman lines —A.C.Whitehead⟩ **5** [²*press*] **:** the properly smoothed and creased condition of a freshly pressed garment ⟨a fabric that keeps its ~⟩ ⟨a good ~ on these trousers⟩ **6 a :** PRINTING PRESS **b** *chiefly Brit* **:** HANDPRESS — compare MACHINE **c :** the act or the process of printing ⟨to see a book through the ~⟩ **d :** a printing or publishing establishment ⟨a university ~⟩; *also* **:** its personnel **7 a :** the gathering and publishing or broadcasting of news **:** JOURNALISM ⟨freedom of the ~⟩ **b :** newspapers, periodicals, and often radio and television news broadcasting regarded as a group ⟨the ~ has three functions: to inform, to influence, and to entertain —R.E. Wolseley⟩ ⟨the American ~⟩ ⟨the Democratic ~⟩ ⟨the religious ~⟩ **c :** news reporters, publishers, and broadcasters as a group ⟨the ~ . . . is very apt to think in the local terms of the papers that they represent —F.D.Roosevelt⟩ **d :** comment or notice in newspapers and periodicals ⟨the navy . . . is enjoying a good ~ —*Atlantic*⟩ **8 a :** any of various pressure devices (as the standing press) used to compress or hold books **b :** any of various devices used to keep sporting gear (as rackets and skis) from warping when not in use **9** [²*press*] **a :** a lift in weight lifting in which the weight is raised from the floor to shoulder height and then smoothly extended overhead — called also *military press*; compare CLEAN AND JERK, SNATCH **b :** a fencer's applying of pressure against an opponent's blade in order to force an opening for an attack **c :** a method by which a gymnast raises the body into a hand balance by using the muscles only without the aid of a kick or throw **d :** a pressuring defense (as in basketball) employed over a part or all of the court to hinder movement of the ball and as an intensive effort to gain possession **10 :** a pair of rolls between which the wet web of paper is passed to remove water and compact the sheet in papermaking **syn** see CROWD
— **in press :** in the process of printing or manufacture — used of books or other printed matter
²press \"\ *vb* -ED/-ING/-ES [ME *pressen*, fr. MF *presser*, fr. OF,

fr. L *pressare*, fr. *pressus*, past part. of *premere* to press; akin to L *prelum* press, wine press and perh. to Russ *peret'* to press] *vt* **1 a :** to bring pushing or thrusting force to bear on by means of something in direct contact **:** FORCE, THRUST **:** exert steady pressure on ⟨found that if a telegraph key was ~*ed* down hard a stronger current ran through the wires —Roger Burlingame⟩ **b :** to torture or put to death by the press **2 a :** to make a hostile assault on **:** ASSAIL, BESET, HARASS ⟨enemy forces ~*ed* the town hard on all sides⟩ ⟨single lions, past their prime . . . become now and then the quarry of a pack hard ~*ed* by hunger —James Stevenson-Hamilton⟩ **b :** to reduce to misery or distress **:** AFFLICT, OPPRESS ⟨the bondslaves of our day, whom dirt and danger ~ —Rudyard Kipling⟩ **c :** to weigh upon (as mind or body) so as to cause distress or pain **:** DEPRESS **3 a :** to squeeze out the juice or contents of **:** EXPRESS ⟨~ grapes⟩ **b :** to squeeze with apparatus or instruments to a desired density, smoothness, or shape **c :** to compact (as paper or bound or unbound books) in a press **4 a :** to exert influence on **:** CONSTRAIN, URGE ⟨my host ~*ed* me to drink —Allen Upward⟩ ⟨came from the dance for a few minutes to ~ his friend to join it —Jane Austen⟩ **b :** to importune urgently **:** try hard to persuade **:** BESEECH, ENTREAT **5 :** to move by means of pressure **6 a :** to inculcate strongly (as an attitude or opinion) **:** present (a claim) earnestly **:** EMPHASIZE, STRESS ⟨~*es* upon us similar reflections —G.G. Coulton⟩ **b :** to insist on or request urgently (an act or procedure) ⟨~ a conciliatory approach on him⟩ **7 :** to follow through (a course of action) **:** PROSECUTE ⟨the bridge trains were ordered to ~ the march at highest possible speed —P.W. Thompson⟩ ⟨must ~ action wherever I can, show people that I mean business when I talk about a flight across the ocean —C.A.Lindbergh b. 1902⟩ **8 :** to clasp in affection or courtesy **:** EMBRACE ⟨~*ed* the visitor's hand⟩ ⟨~*ed* the well loved woman to him⟩ **9 :** to make or reproduce (a phonograph record) from a matrix ~ *vi* **1 :** to crowd closely against or around someone or something **:** MASS ⟨hundreds ~*ed* about the performer after the show⟩ **2 :** to force or push one's way (as through a crowd or against obstruction) **:** strain onward **:** advance energetically or eagerly **3** *obs* **:** to strive earnestly **:** ATTEMPT, UNDERTAKE **4 a :** to seek urgently **:** ARGUE, CONTEND ⟨was now ~*ing* for eight dreadnoughts, rather than six —Virginia Cowles⟩ **b :** to exert effort **:** apply pressure **:** WORK ⟨~*ed* aggressively for power development⟩ **5 :** to require promptitude **:** call for action **:** create urgency ⟨time ~*es*⟩ ⟨let me know if anything ~*es*⟩ **6 :** to impose a weight or burden **:** lie heavily ⟨care ~*ed* upon his mind⟩ **7 :** to take or hold a press ⟨a fabric that ~*es* well⟩ **8 :** to hit a golf ball with excessive impact that impairs smoothness and coordination of the stroke

syn BEAR, SQUEEZE, CROWD, JAM: PRESS indicates application of pressure; it may apply to weighing down, pushing, thrusting, stamping, driving, or to constraining, compelling, persecuting, promoting, or urging ⟨*pressed* the crowd back⟩ ⟨*press* out the grapes⟩ ⟨he *pressed* the agitated girl into a seat —Thomas Hardy⟩ ⟨determined to *press* the matter —Rose Macaulay⟩ ⟨when *pressed* for details he always closed his eyes —L.C.Douglas⟩ ⟨construction was therefore *pressed* at feverish speed —*Amer. Guide Series: Fla.*⟩ ⟨the Conservatives, fearing for imperial security, *pressed* the Labor government hard —*Collier's Yr. Bk.*⟩ BEAR in the sense here discussed may apply to the application of any pressure or force, often actually or figuratively downward or backward ⟨the weight of the roof *bears* on these pillars⟩ ⟨his debts *bore* heavily on him⟩ ⟨his activity and zeal *bore* down all opposition —T.B.Macaulay⟩ ⟨Clan Alpine's best are backward *borne* —Sir Walter Scott⟩ SQUEEZE applies to pressure on all sides to flatten or crush, to force in pressing into a small circumscribed space, to pressure, to extract, elicit, or compel ⟨*squeeze* an orange⟩ ⟨to make newly joined officers *squeeze* through the narrowest shelves of a dinner wagon —J.S.Bradford⟩ ⟨to *squeeze* more education out of the G. I. bill —Louis Auchincloss⟩ ⟨large scale immigration during the 19th century *squeezed* Negro artisans and laborers out of industry —*Amer. Guide Series: N.J.*⟩ CROWD may indicate forceful pushing, pressing, or packing together of people ⟨never have more startling twists been *crowded* into the concluding scene of a melodrama —John Mason Brown⟩ ⟨I hope not too many try to *crowd* in here at once. It isn't a very big room —John Steinbeck⟩ ⟨at first volunteers *crowded* the recruiting stations, could not be used —Elsie Singmaster⟩ JAM suggests wedging in with great pressure or force, sometimes so that subsequent movement is impossible or difficult ⟨*jam* the shirts into the suitcase⟩ ⟨an upturned boat *jammed* by the current against the timbers —H.G.Wells⟩ ⟨*jammed* in the schoolhouse and standing about fifty deep outside —*Amer. Guide Series: Md.*⟩

— press one's luck : to push one's luck

³press \ˈ"\ *vb* -ED/-ING/-ES [alter. (influenced by ²*press*) of obs. E *prest* to enlist (someone) as a soldier or sailor by giving some pay in advance, fr. E ²*prest*] *vt* **1 :** to force (men) into service esp. in the army or navy **:** IMPRESS ⟨the cutter is often mentioned . . . with regard to revenue work and law enforcement, in seizing illegal goods, or in ~*ing* men for naval service —H.I.Chapelle⟩ **2 a :** to take by authority (as for public or emergency use) **:** COMMANDEER ⟨~*ed* a passing car to give chase⟩ **b :** to enlist the help of ⟨~*ed* a passerby into service to warn off traffic⟩ ~ *vi* **:** to impress men as soldiers or sailors

⁴press \ˈ"\ *n* -ES **1 :** impressment into service esp. in a navy **2** *obs* **:** a warrant for impressing recruits

⁵press *adj* [L *pressus*, past part. of *premere* to press — more at ²PRESS] *obs* **:** CONCISE, PRECISE, EXACT

⁶press \ˈpres\ *n* -ES [origin unknown] **:** an East Indian tree shrew (*Tupaia ferruginea*)

press *abbr* pressure

press·able \ˈpresəbəl\ *adj* **:** capable of being pressed

press agent *n* [¹*press* + *agent*] **:** an agent employed by an individual, organization, or group to establish and maintain good public relations through publicity

press–agent \ˈ⸗,⸗⸗\ *vb* -ED/-ING/-S [*press agent*] *vt* **:** to serve as press agent to **:** provide publicity for **:** PUBLICIZE ⟨press-agented him as a popular hero —G.F.Milton⟩ ~ *vi* **:** to serve as press agent ⟨was *press-agenting* for several large companies⟩

press–agent·ry \ˈ⸗,⸗⸗⸗\ *n* **:** the function or activities of press agents **:** PROMOTION, PUBLICITY ⟨this reputation is not wholly the product of *press-agentry* —Egon Glesinger⟩

press association *n* **:** an association of newspapers formed to gather and distribute news to its members — compare NEWS AGENCY

press bed *n* **:** a bed that is set wholly within or folds into a press or cupboard with doors

pressboard \ˈ⸗,⸗\ *n* [¹*press* + *board;* fr. its use in presses for pressing and finishing knit underwear] **1 :** a strong highly glazed board resembling vulcanized fiber **2** [²*press* + *board*] **:** FULLERBOARD **3** [²*press* + *board*] **:** an ironing board; *esp* **:** a small one for sleeves

press box *n* **:** a space reserved for reporters (as at a game)

press brake *n* **:** a press used to bend metal bars or sheets

press bureau *n* **:** a business or a department that acts as a press agent

press–button \ˈ⸗,⸗⸗\ *n* **:** PUSH BUTTON

press cake *n* **:** a cake of compressed substance: as **a :** a filter cake formed in a filter press (as in the manufacture of cane sugar) **b :** an oil cake obtained by expression

press cloth *n* [¹*press* + *cloth*] **1 :** a cloth filter usu. of cotton or linen used in a press **2** [²*press* + *cloth*] **:** a cloth to protect a garment from direct contact with an iron in pressing

press conference *n* **:** an interview given by a public figure to newsmen by appointment

press copy *n* **:** a copy of something written made on a copying press

press cupboard *n* **:** a 16th and 17th century cupboard resembling a court cupboard but having drawers or doors below the main shelf

press cupboard

press drill *n* **:** an agricultural drill having a press wheel attachment for compacting the soil in the seeded furrows

pressed \ˈprest\ *adj* [ME, fr. past part. of *pressen* to press] **1 :** compacted or molded by pressure **:** squeezed together or into some form **2** *of food* **:** shaped, molded, or having liquid or juices extracted under pressure ⟨~ duck⟩ ⟨~ meat loaf⟩

pressed amber *n* **:** AMBEROID

pressed brick *n* **:** bricks subjected to pressure to free them from imperfections of shape and texture before burning

pressed cheese *n* **:** a hard cheese (as cheddar) that has been subjected to pressure to remove the whey, to produce physical conditions essential to ripening, and to give it a form convenient for handling

pressed distillate *n* **:** the oil left in petroleum refining after the paraffin has been separated from the paraffin distillate by cooling and pressing — compare PRESSED OIL

pressed glass *n* **:** glass given its shape in manufacture by being poured under pressure into a mold while still molten or pressed into a mold while still plastic

pressed oil *n* **:** an oil (as a vegetable or petroleum oil) from which the easily solidified substances have been removed by cooling and pressing — compare PRESSED DISTILLATE

pressed steel *n* **:** steel parts made by shaping steel sheet between dies in a mechanical or hydraulic press

pressed ware *n* **:** articles of glass or fired clay formed by pressing

pressed wax *n* **:** PRESS WAX

presse–pâte machine \ˈpreˌspät-\ *n* [prob. fr. F *presse-pâte* presse-pâte machine (fr. *presser* to press + *pâte* paste, pulp, fr. LL *pasta* dough, paste) + E *machine* — more at PASTE] **:** either of two machines used in papermaking: **a :** a machine functioning like the wet end of a paper machine **b :** a wet machine for preparing laps of pulp

press·er \ˈpresə(r)\ *n* -S **:** one that presses **:** a worker or apparatus that presses clothing, food, or an article undergoing an industrial process: as **a :** the operator of a press for forming glassware **b :** an operator who shapes pottery or ceramic ware by hand pressing or in a mechanical press **c :** a bindery worker who stacks completed books in a vertical press after the casing-in operation **d :** a device used in spring-needle knitting to close the barb of the needle so as to permit the yarn loop to be withdrawn

presser bar *n* **:** a bar to which the presser foot of a sewing machine is attached

presser foot *n* **1 :** FOOT 7e **2 :** PRESSER SHOE

presser shoe *n* **:** a machine shoe or foot to hold something down (as lumber during dressing)

presses *pl of* PRESS, *pres 3d sing of* PRESS

press figure *or* **press number** *n* **:** a numeral printed at the foot of a page of some 18th century books perhaps to identify the pressman printing that part of the book — compare SIGNATURE

press fit *n* **:** the fit of a shaft driven into a hole slightly smaller than itself and held tight and motionless — compare LOOSE FIT

press–forge \ˈ⸗,⸗\ *vt* **:** to forge on a forging press — **press forger** *n*

press forging *n* **:** a forging produced between dies by pressure (as of a hydraulic press or a drop hammer)

press gallery *n* **:** a gallery for the press esp. in a legislative chamber; *also* **:** a group or corps of reporters occupying or eligible to occupy such a gallery ⟨the Washington *press gallery*⟩

¹press–gang \ˈ⸗,⸗\ *n* [⁴*press* + *gang*] **:** a detachment of men under command of an officer empowered to force men into military or more commonly naval service

²press–gang \ˈ"\ *vt* **:** to impress by or as if by a press-gang

¹press·ing \ˈpresiŋ, -sēŋ\ *n* -S [ME *pressinge*, fr. gerund of *pressen* to press] **1 :** an exertion of pressure or a process using pressure ⟨requires only the ~ of a button⟩ ⟨the ~ of apples for cider⟩ ⟨the ~ of cheese⟩ **2 :** the product of any of numerous mechanical presses: as **a :** a metal part stamped, pierced, or formed in a press ⟨~*s* for many of the most famous names in the British motor-car industry —*Punch*⟩ **b :** a glass or ceramic article formed by forcing a tempered clay mixture or hot glass into a mold **c** (1) **:** a phonograph record made from a matrix by compression or injection molding (2) **:** the whole number of records made at one time ⟨the first ~ of her song⟩

²pressing \ˈ"\ *adj* [fr. pres. part. of ²*press*] **1 :** urgently important **:** CRITICAL ⟨the ~ necessity of earning a livelihood —*Amer. Guide Series: R.I.*⟩ ⟨I've more ~ things to think about than girls —C.B.Kelland⟩ ⟨a ~ demand⟩ **2 :** EARNEST, WARM ⟨a ~ invitation⟩ ⟨~ attentions⟩

syn PRESSING, URGENT, IMPERATIVE, CRYING, IMPORTUNATE, INSISTENT, EXIGENT, INSTANT can mean, in common, claiming or demanding immediate attention. PRESSING characterizes what makes an unavoidable claim upon one's concern as if pressure were applied ⟨a *pressing* need⟩ ⟨*pressing* problems⟩ URGENT is stronger than PRESSING, suggesting constraint or compulsion of one's attention ⟨his voice was *urgent* and incisive —Elinor Wylie⟩ ⟨an *urgent* seriousness underlay his words —W.H.Wright⟩ ⟨the *urgent* needs of the war —T.B. Costain⟩ ⟨*urgent* expenses⟩ IMPERATIVE puts stress upon the obligatory nature of the task, need, or duty that lays claim to attention ⟨the *imperative* need for a more spacious home —Havelock Ellis⟩ ⟨a remonstrance had become *imperative* —Samuel Butler †1902⟩ ⟨*imperative* orders —Sir Winston Churchill⟩ CRYING puts stress upon the extreme, often shocking, conspicuousness of the thing claiming attention ⟨a *crying* need to make American cities better places in which to live and work —L.E.Cooper⟩ ⟨a *crying* scandal of the times —J.T. Farrell⟩ ⟨*crying* disproportion between ambition and accomplishment —W.C.Brownell⟩ IMPORTUNATE stresses pertinacity in demanding, often to the point of annoyance or nagging ⟨a thick fringe of *importunate* hangers-on —Claudia Cassidy⟩ ⟨the troublesome and *importunate* monk —H.T.Buckle⟩ ⟨hundreds of *importunate* requests to submit to the monarch —*Time*⟩ INSISTENT is not as strong as IMPORTUNATE; it implies, however, an insisting or an unremitting claiming on attention ⟨the *insistent* friendliness of sextons —Robert Lynd⟩ ⟨the clamor of his *insistent* admirers —Saxe Commins⟩ ⟨*insistent* problems⟩ EXIGENT is close to URGENT or PRESSING but implies more an imperative demand for action than a claim upon attention ⟨outlasting the adverse circumstance, however *exigent* and oppressive —*Times Lit. Supp.*⟩ ⟨*exigent* foreign diplomats —Janet Flanner⟩ ⟨the *exigent* demands of war —Allan Nevins⟩ INSTANT is an older form in general interchangeable with INSISTENT, or esp. URGENT or IMPORTUNATE, but sometimes suggesting perseverance ⟨was *instant* that I should continue at Oxford —A.T.Quiller-Couch⟩ ⟨the *instant* need —John Buchan⟩ ⟨down the other side of High Street he walked, his eyes *instant* for suggestion and opportunity —Arthur Morrison⟩ ⟨they would teach in Sunday schools, and be *instant*, in season and out of season, in imparting spiritual instruction —Samuel Butler †1902⟩

pressing board *n* **:** a hardwood often metal-edged board placed between layers of bound books or between unbound sections during pressing

pressing iron *n* **:** IRON 2b

press·ing·ly *adv* **:** in an urgent or pressing manner

press·ing·ness *n* -ES **:** the quality or state of being pressing **:** URGENCY

pres·sion \ˈpreshən\ *n* -S [L *pression-, pressio*, fr. *pressus* (past part. of *premere* to press) + *-ion-, -io* -ion — more at PRESS] **:** PRESSING, PRESSURE

pres·si·ros·tral \ˌpresəˈrästrəl\ *adj* [NL *Pressirostres* + E *-al*] **:** of or relating to the Pressirostres

pres·si·ros·tres \ˌ⸗⸗ˈrä,strēz\ *n pl, cap* [NL, fr. *pressi-* (fr. L *pressus*, past part. of *premere* to press) + *-rostres* (fr. L *rostrum* beak) — more at ROSTRUM] *in former classifications* **:** a group of birds having a narrow compressed bill

pres·sive \ˈpresiv\ *adj* [obs. F *pressif* urgent, fr. MF, fr. *presser* to press + *-if* -ive] *archaic* **:** marked by pressure, urgency, or oppressiveness

press juice *n* **:** a liquid obtained by pressing ⟨*press juice* of potatoes⟩

pressly *adv* [⁵*press* + *-ly*] *obs* **:** EXACTLY

press·man \ˈpresmən\ *n, pl* **pressmen 1 :** the operator of a press; *esp* **:** the operator of a printing press **2** *Brit* **:** NEWSPAPERMAN ⟨he'd fight off all the other *pressmen* —Ngaio Marsh⟩

pressmark \ˈ⸗,⸗\ *n* [¹*press* (closet) + *mark*] *chiefly Brit* **:** a character or combination of characters assigned to a book to indicate its physical location (as room, case, shelf) in a library — compare CALL NUMBER

pressmaster *n, obs* **:** the officer commanding a press-gang

press mold *n* **:** a cast-iron mold used in glassmaking

press money *n* [by alter.] **:** PREST MONEY

press–off \ˈ⸗,⸗\ *n* -S [fr. the phrase *press off*, fr. ²*press* + *off*] **1 :** the jumping of machine-knitted stitches from the needles (as when yarn breaks) **2 :** defective material (as an uncompleted stocking) formed by a press-off

press of sail *or* **press of canvas :** a greater spread of sail than a ship usu. carries in the breeze prevailing

pres·sor \ˈpresə(r)\ *adj* [LL, one that presses, fr. L *pressus* (past part. of *premere* to press) + *-or*] **:** raising or tending to raise blood pressure ⟨~ substances⟩ **:** involving or producing an effect of vasoconstriction ⟨~ reflexes⟩ ⟨a ~ action⟩

pres·so·receptor \ˌpresō+\ *n* [ISV *presso-* (fr. L *pressura* pressure) + *receptor*] **:** a proprioceptor that responds to alteration of blood pressure

press peach *n, chiefly Midland* **:** CLINGSTONE

press point *n* **:** POINT 6d(1)

press proof *n* **1 :** the last proof submitted before a printing order is sent to press **2 :** a proof made on a printing press that is usu. the press on which the job is to be printed to show general appearance, margins, and color **3 :** REPRO PROOF

press reader *n* **:** a proofreader who reads press proofs

press release *n* **:** HANDOUT 1c

press roll *n* **:** a live roll that presses and holds moving lumber against the roll which feeds it into a planer or other machine

pressroom \ˈ⸗,⸗\ *n* -S **:** a room in a printing plant containing the printing presses

pressrun \ˈ⸗,⸗\ *n* -S **:** a continuous operation of a printing press producing a specified number of copies; *also* **:** the number of copies so printed ⟨a ~ of 1000⟩

press sheet *n* **1 :** CLIPSHEET **2 :** a sheet as printed during a pressrun and before folding

press–stud \ˈ⸗,⸗\ *n, chiefly Brit* **:** SNAP FASTENER

pres·sur·al \ˈpreshərəl\ *adj* **:** of, relating to, or caused by pressure ⟨a ~ tide⟩

¹pres·sure \ˈpreshə(r)\ *n* -S [in sense 1, fr. ME, fr. LL *pressura*, fr. L, action of pressing, pressure, fr. *pressus* (past part. of *premere* to press) + *-ura* -ure; in other senses, fr. L *pressura* — more at PRESS] **1 a :** the burden of physical or mental distress **:** the oppression of adversity, grief, illness, or trouble **b :** the constraint of circumstance **:** the weight of social or economic imposition ⟨the ~ of poverty⟩ ⟨financial ~⟩ **c :** the operation of factor urging toward commitment or decision ⟨the ~ of community disapproval⟩ **2 :** the application of force to something by something else in direct contact with it **:** COMPRESSION, PUSHING, SQUEEZING ⟨felt the quick ~ of her companion's hand⟩ **3** *archaic* **:** a mark impressed on something **:** IMAGE, STAMP ⟨from the table of my memory I'll wipe away all trivial fond records . . . all forms, all ~*s* past that youth and observation copied there —Shak.⟩ **4 a :** the action of a force against some opposing force **:** a force in the nature of a thrust distributed over a surface **b :** the force or thrust exerted over a surface divided by the area of the surface **c :** ELECTROMOTIVE FORCE **5 :** the stress or urgency of matters demanding attention **:** EXACTION, EXIGENCY, OBLIGATION ⟨the ~ of affairs⟩ ⟨the ~ of a family's necessities⟩ **6 :** a factor that tends to reduce a wild animal population; *esp* **:** any such factor arising from human activity ⟨hunting ~⟩ ⟨population ~*s*⟩ **7 :** ATMOSPHERIC PRESSURE **8 :** a touch sensation aroused by moderate compression of the skin — distinguished from *contact* and *pain* **syn** see STRESS

²pressure \ˈ"\ *vt* **pressured; pressured; pressuring** \-sh(ə)riŋ\ **pressures 1 :** to apply pressure to **:** bring influence to bear on **:** CONSTRAIN ⟨several advertisers . . . have *pressured* business papers —C.B.Larrabee⟩ **2 :** to increase or intensify pressure in **:** PRESSURIZE ⟨pressurized cabins are *pressured* at about 5000 feet —G.A.Smathers⟩ **3 :** to cook in a pressure cooker ⟨a box of beef or mutton bones, *pressured* until the marrow is extracted, makes excellent broth —*All-Pets Mag.*⟩

pressure accumulator *n* **:** a tank for storing air or gas under pressure or for absorbing the pulses in a hydraulic or pneumatic system

pressure altimeter *n* **:** an altimeter using an aneroid to determine altitude by measuring differences in atmospheric pressure — compare ABSOLUTE ALTIMETER

pressure altitude *n* **:** the altitude corresponding to a given pressure in a standard atmosphere

pressure angle *n* **:** the angle between the line of force and a line at right angles to the center line of two gears at the pitch point

pressure bandage *n* **:** PRESSURE DRESSING

pressure bar *n* **:** a bar that grips the edge of a metal sheet to prevent buckling or crimping during punching, stamping, or forming on a press

pressure bottle *n* **:** a bottle able to withstand pressures greater than atmospheric (as for holding gas under pressure or for conducting chemical digestions under pressure)

pressure box *n* **:** an elevated cistern fed by a flume, ditch, or pipe, and supplying water under a head

pressure cabin *n* **:** an airplane cabin in which near-normal atmospheric pressure can be maintained by a supercharger during high-altitude flight

pressure canner *n* **:** a pressure cooker for use in home canning

pressure car *n* **:** a tank car carrying a compressed gas (as butane) just behind a gas-fired locomotive and supplying it with fuel — compare TENDER

pressure–cook \ˈ⸗⸗,ku̇k\ *vb* [back-formation fr. *pressure cooker*] **:** to cook in a pressure cooker

pressure cooker *n* [¹*pressure* + *cooker*] **:** an airtight utensil for quick cooking or preserving of foods by means of superheated steam under pressure — compare AUTOCLAVE

pressure cooker

pressure distillate *n* **:** an unrefined distillate remaining after cracking of petroleum under heat and pressure

pressure dressing *n* **:** a thick pad of gauze or other material placed over a wound and affixed firmly so that it will exert pressure — called also *compression dressing*

pressure element *n* **:** a fluid connection (as between an accumulator and a machine)

pressure fan *n* **:** a fan supplying air under pressure

pressure filter *n* **:** a filter in which the pressure on the feed side of the filter medium is greater than that of the atmosphere

pressure flaking *n* [*flaking* fr. gerund of *flake*] **:** the shaping of a stone implement by pressing off flakes with a pointed stick or bone — compare PERCUSSION FLAKING

pressure gauge *n* **:** a gauge for indicating fluid pressure **:** MANOMETER: as **a :** a gauge on a steam boiler to indicate steam pressure — see BOURDON GAUGE **b :** a device to measure the pressure of an explosive (as when fired in a gun)

pressure glide *n* **:** a fencer's attack against an opponent's blade by pressing his own sharply forward and downward toward the opponent's guard

pressure gradient *n* **:** the space rate of variation of pressure in a given direction; *specif* **:** such rate of variation in a direction normal to an isobar

pressure group *n* **1 :** a minority group seeking to influence legislation in its own interest (as by lobbying or propaganda) ⟨political scientists who tend to think that the *pressure groups* are the highest form of political organization of which Americans are capable —E.E.Schatt-Schneider⟩ **2 :** a group using tactics resembling the tactics of political pressure groups to promote its interests or affect public opinion ⟨*pressure groups* which insist that the high school maintain a winning football team —Paul Woodring⟩

pressure gun *n* **:** GREASE GUN 1

pressure head *n* **:** HEAD 14

pressure hull *n* **:** the inner hull of a submarine designed to withstand pressure when submerged

pressure ice *n* **:** ice in rough irregular ridges formed in the arctic seas when large areas of sea ice press against each other

pressure jump line *n* **:** a line along which an atmospheric pressure wave produces a sudden increase of pressure that often results in storms

pressure nozzle *n* **1** *aeronautics* **:** PITOT-STATIC TUBE **2** *aeronautics* **:** a combination of a venturi tube and either a pitot or a static tube in which each of the two tubes is joined to a differential pressure gauge the scale of which is calibrated to indicate the velocity of airflow

pressure plate *n* **:** a plate in an automobile dry disk clutch that is pressed against the flywheel to transmit propulsion torque to the wheels

pressure point *n* **:** a region of the body in which the distribution of soft and skeletal parts is such that a static position (as of a part in a cast or of a bedfast person) tends to cause circulatory deficiency and necrosis due to local compression of blood vessels — compare BEDSORE

pressure ridge *n* **:** a ridge produced on floating ice by buckling or crushing under lateral pressure of wind or tide or on a congealing lava flow by the continued movement of its liquid interior

pressures *pl of* PRESSURE, *pres 3d sing of* PRESSURE

pressure saucepan *n* **:** a small pressure cooker

pressure-sensitive \ˈ=ˈ=,=(=)=\ *adj* **:** responsive to pressure **:** adhering or sealing under the influence of pressure alone ⟨*pressure-sensitive* adhesives are normally used in the form of adhesive tapes —V.N.Morris, C.L.Weidner, & N. St. Landau⟩

pressure shift *n* **:** a change in the wavelengths of the spectrum lines of a gas that results from compressing the gas and is often accompanied by a broadening of the lines

pressure sore *n* **:** BEDSORE

pressure spot *n* **:** one of the spots on the skin peculiarly sensitive to pressure — called also *touch spot*

pressure stage *n* **:** the stage in the process of expansion and of energy transformation in which steam after expanding through a predetermined pressure range in a steam turbine gives up its acquired kinetic energy to the moving blades without further drop in pressure — compare VELOCITY STAGE

pressure stop *n, phonetics* **:** a stop in the formation of which the air behind the articulation is compressed with consequent outrush of air when the articulation is broken — compare SUCTION STOP

pressure suit *n* **:** an inflatable suit for high-altitude flying to protect a flier's body from the dangerous effects of low atmospheric pressure

pressure tank *n* **:** a tank in which a liquid or gas is stored under pressure greater than atmospheric

pressure tube *n* **1 :** a heavy tube containing reagents and hermetically closed so that interaction of the contents can be brought about at a much higher pressure than would be possible in an open tube **2 :** BOURDON TUBE

pressure vessel *n* **:** a container (as a tank, boiler, shell, cylinder) subjected in use to disruptive pressure

pressure wave *n* **:** a wave (as a sound wave) in which the propagated disturbance is a variation of pressure in a material medium — called also *P-wave*

pressure welding *n* **:** welding in which pressure is used to complete the weld

pressuring *pres part of* PRESSURE

pres·sur·iza·tion \ˌpreshərəˈzāshən\ *n* -s **:** the action or process of pressurizing or the state of being pressurized

pres·sur·ize \ˈpreshə,rīz\ *vt* -ED/-ING/-S **1 :** to maintain near-normal atmospheric pressure in (as an aircraft cabin) during high-level flight by means of a supercharger **2 :** to apply pressure to **3 :** to design (as an airplane fuselage or a flier's inflatable suit) to withstand pressure **4 :** to force gas into (an oil well) to increase the flow of an adjacent well — **pres·sur·iz·er** \-zə(r)\ *n*

press warrant *n* **:** a warrant formerly given by the crown as authority to impress men into the navy

press wax *n* **:** the press cake from honeycombs after removal of the molten beeswax by filtration

press wheel *n* **:** a wheel attachment on an agricultural press drill for compacting the soil in the seeded furrows

presswoman \ˈ=,==\ *n, pl* **presswomen** *Brit* **:** a woman news reporter or journalist

presswork \ˈ=,=\ *n* **:** the operation, management, or product of a printing press; *esp* **:** the branch of printing concerned with the actual transfer of ink from printing surface to paper

[1]**prest** *adj* [ME, fr. OF, fr. L *praestus* ready — more at PRESTO] *obs* **:** READY, PROMPT, QUICK, PREPARED

[2]**prest** \ˈprest\ *n* -s [ME, fr. MF, loan, fr. OF, fr. *prester* to lend, give, fr. L *praestare* to be responsible for, perform, pay, give, fr. *praed-, praes* surety, bondsman (fr. *prae-* pre- + *vad-, vas* bail, security) + *stare* to stand — more at WED, STAND] **1** *obs* **a :** a loan of money; *esp* **:** a forced loan to the sovereign **b :** an advance on wages or on the cost of an undertaking **c :** PREST MONEY **2** *Eng law* **:** a duty formerly paid by the sheriff on his account into the exchequer or for money in his hands

[3]**prest** \"\ *archaic var of* PRESSED

pre·stab·i·lism \prēˈstabə,lizəm\ *n* -s [G *prästabilismus*, fr. *prästabilieren* to preestablish (fr. *prä-* pre- + *stabilieren* to establish, fr. L *stabilire*) + *-ismus* -ism — more at ESTABLISH] **1 :** the Leibnizian doctrine of preestablished harmony of body and mind **2 :** the Kantian view that the living organism embodies an initial tendency implanted by the first cause whereby its kind is reproduced

pres·ta·ble \ˈprestəbəl\ *adj* [obs. F, capable of being lent, fr. MF, inclined to grant, fr. *prester* to lend, give + *-able*] *archaic Scot* **:** PAYABLE

prestamp cover \ˈprē,stamp-\ *n* [*prestamp* fr. *pre-* + *stamp*, n.] **:** a philatelic cover of a date previous to the use of adhesive stamps **:** a stampless cover

pres·tant \ˈprestənt\ *n* -s [F, fr. L *praestant-, praestans*, pres. part. of *praestare* to be superior, be excellent, fr. *prae-* pre- + *stare* to stand — more at STAND] **:** PRINCIPAL 2g (1)

pre·state \prēˈstāt\ *vt* [L *praestatus*, past part. of *praestare* to be responsible for, perform, pay, give — more at PREST] **1** *Roman & civil law* **:** PERFORM **:** furnish pursuant to an obligation **:** UNDERTAKE **2** *Roman & civil law* **:** GUARANTEE, INDEMNIFY **3** *Roman & civil law* **:** to support by oath

pres·ta·tion \preˈstāshən\ *n* -s [ME, fr. MF, fr. LL *praestation-, praestatio* required payment, fr. L, warranty, fr. *praestatus* (past part. of *praestare* to be responsible for, perform, pay, give) + *-ion-, -io* -ion] **1** *feudal law* **:** a rent, tax, or due paid in kind or in services (as in return for the lord's warrant or authority for taking wood) **2** *civil law* **:** a performance of something due upon an obligation

prestation money *n* **:** annual dues formerly paid by archdeacons and other dignitaries of the Church of England to their bishop

pres·ter \ˈprestə(r)\ *n* -s [ME, fr. L, venomous snake, scorching whirlwind, fr. Gk *prēstēr* venomous snake, scorching whirlwind, neck vein swollen with anger, fr. *prēthein* to blow up, swell out, spout, blow into a flame — more at FROTH] **1** *obs* **:** a venomous snake **2** *obs* **:** a scorching whirlwind **3** *archaic* **:** a neck vein swollen with anger

pre·sternal \(ˈ)prē+\ *adj* [*presternum* + *-al*] **:** of or relating to the presternum

pre·sternum \"+\ *n* [NL, fr. *pre-* + *sternum*] **1 :** the anterior segment of the sternum of a mammal **:** MANUBRIUM **2 :** the first division of the sternum of a thoracic segment of an insect **:** the sclerite in front of the eusternum of the insect thorax

pres·ti·dig·i·ta·tion \ˌprestə,dijəˈtāshən\ *n* -s [F, fr. *prestidigitateur*, after such pairs as F *créateur* creator (fr. OF *creatour*) **:** *création* creation] **:** SLEIGHT OF HAND, LEGERDEMAIN

pres·ti·dig·i·ta·tor \ˌ==ˈdijə,tād·ə(r), -ātə-\ *n* -s [F *prestidigitateur*, alter. (influenced by *preste* quick, nimble — fr. MF, fr. OIt *presto* — & by L *digitus* finger) of *prestigiateur*, fr. L *praestigiator* — more at TOE] **:** one skilled in legerdemain **:** a performer of sleight of hand ⟨is a sort of literary ~: he can make something out of nothing, and keep any number of verbal notions in the air simultaneously —F.B.Millett⟩ — **pres·ti·dig·i·ta·to·ri·al** \ˌ==ˈ=dijəd·əˈtōrēəl\ *adj* — **pres·ti·dig·i·ta·tory** \-d·ə,tōrē\ *adj*

pres·tige \(ˈ)preˈstēzh *also* -ēj *sometimes* ˈprestij *or* -ˌtēj\ *n* -s [F, fr. LL *praestigium*, irreg. fr. L *praestigiae* (pl.) conjurer's tricks, alter. of (assumed) L *praestrigiae*, fr. L *praestringere* to bind, tie up, blind, fr. *prae-* pre- + *stringere* to draw tight — more at STRAIN] **1** *archaic* **:** a conjurer's trick **:** ILLUSION, DECEPTION **2 :** standing or estimation in the eyes of people **:** weight or credit in general opinion **:** ASCENDANCY, HONOR, INFLUENCE, REPUTATION ⟨the power and ~ of the aristocracy and the landed gentry were unimpaired —Bertrand Russell⟩ ⟨such luster — or ~ or mana — as individual writers possess is usually owed, not to the quality of their work, but to its public acceptance —*Times Lit. Supp.*⟩ **syn** see INFLUENCE

pres·tig·i·a·tion \pre,stijēˈāshən\ *n* -s [LL *praestigiatus* (past part. of *praestigiare* to do conjurer's tricks, fr. L *praestigiae*) + E *-ion*] *archaic* **:** the performance of tricks of magic or illusion

pres·tig·i·a·tor \ˈ=ˈ==,ād·ə(r)\ *n* -s [L *praestigiator*, fr. *praestigiae* + *-ator*] *archaic* **:** CONJURER, MAGICIAN

pres·tig·i·ous \(ˈ)preˈstijəs, -tēj-, *also* ˌprəˈ-\ *adj* [L *praestigiosus* full of tricks, deceitful, fr. *praestigiae* + *-osus* -ose] **1** *archaic* **:** of, relating to, or marked by illusion, conjuring, or trickery **2 :** having an illustrious name or reputation **:** esteemed in general opinion **:** HONORED ⟨the most ~ club in town preserves a tenuous artistic tradition —A.L.Guérard⟩ ⟨the ~ or the desirable things of the earth, craved for by predatory natures —Joseph Conrad⟩ — **pres·tig·i·ous·ly** *adv* — **pres·tig·i·ous·ness** *n* -ES

[1]**pres·tis·si·mo** \preˈstisə,mō\ *adv (or adj)* [It, fr. *presto* quick + *-issimo*, suffix denoting a high degree (fr. L *-issimus*, superl. suffix)] **:** at a very rapid tempo — used as a direction in music

[2]**prestissimo** \"\ *n* -s **:** a movement or passage performed prestissimo

prest money *n* [ME *prest moneye* money paid in advance, fr. [2]*prest* + *moneye* money] *obs* **:** money advanced to men enlisting in the British army or navy **:** IMPREST

[1]**pres·to** \ˈpre(,)stō\ *adv (or adj)* [It, adv. & adj., quickly, quick; It *presto*, adv., fr. L *praesto* at hand, on the spot, fr. *prae-* pre- + *-sto* (perh. akin to L *situs*, past part. of *sinere* to lay, let, leave); It *presto*, adj., fr. L *praestus* ready, fr. *praesto* — more at SITE] **1 :** in haste **:** QUICKLY, IMMEDIATELY — used orig. as a magician's command **2 :** at a rapid tempo — used as a direction in music — compare PRESTISSIMO

[2]**presto** \"\ *n* -s **:** a musical passage or movement in rapid tempo

[1]**presto chan·go** \-ˈchān(,)jō\ *v imper* [[1]*presto* + *chango* (fr. *change* + *-o* — as in [1]*presto*)] **:** change quickly — used orig. as a magician's command

[2]**presto chango** \"\ *n* **:** a sudden transformation as if by magic ⟨suggest that the solution of social and political ills lay in . . . a moral *presto chango* —Irwin Edman⟩

pre·sto·mal \prēˈstōməl\ *adj* [*prestom*um + *-al*] **:** of or relating to a prestomum

pre·sto·mum \-məm\ *n, pl* **presto·ma** \-ōmə\ *also* **presto·mums** [NL, fr. *pre-* + *-stomum*] **:** the cleft between the labellar lobes in front of the oral aperture in insects

pres·ton \ˈprestən\ *adj, usu cap* [fr. *Preston*, Lancashire, England] **:** of or from Preston, Lancashire, England **:** of the kind or style prevalent in Preston

preston salts *n* [prob. fr. the name *Preston*] **:** smelling salts consisting of ammonium carbonate in ammonia water with an essential oil

pre·stress \(ˈ)prē+\ *vt* [*pre-* + *stress*] **:** to introduce internal stresses into (a building material) to counteract the stresses that will result from applied load (as in incorporating wires or cables under tension in concrete)

prests *pl of* PREST

pre·subiculum \ˌprē+\ *n* [NL, fr. *pre-* + *subiculum*] **:** the part of the hippocampal convolution lying between the subiculum and the main olfactory region

pre·sum·able \prēˈz(y)üməbəl, prəˈ-\ *adj* [F *présumable*, fr. MF *presumable*, fr. *presumer* to presume + *-able*] **:** capable of being presumed **:** acceptable as an assumption **:** credible on its face or without close inquiry **:** PROBABLE

pre·sum·ably \-blē, -li\ *adv* **:** by reasonable assumption **:** as a ready supposition **:** PROBABLY

pre·sume \-üm\ *vb* -ED/-ING/-S [ME *presumen* to dare, anticipate, suppose, fr. LL & MF; ME *presumen* to dare, fr. LL *praesumere*, fr. L, to anticipate, suppose, take in advance, fr. *prae-* pre- + *sumere* to take, fr. *sub-* + *emere* to buy, obtain; ME *presumen* to anticipate, suppose, fr. MF *presumer*, fr. L *praesumere* — more at REDEEM] *vt* **1 :** to take upon oneself without leave, authority, or warrant **:** undertake rashly **:** DARE ⟨men who *presumed* to guide human thought —R.E.Coker⟩ **2 :** to look confidently forward to **:** ANTICIPATE, EXPECT ⟨the reading public . . . might be *presumed* to know that dynamite and poison have a certain deadly quality —Norman Birkett⟩ **3 :** to accept as true or credible without proof or before inquiry **:** ASSUME, INFER, SUPPOSE ⟨until a man or an organization has been condemned by due process of law he or it must be *presumed* innocent —R.M.Hutchins⟩ **4 :** to raise a presumption of or that **:** take for granted **:** IMPLY ⟨they ~ a fairly high degree of sensitivity and discernment in the reader —Anthony Quinton⟩ ~ *vi* **:** to take a permission or privilege for granted **:** be brash **:** take liberties **:** act presumptuously ⟨ignorance ~s where understanding is reticent⟩ **syn** see PRESUPPOSE — **presume on** *or* **presume upon 1 :** to base expectations on **:** rely on ⟨it was unsafe to *presume* too much *on* their fidelity —J.A. Froude⟩ **2 :** to place presumptuous reliance on **:** count on brashly **:** dare excessively on the strength of ⟨*presumed* abominably *on* an all too brief acquaintance⟩

pre·sumed \-md\ *adj* **:** ASSUMED, SUPPOSED — **pre·sumed·ly** \-m(ə)dlē\ *adv*

pre·sum·er \-mə(r)\ *n* -s **:** one that presumes

presuming *adj* **:** PRESUMPTUOUS — **pre·sum·ing·ly** *adv*

pre·sump·tion \prēˈzəm(p)shən, prəˈ-\ *n* -s [ME *presumpcioun* presumptuous attitude or conduct, assumption, fr. OF *presumption*, fr. LL *praesumption-, praesumptio* presumptuous attitude or conduct (fr. L) & L *praesumption-, praesumptio* assumption, fr. L *praesumptus* (past part. of *praesumere* to anticipate, suppose, take in advance) + *-ion-, -io* -ion — more at PRESUME] **1 :** presumptuous attitude or conduct **:** the taking of too much on oneself **:** the overstepping of limits of propriety, courtesy, or morality **:** AUDACITY, EFFRONTERY ⟨the two qualities most generally associated with Satan were acuteness of intellect and ~ of Spirit —Irving Kristol⟩ ⟨you know nothing about the . . . law, and yet you have the ~ to attempt to influence me —Kenneth Roberts⟩ **2 a :** an attitude or belief dictated by probability **:** ASSUMPTION ⟨the ~ is on the side of established moral law —J.A.Pike⟩ **b :** the ground, reason, or evidence lending probability to a belief **3** *law* **:** an inference as to the existence of the fact not certainly known from the known or proved existence of some other fact, sometimes operating as evidence, sometimes as a rule of procedure as to who must proceed with evidence on the main issue, or as to who has the burden of proof and sometimes having no effect as evidence, once evidence on the issue is in — distinguished from *fiction*

presumption of fact *law* **:** a presumption founded on a previous experience or general knowledge of connection between a known fact and one inferred from it — called also *logical presumption*

presumption of innocence : a rebuttable presumption in favor of the defendant in a criminal action imposing on the prosecution the burden of proving him guilty beyond reasonable doubt

presumption of law : a presumption (as of innocence) founded on a rule or policy of the law regardless of what the actual fact may be — compare IRREBUTTABLE PRESUMPTION, REBUTTABLE PRESUMPTION

presumption of survivorship : the legal presumption in the absence of direct evidence that of two or more persons dying in a common disaster (as a shipwreck) one survived the others because known to be younger, stronger, or otherwise more likely to survive

pre·sump·tive \-(p)tiv, -tēv *also* -təv\ *adj* [ML *praesumptivus*, fr. LL, presumptuous, fr. L *praesumptus* (past part. of *praesumere* to anticipate, suppose, take in advance) + *-ivus* -ive] **1 a :** giving grounds for reasonable opinion or belief ⟨~ evidence⟩ ⟨an extremely strong ~ case is made out —J.A. Hobson⟩ **b :** based on probability or presumption ⟨the ~ heir⟩ **2** [prob. fr. LL *praesumptivus*] *archaic* **:** PRESUMPTUOUS **3 :** based on inference **:** APPARENT, PRESUMED ⟨the ~ visit cannot be established as certain⟩ **4** *embryol* **a :** expected to develop in a particular direction under normal conditions ⟨~ region of the blastula⟩ **b :** being the embryonic precursor of ⟨~ neural tissue⟩

presumptive evidence *n* **:** CIRCUMSTANTIAL EVIDENCE

pre·sump·tive·ly \-tə̇vlē, -li\ *adv* **:** in a presumptive manner **:** by presumption **:** PRESUMABLY

pre·sump·tu·ous \prēˈzəm(p)chəwəs, prəˈ-, -)chəs, -)sh-\ *adj* [ME, fr. MF *presumptueux*, fr. LL *praesumptuosus*, *praesumptiosus*, fr. *praesumptio* presumptuous attitude or conduct + L *-osus* -ose — more at PRESUMPTION] **:** overstepping due bounds (as of propriety in conduct) **:** assuming a prerogative, privilege, or permission without warrant **:** taking liberties **:** manifesting presumption **:** OVERWEENING ⟨enforced the doctor's orders in a way which seemed to him loud and ~ —Glenway Wescott⟩ **syn** see CONFIDENT

pre·sump·tu·ous·ly *adv* [ME, fr. *presumptuous* + *-ly*] **:** in a presumptuous manner

pre·sump·tu·ous·ness *n* -ES [ME *presumptuousnes*, fr. *presumptuous* + *-nes* -ness] **:** the quality or state of being presumptuous

pre·supervisory \(ˈ)prē+\ *adj* [*pre-* + *supervisory*] **:** preparing for or preliminary to supervisory work

pre·sup·pos·al \ˌprēsəˈpōzəl\ *n* [*presuppose* + *-al*] *archaic* **:** PRESUPPOSITION

pre·sup·pose \-ōz\ *vt* [ME *presupposen*, fr. MF *presupposer*, modif. (influenced by *poser* to put, place) of ML *praesupponere* (perfect stem *praesuppos-*), fr. L *prae-* pre- + ML *supponere* to suppose — more at SUPPOSE] **1 :** to suppose beforehand **:** form an opinion or judgment of in advance **:** EXPECT ⟨~s that we are acquainted with the general outline —Daniel George⟩ **2 :** to require as a necessary antecedent condition in logic or fact **:** IMPLY ⟨true amiability ~s discernment, tact, a sense for what other people really feel and want —George Santayana⟩ ⟨every act of ours . . . ~s a balance of thought, feeling, and will — Joseph Conrad⟩

syn PRESUME, ASSUME, POSTULATE, PREMISE, POSIT: PRESUPPOSE indicates a taking for granted of something as true or existent, ranging from hazy, casual, uncritical acceptance or belief to certainty through the requirements of logical causation ⟨Puritanism *presupposed* an intelligent clergy capable of interpreting Scripture —*Amer. Guide Series: Mass.*⟩ ⟨culture, which exists only through man, who is also a social animal, *presupposes* society —A.L.Kroeber⟩ PRESUME may imply that whatever is taken for granted is entitled to belief until disproved; broadly it may imply casual conjecture ⟨everyone charged with a penal offense has the right to be *presumed* innocent until proved guilty —*U.N. Declaration of Human Rights*⟩ ⟨nobody in Baskul had known much about him except that he had arrived from Persia, where it was *presumed* he had something to do with oil —James Hilton⟩ ASSUME indicates arbitrary or deliberate acceptance of something not proved or demonstrated or susceptible of being proved or demonstrated, or acceptance in accord with what evidence is available ⟨there are many laws at present which are inequitable, because, for example, they *assume* a freedom of choice on the part of one party which under existing social circumstances is not there —Norbert Wiener⟩ ⟨if we take the witness at his word and *assume* that he has this fear —B.N.Meltzer⟩ POSTULATE may suggest assumption acknowledged as indemonstrable but accepted as true because indispensable as the basis for some thought series or procedure ⟨the prevailing theological system is one which *postulates* the reality of guidance by a personal god —Aldous Huxley⟩ ⟨in the field of chemistry the nature philosophers *postulated* that electrical forces were responsible for the combination of chemical substances, a theory which enjoyed a considerable following when experimental evidence for the view was later discovered —S.F.Mason⟩ PREMISE indicates laying down a proposition from which an inference can be drawn or stating facts and principles fundamental to an argument ⟨Bentham's hopes for such a "hedonistic" or "felicific calculus" and for a system of legislation and jurisprudence constructed by its use were *premised* on the assumption that pleasures and pains can be compared quantitatively —Lucius Garvin⟩ POSIT may apply to something premised as a truth or declared conviction ⟨St. Thomas *posits* the composition of substance and accident as the objective basis of mathematical abstraction —F.G.Connolly⟩

pre·sup·po·si·tion \ˌprē,səpəˈzishən\ *n* [MF, fr. ML *praesupposition-, praesuppositio*, fr. *praesuppositus* (past part. of *praesupponere*) + L *-ion-, -io* -ion] **:** an act of presupposing or an assumption made in advance **:** a preliminary supposition **:** POSTULATE

pre·sup·po·si·tion·less \-nləs\ *adj* **:** lacking presuppositions

pre·sup·pres·sion \ˌprēsəˈpreshən\ *n* [*pre-* + *suppression*] **:** effective work in fire control prior to any actual fire **:** forest fire control activities including both prevention and suppression

pre·surgical \(ˈ)prē+\ *adj* [*pre-* + *surgical*] **:** preliminary to surgery ⟨~ procedures⟩

pre·sylvian \(ˈ)prē+\ *adj* [*pre-* + *sylvian* (as in *sylvian fissure*)] **:** in front of the lateral fissure of the brain

pre·systole \"+\ *n* [NL, fr. *pre-* + *systole*] **:** the interval just preceding cardiac systole — **pre·systolic** \ˌprē+\ *adj*

pret *abbr* preterit

pre·ta \ˈprād·ə\ *n* -s [Skt, fr. *pra-* before, forward, away + *ita* gone, past part. of *eti* he goes — more at FOR, ISSUE] **1** *Hinduism* **:** a wandering spirit of a dead person who is not at rest **2** *Buddhism* **:** an unresting ghost tortured incessantly by hunger and thirst

pre·tan \(ˈ)prē+\ *vt* [*pre-* + *tan*] **:** to tan (leather) prior to the main tanning

pre·tarsus \(ˈ)prē+\ *n* [NL, fr. *pre-* + *tarsus*] **:** a terminal outgrowth of the arthropod tarsus **:** DACTYLOPODITE

pre·taste \ˈprē+,-\ *n* [*pre-* + *taste*] **:** FORETASTE

pretaxation *var of* PRAETAXATION

pre·technical \(ˈ)prē+\ *adj* [*pre-* + *technical*] **:** existing prior to technological development

pre·tectal \"+\ *adj* [*pre-* + *tectum* + *-al*] **:** situated in front of the tectum; *esp* **:** lying at the junction of the diencephalon and the tectum and being associated with analysis and distribution of visual impulses ⟨~ nucleus of nerve cells⟩ ⟨~ area⟩

pre·temporal \"+\ *adj* [NL *pretemporalis*, fr. *pre-* + LL *temporalis* temporal, of the temples] **:** situated in front of the temporal bone

[1]**pre·tend** \prēˈtend, prəˈ-\ *vb* -ED/-ING/-S [ME *pretenden*, fr. L *praetendere* to stretch forth, spread before, bring forward as an excuse, allege, fr. *prae-* pre- + *tendere* to stretch — more at THIN] *vt* **1 a :** to hold out the appearance of being, possessing, or performing **:** PROFESS ⟨does not ~ to be a social scientist —R.G.Ross⟩ **b :** ASSERT, CLAIM ⟨in cheap years, it is ~*ed*, workmen are generally more idle —Adam Smith⟩ **2 a :** to make believe **:** FEIGN, SHAM ⟨~ to be angry⟩ ⟨~*ed* to be deaf⟩ **b :** to hold out, represent, or assert falsely **:** put forward or offer as true or real (something untrue or unreal) **:** show hypocritically or deceitfully ⟨man who ~s to be dead so as to evade his creditors and collect on his insurance —P.G. Wodehouse & Guy Bolton⟩ **3 a :** PRESUME, VENTURE ⟨how that vehicle got to Sidney I do not ~ to say —Rachel Henning⟩ **b** *archaic* **:** UNDERTAKE, ATTEMPT ⟨she could not ~ to go into the sea without proper attendants —Tobias Smollett⟩ **c** *archaic* **:** INTEND **4 a** *obs* **:** to hold out before one **:** EXTEND, OFFER **b** *obs* **:** to hold out as a disguise for something else ~ *vi* **1** *obs* **:** to direct one's course or efforts **:** ASPIRE ⟨those persons who ~ toward Heaven —Jeremy Taylor⟩ **2 :** to feign an action, part, or role in or as if in play **:** make believe ⟨never sincere, always ~*ing*⟩ **3 a :** to put in a claim **:** lay claim **:** allege a title — used with *to* ⟨those ~*ing* to office were theorists —C.L.Jones⟩ ⟨for the other sciences . . . I can ~ to no special competence —Stuart Chase⟩ **b** *archaic* **:** to make suit **syn** see ASSUME

[2]**pretend** \"\ *adj* **:** MAKE-BELIEVE, IMAGINARY, PRETENDED ⟨dangle our legs in the water and see who could catch the most ~ fish —H.E.Giles⟩ **:** IMITATION ⟨~ pearls⟩

pre·tend·ant \-dənt\ *n* -s [MF, fr. *pretendant*, pres. part. of *pretendre* to claim, aspire, fr. L *praetendere*] **:** PRETENDER, CLAIMANT

pre·tend·ed \-də̇d\ *adj* [ME, fr. past part. of *pretenden*] **1 a :** SO-CALLED, ALLEGED ⟨~ neutrality⟩ **b :** professed or avowed but not genuine ⟨~ loyalty⟩ ⟨a ~ friend⟩ **2** *obs* **:** INTENDED, PROPOSED ⟨notice of their . . . ~ flight —Shak.⟩ — **pre·tend·ed·ly** *adv*

pre·tend·er \-ndə(r)\ *n* -s **:** one that pretends: as **a :** one who lays claim or asserts a title to something **:** CLAIMANT; *specif* **:** a claimant to a throne who is held to have no just title **b :** one who makes a false or hypocritical show **:** one who simulates or feigns

pre·tend·er·ism \-də,rizəm\ *n* -s [*pretender* + *-ism*; fr. the use of the term "Old Pretender" as a nickname for James Francis Edward Stuart †1766 claimant to the throne of England by virtue of being the only son of the deposed Stuart king James II, and the use of the term "Young Pretender" as a nickname for Charles Edward Louis Philip Casimir Stuart †1788 claimant to the throne of England by virtue of being the elder son of James Francis Edward Stuart] : support or agitation for the deposed Stuart dynasty in England

¹pre·tense *or* **pre·tence** \prē'ten(t)s, prə'-, 'prē,t-\ *n* -s [ME, fr. MF *pretensse*, fr. (assumed) ML *praetensa*, fr. LL, fem. of *praetensus* (L *praetentus*), past part. of L *praetendere*] **1 :** claim made or implied ⟨theory which has made the . . . greatest ~ of having a scientific foundation —John Dewey⟩; *esp* : a claim indicated outwardly but not supported by fact ⟨the ~ that one does not use theater music in religious ceremonies —Virgil Thomson⟩ **2 a :** mere ostentation : PRETENTIOUSNESS ⟨confuse dignity with pomposity and ~ —Bennett Cerf⟩ **b :** a pretentious act or assertion ⟨it would be a delight to talk without ~ —Louis Bromfield⟩ **3 :** an attempt to attain a certain condition or quality ⟨the people were so overwhelmingly ignorant that democracy could only be a ~ —C.L.Jones⟩ ⟨laboring . . . to keep some ~ of order in San Antonio —Green Peyton⟩ — often used with *at* ⟨without ~ at general inclusiveness —Frank Weitenkampf⟩ **4 a** *obs* : INTENTION, PURPOSE **b :** professed rather than real intention or purpose : COVER, PRETEXT, EXCUSE ⟨felt as though he were there under false ~s —Joseph Conrad⟩ ⟨under a ~ of personal devotion to a country in which he was not born —O.S.J. Gogarty⟩ **5 a :** something alleged or believed on slight grounds : an unwarranted assumption ⟨mother's affectionate ~ of his being head of the family —Mary Austin⟩ **b :** MAKE-BELIEVE, FICTION **6 :** the act of offering something false or feigned : presentation of what is deceptive or hypocritical : deception by showing what is unreal and concealing what is real : false show : SIMULATION ⟨made a ~ of searching his pockets for cigarettes⟩ ⟨saw through his ~ of indifference⟩

²pretense *or* **pretence** *vt* -ED/-ING/-S [prob. back-formation fr. *pretensed*] *obs* : PRETEND

pre·tensed \-st\ *adj* [ME, fr. LL *praetensus* (L *praetentus*) (past part. of L *praetendere*) + ME *-ed*] *archaic* : PRETENDED

pre·tense·less \-sləs\ *adj* : not having or making pretenses : STRAIGHTFORWARD, SINCERE

¹pre·ten·sion *also* **pre·ten·tion** \prē'tenchən, prə'-\ *n* -s [*pretension* fr. ML *praetension-*, *praetensio*, fr. LL *praetensus* (L *praetentus*) (past part. of L *praetendere* to stretch forth, spread before, bring forward as an excuse, allege) + L *-ion-*, *-io* -ion; *pretention* fr. ML *praetention-*, *praetentio*, fr. L *praetentus* (past part. of *praetendere*) + *-ion-*, *-io* -ion — more at PRETEND] **1 :** an assertion or declaration whose truth is questioned : an allegation of doubtful value : PRETEXT ⟨this was but an invention and ~ given out by the Spaniards —Francis Bacon⟩ **2 :** a claim or an effort to establish a claim : formal demand for recognition of a title, right, or privilege ⟨~ to the throne⟩ **3 :** a tacit, asserted, or obvious claim, right, or title : claim to attention, consideration, or honor because of real or alleged superiority, merit, or ability ⟨country estate of some ~s⟩ ⟨people of ~ to taste and culture⟩ **4 :** ASPIRATION, INTENTION ⟨serious ~s as a writer⟩ **5 :** PRETENTIOUSNESS, VANITY ⟨a quality of ~ and pseudoculture about the program that I found distasteful —Philip Hamburger⟩ ⟨the class which has the ~s and prejudices and habits of the rich without its money —G.B.Shaw⟩

²pre·tension \(')prē+\ *vt* [*pre-* + *tension*] : to prestress (reinforced concrete) by subjecting the steel reinforcement to tension before the concrete hardens

pre·ten·sion·less \prē'tenchənləs\ *adj* : lacking pretension : UNPRETENTIOUS

pre·ten·sive \prē'ten(t)siv\ *adj* [¹*pretense* + *-ive*] **1 :** having the character of a pretense ⟨~ farming carried on for instruction and experiment⟩ **2 :** PRETENTIOUS

pre·ten·tious \prē'tenchəs, prə'-\ *adj* [F *prétentieux*, fr. *prétention* pretension (fr. ML *praetention-*, *praetentio*) + *-eux* -ous] **1 :** making or possessing claims (as to excellence, superiority, greatness) : OSTENTATIOUS, SHOWY, POMPOUS ⟨~ literary style⟩ ⟨~ country house⟩ : SELF-IMPORTANT ⟨~ fraud who assumes a love of culture that is alien to him —Richard Watts⟩ **2 :** characterized by effort or strain : making demands upon one's skill, ability, or means : AMBITIOUS ⟨the ~ daring of the Green Mountain Boys in crossing the lake —*Amer. Guide Series: Vt.*⟩ — **pre·ten·tious·ly** *adv* — **pre·ten·tious·ness** *n* -ES

preter *adj* [by shortening] *obs* : PRETERIT

preter- *also* **praeter-** *comb form* [L *praeter* past, by, beyond, fr. L *prae* before — more at FOR] **1 :** past : by ⟨*preterist*⟩ **2 :** beyond the range of : surpassing ⟨*preternormal*⟩

pre·te·ri·ent \prē'tirēənt\ *adj* [irreg. fr. L *praetereunt-*, *praeteriens*, pres. part. of *praeterire* to go by, pass over] : TRANSIENT

¹pret·er·ist \'pred·ərəst, -rēd-\ *n* -s [*preter-* + *-ist*] : one who believes the prophecies of the Apocalypse to have been already fulfilled — compare FUTURIST, PRESENTIST

²preterist \"\ *adj* : of or relating to the preterists or their views

¹pret·er·it *or* **pret·er·ite** \'pred·ərət, -etə-, *usu* -əd·+V\ *adj* [ME *preterit*, fr. MF, fr. L *praeteritus*, past part. of *praeterire* to go by, pass over, fr. *praeter* past, by, beyond + *ire* to go — more at ISSUE] **1** *archaic* : belonging wholly to the past : BYGONE, FORMER **2 :** of, relating to, or constituting a verb tense that indicates action in the past without implication as to duration, continuance, or repetition — **pret·er·it·ness** *or* **preteriteness** *n* -ES

²preterit *or* **preterite** \"\ *n* -s **1 :** the preterit tense of a language **2 :** a verb form in the preterit tense

pre·ter·i·tal \prē'terəd·ᵊl\ *adj* : of or relating to the preterit

pret·er·i·tion \,pred·ə'rishən\ *n* -s [LL *praeterition-*, *praeteritio*, fr. L *praeteritus* (past part. of *praeterire*) + *-ion-*, *-io* -ion] **1 :** PRETERMISSION 1 **2 :** PARALEIPSIS **3 :** the Calvinistic doctrine that having elected to eternal life such as he chose God passed over the rest leaving them to eternal death — compare REPROBATION b

¹preterit-present \¦==¦==\ *n* [trans. of NL *praeterito-praesens*] : a preterit-present verb form

²preterit-present *or* **preterite-present** \"\ *adj, of a verb* : preterit in form and origin but present in meaning

pre·ter·la·bent \,prēd·ə(r)'lābənt\ *adj* [L *praeterlabent-*, *praeterlabens*, pres. part. of *praeterlabi* to glide by, fr. *praeter* past, by, beyond + *labi* to glide — more at SLEEP] *of a stream* : flowing beside or by

pre·terminal \(')prē+\ *adj* [*pre-* + *terminal*] : occurring before death ⟨~ rise of body temperature⟩

pre·ter·mis·sion \,prēd·ə(r)'mishən, -ētə(-\ *n* -s [L *praetermission-*, *praetermissio*, fr. *praetermissus* (past part. of *praetermittere*) + *-ion-*, *-io* -ion] **1 :** the act or an instance of pretermitting : OMISSION **2 :** PARALEIPSIS **3** *Roman & civil law* : a passing over in silence by a testator of an apparent heir

pre·ter·mit \-it, *usu* -id·+V\ *vt* **pretermitted**; **pretermitted**; **pretermitting**; **pretermits** [L *praetermittere* to let pass, omit, overlook, fr. *praeter* past, by, beyond + *mittere* to let go, send — more at SMITE] **1 :** to let pass without mention, notice, or attention : pass by or over : OMIT ⟨~ all personal references in an account⟩ ⟨~ children in a will⟩ **2 :** to leave undone, unsaid, unused : NEGLECT **3 :** break off : INTERRUPT, SUSPEND ⟨if only reparations were temporarily *pretermitted* —R.F.Harrod⟩

pre·ter·nat·u·ral \,prēd·ə(r)'nach(ə)rəl, -ētə(r)-\ *adj* [ML *praeternaturalis*, fr. L *praeter naturam* beyond nature (fr. *praeter* past, by, beyond + *naturam*, accus. of *natura* nature) + *-alis* -al] **1 :** existing outside of nature : NONNATURAL; *sometimes* : SUPERNATURAL ⟨thoughts, beliefs, and rituals of mankind . . . ~ origins for these aspects of human activity were still widely postulated —H.J.Fleure⟩ **2 :** exceeding in degree or intensity what is natural or regular in nature : ABNORMAL, EXCEPTIONAL ⟨wits trained to ~ acuteness by the debates of the law courts and the assembly —G.L.Dickinson⟩ ⟨composed her features into an appearance of ~ pleasantness —J.C.Snaith⟩ **3 :** lying beyond or outside ordinary experience : inexplicable by ordinary means ⟨~ phenomena, among which the alleged psychic phenomena are perhaps the most spectacular —Herbert Spiegelberg⟩ ⟨notions that ~ powers and human action were inextricably linked —W.V. O'Connor⟩ — **pre·ter·nat·u·ral·ly** \-rəlē, -li\ *adv* — **pre·ter·nat·u·ral·ness** *n*

pre·ter·nat·u·ral·ism \,==ˈnach(ə)rə,lizəm\ *n* **1 :** the quality or state of being preternatural **2 :** something preternatural **3 :** belief in or recognition of the preternatural

¹pre·test \'prē,test\ *n* [*pre-* + *test*] : a preliminary test serving for exploration rather than evaluation: as **a :** a test given to a class to determine readiness for the material about to be taught **b :** a test given to make students aware of their own needs and prepare them for a final and decisive test **c :** a field trial of those techniques (as questionnaires, interviews, schedules) commonly used in testing the public in order to determine their efficiency as instruments of research ⟨a ~ of a public opinion poll⟩ **d :** the advance testing of something intended for public sale or intended to influence public taste in order to determine its probable reception ⟨a ~ for a new line of merchandise⟩

²pre·test \(')=¦=\ *vt* : to subject to a pretest ~ *vi* : to give a pretest

¹pre·text \'prē,tekst\ *n* -s [L *praetextus*, fr. *praetextus*, past part. of *praetexere* to weave in front, fringe, adorn, assign as a pretext, fr. *prae-* pre- + *texere* to weave — more at TECHNICAL] : a purpose or motive alleged or an appearance assumed in order to cloak the real intention or state of affairs : EXCUSE, PRETENSE, COVER **syn** see APOLOGY

²pretext \='=\ *vt* -ED/-ING/-S : to use or allege as a pretext ⟨~*ing* an early engagement in town next morning —W.S. Maugham⟩

pretexta *var of* PRAETEXTA

pre·thin \(')prē+\ *vt* [*pre-* + *thin*] : to thin (a heavy set of fruit) by hand or by the use of a caustic or a hormone spray in order to increase the quality of the remaining fruit and to stimulate flower bud production for the following year

pre·thoracic \¦prē+\ *adj* [*pre-* + *thoracic*] : situated above or anterior to the thorax; *specif* : lying above or anterior to those vertebrae bearing thoracic ribs ⟨~ vertebrae⟩

pre·thoughtful \(')prē+\ *adj* [*pre-* + *thoughtful*] : FORETHOUGHTFUL, PRUDENT — **pre·thought·ful·ly** *adv* — **pre·thought·ful·ness** *n*

pre·tibial \(')prē+\ *adj* [ISV *pre-* + *tibial*] : lying or occurring in front of the tibia ⟨a ~ skin rash⟩ ⟨~ edema⟩

pretibial fever *n* : a disease characterized by an eruption in the pretibial region, headache, backache, malaise, chills, and fever, and believed to be caused by a virus

pre·til \prä'tēl\ *n* -s [AmerSp, fr. Sp, parapet, railing, irreg. fr. L *pector-*, *pectus* breast — more at PECTORAL] : an adobe wall continued above the roof to form a low parapet

pre·ti·um af·fec·ti·o·nis \'pred·ēəm,əfektē'ōnəs\ *n, pl* **pretia affectionis** \-d·ēə-\ [L, price of affection] : a factitious value placed upon a thing by its owner because of some sentimental association or a whim

prêt-nom \'pre'nōⁿ\ *n, pl* **prêt-noms** \"\ [F *prête-nom*, fr. *prêter* to lend (fr. OF *prester*) + *nom* name, fr. L *nomen* — more at PREST, NAME] *civil law* : one who lends his name to another to use

pre·tone \'prē,tōn\ *n* [*pre-* + *tone*] : a sound or syllable immediately preceding the accented syllable

pre·tonic \(')prē+\ *adj* [ISV *pre-* + *tonic*] **1** *of a sound* : immediately preceding or constituting one of a succession of consonants immediately preceding a vowel having stress **2** *of a syllable* : immediately preceding a syllable having stress

pre·tophaceous \¦prē+\ *adj* [*pre-* + *tophaceous*] : existing before the development of tophi ⟨~ stage of gout⟩

pretor *var of* PRAETOR

pre·to·ria \prē'tōrēə, prə'-, -tȯr-\ *adj, usu cap* [fr. *Pretoria*, Union of So. Africa] : of or from Pretoria, the administrative capital of the Union of So. Africa : of the kind or style prevalent in Pretoria

pretorial *var of* PRAETORIAL

pretorial court *n* : a proprietary court of the Colony of Maryland with jurisdiction of capital crimes

pre·treat \(')prē+\ *vt* [*pre-* + *treat*] : to treat previously ⟨~ water with a coagulant before filtering⟩ — **pre·treat·ment** \prē'trētmənt\ *n*

pre·trial \'prē+,-\ *n* [*pre-* + *trial*] : a conference preliminary to a hearing or trial on the merits where a judge, referee, examiner, arbitrator, or other quasi-judicial officer endeavors to simplify the issues of law or fact in a case by ascertaining what is admitted, what is contested, whether certain matters may be stipulated thereby avoiding the expense of proof in order to save time and expense at the trial

pret·ti·fi·ca·tion \,prid·əfə'kāshən\ *n* -s [fr. *prettify*, after such pairs as E *ossify: ossification*] : the act, process, or result of prettifying ⟨an excess of ~ and sentimentality, a failure to stick to what the composer has written —Howard Taubman⟩

pret·ti·fi·er \'prid·ə,fī(ə)r, -itə,-\ *n* -s : one that prettifies

pret·ti·fy \-fī\ *vt* -ED/-ING/-ES [*pretty* + *-fy*] **1 :** to make pretty : adorn esp. in a petty or overnice way **2 :** SOFTEN, PALLIATE ⟨accounts of this series of battles have often been *prettified*⟩

pret·ti·ly \'prid·ᵊlē, -it|, |ᵊli, |əl-\ *adv* [ME *prattily*, fr. *prety*, *praty*, *pratty* pretty + *-ly*] **1 :** in a pretty manner : CHARMINGLY ⟨blushed ~⟩ **2 :** POINTEDLY, APTLY ⟨~ punished by the Gods for my neglect of you —Robert Graves⟩

pret·ti·ness \|ēnəs, |in-\ *n* -ES **1 :** the quality or state of being pretty **2 a :** a pretty or prettyish action, thing, characteristic, or remark **b :** a pretty ornament : AFFECTATION

¹pret·ty \'prid·ē, |t|, |i *also* 'pu̇r|, *-R sometimes* 'pu̇|\ *adj* -ER/-EST [ME *prety*, *praty*, fr. OE *prættig* tricky, fr. *prætt* trick + *-ig* -y; akin to MD *perte* trick, ON *prettr*] **1 a :** marked by or calling for skillful dexterity or artful care and ingenuity esp. in coping with some difficult or complicated matter ⟨the most consummate of ~ hypocrites —Lafcadio Hearn⟩ ⟨keeping up with the elusive dictators of fashion is a ~ game —A.L.Guérard⟩ **b :** extremely fitting or suitable : PAT, APT ⟨as ~ an example . . . as one can find —Oliver La Farge⟩ **2 a :** pleasing by delicacy or grace : superficially appealing rather than impressively or strikingly beautiful ⟨~ verses⟩ ⟨~ little garden⟩ **b :** having conventionally accepted elements (as proportion, shape, color) of beauty ⟨her ~, rather vapid features⟩ **c :** enjoyable for melody, lilt, or suggestion, but not intense, grand, or complex ⟨charming to the wise youth her ~ laughter sounded —George Meredith⟩ **d :** appearing or sounding pleasant or nice : suggesting charm, grace, or delicacy, but lacking strength, force, manliness, purpose, or intensity ⟨young man with a face that was ~ in a chorus-man way —Dashiell Hammett⟩ ⟨stringing ~ words that make no sense —Elizabeth B. Browning⟩ ⟨~ fancies of snow and moonlight —Nathaniel Hawthorne⟩ **3 a (1) :** FINE, GOOD ⟨a ~ bargain on the car being traded in⟩ (2) : POOR, MISERABLE, INDEFENSIBLE — used ironically ⟨a ~ state of affairs⟩ ⟨~ mess you've made of it⟩ ⟨you're a ~ one to talk about language now —Elinor Wylie⟩ **b** *archaic Scot* : strong and brave : STOUT ⟨six to ten ~ men were chosen as town guard —Mairi A. MacDonald⟩ **4 :** moderately large : CONSIDERABLE ⟨has a ~ collection of books —Tobias Smollett⟩ ⟨it may involve a ~ sum —T.B.Costain⟩ ⟨a very ~ profit⟩ ⟨his house cost him a ~ penny⟩ **5** *of weather* : FAIR, MILD, CLEMENT ⟨a ~ day for a picnic⟩ **syn** see BEAUTIFUL

²pretty \'pu̇(r)|, 'pri|, ,pə(r)|\ *sometimes* 'prü| *or -R* 'pu̇| *before 'near' often* 'prüt *or* 'prit\ *adv* **1 :** in some degree : MODERATELY, CONSIDERABLY, TOLERABLY, RATHER ⟨~ sure of the fact⟩ ⟨~ cold weather⟩ ⟨~ equally matched⟩ ⟨left things ~ much as they were⟩ **2** *chiefly dial* : PRETTILY, FINELY ⟨sang real ~⟩

³pretty *pronunc at* ¹*pretty*\ *n* -ES : a pretty person or thing : a pretty one: as **a** *chiefly South and Midland* : TOY **b pretties** *pl* : dainty clothes; *esp* : LINGERIE

⁴pretty \"\ *vt* **prettied**; **prettied**; **prettying**; **pretties** : to make pretty : make attractive or agreeable — usu. used with *up* ⟨curtains to ~ up the room⟩ ⟨once carefully tended gardens . . . have been hurriedly *prettied* up —Joseph Wechsberg⟩

pretty-by-night \'===¦=\ *n* : FOUR-O'CLOCK 1a

prettyface \'==,=\ *n* **1 :** a Californian herb (*Triteleia ixioides*) sometimes cultivated for its delicate yellow, purple-tinged flowers **2** *Austral* : WHIPTAIL

pret·ty·ish \'prid·ēish\ *adj* : rather pretty

pret·ty·ism \-ē,izəm\ *n* -s : affectation or prettiness in style or manner; *also* : an instance of such affectation

pretty nancy *n, usu cap N* [¹*pretty* + *Nancy* (feminine name)] : LOBEL'S CATCHFLY

¹pretty-pretty \¦==¦==\ *n* [redupl. of ³*pretty*] : a useless ornament : KNICKKNACK

²pretty-pretty \"\ *adj* [redupl. of ¹*pretty*] : aiming at prettiness for its own sake : inanely or inappropriately pretty

pre·tuberculous *or* **pre·tubercular** \¦prē+\ *adj* [*pre-* + *tubercular* or *tuberculous*] **1 :** preceding the development of lesions definitely identifiable as tuberculous **2 :** likely to develop tuberculosis ⟨undernourished and ~ children⟩

pre·typify \(')prē+\ *vt* [*pre-* + *typify*] : to typify earlier : PREFIGURE

pret·zel \'pretsəl\ *n* -s [G *brezel*, fr. OHG *brezitella*, fr. (assumed) ML *brachiatellum* (whence It *bracciatello* ring-shaped bun), fr. L *brachiatus* having branches like arms (fr. *brachium* arm + *-atus* -ate) + *-ellum* -el; perh. fr. the likeness in shape to a pair of folded arms — more at BRACE] : a brittle glazed and salted cracker made of a rope of dough typically twisted into a form resembling the letter B

pretzel

pre·umbonal \¦prē+\ *adj* [*pre-* + *umbonal*] : situated before the umbones of a bivalve shell

preux \'prə\ *adj* [F, fr. OF *prod*, *prud*, *prous* good, capable, valiant — more at PROUD] : CHIVALROUS, GALLANT ⟨while one wants on all occasions to do the ~ thing —P.G.Wodehouse⟩

preux che·va·lier \-shə,val'yā\ *n* [F] : a gallant knight : chivalrous fighter

prev *abbr* previous; previously

pre·vail \prē'vāl, prə'-, *esp before pause or consonant* -āəl\ *vi* -ED/-ING/-S [ME *prevailen*, modif. (prob. influenced by ME *vailen* to avail) of L *praevalēre* to be more able, prevail, fr. *prae-* pre- + *valēre* to be strong — more at WIELD, VAIL] **1** *obs* : to grow strong : increase in vigor **2 :** to gain victory by virtue of strength or superiority : win mastery : TRIUMPH — used with *over* or *against* ⟨gates of hell shall not ~ against it —Mt 16:18 (AV)⟩ ⟨the ungodly o'er the just ~*ed* —Robert Burns⟩ **3 :** to be or become effective or effectual : be successful ⟨the temptation to exploit consumers . . . usually ~*s* unless it is curbed —T.W.Arnold⟩ **4 :** to urge one successfully : succeed in persuading or inducing one — used with *on, upon,* or *with* ⟨could not ~ with her to dance with him again —Jane Austen⟩ ⟨she was ~*ed* upon to sing for the company⟩ **5** *obs* : AVAIL ⟨nothing ~*s*, for she is dead —Christopher Marlowe⟩ **6 :** to be or become common or widespread : be frequent : PREDOMINATE ⟨link between obsolete forms of life and those which generally ~ —Thomas Hardy⟩ **7 :** to be or continue in use or fashion : OBTAIN, PERSIST ⟨a custom that still ~*s* among us⟩ ⟨unable to buy at the prices now ~*ing*⟩ **syn** see INDUCE

pre·vail·ance \-ālən(t)s\ *n* -s [*prevail* + *-ance*] : PREVALENCE

prevailing *adj* **1 :** having superior force or influence : EFFICACIOUS ⟨the ~ doctrine of the age⟩ **2 a :** most frequent ⟨windows facing the ~ wind⟩ **b :** generally current : COMMON ⟨adapted a loose structure of ~ ideas to the needs of his own temperament —M.D.Geismar⟩

syn PREVAILING, PREVALENT, RIFE, CURRENT can apply to what is in general or wide circulation or use or what exists generally, especially in a given place or time. PREVAILING applies to what is predominant or widespread beyond others of its kind or class at a time or place indicated, implicit, or assumed to be the present ⟨the *prevailing* point of view among farmers⟩ ⟨the *prevailing* tendency to obliterate the dividing lines between all the arts —J.L.Lowes⟩ ⟨the predominant English taste, the *prevailing* English authority, of his time —H.L.Mencken⟩ ⟨anyone acquainted with the literature of the first decade after the war must have noticed a *prevailing* tone of disgust —C.D.Lewis⟩ PREVALENT applies to what is general or common over a given area at a given time, stressing less than PREVAILING an implicit comparison with other things of the same kind or class ⟨confined by the classical tradition still *prevalent* in their time —Huntington Hartford⟩ ⟨a *prevalent* feature in these compositions was a nursed and petted melancholy —Mark Twain⟩ ⟨this custom is similar to customs *prevalent* in different parts of Europe —K.D.Upadhyaya⟩ ⟨the disease is most *prevalent* in countries where there are large populations of both sheep and dogs —L.K.Whitten⟩ RIFE adds to PREVALENT the idea of great abundance or rapid spread by increase ⟨when cutthroat competition was *rife* in most industries —*Textbooks in Education*⟩ ⟨for slavery of all kinds was *rife* throughout the island —Alan Villiers⟩ ⟨disease was once more *rife* in the herds —*Farmer's Weekly (So. Africa)*⟩ ⟨literary production is *rife* in Puerto Rico —R.M.Lovett⟩ CURRENT applies especially to something that changes with time and implies existence or prevalence at the time specified or understood, chiefly the present ⟨the present vogue of racialism in the West, however, has really little to do with *current* scientific hypotheses —A.J.Toynbee⟩ ⟨caught in the drift of *current* social thinking —C.A. & Mary Beard⟩ ⟨resisted the temptation to use phrases that are merely *current* usage —L.A.Weigle⟩

pre·vail·ing·ly *adv* : most frequently : most commonly ⟨how far our researches are preferably individual, as they have ~ been —F.N.Robinson⟩

pre·vail·ing·ness *n* -ES : the quality or state of being common, frequent, or predominant

prevailing westerlies *n pl* : the average or normal westerly winds of the middle latitudes

pre·vail·ment \-lmənt\ *n* -s : power to prevail or dominate : VICTORY

prev·a·lence \'prev(ə)lən(t)s\ *also* **prev·a·len·cy** \-nsē, -si\ *n, pl* **prevalences** *also* **prevalencies** [*prevalence* fr. F *prévalence* superiority, fr. LL *praevalentia* greater power, fr. L *praevalent-*, *praevalens* (pres. part. of *praevalēre* to be more able, prevail) + *-ia* -y; *prevalency* fr. LL *praevalentia*] **1 :** the quality, condition, or fact of being prevalent : frequent occurrence : general or widespread acceptance, usage, or dissemination ⟨the ~ of burglaries⟩ ⟨~ of radios⟩ ⟨~ of rumors⟩ **2 :** the degree to which something (as a disease, an infective agent) is prevalent; *sometimes* : the percent of a population being studied that is affected with a particular disease at a given time

¹prev·a·lent \-nt\ *adj* [L *praevalent-*, *praevalens*, pres. part. of *praevalēre* to be more able, prevail — more at PREVAIL] **1** *archaic* : POWERFUL, POTENT, INFLUENTIAL, EFFICACIOUS **2 :** being in ascendancy : VICTORIOUS, DOMINANT ⟨law schools with a nominal college affiliation . . . became the ~ type —W.C.Mallalieu⟩ **3 :** generally or widely accepted, current, practiced, or favored : generally or extensively existing : WIDESPREAD ⟨places where malaria is ~⟩ **syn** see PREVAILING

²prevalent \"\ *n* -s : something prevalent

prev·a·lent·ly *adv* : very frequently : most frequently or commonly : PREVAILINGLY

pre·var·i·cate \prē'varə,kāt prə'- *also* -ver-, *usu* -ād·+V\ *vb* -ED/-ING/-S [L *praevaricatus*, past part. of *praevaricari* to walk crookedly, collude, fr. *prae-* pre- + *varicare* to straddle, fr. *varicus* having the feet spread apart, fr. *varus* bent, knock-kneed; prob. akin to OE *wōh* crooked, OHG *winkil* corner, *wado* calf of the leg, ON *vǫthvi* muscle, Goth *unwāhs* blameless, L *vatius* bowlegged, *vagus* wandering, Skt *vañcati* he goes crooked, *vaṅgati* he limps, and perh. to Skt *ūru* thigh; basic meaning: bending] *vi* **1** *obs* : to swerve from regularity or rectitude : go astray **2 :** to deviate from the truth : speak equivocally or evasively : LIE **3** *law* : to deviate from duty and probity: as **a** *Roman & civil law* (1) : to conceal a crime (2) : to collude with the opposing party to an action in making a sham accusation or defense **b** *Old English law* (1) *of an informer or defendant* : to collude in order to conduct a sham prosecution (2) : to violate a trust secretly ~ *vt* **1** *obs* : TRANSGRESS **2** *obs* : PERVERT **syn** see LIE

pre·var·i·ca·tion \=,==ˈkāshən\ *n* -s [ME *prevaricacioun* deviation from duty, fr. LL *praevarication-*, *praevaricatio*, fr. L, collusion, fr. *praevaricatus* (past part. of *praevaricari*) + *-ion-*, *-io* -ion] **1 :** the act or an instance of prevaricating; *esp* : a perversion of or a deviation from the truth **2 :** a statement that deviates from or perverts the truth; *often* : LIE ⟨the august tribunal of the skies, where no ~*s* shall avail —William Cowper⟩

pre·var·i·ca·tive \='==,kād·iv, -,kəd-\ *adj* : tending to prevaricate ⟨~ writers⟩

pre·var·i·ca·tor \-ād·ə(r), -ātə-\ *n* -s [L *praevaricator* advocate that acts in collusion with the opposing party, fr. *praevaricatus* (past part. of *praevaricari*) + *-or*] **1** : one who evades or perverts the truth **2** : one guilty of a breach of trust ⟨such ~s of tithes were destined to find their part in hell —G.G. Coulton⟩ **3** : one guilty of collusion in a court of law **4 a** : a master of arts at Cambridge University appointed to deliver a satirical oration at commencement according to a custom abandoned since the 18th century — compare TERRAE FILIUS

pre·var·i·ca·to·ry \prē'varəkə,tōrē\ *adj* : marked by or given to prevarication ⟨~ answers⟩

pre·velar \(')prē+\ *adj* [*pre-* + *velar*] : articulated against the front half of the soft palate

pré·ve·nance \,prāvə'nä"s\ *n* -s [F, fr. *prévenant* (pres. part. of *prévenir* to anticipate, fr. L *praevenire* to precede, anticipate), after such pairs as F *abondant* abundant (fr. MF *abundant*): *abondance* abundance (fr. MF *abundance*)] : attentiveness to or anticipation of others' needs or an instance of such anticipation

pre·vene \prē'vēn\ *vt* -ED/-ING/-S [ME (Sc) *prevenen*, fr. L *praevenire* to precede, anticipate, prevent] **1** *obs* : FORESTALL, PREVENT **2** : to come before : PRECEDE

pre·ven·ience \prē'vēnyən(t)s, -nēən-\ *n* -s [fr. *prevenient*, after such pairs as E *intelligent*: *intelligence*] **1** : PRÉVENANCE **2** : prevenient character or action

pre·ven·ient \-yənt\ *adj* [L *praevenient-*, *praeveniens*, pres. part. of *praevenire*] : ANTECEDENT, ANTICIPATORY — **pre·ven·ient·ly** *adv*

prevenient grace *n* : divine grace that is said to operate on the human will antecedent to its turning to God

pre·vent \prē'vent, prə'-\ *vb* -ED/-ING/-S [ME *preventen*, fr. L *praeventus*, past part. of *praevenire* to precede, anticipate, prevent, fr. *prae-* pre- + *venire* to come — more at COME] *vt* **1 a** *archaic* : to anticipate (as an occasion, an appointed time) by preparation or action : be in readiness for **b** *archaic* : to meet or satisfy (as a question, wish, objection) in advance **c** *archaic* : to act ahead of (another's action) **d** *archaic* : to arrive before : PRECEDE, OUTRUN **2** *archaic* : to predispose to repentance and faith by divine grace **3** : to deprive of power or hope of acting, operating, or succeeding in a purpose : FRUSTRATE, CIRCUMVENT ⟨police officials should not ~ police reporters from obtaining the news —Lou Smyth⟩ **4** : to keep from happening or existing esp. by precautionary measures : hinder the progress, appearance, or fulfillment of : make impossible through advance provisions ⟨one may ~ feeding problems quite as readily as some physical diseases —M.J.E. Senn⟩ ⟨authority . . . and purposefulness of his manner . . . ~ the role becoming a minor one —E.R.Bentley⟩ **5** : to hold or keep back (one about to act) : HINDER, STOP ⟨had to catch his arm to ~ him falling —Claud Cockburn⟩ — often used with *from* ⟨there is nothing to ~ us from going⟩ **6** *obs* : to hasten the coming of (an event) **7** *obs* : to take possession of or occupy in advance ~ *vi* **1** *obs* : to act or come before **2** : to make something impossible ⟨we shall come if nothing ~s⟩

syn ANTICIPATE, FORESTALL: PREVENT implies an advance move or provision that blocks the occurrence or possible occurrence of something (as a calamity) or the success of something (as a plan) ⟨the surest way to *prevent* aggression is to remain strong enough to overpower and defeat any who might attack —D.L. Lawrence⟩ ⟨medical science knows how to limit these evils and can do much to *prevent* their destructiveness —C.W. Eliot⟩ ⟨we can cure disease or *prevent* it —W.W.Howells⟩ ANTICIPATE stresses more the foreseeing of something that will or may take place in the future than the provision for handling it or acting appropriately in relation to it ⟨one must foresee, *anticipate* and ratify this suggestion, which will inevitably occur —Juan Gris⟩ ⟨my other architectural friends *anticipate* a great outburst of postwar activity and world-planning —E.M. Forster⟩ ⟨she *anticipated* that he would also become more exacting in his demands on her time —G.B.Shaw⟩ FORESTALL can mean to stop something from happening or to intercept and stop something in its course, but more usually stresses not a stopping but a rendering of something ineffective or harmless by forehanded action ⟨property owners own out to the edge of the sidewalk, effectively *forestalling* street widening if they want to —Hal Burton⟩ ⟨to *forestall* every risk and retain every advantage —*New Republic*⟩ ⟨a new warning device to *forestall* surprise attacks by aircraft —I.I.Rabi⟩

syn PREVENT, PRECLUDE, OBVIATE, AVERT, and WARD (*off*) can mean to hinder or stop (something that may occur) or, in the case of PREVENT and PRECLUDE, to stop (someone about to act, or someone's action) PREVENT implies an insurmountable obstacle or impediment ⟨measures taken to *prevent* disease⟩ ⟨no war was too serious to *prevent* frequent truces for meals or festivals —R.A.Billington⟩ ⟨by solving it he *prevents* an innocent man going to the gallows —*New Books*⟩ PRECLUDE implies a situation or condition or measures taken that effectively shut out all possibility of a thing's occurring or a person's doing something ⟨provide the mechanism to assure that atomic energy is used for peaceful purposes and *preclude* its use in war —B.M.Baruch⟩ ⟨the brevity of his stay would *preclude* the possibility of his enjoying the school pageant —C.H.Grandgent⟩ ⟨in no way *precludes* them from having a vital and extraordinary power —Montgomery Belgion⟩ Whereas PRECLUDE often suggests the operation of chance, OBVIATE usually implies the use of intelligence or forethought in clearing away (as obstacles) or disposing of (as difficulties) ⟨fruits should be washed in order to *obviate* hazard to the consumer —R.N. Shreve⟩ ⟨by reciprocally extending rights and privileges to one another's citizens . . . they may *obviate* jealousies and promote the general well-being —F.A.Ogg & P.O.Ray⟩ ⟨a single administrator can do much to *obviate* the confusion which still exists in this field —H.S.Truman⟩ AVERT and WARD (*off*) always imply the anticipation and deflection or prevention of an approaching or oncoming evil, usually by immediate and effective measures, AVERT suggesting more active measures to force back, WARD (*off*) implying more defensive measures to avoid or counteract ⟨delegates were sent to a peace conference held at Washington in an effort to *avert* hostilities —*Amer. Guide Series: N.C.*⟩ ⟨men seeking to *avert* a revolution they do not understand with weapons they don't know how to wield —H.J.Laski⟩ ⟨despite the increased chances for respiratory illness during the winter, there are many things you can do to help *ward* this *off* —*advt*⟩ ⟨most of the time he did not feel this, he *warded off* the possibility of feeling it —Marcia Davenport⟩

pre·vent·abil·i·ty \prē,ventə'bilәd·ē, prə,-, -ətē, -i\ *n* : the quality or state of being preventable

pre·vent·able *also* **pre·vent·ible** \prē'ventəbəl, prə'-\ *adj* : capable of being prevented : AVOIDABLE, AVERTIBLE ⟨conscious of ~ human suffering —A.L.Guérard⟩

pre·vent·ative \-təd·iv, -ətiv\ *adj or n* [*prevent* + *-ative*] : PREVENTIVE

pre·vent·er \-ntə(r)\ *n* -s : one that prevents: as **a** : one that forestalls or anticipates another **b** : PREVENTIVE **c** : an auxiliary rope, stay, bolt, or other contrivance ⟨~ to keep an oar from slipping through the oarlock⟩ **d** *obs* : PROLEPSIS 2b

preventer plate *n* : a heavy plate for holding the chains to the side of a large ship

preventing *pres part of* PREVENT

pre·vent·ing·ly *adv* [*preventing* (pres. part. of *prevent*) + *-ly*] : so as to prevent or hinder

pre·ven·tion \prē'venchən, prə'-\ *n* -s [LL *praevention-*, *praeventio* action of overtaking or anticipating, fr. L *praeventus* (past part. of *praevenire* to precede, anticipate, prevent) + *-ion-*, *-io* -ion — more at PREVENT] **1 a** : the right under canon law of a superior ecclesiastic to claim jurisdiction over or transact a matter excluding an inferior to whom the matter normally would be entrusted **b** *Scots civil law* : the authority of one of a number of judges of concurrent jurisdiction to exercise that jurisdiction with respect to a cause of which he first takes cognizance **2** *obs* : a going before : state of being before : PRECEDENCE **3** *obs* **a** : ANTICIPATION, FORESTALLMENT **b** : PREVENTIVE, PRECAUTION **c** : OBSTACLE **d** : PRESENTIMENT **e** : PREFACE, INTRODUCTION **4** *obs* : PROLEPSIS 2b **5** : the act of preventing or hindering : obstruction or thwarting of action, access, or approach ⟨~ of forest fires⟩ ⟨~ of disease⟩ ⟨~ of war⟩ ⟨~ of cruelty to animals⟩ ⟨slum ~⟩ **6** *obs* : PREJUDICE, PREPOSSESSION

pre·ven·tion·al \-chən³l\ *adj* **1** *obs* : PRECEDING **2** : PREVENTIVE

pre·ven·tion·ism \-chə,nizəm\ *n* -s : a policy of prevention (as of war, fire, disease)

pre·ven·tion·ist \-,nəst\ *n* -s : one expert in or favoring or employing preventive measures

¹**pre·ven·tive** \prē'ventiv, prə'-,-tēv *also* -təv\ *n* -s [*prevent* + *-ive*, n. suffix] : something that prevents or is preventive; *specif* : something taken to prevent disease : PROPHYLACTIC

²**preventive** \"\ *adj* [*prevent* + *-ive*, adj. suffix] **1** : making or aiming to make unlikely or impossible : devoted to or concerned with prevention : PRECAUTIONARY ⟨a ~ measure against rats⟩ ⟨~ steps against soil erosion⟩ ⟨~ penology⟩ **2** : undertaken in order to forestall or ward off hostile action ⟨~ war⟩ ⟨knock out the enemy air force with a quick ~ thrust⟩ — **pre·ven·tive·ly** \-tәvlē, -lī\ *adv* — **pre·ven·tive·ness** \-tivnəs, -tēv- *also* -təv-\ *n* -ES

preventive detention *n, Eng law* : a sentence passed on a persistent offender under the Criminal Justice Act of 1948 in order to protect the public and to administer medical or psychiatric treatment or corrective training to the offender

preventive law *n* : a branch of law that endeavors to minimize the risk of litigation or to secure more certainty as to legal rights and duties

preventive medicine *n* : a branch of medical science dealing with methods (as vaccination) of preventing the occurrence of disease : PROPHYLAXIS

pre·ven·tor \-ntə(r\ *Brit var of* PREVENTER

pre·ven·to·ri·um \,prēvən-'tōrēəm\ *n, pl* **preventoria** \-ōrēə\ *also* **preventoriums** [*prevent* + *-orium*] : an establishment where persons (as children) liable to develop disease (as tuberculosis) receive preventive care and treatment

prevents *pres 3d sing of* PREVENT

pre·verb \'prē+,-\ *n* [ISV *pre-* + *verb*] : a prefix or particle occurring before a verb base (as *be-* in *become*)

pre·verbal \(')prē+\ *adj* [*pre-* + *verbal*] **1** : occurring before the verb ⟨~ position of a preposition⟩ **2** : existing or occurring before speech ⟨~ stage of random articulation in infants —F.H.Allport⟩

pre·vernal \"+\ *adj* [*pre-* + *vernal*] **1** : early flowering or leafing — used of plants that unfold their leaves or flowers before the rest of the plants in their locality **2** : of or relating to the end of winter and the beginning of spring : occurring early in the growing season ⟨~ activity of a ground spider⟩ ⟨~ group of migratory birds⟩

pre·vertebrate \'prē+,-\ *n* [*pre-* + *vertebrate*] : a hypothetical ancestral form preceding the vertebrates

pre·vesical \(')prē+\ *adj* [*pre-* + *vesical*] : situated in front of a bladder and esp. the urinary bladder

¹**pre·view** \'prē,vyü\ *vt* [*pre-* + *view*] **1** : to see beforehand; *specif* : to view or to show in advance of public presentation **2** : to give an overall presentation of (a subject of study) before beginning systematic instruction

²**preview** *n* **1** : a view of a performance or exhibition before it is open to the public : a showing or viewing of a motion picture before it is released for commercial exhibition **2** *also* **pre·vue** \"\ -s [*prevue* alter. (prob. influenced by *revue*) of *preview*] : a showing of snatches from a motion picture advertised for appearance in the near future **3** : a statement giving advance information : FORETASTE, GLIMPSE **4** : a general survey of a new subject given by a teacher before beginning systematic instruction **5** : a radio or television program rehearsal

pre·villous \(')prē+\ *adj* [*pre-* + *villous*] : occurring before the formation of villi ⟨an embryo in the ~ stage⟩ : not yet having villi ⟨a ~ human embryo⟩

¹**pre·vi·ous** \'prēvēəs\ *adj* [L *praevius* going before, leading the way, fr. *prae-* pre- + *via* way — more at VIA] **1 a** : going or existing before in time : EARLIER ⟨reverted to his ~ position⟩ ⟨the ~ owners of our house⟩ **b** : preceding in spatial order ⟨shown in the photograph on the ~ page —Bernard DeVoto⟩ **2** : acting too soon : IMPATIENT, HASTY, PREMATURE ⟨it turned out that our condemnation of him had been a little ~⟩ ⟨grew ~ and stuck my hand in there just when the wheel was moving forward —*Inland Printer*⟩

²**previous** \"\ *adv* : PREVIOUSLY

previous examination *n* : the first examination taken by a candidate for the B. A. degree at Cambridge University — compare INTERMEDIATE 2c, RESPONSION

pre·vi·ous·ly *adv* **1** : BEFOREHAND, HITHERTO, ANTECEDENTLY ⟨had served ~ in the army⟩ ⟨entered the country two years ~⟩ ⟨better than any solution ~ devised⟩ ⟨his own ~ unquestioned first principle —M.R.Cohen⟩ **2** : too soon : HASTILY, PREMATURELY

pre·vi·ous·ness *n* -ES **1** : ANTECEDENCE, PRIORITY **2** : undue haste : IMPATIENCE

previous question *n* : a parliamentary motion to put the main issue to an immediate vote without further debate or proposal of new amendments that if lost has the effect in English practice of postponing consideration of the issue until it may again be introduced and in American practice of keeping the issue before the body as if the motion had not been made

previous to *prep* : in advance of : BEFORE ⟨his high school diploma was presented to him just *previous to* his departure for France — *Current Biog.*⟩

pre·vise \prē'vīz, prə'-\ *vt* -ED/-ING/-S [L *praevisus*, past part. of *praevidēre*] **1** : FORESEE **2** : to inform beforehand : WARN

pre·vis·i·bil·i·ty \prē,vīzə'biləd·ē\ *n* : FORESEEABILITY, PREDICTABILITY

pre·vis·ible \prē'vīzəbəl\ *adj* [*previse* + *-able*] : capable of being foreseen or predicted — **pre·vis·ibly** \-blē\ *adv*

¹**pre·vi·sion** \prē'vizhən, prə'-\ *n* [LL *praevision-*, *praevisio*, fr. L *praevisus* (past part. of *praevidēre* to foresee, fr. *prae-* pre- + *vidēre* to see) + *-ion-*, *-io* -ion — more at WIT] **1** : FORESIGHT, FOREKNOWLEDGE, PRESCIENCE ⟨over a limited period, which is . . . as far as human ~ can go —M.R.Cohen⟩ **2** : PROGNOSTICATION, FORECAST ⟨taken aback to find in her glance an equal ~ of dislike —Clemence Dane⟩

²**prevision** \"\ *vt* **previsioned; previsioned; previsioning** \-zh(ə)niŋ\ **previsions** **1** : to give or endow with prevision ⟨all who have been ~*ed* by suffering —Thomas Hardy⟩ **2** : FORESEE ⟨~*ed* herself in a position where she could repay slurs —S.H.Adams⟩

pre·vi·sion·al \-zhən³l, -zhnəl\ *adj* : marked by prevision

pre·vi·sion·ary \-zhə,nerē\ *adj* : PREVISIONAL ⟨collections of apparently ~ experiences, largely consisting of dreams —J.B. Rhine⟩

pre·vocalic \¦prē+\ *adj* [ISV *pre-* + *vocalic*] : immediately preceding a vowel : ANTEVOCALIC

pre·vocational \"+\ *adj* [*pre-* + *vocational*] : given or required before admission to a vocational school ⟨~ courses⟩

pre·vomer \"+\ *n* [NL, fr. *pre-* + *vomer*] : the vomer of a nonmammalian vertebrate — **pre·vomerine** \"+\ *adj*

prevue *var of* PREVIEW

¹**pre·war** \(')prē+\ *adj* [*pre-* + *war*, n.] : occurring or existing before a war (as the Civil War, World War I, World War II) ⟨~ levels of industrial production⟩

²**prewar** \"\ *adv* : in a prewar period or era ⟨more people can afford autos than ~ —*Time*⟩

pre·warn \"+\ *vt* [*pre-* + *warn*] : FOREWARN

pre·welt method \'prē,welt-\ *n* [*prewelt* fr. *pre-* + *welt*, v.] : shoe construction used chiefly in infants' and children's shoes in which the welt is sewn to the lasting edge of the upper by means of a chainstitch seam and the outsole is attached to the welt with a lockstitch seam

pre·wrap \(')prē+\ *vt* [*pre-* + *wrap*] : to wrap (a manufactured article) before sale

prexy \'preksē, -si\ *also* **prex** \-ks\ *n* -ES [*prexy* fr. *prex* + *-y*; *prex* by shortening & alter. fr. *president*] *slang* : PRESIDENT — used chiefly of a college president

¹**prey** \'prā\ *n* -s [ME *preye*, fr. OF *preie*, fr. L *praeda*; akin to L *prehendere* to grasp, seize — more at PREHENSILE] **1** *archaic* : something taken or got by violence (as in war) : SPOIL, BOOTY, PLUNDER **2 a** : an animal that is or may be seized by another to be devoured **b** : a person or thing helpless or unable to resist injurious attack ⟨ill fares the land, to hastening ills a ~ —Oliver Goldsmith⟩ ⟨fell a ~ to doubts⟩ **3 a** *archaic* : the act of plundering **b** : the act or habit of seizing animals to devour

syn see VICTIM

²**prey** \"\ *vb* **preyed; preyed; preying; preys** [ME *preyen*, fr. OF *preier*, fr. L *praedari* to plunder, prey, fr. *praeda*] *vi* **1** : to make raids for the sake of booty : commit depredations — used with *on, upon* ⟨pirates ~ upon the coastal shipping⟩ **2 a** : to seize and devour prey ⟨cats ~ upon robins⟩ **b** : to commit violence or robbery or fraud ⟨gamblers and confidence men, who ~*ed* upon the construction workers —*Amer. Guide Series: Ark.*⟩ **3** : to have an injurious, destructive, or wasting effect ⟨grief ~*ed* on his mind⟩ ~ *vt* **1** *obs* : to take as prey : seize and devour **2** *obs* : PLUNDER, RAVAGE, ROB

prey·er \-ā̤ə(r)\ *n* -s : one that preys ⟨who had said, ~s are preyed upon —Elizabeth Bowen⟩

preying *adj* : WASTING, GNAWING ⟨~ anxiety⟩ — **prey·ing·ly** *adv*

pre·zoea \¦prē+\ *n, pl* **prezoeae** [NL, fr. *pre-* + *zoea*] : a newly hatched decapod crustacean larva before it sheds the embryonic cuticle — **pre·zoeal** \"+\ *adj*

pre·zon·al \(')prē¦zōn³l\ *adj* [*pre-* + *zone* + *-al*] : situated anterior to the pelvic girdle

pre·zone \'prē,zōn\ *n* [*pre-* + *zone*] : PROZONE

prf *abbr* proof

PRF *abbr* pulse repetition frequency

pri- *comb form* [NL, fr. Gk *priōn* saw — more at PRION-] : saw : resembling a saw ⟨*Pri*acanthus⟩ ⟨*pri*odont⟩

pri *abbr* **1** primary **2** prison **3** private

¹**pri·a·can·thid** \¦prīə¦kan(t)thəd\ *adj* [NL *Priacanthidae*] : of or relating to the Priacanthidae

²**priacanthid** \"\ *n* -s : a fish of the family Priacanthidae

pri·a·can·thi·dae \,==='thə,dē\ *n pl, cap* [NL, fr. *Priacanthus*, type genus + *-idae*] : a family of small usu. red or rose-colored carnivorous percoid fishes of tropical seas having the body short and covered with rough scales, the eyes large, and the mouth very oblique

pri·a·can·thus \-thəs\ *n, cap* [NL, fr. *pri-* + *-acanthus*] : the type genus of the family Priacanthidae including the bigeye of the American coasts

pri·al \'prīəl\ *n* -s [by alter.] *chiefly dial* : PAIR ROYAL

¹**pri·a·pe·an** \¦prīə¦pēən\ *adj* [L *priapeius* of or relating to Priapus (fr. Gk *priapeios* of Priapus, fr. *Priapos* Priapus, Greco-Roman god of procreation and fertility) + E *-an*] **1** *usu cap* : PRIAPIC **2** *often cap* : of or relating to a priapean

²**priapean** \"\ *n* -s *often cap* [LL *priapeius* (fr. L, of Priapus) + E *-an*; fr. the meter having been used in Roman poems to Priapus] : a verse in classical poetry composed of a glyconic followed by a pherecratic

pri·ap·ic \(')prī¦apik\ *adj* [L *priapus* + E *-ic*] **1** : preoccupied with or employing the phallus symbolically : PHALLIC ⟨~ rites⟩ **2 a** : featuring or stressing the phallus ⟨a ~ statuette⟩ **b** : suggesting a phallus ⟨the ~ golden rocket bursting —William Sansom⟩ **3** : preoccupied with maleness : actively and obviously masculine; *esp* : concerned with male sexual ardor ⟨~ episodes⟩ ⟨~ victories⟩

pri·a·pism \'prīə,pizəm\ *n* -s [F & LL; F *priapisme*, fr. LL *priapismus*, fr. Gk *priapismos*, fr. *priapizein* to be lewd, to be a Priapus (fr. *Priapos*, Greco-Roman god of procreation and fertility usu. portrayed in sculpture with an erect phallus + *-izein* -ize) + *-ismos* -ism] **1** : an abnormal, more or less persistent, and often painful erection of the penis; *esp* : one caused by disease rather than sexual desire **2** : a phallic figure **3** : a lewd act or display — **pri·a·pis·mic** \¦==¦pizmik\ *adj*

pri·a·pi·um \prī'āpēəm\ *n, pl* **pria·pia** \-pēə\ [NL, fr. L *priapus* lecher (fr. *Priapus*, god of fertility) + *-ium* (n. suffix)] : PHALLUS

pri·ap·u·la·cea \prī,apyə'lāsh(ē)ə\ *or* **pri·a·pu·li·da** \,prīə'pyüləda\ [NL, fr. *Priapulus*, genus of marine worms + *-acea* or *-ida*] *syn of* PRIAPULOIDEA

¹**pri·ap·u·lid** \prī'apyələd\ *adj* [NL *Priapulida*] : of or relating to the Priapuloidea

²**priapulid** \"\ *n* -s : a worm of the group Priapuloidea

pri·ap·u·loi·dea \prī,apyə'lȯidēə\ *n pl, cap* [NL, fr. *Priapulus*, genus of marine worms (fr. *priapus* phallus + *-ulus* -ule) + *-oidea*] : a group of marine worms of obscure position that are classed as a division of Gephyrea and that somewhat resemble the Sipunculoidea from which they are distinguished by the absence of tentacles and usu. by the presence of caudal gills

pri·a·pus \prī'āpəs\ *n, pl* **pria·pi** \-ā,pī\ *or* **priapuses** [NL, fr. L, lecher, fr. *Priapus*, god of fertility, fr. Gk *Priapos*] : PHALLUS

pri·a·pu·si·an \,prīə¦pyüsēən\ *adj, usu cap* [*Priapus* (fr. L) + E *-an*] : of or relating to the worship of the ancient Greek god Priapus

prib·ble \'pribəl\ *n* -s [alter. (influenced by *bibble-babble*) of *prabble*] *chiefly dial* : a trivial dispute or discussion

¹**price** \'prīs\ *n* -s *often attrib* [ME *pris*, fr. OF, fr. L *pretium* price, money, value; akin to Gk *proti* near, toward, to, OSlav *protivŭ* against, toward, Skt *prati* against, back, in return, L *per* through; basic meaning: exchange — more at FARE] **1** *archaic* : genuine and inherent value : WORTH, EXCELLENCE, PRECIOUSNESS ⟨her ~ is far above rubies —Prov 31: 10 (AV)⟩ **2 a** : the quantity of one thing that is exchanged or demanded in barter or sale for another : a ratio at which commodities and services are exchanged **b** : the amount of money given or set as the amount to be given as a consideration for the sale of a specified thing ⟨the ~ of wheat is expected to rise⟩ **3** : the terms or consideration for the sake of which something is done or undertaken: as **a** : an amount or gain sufficient to bribe one : something for which one is prepared to sacrifice probity, responsibility, or other quality or duty ⟨not always easy to guess a man's ~⟩ **b** : a sum offered in reward for the apprehension or death of a person ⟨outlaws with ~s on their heads⟩ **4** : the cost at which something is obtained ⟨the ~ of liberty is eternal vigilance⟩ or offered ⟨the ~ of peace was more than their spirit could stomach⟩ **5** : ODDS 4b — **at a price** *adv* **1** : through heavy sacrifice : with a great or considerable cost ⟨he won but only *at a price*⟩ **2** : at more than the normal or market price ⟨housing could be obtained *at a price*⟩ — **of price** : having great value or worthiness : PRECIOUS ⟨things *of price*⟩ — **what price** : of what value or use is — used interrogatively ⟨*what price* isolation now⟩ — **without price** : beyond price : PRICELESS

²**price** \"\ *vb* -ED/-ING/-S [ME *prisen* to price, prize — more at PRIZE] *vt* **1** : to set a price on : fix the price of ⟨*pricing* his goods high⟩ **2** *obs* : to rate highly : VALUE **3** *obs* : to pay the price of **4** : to ask the price of ⟨*priced* table linens at several stores **5** : to drive by raising prices to a level at which people refuse to buy or which is too high to meet competition — usu. used with the phrase *out of the market* ⟨*priced* themselves out of the world market⟩ ⟨*priced* coal out of the competitive market⟩ ~ *vi* : to set prices

price·able \'prīsəbəl\ *adj* : capable of being priced : having a determinable price

price concession *n* : CONCESSION 2d

price current *n, pl* **prices current** : PRICE LIST — often used in pl.

price-cutter \'=,==\ *n* : one that reduces prices esp. to a level designed to cripple competition

priced \¦prīst\ *adj* [fr. past part. of ²*price*] : having a price set — often used in combination ⟨high-*priced* goods⟩ ⟨a modestly-*priced* line⟩

price discrimination *n* **1** : the offering of similar or identical goods at different prices to different buyers **2** : the setting of a price differential on similar goods that is not based on differences in the cost of production

price-fixing \'=,==\ *n* : the process by which prices are set in advance (as by agreement among producers or by governmental edict) rather than by operation of a free market

price index *n* **1** *or* **price relative** : a price expressed as a percentage of itself in some arbitrarily chosen base period **2** : the weighted average of a group of price indexes used to indicate changes in the level of prices from one period to another

price·ite \'prī,sīt\ *n* -s [Thomas *Price* 19th cent. Am. metallurgist + E *-ite*] : a mineral $Ca_4B_{10}O_{19}.7H_2O$(?) occurring as a snow-white massive calcium borate

price leadership *n* : leadership by a dominant firm in the determination of prices in an industry with other firms following the pattern established by the leader

price·less \'prīsləs\ *adj* **1 a** : having a value beyond any price : too valuable to be appraised, estimated, or adequately appreciated ⟨the ~ boon of good health⟩ **b** : excessively high-priced ⟨a sale of ~ jewels⟩ **2 a** : of intangible value : having worth in terms of other than market value ⟨such a pair of well-worn comfortable walking shoes is ~⟩ **b** : having no market value : UNSALABLE **3** : surprisingly amusing, odd, or absurd

syn see COSTLY

price·less·ness *n* -ES **:** the quality or state of being priceless
price level *n* **:** an average of prices at a particular time relative to that at some other time — compare PRICE INDEX
price line *n* **:** a line of merchandise available at a fixed price under a price-lining system ⟨an excellent $7.95 *price line* of sport shoes⟩
price lining *n* **:** a system of retail merchandising under which a merchant sets up fixed prices for various categories of goods and plans his buying and other expenses so as to be able to supply goods regularly at such prices ⟨*price lining* is esp. practical in stores that employ comparison shoppers
price list *n* **:** a statement or list of the prevailing prices of the merchandise, stocks, specie, bills of exchange, or other matter dealt in issued statedly or occasionally by dealers to their customers and often giving other particulars (as import or export duties and drawbacks)
pricemaker \ˈ=,==\ *n* [¹*price* + *maker*] **:** a determiner of betting odds (as at a racetrack)
price-mark \ˈ=,=\ *vt* **:** to mark the retail price on (merchandise)
price mechanism *or* **price system** *n* **:** a system of price determination and allocation of goods by free market forces
price of money : the net rate of interest paid for borrowed money
pric·er \ˈprīsə(r)\ *n* -S **:** one that prices something: as **a :** a person that fixes prices of merchandise; *esp* **:** an expert that values and sets a price on specialty items (as jewels or antiques) **b :** a shopper that inquires about and compares prices often with little intention of buying **c :** a clerk who marks prices on stock and quotes prices to inquirers
price range *n* **:** the highest and lowest prices recorded within a given time on a market
price-ring \ˈ=,=\ *n* **:** a group (as of producers) acting in concert to fix or control prices
prices *pl of* PRICE, *pres 3d sing of* PRICE
price support *n* **1 :** artificial maintenance of prices (as of a particular raw material) at some predetermined level usu. through government action **2 :** an amount paid out in purchases or loans by which a price is maintained
price tag *n* **1 :** a tag on merchandise showing the price at which it is offered for sale **2 :** PRICE, COST ⟨the *price tag* is becoming the most important thing in medicine —Milton Silverman⟩ ⟨the *price tag* on dissent can be awfully high —J.B. Martin⟩
price war *n* **:** a period of intensive industrial or commercial competition characterized by repeated price cutting and designed to cripple or gravely handicap financially insecure competitors
pricey \ˈprīsi\ *adj* [¹*price* + *-y*] *Austral* **:** high in price **:** charging high prices
pricier *comparative of* PRICY
priciest *superlative of* PRICY
¹**prick** \ˈprik\ *n* -S [ME *prikke, prik,* fr. OE *prica;* akin to MD *pric, pricke* prick, ON *prik* short stick, point and perh. to ON *pikka* to peck, hack — more at PICK] **1 :** a mark or shallow hole made by a pointed instrument **:** PUNCTURE, POINT, DOT: as **a :** a wound or flaw consisting of such a mark or hole; *esp* **:** an injury to a horse's hoof resulting from driving a nail into the quick in shoeing **b :** the footprint of a hare **2 :** any of various small marks or points resembling a prick made by a pointed instrument: as **a** *archaic* **:** PUNCTUATION MARK **:** a diacritical mark **b** *obs* **:** a minute part or particle **:** a point in space or time **c** (1) **:** a mark fixed for shooting with bow and arrow **:** BULLSEYE, TARGET (2) *obs* **:** something at which one directs one's aim **:** OBJECTIVE, INTENT **d** (1) **:** a note used in medieval music (2) **:** a dot placed after a note or rest in musical notation **e** *obs* **:** a mark on the dial of a sundial or clock noting the divisions of time **3 :** something that pricks or is capable of making punctures (as a pointed instrument or weapon): as **a** (1) **:** a sharp projecting organ or part of a plant or animal (as a thorn, prickle, or spine) (2) *obs* **:** the sting of a bee or other arthropod **b** *obs* **:** a goad for oxen **c** *obs* **:** a usu. nonmaterial source of distress or stimulation (as a cause of remorse or vexation or an incentive) **d** *dial chiefly Eng* **:** SKEWER **e** *obs* **:** an upright tapering object (as a spire, a tent pole, or the pricket of a candlestick) **4 :** an instance of pricking or the sensation of being pricked: as **a :** a nagging or sharp feeling of remorse, regret, or sorrow (as for past deeds or omissions) **b :** a slight sharply localized discomfort ⟨felt only a ~ as the doctor made the injection⟩ **c :** a brief sharp attack **:** STAB ⟨a ~ of conscience⟩ **5 :** PENIS — usu. considered vulgar **6 :** a roll of tobacco suitable for carrying on the person **7** *slang* **:** a disagreeable or contemptible person
²**prick** \"\ *vb* -ED/-ING/-S [ME *prikken, priken,* fr. OE *prician;* akin to MHG *pfrecken* to prick, OE *priccan,* ON *prika;* all fr. the root of E ¹*prick*] *vt* **1 :** to pierce slightly with something sharp-pointed **:** make a puncture in **:** drive a fine point into ⟨~ holes in paper⟩: as **a** (1) **:** to wound usu. slightly with a pointed instrument ⟨~*ed* his finger with a pin⟩ (2) **:** to give a slight piercing wound to ⟨the pin ~*ed* his finger⟩ **b :** to drive a nail into the quick of (a horse) in shoeing **c :** to pierce the skin of (a suspected witch) repeatedly to prove the status by finding spots that fail to bleed **2 :** to affect with anguish or grief **:** sting with or as if with remorse **3 a :** to ride or guide with spurs or a goad **b :** to urge as if with spurs **:** INCITE, IMPEL — sometimes used with *on* or *off* ⟨my duty ~*s* me on to utter that —Shak.⟩ **4 a** *archaic* **:** to write down (music) in notes **b :** to mark, distinguish, or note (as an item in a list) by means of a small mark — sometimes used with *down* ⟨~*s* down each item⟩ **c :** to select (as a candidate) by such pricking **d :** to mark or outline with punctures **:** trace or form by pricking ⟨~ an embroidery pattern⟩ **5** *dial chiefly Eng* **:** to adorn the person or dress of esp. by adding some fancy bauble **:** PRINK — often used with *up* **6 :** to search for the tracks of (a hare) **:** track (a hare) by its footprints **7** *obs* **a :** to make fast or take up on the point of an implement **b :** to fix or insert by the point **:** thrust or drive (a pointed implement) into something **c :** to fasten with a pointed implement **8 a** *obs* **:** to bring into a desired position or relation by or as if by pricking **b :** to remove (a young seedling) from the original container to another suitable for further growth — used with *out* or *off* or formerly with *forth* or *in* **9 :** to cause to be or stand erect; *esp* **:** to raise or bend (the ears) into a position for optimum hearing — usu. used with *up* and esp. of a dog or horse **10 :** to run a middle seam through (a sail) **11 :** to cause (as wine) to undergo an acetic fermentation **:** spoil by acidifying ~ *vi* **1 a :** to prick something or cause a pricking sensation ⟨how those briers ~*ed*⟩; *also* **:** to be prickly ⟨short spines that ~ all over the back⟩ **b** (1) **:** to become punctured (2) **:** to feel a sharp pain as if from being punctured ⟨the elbow ~*ed* and tingled⟩ (3) **:** to give rise to such a sensation ⟨a healing wound often ~*s*⟩ **2 :** to urge a horse with the spur; *also* **:** to ride fast **:** GALLOP ⟨~*ing* through the night⟩ **3 :** THRUST — usu. used with *at* ⟨his neglect ~*ed* at his conscience⟩ **4 :** to become sharp or acid **:** spoil by souring — used of beverages (as wine) **5 a :** to point or become directed upward ⟨steeples ~*ing* toward the sky⟩ **b** *of an ear* **:** to be in a position of attention ⟨the dog's ears ~*ed* up at the sound⟩ **6** *chiefly dial* **:** PRINK
syn see PERFORATE, URGE — **prick up one's ears :** to begin to listen intently or with increased interest
³**prick** \"\ *adj* **:** standing erect ⟨~ ears are a disqualification for this breed⟩ **:** erected in a position of attention ⟨a startled horse with sharply ~ ears⟩ **:** LISTENING ⟨keep your ears ~ for any information we can use⟩
prick ear *n* [back-formation fr. *prick-eared*] **:** an ear carried stiffly erect ⟨*prick ears* are required of most terriers by the breed standards⟩
prick-eared \(ˈ)=ˈ=\ *adj* **1 :** having erect pointed ears — used esp. of a dog; compare CROP-EARED 2 **2 :** having conspicuous ears
pricked \ˈprikt\ *adj* [ME *prikked,* fr. past part. of *prikken* to prick] **:** having pricks: as **a :** POINTED, DOTTED, PUNCTURED **b** *of a game bird* **:** slightly wounded with shot **:** WINGED
pricked-up coat *n, Brit* **:** SCRATCH COAT
prick·er \ˈprikə(r)\ *n* -S [ME *priker,* fr. *priken* to prick + *-er* — more at PRICK] **1 :** one that pricks: as **a :** a rider of horses **b :** a military light horseman **c :** a mounted helper at a hunt **:** WHIPPER-IN — used in the phrase *yeoman pricker* **d :** one who pricks suspected witches to determine their guilt or innocence **e :** one who uses a prick or pricker in various occupations **2 :** something that pricks, is prickly, or is used to prick or puncture something: as **a :** any of various sharp-pointed instruments for pricking holes **:** AWL; *esp* **:** a steel spike having the form of a small fid or marlinespike and used for punching eyelets in sailcloth **b :** BRIAR, PRICKLE, THORN **c :** a toothed roller for marking off a uniform dotted line or for pricking holes in tough material (as leather) prior to sewing **d** (1) *Brit* **:** a pointed bar used by miners esp. for bringing down coal from overhead (2) **:** ¹SNUFFER 3 **e :** an iron rod for sounding (as in a bog) **f :** CLIMBING IRON **g :** NEEDLE 8b **h** (1) **:** a founder's vent wire (2) **:** a pointed projection (as on a covering plate for a loam mold) to hold sand
prick·et \ˈprikət, *usu* -əd·+V\ *n* -S [ME *priket,* fr. *prik* prick + *-et* — more at PRICK] **1 a :** a spike or point on which a candle is stuck to hold it upright **b :** a candlestick with such a point **c** *obs* **:** a candle or taper esp. for use with a pricket holder **2** [prob. so called fr. the straightness of his horns] **a :** a buck in his second year — compare BROCKET **b :** the unbranched horn of a young male deer — called also *dag* **3** *obs* **:** a pointed finial or small spire

pricket 1b

prickfoot \ˈ=,=\ *n* **:** a low-growing prickly Australasian plant (*Eryngium vesiculosum*)
prickier *comparative of* PRICKY
prickiest *superlative of* PRICKY
pricking *n* -S [ME *priking,* fr. gerund of *priken* to prick] **1 :** an act or instance of piercing or puncturing with or as if with a sharp point **2 :** the condition or result of being pricked; *esp* **:** a sharp tingling sensation
prick·ing·ly *adv* **:** in a pricking manner **:** so as to prick
pricking-up \ˌ==ˈ=\ *n* -S **:** SCRATCH COAT
pricking wheel *n* **:** PRICKER 2c
prick·ish \ˈprikish, kēsh\ *adj* **:** easily irritated
¹**prick·le** \ˈprikəl\ *n* -S [ME *prikle, prikel,* fr. OE *pricle, pricel;* akin to MD *prikel* prickle; all fr. the root of E ¹*prick*] **1 :** a little prick **:** a small sharp point **:** a fine sharp process or projection (as from the skin of an animal) **:** a small spine or thorn; *esp* **:** a sharp pointed emergence arising from the epidermis or bark of a plant **2 a :** a prickling sensation **b prickles** *pl* **:** a stinging discomfort (as from prickly heat) ⟨decided, with hot ~*s* at the back of his neck, that a girl customer was giggling at him —Sinclair Lewis⟩
²**prickle** \"\ *vb* **prickled; prickled; prickling** \-k(ə)liŋ\ **prickles** *vt* **:** to prick slightly (as with a prick or prickles); *also* **:** to produce pricks, prickles, or prickings in ~ *vi* **:** to pierce, prod, or cause tingling with or as if with a prick or prickles ⟨how those burrs *prickled*⟩
³**prickle** \"\ *n* -S [origin unknown] **1 :** a wicker or willow basket orig. for fruit or flowers **2 :** a unit of weight that equals the weight of the contents of one prickle and usu. varies about 50 pounds
prickleback \ˈ==,=\ *n* [¹*prickle* + *back*] **:** STICKLEBACK
prickle cell *n* **:** a cell found in the germinal layer of the skin having numerous spines or radiating processes ⟨*prickle-cell* layer⟩
prickle-cone pine \ˈ==,=-\ *also* **prickly-cone pine** \ˈ==,=-\ *n* **:** BISHOP PINE
prick·led \ˈprikəld\ *adj* **:** having prickles
prickle grass *n* **:** a weedy tropical grass (*Tragus racemosus*) with prickly burs introduced into Texas and Arizona
prickle palm *var of* PRICKLY POLE
prick·less \ˈprikləs\ *adj* **1 :** free from prickles ⟨a ~ rose⟩ **2 :** not subjected to pricking **:** UNPRICKED ⟨escape ~ from the briars⟩
prick·li·ness \ˈpriklēnəs, -lin-\ *n* -ES **:** the quality or state of being prickly
prick·ling \ˈprik(ə)liŋ, -lēŋ\ *adj* **:** PRICKLY
pricklouse *n* [¹*prick* + *louse*] *obs* **:** TAILOR
prick·ly \ˈpriklē, -li\ *adj* -ER/-EST [¹*prickle* + *-y*] **1 a :** full of sharp points or prickles **:** covered with prickles ⟨a ~ shrub⟩ **b :** distinguished from related kinds by the presence of prickles **2 :** PRICKLING, STINGING ⟨a ~ sensation⟩ **3 a :** containing points likely to give rise to controversy **:** VEXATIOUS **b :** easily irritated **:** highly sensitive ⟨his ~ originality and sturdy independence —J.G.Robertson⟩
prickly apple *n* **:** a common West Indian thorny shrub or small tree (*Catesbaea spinosa*) — called also *lily thorn*
prickly ash *n* **1 a :** a prickly aromatic shrub or small tree (*Zanthoxylum americanum*) with yellowish flowers appearing with the pinnate leaves **b :** HERCULES'-CLUB 1a **2** *or* **prickly elder :** HERCULES'-CLUB 3 **3 :** an Australian tree (*Orites excelsa*) of the family Proteaceae having alternate lanceolate or obovate leaves, slender axillary spikes of flowers, and woody follicles
pricklyback \ˈ==,=\ *n* **:** STICKLEBACK
prickly beaver *n* **:** PORCUPINE
prickly broom *n* **:** FURZE
prickly bur *n* **:** the fruit of a common American chestnut (*Castanea dentata*)
prickly comfrey *n* **:** a rough-leaved European herb (*Symphytum asperum*) with bluish-purple flowers that is adventive in the eastern U.S. and is sometimes used for forage
prickly fern *n* **:** PRICKLY SHIELD FERN
prickly-fruited \ˌ==ˈ==\ *adj* **:** having the fruit covered with prickles or bristles ⟨a *prickly-fruited* cactus⟩
prickly fungus *n* **:** a fungus of the family Hydnaceae
prickly glasswort *n* **:** GLASSWORT 2
prickly gooseberry *n* **:** a wild gooseberry (*Ribes cynosbati*)
prickly heat *n* **:** a miliaria that is a noncontagious cutaneous eruption of red pimples attended with intense itching and tingling, occurring usu. in hot humid weather, and caused by inflammation of the skin around the sweat ducts
prickly juniper *n* **:** an evergreen shrub or small tree (*Juniperus oxycedrus*) with spine-tipped leaves
prickly lettuce *n* **:** a European annual wild lettuce (*Lactuca scariola*) having prickly stems and yellow flower heads and being a troublesome weed in parts of the U. S.
prickly mimosa *n* **1** *or* **prickly wattle :** a prickly-stemmed Australian acacia (*Acacia juniperina*) **2 :** KANGAROO ACACIA
prickly moses *n, Austral* **:** PRICKLY MIMOSA 1
prickly nightshade *n* **:** BUFFALO BUR
prickly pear *n* **1** *also* **prickly-pear cactus :** a flat-jointed cactus of the genus *Opuntia* often used as food for stock **2 :** the round, pear-shaped, or barrel-shaped fruit of prickly pear widely used as food esp. in tropical America — see TUNA
prickly pine *n* **1** *Austral* **:** LEOPARD TREE **2 a :** LODGEPOLE PINE **b :** TABLE-MOUNTAIN PINE
prickly poison *n* **:** an Australian poison bush (*Gastrolobium spinosum*)
prickly pole *also* **prickly palm** *or* **prickle palm** *n* **:** a West Indian palm (*Bactris plumeriana*) having a slender trunk with many rings of long black prickles
prickly poppy *n* **:** a plant of the genus *Argemone; esp* **:** an annual herb (*A. mexicana*) with large yellow flowers
prickly potato *n* **:** BUFFALO BUR
prickly saltwort *n* **:** GLASSWORT 2
prickly-seeded spinach \ˌ==ˈ==-\ *n* **:** SPINACH 1 — compare ROUND-SEEDED SPINACH
prickly shield fern *n* **:** a No. American fern (*Polystichum braunii*) having its almost coriaceous more or less evergreen fronds densely chaffy with pale brown scales
prickly sida *n* **:** INDIAN MALLOW 2
prickly sow thistle *n* **:** an annual European sow thistle (*Sonchus asper*) naturalized in No. America and having clasping spiny-toothed leaves with rounded basal auricles, lemon-yellow flower heads, and 3-nerved achenes
prickly spruce *n* **:** COLORADO SPRUCE
prickly tang *n* **:** a seaweed (*Fucus serratus*) — see ³TANG
prickly tea tree *n* **:** an Australian shrub (*Melaleuca styphelioides*) with pubescent spikes of white flowers
prickly thatch *n* **:** SILVERTOP 2a
prickly thrift *n* **:** a plant of the genus *Acantholimon* having stiff and prickly foliage (esp. *A. glumaceum*)
prickly yellowwood *or* **prickly yellow** *n* **:** any of several chiefly tropical American trees of the genus *Zanthoxylum; esp* **:** PRICKLY ASH
prick·mad·am \ˈprik,madəm\ *n* -S [modif. (influenced by ¹*prick*) of MF *trique-madame*] *dial chiefly Eng* **:** any of several stonecrops used chiefly in folk medicine as anthelmintics
¹**prickmedainty** \ˈ=(,)=ˈ==\ *adj* [²*prick* + *me* + *dainty*] *chiefly Scot* **:** affectedly nice **:** GOODY-GOODY
²**prickmedainty** \"\ *n, chiefly Scot* **:** an affectedly nice person **:** FOP
prick post *n* **:** a secondary or side post in a framed structure; *sometimes* **:** QUEEN POST
prick punch *n* **:** a pointed steel punch used to mark a reference point on metal or to puncture sheet metal for the insertion of rivets or bolts
prick-punch \ˈ=,=\ *vt* [*prick punch*] **:** to mark (as machine work) with a prick punch
pricks *pl of* PRICK, *pres 3d sing of* PRICK
prickseam \ˈ=,=\ *or* **prix·seam** \"\ *n* [*prickseam* fr. ¹*prick* + *seam; prixseam* alter. of *prickseam*] **:** a seam stitched on the outside (as of a glove) so that both raw edges show
prick shooting *n* **:** shooting (as an arrow) at a prick
prick song *n* [ME *prikked song,* fr. *prikked* pricked (i.e., dotted or written) + *song* — more at PRICKED] **1** *obs* **:** music that is written down **2 a :** descant as distinguished from the cantus firmus **b :** contrapuntal music
prickspur \ˈ=,=\ *n* **:** an ancient spur with a single point
prick stitch *n* **:** a short backstitch used chiefly on bulky materials and covering only a thread or two on the surface of the fabric
prick up *vt* **:** to apply a scratch coat of plaster to (as a wall)

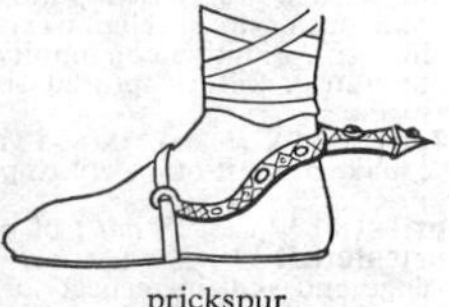

prickspur

prickwood \ˈ=,=\ *n* **1 :** SPINDLE TREE **2 :** RED DOGWOOD
pricky \ˈprikē, -ki\ *adj* -ER/-EST [¹*prick* + *-y*] **:** PRICKLY
pricy \ˈprīsi\ *adj* -ER/-EST [¹*price* + *-y*] *Austral* **:** LUXURIOUS, EXPENSIVE
¹**pride** \ˈprīd\ *n* -S [ME *pride, prude, prute,* fr. OE *prȳte, prȳde* pride, fr. *prūt, prūd* proud — more at PROUD] **1 :** the quality or state of being proud: as **a** (1) **:** inordinate self-esteem **:** an unreasonable conceit of superiority (as in talents, beauty, wealth, rank) (2) *usu cap* **:** such pride personified as one of the deadly sins **b :** a sense of one's own worth and abhorrence of what is beneath or unworthy of oneself **:** lofty self-respect **:** a reasonable or justifiable feeling of one's position ⟨a people which takes no ~ in the noble achievements of remote ancestors —T.B.Macaulay⟩ ⟨took a proper ~ in his skill⟩ **c :** a sense of delight or elation arising from some act or possession ⟨parental ~⟩ **2 :** proud or disdainful behavior or treatment **:** insolence or arrogance of demeanor **:** haughty bearing **:** DISDAIN ⟨let not the foot of ~ come against me —Ps 36:11 (AV)⟩ **3 a :** inordinate show **:** ostentatious display **:** MAGNIFICENCE ⟨~, pomp, and circumstance of glorious war —Shak.⟩ **b :** showy decoration or adornment **:** magnificent or splendid ornamentation — used of a bird (as a peacock) in full display **c :** highest pitch **:** elevation reached **:** LOFTINESS, PRIME ⟨in the ~ of one's life⟩ **4 a :** something of which one is proud or which excites pride **:** the best in a group or class **:** PICK ⟨a bold peasantry their country's ~ —Oliver Goldsmith⟩ **b** *obs* **:** exalted position **:** place such as may reasonably incite to pride **5 a** *obs* **:** a sense of power **:** fullness of animal spirits **:** METTLE **b :** sexual desire **:** LUST, HEAT — used chiefly of a female domestic animal **c** *obs* **:** WANTONNESS, EXCESS, EXTRAVAGANCE, OVERBOLDNESS **6 a** *of lions* **:** COMPANY **b :** a showy or pretentious group ⟨the queen surrounded by a ~ of gaily dressed ladies⟩ ⟨a pompous ~ of civic notables⟩ **7 prides** *pl, chiefly Midland* **:** the male genitals
syn VANITY, VAINGLORY: PRIDE may be commendatory in indicating a justified self-esteem, proper self-respect, or dislike of falling below one's standards that spurs one on, buoys one up, or checks one from base decisions ⟨civic *pride* that brings them great satisfaction and strengthens their character —J.C. Penney⟩ ⟨this *pride* as an integral feeling of self-respect —J.C. Powys⟩ It may be uncomplimentary in designating an unjustified self-esteem arising from a false, inflated, and pretentious sense of one's worth culminating in arrogant conceit ⟨it is not exactly *pride;* there is no strut or swagger in it though perhaps just a little condescension —John Burroughs⟩ ⟨this race so admirably endowed, with ambitions ever unsatisfied, modeling, in insatiable *pride,* its gods after its own likeness —Agnes Repplier⟩ VANITY indicates an unsound, ill-based false pride and self-glorifying or self-centering with specious concern about trivialities ⟨one of the troubles about *vanity* is that it grows with what it feeds on. The more you are talked about, the more you will wish to be talked about —Bertrand Russell⟩ ⟨her face was intent and fixed upon her image in the mirror; *vanity* had superseded shyness in her innocent mind —Elinor Wylie⟩ VAINGLORY may suggest excessive or meretricious pride flaunted with boastful arrogance ⟨*vainglorie* , rivalries, and earthly heats that spring and sparkle out among us in the jousts —Alfred Tennyson⟩
²**pride** \"\ *vb* -ED/-ING/-S [ME *priden, pruden,* fr. *pride, prude,* n.] *vt* **1 :** to indulge (as oneself) in pride **:** take credit to **:** rate highly **:** PLUME ⟨~ herself upon her skill⟩ **2 :** to make (as a person) feel proud **:** infect or fill with pride **3** *obs* **a :** ADORN, GLORIFY **b** *of a bird* **:** to cause (the feathers) to spread in display ~ *vi* **1 :** to be or grow proud — sometimes used with *it* **2 :** to pride oneself or take pride in or over something
³**pride** \"\ *n* -S [origin unknown] **:** SAND PRIDE; *also* **:** a larval lamprey
pride·ful \-fəl\ *adj* [ME *pridefulle,* fr. *pride* + *-fulle* -ful] **:** full of pride: as **a :** HAUGHTY **b :** ELATED — **pride·ful·ly** \-fəlē, -li\ *adv* — **pride·ful·ness** \-lnəs\ *n* -ES
pride·less \ˈprīdləs\ *adj* [ME *pridelees,* fr. *pride* + *-lees* -less] **:** lacking in pride; *often* **:** having no proper self-respect — **pride·less·ly** *adv*
pride of barbados *usu cap B* **:** a thorny shrub or small tree (*Poinciana pulcherrima*) with showy yellow to bright orange-red flowers
pride of california *usu cap C* **:** a Californian wild pea (*Lathyrus splendens*) that is cultivated for ornament and has long climbing stems and large pink or violet flowers
pride of china *usu cap C* **:** CHINABERRY 2
pride-of-india \ˌ==ˈ=(=)=\ *n, usu cap I* **:** CHINABERRY 2
pride of ohio *usu cap 2d O* **:** the common American shooting star (*Dodecatheon meadia*)
pride of place : the highest or first position
pride of the morning : a light fog or misty dew such as often precedes a fine day
pride-of-the-peak \ˌ===ˈ=\ *n* **:** an orchid (*Habenaria paramoena*) chiefly of southeastern U.S. that has rose-purple to violet flowers with the lip shallowly erose and the terminal lobe deeply emarginate
prides *pl of* PRIDE, *pres 3d sing of* PRIDE
prideweed \ˈ=,=\ *n* **1 :** HORSEWEED 1 **2 :** HORSETAIL 2
prideworthy \(ˈ)=ˈ==\ *adj* **:** of a kind or quality in which one may take pride
prid·i·an \ˈprideən\ *adj* [L *pridianus,* fr. *pridie* on the day before (fr. *pri-* before — as in L *prior* — + *dies* day) + *-anus* -an — more at PRIOR, DEITY] **:** of or relating to a previous day or to yesterday; *also* **:** FORMER ⟨a ~ monarchy —Hugh McCrae⟩
prid·ing·ly \ˈprīdiŋlē\ *adv* **:** with a show of pride **:** VAUNTINGLY, PROUDLY
pridy \ˈprīdē, ˈprid-, -di\ *adj* [ME (Sc), fr. *pride* + *-y*] *chiefly dial* **:** PROUD
prie \ˈprē\ *var of* PREE
pried *past of* PRY
prie-dieu \(ˈ)prēd¦y|ə(r), ˈprēdē¦, |ə\ *n, pl* **prie-dieus** *or* **prie-dieux** \-(z)\ *also* **prie-dieu** [F *prie-Dieu,* lit., pray God] **1 :** a small kneeling bench designed for use by a person at prayer and fitted often with a raised shelf on which the elbows or a book may be rested and sometimes with storage space (as for articles of devotion) **2 :** a low upholstered chair without arms and with a high straight back

prie-dieu 1

pri·er *also* **pry·er** \ˈprī(ə)r, ˈprīə\ *n* -S [¹*pry* + *-er*] **:** one that pries **:** a close inquirer **:** an inquisitive person
pries *pres 3d sing of* PRY, *pl of* PRY
¹**priest** \ˈprēst\ *n* -S [ME *prest, preist,* fr. OE *prēost,* modif. of LL *presbyter,* fr. Gk *presbyteros* priest,

elder, older, fr. compar. of *presbys* old, fr. a prehistoric compound whose first constituent is akin to Gk *paros* before, OE *first* period, interval, delay, OHG *frist*, ON *frest* period, interval, delay, Gk *pro* before, ahead and whose second constituent is akin to Gk *bous* head of cattle; basic meaning: leader of the herd — more at FOR, COW] **1 :** one who performs sacrificial, ritualistic, mediatorial, interpretative, or ministerial functions esp. as an authorized or ordained religious functionary or official minister of a particular religion: **a** (1) **:** a member of the second order of clergy in the ancient Christian and Anglican communions ranking below a bishop and above a deacon (2) **:** a member of the highest order of clergy in the Roman Catholic Church since the Reformation and in the Eastern Orthodox Church (3) **:** a professional clergyman of a religious denomination **:** a minister of religion (4) **:** a member of the Aaronic priesthood of the Mormon Church ranking above deacon and teacher and authorized to administer the sacrament of the Lord's Supper and to baptize **b :** a religious functionary who serves at the altar or performs sacrifices at the altar of a pre-Christian or non-Christian religion ⟨ordained that the Levites should be the ~*s* of the tabernacle⟩ ⟨a ~ of Apollo⟩ **c :** a person having a specific religious or quasi religious status (as a witch doctor or seer) in his usu. primitive community **2 :** a short club used by anglers to stun or kill a captured fish **3** *often cap* **:** a breed of fancy pigeons

²**priest** \"\ *vb* -ED/-ING/-S *vt* **:** to ordain (a person) as priest **:** make a priest of ~ *vi* **:** to perform priestly offices **:** serve as a priest

priest·al \'prēst³l\ *adj* **:** of priests **:** PRIESTLY

priestcraft \'ˌ=,=\ *n* [¹*priest* + *craft*] **1 :** professional knowledge and skill in respect to the exercise of priestly functions **2 :** the scheming and machinations of priests **:** priestly intriguing

priest·dom \'prēs(t)dəm\ *n* -S [¹*priest* + *-dom*] **:** the dominion of priests **:** religious rule

priest·ess \'prēstəs\ *n* -ES [¹*priest* + *-ess*] **:** a female priest

priestfish \'=,=\ *n* **:** a common rockfish (*Sebastodes mystinus*) of the Pacific coast of No. America that is slaty or bluish black above fading to white on the belly and is a leading sport fish of shallow waters

priest hole *or* **priest's hole** *n* **:** a secret room or place of concealment for a priest (as in an English house during the proscription of Roman Catholic priests)

priest·hood \'prēst,hu̇d, -,stu̇d\ *n* -S [ME *presthod*, fr. OE *prēosthād*, fr. *prēost* priest + *-hād* -hood] **1 :** the office of a priest **:** priestly function **:** sacerdotal character **2 :** the order of priests **:** PRIESTS **3 :** the authority to speak and administer in the name of the Deity given in the Mormon Church by ordination; *also* **:** the body of those so ordained including those of the Aaronic as well as the Melchizedek orders

priesthood of all believers : a doctrine of the Protestant Christian Church: every individual has direct access to God without ecclesiastical mediation and each individual shares the responsibility of ministering to the other members of the community of believers

priest·ian·i·ty \ˌprēs(h)chē'anəd·ē *also* ˌprēstē'a- *or* prēs(h)-'cha- *sometimes* prēst'ya-\ *n* -ES [¹*priest* + *-ianity* (as in *christianity*)] **:** religion that emphasizes the office or power of the priest — usu. used disparagingly

priest·ish \'prēstish\ *adj* **:** PRIESTLIKE

priest·ism \-,stizəm\ *n* -S **:** the influence, doctrines, or principles of priests — usu. used disparagingly

priest·ist \-,stəst\ *n* -S *usu cap* [trans. of Russ *popovets*] **:** POPOVETS

priest-king \(')=¦=\ *n* -S **:** a sacerdotal ruler **:** one who rules as king by right of his priestly office functioning as vice-regent of a deity

¹**priest·less** \'prēs(t)ləs\ *adj* **:** having no priest ⟨a ~ religion⟩

²**priestless** \"\ *n* -ES *usu cap* [trans. of Russ *bezpopovets*] **:** BEZPOPOVETS

priest·let \'s(t)lət\ *n* -S [¹*priest* + *-let*] **:** a young, new, or unimportant priest **:** PRIESTLING

priestlike \'=,=\ *adv* (*or adj*) [ME *preistlik*, fr. *preist* priest + *lik* like — more at PRIEST, LIKE] **:** like a priest **:** in the manner or character of or befitting to a priest **:** PRIESTLY

priest·li·ness \'prēs(t)lēnəs, -lin-\ *n* -ES [*priestly* + *-ness*] **:** the professional quality or manner of a priest **:** priestly characteristics

priest·ling \'prēs(t)liŋ, -lēŋ\ *n* -S [*priest* + *-ling*] **1 a :** a young priest **b :** a petty priest **2 :** one devoted to or under the influence of priests

priest·ly \-s(t)lē, -li\ *adj* -ER/-EST [ME, fr. OE *prēostlic*, fr. *prēost* priest + *-lic* -ly] **:** of or relating to a priest or the priesthood **:** SACERDOTAL **:** resembling or characteristic of a priest **:** befitting or becoming to a priest

priestly blessing *n* [trans. of LHeb *birkhāt kōhănīm*] **:** a Hebrew blessing of the people pronounced by a cohen or cohanim in a synagogue on festival days in accordance with the command and formula of Num 6: 22–27; *also* **:** an English translation of this blessing pronounced by a rabbi at various occasions (as at a bar mitzvah)

priest-ridden \(')=¦==\ *adj* **:** controlled or oppressed by a priest

prests *pl of* PRIEST, *pres 3d sing of* PRIEST

priest's-crown \(')=¦=\ *n*, *pl* **priest's-crowns** [ME *prestes crowne*, fr. *prestes*, gen. of *prest* priest + *crowne* crown; fr. the bald appearance of the receptacle — more at PRIEST, CROWN] **:** DANDELION 1

priest·ship \'prēs(t),ship, -ēs,chip, -ēsh,ship\ *n* **:** the office of a priest

priestshire *n* [OE *prēost-scīr*, fr. *prēost* priest + *scīr* shire — more at PRIEST, SHIRE] *obs* **:** an ecclesiastical parish

priest's hole *var of* PRIEST HOLE

priest vicar *n* **:** a vicar choral of the Church of England in priest's orders **:** MINOR CANON

¹**prig** *n* -S [ME, alter. of *sprig*] *obs* **:** a small nail **:** BRAD

²**prig** \'prig\ *vb* **prigged**; **prigged**; **prigging**; **prigs** *vt* [origin unknown] *chiefly Brit* **:** STEAL, FILCH, PILFER ~ *vi* **1** *chiefly Scot* **:** to haggle about or over something **:** quibble over money or price **:** drive a hard bargain **2** *chiefly Scot* **:** ENTREAT, PLEAD, BEG

³**prig** \"\ *n* **1** *obs* **:** TINKER **2 :** THIEF, PILFERER

⁴**prig** \"\ *n* [prob. fr. ³*prig*] **1** *archaic* **:** FELLOW, PERSON **2** *archaic* **:** FOP, BUCK, DANDY **3 a :** a notably or excessively punctilious person **b** *obs* **:** a nonconformist minister; *broadly* **:** PURITAN **4 :** one who offends or irritates by obvious or rigid observance of the proprieties (as in speech, manners, or conduct) **:** one self-sufficient in virtue, culture, or propriety often in a pointed manner or to an obnoxious degree

⁵**prig** \"\ *adj* **:** PRIGGISH

prig·ger \'prigə(r)\ *n* -S [²*prig* + *-er*] *archaic* **:** THIEF

prig·gery \-gərē, -ri\ *n* -ES [⁴*prig* + *-ery*] **:** PRIGGISHNESS

prig·gish \'prigish, -gēsh\ *adj* [⁴*prig* + *-ish*] **:** characteristic or suggestive of a prig; *esp* **:** marked by overvaluing oneself or one's ideas, habits, notions, by precise or inhibited adherence to them, and by small disparagement of others ⟨the instructor must not act like a ~ moderator with a gavel —J.M.Barzun⟩

syn see COMPLACENT

prig·gish·ly *adv* **:** in a priggish manner

prig·gish·ness *n* -ES **1 :** the quality or state of being priggish **2 :** a priggish act or piece of conduct

¹**prig·gism** \'pri,gizəm\ *n* -S [³*prig* + *-ism*] *archaic* **:** THIEVISHNESS, ROGUERY

²**priggism** \"\ *n* -S [⁴*prig* + *-ism*] **:** self-conscious propriety of conduct **:** stilted correctness of behavior **:** prim adherence to conventionality **:** PRIGGISHNESS

¹**prill** \'pril\ *n* -S [alter. of ³*purl*] *dial chiefly Eng* **:** a running stream

²**prill** \"\ *vt* -ED/-ING/-S [perh. fr. ¹*prill*] **1 :** to convert (a solid) into spherical pellets (as by forcing a melt through a nozzle and allowing the molten drops to solidify while falling) **2 :** to make (a granular or crystalline material) free flowing

³**prill** \"\ *n* -S **:** a pellet made by prilling

⁴**prill** \"\ *n* -S [origin unknown] **:** rich copper ore selected for excellence

pril·lion \'prilyən\ *n* -S [alter. (influenced by ⁴*prill*) of *pillion*] **:** tin extracted from slag — compare PILLION

¹**prim** \'prim\ *n* -S [short for obs. *primprint* privet, of unknown origin] **:** PRIVET 1a

²**prim** \"\ *vb* **primmed**; **primmed**; **primming**; **prims** [origin unknown] *vi* **:** to make oneself or one's expression prim **:** assume a prim manner or appearance ⟨they mince and ~ and pout —George Meredith⟩ ~ *vt* **1 :** to give a prim or demure expression to ⟨*primming* her thin lips after every mouthful of tea —John Buchan⟩ **2 :** to arrange or dress affectedly or demurely — usu. used with *up* or *out* ⟨~ her up in an old-fashioned gown⟩

³**prim** \"\ *adj*, *usu* **primmer**; *usu* **primmest 1 a :** formal and precise in manner or appearance **:** stiffly decorous ⟨a ~ and slightly sardonic man —W.J.Locke⟩ ⟨*prim*-lipped⟩ **b :** PRUDISH ⟨was at heart intensely ~, easily shocked —*Time*⟩ **2 :** NEAT, TRIM ⟨~ little egg saucers —Sheila Hibben⟩ ⟨~ little spicy gardens —*Amer. Guide Series: Texas*⟩

prim *abbr* **1** primary **2** primate **3** primitive

¹**pri·ma** \'prēmə\ *adj* [It, fem of *primo*, fr. L *primus* — more at PRIME] **:** FIRST, LEADING

²**prima** *var of* PRIMA VOLTA

³**pri·ma** \'prīmə\ *n* -S [L, fem. of *primus* first] **:** the first word of the next galley proof or page of copy marked on the corresponding page or galley; *also* **:** the word at which reading is to be resumed after an interruption — compare MARKOFF

prima ballerina *n* **:** the leading female dancer in a ballet company

pri·ma·cy \'prīməsē, -si\ *n* -ES [ME *primacie*, fr. MF, fr. ML *primatia*, fr. L *primat-*, *primas* one of the first, leader + *-ia* -y — more at PRIMATE] **1 :** the state of being first (as in importance, order, or rank) **:** PRECEDENCE, PREEMINENCE, SUPERIORITY ⟨the ~ of the deed over word and thought —Gilbert Highet⟩ ⟨too proud of the ~ of his intelligence to listen —Eliseo Vivas⟩ **2 :** the office, rank, or character of an ecclesiastical primate **:** the chief ecclesiastical station or dignity in a church; *also* **:** supreme episcopal jurisdiction

prima don·na \ˌprimə'dänə, -rēm-\ *n*, *pl* **prima donnas** [It, lit., first lady] **1 :** the leading or a principal female singer in an opera or concert organization **2 :** a person who finds it difficult to work under direction or as part of a team **:** one who is impatient of restraint or criticism ⟨we are looking for good teammates, rather than *prima donnas* —*Farm Chemicals*⟩

primaeval *var of* PRIMEVAL

¹**pri·ma fa·cie** \ˌprīmə'fāshē,ē, -shē\ *adv* [L] **:** at first view **:** on the first appearance ⟨bears out what is *prima facie* probable —D.M.Davin⟩

²**prima facie** \"\ *adj* **1 :** based on immediate impression **:** APPARENT ⟨*prima facie* plausibility⟩ **2 :** generally applicable but admitting of suspension in a given case ⟨a *prima facie* right⟩

prima facie case *n* **:** a case established by prima facie evidence

prima facie evidence *n* **:** evidence sufficient in law to raise a presumption of fact or establish the fact in question unless rebutted

pri·mage \'prīmij, -mēj\ *n* -S [prob. fr. ⁴*prime* + *-age*] **1 a :** a small payment made by shippers to the captain of a ship for his special care of their goods — called also *hat money* **b :** a small percentage added to the freight charge and paid to the owner of a ship as extra compensation **2 :** a primary ad valorem revenue duty laid by the Australian government on imports

pri·mal \'prīməl\ *adj* [ML *primalis*, fr. L *primus* first + *-alis* -al] **1 :** of or relating to the first period or state **:** ORIGINAL, PRIMITIVE ⟨village life continued in its ~ innocence —Van Wyck Brooks⟩ **2 :** first in importance **:** FUNDAMENTAL, PRINCIPAL ⟨paper money was a ~ necessity to the colonists —J.C.Fitzpatrick⟩

primal cut *n* **:** any of various wholesale cuts (as a quarter, side, or ham) into which the carcass of a food animal is divided

pri·mal·i·ty \prī'maləd·ē\ *n* -ES **:** the quality or state of being primal

primal scene *n* **:** sexual intercourse performed by parents and observed by their child ⟨permitted to . . . witness parental nakedness and *primal scenes* —Victor Eisenstein⟩

pri·ma·quine \'prēmə,kwēn, 'prīm-, -,kwən\ *n* -S [¹*prima* + *-quine* (fr. *quinoline*)] **:** an antimalarial drug $C_{15}H_{21}N_3O$ derived from a methoxy-quinoline and used in the form of its diphosphate

pri·maried \'prī,merēd, -,m(ə)rēd\ *adj* [²*primary* + *-ed*] *of a bird* **:** having primaries — usu. used in combination ⟨ten-*primaried*⟩

pri·mar·i·ly \(')prī'merəlē, ˌprə'm-, -li\ *adv* **1 :** first of all **:** FUNDAMENTALLY, PRINCIPALLY ⟨has now become ~ a residential town —S.P.B.Mais⟩ **2 :** in the first place **:** ORIGINALLY ⟨~ nomads, they eventually settled down to farming⟩

pri·mari·ness \(')prī'merēnəs, 'prīm(ə)rē-\ *n* -ES **:** the quality or state of being primary ⟨this ~ of elements, these gaseous atoms —Saul Levitt⟩

¹**pri·mary** \'prī,merē, -,m(ə)rē, -ri\ *adj* [LL *primarius* basic, primary, fr. L, principal, fr. *primus* first + *-arius* -ary — more at PRIME] **1 a :** first in order of time or development **:** INITIAL **:** PRIMITIVE ⟨the ~ forest⟩ ⟨the ~ stage of civilization⟩ ⟨~ tuberculosis⟩ **b** (1) **:** of or relating to geological formations of the Paleozoic and earlier periods (2) *of minerals or ore deposits* **:** formed first; *esp* **:** formed under igneous, pneumatolytic, or hydrothermal conditions **:** HYPOGENE **2 a :** first in rank or importance **:** CHIEF, PRINCIPAL ⟨the ~ duty of safeguarding the peace of the world —P.J.Noel-Baker⟩ ⟨the ~ member of the cabinet⟩ **b :** BASIC, FUNDAMENTAL ⟨man has always used the most durable materials available for his ~ tools —R.W.Murray⟩ ⟨the family is still the ~ human association —Kimball Young⟩ **c :** of, relating to, or constituting the principal quills of a bird's wing **d :** of or relating to agriculture, forestry, and the extractive industries or their products ⟨~ economic activities⟩ ⟨~ goods⟩ ⟨world ~ prices have dipped significantly below their recent peaks —W.T.C.King⟩ **e :** expressive of present or future time — used of a grammatical tense ⟨the present, future, perfect, and future perfect indicative are the Greek ~ tenses⟩ **f :** of, relating to, or constituting the strongest of the three or the four degrees of stress recognized by most linguists **3 :** functioning or transmitted without intermediary **:** DIRECT ⟨require ~ assistance if they are to be kept from starving and freezing to death —*N.Y. Times*⟩ **4 a :** not derived from or dependent on something else **:** FIRSTHAND, INDEPENDENT, ORIGINAL ⟨a very useful ~ historical source —R.A.Hall b.1911⟩ ⟨~ research⟩ **b** *of a color* **:** not derivable from other colors **c :** preparatory to something else **:** belonging to the first stage of some continuing process or series; *specif* **:** of or relating to a primary school ⟨~ education⟩ ⟨~ grades⟩ ⟨~ instruction⟩ **d :** belonging to the first group or order in successive divisions, combinations, or ramifications ⟨~ nerves⟩ ⟨~ compounds⟩ **e :** of, relating to, or constituting the inducing current or its circuit in an induction coil or transformer ⟨the ~ voltage⟩ ⟨~ current⟩ **f :** directly derived from ore **:** VIRGIN ⟨~ aluminum⟩ ⟨~ copper⟩ **5 :** characterized by replacement in the first degree **:** resulting from the substitution of one of two or more atoms or groups in a molecule ⟨a ~ phosphate⟩; *esp* **:** being or characterized by a carbon atom united by a single valence to only one chain or ring member ⟨a ~ radical RCH_2– such as ethyl or benzyl⟩ — compare SECONDARY, TERTIARY

²**primary** \"\ *n* -ES **1 :** something that stands first in order, rank, or importance **:** FUNDAMENTAL — usu. used in pl. **2** [short for *primary planet*] **a :** a planet as distinguished from its satellites **b :** the brighter component of a double star **3 a** *also* **primary quill :** one of the quills on the distal joint of a bird's wing that are attached to the bones of the hand and its fingers and are usu. 9 or 10 in number — see BIRD illustration **b :** either of the forewings of an insect **c** (1) **:** one of the first formed plates in the development of the skeleton of an echinoderm after metamorphosis (2) **:** an ambulacral plate of a sea urchin extending half across the ambulacral area; *also* **:** the largest spine or one of the largest spines on any plate of the test or the tubercle bearing it — compare SECONDARY 6c **4 a :** PRIMARY COLOR **b :** a primary-color sensation **5 :** PRIMARY COIL **6** [trans. of F (*assemblée*) *primaire*] **a :** CAUCUS 1b **b** *or* **primary election :** an election in which qualified voters nominate or express a preference for a particular candidate or group of candidates for political office, choose party officials, or select delegates for a party convention — see CLOSED PRIMARY, DIRECT PRIMARY, NONPARTISAN PRIMARY, OPEN PRIMARY, PRESIDENTIAL PRIMARY

primary accent *n* **:** the first and chief accent or beat of a musical measure

primary air *n* **:** air admitted to the fuel stream or area ahead of the combustion zone in a burner or furnace

primary alcohol *n* **:** an alcohol that possesses the group $-CH_2OH$ and can be oxidized so as to form a corresponding aldehyde and acid having the same number of carbon atoms

primary alphabet *n* **:** an alphabetic sequence serving as a component of a substitution alphabet; *esp* **:** a mixed sequence serving as a cipher component

primary amine *n* **:** an amine RNH_2 (as methylamine) having one organic substituent attached to the nitrogen atom

primary atypical pneumonia *n* **:** a usu. mild pneumonia caused by a virus or a pleuropneumonia-like organism

primary battery *n* **:** an assembly of two or more primary cells

primary benefit *n* **:** the retirement benefit to which a worker is entitled at age 65 based upon credits earned in employment covered under Federal Old Age and Survivors Insurance

primary body *n* **:** the parts and appendages of the root and stem of a plant that are built up from apical meristems — compare SECONDARY BODY

primary body cavity *n* **:** BLASTOCOEL

primary burial *n* **:** the initial burial of a human corpse or the buried remains — contrasted with *secondary burial*

primary cause *n* **:** FIRST CAUSE

primary cell *n* **:** a cell that converts chemical energy into electrical energy by irreversible chemical reactions and that cannot be recharged by passing an electric current through it — compare STORAGE CELL

primary circle *n* **:** one of the four fundamental great circles of the celestial sphere ⟨the horizon, celestial equator, ecliptic, and galactic equator are *primary circles*⟩

primary coil *n* **:** the coil through which the inducing current passes in an induction coil or transformer

primary color *n* **:** any of a set of colors from which all other colors may be derived — see ADDITIVE PRIMARY, PSYCHOLOGICAL PRIMARY, SUBTRACTIVE PRIMARY

primary commercial blanket bond : a blanket bond covering any loss up to a stated amount caused by the dishonest act of an employee or group of employees

primary constriction *n* **:** CENTROMERE

primary covert *n* **:** a wing covert covering the base of a primary of a bird

primary deposit *n* **:** a bank deposit consisting of cash, checks, or other demands for payments — compare DERIVATIVE DEPOSIT

primary endosperm nucleus *n* **:** the nucleus formed by the fusion of two polar nuclei in the embryo sac of a seed plant prior to fertilization — called also *secondary nucleus;* compare ENDOSPERM NUCLEUS

primary evidence *n* **1 :** the evidence usu. of self-validating written documents primarily required by law as the best evidence of a fact to be proved **2 :** PRIMA FACIE EVIDENCE

primary explosive *n* **:** an explosive (as mercury fulminate or lead azide) that is sensitive to friction, blows, shock, or heat

primary group *n* **:** a social group (as a family or circle of friends) characterized by a high degree of affective interpersonal contact and exerting a strong influence on the social attitudes and ideals of the individual — contrasted with *secondary group;* compare GEMEINSCHAFT

primary growth *n* **:** growth by the activity of a primary meristem resulting mainly in an increase in length and the addition of appendages — compare SECONDARY GROWTH

primary host *n* **:** DEFINITIVE HOST

primary humor *n* **:** HUMOR 1b(1)

primary infection *n* **:** the initial infection of a host by a pathogen that has completed a resting or dormant period

primary intention *n* **:** FIRST INTENTION

primary jurisdiction *n* **:** the right or responsibility of an administrative or regulatory agency to pass initially on controversies involving matters of fact or discretion within its sphere before relief is sought in the courts

primary lesion *n* **:** the initial lesion of a disease (as of cancer); *specif* **:** the chancre of syphilis

primary lookout *n* **:** LOOKOUT 2b

primary market *n* **1 :** a wholesale market large enough to dominate the trade in some goods over a large area **2 :** PRIMARY POINT

primary meeting *n* **:** CAUCUS 1b

primary memory *n* **:** memory of what has just occurred

primary meristem *n* **:** a meristem consisting of direct derivatives of embryonic cells that are always active in growth — compare SECONDARY MERISTEM

primary minimum *n* **:** a depression in the light curve of an eclipsing variable that occurs when the brighter in surface brightness of the two stars is eclipsed by the fainter one

primary narcissism *n* **:** the stage of a child's primary concern with himself as an organism prior to awareness of external reality as a mediating factor

primary phloem *n* **:** the first-formed phloem; *specif* **:** phloem developed from an apical meristem

primary pit field *n* **:** a thin area in the walls of many cells which is esp. conspicuous in cambium initials and in which one or more pits usu. develop

primary point *n* **:** a large city that receives agricultural products in considerable quantities direct from country shippers

primary protective layer *n* **:** a layer developed within the separation layer in leaves of deciduous plants at the time of leaf fall that protects the exposed cells from desiccation and infection until the periderm forms

primary quality *n* **:** a quality (as bulk) that is inseparable from a physical object and is in it as in our perception of it ⟨these I call original or *primary qualities* of body, which I think we may observe to produce simple ideas in us, viz. solidity, extension, figure, motion or rest, and number —John Locke⟩ — contrasted with *secondary quality*

primary quill *n* **:** PRIMARY 3a

primary rainbow *n* **:** a rainbow in which the effective rays are refracted on entering each drop, reflected from its interior surface, and refracted again on emerging to pass to the observer's eye and in which the red is seen on the outside edge of the bow

primary ray *n* **:** a vascular ray developed during primary growth

primary receipts *n pl* **:** the daily receipt of goods at a primary point

primary release *n* **:** an arrow release in which the arrow and bowstring are held between the thumb and forefinger

primary reserve *n* **:** a bank's cash on hand and deposits in other banks

primary road *n* **:** a principal usu. state-maintained road in a recognized system of highways

primary rocks *n pl* **:** the rocks believed to have been first formed — called also *primitive rocks*

primary root *n* **:** the root of a plant that is the first to develop and that originates from the radicle

primary salt *n* **:** a salt derived from a polyacid in which only one acid hydrogen atom has been replaced by a base or basic radical

primary school *n* **1 a :** a school at which children receive their first formal education usu. comprising the first three grades of elementary school but sometimes also including kindergarten **b :** ELEMENTARY SCHOOL **2** *Brit* **:** a school for children from five to eleven years of age

primary shipments *n pl* **:** the daily shipments from a primary point

primary spermatocyte *n* **:** a cell of the next to last generation preceding the spermatozoon

primary substance *n* **:** SUBSTANCE 2a(1), 2a(4)

primary succession *n* **:** PRISERE

primary syphilis *n* **:** the first stage of syphilis marked by the development of the chancre and the spread of the causative spirochete in the tissues and organs of the body

primary tissue *n* **:** plant tissue developed during primary growth — compare MERISTEM

primary triad *n* **:** one of the triads on the first, fourth, or fifth note or tone of any major or minor musical scale

primary type *n* **:** one of the specimens upon which the description of a new biological species is actually based

primary wall *n* **:** the first-formed wall of a plant cell that is produced around the protoplast next to the middle lamella, is usu. anisotropic in polarized light, and possesses plasmodesmata — compare SECONDARY WALL

primary xylem *n* **:** the first-formed xylem; *specif* **:** xylem developed from an apical meristem

¹pri·mate \'prī,māt, -,mət, *usu* -d·+V\ *n* -s [ME *primat*, fr. OF, fr. ML *primat-, primas* archbishop, fr. LL, archbishop, head, leader, fr. L, one of the first, leader, fr. *primus* first — more at PRIME] **1** *often cap* **:** a bishop who has precedence in a province, group of provinces, or a nation **2** *archaic* **:** one who is first in authority or rank **:** LEADER ⟨the prince . . . is the ~ and pearl of nobility —Richard Mulcaster⟩ **3 :** a mammal of the order Primates

²primate \"\ *adj* **:** PRINCIPAL ⟨another bid for recognition as the world's ~ city —*Focus*⟩

pri·ma·tes \prī'mād·(,)ēz, -ā,tēz\ *n pl, cap* [NL, fr. pl. of L *primat-, primas* one of the first] **:** an order of eutherian mammals including man, apes, monkeys, lemurs, and living and extinct related forms that are all thought to be derived from generalized arboreal ancestors descended in turn from shrewlike precursors during the Paleocene and that are in general characterized by increasing perfection of binocular vision, specialization of the appendages for grasping, and enlargement and differentiation of the brain

pri·mate·ship \'=(,)=,ship\ *n* **1 :** the office, dignity, or position of a primate **2 :** PRIMACY

pri·ma·tial \prī'māshəl\ *adj* [F, fr. MF, fr. ML *primatialis*, fr. *primatia* primacy + L *-alis* -al — more at PRIMACY] **1 :** of, relating to, or characteristic of a primate ⟨was deprived of his ~ authority —F.M.Stenton⟩ **2 :** having primacy **:** PRINCIPAL ⟨the ~ city of ancient Ireland —W.G.Carleton⟩

primatial council *n* **:** an assembly of church officials composed of representatives of an ecclesiastical province, a primatial jurisdiction, or an entire nation

pri·mat·i·cal \(')prī¦mad·ə̇kəl\ *adj* [¹*primate* + *-ical*] **:** PRIMATIAL

pri·ma·tol·o·gist \,prīmə'täləjə̇st\ *n* -s **:** a specialist in primatology

pri·ma·tol·o·gy \-jē, -ji\ *n* -ES [NL *Primates* + E *-o-* + *-logy*] **:** the study of members of the order Primates esp. other than recent man

pri·ma·ve·ra \,prēmə'verə\ *n* -s [AmerSp, lit., spring, fr. Sp, spring, fr. LL *prima vera*, fr. fem. of L *primum ver* early spring, fr. *primus* first + *ver* spring; fr. its early flowering — more at VERNAL] **1 :** a Central American timber tree (*Cybistax donnellsmithii*) with brilliant yellow flowers **2 :** the hard light wood of the primavera — called also *white mahogany*

pri·ma·ve·ral \¦prīmə¦virəl\ *adj* [Sp, fr. *primavera* spring + *-al* (fr. L *-alis* -al)] **:** of or relating to early spring ⟨took full advantage of the ~ weather —*Time*⟩

¹pri·ma vol·ta \¦prēmə¦vōltə\ *also* **pri·ma** \'prēmə\ *adv (or adj)* [It] **:** at the first time — used as a direction in music to perform the first time but omit at the repetition

²prima volta \"\ *also* **prima** \"\ *n* **:** a part performed or to be performed prima volta in a piece of music

¹prime \'prīm\ *n* -s [ME, fr. OE *prīm*, fr. L *prima (hora)* first hour, fr. *prima*, fem. of *primus* first + *hora* hour — more at HOUR] **1 a** *often cap* **:** a religious office constituting the first of the daytime canonical hours — compare LAUD, MATINS **b :** the first hour of the day usu. considered either as 6 a.m. or the hour of sunrise **2 a :** the beginning or earliest stage of something **:** the first part or age ⟨saurians of the ~ —Henry Adams⟩ **b :** SPRING ⟨the ~ of the year⟩ **c :** the spring of life **:** YOUTH ⟨in her ~, pretty as a lamb, a laughing girl —A.E. Coppard⟩ **3 a :** the most active, thriving, or successful stage of something ⟨patent medicines were in their ~ —Thérèse S. Westermeier⟩ ⟨the ~ of his musical career —Terry de Valera⟩ **b :** the period of greatest vigor and productivity in a person's life ⟨these two home-run sluggers, who were tremendous crowd pullers in their ~ —*Collier's Yr. Bk.*⟩ **4 a :** the chief or best individual of a group ⟨~ of the flock, and choicest of the stall —Alexander Pope⟩ **b :** the best part of something ⟨give him always of the ~ —Jonathan Swift⟩ **c :** an export grade of yellow pine lumber of very high quality that is free from defects and largely heartwood **d :** sheet metal products of the highest commercial quality **5 :** PRIME NUMBER **6 a :** PRIMERO **b :** the second-highest hand in primero and related games consisting of one card of each suit **c :** a block in backgammon formed by a series of six closed points **7 :** a parry in fencing defending the upper inside target in which the hand is to the left at head height in a position of pronation with the point of the blade directed downward and the forearm is across the body parallel to the ground — called also *first;* compare QUARTE **8 a :** the first note or tone of a musical scale **:** TONIC **b :** a tone represented by the same staff degree as a given tone **c :** the pitch relation between two such musical notes or tones or their simultaneous combination **d :** PRIME TONE **9 :** a symbol or accent ′ suffixed in writing or printing to distinguish one character from a related character (as *a′* from *a* or from *a″*), to indicate a relative unit (as a minute of angle or a foot), or to differentiate a mathematical function — compare DOUBLE PRIME

²prime \"\ *adj* [ME, fr. MF, fem. of *prin* prime, fr. L *primus;* akin to L *prior* former, prior — more at PRIOR] **1 a :** first in order of time **:** ORIGINAL, PRIMITIVE ⟨high heaven and earth ail from the ~ foundation —A.E.Housman⟩ **b :** having the vigor and freshness of youth **:** YOUTHFUL ⟨our manhood's ~ vigor —Robert Browning⟩ **2 a** (1) **:** of, relating to, or constituting a prime number (2) **:** having no common integral divisor greater than 1 ⟨12 is ~ to 25⟩ ⟨12 and 25 are relatively ~⟩ **b** (1) *of a polynomial* **:** not factorable (2) **:** having no common polynomial divisors with coefficients in the same field other than constants ⟨these two polynomials are relatively ~⟩ **3** *obs* **:** LECHEROUS, LUSTFUL ⟨as ~ as goats —Shak.⟩ **4 a :** first in rank or authority **:** CHIEF, LEADING ⟨made you the ~ man of the state —Shak.⟩ **b :** first in significance or urgency **:** PRINCIPAL ⟨a ~ requisite⟩ ⟨a ~ example⟩ ⟨a ~ need⟩ **c** (1) **:** first in excellence or importance **:** having the highest quality or value ⟨a ~ new plow —M.A.Hancock⟩ ⟨~ farming land —J.D.Adams⟩ ⟨a ~ fish⟩ ⟨~ television time⟩ (2) **:** of the highest grade — used of meat, esp. beef; compare CHOICE, COMMERCIAL, GOOD 1f(5) (3) **:** being in the best condition — used esp. of fur skins and hides ⟨when the deer hides are ~ —Farley Mowat⟩ **d :** having the highest credit rating ⟨~ borrowers⟩ ⟨~ commercial loans⟩ **5 :** not deriving from something else **:** PRIMARY ⟨the ~ postulate of his philosophy⟩

³prime \"\ *adv* [²*prime*] **:** PRIMELY

⁴prime \"\ *vb* -ED/-ING/-S [prob. fr. ¹*prime*] *vt* **1 :** FILL, LOAD ⟨*primed* the lamp with oil⟩ ⟨came to these encounters well *primed* with wine —J.B.Cabell⟩ **2 :** to prepare for firing by supplying with priming or a primer ⟨~ a cannon⟩ ⟨~ a mine⟩ **3 a :** to lay the first color, coating, or preparation upon ⟨*primed* the wall with white paint⟩ ⟨an undercoater for sealing and *priming* inside surfaces —*Wall Street Jour.*⟩ **b** *archaic* **:** to put cosmetics on **:** make up ⟨every morning ~*s* her face —John Oldham⟩ **4 :** to put into working order by filling or charging with something: as **a :** to pour water into the barrel or bucket of (a pump) **b :** to pour gasoline into the carburetor of (an engine) **c :** to impart a charge of static electricity to one armature of (an induction electric machine) **5 a :** to instruct beforehand **:** COACH ⟨*primed* the witness⟩ **b :** to make ready **:** PREPARE ⟨keeping their eyes *primed*, their cameras ready —Barbara B. Jamison⟩ ⟨a livestock dipping vat was *primed* with a fresh solution —F.B.Gipson⟩ **6 :** to harvest (tobacco) by picking the leaves a few at a time as they ripen **7 :** STIMULATE ⟨loses money in attempting to ~ the sugarcane industry —Sidney Shalett⟩ **~** *vi* **1** *archaic* **:** to assume precedence **:** DOMINEER **2 :** to operate so that steam is liberated in small portions with the result that fine water particles are entrained with and carried over by steam **3 :** to have a shortened tide day **4 :** to become prime ⟨the hides were *priming* towards winter, heavy and well-furred —Mari Sandoz⟩ — **prime the pump :** to take steps to encourage the growth, functioning, or expression of something; *specif:* to attempt to stimulate employment or economic activity by government spending ⟨this spending has not yet *primed the pump* —T.W.Arnold⟩ — compare PUMP PRIMING

⁵prime \"\ *n* -s **:** the priming of a gun

⁶prime \"\ *vi* -ED/-ING/-S [origin unknown] *of a fish* **:** to leap from the water

prime cost *n* **1 :** the combined total of raw material and direct labor costs incurred in production **2 :** the direct or immediate cost of a commodity; *specif* **:** the cost or expenses of producing or obtaining a commodity exclusive of general expenses of management involved and of profit on capital

prime factor *n* **:** a factor that is a prime number

prime·ly *adv* **:** in a prime manner **:** EXCELLENTLY

prime matter *n* **:** MATTER 3b(5)

prime meridian *n* **:** the meridian of 0 degrees longitude which runs through the original site of the Royal Observatory at Greenwich, England, and from which other longitudes are reckoned east and west around the world to 180 degrees — compare NATIONAL MERIDIAN

prime minister *n* **1 :** the chief minister of a ruler or state **2 :** the official head of a cabinet **:** the chief executive of a parliamentary government

prime ministerial *adj* **:** of or relating to a prime minister

prime ministership *n* **:** PRIME MINISTRY

prime ministry *n* **1 :** the office of prime minister **2 :** the term of office of a prime minister

prime mover *n* [trans. of ML *primus motor*] **1** *in some philosophies* **a :** the self-moved being to which all motion must ultimately go back **b** *cap P&M* **:** GOD — compare FIRST CAUSE **2 a** (1) **:** an initial source of motive power (as an engine) designed to receive and modify force and motion as supplied by some natural source and apply them to drive other machinery (as a waterwheel, turbine, or steam engine) (2) **:** a powerful tractor or truck usu. with all-wheel drive for hauling artillery or moving stalled vehicles **b :** the original or most effective force in an undertaking or work ⟨see the *prime mover* of our increased growth in physical environment —Lawrence Farmer⟩ ⟨he was a *prime mover* in the evolution of progressive ensemble jazz —Bill Simon⟩ **3 :** AGONIST **syn** see ORIGIN

prime·ness *n* -ES **:** the quality or state of being prime

prime number *n* **:** an integer other than 0 or ±1 that is not divisible without remainder by any other integers except ±1 and ± the integer itself

¹prim·er \'primə(r) *also chiefly Brit* 'prīm-\ *n* -s [ME, fr. ML *primarium*, fr. neut. of *primarius* basic, primary, fr. LL — more at PRIMARY] **1 :** a layman's prayer book of the 14th to 17th centuries containing miscellaneous prayers, psalms, and offices orig. written or printed in Latin but later mainly in English and used also in teaching children to read **2 a :** a small elementary book for teaching children to read ⟨a ~ for the first grade⟩ **b :** a usu. small introductory book on a specific subject ⟨a ~ of modern art⟩ ⟨a ~ of chemistry⟩ **3 :** something that gives or is a means of giving elementary instruction or training ⟨his year as a precinct worker served as his ~ of politics⟩

²primer *adj* [ME, fr. MF, fr. LL *primarius*] *obs* **:** PRIMARY

³prim·er \'prīmə(r)\ *n* -s [⁴*prime* + *-er*] **1 :** an instrument or device for priming: as **a :** a contrivance (as a cap, tube, or wafer containing percussion powder or other compound) used to ignite an explosive charge and itself ignited by friction, percussion, or electricity **b :** a small copper cup containing a charge of some shock-sensitive high explosive (as mercury fulminate) that initiates the propelling charge in a firearm when ignited (as in a percussion cap) by a blow from the hammer or (as in a modern cartridge or shot-shell case) by impact of the firing pin **2 :** PRIMING **3 a :** one who applies priming (as of paint or varnish) **b :** a worker who gathers the prime leaves from tobacco plants **4 :** a plasmagene that acts as a priming device for various reactions

pri·mero \prə̇'me(,)rō, -mi(,)rō\ *n* -s [modif. of Sp *primera*, fr. fem. of *primero* first, fr. L *primarius* principal — more at PRIMARY] **:** an old card game popular esp. in the 16th century in which each player holds three or four cards ⟨never prospered since I forswore myself at ~ —Shak.⟩

prim·er seisin \'primə(r), -īmə(r)-\ *n* [ME *primer cession, primer season*, fr. ²*primer* + *cession, season*, alter. of *seisine* seisin — more at SEISIN] **:** a right of the crown to exact from the heir of a tenant in capite seised of a knight's fee one year's profits of the land in addition to the ordinary relief if the lands were in immediate possession or half a year's profits if the lands were in reversion expectant on a life estate

primes *pl of* PRIME, *pres 3d sing of* PRIME

prime tone *n* **:** the lowest tone of a group of overtones

pri·meur \(')prē¦mər, -mə̄\ *n* -s [F, fr. MF, fr. *prime* first + *-eur* -or — more at PRIME] **:** an early fruit or vegetable **:** FIRSTLING

pri·me·val *also* **pri·mae·val** \(')prī¦mēvəl\ *adj* [L *primaevus* of the first period of life (fr. *primus* first + *aevum* age) + E *-al* — more at PRIME, AYE] **:** of or relating to the earliest ages of the world or human history **:** ABORIGINAL, PRIMITIVE ⟨had lapsed into nearly its ~ state of wilderness —Nathaniel Hawthorne⟩ ⟨a splendid ~ rustic figure —Osbert Lancaster⟩ — **pri·me·val·ly** \-vəlē, -li\ *adv*

pri·me·verin \,primə'virə̇n, -ver-\ *n* -s [ISV *primever-* (fr. F *primevère* cowslip, fr. OF *primevoire*, lit., spring, prob. short for *flour de primevoire* spring flower, fr. *flour* flower + *de* of — fr. L, from — + *primevoire* — fr. LL *prima vera* early spring —) + *-in* — more at FLOWER, DE-, PRIMAVERA] **:** a crystalline glycoside $C_{20}H_{28}O_{13}$ that is found in the cowslip (*Primula veris*) and that on hydrolysis yields primeverose and a derivative of salicylic acid

pri·me·verose \-,rōs\ *n* -s [*primeverin* + *-ose*] **:** a crystalline disaccharide $C_{11}H_{20}O_{10}$ obtained by hydrolysis of primeverin, primulaverin, and other glycosides that yields glucose and xylose on hydrolysis

prime vertical *n* **:** the vertical circle at right angles to the celestial meridian and passing through the east and west points of the horizon

prime vertical dial *n* **:** a sundial in which the shadow is projected on the plane of the prime vertical **:** a vertical south dial

prime–vertical transit *n* **:** a transit instrument mounted so that its telescope revolves in the plane of the prime vertical

pri·me·vous \(')prī¦mēvəs\ *adj* [L *primaevus*] **:** of the first period of life] **:** PRIMEVAL

prim·i·ces \'priməsəz\ *n pl* [ME, fr. OF, fr. L *primiciae, primitiae* — more at PRIMITIAE] **:** FIRSTFRUITS

pri·mie·ra \prē'myerə\ *n* -s [It, prob. fr. Sp *primera* — more at PRIMERO] **1 :** a form of primero popular in Italy **2 :** PRIME 6 b

primigenial *var of* PRIMOGENIAL

pri·mi·grav·id \¦prīmə̇¦gravə̇d\ *adj* [NL *primigravida*] **:** pregnant for the first time

pri·mi·grav·i·da \,=='gravədə\ *n, pl* **primigravi·das** \-dəz\ *or* **primigravi·dae** \-,dē\ [NL, fr. *primi-* (fr. L, fr. *primus* first) + L *gravida* pregnant woman — more at PRIME, GRAVIDA] **:** an individual pregnant for the first time

primi inter pares *pl of* PRIMUS INTER PARES

priming *n* -s [fr. gerund of ⁴*prime*] **1 a :** the act or action of one that primes: as (1) **:** the placing in position of an explosive used to fire a charge (2) **:** the application of a first coating (as of paint, varnish, or size) to a surface that is to be painted (3) **:** the action of a boiler or still in carrying water globules over with the steam generated (4) **:** the action of boiling over — used esp. of a still in gas manufacturing (5) **:** the pulling of tobacco leaves from the growing plant as they mature **b** (1) **:** the explosive used in priming a charge (2) **:** the material used in priming a surface (3) **:** the tobacco leaves removed by priming **2 :** a strong solution of sugar added to beer to give it body and make it more palatable

priming charge *n* **:** a small charge of easily detonated explosive used to ignite a main charge (as a propelling charge in a gun)

priming illumination *n* **:** a constant low-intensity illumination of a photocathode that is used to bring the sensitivity of the cell up to a maximum

priming needle *n* **:** NEEDLE 8 b

priming of the tide : acceleration of the time of high or low water in the 1st and 3d quarters of the moon — opposed to *lag of the tide*

priming wire *n* **:** a pointed wire used to penetrate the vent of a firearm and pierce the cartridge before priming

pri·mip·a·ra \prī'mipərə\ *n, pl* **primiparas** *or* **primiparae** [NL, individual having only one child, fr. L, individual bearing for the first time, fr. *primi-* (fr. *primus* first) + *-para* (fem. of *-parus* -parous)] **1 :** an individual that has borne only one offspring **2 :** an individual bearing a first offspring — **pri·mi·par·i·ty** \,prīmə'parəd·ē\ *n*

pri·mip·a·rous \(')prī¦mipərəs\ *adj* [in sense 1, fr. NL *primipara* + E *-ous;* in sense 2, fr. L *primipara* + E *-ous*] **1 :** of or relating to a primipara **2 :** bearing young for the first time — compare MULTIPAROUS

pri·mip·i·lar \(')prī¦mipələ(r), ¦primə¦pīlə(r)\ *adj* [L *primipilaris*, fr. *primipilus* chief centurion of the third division (fr. *primus* first + *pilus* division of the third division — fr. *pilum* javelin, pestle, javelin of the Roman infantry — after the phrase *primi pili (centurio)* centurion of the third division) + *-aris* -ar — more at PESTLE] **:** of, relating to, or constituting the chief centurion of the third division of a Roman legion

pri·mite \'prī,mīt\ *n* -s [L *primus* + E *-ite*] **:** the anterior member of a pair of gregarines in syzygy — compare SATELLITE

pri·mi·ti·ae \prī'mishē,ē\ *n pl* [ML, fr. L, firstlings, firstfruits, fr. *primus* first + *-itiae*, fem. pl. of *-itius* -ice] **:** ANNATES

pri·mi·tial \prī'mishəl\ *adj* [ML *primitialis* original, principal, fr. L *primitus* firstly + *-ialis* -ial] **:** ORIGINAL, PRIMITIVE

¹prim·i·tive \'primə̇d·iv, -ə̇tiv\ *adj* [ME *primitif*, fr. L *primitivus*, fr. *primitus* firstly, originally (fr. *primus* first + *-itus*, adv. suffix) + *-ivus* -ive — more at PRIME] **1 a :** not derived from or reducible to something else **:** ORIGINAL, PRIMARY ⟨seeks excellence at its ~ source — nature —John Dewey⟩ ⟨an acre of one ~ color alone —J.A.Michener⟩ ⟨~ verbs⟩ **b :** AXIOMATIC, POSTULATIONAL ⟨~ formula⟩ ⟨~ concept⟩ **c :** of, relating to, or constituting the smallest possible unit cell of a space lattice; *esp* **:** of, relating to, or constituting such a cell having its axes normal to planes and parallel to axes of symmetry **2 a :** of or relating to the earliest age or period of something ⟨had generally shown a desire to have the church become its ~ self again —Stringfellow Barr⟩ ⟨from the moment when ~ human creatures shaped the first tools —Jacquetta & Christopher Hawkes⟩ ⟨~ Norse⟩ **b** (1) **:** PRIMORDIAL — opposed to *definitive* (2) **:** closely approximating an early ancestral type **:** little evolved **:** ARCHAIC, PERSISTENT ⟨the opossums are ~ mammals⟩ **c :** belonging to or characteristic of an early stage of development **:** CRUDE, RUDIMENTARY ⟨a health resort with ~ facilities has been built here —*Amer. Guide Series: Texas*⟩ ⟨a ~ but effective police inquiry —T.S.Eliot⟩ **d :** of, relating to, or constituting the assumed parent speech of related languages ⟨~ Germanic⟩ **3 a :** of or relating to the beginning of things **:** PRIMEVAL ⟨it runs through resort areas, rolling and rocky farmland, through ~ forests —*Amer. Guide Series: Maine*⟩ **b :** earliest formed **:** FUNDAMENTAL — used esp. of the Archean in geology **4 a :** of or relating to a state of nature **:** ELEMENTAL ⟨the noble savage endowed with ~ virtue —Oscar Handlin⟩ ⟨our ~ feelings of vengeance —John Mackwood⟩ **b :** of or relating to any unindustrialized people or culture not possessing a written language and commonly having a relatively simple technology and material culture **:** NONLITERATE, PRELITERATE **c :** lacking in sophistication or subtlety of thought, feeling, or expression **:** NAÏVE, SIMPLE ⟨neither staunchly ~ nor confidently au courant, she rarely knew where she was at —Jean Stafford⟩ **d** (1) **:** SELF-TAUGHT, UNTUTORED ⟨a ~ painter who has never been inside a museum or art school⟩ (2) **:** produced by a self-taught artist ⟨a ~ portrait⟩ **5 :** of, relating to, or holding the doctrines of any of several small Protestant religious groups

²primitive \"\ *n* -s **1 a :** something that is primitive ⟨involves no cult of the instinctive and ~ —F.R.Leavis⟩; *specif* **:** a primitive idea, term, or proposition ⟨limit the number of undefined concepts to a few simple ~*s* —K.F.Leidecker⟩ **b :** a root word **:** RADICAL — compare DERIVATIVE **2** *often cap* **:** a member of any of several small Protestant religious groups; *esp* **:** PRIMITIVE METHODIST **3 a** (1) **:** an artist active in the early period of a culture or artistic movement (2) **:** a later imitator or follower of such an artist **b** (1) **:** a self-taught artist (2) **:** an artist whose work is marked by directness and naïveté ⟨the simplicity of vision and of purpose that make the true ~ —Cyril Ray⟩ **c :** a work of art produced by a primitive artist **4 :** a relation from which a differential equation is derived **5 a :** a member of a nonliterate or preliterate people ⟨the anthropology of the future will not be concerned above all else with ~*s* —A.L.Kroeber⟩ **b :** a simple and unsophisticated person ⟨this grand ~, shaggy and good as a dog —J.H. Allen⟩ **c :** a person whose attitudes, behavior, or mentality are those of an earlier stage of society or human development ⟨a revolt of the ~*s*, goaded by demagogues —*New Republic*⟩ ⟨a handsome, tough tavern brawler with a law degree, a kind of lowbrow intellectual ~ —*Time*⟩ **6 :** a postage stamp of early issue; *also* **:** a philatelic cover of early date

primitive area *n* **:** a large tract within a U. S. national forest set aside for preservation in natural condition with no alteration or development beyond measures for fire prevention being permitted

primitive axis *n* **:** an elongated thickening of the mesoblastic and hypoblastic layers of the blastoderm extending forward from the anterior end of the primitive streak

primitive baptist *n, usu cap P&B* **:** a member of an ultraconservative Baptist religious group that dates from early in the 19th century but has never been formally organized as a denomination and that from its origin has represented a protest movement against missions and Sunday schools

primitive church *n, often cap P&C* **:** the early Christian church as it existed in its original character and organization for about the first three centuries A.D.

primitive friends *n pl, cap P&F* **:** a conservative group of Friends in the U. S. who in 1861 separated from the Wilburites

primitive green *n* **:** a strong green that is bluer and stronger than mintleaf (sense 1) or pepper green and yellower, lighter, and stronger than viridian

primitive groove *n* **:** a depression or groove in the epiblast of the primitive streak that extends forward to the primitive knot

primitive knot *n* **:** a knob of cells at the anterior end of the primitive streak that is the point of origin of the embryonic head process — see END BUD 2

prim·i·tive·ly \'primə̇d·ə̇vlē, -ə̇tə̇-, -li\ *adv* **1 :** at first **:** in the beginning **:** ORIGINALLY ⟨the two case endings may have been ~ different —Robert Shafer⟩ **2 :** PRIMARILY **3 :** in a primitive style or manner ⟨rather ~ operated quarries —*Amer. Guide Series: Minn.*⟩

primitive methodist *n, usu cap P&M* **:** a member of the nonepiscopal Primitive Methodist Church organized in 1812 in England and later extended to the U. S. where it now continues to emphasize basic Wesleyan doctrines and greater congregational participation in its government

prim·i·tive·ness \-ivnə̇s\ *n* -ES **:** the quality or state of being primitive

primitive pit *n* **:** a depression immediately behind the primitive knot in which the primitive groove ends

primitive rocks *n pl* **:** PRIMARY ROCKS

primitive segment *n* **:** any one of the transverse segments into which the body of the embryo of vertebrates becomes marked off by the formation beginning first in the neck region of a series of distinctly limited masses of mesoblast cells on each side of the neural tube — called also *protovertebra*

primitive streak *n* **:** an opaque band that appears in the blastoderm in the axial line of the future embryo but somewhat behind the place where the embryo proper begins to develop and that represents a highly modified blastopore through which the involution of chordamesoderm takes place

primitive water *n* **:** water originating within the earth

prim·i·tiv·ism \'primə̇d·ə,vizəm, -mətə,-\ *n* -s **1 :** primitive practices or procedures ⟨the final stage of the transition from ~ to modernism —Farley Mowat⟩ **2 a :** a belief in the superiority of a simple unsophisticated way of life esp. close to nature **b :** a belief in the superiority of early esp. nonindustrial society to that of the present **3 a :** the style of self-taught artists usu. marked by imaginative naïveté and formal simplicity and directness **b :** the style of the art of primitive peoples usu. marked by vitality, boldness, and deliberate distortion **c :** a conscious imitation by a sophisticated artist of the style of primitive artists or primitive art

¹prim·i·tiv·ist \-və̇st\ *n* -s **:** an adherent of primitivism

²primitivist \"\ *or* **prim·i·tiv·is·tic** \¦===¦vistik, -tēk\ *adj* **:** of, relating to, or characteristic of primitivism or primitivists — **prim·i·tiv·is·ti·cal·ly** \-tə̇k(ə)lē\ *adv*

prim·i·tiv·i·ty \,primə'tivəd·ē\ *n* -ES **:** PRIMITIVENESS

prim·i·tiv·i·za·tion \,primə̇d·ivə̇'zāshən, -,vī'z-\ *n* -s **:** the process of becoming primitive

prim·ly *adv* **:** in a prim manner
primmed *past of* PRIM
primmer *comparative of* PRIM
primmest *superlative of* PRIM
primming *pres part of* PRIM
prim·ness *n* -ES **:** the quality or state of being prim
¹pri·mo \'prē(,)mō, 'prī(,)-\ *adv* [L, fr. *primus* first — more at PRIME] **:** in the first place **:** FIRST ⟨in danger, ~, of setting down material perhaps distasteful to the reader —Lawrence Durrell⟩
²pri·mo \'prē(,)mō\ *n* -S [It, fr. *primo* first, fr. L *primus*] **:** the first or leading part (as in a duet or trio)
pri·mo·cane \'prīmə,kān\ *n* [¹*primo* + *cane*] **:** a new cane on a bramble fruit (as a blackberry or raspberry) that will flower and fruit the following year
pri·mo·fil·i·ces \,prī(,)mō'filə,sēz\ *n pl, cap* [NL, fr. L *primo* + NL *Filices*] *in some classifications* **:** a subclass of Filicineae comprising fossil forms with the axis usu. protostelic, the fronds but slightly developed, terminal or subterminal sporangia, and usu. isospores and including the order Coenopteridales and sometimes other forms of somewhat uncertain relationships
pri·mo·genial \¦prī(,)mō, -mə+\ *adj* [modif. (influenced by LL *primogenitalis* primogenital) of L *primigenius* primogenial (fr. *primus* first + *-genius* — fr. *gignere* to beget —) + E *-al*] **1** *also* **pri·mi·genial** \¦prīmə+\ **:** first formed or generated **:** ORIGINAL, PRIMITIVE **2 :** PRIMOGENITARY
pri·mo·genital \¦=(,)=+\ *adj* [LL *primogenitalis,* fr. *primogenitus* state of being firstborn (fr. L, firstborn, fr. *primus* first + *genitus,* past part. of *gignere* to beget) + L *-alis* -al] **:** PRIMOGENITARY
pri·mo·gen·i·tary \-əd·,erē\ *adj* [LL *primogenitus* state of being firstborn + E *-ary*] **:** of, relating to, or based on primogeniture ⟨~ rules⟩ ⟨~ succession⟩
pri·mo·gen·i·tor \,=(,)=¦jenəd·ə(r)\ *n* [LL, fr. L *primus* first + *genitor* begetter — more at GENITOR] **:** first ancestor ⟨this tiny, nameless ~ of all living matter —*Time*⟩; *broadly* **:** ANCESTOR, FOREFATHER ⟨our distant ~*s*⟩
pri·mo·gen·i·ture \¦prīmō¦jenə,chů(ə)r, -ůə, -nəchə(r)\ *n* [LL *primogenitura,* fr. L *primus* first + *genitura* birth, fr. *genitus* (past part. of *gignere* to beget) + *-ura* -ure — more at KIN] **1 :** the state of being the firstborn of the children of the same parents **2 :** an exclusive right of inheritance; *specif* **:** a right belonging under English law to the eldest son or failing lineal descendants the eldest male in the next degree of consanguinity to take all the real estate of which an ancestor died seized and intestate to the exclusion of all female and younger male descendants of equal degree
pri·mo·gen·i·ture·ship \-,ship\ *n* **:** PRIMOGENITURE 2
¹pri·mor·di·al \(')prī¦mȯ(r)dēəl\ *adj* [ME, fr. LL *primordialis,* fr. L *primordium* beginning, origin (fr. neut. of *primordius* original, fr. *primus* first + *ordiri* to begin, begin a web) + *-alis* -al — more at PRIME, ORDER] **1 a :** existing at or from the beginning **:** first created or developed **:** EARLIEST, PRIMEVAL ⟨assuming that the sun, planets, and their satellites had all originated from a ~ mass of gas —S.F.Mason⟩ ⟨the child's ~ subconscious world —Louise Bogan⟩ **b :** earliest formed in the growth of an individual or organ **:** PRIMITIVE **c :** CRUDE, UNDEVELOPED ⟨a ~ theologian of the hellfire and brimstone variety —Carey McWilliams⟩ **2 :** constituting a basis or starting point **:** existing independently **:** ELEMENTARY, FUNDAMENTAL, PRIMARY ⟨life's ~ reality is spirit —H.O.Taylor⟩ — **pri·mor·di·al·ly** \-əlē, -li\ *adv*
²primordial \"\ *n* -S **:** something original or fundamental **:** a first principle or element
primordial meristem *n* **:** PRIMARY MERISTEM
primordial ovum *n* **:** one of the large cells in the germinal epithelium and in the sexual cords or egg tubes derived from it which occur in embryos of both sexes but more abundantly in the female and from which the true eggs are believed to be derived
primordial utricle *n* **:** the cytoplasmic lining of the cell wall in a fully developed vacuolated cell
pri·mor·di·um \prī'mȯ(r)dēəm\ *n, pl* **primor·dia** \-dēə\ [L] **1 :** the earliest part or stage **:** BEGINNING, ORIGIN ⟨regards the solar system as resulting by evolution from a ~ —H.S. Jones⟩ **2 :** the rudiment or commencement of a part or organ **:** ANLAGE
pri·mork \(')prē¦mȯrk\ *n, pl* **primork** *or* **primorks** *usu cap* **1 :** a people formerly occupying the region of the Sikhote Alin mountains and the adjoining Ussuri-Amur lowlands of Siberia **2 :** a member of the Primork people
primos *pl of* PRIMO
pri·most \'prē,mȯst, -mōst\ *n* -S [Norw, fr. *prim* whey + *ost* cheese] **:** MYSOST
primp \'primp\ *vb* -ED/-ING/-S [perh. alter. of ²*prim*] *vt* **:** to dress, adorn, or arrange in a careful or finicky manner ⟨she ~*ed* her hair —Walt Sheldon⟩ ⟨seems afraid to trust the strength of his material; he ~*s* it with cute comment —*Time*⟩ ⟨~ herself⟩ ~ *vi* **1** *chiefly Scot* **:** to behave in a prim or affected manner **2 a :** to dress up or groom oneself carefully ⟨she's always ~*ing* in front of the mirror⟩ ⟨~*s* for hours before a date⟩ **b :** to smarten things up **:** arrange things neatly ⟨rearrange her magazine basket as she ~*s* for callers —W.H.Whyte⟩
¹prim·rose \'prim,rōz\ *n* [ME *primerose,* fr. MF, fr. OF, prob. fr. *prime* (fem. of *prin* first, prime) + *rose,* fr. L *rosa* — more at PRIME, ROSE] **1 a :** a plant of the genus *Primula* (as the cowslip or the English primrose); *esp* **:** any of the numerous often hybrid plants of Asiatic or European origin that are cultivated for their bright and varied flowers — see CHINESE PRIMROSE **b :** EVENING PRIMROSE **2 :** the best or fairest part or example **:** FLOWER ⟨the Lord was pleased to work upon him in the ~ of his life —Samuel Clarke⟩ **3 :** PRIMROSE YELLOW
²primrose \"\ *adj* **1 :** of, relating to, or resembling the primrose ⟨~ color⟩ **2 :** abounding in primroses **:** FLOWERY, GAY ⟨the ~ way⟩ ⟨a ~ bank⟩
³primrose \"\ *vi* -ED/-ING/-S **:** to look for or gather primroses ⟨*primrosing* and promise of good sport —Edmund Blunden⟩
primrosed *adj* **:** abounding in primroses
primrose family *n* **:** PRIMULACEAE
primrose green *n* **:** a pale greenish yellow that is very slightly deeper than tilleul
primrose jasmine *n* **:** an evergreen rambling Chinese shrub (*Jasminum mesnyi*) having yellow flowers with a darker eye and cultivated as an ornamental
primrose path *n* **1 :** a path of ease or pleasure ⟨had made some progress in the *primrose path* of Epicurean wisdom —George Santayana⟩; *esp* **:** a path of sensual pleasure ⟨the *primrose path* of dalliance treads —Shak.⟩ **2 :** a path of least resistance; *esp* **:** one leading to disaster ⟨leading them down the *primrose path* of military economy —*Newsweek*⟩
primrose peerless *or* **primrose peerless narcissus** *n* **:** a southern European narcissus (*Narcissus biflorus*) that is sometimes cultivated as an ornamental and has grasslike leaves and usu. paired white to greenish white flowers
primrose willow *n* **:** an annual or perennial herb of the genus *Jussiaea* with yellow flowers and principal leaves resembling those of willows — called also *water primrose*
primrose yellow *n* **1 :** a light to moderate greenish yellow **2 :** a light to moderate yellow
prim·rosy \'prim,rōzē\ *adj* [¹*primrose* + *-y*] **:** PRIMROSE
prims *pl of* PRIM, *pres 3d sing of* PRIM
prim·sie \'primsi,-mzi\ *adj* [²*prim* + connective *-s-* + *-ie*] *Scot* **:** PRIM
prim·u·la \'primyələ\ *n* [NL, fr. ML, primrose, cowslip, fr. *primula veris,* lit., firstling of spring, fr. *primula* firstling (fr. L, fem. of *primulus* first, fr. *primus* first + *-ulus* -ule) + L *veris,* gen. of *ver* spring — more at VERNAL] **1** *cap* **:** a genus (the type of the family Primulaceae) of chiefly European and Asiatic perennial acaulescent herbs having large tufted basal leaves and showy variously colored flowers with a salver-shaped corolla bearing five stamens within its tube — see AURICULA, CHINESE PRIMROSE, COWSLIP, OXLIP, POLYANTHUS **2** -S **:** any plant of the genus *Primula*
prim·u·la·ce·ae \,==¦lāsē,ē\ *n pl, cap* [NL, fr. *Primula,* type genus + *-aceae*] **:** a family of herbs (order Primulales) having perfect regular flowers with a deciduous rotate or campanulate corolla and a superior ovary and being widely distributed chiefly in the northern hemisphere — **prim·u·la·ceous** \¦==¦lāshəs\ *adj*
prim·u·la·les \,==ˈlā(,)lēz\ *n pl, cap* [NL, fr. *Primula* + *-ales*] **:** an order of gamopetalous pentamerous dicotyledonous herbs, shrubs, or trees that includes the families Primulaceae, Theophrastaceae, and Myrsinaceae and is distinguished by the one-celled ovary with free-central placentation — see PLUMBAGINALES
prim·u·lav·er·in \,primyə'lavərən\ *n* -S [alter. (influenced by NL *Primula*) of ISV *primeverin*] **:** a crystalline glycoside $C_{20}H_{28}O_{13}$ that is isomeric with primeverin and occurs with it and that on hydrolysis yields primeverose and a derivative of gentisic acid
prim·u·line \'primyə,lēn, -,lən\ *n* -S [ISV *primul-* (fr. NL *Primula*) + *-ine*] **:** a fugitive yellow dye made by heating para-toluidine and sulfur together and sulfonating the product that can be diazotized on the fiber and coupled with a phenol or amine to yield various developed dyes (as red colors of good fastness to washing but not to light) — see DYE table I (under *Direct Yellow 59*)
primuline yellow *n* **:** YOLK YELLOW
prim·u·li·nus \,primyə'līnəs\ *n* -ES [NL *primulinus* (specific epithet of *Gladiolus primulinus*), fr. L *primula* (fem. of *primulus* first) + *-inus* -ine] **1 :** a gladiolus (*Gladiolus primulinus*) of southeastern tropical Africa having clear primrose yellow flowers with the uppermost perianth segment much curved in a hood **2** *or* **primulinus hybrid :** any of numerous cultivated gladioli produced by hybridizing from the species primulinus and possessing its characteristic hood
pri·mum mob·i·le \¦prīməm'mōbə(,)lē\ *n, pl* **primum mobiles** [ME, fr. ML, lit., first moving thing] **1 a :** the ninth or in later numbering the tenth and outermost concentric sphere added in the middle ages to the system of Ptolemaic astronomy and conceived as carrying the spheres of the fixed stars and the planets in its daily revolution — compare CRYSTALLINE HEAVEN **b** *Aristotelianism* **:** the highest physical sphere that derives its circular motion directly from God the unmoved mover **2 :** something that is a first source of motion or activity **:** PRIME MOVER ⟨regarded self-interest as the *primum mobile* of all human activity⟩
pri mus \'prīməs\ *n* -ES *often cap* [ML, one who is first, magnate, fr. L first — more at PRIME] **:** the first in dignity of the bishops of the Episcopal Church in Scotland who has various privileges but no metropolitan authority
Primus \"\ *trademark* — used for a portable oil-burning stove
primus in·ter pa·res \¦==,intər'pär,ēz\ *n, pl* **pri·mi inter pares** \¦prē,mī,-\ [L] **:** the first among equals ⟨the prime minister's place among his colleagues as *primus inter pares* —F.A.Ogg & Harold Zink⟩
primwort \'=,=\ *n* [prob. fr. ¹*prim* + *wort*] **:** PRIVET 1a(1)
prin \'prin\ *chiefly Scot var of* ¹PREEN
prin *abbr* **1** principal; principally **2** principle
princ *abbr* **1** principal **2** principle
¹prince \'prin(t)s\ *n* -S [ME, fr. OF, fr. L *princip-, princeps* first person, chief, prince, lit., one who takes the first part, fr. *prin-* (fr. *primus* first) + *-cip-, -ceps* (fr. *capere* to take) — more at HEAVE] **1 a :** a sovereign ruler **:** MONARCH ⟨noblemen passed from court to court, seeking service with one ~ or another —W.M.Thackeray⟩ **b :** the ruler of a principality or state ⟨New Delhi has promised the ~*s* . . . the right to be called Your Highness —*Time*⟩ ⟨the *Prince* of Monaco⟩ **2 a :** a male member of a royal family; *esp* **:** a son or a grandson in the male line of the British king or queen **3 :** a nobleman whose rank and status vary from one part of the world to another ⟨Polynesian ~*s*⟩ ⟨a Chinese ~ of the first degree⟩ **4 :** an ecclesiastic of high rank; *specif* **:** CARDINAL **5 a :** a person at the head of a class or profession **:** one very outstanding in a specified respect ⟨a ~ among men⟩ ⟨that ~ of hosts who left nothing undone for the comfort of his guests⟩ ⟨a very ~ of poets⟩ — compare MERCHANT PRINCE **b :** a jolly good fellow **:** an open-handed and genial friend ⟨he's a real ~⟩
²prince \"\ *vi* -ED/-ING/-S *obs* **:** to play or act the part of a prince — often used with *it* ⟨showed a disposition to ~ it⟩
prince al·bert \-'albə(r)t, *usu* -)d·+V\ *n, pl* **prince alberts** *usu cap P&A* [after *Prince Albert* Edward (later Edward VII king of England) †1910 who set the fashion of wearing it] **1** *or* **prince albert coat :** a long double-breasted frock coat for men **2 :** a man's house slipper with a low counter and goring on each side

Prince Albert 1

prince albert fir *also* **prince albert's fir** *or* **prince albert spruce** *n, usu cap P&A* **:** WESTERN HEMLOCK
prince albert's yew *also* **prince albert yew** *n, usu cap P&A* **:** a small evergreen tree (*Saxe-gothaea conspicua*) of the family Taxaceae that resembles the common yews, is native to mountainous southern Chile, and is sometimes cultivated as an ornamental
prince-bishop \(')=¦==\ *n* **:** a bishop of princely rank; *esp* **:** one with a see constituting a feudal principality of the Holy Roman Empire
prince charles spaniel *n, usu cap P&C* [alter. of *King Charles spaniel*] **:** an English toy spaniel having a black, tan, and white coat
prince charming *n, sometimes cap P&C* [after *Prince Charming,* hero of the fairy tale *Cinderella* (1729), translation, by Robert Samber *fl*1729 Eng. writer, of *Cendrillon* (1697) by Charles Perrault †1703 Fr. writer] **:** a suitor who fulfills the dreams of his beloved; *also* **:** a man of often specious affability and charm toward women
prince consort *n, pl* **princes consort :** the husband of a reigning female sovereign
prince·dom \'prin(t)sdəm, -stəm\ *n* -S [*prince* + *-dom*] **1 :** the jurisdiction, sovereignty, rank, or estate of a prince **2 :** PRINCIPALITY
prince ed·ward island \-¦edwə(r)d-\ *adj, usu cap P&E&I* [fr. *Prince Edward Island,* maritime province in the Gulf of St. Lawrence in southeastern Canada] **:** of or from the province of Prince Edward Island **:** of the kind or style prevalent in Prince Edward Island
prince elector *n* **:** ELECTOR a
prince gray *n, often cap P* **:** CRANE 4
prince·kin \'prin(t)skən\ *n* -S [*prince* + *-kin*] **:** a diminutive prince
prince·less \-sləs\ *adj* **:** having no prince
prince·let \-slət\ *n* -S [*prince* + *-let*] **:** a petty prince
prince·li·ness \-slēnəs, -slin-\ *n* -ES **1 :** princely conduct or character ⟨the ~ of his outlook⟩ **2 :** LUXURY, MAGNIFICENCE, SPLENDOR ⟨the ~ of our accommodations⟩
prince·ling \-sliŋ, -slēŋ\ *n* -S [*prince* + *-ling*] **:** a petty or insignificant prince
¹prince·ly \-slē, -sli\ *adj, often* -ER/-EST [*prince* + *-ly* (adj. suffix)] **1 :** of, relating to, or descended from a prince **:** ROYAL, KINGLY **:** of high rank or authority ⟨~ birth⟩ ⟨~ power⟩ **2 :** resembling, befitting, or having the characteristics of a prince **:** STATELY, NOBLE **:** MAGNIFICENT, MUNIFICENT ⟨a message of thanks for this ~ gift —Thomas Cadett⟩ ⟨those ~ ships with long black hulls —Robert Payne⟩
²princely \"\ *adv* [*prince* + *-ly* (adv. suffix)] **:** in a princely manner **:** in a manner befitting a prince
prince of wales \-'wā(ə)lz\ *cap P&W* [ME] **:** the male heir apparent to the British throne — used as a title only after it has been specif. conferred by the sovereign
prince-of-wales'-feather \-lz(əz)-\ *n, usu cap P&W* **1 :** PRINCE'S-FEATHER **2 :** CRAPE FERN
prince of wales feathers *or* **prince of wales plumes** *usu cap 1st P&W* **:** a decorative motif used esp. on chair backs and consisting of three feathers derived from the crest of the Prince of Wales
prince-of-wales'-heath *n, usu cap P&W* **:** a southern African shrub (*Erica perspicua*) grown for its profusion of white flowers
prin·ceps \'prin,seps, -iŋ,ke-\ *n, pl* **princi·pes** \-n(t)sə,pēz, -ŋkə,pās\ [L — more at PRINCE] **:** one that is first: as **a :** the head of the state under the Roman Empire **b :** any of various chief officials (as the headman of a tribe) among the ancient Teutons and Anglo-Saxons **c :** a first edition of a work; *also* **:** a copy of this edition
prince regent *n, pl* **prince regents :** a prince who rules a country during the minority, absence, or disability of the nominal sovereign
prince royal *n, pl* **princes royal :** the eldest son of a sovereign
prince rupert drop *also* **prince rupert's drop** *n, usu cap P&R* [after *Prince Rupert* of Germany †1682 who first brought it to England] **:** RUPERT'S DROP
prince ru·pert's metal \-'rüpə(r)ts-\ *n, usu cap P&R* [after *Prince Rupert* †1682, its inventor] **:** PRINCE'S METAL
princes *pl of* PRINCE, *pres 3d sing of* PRINCE
prince's-feather \¦==¦==\ *n, pl* **prince's-feathers 1 :** a showy annual plant (*Amaranthus hybridus hypochondriacus*) often cultivated for its dense usu. red spikes of bloom **2 :** a plant (*Polygonum orientale*) with broadly ovate leaves and slender drooping crimson spikes — called also *gentleman's-cane, prince's-plume* **3 :** LILAC 1 a **4 :** LONDON PRIDE 1
prince·ship \'prin(t)s,ship, -n,sh-\ *n* [*prince* + *-ship*] **1 :** the dignity or position of a prince **2 :** the period during which a prince (as an heir apparent) is such
prince's lengths *n pl, often cap P* [after *Prince* George Augustus Frederick (later George IV king of England) †1830 who prescribed them] **:** the three distances of 100, 80, and 60 yards in the York round at archery
prince's metal *n, usu cap P* [after *Prince* Rupert of Germany †1682, its inventor] **:** an alloy of the appearance of brass believed to be made of copper and zinc or copper and bismuth and formerly used for cheap jewelry — called also *Prince Rupert's metal*
prince's pine *n* **1 :** JACK PINE 1 **2 :** PIPSISSEWA
prince's-plume \¦==¦=\ *n, pl* **prince's-plumes 1 :** PRINCE'S-FEATHER **2 :** DESERT PLUME
prince's reckoning *n, often cap P* [after *Prince* George Augustus Frederick (later George IV king of England) †1830 who prescribed it] **:** the standard of counting hits in archery on the target as gold 9, red 7, blue 5, black 3, white 1
¹prin·cess \'prin(t)səs (*before a voiced consonant sometimes* -əz), 'prin,ses, prin'ses\ *n* -ES [ME *princesse,* fr. MF, fr. OF *prince* + *-esse* -ess — more at PRINCE] **1** *archaic* **:** a female prince **:** a woman having sovereign power or the rank of a prince ⟨so excellent a ~, as the present queen —Jonathan Swift⟩ **2 :** a female member of a royal family; *esp* **:** a daughter or a granddaughter of a sovereign ⟨the Duchess of Kent was safely delivered . . . of a ~ —*London Times*⟩ **3 :** the consort of a prince **4 a :** a woman outstanding in some usu. specified respect ⟨that ~ of seamstresses⟩ **b :** something personified as female and outstanding of its kind ⟨a winding ~ of a river⟩ **5 :** an attractive young woman selected to represent a commercial product, special group, or other interest publicly or to preside (as at a fair or college homecoming celebration) ⟨the new potato ~⟩ — compare QUEEN
²princess \"\ *vi* -ED/-ING/-ES **:** to act or play the princess — often used with *it*
³princess \"\ *or* **prin·cesse** \(')prin¦ses\ *adj* [*princesse* fr. F, princess] **1 :** close-fitting and usu. with gores from neck to flaring hemline — used esp. of women's full-length garments **2** *usu* **princesse :** served with a garnish of asparagus usu. with artichoke hearts or truffles
princess feather *n* **:** PRINCE'S-FEATHER 2
princess flower *n* **:** TIBOUCHINA 2
prin·cess·ly *adj* **:** like, befitting, or having the characteristics of a princess
princess pine *n* **:** PRINCE'S PINE
princess post *n* **:** a post in a roofing truss that is framed in a position intermediate between the queen post and the tie beam
princess regent *n, pl* **princess regents 1 :** a princess who rules a country during the minority, absence, or disability of the nominal sovereign **2 :** the wife of a prince regent
princess ring *n* **:** a finger ring with three to five stones along the band often surrounded by smaller stones
princess royal *n, pl* **princesses royal :** the eldest daughter of a British or Prussian sovereign — a designation granted for life and used only after the title has been specif. conferred by the sovereign

princess ring

princess tree *n* **:** a Chinese tree (*Paulownia tomentosa*) that has soft pubescent leaves and terminal clusters of large purple irregular flowers and is introduced and naturalized esp. in eastern No. America — called also *karri-tree*
prince·ton orange \'prinztən-, -in(t)stən-\ *n, often cap P* [fr. *Princeton* University, N.J.] **:** a strong orange that is yellower, stronger, and slightly lighter than pumpkin and redder, darker, and slightly less strong than cadmium orange
princewood \'=,=\ *n* **1 a :** either of two tropical American timber trees (*Cordia gerascanthus* and *C. alliodora*) **b :** the hard heavy smooth elastic dark-streaked brown wood of either tree **2 :** a tropical American shrub (*Exostema caribaeum*) with a bark used in the preparation of bitters
princing *pres part of* PRINCE
¹prin·ci·pal \'prin(t)səpəl, -səbəl *also* -inzp- *or* -in(t)sp-\ *adj* [ME, fr. OF, fr. L *principalis* first, principal, fr. *princip-, princeps* first person, chief + *-alis* -al — more at PRINCE] **1 :** most important, consequential, or influential **:** relegating comparable matters, items, or individuals to secondary rank **:** CONTROLLING, PRECEDING, SALIENT ⟨his chief friend and ~ ally —Anthony Trollope⟩ ⟨a chicken stew of which the ~ ingredient was not chicken but sea cucumber —John Steinbeck⟩ **2** *obs* **:** of or relating to a prince **:** PRINCELY **3 :** of, relating to, or constituting principal or a principal. as **a :** CAPITAL ⟨~ costs⟩ ⟨invested a ~ sum⟩ **b :** being the person chiefly concerned in some legal proceeding **4 :** MAIN 6 **syn** see CHIEF
²principal \"\ *n* -S [ME, fr. MF, fr. LL *principalis,* fr. L, adj., principal] **1 :** a person who has controlling authority or is in a position to act independently **:** one who has a leading position or takes the lead: as **a :** a chief or head man or woman **:** one presiding as ruler, leader, superior, or lord **b :** the chief executive officer of various educational institutions ⟨the ~ of our grade school⟩ ⟨the vice-chancellor of some British universities is known as the ~⟩ **c :** one who employs another to act for him subject to his general control and instruction **:** the person from whom an agent's responsibility derives **d :** the chief actor or an actual participant in a crime including anyone present and actively abetting or assisting therein as distinguished from an accessory either before or after the fact **e :** the person primarily liable on a legal obligation or the one who will ultimately bear the burden because of a duty to indemnify another as distinguished from one secondarily liable (as an endorser, surety, or guarantor) **f :** one fighting or pledged to fight a duel — compare SECOND **g :** a leading performer (as in a drama, opera, orchestra, or ballet) **:** a person taking a chief part in a theatrical performance **:** STAR **h :** OFFICIAL 1 **2 :** a matter or thing of primary importance **:** a main or most important element: as **a** (1) **:** a capital sum placed at interest, due as a debt, or used as a fund (2) **:** the corpus or main body of an estate, portion, devise, or bequest — distinguished from *income* **b :** the construction that gives shape and strength to a roof and that is generally one of several trusses of timber or iron; *also* **:** the most important member of a piece of framing **c** *archaic* **:** a fundamental point **:** PRINCIPLE **d :** one of the taper-bearing pillars formerly used to decorate a hearse **e :** an original (as of a writing or work of art) from which copies are, may be, or have been made **f :** either of the two outermost primaries of a hawk's wing **g** (1) **:** the chief open metallic stop in an English pipe organ that is an octave above the open diapason and consists of a 4-foot stop on the manual, an 8-foot stop on the pedal (2) *usu cap* **:** an octave or 4-foot stop — used in combination ⟨dulciana *Principal*⟩ **h** (1) **:** the chief motif or feature in a work of art (2) **:** a fugue subject — compare ANSWER **i :** a trumpet of a kind used prominently in old orchestral music (as of Handel)
³prin·ci·pal \¦prin(t)sə¦päl\ *n, pl* **principa·les** \,==ˈpä(,)lās\ [Sp, fr. LL *principalis* chief, leading person] **:** a leading man or one of the first citizens of a Philippine or Latin American community
principal axis *n* **1 a :** any of three mutually perpendicular axes through a given point of a rigid body with respect to which the moment of inertia is either a maximum or a minimum — com-

pare PERMANENT AXIS **b :** the line with respect to which a spherical mirror or lens system is symmetrical and which passes through both the center of the surfaces and their centers of curvature **2 :** the line through a focus of a conic perpendicular to a directrix
principal boy *n* **:** a male character in English pantomime usu. played by a woman — compare DAME 5
principal challenge *n* **:** a challenge to a juror on a ground assigned that if proved true renders the juror incompetent to serve as such in the case because of his presumed malice or favor **:** a challenge for cause
principal distance *n* **:** the length of a perpendicular from a station point to a perspective plane taken along the principal visual ray
principal focus *n* **:** the focus for a beam of incident rays parallel to the axis
principal form *n* **:** the form that constitutes or determines a philosophical species
principal function *n* **:** the temporal integral of the kinetic potential **:** the integral of the kinetic less the potential energy
prin·ci·pal·i·ty \ˌprin(t)sə'paləd·ē, -lətē, -i\ *n* -ES [ME *principalite*, fr. MF, fr. LL *principalitat-, principalitas* preeminence, excellence, fr. L *principalis* first, principal + *-itat-, -itas* -ity] **1 :** the quality or state of being principal **:** supreme station or power **:** HEADSHIP, PREEMINENCE ⟨your *principalities* shall come down, even the crown of your glory —Jer 13: 18 (AV)⟩ **2 a :** the state, office, or authority of a prince **:** princely dominion **:** SOVEREIGNTY **b :** the position or responsibilities of a principal (as of a school) **3 :** the territory or jurisdiction of a prince **:** the country that gives title to a prince ⟨the ~ of Wales⟩; *often* **:** a minor semi-independent state under the rule of a prince ⟨the ~ of Monaco⟩ — compare KINGDOM 2 **4** [trans. of LL *principatus*, trans. of Gk *archē*] **a :** a good or evil spiritual being of a high order ⟨for I am sure that neither death, nor life, nor angels, nor *principalities* . . . will be able to separate us from the love of God in Christ Jesus our Lord —Rom 8:38 (RSV)⟩ **b :** one of the nine orders of angels in medieval angelology
principal line *n* **:** the first and most intense line of a spectral line series
prin·ci·pal·ly \'prin(t)səp(ə)lē, -səb(-, -li *also* -inzp(ə)l- *or* -in(t)sp-\ *adv* [ME, fr. [1]*principal* + *-ly*] **:** in a principal manner **:** in the chief place or degree **:** PRIMARILY, CHIEFLY, MAINLY
principal meridian *n* **:** any of the true geographical meridians established by authority of the surveyor general of the U.S. that serves as the meridian of reference for subdividing public lands in a given region — compare GUIDE MERIDIAN
principal moment *n* **:** one of the three moments of inertia of a body about its principal axes of inertia at a given point
prin·ci·pal·ness \-pəlnəs, -bəl-\ *n* -ES **:** the quality or state of being principal
principal parts *n pl* **:** a series of verb forms from which all the other forms of a verb can be derived including in English the infinitive, the past tense, and the past participle (as *play, played, played* or *sing, sang, sung*)
principal plane *n* **:** any of the planes perpendicular to the axis and passing through the principal points of an optical system
principal plane of symmetry : a plane of symmetry in a crystal that includes two or more axes of symmetry
principal planet *n* **:** any of the nine known planets of the solar system that comprise the four terrestrial and the five major planets — distinguished from *minor planet*
principal point *n* **1 :** the point at which a principal visual ray intersects a perspective plane **2 :** either of two points on the axis of a lens so related that a ray from any point of the object directed toward one principal point will emerge from the lens in a parallel direction but directed through the other principal point **3 :** the point where the optical axis of the lens meets the film plane in an aerial camera
principal quantum number *n* **:** an integer associated with the energy of an atomic electron in any one of its possible stationary states and including both the azimuthal and the radial quantum number — called also *total quantum number*
principal rafter *n* **:** one of the upper diagonal members of a roof truss supporting the purlins and common rafters or those joints to which the roof boarding is secured — see ROOF illustration
principal ray *n* **1 :** PRINCIPAL VISUAL RAY **2 :** the one ray of the rays entering an optical instrument from any given point of the object that passes through the exact center of the aperture stop
principals *pl of* PRINCIPAL
principal section *n* **1 :** a plane passing through the optical axis of a crystal; *specif* **:** the principal plane that contains either the wave normal or the ray of light under discussion **2 :** a plane perpendicular to the edge of an optical prism
prin·ci·pal·ship \-pəlˌship, -bəl-\ *n* [[2]*principal* + *-ship*] **:** the office or condition of a principal; *esp* **:** the position of an academic principal ⟨will be asked to assume the ~ of the new high school⟩
principal sum *n* **:** the sum specified to be paid under the terms of an accident or health insurance policy in case of the death of the insured or the loss of limb or sight due to an accidental injury
principal visual ray *n* **:** a perpendicular that extends from a station point to a perspective plane and theoretically passes precisely along the visual axis of a viewing eye
principal work *n* **:** the open cylindrical pipes of a pipe organ that give the typical organ quality of tone
prin·ci·pate \'prin(t)səˌpāt, -səpət\ *n* -S [ME *principat*, fr. L *principatus*, fr. *princip-, princeps* first person, prince + *-atus* -ate — more at PRINCE] **1 :** princely power **:** supreme rule **2** *obs* **a :** PRINCIPALITY 4b **b :** a principal person **:** PRINCE **3 :** PRINCIPALITY 3 **4 :** the power or term of a Roman princeps
prin·ci·pe *It* 'prēnchēˌ(ˌ)pā, *Sp* 'prēnsēˌ(ˌ)pā *or* -nthē-, *Pg* 'prī"(n)sēpə\ *n* -S [It *principe* & Sp & Pg *príncipe*, fr. L *princip-, princeps* prince] **:** PRINCE; *esp* **:** the eldest son of a Spanish or Portuguese king — compare INFANTE
[1]**principes** *pl of* PRINCEPS
[2]**prin·ci·pes** \'prin(t)səˌpēz, -iŋkəˌpās\ [NL, fr. L, princes] *syn of* PALMALES
prin·cip·i·al \(')prin'sipēəl\ *adj* [L *principium* beginning + E *-al*] **:** INITIAL, PRIMARY
principiant *adj* [LL *principiant-, principians*, pres. part. of *principiare* to begin, fr. L *principium* beginning] *obs* **:** relating to or dealing with first principles or beginnings
prin·cip·i·um \prin'sipēəm\ *n, pl* **princip·ia** \-ēə\ [L, beginning, origin, basis] **1 :** a fundamental principle **:** ultimate origin **:** BASIS, ELEMENT, FOUNDATION ⟨the *principia* of ethics⟩ **2 :** INCEPTION 2a **3 :** a general's quarters in an ancient Roman military encampment
[1]**prin·ci·ple** \'prin(t)səpəl, -səbəl *also* -inzp- *or* -in(t)sp-\ *n* -S [ME, modif. of MF *principe*, fr. L *principium* beginning, origin, basis (in pl. *principia*, first principles, fundamentals), fr. *princip-, princeps* first, original, lit., taken as first, fr. *prin-* (fr. *primus* first) + *-cip-, -ceps* (fr. L *capere* to take) — more at PRIME, HEAVE] **1 a :** a general or fundamental truth **:** a comprehensive and fundamental law, doctrine, or assumption on which others are based or from which others are derived **:** elementary proposition ⟨the ~*s* of physics⟩ **b** (1) **:** a governing law of conduct **:** an opinion, attitude, or belief that exercises a directing influence on the life and behavior **:** rule or code of usu. good conduct by which one directs one's life or actions ⟨a man of no ~⟩ ⟨the honorable ~*s* to which my father reared me⟩ (2) **:** devotion to what is right and honorable esp. as a trait of character **c** (1) **:** natural law or laws applied to achieve a purpose or produce a result by an artificial device (as a mechanical-contrivance) **:** the laws or facts of nature underlying and exemplified in the working of an artificial device ⟨the ~ of the internal-combustion engine⟩ (2) **:** the mode of construction or working of an artificial device **2 a :** something from which another thing takes its origin **:** a basic or primary source of material or energy **:** ultimate basis or cause ⟨the ancients recognized opposed governing ~*s* as of heat and cold, moisture and dryness⟩ **b :** an original faculty or endowment **:** underlying or basic quality that motivates behavior or other activities ⟨such ~*s* of human nature as greed and curiosity⟩ **c** *obs* **:** original state **:** COMMENCEMENT, BEGINNING **3** *obs* **a principles** *pl* **:** RUDIMENTS **b :** SEED, EMBRYO **4 :** a component part **:** CONSTITUENT: as **a** *archaic* **:** ELEMENT 1a, 1b **b :** a distinguishable ingredient that exhibits or imparts a characteristic quality ⟨the bark contains a bitter ~ used in medicine⟩ ⟨the active ~ of this drug⟩ **5** *cap, Christian Science* **:** a divine principle **:** GOD ⟨the triune *Principle* of Life, Truth, and Love⟩

syn PRINCIPLE, AXIOM, FUNDAMENTAL, LAW, and THEOREM can mean, in common, a proposition or other formulation stating a fact, or a generalization accepted as true and basic. PRINCIPLE applies to any generalization that provides a basis for reasoning or a guide for conduct or procedure ⟨the *principle* of free speech⟩ ⟨his remarkable grasp of *principle* in the remaining field, that of historical geography —Benjamin Farrington⟩ ⟨the same hankering as their pious ancestors for a cozy universe, a closed system of certainties erected upon a single *principle* —H.J.Muller⟩ ⟨the *principle* was established that no officer or employee . . . was entitled to any classified information whatever unless it was necessary for the performance of his duties —J.P.Baxter b.1893⟩ ⟨I do not mean to assert this pedantically as an absolute rule, but as a *principle* guiding school authorities —Bertrand Russell⟩ AXIOM in an older sense applies to a principle not open to dispute because self-evident, usu. one upon which a structure of reasoning is or may be erected; in more common current usage it implies a principle universally accepted or regarded as worthy of acceptance rather than one necessarily true ⟨the journalistic *axiom* that there is nothing as dead as yesterday's newspaper —G.W.Johnson⟩ ⟨one of the *axioms* of U.S. business is that efficiency is increased by specialization —*Time*⟩ FUNDAMENTAL usu. applies to a principle, but sometimes a fact, so essential to a philosophy, religion, science, or art that its rejection would destroy the intellectual structure resting upon it ⟨the *fundamentals* of scientific research⟩ ⟨the *fundamentals* of Christian belief⟩ ⟨the simple economics *fundamental* that mechanization is the secret of America's greatness —*advt*⟩ LAW in this comparison applies to a formulation stating an order or relation of phenomena which is regarded as always holding good ⟨the conquest of nature's procreative forces, through the discovery of the *laws* of agriculture and animal husbandry —R.W.Murray⟩ ⟨the *laws* of the rain and of the seasons here are tropic laws —Marjory S. Douglas⟩ ⟨it is a *law* that no two electrons may occupy the same orbit —A.S.Eddington⟩ THEOREM applies to a proposition that admits of rational proof and, usu., is logically necessary to succeeding logical steps in a structure of reasoning ⟨theoretical economics puts the patterns of uniformity in a coherent system [of which] the basic propositions are called assumptions or postulates, the derived propositions are called *theorems* —Oscar Lange⟩ ⟨the error that was to prove most durable of all, the *theorem* that only a very short land traverse would be found necessary from Missouri to Pacific waters —Bernard DeVoto⟩

—in principle *adv* **:** in regard to fundamentals ⟨the idea was sound *in principle*⟩ **:** with respect to basic elements but not with respect to details ⟨prepared to accept the proposition *in principle*⟩
[2]**principle** \"\ *vt* -ED/-ING/-S *archaic* **:** to instill principles into **:** ground or fix in a principle **:** incite or move as an animating principle
prin·ci·pled \-pəld,-bəld\ *adj* [[1]*principle* + *-ed*] **:** exhibiting, based on, or characterized by principle that is usu. high, righteous, or proper ⟨unprincipled expediency and ~ pragmatism —*Time*⟩ ⟨could find no ~ reason for refusing —William Phillips b.1907⟩ — often used in combination ⟨high-*principled*⟩ ⟨low-*principled*⟩
principle of acceleration : LAW OF ACCELERATION
principle of association : ASSOCIATIVE LAW
principle of causality : LAW OF CAUSATION
principle of contradiction : LAW OF CONTRADICTION
principle of duality : a principle in projective geometry: from a geometric theorem another theorem may be derived by substituting in the original theorem the word *point* for the word *line* in the case of a point or line in the plane or the word *point* for the word *plane* in the case of a point or plane in space and conversely
principle of equivalence : a principle in the general theory of relativity: the mass of a body as measured by its resistance to acceleration under the action of a force is equal to the mass as measured by the effect of a gravitational field on the body
principle of excluded middle : LAW OF EXCLUDED MIDDLE
principle of identity : LAW OF IDENTITY
principle of least action : a principle in physics: if the passage of a dynamic system from one configuration to another is spontaneous and without change in total energy the corresponding action has a minimum value
principle of segregation : the first of Mendel's laws
principle of sufficient reason : LAW OF SUFFICIENT REASON
principle of utility : GREATEST HAPPINESS PRINCIPLE
principle of war : any of the basic elements considered essential to success in war usu. including objective, offensive, surprise, mass or concentration, economy of force, security, movement or mobility, cooperation, and simplicity
prin·cox \'prinˌkäks, -iŋˌkä-\ *or* **princock** \-äk\ *n, pl* **princoxes** *or* **princocks** [*prin-* of unknown origin + *cox*, alter. of *cock*] *archaic* **:** a pert youth **:** COXCOMB
prine \'prīn\ *n* -S [origin unknown] *dial Eng* **:** BAR-TAILED GODWIT
prin·gle \'priŋgəl\ *vb* -ED/-ING/-S [prob. blend of *prinkle* and *tingle*] *vi* **:** to tingle persistently or annoyingly **~** *vt* **:** to cause a tingling in
[1]**prink** \'priŋk\ *vi* -ED/-ING/-S [ME *prinken*] *archaic* **:** WINK
[2]**prink** \"\ *vb* -ED/-ING/-S [prob. alter. of [4]*prank*] *vt* **:** to dress up **:** bedeck with finery ⟨the thousand and one emporiums which patch and ~ us —John Galsworthy⟩ **~** *vi* **:** to dress or arrange oneself for show — often used with *up*
[3]**prink** \"\ *vi* [perh. modif. of D *pronken* to strut — more at PRANK] *dial chiefly Eng* **:** to act or walk in an affected or mincing manner
prink·er \-kə(r)\ *n* -S **:** one that prinks
prin·kle \-kəl\ *vb* -ED/-ING/-S [prob. alter. of *prickle*] *Scot* **:** PRICKLE, TINGLE
prinky \-kē\ *adj* -ER/-EST [[2]*prink* + *-y*] **:** spruce-looking and showy **:** BEDECKED
pri·nos \'prīˌnäs, -rēˌn-\ *n, pl* **prinos** [Gk, holm oak] **1 :** WINTER BERRY **2 :** the bark of winterberry
[1]**print** \'print\ *n* -S [ME *printe, prente, preinte*, fr. OF *preinte*, fr. *preint*, past part. of *preindre* to press, fr. L *premere* — more at PRESS] **1 a** (1) **:** a mark made by impression **:** a line, character, figure, or indentation made by the pressure of one thing on another ⟨sealed with a ~ of his thumb in soft wax⟩ ⟨the delicate ~*s* of a squirrel in snow⟩ (2) **:** a mental impression **:** IMPRINT ⟨these sorrows left their ~ on his spirit⟩ **b** *obs* **:** VESTIGE **c :** something impressed with a print or formed in a mold ⟨obtained an accurate plaster ~ of the convolutions of the skull⟩ ⟨a ~ of butter⟩ **d :** an intaglio impression reproducing in reverse an original having somewhat slight relief; *also* **:** a cast or impression in relief taken from such an intaglio **e :** CORE PRINT **f :** TRACING 2c **2 :** a device or instrument (as a stamp, die, or mold) for impressing or forming a print **3 a :** printed state or form ⟨to see his name in ~⟩ ⟨put a poem into ~⟩ **b :** the printing craft or industry ⟨wise in the ways of ~⟩ **c :** TYPE ⟨set it up in ~⟩ **4 a** (1) **:** printed matter; *esp* **:** a printed publication (2) **prints** *pl* **:** printed papers or cards (as newspapers, pamphlets, sheet music, address cards, printing proofs, engravings) of the specifications set forth in U.S. postal regulations **b :** NEWSPRINT **5 :** printed letters **:** printed matter with regard to quality, size, or form ⟨clear ~⟩ ⟨large ~⟩ ⟨small ~⟩ **6 a :** a copy made by any printing process ⟨color ~*s*⟩ ⟨sporting ~*s*⟩ **b** (1) **:** a reproduction of an original painting or other work of art obtained usu. by a photomechanical process (2) **:** an artistic work sometimes with accompanying text published on a page of not more than four folds in a periodical or separately to advertise merchandise and entitled to copyright registration under English copyright law **c :** cloth with a pattern or figured design applied by printing **d :** a product of the silk-screen process **e** (1) **:** a photographic copy made on a sensitized surface (as from a negative or from a drawing on transparent paper) (2) **:** a photographic negative made from a positive, a negative made from a negative, or a positive made from a positive (3) **:** a developed motion picture-film containing positive images as printed from a negative **7 :** something (as a dress) made of a print fabric ⟨ruffled ~*s* for your kitchen windows⟩ **— in print 1** *chiefly dial* **:** to the letter **:** with accurateness, nice adjustment, or precision ⟨I will do it sir, *in print* —Shak.⟩ **2 :** procurable from the publisher — used esp. of a book **— out of print :** not procurable from the publisher or from ordinary new-book sources because the printed edition has been exhausted — used esp. of a book
[2]**print** \"\ *vb* -ED/-ING/-S [ME *imprenten, prenten*, fr. *printe, prente* print] *vt* **1 a :** to make an impression in or upon **:** mark with a print ⟨two small light feet that barely ~*ed* the soft soil⟩ ⟨fresh butter worked, salted, and ~*ed*⟩ **b :** to cause (as a mark) to be stamped **:** make (an impression or mark) by or as if by pressure ⟨~ his seal in wax⟩ **c :** to apply pressure with (as a stamp of the foot) so as to leave an impression **2 a :** to make a copy of by impressing paper against an inked printing surface or by an analogous method ⟨~*ing* columned pages⟩ ⟨~ bank notes⟩ — often used with *up* **b :** to perform or cause to be performed all or some of the operations necessary to the production of (as a publication, a piece of printed matter, a picture) ⟨~ greeting cards⟩ ⟨~ an edition of a newspaper⟩ **c :** to impress (as wallpaper or cloth) with a design or pattern ⟨~ cloth with linoleum blocks⟩ ⟨this air-dried tub-sized paper is easy to ~ —*Graphic Arts Monthly*⟩ **:** impress (a pattern or design) on something ⟨~*ed* gay foliage on sheer linen⟩ **d :** to publish in print ⟨"all the news that's fit to ~" —*N.Y.Times*⟩ **3 :** to form manually in unjoined characters resembling those of ordinary type ⟨~ the name and address clearly⟩ **4 a :** to make (a positive picture) on sensitized photographic paper, film, plate, or other material from a negative or a positive **b :** to make (a negative) from a negative or a positive **~** *vi* **1 a :** to use or practice the art of typography **:** work as a printer **b :** to produce printed matter ⟨the new rotary press ~*s* very rapidly⟩ **c :** to make a printed copy ⟨badly worn type ~*s* poorly⟩ **d :** to be susceptible of printing ⟨this paper ~*s* badly⟩ **2** *archaic* **:** PUBLISH; *esp* **:** to publish an article or a book **3 :** to write or hand-letter in imitation of unjoined printed characters **4** *of a firearm or a bullet* **:** to puncture a paper target
print·abil·i·ty \ˌprintə'biləd·ē\ *n* **:** the quality or state of being printable **:** printable condition ⟨the ~ of a story⟩ ⟨~ of type⟩
print·able \'printəbəl\ *adj* **1 :** capable of being printed or of being printed from ⟨~ paper⟩ ⟨a ~ halftone⟩ **2 :** considered fit to print or publish because free from matter that is morally or legally objectionable
prin·ta·nier \prä"tányā\ *or* **prin·ta·nière** \-yeer\ *adj* [*printanier* fr. F, fr. *printanier* vernal, fr. MF, fr. *printemps* spring (fr. *prin* prime + *temps* time — fr. L *tempus*—) + *-ier* -er; *printanière* fr. F, fem. of *printanier* — more at PRIME, TEMPORAL] **:** made or dressed with diced spring vegetables ⟨a ~ soup⟩
printcloth \'=,=\ *n* [[1]*print* + *cloth*] **:** plainwoven cotton gray goods suitable for converting into white fabrics (as muslin or cambric), for printing as dress or drapery goods, or for use as bagging
print down *vt* **:** to transfer the image from (a photographic negative) to a printing plate (as in photo-offset or gravure)
printed circuit *n* **:** a circuit for electronic apparatus made by depositing conductive material in continuous paths from terminal to terminal on an insulating surface
printed matter *n* **:** matter that is printed by any of various mechanical processes (as letterpress, lithography) and is eligible for mailing at a special rate by postal regulation which specifically excludes matter produced by various other duplicating processes (as carbon and copying-press copies)
printed page *n* **:** published writing — used with *the* ⟨the importance of the *printed page* in backward areas⟩
printed paper *n* **1 :** a class of mail in the United Kingdom comprising printed matter exclusive of newspapers not exceeding two pounds in weight **2 printed papers** *pl* **:** pieces of mail matter in international mail resembling printed paper but including newspapers and having different weight limits — compare COMMERCIAL PAPERS
print·er \'printə(r)\ *n* -S **1 :** one whose work is printing: as **a :** one that is engaged in the art or business of printing ⟨a small commercial ~⟩; *esp* **:** a practitioner of one of the constituent skilled printing crafts (as a compositor or pressman) **b :** one who decorates materials (as textiles, pottery, wallpaper) with printed designs **2 :** a device used in printing or to print reproductions: as **a** (1) **:** a device containing a light source for exposing sensitive photographic material to light transmitted by a negative or positive that is either held in contact with the material (as in making a contact print) or that is not in contact with it so that a lens is used to project the image onto the material (as in making a projection print) (2) **:** a machine for printing motion-picture positives from negatives or vice versa either by contact or by optical projection **b :** an instrument that records a telegraphic message at the receiving end in printed characters
print·ers \-təz\ *n pl but sing or pl in constr* [fr. pl. of earlier *printer* printcloth, fr. [1]*print* + *-er*] *Brit* **:** PRINTCLOTH
print·er's devil \-tə(r)z-\ *n* [prob. so called fr. his becoming often black with ink] **:** a young apprentice or errand boy in a printing office
printer's ink *n* **1 :** ink for use in printing; *esp* **:** one of the semi-solid quick-drying black inks ordinarily used in letterpress or offset printing **2 :** printed matter ⟨the power of *printer's ink*⟩
printer's mark *n* **:** IMPRINT b(2)
printer's reader *n, chiefly Brit* **:** PROOFREADER
printer's ream *n* **:** a ream of 516 sheets
printer's waste *n* **:** imperfect or experimental postal or other official stamps that are supposed to be destroyed by the printer
print·ery \'printərē\ *n* -ES [[2]*print* + *-ery*] **:** PRINTING OFFICE
printing *n* -S *often attrib* [ME *printing, prenting*, fr. gerund of *printen, prenten* to print — more at PRINT] **1 a :** reproduction (as on paper or cloth) of an image from a printing surface made typically by a contact impression that causes a transfer of ink — compare LETTERPRESS, INTAGLIO, PLANOGRAPHY, STENCIL, ELECTRONOGRAPHY **b :** the process of producing a positive or negative photographic image on a light-sensitive material from a negative or positive by contact or projection **:** the process of making photographic prints **c :** the process or act of decorating pottery by means of transfer papers printed with mineral colors or of gelatin sheets printed in oil with the colors being fixed by firing **2 :** the art, practice, or business of a printer **3 :** the number of copies or the amount of material printed in one continuous operation **:** IMPRESSION 6c **4 printings** *pl* **:** paper to be printed on
printing frame *n* **:** a holder in which a photographic negative or positive is held in uniform close contact with sensitized material for exposing the latter to light in order to make a print
printing-in \'==,=\ *n* -S **:** a process by which cloud effects or other features not in the original negative are introduced into a photograph by printing from another negative
printing ink *n* **:** an ink used in printing and consisting of a pigment or pigments of the required color mixed with oil or varnish; *esp* **:** a black ink made from carbon blacks and thick linseed oil or some similar oil often with rosin oil and rosin varnish added
printing machine *n, chiefly Brit* **:** a power-driven printing press
printing office *n* **:** a business establishment in which printing (as of books, newspapers) is done
printing-out \'==,=\ *adj* **:** relating to, used in, or being a method of photographic printing in which the image is fully brought out by the direct actinic action of light without subsequent development by means of chemicals ⟨*printing-out* paper requires fixing and toning to make the image permanent and give it a satisfactory color⟩
printing plate *n* **:** PLATE 4b(1), 4b(2), 4b(3)
printing press *n* **:** a machine that produces printed copies (as of graphic images or letterpress); *esp* **:** one that is power driven — compare COPPERPLATE PRESS, CYLINDER PRESS, PLATEN PRESS, ROTARY PRESS, WEB PRESS
printing surface *n* **:** a prepared surface (as set type, an electrotype, a lithographic stone, an offset or gravure plate) from which printing is done
printing telegraph *n* **:** PRINTER 2b
print·less \'printləs\ *adj* **1 :** making no imprint **:** passing without a trace **2 :** bearing or taking no imprint **:** unmarked or unmarred by traces of what has passed
printmaker \'=,==\ *n* **:** one that makes prints; *esp* **:** an artist working in a graphic medium (as etching, engraving, lithography, or woodcutting)

print-out \'ˌ=ˌ=\ *adj* : PRINTING-OUT
prints *pl of* PRINT, *pres 3d sing of* PRINT
printscript \'=ˌ=\ *n* [¹*print* + *script*] : writing done in unjoined letters resembling print
printseller \'=ˌ==\ *n* : a seller of graphic art works; *esp* : the proprietor of a printshop (sense 1)
printshop \'=ˌ=\ *n* **1** : a shop in which products of the graphic arts are sold **2** : a printing establishment; *esp* : a small one that does not have a regular schedule of publishing (as of a periodical)
printworks \'=ˌ=\ *n pl but sing or pl in constr* [¹*print* + *works*] : a factory at which cloth, wallpaper, or other material is printed
printz wood *or* **prinz·wood** \'prin(t)sˌ=\ *n* [prob. fr. the name *Printz* or *Prinz* + E *wood*] : quartered veneer of elm
pri·odont \'prīəˌdänt\ *adj* [*pri-* + *-odont*] : having small mandibles — used of some polymorphic insects (as various stag beetles); compare TELEODONT
pri·odon·tes \ˌprīə'dänt(ˌ)ēz, -n(ˌ)tēz\ *n, cap* [NL, fr. *pri-* + *-odontes*] : a genus of mammals including solely the giant armadillo
pri·on \'prīˌän\ *n* -S [NL, fr. Gk *priōn* saw] : any of several petrels of the southern hemisphere (genus *Pachyptila*) that are bluish gray above and white below and somewhat resemble doves — see FAIRY PRION
prion- *or* **priono-** *comb form* [NL, fr. Gk *prion-*, fr. *priōn* saw, fr. *priein* to saw — more at PRISM] : saw : having an action or appearance like that of a saw ⟨*Prionodesmacea*⟩ ⟨*prionodont*⟩
-pri·on \'prīˌän, ˌprēˌän\ *n comb form* [NL, fr. Gk *priōn* saw] : creature with a (specified) kind of sawlike part — in generic names ⟨*Diprion*⟩
pri·o·na·ce \ˌprīə'nā(ˌ)sē\ *n, cap* [NL, fr. *prion-* + *-ace*] : a genus of sharks (family Carcharhinidae) that contains the cosmopolitan blue shark
¹**pri·onid** \(')prī'ōnəd, -'ān-; 'prīənəd, -(ˌ)nid\ *adj* [NL *Prionidae*] : of or relating to the Prionidae
²**prionid** \"\ *n* -S : a beetle of the family Prionidae
pri·on·i·dae \prī'änəˌdē\ *n pl, cap* [NL, fr. *Prionus*, type genus + *-idae*] : a family of large brown or black beetles having the prothorax prolonged outward into a thin more or less toothed margin and developing from larvae that burrow into the roots or wood of plants
pri·ono·des·ma·cea \ˌprīə(ˌ)nōˌdez'māsēə; prīˌänō-, prīˌōnō-\ *n pl, cap* [NL, fr. *prion-* + *desm-* + *-acea*] *in some classifications* : a division of Lamellibranchia comprising comparatively primitive bivalve mollusks that typically have the hinge prionodont and being approximately equal to the combined orders Protobranchia and Filibranchia — **pri·ono·des·ma·cean** \ˌ==(ˌ)=¦=¦māshən, =¦==¦=¦==\ *n or adj* — **pri·ono·des·ma·ceous** \-shəs\ *adj*
¹**pri·on·odon** \prī'änəˌdän\ *n, cap* [NL, fr. *prion-* + *-odon*] : a genus of mammals (family Viverridae) comprising the Asiatic linsangs
²**prionodon** \"\ [NL, alter. of *Priodontes*] *syn of* PRIODONTES
pri·on·odont \-dänt\ *adj* [*prion-* + *-odont*] : having a sawlike row of many simple and similar teeth
pri·o·nop·i·dae \ˌprīə'näpəˌdē\ *n pl, cap* [NL, fr. *Prionops*, type genus (fr. *prion-* + *-ops*) + *-idae*] : a family of African passerine birds consisting of the helmet shrikes
pri·o·no·tus \ˌprīə'nōd·əs\ *n, cap* [NL, fr. *prion-* + *-notus*] : a genus of gurnards comprising the typical sea robins
pri·on·urus \ˌprīə'n(y)u̇rəs\ *n, cap* [NL, fr. *prion-* + *-urus*] : a genus of scorpions including several large venomous African scorpions of medical importance
pri·o·nus \prī'ōnəs, 'prīən-\ *n* [NL, fr. Gk *priōn* saw] **1** *cap* : the type genus of Prionidae including beetles whose larvae are economically important borers in the roots of various trees and shrubs and often completely hollow out the woody tissues **2** -ES : any beetle of the genus *Prionus*
¹**pri·or** \'prī(ə)r, -īə\ *n* -S [ME *prior, priour*, fr. OE *prior* & MF *prior, priour*, fr. ML *prior*, fr. LL, administrator, predecessor, fr. L, former, previous, superior] **1 a** : the superior ranking next to the abbot of a given monastery : CLAUSTRAL PRIOR **b** : the superior of a priory — called also *conventual prior* **c** : the superior of a house or group of houses of any of various religious communities **2 a** : the head of a guild **b** *Brit* : the head of a business firm
²**prior** \"\ *adj* [L, former, previous, first, superior, compar. of OL *pri* before; akin to L *priscus* ancient, *pristinus* primitive, pristine, *prae* before — more at FOR] **1** : earlier in time or order : preceding temporally, causally, or psychologically : ANTECEDENT, PREVIOUS ⟨a ~ appointment⟩ ⟨~ consideration⟩ **2 a** : taking precedence logically, methodologically, or in importance or value — usu. followed by *to* ⟨a responsibility ~ to all others⟩ **b** *of a security* : having priority as to earnings or assets over other issues of the same firm
pri·or·able \'prī(ə)rəbəl\ *adj* [²*prior* + *-able*] : LEGITIMATE 4b
pri·or·al \-ī(ə)rəl\ *adj* [¹*prior* + *-al*] : of or relating to a prior ⟨~ responsibilities⟩
prior art *n* : the processes, devices, and modes of achieving the end of an alleged invention that were known or knowable by reasonable diligence before and at its date — used chiefly in patent law
pri·or·ate \-ī(ə)rət\ *n* -S [ML *prioratus*, fr. *prior* + L *-atus* -ate] **1 a** : the office and dignity of a prior **b** : the term of office of a prior **2 a** : PRIORY **b** : a religious community under a prior
pri·or·ess \-ī(ə)rəs\ *n* -ES [ME *prioresse*, fr. OF, fr. ML *priorissa*, fr. *prior* + LL *-issa* -ess] : a nun whose rank in an order of women corresponds to that of prior in an order of men
pri·or·ite \-īəˌrīt\ *n* -S [G *priorit*, fr. Granville T. *Prior* †1936 Eng. mineralogist + G *-it* -ite] : a titano-niobate of yttrium, cerium, and other rare-earth metals that is isomorphous with eschynite — called also *blomstrandine*
pri·or·i·tied \prī'ȯrəd·ēd\ *adj* : having a priority — usu. used in combination ⟨low-*prioritied* shipments⟩
pri·or·i·ty \prī'ȯrəd·ē, -rətē, -i\ *n* -ES [ME *priorite*, fr. MF, fr. ML *prioritat-, prioritas*, fr. L *prior* former, prior + *-itat-, -itas* -ity] **1** : the quality or state of being prior: as **a** (1) : antecedence in time (2) : precedence in date or position of publication — used of taxa; see LAW OF PRIORITY (3) : the quality or state of being prior logically, methodologically, or epistemologically **b** : superiority in rank, position, privilege, or other quality ⟨the ~ in law of liens on a property⟩ **2** : something that is prior or that conveys precedence: as **a** : a wartime preferential rating assigned by a government for the delivery of products according to the relative need of each for national defense and the proportionate allocation of scarce materials **b** : any preferential rating assigning rights to scarce products or materials, limited services, transportation, or surplus property or prescribing the order in which assignments are to be attended to **c** : something requiring or meriting attention prior to competing alternatives ⟨a ~ project⟩ ⟨high on our list of *priorities* is a trip to New York⟩
pri·or·ly \'prī(ə)rlē, -īəl-, -li\ *adv* [²*prior* + *-ly*] : in advance : PREVIOUSLY
pri·or·ship \-ī(ə)rˌship, -īəˌsh-\ *n* [¹*prior* + *-ship*] : the office and dignity of a prior
prior to *prep* : in advance of : BEFORE ⟨pay the balance due *prior to* receiving the goods⟩
pri·o·ry \'prī(ə)rē, -ri\ *n* -ES [ME *priorie*, fr. AF, fr. ML *prioria*, fr. *prior* monastic superior + L *-ia* -y] **1** : a religious house that ranks immediately below an abbey and is either self-sustaining or dependent upon an abbey **2** : PRIORATE 1
pris *abbr* prisoner
pris·able \'prīzəbəl\ *adj* [*prise* + *-able*] : subject to prisage
pri·sage \'prīzij, prē'zäzh\ *also* **prise** \'prīz, -rēz\ *n* -S [*prisage* fr. ME *prise* prisage + *-age; prise* fr. ME, fr. OF, act of taking, seizure — more at PRIZE (booty)] **1 a** : the right of the crown under old English law to take one tun of wine from every ship importing from 10 to 20 tuns and 2 tuns from every ship importing 20 or more — compare BUTLERAGE **b** : wine so taken **2** : the share of merchandise taken as lawful prize at sea that belongs to the king under old English law
pri·sal \'prīzəl\ *n* -S [AF *prisel*, fr. MF *prise* seizure (fr. OF) + AF *-el* -al] **1** *obs* : seizure (as of goods) under legal or customary privilege **2** *obs* **a** : the action of taking something as a prize of war **b** : something taken as a prize
pris·can \'priskən\ *adj* [L *priscus* ancient, old + E *-an* — more at PRIOR] : dealing with or existing in ancient times

pris·cil·la \prə̇'silə\ *n* -S *sometimes cap* [fr. *Priscilla*, a feminine name] : one of a pair of ruffled curtains with short ruffled valance attached and with tiebacks of the same material

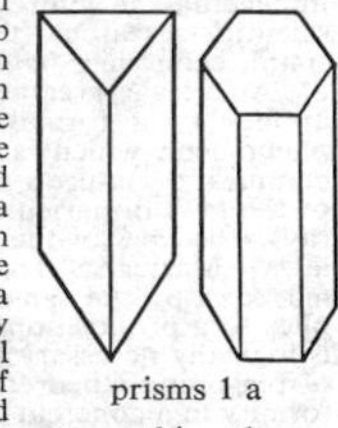
priscillas

pris·cil·lian \prə̇'silyən\ *n* -S *usu cap* [back-formation fr. *priscillianism*] : PRISCILLIANIST 1
pris·cil·lian·ism \-yəˌnizəm\ *n* -S *usu cap* [*Priscillian* †A.D. 385 Span. religious reformer + E *-ism*] : the teachings of Priscillian, bishop of Avila, who was condemned, put to torture, and beheaded with four companions on charges of heresy involving leanings toward Manichaeism, docetism, and modalism — see PRISCILLIANIST
¹**pris·cil·lian·ist** \-yənə̇st\ *n* -S *usu cap* [*Priscillian* †A.D.385 + E *-ist*] **1** : an adherent of Priscillianism or a follower of Priscillian **2** [*Priscilla*, prophetess associated with the founder of Montanism + E *-ist*] : MONTANIST
²**priscillianist** \"\ *adj, usu cap* : of or relating to the Priscillianists or their beliefs
prise *var of* PRIZE
pri·sere \'prī+ˌ-\ *n* [¹*primary* + *sere* (cycle)] : the succession of vegetational stages that occurs in passing from bare earth or water to a climax community — compare SUBSERE
pris·iad·ka *or* **pris·jad·ka** \pris'yädkə\ *n* -S [Russ *prisyadka*] : a Slavic male dance step executed by extending the legs alternately forward from a squatting position
prism \'prizəm\ *n* -S [LL *prisma*, fr. Gk, anything sawn, prism, fr. *priein* to saw *pristēs* saw; akin to Gk *pristis* sawfish and perh. to Alb *priš* to break, spoil] **1 a** : a polyhedron having two faces that are polygons in parallel planes while the other faces are parallelograms — see VOLUME table **b** : something shaped like such a solid figure; *specif* : the volume of water in a stream in motion considered as a prism of chosen length in conjunction with the cross section of the channel **2 a** : a transparent body bounded in part by two plane faces that are not parallel used to deviate or disperse a beam of light **b** : an electric or magnetic field similarly used for a beam of electrons **c** : something that refracts light or produces an effect suggestive of a spectrum; *specif* : a more or less prism-shaped decorative glass luster (as for a chandelier) **3 a** : a crystal form whose faces are parallel to one axis; *specif* : one whose faces are parallel to the vertical axis — compare DOME **b** : a crystal form whose number of faces is three or more and whose intersection edges are all parallel

prisms 1 a

pris·mal \-zməl\ *adj* : PRISMATIC
pris·mat·ic \(')priz¦mad·|ik, -at|, |ēk\ *adj* [F *prismatique*, fr. Gk *prismat-, prisma* prism + F *-ique* -ic] **1** : of, relating to, resembling, or constituting a prism ⟨a ~ form or cleavage⟩ ⟨~ lusters on a chandelier⟩ **2 a** : formed by a prism : resembling the colors formed by the refraction of light through a prism ⟨~ effects⟩ ⟨~ spectrum colors⟩ **b** : consisting of prisms ⟨~ soil aggregates⟩ **3** : resembling a prism or its refraction of light ⟨a ~ book, sharply faceted, receiving light from many aspects and refracting the actual into the prophetic —Warren Beck⟩ : highly colored : BRILLIANT, SHOWY ⟨the ~ life⟩ ⟨~ splendor⟩ **4** : having such symmetry that a general form with faces cutting all axes at unspecified intercepts is a prism — used of a class of crystals with the highest symmetry in the monoclinic system
pris·mat·i·cal \|ə̇kəl, |ēk-\ *adj, archaic* [Gk *prismat-, prisma* + E *-ical*] : PRISMATIC
pris·mat·i·cal·ly \|ə̇k(ə)lē, |ēk-, -li\ *adv* : in a prismatic manner : so as to be prismatic : as if refracted by a prism
prismatic astrolabe *n* : a portable instrument consisting of a small telescope, a 60-degree prism, and a mercury reflecting basin by which determinations of time, latitude, and azimuth may be obtained from star observations
prismatic coefficient *n* : the ratio of the volume of displacement of a ship to that of a prism equal in length to the distance between perpendiculars of the ship and in cross section to that of the immersed midship section
prismatic compass *n* : a surveyor's hand compass provided with a triangular glass prism so adjusted that the compass can be read while taking a sight
prismatic glass *n* : PRISM GLASS
prismatic layer *n* **1** *also* **prismatic tissue** : a layer of secondary tissue developed internally by the cambium of some lycopods (as the quillworts) and interpreted as xylem, phloem, or both **2** : the middle layer of the shell of a mollusk consisting essentially of calcium carbonate arranged in prisms
prismatic reflector *n* : a totally reflecting prism that is usu. right-isosceles in form
prismatic spectrum *n* : PRISM SPECTRUM
pris·ma·tize \'prizməˌtīz\ *vt* -ED/-ING/-S [*prismatic* + *-ize*] : to alter into prisms ⟨*prismatized* lava⟩
pris·ma·toid \-tȯid\ *n* -S [NL *prismatoides*, fr. Gk *prismat-, prisma* prism + L *-oides* -oid] : a polyhedron having all of its vertices in two parallel planes — **pris·ma·toi·dal** \¦==¦tȯidᵊl\ *adj*
prism binocular *n* : a binocular with shortened telescopic tubes in each of which light rays entering through the objective lens are reflected by two Porro prisms before passing through the eyepiece where finally an erect virtual image is formed — often used in pl.; compare FIELD GLASS

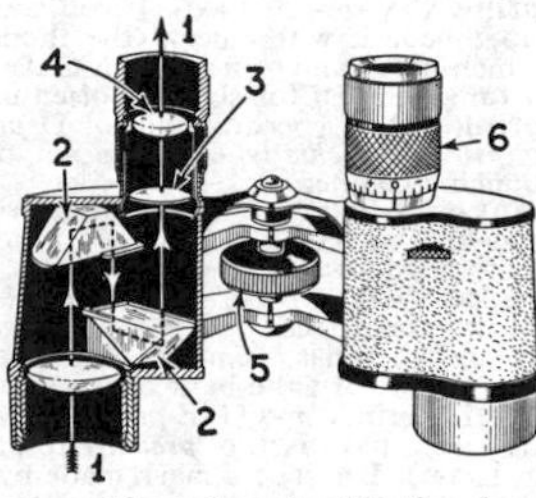

prism binocular: *1* objective lens, *2* Porro prism, *3* concave lens, *4* eyepiece, *5* focusing screw, *6* lens adjustment

prism diopter *n* : an arbitrary standard of prismatic deflection equal to that of a prism that deflects a beam of light one centimeter on a plane placed at a distance of one meter
prism glass *n* : glass with one side smooth and the other side formed into sharp-edged ridges so as to reflect the light that passes through
prism level *n* : a dumpy level with a mirror over the level tube and a pair of prisms so placed that the position of the level bubble can be determined by the levelman without moving his head from the eyepiece
pris·moid \'prizˌmȯid\ *n* -S [prob. fr. (assumed) NL *prismoides*, fr. LL *prisma* prism + L *-oides* -oid] : a prismatoid whose bases have the same number of sides — **pris·moi·dal** \(')priz¦mȯidᵊl\ *adj*
prism spectroscope *n* : a spectroscope in which light is decomposed by a single prism
prism spectrum *n* : a spectrum obtained by use of a prism or train of prisms
prismy \'priz(ə)mē\ *adj* [*prism* + *-y*] : PRISMATIC — not used technically ⟨the ~ feathers of his breast —Audrey A. Brown⟩
¹**pris·on** \'prizᵊn\ *n* -S *often attrib* [ME *prison, prisoun, prisun*, fr. OF *prison, prisun*, fr. L *prehension-, prehensio* act of seizing, fr. *prehensus* (past part. of *prehendere* to seize, grasp) + *-ion-, -io* -ion — more at PREHENSILE] **1** : a place or condition of confinement or restraint (as of a person) : IMPRISONMENT ⟨put in ~⟩ ⟨~ seldom cures the criminal⟩ **2** : a building or other place for the safe custody or confinement of criminals or others (as formerly debtors) committed by lawful authority; *often* : an institution for the imprisonment of persons convicted of major crimes or felonies : a penitentiary as distinguished from a reformatory, local jail, or detention home
²**prison** \"\ *vt* -ED/-ING/-S [ME *prisonen*, fr. *prison*, n.] *chiefly dial* : to put or keep in restraint : IMPRISON, CONFINE
prison bars *n pl but sing or pl in constr* : PRISONER'S BASE

prison bird *n* : JAILBIRD
prison breach *or* **prison breaking** *n* : a common law crime that is now often modified by statute and that involves escape of a prisoner by force and violence from a place in which he is lawfully in custody — compare RESCUE
prison camp *n* **1** : a camp with minimum security for the confinement of reasonably trustworthy prisoners who are employed on farm, road, forestry, or general maintenance projects of the state or federal government **2** : a camp for prisoners of war
pris·on·er \-z(ᵊ)nə(r)\ *n* -S [ME, fr. MF *prisonier*, fr. OF, fr. *prison* + *-ier* -er] **1** : a person held under arrest: as **a** : a person held under arrest or in prison **b** : PRISONER OF WAR, CAPTIVE **c** : a person involuntarily restrained (as by duties, responsibilities, or possessions) ⟨the . . . star becomes the ~ of her own stardom —Delmore Schwartz⟩ ⟨was the ~ of his own suspicious nature⟩ **d** : a convert to Salvationism ⟨~s . . . or persons captured for the Kingdom —*Salvation Army Orders for Officers*⟩ **2 a** : a piece of metal fitted into the segments of a flywheel rim so as to hold them together and usu. held in place by taper keys or close-fitting bolts **b** : a metal link recessed on both sides so that when fitted hot into an appropriate opening in two segments of a flywheel rim the contraction of the link draws the segments together — called also *shrink link* **3** : something that is restrained as if in a prison ⟨made ~s of her little hands in his⟩
prisoner at large : a member of a naval force who is under arrest and restricted to his ship or barracks
prisoner of war : a person captured or interned by a belligerent power because of war with several exceptions provided by international law or agreements
prisoner's base *or* **prison base** *n* : a game of many variations in which players of one team seek to tag and imprison players of the other team who have ventured out of their home territory
prison fever *n* : TYPHUS 1a
prison house *n* : PRISON ⟨the idea that her present life was a *prison house* of which he held the key of escape —H.G.Wells⟩
prisonlike \'==ˌ=\ *adj* : resembling a prison : dreary and confining or rigidly controlled : suitable to a prison ⟨a ~ atmosphere⟩ ⟨these ~ tasks⟩
pris·on·ment \'prizᵊnmənt\ *n* -S [ME, fr. *prison* + *-ment*] : IMPRISONMENT
pris·on·ous \-z(ᵊ)nəs\ *adj* [¹*prison* + *-ous*] : PRISONLIKE
prison psychosis *n* : an apparent mental disturbance brought on by imprisonment and often manifested by pseudohallucinations, mild delusions, and paranoid trends
¹**priss** \'pris\ *vi* -ED/-ING/-ES [back-formation fr. *prissy*] *chiefly Midland* : to act or dress in a prissy or fussy manner — often used with *up* ⟨~*ing* up to impress the teacher⟩
²**priss** \"\ *n* -ES *chiefly Midland* : a prissy person — usu. used of a woman or girl
pris·si·fied \'prisəˌfīd\ *adj* [fr. *prissy*, after such pairs as E *pretty: prettified*] : marked by prissiness ⟨~ diplomatic circles⟩
pris·si·ly \-sə̇lē, -li\ *adv* : in a prissy manner : with prissiness
pris·si·ness \-sēnə̇s, -sin-\ *n* -ES : the quality or state of being prissy
pris·sy \-sē,-si\ *adj* -ER/-EST [prob. blend of ³*prim* and *sissy*] **1** : prim and precise : affectedly proper : PRIGGISH, FINICKY **2** : lacking in masculine vigor : SISSIFIED ⟨the elevated little finger of the ~ tea drinker —Fred Majdalany⟩
pris·tane \'prisˌtān\ *n* -S [L *pristis* shark, sawfish + E *-ane*] : a saturated liquid hydrocarbon $C_{19}H_{40}$ obtained from the liver oils of various sharks and from ambergris
pris·tav *also* **pris·taw** \'priˌstäf, -ˌstəf\ *n* -S [Russ *pristav*] : a former Russian supervisory official (as of a police force)
pris·tel·la \pri'stelə\ *n, cap* [NL, fr. *prist-* (prob. fr. L *pristinus* pristine) + *-ella*] : a genus of small often brightly colored So. American characin fishes that are sometimes kept in the tropical aquarium
pris·ti·dae \'pristəˌdē\ *n pl, cap* [NL, fr. *Pristis*, type genus + *-idae*] : a small family of cartilaginous fishes closely related to the skates and rays but having the body elongated rather than flattened and distinguished by a snout elongated into a flat blade with teeth along each side and comprising the economically important sawfishes of warm seas and estuaries some of which are reputed to exceed 20 feet in length
pris·tine \'priˌstēn *sometimes* pri'stēn *or* 'pristə̇n *or* 'priˌstīn\ *adj* [L *pristinus* — more at PRIOR] **1** : belonging to the earliest period or state : ORIGINAL, PRIMITIVE ⟨a ~ form of air conditioning —Lewis Mumford⟩ **2 a** : uncorrupted by civilization or the world ⟨~ innocence⟩ ⟨~ freshness⟩ **b** : free from drabness, soil, or decay : fresh and clean ⟨a ~ and fabulously wealthy residential area —Bentz Plagemann⟩ ⟨the snow which is ~ powder —*Holiday*⟩ ⟨a ~ dawn in spring⟩ — **pris·tine·ly** *adv*
pris·tio·phor·i·dae \ˌpristēə'fȯrəˌdē\ *n pl, cap* [NL, fr. *Pristiophorus*, type genus (fr. *pristio-* — fr. Gk *pristēs* saw — + *-phorus*) + *-idae* — more at PRISM] : a small family of chiefly tropical sharks (suborder Squaloidea) comprising the saw sharks
pris·tiph·o·ra \pri'stifərə\ *n, cap* [NL, fr. *pristi-* (prob. fr. Gk *pristes* saw) + *-phora*] : a genus of sawflies (family Tenthredinidae) that includes many economic pests of forest trees — see LARCH SAWFLY
pris·tis \'pristə̇s\ *n, cap* [NL, fr. L, sawfish, fr. Gk — more at PRISM] : the type and sole recent genus of Pristidae
¹**pritch** \'prich\ *vt* -ED/-ING/-ES [ME *pricchen*, prob. alter. of *prikken, priken* to prick — more at PRICK] *chiefly dial* : to poke holes in : PRICK
²**pritch** \"\ *n* -ES [prob. alter. (influenced by ¹*pritch*) of ¹*prick*] : a pointed spike or staff put to various uses as an implement
pritch·ar·dia \pri'chärdēə\ *n* [NL, fr. William T. *Pritchard*, 19th cent. Eng. diplomat + NL *-ia*] **1** *cap* : a genus of showy fan palms of the Pacific islands distinguished by cuneate or flabelliform leaves having bifid segments and used for making fans and hats **2** -S : any plant of the genus *Pritchardia*
pritch·el \'prichəl\ *n* -S [alter. (influenced by ¹*pritch*) of ¹*prickle*] : any of various iron-pointed tools; *esp* : one used by blacksmiths for punching or enlarging nail holes in a horseshoe
prith·ee \'prithē, -ithē\ *interj* [fr. earlier *preythe*, fr. (*I*) *pray thee*] *archaic* — used to express a wish or request for something to be done; compare PLEASE *vt* 4
¹**prittle–prattle** \¦prid·ᵊl¦prad·ᵊl\ *vi* [redupl. of ¹*prattle*] : PRATTLE, CHATTER
²**prittle–prattle** \"\ *n* : empty talk : PRATTLE; *also* : CHATTERER
pri·us \'prīəs\ *n* -ES [L, former, previous, neut. of *prior* — more at PRIOR] : something that precedes or takes precedence : PRECONDITION
priv *abbr* **1** private; privately **2** privative
pri·va·cy \'prīvəsē, -si, *Brit sometimes* 'priv-\ *n* -ES [ME *privacie*, fr. *private* + *-cie* -cy] **1 a** : the quality or state of being apart from the company or observation of others : SECLUSION ⟨unwilling to disturb his ~⟩ **b** : isolation, seclusion, or freedom from unauthorized oversight or observation ⟨protected by law in the enjoyment of ~⟩ **2** *archaic* : a place of seclusion or retreat : private apartment ⟨remote woodland *privacies*⟩ **3 a** : private or clandestine circumstances : SECRECY **b** *archaic* : a private or personal matter : SECRET **4** *obs* : FAMILIARITY, INTIMACY **5 privacies** *pl, archaic* : GENITALIA, PRIVATES
pri·va·do \prə̇'vä(ˌ)dō\ *n, pl* **privadoes** *also* **privados** [Sp, private, familiar, favorite, fr. L *privatus* private] *archaic* : INTIMATE, CONFIDANT
pri·vat·do·cent *also* **pri·vat·do·zent** \prē¦vätdō¦sent\ *n, pl* **privatdocents** \-nts\ *or* **privatdocen·ten** \-ntᵊn\ [G *privatdozent* (formerly spelled *privatdocent*), fr. *privat* private (fr. L *privatus*) + *dozent* (formerly spelled *docent*) teacher, lecturer — more at DOCENT] : an unsalaried university lecturer or teacher in German-speaking countries remunerated directly by students' fees
¹**pri·vate** \'prīvə̇t, *usu* -əd+V\ *adj, sometimes* -ER/-EST [ME *privat*, fr. L *privatus* apart from the state, deprived of office, of or belonging to oneself, private, fr. past part. of *privare* to deprive, release, fr. *privus* single, private, set apart, for himself; akin to L *pro* for — more at FOR] **1 a** : intended for or restricted to the use of a particular person or group or class of persons : not freely available to the public ⟨a ~ park⟩ ⟨a ~ party⟩ **b** : belonging to or concerning an individual person,

company, or interest ⟨our ~ goods⟩ ⟨~ property⟩ ⟨a ~ house⟩ ⟨~ means⟩ **c** (1) **:** restricted to the individual or arising independently of others ⟨~ views⟩ ⟨a ~ opinion⟩ (2) **:** carried on by an individual independently rather than under institutional or organizational direction or support ⟨~ research⟩ (3) **:** being educated by independent study, under the direction of a tutor, or in a private school ⟨~ students⟩ **d** (1) **:** affecting an individual or small group **:** RESTRICTED, PERSONAL ⟨~ malice⟩ ⟨for your ~ satisfaction⟩ (2) **:** affecting the interests of a particular person, class or group of persons, or locality **:** not general in effect ⟨~ act⟩ — see PRIVATE BILL **e :** of, relating to, or receiving hospital service in which the patient has more privileges than a semiprivate or ward patient (as in having his own doctor, a room to himself, and extended visiting hours) **2 a** (1) **:** not invested with or engaged in public office or employment ⟨a ~ citizen⟩ (2) **:** not related to or dependent on one's official position **:** PERSONAL ⟨~ correspondence⟩ **b** *of military personnel* **:** of the lowest rank **:** having attained no title of rank or distinction ⟨fought through the revolution as a ~ soldier⟩ **c** (1) **:** manufactured, made, or issued by other than government means ⟨~ mailing card⟩ ⟨~ stamp⟩ (2) **:** issued by private not public authority but acceptable as money either because of intrinsic value or exchange value guaranteed by issuer ⟨a ~ coin⟩ ⟨~ currency⟩ **d** *of clothing* **:** CIVILIAN — used esp. by the Salvation Army **3 a :** sequestered from company or observation **:** withdrawn from public notice ⟨a ~ retreat⟩ **b :** free from the company of others **:** ALONE ⟨let us go where we can be ~⟩ **c :** not known publicly or carried on in public **:** not open **:** SECRET ⟨~ negotiations⟩ ⟨a ~ understanding⟩ ⟨~ prayer⟩; *esp* **:** intended only for the persons involved ⟨a ~ conversation⟩ — compare CONFIDENTIAL **d :** having knowledge not publicly available **:** holding a confidential relationship to something ⟨you are ~ to all my affairs⟩ **e** *obs* **:** peculiar to a particular person **f :** being or considered unsuitable for public mention, use, or display — used esp. of the genital organs

²private \"\ *n* -s [ME, fr. L *privatus*, fr. *privatus*, adj., private] **1** *archaic* **:** one not in public life or office **2** *obs* **a :** a secret message **:** a private communication **b :** personal interest **:** particular business **c :** PRIVACY, RETIREMENT **d :** INTIMATE **3 privates** *pl* **:** GENITALIA, PART 1 d (3) **4 :** a person having neither commissioned nor noncommissioned rank in a group organized along military lines **:** a private soldier: as **a :** an enlistee or draftee in the army just below a private first class and above a recruit or in the marine corps at the lowest level **b :** a fire fighter in an organized force below officer rank **5 :** civilian dress for use when off duty — used by the Salvation Army — **in private** *adv* **:** PRIVATELY, SECRETLY **:** not openly or in public ⟨usurp *in private* the authority she could never assert in public —Edith Wharton⟩

private attorney *n* **:** one employed by a private person rather than by a government or a subdivision thereof **:** ATTORNEY-IN-FACT

private bag *n, Brit* **:** a locked bag for the conveyance of postal matter between an individual and the post office esp. where direct delivery is unavailable — often used as part of a postal address ⟨The Extension Officer, *Private Bag* 602, Oudtshoorn —*Farmer's Weekly (So. Africa)*⟩

private bank *n* **:** an unincorporated bank conducted by an individual or a partnership

private bed *n* **:** a bed in a hospital provided in a private room to a patient who is attended by a personal physician rather than staff physicians of the hospital

private bill *n* **:** a legislative bill affecting a particular individual, organization, or locality as distinguished from all the people or the whole area of a political unit (as a nation or state) ⟨the power of the House of Lords to veto *private bills* —F.A. Magruder⟩ ⟨three principal categories of *private bills* introduced in Congress —S.K.Bailey & H.D.Samuel⟩ — compare PUBLIC BILL

private calendar *n* **:** a legislative calendar listing private bills ⟨241 bills on the *private calendar* —C.V.Woodward⟩

private car *n* **1 :** a car operated but not owned by a railroad **2 :** a passenger car assigned for private use (as of company officials)

private carrier *n* **:** a carrier of passengers or goods who does not hold himself out for public employment so as to be legally a common carrier

private climate *n* **:** the layer of air immediately surrounding and modified as to temperature and moisture by the body of a warm-blooded animal

private company *n* **:** a company under British law restricting the right of its stockholders to transfer their shares, limiting its members to 50 exclusive of shareholders who are present or former employees, and not inviting the public to subscribe for any shares or debentures

private convention *n* **:** a convention in a card game that has a meaning not revealed to the opponents and that is in most games considered unethical

private corporation *n* **1 :** a corporation that is not a public corporation **:** a corporation organized for the profit of its members or in which the entire interest is not held by the state **2 :** PRIVATE COMPANY

private detective *or* **private investigator** *n* **:** a person concerned with the maintenance of lawful conduct or the investigation of crime or other irregularities either as the regular employee of a private interest (as a hotel or store) or as contractor for fees ⟨obtained a *private detective* to report on his wife's associates⟩

private–duty \ˈ==ˈ==\ *adj, of a nurse* **:** caring for a single patient either in the home or in a hospital

private enterprise *n* **:** FREE ENTERPRISE 2

¹pri·va·teer \ˌprīvəˈti(ə)r, -tiə\ *n* -s [¹*private* + *-eer*] **1 :** an armed private ship bearing the commission of the sovereign power to cruise against the commerce or warships of an enemy **2 :** the commander or one of the crew of a privateer **3** *archaic* **:** one fighting voluntarily as a soldier but not formally enlisted in an organized armed force **:** a free-lance soldier

²privateer \"\ *vi* -ED/-ING/-S **:** to cruise in or as a privateer

privateering *n* -s [fr. gerund of ²*privateer*] **:** the career or business of a privateer ⟨the narrow line between ~ and piracy⟩

pri·va·teers·man \ˌ==ˈtirzmən, -iəz-\ *n, pl* **privateersmen** [*privateers* (gen. of ¹*privateer*) + *man*] **:** PRIVATEER 2

private eye *n, slang* **:** a detective who is not a member of an official police force **:** PRIVATE DETECTIVE

private first class *n* **:** an enlistee or draftee in the army just below a corporal and above a private or in the marine corps just below a lance corporal and above a private

private gold *n* **:** gold coins and stamped ingots issued in the U.S. in the 19th century before the Civil War by private authority (as by the Mormons or various mining companies) — called also *pioneer gold, territorial gold*

private insurance *n* **:** insurance organized under private aegis — compare SOCIAL INSURANCE

private judgment *n* **:** the reaching of a conclusion (as in matters of religion) on the basis of personal thought and insight unhindered by political or ecclesiastical interference ⟨the right of *private judgment*⟩

private law *n* **:** a branch of law treating of private matters, involving private persons, property, and relationships, and excluding those matters treated in public law

pri·vate·ly *adv* **1 :** in a private way **:** so as to be private **:** in private **:** SECRETLY, UNOFFICIALLY ⟨some leaders of his own party hoped ~ for his defeat⟩ **2 :** by a private person or interest ⟨~ owned utilities⟩

private mark *n* **:** a distinctive and often secret identifying mark (as on an ingot of bullion or a work of art) **:** PRIVY MARK

private member *n, often cap P&M* **:** a member of a legislative body (as the British House of Commons) who does not belong to the ministry ⟨the right of *private members* to introduce bills —D.G.Hitchner⟩

private member's bill *n, sometimes cap P&M&B* **:** a public or private bill prepared, introduced, and sponsored in the legislature by a private member ⟨in New Zealand . . . *private members' bills* occasionally reach the Statute Book —Walter Nash⟩ — compare GOVERNMENT BILL

pri·vate·ness *n* -ES **:** the quality or state of being private **:** PRIVACY

private notice question *n* **:** a parliamentary question raised following notice given privately to the speaker and the minister concerned when urgency on matters of public importance or the arrangement of business prevents scheduling on the order paper

private nuisance *n* **:** something constituting a nuisance in law but affecting some particular person or persons and not the general public — compare MIXED NUISANCE, PUBLIC NUISANCE

private parts *n pl* **:** PART 1 d (3)

private placement *n* **:** the sale of an issue of securities directly by the issuer to one or a few large investors (as life insurance companies) without public offering through investment bankers

private practice *n* **1 :** practice of a profession (as medicine or architecture) independently and not as an employee **2 :** the circle of patients depending on and availing themselves at need of the services of a physician in private practice

privater *comparative of* PRIVATE

private school *n* **:** a school that is established, conducted, and primarily supported by a nongovernmental agency — compare PUBLIC SCHOOL

private secretary *n* **:** a secretary who serves a single individual **:** a confidential secretary

private siding *n* **:** SIDING 3b

private signal *n* **:** a flag of unique design displayed on a yacht to identify the owner

privatest *superlative of* PRIVATE

private station *n* **:** a radio transmitting station carrying on a message service for business purposes but not open to the public

private sweepstake *n* **:** a sweepstake to which no money or other prize is added and which has not been advertised previous to closing

private time *n* **:** SUBJECTIVE TIME

private treaty *n* **:** a sale of property on terms determined by conference of the seller and buyer ⟨got better prices by *private treaty* than his neighbors did at auction⟩ — distinguished from *auction*

private view *n* **:** an invitation exhibition (as of works of art)

private way *n* **1 :** a right of way classified as an incorporeal hereditament of a real nature for the benefit of a person or group of persons and not the public at large to pass over land owned by another **2 a :** a way laid out by a private owner or owners and maintained at their expense, dedicated to public use, but not accepted as a public way **b :** a way laid out by public authority in New England at the request and expense of a private owner or owners, maintained by them and dedicated to public use, but not accepted as a public way

private wrong *n* **:** a civil injury affecting an individual or person but not the community generally **:** a wrong for which an individual has legal redress — compare PUBLIC WRONG

pri·va·tim \prīˈvādəm *sometimes* -vad·\ *adv* [L, fr. *privatus* private — more at PRIVATE] **:** in private **:** PRIVATELY

pri·va·tion \prīˈvāshən\ *n* -s [ME *privacion*, fr. MF *privation*, fr. L *privation-, privatio*, fr. *privatus* (past part. of *privare* to deprive) + *-ion-, -io* -ion — more at PRIVATE] **1 a :** an act or instance of depriving **:** DEPRIVATION ⟨the physiological effects of complete ~ of protein⟩ **b :** a taking away of rank or office **:** SUSPENSION 1f **2 a** (1) **:** a condition characterized by the loss of something previously or normally possessed ⟨evil is a ~ of good⟩ (2) **:** a condition characterized by the absence of a positive character ⟨darkness is a negative state, a mere ~⟩ **b :** lack of what is desired for comfort or needed for existence **:** DESTITUTION, HARDSHIP, WANT ⟨a winter of hunger and ~⟩ — usu. used in pl. ⟨in spite of grief and ~*s*⟩ **syn** see ABSENCE

pri·va·tion·al \(ˈ)prīˈvāshənᵊl, -shnəl\ *adj* **:** of or relating to privation; *esp* **:** resulting from deprivation of something

¹priv·a·tive \ˈprivəd·iv\ *n* -s [L *privativus*, fr. *privatus* (past part. of *privare* to deprive) + *-ivus* -ive] **1 :** something characterized by privation **2 a :** a privative attribute, term, expression, or proposition **b :** a privative prefix or suffix **c :** a word denoting the negation of a quality otherwise inherent ⟨*deaf* is a ~⟩

²privative \"\ *adj* **1 :** causing privation **:** DEPRIVING ⟨exercise ~ power⟩ **2 :** characterized by privation **:** not positive **:** NEGATIVE **3 :** constituting, signifying, or predicating privation, negation, or absence of a quality ⟨a ~ prefix (as *a-*, *un-*, *non-*)⟩ ⟨*blind* is a ~ term⟩

privative intercession *n* **:** the assumption under Roman or civil law of a liability for a debt or obligation by the substitution of a new debtor or obligor for the old one **:** an expromission that resembles common-law novation

privative jurisdiction *n, Scots law* **:** exclusive jurisdiction

priv·a·tive·ly \-d·əvlē\ *adv* **:** in a privative manner so as to deprive **:** NEGATIVELY

privative proposition *n* **:** a proposition in logic stating that a particular attribute is removed from or absent from the subject

pri·vat·iza·tion \ˌprīvəd·əˈzāshən, -d·ˌīˈz-\ *n* -s [¹*private* + *-ization*] **:** the tendency for an individual to withdraw from participation in social and esp. political life into a world of personal concerns usu. as a result of a feeling of insignificance and lack of understanding of complex social processes

pri·vat·ize \ˈprīvəd·ˌīz\ *vt* -ED/-ING/-S [¹*private* + *-ize*] **:** to alter the status of (as a business or industry) from public to private control or ownership

priv·et \ˈprivət, *usu* -əd·+V\ *n* -s [origin unknown] **1 a** (1) **:** an ornamental Eurasian and northern African shrub (*Ligustrum vulgare*) that is used extensively for hedges and has half-evergreen leaves and small white flowers — called also *common privet* (2) **:** any of various other plants of the genus *Ligustrum* several of which are cultivated as ornamental or hedge plants — see AMUR PRIVET, CALIFORNIA PRIVET, IBOLIUM PRIVET, JAPANESE PRIVET **b** *also* **privet adelia :** SWAMP PRIVET **2 :** a grayish olive green that is greener and less strong than average ivy green and yellower, less strong, and slightly darker than bronze green

privet andromeda *n* **:** a much-branched shrub (*Lyonia ligustrina*) of the family Ericaceae with small white bell-shaped flowers in panicled racemes

privet borer *n* **:** a grub that is the larva of a cerambycid beetle (*Tylonotus bimaculatus*) and that mines twigs of ash and privet

privet hawk *n* **:** a showy Old World hawkmoth (*Sphinx ligustri*) with a larva that feeds chiefly on privet and lilac

privet honeysuckle *n* **:** a low Chinese evergreen shrub (*Lonicera pileata*) having foliage resembling that of a privet and violet-purple fruit

privet mite *n* **:** a common mite (*Brevipalpus obovatus*) that feeds on various host plants and is esp. destructive on azaleas

-priv·ic \ˈprivik, -vēk\ *adj comb form* [L *privus* deprived of, without, private + E *-ic*] **:** deficient in a (specified) thing or element ⟨parathyro*privic*⟩

privier *comparative of* PRIVY

privies *pl of* PRIVY

privies in blood : persons related by blood and having a mutual interest in or successive relationship to the same estate or right in the same property ⟨an heir and his ancestor are *privies in blood* as are coparceners among themselves⟩

privies in estate : persons having a mutual interest in or successive relationship derived at the same time out of the same original seisin to the same estate or right in the same property ⟨the relationship existing between an original owner of an estate in property and one who succeeds to the same estate therein by grant or by testate or intestate succession or succession by operation of law is that of *privies in estate*⟩

privies in law : persons having by operation of special doctrines of law a mutual interest in or successive relationship to the same estate or right in the same property (as where one takes property from another by escheat) and succeeding to property with its attendant benefits and burdens

privies in representation : persons having by the doctrine of representation a mutual interest in or successive relationship to the same estate or right in the same property ⟨an executor and his testator are *privies in representation* as are an administrator and the intestate⟩

priviest *superlative of* PRIVY

¹priv·i·lege \ˈpriv(ə)lij, -lēj\ *n* -s [ME, fr. OF, fr. L *privilegium* law against or in favor of a private person, fr. *privus* private + *leg-, lex* law — more at PRIVATE, LEGAL] **1 a :** a right or immunity granted as a peculiar benefit, advantage, or favor **:** special enjoyment of a good or exemption from an evil or burden **:** a peculiar or personal advantage or right esp. when enjoyed in derogation of common right **:** PREROGATIVE **b :** such right or immunity attaching specif. to a position or an office ⟨pled the ~ of his clergy⟩ ⟨the peculiar ~*s* of the diplomatic corps⟩; *esp* **:** the immunity from arrest in a civil case and enjoyment of freedom of speech during a session that is accorded to members of most legislative assemblies **c** *obs* **:** a right of asylum or sanctuary **d :** any of various fundamental or specially sacred rights considered as peculiarly guaranteed and secured to all persons by modern constitutional governments (as the enjoyment of life, liberty, and reputation, the right to acquire and possess property, the right to pursue happiness) ⟨no State shall make or enforce any law which shall abridge the ~*s* and immunities of citizens of the United States —*U.S. Constitution*⟩ **e :** a condition of legal nonrestraint of natural powers either generally or in respect to a particular case — compare LIBERTY **2 a :** a grant of a special right or immunity **:** FRANCHISE, PATENT ⟨a ~ of printing a book⟩ ⟨a ~ granted a manor or town⟩ **b** (1) **:** a law in ancient Rome in favor of or against a private person or after the time of Augustus a law granting a favor or immunity to some person or class of persons (2) **:** a preference to priority belonging under Roman and civil law to a creditor by reason of the nature of his claim **3 :** a customary payment or gratuity to the master of a ship by way of primage **4 :** a call, put, spread, straddle, or comparable maneuver on a stock or produce exchange; *also* **:** RIGHT 14a **syn** see RIGHT

²privilege \"\ *vt* -ED/-ING/-S [ME *privilegen*, fr. *privilege*, n.] **1 a :** to grant a privilege or privileges to **:** invest with a peculiar right, immunity, prerogative, or other benefit ⟨the *privileged* classes⟩ ⟨some *privileged* institutions⟩ **b :** to take a privilege to (oneself) ⟨I ~ myself to believe⟩ **2 :** to exempt as a privilege **:** deliver by special grace or immunity — used with *from* ⟨~ legislators from arrest⟩ **3** *archaic* **:** to give authorization for **:** EXCUSE ⟨kings cannot ~ what God forbade —Samuel Daniel⟩ ⟨~ without penance or disturbance an odious crime —John Milton⟩

priv·i·leged \-jd\ *adj* [ME, fr. past part. of *privilegen* to privilege] **:** having or endowed with a privilege **:** enjoying or honored with a privilege ⟨open only to the ~ few⟩: as **a :** not subject to the usual rules or penalties because of some special circumstance ⟨a ~ statement⟩ **b :** having a plenary indulgence attached to a mass celebrated thereon ⟨~ altar⟩ **c :** having a right of conversion or bearing a stock purchase warrant — used of a bond or preferred stock **d** *of a boat* **:** having the right of way or the right to maintain a speed and course capable of causing collision with another boat if that boat maintains its speed and course — contrasted with *burdened*

privileged communication *n* **1 :** a communication between parties to a confidential relation such that the recipient cannot be legally compelled to disclose it as a witness (as a communication between lawyer and client, physician and patient, husband and wife) — called also *confidential communication* **2 :** a defamatory communication the making of which does not expose the party making it to the civil or criminal liability that would follow from it if not privileged — called also *absolutely privileged communication* **3 :** a defamatory statement made by one person to another who is in a confidential relation (as that of prospective employer) or who has an interest therein that may upon proof of bad faith with actual malice be deprived of its privileged character — called also *conditionally privileged communication*

privileged debt *n* **:** a debt to which a preference in payment is given under civil and Scots law **:** a preferred debt

privileged deed *n* **:** a holograph deed that is exempted under Scots law from the statute requiring deeds to be signed before witnesses

privileged familiarity *n* **:** culturally sanctioned familiarity (as in a joking relationship) between persons of particular familial relations — compare AVOIDANCE

privilege of the floor : the right of a person to be admitted onto the floor of a legislative chamber while the legislature is in session ⟨a former senator has the *privilege of the floor*⟩

privilege tax *n* **:** EXCISE 1d

priv·i·ly \ˈprivəlē, -li\ *adv* [ME *prively*, fr. *prive* privy + *-ly*] **:** in a privy manner **:** PRIVATELY, SECRETLY

Priv·ine \ˈprivən, -ˌvēn\ *trademark* — used for naphazoline

priv·i·ty \ˈprivəd·ē, -ətē, -i\ *n* -ES [ME *privete, privite*, fr. OF, fr. ML *privitat-, privitas*, fr. L *privus* private + *-itat-, -itas* -ity] **1 :** something that is not made public or openly displayed: as **a** *obs* **:** a private matter (as a plan or affair) **:** SECRET **b** *obs* **:** one's private business **c privities** *pl* **:** the external genitals **:** PART 1d(3) **2** *obs* **:** private condition (as of life or position) **:** SECLUSION, PRIVACY **3 :** private knowledge or joint knowledge with another of a private matter; *esp* **:** cognizance implying concurrence ⟨all the doors were laid open for his departure, not without the ~ of the Prince of Orange —Jonathan Swift⟩ ⟨mere ~ to a crime may involve legal penalties⟩ **4 a :** a connection between parties (as to some particular transaction) **b:** mutual or successive relationship to the same rights of property **:** the relationship between privies whereby they succeed to the same legal right or duty derived from a common source

¹privy \ˈprivē, -vi\ *adj* -ER/-EST [ME *prive*, fr. OF *privé*, fr. L *privatus* private — more at PRIVATE] **1** *obs* **:** holding a close relation usu. to a person **:** INTIMATE, FAMILIAR **2 :** of, or relating to some person exclusively **:** assigned for private use or personal service esp. to an official **:** not public **:** PERSONAL ⟨a ~ symbol⟩ **3 a :** not manifest or apparent **:** withdrawn from the common knowledge or use **:** CONCEALED, PRIVATE ⟨sought a ~ place to rest and think⟩ **b :** done secretly **:** furtive in action **:** CLANDESTINE, STEALTHY ⟨the grim wolf with ~ paw —John Milton⟩ **4 :** admitted as one participating secretly or in a secret **:** privately aware as a party ⟨~ to their secret⟩

²privy \"\ *n* -ES [ME *prive*, fr. AF, fr. OF *privé* intimate, confidant, fr. *privé*, adj.] **1 a :** any of the persons having mutual or successive relationship to the same right of property **b :** a person having an interest in any action or thing esp. deriving from a contract or conveyance to which he is not himself a party **2 a :** a small often detached building having a bench with one or more round or oval holes through which the user may defecate or urinate (as into a pit or tub) and ordinarily lacking any means of automatic discharge of the matter deposited **b :** TOILET 5b **3** *dial* **:** MATRIMONY VINE — **in privy** *adv* **:** in private **:** SECRETLY

privy council *n* [ME *prive counseil*, fr. *prive* privy + *counseil* council — more at COUNCIL] **1** *archaic* **:** a secret or private council ⟨they'll admit me as one of their *privy council* —Oliver Goldsmith⟩ **2** *usu cap P&C* **a :** a body of officials and dignitaries chosen by the British monarch to constitute an advisory council to the Crown that although of great historical importance now seldom meets as a body and functions principally through its committees (as the cabinet and the judicial committee) ⟨His Majesty . . . by and with the advice of His *Privy Council* —E.C.E.Leadbitter⟩ ⟨the *Privy Council* in London granted him dictatorial emergency powers —S.P.Brewer⟩ — see ORDER-IN-COUNCIL **b :** a body of officials in Canada similar in power and function to the British Privy Council ⟨Canadian cabinet ministers are members of the *Privy Council*⟩ — see GOVERNOR-GENERAL-IN-COUNCIL **3 :** a council usu. constituted by appointment to advise or assist a ruler or an executive ⟨the governor of New Caledonia . . . is aided by a *privy council* —*Americana Annual*⟩ ⟨the Constitution granted Jamaica in 1944 provides for . . . a small *privy council* —A.P.Zeidenfelt⟩

privy councillor *n* **1 :** a confidential adviser **2 :** a member of a privy council

privy mark *or* **privy symbol** *n* **:** a symbol on a coin that identifies the minter or mintmaster — called also *private mark*

privy parts *n pl* **:** PART 1d(3)

privy purse *n* **1 :** an allowance from public revenues for the private expenses of a monarch; *esp* **:** an allowance for the private expenses of the British sovereign forming part of the civil list **2** *usu cap both Ps* **:** an officer of the British royal household who pays the private expenses of the sovereign from the civil list — called also *keeper of the privy purse*

privy seal *n* [ME *prive seal*, fr. *prive* privy + *seal* — more at SEAL] **1 :** a private seal: as **a :** a British royal seal used before 1885 to authorize use of the great seal (as on letters patent or pardons) or on documents not requiring the great seal (as discharges of debts) **b :** a seal used in Scotland to authenticate royal grants of personal or assignable rights **2 :** a document bearing a privy seal; *esp* **:** a warrant used by English monarchs in Stuart and earlier periods to exact a forced loan **3** *usu cap P&S* **:** LORD PRIVY SEAL

privy verdict *n* **:** an unsealed verdict given privily to the judge out of court, subject to later confirmation in open court, and now usu. replaced by a sealed verdict

prix \'prē\ *n, pl* **prix** \-ē(z)\ [F, fr. OF *pris* prize, price] **:** PRIZE

prix fixe \'prē¦fiks\ *n, pl* **prix fixes** \"\ [F, fixed price] **1 :** TABLE D'HÔTE **2 :** the price charged for a table d'hôte meal

prixseam *var of* PRICKSEAM

priz·able *or* **prize·able** \'prīzəbəl\ *adj* [1*prize* + *-able*] **:** worthy to be prized **:** VALUABLE

1prize \'prīz\ *n* -S [ME *pris* prize, price — more at PRICE] **1 :** something offered or striven for in competition or in contests of chance: as **a :** an honor or reward striven for in a competitive contest **:** something offered to be competed for or as an inducement to or a reward of effort ⟨a school ~⟩ ⟨the ~*s* given at an agricultural show⟩ **b :** something that may be won by chance (as in a lottery); *also* **:** a novelty or other premium given with merchandise as an inducement to buy **2 a :** something worth striving for **:** a valuable possession held or in prospect **:** ADVANTAGE, PRIVILEGE ⟨methinks, 'tis ~ enough to be his son —Shak.⟩ **b :** something exceptionally good or desirable of its kind **:** GEM ⟨this puppy is the ~ of the litter⟩ ⟨described her as a ~ of a wife⟩ **3** *archaic* **:** a contest for a reward **:** COMPETITION

2prize \"\ *adj* **1 a :** having been awarded or being worthy of a prize ⟨a ~ essay⟩ ⟨a display of ~ pumpkins⟩ **b :** awarded or intended to be awarded as a prize ⟨a ~ medal⟩ **c :** held or entered for the sake of an offered prize ⟨a ~ competition⟩ ⟨a ~ drawing⟩ **2 :** of great value ⟨the ~ argument⟩ **:** outstanding of its kind ⟨a ~ idiot⟩

3prize \"\ *vt* -ED/-ING/-S [ME *prisen*, fr. MF *preiser, prisier*, fr. OF, fr. LL *pretiare* to prize, fr. L *pretium* price, money, value — more at PRICE] **1 :** to set or estimate the relative or formerly the money value of **:** APPRAISE, PRICE, RATE ⟨~ his life highly⟩ **2 :** to regard as of exceptional or great worth or excellence **:** esteem highly **:** hold as highly desirable or very precious ⟨if only rare, how this butterfly would be *prized* —Richard Jefferies⟩ ⟨~ the blessings of life around us —George Borrow⟩ **syn** see APPRECIATE

4prize \"\ *n* -S *obs* **:** ESTIMATE, VALUATION

5prize \"\ *n* -S [ME *prise, pris*, fr. OF *prise* act of taking, seizure, fr. *pris*, past part. of *prendre* to take, fr. L *prehendere* to seize, grasp — more at PREHENSILE] **1 a** (1) **:** something taken (as in war) by force, stratagem, or superior power **:** a captured thing or person **:** BOOTY, PREY; *esp* **:** property (as a ship) lawfully captured in time of war (2) **:** property seized under revenue, excise, or other laws to be taken to a court of prize jurisdiction to be forfeited **b :** an act of capturing or taking: as (1) **:** the capture of something by a belligerent exercising the rights of war; *esp* **:** the capture of a ship and its cargo at sea (2) **:** the taking from a merchant under old English law of a quantity of commodities varying from time to time for the use of the sovereign; *also* **:** the right to make such a seizure — compare PRISAGE **2** *or* **prise** \"\ **a :** a metal bar for moving heavy objects **:** LEVER, PRY **b :** PURCHASE, LEVERAGE **c :** a lever-operated press for tobacco **3** *or* **prise :** a signal blown on the horn to announce the killing or capture of game on a medieval hunt

6prize \"\ *also* **prise** \"\ *vb* -ED/-ING/-S *vt* **1 :** to press, force, or move with or as if with a lever ⟨trying to ~ himself out of sleep —Rebecca Caudill⟩; *esp* **:** to move in a usu. indicated direction by prying ⟨*prized* up the lid of the box⟩ ⟨*prizing* the old shingles off the roof⟩ **2 :** to force or pack (tobacco leaves) into a cask usu. by means of a prize ~ *vi* **:** to exert leverage ⟨*prizing* up with all his strength⟩

7prize \"\ *vt* -ED/-ING/-S **:** to make a prize of **:** seize as a prize ⟨the ship was *prized* for violating neutrality⟩

prize court *n* **1 :** a court having jurisdiction to adjudge upon captures at sea in time of war **2 :** a court having jurisdiction over seizures by revenue officers and other officials with similar authority

prize crew *n* **:** a detail of officers and men from the captor placed aboard a naval prize to take her into port for adjudication

prizefight \'⸗,⸗\ *n* [back-formation fr. *prizefighter*, fr. 1*prize* + *fighter*] **1 :** a contest between pugilists for a stake or wager **2 :** a contest between professional boxers usu. for a fixed fee or for a percentage of the money taken in (as at the gate or for radio or television rights) — **prizefighter** \'⸗,⸗⸗\ *n*

prizefighting \'⸗,⸗⸗\ *n* [1*prize* + *fighting*] **:** BOXING; *esp* **:** professional boxing

prizegiving \'⸗,⸗⸗\ *n, chiefly Brit* **:** a formal assembly for the presentation of prizes (as at a school)

prize·less \'prīzləs\ *adj* **:** having won no prize **:** lacking distinction ⟨a ~ scholar⟩

prize·man \-zmən\ *n, pl* **prizemen :** a winner of a prize (as an academic prize)

prize master *n* **:** an officer in charge of a prize crew or the prize it is handling

prize money *n* **1 a :** a part of the proceeds of a captured ship or other property taken as a prize that was formerly divided among the officers and men of the ship making the capture **b :** a sum formerly granted by a government to the officers and men of a ship participating in the destruction of an enemy's ship in battle **2 :** money offered in prizes

prize package *n* **:** something unexpectedly and surprisingly good ⟨the *prize package* was . . . when a chemical officer actually dropped a round of HE from one of his mortars into the open turret of a German tank —*Infantry Jour.*⟩

1priz·er \'prīzə(r)\ *n* -S [ME *priser*, fr. *prisen* to prize + *-er*] **1** *obs* **:** APPRAISER **2 :** one that prizes something

2prizer \"\ *n* -S [1*prize* + *-er*] **1** *archaic* **:** one that contends for a prize (as in boxing or wrestling) **2 :** PRIZEWINNER

3prizer \"\ *n* -S [6*prize* + *-er*] **:** one that exerts leverage; *esp* **:** a worker who prizes tobacco into hogsheads

prize ring *n* [*prize* short for *prizefight*] **1 :** a ring for a prizefight **2 a :** the system and practice of prizefighting **b :** prizefighters and their followers

prize ring 1

priz·ery \'prīzərē\ *n* -ES [6*prize* + *-ery*] **:** a place (as a room) adjacent to a market where recently purchased tobaccos are assembled and prized in hogsheads for shipment to redrying plants

prizes *pl of* PRIZE, *pres 3d sing of* PRIZE

prizetaker \'⸗,⸗⸗\ *n* **:** PRIZEWINNER

prizewinner \'⸗,⸗⸗\ *n* **:** a winner of a prize

prizewinning \'⸗,⸗⸗\ *adj* **:** having won or of a quality to win a prize ⟨a ~ design⟩

prizeworthy \'⸗,⸗⸗\ *adj* **:** meriting a prize; *often* **:** genuinely deserving of a prize won

prizing *pres part of* PRIZE

prje·valsky's horse *usu cap P, var of* PRZHEVALSKI'S HORSE

prk *abbr* park

prm *abbr* premium

PRN *abbr, often not cap* [L *pro re nata*] for the emergency; as occasion arises

prntr *abbr* printer

1pro \'prō\ *n* -S [ME, fr. L, prep., for — more at FOR] **1 :** the arguments or evidence favoring a statement, proposition, or position **2 :** the affirmative position or one holding it **:** the affirmative side — opposed to *con* ⟨weighing the ~*s* and cons⟩

2pro \"\ *adj* [*pro-*] **:** taking the affirmative side **:** FAVORING — opposed to *con* ⟨considered the ~ and con arguments⟩

3pro \"\ *adv* [*pro-*] **:** on the affirmative side **:** in favor **:** FAVORABLY — opposed to *con* ⟨much has been written on the subject ~ and con⟩

4pro \"\ *prep* [L] **:** in favor of **:** on the supporting or affirmative side of **:** FOR — opposed to *con* ⟨advanced arguments ~ and con the proposal⟩

5pro \"\ *n* -S [by shortening] **:** PROFESSIONAL ⟨a golf ~⟩

6pro \"\ *adj* [by shortening] **:** PROFESSIONAL ⟨a ~ athlete⟩

7pro \"\ *n* -S [by shortening] **:** PROPHYLACTIC

1pro- *prefix* [ME, fr. OF, fr. L, fr. Gk, fr. *pro* — more at FOR] **1 a :** earlier than **:** prior to **:** before ⟨*pro*baptismal⟩ **b :** rudimentary **:** PROT- ⟨*pro*anthropus⟩ ⟨*Pro*mammalia⟩ ⟨*pro*embryo⟩ **2 a :** situated before **:** located in front of **:** anterior to ⟨*pro*cerebrum⟩ **b :** front **:** anterior ⟨*pro*thorax⟩ **3 :** projecting ⟨*pro*gnathous⟩

2pro- *prefix* [L (also used esp. with verbs to mean "before", "forward", "forth", "down", "on behalf of"), fr. *pro* before, in front of, in behalf of, for, on account of — more at FOR] **1 :** taking the place of **:** substituting for ⟨*pro*cathedral⟩ ⟨*pro*-regent⟩ ⟨*pro*-treasurer⟩ **2 :** siding with **:** advocating **:** favoring **:** supporting **:** championing ⟨*pro*-British⟩ ⟨*pro*-liberalism⟩

pro *abbr* **1** progressive **2** pronoun **3** provost

PRO \¦pē¦är¦ō\ *abbr or n* -S **1** public records office **2** public relations officer **3** public relations office

proa *var of* PRAU

pro·ac·cel·er·in \,prō,ak'selərən\ *n* -S [2*pro-* + *accelerate* + *-in*] **:** ACCELERATOR GLOBULIN

pro·actinomyces \(¦)prō+\ *n* [NL, fr. 1*pro-* + *Actinomyces*] **1** *cap, in some classifications* **:** a genus comprising various actinomycetes that are now usu. included in *Nocardia* **2** *pl* **proactinomycetes** *also* **proactinomyces :** any actinomycete now or formerly included in the genus *Proactinomyces*

pro·actinomycete \"+\ *n* -S [1*pro-* + *actinomycete*] **:** PROACTINOMYCES 2

pro·al \'prōəl\ *adj* [Gk *pro* before, forward + E *-al* — more at FOR] *of mastication* **:** effected by forward motion — compare ORTHAL, PALINAL, PROPALINAL

pro·amnion \(')prō+\ *n* [1*pro-* + *amnion*] **:** an area in the anterior part of the blastoderm of an early amniote embryo that lacks mesoblast and gives rise to the head fold of the amnion

pro·amniotic \(¦)prō+\ *adj* [*proamnion* + *-tic* (as in *amniotic*)] **:** of or relating to a proamnion

pro·anaphora \(¦)prō+\ *n* -S *often cap* [MGk, fr. Gk *pro-* 1*pro-* + LGk *anaphora* — more at ANAPHORA] **:** the part of the liturgy of the Eastern Church preceding the anaphora — **pro·anaphoral** \¦prō+\ *adj*

pro-and-con \¦⸗⸗¦⸗\ *vb* **pro-and-conned; pro-and-conned; pro-and-conning; pro-and-cons :** DEBATE ⟨can discuss it and *pro-and-con* it —Gilbert Highet⟩

pro·andric \(')prō+\ *adj* [1*pro-* + *andric*] *of an annelid worm* **:** retaining only the anterior pair of the primitive two pairs of testes — compare METANDRIC, PROTANDRIC

pro·angiosperm \"+\ *n* [1*pro-* + *angiosperm*] **:** a fossil of a plant type held to be ancestral to the modern angiosperms — **pro·angiospermic** *or* **pro·angiospermous** \(¦)prō+\ *adj*

pro·an·thro·pus *or* **pro·an·thro·pos** \(')prō¦an(t)thrəpəs, ¦prō,an¦thrō-\ *n* -ES [NL, fr. 1*pro-* + *-anthropus* or Gk *anthrōpos* man — more at ANTHROP-] **:** a hypothetical prehuman primate

pro·ar·thri \prō'är,thrī\ *n pl, cap* [NL, fr. 1*pro-* + *-arthri* (fr. Gk *arthron* joint) — more at ARTHR-] *in some classifications* **:** a suborder of Cestraciontes that includes the Heterodontidae and related forms having the palatoquadrate apparatus articulated with the preorbital part of the skull

pro·atlas \(')prō+\ *n* [NL, fr. 1*pro-* + *atlas*] **:** a rudimentary vertebra that lies between the atlas and the occipital bone and that occurs as a regular feature of the structure of reptiles and may occur as an anomaly in the structure of man

pro·au·li·on \prō'ōlēən, -ē,än\ *n, pl* **proaulions** \-nz\ *or* **proau·lia** \-ēə\ [LGk, fr. Gk, vestibule, fr. *pro* 1*pro-* + *aulion* cottage, chamber, dim. of *aulē* court, hall — more at AULA] **:** a portico or colonnade that opens into the narthex of a church or temple

pro·avis \(')prō¦āvəs, -¦äv-\ *n* -ES [NL, fr. 1*pro-* + L *avis* bird — more at AVIARY] **:** a hypothetical primitive animal intermediate between a reptile and a bird

prob *abbr* **1** probable; probably **2** probate **3** problem

prob·a·bil·i·o·rism \,präbə'bilēə,rizəm\ *n* -S [F *probabiliorisme*, fr. L *probabilior* (comp. of *probabilis* probable) + F *-isme* -ism — more at PROBABLE] **:** a theory that in moral questions where certainty is impossible only the more probable course may be followed

prob·a·bil·i·o·rist \-,rəst\ *n* -S [F *probabilioriste*, fr. L *probabilior* + F *-iste* -ist] **:** an adherent or advocate of probabiliorism

prob·a·bi·lism \'präbəbə,lizəm\ *n* -S [F *probabilisme*, fr. L *probabilis* probable + F *-isme* -ism — more at PROBABLE] **1 :** a theory that certainty is impossible esp. in the physical and social sciences and that probability suffices to govern belief and action **2 :** a theory that in moral questions where certainty is impossible any course may be followed that is seen as solidly probable either through clear perception of the principles involved or through awareness of the support of judicious sound authority; *esp* **:** the theory that in moral questions where certainty is impossible any solidly probable course may be followed even though an opposed course is or appears to be more probable — compare EQUIPROBABILISM, LAXISM, PROBABILIORISM, TUTIORISM

1prob·a·bi·list \-ləst\ *n* -S [F *probabiliste*, fr. L *probabilis* + F *-iste* -ist] **:** an adherent or advocate of probabilism

2probabilist \"\ *adj* **:** PROBABILISTIC

prob·a·bi·lis·tic \¦⸗⸗bə¦listik\ *adj* **1 :** of, relating to, or based on probabilism **2 :** of, relating to, or typical of a probabilist **3 :** of, relating to, or based on probability

prob·a·bil·i·ty \,präbə'biləd·ē, -lətē, -i\ *n* -ES [MF *probabilité*, fr. L *probabilitat-, probabilitas*, fr. *probabilis* probable + *-itat-, -itas* -ity — more at PROBABLE] **1 :** the quality or state of being probable ⟨such an incredible turn of events lacks ~⟩ **2 :** something (as an occurrence, circumstance) that is probable ⟨that this will happen is a ~⟩ ⟨felt that the appointment was a decided ~⟩ **3 a** (1) **:** the ratio of the number of outcomes in an exhaustive set of equally likely outcomes that produce a given event to the total number of possible outcomes (2) **:** the chance that a given event will occur **b :** a branch of mathematics concerned with the study of probabilities **4 :** a logical relation between statements such that any evidence confirming one necessarily confirms the other to some degree — **in all probability** *adv* **:** quite probably **:** almost certainly

probability curve *n* **:** a curve that represents a probability density function **:** FREQUENCY CURVE

probability density function *n* **1 :** PROBABILITY FUNCTION **2 :** a function of a continuous random variable whose integral over an interval gives the probability that its value will fall within the interval

probability function *n* **:** a function of a discrete random variable that gives the probability that a specified value will occur

prob·a·bi·lize \'präbəbə,līz\ *vt* -ED/-ING/-S [L *probabilis* + E *-ize*] **:** to cause to be probable or to seem probable

1prob·a·ble \'präbəbəl, *in rapid speech sometimes* -bbəl\ *adj* [ME, fr. MF, fr. L *probabilis*, fr. *probare* to try, test, approve, prove + *-abilis* -able — more at PROVE] **1 a :** that is based on or arises from adequate fairly convincing though not absolutely conclusive intrinsic or extrinsic evidence or support ⟨a ~ hypothesis⟩ ⟨a ~ conclusion⟩ **b :** that can reasonably and fairly convincingly be accepted as true, factual, or possible without being undeniably so ⟨something else will seem more ~ later on —Elmer Davis⟩ ⟨indicate the ~ course of events —G.L.Dickinson⟩ ⟨pointed to him as the ~ author of the book⟩ **c :** that reasonably and fairly convincingly establishes something as true, factual, or possible but not with absolute conclusiveness ⟨advanced some highly ~ evidence⟩ **2** *archaic* **:** capable of being proved **:** DEMONSTRABLE ⟨neither proved nor ~ —George Grote⟩ **3 :** that almost certainly is or will prove to be something indicated ⟨seems to be a ~ candidate⟩

syn POSSIBLE, LIKELY: PROBABLE applies to that which is so supported by evidence that is adequate although not conclusive or by reason that it is worthy of belief or acceptance ⟨the *probable* cause of the explosion⟩ ⟨his actual condition or his *probable* future —George Grote⟩ ⟨far from being a madman's dream, he concluded with alarm that Burr's chance of success was uncomfortably *probable* —Hervey Allen⟩ ⟨in the light of the parallels which I have adduced the hypothesis appears legitimate, if not *probable* —J.G.Frazer⟩ POSSIBLE refers to that which is within the limit of what may happen or of what a person or thing may do, although it may not seem probable ⟨to give up the *possible* saving of millions for the immediate saving of thousands —Sinclair Lewis⟩ ⟨the stability statesmen talk about would be *possible*, there could be a new order based on vital harmony, and the earthly millennium might approach —E.M.Forster⟩ LIKELY applies to what seems to be true or to be as alleged, suggested, or represented, the chances being considerably in favor of the thing or person being as indicated ⟨a dearth of factual information to guide them in the choice of a *likely* locale for their operations —K.E. Read⟩ ⟨must the Middle East continue to be a *likely* field for the workings of Communist pressure —H.L.Hoskins⟩

2probable \"\ *n* -S **:** something probable: **a :** a probable situation, circumstance, or event ⟨distinguish between certainties, almost certainties, ~*s*, and possibles —S.A.B.Mercer⟩ **b :** a probable participant or candidate ⟨looked over the list of ~*s* that might be up for reelection⟩ **c :** an almost certainly destroyed airplane, ship, or other object of attack ⟨claimed thirteen kills, nine ~*s* —Wirt Williams⟩

probable cause *n* **:** a reasonable ground for supposing that a criminal charge is well-founded

probable error *n* **:** regular deviation within a determined distance on each side of the mean of a frequency curve

probable word *n* **:** a word whose presence in the plaintext is assumed as a step in cryptanalysis

prob·a·bly \'präbəblē, -⸗·əblē, -li\ *adv* **1** *archaic* **:** in a fairly convincing way ⟨your hypothesis . . . by which you have so ~ solved the problem of gravity —Thomas Hobbes⟩ **2 a :** insofar as seems reasonably true, factual, or to be expected **:** so far as fairly convincing evidence or indications go ⟨will ~ succeed⟩ ⟨is ~ quite happy⟩ **b :** without much doubt **:** with practical certainty **:** very likely **:** in all probability ⟨will ~ be here soon⟩

pro·bacteriophage \¦prō+\ *n* [1*pro-* + *bacteriophage*] **:** PROPHAGE

pro·band \'prō,band\ *n* -S [L *probandus*, gerundive of *probare* to try, test — more at PROVE] **:** an individual actually being studied (as in a genetic investigation) ⟨the ~ had four negative sibs⟩

pro·bang \'prō,baŋ\ *n* -S [alter. (influenced by 1*probe*) of earlier *provang*, of unknown origin] **:** a slender flexible rod (as of whalebone) with a small piece of sponge on one end that is used for removing obstructions from the esophagus or for applying medicinal preparations or for similar medical purposes

pro·basidium \¦prō +\ *n* [NL, fr. 1*pro-* + *basidium*] **:** a cell in which two haploid nuclei fuse to form a diploid nucleus from which the basidium arises in some basidiomycetes

probata *pl of* PROBATUM

1pro·bate \'prō,bāt, *usu* -ād·+V; *chiefly Brit* -bit\ *n* -S *often attrib* [ME *probat*, fr. L *probatum*, neut. of *probatus*, past part. of *probare* to try, test, approve, prove — more at PROVE] **1 a :** the action or process of proving before a competent judicial officer or tribunal that a document offered for official recognition and registration as the last will and testament of a deceased person is genuine — compare COMMON FORM 2, SOLEMN FORM **b :** the judicial determination of the validity of a will; *specif* **:** the establishment of the prima facie validity of a will both as to manner and form of execution and as to the testator's capacity although not the validity of its provisions and also the authorization of an executor or a testamentary trustee to act **c :** the right or jurisdiction of hearing and determining questions or issues arising in matters concerning the probate of wills and the administration of decedents' estates **2 :** the officially authenticated copy of a will that together with a certificate of its having been proved is usu. delivered to the executor or administrator **3** *archaic* **:** something that proves **:** a piece of evidence **:** DEMONSTRATION, PROOF, TESTIMONY

2probate \"\ *vt* -ED/-ING/-S **1 a :** to make probate of (an instrument purporting to be the last will and testament of a person) **:** establish (a will) by probate as genuine and valid **b :** to grant probate of (a will) **:** determine judicially the validity of **2 :** to put (a convicted offender) on probation

probate bond *n* **:** a bond legally required to be given to a probate court or judge by an administrator, executor, guardian, or other fiduciary to secure the faithful performance of his duties

probate court *n* **1 :** a court having jurisdiction over the probate of wills and the administration of decedents' estates and in some states over the estates of minors and other legally incompetent persons and in some states having a limited jurisdiction in civil and criminal cases — called also *court of probate;* compare ORDINARY'S COURT, ORPHANS' COURT, PREFECT'S COURT, SURROGATE 1c **2 :** a British court established in 1857 with jurisdiction over the probate of wills and administration of decedents' personal estates formerly exercised by the ecclesiastical courts and also in probate matters over realty and now forming part of the probate, divorce, and admiralty division of the High Court of Justice

probate duty *n* **1 :** a British tax on the gross value of the personal estate of a deceased testator introduced in 1694 and merged in the estate duty in 1894 **2 :** an estate tax in some U.S. jurisdictions

probate homestead *n* **:** a homestead set apart by a court for the use of a surviving husband or wife and minor children out of the common property or out of the real estate belonging to the deceased

pro·ba·tion \prō'bāshən\ *n* -S [ME *probacioun*, fr. MF *probation*, fr. L *probation-, probatio*, fr. *probatus* (past part. of *probare* to try, test, approve, prove) + *-ion-, -io* -ion — more at PROVE] **1 a** (1) **:** the action of critically testing and evaluating **:** critical investigation or examination ⟨our statements about them will never sustain empirical ~ —A.C.Danto⟩ (2) **:** the condition of being subjected to such testing, examination, and evaluation ⟨an educational system that has been through a long period of ~⟩ **b** (1) **:** the action of subjecting an individual to a period of testing and trial so as to be able to ascertain the individual's fitness or lack of fitness for something (as a particular job, membership in a particular organization, retention of a particular academic classification, enrollment in a particular school) ⟨an engineering company that submits all candidates for jobs to a rigorous ~⟩ (2) **:** the condition of being subjected to such testing and trial ⟨was put on ~⟩ (3) **:** the period during which an individual is subjected to such testing and trial **:** a trial period ⟨his ~ was to last one year⟩ **c** (1) **:** the action of suspending the sentence of a convicted offender in such a way that the offender is given freedom after promising good behavior and agreeing to a varying degree of supervision, to the usu. imposed condition of making a report to a particular officer or court at stated intervals, and to any other additionally specified conditions ⟨hoped that the judge would grant him ~⟩ (2) **:** the condition of one whose sentence has been suspended in such a way **:** the status of one that is being so tested ⟨knew that prison faced him if he got in trouble again during his ~⟩ (3) **:** the period during which one whose sentence has been suspended in such a way is required to fulfill the specified conditions ⟨a long ~⟩ **2** *archaic* **a :** something that constitutes proof **:** EVIDENCE **b :** the action of proving that something is what it is asserted to be **:** DEMONSTRATION

pro·ba·tion·al \-shənᵊl, -shnəl\ *adj* **:** PROBATIONARY — **pro·ba·tion·al·ly** \-ᵊl|ē, -əl|, |i\ *adv*

1pro·ba·tion·ary \-shə,nerē, -ri\ *adj* [*probation* + *-ary*] **1 a :** of, relating to, or contributing toward probation ⟨a candidate for the job who has not yet completed his ~ period⟩ **b :** granted or assigned in connection with probation ⟨a ~ salary⟩ ⟨a ~ appointment⟩ **c :** done by way of or in connection with probation ⟨~ service⟩ **2 :** being tried out **:** being on a trial basis or on probation ⟨~ employees⟩

2probationary \"\ *n* -ES **:** PROBATIONER

pro·ba·tion·er \-sh(ə)nə(r)\ *n* -S **:** one that is being tried out **:** one that is on a trial basis **:** one that is on probation: as **a :** one (as a scholarship candidate, a student nurse) whose fitness is being tested during a trial period **b :** a convicted offender who has been granted freedom under the conditions of probation **syn** see NOVICE

pro·ba·tion·er·ship \-sh(ə)nə(r),ship\ *n* **:** the condition or position of being a probationer

probation officer *n* **:** an officer appointed to keep under supervision and to report on a convicted offender who is free on probation

pro·ba·tion·ship \-shən,ship\ *n* **1 :** the condition of being a probationer **2 :** a period of probation **:** trial period

proba·tive \'prōbəd·iv, -räb-\ *adj* [ME *probatiffe*, fr. L *probativus* of proof, fr. *probatus* (past part. of *probare* to try, test, approve, prove) + *-ivus* -ive — more at PROVE] **1 :** serving to try out or test : EXPLORATORY ⟨a blind forward movement . . . ~ but incisive —J.K.Feibleman⟩ **2 :** that furnishes, establishes, or contributes toward proof : SUBSTANTIATING ⟨has considerable ~ force —B.N.Meltzer⟩ ⟨reasonably ~ evidence —W.W.Werntz⟩ ⟨little or no ~ value —Nathan Schachner⟩ — **proba·tive·ly** *adv* — **proba·tive·ness** *n* -ES

pro·ba·tor \(ˈ)prō¦bād·ə(r)\ *n* -S [L, fr. *probatus* + *-or*] : ²APPROVER

pro·ba·to·ry \ˈprōbə,tōrē\ *adj* [L *probatus* (past part. of *probare* to try, test, approve, prove) + E *-ory* — more at PROVE] : PROBATIVE

pro·ba·tum \prōˈbād·əm, -ˈbäd·-\ *n, pl* **proba·ta** \-d·ə\ [L — more at PROBATE] : something conclusively established : something proved

1probe \ˈprōb\ *n* -S [ML *proba* examination, fr. LL, proof, test, fr. L *probare*] **1 a :** a surgical instrument that consists typically of a light slender fairly flexible pointed metal instrument like a small rod that is used typically for locating a foreign body (as a bullet embedded in a part of the body), for exploring a wound or suppurative tract by prodding or piercing, or for penetrating and exploring bodily passages and cavities **b :** something usu. pointed and slender that resembles or is suggestive of such an instrument and that is used to penetrate, poke, or prod in an exploratory way ⟨used a stick as a ~ to test the ice on the lake⟩ **2 a :** one of several testing devices used in electronics or other physical sciences: as **(1) :** a pointed metal tip that is attached to the free end of a conductor leading to or from an electronic instrument so as to make contact with a circuit element that is being checked **(2) :** a slender wire or some other small slender object that is inserted into something (as a flame, a discharge tube) so as to test conditions (as potential differences) at a given point **(3) :** a device (as a small special microphone attached to a larger conventional microphone) used to test a sound field with minimum disturbance of the field being tested **b :** a device (as a telescope, rocket, artificial satellite) used to penetrate into or scan an otherwise inaccessible area (as of space) **c (1) :** FLYING BOOM **(2) :** a pipe attached to the end of a long flexible hose which is suspended from a tanker airplane in flight and to which another plane in flight connects its gas coupling for refueling **(3) :** a pipe projecting forward from the nose of an airplane in flight that is connected with the drogue of a tanker airplane to receive fuel **d :** a small rod or similar object inserted into something as a medium of transmission or reception; *specif* **:** a metal rod used to draw energy from or inject energy into a klystron **3** [²*probe*] **a :** the action of probing ⟨in the midst of a leisurely ~ of his trouser pockets —Earle Birney⟩ **b :** a penetrating investigation or critical inquiry into something; *esp* **:** an investigation (as by a legislative body or specially appointed committee) designed to ferret out any evidence of illegal or corrupt practices on the part of some individual or group ⟨coupled with grand jury and legislative ~*s* —Ed Wall⟩ ⟨expected another ~ would result merely in a reshuffle in police and political circles —*Newsweek*⟩ **c :** a tentative forward exploratory push, advance, or survey (as of a reconnaissance division, a group of explorers) ⟨in three ~*s*, we covered 1383 miles in five and a half days —W.R. Anderson & Clay Blair⟩ ⟨the battalion made a couple of ~*s* to test the strength and location of the enemy⟩ **syn** see INQUIRY

2probe \"\ *vb* -ED/-ING/-S *vt* **1 a (1) :** to search into, search through, or explore with great thoroughness by or as if by penetrating or trying to penetrate deeply into unknown or obscure points or parts : investigate the points, parts, details, or nature of in this way : subject to intense close penetrating examination ⟨~*s* every detail of his early life and education —Stuart MacClintock⟩ ⟨*probing* the subconscious —Vance Packard⟩ ⟨attempt to ~ his sensations —Stephen Crane⟩ : carefully explore by penetrating into each section ⟨*probed* every part of the island —J.A.Michener⟩ ⟨*probed* the coastlines of both North and South America —L.A.Brown⟩ **(2) :** to subject to a penetrating investigation designed esp. to ferret out any evidence of illegal or corrupt practices : conduct a probe of ⟨spend considerable time in *probing* the actions of administrative officials —C.A.Herter⟩ **b :** to subject to one or more penetrating exploratory questions or remarks designed to elicit from another something that would otherwise remain unknown or obscure : sound out ⟨*probed* them on the matter but got no satisfactory answer⟩ ⟨~ me with that remark —Thomas Hardy⟩ ⟨I'll ~ him on the subject —W.S.Gilbert⟩ **c (1) :** to reach deeply into and search about all parts in a tentative exploratory way ⟨*probed* his pockets but couldn't find the keys⟩ **(2) :** to penetrate or push ahead into unknown or obscurely known parts of ⟨*probing* space with rockets and artificial satellites⟩ ⟨*probing* the wilderness with new roads⟩ **(3) :** RECONNOITER ⟨*probing* an enemy outpost⟩ **(4) :** to launch a small attack or esp. a series of small attacks against so as to discover an opponent's strength or weakness or gain some other strategic or tactical advantage ⟨*probed* enemy territory and withdrew after two or three skirmishes⟩ **2 a :** to penetrate into (as a wound, a cavity of the body) with a surgical probe (as in searching for or removing an embedded bullet, exploring the depth and direction of a sinus) ⟨*probing* a gunshot wound⟩ **b :** to penetrate into with something sharp or pointed or otherwise resembling or suggestive of a probe usu. so as to test, examine, or explore ⟨kept *probing* the crusty snow with a pole⟩ **c :** to poke esp. searchingly with some slender usu. pointed object : PROD ⟨*probed* the glowworms with a bit of stick, and rolled them over —Thomas Hardy⟩ ⟨fingered his heavy underlip as if *probing* it for a cold sore —Kenneth Roberts⟩ **3 :** to cause to move ahead with sudden force : THRUST ⟨*probed* the blade of the knife in between the logs⟩ **~** *vi* **1 :** to probe something ⟨the surgeon kept *probing* until he located the bullet in the soldier's leg⟩ **2 a :** to make a searching exploratory investigation ⟨without being able to ~ into the real nature of it —Liam O'Flaherty⟩ ⟨~ into things a little deeper —Edith Wharton⟩ ⟨always *probed* below the surface of whatever aspect of his subject he discussed —J.D. Adams⟩ **b :** to search about in a tentative exploratory way ⟨was *probing* for some way to discomfort me —Lloyd Alexander⟩ **3 a :** to reach out into something in a tentative exploratory way ⟨as far as our telescopes can ~ —George Gamow⟩ **b :** to penetrate or push ahead into unknown or obscurely known parts of something ⟨new highways are *probing* deeper into the fastnesses of the north —Harold Griffin⟩ **4 :** to force one's way forward with or as if with thrusting movements in spite of resistance : stab ahead or through : push forward ⟨were *probing* to within 20 miles of Moscow —*Time*⟩ **syn** see ENTER

probeagle *var of* PORBEAGLE

prob·er \-bə(r)\ *n* -S : one that probes

prob·ert·ite \ˈpräbə(r),tīt\ *n* -S [Frank H. *Probert* †1940 Am. mining engineer born in England + E *-ite*] : a mineral $NaCaB_5O_9.5H_2O$ consisting of hydrous calcium sodium borate

1probing *n* -S [fr. gerund of ²*probe*] : PROBE 3 ⟨questionings and ~*s* —Barbara Ward⟩

2probing *adj* [fr. pres. part. of ²*probe*] **1 :** that investigates something in a tentative way : that tests or tries out something experimentally ⟨a ~ procedure⟩ **2 :** that penetrates deeply in an exploratory way to the essence of something : keen and to the point : sharply analytical : SEARCHING ⟨a ~ question⟩ ⟨a ~ study⟩

prob·it \ˈpräbət\ *n* -S [*probability unit*] : a statistical unit of measurement of probability based on deviations from the mean of a normal frequency distribution

probi·ty \ˈprōbəd·ē, -ətē, *-i also* -räb-\ *n* -ES [MF *probité*, fr. L *probitat-, probitas*, fr. *probus* honest, upright, virtuous + *-itat-, -itas* -ity — more at PROVE] : uncompromising adherence to the highest principles and ideals : unimpeachable integrity : UPRIGHTNESS, RECTITUDE ⟨a man of indisputable ~ —A.T. Quiller-Couch⟩ ⟨~ in domestic policy and wise judgment in foreign policy —A.E.Stevenson †1965⟩ ⟨accepted standards of sound scholarship and intellectual ~ —H.N.Fairchild⟩

1prob·lem \ˈpräbləm *sometimes* -,blem *or* -,blim; *in rapid speech often* -bᵊm *or with syllabic* l *& syllabic* m *simultaneously articulated*\ *n* -S [ME *probleme*, fr. MF, fr. L *problema*, fr. Gk *problēma* projection, protecting wall, excuse, problem, fr. *proballein* to throw forward, put forward, fr. *pro-* ¹pro- + *ballein* to throw — more at DEVIL] **1** *obs* **:** a formal public disputation based on a question proposed for academic discussion **2 a :** a question raised or to be raised for inquiry, consideration, discussion, decision, or solution ⟨mentioned the ~*s* that the speakers would discuss⟩ **b :** a proposition in mathematics or physics stating something that is to be done ⟨~: to bisect a line⟩ **c :** a constructed position in the game of chess in which a specified result (as a checkmate) is to be accomplished in a specified number of moves **3 a :** an unsettled matter demanding solution or decision and requiring usu. considerable thought or skill for its proper solution or decision : an issue marked by usu. considerable difficulty, uncertainty, or doubt with regard to its proper settlement : a perplexing or puzzling question ⟨~*s* of history —Lewis Mumford⟩ ⟨what to do now is a ~⟩ ⟨social ~*s*⟩ ⟨what happened to them remained a ~⟩ **b :** something that is a source of usu. considerable difficulty, perplexity, or worry : something that presents a perplexing or vexing situation ⟨there are no more serious ~*s* than these immature people —P.B. Gilliam⟩ **syn** see MYSTERY

2problem \"\ *adj* **1 :** that treats of or is centered about a problem of human conduct or social relationship ⟨a ~ novel⟩ **2 :** that presents a problem : that is very difficult to deal with : PROBLEMATIC ⟨a ~ neighborhood⟩ ⟨a good many ~ children who were too tough for the other schools in town —Green Peyton⟩ ⟨~ behavior⟩

prob·lem·at·ic \¦präblə¦mad·|ik, |at|, |ēk\ *or* **prob·lem·at·i·cal** \|əkəl, |ēk-\ *adj* [*problematic* fr. F *problématique*, fr. LL *problematicus*, fr. Gk *problēmatikos*, fr. *problēmat-, problēma* problem + *-ikos* -ic; *problematical* fr. MF *problematique* + E *-al*] **1 a (1) :** constituting or presenting a problem : difficult to solve or to come to a decision about or to deal with : PERPLEXING, PUZZLING ⟨a ~ situation⟩ **(2) :** so full of difficulty as to make only tentative and uncertain solutions or decisions possible ⟨have arrived at a ~ impasse⟩ **b :** unclear and unsettled : being by no means definite : DUBIOUS ⟨the future remains ~⟩ **c :** open to question or debate : QUESTIONABLE ⟨whether we should do it or not is ~⟩ **2** *logic* **:** that enunciates or supports what may be but is not necessarily true ⟨a ~ proposition⟩ ⟨~ judgments concerning the existence of unicorns and zebras⟩ **syn** see DOUBTFUL

prob·lem·at·i·cal·ly \|ək(ə)lē, |ēk-, -li\ *adv* : in such a way as to present a problem

prob·lem·a·tist \präˈblemətəst\ *n* -S [L *problemat-, problema* problem + E *-ist*] : PROBLEMIST

prob·lem·ist \ˈpräbləməst\ *n* -S : one that specializes in studying or composing problems; *esp* **:** a composer or solver of chess problems

prob·lem·ize \-,mīz\ *vi* -ED/-ING/-S : to raise or discuss problems

prob·o·la \ˈpräbələ\ *n, pl* **probo·lae** \-,lē, -,lī\ *or* **probolas** [NL, fr. Gk *probolē* projection, prominence, fr. *proballein* to throw forward, put forward — more at PROBLEM] : one of the processes projecting from the lips of certain soil nematodes

pro·bos·ci·dal \prōˈbäsədᵊl\ *adj* [L *proboscid-, proboscis* + E *-al*] : PROBOSCIDIFORM

pro·bos·ci·date \-,dāt\ *adj* [L *proboscid-, proboscis* + E *-ate*] : having a proboscis

pro·bos·cide \-ˈäsəd\ *n* -S [F, fr. L *proboscid-, proboscis*] : PROBOSCIS 1c

1pro·bos·ci·dea \,prōbəˈsidēə, -,bä's-; prō,bäsəˈd-\ *n pl, cap* [NL, fr. L *proboscid-, proboscis*] : an order of large gravigrade mammals comprising the elephants and extinct related forms that typically have some of the teeth enlarged into tusks with corresponding modifications of the skull, that often have the nose drawn out into a trunk, and that are now limited to Africa and parts of Asia though formerly present in most parts of the world — compare MAMMOTH, MASTODON

2proboscidea \"\ [NL, fr. L *proboscid-, proboscis*] *syn of* MARTYNIA

1pro·bos·ci·de·an \,prō¦bäsə¦dēən; ¦prōbə¦sidēən, -,bä¦s-\ *or* **pro·bos·cid·i·an** \¦prōbə¦sidēən, -,bä¦s-\ *adj* [NL *Proboscidea* + E *-an* or *-ian*] **1 :** of or relating to the order Proboscidea **2** [L *proboscid-, proboscis* + E *-ean* or *-ian*] : having, relating to, or resembling a proboscis

2proboscidean \"\ *n* -S : a mammal of the order Proboscidea

pro·bos·cid·i·al \¦prōbə¦sidēəl, -,bäs'e-\ *adj* [L *proboscid-, proboscis* + E *-ial*] : PROBOSCIDATE

pro·bos·ci·dif·er·ous \¦prō,bäsə¦dif(ə)rəs\ *adj* [L *proboscid-, proboscis* + E *-i-* + *-ferous* — more at PROBOSCIS] : PROBOSCIDATE

pro·bos·cid·i·form \¦prōbə¦sidə,fȯrm, -,bä¦s-\ *adj* [L *proboscid-, proboscis* + E *-iform*] : resembling a proboscis

pro·bos·ci·ger \prōˈbäsəjə(r)\ *n, cap* [NL, fr. *proboscis* + *-ger* -gerous] : a genus of parrots that includes the great black cockatoo

pro·bos·cis \prōˈbäsəs, -äsk-\ *n, pl* **proboscis·es** \-äsəsəz, -äsk-\ *also* **probosci·des** \-äsə,dēz\ [L, fr. Gk *proboskis*, fr. *pro-* ¹pro- + *boskein* to feed — more at BOTANICAL] **1 a :** the flexible conspicuously long snout of some mammals (as tapirs, shrews); *esp* **:** the trunk of an elephant **b :** a tubular organ of varying form and use that extends or that is capable of being extended usu. from or near the oral region of many insects and some other invertebrates: as **(1) :** a sucking organ of insects (as butterflies, houseflies, mosquitoes) that is often also adapted for piercing **(2) :** the anterior muscular protrusible part of the alimentary canal of many annelids **(3) :** a prob. tactile and defensive organ of nemertean worms that can be everted through an opening above the mouth **c :** one of the complex protrusible holdfasts on the scolex of certain tapeworms — compare TRYPANORHYNCHA **2 :** the human nose esp. when very long or otherwise prominent

proboscis flower *n* : UNICORN PLANT

proboscis monkey *n* : a large Bornean monkey (*Nasalis larvatus*) with a long nose and a long tail

pro·bou·leu·tic \¦prōbü¦lüd·ik, -bə¦l-\ *adj* [fr. (assumed) Gk *probouleutos* (verbal of *probouleuein* to pass a preliminary decree, fr. *pro-* ¹pro- + *bouleuein* to take counsel, deliberate, fr. *boulē* will, counsel) + E *-ic* — more at BOULE] *adj* : concerned with preliminary discussion of and deliberation on something (as a legal measure) later to be submitted to another body of voters ⟨the ~ senate of ancient Athens⟩

proc *abbr* **1** proceedings **2** process **3** proclamation **4** proctor

pro·ca·cious \prōˈkāshəs\ *adj* [L *procac-, procax* impudent (fr. *procare* to ask, demand, fr. *procus* suitor) + E *-ious;* akin to L *precari* to pray, entreat — more at PRAY] : IMPUDENT — **pro·ca·cious·ly** *adv*

pro·cac·i·ty \-ˈkasəd·ē\ *n* -ES [F *procacité*, fr. L *procacitat-, procacitas*, fr. *procac-, procax* + *-itat-, -itas* -ity] : IMPUDENCE

pro·cain·amide \prōˈkānə,mīd, -ə məd, ,prō,kāˈna,mīd\ *n* [*procaine* + *amide*] : a base $C_{13}H_{21}ON_3$ of an amide related to procaine that is used in the form of its crystalline hydrochloride as a cardiac depressant in the treatment of ventricular and auricular arrhythmias — called also *procaine amide*

pro·caine \ˈprō,kān\ *n* -S [ISV ²*pro-* + *-caine*] : a basic ester $H_2NC_6H_4COOCH_2CH_2N(C_2H_5)_2$ of *para*-aminobenzoic acid; *also* **:** its crystalline hydrochloride that is a local anesthetic less toxic than cocaine — called also *novocaine*

pro·cambial \(ˈ)prō+\ *adj* [NL *procambium* + E *-al*] : of, relating to, resembling, or derived from procambium

pro·cambium \"+\ *n* [NL, fr. ¹*pro-* + *cambium*] : the part of a plant meristem that gives rise to cambium and other primary vascular tissues

pro·carp \ˈprō,kärp\ *n* -S [NL *procarpium*, fr. ¹*pro-* + *-carpium*] : a specialized female reproductive branch that is found in many red algae and that consists of carpogonium and trichogyne and usu. also auxiliary cells — compare ARCHICARP, CARPOSPORE, GONIMOBLAST

pro·car·pi·um \prōˈkärpēəm\ *n, pl* **procarpiums** \-ēəmz\ *also* **procar·pia** \-ēə\ [NL] : PROCARP

pro·catalectic \(¦)prō+\ *adj* [¹*pro-* + *catalectic*] *prosody* : lacking the unaccented part of the first foot

pro·cat·a·lep·sis \(,)prō,kad·ᵊlˈepsəs\ *n* -ES [ML, fr. Gk *prokatalēpsis*, lit., art of seizing beforehand, fr. *prokatalambanein* to seize beforehand, fr. *pro-* ¹pro- + *katalambanein* to seize — more at CATALEPSY] : PROLEPSIS 2b

pro·cat·arc·tic \¦prō,kad·¦ärktik, -ōkə¦tä-\ *adj* [Gk *prokatarktikos*, fr. (assumed) *prokatarktos* (verbal of *prokatarchein* to begin first, fr. *pro-* ¹pro- + *katarchein* to make a beginning, fr. *kat-* cata- + *archein* to begin) + *-ikos* -ic — more at ARCHI-] **1** *archaic* **:** that is the immediately antecedent cause of some indicated effect **2** *archaic* **:** that is the primary cause of some indicated effect

pro·cathedral \¦prō+\ *n* [²*pro-* + *cathedral*] : a parish church that is used as a temporary substitute for a cathedral (as in a newly created diocese)

pro·cavia \(ˈ)prō+\ *n, cap* [NL, fr. ¹*pro-* + *Cavia*] : a genus (the type of the family Procaviidae) that comprises all or most of the hyraxes

1pro·ca·vi·id \(ˈ)prō¦kāvēəd\ *adj* [NL *Procaviidae*] : of or relating to the Procaviidae

2procaviid \"\ *n* -S : a mammal of the family *Procavia*

pro·ca·vi·idae \,prōkəˈvīə,dē\ *n pl, cap* [NL, fr. *Procavia*, type genus + *-idae*] : a family of Old World ungulate mammals that includes all recent members of the order Hyracoidea

pro·ce·den·do \,prōsəˈden(,)dō\ *n* -S [L, abl. of *procedendum*, gerund of *procedere* to proceed — more at PROCEED] : a writ issuing out of a superior court to an inferior court authorizing or directing the inferior court to act upon certain matters (as the remitting of a cause for trial or the entry of a judgment in accordance with a mandate of the superior court)

pro·ce·dur·al \prəˈsējərəl, prōˈs-\ *adj* : of or relating to procedure ⟨~ details⟩; *esp* **:** of or relating to the procedure used by courts or other bodies (as governmental agencies) in the administration of substantive law ⟨~ due process⟩ — **pro·ce·dur·al·ly** \-rəlē, -li\ *adv*

pro·ce·dure \-jə(r)\ *n* -S [F *procédure*, fr. MF *procedure*, fr. *proceder* to proceed + *-ure* — more at PROCEED] **1 a :** a particular way of doing or of going about the accomplishment of something ⟨the book is lucid in its ~ —H.B.Wehle⟩ ⟨democratic ~⟩ ⟨told me he didn't especially like my ~⟩ **b (1) :** a particular course of action ⟨a ~ that respects the dignity and worth of the individual —W.O.Douglas⟩ **(2) :** a particular step adopted for doing or accomplishing something ⟨one of his first ~*s* was to investigate the reports⟩ **(3) :** a series of steps followed in a regular orderly definite way : METHOD ⟨surgical ~⟩ ⟨therapeutic ~⟩ ⟨scientific ~⟩ **c (1) :** a traditional, customary, or otherwise established or accepted way of doing things ⟨told him it was not the ~ of citizens of that country to act in that way⟩ **(2) :** PROTOCOL 4 ⟨sticklers for ~ —*Time*⟩ **d :** an established way of conducting business (as of a deliberative body): as **(1) :** the accepted usage of parliamentary bodies : established parliamentary practice : parliamentary order ⟨rules of ~⟩ **(2) :** the established manner of conducting judicial business and litigation including pleading, evidence, and practice **2 a** *obs* **:** the progress or continuation of some action or process **b** *archaic* **:** the fact of issuing from a source

1pro·ceed \prōˈsēd, prəˈs-\ *vi* -ED/-ING/-S [ME *proceden, proceeden*, fr. MF *proceder*, fr. L *procedere*, fr. *pro-* before, forward, forth + *cedere* to go, proceed — more at PRO-, CEDE] **1 :** ISSUE: as **a :** to come forth from a usu. specified place or thing ⟨his lips began to form some words, though no sound ~*ed* from them —Charles Dickens⟩ **b :** to come into being : take origin : ORIGINATE ⟨assuring her that his seeming inattention had only ~*ed* from his being involved in a profound meditation —T.L.Peacock⟩ **c :** to come forth by way of descent from a specified parent or ancestor ⟨a family that ~*s* from a long line of royalty⟩ **2 :** CONTINUE: as **a (1) :** to go on (as after a pause or an interruption) with what has been begun : go forward from a point already arrived at : go ahead ⟨let us ~ with the examination of our second main question —W.J.Reilly⟩ ⟨said he would ~ only when there was silence⟩ **(2) :** to go on with one's movement or traveling : go forward on one's way : make one's way forward ⟨had ~*ed* to the Polish capital —*Current Biog.*⟩ ⟨~*ed* from one city to another⟩ ⟨~*ed* into the next room⟩ **(3) :** to go on with what one is saying or writing : move along with the thread of one's discourse or the development of one's ideas **b :** to go on from one point to another : move along from one part of a series or sequence of things to another : pass along in an orderly regulated way usu. decided upon in advance ⟨later we shall ~ to a detailed discussion of the various parts of the country —P.E.James⟩ **3 a :** to begin and carry on some action, process, or movement : set out on a course ⟨~*ed* to wage the bloodiest war in history —M.W.Straight⟩ ⟨~*ed* to walk up and down the big and half-lit chamber —William Black⟩ ⟨~*ed* to examine his new acquaintance —W.M.Thackeray⟩ **b :** to deal with something or act toward something in a particular way ⟨~ rather harshly with themselves⟩ **c (1) :** to go to law : take legal action : enter upon a lawsuit ⟨threatened to ~ against him⟩ : engage in legal prosecution ⟨decided to ~ against war criminals in a more thorough fashion —R.G. Neumann⟩ **(2) :** to carry on a legal action or process ⟨the courts are now ~*ing* with the case⟩ **4 a (1) :** to become progressively effected or moved toward completion ⟨the job ~*ed* in the eerie glow of portable floodlights —E.J.Long⟩ ⟨an understanding of how lawmaking ~*s* —F.A.Ogg & Harold Zink⟩ **(2) :** to be in the process of being done, accomplished, or furthered : be under way ⟨negotiations now ~*ing* in the printing trade —Jack Morpurgo⟩ **b** *obs* **:** HAPPEN, OCCUR ⟨he will . . . tell you what hath ~*ed* worthy note today —Shak.⟩ **5** *Brit* **a :** to graduate as the recipient of an indicated academic degree usu. higher than a B.A. ⟨had ~*ed* M.A. at the age of 18 —*Times. Lit. Supp.*⟩ **b :** to work toward an academic degree ⟨undergraduates ~*ing* to a degree in the university —*Univ. of Toronto Cat.*⟩ **6 a :** to move along on a particular course or in a particular way or direction or toward a particular thing : move on : go along : ADVANCE ⟨her thinking probably does not ~ exactly this way —S.L.Payne⟩ ⟨as the conference ~*ed* —Vera M. Dean⟩ ⟨the highway ~*s* due south through a prosperous farm country —*Amer. Guide Series: Mich.*⟩ : make progress ⟨~*ing* steadily towards the beginning of a truly national literature —*Report: (Canadian) Royal Commission on Nat'l Development*⟩ ⟨the organization of towns ~*ed* rapidly under his jurisdiction —W.E.Stevens⟩ **b** *archaic* **:** to make out : get along : FARE ⟨make inquiry what family he has, and how they ~ —Samuel Johnson⟩ **syn** see SPRING

2pro·ceed \ˈprō,sēd\ *n* -S *archaic* : PROCEEDS

proceeding *n* -S [ME *procedyng*, fr. gerund of *proceden* to proceed — more at PROCEED] **1 :** the action of proceeding **2 a :** a particular way of doing or accomplishing something ⟨is a convenient ~, but it leaves certain questions . . . unanswered —John Lardner⟩ **b :** a particular action or course of action ⟨was not quite so reckless a ~ as it might seem —G.F.Hudson⟩ : a particular way of acting ⟨his ~*s* were enough in themselves to make anyone odious —Joseph Conrad⟩ ⟨I've given up all my wild ~*s* —W.S.Gilbert⟩ : ACT, DEED ⟨everyone who took any notice of my ~*s* —H.L.Mencken⟩ **c :** a particular step or series of steps adopted for doing or accomplishing something ⟨studied each ~ necessary for bringing the case to a successful conclusion⟩ **d proceedings** *pl* **:** DOINGS, GOINGS-ON ⟨through his drunken brain the whole memory of the evening's ~*s* rushed back —Liam O'Flaherty⟩ **e (1) proceedings** *pl* **:** the course of procedure in a judicial action or in a suit in litigation : legal action ⟨took divorce ~*s* against him —O.S.J.Gogarty⟩ ⟨during the court ~*s*⟩ **(2) :** a particular action at law or case in litigation ⟨prosecutions and other judicial ~*s* —Zechariah Chafee⟩ **f :** a particular thing done : AFFAIR, TRANSACTION, NEGOTIATION ⟨an illegal ~⟩ ⟨business ~*s*⟩ **3 proceedings** *pl* **:** an official record or account (as in a book of minutes) of things said or done (as at a meeting or convention of a society) ⟨brought a copy of the club's ~*s* with him⟩

pro·ceeds \ˈprō,sēdz\ *n pl* [fr. pl. of ²*proceed*] **1 a :** what is produced by or derived from something (as a sale, investment, levy, business) by way of total revenue : the total amount brought in : YIELD, RETURNS ⟨the ~ from the sale of the paintings were considerable⟩ ⟨estimated that the ~ from such taxes would be enormous⟩ **b :** the net profit made on something ⟨took the ~ from the sale of his business and invested in stocks⟩ **2 :** the net sum received (as for a check, a negotiable note, an insurance policy) after deduction of any discount or charges

1pro·ce·leus·mat·ic \,prōsə,lüzˈmad·ik, -ü'sm-\ *n* -S [LL *proceleusmaticus*, fr. Gk *prokeleusmatikos*, adj. & n., fr. (assumed) *prokeleusmat-, prokeleusma* incitement (fr. *prokeleuein* to urge on, give orders to, fr. *pro-* ¹pro- + *keleuein* to urge, drive on, command) + *-ikos* -ic; prob. fr. the use of proceleusmatics in ancient Greek rowing songs; akin to Gk *kellein* to beach a ship — more at CELERITY] : a metrical foot used esp. in ancient quantitative verse and consisting of four short syllables

²**proceleusmatic** \¦==¦==\ *adj* [Gk *prokeleusmatikos*] **:** of, relating to, or marked by the use of proceleusmatics

pro·cel·lar·ia \ˌprōsəˈla(a)rēə\ *n, cap* [NL, fr. L *procella* storm (fr. *procellere* to throw down, fr. *pro-* forward, forth, down + *-cellere* to rise, project) + *-aria;* fr. the association of the petrels with storms at sea — more at PRO-, EXCEL] **:** a genus of petrels that includes the white-chinned petrels and related forms and in some classifications the shearwaters and that is the type of the family Procellariidae

pro·cel·la·ri·idae \ˌprōsələˈrīəˌdē, prōˌsel-\ *n pl, cap* [NL, fr. *Procellaria,* type genus + *-idae*] **:** a family of oceanic birds (order Procellariiformes) comprising the fulmars, shearwaters, and related birds

pro·cel·lar·ii·for·mes \ˌprōsəˌla(a)rēəˈfȯr(ˌ)mēz\ *n pl, cap* [NL, fr. *Procellaria* + *-iformes*] **:** an order of predominantly pelagic birds comprising the petrels, shearwaters, albatrosses, and diving petrels

pro·cel·lous \prōˈseləs\ *adj* [L *procellosus,* fr. *procella* + *-osus* -ous] **:** STORMY ⟨the dangers of that ~ sea —Rafael Sabatini⟩

pro·cephalic \¦prō+\ *adj* [¹*pro-* + *cephalic*] **1 :** relating to, forming, or situated on or near the front of the head ⟨~ antennae⟩ **2** [Gk *prokephalos* (fr. *pro-* ¹pro- + *kephalē* head) + E *-ic* — more at CEPHALIC] *of a dactylic hexameter* **:** having actually or apparently an extra syllable at the beginning

pro·cephalon \(ˈ)prō+\ *n* -S [NL, fr. ¹*pro-* + *-cephalon* (fr. Gk *kephalē* head)] **:** the part of an insect's head that is in front of the segment in which the mandibles are located

pro·ceph·a·lous \(ˈ)prō¦sefələs\ *adj* [Gk *prokephalos*] **:** marked by anacrusis (sense 1)

pro·cer·coid \(ˈ)prō¦sərˌkȯid\ *n* -S [¹*pro-* + *cerc-* + *-oid*] **:** the solid first parasitic larva of pseudophyllidean and some other tapeworms that develops usu. in the body cavity of a copepod — compare PLEROCERCOID

pro·cerebral \(¦)prō+\ *adj* [NL *procerebrum* forebrain (fr. ¹*pro-* + L *cerebrum*) + E *-al*] **:** of or relating to the forebrain

proc·er·ite \ˈpräsəˌrīt\ *n* -S [ISV ¹*pro-* + Gk *keras* horn + ISV *-ite* — more at HORN] **:** the flagellum of the antenna of a crustacean

proc·er·it·ic \¦==¦rid·ik\ *adj* **:** of or relating to a procerite

pro·cer·i·ty \prōˈserəd·ē\ *n* -ES [L *proceritas,* fr. *procerus* high, tall (fr. *pro-* forward + *-cerus,* fr. the stem of *crescere* to grow) + *-itas* -ity — more at CRESCENT] *archaic* **:** HEIGHT, TALLNESS

pro·ce·rus \prōˈsirəs\ *n, pl* **pro·ce·ri** \-ˌrī\ *or* **proceruses** [NL, fr. L, high, tall] **:** a facial muscle arising from the nasal bone and lateral nasal cartilage and inserting in the skin at the root of the nose

¹**pro·cess** \ˈprä¦ˌses *also* ˈprō¦ *or* ¦səs\ *n, pl* **processes** \"+əz *also* ÷¦ˌsəˌsēz *sometimes* ÷¦ˌse(ˌ)sēz\ [ME *proces, processe, process,* fr. MF *proces,* fr. L *processus,* fr. *processus,* past part. of *procedere* to proceed — more at PROCEED] **1 a :** a progressive forward movement from one point to another on the way to completion **:** the action of passing through continuing development from a beginning to a contemplated end **:** the action of continuously going along through each of a succession of acts, events, or developmental stages **:** the action of being progressively advanced or progressively done **:** continued onward movement ⟨the job is not yet finished but is still in ~⟩ ⟨many other questions are in ~ of discussion —Vera M. Dean⟩ ⟨social ~⟩ ⟨links in the endless interlocking chain of causation and concomitance that constitutes the ~ of history —Max Lerner & Edwin Mims⟩ ⟨in the ~ of governing people of so many races —Vernon Bartlett⟩ ⟨did his best to educate himself, and in the ~ he developed a profound respect for education —Oscar Schisgall⟩ **b :** continued onward flow **:** COURSE ⟨in the ~ of time⟩ **c :** something (as a series of actions, happenings, or experiences) going on or carried on **:** PROCEEDING ⟨standing in the cold was not a pleasant ~⟩ ⟨behind the arras I'll convey myself to hear the ~ —Shak.⟩ **d** (1) **:** a natural progressively continuing operation or development marked by a series of gradual changes that succeed one another in a relatively fixed way and lead toward a particular result or end ⟨the ~ of growth⟩ ⟨the ~ of digestion⟩ **:** a natural continuing activity or function ⟨such life ~*es* as breathing and the circulation of the blood⟩ (2) **:** an artificial or voluntary progressively continuing operation that consists of a series of controlled actions or movements systematically directed toward a particular result or end ⟨the ~ governing the mechanism of a clock⟩ ⟨cannot be achieved by any deductive ~ —J.H.Steward⟩ ⟨explanations of . . . how the editorial ~ worked —A.S.Link⟩ (3) **:** a set of facts, circumstances, or experiences that are observed and described or that can be observed and described throughout each of a series of changes continuously succeeding each other **:** a phenomenon or condition marked by a series of slow or rapid changes throughout a period of time ⟨the ~ of decay⟩ ⟨a pathological ~⟩ ⟨tuberculous ~⟩ (4) **:** a succession of related changes by which one thing gradually becomes something else ⟨a new theory of evolutionary ~⟩ **e :** a particular method or system of doing something, producing something, or accomplishing a specific result; *esp* **:** a particular method or system used in a manufacturing operation ⟨a ~ of making steel⟩ or other technical operation ⟨a chemical ~⟩ **2** [ME *proces, processe,* fr. MF *proces,* fr. ML *processus,* fr. L] **a :** the course of procedure in a judicial action or in a suit in litigation **:** legal action ⟨changed his name by legal ~ —*Current Biog.*⟩ ⟨federal ~ . . . does not have to be confined to state borders —*Va. Law Rev.*⟩ **b** (1) **:** a summons, mandate, or writ that serves as the means used to bring a defendant into court to answer in a judicial action or in a suit in litigation; *also* **:** a writ by which a court exercises its jurisdiction over the parties or subject matter of judicial action or of a suit in litigation ⟨~ for their appearance has been duly issued —*Detroit Law Jour.*⟩ (2) **:** the whole body of such summonses, mandates or writs **3** *obs* **:** REPORT, ACCOUNT ⟨the whole ear of Denmark is by a forged ~ of my death rankly abused —Shak.⟩ **4 :** a part of the mass of an organism or organic structure that projects outward from the main mass ⟨a bone ~⟩ ⟨a parasite that puts forth ~*es* resembling tentacles⟩ **5** *obs* **:** a royal edict **6** *Roman Catholicism* **:** the canonical procedure followed in beatification or canonization

²**process** \"\ *vb* **processed** \"+t\ **processed** \"+t\ **processing** \"+iŋ\ **processes** \"+əz\ [in sense 1, fr. MF *processer,* fr. *proces;* in other senses, fr. ¹*process*] *vt* **1 a :** to proceed against by law **:** PROSECUTE ⟨the debt for which they were ~*ed* —H.W.V.Stuart⟩ **b** (1) **:** to take out a summons against (2) **:** to serve a summons on ⟨warned that they would ~ him⟩ **2 :** to subject to a particular method, system, or technique of preparation, handling, or other treatment designed to effect a particular result **:** put through a special process**:** as **a** (1) **:** to prepare for market, manufacture, or other commercial use by subjecting to some process ⟨~*ing* cattle by slaughtering them⟩ ⟨~*ed* the milk by pasteurizing it⟩ ⟨~*ing* grain by milling⟩ ⟨~*ing* cotton by spinning⟩ (2) **:** to make usable by special treatment ⟨~*ing* rancid butter⟩ ⟨~*ing* waste material⟩ ⟨~*ed* the water to remove impurities⟩ **b** (1) **:** to subject to rapid examination and handling designed to dispose of routine details (as by recording preliminary data of or about) ⟨~*ing* books for a library⟩ ⟨efficiently ~*ed* the invoices⟩ (2) **:** to subject to a preliminary classification based on apparent skills, aptitudes, and other qualifications ⟨~*ing* applicants⟩ ⟨~*ing* army recruits⟩ (3) **:** to take care of, attend to, or dispose of by some largely routine procedure ⟨quickly ~*ed* the loan requested by the firm⟩ (4) **:** to subject to examination and analysis ⟨~*ing* data radioed by a space rocket⟩ ⟨where news from everywhere is ~*ed* —F.L.Mott⟩ **3 :** to produce a copy of by a mechanical or photomechanical duplicating process ⟨a ~*ed* publication⟩ **~** *vi* **:** to prosecute something

³**process** \"\ *adj* [¹*process*] **1 :** prepared, handled, treated, or produced by a special process: as **a :** made by some special synthetic process ⟨~ fuels⟩ ⟨~ sugar⟩ **b :** made by or used in a mechanical or photomechanical duplicating process ⟨~ publications⟩ ⟨~ ink⟩ **c :** made by special equipment or techniques so as to produce an optical effect not otherwise attainable ⟨a motion picture that has a number of remarkable ~ scenes⟩ **2 a :** used in producing special effects ⟨a ~ motion-picture camera⟩ **b :** used in making colored reproductions in almost any hue or shade by printing from halftone plates in usu. three or more colors (as red, yellow, blue)

⁴**pro·cess** \prəˈses, prōˈs-\ *vi* -ED/-ING/-ES [back-formation fr. ¹*procession*] **:** to move along **:** GO; *esp* **:** to move along in or as if in a procession ⟨~*ed* slowly through the town, conversing amiably —Thomas Wood †1950⟩

process annealing *n* **:** the process of softening steel by heating it to a temperature near but below the transformation range and then cooling slowly

process butter *or* **processed butter** *n* **:** butter that has been melted, refined, and reworked

process chart *n* **:** a chart on which are graphically shown in sequence the separate details that make up a complete process (as of a particular job operation)

process cheese *or* **processed cheese** *n* **:** a cheese made by blending several lots of cheese by heating, stirring, and emulsifying and often smoked or otherwise flavored

processer *var of* PROCESSOR

processes *pl of* PROCESS, *pres 3d sing of* PROCESS

¹**pro·ces·sion** \prəˈseshən, prōˈs-\ *n* -S [ME *processioun,* fr. OF *procession,* fr. LL & L; LL *procession-, processio* religious procession, fr. L, act of proceeding, fr. *processus* (past part. of *procedere* to proceed) + *-ion-, -io* -ion — more at PROCEED] **1 :** the action of proceeding: **a :** the action of moving along on a particular course esp. in a continuous orderly regulated often formal or ceremonial way **:** continuous forward movement **:** PROGRESSION ⟨watched the constant ~ of people passing by the building⟩ ⟨it happened during the ~⟩ ⟨the uninterrupted ~ of the clergy down the aisle⟩ **b :** the action of issuing forth; *specif* **:** the action of the Holy Spirit in issuing forth from another of the persons of the Trinity — see DOUBLE PROCESSION, SINGLE PROCESSION **2 a** (1) **:** a group of individuals (as people, animals, vehicles) moving along or about to move along on a particular course esp. in a continuous orderly regulated often formal or ceremonial way and usu. arranged in a long line ⟨formed a ~⟩ ⟨the ~ moved slowly⟩ ⟨a funeral ~⟩ (2) **:** the formation proper to or typical of such a group ⟨walked along in ~⟩ ⟨go in ~ round the fields —J.G.Frazer⟩ **b :** a succession, sequence, or series of things arranged or occurring in a formation or alignment like that of such a group ⟨a ~ of stately trees on each side of the avenue⟩ ⟨an endless ~ of fields broken now and then by a strip of woodland —Sherwood Anderson⟩ **3** *obs* **:** something (as a hymn, prayer) sung or recited during a religious procession

²**pro·ces·sion** \prəˈseshən, prōˈs-\ *vb* -ED/-ING/-S *vi, archaic* **:** to move along or about in or as if in a procession **~** *vt, Midland* **:** to move in procession around (land, boundaries) in formally determining the limits of

¹**pro·ces·sion·al** \-shənᵊl, -shnəl\ *n* -S [ME, fr. ML *processionale,* fr. neut. of *processionalis,* adj., fr. LL *procession-, processio* + *-alis* -al] **1 a :** a book containing material (as hymns, litanies) to be sung or recited during a religious procession and often containing regulations for conducting various types of religious procession **b :** a musical composition designed for a procession: as (1) **:** a hymn sung during a religious procession; *esp* **:** a hymn sung at the entrance of a procession (as of clergy and choir) into a church at the beginning of a service (2) **:** an instrumental composition typically solemn in character and written as an accompaniment for a religious or other ceremonial procession **c :** the first part of a church service or some other solemn function during which a procession (as of clergy and choir) enters the place in which the service or function is being held **2 :** PROCESSION 1a,2 ⟨marched in a Sunday School ~ —K.D.Miller⟩ ⟨slow ~ of years —R.W.Howard⟩

²**processional** \"\ *adj* [F or ML; F *processionel,* fr. ML *processionalis*] **1 a :** of, relating to, or typical of a procession ⟨moved along in good ~ order⟩ ⟨the car slowed down, and at ~ pace we crept along the road —Richard Church⟩ **b :** designed for or used in a procession ⟨~ music⟩ ⟨a ~ cross⟩ ⟨~ vestments⟩ **2 :** grouped or moving in or as if in a procession ⟨automobiles poking along in ~ lines of traffic⟩ — **pro·ces·sion·al·ly** \-ᵊl¦ē, -əl¦, ¦i\ *adv*

pro·ces·sion·ary \-shəˌnerē\ *adj* **:** PROCESSIONAL

processionary caterpillar *n* **:** the larva of a processionary moth

processionary moth *also* **processional moth** *or* **procession moth** *n* **:** a moth of the genus *Thaumetopoea* whose larvae make large webs on oak trees and go out in columns to feed

pro·ces·sion·er \-sh(ə)nə(r)\ *n* -S *chiefly Midland* **:** one appointed to examine and formally determine the limits of an area of land

procession flower *n* **:** any of various plants of the genus *Polygala; esp* **:** a milkwort (*P. incarnata*) of No. America

pro·ces·sion·ist \-sh(ə)nə̇st\ *n* -S **:** one that takes part in a procession

pro·ces·sion·ize \-shəˌnīz\ *vi* -ED/-ING/-S **:** to move along in a procession **:** go in procession

pro·ces·sive \prəˈsesiv, prōˈs-\ *adj* [L *processus* (past part. of *procedere* to proceed) + E *-ive* — more at PROCEED] **:** moving forward **:** PROGRESSIVE

process of tomes \-ˈtōmz\ *usu cap T* [after Sir John *Tomes* †1895 Eng. dental surgeon] **:** one of the fine fibrils of the ameloblasts that project from the pulp of a tooth into the dentine

proces·sor \ˈprä¦ˌsesə(r) *also* -rō¦ *or* ¦səsə(r) *or* ¦səˌsȯ(ə)r *or* ¦səˌsȯ(ə)\ *also* **process·er** \-ə(r)\ *n* -S **:** one that processes: as **a :** one that processes agricultural products, foods, or similar products **b :** one that processes films, paper, chemicals, or similar products **c :** one that processes individuals (as applicants, recruits) or data forms

process philosophy *n* **:** a theistic philosophy that views being as primarily relational, stresses emergent evolution, and criticizes or rejects nonreligious naturalism — compare NEONATURALISM

process photography *n* **1 :** the photographic steps involved in any photomechanical reproduction process **2** *cinematography* **:** special printing methods or use of a background projection screen in front of which live action is photographed

process plate *n* **:** a photographic plate usu. slow in speed having the characteristics of high contrast and very fine grain and used chiefly in reproducing line drawings or in photomechanical processing

process printer *n* **:** one that does process printing

process printing *n* **:** a method of printing from halftone plates in usu. three or more colors so that nearly any hue may be reproduced

process projection *n* **:** BACKGROUND PROJECTION

process shot *n* **:** a shot made with a trick camera incorporating in the completed film matter not present in the actual scene photographed — compare PROCESS PHOTOGRAPHY 2

process steam *n* **:** steam used for heat and moisture rather than for power

process theology *n* **:** NEONATURALISM

pro·ces·su·al \(ˈ)prä¦seshəwəl, -rō¦s-\ *adj* [ML *processus* legal process + E *-al* — more at PROCESS] **1 :** of or relating to a legal process ⟨a ~ code⟩ **2 :** FUNCTIONAL, OPERATIONAL — **pro·ces·su·al·ly** \-wəlē\ *adv*

pro·ces·sus \prōˈsesəs\ *n, pl* **processus** [L — more at PROCESS] **1 :** FUNCTIONING, OPERATION ⟨the ~ of the mind —H.F. Muller⟩ **2 :** PROCESS 4

pro·cès–verbal \¦präˌsāˌverˈbäl, -rōˌs-, prō¦s-, -bal\ *n, pl* **pro·cès–verbaux** \-bō\ [F, lit., verbal trial] **:** a detailed written account of things said or done that is official and authenticated: as **a :** a written statement of attested facts brought up during a legal action in court together with the official procedures adopted by the court **b :** a written record (as in a book of minutes) of the proceedings of an organized group (as a society, assembly) **c :** a written record of diplomatic negotiations

pro·chancellor \(ˈ)prō+\ *n* [²*pro-* + *chancellor*] **:** an officer of a British university who in the absence of the vice-chancellor may represent the chancellor

pro·chein ami *or* **pro·chein amy** \¦prōˌsheˌnaˈmē, prō¦sh-, -nä¦-\ *n* [ME *prochein amy,* fr. AF *prochein ami,* lit., near friend] **:** one not regularly appointed that acts (as in a suit at law) for one not sui juris (as an infant, married woman) **:** NEXT FRIEND

pro·chlorite \(ˈ)prō+\ *n* [¹*pro-* + *chlorite;* fr. its being the earliest variety of chlorite distinguished] **:** RIPIDOLITE

pro·cho·os \ˈprōkəˌwäs, -räk-\ *n, pl* **procho·oi** \-wȯi\ [Gk *prochoos, prochous,* fr. *procheîn* to pour forth, fr. *pro-* ¹pro- + *chein* to pour — more at FOUND] **:** a tall slender ancient Greek jug used esp. to hold water for washing the hands

pro·chorda \(ˈ)prō+\ *or* **pro·chordata** \¦prō+\ [NL, fr. ¹*pro-* + *Chorda* or *Chordata*] *syn of* PROTOCHORDATA

pro·chordal \(ˈ)prō +\ *adj* [¹*pro-* + *chordal*] **:** anterior to the notochord

¹**pro·chordate** \"+\ *adj* [NL *Prochordata*] **:** PROTOCHORDATE

²**prochordate** \"\ *n* **:** PROTOCHORDATE

pro·chorion \(ˈ)prō+\ *n, pl* **prochorions** *or* **prochoria** [NL, fr. ¹*pro-* + *chorion*] **:** any of several structures surrounding the blastodermic vesicle in some animals (as rodents); *esp* **:** a gelatinous coat that is prob. a secretion of the uterine glands — **pro·chorionic** \(¦)prō+\ *adj*

pro·chromosome \(ˈ)prō+\ *n* [ISV ¹*pro-* + *chromosome*] **:** a condensed heterochromatic portion of a chromosome visible in the resting nucleus

prochro·nism \ˈprōkrəˌnizəm, ˈpräk-\ *n* -S [Gk *prochronos* anticipatory (fr. *pro-* ¹pro- + *chronos* time) + E *-ism*] **:** an anachronism marked by the assignment of something (as an event) to a date earlier than the actual historical one

proci·den·tia \ˌprōsəˈdench(ē)ə, ˌpräs-\ *n* -S [L, fr. *procident-, procidens* (pres. part. of *procidere* to fall forward, fall down, fr. *pro-* forward, down + *-cidere,* fr. *cadere* to fall) + *-ia* -y — more at PRO-, CHANCE] **:** prolapse of an organ; *esp* **:** severe prolapse of the uterus in which the cervix projects from the vaginal opening

¹**procinct** *n* [ME *procincte,* fr. ML *procinctum,* alter. of *praecinctum* — more at PRECINCT] *obs* **:** PRECINCT

²**procinct** *n* [L *procinctus,* fr. *pro-* before, in front + *cinctus,* past part. of *cingere* to gird — more at PRO-, CINCTURE] *obs* **:** READINESS ⟨war he perceived, war in ~ —John Milton⟩

pro·ci·on dye \ˈprōsēən\ *n* [fr. *Procion,* a trademark] **:** any of several fiber-reactive dyes — see DYE table I

prock \ˈpräk\ *n* -S [origin unknown] **:** GYASCUTUS

¹**pro·claim** \prōˈklām, -rəˈk-\ *vb* -ED/-ING/-S [ME *proclamen, proclaimen,* fr. MF or L; MF *proclamer,* fr. L *proclamare,* fr. *pro-* before + *clamare* to cry out, call — more at PRO-, CLAIM] *vt* **1 a** (1) **:** to declare openly or publicly **:** make widely known through speech or writing **:** ANNOUNCE ⟨the newspaper ~*ed* its adherence to the government's policy⟩ ⟨~*ed* that he would be a candidate⟩ (2) **:** to assert openly or publicly and with conviction ⟨in ringing words . . . ~*ed* the . . . right of the opposition to voice its protests —A.C.Cole⟩ **b :** to give an unmistakable indication of **:** clearly reveal **:** SHOW ⟨all these things ~ the actor in him —James Hanley⟩ **c :** to make clearly evident **:** demonstrate undeniably **:** PROVE — usu. used with a complement ⟨such conduct ~*s* him a fool⟩ **2 a :** to declare solemnly, officially, or formally ⟨~*ed* an amnesty —*Collier's Yr. Bk.*⟩ ⟨~*ed* a state of war⟩ **b :** to declare to be by solemn, official, or formal announcement ⟨is ~*ed* the panacea for many of the ills of life —E.J.Banfield⟩ ⟨~*ed* the country a republic⟩ **3 a** *archaic* **:** DENOUNCE **b** *archaic* **:** to place (as a district) under some legal restriction by official decree **4 :** to bring (banns of marriage) to public notice **:** PUBLISH **5 :** to recognize officially and publicly; *specif* **:** to recognize the accession of ⟨was going to help ~ a queen of Britain —John Strachey⟩ **6 :** to praise or glorify openly or publicly **:** EXTOL ⟨loudly ~*ing* their master —*Times Lit. Supp.*⟩ ⟨had loudly ~*ed* the quality of his wife —Compton Mackenzie⟩ **~** *vi* **:** to make a proclamation **syn** see DECLARE

²**proclaim** \"\ *n, archaic* **:** the action of calling out ⟨voices of soft ~ —John Keats⟩

pro·claim·er \-mə(r)\ *n* -S **:** one that proclaims

proc·la·ma·tion \ˌprälkləˈmāshən\ *n* -S [ME *proclamacioun,* fr. MF *proclamation,* fr. L *proclamation-, proclamatio,* fr. *proclamatus* (past part. of *proclamare* to proclaim) + *-ion-, -io* -ion — more at PROCLAIM] **1 a :** the action of proclaiming ⟨laid down as a policy by ~ —Oscar Handlin⟩ **b :** the condition of being proclaimed ⟨becomes legal upon ~ —W.S.Sayre⟩ **2 :** something proclaimed; *specif* **:** an official formal public announcement (as a public notice, edict, decree) ⟨issued a ~ announcing the cessation of war —*Amer. Guide Series: N.C.*⟩

proclamation piece *n* **:** a medal or coin issued at the same time as a proclamation (as at the accession of a ruler)

pro·clam·a·to·ry \prōˈklaməˌtōrē\ *adj* [L *proclamatus* + E *-ory*] **:** of or relating to proclamation or a proclamation **:** proclaiming or like that of one proclaiming ⟨a ~ style of speaking⟩

pro·climax \(ˈ)prō+\ *n* [¹*pro-* + *climax*] **:** an ecological community that suggests a climax in stability and permanence but is not primarily the product of climate — compare CLIMATIC CLIMAX

proc·li·nate \ˈprälkləˌnāt\ *adj* [L *proclinatus,* past part. of *proclinare* to bend forward, fr. *pro-* forward + *clinare* to bend, incline — more at PRO-, LEAN] **:** directed forward ⟨an insect with ~ ocellar bristles⟩

procli·sis \ˈprōkləsə̇s, ˈpräk-\ *n, pl* **procli·ses** \-ləˌsēz\ [NL, fr. ¹*pro-* + LL *-clisis* (as in *enclisis*) — more at ENCLISIS] **:** pronunciation as a proclitic **:** combination in pronunciation of an unaccented word or particle with a following accented word

¹**pro·clit·ic** \(ˈ)prō¦klid·¦ik, -lit¦, ¦ēk\ *adj* [NL *procliticus,* fr. ¹*pro-* + LL *-cliticus* (as in *encliticus* enclitic) — more at ENCLITIC] **:** of, relating to, or constituting a word or particle without sentence stress that is accentually dependent upon the immediately following stressed word and is pronounced with it as a phonetic unit — compare ENCLITIC — **proclitically** *adv*

²**proclitic** \"\ *n* -S **:** a proclitic word or particle

proclive *adj* [L *proclivis,* lit., sloping, fr. *pro-* forward, down + *-clivis* (fr. *clivus* slope, hill) — more at PRO-, DECLIVITY] *obs* **:** inclined toward something by disposition or circumstances

pro·cliv·i·ty \prōˈklivəd·ē, -rəˈk-, -vətē, -i\ *n* -ES [L *proclivitas,* fr. *proclivis* + *-itas* -ity] **:** an inclination or predisposition toward something ⟨must not be forced into social activities for which they have no ~ —Philip Toynbee⟩; *esp* **:** a strong inherent inclination or predisposition toward something objectionable that is difficult to control and that arises from a natural tendency in that direction and esp. from particular characteristics of constitution or temperament or from frequent or habitual experience with or indulgence in the thing indicated ⟨man's ~ for violence —H.N.Maclean⟩ **syn** see LEANING

pro·cnemial \(ˈ)prō+\ *adj* [¹*pro-* + *cnemial*] **:** of, relating to, or formed on the ventral surface of the tibia

pro·coe·la \prōˈsēlə\ *n pl, cap* [NL, fr. ¹*pro-* + *-coela,* neut. pl. of *-coelus* -coelous] **:** a suborder of Salientia that includes Bufonidae, Hylidae, and some families of extinct amphibians and that comprises frogs and toads with vertebrae uniformly concave in front and with sacral vertebrae united with the urostyle by a double condyle

¹**pro·coe·lia** \-lēə\ *n* -S [NL, fr. ¹*pro-* + Gk *koilia* bodily cavity — more at COELIAC] **:** LATERAL VENTRICLE

²**procoelia** \"\ *n pl, cap* [NL, fr. ¹*pro-* + Gk *koilia*] *in some classifications* **:** a division of Loricata that includes recent forms and some late fossils with dorsal vertebrae mostly concave in front

¹**pro·coe·li·an** \(ˈ)=¦=lēən\ *adj* [NL ¹*procoelia* + E *-an*] **1 :** PROCOELOUS **2** [NL ²*Procoelia* + E *-an*] **:** of or relating to the Procoelia

²**procoelian** \"\ *n* -S **:** an animal of the division Procoelia

pro·coe·lous \(ˈ)prō¦sēləs\ *adj* [ISV ¹*pro-* + *-coelous*] **1** *of a vertebra* **:** concave at the anterior end of the centrum and usu. convex at the posterior end of the centrum **2 :** having procoelous vertebrae

pro con·fes·so \¦prōkənˈfe(ˌ)sō\ *adv (or adj)* [L, as (if) confessed] *law* **:** in the category of what may be considered as true, factual, or valid by reason of not having been denied or rejected ⟨the matter was taken *pro confesso* since the defendant did not file an answer⟩ **:** as though admitted **:** as though confessed **:** on the basis of what is implicitly admitted or confessed ⟨the individual defendant was directed to appear and answer the complaint or suffer judgment to be taken *pro confesso* —*Corporation Jour.*⟩

¹**pro·consul** \(ˈ)prō+\ *n* -S [ME, fr. L, fr. the phrase *pro consule* (acting) for a consul, fr. *pro* for + *consule,* abl. of *consul* — more at FOR, CONSUL] **1 :** an official in an ancient Roman province who was entrusted with most of the authority of a consul and who acted as governor or military commander in the province **2 :** an official in a modern colony, dependency, or occupied area who acts as an administrator usu. with extensive powers

²**proconsul** \"\ *n* [NL, fr. L *pro-* ¹pro- + *Consul,* a chimpanzee in the London zoo] **1** *cap* **:** a genus of extinct primitive African Miocene anthropoid apes related to those of the genus *Dryopithecus* **2** -S **:** an ape of the genus *Proconsul*

pro·consular \"+\ *adj* [L *proconsularis*, fr. *proconsul* + *-aris* -ar] **1** : of, relating to, or typical of a proconsul ⟨~ powers⟩ ⟨~ administration⟩ ⟨has that reserved ~ look —*Time*⟩ **2** : governed, administered, or commanded by a proconsul ⟨a ~ province⟩

pro·consulate \"+\ *n* [L *proconsulatus*, fr. *proconsul* + *-atus* -ate] **1 a** : the office or position of a proconsul **b** : the term of office of a proconsul **2** : the district governed or administered by a proconsul

pro·consulship \"+\ *n* : PROCONSULATE 1

pro·cras·ti·nate \prō'krastə,nāt, prə'k-, -raas-, *usu* -ād·+V\ *vb* -ED/-ING/-S [L *procrastinatus*, past part. of *procrastinare*, fr. *pro-* forward + *-crastinare* (fr. *crastinus* of tomorrow, fr. *cras* tomorrow) — more at PRO-] *vt* : to put off intentionally and usu. habitually and for a reason held to be reprehensible (as laziness, indifference to responsibility) : POSTPONE, DEFER ⟨*procrastinated* his return on various pretexts —W.H.Prescott⟩ ⟨a *procrastinated* attack⟩ ~ *vi* : to put off intentionally and usu. habitually and reprehensibly the doing of something that should be done : delay attending to something until some later time : be slow or late in doing or attending to things ⟨one yawns, one ~*s*, one can do it when one will, and therefore one seldom does it at all —Earl of Chesterfield⟩ **syn** see DELAY

procrastinating *adj* : given to, inclined toward, or marked by procrastination ⟨a most annoyingly ~ individual⟩ — **pro·cras·ti·nat·ing·ly** *adv*

pro·cras·ti·na·tion \=,==ˈnāshən\ *n* -S [L *procrastination-*, *procrastinatio*, fr. *procrastinatus* + *-ion-*, *-io* -ion] : the action, habit, or characteristic of procrastinating ⟨was infuriated by their constant ~⟩

pro·cras·ti·na·tive \=ˈ==,nād·|iv, -āt|, |ēv *also* |əv\ *adj* : PROCRASTINATING — **pro·cras·ti·na·tive·ly** \|əvlē, -li\ *adv*

pro·cras·ti·na·tor \|ə(r)\ *n* -S : one that procrastinates

pro·cras·ti·na·to·ry \-_nə,tōrē\ *adj* : PROCRASTINATING

1**pro·cre·ant** \ˈprōkrēənt\ *adj* [L *procreant-*, *procreans*, pres. part. of *procreare* to procreate] : PROCREATIVE ⟨the ~ urge of the world —Walt Whitman⟩

2**procreant** \"\ *n* -S *obs* : PROCREATOR

pro·cre·ate \-ē,āt, *usu* -ād·+V\ *vb* -ED/-ING/-S [L *procreatus*, past part. of *procreare*, fr. *pro-* forward, forth + *creare* to create — more at PRO-, CREATE] *vt* **1** : to produce (offspring) by generation : BEGET, PROPAGATE, GENERATE, REPRODUCE ⟨*procreating* their kind⟩ **2** : to give rise to : ORIGINATE, OCCASION ⟨*procreating* one rumor after another⟩ ~ *vi* : to produce offspring

pro·cre·ation \,==ˈāshən\ *n* [ME *procreacioun*, fr. MF *procreation*, fr. L *procreation-*, *procreatio*, fr. *procreatus* + *-ion-*, *-io* -ion] : the action of procreating or condition of being procreated ⟨with animals we share eating, sleeping, ~ —A.A. Hill⟩

pro·cre·ation·al \¦==¦āshən°l, -shnəl\ *adj* : PROCREATIVE

pro·cre·ative \ˈ==,ād·|iv, -,at|, |ēv *also* |əv\ *adj* **1** : that procreates or is capable of procreating : GENERATIVE ⟨a remarkably ~ people⟩ **2** : of, relating to, or directed toward procreation ⟨the ~ process⟩ ⟨~ instincts⟩ — **pro·cre·ative·ness** \|ivnəs, |ēv- *also* |əv-\ *n*

pro·cre·ator \|ə(r)\ *n* [L, fr. *procreatus*, past part. of *procreare* to procreate + *-or* — more at PROCREATE] : one that procreates

1**pro·crus·te·an** \prōˈkrəstēən\ *adj*, *often cap* [*Procrustes* (fr. L, fr. Gk *Prokroustēs*), legendary robber of ancient Greece who forced his victims to fit a certain bed by stretching or lopping off their legs + E *-an*] **1** : of, relating to, or typical of Procrustes ⟨the ~ legend⟩ ⟨*Procrustean* reasoning —Nathaniel Peffer⟩ ⟨~ determination to make the evidence fit the theory —Walter Lippmann⟩ **2** : that is marked by complete disregard of individual differences or special circumstances and that arbitrarily often ruthlessly or violently forces into conformity with or subservience to something (as a system, policy, doctrine) ⟨~ methods⟩ ⟨~ techniques⟩ ⟨~ legislation —*Wall Street Jour.*⟩

2**procrustean** \"\ *n* -S *often cap* : one that is procrustean (as in actions, methods)

procrustean bed \"-\ *or* **pro·crus·tes bed** \-(,)stēz-\ *n*, *often cap P* : something (as a system, policy, doctrine) into conformity with which or subservience to which someone or something is arbitrarily and often ruthlessly or violently forced ⟨a *Procrustean bed* wherein the unsuspecting student would be cut or stretched to a preconceived pattern —Benjamin Fine⟩ ⟨might be broken by the implacable *procrustes bed* of government machinery —John Gunther⟩

pro·cryp·sis \prōˈkripsəs\ *n* -ES [NL, fr. E *procryptic*, after E *cryptic*: Gk *krypsis* act of hiding, concealment (fr. *kryptein* to hide + *-sis*) — more at CRYPT] : a pattern or shade of coloring in insects that is adapted to concealing the insects from their natural enemies : protective coloration in insects

pro·cryptic \prō+\ *adj* [*pro-* (as in *protect*) + *cryptic*] : of, relating to, or marked by procrypsis ⟨~ coloration⟩ ⟨a ~ beetle⟩ — compare APOSEMATIC

proct- *or* **procto-** *also* **procti-** *comb form* [NL, fr. Gk *prōkt-*, *prōkto-*, fr. *prōktos*; perh. akin to Arm *erastank'* buttocks] **1** : anus ⟨*proct*iger⟩ **2** : rectum ⟨*proct*algia⟩ : rectum and ⟨*proto*sigmoidectomy⟩ **3** : anus and rectum ⟨*procto*logy⟩

1**-proc·ta** \ˈpräktə\ *n pl comb form* [NL, fr. Gk *prōktos*] : animals having a (specified) type of anus — in names of higher taxa ⟨Ento*procta*⟩ ⟨Ecto*procta*⟩

2**-procta** \"\ *n comb form* [NL, fr. Gk *prōktos*] : animal having a (specified) type of anus or buttocks — in generic names of animals ⟨Dasy*procta*⟩

proc·tal \ˈpräkt°l\ *adj* [*proct-* + *-al*] : situated immediately in front of the cloaca ⟨a fish with a ~ pelvic fin⟩

proct·algia \präkˈtalj(ē)ə\ *n* -S [NL, fr. *proct-* + *-algia*] : rectal pain

proc·ti·ger \ˈpräktəjə(r)\ *n* -S [NL, fr. *proct-* + *-ger* -gerous] : the conical reduced terminal abdominal segment of an insect in which the anus is located

proc·ti·tis \präkˈtīd·əs\ *n* -ES [NL, fr. *proct-* + *-itis*] : inflammation of the anus and rectum

proc·to·clysis \¦präktə+\ *n*, *pl* **proctoclyses** [NL, fr. *proct-* + *clysis*] : slow injection of large quantities of a fluid (as a solution of salt) into the rectum in supplementing the liquid intake of the body

proc·to·dae·al *or* **proc·to·de·al** \¦präktə¦dēəl\ *adj* [NL *proctodae*um, *proctode*um + E *-al*] : of, relating to, or connected with the proctodaeum

proc·to·dae·um *or* **proc·to·de·um** \,==ˈdēəm\ *n*, *pl* **proctodaea** \-ēə\ *or* **proctodae·ums** \-ēəmz\ *or* **procto·dea** *or* **proctode·ums** [NL, fr. *proct-* + *-odaeum*, *-odeum* (fr. Gk *hodaios* on the way, fr. *hodos* way) — more at CEDE] : the posterior ectodermal part of the alimentary canal formed in the embryo by invagination of the outer body wall — compare MESENTERON, STOMODAEUM

proc·to·log·ic \¦präktə¦läjik\ *or* **proc·to·log·i·cal** \-jəkəl\ *adj* : of or relating to proctology ⟨a ~ disorder⟩

proc·tol·o·gist \präkˈtäləjəst\ *n* -S : a specialist in proctology

proc·tol·o·gy \-jē\ *n* -ES [*proct-* + *-logy*] : a branch of medicine dealing with the structure and diseases of the anus, rectum, and sigmoid colon

proc·to·phyl·lod·i·dae \,präk(,)tōfəˈlädə,dē\ *n pl*, *cap* [NL, fr. *Proctophyllodes*, type genus (fr. *proct-* + Gk *phyllōdēs* resembling a leaf, fr. *phyll-* + *-ōdēs* -ode) + *-idae*] : a widely distributed family of feather mites

1**proc·tor** \ˈpräktə(r)\ *n* -S [ME *proctour*, *procutour* procurator, proctor, alter. of *procuratour* — more at PROCURATOR] **1** : one that by profession or by special authorization manages another's affairs or conducts proceedings for another in a court of civil or canon law : an attorney acting in a court of civil or canon law **2 a** : one of two officers in a British university who discharge various functions and who are esp. entrusted with the maintenance of order and the enforcement of obedience to the laws of the institution **b** : one that supervises, guides, or advises : SUPERVISOR, MONITOR; *specif* : an officer or student (as in a college or university) appointed to supervise students (as at an examination and in the dormitories) or to check on attendance or perform some similar duty **3** : an elected representative of the clergy at a convocation in the Church of England **4** : a collector of tithes or other ecclesiastical dues for another

2**proctor** \"\ *vb* -ED/-ING/-S : SUPERVISE, MONITOR

3**proctor** \"\ *adj*, *usu cap* [after Ralph R. *Proctor* †1962 Amer. civil engineer] : of, relating to, or determined by a procedure designed to sample and test soil to be used in fills and embankments ⟨the *Proctor* method . . . of determining the moisture content —*Military Engineer*⟩ ⟨the *Proctor* density of soil⟩

proc·to·ri·al \(ˈ)präk¦tōrēəl\ *adj* : of or relating to a proctor ⟨in defiance of ~ regulations —Max Beerbohm⟩ — **proc·to·ri·al·ly** \-əlē\ *adv*

proc·tor·iza·tion \,präktərəˈzāshən, -,rīˈz-\ *n* -S **1** *archaic* : the action of exercising proctorial authority or of serving as a proctor **2** *archaic* : the condition of being subjected to proctorial authority

proc·tor·ize \ˈ==,rīz\ *vb* -ED/-ING/-S *see -ize in Explan Notes* [1*proctor* + *-ize*] *vt*, *archaic* : to subject to proctorial authority (as by reprimanding, disciplining) ~ *vi*, *archaic* : to serve in the position of a proctor

proc·tor·ship \ˈpräktə(r),ship\ *n* : the office or function of a proctor

1**proc·to·scope** \ˈpräktə,skōp\ *n* [ISV *proct-* + *-scope*] : an instrument used for dilating and visually inspecting the rectum

2**proctoscope** \"\ *vt* -ED/-ING/-S : to use a proctoscope on

proc·to·scop·ic \¦==¦skäpik\ *adj* : of or relating to a proctoscope or proctoscopy — **proc·to·scop·i·cal·ly** \-pək(ə)lē\ *adv*

proc·tos·co·py \präkˈtäskəpē\ *n* -ES [ISV *proct-* + *-scopy*] : dilation and visual inspection of the rectum

proc·to·sigmoidectomy \,präk(,)tō+\ *n* -ES [*proct-* + *sigmoid* (n.) + *-ectomy*] : complete or partial surgical excision of the rectum and sigmoid colon

proc·to·sigmoidoscope \"+\ *n* [*proct-* + *sigmoid* + *-o-* + *-scope*] : SIGMOIDOSCOPE — **proc·to·sig·moi·do·scop·ic** \,präk(,)tō,sig¦mȯidə¦skäpik\ *adj* — **proc·to·sigmoidoscopy** \,präk(,)tō+\ *n*

proc·to·tru·pid \¦präktə·¦trüpəd\ *or* **proc·to·tryp·id** \-·¦trip-\ *adj or n* [NL *Proctotrupidae*, *Proctotrypidae*] : SERPHID

proc·to·tru·pi·dae *or* **proc·to·tryp·i·dae** \,==ˈ=pə,dē\ [*Proctotrupidae*, NL, fr. *Proctotrupes*, type genus (fr. *proct-* + *-trupes*, irreg. fr. Gk *trypan* to bore through, pierce) + *-idae*; *Proctotrypidae*, NL, fr. *Proctotypes*, type genus (syn. of *Proctotrupes*; alter. of *Proctotrupes*) + *-idae* — more at TRYPAN-] *syn of* SERPHIDAE

proc·to·tru·poid *or* **proc·to·tryp·oid** \¦==¦=,pȯid\ *adj or n* [NL *Proctotrupoidea*, *Proctotrypoidea*] : SERPHOID

proc·to·tru·poi·dea \,==·(,)trüˈpȯidēə\ *or* **proc·to·try·poi·dea** \-·_trəˈp-\ [NL, fr. *Proctotrupes* or *Proctotrypes* + *-oidea*] *syn of* SERPHOIDEA

-proc·tous \¦präktəs\ *adj comb form* [*proct-* + *-ous*] : of, relating to, or having a (specified) type of anus ⟨ento*proctous*⟩

-proc·tus \ˈpräktəs\ *n comb form* [NL, fr. Gk *prōktos* anus — more at PROCT-] : animal having a (specified) type of anus — in generic names ⟨Mastigo*proctus*⟩

pro·cum·bent \(ˈ)prō¦kəmbənt\ *adj* [L *procumbent-*, *procumbens*, pres. part. of *procumbere* to fall, bend, or lean forward, fr. *pro-* forward, down + *-cumbere* to lie down — more at PRO-, INCUMBENT] **1 a** : being or having stems that trail along the ground without putting forth roots ⟨a ~ plant⟩ ⟨~ stems⟩ **b** : having the longest axis radial ⟨~ cells in a vascular ray⟩ **2 a** : lying stretched out : RECUMBENT ⟨the sight of this gleaming city in a lazy blue haze, ~ by the Tiber —Francis Hackett⟩ **b** : lying face down : PRONE, PROSTRATE ⟨~ slaves⟩ **3** : slanting forward ⟨the ~ incisor teeth of a horse⟩

pro·cur·abil·i·ty \prə,kyu̇rəˈbiləd·ē, prō,k-, -lətē, -i\ *n* : the quality or state of being procurable

pro·cur·able \=ˈ==_bəl\ *adj* : capable of being procured

proc·u·ra·cy \ˈpräkyərəsē\ *n* -ES [ME *procuracie*, fr. AF, fr. ML *procuratia*, alter. of L *procuratio* procuration — more at PROCURATION] **1** *archaic* : the office or functions of a proctor or procurator **2** *archaic* : management or direction of affairs for another

pro·cur·al \prəˈkyu̇rəl, prōˈk-\ *n* -S [*procure* + *-al*] : PROCUREMENT; *esp* : the action of acquiring something ⟨the ~ of new books for the library⟩

pro·cur·ance \-rən(t)s, ˈpräkyər-\ *n* -S : PROCUREMENT; *esp* : the action of furthering or bringing about the achievement of something (as by one's intervention or influence)

proc·u·ra·tion \,präkyəˈrāshən\ *n* -S [ME *procuracioun*, fr. MF *procuration*, fr. L *procuration-*, *procuratio*, fr. *procuratus* (past part. of *procurare* to take care of) + *-ion-*, *-io* -ion — more at PROCURE] **1** *archaic* : management or direction of affairs for another **2 a** : POWER OF ATTORNEY **b** (1) : the action of appointing someone as one's agent or attorney (2) : the authorized action or function of one appointed as an agent or attorney **c** : the authority proper to one appointed as an agent or attorney **d** : MANDATE 2c **3** : a particular quota of provisions or a fixed sum of money given by parochial churches of the Church of England to a bishop or archdeacon at the time of his visitation **4 a** : PROCUREMENT; *esp* : the action of obtaining something **b** (1) : the action of obtaining a loan for a client or of executing a bond for a client (2) *or* **procuration fee** *or* **procuration money** : a sum of money paid (as to a broker) by a client for a loan obtained or bond executed **c** : the act of pimping

pro·cur·a·tive \prəˈkyu̇rəd·iv, prōˈk-\ *adj* [*procure* + *-ative*] *archaic* : that procures or tends to procure

proc·u·ra·tor \ˈpräkyə,rād·ə(r), -ātə-\ *n* -S [ME *procuratour*, fr. OF, fr. L *procurator*, fr. *procuratus* (past part. of *procurare* to take care of) + *-or* — more at PROCURE] **1** : one that manages the affairs of another esp. by acting as the agent, deputy, proxy, or representative of the other: as **a** : one of several imperial officers of the ancient Roman empire entrusted with the management of the financial affairs of a province and often having administrative powers in a province as agents of the emperor **b** : PROCTOR 1 **c** : one that has power of attorney **d** [ML, fr. L] (1) : one of two or more representative officers in a medieval university having financial, electoral, and disciplinary functions (2) : one of several student representatives in some Scottish universities chosen to preside over the election of a rector **2 a** : one of several public magistrates or administrators (as in Italy) with varying functions **b** : PUBLIC PROSECUTOR: as (1) : PROCURATOR FISCAL (2) : PROCUREUR 2 **3** : one that obtains or gets something esp. regularly or in an official capacity; *esp* : one of a group of individuals living a common life together (as in a monastic community) who is appointed to buy supplies for the group

proc·u·ra·tor·ate \-ərət\ *n* -S : the office or functions of a procurator

procurator fiscal *or* **procurator of the fisk** *n* : the public prosecutor of a local district (as a shire) in Scotland

procurator–general \¦==,==¦=(=)=\ *n*, *pl* **procurators–general** *or* **procurator–generals** : a procurator of high rank

proc·u·ra·to·ri·al \¦präkyərə¦tōrēəl\ *adj* [LL *procuratori*us procuratorial (fr. L *procurator*) + E *-al*] **1** : of or relating to a procurator **2** : PROCTORIAL

proc·u·ra·tor·ship \ˈprakyə,rād·ə(r),ship, -ātə-\ *n* : the office or function of a procurator

proc·u·ra·to·ry \-_rə,tōrē\ *n* -ES [LL *procuratorius*] **1** *civil law* : authorization of one individual to act for another **2** : POWER OF ATTORNEY

proc·u·ra·trix \¦präkyə¦ra·triks\ *n* -ES [L, fem. of *procurator*] : a female procurator

pro·cure \prəˈkyu̇(ə)r, prōˈk-, -u̇ə\ *vb* -ED/-ING/-S [ME *procuren* to take care of, bring about, obtain, fr. LL & L; LL *procurare* to obtain, fr. L, to take care of, fr. *pro-* for, on behalf of + *curare* to take care of — more at PRO-, CURE] *vt* **1 a** (1) : to get possession of : OBTAIN, ACQUIRE ⟨*procuring* extra equipment and supplies —H.G.Armstrong⟩; *esp* : to get possession of by particular care or effort ⟨it fell to my lot . . . to scurry around and ~ manuscripts —A.W.Long⟩ and sometimes by devious means ⟨*procured* enormous wealth by such dealings⟩ (2) : GAIN, WIN ⟨the judicial qualities he developed . . . *procured* for him universal confidence and respect —H.W.H. Knott⟩ **b** : to get possession of (women) and make available for promiscuous sexual intercourse (as in a house of prostitution) **2 a** (1) : to cause to happen or be done : bring about : EFFECT ⟨*procured* temporary agreement⟩ : ACHIEVE ⟨failed to ~ a coherent theory —Joseph Conrad⟩; *esp* : to bring about by particular care or effort ⟨had *procured* the enactment of a more complete system of defense laws —F.L.Paxson⟩ ⟨*procuring* the release of a man in jail —Peggy Durdin⟩ and sometimes by devious means ⟨on trial for *procuring* perjury —*Time*⟩ (2) : to bring about by scheming and plotting : CONTRIVE ⟨*procured* the downfall of the government⟩ ⟨did not hesitate to ~ murder —Will Irwin & T.M.Johnson⟩ **b** *archaic* : to cause to be treated in an indicated way or to undergo something indicated ⟨intended by one who ~*s* another to be indicted —O.W.Holmes †1935⟩ **3 a** : to prevail upon to do something indicated : INDUCE ⟨*procuring* a witness to commit perjury⟩ **b** *obs* : to cause (as by persuading or alluring) to come to an indicated place : BRING ⟨what unaccustomed cause ~*s* her hither —Shak.⟩ ~ *vi* : to procure women for promiscuous sexual intercourse ⟨arrested on charges of *procuring* —Joachim Joesten⟩ **syn** see GET

pro·cure·ment \-u̇(ə)rmənt, -u̇əm-\ *n* -S [ME, fr. MF, fr. *procurer* + *-ment*] **1** : the act of procuring ⟨~ of materials and supplies⟩ ⟨~ of personnel⟩ ⟨~ of a loan⟩ **2** : the condition of being procured ⟨knew about the ~ of the books⟩

procurement clerk *n* **1** : a clerk who edits purchase requests, invites bids from suppliers, and makes out orders for procurement of materials by an organization — called also *award clerk* **2** : PURCHASING AGENT 1

pro·cur·er \-u̇rə(r)\ *n* -S [ME *procurour*, fr. MF *procureur*, fr. L *procurator* — more at PROCURATOR] **1** : one that procures; *esp* : a man who procures women for promiscuous sexual intercourse **2** *obs* : PROCUREUR

pro·cur·ess \-u̇rəs\ *n* -ES [ME *procuresse*, modif. of MF *procureresse*, fr. *procureur* + *-esse* -ess] : a female procurer

pro·cu·reur \prȯkūerœr\ *n* -S [MF] **1** : an agent or representative in a French court of law **2** : a public prosecutor in a French court of law

pro·current \(ˈ)prō+\ *adj* [L *procurrent-*, *procurrens*, pres. part. of *procurrere* to run forward, jut out, fr. *pro-* forward + *currere* to run — more at PRO-, CURRENT] *of a fish's fin* : marked by a progressively farther forward placement of rays ⟨the ~ fin of some cottids⟩

pro·curved \ˈprō+¦-\ *adj* [L *pro-* forward + E *curved* — more at PRO-] : curved forward

pro·cuticle \(ˈ)prō+\ *n* [1*pro-* + *cuticle*] : the chitinized part of the cuticle of an insect

pro·cy·on \ˈprōsē,än\ *n*, *cap* [NL, fr. *Procyon*, a star, fr. Gk *Prokyōn*] : a genus (the type of the family Procyonidae) consisting of the raccoons

pro·cy·on·i·dae \,prōsēˈänə,dē\ *n pl*, *cap* [NL, fr. *Procyon*, type genus + *-idae*] : a family of plantigrade carnivorous mammals consisting of the raccoons, coatis, cacomistles, kinkajous, and sometimes the pandas

pro·cy·on·i·for·mia \,==,änəˈfȯ(r)mēə\ *n pl*, *cap* [NL, fr. *Procyon* + L *-iformia*, neut. pl. of *-iformis* -iform] *in former classifications* : a subdivision of Arctoidea coextensive with Procyonidae

1**prod** \ˈpräd\ *vb* **prodded**; **prodded**; **prodding**; **prods** [origin unknown] *vt* **1 a** : to thrust a pointed instrument into : prick with something sharp or blunted ⟨the animals were . . . ruthlessly *prodded* —V.G.Heiser⟩ **b** : to incite to action or thought : jog lightly : stir up : JOSTLE, NUDGE ⟨discretion and good judgment can be cultivated and *prodded* —*Saturday Rev.*⟩ ⟨the student was . . . *prodded* to master something —W.H. White⟩ **2** : to poke about or stir as if with a prod ⟨refilling his pipe . . . he *prodded* the bowl with his thumb —Ellen Glasgow⟩ ⟨a fine cock rail . . . stopping to ~ the mud —D.C. Peattie⟩ ~ *vi* : to go poking — usu. used with *in* or *at* ⟨it is not the facts . . . which drive and ~ at my imagination —Marcia Davenport⟩ **syn** see URGE

2**prod** \"\ *n* -S **1** : a pointed instrument used to impel, move, poke, stir, or make an electrical contact **2** : an incitement to act : a sharp reminder : THRUST ⟨under the ~ of skepticism, there have been refinements in technique —Roland Walker⟩ ⟨a ~ on the subject of church attendance —Compton Mackenzie⟩ — **on the prod** *chiefly West* : in an irritable mood and ready to fight ⟨this man was *on the prod* . . . and as dangerous as a cornered cougar —P.E.Lehman⟩

3**prod** \"\ *var of* PRAD

prod *abbr* **1** produce; producer; produced **2** product; production

prod·der \-də(r)\ *n* -S : one that prods

prod·dle \ˈpräd°l\ *vb* -ED/-ING/-S [freq. of 1*prod*] *dial Eng* : POTTER, FUMBLE, POKE

prod·e·li·sion \,präd°lˈizhən\ *n* -S [L *prod-* (var. of *pro-* before) + E *elision* — more at PRO-] : elision of the initial vowel of a word ⟨Latin *bonum'st* for *bonum est* is an example of ~⟩

pro·del·phic \(ˈ)prō¦delfik\ *also* **pro·del·phous** \-fəs\ *adj* [1*pro-* + Gk *delphys* womb + E *-ic* or *-ous* — more at DOLPHIN] *of a nematode worm* : having the uteri parallel and anteriorly directed

pro·democratic \(¦)prō+\ *adj* [2*pro-* + *democratic*] : favoring democracy ⟨acute difficulties experienced by the ~ parties in trying to achieve governing majorities —W.R.Sharp⟩

pro·de·nia \prōˈdēnēə\ *n*, *cap* [NL] : a common and widespread genus of moths (family Noctuidae) whose larvae are destructive to a great variety of plants

pro·dentine \(ˈ)prō+\ *n* -S [1*pro-* + *dentine*] : a cap of uncalcified tissue over the tooth cusps previous to the formation of dentin

1**prod·i·gal** \ˈprädəgəl, -dēg-\ *adj* [L *prodig*us prodigal (fr. *prodigere* to drive away, squander, fr. *prod-* — var. of *pro-* forward, forth — + *-igere*, fr. *agere* to drive) + E *-al* — more at PRO-, AGENT] **1** : given to reckless extravagance : unrestrained in spending or using up one's means ⟨he had been ~ with his money —Cliff Farrell⟩ **2** : characterized by profuse or wasteful expenditure : LAVISH ⟨make as much money as the most ~ editors will give him —Harrison Smith⟩ **3** : profusely liberal : giving or yielding abundantly : LUXURIANT ⟨the lush ~ way in which the tropics announced spring —William Beebe⟩ **syn** see PROFUSE

2**prodigal** \"\ *n* -S **1 a** : one who spends or gives lavishly : one who is foolishly extravagant : SPENDTHRIFT, SQUANDERER ⟨explained what a ~ this was, what a waster —Francis Hackett⟩ **b** : a repentant wastrel **2** : one adjudged legally incompetent to manage his property or to incur debts because of a propensity to waste his capital

3**prodigal** *adv*, *obs* : PRODIGALLY ⟨when the blood burns, how ~ the soul lends the tongue vows —Shak.⟩

prod·i·gal·i·ty \,prädəˈgaləd·ē, -lətē, -i\ *n* -ES [ME *prodigalite*, fr. MF *prodigalité*, fr. LL *prodigalitat-*, *prodigalitas*, L *prodigus* prodigal + *-alis* -al + *-itat-*, *-itas* -ity — more at PRODIGAL] **1** : extravagance or an extravagant act in expenditure esp. of money : reckless spending of resources : WASTEFULNESS ⟨his ~ became a legend⟩ **2** : profuse liberality : lavish supply : excessive abundance ⟨a sound understanding of the earth's ~ —J.R.Caceres⟩ ⟨our truly wonderful ~ of talent —J.A. Michener⟩

prod·i·gal·ize \ˈprädəgə,līz\ *vt* -ED/-ING/-S : to expend extravagantly

prod·i·gal·ly \-gəlē\ *adv* : in a prodigal manner : EXTRAVAGANTLY ⟨we are still ~ rich in natural beauty —S.P.B.Mais⟩

prodigal son *n* [after the *Prodigal Son* of the Biblical parable (Luke 15:11–32), who squandered his father's money] **1** : PRODIGAL 1b **2** : either of two marine food fishes: **a** : COBIA **b** : RAINBOW RUNNER

pro·dig·i·o·sin \prō,dijēˈōs°n\ *n* -S [NL *prodigiosus* (specific epithet of *Bacillus prodigiosus*, syn. of *Serratia marcescens*) (fr. L *prodigiosus* prodigious) + E *-in*] : a red antibiotic pigment $C_{20}H_{25}N_3O$ that is produced by a bacterium (*Serratia marcescens*), has shown activity on an experimental basis against protozoans (as the parasite of amebic dysentery) and against fungi (as the parasite of coccidioidomycosis), and is a derivative of tri-pyrryl-methane

pro·di·gious \prəˈdijəs, prōˈ-\ *adj* [L *prodigiosus*, fr. *prodigium* omen, portent, monster + *-osus* -ous — more at PRODIGY] **1 a** *obs* : having the nature of an omen : PORTENTOUS ⟨never mole, harelip, nor scar, nor mark ~ . . . shall upon their children be —Shak.⟩ **b** *archaic* : having the appearance of a prodigy : ABNORMAL, STRANGE **2** : exciting amazement or wonder : causing one to marvel : AMAZING ⟨from childhood precocious and ~ in everything —Willa Cather⟩ ⟨a ~ vision —Christopher Rand⟩ **3** : extraordinary in bulk, extent, quantity, or degree : ENORMOUS, IMMENSE, VAST ⟨a ~ noise of wheels —Elinor Wylie⟩ ⟨have done a ~ amount of work —John Sparkman⟩ ⟨the amount of food provided at a party of this kind was ~ —W.S.Maugham⟩ **syn** see MONSTROUS

pro·di·gious·ly *adv* : in a prodigious manner : AMAZINGLY, EXTREMELY ⟨beef cattle were much in evidence . . . black and shiny, and ~ broad and fat —Christopher Rand⟩ ⟨a ~ wealthy nation —G.B.Shaw⟩

pro·di·gious·ness *n* -ES **:** the quality or state of being prodigious

prod·i·gus \'prädəgəs\ *n* -ES [L, fr. *prodigus*, adj., prodigal — more at PRODIGAL] *Roman law* **:** PRODIGAL 2

prod·i·gy \'prädəjē, -ji\ *n* -ES [L *prodigium* omen, portent, monster, fr. *prod-* (var. of *pro-* before) + *-igium* (akin to *aio* I say) — more at PRO-, ADAGE] **1 a** *archaic* **:** something out of the usual course of nature (as an eclipse or meteor) that is a portent **:** OMEN, SIGN **b :** something extraordinary or inexplicable **:** one that is abnormal or monstrous ⟨the name of the ~ was the "Ferris wheel" and thousands were scrambling to get a ride —John Kobler⟩ **2 :** one that excites admiration or wonder: as **a :** an extraordinary, marvelous, or unusual accomplishment, deed, or instance — often used with *of* ⟨regarded as a worker of *prodigies* —T.B.Macaulay⟩ **b :** a highly gifted or academically talented child ⟨he was what is called an infant ~ —Bruce Bliven b.1889⟩ **syn** see WONDER

pro·dissoconch \(ˈ)prō+\ *n* [¹*pro-* + *dissoconch*] **:** the rudimentary or embryonic shell of a bivalve mollusk

pro·di·tion \prō'dishən\ *n* -S [ME *prodycyon*, fr. MF *prodition*, fr. L *prodition-, proditio*, fr. *proditus* (past part. of *prodere* to bring forth, report, betray, fr. *pro-* forth + *-dere*, fr. *dare* to give) + *-ion-, -io* -ion — more at PRO-, DATE] **:** BETRAYAL, TREASON

proditor *n* -S [ME *proditour*, fr. MF *proditeur*, fr. L *proditor*, fr. *proditus* + *-or*] *obs* **:** TRAITOR ⟨thou most usurping ~ and not protector of the king —Shak.⟩

prod·i·to·ri·ous \ˌprädəˌtōrēəs\ *adj* [ME, fr. L *proditus* + ME *-orious*] *archaic* **:** apt to betray secret thoughts

prod·ro·ma \'prädrəmə\ *n, pl* **prodromas** \-məz\ *or* **pro·dro·ma·ta** \prō'drōmədə\ [NL, fr. F *prodrome*] **:** PRODROME

prod·ro·mal \-məl\ *or* **pro·drom·ic** \prō'drämik\ *adj* [*prodrome* + *-al* or *-ic*] **:** PRECURSORY; *esp* **:** of, relating to, or marked by prodromes ⟨the ~ stages of a disease⟩

pro·drome \'prōˌdrōm\ *n* -S [F, precursor, prodrome, fr. Gk *prodromos* precursor, fr. *prodromos*, adj., running ahead, fr. *pro-* ¹pro- + *dromos* -drome] **:** a premonitory symptom of a disease

prod·ro·mus \'prädrəməs\ *n* -ES [NL, fr. Gk *prodromos* precursor] **1** *obs* **:** something that alerts or forewarns **2 :** a preliminary publication or introductory work

prods *pres 3d sing of* PROD, *pl of* PROD

¹**pro·duce** \prə'dyüs, prō'-\ *vb* -ED/-ING/-S [ME (Sc dial.) *producen*, fr. L *producere*, fr. *pro-* forward + *ducere* to lead — more at PRO-, TOW] *vt* **1 :** to bring forward **:** lead forth **:** offer to view or notice **:** EXHIBIT, SHOW ⟨the State Department *produced* the transcript —*New Republic*⟩ ⟨required to ~ his licence for inspection —Priscilla Hughes⟩ **2 :** to bring forth **:** give birth to **:** BEAR, GENERATE, YIELD ⟨the greatest scientist the world has *produced* —T.B.Costain⟩ ⟨the rains ~ a quick-growing and lush herbage —N.C.Wright⟩ **3 :** to extend geometrically **:** PROLONG — used of a line, surface, or solid ⟨~ the side of a triangle⟩ **4 :** to introduce to the public **:** bring out as a dramatic production ⟨five new plays which were *produced* —*Current Biog.*⟩ ⟨said she would like me to ~ her in something —Mrs. Patrick Campbell⟩ **5 :** to cause to have existence or to happen **:** bring about **:** ORIGINATE ⟨the sting . . . ~*s* violent inflammation —Richard Semon⟩ ⟨*produced* an indulgent smile —Edith Wharton⟩ **6** *obs* **:** ADVANCE, PROMOTE **7 :** to compose, create, or bring out by intellectual or physical effort ⟨*produced* a group of poems —Naomi Lewis⟩ ⟨regularly ~*s* articles and drawings —*Current Biog.*⟩ **8 a :** to give being, form, or shape to **:** make often from raw materials **:** MANUFACTURE ⟨*produced* 5,002 cars in three years —*Amer. Guide Series: Mich.*⟩ **b :** to make economically valuable **:** make or create so as to be available for satisfaction of human wants **9 :** to cause to accrue **:** bring in as profit ⟨money at interest ~*s* an income⟩ ~ *vi* **:** to bring forth a product or production **:** bear, make, or yield that which is according to nature or intention **:** grow, make, or furnish economically valuable products ⟨labored literally day and night to ~ —Vera M.Dean⟩ **syn** see BEAR

²**prod·uce** \'präˌd(y)üs, 'prō,-\ *n* -S **1 a** (1) **:** something that is brought forth or yielded either naturally or as a result of effort and work (2) **:** a result produced **:** CONSEQUENCE ⟨the ~ of . . . knowledge extends to the individual and to the community —Curt Stern⟩ **b :** the amount that is produced **:** YIELD ⟨worth about twice as much as the annual ~ of all English mines —T.B.Macaulay⟩ **2 :** agricultural products (as fresh fruits and vegetables) ⟨wagons bringing ~ . . . from farms round about —Sidney Lovett⟩ **3 :** the progeny usu. of a female animal **:** OFFSPRING — distinguished from *get* ⟨the ~ of this fine mare includes the get of several leading stallions⟩

produced *adj* **:** extended esp. in one direction **:** drawn out **:** disproportionately elongated ⟨a ~ leaf⟩ ⟨a scale ~ into spines⟩

¹**pro·du·cent** \prə'd(y)üs°nt\ *adj* [L *producent-, producens*, pres. part. of *producere* to produce — more at PRODUCE] **:** PRODUCING

²**producent** \"\ *n* -S **:** one that produces (as a witness or a document)

produce-of-dam \'=,=+'=\ *n* **1 :** the entire progeny of a dam or a representative sample **2 :** a show class for judging progenies

pro·duc·er \prə'd(y)üsə(r), prō'-\ *n* -S **1 :** one that produces, brings forth, or generates ⟨the state is rated as the largest ~ of northern partridge —*Amer. Guide Series: Mich.*⟩ **2 :** one that grows agricultural products or manufactures crude materials into articles of use — compare CONSUMER **3 :** a furnace or apparatus that produces combustible gas to be used for fuel and is usu. of the updraft type which forces or draws air or a mixture of air and steam through a layer of incandescent fuel (as coke) with the resulting gas consisting chiefly of carbon monoxide, hydrogen, and nitrogen — compare GENERATOR 2b **4 a :** one who assumes responsibility for the public presentation of a theatrical entertainment (as an opera, motion picture, or play for stage or television) as an artistic and usu. also as a financial venture — compare DIRECTOR 1c **b** *Brit* **:** DIRECTOR 1c **5 :** a well that produces ⟨the ~ is one mile east of the . . . oil pool —*Ochiltree County (Texas) Herald*⟩

produce race *n* **:** a race to be run by the produce of horses named or described at the time of entry — compare FUTURITY RACE

producer gas *n* **:** gas made in a producer, consisting chiefly of carbon monoxide, hydrogen, and nitrogen, and having an average heating value of about 150 Btu — compare MOND GAS, SYNTHESIS GAS, WATER GAS

producer goods *n pl* **:** goods (as tools and raw material) that are factors in the production of other goods and that satisfy wants only indirectly — called also *auxiliary goods, instrumental goods, intermediate goods;* compare CONSUMER GOODS

producer's surplus *also* **producer's rent** *n* **:** the payment received by a producer or seller in excess of the least sum he would have been willing to accept to make the sale — compare CONSUMER'S SURPLUS

produces *pres 3d sing of* PRODUCE, *pl of* PRODUCE

pro·duc·ibil·i·ty \prəˌd(y)üsə'bilədē\ *n* -ES **:** the character, state, or fact of being producible

pro·duc·ible \prə'd(y)üsəbəl, prō'-\ *adj* [LL *producibilis*, fr. L *producere* to produce + *-ibilis* -ible] **1 :** capable of being produced or brought forth or forward **2 :** capable of being brought about or made **:** MANUFACTURABLE **3 :** PRESENTABLE

producing *pres part of* PRODUCE

¹**prod·uct** \'prä(ˌ)dəkt *sometimes* -ˌdikt *or* -ˌdĕkt\ *n* -S [in sense 1, fr. ME, fr. ML *productum*, fr. L, something produced, fr. neut. of *productus*, past part. of *producere* to produce; in other senses, fr. L *productum* something produced — more at PRODUCE] **1 :** the number or magnitude resulting from the multiplication together of two or more numbers or magnitudes **:** the result of any kind of multiplication **2 a :** something produced by physical labor or intellectual effort **:** the result of work or thought ⟨use for hammocks and other ~*s* —P.E.James⟩ ⟨even the simplest poem is the ~ of much . . . work —Gilbert Highet⟩ **b :** a result of the operation of involuntary causes or an ensuing set of conditions **:** CONSEQUENCE, MANIFESTATION ⟨a ~ of liberal arts education —B.W. Hayward⟩ ⟨he was a ~ of his time —Allan Nevins⟩ **c :** something produced naturally or as the result of a natural process (as by generation or growth) ⟨major ~*s* from forest lands . . . are mahogany and chicle —*Americana Annual*⟩ **3 :** the amount, total, or quantity produced **:** the output of an industry or firm ⟨our national ~ . . . has quickly risen to an enormous volume —George Soule⟩ **4 :** a substance produced from one or more other substances as a result of chemical change **5 :** CONJUNCTION 7 — usu. used in the algebra of classes

²**pro·duct** \prə'dəkt\ *vt* -ED/-ING/-S [L *productus*, past part. of *producere*] **1 :** PRODUCE **2 :** to lengthen out

³**product** *n* -S [by folk etymology fr. *pratique*] *obs* **:** PRATIQUE

product engineer *n* **:** an engineer who specializes in designing, building, and testing the prototype of a fabricated product and controls subsequent changes in the construction and material of the product

pro·duct·ibil·i·ty \prəˌdəktə'bilədē\ *n* -ES [L *productus* + E *-ibility*] **:** the quality or state of being producible

pro·duc·tile \prə'dəkt°l\ *adj* [LL *productilis*, fr. L *productus* + *-ilis* -ile] **:** PRODUCIBLE

¹**pro·duc·tion** \prə'dəkshən, prō'-\ *n* -S [ME *produccioun*, fr. ML *production-, productio*, fr. L *productus* (past part. of *producere* to produce) + *-ion-, -io* -ion — more at PRODUCE] **1 a :** something that is produced naturally or as the result of labor and effort **:** PRODUCT ⟨acrid ~*s* poisonously irritant to throat, lungs —Emily Holt⟩ ⟨skillful artisans, whose choice ~*s* could secure a ready sale —H.T.Buckle⟩ **b** (1) **:** a literary or artistic work (2) **:** a theatrical representation **:** the staging or performing of a theatrical entertainment **c :** an action resembling an elaborate theatrical performance **:** one exaggerated out of all proportion to its importance ⟨taking a small child visiting . . . can be quite a ~ —Nell Dunkin⟩ ⟨have lunch and still not make a ~ of it —Richard Joseph⟩ **2 a :** the act or process of producing, bringing forth, or making ⟨chief activities . . . are maple sugar ~ and farming —*Amer. Guide Series: Pa.*⟩ ⟨lead ore was worked . . . but they ceased ~ before 1776 —T.T.Read⟩ **b :** the creation of utility **:** the making of goods available for human wants **3 :** the act of exhibiting; *esp* **:** exhibiting in a court of law ⟨the appellate court went so far as to demand ~ of the grounds for refusal —*Report: Amer. Civil Liberties Union*⟩ **4 :** a lengthening out or prolonging **:** ELONGATION, EXTENSION **5 :** the total output of a commodity

²**production** \"\ *adj* **:** designed to provide nutrients to an animal in proportion to its production (as of milk or eggs) and being in addition to those supplied to maintain bodily condition ⟨a ~ ration of two pounds of grain for each additional gallon of milk⟩

pro·duc·tion·al \-shən°l\ *adj* **:** of or relating to production

production control *n* **:** systematic planning, coordinating, and directing of all manufacturing activities and influences to insure having goods made on time, of adequate quality, and at reasonable cost

production cost *n* **:** the combined total of raw material and direct labor costs and burden incurred in production

production curve *n* **:** a curve plotted to show the relation between quantities produced during definite consecutive time intervals

production function *n* **:** the technical relationship between product output and the input of factors of production

production goods *n pl* **:** PRODUCER GOODS

pro·duc·tion·ist \-shənəst\ *n* -S **:** PRODUCER

production line *n* **:** LINE 6j

production standard *n* **:** a unit of measurement that indicates the normal level of performance for an industrial operation and that is expressible as time per unit or units per hour or day

pro·duc·tive \prə'dəktiv, prō'-, -tēv *also* -təv\ *adj* [ML *productivus*, fr. L *productus* + *-ivus* -ive] **1 :** having the quality or power of producing **:** bringing forth or able to bring forth esp. in abundance **:** CREATIVE, GENERATIVE ⟨thousands of fishermen . . . can reach some of the most ~ water —*Ford Times*⟩ ⟨more ~ ideas followed —*Phoenix Flame*⟩ **2 :** effective in bringing about **:** CAUSATIVE, ORIGINATIVE — used with *of* ⟨their knowledge and methods were enormously ~ of new weapons —J.P.Baxter b.1893⟩ ⟨investigating committees have been ~ of much good —R.K.Carr⟩ **3 :** yielding or furnishing results, benefits, or profits ⟨a ~ program of education⟩ **4 a :** effecting or contributing to effect production **b :** yielding or devoted to the satisfaction of wants or the creation of utilities **5 a :** continuing to be used in the formation of new words and constructions ⟨*un-, non-,* and *re-* are ~ prefixes⟩ **b :** of or relating to a productive word element **6 :** raising mucus or sputum (as from the bronchi) — used of a cough ⟨had slight ~ cough and chest pain —*California Medicine*⟩

productive labor *n* **:** DIRECT LABOR

pro·duc·tive·ly \-təvlē, -li\ *adv* **:** in a productive manner ⟨free to think ~ —D.H.Jenkins⟩

pro·duc·tive·ness \-tivnəs, -tev- *also* -təv-\ *n* -ES **:** the quality or state of being productive ⟨the prodigious ~ of great workers —C.W.Eliot⟩

pro·duc·tiv·i·ty \ˌprōˌdək'tivədē, ˌprä,-, -vətē, -i *also* prəˌ- *or* prōˌ- *sometimes* ˌpräd-\ *n* -ES **:** the ability or capacity to produce **:** PRODUCTIVENESS: as **a :** abundance or richness in output ⟨the remarkable ~ of novelists —E.A.Bloom⟩ **b :** the physical output per unit of productive effort **c :** the ability of land to produce a given yield of a particular crop **d :** the degree of effectiveness of industrial management in utilizing the facilities for production; *esp* **:** the effectiveness in utilizing labor and equipment

product line *n* **1 :** all goods made by a manufacturing firm **2 :** a group of closely related commodities made by the same process and for the same purpose and differing only in style, model, or size

pro·duc·tor \prə'dəktə(r)\ *n* -S [²*product* + *-or*] **:** PRODUCER; *specif* **:** a producing cause

pro·duc·to·ry \prə'dəktərē\ *adj* [*production* + *-ory*] **:** of, relating to, or characterized by production

products *pl of* PRODUCT, *pres 3d sing of* PRODUCT

pro·duc·tus \prə'dəktəs\ *n, cap* [NL, fr. L, lengthened, protracted, fr. past part. of *producere* to bring forth, produce, pull out — more at PRODUCE] **:** a genus of extinct articulate brachiopods characteristic of Carboniferous and Permian strata, lacking a pedicle but often anchored by spines on the shell, and including the largest known brachiopods some of which (as *P. giganteus*) attain a width of one foot

pro·em \'prōˌem\ *n* -S [ME *proheme*, fr. MF *proheme, proeme*, fr. L *prooemium*, fr. Gk *prooimion*, fr. *pro-* ¹pro- + *oimē, oimos* song + *-ion*, dim. suffix] **1 :** a preliminary discourse to a longer piece of writing **2 :** an introductory comment before a speech **3 :** something that opens or begins — compare PREFACE

pro·embryo \(ˈ)prō+\ *n* [¹*pro-* + *embryo*] **:** an embryonic structure developed during the segmentation of the egg or oospore before the formation of the true embryo — **pro·embryonal** \"+\ *adj* — **pro·embryonic** \(ˌ)prō+\ *adj*

pro·emi·al \(ˈ)prō¦ēmēəl\ *adj* [ME *prohemyal*, fr. *proheme* + *-yal, -iol*] **:** of the nature of a proem **:** INTRODUCTORY, PREFATORY

pro·enzyme \(ˈ)prō+\ *n* [ISV ¹*pro-* + *enzyme*] **:** ZYMOGEN

pro·epimeron \ˌ¦prō+\ *n* [NL, fr. ¹*pro-* + *epimeron*] **:** the epimeron of the prothorax of an insect

pro·episternum \"+\ *n* [NL, fr. ¹*pro-* + *episternum*] **:** the episternum of the prothorax of an insect

pro·erythroblast \"+\ *n* [¹*pro-* + *erythroblast*] **:** a hemocytoblast that gives rise to erythroblasts — **pro·erythroblastic** \"+\ *adj*

pro·estrous *also* **pro·oestrous** \(ˈ)prō+\ *adj* [¹*pro-* + *estrous, oestrous*] **:** of or relating to proestrus

pro·estrus *or* **pro·estrum** *also* **pro·oestrus** *or* **pro·oestrum** \"+\ *n, pl* **proestruses** *or* **proestrums** [NL, fr. ¹*pro-* + *estrus, estrum, oestrus, oestrum*] **:** a preparatory period immediately preceding estrus and characterized by growth of graafian follicles, increased estrogenic activity, and alteration of uterine and vaginal mucosa

pro·ethical \"+\ *adj* [²*pro-* + *ethical*] **:** serving the end of ethics but not ethical in nature

pro·ethnic \"+\ *adj* [¹*pro-* + *ethnic*] **:** prior to a division into ethnic groups (as a race into peoples or a people into tribes) — **pro·ethnically** \"+\ *adv*

pro·e·tus \prō'ēd·əs\ *n, cap* [NL] **:** a genus (the type of the family Proetidae) comprising small trilobites with nearly equal shields, smooth depressed glabella, and narrow cheeks and being common throughout the Paleozoic after the Cambrian

pro·eutectoid \ˌ¦prō+\ *adj* [¹*pro-* + *eutectoid*] **:** separating from solid solution at a temperature higher than the eutectoid

prof \'präf\ *n* -S [by shortening] *slang* **:** PROFESSOR

prof *abbr* **1** profession; professional **2** *often cap* professor

pro·face \prō'fās\ *interj* [MF (*bon*) *prou* (*vous*) *fasse*, lit., may it make you good profit] *obs* — used as a salutation in welcoming or drinking healths ⟨*Proface!* What you want in meat, we'll have in drink —Shak.⟩

prof·a·na·tion \ˌpräfə'nāshən\ *n* -S [MF *prophanation, profanation*, fr. LL *profanation-, profanatio*, fr. L *profanatus* (past part. of *profanare* to profane) + *-ion-, -io* -ion — more at PROFANE] **1 :** an act of profaning **:** an act of violating sacred things or of treating them with contempt or irreverence **:** irreverent or too familiar treatment or use of what is sacred **2 :** debasement or vulgarization esp. by misuse or disclosure ⟨music may be contemplated . . . happily free from all danger of ~ —C.C.Riker⟩

syn DESECRATION, SACRILEGE, BLASPHEMY: PROFANATION applies to any irreverent outrage shocking to those who cherish and hold sacred the thing treated; although it may suggest base callousness, it often applies to vulgar, insensible irreverence as of vandals ⟨these sages attribute the calamity to a *profanation* of the sacred grove —J.G.Frazer⟩ DESECRATION may apply to any action whereby sacred character is impaired or lost; often it indicates loss of that character through defilement, often malicious or malign and culpable ⟨*desecration* of the cathedrals by the invading barbarians⟩ ⟨the last priest, feeling there was no work to be done in such a dreary outpost, burned the chapel in 1706 to prevent its *desecration* —*Amer. Guide Series: Mich.*⟩ SACRILEGE may refer technically to reception or administration of a religious sacrament by one unworthy; it refers commonly to any outrageous profanation ⟨the execution was not followed by any *sacrilege* to the church or defiling of holy vessels —Willa Cather⟩ ⟨above all things they dread any contact with the spirits of the dead. Only a sorcerer would dare to commit such a *sacrilege*, an offense punishable with death —J.G.Frazer⟩ BLASPHEMY may refer to any strong irreverence, often one involving or suggesting reviling, defying, mocking, or otherwise treating with indignity something sacred ⟨he cooperated with me in sending the pious elders to unspeakable corners of hell; we arranged a wordless language of *blasphemy* and signaled to each other across the laps of the godly —G.W.Brace⟩

pro·fan·a·tory \prō'fanəˌtōrē, prə'-, -tȯr-, -ri\ *adj* [*profanation* + *-ory*] **:** tending to profane **:** DESECRATING

¹**pro·fane** \prō'fān, prə'-\ *vb* -ED/-ING/-S [ME *prophanen*, fr. L *profanare*, fr. *profanus*] *vt* **1 :** to violate or treat with abuse, irreverence, obloquy, or contempt (something sacred) **:** treat as not sacred **:** DESECRATE, POLLUTE ⟨the priests in the temple ~ the sabbath —Mt 12:5 (RSV)⟩ **2 :** to debase by a wrong, unworthy, or vulgar use **:** ABUSE, DEFILE, VULGARIZE ⟨its borders have not been *profaned* by the clutter of outdoor advertising signs —Malcolm Bauer⟩ ~ *vi* **:** to indulge in profanity ⟨we heard a yell and then a loud *profaning*⟩

²**pro·fane** \(ˈ)prō¦fān, prə'f-\ *adj* [ME *prophane*, fr. MF, fr. L *profanus*, fr. *pro-* before + *fanum* temple — more at PRO-, FEAST] **1 :** unconcerned with that which is religious or with the purposes of religion **:** not devoted to the sacred and the holy **:** SECULAR ⟨Jeremiah has been likened to several characters in ~ history —A.W.Streane⟩ ⟨the ~ world of spectators —James Joyce⟩ **2 :** not holy because unconsecrated, impure, or defiled **:** not fit or fitted for religious uses **:** UNSANCTIFIED; *sometimes* **:** HEATHEN ⟨~ rites⟩ **3 a :** serving to debase or defile that which is holy or worthy of reverence **:** contemptuous of beautiful or sacred things **:** IRREVERENT **b** (1) **:** characterized by abusive language directed esp. against the name of God (2) **:** indulging in cursing or vituperation **:** marked by insulting or perverted utterance ⟨the ~ old rascal —Herman Melville⟩ **4 a :** not among the initiated esp. to religious rites **b :** not possessing esoteric or expert knowledge ⟨if a picture . . . had been injured by cleaning, or retouched by some ~ hand —Nathaniel Hawthorne⟩

syn PROFANE, SECULAR, LAY, and TEMPORAL can all signify not dedicated to religious ends or uses. PROFANE is mainly descriptive in opposing *sacred* and sometimes *holy, religious,* or *spiritual* ⟨the *profane* poet is by instinct a naturalist. He loves landscape, he loves love, he loves the humor and pathos of earthly existence. But the religious prophet loves none of these things —George Santayana⟩ ⟨*profane* men living in ships, like the holy men gathered together in monasteries, develop traits of profound resemblance —Joseph Conrad⟩ ⟨that little allegory of sacred and *profane* love —John Galsworthy⟩ SECULAR implies a relation to the world as distinguished from the church, religion, or the religious life ⟨believing that no creed, religious or *secular*, can be justified except on the basis of reason and evidence —*Times Lit. Supp.*⟩ ⟨the *secular* critics of religion —Reinhold Niebuhr⟩ ⟨anarchy in the religious society is as undesirable as it is in the *secular* world —Leo Pfeffer⟩ and is close to PROFANE ⟨*secular* and religious music⟩ but sometimes it opposes *regular* in the sense of governed by monastic rule ⟨a *secular* priest does not belong to a religious order⟩ and usu. it opposes *religious* in the sense of belonging to or serving the ends of religion or a church ⟨the parochial and *secular* schools⟩ LAY commonly applies to a person who does not belong to the clergy or sometimes to such a person's activities, interests, or duties, usu. opposing *clerical* or *ecclesiastic* ⟨the priests met with *lay* members of the parish⟩ Often the term extends to signify nonprofessional ⟨a *lay* opinion on a medical question⟩ or is often close to *average, mundane*, sometimes *untrained* ⟨facts in a war which either are based on military information or which cannot be explained to the *lay* mind —F.D.Roosevelt⟩ TEMPORAL, opposing *spiritual* in designating what belongs to material or worldly concerns, applies chiefly to sovereigns, rulers, or dignitaries having political authority or civil power ⟨to be ruled in *temporal* things by clerical authority —Agnes Repplier⟩ ⟨the superiority of the spiritual and eternal over the carnal and *temporal* —H.O.Taylor⟩ ⟨our *temporal* and ecclesiastical overlords⟩ **syn** see in addition IMPIOUS

³**pro·fane** \prō'fān, prə'-\ *n* -S **:** one that is not initiated — usu. used with *the* ⟨appear . . . ridiculous to the ~ —Ramon Guthrie⟩

pro·fane·ly *adv* **:** in a profane manner ⟨kept wondering ~ why everything had to happen to him —Henry LaCossitt⟩

pro·fane·ness \-ānnəs\ *n* -ES **:** the quality or state of being profane ⟨did frown upon church music which savored of . . . ~ —Douglas Bush⟩

pro·fan·er \-ānə(r)\ *n* -S **:** one that profanes

pro·fan·i·ty \prō'fanədē, prə'-, -ətē, -i\ *n* -ES [LL *profanitas*, fr. L *profanus* profane + *-itas* -ity] **1 a :** the quality or state of being profane ⟨exploitations of the Christian religion . . . would be the ultimate ~ —Walter Moberly⟩ **b :** the use of profane language ⟨banged his gavel and fined him for ~ in court —*Amer. Guide Series: Pa.*⟩ **2 :** something profane: as **a :** secular science or art ⟨a small minority studied the *profanities* —H.O.Taylor⟩ **b :** profane language

profection *n* -S [ML *profection-, profectio*, fr. L *profectus* (past part. of *proficere* to go forward, advance) + *-ion-, -io* -ion — more at PROFICIENT] **1** *obs* **:** the act of progressing **:** a movement forward **2** *obs* **:** an advance or the degree of advancement

pro·fec·ti·tious \ˌ¦prōˌfek¦tishəs\ *adj* [LL *profecticius, profectitius*, fr. *profectus* (past part. of *proficisci* to set out, come forth, proceed (from), fr. *pro-* forward + *-ficisci* (fr. pass. of *facere* to do, make) + *-icius, -itius* -itious — more at PRO-, DO] *Roman law* **:** DERIVED — used of property derived from an ancestor or ascendant

profer *vt* -ED/-ING/-S [ME *proferen*, fr. MF *proferer*, fr. L *proferre*, fr. *pro-* before + *ferre* to carry — more at PRO-, BEAR] *obs* **:** to put forth or before **:** bring forth or out

pro·ferment \(ˈ)prō+\ *n* -S [ISV ¹*pro-* + *ferment*] **:** an inactive precursor of a ferment **:** ZYMOGEN

pro·fert \'prōfə(r)t\ *n* -S [L, he brings forward, 3d pers. pres. indic. of *proferre*] **1 :** an allegation in a pleading or on the record that the pleader produces in open court an instrument relied upon and set forth therein **2 :** the actual exhibition in court of an instrument — see DECLARATION 2a

pro·fess \prə'fes, prō'-\ *vb* -ED/-ING/-ES [in sense 1, fr. ME *professen*, fr. *profes*, adj., having professed one's vows, fr. OF, fr. LL *professus*, fr. L, past part. of *profitērī* to profess, confess, fr. *pro-* before + *-fitērī* (fr. *fatērī* to acknowledge, confess); in other senses, fr. L *professus*, past part. of *profitērī* — more at PRO-, CONFESS] *vt* **1 a :** to receive formally into membership in a religious community through the authorized acceptance of the candidate's vows ⟨the abbot ~*ed* three of the young monks⟩ ⟨he was ~*ed* when 18 years old⟩ **b :** to take (vows) as a member of a religious community or order **2 a :** to declare or admit openly or freely **:** acknowledge without concealment **:** AFFIRM, CONFESS ⟨~*ed* great admiration for his scholarship —H.E.Starr⟩ ⟨gave me a copy of the book whose authorship he modestly ~*ed* —Sidney Lovett⟩ **b :** to declare or admit in words or appearances only **:** imply outwardly **:** aver insincerely **:** PRETEND, PURPORT ⟨they have become what they ~ to scorn —W.L.Sullivan⟩ ⟨doctrines that ~ to explain the human situation —D.W.Brogan⟩ **3 :** to confess one's faith in or allegiance to **:** recognize or embrace as a belief **:** FOLLOW, PRACTICE ⟨~*es* a Protestant faith —*Current Biog.*⟩ **4 a :** to proclaim oneself versed in (as a calling) **:** practice the profession of **b :** to teach as a professor ⟨those learned intellectual historians . . . all ~ literature —H.S.Commager⟩ ~ *vi* **1 a :** to make a profession or one's profession **: b** *obs* **:** to profess friendship ⟨he is dishonored by a man which ever ~*ed* to him —Shak.⟩ **2 :** to follow the calling of professor **syn** see ASSERT

pro·fess·ant \-sᵊnt\ *n* -s **:** one who professes ⟨depends on the vitality of a religion in the lives of its ~*s* —P.W.Tappan⟩

pro·fessed \prə'fest, prō'-\ *adj* [ME, fr. *profes* professed + *-ed* — more at PROFESS] **1 :** characterized by having taken the vows of a religious order ⟨nine ~ nuns, a novice, and two postulants arrived —*Amer. Guide Series: La.*⟩ **2 a :** openly and freely declared or acknowledged **:** AFFIRMED ⟨failed in its ~ task —T.S.Eliot⟩ **b :** avowed with intent to deceive **:** HYPOCRITICAL, INSINCERE **3 :** professing to be qualified **:** not amateur **:** EXPERT ⟨a ~ philosopher —John Buchan⟩

pro·fessed·ly \-sədlē\ *adv* **1 :** by profession or declaration **:** AVOWEDLY **2 :** with pretense **:** ALLEGEDLY

pro·fes·sion \prə'feshən, prō'-\ *n* -s [ME *professioun*, fr. OF *profession*, fr. LL & L; LL *profession-*, *professio* religious profession, fr. L, public declaration, fr. *professus* (past part. of *profitērī* to profess, confess) + *-ion-*, *-io* -ion — more at PROFESS] **1 :** the act of taking the vows that consecrate oneself to special religious service **2 :** an act of openly declaring or publicly claiming a belief, faith, or opinion **:** an avowed statement or expression of intention or purpose **:** PROTESTATION ⟨his frequent ~*s* about love and friendships belie a good deal of . . . his behavior —Joseph Chiari⟩ ⟨his ~ that logic is not the sole criterion of art —Lee Strasberg⟩ ⟨welcomed by her two friends with many ~*s* of pleasure —Jane Austen⟩ **3 a :** Christian or religious conviction and purpose openly avowed **b :** the faith in which one is professed **:** a religion or religious system; *also* **:** a religious body **4 a :** a calling requiring specialized knowledge and often long and intensive preparation including instruction in skills and methods as well as in the scientific, historical, or scholarly principles underlying such skills and methods, maintaining by force of organization or concerted opinion high standards of achievement and conduct, and committing its members to continued study and to a kind of work which has for its prime purpose the rendering of a public service — see LEARNED PROFESSION **b :** a principal calling, vocation, or employment ⟨preferred to move and move again, rather than give up their old ~ of farming —G.W.Pierson⟩ ⟨men who make it their ~ to hunt the hippopotamus —J.G.Frazer⟩ **c :** the whole body of persons engaged in a calling ⟨form an association that will reflect a credit on the ~ —Thomas Pyles⟩ **5** *archaic* **:** professorial teaching or status

[1]pro·fes·sion·al \-shənᵊl, -shnəl\ *adj* [*profession* + *-al*] **1 a** (1) **:** of, relating to, or characteristic of a profession or calling ⟨a ~ degree⟩ (2) **:** concerned or occupied with the training of professionals ⟨universities are ~ institutions —J.B. Conant⟩ **b** (1) **:** engaged in one of the learned professions or in an occupation requiring a high level of training and proficiency ⟨the ~ man or woman is expected to possess several distinctive . . . qualifications —A.E.Bestor⟩ (2) **:** characterized by or conforming to the technical or ethical standards of a profession or an occupation **:** manifesting fine artistry or workmanship based on sound knowledge and conscientiousness **:** reflecting the results of education, training, and experience ⟨~ courtesy⟩ ⟨they are afraid of . . . their own ~ or business standing —John Lodge⟩ ⟨it was a competent ~ job⟩ **2 a :** participating for gain or livelihood in an activity or field of endeavor often engaged in by amateurs ⟨a ~ baseball player⟩ **b :** engaged or participated in by persons receiving financial return ⟨~ football⟩ **3 :** following a line of conduct or assuming a role as though it were a profession ⟨comes at times close to deserving the name of ~ southerner —Tarleton Collier⟩ ⟨become so much the ~ celebrity —Van Wyck Brooks⟩

[2]professional \"\ *n* -s **1 a :** one that engages in a particular pursuit, study, or science for gain or livelihood ⟨a small standing army largely made up of ~*s*⟩ **b :** one that competes in sports or athletics for gain or livelihood or who has taught or trained for money ⟨a golf ~⟩ — compare AMATEUR **c :** one who receives money for appearing in theatrical productions **:** one who is engaged professionally **2 a :** one who belongs to one of the learned professions or is in an occupation requiring a high level of training and proficiency ⟨many highly trained salaried ~*s* —R.K.Burns⟩ ⟨large corporations are absorbing more and more ~*s* —M.L.Cogan⟩ **b :** one with sufficient authority or practical experience in an area of knowledge or endeavor to resemble a professional ⟨though an amateur in politics he had been a ~ in diplomacy —*Time*⟩

pro·fes·sion·al·ism \-shənᵊl,izəm, -shnə,li-\ *n* -s **1 a :** the conduct, aims, or qualities that characterize or mark a profession or a professional person ⟨a moral code is the basis of ~ —Roy Lewis & Angus Maude⟩ **b :** extreme competence in an occupation or pursuit sometimes marked by absence of originality ⟨lose sight of general cultivation and fall into stark ~ —*Educational Rev.*⟩ **2 :** the following of a profession (as athletics) for gain or livelihood **:** the characteristics, standards, or methods of professionals esp. in sports or athletics ⟨the acceptance of money for professional services . . . is the criterion by which ~ is determined —Virgil Thomson⟩ — compare AMATEURISM

pro·fes·sion·al·ist \-shənᵊləst, -shnələ-\ *n* -s **:** one who professionalizes an occupation

pro·fes·sion·al·iza·tion \prə,feshənᵊlə'zāshən\ *n* -s **:** the act or process of making or becoming professionalized ⟨the ~ of college athletics⟩

pro·fes·sion·al·ize \prə'feshənᵊl,īz, prō'-, -shnə,līz\ *vb* -ED/-ING/-S [[1]*professional* + *-ize*] *vt* **:** to give a professional character to **:** treat as or convert into a profession ⟨*professionalizing* the area of law dealing with civil rights —W.H. Hastie⟩ ~ *vi* **:** to assume a professional character **:** become professional

pro·fes·sion·al·ly \-shənᵊlē, -shnəlē, -i\ *adv* **:** in a professional manner ⟨a ~ equipped stage —*Key Reporter*⟩ ⟨the first ~ trained and experienced librarian to fill this position —*Current Biog.*⟩

pro·fes·sion·ary \-shə,nerē\ *adj* [*profession* + *-ary*] **:** of or relating to a profession **:** PROFESSIONAL

pro·fes·sion·ist \-sh(ə)nəst\ *n* -s [G, fr. *profession* (fr. MF) + *-ist*] **1 :** one pursuing a profession or trade **2** *chiefly Scot* **:** one who makes an insincere profession of religion

pro·fes·sion·less \-shənləs\ *adj* **:** lacking a profession

pro·fes·sor \prə'fesə(r), prō'-\ *n* -s [LL & L; LL, one that professes Christianity, fr. L, public teacher, teacher, fr. *professus* (past part. of *profitērī* to profess, confess, declare publicly, be a teacher) + *-or* — more at PROFESS] **1 a :** one who professes, avows, or declares **b** *chiefly dial* **:** one who professes the Christian religion openly or conspicuously and ardently **2 a :** a faculty member of the highest academic rank at an institution of higher education usu. dividing his time between scholarship and lecturing and teaching mainly advanced students — often used as an academic title with *of* ⟨~ of ancient history⟩ **b :** a teacher at a university, college, or secondary school **:** PEDAGOGUE **c :** one who teaches or professes special knowledge of an art, sport, or occupation requiring skill ⟨a ~ of the machine⟩ ⟨the artist was the unchallenged ~ of his art —W.A.Martin⟩ **d :** one who is conspicuous for being quiet and overly serious **:** one who is bookish

pro·fes·sor·ate \-sərət\ *n* -s [F *professorat*, fr. *professeur* professor (fr. L *professor*) + F *-at* -ate] **1 :** the office, term of office, or position of a professor **2 :** PROFESSORIAT ⟨countless services to art history which have set you apart from the ~ —F.H.Taylor⟩

pro·fes·sor·dom \-sə(r)dəm\ *n* -s [*professor* + *-dom*] **:** the realm of professors; *also* **:** PROFESSORS

pro·fes·so·ri·al \¦prōfə¦sōrēəl, ¦präf-, -sȯr-\ *adj* [L *professorius* of a teacher (fr. *professor*) + E *-al*] **:** of, relating to, or possessing qualities thought to resemble those of a professor: as **a :** having the manner or characteristics of a professor **:** DIDACTIC, LEARNED ⟨eminently ~ volume —Ezra Pound⟩ **b :** composed of or produced by professors as a body ⟨the ~ board⟩ ⟨~ opinion⟩ **c :** relating to the office of professor ⟨~ duties⟩ — **pro·fes·so·ri·al·ly** \-ēəlē, -li\ *adv*

pro·fes·so·ri·at *or* **pro·fes·so·ri·ate** \,==ˈsōrēət, -sȯr-\ *n* -s [modif. (influenced by *professorial*) of F *professorat*] **1 :** the body of college and university teachers at an institution or in society at large **2 :** the profession of college or university teaching ⟨special duty of the ~ to pursue and advance pure learning —Ernest Barker⟩ ⟨to a young man bent on entering the ~ —*Atlantic*⟩

professor or·di·nar·i·us \-,ȯ(r)dᵊn'a(a)rēəs\ *n* [NL, lit., regular professor] **:** a professor of the highest rank at a German university **:** the occupant of a chair with control over the teaching of his subject and a share in the government of the university

pro·fes·sor·ship \prə'fesə(r),ship, prō'-\ *n* **:** the office, duties, or position of an academic professor

[1]prof·fer \'präfə(r)\ *vb* **proffered; proffered; proffering** \-f(ə)riŋ\ **proffers** [ME *profren*, fr. AF *profrer*, fr. OF *poroffrir*, fr. *por-* forth (fr. L *pro-*) + *offrir* to offer — more at PRO-, OFFER] *vt* **1 :** to present for acceptance **:** tentatively advance for consideration **:** suggest as a proposal **:** TENDER ⟨hovered round me . . . with their hands full of fading flowers, which they at length ~*ed* me —Samuel Butler †1902⟩ ⟨was ~*ed* the leadership but declined it —J.G.Smith⟩ ⟨return ~*ed* smiles —*Newsweek*⟩ **2 :** to propose or suggest a readiness and willingness ⟨~*ed* to lend him one —D.D.Martin⟩ ~ *vi*, *obs* **:** to move as if about to act **:** HESITATE ⟨when you see him ready to enter water, say he ~*eth* —H.J.Pye⟩ **syn** see OFFER

[2]proffer \"\ *n* -s [ME *profre*, *profer*, fr. AF *profre*, fr. *profrer*] **1 :** an offer made **:** something proposed for acceptance **:** SUGGESTION ⟨her more than generous ~ —C.G.Bowers⟩ ⟨his ~ of hospitality —Irving Bacheller⟩ **2** *obs* **:** a display of willingness **:** ATTEMPT, ESSAY

profferer *n* -s *obs* **:** one that proffers something

pro·fibrinolysin \¦prō+\ *n* [[1]*pro-* + *fibrinolysin*] **:** PLASMINOGEN

pro·fi·chi \prō'fēkē\ *n, pl* **profichi** *or* **profichis** [It, pl. of *profico* caprifig, fr. L *caproficus*, alter. of *caprificus* — more at CAPRIFICATION] **:** the spring crop of the caprifig — compare MAMME, MAMMONI

pro·fi·cience \prə'fishən(t)s, prō'-\ *n* -s **1** *archaic* **:** an advance forward **:** PROGRESS **2** *archaic* **:** the state of progress attained **:** PROFICIENCY

pro·fi·cien·cy \-nsē, -si\ *n* -ES **1 :** advancement toward the attainment of a high degree of knowledge or skill **:** PROGRESS ⟨made little ~ in fashionable or literary accomplishments —T. B.Macaulay⟩ **2 :** the quality or state of being proficient **:** ADEPTNESS, EXPERTNESS ⟨aim at giving their students a certain ~ —W.F.Mackey⟩

proficiency badge *n* **:** a badge awarded to an intermediate girl scout for achieving knowledge or skill (as in citizenship, nutrition, dressmaking)

[1]pro·fi·cient \-nt\ *adj* [L *proficient-*, *proficiens*, pres. part. of *proficere* to go forward, make progress, accomplish, be advantageous, fr. *pro-* forward + *-ficere* (fr. *facere* to make, do) — more at PRO-, DO] **:** well advanced in an art, occupation, skill, or a branch of knowledge **:** unusually efficient ⟨an experienced person, trained and ~ in his job —F.G.Nesbitt⟩

syn ADEPT, SKILLED, SKILLFUL, EXPERT, MASTERLY: these adjectives all mean having the knowledge and experience to be extremely competent in a given line of work or endeavor. PROFICIENT stresses a competence derived from training and practice ⟨a technically *proficient* pianist —Edward Sackville-West & Desmond Shawe-Taylor⟩ ⟨*proficient* in mathematics and philosophy —H.H.Shenk⟩ ⟨*proficient* in the art of self-defense —G.B.Shaw⟩ ADEPT usu. adds to PROFICIENT the idea of aptitude or cleverness ⟨*adept* at speechmaking⟩ ⟨newspapers became *adept* at handling crime news —*Amer. Guide Series: Calif.*⟩ ⟨*adept* at making up with cosmetics and dress for what nature may not have given her —Walter Le Beau⟩ SKILLED, for the most part interchangeable with PROFICIENT, usu. suggests a proficiency in the technique of an art or profession but often in industrial use signifying only that one has met a minimum standard set up for a special type of work or job ⟨contribute many *skilled* performers to the figure-skating troupes —*Amer. Guide Series: Minn.*⟩ ⟨a *skilled* musician⟩ ⟨*skilled* artisans⟩ SKILLFUL stresses dexterity in execution or performance ⟨*skillful* in sketching, pen portraiture and caricature —H.H.Reichard⟩ ⟨a fast, energetic and *skillful* campaign —G.W.Johnson⟩ ⟨*skillful* in the use of the hand tools —H.D.Burghardt & Aaron Axelrod⟩ EXPERT stresses extraordinary proficiency or adeptness ⟨an *expert* mimic —Alexander Forbes⟩ ⟨an *expert* horseman⟩ ⟨*expert* and inept raconteurs —*Yale Rev.*⟩ MASTERLY, usu. applying to the thing executed or accomplished, adds to the idea of competence and adeptness that of confident control ⟨his command of English was so *masterly* —Lucien Price⟩ ⟨in two *masterly* sentences he summed up Captain Guy's character —Herman Melville⟩ ⟨a *masterly* accomplishment in workmanship, detail, and symbolism —*Amer. Guide Series: N.Y.City*⟩

[2]proficient \"\ *n* -s **1** *obs* **:** one that shows signs of definite progress to his objective **2 :** one well advanced in any business, art, science, or branch of learning **:** ADEPT, EXPERT ⟨Shakespeare is their true ~ —I.A.Richards⟩ ⟨she was a ~ in music —T.L.Peacock⟩

pro·fi·cient·ly *adv* **:** in a proficient manner ⟨completely handed over to the experts and . . . ~ dealt with —Albert Dasnoy⟩

proficuous *adj* [LL *proficuus*, fr. L *proficere*] *obs* **:** PROFITABLE, USEFUL

[1]pro·file \'prō,fīl\ *n* -s [It *profilo*, fr. *profilare* to draw in outline, fr. *pro-* forward (fr. L) + *filare* to spin, draw a line, fr. LL, to spin — more at PRO-, FILE] **1 :** a representation of something in outline; *esp* **:** a human head or face represented or seen in a side view ⟨his handsome, blunt ~ —Susan Ertz⟩ ⟨his face presented to us in ~ —Christopher Isherwood⟩ **2 :** an outline seen or represented in sharp relief **:** a distinctive exterior line **:** CONTOUR ⟨from the river as he was seeing it now, the city's ~ seemed all flat planes —Harold Sinclair⟩ ⟨some ~ of the mountains —E.H.Spicer⟩ **3 :** a side or sectional elevation: as **a :** a drawing used in civil engineering to show a vertical section of the ground along a surveyed line or graded work **b :** a drawing of the side elevation of a ship's lines or of its structure **4 :** a ceramics shaping tool **5 :** wooden frames from which lines are stretched to establish the alignment of the face of a wall or the slope of a drainpipe or tile **6 :** a flat piece of theatrical scenery or property cut in outline **7 a :** a vertical section of a soil showing the nature and sequence of its various zones **b :** a vertical section of an organic deposit (as a peat bog) showing the sequence of its flora ⟨pollen ~*s* —*Amer. Jour. of Science*⟩ **c :** a vertical section cut through an archaeological unit (as a burial mound or village site) **8 :** a graph or curve: as **a :** a group of data representing quantitatively the extent to which an individual exhibits traits or abilities as determined by tests or ratings and usu. presented in the form of a graph **b :** a linear series of data recording the position of the piezometric surface in an artesian aquifer or groundwater basin or of the elevations of the bottom and the energy line along the axis of flow of a stream or conduit **9 a :** a concise biographical sketch depicting a personality by vivid outlining and sharp contrast **b :** a concise geographical, historical, or political sketch **c :** a concise analysis of a subject **10 a :** a linear series of recording stations or observation points for geophysical phenomena **b :** a graph or curve showing the data thus obtained **11 :** a recognizable rhythmic line characterizing a musical composition or speech utterance ⟨the classic symphonist selects a subject matter that . . . has a sharp melodic and rhythmic ~ —P.H. Lang⟩ ⟨~ of sounds⟩ **syn** see OUTLINE

profile 1

[2]profile \"\ *vb* -ED/-ING/-S [It *profilare*] *vt* **1 a :** to draw the vertical outline of **:** represent in profile **:** draw a profile of **b :** to study and design the exterior shape of (as a molding) **c :** to give a profile to **2 :** to shape the outline of (an object) by means of a cutting instrument — compare PROFILING MACHINE **3 :** to give or write a profile of ⟨try to ~ a man . . . so typical of New York —Alistair Cooke⟩ ~ *vi* **:** to turn in profile **:** present a profile; *esp* **:** to turn the left shoulder toward a bull in a bullfight ⟨the matador *profiled*, his thin silver blade raised —William Sansom⟩

profile board *n* **:** TEMPLATE 2

profile cutter *n* **:** a knife or machine cutter with an edge shaped to cut a definite form

profile drag *n, aeronautics* **:** the portion of the wing drag that is due to friction and turbulence in the fluid and that would be absent if it were nonviscous

profile machine *n* **:** PROFILING MACHINE

profile of equilibrium **1 :** the longitudinal profile of a stream whose smooth gradient is so adjusted to volume of water and amount and nature of load as to be maintained in approximate equilibrium while erosion and transportation continue **:** a graded profile **2 :** the slope away from shore of a sea floor or lake bottom having a gradient such that waves and currents neither erode it downward nor deposit sediment upon it

profile paper *n* **:** graph paper used for convenience in drawing profiles

pro·fil·er \-lə(r)\ *n* -s **:** one that profiles: as **a :** a profiling machine **b :** one that profiles metal objects by hand or on a profiling machine

profiling machine *n* **:** a vertical milling machine for milling irregular profiles by causing the spindle to move laterally by the cam action of a guide or dummy that serves as a model at the same time that the worktable moves at right angles to the travel of the spindle

pro·fil·ograph \prō'filə,graf, -fīl-, -raf\ *n* [ISV [1]*profile* + *-o-* + *-graph;* orig. formed as F *profilographe*] **1 :** an instrument borne on wheels for recording automatically the profile of the land over which it travels **2 :** an instrument for measuring smoothness of a surface (as of a metal casting) by amplification of the minute variations from the plane or arc of smoothness

pro·fi·lom·e·ter \,prōfə'lämәd·ə(r)\ *n* [ISV [1]*profile* + *-o-* + *-meter;* orig. formed as F *profilomètre*] **:** PROFILOGRAPH

[1]prof·it \'präfət, *usu* -əd·+V\ *n* -s *often attrib* [ME, fr. MF, fr. L *profectus* advance, progress, profit, success, fr. *profectus*, past part. of *proficere* to go forward, make progress — more at PROFICIENT] **1 :** an advantage, benefit, accession of good, gain, or valuable return esp. in financial matters, education, or character development ⟨found moral ~ also in this self-study —L.P. Smith⟩ ⟨reading with ~ and delight —Havelock Ellis⟩ **2 :** the excess of returns over expenditure in a transaction or series of transactions: as **a :** the excess of the price received over the price paid for goods sold — opposed to *loss* **b :** the excess of the price received over the cost of purchasing and handling or of producing and marketing goods **3 a** (1) **:** net income (as in a business) usu. for a given period of time (2) **:** a benefit or advantage accruing from the management, use, or sale of property, from the carrying on of any process of production, or from the conduct of business **b :** the income of invested property not including an appreciation in market value **4 :** the ratio of profit for a given year to the amount of capital invested or to the value of sales **5 a :** the distributive share or compensation accruing to entrepreneurs for the assumption of risk in business enterprise **b :** entrepreneurial or employer income as distinguished from wages or rent **6 :** PROFIT A PRENDRE **syn** see USE

[2]profit \"\ *vb* -ED/-ING/-S [ME *profiten*, fr. MF *profiter*, fr. *profit*] *vi* **1 :** to make progress **:** become proficient **:** ADVANCE, IMPROVE ⟨morale, always a problem . . . has ~*ed* greatly —Greg MacGregor⟩ **2 :** to be of service or advantage **:** AID, FURTHER ⟨nothing ~*s* like an inquiring mind⟩ **3 :** to take advantage **:** make good use **:** derive benefit **:** GAIN — usu. used with *by* or *from* ⟨everyone should get as much liberal education as he can . . . absorb and ~ by —Cormac Philip⟩ ⟨would ~ greatly from a more painstaking examination of manuscripts —E.S. McCartney⟩ ~ *vt* **:** to be of service to **:** ADVANTAGE, AID, BENEFIT ⟨do not think we should ~ ourselves well if we tarried . . . to examine and dissect —Sir Winston Churchill⟩ ⟨hurry by and disregard what does not seem to ~ our own existence —Laurence Binyon⟩

prof·it·abil·i·ty \,präfəd·ə'biləd·ē\ *n* **:** the quality or state of being profitable ⟨getting things done that contribute to the ~ of the company —G.B.Hurff⟩

prof·it·able \'präfəd·əbəl, -f(ə)təb-\ *adj* [ME, fr. MF, fr. *profiter* to profit + *-able* — more at PROFIT] **:** affording profits **:** bringing or yielding benefits or gains **:** HELPFUL, LUCRATIVE, REMUNERATIVE, USEFUL ⟨he had an instinct for noting and retaining ~ detail —Audrey Barker⟩ ⟨cotton growing became increasingly ~ —*Amer. Guide Series: La.*⟩ ⟨the Press Conference . . . was a political innovation and a ~ one —Frances Perkins⟩ **syn** see BENEFICIAL

prof·it·able·ness *n* -ES [ME *profitablenes*, fr. *profitable* + *-nes* -ness] **:** PROFITABILITY

prof·it·ably \-blē, -li\ *adv* [ME, fr. *profitable* + *-ly*] **:** in a profitable manner **:** BENEFICIALLY ⟨very ~ study the events of Scandinavian history —L.B.Burbank⟩

profit and loss *n* **1 :** a summary account used at the end of an accounting period to collect the balances of the nominal accounts that the net profit or loss may be shown **2 :** a nominal account or statement of profit and loss

profit and loss statement *n* **:** INCOME ACCOUNT 2

profit a pren·dre *or* **profit à pren·dre** \-à'präⁿdr(ᵊ), -d(rə)-\ *n, pl* **profits a prendre** *or* **profits à prendre** [AF, lit., profit to be taken] **:** a legal right to take a profit from something yielded or produced by land **:** a right to take from land a part of its soil — distinguished from *easement*

[1]prof·i·teer \¦präfə¦ti(ə)r, -iə\ *n* -s [[1]*profit* + *-eer*] **:** one who makes what is considered an unreasonable profit esp. on the sale of essential goods during times of emergency

[2]profiteer \"\ *vi* -ED/-ING/-S **:** to be a profiteer **:** to engage in the practice of selling essential goods for exorbitant profit

prof·it·er \'präfəd·ə(r)\ *n* -s **:** one that profits

pro·fit·er·ole \prə'fid·ə,rōl\ *n* -s [F, fr. *profiter* to profit — more at PROFIT] **:** a miniature cream puff with sweet or savory filling

prof·it·less \'präfətləs\ *adj* **:** having no profit **:** without benefit or value **:** GAINLESS ⟨let us have no part in ~ quarrels —D.D. Eisenhower⟩ — **prof·it·less·ly** *adv* — **prof·it·less·ness** *n* -ES

profit margin *n* **:** the percentage of profit realized by a business per dollar of sales — compare MARGIN 5a

profits *pl of* PROFIT, *pres 3d sing of* PROFIT

profit sharing *n* **:** a system or process under which employees receive a part of the profits of an industrial or commercial enterprise

profit system *n* **:** FREE ENTERPRISE

profit taking *n* **:** the selling of commodities or securities at prices in excess of cost to realize profits

pro·flavine \(')prō+\ *also* **pro·flavin** \"+\ *n* [[2]*pro-* + *flavine*] **:** a yellow crystalline acridine dye $C_{13}H_7N(NH_2)_2$; *also* **:** the orange to brownish red hygroscopic crystalline sulfate used as an antiseptic esp. for wounds — compare ACRIFLAVINE

prof·li·ga·cy \'präfləgəsē, -lēg-, -si\ *n* -ES [*profligate* + *-cy*] **1 :** the quality or state of being profligate ⟨the ~ of the English plays . . . and novels of that age is a deep blot on our national fame —T.B.Macaulay⟩ **2 :** a thoroughly dissolute character or way of life **:** continuous dissipation **3 :** reckless wastefulness and extravagance

[1]prof·li·gate \-gət, -lə,gāt, *usu* -d·+V\ *adj* [L *profligatus*, fr. past part. of *profligare* to strike down, destroy, ruin, fr. *pro-* forward, down + *-fligare* (fr. *fligere* to strike); akin to W *blif* catapult, Gk *thlibein*, (Aeol. & Ionic dial.) *phlibein* to squeeze, Latvian *blaîzît* to squeeze, crush — more at PRO-] **1 :** completely given up to dissipation and licentiousness : abandoned to vice and corruption : shamelessly immoral ⟨you will find us neither ~ nor ascetic —James Hilton⟩ **2** : wildly extravagant : criminally excessive in spending or using : recklessly wasteful ⟨rescue the Empire from being gambled away by incapable or ~ aristocrats —J.A.Froude⟩ ⟨the ~ profusion with which they carried on bribery —Hartley Withers⟩

²prof·li·gate \-lə,gāt\ *vt* -ED/-ING/-S [L *profligatus*, past part.] *archaic* : to drive away : DEFEAT, OVERCOME

³prof·li·gate \-lə̇gə̇t, -lēg-, -lə,gāt, *usu* -d·+V\ *n* -S [¹*profligate*] : a profligate person

profligated *adj* **1** *obs* : OVERTHROWN **2** *obs* **a** : wastefully squandered **b** : abandoned to vice

prof·li·gate·ly *adv* : in a profligate manner ⟨has wealth of land and tills it ~ for yields so low —Harry Schwartz⟩

prof·li·gate·ness *n* -ES : the quality or state of being profligate

prof·lu·ence \'prä,flüən(t)s, -äflǝwən-\ *n* -S [L *profluentia*, fr. *profluent-, profluens* + *-ia* -y] **1** : a copious or smooth flowing **2** : the quality or state of being profluent : FLUENCY

prof·lu·ent \-nt\ *adj* [ME, fr. L *profluent-, profluens*, pres. part. of *profluere* to flow forth, flow along, fr. *pro-* forward, forth + *fluere* to flow — more at PRO-, FLUENT] : flowing copiously or smoothly in or as if in a stream : FLUENT

pro·flu·vi·um \prō'flüvēəm\ *n, pl* **proflu·via** \-ēə\ *or* **profluviums** [L, fr. *profluere*] : a flowing out : DISCHARGE

pro·fonde \prō'fō̃d\ *n* -S [F, fr. *profonde*, adj., fem. of *profond* deep, fr. L *profundus* — more at PROFOUND] : a special pocket in the tail of a magician's coat

pro for·ma \(')prō'fȯrmə\ *adj* [L] **1** : for the sake of form : as a matter of form ⟨eleven years of strictly *pro forma* equality —George Bailey⟩ **2** : set up in advance to prescribe form or describe items ⟨a *pro forma* financial statement⟩ **3** : consisting of a memorandum invoice sent to a customer for his use or as a notice prior to actual shipment of goods ⟨a *pro forma* invoice for customs⟩

pro forma balance sheet *n* **1** : a balance sheet containing imaginary accounts or figures for illustrative purposes **2** : a balance sheet that gives retroactive effect to new financing, combination, or other change in the status of a business concern or concerns

¹pro·found \prə'faünd, prō'-\ *adj, usu* -ER/-EST [ME, fr. MF *profond* deep, fr. L *profundus*, fr. *pro-* before + *fundus* bottom — more at PRO-, BOTTOM] **1 a** : having intellectual depth : going thoroughly and penetratingly into a problem : possessing knowledge and insight ⟨one of the most ~ minds of this generation⟩ **b** : characterized by, exhibiting, or requiring for comprehension deep learning and insight : difficult to fathom or understand ⟨are, in their meditative depths, among the few ~ poems of our day —Louis Untermeyer⟩ **2 a** : having very great depth : extending far below the surface **b** : coming from, reaching to, or situated at a depth : not superficial : deeply seated ⟨a ~ sigh⟩ **c** (1) *of a bow* : made with the head or body bent low ⟨made a ~ bow to the assembled company⟩ (2) : characterized by admiration ⟨the most ~ respect⟩ **3 a** : characterized by intensity of emotion : deeply realized or felt ⟨my spirit . . . felt a ~*er* fear than ever it knew —Robert Bridges †1930⟩ ⟨have a ~ sympathy —T.S.Eliot⟩ **b** : all encompassing : COMPLETE, THOROUGH ⟨fell into a ~ sleep⟩ **c** : very deep ⟨exerts a ~ influence on legislation —S.K.Padover⟩ **syn** see DEEP

²profound \"\ *n* -S : something that is very deep: as **a** : the deeps of the sea **b** : the depth of a human mind or spirit

pro·found·ly *adv* [ME, fr. *profound* + *-ly*] **1** : with keen penetration and intellectual insight ⟨inability to deal ~ with life —John Portz⟩ **2** : at or as if at a great depth from the surface ⟨why sigh you so ~ —Shak.⟩ **3** : very deeply ⟨I was ~ glad to see it —D.L.Busk⟩ **4** : TOTALLY — used to indicate a degree of deafness ⟨~ deaf children go through the babbling stage —I.J. Hirsh⟩ ⟨from the ~ deaf to the partially deaf —Minnie Hill⟩

pro·found·ness \-n(d)nə̇s\ *n* -ES : PROFUNDITY

profs *pl of* PROF

pro·fun·da \prə'fəndə\ *n, pl* **profun·dae** \-n,dē\ [NL, fr. L, fem. of *profundus* deep — more at PROFOUND] : any of various deep-seated arteries or veins: as **a** : the largest branch of the brachial artery in the upper part of the arm **b** : the deep femoral artery **c** : a tributary of the femoral vein a short distance below Poupart's ligament

pro·fun·dal \prə'fənd°l\ *adj* [L *profundus* deep + E *-al*] : of, relating to, being, or living in the part of a thermally stratified lake that extends downward from the upper part of the hypolimnion to the bottom of the lake or in very deep lakes to 600 meters

profunditude *n* -S [L *profundi-* (fr. *profundus* deep) + E *-tude*] *obs* : PROFUNDITY

pro·fun·di·ty \prə'fəndəd·ē, prō'-, -ətē, -i\ *n* -ES [ME *profundite*, fr. MF *profundité*, fr. L *profunditat-, profunditas* depth, fr. *profundus* deep + *-itat-, -itas* -ity — more at PROFOUND] **1 a** : intellectual depth : penetrating knowledge : keen insight and understanding ⟨the wisest theologians could not match her in ~ —Willa Cather⟩ ⟨the timeless ~ in Jesus —H.E.Fosdick⟩ **b** : a profound or abstruse matter, problem, or theory — often used in pl. ⟨mythology runs into . . . philosophical speculation, sometimes grappling with *profundities* —A.L.Kroeber⟩ **c** : a significant thought : wise saying — often used in pl. ⟨fitting either to formulate or to revere undergraduate *profundities* —F.J.Hoffman⟩ **2 a** *obs* : depth as a dimension or a physical feature **b** : the quality or state of being very deep ⟨the ~ of an abyss⟩ **c** : something resembling a very deep place ⟨through the vast ~ obscure —John Milton⟩ ⟨the ~ of the surrounding shadow —Rebecca West⟩ **3** : extreme thoroughness : INTENSITY ⟨whether or not he understood fully the ~ of his action —M.W.Straight⟩

¹pro·fuse \prə'fyüs, prō'-\ *adj* [ME, fr. L *profusus*, past part. of *profundere* to pour forth, pour out, fr. *pro-* forth + *fundere* to pour — more at PRO-, FOUND] **1** : pouring forth liberally : exceedingly or excessively generous : EXTRAVAGANT ⟨were both ~ in their thanks —*Collier's Yr. Bk.*⟩ **2** : exhibiting great abundance : overly plentiful : BOUNTIFUL ⟨contains the most valuable minerals, in a ~ variety —H.T.Buckle⟩

syn LAVISH, PRODIGAL, LUXURIANT, LUSH, EXUBERANT: PROFUSE suggests an unrestrained abundance, often as of something poured out or gushing out very fully, freely, or copiously ⟨the milk is scanty during the first two or three days, but becomes *profuse*, in most cases, by the third and fourth day —Morris Fishbein⟩ ⟨pourest thy full heart in *profuse* strains of unpremeditated art —P.B.Shelley⟩ ⟨his court became as crowded and *profuse* as his grandfather's. Money was recklessly borrowed and as recklessly squandered —J.R.Green⟩ LAVISH may suggest an unstinted, extravagant, or munificent profusion or outpouring ⟨the *lavish* box lunch where baked ham, fried chicken, and home-baked bread are routine fare —C.W.Morton⟩ ⟨every comfort and luxury that a wealthy and *lavish* old grandfather thought fit to provide —W.M.Thackeray⟩ ⟨five hundred million dollars a year, which go into *lavish* expenditure on health, education, and economic development —Andrew Boyd⟩ PRODIGAL may apply to reckless lavishness and extravagance seeming to lead to depletion or exhaustion of supplies ⟨wildly *prodigal* of color, the new sun then sketched a wide band of throbbing red-gold across less lofty glaciers and snow fields —F.V.W.Mason⟩ ⟨the table spread with opulent hospitality and careless profusion — the baked ham at one end and the saddle of roast mutton at the other, with fried chicken, oysters, crabs, sweet potatoes, jellies, custards — a *prodigal* feast that only outdoor stomachs could manage —V.L.Parrington⟩ LUXURIANT may suggest a splendid, colorful, pleasing rich abundance ⟨a *luxuriant* growth of native iris, trumpet vines, and water hyacinths line its banks —*Amer. Guide Series: La.*⟩ ⟨rich and *luxuriant* beauty; a beauty that shone with deep and vivid tints; a bright complexion, eyes possessing intensity both of depth and glow, and hair already of a deep, glossy brown —Nathaniel Hawthorne⟩ LUSH may suggest a rich, easy, soft luxuriance ⟨a Jersey cow standing belly-deep in a *lush* meadow —Joseph Mitchell⟩ ⟨the fabulous period of the Nineties, that *lush*, plush, glittering era with all its sentimentality and opulence and ostentation —Sara H. Hay⟩ EXUBERANT suggests fruitful abundance marked by vivacity or rampant vitality ⟨an *exuberant* nature pouring out its wealth in spendthrift fashion —V.L.Parrington⟩ ⟨she was in *exuberant* spirits, and the softest colors of flame danced in her lips and eyes and informed the texture of her hair —Elinor Wylie⟩ ⟨houses frescoed, antlered, flowered and curlicued in *exuberant* outburst of Tyrolean design —Claudia Cassidy⟩

²profuse *vt* -ED/-ING/-S [L *profusus*, past part.] **1** *obs* : to pour forth or give freely **2** *obs* : to spend too liberally : LAVISH, SQUANDER

pro·fuse·ly *adv* : in a profuse manner : without limitation : ABUNDANTLY ⟨a ~ illustrated book⟩ ⟨the bush blossoms all too ~ —J.W.Krutch⟩

pro·fuse·ness *n* -ES : the quality or state of being profuse : PROFUSION ⟨it is Elizabethan in its ~ —Owen & Eleanor Lattimore⟩

pro·fu·sion \prə'fyüzhən, prō'-\ *n* [L *profusion-, profusio*, fr. *profusus* (past part. of *profundere* to pour forth) + *-ion-, -io* -ion — more at PROFUSE] **1** : the act of bestowing money or treasures without restraint : lavish expenditure : excessive liberality : EXTRAVAGANCE ⟨made himself popular by his ~ . . . in providing shows for the mob —J.A.Froude⟩ ⟨bountiful even to ~ where the interest of the navy was concerned —T.B. Macaulay⟩ **2** *obs* : the act of pouring forth or discharging **3** : the quality or state of being profuse : a condition of superabundance : PRODIGALITY ⟨noted for their taste, hospitality, and ~ —C.G.Bowers⟩ **4** : an overpowering quantity or amount : lavish display or supply ⟨into its columns he poured a ~ of prose and verse —Brander Matthews⟩ ⟨a ~ of clocks, tapestries, and chairs —Carlton Lake⟩ — often used with *in* ⟨grapes grow in ~ along . . . back roads —*Amer. Guide Series: N.H.*⟩ ⟨objects are piled in a chaotic ~ —David Sylvester⟩

pro·fu·sive \-üsiv\ *adj* : LAVISH — **pro·fu·sive·ly** \-sə̇vlē\ *adv*

¹prog \'präg\ *n* -S [origin unknown] *dial Brit* : a pointed instrument (as a goad or skewer)

²prog \"\ *vt* **progged; progged; progging; progs 1** *dial Brit* : GOAD, PROD **2** *dial Brit* : to poke at (a hole, a log)

³prog \", 'prȯg\ *vi* **progged; progged; progging; progs** [origin unknown] *chiefly dial* : to poke or search about esp. in order to steal, beg, or chance upon something profitable : FORAGE, PROWL

⁴prog *n* -S *chiefly dial* : food esp. when obtained by foraging, filching, or as a handout

⁵prog \'präg\ *n* -S [by shortening & alter.] *slang Brit* : PROCTOR 2a

⁶prog \"\ *vt* **progged; progged; progging; progs** *slang Brit* : to subject to proctorial authority ⟨if I came in here by myself I'd get *progged* —Thomas Wolfe⟩

prog *abbr* **1** program **2** progress; progressive

pro·gametangium \¦prō+\ *n* [NL, fr. ¹*pro-* + *gametangium*] : a hyphal thread in fungi (as of the order Mucorales) at whose tip will be produced a gametangium and subsequently a gamete

pro·gamete \(')prō+; ,prōgə'mēt\ *n* [ISV ¹*pro-* + *gamete*] : an oocyte or a spermatocyte

pro·gam·ic \(')prō¦gamik\ *adj* [¹*pro-* + Gk *gamos* marriage + E *-ic* — more at BIGAMY] : preceding fertilization

prog·a·mous \'prägəməs\ *adj* [¹*pro-* + Gk *gamos* marriage] : PROGAMIC

pro·gan·o·chel·i·dae \prō,ganə'kelə,dē\ *n pl, cap* [NL, fr. *Proganochelys*, type genus (fr. ¹*pro-* + Gk *ganos* brightness + *chelys* tortoise) + *-idae* — more at CHELYS] : a family of extinct Triassic turtles that are the earliest known representatives of the Thecophora

pro·gan·o·saur \prō'ganə,sȯ(ə)r\ *n* -S [NL *Proganosauria*] : MESOSAUR

pro·gan·o·sau·ria \¦=,==¦sȯrēə\ [NL, fr. ¹*pro-* + Gk *ganos* brightness + NL *-sauria*] *syn of* MESOSAURIA

pro·gen·er·ate \prō'jenə,rāt\ *vt* [L *progeneratus*, past part. of *progenerare*, fr. *pro-* forward, forth + *generare* to beget, procreate — more at PRO-, GENERATE] : BEGET, PROCREATE

pro·genesis \(')prō+\ *n* [NL, fr. ¹*pro-* + *genesis*] : precocious sexual reproduction in a trematode worm in which metacercariae or sometimes cercariae may lay eggs capable of repeating the life cycle — compare NEOTENY, PAEDOGENESIS

pro·genetic \¦prō+\ *adj* [¹*pro-* + *genetic*] : of, relating to, or characterized by progenesis

pro·gen·i·tal \prō'jenəd·°l\ *adj* [*progenit*or + *-al*] : PROGENITIVE

pro·gen·i·tive \-d·iv\ *adj* [*progenit*or + *-ive*] : tending to or able to reproduce itself : REPRODUCTIVE — **pro·gen·i·tive·ness** *n* -ES

pro·gen·i·tor \prō'jenəd·ə(r), prə'-, -nətə-\ *n* -S [ME *progenitour*, fr. MF *progeniteur*, fr. L *progenitor*, fr. *progenitus* (past part. of *progignere* to beget, fr. *pro-* before, forward, forth + *gignere* to beget) + *-or* — more at PRO-, KIN] **1 a** : an ancestor in the direct line : FOREFATHER **b** : a biologically ancestral form **2** : one that originates or precedes : one that serves as a guide or pattern : ORIGINATOR, PRECURSOR ⟨biographical study of the ~ of the atmospheric story —*New Yorker*⟩ ⟨~*s* of socialist ideas —*Times Lit. Supp.*⟩ **syn** see ANCESTOR

pro·gen·i·to·ri·al \prō¦jenə¦tōrēəl\ *adj* : of or relating to a progenitor : ANCESTRAL

pro·gen·i·tor·ship \prō'jenəd·ə(r),ship\ *n* : a position as a progenitor

pro·gen·i·trix \-nə·triks\ *also* **pro·gen·i·tress** \-rə̇s\ *n, pl* **progenitri·ces** \prō,jenə·'trī,sēz\ *also* **progenitresses** [LL, fem. of L *progenitor*] : a female progenitor

pro·gen·i·ture \prō'jenəchə(r)\ *n* [F *progéniture*, fr. MF, fr. L *progenitus* + MF *-ure*] **1** : a begetting of offspring **2** : PROGENY

prog·e·ny \'präjənē, -ni\ *n* -ES [ME *progenie*, fr. OF, fr. L *progenies*, fr. *progignere* to beget] **1 a** (1) : descendants of human kind : CHILDREN (2) : a line descended from a common ancestor : CLAN, KIN (3) *archaic* : LINEAGE, PARENTAGE **b** : offspring of animals or plants — used esp. in connection with controlled breeding ⟨the ~ of a wheat cross⟩ ⟨the total ~ of a prepotent sire⟩ **2** : something that is originated or produced : OUTCOME, PRODUCT ⟨examined one by one the marvelous ~ of the workman's art —Elinor Wylie⟩ **3** : a body of followers, disciples, or successors

progeny test *n* : a test of the worth of a sire or sometimes of a dam based on the performance of its early progeny : an evaluation of the genotype of an animal in terms of its offspring — compare SIB TEST

progeny-test \'===,=\ *vt* [*progeny test*] : to perform a progeny test on

pro·ge·ria \prō'jirēə\ *n* -S [NL, fr. ¹*pro-* + Gk *gēras* old age + NL *-ia* — more at CORN] : premature senility; *specif* : an abnormal state showing the symptoms both of infantilism and of a developing senility

pro·gestational \¦prō+\ *adj* [¹*pro-* + *gestational*] : preceding pregnancy or gestation : of, relating to, or constituting the hormonal and tissue modifications of the female mammalian system associated with ovulation and corpus luteum formation

pro·ges·ter·one \prō'jestə,rōn\ *n* -S [*progestin* + *ster*ol + *-one*] : a crystalline ketonic steroid progestational hormone $C_{21}H_{30}O_2$ that is obtained from corpus luteum or made synthetically, that is regarded as a biological precursor of corticoid and androgenic hormones, and that is used chiefly in treating functional uterine bleeding; 4-pregnene-3,20-dione

pro·ges·ter·on·ic \¦=¦==¦ränik\ *adj* : induced by progesterone

pro·ges·tin \prō'jestə̇n\ *n* -S [¹*pro-* for + *gest*ation + *-in*] : a progestational hormone; *esp* : PROGESTERONE

progged *past of* PROG

progging *pres part of* PROG

pro·glacial \(')prō+\ *adj* [¹*pro-* + *glacial*] : in front of, at, or immediately beyond the margin of a glacier or ice sheet ⟨a ~ lake⟩

pro·glot·tic \prō'gläd·ik\ *adj* [*proglott*id + *-ic*] : of or relating to proglottids

pro·glot·tid \-d·ə̇d\ *n* -S [NL *proglottid-, proglottis*] : any of the segments of a tapeworm formed by a process of strobilation in the neck region of the worm, containing both male and female reproductive organs, and surviving briefly after breaking away from the strobila — see ECHINOCOCCUS illustration — **pro·glot·tid·e·an** \¦prō,glä¦tidēən\ *adj*

pro·glot·tis \prō'gläd·ə̇s\ *n, pl* **proglotti·des** \-d·ə,dēz\ [NL, fr. Gk *proglōssis, proglōttis* tip of the tongue, fr. *pro-* ¹*pro-* + *glōssa, glōtta* tongue — more at GLOSS] : PROGLOTTID

prog·nath·ic \(')präg¦nathik, -thēk\ *adj* [*prognath*ous + *-ic*] : PROGNATHOUS

prog·na·thism \'prägnə,thizəm\ *also* **prog·na·thy** \-nəthē\ *n, pl* **prognathisms** *also* **prognathies** [*prognath*ous + *-ism* or *-y*] : prognathic condition : the state of having protruding jaws

prog·na·thous \-nəthəs\ *adj* [¹*pro-* + *-gnathous*] **1** : having the jaws projecting beyond the upper part of the face with a gnathic index above 98 — opposed to *opisthognathous* **2** *of an insect* : having the mouthparts in front of the cranium — compare HYPOGNATHOUS

prog·ne \'prägnē\ *n, cap* [NL, irreg. after *Procne*, a woman in Greek mythology who was transformed into a swallow, fr. L, fr. Gk *Proknē*] : a genus of swallows including the purple martin and its related forms

prog·no·sis \präg'nōsə̇s\ *n, pl* **prog·no·ses** \-ō,sēz\ [LL, fr. Gk *prognōsis*, foreknowledge, prognosis, fr. *progignōskein* to know beforehand, prognosticate, fr. *pro-* ¹pro- + *gignōskein* to know — more at KNOW] **1 a** : the act or art of foretelling the course of a disease **b** : the prospect of survival and recovery from a disease as anticipated from the usual course of that disease or indicated by special features of the case in question ⟨the ~ is grave; death usually occurs within one year⟩ **2** : FORECAST, PROGNOSTICATION ⟨that ~, though wrong, then seemed justified —F.L.Schuman⟩

¹prog·nos·tic \präg'nästik, -tēk\ *n* -S [alter. (influenced by L *prognosticum*) of ME *pronostyke, pronostique*, fr. MF *pronostique*, fr. L *prognosticon, prognosticum*, fr. Gk *prognōstikon*, fr. neut. of *prognōstikos*] **1** : something that foretells : a warning omen : PORTENT, SIGN ⟨that choice would inevitably be considered by the country as a ~ of the highest import —T.B. Macaulay⟩ **2** : a forecast of the future based on a prognostic : PROPHECY ⟨events have caught up with his ~ —Cyril Connolly⟩

²prognostic \(')=¦==\ *adj* [ML *prognosticus*, fr. Gk *prognōstikos* foreknowing, prognostic, fr. (assumed) *prognōstos* (verbal of *progignōskein* to know beforehand, prognosticate) + *-ikos* -ic — more at PROGNOSIS] : of, relating to, or serving as ground for prognostication or a prognosis : FORETELLING, PREDICTIVE ⟨~ weather charts⟩

prog·nos·ti·ca·ble \-tə̇kəbəl\ *adj* [ML *prognosticare* + E *-able*] : capable of being foretold

prog·nos·ti·cal \-kəl\ *adj* : PROGNOSTIC

prognostically *adv, obs* : in a prognostic manner

prog·nos·ti·cate \präg'nästə,kāt, *usu* -ād·+V\ *vb* -ED/-ING/-S [ML *prognosticatus*, past part. of *prognosticare*, fr. *prognosticus* prognostic — more at PROGNOSTIC] *vt* **1** : to foretell from signs or symptoms : PREDICT, PROPHESY ⟨*prognosticating* . . . future relations —T.S.Eliot⟩ **2** : to give an indication of in advance : FORESHOW, PRESAGE ⟨opening new trails, they ~ renaissance and revival —Stephen Crane⟩ ~ *vi* to make a prognostication **syn** see FORETELL

prog·nos·ti·ca·tion \(,)präg,nästə'kāshən *sometimes* prəg-\ *n* -S [alter. (influenced by ML *prognosticatio*) of ME *pronosticacioun*, fr. MF *pronostication*, fr. ML *prognostication-, prognosticatio*, fr. *prognosticatus* + L *-ion-, -io* -ion] **1** : a manifestation of something that is to happen : an indication in advance : FORETOKEN ⟨if an oily palm be not a fruitful ~ —Shak.⟩ **2 a** : an act, the fact, or the power of prognosticating : a prediction of something to come : FORECAST, PROPHECY ⟨the tremendous breadth of his vision . . . as evidenced by his ~*s* and their eventual fulfillment —F.S.Crafford⟩ **b** : a premonition of something that is to or may happen : FOREBODING **3** : PROGNOSIS 1a

prog·nos·ti·ca·tive \=¦==,kād·iv, -,kəd·iv\ *adj* [MF or ML; MF *prognosticatif*, fr. ML *prognosticativus*, fr. *prognosticatus* + L *-ivus* -ive] : characterized by prognosticating : PROPHETIC ⟨her politically ~ husband —*Time*⟩

prog·nos·ti·ca·tor \-,kād·ə(r), -ātə-\ *n* -S [MF *prognosticateur*, fr. ML *prognosticatus* + MF *-eur* -or] : one that prognosticates ⟨weather ~*s* —G.S.Perry⟩ — **prog·nos·ti·ca·to·ry** \-,kə,tōrē\ *adj*

pro·go·ne·a·ta \prō,gōnē'ād·ə, -'ädə\ *n pl, cap* [NL, fr. ¹*pro-* + Gk *gonē* genitals (fr. the stem of *gignesthai* to be born) + NL *-ata* — more at KIN] *in some classifications* : a primary division of Arthropoda comprising forms with the genital apertures near the anterior end of the body and including the classes Diplopoda, Pauropoda, and Symphyla

pro·go·ne·ate \prō'gōnēət, -ē,āt\ *adj* [¹*pro-* + Gk *gonē* + E *-ate*] **1** : having the genital opening placed near the anterior part of the body — distinguished from *opisthogoneate* **2** [NL *Progoneata*] : of or relating to the Progoneata

pro·gra·da·tion \,prōgrā'dāshən\ *n* [*prograde* + *-ation*] : the process of prograding — contrasted with *retrogradation*

pro·grade \prō'grād\ *vi* [L *pro-* forward + E *grade* — more at PRO-] : to build outward toward the sea by deposition of sediment ⟨the shoreward transportation will be the dominating force, and the beach will ~ —F.P.Shepard⟩ ⟨on advancing, or *prograding*, coasts where the waves are throwing up sand —C.A.Cotton⟩

¹pro·gram \'prō,gram, -raam, -ōgrəm\ *or* **pro·gramme** \-,gram\ *n* -S [in sense 1, fr. LL *programma*, fr. Gk, public notice, agenda, fr. *prographein* to write before, set forth as a public notice, fr. *pro-* ¹pro- + *graphein* to write; in sense 3, fr. NL *programma*, fr. LL; in other senses, fr. F *programme*, fr. LL *programma* — more at CARVE] **1** : a public notice **2 a** (1) : a brief outline or explanation of the order to be pursued or the subjects embraced in a public exercise, performance, or entertainment; *esp* : a printed or written list of the acts, scenes, selections, or other features composing a dramatic, musical, or other performance with the names of the performers ⟨handed me the ~ of the concert⟩ ⟨a theater ~⟩ (2) : an order of exercises or numbers **b** : the performance or execution of a program; *esp* : a performance broadcast on radio or television ⟨listen to a brilliant ~⟩ **3** : PROGRAMMA 2 **4 a** : a plan of procedure : a schedule or system under which action may be taken toward a desired goal : a proposed project or scheme ⟨had no ~ except to retain his job —John Gunther⟩ ⟨sets up a buying ~ —A.M.Sullivan⟩ ⟨significant characteristics of a leader are a . . . grasp of the current situation and a ~ for its solution —V.L.Albjerg⟩ ⟨the party's ~ toward socialism⟩ **b** (1) : a plan determining the offerings of an educational institution : CURRICULUM ⟨a school . . . attractive and comfortable but unsuited to the educational ~ —*Education Digest*⟩ ⟨the core ~⟩ (2) : a plan of study for an individual student over a given period : SCHEDULE ⟨had a heavy ~ in his freshman year⟩ **5** : a catalog of projected proceedings or features : PROSPECTUS, SYLLABUS **6** : a printed bill, card, or booklet giving a program; *specif* : a dance order ⟨a box full of yellowed ball ~*s* with faded ribbons —Marcia Davenport⟩ **7** : a statement of an architectural problem and of the requirements to be met in offering a solution **8** : a coherent sequence of incidents, images, thoughts, or feelings providing the background for an instrumental composition that may be inferred by an interpreter or listener, or suggested by the title of the work, or supplied in the form of a poem or exposition **9 a** : a plan for the programming of a mechanism (as a computer) **b** : a sequence of coded instructions that can be inserted in a mechanism (as a computer)

²program \"\ *also* **programme** \"\ *vt* **programmed** *or* **programed; programmed** *or* **programed; programming** *or* **programing; programs** *also* **programmes 1 a** : to arrange or furnish a program of or for : BILL ⟨amount of material needed to ~ these new stations will be tremendous —*Christian Science Monitor*⟩ ⟨capable of *programming* social action with . . . confidence —R.T.La Piere⟩ **b** : to enter in a program **2 a** : to work out a sequence of operations to be performed by (a mechanism) : provide with a program **b** : to insert a program for (a particular action) into or as if into a mechanism

program clock *n* : a master clock that rings bells or other signals at predetermined times

program director *n* : one that is in charge of planning and scheduling program material for a radio or television station or network

pro·gram·ist *or* **pro·gram·mist** \-mə̇st\ *n* -S **1** : a composer or advocate of program music **2** : one who prepares or advocates a program

pro·gram·is·tic *or* **pro·gram·mis·tic** \¦prōgrə¦mistik\ *adj* : relating to a programist — **pro·gram·is·ti·cal·ly** \-tə̇k(ə)lē\ *adv*

pro·gram·ma \prō'gramə\ *n, pl* **programma·ta** \-məd·ə\ [LL — more at PROGRAM] **1** : a public notice esp. if posted : DECREE, EDICT **2** [NL, fr. LL] : a preface esp. to a learned literary work **3** [NL, fr. LL] : PROGRAM 2

pro·gram·mat·ic \¦prōgrə¦mad·|ik, -at|, |ēk\ *adj* [Gk *programmat-, programma* + E *-ic*] **1 :** relating to program music ⟨as is found to be the case in all romantic music, ~ allusions play a big part —Beatrice Maier⟩ **2 :** of, resembling, or having a program ⟨his writing is ~ and pioneering rather than definitive —D.G.Mandelbaum⟩ ⟨the one and only party is bound to degenerate, regardless of its ~ intentions —Philip Rahv⟩ — **pro·gram·mat·i·cal·ly** \|ək(ə)lē, |ēk-, -li\ *adv*

pro·gram·ma·tist \prō'gramədəst\ *n* -s [Gk *programmat-, programma* + E *-ist*] **:** PROGRAMIST

programme *var of* PROGRAM

pro·gram·mer \'prō,gramə(r), -raam-, -ōgrəm-\ *n* -s **:** one that programs **:** as **a :** one that prepares and tests programs for mechanisms **b :** a person or device that programs a mechanism

programming *or* **programing** *n* -s **:** the planning, scheduling, or performing of a program ⟨the listeners alone, can . . . actually correct shoddy or inadequate ~ —A.N.Williams b.1914⟩ ⟨more ~ is only one of many problems facing television —*Advertising Age*⟩

program music *n* **1 :** music that is inspired by or that suggests or characterizes something other than a musical idea or thing **:** descriptive music — compare ABSOLUTE MUSIC **2 :** instrumental music that follows the moods of a program

program picture *n* **:** a motion picture produced cheaply, acted by studio feature players, and usu. shown second on a double-feature program

programs *pl of* PROGRAM, *pres 3d sing of* PROGRAM

pro·gravid \(')prō+\ *adj* [¹*pro-* + *gravid*] **:** PROGESTATIONAL

pro·gre·di·en \prō'grēdēən\ *or* **pro·gre·di·ens** \-nz\ *n, pl* **progrediens** \-nz\ *or* **progredien·tes** \=,=dē'en·,tēz\ [NL *progrediens*, fr. L, pres. part. of *progredi*] **:** a wingless form of an adelgid bug

¹**prog·ress** \'präg|rəs, |,gres, *sometimes* 'prō|\ *n* -ES [ME *progresse*, fr. L *progressus* advance, fr. *progressus*, past part. of *progredi* to go forth, go forward, advance, fr. *pro-* forward + *-gredi* (fr. *gradi* to step, go) — more at PRO-, GRADE] **1 a** (1) **:** a royal journey or tour marked by pomp and pageant ⟨a staff of clerks accompanied the king on his ~*es* —F.M.Stenton⟩ (2) **:** a state procession ⟨at last all was ready for my ~ —George VI⟩ **b :** an official journey or circuit ⟨these men of law . . . on a ~ from court to court —Van Wyck Brooks⟩ **c :** a journeying forward **:** an expedition, journey, or march through a region **:** TOUR ⟨balls, dinners and crowds of beautiful women attended his ~ —*Time*⟩ **2 a :** an advance or movement to an objective or toward a goal **:** purposeful getting or going ahead ⟨when impeded in their ~, these people suddenly ceased muttering —E.A.Poe⟩ ⟨a fishing boat made a slow ~ —Elizabeth Bowen⟩ ⟨~ to the presidency and chairmanship of the board —*Current Biog.*⟩ **b :** a movement onward (as in time or space) **:** a forward course **:** PROGRESSION ⟨the daily ~ of the sun⟩ ⟨the ~ of a disease⟩ ⟨we make ~ — we pass from night to morning —Edmund Wilson⟩ **3** *Scots law* **:** succession in right to a feudal estate **:** the abstract of title with the deeds evidencing such succession **4 a :** the action or process of advancing or improving by marked stages or degrees **:** gradual betterment; *esp* **:** the progressive development or evolution of mankind ⟨there was a general belief in inevitable and universal ~ —John Berger⟩ ⟨found in civil law principles . . . the analogies that were needed to smooth the path of ~ —B.N. Cardozo⟩ **b :** a theory that change from old to new is essential to progress — **in progress :** going on **:** OCCURRING ⟨entertained troops . . . while the fighting was still *in progress* —*Current Biog.*⟩ ⟨with the beginning of healing already *in progress* —Morris Fishbein⟩

²**pro·gress** \prə'gres, prō'-\ *vb* -ED/-ING/-ES [partly fr. ¹*progress*; partly fr. L *progressus*, past part. of *progredi*] *vi* **1 :** to make a journey; *esp* **:** to make a royal progress **2 :** to move forward **:** to proceed or advance from place to place, point to point, or step to step ⟨simply ~ from one place to another as her fancy dictated —Louis Bromfield⟩ ⟨the fireplace is ~*ing*, but not finished yet —Rachel Henning⟩ **3 :** to develop to a higher, better, or more advanced stage **:** make continual improvements ⟨deductive reasoning had to be combined with the methods of experimentation . . . before science could ~ —J.B.Conant⟩ **4 :** to proceed from one musical note or tone to the next ~ *vt* **1** *obs* **:** to pass over or through **2 :** to cause to progress **:** push forward **:** ADVANCE ⟨a really big housing program cannot be successfully ~*ed* —*Americana Annual*⟩

progress chart *n* **:** a chart showing actual performance in comparison with a predetermined schedule or estimate of expected performance

progress clerk *n* **:** a clerk employed to plot out and trace the progress of work from operation to operation in manufacture

pro·gres·sion \prə'greshən, prō'-\ *n* -s [ME *progressioun*, fr. MF *progression*, fr. L *progression-, progressio* action of going forward, advancement, progress, fr. *progressus* (past part. of *progredi* to go forward, advance) + *-ion-, -io* -ion — more at PROGRESS] **1 :** a sequence of mathematical terms in which the terms after the first are determined according to a rule **2 a :** an action of progressing **:** a movement forward **:** ADVANCE ⟨the train . . . is the most amusing means of ~ —*Nat'l Geographic*⟩ **b :** a continuous proceeding **:** a connected series (as of acts, events, steps) **:** a sequence whose continuity suggests movement or flow ⟨all the events and ~*s* of . . . life were gathered up and recorded —Victoria Sackville-West⟩ **c :** the process of advancing esp. to a better or higher condition **:** gradual development **:** PROGRESS ⟨a sphere in which spiritual ~ is impossible —Matthew Arnold⟩ ⟨an inner ~ . . . from apprehension to understanding —R.W.Southern⟩ **3 a :** succession of musical tones or chords **b :** the movement of musical parts in harmony **c :** SEQUENCE 2c **4 :** a betting system in which a player increases his bet by a given sum after each loss and decreases it after each win

pro·gres·sion·al \-shənᵊl\ *adj* **:** of, relating to, or characterized by progression

pro·gres·sion·ist \-sh(ə)nəst\ *n* -s **:** one who believes in progress; *esp* **:** one who believes in the continuous progress of the human race or of society

prog·ress·ism \¦prägrə,sizəm\ *n* -s [F *progressisme*, fr. *progrès* progress (fr. L *progressus*) + *-isme* -ism — more at PROGRESS] **:** advocacy of or devotion esp. to progressive action or social and political reform ⟨illuminating observations on the political ~ of . . . the Northwest —*N. Y. Herald Tribune*⟩

prog·ress·ist \-səst\ *n* -s [F *progressiste*, fr. *progrès* + *-iste* -ist] **1 :** PROGRESSIONIST **2 :** a member of a political party holding views assumed to be progressive

¹**pro·gres·sive** \prə'gresiv, prō'-, -sēv *also* -səv\ *adj* [²*progress* & *progression* + *-ive*] **1 a :** of, relating to, or characterized by progress **:** devoted to or evincing continuous improvement **:** making use of or interested in new ideas, inventions, or opportunities ⟨a young man of ~ tastes —H.S.Canby⟩ ⟨he was . . . of ~ tendencies —E.H.Jenkins⟩ ⟨a practical, ~, hard-driving American city —*Amer. Guide Series: La.*⟩ ⟨the art of stage design is ~ —*Times Lit. Supp.*⟩ **b :** of, relating to, or constituting an educational theory or doctrine that opposes itself to traditional education proposing greater emphasis on the individual child, the use of projects and activities for teaching purposes, informality of classroom procedure, and encouragement of self-expression **2 :** of, relating to, or characterized by progression **:** occurring or arranged in a series **:** advancing or becoming effective by successive stages ⟨the price may be the ~ deterioration of our faculties —W.R.Inge⟩ ⟨~ changes of compressed decaying plant materials to peat . . . and finally anthracite coal —R.W.Murray⟩ ⟨the ~ complexity of business relationship —Helen Sullivan⟩ ⟨the ~ forms of that animal life were struggling for a foothold on the land —W.E. Swinton⟩ **3 :** moving forward or onward **:** ADVANCING ⟨the ~ currents, drifts, and eddies of the wide ocean —R.E.Coker⟩ **4 :** increasing in extent or severity — used of a disease, lesion, or symptom **5** *often cap* **:** of, relating to, or constituting a political party advocating or associated with the principles of political progressivism **6 :** marked by progression from one place to another: as **a** *of a card party* **:** characterized by the moving between rounds of the winners at each table to a higher or next table and the changing of partners **b** *of a meal* **:** having its courses served at different locations **7 :** of, relating to, or constituting a verb form that expresses action or state in progress or continuance at the time of speaking or a time spoken of ⟨*am seeing, had been seeing, is being seen* are ~ forms⟩ **8 :** having the nature of the second of two sounds dependent on the nature of the first ⟨~ assimilation or palatalization⟩ **9 :** of or relating to a tax or taxation imposed on an individual that increases by a given amount with increases in the tax base — used chiefly of income and death taxes **10 :** relating to or characterized by burning (as of perforated grains of smokeless powder) in which the surface increases as the burning advances — opposed to *degressive* **syn** see LIBERAL

²**progressive** \"\ *n* -s **1 a :** one that is progressive **b :** one holding political convictions based on a belief in moderate change designed to improve the condition of the majority of the people and willing to use governmental power to bring about change **:** one believing in change as a desirable means of achieving specified goals — compare CONSERVATIVE, LIBERAL **2** *usu cap* **a :** a member of a U.S. political party: as (1) **:** a member of a predominantly agrarian minor party split off from the Republicans in the early 20th century and advocating domestic reforms designed primarily to reduce the power of and eliminate abuses alleged to be perpetrated by the great industrial and financial interests; *specif* **:** BULL MOOSE (2) **:** a follower of Robert M. La Follette in the presidential campaign of 1924 (3) **:** a follower of Henry A. Wallace in the presidential campaign of 1948 (4) **:** a member of a left-wing minor party split off from the Democrats and usu. associated with essentially socialist domestic policies and a pro-Russian foreign policy **b :** a member of a primarily agrarian Canadian political party advocating low tariffs, nationalization of railways, and direct democracy (as through the use of the initiative, referendum, and recall) and achieving its chief strength in the early 1920s

progressive-alphabet cipher *n* **:** polyalphabetic substitution in which the choice of alphabets runs through them all in a definite order — compare MULTIPLE-ALPHABET CIPHER

¹**progressive conservative** *adj, usu cap P&C* **:** of, relating to, or constituting a major political party in Canada traditionally associated with economic nationalism and esp. a protective tariff and with advocacy of close ties with the United Kingdom and the Commonwealth

²**progressive conservative** *n, usu cap P&C* **:** a member or supporter of the Progressive Conservative party

progressive dies *n* **:** a compound tool used in a punch press for performing several operations (as drawing, punching, bending) in a single movement or in as few as possible successive movements

progressive dunker *n, usu cap P&D* **:** a member of a religious group of Brethren who because of their desire for more stress on education, a church polity that was congregational, and less rigid rules regarding plain dress left the Church of the Brethren in 1882 and formed the Brethren Church

progressive jazz *n* **:** jazz of the 1950s characterized by harmonic, contrapuntal, and rhythmic experimentation

pro·gres·sive·ly \-səvlē, -sēv-, -li\ *adv* **:** in a progressive manner **:** continuously step by step ⟨mechanization ~ opened up ever more places for the unskilled —Oscar Handlin⟩ ⟨expect little from government and ~ rely on it more —Felix Frankfurter⟩

progressive muscular dystrophy *n* **:** MUSCULAR DYSTROPHY

pro·gres·sive·ness \-sivnəs\ *n* -ES **:** the quality or state of being progressive

progressive proof *n* **:** a proof of a set made from plates for color printing showing each color separately and then the colors combined with one color being added at a time in the order in which they are to print

progressive rummy *n* **:** a variety of contract rummy

progressive scanning *n* **:** television scanning in which each successive line is scanned in sequence — compare INTERLACED SCANNING

progressive sorites *n* **:** a sorites arranged so that the predicate of each proposition that precedes forms the subject of each one that follows and the conclusion unites the subject of the first proposition with the predicate of the last proposition — compare GOCLENIAN SORITES

progressive system *n* **:** ALEMBERT

pro·gres·siv·ism \-sə,vizəm\ *n* -s **1 :** the principles or beliefs of progressives **2 :** PROGRESS 4a **3** *usu cap* **:** the political and economic doctrines advocated by the Progressives **4 :** the theories of progressive education — contrasted with *essentialism*

¹**pro·gres·siv·ist** \-,vəst\ *n* -s [¹*progressive* + *-ist*] **:** PROGRESSIVE

²**progressivist** \"\ *adj* **:** of or relating to progressivism or progressivists ⟨a tension between . . . ~ tendencies of thought and conservative . . . ones —Douglas Knight⟩

pro·gres·siv·i·ty \,prō,gre'sivəd·ē\ *n* -ES **:** PROGRESSIVENESS

progress payment *n* **:** a partial payment made under a construction contract as the project goes forward

progs *pres 3d sing of* PROG, *pl of* PROG

pro·guan·il \prō'gwänəl\ *n* -s [*isopropyl* + *guanine* + *-il*] **:** CHLOROGUANIDE

progue \'prōg\ *var of* PROG

pro·gymnosperm \(')prō+\ *n* [¹*pro-* + *gymnosperm*] **:** one of the ancestral fossil types from which modern gymnosperms are thought to have been derived — **pro·gymnospermic** \(¦)prō+\ *adj* — **progymnospermous** \"+\ *adj*

pro·haptor \(')prō+\ *n* -s [NL, fr. ¹*pro-* + *haptor*] **:** the complex anterior attachment organ of a typical monogenetic trematode

pro·hib·it \prō'hibət, prə'-, *usu* -bəd.+V\ *vt* -ED/-ING/-s [ME *prohibiten*, fr. L *prohibitus*, past part. of *prohibēre* to hold back, hinder, forbid, fr. *pro-* forward, forth + *-hibēre* (fr. *habēre* to hold, have) — more at PRO-, GIVE] **1 :** to forbid by authority or command **:** ENJOIN, INTERDICT ⟨the statute . . . ~*ed* the employment of workers under 16 years — *Amer. Guide Series: N.C.*⟩ **2 a :** to prevent from doing or accomplishing something **:** effectively stop ⟨children should be ~*ed* from riding bicycles on the sidewalk⟩ **b :** to make impossible **:** DEBAR, HINDER, PRECLUDE ⟨family finances ~*ed* his going to college —*Current Biog.*⟩ **syn** see FORBID

prohibited degree *n* **:** FORBIDDEN DEGREE

pro·hib·it·er \-bəd·ə(r), -bətə-\ *n* -s **:** one that prohibits

pro·hi·bi·tion \,prōə'bishən, ,prōhə'-\ *n* -s [ME *prohibicioun*, fr. MF *prohibition*, fr. L *prohibition-, prohibitio*, fr. *prohibitus* (past part of *prohibēre* to prohibit) + *-ion-, -io* -ion — more at PROHIBIT] **1 :** WRIT OF PROHIBITION **2 :** the act of prohibiting by or as if by authority **3 :** a declaration or injunction forbidding an action **:** an order to restrain or stop ⟨enforcing many ~*s* against his settlers concerning trade, crops, and occupations —*Amer. Guide Series: Del.*⟩ ⟨don't often issue positive ~*s* in my capacity of superior officer —S.E.White⟩ **4 a :** the forbidding by law of the sale and sometimes the manufacture of alcoholic liquors as beverages **b :** the forbidding by law of the transportation as well as the manufacture and sale of intoxicating liquors except for medicinal and sacramental purposes

pro·hi·bi·tion·ist \-sh(ə)nəst\ *n* -s **:** one who favors the prohibition of the sale or manufacture of alcoholic liquors as beverages: as **a** *usu cap* **:** a member of a minor U.S. political party that has as its fundamental platform the prohibition by law of the manufacture, importation, transportation and sale of alcoholic beverages **b :** a supporter of the 18th Amendment to the Constitution

pro·hib·i·tive \prō'hibəd·iv, prə'-, -bətiv\ *adj* [F *prohibitif*, fr. LL *prohibitivus*, fr. L *prohibitus* (past part. of *prohibēre* to prohibit) + *-ivus* -ive — more at PROHIBIT] **1 :** tending to prohibit or interdict **:** restraining from a desired course or action ⟨the ~ power of the police⟩ ⟨can be expressed without meeting anger or ridicule in a ~ measure —Christopher Sykes⟩ **2 :** serving to preclude the use of something — usu. used of a price or a tax ⟨the price . . . was almost ~ —A.G.DuMez⟩ ⟨the rise of ~ taxes and inheritance dues —F.B.Millett⟩

prohibitive impediment *n* **:** the impediment to a marriage whose existence does not nullify the marriage but subjects the parties to punishment

pro·hib·i·tive·ly \-əvlē\ *adv* **:** in a prohibitive manner ⟨it is ~ time-consuming —*Biol. Abstracts*⟩

pro·hib·i·tive·ness \-ivnəs\ *n* -ES **:** the quality or state of being prohibitive

pro·hib·i·tor \-bəd·ə(r), -bətə-\ *n* -s [L fr. *prohibitus* (past part. of *prohibēre* to prohibit) + *-or* — more at PROHIBIT] **:** one that prohibits

pro·hib·i·to·ry \-bə,tōrē, -tòr-, -ri\ *adj* [L *prohibitorius*, fr. *prohibitus* (past part. of *prohibēre* to prohibit) + *-orius* -ory — more at PROHIBIT] **:** PROHIBITIVE

prohibitory injunction *n* **:** a legal injunction granted before the merits of a case are heard restraining one party from doing some act or threatened act to the injury of another party — compare MANDATORY INJUNCTION

pro in·di·vi·so \(¦)prō,ində'vī(,)zō\ *adv* [L] **:** for or as undivided **:** in common **:** in joint tenancy or coparcenary

pro·japygidae \¦prō+\ *n pl, cap* [NL, fr. *Projapyg-, Projapyx*, type genus (fr. ¹*pro-* + *Japyg-, Japyx*) + *-idae*] **:** a small but widely distributed family of the order Entotrophi comprising minute chiefly tropical subterranean insects

pro·jeck \prō'jek, prə'-\ *dial var of* PROJECT *vi* 1

¹**proj·ect** \'prä,jekt, 'prō-, -jəkt\ *n* -s [ME *proiecte*, modif. (influenced by L *projectus*, past part. of *proicere, projicere* to throw forth) of MF *pourjet, porjet, pourject*, fr. *pourjeter, porjeter, pourjecter* to throw out, spy, get the lay of the land, plan, fr. *pour-, por-* (fr. L *porro* forward, onward) + *jeter* to throw; akin to Gk *porrō* away, forward, *pro* forward, ahead — more at PROJECTION, FOR, JET] **1 :** a specific plan or design: as **a** *obs* **:** a tabular outline **:** DRAFT, PATTERN **b :** a devised or proposed plan **:** a scheme for which there seems hope of success **:** PROPOSAL ⟨presented his ~ to the committee⟩ ⟨he discusses his ~*s* with her —*Current Biog.*⟩ **2** *obs* **:** a mental conception **:** IDEA **3 :** a planned undertaking: as **a :** a definitely formulated piece of research **b** (1) **:** an undertaking devised to effect the reclamation or improvement of a particular area of land ⟨the construction of small irrigation ~*s* —W. O.Douglas⟩ (2) **:** the area of land involved **c :** a systematically built group of houses or apartment buildings; *esp* **:** one that includes community facilities and has been socially planned with government support to serve low-income families **d :** a vast enterprise usu. sponsored and financed by a government ⟨tax money made for setting up public work ~*s* —*Amer. Guide Series: N.Y.*⟩ ⟨the ~, as authorized by Congress . . . provided for a ten-year expenditure of $88 million —*Current Biog.*⟩ **4 :** PROJET 2 **5 :** a task or problem that is engaged in usu. by a group of students to supplement and apply classroom studies and that often involves a variety of mental and physical activities related to the center of interest ⟨making a model of the Shakespearean stage is a good ~ for an English class⟩ **6 :** PROJECTION 8b (1) **syn** see PLAN

²**pro·ject** \prə'jekt, prō'-\ *vb* -ED/-ING/-s [modif. (influenced by L *projectus*) of MF *pourjeter, porjeter, pourjecter*] *vt* **1 :** to devise in the mind **:** plan for **:** CONTRIVE, DESIGN ⟨a road is now ~*ed* all the way along the south side —G.R.Stewart⟩ ⟨support . . . is mighty important in ~*ing* school building programs —*Education Digest*⟩ ⟨ridiculed plants of this size when they were first ~*ed* —M.W.Straight⟩ **2 :** to throw or cast forward **:** shoot forth ⟨a fountain that ~*s* its slender column of water about 75 feet in the air —*Amer. Guide Series: N.C.*⟩ ⟨plans were made to ~ iron missiles —*Current Biog.*⟩ **3 :** to put or set forth **:** present for consideration **:** exhibit the characteristics of ⟨in these volumes I was trying to ~ how this world would have appeared —F.M.Ford⟩ ⟨doing a grand job ~*ing* Britain overseas —Asher Lee⟩ **4 :** to conceive of mentally **:** IMAGINE **5 :** to cause to protrude ⟨a tiny kitchen which had no equipment . . . visibly ~*ed* —Martin Flavin⟩ **6 a :** to cause (light or shadow) to fall into space or (an image) upon a surface ⟨these pictures have been ~*ed* on screens throughout the U.S. —*Current Biog.*⟩ **b :** to cause (a figure) to stand out distinctly against a background ⟨appeared on his doorstep, darkly ~*ed* against a blaze of light —Edith Wharton⟩ **7 a :** to move in a prescribed direction (as a point, line, or area) so as to depict on a curve, a plane, or a cylindrical, spherical, or other surface so that the picture thus represented on the curve or surface is the shadow of the points, lines, or areas that would be thrown by parallel, diverging, or converging rays of light ⟨the map maker ~*ed* the world as the section of a cylinder suspended in the center of the circular vault of heaven —Tad Szulc⟩ **b :** to depict (one figure) by another figure according to a fixed correspondence between the points of the two **8 a :** to communicate or convey vividly esp. to an audience ⟨not only sang beautifully, but ~*ed* the drama very well —Robert Evett⟩ **b :** to produce with exceptional clarity and distinctness ⟨a particularly brilliant example of the singer who knows how to ~ our language —Howard Taubman⟩ ⟨his voice is not large but . . . is ~*ed* well —W.M.Clark⟩ **9 :** to externalize and regard as objective or outside oneself (as a sensation, image, or emotion) ⟨a nation is an entity on which one can ~ many of the worst of one's instincts —*Times Lit. Supp.*⟩ — opposed to *introject* ~ *vi* **1** *chiefly dial* **a :** to form a project **:** SCHEME **b :** to go about idly with no particular purpose **:** fool around ⟨I wouldn't go ~*ing* off into the woods alone —C.B.Kelland⟩ — often used with *around* **2 :** to jut out **:** extend beyond a given line **:** PROTRUDE ⟨the walls in places ~ into massive buttresses —Andrew Finn⟩ ⟨hands ~*ed* a little too far from the sleeves —J.P.Marquand⟩ **3 a :** to communicate or convey an idea or conception vividly esp. to an audience **b :** to speak with exceptional clarity and distinction ⟨a young actor who had no idea how to ~ to the last row⟩ **syn** see BULGE, ¹PLAN

³**project** *adj* [L *projectus*, past part. of *proicere, projicere* to throw forth, reject — more at PROJECTION] *obs* **:** ABANDONED

pro·ject·able \-təbəl\ *adj* **:** capable of being projected ⟨results of the random sampling must be ~ to national totals⟩

projected *adj* **1 :** thrown or as if thrown or cast forward ⟨the ~ scene of the mountains brought scattered applause from the audience⟩ **2 :** planned for future execution **:** CONTRIVED, PROPOSED ⟨a ~ excursion a full day long —W.F.DeMorgan⟩ ⟨~ outlays for new plant and equipment —J.G.Forrest⟩

¹**pro·jec·tile** \prə'jektᵊl, -k,tīl, -k(,)til, prō'-\ *n* -s [NL, fr. neut. of *projectilis*, adj.] **1 :** a body projected by external force and continuing in motion by its own inertia (subatomic particles used as ~*s* in atom smashing); *specif* **:** a missile for a firearm, cannon, or other weapon **2 :** a self-propelling weapon (as a rocket, torpedo, or guided missile)

²**projectile** \"\ *adj* [NL *projectilis*, fr. L *projectus* (past part. of *proicere, projicere* to throw forth) + *-ilis* -ile — more at PROJECTION] **1 :** caused or imparted by impulse or projection **:** impelled forward ⟨~ motion⟩ **2 :** projecting or impelling forward ⟨the great injury . . . was more owing to the gravity of the stone . . . than to the ~ force of it —Laurence Sterne⟩ ⟨his family was getting on in the world and . . . he was to receive a ~ push from them —John Dollard⟩ **3 :** capable of being hurled, thrown, or projected with force similar to a missile **4 :** capable of being thrust forward — **pro·jec·tile·ly** \-l(l)ē\ *adv*

projectile lathe *n* **:** a lathe for turning and pointing projectiles

projectile point *n* **:** a point that constitutes a projectile or projectile head (as a dart or arrowhead)

projectile vomiting *n* **:** vomiting that is sudden, usu. without nausea, and so sufficiently vigorous that the vomitus is forcefully projected to a distance

projecting *adj* **:** PROTRUSIVE ⟨low ~ eaves which keep out summer heat —D.C.Buchanan⟩

pro·jec·tion \prə'jekshən, prō'-\ *n* -s [MF, fr. L *projection-, projectio*, fr. *projectus* (past part. of *proicere, projicere* to throw forth, throw down, stretch out, jut out, fr. *pro-* forward, down + *-icere, jicere*, fr. *jacere* to throw) + *-ion-, -io* -ion — more at PRO-, JET] **1 :** a systematic presentation of intersecting coordinate lines on a flat surface upon which features from the curved surface of the earth or the celestial sphere may be mapped — compare CONIC PROJECTION, CYLINDRICAL PROJECTION, GNOMONIC PROJECTION, MERCATOR PROJECTION, ORTHOGRAPHIC PROJECTION, STEREOGRAPHIC PROJECTION **2 a :** the casting by an alchemist of a powder into a crucible containing a metal to effect its transmutation **b :** a transforming change **3 a :** the act of throwing or shooting forward **:** EJECTION ⟨watched the ~ of the arrow⟩ **b :** the state of being thrown or shot forward **4 a :** the forming of a plan **:** SCHEMING **b :** something that is planned **:** DESIGN **5 :** the representation of something against a background (as an image or shadow) **6 a** (1) **:** a jutting out or causing to jut out (2) **:** a part that projects or juts out **:** an extension beyond something else ⟨~ of earth above its natural level —Thomas Hardy⟩ ⟨~*s* . . . in the corners reveal the heavy timber framework —*Amer. Guide Series: Mich.*⟩ **b :** a view of a building or architectural element (as a front elevation) — used esp. of architectural drawings **7 a :** the operation of projecting b : the picture so formed — see AXONOMETRIC PROJECTION, OBLIQUE PROJECTION, ORTHOGRAPHIC PROJECTION, TRIMETRIC PROJECTION **c** : a segment joining the projections of the ends of a given segment upon a given line or plane **d** : the foot of a perpendicular from a point upon a line or plane **8 a** (1) : the act of perceiving a mental object as spatially and sensibly objective or of objectifying what is primarily subjective (2) : a mental object or image so perceived ⟨writing from experience or from an imaginative ~ of experience —Malcolm Cowley⟩ **b** : the act of externalizing: as (1) : the spontaneous localization of a sensory impression or memory image either upon the surface of the body or outside in space ⟨the ~ of an afterimage upon a wall⟩ (2) : the attribution to other people and to objects of one's own ideas, feelings, or attitudes; *esp* : the externalization of blame, guilt, or responsibility for one's thoughts or actions as an unconscious mechanism to defend the ego against anxiety ⟨delusions of persecution are based on the mechanism of ~⟩ **9 a** : the display of motion pictures by projecting an image from them upon a screen for either visual or aural review **b** : the process of projecting the image of a negative or positive for viewing on a screen or for exposing a print on a light-sensitive material **10 a** : the act of communicating or conveying a vivid image esp. to an audience ⟨she excels in genuine stage ~ —Stark Young⟩ **b** : clarity and distinctness esp. of a voice ⟨sings . . . with the rugged, compelling ~ that has brought him such success —J.S.Wilson b. 1913⟩ **11** : the functional correspondence and connection of parts of the cerebral cortex with parts of the organism ⟨the ~ of the retina upon the visual area⟩ **12 a** : the carrying forward of a trend into the future **b** : an estimate of future possibilities based on a current trend ⟨~s of increases in number of households —M.D.Ketchum⟩

pro·jec·tion·al \-shənᵊl, -shnəl\ *adj* : of, relating to, or making use of projection

projection area *n* : an area of the cerebral cortex having connection through projection fibers with subcortical centers that in turn are linked with peripheral sense or motor organs

projection booth *n* : a usu. fireproof booth in a theater or assembly hall for housing a motion-picture or other projector

projection fiber *n* : a nerve fiber connecting some part of the cerebral cortex with lower sensory or motor centers — distinguished from *association fiber*

projection formula *n* : a perspective formula projected so as to represent it in two dimensions — compare STRUCTURAL FORMULA

COOH / H–C–NH_2 / CH_2OH — D-serine; COOH / H_2N–C–H / CH_2OH — L-serine

projection formula

pro·jec·tion·ist \-sh(ə)nəst\ *n* -s : one who projects or makes projections: as **a** : one skilled in the process of making projections; *esp* : a map maker **b** : one who operates a motion-picture projector **c** : an operator of television equipment

projection print *n* : a photographic print made by projecting the image of the negative upon light-sensitive paper — compare CONTACT PRINT

projection television *n* : a television picture that is picked up from a picture tube of relatively small size and that by means of an optical system is greatly magnified and projected on a large screen

projection welding *n* : a resistance welding made by joining embossments on one or both of the parts being welded

pro·jec·tive \prə'jektiv, prō'-, -tēv\ *adj* [²*project* + *-ive*] **1** : relating to or produced by projection: as **a** : of or relating to such properties of curves or surfaces as are unaltered by projection **b** : not metrical : not involving size and measurement but only relative position, incidences, and coincidences **c** : transformable into one another by repeated projections and sections **2** : jutting out : PROJECTING **3 a** : externalizing esp. images or ideas ⟨a victim of his own ~ imagination⟩ **b** : revealing a subjective opinion ⟨~ adjectives of approval and disapproval —N.C.Stageberg⟩ **4** : of or relating to a technique, test, or device designed to analyze the psychodynamic constitution of an individual by presenting to him unstructured or ambiguous material (as inkblots, pictures, and sentence elements) that will elicit interpretive responses revealing his personality structure — compare RORSCHACH TEST **5** : relating to a social mechanism through which personality traits are given expression ⟨evidence of ~ material in folklore and legends⟩

projective geometry *n* : a branch of geometry that deals with the properties of geometric configurations that are unaltered by projective transformation and in which the notion of length does not appear

pro·jec·tive·ly \-təvlē\ *adv* : in a projective manner

projective transformation *n* : a transformation of space that sends points into points, lines into lines, planes into planes, and any two incident elements into two incident elements

pro·jec·tiv·i·ty \ˌprōˌjek'tivəd·ē, ˌprä,-\ *n* -ES : projective character or relation : the quality in one geometric figure of being derivable from another by projection : PROJECTIVE TRANSFORMATION

pro·jec·tor \prə'jektə(r), prō'-\ *n* -s [²*project* + *-or*] **1 a** : one that plans a project **b** : one that promotes a chimerical project : SCHEMER **2** : one that projects: as **a** : a device for projecting a beam of light ⟨a searchlight ~⟩ **b** : an optical instrument for projecting an image upon a surface (as a screen) by means of the transmission of light through a transparent slide or film or the reflection of light from an opaque object (as a photograph or postcard) **c** : a machine for projecting and showing motion pictures on a screen — compare SOUND PROJECTOR **d** : a smooth bore weapon usu. used for launching grenades or pyrotechnic signals **3** : a projection line (as from an object to a plane of projection) — used esp. in mechanical drawing

projects *pl of* PROJECT, *pres 3d sing of* PROJECT

pro·jec·ture \prə'jekchə(r)\ *n* -s [²*project* + *-ure*] : the state or fact of projecting or jutting out : PROJECTION

pro·jet \(')prō¦zhā\ *n* -s [F, project, plan, sketch — more at PROJECT] **1** : PLAN; *esp* : a draft of a proposed measure or treaty **2** : a projected or proposed design esp. when developed beyond the stage of a sketch

pro·ji·cience \prō'jishən(t)s\ *n* -s **1** : the property of being projicient : reference of a perceived quality or modification of consciousness to an external reality **2** : PROJECTION 8b(1)

pro·ji·cient \-nt\ *adj* [L *projicient-, projiciens*, pres. part. of *proicere, projicere* to jut out — more at PROJECTION] : serving to bring an organism into relation with the environment ⟨the ~ senses⟩ ⟨~ neuromuscular system⟩ — **pro·ji·cient·ly** *adv*

proke \'prōk\ *vb* -ED/-ING/-S [ME *proken*; akin to LG *proken* to prod, poke] *dial Brit* : POKE, STIR

pro·kei·me·non \prō'kīmə,nän\ *n, pl* **prokeime·na** \-,nə\ [LGk, fr. Gk, neut. of *prokeimenos*, pres. part. of *prokeisthai* to lie before, precede, fr. *pro-* ¹pro- + *keisthai* to lie — more at CEMETERY] : a short anthem sung in Eastern churches before the reading of a passage from the Acts, the Epistles, or the Apocalypse

pro·ko·pevsk \prə'kōp(y)əfsk\ *adj, usu cap* [fr. *Prokopevsk*, U.S.S.R.] : of or from the city of Prokopevsk, U.S.S.R. : of the kind or style prevalent in Prokopevsk

prol *abbr* prologue

pro·la·bi·um \prō'lābēəm\ *n* [NL, fr. ¹*pro-* + L *labium* lip — more at LIP] : the exposed part of a lip; *esp* : the protuberant central part of the upper lip

pro·labor \(')prō+\ *adj* [²*pro-* + *labor*] : favoring or supporting a labor union or organized labor ⟨~ legislation⟩

pro·lac·tin \prō'laktən\ *n* -s [²*pro-* + *lact-* + *-in*] : LACTOGENIC HORMONE

pro·lam·in \prō'lamən, 'prōləmən\ *or* **pro·lam·ine** \-mən, -,mēn\ *n* -s [ISV *proline* + *ammonia* + *-in, -ine*] : any of a class of simple proteins (as zein, gliadin, hordein) that are found esp. in seeds and are soluble in relatively strong alcohol but insoluble in absolute alcohol, water, and neutral solvents

pro·lan \'prō,lan\ *n* -s [G, fr. L *proles* offspring, progeny — more at PROLETARIAN] : either of two gonadotropic hormones: **a** *or* **prolan A** : FOLLICLE-STIMULATING HORMONE **b** *or* **prolan B** : LUTEINIZING HORMONE

¹**pro·lapse** \prō'laps, '=,=\ *n* [NL *prolapsus*, fr. LL, fall, fr. L *prolapsus*, past part. of *prolabi* to slide forward, fall down, fr. *pro-* forward, down + *labi* to slide, fall — more at PRO-, SLEEP] **1** : the falling down of an internal part of the body ⟨~ of the uterus⟩ **2** : the slipping of a body part from its usual position in relation to other parts ⟨~ of an intervertebral disk⟩

²**prolapse** \"\ *vi* : to fall or slip forward, down, or out (as in a prolapse)

pro·lap·sis \prō'lapsəs\ *n* -ES [alter. of NL *prolapsus*] : PROLAPSE

pro·lap·sus \-səs\ *n* -ES [NL — more at PROLAPSE] : PROLAPSE

pro·larva \(')prō+\ *n* [¹*pro-* + *larva*] : a newly hatched fish in which the mouth parts are undeveloped and nutrition is from the yolk sac — **pro·larval** \"+\ *adj*

¹**pro·late** \prō'lāt\ *vt* [L *prolatus*, suppletive past part. of *proferre* to utter, extend] *archaic* : to utter or pronounce esp. with prolonged or drawling enunciation ⟨for the sake of . . . solemnity, every note was *prolated* in one uniform mode of intonation —William Mason⟩

²**pro·late** \(')prō¦lāt\ *adj* [L *prolatus* (suppletive past part. of *proferre* to bring forward, utter, extend), fr. *pro-* forward + *latus*, suppletive past part. of *ferre* to bear — more at PRO-, TOLERATE] **1** : stretched out : EXTENDED; *esp* : elongated in the direction of a line joining the poles — opposed to *oblate* **2** : PROLATIVE — **pro·late·ly** *adv* — **pro·late·ness** *n* -ES

prolate spheroid *n* [²*prolate*] : an ellipsoid of revolution generated by revolving an ellipse about its major axis

pro·la·tion \prō'lāshən\ *n* -s [L *prolation-, prolatio*, fr. *prolatus* + *-ion-, -io* -ion] **1** *obs* : UTTERANCE ⟨the ~ of the words of benediction —John Lloyd⟩ **2** : the division of musical notes in mensural notation into duple or triple time

pro·la·tive \prō'lād·iv\ *adj* [L *prolatus* + E *-ive*] : serving to extend or complete the predication — **pro·la·tive·ly** \-əvlē\ *adv*

prole \'prōl(ə)\ *n* -s [short for *proletarian*] *chiefly Brit* : a member of the proletariat ⟨the ~s . . . perform routine tasks of work —Irving Howe⟩

pro·leg \'prō+,=\ *n* [²*pro-* + *leg*] : a fleshy leg found on the abdominal segments of the larvae of lepidopterans, sawflies, and some other insects

pro·le·gom·e·non \ˌprōlə'gämə,nän, -,nən\ *n, pl* **prolegome·na** \-,nə\ *sometimes sing in constr* [Gk, neut. pres. passive part. of *prolegein* to say beforehand, fr. *pro-* ¹pro- + *legein* to say — more at LEGEND] **1** : prefatory remarks or introductory observations; *specif* : a formal essay or critical discussion serving to introduce and interpret an extended work ⟨the *prolegomena* to a work on Shakespeare's dramatic structure —E.T.Sehrt⟩ **2** : a reading or group of readings or intellectual exercises leading to further understanding, development, or advance in knowledge or technique in a subject matter field : INTRODUCTION ⟨fundamental points . . . constitute a ~ to any future philosophy of criticism —Morris Weitz⟩ ⟨working out the *prolegomena* to a new technique of communication —*Monthly*⟩ ⟨serves as a full-length *prolegomena* to a new phase in our way of thinking about the relation of science to society —*Times Lit. Supp.*⟩

pro·le·gom·e·nous \;==;==,nəs\ *adj* [*prolegomenon* + *-ous*] : of, relating to, or having the characteristics of a prolegomenon

pro·lep·sis \prō'lepsəs *chiefly Brit* -lēp-\ *n, pl* **prolep·ses** \-p,sēz\ [Gk *prolēpsis* anticipation, preconception, fr. *prolambanein* to take beforehand, anticipate, fr. *pro-* ¹pro- + *lambanein* to take — more at LATCH] **1** : the representation or assumption of a future act or development as being presently existing or accomplished : PROCHRONISM ⟨that ~, or prevision and apprehension of holiness which we call faith —Wilham Sunday⟩ **2 a** : a figure in which a matter is set forth in summary before being stated or related in detail ⟨a relation by ~, anticipation of the story —L.D.Lerner⟩ **b** : a figure by which objections are anticipated in order to weaken their force ⟨thought it needful . . . by way of ~, to prevent whatsoever might be surmised in that kind —Robert Sanderson⟩ **c** : the use of an attribute to denote a future condition or development as existing or occurrent when it is actually consequential (as in "ere humane statute purged the *gentle* weal") : anticipative use of an adjective **3 a** : a conception or belief derived from sense perception and therefore regarded as not necessarily true **b** : an empirical general conception — used esp. in Stoicism and Epicureanism **4** : PRESUPPOSITION, POSTULATE ⟨that nature should form real shells, without any design of covering an animal, is contrary to that innate ~ we have of the prudence of nature —John Ray⟩

pro·lep·tic \(')prō¦leptik *chiefly Brit* -lēp-\ *also* **pro·lep·ti·cal** \-təkəl\ *adj* [*proleptic* fr. Gk *prolēptikos*, fr. (assumed) *prolēptos* (verbal of *prolambanein* to anticipate) + *-ikos* -ic; *proleptical* fr. Gk *prolēptikos* + E *-al*] : of, relating to, or exemplifying prolepsis ⟨a ~ justification of the line he was to take —R.F.Harrod⟩ ⟨a ~ interpretation by the prophet of the future events —Georges Florovsky⟩ ⟨and he will move breathing through us wing-linked ~ of what Eden —Denis Devlin⟩ — **pro·lep·ti·cal·ly** \-tək(ə)lē\ *adv*

¹**pro·le·tar·i·an** \ˌprōlə¦terēən, -ta(a)r-, -tār-\ *n* -s [L *proletarius* proletarian (fr. *proles* offspring, progeny, fr. *pro-* forth + root of *-olescere* to grow) + E *-an* — more at PRO-, ADULT] : a member of the proletariat

²**proletarian** \"\ *adj* [¹*proletarian*] : of, relating to, or representative of the proletariat ⟨~ policy⟩ ⟨~ party⟩ ⟨~ literature⟩ ⟨~ background⟩ — opposed to *proprietarian*

proletarian dictatorship *n* : DICTATORSHIP OF THE PROLETARIAT

pro·le·tar·i·an·ism \ˌ==¦'==,nizəm\ *n* -s [*proletarian* + *-ism*] : the condition or political position of a proletarian

pro·le·tar·i·an·i·za·tion \ˌ==;==nə'zāshən, -,nī'z-\ *n* -s [*proletarianize* + *-ation*] : a change or shift to the status or level of the proletariat ⟨the ~ of the middle class —Daniel Lang⟩ ⟨a ~ of taste both in language and literature —Gilbert Murray⟩

pro·le·tar·i·an·ize \ˌ==;'==,nīz\ *vt* -ED/-ING/-S [¹*proletarian* + *-ize*] : to cause to undergo proletarianization ⟨has *proletarianized* the ruling minority —*Atlantic*⟩

pro·le·tar·i·an·ly *adv* : in a proletarian manner : according to proletarian sympathies or predilections

pro·le·tar·i·an·ness \-n(n)əs\ *n* -ES : the quality or state of being proletarian

¹**pro·le·tar·i·at** *also* **pro·le·tar·i·ate** \ˌprōlə'terēə|t, -ta(a)r-, -tār-, *sometimes* -ē,a|; *usu* |d·+V\ *n* -s [F *prolétariat*, fr. L *proletarius* proletarian + F *-at* -ate] **1** : the lowest social and economic class in ancient Rome **2** : the lowest social or economic class of a community ⟨a discontented ~ —*No. Amer. Rev.*⟩ ⟨savage ~ —Count Moffie⟩ **3** : the laboring class : WAGE EARNERS; *specif* : the industrial workers — compare ARISTOCRACY, BOURGEOISIE **4** *in Marxist doctrine* : the class of wage earners who lack their own means of production and hence sell their labor to live

²**proletariat** *or* **proletariate** \"\ *adj* [¹*proletariat*] : PROLETARIAN

pro·le·tar·i·za·tion \ˌprōlə,terə'zāshən, -,rī'z-\ *n* -s [*proletarize* + *-ation*] : PROLETARIANIZATION

pro·le·tar·ize \ˌprōlə'te,rīz\ *vt* -ED/-ING/-S [*proletary* + *-ize*] : PROLETARIANIZE

pro·le·tary \'prōlə,terē\ *n or adj* [L *proletarius* — more at PROLETARIAN] : PROLETARIAN

pro·let·cult *also* **pro·let·kult** \prō'let,kəlt\ *n* -s [Russ *proletkul't*, fr. *proletarskaya kul'tura*, proletarian culture] : a movement in the U. S. S. R. to foster an art and a culture expressive of proletarian interests and activities

pro·leucocyte *or* **pro·leukocyte** \(')prō+\ *n* [F, fr. *pro-* ¹pro- + *leucocyte*] **1** : LEUKOBLAST **2** : a basophilic immature cell of insect blood that gives rise to other kinds of blood cells

proli- *comb form* [L *proles* offspring, progeny — more at PROLETARIAN] : offspring ⟨*prolicidal*⟩ ⟨*proligerous*⟩

pro·lif·er·ant \prō'lifərənt\ *adj* [fr. *proliferate*, after such pairs as E *militate*: *militant*] : PROLIFIC

¹**pro·lif·er·ate** \-ə,rāt, *usu* -ād·+V\ *vb* -ED/-ING/-S [back-formation fr. *proliferation*] *vi* **1** : to grow by proliferation ⟨the nerve tips ~ —F.A.Geldord⟩ **2** : to increase in numbers as if by proliferation : BURGEON, EXPAND, MULTIPLY, SPREAD ⟨had *proliferated* into eleven subsidiary agencies —*Time*⟩ ⟨fantasies — where facts are few —Weston La Barre⟩ ⟨buildings which . . . ~ farther back —*Fortune*⟩ ~ *vt* **1** : to cause to grow by proliferation **2** : to cause to increase in numbers as if by proliferation : produce abundantly ⟨that fellow *proliferated* ideas —H.J.Laski⟩ ⟨tendency to ~ jobs and men —J.K.Galbraith⟩

²**pro·lif·er·ate** \-,rət, -,rāt, *usu* -d·+V\ *adj* [back-formation fr. *proliferation*] : developing a leafy shoot from a normally terminal organ — used esp. of a flower

pro·lif·er·a·tion \=,=='rāshən\ *n* -s [F *prolifération*, fr. *proliférer* to proliferate (fr. *prolifère* proliferous, fr. *proli-* + *-fère* -ferous) + *-ation*] **1 a** : rapid and repeated production of new parts or of buds or offspring (as in a mass of cells by a rapid succession of cell divisions or in a coral by the production of buds in quick succession) **b** : a growth so formed **2** : the action, process, or result of increasing by or as if by proliferation ⟨the ~ of subjects taught —S.A.Rice⟩ ⟨the ~ of error —Norman Cousins⟩ ⟨~ and fragmentation of parties —Geoffrey Sawer⟩

pro·lif·er·a·tive \=¦'==,rād·iv, -ātiv\ *adj* [¹*proliferate* + *-ive*] **1** : capable of or engaged in proliferation **2** : of, marked by, or tending to proliferation

pro·lif·er·ous \-f(ə)rəs\ *adj* [*proli-* + *-ferous*] **1** *obs* : PROLIFIC 1a **2 a** : reproducing freely by offsets, bulbils, gemmae, or other vegetative means **b** : PROLIFERATE **3** : PROLIFERATING; *specif* : producing a cluster of branchlets from a larger branch — used of coral — **pro·lif·er·ous·ly** *adv*

pro·lif·ic \prə|'lifik, prō|, |fēk\ *adj* [F *prolifique*, fr. L *proles* offspring + F *-fique* -fic — more at PROLETARIAN] **1 a** : capable of reproducing or generating ⟨the domestic cat begins . . . to reproduce by the end of the first year of her life, and she is ~ to her ninth —S.G.J.Mivart⟩ **b** (1) : abundantly and quickly reproductive or generative : FECUND, FRUITFUL ⟨flying foxes are extremely ~ —J.G.Frazer⟩ ⟨the ~ hyacinth . . . is a curse to boatmen —*Lamp*⟩ (2) : marked by an abundance : copiously productive — usu. used with *in* or *of* ⟨~ of ferns —*Amer. Guide Series: Ark.*⟩ ⟨~ of illusion —H.J. Muller⟩ ⟨the waterside is ~ of such heroes —G.B.Shaw⟩ ⟨~ in the production of scientists —W.A.Noyes b. 1898⟩ **2** : occurring or existing in large numbers : ABUNDANT, PROFUSE ⟨contour leather belts . . . are ~ here —Lois Long⟩ ⟨the achievements of . . . western art are both ~ and illustrious —P.A.Sorokin⟩ ⟨both books contain ~ references —W.G.V. Balchin⟩ **3** *archaic* : helpful to or causing abundant growth, generation, or reproduction ⟨the ~ sun, and the sudden and rank plenty which his heat engenders —R.W.Emerson⟩ **4** : marked by abundant and often rapid productivity ⟨his ~ output as a research worker —*Chronica Botanica*⟩ ⟨a ~ writer —J.T.Adams⟩ ⟨the most ~ contributor —Lucile E. Hoyme⟩ **syn** see FERTILE

pro·lif·i·ca·cy \-fəkəsē, -fēk-, -si\ *n* -ES [*prolific* + *-acy* (as in *efficacy*)] : the quality or state of being prolific ⟨the emergence of paperback books in a ~ unknown on these shores —*Times Lit. Supp.*⟩; *esp* : the quality or state of producing young in large numbers or at frequent intervals ⟨the ~ of rabbits⟩

prolifical *adj* [F *prolifique* + E *-al*] *obs* : PROLIFIC

pro·lif·i·cal·ly \prə'lifək(ə)lē, prō'-, -fēk-, -li\ *also* **pro·lif·ic·ly** \-klē, -li\ *adv* [*prolifically* fr. *prolifical* + *-ly*; *prolificly* fr. *prolific* + *-ly*] : in a prolific manner

pro·lif·i·cal·ness *n* -ES : PROLIFICACY

pro·lif·i·cate \='==,kāt\ *vt* -ED/-ING/-S [*prolific* + *-ate*] : to make prolific : FERTILIZE

pro·lif·i·ca·tion \=,=='kāshən\ *n* -s [ML *prolification-, prolificatio*, fr. *prolificatus* (past part. of *prolificare* to generate young, fr. L *proles* offspring + *-ficare* to move) + L *-ion-, -io* -ion — more at PROLETARIAN, -FICATION] **1 a** : the generation of young **b** : FECUNDITY **2** : the quality or state of being proliferous **3** : an apical branch arising from within an inflorescence and continuing the terminal growth of the stem (as in the male inflorescence of mosses of the genus *Polytrichum*) — compare INNOVATION

pro·li·fic·i·ty \ˌprōlə'fisəd·ē\ *n* -ES [*prolific* + *-ity*] : prolific power or character

pro·lif·ic·ness *n* -ES [*prolific* + *-ness*] : PROLIFICACY

pro·lig·er·ous \prō'lijərəs\ *adj* [ISV *proli-* + *-gerous*] **1** : producing or believed to produce living beings **2** : PROLIFERATIVE ⟨the cyst is typically lined with a ~ membrane that buds off daughter cysts or infective scolices⟩

pro·line \'prō,lēn, -,lən\ *n* -s [G *prolin*, fr. *pyrrolidin* pyrrolidine] : a heterocyclic amino acid C_4H_8NCOOH that is a constituent of many proteins (as gliadin, casein, zein) and is obtained therefrom by hydrolysis; 2-pyrrolidine-carboxylic acid

pro·lix \(')prō¦liks\ *adj* [ME, fr. MF & L; MF *prolixe*, fr. L *prolixus* extended, copious, fr. *pro-* forward + *-lixus* (akin to *liquēre* to be fluid) — more at PRO-, LIQUID] **1** *obs* : marked by long duration : PROTRACTED ⟨if the chain of consequences be a little ~ —Isaac Watts⟩ **2 a** : unduly prolonged or drawn out : DIFFUSE, REPETITIOUS, VERBOSE ⟨very ~, and bursting with subordinate sentences and clauses —Arnold Bennett⟩ ⟨a sprawling book, discursive and ~ —Brendan Gill⟩ ⟨~ and often loose statements —Gail Kennedy⟩ **b** : given to verbosity and diffuseness in speaking or writing : LONG-WINDED ⟨the author can be awkward, stiff, and ~ —*Newsweek*⟩ ⟨was ~ with his pen —J.L.Motley⟩ **3** *archaic* : long or extensive in measurement ⟨with wig ~, downflowing to his waist —William Cowper⟩ **syn** see WORDY

prolixious *adj* [irreg. fr. L *prolixus*] *obs* : PROLIX

pro·lix·i·ty \prō'liksəd·ē, -sətē, -i\ *n* -ES [ME *prolixite*, fr. MF *prolixité*, fr. L *prolixitat-, prolixitas*, fr. *prolixus* + *-itat-, -itas* -ity] : the quality or state of being prolix; *esp* : undue lengthiness in speaking or writing ⟨his facility carried him . . . into ~ —Sir Winston Churchill⟩

pro·lix·ly *adv* : in a prolix manner

pro·lix·ness *n* -ES [*prolix* + *-ness*] : PROLIXITY

pro·lo·bous \(')prō¦lōbəs\ *adj* [¹*pro-* + *lobe* + *-ous*] : set off — used of the prostomium of an annelid worm when separated by a groove from the first true segment

pro·loc·u·lum \prō'läkyələm\ *or* **pro·loc·u·lus** \-ləs\ *n, pl* **proloc·u·la** \-lə\ *or* **proloc·u·li** \-ə,lī\ [NL, fr. ¹*pro-* + *loculus*] : the initial chamber of a foraminiferan test

pro·lo·cu·tion \ˌprōlə'kyüshən, ˌpräl-\ *n* [LL *prolocution-, prolocutio* preamble, fr. L *pro-* before + *locution-, locutio* speech — more at PRO-, LOCUTION] **1** *archaic* : a prefatory statement **2** [²*pro-* + *locution*] *obs* : intentionally ambiguous language

pro·loc·u·tor \prō'läkyə|d·ə(r), |tə(r)\ *n* -s [L, fr. *pro-* ²pro- + *locutor* speaker, fr. *locutus* (past part. of *loqui* to speak) + *-or*] **1 a** : one who speaks, pleads, or interprets for another : SPOKESMAN ⟨in a national crisis one . . . ~ who spoke in the name of all the estates —T.E.May⟩ **b** *Scot* : an advocate or legal spokesman in a court of law **2 a** : the speaker or presiding officer of the lower house of a convocation of the Church of England through whom all resolutions of the lower house are communicated to the upper house **b** : the presiding officer or chairman of a meeting or assembly

pro·loc·u·tor·ship \-,ship\ *n* : the office of a prolocutor

pro·log·ist \'prō,lȯgəst *also* -,läg- *or* -,ləjəst\ *also* **pro·logu·ist** \'prō,lȯgəst *also* -läg-\ *n* -s [*prologue* + *-ist*] : one who writes or delivers a prologue

pro·log·ize \-,gīz, -,jīz\ *or* **pro·logu·ize** \-,gīz\ *vi* -ED/-ING/-S [Gk *prologizein* to speak a prologue, fr. *prologos* prologue + *-izein* -ize] : to write or speak a prologue

pro·lo·gos \prō'lō,gäs\ *also* **pro·lo·gus** \-,gəs\ *n, pl* **prolo·goi** \-,gȯi\ *also* **prolo·gi** \-,jī\ [Gk *prologos*, fr. *pro-* ¹pro- + *-logos* (fr. *legein* to speak) — more at LEGEND] : the entire part of an ancient Greek play preceding the parodos

¹**pro·logue** *also* **pro·log** \'prō,lȯg *also* -,läg\ *n* -s [ME *prolog, prologe*, fr. OF *prologue, prologe*, fr. L *prologus* preface to a play, speaker of the preface, fr. Gk *prologos* prologos] **1** : the preface or introduction to a discourse, performance, or nondramatic literary work **2 a** (1) : a speech often in verse addressed to the audience by one or more of the actors at the opening of a play — compare EPILOGUE (2) : the actor speaking such a prologue **b** : the opening scene of a play whose main action is set within a separate frame **3** : an introductory

or preceding act, event, or development ⟨in the ~ of life —W.E.Swinton⟩ ⟨a ~ to her own . . . history —Hugh Walpole⟩ ⟨sacred and solemn ~*s* to . . . Easter Sunday are planned Maundy Thursday and Good Friday —*Springfield* (*Mass.*) *Union*⟩

2prologue \"\ *vt* -ED/-ING/-S **:** to introduce or provide with a prologue or preface ⟨~*s* and epilogues the selection —*Saturday Rev.* (*London*)⟩

1pro·long \prə'lȯŋ, prō'- *also* -läŋ\ *vt* -ED/-ING/-S [ME *prolongen*, fr. MF *prolonguer*, fr. LL *prolongare*, fr. L *pro-* forward + *longus* long — more at PRO-, LONG] **1 :** to lengthen in time **:** extend in duration **:** draw out **:** CONTINUE, PROTRACT ⟨the candidacy period for party membership can be ~*ed* one year —*Americana Annual*⟩ ⟨a chance of ~*ing* his life indefinitely —J.G.Frazer⟩ ⟨enjoying the situation and wanting to ~ it —Rose Macaulay⟩ ⟨~*ed* this anxiety⟩ **2** *archaic* **:** to put off **:** DELAY, POSTPONE ⟨and the word that I shall speak shall come to pass; it shall be no more ~*ed* —Ezek 12: 25 (AV)⟩ **3 :** to lengthen or draw out the pronunciation of (as a syllable or sound) ⟨no matter how long you ~ the "i" of "bit" — "b-i-i-i-t" — you never get the "i" of "police" —Weston LaBarre⟩ **4 :** to lengthen in extent, scope, or range ⟨habitually ~*s* a sentence thus until it has covered the unit of its subject —R.M. Weaver⟩ ⟨the boundary . . . has . . . ~*ed* itself northward —Herbert Agar⟩ ⟨~ the list —F.L.Mott⟩ ⟨~*ing* the runways of the airfield —*Weekly Overseas Mail* (*London*)⟩ ⟨education . . . should be ~*ed* through adult years —C.W.Eliot⟩ **syn** see EXTEND

2pro·long \'prō,lȯŋ *also* -läŋ\ *n* -S **:** a prolonged part; *specif* **:** a cone of sheet iron placed over the end of the condenser in a furnace for recovering zinc by distillation

pro·long·able *pronunc at* 1PROLONG + əbəl\ *adj* **:** capable of being prolonged

pro·lon·gate \prə'lȯŋ,gāt, prō'- *also* -läŋ- *sometimes* 'prō,=,=; *usu* -ād·+V\ *vt* -ED/-ING/-S [LL *prolongatus*, past part. of *prolongare* to prolong] **:** PROLONG

pro·lon·ga·tion \(,)prō,lȯŋ'gāshən prə,- *also* -läŋ-\ *n* -S [MF, fr. LL *prolongation-*, *prolongatio*, fr. *prolongatus* + L *-ion-*, *-io* -ion] **1 a :** an extension or lengthening in time or duration ⟨the indefinite ~ of the Korean truce talks —Joseph & Stewart Alsop⟩ **b :** the continuation or protraction of a spoken syllable or sound ⟨the principle of ~ —H.W.Smyth⟩ **2 :** an expansion or continuation in extent, scope, or range ⟨a northwesterly ~ into the plain of Lancastria —L.D. Stamp⟩ ⟨a ~ of ourselves —*Time Lit. Supp.*⟩ ⟨water and plants . . . became a part and ~ of the structures conceived by the architect —José Gómez-Sicre⟩ ⟨treats literature . . . as a ~ (of the past) rather than as an original creation —Wallace Fowlie⟩

pro·longe \prō'länj\ *n* -S [F, fr. *prolonger* to prolong, draw out, fr. MF *prolonguer*] **:** a rope with a hook and a toggle used chiefly for dragging a gun carriage or attaching it to the limber

pro·long·er \prə'lȯŋə(r), prō'-\ *n* -S [*prolong* + *-er*] **:** one that prolongs

pro·long·ment \-mənt\ *n* -S [*prolong* + *-ment*] **:** PROLONGATION

pro·lo·ther·a·py \ˌprōlōˌtherəpē, -pi\ *n* [L *prol*es progeny + E *-o-* + *therapy* — more at PROLETARIAN] **:** the rehabilitation of an incompetent structure (as a ligament or tendon) by the induced proliferation of new cells

pro·lu·sion \prō'lüzhən *also* prōl'yü-\ *n* -S [L *prolusion-*, *prolusio* prelude, preliminary exercise, fr. *prolusus* (past part. of *proludere* to play or practice beforehand, fr. *pro-* before + *ludere* to play) + *-ion-*, *-io* -ion — more at LUDICROUS] **1 :** an exercise or trial preliminary to a contest or performance **:** PRELUDE, WARM-UP ⟨useth . . . no ~ after the manner of fencers —Daniel Featley⟩ **2 :** an introductory and often tentative discourse **:** PREFACE, PROLOGUE ⟨~*s* on the Pentateuch —J.R.Lowell⟩ ⟨all this . . . ~ is only to enable you to understand —W.H.Hudson †1922⟩ ⟨his ~ on the style of the most famous among the ancient Latin poets —Joseph Addison⟩

pro·lu·so·ry \-üs(ə)rē, -üz(-, -ri\ *adj* [LL *prolusorius* (MS var. of *perlusorius* sportive), fr. L *prolusus* + *-orius* -ory] **:** of, relating to, or having the characteristics of a prolusion

pro·lyl \'prō,lil\ *n* -S [ISV *prol*ine + *-yl*] **:** the univalent acid radical C_4H_8NCO- of proline

pro·lymphocyte \(')prō+\ *n* [1*pro-* + *lymphocyte*] **:** LYMPHOBLAST

prom \'präm\ *n* -S [short for *promenade*] **1 :** a formal dance given by a high school or college class ⟨junior ~⟩ **2** *chiefly Brit* **:** PROMENADE CONCERT

prom *abbr* **1** prominent **2** promontory **3** promoted

pro·mammal \(')prō+\ *n* [1*pro-* + *mammal*] **1 :** an extinct reptile exhibiting definite mammalian characteristics; *esp* **:** a synapsid reptile **2 a :** a primitive mammal (as a platypus) not exhibiting all the characteristics of the group **b :** one of the Protomammalia

pro·mammalia \ˌprō+\ *n pl*, *cap* [NL, fr. 1*pro-* + *mammalia*] **:** a hypothetical group often treated as a subclass and comprising animals immediately ancestral to the true mammals — **promammalian** \"+\ *adj*

pro·ma·zine \'prōmə,zēn\ *n* -S [*prometh*azine] **:** a basic compound $C_{17}H_{20}N_2S$ derived from phenothiazine and administered as the hydrochloride similarly to chlorpromazine

pro·megaloblast \(')prō+\ *n* [1*pro-* + *megaloblast*] **:** a cell that produces megaloblasts and is possibly equivalent to a hemocytoblast

pro me·mo·ria \ˌprōmə'mōrēə, -'mȯr-\ *n*, *pl* **pro memoria** [L, for the sake of memory] **:** a formal note embodying the written record of a diplomatic discussion

1prom·e·nade \ˌpräməˌnād, -näd,-nȧd\ *n* -S [F, fr. *promener* to take for a walk (fr. L *prominare* to drive forward, fr. *pro-* forward + *minare* to drive) + *-ade* — more at PRO-, AMENABLE] **1 :** a leisurely walk or ride esp. in a public place for pleasure, display, or exercise ⟨daily ~ through the park⟩ **2 a :** a place for strolling **:** a public walk **b :** a passage, gallery, or extended balcony on a building **c :** PROMENADE DECK **3 a :** a ceremonious opening of a formal ball consisting of a grand march or polonaise in which all the guests participate **b :** a square-dance figure in which the couples walk counterclockwise around the square usu. side by side with the woman on the outside **c :** PROM 1 **4 :** PROMENADE CONCERT

2promenade \"\ *vb* -ED/-ING/-S *vi* **1 :** to take or go on a promenade **:** stroll esp. in public **2 :** to perform a promenade in a dance ~ *vt* **1 :** to walk about in or on ⟨had the privilege of *promenading* the gardens —C.G.Bowers⟩ **2 :** to display in or as if in a promenade **:** PARADE

promenade concert *n* **:** an orchestral concert during which the audience stands or promenades

promenade deck *n* **:** an upper deck or an area on a deck of a passenger ship where passengers promenade — called also *hurricane deck;* see DECK illustration

prom·e·nad·er \,==''=də(r)\ *n* -S **:** one who promenades

promenade tile *n* **:** QUARRY TILE

pro·meristem \(')prō+\ *n* [1*pro-* + *meristem*] **:** the portion of a primary meristem that contains actively dividing, undifferentiated, isodiametric thin-walled cells and their most recent derivatives — compare DERMATOGEN, GROUND MERISTEM, PROCAMBIUM

promerit *vt* [L *promeritus*, past part. of *promerēre*, *promerēri* to deserve, merit, fr. *pro-* in behalf of + *merēre*, *merēri* to earn — more at PRO-, MERIT] *obs* **:** to win or deserve the favor of (God)

pro·metaphase \(')prō+\ *n* [*pro-* + *metaphase*] **:** a stage sometimes distinguished between the prophase and metaphase of mitosis and characterized by disappearance of the nuclear membrane and formation of the spindle

pro·methazine \"+\ *n* -S [*pro*pyl + di*meth*ylamine + phenothi*azine*] **:** a crystalline antihistaminic drug $C_{17}H_{20}N_2S$ derived from phenothiazine and used chiefly in the form of its hydrochloride

pro·me·thea moth \prə|'mēthēə-,prō|\ *also* **pro·me·theus moth** \-thēəs-, -,th(y)üs-\ *n* [*promethea* fr. NL, fr. L, fem. of *prometheus* Promethean; *prometheus* fr. Gk *Promētheus*] **:** a large American saturniid silkworm moth (*Callosamia promethea*) having the wings and body chiefly smoky brown in the male and reddish brown in the female and a larva that feeds on sassafras, wild cherry, and other trees and suspends its cocoon from a branch by a silken band — compare CECROPIA MOTH

pro·me·thean \-thēən, -thyən\ *adj*, *usu cap* [L *prometheus* Promethean (fr. Gk *promētheios*, fr. *Promētheus* Prometheus, the Titan pioneer of civilization) + E *-an*] **:** of, relating to, or resembling Prometheus, his experiences, or his art; *esp* **:** daringly original or originative ⟨the painter's true *Promethean* craft —William Wordsworth⟩ ⟨there will always be nonconformists, bitter rebels, *Promethean* pioneers —C.I.Glicksberg⟩

pro·me·thi·um \-thēəm\ *n* -S [NL, fr. *Prometheus* + NL *-ium*] **:** a metallic element of the rare-earth group with no stable isotope occurring naturally that was discovered in radioactive form as a fission product of uranium, that has been obtained also from neutron-irradiated neodymium, and that shows chemical properties of other rare-earth elements — symbol *Pm;* see ELEMENT table

pro mil·le \(')prō'mi(,)lē\ *adv* (*or adj*) [LL] **:** per thousand

Pro·min \'prōmən\ *trademark* — used for glucosulfone

prom·i·nence \'prämənən(t)s *sometimes* -mnə-\ *n* -S [F, fr. L *prominentia*, fr. *prominent-*, *prominens* prominent + *-ia* -y] **1 :** the quality, state, or fact of being prominent or conspicuous **:** SALIENCE ⟨as the war progressed, the doctrine of national self-determination acquired greater ~ —Oscar Handlin⟩ **:** DISTINCTION, IMPORTANCE ⟨men of considerable ~ in the world of letters were offered the editorship —*Saturday Rev.*⟩ ⟨which syllable has the greater ~ in ordinary pronunciation⟩ **2 :** something prominent **:** a salient point **:** PROJECTION, PROTUBERANCE ⟨ricochet of the whole over pits and ~*s* —Thomas Hardy⟩ **3 a :** a mass of gas that resembles a cloud, arises or erupts from the chromosphere of the sun, and is seen in monochromatic light of hydrogen or calcium as dark against the solar surface or bright if protruding from the sun's limb **b :** a similar feature of any star

prom·i·nen·cy \-nənsē\ *n* -ES [L *prominentia*] **:** PROMINENCE

1prom·i·nent \-nənt\ *adj* [L *prominent-*, *prominens*, fr. pres. part. of *prominēre* to jut out, project, fr. *pro-* forward + *-minēre* (akin to L *mont-*, *mons* mountain) — more at PRO-, MOUNT] **1 :** standing out or projecting beyond a surface or line **:** appearing in high relief **:** JUTTING, PROTUBERANT ⟨a very ~ nose⟩ ⟨eyes sunken under ~ brows⟩ ⟨the most ~ peak in a range⟩ **2 :** distinctly manifest to the senses **:** readily noticeable **:** CONSPICUOUS, STRIKING ⟨the tower forms a ~ landmark⟩ ⟨~ diagnostic symptom⟩ ⟨~ fault in our reading and thinking —F.L.Mott⟩ **3 :** NOTABLE, LEADING, EMINENT ⟨~ men of the town⟩ ⟨~ singers⟩ ⟨a family long ~ in that region⟩ **syn** see NOTICEABLE

2prominent \"\ *n* -S [1*prominent;* fr. the hump or prominence on the back of the larva] **:** a moth of the family Notodontidae

prom·i·nent·ly *adv* **:** in a prominent manner ⟨his picture was ~ displayed in newspapers⟩

prom·is·cu·i·ty \,prämə'skyüəd·ē, ,prō,mi'-, -ətē, -i\ *n* -ES [F *promiscuité*, fr. L *promiscuus* + F *-ité* -ity] **1 a :** indiscriminate mingling **:** PROMISCUOUSNESS ⟨why do we not find indicative and subjunctive interchanging in complete ~ —Adelaide Hahn⟩ **b :** a brief or random social exchange or relation ⟨in the informal *promiscuities* which followed the prize distribution —Arnold Bennett⟩ **2 :** promiscuous sexual union

pro·mis·cu·ous \prə'miskyəwəs\ *adj* [L *promiscuus*, fr. *pro-* forward + *miscēre* to mix — more at PRO-, MIX] **1 :** consisting of a heterogeneous or haphazard mixture of persons or things **:** composed of all sorts and conditions ⟨~ crowd of people⟩ ⟨~ collection of curios⟩ ⟨involving plates, cups and saucers, in one ~ ruin —T.L.Peacock⟩ **2 :** not restricted to one class, sort, or person **:** INDISCRIMINATE ⟨~ soliciting of funds⟩ ⟨rather than a ~ acceptance of all our impulses as good —M. R.Cohen⟩ ⟨~ destruction by bombing⟩; *specif* **:** not restricted to one sexual partner ⟨cases where women who have abandoned the habit of ~ intercourse confine themselves to one man by marriage or cohabitation —W.W.Sanger⟩ ⟨gray squirrels are ~ in their breeding habits —R.E.Trippensee⟩ **3 :** CASUAL, CARELESS, IRREGULAR, RANDOM ⟨~ eating habits⟩ — **pro·mis·cu·ous·ness** *n* -ES

pro·mis·cu·ous·ly *adv* **:** in a promiscuous manner **:** INDISCRIMINATELY ⟨read continually and ~⟩ ⟨cautioned about . . . riding ~ across country —W.F.Brown b. 1903⟩

1prom·ise \'präməs\ *n* -S [ME *promis*, *promisse*, fr. L *promissum*, fr. neut. of *promissus*, past part. of *promittere* to send forth, promise, fr. *pro-* forth + *mittere* to send — more at PRO-, SMITE] **1 a :** a declaration that one will do or refrain from doing something specified ⟨never gave a ~ that he did not intend to keep⟩ ⟨miserable record of broken ~*s*⟩ ⟨effort of the Conservative government to validate its ~ to denationalize the steel industry —Alzada Comstock⟩ **b :** an undertaking however expressed that something will happen or that something will not happen in the future; *specif* **:** a declaration that gives the person to whom it is made a right to expect or to claim the performance or forbearance of a specified act — compare AGREEMENT, CAUSE, CONSIDERATION, CONTRACT, PACT **c :** a formal pledge of loyalty to various aims required by an organization ⟨the Girl Scout ~⟩ **2 a :** ground for expectation usu. of success, improvement, or excellence ⟨young poets of ~⟩ ⟨our time is . . . poised between ~ and despair —Norman Cousins⟩ **b :** appearance, character, or quality that gives or seems to give such ground of expectation ⟨book shows ~ of popular appeal —R.G. Albion⟩ **3 :** something that is promised ⟨I'll claim that ~ at your Grace's hand —Shak.⟩

2promise \"\ *vb* -ED/-ING/-S [ME *promisen*, fr. *promis*, n.] *vt* **1 :** to engage to do or bring about (as something desired or pleasing) **:** give assurance or promise of ⟨*promised* to be careful⟩ ⟨*promised* assistance whenever it should be needed⟩ ⟨*promised* his son a new bicycle⟩ ⟨*promised* the court to be ready⟩ ⟨~ me that you will tell no one⟩ **2** *archaic* **:** to affirm to someone the truth or certainty of (something stated) **:** WARRANT, ASSURE ⟨I do not like thy look, I *promise* thee —Shak.⟩ **3** *chiefly dial* **:** BETROTH ⟨she was happy, bein' *promised* to the son o' Farmer Brown —J. W. Riley⟩ **4 :** to give ground for expecting **:** FORETOKEN ⟨gray skies *promising* rain⟩ ⟨~*s* to be the best game of the season⟩ **5 :** to execute (as a note) as promisor ~ *vi* **1 :** to give one's word to do or refrain from doing something ⟨you always ~, and you never do it⟩ **2 :** to give ground for expectation **:** be imminent or threatening ⟨there had been a little rain, and more was *promising* —George Farwell⟩ ⟨the venture ~*s* well⟩

syn ENGAGE, PLEDGE, PLIGHT, COVENANT, CONTRACT: PROMISE indicates the giving of a stated assurance about some future act or action ⟨he *promised* to pay the bill⟩ ⟨she *promised* the child a new toy⟩ ⟨the amnesty *promised* by the king to political prisoners —*Current Biog.*⟩ Sometimes it signifies a giving of evidence or indication rather than a granting of one's word ⟨the child *promises* to be tall⟩ ⟨the night before it had rained and more rain was *promised* —Sherwood Anderson⟩ ENGAGE is used in formal or consequential situations to indicate a promising regarded as binding and one to be relied on, often concerning conduct over a period of time ⟨"You couldn't make some arrangement?" she asked. "*Engage* somebody to stay with him, or — or send him away?" —Ellen Glasgow⟩ ⟨*engaged* to be married⟩ PLEDGE, aside from uses in connection with drives and charities ⟨to *pledge* a dollar to a special church fund⟩, may apply to solemn binding assurance concerning a consequential matter ⟨I *pledge* allegiance to the Flag of the United States of America and to the Republic for which it stands —Francis Bellamy⟩ ⟨thirteen of the 26 delegates were *pledged* to bolt the convention —*Collier's Yr. Bk.*⟩ ⟨Austria swarmed with excited and angry men *pledged* to destroy the Church —Hilaire Belloc⟩ PLIGHT, indicating solemn promise, now exists mainly in stereotyped phrases ⟨to *plight* one's troth⟩ although it is occasionally used elsewhere ⟨if for America it is too violent a wrench to *plight* its fate with Europe —Nathaniel Peffer⟩ COVENANT stresses formality and seriousness of intent in promises ⟨*covenanted* to defeat the present conspiracy to set up a Home Rule Parliament in Ireland —Rose Macaulay⟩ ⟨the seller *covenants* to indemnify the purchaser if these provisions cannot be fulfilled⟩ CONTRACT may suggest definite agreements to be relied on in business and legal affairs ⟨the John Doe company has *contracted* to supply the equipment⟩ ⟨he *contracted* to pay the interest on his brother's debts⟩

promised land *n* [fr. past part. of 2*promise;* fr. the promise made to Abram in Gen 12:7] **:** a better country or condition **:** some place or thing that seems to promise final satisfaction or realization of hopes or dreams ⟨had himself explored the whole of the *promised land* to which he had led Italian painting —Roger Fry⟩

prom·is·ee \ˌpräməˌsē\ *n* -S [2*promise* + *-ee*] **:** a person to whom a promise is made — contrasted with *promisor*

prom·ise·ful \'präməsfəl\ *adj* [1*promise* + *-ful*] **:** PROMISING **:** full of promise ⟨~ of better times to come⟩

prom·is·er \'präməsə(r)\ *n* -S [2*promise* + *-er*] **:** one that promises

promising *adj* [fr. pres. part. of 2*promise*] **:** full of promise **:** likely to succeed or to yield good results **:** APT, AUSPICIOUS, LIKELY — **prom·is·ing·ly** *adv* — **prom·is·ing·ness** *n* -ES

prom·i·sor \ˌpräməˌsȯ(ə)r, -ȯ(ə)\ *n* -S [2*promise* + *-or*] **:** one who engages or undertakes — contrasted with *promisee*

pro·mis·sor \prə'misə(r)\ *n* -S [L, promiser, fr. *promissus* + *-or*] **1** *obs* **:** PROMISOR **2 :** PROMITTOR

prom·is·so·ry \'prämə,sōrē, -sȯr-, -ri\ *adj* [ML *promissorius*, fr. L *promissus* (past part. of *promittere* to promise) + *-orius* -ory — more at PROMISE] **1 :** containing or conveying a promise or assurance that something will be done or forborne or will probably be or happen ⟨~ oath⟩ ⟨~ speech⟩ **2 :** stipulating or representing what is to happen or to be done subsequent to the time of making the contract of insurance — used of a representation, a warranty; compare AFFIRMATIVE

promissory note *n* **:** an unconditional written promise to pay on demand or at a fixed or determined future time a given sum of money to or to the order of a specified person or to bearer

pro·mitosis \ˌprō+\ *n* [NL, fr. 1*pro-* + *mitosis*] **:** a primitive intranuclear mitosis in protistans characterized by absence of asters and the presence of a karyosome — compare HAPLOMITOSIS

pro·mitotic \"+\ *adj* [fr. NL *promitosis*, after NL *mitosis:* E *mitotic*] **:** of, relating to, or involving promitosis

pro·mit·tor \prō'mid·ə(r)\ *n* -S [obs. *promit* to promise (fr. ME *promitten*, fr. L *promittere*) + *-or*] **:** a planet that promises in the root of a nativity something to be fulfilled when the time of direction shall be accomplished

Promi·zole \'prōmə,zōl, 'präm-\ *trademark* — used for thiazolsulfone

prom·ne·sia \präm'nēzhə\ *n* -S [NL, fr. 1*pro-* + *-mnesia*] **:** PARAMNESIA b

pro·monarchic \ˌprō+\ *or* **pro·monarchical** \"+\ *adj* [2*pro-* + *monarchy* + *-ic*, *-ical*] **:** favoring monarchy

pro·monocyte \(')prō+\ *n* [1*pro-* + *monocyte*] **:** a cell that produces monocytes **:** MONOBLAST

promont *n* -S [by shortening] *obs* **:** PROMONTORY

prom·on·to·ried \'prämən·,tōrēd, -tȯr-, -rid\ *adj* [*promontory* + *-ed*] **:** furnished with or as if with a promontory

prom·on·to·ry \-rē, -ri\ *n* -ES [L, alter. (infl. by *mont-*, *mons* mountain & *-orium* -ory) of *promunturium;* akin to *prominēre* to jut out — more at PROMINENT] **1 a :** a high point of land or rock projecting into a body of water beyond the line of coast **:** HEADLAND **b :** a bluff or prominent hill overlooking or projecting into a lowland **c :** a low-lying cape **2 :** a bodily prominence: as **a :** the angle of the ventral side of the sacrum where it joins the vertebra **b :** a prominence on the inner wall of the tympanum of the ear

pro·morphology \ˌprō+\ *n* [G *promorphologie*, fr. *pro-* 1pro- + *morphologie* morphology] **:** the study of the organization of the egg esp. with reference to localization of subsequently developed embryonic structures

pro·mot·abil·i·ty \prə,mōd·ə'biləd·ē\ *n* [*promotable* + *-ity*] **:** the quality or state of deserving promotion

pro·mot·able \='mōd·əbəl, -ōtə-\ *adj* [*promote* + *-able*] **:** likely to be or deserving to be advanced in rank or position

pro·mote \prə'mōt, *usu* -ōd·+V\ *vb* -ED/-ING/-S [L *promotus*, past part. of *promovēre* to move forward, promote, fr. *pro-* forward + *movēre* to move — more at PRO-, MOVE] *vt* **1 a :** to advance in station, rank, or honor **:** RAISE — opposed to *demote* **b :** to change (a pawn) into a piece by moving to the eighth rank **c :** to advance (a student) from one grade or class to the next usu. at the end of an academic year or semester **2** *obs* **a :** to inform against **b :** to put forward (as a claim) **3** *law* **:** to institute (as a prosecution or suit) as a common informer, or as one permitted by the ordinary to inaugurate a criminal proceeding — used chiefly in the phrase *to promote the office of the ordinary* **4 a :** to contribute to the growth, enlargement, or prosperity of **:** FURTHER, ENCOURAGE ⟨~ international understanding⟩ ⟨the fixity of inheritance laws . . . *promoted* extreme jealousy among potential heirs —Ralph Linton⟩ **b :** to bring or help to bring (as a business enterprise) into being **:** LAUNCH ⟨~ a mining company⟩ ⟨~ a prize fight⟩ **c :** to present (merchandise) for public acceptance through advertising and publicity **d :** to increase the activity of (a catalyst) by adding a small percentage of another substance; *also* **:** to accelerate (a reaction) by such an addition — opposed to *poison* **5** *slang* **:** to get possession of by doubtful means or by ingenuity ⟨see what he could ~ by a little personal string pulling —J.G.Cozzens⟩ ⟨able to ~ a bottle of wine —R.M.Ingersoll⟩ ~ *vi* **1** *obs* **:** to incite someone (as to strife) **2** *obs* **:** to inform against someone **3 :** to become a queen or other piece in chess ⟨a pawn automatically ~*s* when it reaches the eighth rank⟩ **syn** see ADVANCE

pro·mot·ee \prə,mō'tē\ *n* -S [*promote* + *-ee*] **:** one who is raised in rank or position ⟨each man in the outfit punches the ~ in the arm, once for each pay grade —L.M.Uris⟩

pro·mot·er \prə'mōd·ə(r), -ōtə-\ *n* -S [partly fr. earlier *promotor* (fr. MF & ML; MF *promoteur*, fr. ML *promotor*, fr. L *promotus* + *-or*); partly fr. *promote* + *-er*] **1 a :** one that forwards or advances **:** ENCOURAGER, ABETTOR ⟨~ of discord⟩ ⟨chief ~*s* of a congressional bill⟩ **b :** a person who alone or with others sets on foot and takes the preliminary steps in a scheme or undertaking for the organization of a company or the carrying out of a business project **c :** one who assumes the financial responsibilities of a sporting event (as a boxing match) including contracting with the principals, renting the site, collecting gate receipts **2** *obs* **a :** PROSECUTOR **b :** INFORMER 3 **3** *Eng law* **:** one who promotes a prosecution **4** *or* **pro·mo·tor** \"\ **:** an officer at various British universities who supervises the work of a student and presents him for a degree **5 a :** a substance that in very small amounts is able to increase the activity of a catalyst **b** *or* **promotor :** COLLECTOR 5

promoter of the faith [trans. of NL *promotor fidei*] **:** DEVIL'S ADVOCATE 1

pro·mo·tion \prə'mōshən\ *n* -S [ME, fr. MF, fr. LL *promotion-*, *promotio*, fr. L *promotus* (past part. of *promovēre* to promote) + *-ion-*, *-io* -ion — more at PROMOTE] **1 :** the act or fact of being raised in position or rank **:** PREFERMENT ⟨next in line for a ~⟩ ⟨the problem is solved by the ~ of a pawn to knight instead of queen⟩ **2 a :** the act of setting up or furthering a business enterprise ⟨~ of a stock company⟩ **b :** active furtherance of sale of merchandise through advertising or other publicity **syn** see PUBLICITY

pro·mo·tion·al \-shənᵊl, -shnəl\ *adj* **:** of, relating to, or serving the end of promotion ⟨~ civil service examinations⟩ ⟨fiercely accelerated advertising and ~ campaigns —Charles Lee⟩ ⟨~ pamphlets to attract settlers and investors —*Amer. Guide Series: N.Y.*⟩

pro·mo·tive \prə'mōd·|iv, -ōt|, |ēv *also* |əv\ *adj* [*promote* + *-ive*] **1 :** tending to further or encourage **2 :** PROMOTIONAL — **pro·mo·tive·ness** *n* -ES

pro·mo·tor \prō'mōd·ə(r)\ *n* -S [NL, fr. ML, one that advances — more at PROMOTER] **:** a muscle connected anteriorly to the base of each locomotor appendage in an onychophoran

promotor fi·dei \-'fīdē,ī\ *n*, *pl* **pro·mo·to·res fidei** \,prō-,mō'tōr,ēz, -tȯ,rēz\ [NL, lit., promoter of the faith] **:** DEVIL'S ADVOCATE 1

pro·mo·to·ri·al \ˌprō,mōˌtōrēəl, -tȯr-\ *adj* [ML *promotor* promoter, prosecutor + E *-ial*] **:** of or relating to a promoter

promove *vt* [ME *promoven*, fr. L *promovēre* — more at PROMOTE] *obs* **:** PROMOTE

pro·mo·vent \'prōməvənt\ *n* -S [L *promovent-*, *promovens*, pres. part. of *promovēre* to promote] **:** a person who promotes a suit in an ecclesiastical court

1prompt \'präm(p)t\ *vt* -ED/-ING/-S [ME *prompten*, fr. ML *promptare*, fr. L *promptus* prompt] **1 :** to move to action **:** INCITE, PROVOKE ⟨~*ed* by curiosity to open the closet⟩ ⟨his wife ~*ed* him to ask for a transfer to a new job⟩ **2 :** to remind (one acting or reciting) of words or topics forgotten **:** assist by suggesting or uttering the next words of something forgotten or imperfectly learned : give a cue to **3** : to serve as the inciting cause of (an act or thought) : URGE, SUGGEST ⟨the answer shown by the . . . bank and turn indicator instead of the answer ~*ed* by his senses —H.G.Armstrong⟩ ⟨~*s* the question: has the danger of a severe recession passed —S.H.Slichter⟩

²prompt \"\ *adj* -ER/-EST [ME, fr. MF or L; MF *prompt*, fr. L *promptus* visible, ready, prompt, fr. past part. of *promere* to bring forth, take out, fr. *pro-* forth + *emere* to take, buy — more at PRO-, REDEEM] **1** : ready and quick to act as occasion demands : responding instantly : ALERT ⟨~ to retort to insults⟩ ⟨~ in obedience⟩ **2** : performed readily or immediately : given without delay or hesitation ⟨~ assistance⟩ ⟨~ decisions⟩ ⟨~ payment of bills⟩ ⟨~ delivery of goods⟩ **3** : of or relating to prompting actors ⟨as the young actor bowed and withdrew to the ~ corner —Laurence Irving⟩ **syn** see QUICK

³prompt \"\ *adv* : on time : PUNCTUALLY

⁴prompt \"\ *n* -S [in sense 1, fr. ¹*prompt;* in sense 2, fr. ²*prompt*] **1** : the act or an instance of prompting or reminding : REMINDER ⟨so regularly performed that there was no need of written ~*s* —Iona & Peter Opie⟩ **2** : a limit of time usu. equaling the free credit period given for payment of an account for goods purchased; *also* : the contract by which this time is fixed **3** : PROMPT SIDE

promptbook \ˈ=,=\ *n* [¹*prompt* + *book*] : a copy of a play with directions for performance used by a theater prompter

prompt box *n* [¹*prompt*] : a low box projecting above the floor of a stage with its opening toward the actors

prompt call *n* : a short simple square dance call serving as a reminder

prompt copy *n* : PROMPTBOOK

prompt day *n* [⁴*prompt*] : a day of settling accounts

prompt·er \ˈpräm(p)tə(r)\ *n* -S [¹*prompt* + *-er*] **1** : one that prompts : one who reminds another (as a reciter) of the words to be spoken next; *specif* : one responsible for prompting actors during performance **2** : CALLER a

promp·ti·tude \ˈpräm(p)tə,tüd, -tə,tyüd\ *n* -S [ME, fr. MF or LL; MF *promptitude*, fr. LL *promptitudo*, fr. L *promptus* prompt + *-i-* + *-tudo* -tude] : the quality or habit of being prompt : promptness or an instance of it : quickness in deciding, acting, or meeting obligations : ALACRITY ⟨reacted with exceptional ~ . . . to the challenge of another will —Hilaire Belloc⟩ ⟨the texts . . . should be published with the utmost ~ —*U.N. Dept. of Public Information*⟩

promp·tive \ˈpräm(p)tiv\ *adj* [¹*prompt* + *-ive*] : tending to prompt : PROVOCATIVE ⟨~ of very serious reflection⟩

prompt·ly \ˈpräm(p)tlē, -li, *rapid* -mpl-\ *adv* : in a prompt manner : at once : IMMEDIATELY, QUICKLY

prompt·ness \-nəs\ *n* -ES : the quality or habit of being prompt

prompt note *n* [⁴*prompt*] : a memorandum of a sale given by a seller to a purchaser specifying the sum to be paid and the time when payment is due

promptscript \ˈ=,=\ *n* [¹*prompt* + *script*] : PROMPTBOOK

prompt side *n* [¹*prompt;* fr. its being the usual station of the prompter] : the side of the stage to the right of an actor facing the audience; *broadly* : the side of the stage adjacent to the prompter's corner — abbr. *P.S.*

promp·tu·ary \ˈprämpchə,werē\ *n* -ES [LL *promptuarium* storehouse, fr. L, neut. of *promptuarius* serving for distribution, fr. *promptus* act of taking out (in the phrase *in promptu* visible, at hand) (fr. *promptus*, past part. of *promere* to take out) + *-arius* -ary — more at PROMPT] **1** *obs* : STOREHOUSE, REPOSITORY **2** : a book of ready reference

promp·ture \ˈpräm(p)chə(r)\ *n* -S [¹*prompt* + *-ure*] *archaic* : URGING, INCITEMENT ⟨hath fallen by ~ of the blood —Shak.⟩

proms *pl of* PROM

promul·gate \ˈpräməl,gāt, prəˈm-,prōˈm- *also* ˈprō(,)m-; *usu* -ād.+V\ *vt* -ED/-ING/-S [L *promulgatus*, past part. of *promulgare* to make public, perh. alter. of *provulgare*, fr. *pro-* forth + *vulgare* to publish — more at PRO-, VULGATE] **1** : to make known (as a decree, a dogma) by open declaration : PROCLAIM **2 a** : to make known or public the terms of (a proposed law) **b** : to issue or give out (a law) by way of putting into execution **c** : to make public as having the force of law **d** : to announce officially **syn** see DECLARE

promul·ga·tion \,präməlˈgāshən, ,prō(,)m\ *n* -S [F, fr. L *promulgation-, promulgatio*, fr. *promulgatus* + *-ion-, -io* -ion] : an act of promulgating : open declaration : public and official announcement

promul·ga·tor \ˈpräməl,gād.ə(r), prəˈm-, prōˈm-, ˈprō(,)m-, -ātə-\ *n* -S [LL, fr. L *promulgatus* + *-or*] : one that promulgates or publishes ⟨the original and systematic ~ of the doctrine of free, self-governing institution —John Dewey⟩

pro·mulge \prōˈməlj\ *vt* -ED/-ING/-S [ME *promulgen*, fr. L *promulgare*] *archaic* : PROMULGATE

pro·mulg·er \-jə(r)\ *n* -S [*promulge* + *-er*] *archaic* : PROMULGATOR

pro·mus·ci·date \(ˈ)prō;məsə,dāt\ *adj* [LL *promuscid-, promuscis* + E *-ate*] *of an insect* : having a proboscis

pro·mus·cis \prōˈməsəs\ *n, pl* **promus·ces** \-ə,sēz\ *or* **pro·mus·ci·des** \-,sə,dēz\ [LL *promuscid-, promuscis*, alter. of *proboscis*] : PROBOSCIS; *specif* : the proboscis of a hemipterous insect

pro·mycelial \;prō+\ *adj* [NL *promycelium* + E *-al*] : of, relating to, or being a promycelium

pro·mycelium \(;)prō+\ *n, pl* **promycelia** [NL, fr. ¹*pro-* + *mycelium*] : a short usu. 4-celled hyphal filament that constitutes the basidium of various heterobasidiomycetous fungi, is formed by germination of a teliospore in rusts or of a chlamydospore in smuts, and bears sporidia — called also *epibasidium;* compare AUTOBASIDIUM

pro·myelocyte \(ˈ)prō+\ *n* [ISV ¹*pro-* + *myelocyte*] : PREMYELOCYTE — **pro·myelocytic** \(;)=+\ *adj*

pro·my·shlen·nik \,prəmə'shlenək\ *n, pl* **promyshlenni·ki** \-nəkē\ [Russ, lit., trader, industrialist, fr. *promyshlyat'* to trade, engage in business, fr. *promysl'* business, fr. *pro* for + *mysl'* thought; akin to L *pro* for and to OSlav *mysli* thought — more at FOR, MYTH] : a Russian trapper and fur trader of Siberia and Alaska

pron *abbr* **1** pronominal **2** pronoun **3** pronounced **4** pronunciation

pro·naos \(ˈ)prō+\ *n, pl* **pronaoi** [L, fr. Gk, fr. *pronaos* situated in front of a temple, fr. *pro-* ¹pro- + *naos* temple — more at NAOS] : the outer part of an ancient Greek temple forming a portico immediately in front of the cella and delimited by the front wall of the cella and the columns or the antae and columns; *also* : the narthex of an early church

pro·na·tal·ist \(ˈ)prō;nād.ᵊləst\ *adj* [¹*pro-* + L *natus* (past part. of *nasci* to be born) + E *-al* + *-ist* — more at NATION] : encouraging an increased birthrate ⟨~ policies⟩

pro·nate \ˈprō,nāt, *usu* -ād.+V\ *vb* -ED/-ING/-S [LL *pronatus*, past part. of *pronare* to bend forward, bow, fr. L *pronus* prone] *vt* : to rotate (as the hand or forearm) so as to bring the palm facing downward or backward ~ *vi* : to assume a position of pronation

pro·na·tion \prōˈnāshən\ *n* -S [*pronate* + *-ion*] **1 a** : a medial rotation of the hand and radius around the ulna so that the palm is turned backward or downward; *also* : the position resulting from this movement — opposed to *supination* **b** : the act or state of lying face downward **2** : a faulty foot posture characterized by toeing out and usu. associated with sagging of the inner arch and inward tipping of the ankle joint

pro·na·to·flexor \prō;nād.ō+\ *n* [NL, fr. *pronator* + *-o-* + *flexor*] : one of a group of muscles on the volar aspect of the forearm acting both as pronator and flexor

pro·na·tor \ˈprō,nād.ə(r), =ˈ==\ *n* -S [NL, fr. LL *pronatus* + L *-or*] : a muscle that produces pronation

pronator qua·dra·tus \-kwäˈdrād.əs\ *n* [NL, lit., squared pronator] : a deep muscle of the forearm passing transversely from the ulna to the radius and serving to pronate the forearm

pronator te·res \-ˈti,rēz\ *n* [NL, lit., smooth or rounded pronator] : a muscle of the forearm, arising from the medial epicondyle of the humerus, inserting into the lateral surface of the middle third of the radius, and serving to pronate and flex the forearm

¹prone \ˈprōn\ *adj* [ME, fr. L *pronus* bent forward, inclined, tending; akin to L *pro* before, forward — more at FOR] **1** : having a tendency, propensity, or inclination : DISPOSED, PREDISPOSED ⟨drivers suspected of being accident ~⟩ — used with *to* ⟨man is ~ to error⟩ ⟨those industries that are most ~ to periods of depression —J.A.Hobson⟩ ⟨when courts are so very ~ to stand upon their dignity —H.G.Wells⟩ **2** *obs* : readily followed or yielded to : EASY **3** *archaic* : ready or willing to do something specified or implied ⟨~ submission to the heavenly will —Robert Browning⟩ **4** : DOWNWARD: as **a** : having the front or ventral surface downward : standing, lying, or placed so that the face and belly are facing or upon the earth or other supporting base ⟨a ~ position⟩ ⟨the upper side of a ~ or horizontal animal —W.E.Swinton⟩ — distinguished from *supine* **b** : lying flat or prostrate — contrasted with *erect* **5** *archaic* : ANIMALLIKE, BEASTLY, BESTIAL ⟨a ~ and savage necessity, not worth the name of marriage —John Milton⟩

syn SUPINE, PROSTRATE, RECUMBENT, COUCHANT, DORMANT: PRONE may apply to a position with the face, chest, or abdomen lying on or turned toward the ground, floor, or other surface ⟨if we ourselves lie *prone* upon the floor we can exemplify the characteristic relationship, for our internal cavity is nearest to the floor, above it is our backbone —W.E.Swinton⟩ ⟨Her Majesty, *prone* but queenly, stretched out on the deck . . . to try her hand at target shooting —*Time*⟩ SUPINE applies to a position with the back against a supporting surface, the face upward, and suggests lethargic abjectness or inertness ⟨lying *supine* in the bottom of the canoe and staring upward at the immaculate azure of the sky —Elinor Wylie⟩ ⟨jaded people lolling *supine* in carriages —G.B.Shaw⟩ PROSTRATE applies to full-length proneness as in submission, fear, or helplessness; it may also apply to any horizontal position brought about by fall, weakness, or shock and inability to use and act ⟨*prostrate* in homage, on her face, silent —Gordon Bottomley⟩ ⟨lying *prostrate* on my chest, I took a long draught of clear cold water —W.H.Hudson †1922⟩ ⟨stood over the bloody and *prostrate* form —C.B.Nordhoff & J.N.Hall⟩ RECUMBENT may apply to lying down in any position of comfortable repose ⟨if the patient is greatly weakened or prostrated, he must be kept reasonably warm, *recumbent* —Morris Fishbein⟩ ⟨*recumbent* upon the brown pine-droppings —George Meredith⟩ COUCHANT and DORMANT, mainly technical heraldic terms in the senses here involved, apply to a prone body position, the former suggesting that the head is raised as if in watchfulness, the latter that it is lowered in sleep. **syn** see in addition LIABLE

²prone \"\ *n* -S [F *prône*, lit., choir screen (where the instruction was orig. delivered), fr. (assumed) VL *protinum* vestibule, screen before an entrance, alter. of L *prothyra* (pl.), fr. Gk *prothyron* space before a door, fr. *pro-* ¹pro- + *thyra* door — more at DOOR] : a short religious instruction delivered in church preceding the sermon : a brief pedagogical, hortatory, or homiletical introduction to the sermon

prone float *n* : DEAD MAN'S FLOAT

prone·ly *adv* [*prone* + *-ly*] : in a prone manner or position

prone·ness \ˈprōnnəs\ *n* -ES : the condition or fact of being prone ⟨~ to disease⟩ ⟨possible reason for accident ~⟩

pro·neph·ric \(ˈ)prō;nefrik\ *adj* [NL *pronephros* + E *-ic*] : of or relating to a pronephros

pro·nephridiostome \;=+\ *n* -S [NL ¹*pro-* + *nephridium* + *-o-* + E *-stome*] : FLAME CELL

pro·neph·ros \(ˈ)prō;nefrəs, -,fräs\ *also* **pro·neph·ron** \-,frən, -,frän\ *n, pl* **proneph·roi** \-,frȯi\ *also* **proneph·ra** \-,frə\ [NL, fr. ¹*pro-* + Gk *nephros* kidney — more at NEPHRITIS] : one of the anterior of the three pairs of embryonic renal organs of higher vertebrates

prone pressure method *n* : a method of artificial respiration consisting essentially of alternate pressure and release of pressure on the back of the thorax of the prone patient by means of which water if present is expelled from the lungs and air is allowed to enter

pro·neur \prōˈnər(·)\ *n* -S [F *prôneur*, fr. *prôner* to exhort, praise to excess (fr. *prône* religious instruction) + *-eur* -or — more at PRONE] : FLATTERER, EULOGIST

¹prong \ˈprȯŋ, ˈpräŋ\ *n* -S [ME *pronge, prange;* perhaps akin to MHG *pfrengen* to press, Goth *anaprangan* to afflict, Lith *branktas* whiffletree] **1** : FORK ⟨hay ~⟩ ⟨dung ~⟩ **2** : a tine of a fork **3** : a slender pointed or projecting part: as **a** : a fang of a tooth **b** : a point of an antler **c** *South & Midland* : a branch of a stream or inlet **d** : ¹SPUR 6b **e** : a branch of a tree **f** : the projecting part or edge of a jewelry setting that holds a stone in place

²prong \"\ *vt* -ED/-ING/-S : to stab, pierce, or break up (as soil) with a prong : FORK

prongbuck \ˈ=,=\ *n* [*prong* + *buck*] **1** : SPRINGBOK **2** : PRONGHORN

prong budding *n* : shield budding in which a bud-bearing prong or spur is used instead of a simple bud

prong die *n* **1** : SPRING DIE **2** : SPLIT DIE

pronged \;prȯŋd, ;präŋd\ *adj* [¹*prong* + *-ed*] : having or divided into prongs : FORKED — often used in combination

prong hoe *n* : a hand implement equipped with two or more curved prongs and used for garden hoeing or cultivation

pronghorn \ˈ=,=\ *also* **pronghorn antelope** \ˈ=,=-\ *or* **prong-horned antelope** \(ˈ)=ˈ=-\ *n, pl* **pronghorn** *also* **pronghorns** [*pronghorn* fr. *prong-horned* (*antelope*), fr. ¹*prong* + *horned*] : a ruminant mammal (*Antilocapra americana*) of unforested parts of western No. America that is yellowish tawny above and about the neck and white below with a white rump patch and that has slightly curved horns with a lateral prong which are present in both sexes and which resemble the bovine horns in having a bony core but have a deciduous horny sheath that is replaced annually

pronghorn

prong key *n* [¹*prong*] : a key or spanner having two projecting pins to fit holes in the face of a circular nut : FACE SPANNER

prongy \ˈprȯŋē, ˈpräŋē\ *adj* [¹*prong* + *-y*] : FORKED, DIVIDED ⟨horseradish grown in poor soil may develop ~ roots⟩

pro·no·grade \ˈprōnə,grād\ *adj* [L *pronus* leaning forward + E *-o-* + *-grade* — more at PRONE] : walking with the body approximately horizontal ⟨most mammals except man and the higher apes are ~⟩ — compare ORTHOGRADE

¹pro·nom·i·nal \prōˈnämənᵊl, prəˈ-\ *adj* [LL *pronominalis*, fr. L *pronomin-, pronomen* pronoun + *-alis* -al — more at PRONOUN] **1** : of, relating to, or constituting a pronoun **2** : resembling a pronoun : having a meaning that resembles that of a pronoun in identifying or specifying without describing ⟨the adverb *here* is ~ in *come here*⟩

²pronominal \"\ *n* -S : a pronominal word

pro·nom·i·nal·ly \-nəlē, -li\ *adv* [¹*pronominal* + *-ly*] : in the manner of a pronoun

pro·normoblast \(ˈ)prō+\ *n* [ISV ¹*pro-* + *normoblast;* prob. orig. formed in G] : a cell recognized in some theories of erythropoiesis that arises from a myeloblast and gives rise to normoblasts and is approximately equivalent to the erythroblast of other theories

pronotary *n* -ES [by contr.] *obs* : PROTHONOTARY

pro·notum \(ˈ)prō+\ *n, pl* **pronota** [NL, fr. ¹*pro-* + *notum*] : the dorsal plate of an insect's prothorax

pro·noun \ˈprō,naůn\ *n* [MF *pronom*, fr. L *pronomin-, pronomen*, fr. *pro-* ²pro- + *nomin-, nomen* name, noun — more at NAME] **1** : a word belonging to one of the major form classes in any of a great many languages that is used as a substitute for a noun or noun equivalent, takes noun constructions and is declined, refers to persons or things named, asked for, or understood in the context, and has little or no fixed meaning except one of relation or limitation **2** : PRONOMINAL

STANDARD SIMPLE PERSONAL PRONOUNS

	SINGULAR	
1st person	*2d person*	*3d person*
I	you	he, she, it
(mine)	(yours)	(his) (hers) (its)
me	you	him, her, it
	PLURAL	
we	you	they
(ours)	(yours)	(theirs)
us	you	them

The pronouns in parentheses normally do not show possessive-case relation but function nominatively (as *mine* in "mine is on the table" and "this book is mine") or objectively (as *mine* in "bring me mine" and "he mistook his coat for mine").

The forms *my, our, your,* and *their* are possessive adjectives, as are also *his, her,* and *its* when used to modify nouns.

pro·nounce \prəˈnaůn(t)s\ *vb* -ED/-ING/-S [ME *pronuncen, pronouncen*, fr. MF *prononcier*, fr. L *pronuntiare* to proclaim, articulate, fr. *pro-* forth + *nuntiare* to report, relate, fr. *nuntius* messenger — more at PRO-] *vt* **1** : to utter officially or ceremoniously ⟨~ a eulogy⟩ ⟨~ a death sentence⟩ : declare solemnly ⟨I now ~ you man and wife⟩ ⟨have been officially *pronounced* to be exemplars of the Christian faith —K.S. Latourette⟩ ⟨the weightiest judgment which he could ~ —H.E.Scudder⟩ **2** : to declare authoritatively or by way of a judgment, opinion, or conclusion ⟨doctors *pronounced* him fit to resume his duties⟩ ⟨*pronounced* the meeting adjourned⟩ **3 a** : to employ the organs of speech to produce (as a variety or a component of spoken language) or to produce the spoken counterpart of (as an orthographic representation of a word, syllable, speech sound, phrase) ⟨to ~ German well⟩ ⟨*chimpanzee* is *pronounced* in several ways⟩ **b** : to represent in printed or written characters the spoken counterpart of (an orthographic representation) ⟨both dictionaries ~ *clique* the same⟩ **4** : to deliver (a speech) with regard to sound or manner of utterance : RECITE ⟨speak the speech, I pray you, as I *pronounced* it to you —Shak.⟩ ~ *vi* **1** : to declare one's opinion or conclusion definitely or authoritatively : pass judgment ⟨the speaker was twice required to ~ on the subject of free speech —Guy Eden⟩ ⟨liberal platforms regularly ~ in favor of . . . antitrust enforcement —Carl Kaysen⟩ **2** : to produce the components of spoken language ⟨to ~ faultlessly⟩ ⟨why radio announcers . . . are continually under attack for the way they ~ —David Abercrombie⟩

pro·nounce·able \-səbəl\ *adj* : capable of being pronounced ⟨~ group of letters⟩ — **pro·nounce·able·ness** *n* -ES

pronounced *adj* [fr. past part. of *pronounce*] : strongly marked : DECIDED, UNMISTAKABLE ⟨~ limp⟩ ⟨~ aptitude for languages⟩ ⟨a ~ odor of fish hung about⟩ ⟨the symptoms of the disease have become steadily more ~⟩ — **pro·nounced·ly** \-n(t)sədlē, -n(t)stlē, -li\ *adv*

pro·nounce·ment \-n(t)smənt\ *n* -S [*pronounce* + *-ment*] **1 a** : usu. formal declaration of opinion or judgment or estimation ⟨confident ~*s* of generations of literary critics⟩ ⟨~*s* of persons who know something about music but not much —Virgil Thomson⟩ **2** : an authoritative or official announcement ⟨had been making all of the important ~*s* on government policy —Don Dallas⟩

pro·nounc·er \-(t)sə(r)\ *n* -S [ME *pronouncere*, fr. *pronouncen* to pronounce + *-ere* -er] : one that pronounces

pronouncing *adj* [fr. gerund of *pronounce*] : relating to or indicating pronunciation : serving as a guide to pronunciation ⟨~ dictionary⟩ ⟨~ alphabet⟩

pron·to \ˈprän·(,)tō\ *adv* [Sp, quick, prompt, quickly, fr. L *promptus* prompt] : QUICKLY, PROMPTLY — not often in formal use

pron·to·sil \ˈpräntə,sil\ *n* -S [G] : any of three sulfonamide drugs: **a** *or* **prontosil rubrum** : a red azo dye $H_2NSO_2C_6H_4N{=}NC_6H_3(NH_2)_2$ that was the first sulfa drug tested clinically **b** *or* **prontosil album** : SULFANILAMIDE **c** *or* **prontosil soluble** : AZOSULFAMIDE

¹pron·u·ba \ˈprӓnyəbə, ˈprōn-\ [NL, fr. L, matron who attended the bride in a Roman marriage, fr. fem. of *pronubus* relating to or for marriage, fr. *pro-* ²pro- + *nubere* to marry a man — more at NUPTIAL] *syn of* TEGETICULA

²pronuba \"\ *n* -S [NL *Pronuba*] : YUCCA MOTH

pro·nuclear \(ˈ)prō+\ *adj* [NL *pronucleus* + E *-ar*] : of, relating to, or resembling a pronucleus

pro·nucleus \"+\ *n* [NL, fr. ¹*pro-* + *nucleus*] : a gamete nucleus after completion of maturation and entry of a sperm into the egg — compare CLEAVAGE, FERTILIZATION

pro number \ˈprō-\ *n* [*progressive* + *number*] : a number in a single continuous series of numbers assigned by a motor transportation company to successive shipments regardless of classification

pro·nun·cia·men·to \prō,nənchēəˈmen(,)tō, -nən(t)sēə-\ *n, pl* **pronunciamentos** *or* **pronunciamentoes** [Sp *pronunciamiento* proclamation, fr. *pronunciar* to pronounce (fr. L *pronuntiare*) + *-miento* -ment — more at PRONOUNCE] **1 a** : PROCLAMATION, EDICT, MANIFESTO; *esp* : an edict announcing a change in government **b** : military revolt **2** : PRONOUNCEMENT ⟨novels, lectures, and ~*s* on life, politics, and art —Brendan Gill⟩

pro·nun·ci·a·tion \prə,nən(t)sēˈāshən, *chiefly in substand speech* -naůn(t)s- *or* -nənchē-\ *n* -S [ME *pronunciacion*, fr. MF *prononciation*, fr. L *pronuntiation-, pronuntiatio*, fr. *pronuntiatus* (past part. of *pronuntiare* to pronounce) + *-ion-* *-io* -ion — more at PRONOUNCE] **1 a** : the act or manner of pronouncing something : articulate utterance ⟨changes in the ~ of English⟩ **b** : the way or ways in which a unit of language is usu. spoken or on the basis of analogy probably would be spoken by persons qualified by education or otherwise to be speakers worthy of imitation **2** *obs* : DECLARATION, PRONOUNCEMENT **3** *obs* : ELOCUTION, DELIVERY

pro·nun·ci·a·tion·al \=;==;āshənᵊl, -shnəl\ *adj* : relating to or dealing with pronunciation ⟨~ hints⟩ ⟨~ puns⟩

pro·nun·ci·a·tive \=ˈ==,ād.iv\ *adj* [L *pronuntiatus*, past part. of *pronuntiare* to declare, pronounce + E -ive — more at PRONOUNCE] : DOGMATIC

pro·nun·ci·a·tor \-,ād.ə(r)\ *n* -S [L *pronuntiatus* + E *-or*] : one that pronounces; *esp* : one who prescribes pronunciations

pro·nun·ci·a·to·ry \=ˈ==ə,tōrē\ *adj* [L *pronuntiatus* + E *-ory*] : of or relating to pronunciation

pro·ny brake \ˈprōnē-\ *n, usu cap P* [after G. C. F. M. Riche, Baron de *Prony* †1839 French engineer] : a friction brake or absorption dynamometer in which the pull on the flywheel friction blocks is measured by a spring balance or weighted lever — compare ROPE BRAKE

pro·nymph \(ˈ)prō+\ *n* [¹*pro-* + *nymph*] : the first postembryonic form of some insects (as the dragonfly) in which the larva is encased in a thin temporary membrane — **pronymphal** \(ˈ)=+\ *adj*

pro·ode \ˈprō,ōd\ *n* [Gk *proōidos*, fr. *pro-* ¹pro- + *ōidē* ode — more at ODE] **1** : a distich with the first line shorter than the second — opposed to *epode* **2** : a strophic unit in an ancient ode preceding the strophe and antistrophe and differing from them in structure

pro·od·ic \(ˈ)prō;ädik\ *adj* [Gk *proōidikos* of or relating to a prelude, fr. *proōidos* prelude, proode + *-ikos* -ic] **1** : preceding and differing in metrical pattern from the first strophe of an ode **2** *of an ode* : preceded or introduced by a group of lines of different pattern

pro·oe·mi·ac \(ˈ)prō;ēmē,ak\ *adj* [LGk *prooimiakos*, fr. Gk *prooimion* proem] : PROEMIAL

pro·oe·mi·um \prōˈēmēəm\ *or* **pro·oe·mi·on** \-ən\ *n, pl* **prooemiums** *or* **prooe·mia** \-ˈēmēə\ [*prooemium* fr. ME(Sc) *prohemium*, fr. L *prooemium*, fr. Gk *prooimion;* *prooemion* fr. Gk *prooimion* — more at PROEM] : PROEM

proestrous *var of* PROESTROUS

proestrus *or* **proestrum** *var of* PROESTRUS

¹proof \ˈprüf\ *n* -S [ME *proof, prove*, alter. (influenced by *proven* to prove) of *preef, preve, preove*, fr. OF *preuve*, fr. LL *proba*, fr. L *probare* to test, prove — more at PROVE] **1 a** : the cogency of evidence or of demonstrated relationship that compels acceptance by the mind of a truth or a fact : DEMONSTRATION ⟨one who believes in you doesn't need any ~ at all —W.J. Reilly⟩ **b** : the derivation of one or more propositions or statements from one or more others in accordance with either generally recognized or specif. stipulated principles of validity **2** *obs* : something proved by common experience : knowledge acquired by experience ⟨'tis a common ~ that lowliness is young ambition's ladder —Shak.⟩ **3** : something that induces certainty or establishes validity: as **a** : a chain of statements or formulas leading logically from axioms and theorems previously established to the theorem which is the conclusion of the demonstration **b** : a mathematical process that establishes the validity of a theorem or statement **c** : an act, effort, or operation designed to establish or discover a fact or truth ⟨prepared to put his theories to the ~⟩ ⟨laboratory ~ of the presence of gold in the sample⟩ **4** *obs* **:** OUTCOME, RESULT **5 a** *obs* **:** WITNESS **b :** a leaf having its original rough outer edge or a pair of adjacent leaves still joined together at one or more edges regarded as proof that the book containing it is untrimmed — called also *witness* **6** *dial chiefly Eng* **:** good condition or quality **:** GOODNESS **7 a** *archaic* **:** the quality or state of having been tested or tried; *esp* **:** unyielding hardness or firmness ⟨armor of ~⟩ **b** *obs* **:** ARMOR **8 :** evidence operating to determine the finding or judgment of a tribunal: as **a** *Eng law* **:** a written statement of the testimony which a proposed witness will give in court **b** *civil law* **:** a document or number of documents so established as to be legally receivable as evidence **c** *Scots law* **:** the evidence upon a point at issue taken before a judge or judge's representative; *also* **:** the taking of the evidence **d** *Scots law* **:** a trial by a court without a jury **9** *obs* **:** ATTEMPT **10 a :** an impression (as from type) taken for correction or examination; *also* **:** a comparable print or impression made by some other composing or printing process **b :** a proof impression of an engraving, etching, or lithograph — see OPEN-LETTER PROOF, PROOF BEFORE LETTER, REMARQUE PROOF **c :** PROOF COIN **d :** a test photographic print made from a negative **11 a :** a test applied to articles or substances to determine whether they are of standard or satisfactory quality ⟨the ~ of the pudding is in the eating⟩ **b :** a trial of ordnance, projectiles, armor, or powder to determine suitability for acceptance **c :** the process of bringing dough to a standard lightness **12 a :** the minimum alcoholic strength of proof spirit **b :** strength with reference to the standard for proof spirit **syn** see REASON

²proof \"\ *adj* **1 :** firm or successful in resisting or repelling ⟨~ against your own moods —William Sansom⟩ **:** IMPENETRABLE, IMPREGNABLE — often used in combination ⟨burglar-*proof* windows⟩ ⟨bomb*proof*⟩; sometimes distinguished from *resistant* **2 :** used in proving or testing **:** serving as a proof: as **a :** measuring or producing the greatest strain in a piece or member consistent with safety ⟨~ stress⟩ ⟨~ strength⟩ **b** *of gold or silver* **:** perfectly pure and kept (as in a mint or assay office) as a standard of comparison or for experiment **3 :** of standard strength or quality or alcoholic content ⟨~ whiskey⟩

³proof \"\ *adv* [²*proof*] *archaic* **:** CONFIRMEDLY, THOROUGHLY, UTTERLY

⁴proof \"\ *vt* -ED/-ING/-S [¹*proof*] **1 a :** to make or take a proof or test of ⟨~ an etching⟩ ⟨~ a negative⟩ ⟨~ a galley of set type⟩ **b :** PROOFREAD ⟨books which I edited, ~*ed*, and supervised in production —E.G.Berenson⟩ **2 :** to bring (dough) to the proper lightness **3** [²*proof*] **:** to give a resistant quality to **:** make impervious to water, gas, weather, or chemical action

proof before letter : a proof taken before the title or inscription has been engraved

proof box *n* **:** a cabinet for proofing dough

proof coin *n* **:** a coin not intended for circulation but struck from a new, highly-polished die on a polished planchet and sometimes in a metal different from a coin of identical denomination struck for circulation

proof·er \-fə(r)\ *n* -S **1 :** one that pulls or makes proofs (as in letterpress printing and lithography) **2 :** a bakery worker who controls the raising of dough (as in a proofer) — called also *raiser* **3 :** a machine in which leavened dough is kept at a controlled temperature for raising

proof gallon *n* **:** a gallon of proof spirit

proofhouse \ˈ=,=\ *n* **:** a place for testing the barrels of firearms

proofing *n* -S **1 :** the act or process of making proof **2 :** a chemical or other substance used in proofing; *specif* **:** a preparation applied to fabric or incorporated in it at the time of manufacture to make it proof against weather or to prevent the passage of gas

proof·less \ˈprüfləs\ *adj* **:** lacking proof **:** not supported by proof ⟨~ charges⟩

proof load *n* **:** a cartridge made with a heavier charge of powder than normal ammunition for the piece and used to test the strength of chamber, barrel, and action

proofmark \ˈ=,=\ *n* **:** a distinctive symbol stamped into the metal of the barrel or other part of a firearm to indicate that testing of the part bearing the stamp by firing proof loads has been carried out

proof·ness *n* -ES **:** the state or property of being proof ⟨tested for ~ against water and corrosion⟩ **:** degree of being proof

proof paper *n* **1 :** paper (as printing-out paper) for making proofs **2 :** paper used in timing an exposure

proof plane *n* **:** a small metal disk attached to an insulating handle, used in testing the nature of the electrification of a body

proof positive *n, pl* **proofs positive :** conclusive proof

proof press *n* **:** a press used for the pulling or making of proofs

proof·read \ˈprü,frēd\ *vt* [back-formation fr. *proofreader*] **:** to read and mark corrections in (a proof or other printed or written matter)

proofreader \ˈ=,==\ *n* [¹*proof* + *reader*] **:** one that proofreads; *esp* **:** one whose regular occupation is proofreading — called also *corrector of the press, printer's reader, reader*

proofroom \ˈ=,=\ *n* **1 :** a room in which proofreading is done **2 :** the room where formed bread doughs are kept to rise (as in a proofer)

proofs *pl of* PROOF, *pres 3d sing of* PROOF

proof spirit *n* **:** alcoholic liquor or mixture of alcohol and water that contains a standard percentage of alcohol: **a :** liquor that contains nearly half alcohol by volume **b** *Brit* **:** liquor that weighs ¹²⁄₁₃ of an equal measure of distilled water or contains 57.10 percent by volume of alcohol — compare OVERPROOF, UNDERPROOF

proof stress *n* **:** stress that causes a specified amount of permanent deformation in a test specimen

proof–test \ˈ=,=\ *vt* **:** to fire proof loads in (a firearm)

proof text *n* **:** a Scriptural passage adduced as proof for a theological doctrine, belief, or principle

proof with open–letter : OPEN-LETTER PROOF

proof with remarque : REMARQUE PROOF

proofy \ˈprüfi\ *adj* [¹*proof* + -*y*] *dial Eng* **:** LIKELY, PROMISING

pro·op·ic \(ˈ)prō¦äpik, -¦ōpik\ *adj* [¹*pro-* + Gk *ōp-*, *ōps* face, eye + E *-ic* — more at EYE] **:** having a face in which the nose and central line are prominent

pro·os·tra·cum \prōˈästrəkəm\ *n, pl* **proostra·ca** \-kə\ [NL, fr. ¹*pro-* + Gk *ostrakon* earthen vessel, potsherd, shell — more at OYSTER] **:** the anterior horny or calcareous prolongation of the phragmocone of belemnites and related cephalopods

¹pro·otic \(ˈ)prō+\ *adj* [*pro-* + *-otic* (of the ear)] **:** of or relating or adjacent to a prootic bone or center **:** being a prootic part

²prootic *n* -S **:** a prootic part (as a bone or cartilage)

prootic bone *n* **:** a bone or center of ossification in the front of the periotic capsule in special relation with the anterior semicircular canal

pro·oxidant \(ˈ)prō+\ *n* [²*pro-* + *oxidant*] **:** a substance that accelerates the oxidation of another substance — compare ANTIOXIDANT

pro·oxygen \"+\ *n* [ISV ²*pro-* + *oxygen*] **:** PROOXIDANT — **pro·oxygenic** \(¦)prō+\ *adj*

¹prop \ˈpräp\ *n* -S [ME *proppe*, fr. MD, stopper; akin to MLG *proppe* stopper] **1 :** a rigid usu. independent and often auxiliary vertical support: as **a :** a timber for holding up the roof of a mine **b :** a pole for keeping a clothesline from sagging down **c :** a pole or stake for holding up a plant **d props** *pl* **:** LEGS **e :** a fired-clay piece used as a support for a shelf in a kiln **2 :** something on which one leans or depends for support or strength **:** STAY ⟨his son was his chief ~ in old age⟩ ⟨this side of religion which has . . . become the ~ of advanced cultures and complex societies —W.W.Howells⟩ ⟨a government ~ keeping wheat from falling below a set level⟩ ⟨knocks the ~*s* from under some critical theories —B.R.Redman⟩ **3 :** PROP FORWARD

²prop \"\ *vb* **propped; propped; propping; props** [ME *proppen*, fr. *proppe*, n.] *vt* **1 a :** to prevent from falling, collapsing, sagging, or slipping by placing something under or against **:** shore up ⟨sat with his chin *propped* in his hands⟩ ⟨frame houses, some *propped* on stilts —*Amer. Guide Series: Pa.*⟩ — often used with *up* ⟨lay with his head *propped* up on a pillow⟩ **b :** to support by placing against something ⟨~ a ladder against a wall⟩ ⟨photographs on the mantel, *propped* up amid a clutter of china ornaments —Hamilton Basso⟩ **2 :** to give support to (as by assisting, encouraging, upholding) **:** SUSTAIN, STRENGTHEN ⟨emphasis on *propping* economic structures abroad, rather than unduly expanding military power —*Biddle Survey*⟩ ⟨to ~ up my morale . . . a top designer had done over my office —Gary Cooper⟩ **~** *vi, Austral & Africa, of a draft animal, esp a horse* **:** BALK **syn** see SUPPORT

³prop \"\ *n* -S [origin unknown] **:** one of the seashells used in the game of props

⁴prop \"\ *n* -S [by shortening] **1 :** PROPERTY 4a **2 :** an article, object, or device used to provide or aid in creating a realistic effect (as of a performance, exhibit, or narrative) ⟨all the ~*s* of an espionage case are there — foreign agents, household traitors, stolen documents —J.P.Marquand⟩ ⟨camels, which they hire to visitors as ~*s* for exotic snapshots —Mollie Panter-Downes⟩

⁵prop \"\ *n* -S [by shortening] **:** PROPELLER

prop- *comb form* [ISV, fr. *propionic* (in *propionic acid*)] **:** related to propionic acid ⟨*prop*ane⟩ ⟨*prop*yl⟩

prop *abbr* **1** propeller **2** proper; properly **3** property **4** proposed; proposition **5** proprietary; proprietor

pro·pa·di·ene \¦prōpə¦dī,ēn\ *n* -S [ISV *propane* + *-diene*] **:** ALLENE

Pro·pa·drine \ˈprōpədrən\ *trademark* — used for racemic norephedrine used in the form of its hydrochloride as a nasal vasoconstrictor

¹pro·pae·deu·tic \,prōpēˈd(y)üd·|ik, -üt|, |ēk\ *n* -S [fr. Gk *propaideuein* to teach beforehand (fr. *pro-* ¹*pro-* + *paideuein* to rear a child, educate, teach, fr. *paid-*, *pais* child), after Gk *paideuein*: *paideutikē* education, fr. fem. of *paideutikos* of teaching, fr. *paideutos* (verbal of *paideuein*) + *-ikos* -ic — more at FEW] **:** preparatory study or instruction **:** INTRODUCTION ⟨an essential ~ to this more philosophical task will be accomplished by our analysis —Donald Walhout⟩

²propaedeutic \¦==¦==\ *adj* [fr. Gk *propaideuein* to teach beforehand, after Gk *paideuein* to teach: *paideutikos* of teaching] **:** needed as preparation for learning or study **:** introductory to an art or science ⟨logic is not philosophy; it is a ~ discipline —*Times Lit. Supp.*⟩

prop·a·ga·bil·i·ty \,präpəgəˈbiləd·ē\ *n* **:** the quality or state of being propagable

prop·a·ga·ble \ˈpräpəgəbəl\ *adj* [ML *propagabilis*, fr. L *propagare* to propagate + *-abilis* -able] **:** capable of being propagated

prop·a·gand \ˈpräpə,gand\ *vb* -ED/-ING/-S [prob. fr. F *propagander*, fr. *propagande* propaganda] **:** PROPAGANDIZE

prop·a·gan·da \,präpəˈgandə, -gaan- *also* ,prōp- *sometimes* ˈ==,==\ *n* -S [NL (in *Congregatio de propaganda fide* Congregation for propagating the faith — an organization established by Pope Gregory XV in 1622 to take charge of Catholic missionary activity), fr. L, abl. sing. fem. of *propagandus*, gerundive of *propagare* to propagate] **1** *archaic* **:** a group or movement organized for spreading a particular doctrine or system of principles **2 :** dissemination of ideas, information, or rumor for the purpose of helping or injuring an institution, a cause, or a person ⟨steady erosion of Socialist ~ about the wrongs done to the people —Roy Lewis & Angus Maude⟩ **3 a :** doctrines, ideas, arguments, facts, or allegations spread by deliberate effort through any medium of communication in order to further one's cause or to damage an opposing cause ⟨brushed aside the peace proposals as mere ~⟩ **b :** a public action or display having the purpose or the effect of furthering or hindering a cause ⟨distribution of free food parcels . . . is the first successful piece of ~ that the Western Powers have thought up —*New Statesman & Nation*⟩ **syn** see PUBLICITY

prop·a·gan·dee \¦==gan¦dē\ *n* -S [*propagand* + *-ee*] **:** one subjected to propagandizing

prop·a·gan·dism \,==ˈgan,dizəm\ *n* -S [F *propagandisme*, fr. *propagande* propaganda (fr. NL *propaganda*) + *-isme* -ism] **:** the action, practice, or art of propagating doctrines or of spreading or employing propaganda ⟨untiring ~ on behalf of French contemporary music —*New Internat'l Yr. Bk.*⟩

¹prop·a·gan·dist \-dəst *sometimes* ˈ==,==\ *n* -S [F *propagandiste*, fr. *propagande* propaganda + *-iste* -ist] **:** one engaged in propagating a belief or in producing or spreading propaganda ⟨democratic and humanitarian ~*s* succeeded in popularizing the ideal of universal elementary education —Helen Sullivan⟩

²propagandist \¦==¦==\ *or* **prop·a·gan·dis·tic** \¦präpə,gan¦distik\ *adj* **:** of, relating to, or characterized by propaganda ⟨~ writing⟩ ⟨~ plays⟩

prop·a·gan·dis·ti·cal·ly \-tək(ə)lē\ *adv* **:** in a propagandist manner **:** by way of propaganda ⟨~ effective play⟩

prop·a·gan·dize \,präpəˈgan,dīz, -gaan- *also* ,prōp- *sometimes* ˈ==,=dīz *or* -gən-\ *vt* -ED/-ING/-S [*propaganda* + *-ize*] **1 :** to disseminate (ideas, beliefs, principles) by propaganda ⟨~ the cause of states' rights⟩ **2 :** to subject to propaganda ⟨~ a country⟩ **~** *vi* **:** to carry on propaganda

prop·a·gant \ˈpräpəgənt\ *n* -S [*propagate* + *-ant*] **:** a plant part used for vegetative propagation

prop·a·gate \ˈpräpə,gāt *sometimes* ˈprōp-, *usu* -ād·+V\ *vb* -ED/-ING/-S [L *propagatus*, past part. of *propagare* to set slips, propagate, extend, enlarge, fr. *propages* layer (of a plant), slip, offspring, fr. *pro* before + *-pages* (akin to L *pangere* to fix, fasten) — more at FOR, PACT] *vt* **1 :** to cause to continue or increase by natural reproduction ⟨~ a breed of horses⟩ ⟨a plant unable to ~ itself in a new region⟩ ⟨~ a tree vegetatively⟩ **2 :** to transmit to offspring **:** pass along to succeeding generations **3 a :** to cause to spread out and affect a greater number or greater area **:** foster the spread of **:** EXTEND ⟨this vast area . . . through which the Greco-Roman civilization has been *propagated* —A.J.Toynbee⟩ ⟨the evil *propagated* itself —T.B.Macaulay⟩ **b :** to make known or familiar **:** foster growing knowledge of, familiarity with, or acceptance of **:** PUBLICIZE ⟨~ the Gospel⟩ ⟨the revival meeting method of *propagating* the faith —W.P.Webb⟩ ⟨the Rights of Man, rights which the French Revolution had *propagated* —Stringfellow Barr⟩ **c :** to reproduce or accomplish incidence of elsewhere **:** expand the activity, intensity, or transmission of **:** TRANSMIT ⟨radio waves *propagated* over long distances by alternate reflections at the ground and in the ionosphere —*Technical News Bull.*⟩ ⟨sufficient to ~ the detonation through the wet earth and set off the whole line of charges —*Blasters' Handbook*⟩ ⟨~ a chain reaction⟩ **~** *vi* **1 :** to have young or issue **:** multiply by sexual generation or by seeds, shoots, cuttings ⟨rabbits ~ rapidly⟩ **2 :** to increase in extent, numbers, or influence **:** EXTEND ⟨cause the flame to ~ along the fiber —W.E.Shinn⟩ **syn** see SPREAD

propagating frame *n* **:** an opaque enclosed case with artificial controlled light and heat that is used for propagating plants; *broadly* **:** any enclosure so used **:** HOTBED, COLD FRAME

propagating pit *n* **:** an excavation often covered with a glass frame used for the protection of plants in cold weather or for forwarding early growth

prop·a·ga·tion \,==ˈgāshən\ *n* -S [ME *propagacyon*, fr. MF *propagation*, fr. L *propagation-*, *propagatio*, fr. *propagatus* (past part. of *propagare*) + *-ion-*, *-io* -ion] **1 :** the act or action of propagating: as **a :** natural reproduction **:** production of young **:** natural increase (as a kind of organism) in numbers **:** PROCREATION ⟨~ of a pure culture of bacteria⟩ ⟨vegetative ~ of chrysanthemums⟩ **b :** the spreading of something (as a belief, ideal, practice) abroad or into new regions **:** DISSEMINATION **c :** the transmission of a form of wave energy (as light, sound, radio wave) through space or along a path **d :** enlargement or extension (as of a crack) in a solid body ⟨~ under stress of a flaw in glass⟩ **2** *obs* **:** OFFSPRING, BREED — **prop·a·ga·tion·al** \¦==¦gāshən³l, -shnəl\ *adj*

prop·a·ga·tive \ˈ==,gād·|iv, -āt|, |ēv *also* |əv\ *adj* **:** characterized by propagation ⟨spirochetes . . . undergo . . . a ~ type of development —K.F.Maxcy⟩ **:** tending to propagate **:** relating to propagation

prop·a·ga·tor \|ə(r)\ *n* -S [L, fr. *propagatus* (past part. of *propagare* to propagate) + *-or*] **1 :** one that propagates or disseminates ⟨find the ~ of this slander⟩ ⟨war has been the chief ~ of the machine —Lewis Mumford⟩ **2 :** one that propagates plants under glass or other special structures or in the open

prop·a·ga·tory \ˈpräpəgə,tōrē\ *adj* **1 :** PROPAGATIVE **2 :** PROPAGABLE

pro·pag·u·lum \prōˈpagyələm\ *or* **prop·a·gule** \ˈpräpə,gyül\ *n, pl* **propag·ula** \-lə\ *or* **propagules** [NL *propagulum*, fr. L *propages* layer (of a plant), slip + *-ulum*] **1 :** a propagable shoot (as an offset) **2 :** a reproductive structure in brown algae

pro·pale \prōˈpā(ə)l\ *vt* -ED/-ING/-S [LL *propalare*, fr. L *propalam* openly, publicly, fr. *pro* before + *palam* openly; akin to OSlav *polje* field — more at FOR, FLOOR] *archaic* **:** DIVULGE

pro·pal·i·nal \(ˈ)prō¦palən³l\ *adj* [Gk *pro* before, forward + *palin* back + E *-al* — more at FOR, PALI-] *of mastication* **:** effected by forward and backward motion — compare ORTHAL, PALINAL, PROAL

pro·pam·i·dine \prōˈpamə,dēn, -dən\ *n* [*propane* + *amidine*] **:** an antiseptic $CH_2[CH_2OC_6H_4C(-NH)NH_2]_2$ structurally related to propane and the amidine of benzoic acid and used chiefly in surgery for inhibiting the growth of hemolytic streptococci and staphylococci

pro·pa·nal \ˈprōpə,nal\ *n* -S [ISV *propane* + *-al*] **:** PROPIONALDEHYDE

pro·pane \ˈprō,pān\ *n* -S [ISV *prop-* + *-ane*] **:** a flammable gaseous paraffin hydrocarbon $CH_3CH_2CH_3$ that is heavier than air, occurs naturally in crude petroleum and natural gas and is also obtained by cracking, and is used chiefly as a fuel (as in liquefied petroleum gas) and in the manufacture of chemicals (as the lower nitroparaffins)

pro·pa·no·ic acid \¦prōpə¦nōik-\ *n* [*propanoic* ISV *propane* + *-oic*] **:** PROPIONIC ACID

pro·pa·nol \ˈprōpə,nōl, -nōl\ *n* -S [ISV *propane* + *-ol*] **:** PROPYL ALCOHOL

pro·pa·none \-nōn\ *n* -S [ISV *propane* + *-one*] **:** ACETONE

pro·par·gyl \prōˈpärjəl\ *n* -S [ISV *prop-* + *arg-* (fr. Gk *argyros* silver) + *-yl*; fr. the possible replacement of a hydrogen atom by one of silver — more at ARGENT] **:** a univalent unsaturated radical HC≡CCH₂— derived from methylacetylene by removal of one hydrogen atom ⟨~ alcohol⟩

pro·par·ia \prōˈpa(a)rēə\ *n pl, cap* [NL, fr. ¹*pro-* + Gk *pareia* cheek, cheekpiece of a helmet, prob. fr. *para-* + *-eia* (akin to Gk *ous* ear) — more at EAR] **:** an order of trilobites in which the posterior branch of the facial suture cuts the lateral margin of the cephalon — **pro·par·i·an** \-ēən\ *n or adj*

¹pro·par·oxy·tone \¦prōpə¦räksə,tōn\ *adj* [Gk *proparoxytonos*, fr. *pro-* ¹*pro-* + *paroxytonos* having an acute accent on the penultimate syllable — more at PAROXYTONE] **1 :** having or characterized by an acute accent on the antepenult **2 :** having or characterized by heavy stress on the antepenult

²proparoxytone \"\ *n* **:** a proparoxytone word — **pro·par·oxy·ton·ic** \-sə¦tänik\ *adj*

pro·pa·ta·gi·al \¦prōpə¦tājēəl\ *also* **pro·pa·ta·gi·an** \-ēən\ *adj* [NL *propatagium* + E *-al* or *-an*] **:** relating to or situated in a propatagium ⟨~ muscle⟩

pro·patagium \¦prō+\ *n, pl* **propatagia** [NL, fr. ¹*pro-* + *patagium*] **:** the membrane of a wing in front of the arm in a bird or bat; *also* **:** a corresponding fold of skin in a flying lemur

prop boy *n* **:** PROPERTY MAN

pro·pel \prəˈpel, prō'-\ *vt* **propelled; propelled; propelling; propels** [ME *propellen*, fr. L *propellere*, fr. *pro* before + *pellere* to drive — more at FOR, FELT] **1** *obs* **:** to drive away **:** drive out **:** EXPEL **2 :** to impel forward or onward **:** push ahead by imparting motion **:** give motive power to **:** drive onward ⟨a locomotive *propelled* by electricity⟩ ⟨the use of steam to ~ ships⟩ **3 :** to give an impelling motive or impetus to **:** urge on ⟨had long been *propelled* by greed and ambition⟩ **syn** see PUSH

pro·pel·la·ble \-ləbəl\ *adj* **:** capable of being propelled ⟨~ by oars or sail⟩

¹pro·pel·lant *or* **pro·pel·lent** \-lənt\ *adj* [*propellant* fr. *propel* + *-ant*, adj. suffix; *propellent* fr. L *propellent-*, *propellens*, pres. part. of *propellere* to propel] **:** capable of propelling **:** used for propelling ⟨~ fuel for submarines⟩

²propellant *also* **propellent** \"\ *n* -S **1 :** something that propels **:** a driving force or motive **:** STIMULUS **2 a :** an explosive for propelling projectiles **b :** the fuel and oxidizer carried separately or in physical combination which combine chemically to provide rocket propulsion **c :** a gas (as propane, nitrous oxide, nitrogen) placed in a pressure bottle for expelling the contents of the bottle when the pressure is released

pro·pel·ler *also* **pro·pel·lor** \-lə(r)\ *n* -S **:** one that propels: as **a :** SCREW PROPELLER **b** *obs* **:** a ship driven by a propeller **c :** a mechanical device having one or more blades which when rotated about a central shaft produce a forward thrust due to the aerodynamic forces acting upon them

propeller cuff *n* **:** a fairing of suitable airfoil shape used to cover the shanks of propeller blades in order to reduce the aerodynamic losses

propeller race *n* **:** SLIPSTREAM

propeller shaft *n* **1 :** a shaft that carries a screw propeller at its end and transmits power from engine to propeller **2 :** a shaft that transmits power from the transmission to the rear axle of an automotive vehicle **:** DRIVE SHAFT

propeller turbine engine *n* **:** TURBO-PROPELLER ENGINE

propelling pencil *n, Brit* **:** MECHANICAL PENCIL

pro·pel·ment \-lmənt\ *n* -S **1 :** PROPULSION **2 :** a propelling device in a mechanism

propend *vi* -ED/-ING/-S [L *propendēre*, fr. *pro* before + *pendēre* to hang — more at PENDANT] **1** *obs* **:** to hang downward or forward **:** INCLINE **2** *obs* **:** to become favorably inclined or disposed **:** TEND

pro·pen·dent \prōˈpendənt\ *adj* [L *propendent-*, *propendens*, pres. part. of *propendēre*] **:** hanging forward or down

pro·pene \ˈprō,pēn\ *n* -S [ISV *prop-* + *-ene*] **:** PROPYLENE

pro·pe·no·ic acid \¦prōpə¦nōik-\ *n* [*propenoic* ISV *propene* + *-oic*] **:** ACRYLIC ACID

pro·pense \prōˈpen(t)s\ *adj* [L *propensus*, past part. of *propendēre*] *archaic* **:** leaning or inclining toward **:** INCLINED, PRONE, DISPOSED

pro·pen·sion \-nchən\ *n* -S [L *propension-*, *propensio*, fr. *propensus* (past part. of *propendēre*) + *-ion-*, *-io* -ion] *archaic* **:** PROPENSITY

pro·pen·si·ty \prəˈpen(t)səd·ē, prō'-, -sətē, -i\ *n* -ES [*propense* + *-ity*] **:** a natural inclination **:** innate or inherent tendency ⟨~ for versifying⟩ ⟨~ to alcoholic sprees⟩ ⟨function of the wife was . . . to curb the roving *propensities* of the male —C.W. Cunnington⟩ ⟨often twitted about his ~ for having his picture taken —E.J.Kahn⟩ **syn** see LEANING

pro·pe·nyl \ˈprōpə,nil\ *n* -S [ISV *propene* + *-yl*] **:** a univalent unsaturated radical $CH_3CH{=}CH$— derived from propylene by removal of one hydrogen atom — compare ALLYL, ISOPROPRENYL — **pro·pe·nyl·ic** \¦==¦nilik\ *adj*

¹prop·er \ˈpräpə(r)\ *adj, sometimes* -ER/-EST [ME *propre* proper, own, fr. OF, fr. L *proprius* own, particular] **1 :** marked by suitability, fitness, accord, compatibility: as **a :** naturally suiting, complying with, or relevant to ⟨something mysterious, unreal . . . something ~ to the night —W.H.Hudson †1922⟩ ⟨keeping the body tissues in ~ condition —Morris Fishbein⟩ **b :** sanctioned as according with equity, justice, ethics, or rationale ⟨to administer ~ punishment to the perpetrators of these crimes —F.D.Roosevelt⟩ ⟨an adverse wind had so delayed him that his cargo brought but half its ~ price —Amy Lowell⟩ **c :** socially appropriate **:** according with established traditions and feelings of rightness and appropriateness ⟨a ~ reluctance to pronounce final judgments —*Times Lit. Supp.*⟩ ⟨the ~ ceremony, accompanied by the appropriate spell —J.G.Frazer⟩ **d :** acceptable as being qualified or competent **:** marked by adequate qualification, knowledge, or standards ⟨virtually all fields of human knowledge, necessary for the ~ reporting of Washington —F.L.Mott⟩ **e :** adequate to the purpose **:** SATISFACTORY, GOOD, PRAISEWORTHY ⟨discovered the true murderer and worked out a ~ revenge —*Time*⟩ ⟨amount of spirit . . . to give him the feeling of a ~ drink —Frank O'Connor⟩ ⟨the Department of Parks will undoubtedly build some ~ parks out there —Joseph Mitchell⟩ **f :** special to or appointed for a particular religious day or festival **2 a :** belonging to one **:** OWN ⟨the evidence of one's ~ nose —J.L.Lowes⟩ ⟨in the early days a leader had to be everything . . . in his own ~ person —G.W.Johnson⟩ **b :** belonging or applying to one individual only **:** distinguishing a person or a thing or a place from all others of the same class **:** naming without describing ⟨~ noun⟩ ⟨~ name⟩ —

opposed to *common* **c** *heraldry* **:** represented in natural color — abbr. *ppr.* **3 :** belonging characteristically to a species or individual **:** DISTINCTIVE, PECULIAR ⟨those high and peculiar attributes . . . which constitute our ~ humanity —S.T. Coleridge⟩ ⟨insidious ailments ~ to tropical climates —George Santayana⟩ **4 :** very good **:** EXCELLENT, CAPITAL ⟨that girl will make a ~ wife for some man⟩ **5** *chiefly Brit* **:** marked by ascribed or designated characterization to a remarkable or extreme degree **:** UTTER, ABSOLUTE ⟨that child is a ~ terror⟩ ⟨a ~ man the champion, for sure⟩ ⟨the roads are getting ~ death traps —*Time*⟩ **6** *chiefly dial* **:** becoming in appearance **:** well-formed and handsome **7 :** strictly limited or isolated to a specified thing, place, or idea **:** excluding adjuncts, concomitants, extensions, or allied matters — often used postpositively ⟨the expression "China ~" . . . applies to the eighteen provinces that lie south of the Great Wall —Owen & Eleanor Lattimore⟩ ⟨their animosity dated back to the Civil War, but the feud ~ began in 1880 —A.F.Harlow⟩ **8 :** marked by rightness, correctness, or rectitude: as **a :** strictly accurate **:** precisely applicable or pertinent **:** entirely in accordance with authority, observed facts, or other sanction **:** CORRECT ⟨various ~ ways of pronouncing a large number of words in our language —M.M.Mathews⟩ ⟨it was ~ to say that . . . most Americans belonged to the middle class —H.S.Commager⟩ **b** *archaic* **:** VIRTUOUS, RESPECTABLE ⟨a ~ gentlewoman —Shak.⟩ **c :** marked by occasionally prissy and too strict conformity to ethical standards, social conventions, or sanctioned usages ⟨mustn't sing that sort of song in company. We're oh! so ~ —George Meredith⟩ ⟨their women so ~ that no one mentioned babies until they arrived —H.S.Canby⟩ **d :** of the upper classes and correct to the point of smug priggishness ⟨she realized that ~ people go to sea as passengers on a liner, not as sailors —Hugh MacLennan⟩ ⟨ostracized by ~ folk —*Amer. Guide Series: Mass.*⟩ **9 :** being a mathematical subset that does not contain all the elements of the inclusive set from which it is derived **syn** see DECOROUS, FIT

²**proper** \"\ *n* -s [ME *propre*, fr. *propre*, adj.] **1** *obs* **:** PROPERTY, POSSESSIONS **2** *obs* **:** essential attribute **3** *sometimes cap* **a :** the special divine office for a particular day or festival ⟨the ~ for Christmas⟩ — compare COMMON 6 **b :** the parts of the mass that vary according to the day or the feast **c :** the part of a missal or breviary containing the offices proper to certain feasts or saints ⟨the ~ of the saints⟩

³**proper** \"\ *adv* [ME *propre*, fr. *propre*, adj.] **1** *chiefly dial* **:** PROPERLY **2** *chiefly dial* **:** THOROUGHLY ⟨scolded good and ~⟩

proper adjective *n* **:** an adjective that is formed from a proper noun, takes its meaning from what is characteristic of the being or thing named by the noun, and is usu. capitalized in English

properate *vb* [L *properatus*, past part. of *properare*, fr. *properus* speedy] *obs* **:** HASTEN — **properation** *n* -s *obs*

pro·per·din \ˈprōpə(r)dən\ *n* -s [prob. fr. ¹*pro-* + L *perdere* to destroy + E *-in* — more at PERDITION] **:** a serum protein that acting together with complement and magnesium ions participates in the destruction of bacteria, the neutralization of viruses, and the lysis of red blood cells

properer *comparative of* PROPER

properest *superlative of* PROPER

proper fraction *n* **:** a fraction in which the numerator is less or of lower degree than the denominator

pro·per·i·spome \prōˈperə,spōm\ *n* -s [by shortening & alter.] **:** PROPERISPOMENON

pro·per·i·spom·e·non \ˌprō,perəˈspämə,nän, -spōm-, -ˌnən\ *n, pl* **properispome·na** \-mənə\ [Gk *properispōmenon*, fr. neut. of *properispōmenos*, pres. pass. part. of *properispan* to pronounce the penultimate syllable with a circumflex accent, fr. *pro-* ¹pro- + *perispan* to pronounce with a circumflex accent — more at PERISPOMENON] **:** a word having the circumflex accent on the penult

pro·peritoneal \(ˌ)prō+\ *adj* [¹*pro-* + *peritoneal*] **:** lying between the parietal peritoneum and the ventral musculature of the body cavity ⟨a ~ herniated mass⟩

prop·er·ly \ˈpräpə(r)lē, -li, *in rapid -R speech sometimes* -pl-\ *adv* [ME *proprely*, fr. *propre* proper + *-ly*] **1 :** SUITABLY, FITLY, RIGHTLY, CORRECTLY ⟨tool ~ used⟩ ⟨~ dressed for the ceremony⟩ ⟨~ assembled machine⟩ **:** STRICTLY ⟨not ~ part of his duties⟩ **2 a :** INDIVIDUALLY **b :** INTRINSICALLY, INHERENTLY **3 a :** in an excellent or fine manner **b** *chiefly Brit* **:** EXCEEDINGLY, UTTERLY, EXTREMELY

proper motion *n* **:** the apparent change in position of a star usu. expressed in seconds of arc per year that results from the projection on the celestial sphere of its motion with respect to the solar system — see TANGENTIAL MOTION

proper name [ME *propre name*, fr. *propre* proper + *name*] *n* **1 :** PROPER NOUN **2 :** a symbol that indicates a logical subject and uniquely designates a logical simple; *specif* **:** a symbol that designates a sense-datum present and observed at the moment of the utterance of the symbol ⟨only two words which are strictly *proper names* of particulars, namely, 'I' and 'this' —Bertrand Russell⟩ — compare DESCRIPTION 1b, INCOMPLETE SYMBOL

prop·er·ness *n* -ES **:** the quality or state of being proper

proper noun *n* **:** a noun that designates a particular being or thing, does not take a limiting modifier, and is usu. capitalized in English

prop·er·tied \ˈpräpə(r)d·ēd, -)tēd\ *adj* [*property* + *-ed*] **1 :** possessing property **:** holding real estate or securities ⟨~ classes of society⟩ **2** *of a stage or scene* **:** requiring or using properties

¹**prop·er·ty** \ˈpräpə(r)d·ē, -)t|, |i, *in rapid -R speech sometimes* -pt|\ *n* -ES [ME *proprete*, fr. MF *propreté, propriété*, fr. L *proprietat-, proprietas*, fr. *proprie-* (fr. *proprius* own, particular) + *-tat-, -tas* -ty] **1 a :** a quality or trait belonging to a person or thing; *esp* **:** a quality peculiar to an individual person or thing ⟨the eye has this strange ~: it rests only in beauty —Virginia Woolf⟩ **b :** an effect that a material object or substance has on another object or on one or more of the senses of an observer ⟨the *properties* of the objects of nature do not signify . . . anything proper to the particular objects in and for themselves, but always a relation to a second object (including our sense organs) —H.L.F. von Helmholtz⟩ ⟨alkaline *properties* of ammonia⟩ ⟨optical *properties* of a mineral⟩ **c :** special power or capability **:** VIRTUE ⟨health resort . . . popular because of the healing *properties* attributed to the water of its spring —*Amer. Guide Series: Md.*⟩ ⟨rhythm is a ~ of words —C.H.Rickword⟩ **d** (1) **:** an attribute, characteristic, or distinguishing mark common to all members of a class or species ⟨protein molecules . . . have the extraordinary ~ of being able to reproduce themselves —Gerard Piel⟩ — called also *essential property* (2) *Aristotelian logic* **:** an attribute that is common and peculiar to a species but not a part of its essence nor contained in its definition **:** PROPRIUM — called also *nonessential property*; compare PREDICABLE **2 a :** something that is or may be owned or possessed **:** WEALTH, GOODS; *specif* **:** a piece of real estate ⟨the house . . . surrounded by the ~ —G.G.Weigend⟩ **b :** the exclusive right to possess, enjoy, and dispose of a thing **:** a valuable right or interest primarily a source or element of wealth **:** OWNERSHIP ⟨all individual ~ is . . . a form of monopoly —Edward Jenks⟩ **c :** something to which a person has a legal title **:** an estate in tangible assets (as lands, goods, money) or intangible rights (as copyrights, patents) in which or to which a person has a right protected by law **3** *obs* **:** PROPRIETY, FITNESS **4 a :** any article or object used in a play or motion picture except painted scenery and actors' costumes **b** *obs* **:** a means to an end **:** TOOL ⟨impossible I should love thee, but as a ~ —Shak.⟩ **syn** see QUALITY

²**property** *vt* -ED/-ING/-ES **1** *obs* **:** to make a tool of **:** EXPLOIT **2** *obs* **:** APPROPRIATE

property damage insurance *n* **:** protection against the legal liability of the insured for damage caused by his automobile to the property of others

property-increment tax *n* **:** a tax on increase in the value of the principal of an estate as distinct from income actually realized

property insurance *n* **:** insurance against direct loss or damage, consequential loss, loss due to liability for damages, or loss due to dishonesty or failure of others to perform their duty

prop·er·ty·less \ˈpräpə(r)d·ēlə̇s\ *adj* **:** lacking property ⟨party of the ~ proletariat —G.B.Shaw⟩

property man *n* **1** *or* **property master :** one who is in charge of the procuring and handling of theater or motion-picture stage properties **2 :** one who is in charge of equipment used at a coal mine

property right *n* **1 :** a right protected by a constitution to make contracts, conduct a business, labor, or use, enjoy, and dispose of property **2 :** a legal right or interest in or against specific property as opposed to a right enforceable against a person

prop forward *n* **:** either of the forwards to the right and left of the hooker in the front row of the rugby league scrum

pro·phage \ˈprō,fāj\ *n* -s [¹*pro-* + *phage*] **:** an intracellular form of various bacterial viruses in which the virus is harmless to the host and protects it from the attack of active viruses

prophane *obs var of* PROFANE

pro·phase \ˈprō,fāz\ *n* [ISV ¹*pro-* + *phase*; orig. formed in G] **:** the initial phase of mitosis in which chromosomes are condensed from the resting form and split into paired chromatids — **pro·pha·sic** \(ˈ)prō¦fāzik\ *adj*

proph·e·cy *also* **proph·e·sy** \ˈpräfəsē, -si\ *n* -ES [ME *prophecie, prophesie*, fr. OF, fr. LL *prophetia*, fr. Gk *prophēteia*, fr. *prophētēs* prophet + *-eia* -y] **1 :** the function or vocation of a prophet **:** utterance under the inspiring influence of religious experience; *specif* **:** the declaration of divine will and purpose **2 :** spoken or recorded utterance of a prophet **:** divinely inspired moral teaching (as by warning, exhorting, consoling) **:** apocalyptic revelation **3 :** a declaration of something to come **:** FORETELLING, PREDICTION **4** *obs* **:** public interpretation of Scripture **5 :** an Old Testament lection preceding the Epistle in various Christian liturgies

proph·e·si·er \ˈpräfə,sī(ə)r\ *n* -s **:** one that prophesies

proph·e·sy *also* **proph·e·cy** \-sī\ *vb* -ED/-ING/-ES [ME *prophecien, prophesien*, fr. MF *prophecier, prophesier*, fr. OF, fr. *prophecie, prophesie*, n.] *vt* **1 :** to utter or announce by or as if by divine inspiration **:** PREDICT ⟨~ general disaster⟩ ⟨~ a fall in prices⟩ **2 :** FORESHOW, PREFIGURE ⟨thy very gait did ~ a royal nobleness —Shak.⟩ ~ *vi* **:** to do the work or office of a prophet: as **a :** to speak for God or a deity **:** speak under the inspiring influence of religious experience **:** speak as or as if divinely inspired **b :** to give instruction in religious matters **:** interpret or expound Scripture or religious subjects **:** PREACH, EXHORT **c :** to speak or write under strong excitement or enthusiasm **:** speak or act with prophetic frenzy **d :** to make a prediction ⟨to be a successful prophet you had to ~ —Ernest Hemingway⟩ **syn** see FORETELL

proph·et \ˈpräfə̇t, *usu* -əd·+V\ *n* -s [ME *prophete*, fr. OF, fr. L *propheta*, fr. Gk *prophētēs*, fr. *pro* before, for + *-phētēs* (fr. *phanai* to say, speak) — more at FOR, BAN] **1 :** one who speaks for God or a deity **:** a divinely inspired revealer, interpreter, or spokesman: as **a :** an individual believed in ancient Israel to be possessed of clairvoyance ⟨is there no ~ of the Lord here, through whom we may inquire of the Lord? —2 Kings 3:11 (RSV)⟩ **b :** a member of a band of religious ecstatics believed in ancient Israel to be wonder workers and soothsayers ⟨a band of ~s coming down from the high place with harp, tambourine, flute, and lyre before them, prophesying —1 Sam 10:5 (RSV)⟩ **c** *often cap* **:** the writer of one of the prophetic books of the Old Testament **d :** an officer in a Christian church; *specif* **:** one in the early church interpreting God's will under the inspiration of the Holy Spirit **e** *usu cap* **:** a person regarded by a group of followers as the final authoritative revealer of God's will ⟨Muhammad, the *Prophet* of Allah to Muslims⟩ ⟨to all his followers, Zoroaster is the *Prophet*⟩ **f** *usu cap* **:** the accredited leader of a religious group (as the Mormons) **2 :** one gifted with more than ordinary spiritual and moral insight **:** SEER ⟨mighty ~ . . . on whom those truths do rest which we are toiling all our lives to find —William Wordsworth⟩; *esp* **:** an inspired poet **3 :** one who foretells future events **:** PREDICTOR ⟨in defiance of all the ~s of doom⟩ ⟨weather ~⟩ **4 :** an effective or leading spokesman for a cause, doctrine, or group ⟨the ~ of higher education for the many —J.S.Reeves⟩ ⟨one of the ~s of socialism⟩ ⟨~ of literary realism⟩ **5** *Christian Science* **a :** a spiritual seer **b :** disappearance of material sense before the conscious facts of spiritual Truth

proph·et·ess \-əd·ə̇s, -ə̇tə̇s\ *n* -ES [ME *prophetesse*, fr. MF, fr. LL *prophetissa*, fr. L *propheta* prophet + LL *-issa* -ess] **1 :** a female prophet **2 :** the wife of a prophet

prophet flower *n* [trans. of Per *guli paighāmbar* flower of the Prophet (Muhammad †A.D.632 Arabian prophet and founder of Islam)] **:** an East Indian perennial herb (*Arnebia echioides*) having yellow flowers marked with five spots that fade after a few hours; *also* **:** a related annual (*A. griffithii*)

proph·et·hood \-ət,hu̇d\ *n* **:** the position or career of a prophet

pro·phet·ic \prəˈfed·|ik, prōˈ-, -et|, |ēk\ *adj* [MF *prophetique*, fr. LL *propheticus*, fr. Gk *prophētikos*, fr. *prophētēs* prophet + *-ikos* -ic] **1 :** of, relating to, or characteristic of a prophet or prophecy **:** containing or resembling prophecy **:** INTERPRETATIVE, REVELATORY ⟨~ powers⟩ ⟨~ writings⟩ **2 :** foretelling events **:** tending to indicate what is going to happen **:** PRESAGEFUL ⟨~ skirmishes on the eve of a great battle⟩

pro·phet·i·cal \|ə̇kəl, |ēk-\ *adj* [ME, fr. MF *prophetique* + E *-al*] **:** of, pertaining to, or like a prophet or prophecy **:** containing prophecy ⟨~ books of the Old Testament⟩

pro·phet·i·cal·i·ty \prə,fed·əˈkaləd·ē\ *n* -ES **:** prophetical quality

pro·phet·i·cal·ly \prəˈfed·|ək(ə)lē, prōˈ-, -et|, |ēk-, -li\ *adv* **:** in a prophetic manner **:** like or characteristic of a prophet

pro·phet·i·cal·ness *n* -ES **:** prophetic quality

pro·phet·i·cism \|ə,sizəm\ *n* -s **1 :** an idea or form of words characteristic of the prophets **2 :** PROPHETISM

prophetic lesson *n* **:** PROPHECY 5

proph·e·tism \ˈpräfə,tizəm\ *n* -s **:** prophetic character, function, or authority; *specif* **:** the system or doctrines of the Hebrew prophets

¹**pro·phy·lac·tic** \¦prōfə¦laktik, -tēk *also* ¦präf-\ *adj* [Gk *prophylaktikos*, fr. (assumed) Gk *prophylaktos* (verbal of Gk *prophylassein* to keep guard before, take precautions against, fr. *pro-* ¹pro- + *phylassein* to guard, preserve, fr. *phylak-, phylax* guard) + Gk *-ikos* -ic] **1 :** guarding from disease **:** preventing or contributing to the prevention of disease **2 :** tending to prevent or ward off **:** PREVENTIVE, CAUTIONARY ⟨the swastika . . . a very ancient ~ symbol occurring among all peoples —Victor Schultze⟩ ⟨the purpose of this volume is ~ rather than remedial —Knight Dunlap⟩

²**prophylactic** \"\ *n* -s **1 :** something (as a medicinal preparation) that prevents or helps to prevent disease **:** PREVENTIVE **2 a :** a device (as a condom) for preventing venereal infection **b :** any of a number of devices for the prevention of conception

pro·phy·lac·ti·cal·ly \-tə̇k(ə)lē, -tēk-, -li\ *adv* **:** with a preventive purpose **:** so as to prevent ⟨the hotel seems to have been ~ insulated against any form of mirth —Robert Craft⟩

pro·phy·lax·is \ˌ≈≈ˈlaksə̇s\ *n, pl* **prophylax·es** \-k,sēz\ [NL, fr. Gk *prophylaktikos* prophylactic, after such pairs as Gk *praktikos* practical **:** *praxis* doing, action] **:** the prevention of disease **:** measures necessary to preserve health and prevent the spread of disease **:** protective, preservative, or preventive treatment

pro·phy·laxy \ˈ≈≈,laksē\ *n* -ES [F *prophylaxie*, fr. NL *prophylaxis*] **:** PROPHYLAXIS

pro·phyll \ˈprō,fil\ *also* **pro·phyl·lum** \prōˈfiləm\ *n, pl* **prophylls** \-lz\ *also* **prophyl·la** \-lə\ [NL *prophyllum*, fr. ¹*pro-* + *-phyllum*] **:** a plant structure resembling a leaf (as a bracteole) or consisting of a modified or rudimentary leaf (as a foliar primordium)

propination *n* -s [L *propination-, propinatio*, fr. *propinatus* (past part. of *propinare*) + *-ion-, -io* -ion] *obs* **:** the act of drinking to someone's health

¹**pro·pine** \prəˈpēn, -pīn\ *vt* -ED/-ING/-S [ME *propinen*, fr. MF *propiner*, fr. L *propinare* to present, procure, give to drink, drink to someone's health, fr. Gk *propinein* to present, drink to someone's health, drink first, fr. *pro-* ¹pro- + *pinein* to drink — more at POTABLE] **1** *chiefly Scot* **:** to present or give esp. as a token of friendship **2** *obs* **:** to pledge in drinking

²**propine** \"\ *n* -s [ME (Sc) *propyne*, fr. MF *propine*, fr. ML *propina*, fr. L *propinare*] *n, Scot* **:** a gift in return for a favor **:** TIP

³**propine** [ISV *prop-* + *-ine*] *var of* PROPYNE

pro·pin·quant \prōˈpiŋkwənt\ *adj* [L *propinquant-, propinquans*, pres. part. of *propinquare* to draw near, approach, fr. *propinquus* near, neighboring] **:** being in propinquity **:** NEARBY

pro·pinque \prōˈpiŋk\ *adj* [L *propinquus*] *archaic* **:** NEAR

pro·pin·qui·ty \prōˈpiŋkwəd·ē, prəˈ-, -ink-, -wəte, -i\ *n* -ES [ME *propinquite*, fr. L *propinquitat-, propinquitas* kinship, proximity, fr. *propinquus* near, neighboring, akin (fr. *prope* near) + *-itat-, -itas* -ity — more at APPROACH] **1 :** nearness of blood **:** KINSHIP ⟨degrees of ~⟩ **2 a :** nearness in place **:** PROXIMITY ⟨trees in close ~ to the house⟩ **b :** nearness in time **3** *archaic* **:** closeness in nature, disposition, or interests

pro·pin·quous \-wəs\ *adj* [L *propinquus*] **:** PROPINQUANT

pro·pio·lactone \¦prōpēō+\ *or* **pro·pi·ono-lactone** \¦prōpē¦äno, -¦ōnō+\ *n* [*propiolactone* ISV *propion-* + *lactone*; *propiono-lactone* fr. *propion-* + *lactone*] **:** a liquid beta-lactone $C_3H_4O_2$ made by condensation of ketene and formaldehyde

pro·pi·ol·aldehyde \¦prōpē,ōl, -¦ōl+\ *n* [ISV *propiolic* (in *propiolic acid*) + *aldehyde*] **:** a mobile liquid aldehyde HC≡CCHO made synthetically

pro·pi·o·late \ˈprōpēə,lāt\ *n* -s [ISV *propiolic* (in *propiolic acid*) + *-ate*] **:** a salt or ester of propiolic acid

pro·pi·olic acid \¦prōpē¦ōlik-, -¦älik-\ *n* [*propiolic* ISV *propionic* (in *propionic acid*) + *-ol-* (prob. fr. *stearolic acid*) + *-ic*; prob. fr. the fact that the relation of propiolic acid to propionic acid is analogous to that of stearolic acid to stearic acid] **:** a pungent liquid acetylenic acid HC≡CCOOH made by carbonation of sodium acetylide that forms not only salts but also metallic derivatives like those of acetylene

propion- *or* **propiono-** *also* **propi-** *or* **propio-** *comb form* [ISV, fr. *propionic* (in *propionic acid*)] **:** propionic acid **:** related to propionic acid ⟨*propionyl*⟩ ⟨*propionitrile*⟩ ⟨*propiono*-lactone⟩

pro·pi·on·aldehyde \¦prōpē,än+\ *n* [ISV *propion-* + *aldehyde*] **:** a volatile pungent liquid aldehyde C_2H_5CHO made usu. by dehydrogenation of propyl alcohol or as a by-product in the Fischer-Tropsch synthesis of higher hydrocarbons and used in organic synthesis

pro·pi·o·nate \ˈprōpēə,nāt\ *n* -s [ISV *propion-* + *-ate*] **:** a salt or ester of propionic acid

pro·pi·one \ˈprōpē,ōn\ *n* -s [ISV *propion-* + *-one*] **:** PENTANONE b

pro·pi·oni·bacterium \¦prōpē¦äno, -¦ōnə+\ *n* [NL, fr. ISV *propion-* + NL *-i-* + *bacterium*] **1** *cap* **:** a genus (the type of the family Propionibacteriaceae) of gram-positive nonmotile usu. anaerobic eubacteria that form propionic acid by fermenting lactic acid, carbohydrates, and polyalcohols and that include forms associated with the ripening of dairy products (as some hard cheeses) **2** *pl* **propionibacteria :** any bacterium of the genus *Propionibacterium*

pro·pi·on·ic acid \¦prōpē¦änik-\ *n* [*propionic* ISV ¹*pro-* + *pion-* (fr. Gk *pion-, piōn* fat) + *-ic*; orig. formed as F (*acide*) *propionique* — more at PIOPHILIDAE] **:** a liquid fatty acid C_2H_5COOH that has a sharp odor and is miscible with water, that occurs in milk and milk products and in distillates of wood, coal, and petroleum but that is usu. made by oxidation of propionaldehyde or propyl alcohol, and that is used chiefly in making salts (as the fungistatic calcium and sodium salts) and esters (as used for fruity and floral odors in perfumes)

pro·pio·nitrile \¦prōpēō+\ *n* [ISV *propion-* + *nitrile*] **:** a toxic volatile liquid nitrile C_2H_5CN that yields propionic acid and ammonia on hydrolysis and is used chiefly as a solvent — called also *ethyl cyanide*

pro·pi·o·nyl \ˈprōpēə,nil, -nēl\ *n* -s [ISV *propion-* + *-yl*] **:** the univalent radical $C_2H_5CO—$ of propionic acid

pro·pi·on·y·late \ˌprōpēˈänᵊl,āt\ *vt* -ED/-ING/-S [*propionyl* + *-ate*] **:** to introduce propionyl into (a compound) usu. by reaction with propionic acid or a derivative of it

pro·pi·the·cus \ˌprōpəˈthēkəs\ *n, cap* [NL, fr. ¹*pro-* + *-pithecus*] **:** a genus of lemurs consisting of the sifakas

pro·pi·ti·a·ble \prəˈpishēəbəl, prōˈ- *sometimes* -isē-\ *adj* [L *propitiabilis*, fr. *propitiare* to propitiate + *-abilis* -able] **:** capable of being propitiated

pro·pi·ti·ate \-ē,āt, *usu* -ād·+V\ *vt* -ED/-ING/-S [L *propitiatus*, past part. of *propitiare*, fr. *propitius* propitious] **:** to appease and make favorable **:** CONCILIATE ⟨the savage hunter and fisher is careful to ~ the animals and fish which he kills —J. G.Frazer⟩ **syn** see PACIFY

pro·pi·ti·at·ing·ly *adv* **:** in a propitiating manner **:** so as to appease or conciliate

pro·pi·ti·a·tion \≈,≈ˈāshən\ *n* -s [ME *propiciacioun*, fr. LL *propitiation-, propitiatio*, fr. L *propitiatus* (past part. of *propitiare*) + *-ion-, -io* -ion] **1 :** the act of propitiating, appeasing, or conciliating **2 :** something that appeases or conciliates a deity **:** ATONEMENT; *specif* **:** the self-sacrifice and death of Jesus Christ to appease divine justice and to effect reconciliation between God and man

pro·pi·ti·a·tive \≈ˈ≈≈,ād·|iv, -āt|, |ēv *also* |əv\ *adj* **:** tending to propitiate

pro·pi·ti·a·tor \|ə(r)\ *n* -s [LL, fr. L *propitiatus* (past part. of *propitiare*) + *-or*] **:** one that propitiates

pro·pi·ti·a·to·ri·ly \prəˈpishēə¦tōrəlē, prōˈ-, -tȯr-, -li *sometimes* -isē-\ *adv* **:** by way of propitiation

¹**pro·pi·ti·a·to·ry** \≈ˈ≈≈,tōrē, -tȯr-, -ri\ *n* -ES [ME *propiciatorie*, fr. LL *propitiatorium* means of atonement, mercy seat, fr. neut. of *propitiatorius*, adj.] **1 :** MERCY SEAT **2** *obs* **:** a sacrifice made in propitiation

²**propitiatory** \"\ *adj* [LL *propitiatorius*, fr. L *propitiatus* (past part. of *propitiare*) + *-orius* -ory] **1 :** of or relating to propitiation **:** EXPIATORY ⟨~ sacrifice⟩ **2 :** intended to appease or conciliate ⟨sent her flowers as a ~ gesture⟩

pro·pi·tious \prəˈpishəs, prōˈ-\ *adj* [ME *propicious*, fr. L *propitius*, fr. *pro* before + *-pitius* (akin to L *petere* to go to or toward, seek) — more at FOR, FEATHER] **1 :** favorably disposed **:** graciously inclined **:** BENEVOLENT ⟨we may succeed if the gods are ~⟩ **2 :** being of good omen **:** AUSPICIOUS, ENCOURAGING, FAVORABLE ⟨no conditions seem so ~ for a practical confederation as those of South America —Norman Angell⟩ **3 :** tending to favor or assist **:** HELPFUL, ADVANTAGEOUS, OPPORTUNE ⟨conditions ~ to the development of democracy —A.N.Christensen⟩ **syn** see FAVORABLE

pro·pi·tious·ly *adv* **:** in a propitious manner

pro·pi·tious·ness *n* -ES **:** the quality or state of being propitious

propjet \ˈ≈,≈\ *n* [⁵*prop* + *jet*] **:** TURBOPROP

propjet engine *n* **:** TURBO-PROPELLER ENGINE

prop joint *n* **:** RULE JOINT

propl *abbr* proportional

pro·plasm \ˈprō,plazəm\ *n* -s [L *proplasma*, fr. Gk, fr. *proplassein* to form or mold before, fr. *pro-* ¹pro- + *plassein* to form, mold — more at PLASTER] **:** a preliminary model (as made by a sculptor) **:** MOLD, MATRIX

pro·plastid \prō+\ *n* -s [ISV ¹*pro-* + *plastid*] **:** a minute cytoplasmic body from which a plastid is formed

prop·less \ˈpräplə̇s\ *adj* **:** having no support

pro·pleu·ral \prōˈplu̇rəl\ *adj* [*propleuron* + *-al*] **:** situated in or relating to a propleuron ⟨~ bristle⟩

pro·pleuron \prō+\ *n* [NL, fr. ¹*pro-* + *pleuron*] **:** a pleuron of the prothorax of an insect

pro·plexus \prō+\ *also* **pro·plex** \ˈprō,pleks\ *n* [NL *proplexus*, fr. ¹*pro-* + *plexus*] **1 :** BRACHIAL PLEXUS **2 :** CHOROID PLEXUS

pro·pliopithecus \prō+\ *n, cap* [NL, fr. ¹*pro-* + *Pliopithecus*] **:** a genus of small primitive short-jawed anthropoids from the Lower Oligocene of Egypt related to the gibbon but having the same dental formula as man

propman \ˈ≈,≈\ *n, pl* **propmen :** PROPERTY MAN

propn *abbr* proportion

pro·pneus·tic \prōˈn(y)üstik\ *adj* [¹*pro-* + Gk *pneustikos* of or for breathing, fr. (assumed) Gk *pneustos* (verbal of Gk *pnein* to breathe) + Gk *-ikos* -ic — more at SNEEZE] *of an insect larva* **:** having only the anterior pair of spiracles functional

pro·po·de·al \prōˈpōdēəl\ *adj* [*propodeum* + *-al*] **:** relating to or situated at a propodeum

pro·po·de·um \-ēəm\ *also* **pro·po·de·on** \-ēən\ *n, pl* **propodeums** *also* **propo·dea** \-ēə\ [*propodeum* fr. NL, alter. of *propodeon*, fr. ¹*pro-* + *podeon*; *propodeon* fr. NL] **:** the part of the thorax of a hymenopteran that lies immediately over and partly surrounding the insertion of the petiole of the abdomen and represents a basal abdominal segment which has become fused with the thorax

pro·po·di·al \-ēəl\ *adj* [NL *propodialis*, fr. *propodium* + L *-alis* -al] **1 :** of or relating to the propodium **2 :** of or relating to a propodiale or the propodialia

pro·po·di·a·le \prō,pōdē'ālē\ *n, pl* **propodia·lia** \-lēə\ [NL, fr. neut. of *propodialis*] **:** the proximal bone of a limb **:** HUMERUS, FEMUR
prop·o·dite \'präpə,dīt\ *n* -S [ISV ¹*pro-* + *-podite*] **:** the sixth or penultimate joint of a leg (as a walking leg) of a crustacean (as a decapod) — **prop·o·dit·ic** \;==;did·ik\ *adj*
pro·podium \prō+\ *n, pl* **propodia** [NL, fr. ¹*pro-* + *podium*] **:** the anterior portion of the foot of a mollusk
prop·o·dus \'präpədəs\ *n, pl* **propo·di** \-pə,dī\ [NL, fr. ¹*pro-* + *-podus* (fr. Gk *pod-, pous* foot — more at FOOT)] **:** PROPODITE
prop·o·lis \'präpələs\ *n* -ES [L, fr. Gk, fr. *pro-* ¹pro- + *polis* city — more at POLICE] **:** a brownish resinous material of waxy consistency collected by bees from the buds of trees and used as a cement — called also *bee glue*
prop·o·lize \'präpə,līz\ *vt* -ED/-ING/-S [F *propoliser,* fr. *propolis* (fr. L) + *-iser* -ize] **:** to fill or cover up with propolis
pro·pone \prō'pōn\ *vt* -ED/-ING/-S [ME (Sc) *proponen,* fr. L *proponere* to display, declare, propound — more at PROPOUND] **1** *Scot* **:** PROPOSE, PROPOUND **2** *Scot* **:** to bring or put forward (a defense, an excuse) **:** set forth
¹**pro·po·nent** \prə'pōnənt, prō'-\ *n* -S [L *proponent-, proponens,* pres. part. of *proponere*] **1 :** one who makes a proposal **:** one who lays down and defends a proposition **:** one who argues in favor of something (as an institution, a policy, a legislative measure, a doctrine) **:** ADVOCATE, SUPPORTER — opposed to *opponent* **2 :** the propounder of a legal instrument (as a will for probate)
²**proponent** \"\ *adj* [L *proponent-, proponens,* pres. part. of *proponere*] **:** that proposes, advocates, or defends ⟨peculiar element in Zionism is that its ~ Jews are not a full nationality —A.L.Kroeber⟩
pro·pons \'prō,pänz\ *n, pl* **propon·tes** \prō'pän.,tēz\ [NL *propont-, propons,* fr. ¹*pro-* + *pont-, pons* pons] **:** PONTICULUS 2
pro·pon·tic \prō'päntik\ *adj, cap* [*Propontis,* sea in northwest Turkey between Europe and Asia + E *-ic*] **:** of or relating to the ancient Propontis or modern Sea of Marmara
¹**pro·por·tion** \prə'pōrshən, prō'-, -pȯr-, -pōəsh-, -pȯ(ə)sh- *sometimes by* r-*dissimilation* pə'-\ *n* -S [ME *proporcioun,* fr MF *proportion,* fr. L *proportion-, proportio,* fr. *pro* for + *portion-, portio* part, share, portion — more at FOR, PORTION] **1 a :** the relation of one part to another or to the whole with respect to magnitude, quantity, or degree **:** relative size **:** RATIO ⟨the ~*s* of local, domestic, governmental, and foreign news have never been set —F.L.Mott⟩ ⟨winter rainfall decreases, and . . . summer rainfall increases, until at the eastern margin the ~ is reversed —F.E.Egler⟩ **b** *archaic* **:** COMPARISON, ANALOGY **2 a :** harmonious relation of parts to each other or to the whole **:** BALANCE, SYMMETRY ⟨finely molded cornice in correct classic ~ —*Amer. Guide Series: Minn.*⟩ **b :** reasonable or desirable estimation or assignment of relative value ⟨the more responsible . . . journals will either redress the wrong or treat it with ~ and humor —Jean Hills⟩ **3 :** the equality of two ratios **:** a relation among quantities such that the quotient of the first divided by the second equals that of the third divided by the fourth (as 4:2=10:5 or 4/2=10/5 or 4:2::10:5) — called also *geometrical proportion* **4 a :** proper or equal share **:** LOT ⟨the ~ of sago flour allotted to different members of the . . . labor group —R.W.Firth⟩ **b :** a portion or share of an actual or implied whole having a size or value relative to other portions or shares **:** QUOTA, PERCENTAGE ⟨felt anger and fear in equal ~*s*⟩ ⟨a much higher ~ of young people are going to high school and beyond —Walter Lippmann⟩ **5 a** *archaic* **:** FORM, SHAPE **b :** SIZE, DEGREE, DIMENSION ⟨eddies, some of which are small and some of oceanic ~*s* —R.E.Coker⟩ **6 :** the act of dividing proportionately; *specif* **:** the modification of the normal note values in mensural notation of music by diminution or augmentation according to a fractional arithmetic ratio — **in proportion 1 :** of the extent, size, or degree demanded (as by a relationship, comparison, or sense of fitness) ⟨a large house, with rooms *in proportion*⟩ **2 :** to the same degree **:** INSOFAR ⟨man is free *in proportion* as his surroundings have a determinate nature —R.M.Weaver⟩ — **out of proportion :** DISPROPORTIONATELY, EXCESSIVELY ⟨as the speed of a plane approaches . . . 750 miles an hour the amount of power needed . . . increases *out of* all *proportion* —G.R.Harrison⟩
²**proportion** \"\ *vt* **proportioned; proportioned; proportioning** \-sh(ə)niŋ\ **proportions** [ME *proporciounen,* fr. MF *proportionner,* fr. *proportion,* n.] **1 :** to adjust (a part or thing) in size relative to other parts or things **:** regulate the relative size of the parts of ⟨the duty of the older man to ~ his pace to the . . . course of his master —Francis Hackett⟩ **2 :** to make the parts of harmonious or correspondent or symmetrical **:** give pleasing or appropriate proportions to **3** *obs* **:** to be proportionate to **:** equal in value or importance ⟨his ransom, which must ~ the losses we have borne —Shak.⟩ **4** *obs* **:** to divide into or distribute in shares **5** *obs* **:** APPORTION **6** *obs* **:** to estimate the proportions of **:** COMPARE
pro·por·tion·able \-nəbəl\ *adj* [ME *proporcionable,* fr. LL *proportionabilis,* fr. L *proportion-, proportio* proportion + *-abilis* -able] *archaic* **:** PROPORTIONAL, PROPORTIONATE
pro·por·tion·ably \-blē\ *adv* [ME *proporcionably,* fr. *proporcionable* + *-ly*] *archaic* **:** in proportion **:** PROPORTIONATELY ⟨to make the being of a gigantic stature, . . . about eight feet in height, and ~ large —Mary W. Shelley⟩
¹**pro·por·tion·al** \-shənᵊl, -shnəl\ *adj* [ME *proporcional,* fr. L *proportionalis,* fr. *proportion-, proportio* proportion + *-alis* -al] **1 a :** being in proportion **:** corresponding in size, degree, or intensity **:** PROPORTIONATE — used with *to* ⟨rushed into freedom and enjoyment . . . with an energy ~ to their previous restraint —G.L.Dickinson⟩ **b :** having the same or a constant ratio **2 :** of, relating to, or used in determining proportions ⟨windows were widened for ~ consideration⟩ ⟨~ compasses⟩ **3 :** regulated or determined in size or degree with reference to proportions ⟨~ system of immigration quotas⟩ — **pro·por·tion·al·ly** \-shənᵊlē, -shnəlē, -i\ *adv*
²**proportional** \"\ *n* -S **1 :** a number or quantity in a proportion **2** *obs* **:** EQUIVALENT 2
proportional counter *n* **:** a counting tube operated at voltages below the threshold voltage whose discharge pulses are proportional to the amount of ionization produced by the ionizing particles
proportional dividers *n pl* **:** dividers having two legs pointed at both ends and joined by an adjustable pivot so that distances measured between the points at one end can be laid off in the same proportion by the points at the opposite end

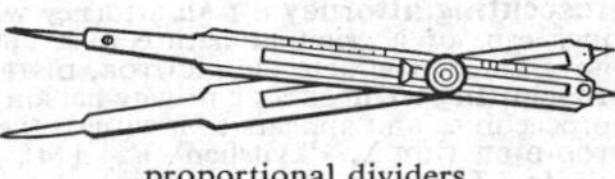
proportional dividers

pro·por·tion·al·ism \-shənᵊl,izəm, -shnə,li-\ *n* -S **:** the principle or practice of electing officials by proportional representation
pro·por·tion·al·ist \-shənᵊləst, -shnələ-\ *n* -S **:** a believer in or advocate of proportional representation
pro·por·tion·al·i·ty \prə,pōrshə'naləd·ē\ *n* -ES [LL *proportionalitat-, proportionalitas,* fr. L *proportionalis* proportional + *-tat-, -tas* -ty] **:** the quality, state, or fact of being proportional
proportionality constant *n* **:** the constant ratio of one variable quantity to another to which it is proportional
proportional limit *n* **:** ELASTIC LIMIT 2
proportional parts *n pl* **:** fractional parts of the difference between successive entries in a table that are arranged in a supplementary table for use in linear interpolation
proportional rate *n* **:** a freight rate for use only as a factor in making a combination through rate
proportional representation *n* **:** an electoral system designed to represent in a legislative body each political group or party in optimum proportion to its actual voting strength in a community — abbr. *P.R.;* see CUMULATIVE VOTING, HARE SYSTEM, LIST SYSTEM; compare PREFERENTIAL VOTING, SINGLE-MEMBER DISTRICT
proportional tax *n* **:** a tax in which the tax rate remains constant regardless of the amount of the tax base
¹**pro·por·tion·ate** \prə'pōrsh(ə)nət, prō'-, -pȯr-, -pōəsh-, -pȯ(ə)sh-, *sometimes by* r-*dissimilation* pə'-, *usu* -əd.+V\ *adj* [ME *proporcionate,* fr. LL *proportionatus,* fr. L *proportion-, proportio* proportion + *-atus* -ate] **:** being in proportion **:** proportionally adjusted **:** adequately proportioned ⟨representation ~ to the population⟩ ⟨returns ~ to your efforts⟩ ⟨additions to his family meant a ~ increase in his expenses⟩ — **pro·por·tion·ate·ly** *adv* — **pro·por·tion·ate·ness** *n* -ES
²**proportionate** \-shə,nāt, *usu* -ād.+V\ *vt* -ED/-ING/-S **:** to make proportionate **:** distribute or determine proportionally **:** give due proportions to **:** PROPORTION ⟨~ punishments to crimes⟩
pro·por·tioned \-shənd\ *adj* [ME *proporciouned,* fr. past part. of *proporciounen* to proportion] **:** having such proportions ⟨he was small and slight . . . but well-*proportioned,* and his short stature did not catch the eye —John Buchan⟩ **:** made or treated with regard for proper proportion ⟨give their readers a ~ and honest view of the world —Alan Barth⟩; *specif* **:** made in several standard lengths suited to body height classifications ⟨women's slips ~ for tall, medium, short⟩
pro·por·tion·er \-sh(ə)nə(r)\ *n* -S **:** one that proportions **:** a device for securing proportions in a mixture ⟨pumping liquid foam through a ~ and smothering the fire in the gasoline hatch —K.M.Dodson⟩
proportioning *pres part of* PROPORTION
pro·por·tion·less \-shənləs\ *adj* **:** lacking in proportion **:** UNSYMMETRICAL, DISTORTED
pro·por·tion·ment \-nmənt\ *n* -S **:** a state of being proportioned **:** PROPORTIONING
proportions *pl of* PROPORTION, *pres 3d sing of* PROPORTION
pro·pos·al \prə'pōzəl, prō'-\ *n* -S [*propose* + *-al*] **1 :** an act of putting forward or stating (a scheme, an offer, an intention) for consideration ⟨sincere ~ of friendship⟩ **2 a :** something put forward for consideration or acceptance **:** SUGGESTION, MOTION ⟨~*s* for mutual disarmament⟩ ⟨~ to build a new bridge⟩ ⟨legislative ~*s*⟩ **b :** an offer to perform or undertake something **:** BID ⟨~ of marriage⟩ ⟨the union rejected the companies' wage ~*s*⟩
proposal bond *n* **:** BID BOND
pro·pos·ant \-z°nt\ *n* -S [F, candidate for the Protestant ministry, fr. *proposant,* pres. part. of *proposer* to propose] **:** one who proposes himself as a candidate (as for the ministry)
pro·pose \prə'pōz, prō'-\ *vb* -ED/-ING/-S [ME *proposen,* fr. MF *proposer,* modif. (influenced by *poser* to put, place) of L *proponere* to display, declare, propound (perfect stem *propos-*) — more at PROPOUND, POSE] *vi* **1 :** to form or declare a plan or intention ⟨man ~*s,* but God disposes⟩ **2** *obs* **:** to engage in talk or discussion **:** CONVERSE ⟨there shalt thou find my cousin . . . *proposing* with the prince —Shak.⟩ **3 :** to make an offer of marriage **4 :** to make a prescribed statement in a card game indicating that one's hand is weak: as **a :** to undertake the lowest contract in solo **b :** to offer the drawing of additional cards in écarté ~ *vt* **1 a :** to set before the mind **:** bring forward **:** PROPOUND **b :** INTEND ⟨to China, where she *proposed* to spend some time with her friends —H.E.Salisbury⟩ **c** *obs* **:** CONFRONT, FACE **d** *obs* **:** SUPPOSE, IMAGINE ⟨be now the father, and ~ a son —Shak.⟩ **e :** to picture in the mind **:** IMAGE **2** *obs* **:** to set forth **:** EXHIBIT, SHOW **3 :** to offer for consideration, discussion, acceptance, or adoption ⟨~ terms of peace⟩ ⟨~ a legislative measure⟩ ⟨~ a topic for debate⟩ ⟨~ an alliance⟩ ⟨~ a friend for a club⟩ **4 :** to set up or declare as a formed purpose ⟨*proposed* to himself to achieve what hitherto he had been promised in vain, the title of cardinal —Hilaire Belloc⟩ **5 a :** to offer as a toast ⟨*proposed* the health of all the ladies present⟩ **b :** to suggest drinking (a toast) **6 :** to use (a taxonomic name for a new or reclassified species) for the first time in a publication **syn** see INTEND
pro·pos·er \-zə(r)\ *n* -S **:** one that proposes ⟨the original ~ of this theory —L.C.Douglas⟩; *specif* **:** one who applies for life insurance
pro·pos·i·ta \prō'päzəd·ə\ *n, pl* **proposi·tae** \-zə,tē\ [NL, fem. of *propositus*] **:** a female propositus
pro·po·si·tio \,prōpə'sid·ē,ō\ *n, pl* **propositi·o·nes** \,==,==-'ō,nās\ *or* **propositios** [L *proposition-, propositio*] **:** PROPOSITION 3
¹**prop·o·si·tion** \,präpə'zishən\ *n* -S [ME *proposicioun,* fr. MF *proposition,* fr. L *proposition-, propositio* representation, proposition, major premise, fr. *propositus* (past part. of *proponere* to display, declare, propound) + *-ion-, -io* -ion — more at PROPOUND] **1 a** *obs* **:** the act of proposing something for discussion or development (as by argument, narration) **b :** something proposed or offered for consideration, acceptance, or adoption **:** PROPOSAL ⟨the ~ to extend the . . . act spurred him to a defense of . . . institutions —S.H.Adams⟩ **c :** the point to be discussed or maintained in argument usu. stated in sentence form near the outset **d** (1) **:** a formal statement of a mathematical truth to be proved or demonstrated **:** THEOREM (2) **:** a mathematical statement of an operation to be performed **:** PROBLEM **2 a** *obs* **:** the act of setting or showing forth **b** *obs* **:** the act of offering **:** OFFER ⟨allures us by the ~ of rewards —Jeremy Taylor⟩ **3 a :** a declarative sentence **:** an expression in language, symbols, or signs of something capable of being believed, doubted, or denied **:** a verbal expression that is either true or false — called also *statement* **b :** the objective meaning of a statement **c :** a statement together with its objective meaning **4 a :** a project, plan, undertaking, or situation requiring some action (as dealing with, managing, operating, carrying out) with reference to it **:** BUSINESS, AFFAIR ⟨a wounded bull is a nasty ~ to tackle —*Manchester Guardian Weekly*⟩ ⟨writing is essentially a two-way ~ —S.E. Fitzgerald⟩ ⟨the scheme . . . has come up against a political snag and is at the moment not a practical ~ —W.B.Fisher⟩ ⟨it looked as if the mine would never become a paying ~⟩ **b :** a person requiring to be dealt with ⟨a tough ~⟩ ⟨a queer ~⟩ **c :** a proposed conditional bargain, agreement, deal, or settlement of a difficulty
²**proposition** \"\ *vt* -ED/-ING/-S **:** to make a proposal to **:** offer a scheme to; *specif* **:** to suggest sexual intercourse to ⟨had a habit of pinching and ~*ing* the nurses —Alan Hynd⟩
prop·o·si·tion·al \;==;zishənᵊl, -shnəl\ *adj* **:** of, relating to, or resembling a proposition ⟨these poems are sometimes too thinly ~ —David Daiches⟩ — **prop·o·si·tion·al·ly** \-shənᵊlē, -shnəlē, -i\ *adv*
propositional calculus *n* **:** a fundamental branch of symbolic logic dealing with propositions or statements as wholes, with their combinations, with the connectives that interrelate them, and with their transformation rules — compare TRANSFORMATION RULE, TRUTH TABLE
propositional function *n* **1 :** SENTENTIAL FUNCTION **2 :** something that is designated or expressed by a sentential function
proposition bet *n* **:** a bet in craps that a certain number or combination of numbers will or will not appear during a specified series of rolls
pro·pos·i·tus \prō'päzəd·əs\ *n, pl* **proposi·ti** \-zə,tī\ [NL, fr. L, past part. of *proponere* to display, declare, propound] **1 a :** one whose relations and pedigree are sought to be ascertained by a genealogical table **b :** PROBAND **2 :** the person immediately concerned **:** SUBJECT ⟨the personal law of persons domiciled in India varies with the religion of the ~ —J.H.C. Morris⟩
pro·pound \prə'pau̇nd, prō'-\ *vb* -ED/-ING/-S [alter. of earlier *propoun,* alter. (influenced by obs. E *compoun* — var. of E ¹*compound* — & obs. E *expoun* — var. of E *expound*) of *propone,* fr. ME (Sc) *proponen,* fr. L *proponere* to display, declare, propound, fr. *pro* before + *ponere* to put, place — more at FOR, POSITION] *vt* **1 :** to offer for consideration, deliberation, or debate **:** put for solution **:** set forth ⟨~ a doctrine⟩ **:** PROPOSE ⟨~ a question⟩ ⟨~ a hypothesis⟩ **2 :** to propose or name as a candidate (as for admission to communion with a church or for an office) **3** *obs* **:** to set before one's own mind or another's as an incentive, motive, aim, representation, or idea ⟨darest thou to the Son of God ~ to worship thee —John Milton⟩ ~ *vi* **:** to make a proposal **:** put a question
pro·pound·er \-də(r)\ *n* -S **:** one that propounds
propoxy- *comb form* [*prop-* + *oxy-*] **:** containing the univalent group $CH_3CH_2CH_2O$— composed of propyl united with oxygen ⟨*propoxy*acetanilide⟩
propped *past of* PROP
prop·per \'präpə(r)\ *n* -S **:** one that props **:** SUPPORTER
propping *pres part of* PROP
propr *abbr* proprietor
pro·prae·tor *or* **pro·pre·tor** \prō'prēd·ə(r)\ *n* [L *propraetor,* fr. *pro-* (as in *proconsul*) + *praetor*] **:** a praetor of ancient Rome sent out to govern a province
pro·prae·to·ri·al *or* **pro·pre·to·ri·al** \;prōprē;tōrēəl, -tȯr-\ *adj* **:** of or relating to a propraetor — **pro·prae·to·ri·an** \-ēən\ *adj*
propria *pl of* PROPRIUM
propriate *adj* [L *propriatus,* past part. of *propriare* to make one's own, fr. *proprius* own, particular] **1** *obs* **:** APPROPRIATED **2** *obs* **:** PARTICULAR, PECULIAR
pro·pri·e·tage \prə'prīəd·ij\ *n* -S [*proprietor* + *-age*] **:** the body of property owners
¹**pro·pri·e·tar·i·an** \prə,prīə'ta(a)rēən\ *n* -S [¹*proprietary* + *-an*] **1 :** an advocate of proprietary government **2** [*propriety* + *-arian*] **:** a stickler for the proprieties
²**proprietarian** \;=;==;==\ *adj* [fr. *proprietariat,* after E *proletariat: proletarian*] **:** relating or belonging to or characteristic of the propertied class — opposed to *proletarian* ⟨sending proletarian winners of scholarships to ~ public schools . . . and absorbing them into the service of the capitalist class —G.B. Shaw⟩
pro·pri·e·tar·i·at \=,==ta(a)rēət\ *n* -S [¹*proprietary* + *-at* (as in *proletariat*)] **:** the proprietorial class — opposed to *proletariat*
pro·pri·e·tar·i·ly \=;==;terəlē\ *adv* **:** in a proprietary manner
¹**pro·pri·e·tary** \prə'prīəterē, prō'-, -ri, *by* r-*dissimilation* pə'-\ *n* -ES [ME *proprietarie,* fr. LL *proprietarius,* fr. *proprietarius,* adj.] **1 :** one who has exclusive title to a thing in his own right **:** one who possesses the ownership of a thing in his own right **:** PROPRIETOR, OWNER; *specif* **:** an owner or grantee of a proprietary colony **2** [ME *proprietarie,* fr. ML *proprietarius,* fr. LL] *obs* **:** a monk holding property in violation of his vow of poverty **3 a :** a privately owned piece of property **b :** PROPRIETARY COMPANY **4 :** right of property **:** OWNERSHIP **5 :** a body of proprietors **6** [²*proprietary*] **a :** a drug that is protected by secrecy, patent, or copyright against free competition as to name, product, composition, or process of manufacture **b :** an ethical drug **c :** a nonprescription drug or medicine designed for self-medication and required to be accompanied by a list of all active ingredients and directions for safe use ⟨aspirin is a ~⟩
²**proprietary** \"\ *adj* [LL *proprietarius,* fr. L *proprietas* property + *-arius* -ary — more at PROPERTY] **1 a :** held as the property of a private owner ⟨~ right of manufacture⟩ **:** relating or belonging to a proprietor ⟨~ control of mineral resources⟩ ⟨~ government⟩ **b :** characteristic of or appropriate to an owner ⟨the lawyers' . . . normal ~ feeling about the law courts —Walter Goodman⟩ **2 :** made and marketed by a person or persons having the exclusive right to manufacture and sell ⟨~ baby food⟩ ⟨~ medicine⟩ **3 :** privately owned and managed usu. without public control or supervision ⟨in the 19th century there were many ~ medical schools in America⟩ ⟨~ hospital⟩
proprietary colony *n* **:** a colony granted to some individual or individuals with the fullest prerogatives of government — compare CHARTER COLONY, ROYAL COLONY
proprietary company *n* **1 :** a corporation owning all or a controlling number of the shares of another corporation **2 :** a company owning land that it leases or sells to other corporations **3** *Brit* **:** a privately owned company the shares of which are not offered to the public **:** CLOSE CORPORATION
proprietary library *n* **:** a library supported and usu. controlled by stockholding proprietors as well as by subscribers
proprietary stamp *n* **:** a revenue stamp for use on proprietary articles
pro·pri·e·tor \prə'prīəd·ə(r), prō'-, -ətə-, *by* r-*dissimilation* pə'-\ *n* -S [alter. (influenced by *-or*) of ¹*proprietary*] **1 :** an owner or grantee of a proprietary colony **:** PROPRIETARY **2 a :** one who has the legal right or exclusive title to something whether in possession or not **:** OWNER ⟨~ of a store⟩ ⟨protection of the rights of authors and other copyright ~*s* —*Universal Copyright Convention*⟩ **b :** one having an interest (as control, present use, or usufruct) less than absolute and exclusive right
pro·pri·e·to·ri·al \prə;prīə;tōrēəl, prō;p-, -tȯr-\ *adj* **1 :** of or relating to a proprietor or proprietorship **:** PROPRIETARY ⟨~ rights⟩ **2 :** arising from or manifesting consciousness of ownership **:** appropriate to an owner ⟨showed them around the place with ~ pride⟩ ⟨adopted a ~ attitude towards the entire hill —John Morrison⟩
pro·pri·e·to·ri·al·ly \-ēəlē\ *adv* **:** in a proprietorial capacity or manner
pro·pri·e·tor·ship \prə'prīəd·ə(r),ship\ *n* **1 a :** the state or fact of being a proprietor **:** OWNERSHIP **b :** an exclusive legal right for a definite or indefinite time to the profitable use of corporeal or incorporeal property upon agreed terms ⟨~ of a drug product⟩ ⟨~ of a copyright⟩ **2 :** a holding in land ⟨numerous small pleasant ~*s*⟩ **3 :** proprietor's equity **:** NET ASSETS
pro·pri·e·to·ry \-ə,tōrē\ *n or adj* [by alter. (influence of *-ory*)] **:** PROPRIETARY
pro·pri·e·tous \-ədəs\ *adj* [*proprietor* + *-ous*] **:** disposed to assume a proprietor's rights **:** PROPRIETORIAL ⟨now look . . . old girl, I won't have you adopting that ~ tone —G.J.W. Goodman⟩
pro·pri·e·tress \-ə·trəs\ *also* **pro·pri·e·trix** \-riks\ *n* -ES [*proprietress* fr. *proprietor-* + *-ess; proprietrix* fr. *proprietor,* after such pairs as E *executor: executrix*] **:** a female proprietor ⟨~ of a school for girls⟩
pro·pri·e·ty \prə'prīəd·ē, prō'-, -ətē, -i, *by* r-*dissimilation* pə'-\ *n* -ES [ME *propriete,* fr. MF *proprieté* quality or trait belonging to a person or thing, property — more at PROPERTY] **1 a** *obs* **:** peculiar, proper, or true nature, character, or condition ⟨the baseness of thy fear that makes thee strangle thy ~ —Shak.⟩ **b** *obs* **:** special nature **:** PECULIARITY **2 a** *obs* **:** private ownership **:** PROPRIETORSHIP **b** *obs* **:** privately owned possessions **:** PROPERTY **3 a** *obs* **:** a special characteristic of a language **:** IDIOM **b** *obs* **:** precise literal or strict sense **4 :** the quality or state of being proper or fitting **:** SUITABILITY, FITNESS, APPROPRIATENESS ⟨not so easy to see the ~ in an image which divests a snake of "winter weeds" —T.S.Eliot⟩ ⟨~ and necessity of preventing interference with the course of justice by premature statement, argument, or intimidation —O.W. Holmes †1935⟩ **5 a :** the standard of what is socially acceptable in conduct, behavior, speech **:** DECORUM ⟨passionately, deeply devoted to ~ . . . one of the most formal high U.S. officers in Europe —*Time*⟩ ⟨many of the topics denied by ~ to the newspaper's columns are considered suitable in a barbershop atmosphere —G.S.Perry⟩; *often* **:** prudent regard for or fear of offending against conventional rules of behavior esp. as between the sexes ⟨a long-ago love affair and the dead Welsh girl who was too innocent-hearted for his ~ —*Time*⟩ ⟨in her re-creation of the Victorian age she antedates . . . the victory of bourgeois ~ over the more raffish and glaring manners of the Regency —R.E.Roberts⟩ **b proprieties** *pl* **:** the customs and manners of polite society **:** conventionally correct behavior — used with *the* ⟨they talked the stupid, polite conversation that occurs between strangers; and then, the *proprieties* satisfied, . . . drifted back into the realm of music —Louis Bromfield⟩ ⟨feels compelled to observe the established *proprieties* of textbook writing —J.C.Cooley⟩
pro·pri·o·cep·tion \,prōprēō'sepshən\ *n* -S [fr. *proprioceptive,* after E *receptive: reception*] **:** the reception of stimuli produced within the organism — see PROPRIOCEPTOR
pro·pri·o·cep·tive \;===;septiv\ *adj* [*proprio-* (fr. L *proprius* own, particular) + *-ceptive* (as in *receptive*)] **:** activated by, relating to, or being stimuli produced within the organism (as by movement or tension in its own tissues) — compare EXTEROCEPTIVE, INTEROCEPTIVE
pro·pri·o·cep·tor \-tə(r)\ *n* -S [*proprio-* (fr. L *proprius* own, particular) + *-ceptor* (as in *receptor*)] **:** a sensory receptor that is located deep in the tissues (as in skeletal or heart muscle, tendons, the gastrointestinal wall, or the carotid sinus) and that functions in proprioception (as in response to changes of physical tension or chemical condition within the body proper)
pro·prio mo·tu \'prōprē,ō'mō(,)tü\ *adv* [L, by one's own motion] **:** by one's own motion **:** on one's own initiative
pro·prio·spinal \;prōprēō+\ *adj* [*proprio-* (fr. L *proprius* own, particular) + *spinal*] **:** distinctively or exclusively spinal ⟨a ~ reflex⟩
proprio vi·gore \-vəˈgō(,)rā\ *adv* [L, by its own force] **:** of or by its own force independently
pro·pri·um \'prōprēəm\ *n, pl* **pro·pria** \-ēə\ [L, possession, characteristic, fr. neut. of *proprius* own, particular] **1 :** PROP-

ERTY, ATTRIBUTE; *esp* : an attribute belonging inseparably to every member of a species **2** : the principle of individuation in personality : SELFHOOD

pro·proctor \prō+\ *n* [²*pro-* + *proctor*] : an assistant or deputy proctor (as at an English university)

prop root *n* : a root that serves as a prop or support to the plant (as in maize or mangrove) — called also *brace root;* see ROOT illustration

¹props *pl of* PROP, *pres 3d sing of* PROP

²props *n pl but sing in constr* [fr. pl. of ³*prop*] : a game similar to dicing played with four sea shells

³props *n pl but sing in constr* [fr. pl. of ⁴*prop*] : PROPERTY MAN

prop·ter af·fec·tum \ˈpräptərəˈfektəm\ *adv* [ML] : on account of partiality ⟨challenge a juror *propter affectum*⟩

propter de·fec·tum \-dəˈfektəm\ *adv* [ML] : on account of a defect ⟨the disqualification of a juror *propter defectum*⟩

propter defectum san·gui·nis \-ˈsaŋgwənəs\ *adv* [ML, on account of lack of blood kin] : for lack of an heir ⟨escheat an estate *propter defectum sanguinis*⟩

propter de·lic·tum \-dəˈliktəm\ *adv* [ML, on account of a crime] : on account of conviction for a crime ⟨disqualify a juror *propter delictum*⟩

propter delictum te·nen·tis \-təˈnentəs\ *adv* [ML] : on account of the tenant's crime ⟨property declared forfeit *propter delictum tenentis*⟩

propter hoc \-ˈhäk\ *adv* [L] : because of this — compare POST HOC

propter ho·no·ris re·spec·tum \-həˈnōrəsrəˈspektəm\ *adv* [ML] : on account of respect for rank ⟨a lord may claim exemption from ordinary jury duty *propter honoris respectum*⟩

prop·ter·yg·i·al \ˌpräptəˈrijēəl\ *adj* [*propterygium* + *-al*] : of, relating to, or being a propterygium

prop·ter·yg·i·um \ˌ=ˈ=ˈrijēəm\ *n, pl* **propteryg·ia** \-ēə\ [NL, fr. ¹*pro-* + Gk *pterygion* fin, lit., small wing — more at PTERYGIUM] : the anterior of the three principal basal cartilages in the paired fins of some fishes (as sharks and rays) — compare BASIPTERYGIUM

prop·tosed \ˈpräpˌtōst\ *adj* [*proptosis* + *-ed*] : affected by proptosis ⟨a ~ eye⟩

prop·to·sis \präpˈtōsəs\ *n, pl* **propto·ses** \-ōˌsēz\ [NL, fr. LL, prolapse, falling forward, fr. Gk *proptōsis,* fr. *propiptein* to fall forward, fr. *pro-* ¹pro- + *piptein* to fall — more at FEATHER] : forward projection or displacement esp. of the eyeball : EXOPHTHALMOS

propugnation *n* -s [L *propugnation-, propugnatio,* fr. *propugnatus* (past part. of *propugnare* to fight for, defend, fr. *pro* before, for + *pugnare* to fight) + *-ion, -io* -ion — more at FOR, PUGNACIOUS] *obs* : means of defense : DEFENSE ⟨what ~ is in one man's valor —Shak.⟩

propugnator *n* -s [ME *propugnatoure,* fr. L *propugnator,* fr. *propugnatus* (past part. of *propugnare*) + *-or*] *obs* : DEFENDER, VINDICATOR

pro·pul·sion \prəˈpəlshən, prōˈ-\ *n* -s [L *propulsus* (past part. of *propellere* to drive away, propel) + E *-ion* — more at PROPEL] **1** *obs* : the action of driving out or forth : EXPULSION, EJECTION **2** : the action of driving forward or ahead : action or process of propelling ⟨~ of ships by steam turbine⟩ ⟨problems of rocket ~⟩ **3** : something that propels : a driving or inciting force or influence ⟨in the ~ and in the excitement that can be provoked by forceful and expert pianists —Arthur Berger⟩ **4** : tendency to fall forward in walking (as in paralysis agitans)

pro·pul·sive \-lsiv, -sēv *also* -səv\ *adj* [L *propulsus* (past part. of *propellere*) + E *-ive*] : tending or having power to propel : driving onward or forward : impelling to action or motion ⟨gunpowder was well established as a ~ agent in war weapons —H.J.J.Winter⟩ ⟨the faster the jet plane goes, the greater its ~ efficiency —Harland Manchester⟩ ⟨universities . . . have . . . been the seats of ~ thought —Amy Loveman⟩ — **pro·pul·sive·ness** *n* -ES

propulsive coefficient *n* : the ratio between the indicated horse power of a ship's engine and the effective horsepower

pro·pul·sor \-sə(r)\ *n* -s [L *propulsus* (past part. of *propellere*) + E *-or*] : one that propels or produces a propulsive force ⟨use of hydrazine as a rocket ~⟩

pro·pul·so·ry \-sərē\ *adj* [L *propulsus* (past part. of *propellere*) + E *-ory*] : PROPULSIVE

pro·pupa \(ˈ)prō+\ *n* [NL, fr. ¹*pro-* + *pupa*] **1** : PREPUPA **2** : any of various insects in the late stage of incomplete metamorphosis in which the rudiments of external wings appear — **pro·pupal** \ˈ"+\ *adj*

prop wash *n* : SLIPSTREAM

prop word *n* : a noun or pronoun of very indefinite meaning that takes the qualification of an adjective with the effect of giving the latter a virtual noun construction (as *things* in "review books, manuscripts, and other literary things" or *one* in "two apples, a red and a green one")

pro·pygidium \ˌprō +\ *n* [NL, fr. ¹*pro-* + *pygidium*] : the dorsal plate of the segment that precedes the pygidium in beetles and some other insects

pro·pyl \ˈprōpəl, -ōˌpil\ *n* -s [ISV *prop-* + *-yl*] : either of two isomeric alkyl radicals C_3H_7 derived from propane and isopropane: **a** : the normal radical $CH_3CH_2CH_2$— — called also *n-propyl* **b** : ISOPROPYL

prop·y·lae·um \ˌpräpəˈlēəm\ *n, pl* **propy·laea** \-ēə\ [L, fr. Gk *propylaion* (usu. in pl. *propylaia*), fr. neut. of *propylaios* situated before the gate, fr. *pro-* ¹pro- + *pylē* gate] : a vestibule or entrance of architectural importance before a building or enclosure — often used in pl.

propyl alcohol *n* : either of two isomeric liquid alcohols C_3H_7OH: **a** : the normal alcohol $CH_3CH_2CH_2OH$ occurring in fusel oil but usu. obtained synthetically (as by oxidation of mixtures of propane and butane) that is used chiefly as a solvent (as in brake fluid compositions) and in organic synthesis; 1-propanol **b** : ISOPROPYL ALCOHOL

pro·pyl·amine \ˌprōpəlˈəˈmēn, -pəˈlamən\ *n* [ISV *propyl* + *amine*] **1** : either of two flammable isomeric liquid bases $C_3H_7NH_2$ of ammoniacal fishy odor; *esp* : the normal amine $CH_3CH_2CH_2NH_2$ **2** : an amine in which propyl is attached to the nitrogen atom

pro·pyl·ate \ˈprōpəˌlāt\ *vt* -ED/-ING/-S [*propyl* + *-ate*] : to introduce propyl into (a chemical compound) — **pro·pyl·ation** \ˌ=ˈ=ˈlāshən\ *n* -s

pro·pyl·ene \ˈprōpəˌlēn\ *n* -s [*propyl* + *-ene*] **1** : a flammable gaseous olefin hydrocarbon $CH_3CH{=}CH_2$ obtained usu. in petroleum refineries by cracking petroleum hydrocarbons and used chiefly in organic synthesis of compounds (as isopropyl alcohol, allyl chloride, cumene, propylene tetramer) with which benzene is alkylated for making detergents — called also *propene;* see POLYPROPYLENE **2** : the bivalent radical $-CH(CH_3)CH_2-$ derived from propane by removal of two hydrogen atoms from adjacent carbon atoms or from propylene by breaking of the double bond — compare TRIMETHYLENE

propylene glycol *n* : a sweet hygroscopic viscous liquid $CH_3CHOHCH_2OH$ made usu. from propylene or propylene oxide and used chiefly as a solvent, humectant, and preservative, as an antifreeze, and in hydraulic brake fluids; 1,2-propane-diol

propylene oxide *n* : a flammable liquid cyclic ether C_3H_6O similar to ethylene oxide that is made by chlorinating propylene to its chlorohydrin then adding alkali and is used chiefly as a solvent and in organic synthesis

pro·pyl·ic \(ˈ)prōˈpilik\ *adj* [ISV *propyl* + *-ic*] : of, relating to, or containing propyl

pro·pyl·i·dene \prōˈpiləˌdēn, ˈprōpələ-,\ *n* -s [ISV *propyl* + *-idene*] : a bivalent hydrocarbon radical CH_3CH_2CH< analogous to ethylidene — compare ISOPROPYLIDENE

prop·y·lite \ˈpräpəˌlīt\ *n* -s [*propylon* + *-ite*] : an altered form of andesite important for its connection with certain ore deposits and orig. supposed to mark the beginning of Tertiary eruptive activity — **prop·y·lit·ic** \ˌ=ˈ=ˈlid·ik\ *adj*

prop·y·lit·iza·tion \ˌpräpəˌlid·əˈzāshən\ *n* -s [*propylite* + *-ization*] : the alteration of an igneous rock to propylite

prop·y·lon \ˈpräpəˌlän\ *n, pl* **propy·la** \-lə\ [L, fr. Gk, fr. *pro-* ¹pro- + *pylē* gate] : an outer monumental gateway standing before a main gateway (as of a temple)

pro·pyl·par·a·ben \ˌprōpəlˈparəˌben\ *n* -s [*propyl* + *-paraben* (as in *methylparaben*)] : a crystalline ester $HOC_6H_4COOC_3H_7$ used as a preservative in pharmaceutical preparations; propyl *para*-hydroxy-benzoate

pro·pyl·thiouracil \ˌprōpəl+\ *n* [*propyl* + *thiouracil*] : a crystalline compound $C_7H_{10}N_2OS$ used as an antithyroid drug in the treatment of goiter — called also *6-propyl-2-thiouracil*

pro·pyne *also* **pro·pine** \ˈprōˌpīn\ *n* -s [ISV *prop-* + *-yne* or *-ine*] : METHYLACETYLENE

pro·quaes·tor \prōˈkwestə(r)\ *n* [LL, fr. L *pro quaestore,* fr. the phrase *pro quaestore* (acting) for a quaestor, fr. *pro* for + *quaestore,* abl. of *quaestor* — more at FOR, QUAESTOR] : one acting for a quaestor; *esp* : a magistrate associated with a proconsul in the administration of an ancient Roman province

¹pro ra·ta \(ˈ)prōˈrād·ə, -räl, -rā|, |tə\ *adv* [L] : proportionately according to some exactly calculable factor (as share, liability, period of time) : in proportion

²pro rata \ˈ"\ *adj* : divided, distributed, or assessed pro rata

¹pro·rate \(ˈ)prōˈrāt, *usu* -ād·+V\ *vb* -ED/-ING/-S [¹*pro rata*] *vt* : to divide, distribute, or assess proportionately ⟨in the sale of real estate, it is usual to ~ the taxes between the seller and the buyer —*Jour. of Accountancy*⟩ ~ *vi* : to make a pro rata distribution **syn** see APPORTION

²prorate \ˈ=ˌ=\ *n* -s : an amount determined pro rata

pro·rat·er \(ˈ)prōˈrād·ə(r)\ *n* -s : one that prorates; *specif* : one who acts as an agent for a debtor in making payments to his creditors

pro·ra·tion \prōˈrāshən\ *n* -s [¹*prorate* + *-ion*] : the act or an instance of prorating; *specif* : the limitation of production of crude oil or gas to some fractional part of the total productive capacity of each producer

prore \ˈprō(ə)r\ *n* -s [prob. fr. MF, fr. L *prora* — more at PROW] *archaic* : PROW

pro·rec·tor \prōˈrektə(r)\ *n* [NL, fr. ²*pro-* + ML *rector*] : a deputy rector in a university

pro·rec·tor·ate \-tərət\ *n* [ISV *prorector* + *-ate*] : the office of prorector

pro·rep·til·ia \ˌprōˌrepˈtilēə\ *n pl, cap* [NL, fr. ¹*pro-* + *Reptilia*] *in some classifications* : a division of reptiles containing various extinct forms regarded as connecting the reptiles and amphibians — **pro·rep·til·i·an** \ˌ=ˌ=ˈtilēən\ *adj*

pro·rhinal \(ˈ)prō+\ *adj* [¹*pro-* + *rhinal*] : in front of the nasal cavities

pro·rhip·i·do·glos·so·mor·pha \prōˌripədōˌgläsəˈmȯrfə\ *n pl, cap* [NL, fr. ¹*pro-* + *Rhipidoglossa* + *-o-* + *-morpha*] *in some classifications* : a primary division of Mollusca including the classes Gastropoda, Scaphopoda, and Lamellibranchia

pro·ro·cen·trum \ˌprōrəˈsentrəm\ *n, cap* [NL, fr. *proro-* (fr. L *prora* prow) + L *centrum* center — more at CENTER] : a genus of marine dinoflagellates that occas. cause local outbreaks of red water

pro·ro·gate \ˈprōrəˌgāt\ *vt* -ED/-ING/-S [ME *prorogaten,* fr. L *prorogatus,* past part. of *prorogare*] **1** : PROROGUE **2** *Scots law* : to extend (a judge's jurisdiction) by consent

pro·ro·ga·tion \ˌ=ˈ=ˈgāshən\ *n* -s [ME *prorogacion,* fr. L *prorogation-, prorogatio* prolongation, deferring, fr. *prorogatus* (past part. of *prorogare*) + *-ion-, -io* -ion] : the act of proroguing or state of being prorogued ⟨only one debate, that on foreign affairs, before the ~ on Friday —*Manchester Guardian Weekly*⟩

pro·ro·ga·tor \ˈ=ˌ=ˌgād·ə(r)\ *n* -s [LL, dispenser, fr. *prorogatus* (past part. of *prorogare* to pay in advance, fr. L, to prolong, defer) + L *-or*] : HYLEG

pro·rogue \prōˈrōg, prəˈ-\ *vb* -ED/-ING/-S [ME *prorogen,* fr. MF *proroguer,* fr. L *prorogare* to prolong, defer, fr. *pro* before + *rogare* to ask — more at FOR, RIGHT] *vt* **1** *archaic* : to extend the duration of : PROLONG, PROTRACT **2** : DEFER, POSTPONE ⟨this discussion was *prorogued* until those troubles were over and the Court had been reconstructed —C.P.Curtis⟩ **3 a** : to adjourn (as a parliament) to a specific day by prerogative act of the British crown **b** : ADJOURN 2 ⟨Massachusetts legislative leaders are apparently giving up on previous plans to ~ the 1951 legislative session by the coming weekend —*Christian Science Monitor*⟩ ~ *vi* : to suspend or end a legislative session ⟨the Vermont Legislature *prorogued* yesterday after setting a number of new records —*Springfield (Mass.) Daily News*⟩

pro·ruminal \(ˈ)prō+\ *adj* [¹*pro-* + *ruminal*] : situated in front of or coming before the rumen

pro·rupt \prōˈrəpt\ *or* **pro·rupt·ed** \-təd\ *adj* [*prorupt* fr. L *proruptus,* past part. of *prorumpere* to burst forth, fr. *pro* before + *rumpere* to break; *prorupted* fr. L *proruptus* + E *-ed* — more at FOR, REAVE] : not compact : PROTUBERANT ⟨possesses not only a panhandle but two additional protuberances as well, making that state markedly *prorupted* in form —C.L. White & G.T.Renner⟩

pro·rup·tion \-pshən\ *n* -s [LL *proruption-, proruptio* action of bursting forth, fr. L *proruptus* (past part. of *prorumpere*) + *-ion-, -io* -ion] : a bursting forth : the state of being protuberant or distended ⟨~ in form reduces the labor efficiency of the state —C.L.White & G.T.Renner⟩

pros *pl of* PRO

pros *abbr* **1** prosecuting; prosecutor **2** prosody

pros- *prefix* [LL, fr. Gk, fr. *pros* near, toward, to, prob. alter. (influenced by Gk dial. *pos* toward) of *proti* — more at PRICE, POST-] **1** : near : toward ⟨*pros*enchyma⟩ **2** [prob. influenced in meaning by Gk *pro* before — more at FOR] : in front ⟨*pros*encephalon⟩

pro·sa·ic \prōˈzāik, prəˈ-, -āek\ *adj* [LL *prosaicus,* fr. L *prosa* prose + *-icus* -ic — more at PROSE] **1 a** : of or relating to prose : written in prose **b** : belonging to or characteristic of prose as distinguished from poetry : FACTUAL, LITERAL ⟨the poetic is in the same way an exacter speech than the ~ —Hugh Kenner⟩ ⟨the intention is a ~ statement of weather conditions —John Dewey⟩ **c** : having a dull, flat, unimaginative quality of style or expression ⟨~ dullness, excessive and mere factuality —E.R.Bentley⟩ ⟨something provincial, mean, and ~ —Matthew Arnold⟩ **2** : belonging to or suitable for the everyday world : COMMONPLACE, DOWN-TO-EARTH, MATTER-OF-FACT ⟨the more ~ business of testing boilers —Richard Thruelsen⟩ ⟨a far more robust, more religious and, in a good sense, more ~ heritage —Douglas Bush⟩ — **pro·sa·ic·ness** *n* -ES

pro·sa·i·cal \-āəkəl, -āek-\ *adj* [LL *prosaicus* + E *-al*] : PROSAIC — **pro·sa·i·cal·ness** *n* -ES

pro·sa·i·cal·ly \-āək(ə)lē, -āek-, -li\ *adv* : in a prosaic manner : MATTER-OF-FACTLY ⟨apply my attention ~ to my routine at the museum —Edmund Wilson⟩

pro·sa·i·cism \-āəˌsizəm\ *n* -s : PROSAISM

pro·sa·ism \-āˌizəm\ *n* -s [F *prosaïsme,* fr. *prosaïque* prosaic (fr. LL *prosaicus*), after such pairs as F *archaïque* archaic: *archaïsme* archaism (fr. NL *archaismus*)] **1** : a prosaic manner, style, or quality ⟨a disinclination to interest himself in what may be called the ~s of the female world —Carlos Baker⟩ **2** : a prosaic phrase or expression ⟨prose in a poem seems offensive to me when . . . the ~s are sharp, obvious, individual —F.A.Pottle⟩

pro·sa·ist \-āəst\ *n* -s [L *prosa* prose + E *-ist*] **1** : a prose writer ⟨a beauty no present-day poet or ~ has yet attained —Kate W. Tibbals⟩ **2** : a prosaic person

pros·ar·thri \präˈsärˌthrī\ [NL, alter. (influenced by *pros-*) of *Proarthri*] *syn of* PROARTHRI

pro·sa·teur \ˌprōzəˈtər\ *n* -s [F, fr. It *prosatore,* fr. ML *prosator,* fr. L *prosa* prose + *-ator*] : a writer of prose ⟨other literary vices quite as widespread among our representative ~s —*Yale Rev.*⟩

¹pro·sau·ro·pod \prōˈsȯrəˌpäd\ *adj* [NL *Prosauropoda*] : of or relating to the Prosauropoda

²prosauropod \ˈ"\ *n* -s [NL *Prosauropoda*] : a reptile of the division Prosauropoda

pro·sauropoda \ˌprō+\ *n pl, cap* [NL, fr. ¹*pro-* + *Sauropoda*] : a division of Saurischia comprising bipedal Triassic reptiles ancestral to the sauropod dinosaurs

pros·bul \ˈprazˌbu̇l\ *n* -s [Mishnaic Hebrew *pĕrōzbōl, pĕrōsbōl,* prob. fr. Gk *prosbolē* application, approach, fr. *prosballein* to strike against, apply, fr. *pros-* + *ballein* to throw — more at DEVIL] : a rabbinical enactment circumventing the biblical law remitting debts during the sabbatical year by transferring a creditor's claims to the court

pro·scap·u·la \prōˈskapyələ\ *n* [NL, fr. ¹*pro-* + L *scapula*] : the clavicle of a teleost fish — **pro·scap·u·lar** \-lə(r)\ *adj*

pro·sce·ni·um \prəˈsēnēəm, prōˈ-\ *n* -s [L, fr. Gk *proskēnion,* fr. *pro-* ¹pro- + *skēnē* tent, scene — more at SHINE] **1 a** : the stage of an ancient theater — see THEATER illustration **b** : the part of a modern stage in front of the curtain : FORESTAGE **c** : the wall that separates the stage from the auditorium in a modern theater ⟨as a frame is to a painting, as a ~ to a play —*Atlantic*⟩ **2** : the front part : FOREGROUND ⟨these thoughts . . . kept possession of the ~ of his mind —Thomas Carlyle⟩

proscenium arch *n* : the arch that encloses the opening in the proscenium wall through which the spectator sees the stage : the frame of the stage picture

proscenium box *n* : a box in or near the proscenium : STAGE BOX

pro·sciut·to \prōˈshü(ˌ)tō\ *n, pl* **prosciut·ti** \-d·ē\ *or* **prosciuttos** [It, alter. (influenced by It *pro-* before, fr. L) of obs. It *presciutto,* fr. *pre-* (fr. L *prae-* pre-) + *-sciutto* (fr. L *exsuctus* dried up, sucked out, past part. of *exsugere* to suck out, fr. *ex-* + *sugere* to suck) — more at PRO-, SUCK] : dry-cured spiced ham

pro·scolex \prō+\ *n* [NL, fr. ¹*pro-* + *scolex*] : ONCHOSPHERE

pros·cop·i·nous \(ˈ)präˈskäpənəs\ *adj* [*proscopin-* (irreg. fr. Gk *proskopion* visor) + *-ous*] : having supraorbital ridges ⟨most primitive hominids are ~⟩

pros·cop·i·ny \=ˈ==nē\ *n* -ES [*proscopinous* + *-y*] : the condition of being proscopinous

pro·scribe \prōˈskrīb\ *vt* -ED/-ING/-S [L *proscribere* to publish, proscribe, fr. *pro* before + *scribere* to write — more at FOR, SCRIBE] **1 a** *Roman & civil law* : to post or publish the name of (a person) as condemned to death with his property forfeited to the state **b** : to put outside the law : OUTLAW ⟨lasting pacts *proscribing* warfare exist between many primitive societies —*Notes & Queries on Anthropology*⟩ **2** : to condemn or forbid as harmful : PROHIBIT ⟨any definition of security gets to be so broad as to ~ practically any free-flowing news —J.S.Pope⟩ — **pro·scrib·er** \-bə(r)\ *n* -s

pro·script \ˈprōˌskript\ *n* [L *proscriptus,* fr. *proscriptus,* past part. of *proscribere*] : one that is proscribed : OUTLAW

pro·scrip·tion \prōˈskripshən\ *n* -s [ME *proscripcioun,* fr. L *proscription-, proscriptio,* fr. *proscriptus* (past part. of *proscribere*) + *-ion-, -io* -ion] **1** : the act of proscribing or state of being proscribed : condemnation to death or exile : OUTLAWRY ⟨by ~ and bills of outlawry —Shak.⟩ **2** : an imposed restraint or restriction : INTERDICTION, PROHIBITION ⟨the ~ of solicitation and advertising and of enticing another's clients —H.S.Drinker⟩

pro·scrip·tive \-ptiv, -tēv *also* -təv\ *adj* [L *proscriptus* (past part. of *proscribere*) + E *-ive*] : given to proscribing or serving to proscribe ⟨a ~ tribunal⟩ ⟨a ~ law⟩ — **pro·scrip·tive·ly** \-təvlē\ *adv* — **pro·scrip·tive·ness** \-tivnəs\ *n* -ES

pro·scu·tel·lar \ˌprōskyüˈtelə(r)\ *adj* [*proscutellum* + *-ar*] : of, relating to, or constituting a proscutellum

pro·scu·tel·lum \ˌ=ˌ=ˈteləm\ *n* [NL, fr. ¹*pro-* + *scutellum*] : the scutellum of the prothorax of an insect

¹prose \ˈprōz\ *n* -s [ME, fr. MF, fr. L *prosa,* fr. fem. of *prosus* straightforward, direct, being in prose, fr. *prorsus,* fr. *proversus,* past part. of *provertere* to turn forward, fr. *pro* before + *vertere* to turn — more at FOR, WORTH] **1 a** : the ordinary language of men in speaking or writing : language intended primarily to give information, relate events, or communicate ideas or opinions **b** : a literary medium distinguished from poetry by its greater irregularity and variety of rhythm, its closer correspondence to the patterns of everyday speech, and its more detailed and factual definition of idea, object, or situation — compare VERSE **2** [ME, fr. ML *prosa,* fr. L] : SEQUENCE 1 **3** : a prosaic style, quality, character, or condition : ORDINARINESS, MATTER-OF-FACTNESS, PLAINNESS ⟨it was to escape from the ~ of existence that they had left America —Van Wyck Brooks⟩ **4 a** : a piece of prose : a prose exercise or composition ⟨got his ~s past . . . the heavy-lidded cold grey eye —Thomas Wood †1950⟩ **b** : a flat, tedious, unimaginative speech or piece of writing ⟨delivered a long ~, full of platitudes⟩ **c** : a friendly conversation : CHAT

²prose \ˈ"\ *vb* -ED/-ING/-S [ME *prosen,* fr. *prose,* n.] *vt* **1** : to write, translate, or paraphrase in prose **2** : to lecture, write, or talk into a specified state ⟨*prosed* them to death⟩ ~ *vi* **1** : to write prose ⟨*prosing* or versing —John Milton⟩ **2** : to write or speak in a dull, prosy manner ⟨don't ~ to me about duty and stuff —W.A.Butler †1902⟩

³prose \ˈ"\ *adj* [¹*prose*] **1** : of, relating to, or written in prose ⟨~ style⟩ ⟨~ drama⟩ **2** : MATTER-OF-FACT, PROSAIC ⟨dry, ~ people of superior intelligence object to feeling what they are supposed to feel in the presence of marvels —Mary McCarthy⟩

pro·sect \prōˈsekt\ *vt* -ED/-ING/-S [back-formation fr. *prosector*] : to dissect (an anatomic specimen) for demonstration — **pro·sec·tion** \-kshən\ *n*

pro·sec·tor \-ktə(r)\ *n* -s [prob. fr. F *prosecteur,* fr. LL *prosector* anatomist, fr. L *prosectus* (past part. of *prosecare* to cut away, cut off, fr. *pro* before + *secare* to cut) + *-or* — more at SAW] : one that makes dissections for anatomic demonstrations — **pro·sec·to·ri·al** \ˌprōsekˈtōrēəl\ *adj*

pro·sec·tor·ship \prōˈsektə(r)ˌship\ *n* -s : the position of prosector

pros·e·cut·able \ˈpräsəˌkyüd·əbəl, ˌ=ˈ=ˈ===\ *adj* : subject to prosecution ⟨a ~ offense⟩

pros·e·cute \ˈpräsəˌkyüt, -sē,-, *usu* -üd·+V\ *vb* -ED/-ING/-S [ME *prosecuten,* fr. L *prosecutus,* past part. of *prosequi* to follow, follow after, pursue — more at PURSUE] *vt* **1 a** : to follow to the end : press to execution or completion : pursue until finished ⟨was now ordered to ~ the war with the utmost vigor —Marjory S. Douglas⟩ ⟨determined to ~ the investigation⟩ **b** : to develop in detail : go further into : INVESTIGATE ⟨its central topic, sensation . . . continued to be *prosecuted* wherever the young science took root —F.A.Geldard⟩ **2** : to engage in or proceed with : carry on : PERFORM ⟨long-lining is *prosecuted* mainly by Cornish fishermen —G.A.Steven⟩ ⟨*prosecuted* wool-growing on a large scale —H.E.Starr⟩ **3** [LL *prosecutus,* past part. of *prosequi,* fr. L] **a** : to institute legal proceedings against; *esp* : to accuse of some crime or breach of law or to pursue for redress or punishment of a crime or violation of law in due legal form before a legal tribunal ⟨*prosecuted* them for fraud⟩ **b** : to institute legal proceedings with reference to ⟨~ a claim⟩ ⟨~ an application⟩ ⟨~ an action⟩ ⟨~ a crime⟩ ~ *vi* : to institute and carry on a legal suit or prosecution : SUE ⟨~ for public offenses⟩

prosecuting attorney *n* : an attorney who conducts proceedings esp. of a criminal nature in a court on behalf of the government : PUBLIC PROSECUTOR, DISTRICT ATTORNEY

prosecuting witness *n* : a private person who initiates criminal proceedings and appears as a witness therein

pros·e·cu·tion \ˌ=ˈ=ˈkyüshən\ *n* -s [ML *prosecution-, prosecutio,* fr. LL, continuation, retinue, fr. L *prosecutus* (past part. of *prosequi*) + *-ion-, -io* -ion] **1 a** : the carrying out of a plan, project, or course of action to or toward a specific end ⟨the successful ~ of a policy of developing the primary industries —George O'Brien⟩ ⟨the feverish ~ of expansion and internal improvement —*Amer. Guide Series: N.Y.*⟩ **b** : the performance or management of an occupation or activity ⟨salmon-spearing is a culturally higher type of activity . . . because there is normally no sense of spiritual frustration during its ~ —Edward Sapir⟩ **2** *obs* : PURSUIT ⟨see behind me the inevitable ~ of disgrace and horror —Shak.⟩ **3** : INVESTIGATION, STUDY ⟨facilities are provided for the ~ of research problems by qualified medical students —*Bull. of Meharry Med. Coll.*⟩ **4 a** : the institution and carrying on of a suit or proceeding in a court of law or equity to obtain or enforce some right or to redress and punish some wrong : the carrying on of a judicial proceeding in behalf of a complaining party; *specif* : the institution and continuance of a criminal suit involving the process of exhibiting formal charges against an offender before a legal tribunal and pursuing them to final judgment on behalf of the state or government (as by indictment or information) — compare DEFENSE **b** : the party by whom criminal proceedings are instituted or conducted

¹pros·e·cu·tive \ˌ=ˈ=ˈkyüd·iv\ *adj* [*prosecute* + *-ive*] : of or relating to prosecution ⟨a ~ action⟩ ⟨~ function⟩

²prosecutive \ˈ"\ *adj* [LL *prosecutus* (past part. of *prosequi* to follow after, pursue, proceed, continue) + E *-ive*] : of, relating to, or constituting a grammatical case (as in Eskimo) that denotes motion along

³prosecutive \ˈ"\ *n* -s : the prosecutive case of a language or a prosecutive form

pros·e·cu·tor \-ūd·ə(r), -ūtə-\ *n* -s [ML, fr. LL, escort of goods in transit, fr. L *prosecutus* (past part. of *prosequi*) + *-or*] **1 :** a person who institutes an official prosecution before a court often by appearing as the chief witness before a grand or petit jury or before a magistrate **2 :** PROSECUTING ATTORNEY

pros·e·cu·to·ry \ˈpräsəkyəˌtōrē\ *adj* [*prosecute* + *-ory*] **:** of, relating to, or concerned with prosecution ⟨~ functions⟩ ⟨~ officials⟩

pros·e·cu·trix \ˌpräsəˈkyü·triks\ *n, pl* **prosecutri·ces** \-rəˌsēz\ *or* **prosecutrixes** [fr. *prosecutor*, after such pairs as E *executor: executrix*] **:** a female prosecutor

prosed *past of* PROSE

¹pros·e·lyte \ˈpräsəˌlīt, *usu* -īd.+V\ *n* -s [ME *proselite*, fr. LL *proselytus* proselyte, alien resident, fr. Gk *prosēlytos*, fr. *pros* near, toward, to + *-ēlytos* (akin to *elthein* to come, go, suppletive aor. of *erchesthai* to come, go); akin to Gk *elan* to drive — more at PROS-, ELASTIC] **1 :** one who has been converted from one religious faith to another **:** NEOPHYTE; *specif* **:** a convert to Judaism who performs all the religious duties required of Jews and enjoys all the privileges **2 :** one who has been converted from one belief, attitude, or party to another **:** CONVERT ⟨a ~, a traditionalist who has only recently been converted to the modern credo of the glossematicians —Bjarne Ulvestad⟩

²proselyte \"\ *vb* -ED/-ING/-s *vt* **:** to convert from one religion, belief, opinion, or party to another **:** make a proselyte of ⟨the efforts of early missionaries to ~ Minnesota Indians were largely unproductive —*Amer. Guide Series: Minn.*⟩ ~ *vi* **1 :** to make or attempt to make proselytes ⟨left . . . to secure religious liberty and to ~ among heathen —A.D.Graeff⟩ **2 :** to recruit members for an institution, team, or group esp. by the offer of special inducements ⟨though it does not engage in *proselyting*, the college usually turns out fine basketball teams⟩

pros·e·lyt·er \-īd·ə(r)\ *n* -s **:** PROSELYTIZER

pros·e·lyt·i·cal \ˌ;==;lid·əkəl\ *adj* **:** of, relating to, or given to proselytism

pros·e·lyt·ism \ˈ==ˌlīˌtizəm, -ˌlə-,\ *n* -s **1 :** the act of becoming or condition of being a proselyte **:** CONVERSION ⟨his ~ inspired him to convert others⟩ **2 :** the act or process of proselyting ⟨represent sections detached from these ancient Churches, sometimes by ~ —B.J.Kidd⟩

pros·e·lyt·ist \ˈ==ˌlīd·əst, -ləd-\ *n* -s **:** PROSELYTIZER — **pros·e·lyt·is·tic** \ˌ==ˌlīˈtistik, -ləˈ-\ *adj*

pros·e·lyt·iza·tion \ˌ==ˌlīd·əˈzāshən\ *n* -s **:** PROSELYTISM

pros·e·lyt·ize \ˈpräs(ə)ləˌtīz\ *vb* -ED/-ING/-s *see -ize in Explan Notes* **:** PROSELYTE

pros·e·lyt·iz·er \-zə(r)\ *n* -s **:** one that proselytizes **:** one that makes or tries to make proselytes

prose·man \ˈprōzmən\ *n, pl* **prosemen :** a prose writer — opposed to *poet* ⟨our 18th century *prosemen* whom some uphold as our greatest —H.E.Cory⟩

pro·seminar \(ˈ)prō+\ *n* [ˈ*pro-* + *seminar*] **:** a directed course of study conducted in the manner of a graduate seminar but often open to advanced undergraduate students

pros·en·ce·phal·ic \ˌ;präsˈnsəˈfalik\ *adj* [*prosencephalon* + *-ic*] **:** of, relating to, or derived from the forebrain

pros·en·ceph·a·lon \ˌpräsˈnˈsefəˌlän\ *n* [NL, fr. *pros-* + *encephalon*] **:** FOREBRAIN

pros·en·chy·ma \präˈseŋkəmə\ *n, pl* **prosenchym·a·ta** \ˌpräsˈnˈkimad·ə\ *or* **prosenchymas** [NL, fr. *pros-* + *-enchyma*] **:** any of various tissues of higher plants composed of elongated usu. pointed cells mostly with little or no protoplasm and including tissues specialized for conduction and support — compare PARENCHYMA, PLECTENCHYMA — **pros·en·chym·a·tous** \ˌ;präsˈnˈkimad·əs\ *adj*

prose poem *n* **:** a work in prose that has some of the technical or literary qualities of a poem (as regular rhythm, definitely patterned structure, or emotional or imaginative heightening)

prose poet *n* **:** a writer of prose poems

pros·er \ˈprōzə(r)\ *n* -s **1 :** a writer of prose **:** PROSAIST 1 ⟨the outsider, the ~, even if he is modest and sensitive, goes wrong in the poetry world very quickly —E.M.Forster⟩ **2 :** one who talks or writes tediously ⟨an insufferable ~ who bored everyone⟩

pro·ser·pi·na·ca \prōˌsərpəˈnäkə\ *n, cap* [NL, fr. L, a plant, prob. knotweed, fr. *Proserpina*, goddess of the subterranean world of the dead, fr. Gk *Persephonē*] **:** a genus of No. American aquatic or marsh herbs (family Haloragaceae) having finely divided or pinnatifid leaves, tiny perfect but apetalous axillary flowers, and small bony angled fruit — see MERMAID WEED

proses *pl of* PROSE, *pres 3d sing of* PROSE

pros·ethmoid \(ˈ)präs+\ *or* **prosethmoid bone** *n* [*pros-* *ethmoid* fr. *pros-* + *ethmoid*] **:** the median anterior bone of the upper part of the skull of a teleost fish **:** ETHMOID

pro·seu·che \prōˈs(y)ükē\ *or* **pro·seu·cha** \-kə\ *n, pl* **proseu·chae** \-ü,kē\ [L & Gk; L *proseucha*, fr. Gk *proseuchē* proseuche, prayer, fr. *proseuchesthai* to pray to, fr. *pros* near, toward, to + *euchesthai* to pray — more at PROS-, VOW] **1 :** an ancient place of prayer **:** ORATORY **2 :** an ancient synagogue

prosier *comparative of* PROSY

prosiest *superlative of* PROSY

pros·i·fy \ˈprōzəˌfī\ *vb* -ED/-ING/-ES [ˈ*prose* + *-ify*] *vt* **:** to make prosaic ⟨his summary *prosifies* the poem⟩ ~ *vi* **:** to write prose ⟨*prosifies* as well as versifies⟩

pros·i·ly \-zəlē\ *adv* **:** in a prosy manner ⟨somewhat ~ and repetitively expounded —Anthony Quinton⟩

pro·sim·ia \prōˈsimēə\ *or* **prosimi·ae** \-ēˌē\ [NL, fr. ˈ*pro-* + *-simia* or *-simiae* (fr. L *simia* ape)] *syn of* PROSIMII

¹pro·sim·i·an \-ēən\ *adj* [ISV *prosimi-* (fr. NL *Prosimii*) + *-an*, adj. suffix] **:** of or relating to the Prosimii

²prosimian \"\ *n* -s [ISV *prosimi-* (fr. NL *Prosimii*) + *-an*, n. suffix] **:** one of the Prosimii

prosim·ii \-mēˌī\ *n pl, cap* [NL, fr. ˈ*pro-* + *-simii* (fr. L *simia* ape) — more at SIMIAN] *in some classifications* **:** a suborder of Primates that includes the less progressive primates (as the tarsiers and lemurs) and is coextensive with Lemuroidea and Tarsioidea of other classifications

pro·simulium \ˌprō+\ *n, cap* [NL, fr. ˈ*pro-* + *Simulium*] **:** a genus of blackflies

pros·i·ness \ˈprōzēnəs\ *n* -ES **:** the quality or state of being prosy ⟨his occasional ~, his lapses into mere talk —*Quarterly Rev.*⟩

¹prosing *n* -s [fr. gerund of ²*prose*] **1 :** writing in prose ⟨has poetic ambitions but ~ suits him better⟩ **2 :** tedious discourse ⟨half-baked opinionating and self-consciously . . . awkward ~s on life —John Farrelly⟩

²prosing *adj* [fr. pres. part. of ²*prose*] **:** PROSY — **pros·ing·ly** *adv*

pros·ist \ˈprōzəst\ *n* -s **:** a prose writer **:** PROSAIST

pro·sit \ˈprōsət, -ōzət\ *or* **prost** \ˈprōst\ *interj* [G, fr. L *prosit* may it be beneficial, 3d pers. sing. pres. subj. of *prodesse* to be useful, be beneficial — more at PROUD] — used to wish good health esp. before drinking

pro·slavery \(ˈ)prō+\ *adj* [²*pro-* + *slavery*] **:** favoring slavery; *specif* **:** favoring the continuance of or noninterference with Negro slavery ⟨the ~ states of the era before the Civil War⟩

pro·slav·ery·ism \prōˈslāv(ə)rēˌizəm\ *n* -s [*proslavery* + *-ism*] **:** the advocacy of slavery

pro·so \ˈprō(ˌ)sō\ *or* **proso millet** *n* -s [Russ *proso*; perh. akin to Gk *perknos* dusky, dark colored — more at PERCH] **:** MILLET 1a

proso- *comb form* [NL, fr. Gk *prosō* forward, fr. *proti* near, toward, to — more at PRICE] **1 :** in front ⟨*Proso*branchia⟩ **2 :** in a forward direction **:** onward ⟨*proso*plasia⟩

¹pros·o·branch \ˈpräsəˌbraŋk\ *adj* [NL *Prosobranchia*] **:** of or relating to the Streptoneura

²prosobranch \"\ *n* -s [NL *Prosobranchia*] **:** a gastropod of the subclass Streptoneura

pros·o·bran·chia \ˌ==ˈbraŋkēə\ *or* **pros·o·bran·chi·a·ta** \ˌ==ˌbraŋkēˈäd·ə\ [*Prosobranchia* fr. NL, fr. *proso-* + *-branchia*; *Prosobranchiata* fr. NL, fr. *proso-* + L *branchia* gill + NL *-ata*; fr. the usual location of the gills anterior to the heart — more at BRANCHIA] *syn of* STREPTONEURA

pros·o·bran·chi·ate \ˌ==ˈbraŋkēət, -ēˌāt\ *adj or n* [NL *Prosobranchiata*] **:** PROSOBRANCH

pros·o·coel *also* **pros·o·cele** *or* **pros·o·coele** \ˈpräsəˌsēl\ *n* -s [*proso-* + *-coele*] **:** the primitive undivided cavity of the forebrain of an early vertebrate embryo

pros·o·deme \ˈpräsəˌdēm\ *n* -s [*prosody* + *-eme*] **:** SUPRASEGMENTAL PHONEME

pros·o·det·ic \ˌ;präsəˈded·ik\ *adj* [*proso-* + *-detic* (as in *amphidetic*)] **:** situated in front of the beak — used of the ligament of a bivalve mollusk; compare AMPHIDETIC, OPISTHODETIC

¹pro·so·di·ac \prəˈsōdēˌak\ *or* **pros·o·di·a·cal** \ˌ;präsəˈdīəkəl\ *adj* [*prosodiac* fr. LL *prosodiacus*, fr. Gk *prosōidiakos* (perh. only a MS var. of *prosodiakos*), fr. *prosōidia*; *prosodiacal* fr. LL *prosodiacus* + E *-al*] **:** PROSODIC — **pros·o·di·a·cal·ly** \-ək(ə)lē\ *adv*

²prosodiac \"\ *n* -s [Gk *prosodiakos*, adj., used in a prosodion, fr. *prosodion*] **:** the verse used in a prosodion consisting of an enoplion followed by a long or short syllable

pro·so·di·al \prəˈsōdēəl\ *adj* [*prosody* + *-al*] **:** PROSODIC — **pro·so·di·al·ly** \-ēəlē\ *adv*

pro·so·di·an \-ēən\ *n* -s [*prosody* + *-an*] **:** PROSODIST

pro·sod·ic \prəˈsädik, prōˈ-, -dēk\ *or* **pro·sod·i·cal** \-dəkəl, -dēk-\ *adj* [*prosodic* fr. F *prosodique*, fr. *prosodie* prosody (fr. L *prosodia*) + *-ique* -ic; *prosodical* fr. *prosodic* + *-al*] **1 :** of or relating to prosody **2 :** of or relating to suprasegmental phonemes — **pro·sod·i·cal·ly** \-dək(ə)lē\ *adv*

pro·so·di·on \prəˈsōdēˌän\ *n, pl* **proso·dia** \-ēə\ [Gk, fr. neut. of *prosodios* processional, fr. *prosodos* procession, fr. *pros-* + *hodos* way, journey — more at CEDE] **:** an ancient Greek processional hymn sung by a chorus approaching the temple or altar of a god

pros·o·dist \ˈpräsədəst\ *n* -s [*prosody* + *-ist*] **:** a specialist in prosody

pros·o·dus \ˈpräsədəs\ *n, pl* **proso·di** \-səˌdī\ *or* **prosoduses** [NL, fr. Gk *prosodos* approach, procession] **:** a small canal in a sponge leading from an incurrent canal to a flagellated chamber

pros·o·dy \ˈpräsədē, -di\ *n* -ES [ME *prosodye*, fr. L *prosodia* accent of a syllable, fr. Gk *prosōidia* song sung to instrumental music, modulation of the voice, accent, fr. *pros* near, toward, to, in addition to + *ōidē* song, ode — more at PROS-, ODE] **1 a :** the study of versification; *esp* **:** the systematic study of metrical structure **:** METRICS — compare CADENCE, FOOT, METER, RHYTHM **b :** a treatise on versification ⟨the best ~ yet written⟩ **c :** a particular system or theory of versification ⟨although the nominal basis of his ~ is both accentual and syllabic, the latter element is really its defining principle —A.D.Culler⟩ **d :** method or style of versification ⟨the ~ of Milton⟩ ⟨the ~ of Gerard Manley Hopkins⟩ **2 :** the rhythmic aspect of language ⟨the ~ of the English language —H.H.J.Murrill⟩

pros·o·gas·ter \ˌ;präsəˈgastə(r)\ *n* -s [NL, fr. *proso-* + *-gaster*] **:** FOREGUT

proso·gyrate \ˌ;präsə+\ *adj* [*proso-* + *gyrate*] **:** curving toward the anterior — used esp. of the umbones of a bivalve mollusk; compare MESOGYRATE, OPISTHOGYRATE

pro·so·ma \prōˈsōmə\ *n* -s [NL, fr. ˈ*pro-* + *-soma*] **:** the anterior region of the body of various invertebrates (as of some mollusks) when it cannot readily be analyzed into its primitive segmentation; *esp* **:** CEPHALOTHORAX — **pro·so·mal** \-məl\ *adj*

proso millet *var of* PROSO

prosop- *or* **prosopo-** *comb form* [LL *prosopo-*, fr. Gk *prosōp-*, *prosōpo-* person, face, fr. *prosōpon*, fr. *pros-* + *-ōpon* (fr. *ōp-*, *ōps* face, eye) — more at EYE] **1 :** person ⟨*prosopo*graphy⟩ **2 :** face ⟨*prosop*algia⟩ ⟨*Prosopo*thrips⟩

pro·sop·ic \prəˈsäpik, -sōp-\ *adj* [*prosop-* + *-ic*] **:** of or relating to the face — **pro·sop·i·cal·ly** \-pək(ə)lē\ *adv*

pros·o·pid·i·dae \ˌpräsəˈpidəˌdē\ *n pl, cap* [NL, fr. *Prosopid-*, *Prosopis*, type genus + *-idae*] **:** a small but widely distributed family of small black hairy bees

¹pro·so·pis \prəˈsōpəs\ *n, cap* [NL, fr. Gk *prosōpis* burdock, perh. fr. *prosōpon* face] **:** a genus of tropical or subtropical branching shrubs or trees (family Leguminosae) having small flowers in axillary cylindrical spikes succeeded by large pods — see MESQUITE

²prosopis \"\ *n, cap* [NL *Prosopid-*, *Prosopis*, perh. irreg. fr. Gk *prosōpon* face] **:** the type genus of Prosopididae

pros·o·pite \ˈpräsəˌpīt\ *n* -s [G *prosopit*, fr. *prosop-* (fr. Gk *prosōpeion* mask, fr. *prosōpon* face) + *-it* -ite; fr. its occurrence as a pseudomorph] **:** a mineral $CaAl_2(F,OH)_8$ consisting of a basic fluoride of calcium and aluminum

pro·so·pi·um \prəˈsōpēəm\ *n, cap* [NL, fr. Gk *prosōpeion* mask] **:** a genus of whitefishes including the Menominee whitefish, Rocky Mountain whitefish, and related forms

pros·o·pla·sia \ˌpräsəˈplāzh(ē)ə\ *n* -s [NL, fr. *proso-* + *-plasia*] **1 :** differentiation of tissue; *esp* **:** abnormal differentiation **2 :** organization of tissue toward a more complex state

pros·o·plas·tic \ˌ;==ˈplastik\ *adj* [*proso-* + *-plastic*] **:** relating to or produced by prosoplasia

pros·o·pog·ra·phy \ˌpräsəˈpägrəfē\ *n* -ES [NL *prosopographia*, fr. LL *prosopo-* prosop- + L *-graphia* -graphy] **1 :** a description of a person's appearance, character, and career **2 a :** a collection of biographical sketches **b :** the activity of producing such a collection

pros·o·po·lep·sy \prəˈsōpəˌlepsē\ *n* -ES [Gk *prosōpolēpsia*, fr. *prosōpon* person, face + *-lēpsia* (fr. *lēpsis* act of taking hold or receiving, acceptance + *-ia* -y) — more at -LEPSY] **:** PARTIALITY

pro·so·pon \prəˈsōˌpän\ *n* -s [NL, fr. Gk *prosōpon*] **:** the younger nymphal stage of an insect that undergoes an incomplete metamorphosis

pros·o·po·poe·ia \prəˌsōpəˈpēə\ *n* -s [L, fr. Gk *prosōpopoiia* dramatization, prosopopoeia, fr. *prosōpon* person, face + *-poiia* (fr. *poiein* to make + *-ia* -y) — more at POET] **1 :** a figure of speech in which an absent person is represented as speaking or a dead person as alive and present ⟨the whole speech, a ~ spoken as by the poor man —*Quarterly Jour. of Speech*⟩ **2 :** PERSONIFICATION ⟨a ~ by which virtue becomes a knight in shining armor⟩

pros·o·po·thrips \ˌ;präsəpō+\ *n, cap* [NL, fr. *prosop-* + *Thrips*] **:** a genus of thrips including several that attack wheat

pros·o·pyle \ˈpräsəˌpīl\ *n* -s [*proso-* + *-pyle*] **:** the aperture between incurrent and radial canals in some sponges

pro·sorus \prə+\ *n* [NL, fr. ˈ*pro-* + *sorus*] **:** the initial thallus cell that produces a vesicle in which the sporangia are formed in some Chytridiales

pros·o·sto·ma·ta \ˌpräsəˈstōmad·ə\ *n pl, cap* [NL, fr. *proso-* + *-stomata*] *in some classifications* **:** an order of Digenea comprising trematode worms with the mouth at or near the anterior end of the body and including all the Digenea except members of the family Bucephalidae

pros·o·stome \ˈ==ˌstōm\ *n* -s [NL *Prosostomata*] **:** a worm of the order Prosostomata

¹pros·pect \ˈpräˌspekt *sometimes* -ˌspikt *or* -ˌspēkt\ *n* -s [ME *prospecte*, fr. L *prospectus* lookout, distant view, sight, fr. *prospectus*, past part. of *prospicere* to look forward, look into the distance, exercise foresight, fr. *pro* before + *specere* to look — more at FOR, SPY] **1 :** relative aspect **:** EXPOSURE 2d ⟨their ~ was toward the south —Ezek 40: 44 (AV)⟩ **2 a (1) :** an extensive view **:** a sight from a commanding position ⟨here, just above 1000 feet above sea level, our ~ embraces a dozen counties —S.W.Wooldridge⟩ **(2) :** a mental consideration **:** SURVEY ⟨on a nearer ~, all the circumstance of greatness vanished into shadow —A.C.Benson⟩ **b :** a place or station that commands an extensive view **:** LOOKOUT ⟨God beholding from his ~ high —John Milton⟩ **c :** something extended to the view **:** SCENE ⟨climbing onto a huge block of stone, began gazing at the wide ~ spread out before me —W.H.Hudson †1922⟩ **d** *archaic* **:** a sketch or picture of a scene ⟨a ~ of Yale College in New Haven, neatly engraved —*Boston Evening Post*⟩ **3** *obs* **:** an appearance presented by something ⟨it were a tedious difficulty . . . to bring them to that ~ —*Shak.*⟩ **4 a :** act of looking forward **:** ANTICIPATION, FORESIGHT ⟨its later development justified his ~ of its future value⟩ **b :** a mental picture of something to come **:** VISION ⟨attracted by the fascination of discovery and the ~ of spiritual conquest —*Amer. Guide Series: Minn.*⟩ **c :** something that is awaited or expected **:** POSSIBILITY ⟨air-conditioned cars are a happy ~ for some commuters —*Collier's Yr. Bk.*⟩ ⟨her sadness at the small ~ of seeing him again, old as she was —Archibald Marshall⟩ **d prospects** *pl* **(1) :** financial expectations ⟨as a young man with ~s he married the girl —Dixon Wecter⟩ ⟨without any ~s in the world except those which he could make for himself —R.W.Southern⟩ **(2) :** CHANCES ⟨improved corn ~s in other areas —*Wall Street Jour.*⟩ **5 a :** a place showing signs of containing a mineral deposit **b :** a partly developed mine **c (1) :** a sample of ore or gravel tested for mineral content **(2) :** the mineral yield of such sample **6 a :** a potential buyer or customer ⟨called on ten ~s but failed to make a sale⟩ **b :** a likely candidate for some appointment, job, or position ⟨a good ~ for the Supreme Court⟩ ⟨the coach has come up with several fine ~s for the team⟩ — **in prospect :** in view **:** ANTICIPATED, EXPECTED ⟨new medical advances are *in prospect*⟩

²pros·pect \ˈpräˌspekt *sometimes* prəˈs-\ *vb* -ED/-ING/-s *vi* **1 a :** to explore an area for mineral deposits ⟨~*ing* for gold⟩ ⟨~*ing* for uranium⟩ **b :** to make a search or investigation ⟨fat robins ~*ing* in the spaded earth of the flower beds —John & Ward Hawkins⟩ **2 :** to give indications of mineral yield ⟨this ore ~s well⟩ ~ *vt* **1 a :** to explore or inspect (a region) for mineral deposits **b :** to make preliminary developments and tests of (as a mine, an ore deposit) to determine its probable value **2 :** to make a careful investigation of **:** EXPLORE ⟨cautiously ~*ed* the highway —John Buchan⟩ ⟨today the principal tools for ~*ing* the brain are electrical —G W.Gray b.1886⟩

prospect glass *n, dial chiefly Eng* **:** TELESCOPE

pro·spec·tion \prəˈspekshən\ *n* -s [LL *prospection-*, *prospectio*, fr. L *prospectus* (past part. of *prospicere*) + *-ion-*, *-io* -ion] **1 :** the act of anticipating **:** FORESIGHT **2 :** the act of viewing **3 :** the act of exploring (as for gold)

¹pro·spec·tive \prəˈspektiv, -tēv *also* (ˈ)präˈs- *or* -təv *sometimes* prōˈs-\ *adj* [LL *prospectivus*, fr. L *prospectus* (past part. of *prospicere*) + *-ivus* -ive] **1** *archaic* **:** commanding an extensive view **2** *archaic* **:** FORESIGHTED, FORWARD-LOOKING **3 :** concerned with or relating to the future **:** effective in the future ⟨the statute which I have proposed is solely ~ in its operation —*Jour. of Accountancy*⟩ **4 :** of the future **:** in prospect **:** EXPECTANT, EXPECTED ⟨a ~ mother⟩ ⟨a ~ teacher⟩ ⟨a ~ heir⟩ ⟨the announcement declaring his candidacy is ~⟩ — **pro·spec·tive·ly** \-təvlē, -tēv-, -li\ *adv* — **pro·spec·tive·ness** \-tivnəs\ *n* -ES

²prospective \"\ *n* -s **1** *obs* **:** PROSPECTIVE GLASS **2 :** a scenic picture **:** PERSPECTIVE ⟨the scene again changed to a ~ of porticoes —E.K.Chambers⟩

prospective glass *n* **1** *obs* **:** a crystal or mirror used to predict the future ⟨in Time's long and dark *prospective glass*, foresaw what future days should bring to pass —John Milton⟩ **2 :** a small portable telescope

pros·pect·less \ˈpräˌspektləs\ *adj* **:** having no prospect

pros·pec·tor \ˈpräˌspektə(r) *sometimes* prəˈs-\ *n* -s [²*prospect* + *-or*] **:** one that prospects; *esp* **:** a person who explores a region for valuable mineral deposits

prospects *pl of* PROSPECT, *pres 3d sing of* PROSPECT

pro·spec·tus \prəˈspektəs\ *n* -ES [L, lookout, distant view, sight — more at PROSPECT] **:** a preliminary printed statement describing a business or other enterprise and distributed to prospective buyers, investors, or participants: as **a (1) :** a booklet or leaflet describing a forthcoming publication **(2) :** a book containing samplings and descriptions of the contents of a set of books (as of an encyclopedia) **b :** a description of a new security issue supplied to prospective purchasers and giving detailed information concerning the company's business and financial standing **c** *Brit* **:** a school catalog

pros·per \ˈpräsp(ə)r\ *vb* **prospered; prospered; prospering** \-p(ə)riŋ\ **prospers** [ME *prosperen*, fr. MF *prosperer*, fr. L *prosperare* to cause to succeed, fr. *prosperus*, adj., favorable, prob. fr. *prospere*, adv., favorably, according to hope, prob. fr. (assumed) OL *pro spere* according to hope, fr. L *pro* before, for, according to + (assumed) OL *spere*, abl. of L *spes* hope — more at FOR, SPEED] *vi* **1 a :** to succeed in an enterprise or activity **:** do well ⟨again reunited in spirit, the church ~*ed* from that time on —*Amer. Guide Series: Conn.*⟩; *esp* **:** to achieve economic or financial success ⟨after years of poverty, began to ~⟩ **b :** to turn out successfully ⟨his first venture into politics ~*ed* and he was soon considered for higher office⟩ **2 :** to become strong and flourishing **:** THRIVE ⟨there are lawns which do not ~ —R.M.Yoder⟩ ⟨moist yeast ~s at around 80 to 83 degrees —Dorothy Dean⟩ ~ *vt* **:** to cause to succeed or thrive ⟨whatever ~s my business is good —Lincoln Steffens⟩ **syn** see SUCCEED

pros·per·i·ty \präˈsperəd·ē, -ətē, -i\ *n* -ES [ME *prosperite*, fr. OF *prosperité*, fr. L *prosperitat-*, *prosperitas*, fr. *prosperus* favorable + *-itat-*, *-itas* -ity] **1 a :** the condition of being successful or thriving **:** a state of good fortune; *esp* **:** financial success ⟨since ~ has come to him he has added some conveniences to his cottage —*Current Biog.*⟩ **b :** a state of vigorous and healthy growth **:** WELL-BEING ⟨chlorophyll, apparently essential to plant ~ —*Crops in Peace & War*⟩ **2 :** a state of high general economic activity marked by relatively full employment, an increasing use of resources, and a high level of investment — compare DEPRESSION 3c

pros·per·ous \ˈpräsp(ə)rəs\ *adj* [ME, fr. MF *prospereux*, fr. *prosperer* to prosper + *-eux* -ous] **1 :** conducive to success **:** AUSPICIOUS, FAVORABLE ⟨await a more ~ moment⟩ **2 a :** attended with or marked by good fortune **:** SUCCESSFUL, THRIVING ⟨was longing to publish his ~ love —Jane Austen⟩ ⟨a ~ voyage⟩ **b :** attended with or marked by economic well-being ⟨~ times⟩ ⟨a ~ businessman⟩ ⟨a ~ nation⟩ **c :** enjoying a vigorous and healthy growth **:** FLOURISHING ⟨never had leaves been more green or ~ —Osbert Sitwell⟩ — **pros·per·ous·ly** *adv* — **pros·per·ous·ness** *n* -ES

pros·pho·ra \ˌ;präsfəˈrä\ *n, pl* **prospho·rae** \-ˈrä, ˈrē\ [LGk, fr. Gk, offering, fr. *prospherein* to present, offer, fr. *pros-* + *pherein* to carry — more at BEAR] **:** one of several loaves of bread each with special seals on the upper side used in the Eastern Church in the preparation of the Eucharistic elements

pro·spi·cience \prōˈspishən(t)s\ *n* -s [L *prospicientia*, fr. *prospicient-*, *prospiciens* (pres. part. of *prospicere* to look forward) + *-ia* -y — more at PROSPECT] **:** the act of looking forward **:** FORESIGHT

pro·sporangium \ˌprō+\ *n* [NL, fr. ˈ*pro-* + *sporangium*] **:** the initial cell that gives rise to a thin-walled vesicle in which the zoospores are formed in some fungi

pross \ˈpräs\ *vi* -ED/-ING/-ES [origin unknown] *chiefly Scot* **:** to put on airs

prost *var of* PROSIT

pros·tal \ˈprästˈl\ *n* -s [NL *prostalia* (pl.) prostals, fr. ˈ*pro-* + *-stalia* (fr. L *stare* to stand + *-alia*, neut. pl. of *-alis* -al) — more at STAND] **:** a spicule that projects beyond the body of a living sponge

pro·sta·sis \prōˈstāsəs\ *n* -ES [Gk, portico, fr. *proïstanai* to put in front, fr. *pro-* ˈpro- + *histanai* to cause to stand — more at STAND] **:** the space between the antas of a portico in antis

prostat- *or* **prostato-** *comb form* [NL, fr. *prostata*] **1 :** prostate ⟨*prostat*ectomy⟩ ⟨*prostat*itis⟩ **2 :** prostate and ⟨*prostato*vesical⟩

¹pros·tate \ˈpräˌstāt, *chiefly in substandard speech* -trāt, *usu* -ād.+V\ *n* -s [NL *prostata*, fr. Gk *prostatēs*, fr. *proïstanai* to put in front] **:** PROSTATE GLAND

²prostate \"\ *also* **pros·tat·ic** \(ˈ)präˌ;stad·ik\ *adj* [*prostate* fr. ˈ*prostate*; *prostatic* prob. fr. (assumed) NL *prostaticus*, fr. NL *prostata* + L *-icus* -ic] **:** of or relating to or being the prostate gland

pros·ta·tec·to·my \ˌprästəˈtektəmē\ *n* -ES [ISV *prostat-* + *-ectomy*] **:** surgical removal of the prostate gland

prostate gland *n* **1 a :** a pale firm partly muscular partly glandular body that surrounds the base of the male urethra in man and other mammals and discharges its viscid opalescent secretion through ducts opening into the floor of the urethra **b :** a corresponding group of glands about the female urethra of some mammals commonly considered a rudimentary or vestigial homologue of the male gland **2 :** any of various glandular bodies associated with genital ducts of male invertebrates and like or likened to the mammalian prostate

pros·tat·i·co·vesical \präˌ;stad·əkō+\ *or* **pros·ta·to·vesical** \ˌ;prästəd·ō+\ *adj* [*prostaticovesical* fr. *prostatic* + *-o-* + *vesical*; *prostatovesical* fr. *prostat-* + *vesical*] **:** of, relating to, or adjoining the prostate and the bladder ⟨the ~ venous plexus about the base of the bladder and prostate⟩

prostatic utricle *n* **:** a small blind pouch that projects from the posterior wall of the urethra into the prostate

pros·ta·tism \ˈprästəˌtizəm\ *n* -s [ISV *prostat-* + *-ism*] **:** disease of the prostate; *esp* **:** a condition resulting from obstruction of the bladder neck by an enlarged prostate

pros·ta·ti·tis \ˌ==ˈtīd·əs\ *n* -ES [NL, fr. *prostat-* + *-itis*] **:** inflammation of the prostate gland

pro·stem·mat·ic \ˌprō,steˈmad·ik\ *also* **pro·stem·mate** \prōˈste,māt\ *adj* [*prostemmatic* fr. ¹*pro-* + NL *stemmat-, stemma* one of the simple eyes of an insect, ocellus + E *-ic; prostemmate* fr. ¹*pro-* + *-stemmate* (fr. NL *stemmat-, stemma*) — more at STEMMA] **:** of, relating to, or constituting a minute sense organ in front of the eyes of collembolan insects

pro·ster·nal \prōˈstərnᵊl\ *adj* [ISV *prosternum* + *-al*] **:** of or relating to the prosternum

pros·ter·na·tion \ˌprästə(r)ˈnāshən\ *n* -s [ML *prosternation-, prosternatio*, fr. L *prosternere* to prostrate + *-ation-, -atio* -ation — more at PROSTRATE] **:** PROSTRATION

pro·sternum \prō+\ *n* [NL, fr. ¹*pro-* + *sternum*] **:** the ventral plate of the prothorax of an insect

pros·the·ca \prässˈthēkə\ *n, pl* **prosthe·cae** \-ē(,)sē\ *or* **prosthecas** \-ēkəz\ [NL, fr. Gk *prosthēkē* appendage, addition, fr. *prostithenai* to put to, add] **:** a small sclerite articulated to the base of the mandible in some insects

pros·the·sis \ˈprästhəsəs, *in sense 2* präsˈthēsəs\ *n, pl* **prosthe·ses** \-thə,sēz, -ˈthē,sēz\ [LL, fr. Gk, lit., addition, fr. *prostithenai* to put to, add, fr. *pros* near, toward, to + *tithenai* to place, put — more at PROS-, DO] **1 a :** the addition of a sound or syllable to a word esp. by prefixing (as in *newt, beloved*) **b :** the addition of one or more syllables at the beginning of a member or verse — used esp. in ref. to Greek and Latin prosody; compare APHAERESIS **2 :** an artificial device to replace a missing part of the body (as a suction socket to replace a lower leg or a dental restoration)

pros·thet·ic \(ˈ)präsˈthed·ik, -et\, \ēk\ *adj* [Gk *prosthetikos* adding, furthering, fr. *prosthetos* put to, added (fr. *prostithenai* to add) + *-ikos* -ic] **1 :** added to a word esp. by prefixing ⟨a ~ letter⟩ ⟨a ~ sound⟩ **2 :** of or relating to prosthesis or prosthetics ⟨~ hand⟩ ⟨~ research⟩ **3 :** of, relating to, or constituting a group or radical of a different kind attached to or substituted in a compound; *esp* **:** of, relating to, or constituting a nonprotein group of a conjugated protein ⟨the ~ nucleic acid group of a nucleoprotein⟩ — compare COENZYME — **pros·thet·i·cal·ly** \|ək(ə)lē\ *adv*

prosthetic dentistry *n* **:** PROSTHODONTICS

pros·thet·ics \präsˈthed·iks, -et\, \ēks\ *n pl but sing or pl in constr* [fr. *prosthetic*, after such pairs as E *economic: economics*] **:** the surgical and dental specialties concerned with the artificial replacement of missing parts — compare PROSTHODONTICS, RECONSTRUCTIVE SURGERY

pros·the·tist \ˈprästhəd·əst\ *n* -s [*prosthetic* + *-ist*] **:** a specialist in prosthetics

pros·thi·on \ˈprästhē,än\ *n* -s [NL, fr. Gk, neut. of *prosthios* foremost, fr. *prosthen* before, in front; akin to Gk *proti* near, toward, to — more at PRICE] **:** ALVEOLAR POINT — see CRANIOMETRY illustration

pros·tho·don·tia \ˌprästhəˈdänch(ē)ə\ *n* -s [NL, fr. *prosth-* (as in *prosthesis*) + *-odontia*] **:** PROSTHODONTICS

pros·tho·don·tics \-ntiks\ *n pl but sing or pl in constr* [*prosthodontia* + *-ics*] **:** the dental specialty concerned with the making of artificial replacements of missing parts of the mouth and jaws

pros·tho·don·tist \ˌ≈≈ˈdäntəst\ *n* -s [*prosthodontia* + *-ist*] **:** a specialist in prosthodontics

pros·tho·gon·i·mus \ˌprästhəˈgänəməs\ *n, cap* [NL, fr. *prosth-* (fr. Gk *prosthen* before, in front) + *-o-* + Gk *gonimos* productive, fertile; akin to Gk *gignesthai* to be born — more at KIN] **:** a genus of trematode worms (family Plagiorchiidae) parasitic in the oviducts and bursa of Fabricius and rarely in the intestine or esophagus of domestic and other birds

pros·tho·mere \ˈprästhə,mi(ə)r\ *n* -s [*prosth-* (fr. Gk *prosthen* before, in front) + *-o-* + *-mere*] **:** a segment anterior to the mouth in arthropods

pro·stig·ma·ta \ˌprō,stigˈmäd·ə, -mād·ə\ *n pl, cap* [NL, fr. ¹*pro-* + *stigma* + *-ata*] **:** a large group of mites having a respiratory system with the stigmal opening near the base of the chelicerae — **pro·stig·mat·ic** \ˌ≈≈ˈmad·ik\ *or* **pro·stig·mat·id** \-d·əd\ *adj*

pro·stig·min *or* **pro·stig·mine** \prōˈstigmən, -g,mēn\ *n* -s [fr. *Prostigmin*, a trademark] **:** NEOSTIGMINE

¹**pros·ti·tute** \ˈprästə,tüt, -ə,tyüt, *usu* -üd·+V\ *vb* -ED/-ING/-S [L *prostitutus*, past part. of *prostituere* to expose publicly to prostitution, prostitute, fr. *pro* before + *statuere* to set, station — more at FOR, STATUTE] *vt* **1 :** to offer indiscriminately for sexual intercourse esp. for payment ⟨do not ~ thy daughter, to cause her to be a whore —Lev 19:29 (AV)⟩ ⟨~ herself⟩ **2 :** to devote to corrupt or unworthy purposes or ends **:** DEBASE ⟨to mix culture with personal charm or advertisement is to ~ culture —Virginia Woolf⟩ ⟨men who ~ science in the name of profits —Harrison Brown⟩ ~ *vi* **:** to act as a prostitute **:** prostitute oneself ⟨while she was *prostituting* for him he married another woman —*Washington Post*⟩

²**prostitute** \"\ *adj* [L *prostitutus*, past part. of *prostituere*] **1** *archaic* **:** sexually promiscuous **:** LICENTIOUS **2 :** devoted to corrupt purposes or ends **:** PROSTITUTED

³**prostitute** \"\ *n* -s [L *prostituta*, fr. fem. of *prostitutus*, past part. of *prostituere*] **1 a :** a woman who engages in promiscuous sexual intercourse esp. for payment **:** HARLOT, STRUMPET, WHORE **b :** a male who engages in homosexual practices for payment **c :** a member of a group of women or sometimes men dedicated to a god who practice prostitution in association with the temple rites of the cult **2 :** a person who deliberately debases himself for money or other consideration; *specif* **:** a creatively gifted person (as a writer or painter) who deliberately lowers his standards for financial gain ⟨turns literary ~ and starts writing "poisoned pap" that sells well —*Time*⟩

pros·ti·tu·tion \ˌprästəˈtüshən, -əˈtyü-\ *n* -s [LL *prostitution-, prostitutio*, fr. L *prostitutus* (past part. of *prostituere*) + *-ion-, -io* -ion] **1 :** the act or practice of indulging in promiscuous sexual relations esp. for payment **2 :** the state of being prostituted **:** CORRUPTION, DEBASEMENT ⟨early-nineteenth-century houses, in various stages of destitution and ~ —Lewis Mumford⟩ ⟨political ~⟩ ⟨literary ~⟩

pros·ti·tu·tor \ˈprästə,tüd·ə(r)\ *n* -s [LL, fr. L *prostitutus* (past part. of *prostituere*) + *-or*] **:** one that prostitutes

pro·sto·mi·al \prōˈstōmēəl\ *adj* [*prostomium* + *-al*] **:** of or relating to the prostomium

pro·sto·mi·ate \-ē,āt\ *adj* [*prostomium* + *-ate*] **:** having a prostomium

pro·sto·mi·um \-ēəm\ *n, pl* **prosto·mia** \-ēə\ [NL, fr. ¹*pro-* + *-stoma* + *-ium*] **:** the portion of the head of various worms and mollusks situated in front of the mouth and commonly held to be nonmetameric

¹**pros·trate** \ˈprä,strāt *sometimes* -ästrət, *usu* -d·+V\ *adj* [ME *prostrat*, fr. L *prostratus*, past part. of *prosternere* to prostrate, fr. *pro* before + *sternere* to spread out, throw down — more at STREW] **1 a :** stretched out with face on the ground in adoration or submission ⟨smite the tax-gatherer, but fall ~ at the feet of the contemptible prince for whom the tax-gatherer plies his trade —H.T.Buckle⟩ **b :** lying prone or supine **:** extended in a horizontal position **:** FLAT ⟨quickly stooping I once more drove my weapon to the hilt in his ~ form —W.H.Hudson †1922⟩ **c :** knocked down **:** OVERTHROWN ⟨clambered over half-visible rocks, fell over ~ trees —Willa Cather⟩ **2 :** lacking in vitality or will **:** powerless to rise **:** laid low **:** OVERCOME ⟨~ with fear⟩ ⟨a whole continent ~ and impoverished —Andrew Shonfield⟩ **3 :** trailing on the ground **:** PROCUMBENT ⟨a subalpine species, usually shrubby or ~ in habit —William Dallimore & A.B.Jackson⟩ **syn** see PRONE

²**pros·trate** \ˈprä,strāt, *usu* -ād·+V\ *vt* -ED/-ING/-S [ME *prostraten* to prostrate oneself, fr. L *prostratus*, past part. of *prosternere* to prostrate] **1 :** to throw into a prostrate position **:** knock down **:** lay flat ⟨*prostrated* his opponent with one blow⟩ **2 a :** to extend (oneself) in a prostrate position ⟨half *prostrated* himself in something between an obeisance and an embrace —Claud Cockburn⟩ **b :** to put (oneself) in a humble and submissive posture or state ⟨the whole town had to ~ itself in official apology —Claudia Cassidy⟩ **3 a :** to reduce to submission or helplessness **:** render powerless **:** lay low ⟨the financial panic that had *prostrated* the East with the suddenness of a natural catastrophe —*Amer. Guide Series: Mich.*⟩ **b :** to subject to an emotional shock **:** OVERCOME ⟨*prostrated* with grief⟩ ⟨*prostrated* by the loss of his wife —C.S.Lewis⟩ **c :** to put into a state of extreme bodily exhaustion **:** DEBILITATE, WEAKEN ⟨*prostrated* by an attack of bilious fever —E.S.Bates⟩

prostrate juniper *n* **:** DWARF JUNIPER b

prostrate pigweed *n* **:** a prostrate or decumbent annual plant (*Amaranthus blitoides*) native to western No. America but established as a weed elsewhere esp. in waste places and neglected fields having alternate simple spatulate leaves and small greenish flowers in axillary clusters

pros·tra·tion \präˈstrāshən\ *n* -s [MF, fr. ML *prostration-, prostratio*, fr. LL, overthrow, defeat, fr. L *prostratus* (past part. of *prosternere*) + *-ion-, -io* -ion] **1 a :** the act of assuming a prostrate position esp. as a ceremonial or submissive gesture ⟨a number of young girls enter, make the customary ~ of greeting —Lafcadio Hearn⟩ **b :** the state of being in a prostrate position **:** ABASEMENT, SUBMISSIVENESS **2 a :** complete physical or mental exhaustion **:** COLLAPSE ⟨~ in influenza⟩ **b :** SHOCK, STUPEFACTION ⟨brought no incoherent cry of pity or ~ —C.E.Montague⟩ ⟨leaves the lay reader with a sense of ~ —A.G.Mazour⟩ **3 :** the process of being made powerless or the condition of powerlessness ⟨the ~ of the country before any invading and conquering army —Hilaire Belloc⟩ ⟨the general ~ of business after the war —Samuel Van Valkenburg & Ellsworth Huntington⟩

pros·tra·tor \ˈprä,strād·ə(r)\ *n* -s [LL, fr. L *prostratus* (past part. of *prosternere*) + *-or*] **:** one that prostrates

¹**pro·style** \ˈprō,stīl\ *adj* [L *prostylos* having pillars in front, fr. Gk, fr. *pro-* ¹pro- + *stylos* pillar — more at STEER] **:** marked by columniation consisting of free columns in a front portico only and across the full front of the structure — compare AMPHIPROSTYLE, PSEUDOPROSTYLE; see COLUMNIATION illustration

²**prostyle** \"\ *n* -s **:** a prostyle building

pro·suspensor \ˌprō+\ *n* [NL, fr. ¹*pro-* + *suspensor*] **:** the portion of the undifferentiated proembryo that gives rise to the suspensor

prosy \ˈprōzē, -zi\ *adj* -ER/-EST [¹*prose* + *-y*] **1 :** of, relating to, or having the characteristics of prose **:** COMMONPLACE, PROSAIC ⟨a dull ~ description of some of the exhibits —Sam Pollock⟩ ⟨the ~, shapeless frame houses without architectural charm or dignity —C.G.Bowers⟩ **2 :** tedious in speech or manner ⟨all ~ dull society sinners, who chatter and bleat and bore —W.S.Gilbert⟩

pro·syl·lo·gism \prōˈsilə,jizəm\ *n* [ML *prosyllogismus*, fr. Gk *prosyllogismos*, fr. *pro-* ¹pro- + *syllogismos* syllogism] **:** a syllogism with a conclusion that becomes a premise of a following syllogism

prot- *or* **proto-** *comb form* [ME *protho-*, fr. MF, fr. LL *proto-*, fr. LGk *prōt-, prōto-*, fr. Gk, fr. *prōtos*; akin to Gk *pro* before, ahead — more at FOR] **1 a :** first in time ⟨*proto*historic⟩ ⟨*proto*nymph⟩ **b :** first in status **:** chief in rank or importance **:** principal ⟨*proto*cerebrum⟩ ⟨*proto*cone⟩ **c :** beginning **:** tending toward **:** giving rise to ⟨*proto*fascism⟩ ⟨*proto*planet⟩ **2** *chem* **a :** first or lowest of a series **:** member of a series having or supposed to have the smallest relative amount of the element or radical indicated in the name to which it is prefixed ⟨*prot*oxide⟩ ⟨*proto*chloride⟩ **b :** substance held to be the parent of the substance to the name of which it is prefixed ⟨*prot*actinium⟩ **c :** first or primary product of decomposition ⟨*proto*proteose⟩ **3** *biol* **a :** archetypal ⟨*proto*morph⟩ ⟨*proto*nephros⟩ **b :** first formed **:** primary ⟨*proto*derm⟩ ⟨*proto*xylem⟩ **4** *usu cap* **:** belonging to or constituting the recorded or assumed language that is ancestral to a language or to a group of related languages or dialects — usu. spelled *proto-* and joined to a capitalized second element with a hyphen ⟨*Proto*-Arabic⟩ ⟨*Proto*-Indo-European⟩

prot *abbr* **1** protected; protection **2** protectorate **3** *usu cap* Protestant

prot·actinium \ˌprōd·+\ *or* **pro·to·actinium** \ˌprōd·(,)ō+\ *n* [NL, fr. *prot-* + *actinium*] **:** a shiny metallic radioelement of relatively short life that is formed in nature by loss of an alpha-particle and a beta-particle from uranium 235, that disintegrates into actinium and ultimately into lead, and that is pentavalent in compounds and shows close chemical resemblance to tantalum but differs in that its pentoxide is exclusively basic with no acidic characteristics — symbol *Pa;* see ACTINIUM SERIES, URANIUM SERIES; ELEMENT table

pro·ta·gon \ˈprōd·ə,gän\ *n* -s [G, fr. *prot-* + Gk *agōn* gathering, assembly] **:** a white crystalline powder consisting of a mixture of lipides obtained from the brain

pro·tag·o·nism \prōˈtagə,nizəm\ *n* -s [*protagonist* + *-ism*] **:** the state, character, or activity of a protagonist

pro·tag·o·nist \-ˌnəst\ *n* -s [Gk *prōtagōnistēs*, fr. *prōt-* prot- + *agōnistēs* competitor at games, debater, actor, fr. *agōnizesthai* to compete for a prize, contend, fr. *agōn* gathering, assembly at games, contest — more at AGONY] **1 a :** one who takes the leading part in a drama — opposed to *antagonist* **b :** the chief character of a novel or story in or around whom the action centers **2 a :** the spokesman or leader for a cause **:** the principal mover **:** CHAMPION ⟨was not only the ~ of his age; he was the symbol of all its inner meaning —W.O.Douglas⟩ **b :** an active participant **:** the supporter of an idea or action **:** ADVOCATE ⟨there remains a problem of market power that the ~*s* of big business . . . have not understood —E.S.Mason⟩ **3 :** a muscle that by its contraction actually causes a particular movement

pro·tag·o·re·an \prōˌtagəˈrēən\ *adj, usu cap* [*Protagoras*, 5th cent. B.C. Greek philosopher + E *-an*] **:** of or relating to Protagoras or his teachings

pro·tag·o·re·an·ism \-ə,nizəm\ *n* -s *usu cap* **:** the teachings of the Sophist Protagoras of Abdera — compare HOMO MENSURA

prot·amine \(ˌ)prōd·+\ *n* [ISV *prot-* + *amine;* orig. formed in G] **:** any of a class of simple proteins (as clupeine or salmine) that are strongly basic, not coagulable by heat, and soluble in water and dilute ammonia, that yield large amounts of basic amino acids on hydrolysis, and that occur combined with nucleic acid in the sperm of fish; *esp* **:** SALMINE — compare HISTONE

protamine zinc insulin *n* **:** a combination of protamine, zinc, and insulin used in suspension in water for subcutaneous injection in place of insulin because of its prolonged effect

prot·an·dric \prōdˈandrik, -aan-\ *adj* [ISV *protandry* + *-ic*] **:** PROTANDROUS

prot·an·drous \-drəs\ *adj* [*prot-* + *-androus*] **:** exhibiting protandry

prot·an·dry \-drē\ *n* -ES [ISV *prot-* + *-andry*] **1 :** a state in hermaphroditic systems that is characterized by the development of male organs or maturation of their products before the appearance of the corresponding female product thus inhibiting self-fertilization and that is encountered commonly in mints, legumes, and composites and among diverse groups of invertebrate animals — compare PROTOGYNY **2** [*prot-* + *andr-* + *-y*] **:** the appearance of male insects earlier in the season than females of the same species

prot·anomalous \ˌprōd·+\ *adj* [*prot-* + *anomalous*] **:** exhibiting protanomaly

prot·anomaly \"+\ *n* [ISV *prot-* + *anomaly;* prob. orig. formed as G *protanomalie*] **:** trichromatism in which an abnormally large proportion of red is required to match the spectrum — compare DEUTERANOMALY, TRICHROMAT

pro·ta·nope \ˈprōd·ə,nōp\ *n* -s [back-formation fr. NL *protanopia*] **:** an individual affected with protanopia

pro·ta·no·pia \ˌ≈≈ˈnōpēə\ *n* -s [NL, fr. *prot-* + ²*a-* + *-opia*] **:** red-green blindness believed due to a defect in the receptive mechanism of the retina of the eye and marked by confusion of red and blue-green — compare DEUTERANOPIA

pro·ta·nop·ic \ˌ≈≈ˈnäpik\ *adj* [ISV *protanop-* (fr. NL *protanopia*) + *-ic*] **:** characterized by or affected by protanopia ⟨~ vision⟩ ⟨a ~ person⟩

pro tan·to \prōˈtan·(ˌ)tō\ [LL] **:** for so much **:** to a certain extent

prot·argentum \ˌprōd·+\ *n* [NL, fr. *prot-* (fr. ISV *protein*) + L *argentum*] **:** SILVER PROTEIN b

pro·tar·gin \prōˈtärjən\ *n* -s [NL *protargentum* + ISV *-in*] **:** SILVER PROTEIN

Pro·tar·gol \-ˌgōl, -gōl\ *trademark* — used for strong silver protein

pro·tarsal \(ˈ)prō+\ *adj* [NL *protarsus* + E *-al*] **:** of or relating to a protarsus

pro·tarsus \"+\ *n, pl* **protarsi** [NL, fr. ¹*pro-* + *tarsus*] **1 :** the tarsus of the front leg of an insect **2 :** the tibia of the leg of a spider

prot·a·sis \ˈprädəsəs\ *n, pl* **prota·ses** \-ə,sēz\ [LL, fr. Gk, fr. *proteinein* stretch out before, put forward, fr. *pro-* ¹pro- + *teinein* to stretch — more at THIN] **1 a :** the first part of an ancient drama in which the characters are introduced and the argument explained **b :** the opening lines esp. of a drama or narrative poem **:** the part preceding the epitasis **:** INTRODUCTION — compare CATASTASIS **2 :** CONDITION 2a(2) — contrasted with *apodosis* **3 :** a proposition that serves esp. as a premise in a syllogism or in reasoning **:** ANTECEDENT, CONDITIONAL

pro·tas·pid \prōˈtaspəd\ *adj* [NL *protaspid-, protoaspis*] **:** relating to or being a protaspis

pro·tas·pis \-pəs\ *n, pl* **protaspi·des** \-pə,dēz\ [NL, fr. *prot-* + *-aspis*] **:** the minute discoid or oval first larval form of a trilobite that has a well-marked axial lobe, large head region, and but little segmentation

pro·tat·ic \prōˈtad·ik\ *adj* [LL *protaticus*, fr. Gk *protatikos*, fr. *protasis* + *-ikos* -ic] **:** of or relating to the protasis of a play **:** INTRODUCTORY — **pro·tat·i·cal·ly** \-ək(ə)lē\ *adv*

prot·axial \(ˈ)prōd·+\ *adj* [NL *protaxis* + E *-al*] **:** of or relating to the protaxis

prot·axis \"+\ *n* [NL, fr. *prot-* + *axis*] **:** the line of initial uplift or the core in a mountain system or range

prote- *or* **proteo-** *comb form* [ISV, fr. F *protéine* protein — more at PROTEIN] **:** protein ⟨*proteo*lysis⟩ ⟨*prote*ose⟩

pro·tea \ˈprōd·ēə\ *n* [NL, fr. *Proteus*, sea god who had the power of assuming different shapes, fr. L; fr. the great variety of forms it exhibits] **1** *cap* **:** a genus (the type of the family Proteaceae) of shrubs with alternate rigid leaves, dense flower heads resembling cones, and a fruit that is a hairy nut — see HONEYFLOWER b **2** -s **:** any plant of the genus *Protea*

pro·te·a·ce·ae \ˌprōd·ēˈāsē,ē\ *n pl, cap* [NL, fr. *Protea*, type genus + *-aceae*] **:** a family of chiefly Australian and southern African dicotyledonous shrubs and trees (order Proteales) that has coriaceous leaves and clustered bracteate mostly tetramerous flowers — **pro·te·a·ceous** \ˌ≈≈ˈāshəs\ *adj*

pro·te·a·les \ˌ≈≈ˈā(,)lēz\ *n pl, cap* [NL, fr. *Protea* + *-ales*] **:** an order of plants that is coextensive with the family Proteaceae

¹**pro·te·an** \ˈprōd·ēən, -ōtē-, prōˈtēən\ *adj, sometimes cap* [*Proteus*, legendary sea god in the service of Neptune who had the power of assuming different shapes (fr. L, fr. Gk *Prōteus*) + E *-an*] **1 :** characteristic of or resembling Proteus **:** capable of change **:** exceedingly variable ⟨the eyes . . . were of that baffling ~ gray which is never twice the same —Jack London⟩ **2 :** readily assuming different shapes or forms ⟨an amoeba is a ~ animalcule⟩ **3 :** capable of acting many different roles ⟨the company was led by a ~ actor⟩ **4 :** displaying great diversity **:** possessed of infinite variety ⟨one of our most ~ artists; he has been an architect, a painter, an engraver —*New Yorker*⟩ ⟨he is so many-sided, so ~ that he refuses to be pigeonholed —*Times Lit. Supp.*⟩

²**pro·te·an** \ˈprōd·ēən\ *n* -s [*prote-* + *-an*] **:** any of various insoluble primary protein derivatives that result from a slight modification of the protein molecule esp. by the incipient action of water, very dilute acids, or enzymes

pro·te·ase \ˈprōd·ē,ās, -āz\ *n* -s [ISV *prote-* + *-ase*] **:** any of the class of proteolytic enzymes comprising the proteinases and the peptidases

protea veld *n* **:** BUSHVELD

pro·tect \prəˈtekt\ *vt* -ED/-ING/-S [L *protectus*, past part. of *protegere* to cover in front, to defend, protect, fr. *pro-* ¹pro- + *tegere* to cover — more at THATCH] **1 :** to cover or shield from that which would injure, destroy, or detrimentally affect **:** secure or preserve usu. against attack, disintegration, encroachment, or harm **:** GUARD ⟨the ring of old forts which so far had ~*ed* the city successfully —P.W.Thompson⟩ ⟨hands half ~*ed* by shabby woolen mittens —F.V.W.Mason⟩ ⟨his invention was ~*ed* by a patent⟩ ⟨the scanty vegetation was insufficient to ~ the light soil from blustery winds —R.H. Billington⟩ ⟨both led happy ~*ed* lives —Kathleen Freeman⟩ **2** *obs* **:** to act as protector for ⟨the King had virtuous uncles to ~ his Grace —Shak.⟩ **3 :** to guard, shield, or foster by a protective tariff or other form of trade control **4 :** to render (a lyophobic colloid) stable by the addition of a protective colloid **5 a :** to warn (the crew of an approaching train) that the track ahead is not clear **b :** to flag or signal to stop **syn** see DEFEND

pro·tect·ant \-tənt\ *n* -s [*protect* + *-ant*] **:** a protecting agent; *specif* **:** a pesticidal spray that is applied to a plant before the arrival of the spore or other agent of infection — compare ERADICANT

protected *adj* [fr. past part. of *protect*] **:** guarded or shielded to prevent accidental contact or injury — used esp. of machinery

protected state *n* **:** an internationally recognized state under the protection of another usu. larger and more powerful state; *specif* **:** a state having a relatively stable and traditional government that has entered into treaty relations with the British Crown to avail itself of British protection and that while giving the British government certain rights and responsibilities usu. retains supervision of its domestic affairs while placing its foreign relations under British control ⟨the two British Settlements and the nine *protected states* which together form the Federation of Malaya —M.E.Cooper⟩ — compare PROTECTORATE

protecting *adj* **1 :** serving to protect or shield ⟨a good part of this game-filled plain lies within the ~ confines of the . . . National Park —Tom Marvel⟩ **2 :** serving to prevent sale at a price below a minimum — **pro·tect·ing·ly** *adv*

pro·tec·tion \prəˈtekshən\ *n* -s [ME *proteccioun*, fr. MF *protection*, fr. LL *protection-, protectio*, fr. L *protectus* (past part. of *protegere* to protect) + *-ion-, -io* -ion] **1 :** a writing that protects or secures from molestation or arrest **:** PASSPORT, SAFE-CONDUCT **2 :** the act of protecting **:** the state or fact of being protected **:** shelter from danger or harm ⟨a sense of ~ and security in the life of his home —Archibald Marshall⟩ ⟨huddled in the lee of the rock, trying to get a little ~ from the wind —H.D.Quillin⟩ **3 a :** one that protects ⟨an umbrella is ~ in a sudden shower⟩ **b :** the oversight or support usu. of one that is smaller and weaker ⟨government ~ for small business⟩ ⟨her brother's ~ was very welcome on the way home from school⟩ **4 a :** the freeing of the producers of a country from foreign competition in their home market by the imposition of high duties, quantitative trade controls, or exchange controls to restrict the importation of goods of foreign origin **b :** the theory, policy, or system favoring or practicing the imposition of such controls — compare AMERICAN SYSTEM, FREE TRADE **5 a :** immunity from prosecution obtained by some criminal classes (as proprietors of gambling houses) through bribes to officials or political bosses **b :** money paid to racketeers under threat of depredation ⟨sold ~ to everyone from the proprietors of the neighborhood delicatessens to the owners of the town's plushiest clubs —Polly Adler⟩ **6 :** COVERAGE 2c **7 :** a plant-disease control measure in which a protectant is used

pro·tec·tion·al \-shənᵊl, -shnəl\ *adj* **:** of, relating to, or serving for protection

protection and indemnity insurance *n* **:** insurance for ship owners against loss due to legal liability arising from damage to cargo, injury to passengers and crew, and other legal liabilities not assumed under the regular forms of hull insurance

protection forest *n* **:** a forest whose value lies in the regulating of stream flow and the preventing of erosion and avalanches rather than in its timber

pro·tec·tion·ism \-shə,nizəm\ *n* -s [¹*protectionist* + *-ism*] **:** the doctrine or policy of protectionists

¹**pro·tec·tion·ist** \-sh(ə)nəst\ *n* -s [*protection* + *-ist*] **:** one who favors protection; *esp* **:** one who advocates or supports a governmental policy that imposes trade restrictions on competitive foreign goods

²**protectionist** \"\ *adj* **:** favoring or maintaining protection; *esp* **:** favoring trade restrictions on competitive foreign goods ⟨the surprise when the voting began was the extent of new ~ sentiment —*Atlantic*⟩

protection line *n, usu cap P* **:** LINE OF MARS

¹**pro·tec·tive** \prəˈtektiv, -tēv *also* -əv\ *adj* [*protect* + *-ive*] **1 :** protecting or intended to protect **:** affording or serving as a safeguard **:** providing a defense or shelter against danger or harm **:** tending to shield ⟨many shore animals have ~ color and patterns which enable them to blend with their surround-

ings —W.H.Dowdeswell⟩ ⟨failure to use ~ masks in the numerous grinding operations —Lewis Mumford⟩ ⟨she felt ~ towards him —Olive Johnson⟩ **2 :** based on or relating to the economic principles of protection **:** affording or designed to afford protection ⟨~ duties⟩ **3 :** imposed as a means of or under the guise of insuring protection from public hostility ⟨~ arrest⟩ ⟨if he's tight, return him to his ship under ~ custody —D.R.Morris⟩

²protective \"\ *n* -s **1 :** something that serves for protection **2 :** an agent (as a medicine or a dressing) that protects the body or one of its parts (as from irritation or injury) ⟨vitamins are ~s against certain deficiency diseases⟩

protective coating *n* **:** a type of paint, varnish, or lacquer used more to protect than decorate

protective colloid *n* **:** a lyophilic colloid (as gelatin, a natural gum, or a cellulose derivative) that when present in small quantities renders lyophobic colloids stable toward the coagulating action of electrolytes ⟨gelatin acts in part as a *protective colloid* in photographic emulsions⟩

protective coloration *n* **:** coloration by which an organism is actually or apparently made less visible or less attractive to predators

protective cover *n* **:** a permanent outer container used to protect a book against atmospheric and handling damage

protective deck *n* **:** the most heavily armored and usu. convexly shaped deck of a warship

protective department *n* **:** SALVAGE CORPS

protective foods *n* **:** foods (as leafy or yellow vegetables, citrus fruits, meat, milk, eggs) that contain adequate amounts of vitamins, minerals, and high quality proteins and that protect against development of a deficiency disease (as pellagra, beriberi, scurvy)

protective liability insurance *n* **:** insurance that protects an owner or contractor against liability for injury or damage caused by independent contractors doing work in his behalf

pro·tec·tive·ly \-tәvlē, -li\ *adv* **:** in a protective manner

pro·tec·tive·ness \-tivnәs, -tēv- *also* -әv-\ *n* -ES **:** the quality or state of being protective ⟨could not escape his mother's ~⟩

protective resemblance *n* **:** resemblance of an animal to its environment (as by coloration) that causes it to blend with the substrate and become hidden from its enemies

protective system *n* **:** PROTECTION 4b

protective tariff *n* **:** a tariff that protects domestic producers; *esp* **:** one primarily designed to secure protection and not revenue — compare REVENUE TARIFF

pro·tec·tor \prә'tektә(r)\ *n* -s [ME *protectour,* fr. MF, fr. LL *protector,* fr. L *protectus* (past part. of *protegere* to protect) + *-or* — more at PROTECT] **1 a :** one that protects or shields esp. from danger or harm **:** GUARDIAN, PATRON **b :** something serving or designed to protect **:** a device used to prevent injury **:** GUARD ⟨the chest ~ of the baseball catcher —J.H.Shaw⟩ **2 :** one having the care of the kingdom (as during the king's minority) **:** REGENT

pro·tec·tor·al \-t(ә)rәl\ *adj* **:** of or relating to a protector or protectorate

pro·tec·tor·ate \-t(ә)rәt *sometimes* -tә,rāt, *usu* -d·+V\ *n* -s **1 a :** government by a protector (as of a kingdom) ⟨conditions in England under the Cromwellian ~⟩ **b :** the rank, office, or period of rule of a protector ⟨during the ~⟩ ⟨succeeded to the ~⟩ **2 a :** the relationship of superior authority assumed by one power or state over a dependent political unit ⟨conceded to Russia a virtual ~ over Manchuria —J.A.S.Grenville⟩ **b :** the period during which such a relationship is maintained **c :** the authority assumed by the predominant state in such a relationship **d :** the dependent political unit in such a relationship: (1) **:** a territorial unit under the political control and protection of a larger and more powerful state esp. in the areas of defense and foreign relations (2) **:** a dependent territory usu. having only rudimentary political institutions over which a larger and more powerful country exercises the powers of government without having legal possession; *specif* **:** one having in effect although not in law the status of a British colony and as a result governed in both internal and external affairs by the British government although technically not constituting a part of the dominions of the crown (3) **:** PROTECTED STATE

protectorian *adj, obs* **:** of or relating to a protector **:** PROTECTORAL

pro·tec·to·ry \prә'tekt(ә)rē\ *n* -ES **:** an institution for the protection and care usu. of homeless or delinquent children

pro·tec·tress \-trәs\ *n* -ES [*protector* + *-ess*] **:** a female protector

pro·tec·trix \-triks\ *n* -ES [ML, fem. of *protector,* fr. LL] **:** PROTECTRESS

protects *pres 3d sing of* PROTECT

pro·té·gé \'prōd·ә,zhā, -ōtә-, ,==\'=\ *n* -s [F, fr. past part. of *protéger* to protect, fr. L *protegere*] **1 :** a man under the care and protection of an influential person (as a sponsor, instructor, or patron) usu. for the furthering of his career (as in art, politics, sport) **:** PUPIL ⟨big-business ~s —*Harper's*⟩ ⟨a ~ of the Institute's famous professor —Jack Goodman⟩ ⟨~ of many popes —*Mentor*⟩ **2 a :** a resident of one country (as a colony or a protectorate) under the juridical protection of another government **b :** one protected by a foreign country under extraterritorial rights

pro·té·gée \"\ *n* -s [F, fem. of *protégé*] **:** a female protégé ⟨by way of example to her ~s, won more national championships than any other player in the history of the sport —H.W. Wind⟩

pro·tegulum \(')prō+\ *n* -s [NL, fr. ¹*pro-* + L *tegulum* covering, fr. *tegere* to cover + *-ulum* (neut. of *-ulus* -ule) — more at THATCH] **:** the embryonic shell of a brachiopod that is biconvex and smooth and has a wide posterior gape

protei *pl of* PROTEUS

pro·te·ic \prō'tēik\ *adj* [ISV *prote-* (fr. F *protéine* protein) + *-ic*] **:** PROTEINACEOUS

pro·teid \'prō,tēd, -ōd·ēәd\ *n* -s [ISV *prote-* + *-id;* orig. formed in G] **:** PROTEIN 2

pro·te·i·da \prō'tēәdә\ *n pl, cap* [NL, fr. *Proteus* (genus of olms) + *-ida*] **:** a suborder of Caudata comprising aquatic salamanders with persistent gills and two pairs of weak limbs and usu. regarded as including the single family Proteidae and consisting of the European olms and the American mud puppies

pro·te·i·dae \-ә,dē\ *n pl, cap* [NL, fr. *Proteus* (genus of olms) + *-idae*] **:** a family of amphibians coextensive with the suborder Proteida

pro·te·ide \'prōd·ē,īd, -ēәd\ *n* -s [ISV *prote-* + *-ide;* orig. formed as G *proteid*] **:** PROTEIN 2 — used of a subdivision of protides

pro·te·i·form \prō'tēә,fȯrm\ *adj* [F *protéiforme,* fr. *Protée* Proteus (fr. L *Proteus*) + *-iforme* -iform — more at PROTEAN] **:** PROTEAN

¹pro·tein \'prō,tēn *also* -ōd·ēәn *or* -ōtēәn\ *n* -s [F *protéine,* fr. LGk *prōteios* primary (fr. Gk *prōtos* first) + F *-ine* — more at PROT-] **1** *archaic* **:** an alkali metaprotein supposed to be the basis of all albuminous substances **2 :** any of a very large class of naturally occurring extremely complex combinations of amino acids containing the elements carbon, hydrogen, nitrogen, oxygen, usu. sulfur, occasionally phosphorus, iron, or other elements that are essential constituents of all living cells both animal and vegetable and also of the diet of the animal organism, that are both acidic and basic and usu. colloidal in nature although many have been crystallized, that are hydrolyzable by acids, alkalies, proteolytic enzymes, and putrefactive bacteria to polypeptides, to simpler peptides, and ultimately to alpha-amino acids, that have been classified by biological functions, by chemical composition as simple or conjugated, by solubility in water and salt solutions, or by the shape of the molecule as fibrous or fibrillar (as those forming structural elements of animal tissue) or as corpuscular or globular (as those involved in metabolism) — compare CONJUGATED PROTEIN, DENATURE 2, ENZYME, SCLEROPROTEIN, SIMPLE PROTEIN **3 :** the total nitrogenous material in vegetable or animal substances; *esp* **:** CRUDE PROTEIN

²protein \"\ *adj* **:** of or containing protein

pro·tein·a·ceous \¦prō,tē¦nāshәs, ¦prōd·ēә¦n-\ *adj* [¹*protein* + *-aceous*] **:** of, relating to, or of the nature of a protein

pro·tein·ase \'prō,tē,nās, -ōd·ēә,n-, -āz\ *n* -s [ISV ¹*protein* + *-ase*] **:** any of a group of enzymes (as pepsin, papain) that hydrolyze proteins esp. to peptides **:** ENDOPEPTIDASE — often distinguished from *peptidase;* compare PROTEASE

pro·tein·ate \-,nāt\ *n* -s [ISV ¹*protein* + *-ate*] **:** a compound of a protein — not used systematically ⟨silver ~⟩

protein-bound iodine *n* **:** the amount of iodine expressed in micrograms per 100 milliliters of blood serum that is precipitated with serum proteins and that serves as a measure of the activity of the thyroid gland ⟨the *protein-bound iodine* in the normal human being ranges from 4 to 8 micrograms, in hypothyroidism falls below this range, and in hyperthyroidism rises above it⟩

protein crystal *n* **:** CRYSTALLOID 2

protein hydrolysate *n* **:** a mixture containing amino acids and often other substances (as peptides) obtained by the hydrolysis of various animal and vegetable proteins (as lactalbumin or soybean protein) and used as sources of amino acids, as seasoning agents, and in nutrition

pro·tein·ic \(')prō¦tēnik, ¦prōd·ē¦inik\ *adj* [¹*protein* + *-ic*] **:** PROTEINACEOUS

protein milk *n* **:** a modified milk having a relatively high content of protein and low content of carbohydrate and fat

pro·tei·nous \prō'tēәnәs\ *adj* [¹*protein* + *-ous*] **:** PROTEINACEOUS

protein paint *n* **:** a paint that may be either powder, paste, or ready-mixed with casein or protein for its binder

protein shock *n* **:** a severe reaction produced by the injection of protein (as bacterial, animal, or plant proteins or protein-containing organic extracts) and marked by chill, fever, bronchial spasm, acute emphysema, and vomiting and diarrhea

protein silver *n* **:** SILVER PROTEIN

protein therapy *n* **:** therapeutic injection of protein (as casein or a bacterial vaccine)

pro·tein·uria \,prō,tē'n(y)ůrēә, ,prōd·ēә'n-\ *n* -s [NL, fr. ISV ¹*protein* + NL *-uria*] **:** the presence of protein in the urine — **pro·tein·uric** \¦=,=¦rik, ¦===¦-\ *adj*

prot·e·les \'präd·ә,lēz\ *n, cap* [NL, fr. ¹*pro-* + *-teles* (fr. Gk *telos* completion, maturity, end); fr. the degree of development of the forefeet — more at WHEEL] **:** a genus of mammals (family Hyaenidae) consisting of the aardwolf — compare PROTELIDAE

¹pro·tel·id \prә'telәd\ *adj* [NL *Protelidae*] **:** of or relating to the Protelidae

²protelid \"\ *n* -s **:** a mammal of the family Protelidae **:** AARDWOLF

pro·tel·i·dae \prә'telә,dē\ *n pl, cap* [NL, fr. *Proteles,* type genus + *-idae*] *in some esp. former classifications* **:** a family closely related to and now usu. included in the Hyaenidae that includes the aardwolf and related extinct mammals

pro·tely·trop·tera \prә,telē·'träpt(ә)rә\ *n pl, cap* [NL, fr. *prot-* + *elytron* + *-ptera*] **:** an order of extinct insects related to the Dermaptera, known only from the Permian, and characterized by slender elytra with a reduced venation and by broad hind wings resembling those of the Dermaptera — **pro·tely·trop·ter·an** \-t(ә)rәn\ *n or adj* — **pro·tely·trop·ter·on** \-tә,rän\ *n* -s — **pro·tely·trop·ter·ous** \-t(ә)rәs\ *adj*

¹pro tem \(')prō¦tem\ *adj* [by shortening] **:** PRO TEMPORE

²pro tem \"\ *adv* **:** for the time being ⟨accepting *pro tem* that hypothesis consistent with the facts —J.W.Krutch⟩

pro tem·po·re \-'tempә(,)rē\ *adj* [L, for the time being] **:** chosen to occupy a position either temporarily or during the absence of a regularly elected official **:** appointed for the time being ⟨designated him to act as consul *pro tempore* —H.H. Fiske⟩ — compare PRESIDENT PRO TEMPORE

pro·tend \prō'tend\ *vb* -ED/-ING/-S [ME *protenden,* fr. L *protendere,* fr. *pro-* ¹*pro-* + *tendere* to stretch — more at THIN] *vt* **1 :** to hold out **:** stretch forth **2 :** EXTEND ~ *vi* **:** to stick out **:** PROTRUDE ⟨his staff ~*ing* like a hunter's spear —William Wordsworth⟩

pro·ten·sion \-'tenchәn\ *n* -s [LL *protension-, protensio,* fr. L *protensus* (past part. of *protendere* to protend) + *-ion-, -io* -ion] **:** a protending esp. forward

pro·ten·si·ty \-n(t)sәd·ē\ *n* -ES [L *protensus* (past part. of *protendere*) + E *-ity*] **1 :** the quality or character of being protensive **2 :** the duration of a sensation — compare EXTENSITY

pro·ten·sive \-n(t)siv\ *adj* [L *protensus* (past part.) + E *-ive*] **1 :** having continuance in time **:** having duration even though very slight **2 :** having lengthwise extent or extensiveness — **pro·ten·sive·ly** \-sәvlē\ *adv*

proteo- — see PROTE-

¹pro·teo·ceph·a·lid \¦prōd·ē(,)ō¦sefәlәd, -,lid\ *adj* [NL *Proteocephalidae*] **:** of or relating to the Proteocephalidae

²proteocephalid \"\ *n* -s **:** a tapeworm of the family Proteocephalidae

pro·teo·ce·phal·i·dae \,===sә'falә,dē\ *n pl, cap* [NL, fr. *Proteocephalus,* type genus + *-idae*] **:** a family of tapeworms that are parasites of fishes, have scolices resembling those of members of the Cyclophyllidea and reproductive organs like those of members of the Tetraphyllidea, and are sometimes placed in either of these orders but now more usu. isolated in a separate order

pro·teo·ceph·a·loid \¦==(,)=¦sefә,lȯid\ *adj* [NL *Proteocephalus* + E *-oid*] **:** resembling or related to *Proteocephalus* or to the Proteocephalidae

pro·teo·ceph·a·lus \,==(,)='sefәlәs\ *n, cap* [NL, fr. *Proteus,* sea god who could assume different shapes (fr. L) + NL *-cephalus* — more at PROTEAN] **:** a very large genus comprising tapeworms parasitic in the intestines of various fishes and being the type of the family Proteocephalidae

pro·teo·clas·tic \¦prōd·ēә¦klastik\ *adj* [*prote-* + *-clastic*] **:** PROTEOLYTIC

pro·te·og·e·nous \¦prōd·ē¦äjәnәs\ *adj* [*prote-* + *-genous*] **:** of or relating to a substance obtained from a protein ⟨a ~ amine⟩

pro·teo·lipid \¦prōd·ēō+\ *also* **pro·teo·lipide** \"+\ *n* [*prote-* + *lipid, lipide*] **:** any of a class of proteins that contain a considerable percentage of lipid and are soluble in lipids and insoluble in water — compare LIPOPROTEIN

pro·te·ol·y·sin \,prōd·ē'älәsәn, ¦==ә¦līsᵊn\ *n* [ISV *prote-* + *lysin*] **:** a lysin (as an enzyme) producing proteolysis

pro·te·ol·y·sis \,=='älәsәs\ *n* [NL, fr. *prote-* + *-lysis*] **:** the hydrolysis of proteins or peptides with formation of simpler and soluble products (as in digestion)

pro·teo·lyt·ic \¦==ә¦lid·ik\ *adj* [ISV *prote-* + *-lytic*] **:** of, relating to, or producing proteolysis

pro·teo·myxa \,==='miksә\ *n pl, cap* [NL, fr. *Proteus,* sea god who could assume different shapes + NL *-myxa*] **:** a small order of obscure rhizopods of uncertain relationships usu. possessing flagella at some stage of their life

pro·te·ose \'prōd·ē,ōs, -ōtē-\ *n* -s [ISV *prote-* + *-ose*] **:** any of various protein derivatives that are formed by the partial hydrolysis of proteins (as by enzymes of the gastric and pancreatic juices), that are not coagulated by heat, and that are soluble in water but are precipitated from solution by saturation with ammonium sulfate — compare ALBUMOSE, PEPTONE

¹prot·ephemerid \¦prōd·+\ *adj* [NL *Protephemerida*] **:** of or relating to the Protephemerida

²protephemerid \"\ *n* -s **:** an insect of the order Protephemerida

prot·ephemerida \(¦)prōd·+\ *n pl, cap* [NL, fr. *prot-* + *Ephemerida*] **:** an order of extinct insects related to the Plectoptera, known only from the Upper Carboniferous, and characterized by long cerci and homonomous wings with numerous crossveins

prot·ephem·er·oi·dea \,prōd·ә,femә'rȯidēә\ [NL, fr. *prot-* + *Ephemera* + *-oidea*] *syn of* PROTEPHEMERIDA

proter- *or* **protero-** *comb form* [NL, fr. Gk *proter-, protero-,* fr. *proteros;* akin to Gk *pro* before, ahead — more at FOR] **:** before **:** earlier **:** former ⟨*proterozoic*⟩ ⟨*proteranthous*⟩

proter·an·dric \¦präd·ә¦randrik, ¦prōd·ә¦-, -raan-\ *adj* [ISV *proterandr-* (fr. *proterandry*) + *-ic*] **:** PROTANDROUS

proter·an·dri·ous \-drēәs\ *adj* [*proter-* + *andr-* + *-ious*] **:** PROTANDROUS

proter·an·drous \-drәs\ *adj* [ISV *proter-* + *-androus*] **:** PROTANDROUS — **proter·an·drous·ly** *adv* — **proter·an·drous·ness** *n* -ES — **proter·an·dry** \'==,=drē\ *n* -ES

proter·an·thous \¦==¦ran(t)thәs\ *adj* [*proter-* + *-anthous*] **:** having flowers appearing before the leaves — **proter·an·thy** \'==,ran(t)thē\ *n* -ES

¹protero·glyph \'präd·әrә,glif, prō'terә,-\ *adj* [NL *Proteroglypha*] **:** of or relating to the Proteroglypha

²proteroglyph \"\ *n* -s **:** a snake of the group Proteroglypha

protero·glypha \,==='glifә\ *n pl, cap* [NL, fr. *proter-* + *-glypha* (fr. Gk *glyphē* carved work); fr. the grooved fangs — more at GLYPH] **:** a group of venomous snakes comprising forms that have in the front of the upper jaw and preceding the ordinary teeth permanently erect fangs with an open or a nearly closed groove associated with a venom gland and including the families Elapidae and Hydrophidae widely distributed in the warmer parts of the world — compare OPISTHOGLYPHA — **protero·glyph·ic** \¦===¦glifik\ *adj* — **protero·glyph·ous** \-fәs\ *adj*

proterog·y·nous \¦präd·ә¦räjәnәs\ *adj* [ISV *proter-* + *-gynous*] **:** PROTOGYNOUS — **proterog·y·ny** \-nē\ *n* -ES

protero·saur \'präd·әrә,sȯ(ә)r\ *var of* PROTOROSAUR

protero·sau·ria \-rēә\ [NL, fr. *proter-* + *-sauria*] *syn of* PROTOROSAURIA

protero·sau·rus \,==='sȯrәs\ [NL, alter. of *Protorosaurus*] *syn of* PROTOROSAURUS

proteroth·e·sis \,=='räthәsәs\ *n* -ES [NL, fr. *proter-* + Gk *thesis* setting, position — more at THESIS] **:** the laying of female-producing eggs in the first cells constructed by some solitary wasps and bees after which male-producing eggs are laid

protero·type \'==rә,tīp\ *n* [*proter-* + *type*] **:** a primary type

¹protero·zo·ic \¦===¦zōik\ *adj, usu cap* [ISV *proter-* + *-zoic*] **:** of or relating to a grand division of geological history that includes the entire interval from the beginning of the Huronian to the close of the Keweenawan, perhaps exceeds in length all of subsequent geological time, and is marked by rocks that contain a few fossils indicating the existence of animals as highly organized as annelid worms and of blue-green and brown algae — see GEOLOGIC TIME table

²proterozoic \"\ *n* -s *usu cap* **:** the Proterozoic era or system of rocks

pro·ter·vi·ty \prō'tәrvәd·ē\ *n* -ES [L *protervitas,* fr. *protervus* forward, bold, impudent, flighty (prob. alter. of *proptervus,* fr. *pro-* forward + *-ptervus* — akin to Gk *petesthai* to fly) + *-itas* -ity — more at PRO-, FEATHER] **1 :** a petulant manner **:** PEEVISHNESS **2 :** insolent sauciness

¹pro·test \'prō,test\ *n* -s *often attrib* [ME, fr. MF, fr. *protester* to protest] **1 :** an affirmative statement **:** a frank and open avowal **:** ACKNOWLEDGMENT **2 a** (1) **:** a solemn declaration in writing made in due form usu. by a notary public under his notarial seal on behalf of the holder of a bill or note announcing refusal of payment or acceptance upon presentment and protesting against all parties to the instrument and declaring their liability for any loss or damage arising from such action (2) **:** a formal notarial notice to all parties of the insolvency or other condition of the acceptor of a bill warranting the supposition that payment will not be made when due that is employed for better security against the drawer and endorsers — used chiefly in English practice (3) **:** the action of making or procuring to be made such a declaration with due service of notice of dishonor **b :** a declaration made by the master of a ship before a notary, consul, or other authorized officer upon his arrival in port after a disaster stating the particulars of it and showing that any damage or loss sustained was not owing to the fault of the ship, her officers, or crew but to the perils of the sea and protesting against them **c :** a declaration made by a party esp. before or while paying a tax or duty or performing an act demanded of him which he deems illegal, denying the justice of the demand, and asserting his rights and claims to show that his action is not voluntary **3 a :** a solemn declaration of disapproval **:** a formal or public remonstrance ⟨saved from execution by ~s from other countries —*Current Biog.*⟩ ⟨the constitutional right of the opposition to voice its ~s —A.C. Cole⟩ **b :** a complaint, objection, or display of unwillingness usu. to an idea or a course of action ⟨went . . . under ~ to hear some Negro spirituals —H.J.Laski⟩ **c :** a gesture of extreme disapproval ⟨always threatening to resign in ~ of what he considered to be the radical views of some of the club members —*Saturday Rev.*⟩ **4 :** an objection lodged with a sports official or a governing body (as against a player because of ineligibility, a play because of illegality, a referee or umpire because of a decision)

²pro·test \prә'test, (')prō¦test\ *vb* -ED/-ING/-S [ME *protesten,* fr. MF *protester,* fr. L *protestari,* fr. *pro-* + *testari* to be a witness — more at TESTAMENT] *vt* **1 :** to make solemn declaration or affirmation of **:** AVER ⟨he would have to ~ his affection —Robertson Davies⟩ ⟨he never ~*ed* his friendship —Morley Callaghan⟩ **2** *obs* **:** to declare publicly **:** PROCLAIM, PUBLISH ⟨do me right or I will ~ your cowardice —Shak.⟩ **3 :** to promise solemnly **:** VOW ⟨if you entreat me . . . I will ~ you with my favorite vow —Edna S. V. Millay⟩ **4 :** to make or procure to be made a notarial protest of (as a bill) **5 :** to make a protest against ⟨~ a witness or a commercial instrument⟩ **6 :** to object to **:** remonstrate against ⟨some of the subscribers complained of their inadequacy while others ~*ed* their cost —John Lawler⟩ ⟨it has become customary . . . to ~ the seating —P.C.Jessup⟩ ~ *vi* **1 :** to make a protestation **:** declare the truth solemnly ⟨you don't have to ~ so much —Saul Bellow⟩ **2 :** to enter a protest **:** object formally and often strongly ⟨she ~*ed* about the expense —Edmund Wilson⟩ ⟨noted the number of people who were ~*ing* against the morals of the time —Gilbert Seldes⟩ **syn** see ASSERT, OBJECT

prot·es·tan·cy \'präd·әstәnsē\ *n* -ES [¹*protestant* + *-cy*] **:** PROTESTANTISM

¹prot·es·tant \'präd·әstәnt, 'prätә-; *also* prә'testәnt *in sense 2b*\ *n* -s [MF, fr. L *protestant-, protestans,* pres. part. of *protestari* to protest] **1** *usu cap* **a :** one of the German princes favoring the Lutheran movement who presented at the Diet of Spires in 1529 a protest opposing the annulment of an earlier decree allowing each prince to manage the religious affairs of his territory and defending freedom of conscience and the right of minorities **b** *archaic* **:** a member of the Anglican Church **c :** a member of a Protestant religious body **d :** a Christian not of a Roman Catholic or an Eastern church **2 a :** one who makes a declaration ⟨a ~ on behalf of the life of reason —J.M.Grossman⟩ **b :** one who makes or enters a protest ⟨the percentage of ~s seems pitifully inadequate for the needs of the hour —M.L.Cooke⟩ ⟨~s against these books —W.M.Houghton⟩ ⟨the ~s against war throughout the country —W.A.White⟩ **3** *sometimes cap* **:** one who applies Protestant principles elsewhere than in religion ⟨a history which reflects a peculiarly ~ attitude . . . evolved, quite peacefully, from liberal theology —*Times Lit. Supp.*⟩ ⟨moral ~s like their religious counterparts —H.D.Aiken⟩

²protestant *see pronunc of noun*\ *adj* [F, fr. MF, fr. *protestant,* n.] **1** *usu cap* **:** of or relating to one of the Christian churches separating from the Roman Catholic Church in the Reformation of the 16th century or from another Protestant church to defend beliefs and practices held vital (as the Reformation principles of justification by faith, the priesthood of all believers, the authority and sufficiency of the Bible, and the right and duty of individual judgment in matters of faith), usu. rejecting as unscriptural the ceremonial reverence of the saints, monasticism, clerical celibacy, and all but two sacraments, and marked by nonliturgical worship featuring preaching, emphasis on individual salvation or morality or on social reform, and sectarian divisions based on points of doctrine or observance **2 :** making or sounding a protest ⟨the two ~ ladies up and marched out —*Time*⟩ ⟨it is still merely a ~ movement . . . whereby students mass themselves to protest —Nathaniel Peffer⟩

protestant existentialism *n, usu cap P* **:** CHRISTIAN EXISTENTIALISM

prot·es·tant·ish \'präd·әstәntish, 'prätә-\ *adj, often cap* [¹*protestant* + *-ish*] **:** inclined to Protestant Christianity — **prot·es·tant·ish·ly** *adv, often cap*

prot·es·tant·ism \-n·,tizәm\ *n* -s [F *protestantisme,* fr. *protestant* + *-isme* -ism] **1 a :** the quality or state of being protestant **b** *usu cap* **:** Protestant principles or practice ⟨distinguish classical from radical *Protestantism*⟩ — compare FUNDAMENTALISM, LIBERALISM, MODERNISM **2** *usu cap* **:** the body of Protestant Christians ⟨representatives of American *Protestantism*⟩

prot·es·tant·ize \-n·,tīz\ *vt* -ED/-ING/-S *sometimes cap* [¹*protestant* + *-ize*] **:** to make Protestant **:** convert to Protestantism

protestant reformation *n, usu cap P&R* **:** REFORMATION 2
protes·ta·tion \ˌprät|də'stāshən, -rō|, |tə-, -rō,te's- *sometimes* -rä,te- *or* -räd·,e- *or* -rōd·,e-\ *n* -s [ME *protestacioun*, fr. MF *protestation*, fr. LL *protestation-, protestatio*, fr. L *protestatus* (past part. of *protestari* to protest) + *-ion-, -io* -ion — more at PROTEST] **1 :** the act of protesting or solemnly declaring existent or true **:** a public avowal **:** serious assertion ⟨with some proper ~s of modesty —W.A.White⟩ **2 :** a declaration in common-law pleading by which the party interposes an oblique allegation or denial of some fact protesting that it does or does not exist or is or is not sufficient in law and at the same time avoiding the duplicity of a direct affirmation or denial **3 :** a formal or documentary declaration of dissent, disapproval, or objection ⟨organizes these data around eight specific ~s —R.L.Roy⟩
protested *adj* [fr. past part. of ²*protest*] **:** PROTESTANT
pro·test·er \prə'testə(r), (')prō¦t-\ *n* -s **1** *obs* **:** one that makes an affirmation ⟨state with ordinary oaths my love to every new ~ —Shak.⟩ **2 :** one that disagrees or disapproves ⟨all their friends were ~s and rebels and seceders —H.G.Wells⟩ ⟨even the town ~ thinks of things he would have liked in school —*Education Digest*⟩ **3** *usu cap* **:** one of a party among the Covenanters that protested against the resolution of 1650 that all persons not professed enemies to the Covenant or excommunicated should be allowed to serve in the army — compare RESOLUTIONER **4 :** one that protests a bill of exchange or a note
pro·tes·tor \"\ *n* -s [MF *protesteur*, fr. *protester* to protest + *-eur* -or — more at PROTEST] **:** PROTESTER
pro·teus \'prōd·ēəs, -ō,tüs, -ō·,tyüs\ *n* [fr. *Proteus*, sea god who could assume different shapes, fr. L — more at PROTEAN] **1** -ES *often cap* **:** one that is capable of infinite change **:** one having a great diversity of interests or abilities ⟨a true *Proteus* of literature . . . has been successively a dramatist, a sociologist, a highly successful writer of historical novels —William Du Bois⟩ ⟨a *Proteus*, a master of disguise, an impersonator —*Times Lit. Supp.*⟩ **2** [NL, fr. *Proteus*, sea god, fr. L] **a** (1) *cap* **:** the type genus of the family Proteidae comprising solely the olm (2) -ES **:** OLM **b** -ES **:** AMOEBA **3** *cap* [NL, fr. *Proteus*, sea god] **a :** a genus of aerobic gram-negative bacteria (family Enterobacteriaceae) that ferment glucose but not lactose, decompose urea, that are usu. motile by means of peritrichous flagella, and that include saprophytes in decaying organic matter as well as forms obscurely related to gastrointestinal disorders and several strains antigenically linked to the rickettsias of typhus **b** *pl* **pro·tei** \-d·ē,ī\ **:** any bacterium of the genus *Proteus*
prot·evan·gel·i·um \ˌprōd·,ē,van'jelēəm\ *n* -s [NL, fr. *prot-* + LL *evangelium* evangel — more at EVANGEL] **:** a messianic interpretation of a text (as Gen 3:15 RSV) presaging man's ultimate triumph over sin through a coming Savior — used as the first anticipation of the gospel
pro·tha·la·mi·on \ˌprōthə'lāmēən, -ē,än\ *or* **pro·tha·la·mi·um** \-mēəm\ *n, pl* **prothala·mia** \-mēə\ [NL, fr. ¹*pro-* + *-thalamion* (as in *epithalamion*)] **:** a song in celebration of an approaching marriage
pro·thal·li·al \(')prō¦thalēəl\ *also* **pro·thalline** \(')prō+\ *adj* [NL *prothallium* + E *-al* or *-ine*] **:** of or relating to a prothallium
prothallial cell *n* **:** one of the cells produced by the first division of the microspore in a gymnosperm and believed to be a vestige related to the fern prothallus
pro·thal·lic \(')prō+\ *adj* [NL *prothallium* + E *-ic*] **:** PROTHALLOID
pro·thallium \(')prō+\ *n, pl* **prothallia** [NL, fr. ¹*pro-* + *thallus* + *-ium*] **1 :** the gametophyte of a fern or other pteridophyte that is typically a small flat green thallus attached to the soil by rhizoids but is sometimes filamentous and branching, that occasionally forms a subterranean tuberous mass, or that rarely (as in the club mosses) develops within the megaspore by which it is produced **2 :** any of various structures (as several cells of the pollen grain or in gymnosperms of the megaspore) that in seed plants correspond to the pteridophyte prothallium
pro·thalloid \"+\ *adj* [NL *prothallium* + *-oid*] **:** resembling a prothallium
pro·thallus \"+\ *n, pl* **prothalli** [NL, fr. ¹*pro-* + *thallus*] **:** PROTHALLIUM
¹**pro·than·ic** \(')prō¦thanik\ *adj* [¹*pro-* + *than-* (fr. *thanat-*) + *-ic*] **:** subject to early death — used of an embryo that fails to complete development due to severe anomalies
²**prothanic** \"\ *n* -s **:** a prothanic embryo
pro·theca \"+\ *n, pl* **prothecae** [NL, fr. ¹*pro-* + *theca*] **:** the basal and first-formed part of the calyculus of a coral
proth·e·sis \'präthəsəs\ *n, pl* **prothe·ses** \-ə,sēz\ [Gk, presentation of the shewbread, lit., act of placing before, fr. *protithenai* to put before, fr. *pro-* ¹pro- + *tithenai* to place, put — more at DO] **1 a :** the preparation of the bread and the wine in the liturgy of the Eastern Church **b :** the table on which this preparation is done **:** CREDENCE **c :** the northern part of the bema where this preparation occurs **2** [LL, fr. Gk, prefixation, act of placing before] **:** PROSTHESIS 2 **3 :** the addition of an inorganic sound to the beginning of a word (as in Old French *estat* and English *estate* from Latin *status*)
pro·the·tely \'prōthə,telē\ *n* -ES [fr. (assumed) Gk *prothetos* (verbal of Gk *protithenai* to put before) + Gk *telos* end, completion, maturity + E *-y* — more at WHEEL] **:** relatively precocious differentiation of a structure that is usu. associated with a later stage of development — compare HYSTEROTELY, NEOTENY
pro·thet·ic \prə'thed·ik\ *adj* [Gk *prothetikos*, fr. (assumed) Gk *prothetos* + Gk *-ikos* -ic] **:** of, relating to, or exhibiting prothesis ⟨a ~ vowel⟩ — **pro·thet·i·cal·ly** \-ək(ə)lē\ *adv*
pro·thono·tar·i·al \prə¦thänə¦ta(a)rēəl, -¦terē-\ *adj* **:** of or relating to a prothonotary
pro·thono·tary \prə'thänə,terē, ˌprōthə'nōd·ərē, -ri\ *or* **pro·tono·tary** \prə'tän-, ˌprōd·ə'-\ *n* [ME *prothonotarie*, fr. LL *protonotarius*, fr. *prot-* + L *notarius* notary, secretary — more at NOTARY] **1 a :** a chief clerk in the English Court of King's Bench or in a court of common pleas **b :** a similar official of the supreme court of New South Wales, Australia, and Nova Scotia **c :** a register or chief clerk of a court in some states of the U.S. **2** *usu protonotary* **:** any of various high ecclesiastical officials: **a :** one of the seven members of the College of Protonotaries Apostolic of the curia of the Roman Catholic Church whose chief duties are to keep the records of consistories and canonizations and to sign papal bulls **b :** the chief secretary of the ecumenical patriarch of Constantinople **3 :** a principal court secretary in some European countries
pro·thono·tary·ship \-,ship\ *n* **:** the office of a prothonotary
prothonotary warbler *n* **:** a showy chiefly rich orange-golden warbler (*Protonotaria citrea*) of the southeastern U.S. with olivaceous back and blue-gray wings
pro·thoracic \¦prō+\ *adj* [NL *prothorac-, prothorax* + E *-ic*] **:** of or relating to the prothorax
pro·thorax \(')prō+\ *n* [NL, fr. ¹*pro-* + *thorax*] **:** the first or anterior segment of the thorax of an insect bearing the first pair of legs — see INSECT illustration
pro·thrombase \(')prō+\ *n* [ISV ¹*pro-* + *thrombase*] **:** PROTHROMBIN
pro·thrombic \"+\ *adj* [*prothrombin* + *-ic*] **:** of or resembling that of a prothrombin
pro·thrombin \"+\ *n* [ISV ¹*pro-* + *thrombin*] **:** a protein that is produced in the liver in the presence of vitamin K, is present in blood plasma, and is converted into thrombin by the action of various activators (as thromboplastin, blood platelet factors, accelerator globulin, and calcium ions) in the course of the clotting of blood — compare ANTIPROTHROMBIN
prothrombin time *n* **:** the time required for a particular specimen of prothrombin to induce blood-plasma clotting under standardized conditions in comparison with a time of between 11.5 and 12 seconds for normal human blood
pro·tide \'prō,tīd, -,təd\ *n* -s [ISV, alter. of *proteide;* orig. formed in F] **:** any of a class of compounds comprising the amino acids and the proteides
pro·tist \'prōd·əst\ *n* -s [NL *Protista*] **:** one of the Protista
pro·tis·ta \prə'tistə\ *n pl, cap* [NL, fr. Gk *prōtista*, neut. pl. of *prōtistos* primary, principal, superl. of *prōtos* first — more at PROT-] **:** the unicellular and acellular organisms comprising bacteria, protozoa, many algae and fungi, and sometimes viruses and constituting a kingdom or other division of living beings distinct from multicellular plants and animals — compare ANIMALIA, PLANTAE, PROTOZOA — **pro·tis·tan** \-tən\ *adj or n* — **pro·tis·tic** \-tik\ *adj* — **pro·tis·ton** \-tən\ *n* -s
pro·tis·to·logical \ˌprō¦tistə¦läjəkəl\ *adj* [*protistology* + *-ical*] **:** of or relating to protistology
pro·tis·tol·o·gist \ˌprō,ti'stäləjəst\ *n* -s [*protistology* + *-ist*] **:** one who specializes in protistology
pro·tis·tol·o·gy \-jē\ *n* -ES [ISV *protisto-* (fr. NL *Protista*) + *-logy*] **:** biology dealing with the Protista
¹**pro·ti·um** \'prōd·ēəm, -ōshē-\ *n, cap* [NL, perh. fr. *prot-* + *-ium*] **:** a large genus of chiefly tropical American trees (family Burseraceae) having pinnate leaves and slender-pediceled paniculate flowers that are succeeded by globose drupes — see CARANNA, ELEMI
²**protium** \"\ *n* -s [ISV *prot-* + *-ium*] **:** the ordinary light hydrogen isotope of atomic mass 1 — symbol H^1 or ^1H; compare DEUTERIUM, PROTON, TRITIUM
proto- — see PROT-
protoactinium *var of* PROTACTINIUM
pro·to·as·ca·les \ˌprōd·(ˌ)ōə'skā(ˌ)lēz\ *n pl, cap* [NL, fr. *prot-* + *asc-* + *-ales*] *in some classifications* **:** an order of fungi coextensive with the subclass Hemiascomycetes
pro·to·as·co·my·ce·tae \ˌ=(ˌ)=,a,skōmī'sēd·,ē\ [NL, alter. of *Protoascomycetes*] *syn of* PROTOASCOMYCETES
pro·to·ascomycetes \¦==+\ *n pl, cap* [NL, fr. *prot-* + *Ascomycetes*] *in some classifications* **:** a subclass of Ascomycetes characterized by the lack of an ascocarp, by the production of asci directly from the fertilized ascogonium, and by a small and definite number of spores in each ascus — compare EUASCOMYCETES, HEMIASCOMYCETES
¹**pro·to-australoid** \¦==+\ *adj, usu cap A* **:** of, relating to, or constituting a generalized type of prehistoric man characterized by long narrow head, broad nose, and medium long face
²**proto-australoid** \"\ *n* -s *usu cap A* **:** an individual of the proto-Australoid type
pro·to·ba·sid·i·ae \ˌprōd·(ˌ)ōbə'sidē,ē\ *or* **pro·to·ba·sid·ii** \-dē,ī\ [NL, fr. *prot-* + *basidiae* or *basidii* (fr. *basidium*)] *syn of* HETEROBASIDIOMYCETES
pro·to·basidiomycetes \¦prōd·(ˌ)ō+\ [NL, fr. *prot-* + *Basidiomycetes*] *syn of* HETEROBASIDIOMYCETES
pro·to·basidium \"+\ *n, pl* **protobasidia** [NL, fr. *prot-* + *basidium*] **:** a basidium (as a promycelium) that is divided into four cells each of which gives rise to a single basidiospore and that is characteristic of the subclass Heterobasidiomycetes — compare AUTOBASIDIUM, HEMIBASIDIUM
pro·to·blast \'prōd·ə,blast\ *n* [ISV *prot-* + *-blast;* prob. orig. formed in G] **1 :** a naked cell without a cell wall **2 :** a blastomere of the segmenting egg that is the parent cell of a definite part or organ — **pro·to·blas·tic** \¦=¦blastik\ *adj*
pro·to·blat·toid \¦=(ˌ)=¦bla,tȯid\ *adj* [NL *Protoblattoidea*] **:** of or relating to the Protoblattoidea
pro·to·blat·toi·dea \ˌ=(ˌ)=bla'tȯidēə\ *n pl, cap* [NL, fr. *prot-* + *Blatta* + *-oidea*] **:** a polyphyletic group of extinct families of insects related to the Blattaria and Protorthoptera, known only from the Upper Carboniferous and Permian, and formerly regarded as an order
pro·to·branchia \ˌ=(ˌ)=+\ *n pl, cap* [NL, fr. *prot-* + *-branchia*] **:** an order of Lamellibranchia comprising primitive bivalve mollusks in which the gills consist of a double row of simple lamellae not reflected or united — **pro·to·branchiate** \¦=(ˌ)=+\ *adj*
pro·to·branchiata \¦=(ˌ)=+\ [NL, fr. *prot-* + *branchiata*] *syn of* PROTOBRANCHIA
pro·to·canonical \¦prōd·(ˌ)ō+\ *adj* [NL *protocanonicus* protocanonical (fr. *prot-* + LL *canonicus* belonging to the canon of Scripture) + E *-al* — more at CANONIC] **:** of, relating to, or constituting those books of the Bible accepted early into the biblical canon without serious controversy — compare DEUTEROCANONICAL
pro·toc·a·ris \prə'täkərəs\ *n, cap* [NL, fr. *prot-* + *-caris*] **:** the oldest known branchiopod genus found in the Lower Cambrian of Vermont and consisting of small crustaceans resembling *Triops*
pro·to·catechualdehyde \¦prōd·(ˌ)ō+¦==,=¦==,=\ *or* **pro·to·cat·e·chu·ic aldehyde** \"+¦kad·ə¦chüik, -¦shüik, -¦kyüik-\ *n* [*protocatechualdehyde* ISV *protocatechuic* acid + *aldehyde*] **:** a crystalline compound $C_6H_3(OH)_2CHO$ which is synthetically prepared and the monomethyl ether of which is vanillin; 3,4-dihydroxy-benzaldehyde
protocatechuic acid *n* [*protocatechuic* ISV *prot-* + *catechu* + *-ic*] **:** a crystalline acid $C_6H_3(OH)_2CO_2H$ produced from various resins and other plant products by fusion with alkali; 3,4-dihydroxy-benzoic acid
pro·to·cephalon \¦prōd·(ˌ)ō+\ *n, pl* **protocephala** [NL, fr. *prot-* + *cephalon*] **1 :** the part of an insect embryo that consists of the prostomium and the first postoral somite **2 :** the primitive arthropod head corresponding to the sensory as distinguished from the feeding portion of the head of higher forms — compare GNATHOTHORAX
pro·toc·er·as \prə'täsərəs\ *n, cap* [NL, fr. *prot-* + *-ceras*] **:** a No. American Miocene genus of ungulates related to the chevrotains
pro·to·ceratops \¦prōd·(ˌ)ō+\ *n, cap* [NL, fr. *prot-* + *Ceratops*] **:** a genus of small hornless ceratopsian dinosaurs from the Cretaceous of Mongolia that is unique in that all stages of growth from the egg to the adult are represented by fossils
pro·to·cerebral \¦prōd·(ˌ)ō+\ *adj* [NL *protocerebrum* + E *-al*] **:** of or relating to the protocerebrum
pro·to·cerebrum \"+\ *n* [NL, fr. *prot-* + *cerebrum*] **1 :** the first segment of the brain in an insect innervating the compound eyes **2 :** the ganglion in a lower crustacean giving rise to the optic nerve
pro·to-chimu \"+\ *adj, usu cap C* **:** MOCHICA
pro·to·chlorophyll \"+\ *n* [*prot-* + *chlorophyll*] **:** a green magnesium-containing pigment that is present in etiolated leaves and seedlings which develop in the dark and that is converted to chlorophyll by reduction under the influence of light
pro·to·chorda \"+\ [NL, fr. *prot-* + *chorda* (fr. *Chordata*)] *syn of* PROTOCHORDATA
pro·to·chordata \"+\ *n pl, cap* [NL, fr. *prot-* + *Chordata*] *in some classifications* **:** a major division of Chordata comprising the Hemichordata, Urochorda, and usu. the Cephalochordata — **pro·to·chordate** \"+\ *adj or n*
pro·to·ciliata \"+\ *n pl, cap* [NL, fr. *prot-* + *Ciliata*] **:** a subclass of Ciliata comprising endozoic forms that have two to many similar nuclei and that reproduce sexually through fusion of gametes — compare EUCILIATA — **pro·to·ciliate** \"+\ *adj or n*
pro·to·clas·tic \¦prōd·ə¦klastik\ *adj* [G *protoklastisch*, fr. *prot-* + *-klastisch* -clastic] **:** of, relating to, or constituting the texture of an igneous rock whose earlier crystals show deformation and granulation produced before the complete solidification of the magma
pro·toc·neme \'prō,täk,nēm\ *n* -s [NL, fr. *prot-* + Gk *knēmē* shin — more at HAM] **:** one of the 12 primary mesenteries recognizable in an actinozoan
pro·to·coccaceae \¦prōd·(ˌ)ō+\ *n pl, cap* [NL, fr. *Protococcus*, type genus + *-aceae*] **:** a family of unicellular green algae that is coextensive with the genus *Protococcus* and is now usu. placed in the order Ulotrichales but is sometimes isolated in a separate order or esp. formerly included in Chlorococcales or Chaetophorales
pro·to·coc·cal \¦prōd·ə¦käkəl\ *adj* [NL *Protococcus* + E *-al*] **:** of or relating to the genus *Protococcus*
pro·to·coc·ca·les \ˌprōd·(ˌ)ōkə'kā(ˌ)lēz, -kä'k-\ *n pl, cap* [NL *Protococcus* + *-ales*] *in some classifications* **:** an order of algae coextensive with the family Protococcaceae
pro·to·coc·coid \¦prōd·ə¦kä,kȯid\ *adj* [NL *Protococcus* + E *-oid*] **:** resembling the genus *Protococcus*
pro·to·coc·cus \ˌ=='käkəs\ *n, cap* [NL, fr. *prot-* + *-coccus*] **:** a genus of unicellular globose chiefly terrestrial green algae (family Protococcaceae) that in former classifications included most such aerial algae but is now usu. restricted to forms with a single large peripheral chloroplast that divide in two planes to form thin filmy colonies (as on damp rocks or the bark of trees) — compare CHLOROCOCCUM
¹**pro·to·col** \'prōd·ə,kȯl, 'prōt| *also* -,käl *or* -,kōl *or* |ōkəl *or* |ēkəl\ *n* -s *often attrib* [earlier *prothocoll*, fr. MF *prothocole*, fr. ML *protocollum*, fr. LGk *prōtokollon* first sheet of a papyrus roll bearing the authentication and date of manufacture of the papyrus, fr. Gk *prōt-* prot- + LGk *-kollon* (fr. Gk *kollēma* papyrus roll, sheets of papyrus glued together, lit., that which is glued together, fr. *kollan* to glue together, fr. *kolla* glue); akin to OSlav *klějī* glue, MD *helen* to glue] **1 :** an original draft, minute, or record of a document or transaction; *specif* **:** the original record kept by a notary of documents or transactions from which he certifies copies **2 a :** a preliminary memorandum (as of discussions and resolutions arrived at in negotiation) often signed by diplomatic negotiators as a basis for a final convention or treaty **b :** the records or minutes of a diplomatic conference or congress that show officially the agreements arrived at by the negotiators **3 a :** an official account of a proceeding; *esp* **:** the notes or records relating to a case, an experiment, or an autopsy **b :** the plan of a scientific or medical experiment or treatment **4 :** a rigid long-established code prescribing complete deference to superior rank and strict adherence to due order of precedence and precisely correct procedure (as in diplomatic exchange and ceremonies and in the military services) **5 :** PROTOCOL STATEMENT
²**protocol** \"\ *vb* **protocolled** *or* **protocoled; protocolled** *or* **protocoled; protocolling** *or* **protocoling; protocols** *vi* **:** to write or issue protocols ~ *vt* **:** to state in a protocol
pro·to·col·ar \¦==¦kälə(r)\ *or* **pro·to·col·a·ry** \-lərē\ *also* **pro·to·col·ic** \-lik\ *adj* [¹*protocol* + *-ar* or *-ary* or *-ic*] **:** of or relating to a protocol
pro·to·coleoptera \¦prōd·(ˌ)ō+\ *n pl, cap* [NL, fr. *prot-* + *Coleoptera*] *in some classifications* **:** an order of extinct insects that are now usu. regarded as belonging to the order Protelytroptera — **pro·to·co·le·op·ter·an** \-tərən\ *adj or n* — **pro·to·coleopteron** \¦prōd·(ˌ)ō+\ *n* -s — **pro·to·coleop·terous** \"+\ *adj*
pro·to·col·ist *pronunc at* PROTOCOL + əst\ *n* -s [¹*protocol* + *-ist*] **1 :** one who drafts protocols **2 :** a stickler for protocol
pro·to·col·ize \-,līz\ *vb* -ED/-ING/-S [¹*protocol* + *-ize*] **:** PROTOCOL
protocol statement *n* [trans. of G *protokollsatz*] **:** a basic observational sentence; *esp* **:** a statement that reports the uninterpreted results of observations and provides the basis for scientific confirmation
pro·to·conch \'prōd·ə+,-\ *n* [ISV *prot-* + *conch*] **1 :** the embryonic shell of a mollusk (as a univalve) **2 :** the apical chamber or whorl of an ammonite or gastropod — **pro·to·conchal** \¦==+\ *adj*
pro·to·cone \"+,-\ *n* [*prot-* + *cone*] **:** the central of the three cusps of a primitive upper molar that in higher forms is the principal anterior and external cusp
pro·to·co·nid \"+¦kōnəd\ *n* -s [*protocone* + *-id* (structural element)] **:** an anterior and external cusp of a lower molar that corresponds to the protocone
pro·to·conule \¦prōd·(ˌ)ō+\ *n* [*protocone* + *-ule*] **:** the anterior intermediate cusp between protocone and paracone of an upper molar
pro·to·cooperation \"+\ *n* [*prot-* + *cooperation*] **:** automatic or involuntary interaction by different kinds of organisms through which they mutually benefit (as by provision of debris habitats by trees and stirring of the forest floor by microfauna living in or on the debris) — **pro·to·cooperative** \"+\ *adj*
pro·to-corinthian \"+\ *adj, usu cap C* **:** primitively Corinthian — used of a type of decoration on painted vases
pro·to·corm \'prōd·ə+,-\ *n* [ISV *prot-* + *corm*] **1 :** a tuber-shaped body with rhizoids that is produced by the young seedlings of various orchids and some other plants having associated mycorhizal fungi **2** [*prot-* + *-corm* (fr. NL *cormus*) — more at CORMUS] **:** the part of an insect embryo posterior to the protocephalon — **pro·to·cor·mic** \¦==¦kȯrmik\ *adj*
protocorm theory *n* **:** a theory in botany: the sporophyte of a vascular plant is derived from a transition form comparable to the protocorm of some club mosses — compare CAULOID THEORY
pro·to·derm \'prōd·ə,dərm\ *n* -s [ISV *prot-* + *-derm*] **:** DERMATOGEN — **pro·to·der·mal** \¦==¦dərməl\ *adj*
prot·odonata \(¦)prōd·+\ *n pl, cap* [NL, fr. *prot-* + *Odonata*] **:** an order of extinct insects related to the Odonata, known mainly from the Upper Carboniferous and Permian, and characterized by a full but specialized venation with numerous crossveins — **prot·odona·tan** \-d·ən\ *adj or n* — **prot·odonate** \(')prōd·+\ *adj*
pro·to-doric \¦prōd·(ˌ)ō+\ *adj, usu cap D* **:** primitively Doric ⟨*proto-Doric* capital⟩ ⟨*proto-Doric* column⟩
pro·to·dynastic \"+\ *adj* [*prot-* + *dynastic*] **:** of or relating to the earliest dynasties of Egypt
pro·to·enstatite \"+\ *n* [G *protoenstatit*, fr. *prot-* + *enstatit* enstatite] **:** an unstable product of the decomposition of talc by heating that has the composition of enstatite and is convertible thereto esp. by grinding or by heating to a high temperature
pro·to·fascism \"+\ *n* [*prot-* + *fascism*] **:** a political movement or program tending toward or imitating fascism
pro·to·fascist \"+\ *n, often attrib* [*protofascism* + *-ist*] **:** one who adheres to, advocates, or practices protofascism
pro·to·gas·ter·a·ce·ae \ˌprōd·(ˌ)ō,gastə'rāsē,ē\ *n pl, cap* [NL, fr. *Protogaster*, type genus (fr. *prot-* + *-gaster*) + *-aceae*] **:** a family of homobasidiomycetous fungi (order Hymenogastrales) characterized by having only one glebal cavity in each basidiocarp
pro·to·gas·tra·les \ˌprōd·(ˌ)ō(ˌ)ga'strā(ˌ)lēz\ *n pl, cap* [NL, fr. *Protogaster* + *-ales*] *in some classifications* **:** an order of fungi coextensive with the family Protogasteraceae
pro·to·gen \'prōd·əjən, -,jen\ *n* -s [*proto-* (fr. *protozoa*) + *-gen;* fr. its being a microbial growth factor] **:** LIPOIC ACID
pro·tog·e·nal \prō'täjən°l\ *adj* [NL *protogenes* + E *-al*] **:** of or relating to a protogene
pro·to·gene \'prōd·ə+,-\ *n* [*prot-* + *gene*] **1 :** a dominant gene or factor **2** [ISV, fr. NL *protogenes* primeval, firstborn, fr. Gk *prōtogenēs*, fr. *prōt-* prot- + *-genēs* born — more at -GEN] **:** a hypothetical mutable primary unit that is capable of reduplication, is held to have differentiated from nonliving matter, and is regarded as a precursor of living beings
pro·to·genesis \¦prōd·ə+\ *n* [NL, fr. *prot-* + *genesis*] **1 :** ABIOGENESIS **2 :** reproduction by budding
pro·to·genetic \"+\ *adj* **:** of, relating to, or exhibiting protogenesis
pro·to·gen·ic \¦prōd·ə¦jenik\ *adj* [*prot-* + *-genic*] **:** formed by crystallization or solidification of molten magma
pro·to·geometric \¦prōd·(ˌ)ō+\ *adj, often cap* [*prot-* + *geometric*] **:** of, relating to, or characteristic of the earliest phase of geometric art in Greece
¹**pro·to-germanic** \"+\ *n, cap P&G* **:** the assumed ancestral language of the Germanic languages
²**proto-germanic** \"\ *adj, usu cap P&G* **:** of or belonging to Proto-Germanic
pro·to·gine *also* **pro·to·gene** \'prōd·ə,jēn\ *n* -s [*protogine* fr. F, fr. *prot-* + *-gine* (fr. Gk *-genēs* born); *protogene* alter. (influenced by *-gene*) of *protogine*] **1 :** a granite that is esp. prevalent in the central Alps and that has a gneissoid texture prob. due to dynamic action **2 :** a rock with authigenic constituents
pro·to·graph \'prōd·ə,graf\ *n* [*prot-* + *-graph*] **:** an original writing **:** HOLOGRAPH
pro·tog·y·ne \prə'täjə(ˌ)nē\ *n* -s [back-formation fr. *protogynous*] **:** a protogynous individual
pro·to·gy·nous \¦prōd·ə¦jīnəs, -¦gī-\ *also* **pro·to·gynic** \¦==-¦jinik, -jin-\ *adj* [*protogynous* ISV *prot-* + *-gynous; protogynic* fr. *protogyny* + *-ic*] **:** characterized by protogyny
pro·tog·y·ny \prō'täjənē\ *n* -ES [ISV *protogynous* + *-y*] **:** a state in hermaphroditic systems that is characterized by development of female organs or maturation of their products before the appearance of the corresponding male product thus inhibiting self-fertilization and that is encountered in apples, pears, figworts, and among several groups of invertebrate animals — compare PROTANDRY
pro·to-hattic \¦prōd·(ˌ)ō+\ *n, usu cap H* **:** HATTIC
pro·to·hematin \"+\ *n* [ISV *prot-* + *hematin*] **:** HEMATIN 2a
pro·to·heme \'prōd·ə+,-\ *n* [*prot-* + *heme*] **:** HEME 1
pro·to·hemin \¦prōd·ə+\ *n* [ISV *prot-* + *hemin*] **:** HEMIN 1a
pro·to·hemiptera \"+\ *n pl, cap* [NL, fr. *prot-* + *Hemiptera*] **:** an order of extinct insects known only from the Upper Carboniferous and Permian, formerly considered ancestral to

the Hemiptera but now usu. regarded as closely related to the Palaeodictyoptera, and characterized by suctorial mouthparts and by a wing venation like that of the Palaeodictyoptera — **pro·to·hemipteran** \"+\ *adj or n* — **pro·to·hemipteron** \"+\ *n* -s — **pro·to·hemipterous** \"+\ *adj*

pro·to·hip·pus \ˌprōd·ə'hipəs\ *n, cap* [NL, fr. *prot-* + *-hippus*] : a genus of Pliocene horses approximating donkeys in size and having two small vestigial lateral toes that do not touch the ground

pro·to·historian \ˌprōd·(ˌ)ō+\ *n* [*protohistory* + *-an*] : a specialist in protohistory

pro·to·historic \"+\ *adj* [ISV *prot-* + *historic*] : of or relating to the times just preceding the period of recorded history ⟨artifacts from ~ Indian sites —F.M.Setzler⟩

pro·to·history \"+\ *n* [ISV *prot-* + *history*] **1** : the study of man during the times that just antedate the beginning of recorded history **2** : the times immediately preceding historical times

pro·to–hittite \"+\ *n, usu cap H* : HATTIC

¹pro·to·human \"+\ *adj* [*prot-* + *human*] : of, relating to, or resembling an early primitive human or a prehominid

²protohuman \"\ *n* : a primitive human individual

pro·to·hydra \"+\ *n, cap* [NL, fr. *prot-* + *Hydra*] : a genus of marine coelenterates similar to *Hydra* but having no tentacles

pro·to·hymenoptera \"+\ *n pl, cap* [NL, fr. *prot-* + *Hymenoptera*] *in some classifications* : an order of extinct insects known only from the Permian and now usu. included in the order Megasecoptera — **pro·to·hymenopteran** \"+\ *adj or n* — **pro·to·hymenopteron** \"+\ *n* — **pro·to·hymenopterous** \"+\ *adj*

¹pro·to–indo–european \"+\ *n, cap P&I&E* : the assumed ancestral language of the Indo-European languages

²proto–indo–european \"\ *adj, usu cap P&I&E* : of or relating to Proto-Indo-European

pro·to·language \"+\ *n* [*prot-* + *language*] : the assumed or recorded ancestral language of a language or group of languages ⟨in reconstructing the vocabulary of a ~ —H.M. Hoenigswald⟩ ⟨must have been a suffix verb form in the ~ —C.T.Hodge⟩ — compare URSPRACHE

pro·to·lignin \ˌprōd·(ˌ)ō+\ *n* [*prot-* + *lignin*] : LIGNIN 1

pro·to·lith·ic \ˌprōd·əˌlithik\ *adj* [*prot-* + *-lithic*] : of or relating to the earliest period of the Stone Age : EOLITHIC

pro·to·log \'prōd·ᵊlˌȯg *also* -ˌäg\ *n* -s [*prot-* + *-log*] : the original description of a species

pro·to·loph \'prōd·ᵊlˌäf\ *n* -s [*prot-* + *-loph*] : a crest on a lophodont molar that extends from the ectoloph to the protocone

pro·to·ma \prə'tōmə\ *or* **pro·to·me** \-(ˌ)mē\ *n* -s [NL, fr. Gk *protomē* head of a decapitated animal, lit., front part cut off, fr. *protemnein* to cut off in front, fr. *pro-* ¹pro- + *temnein* to cut — more at TOME] : the representation of the head and neck of an animal often used decoratively in architecture

pro·to–malay \ˌprōd·(ˌ)ō+\ *n* -s *usu cap M* : a Malaysian whose physical appearance distinguishes him from the more Mongoloid deutero-Malay and from Veddoid or negritoid types but who is sometimes described as having early Asiatic characteristics — called also *Indonesian* — **pro·to–malayan** \"+\ *adj, usu cap M*

pro·to·mammal \ˌprōd·(ˌ)ō+\ *n* [*prot-* + *mammal*] : PROMAMMAL — **pro·to·mammalian** \"+\ *adj*

pro·to·martyr \"+\ *n* [ME *prothomartir,* fr. MF, fr. LL *protomartyr,* fr. LGk *prōtomartyr-, prōtomartys,* fr. Gk *prōt-* prot- + *martyr-, martys* martyr — more at MARTYR] : the first martyr in any cause — used esp. of the Christian martyr Stephen

pro·to·mas·tig·i·da \ˌ=(ˌ)=ma'stijədə\ [NL, fr. *prot-* + *mastig-* + *-ida*] *syn of* PROTOMONADINA

pro·to·meristem \"+\ *n* [*prot-* + *meristem*] : primary meristem

pro·tom·er·ite \prō'tämə,rīt\ *n* -s [ISV *prot-* + *mer-* + *-ite*] : the smaller anterior part of the trophozoite of a gregarine that is subdivided into two sections and is often prolonged anteriorly by an epimerite on which attachment organelles are located

¹pro·tom·o·nad \prō'tämə,nad\ *adj* [NL *Protomonadina*] : of or relating to the Protomonadina

²protomonad \"\ *n* : one of the Protomonadina

pro·to·mo·nad·i·da \ˌprōd·(ˌ)ōmə'nadədə\ [NL, fr. *Protomonad-, Protomonas,* genus of flagellates + *-ida*] *syn of* PROTOMONADINA

pro·to·mon·a·di·na \-ˌmänə'dīnə, -dēnə\ *n pl, cap* [NL, fr. *Protomonad-, Protomonas,* genus of flagellates (fr. *prot-* + *-monad-, -monas*) + *-ina*] : an order comprising small plastic flagellates (subclass Zoomastigina) with one or two flagella and including many colonial or solitary and naked or loricate free-living freshwater forms as well as numerous species (family Trypanosomatidae) of medical or veterinary importance — compare LEISHMANIA, TRYPANOSOMA

pro·to·mor·phic \ˌprōd·əˌmȯrfik\ *adj* [*prot-* + *-morphic*] : PRIMITIVE

pro·to·my·ce·ta·les \ˌ=(ˌ)=ˌmīsə'tā(ˌ)lēz\ [NL, fr. *prot-* + *mycet-* + *-ales*] *syn of* HEMIASCOMYCETES

pro·ton \'prōˌtän\ *n* -s [Gk *prōton,* neut. of *prōtos* first — more at PROT-] **1** : ANLAGE **2** : an elementary particle that is identical with the nucleus of the hydrogen atom, that along with neutrons is a constituent of all other atomic nuclei, that carries a positive charge numerically equal to the charge of an electron, and that has a mass of 1.672×10^{-24} gram — **pro·ton·ic** \prō'tänik\ *adj*

pro·ton·ate \'prōtᵊnˌāt\ *vt* -ED/-ING/-S [*proton* + *-ate* (v. suffix)] : to add a proton to

pro·to·ne·ma \ˌprōtᵊn'ēmə\ *n, pl* **protonema·ta** \-mədə\ [NL, fr. *prot-* + *-nema*] : the primary and usu. transitory growth or thalloid stage of the gametophyte in mosses and in some liverworts that corresponds somewhat to the prothallium in ferns, that is usu. a filamentous body resembling an alga though sometimes flat and platelike, that originates from the germination of an asexual spore, that is capable of independent growth, and that gives rise by budding to the moss plant proper or to the second stage of the gametophyte — **pro·to·ne·mal** \ˌ=='ēməl\ *adj* — **pro·to·ne·ma·tal** \-məd·ᵊl\ *adj* — **pro·to·ne·ma·toid** \-məˌtȯid\ *adj*

pro·to·nemertini \ˌprōd·(ˌ)ō+\ *n pl, cap* [NL, fr. *prot-* + *Nemertini*] *in some classifications* : an order of unarmed nemertine worms in which the brain and lateral nerves lie outside the musculature

pro·to·nephridial \"+\ *adj* [NL *protonephridium* + E *-al*] : resembling a protonephridium in nature or function

pro·to·nephridium \"+\ *n* [NL, fr. *prot-* + *nephridium*] **1** : the duct of a flame cell **2** : a nephridium equipped with a solenocyte — compare METANEPHRIDIUM

protonotary *var of* PROTHONOTARY

proton–synchrotron \'=ˌ=='=ˌ=\ *n* : a synchrotron in which protons are accelerated by means of frequency modulation of the radio-frequency accelerating voltage so that they have energies of billions of electron volts

pro·to·nymph \'prōd·ə+ˌ-\ *n* [*prot-* + *nymph*] : any of various acarids in their first developmental stage — compare DEUTONYMPH — **pro·to·nymphal** \ˌ==+\ *adj*

pro·to·papas \ˌprōd·ə'papəs, -pāp-\ *n* -ES [MGk *prōtopapas* chief priest — more at PROTOPOPE] : PROTOPOPE

pro·to·par·ce \ˌprōd·ə'pärsē\ *n, cap* [NL, fr. *prot-* + *-parce* (perh. fr. L *parcus* sparing, frugal) — more at PARSIMONY] : a genus of New World hawkmoths with larvae that are hornworms — see TOBACCO HORNWORM, TOMATO HORNWORM

pro·to·par·ia \ˌprōd·ə'pa(a)rēə\ *n pl, cap* [NL, fr. *prot-* + Gk *pareia* cheek — more at PROPARIA] : a cosmopolitan order of Lower Cambrian trilobites with the facial suture marginal, the eyes large, and the pygidium small and rudimentary

pro·to·path·ic \ˌ=='pathik\ *adj* [ISV *protopath-* (fr. MGk *prōtopathēs* affected first, fr. Gk *prōt-* prot- + *-pathēs* — fr. *pathos* experience, suffering) + *-ic* — more at PATHOS] **1** *of cutaneous reception* : responsive only to rather gross stimuli (as of heat, cold, and pain) **2** *of a cutaneous sensory receptor* : adapted to or subserving protopathic reception **3** *of cutaneous reactivity* : dependent on protopathic reception or receptors — compare EPICRITIC

pro·to·pectin \"+\ *n* [ISV *prot-* + *pectin*] : any of a group of water-insoluble pectic substances occurring in plants and yielding pectin or pectinic acids on hydrolysis

pro·to·pectinase \"+\ *n* -s [*protopectin* + *-ase*] : an enzyme that accelerates the change of protopectin into soluble pectin or pectinic acids with the resultant separation of plant cells from one another

pro·to·perithecium \ˌprōd(ˌ)ō+\ *n* [NL, fr. *prot-* + *perithecium*] : a primordium that when fertilized develops into a perithecium

pro·to·perlaria \"+\ *n pl, cap* [NL, fr. *prot-* + *Perlaria*] : an order of extinct insects related to the Plecoptera, known only from the Permian, and characterized by primitive plecopterid features and a pair of prothoracic lobes resembling small wings — **pro·to·perlarian** \"+\ *adj or n*

pro·to·phloem \ˌprōd·ə+\ *n* [*prot-* + *phloem*] : the first-formed part of the primary phloem that develops from the procambium and consists of narrow thin-walled cells usu. capable of a limited amount of stretching and usu. associated with a region of rapid growth in length — compare METAPHLOEM

pro·toph·y·ta \prə'täfədə\ *n pl, cap* [NL, fr. *prot-* + *-phyta*] : a major category of lower plants: as **a** *in former classifications* : a division or other group comprising the algae, fungi, and lichens **b** *in some esp. former classifications* : a division or other group comprising unicellular plants and including bacteria, yeasts, slime molds, blue-green algae, and various simple green algae — often used as a term of convenience rather than strict taxonomy; compare PROTISTA **c** *in some classifications* : a division comprising unicellular and noncellular organisms and including blue-green algae, bacteria, rickettsias and related organisms, and viruses — used chiefly in bacteriological taxonomy

pro·to·phyte \'prōd·əˌfīt\ *n* -s [NL *Protophyta*] **1** : a plant of the Protophyta **2** : a unicellular plant — compare METAPHYTE — **pro·to·phyt·ic** \ˌ=='fid·ik\ *adj*

pro·to·pine \'prōd·əˌpēn, -pən\ *n* -s [ISV *prot-* + *opium* + *-ine*] : a crystalline alkaloid $C_{20}H_{19}NO_5$ found in small quantities in opium and in many papaveraceous plants

pro·to·planet \ˌprōd·ə+\ *n* [*prot-* + *planet*] : a whirling gaseous eddy within a giant cloud of gas and dust rotating around a sun believed to give rise to a planet

pro·to·plasm \'prōd·ə, -ōtə+,-\ *also* **pro·to·plasma** \"+\ *n* [G *protoplasma,* fr. *prot-* + *-plasma* -plasm (fr. NL *plasma*) — more at PLASMA] **1** : organized living matter : the more or less fluid colloidal complex of protein, other organic and inorganic substances, and water that constitutes the living nucleus, cytoplasm, plastids, and mitochondria of the cell, that is regarded as the only form of matter in which or by which the vital phenomena (as metabolism and reproduction) are manifested, that is often designated the physical basis of life, and that sometimes exhibits under the microscope a variety of appearances but typically shows a relatively fluid hyaline ground substance in which various granules and formed elements are suspended — see ALVEOLAR THEORY, GRANULAR HYPOTHESIS, RETICULAR THEORY **2** : CYTOPLASM 2

pro·to·plasmal \ˌ==+\ *or* **pro·to·plasmatic** \"+\ *adj* [*protoplasmal* fr. *protoplasm* + *-al; protoplasmatic* ISV *protoplasm* + *-atic* (as in *plasmatic*)] : PROTOPLASMIC

pro·to·plasmic \ˌ==+\ *adj* [ISV *protoplasm* + *-ic*] : of, relating to, consisting of, or resembling protoplasm ⟨some chemicals . . . tend to damage tissue universally and are referred to as ~ poisons —W.W.Jetter⟩

¹pro·to·plast \'prōd·əˌplast, -aa(ə)st, -aist, 'prōtə,-\ *n* -s [MF *protoplaste,* fr. LL *protoplastus* first man, fr. Gk *prōtoplastos* first formed, created first, fr. *prōt-* prot- + *plastos* formed, molded, fr. *plassein* to mold — more at PLASTER] **1** : one that is formed first : PROTOTYPE **2 a** : the living content of a cell : the nucleus, cytoplasm, and plasma membrane constituting a living unit distinct from ergastic substances and inert walls **b** : ENERGID **c** *archaic* : PLASTID — **pro·to·plas·tic** \ˌ=='plastik, -aas-, -tēk\ *adj*

²protoplast \"\ *n* -s [NL *protoplastes,* fr. *prot-* + Gk *plastēs* molder, modeler, fr. *plassein* to mold] *archaic* : the original maker or creator ⟨a complete imitation of the copy set by the Protoplast —Isaac Newton⟩

¹pro·to·pod \'prōd·əˌpäd\ *n* -s [*prot-* + *-pod*] : PROTOPODITE — **pro·to·po·di·al** \ˌ=='pōdēəl\ *adj*

²protopod \"\ *adj* [NL *protopoda*] : of or relating to the early undifferentiated stage of an insect embryo

pro·top·o·da \prə'täpədə\ *n pl, usu cap* [NL, fr. *prot-* + *-poda*] : a category of insect larvae that emerge early in their embryological development and that are then only partially differentiated

pro·top·o·dite \-ˌdīt\ *n* -s [*prot-* + *-podite*] : the basal part of a typical limb of a crustacean consisting of two more or less consolidated segments and bearing at its distal extremity an exopodite or endopodite or both — **pro·top·o·dit·ic** \ˌ=;=='did·ik\ *adj*

pro·to·pope \'prōd·əˌpōp\ *n* [Russ *protopop,* fr. MGk *prōtopapas* chief priest, fr. Gk *prōt-* prot- + MGk *papas* priest, fr. Gk, title of bishops, lit., papa — more at PAPA] : the first in rank of the priests of a cathedral in the Eastern Church who administers the diocese during the absence of the bishop or a vacancy in the see

pro·to·porphyrin \ˌprōd·(ˌ)ō+\ *n* [ISV *prot-* + *porphyrin*] : a purple porphyrin acid $C_{32}H_{32}N_4(COOH)_2$ that is obtained from hemin or heme by removal of bound iron (as with formic acid and iron filings); tetramethyl-divinyl-porphin-di-propionic acid

pro·to·presbyter \"+\ *n* -s [NGk *prōtopresbyteros,* fr. Gk *prōt-* prot- + *presbyteros* priest — more at PRIEST] : PROTOPOPE

pro·to·proteose \"+\ *n* [ISV *prot-* + *proteose*] : any of a class of proteoses formed as primary products in digestion of proteins

¹pro·top·ter·an \prə'täptərən\ *or* **pro·top·ter·ous** \-t(ə)rəs\ *adj* [NL *Protopterus* + E *-an* or *-ous*] : of or relating to the genus *Protopterus* or a protopterus

²protopteran \"\ *n* -s : PROTOPTERUS 2

pro·top·ter·us \-rəs\ *n* [NL, fr. *prot-* + *-pterus*] **1** *cap* : a genus of dipnoan fishes of the rivers and swamps of central and western Africa that reach a length of six feet, that bury themselves in the mud during the dry season, that are closely related to lepidosirens but have a stouter body and five branchial clefts and differently constructed paired fins, and that are sometimes placed in a separate family but are usu. placed in the same family as *Lepidosiren* **2** -ES : any fish of the genus *Protopterus*

pro·top·tile \(')prō¦täptᵊl\ *n* -s [*prot-* + *-ptile*] : one of the first set of down feathers in young birds having two sets of down

prot·ore \'prōd·+ˌ-\ *n* [*prot-* + *ore*] : metalliferous material before it becomes ore through enrichment

¹pro·to–romance \ˌprōd·(ˌ)ō+\ *n, cap P&R* : the partly recorded and partly assumed ancestral language of the Romance languages : VULGAR LATIN

²proto–romance \"\ *adj, usu cap P&R* : of or relating to Proto-Romance

pro·to·ro·saur \'prōd·ərəˌsȯ(ə)r\ *or* **pro·to·ro·sau·ri·an** \ˌ=;==='sȯrēən\ *also* **pro·te·ro·saur** \'===ˌsȯ(ə)r\ *n* -s [NL *Protorosauria*] : a reptile or fossil of the order Protorosauria

pro·to·ro·sau·ria \ˌ==='sȯrēə\ *n pl, cap* [NL, fr. *Protorosaurus* + *-ia*] : an order of Synaptosauria comprising rather small Permian and Triassic reptiles — see PROTOROSAURUS

pro·to·ro·sau·ri·an *or* **pro·tero·sau·ri·an** \ˌ==='sȯrēən\ *adj* [NL *Protorosauria, Proterosauria* + E *-an*] : of or relating to the Protorosauria

pro·to·ro·sau·roid *also* **pro·tero·sau·roid** \-ˌrȯid\ *adj* [NL *Protorosaurus, Proterosaurus* + E *-oid*] : resembling or related to the Protorosauria

pro·to·ro·sau·rus \ˌ==='sȯrəs\ *n, cap* [NL, irreg. fr. *proter-* + *-saurus*] : a genus of upper Permian reptiles (order Protorosauria) resembling lizards and attaining a length of several yards

prot·orthoptera \ˌprōd·+\ *n pl, cap* [NL, fr. *prot-* + *Orthoptera*] : an order of extinct insects related to the Orthoptera, known only from the Upper Carboniferous and Permian, and characterized by numerous venational features recalling the Orthoptera — **prot·orthopteran** \"+\ *adj or n* — **prot·orthopteron** \"+\ *n* — **prot·orthopterous** \"+\ *adj*

pro·to·selachii \ˌprōd·(ˌ)ō+\ [NL, fr. *prot-* + *Selachii*] *syn of* NOTIDANI

¹proto–semitic \"+\ *n, cap P&S* : the assumed ancestral language of the Semitic languages

²proto–semitic \"\ *adj, usu cap P&S* : of or relating to Proto-Semitic

pro·to–sinaitic \"+\ *adj, usu cap S* : of or relating to an early Semitic alphabet known only from fragmentary inscriptions from Sarabit el Khadem in the Sinai peninsula and thought to date from about 1500 B.C.

pro·to·siphon \"+\ *n, cap* [NL, fr. *prot-* + Gk *siphōn* siphon, tube, pipe] : a genus (the type of the family Protosiphonaceae) of unicellular multinucleate freshwater green algae consisting of a single form (*P. botryoides*) that is broadly tubular or more or less balloon-shaped and grows often confusingly mingled with *Botrydium* attached to mud by a single rarely branching rhizoid — **pro·to·siphonaceous** \"+\ *adj*

pro·to·sphargis \"+\ *n, cap* [NL, fr. *prot-* + *Sphargis*] : a genus of gigantic turtles from the Upper Cretaceous of Italy including one form (*P. veronensis*) with a shell about nine feet long

pro·to·spon·dy·li \ˌ=(ˌ)='spändəˌlī\ [NL, fr. *prot-* + *-spondyli*] *syn of* CYCLOGANOIDEI

pro·to·spon·dy·lous \ˌ=(ˌ)=¦==ləs\ *adj* [NL *Protospondyli* + E *-ous*] : of or relating to the Cycloganoidei

pro·to·star \'prōd·ə+ˌ-\ *n* [ISV *prot-* + *star*] : a hypothetical flat circular gaseous cloud of dust and atoms in space believed to develop into a star

pro·tos·te·ga \prə'tästəgə\ *n, cap* [NL, fr. *prot-* + Gk *stegē* roof; akin to L *tegere* to cover — more at THATCH] : a genus of large marine turtles from the Upper Cretaceous of No. America having a carapace and plastron somewhat like those of the leatherback

pro·to·stele \'prōd·əˌstēl, ˌ==¦stēlē\ *n* [*prot-* + *stele*] : a stele that has the form of a solid rod or column with the phloem surrounding the xylem — called also *monostele;* compare SIPHONOSTELE — **pro·to·ste·lic** \ˌ=='stēlik\ *adj*

¹pro·to·stome \'prōd·əˌstōm\ *adj* [NL *Protostomia*] : of or relating to the Protostomia

²protostome \"\ *n* -s [NL *Protostomia*] : one of the Protostomia

pro·to·sto·mia \ˌ=='stōmēə\ *n pl, cap* [NL, fr. *prot-* + *-stomia*] : animals in which the definitive mouth develops directly from the blastopore (as most worms, bryozoans, brachiopods, mollusks, and arthropods) — compare DEUTEROSTOMIA

pro·to·strongyle \ˌ==+\ *n* -s [NL *Protostrongylus*] : a worm of the genus *Protostrongylus*

pro·to·strongylin \"+\ *n* -s [NL *Protostrongylus* + E *-in*] : PROTOSTRONGYLE

pro·to·strongyline \"+\ *adj* [NL *Protostrongylus* + E *-ine*] : of or relating to the genus *Protostrongylus*

pro·to·strongylus \"+\ *n, cap* [NL, fr. *prot-* + *Strongylus*] : a genus of lungworms (family Metastrongylidae) parasitic in ruminants and rodents

pro·to·syllabic \ˌprōd·ə+\ *adj* [*prot-* + *syllabic*] *of the heaviest stress in a word* : falling on the first syllable

pro·to·symphyla \"+\ *n pl, cap* [NL, fr. *prot-* + *Symphyla*] : a hypothetical class of arthropods held to be ancestral to the Insecta and Symphyla

pro·to·taxic \"+\ *adj* [*prot-* + *-taxic* (as in *parataxic*)] : lacking in self-awareness and in perception of temporal sequence : cognitively inchoate : PRECONCEPTUAL ⟨~ symbols⟩ ⟨in the first year of life the ~ mode is operating —G.S. Blum⟩ — contrasted with *parataxic* and *syntaxic*

pro·to·taxites \ˌ==+\ *n, pl* **prototaxites** [NL, fr. *prot-* + *tax-* + *-ites*] : NEMATOPHYTON

pro·to–teutonic \ˌprōd·(ˌ)ō+\ *adj or n, cap P&T* : PROTO-GERMANIC

pro·to·the·ca \ˌprōd·ə'thēkə\ *n, pl* **protothe·cae** \-ē(ˌ)sē\ [NL, fr. *prot-* + *theca*] : the cup-shaped structure forming the first part of the skeleton in the Madreporaria — **pro·to·the·cal** \ˌ=(ˌ)=¦thēkəl\ *adj*

pro·to·there \'prōd·əˌthi(ə)r\ *n* -s [NL *Prototheria*] : one of the Prototheria

pro·to·the·ria \ˌ=='thirēə\ *n pl, cap* [NL, fr. *prot-* + *-theria*] : a subclass of Mammalia that is coextensive with Monotremata or in some classifications includes both Monotremata and Allotheria and that is represented in the recent fauna solely by the egg-laying platypus and echidnas

pro·to·tonic \ˌprōd·ə+\ *adj* [*prot-* + *tonic*] : characterized by accent on the first syllable — contrasted with *deuterotonic*

pro·to·tracheata \ˌprōd·(ˌ)ō+\ [NL, fr. *prot-* + *Tracheata*] *syn of* ONYCHOPHORA

pro·to·troch \'prōd·əˌträk\ *n* -s [*prot-* + *-troch*] : the ciliated band or ring characteristic of trochophore larvae — **pro·tot·ro·chal** \prō'tä·trəkəl\ *adj*

pro·to·troph \'prōd·əˌträf, -rōf\ *n* -s [back-formation fr. *prototrophic*] : a prototrophic individual

pro·to·trophic \ˌ=='träfik, -rōf-\ *adj* [ISV *prot-* + *-trophic*] **1** : deriving nutriment from inorganic sources — used esp. of those bacteria that do not require organic media for growth **2** : requiring no specific growth substances for normal metabolism and reproduction — used esp. of the wild types of various molds

pro·to·trop·ic \ˌ=='träpik\ *adj* [*prototropy* + *-ic*] : of or relating to prototropy

pro·tot·ro·py \prə'tä·trəpē\ *n* -ES [*proton* + *-tropy*] : tautomerism involving the migration of a proton esp. to a location three atoms distant in an organic molecule — compare ANIONOTROPY, KETO-ENOL TAUTOMERISM

pro·to·typ·al \ˌprōd·ə¦tīpəl\ *adj* [*prototype* + *-al*] : of, relating to, or constituting a prototype : ARCHETYPAL

pro·to·type \'==ˌtīp\ *n* [F, fr. MF, fr. Gk *prōtotypon* archetype, fr. neut. of *prōtotypos* original, primitive, fr. *prōt-* prot- + *typos* type — more at TYPE] **1 a** (1) : an original on which a thing is modeled : PATTERN ⟨consciously identifying the new republic with the ancient ~ —*Amer. Guide Series: N.Y.*⟩ (2) : one of the ideas or patterns in the divine mind after the likeness of which created things are made — compare ARCHETYPE, IDEA 1a **b** : an individual that exhibits the essential features of a later individual or species : PRECURSOR ⟨metal-wheeled chariots, the ~ of the tanks of modern warfare —R.W.Murray⟩ **c** : an individual, quality, or complex that exemplifies or serves as a standard of the essential features of a group or type : EXEMPLAR ⟨the gangster ~ the movies have shown the world —Polly Adler⟩ ⟨mathematics is the ~ of logical thinking⟩ ⟨~ kilogram⟩ **d** (1) *also* **prototype airplane** : the first full-scale piloted flying model of a new type of airplane (2) : the first full-scale model of a new type or design of furniture, machinery, or vehicle ⟨~ chair⟩ ⟨~ of a new tractor engine⟩ ⟨~ of a new medium tank⟩ **2 a** : an ancestral form **b** : primary type **3** : an individual that exemplifies an earlier prototype ⟨the modern ~ of Catherine the Great —Thomas Wolfe⟩

pro·to·typ·i·cal \ˌ=='tipəkəl, -pēk-\ *also* **pro·to·typ·ic** \-pik, -pēk\ *adj* [*prototypical* fr. *prototype* + *-ical; prototypic* ISV *prototype* + *-ic*] : PROTOTYPAL — **pro·to·typ·i·cal·ly** \-pək(ə)lē, -ēk-, -li\ *adv*

pro·to·veratrine \ˌprōd·(ˌ)ō+\ *n* [ISV *prot-* + *veratrine*] : a toxic crystalline alkaloid or a mixture of two closely related alkaloids distinguished as protoveratrine A and B obtained from the white hellebore and used in the treatment of hypertension

pro·to·vertebra \"+\ *n* [NL, fr. *prot-* + *vertebra*] **1** : PRIMITIVE SEGMENT **2** : MYOTOME — **pro·to·vertebral** \"+\ *adj*

prot·oxide \(')prōd·+\ *n* [ISV *prot-* + *oxide*] : the one of a series of oxides exclusive of suboxides that has the lowest proportion of oxygen

pro·to·xylem \ˌprōd·(ˌ)ō+\ *n* [*prot-* + *xylem*] : the first part of the primary xylem that differentiates from the procambium and that is distinguished from the metaxylem by smaller diameter and the annular, spiral, or occasionally scalariform wall thickenings

protoxylem point *n* : the protoxylem strand in cross section

protoxylem strand *n* : a group of protoxylem elements forming a longitudinal strand in the stele

pro·to·zoa \ˌprōd·ə'zōə, -ōtə-\ *n pl, cap* [NL, fr. *prot-* + *-zoa*] : a phylum or subkingdom of animals that have an essentially acellular structure though varying from simple uninucleate protoplasts (as most amoebas) to cell colonies (as volvox), syncytia (as pelomyxa), or highly organized protoplasts (as various higher ciliates) far more complex in organization and differentiation than most metazoan cells, that consist of a protoplasmic body either naked or enclosed in a test, fixed to the substrate or free, and immobile, creeping by means of pseudopodia or protoplasmic flow, or freely motile by cilia or flagella, that are similarly varied in physiological characteristics with nutrition holophytic, saprophytic, or holozoic, with reproduction asexual involving nuclear division usu. by more or less modified mitosis associated with cytoplasmic binary fission or with multiple fission or exogenous or endogenous budding or sexual by means of conjugation, of isogamous or anisogamous hologamy or of processes approaching the fertilization processes of metazoans, and with a life cycle simple (as in an amoeba) or extremely complex (as in many sporozoans), that are represented by one form or another in almost every kind of habitat (as fresh or salt water, soil, sewage, the latex of plants, and the bodies of living animals), and that include parasitic forms which are among the gravest plaguers of man and his domestic animals — compare MALARIA PARASITE, TRYPANOSOME; CILIOPHORA, PLASMODROMA; EIMERIA, METAZOA, PARAZOA, PROTISTA

pro·to·zo·a·ci·dal \¦==¦==¦sīdᵊl\ *adj* [*protozoacide* + *-al*] **1 :** destroying protozoans **2 :** of or relating to a protozoacide

pro·to·zo·a·cide \,==ˈ=ə,sīd\ *n* -s [NL *Protozoa* + E *-cide*] **:** an agent that destroys protozoans

pro·to·zo·al \¦==¦zōəl\ *adj* [NL *Protozoa* + E *-al*] **:** PROTOZOAN

¹pro·to·zo·an \-ən\ *n* -s [NL *Protozoa* + E *-an*] **:** one of the Protozoa

²protozoan \"\ *adj* **:** of or relating to the Protozoa

pro·to·zoea \¦prōd·ə+\ *n* [NL, fr. *prot-* + *zoea*] **:** a larval stage preceding the zoea in some decapod Crustacea — **pro·to·zoean** \"+\ *adj*

pro·to·zo·i·a·sis \,prōd·ə(,)zōˈīəsəs\ *n, pl* **protozoia·ses** \-ə,sēz\ [NL, fr. *Protozoa* + *-iasis*] **:** infection with or disease caused by protozoan parasites

pro·to·zo·ic \¦prōd·ə¦zōik\ *adj* [NL *Protozoa* + E *-ic*] **1 :** PROTOZOAN **2 :** containing or belonging to the period of remains of the earliest discovered life

pro·to·zoological \"+\ *adj* [*protozoology* + *-ical*] **:** of or relating to protozoology

pro·to·zoologist \"+\ *n* [*protozoology* + *-ist*] **:** a specialist in protozoology

pro·to·zoology \"+\ *n* [ISV *protozoo-* (fr. NL *Protozoa*) + *-logy*] **:** a branch of zoology concerned with the study of the Protozoa

pro·to·zo·on \,prōd·əˈzō,än, -ōtə'-\ *n, pl* **protozoa** [NL, sing. of *Protozoa*] **:** PROTOZOAN — **pro·to·zo·on·al** \¦==¦zōənᵊl\ *adj*

pro·tracheata \(¦)prō+\ [NL, fr. ¹*pro-* + *Tracheata*] *syn of* ONYCHOPHORA

pro·tracheate \(ˈ)=+\ *adj or n* [NL *Protracheata*] **:** ONYCHOPHORAN

pro·tract \prōˈtrakt, prə'-\ *vt* -ED/-ING/-S [L *protractus*, past part. of *protrahere* to draw before, protract, fr. *pro-* ¹pro- + *trahere* to draw — more at TRACE] **1** *archaic* **:** to put off to a later time **:** DELAY, DEFER ⟨attempted, however, to prevent, or at least to ~, his ruin —Edward Gibbon⟩ **2 :** to draw out or lengthen in time or space **:** CONTINUE, PROLONG ⟨the trial must not be ~*ed* in duration by anything that is obstructive or dilatory —R.H.Jackson⟩ **3 :** to draw to a scale **:** lay down the lines and angles of with scale and protractor **:** PLOT **syn** see EXTEND

pro·tract·ed·ly *adv* **:** in a protracted manner

protracted meeting *n* **:** a series of revival meetings extending over a period of time ⟨in the spring when they had the big *protracted meetings* and the foot washings —J.H.Stuart⟩

pro·tract·ed·ness *n* -ES **:** the quality or state of being protracted

pro·tract·er \-tə(r)\ *n* -s [by alter.] **:** PROTRACTOR

pro·tract·ible \-təbəl\ *adj* **:** capable of being protracted

pro·trac·tile \prōˈtrakt ᵊl, prə'-, -,tīl, -(,)til\ *adj* **:** capable of being thrust out **:** PROTRUSILE — compare RETRACTILE — **pro·trac·til·i·ty** \,prō,trakˈtiləd·ē, -lətē, -i\ *n* -ES

pro·trac·tion \-ˈtrakshən\ *n* -s [LL *protraction-, protractio*, fr. L *protractus* (past part. of *protrahere* to protract) + *-ion-, -io* -ion] **1 :** the act or an instance of protracting **:** EXTENSION, PROLONGATION, DELAY ⟨the ~ of a debate⟩ **2 a :** the drawing to scale of an area of land **b :** a plan drawn to scale of an area **:** PLOT **3 :** the prolonging of a syllable in a Greek or Latin poem beyond its normal length

pro·trac·tive \-ktiv\ *adj* [L *protractus* + E *-ive*] **:** that protracts **:** DELAYING

pro·trac·tor \-tə(r)\ *n* -s [ML, fr. L *protractus* (past part. of *protrahere* to protract) + *-or*] **1 :** one that protracts **:** as **a** *obs* **:** one that prolongs **:** RETARDER, DELAYER **b :** a muscle that extends a part — opposed to *retractor* **2 a :** an instrument made for laying down and measuring angles on paper and used in drawing and plotting **b :** a similar instrument for locating distant forest fires

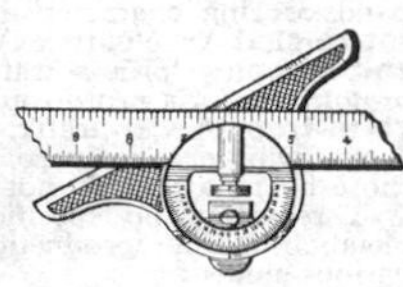

bevel protractor

pro·trema·ta \prōˈtremәd·ə, -rēm-\ *n pl, cap* [NL, fr. ¹*pro-* + *-tremata*] **:** an order of articulate brachiopods having the peduncle opening restricted to the ventral valve or absent — **pro·tremate** \-māt\ *n* -s — **pro·trema·tous** \(ˈ)=¦tremәd·əs, -rēm-\ *adj*

¹pro·trep·tic \prōˈtreptik\ *n* -s [LL *protrepticus* hortatory, encouraging, fr. Gk *protreptikos*, fr. (assumed) Gk *protreptos* (verbal of *protrepein* to turn forward, urge on, fr. *pro-* ¹pro- + *trepein* to turn) + *-ikos* -ic — more at TROPE] **:** EXHORTATION

²protreptic \"\ *also* **pro·trep·ti·cal** \-tәkәl\ *adj* [*protreptic* fr. LL *protrepticus; protreptical* fr. LL *protrepticus* + E *-al*] **:** HORTATORY, PERSUASIVE

pro·triaene \(ˈ)prō+\ *n* [¹*pro-* + *triaene*] **:** a triaene in which the cladi point in a direction opposite to that of the shaft

pro·troch·u·la \prōˈträkyələ\ *n* -s [NL, fr. ¹*pro-* + *troch-* + *-ula* (fem. of *-ulus* -ule)] **:** a hypothetical free-swimming primitive organism resembling a simple trochophore and regarded as indicating the way of transition from radial to bilateral symmetry

pro·trud·able \prōˈtrüdәbәl\ *adj* **:** PROTRUSIBLE

pro·trude \-ˈtrüd\ *vb* -ED/-ING/-S [L *protrudere*, fr. *pro-* ¹pro- + *trudere* to thrust — more at THREAT] *vt* **1** *archaic* **:** to thrust forward **:** drive or force along **2 :** to thrust out through or as if through a narrow orifice **:** cause to project or stick out ⟨to ~ one's tongue⟩ ~ *vi* **:** to jut out beyond the surrounding surface or context ⟨tall apartment buildings perch on the top of rocky cliffs or ~ from hillsides —*Amer. Guide Series: N.Y. City*⟩ ⟨memories *protruded* into his consciousness⟩ **syn** see BULGE

pro·trud·ent \-dᵊnt\ *adj* [L *protrudent-, protrudens*, pres. part. of *protrudere* to protrude] **:** PROTRUDING, PROJECTING, BULGING

pro·tru·si·ble \prōˈtrüsәbәl, -üzә-\ *adj* [*protrusion* + *-ible*] **:** capable of being protruded

pro·tru·sile \prōˈtrü,|s|īl, -,|s|әl, -(,)|s|il, |z|\ *adj* [*protrusion* + *-ile*] **:** so made that it can be protruded ⟨a ~ proboscis⟩ — **pro·tru·sil·i·ty** \,prō,trüˈsilәd·ē, -ˈzil-\ *n* -ES

pro·tru·sion \prōˈtrüzhәn\ *n* -s [L *protrusus* (past part. of *protrudere* to protrude) + E *-ion*] **1 :** the quality or state of protruding **:** PROJECTION ⟨the ~ of a jaw⟩ **2 :** something that protrudes ⟨a roof with many ~*s*⟩

pro·tru·sive \prōˈtrüsiv, (ˈ)prō¦t-, -üziv\ *adj* [L *protrusus* (past part. of *protrudere* to protrude) + E *-ive*] **1** *archaic* **:** that thrusts forward or pushes along **:** PROPULSIVE **2 :** that protrudes **:** PROTUBERANT ⟨a ~ jaw⟩ ⟨to pull a ~ manuscript from one's pocket⟩ **3 :** characterized by obtrusiveness **:** that forces attention ⟨a ~ boisterous manner⟩ — **pro·tru·sive·ly** \-әvlē\ *adv* — **pro·tru·sive·ness** \-ivnәs\ *n* -ES

pro·tu·ber·ance \prōˈt(y)üb(ә)rәn(t)s\ *n* -s [LL *protuberare* to bulge out + E *-ance*] **1 :** the quality or state of being protuberant ⟨lessen the ~ of an underjaw by an operation⟩ **2 :** something that is protuberant **:** PROTRUSION, BULGE ⟨a ~ on the forehead⟩ ⟨a cancerous ~⟩

pro·tu·ber·an·cy \-nsē, -si\ *n* -ES [LL *protuberare* + E *-ancy*] *archaic* **:** PROTUBERANCE

pro·tu·ber·ant \-nt\ *adj* [LL *protuberant-, protuberans*, pres. part. of *protuberare* to bulge out] **1 :** bulging beyond the surrounding or adjacent surface **:** PROMINENT ⟨a ~ joint⟩ ⟨~ eyes⟩ **2 :** forcing itself into consciousness **:** OBTRUSIVE ⟨one of the most ~ facts of the history of the past twenty years — Elmer Davis⟩ — **pro·tu·ber·ant·ly** *adv*

pro·tu·ber·ate \-ә,rāt\ *vi* -ED/-ING/-S [LL *protuberatus*, past part. of *protuberare* to bulge out, fr. L *pro-* ¹pro- + *tuber* bump, swelling, tumor — more at TUBER] **:** to swell beyond a surface **:** form a protuberance **syn** see BULGE

prot·ungulata \(¦)prōd·+\ *n pl, cap* [NL, fr. *prot-* + *Ungulata*] **1 :** a hypothetical group ancestral to the ungulate mammals **2** *in some classifications* **:** a major division of Eutheria comprising extinct mammals of the orders Condylarthra, Litopterna, Notoungulata, and Astrapotheria together with the recent and extinct Tubulidentata — **prot·ungulate** \(ˈ)=+\ *adj or n*

pro·tu·ra \prәˈtyůrә\ *n pl, cap* [NL, fr. *prot-* + *-ura*] **:** a group of very minute primitive wingless blind arthropods that lack antennae, have the mouth parts concealed within the head, undergo no noticeable metamorphosis except an increase in the number of abdominal segments, and are sometimes considered to form an order of Insecta or more often in current classification treated as a distinct class — **pro·tu·ran** \-rәn\ *adj or n*

pro·tutor \(ˈ)prō+\ *n* [LL *protutela* vice-tutelage (fr. L *pro-* ¹pro- + *tutela* tutelage) + E *-or* (as in *tutor*)] **:** one who acts as tutor without legal appointment or one who marries a tutoress and is equally responsible with her

pro·tu·tory \-üd·әrē\ *n* -ES [*protutor* + *-y*] **:** the office or tenure of office of a protutor

pro·tyl·o·pus \prәˈtilәpәs\ *n, cap* [NL, fr. ¹*pro-* + *-tylopus* (fr. *Tylopoda*)] **:** a genus of camels no larger than jackrabbits found in the Upper Eocene of No. America and having teeth that form a continuous series, unfused lower leg bones, and four functional toes on the front feet

pro·type \ˈprō+,\ *n* [¹*pro-* + *type*] **:** the first intact described specimen of a fossil species previously known only from an incomplete type

proud \ˈpraůd\ *adj* -ER/-EST [ME, fr. OE *prūd, prūt*, prob. fr. OF *prod, prud, prut, prou* good, capable, brave, fr. LL *prode* advantageous, advantage, fr. L *prodesse* to be useful, be beneficial, fr. *prod-* (var. of *pro-* before, forward) + *esse* to be — more at PRO-, IS] **1 :** feeling or showing pride: as **a :** having or displaying inordinate self-esteem ⟨goaded the ~ baronage —J.R.Green⟩ ⟨his cold and ~ nature —A. Conan Doyle⟩ **b :** highly satisfied or pleased **:** deeply gratified **:** ELATED, EXULTANT ⟨~ to have such men —Sherwood Anderson⟩ ⟨a ~ boy . . . he has made something with his own hands —*Better Homes & Gardens*⟩ — often used with *of* ⟨~ of his success⟩ ⟨a record to be ~ of⟩ **c** *chiefly Midland* **:** GLAD, DELIGHTED ⟨we'd be ~ to have you stay for supper⟩ **d :** marked by a proper or becoming self-respect ⟨too ~ to fight —Woodrow Wilson⟩ ⟨brought a ~ . . . efficiency to everything she did — Fred Majdalany⟩ **2 a :** marked by stateliness or magnificence **:** SPLENDID ⟨~ princes and humble peasants —Vicki Baum⟩ ⟨~ old castles —E.O.Hauser⟩ **b :** giving reason or occasion for pride **:** GLORIOUS ⟨a ~ heritage⟩ ⟨our ~*est* feat —Joyce Cary⟩ ⟨his ~*est* moment —Paul Pickrel⟩ **3 :** marked by great vitality or power **:** VIGOROUS, EXUBERANT: as **a** *of an animal* **:** full of spirit **:** METTLESOME ⟨a ~ steed⟩ **b** *of a body of water* **:** overflowing its banks **:** SWOLLEN ⟨the ~ stream⟩ **c** (1) *of granulation tissue* **:** growing exuberantly ⟨~ growth in an old wound⟩ (2) *of a plant, Brit* **:** LUXURIANT ⟨~ corn⟩ **4 :** arising from or produced by pride ⟨a ~ look⟩ **5** *chiefly dial, of a female animal* **:** sexually excited **:** in heat **6 a** *chiefly dial Brit* **:** PROTUBERANT — used esp. of construction ⟨~ . . . jointings may have to be pared down —*Choice of Careers: Furniture Manufacturing*⟩ ⟨~ base edges —F.W.Mann⟩ **b** *of a cutting tool* **:** having a large amount of top rake

syn PROUD, ARROGANT, HAUGHTY, LORDLY, INSOLENT, OVERBEARING, SUPERCILIOUS, DISDAINFUL can mean in common showing a sense of one's superiority and scorn for what one regards as beneath him. PROUD may stress less the idea of one's sense of superiority than the idea of one's sense of accomplishment, often genuine, or strong self-respect, often justified, although it often implies an assumed superiority or suggests a loftiness or manifest self-congratulation in manner or appearance ⟨*proud* to publish a group of excellent reference works —*Saturday Rev.*⟩ ⟨he was too *proud* to admit failure and withdraw —Aldous Huxley⟩ ⟨he had a mild impersonal manner and was *proud* of having no rancor for any of the criminals he arrested —Morley Callaghan⟩ ⟨she is *proud* of everything of which she should be ashamed —H.T.Buckle⟩ ⟨a *proud* and objectionable bearing toward colleagues⟩ ARROGANT implies a claiming for oneself, often domineeringly or offensively, more consideration, importance, or worth than is warranted ⟨he was not, however, disagreeably *arrogant* or contemptuous in a cutting way as I am afraid I had been at that age —Edmund Wilson⟩ ⟨vain, *arrogant*, blustering, trying to keep leadership of his associates —Amy Loveman⟩ ⟨an *arrogant* disregard for the popular will —D.D.McKean⟩ HAUGHTY stresses an obvious consciousness of superior position or character and an obvious scorn of things regarded as beneath one ⟨supercilious and *haughty*, they turn this way and that, like the dowagers of very aristocratic families at a plebeian evening party —Aldous Huxley⟩ ⟨a cold and *haughty* stare⟩ LORDLY implies behavior or bearing befitting a nobleman but can also suggest pure pompousness or an arrogant display of power or magnificence ⟨these *lordly* archbishops who once ranked second to the emperor himself —Claudia Cassidy⟩ ⟨she had collected — or rather had received — almost with the air of a domestic, four= fifty per week from a *lordly* foreman in a shoe factory — a man who, in distributing the envelopes, had the manner of a prince doling out favors to a servile group of petitioners —Theodore Dreiser⟩ ⟨a *lordly* condescension⟩ INSOLENT implies an improper and manifest contemptuousness, suggesting a will to insult or affront ⟨vile food, vile beyond belief, slapped down before their sunken faces by *insolent* waiters —Katherine A. Porter⟩ ⟨searching the crowd until he found the face from which that *insolent* jeering came —O.E.Rölvaag⟩ ⟨an *insolent* familiarity⟩ OVERBEARING suggests a bullying or tyrannical disposition or manifest preemption of power, or an intolerable insolence ⟨backcountry militiamen whose rough *overbearing* manners sorely tried the Indians' patience —*Amer. Guide Series: Tenn.*⟩ ⟨he was arrogant, *overbearing*, conceited, and passionate — without any rank which could excuse pride, or any acquirement that could justify conceit —Anthony Trollope⟩ ⟨whose temper was so *overbearing*, that he could not restrain himself from speaking disrespectfully of that young lady at this desk —Charles Dickens⟩ SUPERCILIOUS stresses an outward appearance of patronizing haughtiness though it also suggests inner conceit and often not only scorn but also incivility ⟨he looks upon the whole struggle with the *supercilious* contempt of an indifferent spectator —Leslie Stephen⟩ ⟨his dislike of me gleamed in his blue eyes and in his *supercilious*, cold smile —Rose Macaulay⟩ DISDAINFUL implies a more contemptuous and more manifest scorn than SUPERCILIOUS ⟨nor grandeur hear with a *disdainful* smile the short and simple annals of the poor —Thomas Gray⟩ ⟨a little vanity and a little sensuality, says a *disdainful* French moralist, is about all that enters into the makeup of the average man —Irving Babbitt⟩

proud flesh *n* [ME] **:** an exuberant growth of granulation tissue in a wound or ulcer

proud·ful \-dfәl\ *adj* [ME, fr. *proud* + *-ful*] *chiefly dial* **:** marked by or full of pride ⟨a delegation of ~ citizens — Bennett Cerf⟩

proudhearted \ˈ=,==\ *adj* [ME *proudherted*, fr. *proud* + *herted* hearted — more at HEARTED] **:** proud in spirit **:** HAUGHTY ⟨~ wretch⟩

proud·ish \ˈpraůdish\ *adj* **:** somewhat proud

proud·ly *adv* [ME, fr. OE *prūtlīce*, fr. *prūd, prūt* proud + *-līce* -ly — more at PROUD] **:** in a proud manner **:** with elation ⟨a ceremonial dish . . . borne ~ into a banquet —Geoffrey Boumphrey⟩

proust·ian \ˈprüstēәn\ *adj, usu cap* [Marcel *Proust* †1922 Fr. novelist + E *-ian*] **:** of, relating to, or having the characteristics of Proust or his writings ⟨the familiar atmospheres of the *Proustian* world —J.M.O'Brien⟩ ⟨*Proustian* resonances of the recalled past —Irwin Edman⟩

proust·ite \ˈprü,stīt\ *n* -s [F, fr. Joseph L. *Proust* †1826 Fr. chemist + F *-ite*] **:** a mineral Ag_3AsS_3 that is isomorphous with pyrargyrite and consists of a silver arsenic sulfide of a cochineal red occurring in rhombohedral crystals and also massive

proust's law \ˈprüsts-\ *n, usu cap P* [after J. L. *Proust*] **:** LAW OF DEFINITE PROPORTIONS

prout's brown \ˈpraůts-\ *n, often cap P* [after Samuel *Prout* †1852 Eng. artist] **:** BROWN SUGAR 2

prout's hypothesis \ˈpraůts-\ *n, usu cap P* [after William *Prout* †1850 Eng. chemist and physician] **:** a hypothesis in chemistry: the atomic weights of all other elements are exact multiples of that of hydrogen and hence hydrogen is the primary substance from which the other elements have been formed

prov *abbr* **1** proverb; proverbial **2** provided **3** province; provincial **4** provision **5** provisional **6** provost

prov·abil·i·ty \,prüvәˈbilәd·ē\ *n* -ES **:** the quality or state of being provable

prov·able \ˈprüvәbәl\ *adj* [ME, fr. MF, fr. L *probabilis* that which may be believed, fr. *probare* to test, prove + *-abilis* -able — more at PROVE] **:** capable of being proved ⟨practical truth ~ to all men —Walter Bagehot⟩ — **prov·able·ness** *n* -ES — **prov·ably** \-blē\ *adv*

prov·and \ˈprävәnd\ *or* **prov·ant** \-nt\ *n* -s [ME *provande, provant*, fr. MD & MLG; MD *provande* & MLG *provande, provant*, fr. OF *provende* — more at PROVENDER] **1** *archaic* **:** supply of food **:** PROVISIONS **2** *chiefly dial* **:** PROVENDER 2

pro·vascular \(ˈ)prō+\ *adj* [¹*pro-* + *vascular*] **:** of or relating to procambial tissue

prove \ˈprüv\ *vb* **proved; proved** \-vd\ *or* **prov·en** \-vәn\ **proving; proves** [ME *proven*, fr. OF *prover*, fr. L *probare* to test, prove, fr. *probus* good, fr. *pro-* before, forward + *-bus* (fr. the root of *fui* I have been) — more at PRO-, BE] *vt* **1** *archaic* **:** to know by trial **:** EXPERIENCE, SUFFER ⟨be my love and we will all the pleasures ~ —Christopher Marlowe⟩ **2 a :** to test the quality of **:** try out ⟨~ all things; hold fast that which is good —1 Thess 5:21 (AV)⟩ **b :** to subject to a technical testing process **:** ascertain (as by analysis or experiment) conformity with a standard or with stipulated requirements ⟨~ coal⟩ ⟨~ gold⟩ ⟨~ a new weapon⟩ ⟨~ a meter⟩ ⟨~ a new car model⟩ **c :** PROOF 1a — often used with *up* ⟨decided to draw and ~ up a small section —*Publishers' Weekly*⟩ **d :** to determine the alcoholic content of (a liquid) **e :** to determine the worth of (a sire) by progeny testing **f** (1) **:** to make a test of (as a mineral vein) — usu. used with *up* or *out* ⟨*proved* up the . . . copper deposit —*Time*⟩ (2) **:** to establish the presence of oil under — often used with *up* (3) **:** to establish the presence of (oil) — often used with *up* ⟨*proved* up . . . 12 billion in reserves —*Time*⟩ **3 a :** to establish the truth of (as by argument or evidence) **:** DEMONSTRATE, SHOW ⟨these . . . statements can be *proved* —*William & Mary Quarterly*⟩ ⟨no charge against him was ever *proven* in court —S.H.Adams⟩ **b :** to establish the validity of (as by mathematical demonstration) ⟨could ~ the forty-seventh proposition —R.L. Stevenson⟩ **c :** to verify the correctness of (as an arithmetic operation) ⟨showed her pupils how to ~ their answers⟩ **4 :** to ascertain the genuineness of **:** VERIFY ⟨such acts, records, and proceedings shall be *proved* —*U.S.Constitution*⟩ ⟨photographic copies of the check . . . were then *proved* and admitted in evidence —*Criminal Law Rev.*⟩; *specif* **:** to obtain probate of (a will) **5 :** to raise (dough) to a desired lightness ~ *vi* **:** to turn out esp. after trial or test ⟨the medicine *proved* to be salutary⟩; *also* **:** to turn out to be ⟨the report of the war's end *proved* false⟩

syn TRY, TEST, DEMONSTRATE: PROVE is now likely to stress ascertainment as certain, true, genuine, or worthy by means of evidence, tests, or logic ⟨to become a writer was, however, in Thoreau's mind; his verses *prove* it, his Journal *proves* it — H.S.Canby⟩ ⟨he *proves* the superior importance of plot over other elements in dramatic poetry —Irving Babbitt⟩ TRY in this sense is now likely to stress subjection to experiences or tests calculated to discern the good from the bad, the strong from the weak ⟨I crumbled common crackers into the pea soup and *tried* it. It was good pea soup —Kenneth Roberts⟩ ⟨the young man should be *tried* and tested —George Meredith⟩ TEST likewise stresses subjection to tests and trials, in general to specific, planned, and regular tests calculated to reveal any deficiencies ⟨the first time he made a helmet, he *tested* its capacity for resisting blows, and battered it out of shape — Bertrand Russell⟩ ⟨he gives us the background of these witnesses, *tests* their reliability, shifts, summarizes, and collates the main portions of their evidence —*Christian Science Monitor*⟩ DEMONSTRATE is likely to stress conclusive proof or resolution and its orderly presentation with many details ⟨to *demonstrate* and popularize the Copernican hypothesis —Stringfellow Barr⟩ ⟨*demonstrated* that art did not imitate nature —F.B.Millet⟩ **syn** see INDICATE

pro·vect \prōˈvekt\ *vt* -ED/-ING/-S [L *provectus*, past part. of *provehere* to carry forward, convey onward, fr. *pro-* forward + *vehere* to carry, convey — more at PRO-, VEHICLE] **:** to change (a consonant) by provection

pro·vec·tion \-kshәn\ *n* -s [L *provectus* + E *-ion*] **1 :** CONSONANT SHIFT **2 a :** a phonetic change in Celtic languages whereby in contact with other consonants (as homorganic sonants) fricatives become the corresponding homorganic stops and voiced stops become voiceless **b :** a mutation in some Celtic languages (as Breton and Cornish) whereby a voiced consonant becomes unvoiced **3 :** the carrying forward of a final sound or letter to a following word (as in *a nickname* for *an ekename*)

proved *past of* PROVE

pro·ved·i·tor \prōˈvedәd·ә(r)\ *n* -s [It *proveditore, provveditore*, fr. *provedito, provveduto* (past part of *provedere, provvedere* to provide, purvey, fr. L *providēre* to provide) + *-ore* -or — more at PROVIDE] **1 :** a functionary in the Venetian republic having oversight of public services and government of provinces or acting as military adviser **2 :** one employed to procure supplies (as for an army, company, ship) **:** PURVEYOR

prov·e·dore *also* **provedor** *or* **prov·i·dore** \ˈprävә,dō(ә)r, -dȯ(ә)r\ *n* -s [It dial (Venice) *providore*, var. of *proveditore*] **:** PURVEYOR, PROVEDITOR

proven *past part of* PROVE

prov·e·nance \ˈprävәnәn(t)s\ *n* -s [F, fr. *provenant* coming from, originating in, fr. pres. part. of *provenir* to originate, come (from), fr. L *provenire* to come forth, originate — more at PROVENIENCE] **:** place of origin **:** SOURCE, PROVENIENCE ⟨the ~ of a lot of seed⟩ ⟨the ~ of the minerals⟩ ⟨tapestry . . . of Italian ~ —W.M.Milliken⟩ ⟨the date and ~ of the scrolls — Harold Roberts⟩ ⟨the ~ of these concepts —Gilbert Ryle⟩ **syn** see ORIGIN

¹pro·ven·çal \¦prōvәn¦säl, ¦präv-\ *adj, usu cap* [MF, fr. *Provence*, region of southeastern France (fr. L *Provincia*, lit., province) + *-al* — more at PROVINCE] **1 :** of, relating to, or characteristic of Provence, a region of France **2 :** of, relating to, or characteristic of the people of Provence

²provençal \"\ *n, pl* **provençals** *or* **proven·çaux** \-sō(z)\ *cap* [MF, fr. *provençal*, adj.] **1 a :** a native or inhabitant of Provence in France **b :** a native speaker of the Provençal language **2 :** a Romance language spoken in southeastern France

pro·ven·çale \"\ *adj, usu cap* [F, fem. of *provençal*] **:** cooked with garlic, onion, olive oil, mushrooms, and herbs ⟨frogs' legs ~⟩ ⟨~ sauce⟩

prov·ence rose \ˈprä,ven(t)s-\ *n, usu cap P* [*Provence* alter. of *Provins*, town in northern France; trans. of F *rose de Provins*] **:** CABBAGE ROSE

pro·ven·cial \prōˈvenchәl\ *archaic var of* PROVENÇAL

prov·end \ˈprävәnd\ *n* -s [ME *provende*, fr. MF — more at PROVENDER] **1** *archaic* **:** PREBEND 1 **2 :** PROVENDER

¹prov·en·der \ˈprävәndә(r)\ *n* -s [ME *provendre, provender*, fr. MF *provende, provendre*, fr. ML *provenda*, alter. (influenced by L *providēre* to provide) of *praebenda* prebend — more at PROVIDE, PREBEND] **1 :** FOOD, PROVISIONS ⟨how much ~ a . . . girl of fifteen could pack into her slender person —Harvey Fergusson⟩ **2 :** dry food for domestic animals (as hay, straw, corn, oats, or a mixture of ground grain) **:** FEED

²provender \"\ *vt* -ED/-ING/-S **:** to provide with provender

pro·ve·nience \prōˈvēnyәn(t)s, prә'-, -nēәn-\ *n* -s [by alter. (influence of L *provenient-, proveniens*, pres. part. of *provenire* to come forth, originate, fr. *pro-* forth + *venire* to come) — more at PRO-, COME] **:** PROVENANCE **syn** see ORIGIN

prov·en·ly *adv* : in a proven manner ⟨~ valuable methods —*Atlantic*⟩

pro·ven·tric·u·lar \ˌprōven·ˌtrikyələ(r)\ *adj* [NL *proventriculus* + E *-ar*] : of or relating to a proventriculus

pro·ven·tric·u·li·tis \ˌ==ˌtrikyəˈlīd·əs\ *n* -ES [NL, fr. *proventriculus* + *-itis*] : inflammation of the proventriculus of a bird usu. due to nutritional deficiencies or to parasitism

pro·ven·tric·u·lus \ˌ==ˈtrikyələs\ *also* **pro·ven·tri·cule** \prōˈven·trəˌkyül\ *n, pl* **proventricu·li** \-yəˌlī\ *also* **proventricules** [NL *proventriculus*, fr. ¹*pro-* + *ventriculus*] **1** : the glandular or true stomach of a bird situated between the crop when a crop is present and the gizzard and usu. separated from the gizzard by a constriction **2** : a muscular dilatation of the foregut in front of the midgut in most mandibulate insects that is usu. armed internally with chitinous teeth or plates for triturating food **3** : the thin-walled sac in front of the gizzard of an earthworm : CROP

prove out *vi* : to turn out to be as stated, believed, planned, expected, hoped : measure up esp. under testing ⟨in the face of the sternest handicaps, down east individualism was still *proving out* —*Time*⟩ ⟨if . . . the selected key word does not *prove out*, the compilations on possible key letters can be carried farther —Fletcher Pratt⟩ : turn out well : PROSPER, SUCCEED, THRIVE ⟨wants to wait until the five now on order . . . *prove out* —*Newsweek*⟩

prov·er \ˈprüvə(r)\ *n* -S [ME, fr. *proven* to prove + *-er* — more at PROVE] : one that proves; *specif* : PROOFER

¹**prov·erb** \ˈprä,vərb, -vəb, -vəib *sometimes* -ä,və(r)b\ *n* -S [ME *proverbe*, fr. MF, fr. L *proverbium*, fr. *pro-* before + *verbum* word — more at PRO-, WORD] **1 a** : a brief epigrammatic saying that is a popular byword : an oft-repeated pithy and ingeniously turned maxim : ADAGE, SAW ⟨referred her to the ~ "marry in haste, repent at leisure"⟩ **b** : a profound or oracular maxim; *esp* : a truth couched in obscure language : PARABLE **2** : one (as a name or person) that has become a matter of common talk : BYWORD ⟨~*s* for places no one could ever see —*Manchester Guardian Weekly*⟩ **3 proverbs** *pl but sing or pl in constr* : a game in which one player tries to guess a proverb that the others have chosen by asking questions and finding one word of the proverb in each answer — **to a proverb** *adv* : in a degree that is proverbial : PROVERBIALLY ⟨ridiculous even *to a proverb* —Tobias Smollett⟩

²**proverb** \"\ *vt* -ED/-ING/-S **1** *obs* : to provide with a proverb ⟨I am ~*ed* with a grandsire phrase —Shak.⟩ **2** : to turn into a proverb or byword ⟨~*ed* for a fool in every street —John Milton⟩

pro–verb \ˈprō+,-\ *n* [²*pro-* + *verb*] : a form of the verb *do* used to avoid repetition of a full verb (as *do* in "my brother smokes and I do too")

pro·ver·bi·al \prəˈvərbēəl, -vəb-, -vəib-\ *adj* [L *proverbialis*, fr. *proverbium* proverb + *-alis* -al — more at PROVERB] **1** : of, relating to, or resembling a proverb ⟨the ~ style⟩ ⟨~ wisdom⟩ ⟨~ comparisons⟩ **2** : that has become a proverb or byword : commonly spoken of ⟨the ~ restlessness of sailors —Herman Melville⟩ — **pro·ver·bi·al·ly** \-ēəlē, -li\ *adv*

pro·ver·bi·al·ist \-ləst\ *n* -S : one that makes, collects, or uses proverbs

proves *pres 3d sing of* PROVE

prove up *vi* **1** : to measure up to expectations : turn out well : prove out ⟨the spots where these prospector dreams *proved up* —*Amer. Guide Series: Ariz.*⟩ **2** : to bring proof of one's right to something; *specif* : to show that the requirements for receiving a patent for government land have been satisfied

prov·i·ant \ˈprävēənt\ *n* -S [G, fr. It *provianda*, fr. ML *provenda* — more at PROVENDER] : PROVENDER 1

pro·vicar \(ˈ)prō+\ *n* [²*pro-* + *vicar*] : an administrator of a vicariate apostolic

pro–vice–chancellor \ˈprō+\ *n* [²*pro-* + *vice-chancellor*] : a deputy appointed by the vice-chancellor of a British university on his election

pro·vide \prəˈvīd, prōˈ-\ *vb* -ED/-ING/-S [ME *providen*, fr. L *providēre*, to foresee, provide, provide for, fr. *pro-* before, forward + *vidēre* to see — more at PRO-, WIT] *vi* **1 a** : to take precautionary measures : make provision — used with *against* or *for* ⟨~ against an inflationary economy⟩ ⟨~ for the common defense —*U.S.Constitution*⟩ **b** *obs* : to make ready : make preparation ⟨men . . . *providing* to live another time —Alexander Pope⟩ **2** : to make a proviso or stipulation ⟨*provided* for the adoption of collective measures —Vera M. Dean⟩ **3** : to supply what is needed for sustenance or support ⟨the Lord will ~⟩ ⟨we'll have to ~ for him —Ellen Glasgow⟩ ~ *vt* **1** *archaic* : to procure in advance : get ready beforehand : PREPARE ⟨~ us all things necessary —Shak.⟩ **2 a** : to fit out or fit up : EQUIP — used with *with* ⟨*provided* the children with the books they needed⟩ ⟨~ the car with a radio⟩ **b** : to supply for use : AFFORD, YIELD ⟨olives . . . ~ an important item of food —W.B.Fisher⟩ ⟨the preface . . . ~*s* a hint —L.R.McColvin⟩ **3** : STIPULATE ⟨the contract ~*s* that the work be completed by a given date⟩ **4** *obs* : to appoint to an ecclesiastical benefice esp. before it is vacant

syn SUPPLY, FURNISH: PROVIDE and SUPPLY are often interchangeable. PROVIDE may suggest equipping, stocking, or giving in the interest of preparing with foresight ⟨to *provide* for one's wife and children⟩ ⟨*provide* the safeguard we need against the abuse of mankind's scientific genius for destructive ends —Vera M. Dean⟩ ⟨to *provide* military aid and missions for friendly countries —*Current Biog.*⟩ SUPPLY may apply to providing what is needed, sometimes to making up a deficiency, replacing losses or depletions, filling a gap ⟨the book would be incomplete without some such discussion as I have tried to *supply* —W.R.Inge⟩ ⟨an age which *supplied* the lack of moral habits by a system of moral attitudes and poses —T.S.Eliot⟩ ⟨doctors or others *supplying* medical care to assistance recipients —*Americana Annual*⟩ FURNISH, also often interchangeable with PROVIDE and SUPPLY, may sometimes apply to equipping or giving something needed in a particular situation ⟨the first attempt in history to *furnish* the international society of nations with a permanent and organic system of international political institutions —P.J.Noel-Baker⟩ ⟨our failure, he believes, is not a failure to furnish education for the average —*College English*⟩

¹**provided** *adj* [fr. past part. of *provide*] **1** *obs* : PREPARED, READY ⟨a sharp ~ wit —Shak.⟩ **2** : supplied with necessaries : EQUIPPED, FURNISHED ⟨although he never did a lick of work, was always well ~ —J.F.Dobie⟩

²**provided** *conj* [fr. past part. of *provide*] : on condition that : with the understanding : if only ⟨~ the deductions are logical —G.H.Lewes⟩ ⟨~ benefits are not claimed under any other part of this policy —*Mutual of Omaha*⟩ ⟨any hole . . . ~ only it be small and narrow —J.G.Frazer⟩

provided school *n, Brit* : COUNCIL SCHOOL

¹**prov·i·dence** \ˈprävədən(t)s *also* -dᵊn- *or* -,den-\ *n* -S [ME, fr. MF, fr. L *providentia*, fr. *provident-*, *providens* (pres. part. of *providēre* to foresee, provide, provide for) + *-ia* -y — more at PROVIDE] **1** *often cap* **a** : divine guidance or care ⟨the notion of the detailed ~ of a rational personal God —A.N.Whitehead⟩ **b** : an act or instance of such guidance or care ⟨a special ~ in the fall of a sparrow —Shak.⟩ **2** : the quality or state of being provident or of exercising foresight : PRUDENCE, THRIFT ⟨the intellectual ~ to acquire . . . vast stores of dry information —Walter Bagehot⟩ ⟨the peasant in his traditional ~ —Bernard Pares⟩ **3 a** *usu cap* : one who exercises providential power **b** *cap* : God conceived as that ultimate reality whose sustaining power and ordering activity provide continual guidance over the matters of human destiny ⟨a redeeming *Providence* presides over the rise and fall of civilizations —S.P.Cadman⟩ **syn** see PRUDENCE

²**providence** \"\ *adj, usu cap* [fr. *Providence*, Rhode Island] : of or from Providence, the capital of Rhode Island ⟨a *Providence* silversmith⟩ : of the kind or style prevalent in Providence

prov·i·dent \-nt\ *adj* [ME, fr. L *provident-*, *providens*, pres. part. of *providēre* to foresee, provide, provide for — more at PROVIDE] **1** : taking thought of the end in view : making provision for the future : prudent in anticipating conditions or needs : THRIFTY ⟨wild squirrels are ~⟩ ⟨the ~ and subtle statesman —John Buchan⟩ **2** : prudent in the use of resources : FRUGAL, SAVING ⟨can say with certainty that he is both ~ and generous —Eric Linklater⟩

prov·i·den·tial \ˌprävəˈdenchəl\ *adj* [L *providentia* providence + E *-al* — more at PROVIDENCE] **1** *archaic* : FORESIGHTED, PRUDENT ⟨the ~ raven —Thomas Hood †1845⟩ **2** : of, relating to, or determined by Providence ⟨~ guidance⟩ ⟨~ mission⟩ ⟨~ disposition of events⟩ ⟨theologic assumption that nature operates only according to a ~ plan —M.R.Cohen⟩ **3** : occurring by or as if by an intervention of Providence : highly opportune : MIRACULOUS, LUCKY ⟨~ escape⟩ ⟨seemed ~ that he should arrive at just that moment⟩ ⟨what a ~ return to sanity —W.J.Locke⟩ **syn** see LUCKY

prov·i·den·tial·ly \-chəlē, -li\ *adv* : in a providential manner: as **a** : by divine foresight ⟨a ~ destined role —H.P.Van Dusen⟩ **b** : PRUDENTLY ⟨~ absented himself —*Time*⟩ **c** : LUCKILY ⟨the weather ~ remained clear —*Saturday Rev.*⟩

prov·i·dent·ly *adv* [ME, fr. *provident* + *-ly*] : in a provident manner : PRUDENTLY

pro·vid·er \prəˈvīd·ə(r), prōˈ-\ *n* -S **1** : one that provides : PURVEYOR ⟨the government . . . is a reluctant subsidy ~ —M.H.Curtis⟩ ⟨famed ~ of borrowed finery —*Time*⟩; *esp* : one that provides for his family ⟨a man might be a great lover but a poor ~ —W.J.Reilly⟩ **2** : an iron or steel worker who makes up production schedules based on the amounts of materials needed to fill outstanding orders

providing *conj* [fr. pres. part. of *provide*] : on condition that : in case : PROVIDED ⟨~ they pay the fixed rent —John Ruskin⟩ ⟨deal with whomever they wish ~ they conform to the agreement —*Canadian Forum*⟩ ⟨~ he decided not to keep it a secret —J.F.Powers⟩

providore *var of* PROVEDORE

prov·ince \ˈprävən(t)s *sometimes* -ä,vin-\ *n* -S [F, fr. L *provincia*; perh. akin to Goth *frauja* lord, master — more at FRAU] **1 a** : a country or a more or less remote region brought under the control of the ancient Roman government **b** : an administrative district or division of a country or empire ⟨the ~*s* of old Spain⟩ ⟨the ~*s* of Canada⟩ **c** (1) : a portion of a country; *esp* : one remote from or outside of the capital or largest city (2) **provinces** *pl* : all of a country outside of the metropolis — usu. used with *the* ⟨a shabby theatrical troupe which tours *the provinces* —Donald Heiney⟩ **2** [ME, fr. MF, fr. ML *provincia*, fr. L] **a** : any of the principal ecclesiastical divisions of a country forming the jurisdiction of an archbishop or metropolitan ⟨the ~ of Canterbury⟩ **b** : a territorial division of a religious order ⟨the general of the order administers several ~*s*⟩ **c** : a Salvation Army administrative unit smaller than a territory and larger than a division **3 a** : a biogeographic division of less rank than a region; *esp* : a primary division of a subregion **b** : an area throughout which geological history has been essentially the same or which is characterized by particular structural, petrographical, or physiographical features **4 a** : proper or appropriate business or scope (as of a person or body) : SPHERE, JURISDICTION ⟨semantic questions . . . are outside his ~ —*English Language Teaching*⟩ **b** : a department of knowledge or activity ⟨humanitarianism invaded one ~ of life after another —G.M.Trevelyan⟩ **syn** see FIELD, FUNCTION

¹**pro·vin·cial** \prəˈvinchəl, prōˈ-\ *n* -S [in sense 1, fr. ME, fr. MF or ML; MF, fr. ML *provincialis*, fr. *provincia* ecclesiastical province + L *-alis* -al; in other senses, fr. L *provincialis*, fr. *provincia* province + *-alis* -al — more at PROVINCE] **1** *sometimes cap* : a religious superior in the Roman Catholic Church who has direction under the general of his order of all religious houses in a province of the order **2 a** : one living in or coming from a province ⟨delegations of ~*s* —Robert Graves⟩; *specif* : a soldier recruited from a province (as a Roman province or an American colony before the Revolution) — usu. used in pl. ⟨3500 ~*s* . . . moved north against Crown Point —Arthur Pound⟩ **b** : a person of local or restricted interests or outlook ⟨the true ~'s attachment to a region —Milton Rugoff⟩ **c** : one who exhibits markedly the special characteristics (as of speech and customs) of a section of a country ⟨classifies the four novelists as ~*s* —James Gray⟩ **d** : a person lacking the polish and refinement of urban society

²**provincial** \"\ *adj* [ME, fr. *provincial*, adj.] **1 a** : of or relating to a province ⟨a ~ government⟩ ⟨a ~ dialect⟩ ⟨our greater ~ libraries —*Notes & Queries*⟩ **b** *obs* : having the subordinate relationship of a province ⟨the aforesaid country . . . now ~ to Denmark —William Warner⟩ **2** : confined to a province or region : limited in scope : NARROW, SECTIONAL ⟨~ interests⟩ ⟨a ~ attitude of mind⟩ ⟨helps free us from the ~ and the merely local —E.J.McGrath⟩ **3 a** : exhibiting the ways and manners of a province or rural district : COUNTRIFIED, UNSOPHISTICATED ⟨~ airs and graces —T.B.Macaulay⟩ ⟨no ~ twang in their writings —H.O.Taylor⟩ **b** : of, relating to, or constituting a decorative style (as in furniture and architecture) that is of country rather than courtly origin and is usu. marked by simplicity in design, informality in character, and relative plainness in decoration ⟨a French ~ style house⟩ ⟨~ chest of . . . faded walnut —*Antiques*⟩ ⟨~ designs . . . in hooked rugs —Mildred J. O'Brien⟩

pro·vin·cial·ate \-chələt, -chə,lāt\ *n* -S **1 a** : the office of a provincial **b** : the term of office of a provincial **2** : the motherhouse of a provincial

provincial court *n* : the court of an archbishop within his province or jurisdiction ⟨the *provincial court* of Canterbury⟩

pro·vin·cial·ism \-chə,lizəm\ *n* -S **1** : a dialectal or local word, phrase, or idiom ⟨answers come back in . . . slang, ~*s*, profanity —S.L.Payne⟩ **2** : the quality or state of being provincial: as **a** : exclusive attachment to one's own province, region, or country ⟨tourists shedding their ~⟩; *specif* : devotion to provincial autonomy ⟨went back to the pub to argue ~ —*Sunday Express (Johannesburg) So. Africa*⟩ **b** : indifference to what is alien, unfamiliar, or diverse : narrowness or limitation (as in interests, views, or thought) — contrasted with *cosmopolitanism* ⟨intellectual ~⟩ ⟨relation between temporal . . . cultural or national ~ —*Jour. of Philosophy*⟩ ⟨a newspaper steeped in biased ~ —Herbert Brucker⟩

pro·vin·cial·ist \-ləst\ *n* -S **1** : a native or inhabitant of a province : PROVINCIAL **2** : an advocate of provincialism esp. in politics ⟨the electorate was divided into centralists and ~*s* —Alexander Brady⟩

pro·vin·ci·al·i·ty \prə,vinchēˈaləd·ē, prō,- , -ətē, -i\ *n* -ES **1** : the quality or state of being provincial : PROVINCIALISM ⟨lack of intercourse with others . . . with a consequent increase in his aloofness and ~ —J.T.Adams⟩ ⟨the ~ of his thought —Winthrop Sargeant⟩ ⟨the whole scene, paltry, confined, and dull . . . the extreme of ~ —Arnold Bennett⟩ **2** : an act or instance of provincialism ⟨biased . . . by the *provincialities* of groups —A.N.Whitehead⟩

pro·vin·cial·iza·tion \prə,vinchələˈzāshən\ *n* -S : the act or process of provincializing ⟨practiced a further ~ of provincial styles —*Antiques*⟩

pro·vin·cial·ize \prəˈvinchə,līz, prōˈ-\ *vt* -ED/-ING/-S [¹*provincial* + *-ize*] : to make provincial : bring under provincial influence or control ⟨tended to divide, to ~, and to brutalize mankind —*Harper's*⟩ ⟨every branch of expenditure . . . was *provincialized* —*Pall Mall Gazette*⟩

pro·vin·ci·ate \prəˈvinchē,āt\ *vt* -ED/-ING/-S [L *provincia* province + E *-ate* — more at PROVINCE] : to convert into a province : give a provincial status to

pro·vinculum \prō+\ *n* [NL, fr. ¹*pro-* + *vinculum*] : a primitive hinge composed of minute teeth developed before the permanent dentition in some bivalve mollusks

pro·vine \prōˈvīn\ *vt* -ED/-ING/-S [ME *provinen*, fr. MF *provigner*, fr. *provain* layer (of plants), fr. L *propagin-*, *propago*, fr. *propages* — more at PROPAGATE] : LAYER

proving *pres part of* PROVE

proving ground *n* **1** : a place or area for scientific experimentation or testing (as of aircraft, vehicles, weapons) ⟨the laboratories, pilot plants, and *proving grounds* of the nation —H.S.Truman⟩ **2** : a place where something new is tried out ⟨the *proving ground* for one of the most comprehensive social experiments —*Amer. Guide Series: Tenn.*⟩

proving press *n* : a small usu. hand-operated press for pulling printer's proofs

proving ring *n* : an elastic-shell ring used to calibrate testing machines by means of change in diameter undergone upon application of force along the diameter

pro·virus \(ˈ)prō+\ *n* [NL, fr. ¹*pro-* + *virus*] : a noninfectious intracellular form of a virus that behaves in the host cell as though it were a plasmagene

¹**pro·vi·sion** \prəˈvizhən, prōˈ-\ *n* [ME, fr. MF, fr. LL & L; LL *provision-*, *provisio* action of providing, provisions, fr. L, foresight, fr. *provisus* (past part. of *providēre* to foresee, provide, provide with) + *-ion-*, *-io* -ion — more at PROVIDE] **1 a** : promotion to office by an ecclesiastical superior; *esp* : appointment to a benefice not yet vacant ⟨through . . . a papal ~ he was made bishop —G.C.Sellery⟩ **b** : *Scots law* : a gift by will or deed to one as heir who would not be heir otherwise — compare HEIR OF PROVISION **c** *usu cap* : any of various laws enacted in the 13th and early 14th centuries by the assemblies of the English prelates and nobles or issued by the king with their consent ⟨*Provisions* of Oxford⟩ **2 a** : the act or process of providing ⟨the ~ of a play area for the children⟩ ⟨the ~ of free speech is . . . a weapon of enlightenment —Lucius Garvin⟩ **b** : the quality or state of being prepared beforehand ⟨cast upon the world without ~ —J.H.Newman⟩ **c** : a measure taken beforehand : PREPARATION ⟨~ . . . for decentralization —Vera M. Dean⟩ ⟨~ for inserting . . . die slings —*Steel*⟩ **3** : a stock of needed materials or supplies ⟨caravans expecting water or ~ at a designated spot —Irving Stone⟩; *esp* : a stock of food : VICTUALS — usu. used in pl. ⟨a basket of ~*s* — Green Peyton⟩ **4** : a stipulation (as a clause in a statute or contract) made in advance : PROVISO ⟨bequeathed the house with the ~ that it be preserved⟩ ⟨this ~ is one of fundamental importance in our legal . . . system —E.N.Griswold⟩ **syn** see CONDITION

²**provision** \"\ *vt* : to supply with provisions : VICTUAL ⟨trips to ~ the island —Ben Holt⟩ ⟨have an amply ~*ed* look that betrays their bucolic childhood —*Amer. Mercury*⟩

provision account *n* : RESERVE ACCOUNT 1

¹**pro·vi·sion·al** \-zhənᵊl, -zhnəl\ *adj* [¹*provision* + *-al*] **1** : provided for a temporary need : suitable or acceptable in the existing situation but subject to change or nullification : TENTATIVE, CONDITIONAL ⟨a ~ government set up in territory freed from enemy control⟩ ⟨a ~ appointment⟩ ⟨a ~ classification⟩ ⟨a ~ interpretation of the data⟩ ⟨their beliefs are relative and ~ —Walter Lippmann⟩ **2** *archaic* : marked by foresight : PROVIDENT ⟨this ~ care in every species —Oliver Goldsmith⟩ **3** : of or relating to special or extraordinary legal acts or proceedings allowed before final judgment to protect the interests of one or more parties to an action at law (as under the code procedure of New York and some other states remedies had by order of arrest, warrant of attachment, temporary injunction, or appointment of a receiver) **4** *of a postage stamp* : overprinted or issued for temporary use esp. as a substitute for a regular issue that has not yet been made or that has not yet been received in the country or territory where it is to be used — contrasted with *definitive* — **pro·vi·sion·al·ly** \-zhənᵊlē, -zhnəlē, -i\ *adv*

²**provisional** \"\ *n* -S : a provisional postage stamp

provisional order *n* : an order (as on a matter of local concern normally dealt with by a private bill) issued by a British governmental agency under powers granted by parliament and having the force of law subject to specific parliamentary confirmation by means of a provisional orders confirmation bill

pro·vi·sion·ary \-zhə,nerē, -ri\ *adj* [¹*provision* + *-ary*] : PROVISIONAL

pro·vi·sion·er \-zh(ə)nə(r)\ *n* -S : a furnisher of provisions : PURVEYOR, VICTUALLER ⟨the . . . farmers were the chief ~*s* of the armies —A.D.Graeff⟩

pro·vi·sion·ment \-zhənmənt\ *n* -S : supply of provisions ⟨carrying little ~ —Willa Cather⟩

provision tree *n* : a tropical American tree (*Pachira aquatica*) of the family Bombacaceae having large heavy russet fruits with edible brown seeds

pro·vi·so \prəˈvī(,)zō, prōˈ-\ *n, pl* **provisos** *or* **provisoes** [ME, fr. L, provided (abl. of *provisum*, neut. of *provisus*, past part. of *providēre* to provide), in *proviso quod* provided that, a phrase with which clauses in medieval legal documents often began — more at PROVIDE] **1** : an article or clause (as in a statute, contract, or grant) that introduces a condition, qualification, or limitation and usu. begins with the word *provided* ⟨a ~ . . . to modify the operation of that part of the statute —G.D.Oxner⟩ — compare PURVIEW **2** : a conditional stipulation : RESERVATION ⟨expresses the belief only with a skeptical ~ —H.R.Finch⟩ **syn** see CONDITION

pro·vi·sor \prəˈvīzə(r)\ *n* -S [ME *provisour*, fr. AF, ML, & L; AF *provisour* ecclesiastical provisor, fr. ML *provisor* ecclesiastical provisor, guardian, administrator, fr. L, one that provides, fr. *provisus* (past part. of *providēre* to provide) + *-or* — more at PROVIDE] **1** : one having a provision esp. papal to a benefice not yet vacant — compare PROVISION 1a **2** : one having charge of getting provisions (as for an army or a religious house) : PURVEYOR, STEWARD **3** *obs* : one who provides (as care, protection, sustenance) : GUARDIAN **4** : a cleric acting as an assistant to or vicar for an archbishop or bishop : an ecclesiastical deputy

pro·vi·so·ri·ly \-zərəlē\ *adv* : in a provisory manner

pro·vi·so·ry \-zərē, -ri\ *adj* [F or ML; F *provisoire*, fr. ML *provisorius*, fr. L *provisus* (past part. of *providēre* to provide) + *-orius* -ory — more at PROVIDE] **1** : containing or subject to a proviso : CONDITIONAL ⟨a ~ clause⟩ **2** : PROVISIONAL 1 ⟨human institutions as ~ and precarious —Edmund Wilson⟩

pro·vitamin \(ˈ)prō+\ *n* [¹*pro-* + *vitamin*] : a precursor of a vitamin that can be converted into a vitamin in the organism ⟨ergosterol is a ~ of vitamin D_2⟩

provitamin A *n* : a provitamin of vitamin A; *esp* : CAROTENE

provn *abbr* provision

pro·vo \ˈprō(,)vō\ *archaic var of* PROVOST

provocateur *n* [F (*agent*) *provocateur*] : AGENT PROVOCATEUR

prov·o·ca·tion \,prävəˈkāshən\ *n* -S [ME *provocacioun*, fr. MF *provocation*, fr. L *provocation-*, *provocatio*, fr. *provocatus* (past part. of *provocare* to call forth, provoke) + *-ion-*, *-io* -ion — more at PROVOKE] **1** : the act or process of provoking : STIMULATION, INCITEMENT ⟨~*s* to further thought about our own dilemmas —E.R.May⟩ ⟨ready to smash them to pieces on the slightest ~ —Havelock Ellis⟩ ⟨her every movement was a ~ —S.B.Kaiser⟩ **2 a** *archaic* : APPEAL; *esp* : an appeal to a higher court **b** : the right of a Roman citizen condemned in a criminal action to appeal to the Roman people or the emperor

¹**pro·voc·a·tive** \prəˈväkəd·iv, prōˈ-, -ət| *also* |əv\ *n* -S [ME, fr. MF *provocatif*, adj.] **1** *archaic* : something that arouses desire or appetite; *esp* : APHRODISIAC ⟨greedy after vicious ~*s* —S.T. Coleridge⟩ **2** : something that provokes : STIMULUS, INCENTIVE ⟨a ~ to mirth —A.D.White⟩ ⟨his society tends to supply few ~*s* —Abram Kardiner⟩ ⟨prove suitable . . . as a ~ for allergic tests —R.T.Leiper⟩

²**provocative** \"\ *adj* [F *provocatif*, fr. LL *provocativus* calling forth, eliciting, fr. L *provocatus* + *-ivus* -ive] : serving or tending to provoke: as **a** : calling forth a desired feeling or action ⟨~ Irish tunes which . . . compel the hearers to dance —Anthony Trollope⟩ **b** : pleasantly stimulating : APPEALING, PIQUANT ⟨her features are ~ and lively —J.K.Newnham⟩ **c** : exciting sexual desire ⟨her gestures and postures became . . . more wanton and ~ —C.B.Nordhoff & J.N.Hall⟩ **d** : exciting irritation, resentment, or anger ⟨prepared for war without being ~ —*Atlantic*⟩ **e** : arousing curiosity or anticipation ⟨~ glimpses of characters —Carol Field⟩ **f** : stimulating discussion or controversy ⟨one of the most ~ . . . novels —*Saturday Rev.*⟩ ⟨toss a ~ political comment into the conversation —R.C.Doty⟩ — **pro·voc·a·tive·ly** \|əvlē, -li\ *adv* — **pro·voc·a·tive·ness** \|ivnəs\ *n* -ES

pro·voc·a·to·ry \-kə,tōrē\ *adj* [L *provocatorius*, fr. *provocatus* + *-orius* -ory] : PROVOCATIVE

pro·voke \prəˈvōk, prōˈ-\ *vt* -ED/-ING/-S [ME *provoken*, fr. MF *provoquer*, fr. L *provocare*, fr. *pro-* forth + *vocare* to call — more at PRO-, VOCATION] **1 a** *archaic* : to stir to a desired feeling or action : move deeply : AROUSE ⟨your zeal hath *provoked* very many —2 Cor 9:2 (AV)⟩ **b** : to incite to anger : INCENSE ⟨enough to ~ a saint⟩ ⟨loved to . . . make his brakes screech just to ~ her —H.H.Reichard⟩ **2** *archaic* : SUMMON, EVOKE ⟨can honor's voice ~ the silent dust? —Thomas Gray⟩ **3 a** : to call forth (an emotion, action, activity) : bring on : EVOKE ⟨a device that *provoked* an unfailing roar of laughter —*Saturday Rev.*⟩ ⟨his candor *provoked* a storm of controversy —*Times Lit. Supp.*⟩ ⟨no area of school learning ~*s* as much concern —*Education Digest*⟩ **b** : to stir up on purpose : bring about deliberately ⟨had foreseen and even *provoked* this invasion —Francis Hackett⟩ ⟨did his best to ~ an argument —Lester Atwell⟩ **c** : to provide the needed stimulus for : call into being ⟨*provoking* a vigorous development of logical studies —*Times Lit. Supp.*⟩ ⟨not merely anticipated the new methods but actually *provoked* them —Bryan Morgan⟩ **d :** to induce (a physical reaction) ⟨~ vomiting by tickling the throat⟩ ⟨the hit . . . may ~ the nucleus to eject a particle —G.W.Gray b. 1886⟩

syn EXCITE, STIMULATE, PIQUE, QUICKEN: PROVOKE may center attention on the fact of rousing to action or calling forth a response; often it implies little about cause, manner, or result, but is often used in connection with angry or vexed reactions ⟨his personal emotions, the emotions *provoked* by particular events in his life —T.S.Eliot⟩ ⟨to imagine the emotions and the actions of which she might *provoke* a man —B.A.Williams⟩ ⟨it was not until the end of October that Turkey, by bombarding Russian Black Sea ports, *provoked* the Allies into declaring war on her —C.E.Black & E.C.Helmreich⟩ EXCITE, sometimes close to provoke, may suggest a more active stirring up, moving profoundly, awakening lively interest, or rousing to marked activity ⟨feeling, which had drugged her until only half of her being was awake, had *excited* him into an unusual mental activity. He was animated, eager, weaving endless impracticable schemes —Ellen Glasgow⟩ ⟨they were interested and *excited* by this prophetic voice calling for a renaissance in American political life —Bruce Bliven b. 1889⟩ ⟨your letter as usual *excites* my envy at the description of your finds —O.W.Holmes †1935⟩ STIMULATE applies to the heightening of activity or the rousing of the dominant or quiescent by something that spurs or incites or overcomes whatever makes for inactivity ⟨increasing the supply of liquid assets in order to *stimulate* spending —W.M.Dacey⟩ ⟨extra iron may be supplied to *stimulate* the formation of red blood cells —Morris Fishbein⟩ ⟨his own thought was clarified by the impulse to coherent intelligibility which good teaching *stimulates* —M.R.Cohen⟩ PIQUE suggests provoking by mild irritation, slight, challenge, rebuff, or inciting curiosity or jealousy ⟨one's interest is *piqued* but not captured by the chronicle of this weak-willed man —*N.Y.Times*⟩ ⟨the contrast between the pair held puzzles that *piqued* the inquisitive —Arnold Bennett⟩ QUICKEN applies to a general vivifying, stimulating, or making active, often beneficially ⟨the sound of tuning strings combined with the hum of voices and the flutter of programs to *quicken* yet more the thrill of expectancy that ran down her veins —Clive Arden⟩ ⟨his response was *quickened* and deepened by his mystical temperament —*Times Lit. Supp.*⟩ ⟨with his feeling of history *quickened* and sharpened, he was to find another stimulus to follow up this interest —Van Wyck Brooks⟩ **syn** see in addition IRRITATE

pro·vok·ing *adj* **:** PROVOCATIVE; *esp* **:** EXASPERATING ⟨will find the lack of any index . . . ~ —L.S.Hall⟩ — **pro·vok·ing·ly** *adv*

pro·vo·la \ˈprōvələ\ *n* -s [It, prob. fr. ML *probula* cheese made from buffalo milk] **:** a small round flaky cheese made of plastic curd and hung in a net to cure

pro·vo·lette \ˌprōvəˈlet\ *n* -s [*provola* + *-ette*] **:** a small round or pear-shaped cheese of stringy texture hung in a net to cure

pro·vo·lo·ne \ˌprōvəˈlōnē\ *also* **provolone cheese** *n* -s [It *provolone*, aug. of *provola*] **:** an often pear-shaped cheese of stringy texture made of plastic curd, molded in various forms, and hung in a net to cure

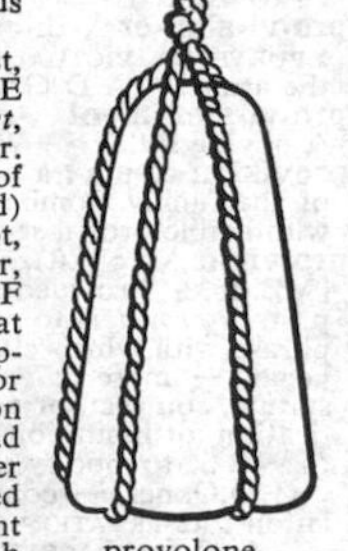
provolone

pro·vost \ˈprōˌvōst, ˈprävəst, ˈprōvəst, *esp as attributive* ˈprō(ˌ)vō\ *n* -s [ME *provost, provest*, partly fr. OE *prafost, profast, profost*, fr. ML *propositus*, alter. (influenced by L *propositus*, past part. of *proponere* to display, declare, propound) of ML *prepositus, praepositus* abbot, prior, provost & L *praepositus* director, chief, man in charge; partly fr. OF *provost*, fr. ML *propositus* — more at PROPOSE, PREPOSITUS] **1 :** a person appointed to superintend, preside over, or be the official head of (as an institution or corporate body): as **a** (1) **:** the head of a cathedral or collegiate chapter (2) **:** the head of a newly-constituted cathedral church (3) **:** a Protestant clergyman in charge of the chief church of a region in Germany (4) **:** an ecclesiastic whose duties approximate those of a dean or prior but who at times is second in authority to a dean, prior, or abbot **b :** the chief magistrate of a Scottish burgh corresponding to the mayor of an English city **c** (1) **:** the steward or bailiff of a feudal manor (2) **:** the reeve of a medieval tithing borough or town (3) **:** the officer in charge of a royal establishment (as a mint) **d :** the keeper of a prison **e** (1) **:** the head of any of several British colleges (2) **:** a high-ranking administrative officer of an American university **f :** PROVOST MARSHAL **2 :** a fencer of lower rank than a maître d'armes — **prov·ost·al** \ˈprävəstᵊl\ *adj*

provost court *n* **:** a military court usu. for the trial of minor offenses and of limited jurisdiction within an occupied hostile territory

provost guard *n* **:** a police detail of soldiers under the authority of the provost marshal — compare MILITARY POLICE

provost marshal *n* **:** an officer who supervises the military police of a command esp. in keeping order among military personnel outside areas patrolled by an interior guard and who as a staff officer advises the commander on military police matters

prov·ost·ry \ˈprävəstrē\ *n* -ES [ME *provostrie*, fr. *provost, provest* provost + *-rie* -ry — more at PROVOST] **1 :** the office or authority of a provost of a cathedral or collegiate church **2 a :** an ecclesiastical foundation (as a cathedral or collegiate church) **b :** the revenue from such a foundation

pro·vost·ship *pronunc at* PROVOST + ˌship\ *n* **:** the office or jurisdiction of a provost (as of the provost of an ecclesiastical or educational college or of a Scottish burgh)

¹prow \ˈprau̇\ *adj* -ER/-EST [ME, fr. MF *prou, preu*, like MF *prou, preu* profit, advantage fr. LL *prode* — more at PROUD] *archaic* **:** VALIANT, GALLANT ⟨the ~*est* knight that ever field did fight —Edmund Spenser⟩

²prow \"\ *n* -s [MF, fr. OF *proe*, prob. fr. OIt (Genoese dial.) *prua*, fr. L *prora*, fr. Gk *prōira*; perh. akin to Gk *peran* to pass through — more at FARE] **1 :** the bow of a ship **:** STEM, BEAK ⟨stepped firmly to the boat's ~ —Charles Spielberger⟩ **2 :** a pointed projecting front part (as of a racing skate, airplane, chariot) ⟨turned the snowshoe sled so its ~ was headed down canyon —W.V.T.Clark⟩ ⟨other toques . . . have visor ~*s* —Lois Long⟩

³prow \"\ *var of* PRAU

prow·ess \ˈprau̇əs\ *n* -ES [ME *prouesse, prowesse*, fr. OF *proece, proesse*, fr. *prod, prud, prou* good, capable, brave — more at PROUD] **1 :** distinguished bravery **:** GALLANTRY; *esp* **:** military valor and skill ⟨supposed warlike exploits . . . details of their imaginary ~ —J.G.Frazer⟩ **2 :** extraordinary ability **:** EXCELLENCE ⟨the politician's ~ in debate⟩ ⟨his ~ on the football field⟩ ⟨power derived from . . . technical ~ —Raymond Aron⟩ ⟨his ~ with a forty-five —Green Peyton⟩

¹prowl \ˈprau̇l, *esp before pause or consonant* -au̇əl\ *vb* -ED/-ING/-S [ME *prollen*] *vi* **:** to move about or wander stealthily in the manner of a wild beast seeking prey **:** roam in search or as if in search of whatever may be found **:** pace restlessly back and forth ⟨submarines were ~*ing* along our coast —Owen Wister⟩ ⟨the fear still ~*s* in her consciousness —Ellen Glasgow⟩ ⟨the foreman . . . ~*ing* constantly about —Theodore Dreiser⟩ ⟨~*s* as he talks —T.R.Ybarra⟩ ⟨loved to ~ about the city⟩ ~ *vt* **:** to roam over (an area) in a predatory manner ⟨wolves ~ the forest⟩ ⟨the bloodthirstiest villain that ever ~*ed* the Western highways —Herbert Asbury⟩

²prowl \"\ *n* -s **:** an act or instance of prowling ⟨his jubilant ~ through . . . attics —C.G.Poore⟩ — often used in the phrase *on the prowl* ⟨a rapacious divorcee on the ~ —Helen Howe⟩

prowl car *n* **:** SQUAD CAR

prowl·er \-lə(r)\ *n* -s **:** one that prowls ⟨a ~ through junk shops —H.H.Martin⟩ ⟨car ~*s* . . . agog for a pickup —*Harper's*⟩; *esp* **:** SNEAK THIEF ⟨~*s* made off with . . . men's clothing —*Edmonton (Alberta) Jour.*⟩

prox \ˈpräks\ *n* -ES [short for *proxy*] *NewEng* **:** BALLOT

prox *abbr* proximo

prox·e·nete \ˈpräksəˌnēt\ *also* **prox·e·net** \-net\ *n* -s [F or L; F *proxénète*, fr. L *proxeneta*, fr. Gk *proxenētēs*, fr. *proxenein* to do something for someone else, fr. *proxenos*] **:** a person who negotiates on another's behalf; *specif* **:** MARRIAGE BROKER

prox·e·nus \ˈpräksənəs\ *also* **prox·e·nos** \-ksəˌnäs\ *n, pl* **prox·e·ni** \-ksəˌnī\ *also* **prox·e·noi** \-ksəˌnoi\ [NL, fr. Gk *proxenos*, fr. *pro* before, for + *xenos* stranger, guest — more at FOR] **:** a citizen of a city state in ancient Greece appointed by another state to have charge of its interests and the welfare of its citizens while in his state

proxied *past of* PROXY

proxies *pl of* PROXY, *pres 3d sing of* PROXY

prox·i·mad \ˈpräksəˌmad\ *adv* [L *proximus* + E *-ad*] **:** PROXIMALLY

prox·i·mal \ˈpräksəməl\ *adj* [L *proximus* + E *-al*] **1 :** situated close to ⟨the magnetic compass . . . in ~ polar areas —*Scientific Monthly*⟩ **2 :** next to or nearest the point of attachment or origin, a point conceived of as central, or the point of view ⟨the ~ was . . . better than the peripheral stump for a graft —*Annual Rev. of Med.*⟩ ⟨more sediment is deposited on the ~ . . . slopes —P.H.Kuenen⟩; *esp* **:** located toward the center of the body ⟨the ~ end of a bone⟩ — opposed to *distal* **3 :** sensory rather than physical or social ⟨~ stimuli —D.W.Hamlyn⟩ — opposed to *distal*

proximal convoluted tubule *n* **:** the convoluted portion of the vertebrate nephron that lies between the Malpighian corpuscle and the loop of Henle, is made up of a single layer of cuboidal cells with striated borders, and is believed to be concerned esp. with the resorption of sugar, sodium and chloride ions, and water from the glomerular filtrate — see DISTAL CONVOLUTED TUBULE

prox·i·mal·ly \-məlē, -li\ *adv* **:** toward or near a proximal part or point

prox·i·mate \ˈpräksəmət, *usu* -əd·+V\ *adj* [L *proximatus*, past part. of *proximare* to come near, approach, fr. *proximus*, nearest, next, superl. of *prope* near — more at APPROACH] **1 a :** very near **:** immediately adjoining **:** CLOSE ⟨singed . . . at the too ~ candle —J.W.Krutch⟩ ⟨a playwright so ~ to the century mark —Dan Laurence⟩ **b :** soon forthcoming **:** IMMINENT, NEXT ⟨news of his ~ arrival⟩ ⟨the ~ possibility of space travel —Pius Walsh⟩ ⟨on Tuesday ~ —George Meredith⟩ **2 :** next immediately preceding or following (as in a chain of causes or effects) ⟨an interest in ~, rather than ultimate, goals —Reinhold Niebuhr⟩ ⟨the ~ cause of their disaster —Elmer Davis⟩ ⟨one of the ~ effects will be to increase consumer spending —James Tobin⟩ — compare REMOTE, ULTIMATE **3 :** nearly accurate or correct **:** APPROXIMATE ⟨make a ~ estimate⟩ ⟨a ~ graduation scale —H.J.Wegrocki⟩ ⟨the figures . . . give at least a ~ explanation of price behavior —James Tobin⟩ **4 :** determined by proximate analysis as opposed to ultimate analysis ⟨~ composition⟩ **5** *of a grammatical form* **:** denoting the first of two third persons referred to in a context (as in the construction in some languages corresponding to "John caught sight of Albert and *he* [John] told him the news") — compare OBVIATIVE — **prox·i·mate·ly** *adv* — **prox·i·mate·ness** *n* -ES

proximate analysis *n* **:** quantitative analysis of a mixture (as food, coal) in which the percentage of components is determined

proximate cause *n* **:** a cause that directly or with no mediate agency produces an effect; *specif* **:** a cause arising out of a wrongdoer's negligence or conduct deemed under the rules of law applicable to the case and under the extent of his duty sufficient to hold him liable for the particular harm in fact resulting therefrom as distinguished from a remote cause or any supervening or concurring cause for which he is not deemed chargeable under those rules

proximate matter *n* **1 :** matter ready for the reception of a form — compare MATTER 3b **2 :** MATTER OF A SYLLOGISM 1

proximate principles *or* **proximate substances** *n pl* **:** compounds occurring naturally in animal and vegetable tissues and separable by analytical methods ⟨the *proximate principles* of food are proteins, fats, carbohydrates, mineral salts, and water⟩

prox·ime \ˈpräksəm\ *adj* [L *proximus* nearest, next — more at PROXIMATE] *archaic* **:** PROXIMATE

prox·im·i·ty \präkˈsimədē, -ətē, -i\ *n* -ES [MF *proximité*, fr. L *proximitat-, proximitas*, fr. *proximus* nearest, next + *-itat-, -itas* -ity — more at PROXIMATE] **:** the quality or state of being proximate, next, or very near (as in time, place, relationship) **:** immediate or close propinquity **:** NEARNESS ⟨research facilitated by ~ to a great library⟩ ⟨marriages in ~ of blood⟩

proximity effect *n* **:** the mutual effect of the currents in closely adjacent conductors (as the turns of a coil) producing an apparent increase in resistance esp. with high-frequency alternating current

proximity fuze *n* **:** an electronic device that detonates a projectile within effective range of the target by means of the radio waves sent out from a tiny radio set in the nose of the projectile and reflected back to the set from the target — called also *radio proximity fuze, variable time fuze, VT fuze*

prox·i·mo \ˈpräksəˌmō\ *adj* [L *proximo* (*mense*) in the next (month), fr. abl. sing. masc. of *proximus* nearest, next — more at PROXIMATE] **:** of or occurring in the next month after the present — abbr. *prox.* ⟨to be held on the 6th *prox.*⟩; compare INSTANT, ULTIMO

proximo- *comb form* [*proximal*] **:** proximal ⟨*proximo*buccal⟩ — opposed to *dist-*

¹proxy \ˈpräksē, -si\ *n* -ES [ME *procusie, prokecye, proccy*, contr. of *procuracie* procuracy — more at PROCURACY] **1 :** the act or practice of a person serving (as in voting or marrying) as an authorized agent or substitute for another **:** the agency, function, or office of a deputy or procurator — used chiefly in the phrase *by proxy* ⟨vote by ~⟩ ⟨appear by ~⟩ ⟨marriage by ~⟩ **2 a :** authority or power to act for another **b :** a document giving such authorization; *specif* **:** a power of attorney given and signed by a stockholder authorizing a specified person or persons to vote corporate stock ⟨send *proxies* for the directors' meeting⟩ **3 a :** a person authorized to act for another **:** PROCURATOR **b :** something serving to replace another thing or substance **:** SUBSTITUTE ⟨books . . . were not *proxies* for experience —Frederick Mayer⟩ **4 :** PROCURATION 3 **5** *NewEng* **a :** BALLOT **b proxies** *pl* **:** ELECTION

²proxy \"\ *adj* **1 a :** taking the place of another ⟨a ~ mother of several large families —Booth Tarkington⟩ **b** *of a mineral* **:** occurring where another mineral would normally be expected **2 :** carried on by proxy ⟨~ voting⟩ or by solicitation and control of proxies ⟨a ~ war for control of a corporation⟩

³proxy \"\ *vi* -ED/-ING/-ES **:** to occur as a proxy mineral ⟨the gold . . . may ~ for iron ions in a growing pyrite crystal —*Economic Geology*⟩

proxy marriage *n* **:** a marriage that is celebrated in the absence of one of the contracting parties who however authorizes a proxy or substitute to represent him at the ceremony for the purpose of entering into marriage with the other and is valid in some, voidable in some, and void in other states of the U.S.

pro·zone \ˈprōˌzōn\ *n* [¹*pro-* + *zone*] **:** the portion of the range of concentration of antibody-antigen mixtures in which one of them although present in excess does not produce its characteristic effect (as agglutination or precipitation)

prs *abbr* present

prsfdr *abbr* press feeder

prsmn *abbr* pressman

prtr *abbr* printer

PRU *abbr* photographic reconnaisance unit

¹prude \ˈprüd\ *n* -s [F, wise or good woman, prudish woman, short for *prudefemme* wise or good woman, fr. MF, alter. of *preudefemme*, fr. OF *prode femme*, fr. *prode* (fem. of *prod, prud, prou* good, capable, brave) + *femme* woman — more at PROUD, FEMME] **:** a person who is excessively or priggishly attentive to propriety or oversensitive to slight breaches of decorum ⟨not a book for ~*s* —*Saturday Rev.*⟩ ⟨"you're ~*s* . . . this and that can't be discussed before you" —Henry Green⟩; *esp* **:** a woman who shows or affects extreme modesty or reticence (as in speech, behavior, or dress) ⟨cold, heartless, a ~, he called her —Virginia Woolf⟩ ⟨a ~ . . . virtuously flies from the temptation of her desires —Ambrose Bierce⟩

²prude \"\ *adj* [F, back-formation fr. *prudefemme*] *archaic* **:** PRUDISH

pru·dence \ˈprüdᵊn(t)s\ *n* -s [ME, fr. MF, fr. L *prudentia*, alter. of *providentia* foresight, providence — more at PROVIDENCE] **:** the quality or state of being prudent: as **a :** wisdom shown in the exercise of reason, forethought, and self-control ⟨the blessed virtue of ~ —*Liturgical Arts*⟩ **b :** sagacity or shrewdness in the management of affairs (as of government or business) shown in the skillful selection, adaptation, and use of means to a desired end **:** DISCRETION ⟨acted with considerable ~ —W.M.Thackeray⟩ ⟨the hard ~ of statesmen —G.M. Trevelyan⟩ **c :** providence in the use of resources **:** ECONOMY, FRUGALITY ⟨wealth due to ~ during prosperous times⟩ ⟨the ~ and economic value of the extended coverage —J.V.Herd⟩ **d :** attentiveness to possible hazard or disadvantage **:** CIRCUMSPECTION, CAUTION ⟨~ not to go . . . unescorted —W.A. Swanberg⟩ ⟨conservative from ~ —T.S.Eliot⟩ ⟨~ dictated by self-regard —Felix Frankfurter⟩

syn PRUDENCE, PROVIDENCE, FORESIGHT, FORETHOUGHT, and DISCRETION can apply in common to a quality in a person that enables him to choose a sensible course, especially in managing his practical affairs. PRUDENCE, the most comprehensive, implies a habitual deliberateness, caution, and circumspection in action ⟨she had not *prudence* enough to hold her tongue before the servants —Jane Austen⟩ ⟨we can dream that the future will realize all our hopes, though *prudence* might suggest that as it is not yet born, it is too early to baptize it —W.R.Inge⟩ ⟨man is believed to show the highest degree of pecuniary *prudence*, scheming craftily to get the most for his money at every turn —C.E.Ayres⟩ PROVIDENCE implies thought for and provision in advance for the difficulties and needs of the future ⟨enough *providence* to save something out of one's pay for emergencies⟩ FORESIGHT stresses the ability to divine and prepare for what is going to happen ⟨not want of feeling so much as want of *foresight*. They will not look ahead. A famine ceasing, a rebellion crushed, they jog on as before —George Meredith⟩ ⟨it is essential to remember . . . that no man, whatever his diplomatic genius and *foresight*, can conceive the future —Hilaire Belloc⟩ FORETHOUGHT suggests due consideration for contingencies ⟨*forethought*, which involves doing unpleasant things now for the sake of pleasant things in the future —Bertrand Russell⟩ ⟨dry clothes . . . which . . . *forethought* had provided —B.A.Williams⟩ DISCRETION implies such qualities as good judgment, caution, and self-control that make for prudence or prudent action ⟨she administered her little patrimony and her savings with shrewd *discretion* and had enough put by for any number of rainy days that might occur —Gamaliel Bradford⟩ ⟨permitted her sympathy to outrun her *discretion*⟩ ⟨to administer public funds with fairness and *discretion*⟩

pru·dent \-ᵊnt\ *adj* [ME, fr. MF, fr. L *prudent-, prudens*, alter. of *provident-, providens*, pres. part. of *providēre* to foresee, provide — more at PROVIDE] **:** characterized by, arising from, or showing prudence: as **a :** marked by wisdom or judiciousness ⟨~ rulers⟩ ⟨~ laws⟩ ⟨the wise in heart shall be called ~ —Prov 16:21 (AV)⟩ ⟨a man . . . of notably liberal, ~, and humane views —*Times Lit. Supp.*⟩ **b :** shrewd in the management of practical affairs ⟨a ~ politician⟩ ⟨a ~ . . . businessman who never does anything except for a useful end —M.R. Cohen⟩ **c :** circumspect (as in conduct) **:** DISCREET, CAUTIOUS ⟨~ hesitation —Derek Patmore⟩ ⟨more ~ to hide than to fight —V.G.Heiser⟩ **d :** PROVIDENT, FRUGAL ⟨the ~ use and development of . . . resources —D.D.Eisenhower⟩ ⟨had been a ~ and thrifty wife —W.M.Thackeray⟩ **syn** see WISE

¹pru·den·tial \prüˈdenchəl\ *adj* [L *prudentia* prudence + E *-al*] **1 :** of, relating to, or proceeding from prudence ⟨the use of ~ in addition to scientific judgment —David Easton⟩ ⟨code of ~ morality —*Saturday Rev.*⟩ ⟨the ~ timidity of their . . . representative —W.L.Sperry⟩ **2 :** exercising prudence **:** having administrative discretion esp. in business matters ⟨some churches turn over their business affairs to ~ committees⟩ — **pru·den·tial·ly** \-chəlē, -li\ *adv*

²prudential \"\ *n* -s **1 :** a matter involving the exercise of administrative or financial discretion — usu. used in pl. ⟨the ~*s* of the college⟩ **2** *archaic* **:** a prudential consideration — usu. used in pl. ⟨~*s* restrain him —Daniel Defoe⟩

pru·den·tial·ism \-chəˌlizəm\ *n* -s **:** a prudential philosophy or doctrine

prudent investment *n* **:** investment valuation esp. for rate-making purposes (as of a public utility) on the basis of original cost subject to adjustment for unwise investment decision as distinguished from cost of reproduction

pru·dent·ly *adv* [ME, fr. *prudent* + *-ly*] **:** in a prudent manner ⟨~ desisted in view of the damaging evidence —*Times Lit. Supp.*⟩ ⟨bear themselves ~ —E.C.Marchant⟩

prudent man rule *n* **:** a rule that gives a large measure of discretion to trustees in selecting investments for trust funds where the trust agreement calls for purchase of legal investments and that allows stocks to be purchased as well as bonds though in some states only up to a specified limit

prud·ery \ˈprüd(ə)rē, -ri\ *n* -ES [F *pruderie*, fr. *prude* prudish + *-erie* -ery — more at PRUDE] **:** the quality or state of being prudish **:** excessive or priggish modesty or decorousness **:** PRIMNESS ⟨sexual ~⟩ ⟨a ~ which wished to conceal the body —*Horizon*⟩

prud·ish \-dish, -dēsh\ *adj* [¹*prude* + *-ish*] **:** marked by prudery **:** PRIM, PRIGGISH ⟨a very straight-laced, ~ girl⟩ ⟨is sexually not so much chaste as ~ —Virginia Woolf⟩ ⟨~ contemporary criticism —W.C.DeVane⟩ — **prud·ish·ly** *adv* — **prud·ish·ness** *n* -ES

pru·i·nate \ˈprüəˌnāt\ *adj* [L *pruina* hoarfrost + E *-ate*] **:** PRUINOSE

pru·i·nes·cence \ˌprüəˈnesᵊn(t)s\ *n* -s [L *pruina* + E *-escence*] **:** the state of being pruinose; *also* **:** the dust or bloom causing this condition

pru·i·nose \ˈprüəˌnōs\ *adj* [L *pruinosus* covered with frost, fr. *pruina* hoarfrost + *-osus* -ose — more at FREEZE] **:** covered with whitish dust or bloom

pru·i·nos·i·ty \ˌprüəˈnäsədē\ *n* -ES **:** PRUINESCENCE

pru·i·nous \ˈprüənəs\ *adj* [L *pruinosus* covered with frost] **:** FROSTY, PRUINOSE

pru·lau·ra·sin \prüˈlȯrəsən\ *n* -s [ISV *prulauras-* (fr. NL *Prunus laurocerasus* cherry laurel) + *-in*] **:** a crystalline beta-glucoside $C_6H_5CH(CN)OC_6H_{11}O_5$ that is the chief active component of the leaves of the cherry laurel and is derived from glucose and racemic benzaldehyde cyanohydrin — compare AMYGDALIN

pru·na·ce·ae \prüˈnāsēˌē\ [NL, fr. *Prunus*, type genus + *-aceae*] *syn of* AMYGDALACEAE

pru·nase \ˈprüˌnās\ *n* -s [ISV *prunasin* + *-ase*] **:** an enzyme that accelerates the hydrolysis of prunasin, is found in yeast and in bitter almonds, and is one of two enzymes concerned in the hydrolysis of amygdalin

pru·na·sin \ˈprünəsən\ *n* -s [ISV *prunas-* (fr. NL *Prunus serotina* black cherry) + *-in*] **:** a crystalline beta-glucoside $C_6H_5CH(CN)OC_6H_{11}O_5$ found in various plants of the genus *Prunus* and obtained by partial hydrolysis of amygdalin by the enzyme prunase

¹prune \ˈprün\ *n* -s [ME, fr. MF, fr. (assumed) VL *pruna*, fr. L, pl. of *prunum* plum — more at PLUM] **1 :** a plum that is capable of being dried or that has been dried without the development of fermentation even though the pit is not removed from the fruit and that when fresh is typically a moderate sized fruit with firm dark blue pruinose skin and a rather solid somewhat bland pulp **2 :** a variable color averaging a dark purple that is redder and duller than mulberry, mulberry purple, or plum and less strong and slightly redder than prune purple **3 :** a dull, unattractive, or stupid person

²prune \"\ *vt* -ED/-ING/-S [ME *proinen, preinen, prunen*] *archaic* **:** PREEN

³prune \"\ *vb* -ED/-ING/-S [ME *prouynen*, fr. MF *proignier, proongier*, prob. alter. of *provigner* to layer — more at PROVINE] *vt* **1 a :** to cut down or reduce (as a literary composition) by eliminating what is useless, burdensome, or superfluous ⟨~ an essay⟩ ⟨a severely *pruned* style⟩ ⟨*pruned* of its redundancies —Samuel Butler †1902⟩ **b :** to remove (something) as superfluous ⟨~ away all ornamentation⟩ **c :** to cut back or reduce (as a budget) **:** RETRENCH ⟨the drive to ~ appropriations —Gardner Patterson & J.N.Behrman⟩ **2 :** to lop or cut off the superfluous parts, branches, or shoots of (a plant) for better shaped or more fruitful growth **:** shape or smooth by trimming **:** TRIM ⟨*pruned* all the trees along the boulevard⟩ ⟨vines were *pruned* —*Experiment Station Record*⟩ **3 :** to cut off or cut out (as dead branches from a rosebush) — see ROOT-PRUNE ~ *vi* **:** to cut away what is superfluous or excessive ⟨selfishness plants best, ~*s* best —R.W.Emerson⟩ ⟨the best time to ~⟩

1pru·nel·la \prü'nelə\ *n, cap* [NL, fr. *prunella, brunella* quinsy, angina (trans. of G *bräune,* fr. *braun* brown), fr. ML *brunus* brown (fr. OHG *brūn*) + L *-ella,* dim. suffix; fr. the belief that herbs of this genus healed quinsy — more at BROWN] **:** a small genus of perennial largely Eurasian herbs (family Labiatae) having terminal spikes or heads of small purple or white flowers with the corolla tube inflated and its limb strongly 2-lipped — see SELF-HEAL

2prunella \"\ *also* **pru·nelle** \-el\ *n* -s [F *prunelle,* lit., sloe; fr. the dark color — more at PRUNELLE] **1 a :** a silk or woolen fabric formerly in use for gowns (as of clerics, scholars, barristers) **b :** a twilled woolen dress fabric **2 a :** a heavy woolen fabric used for the uppers of shoes **b prunellas** *pl* **:** a pair of shoes made of prunella

3prunella \"\ *n, cap* [NL] **:** a genus (the type of the family Prunellidae) of passerine birds that resemble thrushes and comprise the accentors — see HEDGE SPARROW

pru·nelle \prü'nel\ *n* -s [F, sloe, wild plum, sloe-flavored brandy, dim. of *prune* plum, prune — more at PRUNE] **1 :** a small yellow dried plum packed without the skin **2 :** a sweet brown French liqueur having a grape brandy base and flavored chiefly with the sloe

pru·nel·lo \prü'ne(,)lō\ *n* -s [modif. of It *prunella* small plum, dim. of *pruna* plum, fr. (assumed) VL — more at PRUNE] **:** PRUNELLE 1

prune purple *n* **:** a dark purple that is stronger and slightly bluer than average prune, redder and deeper than mulberry or plum, and redder and duller than mulberry purple — called also *loganberry*

prun·er \'prünə(r)\ *n* -s [3*prune* + *-er*] **:** one that prunes: as **a :** a worker employed to prune dead and excess branches from trees **b :** a tool for use in pruning operations **c :** any of several beetles whose larvae gnaw the branches of trees so as to cause them to fall; *esp* **:** OAK PRUNER

prunes and prisms *n pl* **:** affected, primly precise, or priggish speech or behavior ⟨go atiptoe and talk *prunes and prisms* — C.G.D.Roberts⟩ ⟨their *prunes and prisms* young daughters — Bruce Marshall⟩

pru·ne·tin \'prünəd·ən\ *n* -s [ISV *prunet-* (fr. NL *Prunus emarginata*) + *-in*] **:** a crystalline phenolic isoflavone $C_{15}H_7O_2(OH)_2OCH_3$ obtained by hydrolysis of prunitrin

pru·ne·tol \-ünə,tōl, -tȯl\ *n* -s [ISV *prunet*in + *-ol*] **:** GENISTEIN

prune tree *n* **:** a tree yielding fruits that are or are used for prunes

prune worm *n* **:** a larva of a phycitid moth (*Mineola scitulella*) that infests plum, prune, and other fruit trees

1pruning *n* -s [fr. gerund of 3*prune*] **1 :** the act or process of one that prunes **2 :** something pruned off — usu. used in pl.

2pruning *adj* [fr. pres. part. of 3*prune*] **:** that prunes

pruning hook *n* **:** a pole or rod with curved blade attached for removing spent or superfluous bramble canes

pruning knife *n* **:** a knife resembling a common jackknife but having a curved or hooked blade

pruning saw *n* **:** a saw that has a usu. tapering straight or curved blade and either a closed or an open and sometimes folding handhold and that may or may not be attached to a pole

pruning shears *n pl* **:** shears with strong blades used in the light pruning of any kind of woody plant

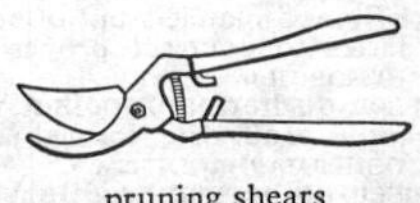
pruning shears

pru·ni·trin \'prünə·trən\ *n* -s [ISV *pruni* (fr. NL *prunus,* genus name of *prunus emarginata*) + *-trin* (as in *dextrin*)] **:** a crystalline glucoside $C_{22}H_{24}O_{11}$ found in the bitter cherry of western and in the chokecherry of eastern No. America that on hydrolysis yields glucose and prunetin

prunt \'prənt\ *n* -s [origin unknown] **:** a small glass ornament attached by fusing to a glass pattern (as on a vase)

prunt·ed \-təd\ *adj* **:** ornamented with prunts

pru·nus \'prünəs\ *n, cap* [NL, fr. L, plum tree, fr. Gk *proumnē*] **:** a genus of trees and shrubs (family Rosaceae) widely distributed in temperate regions that have usu. serrate leaves often with glands along the petiole or at the base of the blade and have flowers usu. in umbellate clusters or racemes which appear in spring and often before the leaves and are succeeded by a smooth globose fruit often with a bloom on its surface — see ALMOND, APRICOT, CHERRY, PEACH

pru·ri·ence \'prürēən(t)s, 'prür-\ *n* -s **:** the quality or state of being prurient

pru·ri·en·cy \-nsē, -si\ *n* -ES **:** PRURIENCE ⟨the ~ of curious ears —Edmund Burke⟩

pru·ri·ent \-nt\ *adj* [L *prurient-, pruriens,* pres. part. of *prurire* to itch, long for, be wanton; akin to L *pruna* glowing coal, Skt *ploṣati* he singes, burns, and prob. to L *pruina* hoarfrost — more at FREEZE] **1 a :** marked by restless craving **:** itching with curiosity ⟨the reading public . . . in its usual ~ longing after anything like personal gossip —Charles Kingsley⟩ **b :** having or easily susceptible to lascivious thoughts or desires ⟨titillated ~ people by its frank discussion of sexual experience⟩ **c :** tending to excite lasciviousness ⟨the japes about sex . . . being ~ rather than funny —John McCarten⟩ **2 :** exhibiting abnormally rapid or excessive growth ⟨pinching off the ~ bud —Nathaniel Paterson⟩ — **pru·ri·ent·ly** *adv*

pru·rig·i·nous \prü'rijənəs\ *adj* [LL *pruriginosus,* fr. L *prurigin-, prurigo* + *-osus* -ous] **:** like or caused by prurigo **:** affected by prurigo **:** constituting prurigo

pru·ri·go \prü'rī(,)gō\ *n* -s [NL, fr. L, itching, itch, fr. *prurire* to itch — more at PRURIENT] **:** a chronic inflammatory skin disease marked by a general eruption of small itching papules

pru·rit·ic \prü'rid·ik\ *adj* [*pruritus* + *-ic*] **:** relating to, marked by, or producing pruritus

pru·ri·tus \-rīd·əs\ *n* -ES [L, fr. *prurire* to itch] **:** localized or generalized itching due to irritation of sensory nerve endings from organic or psychogenic causes

pru·si·a·no \,prüsē'ä(,)nō\ *n* -s [MexSp, fr. Sp, Prussian, fr. *Prusia* Prussia + *-ano* -an] **:** VARIED BUNTING

prus·ik knot \prəsik-\ *n, usu cap P* [fr. the name *Prusik*] **:** a knot that is used in mountaineering for tying a small sling to a climbing rope as an aid to one who has fallen into a crevasse and that holds fast when weighted but is movable when unweighted

prusik sling *n, usu cap P* **:** a small movable sling fastened to a climbing rope by means of a Prusik knot

1prus·sian \'prəshən\ *adj, usu cap* [*Prussia,* region in northern Germany + E *-an*] **1 :** of, relating to, or characteristic of Prussia **2 :** of, relating to, or characteristic of the Prussians

Prusik knot

2prussian \"\ *n* -s *cap* **:** a native or inhabitant of Prussia: **a :** one of a people once living in Prussia esp. in the old provinces of West and East Prussia and related to the Lithuanians **b :** a native or inhabitant of modern Prussia

prussian blue *n* [trans. of F *bleu de Prusse*] **1** *usu cap P* **a :** any of numerous iron blue pigments formerly regarded as ferric ferrocyanide; *esp* **:** one characterized by dark masstones and reddish tints — compare CHINESE BLUE 1a, TURNBULL'S BLUE **b :** a dark blue crystalline salt $Fe_4[Fe(CN)_6]_3.xH_2O$ obtained by precipitation from a solution of ferrocyanic acid or a ferrocyanide treated with a ferric salt and used as a test for ferric iron; ferric ferrocyanide **2** *often cap P* **:** any of the colors produced with Prussian blue, averaging a moderate to strong blue that is greener than orient — called also *Berlin blue, bronze blue, Brunswick blue, Chinese blue, Hortense blue, Milori blue, Paris blue, steel blue*

prussian brown *n* **1** *usu cap P* **:** an orange-brown iron oxide pigment obtained by calcining Prussian blue **2** *often cap P* **:** GOLD PHEASANT

prussian carp *n, usu cap P* **:** CRUCIAN CARP

prus·sian·ism \-shə,nizəm\ *n* -s *usu cap* **:** the ideas, practices, or policies (as the advocacy of militarism, ruthless discipline, and despotism) commonly held to be typically Prussian; *also* **:** allegiance to or partiality for such ideas, practices, or policies

prus·sian·ize \-nīz\ *vt* -ED/-ING/-S *often cap* **:** to make Prussian in character or principle (as in authoritarian control or rigid discipline) ⟨~ education⟩

prussian knight *n, usu cap P&K* **:** NOACHITE

prussian red *n, often cap P* **1 :** INDIAN RED 2a **2 :** COLCOTHAR 2

prus·si·ate \'prəs(h)ēət, -ē,āt\ *n* -s [F, fr. (*acide*) *prussique* prussic acid + *-ate*] **1 :** a salt of hydrocyanic acid **:** CYANIDE **2 a :** FERROCYANIDE **b :** FERRICYANIDE

prussiate of potash : POTASSIUM CYANIDE

prus·sic acid \'prəsik-, -sēk-\ *n* [part trans. of F *acide prussique,* fr. *acide* acid + *prussique* prussic, fr. (*bleu de*) *Prusse* Prussian blue + *-ique* -ic] **:** HYDROCYANIC ACID

pru·tah *or* **pru·ta** \prü'tä\ *n, pl* **pru·toth** *or* **pru·tot** \-tōt(h), -tōs\ [NHeb *pĕrūṭāh,* fr. Mishnaic Heb, lepton] **1 :** a former monetary unit of the Republic of Israel equal to 1/1000 of a pound **2 :** a coin representing one prutah

pruve \'prüv\ *chiefly Scot var of* PROVE

1pry \'prī\ *vi* **pried; pried; prying; pries** [ME *prien*] **:** to look closely or inquisitively **:** peer curiously **:** PEEP ⟨~ into every corner of the house⟩; *esp* **:** to make a searching or presumptuous inquiry or investigation ⟨no need to ~ for psychopathological causes —T.S.Eliot⟩ — usu. used with *into* ⟨~ into people's secrets —Virginia Woolf⟩ ⟨*pried* curiously into the meaning of nature —V.L.Parrington⟩

2pry \"\ *vt* **pried; pried; prying; pries** [back-formation (*prize* being taken as 3d sing. pres.) fr. 6*prize*] **1 :** to raise, move, or pull apart with a pry or lever **:** PRIZE ⟨~ up a floorboard⟩ ⟨~ the lid off a can⟩ ⟨~ away a large stone blocking the entrance⟩ ⟨~*ing* the heavy slabs apart⟩ **2 :** to extract, detach, or open with difficulty ⟨~ military information out of a prisoner⟩ ⟨deputies he was able to ~ away from the . . . leadership —Paul Johnson⟩ ⟨try to ~ loose that 10 percent on the . . . deal —Bennett Cerf⟩ ⟨have *pried* open enough pocketbooks —D.C.Morrill⟩

3pry \"\ *n* -ES [back-formation (*prize* being taken as pl.) fr. 5*prize*] **1 :** a tool (as a lever or crowbar) for prying or prizing; *esp* **:** one with a claw end for removing spikes **2 :** LEVERAGE

pryer *var of* PRIER

prying *adj* [fr. pres. part. of 1*pry*] **:** inspecting closely or impertinently **:** officiously curious **:** PEEPING ⟨will not bare my soul to their shallow ~ eyes —Oscar Wilde⟩ ⟨adopt a ~, suspicious, inquisitorial attitude —*Orient Bk. World*⟩ **syn** see CURIOUS

pry·ing·ly *adv* **:** in a prying manner **:** INQUISITIVELY

pry·ler \'prīlə(r)\ *n* -s [origin unknown] **:** one who sweeps scale from bars and sheets in a sheet rolling mill

prypole \'=,=\ *n* [2*pry* + *pole*] **:** a pole that forms the prop of a hoisting gin and stands facing the windlass

pryt·a·ne·um \,pritᵊn'ēəm\ *n* -s [L, fr. Gk *prytaneion,* fr. *prytaneia*] **:** a public building or hall in an ancient Greek city containing the state hearth and serving as the place of meeting and dining for the prytanes and sometimes of official hospitality for distinguished citizens and visitors

pryt·a·nis \'pritᵊnəs\ *n, pl* **pryta·nes** \-ᵊn,ēz\ [L, fr. Gk, ruler, lord, prytanis, of non-IE origin] **1 :** a member of a prytany **2 :** a chief official in various ancient Greek states (as Lycia, Miletus, or Rhodes) after the abolition of monarchies

pryt·a·ny \-ᵊnē\ *n* -ES [Gk *prytaneia,* fr. *prytanis* + *-eia* -y] **1 :** the presidential office of the Athenian senate held successively during the year by each of the ten sections into which the senate was divided **2 :** one of the ten divisions of the Athenian senate during its presidency **3 :** the period during which a section of the senate held the office of president

przhe·val·ski's horse *or* **prze·wal·ski's horse** *or* **pre·je·val·sky's horse** *or* **prje·val·sky's horse** \,pərzhə¦välzkēz-, ¦prezhə¦|, (p)she¦\ *n, usu cap P* [after Nikolai M. *Przhevalski* †1888 Russian soldier and explorer] **:** a wild horse (*Equus przewalskii*) of central Asia intermediate between the true horse and the ass and having a dun-colored coat with a brown mane, the lower half of the tail covered with long hairs, callosities on all four legs, and broad hoofs

ps *abbr* **1** pieces **2** pseudo **3** pseudonym

PS *abbr* **1** passenger steamer **2** permanent secretary **3** police sergeant **4** [L *postscriptum*] postscript **5** private secretary **6** privy seal **7** prompt side **8** public sale **9** public school **10** public stenographer

p's *or* **ps** *pl of* P

psal·li·o·ta \,salē'ōd·ə\ [NL, prob. fr. Gk *psallion* chain (perh. akin to Gk *psallein* to pull) + L *-ota* -ote] *syn of* AGARICUS

psal·loid *also* **psal·oid** \'sa,lȯid\ *adj* [NL *psalloides,* fr. Gk *psallein* to play upon a stringed instrument + L *-oides* -oid; fr. the lines on the fornix suggesting strings] **:** of, relating to, or constituting the fornix (sense 1c)

1psalm \'säm, 'sȧl\ *also* \ȧlm, *archaic* 'sam\ *n* -s [ME *psalm, salm,* fr. OE *psealm, salm,* fr. LL *psalmus,* fr. Gk *psalmos* song sung to the harp, psalm (trans. of Heb. *mizmōr* song, psalm), fr. *psallein* to pull, twitch, play upon a stringed instrument; prob. akin to L *palpare* to caress — more at FEEL] **:** a sacred song, poem, or poetical composition used in the praise or worship of the Deity: as **a** *often cap* **:** one of the biblical hymns collected in the Book of Psalms **b** *often cap* **:** a modern metrical version of one of the biblical psalms used as a liturgical hymn in public worship

2psalm \"\ *vt* -ED/-ING/-S [ME *psalmen, salmen,* fr. *psalm, salm* psalm] **:** to sing or extol in psalms **:** pray over with psalms ~ *vi* **:** to sing psalms **:** HYMN ⟨walk in the fields, ~ with the birds —C.E.S.Wood⟩

psalmbook \'=,=\ *n* [ME *salm boc,* fr. *salm* psalm + *boc* book, fr. OE *bōc* — more at BOOK] **1 :** a book consisting of a version of the Psalms **:** PSALTER **2 :** any book of sacred poems or songs for use in public worship

psalm·ic \-mik\ *adj* [*psalm* + *-ic*] **:** of, relating to, or like a psalm ⟨~ wails —Israel Zangwill⟩

psalm·ist \-məst\ *n* -s [LL *psalmista,* fr. LGk *psalmistēs,* fr. *psalmizein* to sing psalms, fr. Gk *psalmos* psalm + *-izein* -ize] **1 :** a writer or composer of sacred songs; *esp* **:** one of the authors of the Psalms **2 :** a precentor, cantor, or member of the lower ranks of the clergy who leads or sings the music in public worship (as in the Eastern Orthodox Church)

psalm·is·ter \-məstə(r)\ *n* -s [ME *psalmistre,* fr. MF, fr. LL *psalmista* psalmist + MF *-re* -er] **:** PSALMIST 2

psalm·ist·ry \-trē\ *n* -ES [*psalmist* + *-ry*] **:** use of psalms in devotion **:** PSALMODY

psalm·less \-mləs\ *adj* **:** unaccompanied by a psalm

psal·mo·di·al \(')sä(l)¦mōdēəl, (')sä(l)¦m-, (')sal¦m-\ *adj* [*psalmody* + *-ial*] **:** PSALMODIC

psal·mod·ic \-'mädik\ *also* **psalmod·i·cal** \-dəkəl\ *adj* [*psalmody* + *-ic* or *-ical*] **:** of or relating to psalmody ⟨repetitive ~ plainsong —M.F.Bukofzer⟩

psalmo·dist \'=,mədəst\ *n* -s **1 :** one versed in psalmody **2 :** one that composes psalms or sacred songs **:** PSALMIST

psalmo·dize \-,mə,dīz\ *vi* -ED/-ING/-S [ML *psalmodizare,* fr. LL *psalmodia* psalmody + *-izare* -ize] **:** to practice psalmody

1psalmo·dy \-,mədē\ *n* -ES [ME *psalmodie,* fr. LL *psalmodia,* fr. LGk *psalmōdia,* fr. Gk, singing to the harp, fr. *psalmos* psalm + *ōidē* song, ode + *-ia* -y — more at ODE] **1 :** the act, practice, or art of singing psalms or sacred songs in worship **2 :** a collection of psalms (as for liturgical use)

2psalmody \"\ *vb* -ED/-ING/-ES [ME *psalmodien,* fr. *psalmodie* psalmody] *vt* **:** HYMN ~ *vi* **:** PSALMODIZE, HYMN

psalm of ascents *usu cap P&A* **:** SONG OF ASCENTS

psalmograph *n* [LL *psalmographus,* fr. LGk *psalmographos,* fr. Gk *psalmos* psalm + *-graphos* -grapher (fr. *graphein* to WRITE) — more at PSALM, CARVE] *obs* **:** PSALMIST 1

psal·mog·ra·phy \sä(l)'mägrəfē, sȧ(l)'m-, sal'm-\ *n* -ES **:** the act or practice of writing psalms

psalm singer *n* **:** one holding that the Psalms and not hymns should be sung in worship

psalm tone *n* **:** a tone or melody in Gregorian chant used for the singing of the Psalms

psalm tune *n* **:** the melody to which a metrically arranged psalm is sung

psaloid *var of* PSALLOID

psal·ter \'sȯltə(r)\ *n* -s [ME *psalter, salter, sauter,* fr. OE & OF; OE *psaltere, saltere* & OF *psautier, sautier, psaltier,* fr. LL *psalterium,* fr. LGk *psaltērion,* fr. Gk, stringed instrument, psaltery, fr. *psallein* to play upon a stringed instrument — more at PSALM] **1 :** a translation or version of the Psalms ⟨an English ~⟩ ⟨a metrical ~⟩ **2 :** a book containing the Psalms separately printed or esp. arranged for liturgical or devotional use: as **a** *sometimes cap* **:** the Psalms as printed in the Book of Common Prayer **b** *sometimes cap* **:** the part of a breviary containing the Psalms set for each day of the week **3** *archaic* **:** PSALTERY **4 :** PSALTERIUM

psal·ter·er \-tərə(r)\ *n* -s [ME *sawtrer,* fr. *sautre* psaltery + *-er*] **:** a player on the psaltery

psal·teri·al \(')sȯl¦tirēəl, -ter-\ *adj* [NL *psalterium* + E *-al*] **:** of or relating to the psalterium

psal·teri·on \=ˈ=rēən, -ē,än\ *n* -s [Gk *psaltērion*] **:** PSALTERY

psal·teri·um \-ēəm\ *n, pl* **psal·teria** \-ēə\ [NL, fr. LL, psalter; fr. the resemblance of the folds to the pages of a book] **1 :** OMASUM **2 :** LYRA 2

psal·tery \'sȯltərē, -l·trē\ *also* **psal·try** \-l·trē\ *n* -ES [ME *psalterie, sautre,* fr. MF *psalterie, sautere,* fr. L *psalterium,* fr. Gk *psaltērion*] **:** an ancient and medieval stringed musical instrument that consists of a soundboard over which a number of strings are stretched and that is played by plucking with or without a plectrum ⟨praise him with the ~ and harp —Ps 150:3 (AV)⟩

psal·tress \-l·trəs\ *n* -ES [*psalterer* + *-ess*] **:** a female psalterer

psamm- *or* **psammo-** *comb form* [Gk, fr. *psammos* — more at SAND] **:** sand ⟨*psammo*biotic⟩ ⟨*psammo*phile⟩

psam·mite \'sa,mīt\ *n* -s [F, fr. *psamm-* + *-ite*] **:** a rock composed of sandy particles **:** SANDSTONE — compare PELITE, PSEPHITE — **psam·mit·ic** \(')sa¦mid·ik\ *adj*

psam·mo·biotic \¦sa(,)mō+\ *adj* [*psamm-* + *-biotic*] **:** living or thriving in sandy areas or in the psammon

1psam·moch·a·rid \(')sa¦mäkərəd\ *adj* [NL *Psammocharidae*] **:** of or relating to the Pompilidae

2psammocharid \"\ *n* -s **:** a wasp of the family Pompilidae

psam·mo·char·i·dae \,samə'karə,dē\ [NL, fr. *Psammochares,* genus of wasps (fr. *psamm-* + Gk *chairein* to rejoice) + *-idae* — more at YEARN] *syn of* POMPILIDAE

psam·mo·ma \sa'mōmə\ *n, pl* **psammomas** \-ōməz\ *or* **psammoma·ta** \-ōməd·ə\ [NL, fr. *psamm-* + *-oma*] **:** a hard fibrous tumor of the meninges of the brain and spinal cord containing calcareous matter — **psam·moma·tous** \(')sa¦mōməd·əs, -mäm-\ *adj*

psam·mon \'sa,män\ *n* -s [NL, fr. Gk *psammos* sand] **:** an ecological community consisting of the typically minute plants and animals that live in the water filling the interstices of sand adjacent to a body of fresh water; *also* **:** the habitat utilized

psam·mo·phile \'samə,fīl\ *n* -s [ISV *psamm-* + *-phile*] **:** an organism that prefers or thrives in sandy soils or areas — **psam·moph·i·lous** \(')sa¦mäfələs\ *adj*

psam·mo·phis \'saməfəs\ *n, cap* [NL, fr. *psamm-* + *-ophis*] **:** a genus of No. African and Asiatic back-fanged snakes comprising the sand snakes

psam·mo·phyte \'samə,fīt\ *n* -s [ISV *psamm-* + *-phyte*] **:** a plant thriving on or requiring sandy soil — **psam·mo·phyt·ic** \¦==¦fid·ik\ *adj*

psam·mo·sere \'samə,si(ə)r\ *n* [*psamm-* + *sere*] **:** a sere that originates in sand

p's and q's \¦pēz'n¦kyüz\ *n pl* **:** something (as one's manners) about which one ought to be careful or circumspect **:** best behavior — usu. used with *mind* or *watch* ⟨exhorting the older democracies to mind their *p's and q's* —A.S.Bokhari⟩ ⟨just better watch his *p's and q's* when I get a six-gun of my own —Jean Stafford⟩ ⟨being on her *p's and q's* for two solid days was too much for her —Guy McCrone⟩

psa·ro·ni·us \sə'rōnēəs\ *n, cap* [NL, fr. L, a precious stone; fr. its speckled appearance when polished] **:** a genus of fossil ferns based on tree fern trunks with a vascular system that is a polycyclic dictyostele — see STARLING STONE

PSC *abbr* **1** *often not cap* per standard compass **2** public service commission

pschent \'(p)skent\ *n* -s [Gk, fr. Egypt *p-skhent,* fr. *p* the + *skhent* double crown] **:** the headdress of the later Egyptian pharaohs formed of the two crowns worn by the respective pharaohs of Upper Egypt and Lower Egypt before the union of the country under one rule

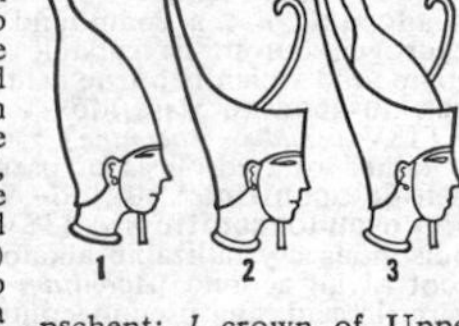

pschent: *1* crown of Upper Egypt, *2* crown of Lower Egypt, *3* double crown of Egypt

psech·ri·dae \'sekrə,dē\ *n pl, cap* [NL, fr. *Psechrus,* type genus (fr. Gk *psēchros* ground fine, fr. *psēchein* to rub down) + *-idae*; akin to Gk *psēn* to rub — more at SAND] **:** a family of chiefly Old World spiders

pse·de·ra \sə'dirə, 'sedərə\ [NL] *syn of* PARTHENOCISSUS

1psel·a·phid \'seləfəd\ *adj* [NL *Pselaphidae*] **:** of or relating to the Pselaphidae

2pselaphid \"\ *n* -s **:** a beetle of the family Pselaphidae

pse·laph·i·dae \sə'lafə,dē\ *n pl, cap* [NL, fr. *Pselaphus,* type genus + *-idae*] **:** a family of small beetles related to the rove beetles but with abdomen inflexible

pse·laph·ognath \sə'lafə(g),nath\ *n* -s [NL *Pselaphognatha*] **:** a millipede of the subclass Pselaphognatha

psel·a·phog·na·tha \,selə'fägnəthə\ *n pl, cap* [NL, fr. *pselapho-* (fr. Gk *psēlaphan* to grope about) + *-gnatha*] **:** a small subclass of soft-bodied millipedes with tufts and rows of bristles — compare CHILOGNATHA, POLYXENUS

psel·a·phog·na·thous \¦==¦fägnəthəs\ *adj* [NL *Pselaphognatha* + E *-ous*] **:** of or relating to the Pselaphognatha

psel·a·phus \'seləfəs\ *n, cap* [NL, fr. Gk *psēlaphan* to grope about, feel, touch; akin to Gk *psallein* to pull, twitch — more at PSALM] **:** a genus (the type of the family Pselaphidae) of small beetles

pse·phism \'sē,fizəm\ *also* **pse·phis·ma** \sə'fizmə\ *n, pl* **psephisms** \-,fizəmz\ *also* **psephismas** \-'fizməz\ *or* **psephis·ma·ta** \-'fizməd·ə\ [Gk *psēphisma,* fr. *psēphizein* to count, reckon, cast one's vote with a pebble, fr. *psēphos* pebble + *-izein* -ize — more at SAND] **:** a decree of an ancient popular assembly (as of the ecclesia of Athens)

pse·phite \'sē,fīt\ *n* -s [F *pséphite,* fr. *pséph-* (fr. Gk *psēphos* pebble) + *-ite*] **:** a coarse fragmental rock composed of rounded pebbles (as conglomerate) — compare PELITE, PSAMMITE — **pse·phit·ic** \(')sē¦fid·ik\ *adj*

pse·pho·log·i·cal \¦sēfə¦läjəkəl\ *adj* **:** of or relating to psephology

pse·phol·o·gist \sē'fäləjəst\ *n* -s **:** one who specializes in psephology

pse·phol·o·gy \-jē\ *n* -ES [Gk *psēphos* pebble + E *-logy*; fr. the use of pebbles by the ancient Greeks in voting] **:** the scientific study of elections

pse·pho·man·cy \'sēfə,man(t)sē\ *n* -ES [Gk *psēphos* pebble + E *-mancy*] **:** divination by pebbles

pse·phu·rus \sə'fyürəs\ *n, cap* [NL, fr. Gk *psēphos* pebble + NL *-urus*] **:** a genus of ganoid fishes of the larger rivers of China that includes solely the Chinese paddlefish (*P. gladius*), is closely related to the American genus *Polyodon,* and is distinguished by a narrow high snout and greatly developed caudal fulcra

pset·ta \'sed·ə\ *n, cap* [NL, fr. Gk *psētta,* a flatfish; perh. akin to Gk *psēchein* to rub down] **:** a genus of large flatfishes including the European turbot

1pset·to·did \'sed·ədəd\ *adj* [NL *Psettodidae*] **:** of or relating to the Psettodidae

2psettodid \"\ *n* -s **:** a flatfish of the family Psettodidae

pset·tod·i·dae \se'tädə,dē\ *n pl, cap* [NL, fr. *Psettodes,* type genus (fr. Gk *psētta* flatfish + NL *-odes*) + *-idae*] **:** a small family (coextensive with the genus *Psettodes*) of tropical flatfishes that are in several respects intermediate between the more specialized flatfishes and the typical bony fishes

pseud- *or* **pseudo-** *comb form* [ME *pseudo-,* fr. LL *pseud-, pseudo-,* fr. Gk, fr. *pseudēs,* fr. *pseudein* to lie, cheat, falsify] **1 :** false: **a :** sham **:** feigned **:** fake ⟨*pseudo*dramatic⟩ ⟨*pseudo*serious⟩ **b :** counterfeit **:** spurious ⟨*pseudo*antique⟩ **c :** quack ⟨*pseudo*analyst⟩ **d :** fictitious ⟨*pseudo*biography⟩ **e :** unreal **:** illusory ⟨*pseudo*hallucination⟩ **2 a :** substance deceptively resembling (a specified thing) ⟨*pseudo*malachite⟩ **b :** temporary or substitute formation similar to (a specified thing) ⟨*pseudo*branchia⟩ ⟨*pseudo*podium⟩ **3 :** chemical compound resembling, isomeric with, or related to (a specified compound) ⟨*pseudo*cumene⟩ **4 :** abnormal **:** aberrant ⟨*pseud*arthrosis⟩ ⟨*pseud*embryo⟩ ⟨*pseudo*vum⟩

pseud *abbr* pseudonym; pseudonymous
pseudaconine *var of* PSEUDOACONINE
pseudaconitine *var of* PSEUDOACONITINE
pseu·da·le·tia \ˌsüdəˈlēsh(ē)ə\ *n, cap* [NL, fr. *pseud-* + Gk *aletēs* grinder + NL *-ia*] : a genus of noctuid moths whose larvae are armyworms
pseud·amphora \(ˈ)süd+\ *n* [NL, fr. *pseud-* + *amphora*] : a Mycenaean vase with a spheroidal body, an arched handle at the top supported by a false neck, and a spout in the shoulder

pseudamphora

pseud·an·dry \ˈsüˌdandrē\ *n* -ES [*pseud-* + *andr-* + *-y*] : use of a masculine name by a woman as a pseudonym — compare PSEUDOGYNY
pseud·aposematic \(ˌ)süd+\ *adj* [*pseud-* + *aposematic*] : imitating in coloration or form another animal having dangerous or disagreeable qualities
pseud·apospory \"+\ *n* [*pseud-* + *apospory*] : production of diploid spores by the sporophytes (as in ferns of the genus *Marsilea*) — compare APOSPORY
pseud·apostle \ˌsüd+\ *n* [LL *pseudapostolus,* fr. Gk *pseudapostolos,* fr. *pseud-* + *apostolos* apostle — more at APOSTLE] : one falsely claiming to be an apostle
pseud·arthrosis \"+\ *also* **pseu·do·arthrosis** \ˌsü(ˌ)dō+\ *n* [NL, fr. *pseud-* + *arthrosis*] : the formation of a false joint (as by fibrous tissue between the ends of a fractured bone which has not perfectly united); *also* : a false joint or abnormal union between parts of bone
pseud·atoll \(ˌ)süd+\ *n* [*pseud-* + *atoll*] : an island or reef shaped like an atoll but not formed of true coral-reef limestone
pseud·axis \(ˈ)süd+\ *n* [NL, fr. *pseud-* + *axis*] : SYMPODIUM
pseud·echis \"+\ *n, cap* [NL, fr. *pseud-* + Gk *echis* viper — more at ECHIS] : a genus of large Australian elapid snakes including the semiaquatic black snake (*P. porphyriacus*)
pseud·emys \"+\ *n, cap* [NL, fr. *pseud-* + *Emys*] : a genus of turtles (family Testudinidae) comprising the sliders and including several species used for food in the southeastern U.S.
pseud·epigraph \"+\ *n* [NL *pseudepigrapha*] : one of the pseudepigrapha
pseud·epig·ra·pha \ˌsüdəˈpigrəfə\ *n pl, sometimes cap* [NL, fr. Gk, neut. pl. of *pseudepigraphos* falsely ascribed, with a false title, fr. *pseud-* + *epigraphein* to ascribe, inscribe — more at EPIGRAM] : spurious works purporting to emanate from biblical characters — compare ¹CANON 3a, APOCRYPHA
pseud·epigraphic \(ˌ)süd+\ *or* **pseud·epig·ra·phal** \ˌsüdəˈpigrəfəl\ *also* **pseud·epigraphical** \(ˌ)süd+\ *or* **pseud·epig·ra·phous** \ˌsüdəˈpigrəfəs\ *adj* [NL *pseudepigrapha* + E *-ic* or *-al* or *-ical,* or *-ous*] : of or relating to pseudepigraphy or pseudepigrapha : falsely or wrongly attributed
pseud·epigraphy \ˌsüd+\ *n* -ES [NL *pseudepigrapha* + E *-y*] : the ascription of false names of authors to works
pseud·episcopacy \"+\ *n* [alter. (influenced by *episcopacy*) of *pseudepiscopy*] : spurious episcopacy
pseud·epis·co·py \ˌsüdəˈpiskəpē\ *n* -ES [LGk *pseudepiskopos* false bishop (fr. Gk *pseud-* + *episkopos* bishop) + E *-y* — more at BISHOP] *archaic* : PSEUDEPISCOPACY ⟨a long usurpation and convicted ~ of prelates —John Milton⟩
pseud·imago \"+\ *n* [NL, fr. *pseud-* + *imago*] : SUBIMAGO
pseu·do \ˈsü(ˌ)dō\ *adj* [ME, fr. *pseudo-*] : SHAM, FEIGNED, SPURIOUS ⟨decorative ribbing of ~ wirework —*Univ. of Ariz. Record*⟩ ⟨the delicious and sometimes ~ rusticity of the eighteenth century —Christopher Morley⟩ ⟨distinction between true and ~ humanism —K.F.Reinhardt⟩ ⟨~ literary mannerisms —E.D.Radin⟩ ⟨~ candor⟩ **syn** see COUNTERFEIT
pseudo- — see PSEUD-
pseudo acid *n* : a compound believed not to contain acid hydrogen but to be capable of changing into an isomeric compound which is a true acid
pseu·do·aconine \ˌsü(ˌ)dō+\ *or* **pseud·aconine** \(ˈ)süd+\ *n* [ISV *pseud-* + *aconine*] : a crystalline base $C_{25}H_{41}NO_8$ obtained by hydrolysis of pseudoaconitine and indaconitine
pseu·do·aconitine \ˌsü(ˌ)dō+\ *or* **pseud·aconitine** \ˌsüd+\ *also* **pseudoaconitin** *n* -S [ISV *pseud-* + *aconitine*] : a very poisonous crystallizable alkaloid $C_{36}H_{51}NO_{12}$ found in the root of an aconite (*Aconitum ferox*) that yields acetic acid, veratric acid, and pseudoaconine on alkaline hydrolysis
pseu·do·adiabatic \ˌsü(ˌ)dō+\ *adj* [*pseud-* + *adiabatic*] : of or relating to processes whereby the temperature of a rising sample of saturated air as it undergoes volume or pressure variations changes without loss or gain of heat except that due to condensation of water vapor and all condensed material drops out as soon as formed — used of the cooling of rising air in which precipitation occurs
pseu·do·aethalium \"+\ *n* [NL, fr. *pseud-* + *aethalium*] : the densely clustered group of distinct sporangia in various myxomycetes
pseu·do·allele \"+\ *n* [*pseud-* + *allele*] : one of two or more closely linked genes that appear to act as a single member of an allelic pair — **pseu·do·allelic** \"+\ *adj* — **pseu·do·allelism** \"+\ *n*
pseu·do·alum \"+\ *n* [*pseud-* + *alum*] : any of various double sulphates of aluminum and a bivalent metal (as magnesium or zinc) that are not isomorphous with common alum
pseu·do·aquatic \"+\ *adj* [*pseud-* + *aquatic*] : growing in moist or wet places but not truly aquatic
pseudoarthrosis *var of* PSEUDARTHROSIS
pseudo base *n* : a compound that though not itself containing basic hydroxyl ion is capable of isomerizing into a true base that does contain hydroxyl ion
pseu·do·benthonic \ˌsü(ˌ)dō+\ *adj* [NL *pseudobenthos* + E *-on* (as in *plankton*) + *-ic*] : of, relating to, or being pseudobenthos
pseu·do·benthos \"+\ *n* [NL, fr. *pseud-* + *benthos*] : PSEUDOPLANKTON
pseu·do·boleite \"+\ *n* [F *pseudoboléite,* fr. *pseud-* + *boléite* boleite] : A hydrous basic chloride of lead and copper $Pb_5Cu_4Cl_{10}(OH)_8.2H_2O$
pseu·do·branch \ˈsüdōˌbraŋk\ *or* **pseu·do·bran·chia** \ˌ==ˈbraŋkēə\ *or* **pseu·do·bran·chi·um** \-ēəm\ *n, pl* **pseudobranchs** \-ks\ *or* **pseudobranchi·ae** \-kēˌē\ *or* **pseudo·bran·chia** \-kēə\ [*pseudobranch* fr. NL *pseudobranchia; pseudobranchia* fr. NL, fr. *pseud-* + ²*-branchia; pseudobranchium* fr. NL, fr. *pseudobranchia*] : an accessory or spurious gill (as on the inner surface of the operculum in various fishes) that is usu. small and is sometimes completely hidden beneath the epithelium — **pseu·do·bran·chi·al** \ˌ==ˈbraŋkēəl\ *or* **pseu·do·bran·chi·ate** \-ēət,-ēˌāt\ *adj*
pseu·do·bran·chus \ˌ==ˈbraŋkəs\ *n, cap* [NL, fr. *pseud-* + *-branchus* -branch] : a genus comprising amphibians closely related to the sirens but with thickened functionless gills and with only three toes on each foot and consisting of a single form (*P. striatus*) of Georgia and Florida that reaches a length of about 18 inches
pseu·do·brookite \ˌsü(ˌ)dō+\ *n* [G *pseudobrookit,* fr. *pseud-* + *brookit* brookite] : an iron titanium oxide Fe_2TiO_5 occurring in small brown or black orthorhombic crystals (sp. gr. 4.4–4.98)
pseu·do·bulb \ˈsüdō+,-\ *n* [*pseud-* + *bulb*] : a solid bulbous enlargement of the stem (as found in many epiphytic orchids)
pseu·do·bulbar \ˌsü(ˌ)dō+\ *adj* [ISV *pseud-* + *bulbar*] : simulating that caused by lesions of the medulla oblongata
pseu·do·bulbil \ˌsü(ˌ)dō+\ *n* [*pseud-* + *bulbil*] : a pear-shaped oophytic outgrowth in various ferns replacing the sporangia and characterizing a phase of apospory
pseu·do·bulbous \"+\ *adj* [*pseudobulb* + *-ous*] : relating to or having a pseudobulb
pseu·do·carbamide \"+\ *n* [*pseud-* + *carbamide*] : PSEUDOUREA
pseu·do·carp \ˈsüdō +,-\ *n* -S [*pseud-* + *-carp*] : ACCESSORY FRUIT — **pseu·do·car·pous** \ˌ==ˈkärpəs\ *adj*
pseud·ocel·lus \ˌsüd+\ *n, pl* **pseudocelli** [NL, fr. *pseud-* + *ocellus*] **1** : one of a pair of minute structures of unknown function on the head of a proturan **2** : one of the simple eyes of a larval insect
pseu·do·cen·trous \ˌsüdōˈsen·trəs\ *adj* [NL *pseudocentrum* + E *-ous*] : having a pseudocentrum
pseu·do·centrum \ˌ=(ˌ)=+\ *n, pl* **pseudocentra** [NL, fr. *pseud-* + *centrum*] : the body of a vertebra formed by fusion of the dorsal or dorsal and ventral arcualia (as in tailed amphibians)
pseu·do·ceratite \"+\ *n* [NL *Pseudoceratites*] : an ammonite of the group Pseudoceratites
pseu·do·ceratites \"+\ *n pl, cap* [NL, fr. *pseud-* + *Ceratites*] *in some classifications* : a group of Cretaceous ammonites with sutures similar to those of Ceratites — **pseu·do·ceratitic** \"+\ *adj*
pseu·do·cercus \"+\ *n* [NL, *pseud-* + *cercus*] : a process on the terminal segments of various insect larvae — called also *urogomphus*
pseu·do·ceryl alcohol \"+. . .-\ *n* [*pseud-* + *ceryl alcohol*] : CERYL ALCOHOL
pseu·do·chromesthesia \ˌsü(ˌ)dō+\ *n* [NL, fr. *pseud-* + *chromesthesia*] : association of sounds with certain colors; *specif* : the production of a colored visual sensation in response to certain sounds
pseu·do·cilium \"+\ *n* [NL, fr. *pseud-* + *cilium*] : one of two or four long hairlike immobile protoplasmic processes extending from the outer surface of each vegetative cell in various colonial algae (as of the genus *Tetraspora*) and often having a dense mucilaginous sheath that may extend beyond the envelope of the colony
¹**pseu·do·classic** *also* **pseu·do·classical** \"+\ *adj* [*pseud-* + *classic* or *classical*] : pretending to be or erroneously regarded as classic
²**pseudoclassic** \"+\ *n* : something (as a work of art) that is pseudoclassic
pseu·do·classicism \"+\ *n* [*pseud-* + *classicism*] : imitative representation of classicism in literature and art (as in the 18th century)
pseudo-clementine \"+\ *adj, usu cap P&C* [*pseud-* + *clementine*] : CLEMENTINE a
pseu·do·coccidae \"+\ *n pl, cap* [NL, fr. *Pseudococcus,* type genus + *-idae*] : a family of hemipterous insects (suborder Homoptera) comprising the mealybugs — see PSEUDOCOCCUS
pseu·do·coccus \"+\ *n, cap* [NL, fr. *pseud-* + *Coccus*] : a genus (type of the family Pseudococcidae) of mealybugs including several that are economically important — see CITROPHILUS MEALYBUG, CITRUS MEALYBUG, COMSTOCK MEALYBUG
pseu·do·coel *also* **pseu·do·cele** *or* **pseu·do·coele** \ˈsüdōˌsēl\ *or* **pseu·do·coelom** \ˌsü(ˌ)dō+\ *n* -S [*pseud-* + *-coel, -cele, -coele* or *coelom*] : a body cavity that is not the product of gastrulation and is not lined with a well-defined mesodermal membrane (as in rotifers and various worms) — compare COELOM — **pseu·do·coe·lic** \ˌ==ˈsēlik\ *adj*
pseu·do·coelomata \ˌsü(ˌ)dō+\ *n pl, cap* [NL, fr. *pseud-* + *Coelomata*] *in some classifications* : a group comprising lower invertebrates in which there is a body cavity that either lacks a mesodermal lining or has one derived from wandering mesenchymal cells, including rotifers, nematodes, bryozoans, and related forms, and being basically equivalent to Aschelminthes
pseu·do·coelomate \ˌsü(ˌ)dō+\ *adj* [*pseudocoelom* + *-ate*] : having a body cavity that is a pseudocoel ⟨~ animals⟩ — compare EUCOELOMATE
pseu·do·conch \ˈsüdō+,-\ *n* -S [*pseud-* + *conch*] : an eminence found above and dorsal to the concha in crocodiles
¹**pseu·do·cone** \"+,-\ *adj* [*pseud-* + *cone*] : being an insect eye in which the crystalline cone is formed by a vitreous secretion of the cone cells — compare EUCONE
²**pseudocone** \"\ *n* : a pseudocone eye
pseu·do·conhydrine \ˌsü(ˌ)dō+\ *n* [*pseud-* + *conhydrine*] : a poisonous crystalline alkaloid $C_8H_{17}NO$ that is found in hemlock and is isomeric with conhydrine which it closely resembles
pseu·do·copulation \"+\ *n* [*pseud-* + *copulation*] : close association of individuals of opposite sex for the bringing together (as in the amplexus of a frog) of the eggs and sperm without actual intromission
pseu·do·cortex \"+\ *n* [NL, fr. *pseud-* + *cortex*] : CORTEX 3c, 3d
pseu·do·cotunnite \"+\ *n* [It, fr. *pseud-* + *cotunnite*] : a mineral consisting of potassium lead chloride K_2PbCl_4(?) found in Vesuvian fumaroles after the volcanic eruptions of 1872 and 1906
pseu·do·crystal \"+\ *n* [ISV *pseud-* + *crystal*] : a solid body that looks crystalline even under a microscope but fails to produce a diffraction pattern indicating true crystallinity ⟨the carbon film . . . is made up of sharply oriented ~s —L.H.Germer⟩ — **pseu·do·crystalline** \"+\ *adj*
pseu·do·cumene \"+\ *n* [ISV *pseud-* + *cumene*] : a liquid hydrocarbon $C_6H_3(CH_3)_3$ isomeric with mesitylene and cumene that is found in coal tar and petroleum; 1,2,4-trimethyl-benzene
pseu·do·cumidine \"+\ *n* [ISV *pseud-* + *cumidine*] : a crystalline base $C_6H_2(CH_3)_3NH_2$ isomeric with cumidine; 2,4,5-trimethyl-aniline
pseu·do·cumyl \"+\ *n* [*pseud-* + *cumyl*] : any of three trimethyl-phenyl radicals $(CH_3)_3C_6H_2$ that are derived from cumene
pseu·do·cyesis \"+\ *n* [NL, fr. *pseud-* + *cyesis*] : a psychosomatic state marked by involuntary simulation of pregnancy and often accompanied by clear-cut physical symptoms (as cessation of menses, enlargement of the abdomen, and apparent fetal movements) and changes in endocrine balance of the same type as but less marked than those accompanying pregnancy — called also *false pregnancy*
pseu·do·cyst \ˈsüdō+,-\ *n* [*pseud-* + *cyst*] **1** : a cluster of toxoplasms in an enucleate host cell **2** : CYSTOID 1
pseu·do·deltidium \ˌsü(ˌ)dō+\ *n* [NL, fr. *pseud-* + *deltidium*] : DELTIDIUM 1
pseu·do·derm \ˈsüdōˌdərm\ *n* -S [*pseud-* + *-derm*] : an outer covering in various sponges of the class Calcispongiae formed by outgrowth from the peripheral portions of the incurrent canals — **pseu·do·der·mic** \ˌ==ˈdərmik\ *adj*
pseu·do·diphtheria bacillus \ˌsü(ˌ)dō+. . .-\ *n* [*pseudodiphtheria* fr. NL, fr. *pseud-* + *diphtheria*] : a nonpathogenic bacterium (*Corynebacterium pseudodiphthericum*) that closely resembles the organism causing diphtheria but occurs in healthy throats
pseu·do·dipteral \ˌsü(ˌ)dō+\ *adj* [Gk *pseudodipteros* + E *-al*] : marked by columniation that is falsely or imperfectly dipteral in that the inner row of columns is omitted but the space for them is preserved — see COLUMNIATION illustration
pseu·do·dipteros \"+\ *n* [NL, fr. Gk, pseudodipteral, fr. *pseud-* + *dipteros* dipteral — more at DIPTERA] : a pseudodipteral building
pseu·do·dominance \"+\ *n* [*pseud-* + *dominance*] : appearance of a recessive phenotype in a heterozygote containing the dominant factor on one chromosome and a deficiency on the other — called also *mock-dominance*
pseud·odont \ˈsüdōˌdänt\ *adj* [*pseud-* + *-odont*] : having spurious or horny teeth ⟨monotremes are ~⟩
¹**pseu·do·dox** \-ˌäks\ *n* -ES [Gk *pseudodoxos* holding a false opinion, fr. *pseudodoxein* to hold a false opinion, fr. *pseud-* + *doxa* opinion — more at DOXOLOGY] : a false opinion or doctrine
²**pseudodox** \"\ *adj* : false esp. in opinion or doctrine
pseu·do·doxy \-sē\ *n* -ES [Gk *pseudodoxia* false opinion, fr. *pseudodoxein* to hold a false opinion + *-ia* -y] : an erroneous belief; *also* : the holding of erroneous beliefs ⟨a splendid list of contemporary *pseudodoxies,* mostly old-country beliefs —*Times Lit. Supp.*⟩
pseu·do·ephedrine \ˌsü(ˌ)dō+\ *n* [*pseud-* + *ephedrine*] : a poisonous crystalline alkaloid $C_{10}H_{15}NO$ occurring with ephedrine and isomeric with it
pseu·do·farcy \"+\ *n* [*pseud-* + *farcy*] : EPIZOOTIC LYMPHANGITIS
pseu·do·fertilization \"+\ *n* [*pseud-* + *fertilization*] : a process substituting for normal fertilization (as fusion of egg and polar body in various coccids or pseudogamy in a nematode)
pseudo-foot-and-mouth disease *n* : VESICULAR STOMATITIS
pseudo-fowl pest *n* : NEWCASTLE DISEASE
pseu·do·galena \ˌsü(ˌ)dō+\ *n* [NL, fr. *pseud-* + *galena*] : SPHALERITE
pseu·do·gam·ic \ˌsüdōˈgamik\ *adj* : of, relating to, or being pseudogamy
pseu·dog·a·my \süˈdägəmē\ *n* -ES [ISV *pseud-* + *-gamy*] **1** : activation of an egg by a sperm without accompanying nuclear fusion **2** : diploid parthenogenesis
pseu·do·gastrula \ˌsü(ˌ)dō+\ *n* [NL, fr. *pseud-* + *gastrula*] : AMPHIBLASTULA
pseu·do·generic name \"+. . .-\ *n* [*pseudogeneric* fr. *pseud-* + *generic*] : a designation used in the manner of a generic name but without taxonomic validity to group organisms too imperfectly known to permit valid classification ⟨*Sparganum, Tornaria, Cysticercus* are *pseudogeneric names*⟩ — compare FORM GENUS
pseu·do·glanders \"+\ *n pl but sing or pl in constr* [*pseud-* + *glanders*] : an infectious lymphangitis of horses and other equines caused by the bacterium (*Corynebacterium pseudotuberculosis*) responsible for caseous lymphadenitis of sheep, marked by ulcerating nodules of the lymph nodes of the legs, and readily mistaken for cutaneous glanders
pseu·do·globulin \"+\ *n* [ISV *pseud-* + *globulin*] : a simple protein insoluble in half-saturated ammonium sulfate or sodium sulfate solutions but soluble in pure water — distinguished from *euglobulin*
pseu·do·glottis \"+\ *n* [NL, fr. *pseud-* + *glottis*] : the space between the false vocal cords
pseu·do·graph \ˈsüdōˌgraf, -ˌräf\ *n* [LL *pseudographus,* fr. LGk *pseudographos* writer of falsehoods, fr. Gk *pseudographein* to write false statements, fr. *pseud-* + *graphein* to write — more at CARVE] : a false writing : a spurious document : FORGERY, PSEUDEPIGRAPH — **pseu·dog·ra·pher** \süˈdägrəfə(r)\ *n* -S
pseu·dog·ra·phy \süˈdägrəfē\ *n* -ES [*pseud-* + *-graphy*] *archaic* : incorrect writing or printing of words : wrong or bad spelling
pseu·do·grasserie \ˌsü(ˌ)dō+\ *n* [*pseud-* + *grasserie*] : a disease of the gypsy moth and other caterpillars thought to be due to a virus
pseu·do·gry·phus \ˌsüdōˈgrīfəs\ [NL, fr. *pseud-* + L *gryphus* griffin — more at GRIFFIN] *syn of* GYMNOGYPS
pseu·do·gyne \ˈsüdōˌjīn\ *n* -S [ISV *pseud-* + *-gyne*] **1** : an insect (as an aphid) that reproduces parthenogenetically **2** : an abnormal form of worker ant with a well-developed body approaching that of the fertile female esp. in the shape of the thorax — **pseu·dog·y·nous** \(ˈ)süˈdäjənəs\ *adj*
pseu·dog·y·ny \süˈdäjənē\ *n* -ES [*pseud-* + *-gyn* + *-y*] : use of a feminine name by a man as a pseudonym — compare PSEUDANDRY
pseu·do·halide \ˌsü(ˌ)dō+\ *n* [*pseud-* + *halide*] : a binary compound of a pseudohalogen analogous to a halide
pseu·do·hallucination \"+\ *n* [ISV *pseud-* + *hallucination*] : an externalized sensory image vivid enough to be a hallucination but recognized as unreal
pseu·do·hallucinatory \"+\ *adj* [*pseudohallucination* + *-ory*] : characterized by or tending to produce pseudohallucinations
pseu·do·halogen \"+\ *n* [ISV *pseud-* + *halogen*] : any of several radicals (as cyanogen and the cyanate, thiocyanate, and azide groups) that resemble halogens in reactions
pseu·do·hemophilia \"+\ *n* [NL, fr. *pseud-* + *hemophilia*] : a bleeding tendency occurring in both males and females marked by a prolonged bleeding time despite a normal number of blood platelets but often with an inability of injured capillaries to contract properly after minor injury — compare HEMOPHILIA
pseu·do·hermaphrodism \"+\ *n* [ISV *pseud-* + *hermaphrodism;* prob. orig. formed as F *pseudohermaphrodisme*] : PSEUDOHERMAPHRODITISM
pseu·do·hermaphrodite \"+\ *n* [ISV *pseud-* + *hermaphrodite;* prob. orig. formed in F] : an individual exhibiting pseudohermaphroditism
pseu·do·hermaphroditic \"+\ *adj* [*pseudohermaphrodite* + *-ic*] : relating to or exhibiting pseudohermaphroditism
pseu·do·hermaphroditism \"+\ *n* [ISV *pseud-* + *hermaphroditism*] : the condition of having the gonads of one sex and the external genitalia and other sex organs so variably developed that the sex of the individual is uncertain
pseu·do·hexagonal \"+\ *adj* [*pseud-* + *hexagonal*] *of a crystal or axis* : approximating in form to the hexagonal type
pseu·do·hieroglyphic script \"+. . .-\ *n* [*pseud-* + *hieroglyphic*] : a syllabic form of writing related to Egyptian hieroglyphics and used esp. at Byblos before 1500 B.C.
pseu·do·hyoscyamine \"+\ *n* [*pseud-* + *hyoscyamine*] : an alkaloid $C_{17}H_{23}NO_3$ obtained from the leaves of a corkwood (*Duboisia myoporoides*) and used as a sedative and antispasmodic like atropine
pseu·do·hypertrophic \"+\ *adj* [ISV *pseud-* + *hypertrophic*] : falsely hypertrophic : exhibiting increase in size without true hypertrophy — **pseu·do·hypertrophy** \"+\ *n*
pseu·do·insoluble \"+\ *adj* [*pseud-* + *insoluble*] : of, relating to, or constituting a substance that is not dissolved by the usual acid reagents but that is soluble in some specific solvent
pseu·do·is \ˈsüdəwəs, ˈsüˌdōis, süˈdōəs\ *n, cap* [*pseud-* + *ois* (perh. contr. of *Ovis*)] : a genus that comprises the bharal
pseu·do·isatin \ˌsü(ˌ)dō+\ *n* [*pseud-* + *isatin*] : the isomeric lactam form of isatin
pseudo-isidorian *or* **pseudo-isidorean** \"+\ *or* **pseudo-isidoran** \ˌ=(ˌ)=ˌizəˈdōrən\ *adj, often cap P & usu cap I* : of, relating to, or constituting a 9th century collection of decretals, decisions of councils, and letters consisting chiefly of forged documents held to have been compiled by St Isidore of Seville
pseu·do·isochromatic plate \ˌsü(ˌ)dō+. .-\ *n* [*pseudo-isochromatic* fr. *pseud-* + *isochromatic*] : one of a set of colored plates that include some which appear isochromatic to individuals with color-vision abnormality and that are widely used as a test for color blindness — compare ISHIHARA TEST
pseu·do·jervine \ˌsü(ˌ)dō+\ *n* [*pseud-* + *jervine*] : a crystalline alkaloid $C_{29}H_{43}NO_7$ resembling jervine and occurring with it
pseu·do·keratin \"+\ *n* [ISV *pseud-* + *keratin*] : a protein (as neurokeratin) that occurs esp. in the skin and nerve sheaths and that like keratins is insoluble but is less resistant to enzyme action than keratins
pseu·do·labial \"+\ *adj* [NL *pseudolabium* + E *-al*] : simulating a lip : having or being a pseudolabium ⟨a ~ process⟩
pseu·do·labium \"+\ *n* [NL, fr. *pseud-* + *labium*] : a liplike process esp. on a nematode worm
pseu·do·lamellibranchia \"+\ *n pl, cap* [NL, fr. *pseud-* + *Lamellibranchia*] *in some classifications* : an order of Lamellibranchia comprising bivalve mollusks (as scallops, pearl oysters, true oysters) having gills with interfilamentary and interlamellar junctions poorly developed, the mantle edges entirely open, and the anterior adductor muscle usu. wanting — **pseu·do·lamellibranchiate** \"+\ *adj*
pseu·do·lamellibranchiata \"+\ *n pl, cap* [NL, fr. *pseud-* + *Lamellibranchiata*] *syn of* PSEUDOLAMELLIBRANCHIA
pseu·do·larix \"+\ *n, cap* [NL, fr. *pseud-* + *Larix*] : a genus of Chinese coniferous deciduous trees (family Pinaceae) having the staminate flowers clustered and the cone scales deciduous — compare LARIX; see GOLDEN LARCH
pseu·do·leucite \"+\ *n* [ISV *pseud-* + *leucite*] : a mixture of orthoclase and nepheline pseudomorphic after leucite
pseu·do·leukemia \"+\ *n* [NL, fr. *pseud-* + *leukemia*] : any abnormal state (as Hodgkin's disease) resembling leukemia in its anatomical changes but lacking the changes in the circulating blood characteristic of the latter — **pseu·do·leukemic** \"+\ *adj*
pseu·do·log·i·cal \ˌsüdᵊlˈäjəkəl\ *adj* [*pseudology* + *-ical*] : fantastically or romantically falsified ⟨accounts of it are doubtless somewhat ~ —F.C.Prescott⟩
pseu·dol·o·gist \süˈdäləjəst\ *n* -S [Gk *pseudologistēs,* fr. *pseudologein* to speak falsely (fr. *pseudologos* speaking falsely) + *-istēs* -ist] : LIAR
pseu·do·logue \ˈsüdᵊlˌȯg *also* -ˌäg\ *n* -S [prob. fr. F, fr. Gk *pseudologos*] : a pathological liar
pseu·dol·o·gy \süˈdäləjē\ *n* -ES [Gk *pseudologia,* fr. *pseudologos* speaking falsely (fr. *pseud-* + *logos* speech) + *-ia* -y — more at LEGEND] : FALSEHOOD, LYING

pseu·do·looper \ˈsü(ˌ)dō+\ n [pseud- + looper] : the caterpillar of a moth (*Plusia argentifera*) that damages tobacco and other plants in Australia

pseu·do·lyn·chia \ˌsüdōˈliŋkēə\ n, cap [NL, fr. *pseud-* + *Lynchia*, genus of flies] : a genus of hippoboscid flies including the pigeon fly

pseu·do·malachite \ˈsü(ˌ)dō+\ n [G *pseudomalachit*, fr. *pseud-* + *malachit* malachite] : a hydrous basic copper phosphate $Cu_5(PO_4)_2(OH)_4.H_2O(?)$ resembling malachite — called also *dihydrite*

pseu·do·man·cy \ˈsüdəˌman(t)sē\ n -ES [LGk *pseudomanteia*, fr. *pseud-* + Gk *manteia* divination — more at -MANCY] : false or counterfeit divination — **pseu·do·man·tic** \ˌ==ˈmantik\ adj

pseu·do·mat \ˈsüdō+,-\ adj [*pseud-* + *mat*] *of a ceramic glaze* : having a mat surface because of incomplete fusion

pseu·do·membrane \ˈsü(ˌ)dō+\ n [*pseud-* + *membrane*] : FALSE MEMBRANE — **pseu·do·membranous** \"+\ adj

pseu·do·metameric \"+\ adj [*pseudometamerism* + *-ic*] : of, relating to, or exhibiting pseudometamerism ⟨a ~ worm⟩

pseu·do·metamerism *also* **pseu·do·metamery** \"+\ n [*pseud-* + *metamerism* or *metamery*] : false segmentation

pseu·do·mix·is \ˌ=(ˌ)=ˈmiksəs\ n, pl **pseudomix·es** \-k(ˌ)sēz\ [NL, fr. *pseud-* + *-mixis*] : pseudofertilization involving fusion of cells other than gametes and resulting in embryo formation

pseu·dom·o·nad \süˈdäməˌnad\ n [NL *Pseudomonad-, Pseudomonas*] : PSEUDOMONAS 2

pseu·dom·o·na·da·ce·ae \sü,dämənəˈdāsē,ē, ˌsüdə,mänəˈd-\ n pl, cap [NL, fr. *Pseudomonad-, Pseudomonas*, type genus + *-aceae*] : a large family of rod-shaped or somewhat spiral usu. aerobic and gram-negative bacteria (order Pseudomonadales) that do not form endospores, are commonly motile by polar flagella, and include saprophytes in soil and water and important plant and animal pathogens — see PSEUDOMONAS, XANTHOMONAS

pseu·dom·o·na·da·les \sü,dämənəˈdā(ˌ)lēz, ˌsüdəmänəˈd-\ n pl, cap [NL, fr. *Pseudomonad-, Pseudomonas* + *-ales*] : a large order of spherical, rod-shaped or spiral eubacteria which are usu. motile by polar flagella and some of which contain photosynthetic pigments — compare ATHIORHODACEAE, CAULOBACTERACEAE, NITROBACTERIACEAE, PSEUDOMONADACEAE, SPIRILLACEAE, THIORHODACEAE

psue·dom·o·nas \ˌsüdəˈmōnəs *also* süˈdämənəs\ n [NL, fr. *pseud-* + *-monas*] **1** *cap* : a genus (the type of the family Pseudomonadaceae) comprising short rod-shaped bacteria many of which produce greenish fluorescent water-soluble pigment and including saprophytes, a few animal pathogens, and numerous important plant pathogens — see XANTHOMONAS **2** *pl* **pseudo·mon·a·des** \ˌsüdəˈmänəˌdēz\ : any bacterium of the genus *Pseudomonas*

pseu·do·monocotyledonous \ˈsü(ˌ)dō+\ adj [*pseud-* + *monocotyledonous*] : having the two cotyledons coalesced or one of them aborted — used of a normally dicotyledonous embryo

pseu·do·monotropy \"+\ n [*pseud-* + *monotropy*] : monotropy in which the transition point lies below the melting points of the two forms

¹pseu·do·morph \ˈsüdəˌmȯrf\ n -s [prob. fr. F *pseudomorphe*, fr. *pseud-* + *-morphe* -morph] **1** : a mineral (as a piece of quartz) having the characteristic outward form of another species (as the cubic form of fluorite) or of some object (as a shell) ⟨limonite occurs as a ~ after pyrite⟩ ⟨unidentified trunks are preserved as ~s —G.W.Sinclair⟩ **2** : something formed in the manner of a pseudomorph ⟨the concept of the cultural ~ —Lewis Mumford⟩

²pseudomorph \"\ vt -ED/-ING/-S : PSEUDOMORPHOSE ⟨glauberite ~ed to selenite —*Ward's Natural Science Bull.*⟩

pseu·do·morphine \ˈsü(ˌ)dō+\ n [ISV *pseud-* + *morphine*; orig. formed in F] : a nonpoisonous crystalline alkaloid $C_{34}H_{36}N_2O_6$ obtained from opium and by oxidation of morphine

pseu·do·mor·phism \ˌsüdəˈmȯrˌfizəm\ n -s [prob. fr. F *pseudomorphisme*, fr. *pseudomorphe* pseudomorph + *-isme* -ism] : the property of crystallizing as a pseudomorph

pseu·do·mor·phose \ˌ==ˈmȯrˌfōz, -ōs\ vt -ED/-ING/-S [F *pseudomorphose*, n., mineral form resulting from pseudomorphosis, fr. *pseudomorphe* + *-ose* -osis] : to transform into a pseudomorph

pseu·do·mor·pho·sis \ˌsüdəˈmȯrfəsəs, -ˌmȯrˈfōs-\ n, pl **pseudomorpho·ses** \-ōˌsēz\ [NL, fr. ISV *pseudomorph* + NL *-osis*] : transformation into a pseudomorph

pseu·do·mor·phous \ˌ==ˈmȯrfəs\ *or* **pseu·do·mor·phic** \-fik\ [*pseudomorphous*, fr. *pseud-* + *morph-* + *-ous*; *pseudomorphic* prob. fr. F *pseudomorphique*, fr. *pseud-* + Gk *morphē* form + F *-ique* -ic — more at FORM] : of, relating to, or being a pseudomorph : exhibiting pseudomorphism

pseu·do·mycelial \"+\ adj [NL *pseudomycelium* + E *-al*] : of, relating to, or producing pseudomycelium

pseu·do·mycelium \"+\ n [NL, fr. *pseud-* + *mycelium*] : a cellular association occurring in various higher bacteria and yeasts in which cells cling together in chains resembling small true mycelia

pseu·do·myr·mex \ˌsüdōˈmərˌmeks\ n, cap [NL, fr. *pseud-* + Gk *myrmēx* ant] : a neotropical genus of ants

pseu·do·neuroma \ˈsü(ˌ)dō+\ n [NL, fr. *pseud-* + *neuroma*] : NEUROMA 2

pseu·do·neuropter \ˈsü(ˌ)dō+\ n -s [NL *Pseudoneuroptera*] : an insect of the division Pseudoneuroptera

pseu·do·neuroptera \"+\ n pl, cap [NL, fr. *pseud-* + *Neuroptera*] *in some esp former classifications* : a division of insects having reticulate wings like those of the Neuroptera among which they have sometimes been included but undergoing an incomplete metamorphosis and including the dragonflies, mayflies, termites, psocids and book lice, bird lice, caddis flies, scorpion flies, stone flies, and others that are now placed in separate orders — **pseu·do·neuropteran** \"+\ adj or n — **pseu·do·neuropterous** \"+\ adj

pseu·do·ni·trole \ˌ==ˈnīˌtrōl\ n -s [G *pseudonitrol*, fr. *pseud-* + *nitr-* + *-ole*] : any of a class of compounds of the general formula $RR'C(NO)NO_2$ formed by the action of nitrous acid on a disubstituted nitromethane $RR'CHNO_2$ as pungent-odored, colorless, solid dimers that when fused or dissolved depolymerize into the monomers of intense and characteristic blue color — compare NITROLIC ACID

pseu·do·nitrosite \ˈsü(ˌ)dō+\ n [*pseud-* + *nitrosite*] : any of a class of compounds isomeric with nitrosites and characterized by the grouping $-C(NO)C(NO_2)$

pseu·do·nucleolus \"+\ n [NL, fr. *pseud-* + *nucleolus*] : KARYOSOME

pseud·onychium \ˈsüd+\ n, pl **pseudonychia** [NL, fr. *pseud-* + *-onychium*] : PARONYCHIUM

pseu·do·nym *also* **pseu·do·nyme** \ˈsüdᵊnˌim\ n -s [F *pseudonyme*, fr. Gk *pseudōnymos* falsely named, fr. *pseud-* + *onyma, onoma* name — more at NAME] : a fictitious name assumed (as by an author) for the time : PEN NAME

pseu·do·nym·i·ty \ˌsüdᵊnˈiməd·ē, -mətē, -i\ n -ES [*pseudonym* + *-ity*] : the use (as by an author) of a pseudonym; *also* : the fact or state of being signed (as of a book or other writing) with a pseudonym

pseu·don·y·mous \(ˈ)süˈdänəməs\ *also* **pseu·do·nym·ic** \ˌsüdᵊnˈimik\ adj [*pseudonymous* fr. Gk *pseudōnymos*; *pseudonymic* fr. F *pseudonyme* + E *-ic*] : bearing or using a false or fictitious name : identified by a pseudonym ⟨a ~ work⟩ ⟨a ~ author⟩; *also* : being a pseudonym — **pseu·don·y·mous·ly** adv — **pseu·don·y·mous·ness** n -ES

pseu·do·paralysis \ˈsü(ˌ)dō+\ n [NL, fr. *pseud-* + *paralysis*] : apparent lack or loss of muscular power (as that produced by pain) unattended by paralysis

pseu·do·parasite \"+\ n [ISV *pseud-* + *parasite*] : something (as a normally free-living organism, a spore, or a bit of food debris) that appears in a specimen (as of blood or feces) and is mistaken for a parasite — **pseu·do·parasitic** \"+\ adj

pseu·do·parenchyma \"+\ n [NL, fr. *pseud-* + *parenchyma*] : a tissuey aggregation of compactly interwoven short-celled filaments in a thallophyte that somewhat resembles the parenchyma of higher plants — compare PLECTENCHYMA — **pseu·do·parenchymatous** \"+\ adj

pseu·do·pelletierine \"+\ n [ISV *pseud-* + *pelletierine*] : a crystalline bicyclic alkaloid $C_9H_{15}NO$ found with pelletierine

pseud·opercular *or* **pseud·operculate** \ˈsüd+\ adj [NL *pseudoperculum* + E *-ar* or *-ate*] : of or relating to a pseudoperculum

pseud·operculum \"+\ n [NL, fr. *pseud-* + *operculum*] : EPIPHRAGM 1

pseu·do·perianth \ˈsü(ˌ)dō+\ n [*pseud-* + *perianth*] : a thin cuplike or saclike protective envelope one cell thick that develops after fertilization around the archegonium in some liverworts

pseu·do·peridium \"+\ n [NL, fr. *pseud-* + *peridium*] : a membranous cup enclosing the aeciospores in various rust fungi

pseu·do·peripteral \"+\ adj [*pseud-* + *peripteral*] : marked by columniation that is falsely or imperfectly peripteral with the lateral or lateral and rear columns engaged — compare PERISTYLAR; see COLUMNIATION illustration

pseu·do·peziza \"+\ n, cap [NL, fr. *pseud-* + *Peziza*] : a genus of fungi (family Mollisiaceae) having smooth waxy ascocarps and thin-walled asci that bear hyaline unicellular spores, containing one form (*P. medicaginis*) that causes a leaf spot of alfalfa and another (*P. ribis*) that causes anthracnose of currants, and including some species that were formerly included in the form genera *Colletotrichum, Gloeosporium*, and *Marssonina*

pseu·do·phyl·lid·ea \ˌsü(ˌ)dōfəˈlidēə\ n pl, cap [NL, fr. *pseud-* + *phyll-* + *-idea*] : an order of Cestoda comprising tapeworms with two sucking grooves on the unarmed scolex and the vitelline glands scattered throughout the parenchyma and including numerous parasites of fish-eating vertebrates (as the medically important fish tapeworm of man) — **pseu·do·phyl·lid·e·an** \ˌ=(ˌ)==ˈ=dēən\ adj or n

pseudo-pindaric ode \ˈsü(ˌ)dō+. . .-\ n, *usu cap 2d P* : IRREGULAR ODE

pseu·do·pionnotes \ˈsü(ˌ)dō+\ n pl but sing or pl in constr [NL, fr. *pseud-* + *pionnotes*] : pionnotes that are buttery instead of gelatinous

pseu·do·placenta \"+\ n [NL, fr. *pseud-* + *placenta*] : a membranous organ occurring in a few insects and functioning as a placenta — **pseu·do·placental** \"+\ adj

pseu·do·plague \ˈsüdō+,-\ n [*pseud-* + *plague*] : NEWCASTLE DISEASE

pseu·do·plankton \ˈsü(ˌ)dō+\ n [NL, fr. *pseud-* + *plankton*] : organisms (as bryozoans, barnacles, corals, or corallines) that attach themselves to floating vegetation or debris and are thus effectively a part of the plankton — **pseu·do·planktonic** \"+\ adj

pseu·do·plasm \ˈsüdōˌplazəm\ n [ISV *pseud-* + *plasm*; prob. orig. formed in G] : an apparent neoplasm that disappears spontaneously : PHANTOM TUMOR

pseu·do·plasmodium \ˈsü(ˌ)dō+\ n [NL, fr. *pseud-* + *plasmodium*] : an aggregation of myxamoebas resembling a plasmodium but without protoplasmic fusion (as in members of the genus *Acrasia*)

pseu·do·plastic \"+\ adj [*pseud-* + *plastic*] **1** : lacking the capacity for major modification or evolutionary differentiation — compare EURYPLASTIC, STENOPLASTIC **2** : characterized by or being flow in which the rate of flow (as of solutions of rubber or gelatinous substances) increases faster than normally in relation to the shearing stress — **pseu·do·plasticity** \"+\ n

pseu·do·pod \ˈsüdəˌpäd\ *also* **pseu·do·pode** \-ˌpōd\ n [in sense 1, fr. NL *pseudopodium*; in other senses, fr. *pseud-* + *-pod, -pode*] **1** *also* **pseudopode** : PSEUDOPODIUM **2** : a supposed or apparent psychic projection (as from a medium's body) **3** : something resembling a pseudopodium: as **a** : a slender extension from the edge of a wheal at the site of injection of an allergen **b** : one of the slender processes of some tumor cells extending out from the main mass of a tumor **4** : the paired unsegmented abdominal legs of caterpillars and sawfly larvae

pseu·dop·o·dal \(ˈ)süˈdäpədᵊl\ *or* **pseu·do·po·di·al** \ˌsüdəˈpōdēəl\ adj : of, relating to, or resembling a pseudopod or pseudopodium

pseu·do·pod·ic \ˌsüdəˈpädik\ adj [ISV *pseudopod* + *-ic*] : PSEUDOPODAL

pseu·do·po·di·um \ˌsüdəˈpōdēəm\ n, pl **pseudopo·dia** \-ēə\ [NL, fr. *pseud-* + *-podium*] **1 a** : a temporary protrusion or retractile process of the protoplasm of a cell (as a unicellular organism or a leukocyte of a higher organism) often having a fairly definite filamentous form, sometimes fusing with others to form a network, and serving esp. as an organ of locomotion or for taking up food — see AXOPODIUM, FILOPODIUM, LOBOPODIUM, MYXOPODIUM **b** : one of the amoeboid protrusions of an active myxomycete plasmodium **2** : a slender leafless branch of the gametophyte in various mosses that often bears gemmae **3** : the foot of a rotifer

pseu·do·pore \ˈsüdəˌpō(ə)r\ n [ISV *pseud-* (in *pseudoderm*) + *pore*; prob. orig. formed in F] : a pore in the pseudoderm of a sponge

pseu·do·porphyritic \ˈsü(ˌ)dō+\ adj [*pseud-* + *porphyritic*] *of a rock* : having a porphyritic appearance caused by the more rapid growth of various crystals but not being a true porphyry

pseu·do·pregnancy \"+\ n [*pseud-* + *pregnancy*] **1** : PSEUDOCYESIS **2** : an anestrous state resembling pregnancy that occurs in various mammals (as the dog, ferret, rabbit) usu. following an infertile copulation — compare CLOUDBURST 3, PSEUDOCYESIS — **pseu·do·pregnant** \"+\ adj

pseu·do·proposition \"+\ n [*pseud-* + *proposition*] : PSEUDOSTATEMENT

pseu·do·prostyle \"+\ adj [*pseud-* + *prostyle*] : marked by columniation that is falsely or imperfectly prostyle with the portico columns less than an intercolumniation from the front wall or engaged in it

pseud·optics \(ˈ)süd+\ n pl but usu sing in constr [*pseud-* + *optics*] : the study of optical illusions

pseu·do·pupa \ˈsü(ˌ)dō+\ n [NL, fr. *pseud-* + *pupa*] : resting stage that intervenes in any of various insects between two of the larval stages of hypermetamorphosis; *also* : an individual in this stage — **pseu·do·pupal** \"+\ adj

pseu·do·purpurin \"+\ n [ISV *pseud-* + *purpurin*] : a red crystalline compound $C_{14}H_4O_2(OH)_3COOH$ obtained from madder root and also made synthetically that decomposes in boiling water into purpurin and carbon dioxide and whose alumina lake is a fine red pigment; purpurin-carboxylic acid

pseu·do·rabies \"+\ n [NL, fr. *pseud-* + *rabies*] : an acute febrile virus disease of domestic animals (as cattle, swine) marked by cutaneous irritation and intense itching followed by encephalomyelitis and pharyngeal paralysis and commonly terminating in death within 48 hours — called also *mad itch*; see BULBAR PARALYSIS

pseu·do·racemic \"+\ adj [*pseud-* + *racemic*] : of or relating to optically inactive mixed crystals containing equal quantities of the dextro and levo forms of an active compound

pseu·do·ramose \"+\ adj [*pseud-* + *ramose*] : forming false branches

pseu·do·raphe \"+\ n [NL, fr. *pseud-* + *raphe*] : an axial area on the valve of various diatoms that lacks markings but simulates the true raphe

pseu·do·reduction \"+\ n [*pseud-* + *reduction*] : an apparent halving of the number of chromosomes by synapsis

pseu·do·reminiscence \"+\ n [*pseud-* + *reminiscence*] : an error of memory consisting in illusory recall of an experience that one has not had — compare CONFABULATION

pseu·do·saccharomycetaceae \"+\ n pl, cap [NL, fr. *Pseudosaccharomycet-, Pseudosaccharomyces*, type genus (fr. *pseud-* + *sacchar-* + *mycet-, -myces*) + *-aceae*] : a family of yeastlike fungi (order Moniliales) that do not germinate by repetition

pseu·do·salt \ˈsüdō+,-\ n [*pseud-* + *salt*] : a compound (as stannic chloride or mercuric cyanide) analogous in formula to a salt and sometimes called a salt but not ionized as such

pseu·do·scarus \ˈsü(ˌ)dō+\ n, cap [NL, fr. *pseud-* + *Scarus*] : a widely distributed genus of parrot fishes

pseu·do·science \"+\ n [*pseud-* + *science*] : a system of theories, assumptions, and methods erroneously regarded as scientific

pseu·do·scientific \"+\ adj [*pseud-* + *scientific*] : of, relating to, or having the characteristics of a pseudoscience or pseudoscientists

pseu·do·scientist \"+\ n [*pseud-* + *scientist*] : a practitioner of a pseudoscience

pseud·oscines \(ˈ)süd+\ n pl, cap [NL, fr. *pseud-* + *Oscines*] *in some classifications* : a superfamily equivalent to the suborder *Menurae* — **pseud·oscinine** \"+\ adj

pseu·do·scolex \ˈsü(ˌ)dō+\ n [NL, fr. *pseud-* + *scolex*] : an altered group of anterior segments that in some tapeworms replaces the scolex and serves as a holdfast

pseu·do·scope \ˈsüdəˌskōp\ n [*pseud-* + *-scope*] : an optical instrument that exhibits objects with their proper relief reversed, thus producing an effect opposite to that of the stereoscope — **pseu·do·scop·ic** \ˌ==ˈskäpik\ adj — **pseu·do·scop·i·cal·ly** \-pək(ə)lē\ adv

pseu·dos·co·py \süˈdäskəpē\ n -ES [ISV *pseudoscope* + *-y*] : the production of the effect of reversed relief (as by the pseudoscope)

pseu·do·scorpion \ˈsü(ˌ)dō+\ n [NL *Pseudoscorpiones*] : an arachnid of the order Pseudoscorpiones

pseu·do·scorpiones \"+\ n pl, cap [NL, fr. *pseud-* + *Scorpiones*] : an order of Arachnida comprising the book scorpions

pseu·do·scorpionida *or* **pseu·do·scorpionidea** \"+\ [NL, fr. *pseud-* + *Scorpionida* or *Scorpionidea*] *syn of* PSEUDOSCORPIONES

pseu·do·segmentation \"+\ n [*pseud-* + *segmentation*] : external annulation of the body of a nonmetameric animal (as a nematode) so that it appears segmented

pseu·do·segmented \"+\ adj [*pseud-* + *segmented*, past part. of ²*segment*] : having a superficial annulation that simulates metameric segmentation ⟨~ nematodes of the genus *Desmoscolex*⟩

pseu·do·septate \"+\ adj [*pseud-* + *septate*] : apparently septate ⟨~ spores⟩

pseu·do·septum \"+\ n [NL, fr. *pseud-* + *septum*] : a septum that is perforated by one or more openings (as in various algae and fungi)

pseu·do·skeleton \"+\ n [*pseud-* + *skeleton*] : a sponge skeleton consisting of foreign bodies not secreted by the animal — opposed to *autoskeleton*

pseu·do·social \"+\ adj [*pseud-* + *social*] : marked by or reflecting loyalty to a small group that is usu. predatory and parasitic on society

pseu·do·solution \"+\ n [*pseud-* + *solution*] : a colloidal solution

pseu·do·sophisticated \"+\ adj [*pseud-* + *sophisticated*] : marked by a false or feigned sophistication

pseu·do·sperm \ˈsüdōˌspərm\ n [NL *pseudospermium*] : PSEUDOSPERMIUM

pseu·do·sper·mi·um \ˌsüdōˈspərmēəm\ n, pl **pseudospermia** [NL, fr. *pseud-* + *-spermium* (fr. Gk *sperma* seed) — more at SPERM] : a small indehiscent seedlike fruit (as an achene) — **pseu·do·sper·mous** \ˌ==ˈ=məs\ adj

pseu·do·sphaeriaceae \ˈsü(ˌ)dō+\ n pl, cap [NL, fr. *pseud-* + *Sphaeriaceae*] : a family of ascomycetous fungi (order Dothideales) having separate stromata resembling perithecia and each bearing a single ascus

pseu·do·sphaeriales \"+\ n pl, cap [NL, fr. *pseud-* + *Sphaeriales*] *in some classifications* : an order of ascomycetous fungi including forms (as those of the family Pseudosphaeriaceae) in which one ascus develops in each stromatic cavity

pseu·do·sphere \ˈsüdō+,-\ n [ISV *pseud-* + *sphere*; prob. orig. formed as It *pseudosfera*] : a surface of constant negative curvature (as generated by the revolution of a tractrix about its axis)

pseu·do·statement \ˈsü(ˌ)dō+\ n [*pseud-* + *statement*] **1** : a statement that cannot be empirically verified; *esp* : a statement made in a poem **2** : a sentence that is grammatically correct yet fails to express a total sense (as in the sentence "the true is more identical than the beautiful")

pseu·do·stereoscopic \"+\ adj [*pseud-* + *stereoscopic*] : giving the impression of three-dimensional relief by other means (as movement, color, perspective) than binocular vision

pseu·dos·to·ma \süˈdästəmə\ n [NL, fr. *pseud-* + *stoma*] **1** : a stigma in serous membrane filled by intercellular substance or otherwise closed **2** : the temporary mouth of a larval echinoderm **3** : the osculum of a sponge — **pseu·do·stoma·tous** \ˌsüdəˈstōmədəs, -täm-\ *or* **pseu·dos·to·mous** \(ˈ)süˈdästəməs\ adj

pseu·do·succinea \ˈsü(ˌ)dō+\ n, cap [NL, fr. *pseud-* + *Succinea*] : a genus of freshwater snails (family Lymnaeidae) including important New World intermediate hosts of a liver fluke (*Fasciola hepatica*)

pseu·do·su·chia \ˌsüdōˈsükēə\ n pl, cap [NL, fr. *pseud-* + Gk *souchos* crocodile + NL *-ia*] : a suborder of Thecodontia comprising small slender generalized Triassic reptiles probably near the common ancestry of dinosaurs, birds, and crocodilians — **pseu·do·su·chi·an** \ˌ==ˈ=kēən\ adj or n

pseu·do·syllogism \ˈsü(ˌ)dō+\ n [*pseud-* + *syllogism*] : a formal fallacy in which the conclusion does not follow from the premises

pseu·do·symmetric *or* **pseu·do·symmetrical** \"+\ adj [*pseudosymmetry* + *-ic* or *-ical*] : exhibiting pseudosymmetry

pseu·do·symmetry \"+\ n [ISV *pseud-* + *symmetry*] : the apparent symmetry in crystals that come to resemble (as in the apparently hexagonal prisms of aragonite) forms of another system

pseu·do·tachylyte \"+\ n [ISV *pseud-* + *tachylyte*] : a rock consisting of glass in which are included numerous fragments of the adjacent rock and which is supposed to have been formed by the partial fusion of crush breccia or mylonite

pseu·do·tetramera \"+\ n pl, cap [NL, fr. *pseud-* + *Tetramera*] : a division of beetles having the fifth tarsal joint minute and obscure so that there appear to be but four joints — **pseu·do·tetrameral** *or* **pseu·do·tetramerous** \"+\ adj

pseu·do·trachea \"+-\ n [NL, fr. *pseud-* + *trachea*] : one of a series of chitinous tubes in the labella of dipterans (suborder Brachycera) through which liquid food is taken into the mouth — **pseu·do·tracheal** \"+-\ adj

pseu·do·trim·era \ˌsüdōˈtrimərə\ n pl, cap [NL, fr. *pseud-* + *tri-* + Gk *meros* part — more at MERIT] : a division of beetles having 4-jointed tarsi but with the 4th joint very small and hidden by the 3d — **pseu·do·trim·er·al** \ˌ==ˈ=mərəl\ *or* **pseu·do·trim·er·ous** \-mərəs\ adj

pseu·do·tropine \ˈsü(ˌ)dō+-\ n [*pseud-* + *tropine*] : a crystalline alkaloid $C_8H_{15}NO$ stereoisomeric with tropine and formed by hydrolysis of tropacocaine

pseu·do·trunk \ˈsüdō+,-\ n [*pseud-* + *trunk*] : a column like a trunk formed by overlapping leafstalks (as in the abaca)

pseu·do·tsu·ga \ˈsü(ˌ)dō(t)ˈsügə\ n, cap [NL, fr. *pseud-* + *Tsuga*] : a genus of American and Asiatic evergreen trees (family Pinaceae) having whorled branches, linear flat leaves, monoecious flowers, and pendulous rather large cones that have the bracts longer than the cone scales and the midrib of each produced into a rigid awn and two pointed lobes — see BIG-CONE SPRUCE, DOUGLAS FIR

pseu·do·tubercle \ˈsü(ˌ)dō+\ n [*pseud-* + *tubercle*] : a nodule or granuloma resembling a tubercle of tuberculosis but due to other causes

pseu·do·tuberculosis \"+\ n [NL, fr. *pseud-* + *tuberculosis*] : any of several diseases characterized by the formation of granulomas resembling tubercular nodules but not caused by the tubercle bacillus: as **a** : SARCOIDOSIS **b** : CASEOUS LYMPHADENITIS **c** : any of various pasteurelloses of birds and mammals **d** : JOHNE'S DISEASE

pseu·do·turbinal \"+\ n [*pseud-* + *turbinal*] : an inversion of the lateral wall of the nose of a reptile or bird

pseu·do·type \ˈsüdōˌtīp\ n [*pseud-* + *type*] : an invalid type in biology; *esp* : an invalid genotype — **pseu·do·typ·ic** \ˌ==ˈtipik\ adj

pseu·do·urea \ˈsü(ˌ)dō+\ n [NL, fr. *pseud-* + *urea*] : the tautomeric enol form $HN{=}C(OH)NH_2$ of urea known in the form of its esters — called also *isourea*

pseu·do·uric acid \"+...-\ n [*pseudouric* ISV *pseud-* + *uric*] : a crystalline acid $C_5H_6N_4O_4$ related to uric acid; 5-ureido-barbituric acid

pseu·do·vitellus \"+\ n [NL, fr. *pseud-* + *vitellus*] : a mycetome consisting of a mass of fatty cells in the abdomen of an aphid

pseu·do·volcano \"+\ n [*pseud-* + *volcano*] : a false volcano : an eruptive vent not emitting lava like a true volcano

pseud·ovum \(ˈ)süd+\ n [NL, fr. *pseud-* + *ovum*] : an egg capable of developing without fertilization : a parthenogenetic egg

pseu·do·wavellite \ˌsü(ˌ)dō+\ *n* [*pseud-* + *wavellite*] : CRANDALLITE

pseu·do·yohimbine \"+\ *n* [*pseud-* + *yohimbine*] : a crystalline alkaloid $C_{21}H_{26}N_2O_3$ isomeric with yohimbine and occurring with it

pseu·do·zoea *also* **pseu·do·zoaea** \"+\ *n* [NL, fr. *pseud-* + *zoea, zoaea*] : a larval stage in the Stomatopoda similar to the decapod zoea

PSF *abbr, often not cap* pounds per square foot

psgr *abbr* passenger

pshav \'(p)shäv, -äf\ *n, pl* **pshav** *or* **pshavs** *usu cap* : a member of a mountain people of the Caucasus

psha·vi·an \-ävēən\ *adj, usu cap* : of or relating to the Pshav

¹pshaw *any of various sounds or successions of sounds expressing any of the emotions named in the definition, among them* 'shȯ *esp when* ō *precedes; usu read as* 'shȯ\ *interj* — used to express irritation, disapproval, contempt, or disbelief

²pshaw \'shȯ\ *n* -s : an exclamation of *pshaw* ⟨a few episodical poohs and ~s —Sir Walter Scott⟩

³pshaw \"\ *vb* -ED/-ING/-S *vi* : to express irritation, disapproval, or disbelief by saying *pshaw* ⟨no doubt the government contractors ~*ed* and pished over it —Charles Hasler⟩ ~ *vt* : to say *pshaw* at

psi \'(p)sī, 'psē\ *n* -s [LGk, fr. Gk *psei*] **1** : the 23d letter of the Greek alphabet — symbol Ψ or ψ; see ALPHABET table **2** : PSI PHENOMENA

PSI *abbr, often not cap* pounds per square inch

PSIA *abbr, often not cap* pounds per square inch absolute

psi·cose \'sīˌkōs *also* -ōz\ *n* -s [alter. (influenced by *psi*) of *pseudofructose*, fr. *pseud-* + *fructose*] : ALLULOSE

psid·i·um \'sidēəm\ *n, cap* [NL, prob. fr. Gk *psidion* armlet] : a genus of tropical American trees (family Myrtaceae) having pubescent leaves and cymose flowers with broad calyx tube and 4- or 5-celled ovary becoming in fruit a pulpy, many-seeded berry — see GUAVA

PSIG *abbr, often not cap* pounds per square inch gauge

psil- *or* **psilo-** *comb form* [Gk, fr. *psilos*; akin to Gk *psēn* to rub, wipe — more at SAND] : mere : bare ⟨*psilomelane*⟩ ⟨*Psilopsida*⟩

psi·la \'sīlə\ *n, cap* [NL, fr. L, shaggy covering, fr. Gk *psilos* bare] : a genus of small slender two-winged flies some of whose larvae attack the roots and crown of umbelliferous plants — see CARROT RUST FLY

psil·anthropic \ˌsīl+\ *adj* [*psilanthropist* + *-ic*] : relating to or embodying psilanthropy

psil·an·thro·pism \sī'lan(t)thrəˌpizəm\ *n* -s [LGk *psilanthrōpos* + E *-ism*] : PSILANTHROPY

psil·an·thro·pist \-ˌpəst\ *n* -s [LGk *psilanthrōpos* merely human (fr. Gk *psil-* + *anthrōpos* human being) + E *-ist* — more at ANTHROP-] : one who believes that Christ was a mere man

psil·an·thro·py \-ˌpē\ *n* -ES [fr. *psilanthropist*, after such pairs as E *philanthropist: philanthropy*] : a doctrine of the merely human existence of Christ

psi·late \'sīˌlāt\ *adj* [*psil-* + E *-ate*] : lacking ornamentation — used esp. of pollen grain walls

psi·lo·mel·ane \ˌsīlō'meˌlān\ *n* -s [*psil-* + *-melane*] : a basic oxide of barium and bivalent and quadrivalent manganese probably $BaMnMn_8O_{16}(OH)_4$ — compare HOLLANDITE, CORONADITE

psi·lo·pae·des \ˌsīlō'pē(ˌ)dēz\ *n pl* [NL, fr. *psil-* + Gk *paides*, pl. of *pais* child — more at FEW] *archaic* : ALTRICES

psi·lo·phy·ta·ce·ae \ˌsīlōˌfī'tāsēˌē\ *n pl, cap* [NL, fr. *Psilophyton*, type genus + *-aceae*] : a family of Paleozoic plants (order Psilophytales)

psi·lo·phy·ta·les \-ā(ˌ)lēz\ *n pl, cap* [NL, fr. *Psilophyton* + *-ales*] : an order of Paleozoic simple dichotomously branched plants of Europe and eastern Canada including the oldest known land plants with vascular structure

psi·lo·phyte \'==ˌfīt\ *n* -s [NL *Psylophyton*] **1** : a plant of the order Psilophytales **2** : a savanna plant

psi·loph·y·ton \sī'läfəˌtän\ *n* [NL, fr. *psil-* + *phyton*] **1** *cap* : a genus (the type of the family Psilophytaceae) of small wiry herbaceous Paleozoic plants with underground rhizomes and apical sporangia **2** -s : any plant or fossil of the genus *Psilophyton*

¹psi·lop·sid \(')sī¦läpsəd\ *adj* [NL *Psilopsida*] : of or relating to the Psilopsida ⟨~ land plants⟩

²psilopsid \"\ *n* -s : a plant of the subdivision Psilopsida

psi·lop·si·da \sī'läpsədə\ *n pl, cap* [NL, fr. *psil-* + *-opsida* (as in *lycopsida*)] : a subdivision of Tracheophyta comprising vascular plants with no roots, leaves only partially differentiated or lacking, no leaf traces, a usu. protostelic vascular cylinder, and the sporangia merely terminal enlargements of the stem — compare LYCOPSIDA, PTEROPSIDA, SPHENOPSIDA

psi·lo·sis \sī'lōsəs\ *n, pl* **psilo·ses** \-ōˌsēz\ [NL, fr. Gk *psilōsis*, fr. *psiloun* to strip bare, leave naked, pronounce without aspiration, (fr. *psilos* bare) + *-sis*] **1 a** : a falling out of hair **b** : SPRUE **2** : failure to pronounce aspirate sounds

psi·los·tro·phe \sī'lästrə(ˌ)fē\ *n, cap* [NL, fr. *psil-* + Gk *strophē* act of turning — more at STROPHE] : a genus of herbs or low shrubs (family Compositae) of the rangelands of southwestern U.S. having persistent papery yellow flowers

psi·lo·ta·ce·ae \ˌsīlō'tāsēˌē\ *n pl, cap* [NL, fr. *Psilotum*, type genus + *-aceae*] : a family of plants that are usu. placed in order Psilotales and are characterized by nearly naked stems, minute scalelike leaves, and 2- or 3-celled sporangia — compare PSILOTUM, TMESIPTERIS — **psi·lo·ta·ceous** \¦==¦tāshəs\ *adj*

psi·lo·ta·les \ˌ=='tā(ˌ)lēz\ *n pl, cap* [NL, fr. *Psilotum* + *-ales*] : an order of lower tracheophytes (subdivision Psilopsida) having a dichotomously branched sporophyte that is divided into aerial shoot and rhizome, lacks true roots, and has few or minute leaves, and having a gametophyte that is subterranean and free from chlorophyll — see PSILOTACEAE

psi·lot·ic \(')sī¦läd·ik, -lōd-\ *adj* [Gk *psilōtikos*, fr. (assumed) *psilōtos* (verbal of Gk *psiloun* to strip bare) + *-ikos* -ic] : of or relating to psilosis

psi·lo·tum \sī'lōd·əm\ *n, cap* [NL, prob. fr. LGk *psilōton*, a plant, perh. fr. Gk *psilon* down, soft feather, alter. of *ptilon*; akin to Gk *pteron* wing, feather — more at FEATHER] : a genus (the type of the family Psilotaceae) of chiefly tropical fern allies with terrestrial or epiphytic habit, slender branching stems, and sessile 3-celled sporangia usu. in spikes

psi phenomena *n pl* : the aggregate of parapsychological functions of the mind including extrasensory perception, precognition, and psychokinesis

psis *pl of* PSI

psith·y·rus \'sithərəs\ *n* [NL, fr. Gk *psithyros* whispering, twittering] **1** *cap* : a genus of large bees resembling bumblebees but lacking the pollen-collecting apparatus and the worker caste and being parasitic in the nests of bumblebees **2** *pl* **psithy·ri** \-ˌrī\ : any bee of the genus *Psithyrus*

psit·ta·ceous \sə'tāshəs\ *adj* [NL *Psittacus* + E *-eous*] **1** : PSITTACINE **2** : like a parrot ⟨~ chatter⟩

psit·ta·ci \'sid·əˌsī, -əˌkī\ [NL, fr. *Psittacus*] *syn of* PSITTACIFORMES

psit·tac·i·dae \sə'tasəˌdē, -akə-\ *n pl, cap* [NL, fr. *Psittacus*, type genus + *-idae*] : a family of parrots coextensive with the order Psittaciformes

psit·ta·ci·for·mes \ˌsid·əsə'fȯr(ˌ)mēz, -əkə-\ *n pl, cap* [NL, fr. *Psittacus* + *-iformes*] : an order of zygodactyl birds comprising the parrots and related birds (as the amazons, cockatoos, lorikeets, lories, macaws, parrakeets)

¹psit·ta·cine \'sid·əˌsīn, -ˌkīn\ *adj* [L *psittacinus* of or relating to a parrot, fr. *psittacus* parrot + *-inus* -ine] : of or relating to the Psittacidae

²psittacine \"\ *n* -s : a bird of the family Psittacidae

psit·ta·cism \'sid·əˌsizəm\ *n* -s [NL *psittacismus*, fr. L *psittacus* parrot + *-ismus* -ism] : automatic speech without thought of the meaning of the words spoken

psit·ta·co·mor·phae \ˌsid·əkō'mȯr(ˌ)fē\ [NL, fr. *Psittacus* + *-morphae*] *syn of* PSITTACIFORMES

psit·ta·co·sis \ˌsid·ə'kōsəs, -dē'k-\ *n, pl* **psittaco·ses** \-ōˌsēz\ [NL, fr. L *psittacus* parrot + *-osis*] : an infectious disease of birds that is caused by a rickettsia of the genus *Chlamydia* (*C. psittaci*), is marked by diarrhea and wasting, and is transmissible to man in whom it is usu. manifested as an atypical pneumonia accompanied by high fever; *esp* : the form of this disease that originates in psittacine birds — see ORNITHOSIS

psit·ta·cot·ic \¦==¦käd·ik\ *adj* [fr. NL *psittacosis*, after such pairs as NL *narcosis*: E *narcotic*] : of, relating to, characteristic of, or affected with psittacosis

psit·ta·cus \'sid·əkəs\ *n, cap* [NL, fr. L, parrot, fr. Gk *psittakos*] : a type genus of Psittacidae formerly extensive but now usu. restricted to the African gray

p slip *n* [*p* prob. abbr. of *postal*; fr. its being the same size as former small-sized U.S. postal cards] : a slip of paper approximately three by five inches in size used in library filing

psn *abbr* position

pso·as \'sōəs\ *n, pl* **pso·ai** \-ōˌī\ *or* **pso·ae** \-ōˌē\ [NL, fr. pl. of *psoa* psoas, fr. Gk, muscle of the loins] : either of two internal muscles of the loin that together form the tenderloin of animals used as food of which the larger arises from the anterolateral surfaces of the lumbar vertebrae and passes beneath Poupart's ligament to insert with the iliacus into the lesser trochanter of the femur and of which the smaller muscle often absent arises from the last dorsal and first lumbar vertebrae and inserts into the brim of the pelvis — called also respectively *psoas major* or *psoas magnus* and *psoas minor* or *psoas parvus*

pso·at·ic \(')sō¦ad·ik\ *adj* : of or relating to a psoas

¹pso·cid \'sōsəd, 'säs-\ *adj* [NL *Psocidae*] : of or relating to the Psoidae or to psocids

²psocid \"\ *n* -s : an insect of the family Psocidae; *broadly* : any of various usu. winged insects of the order Corrodentia

psoci·dae \-ōsəˌdē, -äs-\ *n pl, cap* [NL, fr. *Psocus*, type genus + *-idae*] : a family of small soft-bodied winged insects (order Corrodentia) related to the book lice, widely distributed, and feeding upon lichens, fungi, and decaying vegetation — **pso·cine** \-ōˌsīn, ä,s-\ *adj*

pso·cop·tera \sō'käptərə\ [NL, fr. *Psocus* genus of book lice + *-ptera*] *syn of* CORRODENTIA

pso·pho·car·pus \ˌsäfə'kärpəs\ *n, cap* [NL, fr. Gk *psophos* noise + NL *-carpus*; fr. the sound made by the ripe pod when it springs open] : a genus of tropical Asiatic and African tuberous-rooted herbs (family Leguminosae)

pso·phom·e·ter \sō'fäməd·ə(r)\ *n* [Gk *psophos* noise + E *-meter*] : a device for measuring the volume of noise — **psopho·met·ric** \¦säfə¦me·trik, ¦sōf-\ *adj*

psor- *or* **psoro-** *comb form* [NL, fr. L, fr. Gk, *psōra*] : itch ⟨*psorergates*⟩ ⟨*psorosperm*⟩

pso·ra \'sōrə\ *n* -s [L, itch, mange, fr. Gk *psōra*] : PSORIASIS

pso·ralea \sə'rālēə, -ral-\ *n, cap* [NL, fr. Gk *psōraleos* scabby, itchy, fr. *psōra* itch] : a large widely distributed genus of herbs and shrubs (family Leguminosae) with glandular compound leaves and spicate or racemose purple or white flowers — see BREADROOT

psor·er·gates \sə'rərgəˌtēz\ *n, cap* [NL, fr. *psor-* + Gk *ergatēs* worker — more at ERGAT-] : a genus of parasitic mites including an itch mite (*P. ovis*) troublesome to sheep in Australia

pso·ri·a·si·form \sə'rīəsəˌfȯrm\ *adj* [ISV *psorias-* (fr. NL *psoriasis*) + *-iform*] : like psoriasis

pso·ri·a·sis \sə'rīəsəs\ *n, pl* **psoria·ses** \-īəˌsēz\ [NL, fr. Gk *psōriasis*, fr. *psōrian* to have the itch (fr. *psōra* itch, mange) + *-iasis*; prob. akin to Gk *psēn* to rub — more at SAND] : a chronic skin disease characterized by circumscribed red patches covered with white scales

¹pso·ri·at·ic \ˌsōrē¦ad·ik\ *adj* [fr. NL *psoriasis*, after such pairs as L *emphasis*: E *emphatic*] : of, relating to, affected with, or accompanied by psoriasis

²psoriatic \"\ *n* -s : one affected with psoriasis

pso·ric \'sōrik\ *adj* [L *psoricus*, fr. Gk *psōrikos*, fr. *psōra* psora + *-ikos* -ic] : of or relating to psoriasis

pso·roph·o·ra \sə'räfərə\ *n, cap* [NL, fr. *psor-* + *-phora*] : a genus of large showy mosquitoes having the palpi of dissimilar length in the two sexes and the scutellum 3-lobed

pso·rop·tes \sə'räp(ˌ)tēz\ *n, cap* [NL, fr. *psor-* + *-optes* (as in *Sarcoptes*)] : a genus (the type of the family Psoroptidae) of mites having piercing mandibles and suckers with jointed pedicels, living on and irritating the skin of various mammals, and resulting in the development of scab — **pso·rop·tic** \sə'räptik\ *adj*

psoroptic mange *n* : mange caused by mites of the genus *Psoroptes*

pso·ro·sis \sə'rōsəs\ *n, pl* **psoro·ses** \-ōˌsēz\ [NL, fr. *psor-* + *-osis*] : a virus disease of citrus trees affecting sweet oranges, tangerines, and grapefruit and characterized by scaly bark and exudation of gum and in the later stages retarded growth, small yellow leaves, and dieback of twigs — called also *scaly bark*; compare LEPROSIS

pso·ro·sperm \'sōrəˌspərm\ *n* [*psor-* + *sperm*] **1** : a myxosporidian spore **2** : any of various minute parasitic organisms probably mostly sporozoans — **pso·ro·sper·mi·al** \¦==-spərmēəl\ *or* **pso·ro·sper·mic** \-mik\ *adj*

PSS *abbr* [L *postscripta*] postscripts

PSSO *abbr, often not cap* pass slip stitch over

PST *abbr* Pacific standard time

psych *also* **psyche** \'sīk\ *vt* -ED/-ING/-S [short for *psychoanalyze*] **1** *slang* : PSYCHOANALYZE **2** *slang* : to analyze (as a problem or opponent) psychologically [I ~*ed* it all out by myself and decided —David Hulburd⟩; *also* : to overcome (an opponent) as the result of analyzing psychologically ⟨~ a tennis opponent⟩

psych *abbr* **1** psychic; psychical **2** psychological; psychologist; psychology

psych- *or* **psycho-** *comb form* [Gk, fr. *psychē* life, spirit, soul, self] **1** : soul : spirit ⟨*psycho*gram⟩ ⟨*psycho*pannychism⟩ ⟨*psych*otheism⟩ **2 a** : mind : mental processes and activities ⟨*psycho*dynamic⟩ ⟨*psycho*logy⟩ ⟨*psycho*metric⟩ **b** : psychological methods ⟨*psycho*analysis⟩ ⟨*psycho*therapy⟩ **c** : cerebral ⟨*psycho*surgery⟩ ⟨*psycho*tropic⟩ **d** : mental and : psychic and ⟨*psycho*galvanic⟩ ⟨*psycho*physical⟩

psy·cha·gog·ic \ˌsīkə¦gäjik\ *adj* [Gk *psychagōgikos*, fr. *psychagōgia* persuasion, winning of souls + *-ikos* -ic] **1** : ATTRACTIVE, PERSUASIVE, INSPIRING **2** : of or relating to psychagogy

psy·cha·gogue \'sīkəˌgäg *sometimes* -ˌgȯg\ *n* -s [Gk *psychagōgos* leading souls to the lower world, fr. *psych-* + *agōgos* leading, fr. *agein* to lead — more at AGENT] : a believer in or practicer of psychagogy

psy·cha·gogy \-ˌgäjē, -ˌgōjē\ *n* -ES [LGk *psychagōgia* evocation of souls from the lower world, fr. Gk, persuasion, winning of souls, fr. *psychagōgos* leading the soul + *-ia* -y] **1** : guidance of the soul esp. of a departed one **2** [Gk *psychagōgia* persuasion, winning of souls] : a method of influencing behavior by suggesting desirable life goals

psy·chal \'sīkəl\ *adj* [*psych-* + *-al*] : PSYCHICAL ⟨whatever the ~ reactions to the camera and the moving picture —Lewis Mumford⟩ — **psy·chal·ly** \-əlē\ *adv*

psy·chal·gia \sī'kalj(ē)ə\ *n* -s [NL, fr. *psych-* + *-algia*] : mental distress

psychanalysis *var of* PSYCHOANALYSIS

psych·asthenia \(¦)sīk+\ *n* [NL, fr. *psych-* + *asthenia*] : a state of characterological weakness such that one feels unable to resolve doubts or uncertainties or to resist phobias, obsessions, or compulsions even though aware of their irrational nature ⟨most cases formerly classed as ~ are today considered psychoneuroses⟩ — **psychasthenic** *adj or n*

psy·che \'sī(ˌ)kē\ *n* [Gk *psychē* life, spirit, soul, self; akin to Gk *psychein* to breathe, blow, make cold, Skt *babhasti* he blows] **1** -s **a** : the vital principle of corporeal matter that is a distinct mental or spiritual entity coextensive with but independent of body or soma : SOUL, SELF, PERSONALITY — compare ÉLAN VITAL **b** : the specialized cognitive, conative, and affective aspects of a psychosomatic unity : MIND; *specif* : the totality of the id, ego, and superego including both conscious and unconscious components **2** -s [F *psyché*, fr. *Psyché*, in Greco-Roman mythology a beautiful maiden personifying the soul who was loved by the god of love Eros, fr. L *Psyche*, fr. Gk *Psychē*, fr. *psychē* soul; perh. fr. the full-length painting of Psyche by Raphael †1520 Ital. painter] : CHEVAL GLASS **3** *cap* [NL, fr. Gk *psychē* butterfly, moth, soul] : the type genus of Psychidae **syn** see MIND

psy·che·an \'sīkēən, (')sī¦k-\ *adj, usu cap* [*Psyche*, beloved of Eros + E *-an*] : of or relating to Psyche

psyche knot *n, usu cap P* [after *Psyche*, who in works of art is often represented with this hair style] : a woman's hair style in which the hair is brushed back and twisted into a conical coil usu. just above the nape — compare CHIGNON

psy·chi·ana \ˌsīkē'anə, -'änə *also* -'ānə\ *n* -s *cap* [NL, fr. *psych-* + *-ana*] : a religion disseminated principally through lessons and publications sent out on a mail-order basis from its headquarters in Moscow, Idaho and based on a central message that each individual is capable of discovering and utilizing the spiritual power within him to achieve his own requisites (as health, happiness, and financial success)

psy·chi·a·ter \sə'kīəd·ə(r), sī'k-\ *n* -s [prob. fr. F *psychiatre*, fr. *psych-* + Gk *iatros* healer, physician — more at IATRIC] *archaic* : PSYCHIATRIST

psy·chi·at·ric \ˌsīkē¦a·trik, -rēk\ *also* **psy·chi·at·ri·cal** \-rəkəl, -rēkəl\ *adj* [*psychiatric* ISV *psychiatr-* (fr. — assumed — NL *psychiatria*) + *-ic*; orig. formed as G *psychiatrisch*; *psychiatrical* fr. *psychiatry* + *-ical*] **1** : relating to, employed in, or of concern to psychiatry ⟨~ disorders⟩ ⟨~ rejections⟩ ⟨~ drugs⟩ ⟨~ immaturity —Weston LaBarre⟩ **2** : engaged in the practice of psychiatry : dealing with cases of mental disorder ⟨~ experts⟩ ⟨~ nursing⟩ ⟨~ ward⟩ — **psy·chi·at·ri·cal·ly** \-rək(ə)lē, -rēk-, -li\ *adv*

psy·chi·a·trist \sə'kīə·trəst *also* sī'k-\ *n* -s [*psychiatry* + *-ist*] : a physician specializing in psychiatry — distinguished from *neurologist*

psy·chi·a·try \-trē, -ri\ *n* -ES [prob. fr. (assumed) NL *psychiatria*, fr. *psych-* + *-iatria* -iatry] **1** : a branch of medicine that deals with the science and practice of treating mental, emotional, or behavioral disorders esp. as originating in endogenous causes or resulting from faulty interpersonal relationships **2** : a treatise or text on or theory of the etiology, recognition, treatment, or prevention of mental, emotional, or behavioral disorder or the application of psychiatric principles to any area of human activity ⟨social ~⟩ **3** : the psychiatric service in a general hospital ⟨this patient should be referred to ~⟩

¹psy·chic \'sīkik, -kēk\ *adj* [Gk *psychikos* of the soul, of life, fr. *psychē* soul, life + *-ikos* -ic] **1** : of, arising in, or relating to the psyche : PSYCHOGENIC ⟨terrorism and fear create a low ~ state —Lewis Mumford⟩ ⟨~ disturbances⟩ **2** : not physical or organic : lying outside the sphere of physical science or knowledge : governed by, concerned with, or acting on the psyche or self ⟨a momentary fusion of my own being with the souls of others brought into a ~ intimacy by some affinity of emotion or thought —G.W.Russell⟩ **3** : sensitive to nonphysical forces and influences : marked by extraordinary or mysterious sensitivity, perception, or understanding ⟨the naval battle . . . was recorded in all the guide books and required no ~ powers to reveal —Upton Sinclair⟩ **4** : physically delicate; *specif, of a hand* : long and narrow often fragile in appearance with slender tapering fingers and long almond-shaped nails usu. held by palmists to indicate a visionary gentle trusting nature lacking in practical or worldly qualities — compare MIXED **syn** see MENTAL

²psychic \"\ *n* -s **1 a** : a person apparently sensitive to nonphysical forces **b** : one serving or capable of serving as a spiritualistic medium **c** : MENTALIST **2 a** : psychic phenomena **b psychics** *pl but sing in constr* : the study of purely psychic, mental, or spiritual phenomena and laws **3** *Gnosticism* : a being endowed with soul and belonging to the second of the three classes into which mankind was divided — compare PNEUMATIC 1 **4** : PSYCHIC BID

psy·chi·cal \'sīkəkəl, -kēk-\ *adj* [Gk *psychē* life, soul + E *-ical* — more at PSYCHE] **1** : PSYCHIC **2** : of or relating to the mind : MENTAL — contrasted with *physical*

psychical distance *or* **psychic distance** *n* : AESTHETIC DISTANCE

psy·chi·cal·ly \-ik(ə)lē, -ēk-, -li\ *adv* : in a psychic manner

psychical research *or* **psychic research** *n* : the investigation of phenomena that appear to be contrary to physical laws and that suggest the possibility of mental activity existing apart from body

psychic bid *n* : a bid in contract bridge made on a hand or suit that is not conventionally strong enough to bid for the purpose of misleading the opponents

psych·ich·thys \sī'kikthəs\ *n, cap* [NL, fr. *psych-* + *-ichthys*] : a genus of chimaeras differing from *Chimaera* in having no anal fin

psychic income *n* **1** : imputed income **2** : rewards (as in prestige, leisure, or pleasant surroundings) not measurable in terms of money or goods but serving as an incentive to work in certain occupations or situations ⟨a creative artist can reap a *psychic income* that money cannot match⟩

psy·chi·cism \'sīkəˌsizəm\ *n* -s [*psychic* + *-ism*] : PSYCHICAL RESEARCH

psy·chi·cist \-kəsəst\ *n* -s : one interested in or concerned with psychical research

psychic monism *n* : a view that the psychic, spiritual, or mental constitutes the only ultimate reality

psychic unity *n* : a posited unity of mental structure in mankind that leads to the independent development of similar technologies, traits, and institutions

¹psy·chid \'sīkəd\ *adj* [NL *Psychidae*] : of or relating to the Psychidae

²psychid \"\ *n* -s : a moth of the family Psychidae

psychi·dae \'sīkəˌdē, 'sik-\ *n pl, cap* [NL, fr. *Psyche*, type genus + *-idae*] : a family of moths the males of which have thinly scaled or nearly transparent wings while the females are wingless and wormlike

psy·chism \'sīˌkizəm\ *n* -s [F *psychisme*, fr. *psych-* + *-isme* -ism] **1** : a doctrine that there is a fluid universally diffused and equally animating all living beings **2** [*psych-* + *-ism*] : psychic nature or character : mental fact or process **3** : PSYCHICAL RESEARCH

psy·chis·tic \(')sī¦kistik\ *adj* : of or related to psychism

¹psy·cho \'sī(ˌ)kō\ *n* -s [by shortening] **1** : PSYCHOANALYSIS **2** [short for *psychoneurotic*] : one who has developed an emotional disorder (as a psychoneurosis) ⟨most of your clients are pimps, drug dealers, and ~s⟩

²psycho \"\ *adj* [by shortening] **1** : PSYCHIATRIC ⟨~ ward⟩ **2** : PSYCHONEUROTIC ⟨~ cases⟩

³psycho \"\ *vt* -ED/-ING/-S *slang* : PSYCHOANALYZE

psycho- — see PSYCH-

psy·cho·acoustic \¦sī(ˌ)kō+\ *adj* [ISV *psych-* + *acoustic*] : of or relating to psychoacoustics

psy·cho·acoustics \"+\ *n pl but sing in constr* : a branch of science dealing with hearing, the sensations produced by sounds, and the problems of communication

psy·cho·analysis \"+\ *also* **psych·analysis** \¦sik+\ *n* [ISV *psych-* + *analysis*; orig. formed as G *psychoanalyse*] **1** : a method of investigating (as through free association and dream analysis) psychic content and mechanisms not readily accessible to voluntary exploration by the conscious mind **2** : a method of psychotherapy esp. with psychoneurotics designed to bring unconscious and preconscious material into consciousness and carried out largely through the analysis of resistance and through the establishment and analysis of a transference neurosis **3** : a body of empirical findings and a set of theories on human motivation, behavior, and personality development : METAPSYCHOLOGY **4** : an area of psychotherapeutic practice : an institutionalized school (as founded by Sigmund Freud) of psychology, psychiatry, and psychotherapy **5** : a method or the practice of interpreting data obtained from nonpsychiatric sources (as from anthropology, art, literature) in the light of theories based on clinical observation

psy·cho·analyst \¦sī(ˌ)kō+\ *also* **psych·analyst** \(')sīk+\ *n* [ISV, fr. *psychoanalysis, psychanalysis*, after such pairs as ISV *analysis: analyst*] : one who practices or adheres to the principles of psychoanalysis; *specif* : a psychotherapist trained at an established psychoanalytic institute

psy·cho·analytic \¦sī(ˌ)kō+\ *also* **psych·analytic** *or* **psy·cho·analytical** \¦sī(ˌ)kō+\ *also* **psych·analytic** *or* **psych·analytical** \(¦)sīk+\ *adj* [*psychoanalytic*, *psychanalytic* ISV, fr. *psychoanalysis*, *psychanalysis*, after such pairs as ISV *analysis: analytic*; orig. formed as G *psychoanalytisch*; *psychoanalytical, psychanalytical* fr. *psychoanalysis, psychanalysis* after such pairs as E *analysis: analytical*] : of or relating to psychoanalysis : employing the principles or techniques of psychoanalysis — **psychoanalytically** *adv*

psy·cho·analyze \¦sī(ˌ)kō+\ *vt* [ISV, fr. *psychoanalysis*,

after such pairs as ISV *analysis: analyze*] **:** to treat in accordance with the principles of psychoanalysis
psy·cho·biochemistry \"+\ *n* [*psych-* + *biochemistry*] **:** biochemistry applied to the problems of psychology and psychiatry
psy·cho·biological *or* **psy·cho·biologic** \"+\ *adj* [*psychobiology* + *-ical* or *-ic*] **:** of or relating to psychobiology
psy·cho·biologist \"+\ *n* [*psychobiology* + *-ist*] **:** a specialist in psychobiology
psy·cho·biology \"+\ *n* [ISV *psych-* + *biology;* orig. formed as G *psychobiologie*] **:** the study of mental life and behavior in relation to other biological processes
psy·cho·catharsis \"+\ *n* [NL, fr. *psych-* + *catharsis*] **:** CATHARSIS 3
psy·cho·cultural \"+\ *adj* [*psych-* + *cultural*] **:** of or relating to the interaction of psychological and cultural factors in the individual's personality or in the characteristics of a group ⟨a ~ study of suicide⟩ ⟨the ~ approach in ethnology⟩ — **psy·cho·culturally** \"+\ *adv*
psy·cho·da \sīˈkōdə\ *n, cap* [NL, fr. Gk *psychē* butterfly, moth + NL *-oda* (prob. fr. Gk *-ōdēs* -ode) — more at PSYCHE] **:** the type genus of Psychodidae
psy·cho·diagnosis \ˌsī(ˌ)kō+\ *n* [NL, fr. *psych-* + *diagnosis*] **:** diagnosis employing the principles and techniques of psychodiagnostics
psy·cho·diagnostic \"+\ *adj* [*psych-* + *diagnostic*] **:** of, relating to, or employing psychodiagnostics
psy·cho·diagnostics \"+\ *n pl but sing in constr* [ISV *psych-* + *diagnostics;* orig. formed as G *psychodiagnostik*] **:** the science or practice of accomplishing a personality evaluation or of diagnosing a mental disorder esp. by the techniques of clinical psychology
¹**psy·chodid** \(ˈ)sīˌkōdəd, -kädˈ\ *adj* [NL *Psychodidae*] **:** of or relating to the Psychodidae
²**psychodid** \"\ *n* -s **:** a fly of the family Psychodidae
psy·chodi·dae \sīˈkädəˌdē, -kōd-\ *n pl, cap* [NL, fr. *Psychoda*, type genus + *-idae*] **:** a family of very small two-winged flies (suborder Nematocera) having hairy wings resembling those of moths and larvae that develop in moss and damp vegetable matter — see PHLEBOTOMUS
psy·cho·drama \"+\ *n* [*psych-* + *drama*] **:** a usu. unrehearsed dramatic play designed to afford catharsis and social relearning for one or more of the participants from whose life history the plot is abstracted — compare SOCIODRAMA — **psy·cho·dramatic** \"+\ *adj*
psy·cho·dynamic \"+\ *adj* [*psych-* + *dynamic*] **:** relating to or concerned with mental or emotional forces or processes developing esp. in early childhood and their effects on behavior and mental states — **psy·cho·dynamically** \"+\ *adv*
psy·cho·dynamics \"+\ *n pl but sing in constr* [*psych-* + *dynamics*] **1 :** the study of psychology from a psychodynamic point of view **2 :** explanation or interpretation (as of behavior or of mental states) in terms of mental or emotional forces or processes **3 :** motivational forces acting esp. at the unconscious level
psy·cho·dynamism \"+\ *n* [*psych-* + *dynamism*] **:** a dynamism that is psychological
psychoed *past of* PSYCHO
psycho–ethical \"+\ *adj* [*psych-* + *ethical*] **:** of or relating to innate ethical principles
psy·cho·galvanic \"+\ *adj* [ISV *psych-* + *galvanic*] **:** relating to or involving electrical changes in the body as dependent on mental or emotional processes
psychogalvanic reflex *or* **psychogalvanic response** *n* **:** a momentary decrease in the apparent electrical resistance of the skin resulting from activity of the sweat glands in response to exciting stimuli
psy·cho·galvanometer \"+\ *n* [*psych-* + *galvanometer*] **:** a galvanometer used to detect the psychogalvanic reflex — **psy·cho·galvanometric** \"+\ *adj*
psy·cho·genesis \ˌsīkō+\ *n* [NL, fr. *psych-* + *genesis*] **1 :** the origin and development of the mind or of a mental function or trait **2 :** development from psychic as distinguished from somatic origins **3 :** development from mental factors operating through the central nervous system ⟨the ~ of an illness⟩ — compare PSYCHOSOMATICS
psy·cho·genetic \ˌsīkō+\ *adj* [fr. NL *psychogenesis*, after such pairs as L *genesis:* E *genetic*] **1 :** of or relating to psychogenesis **2 :** PSYCHOGENIC — **psy·cho·genetically** \"+\ *adv*
psy·cho·genetics \"+\ *n pl but sing in constr* **:** the study of psychogenesis
psy·cho·gen·ic \ˌsīkōˈjenik\ *adj* [*psych-* + *-genic*] **:** originating in the mind or in mental or emotional conflict ⟨hysterical paralyses are thought to be ~ in origin⟩ — distinguished from *somatogenic;* compare FUNCTIONAL, HYSTERICAL, ORGANIC, PSYCHOSOMATIC — **psy·cho·gen·i·cal·ly** \-nək(ə)lē\ *adv* — **psy·cho·ge·nic·i·ty** \ˌ==jəˈnisəd·ē\ *n* -ES
psy·chog·e·ny \sīˈkäjənē\ *n* -ES [ISV *psych-* + *-geny*] **:** PSYCHOGENESIS 1
psy·chog·no·sis \ˌsīkägˈnōsəs\ *also* **psy·chog·no·sy** \sīˈkägnəsē\ *n, pl* **psychogno·ses** \-ōˌsēz\ *also* **psychognosies** \-əsēz\ [*psych-* + *-gnosis* or *-gnosy*] **:** the study of the psyche esp. as concerned with the individual character ⟨the biognosis and ~ of group life —J.W.Powell⟩ — compare PSYCHOANALYSIS
psy·chog·nos·tic \ˌsīkəgˈnästik\ *adj* **:** of or relating to psychognosis
psy·cho·gram \ˈsīkəˌgram\ *n* [*psych-* + *-gram*] **1 :** a message supposed to have been sent by a spirit **2 :** a description of the mental life of an individual; *esp* **:** the pattern of responses to a projective technique (as the Rorschach test) **3 :** PROFILE 8a
psy·cho·graph \-raf,-räf\ *n* [*psych-* + *-graph*] **1 a :** an instrument intended to record psychic processes; *esp* **:** an instrument for spirit writing **b :** a device used in automatic writing or drawing **:** AUTOSCOPE, PLANCHETTE **2 :** an image felt to have been produced upon a photographic plate without a camera by the influence of a spirit **3 :** PROFILE 8a **4 :** a biography written from a psychodynamic point of view **:** a character analysis ⟨not to treat them too seriously but rather to expose them to pitiless publicity in ~*s* which reveal their essential absurdity —*N. Y. Herald Tribune Bk. Rev.*⟩
psy·chog·ra·pher \sīˈkägrəfə(r)\ *n* -s [*psych-* + *-grapher*] **:** the writer of a psychograph **:** a psychological biographer
psy·cho·graph·ic \ˌsīkəˈgrafik\ *adj* [*psychography* + *-ic*] **1 :** of or relating to the psychograph **2 :** of or relating to psychography — **psy·cho·graph·i·cal·ly** \-fək(ə)lē\ *adv*
psy·chog·ra·phy \sīˈkägrəfē\ *n* -ES [*psych-* + *-graphy*] **1 :** automatic writing used for spiritualistic purposes **2 :** the production of images of spirits upon sensitive plates without the use of a camera held to be accomplished by means of spiritualistic forces **3** [F *psychographie*, fr. *psych-* + *-graphie* -graphy] **:** the description of an individual's mental characteristics and their development **:** psychological biography
psy·choid \ˈsīˌkȯid\ *n* -s [ISV *psych-* + *-oid*] **:** a hypothetical vital principle directing the behavior of an organism
psychoing *pres part of* PSYCHO
psy·cho·ki·ne·sia \ˌsī(ˌ)kōkəˈnēzh(ē)ə, -ōˌkīˈn-\ *n* -s [NL, fr. *psych-* + *-kinesia*] **:** a fit of violent maniacal action resulting from defective inhibition
psy·cho·kinesis \ˌsī(ˌ)kō+\ *n* [NL, fr. *psych-* + *-kinesis*] **:** the production or alteration of motion by influence of the mind without somatic intervention in objects discrete from the subject's body — compare PRECOGNITION, TELEKINESIS
psy·cho·kinetic \ˌsī(ˌ)kō+\ *adj* [fr. NL *psychokinesis*, after such pairs as NL *kinesis:* E *kinetic*] **:** of or relating to psychokinesis or to psychokinetics — **psy·cho·kinetically** \"+\ *adv*
psy·cho·kinetics \"+\ *n pl but sing in constr* **:** the science that deals with psychokinesis
psy·cho·kyme \ˈsīkōˌkīm\ *n* -s [*psych-* + Gk *kyma* wave — more at CYME] **:** the neural energy operative in any mental activity
psy·cho·lep·sy \ˈsīkōˌlepsē\ *n* -ES [ISV *psych-* + *-lepsy*] **:** an attack of hopelessness and mental inertia esp. following elation and occurring typically in psychasthenic individuals
psy·cho·lep·tic \ˌ==ˈleptik\ *adj* **:** of or relating to psycholepsy
psy·cho·linguistic \ˌsī(ˌ)kō+\ *adj* [*psych-* + *linguistic*] **1 :** of or relating to psycholinguistics **2 :** of or relating to the psychological aspects of language
psy·cho·linguistics \"+\ *n pl but usu sing in constr* [*psych-* + *linguistics*] **:** the study of linguistic behavior as conditioning and conditioned by psychological factors including the speaker's and hearer's culturally determined categories of expression and comprehension
psy·cho·log·i·cal \ˌsīkəˈläjəkəl, -jēk-\ *also* **psy·cho·log·ic** \-jik\ *adj* [*psychology* + *-ic* or *-ical*] **1 a :** relating to, characteristic of, directed toward, influencing, arising in, or acting through the mind esp. in its affective or cognitive functions ⟨~ phenomena⟩ ⟨the ~ aspects of a problem⟩ ⟨~ climate⟩ ⟨organize the material on a ~ rather than a logical basis —A.G.Schmidt⟩ **b :** directed toward the will or toward the mind specif. in its conative function ⟨~ warfare⟩ ⟨~ strategy⟩ **2 :** relating to, concerned with, deriving from, or used in psychology ⟨~ research⟩ ⟨~ tests⟩ ⟨~ criticism⟩ ⟨~ clinic⟩ ⟨~ assistant⟩ **3 :** dealing with mental phenomena esp. as interpreted or elucidated by the application of principles of psychology ⟨~ drama⟩ ⟨~ films⟩ ⟨~ novels⟩
psychological act *n* **:** ACT 1c
psychological distance *n* **:** AESTHETIC DISTANCE
psychological hedonism *n* **:** the theory that conduct and esp. all human behavior is fundamentally motivated by the pursuit of pleasure or the avoidance of pain — distinguished from *hedonism*
psy·cho·log·i·cal·ly \ˌsīkəˈläjək(ə)lē, -jēk-, -li\ *adv* [*psychological* + *-ly*] **1 :** in a psychological manner ⟨solve a problem ~⟩ ⟨a ~ sound practice⟩ **2 :** MENTALLY ⟨war which caught them in its toils either ~ or physically —G.P.Meyer⟩ **3 a :** from the standpoint of psychology **:** in terms of psychology ⟨attempt to classify poetry ~ —Gerald Brenan⟩ ⟨a drastic and a ~ dangerous experiment in planned migration —Stuart Chase⟩ **b :** by employing psychology ⟨has all the time to nurse them ~ —*Trained Nurse & Hospital Rev.*⟩
psychological medicine *n* **1 :** medicine studied or practiced from the standpoint of the patient as an individual **:** PSYCHOSOMATICS **2 :** PSYCHIATRY
psychological moment *n* **:** the occasion when the mental atmosphere is most certain to be favorable to the full effect of an action or event ⟨wait for the *psychological moment* to present a bold proposal⟩
psychological primary *n* **:** one of a set of six object colors comprising red, yellow, green, blue, black, and white in terms of which all other object colors may be described
psy·chol·o·gism \sīˈkäləˌjizəm *sometimes* səˈk-\ *n* -s [ISV *psychology* + *-ism*] **1 :** a doctrine or theory that emphasizes psychological conceptions outside the field of psychology proper (as in history or in philosophy) **2 :** an expression or term used in psychology **3 :** a theory that explains the usual normative formal principles of logic as psychological and descriptive laws — opposed to *logicism*
psy·chol·o·gist \-jəst\ *n* -s [*psychology* + *-ist*] **1 :** a student of the mind or of behavior **2 :** a specialist in one or more branches of psychology; *esp* **:** a practitioner of clinical psychology, counseling, or guidance
psy·chol·o·gis·tic \(ˌ)sīˌkäləˈjistik *sometimes* səˌk-\ *adj* [ISV *psychologism* + *-istic*] **:** tending toward psychologism; *specif* **:** attempting to introduce psychological explanations of social phenomena
psy·chol·o·gize \sīˈkäləˌjīz *sometimes* səˈk-\ *vb* -ED/-ING/-S *see -ize in Explan Notes* [*psychology* + *-ize*] *vt* **:** to explain or interpret in mentalistic, psychological, or psychodynamic terms ⟨~ religion⟩ ~ *vi* **:** to speculate in psychological terms or upon psychological motivations
psy·cho·logue \ˈsīkəˌlȯj *also* -läg\ *n* -s [F, prob. fr. *psych-* + *-logue*] **:** one devoted to psychology or to psychologism
psy·chol·o·gy \sīˈkäləjē, -ji *sometimes* səˈk-\ *n* -ES [NL *psychologia*, fr. *psych-* + *-logia* -logy] **1 a :** the science of mind or of mental phenomena and activities **:** systematic knowledge about mental processes **:** a method of obtaining knowledge about mental processes **b :** the science of behavior **:** the study of the interactions between the biological organism (as man) and its physical and social environment; *also* **:** systematic knowledge gained through such study **2 :** the mental, attitudinal, motivational, or behavioral characteristics of an individual or of a type, class, or group of individuals ⟨the ~ of the fighting man⟩ ⟨mob ~⟩; *also* **:** such principles pertinent to a particular field of knowledge or activity ⟨color ~⟩ ⟨the ~ of power and leadership —Norman Cousins⟩ ⟨the ~ of learning⟩ **3 :** a treatise on or a school, system, or branch of psychology
psy·chom·a·chy \-ämәkē\ *n* -ES [LL *psychomachia* conflict of the soul, prob. fr. Gk *psych-* + *-machia* -machy] **:** a conflict of the soul (as with the body or between good and evil)
psy·chom·e·ter \-məd·ə(r)\ *n* [back-formation fr. *psychometry*] **1 :** one who practices the occult art of psychometry **2** [ISV *psych-* + *-meter*] **:** a timing or measuring instrument used in mental measurement
psy·cho·met·ric \ˌsīkəˈme·trik\ *adj* [ISV *psych-* + *-metric*] **1 :** relating to the measurement of mental or subjective data **2 :** relating to or being a mental test or psychological method whose results are expressed quantitatively rather than qualitatively — **psy·cho·met·ri·cal·ly** \-rək(ə)lē\ *adv*
psy·chom·e·tri·cian \(ˌ)sīˌkäməˈtrishən *sometimes* səˌk-\ *n* -s [*psychometric* + *-an*] **1 :** a person (as a clinical psychologist) who is skilled in the administration and interpretation of objective psychological tests (as of intelligence or of personality) **2 :** a psychologist who devises, constructs, and standardizes psychometric tests — compare PSYCHOTECHNICIAN
psy·cho·met·rics \ˌsīkəˈme·triks\ *n pl but sing in constr* [*psychometric* + *-s*] **1 :** a branch of clinical or applied psychology dealing with the use and application of mental measurement **2 :** the technique of mental measurements **:** the use of quantitative devices for assessing psychological trends
psy·chom·e·trist \sīˈkämə·trəst *sometimes* səˈk-\ *n* -s [*psychometry* + *-ist*] **:** PSYCHOMETRICIAN
psy·chom·e·trize \-ˌtrīz\ *vb* -ED/-ING/-S [*psychometry* + *-ize*] *vt* **:** to interpret by the occult art of psychometry ~ *vi* **:** to practice divination by means of psychometry
psy·chom·e·try \-ˌtrē\ *n* -ES [*psych-* + *-metry*] **1 :** divination of facts concerning an object or its owner through contact with or proximity to the object **2 :** PSYCHOMETRICS
psy·cho·mi·idae \ˌsīkəˈmīəˌdē\ *n pl, cap* [NL, fr. *Psychomia*, type genus (fr. *psych-* + *-myia*) + *-idae*] **:** a small family of caddis flies
psy·cho·mor·phism \-ˈmȯrˌfizəm\ *n* -s [*psych-* + *-morphism* (as in *anthropomorphism*)] **:** the attribution of mental processes (as feeling and purpose) to animals or to inanimate objects
psy·cho·motility \ˌsī(ˌ)kō+\ *n* [ISV *psych-* + *motility*] **:** the power of bodily movement as dependent on mental processes
psy·cho·motion \"+\ *n* [*psych-* + *motion*] **:** PSYCHOMOTILITY
psy·cho·motor \ˌsīkə+\ *adj* [ISV *psych-* + *motor*] **:** of or relating to muscular action believed to ensue from prior esp. conscious mental activity
psy·chon \ˈsīˌkän\ *n* -s [*psych-* + *-on*] **:** an ultimate particle of psychic nature
psy·cho·neural \ˌsī(ˌ)kō+\ *adj* [*psych-* + *neural*] **:** of or relating to the interrelationship of nervous system and consciousness **:** relating to the mental functions of the central nervous system
psy·cho·neurosis \"+\ *n* [NL, fr. *psych-* + *neurosis*] **1 :** a neurosis based on emotional conflict in which an impulse that has been blocked seeks expression in a disguised response or symptom — distinguished from *actual neurosis* **2 :** NEUROSIS 1
¹**psy·cho·neurotic** \"+\ *adj* [fr. NL *psychoneurosis*, after such pairs as NL *neurosis:* E *neurotic*] **1 :** of or relating to psychoneurosis **2 :** affected with psychoneurosis
²**psychoneurotic** \"\ *n* **:** one who is psychoneurotic
psy·cho·nom·ic \ˌsīkəˈnämik\ *adj* [*psychonomy* + *-ic*] **:** relating to or constituting the laws of mental life
psy·cho·nom·ics \ˌ==ˈnämiks\ *n pl but sing in constr* **:** the science of the laws relating the mind to the organism's internal and external environment **:** PSYCHOLOGY
psy·chon·o·my \sīˈkänəmē\ *n* -ES [*psych-* + *-nomy*] **:** PSYCHONOMICS
psy·cho·pan·nych·i·an \ˌsīkōpaˈnikēən\ *n* -s [*psychopannychy* + *-an*] **:** PSYCHOPANNYCHIST
psy·cho·pan·ny·chism \ˌ==ˈpanəˌkizəm\ *n* -s [*psychopannychy* + *-ism*] **:** the theological doctrine that the soul falls asleep at death and does not wake until the resurrection of the body
psy·cho·pan·ny·chist \ˌ==ˈpanəkəst\ *or* **psy·cho·pan·ny·chite** \-nəˌkīt\ *n* -s [NL *psychopannychia* + *-ist* or *-ite*] **:** one who believes in or supports the doctrine of psychopannychism
psy·cho·pan·ny·chis·tic \ˌ==ˌpanəˈkistik\ *adj* **:** of or relating to psychopannychism
psy·cho·pan·ny·chy \-nəkē\ *n* -ES [NL *psychopannychia*, fr. *psych-* + Gk *pannychios* all night long, (fr. *pan-* + *nychios* nightly, of the night, fr. *nykt-, nyx* night) + NL *-ia* -y — more at NIGHT] **:** psychopannychistic slumber
psy·cho·path \ˈsīkəˌpath, -paa(ə)th, -paith\ *n* -s [ISV *psych-* + *-path*] **1 :** a mentally ill or unstable person **:** one with a poorly balanced personality structure **:** ECCENTRIC **2 :** PSYCHOPATHIC PERSONALITY 2
psy·cho·path·ia \ˌ==ˈpathēə\ *n* -s [NL, fr. *psych-* + *-pathia* -pathy] **:** PSYCHOPATHY
¹**psy·cho·path·ic** \ˌ==ˈpathik, -ˈpaath-, -ˈpaith-, -thēk\ *adj* [ISV *psych-* + *-pathic;* orig. formed as G *psychopathisch*] **:** of, relating to, or characterized by psychopathy — **psy·cho·path·i·cal·ly** \-thək(ə)lē, -thēk-, -li\ *adv*
²**psychopathic** \"\ *n* -s **:** PSYCHOPATH
psychopathic hospital *n* **:** a hospital for the observation, examination, treatment, or temporary retention of patients showing evidence of mental disturbance
psychopathic personality *n* **1 :** a disorder of behavior toward other individuals or toward society in which reality is usu. clearly perceived except for an individual's social responsibilities or moral obligations, which is often manifested hedonistically (as by criminal acts, drug addiction, sexual perversion, or activity leading to immediate personal gratification esp. when it is believed that punishment can be avoided), by passive indifference (as by shiftlessness, untrustworthiness, or vagabondism), or in contrast by fanatical pseudosocial zealousness, and which is usu. a more or less permanent way of life refractory to treatment and hence often considered a constitutional disorder **2 :** an individual having a psychopathic personality
psychopathic ward *n* **:** a ward in a general or other hospital serving the same purpose as a psychopathic hospital
psy·chop·a·thist \sīˈkäpəthəst\ *n* -s [*psychopathy* + *-ist*] **:** PSYCHOPATHOLOGIST
psy·cho·pathological *or* **psy·cho·pathologic** \ˌsī(ˌ)kō+\ *adj* [*psychopathology* + *-ical* or *-ic*] **:** of, relating to, or exhibiting psychopathology
psy·cho·pathologist \"+\ *n* [*psychopathology* + *-ist*] **:** a specialist in psychopathology
psy·cho·pathology \"+\ *n* [ISV *psych-* + *pathology;* orig. formed as G *psychopathologie*] **1 :** the study of psychologic and behavioral dysfunction occurring in mental disorder or in social disorganization **2 :** disordered psychologic and behavioral functioning (as in a mental disease)
psy·chop·a·thy \sīˈkäpəthē\ *n* -ES [ISV *psych-* + *-pathy;* orig. formed as G *psychopathie*] **1 :** mental disorder **2 :** PSYCHOPATHIC PERSONALITY 1
psy·cho·pharmacologic *or* **psy·cho·pharmacological** \ˌsī(ˌ)kō+\ *adj* [*psychopharmacology* + *-ic* or *-ical*] **:** of, relating to, or used in psychopharmacology ⟨~ agent⟩ ⟨tranquilizers are ~ drugs⟩
psy·cho·pharmacology \"+\ *n* [*psych-* + *pharmacology*] **:** the study of the effects of drugs on mental states
psy·cho·pho·bia \ˌsīkəˈfōbēə\ *n* [NL, fr. *psych-* + *-phobia*] **:** an aversion to psychological considerations
psy·cho·phon·asthenia \ˌsī(ˌ)kōˌfōn+\ *n* [*psych-* + *phon-* + *asthenia*] **:** a hysterical symptom in which the voice becomes tremulous, choked, and irregular in pitch with overall difficulty in vocalization
psy·cho·physical \ˌsī(ˌ)kō+\ *adj* [*psychophysics* + *-al*] **1 :** of or relating to psychophysics **2 :** interrelating or existing between the physical and the psychic **3 :** partaking of both physical and psychical ⟨the ~ organism⟩ ⟨a ~ disposition⟩ — compare PSYCHOSOMATIC — **psy·cho·physically** \"+\ *adv*
psychophysical method *n* **:** any of the experimental and statistical methods (as of just-noticeable differences, of constant stimuli, or of average error) developed for studying the perception of physical magnitudes
psychophysical parallelism *n* **1 :** a philosophical theory that the parallel physical and psychical events do not interact — compare DOUBLE-ASPECT THEORY, INTERACTIONISM **2 :** DOUBLE-ASPECT THEORY 2
psy·cho·physicist \ˌsī(ˌ)kō+\ *n* [*psychophysics* + *-ist*] **:** a specialist in psychophysics
psy·cho·physics \"+\ *n pl but sing in constr* [ISV *psych-* + *physics;* orig. formed as G *psychophysik*] **:** a branch of science that deals with the problems (as the interrelations of the physical processes that constitute stimuli and the mental processes that result from their impingement on the living organism) common to physics and psychology — compare PHYSIOLOGICAL PSYCHOLOGY, PSYCHOSOMATICS
psy·cho·physiological *or* **psy·cho·physiologic** \"+\ *adj* [*psychophysiological* fr. *psychophysiology* + *-ical; psychophysiologic* ISV *psychophysiology* + *-ic*] **1 :** of or relating to physiological psychology **2 :** combining, interrelating, or involving mental and bodily processes — **psy·cho·physiologically** \"+\ *adj*
psy·cho·physiologist \"+\ *n* [ISV *psychophysiology* + *-ist*] **:** a specialist in physiological psychology
psy·cho·physiology \"+\ *n* [ISV *psych-* + *physiology*] **:** PHYSIOLOGICAL PSYCHOLOGY
psy·cho·plasm \ˈsīkōˌplazəm\ *n* [ISV *psych-* + *-plasm*] **:** a primordial substance held to supply the basis of the psychical as well as of the physical
psy·cho·pomp \ˈsīkōˌpämp\ *or* **psy·cho·pom·pos** \ˌ==ˈpämpəs, -m,päs\ *n, pl* **psychopomps** \ˈ==ˌpämps\ *or* **psychopompoi** \ˌ==ˈpämˌpȯi\ [Gk *psychopompos*, fr. *psych-* + *pompos* conductor, fr. *pempein* to send, conduct] **:** a conductor of souls to the afterworld
¹**psy·chop·sid** \(ˈ)sīˈkäpsəd\ *adj* [NL *Psychopsidae*] **:** of or relating to the Psychopsidae
²**psychopsid** \"\ *n* -s **:** a lacewing of the family Psychopsidae
psy·chop·si·dae \sīˈkäpsəˌdē\ *n pl, cap* [NL, fr. *Psychopsis*, type genus (fr. Gk *psychē* butterfly + NL *-opsis*) + *-idae* — more at PSYCHE] **:** a small family of chiefly tropical lacewings occurring in Australia and part of So. America
psy·chor·rhag·ic \ˌsīkəˈrajik\ *adj* [*psychorrhagy* + *-ic*] **:** of or relating to psychorrhagy
psy·chor·rha·gy \sīˈkȯrəjē\ *n* -ES [*psych-* + *-rrhagy*] **:** temporary manifestation of a person's soul to other persons at a distance from his body
psychos *pl of* PSYCHO, *pres 3d sing of* PSYCHO
psy·cho·scope \ˈsīkəˌskōp\ *n* [*psych-* + *scope*] **:** a means of observing mental processes
psy·cho·sensorial \ˌsī(ˌ)kō+\ *adj* [ISV *psychosensory* + *-al*] **:** PSYCHOSENSORY
psy·cho·sensory \"+\ *adj* [*psych-* + *sensory*] **1 :** of, relating to, or constituting sensory consciousness not directly mediated by the sense organs **:** HALLUCINATORY **2 :** of or relating to sense perception
psy·cho·sexual \"+\ *adj* [*psych-* + *sexual*] **1 :** of or relating to the mental, emotional, and behavioral aspects or consequences of the biological process of sexual differentiation **2 :** of or relating to the complex of mental or emotional attitudes concerning sexual activity **3 :** of or relating to the physiological psychology of sex — **psy·cho·sexually** \"+\ *adv*
psy·cho·sexuality \"+\ *n* [*psych-* + *sexuality*] **:** the psychic factors of sex
psy·cho·sis \sīˈkōsəs\ *n, pl* **psycho·ses** \-ōˌsēz\ [NL, fr. *psych-* + *-osis*] **1 :** profound disorganization of mind, personality, or behavior that results from an individual's inability to tolerate the demands of his social environment whether because of the enormity of the imposed stress or because of primary inadequacy or acquired debility of his organism esp. in regard to the central nervous system or because of combinations of these factors and that may be manifested by disorders of perception, thinking, or affect symptoms of neurosis, by criminality, or by any combination of these —distinguished from *neurosis;* compare INSANITY **2 :** extreme mental unrest of an individual or of a social group esp. in regard to situational factors of grave import ⟨war ~⟩ ⟨mass ~⟩ — compare HYSTERIA 2 **syn** see INSANITY
psy·cho·social \ˌsī(ˌ)kō+\ *adj* [*psych-* + *social*] **1 :** involving both psychological and social aspects ⟨a stable marriage requires ~ adjustment⟩ **2 :** combining clinical psychological and social services ⟨the ~ team of a child

guidance clinic⟩ **3 :** relating social conditions to mental health ⟨~ medicine⟩

psy·cho·sociological \"+\ *adj* [*psych-* + *sociological*] **:** dealing with or measuring both psychological and sociological variables ⟨a ~ survey⟩ **:** concerned with the psychological characteristics of a race or people

psy·cho·sociologist \"+\ *n* **:** a specialist in psychosociology

psy·cho·sociology \"+\ *n* **:** a study of problems common to psychology and sociology

psy·cho·so·ma \ˌsīkə'sōmə\ *or* **psy·cho·some** \'⸗⸗ˌsōm\ *n* -s [*psychosoma* fr. NL, fr. *psych-* + *-soma; psychosome* fr. *psych-* + *-some*] **:** the mental and physical organism **:** mind and body as a functional unit

[1]**psy·cho·somatic** \¦sī(ˌ)kō+\ *adj* [ISV *psych-* + *somatic*] **1 :** relating to, involving, or resulting from the interaction between mind or emotions and body **:** relating to or involving both mind and body ⟨~ medicine⟩ **2 :** resulting from the influence of emotional stress or conflict on a predisposed somatic area, organ, or bodily system ⟨a ~ disorder⟩ **3 :** evidencing bodily symptoms or bodily and mental symptoms as a result of emotional conflict ⟨a ~ patient⟩ — **psy·cho·somatically** \"+\ *adv*

[2]**psychosomatic** \"\ *n* -s **:** one who evidences bodily symptoms or bodily and mental symptoms as a result of mental conflict

psy·cho·so·mat·i·cist \ˌsī(ˌ)kōsə'mad·əsəst\ *n* -s [[1]*psychosomatic* + *-ist*] **:** a specialist in psychosomatics

psy·cho·so·mat·ics \-d·iks\ *n pl but sing in constr* [ISV *psychosomat-* (fr. [1]*psychosomatic*) + *-ics*] **:** a branch of medical science that deals with the interrelationships between mental or emotional and somatic processes and esp. with the manner in which intrapsychic conflict influences somatic symptomatology **:** psychosomatic medicine — compare PHYSIOLOGICAL PSYCHOLOGY, PSYCHOPHYSICS

psy·cho·sta·sia \ˌsīkō'stāzh(ē)ə\ *n* -s [Gk, fr. *psych-* + *stasis* act of weighing, (fr. *histanai* to make to stand, weigh) + *-ia* -y — more at STAND] **:** a weighing of lives or souls ⟨the judgment of Osiris under the New Kingdom consisted essentially of the ceremony of the ~ —J.E.M.White⟩

psy·cho·static *also* **psy·cho·statical** \¦sīkō+\ *adj* [*psychostatic* back-formation fr. *psychostatics; psychostatical* fr. *psychostatics* + *-al*] **:** of or relating to psychostatics — **psy·cho·statically** \"+\ *adv*

psy·cho·statics \ˌsīkō+\ *n pl but sing in constr* [*psych-* + *statics*] **1 :** the study of the conditions of mental processes **2 :** a theory that conscious states consist of elements subject to separation and fusion without loss of essential character

psy·cho·surgery \¦sī(ˌ)kō+\ *n* [*psych-* + *surgery*] **:** cerebral surgery (as frontal lobotomy) employed in treating psychic symptoms

psy·cho·synthesis \"+\ *n* [NL, fr. *psych-* + *synthesis*] **1 :** the integrative or synthetic process in psychotherapy as contrasted with the abreactive or cathartic **2 :** a form of psychotherapy combining psychoanalytic techniques with meditation and exercise

psy·cho·synthetic \"+\ *adj* **:** of or relating to psychosynthesis

psy·cho·taxis \ˌsīkō+\ *n* [NL, fr. *psych-* + *-taxis*] **:** an involuntary adjustment of one's modes of thought and action for keeping the agreeable and avoiding the disagreeable as a mechanism of ego defense

psy·cho·technical *also* **psy·cho·technic** \¦sī(ˌ)kō+\ *adj* [*psych-* + *technical* or *technic*] **:** of or relating or devoted to the practical applications (as industrial or military problems) of psychology

psy·cho·technician \"+\ *n* [*psych-* + *technician*] **:** one specializing in the practical application of psychology (as in the use of psychological tests) — compare PSYCHOMETRICIAN

psy·cho·technics \ˌsīkō+\ *n pl but sing in constr* [ISV *psych-* + *technics;* prob. orig. formed as G *psychotechnik*] **:** PSYCHOTECHNOLOGY

psy·cho·technological \¦sī(ˌ)kō+\ *adj* [*psychotechnology* + *-ical*] **:** of or relating to psychotechnology

psy·cho·technologist \"+\ *n* [*psychotechnology* + *-ist*] **:** a specialist in psychotechnology

psy·cho·technology \"+\ *n* [*psych-* + *technology*] **:** the application of psychological methods and results to the solution of practical problems esp. in industry — compare INDUSTRIAL PSYCHOLOGY

psy·cho·the·ism \'sīkō(ˌ)thēˌizəm\ *n* [*psych-* + *theism*] **:** the doctrine that God is pure spirit

psy·cho·therapeutic \¦sī(ˌ)kō+\ *adj* [ISV *psych-* + *therapeutic*] **:** relating to or involving psychotherapeutics or psychotherapy ⟨psychological and ~ means of behavior control —Robert Michels⟩ ⟨a drug used for ~ purposes on human beings⟩ — **psy·cho·therapeutically** \"+\ *adv*

psy·cho·therapeutics \"+\ *n pl but usu sing in constr* **:** the science and art of psychotherapy

psy·cho·therapeutist \"+\ *n* **:** PSYCHOTHERAPIST

psy·cho·therapist \"+\ *n* [*psychotherapy* + *-ist*] **:** one (as a psychiatrist, clinical psychologist, psychiatric social worker, or clergyman) who is a practitioner of psychotherapy

psy·cho·therapy \"+\ *n* [ISV *psych-* + *therapy*] **1 a :** treatment of mental or emotional disorder or maladjustment by psychological means esp. involving verbal communication (as in psychoanalysis, nondirective psychotherapy, reeducation, hypnosis, or prestige suggestion) **b :** a particular school or method (as Freudian psychoanalysis) of psychotherapy ⟨the bewildering proliferation of self-improvement manuals and popular *psychotherapies* —R.D.Rosen⟩ **2 :** any alteration in an individual's interpersonal environment, relationships, or life situation brought about esp. by a qualified therapist and intended to have the effect of alleviating symptoms of mental or emotional disturbance

[1]**psy·chot·ic** \(')sī¦käd·|ik, -ät|, |ēk\ *adj* [ISV, fr. NL *psychosis,* after such pairs as NL *narcosis:* E *narcotic*] **:** of, relating to, or marked by psychosis ⟨suffered a ~ break from reality —K.S.Felton⟩ ⟨he is ~ and unable to stand trial —David Abrahamsen⟩ — **psy·chot·i·cal·ly** \|ək(ə)lē, |ēk-, -li\ *adv*

[2]**psychotic** \"\ *n* -s **:** a psychotic individual

psy·chotria \sī'kō·trēə, -kä·-\ *n, cap* [NL, prob. fr. MGk *psychōtria* vivifying, fr. Gk *psychē* life — more at PSYCHE] **:** a very large genus of chiefly So. American shrubs, trees, or rarely herbs (family Rubiaceae) having corymbose flowers with a 5-lobed corolla and a fruit that is a berrylike drupe with two nutlets

psy·cho·trine \'sīkə·ˌtrēn, -·ˌtrən\ *n* -s [ISV *psychotr-* (fr. NL *Psychotria*) + *-ine*] **:** a yellow crystalline alkaloid $C_{28}H_{36}N_2O_4$ having a blue fluorescence and found in ipecac

[1]**psy·cho·trop·ic** \¦sīkə·¦träpik\ *adj* [*psych-* + *-tropic*] **:** acting on the mind ⟨~ plants⟩ ⟨~ drugs⟩ ⟨~ activity⟩

[2]**psychotropic** *n* **:** a psychotropic substance (as a drug) — compare TRANQUILIZER

psy·cho·zo·ic \¦sīkə¦zōik\ *adj, usu cap* [*psych-* + *-zoic*] **:** of or relating to the period beginning with the appearance of man on the earth **:** QUATERNARY

psychro- *comb form* [Gk, fr. *psychros,* fr. *psychein* to make cold — more at PSYCHE] **:** cold ⟨*psychro*meter⟩

psy·chro·energetic \¦sī(ˌ)krō+\ *adj* [*psychro-* + *energetic*] **:** of or relating to the relationship between environmental climatic conditions and the efficiency of utilization of foodstuffs esp. by domestic animals

psy·chro·graph \'sīkrōˌgraf, -råf\ *n* [*psychro-* + *-graph*] **:** a self-recording psychrometer giving simultaneous readings of the dry-bulb and wet-bulb thermometer

psy·chrom·e·ter \sī'krämәd·ә(r)\ *n* [ISV *psychro-* + *-meter*] **:** a hygrometer whose operation depends on two similar thermometers with the bulb of one being kept wet so that it is cooled as a result of evaporation and shows a temperature lower than that of the dry-bulb thermometer and with the difference between the thermometer readings constituting a measure of the dryness of the surrounding air — **psy·chro·met·ric** \¦sīkrō¦me·trik\ *adj*

psychrometric chart *n* [*psychrometric* fr. *psychrometry* + *-ic*] **:** a graphic representation of the properties of mixtures of air and water vapor

psy·chrom·e·try \sī'krämə·trē\ *n* -ES [ISV *psychrometer* + *-y*] **1 :** the use of the psychrometer **2 :** a science dealing with the physical laws governing air and water mixture — compare HYGROMETRY

psy·chro·phile \'sīkrōˌfīl\ *n* -s [ISV *psychro-* + *-phile*] **:** a psychrophilic organism — compare MESOPHILE, THERMOPHILE

psy·chro·phil·ic \¦sīkrō¦filik\ *also* **psy·chro·phile** \'⸗⸗ˌfīl\ *adj* [*psychrophilic* fr. *psychro-* + *-phil* + *-ic; psychrophile* fr. *psychro-* + *-phile*] **:** thriving at a relatively low temperature ⟨~ bacteria⟩

psy·chro·phyte \'⸗⸗ˌfīt\ *n* -s [ISV *psychro-* + *-phyte*] **:** a plant suited to arctic or alpine conditions

psy·dra·cious \(')sī¦drāshəs\ *adj* [NL *psydracium* + E *-ous*] *archaic* **:** of or relating to a psydracium

psy·dra·cium \sī'drāsh(ē)əm\ *n, pl* **psydra·cia** \-)ə\ [NL, fr. Gk *psydrakion,* fr. *psydrak- psydrax* blister on the tongue (fr. *psydros* lying, untrue, fr. *pseudein* to lie, falsify) + *-ion* (n. suffix)] *archaic* **:** PIMPLE, PUSTULE

psyk·ter *also* **psyc·ter** \'siktə(r)\ *n* -s [Gk *psyktēr,* fr. *psychein* to make cold — more at PSYCHE] **:** a jar used in ancient Greece for cooling wine

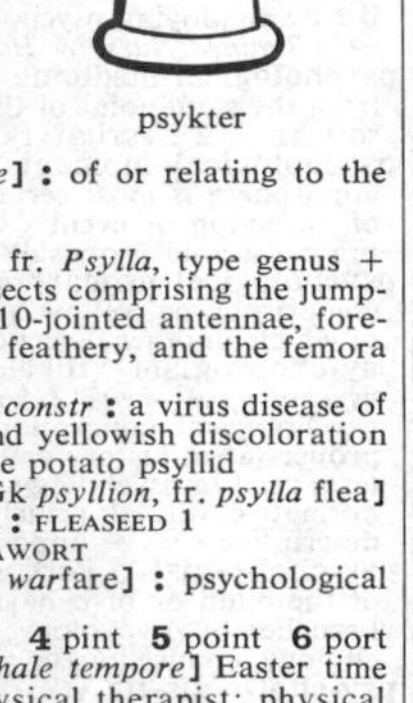

psykter

psyl·la \'silə\ *n* [NL, fr. Gk, flea; akin to L *pulex* flea, Lith *blusà,* Skt *pluṣi*] **1** *cap* **:** a genus of jumping plant lice that is often considered synonymous with *Chermes* **2** -s **:** any insect of the family Psyllidae **:** JUMPING PLANT LOUSE

psylla wax *n* **:** a waxy varnish deposited on alder branches by a psyllid (*Psyllia alni*)

psyl·lia \'silēə\ *n, cap* [NL, fr. *Psylla* + *-ia*] **:** a genus of jumping plant lice containing many economically important pests of cultivated plants — see PEAR PSYLLA

[1]**psyl·lid** \'siləd\ *adj* [NL *Psyllidae*] **:** of or relating to the Psyllidae

[2]**psyllid** \"\ *n* -s **:** PSYLLA 2

psyl·li·dae \-ləˌdē\ *n pl, cap* [NL, fr. *Psylla,* type genus + *-idae*] **:** a family of homopterous insects comprising the jumping plant lice and having long usu. 10-jointed antennae, forewings that are thickened and often feathery, and the femora thickened and adapted for leaping

psyllid yellows *n pl but sing or pl in constr* **:** a virus disease of potatoes characterized by rolling and yellowish discoloration of the leaflets and transmitted by the potato psyllid

psyl·li·um \'silēəm\ *n* -s [NL, fr. Gk *psyllion,* fr. *psylla* flea] **1 :** FLEAWORT **2** *or* **psyllium seed :** FLEASEED 1

psylly *n* -ES [NL *psillium*] *obs* **:** FLEAWORT

psy·war \'sī+ˌ-\ *n* [*psy*chological *war*fare] **:** psychological warfare

pt *abbr* **1** part **2** payment **3** peseta **4** pint **5** point **6** port

PT *abbr* **1** Pacific time **2** [L *Paschale tempore*] Easter time **3** *often not cap* past tense **4** physical therapist; physical therapy **5** physical training **6** postal telegraph **7** *often not cap* post town **8** private terms **9** pro tempore **10** *often not cap* pupil teacher

Pt *symbol* platinum

pta *abbr* peseta

PTA *abbr or n* -s **1 :** PARENT-TEACHER ASSOCIATION **2 :** a member of a parent-teacher association

[1]**ptar·mic** \'tärmik\ *n* -s [LL *ptarmicum,* fr. Gk *ptarmikon,* neut. of *ptarmikos* causing to sneeze, fr. *ptarmos* act of sneezing + -ikos -ic — more at STERNUTATION] **:** a substance that causes sneezing

[2]**ptarmic** \"\ *or* **ptar·mi·cal** \-məkəl\ *adj* [*ptarmic* fr. LL *ptarmicus,* fr. Gk *ptarmikos; ptarmical* fr. [1]*ptarmic* + *-al*] **:** STERNUTATORY

[1]**ptar·mi·ca** \-məkə\ *n* -s [NL, fr. Gk *ptarmikē,* fr. *ptarmikos* causing to sneeze] **:** SNEEZEWORT

[2]**ptarmica** \"\ [NL, lit., sneezewort] *syn of* ACHILLEA

ptar·mi·gan \'tärməgən, -mēg-\ *n, pl* **ptarmigan** *or* **ptarmigans** [modif. of ScGael *tārmachan*] **:** any of various grouses of the genus *Lagopus* of northern regions having completely feathered feet, winter plumage that is chiefly or wholly white except in the British red grouse, and summer plumage that is largely grayish, brownish, or blackish and variously barred and vermiculated

ptbl *abbr* portable

pt boat \'pē'tē-\ *also* **pt** [*p*atrol *t*orpedo] *n* -s *usu cap P&T* **:** MOTOR TORPEDO BOAT

PTC *abbr* postal telegraph cable

ptd *abbr* **1** painted **2** pointed **3** printed

pte *abbr, often cap* private

ptelea \'telēə, 'tēl-\ *n, cap* [NL, fr. Gk *ptelea* elm; perh. akin to L *tilia* linden] **:** a small genus of No. American shrubs or small trees (family Rutaceae) having 3- to 5-foliolate leaves and panicles of small greenish flowers with 4 or 5 imbricated petals and a rounded samara — see HOP TREE

pteno·glos·sa \ˌtenə'gläsə, ˌtēn-, -lȯsə\ *n pl, cap* [NL, fr. Gk *ptēnos* winged (akin to Gk *petesthai* to fly) + NL *-glossa* — more at FEATHER] *in some classifications* **:** a division of Pectinibranchia comprising the gastropod families Janthinidae and Epitoniidae in which the median tooth is very small or wanting and the lateral teeth are strong and hooked and largest at the outside of each row — **pteno·glos·sate** \¦⸗⸗¦⸗ˌsāt, -ˌsət\ *adj*

pter- *or* **ptero-** *comb form* [NL, fr. Gk, fr. *pteron* — more at FEATHER] **:** feather **:** wing ⟨*pter*idium⟩ ⟨*ptero*dactyl⟩

-p·tera \-pt(ə)rə\ *n comb form* [NL, fr. Gk, neut. pl. of *-pteros* -pterous] **:** organism or organisms having (such or so many) wings or winglike parts — in taxonomic names esp. in zoology ⟨Hemi*ptera*⟩ ⟨Physalo*ptera*⟩

pte·ra·li·um \tə'rālēəm, te'r-\ *n, pl* **ptera·lia** \-ēə\ [NL, irreg. fr. Gk *pteron* feather, wing] **:** a sclerite in the articular region of an insect's wing

pter·an·o·don \-'ranəˌdän\ *n* [NL, fr. *pter-* + Gk *anodont-, anodōn* toothless, fr. *an-* + *odōn* tooth — more at TOOTH] **1** *cap* **:** a genus of Cretaceous pterosaurs having a long toothless beak, a backwardly directed bony crest on the skull, and a wingspread of up to 25 feet **2** -s **:** any pterosaur of *Pteranodon* or a closely related genus

[1]**pter·an·o·dont** \-nt\ *adj* [NL *Pteranodont-, Pteranodon*] **:** of or relating to *Pteranodon* or a closely related genus

[2]**pteranodont** \"\ *n* -s **:** PTERANODON 2

[1]**pte·ras·pid** \-'raspəd\ *adj* [NL *Pteraspidae*] **:** of or relating to the Pteraspidae

[2]**pteraspid** \"\ *n* -s **:** an ostracoderm of the family Pteraspidae

pte·ras·pi·dae \-pəˌdē\ *n pl, cap* [NL, fr. *Pteraspid-, Pteraspis,* type genus + *-idae*] **:** a family of widespread Silurian and Lower Devonian ostracoderms (class Heterostraci) — see PTERASPIS

pte·ras·pis \-pəs\ *n, cap* [NL, fr. *pter-* + *-aspis*] **:** the type genus of Pteraspidae comprising small ostracoderms in which the dorsal armor is made up of 7 large plates

pter·ergate \tər, (')ter+\ *n* [*pter-* + *ergate*] **:** an abnormal worker ant with minute wings

pte·re·tis \tə'rēd·əs\ *n, cap* [NL, irreg. fr. *pteris* fern] **:** a genus of ferns (family Polypodiaceae) that are sometimes included in *Onoclea* but distinguished by the vaselike clumps of fronds with feathery pinnate fertile fronds surrounded by or clustered among much taller sterile lanceolate fronds — see OSTRICH FERN

pter·ic \'terik\ *adj* [ISV *pter-* + *-ic*] **:** of, relating to, or resembling a wing

pter·ich·thy·o·des \təˌrikthē'ō(ˌ)dēz, (ˌ)teˌr-\ *n, cap* [NL, fr. *pter-* + *ichthy-* + *-odes*] **:** a genus of ostracoderms (subclass Antiarcha) from the Devonian rocks of Scotland having the head covered with bony plates and bearing the orbits close together on its dorsal surface with the anterior half of the body encased in a buckler of large bony plates

pterid- *or* **pterido-** *comb form* [Gk *pterid-, pteris* — more at PTERIS] **:** fern ⟨*pterido*graphy⟩ ⟨*pterid*oid⟩

pte·rid·e·ous \tə'ridēəs, (')te¦r-\ *adj* [NL, fr. *Pterid-, Pteris* + E *-eous*] **:** of or relating to *Pteris* or a closely related genus

pter·i·dine \'terəˌdēn, -ˌdᵊn\ *n* -s [ISV *pter-* + *-id* + *-ine;* orig. formed as G *pteridin;* fr. its being a factor in the pigments of butterfly wings] **:** a yellow crystalline bicyclic base $C_6H_4N_4$ that is a fundamental constituent in important natural products (as folic acid, leucopterin, xanthopterin); 1,3,5,8-tetra-aza-naphthalene

pte·rid·i·um \tə'ridēəm, te'r-\ *n, cap* [NL, fr. *Pterid-, Pteris* + *-ium*] **:** a genus of ferns that are related to and sometimes included in *Pteris* and that have in addition to the false indusium formed by the frond margin a true indusium on the inner side of the sori — see BRACKEN

pter·i·dog·ra·phy \ˌterə'dägrəfē\ *n* -ES [ISV *pterid-* + *-graphy*] **:** the description of ferns

pter·i·doid \'terəˌdȯid\ *adj* [*pterid-* + *-oid*] **:** of, relating to, or resembling a fern

pter·i·do·log·i·cal \¦terədə¦läjəkəl\ *adj* [*pteridology* + *-ical*] **:** of or relating to pteridology or pteridologists

pter·i·dol·o·gist \ˌterə'däləjəst\ *n* -s [*pteridology* + *-ist*] **:** a specialist in pteridology

pter·i·dol·o·gy \-jē\ *n* -ES [*pterid-* + *-logy*] **:** the study of ferns

pter·i·doph·y·ta \ˌterə'däfəd·ə\ *n pl, cap* [NL, fr. *pterid-* + *-phyta*] *in some classifications* **:** a division of vascular plants coordinate with Bryophyta and Spermatophyta and coextensive with the subdivisions Psilopsida, Lycopsida, Sphenopsida and the class Filicineae of the Pteropsida

pte·rid·o·phyte \tə'ridəˌfīt, 'terəd-\ *n* -s [NL *Pteridophyta*] **:** a plant of the division Pteridophyta **:** a fern or fern ally

pte·rid·o·phyt·ic \tə¦ridə¦fid·ik, ¦terəd-\ *or* **pter·i·doph·y·tous** \¦terə¦däfəd·əs\ *adj* [NL *Pteridophyta* + E *-ic* or *-ous*] **:** of, relating to, or characteristic of the Pteridophyta

pte·rido·sperm \tə'ridəˌspərm, 'terəd-\ *n* [ISV *pterid-* + *sperm*] **:** a fossil plant of the order Cycadofilicales **:** SEED FERN

pter·i·do·sper·mae \ˌterədō'spər(ˌ)mē\ [NL, fr. *pterid-* + *-spermae*] *syn of* PTERIDOSPERMAPHYTA

pter·i·do·spermaphyta \¦terə(ˌ)dō+\ *n pl, cap* [NL, fr. *pterid-* + *Spermaphyta*] *in some classifications* **:** a group of fossil plants coextensive with the order Cycadofilicales but treated as coordinate with Gymnospermae and Angiospermae — **pter·i·do·sper·ma·phyt·ic** \¦⸗⸗(ˌ)⸗¦spərmə¦fid·ik\ *adj* — **pter·i·do·sper·mous** \-məs\ *adj*

pte·ri·idae \tə'rīəˌdē, te'r-\ *n pl, cap* [NL, fr. *Pteria,* type genus (fr. *pter-* + *-ia*) + *-idae*] **:** a family of bivalve mollusks (group Pectinaceae) most prominent in the Paleozoic and surviving chiefly in warm seas, including the pearl oysters, and having the right valve smaller and lower, the hinge line long and straight, the shell attached by a byssus, and the foot reduced

pter·in \'terən\ *n* -s [ISV *pter-* + *-in;* orig. formed in G; fr. its being a factor in the pigments of butterfly wings] **:** a compound containing the pteridine ring system

pteri·on \'terēˌän, 'tir-\ *n* -s [NL, fr. *pter-* + *-ion* (as in *inion*)] **:** the suture of the frontal, parietal, and temporal bones with the greater wing of the sphenoid — see CRANIOMETRY illustration

pteris \'terəs, 'tir-\ *n, cap* [NL, fr. Gk *pterid-, pteris* fern; akin to Gk *pteron* feather, wing — more at FEATHER] **1 :** a genus of coarse ferns (family Polypodiaceae) having variously divided or rarely simple fronds with a marginal linear continuous sorus and an indusium composed of the reflexed margin of the frond — see PTERIDIUM **2** -ES **:** RIBBON FERN

-p·ter·is \pt(ə)rəs\ *n comb form* [NL, fr. Gk, fr. *pteris*] **:** fern — in generic names ⟨Glosso*pteris*⟩ ⟨Ornitho*pteris*⟩

ptero- — see PTER-

ptero·branch \'terəˌbraŋk\ *n* -s [NL *Pterobranchia*] **:** a member of the order Pterobranchia

ptero·bran·chia \ˌterə'braŋkēə\ *n pl, cap* [NL, fr. *pter-* + *-branchia*] **:** an order of Hemichordata or an independent phylum of uncertain affinities that comprises two genera (*Cephalodiscus* and *Rhabdopleura*) of small deep-sea tube-dwelling animals that commonly reproduce by budding

ptero·car·pous \¦terə¦kärpəs\ *adj* [*pter-* + *-carpous*] **:** having winged fruit

ptero·car·pus \ˌterə'kärpəs\ *n, cap* [NL, fr. *pter-* + *-carpus*] **:** a genus of tropical trees (family Leguminosae) with alternate pinnate leaves, yellow flowers, and a broad legume having a membranous-winged margin — see KINO

ptero·car·ya \-'ka(a)rēə\ *n, cap* [NL, fr. *pter-* + Gk *karya* nut tree, fr. *karyon* nut — more at CAREEN] **:** a genus of Asiatic trees (family Juglandaceae) having thin-shelled nuts subtended by bracteoles that become enlarged in the two-winged fruit

ptero·cau·lon \ˌterə'kȯlən, -ˌlän\ *n, cap* [NL, fr. *pter-* + *-caulon* (fr. Gk *kaulos* stem, stalk — more at COLE] **:** a small genus of vigorous woolly or downy perennial herbs (family Compositae) with alternate decurrent leaves and flower heads in dense terminal clusters — see BLACK ROOT, GOLDEN CUDWEED

pte·roc·era \tə'räsərə, te'r-\ *also* **pte·roc·er·as** \-sərəs, -ˌras\ [NL, fr. *pter-* + *-cera* or *-ceras*] *syn of* LAMBIS

ptero·cla·dia \ˌterə'klādēə\ *n, cap* [NL, fr. *pter-* + *clad-* + *-ia*] **:** a genus of red algae (family Gelidiaceae) having thalli suggestive of fern fronds

ptero·cle·tes \ˌterə'klēd·(ˌ)ēz\ *n pl, cap* [NL, irreg. fr. *Pterocles,* genus of sandgrouse] **:** a suborder of Columbiformes coextensive with the Pteroclididae

ptero·clid·i·dae \ˌterə'klidəˌdē\ *n pl, cap* [NL, fr. *Pteroclid-, Pterocles,* type genus (fr. *pter-* + Gk *kleid-, kleis* key) + *-idae* — more at CLEID-] **:** a family of birds (suborder Pterocletes) consisting of the sandgrouses

ptero·dac·tyl \¦terə¦daktəl\ *n* -s [NL *Pterodactylus*] **:** any of numerous extinct flying reptiles constituting the order Pterosauria, known from the Lower Jurassic nearly to the close of the Mesozoic, and having no feathers, a wing membrane extending from the side of the body along the arm to the end of the greatly enlarged fourth digit, and a tail usu. rather short but sometimes expanded and resembling a rudder — **ptero·dac·tyl·i·an** \¦⸗⸗¦⸗¦tilēən\ *adj or n* — **ptero·dac·tyl·ic** \-lik\ *adj* — **ptero·dac·ty·lid** \¦⸗⸗¦⸗ˌtələd\ *adj or n* — **ptero·dac·ty·loid** \-ˌlȯid\ *adj* — **ptero·dac·ty·lous** \-ˌləs\ *adj*

ptero·dac·ty·li \ˌterə'daktəˌlī\ [NL, fr. *pter-* + *dactyli*] *syn of* PTEROSAURIA

ptero·dac·ty·lus \-ˌləs\ [NL, fr. *pter-* + *dactylus*] *syn of* ORNITHOCEPHALUS

pte·rod·ro·ma \tə'rädrəmə, te'r-\ *n, cap* [NL, fr. *pter-* + *-droma* (fr. Gk *dromos* course, race) — more at -DROME] **:** a large genus of petrels found chiefly in southern seas that are dark-colored often with a white tail and under parts

pte·rog·ra·pher \-ägrəfə(r)\ *n* -s [*pterography* + *-er*] **:** a specialist in pterography

ptero·graph·ic \¦terə¦grafik\ *or* **ptero·graph·i·cal** \-fəkəl\ *adj* [*pterography* + *-ic* or *-ical*] **:** of or relating to pterography

pte·rog·ra·phy \tə'rägrəfē, te'r-\ *n* -ES [*pter-* + *-graphy*] **:** the description of feathers

pte·ro·ic acid \tə'|rōik-, (')te¦|\ *n* [*pteroic* fr. *pter*in + *-oic*] **:** a crystalline amino acid $H_2NC_6HN_4(OH)CH_2NHC_6H_4COOH$ derived from *para*-aminobenzoic acid and pteridine and formed along with glutamic acid by hydrolysis of folic acid or other pteroylglutamic acids

pteroid \'teˌrȯid, 'tiˌr-\ *adj* [*pter-* + *-oid*] **1 :** WINGLIKE **2** [Gk *pter*is fern + E *-oid* — more at PTERIS] **:** FERNLIKE

pter·ois \'terəwəs, -eˌrȯis\ *n, cap* [NL, prob. fr. Gk *pteroeis* feathered, winged, fr. *pteron* feather, wing] **:** a genus of small brilliantly colored scorpion fishes including the lion-fishes

pter·o·li·chus \ˌterə'līkəs\ *n, cap* [NL, fr. *pter-* + *-lichus* (prob. irreg. fr. Gk *lichēn* lichen) — more at LICHEN] **:** a genus of feather mites occurring on various birds

pte·ro·ma \tə'rōmə, te'r-\ *n, pl* **pteroma·ta** \-məd·ə\ [L, fr. Gk *pterōma* fr. *pteron* feather, wing + *-ōma* -ome] **:** the enclosed space of a stoa, portico, or peristyle including the stylobate and the space to the solid wall behind the portico (as in a Greek temple)

[1]**pte·rom·a·lid** \tə'räməlәd, ¦terə¦mal-\ *adj* [NL *Pteromalidae*] **:** of or relating to the Pteromalidae

[2]**pteromalid** \"\ *n* -s **:** a chalcid fly of the family Pteromalidae

pter·o·mal·i·dae \ˌterə'maləˌdē\ *n pl, cap* [NL, fr. *Pteromalus,* type genus (fr. *pter-* + Gk *homalos* even, level) + *-idae;* akin to Gk *homos* same — more at SAME] **:** a large family of chalcid flies having larvae that are parasitic on the larvae of other insects (as of the orders Lepidoptera and Coleoptera) and some that are hyperparasites

ptero·mys \'terəˌmis\ [NL, fr. *pter-* + *-mys*] *syn of* PETAURISTA

pteron \'teˌrän, 'tiˌr-\ *n* -s [L, fr. Gk, lit., wing, feather — more at FEATHER] **:** a side (as of a temple) in classical architecture

[1]**ptero·nar·cid** \¦terə¦närsəd\ *adj* [NL *Pteronarcidae*] **:** of or relating to the Pteronarcidae

[2]**pteronarcid** \"\ *n* -s **:** a stone fly of the family Pteronarcidae

ptero·nar·ci·dae \\,==ˈnärsə,dē\\ *n pl, cap* [NL, fr. *pter-* + *narc-* + *-idae;* fr. the sluggish flight] **:** a widely distributed family of stone flies

ptero·pae·des \\,terəˈpē(,)dēz\\ *n pl* [NL, fr. *pter-* + Gk *paides,* pl. of *pais* child — more at FEW] **:** birds (as the megapodes) able to fly shortly after hatching

ptero·pae·dic \\¦==¦pēdik\\ *adj* [NL *pteropaedes* + E *-ic*] **:** of or relating to the pteropaedes

ptero·pe·gal \\¦terə¦pēgəl\\ *or* **ptero·pe·gous** \\-gəs\\ *adj* [NL *pteropegum* + E *-al* or *-ous*] **:** of or relating to the pteropegum

ptero·pe·gum \\,==ˈ==gəm\\ *n* -s [NL, fr. *pter-* + Gk *pēgon,* neut. of *pēgos* solid, strong, fr. *pēgnynai* to fasten together — more at PACT] **:** an articular socket of the wing of an insect

[1]**pte·roph·o·rid** \\təˈräfərəd, (ˈ)te¦r-; ¦terə¦fōr-\\ *adj* [NL *Pterophoridae*] **:** of or relating to the Pterophoridae

[2]**pterophorid** \\"\\ *n* -s **:** a plume moth of the family Pterophoridae

pter·o·phor·i·dae \\,terəˈfōrə,dē\\ *n pl, cap* [NL, fr. *Pterophorus,* type genus (fr. *pter-* + *-phorus*) + *-idae*] **:** a family of moths comprising the plume moths and having larvae that are usu. leaf rollers

pte·rop·i·dae \\təˈräpə,dē, teˈr-\\ [NL, fr. *Pteropus* + *-idae*] *syn of* PTEROPODIDAE

[1]**ptero·pod** \\ˈterə,päd\\ *adj* [NL *Pteropoda*] **:** of or relating to the Pteropoda

[2]**pteropod** \\"\\ *n* -s **:** a mollusk of the division Pteropoda

pte·rop·o·da \\təˈräpədə, teˈr-\\ *n pl, cap* [NL, fr. *pter-* + *-poda*] **:** a division of Tectibranchia formerly ranked as a separate class of Mollusca comprising small hermaphroditic gastropod mollusks having the anterior lobes of the foot developed in the form of broad thin winglike organs with which they swim at or near the surface of the sea, usu. lacking gills, and frequently lacking a shell

ptero·pod·i·dae \\,terəˈpädə,dē\\ *n pl, cap* [NL, fr. *Pteropod-, Pteropus,* type genus + *-idae*] **:** a family of fruit bats coextensive with the suborder Megachiroptera

ptero·po·di·um \\,terəˈpōdēəm\\ *n, pl* **pteropo·dia** \\-ēə\\ [NL *pterop-* (fr. *Pteropoda*) + *-podium*] **:** a pteropod's foot

pte·rop·o·dous \\təˈräpədəs, (ˈ)te¦r-\\ *adj* [NL *Pteropoda* + E *-ous*] **:** of or relating to the Pteropoda

pte·rop·sid \\təˈräpsəd, teˈr-\\ *n* -s [NL *Pteropsida*] **:** a plant of the subdivision Pteropsida

pte·rop·si·da \\-sədə\\ *n pl, cap* [NL, fr. *Pteropsis,* genus of ferns (fr. *pter-* + *-opsis*) + *-ida*] **:** a subdivision of Tracheophyta comprising vascular plants (as the ferns and flowering plants) with well-developed and typically large leaves, leaf gaps usu. present in the primary vascular cylinder, and sporangia abaxial on normal or modified leaves and including the classes Filicineae, Gymnospermae, and Angiospermae — compare LYCOPSIDA, PSILOPSIDA, SPHENOPSIDA

ptero·pus \\ˈterəpəs\\ *n, cap* [NL, fr. Gk *pteropous* wing-footed, fr. *pter-* + *pous* foot — more at FOOT] **:** the type genus of Pteropodidae comprising the common fruit bats

ptero·saur \\ˈterə,sȯ(ə)r\\ *n* -s [NL *Pterosauria*] **:** one of the Pterosauria **:** a flying reptile

ptero·sau·ria \\,==ˈsȯrēə\\ *n pl, cap* [NL, fr. *pter-* + *-sauria*] **:** an order of Archosauria comprising flying reptiles flourishing from the Jurassic to late Cretaceous times and including the pterodactyls and related forms

ptero·sper·mum \\-ˈspərməm\\ *n, cap* [NL, fr. *pter-* + *-spermum*] **:** a genus of shrubs and trees (family Sterculiaceae) of southeastern Asia and the East Indies including several that yield economically important timbers — see MAYENG

ptero·ste·mon \\-ˈstēmən\\ *n, cap* [NL, fr. *pter-* + Gk *stēmōn* warp, thread — more at STAMEN] **:** a genus of Mexican shrubs (family Saxifragaceae) having pubescent twigs, alternate dentate leaves, showy white perfect flowers in cymes, and capsular fruit

ptero·stigma \\,terə+\\ *n, pl* **pterostigmata** [NL, fr. *pter-* + L *stigma*] **:** an opaque thickened spot on the costal margin of the wing of an insect — **ptero·stigmal** *adj* — **ptero·stigmatic** *or* **ptero·stigmatical** \\¦terə+\\ *adj*

ptero·theca \\¦terə+\\ *n* [NL, fr. *pter-* + *theca*] **:** the part of the pupa case that covers the rudimentary wing of an insect

ptero·thorax \\"+\\ *n* [NL, fr. *pter-* + *thorax;* fr. its being the wing-bearing segment] **:** the mesothorax and metathorax of an insect

[1]**pte·rot·ic** \\təˈräd·ik, (ˈ)te¦r-\\ *adj* [*pter-* + [2]*-otic;* fr. the bone being winglike] **:** of, relating to, or constituting a bone between the prootic and epiotic in the dorsal and outer part of the periotic capsule of a fish

[2]**pterotic** \\"\\ *n* -s **:** the pterotic bone

-p·ter·ous \\pt(ə)rəs\\ *adj comb form* [Gk *-pteros* -winged, fr. *pteron* wing, feather — more at FEATHER] **:** having (so many or such) wings or winglike parts ⟨anisopterous⟩ ⟨hexapterous⟩ ⟨trichopterous⟩

pter·o·yl \\ˈterəwəl, -,wil\\ *n* -s [*pter-* (in *pteroic acid*) + *-yl*] **:** the radical ($C_{13}H_{11}N_6O$)CO— of pteroic acid

pter·o·yl·glutamic acid \\¦==(,)=+…-\\ *n* [*pteroylglutamic* ISV *pteroyl* + *glutamic*] **1 :** an acid that is a conjugate of one molecule each of pteroic acid and glutamic acid; *esp* **:** FOLIC ACID 1 **2 :** any of several acids (as pteroyl-hepta-glutamic acid found in yeast) that are conjugates of pteroic acid with more than one molecule of glutamic acid

pter·o·yl·mono·glutamic acid \\¦==(,)=¦==+…-\\ *n* [*pteroylmonoglutamic* fr. *pteroyl* + *mon-* + *glutamic*] **:** FOLIC ACID 1

-p·ter·us \\pt(ə)rəs\\ *n comb form* [NL, fr. Gk *-pteros* -pterous] **:** one having (such) wings or winglike structures — in generic names ⟨*Chaetopterus*⟩ ⟨*Trachypterus*⟩

pteryg- *or* **pterygo-** *comb form* [Gk, fr. *pteryg-, pteryx;* akin to Gk *pteron* wing, feather — more at FEATHER] **1 :** wing **:** fin ⟨*pterygoblast*⟩ ⟨*pterygobranchiate*⟩ **2 :** pterygoid and ⟨*pterygomalar*⟩

[1]**pte·ryg·ial** \\təˈrij(ē)əl, (ˈ)te¦r-\\ *adj* [NL *pterygium* + E *-al*] **:** of or relating to a pterygium

[2]**pterygial** \\"\\ *n* -s **:** a pterygial bone or cartilage; *specif* **:** ACTINOST

-p·te·ryg·ii \\ptəˈrijē,ī\\ *n pl comb form* [NL, fr. Gk *pteryg-, pteryx* wing, fin] **:** winged ones **:** finned ones — in taxonomic names ⟨Chrondro*pterygii*⟩ ⟨Neo*pterygii*⟩ ⟨Pleuro*pterygii*⟩

pte·ryg·io·phore \\təˈrijēə,fō(ə)r, teˈr-\\ *n* -s [*pteryg-* + *-phore*] **:** one of the cartilaginous or bony elements (as basalia and radialia) by which rays of the fin of a fish are supported **:** ACTINOST

pte·ryg·i·um \\-jēəm\\ *n, pl* **pterygiums** \\-mz\\ *or* **pteryg·ia** \\-ēə\\ [NL, fr. Gk *pterygion* little wing, fin, fr. *pteryg-* + *-ion* (dim. suffix)] **1 a :** a triangular fleshy mass of thickened conjunctiva occurring usu. at the inner side of the eyeball, covering part of the cornea, and causing a disturbance of vision **b :** a forward growth of the cuticle over the nail **2 :** a generalized limb of a vertebrate **3 :** one of the lobes at the end of the snout of a weevil

pter·y·go·branchiate \\¦terəgō+\\ *adj* [*pteryg-* + *branchiate*] **:** having plumose gills — used of an isopod crustacean

pter·y·gode \\ˈterə,gōd\\ *n* -s [NL *pterygoda*] **:** PATAGIUM 2a

pter·y·go·dum \\,terəˈgōdəm\\ *n, pl* **pterygo·da** \\-də\\ [NL, fr. Gk *pterygōdēs* winglike, fr. *pteryg-* + *-ōdēs* -ode] **:** PATAGIUM 2a

pter·y·go·ge·nea \\,terəgōˈjēnēə\\ [NL, fr. *pteryg-* + *-genea* (fr. Gk *genos* race, kind) — more at GEN-] *syn of* PTERYGOTA

[1]**pter·y·goid** \\ˈterə,gȯid\\ *also* **pter·y·goi·dal** \\¦==¦gȯidᵊl\\ *adj* [*pterygoid* prob. fr. (assumed) NL *pterygoides,* fr. Gk *pterygoeidēs* winglike, fr. *pteryg-* + *-oeidēs* -oid; *pterygoidal* fr. [2]*pterygoid* + *-al*] **:** of, relating to, being, or lying in the region of the inferior part of the sphenoid bone of the vertebrate skull — see PTERYGOID BONE

[2]**pterygoid** \\"+\\ *n* -s **:** a pterygoid element (as a muscle, nerve, or bone)

pterygoid artery *n* **:** a branch of the internal maxillary artery supplying the pterygoid muscles

pterygoid bone *n* **:** a horizontally placed often more or less rodlike bone or group of bones of the upper jaw or roof of the mouth in most lower vertebrates connecting the palatine in front and the quadrate behind and forming part of the palatoquadrate arch

pterygoid canal *n* **:** a canal in the sphenoid bone transmitting the Vidian nerve and artery

pter·y·goi·de·us \\,terəˈgȯidēəs\\ *n, pl* **pterygoi·dei** \\-ē,ī\\ [NL, fr. (assumed) NL *pterygoides* pterygoid] **:** PTERYGOID MUSCLE

pterygoid fossa *n* **1 :** a depression on the outer and posterior aspect of the pterygoid process of the sphenoid bone **2 :** a depression on the lower jawbone for the insertion of the external pterygoid muscle

pterygoid lamina *n* **:** one of the two vertical plates making up a pterygoid process of the mammalian sphenoid bone

pterygoid muscle *n* **:** either of two muscles extending from the sphenoid bone to the lower jaw: **a :** an external muscle that arises from the greater wing of the sphenoid and from the outer surface of the lateral pterygoid lamina, is inserted into the condyle of the mandible and the interarticular disk, and acts as an antagonist of the masseter, temporal, and internal pterygoid muscles **b :** an internal muscle that arises from the inner surface of the lateral pterygoid lamina and the palatine and maxillary bones, is inserted into the angle and ramus of the mandible, cooperates with the masseter and temporal in elevating the lower jaw, and controls certain lateral and rotary movements of the jaw

pterygoid nerve *n* **:** either of two branches of the mandibular nerve chiefly supplying the pterygoid muscles and other muscles of mastication

pterygoid notch *n* **:** an angular notch separating the pterygoid laminae of each pterygoid process

pterygoid plate *n* **:** PTERYGOID LAMINA

pterygoid plexus *n* **:** a plexus of veins draining the region of the pterygoid muscles and emptying chiefly into the internal maxillary and anterior facial veins

pterygoid process *n* **1 :** a process extending downward from each side of the sphenoid bone in man and other mammals consisting of a pair of pterygoid laminae separated by a pterygoid notch and having a deep depression on its outer and posterior aspect **2 :** PTERYGOID LAMINA **3 :** a process on the palatine bone fitting into the pterygoid notch

pterygoid ridge *n* **:** a transverse ridge on the sphenoid bone marking the separation of the temporal and infratemporal fossae

pter·y·go·mandibular \\¦terə(,)gō+\\ *adj* [*pteryg-* + *mandibular*] **:** of, relating to, or linking the pterygoid process and mandible

pter·y·go·palatine fossa \\"+…-\\ *n* [*pterygopalatine* ISV *pteryg-* + *palatine*] **:** a small triangular space beneath the apex of the orbit bounded in front by the maxilla, medially by the palatine bone, and behind by the pterygoid process of the sphenoid and lodging among other structures the sphenopalatine ganglion

pte·rygo·phore \\təˈrigə,fō(ə)r, ˈterəgō,f-\\ *n* -s [*pteryg-* + *-phore*] **:** ACTINOST

pter·y·go·po·di·um \\,terəgōˈpōdēəm\\ *n, pl* **pterygopo·dia** \\-ēə\\ [NL, fr. *pteryg-* + *-podium*] **:** a clasper of an elasmobranch

pter·y·go·quadrate \\¦terə(,)gō+\\ *adj* [*pteryg-* + *quadrate*] **:** of, relating to, or constituting the upper half of the first branchial arch that gives rise in lower vertebrates to most of the upper jaw

[1]**pter·y·go·so·mal** \\+¦sōməl\\ *n* -s [NL *Pterygosoma* + E *-al*] **:** a mite of the family Pterygosomidae

[2]**pterygosomal** \\"\\ *adj* **:** of or relating to the Pterygosomidae

pter·y·go·so·mi·dae \\,==(,)=ˈsōmə,dē\\ *n pl, cap* [NL, fr. *Pterygosoma,* type genus (fr. *pteryg-* + *-soma*) + *-idae*] **:** a family of mites mostly parasitic on lizards

pter·y·go·ta \\,terəˈgōd·ə\\ *n pl, cap* [NL, fr. Gk, neut. pl. of *pterygōtos* winged, fr. *pteryg-, pteryx* wing — more at PTERYG-] **:** a subclass of Insecta consisting of the winged and secondarily wingless insects — compare APTERYGOTA

pter·y·gote \\ˈterə,gōt\\ *or* **pter·y·go·tous** \\¦==¦gōd·əs\\ *adj* [*pterygote* fr. NL *Pterygota; pterygotous* fr. NL *Pterygota* + E *-ous*] **:** of or relating to the subclass Pterygota

pter·y·la \\ˈterələ\\ *n, pl* **pter·y·lae** \\-,lē, -,lī\\ [NL, fr. *pter-* + Gk *hylē* wood, forest — more at HYLE] **:** one of the definite areas of the skin of a bird on which feathers grow — called also *feather tract;* contrasted with *apterium*

pter·y·lo·graph·ic \\¦terəlō¦grafik\\ *or* **pter·y·lo·graph·i·cal** \\-fəkəl\\ *adj* [*pterylography* + *-ic* or *-ical*] **:** of or relating to pterylography

pter·y·log·ra·phy \\,terəˈlägrəfē\\ *n* -ES [ISV *pterylo-* (fr. NL *pteryla*) + *-graphy;* orig. formed as G *pterylographie*] **:** the study or description of the pterylae of birds

pter·y·lo·log·i·cal \\¦terəlō¦läjəkəl\\ *adj* [*pterylology* + *-ical*] **:** of or relating to pterylology

pter·y·lol·o·gy \\,terəˈläləjē\\ *n* -ES [NL *pterylosis* + *-logy*] **:** the study of pterylosis

pter·y·lo·sis \\,terəˈlōsəs\\ *n, pl* **pterylo·ses** \\-ō,sēz\\ [NL, fr. *pteryla* + *-osis*] **:** the arrangement of feathers in definite areas of growth ⟨birds . . . at least three years old judging from the ~ of the head —*Amer. Midland Naturalist*⟩

-p·ter·yx \\pt(ə)riks\\ *n comb form* [NL, fr. Gk, fr. *pteryx* wing — more at PTERYG-] **:** winged one **:** finned one — in generic names ⟨*Dipteryx*⟩ ⟨*Odontopteryx*⟩

ptg *abbr* printing

ptil- *or* **ptilo-** *comb form* [NL, fr. Gk *ptilon;* akin to Gk *pteron* feather — more at FEATHER] **:** down **:** feather ⟨*Ptilocercus*⟩

-p·tile \\ptəl, p,tīl\\ *n comb form* -s [Gk *ptilon*] **:** feather ⟨neossoptile⟩ ⟨teleoptile⟩ ⟨protoptile⟩

ptil·ich·thy·i·dae \\,ti,likˈthīə,dē\\ *n pl, cap* [NL, fr. *Ptilichthys,* type genus (fr. *ptil-* + *-ichthys*) + *-idae*] **:** a family of blennies comprising the quillfishes

pti·li·i·dae \\təˈliə,dē\\ [NL, fr. *Ptilium,* genus of beetles (fr. *ptil-* + *-ium*) + *-idae*] *syn of* TRICHOPTERYGIDAE

pti·lim·ni·um \\təˈlimnēəm\\ *n, cap* [NL, fr. *ptil-* + *limn-* + *-ium*] **:** a genus (family Umbelliferae) of widely distributed annual herbs having finely dissected leaves, compound umbels of minute white flowers, and angled or winged fruits — see MOCK BISHOP'S-WEED

pti·li·nal \\təˈlīnᵊl\\ *adj* [NL *ptilinum* + E *-al*] **:** of or relating to the ptilinum

pti·li·num \\-nəm\\ *n, pl* **ptili·na** \\-nə\\ [NL, prob. fr. *ptil-* + L *-inum* (neut. of *-inus* -ine)] **:** a vesicular organ on the front of the head of flies that assists in rupturing the pupa case and shortly afterward shrinks away

ptilo·cer·cus \\,tilōˈsərkəs, ,tīl-\\ *n, cap* [NL, fr. *ptil-* + Gk *kerkos* tail] **:** a genus of insectivores comprising the pentails

ptil·o·no·rhyn·chi·dae \\,tilənōˈriŋkə,dē\\ *n pl, cap* [NL, fr. *Ptilonorhynchus,* type genus (fr. Gk *ptilon* feather, down + *-rhynchus*) + *-idae*] **:** a family of passerine birds that comprises the bowerbirds and is often included as a subfamily in Paradiseidae

ptilo·pod \\ˈtilə,päd, ˈtīl-\\ *adj* [*ptil-* + *-pod*] **:** having the feet feathered ⟨~ domestic fowls⟩

pti·lo·sis \\təˈlōsəs, tīˈl-\\ *n, pl* **ptilo·ses** \\-ō,sēz\\ [NL, fr. Gk *ptilōsis* plumage, fr. *ptil-* + *-ōsis* -osis] **:** plumage irrespective of pterylosis

pti·lo·ta \\-ōd·ə\\ *n, cap* [NL, fr. Gk, fem. sing. of *ptilōtos* winged, feathered, fr. *ptilon* feather] **:** a genus of marine red algae (family Ceramiaceae) having flat feathery fronds

[1]**pti·nid** \\ˈtīnəd\\ *adj* [NL *Ptinidae*] **:** of or relating to the Ptinidae

[2]**ptinid** \\"\\ *n* -s **:** a serricorn beetle of the family Ptinidae

ptin·i·dae \\ˈtinə,dē\\ *n pl, cap* [NL, fr. *Ptinus,* type genus + *-idae*] **:** an extensive family of serricorn beetles of small size and usu. brown color that live mostly on dead animal and vegetable matter

pti·nus \\ˈtīnəs\\ *n, cap* [NL, perh. fr. Gk *phthinein* to decay, wane — more at PHTHISIS] **:** the type genus of Ptinidae comprising predominantly brown often hirsute beetles and including several pests of stored products — see SPIDER BEETLE

pti·san \\təˈzan, ˈtiz°n\\ *n* -s [ME *tisane,* fr. MF, fr. L *ptisana* peeled barley, barley water, fr. Gk *ptisanē,* fr. *ptissein* to peel, crush — more at PESTLE] **:** a decoction of barley with other ingredients; *broadly* **:** TEA, TISANE

PTM *abbr* pulse-time modulation

PTO *abbr* please turn over

ptol·e·ma·ic \\¦tälə¦māik, -āēk\\ *also* **ptol·e·mae·an** \\-mēən\\ *adj, usu cap* [in sense 1, fr. L *Ptolemaeus* Ptolemy 2d cent. A.D. geographer and astronomer of Alexandria (fr. Gk *Ptolemaios*) + E *-ic* or *-an;* in sense 2, *ptolemaic* fr. Gk *ptolemaikos,* fr. *Ptolemaios* Ptolemy, any of the Greco-Egyptian rulers of Egypt + *-ikos* -ic; *ptolemaean* fr. L *ptolemaeus* Ptolemaean (fr. *Ptolemaeus* Ptolemy, Greco-Egyptian ruler of Egypt, fr. Gk *Ptolemaios*) + E *-an*] **1 :** of or relating to Ptolemy the geographer and astronomer **2 :** of or relating to the Greco-Egyptian rulers of Egypt from 323 B.C. to 30 B.C.

ptolemaic system *n, usu cap P* [after Ptolemy *fl* 2d cent. A.D. who maintained it] **:** the system of planetary motions according to which the earth is at the center with the sun, moon, and planets revolving around it and each orbit except for the sun and moon is composed of a principal circle upon which moves a smaller circle carrying the planet — compare COPERNICAN SYSTEM, DEFERENT, ECCENTRIC 1, EPICYCLE

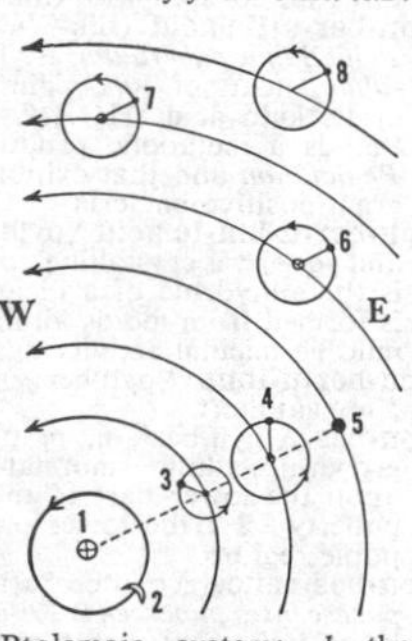

Ptolemaic system: *1* the Earth, *2* Moon, *3* Mercury, *4* Venus, *5* Sun, *6* Mars, *7* Jupiter, *8* Saturn

ptol·e·ma·ism \\¦==¦mā,izəm\\ *n* -s *usu cap* [*ptolemaic* + *-ism*] **:** the principles of the Ptolemaic system

ptol·e·ma·ist \\-āəst\\ *n* -s *usu cap* [*ptolemaic* + *-ist*] **:** a supporter of the Ptolemaic system

ptol·e·my \\ˈ==,mē, -mi\\ *n* -ES *cap* [after *Ptolemy,* name given to various kings of Egypt, esp. fr. 323–30 B.C., fr. L *Ptolemaeus,* fr. Gk *Ptolemaios*] **:** a ruler of the Macedonian dynasty of Egypt

pto·maine \\(ˈ)tō¦mān\\ *n* -s [It *ptomaina,* fr. Gk *ptōma* fall, fallen body, corpse (fr. *piptein* to fall) + It *-ina* -ine — more at FEATHER] **:** any of various organic bases some of which (as cadaverine or putrescine) are poisonous and which are formed by the action of putrefactive bacteria on nitrogenous matter — compare LEUCOMAINE

ptomaine poisoning *n* **:** FOOD POISONING

pto·ma·tine \\ˈtōmə,tēn, -,tən\\ *n* -s [ISV *ptomat-* (fr. Gk *ptōmat-, ptōma* corpse) + *-ine*] **:** PTOMAINE

ptosed \\ˈtōzd\\ *or* **ptot·ic** \\ˈtäd·ik\\ *adj* [*ptosed* fr. NL *ptosis* + E *-ed; ptotic* ISV, fr. NL *ptosis,* after such pairs as L *synthesis:* E *synthetic*] **:** affected with or subject to ptosis

pto·sis \\ˈtōsəs\\ *n, pl* **pto·ses** \\-ō,sēz\\ [NL, fr. Gk *ptōsis* fall, falling, fr. *piptein* to fall] **:** a sagging or prolapse of an organ or part (as one of the abdominal viscera) ⟨renal ~⟩; *specif* **:** drooping of the upper eyelid (as from paralysis of the oculomotor nerve)

ptr *abbr* **1** painter **2** printer

p trap *n, cap P* **:** a P-shaped trap used esp. for sinks and lavatories

ptrnmkr *abbr* patternmaker

pty *abbr* **1** party **2** *often cap* proprietary

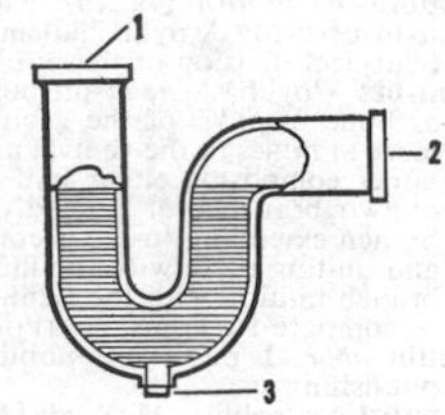

P trap: *1* intake, *2* outlet, *3* cleanout

ptyal- *or* **ptyalo-** *comb form* [NL, fr. Gk, fr. *ptyalon* spittle, saliva, fr. *ptyein* to spit — more at SPEW] **:** saliva ⟨*ptyal*agogue⟩ ⟨*ptyalo*rrhea⟩

pty·al·a·gogue \\tīˈalə,gäg *sometimes* -gȯg\\ *n* -s [ISV *ptyal-* + *-agogue*] **:** SIALAGOGUE

pty·a·lin \\ˈtīələn\\ *n* -s [ISV *ptyal-* + *-in*] **:** an alpha-amylase found in the saliva of many animals including man but not in that of horses, dogs, or cats **:** salivary amylase

pty·a·lism \\ˈtīə,lizəm\\ *n* -s [NL *ptyalismus,* fr. Gk *ptyalismos,* fr. *ptyalizein* to salivate, fr. *ptyalon* spittle, saliva + *-izein* -ize] **:** an excessive flow of saliva

pty·as \\ˈtīəs\\ *n, cap* [NL, fr. Gk, spitter, fr. *ptyein* to spit] **:** a genus of Colubridae comprising the Indian rat snake

ptych- *or* **ptycho-** *comb form* [Gk *ptych-,* fr. *ptychē,* fr. *ptyssein* to fold] **:** fold **:** layer ⟨*Ptycho*sperma⟩

pty·chod·era \\tīˈkädərə\\ *n, cap* [NL, prob. fr. *ptych-* + Gk *derē* neck, throat] **:** a widely distributed genus (the type of the family Ptychoderidae) of enteropneusts

[1]**pty·choder·id** \\(ˈ)tī¦kädərəd, ¦tīkō¦der-\\ *adj* [NL *Ptychoderidae*] **:** of or relating to the Ptychoderidae

[2]**ptychoderid** \\"\\ *n* -s **:** an enteropneust of the family Ptychoderidae

pty·cho·der·i·dae \\,tīkōˈderə,dē\\ *n pl, cap* [NL, fr. *Ptychodera* + *-idae*] **:** a nearly cosmopolitan family of enteropneusts that includes *Balanoglossus* and related genera

pty·cho·par·ia \\,tīkōˈpa(a)rēə\\ *n, cap* [NL, fr. *ptych-* + Gk *pareia* cheek] **:** a genus of Middle and Upper Cambrian trilobites with small prominent glabella, long narrow thorax, and strongly segmented pygidium

[1]**pty·cho·par·i·id** \\-rēəd\\ *n* -s [NL *Ptychoparia* + E *-id*] **:** a trilobite of the genus *Ptychoparia*

[2]**ptychopariid** \\¦==¦=rēəd\\ *adj* **:** of or relating to the genus *Ptychoparia*

pty·chop·ter·i·dae \\,tī,käpˈterə,dē\\ *n pl, cap* [NL, fr. *Ptychoptera,* type genus (fr. *ptych-* + *-ptera*) + *-idae*] **:** a family of very delicate two-winged flies (suborder Nematocera) with long black white-barred legs and larvae with a prolonged caudal respiratory tube comprising the phantom crane flies

pty·cho·pterygial \\¦tīkō+\\ *adj* [NL *ptychopterygium* + E *-al*] **:** of or relating to a ptychopterygium

pty·cho·pterygium \\"+\\ *n, pl* **ptychopterygia** [NL, fr. *ptych-* + Gk *pterygion* little wing, fin — more at PTERYGIUM] **:** a primitive fin consisting of a low triangular flap supported by a series of unbranched rays

pty·cho·sper·ma \\,tīkōˈspərmə\\ *n, cap* [NL, fr. *ptych-* + *-sperma*] **:** a genus of pinnate-leaved palms that are native chiefly to Australasia and have pinnatisect leaves with segments cuneate and erose on the margin and small monoecious flowers borne in a slender branched spadix

pty·cho·tis oil \\(ˈ)tī¦kōd·əs-\\ *n* [ISV *ptychotis* (fr. NL *ptychotis,* of unknown origin) + *oil*] **:** AJOWAN OIL

-p·ty·sis \\ptəsəs\\ *n comb form, pl* **-pty·ses** \\-ptə,sēz\\ [NL, fr. Gk, act of spitting, fr. *ptyein* to spit — more at SPEW] **:** spittle **:** spit ⟨hemo*ptysis*⟩ ⟨plasmo*ptysis*⟩

ptyx·is \\ˈtiksəs\\ *n, pl* **ptyx·es** \\-k,sēz\\ [NL, fr. Gk, act of folding, fr. *ptyssein* to fold] **:** the disposition of a single leaf in the bud

pu \\ˈpü\\ *chiefly Scot var of* PULL

PU *abbr* pickup

Pu *symbol* plutonium

pua hemp \\ˈpüə-\\ *n* [*pua* of unknown origin] **1 :** an East Indian shrub (*Maoutia puya*) of the family Urticaceae the bast fiber of which is used for cordage **2 :** the fiber of the pua hemp shrub

pub \\ˈpəb\\ *n* -s [short for *public*] **1** *chiefly Brit* **:** PUBLIC HOUSE **2 :** any of various establishments (as bars, taverns, cocktail lounges) where alcoholic beverages are sold and consumed

pub *abbr* **1** public **2** publication **3** published; publisher; publishing

pub·ble \\ˈpəbəl\\ *adj* [origin unknown] *dial chiefly Eng* **:** FAT, PLUMP

pub crawl *n* **:** a tour of bars and public houses usu. with a pause for one drink at each ⟨moved from café to café in a regular *pub crawl* —A.L.Mikhelson⟩

pub-crawl \\ˈ=,=\\ *vi* **:** to make a pub crawl ⟨went *pub-crawling* again, and by night . . . had a fine load on —T.G.Horton⟩ ~ *vt* **:** to make the rounds of (a series of bars) ⟨took off to *pub-crawl* the cafés of flag-decked Omdurman —*Time*⟩

pub crawler *n* **:** one that goes from bar to bar

pu·ber·tal \\ˈpyübə(r)d·ᵊl, -)tᵊl *sometimes* ˈpüb-\\ *also* **pu·ber·al** \\-ərəl\\ *adj* [*pubertal* fr. *puberty* + *-al; puberal* fr. ML *puberalis,* fr. L *puber* + *-alis* -al] **:** of or relating to puberty

pu·ber·ty \\-ə(r)d·ē, -)tē, -i\\ *n* -ES [ME *puberte,* fr. L *pubertas,* fr. *puber* grown up, adult + *-tas* -ty; perh. akin to L *puer* boy — more at PUERILE] **:** the condition of being or the period of becoming first capable of reproducing sexually marked by maturing of the genital organs, development of secondary sex characteristics, and in the human and in higher primates by the first occurrence of menstruation in the female; *broadly* **:** the age at which puberty occurs being typically between 13 and 16 years in boys and 11 and 14 in girls and often construed legally as 14 in boys and 12 in girls **syn** see YOUTH

pu·ber·u·lent \pyü'ber(y)ələnt\ *adj* [L *puber* grown up, adult, downy + E *-ulent* (as in *pulverulent*)] *biol* **:** minutely downy **:** covered with fine pubescence
pu·ber·u·lic acid \-lik-\ *n* [NL *puberulum* (specific epithet of *Penicillium puberulum*, fr. L *puber* grown up, adult, downy + *-ulum*, neut. of *-ulus*, dim. suffix) + E *-ic*] **:** a crystalline cyclic keto acid $(HO)_3(C_7H_2O)COOH$ related to tropolone that is a metabolic product of several molds of the genus *Penicillium* and that exhibits some germicidal activity against gram-positive bacteria
pu·ber·u·lon·ic acid \pyü¦berya¦länik-\ *n* [blend of *puberulic* and *-one*] **:** a crystalline compound $(HO)_3C_7HO(CO)_2O$ that is the anhydride of a dicarboxylic acid related to tropolone, is formed from molds along with puberulic acid, and exhibits mild germicidal activity against gram-positive bacteria
pu·ber·u·lous \pyü'ber(y)ələs\ *adj* [L *puber* + E *-ulous*] **:** PUBERULENT
pu·bes \'pyü,bēz\ *n, pl* **pubes** [L; akin to L *puber, pubes* grown-up, adult — more at PUBERTY] **1 :** the hair that appears upon the lower part of the hypogastric region at the age of puberty **2 :** the lower part of the hypogastric region **:** the pubic region
pu·bes·cence \pyü'bes°n(t)s\ *n* -s [ML *pubescentia*, fr. L *pubescent-, pubescens* + *-ia* -y] **1 :** the quality or state of being pubescent; *esp* **:** pubertal development of genital hair **2 a :** an epidermal covering of soft short hairs or down (as on the surfaces of leaves and stems or the bodies of insects) **b :** FUZZINESS **syn** see YOUTH
pu·bes·cent \-nt\ *adj* [L *pubescent-, pubescens*, pres. part. of *pubescere* to reach puberty, fr. *puber* grown up, adult + *-escere* (suffix forming inchoative verbs) — more at PUBERTY] **1 :** arriving at or having reached puberty **:** characteristic of or relating to this state — compare ADOLESCENT **2 :** having a fuzzy surface; *specif* **:** covered with fine soft short hairs — compare HIRSUTE, HISPID, LANATE, SERICEOUS, TOMENTOSE, VILLOUS
pu·bic \'pyübik, -bēk\ *adj* [*pubes* + *-ic*] **:** of, relating to, or lying in the region of the pubes or the pubis
pubic arch *n* **:** the arch formed at the front of the pelvis by the conjoined pubic bones
pubic bone *n* **:** PUBIS
pubic crest *n* **:** the border of the pubis between the pubic tubercle and the pubic symphysis
pubic louse *n* **:** CRAB LOUSE
pubic symphysis *n* **:** the rather rigid articulation of the two pubic bones in the midline of the lower anterior part of the abdomen
pubic tubercle *also* **pubic spine** *n* **:** a rounded eminence on the upper margin of each pubic bone near the symphysis
pubio- *comb form* [NL, fr. *pubis*] **:** pubis
pu·bi·ot·o·my \,pyübē'ädəmē\ *n* -ES [ISV *pubio-* + *-tomy*] **:** surgical division of the pubic bone to facilitate delivery
pu·bis \'pyübəs\ *n, pl* **pu·bes** \-,bēz\ [NL (*os*) *pubis*, fr. L *os* bone + *pubis* of the groin, gen. of *pubes* pubes, groin — more at PUBES] **:** the ventral and anterior of the three principal bones composing either half of the pelvis, in man consisting of two branches or rami diverging posteriorly, the superior branch extending to the acetabulum, of which it forms a part, and uniting there with the ilium and ischium, and the inferior branch uniting with the ischium below the obturator foramen — compare PREPUBIS, POSTPUBIS
publ *abbr* **1** public **2** publication **3** published; publisher; publishing
¹pub·lic \'pəblik, -lēk\ *adj* [ME *publique*, fr. MF *public, publique*, fr. L *publicus*, prob. alter. (influenced by *puber, pubes* grown up, adult) of *poplicus*, fr. *populus* people + *-icus* -ic — more at PUBERTY, PEOPLE] **1 a :** of, relating to, or affecting the people as an organized community **:** CIVIC, NATIONAL ⟨~ affairs⟩ ⟨~ holiday⟩ ⟨~ authority exists primarily to regulate . . . social and economic life —M.S.Kendrick⟩ — compare PUBLIC LAW **b :** of or relating to the international community or to mankind in general **:** COMMON, UNIVERSAL ⟨~ philosophy has . . . always been a political ideology —H.J.Morgenthau⟩ **c :** authorized or administered by or acting for the people as a political entity **:** GOVERNMENT ⟨~ expenditures⟩ ⟨~ subsidy⟩ ⟨~ agency⟩ ⟨~ prosecutor⟩ **d :** provided for, used by, or containing the records of a government agency ⟨the post office and other ~ buildings⟩ ⟨~ documents⟩ **2** *Brit* **:** of, relating to, or representing a university as a whole rather than one of its colleges or departments ⟨the office of . . . ~ Orator —*Cambridge Univ. Cal.*⟩ **3 a :** of or relating to business or community interests as opposed to private affairs **:** SOCIAL, IMPERSONAL ⟨~ morality⟩ ⟨leading from these private confessions of his poetry . . . toward a more ~ form of expression —Hans Meyerhoff⟩ **b :** of, relating to, or in the service of the community or nation ⟨an eminent figure in ~ life⟩ ⟨housewives volunteering for ~ work in charitable institutions⟩; *specif* **:** holding political office ⟨~ official⟩ **c :** devoted to the general or national welfare **:** PATRIOTIC, HUMANITARIAN ⟨debt the legal profession . . . owe to the publishers for their ~ spirit in producing these records —Norman Birkett⟩ ⟨all Greek thinkers were ~ men —C.P.Rodocanachi⟩ **4 a :** accessible to or shared by all members of the community ⟨~ hearing⟩ ⟨~ park⟩ ⟨~ water supply⟩ ⟨tourist passengers enjoy 16 ~ rooms aboard the magnificent new . . . flagship —*N.Y.Times*⟩ **b :** supported by or for the benefit of the people as a whole ⟨~ education⟩ ⟨~ welfare agencies⟩ **c :** COMMON 2d **d :** of, by, for, or directed to the people **:** GENERAL, POPULAR ⟨~ sentiment⟩ ⟨~ spokesman⟩ ⟨~ address⟩ ⟨a book which increases ~ awareness—E.S.Furniss b. 1918⟩ ⟨effective use of the property in the ~ interest —C.V.Shields⟩ ⟨philanthropic activities keep him in the ~ eye⟩ **e :** providing services to the people on a business basis under some degree of civic or state control ⟨wrote with force on . . . railroads as ~ agents —W.C.Ford⟩ ⟨right of women to smoke in restaurants and other ~ places —Frances Perkins⟩ **5 a :** exposed to general view **:** CONSPICUOUS, OPEN ⟨a rather too ~ affair with another woman —William Sansom⟩ **b :** WELL-KNOWN, PROMINENT ⟨stage stars and ~ figures —James Dowdall⟩ **c :** of an observable or perceptible nature **:** EXTERNAL, MATERIAL ⟨belief in tables and chairs existing as ~ . . . objects independently of his sense impressions of them —F.S.C.Northrop⟩ ⟨the conventional or ~ aspect of language can encroach upon the . . . symbolical aspect —R.M.Weaver⟩
²public \"\ *n* -s [ME *publique*, fr. *publique*, adj.] **1 :** a place accessible or visible to all members of the community — usu. used in the phrase *in public* ⟨resent the . . . attempt to usurp in private the authority she could never assert in ~ —Edith Wharton⟩ **2 a :** an organized body of people **:** COMMUNITY, NATION ⟨the western European statesmen and ~*s* alike seem equally agreed that the slightest infringement of their national sovereignty is . . . abhorrent —Patrick McMahon⟩ **b :** the people as a whole **:** POPULACE, MASSES ⟨the ~ . . . in many cities have become apathetic to hit-and-run accidents —Ray Ashworth⟩ **3 :** a group of people distinguished by common interests or characteristics ⟨protecting movie stars from their ~*s* —*New Yorker*⟩ ⟨two books . . . different in scope, and aimed at different ~*s* —T.G.Bergin⟩ ⟨places before farmers, homemakers, and the rural ~ information on currently important agricultural situations —*U.S. Govt. Manual*⟩ **4** *Brit* **:** PUBLIC HOUSE
public accountant *n* **:** an accountant whose services are available to the public — compare CERTIFIED PUBLIC ACCOUNTANT
public accounting *n* **:** accounting performed by a public accountant
public account system *n* **:** a system under which the state buys raw materials for processing in prison factories and sells the products in the open market — compare CONVICT LABOR SYSTEM
public act *n* **:** PUBLIC LAW
public–address system \¦==¦=-\ *n* **:** an apparatus including one or more microphones or other pickup devices, an audio-frequency amplifier, and one or more loudspeakers used for broadcasting speech, music, or other sounds to a large audience (as in an auditorium or out of doors) — called also *PA system*
public administration *n* **:** a branch of political science dealing primarily with the structure and workings of agencies charged with the administration of governmental functions
public administrator *n* **1** *in many jurisdictions* **:** an officer appointed to administer the estate of a decedent where there is no one else entitled and willing to act — compare GENERAL ADMINISTRATOR **2** *in some states* **:** the custodian of an estate pending settlement of a dispute or doubt as to the person entitled to letters
publically *var of* PUBLICLY
pub·li·can \'pəblәkən, -lēk-\ *n* -s [ME, fr. MF *publicain, publican*, fr. L *publicanus*, fr. *publicum* public revenue (fr. neut. of *publicus* public) + *-anus* -an — more at PUBLIC] **1 a :** a Jewish tax collector for the ancient Romans ⟨~*s* were outcasts among the Jews, because, having accepted the office under the Roman government . . . they were regarded as traitors —F.W. Robertson⟩ **b :** one estranged from the church ⟨I firmly believe this church . . . has power to exclude him and to hold him as a ~ and heathen —A.C.McGiffert⟩ **c :** any collector of taxes or tribute ⟨outrages and exactions such as have, in every age, made the name of ~ a proverb for all that is most hateful —T.B.Macaulay⟩ **2** *chiefly Brit* **:** the keeper of a public house ⟨the local ~ produced trays of foaming stout —E.J.Gates⟩
public assistance *n* **:** aid provided to the needy aged, dependent children, and blind and disabled persons under the Federal Social Security Act of the U.S.
pub·li·cate \'pəblə,kāt\ *vt* -ED/-ING/-S [L *publicatus*, past part. of *publicare* — more at PUBLISH] *archaic* **:** PUBLISH
pub·li·ca·tion \,pəblə'kāshən, -blē'-\ *n* -s [ME *publicacioun*, fr. MF *publication*, fr. LL *publication-, publicatio*, fr. L *publicatus* (past part. of *publicare* to announce, proclaim, publish) + *-ion-, -io* -ion — more at PUBLISH] **1 :** communication (as of news or information) to the public **:** public announcement **:** PROCLAMATION ⟨radio is a . . . great method of communication and ~ —G.C.Chandler⟩; *specif* **:** legal notification **2 a :** the act or process of issuing copies (as of a book, photograph, or musical score) for general distribution to the public ⟨the firm is engaged in the ~ of text books⟩ ⟨the date of ~⟩ ⟨prior to the first general ~ the owner of the common law copyright . . . may enjoy the benefit of a restricted publication —R.R.Shaw⟩ **b :** a published work ⟨study of . . . the journals of social science, the ~*s* of the learned generally —B.N. Cardozo⟩ ⟨among his many ~*s* was a volume of light verse⟩ **3 :** the distribution in print esp. in technical journals of a taxonomic name (as of a species or genus) together with such descriptive or illustrative material as will characterize and distinguish the organism or group named
public bill *n, sometimes cap P&B* **:** a legislative bill affecting the community (as a nation or state) at large ⟨the First Reading of a *public bill* . . . is usually a formality —*Brit. Parliament*⟩ — compare PRIVATE BILL
public bond *n* **:** a bond issued by a government (as a nation or state) or by a subsidiary incorporated governmental authority or by a municipality
public charge *n* **:** one that is supported at public expense
public corporation *n* **1 :** MUNICIPAL CORPORATION **2 :** a government-owned corporation organized to carry on a particular governmental activity, managed according to business principles by an appointed board, and often to some extent financially independent of the government — called also *government corporation*
public day *n* **1 :** a day when a private institution is opened to the public or when an official devotes himself to hearing direct public business **2 :** HOLIDAY 3a
public debt *n* **:** NATIONAL DEBT
public defender *n* **:** a lawyer usu. holding public office whose duty is to defend accused persons unable to pay for legal assistance
public domain *n* **1 :** land owned or controlled by the U.S. government ⟨on this *public domain* the national government, as proprietor, can lease grazing lands —F.A.Ogg & P.O.Ray⟩ **2 :** the realm embracing property rights belonging to the community at large, subject to appropriation by anyone; *specif* **:** status unprotected by copyright or patent
public enemy *n* **:** one that constitutes a menace to society; *specif* **:** a criminal whose crimes have so aroused the police or public as to result in an intensive effort to apprehend him with the aid of wide publicity
public funds *n pl* **:** FUND 4d
public health *n* **:** the art and science dealing with the protection and improvement of community health by organized community effort and including preventive medicine and sanitary and social sciences
public highway *n* **:** HIGHWAY 1a
public house *n* **1 :** INN, HOSTELRY **2** *chiefly Brit* **:** a licensed saloon or bar
public housing *n* **:** low-rent housing owned, sponsored, or administered by a government
pu·bli·ci ju·ris \¦pəblə,sī'jurəs, -jür-\ *adj* [L] **:** belonging to the public **:** subject to a right of the public to enjoy
pub·li·cist \'pəbləsəst\ *n* -s [F *publiciste*, fr. *public* + *-iste* -ist] **1 a :** an expert in international law ⟨judicial decisions of the most highly qualified ~*s* of the various nations —*Basic Facts about the U.N.*⟩ **b :** an expert or commentator on public affairs **:** political pundit ⟨the self-constituted party of property owners, ~*s*, and professional men that framed the Federal Constitution —S.E.Morison & H.S.Commager⟩ ⟨cocksure materialist at whom . . . contemporary ~*s* are wont to fling their dialectical brickbats —Aldous Huxley⟩ **2 :** one that publicizes ⟨effective ~ of the slum problem —J.G.Hill⟩ ⟨task of the scientist as ~ to make sure that science is science, and not magic, to the public at large—Irwin Edman⟩; *specif* **:** PRESS AGENT ⟨something more lasting than a pretty face, attractive figure or a persuasive ~ —J.K.Newnham⟩
pub·lic·i·ty \(,)pə'blisəd·ē, -sətē, -i\ *n* -ES *often attrib* [F *publicité*, fr. *public* + *-ité* -ity] **1 :** the quality or state of being obvious or exposed to the general view **:** accessibility to the public ⟨wide open ranks . . . of desks kept everyone working by mere ~ —Christopher Morley⟩ ⟨the ~ of the courtroom —*Saturday Rev.*⟩ **2 a :** an act or device designed to attract public interest ⟨regards a whistle-stop tour as good ~⟩; *specif* **:** information with news value issued as a means of gaining public attention or support ⟨his job is producing ~ for child welfare organizations⟩ ⟨the flood of ~ and promotional material that now overloads the desk of everybody in the news business —Elmer Davis⟩ **b :** the dissemination of information or promotional material esp. by the press and other mass media ⟨felt that the recent wave of ~ on her work . . . had hurt her professionally —*Time*⟩ **c :** paid advertising ⟨the object of all commercial ~ is to persuade someone to exchange his money for what the advertiser has for sale —H.H.Smith⟩ **d :** public attention or acclaim ⟨~ came . . . unsought; he was a man who attracted attention —V.G.Heiser⟩ ⟨received considerable ~ because of their refusal to accept a . . . grant for school purposes —*Amer. Guide Series: Pa.*⟩ **e :** the practice or profession of producing promotional material ⟨~ is a one-way street; public relations, a two-way street —E.L.Bernays⟩
syn BALLYHOO, PROMOTION, PROPAGANDA: PUBLICITY refers to any effort to attract public attention whether by furnishing information for dissemination through regular news channels or by paid advertising ⟨recipients of this announcement are requested to give it immediately the widest possible *publicity* —*Amer. Council of Learned Soc. Scholars*⟩ ⟨"*publicity*" was not mainly an art for causing the world to take notice of, and think well of, goods; or of policies which the makers of goods wished to make popular. The word was coming to be synonymous with advertising —Mark Sullivan⟩ ⟨actresses bathing in champagne and other *publicity* stunts⟩ BALLYHOO may refer to sensational, strident, or noisy publicity ⟨the patient blindly follows the *ballyhoo* of the medical charlatan —*Police Gazette*⟩ PROMOTION suggests concentrated efforts to publicize something new or persuade the public to accept it ⟨attractive *promotions* of spring clothing helped to allay the usual post-Easter drop in retail volume —*Dun's Rev.*⟩ PROPAGANDA, the strongest term, usu. carries the suggestion of manipulation of public opinion whether through acceptable educational processes or by direct and coercive indoctrination ⟨*propaganda* means the planned use of all kinds of communications to influence the actions of other peoples —*Combat Forces Jour.*⟩
pub·li·cize \'pəblə,sīz\ *vt* -ED/-ING/-S ['*public* + *-ize*] **:** to bring to the attention of the public **:** give publicity to **:** ADVERTISE
public land *n* **:** land owned by a government, esp. a national government; *specif* **:** that part of the U.S. public domain subject to sale or disposal under the homestead laws
public law *n* **1 a :** an enactment of a legislature affecting the public at large throughout the entire territory (as state or nation) subject to the jurisdiction of the legislature **:** GENERAL LAW — called also *public act, public statute* **b :** an enactment of a legislature (as a municipal charter) affecting the public at large within a particular subdivision of the legislative jurisdiction **2 :** the division of law that adjusts the relations of individuals with the state and regulates the organization and conduct of the machinery of government — contrasted with *private law* **3 :** international law regulating the relations among sovereign states or nations as distinguished from private international law
public liability insurance *n* **:** insurance to protect businessmen (as owners or landlords) against loss due to legal liability for injury or damage to the persons or property of the public
public library *n* **:** a nonprofit library maintained for public use and usu. supported in whole or in part by local taxation
pub·lic·ly \'pəbliklē, -lēk-, -li\ *also* **pub·li·cal·ly** \-lək(ə)lē, -lēk-, -li\ *adv* **1 :** in public **:** in a manner observable by or a place accessible to the public **:** OPENLY, OBVIOUSLY ⟨claims that many of them are privately on his side, but cannot support him ~ —*Time*⟩ ⟨attributes . . . directly and ~ observable —C.G.Hempel⟩ **2 :** by the public **:** by the people generally **:** COMMUNALLY ⟨every corporation is deemed ~ held unless 10 or fewer shareholders own stock —*U.S.Code*⟩; *specif* **:** by a government ⟨~ provided medical care starts with the school medical service —Moses Abramovitz & Vera Eliasberg⟩
public member *n* **:** a member (as of a labor relations board) not representing the special interest groups involved
pub·lic·ness *n* -ES **:** the quality or state of being public
public nuisance *n, law* **:** a nuisance (as obstructing a highway) that causes harm or annoyance to persons in a particular locality in violation of their rights as members of the community — compare MIXED NUISANCE, PRIVATE NUISANCE
public officer *n* **:** a person holding a post to which he has been legally elected or appointed and exercising governmental functions
public official bond *n* **:** a surety bond providing indemnity for failure of a public official to perform faithfully the duties of his office
public opinion *n* **1 :** the predominant attitude of a community **:** the collective will of the people ⟨a fluctuation in *public opinion* may redirect national policy⟩ **2 :** a summation of public expression regarding a specific issue or event ⟨*public opinion* on racial segregation falls into two main categories⟩
public policy *n* **1 :** the governing policy within a community as embodied in its legislative and judicial enactments which serve as a basis for determining what acts are to be regarded as contrary to the public good **2 :** the principle of law by virtue of which acts contrary to the public good are held invalid
public prints *n pl* **:** newspapers and periodicals ⟨led to much talk in the *public prints*⟩
public prosecutor *n* **:** a public official charged with the investigation and prosecution of punishable acts on behalf of the state or an international commission
public record *n* **:** a record required by law to be made and kept: **a :** a record made by a public officer in the course of his legal duty to make it **b :** a record filed in a public office and open to public inspection
public relations *n pl but usu sing in constr* **1 :** the promotion of rapport and goodwill between a person, firm, or institution and other persons, special publics, or the community at large through the distribution of interpretative material, the development of neighborly interchange, and the assessment of public reaction ⟨*public relations* are designed . . . to give a business a good reputation with the public —A.W.Page⟩ ⟨*public relations* of a resort may be only a portion of the duties of the . . . general manager —*Jour. Amer. Med. Assoc.*⟩ ⟨if the officer is civil . . . he gets a lot more done, both in correcting the driver and in doing good *public relations* for his town —Fred Sharpe⟩ ⟨took a pioneering step in *public relations* by asking . . . brokers to report the various attitudes toward the exchange they encountered generally —*Newsweek*⟩ **2 a :** the degree of understanding and goodwill achieved between an individual, organization, or institution and the public ⟨little favors, a helping hand, a brief visit, a kindly word, all add up to good *public relations* —S.I.Stuber⟩ ⟨in a sense *public relations* is the measure of the extent to which an organization has adapted itself . . . to society —E.A. Cunningham⟩ **b :** application of the techniques for achieving this relationship ⟨persuaded the President that it would be bad *public relations* to stay away from his White House desk more than two weeks at a time —*New Republic*⟩ **3 a :** the art or science of developing reciprocal understanding and goodwill ⟨universities offered courses in *public relations* —E.L.Bernays⟩ **b :** the professional staff entrusted with this task ⟨*public relations* collects, prepares and distributes information to . . . the consuming public —*Preview of Amer. Viscose Corp.*⟩ ⟨why do the Air Forces Group people in *public relations* fire that upstairs when they don't know whether it's true or not —J.G. Cozzens⟩
public rights *n pl* **:** the rights under law of the state over the subject and of the subject against the state
publics *pl of* PUBLIC
public sale *n* **:** AUCTION 1
public school *n* **1 a :** any of various endowed secondary boarding schools in Great Britain offering a classical curriculum and preparing boys esp. for the ancient universities or for public service **b :** a similar school for girls **2 a :** a tax-supported school controlled by a local governmental authority; *specif* **:** an elementary or secondary school in the U.S. providing free education for the children of residents of a specified area **b :** the building housing a public school
public servant *n* **1 :** a holder of public office **2 :** an individual or corporation (as a bus company) rendering a public service
public service *n* **1 a :** a publicly or privately owned enterprise (as a waterworks, railway, telephone company) conducted for the benefit of the community as a whole **b :** a service rendered in the public interest ⟨the program is not sponsored but is presented by the network as a *public service*⟩ **2 :** governmental employment; *esp* **:** CIVIL SERVICE ⟨first appointment to the *public service* is usually on a temporary basis —*Employment Opportunities in the Civil Service*⟩
public–service corporation *n* **:** a corporation providing services essential to the general public convenience or safety
public speaker *n* **:** one skilled in public speaking
public speaking *n* **1 :** the act or process of making speeches in public **2 :** the art or science of effective oral communication with an audience ⟨took a course in *public speaking*⟩
public–spirited \¦==¦===\ *adj* **:** motivated by devotion to the general or national welfare ⟨the trustees of our American universities are, as a class, *public-spirited* citizens . . . trying to promote the public good —M.R.Cohen⟩ — **public–spiritedness** *n* -ES
public statute *n* **:** PUBLIC LAW 1
public store *n* **:** a warehouse where dutiable goods are appraised or held under bond
public time *n* **:** OBJECTIVE TIME
public utility *n* **1 :** a business organization deemed by law to be vested with public interest usu. because of monopoly privileges and so subject to public regulation such as fixing of rates, standards of service and provision of facilities **2 :** a stock or bond issued by a public utility
public vessel *n* **:** a ship belonging to a government and not engaging in trade
public warehouse *n* **:** a privately owned warehouse for public use
public waters *n pl* **:** waters open of right to the use of the general public; *specif* **:** navigable waters
public way *n* **:** any passageway (as an alley, road, highway, boulevard, turnpike) or part thereof (as a bridge) open as of right to the public and designed for travel by vehicle, on foot, or in a manner limited by statute (as by excluding pedestrians or commercial vehicles) — compare PRIVATE WAY
public works *n pl* **:** fixed works (as schools, highways, docks) constructed for public use or enjoyment esp. when financed and owned by the government; *specif* **:** government sponsored public improvements (as parks or playgrounds) as distinguished from work of a routine nature such as the grading and lighting of streets

public works and ways system *n* **:** a plan or system for employing convict labor on public works and highways — compare CONVICT LABOR SYSTEM

public wrong *n* **1 :** a crime, misdemeanor, tort, or breach of a duty owed to and prejudicing the interests of the community at large — compare PRIVATE WRONG **2 :** a breach of duty owed to any person by the state or one of its political subdivisions

pub·lish \'pəblish, *esp in pres part* -ləsh\ *vb* -ED/-ING/-ES [ME *publishen*, modif. of MF *publier*, fr. L *publicare*, fr. *publicus* public — more at PUBLIC] *vt* **1 a :** to declare publicly **:** make generally known **:** DISCLOSE, CIRCULATE ⟨~ glad tidings, tidings of peace —Mary A. Thomson⟩ ⟨the plan of action has not been ~*ed* in detail —D.S.Campbell⟩; *specif* **:** to impart or acknowledge to one or more persons ⟨a slander is not actionable unless it is ~*ed* to a third person —T.F.T.Plucknett⟩ ⟨do ~ and declare this to be my last will and testament⟩ **b :** to proclaim officially **:** PROMULGATE ⟨~ an edict⟩ **c :** to make public announcement of (banns of marriage) **d :** PUBLICIZE ⟨mourning . . . by which a widow ~*ed* her single-minded grief —Margery Sharp⟩ ⟨first Neolithic site to be thoroughly excavated and ~*ed* in Macedonia —G.E.Mylonas⟩; *specif* **:** to give publication to (a taxonomic name) **2 a :** to make a public evaluation of; *specif* **:** CENSURE ⟨stewards have power to ~ at their discretion any person subject to their control either by suspension . . . or by fine —Dan Parker⟩ **b** *obs* **:** to call to the attention of the public **:** ADVERTISE ⟨goods found shall be ~*ed* by the finder —Nathaniel Bacon⟩ **3 a :** to place before the public (as through a mass medium) **:** DISSEMINATE ⟨adopted and ~*ed* a statement of principles —H.E.Starr⟩ ⟨does not pay but ~*es* significant poetry —*Author & Journalist*⟩; *specif* **:** UTTER ⟨~ a forgery⟩ **b :** to produce for publication or allow to be issued for distribution or sale ⟨they write brilliantly at times, have ~*ed* long passages that . . . interest the intelligent reader —H.C. Webster⟩ **c :** to reproduce for public consumption ⟨the number of companies . . . ~*ing* LP recordings —Roland Gelatt⟩; *specif* **:** PRINT ⟨the pictures and stories ~*ed* in these pages are selections from previous issues —*New England Journeys*⟩ **d :** to release (a product of creative work) for public distribution or sale usu. with the consent of the copyright holder ⟨a shilling volume of 96 pages written, printed and ~*ed* within a month —*Modern Churchman*⟩ ⟨in 1837 were ~*ed* four engraved charts, the first issued by the Navy Department —C.L.Lewis⟩ ⟨his five ~*ed* symphonies —Irving Kolodin⟩ ⟨~*ed* in manuscript the first Lusatian grammar —R. G. A. De Bray⟩ **e :** to issue the work of (as an author) ⟨latest of the younger Italian novelists to be ~*ed* in the U.S. —*Time*⟩ ~ *vi* **1 :** to put out an edition or circulate it to the public ⟨the only daily newspaper in the borough did not ~ yesterday because of a strike —*N.Y.Times*⟩ **2 a :** to have one's work accepted for publication or allow it to be reproduced for public consumption ⟨pressure put on faculty members . . . to ~ as a condition of appointment or promotion —H.M.Silver⟩ **b :** to reproduce the work of an author and release it to the public ⟨his first novel became a best seller and several firms offered to ~ for him⟩ **3 :** to become manifest **:** give public witness ⟨so much joy . . . I felt it ~ in my eye —Emily Dickinson⟩ **syn** see DECLARE

pub·lish·able \-shəbəl\ *adj* **:** allowable or suitable for publication ⟨there must not . . . be any censorship of legally ~ materials —D.H.Clift⟩ ⟨investigations have not been carried far enough to yield ~ results —T.H.Johnson⟩ ⟨it was not a ~ book —Harrison Smith⟩

pub·lish·er \-shə(r)\ *n* -s [ME, fr. *publishen* + *-er*] **1 a** *archaic* **:** one that makes public **:** ANNOUNCER, PROCLAIMER; *specif* **:** TOWN CRIER **b :** a member of Jehovah's Witnesses who is expected to devote at least 60 hours of his time each month to the propagation of his faith on a house-to-house visitation basis **2 a :** the reproducer of a work intended for public consumption ⟨found it impossible to trace the ~ of the underground pamphlet⟩ **b** (1) **:** one whose business is publishing ⟨textbook ~⟩ ⟨greeting-card ~⟩ ⟨two new record ~*s* have recently become active —Edward Sackville-West & Desmond Shawe-Taylor⟩; *specif* **:** the owner and operator of a publishing firm ⟨editorials tend to reflect the views of the ~⟩ (2) *Brit* **:** a newspaper circulation manager

publisher's binding *n* **:** EDITION BINDING

publisher's statement *n* **:** a sworn statement of circulation for a specified period (as a year) made by a publisher of a newspaper or periodical

publishing *n* -s **:** the business or profession of the commercial production and issuance of literature esp. in book form for public distribution or sale ⟨~ as a business apart from book selling is of comparatively modern date —J.A.Holden⟩ ⟨entered ~ with the Oxford University Press —*Publishers' Weekly*⟩

pub·lish·ment \'==mənt\ *n* -s *archaic* **:** PUBLICATION; *specif* **:** public announcement of banns of marriage

pubs *pl of* PUB

PUC *abbr* public utilities commission

pu·ca·ra \,pükə'rä\ *adj, usu cap* [Sp *pucará*, fr. *Pucará*, district in Peru, fr. Quechua *pukára* fort] **:** of or relating to a culture of the southern Andes in Peru during the Tiahuanaco period characterized by a black and yellow-on-red pottery with sharp narrow incisions outlining the color areas

pucca *var of* PUKKA

puc·cin·ia \,pək'sinēə\ *n, cap* [NL, fr. Tommaso *Puccini* †1735 It. anatomist + NL *-ia*] **:** a very large genus (the type of the family Pucciniaceae) that is sometimes separated into four genera and consists of heteroecious parasitic fungi having 2-celled teliospores whose pedicels do not gelatinize and aecia with a pseudoperidium and including many forms that are destructive to various economic plants — see WHEAT RUST — **puc·cin·oid** \-,nȯid\ *adj*

puc·cin·i·a·ce·ae \,pək,sinē'āsē,ē\ *n pl, cap* [NL *Puccinia*, type genus + *-aceae*] **:** a large important family of rust fungi (order Uredinales) having stalked teliospores either separate or united in sori, being mostly heteroecious, and exhibiting in the complete forms four spore stages usu. upon two or more distinct hosts followed by an independent promycelial stage upon the germination of the teliospores — see PUCCINIA; compare SHORT-CYCLED — **puc·cin·i·a·ceous** \(,)=;==;āshəs\ *adj*

puc·coon \pə'kün\ *n* -s [fr. *puccoon* (in some Algonquian language of Virginia)] — more at POKE] **1 :** any of several American plants yielding a red or yellow pigment: as **a :** BLOODROOT 1 **b :** any of several plants of the genus *Lithospermum* (as *L. carolinense* or *L. canescens*) — see HOARY PUCCOON **c :** GOLDENSEAL 1 **2 :** the pigment obtained from a puccoon plant

puce \'pyüs\ *n* -s [F, lit., flea, fr. L *pulic-, pulex* — more at PSYLLA] **:** a dark red that is yellower and less strong than cranberry, paler and slightly yellower than average garnet, bluer, less strong, and slightly lighter than pomegranate, and bluer and paler than average wine — called also *eureka red, flea, Victoria lake*

pu·cel·las \pyə'seləs\ *n pl but sing or pl in constr* [modif. of It

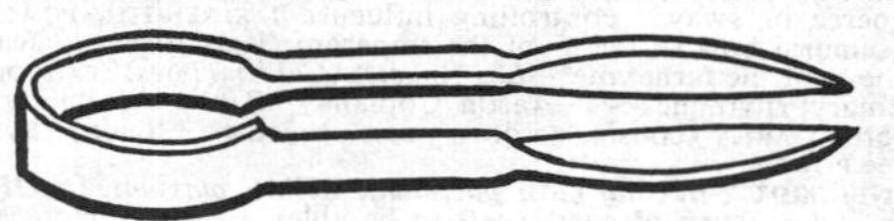

pucellas

procello] **:** a spring tool resembling tongs and used for shaping molten glass — called also *steel jack* ⟨next in importance to the blowpipe is the ~ —F.W.Hunter⟩ ⟨the top of the glass may be opened up with ~ —Karen Gillespie⟩

pu·cher·ite \'pükə,rīt\ *n* -s [G *pucherit*, fr. the *Pucher* mine, Schneeberg, Saxony + G *-it* -ite] **:** a mineral $BiVO_4$ consisting of a bismuth vanadate occurring in small reddish brown orthorhombic crystals

pu·che·ro \pü'che,rō\ *n* -s [Sp, lit., pot, fr. L *pultarius* vessel for porridge, cooking or drinking vessel, fr. *pult-, puls*, a kind of thick porridge + *-arius* -ary — more at PULSE] **:** a Latin American boiled dinner or stew containing beef, sausage, bacon, and various vegetables

¹puck \'pək\ *n* -s *often cap* [ME *puke, pouke*, fr. OE *pūca*; akin to Fris *puk* goblin, ON *pūki* devil, Norw & Sw dial. *puke* goblin, and prob. to OE *pocc* pock — more at POCK] **1 a** *archaic* **:** an evil or malicious spirit **:** DEVIL, DEMON ⟨nor let the ~, nor other evil spirits . . . fright us —Edmund Spenser⟩ **b :** a mischievous or rascally sprite **:** IMP, HOBGOBLIN **2 :** a prankish person ⟨was also a ~ who loved to disconcert any classification —Ernest Barker⟩

²puck \"\ *vt* -ED/-ING/-S [alter. of ²*poke*] *dial chiefly Brit* **:** POKE, STRIKE

³puck \"\ *n* -s **1** *dial chiefly Brit* **:** BLOW, POKE ⟨hit him a ~ in the jaw —Liam O'Flaherty⟩ **2 a :** a vulcanized rubber disk 3 inches in diameter used in the game of ice hockey as the object to be driven through the goals **b :** a disk of resilient material used on a vehicle or a reciprocating machine to absorb shock and vibration **c :** a pressure roller in a magnetic recorder

pucka *var of* PUKKA

¹puck·er \'pəkə(r)\ *vb* **puckered; puckered; puckering** \-k(ə)riŋ\ **puckers** [prob. alter. of ¹*poke* + *-er* (freq. suffix)] *vi* **1 :** to become wrinkled or constricted **:** present an uneven appearance **:** CONTRACT, FURROW, WRINKLE ⟨lips ~*ed* into a low whistle —Don Davis⟩ ⟨in humid weather . . . the finished print may have a tendency to ~ —C.E.Dunn⟩ **2 :** to assume an expression of earnest concentration **:** FROWN ⟨an envious body will ~ as if he had never heard the name —G.D.Brown⟩ ~ *vt* **1 :** to contract into folds or corrugations **:** draw together so as to wrinkle or crimp **:** CONSTRICT, FURROW ⟨spasms gnarl the hands . . . and ~ the face —A.C.Fisher⟩ ⟨the effort of thought ~*ed* his brow⟩ — often used with *up* ⟨~*ed up* my lips for . . . a good-bye kiss —Glenway Wescott⟩; *esp* **:** to produce (an uneven surface consisting of a series of small bulges and depressions) in a fabric by alternating groups of slack and tight yarns or by finishing with a shrinking treatment that affects only one set of yarns ⟨~*ed* nylon sport shirts need no ironing —*advt*⟩ **2 :** to produce fullness in (a sewn article) by drawing stitches tight or by gathering a longer edge to a shorter one ⟨~ a blouse for smocking⟩ ⟨moccasins . . . ~*ed* to a single seam in front —*Museum of the Amer. Indian (N.Y.)*⟩

²pucker \"\ *n* -s **1 a :** a crimp in a normally even surface **:** WRINKLE, FURROW ⟨screwed her pretty mouth into a ~ of exasperation —Walter O'Meara⟩ ⟨the folds and ~*s* of the unexpanded wings of certain moths —E.B.Ford⟩; *specif* **:** a slight unevenness in a fabric ⟨~*s* are usually due to the presence of nonuniformly drawn yarns —C.M.Whittaker & C.C. Wilcock⟩ **b :** a fabric having a puckered finish ⟨the newest all-nylon cloth to be added is a ~ in a plaid design —*Women's Wear Daily*⟩ **2** *archaic* **:** a state of agitation or distraction **:** TIZZY

puckerbush \'==,=\ *n* **:** WAX MYRTLE

puck·ery \'pək(ə)rē, -ri\ *adj, sometimes* -ER/-EST **1 :** characterized by puckers or having a tendency to pucker ⟨~ cloth⟩ **2 :** causing puckers or puckering ⟨a ~ quince⟩

puck·fist \'pək,fist, -fist\ *n* [¹*puck* + *fist*] **1 :** PUFFBALL 1 **2 :** BRAGGART

puck·ish \'pəkish, -kēsh\ *adj* [¹*puck* + *-ish*] **:** of, relating to, characteristic of, or resembling a puck **:** IMPISH, WHIMSICAL ⟨is wayward, ~, inconsistent —Gerald Abraham⟩ ⟨takes a ~ delight in shocking the smug and complacent —S.E.Morison⟩ ⟨her little heart-shaped face, with its . . . pointed chin and ~ nose —Sheila Kaye-Smith⟩ — **puck·ish·ly** \-kəshlē, -kēsh-, -li\ *adv*

puck·ish·ness \-kishnəs, -kēsh-\ *n* -ES **:** the quality or state of being puckish ⟨a charming ~ which helps to explain the wide range of his friendships —Mason Wade⟩

puck·le \'pəkəl\ *Scot var of* ⁴PICKLE 2

pucksey *var of* PUXY

puck·ster \'pəkstə(r)\ *n* -s [³*puck* + *-ster*] **:** an ice hockey player

¹pud *var of* POOD

²pud \'pəd\ *n* -s [origin unknown] **:** the hand of a child or the paw of an animal

³pud \'pud\ *n* -s [short for *pudding* "sausage," "penis"] **1 :** PENIS — usu. considered vulgar **2** *Brit* **:** PUDDING ⟨a tin of steak and kidney ~ —Fred Majdalany⟩

PUD *abbr* **1** pickup and delivery **2** public utility district

pud·den·ing \'pud(ᵊ)niŋ\ *n* -s [*pudden* (alter. of *pudding*) + *-ing*] *chiefly Brit* **:** PUDDING 3

pud·der \'pədə(r)\ *archaic var of* POTHER

pud·ding \'pudiŋ, -dēŋ\ *n* -s *often attrib* [ME; perh. akin to OE *puduc* wart, LG *puddek* sausage, *puddig* swollen] **1 a :** BLOOD SAUSAGE **b** *obs* **:** sausage stuffing for roast meat ⟨that roasted . . . ox with the ~ in his belly —Shak.⟩ **c** *dial Eng* **:** GUTS — usu. used in pl. **2 a** (1) **:** a boiled or baked unsweetened soft food usu. having a cereal base and a texture resembling custard and eaten either as a main course or as a side dish ⟨Virginia chicken ~⟩ ⟨corn ~⟩ — compare HASTY PUDDING, YORKSHIRE PUDDING (2) **:** a usu. boiled or baked sweetened dessert of a soft, spongy, or thick creamy consistency ⟨bread ~⟩ ⟨rice ~⟩ ⟨chocolate ~⟩ **b :** an unsweetened dish often containing suet or having a suet crust and orig. boiled in a bag but now often steamed or baked ⟨fig ~⟩ ⟨beefsteak and kidney ~⟩ — compare PLUM PUDDING **c :** something that resembles a pudding ⟨~ bolster⟩ ⟨the low bogs . . . had been churned to chocolate-colored ~*s* of ancient peat —Farley Mowat⟩ **3 a :** a tapered fender usu. made of rope yarn or canvas and attached to the stern of a ship ⟨the bow of your dinghy should be protected by a big, soft ~ —H.A.Calahan⟩ **b :** a soft padding esp. a binding around a metal ring used to prevent parts of a ship's rigging from chafing **4 a :** inherent quality **:** ability to measure up to expectations **:** ADEQUACY, MERIT ⟨proved his ~ commercially —*Newsweek*⟩ ⟨the proof of the ~ is in the eating⟩ **b :** tangible support or profit ⟨truth with gold she weighs, and solid ~ against empty praise —Alexander Pope⟩

puddingberry \'==- — *see* BERRY\ *n* **1 :** DWARF CORNEL **2 :** the fruit of a dwarf cornel

pudding grass *n* **:** a pennyroyal (*Hedeoma pulegioides*) formerly used to flavor stuffing for roast meat

puddingheaded \'==;==\ *adj* **:** FATHEADED

pudding-pipe tree \'==,=-\ *n* **:** DRUMSTICK TREE

pudding stone *n* **:** CONGLOMERATE

pudding time *n* **1** *archaic* **:** DINNERTIME ⟨as it was *pudding time* with us, our visitor was . . . invited to sit and eat —J.K. Townsend⟩ **2** *archaic* **:** an auspicious moment ⟨here he comes in *pudding time* to resolve the question —John Dryden & W.C. Newcastle⟩

puddingwife \'==,=\ *n, pl* **puddingwives** [fr. obs. E, woman who sells sausage, fr. ME *podyngwyf*, fr. *podyng, pudding* blood sausage + *wyf, wif* woman — more at PUDDING, WIFE] **:** a large blue and bronze wrasse (*Iridio radiata*) of Florida and the West Indies south to Brazil

pud·dingy \'pùdiŋē, -dēŋē\ *adj* **:** resembling a pudding

¹pud·dle \'pədᵊl\ *n* -s *often attrib* [ME *podel, pothel*; akin to OE *pudd* ditch, LG *pudel* puddle, and perh. to OE *puduc* wart — more at PUDDING] **1 a** (1) **:** a shallow depression full of water and esp. of muddy or dirty water ⟨a hard rain leaves ~*s* in the road⟩ (2) **:** a little pool of any kind ⟨prodded a little ~ of beer by his glass —Earle Birney⟩ ⟨~*s* of moonlight on the floor —T.W.Duncan⟩ **b** *archaic* **:** ditch water ⟨hard roots my only food, foul ~ all my drink —John Crowne⟩ **c** *obs* **:** POND, MARSH ⟨near to a long ~ or moorish ground, of some four miles long —Edward Barton⟩ **2 a** (1) **:** something that resembles a puddle in form ⟨most men live in a little ~ of light thrown by the gig-lamps of habit —Aldous Huxley⟩ ⟨a small ~ of minced veal on toast —Robert Standish⟩ (2) **:** something suggestive of a puddle of foul or dirty liquid **:** a contaminating circumstance or condition **:** MESS, SINK ⟨would have us believe . . . that in spite of all the ~*s* through which the priestly politician splashed to reach his ends, no spot or stain ever smutched his gown —V.L.Parrington⟩ **b :** MUDDLE ⟨stand and look over the little ~ of empty desks —W.A.White⟩ **3 a** (1) **:** an earthy mixture (as of clay, sand and gravel) worked while wet into a compact mass that becomes impervious to water when dry (2) **:** TAMPER **c b :** a thin mixture of soil and water for puddling plants **4 :** the molten portion of a weld

²puddle \"\ *vb* **puddled; puddled; puddling** \-d(ᵊ)liŋ\ **puddles** [ME *podelen, pothelen*, fr. *podel, pothel*, n.] *vi* **1 a :** to dabble or wade around in a puddle ⟨in the ooze . . . a brood of goslings *puddled* —Rockwell Kent⟩ **b :** to dawdle or mess around **:** PUTTER ⟨children spent yesterday afternoon *puddling* in paint, plasticene, and paste —*Springfield (Mass.) Union*⟩ **2 a :** to make a puddle ⟨spray heaved in over the side, *puddling* on the slippery deck —Irwin Shaw⟩; *specif* **:** URINATE ⟨baby . . . alternately dozed and *puddled* —Ann Leighton⟩ **b :** to become a puddle ⟨slithering on the *puddling* brown snow —William Sansom⟩ ~ *vt* **1 a :** to stir up **:** make muddy or turbid **:** MUDDLE, ROIL ⟨great pails of *puddled* mire —Shak.⟩ ⟨the bartender went on *puddling* an old-fashioned —E.B. White⟩ **b** *archaic* **:** to make murky **:** BEFUDDLE, CONFUSE ⟨something sure of state . . . hath *puddled* his clear spirit —Shak.⟩ **c :** to immerse in a liquid ⟨the crystals are *puddled* with syrup to make a fluid mass —*Oil-Power*⟩; *specif* **:** to separate (ore) from sticky clay by washing in a shallow tank **2 a** (1) **:** to work (a wet mixture of earth or concrete) into a dense impervious mass ⟨hand methods of compacting concrete mixtures include *puddling*, spading, and tamping —J.H. Bateman⟩; *specif* **:** to combine with water into an impervious cover or lining ⟨a dew pond . . . constructed of straw and *puddled* clay —Norman Wymer⟩ (2) *archaic* **:** to cover or line with puddle ⟨~ the seams of the rock on that side of the well —Henry Stephens⟩ **b** (1) **:** to work (metal) while molten ⟨enabling the iron to be *puddled* into a bloom —Juliusz Slaski⟩; *specif* **:** to form (molten metal) into a desired shape ⟨carefully *puddled* ingots of aluminum into "contemporary amorphic baroque" blobs, then welded them to the steeple's base —*Time*⟩ (2) **:** to subject (iron) to the process of puddling **c :** to texture (stage scenery) by running together small colored puddles of paint **3 a :** to strew or pock with puddles ⟨meltwater ~*s* the flat sea ice⟩ ⟨cattle ~ the soft ground around the water hole with their hooves⟩ **b :** to render (soil) hard and dense by compacting ⟨splash erosion . . . ~*s* surface soils and causes surface seals —*Scientific Monthly*⟩ ⟨once soils are *puddled* badly, it may require several seasons to restore them to good tilth —A.F.Gustafson⟩ **c** (1) **:** to dip the roots of (a plant) in a thin mud before transplanting (2) **:** to saturate the soil around (a plant) in order to settle the dirt around the roots or to supply moisture, nutriment, or an insecticide

puddle ball *n* **:** the lump of pasty wrought iron taken from the puddling furnace to be hammered or rolled

puddle bar *n* **:** an iron bar made at a single heat from a puddle ball by hammering and rolling

puddle duck *n* **:** DABBLER 2

puddle jumper *n* **1** *slang* **a :** a small usu. antiquated car or truck **b :** LIGHTPLANE; *esp* **:** a military airplane used for low level observation or liaison and sometimes equipped with bazookas **2** *slang* **:** an outboard motorboat

pud·dler \'pəd(ᵊ)lə(r)\ *n* -s **:** one that puddles: as **a :** one who converts pig iron into wrought iron by puddling **b :** a rabble used in puddling **c :** PUDDLING FURNACE

puddle wall *or* **puddle core wall** *n* **:** a core wall of a dam made of puddled clay — called also *hearting*

puddling *n* -s **1 a :** the act or process of working a wet mixture of earth or concrete into a solid impervious mass **b** (1) **:** the compacting of a soil surface by water (2) **:** the dipping of roots into thin mud before transplanting **2 :** the art or process of converting pig iron into wrought iron or now rarely steel by subjecting it to heat and frequent stirring in a small reverberatory furnace in the presence of oxidizing substances by which it is freed from most of its carbon and other impurities

puddling furnace *n* **:** a small reverberatory furnace in which iron is puddled

pud·dly \'pəd(ᵊ)lē, -li\ *adj* -ER/-EST **1** *archaic* **:** MUDDY, MURKY **2 :** full of puddles ⟨considering a dash down the ~ path to the stable —Nora Waln⟩

pud·dock \'pədək\ *chiefly dial var of* ¹PADDOCK

pud·dy \'pədē\ *adj* -ER/-EST [perh. akin to LG *puddig* swollen, pudgy — more at PUDDING] **:** PUDGY

pu·den·cy \'pyüdᵊnsē\ *n* -ES [L *pudentia*, fr. *pudent-, pudens* (pres. part. of *pudēre* to be ashamed) + *-ia* -y — more at PUDIC] **:** MODESTY, PRUDISHNESS

pu·den·dal \pyü'dendᵊl\ *adj* [NL *pudendum* + E *-al*] **:** of, relating to, or lying in the region of the external organs of generation ⟨a ~ artery⟩ ⟨~ nerve⟩ ⟨~ veins⟩

pu·den·dum \-dəm\ *n, pl* **puden·da** \-də\ [NL, back-formation fr. LL *pudenda*, fr. L, neut. pl. of *pudendus*, gerundive of *pudēre* to be ashamed — more at PUDIC] **:** the external genital organs of a human being and esp. of a woman — usu. used in pl.

pudge \'pəj\ *n* -s [origin unknown] **:** one that is pudgy

pudg·i·ly \'pəjəlē, -li\ *adv* **:** in a pudgy manner

pudg·i·ness \'pəjēnəs, -jin-\ *n* -ES **:** the quality or state of being pudgy

pudgy \-jē, -ji\ *adj* -ER/-EST [*pudge* + *-y*] **1 :** short and plump **:** tending toward corpulence **:** CHUBBY, SQUAT ⟨has its share of ~ cupids —Sheila Hibben⟩ ⟨the man behind the lectern was ~ and stocky, with a fleshy face —Hans Meyerhoff⟩ **2 :** BULKY ⟨a good winter glove, warm but not ~ —*New Yorker*⟩

pu·di·bund \'pyüdə,bənd\ *adj* [L *pudibundus*, fr. *pudēre* to be ashamed + *-bundus* (as in *moribundus* moribund) — more at PUDIC, MORIBUND] **:** PRUDISH

pu·di·bun·di·ty \,==='bəndəd·ē\ *n* -ES **:** PRUDISHNESS

pu·dic \'pyüdik\ *adj* [F *pudique*, fr. L *pudicus* modest, fr. *pudēre* to be ashamed; perh. akin to L *pavire* to beat, strike — more at PAVE] **:** PUDENDAL

pu·dic·i·ty \pyü'disəd·ē\ *n* -ES [MF *pudicité*, fr. L *pudicus* + MF *-ité* -ity] **:** MODESTY, CHASTITY

pu·dor \'pyü,dȯr, -ə̇ə\ *n* -s [L, fr. *pudēre* + *-or*] **:** MODESTY

pu·du \'pü,dü\ *n* -s [Sp, fr. Mapuche] **:** a small reddish deer (*Pudu pudu*) of the Chilean Andes having simple antlers resembling spikes and standing only 12 or 13 inches high

pue \'pyü\ *n* -s [ME — more at PEW] *archaic* **:** ¹PEW

pueb·la \p(y)ü'eblə, 'pweblə\ *adj, usu cap* [fr. *Puebla*, Mexico] **:** of or from the city of Puebla, Mexico **:** of the kind or style prevalent in Puebla

¹pueb·lo \p(y)ü'e(,)blō, 'pwe(,)-\ *n* -s [Sp, people, village, fr. L *populus* people — more at PEOPLE] **1 a :** a Latin-American community; *esp* **:** an Indian town or village ⟨typical street in a ~ of northwestern Venezuela —W.E.Rudolph⟩ **b :** a town founded by Mexican Spanish settlers in the southwestern U.S. esp. in California ⟨it was founded as San Jose de Guadalupe . . . the first ~ to be established in Alta California —Aubrey Drury⟩ **2 a :** the communal dwelling of an Indian village of Arizona, New Mexico, and adjacent parts of Mexico and Texas typical of the Anasazi culture and consisting of contiguous flat-roofed stone or adobe houses in groups sometimes several stories high and built in receding terraces with access to the lowest story orig. only by trap doors in the roof which was reached by ladders that could be drawn up for defense **b :** an Indian village of the southwestern U.S. ⟨all ~*s* have their religious societies, priests, warriors, medicine men and women —*Amer. Guide Series: N.Mex.*⟩ ⟨many members of modern ~*s* are abandoning the imposing citadels of their ancestors in favor of individual housing⟩ **3** *usu cap* **a :** a group of Indian peoples of Arizona and New Mexico **b :** a member of any of such peoples **4** *usu cap* **:** the languages spoken by the Pueblo peoples comprising the Keresan, Shoshonean, Tanoan, and Zuñian language families

²pueblo \"\ *adj, usu cap* **1 :** of or relating to a culture of the plateau area of the southwestern U.S. following and forming one cultural development with the Basket Maker, developing in five stages, and characterized in its earliest stage by true masonry buildings and loom weaving and at its zenith by fine masonry, large communal towns, and buildings set under overhanging cliffs or in the open — see ANASAZI, DEVELOPMENTAL PUEBLO, GREAT PUEBLO **2 :** of, relating to, or imitating the decorative and architectural style of the Pueblo Indians of New Mexico

pueb·lo·an \-ləwən\ *adj or n, usu cap* [¹*pueblo* + *-an*] **:** PUEBLO

pueb·loid \-,blȯid\ *adj* [¹*pueblo* + *-oid*] **1 :** resembling a pueblo **2 :** having characteristics similar to those of the Pueblo people or their culture

puel·che \'pwelchē\ *n, pl* **puelche** *or* **puelches** *usu cap* [Sp, fr. Araucanian] **1 a :** a people of the Argentine pampas **b :** a member of such people **2 a :** the language of the Puelche people **b :** a language stock comprising the Puelche language — **puel·che·an** \-chēən\ *adj, usu cap*

¹pu·er \'pyü(ə)r\ *n* -s [alter. of ⁴*pure*] **:** a mixture (as of dogs' dung in water) formerly used by tanners for bating hides and skins after liming

²puer \"\ *vt* -ED/-ING/-S [alter. of ³*pure*] **:** to bate (hides) in a solution of fermented dog dung

pu·e·rar·ia \ˌpyüə'ra(a)rēə\ *n, cap* [NL, fr. Marc N. *Puerari* †1845 Swiss botanist + NL -*ia*] **:** a genus of chiefly Asiatic herbaceous or woody vines (family Leguminosae) with trifoliolate leaves, blue or purple racemose flowers, and long narrow many-seeded pods — see KUDZU

pu·er·er \'pyü(ə)rə(r)\ *n* -S **:** BATER

pu·er·i·cul·ture \'pyü(ə)rə,kəlchə(r)\ *n* [F *puériculture*, fr. L *puer* + F -*iculture* (as in *agriculture*) — more at AGRICULTURE] **:** the rearing or hygienic care of children; *specif* **:** the prenatal care of unborn children through attention to the health of pregnant women

pu·er·ile \'pyü(ə)rəl, -ˌrīl\ *adj* [F or L; F *puéril*, fr. L *puerilis*, fr. *puer* boy, girl, child + -*ilis* -ile; akin to Gk *pais* child — more at FEW] **1 a :** of or relating to childhood **:** BOYISH ⟨~ humility . . . we used to show to the world —Corra Harris⟩ ⟨mocking is the first ~ form of wit, playing with surfaces without sympathy —George Santayana⟩ **b :** unworthy of an adult **:** IMMATURE, CHILDISH ⟨the ~ and half-educated mind —Bernhard Berenson⟩ ⟨great affairs of men in society are carried on as if they were . . . ~ and degrading farces —R.P.Blackmur⟩ **2 :** characteristic of or resembling that of children — used of respiration ⟨~ breathing is louder than normal vesicular breathing —R.M.Goepp & H.F.Flippin⟩ **syn** see YOUTHFUL

pu·er·ile·ly \-l(l)ē\ *adv* **:** in a puerile manner

pu·er·il·ism \-ˌrəˌlizəm\ *n* -S [ISV *puerile* + -*ism*] **:** childish or infantile behavior esp. as a psychiatric symptom of mental disorder

pu·er·il·i·ty \ˌpyüə'riləd·ē, -lətē, -i\ *n* -ES [MF or L; MF *puerilité*, fr. L *puerilitat-, puerilitas*, fr. *puerilis* + -*itat-*, -*itas* -ity] **1 a :** the quality or state of being a child; *specif* **:** the status under civil law of a child between infancy and puberty defined as from 7 to 14 years of age in boys and from 7 to 12 years of age in girls **b :** IMMATURITY, CHILDISHNESS ⟨the ballet comic in its ~ and ugliness —Arnold Bennett⟩ **2 a :** an act, instance, or product of an immature mind ⟨where he has committed the ~ of employing more words than are necessary, he now has the one correct word —*College English*⟩ ⟨pettiness, juvenilities, and . . . *puerilities* become not a great assembly like this —John Adams⟩

pu·er·pera \pyü'ərp(ə)rə\ *n, pl* **puerper·ae** \-pəˌrē\ [L] **:** a woman in childbirth or in the period immediately succeeding

pu·er·per·al \(')=ˌ=rəl\ *adj* [L *puerpera* woman in childbirth (fr. *puer* child + -*pera*, fr. *parere* to give birth to) + E -*al* — more at PUERILE, PARE] **:** of or relating to parturition ⟨~ infection⟩

puerperal fever *or* **puerperal sepsis** *n* **:** an abnormal condition that results from infection of the placental site following delivery or instrumental abortion and is characterized in mild form by fever of not over 100.4°F but may progress to a localized endometritis or spread through the uterine wall and develop into peritonitis or pass into the blood stream and produce septicemia — called also *childbed fever*

pu·er·pe·ri·um \ˌpyüə(r)'pirēəm\ *n, pl* **puerpe·ria** \-rēə\ [L, fr. *puerpera*] **1 :** the condition of a woman immediately following childbirth **2 :** the period between childbirth and the return of the uterus to its normal size

¹puer·to ri·can \ˌpwerd·(ˌ)ō'rēkən, -rd·ə'-\ *also* **por·to rican** \ˌpōrd·(ˌ)ō-, -rd·ə'-\ *adj, usu cap P&R* [*Puerto Rico* or *Porto Rico*, island in the West Indies + E -*an*] **1 :** of, relating to, or characteristic of Puerto Rico **2 :** of, relating to, or characteristic of Puerto Ricans

²puerto rican \"\ *also* **porto rican** \"\ *n, pl* **puerto ricans** *also* **porto ricans** *cap P&R* **:** a native or inhabitant of Puerto Rico

puer·to ri·co \-'rē(ˌ)kō\ *adj, usu cap P&R* [fr. *Puerto Rico*, island in the West Indies] **:** of or from Puerto Rico **:** of the kind or style prevalent in Puerto Rico **:** PUERTO RICAN

¹puff \'pəf\ *vb* -ED/-ING/-S [ME *puffen*, fr. OE *pyffan*, of imit. origin] *vi* **1 a :** to blow in short gusts **:** exhale forcibly or escape in a cloud ⟨a fresh salt breeze ~*s* across the bay⟩ ⟨the gatherer ~*s* lightly into the blowpipe to shape the molten glass⟩ ⟨the dust almost ~*ed* out of the door when we opened it —Molly L. Bar-David⟩ **b :** to breathe hard because of exertion **:** PANT ⟨was ~*ing* heavily when he reached the top⟩ **c :** to emit a series of little whiffs or clouds (as of smoke or steam) often as an accompaniment to vigorous action ⟨~ at a pipe⟩ ⟨the kettle ~*ing*, and the tea all set out —Adrian Bell⟩ ⟨snorting, ~*ing* river steamers that churned their way to the city —*Amer. Guide Series: Maine*⟩ **d :** to discharge a powdery cloud of spores ⟨changes in temperature or humidity may cause some ascomycetes to ~⟩ **2 :** to speak or act in a scornful or conceited manner **:** BLUSTER, POOH-POOH ⟨a ~*ing* turkey-cock of a man, full of himself and of false patriotism —E.S.Morgan⟩ ⟨it is . . . to defy Heaven to ~ at damnation —Robert South⟩ **3 a :** to become distended **:** SWELL — usu. used with *up* ⟨a sprained ankle ~*s* up⟩ **b :** to open or appear in or as if in a puff **:** ERUPT, EXPLODE, EXPAND, POP ⟨the spin chute ~*s* out behind the hurtling plane⟩ ⟨flak was ~*ing* all around —F.V. Drake⟩ ⟨twice, little spot fires ~*ed* up on the wrong side —G.R.Stewart⟩ **c :** to make exaggerated statements or claims **:** BRAG ⟨a considerable amount of ~*ing* . . . was part of the sales talk that induced the marriage —Morris Ploscowe⟩; *specif* **:** to advertise in glowing terms ⟨~*ing* . . . is well understood by a public immunized to the superlatives of the marketplace —F.V.Harper⟩ **~** *vt* **1 a :** to propel or agitate by means of short gusts **:** blow in whiffs or spurts **:** WAFT ⟨people who eat peppermint and ~ it in your face —W.S.Gilbert⟩ ⟨a brisk breeze ~*s* the clouds away⟩ ⟨bullets . . . ~*ed* up the white dust all around him —A. Conan Doyle⟩ **b :** to extinguish by blowing — used with *out* ⟨~ out a candle⟩ **c** (1) **:** to say breathlessly **:** PANT ⟨"wait for me," he ~*ed*, doing his best to keep up with the bigger boys⟩ (2) **:** to render breathless **:** wear out ⟨twisted the rope round faster and faster, until he was ~*ed* —Dannie Abse⟩ **d :** to draw on (as a pipe or cigarette) with intermittent exhalations of smoke ⟨found that when people ~ two cigarettes alternately, they cannot in fact tell the difference between them —Martin Mayer⟩ **e :** to apply with a diffusing device (as a powder puff) ⟨neck, still white with the powder she had ~*ed* there after her bath —Wright Morris⟩ **2 a** (1) **:** to distend with or as if with air or gas **:** INFLATE, SWELL ⟨green lizards ~ out their throats like thin red bubbles —Marjory S. Douglas⟩ ⟨~*ed* out his chest and pranced around the chair —Daniel Curley⟩ (2) **:** to fluff up or pad out **:** EXPAND, STUFF ⟨the ~*ed* and tufted furniture —Norman Mailer⟩ ⟨the manuscript of her work had been submitted . . . for this one to prune and that one to ~ out —Wilfred Partington⟩; *specif* **:** to arrange (hair) in puffs **b** (1) **:** to make proud or conceited **:** ELATE, GRATIFY ⟨public acclamation ~*s* his ego⟩ ⟨might have become morally ~*ed* up if a healthy corrective had not been administered —A.W.Long⟩ (2) **:** to cause to swell with anger **:** ROUSE ⟨audience ~*s* itself to storm the gates —D.M.Friedenberg⟩ **c :** to praise extravagantly **:** OVERRATE, EXTOL ⟨hit too many homers and people start ~*ing* you up —Willie Mays⟩ ⟨do not ~ impossible trash, but they do let people . . . know what is interesting and worth reading —Mary C. Fair⟩; *specif* **:** ADVERTISE ⟨traders . . . still ~ their goods as if the whole aim of their toils were just to achieve a single transaction —C.E. Montague⟩

²puff \"\ *n* -S [ME *puf, puffe*, fr. OE *pyff*, fr. *pyffan*] **1 a :** an act or instance of puffing **:** WHIFF, GUST ⟨storm which set out as a mere ~ of wind thousands of miles away —Carey Longmire⟩; *specif* **:** CAT'S-PAW 1 ⟨when you reef for a land breeze study the duration of the ~*s* —Peter Heaton⟩ **b :** a slight explosive sound accompanying a puff **:** HUFF ⟨let out an irrepressible little ~ of laughter —Marguerite Steen⟩ ⟨listen to the ~ of a distant locomotive⟩ **c :** a perceptible cloud or aura emitted in a puff ⟨let ten ~*s* of his pipe eddy away —F.M.Ford⟩ ⟨sat back . . . in a fluff of soft fur and a ~ of expensive scent —Anne Panish⟩ **d :** something that resembles a puff ⟨a clear blue sky with only a few ~*s* of cloud sailing in it —Clifton Cuthbert⟩ ⟨can all be blown away with one ~ of clear common sense —Stuart Hampshire⟩ **e :** PUFFBALL **2 a :** a hollow or airy substance: as (1) **:** a dish that puffs in cooking ⟨corn ~⟩ ⟨potato ~⟩; *esp* **:** a light pastry that rises high in baking (2) **:** a tall drink that consists of an alcoholic liquor, milk, and soda water ⟨brandy ~⟩ ⟨gin ~⟩ **b** (1) **:** a disease of the tomato characterized by light hollow fruits and thought to be caused by environmental or nutritional factors (2) **:** WINDGALL 1 **3 a :** a slight swelling **:** PROTUBERANCE **b :** a fluffy mass: as (1) **:** POUF b ⟨a dainty ~ of sleeve at the shoulder⟩ ⟨great ~*s* of blue hydrangea blossoms —Placide Martin⟩ ⟨bird didn't even have time to get its wings open before pellets ripped it into a ~ of feathers —Barnaby Conrad⟩ (2) **:** POWDER PUFF (3) **:** a soft loose roll of hair usu. wound over a pad and pinned in place — called also *pouf* (4) **:** a quilted or tufted bed covering filled with down or fiber — called also *pouf* **c :** a padded ridge or piece of wadding; *specif* **:** TOE PUFF **4 a :** an exhibition of arrogance or ostentation **:** BLUFF, SHOW ⟨showing off for each other . . . like housewives putting on a ~ at a party —John Steinbeck⟩ **b** *archaic* **:** one that exhibits arrogance or ostentation **:** BRAGGART, SHOW-OFF **5 :** a commendatory notice or review ⟨pleasant letters came to me on my birthday . . . and one or two ~*s* in the newspapers —O.W. Holmes †1935⟩ ⟨interested in political ~*s*, not news —W.A. Swanberg⟩ ⟨the play got ~*s* from several critics⟩; *specif* **:** BLURB ⟨~*s* . . . with which booksellers sometimes embroider their catalogs —John Carter⟩ ⟨firm does not favor . . . publicity stunts or ~*s* for goods on sale —*Persuasion*⟩

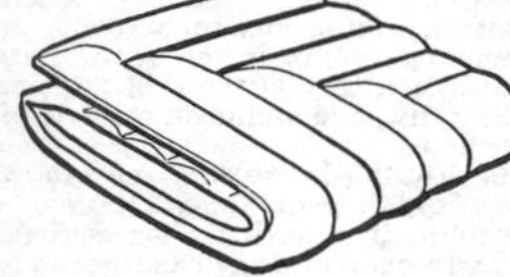
puff 3b(4), folded

³puff \"\ *adj* **1 :** PUFFED ⟨~ sleeve⟩ **2 :** of, relating to, or designed for promotion or flattery ⟨aren't all autobiographies essentially ~ jobs —Thomas Goldwasser⟩

⁴puff *a strongly articulated* p-*sound sometimes trilled & sometimes with a vowel sound following; usu read as* 'pəf\ *interj* [ME *puf*] — used to express disdain or to indicate transience

puff adder *n* **1 a :** a thick-bodied exceedingly venomous widely distributed African viper (*Bitis arietans*) that inflates its body and hisses loudly when disturbed **b :** a similar smaller snake (*B. inornata*) that occurs only in southern Africa **2 :** HOGNOSE SNAKE

puffback \'=ˌ=\ *n* **1** *or* **puffback shrike :** any of several African shrikes of the genus *Dryoscopus* that are chiefly black and white or buffy in color and have the feathers of the lower back long, fluffy, and erectile **2 :** a strike-back of the flame in a stove or oil burner

puffball \'=ˌ=\ *n* **1 a :** any of various basidiomycetous fungi of the family Lycoperdaceae that have a globose shape, discharge the ripe spores in a smokelike cloud when pressed or struck, and are often edible **b :** any of various similar fungi (as of the families Sclerodermataceae and Tulostomaceae) **2 :** the feathery head of achenes in the dandelion

puffbird \'=ˌ=\ *n* **:** any of numerous So. American and Central American zygodactyl birds of the family Bucconidae that are related to the jacamars and often sit with the feathers of the head fluffed out — called also *barbet*

puffed *adj* **1 a** (1) **:** BLOATED, SWOLLEN ⟨her face pale, ~, streaked with weeping —Ethel Wilson⟩ (2) **:** gathered or stiffened for protruding fullness ⟨~ sleeves⟩ **b** (1) **:** INFLATED (2) **:** heated in a closed container until the moisture in the grain turns to steam that causes the kernel to expand when the pressure is suddenly released ⟨~ rice⟩ ⟨~ wheat⟩ **2 :** exhibiting or expressive of vanity or conceit **:** PRETENTIOUS, ARROGANT ⟨are but ~ minds that bubble thus above inferiors —Owen Feltham⟩

puff·er \'pəfə(r)\ *n* -S **1 a :** one that emits puffs: as (1) **:** SMOKER 1b (2) *chiefly Scot* **:** a small steam-powered cargo ship used in coastal trade (3) **:** a small engine used in coal mines for hoisting and hauling **b :** the operator of a small engine for hauling mine cars or hoisting coal or rock **2 a :** one that extols; *esp* **:** a writer of commendatory or promotional material ⟨reviewing is done largely by people who are not critics but simply ~*s* —James Laughlin⟩ **b :** BY-BIDDER **3 a :** one that stuffs or swells; *specif* **:** an operator of a machine for raising designs on manufactured articles (as leather goods, gloves, draperies) **b** (1) **:** PUFF IRON (2) **:** BALLER 2 **4 a** (1) **:** GLOBEFISH 1 (2) **:** any of various other fishes of the order Plectognathi **b :** HARBOR PORPOISE

puff·ery \-fərē, -ri\ *n* -ES **:** flattering publicity **:** extravagant commendation esp. for promotional purposes; *specif* **:** ADVERTISING

puff-fish \'=ˌ=\ *n* **:** PUFFER 4a

puff·i·ly \'pəfəlē, -li\ *adv* **:** in a puffy manner

puf·fin \'pəfən\ *n* -S [ME *poffoun, pophyn*] **1 :** any of several seabirds of the genera *Fratercula* and *Lunda* (family Alcidae) having a short neck and a deep grooved parti-colored laterally compressed bill, nesting in burrows or crevices, and laying a single white or nearly white egg **2 :** SHEARWATER; *esp* **:** MANX SHEARWATER

puff·i·ness \'pəfēnəs, -fin-\ *n* -ES **:** the quality or state of being puffy

puffing *n* -S **1 :** an act or instance of puffing: as **a :** puffed decoration or trimming esp. on clothing **b :** extravagant praise or commendation; *specif* **:** seller's or dealer's talk in praise of the virtues of something offered for sale **c :** the action of a puffer in bidding up the price at an auction **2 :** PUFF 2b (1)

puffing adder *n* **:** HOGNOSE SNAKE

puff·ing·ly *adv* **:** with puffing ⟨labored ~ up one flight of stairs —J.B.Benefield⟩

puffing pig *n* **:** HARBOR PORPOISE

puf·fi·nus \'pəfənəs\ *n, cap* [NL, fr. E *puffin*] **:** a genus of oceanic birds (family Procellariidae) that comprises the shearwaters and is sometimes included in the genus *Procellaria*

puff iron *n* **:** an electrically heated metal form of irregular shape used by dry cleaners to press parts of garments (as gathers or flounces) difficult to iron by hand

puff-leg \'=ˌ=\ *n* **:** any of numerous hummingbirds of the genus *Eriocnemis* having tufts of downy feathers on the legs

puff paste *n* **:** a very rich flaky pastry composed usu. of equal parts of flour and butter, processed by repeated rolling and folding after each addition of butter, and baked at high temperature which causes it to puff in leaves or flakes ⟨make patty shells of *puff paste*⟩

puffs *pl of* PUFF, *pres 3d sing of* PUFF

puffy \'pəfē, -fi\ *adj* -ER/-EST **1 :** characterized by vanity or ostentation **:** POMPOUS, SHOWY ⟨a ~ pretentious man⟩ ⟨the scenes are more ~ than pointed —Leslie Rees⟩ **2 a :** blowing in puffs **:** GUSTY ⟨a ~ northeast wind⟩ **b :** BREATHLESS, SHORT-WINDED ⟨were ~ long before they reached the summit⟩ **3 a :** swollen or tending to swell in size **:** BLOATED, CHUBBY ⟨his face . . . aside from a few ~ bruises, looked fit —Gordon Merrick⟩ ⟨two Englishmen, one ~, one rangy —Sinclair Lewis⟩ **b :** resembling a puff **:** BOUFFANT, FLUFFY ⟨a ~, floor-length underskirt —Lois Long⟩ ⟨~ pillow⟩ ⟨~ clouds⟩

¹pug \'pəg, 'pu̇g\ *n* -S [ME *pugge*] *archaic* **:** ¹CHAFF 1

²pug \'pəg\ *n* -S [perh. alter. of ¹*puck*] **1** *obs* **a :** a dear one **:** SWEETHEART, PET **b :** MISTRESS, PROSTITUTE **2** *obs* **a :** HOBGOBLIN **b :** MONKEY **3 a :** a small sturdy compact dog of a breed introduced from Asia into Europe by the Dutch with a short sleek coat silvery or fawn marked with black or all black, a tightly curled tail, broad wrinkled face and rounded head with button ears, and strong straight legs **b :** something that is short and squat: as (1) **:** PUG NOSE (2) **:** a close knot or coil of hair **:** BUN **4 :** PUG MOTH

³pug \"\ *vt* **pugged; pugged; pugging; pugs** [perh. alter. of ²*puck*] **1 :** to plug or pack with a compacted substance (as clay or mortar); *esp* **:** to fill (the space under a floor) with sound-deadening material **2 :** to work into a desired consistency by kneading or churning; *esp* **:** to wedge (clay) for making bricks or pottery **3** *chiefly Brit* **:** to trample (wet ground) into a sticky mass — used of cattle

⁴pug \"\ *n* -S **1 a :** a compacted mass of a plastic substance; *esp* **:** a large lump of tempered clay for making pottery **b :** a mixture of clay and manure sometimes with chopped hay or cow hair added used for covering grafts **c :** GOUGE 4 **2 :** PUG MILL

⁵pug \"\ *n* -S [by shortening & alter. fr. *pugilist*] **:** BOXER, PRIZEFIGHTER

⁶pug \"\ *n* -S [Hindi *pag* foot] **:** FOOTPRINT; *esp* **:** a print of a wild mammal **:** TRACK, SPOOR ⟨the great ~*s*, pressed deep, led from the trees on their left —Jon Godden⟩

⁷pug \"\ *vt* **pugged; pugged; pugging; pugs :** to track by pugs ⟨~ a tiger⟩ ⟨~ a criminal⟩

pug-dog \'=ˌ=\ *n* **:** ²PUG 3a

pu·get sound pine \'pyüjət-\ *n, usu cap 1st P & S* [fr. *Puget Sound*, arm of the Pacific ocean extending southward into Washington state] **:** DOUGLAS FIR

pu·get·tia \pyü'ged·ēə\ *n, cap* [NL, fr. *Puget* Sound + NL -*ia*] **:** a genus of spider crabs (family Majidae) common along the Pacific coast of No. America

pug·a·ree *or* **pug·a·ree** \'pəg(ə)rē\ *or* **pug·gree** *also* **pug·ree** *or* **pa·gri** \'pəgrē\ *n* -S [Hindi *pagṛī*] **1 :** a turban worn in India **2 :** a light usu. printed or colored scarf wrapped around a sun helmet often with a piece hanging down in back as a protection from the sun or used as a hatband esp. for a straw hat

pug·ger \'pəgə(r)\ *n* -S [³*pug* + -*er*] **:** one that pugs clay (as for pottery or brick); *esp* **:** an operator of a pug mill

pugging *n* -S [fr. gerund of ³*pug*] **1 :** the working and tempering of clay usu. by machine to make it plastic and of uniform consistency **2 :** DEAFENING 2

pug·gish \'pəgish\ *adj* [²*pug* + -*ish*] **1** *archaic* **a :** characteristic of a monkey **b :** PUCKISH **2 :** SNUBBY

pug·gle \'pəgəl\ *vt* -ED/-ING/-S [freq. of ³*pug*] *chiefly dial* **:** to clear out or stir up by poking

¹pug·gy \'pəgē, -gi\ *n* -ES [²*pug* + -*y* (n. suffix)] **1 :** SWEETHEART, PET **2** *Scot* **:** MONKEY

²puggy \"\ *adj* -ER/-EST [²*pug* + -*y* (adj. suffix)] **:** PUGGISH 2

³puggy \"\ *adj* [E dial. *pug* to sweat + -*y*] **1** *dial Eng* **:** perspiring or causing perspiration **:** SWEATY **2** *dial Brit* **:** clammy, damp, and sticky ⟨tuberous plants won't do well in soggy, ~ soils —*Sydney (Australia) Bull.*⟩

⁴pug·gy *also* **pug·gi** \'pəgē\ *n, pl* **puggies** [Hindi *pagī*, fr. *pag* foot] **:** TRACKER; *esp* **:** a member of a caste in India trained to track criminals by their footprints

¹pugh *a strongly articulated* p-*sound sometimes trilled & sometimes with a vowel sound following; usu read as* 'pü\ *interj* [imit. of the sniff of disdain caused by a bad smell] — used to express disgust or disdain

²pugh \'pyü\ *n* -S [by alter.] **:** ⁵PEW

pugil *n* -S [L *pugillus* handful, fr. *pugnus* fist — more at PUGNACIOUS] *archaic* **:** ²PINCH 2b

pu·gi·lant \'pyüjələnt\ *adj* [L *pugilant-, pugilans* pres. part. of *pugilare, pugilari* to fight with fists, fr. *pugil* boxer — more at PUGILISM] **:** PUGILISTIC

pu·gi·lism \-jəˌlizəm\ *n* -S [L *pugil* pugilist, boxer + E -*ism*; akin to L *pugnus* fist — more at PUGNACIOUS] **:** ²BOXING

pu·gi·list \-ˌləst\ *n* -S [L *pugil* + E -*ist*] **:** FIGHTER; *esp* **:** a professional boxer

pu·gi·lis·tic \ˌ=ˌ='listik, -tēk\ *adj* **:** of or relating to pugilism ⟨ended his ~ career by retiring undefeated⟩ — **pu·gi·lis·ti·cal·ly** \-tək(ə)lē, -li\ *adv*

pugmark \'=ˌ=\ *n* [⁶*pug* + *mark*] **:** ⁶PUG ⟨your eye notes ~*s* telling of a hungry wolf or lynx that climbed the dome —W.J.Long⟩

pug mill *n* [³*pug*] **:** a machine consisting of a shaft armed with blades revolving in a drum or trough and used for mixing or tempering a plastic substance into a desired consistency ⟨brick= clay . . . might need sieving, weathering, and mincing in the *pug mill* before it could be worked —Katharine S. Woods⟩ ⟨clay . . . and mixed by hand, foot, or *pug mill* to the right consistency for throwing —Bernard Leach⟩ ⟨rubber compound . . . thinned down with naphtha to suitable consistency in a *pug mill* —H.P.Stevens & Clayton Beadle⟩; *esp* **:** CEMENT MIXER

pug moth *n* [²*pug*] **:** any of various small geometrid moths of *Chloroclystis* and related genera

pug·na·cious \ˌpəg'nāshəs\ *adj* [L *pugnac-, pugnax* pugnacious (fr. *pugnare* to fight, fr. *pugnus* fist) + E -*ious* — more at PUNGENT] **:** having a quarrelsome or belligerent nature **:** thriving on challenge **:** AGGRESSIVE, TRUCULENT ⟨bushpigs are most courageous and ~ animals . . . capable of putting up a successful fight even against a leopard —James Stevenson= Hamilton⟩ ⟨~ spirits . . . lamented that there was so little prospect of an exhilarating disturbance —Herman Melville⟩ ⟨equally ~ when it came to fighting for human rights —P.V.D. Stern⟩ ⟨not a ~ enough mediocrity to earn a larger salary —V.A.Young⟩ **syn** see BELLIGERENT

pug·na·cious·ly *adv* **:** in a pugnacious manner

pug·na·cious·ness *n* -ES **:** PUGNACITY

pug·nac·i·ty \ˌpəg'nasəd·ē, -sətē, -i\ *n* -ES [L *pugnacitas*, fr. *pugnac-, pugnax* + -*itas* -ity] **:** fighting instinct **:** ready response to challenge **:** COURAGE, AGGRESSIVENESS, TRUCULENCE ⟨some children . . . seem to be born fighting and never wish to repudiate their native ~ —Margaret Hay⟩ ⟨retain . . . the ~ developed in their struggle for full civil status —William Petersen⟩

pug nose *n* [²*pug*] **:** a nose having a slightly concave bridge and flattened nostrils **:** SNUB NOSE

pug-nosed \(')=ˌ=\ *adj* **:** having a blunt nose

pug-nosed eel *n* **:** a deep-sea eel (*Simenchelys parasiticus*) having a shorter and stouter body than the common eel and a short blunt nose and burrowing into the bodies of other fishes

pugree *var of* PUGGAREE

pugs *pl of* PUG, *pres 3d sing of* PUG

pu·ha \'pühə\ *n* -S [Maori] *New Zealand* **:** a sow thistle (*Sonchus oleraceus*) that is commonly used as a potherb ⟨~ turned up with practically everything, corned beef, boiled bacon, baked rabbit —Ruth Park⟩

pu·hoe \(')pü'hōē\ *n* -S [*Tahitian*] **:** an outrigger paddling canoe of the Society islands

pui·na·ve \pwē'nävē\ *n, pl* **puina·ve** \"\ *or* **puina·vis** \-vēz\ *usu cap* **1 a :** a people of eastern Colombia **b :** a member of such people **2 a :** the language of the Puinave people **b :** the Puinavean language family comprising Puinave and Macú

pui·na·ve·an \-vēən\ *adj, usu cap* **:** of or relating to the Puinave or their language

puir \'pyü(ə)r\ *Scot var of* POOR

puis dar·rein continuance \pwis'darən-, -ˌda'rān-\ *n* [AF, lit., since the last continuance] **:** a pleading introducing new matter after plea has already been made and issue joined but preceding trial

¹puis·ne \'pyünē, -ni\ *adj* [AF, fr. OF *puisné* born afterwards — more at PUNY] **1** *or* **puisny** \"\ *obs* **:** of little consequence or experience **:** INSIGNIFICANT, PETTY ⟨a ~ tilter, that spurs his horse but on one side —Shak.⟩ **2 a :** of lesser age or importance **:** JUNIOR, SUBORDINATE **b** *law* **:** ASSOCIATE ⟨a ~ judge of the superior court⟩ **3** *law* **:** of subsequent date **:** LATER

²puisne \"\ *n* -S [AF, fr. *puisne*, adj.] **1 :** one who is a junior or subordinate **2 :** a puisne judge ⟨the other ~ doubted, but agreed that the case must be discussed —O.W.Holmes †1935⟩

pu·is·sance \'pyüəsᵊn(t)s, pyü'is-, 'pwis-\ *n* -S [ME *puissaunce*, fr. MF *puissance*, fr. OF, fr. *puissant*] **1 :** ability to coerce or sway **:** controlling influence **:** STRENGTH, POWER ⟨samurai bow to the ~ of the emperor⟩ ⟨legislators . . . fear the ~ of the farm vote —*Los Angeles (Calif.) Times*⟩ ⟨extraordinary rhythmic ~ —Aaron Copland⟩ **2** *obs* **:** a military force **:** ARMY ⟨cousin, go draw our ~ together —Shak.⟩ **syn** see POWER

pu·is·sant \-nt\ *adj* [ME *puissaunt*, fr. MF *puissant*, fr. OF, fr. *puiss-* (stem of *poer, poeir* to be able) + -*ant* — more at POWER] **:** of great force or vigor **:** STRONG, POWERFUL ⟨one of the nation's most ~ labor leaders —*Time*⟩ ⟨called on all the ~ stamina of her mother —Adria Langley⟩ ⟨though not a ~ colorist, secured some . . . beautiful effects —Royal Cortissoz⟩ — **pu·is·sant·ly** *adv*

pu·ja *also* **poo·ja** *or* **poo·jah** \'püjə\ *n* -S [Skt *pūjā*, prob. of Dravidian origin; akin to Tamil *pūcu* to anoint, besmear] **1 :** a Hindu act of worship or propitiation ⟨the priest advised us to do ~ and make offerings . . . for relief from our terrible problem —*New Yorker*⟩ **2 :** a Hindu rite or religious festival ⟨some engage in ~ and some perform salat —J.C.Archer⟩

pu·ju·nan \pü'jünən\ *n* -S *usu cap* **:** a language family of the Penutian stock in California comprising four languages all known as Maidu — called also *Maidu*

¹pu·ka \'pükə\ *n* -S [Maori] **1 :** a rare New Zealand tree (*Meryta sinclairii*) of the family Araliaceae with large resinous leaves and dioecious flowers in panicles **2 :** either of two New Zealand trees of the genus *Griselinia* that are sometimes epiphytic: **a** : a tree (*G. lucida*) with long thick shining leaves and green or yellow flowers in axillary panicles **b** : KAPUKA

²puka \"\ *n* -s [Hawaiian] *Hawaii* : HOLE, TUNNEL ⟨if . . . I ever get the giant African snails out of their favorite ~s, I shall really enjoy the gardening —*Honolulu Star-Bull.*⟩

pu·ka·tea \ˌpükəˈtāə\ *n* -s [Maori] : a lofty New Zealand forest tree (*Laurelia novae-zealandiae*) of the family Monimiaceae having a light-colored wood that is soft but strong

pu·ka·teine \ˌpükəˈtāˌēn, -ˌən\ *n* -s [ISV *pukatea* + *-ine*] : a crystalline alkaloid $C_{18}H_{17}NO_3$ found in pukatea bark

¹puke \ˈpyük\ *n* -s [ME *pewke, puke*, fr. MD *puuc, puyc;* akin to D *puik* excellent, Fris *pûk, pùk*] : a woolen fabric of good quality used esp. for gowns in 15th century England

²puke \"\ *vb* -ED/-ING/-S [perh. of imit. origin] *vi* **1 a** : VOMIT 1 — often considered vulgar **b** : to spill over because of the faulty mixing of slugs of liquid with the expelled vapors — used of a petroleum fractionating column **2** : to become revolted ⟨a frame of mind that makes me ~ —O.W.Holmes †1935⟩ ~ *vt* **1** : to throw up : VOMIT — often considered vulgar **2** : to cause to vomit ⟨purged me and *puked* me and charged me two shillings —S.H.Adams⟩

³puke \"\ *n* -s **1 a** *archaic* : an act of vomiting induced by an emetic **b** *archaic* : EMETIC **c** : an attack of nausea ⟨had the ~s⟩ — often considered vulgar **d** : VOMIT 1b — often considered vulgar **2** *usu cap* : MISSOURIAN — used as a nickname **3** : a disgusting or contemptible person ⟨backboneless little ~s —H.L.Davis⟩

pu·ke·ko \püˈkā(ˌ)kō\ *also* **pu·ke·ka** \-ākə\ *n* -s [Maori] : a handsome blue, black, and white gallinule (*Porphyrio melanotus*) of New Zealand, Australia, and adjacent islands

puk·er \ˈpyükə(r)\ *n* -s [²*puke* + *-er*] **1** *archaic* : EMETIC **2** : one that vomits — often considered vulgar

pukeweed \ˈ=,=\ *n* : INDIAN TOBACCO 1

pukh·tun \pu̇kˈtün\ *n, pl* **pukhtun** *or* **pukhtuns** *cap* [Pashto] : AFGHAN 1

puk·ka *or* **pucka** *also* **puc·ca** \ˈpəkə\ *adj* [Hindi *pakkā* cooked, ripe, solid, fr. Skt *pakva;* akin to Skt *pacati* he cooks — more at COOK] : of a genuine or total nature : absolutely first class : AUTHENTIC, COMPLETE ⟨~ sahib⟩ ⟨never did . . . have ~ quarters, with a swarm of servants —P.A.Waring⟩ ⟨the case is ~, all right. Probably a gift from some wealthy female admirer —Dorothy Sayers⟩

puk·ras \ˈpəkrəs\ *or* **pukras pheasant** *n* -ES [*pukras* fr. native name in India] : any of several pheasants of northern India and the Himalayas constituting the genus *Pucrasia* and being in the males mostly crested with long black ear tufts — called also *koklas*

pu·ku \ˈpü(ˌ)kü\ *also* **po·ku** \ˈpō(ˌ)-\ *or* **poo·koo** \ˈpü(ˌ)kü\ *n* -s [native name in Africa] : a reddish African antelope (*Adenota vardoni*) related to the waterbuck

pul \ˈpül\ *n, pl* **puls** \-z\ *or* **pul** *or* **pu·li** \-ü(ˌ)lē\ **1** [Russ *pulo, pul*, fr. Turk *pul* small coin, fr. LGk *phollis* bellows, a small coin, fr. L *follis* bellows, bag — more at FOOL] : a Russian copper coin issued from the 15th century to 1810 **2** [Per *pūl*, fr. Turk *pul*] **a** : a unit of value of Afghanistan equal to $\frac{1}{100}$ afghani — see MONEY table **b** : a coin representing this unit

pu·la·han \ˌpüləˈhän\ *n, pl* **pulaha·nes** \-(ˌ)näs\ [Tag, fr. *pulá* red; fr. the color of the dress of the insurgents] : a member of a 19th century band of Tagalog insurgents esp. in Leyte and Samar organized in opposition to domination of the Philippines by the Spanish friars

pulas *var of* PALAS

pu·la·san *or* **pu·las·san** \ˌpüləˈsän\ *n* -s [Malay] **1** : an East Indian fruit tree (*Nephelium mutabile*) **2** : the fruit of the pulasan tree that resembles the closely related rambutan but is sweeter and less juicy

pu·las·ki \pəˈlaskē\ *n* -s *usu cap* [after Edward C. *Pulaski*, 20th cent. Am. forest ranger, its inventor] **1** *also* **pulaski tool** : a single-bit axe with an adze-shaped grub hoe extending from the back **2** : HAZEL HOE

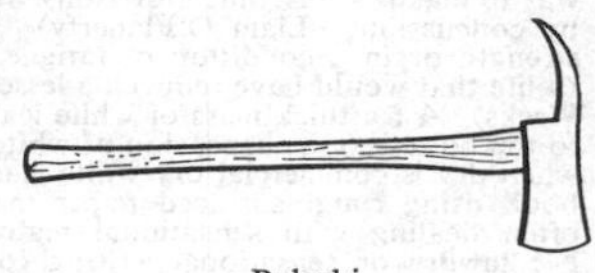
Pulaski

pul·chri·tude \ˈpəlkrəˌtüd, -əˌtyüd\ *n* -s [ME *pulcritude*, fr. L *pulchritudo*, fr. *pulchr-, pulcher* beautiful + *-i-* + *-tudo* -tude; perh. akin to Gk *perknos* dusky, dark — more at PERCH] : physical comeliness : BEAUTY ⟨the May queen and her court making a dazzling assemblage of ~⟩ ⟨a he-man, handsome with a certain bull-like ~ —W.A.White⟩

pul·chri·tu·di·nous \ˌ=ˌ=ˈ=dᵊnəs\ *adj* [L *pulchritudin-, pulchritudo* + E *-ous*] : having or marked by pulchritude ⟨~ movie stars⟩ **syn** see BEAUTIFUL

pule \ˈpyül\ *vb* -ED/-ING/-S [prob. of imit. origin] *vi* **1** : to make a plaintive moaning sound : WHINE, WHIMPER **2** *obs* : to chirp weakly : PEEP ~ *vt, archaic* : to utter in a plaintive manner

pu·le·gol \ˈpyüləˌgōl, -gōl\ *n* -s [ISV *pulegone* + *-ol*] : a viscous liquid alcohol $C_{10}H_{17}OH$ obtained by reduction of pulegone; 2-isopropylidene-5-methyl-cyclohexanol

pu·le·gone \-ˌgōn\ *n* -s [ISV *puleg-* (fr. NL *pulegium*, specific epithet of *Mentha pulegium*, fr. L *puleium, pulegium* pennyroyal) + *-one*] : a fragrant liquid terpenoid ketone $C_{10}H_{16}O$ derived from menthenone that is the principal constituent of pennyroyal oil and yields menthol on hydrogenation

pul·er \ˈpyülə(r)\ *n* -s *archaic* : one that pules

pulesati *usu cap, var of* PURASATI

pu·lex \ˈpyüˌleks\ *n, cap* [NL, fr. L, flea — more at PSYLLA] : a genus (the type of the family Pulicidae) of fleas including the most common flea (*P. irritans*) that regularly attacks man

¹puli *pl of* PUL

²pu·li \ˈpülē, ˈpyülē\ *n, pl* **pu·lik** \-k\ *also* **pulis** [Hung] : an intelligent vigorous medium-sized farm dog of a Hungarian breed with long profuse coat tending to mat into a corded appearance

¹pu·li·cid \ˈpyüləsəd\ *adj* [NL *Pulicidae*] : of or relating to the Pulicidae

²pulicid \"\ *n* -s : a flea of the family Pulicidae

pu·lic·i·dae \pyüˈlisəˌdē\ *n pl, cap* [NL, fr. *Pulic-, Pulex*, type genus + *-idae*] : a large and nearly cosmopolitan family of fleas that includes many of the common fleas attacking man and his domestic animals — see PULEX

pu·li·ci·dal \ˌpyüləˈsīdᵊl\ *adj* [blend of L *pulic-, pulex* flea and E *-cidal* — more at PSYLLA] : destructive to fleas

pu·li·cide \ˈpyüləˌsīd\ *n* -s [blend of L *pulic-, pulex* flea and E *-cide*] : an agent used for destroying fleas

pu·li·cose \-ˌkōs\ *or* **pu·li·cous** \-ləkəs\ *adj* [L *pulicosus*, fr. *pulic-, pulex* + *-osus* -ose, -ous] *archaic* : infested with or caused by the bite of fleas

puling *adj* [fr. pres. part. of *pule*] **1** : of an abject or plaintive nature : SPIRITLESS, WHINING ⟨~ coward⟩ ⟨~ hypochondriac⟩ **2** : of a feeble or sickly nature : SPINDLY, LANGUISHING ⟨~ hybrids between rhododendrons and azaleas —W.H.Camp⟩ ⟨glanced with . . . favor on a ~ milkmaid —W.S.Gilbert⟩ — **pul·ing·ly** *adv*

pulitzer \ˈpu̇lətsə(r), ˈpyül-\ *n* -s *usu cap* [after Joseph *Pulitzer* †1911 Am. newspaper publisher] : any of several annual awards for outstanding literary or journalistic achievement or public service established by the will of Joseph Pulitzer

pulk \ˈpu̇lk\ *n* -s [ME *polk, pulk*, perh. dim. of *pool* — more at POOL] **1** *dial chiefly Eng* : a muddy pond **2** *dial chiefly Eng* : MUDHOLE

pul·ka \ˈpəlkə\ *n* -s [Finn *pulkka* & Lapp *pulkke*] : a one-man Lapp sledge shaped like half a canoe and resting on a broad board or on several runners

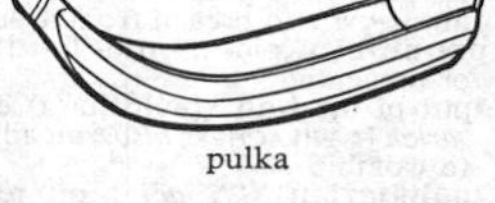
pulka

¹pull \ˈpu̇l\ *vb* -ED/-ING/-S [ME *pullen*, fr. OE *pullian;* prob. akin to Fris *pûlje* to shell, MLG *pulen* to shell, cull, perform a laborious task, MD *pulen, puilen, pullen* to bulge, protrude, Norw dial. *pulla* to bubble up, Icel *pūla* to work hard, push hard] *vt* **1 a** (1) : to draw out from the skin : PLUCK ⟨we'll ~ his plumes —*Shak.*⟩; *specif* : to remove (as the wool or hair) from hides or skins usu. by means of a blunt knife, scraper, or rotating spiral knife ⟨as the wool is ~*ed* it is put into containers by grade —A.L. Anderson⟩ (2) *chiefly dial* : PLUCK ⟨~ poultry⟩ **b** : to pick from a tree or plant : GATHER ⟨handed me a gay bouquet of roses ~*ed* in the rain —Katherine Mansfield⟩ ⟨~ corn from the stalk⟩ **c** (1) : to take out of the ground by the roots ⟨ate plenty of green food, all home-grown and freshly ~*ed;* lettuce and radishes and young onions —Flora Thompson⟩ (2) : to dig out : UPROOT ⟨immigrants were planting garden plots and ~*ing* stumps as the forest wall receded —*Amer. Guide Series: Oregon*⟩ **d** : EXTRACT ⟨had two teeth ~*ed*⟩ **2 a** : to exert force upon so as to cause or tend to cause motion toward the force : tug at ⟨the engine ~*ed* a long line of freight cars⟩ ⟨~*ed* the sled with a rope⟩ ⟨~*ed* his hair⟩ ⟨~ off a ring⟩ — opposed to *push* **b** (1) : to change the state or condition of by exerting a tugging force ⟨the major ~*ed* open a zipper on the corner of the oxygen tent —Raymond Boyle⟩ ⟨~*ed* the door shut behind him⟩ (2) : to stretch (cooling candy) repeatedly in order to produce a desired color, texture, and flavor (3) : to strain or stretch abnormally ⟨~ a muscle⟩ ⟨~ a tendon⟩ **c** : to exert an influence on : IMPEL ⟨driven by ambitions, ~*ed* by private sentiments —Carl Van Doren⟩ ⟨through his affection for his brother, was ~*ed*, now this way, now that —Edith Sitwell⟩ **d** : to hold back (a racehorse) from running at full speed and winning ⟨told track stewards he was approached by gamblers to ~ his mount —*Springfield (Mass.) Daily News*⟩ **e** (1) : to draw (an oar) through the water ⟨~*ed* an oar in the winning shell⟩ (2) : ROW ⟨~*ed* a dinghy across the star-bright water to the lugger —Olaf Ruhen⟩ **f** : to set in action or operation ⟨~*ed* a fire alarm⟩ ⟨some positive safeguard was required against the chance of signalmen ~*ing* the wrong levers —O.S.Nock⟩ ⟨~ the trigger⟩ **g** (1) *baseball* : to hit (a pitched ball) into or toward left field from a right-handed batting stance or into or toward right field from a left-handed batting stance ⟨some left-handed batters are shallow left field hitters but may ~ the ball a mile to right —Lou Boudreau⟩ (2) *cricket* : to hit (a bowled ball) to the on side with a stroke resembling a drive in which the bat swings downward and approximately parallel to the popping crease (3) *golf* : to hit (a ball) toward the left from a right-handed swing or toward the right from a left-handed swing **3** : to draw apart : REND, TEAR ⟨hath turned aside my ways, and ~*ed* me in pieces —Lam 3:11 (AV)⟩ ⟨~*ed* his opponent's arguments to bits⟩ **4 a** : to make (as a proof or impression) by printing **b** : to make a proof or impression of (as a type form, lithographic stone, etching) **5 a** : to remove or cause to be removed from a place, enclosure, or situation ⟨started ~*ing* the wounded out of the vehicles —J.P.O'Neill⟩ ⟨get the prop off, ~ that tail shaft and put in the spare —K.M.Dodson⟩ ⟨~*ed* the pitcher in the third inning⟩ ⟨traveling gagman who ~*s* jokes out of his inside pockets —Lee Rogow⟩ **b** : to bring (a weapon) into the open ready for use esp. by removing from a sheath : DRAW ⟨~*ed* a gun on his partner —Erle Stanley Gardner⟩ ⟨~*ed* a knife on me and tried to slash my face —William Goyen⟩ **c** : to draw from a barrel or other container ⟨~*ing* pints of porter for the men off the boats —Frank Ritchie⟩ **d** : to remove (a bullet) from a cartridge **e** : to remove the old construction from (a book) preparatory to rebinding **f** (1) : to call out on strike ⟨~*ed* all the workers out of the plant⟩ (2) : to call a strike in ⟨~*ed* the plant⟩ (3) : to call (a strike) into effect ⟨~*ed* a strike in the plant⟩ **g** : to break up ⟨they ~*ed* camp and headed for home⟩ **6 a** : to carry out with daring and imagination ⟨~*ed* another coup, sailing his fleet out under cover of darkness —*Amer. Guide Series: Vt.*⟩ ⟨~*ed* a play that was entirely unexpected —F.G.Lieb⟩ **b** (1) : to put (a crime) into execution : COMMIT ⟨concluded that the same bandit probably had ~*ed* all three holdups —Al Spiers⟩ (2) : to be guilty of ⟨~ a boner⟩ (3) : to do, perform, or say with a deceptive intent : PERPETRATE ⟨had been ~*ing* all this stuff for years and getting away with it —Richard Bissell⟩ ⟨~ a fast one⟩ **c** : to draw or carry out as an assignment or duty ⟨was ~*ing* KP when his discharge papers came through —Mack Morriss⟩ ⟨~*ed* 23 combat missions⟩ **7 a** : to put on : ASSUME ⟨~*ed* a reluctant grin as he rode away —L.C. Douglas⟩ **b** *slang* : to act or behave in the manner of ⟨~ a Simon Legree⟩ **8 a** : to draw the support or attention of : ATTRACT ⟨~*ed* more votes than his running mates⟩ ⟨~*ed* the largest crowds in baseball history⟩ **b** : OBTAIN, SECURE ⟨~*ed* an A in his English course⟩ ⟨the motorist who dawdles at less than forty ~*s* a ticket —Noel Houston⟩ **9** : to demand or obtain an advantage over someone by the assertion of (as a real or fancied superiority) ⟨~*ed* his scientific authority on me —Saul Bellow⟩ ⟨liked to ~ his rank on his inferiors⟩ ~ *vi* **1 a** : to exert a pulling force or perform a pulling action ⟨the second button of his dark blue coat . . . was strained, ~*ing* on the threads that held it —Stuart Cloete⟩ ⟨somebody was ~*ing* again and again at the rusty knob —Marcia Davenport⟩ **b** : to move to or from a particular place or in a particular direction esp. through the exercise of mechanical energy or physical force ⟨the train ~*ed* into the platform⟩ ⟨the car ~*ed* out of the driveway⟩ ⟨the rowers ~*ed* clear of the ship⟩ ⟨~*ed* into town last night⟩ ⟨decided to ~ south to avoid pursuit⟩ **c** (1) : to take a drink ⟨~*ed* at rum bottles —S.T. Williamson⟩ (2) : to puff or draw hard in smoking ⟨~*ed* at his pipe and stared at the fire —Kathleen Freeman⟩ **d** *of a horse* : to strain against the bit **e** *of a hawk* : to feed by tearing or snatching ⟨~ upon a stump⟩ **f** : to draw a gun ⟨without warning he ~*ed* and fired⟩ **g** : to pull a ball ⟨he'd be a better hitter if he could learn to ~⟩ **2 a** : to admit of being pulled ⟨these roots ~ easily⟩ **b** *of type* : to become pulled out of a form (as by an ink roller) — often used with *out* **3** : to attract attention or influence people esp. to buy a particular product ⟨this ad ~*ed* better than any other we have run⟩ ⟨the clearance sale is ~*ing* well⟩ **4** : to feel or express strong sympathy : vigorously encourage or support : ROOT ⟨nearly always ~*s* for the underdog —*Time*⟩ ⟨was ~*ing* for his team to win⟩

syn DRAW, DRAG, HAUL, HALE, TUG, TOW: PULL is a general term meaning to move in the direction of the person or thing exerting force ⟨locomotives *pulling* the train⟩ ⟨*pulling* the drowning child from the water⟩ ⟨*pulling* the box off the shelf⟩ DRAW, often interchangeable with PULL, may sometimes apply to lighter action marked by smooth continuity or dexterity ⟨*draw* up a chair⟩ ⟨*draw* the curtains⟩ ⟨*draw* off the fluid with a pipette⟩ DRAG may suggest a slow, heavy, labored, rough pulling against resistance, over an uneven surface, or of something that does not readily roll or glide ⟨*dragging* the overturned car off the road⟩ ⟨a ship *dragging* her anchor⟩ ⟨*dragging* the rocks out of the field⟩ HAUL may apply to steady forceful heavy pulling or dragging; it may apply to transporting of heavy bulky materials, often those undergoing rough handling ⟨*haul* the trunk up the stairs⟩ ⟨he made a rope fast round the body and it was unceremoniously *hauled* aboard —Nevil Shute⟩ ⟨*haul* the coal from the mines⟩ ⟨*hauling* the bricks from the town upon his wheelbarrow —Pearl Buck⟩ ⟨*hauled* in, the fish are dumped into bins partially filled with cracked ice —*Amer. Guide Series: Fla.*⟩ HALE, once a fairly common synonym of HAUL, is now most likely to be used of the constraining, compelling, and dragging involved in arresting someone resisting ⟨natives, *haled* long distances to court as liquor witnesses —Elbridge Colby⟩ TUG applies to strenuous pulling, sometimes steady but more often in marked spasmodic bursts ⟨*tugging* at the ropes⟩ ⟨*tug* the rug out from under the furniture⟩ TOW applies to pulling along behind one with a rope, chain, cable, or bar ⟨tugs *towing* strings of barges⟩ ⟨a plane *towing* a glider⟩ ⟨*towing* the wrecked car to the garage⟩ — **pull a face** : to make a face : GRIMACE ⟨*pulled a face* as he tasted the bitter medicine⟩ — **pull a fast one** : to deceive by a crafty and usu. dishonest trick ⟨tried to *pull a fast one* and got caught⟩ — **pull a lone oar** : to act on one's own : proceed without help ⟨despite offers of assistance, he insists on *pulling a lone oar*⟩ — **pull a punch 1** : to hit an opponent with less than one's full power **2** : to act or express oneself in a cautious or guarded manner : PUSSYFOOT ⟨she has *pulled* no *punches* in coming directly to the extreme issues involved —Sara H. Hay⟩ — **pull caps** : QUARREL — **pull devil, pull baker** — used as a command (as in a tug of war) for each of two opposing sides to do its utmost in pulling against the other ⟨a sorry makeshift, a compromise arrived at by the familiar *pull devil, pull baker* method —S.H.Adams⟩ — **pull fodder** *Midland* : to gather fodder — **pull in one's horns** : draw in one's horns — **pull leather** *chiefly West* : to hang on to the saddle — **pull oneself together** : to regain one's self-possession : collect one's faculties ⟨it took some time for him to recover from the shock and *pull himself together*⟩ — **pull one's freight** *slang* : DEPART, LEAVE — **pull one's leg** : to deceive or hoodwink someone : play a trick or prank upon someone ⟨admit he had been *pulling my leg* —*London Calling*⟩ ⟨unaware that *their legs* were being *pulled* —O.S.J.Gogarty⟩ — **pull one's teeth** : to deprive one of weapons : render one harmless or defenseless — **pull one's weight** : to do one's full share of the work in a joint enterprise ⟨was dropped from the committee because he wasn't *pulling his weight*⟩ — **pull stakes** *or* **pull up stakes** : to move out : LEAVE ⟨*pulled up stakes* and went abroad to live⟩ — **pull strings** *or* **pull wires 1** : to exert influence (as political influence) or control over others without publicity **2** : to employ usu. secret influence or connections in order to accomplish one's ends ⟨*pulled wires* to get the position for his son⟩ — **pull the string** *of a baseball pitcher* : to throw a slow ball or change-of-pace pitch

²pull \"\ *n* -s *often attrib* [ME *pul*, fr. *pullen*, v.] **1 a** : the act or an instance of pulling ⟨gave a quick ~ on the rope⟩ ⟨supposed to hold the man's foot in a certain position and keep a steady straight ~ on it —R.H.Newman⟩ ⟨a candy ~⟩: as (1) : a draft of liquid or an inhalation of smoke : DRAG ⟨paused to take a long ~ on his stein of beer —Warner Bloomberg⟩ ⟨the old man would take a ~ at his pipe —Donn Byrne⟩ ⟨taking a ~ of milk from the can on the window sill —B.T. Cleeve⟩ (2) : a pull on the bridle of a horse to check its speed ⟨in race after race he won in a gallop, under a ~ —*Collier's Yr. Bk.*⟩ ⟨to avoid a collision our young friend has to take a ~ —Geoffrey Brooke⟩ (3) : the act of pulling at an oar; *broadly* : an excursion in a rowboat ⟨enjoyed the ~, though the river is very desolate-looking down there —Rachel Henning⟩ (4) : the act or an instance of pulling a ball (as in golf, cricket) ⟨a powerful ~ to leg⟩ ⟨a ~ stroke⟩ ⟨a ~ shot⟩ (5) : the change of course of a curling stone as it moves down the ice **b** (1) : a force or effort exerted in pulling ⟨its ~ is only one third that of the earth —J.G.Vaeth⟩ ⟨the sun's sideward ~ —*Newsweek*⟩ (2) : the effort expended in moving forward or upward ⟨a long ~ uphill⟩ ⟨his long hard ~ to get where he had got in her uncle's firm —Louis Auchincloss⟩ (3) : the force required to overcome the resistance to pulling of a specific object (as a bow or the trigger of a firearm) ⟨a bow with a 30 pound ~⟩ ⟨a trigger with a four pound ~⟩ (4) : the resistance of a paint to brushing : drag under the brush **2 a** : something (as a quality, attainment, or circumstance) that favors an individual in a comparison or contest : ADVANTAGE ⟨people who have had a classical education do start with a ~ —Archibald Marshall⟩ ⟨the old families, with all the ~ of their name and possessions —A.L.Rowse⟩ **b** : special influence exerted or capable of being exerted on behalf of a person or group ⟨got that job through ~ —W.J. Reilly⟩ ⟨has come up from the ranks without any ~ or family backing —*Current History*⟩ **3** : PROOF 10a **4** : a device (as a knob, cord, handle) for pulling something or for operating (as in opening, closing, or lifting) by pulling ⟨a plastic ~ for a window shade⟩ ⟨a wooden ~ for a desk drawer⟩ **5 a** : a force that attracts, compels, or influences : ATTRACTION ⟨writes of the natural world with scientific accuracy and the ~ of humor —N.J.Berrill⟩ ⟨a being constantly torn between the ~ of desires on the one hand and the demands of reason on the other —O.A.Johnson⟩ **b** : the ability to arouse public interest or stimulate public demand ⟨an actress with great box-office ~⟩ ⟨an advertising slogan with tremendous ~⟩ **c** : a response to an advertisement or advertising campaign ⟨a mail ~ heavy enough to make any sponsor drool —*New Republic*⟩ **6** : the length of a shotgun stock measured by the distance between the front of the trigger and the center of the butt plate **7 a** — used as a skeet shooter's command for the release of the high-house target; compare ¹MARK 1c(7) **b** — used as a trapshooter's command for the release of the target

pull·able \-ləbəl\ *adj* : capable of being pulled

pullaway \ˈ=ˌ=ˌ=\ *n* -s [by shortening] : POM-POM-PULL-AWAY

pull away *vi* : to draw oneself back or away ⟨*pulled away* from a high inside pitch⟩ ⟨was hard for him to *pull away* from the ties of home⟩

pullback \ˈ=ˌ=\ *n* -s [fr. *pull back*, v.] **1 a** : something that holds back : a restraining force : CHECK, DRAWBACK **b** : one that pulls back : REACTIONARY ⟨the diehards, the ~s, the enemies of progress —*Newsweek*⟩ **2** : a pulling or drawing back; *esp* : an orderly withdrawal of troops from a particular position or area ⟨a ~ of troops from the frontier —*Wall Street Jour.*⟩ ⟨the long-awaited, long-planned ~ from overseas of American troops —*Newsweek*⟩ **3 a** : an iron hook fixed to a casement to pull it shut or to hold it partly open at a fixed point **b** : something that returns a machine part to an initial position **c** : HAULBACK 1 **4** : a skirt style marked by fullness drawn to the back

pullboat \ˈ=ˌ=\ *n* : a heavy flatboat provided with winding drums and used to pull logs to the water's edge

pull box *n* : a metal box with a blank cover that is installed in an accessible place in a run of conduit to facilitate the pulling in of wires or cables

pulldevil \ˈ=ˌ=ˌ=\ *n* : a gang of fishhooks fastened back to back to be pulled through the water to catch fish

pull·doo \ˈpu̇lˌdü\ *n* -s [LaF *poule d'eau*, lit., water hen] : AMERICAN COOT

pull down *vt* **1 a** : DEMOLISH, DESTROY ⟨the wreckers *pulled* the building *down*⟩ **b** : to hunt down : OVERCOME ⟨together *pulling down* game too powerful for one to master alone —C.G.D.Roberts⟩ **2 a** : to bring to a lower level (as in price or value) : REDUCE ⟨the panic *pulled* stock prices *down*⟩ **b** : to depress in health, strength, or spirits : ENFEEBLE ⟨since his illness, he is very much *pulled down*⟩ **3** : to catch (a ball) esp. after a hard run ⟨*pulled* the ball *down* in deep right field⟩ **4** : to draw as wages or salary : receive as compensation or reward ⟨he's got to be good to *pull down* that kind of money —Richard Llewellyn⟩ ⟨*pulling down* the highest grades in the academy's history —*Time*⟩

¹pulldown \ˈ=ˌ=\ *n* -s [*pull down*] **1** : a movable arm set over a jigger to hold the profile that shapes ceramic ware on the mold **2** : a mechanism for rapidly moving a series of motion-picture film frames into place successively in the camera gate or at the aperture of a printer or a projector **3** : one of two or more samples of printing ink smeared on paper for purposes of comparison

²pulldown \(ˈ)=ˈ;=\ *adj* [*pull down*] : capable of being pulled down or intended to be pulled down ⟨a ~ bed⟩ ⟨a ~ seat⟩

pulled *past of* PULL

pulled bread *n* : bread pulled from the inside of a loaf in irregular pieces and browned lightly

pulled figs *n pl* : dried figs that are drawn flat by the fingers with the blossom end in the center before they are packed in layers in boxes

pulled wool *n* : wool removed from the pelt of a slaughtered sheep (as by sweating or a depilatory) — called also *skin wool*

pul·len \ˈpu̇lən\ *n* -s [ME *pullan, pullayn*, fr. OF *poleing* young cock, fr. LL *pullinus* of a chicken, fr. L, of a young animal, fr. *pullus* young of an animal, foal, chick + *-inus* -ine — more at FOAL] *dial chiefly Brit* : POULTRY

pull·er \ˈpu̇lə(r)\ *n* -s [ME, fr. *pullen* to pull + *-er* — more at PULL] : one that pulls ⟨proud setter up and ~ down of kings —*Shak.*⟩: as **a** : an instrument or device for pulling or extracting something ⟨a tack ~⟩ ⟨a cork ~⟩ **b** (1) : one that stretches, softens, and removes flesh from fur pelts (2) : one that removes wool from sheepskins (3) : a worker who pulls metal parts from a heat-treating furnace (4) : a shoe worker who stretches and fastens uppers into the proper shape and position for lasting (5) : a laundry worker who pulls articles from a washing machine and takes them to the extractor (6) : a textile worker who bunches bleached yarn skeins **c** : a horse that habitually thrusts its head forward against the bit and so maintains a pull on the reins **d** : one that releases clay targets from a trap for skeet shooters and trapshooters **e** : a long-handled stout elliptical knife used in turpentining for opening a face that is beyond ordinary reach **f** : one that draws business ⟨this ad is an excellent ~⟩

puller-in \'ˌ=ˌ=\ *n, pl* **pullers-in** [*pull in* + *-er*] **:** one that pulls in; *specif* **:** a man who stands in front of a store or place of entertainment and tries sometimes forcibly to get passersby to enter

pull·ery \'pu̇lərē\ *n* -ES [¹*pull* + *-ery*] **:** an establishment for removing wool from sheep skins

pul·let \'pu̇lət, *usu* -əd.+V\ *n* -s [ME *polet, pulett* young chicken, young fowl, fr. MF *poulet, pollet,* fr. OF, dim. of *poul* cock, fr. LL *pullus,* fr. L, young of an animal, foal, chick — more at FOAL] **:** a young hen; *specif* **:** a hen of the common fowl less than a year old

pullet disease *n* **:** BLUE COMB

¹**pul·ley** \'pu̇lē, -li\ *n* -s [ME *poley, pouley,* fr. MF *polie,*

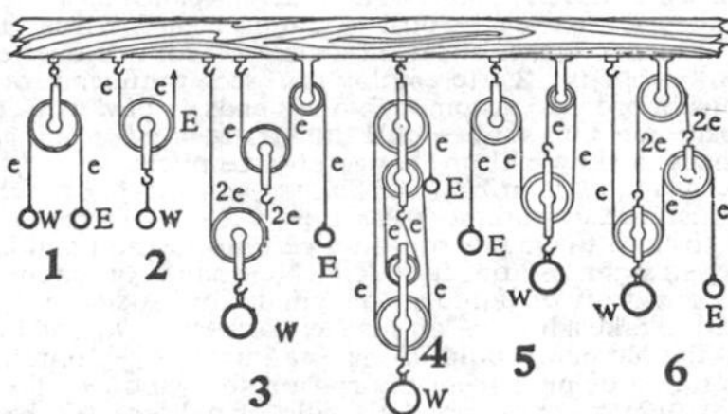

pulley 1b: various tackles showing theoretical ratios of weight lifted, *W,* to effort, *E,* and tensions in various cords, *e: 1* W=E; *2* W=2E; *3, 4, 6,* W=4E; *5* W=3E

poulie, fr. (assumed) VL *polidium,* prob. fr. (assumed) LGk *polidion,* dim. of Gk *polos* pivot, axis, pole — more at POLE (extremity of an axis)] **1 a :** a small wheel with a grooved rim **:** SHEAVE **b :** a sheave with the pin on which it turns, the frame in which it runs, and the flexible rope, cord, or chain passing through the groove that is used singly to change the direction and point of application of a pulling force applied at one end of the rope, cord, or chain and singly or in any of various definite combinations to increase the applied force esp. for lifting weights — see TACKLE **2 a :** a single pulley or a combination of pulleys with the necessary ropes to form a tackle regarded as one of the simple machines or mechanical powers **b :** a wheel of any size with a flat, curved, or grooved rim often of considerable width revolvable on its axis and supported by a bearing or bearings that is used to transmit power by means of a band or belt passing over its rim or a cord, rope, or chain or several of them running in its groove or grooves — see CONE PULLEY, EXPANDING PULLEY, IDLER PULLEY, MULE PULLEY, SPLIT PULLEY, TENSION PULLEY; compare DRUM, SPROCKET WHEEL **3 :** TROCHLEA

²**pulley** \"\ *n* -s [alter. (influenced by ¹*pulley*) of ME *puleyn,* fr. MF *poulain,* lit., foal, fr. LL *pullamen,* fr. L *pullus* young of an animal — more at FOAL] **:** a slideway for barrels

pulley block *n* **:** BLOCK 4a

pulley bone *n* [¹*pull* + *-ey*] *chiefly Midland* **:** WISHBONE

pulley frame *n* **:** HEADFRAME

pulley lathe *n* **:** a lathe for turning and crowning pulleys

pulley stile *n* **:** the upright of a window frame into which a pulley is fixed and along which the sash slides

pulley tap *n* **:** a tap with a long shank for tapping setscrew holes in the hubs of pulleys

pull hitter *n* **:** a baseball batter who consistently pulls the ball

pulli *pl of* PULLUS

pul·li·cat \'pələkət, -lē,kat\ *or* **pul·li·cate** \-ləkət, -lē,kāt\ *n* -s [fr. *Pulicat,* town of the southeastern coast of India] **:** BANDANNA

pull in *vt* **1 :** CHECK, RESTRAIN ⟨*pull* a horse *in*⟩ ⟨begin to *pull in* its expenses without overmuch damaging its charm —Harold Hobson⟩ ⟨*pull in* resolution —Shak.⟩ **2 :** ARREST ⟨was *pulled in* for questioning in connection with the crime⟩ ⟨took one look and *pulled* him *in*⟩ ~ *vi* **:** to arrive at a destination or come to a stop ⟨the train *pulled in* on time⟩ ⟨when a car *pulled in* he would go out to it, dressed in a white coverall —Robert McLaughlin⟩

¹**pull-in** \(')=ˌ=\ *adj* [*pull in*] **:** used for or having the effect of pulling in

²**pull-in** \"\ *n* -s [*pull in*] *Brit* **:** a roadside eating place **:** DRIVE-IN ⟨supposes that you can always stop at any *pull-in* . . . and be given a delicious meal for a small sum —Anthony Powell⟩ — called also *pull-up*

pulling *pres part of* PULL

pulling boat *n* **:** ROWBOAT

pull-in torque *n* **:** the maximum constant torque under which a motor will accelerate from rest to approximate normal speed

¹**pull·man** \'pu̇lmən\ *n* -s *often cap* [after George M. *Pullman* †1897 Am. inventor] **:** a railroad passenger car with specially comfortable furnishings for day or esp. for night travel — used orig. of a parlor or sleeping car operated by a particular manufacturer

²**pullman** \"\ *adj* **1 :** of, relating to, or suitable for use in a pullman ⟨~ ticket⟩ ⟨~ case⟩ **2 :** designed for compactness and efficiency ⟨~ kitchen⟩

pullman conductor *n* **:** a railroad employee who supervises the porter and maid service and provides for the comfort of passengers in the sleeping, parlor, buffet, and observation cars

pull off *vt* **:** to carry out despite difficulties **:** complete successfully against great odds ⟨*pulled* the scheme *off*⟩ ⟨the only man in our time to have *pulled off* the miracle of writing a verse comedy —W.F.Kerr⟩

¹**pull-on** \(')=ˌ=\ *adj* [fr. *pull on,* v.] **:** designed to be put on by being pulled on ⟨*pull-on* sports hat in gaily colored felts —*Women's Wear Daily*⟩

²**pull-on** \"\ *n* -s **:** an article of clothing (as a glove, girdle, sweater) that is pulled on to be worn and is usu. made without a placket or similar opening

pul·lo·rum disease \pə'lōrəm-, -lȯrəm-\ *also* **pullorum** *n* -s [L *pullorum,* gen. pl. of *pullus* young of an animal, foal, chick — more at FOAL] **:** salmonellosis of the chicken and less commonly of other birds that is caused by infection with a bacterium (*Salmonella pullorum*) transmitted both through the egg and from chick to chick, that is highly fatal in the young and is marked by weakness, lassitude, lack of appetite, and commonly by white or yellowish diarrhea, and that is frequently symptomless in mature birds but persists as an infection in the ovary resulting in lowered egg production and infertility and passing of the infection to the next generation — see BACILLARY WHITE DIARRHEA

pull out *vi* **1 :** LEAVE ⟨the troops *pulled out* for home⟩ **2 :** WITHDRAW ⟨one or the other of the two big unions might eventually *pull out* —*N.Y.Times*⟩

¹**pullout** \(')=ˌ=\ *n* -s [*pull out*] **1 :** something that can be pulled out: as **a :** an outsize leaf that is secured between and folded to the same size as the ordinary leaves of a book or magazine ⟨a ~ carrying an illustration 3 pages wide⟩ **b :** readily removable printed matter placed between the leaves of a magazine and often attached by a wire stitch **2 :** the act or an instance of pulling out: as **a :** an instance of the accidental pulling out of type (as by an inking roller) from a form that is being printed or proofed — compare DROPOUT, WORK-UP **b :** a maneuver in which an airplane goes from a dive to horizontal flight **c :** a withdrawal (as of troops) from a particular area

²**pullout** \"\ *adj* [*pull out*] **:** used for or having the effect of pulling out **:** capable of being pulled out ⟨the ~ seat of this new space-saver desk —*Retailing Daily*⟩

pull-out torque *n* **:** the maximum torque a motor will carry without an abrupt drop in speed

pull over *vi* **:** to steer one's vehicle to the side of the road ⟨the trooper ordered him to *pull over*⟩ ~ *vt* **:** to locate (the forepart of a shoe) in correct position on the last and secure to the insole or to the sole in the case of a turned shoe

¹**pullover** \(')=ˌ==\ *adj* [*pull over*] **:** designed to be put on by being pulled over the head ⟨consists of a ~ parka with a hood —Farley Mowat⟩

²**pullover** \"\ *n* -s **:** a garment (as a sweater, shirt, or blouse) that is put on by being pulled over the head and is usu. made without a placket or similar opening

pullover

pull pin *n* **:** a pin that when pulled disconnects or unlocks two parts of a machine and usu. reverses the process when pushed

pull round *vt* **:** to restore to good health ⟨the doctor *pulled* him *round*⟩ ~ *vi* **:** to regain one's health ⟨after two days of high fever, he began to *pull round*⟩

pulls *pres 3d sing of* PULL, *pl of* PULL

pullshovel \'=ˌ==\ *n* **:** BACKHOE

pull socket *n* **:** a lamp socket with a pull switch

pull station *n* **:** a fire-alarm apparatus operated by pulling a handle or hook

pull strap *or* **pull tab** *n* **:** a leather or fabric loop or tab attached to the top of a shoe or boot to help in drawing it on — compare BACKSTRAP

pull switch *n* **:** a snap switch operated by pulling a chain or cord

pull through *vt* **:** to help through a dangerous or difficult period or situation ⟨new capital is needed to *pull* the business *through* its difficulties⟩ ~ *vi* **:** to survive a dangerous or difficult period or situation ⟨was so ill that no one thought he would *pull through*⟩

pull-through \(')=ˌ=\ *n* -s [fr. *pull through,* v.] **:** something that is pulled through; *specif* **:** a cord fitted at one end with a weight and at the other with a brush and used for cleaning the bores of small arms

pull-through torque *n* **:** PULL-IN TORQUE

pull together *vi* **:** to work in harmony **:** COOPERATE ⟨learned to *pull together* for the good of all⟩

pull toy *n* **:** a toy designed to be pulled along the ground and usu. having moving parts that make sounds as it is pulled

pul·lu·lant \'pəlyələnt\ *adj* [L *pullulant-, pullulans,* pres. part. of *pullulare*] **:** SPROUTING, BUDDING

pul·lu·lar·ia \ˌpəlyə'la(a)rēə\ *n, cap* [NL, fr. L *pullulare* + NL *-aria*] **:** a genus of fungi (family Pseudosaccharomycetaceae) forming yeastlike colonies that are at first dirty white, then streaked with dark green or black, and eventually wholly black and more or less leathery and including a form (*P. pullulans*) that causes discoloration of pulp and paper

pul·lu·late \'pəlyəˌlāt, *usu* -ād.+V\ *vi* -ED/-ING/-S [L *pullulatus,* past part. of *pullulare* to sprout, fr. *pullulus* young of an animal, chick, sprout, dim. of *pullus* young of an animal — more at FOAL] **1 a :** to send out shoots or show signs of growth **:** BUD, GERMINATE **b :** to breed rapidly **:** produce abundantly ⟨his muse ~s with dizzying speed —Victor Purcell⟩ **2 a :** to increase rapidly **:** become abundant **:** MULTIPLY ⟨in the course of the argument, the most enormous errors of fact . . . simply ~ —George Saintsbury⟩ **b :** SWARM, TEEM ⟨the bleak ground ~s with jackrabbits —A.J.Liebling⟩ ⟨the pavements of hell ~ with liars, thieves, murderers —Bruce Marshall⟩

pul·lu·la·tion \ˌ==='lāshən\ *n* -s **1 :** the act or an instance of pullulating ⟨I like ~; everything ought to increase and multiply as hard as it can —Aldous Huxley⟩ **2 :** GEMMATION

pull up *vt* **1 :** to bring up short **:** CHECK, REBUKE ⟨*pulled* him *up* for speaking in an insulting tone⟩ **2 :** to bring to a stop **:** HALT ⟨the kids *pulled up* their pony and sat watching —Ross Annett⟩ ~ *vi* **1 a :** to check oneself ⟨was advised by his doctor to *pull up* and take it easy⟩ **b :** to come to a halt **:** STOP ⟨*pulled up* at the gas station⟩ **2 :** to draw even with or to go ahead of others in a race or contest ⟨coming into the stretch, the big horse was third, but he began to *pull up* and won by a nose⟩

pull-up \(')=ˌ=\ *n* -s [fr. *pull up,* v.] **1 :** the act or an instance of pulling up: as **a :** a maneuver in which an airplane in level flight is forced into a short climb **b :** an arm strengthening exercise in which a person pulls himself up from an extended hanging position until his chin is higher than the supporting bar or rings **2** *Brit* **:** PULL-IN ⟨the place used to be a *pull-up* for lorry drivers —*Punch*⟩

pul·lus \'pələs\ *n, pl* **pul·li** \-əˌlī\ [NL, fr. L, young of an animal, chick — more at FOAL] **:** a young bird in the downy stage

pully-haul \'pu̇lē,=\ *vi* [¹*pull* + *-y* + *haul*] **:** to pull and haul with one's full strength or with combined strength

pulmo- *comb form* [L *pulmo* — more at PULMONARY] **1 :** lung ⟨*pulmo*metry⟩ **2 :** pulmonic and ⟨*pulmo*gastric⟩

pul·mo·branchia \ˌpəl(ˌ)mō+\ *n, pl* **pulmobranchiae** [NL, fr. *pulmo-* + *-branchia*] **1 :** a gill or similar organ so modified as to breathe air **2 :** a book lung (as of a spider) — **pul·mo·branchial** \ˌ==+\ *adj* — **pul·mo·branchiate** \"+\ *adj or n*

pul·mo·cutaneous \ˌ=(ˌ)=+\ *adj* [*pulmo-* + *cutaneous*] **:** of or relating to the lungs and the skin

pulmocutaneous artery *or* **pulmocutaneous arch** *n* **:** either of the posterior pair of arterial arches that arise from the truncus arteriosus in amphibians, divide into pulmonary and cutaneous arteries, and transport venous blood to the respiratory surfaces of the skin, buccal cavity, and lungs

pul·mo·gastric \ˌ=(ˌ)=+\ *adj* [*pulmo-* + *gastric*] **:** relating to the lungs and stomach

pul·mom·e·ter \(ˌ)pəl'mäməd·ə(r)\ *n* [*pulmo-* + *-meter*] **:** SPIROMETER

pul·mom·e·try \-ə·trē, -ri\ *n* -ES [*pulmo-* + *-metry*] **:** the determination of the capacity of the lungs

pulmon- *also* **pulmoni-** *or* **pulmono-** *comb form* [L *pulmon-, pulmo* — more at PULMONARY] **:** lung ⟨*pulmon*al⟩ ⟨*pulmoni*ferous⟩ **:** pulmonary and ⟨*pulmono*cardiac⟩

pul·mo·nal \'pəlmənᵊl\ *adj* [*pulmon-* + *-al*] **:** PULMONARY

¹**pul·mo·nar·ia** \ˌpəlmə'na(a)rēə\ *n, cap* [NL, fr. L, fem. of *pulmonarius*] **:** a genus of European herbs (family Boraginaceae) having large basal leaves, cymose blue flowers with a 5-lobed funnel-shaped corolla, and large nutlets — see BETHLEHEM SAGE, LUNGWORT

²**pulmonaria** \"\ *n pl, cap* [NL, fr. L, neut. pl. of *pulmonarius*] *in some esp former classifications* **:** a group comprising the pulmonate arachnids (as the scorpions and spiders)

³**pulmonaria** \"\ [NL, fr. L, neut. pl. of *pulmonarius*] *syn of* PULMONATA

¹**pul·mo·nary** \'pu̇lmə,nerē, 'pəl-, -ri\ *adj* [L *pulmonarius,* fr. *pulmon-, pulmo* lung + *-arius* -ary; akin to Gk *pleumōn* lung, Skt *kloman* right lung, Lith *plaũčiai* lungs, and perh. to Gk *plein* to sail, float; fr. the fact that lungs float in water — more at FLOW] **1 :** of, relating to, or associated with the lungs **2 :** resembling or functioning like a lung **3 :** PULMONATE **4 :** carried on by the lungs

²**pulmonary** \"\ *n* -ES [NL ¹*Pulmonaria*] **:** LUNGWORT

pulmonary arch *n* **:** the fetal left fifth aortic arch that persists as the pulmonary artery

pulmonary artery *n* **:** an artery that conveys venous blood from the heart to the lungs and in man arises from the right ventricle, runs upward and backward, and divides into the right pulmonary artery which passes under the arch of the aorta and goes to the right lung and the left pulmonary artery which goes to the left lung with further division into branches that accompany the bronchial tubes

pulmonary circulation *n* **:** the passage of venous blood from the right auricle of the heart through the right ventricle and pulmonary arteries to the lungs where it is oxygenated and its return via the pulmonary veins to enter the left auricle and participate in the systemic circulation — used of man and animals with a complete double circulation

pulmonary heart *n* **:** the right atrium and right ventricle — compare SYSTEMIC HEART

pulmonary plexus *n* **:** either of two nerve plexuses that are superficial and deep and lie on either aspect of the bronchi and distributing fibers mainly from the vagus to the lungs

pulmonary sac *also* **pulmonary cavity** *n* **:** a hollow organ having a contractile exterior opening and lined with a network of blood vessels that functions as a lung in most land mollusks

pulmonary valve *n* **:** a valve consisting of three crescentic cusps separating the pulmonary artery from the right ventricle

pulmonary vein *n* **:** a valveless vein that returns oxygenated blood from the lungs to the heart and in man is commonly one of a pair for each lung

¹**pul·mo·na·ta** \ˌ=='nād·ə, -ād·ə\ *n pl, cap* [NL, fr. *pulmon-* + *-ata*] **:** a very large order of Gastropoda (subclass Euthyneura) comprising most land snails and slugs and many freshwater snails that are distinguished by lacking gills which are usu. replaced by a lung or respiratory sac formed by the modification of the mantle cavity and communicating with the exterior by a contractile orifice capable of being entirely closed in which blood vessels line the walls and by having no true operculum and a nervous system that is concentrated and not twisted — see BASOMMATOPHORA, STYLOMMATOPHORA

²**pulmonata** \"\ [NL, fr. *pulmon-* + *-ata*] *syn of* PNEUMOBRANCHIA

³**pulmonata** \"\ [NL, fr. *pulmon-* + *-ata*] *syn of* PULMONARIA

¹**pul·mo·nate** \'pəlmənət, -ˌnāt\ *adj* [*pulmon-* + *-ate*] **1 :** having lungs or organs resembling lungs **2** [NL ¹*Pulmonata*] **:** relating to the Pulmonata or Pulmonifera

²**pulmonate** \"\ *n* -s **:** a gastropod of the order Pulmonata

pul·mo·nat·ed \'==ˌnād·əd\ *adj* [*pulmon-* + *-ate* + *-ed*] **:** PULMONATE 1

pul·mo·nec·to·my \ˌ==='nektəmē\ *n* -ES [*pulmon-* + *-ectomy*] **:** PNEUMECTOMY

pulmoni- *or* **pulmono-** — see PULMON-

pul·mon·ic \(ˌ)pəl'mänik, -nēk\ *adj* [F *pulmonique,* fr. MF, fr. *pulmon-* + *-ique* -ic] **1 :** relating to or affecting the lungs **:** PULMONARY **2 :** of or relating to the pulmonary artery or to the junction between this artery and the right ventricle ⟨~ stenosis may be associated with pulmonary atherosclerosis⟩ **3 :** having inner closure at the bottom of the lungs — used of a phonetic stop or stop articulation ⟨consonants which include ejective and ~ variants of the characteristic lateral affricate —W.K.Matthews⟩

pul·mon·i·fer \(ˌ)=ˈmänəfə(r)\ *n* -s [NL *Pulmonifera*] **:** one of the Pulmonifera

¹**pul·mo·nif·era** \ˌpəlmə'nif(ə)rə\ [NL, fr. *pulmon-* + L *-fera* (neut. pl. of *-fer*)] *syn of* PULMONATA

²**pulmonifera** \"\ *n pl, cap* [NL, fr. *pulmon-* + L *-fera*] **:** a group of terrestrial snails (suborder Taenioglossa) having the gill replaced by a pulmonary sac

pul·mo·nif·er·ous \ˌ==ˌnif(ə)rəs\ *adj* [*pulmon-* + *-ferous*] **:** PULMONATE

pul·mo·no·cardiac \ˌpəlmə(ˌ)nō+\ *adj* [*pulmon-* + *cardiac*] **:** of, relating to, or involving both heart and lungs ⟨~ failure⟩

pul·mo·tor \'pu̇lˌmōd·ə(r), 'pəl-, -ōtə-\ *n* [fr. *Pulmotor,* a trademark] **:** a respiratory apparatus for pumping oxygen or air or a mixture of the two into and out of the lungs

pul·mo·trachearia \ˌpəlmō+\ [NL, fr. *pulmo-* + *Trachearia*] *syn of* PULMONARIA

¹**pulp** \'pəlp\ *n* -s *often attrib* [MF *poulpe,* fr. L *pulpa* solid flesh, pulp] **1 :** a moist slightly cohering mass consisting of soft undissolved animal or vegetable matter: as **a** (1) **:** the soft succulent part of fruit ⟨the ~ of a grape⟩ ⟨orange ~⟩ (2) **:** the soft pith of various stems (3) **:** PULPWOOD **b :** a soft mass of vegetable matter (as of apples or sugarcane) from which most of the water has been extracted by pressure **c :** a cellulosic material prepared by chemical or mechanical means chiefly from wood but also from rags and other materials and used in making paper and cellulose products (as rayon and cellulose acetate) — compare STOCK, STUFF **d** (1) **:** a tissue or part resembling pulp; *esp* **:** DENTAL PULP (2) **:** the characteristic somewhat spongy tissue of the spleen (3) **:** the fleshy portion of the fingertip **2 a :** pulverized ore mixed with water so as to resemble mud **b :** dry crushed ore **3 a :** pulpy condition or character **b :** something in such a condition or having such a character ⟨hammering his face in a way to make ~ —Arthur Morrison⟩ ⟨reduced to a shapeless ~ by concussion —Liam O'Flaherty⟩ **c :** something without strength or in a condition of fatigue or nervous exhaustion ⟨a life that would have reduced a lesser woman to a ~ —E.A. Weeks⟩ **4 :** a thick mass of white lead and water that settles to the bottom of a suspension of white lead in water and that when dry is commercial dry white lead **5 a :** a magazine or book using rough-surfaced paper made of wood pulp and often dealing with sensational material — compare SLICK **b :** tawdry or sensational writing ⟨other ~s that give the outside world such an odd picture of the American way of life —Joan Comay⟩

²**pulp** \"\ *vb* -ED/-ING/-S *vt* **1 :** to reduce to pulp **:** cause to appear pulpy **2 :** to form (material) into a pulp **3 :** to deprive of the pulp **4 :** to produce or reproduce (written matter) in pulp form ~ *vi* **:** to become pulp or pulpy

pulp·al \'pəlpəl\ *also* **pulp·ar** \-pə(r)\ *adj* **:** of or relating to pulp esp. of a tooth ⟨a ~ abscess⟩ — **pulp·al·ly** \-pəlē\ *adv*

pulpboard \'=ˌ=\ *n* **:** a solid board or a combination board made from various fibers (as wood)

pulp canal *n* **:** the part of the pulp cavity lying in the root of a tooth

pulp cavity *n* **:** the central cavity of a tooth containing the dental pulp and being made up of the pulp canal and the pulp chamber

pulp chamber *n* **:** the part of the pulp cavity lying in the crown of a tooth — see TOOTH illustration

pulp color *n* **:** a pigment that is prepared by precipitation in water, filtered, and pressed but not dried and that is marketed in the water paste form — compare ⁴DISTEMPER 2c, DRY COLOR, FLUSH COLOR, ⁴LAKE 1b

pulp·ec·to·my \ˌpəl'pektəmē\ *n* -ES [¹*pulp* + *-ectomy*] **:** the removal of the pulp of a tooth

pulp engine *n* **:** BEATER 1n

pulp·er \'pəlpə(r)\ *n* -s **:** one that makes, grinds, mixes, or removes pulp **:** one that reduces something (as fruit or guncotton) to pulp; *specif* **:** a machine that reduces (as broke and waste paper) to pulp in the presence of water in papermaking

pul·pe·ria \ˌpu̇lpə'rēə\ *n* -s [AmerSp *pulperia,* fr. Sp *pulpa* pulp, meat, fruit, candied fruit (fr. L, solid meat, pulp) + *-eria* -ery — more at PULP] **:** a Spanish American rural grocery store often functioning also as a drinking establishment

pulpier *comparative of* PULPY

pulpies *pl of* PULPY

pulpiest *superlative of* PULPY

pulp·ify \'pəlpəˌfī\ *vt* -ED/-ING/-ES [¹*pulp* + *-ify*] **:** to make pulp of **:** PULP ⟨to ~ wood fiber⟩

pulp·i·ly \-pəlē\ *adv* **:** in a pulpy manner

pulp·i·ness \-pēnəs, -pin-\ *n* -ES **:** the quality or state of being pulpy

¹**pul·pit** \'pu̇lˌpit, 'pəl-, -ˌpət, *usu* -d.+V\ *n* -s *often attrib* [ME, fr. LL *pulpitum,* fr. L, scaffold, stage, platform] **1 a :** a usu. enclosed elevated platform or a high reading desk used in preaching or conducting a service of worship ⟨an ornate medieval ~ with a flight of steps and a sounding board⟩ ⟨read from the large Bible on the ~⟩ **b :** an elevated structure for a machine operator ⟨an operator in the control ~ pressed a button —*Newsweek*⟩ **2** [ME, fr. L *pulpitum*] *obs* **:** an elevated platform for a public speaker **3 a :** the clergy as a profession **:** PREACHERS ⟨the power of the ~⟩ **b :** the ministry of preaching a religious faith **:** a preaching position ⟨called to a city ~⟩ **4 :** a support for a harpooner on the end of the bowsprit in a whaling ship

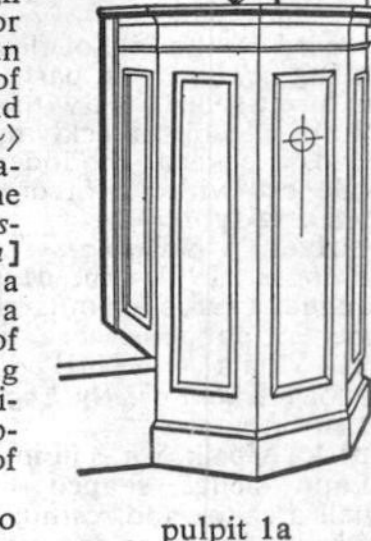

pulpit 1a

²**pulpit** \"\ *vb* -ED/-ING/-S *vt* **:** to supply with a pulpit or with preaching ~ *vi* **:** to preach from a pulpit

pul·pit·al \-ˌpid·ᵊl, -ˌpəd·ᵊl, -tᵊl\ *adj* **:** of or relating to a pulpit or preaching

¹**pul·pi·tar·i·an** \ˌpu̇lpə'ta(a)rēən, ˌpəl-, -ter-\ *n* -s [¹*pulpit* + *-arian*] **:** PREACHER; *also* **:** an advocate of preaching as essential to worship

²**pulpitarian** \"\ *adj* **:** of, relating to, or characteristic of preaching

pulpit bible *n, usu cap B* **:** a large Bible traditionally kept open on the pulpit or lectern of many Protestant churches

pulpit cloth *or* **pulpit hanging** *n* **:** the antependium of a pulpit

¹**pul·pi·teer** \ˌpu̇lpəˈti(ə)r, ˌpəl-, -iə\ *n* -s [¹*pulpit* + *-eer*] **:** one who speaks in or delivers sermons from a pulpit **:** PREACHER ⟨an eloquent ~⟩

²**pulpiteer** \"\ *vi* -ED/-ING/-S **:** PREACH, SERMONIZE ⟨~*ed* against the wets —*Newsweek*⟩

pul·pit·er \ˈpu̇l,pid·ə(r), ˈpəl-, -ˌpəd-\ *n* -s [¹*pulpit* + *-er*] **:** PREACHER

pulp·i·tis \ˌpəlˈpīd·əs\ *n, pl* **pulpit·i·des** \-pid·ə,dēz\ [NL, fr. E ¹*pulp* + NL *-itis*] **:** inflammation of pulp esp. of a tooth

pul·pit·ism \ˈpu̇l,pid·,izəm, ˈpəl-, -pəd-\ *n* -s **:** a characteristic, idea, or custom of preachers or preaching

pul·pit·less *pronunc at* PULPIT + ləs\ *adj* **:** having no pulpit

pulpit man *n* **:** an operator of a steel and iron rolling mill

pulpit rock *n* **:** CHIMNEY ROCK

pul·pit·ry \ˈpu̇l,pitrē, ˈpəl-, -pətrē\ *n* -ES **:** the teaching of the pulpit **:** PREACHING ⟨the platitudes of conventional ~ —John Beaufort⟩

pulp·less \ˈpəlpləs\ *adj* **:** having no pulp ⟨~ teeth⟩

pulp·ot·o·my \ˌpəlˈpäd·əmē\ *n* -ES [*pulp* + *-o-* + *-tomy*] **:** removal in a dental procedure of the coronal portion of the pulp of a tooth in such a manner that the pulp of the root remains intact and viable

pulp·ous \ˈpəlpəs\ *adj* [L *pulposus* fr. *pulpa* solid flesh, pulp + *-osus* -ous — more at PULP] **:** PULPY — **pulp·ous·ness** *n* -ES

pulps *pl of* PULP, *pres 3d sing of* PULP

pulpstone \ˈ=,=\ *n* **1 :** a massive grindstone used in the mechanical reduction of wood to pulp in papermaking **2 :** a lump of calcified tissue within the dental pulp

pulpwood \ˈ=,=\ *n* **1 :** any of various woods (as aspen, hemlock, pine, spruce) used in making pulp for paper; *also* **:** this wood after being macerated **2 :** the trees used for pulpwood

¹**pulpy** \ˈpəlpē, -pi\ *adj* -ER/-EST [¹*pulp* + *-y*] **:** resembling or consisting of pulp **:** SOFT, FLABBY, FLESHY ⟨the ~ substance of a peach⟩ ⟨men with streaks of flintlike obstinacy within their ~ exteriors —C.S.Forester⟩

²**pulpy** \"\ *n* -ES **:** PULP 5a

pulpy kidney disease *or* **pulpy kidney** *n* **:** a destructive enterotoxemia of lambs caused by clostridia (esp. *Clostridium welchii*) and characterized by softening and degeneration of the kidneys and often by accumulation of fluid about the heart

pulpy nucleus *n* **:** a very elastic but somewhat soft body of connective tissue that forms the central part of an intervertebral disk and is surrounded by the fibrous ring

pul·que \ˈpül(,)kā, -kē, ˈpu̇lkē\ *n* -s [MexSp, prob. fr. an obs. Nahuatl word derived fr. *poliuhqui, puliuhqui* decomposed, spoiled; fr. the fact that it spoils 24 to 36 hours after its preparation] **:** fermented drink that is made in Mexico from the juice of various magueys (esp. *Agave atrovirens*) and is the source of mescal

pul·que·ria \ˌpülkəˈrēə, ˌpu̇l-\ *n* -s [MexSp *pulqueria*, fr. *pulque* + Sp *-eria* -ery] **:** a Mexican shop that sells pulque

puls *pl of* PUL

pul·sant \ˈpəlsənt\ *adj* [L *pulsant-, pulsans*, pres. part. of *pulsare*] **:** PULSATING ⟨the hall is . . . ~ with men and women massed in the bonds of the tango —Waldo Frank⟩

pul·sa·tance \ˈpəlsəd·ən(t)s, -sətən-, -setᵊn-\ *n* -s **:** the angular velocity that may be associated with a periodic motion **:** 2 π times the frequency of a periodic motion

pul·sate \ˈpəl,sāt *chiefly Brit* ,=ˈ=, *usu* -ād·+V\ *vi* -ED/-ING/-S [L *pulsatus*, past part. of *pulsare* to beat, strike — more at PUSH] **1 :** to exhibit a pulse **:** BEAT ⟨an artery ~*s*⟩ **2 :** to throb or move rhythmically **:** vibrate esp. with life, activity, feeling ⟨a *pulsating* population which expands and contracts with changes in religious beliefs —M.D.Brockie⟩ ⟨behind every line . . . ~ the rhythms of the authors' hatred or contempt or scorn —L.O.Coxe⟩ ⟨the country is alive and *pulsating* with beauty —Alice Duncan-Kemp⟩ ⟨the river breeze *pulsated* warmly upward —Harriet La Barre⟩

syn PULSE, BEAT, THROB, PALPITATE: PULSATE suggests a rhythmic regular movement, typically that of the heart in alternate dilation and constriction ⟨the heart *pulsating*⟩ ⟨a motor *pulsating*⟩ It is often used figuratively in reference to healthy or vigorous action or inspiration ⟨great effort *pulsating* from the heart of this small island —Sir Winston Churchill⟩ PULSE applies to what flows or is thought of as flowing in a regular spurting rhythm ⟨through the tensed veins on his forehead the blood could be seen to *pulse* in nervous, stacatto bounds —Donn Byrne⟩ ⟨a small fountain *pulsed* in the court —Harry Sylvester⟩ ⟨her excitement, that *pulsed* with interest and curiosity —Robert Hichens⟩ BEAT is a nontechnical term for PULSE or PULSATE; it often applies to rhythmic motion with an audible effect ⟨the *beating* of the patient's heart⟩ ⟨drums *beating*⟩ THROB indicates strong pulsation, often abnormally strong, sometimes as though caused and accompanied by passion or agitation ⟨the planes' motors *throbbed* steadily, powerfully, on the field —Kay Boyle⟩ ⟨western Christendom *throbbed* to the news of the French Revolution —Stringfellow Barr⟩ ⟨the love which fills the letter, which *throbs* and burns in it, which speaks and argues in it —H.O.Taylor⟩ PALPITATE applies to rapid throbbing or vibrating, sometimes quivering or fluttering ⟨planet-ridden space, filled with the ether, *palpitating* with strange vibrations, like light and heat and wireless —W.E.Swinton⟩ ⟨the worshiper, *palpitating* emotionally after the performance of some anthem —A.T.Davison⟩

pul·sa·tile \ˈpəlsəd·ᵊl, -ə,til\ *adj* [ML *pulsatilis*, fr. L *pulsatus* + *-ilis* -ile] **1 :** PULSATING, THROBBING ⟨a ~ vascular tumor⟩ **2 :** vibrating when beaten or struck **:** PERCUSSIVE ⟨drums are ~ instruments⟩

pul·sa·til·la \ˌpəlsəˈtilə\ *n, cap* [NL, fr. L *pulsatus* + *-illa*, dim. suffix] *in some classifications* **:** a genus now usu. included as a section in *Anemone* that comprises the pasqueflowers which differ from the typical anemones chiefly in their very long feathery styles

pulsating current *n* **:** a direct current that has recurring more or less regular variations in magnitude

pulsating organ *n* **:** a minute muscular organ functioning as an accessory heart in various insects

pulsating star *n* **:** a star that alternately increases and decreases in size usu. with corresponding changes in brightness

pulsating vacuole *n* **:** CONTRACTILE VACUOLE

pul·sa·tion \ˌpəlˈsāshən\ *n* -s [L *pulsation-, pulsatio*, fr. *pulsatus* (past part. of *pulsare* to beat, strike) + *-ion-, -io* -ion — more at PUSH] **1 a :** a beating or throbbing esp. of the heart or of an artery **b :** a single beat of the heart or pulse **2 a :** rhythmical throbbing, contraction and expansion, moving, vibration, or undulation ⟨long heavy ~ of aeroplanes passing over —Angela Thirkell⟩ ⟨a ~ of the star as a whole —Leon Campbell & L.G.Jacchia⟩ ⟨at low frequencies, such as 10 per sec., ~ is sensed rather than vibration —R.S.Woodworth⟩ ⟨a slow ~, like the quiver of invisible wings, in the air —Ellen Glasgow⟩ **b :** a distinct step in such a series of rhythmical movements **:** BEAT, VIBRATION ⟨two ~*s* of continental glaciation —J.C.Frye & A.B.Leonard⟩ ⟨the island was elevated in a series of ~*s* —D.J.Miller⟩ ⟨in the course of these ~*s* in dominance the male may not actually move up the social scale —W.C.Allee⟩ ⟨the ~*s* of its engine had died away —Arnold Bennett⟩ **3 :** a periodically recurring alternate increase and decrease of pressure, volume, voltage, or other quantity **4** *Roman law* **:** a touching of another's body willfully or in anger

pul·sa·tion·al \-shənᵊl, -shnəl\ *adj* **:** of, relating to, or characterized by a pulsation

pulsation theory *n* **:** a theory that explains the peculiar features of such stars as the Cepheid variables by assuming an expansion and contraction of the star as a whole in a regular periodic pulsation

pul·sa·tive \ˈpəlsəd·iv\ *adj* [ME *pulsatif*, fr. MF, fr. L *pulsatus* + MF *-if* -ive] **:** BEATING, THROBBING, PULSATILE — **pul·sa·tive·ly** \-əvlē\ *adv*

pul·sa·tor \ˈpəlˈsād·ə(r), ˈ=,==\ *n* -s [L, fr. *pulsatus* + *-or*] **1 :** BEATER, STRIKER **2 :** something that beats or throbs in working: as **a :** PULSOMETER **b :** a device for producing pulsations in a reaction chamber by periodic discharges of gas or vapor

pul·sa·to·ry \ˈpəlsə,tōrē, -tȯr-, -ri\ *adj* **:** capable of pulsating **:** characterized by pulsation **:** THROBBING

¹**pulse** \ˈpəls *also* -l(t)s\ *n* -s [ME *pols, puls*, fr. OF *pols, pouls, pous* porridge, fr. L *pult-, puls* porridge made of meal and pulse, prob. fr. Gk *poltos* porridge — more at POLLEN] **1 :** the edible seeds of various leguminous crops (as peas and beans) **2 a :** a plant yielding pulse **b :** pulse plants

²**pulse** \"\ *n* -s *often attrib* [ME *pous, puls*, fr. MF *pous, pouls, pols*, fr. L *pulsus* beating, striking, pulse, fr. *pulsus*, past part. of *pellere* to drive, beat, push — more at FELT] **1 a :** a regularly recurrent wave of distention in arteries that results from the progress through an artery of blood injected into the arterial system at each contraction of the ventricles of the heart **b :** the palpable beat resulting from such pulse as detected in a superficial artery (as the radial artery) ⟨a very soft ~⟩; *often* **:** the number of such beats in a specified period of time (as one minute) ⟨a resting ~ of 70⟩ **2 a :** underlying sentiment, opinion, or drift esp. as discoverable by tact or skill in perception rather than by open inquiry; *also* **:** an indication of such ⟨one may feel the social, economic, and political ~ of the State —*Amer. Guide Series: Maine*⟩ ⟨one felt the ~ of the village in the pub —S.P.B.Mais⟩ ⟨the ~ of the wisdom and genius of the age —T.L.Peacock⟩ ⟨the ~ of international political purpose —Herbert Feis⟩ ⟨these farmers, owners of their land, are the ~ of anticommunism —George Weller⟩ **b :** feeling of life **:** throb of emotion **:** sensation of excitement **:** VITALITY ⟨new industry has quickened the ~ of the people —*Amer. Guide Series: Texas*⟩ ⟨stirred the ~ of mankind —M.R.Cohen⟩ ⟨awakened love's deep ~*s* —Vachel Lindsay⟩ **3 a :** pulsing movement **:** rhythmical beating, vibrating, or sounding ⟨the driller . . . feels the ~ of a bit far below his feet by the kick in his hand —*Lamp*⟩ ⟨the ~ of its drama is deep and slow —George Farwell⟩ ⟨the ~ of an engine⟩ **b :** PULSATION, BEAT, THROB; *specif* **:** a beat or stress in music or poetry **4 a :** a transient variation of electrical current, voltage, or some other quantity whose value is normally constant — often used of current variations produced artificially and repeated either with a regular period or according to some code **b :** an electromagnetic wave or modulation thereof having brief duration **c :** a brief disturbance transmitted through a medium ⟨a ~ of light⟩ ⟨a ~ of sound⟩ ⟨a ~ of pressure⟩ **5 :** a sudden sharp upswing in numbers (as of a kind of organism) usu. occurring at regular intervals ⟨annual plankton ~*s*⟩

³**pulse** \"\ *vb* -ED/-ING/-S *vi* **:** to exhibit a pulse or pulsation **:** THROB **:** move in pulses, beats, or periodic spurts **:** vibrate with life, sound, light ⟨an environment that ~*s* and glows —H.L.Mencken⟩ ~ *vt* **1 :** to drive by or as if by a pulsation **:** cause to pulsate ⟨the echoes had *pulsed* themselves to silence —Florette Henri⟩ ⟨a gentle surf *pulsed* the air —Ward Taylor⟩ **2 a :** to produce or modulate (as electromagnetic waves) in the form of pulses ⟨*pulsed* waves⟩ **b :** to cause to be emitted in pulses ⟨*pulsed* light⟩ **c :** to cause (an apparatus) to produce pulses ⟨a transmitter *pulsed* by an electron tube⟩ **syn** see PULSATE

pulsebeat \ˈ=,=\ *n* **1 a :** PULSE 1b **b :** regular rhythm ⟨the ~ of the universe⟩ **2 :** an indication of an underlying sentiment, opinion, or drift ⟨every ~ of that distrust which filled the souls of . . . people —Upton Sinclair⟩

pulse code modulation *n* **:** modulation of a radio wave or signal in which the intelligence is conveyed by a code or order of pulses of the wave that are usu. all of the same size and shape and that are transmitted at multiples of a standard time interval

pulse deficit *n* **:** the difference in a minute's time between the number of beats of the heart and the number of beats of the pulse observed in diseases of the heart

pulse duration modulation *n* **:** PULSE LENGTH MODULATION

pulse family *n* **:** LEGUMINOSAE

pulse frequency modulation *n* **:** modulation of a radio wave or signal in which the intelligence is conveyed by varying the frequency or repetition rate of the pulses of the wave

pulse-jet engine \ˈ=,=-\ *n* **:** a jet engine having in its forward end intermittent air-inlet valves designed to produce a pulsating thrust by the intermittent flow of hot gases

pulse length modulation *n* **:** modulation of a radio wave or signal in which the intelligence is conveyed by varying the length or duration of the pulses of the wave

pulse·less \ˈpəlsləs\ *adj* **:** having no pulse **:** lacking energy, animation, or purpose—**pulse·less·ly** *adv*—**pulse·less·ness** *n* -ES

pulse modulation *n* **:** modulation of a radio wave or signal by pulses

pulse position modulation *n* **:** modulation of a radio wave or signal in which the intelligence is conveyed by varying the time relationship of the pulses of the wave

pulse pressure *n* **:** the pressure that is characteristic of the arterial pulse and represents the difference between diastolic and systolic pressures of the heart cycle

puls·er \ˈpəlsə(r)\ *n* -s **:** a device to generate pulses or apply pulses for control

pulse radar *n* **:** radar that operates by emitting and receiving pulses at signal

pulse rate *n* **:** the rate of the arterial pulse usu. observed at the wrist and stated in beats per minute

pulses *pl of* PULSE, *pres 3d sing of* PULSE

pulse time modulation *n* **:** modulation of the time intervals between successive pulses of constant duration and amplitude in accordance with a signal; *specif* **:** a system of multiplex high-frequency transmission using this method of modulation

pulse-warmer \ˈ=,==\ *n* **:** WRISTER 1

pulse wave *n* **:** the wave of increased pressure started by the ventricular systole radiating from the semilunar valves over the arterial system at a rate varying between 20 and 30 feet a second in different arteries

pulse width modulation *n* **:** PULSE LENGTH MODULATION

pul·sif·ic \ˌpəlˈsifik\ *adj* [²*pulse* + *-i-* + *-fic*] **:** exciting the pulse **:** causing pulsation

pul·sim·e·ter \ˌpəlˈsimәd·ə(r)\ *n* [²*pulse* + *-i-* + *-meter*] **:** an instrument for measuring the pulse esp. for force and rate

pulsing *pres part of* PULSE

pul·sion \ˈpəlshən\ *n* -s [LL *pulsion-, pulsio*, fr. L *pulsus* (past part. of *pellere* to beat, drive, push) + *-ion-, -io* -ion — more at FELT] **:** the act or action of pushing or driving **:** PROPULSION ⟨these undirected and hence uncoordinated ~*s*, so prevalent in childhood —H.A.Murray⟩ — opposed to *traction*

pulsion diverticulum *n* **:** a diverticulum pushed out from a hollow organ by pressure from within; *specif* **:** a diverticulum of the esophagus as a result of the pressure from within resulting in herniation of the mucosa

pul·sive \ˈpəlsiv, -sēv *also* -səv\ *adj* [L *pulsus* (past part. of *pellere*) + E *-ive*] **:** impelling or tending to impel **:** PROPULSIVE — **pul·sive·ness** *n* -ES

pul·som·e·ter \ˌpəlˈsämәd·ə(r), -mәtə-\ *n* [ISV ²*pulse* + *-o-* + *-meter*] **1 :** a displacement pump with valves for raising water by steam partly by atmospheric pressure and partly by the direct action of the steam on the water without intervention of a piston — called also *vacuum pump* **2 a :** SPHYGMOGRAPH, PULSIMETER **b :** a watch with special dial used by physicians in determining the pulse rate

pul·ta·ceous \ˌpəlˈtāshəs\ *adj* [L *pult-, puls* porridge made of meal and pulse + E *-aceous* — more at PULSE] **:** having a consistency like that of porridge **:** MACERATED, PULPY

pul·ton *or* **pul·tun** \ˈpəltᵊn *also* -tən\ *n* -s [Hindi *palṭan*, fr. E *battalion*] **:** an infantry regiment in India

pu·lu \ˈpü,lü\ *n* -s [Hawaiian, fr. *pulu* wet, soaked] **:** a soft elastic yellowish brown vegetable wool obtained in Hawaii from the young fronds of tree ferns of the genus *Cibotium* (esp. *C. menziesii*) and formerly exported for mattress and pillow stuffing

pulv *abbr* **1** pulverized; pulverizer **2** [L *pulvis*] powder

pul·ver·a·ble \ˈpəlv(ə)rəbəl\ *adj* [L *pulverare* to bestrew with dust, pulverize (fr. *pulver-, pulvis* dust, powder) + E *-able* — more at POLLEN] **:** capable of being pulverized

pul·ver·ant \ˈpəlvərənt\ *adj* [L *pulverant-, pulverans*, pres. part. of *pulverare*] **:** PULVERIZED ⟨~ gypsum⟩

Pul·ver·a·tor \-,rād·ə(r)\ *trademark* — used for a device that reduces material to fine bits

pul·ver·iz·able \-,rīzəbəl, ,==ˈ===\ *adj* **:** capable of being pulverized

pul·ver·i·za·tion \-,pəlvərəˈzāshən, -,rīˈz-\ *n* -s [F *pulvérisation*, fr. MF *pulverisation*, fr. *pulveriser* + *-ation*] **:** the act or process of pulverizing ⟨avoiding the ~ of individual liberty and dignity —*New Republic*⟩

pul·ver·ize \ˈpəlvə,rīz\ *vb* -ED/-ING/-S *see -ize in Explan Notes* [MF *pulveriser*, fr. LL *pulverizare*, fr. L *pulver-, pulvis* dust, powder + *-izare* -ize — more at POLLEN] *vt* **1 :** to reduce (as by crushing, beating, or grinding) to very small particles (as in fine powder or dust) **:** ATOMIZE ⟨~ the soil with steel implements —Russell Lord⟩ ⟨mower . . . ~*s* grass clippings —*Star Weekly*⟩ **2 :** to destroy by or as if by smashing into fragments **:** DISINTEGRATE, ANNIHILATE, DEMOLISH, VANQUISH ⟨buildings *pulverized* by a tornado⟩ ⟨a bomb that could ~ a city⟩ ⟨if in the East Socialism has been *pulverized* by the totalitarian state —*Times Lit. Supp.*⟩ ⟨started as a slashing journalistic critic . . . joyfully *pulverizing* every kind of conventional nonsense —Edgar Johnson⟩ ~ *vi* **:** to become pulverized

pulverized sugar *n* **:** standard powdered sugar derived from granulated sugar by grinding and usu. after adding flour to prevent caking

pul·ver·iz·er \-zə(r)\ *n* -s **:** one that pulverizes; *specif* **:** ACME HARROW

pul·ver·ous \ˈpəlvərəs\ *adj* [L *pulver-, pulvis*, dust, powder + E *-ous* — more at POLLEN] **:** POWDERY

pul·ver·u·lent \(ˌ)pəlˈveryələnt\ *adj* [L *pulverulentus*, fr. *pulver-, pulvis* dust + *-ulentus* -ulent — more at POLLEN] **:** consisting of or reducible to fine powder **:** covered or looking as if covered with dust or powder **:** DUSTY, CRUMBLY ⟨if a mineral is ~, granular, or splintery —C.S.Hurlbut⟩ ⟨baking powder is a white ~ or finely granular compounded material —C.S. Bryan⟩ — **pul·ver·u·lent·ly** *adv*

pul·vic acid \ˈpəlvik-\ *n* [ISV *pulvic*, anagram of *vulpic*] **:** PULVINIC ACID

pul·vil \ˈpəl(,)vil\ *or* **pul·vil·lio** \ˌpəlˈvilē(,)ō\ *n* -s [It *polviglio*, fr. Sp *polvillo*, dim. of *polvo* dust, powder, fr. (assumed) VL *pulvus*, alter. of L *pulvis* — more at POLLEN] *archaic* **:** cosmetic or perfumed powder

pul·vil·lar \ˌpəlˈvilə(r), ˈpəlvəl-\ *adj* [NL *pulvillus* + E *-ar*] **:** of or relating to a pulvillus

pul·vil·li·form \ˌpəlˈvilə,fȯrm\ *adj* [NL *pulvillus* + E *-iform*] **:** having the shape or appearance of a pulvillus

pul·vil·lus \ˌpəlˈviləs\ *n, pl* **pulvil·li** \-i,lī\ [NL, fr. L, small cushion, dim. of *pulvinus* cushion] **:** a pad often covered with short hairs or an organ or process resembling or functioning like a cushion or sucker that occurs on an insect's foot between the claws of the last segment and often forms an adhesive organ

¹**pul·vi·nar** \ˌpəlˈvīnə(r)\ *n* -s *see sense 2* [L, cushioned seat, couch, fr. *pulvinus* cushion] **1 :** CUSHION **2** *pl* **pul·vi·nar·ia** \ˌpəlvəˈna(a)rēə\ **:** a cushioned couch reserved for the gods in Roman antiquity; *also* **:** a cushioned seat at a public spectacle **3** [NL, fr. L] **:** a prominence on the back of the thalamus

²**pulvinar** \"\ *adj* [NL *pulvinus* + E *-ar*] **:** resembling a cushion; *specif* **:** relating to or resembling a pulvinus

pul·vi·nar·ia \ˌpəlvəˈna(a)rēə\ *n* [NL, fr. L *pulvinus* cushion + NL *-aria*; fr. the appearance of the egg case] **1** *cap* **:** a genus of scales in which the females are large, flat, and nearly circular and secrete a cottony egg case — see COTTONY MAPLE SCALE **2** -s **:** any insect of the genus *Pulvinaria*

pul·vi·nate \ˈpəlvə,nāt, *usu* -ād·+V\ *or* **pul·vi·nat·ed** \-,nād·əd\ *adj* [L *pulvinatus*, fr. *pulvinus* cushion + *-atus* -ate, -ated] **1 :** curved convexly or swelled ⟨a ~ frieze⟩ **2 a :** cushion-shaped **b :** having a pulvinus **:** PULVINAR — **pul·vi·nate·ly** *adv*

pul·vi·na·tion \ˌ==ˈnāshən\ *n* -s **:** a convex curve or swelling (as on a frieze)

pul·vin·ic acid \ˌpəlˈvinik-\ *n* [ISV, blend of *pulvic* and *-in*] **:** an orange crystalline lactonic acid ($C_{17}H_{11}O_3$)COOH obtained from lichens and by hydrolysis of vulpinic acid

pul·vi·no \ˌpəlˈvē(,)nō\ *n, pl* **pulvi·ni** \-,nī\ [It, fr. L *pulvinus* cushion] **:** DOSSERET

pul·vin·u·lus \ˌpəlˈvinyələs\ *n, pl* **pulvinu·li** \-ə,lī\ [NL, dim. of L *pulvinus*] **:** PULVILLUS

pul·vi·nus \ˌpəlˈvīnəs\ *n, pl* **pulvi·ni** \-ī,nī\ [NL, fr. L, cushion] **:** a cushionlike enlargement of the base of a petiole or petiolule consisting of a mass of large thin-walled cells surrounding a vascular strand and functioning in turgor movements of leaves or leaflets by reversible volume changes in the cells

pul·vi·plume \ˈpəlvē+,-\ *n* [L *pulvis* dust, powder + E *plume* — more at POLLEN] **:** POWDER DOWN

pul·war \(,)pəlˈwär\ *n* -s [Hindi *palwār*] **:** a light keelless riverboat used in India

pulwar

pu·ma \ˈp(y)ümə\ *n, pl* **pumas** *also* **puma** [Sp, fr. Quechua] **:** COUGAR; *also* **:** the fur or pelt of a cougar sometimes used for rugs

pumace *var of* POMACE

pumelo *var of* POMELO

pu·mex \ˈpyü,meks\ *n* -ES [L — more at FOAM] **:** PUMICE

¹**pum·ice** \ˈpəməs\ *or* **pumice stone** *n* -s [ME *pomis*, fr. MF *pomis*, fr. L *pumic-, pumex* — more at FOAM] **1 :** a white, gray, yellowish, brownish, or rarely red volcanic glass that is light in weight because it is full of cavities produced by the expulsion of water vapor at a high temperature as lava comes to the surface and that is used esp. in powder form for smoothing and polishing **:** hardened volcanic froth **2 :** a piece of pumice esp. for use in polishing, blotting, or erasing **3** *obs* **:** something that is as dry as pumice

²**pumice** \"\ *vt* -ED/-ING/-S **:** to clean, smooth, or treat with pumice

pumiced sole *or* **pumiced foot** *n* [¹*pumice* + *-ed*] **:** a horse's hoof in which the horny laminae have become spongy and soft

pu·mi·ceous \pyüˈmishəs\ *adj* [L *pumiceus*, fr. *pumic-, pumex* pumice + *-eus* -eous] **1 :** of, relating to, or consisting of pumice **2 :** resembling pumice in structure

pum·ic·er \-sə(r)\ *n* -s **:** one that pumices

pumice soap *n* **:** a hard soap charged with a gritty powder (as silica, alumina, powdered pumice)

pum·i·cite \ˈpəmə,sīt\ *n* -s [*pumice* + *-ite*] **1 :** PUMICE 1 **2 :** a volcanic dust that is similar in composition to pumice and used for abrasive purposes

¹**pum·mel** \ˈpəməl\ *vb* **pummeled** *or* **pummelled**; **pummeled** *or* **pummelled**; **pummeling** *or* **pummelling** \-m(ə)liŋ\ **pummels** [alter. of ²*pommel*] **:** THUMP, POUND, POMMEL ⟨he ~*ed* and slapped and scrubbed the somewhat obese nudity of his companion —John Buchan⟩ ⟨~*ing* away most unmercifully —Samuel Lover⟩ **syn** see BEAT

²**pummel** *var of* POMMEL

pummelo *var of* POMELO

pum·mies \ˈpəmēz\ *n pl but sing or pl in constr* [by alter.] *dial* **:** POMACE 1

¹**pum·my** \ˈpəmē\ *dial var of* ¹PUMICE

²**pummy** \"\ *chiefly dial var of* POMACE

¹**pump** \ˈpəmp\ *n* -s [ME *pumpe, pompe*, fr. MLG *pumpe* or MD *pompe*, prob. fr. Sp *bomba*, of imit. orig.] **1 a :** a device or machine that raises, transfers, or compresses fluids or that attenuates gases esp. by suction or pressure or both — see CENTRIFUGAL PUMP, DISPLACEMENT PUMP, JET PUMP, PISTON PUMP, ROTARY PUMP **b :** a part of an animal organism that functions as a mechanical pump; *specif* **:** HEART ⟨the doctor in Washington said I had a good ~ —O.W.Holmes †1935⟩ **2 a :** an act or the process of pumping **b :** a stroke of a pump **3 :** one that pumps esp. for information **4 :** PUMP GUN

²**pump** \"\ *vb* -ED/-ING/-S *vt* **1 :** to raise (as water) with a pump — often used with *up* or *out* **2 a :** to pour forth, eject, deliver, force, or draw in the manner of a pump or one using a pump ⟨spring ~*s* mildly sulfurous hot water into a deep pool —J.A.Michener⟩ ⟨the blood is ~*ed* into the running and fighting muscles —H.A.Overstreet⟩ ⟨~*ed* bullets into five congressmen —*U.S. News & World Report*⟩ ⟨knowledge ~*ed* into their resisting skulls —H.F. & Katharine Pringle⟩ ⟨~*ed* fresh life into art . . . by using his own raw experiences —L.B. Nicolson⟩ **b :** to direct, assign, or influence the flow of (money) for stimulating or building up something (as agriculture, trade, or a business) ⟨the power of the Federal Reserve system to ~ cash into the commercial banks —R.S.Sayers⟩ ⟨foreign aid programs which have ~*ed* dollars into world trade channels —*Introduction to Doing Import & Export Business*⟩ ⟨~ extra capital into the land —*Economist*⟩ **3 a :** to subject to efforts intended to draw out, obtain, or extract (as

information, secrets, money) **:** ply persistently with urgings and questions in order to elicit something ⟨had been ~*ed* long ago for biographical material —*Times Lit. Supp.*⟩ **b :** to draw out, elicit, or extract by such efforts ⟨tried to ~ out from his memory reminiscences of his youth —H.S.Canby⟩ **4 :** to draw water, air, or other fluid from **:** free from water by means of a pump ⟨~ a well dry⟩ ⟨~ out a ship⟩ **5 a :** to manipulate as or as if a pump handle ⟨he ~*ed* Daniel's hand —Walter O'Meara⟩ ⟨just ~ the lever and shoot it —Ernest Hemingway⟩ **b :** to operate by so manipulating a lever or handle ⟨a parcel-conveying system . . . which he operated by ~*ing* the sewing-machine treadle —Clarence Woodbury⟩ ⟨~ a handcar⟩ ⟨~ a bicycle⟩ **6 :** to reduce by exertion to a breathless or panting condition — often used with *out* ⟨after the race he was all ~*ed* out⟩ **7 :** to fill with air by means of a pump or bellows ⟨~ up a tire⟩ **8 :** to inject a preservative solution into (ham or other meat) by means of a needle and pump **~** *vi* **1 :** to work a pump **:** raise or move water or other fluid with a pump ⟨mill ~*ing* away on an almost still day —Laura Krey⟩ **2 :** to drive, eject, or pour forth contents in the manner of a pump ⟨rifles ~*ed* continuously⟩ **3 a :** to exert oneself to pump something or somebody ⟨constricting the throat muscles, instead of ~*ing* more vigorously with the abdominal muscles —A.T.Weaver⟩ ⟨never tell our secrets to people that ~ for them —O.W. Holmes †1894⟩ **b :** to throb heavily ⟨heart ~*ed* hard —Marcia Davenport⟩ **4 a :** to move up and down like a pump handle ⟨with a ~*ing* of wings the birds were gone —Shirley A. Grau⟩ ⟨bicycled by . . . her knees ~*ing* furiously —Lael Tucker⟩ ⟨a handcar operated by ~*ing*⟩ **b :** to run, fly, or move as the result of such movement esp. of legs or wings ⟨a man came ~*ing* up the road on a bicycle —Nelson Hayes⟩ ⟨we would stand up in the swing and ~ —Gordon Wilson⟩ ⟨runner was rounding second, ~*ing* for third —George Barrett⟩ **5 :** to spurt out intermittently ⟨blood ~*s* from a cut artery⟩ **6** *of a mechanical or electrical device* **:** HUNT 3, PULSATE, SEESAW **7 :** to take a full windup before pitching a baseball — **pump by heads :** to pump (a well producing a small quantity) intermittently by allowing the contents to accumulate to a certain depth and then emptying the well

³pump \"\ *n* -s [origin unknown] **:** a low shoe not fastened on and gripping the foot chiefly at the toe and heel

pump·abil·i·ty \ˌpəmpəˈbilədē\ *n* **:** the quality, state, or degree of being pumpable

pump·able \ˈpəmpəbəl\ *adj* **:** capable of being pumped ⟨a heavy but still ~ mud fluid —F.J.Williams⟩

pump

pump-action \ˈ≈ˌ≈≈\ *adj* [¹*pump* + *action*] *of a shotgun or rifle* **:** having an action that by the backward and forward motion of a sliding lever extracts and ejects the empty case, cocks the piece, and loads in a new round

pump·age \ˈpəmpij\ *n* -s [²*pump* + *-age*] **:** the amount raised by pumping or the work done by pumping ⟨the ~ of an oil well⟩

pump bob *n* [¹*pump*] **:** a bell crank or similar device for converting rotary into reciprocating motion

pump brake *n* **1 :** ⁵BRAKE 2 **2 :** a hydraulic brake (as for controlling the recoil of a gun) operating on the principle of the cataract

pump cylinder *n* **1 :** the cylinder of a pump **2 :** a sliding telescopic gage used by chronometer makers

pump dale *n* **:** the discharge spout of a bilge pump

pump doctor *n* **:** an expert charged with supervision and repair of pumps (as in a coal mine or copper mine)

pump dredge *n* **:** a dredge that delivers excavated material by pipeline usu. for dikes or fill

pump drill *n* **:** a primitive drill in which the shaft is revolved by working up and down a bow or bar carrying a cord attached at the center to the upper end of the shaft

pum·pel·ly·ite \ˌpəmˈpelēˌīt\ *n* -s [Raphael *Pumpelly* †1923 Am. geologist + E *-ite*] **:** a mineral $Ca_4(Al,Mg,Fe)_6Si_6O_{23}(OH)_3.2H_2O$(?) consisting of a hydrous calcium aluminosilicate probably related to clinozoisite

pump·er \ˈpəmpə(r)\ *n* -s **1 :** one that pumps or operates a pump (as for pumping oil) **2 :** an instrument or machine used in pumping; *esp* **:** a fire truck equipped with a pump **3 :** an oil well that has to be pumped

pumper company *n* **:** an engine company of a fire department

pumper-ladder \ˈ≈≈ˈ≈≈\ *n* **:** a fire truck equipped as both a pumper and a ladder truck

pum·per·nick·el \ˈpəmpə(r)ˌnikəl\ *n* -s [G] **:** a sourdough bread made by fermentation using unbolted rye flour for the dark variety and various proportions of rye and wheat flours for the lighter kinds

pum·pet \ˈpəmpət\ *or* **pumpet ball** *n* -s [MF *pompette* wart, pimple, fr. *pompe* tuft of ribbons + *-ette* — more at POMPON] **:** INK BALL

pump gun *n* [²*pump*] **:** a pump-action shotgun or rifle

pump handle *n* [¹*pump*] **1 :** the handle of a pump esp. of a house well or cistern **2 :** a handshake in which the arm is moved as though it were a pump handle

pump house *n* **:** a building in which are located and operated the pumps of an irrigation system (as a spa) **:** a pumping station

pumping *n* -s [fr. gerund of ²*pump*] **:** the action produced by heavy traffic whereby free water rises through joints and cracks in a pavement carrying with it fine-grained soil whose removal causes voids and subsequent subsidence and cracking of the pavement

pumping engine *n* **:** an engine used for pumping: as **a :** a steam engine and pump combined for raising water **b :** a fire truck equipped with a pump

pumping jack *n* **:** a device over a deep well for operating a pump by belt power

pumping of the barometer : a rather rapid rise and fall of the column of the mercurial barometer due to inertia attending changes in the rate of vertical motion **:** a corresponding oscillation of the index of the aneroid barometer or of the recording pen of the barograph due to various causes (as change of pressure)

pump·kin \÷ˈpəŋkən, ˈpəm(p)kən\ *or* **pun·kin** \ˈpəŋkən\ *n* -s *often attrib* [alter. (influenced by *-kin*) of *pumpion, pompion*, modif. of MF *popon, pompon* pumpkin, melon, fr. L *pepon-, pepo*, fr. Gk *pepōn* an edible gourd, fr. *pepōn* cooked by sun, ripe, fr. *peptein, pessein* to cook, ripen, digest — more at COOK] **1 a :** any of various usu. firm-rinded fruits of vines of the genus *Cucurbita* that are widely cultivated as a vegetable, for pies, and for livestock feed: (1) **:** any of numerous usu. large rounded, and deep yellow to orange fruits produced by plants that are horticultural varieties of the natural species (*C. pepo*); *also* **:** SUMMER SQUASH (2) **:** a fruit similarly used that is produced by horticultural varieties of the natural species (*C. moschata*) **:** a winter crookneck squash **:** CUSHAW — called also *squash* (3) *Brit* **:** any of various large-fruited winter squashes that are produced by horticultural varieties of the natural species (*C. maxima*) **b** *or* **pumpkin vine :** a plant that bears pumpkins and is usu. a strong-growing prickly vine with large lobed leaves and with yellow flowers having erect corolla lobes **2 a :** a lumbering person or body **:** CHUMP **b :** a very important person or place — usu. used in pl. and chiefly in the phrase *some pumpkins* ⟨a man of learning is supposed to be some ~*s* —J.F.Dobie⟩ **3 :** a strong orange that is lighter than mandarin orange, redder, less strong, and slightly darker than Princeton orange, redder and duller than cadmium orange, and redder and deeper than cadmium yellow

pumpkin ash *n* **1 :** a timber tree (*Fraxinus tomentosa*) of the central and southeastern U.S. having hairy twigs and leafstalks **2 :** the wood of the pumpkin ash tree

pumpkin ball *n* **:** a solid ball or rifled slug used as shotgun ammunition for large game animals

pumpkin beetle *n* **:** a chrysomelid beetle (*Aulacophora hilaris*) that damages fruits and vegetables in parts of Australia

pumpkin bread *n* **:** bread made of ground dried pumpkin or mashed boiled pumpkin mixed with cornmeal

pumpkin bug *n* **:** SQUASH BUG

pumpkin head *n* **1** *archaic* **:** a New England Puritan **2 :** DOLT, BLOCKHEAD **3 :** a pumpkin-sized head — **pumpkin-headed** \ˈ≈≈ˈ≈≈\ *adj*

pumpkin pine *n* **1 :** the homogeneous close-grained wood of especially fine old trees of the white pine (*Pinus strobus*) **2 :** WHITE PINE 1a

pumpkinseed \ˈ≈≈ˌ≈\ *n* **1 :** a small brilliantly colored No. American freshwater sunfish (*Lepomis gibbosus*) or the related bluegill **2 :** BUTTERFISH a

pumpknot \ˈ≈ˌ≈\ *n* [origin unknown] *Midland* **:** a lump or swelling on the head usu. from a blow

pum·ple \ˈpəmpəl\ *archaic var of* PIMPLE

pump·less \ˈpəmpləs\ *adj* **:** having no pump

pump log *n* [¹*pump*] **:** a hollowed-out log used as a conduit

pump·man \ˈpəmpmən\ *n, pl* **pumpmen** [¹*pump* + *man*] **:** one who tends, operates, or cares for a pump

pump priming *n* [¹*pump*] **:** investment expenditures by government designed to induce a self-sustaining expansion of economic activity

pump rod *n* **:** the rod to which the bucket of a pump is fastened and which is attached to the brake or handle **:** PISTON ROD

pump room *n* **:** PUMP HOUSE; *specif* **:** a hall or casino at a spa provided for the treatment of and as a gathering place for its patrons

pumps *pl of* PUMP, *pres 3d sing of* PUMP

pump sole *n* [³*pump*] **:** a thin single sole generally with beveled edges that is common on men's and women's shoes (as pumps)

pump up *vt* [²*pump*] **:** to work up by artificial means or by great effort ⟨*pumping up* a poem till it means everything —N.E. Nelson⟩ ⟨*pumping up* his smile —Edwin O'Connor⟩

pump well *n* [¹*pump*] **:** WELL 3a

¹pun \ˈpən\ *vt* **punned; punned; punning; puns** [ME *pounen* — more at POUND] *chiefly dial* **:** to beat with telling force **:** POUND ⟨would ~ thee into shivers with his fist —Shak.⟩

²pun \"\ *n* -s [perh. fr. It *puntiglio* quibble, fine point — more at PUNCTILIO] **:** the humorous use of a word in such a way as to suggest different meanings or applications or of words having the same or nearly the same sound but different meanings **:** a play on words ⟨never knew an enemy to ~*s* who was not an ill-natured man —Charles Lamb⟩ ⟨any man who would make such an execrable ~ would not scruple to pick my pocket —John Dennis⟩

³pun \"\ *vb* **punned; punned; punning; puns** *vi* **:** to make puns **~** *vt* **:** to persuade or drive by the use of puns

pun *abbr* puncheon

¹pu·na \ˈpünə\ *also* **pu·no** \ˈpü(ˌ)nō\ *n* -s [AmSp *puna*, fr. Quechua] **1 :** a bleak desolate region; *specif* **:** a treeless windswept tableland or basin in the higher Andes **2 :** a cold mountain wind in Peru

²puna \"\ *n, pl* **puna** *or* **punas** *usu cap* [AmSp, of AmerInd origin] **1 a :** an Indian people chiefly of the island of Puna in the Gulf of Guayaquil, Ecuador **b :** a member of such people **2 :** the language of the Puna people

pu·naise \pyüˈnāz\ *or* **pu·nese** \-ˈnēz\ *n* -s [MF *punaise*, fr. fem. of *punais* stinking, fr. (assumed) VL *putinasius* stinking from the nose, fr. L *putēre* to stink + *nasus* nose — more at FOUL, NOSE] **:** BEDBUG

pu·na·lua \ˌpünəˈlüə\ *n* -s [Hawaiian] **1 :** a group marriage formerly practiced in Hawaii in which a group of brothers is married to a group of sisters or in which the husbands are of the same kinship group and the wives are members of another kinship group **2 :** the two or more husbands of a wife or the two or more wives of a husband in such a group marriage **3 :** the relationship of the persons in such a form of marriage

pu·na·lu·an \ˌ≈≈ˈlüən\ *adj* **:** of or relating to punalua ⟨a ~ family⟩

pu·nan \püˈnän\ *n, pl* **punan** *or* **punans** *usu cap* [native name in Borneo] **1 :** a Dayak people living as forest nomads in the remote interior of Borneo **2 :** a member of the Punan people

punc *abbr* punctuation

punce \ˈpən(t)s\ *dial Eng var of* POUNCE

¹punch \ˈpənch\ *vb* -ED/-ING/-ES [partly fr. ME *punchen*, fr. MF *poinçonner* to prick, stamp, fr. *poinçon* pointed tool; partly fr. ³*punch* — more at PUNCHEON] *vt* **1 a :** to prod with a stick or other blunt object **:** POKE ⟨was ~*ed* with her umbrella⟩ ⟨rod to ~ out the empty shells —W.F.Harris⟩ **b :** to act as herdsman of **:** DRIVE 1c **c :** to push (material) through a foundation piece with a needle ⟨in some carpets the pile is ~*ed* through the foundation⟩ **2 a :** to strike with a hard and usu. quick forward thrust esp. with the fist ⟨the boxer ~*ed* his opponent on the nose⟩ ⟨check the dough temperature, relieve it of excess gases through ~*ing* it —Mary K. Moore⟩ ⟨began to ~ a pillow into shape —Berton Roueché⟩ **b :** to drive or push rapidly and forcibly by or as if by punching ⟨roads ~*ed* out of the wilderness by massive bulldozers —*Spokane* (*Wash.*) *Spokesman Rev.*⟩ ⟨a rocket could ~ its way out of the atmosphere —*N.Y.Times*⟩ ⟨~*ed* over a touchdown —C.B. Wilkinson⟩ ⟨ideals are ~*ed* over in anger —A.L.Guernsey⟩ **3 :** to emboss, cut, or operate on by means of a punch: as **a :** to stamp with perforations **:** PERFORATE, PUNCTURE ⟨a postage stamp ~*ed* with round holes⟩ ⟨~ a ticket⟩ **b :** to record (data) by perforating a card or tape ⟨the machine reads the factors, adds, subtracts . . . and ~*es* the results —H.C. Zeisig & P.T.Martin⟩ **c :** to make by perforating or puncturing ⟨holes can be ~*ed* in glass by forcing a sharp steel pin through —C.J.Phillips⟩ **d :** to make (a foundry-type matrix) by stamping with a punch ⟨most matrices are stamped or ~*ed*, rather than engraved —*Foundry Type*⟩ **4 :** to strike sharply so as to make a printed or other record or produce some other intended effect ⟨~ the keys of a typewriter⟩; *also* **:** to press or strike sharply the activating mechanism (as a button, key, or plunger) of ⟨~ a typewriter⟩ ⟨~ a time clock⟩ ⟨~ the throttle⟩ **5 :** to deliver (as a spoken line) or render (as a musical phrase) with strong emphasis ⟨jokes were ~*ed* with an assist from a thud on the bass drum —Henry Hewes⟩ ⟨lectures on how to ~ their lines —Jane Woodfin⟩ **~** *vi* **1 :** to perform the action of punching something ⟨after the damage to his hand, the fighter could no longer ~⟩ ⟨~*ing* away at a typewriter⟩ **2 :** to penetrate the paper being printed — used of a part of a printing surface ⟨the very first thing a pressman will do when he looks at the back of a printed sheet is to start cutting out the points which ~ —*Graphic Arts Monthly*⟩ **3 :** to conduct oneself esp. against odds or difficulties with continued effort, determination, and morale ⟨after months of discouragement, he was still in there ~*ing*⟩ **syn** see PERFORATE, STRIKE

²punch \"\ *n* -ES **1 :** the action of punching **2 :** a quick thrust or a blow with or as if with the fist ⟨land a ~ on the jaw⟩ ⟨has thrown verbal ~*es* at many a government bigwig —*Time*⟩ ⟨the searing ~ of cloud to ground lightning —J.C.Dillon⟩ ⟨neither could expect to win a one ~ war —H.E.Salisbury⟩ **3 :** energy or vigor that commands or arrests attention **:** effectively aimed force **:** EFFECTIVENESS ⟨this book has a ~ —W.L.Dorn⟩ ⟨put more science and ~ into salesmanship —*Systems Mag.*⟩ ⟨verbs that have ~ —Bruce Westley⟩ ⟨a team with a terrific ~ —*Sporting News* (*St. Louis, Mo.*)⟩ **4 :** PUNCH LINE; *also* **:** a word that has the same effect **syn** see VIGOR — **to the punch :** to the first blow or decisive action in a competition — used esp. with *beat* ⟨beats you *to the* conversational *punch* by having his say before you have a chance to open your mouth —W.J.Reilly⟩

³punch \"\ *n* -ES [prob. short for *puncheon*] **1 a :** a tool usu. in the form of a short rod of steel that is either solid or hollow and sharp-edged and that is variously shaped at one end for different operations (as perforating, blanking, cutting, forming, drawing, bending, coining, embossing, seaming, trimming): as (1) **:** PRICK PUNCH (2) **:** CENTER PUNCH (3) **:** a short tapering steel rod for driving the heads of nails or brads below the surface — called also *nail set* (4) **:** a tool for driving a bolt or other object out of a hole — called also *starting punch* (5) **:** FORCE 8a (6) **:** ²HOB 4a (4) (7) **:** a steel die faced with a letter in relief that is forced into a softer metal (as copper) to form an intaglio matrix from which foundry type is cast **b :** a device or machine for performing the operations of a hand punch: as (1) **:** a hand-operated device for cutting holes or notches in paper or cardboard (2) **:** PUNCH PRESS (3) **:** KEYPUNCH **2 :** a stonecutter's point **3 :** a part having on its surface a figure or design in relief so that it is suitable for impressing an intaglio design on wax or other plastic material **4 :** a hole or notch resulting from a perforating operation esp. of a card or tape

⁴punch \"\ *n* -ES [perh. fr. Hindi *pāc* five, fr. Skt *pañca*; fr. the number of ingredients — more at FIVE] **1 :** a hot or cold beverage varying greatly in composition but usu. composed of wine, spirituous liquor, or ale or a combination thereof and citrus juice, spices, tea, and water and often served from a large bowl ⟨hot rum ~⟩ ⟨whiskey ~⟩; *also* **:** a beverage composed of fruit juices and other nonalcoholic liquids (as tea, ginger ale) and usu. served cold **2 :** a drink or serving of punch **3 :** a social affair at which punch is served

⁵punch \"\ *n* -ES [prob. short for *punchinello*] *dial chiefly Eng* **:** a short stocky person or animal

⁶punch \"\ *adj, dial Brit* **:** SHORT, THICKSET

⁷punch \"\ *n* -ES [by shortening & alter.] **:** PANCHAYAT

punch·able \ˈpənchəbəl\ *adj* **1 :** capable of being punched **2 :** made esp. for being punched — used of a card

punch-and-judy show \ˈpənchənˈjüdē-\ *n, usu cap P&J* [fr. *Punch and Judy*, traditional names of the principal characters] **:** a puppet show in which the principal character quarrels with his wife and does various outrageous and tragic things in a ludicrous way

punchayet *var of* PANCHAYAT

punchball \ˈ≈ˌ≈\ *n* [¹*punch* + *ball*] **:** a game similar to baseball but played with a tennis ball that is struck with a closed fist instead of a bat

punchboard \ˈ≈ˌ≈\ *n* [¹*punch* + *board*] **:** a small board usu. 6″x6″x½″ to 15″x15″x¾″ that has many holes each filled with a rolled-up printed slip to be punched out on payment of a nominal sum in an effort to obtain a slip bearing a lucky name or number that entitles the player to a designated prize — called also *pushcard*

punch bowl *n* [⁴*punch*] **1 :** a large bowl from which a beverage (as punch or lemonade) is served **2 :** something suggestive of a punch bowl; *esp* **:** a cuplike hollow in a hilly region — often used in place names

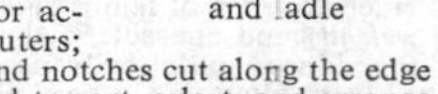
punch bowl with cups and ladle

punch card *or* **punched card** *n* [¹*punch*] **:** a data card with holes punched in particular positions having particular assigned significations singly or in combination for automatic sorting, selecting, arranging, or computing in electrically operated tabulating or accounting equipment or computers; *also* **:** a similar card with holes and notches cut along the edge so that a slender rod may be used to sort, select, and arrange a group of such cards by hand

punch cutter *n* [³*punch*] **:** one that cuts typefounders' punches

punch-drunk \ˈ≈ˌ≈\ *adj* [²*punch* + *drunk*] **1 :** suffering cerebral injury as a result of many minute brain hemorrhages following repeated head blows received in prizefighting **2 :** affected as if punch-drunk **:** DAZED, DAZZLED, CONFUSED ⟨a country *punch-drunk* from war losses⟩ — **punch-drunkenness** \ˈ≈ˌ≈≈≈\ *n*

punched *past of* PUNCH

punched tape *n* [fr. past part. of ¹*punch*] **:** paper tape punched with holes in such a way as to convey information

¹pun·cheon \ˈpənchən\ *n* -s [ME *ponchon, punson, punson* pointed tool, dagger, king post, fr. MF *poinchon, poinçon* pointed tool, king post (perh. fr. its being marked by the builder with a pointed tool), fr. (assumed) VL *punction-, punctio* pointed tool, fr. (assumed) *punctiare* to prick, fr. L *punctus*, past part. of *pungere* to prick — more at PUNGENT] **1 :** a pointed tool for piercing or for working on stone **2 a :** a short upright piece of timber in framing **:** a short post **:** an intermediate stud **b :** a split log or heavy slab with the face smoothed ⟨a ~ floor⟩ ⟨a ~ door⟩ **3 :** a figured stamp, die, or punch used esp. by goldsmiths, cutlers, and engravers

²puncheon \"\ *n* -s [ME *poncion*, fr. MF *ponchon, poinçon*, of unknown origin] **1 :** a large cask of varying capacity **2 :** any of various units of liquid capacity (as a unit equal to 70 gallons or one of 72 gallons)

punch·er \ˈpənchə(r)\ *n* -s **:** one that punches or operates a punch: as **a :** COWBOY **b :** a telegraphic perforator **c :** an operator of a punch press or drill press

punches *pres 3d sing of* PUNCH, *pl of* PUNCH

punch in *vi* [¹*punch*] **:** to record the time of one's presence (as for work) by punching a time clock ⟨arrive at the plant in time for a cup of coffee before *punching in* at eight o'clock —Elizabeth Ward⟩

pun·chi·nel·lo \ˌpənchəˈne(ˌ)lō\ *n, pl* **punchinellos** *or* **punchinelloes** [alter. of earlier *polichinello*, fr. It dial. *polecenella*, dim. of It *pulcino* chicken, fr. LL *pullicenus*, dim. of L *pullus* young of an animal, chicken — more at FOAL] **1 :** a clown or buffoon suggestive of a fat short humpbacked character in Italian puppet shows **2 :** one resembling a punchinello esp. in grotesqueness

punch·i·ness \ˈpənchēnəs\ *n* -ES **:** the quality, condition, or state of being punchy

punching *n* -s [fr. gerund of ¹*punch*] **1 :** a piece or burr removed (as from a steel plate) by a punch **2 :** an ornamental perforation (as in leather)

punching bag *n* **:** a stuffed or inflated bag usu. suspended but sometimes supported on a flexible rod to be punched for exercise or for training in boxing

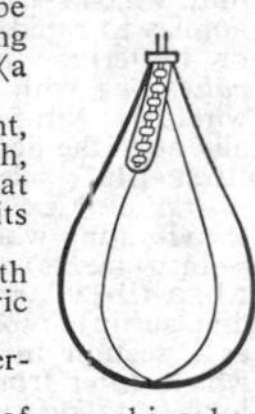
punching bag

punch·less \ˈpənchləs\ *adj* **:** lacking punch ⟨a ~ fighter⟩

punch line *n* [²*punch*] **:** a sentence, statement, or phrase in a play, musical comedy, speech, cartoon, humorous story, or advertisement that drives home the point ⟨a poem that found its *punch line* at the very finish —M.H.Cane⟩

punch loom *n* [¹*punch*] **:** a machine with needles for punching loose fiber or fabric pieces through a mesh fabric background

punch mark *n* [³*punch*] **:** a small counter-stamp on a coin or other metal object

punch out *vi* [¹*punch*] **:** to record the time of one's stopping work or departure by punching a time clock ⟨*punched out* and went home at five o'clock⟩

punch-out \ˈ≈ˌ≈\ *n* -s [¹*punch* + *out*] **:** a part of a surface marked off by perforations so that it may be forced out **:** KNOCKOUT

punch pliers *n pl* [¹*punch*] **:** pliers for perforating material (as leather, paper)

punch press *also* **punching press** *n* **:** a press for working on metal or other materials by the use of cutting, shaping, or combination dies consisting essentially of a frame in which one or more slides or rams are made to move up and down, of a bed to which the die shoe or bolster plate is bolted, and of means for applying power to the slide usu. through a crank, cam, eccentric shaft, toggle joint, knuckle joint, rack and pinion, or other device

punchwork \ˈ≈ˌ≈\ *n* [partly fr. ¹*punch*, partly fr. ³*punch*] **1 a :** an openwork embroidery with patterns of holes formed by separating threads of the cloth and stitching them in place **b :** a tufted embroidery of cut or uncut loops made by pushing a heavy thread through cloth and used esp. for bedspreads **2 :** a small repetitive allover pattern made with a steel punch (as on furniture or for the background on a carved decorative panel)

¹punchy \ˈpənchē, -chi\ *adj* -ER/-EST [⁵*punch* + *-y*] **:** having a short and thick or fat body

²punchy \"\ *adj* -ER/-EST [²*punch* + *-y*] **:** having or characterized by punch **:** FORCEFUL ⟨his characters all converse with the ~ drive of professional wits —*Saturday Rev.*⟩ ⟨thanked the admiral for his ~ interview —Joseph Driscoll⟩ ⟨short, ~ one-sentence paragraphs —*Newsweek*⟩ ⟨~ prose⟩

³punchy \"\ *adj* -ER/-EST [²*punch* + *-y*] **1 :** physically groggy from a punch or series of punches ⟨a ~ fighter⟩ **2 :** PUNCH-DRUNK 2 ⟨tendency of the bull moose to stagger around, ~ but on his feet even with a mortal hit —Warren Page⟩ ⟨men already ~ from combat —*Time*⟩

punct \ˈpəŋkt\ *n* -s [L *punctum* — more at POINT] **1 :** POINT **2 :** an element held in Whitehead's philosophy of nature to be analogous to a point in a geometric system

¹puncta *pl of* PUNCTUM

²punc·ta \ˈpəŋ(k)tə\ *n, pl* **punc·tae** \-ˌ)tē\ [NL, fr. LL, pricking, puncture, fr. *punctus*, past part. of *pungere* to prick — more at PUNGENT] **:** any of various thin places arranged in characteristic pattern in the frustule wall of pennate diatoms — compare AREOLE

punc·tar·i·a·les \ˌpəŋ(k)ˌta(a)rēˈā(ˌ)lēz\ *n pl, cap* [NL, fr. *Punctaria*, type genus (fr. L *punctum* point + *-aria* -ary) + *-ales*] **:** an order comprising brown algae that resemble members of and are sometimes included in the order Dictyosiphonales but are distinguished by the lack of any marked internal tissue differentiation

punc·tate \'pəŋ(k),tāt\ *adj* [NL *punctatus*, fr. L *punctum* point + L *-atus*, -ate — more at POINT] **1 :** ending in a point **:** resembling a point **:** small and round like a dot **2 :** applied to a point ⟨a ~ stimulation of the skin⟩ **3 :** dotted with minute spots or depressions ⟨a ~ leaf⟩ ⟨a ~ fossil shell⟩ **4 :** marked by dots or points — used esp. of a skin lesion or disease

punc·tat·ed \-ād·əd\ *adj* [*punctate* + *-ed*] **:** PUNCTATE

punc·ta·tion \,pəŋ(k)'tāshən\ *n* -s [ML *punctatus* (past part. of *punctare* to point, fr. L *punctum*) + E *-ion*] **1 :** the action of making punctate, perforated, or marked by points or dots **:** the condition of being punctate **2 :** a minute spot or depression (as on a plant, animal, or piece of pottery) **3** *civil law* **:** a preliminary statement in writing presenting matters proposed to be put into a contemplated contract

punc·tic·u·lar \,pəŋ(k)'tikyələ(r)\ *or* **punc·tic·u·late** \-lət, -,lāt\ *adj* [(assumed) NL *puncticulum* (dim. of L *punctum* point) + E *-ar*, *-ate*] **:** PUNCTULATE

punc·ti·form \'pəŋ(k)tə,fȯrm\ *adj* [L *punctum* point + E *-iform*] **1 :** having the form or character of a point **2 :** marked by or composed of points or dots **:** PUNCTATE **3 :** of or relating to tangible points or dots used for representing words for reading by the blind

punc·til·i·ar \,pəŋ(k)'tilēə(r)\ *adj* [*punctilio* + *-ar*] **:** of or relating to a point of time

punc·til·io \,pəŋ(k)'tilē,ō\ *n, pl* **punctilios** [It & Sp; It *puntiglio* small point, point of honor, scruple, fr. Sp *puntillo*, fr. dim. of *punto* point, fr. L *punctum* — more at POINT] **1 a :** an instant of time **b :** a small detail **2 :** a nice detail of conduct in a ceremony, a procedure, or in the observance of a social or moral code **:** a point of behavior about which one is fastidious ⟨his ~, and love of ceremonious manners —Osbert Sitwell⟩ ⟨no ~ would keep him from telling what he knew —Carl Van Doren⟩ ⟨not accustomed to give much regard to the ~*s* of law —Oscar Handlin⟩ ⟨treat them with the ~*s* of the duelist's code —H.F.Armstrong⟩

punc·til·i·ous \,pəŋ(k)'tilēəs\ *adj* [*punctilio* + *-ous*] **:** attentive to punctilios **:** marked by precise exact accordance with the details of codes or conventions ⟨fussy about the ~ observance of orders —Willa Cather⟩ ⟨uncivilized people often pay ~ attention to rules of etiquette about salutations, visits, meetings —W.G.Sumner⟩ **syn** see CAREFUL

punc·til·i·ous·ly *adv* **:** in a punctilious manner

punc·til·i·ous·ness *n* -ES **:** the quality or state of being punctilious

punc·tion \'pəŋ(k)shən\ *n* -s [L *punction-*, *punctio*, fr. *punctus* (past part. of *pungere* to prick) + *-ion-*, *-io*, -ion — more at PUNGENT] **:** PRICKING, PUNCTURE

punc·to·graph·ic \,pəŋ(k)tə'grafik\ *adj* [fr. L *punctum* point + E *-o-* + *-graphic* — more at POINT] **:** of or relating to point writing or printing for the blind

punc·tu·al \'pəŋ(k)ch(əw)əl, -(k)sh-\ *adj* [ML *punctualis*, fr. L *punctus* pricking, point (fr. *punctus*, past part. of *pungere* to prick) + *-alis* -al — more at PUNGENT] **1 a :** of or relating to a point **b :** of or relating to punctuation **2 :** having the nature or a property of a point ⟨a ~ light source⟩: as **a :** belonging to a definite point of time ⟨achievements . . . are of a continuous rather than ~ nature —J.J.Obermann⟩ **b :** having fixity ⟨a ~ point in space⟩ **:** confined to a locale **:** CONCENTRATED ⟨a ~ seat of the soul —James Ward⟩ **c :** lacking extent or duration ⟨the particles which result from a quantizing of a wave equation appear to be ~ —Werner Heisenberg⟩ **3 :** pointed in expression or conception **:** being to the point **:** DEFINITE, EXPLICIT, ACCURATE; *also* **:** dealing or dealt with point by point **:** DETAILED ⟨with ~ care —William Wordsworth⟩ **4 :** marked by attention to small details and nice points **:** particular about minutiae **:** PUNCTILIOUS **5 a :** marked by exact adherence to an appointed time ⟨~, commonplace, keeping all appointments —L.P.Smith⟩ ⟨attracted notice by his ~ discharge of his duties —J.A.Froude⟩ **b :** marked by a regular predictable time schedule without unexpected deviation ⟨in a land of ~ trains —Alzada Comstock⟩ ⟨~ revolution of the seasons —Osbert Sitwell⟩ **6 :** PERFECTIVE 2 **syn** see CAREFUL

punc·tu·al·i·ty \,pəŋ(k)chə'waləd·ē, -(k)sh-, -lətē, -i\ *n* -ES [*punctual* + *-ity*] **1 :** the quality or state of being punctual; *esp* **:** the characteristic of being prompt in keeping engagements **2** *obs* **a :** a fine or nice point **:** an instance of precision, scrupulosity, fastidiousness, or punctiliousness **b :** a requisite of behavior or etiquette **:** PUNCTILIO **3 :** punctilious observance **:** PUNCTILIOUSNESS ⟨strictest ~ to the family hours would be expected —Jane Austen⟩

punc·tu·al·ly \'pəŋ(k)ch(əw)əlē, -(k)sh-, -lī\ *adv* **1 :** in a punctual manner **:** PRECISELY **2 :** PROMPTLY

punc·tu·al·ness *n* -ES [*punctual* + *-ness*] **:** PUNCTUALITY, EXACTNESS

[1]**punc·tu·ate** \'pəŋ(k)chə,wāt, -(k)sh-, *usu* -ād.+V\ *vb* -ED/-ING/-S [ML *punctuatus*, past part. of *punctuare* to point, fr. L *punctus* pricking, point, fr. *punctus*, past part. of *pungere* to prick — more at PUNGENT] *vt* **1 :** to mark or divide (written or printed matter) with punctuation marks in order to clarify the meaning and separate structural units **2 :** to break into or interrupt at intervals ⟨the steady click of her needles *punctuated* the silence —Edith Wharton⟩ ⟨she *punctuated* his petitions with Amens —Alan Paton⟩ ⟨meetings *punctuated* by brief recesses —Lindesay Parrott⟩ ⟨her career was *punctuated* by a series of mishaps —*Harper's*⟩ ⟨the many odysseys which have *punctuated* his life —Polly Adler⟩ **3 :** to set off by contrast **:** ACCENTUATE, EMPHASIZE ⟨her heels . . . *punctuated* the declaration of finality as they clicked along the sidewalk —Helen Howe⟩ ⟨raising of a finger *punctuating* the lively lingo of the auctioneer —*Amer. Guide Series: La.*⟩ ⟨the music . . . with enough beat to ~ it —Harold Sinclair⟩ ⟨copious tears ~ their bitter tale of financial woe —B.B.Seligman⟩ ⟨brilliant solid color is *punctuated* by the blackest black —Rosamund Frost⟩ ⟨dress with beige top and caramel skirt, *punctuated* at the waistline with a black patent belt —*Women's Wear Daily*⟩ ⟨the sun was *punctuating* the sky —Sabine Gova⟩ ~ *vi* **:** to use punctuation marks

[2]**punc·tu·ate** \-wət, -,wāt\ *adj* [L *punctus* point + E *-ate*] **:** PUNCTATE, DOTTED

punc·tu·a·tion \,pəŋ(k)chə'wāshən, -(k)sh-\ *n* -s [ML *punctuation-*, *punctuatio*, fr. *punctuatus* (past part. of *punctuare* to point) + *-ion-*, *-io* -ion — more at PUNCTUATE] **1 :** the act or an instance of punctuating **:** the character of being punctuated ⟨the ~ of the infinite stretch of time by periodic world conflagration —Catherine Rau⟩ ⟨the emotional impact of explosions used as a ~ —*Modern Music*⟩ ⟨the occasional ~ of a siren call, as either a squad car or an ambulance dashes through —Burns Mantle⟩ **2 :** the act, practice, or system of inserting various standardized marks or signs in written or printed matter in order to clarify the meaning and separate structural units **:** the division of written or printed matter (as into sentences or clauses) by means of punctuation marks **3 :** a system of vowel points and accents used in writing Hebrew and other Semitic languages

punc·tu·a·tion·al \;==;wāshən°l, -āshnəl\ *adj* [*punctuation* + *-al*] **:** of or relating to punctuation

punctuation mark *n* **:** any of various standardized marks or signs used in punctuation — compare APOSTROPHE, BRACE, BRACKET, COLON, COMMA, DASH, DIAGONAL, ELLIPSIS, EXCLAMATION POINT, HYPHEN, PARENTHESIS, PERIOD, QUESTION MARK, QUOTATION MARK, SEMICOLON, VIRGULE

punc·tu·a·tive \'==,wād·iv\ *adj* [*punctuate* + *-ive*] **:** PUNCTUATIONAL

punc·tu·a·tor \-d·ə(r)\ *n* -s [*punctuate* + *-or*] **:** one that punctuates

punc·tu·late \'pəŋ(k)chələt, -(k)sh-, -,lāt\ *adj* [NL *punctulatus*, fr. L *punctulum* (dim. of *punctum* puncture, point) + *-atus* -ate — more at POINT] **:** marked with small spots; *specif* **:** minutely punctate

punc·tu·lat·ed \-,lād·əd\ *adj* [*punctulate* + *-ed*] **:** PUNCTULATE

punc·tu·la·tion \,==='lāshən\ *n* -s [*punctulate* + *-ion*] **:** the state of being punctulate

punc·tu·lum \'pəŋ(k)chələm, -(k)sh-\ *n, pl* **punctu·la** \-lə\ [NL, fr. L, small puncture, small point — more at PUNCTULATE] **:** PUNCTURE

punc·tum \'pəŋ(k)təm\ *n, pl* **punc·ta** \-tə\ [L, puncture, point — more at POINT] **1** *obs* **:** POINT **2 :** a small area marked off in any way from a surrounding surface **:** DOT, PUNCTURE ⟨a ~ in a fossil shell⟩ ⟨insect bites . . . may show the central tiny hemorrhagic ~ —*Jour. Amer. Med. Assoc.*⟩ **3 :** a neume indicating a single note which is usu. higher than that preceding

punc·tur·able \'pəŋ(k)chərəbəl, -(k)sh-\ *adj* **:** capable of being punctured

punc·tur·ation \,pəŋ(k)chə'rāshən, -(k)shə'-\ *n* -s [[2]*puncture* + *-ation*] **1 :** an act or process of puncturing or state of being punctured **2 :** form or arrangement of punctures ⟨~ fine, the punctures separated by slightly more than their own diameter —*Jour. of the N.Y. Entomological Society*⟩

[1]**punc·ture** \'pəŋ(k)chə(r), -(k)sh-\ *n* -s [L *punctura*, prick, puncture, fr. *punctus* (past part. of *pungere* to prick) + *-ura* -ure — more at PUNGENT] **1 :** act of puncturing **:** perforation with something pointed **2 :** a hole, slight wound, or other perforation made by puncturing ⟨the ~ of a hypodermic needle⟩ ⟨a ~ wound made by a thorn⟩; *specif* **:** an accidental perforation in a pneumatic tire **3 :** a minute depression like one made by a point ⟨a shallow ~ on an insect's thorax⟩

[2]**puncture** \"\ *vb* **punctured; punctured; puncturing** \-chəriŋ, -sh(ə)riŋ\ **punctures** *vt* **1 :** to pierce with a pointed instrument or object **:** PRICK **:** make a puncture in ⟨~ the skin with a needle⟩ **2 :** to suffer a puncture of ⟨*punctured* his new tire⟩ **3 :** to deflate or make useless or absurd as if by a puncture **:** DESTROY ⟨~ one's ego⟩ ⟨~ an illusion⟩ ⟨~ a fallacy⟩ ⟨~ pretensions⟩ **4 :** to pass a spark discharge through (an insulator) ~ *vi* **:** to become punctured **syn** see PERFORATE

punc·tured \-(r)d\ *adj* [[1]*puncture* + *-ed*] **:** having the surface covered with minute indentations or dots **:** PUNCTATE ⟨an insect with scutellum obsoletely ~⟩

punctured stamp *n* [fr. past part. of [2]*puncture*] **:** a postage stamp with perforated initials

punc·ture·less \-(r)ləs\ *adj* **1 :** being without punctures **2 :** incapable of being punctured

puncture vine *or* **punctureweed** \'==,=\ *n* [[2]*puncture*] **:** a caltrop (*Tribulus terrestris*) having prickly fruits that puncture tires

puncture voltage *n* **:** the voltage at which an insulator is punctured electrically when subjected to a gradually increasing voltage

punc·tus \'pəŋ(k)təs\ *n* -ES [ML, fr. L, point — more at PUNCTUAL] **1 :** melody or melodic division in medieval music **2 :** DOT 2e(1)

punctus con·tra punc·tum \-,kän·trə'pəŋ(k)təm\ *adv* [ML] **:** melody against melody — used of early musical part writing; compare COUNTERPOINT

pund \'pu̇n(d)\ *dial var of* POUND

pun·dit \'pəndət, *usu* -əd.+V\ *n* -s [Hindi *paṇḍit*, fr. Skt *paṇḍita*, fr. *paṇḍita* learned, wise] **1 :** PANDIT **2 :** a learned man **:** TEACHER ⟨the fantastic ~ who was his tutor —John Gunther⟩ **3 :** an authority or one who announces judgments, opinions, or conclusions in an authoritative manner **:** CRITIC ⟨according to the ~*s*, the odds favor a breakout on the low, rather than the high, side of the market —*Wall Street Jour.*⟩ ⟨the ~*s* — most of the nationally known political reporters —*New Republic*⟩ ⟨when . . . the journalistic ~ talks commercial diplomacy —Norman Angell⟩ ⟨a staid and dependable literary ~ —*Times Lit. Supp.*⟩ ⟨musical ~*s* —R.G.Hubler⟩ ⟨the novel . . . has had moments at which the ~*s* have prophesied its decay —*Saturday Rev.*⟩

pun·dit·ic \,pən'did·ik\ *also* **pun·dit·i·cal** \-d·əkəl\ *adj* **:** of or relating to a pundit — **pun·dit·i·cal·ly** \-d·ək(ə)lē\ *adv*

pun·dit·ry \'pəndətrē\ *n* -ES [*pundit* + *-ry*] **:** the learning, methods, or pronouncements of pundits

pun·do·nor \,pu̇ndə'nō(ə)r\ *n, pl* **pundono·res** \-ō,rās\ [Sp, contr. of *punto de honor*] **:** a point of honor

pu·nee \'pünä·ā\ *n* -s [Hawaiian *pūne'e*] *Hawaii* **:** a movable couch

punese *var of* PUNAISE

pung \'pəŋ\ *n* -s [by shortening fr. earlier *tom-pong*, *tow-pong*, of Algonquian origin; akin to Micmac *tobâgun* drag made of skin — more at TOBOGGAN] *NewEng* **:** a rude oblong box on runners **:** a sleigh with a box-shaped body

pun·ga·pung \,pəŋ'gä,pəŋ\ *n* -s [Tag *pungapong*] **:** a Philippine aroid (*Amorphophallus campanulatus*) that has a putrid odor

pun·gence \'pənjən(t)s\ *n* -s [fr. [1]*pungent*, after such pairs as E *benevolent: benevolence*] **:** PUNGENCY ⟨smell, oily and a little fishy, with some ~ in it of herbs —Marjory S. Douglas⟩

pun·gen·cy \-jənsē, -si\ *n* -ES [[1]*pungent* + *-cy*] **1 :** the quality or state of being pungent **:** KEENNESS, SHARPNESS, POIGNANCY ⟨smoldering cigarettes have a harsh ~ of their own —Frances & Richard Lockridge⟩ ⟨the ~ of an aphorism⟩ ⟨~ of dialogue⟩ **2 :** something that is pungent (as an odor, taste, statement)

[1]**pun·gent** \-jənt\ *adj* [L *pungent-*, *pungens*, pres. part. of *pungere* to prick, sting; akin to L *pugio* dagger, *pugnus* fist, *pugnare* to fight, Gk *pygmē* fist, *peukedanos* sharp, piercing, *peukē* pine tree, OHG *fiuhta*] **1 :** having a stiff and sharp point **:** prickly-pointed ⟨a ~ ray on a fish⟩ ⟨~ leaves of holly⟩ **2 :** sharply painful **:** PENETRATING, PIERCING, STABBING, ACUTE ⟨our sympathy becomes so ~ —Leslie Stephen⟩ **3 a :** CAUSTIC, STINGING, BITING ⟨a ~ editorial⟩ ⟨~ humor⟩ ⟨a ~ truth⟩ **b :** POINTED, TELLING, STIMULATING ⟨fewer pages and shorter paragraphs help make it more ~ —H.T.Moore⟩ ⟨compiled a collection which should serve as a ~ antidote to much of the fuzzy thinking —R.B.Morris⟩ ⟨has drawn, with ~ finesse, the interior of a slum bistro —*Books of the Month*⟩ ⟨a place of ~ contrasts — of dull monotony and indiscreet adventure —E.M.Lustgarten⟩ **4 :** causing a sharp sensation **:** PRICKING, IRRITATING, ACRID ⟨the autumn's ~ smell of burning leaves⟩ ⟨tasting the ~ acidulous wood sorrel —John Burroughs⟩ ⟨some half-forgotten but still ~ memories —Virginia Woolf⟩ ⟨singers with coarse, ~ voices —H.F.Mooney⟩

syn PIQUANT, POIGNANT, RACY, SPICY, SNAPPY: PUNGENT may designate a sharp, piercing, stinging, biting, or penetrating quality, esp. of odors; it may suggest power to excite or stimulate keen interest or telling force and cogency ⟨the *pungent* odor of untanned leather⟩ ⟨the *pungent* reek of a strong cigar —A. Conan Doyle⟩ ⟨his *pungent* pen played its part in rousing the nation to its later struggle with the Crown —J.R.Green⟩ ⟨the mob needs concrete goals and the *pungent* thrill of hate in order to give vent to its destructive impulses —M.R.Cohen⟩ PIQUANT may indicate an interesting or appetizing tartness, sharpness, or pungency that stimulates or a zestful, arch, provocative, challenging, or exciting quality that is individual or peculiar ⟨a *piquant* sauce⟩ ⟨*piquant* with the tart-sweet taste of green apples and sugar —Silas Spitzer⟩ ⟨*piquant* touch of innocent malice in his narration —G.G.Coulton⟩ ⟨those *piquant* incongruities, which are the chief material of wit —C.E.Montague⟩ POIGNANT may describe what is sharply or piercingly effective upon the senses or stirring to one's inmost consciousness or deepest emotions ⟨the air of romantic poverty which Rosalie found so tragically *poignant* —Elinor Wylie⟩ ⟨with *poignant* finality, as a lover might put away a rose from a lost romance —Agnes S. Turnbull⟩ ⟨a vague but *poignant* sense of discouragement that the sacrifices of the war had not been justified by its results spread over the country —Oscar Handlin⟩ RACY may suggest verve, dash, tang, or vitality manifested with lively free heartiness ⟨everybody who loves the language enough to want to keep it always young and *racy* ought to turn out too and keep the pedants from running amok —C.E.Montague⟩ ⟨a rare and *racy* sense of humor —W.S.Maugham⟩ SPICY describes what is seasoned or made redolent of spice; in extended uses it may suggest the piquant, smart, spirited, sensational, or scandalous ⟨flair for a *spicy* zestful vernacular in dialogue —Leslie Rees⟩ ⟨*spicy* tales of the type which usually appear in paperbound copies, in which bishops are forced to visit nudist camps in their underwear —Robertson Davies⟩ SNAPPY suggests briskness, animation, dash, wit, or risqué quality ⟨spoken in a *snappy*, matter-of-fact way —Vachel Lindsay⟩ ⟨the renditions, if not especially lovely, were at all times spirited, neat, and *snappy* —Virgil Thomson⟩

[2]**pungent** \"\ *n* -s **:** a pungent substance ⟨surprise is like a thrilling ~ upon a tasteless meat —Emily Dickinson⟩

pun·gent·ly *adv* **:** in a pungent manner ⟨write swiftly and ~, every word doing its work —Robert Payne⟩ **:** so as to be pungent ⟨~ flavored⟩

pung·ey *or* **pungy** \'pəŋgē\ *n, pl* **pungeys** *or* **pungies** [origin unknown] **1 :** a two-masted schooner for oyster dredging or fishing in Chesapeake Bay **2 :** CHESAPEAKE CANOE

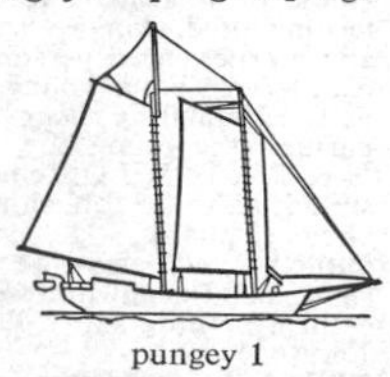

pungey 1

pun·gi \'püŋgē\ *also* **poo·gye** \'pügē\ *n* -s [Hindi *pūgī*, *pūgī*] **:** a Hindu reed pipe with a globular mouthpiece and often a drone — called also *bin*

pungitive *adj* [ME, fr. ML *pungitivus*, irreg. fr. *pungere* to prick + *-ivus* -ive — more at PUNGENT] *obs* **:** tending to prick or sting **:** PUNGENT

pun·gle \'pəŋgəl\ *vb* -ED/-ING/-S [Sp *póngale* put it down] *vt* **:** to make a contribution or payment of (money) — usu. used with *up* ⟨Congress would ~ up that much money —*Time*⟩ ~ *vi* **:** to pay or contribute money — usu. used with *up* ⟨must ~ up for his fare —R.L.Neuberger⟩

pun·gled \'pəŋgəld\ *adj* [origin unknown] **:** SHRIVELED, SHRUNKEN — used esp. of grain robbed of its juices by insects

pungs *pl of* PUNG

[1]**pu·nic** \'pyünik, -nēk\ *adj, usu cap* [L *punicus*, fr. OL *poenicus*, fr. *Poenus* inhabitant of the Phoenician colony of Carthage (irreg. fr. Gk *Phoinix* Phoenician) + *-icus* -ic — more at PHOENICIAN] **1 :** of, relating to, or characteristic of the ancient Carthaginians **:** CARTHAGINIAN **2 :** FAITHLESS, TREACHEROUS

[2]**punic** \"\ *n* -s *usu cap* **:** the Phoenician dialect of ancient Carthage

pu·ni·ca \'pyünəkə\ *n, cap* [NL, fr. L *punicum* pomegranate, fr. *punicum malum*, lit., Punic apple] **:** a genus (coextensive with the family Punicaceae of the order Myrtales) comprising shrubs or small trees with showy solitary white to deep red sometimes double flowers that have numerous stamens and an ovary with the cells in two rows and are followed by an edible fruit which is technically a berry — see POMEGRANATE

pu·nic·ic acid \pyü'nisik-\ *n* [L *punicum* pomegranate + E *-ic*] **:** a crystalline unsaturated fatty acid $C_4H_9(CH{=}CH)_3(CH_2)_7COOH$ that is a geometrical isomer of eleostearic acid and is obtained from oil of pomegranate

pu·ni·cin \'pyünəsən\ *n* -s [L *punicum* + ISV *-in*] **:** PELARGONIN

punie *obs var of* PUNY

punier *comparative of* PUNY

punies *pl of* PUNY

puniest *superlative of* PUNY

pu·ni·ly \'pyün°lē\ *adv* **:** in a puny manner

pu·ni·ness \-nēnəs\ *n* -ES **:** the quality or state of being puny

pun·ish \'pənish, -nēsh, *esp in pres part* -nəsh\ *vb* -ED/-ING/-ES [ME *punissen*, fr. MF *puniss-*, stem of *punir*, fr. L *punire*, fr. OL *poenire*, irreg. fr. *poena* penalty — more at PAIN] *vt* **1 :** to impose a penalty (as of pain, suffering, shame, strict restraint, or loss) upon for some fault, offense, or violation: **a :** to afflict (a person) with such a penalty for an offense ⟨the respectable not only obey the law, but ~ . . . those who refuse to do so —*Times Lit. Supp.*⟩ **b :** to inflict a penalty for (an offense) in retribution or retaliation ⟨the Sedition Act of 1798, designed to ~ attacks on the federal administration —Zechariah Chafee⟩ **2 a :** to deal with roughly or harshly ⟨the wife . . . who ~*ed* him with frenetic fits of nerves —Oscar Handlin⟩ **b :** to inflict injury or loss upon **:** HURT ⟨the ships were considerably ~*ed* by the batteries —P.G.Mackesy⟩ ⟨if you fined or imprisoned a man you ~*ed* his wife and children —Arnold Bennett⟩ **c :** DEPLETE, CONSUME ⟨~ a bottle of port⟩ **3 :** to score freely from (bowling or a bowler) **:** FLOG — used of a batsman in cricket ~ *vi* **:** to inflict punishment ⟨a ~*ing* race⟩ ⟨a ~*ing* defeat⟩

syn CHASTISE, CHASTEN, DISCIPLINE, CORRECT, CASTIGATE: PUNISH indicates some retribution inflicted after a fault, disobedience, or wrongdoing, usu. conscious or purposive; it may refer to any kind of transgression and any kind of penalty ⟨looked after a little more strictly than other children, and perhaps *punished* more —Margaret Deland⟩ ⟨no misdemeanor should be *punished* more severely than the most atrocious felonies —T.B.Macaulay⟩ CHASTISE is likely to suggest infliction of corporal pain, esp. by a parent, elder, or superior, and with the hope of effecting a reformation ⟨the father had to go over and give them a box or two on the ears, to quiet them down, but it turned into skylarking instead of *chastising* —O.E. Rölvaag⟩ CHASTEN is likely to suggest any affliction or trial, ranging from corporal punishment to worry, chagrin, tribulation, or duress, which leaves one humbled, more moderate, less extreme ⟨to devise means for *chastening* the stubborn heart of her husband —Rudyard Kipling⟩ ⟨heavier fines and jail sentences followed by disqualification from driving for life . . . would *chasten* most reckless and drunken drivers — Priscilla Hughes⟩ DISCIPLINE may involve punishing; it always suggests action in the interest of order, regularity, rule, or control by authority ⟨among the first recorded motions of the magistrates of the new court was the *disciplining* of Thomas Williams, who had said he did not see why the Duke of York had been such a fool as to make them the judges —*Amer. Guide Series: Del.*⟩ CORRECT may indicate chastening or punishing in the interest of amending or reforming, of guiding away from errors and lapses ⟨must know how to *correct* without wounding —J.M.Barzun⟩ CASTIGATE is likely to indicate a bitter, tongue-lashing denunciation or reprimand rather than any other form of punishment ⟨courageously patronizes democracy in England, and with equal courage *castigates* it at home —W.C.Brownell⟩

punish·abil·i·ty \,pənishə'biləd·ē\ *n* **:** PUNISHABLENESS

pun·ish·able \'pənishəbəl, -nēsh-\ *adj* [perh. fr. MF *punissable*, fr. *puniss-* (stem of *punir*) + *-able* — more at PUNISH] **:** deserving of, or liable to, punishment **:** capable of being punished by law or right ⟨~ offenders⟩ ⟨a ~ offense⟩ — **pun·ish·ably** \-blē\ *adv*

pun·ish·able·ness *n* **:** the quality or state of being punishable

pun·ish·er \'pənishə(r)\ *n* -s [ME *punisere*, fr. *punissen* to punish + *-ere* -er] **:** one that inflicts punishment

pun·ish·ment \'pənishmənt, -nēsh-\ *n* -s [ME *punisshement*, fr. MF *punissement*, fr. *puniss-* (stem of *punir* to punish) + *-ment*] **1 :** the act of punishing **:** the infliction of a penalty **2 a :** retributive suffering, pain, or loss **:** PENALTY ⟨rewards and ~*s* serve as the incentives to learning —L.W.Doob⟩ **b :** a penalty inflicted by a court of justice on a convicted offender **:** a penalty for an offense and for reformation and prevention; *broadly* **:** any damage or pain inflicted on an offender through judicial procedure aiming at either prevention, retribution, or reformation — compare CRUEL AND UNUSUAL PUNISHMENT **3 :** severe, rough, or disastrous treatment ⟨the fighter had been subjected to heavy ~ in his losing bout —*N.Y.Times*⟩ ⟨parts in your automobile take thousands of miles of ~ without becoming tired —*Hot-Metal Magic*⟩ ⟨the aggressor would receive terrific ~ which might well destroy the whole of his warmaking potential —A.P.Ryan⟩

pu·ni·tion \pyü'nishən\ *n* -s [ME *punicion*, fr. MF *punition*, fr. L *punition-*, *punitio*, fr. *punitus* (past part. of *punire*) + *-ion-*, *-io* -ion — more at PUNISH] **:** PUNISHMENT ⟨smarting from her latest ~ —Rosamond Lehmann⟩

pu·ni·tive \'pyünəd·|iv, -ət|\ *adj* [F *punitif*, fr. ML *punitivus*, fr. L *punitus* + *-ivus* -ive] **1 :** inflicting, awarding, or involving punishment or penalties **:** aiming at punishment ⟨a ~ law⟩ ⟨~ justice⟩ ⟨a ~ expedition⟩ **2 :** constituting or serving as a severe or discriminatory penalty ⟨~ taxes⟩ — **pu·ni·tive·ly** \|əvlē, -li\ *adv* — **pu·ni·tive·ness** \|ivnəs\ *n* -ES

punitive damages *n pl* **:** damages awarded in excess of compensatory damages or nominal damages to punish a defendant for a gross wrong — called also *exemplary damages*

pu·ni·to·ry \'pyünə,tōrē, -tȯr-, -ri\ *adj* [L *punitus* + E *-ory*] **:** having the nature of a punishment **:** PUNITIVE

[1]**pun·ja·bi** \,pən'jäbē, -jabē\ *n* -s *cap* [Hindi *pañjābī*, adj. & n.] **1 :** a native or inhabitant of the Punjab region of northwestern India **2 :** PANJABI 2

[2]**punjabi** \"\ *adj, usu cap* [Hindi *pañjābī*, fr. Per, fr. *Pañjāb* Punjab, region of northwestern India] **:** of or relating to the Punjab or its inhabitants

[1]**punk** \'pəŋk\ *n* -s [origin unknown; in sense 2, prob. partly fr. [3]*punk*] **1** *archaic* **:** PROSTITUTE, STRUMPET **2 a :** something or someone worthless or inferior **b :** NONSENSE, BUNKUM

⟨these flowers are a lot of ~ —Roger Williams⟩ ⟨~ about feeding tired skins —*Books of the Month*⟩ **3 a :** a young and inexperienced person : BEGINNER, NOVICE; *esp* : a young man : BOY **b :** a young gangster, hoodlum, or ruffian : a petty criminal **c** *slang* : a youth used as a homosexual partner ⟨the young boy, known in prison parlance as a ~ —N.K.Teeters & J.O.Reinemann⟩ **d :** a young tramp **e :** a stupid, naïve, or foolish person : JERK **4 :** a young untrained circus elephant

²punk \"\ *adj* -ER/-EST **:** very poor in quality : BAD, INFERIOR, MISERABLE ⟨meanwhile went from poor to ~ —*Time*⟩ ⟨looked ~ in a bathing suit —D.C.Loughlin⟩ ⟨a ~ liar —Josephine Johnson⟩

³punk \"\ *n* -s [perh. alter. (infl. by Delaware *punk* fine ashes, powder) of *spunk*] **1 :** wood that is so decayed as to be very dry, crumbly, and useful for tinder **2 :** a dry spongy substance prepared from the sporophores of various fungi of the genus *Fomes* (esp. *F. fomentarius* and *F. igniarius*) by removing the outer rind, slicing and pounding the sporophore until soft and flexible, dipping or sometimes boiling in a solution of potassium nitrate, and then drying and forming into molded sticks that are used to ignite fuses esp. of fireworks **3 :** the leathery or woody sporophore of a polypore : CONCH

⁴punk \"\ *adj* **1 :** having a dry flavorless flesh — used of fruits and vegetables **2 :** PUNKY

pun·kah *also* **pun·ka** \ˈpəŋkə\ *n* -s [Hindi *pākhā* fan, fr. Skt *pakṣa* wing; akin to Skt *pakṣas* wing — more at PECTORAL] **:** an Indian device for fanning a room consisting of a frame covered with cloth and suspended from the ceiling or a large fan held in the hand; *also* : a fanning device (as an electric fan)

punkah wal·lah \-ˈwälə\ *n* **:** the operator of a punkah

punk·ie *also* **punky** \ˈpəŋkē\ *n, pl* **punkies** [D dial. (New Amsterdam) *punki*, fr. Delaware *punk*, lit., fine ashes, powder] : BITING MIDGE

punkin *var of* PUMPKIN

punk oak *n* [¹*punk*] : POSSUM OAK

punk out *vi* [¹*punk* + *out*] **:** to back out

punk tree *n* [¹*punk*] : CAJEPUT 1

punkwood \ˈ=,=\ *n* **:** rotten wood; *esp* : wood permeated by the mycelium of pore fungi and frequently luminescent — compare ³PUNK 1

punky \ˈpəŋkē\ *adj* -ER/-EST [¹*punk* + *-y*] **1 :** of, relating to, or like punk ⟨a ~ splintering of water-soaked wood —Ruth Moore⟩ **2 :** SMOLDERING : SLOW-BURNING

pun·less \ˈpənləs\ *adj* **:** lacking puns

punned *past of* PUN

¹pun·ner \ˈpənə(r)\ *n* -s [¹*pun* + *-er*] **:** one that rams, tamps, packs, or consolidates by ramming; *specif* : a ramming tool

²punner \"\ *n* -s [³*pun* + *-er*] : PUNSTER

punner bar *n* [¹*punner*] **:** a combined punner and crowbar

pun·net \ˈpənət\ *n* -s [origin unknown] *chiefly Brit* **:** a chip basket or berry basket for fruit (as strawberries)

punning *pres part of* PUN

pun·ning·ly *adv* **:** in a punning manner

pun·ny \ˈpənē\ *adj* -ER/-EST [²*pun* + *-y*] **:** constituting or involving a pun ⟨a ~ slogan⟩ ⟨a ~ farce⟩

puno *var of* PUNA

puns *pl of* PUN, *pres 3d sing of* PUN

pun·ster \ˈpənztə(r), ˈpən(t)st-\ *n* -s [²*pun* + *-ster*] **:** one who puns; *esp* : one who is skilled in or addicted to punning

¹punt \ˈpənt\ *n* -s [fr. (assumed) ME, fr. OE, fr. L *ponton-, ponto* floating bridge, punt — more at PONTOON] **1 a :** a long narrow flat-bottomed boat with square ends usu. propelled with a pole **b :** a flat-bottomed boat esp. of broad beam **2 :** KICK 8 ⟨many bottles . . . have a concave bottom, or ~, to give added strength —O.A.Mendelsohn⟩

²punt \"\ *vb* -ED/-ING/-S *vt* **1 :** to propel (as a punt) by pushing with a pole against the bottom **2 :** to convey in a punt ~ *vi* **:** to boat or hunt in a punt

³punt \"\ *n* -s [F or Sp; F *ponte*, fr. Sp *punto* point, fr. L *punctum* — more at POINT] **1 :** a point in some games of chance (as basset) **2 :** ¹PUNTER a **3 :** a play made against the banker (as in faro)

⁴punt \"\ *vi* -ED/-ING/-S [F *ponter*, fr. *ponte*] **1 :** to play at a gambling game against the banker **2** *Brit* : GAMBLE, BET ⟨in the baccarat room, ~*ing* —Max Beerbohm⟩ ⟨arguing horses in the morning, ~*ing* on them by phone and radio during . . . afternoon —Leslie Rees⟩

⁵punt \"\ *vb* -ED/-ING/-S [origin unknown] *vt* **:** to kick (a ball) in football, soccer, or rugby before the ball dropped from the hands hits the ground ~ *vi* **:** to punt a ball ⟨unable to advance after receiving the kickoff and ~*ed* —*N.Y.Times*⟩

⁶punt \"\ *n* -s **1 :** the act or an instance of punting a ball: as **a :** a kick used by the goalkeeper in soccer to clear the ball **b :** a kick in football made esp. on fourth down to gain ground when relinquishing possession of the ball **2 :** a punted ball ⟨returned a ~ 67 yards for a touchdown —*N.Y.Times*⟩

¹punt·er \ˈpəntə(r)\ *n* -s [⁴*punt* + *-er*] **:** one that gambles: as **a :** a player who bets against the banker in a gambling game **b :** one that bets against a bookmaker ⟨~*s* who keep Britain's £1,500,000-a-week pools booming —*Australian Monthly*⟩ **c** *Brit* : SCALPER c(1)

²punter \"\ *n* -s [¹*punt* + *-er*] **1 :** one that uses a punt for boating or shooting **2 :** SERVITOR 4

³punter \"\ *n* -s [⁵*punt* + *-er*] **:** one that punts a ball (as a football)

punt formation *n* [⁵*punt*] **:** an offensive football formation in which a back making a punt stands approximately 10 yards behind the line and the other backs are in blocking position close to the line of scrimmage

punt gun *n* [¹*punt*] **:** a smooth-bored gun firing a large charge of shot fixed on a swivel in a punt and used in killing waterfowl

pun·til \ˈpənt³l\ *n* -s [F *pontil* — more at PONTIL] : PUNTY

pun·ti·lla \pünˈtē(y)ə\ *n* -s [MexSp, dim. of Sp *punta, punto* point, fr. L *punctum* — more at POINT] **:** a dagger used to sever a bull's spinal cord in bullfighting

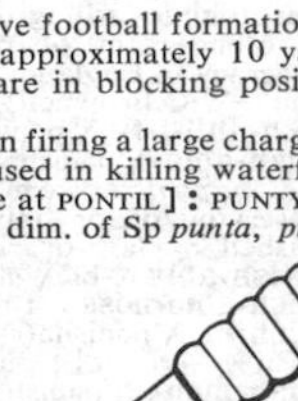

pun·ti·lle·ro \,püntēˈye(,)rō\ *n* -s [MexSp, fr. *puntilla* + Sp *-ero* -er] **:** one who delivers the coup de grace to a dying bull in bullfighting

puntilla

punt·latsh \ˈpənt,lach\ *or* **pent·latch** \ˈpen-\ *n, pl* **puntlatsh** *or* **puntlatshes** *or* **pentlatch** *or* **pentlatches** *usu cap* **1 a :** a Salishan people of the east coast of Vancouver Island, British Columbia **b :** a member of such people **2 :** the language of the Puntlatsh people

punt·man \ˈpəntmən\ *also* **punts·man** \-tsm-\ *n, pl* **puntmen** *also* **puntsmen** [¹*punt* + *man*] : ²PUNTER 1

¹pun·to \ˈpən·(,)tō\ *n* -s [It, fr. L *punctum* — more at POINT] **1 :** a hit in fencing : POINT **2** *obs* **:** a point of punctilio

²punto \ˈpün·(,)tō\ *or* **pon·to** \ˈpän-\ *n* -s [Sp, lit., point, fr. L *punctum*] **:** the ace of trumps when trumps are red (as in ombre)

³pun·to \ˈpün(,)tō\ *n* -s [It, fr. L *punctum* point] : POINT, STITCH — used esp. in combination of lace or embroidery of Spanish or Italian origin

punts *pl of* PUNT, *pres 3d sing of* PUNT

pun·ty *also* **pon·te** *or* **pon·tee** *or* **pun·tee** *or* **pon·ty** \ˈpəntē, ˈpän-\ *n, pl* **punties** *also* **pontes** *or* **pontees** *or* **puntees** *or* **ponties** [F *pontil* — more at PONTIL] **:** a solid metal rod used for fashioning hot glass to which it is attached by a button of glass first gathered on the rod — called also *pontil*

pu·nuk \ˈpü,nu̇k\ *adj, usu cap* [fr. *Punuk*, group of islets southeast of Saint Lawrence Island in the Bering sea] **:** of or belonging to an Eskimo culture of northeastern Siberia, northwestern Alaska, and St. Lawrence Island of about A.D. 500–1000 characterized by sea-mammal hunting, knives and carving tools with iron points, and a circle and dot decorative design

¹pu·ny \ˈpyünē, -ni\ *adj* -ER/-EST [MF *puisné* younger, lit., born afterward, fr. *puis* afterward (fr. — assumed — VL *postius*, compar. of L *post* after, afterward) + *né* born — more at POST-, NÉ] **1** *obs* **a :** PUISNE **b :** JUNIOR **c :** RECENT, SUBSEQUENT **d :** INEXPERIENCED, UNSKILLED **2 :** slight or inferior in power, vigor, size, or importance : lacking in force or vitality : WEAK, INSIGNIFICANT, SICKLY ⟨was cowed by their indifference to him, and felt ~ —G.D.Brown⟩ ⟨man's mechanical skill has permitted him to raise to the nth power his ~ strength —E.A.Hooton⟩ ⟨pitted my ~ opinion against the judgment of the medical world —V.G.Heiser⟩ ⟨the sun is not the only heavenly body which ~ man attempts to coerce by his magic —J.G.Frazer⟩ **syn** see PETTY

²puny *n* -ES [MF *puisné* younger son, fr. *puisné*, adj.] *obs* : PUISNE, JUNIOR, NOVICE, SUBORDINATE

pun·ya \ˈpənyə\ *n* -s [Skt *puṇya*, fr. neut. of *puṇya* auspicious, beautiful, good] *Jainism* : GOOD, MERIT — compare ⁶PAPA

¹pup \ˈpəp\ *n* -s [short for ¹*puppy*] **1 a :** a young dog : PUPPY **b :** one of the young of various other animals esp. of the dog family or of some marine mammals (as seals or sea otters) **2 :** an inexperienced or objectionably brash person ⟨men did the work in those days; these young ~*s* hardly knew the meaning of the word —John Galsworthy⟩ ⟨loathed going to this red-haired young ~ for supplies —Joseph Whitehill⟩ **3** *slang* **:** a prospect of apparent promise that fails of realization; *esp* : an investment that turns out to be relatively worthless ⟨had sold him a racehorse for $1,600 which turned out to be a ~ —*Time*⟩

²pup \"\ *vi* **pupped; pupped; pupping; pups** [short for ²*puppy*] **:** to bring forth pups or young

pu·pa \ˈpyüpə\ *n, pl* **pu·pae** \-ü,pē\ *or* **pupas** [NL, fr. L *pupa* girl, doll — more at PUPIL] **1 :** an insect in an intermediate usu. quiescent form that is assumed by an insect with complete metamorphosis between the larval and the imaginal stages, is enclosed in a hardened cuticle and often in a cocoon or case formed by the larva, and is characterized by internal dedifferentiation of larva structures and their replacement by structures typical of the imago which arise from imaginal disks — see CHRYSALIS; ANT illustration **2 :** the stage in an insect's life cycle in which it is a pupa

pupa co·arc·ta·ta \-,kō,ärkˈtäd·ə\ *n, pl* **pupae coarctatae** \-d·,ē\ [NL, lit., coarctate pupa] **:** a pupa in which the larval skin is retained as a pupal covering — compare COARCTATE

pu·pal \ˈpyüpəl\ *adj* **:** of, relating to, or characteristic of a pupa

pupa li·be·ra \-ˈlibərə\ *n, pl* **pupae libe·rae** \-bə,rē\ [NL, lit., free pupa] **:** a typical pupa in which the limbs are free

pupa ob·tec·ta \-äbˈtektə\ *n, pl* **pupae obtec·tae** \-k,tē\ [NL, lit., obtected pupa] **:** a typical pupa (as the chrysalis of most lepidopterans) in which the appendages are closely bound to the body

pu·par·i·al \pyüˈpa(a)rēəl\ *adj* [NL *puparium* + E *-al*] **:** of, relating to, or having the characteristics of a puparium

pu·par·i·um \-ēəm\ *n, pl* **pupar·ia** \-ēə\ [NL, fr. *pupa* + L *-arium*] **:** the outer shell formed from the larval skin that covers a coarctate pupa

pupa shell *n* **:** a small pupa-shaped shell of the family Pupillidae or a related form

pu·pate \ˈpyü,pāt\ *vi* -ED/-ING/-S [NL *pupa* + E *-ate*] **1 :** to become a pupa **2 :** to pass through a pupal state

pu·pa·tion \pyüˈpāshən\ *n* -s **:** the act or process of pupating

pupfish \ˈ=,=\ *n* [¹*pup* + *fish*] **:** either of two tiny cyprinodont fishes (*Cyprinodon nevadensis* and *C. diabolis*) of warm streams and springs of Nevada

pu·pi·dae \ˈpyüpə,dē\ [NL, fr. *Pupa*, type genus (fr. *pupa*) + *-idae*] *syn of* PUPILLIDAE

pu·pif·er·ous \(ˈ)pyüˈpif(ə)rəs\ *adj* [NL *pupa* + E *-iferous*] **:** producing sexual individuals — used of the parthenogenetic generation of an aphid

pu·pi·form \ˈpyüpə,fȯrm\ *adj* [NL *pupa* + E *-iform*] **:** shaped like a pupa : PUPAL

pu·pig·e·nous \(ˈ)pyüˈpijənəs\ *adj* [NL *pupa* + *-i-* + E *-genous*] : PUPIPAROUS

pu·pig·er·ous \-j(ə)rəs\ *adj* [NL *pupa* + E *-igerous*] **:** bearing or containing a pupa — used of dipterous larvae that do not molt when the pupa is formed within them but retain the larval skin as a pupal covering

¹pu·pil \ˈpyüpəl\ *n* -s [ME *pupille*, fr. MF, fr. L *pupillus* male ward, *pupilla* female ward; L *pupillus* fr. dim. of *pupus* boy; L *pupilla* fr. dim. of *pupa* girl, doll, puppet; prob. akin to L *puer* boy — more at PUERILE] **1 :** *Roman & Scots civil law* **:** a boy or a girl under the age of puberty and in the care of a guardian **2 :** a child or young person in school or in the charge of a tutor or instructor : STUDENT 1a **3 :** one who has been taught or influenced by a person of fame or distinction : DISCIPLE ⟨was a ~ of the great Stoic philosopher . . . and wrote a voluminous commentary to a work of his —Benjamin Farrington⟩

²pupil \"\ *n* -s [MF *pupille* pupil of the eye, fr. L *pupilla*, fr. dim. of *pupa* girl, doll, puppet; fr. the tiny image of oneself seen reflected in another's eye] **1 :** the contractile aperture in the iris of the eye that is round in most vertebrates whether enlarged or contracted but in foxes and cats becomes elliptical like a slit when contracted — see EYE illustration **2 :** the central dark spot of an ocellus

pu·pil·age *or* **pu·pil·lage** \-lij\ *n* -s [¹*pupil* + *-age*] **:** the condition or period of being or of being like a pupil

¹pu·pil·ar *also* **pu·pil·lar** \-lə(r)\ *adj* [¹*pupil* + *-ar*] : ¹PUPILLARY

²pupilar *also* **pupillar** \"\ *adj* [²*pupil* + *-ar*] : ²PUPILLARY

pu·pil·ize *or* **pu·pil·lize** \-pə,līz\ *vb* -ED/-ING/-S [¹*pupil* + *-ize*] *archaic* : TEACH, COACH

pu·pil·lar·i·ty *also* **pu·pi·lar·i·ty** \,pyüpəˈlarəd·ē\ *n* -ES [MF *pupillarité* state of being a minor ward, fr. *pupillaire* pupillary + *-ité* -ity] **:** the period of growth before puberty

¹pu·pil·lary \ˈpyüpə,lerē, -ri\ *adj* [F *pupillaire*, fr. L *pupillaris* of a ward, fr. *pupillus* ward + *-aris* -ar — more at PUPIL] **:** of or relating to a pupil or ward

²pupillary *also* **pu·pi·lary** \"\ *adj* [L *pupilla* pupil of the eye + E *-ary*] **:** of or relating to the pupil of the eye

pupillary reflex *n* [²*pupillary*] **:** the contraction of the pupil in response to light entering the eye

pupillary substitution *n* [trans. of L *substitutio pupillaris*] *Roman & civil Law* **:** the substitution by a father in his will of another heir for his own descendant instituted heir who is below the age of puberty and under the father's power for the purpose of having the substitute heir succeed to his own and the descendant's property if the descendant declines the inheritance or dies before attaining puberty when he could make his own will — compare QUASI-PUPILLARY SUBSTITUTION

pu·pil·late *also* **pu·pil·ate** \ˈpyüpə,lāt, -ˌlət\ *adj* [NL *pupillatus*, fr. L *pupilla* pupil of the eye + *-atus* -ate] : OCELLATED — used of a color spot

pu·pil·less \ˈpyüpəlləs\ *adj* **:** having no pupil

pu·pil·li·dae \pyüˈpilə,dē\ *n pl, cap* [NL, fr. *Pupilla*, type genus (fr. dim. of *pupa*) + *-idae*] **:** a large family of usu. small pulmonate land snails having a long spiral often somewhat cylindrical shell generally with a narrowed and more or less toothed aperture — compare PUPA SHELL

pupillo- *comb form* [L *pupilla* pupil of the eye] **:** pupil ⟨*pupillodilator*⟩

pupil load *n* [¹*pupil*] **:** the total number of pupils assigned to a single teacher in a school for classroom or other instruction

pu·pil·lo·dilator \,pyüpəlō+\ *adj* [*pupillo-* + *dilator*] **:** having a dilative effect on or involving dilation of the pupil of the eye

pu·pil·lom·e·ter \,pyüpəlˈämәd·ə(r)\ *n* [*pupillo-* + *-meter*] **:** an instrument for measuring the diameter of the pupil of the eye — **pu·pil·lom·e·try** \-mə·trē\ *n* -ES

pu·pil·lo·motor \ˈpyüpəlō+\ *adj* [*pupillo-* + *motor*] **:** having a motor influence on or involving alteration of the pupil of the eye ⟨~ nerve fibers⟩ ⟨a ~ reflex⟩

pupil teacher *n* [¹*pupil*] : STUDENT TEACHER

pu·pin system \pyüˈpēn-\ *n, usu cap P* [after Michael I. *Pupin* †1935 Am. physicist and inventor] **:** a telephone communication system in which the fidelity of the transmission is increased by introducing inductance coils in the line at definite equal intervals

pu·pip·a·ra \pyüˈpipərə\ *n pl, cap* [NL, fr. *pupa* + *-i-* + *-para* (fr. L, neut. pl. of *-parus* -parous)] **:** a division of Diptera in which the young are born as mature maggots ready to become pupae (as of the sheep ked or horse tick)

pu·pip·a·rous \-rəs\ *adj* [NL *pupa* + *-i-* + E *-parous*] **1 :** producing mature larvae that are ready to pupate at birth ⟨~ insects⟩ **2 :** of or relating to the Pupipara ⟨~ anatomy⟩

pu·poid \ˈpyü,pȯid\ *adj* [NL *pupa* + E *-oid*] : PUPIFORM

pupped *past of* PUP

pup·pet \ˈpəpət, *usu* -əd·+V\ *n* -s *often attrib* [ME *popet*, fr. MF *poupette* little doll, dim. of (assumed) *poupe* doll (whence F *poupée* doll), fr. (assumed) VL *puppa*, alter. of L *pupa* girl, doll, puppet — more at PUPIL] **1 a :** a small-scale figure of a human or other living being often constructed with jointed limbs, appropriately painted and costumed, and moved usu. on a small stage by a rod or by hand from below or by strings or wires from above — see MARIONETTE **b** *obs* **:** an actor in a play or pantomime **2 a** *archaic* : IDOL 1a **b :** DOLL 1a **3** *archaic* **:** a vain gaudily dressed person **4 :** one whose acts are controlled by an outside force or influence ⟨is no longer the arbiter of his own situation, but rather the ~ of circumstance —Joseph Furphy⟩ ⟨felt that they were after all mere ~*s*, creatures he could use —Sherwood Anderson⟩: **a :** a political or governmental official acting in an ostensibly independent or discretionary capacity but actually carrying out instructions from another authority or source ⟨eager to succeed, yet empty of policy and the ~ of his country's enemies —Hilaire Belloc⟩ ⟨their satellites and ~*s* and collaborators have indisputably recorded the actual nature of their governance —Walter Millis⟩ **b :** a character in literature that serves chiefly as an agent of the author's designs without exhibiting or developing a distinct personality or a logical motivation ⟨his personages are mere ~*s*, or, at best, incarnations of abstract qualities, or idealizations of disembodied grace or beauty —Richard Garnett †1906⟩ ⟨they are not characters; they are ~*s* needed to establish certain information —John Van Druten⟩ **5** *obs* : PUPPY **6 :** a lathe poppet

¹pup·pe·teer \,pəpəˈti(ə)r, -iə\ *n* -s [*puppet* + *-eer*] **:** one who manipulates puppets or marionettes

²puppeteer \"\ *vi* -ED/-ING/-S **:** to perform the functions or work of a puppeteer ⟨in whose show she ~*ed* —Paul McPharlin⟩

puppet government *n* **:** a government which is endowed with the outward symbols of authority but in which direction and control are exercised by another power

pup·pet·ize \ˈpəpə,tīz\ *vt* -ED/-ING/-S **:** to make into or like a puppet ⟨tendency . . . to ~ his characters —*Nineteenth Century*⟩

puppet master *n* **:** one who makes and entertains with puppets

puppet player *n* **:** one that manages puppets in a puppet show

pup·pet·ry \ˈpəpətrē, -ri\ *n* -ES [*puppet* + *-ry*] **1** *archaic* : MUMMERY 2 ⟨the low ~ of thrones —S.T.Coleridge⟩ **2 :** the production or creation of puppets or puppet shows ⟨this yearbook . . . is one of the outstanding contributions to ~ —*Quarterly Jour. of Speech*⟩ ⟨a thriving center of ~ —Barry Carman⟩ **3 :** the creation or presence in a literary work of an inadequately motivated character or group of characters ⟨a great modern writer . . . capable in activity of presenting thoughtful women, thinking men, groaned over his ~, that he dared not animate them —George Meredith⟩

puppet show *or* **puppet play** *n* **:** a usu. dramatic performance staged with puppets with the dialogue or music provided by a puppeteer

puppet valve *n* : LIFT VALVE

pup·pi·ly \ˈpəpəlē\ *adj* [¹*puppy* + *-ly*] *archaic* : PUPPYISH

pupping *pres part of* PUP

¹pup·py \ˈpəpē, -pi\ *n* -ES [ME *popi*, fr. MF *popée, poupée* doll, toy, fr. (assumed) *poupe* doll — more at PUPPET] **1** *obs* **:** a small dog used esp. as a woman's pet **2 a :** a young domestic dog; *specif* : one less than a year old **b :** PUP 1b **3 :** PUP 2 **4 :** a small ball of crude rubber softened by means of kerosine to a gelatinous consistency and used by stampers to clean surplus gold from book covers after finishing or stamping — called also *rubber dog*

²puppy \"\ *vi* -ED/-ING/-ES *archaic* : PUP

pup·py·dom \-dəm\ *n* -s [¹*puppy* + *-dom*] : PUPPYHOOD

puppy drum *n* **:** a young drumfish

puppyfish \ˈ=,=,=\ *n* : MONKFISH

puppyfoot \ˈ=,=,=\ *n, pl* **puppyfeet :** a card of the club suit in a pack of playing cards

pup·py·hood \ˈpəpē,hu̇d\ *n* **:** the state or period of being a puppy

pup·py·ish \-ēish\ *adj* **:** of, relating to, or characteristic of a puppy ⟨whimpering and wailing in a ~ sort of way —Jack London⟩

pup·py·ism \-ē,izəm\ *n* -s **:** the quality or state of being a puppy

puppy love *n* : CALF LOVE

puppy shark *n* **1 :** CUB SHARK **2 :** a young or small shark

puppytrack \ˈ=,=,=\ *n* : PUPPYFOOT

pups *pl of* PUP, *pres 3d sing of* PUP

pup tent *n* **:** a wedge-shaped shelter tent usu. without flooring, sidewalls, or window

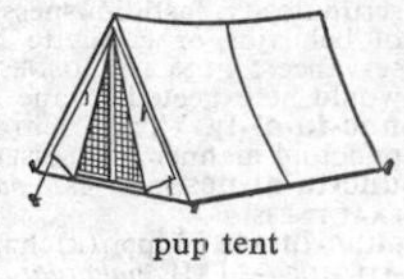

pu·pu·nha \puˈpünyə\ *n* -s [Pg, fr. Tupi] **:** a pinnate-leaved palm (*Guilielma speciosa*) that occurs in northern Brazil and Venezuela and has red starchy edible fruit

pup tent

pu·qui·na \püˈkēnə\ *n, pl* **puquina** *or* **puquinas** *usu cap* **1 a :** a people inhabiting the shores of Lake Titicaca in Bolivia **b :** a member of such people **2 :** the language of the Puquina people

pur *archaic var of* PURR

pur *abbr* **1** purchase; purchaser; purchasing **2** purification **3** pursuit

pu·ra·na \püˈränə\ *n* -s *often cap* [Skt *purāṇa*, lit., ancient, an ancient tale, fr. *purā* formerly; akin to OE ¹*fore*] **1 :** an ancient legendary tale of India **2 :** the third class of shastras or a text of this class — **pu·ra·nic** \-nik\ *adj, often cap*

pu·ra·sa·ti \,p(y)u̇rəˈsäd·ē\ *or* **pu·le·sa·ti** \,p(y)ülə-\ *n, pl* **purasati** *or* **pulesati** *usu cap* [Egypt *prst*] **:** a Mediterranean people wearing a distinctive armor and feather crest believed to have been refugees from Crete migrating to Palestine and there becoming the Philistines

pu·rau \ˈpü,rau̇\ *n* -s [Tahitian] : MAJAGUA a

pur au·tre vie \pu̇,rōd·ə(r)ˈvē, -ō,trə-\ [AF] **:** for the life of another — used of an estate the tenancy of which is measured by the life of a person other than the tenant; compare LIFE ESTATE

¹pur·blind \ˈpər, ˈpə +,-\ *adj* [ME *pur blind, pure blind*, fr. ²*pure* + *blind*] **1 a** *obs* **:** wholly blind ⟨~ Argus, all eyes and no sight —Shak.⟩ **b :** partly blind : DIM-SIGHTED, SHORT-SIGHTED ⟨like a morning eagle . . . ~ amid foggy, midnight wolds —John Keats⟩ ⟨~ with cataracts —Gerald Kersh⟩ **2 :** comprehending or discerning imperfectly or obscurely : lacking in vision, insight, or understanding : characterized by obtuseness ⟨this ~ policy of social legislation⟩ ⟨shooting pheasants . . . in their ~ pomp of pelf and power —James Joyce⟩ — **pur·blind·ly** *adv* — **pur·blind·ness** *n* -ES

²purblind \"\ *vt* **:** to make purblind

pur·chas·able *also* **pur·chase·able** \ˈpərchəsəbəl, ˈpəch-, ˈpəich-\ *adj* [¹*purchase* + *-able*] **1 :** capable of being purchased : available on the market **2 :** VENAL, CORRUPT

¹pur·chase \-chəs\ *vb* -ED/-ING/-S [ME *purchacen*, fr. OF *porchacier, purchacier* to seek to obtain, fr. *por, pur, pour* for (modif. — perh. influenced by L *per* through — of L *pro* for) + *chacier* to pursue, chase — more at FOR, CHASE] *vt* **1 a** *archaic* **:** to get into one's possession : GAIN, ACQUIRE ⟨your accent is something finer than you could ~ in so removed a dwelling —Shak.⟩ **b :** to acquire (real estate) by any means other than descent or inheritance **c** *archaic* **:** to obtain (as a license) from authority **d :** to obtain (as merchandise) by paying money or its equivalent : buy for a price ⟨*purchased* a new suit⟩ **e :** to obtain (something desired) by an outlay (as of labor, danger, sacrifice) ⟨~ one's life at the expense of one's honor⟩ : WIN, EARN ⟨his place was dearly *purchased*⟩ **2** *obs* **:** to cause to occur : EFFECT, PROCURE **3 a :** to haul in or up with or as if with a mechanical device or rope **b :** to apply to (as something to be moved or lifted) a device for obtaining a mechanical advantage : get a purchase upon or apply a purchase to; *also* : to move (as a cannon) by a purchase **4 a** *obs* **:** to serve as a ransom for **b :** to constitute the means or medium for buying (something) ⟨our dollars ~ less each year⟩ ⟨expert flattery may ~ an honest man⟩ ~ *vi* **1 a** *obs* **:** to acquire wealth or property **b :** to make a purchase or purchases : BUY **2** *obs* **:** to exert oneself : expend effort toward some end

²purchase \"\ *n* -s [ME *purchas, porchas*, fr. OF, fr. *porchacier* to purchase] **1 :** an act or instance of purchasing: as **a** *obs* (1) **:** the taking or seizing of prey (as in hunting)

(2) : the taking of something into one's possession violently or with force of arms : PLUNDERING, PILLAGE **b** *obs* : the seeking, procuring, or taking into possession of something : ACQUISITION; *also* : an act of instigating : CONTRIVANCE **c** : the acquiring of lands or tenements by any means other than descent or inheritance **d** : the acquiring of title to or property in anything for a price : a buying for money or its equivalent ⟨the ~ of shares in a business⟩ **2 a** (1) : something gotten into one's possession by any means honest or dishonest : GAIN, BOOTY; *esp* : the prize of a privateer (2) : something obtained for a price in money or its equivalent ⟨showed her ~*s* with pride⟩ **b** (1) : annual yield in rent (2) : value or potentiality for use or service in something or the hypothetical or figurative cash value of such or of a specified increment of such ⟨a life not worth a day's ~⟩ **c** : something bought considered with reference to its price or value : BARGAIN, BUY ⟨will find him a dearer ~ than she thought⟩ ⟨a good ~⟩ **3** *chiefly Scot* : means of acquiring property : RESOURCES **4 a** (1) : a mechanical hold or advantage applied to the raising or moving of heavy bodies (as by a lever, tackle, capstan) (2) : an apparatus or device by which the advantage is gained (as a pulley tackle) **b** (1) : an advantage used in applying one's power in any effort (2) : position or means of exerting power **5** : an unorganized minor territorial division in New Hampshire consisting of land that was originally laid off and sold by the state to an individual or individuals

pur·chase·less \-sləs\ *adj* : giving no purchase ⟨straining through the ~ mud⟩

purchase money *n* : the consideration paid or to be paid by the purchaser of property

purchase–money mortgage *n* : a mortgage to secure part or all of the purchase price of the property mortgaged given by the buyer to the seller or to a third person furnishing a loan to the buyer

purchase prize *n* : an award of being purchased (as by an established collection or museum) conferred upon a work of art in a competitive exhibition

pur·chas·er \-sə(r)\ *n* -s [ME *purchasour*, fr. AF, fr. OF *purchacier* to purchase + AF *-our* -or] : one that purchases: as **a** *obs* : one that makes provision esp. for his material welfare : a mercenary person **b** : one that acquires an estate in lands by his own act or agreement or takes or obtains an estate by any means other than by descent or inheritance **c** (1) : one that acquires property for a consideration (as of money) : BUYER, VENDEE (2) : PURCHASING AGENT

purchase shears *n pl but sing or pl in constr* : very powerful shears with removable steel cutters of rectangular section

purchase tax *n* : a tax imposed in Great Britain upon various commodities at rates graduated according to the degree of luxury or necessity of the particular commodity

purchase warrant *n* : WARRANT 2e(2)

purchasing agent *n* [fr. gerund of ¹*purchase*] **1** : an employee who purchases materials and supplies to be used by a business (as a manufacturer) **2** : a middleman who makes purchases for clients

purchasing power *n* : capacity to buy: as **a** : capacity of an individual, group of individuals, or the aggregate of prospective buyers as determined primarily by current income and savings — called also *buying power* **b** : the worth of money as determined by what it can buy at a given time in comparison with what it could buy at a specified previous time ⟨decline in the *purchasing power* of the dollar⟩

purchasing power parity *n* : the ratio between the currencies of two countries at which each currency when exchanged for the other will purchase the same quantity of goods as it purchases at home excluding customs duties and costs of transport — compare PAR

pur·dah *also* **par·dah** \ˈpərdə\ *n* -s [Hindi *parda*, lit., screen, veil, fr. Per] : a practice inaugurated by Muslims and later adopted by various Hindus and found esp. in India that involves the seclusion of women from public observation by means of concealing clothing including the veil and by the use of high-walled enclosures, screens, and curtains within the home

pur·do·ni·um \ˌpərˈdōnēəm\ *also* **pur·do·ni·an** \-ēən\ *or* **pur·do·ni·on** \-ēən\ *n* -s [prob. fr. *Purdon*, name of its inventor] *Brit* : a container for coal in the form of a box with removable metal lining

pur·dy \ˈpərdi\ *adj* [origin unknown] *dial Eng* : disagreeably self-important

¹**pure** \ˈpyu̇(ə)r, -ůə\ *adj* -ER/-EST [ME *pur*, fr. OF, fr. L *purus* clean; akin to Skt *punāti* he cleanses, MIr *ūr* fresh, green, Welsh *ir*] **1 a** *of physical matter* (1) : unmixed with any other thing : free from admixture : containing no added, substitute, or foreign substance ⟨~ gold⟩ ⟨the *purest* silk obtainable⟩ (2) : free from dust, dirt, or taint : containing nothing that impairs or is hurtful ⟨~ spring water rich in minerals⟩ ⟨~ food and abundant rest⟩ (3) : perfectly clear to the eye : optically clear : SPOTLESS, STAINLESS ⟨a ~ bubbling brook⟩ ⟨fresh ~ linens⟩ **b** (1) : free from harshness or roughness and in tune — used of a musical tone (2) : perfect mathematically ⟨~ harmony⟩ ⟨a ~ interval⟩ — compare TEMPERED (3) : ABSOLUTE 11a **c** *of a vowel* : characterized by no appreciable alteration of articulation or acoustic effect during the utterance : not diphthongized **2 a** (1) : being such and no other : SHEER, SIMPLE ⟨acted so from ~ necessity⟩ ⟨the *purest* malice⟩ (2) : being nothing less than : COMPLETE, UNALLOYED, ⟨~ folly⟩ **b** (1) : taken in its essential character and apart from relations and applications : concerned basically with theory rather than practice or application : ABSTRACT ⟨~ science⟩ ⟨~ mechanics⟩ (2) : neither biased by practical considerations nor directed toward the exposition of demonstrable realities or the solution of practical problems ⟨~ literature⟩; *esp* : nonobjective and to be appraised on formal and technical qualities only — used esp. of a work of art **3 a** (1) : free from what harms, vitiates, weakens, or pollutes : faultless and uncontaminated : PERFECT — used of concepts, actions, and other immaterial matters ⟨the ~ religion of our fathers⟩ ⟨a critic of ~ if somewhat narrow taste⟩ (2) : containing nothing that does not properly belong : free from alteration, error, or foreign increment ⟨the ~ and original text⟩ ⟨spoke a very ~ French⟩ **b** : free from moral fault or guilt : INNOCENT, GUILTLESS ⟨moved only by the *purest* feelings⟩ ⟨a ~ and upright man⟩ **c** : marked by chastity : CONTINENT ⟨a ~ relationship between the sexes⟩ **d** (1) : of pure blood : having an unmixed ancestry ⟨a ~ Arab horse⟩ (2) : HOMOZYGOUS ⟨mice ~ for the dilution factor⟩ (3) : breeding true for one or more characters **e** *obs* : belonging to a religious group that stresses personal purity and precision of conduct — used usu. disparagingly of Puritans and Quakers **f** : ritually clean : suitable for use in holy services **g** : free from empirical elements : A PRIORI ⟨~ intuition⟩ ⟨~ ego⟩ **4** *chiefly dial* : having good health and spirits : FINE

syn ABSOLUTE, SIMPLE, SHEER: these words are alike in stressing the notion that the essential character of a thing, unmixed, unalleviated, and undiminished, is being spoken of. PURE may stress lack of intermixture, adulterating, or obscuring the essence of a matter ⟨the founders of American political democracy were not so naïvely devoted to *pure* theory that they were unaware of the necessity of cultural conditions for the successful working of democratic forms —John Dewey⟩ ⟨a wider opening of the hospitable American doors to the oppressed of Europe seemed to the divines and social reformers an exercise of *pure* magnanimity —Roger Burlingame⟩ ABSOLUTE may further emphasize lack of admixture or stress lack of dependence, relationship, or reservation ⟨for Christianity aims at nothing less than *absolute* truth —W.R.Inge⟩ ⟨the obstinacy, the ferocity, the treachery of the aristocracy, had compelled Caesar to crush them; and the more desperate their struggles the more *absolute* the necessity became —J.A. Froude⟩ ⟨it was horrid, that pitiful, forlorn cry of pain and of *absolute* despair coming from such a giant —Liam O'Flaherty⟩ SIMPLE stresses isolation from complicating or obscuring factors; it may indicate that further resolution or analysis is unnecessary or impossible ⟨the assumption that the exposure of an error is identical with the discovery of the truth — that error and truth are *simple* opposites —H.L.Mencken⟩ ⟨the *simple* truth, so hard to come by anywhere, implies, of course, a lucid statement of it —H.V.Gregory⟩ SHEER has more intensifying force and less suggestion of shades of meaning than others in this group; it may stress the palpable revelation or obvious display of whatever is being spoken of ⟨the "Ancient Mariner," . . . is a work of *sheer* imagination —J.L.Lowes⟩ ⟨is there anything that, for *sheer* simplicity of pathos . . . can be said to equal or even approach the last act of Christ's passion —Oscar Wilde⟩ ⟨the *sheer* dynamism of the totalitarian promise acquires a glistening certainty which few men can stand up against —A.M.Schlesinger b.1917⟩ **syn** see in addition CHASTE

²**pure** \"\ *adv* [ME *pur*, fr. *pur*, adj.] : PURELY: as **a** : without admixture — usu. used in combination with an adjective ⟨a *pure*-white linen⟩ ⟨*pure*-silk shirtings⟩ **b** *chiefly dial* : to a notable degree : EXCEEDINGLY, THOROUGHLY ⟨~ miserable with a toothache⟩ ⟨most of the track was ~ muddy⟩

³**pure** \"\ *vt* -ED/-ING/-S [ME *puren*, fr. *pur*, adj.] **1** *obs* : PURIFY, REFINE **2** : PUER

⁴**pure** \"\ *n* -s [in sense 1, fr. ¹*pure*; in sense 2, fr. ³*pure*] **1 a** : PURITY **b** : something that is pure **2** : PUER

⁵**pure** \ˈpür\ *Scot var of* POOR

pure and simple *adj* : of the clearest kind : MERE, PLAIN, ABSOLUTE — used postpositively for emphasis ⟨a pointer word *pure and simple* —Frederick Bodmer⟩ ⟨he is an adventurer *pure and simple*⟩

¹**pureblood** \ˈ⸗ˌ⸗\ *or* **pure–blooded** \ˈ⸗¦⸗⸗\ *adj* [¹*pure* + *blood*, *blooded*] : of unmixed ancestry : PUREBRED

²**pureblood** \"\ *n* : a pureblood individual : PUREBRED ⟨a beef sire that is a ~ of excellent ancestry⟩; *esp* : a member of one of the non-Caucasian divisions of mankind (as a Negro or American Indian) — compare MIXED-BLOOD

¹**purebred** \ˈ⸗¦⸗\ *adj* [¹*pure* + *bred*] : bred from members of a recognized breed, strain, or kind without admixture of other blood over many generations — used chiefly of livestock ⟨~ cattle⟩ ⟨~ poultry⟩; compare GRADE, THOROUGHBRED

²**purebred** \ˈ⸗ˌ⸗\ *n* -s : a purebred animal esp. of a lineage established by registration records

pure christiania *n, often cap C* : PARALLEL CHRISTIANIA

pure color *n* **1** : a color evoked by homogeneous spectral light **2** : a color of a colorimetric purity approximating that of the colors of the physical spectrum

pure culture *n* **1** : a culture containing a growth of a single kind of organism free from other organisms **2** : a culture containing the descendants of a single organism whether free from all organisms of other kinds or not

puredee *also* **pure–D** \ˈ⸗¦⸗\ *adj* [¹*pure* + *dee*] *South* : THOROUGHGOING, UNMITIGATED ⟨a fit of ~ jealousy —Eudora Welty⟩

pure–dye \ˈ⸗¦⸗\ *adj* [¹*pure* + *dye*] : having very little or no weighting — used of dyed silk

¹**pu·ree** \pyu̇ˈrā, pyüˈ-,pyə'- *sometimes* pə'- *or* -ˈrē\ *n* -s [F, fr. past part. of MF *purer* to cleanse, strain vegetables, fr. L *purare* to cleanse, fr. *purus* clean — more at PURE] **1** : a paste or thick liquid suspension of a food (as liver, peas, chestnuts) usu. produced by rubbing the cooked food through a sieve **2** : a thick soup of smooth texture having pureed vegetables as a base ⟨a tomato ~⟩ ⟨~ of dried peas⟩

²**puree** \"\ *vt* **pureed; pureed; pureeing; purees** : to prepare in the form of a puree : boil soft and then rub through a sieve ⟨~*ing* vegetables for soup⟩

pure endowment *n* : an insurance contract promising to pay the insured a stated sum if he survives a specified period with nothing payable in case of prior death — compare ENDOWMENT INSURANCE

pure experience *n* : experience unqualified by conception or association : immediate apprehension

pure–food law *n* : a legislative act prohibiting the adulteration or misbranding of any article of food

pure forest *n* : a forest in which at least 80 percent of the trees are of the same species

purehearted \ˈ⸗¦⸗\ *adj* [¹*pure* + *hearted*] : having the heart free from guile or evil

pure imaginary *n* : a complex number of the form *ai* where *a* is any real number and $i=\sqrt{-1}$

pure interest *n* : interest on capital excluding payment for risk

pure land *n, usu cap P&L* **1** : a paradise into which according to Amidism anyone is reborn who calls in faith on the name of the deified Buddha Amitabha and in which one can attain Buddhahood free from the hindrances of earth — called also *Sukhavati, Western Paradise* **2** : AMIDISM

pure line *n* [trans. of G *reine linie*] : a homogeneous line of descent: as **a** : a group of closely related individuals of identical genetic constitution (as the offspring of a homozygous self-fertilized parent) : a line of descent theoretically realizable from the inbreeding of completely homozygous and comparable parents **b** : the descendants of a single individual esp. by vegetative multiplication : CLONE

pure·ly *adv* : in a pure manner: as **a** : without admixture of anything injurious, inharmonious, foreign, or otherwise undesirable or divergent ⟨a ~ bred strain⟩ ⟨to speak French ~⟩ **b** : MERELY, SIMPLY, SOLELY ⟨a ~ formal courtesy⟩ **c** : CHASTELY, INNOCENTLY ⟨live ~⟩ **d** (1) : COMPLETELY, WHOLLY ⟨a ~ experimental study⟩ (2) *chiefly dial* : in the highest degree : EXCEEDINGLY — usu. used prepositively ⟨I ~ hate a haircut —Helen Eustis⟩

pure minor scale *n* : NATURAL MINOR SCALE

pure–mixed \ˈ⸗¦⸗\ *adj* : free from related organisms; *esp* : containing the desired organism together with one or more others that are necessary for its growth ⟨a *pure-mixed* culture of paramecium⟩

pure·ness *n* -ES [ME *purenesse*, fr. *pur*, *puer* pure + *-nesse* -ness] : the quality or state of being pure : PURITY

pure premium *n* : NET PREMIUM

pure profit *n* : profit less the unremunerated cost of services furnished by the owner for which payment would be received if supplied elsewhere

pure proposition *n* : a proposition that asserts or denies without qualification

¹**pur·er** \ˈpyu̇rə(r)\ *comparative of* PURE

²**purer** \"\ *n* -s [³*pure* + *-er*] : BATER

pure reason *n, Kantianism* : the faculty that embraces the a priori forms of knowledge and is the source of transcendental ideas — compare INTUITIVE REASON

pures *pres 3d sing of* PURE, *pl of* PURE

pure spectrum *n* : a spectrum in which the dispersion is highly discriminative so that at each point the light is practically monochromatic

purest *superlative of* PURE

pure stand *n* : a plant population consisting exclusively or largely of members of one species, variety, or type ⟨a *pure stand* of oak⟩

pure tone *n* : a musical tone of a single frequency produced by simple harmonic vibrations and without overtones

pure wave *n* : a radio wave produced by a transmitting set that is substantially free from harmonics or any frequency except the fundamental

pur·ey \ˈpyu̇rē\ *n* -s [¹*pure* + *-y*] : a child's solid-colored glass marble

¹**pur·fle** \ˈpərfəl, ˈpə̄f-,ˈpəif-\ *vt* **purfled; purfled; purfling** \-f(ə)liŋ\ **purfles** [ME *purfilen*, fr. MF *porfiler* to interweave, border, fr. (assumed) VL *profilare*, fr. L *pro-* forward + LL *filare* to spin — more at PRO-, FILE] **1** : to ornament the border of : trim the edge or edges of **2** : to decorate with embroidery : ornament with metallic threads, jewels, or fur ⟨a goodly lady clad in scarlet red *purfled* with gold and pearl of rich assay —Edmund Spenser⟩ : to ornament (as cabinetwork) with tracery, inlay, or similar treatment esp. around the edges ⟨~ a violin body⟩

²**purfle** \"\ *n* -s [ME *porfil*, *purfil*, fr. MF *porfil*, fr. *porfiler* to border] **1** : a decorated border; *esp* : an embroidered edge of a garment **2** : a heraldic border (as of fur)

purfled *adj* [ME *purfiled*, fr. past part. of *purfilen* to purfle] : having trimming or decoration (as of embroidery or tracery); *also* : BORDERED

purfled work *n* : delicate esp. Gothic tracery (as in architectural ornamentation)

purfling *n* -s [ME *purfiling*, fr. gerund of *purfilen* to border] : ornamentation on a border; *esp* : an inlaid border of a musical instrument (as a violin)

pur·ga \ˈpu̇(ə)rgə\ *n* -s [Russ, fr. Karelian *purgu* snowstorm; akin to Finn *purku* snowstorm] : an intense arctic snowstorm occurring usu. in flat open country and characterized by severe cold and wind-driven snow

purgament *n* -s [L *purgamentum*, fr. *purgare* + *-mentum* -ment] *obs* : EXCRETION

pur·ga·tion \ˌpərˈgāshən, pə̄ˈg-,pəiˈg-\ *n* -s [ME *purgacioun*, fr. MF *purgation*, fr. L *purgation-*, *purgatio*, fr. *purgatus* (past part. of *purgare* to cleanse) + *-ion-*, *-io* -ion — more at PURGE] **1 a** : the act of purging; *specif* : vigorous evacuation of the bowels (as from the action of a purgative or an infective agent) **b** : administration of or treatment with a purgative **c** *obs* : MENSTRUATION **2** : ceremonial cleansing : PURIFICATION **3 a** : moral or spiritual purification : destruction of the influences of sin : a freeing from moral evil **b** : the first stage in a mystic's progress to perfection consisting of conscious moral purification by self-discipline, subjugation of distracting desires, ascetic practices, and similar measures — called also *purgative way* **4** : the clearing of oneself from alleged guilt ⟨let him put me to my ~ —Shak.⟩ — see CANONICAL PURGATION, VULGAR PURGATION

¹**pur·ga·tive** \ˈpərgəd·|iv, ˈpə̄g-,ˈpəig-, -gət|\ *adj* [ME *purgatif*, fr. MF, fr. LL *purgativus*, fr. L *purgatus* + *-ivus* -ive] **1** : purging or tending to purge : CATHARTIC **2** : cleansing or purifying esp. from sin or sinful inclinations : PURGATORIAL, EXPIATORY ⟨a ~ ceremony⟩ **3** : freeing legally from fault or blame : clearing from guilt ⟨a ~ answer⟩ ⟨~ evidence⟩

²**purgative** \"\ *n* -s : a purging medicine : CATHARTIC — compare LAXATIVE

pur·ga·tive·ly \|əvlē, -li\ *adv* : so as to purge : in a purgative manner

purgative way *n* : PURGATION 3

pur·ga·to·ri·al \ˌ⸗⸗¦tōrēəl, -¦tȯr-\ *adj* [in sense 1, fr. LL *purgatorius* cleansing + E *-al*; in sense 2, fr. ML *purgatorium* purgatory + E *-al* — more at PURGATORY] **1** : cleansing of sin or sinful influences : EXPIATORY, PURIFYING **2** : of, relating to, or resembling purgatory ⟨a ~ experience⟩ ⟨~ fires⟩

¹**pur·ga·to·ri·an** \ˌ⸗⸗¦⸗rēən\ *n* -s [¹*purgatory* + *-an*] : a believer in the existence of a purgatory

²**purgatorian** \ˈ⸗¦⸗⸗\ *adj* [¹*purgatory* + *-an*] : PURGATORIAL 2

¹**pur·ga·to·ry** \ˈpərgəˌtōrē, ˈpə̄g-,ˈpəig-, -tȯr-, -ri\ *n* -ES *sometimes cap* [ME, fr. AF or ML; AF *purgatorie*, fr. ML *purgatorium*, fr. neut. of LL *purgatorius* cleansing, purging, fr. L *purgatus* (past part. of *purgare* to purge) + *-orius* -ory — more at PURGE] **1** : an intermediate state after death for expiatory purification; *specif* : a place or state of punishment wherein according to Roman Catholic doctrine the souls of those who die in God's grace may expiate venial sins or satisfy divine justice for the temporal punishment still due to remitted mortal sin **2 a** : a place or state like purgatory : a condition of prolonged and usu. penitential suffering : temporary torture or punishment : acute misery ⟨the return trip was absolute ~⟩ **b** : an expiation or means of expiation **3 a** : a chasm or cleft in a cliff or wall of rock differing from a flume in not having a stream **b** *chiefly dial* : SWAMP; *esp* : a swamp that is dangerous or difficult to cross

²**purgatory** \"\ *adj* [ME, fr. LL *purgatorius*] *archaic* : PURGATIVE, PURGATORIAL

³**purgatory** \"\ *vt* -ED/-ING/-ES [¹*purgatory*] : to put into a purgatory or a purgatorial situation : subject to prolonged suffering

purgatory hammer *n* [¹*purgatory*] : a prehistoric stone hammer that was formerly popularly supposed to have been buried with the dead for use in knocking at the gates of purgatory

¹**purge** \ˈpərj, ˈpə̄j, ˈpəij\ *vb* -ED/-ING/-S [ME *purgen*, fr. OF *purgier*, fr. L *purgare* to cleanse, purify, purge, fr. OL *purigare*, fr. *purus* clean, pure + *-igare* (fr. *agere* to lead, drive, do) — more at PURE, ACT] *vt* **1 a** (1) : to clear (as oneself or another) from a charge or doubt : remove a stigma from the name of : demonstrate the innocence of : free from a charge by purgation ⟨the committee heard his attempt to ~ himself of a charge of heresy⟩ (2) : to demonstrate (as oneself) to be free from guilt by submission to ordeal under a medieval code of legal procedure **b** : to make free of physical impurities : make clean by removing whatever is foreign, soiling, or superfluous ⟨~ metal of dross⟩ ⟨*purging* water by distillation⟩ **c** : to make morally or spiritually clean : free from moral or ceremonial contamination or defilement **2** : to remove by a process of cleansing : take off or out by or as if by washing ⟨~ away dross from metal⟩ ⟨let us ~ our sins with prayer⟩ **3 a** : to cause evacuation of or from (the bowels) ⟨drugs that ~ the bowels⟩ or of or from the bowel of ⟨*purged* himself with calomel⟩ **b** : to free (itself) of suspended matter usu. by sedimentation : DEFECATE — used of a liquid **c** : to free (as a boiler) of sediment or relieve (as a steampipe) of trapped air by bleeding **d** : to rid (as a state or party) by a purge : get rid of (as disloyal or suspect elements from a group or undesirable material in a publication) : ELIMINATE **4** : to make submission or atonement in order to relieve oneself of (as a legal offence or sentence) ⟨a restitution that *purged* the previous seizure⟩ or in order to relieve (as oneself) from liability or penalty ⟨*purged* himself of contempt of court⟩ ~ *vi* **1** : to become free of impurities, excess, or other unwanted matter (as by clearing, discharging, washing) **2 a** : to have or produce frequent evacuations from the intestines (as by means of a purgative) **b** : to take a purge or purgative **3** : to cause or bring about purgation, purification, or similar effects **syn** see RID

²**purge** \"\ *n* -s **1 a** : an act or instance of purging : PURGATION **b** : a ridding (as of a nation or party) of elements or members regarded as treacherous, disloyal, or suspect **2** : something that purges; *esp* : PURGATIVE

purge·able \-jəbəl\ *adj* : capable of being purged : subject to purging

purg·ee \ˌpər¦jē, (ˈ)pə̄¦-, (ˈ)pəi¦-\ *n* -s [¹*purge* + *-ee*] : a person (as a political opponent) eliminated in a purge

purg·er \ˈ⸗jə(r)\ *n* -s [ME, fr. *purgen* to purge + *-er*] : one that purges ⟨the ~*s* of yesterday have become the purgees of today —Michael Padev⟩

purg·ery \-jərē\ *n* -ES [F *purgerie*, fr. *purger* to purge (fr. OF *purgier*) + *-erie* -ery] : the part of a sugarhouse where molasses is drained from the sugar

purging *n* -s [fr. gerund of ¹*purge*] **1** : the act or process of cleansing or purifying **2** : the evacuation of large amounts of usu. loose or unformed feces whether as a result of disease or of purgation

purging agaric *n* [fr. pres. part. of ¹*purge*] : a common white pore fungus (*Fomes officinalis*) of Europe and America that causes a heart rot of various conifers and has been used as a purgative in human medicine — called also *white agaric*

purging buckthorn *n* : a common arborescent European buckthorn (*Rhamnus cathartica*) that is widely naturalized in the eastern U.S. and has purgative black berries and bark

purging cassia *n* **1** : DRUMSTICK TREE **2** : CASSIA FISTULA

purging croton *n* : an East Indian shrub or small tree (*Croton tiglium*) whose seeds yield croton oil

purging flax *n* : a European annual herb (*Linum catharticum*) with white or yellowish white flowers followed by seeds that are cathartic and diuretic — called also *fairy flax*; see ¹LININ

purging house *n* [fr. gerund of ¹*purge*] : PURGERY

purging root *n* [fr. pres. part. of ¹*purge*] : the root of the flowering spurge

pu·ri \ˈpu̇rē\ *n* -s [Hindi, fr. Skt *pūrī*; akin to Skt *piparti* he fills, nourishes, sates, *pūrṇa* full — more at FULL] : a very light fried wheat cake of India

pu·ri·fi·cant \pyu̇ˈrifəkənt\ *n* -s [L *purificant-*, *purificans*, pres. part. of *purificare*] : a purifying agent

pu·ri·fi·ca·tion \ˌpyu̇rəfəˈkāshən\ *n* -s [MF, fr. L *purification-*, *purificatio*, fr. *purificatus* (past part. of *purificare* to purify) + *-ion-*, *-io* -ion — more at PURIFY] **1** : an act of purifying : the act or operation of removing impure, noxious, or foreign matter **2 a** : the act or operation of cleansing ceremonially by removing any pollution or defilement **b** : a cleansing from guilt or the pollution of sin : extinction of sinful desires or deliverance from their dominating power : spiritual or moral purgation ⟨~ through repentance⟩ **3** : the ceremony of bathing performed by Jewish women after menstruation in accordance with biblical law

pu·ri·fi·ca·tor \ˈ⸗⸗⸗ˌkād·ə(r)\ *n* -s [L *purificatus* + E *-or*] : one that purifies : PURIFIER: as **a** : a linen cloth used to wipe the chalice after celebration of the Eucharist **b** : a cloth⸗wrapped sponge used similarly to wipe the hands of the officiating clergy

¹pu·rifi·ca·to·ry \pyu̇ˈrifəkə,tōrē, ˈpyu̇rəf-, *chiefly Brit* ˌpyu̇(ə)rəfə̇ˈkātəri *or* -ā·tri\ *adj* [LL *purificatorius*, fr. L *purificatus* + *-orius* -ory] : serving, tending, or intended to purify : PURIFYING

²purificatory \"\ *n* -ES [ML *purificatorium*, fr. neut. of LL *purificatorius* serving to purify] : PURIFICATOR

pu·ri·fi·er \ˈpyu̇rə,fī(ə)r, -īə\ *n* -S [ME, fr. *purifien* to purify + *-er*] : one that purifies or cleanses (as an apparatus for purifying coal gas or a machine for separating fine bran particles from flour middlings) : CLEANSER, REFINER

pu·ri·form \ˈpyu̇rə,fȯrm\ *adj* [L *pur-* *pus* pus + E *-iform*] : constituting or resembling pus ⟨a ~ discharge⟩ : PURULENT

pu·ri·fy \ˈpyu̇rə,fī\ *vb* -ED/-ING/-ES [ME *purifien*, fr. MF *purifier*, fr. L *purificare*, fr. *purus* pure + *-ificare* -ify] *vt* **1** : to make pure: as **a** : to clear from material defilement or imperfection : free from impurities or noxious matter ⟨~*ing* air by filtration⟩ ⟨*purified* the house with soap, and water, and sweat⟩ **b** : to free from guilt or moral blemish ⟨~ the heart⟩ **c** : to cleanse ceremonially ⟨and Moses . . . *purified* the altar —Lev 8:15 (RSV)⟩ **d** : to free from anything that is alien, extraneous, improper, corrupting, or otherwise damaging ⟨~ a language of barbarisms⟩ ⟨*purified* the state of traitors⟩ **2** *Scots law* : to free (a condition) from defect or imperfection by performance or fulfillment ~ *vi* : to grow or become pure or clean

pu·rim \ˈpu̇rəm, ˈpü-, ˈ(,)rim, pu̇ˈrim\ *n* -S *usu cap* [Heb *pūrīm*, lit. the lots, fr. pl. of *pūr* lot; fr. the casting of lots by Haman to destroy the Jews, Esth 9:24-26] : a Jewish festival celebrated on the 14th of Adar and instituted to commemorate the deliverance of the Jews from the machinations of Haman — called also *Feast of Lots*

pu·rine \ˈpyu̇,rēn, -rə̇n\ *n* -S [G *purin*, fr. L *purus* pure + NL *uricus* uric (fr. E *uric*) + G *-in* -ine] **1** : a crystalline base $C_5H_4N_4$ composed of a pyrimidine ring fused with an imidazole ring that is prepared from uric acid and is the parent of compounds (as allantoin and alloxan) derived from uric acid — compare STRUCTURAL FORMULA **2** : a derivative of purine; *esp* : PURINE BASE

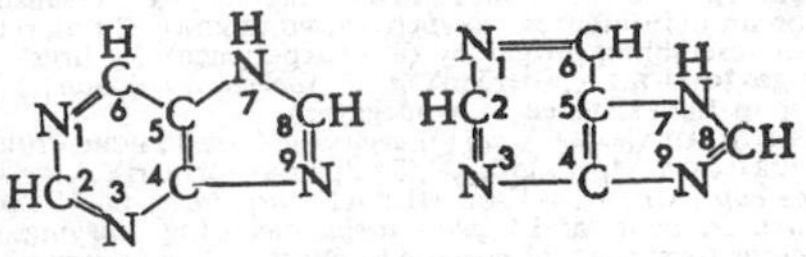

purine

purine base *n* : any of a group of crystalline bases comprising purine and bases derived from it (as adenine, caffeine, guanine, theobromine, or xanthine) some of which are components of nucleosides and nucleotides

pu·ri·ri \pəˈrirē\ *n* -S [Maori] : a New Zealand ironwood (*Vitex littoralis*) yielding a very durable hard strong dark brown wood

puris *pl of* PURI

pur·ism \ˈpyu̇,rizəm\ *n* -S [F *purisme*, fr. *pur* pure (fr. L *purus*) + *-isme* -ism] **1** : rigid adherence to or insistence on purity or nicety (as in literary style or use of words) **2** : an example of purism; *esp* : a word or phrase or a sense of a word or phrase that is used chiefly by purists ⟨readers who find a usage stigmatized as ~ have a right to know the stigmatizer's place in the purist scale —H.W.Fowler⟩ **3** : a theory and practice in art originated about 1918 by Amédée Ozenfant and Le Corbusier that reduces all natural appearances to a geometric simplicity characteristic of machines

¹pur·ist \-rə̇st\ *n* -S [F *puriste*, fr. *pur* + *-iste* -ist] : a person solicitous or oversolicitous about purity or nicety (as of conduct or usage): as **a** : one preoccupied with the purity of a language and its protection from the ingress of foreign or altered forms **b** : a sport fisherman who uses exclusively one method and who will give serious consideration to no other ⟨a dry fly ~⟩ ⟨a squidding ~⟩

²purist \"\ *adj* [¹*purist*] : PURISTIC

pu·ris·tic \pyu̇ˈristik, pyəˈr-, pyüˈr-\ *also* **pu·ris·ti·cal** \-tə̇kəl, -tēk-\ *adj* [¹*purist* + *-ic*, *-ical*] : of, relating to, or characteristic of purists or purism : marked by purism ⟨a ~ outlook⟩ ⟨a ~ style⟩ — **pu·ris·ti·cal·ly** \-tə̇k(ə)lē, -tēk-, -li\ *adv*

¹pu·ri·tan \ˈpyu̇rət°n, -rəd·ən, -rətən\ *n* -S [prob. fr. LL *puritas* purity + E *-an*] **1** *usu cap* : a member of a group of 16th and 17th century Protestant Christians in England opposing the traditional and formal usages of the Church of England who during the Commonwealth period (1649-59) became a powerful political party and who emigrated in large numbers to New England **2** *sometimes cap* **a** : one who (as because of adherence to a religious sect) practices or preaches a more rigorous or professedly purer moral code than that which prevails **b** : one who on religious or ethical grounds inveighs against current practices, pleasures, or indulgences which he regards as lax, impure, or corrupting : PRECISIAN ⟨she would make a ~ of the Devil —Shak.⟩

²puritan \"\ *adj* : of or relating to puritans, the Puritans, or puritanism

puritan father *n, often cap P&F* : one of the early Puritan settlers of New England

puritan gray *n, sometimes cap P* : a bluish gray that is less strong than clair de lune, greener and paler than average dusk (sense 3a), and paler than Medici blue

pu·ri·tan·ic \ˌpyu̇rəˈtanik, -nēk\ *adj* [¹*puritan* + *-ic*] : PURITANICAL

pu·ri·tan·i·cal \-nəkəl, -nēk-\ *adj* [¹*puritan* + *-ical*] **1** *often cap* : of or relating to the Puritans or their doctrines and practice **2** : manifesting the influence of puritan beliefs or practices : morally rigorous : STRICT ⟨a ~ woman⟩ ⟨strict ~ restraint⟩ — **pu·ri·tan·i·cal·ly** \-nək(ə)lē, -nēk-, -li\ *adv* — **pu·ri·tan·i·cal·ness** \-nəkəlnə̇s, -nēk-\ *n* -ES

pu·ri·tan·ism \ˈpyu̇rət°n,izəm, -rəd·ə,ni-, -rətə,ni-\ *n* -S **1** *usu cap* : the beliefs and practices of or characteristic of the Puritans **2** *sometimes cap* : strictness and austerity esp. in matters of religion or conduct

pu·ri·tan·ize \-°n,īz, -ə,nīz\ *vb* -ED/-ING/-S *sometimes cap* [¹*puritan* + *-ize*] *vi* : to practice puritanism : conform to puritan beliefs ~ *vt* : to make puritan : give a puritan character to

pu·ri·tan·ly *adv* : in a puritan manner : toward the Puritans or their beliefs or practices ⟨~ inclined⟩

pu·ri·tano \,p(y)u̇rəˈtä(,)nō, -tä(-\ *n* -S [AmerSp, fr. Sp *puritano* puritan, fr. E *puritan*] : a medium-sized cigar that resembles a perfecto and is pointed at both ends

pu·ri·ty \ˈpyu̇rəd·ē, -ətē, -i\ *n* -ES [ME *purete*, fr. OF *pureté*, fr. LL *puritat-*, *puritas*, fr. L *purus* pure + *-itat-*, *-itas* -ity] **1** : the quality or state of being pure ⟨a chemical of extreme ~⟩ ⟨lead a life of perfect ~⟩ ⟨the ~ of his intent was manifest⟩ ⟨spoke a French of great ~⟩ **2 a** : the fraction of spectrum component in a mixture of achromatic and spectrum colors that is required to match the color being considered and that constitutes an approximate psychophysical correlate of saturation **b** : SATURATION 4a — not used technically **3** : ability to breed true : HOMOZYGOSITY ⟨the ~ of a strain⟩ — compare PURE LINE

purity rubric *n* : an authoritative statement (as in the U.S. Pharmacopoeia and the National Formulary) defining the purity of a drug or chemical for medicinal use

pur·kin·je afterimage \(,)pərˈkin(,)jē-, ˈpu̇rkən,yā-\ *n, usu cap P* [after Johannes E. *Purkinje* †1869 Czech physiologist] : a second positive afterimage in a succession of visual afterimages resulting from a brief light stimulus and appearing most distinctly in a hue complementary to that of the original sensation

pur·kin·je·an \(;)pər¦kinjēən, ¦pu̇rkən¦yāən\ *adj, usu cap* [J. E. *Purkinje* + E *-an*] : relating to, discovered by, or named after the Czech physiologist J. E. Purkinje (1787–1869)

purkinje cell *n, usu cap P* : any of numerous nerve cells occupying the middle layer of the cerebellar cortex and being characterized by a large globose body with massive dendrites that are directed outward and a single slender axon that is directed inward

purkinje fiber *n, usu cap P* : any of the modified cardiac muscle fibers with few nuclei, granulated central cytoplasm, and sparse peripheral striations, that make up the Purkinje's network

purkinje phenomenon *or* **purkinje shift** *also* **purkinje effect** *n, usu cap 1st P* : a shift of the region of apparent maximal spectral luminosity from yellow with the light-adapted eye toward violet with the dark-adapted eye that is presumably associated with predominance of cone vision in bright and rod vision in dim illumination

purkinje's figure *or* **purkinje figure** *n, usu cap P* : any of the shadowy figures of the network of retinal vessels that may be made visible in one's own eye (as by light from a pinhole close to the eye

purkinje's network *or* **purkinje's system** *or* **purkinje's tissue** *n, usu cap P* : a network of intracardial conducting tissue made up of syncytial Purkinje fibers that lie in the myocardium and constitute the atrioventricular bundle and other conducting tracts which spread out from the sinus node — compare SINOVENTRICULAR SYSTEM

¹purl \ˈpərl, *esp before pause or consonant* ˈpər·əl; ˈpəl, ˈpəil\ *n* -S [*pirl*] **1** : gold or silver thread or wire used for embroidering or edging **2** *Brit* : ⁴PEARL **3 a** *obs* : a lace frill on a ruff **b** : a ruffled or indented edge (as on a leaf) **4** : PURL STITCH **5** : the intertwist of thread knotting a stitch usu. along an edge ⟨the single ~ typical of blanket stitch⟩ ⟨the double ~ of buttonhole stitch⟩

²purl \"\ *vb* -ED/-ING/-S *vt* **1 a** : to embroider with gold or silver thread **b** : to edge or border with gold or silver embroidery ⟨cloth . . . powdered with red roses ~*ed* with fine gold —Edward Hall⟩ **2** *Brit* : ⁵PEARL **3** : to knit (as a garment) in purl stitch ~ *vi* : to do knitting in purl stitch

³purl \"\ *n* -S [perh. of Scand origin; akin to Norw *purla* to ripple, Sw *porla*] **1** : a purling or swirling stream or rill **2 a** : a gentle murmuring sound **b** : a gentle movement (as of purling water)

⁴purl \"\ *vi* -ED/-ING/-S [perh. of Scand origin; akin to Norw *purla* to ripple, Sw *porla*] **1** : to run swiftly around (as in ripples or about obstructions) : move in circles or undulations : EDDY, SWIRL, CURL ⟨a brook ~*ing* over mossy stones⟩ ⟨thin winding breath which ~*ed* up to the sky —Shak.⟩ **2** : to make a soft murmuring sound like that of a purling stream

⁵purl \"\ *n* -S [origin unknown] **1** : an infusion of bitter herbs (as wormwood) in hot malt liquor used formerly as a tonic **2** *chiefly Brit* : hot beer or ale mixed with gin and sometimes sugar and spices esp. for use as a pick-me-up

⁶purl \"\ *vb* -ED/-ING/-S [alter. of *pirl*] *vi* **1** *chiefly dial* : to spin like a top : WHIRL, WHEEL **2** *chiefly dial* : to tip over : tumble or plunge forward in a fall (as from a horse) : CAPSIZE, UPSET ~ *vt* : to cause to overturn or take a tumble

⁷purl \"\ *n* -S : a spill that sends one whirling : CAPSIZING, UPSET

¹purl·er \-lə(r)\ *n* -S [⁶*purl* + *-er*] *chiefly Brit* : SPILL, CROPPER, TUMBLE

²purler \"\ *n* -S [²*purl* + *-er*] : a worker who finishes raw edges of knitted garments with decorative stitching

purlhouse \ˈ=,=\ *n* [⁵*purl* + *house*] *chiefly Brit* : a drinking place selling purl

¹pur·li·cue *or* **pur·lie·cue** \ˈpərlə̇,kyü\ *n* -S [origin unknown] *chiefly Scot* : a résumé of a series of sermons or addresses given at the close (as of a communion season) : PERORATION

²purlicue *or* **purliecue** \"\ *vi* -ED/-ING/-S *chiefly Scot* : to give a purlicue

pur·lieu \ˈpərl(,)yü, -(,)lü\ *n* -S [ME *purlewe*, modif. (influenced by MF *lieu* place) of AF *puralé*, *puralee* perambulation, fr. OF, past part. of *puraler*, *poraler* to go through, fr. *pur*, *por* for, through + *aler* to go — more at PURCHASE, ALLEY, LIEU] **1** : afforested land severed from an English royal forest by perambulation and disafforested so as to remit to the former owners their rights subject to various forest laws and restrictions **2 a** : a place of resort : HAUNT **b purlieus** *pl* : CONFINES, BOUNDS **3 a** : a locality, region, or other place just beyond or sometimes just within given bounds : an outlying or adjacent district **b purlieus** *pl* : ENVIRONS, NEIGHBORHOOD

pur·lin \ˈpərlə̇n\ *also* **pur·line** \", -,līn\ *n* -S [origin unknown] : a horizontal member in a roof supported on the principals and supporting the common rafters — see ROOF illustration

pur·loin \pə(r)ˈlȯin, (ˈ)pər¦l-, (ˈ)pə¦l-, (ˈ)pəi¦l-\ *vb* -ED/-ING/-S [ME *purloinen*, fr. AF *purloigner*, fr. OF *porloigner* to put off, delay, fr. *por* for + *loing* at a distance, fr. L *longe*, fr. *longus* long — more at PURCHASE, LONG] *vt* **1** *obs* : to set aside : render inoperative or ineffectual **2** : to take away for oneself : appropriate wrongfully and often under circumstances that involve a breach of trust : FILCH ~ *vi* : to practice theft **syn** see STEAL

pur·loin·er \-nə(r)\ *n* -S : one that purloins : THIEF, PILFERER

purl stitch *n* [¹*purl*] : a basic knitting stitch usu. made with the yarn at the front of the work by inserting the right needle into the front part of a loop on the left needle from the right side, catching the yarn with the point of the right needle, and bringing it through the first loop to form a new loop — compare KNIT STITCH

pu·ro \ˈp(y)u̇(,)rō\ *n* -S [Sp, fr. *puro* pure, fr. L *purus*; fr. its being all tobacco, unlike a cigarette] : CIGAR

pu·ro·my·cin \¦pyu̇rō¦mīs°n\ *n* -S [*purine* + *-o-* + *-mycin*] : a trypanocidal and amebicidal antibiotic $C_{22}H_{29}N_7O_5$ obtained from an actinomycete (*Streptomyces alboniger*)

purp \ˈpərp\ *dial var of* PUP

pur·part \ˈpər,pärt\ *n* [ML *purpart-*, *purpars*, fr. OF *pur* for + L *part-* *pars* part, portion] : PURPARTY

pur·par·ty \-rd·ē\ *or* **pour·par·ty** \ˈpu̇r-\ *n* [ME *purpartie*, *pourpartie*, fr. AF, fr. OF *pur*, *pour*, *por* for + *partie* division — more at PURCHASE, PARTY] : a share or portion of an estate allotted by a partition to a coparcener

¹pur·ple \ˈpərpəl, ˈpəp-ˈpəip-\ *adj, sometimes* -ER/-EST [ME *purpel*, *purpil*, alter. of *purper*, *purpre*, fr. OE *purpuran* of purple, gen. of *purpure* purple color, fr. L *purpura* purple color, purple fish, fr. Gk *porphyra*] **1 a** *archaic* : of a color reserved for the use of a royal or imperial ruler **b** : of, belonging to, or worn by those of royal or imperial rank : IMPERIAL, REGAL ⟨a ~ tyrant⟩; *also* : dressed in royal raiment or colors **2 a** : of a color approaching crimson — presently used almost wholly in vernacular names of plants or animals; compare PURPLE BELLS, PURPLE FINCH **b** : of the color purple **c** *archaic* : colored or stained by or as if by blood ⟨I view a field of blood and Tiber rolling with a ~ flood —John Dryden⟩ **3 a** : marked by brilliant coloring : SHOWY **b** (1) : highly rhetorical : ornately and showily phrased or expressed ⟨a ~ patch of writing⟩ (2) : marked by undue pungency and profanity ⟨his language . . . is so ~ they had to stop broadcasting the meetings —*Newsweek*⟩ **c** : having the countenance overspread with tinting of purple resulting from or as if from ill-suppressed anger

²purple \"\ *n* -S [ME *purpil*, fr. *purpil*, adj.] **1 a** (1) *archaic* : any of various rich deep crimsons or scarlets; *specif* : the crimson obtained by dyeing textile fibers with a dye obtained from mollusks : TYRIAN PURPLE 1 (2) : any of various colors that in hue fall about midway between red and blue; *also* : the hue of such a color (3) : a nonspectral color **b** (1) : cloth dyed purple (2) : a garment of such color; *esp* : a purple robe worn as an emblem of rank or authority (as by a Roman emperor) **c** (1) : a mollusk yielding a purple dye; *specif* : a gastropod mollusk of *Purpura* or a related genus (as *Thais*) with an adrectal gland that yields the Tyrian purple of ancient times (2) : a pigment or dye that colors purple **2 a** : imperial or regal rank or power — compare PORPHYROGENITE **b** : exalted station : great wealth **3** *archaic* : a purplish blotch or discoloration (as of the skin)

³purple \"\ *vb* **purpled; purpled; purpling** \-p(ə)liŋ\ **purples** [¹*purple*] *vt* : to make purple : dye or tint with purple ⟨the setting sun *purpled* the clouds⟩ ~ *vi* : to become or turn purple ⟨*purpling* with fury⟩

purple apricot *n* : a hybrid apricot (*Prunus dasycarpa*) having purplish twigs and white flowers and a dark purple bloomy fruit of inferior quality

purple avens *n* **1** : WATER AVENS **2** : PRAIRIE SMOKE 1

purple azalea *n* : PINXTER FLOWER

purple bacterium *n* : any of various free-living bacteria that contain bacteriochlorophyll marked by purplish or sometimes reddish or brownish pigments — compare PURPLE SULFUR BACTERIUM

purple beech *n* : COPPER BEECH

purple bells *n pl but sing or pl in constr* : a Mexican climbing herb (*Rhodochiton atrosanguineum*) of the family Scrophulariaceae that is sometimes cultivated for its showy dark red bell-shaped flowers

purple bent *n* **1** : RHODE ISLAND BENT **2** : an American grass (*Calamovilfa brevipilis*) found in the pine barrens from New Jersey to No. Carolina

purple betony *n* : a somewhat hairy perennial Old World betony (*Betonica officinalis*) that is sometimes cultivated for its spikes of showy reddish purple flowers

purple bladderwort *n* : an aquatic herb (*Utricularia purpurea*) that is common in ponds of the eastern U.S. and has submerged finely dissected leaves and showy emersed very irregular reddish purple flowers

purple blotch *n* : a fungous disease of onions, garlic, and shallots caused by a fungus (*Alternaria porri*) and characterized at first by small white circular to irregular spots which increase and become large purplish blotches sometimes surrounded by orange or salmon bands

purple boneset *n* : a joe-pye weed (*Eupatorium purpureum*)

purple bonnet *n* : WATER SHIELD 1

purple bottle *n* : a moss of the genus *Splachnum* (esp. *S. ampullaceum*) in which the flask-shaped apophysis is highly colored

purple brown *n* : OXIDE BROWN

purple cane *n* : PURPLE RASPBERRY

purple carmine *n* : MUREXIDE

purple chamber *n* : a royal accouchement chamber — see PORPHYROGENITE

purple chokeberry *n* : a chokeberry (*Aronia prunifolia*) of eastern No. America with a globular purplish black fruit

purple cinquefoil *n* : MARSH CINQUEFOIL

purple clematis *n* : PURPLE VIRGIN'S-BOWER

purple cliff brake *n* : a small cliff brake (*Pellaea atropurpurea*) with purplish stipes

purple clover *n* **1** : RED CLOVER **2** : a western American clover (*Trifolium involucratum*) with purple-flowered heads **3** : an Australian herb (*Kennedya tabacina*) used for forage

purple cockle *n* : CORN COCKLE

purple coneflower *n* : a plant of the genus *Echinacea* (esp. *E. purpurea*)

purple copper ore *n* : BORNITE

purple crab *n* : a small rounded red and purple shallow-water crab (*Randallia ornata*) of the California and Mexican Pacific coast

purple cress *n* : a small perennial herb (*Cardamine douglasii*) of the cooler regions of No. America with dentate roundish leaves and racemose purple flowers

purple cudweed *n* : an annual or biennial cudweed (*Gnaphalium purpureum*) with brown to chestnut or purplish flowers

purpled *past of* PURPLE

purple daisy *n* : either of two coneflowers of the genus *Echinacea* (*E. purpurea* and *E. angustifolia*)

purple dogwood *n* : BLUE DOGWOOD

purple emperor *n* : a large European nymphalid forest butterfly (*Apatura iris*) that in the male has the wings shaded with purple

purple-faced langur \ˈ==,=-\ *n* [*purple* + *faced*] : a common monkey (*Presbytis senex*) of eastern Asia having purplish brown facial skin

purple fig *n* : a rough-leaved Australian fig tree (*Ficus scabra*) with inedible fruit

purple finch *n* : an American finch (*Carpodacus purpureus*) the male of which has the head and breast raspberry red

purple fish *n, archaic* : PURPLE 1c(1)

purple-flowering raspberry \ˈ==,=(=)=-\ *n* : FLOWERING RASPBERRY

purple foxglove *n* : a common biennial foxglove (*Digitalis purpurea*) of western Europe from which most cultivated foxgloves are derived

purple-fringed orchid \ˈ==,=-\ *or* **purple-fringed orchis** *n* : either of two orchids of the genus *Habenaria* with the lip deeply cleft into three lobes and usu. fringed and lacerate: **a** : a No. American orchid (*H. psycodes*) with fragrant purplish-fringed flowers **b** : a closely related orchid (*H. fimbriata*) with larger paler flowers

purple fringeless orchid *also* **purple fringeless orchis** *n* [¹*purple* + *fringe* + *-less*] : an orchid (*Habenaria peramoena*) of northeastern and alpine eastern No. America that is closely related to the large-flowered purple-fringed orchid but has rosy purple to purple violet flowers with the lip divisions denticulate

purple-fruited chokeberry \ˈ==,==-\ *n* [*purple* + *fruit* + *-ed*] : PURPLE CHOKEBERRY

purple gallinule *n* : any of various gallinules with showy blue and greenish plumage: as **a** : a gallinule (*Porphyrio porphyrio*) of southern Europe **b** : a gallinule (*Porphyrula martinica*) of tropical America and the southern U.S.

purple goatsbeard *n* : SALSIFY

purple grackle *n* : a No. American grackle (*Quiscalus quiscula*) with black and in the full-plumaged male purplish iridescent plumage — see BRONZED GRACKLE, FLORIDA GRACKLE

purple granadilla *n* : a commonly cultivated Brazilian passionflower (*Passiflora edulis*) grown all over the tropical world for its edible deep purple fruit which is used for sherbets, icing, confectionery, and beverages

purple grass *n* : any of various herbs (as red clover or spotted medic) having purple flowers or purplish spotted foliage

purple hairstreak *n* : a hairstreak butterfly that has the wings marked with iridescent purple: as **a** : a European forest hairstreak (*Thecla quercus*) **b** : a large American hairstreak (*Atlides halesus*) with metallic spots on the largely bluish purple to greenish wings — called also *giant purple hairstreak*

purple haw *n* : BLUEWOOD 1

purpleheart \ˈ==,=\ *n* : a strong durable elastic purplish timber that is obtained in tropical America from leguminous trees of the genus *Peltogyne* (esp. *P. purpurea*) and that is used esp. in fancy veneers

purple heron *n* : an Old World heron (*Ardea purpurea*) chiefly grayish with a black crown and maroon breast

purple-hinged scallop *n* \ˈ==,=-\ : a rock oyster (*Hinnites giganteus*)

purple lake *n* : BURNT CARMINE

purple laurel *n* : CATAWBA RHODODENDRON

purple laver *n* : an edible red alga (*Porphyra vulgaris*)

purpleleaf sand cherry \ˈ==,=-\ *n* : a hybrid sand cherry that is sometimes cultivated for its reddish leaves, pedicels, and calyces and for its white flowers and blackish purple fruits

purple-leaved plum \ˈ==,=-\ *n* : a plum that is a garden variety (*Prunus cerasifera pissardi*) of the cherry plum and is cultivated chiefly for its showy purplish foliage and white flowers

purple locoweed *or* **purple loco** *n* : WOOLLY LOCOWEED

purple loosestrife *n* : a marsh herb (*Lythrum salicaria*) of Europe and the eastern U.S. having a long spike of purple flowers

purple marshlocks *n pl but sing or pl in constr* : MARSH CINQUEFOIL

purple martin *n* : a large swallow (*Progne subis*) widely distributed in No. America and formerly abundant in towns and villages but tending to disappear from localities where the house sparrow has become abundant

purple meadow parsnip *n* : a perennial usu. yellow-flowered herb (*Thaspium trifoliatum*) of the eastern U.S. with ternately compound leaves

purple melic grass *n* : MOOR GRASS 2

purple milkweed *n* : a tall No. American perennial herb (*Asclepias purpurascens*) with a terminal umbel of red or purple flowers

purple milkwort *n* : a showy low annual herb (*Polygala viridescens*) of eastern No. America with compact spikes of rose-purple or rarely greenish flowers

purple mite *n* : CITRUS RED MITE

purple mombin *n* : MOMBIN

purple moor grass *n* : MOOR GRASS 2

purple mullein *n* : a Eurasian mullein (*Verbascum phoeniceum*) having showy purple or pink flowers

purple navy *n* : MARINE BLUE

purple needlegrass *n* : a tall needlegrass (*Stipa pulchra*) with loose nodding panicles and purplish glumes

pur·ple·ness *n* -ES **:** the quality or state of being purple
purple nightshade *n* **:** TROMPILLO
purple of cas·sius \-ˈkash(ē)əs, -ˈkäsēəs\ *usu cap C* [after Andreas *Cassius* †1673? German physician] **:** a purple pigment prepared usu. by precipitation from solutions of gold chloride and stannous chloride, consisting of colloidal gold and stannic oxide, and used chiefly in coloring ceramic glazes and ruby glass and in a very delicate test for gold
purple of the ancients **:** TYRIAN PURPLE 1
purple orchid *n* **:** a strong reddish purple that is bluer and stronger than average fuchsia purple and bluer and deeper than phlox purple
purple orchis *also* **purple-hooded orchis** \ˈ==,==-\ *n* **:** SHOWY ORCHIS
purple osier *n* **:** PURPLE WILLOW
purple oxide *n* **1 :** a natural or synthetic ferric oxide pigment varying in hue from reddish red-yellow to bluish red **2 :** OXIDE BROWN
purple passage *also* **purple patch** *n* [trans. of L *pannus purpureus* purple patch; fr. the traditional splendor of purple cloth as contrasted with more shabby materials] **1 :** a passage conspicuous for brilliancy or effectiveness in a work that is characteristically dull, commonplace, or uninspired **2 :** a piece of obtrusively ornate writing
purple ragwort *n* **:** a southern African annual herb (*Senecio elegans*) grown for its purple-rayed flowers
purple raspberry *n* **1 :** a raspberry with purplish fruits; *esp* **:** any of several cultivated raspberries that are hybrids between red and black raspberries **2 :** a raspberry with purplish canes
purple rocket *n* **1 :** an American herb (*Iodanthus pinnatifidus*) of the family Cruciferae with purple flowers and long slender fruits **2 :** FIREWEED b
purples *pl of* PURPLE, *pres 3d sing of* PURPLE
purple sage *n* **1 :** a silvery-leaved California herb (*Salvia leucophylla*) having purple flowers **2 :** a shrubby sagebrush (*Artemisia tridentata*) having the silvery leaves mostly 3-toothed at the apex and flowers in panicles
purple sandpiper *n* **:** a sandpiper (*Erolia maritima*) of the coasts of northern Europe and northeastern America that has the upper parts in winter purplish black and the underparts white
purple sandwort *n* **:** a sand spurry (*Spergularia rubra*)
purple saxifrage *n* **:** a low densely tufted perennial saxifrage (*Saxifraga oppositifolia*) growing on cool wet rocks in northern regions and having purplish imbricated keeled leaves and a solitary terminal purple flower
purple scale *n* **:** a brownish or purplish armored scale (*Lepidosaphes beckii*) destructive to citrus fruits
pur·ples·cent \ˌpərpəˈles³nt\ *adj* [¹*purple* + *-escent*] **:** approaching purple **:** growing or becoming purple
purple shell *or* **purple snail** *n* **1 a :** a gastropod mollusk that is a source of purple dye **:** PURPLE 1c(1) **b :** JANTHINA 2 **2 :** the shell of a purple shell
purple shore crab *n* **:** a shore crab (*Hemigrapsus nudus*) of the Pacific coast with variable markings of yellowish green, reddish brown, or esp. purple and red-spotted chelae
purple spurge *n* **:** a devil's milk (*Tithymalus peplus*)
purple star thistle *n* **:** STAR THISTLE a
purple-striped jellyfish \ˈ==,strīpt-\ *n* **:** any of several large scyphozoan jellyfishes (genus *Pelagia*) with the umbrella more or less striped and mottled with purple
purple sulfur bacterium *n* **:** any of numerous sulfur bacteria (as of the family Thiorhodaceae) appearing reddish or purplish due to the combination of bacteriochlorophyll and carotenoid pigments in the cell
purple thorn apple *n* **:** a jimsonweed (*Datura stramonium tatula*) that is sometimes cultivated for its purplish leaves and stems and showy violet purple flowers
purpletop \ˈ==,=\ *also* **purpletop grass** *n* **:** a sticky grass (*Triodia flava*) of the eastern U.S. with purple panicles
purple-top *also* **purple-top wilt** *n* **:** an insect-transmitted and often fatal disease of potato plants caused by the same virus that produces aster yellows and characterized by a purplish or chlorotic discoloration of the top shoots, swelling of axillary branches, and severe wilting
purple trillium *n* **:** a birthroot (*Trillium erectum*) of eastern No. America having pink to purple or rarely white ill-scented flowers and an astringent root sometimes used in folk medicine
purple veil *n* **:** the egg raft of the angler (sense 2) consisting of a gelatinous sheet containing eggs which on hatching give it a purple color
purple vetch *n* **1 :** a European vetch (*Vicia benghalensis*) with whitish purple flowers that is grown for green manure and forage esp. on the Pacific coast of No. America **2 :** AMERICAN VETCH
purple virgin's-bower *n* **:** a partly woody vine (*Clematis verticillaris*) of northeastern No. America with waxy purplish blue flowers — called also *purple clematis*
purple willow *n* **:** a Eurasian osier willow (*Salix purpurea*) having a bark rich in tannin and salicin — called also *purple osier*
purple wine *n* **:** a variable color averaging a dark grayish purple that is bluer than raisin black and bluer and stronger than old lavender (sense 2)
purple wing *n* **:** any of several chiefly tropical small to medium-sized butterflies that constitute a genus (*Eunica*) of the family Nymphalidae and are often dark-colored but with blue or purple iridescence
purple wood *n* **1 :** a So. American tree (*Copaifera bracteata*) the bark of which yields phenin **2 :** PURPLEHEART
purplewort \ˈ==,=\ *n* **1 :** MARSH CINQUEFOIL **2 :** a white clover with dark-colored leaves that is a variant form of the white Dutch clover **3 :** PURPLE GRASS
purple wreath *n* **:** a tropical American woody vine (*Petrea volubilis*) with a profusion of showy racemes of purplish violet or blue flowers
purpling *pres part of* PURPLE
pur·plish \ˈpərp(ə)lish, ˈpə̄p-,ˈpəip-, -lēsh\ *adj* [¹*purple* + *-ish*] **:** being somewhat purple **:** having a tinge of purple ⟨a ~ red⟩
pur·ply \-(ə)lē, -lī\ *adj* [²*purple* + *-y*] **:** PURPLISH
purpoint *archaic var of* POURPOINT
¹**pur·port** \ˈpər,pō(ə)rt, ˈpə̄,-, ˈpəi,-, -,pȯ(ə)rt, -,pōə|, -,pȯ(ə)|, *usu* |d·+V; *chiefly Brit* -,pət\ *n* -S [ME, fr. AF, content, tenor, fr. *purporter* to contain, fr. OF *porporter* to carry, convey, fr. *por* for + *porter* to carry — more at PURCHASE, PORT] **1 a :** meaning conveyed, professed, or implied **:** IMPORT, TENOR ⟨a look so piteous in ~ —Shak.⟩ **b :** meaning synthesized or synopsized **:** SUBSTANCE, GIST ⟨gave the ~ of their talk in a few words⟩ **2** *obs* **:** DISGUISE, COVERING **3 :** INTENTION, PURPOSE, DESIGN
²**pur·port** \,pərˈpō(ə)r|d, -ˈpȯ(ə)r|, -ˈpōə|, -ˈpȯ(r)| *sometimes* ,pər|- *or* (ˈ)pə̄|-*or* (ˈ)pəi|-; *usu* |d·+V; *chiefly Brit* ˈ=,pət\ *vt* -ED/-ING/-S **1 :** to convey, imply, or profess outwardly (as meaning, intention, or true character) **:** have the often specious appearance of being, intending, claiming (something implied or inferred) **:** IMPART, PROFESS ⟨a letter that ~s to express public opinion⟩ ⟨a law that ~s to be in the interest of morality⟩ ⟨men ~*ing* to be citizens⟩ **2 :** to have in mind **:** INTEND, PURPOSE
purported *adj* [fr. past part. of ²*purport*] **:** suspected of being **:** REPUTED, RUMORED ⟨~ foreign spies⟩ ⟨a ~ biography⟩ — **pur·port·ed·ly** *adv*
pur·por·tless *pronunc at* ¹PURPORT *or* ²PURPORT +ləs\ *adj* [¹*purport* + *-less*] **:** lacking purpose or meaning ⟨~ questioning⟩
¹**pur·pose** \ˈpərpəs, ˈpə̄p-,ˈpəip-\ *n, pl* **purposes** \-pəsəs, *in rapid speech sometimes* -psəz\ [ME *porpos, purpos,* fr. OF, fr. *porposer* to purpose] **1 a :** something that one sets before himself as an object to be attained **:** an end or aim to be kept in view in any plan, measure, exertion, or operation **:** DESIGN ⟨it was our ~ to get home before the storm⟩ ⟨his ~ was above reproach⟩ **b :** RESOLUTION, DETERMINATION ⟨infirm of ~ —Shak.⟩ **2 :** an object, effect, or result aimed at, intended, or attained ⟨energy applied to little ~⟩ **3 :** a subject under discussion or an action in course of execution **4** *obs* **a** (1) **:** PROPOSAL, PROPOSITION (2) **purposes** *pl* **:** a game like conundrums or riddles **b :** DISCOURSE, TALK, CONVERSATION **c :** PURPORT, INTENT, MEANING **5 :** an old Scots dance in which the couples talked together in an affectedly secretive manner **syn** see INTENTION — **in purpose** *adv* **1 :** in one's mind as a purpose **2 :** on purpose — **of purpose** *or* **of set purpose :** on purpose — **on purpose** *adv* **1 :** by deliberate intent and not by accident **:** INTENTIONALLY, DESIGNEDLY **2 :** in order to attain an end ⟨did it *on purpose* to fool his friends⟩ — **to the purpose :** to the point ⟨little . . . said that is at all *to the purpose* —Clive Bell⟩
²**purpose** \"\ *vb* -ED/-ING/-S [ME *purposen,* fr. MF *purposer, porposer,* fr. OF, modif. (influenced by *poser* to put, place) of L *proponere* to put forward, propose — more at PROPOSE] *vt* **1 :** to propose as an aim to oneself **:** determine upon **:** resolve to do or bring about ⟨did nothing ~ against the state —Shak.⟩ ⟨*purposing* to write an account of the tragedy⟩ **2** *obs* **:** to set forth **:** PROPOUND **3** *obs* **:** DESIGN, DESTINE ~ *vi* **1 :** to have a purpose **2** *obs* **:** to proceed to a destination **:** to be bound for some place **3** *obs* **:** DISCOURSE, TALK **syn** see INTEND
pur·posed·ly \-pəstlē, -sədlē\ *adv* [*purposed* + *-ly*] **:** PURPOSELY, DELIBERATELY
pur·pose·ful \-pəsfəl\ *adj* **1 :** full of determination **:** guided by a definite aim ⟨he was a ~ man⟩ **2 :** serving as, being directed to, or indicating the existence of a purpose or object **:** not aimless or meaningless ⟨~ activities⟩ ⟨ornament is often both decorative and ~⟩ — **pur·pose·ful·ly** \-fəlē, -li\ *adv* — **pur·pose·ful·ness** *n* -ES
pur·pose·less \-pəsləs\ *adj* **:** having no purpose **:** not purposeful or purposive **:** AIMLESS, MEANINGLESS — **pur·pose·less·ly** *adv* — **pur·pose·less·ness** *n* -ES
pur·pose·like \ˈ==,=\ *adj* [¹*purpose* + *like*] *chiefly Scot* **:** PURPOSEFUL
pur·pose·ly \-pəslē, -li\ *adv* [¹*purpose* + *-ly*] **:** with a deliberate or an express purpose **:** on purpose **:** INTENTIONALLY, DESIGNEDLY, EXPRESSLY
purpose-made \ˈ==ˈ=\ *adj* **:** designed and constructed to serve a particular purpose
pur·pos·er \-sə(r)\ *n* -S **:** one that purposes
pur·pos·ive \-siv\ *adj* [²*purpose* + *-ive*] **1 :** serving or effecting a useful end or function though not necessarily as a result of deliberate design ⟨a work of art may be without a purpose, yet ~⟩ **2 :** having, constituting, or tending to fulfill a conscious purpose or design **:** PURPOSEFUL ⟨~ action⟩ **3 :** of or relating to purposivism ⟨~ psychology⟩ — **pur·pos·ive·ly** \-səvlē, -li\ *adv* — **pur·pos·ive·ness** \-sivnəs\ *n* -ES
pur·pos·iv·ism \-si,vizəm\ *n* -S [*purposive* + *-ism*] **:** any of various theories of nature or of human and animal behavior that regard purpose or conscious intent as a basal fact
pur·pos·iv·ist \-sivəst\ *n* -S [*purposive* + *-ist*] **:** an adherent or proponent of a theory of purposivism
pur·pres·ture \(,)pərˈpres(h)chər\ *or* **pour·pres·ture** \pu̇r-\ *n* -S [ME, fr. MF, alter. of *purpresure, propresure,* fr. *porprendre* to seize, occupy, enclose fr. *por* for + *prendre* to take, fr. L *prehendere* — more at PURCHASE, PREHENSILE] **1 :** wrongful appropriation of land subject to the rights of others: as **a :** an encroachment upon or enclosure of real estate subject to common or public rights (as highways, rivers, harbors, forts) **b** *Brit* **:** encroachment upon the royal domain (as the royal forests) **2 :** property enclosed or seized by purpresture
pur·pri·sion \-ˈprizhən\ *n* -S [ME, fr. MF *porprison,* fr. *porpris* (past part. of *porprendre*) + *-on* -ion] *obs* **:** PURPRESTURE 1
pur·pu·ra \ˈpərpyərə\ *n* [NL, fr. L, purple color — more at PURPLE] **1** -S **:** any of several hemorrhagic states characterized by extravasation of blood into the skin and mucous membranes resulting in patches of purplish discoloration — see PURPURA HEMORRHAGICA **2** *cap* [NL, fr. L, purple fish — more at PURPLE] **:** a genus of marine snails (family Muricidae) including some that yield a purple dye and formerly comprising many forms now usu. placed in the genus *Thais*
purpura hem·or·rhag·i·ca \-,hemˌəˈrajəkə\ *n* [NL, lit., hemorrhagic purpura] **1 :** a condition of unknown cause that is characterized by bleeding into the skin with the production of petechiae or ecchymoses and by hemorrhages into mucous membranes and other tissues and that is associated with a reduction in circulating blood platelets and prolonged bleeding time **2 :** an acute or subacute toxemic state in horses that is commonly secondary to an infectious disease and is characterized by dropsical swellings of the legs, abdomen, and head and by small purple hemorrhages in these swellings and in the mucous membranes — called also *petechial fever*
¹**pur·pu·rate** \ˈpərpyərət, -,rāt\ *adj* [L *purpuratus* clothed in purple, fr. *purpura* purple + *-atus* -ate] *obs* **:** purple-colored; *also* **:** ROYAL
²**pur·pu·rate** \-,rāt\ *vt* -ED/-ING/-S [L *purpuratus,* past part. of *purpurare* to purple, fr. *purpura* purple] *archaic* **:** to make purple **:** robe in purple
³**pur·pu·rate** \-,rət, -,rāt\ *n* -S [*purpuric acid* + *-ate*] **:** a salt or ester of purpuric acid
pur·pure *or* **pur·pur** *also* **pur·pour** \ˈpərp(y)ər\ *n or adj* [ME, fr. OE *purpure* — more at PURPLE] **:** PURPLE — used chiefly in heraldry
pur·pu·re·al \,pərˈpyu̇rēəl\ *also* **pur·pu·re·ous** \-ēəs\ *or* **pur·pu·re·an** \-ēən\ *adj* [*purpureous* fr. L *purpureus,* fr. *purpura* purple color + *-eus* -eous; *purpureal, purpurean* fr. L *purpureus* + E *-al, -an*] **:** PURPLE
purpureo- *comb form* [L *purpureus* purple] **:** of a purple or purple-red color — in names of purple or purple-red coordination complexes (as of cobalt or chromium) containing five molecules of ammonia ⟨*purpureo*-cobaltic chloride [$CoCl(NH_3)_5]Cl_2$⟩
pur·pu·res·cent \,pərpyəˈres³nt\ *adj* [L *purpura* purple color + E *-escent*] **:** tinged with purple **:** PURPLISH
purpuri- *comb form* [L *purpura*] **:** purple ⟨*purpuri*parous⟩ ⟨*purpuri*ferous⟩
pur·pu·ric \,pərˈpyu̇rik\ *adj* [NL *purpura* + E *-ic*] **:** of, relating to, or affected with purpura
purpuric acid *n* [L *purpura* purple + E *-ic*] **:** a nitrogenous acid $C_8H_5N_5O_6$ related to barbituric acid that yields alloxan and uramil on hydrolysis and is known esp. in purple-red salts (as murexide) from which it is obtained as an orange-red powder
pur·pu·rin \ˈpərpyərən\ *n* -S [L *purpura* + E *-in*] **1 :** an orange or red crystalline compound $C_{14}H_5O_2(OH)_3$ obtained from madder root along with alizarin or by oxidation of alizarin and used in dyeing; 1,2,4-trihydroxy-anthraquinone **2** *also* **pur·pu·rine** \",-,rēn\ **:** any of various colored compounds obtained from chlorophyll or related compounds by the action of cold alcoholic alkali and oxygen and closely related to the chlorins
pur·pu·rine \-,rīn, -,rēn\ *adj* [F *purpurin,* fr. L *purpura* + F *-in* -ine] **:** of purple color **:** PURPLISH
pur·pu·rite \-,rīt\ *n* -S [L *purpura* purple + E *-ite*] **:** a mineral $(Mn,Fe)PO_4$, consisting of ferric-manganic phosphate isomorphous with heterosite and having a dark reddish or purple color
pur·pu·ro·gal·lin \,pərpyərōˈgalən\ *n* -S [L *purpura* purple + E *-o-* + *pyrogallol* + *-in*] **:** a red crystalline phenolic ketone dye $C_{11}H_4O(OH)_4$ that occurs naturally in various plant galls as the diglucoside and is made synthetically by oxidation of pyrogallol
pur·pu·rog·e·nous \,pərpyəˈräjənəs\ *adj* [L *purpura* purple + E *-o-* + *-genous*] **:** giving rise to a purple color or producing a purple product ⟨a ~ gland⟩
pur·pu·ro·xan·thin \,pərpyə(,)rō+\ *n* [L *purpura* + ISV *-o-* + *xanthin*] **:** a reddish yellow crystalline compound $C_{14}H_6O_2(OH)_2$ obtained from madder root or by reduction of purpurin; 1,3-dihydroxy-anthraquinone — called also *xanthopurpurin*
¹**purr** *R* ˈpər, + *vowel* ˈpər·; *–R* ˈpə̄, + *suffixal vowel* ˈpər· *also* ˈpər, + *vowel in a following word* ˈpər· *or* ˈpə̄ *also* ˈpər\ *n* -S [imit] **1 a :** a low vibratory murmur of a cat that appears to indicate contentment or pleasure and is believed to result from the streaming of air over the false vocal cords **b :** a similar sound of another animal **2 :** a sound resembling the purr of a cat ⟨the soft ~ of a passing motor⟩
²**purr** \"\ *vb* -ED/-ING/-S [imit.] *vi* **1 :** to utter or give forth a purr **2 a :** to speak as if purring **b :** to speak in a light but catty manner ~ *vt* **:** to signify or express by purring or in a lightly catty manner
purre \"\ *n* -S [imit.] *dial Eng* **:** a dunlin in winter plumage
pur·ree \ˈpu̇rē, ˈpərē\ *n* -S [Hindi *piūrī;* akin to Skt *pīta* yellow] **:** INDIAN YELLOW 2
purre maw *n, dial Eng* **:** ROSEATE TERN
purr·er \ˈpər·ə(r), *–R also* ˈpərə(r\ *n* -S **:** one that purrs
purr·ing·ly *adv* **:** in a purring manner **:** with a purr
purring spider *n* **:** a moderate-sized wolf spider (*Lycosa gulosa* syn. *L. kochii*) of the eastern U.S. that often drums on dead leaves with its palpi
purry \ˈpər·|ē, |ī, *–R also* ˈpər|\ *adj* -ER/-EST [¹*purr* + *-y*] **:** like a purr
pur sang \(ˈ)pu̇(ə)rˈsäⁿ\ *adj* [F *pur-sang* thoroughbred animal, fr. *pur* pure + *sang* blood, fr. L *sanguis*] **:** being such beyond a doubt or to the utmost degree **:** PURE-BLOODED — used postpositively ⟨the contemplative poet *pur sang* —Louise Bogan⟩ ⟨denounce him as a fascist *pur sang* —Thomas Mann⟩
¹**purse** \ˈpərs, ˈpə̄s, ˈpəis, *dial* ˈpəs\ *n* -S [ME *purs,* fr. OE, modif. (perh. influenced by OE *pusa, posa* bag) of ML *bursa,* fr. LL, oxhide, fr. Gk *byrsa*] **1 a :** a small bag closed with a drawstring and used to carry money; *broadly* **:** a receptacle (as a handbag, pocketbook, or wallet) used to carry money and often other small objects about with one **b :** a pouch or other receptacle (as in a fishing net) that suggests a purse in form **c** (1) *archaic* **:** a normal or abnormal bodily structure in the form of a pouch (2) **:** SCROTUM — used chiefly of domestic animals **2 a :** a money purse with its contents; *also* **:** a sum of money **:** MEANS, RESOURCES, FUNDS ⟨live within one's ~⟩ ⟨all shared the common ~⟩ ⟨charities from his private ~⟩ **b** (1) **:** a sum of money offered as a prize or as a present ⟨a race with a ~ of $3000⟩ ⟨collected a ~ to help the flood victims⟩ (2) **:** PURSE RACE **c** *archaic* **:** a definite sum of money in the Muslim Orient ⟨in imperial Turkey a ~ of silver equaled 500 piasters, a ~ of gold, 10,000⟩ **3 :** a splinter or spark that pops from an open fire

purse 1a

²**purse** \"\ *vb* -ED/-ING/-S [ME *pursen,* fr. *purs* purse] *vt* **1 :** to put into a purse ⟨I will . . . ~ the ducats —Shak.⟩ **2** *obs* **:** to enclose and hold as if in a purse **:** shut up or off **:** CONFINE **3 a :** to draw up or contract into folds or wrinkles like the mouth of a purse **:** PUCKER, KNIT ⟨didst contract and ~ thy brow —Shak.⟩ **b :** to draw closed (the mouth of a purse seine) ~ *vi* **:** to become puckered **:** draw some part (as one's lips or brow) up or together
purse bearer *n* [ME *pursberer,* fr. *purs* purse + *berere, berer* bearer] **1 :** the bearer of a purse **:** TREASURER, BURSAR **2 :** an official of the British crown office who bears the great seal before the lord chancellor
purse crab *n* **:** a large anomuran land crab (*Birgus latro*) that is widely distributed about islands of the tropical Indian and Pacific oceans where it burrows in the soil and feeds on coconuts and is related to the hermit crabs but distinguished by its large size and its broad symmetrical abdomen the oily flesh of which is esteemed a delicacy by natives of the region — called also *palm crab, robber crab, tree crab*
purse cutter *n* **:** CUTPURSE
purse-cutting \ˈ=,==\ *n* **:** the practice of a cutpurse **:** thievery or pilfering from the person of the victim
purse·ful \ˈ=,fu̇l\ *n* -S [*purse* + *-ful*] **:** all that is or can be contained in a purse
purse isinglass *n* **:** isinglass made from unopened bladders of fish
purse-leech \ˈ=,=\ *n* **:** one that is excessively greedy for money
purse·less \ˈ=ləs\ *adj* **:** lacking a purse **:** having no money
purselike \ˈ=,=\ *adj* **:** resembling a purse esp. in pouched rounded form ⟨wattles in the form of ~ outgrowths⟩
purse line *n* **:** a rope by which a purse seine is pursed
purse pride *n* **:** pride of money **:** the condition of the purse-proud
purse-proud \ˈ=,=\ *adj* **:** proud or arrogant because of one's wealth esp. in the absence of other distinctions
purs·er \ˈpərsər, ˈpə̄sə(r, ˈpəisə(r\ *n* -S [ME, fr. *purs* purse + *-er*] **1** *archaic* **:** a maker of purses **2 a** *archaic* **:** an official in charge of and keeping records of disbursements and receipts **:** TREASURER **b** *obs* **:** a paymaster in the British or U.S. Navy **c** (1) **:** an official on a ship responsible for all papers and accounts and on a passenger ship also for the comfort and welfare of the passengers (2) **:** a similar official on an airliner
purse race *n* **:** a race for a fixed purse to which entries usu. close less than six weeks before the first day of the meet in which the race is to be run — compare STAKE RACE
purse rat *n* **:** POCKET GOPHER
purse ring *n* **1 :** a ring or one of the rings to which purse strings are attached **2 :** one of the rings on a purse seine through which the purse line passes
purs·er·ship \ˈ==,ship\ *n* [*purser* + *-ship*] **:** the office or duties of a purser
purses *pl of* PURSE, *pres 3d sing of* PURSE
purse seine *also* **purse net** *n* [*purse seine* fr. ¹*purse* + *seine;*

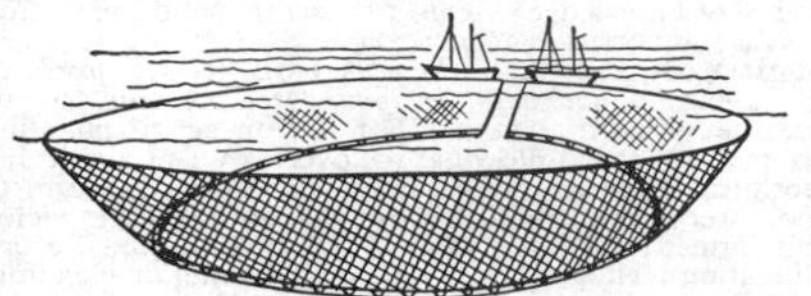

purse seine

purse net fr. ME *pursnette,* fr. *purs* purse + *nette* net] **:** a large seine designed to be set by two boats around a school of fish and so arranged that after the ends have been brought together the bottom can be closed, ranging typically from 250 to 400 yards in length and from 18 to 20 yards in depth, having the upper edge supported by floats and the lower edge weighted by brass rings through which the purse line passes, and being closed below when the ends of the net have been brought together by the dropping of a heavy lead weight that is attached over pulleys to the ends of the purse line and that by its descent puckers together the bottom of the net
purse sein·er \ˈ=,sānə(r)\ *n* [*purse seine* + *-er*] **1** *also* **purse boat :** a usu. power-driven fishing boat equipped or used for fishing with a purse seine **2 :** a fisherman who uses a purse seine **:** a member of the crew of a purse seiner
purse silk *n* **:** a smooth tightly twisted silk thread used esp. for embroidery or knitting
purse string *n* [ME, fr. *purs, purse* purse + *string*] **1 :** one of the drawstrings of a purse by which its mouth is opened or closed **2 purse strings** *pl* **:** financial resources ⟨those who have control of our municipal *purse strings*⟩ ⟨*purse strings* will thus continue to control the distribution of . . . documents —*Economist*⟩
purse-string \ˈ=,=\ *adj* [*purse string*] **1 :** formed or drawn in the manner of a purse string ⟨a wind-tight *purse-string* closure about the neck⟩ — see PURSE-STRING SUTURE **2 :** involving control of financial matters **:** acting through financial control ⟨committee would have *purse-string* power to enforce the decisions —*The Nat'l Jewish Monthly*⟩
purse-string suture *n* **:** a surgical suture passed as a running stitch in and out along the edge of a circular wound in such a way that when the ends of the suture are drawn tight the wound is closed like a purse
pursevant *obs var of* PURSUIVANT
purseweb spider \ˈ=,=-\ *also* **purse spider** *n* **:** a spider (*Atypus abbotti*) that forms a purse-shaped web at the base of tree trunks
purse weight *n* **:** the tom of a purse seine
pur·shia \ˈpərshēə, ˈpu̇r-\ *n, cap* [NL, fr. Frederick *Pursh* †1820 Ger. botanist and horticulturist in America + NL *-ia*] **:** a genus of western American shrubs (family Rosaceae) having small solitary yellow flowers and pubescent achenes and being important browse plants in dry parts of the southwestern U.S.
pursh's plantain \ˈpərshəz-, ˈpu̇|\ *or* **pursh plantain** *n, usu cap 1st P* [after Frederick *Pursh*] **:** a tufted annual plantain (*Plantago purshii*) of central and western No. America with whitish woolly spikes and foliage and small whitish flowers
pursier *comparative of* PURSY

pursiest *superlative of* PURSY

pur·si·ly \'pəsəlē, -li, 'pərs-,'pəs-,pəis-\ *adv* **:** in a pursy manner

pur·si·ness \-sēnəs, -sin-\ *n* -ES [ME *pursynes*, fr. ¹*pursy* + *-nes* -ness] **:** the quality or state of being pursy **:** a condition of being swollen or puffed up (as with pride, self-importance, flatulence)

pursing *pres part of* PURSE

pur·sive \'pərsiv\ *adj* [AF *pursif* — more at PURSY] **:** SHORT-WINDED, PURSY

¹**purs·lane** \'pərslən, 'pəs-,'pəis-, -,slān\ *n* -S [ME *purcelan*, *purslane*, fr. MF *porcelaine*, fr. LL *porcillagin-*, *porcillago*, alter. (influenced by such plant names as *plantagin-*, *plantago* plantain) of L *porcillaca*, alter. of *portulaca*] **:** a plant of the family Portulacaceae; *esp* **:** an annual herb (*Portulaca oleracea*) with fleshy succulent obovate leaves that is widely distributed in both hemispheres, is a troublesome weed in some areas, and is used as a potherb and for salads

²**purslane** *or* **purslaine** *obs var of* PORCELAIN

purslane family *n* **:** PORTULACACEAE

purslane speedwell *n* **:** a No. American annual herb (*Veronica peregrina*) that has small white flowers and is widely naturalized as a weed in So. America and the Old World

purslane sphinx *n* **:** WHITE-LINED SPHINX

purslane tree *n* **:** a southern African fleshy shrub (*Portulacaria afra*) with foliage that is used as fodder

purs·ley \'pə(r)slē, 'pəs-,'pəis-, -li\ *n* -S [by shortening and alter.] **:** PURSLANE

pur·su·able \pə(r)'süəbəl\ *adj* [*pursue* + *-able*] **:** subject to pursuit

pur·su·al \-üəl\ *n* -S [*pursue* + *-al*] **:** the act or an instance of pursuing **:** PURSUIT

pur·su·ance \-üən(t)s\ *n* -S [*pursue* + *-ance*] **1 a :** the act of pursuing (as by chasing, seeking after, continuing, following up) ⟨the ~ of truth⟩ **b :** a carrying out or into effect **:** the action of executing **:** PROSECUTION ⟨engaged in ~ of his researches⟩ ⟨immediate ~ of his orders⟩ **2 a :** something that is pursuant **:** CONSEQUENCE **b :** SEQUENCE; *specif* **:** the body of a discourse

¹**pur·su·ant** \-nt\ *n* -S [ME *poursuiant*, *pursuant*, fr. MF *poursuivant*, *poursuiant* follower, pursuer, prosecutor, fr. OF, fr. pres. part. of *poursivre*, *poursuir* to pursue, prosecute — more at PURSUE] **1** *obs* **:** PROSECUTOR **2 :** PURSUER

²**pursuant** \"\ *adj* [*pursue* + *-ant*] **:** that is in pursuit **:** PURSUING ⟨a ~ and powerful grandee —Lon Tinkle⟩ ⟨a ~ reek of the stables⟩

pur·su·ant·ly *adv* [²*pursuant* + *-ly*] **:** CONSEQUENTLY

pursuant to *prep* [²*pursuant*] **:** in the course of carrying out **:** in conformance to or agreement with **:** according to ⟨*pursuant to* the proposals of this note⟩ ⟨acted *pursuant to* their agreement⟩

pur·sue \pə(r)'sü\ *vb* -ED/-ING/-S [ME *pursuen*, fr. AF *pursuer*, fr. OF *poursivre*, *poursuir*, fr. (assumed) VL *prosequere*, fr. L *prosequi* to follow, follow after, pursue, fr. *pro-* forward + *sequi* to follow — more at PRO-, SUE] *vt* **1 a :** to follow with enmity **:** PERSECUTE, BEDEVIL **:** persist in harassing, afflicting, or aggrieving ⟨*pursued* with peculiar animosity —T.B.Macaulay⟩ **b :** to follow usu. determinedly in order to overtake, capture, kill, or defeat ⟨the hounds *pursued* the stag⟩ ⟨*pursued* the fleeing Indians⟩ **c :** to attend, follow, and seek to attract ⟨was *pursuing* two girls at the time —Oliver La Farge⟩ **2 a :** to seek to follow, obtain, attain to, or accomplish **:** find or employ measures to obtain or accomplish ⟨losing the pearl of great price while *pursuing* lesser ends —W.R.Inge⟩ **b :** to follow or seek by judicial proceedings **:** PROSECUTE ⟨*pursued* his legal remedies⟩ **3 :** to proceed along or act in, according to, or in compliance with **:** FOLLOW ⟨U.S. 220 ~*s* an irregular north-south course —*Amer. Guide Series: Pa.*⟩ ⟨a compact little village, astir with the same activity it has *pursued* . . . since the 17th century —*Amer. Guide Series: N.H.*⟩ **4 :** to follow up or proceed with **:** CONTINUE **:** engage oneself with **:** PRACTICE ⟨the ordinary rigorous canons of scientific evidence *pursued* by the scholarly historian —M.R.Cohen⟩ ⟨*pursuing* the game of high ambition —John Buchan⟩ ⟨placidly *pursuing* her tasks without heeding the surrounding clamor⟩ **5 :** to follow with or as if with one's eyes, senses, or mind ⟨his thoughts also followed or, rather, *pursued* the slim woman —Ethel Wilson⟩ **6 a :** to attempt to arrive at (as a point, a place, an end) ⟨moving toward the point it has so energetically *pursued* —Henry Adams⟩ **b** *obs* **:** to follow in order to avenge or punish **~** *vi* **1 :** to go in pursuit **:** follow after someone or something ⟨where only the strongest dared ~⟩ **2** *Scots & eccl law* **:** to bring suit **:** PROSECUTE — often used with *for* **3 :** to keep on doing or saying **:** press on (as in argument or speech) **syn** see FOLLOW

pur·su·er \-süə(r), -süə)r, -süə\ *n* -S [ME *pursuere*, fr. *pursuen* to pursue + *-ere* -er] **:** one that pursues: as **a :** one that chases or follows after ⟨that canine ~ of the rabbit⟩ ⟨a devoted ~ of knowledge⟩ **b** *obs* **:** PERSECUTOR **c** *chiefly Scots & eccl law* **:** PLAINTIFF, PROSECUTOR

pur·suit \-süt, *usu* -üd.+V\ *n* -S [ME, fr. AF *purseute*, fr. OF *poursieute*, *poursuite*, fr. *poursivre*, *poursuir* to pursue, prosecute — more at PURSUE] **1 a :** an act of pursuing (as with malice) **:** a following to overtake usu. with hurtful intentions **:** a chasing with haste (as to kill or capture) ⟨~ of game⟩ ⟨went out in ~ of the thief⟩ ⟨spent his life in vicious ~ of his former rival⟩ **b (1)** *chiefly Scots & eccl law* **:** a process of litigating **:** PROSECUTION **(2)** *obs* **:** a suing or pleading esp. for mercy or attention **:** ENTREATY **c** *obs* **:** ATTACKING, ASSAULT **2 a :** an activity that one pursues or engages in seriously and continually or frequently as a vocation or profession or as an avocation ⟨except in the arts, letters, or other unprofitable ~*s* —H.S.Canby⟩ **:** a way of life **:** OCCUPATION ⟨the law, being a profession, was accounted a more gentlemanly ~ than business —Edith Wharton⟩ **b :** an end pursued **:** OBJECTIVE **3 :** a following with a view to reach, accomplish, or obtain **:** an endeavor to attain to, gain, or achieve ⟨the ~ of knowledge⟩ ⟨mad ~ of pleasure⟩ **4 :** PURSUIT PLANE **syn** see WORK

pursuit curve *n* **:** the interception curve made by an interceptor maintaining continuous fire on a moving airplane from a position to the rear and side — compare LEAD-COLLISION COURSE

pur·suit·me·ter \=ˈ=,mēd·ə(r)\ *n* [*pursuit* + *-meter*] **:** a device for testing the coordination of eyes and hand in respect to ability to maintain a manually operated test object in a given position or along a changing course

pursuit plane *n* **:** FIGHTER; *esp* **:** a fighter plane designed for pursuit of and attack on enemy airplanes

pursuit race *n* **:** a bicycle race in which riders spaced at equal intervals at the start attempt to eliminate other contestants by overtaking them

¹**pur·sui·vant** \'pərs(w)əvənt, -)ēv-\ *n* -S [ME *pursevant*, fr. MF *poursuivant*, *poursuiant*, lit., follower, pursuer — more at PURSUANT] **1** *also* **pursuivant of arms** *or* **pursuivant at arms a :** an inferior heraldic functionary attendant on medieval European heralds and learning the profession of heraldry **:** a neophyte herald **b :** an officer of arms ranking below a herald but having similar duties **2** *archaic* **:** a royal or state messenger **:** one with power to execute a warrant **3 a** *archaic* **:** FOLLOWER, ATTENDANT **b :** one that seeks out and follows or delves into ⟨the literary ~ of the Renaissance —Delbert Clark⟩; *sometimes* **:** one that seeks out to entrap or seize

²**pursuivant** *vt* -ED/-ING/-S *obs* **:** to deliver to or by a pursuivant **:** PURSUE

¹**pur·sy** \'pəsē, 'pərs-,'pəs-,'pəis-, -si\ *or* **pus·sy** \'pəs-\ *adj* -ER/-EST [ME *pursy*, fr. AF *pursif*, alter. of MF *polsif*, fr. *polser* to push, beat, breathe with difficulty + *-if* -ive — more at PUSH] **1 a :** tending to be or habitually short-winded or asthmatic **:** short-breathed esp. because of corpulence **b :** FAT, PUFFY, OBESE **2 :** made large or self-important with pampering or luxurious living **:** characterized by or arising from arrogance of wealth, self-indulgence, or luxury

²**pursy** \'pərsē, 'pəs-,'pəis-, -si, *dial* 'pəs-\ *adj* -ER/-EST [¹*purse* + *-y*] **1 :** puckered up ⟨a ~ mouth⟩ **2 :** having and usu. excessively aware of having an abundance of material possessions **:** wealthy and purse-proud

pur·te·nance \'pərtᵊnən(t)s\ *n* -S [ME *purtenaunce*, lit., that which belongs to something, modif. (prob. influenced by OF *por*, *pur* for) of MF *partenance*, *pertinence* — more at PURCHASE, PERTINENCE] **:** the heart, liver, and lungs of an animal **:** ENTRAILS, PLUCK

pu·ru·há \,püra'hä, -rə'wä\ *n, pl* **puruhá** \"\ *or* **puruha·es** \,==ˈ=,äs\ *usu cap* [Sp, of AmerInd origin] **1 a :** an Indian people of central Ecuador **b :** a member of such people **2 :** the extinct language of the Puruhá people

pu·ru·lence \'pyür(y)ələn(t)s\ *also* **pu·ru·len·cy** \-nsē,-nsi\ *n* -S [LL *purulentia*, fr. L *purulentus* purulent + *-ia* -y] **1 :** the quality or state of being purulent **2 :** PUS; *also* **:** the formation of pus

pu·ru·lent \-nt\ *adj* [L *purulentus*, fr. *pur-*, *pus* pus + *-ulentus* -ulent — more at FOUL] **1 :** consisting of or being pus ⟨a ~ discharge⟩ **2 a :** containing pus ⟨a ~ lesion⟩ **b :** accompanied by the formation of pus ⟨~ meningitis⟩

pu·ru·loid \-,lȯid\ *adj* [*purulent* + *-oid*] **:** resembling pus

pu·ru·sha \'pürəshə\ *n* -S [Skt *puruṣa*, lit., man] **:** the soul that with prakriti constitutes the primary cause of phenomenal existence according to Sankhya philosophy; *specif* **:** an individual soul of an infinite number of like, discrete, and eternal souls

pur·ves flue *or* **purves tube** \'pərvəs-\ *n, usu cap P* [after *Purves*, 19th cent. Eng. engineer, its inventor] **:** a boiler flue with thickened transverse ribs or corrugations rather widely spaced

¹**pur·vey** \pə(r)'vā *sometimes* ¦pər¦v- *or* (')pə¦v- *or* (')pəi¦v-\ *vb* -ED/-ING/-S [ME *purveien*, *porveien*, fr. MF *porveeir*, *porveioir* to foresee, provide, fr. L *providēre* — more at PROVIDE] *vt* **1 :** to make available (something wanted or needed) **:** obtain or supply for use ⟨information ~*ed* by government bulletins⟩; *esp* **:** to provide (food or other provender) usu. as a matter of business ⟨mine host ~*ed* us a sumptuous feast⟩ **2** *archaic* **:** to provide (as a person) with something needed or wanted (as provisions, supplies, equipment) **~** *vi* **1 :** to make provision or preparations **2 :** to serve as a purveyor; *esp* **:** to supply provisions **3 :** to provide or convey something essential **:** lend necessary assistance **:** serve as a source of supply — used with *to* or *for* ⟨the function of the eye is now purely ministerial; it merely ~*s* for the ear —Sidney Lanier⟩

²**pur·vey** *n* -S *obs* **:** an act of purveying **:** something purveyed

pur·vey·ance \(,)=ˈvāən(t)s\ *also* **pour·vey·ance** \pür'v-\ *n* -S [ME *porveance*, *purveiaunce* foresight, provision for the future, fr. OF *porveance*, fr. *porveeir* to provide + *-ance* — more at PURVEY] **1 a :** the act or fact of providing in advance **:** PREPARATION **:** prudent direction or management **b :** the act or process of purveying or procuring (as provisions) ⟨the ~ of supplies for an army⟩ ⟨dedicated to the ~ of dreams —J.W.Aldridge⟩; *specif* **:** the providing of supplies or services for a sovereign or for the crown by preemption or impressment at a valuation fixed by appraisers appointed by the purveyors or by the purveyors themselves and usu. below the market value as a royal prerogative **2** *obs* **:** something (as supplies or provisions) that is purveyed

pur·vey·or \(,)=ˈvāə(r), ˈ=,==\ *n* -S [ME *purveour*, fr. OF *porveeur*, fr. *porveeir* to provide + *-eur* -or] **:** one who purveys, provides, or procures: as **a :** one who provides victuals or whose business is to make provisions for the table **:** VICTUALER, CATERER **b** *obs* **:** an official functioning in the securing of necessary supplies (as for a city or an army) **c :** a former officer of the British government providing or exacting provision under the right of purveyance

pur·view \'pər,vyü, 'pə,v-, 'pəi,v-\ *n* [ME *purveu*, *purvewe*, fr. AF *purveu (est)* it is provided (opening phrase of a statute), fr. OF *porveu*, past part. of *porveeir* to provide — more at PURVEY] **1 a :** the body of a statute or the part that begins with "*Be it enacted*" and ends before the repealing clause — compare PREAMBLE, PROVISO, SAVING CLAUSE **b :** the limit or scope of a statute **:** the whole extent of its intention or provisions **2 :** the range or limit of authority, competence, responsibility, concern, or intention ⟨actively under the ~ of the Federal Trade Commission —*Jour. Amer. Med. Assoc.*⟩ ⟨the problem in Indonesia . . . does not fall within the ~ of the Security Council —*N.Y.Times*⟩ **3 :** range of sight, vision, understanding, cognizance, or knowledge ⟨persuaded that there is . . . no human destiny outside the ~ of their system —Bertrand Russell⟩ **syn** see RANGE

pur·voe \pə(r)'vō\ *n* -S [Marathi *parbhū*, fr. Skt *prabhu* — more at PRABHU] **:** a writer caste of India

pur·wan·nah \pə(r)'wänə\ *n* -S [Hindi *parwāna*, fr. Per] *India* **:** a written pass or permit **:** ORDER; *also* **:** a royal grant

¹**pus** \'pəs\ *n* -ES [L *pur-*, *pus* — more at FOUL] **:** thick opaque usu. yellowish white fluid matter formed in connection with an inflammation due to the invasion of the body by an infective microorganism (as a bacterium) and composed of fluid exudate containing degenerating leukocytes, tissue debris, and living or dead microorganisms — see SUPPURATION

²**pus** \'püs\ *n, usu cap* [Skt *pusya*] **:** a month of the Hindu year — see MONTH table

-pus \pəs\ *n comb form* [NL *-pod-*, *-pus*, fr. Gk *-pod-*, *-pous*, fr. *pod-*, *pous* foot — more at FOOT] **:** creature having (such) a foot or feet ⟨monopus⟩ ⟨Lycopus⟩ — chiefly in generic names in zoology ⟨mastigopus⟩ ⟨Pygopus⟩; compare -PODA

pu·san \(')pü¦sän\ *adj, usu cap* [fr. *Pusan*, *Fusan*, city of southern Korea] **:** of or from the city of Pusan, Korea **:** of the kind or style prevalent in Pusan

pus basin *n* **:** a kidney-shaped metal basin used in sickrooms and hospitals to catch body discharges (as pus or sputum)

pus basin

pus cell *n* **:** a polymorphonuclear leukocyte

pusch·kin·ia \püsh'kinēə\ *n* [NL, fr. A.A.Mussin-*Puschkin* †1805? Russ. scientist + NL *-ia*] **1** *cap* **:** a small genus of Asiatic spring-blooming bulbous herbs (family Liliaceae) having solitary or racemose flowers with a 6-parted blue-veined white perianth and connate filaments **2** -S **:** any plant of the genus *Puschkinia*

pu·sey·ism \'pyüzē,izəm, -üsē-\ *n, usu cap* [E.B.*Pusey* 1800–1882, Eng. theologian + E *-ism*] **:** TRACTARIANISM

pu·sey·ite \-,īt\ *n* -S *usu cap* [E.B.*Pusey* + E *-ite*] **:** an adherent of Puseyism **:** HIGH CHURCHMAN

¹**push** \'püsh\ *vb* -ED/-ING/-ES [ME *posshen*, *pusshen*, fr. OF *polser*, *poulser* to push, beat, fr. L *pulsare*, fr. *pulsus*, past part. of *pellere* to drive, push — more at FELT] *vt* **1 a :** to exert physical force upon so as to cause or tend to cause motion away from the force **:** to cause to move or tend to move away or ahead by steady pressure in contact ⟨~ a baby carriage⟩ ⟨~ a door open⟩ ⟨~ a boat off⟩ ⟨~ him out of the way⟩ ⟨~*ed* back his chair⟩ ⟨dunes that the ice ~*ed* up⟩ — opposed to *pull* **b** *archaic, of an animal* **:** to butt or thrust against with the head or horns **c :** to force to go (as by driving or displacing) ⟨~ the enemy troops into the sea⟩ ⟨my crew will ~ your cattle across the creek tomorrow —Luke Short⟩ ⟨~*ed* the worry to the back of her mind⟩ ⟨~ the job onto someone else⟩ **:** CROWD ⟨a local sensation that ~*ed* the foreign news off the front page⟩ ⟨cleared fields that ~ back the wilderness⟩ **d :** to make, effect, or accomplish by forcing aside obstacles or opposition ⟨~ his way to the front of the crowd⟩ ⟨~*ed* the new road into the wilderness⟩ **2 a :** to put in a projecting position **:** STICK ⟨~*ed* out his lower lip⟩ ⟨~ her nose into their affairs⟩ **b :** to cause to extend against resistance or with vigorous effort **:** put forth ⟨plants that ~ their roots deep into the soil⟩ **:** send out ⟨~*ed* an army across the river to intercept the enemy⟩ **c :** to cause to change in quantity or extent ⟨costs of municipal government are still rising, ~*ing* up . . . taxes —Ed Cony⟩ ⟨as the frontier was ~*ed* westward —*Amer. Guide Series: Va.*⟩; *esp* **:** INCREASE ⟨~ the production of consumer goods to record levels⟩ **3 a :** to press (a person) to do something ⟨~ her son to pursue a musical career⟩ **b :** to urge or force to greater speed or activity or beyond usual limits ⟨~*es* his horse to the front of the race⟩ ⟨~*ed* the truck to a breakneck speed⟩ ⟨cruises at 200 but can hit 250 if ~*ed*⟩ ⟨~*es* her voice a little too hard —Edward Sackville-West & Desmond Shawe-Taylor⟩ **c :** to bring (a person) to a point, state, or position by severe pressure ⟨fancied slights . . . ~*ed* men to the breaking point —Oscar Handlin⟩ ⟨the students . . . frequently ~ the professors into extreme views —Dallas Finn⟩; *esp* **:** to reduce to straits (as by lack of money, time) ⟨~ smaller companies into bankruptcy⟩ ⟨~*ed* for time⟩ **d :** to bid for the purpose of inducing (an opponent in a card game) to make a higher and possibly unsafe bid **e :** to direct the course of ⟨~*ed* his horse into the opening⟩ ⟨~ a pencil⟩ **:** OPERATE ⟨~*es* a taxi for a living⟩ **4 :** to develop (as an idea or system) more fully or to an extreme ⟨~*es* the argument one step further —Robert Strausz-Hupé⟩ ⟨~*es* his historical interpretation as far as it will go —S.F.Damon⟩ **5 a :** to promote or carry out with vigor **:** urge or press the advancement, adoption, or practice of ⟨~*ed* his protegé in university circles⟩ ⟨~ the bill in the legislature⟩; *specif* **:** to make aggressive efforts to sell ⟨a heavy consumer drive to ~ canned foods —*Printers' Ink*⟩ **b :** to engage in the illicit sale of (narcotics) **6 :** to approach in age or number ⟨the old man was ~*ing* seventy-five —Saul Bellow⟩ ⟨the crowds are ~*ing* 200,000 —Ken Purdy⟩ **~** *vi* **1** *archaic* **a** *of an animal* **:** to butt a person or object with the head or horns **b :** to thrust with a pointed weapon **c :** to make a hostile advance **2 a :** to exert oneself continuously, vigorously, or obtrusively to gain a desired end **:** work or drive hard ⟨unions ~*ing* for higher wages⟩ **b :** to peddle narcotics **3 a :** to exert a steady force against something ⟨watched the crowd ~ against the gate until it broke⟩ **b :** to move by pushing or being pushed ⟨took the raft pole and ~*ed* out into the stream⟩ ⟨the door ~*ed* open —Erle Stanley Gardner⟩ ⟨fillers that ~ out easily⟩ **c :** to make one or more bids that push an opponent **4 :** to press forward against obstacles or opposition or with energy **:** advance persistently or courageously ⟨encouraged adventurous Portuguese captains to ~ out into the Atlantic —G.C.Sellery⟩ **5 a :** to stick out **:** PROJECT ⟨a dock that ~*es* far out into the lake⟩ **:** EXTEND ⟨a road that ~*es* toward the mountains⟩ **b :** to change in quantity or extent; *esp* **:** INCREASE ⟨corn acreage ~*ed* into first place —*Amer. Guide Series: Minn.*⟩ — **push one's luck :** to take a rash risk **:** venture against increasingly adverse odds ⟨*pushed his luck* too far when he deliberately insulted a churchman —Louis Simpson⟩ — **push up daisies** *or* **push daisies** *slang* **:** to lie dead and buried ⟨if a shell has my number on it, I'll soon be *pushing daisies* —Dixon Wecter⟩

syn PUSH, SHOVE, THRUST, and PROPEL can mean, in common, to use force upon a thing so as to make it move ahead or aside. PUSH implies the application of force by a body already in contact with the thing to be moved onward, aside, or out of the way ⟨*push* a wheelbarrow⟩ ⟨*push* a man off a seat⟩ ⟨*push* a card across the table⟩ ⟨*push* a man into a high political position⟩ SHOVE implies a strong, usu. fast or rough, pushing of something usu. along a surface, as the ground or a floor ⟨*shove* a piano a few feet back⟩ ⟨*shove* a handkerchief into one's pocket⟩ ⟨*shove* a plate away from one⟩ THRUST stresses a rapidity or violence rather than any continuousness or steadiness in the application of force, often implying the sudden and forcible pushing of a weapon or instrument into something ⟨*thrust* a hand into a box⟩ ⟨*thrust* a sword through the arras⟩ ⟨*thrust* a grievance out of one's mind⟩ PROPEL implies a driving forward or onward by a force or power ⟨*propel* a hoop along the sidewalk⟩ ⟨boats *propelled* by the wind⟩ ⟨the engine *propels* the car at over a hundred miles an hour⟩ ⟨a man *propelled* by hunger to an enemy's house⟩

²**push** "\ *n* -ES **1 :** a vigorous effort to attain a desired end **:** DRIVE ⟨a strong Congressional ~ for restoring high, rigid supports —Eric Sevareid⟩: **a :** a strong organized military attack **:** ASSAULT, OFFENSIVE ⟨on the Russian front the spring ~ had finally begun —*Time*⟩ **b :** an advance overcoming obstacles ⟨the big scientific ~ into the south polar region —*Springfield (Mass.) Union*⟩ **c :** an active campaign to promote the sale of a product ⟨his sales picture on this product may be influenced by a heavy ~ on another product —J.K. Blake⟩ **2 :** a condition or occasion of stress **:** an urgent state **:** a time for action **:** EMERGENCY, PINCH ⟨when it came to the ~, I found, I had forgot all I intended to say —Thomas Gray⟩ **3 a (1) :** a sudden forcible act of pushing **:** SHOVE ⟨gave the boy ahead of him an impatient ~ and knocked him down⟩ **(2) :** a thrust with a pointed weapon or the horn of an animal **b (1) :** a physical force steadily applied in a direction away from the body exerting it ⟨gave the car a ~ around the block to start it⟩ ⟨driven by the ~ of the wind on the sails⟩ ⟨the ~ of the water against the walls of the tank⟩ **(2) :** a nonphysical pressure **:** INFLUENCE, COMPULSION, URGE ⟨the ~ and pull of conflicting emotions⟩ **c :** aggressive energy **:** vigorous enterprise ⟨it was the ~ . . . of a reinvigorated government that carried the program through —F.A.Ogg & Harold Zink⟩ **4 a :** an exertion of influence to promote another's interests **b :** stimulation or encouragement to vigorous activity **:** BOOST, IMPETUS ⟨war gave weather forecasting a tremendous ~ —J.D.Ratcliff⟩ **5 a :** CROWD, BUNCH ⟨hurry and get ready, . . . the whole ~ of you —*Atlantic*⟩ **b** *Austral* **:** a gang of rowdies or toughs **6 :** a part to be pushed; *esp* **:** PUSH BUTTON **7** *slang* **:** a foreman in a lumber camp **8** *Brit* **:** DISMISSAL — used in the phrase *get the push* or *give the push* ⟨when the Mayor makes his replacements . . . all I do is put the finger on the guy who's to get the ~ —Hartley Howard⟩ **9 :** a bid in a card game that pushes an opponent

³**push** \"\ *adj* **1 :** that pushes **:** used to communicate a push ⟨~ pole⟩ ⟨~ pedal⟩ **2 :** operated or propelled by pushing ⟨a ~ mower⟩ ⟨a ~ feed⟩

⁴**push** \"\ *n* -ES [origin unknown] **1** *dial chiefly Eng* **:** PUSTULE, PIMPLE **2** *dial chiefly Eng* **:** BOIL, CARBUNCLE

push along *vi* **:** to push on ⟨*pushed along* on their journey after a rest of a few hours⟩

push and pull *var of* PUSH-PULL

push around *vt* **:** to subject to impositions, unfair discrimination, or rough or contemptuous treatment **:** impose on **:** HECTOR ⟨serving the public instead of *pushing* it *around* —J.E.Gloag⟩ ⟨a people whose history for centuries has been one continuous resistance to being *pushed around*, dominated, or swallowed —Marcia Davenport⟩

push-away \'==,=\ *n* **:** PUSHOVER 5

pushball \'=,=\ *n* **1 :** a game in which each of two sides endeavors to push an inflated leather-covered ball about six feet in diameter across its opponents' goal **2 :** the ball used in a game of pushball

push bar *n* **:** a bar placed usu. transversely on a door at hand height (as for the protection of a screen or glass panel)

push-bar conveyor *or* **push-bar elevator** *n* **:** an endless-chain conveyor in which crossbars propel or lift the load by direct engagement or push the load over rollers or a flat surface

push-bike \'=,=\ *also* **push bicycle** *or* **push cycle** *n, Brit* **:** a pedal bicycle — distinguished from a motor bicycle

push boat *n* **:** a powerboat used esp. for pushing a tow of barges

push bolt *n* **1 :** a door bolt moved by pushing with the hand instead of with a key **2 :** a cylinder lock (as on a filing cabinet) that locks by pushing but must be unlocked with a key

push broom *n* **:** a brush for sweeping that has a long handle attached and is pushed

push button *n* **:** a small button or knob that when pushed operates something or sets it in operation ⟨lock the door by pressing the *push button* in the center of the knob⟩; *specif* **:** one that actuates a switch by making or breaking an electric circuit ⟨an elevator operated by *push buttons*⟩

push-button \'=,==\ *adj* [*push button*] **1 :** operated, carried on, or done by means of push buttons or as if by such means **2** *of warfare* **:** using complex and more or less self-operating mechanisms that accomplish missions against enemy airplanes, troops, ships, and installations when put in operation by a simple act comparable to pushing a button ⟨the idea formed in the public mind by such phrases as *push-button* war is a war of robots, a war of machines —E.A.Fitzpatrick⟩

push-button yard *n* **:** a mechanized classification yard in which an operator by pushing buttons or levers may accomplish the switching of cars and makeup of trains

push car *n* **1 :** a railway work car for transporting materials that is usu. towed behind a motorcar **2 :** an intermediate car connecting a locomotive and a train to be pushed on to a ferryboat

pushcard \'=,=\ *n* **:** PUNCHBOARD ⟨an order prohibiting the interstate sale of . . . ~*s* and other lottery devices —*Federal Trade Comm. Releases*⟩

push·cart \ˈ=,=\ *n* **:** a cart or barrow pushed by hand ⟨a vendor with a ~ of fresh fruit⟩ ⟨loaded a self-service ~ in the supermarket⟩

pushcart

push·chair \ˈ=,=\ *n, Brit* **:** STROLLER

push-down \ˈ=,=\ *n* -s **:** a maneuver in which an airplane in level flight is forced into a short dive

pushed *past of* PUSH

push·er \ˈpu̇shə(r)\ *n* -s [¹*push* + *-er*] **1 :** one that pushes ⟨ate using a piece of bread as a ~⟩: as **a** (1) **:** a machine part or implement for pushing something ⟨a cuticle ~⟩ (2) **:** a machine with parts having a thrusting action (3) **:** a watchmaker's tool used in a staking set to push friction jewels in place (4) **:** a soft metal rod used to insert or eject bushings (5) **:** a hard-pointed tool used to remove case pins, lugs, or bars (6) **:** a button on top of a watch crown or on the side of a watchcase for activating the hands of a chronograph or stopwatch (7) **:** a slide on the edge of a watch case for releasing an internal action **b** (1) **:** an aggressive person ⟨stiff competition from a réal ~⟩; *esp* **:** a very aggressive salesman (2) **:** an illicit peddler of narcotics **c** (1) **:** an auxiliary locomotive used behind a train on steep grades (2) **:** PUSH BOAT **d :** the foreman of a crew of workers **:** STRAW BOSS **e :** a miner who pushes loaded cars to the place from which they will be hauled to the shaft or surface by locomotive — called also *headsman, putter, trailer, trammer, wheeler* **f :** PLUNGER **2 :** a chamois toe sock worn by a track athlete **3 a :** an airplane with the propeller located behind the wing — compare TRACTOR **b** *or* **pusher engine :** a piston engine with the propeller mounted behind

pusher furnace *n* **:** a continuous furnace in which pieces of work are pushed at proper speed for completion at the exit

pusher grade *n* **:** a railroad grade that is steeper than the ruling grade and requires a pusher locomotive to be used with a train of normal weight

pusher propeller *n* **:** a propeller operating at the trailing rather than the leading edge of the wing

pushes *pres 3d sing of* PUSH, *pl of* PUSH

push fit *n* **:** a fit of mating machine parts that can be made with moderate hand pressure by the assembler and is used where occasional disassembly is expected

push·ful \ˈpu̇shfəl\ *adj* [²*push* + *-ful*] **1 :** marked by push **:** ZEALOUS, ENERGETIC, ENTERPRISING **2 :** intrusively aggressive ⟨a ~ insurance agent⟩ **syn** see AGGRESSIVE

push·ful·ly \-fəlē\ *adv* **:** in a pushful manner

push·ful·ness \-fəlnəs\ *n* -ES **:** the quality or state of being pushful

push hoe *n* **:** SCUFFLE HOE

push·i·ly \-shəlē\ *adv* [*pushy* + *-ly*] **:** PUSHINGLY

push·i·ness \-shēnəs\ *n* -ES [*pushy* + *-ness*] **:** PUSHINGNESS

pushing *adj* [fr. pres. part. of ¹*push*] **1 :** marked by ambition, energy, enterprise, and initiative **2 :** marked by tactless forwardness, officious intrusion, and snobbish aspiration **syn** see AGGRESSIVE

push·ing·ly *adv* **:** in a pushing manner

push·ing·ness *n* -ES **:** the quality or state of being pushing

push joint *n* **:** a joint formed by placing a brick on a thick bed of mortar and pushing the brick against another brick in the same course in such a way as to fill the space between the bricks — called also *shoved joint*

push key *n* **:** a key that operates a lock by inward rather than rotary motion — called also *thrust key*

push·mo·bile \ˈpu̇shmō,bēl\ *n* -s [¹*push* + *-mobile*] **:** a toy vehicle resembling an automobile and propelled by pushing

push money *n* **:** a commission paid (as by a manufacturer) to a sales person to push the sale of a particular item or line of merchandise — called also *PM, spiff*

push moraine *n* **:** a moraine pushed by a glacier into a ridge at its front

push net *n* **:** a small triangular fishing net with a rigid frame that is pushed along the bottom in shallow waters and is used in parts of the southwestern Pacific for taking shrimps and small bottom-dwelling fishes

push off *vi* **:** to go away **:** get out **:** set out ⟨I'd better *push off* and see about it —Dorothy Sayers⟩ ⟨about time to *push off*⟩

push-off \ˈ=,=\ *n* -s [fr. *push off*, v.] **1 a :** the action of pushing off **b :** SEND-OFF **2 :** a rod or tube in compression used for keeping a trolley wire in its proper position

push-off sweep rake *n* **:** a tractor-mounted power sweep rake with a frame that pushes the hay from the teeth instead of merely allowing it to slide off from the force of gravity

push on *vi* **:** to continue on one's way **:** PROCEED ⟨instead of *pushing on* I stayed —Thomas Skelton⟩

pushover \ˈ=,==\ *n* -s [¹*push* + *over*] **1 :** an opponent easy to defeat or a victim capable of no effective resistance and succumbing or sure to succumb readily to force or guile ⟨so kind, warmhearted and open that she's . . . a ~ for rivals —Virginia Bird⟩ **2 :** someone unwilling or unable to resist the power of a particular attraction or appeal **:** SUCKER ⟨I'm a ~ for any pocket-size atlas and buy them as fast as they appear —*Saturday Rev.*⟩ **3 :** something accomplished without resistance or difficulty **:** SNAP ⟨snow is a painting ~, a surefire subject for the amateur —Joseph Alger⟩ **4 :** the beginning of a dive in flying; *specif* **:** the moment at which the control stick is pushed forward **5 :** a canoeing stroke in which the boat is moved broadside away from the paddle by bracing the shaft against the gunwale, the blade parallel to the side of the canoe, then pulling down on the handle — called also *push-away*

push-pad \ˈ=,=\ *n* **:** a circular pad attached to a door at hand height for use in opening it

push-piece \ˈ=,=\ *n* **:** a stud on the side of a watchcase to activate a special mechanism (as a repeater, chronograph) inside the watch

pushpin \ˈ=,=\ *n* **1 :** a children's game in which one player tries to maneuver his pin over that of another player **2 :** a steel point having a projecting glass or metal head for sticking into a wall or board and used chiefly as a picture hook or as an indicator on a map

push plate *n* **:** HAND PLATE

¹push-pull \ˈ=ˈ=\ *adj* [¹*push* + *pull*] **1 :** constituting or relating to an arrangement of two electron tubes such that an alternating input causes them to send current through a load alternately ⟨a *push-pull* circuit⟩ ⟨a *push-pull* amplifier⟩ **2 :** belonging to or being a linkage for exerting both push and pull at somewhat remote distances ⟨*push-pull* rods⟩ ⟨a *push-pull* control system⟩ **3** *or* **push and pull :** that may be pushed or pulled ⟨a *push-pull* toy⟩ ⟨a *push-pull* latch⟩

²push-pull \"\ *n* [¹*push-pull*] **:** a push-pull arrangement ⟨connect electron tubes in *push-pull*⟩

pushrod \ˈ=,=\ *n* **:** a rod actuated by a cam to open or close the valves of an internal combustion engine

push shot *n* **1 :** a billiards or pool shot in which the cue remains in contact with the cue ball until the cue ball has touched the object ball or one in which the cue strikes the cue ball twice **2 :** a golf shot in which a player having his weight forward on the left foot and his wrists firm hits the ball a descending blow thus producing a low ball which stops quickly **3 :** a one-hand basketball shot similar to the lay-up but executed farther from the basket

pushtu *or* **pushto** *cap, var of* PASHTO

push-up \ˈ=,=\ *n* -s **1 :** an exercise for strengthening arm and shoulder girdle muscles that consists of bending and extending the elbows while the body is kept in a prone position with the back flat and is supported only on the hands and toes **2 :** a mass of frozen aquatic vegetation placed by muskrats over a hole in the ice that they use for access to the water

push wave *n* **:** a seismic disturbance consisting of longitudinal vibrations of the earth's crust

pushy \ˈpu̇shē, -shi\ *adj* -ER/-EST [¹*push* + *-y*] **1 :** PUSHING, AGGRESSIVE **2** *chiefly dial* **:** unpleasantly eager or anxious

pu·sil·la·nim·i·ty \,pyüsələˈniməd·ē, -mətē, -i *sometimes* -üzə-\ *n* -ES [ME *pusillanimite*, fr. MF *pusillanimité*, fr. LL *pusillanimitat-, pusillanimitas*, fr. *pusillanimis* pusillanimous + L *-itat-, -itas* -ity] **:** the quality or state of being pusillanimous **:** weakness of spirit **:** COWARDLINESS

pu·sil·lan·i·mous \ˌ==ˈlanəməs\ *adj* [LL *pusillanimis*, fr. L *pusillus* very small (dim. of *pusus* small child) + *animus* soul, mind, spirit; akin to L *puer* child, Skt *putva* child, son — more at FEW, ANIMATE] **:** lacking or showing a lack of courage and manly strength and resolution **:** marked by mean-spirited and contemptible timidity ⟨the policy of watchful waiting denounced as ~ —Allan Nevins & H.S.Commager⟩ **syn** see COWARDLY

pu·sil·lan·i·mous·ly *adv* **:** in a pusillanimous manner

pu·sil·lan·i·mous·ness *n* -ES **:** the quality or state of being pusillanimous **:** PUSILLANIMITY

¹puss \ˈpu̇s\ *n* -ES [origin unknown] **1 a :** CAT **b** *dial Brit* **:** HARE **2 :** a young woman **:** CHILD — usu. used in affection or reproach

²puss \"\ *n* -ES [IrGael *pus* lip, mouth, fr. MIr *bus*, prob. of imit. origin — more at BUSS] *slang* **:** FACE ⟨couple of guys who need a poke in the ~ —Michael Fessier⟩ **syn** see FACE

puss caterpillar *n* [¹*puss*] **:** a caterpillar that is the larva of a flannel moth (*Megalopyge opercularis*) chiefly of the southeastern U.S. and that has urticating hairs

puss in the corner : a game in which all players but one occupy goals (as the corners of a room) and at a signal try to exchange places before the one having no place of his own can reach one of the vacant goals — called also *pussy wants a corner*

puss·ley *or* **pus·ley** *also* **puss·ly** \ˈpəslē, -li\ *n* -s [alter. of *pursley*] **:** PURSLANE

puss moth *n* [¹*puss*] **:** a light-colored stout-bodied European notodontid moth (*Cerura vinula*) whose larva feeds on poplar and willow leaves; *broadly* **:** any moth of the genus *Cerura*

¹pussy \ˈpu̇sē, -si\ *n* -ES [¹*puss* + *-y*, dim. suffix] **1 a :** GIRL **b :** CAT **c** *dial Brit* **:** HARE **2 a :** a catkin of the pussy willow **b :** RABBIT-FOOT CLOVER

²pus·sy \ˈpəsē, -si\ *adj* -ER/-EST [¹*pus* + *-y*, adj. suffix] **:** full of or like pus

³pus·sy \"\ *var of* PURSY

⁴pussy \ˈpu̇sē, -si\ *n* -ES [earlier *puss* vulva (perh. of LG or Scand origin) + *-y*, dim. suffix; akin to ON *pūss* pocket, pouch, Icel *pussa* vulva, LG *pūse* vulva, OE *pusa, posa* bag, Gk *byein* to stuff, plug] **1 :** female genitals; *esp* **:** VULVA — usu. considered vulgar **2 :** SEXUAL INTERCOURSE — usu. considered vulgar

pussycat \ˈ=,=\ *n* [¹*pussy* + *cat*] **1 :** CAT **2 :** PUSSY WILLOW **3 :** RABBIT-FOOT CLOVER

pussy clover *n* [¹*pussy*] **:** RABBIT-FOOT CLOVER

¹pussy·foot \ˈpu̇sē,fu̇t, -si,f-, *usu* -u̇d·+V\ *vi* [¹*pussy* + *foot*] **1 :** to tread or move warily or stealthily **2 :** to refrain from committing oneself (as in regard to a question at issue) **:** make guarded or equivocal statements of one's views

²pussyfoot \"\ *n, pl* **pussyfoots** [fr. *Pussyfoot*, nickname of W. E. Johnson †1945 Am. law enforcement officer and prohibition advocate] **:** PROHIBITIONIST

³pussyfoot \"\ *n, pl* **pussyfoots** [¹*pussy* + *foot*] **:** any of several plants having leaf clusters or flower heads that suggest a cat's foot in shape: as **a :** PUSSY-PAW **b :** PUSSYTOE

pussyfooted \ˈ==,==\ *also* **pussyfoot** \ˈ==,=\ *adj* [*pussyfooted* fr. *pussyfoot*, adj. + *-ed*; *pussyfoot* fr. ¹*pussy* + *foot*] **:** characterized by pussyfooting

pussy·foot·er \ˈ==,=ə(r)\ *n* -s [¹*pussyfoot* + *-er*] **1 :** one that pussyfoots **2 :** an advocate or adherent of prohibition

pussy-paw *also* **pussy's-paw** \ˈ==,=\ *n* **:** a Californian herb (*Calyptridium umbellatum*) of the family Portulacaceae with a scapose spike of pink or white flowers rising from a dense rosette of leaves — usu. used in pl.

pussytoe *or* **pussy's toe** \ˈ==,=\ *n* **:** a cat's-foot of the genus *Antennaria*; *esp* **:** a cat's foot (*A. plantaginifolia*) of eastern and central No. America with foliage suggesting that of a plantain and usu. crimson flower heads subtended by purple white-marked involucres — usu. used in pl.

pussy wants a corner : PUSS IN THE CORNER

pussy willow \ˈ==ˈ=(,)=\ *n* **:** a willow having large cylindrical silky catkins; *esp* **:** a small arboreal American willow (*Salix discolor*) with usu. lanceolate leaves that are bright green above and glaucous to whitish on the undersurface

pussy willow

pussywillow gray *n* **:** a pinkish gray that is redder, lighter, and stronger than gull (sense 2b)

¹pus·tu·lant \ˈpəschələnt, -st(y)ə-\ *adj* [LL *pustulant-, pustulans*, pres. part. of *pustulare* to blister — more at PUSTULATE] **:** producing pustules

²pustulant \"\ *n* -s **:** an agent (as a chemical) that induces pustule formation

pus·tu·lar \-lə(r)\ *adj* [*pustule* + *-ar*] **1 :** of, relating to, or of the character of pustules ⟨~ prominences⟩ ⟨~ eruptions⟩ **2 :** covered with pustular prominences **:** PUSTULATE

¹pus·tu·late \-,lāt\ *vb* -ED/-ING/-S [LL *pustulatus*, past part. of *pustulare* to blister, fr. L *pustula* pustule, blister] *vt* **:** to cause to form into pustules ~ *vi* **:** to become pustulous

²pus·tu·late \-,lət, -,lāt\ *or* **pus·tu·lat·ed** \-,lād·əd\ *adj* [*pustulate* fr. LL *pustulatus* blistered, fr. past part. of *pustulare*; *pustulated* fr. past part. of ¹*pustulate*] **:** covered with pustules or similar prominences

pus·tu·la·tion \,==ˈlāshən\ *n* -s [LL *pustulation-, pustulatio*, fr. *pustulatus* (past part. of *pustulare*) + L *-ion-, -io* ion] **1 :** the action of producing pustules or state of being pustulated **2 :** PUSTULE

pus·tu·la·tous \ˌ==ˈlād·əs, ˈ==,ləd·-\ *adj* [²*pustulate* + *-ous*] **:** PUSTULAR 2

pus·tule \ˈpəs(,)chül, -,st(y)ül\ *n* -s [ME, fr. L *pustula, pussula*; akin to Gk *physa* bellows, bladder, bubble, Lith *puslė* bladder — more at FOG] **1 :** a small circumscribed elevation of the skin containing pus and having an inflamed base **2 :** any small elevation or spot on a plant resembling a blister; *esp* **:** a mark on a leaf due to the rupture of surface tissues overlying spore masses or fruiting structures of a parasitic fungus **3 a :** a wart or dermal excrescence in some amphibians (as toads) **b :** a colored point or a swelling resembling a blister (as on the integument of an insect)

pus·tu·li·form \ˈpəschələ,fȯrm, -st(y)əl-\ *adj* [NL *pustuliformis*, fr. L *pustula* + *-iformis* -iform] **:** having the form of a pustule

pus·tu·lose \-,lōs\ *adj* [L *pustulosus*, fr. *pustula* + *-osus* -ose] **:** PUSTULAR

pus·tu·lous \-,ləs\ *adj* [L *pustulosus*] **:** resembling, covered with, or characterized by pustules **:** PUSTULATE, PUSTULAR ⟨~ skin⟩ ⟨a ~ disease⟩

pusz·ta \ˈpu̇,stȯ\ *n* -s [Hung, fr. *puszta* deserted, bare, bleak] **:** a treeless plain in Hungary **:** STEPPE

¹put \ˈpu̇t *chiefly dial* ˈpət, *usu* |d·+V\ *vb* **put** \"\ *or dial* **put·ten** \-tᵊn\ **put** *or dial* **putten; putting; puts** [ME *putten, puten*; akin to OE *putung* instigation, *potian* to push, MD *poten* to plant, graft, Icel *pota* to poke] *vt* **1 a :** to place or cause to be placed in a specified position or relationship **:** LAY, SET ⟨~ the roof on the house⟩ ⟨~ the plant near the window⟩ ⟨two tumblers of brandy had been enough to ~ him under the table —Van Wyck Brooks⟩ **b :** to move in a specified direction or into or out of a specified place ⟨~ the hands of the clock back⟩ ⟨~ the book down⟩ ⟨~ his arm through the sleeve⟩ ⟨~ the car into the garage⟩ ⟨~ the cat out of the house⟩ **c** (1) **:** to send (as a weapon or missile) into or through something **:** THRUST ⟨a sharpshooter ~ a ball through the old captain's head —Frank Yerby⟩ ⟨~ a knife between his ribs⟩ (2) **:** DRIVE ⟨~ a nail into the wall⟩ (3) **:** to throw with an overhand pushing motion ⟨~ the shot 63 feet 6 inches —*Newsweek*⟩ **d** (1) **:** to bring into or establish in a specified state or condition ⟨when his father had died he had ~ her into mourning —F.M.Ford⟩ ⟨~ one in the proper mood to enjoy the local operettas —Horace Sutton⟩ ⟨~ the motor into working order⟩ ⟨~ her to shame⟩ ⟨~ it to use⟩ ⟨~ the matter right⟩ (2) **:** to bring into a state of dependence esp. upon a specified regimen — usu. used with *on* ⟨~ him on a salt-poor diet⟩ ⟨~ them on bread and water⟩ **e :** to carry or cause to be taken across a body of water ⟨you could ask anybody to ~ you across a river —Archibald Marshall⟩ ⟨the twenty-knot speed that would ~ a ship across the Atlantic in . . . seven days —Edward Ellsberg⟩ **f :** to remove from a specified state, condition, or situation ⟨~ its competitor out of business⟩ ⟨~ the idea from his mind⟩ **g :** FOCUS ⟨~ his glasses on the group —F.W.Booth⟩ **2 a :** to cause to endure or suffer something **:** SUBJECT — usu. used with *to* ⟨~ him to death⟩ ⟨~ them to the sword⟩ ⟨~ him to the expense of a new roof⟩ ⟨~ him to the shame of revealing his poverty⟩ **b :** IMPOSE, INFLICT — usu. used with *on* or *upon* ⟨~ a special tax on luxuries⟩ ⟨~ a heavy strain on his resources⟩ ⟨if I ~ any tricks upon 'em —Shak.⟩ ⟨~ numerous insults on him⟩ **3 a :** to set before one for judgment or decision **:** bring to the attention ⟨~ the question of a special dividend before the board of directors⟩ ⟨~ the problem of downtown parking before the mayor⟩ ⟨it was a question that her life had never permitted her to ~ to herself —Laura Krey⟩ **b :** to call for a formal vote on ⟨the chairman is not supposed to say anything except to ~ the motion —Dorothy C. Fisher⟩ ⟨the question of adjournment was then ~, and carried by a large majority —T.L.Peacock⟩ **4 a** (1) **:** to turn into language or literary form — usu. used with *in* or *into* ⟨found it difficult to ~ his feelings in words⟩ ⟨~ the story of his life into a novel⟩ (2) **:** to translate into another language or style — usu. used with *into* ⟨~ the poem into English⟩ ⟨~ the play into modern idiom⟩ (3) **:** ADAPT ⟨witty lyrics ~ to tuneful music⟩ **b :** EXPRESS, STATE ⟨that's *putting* it mildly⟩ ⟨~ his proposal awkwardly⟩ **5 a :** to devote (oneself) to an activity or end — usu. used with *to* ⟨~ himself to the study of law⟩ ⟨~ himself to winning back their confidence⟩ **b :** to set to use **:** employ actively **:** APPLY ⟨~ his mind to the problem⟩ ⟨~ all his strength into the fight⟩ ⟨~ all his resources behind the candidate⟩ **c :** to set to some employment or function **:** ASSIGN — usu. used with *to* ⟨~ him to mixing the salad⟩ ⟨~ her to filing letters⟩ ⟨~ them to work⟩ **d :** to set in a particular place or position for the purpose of carrying out an activity or performing a function ⟨~ him to school⟩ ⟨~ the children to bed⟩ ⟨~ the play on the stage⟩ **e** (1) **:** to cause to perform an action or clear an obstacle **:** URGE ⟨~ the horse over the fence⟩ ⟨~ the boy through his exercises⟩ (2) **:** to set into sudden or violent movement or activity **:** IMPEL, INCITE ⟨~ the prowler to flight⟩ ⟨~ them into a frenzy⟩ (3) **:** to compel (a person) to some course of action or behavior ⟨you ~ me to forget a lady's manners —Shak.⟩ — now used only in legal phrases ⟨the husky handyman was not immediately ~ to plea and no date was set for the arraignment —*Springfield (Mass.) Union*⟩ **6 a :** to bring into the power or under the protection or care of someone ⟨~ him into the hands of his enemies⟩ ⟨~ themselves in good hands⟩ ⟨~ him under the care of a specialist⟩ **b :** REPOSE, REST — usu. used with *in* ⟨~s his trust in God⟩ ⟨~s his faith in reason⟩ **c :** INVEST — usu. used with *in* or *into* ⟨~ all his money in the company⟩ ⟨~ his savings into stocks⟩ **d** *archaic* **:** to set as a beginner **:** APPRENTICE — usu. used with *to* **7 a :** to give as an estimate ⟨the medical examiner ~ the time as about a quarter past eleven —Mary R. Rinehart⟩ ⟨~ the number at 500,000 —Roy Lewis & Angus Maude⟩ **b :** ATTACH, ATTRIBUTE — usu. used with *on* or *upon* ⟨~s a wrong construction on his actions⟩ ⟨~s a high value on his friendship⟩ ⟨~s a high premium on leisure —H.W.Glidden⟩ **c :** IMPUTE — usu. used with *on* ⟨~ the blame for the illegal actions on his partner⟩ ⟨~ the responsibility for the accident on the other driver⟩ **d :** to ascribe to or base upon a particular cause or foundation — usu. used with *on* or *upon* ⟨~s morality on the basis of self-interest⟩ ⟨~s his conclusion on the evidence of the fossil remains⟩ **e :** to represent as being in a particular place ⟨he ~s "episcopal buildings along the crest" of Quebec before the first bishop set foot in the country —A.L. Burt⟩ ⟨the poet ~s his enemies in hell⟩ **8 :** to establish or cause to take effect (a limit or restraint) ⟨~ an end to his suffering⟩ ⟨~ a limit on the betting⟩ ⟨~ a check on his enthusiasm⟩ **9 :** ASSUME, SUPPOSE ⟨~ the absurd impossible case, for once —Robert Browning⟩ **10 a :** to affix (a signature or other mark) to a written or printed document ⟨they did not dare to ~ their names to what they wrote —Virginia Woolf⟩ ⟨~ a check next to the name of each course he had taken⟩ **b :** to enter as part of a list or group of related items — usu. used with *on* ⟨asked to have his name ~ on the list of candidates⟩ ⟨~ the telephone call on my bill⟩ ⟨let's plan to ~ it on the menu for tomorrow⟩ **11 :** PLACE, SUBSTITUTE ⟨before you condemn him, ~ yourself in his place⟩ **12 :** to bring (an animal) together with one of the opposite sex for breeding — usu. used with *to* ⟨consider seriously *putting* some of your ewes to longwool rams —E.F.Fricke⟩ **13 :** BET, WAGER — usu. used with *on* ⟨~ two dollars on the favorite⟩ ~ *vi* **1** *chiefly dial* **:** BUTT **2 a :** to start out; esp **:** to leave in a hurry **:** make off **:** DECAMP ⟨caught his squaw by one arm and ~ for the timber with her —H.L.Davis⟩ **b** *of a ship* **:** to take a specified course ⟨~ into the bay to avoid the storm⟩ ⟨~ down the river⟩ **3** *chiefly dial* **:** to shoot up **:** GROW, SPROUT — used of plants **4 :** to flow in or out of a body of water ⟨the river ~s into a lake⟩ **syn** see SET — **put forth** [ME *putten forth*, fr. *putten* to put + *forth*] **1 a :** ASSERT, PROPOSE ⟨has *put forth* a new theory of the origin of the solar system⟩ **b :** to make public **:** ISSUE ⟨has *put forth* a new set of parking regulations⟩ **2 :** to bring into action **:** EXERT ⟨had to *put* all his strength *forth* to get the measure through⟩ **3 :** to produce or send out (a growth) ⟨*put forth* leaves⟩ **4 :** to come into leaf, bud, or flower ⟨other things might *put forth*; but never again that wild beauty —Ellen Glasgow⟩ **5 :** to start out **:** begin a voyage ⟨*put forth* alone upon the great inland ocean —Jackson Rivers⟩ — **put forward 1 :** to advance to a position of prominence or responsibility ⟨was *put forward* as spokesman for the party —S.H.Adams⟩ ⟨the shortage of qualified people gave him the opportunity to *put* himself *forward*⟩ **2 :** to offer for consideration **:** PROPOSE ⟨any single fact to *put forward* in support of these fantastic charges —Kathleen Freeman⟩ ⟨the organic theory of nature which I have been tentatively *putting forward* —A.N.Whitehead⟩ — **put in an appearance :** to be present; *esp* **:** to appear at a formal or planned gathering usu. for a brief time only ⟨the candidate *put in an appearance* at five rallies in one night⟩ — **put in mind :** REMIND ⟨*put* him *in mind* of his father⟩ — **put one on to :** to call one's attention to **:** alert one to ⟨it was his suspicious manner that first *put me on to* him⟩ ⟨*put me on to* a good book⟩ — **put one's finger on :** DISCOVER, IDENTIFY ⟨*put his finger on* the cause of the trouble⟩ — **put out of the way 1 :** ¹KILL 1a ⟨hired a gunman to *put* his competitor *out of the way*⟩ **2** *also* **put out of one's way** *Brit* **:** to cause inconvenience or trouble to — often used with a reflexive object ⟨cannot *put* themselves *out of their way* on any account —William Hazlitt⟩ — **put paid to** *Brit* **:** to finish off **:** wipe out ⟨a tempest had *put paid to* their efforts —David Masters⟩ ⟨*puts paid to* whatever chances you had of coming first —Roy Saunders⟩ — **put the arm on** *slang* **1 :** to ask for money ⟨*put the arm on* a rich alumnus and got enough for a new gymnasium⟩ **2 :** to hold up **:** HIJACK ⟨*put the arm on* a big load of furs⟩ — **put the bee on** *or* **put the bite on** *slang* **:** to ask for a loan or to get money from ⟨some smooth hoodlum *puts the bee on* his daughter for two thousand bucks —Hartley Howard⟩ — **put the finger on :** to point out or identify to the police or other authorities **:** inform on ⟨*put the finger on* the other members of the gang⟩ — **put to bed :** to make the final preparations for printing (a newspaper or magazine) — **put to it :** to give difficulty to **:** press hard ⟨had been *put to it* to keep up with her even with her own famous big flat stride —Elizabeth Bowen⟩ — **put to rights :** to put into shape **:** make tidy **:** ARRANGE ⟨a new commanding officer who *put* the company *to rights*⟩ — **put two and two together :** to draw the proper inference from given premises or related circumstances ⟨sharp enough wits to *put two and two together* —T.B.Costain⟩ — **put up to 1 :** INCITE, INSTIGATE ⟨he was the ringleader who *put* the others *up to* mischief⟩ **2 :** to make acquainted with **:** inform of ⟨*put* him *up to* a good buy in stocks⟩ — **put up with 1 :** to suffer (as an insult or injury) without open resentment or attempted reprisal ⟨must live among his unruly parishioners and even *put up with* physical assault from them —Peter Forster⟩ **2 :** to endure (as something harmful or unpleasant) without complaint **:** TOLERATE ⟨we do not *put up with* string quartets playing transcriptions of piano music —Virgil Thomson⟩

²put \"\ *n* -s [ME, fr. *putten, puten* to put — more at ¹PUT] **1 :** a throw made with an overhand pushing motion; *specif* **:** the act or an instance of putting the shot **2** *dial Brit* **:** a thrust made in attack or in coming to someone's assistance **:** PUSH, SHOVE **3 :** an option to sell a specified amount of stock, grain, or other commodity at a fixed price at or within a given time — compare CALL 3d

³put \"\ *adj* [fr. past part. of ¹*put*] **:** being in place **:** FIXED, SET ⟨stayed ~ under the stove —E.B.White⟩

⁴put \ˈpət\ *n* -s [origin unknown] **:** BLOCKHEAD, DOLT

put about *vi, of a ship* **:** to change direction **:** go on another tack ~ *vt* **1 a :** to place (a sailing ship) on another tack ⟨the pinnace was *put about,* and run towards a certain dark speck —William Black⟩ **b :** to cause to change course or direction **:** cause to turn back or around ⟨*put* the horse *about* and headed for the corral⟩ **2 :** to cause to be talked about **:** CIRCULATE, RUMOR ⟨it was *put about* in Paris that he was tired of aristocratic mistresses —Nancy Mitford⟩ **3 a :** to cause difficulty or trouble for **:** INCONVENIENCE ⟨I don't want to *put* you *about,* telling falsehoods for me —John Galsworthy⟩ **b :** DISCONCERT, DISTRESS ⟨I thought the poor man would break down into tears at last, he was so *put about* —Mary Deasy⟩

put across *vt* **1 :** to achieve or carry through by deceit or trickery ⟨acts as a restraint on all the nations from trying to *put across* illicit enterprises —*Harper's*⟩ **2 a :** to convey effectively or forcefully ⟨knows how to *put* a song *across* —*Time*⟩ **b :** to cause to be accepted or acted upon ⟨tells how to *put* yourself *across* as a man of the world —*Saturday Rev.*⟩ ⟨was so heart-and-soul in the project that I was able to *put* the idea *across* to our group of twenty-five women —Winona Sparks⟩

pu·ta·men \pyüˈtāmən\ *n, pl* **putam·i·na** \-tamənə\ [NL, fr. L, that which falls off in pruning, shells, peels, fr. *putare* to cut, prune — more at PAVE] **1 :** an outer reddish layer of gray matter in the lenticular nucleus **2 :** a tough membrane that lines the shell of a bird's egg — **pu·tam·i·nous** \-tamənəs\ *adj*

put-and-take \ˌ≈ˈ≈\ *n* **:** any of various games of chance played with a special top or with dice or cards in which the players contribute to a pool or take from it — see TEETOTUM

top used in put-and-take

pu·ta·tive \ˈpyüd·əd·iv\ *adj* [ME, fr. LL *putativus,* fr. L *putatus* (past part. of *putare* to consider, think) + *-ivus* -ive — more at PAVE] **1 :** commonly accepted or supposed **:** REPUTED ⟨a few of us are a little dubious about these ~ human superiorities —E.A.Hooton⟩ ⟨the ~ father⟩ **2 :** assumed to exist or to have existed **:** HYPOTHESIZED, INFERRED ⟨they can recognize rock strata capable of producing oil, and look for the ~ product —*Time*⟩ ⟨traced back to a postulated form in a ~ parent language —J.B.Carroll⟩ — **pu·ta·tive·ly** \-d·əvlē\ *adv*

putative marriage *n, canon & civil law* **:** a duly formalized marriage that is invalid because of various impediments (as consanguinity) though recognized in some states as valid for certain purposes if contracted in good faith by at least one of the parties to it

put away *vt* [ME *putten away,* fr. *putten* to put + *away*] **1 a :** DISCARD, RENOUNCE ⟨to *put* grief *away* is disloyal to the memory of the departed —H.A.Overstreet⟩ **b :** DIVORCE ⟨incurring the risk of being *put away* by her husband on discovery of her previous immorality —Morris Ploscowe⟩ **2 :** to eat or drink up **:** CONSUME ⟨has been known to *put away* a couple of pounds of sausage at a single sitting —*New Yorker*⟩ **3 a :** to confine esp. in a mental institution ⟨poor demented creature, she thought, how many months would it be before they *put* her *away?* —Ellen Glasgow⟩ **b :** BURY ⟨*put away* their dead in seated position in pits roofed with bark —*Amer. Guide Series: Md.*⟩ **c :** KILL ⟨every man you *put away* has friends —Maxwell Anderson⟩ ⟨take an incurably sick dog to the vet to be *put away* —G.S.Perry⟩

put by *vt* [ME *putten by* to reject, fr. *putten* to put + *by*] **1** *obs* **:** to give up **:** DISCONTINUE ⟨*put by* this barbarous brawl —Shak.⟩ **2** *archaic* **a :** to turn aside **:** AVERT **b :** to cause to abandon a project **3 :** to lay aside **:** SAVE ⟨enough money *put by* for when he retires —M.A.Abrams⟩

putch·er \ˈpəchə(r), ˈpŭch-\ *n* -s [origin unknown] *dial Eng* **:** a wicker trap used in catching salmon

put down *vb* [ME *putten doun,* fr. *putten* to put + *doun* down] *vt* **1 a :** to do away with **:** ABOLISH, DESTROY ⟨indicted on charges of failure to *put down* gambling —Meyer Berger⟩ ⟨assist in *putting down* the pestilences —*Current History*⟩ **b :** to bring to an end by force (as an outbreak against authority) **:** SUPPRESS, CRUSH ⟨stern military measures *put down* the rioting —Jean & Franc Shor⟩ **c** *Brit* **:** to give up **:** discontinue using **2 :** DEGRADE, DEPOSE ⟨has *put down* the mighty from their thrones, and exalted those of low degree —Lk 1:52 (RSV)⟩ **3 :** to make ineffective **:** CHECK, SNUB ⟨*put down* gossip that she will again be a mama by labeling it the truth —*Time*⟩ **4 :** to do away with (as an injured, sick, or aged animal) **:** put to death **:** DESTROY, KILL ⟨with the veterinary means . . . at our disposal, I would always decide to have a sufferer from this disease *put down* —Henry Wynmalen⟩ **5 a :** to write down **:** put in writing ⟨was careful to *put down* only what he knew from first-hand experience —Granville Hicks⟩ **b :** to enter in a list ⟨one of the largest subscribers, *putting* his name *down* initially for £1,000 —W.P.Webb⟩ ⟨*putting down* the industrialist's son at birth for Eton —Roy Lewis & Angus Maude⟩ **6 a :** to place in a specified category ⟨I *put* him *down* as a hypochondriac —O.S.J.Gogarty⟩ ⟨I'd have *put* her *down* as being just on the far side of forty-five —Hamilton Basso⟩ **b :** ATTRIBUTE ⟨prepared to put these "shortcomings" *down* to inexperience —C.H.Dewhurst⟩ **7 :** to make by digging or drilling (as a well or pit) **:** SINK ⟨began *putting down* experimental bores —Margaret Clarke⟩ **8 :** to cause (a fish) to swim near the bottom (as from alarm) ⟨the noisy activity quickly *put down* the fish —F.C.Craighead b.1916 & J.J. Craighead⟩ **9 a :** GROOM ⟨much practice will be needed to *put* your dog *down* properly —Winnie Barber⟩ **b :** to eliminate (a show animal) from consideration in a competition ⟨even the ideal cat may be *put down* if it is not shown in perfect condition —P.M.Soderberg⟩ **10 :** to take in as food or drink ⟨poured a stiff jolt of whiskey and *put* it *down* —Raymond Chandler⟩ ⟨was now *putting down* helping after helping of the dinner —Carson McCullers⟩ **11 :** to pack or preserve for future use (as meats in brine, eggs in waterglass) ⟨*put down* a whole cask of pickles⟩ **12** *cricket* **:** to break (a wicket) with a fielded ball ~ *vi, of an airplane or airplane pilot* **:** LAND ⟨*put down* at the airport on time⟩ ⟨despite the rain, he *put down* in a perfect landing⟩

pute \ˈpyüt\ *adj* [L *putus,* fr. *putare* to cut, prune, cleanse — more at PAVE] **:** PURE, UNADULTERATED ⟨you and I chance to be pure ~ asses —Rudyard Kipling⟩

put·e·lee *or* **put·e·li** \ˈpəd·əlē\ *n* -s [Hindi *paṭelī,* dim. of *paṭelā*] **:** a bulky flat-bottomed boat used on the Ganges river in India

puteng *usu cap, var of* PHUTENG

puth·ery \ˈpŭthərī\ *adj, dial* **:** MUGGY, SULTRY

pu·tid \ˈpyüd·əd\ *adj* [L *putidus,* fr. *putēre* to stink, be rotten — more at FOUL] **:** ROTTEN, WORTHLESS — **pu·tid·ly** *adv*

put in *vb* [ME *putten in,* fr. *putten* to put + *in*] *vt* **1 :** to make a formal offer or declaration of ⟨*put in* a plea of guilty⟩ ⟨*put* his claim *in* for damages⟩ **2 :** to come in with **:** INTERPOSE ⟨blocked his opponent's blows and then *put in* a sudden right to the jaw⟩ ⟨thought it opportune to *put in* a defensive word for his elder brother —L.C.Douglas⟩ — often used with quoted words as object ⟨another *put in,* "Pigmy-minded senators!" —Margaret A. Barnes⟩ **3 :** to lay in a supply of ⟨ran a small store, starting out with selling soft drinks . . . then he *put in* candy, cigarettes and bread —B.J.Siegel⟩ **4 :** to spend (a specified amount of time) esp. at some occupation or job ⟨*put in* their customary six or seven hours at the office —Jerome Weidman⟩ **5 :** PLANT ⟨all we got to do now is *put in* that next year's crop —William Faulkner⟩ ~ *vi* **1 :** to call at or enter a place ⟨a lot of the boys *put in* here on account of the good water —Edwin Corle⟩; *esp* **:** to enter a harbor or port ⟨the dune-locked harbors . . . where vessels frequently *put in* —*Amer. Guide Series: Mich.*⟩ **2 :** to make an application, request, or offer ⟨had to retire and *put in* for a pension —Seymour Nagan⟩ ⟨*put in* for its share of new production —*Time*⟩

put·log \ˈpŭtˌlȯg, ˈpət- *also* -ˌläg\ *also* **put·lock** \-ˌläk\ *n* [*putlog* prob. by folk etymology (influence of *log*) fr. *putlock,* perh. fr. ³*put* + *lock*] **:** one of the short pieces of timber that directly support the flooring of a scaffold and that have one end resting on the ledger of the scaffold and the other in a hole left in the wall temporarily for the purpose

put·nam scale \ˈpətnəm-\ *also* **putnam's scale** *n, usu cap P* [prob. fr. the name *Putnam*] **:** a scale (*Aspidiotus ancylus*) that feeds on various trees and shrubs throughout most of the U.S.

put off *vb* [ME *putten of,* fr. *putten* to put + *of* off] *vt* **1 :** DISCONCERT, REPEL ⟨don't be *put off* by the ghastly jacket —B.C.L.Keelan⟩ ⟨in this way you may *put off* as many as you persuade —A.P.Herbert⟩ **2 a :** DELAY, POSTPONE ⟨many girls tend to *put off* marriage until they are older —Robert Reid⟩ ⟨somehow the time for departure must be *put off* —Lyle Saxon⟩ **b :** to get rid of for the time being or to induce to wait ⟨*put* the bill collector *off* for another month⟩ ⟨I'd forgotten it was that night . . . can't you *put* him *off?* —Nigel Balchin⟩ **c :** to turn the attention of from some design or purpose **:** DISSUADE, ELUDE, FRUSTRATE ⟨had *put* a robber *off* with a show of unconcern⟩ ⟨was so importunate it was impossible to *put* him *off*⟩ **3 a :** to take off **:** rid oneself of ⟨*put* his coat *off*⟩ ⟨you had your choosing, and it's time you'd *put off* your flightiness —Mary Deasy⟩ **b :** to dispose of ⟨second litters can be *put off* in autumn as porkers —A.Longwill⟩ **c :** to sell or pass fraudulently ⟨a moon-eyed roan that some slick trader had *put off* on him —F.B.Gipson⟩ ⟨*put off* a counterfeit ten-dollar bill⟩ **4 :** to push or send off (a boat) from land or another boat ⟨the pinnace was *put off* from the yacht —William Black⟩ ⟨let me cut the cable, and when we are *put off,* fall to their throats —Shak.⟩ ~ *vi* **:** to leave land ⟨the inhabitants then *put off* in boats and salvaged the cargo of the wrecked boat —*Amer. Guide Series: N.J.*⟩

put-off \(ˈ)≈ˈ≈\ *n* -s [*put off*] **:** the act or an instance of evasion or delay **:** EXCUSE, POSTPONEMENT

put on *vb* [ME *putten on,* fr. *putten* to put + *on*] *vt* **1 :** to impose as a burden **:** INFLICT ⟨known for *putting on* heavy fines⟩ **2 a :** to dress oneself in **:** DON ⟨at night would *put on* courtly garb —R.A.Hall b.1911⟩ ⟨*put* her new dress *on*⟩ **b :** to invest oneself with **:** take on ⟨*put on* the flesh and bones of a creature and walked His own earth —Alan Paton & Liston Pope⟩ **c :** to make part of one's appearance or behavior **:** ADOPT ⟨seems to feel the necessity of *putting on* a good deal of professional dignity —A.W.Long⟩ **d :** to assume misleadingly **:** FEIGN ⟨looked so pretty, *putting on* an ugly face —Andrew Young⟩ ⟨*put* a saintly manner *on*⟩ **3 a :** to cause to act or operate **:** APPLY ⟨*put on* a sprint of speed to make it —Donn Byrne⟩ **b :** to assign to some job or activity ⟨were *put on* with mattocks at chipping over the whole of the bare area —A.F. Ellis⟩ ⟨*put* extra salesmen *on* for the holiday rush⟩ **c** *cricket* **:** to direct (a player) to bowl **4 a :** ADD ⟨has been *putting on* weight⟩ **b :** EXAGGERATE, OVERSTATE ⟨he's *putting* it *on* when he makes such claims⟩ **5 :** to push forward (as the hands of a clock) **:** ADVANCE **6 :** PERFORM, PRODUCE ⟨*put on* an entertaining act⟩ ⟨*put on* a spectacular production of the play⟩ **7 :** to deceive in a good-natured way **:** KID ⟨you're *putting* me *on*⟩ ~ *vi, chiefly Scot* **:** to dress oneself ⟨slowly slowly raise she up and slowly *put* she *on* —*Barbara Allen*⟩

¹put-on \(ˈ)≈ˈ≈\ *adj* [fr. past part. of *put on*] **1 :** ASSUMED, PRETENDED ⟨in a *put-on* childish voice —Barnaby Conrad⟩ **2** *Scot* **:** CLOTHED

²put-on \"\ *n* -s [*put on*] **:** a false or pretentious manner, appearance, or mode of behavior **:** AFFECTATION ⟨all the *put-on* had gone out of their faces — they were left with what God gave them at the beginning —Shelby Foote⟩

pu·to·ri·us \pyüˈtōrēəs, -tȯr-\ *n, cap* [NL, fr. L *putēre* to stink + *-orius* -ory — more at FOUL] *in some classifications* **:** a genus of Mustelidae comprising the Old World polecats and now usu. considered a subgenus of *Mustela*

put out *vb* [ME *putten out,* fr. *putten* to put + *out*] *vt* **1 :** EXERT, USE ⟨*put out* all his strength to move the piano⟩ **2 :** EXTINGUISH ⟨*put out* the light⟩ ⟨*put* the fire *out*⟩ **3 a :** PUBLISH, ISSUE ⟨*puts out* the only newspaper in town⟩ ⟨*puts* a new catalog *out* every year⟩ **b :** PRODUCE, PROVIDE ⟨*puts out* an excellent line of inexpensive coats⟩ ⟨*putting out* a table d'hôte tourist menu that will run cheaper than à la carte dinners —Henry Giniger⟩ **4 :** INVEST ⟨couldn't *put* it *out* at profit, now —Joseph Hergesheimer⟩ **5 a :** to upset the composure of **:** DISCONCERT, EMBARRASS ⟨is never *put out* by unexpected problems⟩ ⟨such is outback hospitality that they were not in the least *put out* by our arrival —George Farwell⟩ **b :** to put into a bad temper **:** ANNOY, IRRITATE ⟨nothing *puts* him *out* so much as a chattering bridge partner⟩ **c :** to create difficulties for **:** INCONVENIENCE ⟨don't *put* yourself *out* for us⟩ ⟨will it *put* you *out* to take me to the station?⟩ **6 :** to cause to be out (as in baseball or cricket) **:** RETIRE ~ *vi* **1 :** to set out from shore ⟨a boat *puts out* with fishermen every morning⟩ **2** *slang* **:** to exert oneself **:** make an effort ⟨the only GI who deserves criticizing is the one who isn't *putting out* —*Infantry Jour.*⟩ **3** *slang, of a female* **:** to indulge in promiscuous sexual intercourse

putout \(ˈ)≈ˈ≈\ *n* -s [*put out*] **1 :** the retiring of a base runner or batter by a defensive player in baseball ⟨make the ~ on a throw to first⟩ **2 :** the official credit given a baseball player for making a putout ⟨leads the league in ~s⟩

put over *vt* **1 :** DELAY, POSTPONE ⟨consideration of this bill also was *put over* to the next session —Alzada Comstock⟩ **2 :** to put across ⟨*puts over* a feeling of power and bulk —Rosamund Frost⟩ ⟨*put over* a deliberate deception⟩ ⟨chose an unknown candidate and *put* him *over*⟩

¹put-put *or* **putt-putt** \ˈpətˌpət, *usu* -ˌpəd·+V\ *n* -s [imit.] **1 :** a sound made by or suggestive of the operation of a small gasoline engine ⟨the *put-put* of its motor —Kay Boyle⟩ ⟨occasionally there would be the rapid *put-put* of conversation —Donn Byrne⟩ **2 :** a small gasoline engine or a vehicle or boat equipped with one ⟨a phonograph and a radio and a flivver and a *put-put* for the canoe —Fannie Kilbourne⟩ ⟨experimenting with fast-flying combat planes to replace the slow-flying *put-puts* now used for the job —*Time*⟩

²put-put *or* **putt-putt** \"\ *vi* **put-putted** *or* **putt-putted; put-putted** *or* **putt-putted; put-putting** *or* **putt-putting; put-puts** *or* **putt-putts 1 :** to make put-puts **:** make the flat regularly repeated explosive sound of a small gasoline engine ⟨his angry style, which keeps *put-putting* in a series of equal explosions like a one-cylinder gasoline engine —Malcolm Cowley⟩ **2 :** to proceed or operate with or as if with put-puts **:** travel in a vehicle or boat that put-puts ⟨the launch went *put-putting* across the darkening harbor —William Irish⟩ ⟨*put-put* off across the water to visit the alligators —J.L.Jolley⟩

pu·tre·fa·cient \ˌpyü·trəˈfāshənt\ *adj* [L *putrefacient-, putrefaciens,* pres. part. of *putrefacere*] **:** PUTREFACTIVE

pu·tre·fac·tion \ˌ≈≈ˈfakshən\ *n* -s [ME *putrefaccion,* fr. LL *putrefaction-, putrefactio,* fr. L *putrefactus* (past part. of *putrefacere*) + *-ion-, -io* -ion] **1 :** the decomposition of organic matter; *esp* **:** the typically anaerobic process of splitting of proteins by the agency of bacteria and fungi with the formation of foul-smelling incompletely oxidized products (as mercaptans and alkaloids) — compare DECAY 5a **2 :** the state of being putrefied **:** CORRUPTION, DECAY ⟨his mind was in a state of advanced ~ —Norman Douglas⟩

pu·tre·fac·tive \ˌ≈≈ˈfaktiv, -tēv *also* -təv\ *adj* [MF *putrefactif,* fr. L *putrefactus* (past part. of *putrefacere*) + MF *-if* -ive] **1 :** of or relating to putrefaction **2 :** causing or tending to promote putrefaction

pu·tre·fi·able \ˌpyü·trəˈfīəbəl\ *adj* **:** PUTRESCIBLE

pu·tre·fi·er \ˈ≈≈ˌfī(ə)r, -īə\ *n* -s **:** something (as a bacterium) that causes putrefaction

pu·tre·fy *also* **pu·tri·fy** \-ˌfī\ *vb* -ED/-ING/-ES [ME *putrefien, putryfyen,* fr. MF & L; MF *putrefier,* fr. L *putrefacere,* fr. *putrēre* to be rotten + *facere* to make — more at DO] *vt* **:** to make putrid **:** cause to decay offensively **:** produce putrefaction in ⟨flesh in that long sleep is not *putrefied* —John Donne⟩ ~ *vi* **:** to become putrid ⟨they will not ~ but rather ferment —Jane Nickerson⟩ **syn** see DECAY

pu·tresce \pyüˈtres\ *vi* -ED/-ING/-S [L *putrescere*] **:** to become putrescent or putrid **:** PUTREFY

pu·tres·cence \-sᵊn(t)s\ *n* -s [prob. fr. (assumed) NL *putrescentia,* fr. L *putrescent-, putrescens* + *-ia* -y] **:** the state of being putrescent **:** ROTTENNESS

pu·tres·cen·cy \-nsē\ *n* -ES [prob. fr. (assumed) NL *putrescentia*] **:** PUTRESCENCE

pu·tres·cent \-nt\ *adj* [L *putrescent-, putrescens,* pres. part. of *putrescere* to grow rotten, putrefy, incho. of *putrēre* to be rotten] **1 :** undergoing putrefaction **:** becoming putrid ⟨there was a continuous band of ~ carcasses —Mari Sandoz⟩ ⟨the scandal concerning all the ~ world which contains her intimate friends —W.J.Locke⟩ **2 :** of, relating to, or characteristic of putrefaction ⟨sweetmeats colored violet pink and ~ yellow — Nadine Gordimer⟩

pu·tres·ci·bil·i·ty \(ˌ)pyüˌtresəˈbiləd·ē\ *n* -ES [F *putrescibilité,* fr. *putrescible* + *-ité* -ity] **:** susceptibility to putrefaction

pu·tres·ci·ble \pyüˈtresəbəl\ *adj* [F or LL; F, fr. LL *putrescibilis,* fr. L *putrescere* + *-ibilis* -able] **:** capable of being putrefied **:** liable to become putrid

pu·tres·cine \-ˌsēn, -ˌsən\ *n* -s [ISV *putresc-* (fr. L *putrescere*) + *-ine*] **:** a crystalline slightly poisonous ptomaine $NH_2(CH_2)_4NH_2$ found esp. in putrid fish or flesh and in abnormal urine and also made synthetically; 1,4-butane-diamine

pu·trid \ˈpyü·trəd\ *adj* [L *putridus,* fr. *putrēre* to be rotten, fr. *puter, putris* rotten; akin to L *putēre* to stink, be rotten — more at FOUL] **1 a :** in an advanced state of putrefaction **:** ROTTEN ⟨horrible like raw and ~ flesh —W.S.Maugham⟩ **b :** of, relating to, indicative of, or due to putrefaction or decay **:** FOUL ⟨a ~ smell⟩ ⟨~ decomposition⟩ **2 a :** morally corrupt **:** DEPRAVED, VICIOUS ⟨knows the ~ atmosphere of the Court —Karl Polanyi⟩ ⟨teaches that pacifism is as ~ as Fascism is wicked —M.W.Straight⟩ **b :** totally disagreeable or objectionable **:** LOUSY, VILE ⟨from the practical aspect, it was ~ politics —*Time*⟩ ⟨I wanted to see them look a little more cheerful even if world events did look ~ —Henry Miller⟩ **3** *of soil* **:** easily decomposable **:** FRIABLE ⟨the hoof shakes the ~ field —Aldous Huxley⟩ — **pu·trid·ly** *adv* — **pu·trid·ness** *n* -ES

pu·trid·i·ty \pyüˈtridəd·ē, -ətē, -i\ *n* -ES **:** the quality or state of being putrid ⟨the ~ of vice and crime that reeked up from among the pestilent alleys —Newton Arvin⟩

pu·tri·fact·ed \ˈpyü·trəˌfaktəd\ *adj* [irreg. (influenced by E *putrify*) fr. L *putrefactus* (past part. of *putrefacere*) + E *-ed*] **:** PUTREFIED

pu·tri·lage \ˈpyü·trəlij\ *n* -s [LL *putrilagin-, putrilago* rottenness, fr. L *puter, putris* rotten] **:** matter that is undergoing putrefaction **:** the products of putrefaction — **pu·tri·lag·i·nous** \ˌ≈≈ˈlajənəs\ *adj* — **pu·tri·lag·i·nous·ly** *adv*

puts *pres 3d sing of* PUT, *pl of* PUT

putsch \ˈpŭch\ *n* -ES [G, fr. G (Swiss dial.), lit., thrust, fr. MHG (Swiss dial.), of imit. origin] **:** a secretly plotted and suddenly executed attempt to overthrow a government or governing body ⟨was opposed to opportunistic plots and ~*es* —M.R.Konvitz⟩ — compare COUP D'ETAT **syn** see REBELLION

putsch·ism \-ŭˌchizəm\ *n* -s **:** the advocacy or organization of a putsch

putsch·ist \-ˌchəst\ *n* -s **:** one who advocates or organizes a putsch

¹putt \ˈpət, *usu* -əd·+V\ *n* -s [origin unknown] *dial Eng* **:** a heavy cart used on a farm

²putt \"\ *n* -s [alter. of ²*put*] **:** a golf stroke made on or near a putting green to cause the ball to roll into or near the hole

³putt \"\ *vb* -ED/-ING/-S [alter. of ¹*put*] *vt* **:** to strike (a golf ball) in playing a putt ~ *vi* **:** to play a putt

put·tee \ˌpəˈtē, ˌpŭˈ-, ˈpəd·ē\ *n* -s [Hindi *paṭṭī* strip of cloth, bandage, fr. Skt *paṭṭikā,* fr. *paṭṭa* cloth, silk, bandage] **:** a covering for the leg from ankle to knee consisting of a narrow cloth wrapped spirally around the leg or a fitted leather legging secured by a strap, catch, or laces

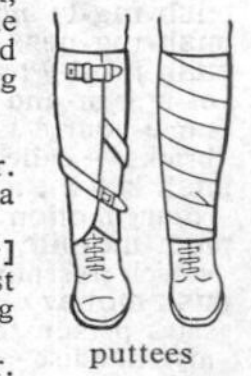
puttees

putten *dial past of* PUT

¹put·ter \ˈpŭd·ə(r), -ŭtə-\ *n* -s [ME *puttere,* fr. *putten* to put + *-ere* -er] **1 :** one that puts ⟨a ~ of questions⟩ **2 :** PUSHER 1e

²putt·er \ˈpəd·ə(r), -ətə-\ *n* -s [³*putt* + *-er*] **1 :** a golf club with a short shaft and almost perpendicular face that is used in putting **2 :** one that putts

³put·ter \ˈpəd·ə(r), -ətə-\ *vi* -ED/-ING/-S [alter. of ²*potter*] **1 a :** to move or act without plan or purpose **:** occupy oneself aimlessly — usu. used with *about* or *around* ⟨rising now and then to ~ about the room —Laura Krey⟩ ⟨if he sold the business, what would he do with himself all day? *Putter* around —*Scribner's*⟩ **b :** to move or act slowly or lackadaisically **:** DAWDLE ⟨a slow train that ~*ed* along on a narrow-gage track —Christopher Rand⟩ ⟨you're always ~*ing* . . . now I want you to hustle —Sherwood Anderson⟩ **2 :** to look casually **:** BROWSE ⟨it is as much fun to ~ through as a family album or a municipal museum —Helen B. Woodward⟩ **3 :** to work at random **:** TINKER ⟨was ~*ing* with a small stove —Joseph Wechsberg⟩ ⟨so enthusiastic are they about the work that they return to ~ even on their days off —*Nat'l Geographic*⟩ — **put·ter·er** \-ərə(r)\ *n* -s

⁴putter \"\ *vi* -ED/-ING/-S [imit.] **:** to proceed or operate by means of a small gasoline engine ⟨motor whaleboats ~*ed* back and forth between the anchorage and the beach —*New Yorker*⟩ ⟨they ~*ed* on upon a steady course towards the west —Nevil Shute⟩ ⟨~*ing* motorcycles —W.H.Hale⟩

putter-in \ˌ≈≈ˈ≈\ *n, pl* **putters-in** [*put in* + *-er*] **:** one that puts in; *esp* **:** a worker engaged in any of various operations (as feeding, filling, or guiding) involving the action of putting in

put·ter·ing·ly *adv* **:** in a puttering manner **:** AIMLESSLY

putter-on \ˌ≈≈ˈ≈\ *n, pl* **putters-on** [*put on* + *-er*] **:** one that puts on; *esp* **:** a worker engaged in any of various operations (as in textile printing or glue making) in which one thing is placed on something else

putter-out \ˌ≈≈ˈ≈\ *n, pl* **putters-out** [*put out* + *-er*] **:** one that puts out; *esp* **:** SETTER 2h

putter-up \ˌ≈≈ˈ≈\ *n, pl* **putters-up** [*put up* + *-er*] **:** one that puts up; *esp* **:** PACKER

put through *vt* **1 :** to carry to a successful conclusion **:** bring to completion ⟨the thing has to be done and the job *put through* and finished —Sir Winston Churchill⟩ ⟨in the latter office he *put through* a number of reforms —*Current Biog.*⟩ **2 a :** to make a telephone connection for ⟨the operator *put* him *through* to his party without delay⟩ **b :** to obtain a connection for (a telephone call) ⟨*put through* a long-distance call one evening —Anna Wright⟩

put·ti·er \ˈpəd·ēə(r), -ətē-\ *n* -s **:** one that putties **:** GLAZIER

putting *pres part of* PUT *or of* PUTT

putting cleek *n* **:** a putter having a long narrow blade with very little loft

putting green *n* **:** a closely cropped and rolled grassy area of a golf course located at the end of a fairway and containing the hole into which the ball must be played

put to *vb* [ME *putten to* to shut, fr. *putten* to put + *to*] *vt* **1** *chiefly dial* **:** SHUT ⟨*put* the door *to*⟩ **2 :** to close off (a fox earth) with the fox inside on the morning of a hunt ~ *vi, of a ship* **:** to put in to shore (as for shelter)

put·to \ˈpüd·(ˌ)ō\ *n, pl* **put·ti** \-üd·(ˌ)ē\ [It, lit., boy, fr. L *putus;* akin to Skt *putra* son, child — more at FEW] **:** a figure of a young boy (as a cupid) frequently used in decorative painting and sculpture esp. of the Renaissance — usu. used in pl.

put·tock \ˈpəd·ək\ *n* -s [ME *puttok*] **:** any of several birds of prey: **a :** a kite (*Milvus milvus*) **b :** BUZZARD **c :** MARSH HARRIER

put together *vt* [ME *putten togeder* to place together, fr. *putten* to put + *togeder, togedere* together] **1 :** to create as a unified whole **:** CONSTRUCT ⟨civilization is *put together* not by machines but by thought —*Saturday Rev.*⟩ ⟨*put* the book *together* in his spare time⟩ **2 :** ADD, COMBINE ⟨thought he knew more than all his teachers *put together*⟩

puttoo *var of* PATTU

putt-putt *var of* PUT-PUT

putts *pl of* PUTT, *pres 3d sing of* PUTT

¹put·ty \ˈpəd·|ē, -ət|, |i\ *n* -ES [F *potée* putty, potful, fr. OF, potful, fr. *pot* — more at POTAGE] **1 :** LIME PUTTY **2 :** PUTTY POWDER **3 a :** a cement usu. made of whiting and boiled linseed oil beaten or kneaded to the consistency of dough and used in fastening glass in sashes and stopping crevices in woodwork **b :** any of various substances resembling such cement in appearance, consistency, or use: as (1) **:** IRON PUTTY (2) **:** RED-LEAD PUTTY (3) **:** the sticky mud at the bottom of shallow navigable water **4 a :** a variable color averaging a grayish yellow green **b :** a pale to grayish yellow **c** *of textiles* **:** a light brownish gray to light grayish brown **5 :** one who is easily manipulated **:** a soft and pliable person

⟨a grotesque fool who foolishly spoilt her, yet refused to be the ~ she desired —Rex Ingamells⟩ ⟨is ~ in her hands⟩

²putty \"\ *vt* -ED/-ING/-ES **:** to use putty on or apply putty to

puttyblower \ˈ==,==\ *n, dial* **:** PEASHOOTER

putty coat *n* **:** HARD FINISH

putty eye *n* **:** an eye surrounded by thick fleshy tissues (as in various pigeons)

putty gloss *n* **:** a high polish imparted to stonework by a final polishing with putty powder

putty knife *n* **:** a knife with a broad flexible steel blade that is used for laying on and smoothing putty

putty knife

putty powder *n* **:** a polishing material (as for glass or marble) containing chiefly stannic oxide — called also *jewelers' putty*

puttyroot \ˈ==,=\ *n* **:** a No. American orchid (*Aplectrum hyemale*) having a slender naked rootstock which produces each year a solid corm of which two or three remain strung together and sending up in late summer a single plaited evergreen leaf and in spring a scape of brown flowers

put up *vb* [ME *putten up*, fr. *putten* to put + *up*] *vt* **1 a :** to place in a container or receptacle ⟨*put* his lunch *up* in a brown paper bag⟩ **b :** to put away (a sword) in its scabbard **:** SHEATHE ⟨*put up* your swords; you know not what you do —Shak.⟩ **c :** to pack with something **:** make up into a container or package ⟨had with him a basket his mother had *put up* —Winston Churchill⟩ **d :** to prepare so as to preserve for later use: as (1) **:** to prepare (perishable foodstuffs) by canning ⟨*put up* several quarts of peaches⟩ ⟨*put* enough preserves *up* to last the year⟩ (2) **:** to cure and store (as hay or fodder) ⟨*put up* hay for wintering my saddle horses —Bruce Siberts⟩ **e :** to make up (as a medicine, prescription) **:** COMPOUND, PREPARE **f :** to put away out of use ⟨*put* her car *up* then and began spending her days cooped in . . . her hundred thousand dollar home —John Faulkner⟩ **2 :** to start (game) from cover **:** ROUSE ⟨saw birds, which my dog *put up* on one side of the river, cross to the other bank —Douglas Carruthers⟩ ⟨*put up* a herd of eleven wild deer who . . . only glided noiselessly a few yards into the woods —S.P.B.Mais⟩ **3** *archaic* **:** to put up with **:** ENDURE ⟨persuaded to *put up* in peace what already I have foolishly suffered —Shak.⟩ **4 a :** to nominate for election to a position or membership in an association ⟨his colleagues *put up* his name for premier —Neal Stanford⟩ ⟨*put* her name *up* for the sorority⟩ **b :** to select for some function or duty ⟨I was *put up*, at eight or nine, to propose some family toast —Joyce Cary⟩ ⟨catechized each man *put up* to serve on the jury —David Masters⟩ **5 :** to offer up (a prayer) **:** present (a petition) for action or consideration ⟨were really *putting up* — and in vain — a supplication for mercy —Havelock Ellis⟩ ⟨he's going to *put up* prayers for rain in church next Sunday —Ellen Glasgow⟩ **6 :** to set (hair) usu. in pin curls **7 a :** to make public or ask to be made public — used esp. of banns ⟨*put up* their banns for the third time⟩ **b :** to offer for public sale ⟨some farmer decides to pull up stakes and *puts* his possessions *up* for auction —*Amer. Guide Series: Texas*⟩ **c :** to present publicly **:** EXPOSE ⟨an idea which has been occupying me of late I would like to *put up* for criticism —Lucien Price⟩ **8 a :** to give food and shelter to (a horse) ⟨*put up* his horse for the night at the only stable in town⟩ **b :** to provide lodgings for **:** ACCOMMODATE ⟨suggested I go to his club, where he was *putting* me *up*, and have the bath —Marcia Davenport⟩ **9 :** to arrange (as a plot or scheme) with others **:** PRECONCERT ⟨*put up* a job to steal the jewels⟩ **10 :** BUILD, ERECT ⟨before the present building was *put up*, a smaller stone structure occupied the same site —C.J.Allen⟩ **11 a :** to make a display of **:** EXHIBIT, SHOW ⟨swallows can *put up* very good flight performances —David Gunston⟩ ⟨desperate as he was, he *put up* a brave front⟩ ⟨*put up* a bluff⟩ **b :** to carry on ⟨has *put up* a bitter struggle against great odds⟩ ⟨had *put up* a losing fight against erosion⟩ **12 a :** CONTRIBUTE, PAY ⟨was supposed to *put up* enough money to finish the film —Moore Raymond⟩ **b :** to offer as a prize or stake ⟨a bet of $25 was *put up* —*Amer. Guide Series: Minn.*⟩ **13 :** to increase the amount of **:** RAISE ⟨this sellers' cartel *put up* the price of rubber for a time —D.W.Brogan⟩ ⟨mechanical handling is one of the things which are *putting up* industrial productivity —Bertram Mycock⟩ ~ *vi* **:** LODGE ⟨two seasons ago I *put up* at a farmhouse —T.H.White b.1906⟩ **syn** see RESIDE

¹**put-up** \(ˈ)=ˈ=\ *adj* [fr. past part. of *put up*] **:** underhandedly arranged esp. with the cooperation of insiders **:** PLOTTED, PRECONCERTED ⟨a *put-up* piece of legal chicanery, fit only to arouse derisive laughter —*Time*⟩ ⟨a *put-up* job⟩

²**put-up** \"\ *n* -S [fr. past part. of *put up*] **:** something that is put up for marketing **:** PACKAGE; *esp* **:** any of various cones, tubes, or bobbins of yarn or thread

put-upon \ˈ=ˈ=ˈ=\ *adj* [fr. the past part. form of the phrase *put upon*] **:** imposed upon **:** taken advantage of **:** ABUSED, VICTIMIZED ⟨a deceived, anguished, *put-upon* girl —Anthony West⟩ ⟨identifies herself with the characters who are most *put-upon*, most noble, most righteous —James Thurber⟩

pu·ture \ˈpyüchə(r)\ *n* -S [AF, food, fr. OF *pouture*, fr. *pou*, *pouls* porridge — more at PULSE] *Eng law* **:** the customary right of keepers of forests and some bailiffs of hundreds to take food for man, horse, and dog from land of various tenants within the forest or hundred

putwari *var of* PATWARI

putz \ˈpu̇ts\ *n* -ES [PaG, fr. G, decoration, finery, fr. *putzen* to adorn, clean] **:** a decoration built around a representation of the Nativity scene and traditionally placed under a Christmas tree in Pennsylvania Dutch homes **:** CRÈCHE

¹**puxy** *also* **puck·sey** \ˈpəksi\ *n* -ES [origin unknown] *dial Eng* **:** swampy ground **:** QUAGMIRE

²**puxy** \"\ *adj, dial Eng* **:** SWAMPY

puy \ˈpwē\ *n* -S [F, fr. L *podium* balcony — more at PEW] **:** one of the hills of volcanic origin common in the Auvergne district of France

pu·ya \ˈpüyə\ *n, cap* [NL, fr. AmerSp *puya* (plant of the genus *Puya*), perh. fr. Sp *puya* goad, perh. fr. (assumed) VL *puga*; akin to L *pungere* to prick, sting — more at PUNGENT] **:** a genus of terrestrial plants (family Bromeliaceae) found mostly in Peru and Chile that have basal spiny leaves and showy bracteate flowers in terminal racemes that may be 30 feet in height — see CHAGUAL GUM

puy·al·lup \pyüˈaləp\ *n, pl* **puyallup** *or* **puyallups** *usu cap* **1 a :** a Salishan people of the east coast of Puget Sound and Vashon Island, Washington **b :** a member of such people **2 :** a dialect related to Skagit

¹**puz·zle** \ˈpəzəl\ *vb* **puzzled; puzzled; puzzling** \-z(ə)liŋ\ **puzzles** [origin unknown] *vt* **1** *obs* **:** to make it difficult for (a person) to choose or carry out a course of action **:** BEWILDER, CONFOUND ⟨more *puzzled* than the Egyptians in their fog —Shak.⟩ **2 a :** CONFUSE, PERPLEX ⟨~ my sad brains about life —L.P.Smith⟩ **b :** to bewilder mentally **:** confuse or nonplus the understanding of ⟨a malignant fever which *puzzled* the doctors —John Buchan⟩ ⟨are often *puzzled* and sometimes annoyed by the ways of other peoples who are strange to us —W.A.Parker⟩ **3** *archaic* **:** to make intricate **:** COMPLICATE, ENTANGLE ⟨disentangle from the *puzzled* skein —William Cowper⟩ **4 :** to proceed along in a mentally laborious manner ⟨teen-age boys who ~ their way through geometry —*Newsweek*⟩ ~ *vi* **1 a :** to be uncertain as to action or choice **:** become bewildered or perplexed ⟨we *puzzled* for two moons about where to put you —Nora Waln⟩ **b :** to exercise one's mind **:** attempt a solution of a puzzle ⟨I *puzzled* over her words and sought to attach to them some intelligent meaning —Rafael Sabatini⟩ **2 :** to search in a confused manner **:** GROPE ⟨*puzzled* about in his desk for the missing file of letters⟩

syn MYSTIFY, PERPLEX, BEWILDER, DISTRACT, NONPLUS, CONFOUND, DUMBFOUND: these verbs in the uses here compared all signify to disturb mentally, baffle, or throw into mental disorder or immobility. PUZZLE and MYSTIFY both suggest a complication or intricacy difficult to understand or explain, MYSTIFY suggesting more often a complication purposely created as by the concealment or obscuring of essential fact ⟨the questions which doubtless *puzzle* most of us —*Town Jour.*⟩ ⟨the secret of the enigma that *puzzled* me —L.P.Smith⟩ ⟨it was the riddle of life that was *puzzling* and killing her —Arnold Bennett⟩ ⟨why more visitors to South America do not take this memorable river trip *mystifies* my wife and me —L.A.Keating⟩ ⟨once prescriptions were written almost altogether in Latin. This was not done to *mystify* the patient —Morris Fishbein⟩ ⟨historical paraphernalia with which to *mystify* their unsuspecting clients —*Amer. Guide Series: N.Y.*⟩ PERPLEX and BEWILDER add the ideas of uncertainty and, often, worry to that of puzzlement, BEWILDER implying a consequent and usually complete intellectual disorder ⟨on their arrival they were *perplexed* by radical differences in language, customs, and environment —*Amer. Guide Series: R.I.*⟩ ⟨Gates was greatly *perplexed* to know what to do —H.E.Scudder⟩ ⟨they were *perplexed*, vexed and worried —Ernie Pyle⟩ ⟨textbooks in *bewildering* variety confronted the pioneer teacher —*Amer. Guide Series: Wash.*⟩ ⟨the *bewildering* confusion of our times —Matthew Arnold⟩ ⟨a character *bewildered* by a confusion of values —R.B.West⟩ DISTRACT suggests the perturbation of an uncertain though not necessarily puzzled or bewildered mind, implying, rather, strongly conflicting preoccupations or interests ⟨his fury is that of a temporarily *distracted* boy —Walter Goodman⟩ ⟨a man *distracted* between two spiritual homes —*Time*⟩ ⟨that conflict of races and religions which had so long *distracted* the island —T.B.Macaulay⟩ NONPLUS suggests a blankness of mind often attendant upon complete bafflement ⟨the pilots wrote: — "It was imperative that we should not find ourselves *nonplussed* in an emergency in the air . . ." —*Times Lit. Supp.*⟩ ⟨the problem which *nonplusses* the wisest heads on this planet . . . What is reality? —L.P.Smith⟩ ⟨she was utterly *nonplussed* by the pair of them . . . What on earth were they? —Elizabeth Goudge⟩ CONFOUND implies a mental confusion attendant upon astonishment or complete abashment ⟨professional critics . . . should be *confounded* by the book's evidence of careful research —Beka Doherty⟩ ⟨someone who can furnish him with the sort of evidence of the authenticity of his picture that would satisfy a special juryman and *confound* a purchasing dealer —Clive Bell⟩ DUMBFOUND may be interchangeable with CONFOUND but usually suggests a stronger effect, a confounding to the point of mental paralysis or wonderment ⟨to be so *dumbfounded* as to be unable to speak for a moment⟩ ⟨apparently too *dumbfounded* by the insane assault to interfere seriously —Al Newman⟩ ⟨his schoolmates are astonished; his fellow-soldiers are *dumbfounded* —J.M.Brinnin⟩

²**puzzle** \"\ *n* -S **1 :** the state of being puzzled **:** mental embarrassment **:** PERPLEXITY ⟨the transition from a state of ~ and perplexity to rational comprehension —William James⟩ **2 a :** something that puzzles **:** a difficult question or problem ⟨it is more a ~ than a comfort to see those children growing so fine and straight —Claudia Cassidy⟩ ⟨this young man was an unaccountable ~ —J.H.Powers⟩ **b :** a question, problem, toy, or contrivance designed for testing ingenuity — see CHINESE PUZZLE, CROSSWORD, JIGSAW PUZZLE **syn** see MYSTERY

puzzle box *n* **:** a cage used in experiments on animal learning from which the animal learns to escape by operating a button, hook, or other device

puzzle canon *n* **:** RIDDLE CANON

puz·zled·ly *adv* **:** in a puzzled manner

puzzleheaded \ˈ=ˈ=ˈ=\ *adj* **:** having or based on confused attitudes or ideas ⟨the professional philosopher is a help and an inspiration even when he is somewhat ~ —J.A.Macy⟩ ⟨a kind of ~ conservatism —*Spectator*⟩ — **puz·zle·head·ed·ness** *n* -ES

puzzle jug *n* **:** a ceramic pitcher or jug with pierced neck that will pour without spilling only if certain holes are covered with the fingers

puzzle lock *n* **:** COMBINATION LOCK

puz·zle·ment \ˈpəzəlmənt\ *n* -S **1 :** the state of being puzzled **:** BEWILDERMENT, PERPLEXITY ⟨frowns of deep ~ —J.D. Williams⟩ ⟨expressing his interest in and frank ~ at the ways of the world —C.L.Sulzberger⟩ **2 :** something that puzzles **:** PUZZLE ⟨the affair . . . will long be a ~ —*New Yorker*⟩

puzzle out *vt* **:** to solve, discover, or work out by mental effort or ingenuity ⟨*puzzled* it *out* and made a translation of it —Van Wyck Brooks⟩ ⟨don't bother to combine the symptoms in their own mind and *puzzle out* the diagnosis —A.J.Cronin⟩

puzzlepated \ˈ=ˈ=ˈ=\ *adj* **:** PUZZLEHEADED

puz·zler \ˈpəz(ə)lə(r)\ *n* -S **1 :** one that puzzles **2 :** a person devoted to solving puzzles

puz·zling·ly *adv* **:** in a puzzling manner ⟨such was the object on which she ~ challenged him —Henry James †1916⟩

puzzolan *or* **puzzolana** *var of* POZZOLANA

PV *abbr* **1** par value **2** pipe ventilated **3** post village **4** priest vicar

PVA *abbr* **1** polyvinyl acetate **2** polyvinyl alcohol

PVC *abbr* polyvinyl chloride

PVP *abbr* polyvinylpyrrolidone

pvt *abbr, often cap* private

PW *abbr* **1** packed weight **2** prisoner of war **3** public works

p-wave \ˈ=,=\ *n, usu cap P* **1 :** PRESSURE WAVE **2** *usu* **p wave** **:** a deflection in an electrocardiographic tracing that represents auricular activity of the heart — compare T WAVE

pwd *abbr* powder

pwe \ˈpwā, ˈpyā\ *n* -S [Burmese] **:** a Burmese open-air festival consisting of dancing, singing, and dramatization

pwo \ˈpwō\ *n, pl* **pwo** *or* **pwos** *usu cap* **1 a :** a Karen people of the Irrawaddy delta region **b :** a member of such people **2 :** the language of the Pwo people

pwr *abbr* power

pwt *abbr* pennyweight

PX \(ˈ)pēˈeks\ *abbr or n, pl* **PXs** \-eksəz\ post exchange

PX *abbr* **1** please exchange **2** private exchange

pxt *abbr* [L *pinxit*] he or she painted it

py- *or* **pyo-** *comb form* [Gk, fr. *pyon* pus — more at FOUL] **1 :** marked by the presence of pus in or with **:** pussy ⟨*pyo*lymph⟩ ⟨*pyo*ureter⟩ ⟨*py*emia⟩ **2 :** due to or associated with a pus-producing infection **:** suppurative ⟨*pyo*nephritis⟩ ⟨*pyo*phthalmia⟩

pya \pēˈä\ *n* -S [Burmese] **1 :** a Burmese monetary unit equal to $^1/_{100}$ kyat — see MONEY table **2 :** a coin representing one pya

pyaemia *var of* PYEMIA

py·al \(ˈ)pīˈäl\ *n* -S [Pg *poyal* mounting stone, stone bench, fr. *poyo* bench, block, fr. L *podium* platform — more at PEW] **:** the raised platform or veranda of an Indian house

py·arthrosis \ˈpī+\ *n* [NL, fr. *py-* + *arthrosis*] **:** the formation or presence of pus within a joint

pycn- *or* **pycno-** *comb form* [L, fr. Gk *pykn-*, *pykno-*, fr. *pyknos*; akin to Gk *pyka* thickly, Alb *puth* kiss, Av *pusā-* headband; basic meaning: pressed together] **:** close **:** compact **:** dense **:** bulky ⟨*pycn*ic⟩ ⟨*pycn*idium⟩ ⟨*pycno*gonid⟩

pyc·nan·the·mum \pikˈnan(t)thəməm\ *n, cap* [NL, fr. *pycn-* + *-anthemum*] **:** a genus of No. American aromatic herbs (family Labiatae) with small white or purple-dotted flowers — see BASIL MINT, MOUNTAIN MINT

pyc·ni·al \ˈpiknēəl\ *adj* [NL *pycnium* + E *-al*] **:** of or relating to a pycnium **:** characterized by the presence or development of pycnia

pycnic *var of* PYKNIC

pyc·nid \ˈpiknəd\ *also* **pyc·nide** \", -,nīd\ *n* -S [ISV, fr. NL *pycnidium*] **:** PYCNIDIUM

pyc·nid·i·al \(ˈ)pikˈnidēəl\ *adj* [NL *pycnidium* + E *-al*] **:** of, relating to, or characterized by the production of pycnidia

pyc·nid·io·spore \pikˈnidēə+,-\ *n* [NL *pycnidium* + E *-o-* + *-spore*] **:** a conidium formed in a pycnidium

pyc·nid·i·um \pikˈnidēəm\ *n, pl* **pycnid·ia** \-ēə\ [NL, fr. *pycn-* + *-idium*] **1 :** a flask-shaped spore fruit that bears conidiophores and pycnidiospores on the interior and is typical of various imperfect fungi (as of the order Phyllostictales) and ascomycetes **2 :** PYCNIUM

pyc·nio·spore \ˈpiknēə+,-\ *n* [NL *pycnium* + E *-o-* + *-spore*] **:** a haploid pycnial spore of a rust fungus that by fusion with a haploid hypha of opposite sex produces aecia and dikaryotic aeciospores — see PYCNIUM

pyc·nite \ˈpik,nīt\ *n* -S [fr. *pycn-* + *-ite*] **:** a massive columnar topaz

pyc·ni·um \ˈpiknēəm\ *n, pl* **pyc·nia** \-ēə\ [NL, fr. *pycn-* + *-ium*] **:** one of the small flask-shaped fruit bodies of a rust fungus formed in clusters just beneath the surface of the host tissue, produced as a result of infection by a single basidiospore, and producing haploid flexuous hyphae and pycniospores

pyc·noc·o·ma \pikˈnäkəmə\ *n, cap* [NL, fr. *pycn-* + *-coma*] **:** a small genus of shrubs or trees (family Euphorbiaceae) of tropical Africa and the Mascarene Islands having monoecious flowers and numerous stamens with hairlike elongated filaments

¹**pyc·no·dont** \ˈpiknə,dänt\ *adj* [NL *Pycnodontidae*] **:** of or relating to the Pycnodontidae

²**pycnodont** \"\ *n* -S **:** a fish or fossil of the family Pycnodontidae

pyc·no·don·ta \,piknəˈdäntə\ *n, cap* [NL, fr. *pycn-* + *-odonta*] **:** a genus of large tropical oysters having strongly scalloped shells with crinkled ridges on each side of the hinge and occurring chiefly on coral reefs

pyc·no·don·ti \,piknəˈdän·,tī\ *n pl, cap* [NL, fr. *Pycnodont-*, *Pycnodus*] *in some classifications* **:** an order or other group coextensive with the family Pycnodontidae

pyc·no·don·ti·dae \-ˈäntə,dē\ *n pl, cap* [NL, fr. *Pycnodont-*, *Pycnodus*, type genus (fr. *pycn-* + *-odont-*, *-odus*) + *-idae*] **:** a large family that is segregated in the order Pycnodonti or now more usu. included in Cycloganoidei and that includes Mesozoic and Tertiary ganoid fishes having a deep compressed body typically covered with rhomboidal scales, a homocercal tail, and strong blunt crushing teeth

¹**pyc·no·don·toid** \ˈ==ˈdän,tȯid\ *adj* [NL *Pycnodont-*, *Pycnodus* + E *-oid*] **:** resembling or related to the family Pycnodontidae

²**pycnodontoid** \"\ *n* -S **:** a pycnodontoid fish or fossil

¹**pyc·nog·o·nid** \(ˈ)pikˈnägənəd, ˈpiknəˈgän-\ *adj* [NL *Pycnogonida*] **:** of or relating to the Pycnogonida

²**pycnogonid** \"\ *n* -S **:** an arthropod of the class Pycnogonida

pyc·no·gon·i·da \,piknəˈgänədə\ *n pl, cap* [NL, fr. *Pycnogonum*, genus of sea spiders (fr. *pycn-* + Gk *gony* knee) + *-ida* — more at KNEE] **:** a class of marine arthropods that superficially resemble spiders with the body relatively very thin and small, the legs usu. excessively long and slender, and the abdomen rudimentary, that have typically seven pairs of appendages of which the posterior four pairs are legs and contain diverticula of the intestine and reproductive organs and of which the first two or three pairs are often absent, a triangular mouth at the end of a tubular proboscis, no organs of respiration, and separate sexes, and that produce young which usu. pass through a metamorphosis

pyc·nom·e·ter *also* **pic·nom·e·ter** *or* **pyk·nom·e·ter** \pikˈnämәd·ə(r)\ *n* [ISV *pycn-* + *-meter*] **:** a standard vessel often provided with a thermometer for measuring and comparing the densities of liquids or solids — **pyc·no·met·ric** \ˈpiknəˈme·trik\ *adj* — **pyc·nom·e·try** \pikˈnämə·trē\ *n* -ES

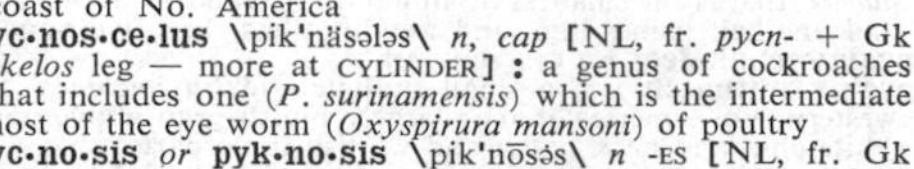

pycnometers

pyc·no·mor·phic \ˈpiknəˈmȯrfik\ *also* **pyc·no·mor·phous** \-fəs\ *adj* [*pycn-* + *-morphic* or *-morphous*] **:** compactly formed **:** characterized by compact arrangement of stainable parts — used esp. of nerve cells

pyc·no·noti·dae \,piknəˈnäd·ə,dē, -nōd-\ *n pl, cap* [NL, fr. *Pycnonotus*, type genus (fr. *pycn-* + *-notus*) + *-idae*] **:** a family of Old World passerine birds consisting of the bulbuls — **pyc·no·no·tine** \ˈ==ˈnō,tīn\ *adj*

pyc·no·po·dia \,piknəˈpōdēə\ *n, cap* [NL, fr. *pycn-* + *-podia*] **:** a genus of starfishes (family Asteriidae) including only the large 20-rayed sunflower star (*P. helianthoides*) of the littoral zone of the western coast of No. America

pyc·nos·ce·lus \pikˈnäsələs\ *n, cap* [NL, fr. *pycn-* + Gk *skelos* leg — more at CYLINDER] **:** a genus of cockroaches that includes one (*P. surinamensis*) which is the intermediate host of the eye worm (*Oxyspirura mansoni*) of poultry

pyc·no·sis *or* **pyk·no·sis** \pikˈnōsəs\ *n* -ES [NL, fr. Gk *pyknōsis* condensation, fr. *pyknoun* to condense (fr. *pyknos* dense, thick) + *-ōsis* -osis — more at PYCN-] **:** a degenerative condition of a cell nucleus marked by clumping of the chromosomes, hyperchromatism, and shrinking of the nucleus

pyc·no·spore \ˈpiknə+,-\ *n* [ISV *pycn-* + *-spore*] **:** PYCNIOSPORE

¹**pyc·no·style** \-,stīl\ *adj* [Gk *pyknostylos* with the pillars close together, fr. *pykn-* pycn- + *stylos* pillar — more at STEER] **:** having or constituting an intercolumniation of one and one-half diameters

²**pycnostyle** \"\ *n* -S **:** a pycnostyle colonnade

pyc·not·ic *or* **pyk·not·ic** \(ˈ)pikˈnäd·ik\ *adj* [ISV, fr. NL *pycnosis*, *pyknosis*, after such pairs as NL *narcosis*: E *narcotic*; orig. formed as G *pyknotisch*] **:** of, relating to, or exhibiting pycnosis

pyc·nox·yl·ic \ˈpik,näkˈsilik\ *adj* [*pycn-* + *oxylic*] **:** having dense hard wood because of a high proportion of secondary xylem

pye *var of* PIE

pye book *n, obs* **:** ³PIE 2

pye-dog *also* **pi-dog** *or* **pie-dog** \ˈpī,=\ *n* [Anglo-Indian, prob. by shortening and alter. fr. *pariah dog*] **:** a half-wild dog of uncertain ancestry and ownership that is common about villages throughout much of southern and eastern Asia

pyel- *or* **pyelo-** *comb form* [NL, fr. Gk, trough, vat, fr. *pyelos*; akin to Gk *plynein* to wash, *plein* to sail, float — more at FLOW] **1 :** pelvis ⟨*pyelo*metry⟩ ⟨*pyel*ic⟩ **2 :** renal pelvis ⟨*pyelo*gram⟩ ⟨*pyel*itis⟩

py·el·ectasis \ˈpīəl+\ *n* [NL, fr. *pyel-* + *ectasis*] **:** dilatation of the pelvis of a kidney

py·el·ic \(ˈ)pīˈelik\ *adj* [ISV *pyel-* + *-ic*] **:** of, relating to, or affecting the renal pelvis

py·elit·ic \ˈpīəˈlid·ik\ *adj* [NL *pyelitis* + E *-ic*] **:** of, relating to, or constituting pyelitis

py·eli·tis \,pīəˈlīd·əs\ *n* -ES [NL, fr. *pyel-* + *-itis*] **:** inflammation of the pelvis of a kidney

py·elo·gram \pīˈelə,gram, ˈpīəlō,-\ *also* **py·elo·graph** \-,raf, -,räf\ *n* [ISV *pyel-* + *-gram* or *-graph*] **:** a roentgenogram made by pyelography

py·elo·graph·ic \pīˈeləˈgrafik, ˈpīəlōˈ-\ *adj* [*pyelography* + *-ic*] **:** of, relating to, or involving the use of pyelography

py·elog·ra·phy \,pīəˈlägrəfē\ *n* -ES [ISV *pyel-* + *-graphy*] **:** roentgenographic visualization of the kidney pelvis after injection of a radiopaque substance through the ureter or into a vein

py·elo·nephritic \ˈpīə(,)lō+\ *adj* [NL *pyelonephritis* + E *-ic*] **:** of, relating to, or caused by pyelonephritis

py·elo·nephritis \"+\ *n* [NL, fr. *pyel-* + *nephritis*] **:** inflammation of both the pelvis and the substance of the kidney

py·elo·nephrosis \"+\ *n* [NL, fr. *pyel-* + *nephrosis*] **:** disease of the kidney and of its pelvis

py·elo·ureterogram \"+\ *n* [*pyel-* + *ureterogram*] **:** a roentgenogram of a kidney pelvis and the corresponding ureter

py·emia *or* **py·ae·mia** \pīˈēmēə\ *n* -S [NL, fr. *py-* + *-emia*] **:** septicemia accompanied by multiple abscesses and secondary toxemic symptoms and caused by pus-forming microorganisms (as the bacterium *Staphylococcus aureus*) — compare BACTEREMIA — **py·emic** \(ˈ)pīˈēmik\ *adj*

py·emo·tes \,pīəˈmōd·(,)ēz\ *n, cap* [NL] **:** a genus of mites that are usu. ectoparasites of insects but that include one (*P. ventricosus*) which causes grain itch in man when transferred (as in harvesting) to the skin

pyengadu *var of* PYINKADO

py·esis \pīˈēsəs\ *n* -ES [NL, fr. *py-* + *-esis*] **:** SUPPURATION

pyg- *or* **pygo-** *comb form* [Gk, fr. *pygē* — more at FOG] **:** rump **:** buttocks ⟨*pyg*algia⟩ ⟨*pygo*style⟩

-py·ga \ˈpīgə\ *or* **-pyg·ia** \ˈpijēə\ *n comb form* [*-pyga* fr. NL, fr. Gk *pygē* rump; *-pygia* fr. NL, fr. Gk *pygē* + NL *-ia*] **:** creature having (such) a rump — in generic names in zoology ⟨Eury*pyga*⟩ ⟨Macro*pygia*⟩

¹**py·gal** \ˈpīgəl\ *adj* [*pyg-* + *-al*] **:** of, relating to, or located in the region of the rump or posterior end of the back ⟨~ plates in the carapace of a turtle⟩

²**pygal** \"\ *n* -S **:** a pygal part

pygarg *also* **pygargus** *n, pl* **pygargs** *also* **pygarguses** [L *pygargus,* an antelope, an eagle, fr. Gk *pygargos,* lit., white rump, fr. *pyg-* + *argos* white — more at ARGENT] **1** *obs* **:** a white-rumped ungulate (as an addax) **2** *obs* **:** SEA EAGLE

py·gid·i·al \(')pī¦jidēəl\ *adj* [NL *pygidium* + E *-al*] **:** of, relating to, or constituting a pygidium

py·gi·di·idae \,pījə'dīə,dē\ *n, cap* [NL, fr. *Pygidium,* type genus (fr. Gk *pygidion*) + *-idae*] *in some classifications* **:** a family of usu. small and often parasitic So. American catfishes that lack an adipose fin and have the dorsal fin located far back toward the tail

py·gid·i·um \pī'jidēəm\ *n, pl* **pygid·ia** \-ēə\ [NL, fr. Gk *pygidion* small rump, fr. *pygē* rump + *-idion* -idium] **:** a caudal structure or the terminal body region of various invertebrates: as **a :** the caudal plate of a trilobite **b :** the terminal tergite of an insect's abdomen

¹pygmaean *or* **pygmean** *n* -s [*pygmaean* fr. L *pygmaeus* dwarfish + E *-an; pygmean* fr. L *pygmaeus* + E *-an*] *obs* **:** PYGMY

²pyg·mae·an *or* **pyg·me·an** \(')pig¦mēən, 'pig,m-\ *adj* **:** PYGMY

pyg·ma·lion \pig'mālyən, -lēən\ *n* -s *often cap* [fr. *Pygmalion,* legendary sculptor of Cyprus] **:** CENTENNIAL BROWN

pyg·ma·lion·ism \-,nizəm\ *n* -s *often cap* [ISV *pygmalion-* (fr. *Pygmalion,* legendary king and sculptor of Cyprus who fell in love with the statue that he had made of a woman and at whose request Aphrodite gave the statue life, fr. Gk *Pygmaliōn*) + *-ism*] **:** sexual responsiveness directed toward a statue or other representation

pyg·moid \'pig,mȯid\ *adj* [*pygmy* + *-oid*] **:** resembling or partaking of the characteristics of the Pygmies

¹pyg·my *also* **pig·my** \'pigmē, -mi\ *n* -ES [ME *pigmei,* fr. L *pygmaeus* of a pygmy, dwarfish (n. pl. *pygmaei,* fr. Gk *pygmaioi*), fr. Gk *pygmaios* of a pygmy, fr. *pygmē* fist, measure of length, distance from the elbow to the knuckles — more at PUNGENT] **1** *often cap* **:** one of a fabled race of dwarfs described by ancient Greek authors **2** *usu cap* **:** one of a small people of equatorial Africa ranging under five feet in height, having dark skin but lighter than that of true Negroes, poorly developed chins, moderately round heads, and broad noses, practicing a crude hunting culture, using the languages of their nearest neighbors, and being prob. most closely related to the Negritos **3 a :** a short insignificant person **:** DWARF **b :** ELF, GNOME, PIXY **c :** a thing very small for its kind **4** *obs* **:** a chimpanzee or other anthropoid ape

²pygmy \"\ *adj* **1 :** of or relating to the Pygmies or a pygmy **2 :** resembling a pygmy **:** DWARFISH **:** very small

³pygmy *also* **pigmy** \"\ *vt* -ED/-ING/-ES **:** to make a pygmy of **:** cause to appear small or insignificant **:** DWARF

pygmy antelope *n* **:** ROYAL ANTELOPE

pygmy elephant *n* **:** a small elephant (*Loxodonta pumilio*) of the Congo region that rarely exceeds six feet at the shoulder

pygmy falcon *n* **:** FALCONET 2a

pygmy flint *n* **:** MICROLITH

pygmy goose *n* **:** any of several very small short-billed extremely aquatic geese (genus *Nettapus*) that have considerable white and green in their plumage and are native to Africa, India, China, and Australia

pygmy hippopotamus *n* **:** a small hippopotamus (*Hippopotamus liberiensis* or *Choeropsis liberiensis*) of Liberia having but one pair of lower incisors

pygmy hog *n* **:** a very small wild pig (*Sus salvanius*) of the forests of Nepal

pyg·my·ish \-mēish, -miish\ *adj* [¹*pygmy* + *-ish*] **:** DWARFISH, STUNTED

pyg·my·ism \-mē,izəm, -mi,iz-\ *n* -s [¹*pygmy* + *-ism*] **:** the condition of a pygmy **:** a stunted or dwarfish state

pygmy lemur *n* **:** a dwarf lemur (esp. *Microcebus murinus*)

pygmy locust *n* **:** GROUSE LOCUST

pygmy marmoset *n* **:** a So. American marmoset (*Callithrix pygmaeus*) that is the smallest of all monkeys standing about two and one half inches high and weighing less than five ounces

pygmy musk deer *n* **:** CHEVROTAIN

pygmy nuthatch *n* **:** a small nuthatch (*Sitta pygmaea*) of western No. America that is largely bluish gray above with white chin and neck patch and whitish underparts

pygmy owl *n* **:** any of various small and usu. rather dark-colored owls (genus *Glaucidium*) that are sometimes day-flying and chiefly insectivorous — called also *gnome owl*

pygmy parrot *n* **:** any of various small parrots (genus *Micropsitta*) of New Guinea and adjacent islands having a thick bill with a cere, very long claws, and brilliant plumage in the male

pygmy-pipes \'=,=\ *n pl but sing or pl in constr* **:** SWEET PINESAP

pygmy possum *n* **:** MOUSE OPOSSUM

pygmy rattler *or* **pygmy rattlesnake** *n* **:** a rattlesnake of the genus *Sistrurus* — see MASSASAUGA

pygmy rose *n* **:** FAIRY ROSE

pygmy shrew *n* **1 :** a small European shrew (*Sorex minutus*) **2 :** a small No. American shrew (*Microsorex hoyi*)

pygmy sperm whale *n* **:** any of several small whales (genus *Kogia*) that are chiefly of southern seas, approximate 15 feet in length, and have a falcate dorsal fin and crescentic blowhole

pygmy squirrel *n* **:** any of numerous minute African and Asiatic tree squirrels (as of the genus *Myosciurus*)

pygmyweed *or* **pigmyweed** \'=,=\ *n* **:** a small annual aquatic herb (*Tillaea aquatica*) of the family Crassulaceae that occurs along the coasts of No. America, Europe, and northern Africa and has very small solitary axillary greenish flowers

pygmy whale *n* **:** a small whalebone whale (*Neobalaena marginata*) of New Zealand waters

pygo- — see PYG-

py·go·fer \'pīgəfə(r)\ *n* -s [*pyg-* + *-fer*] **:** the last segment of the abdomen of some insects; *also* **:** the side margin of this segment

py·gop·a·gus \pī'gäpəgəs\ *n* -ES [NL, fr. *pyg-* + *-pagus*] **:** a twin fetal monster joined in the sacral region

¹py·go·pod \'pīgə,päd\ *adj* [NL *Pygopodes*] **:** of or relating to the Pygopodes

²pygopod \"\ *n* -s **:** a bird of the order Pygopodes

³pygopod \"\ *n* -s [*pyg-* + *-pod*] **:** one of the paired appendages of the tenth abdominal segment of an insect

py·gop·o·des \pī'gäpə,dēz\ *n pl, cap* [NL, fr. *pyg-* + Gk *pod-, pous* foot — more at FOOT] *in some esp former classifications* **:** an order of diving birds comprising the loons, grebes, and sometimes the auks

py·gop·o·did \(')pī¦gäpədəd\ *adj* [NL *Pygopodidae,* family of lizards, fr. *Pygopod-, Pygopus,* type genus + *-idae*] **:** of or relating to the genus *Pygopus* or to the family Pygopodidae

py·go·po·di·um \,pīgə'pōdēəm\ *n, pl* **pygopo·dia** \-ēə\ [NL, fr. *pyg-* + *-podium*] **:** a fleshy process on the terminal abdominal segment of various beetle and fly larvae

py·gop·o·dous \(')pī¦gäpədəs\ *adj* [*pyg-* + *-podous*] **:** having the feet set far back ⟨grebes and penguins are typical ~ birds⟩

py·go·pus \'pīgəpəs\ *n, cap* [NL, fr. *pyg-* + *-pus*] **:** a genus (the type of the family Pygopodidae) of pleurodont snake-shaped Australian and Tasmanian lizards without forelimbs and with rudimentary hind limbs

py·go·style \'pīgə,stīl\ *n* -s [*pyg-* + *-style*] **1 :** a plate of bone that forms the posterior end of the vertebral column in most birds and is formed by the union of vertebrae **2** *obs* **:** VOMER

py·go·styled \-ld\ *adj* [*pygostyle* + *-ed*] **:** having a pygostyle

py·go·sty·lous \,pīgə¦stīləs\ *adj* [*pygostyle* + *-ous*] **:** of, relating to, or constituting a pygostyle **:** PYGOSTYLED

pyin·ka·do \pē'iŋkə,dō, 'pyi-\ *or* **pyin·ga·do** \-ŋgə-\ *or* **pyen·ga·du** \pē'eŋ-,'pyeŋ-\ *n* -s [Burmese *pyeng-kadō*] **1 a :** a tall Asiatic tree (*Xylia dolabriformis*) that is often confused with the acle and that has very heavy hard durable wood **b :** the wood of pyinkado **2 :** ACLE

pyin·ma \pē'in,mä, 'pyi-\ *n* -s [native name in Burma] **:** the light red to reddish brown smooth lustrous and moderately hard heavy durable wood of the queen's crape myrtle

py·ja·mas \pə'jäməz *sometimes* pī'j-, *archaic* pī'j-\ *chiefly Brit var of* PAJAMAS

pyke \'pīk\ *n* -s [Hindi *pāyik, pāyak* messenger, fr. Per] *dial Eng* **:** a civilian at whose expense a soldier is treated or entertained

¹pyk·nic *also* **pyc·nic** \'piknik\ *adj* [ISV *pykn-, pycn-* pycn- + *-ic;* orig. formed as G *pyknisch*] **:** characterized by shortness of stature, broadness of girth, and powerful muscularity **:** ENDOMORPHIC — compare ASTHENIC, ATHLETIC

²pyknic *also* **pycnic** \"\ *n* -s **:** a person of pyknic build

pykno- *comb form* **:** PYCN-

pyk·no·epilepsy \¦pik(,)nō+\ *n* [ISV *pycn-* + *epilepsy;* orig. formed as G *pyknoepilepsie*] **:** PYKNOLEPSY

pyk·no·lep·sy \'piknə,lepsē\ *n* -ES [ISV *pycn-* + *-lepsy;* orig. formed as G *pyknolepsie*] **:** a condition marked by epileptiform attacks resembling petit mal

pyknometer *var of* PYCNOMETER

pyknosis *var of* PYCNOSIS

pyknotic *var of* PYCNOTIC

pyk·rete \'pī,krēt\ *n* -s [Geoffrey *Pyke,* 20th cent. Eng. inventor who invented it + *-rete* (as in *concrete*)] **:** a frozen mixture of water and wood pulp that gives a tough resistant product used experimentally in arctic military structures

pyl- *or* **pyle-** *or* **pylo-** *comb form* [NL, fr. Gk, fr. *pylē* gate — more at PYLON] **:** portal vein ⟨*pyle*thrombophlebitis⟩

py·la \'pīlə\ *n, pl* **pylas** \-ləz\ *or* **py·lae** \-(,)lē\ [NL, fr. Gk *pylē* gate] **:** the opening from the third ventricle into the aqueduct of Sylvius in higher vertebrates including man; *also* **:** a corresponding opening on either side from the cavity of the optic lobe in some lower vertebrates — **py·lar** \-lə(r)\ *adj*

pyla·gore \'pīlə,gō(ə)r, 'pīl-\ *n* -s [Gk *pylagoras,* fr. *Pylai* Pylae, Thermopylae, meeting place of the amphictyonic council + Gk *-agoras* (fr. *ageirein* to collect, assemble) — more at GREGARIOUS] **:** a deputy of a state at the council of the Delphic Amphictyony of ancient Greece

py·lan·gi·um \pī'lanjēəm\ *n, pl* **pylan·gia** \-ēə\ [NL, fr. *pyl-* + *-angium*] **:** the highly muscular portion of the arterial trunk in immediate connection with the ventricle of the heart in some lower vertebrates — compare SYNANGIUM

pyle *chiefly Scot var of* PILE

-pyle \,pīl\ *n comb form* -s [ISV, fr. Gk *pylē* gate] **:** opening **:** orifice ⟨micro*pyle*⟩ ⟨apo*pyle*⟩

py·le·phlebitis \¦pīlə+\ *n* [NL, fr. *pyl-* + *phlebitis*] **:** inflammation of the portal vein usu. secondary to intestinal disease and with suppuration

py·lic \'pīlik\ *adj* [*pyl-* + *-ic*] **:** of or relating to a portal vein

py·lon \'pī,län, -,lən\ *n* -s [Gk *pylōn* gateway, fr. *pylē* gate; perh. akin to Skt *gopura* town-gate, gate] **1 a :** a usu. massive gateway often with flanking towers — compare PROPYLON **b :** an ancient Egyptian gateway building having a truncated pyramidal form; *broadly* **:** two such truncated pyramids with a gateway between **c :** a monumental mass placed so as to flank an entranceway (as an approach to a bridge) **2 :** a tower (as of steelwork) for supporting either end of a wire (as for a telegraph line) over a long span **3 a :** a post, tower, or other projection marking a prescribed course of flight for an airplane **b :** a structure for supporting the propeller on the side of a rigid airship or for attaching an auxiliary fuel tank, a bomb, or other external stores carried by an airplane

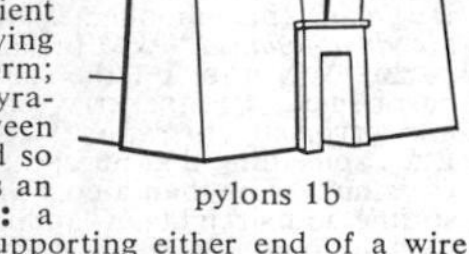

pylons 1b

pylon antenna *n* **:** a slotted tubular radio antenna

pylor- *or* **pyloro-** *comb form* [LL *pylorus* — more at PYLORUS] **:** pylorus ⟨*pylor*algia⟩ ⟨*pyloro*cleisis⟩

py·lor·ic \(')pī¦lȯrik, pə'l-, -lär-, -rēk\ *adj* [*pylor-* + *-ic*] **:** of, relating to, lying in the region of, or involving the pylorus or the part of the stomach from which the intestine leads

pyloric artery *n* **:** a branch of the hepatic artery supplying the pyloric end and lesser curvature of the stomach

pyloric caecum *n* **1 :** one of the tubular pouches opening into the alimentary canal in the pyloric region of most fishes **2 :** one of the tubular pouches opening into the ventriculus of an insect **3 :** one of the paired tubes in each ray of a starfish that have lateral glandular diverticula, that constitute the liver, and that communicate in pairs by a common duct with the pyloric sac

pyloric glands *n* **:** one of the short more or less tortuous glands of the mucous coat of the stomach occurring chiefly near the pyloric end

pyloric ring *n* **:** PYLORUS 1

pyloric sac *n* **:** an aboral division of the stomach of a starfish

pyloric stenosis *n* **:** narrowing of the pyloric opening (as from congenital malformation or contraction of scar tissue)

pyloric valve *or* **pyloric sphincter** *n* **1 :** the circular fold of mucous membrane containing a ring of circularly disposed muscle fibers that closes the vertebrate pylorus **2 :** the valvular fold of the pylorus of an invertebrate

py·lo·ro·plas·ty \pī'lōrə,plastē, pə'l-\ *n* -ES [ISV *pylor-* + *-plasty*] **:** a plastic operation on the pylorus (as to enlarge a stricture)

py·lo·ro·spasm \-rə,spazəm\ *n* [ISV *pylor-* + *-spasm*] **:** spasm of the pylorus often associated with other conditions (as ulcer of the stomach) or occurring in infants and marked by pain and vomiting

py·lo·rus \pī'lōrəs, pə'l-, -lȯr-\ *n, pl* **pylo·ri** \-ō,rī, -ō,rī\ *also* **pyloruses** [LL, fr. Gk *pylōros* gatekeeper, pylorus, fr. *pylē* gate — more at PYLON] **1 :** the opening in a vertebrate from the stomach into the intestine — see PYLORIC VALVE **2 a :** a posterior division of the stomach or midgut in some invertebrates commonly separated from the posterior intestine by a valvular fold or sphincter

pyl·stert \'pīl,stert\ *n* -s [Afrik, fr. D *pijlstaart* pintail duck, lit., arrow-tail, fr. *pijl* arrow (fr. MD *pijl, pile,* fr. L *pilum* javelin) + *staart* tail (fr. MD *start*) — more at PESTLE, START] *southern Africa* **:** any of various rays

pymander *obs var of* POMANDER

pyment *var of* PIMENT

pymt *abbr* payment

pyo \'pī(,)ō\ *n* -s [short for *pyocyanase*] **:** any of several crystalline fractions possessing antibiotic activity that are obtained from pyocyanase and distinguished from each other as pyo Ib, Ic, II, III, IV

pyo- — see PY-

pyo·bacillosis \¦pī(,)ō+\ *n* [NL, fr. *py-* + *bacillosis*] **:** infection with or disease caused in sheep, swine, or rarely cattle by a bacterium (*Corynebacterium pyogenes*) that is usu. marked by abscess formation but in sheep commonly takes the form of chronic purulent pneumonia accompanied by extensive fibrosis, pleurisy, and joint lesions

pyo·cele \'pīə,sēl\ *n* -s [ISV *py-* + *-cele*] **:** a pus-filled cavity (as of the scrotum)

pyo·coc·cus \,pīō'käkəs\ *n* [NL, fr. *py-* + *-coccus*] **:** any coccoid bacterium that tends to form pus

pyo·cy·a·nase \,pīō'sīə,nās, -āz\ *n* -s [NL *pyocyaneus* (specific epithet of *Bacillus pyocyaneus,* syn. of *Pseudomonas aeruginosa*) (fr. *py-* + *cyaneus* cyaneous) + E *-ase*] **:** a mixture of antibiotics once regarded as a specific bacteriolytic enzyme that is obtained from the bacillus of green pus (*Pseudomonas aeruginosa*) and that is a soluble, yellowish green, alkaline, amorphous substance capable of digesting various other bacteria (as those of typhoid fever, diphtheria, and cholera)

pyo·cy·a·ne·ous *or* **pyo·cy·a·ne·us** \¦pīō¦sī¦ānēəs\ *also* **pyo·cy·an·ic** \-ī¦anik\ *or* **pyo·cy·a·ne·al** \-ī¦ānēəl\ *adj* [*pyocyaneous, pyocyaneus* fr. NL *pyocyaneus; pyocyanic* fr. NL *pyocyaneus* + E *-ic; pyocyaneal* fr. NL *pyocyaneus* + E *-al*] **:** of, relating to, or produced by a bacterium (*Pseudomonas aeruginosa*) — compare PYOCYANASE

pyo·cy·a·nin \,pīō'sīənən\ *or* **pyo·cy·a·nine** \", -ī ə,nēn\ *n* -s [ISV *pyocyan-* (fr. NL *pyocyaneus*) + *-in* or *-ine*] **:** a toxic blue crystalline pigment $C_{13}H_{10}N_2O$ found in green pus and formed in the metabolism of a bacterium (*Pseudomonas aeruginosa*) that is a quinone imine related to phenazine and has antibiotic activity esp. toward gram-positive bacteria

pyo·der·ma \-'dərmə\ *also* **pyo·der·mia** \-mēə\ *n* -s [NL, fr. *py-* + *-derma* or *-dermia*] **:** an inflammatory skin disease caused by pus-forming microorganisms (as staphylococci) and marked by pus-containing lesions — **pyo·der·mic** \¦=¦=mik\ *adj*

py·o·gen \'pīəjən, -,jen\ *n* -s [ISV *py-* + *-gen*] **:** a pus-producing microorganism

py·o·gen·ic \¦=¦jenik\ *adj* [ISV *py-* + *-genic*] **:** producing pus ⟨~ staphylococcus⟩ **:** marked or characterized by pus production ⟨~ meningitis⟩

pyogenic membrane *n* **:** the limiting layer of an abscess or other region of suppuration formerly supposed to secrete the pus

py·oid \'pī,ȯid\ *adj* [ISV *py-* + *-oid*] **:** resembling or made up of pus

pyo·me·tra \,pīō'mētrə\ *n* -s [NL, fr. *py-* + *-metra*] **:** an accumulation of pus in the uterine cavity

pyo·nephritis \¦pī(,)ō+\ *n* [NL, fr. *py-* + *nephritis*] **:** inflammation of the kidney attended with suppuration

pyo·nephrosis \"+\ *n* [NL, fr. *py-* + *nephrosis*] **:** a collection of pus in the kidney

pyo·nephrotic \"+\ *adj* [fr. NL *pyonephrosis,* after such pairs as NL *nephrosis:* E *nephrotic*] **:** of, relating to, or affected with pyonephrosis

pyong·yang \pē'ȯŋ¦yäŋ, 'pyȯ|, |əŋ-, -yaŋ\ *adj, usu cap* [fr. *Pyongyang,* No. Korea] **:** of or from Pyongyang, the capital of No. Korea **:** of the kind or style prevalent in Pyongyang

pyopneumo- *comb form* [NL, fr. *py-* + *pneum-*] **:** containing or characterized by the presence of both pus and gas ⟨*pyopneumo*cyst⟩ ⟨*pyopneumo*peritonitis⟩

pyo·pneu·mo·thorax \¦pīə¦n(y)ümə+\ *n* [NL, fr. *pyopneumo-* + *thorax*] **:** a collection of pus and air or other gas in the thorax

pyo·poiesis \,pīə+\ *n* [NL, fr. *py-* + *poiesis*] **:** the formation of pus

py·or·rhea *also* **py·or·rhoea** \,pīə'rēə\ *n* -s [NL, fr. *py-* + *-rrhea, -rrhoea*] **1 :** a discharge of pus **2 :** PYORRHEA ALVEOLARIS

pyorrhea al·ve·o·lar·is \-,alvēə'la(a)rəs\ *n* [NL, alveolar pyorrhea] **:** an inflammatory condition involving the gingival tissues and periodontal membrane often associated with a discharge of pus from the alveoli and loosening of the teeth in their sockets

py·or·rhe·al \¦pīə¦rēəl\ *or* **py·or·rhe·ic** \-rēik\ *also* **py·or·rhet·ic** \-red·ik\ *adj* [*pyorrheal, pyorrhetic* fr. NL *pyorrhea* + E *-al* or *-etic; pyorrheic* ISV *pyorrh-* (fr. NL *pyorrhea*) + *-ic*] **:** of, relating to, or constituting pyorrhea

pyos *pl of* PYO

pyo·salpinx \¦pīō+\ *n* [NL, fr. *py-* + *salpinx*] **:** a collection of pus in an oviduct

pyo·septicemia \¦pī(,)ō+\ *n* [NL, fr. *py-* + *septicemia*] **:** pyemia and septicemia combined — **pyo·septicemic** \"+\ *adj*

pyo·thorax \"+\ *n* [NL, fr *py-* + *thorax*] **:** EMPYEMA

pyo·xan·those \,pīō'zan,thōs *also* -ōz\ *n* -s [ISV *py-* + *xanth-* + *-ose*] **:** a greenish yellow crystalline coloring matter in pus

pyr- *or* **pyro-** *comb form* [ME *pyro-,* fr. MF *pyr-, pyro-,* fr. LL, fr. Gk, fr. *pyr* — more at FIRE] **1 a :** fire **:** heat ⟨*pyro*meter⟩ ⟨*pyr*heliometer⟩ **b :** pyrogenous and ⟨*pyro*magnetic⟩ **2 a :** derivative by the action of heat; *esp* **:** derived from the corresponding ortho acid by loss usu. of one molecule of water from two molecules of acid — in names of inorganic acids ⟨*pyro*phosphoric acid⟩; compare META- 4c, ORTH- 3a **b :** due to or attributed to the action of fire or heat ⟨*pyro*chlore⟩ ⟨*pyro*metamorphism⟩; *also* **:** of fiery color ⟨*pyro*phanite⟩ **3 :** fever **:** fever producing ⟨*pyro*toxin⟩ ⟨*pyro*gen⟩

pyr·acanth \'pīrə,kan(t)th, 'pir-\ *n* -s [LL *pyracanthe,* a tree, prob. fire thorn, fr. Gk *pyrakantha*] **:** FIRE THORN

pyr·acan·tha \,==¦kan(t)thə\ *n* [NL, fr. Gk *pyrakantha,* a tree, prob. fire thorn, fr. *pyr-* + *akantha* thorn — more at ACANTH-] **1** *cap* **:** a small genus of Eurasian thorny evergreen or half-evergreen shrubs (family Rosaceae) with alternate leaves, white flowers in compound corymbs, and small red or orange pomes — see FIRE THORN **2** -s **:** any plant of the genus *Pyracantha*

pyra·cene \'pirə,sēn, 'pīr-\ *n* -s [ISV *pyr-* + *ace-* + *-ene*] **:** a tetracyclic parent hydrocarbon $C_{16}H_{12}$ regarded as derived from acenaphthene

pyr·al \'pīrəl\ *adj* [*pyre* + *-al*] **:** of or relating to a pyre

pyrales [NL, fr. *pyr-* + *-ales*] *obs syn of* PYRALIDOIDEA

py·ral·i·dae \pə'ralə,dē, pī'r-\ [NL, fr. *Pyralis* + *-idae*] *syn of* PYRALIDIDAE

¹py·ral·i·did \-lədəd, ¦pirə¦lidəd\ *or* **pyr·a·lid** \'pirələd\ *adj* [*pyralidid* fr. NL *Pyralididae; pyralid* fr. NL *Pyralidae*] **:** of or relating to the Pyralididae

²pyralidid \"\ *or* **pyralid** \"\ *n* -s **:** a moth of the family Pyralididae

pyr·a·lid·i·dae \,pirə'lidə,dē\ *n pl, cap* [NL, fr. *Pyralid-, Pyralis,* type genus + *-idae*] **1 :** a family of moths comprising a vast and heterogeneous assemblage of small or medium-sized plainly colored slender-bodied and long-legged moths in which the costal vein of the hind wing approaches close to or unites with the subcostal vein near the middle of the wing **2** *in some classifications* **:** a small family of moths comprising typical members of the superfamily Pyralidoidea

pyr·a·li·doi·dea \,pirələ'dȯidēə, pə,ralə'-\ *n pl, cap* [NL, fr. *Pyralid-, Pyralis* + *-oidea*] *in some classifications* **:** a superfamily of moths coextensive with the family Pyralididae (sense 1)

Pyr·a·lin \'pirələn\ *trademark* — used for a plastic

pyr·a·lis \'pirələs\ *n* [L, fr. Gk, fr. *pyr* fire — more at PYR-] **1** *pl* **pyralides** *obs* **:** a fly fabled as born from or living in fire **2** [NL, fr. L] **a** *cap* **:** the type genus of the family Pyralididae — see MEAL MOTH **b** *pl* **pyralis·es** \-ləsəz\ *or* **py·ral·i·des** \pə'ralə,dēz, pī'r-\ **:** any moth of the genus *Pyralis*

pyr·a·loid \'pirə,lȯid\ *adj* [NL *Pyralis* + E *-oid*] **:** related to or resembling the genus Pyralis **:** PYRALIDID

pyr·a·me·is \,pirə'mēəs\ [NL, prob. fr. L *pyramis* pyramid] *syn of* VANESSA

¹pyr·a·mid \'pirə,mid, *in rapid speech sometimes* -r,m-\ *n* -s [L *pyramid-, pyramis,* fr. Gk] **1 a :** an ancient massive structure of huge stone blocks found esp. in Egypt having typically a square ground plan, outside walls in the form of four triangles that meet in a point at the top, and inner sepulchral chambers **b :** any architectural structure (as a spire or pinnacle) of similar form **c :** an ancient truncate pyramidal structure found in Mexico and Central America that served as a foundation for a building or a platform for an altar **2 :** a polyhedron having for its base a polygon and for its other faces triangles with a common vertex — see VOLUME table **3 :** an object or figure of pyramidal form or with the shape or profile of a pyramid ⟨a ~ of cartons⟩ ⟨the frosty ~ of a well-shaped blue spruce⟩: as **a :** a tree pruned and trained in pyramidal shape **b :** a crystal-line form each face of which intersects the vertical axis and either two lateral axes or in a tetragonal system one lateral axis — compare DIPYRAMID **c :** an anatomical structure resembling a pyramid: as (1) **:** a petrous bone (2) **:** a conical projection making up the central part of the inferior vermis of the cerebellum (3) **:** PYRAMID OF THE MEDULLA (4) **:** MALPIGHIAN PYRAMID **d :** one of the five large vertical sections of the Aristotle's lantern of a sea urchin **e :** PYRAMID SHELL **4 a :** verse in which the succeeding lines increase in length **b :** a graphic representation of a statistical distribution (as of a population on the basis of age and sex categories) that has essentially the form of a triangle or wedge **c :** a tridimensional diagrammatic representation representing sensory relationships **5 :** an English pool game played with 15 red balls and a white cue ball in which the player pocketing the most balls wins but loses a point each time he pockets the white ball or misses his aim **6 a :** an immaterial structure built upon a broad supporting base and narrowing gradually to an apex (as of power, dominance, or significance) ⟨families at the base of a socioeconomic ~⟩ **b** (1) **:** a group of holding companies superimposed one on another to give those in control of the top holding company control over the whole pyramid with a small investment (2) **:** the series of operations involved in pyramiding on an exchange **c :** CHAIN LETTER

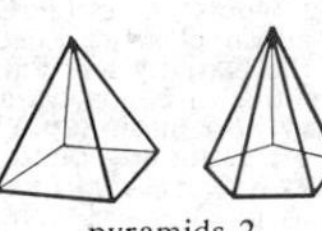

pyramids 2

²pyramid \"\ *vb* -ED/-ING/-S *vi* **1 :** to assume or to become disposed in the form of a pyramid **2 a :** to enlarge one's holdings on an exchange on a continued rise by using paper profits as margin to buy additional amounts **b :** to superimpose holding companies so as to reduce the investment required to control enterprises **3 :** to increase rapidly and progressively step by step on a broadening base that supports a concomitant upward trend ⟨demand for more efficient insecticides continues to ~⟩ ~ *vt* **1 :** to arrange, place, build up, or construct in a pyramidal form or as if upon the base of a pyramid : heap up ⟨~ arguments upon a hypothesis⟩ ⟨~*ed* his gains by careful reinvestment⟩ **2 :** to use or to deal in (as a stock or commodity) in a pyramiding transaction

1py·ram·i·dal \pə'ramədᵊl, ÷ ¦pirə¦midᵊl\ *adj* [ML *pyramidalis*, fr. L *pyramid-*, *pyramis* + *-alis* -al] **1 a :** of, relating to, or having the form of a pyramid **b :** having symmetry such that the general form is a pyramid ⟨a ~ crystal⟩ **2 :** sloping like a face of a pyramid ⟨the sheer ~ side of the cliff⟩ **3 :** HUGE, ENORMOUS, IMPOSING **4 :** affecting, involving, or connecting with an anatomical pyramid esp. of the central nervous system ⟨a crossed ~ lesion⟩ ⟨the inferior ~ tracts⟩

2pyramidal \"\ *n* -s [NL *pyramidale*] **1 :** PYRAMIDAL BONE **2 :** a pyramidal tent

pyramidal bone *n* **:** the third bone in the proximal row of the carpus — called also *triquetrum*

pyramidal cell *n* **:** one of numerous large multipolar cells in the cerebral cortex of higher vertebrates

py·ram·i·dale \pə,ramə'da(,)lē, ,pirəmə'd-, -dā(-, -dä(-\ *n* -s [NL, short for *os pyramidale* pyramidal bone, fr. L *os* bone + ML *pyramidale*, neut. of *pyramidalis* pyramidal — more at OSSEOUS] **:** PYRAMIDAL BONE

py·ram·i·dalis \-ləs\ *n*, *pl* **pyrami·dales** \-(,)lēz\ *or* **pyramidalises** [NL, fr. ML, pyramidal] **:** a small triangular muscle of the lower front part of the abdomen situated in front of and in the same sheath with the rectus

py·ram·i·dal·ism \=ˈ===, ,==ˈ== (*see* 1PYRAMIDAL) + ,izəm\ *n* -s *usu cap* [1*pyramidal* + *-ism*] **:** lore concerned with the Egyptian pyramids

py·ram·i·dal·ist \-əst\ *n* -s *usu cap* **:** an exponent of Pyramidalism; *esp* **:** one who holds positive views as to the mystic and predictional import of the Egyptian pyramids

py·ram·i·dal·ly *pronunc at* 1PYRAMIDAL + ē *or* i\ *adv* **:** in the form or manner of a pyramid

pyramidal tent *n* **:** a pyramidal canvas shelter capable of holding six or more persons

pyramidal tract *n* **:** any of four columns of motor fibers that run in pairs on each side of the spinal cord and that are continuations of the pyramids of the medulla

pyramid ant *n* **:** a common household ant (*Dorymyrmex pyramicus*) of California

pyramided *past of* PYRAMID

1py·ram·i·del·lid \pə¦ramə¦deləd, ¦pirəmə¦d-\ *adj* [NL *Pyramidellidae*] **:** of or relating to the Pyramidellidae

2pyramidellid \"\ *n* -s **:** a snail of the family Pyramidellidae

py·ram·i·del·li·dae \=,=='delə,dē, ,===-\ *n pl*, *cap* [NL, fr. *Pyramidella*, type genus (fr. L *pyramid-*, *pyramis* pyramid + *-ella*) + *-idae* — more at PYRAMID] **:** a large family of marine snails (suborder Taenioglossa) having a conical or turreted dextrally coiled shell but with the apical whorls or embryonic shell sinistrally coiled, a long retractile proboscis, and no radula

pyr·a·mid·er \'pirə,midə(r)\ *n* -s [2*pyramid* + *-er*] **:** one that pyramids (as on a stock exchange)

pyramid flower *n* **1 :** AMERICAN COLUMBO **2 :** the flower of American columbo

pyramid head *n* **:** a printed heading with matter so arranged that the lines form an inverted and truncated pyramid

pyr·a·mid·i·cal \¦pirə¦midəkəl\ *also* **pyr·a·mid·ic** \-dik\ *adj* [*pyramidical* fr. *pyramid* + *-ical; pyramidic* prob. fr. Gk *pyramidikos*, fr. *pyramid-*, *pyramis* + *-ikos* -ic] **:** resembling a pyramid **:** PYRAMIDAL — **pyr·a·mid·i·cal·ly** \-dək(ə)lē\ *adv* — **pyr·a·mid·i·cal·ness** \-kəlnəs\ *n* -ES

pyramiding *pres part of* PYRAMID

pyr·a·mid·i·on \,pirə'midē,än, -ēən\ *n*, *pl* **pyramidions** \-nz\ *also* **pyramid·ia** \-dēə\ [NL, dim. of L *pyramid-*, *pyramis* pyramid — more at PYRAMID] **:** a small pyramid (as at the top of an obelisk or at the apex of a large pyramid)

pyr·a·mid·ist \'pirə,midəst, pə'ramәd-\ *n* -s *often cap* **:** PYRAMIDALIST

pyramido- *comb form* [NL, fr. L *pyramid-*, *pyramis* pyramid] **1 :** pyramidally ⟨*pyramido*attenuate⟩ **2 :** pyramidal and ⟨*pyramido*prismatic⟩

pyramid of numbers : a concept in ecology: an organism forming the base of a food chain is numerically very abundant each succeeding member of the chain being represented by successively fewer individuals and the final large predator being always numerically rare

pyramid of the cerebellum : PYRAMID 3c(2)

pyramid of the medulla : either of two large bundles of motor fibers from the cerebral cortex reaching the medulla through the cerebral peduncles and pons and continuous with the pyramidal tracts of the spinal cord

py·ram·i·doi·dal \pə¦ramə¦dȯidᵊl, ¦pirə(,)mi¦d-\ *adj* [NL *pyramidoides* figure resembling a pyramid (fr. L *pyramid-*, *pyramis* + *-oides* -oid) + E *-al*] **:** like a pyramid

py·ram·i·dol·o·gist \=,=='däləjəst, ,==(,)=-\ *n* -s [*pyramidology* + *-ist*] **:** PYRAMIDALIST

py·ram·i·dol·o·gy \-jē\ *n* -ES *often cap* [*pyramido-* + *-logy*] **:** PYRAMIDALISM

Py·ram·i·don \pə'ramə,dän\ *trademark* — used for aminopyrine

pyramid plant *n* **:** AMERICAN COLUMBO

pyramid roof *n* **:** a roof having four slopes that meet at a peak

pyramids *pl of* PYRAMID, *pres 3d sing of* PYRAMID

pyramid shell *n* [*pyramid* short for 1*pyramidellid*] **:** a mollusk of the family Pyramidellidae or its shell

pyramid roof

pyramidwise \'==,=,=\ *adv* **:** in the manner of or so as to have the form of a pyramid ⟨arranging the bunches of grapes ~ on a platter⟩

pyramis *n*, *pl* **pyramides** [L — more at PYRAMID] **:** PYRAMID 3c(2)

py·ran \'pī,ran\ *n* -s [ISV *pyr-* + *-an*] **:** either of two parent cyclic compounds C_5H_6O that contain five carbon atoms and one oxygen atom in the ring: **a :** the alpha isomer — called also *2H-pyran* **b :** the gamma isomer — called also *4H-pyran;* see PYRONE; compare CHROMAN, XANTHENE

pyra·noid \'pirə,nȯid, 'pīr-\ *adj* [*pyran* + *-oid*] **:** resembling pyran in chemical structure **:** characterized by the presence of the furan ring

pyra·nom·e·ter \,pirə'nämәd·ə(r), ,pīr-\ *n* [ISV *pyr-* + *ano-* + *-meter*] **:** an instrument for measuring radiation from the sky by comparing the heating effect of such radiation upon two blackened metallic strips with that produced in the same strips when heated by means of an electric current

pyra·nose \'pirə,nōs, 'pīr- *also* -ōz\ *n* -s [ISV *pyran* + *-ose*] **:** a glycose sugar in the form of a cyclic hemiacetal containing a 6-member ring

py·ran·o·side \pə'ranə,sīd, pī'r- -səd\ *n* -s [*pyranose* + *-ide*] **:** a glycoside containing the ring characteristic of a pyranose

pyr·an·threne \pə'ran,thrēn, pī'r-\ *n* -s [ISV *pyr-* + *-anthrene*] **:** a green-yellow crystalline aromatic hydrocarbon consisting of eight compactly but unsymmetrically fused benzene rings in three tiers

pyra·nyl \'pirə,nil, 'pīr-\ *n* -s [*pyran* + *-yl*] **:** any of several univalent radicals C_5H_5O derived from the pyrans by removal of one hydrogen atom

pyr·ar·gy·rite \pī'rärjə,rīt, pə'r-\ *n* -s [G *pyrargyrit*, fr. *pyr-* + *argyr-* + *-it* -ite] **:** a silver antimony sulfide Ag_3SbS_3 that is isomorphous with proustite, occurs in rhombohedral crystals or massive, and has a dark-red or black color with a metallic adamantine luster — called also *dark red silver ore*, *ruby silver*

py·raus·ta \pə'rȯstə\ *n*, *cap* [NL, fr. Gk *pyraustēs* moth that gets singed in fire, fr. *pyr-* + *-austēs* (fr. *auein* to get a light, start a fire)] **:** a genus (the type of the family Pyraustidae) of inconspicuously colored moths with larvae that feed on foliage or bore in the stems of plants — see CORN BORER

py·raus·ti·dae \-tə,dē\ *n pl*, *cap* [NL, fr. *Pyrausta*, type genus + *-idae*] **:** a family closely related to Pyralididae and comprising small or medium-sized rather slender moths with larvae that are webworms or leaftiers or that bore in the stems and roots of plants — see PYRAUSTA

pyr·a·zin·amide \,pirə'zinə,mīd, -məd\ *n* [*pyrazine* + *amide*] **:** a tuberculostatic drug $C_4H_3N_2CONH_2$; pyrazine-carboxamide

pyr·azine \'pirə,zēn, -zən\ *n* [ISV *pyr-* + *azine*] **:** a crystalline feeble heterocyclic base $C_4H_4N_2$ obtained usu. by distilling piperazine with zinc dust — called also *paradiazine*

pyr·azole \'pirə,zōl, -zȯl\ *n* [ISV *pyr-* + *azole;* orig. formed as G *pyrazol*] **1 :** a crystalline feeble heterocyclic base $C_3H_4N_2$ isomeric with imidazole obtained usu. by action of acetylene on diazomethane; 1,2-diazole **2 :** a derivative of pyrazole

py·raz·o·line \pə'razə,lēn, pī'r-, -lən\ *n* -s [ISV *pyrazole* + *-ine*] **1 :** a dihydro derivative $C_3H_6N_2$ of pyrazole; *esp* **:** a liquid compound obtained usu. by the action of hydrazine on acrolein **2 :** a derivative of pyrazoline

py·raz·o·lone \-,lōn\ *n* -s [ISV *pyrazole* + *-one*] **1 :** any of three isomeric carbonyl compounds $C_3H_4N_2O$ derived from pyrazoline **2 :** any of numerous derivatives of the pyrazolones some of which (as antipyrine) are used as analgesics and antipyretics and others (as 3-methyl-1-phenyl-5-pyrazolone) in making azo dyes and as developers

py·raz·o·lyl \-,lil\ *n* -s [*pyrazole* + *-yl*] **:** any of four univalent radicals $C_3H_3N_2$ derived from pyrazole by removal of one hydrogen atom

pyre \'pī(ə)r, -īə\ *n* -s [L *pyra*, fr. Gk, fr. *pyr* fire — more at FIRE] **:** a combustible heap (as of wood) for burning a dead body as a funeral rite; *broadly* **:** a pile to be burnt

pyren- *or* **pyreno-** *comb form* [NL, fr. Gk *pyrēn-*, *pyrēno-*, fr. *pyrēn* — more at FURZE] **1 :** stone of a fruit ⟨*pyreno*carp⟩ **2 :** nucleolus ⟨*pyren*ematous⟩ ⟨*pyren*in⟩

py·re·na \pī'rēnə\ *n*, *pl* **pyre·nae** \-(,)nē\ [NL, fr. Gk *pyrēn*] **:** PYRENE

1py·rene \'pī,rēn, ='=\ *n* -s [NL *pyrena*] **:** the stone of a drupelet (as in the fruit of the huckleberry); *broadly* **:** a small hard nutlet

2py·rene \'pī,rēn\ *n* -s [*pyr-* + *-ene*] **:** a pale yellow crystalline hydrocarbon $C_{16}H_{10}$ that fluoresces blue in solution, that is obtained from coal-tar distillation, from petroleum cracking, and from stupp and is also made synthetically, and that consists structurally of a cluster of four compactly fused benzene rings

1pyr·e·ne·an \¦pirə¦nēən\ *adj*, *usu cap* [L *pyren*aeus Pyrenean (fr. *Pyrene*, the Pyrenees, mountain range along the French-Spanish border from the Bay of Biscay to the southwestern coast of the Gulf of Lions, fr. Gk *Pyrēnē*, beloved of Hercules in Greek mythology who was believed to be buried upon the Pyrenees) + E *-an*] **:** of or relating to the Pyrenees separating France and Spain

2pyrenean \"\ *n* -s *cap* **:** a native or inhabitant of the Pyrenees

pyrenean mountain dog *n*, *usu cap P* **:** GREAT PYRENEES

py·ren·em·a·tous \¦pīrə¦nemәd·əs\ *adj* [*pryen-* + *hemat-* + *-ous*] **:** having nucleated red blood corpuscles

py·renic acid \(')pī¦rē|nik-, -re|\ *n* [*pyrenic* ISV *pyrene* + *-ic*] **:** a yellow crystalline tricyclic keto dicarboxylic acid $C_{13}H_6O(COOH)_2$ formed by the oxidation of pyrene

py·ren·i·dae \pī'renə,dē\ [NL, fr. *Pyrena*, genus of dove shells (fr. Gk *pyrēn* pit of a fruit) + *-idae*] *syn of* COLUMBELLIDAE

py·re·nin \pī'rēnən\ *n* -s [*pyren-* + *-in*] **:** PLASTIN

py·re·no·carp \pī'rēnə,kärp\ *n* -s [*pyren-* + *-carp*] **1 :** PERITHECIUM **2 :** DRUPE — **py·re·no·car·pic** \(¦)=¦==¦kärpik\ *or* **py·re·no·car·pous** \-pəs\ *adj*

py·re·no·car·pe·ae \=,=='kärpē,ē\ *n pl*, *cap* [NL, fr. *pyren-* + *-carpeae* (fr. *-carpus* -carpous)] *in some classifications* **:** a group of lichens comprising those whose fruiting body is closed — compare GYMNOCARPEAE

py·re·no·chae·ta \-'kēd·ə\ *n*, *cap* [NL, fr. *pyren-* + *-chaeta*] **:** a genus of imperfect fungi (family Sphaeropsidaceae) characterized by setose pycnidia and unicellular hyaline ovate to elongate or cylindric pycnospores

py·re·noid \pī'rē,nȯid, 'pīrə,n-\ *n* -s [ISV *pyren-* + *-oid;* prob. orig. formed in G] **:** one of the colorless highly refractive proteid bodies found within the chromatophores of various low organisms (as algae of the order Zygnematales) and serving as centers for the deposition of starch

py·re·no·lichen \pī¦rēnə+\ *n* [ISV *pyren-* + *lichen*] **:** an ascolichen of the subgroup Pyrenolichenes — compare BASIDIOLICHEN

py·re·no·lichenes \"+\ *n pl*, *cap* [NL, fr. *pyren-* + *Lichenes*] **:** a subgroup of ascolichens having a closed spore fruit — compare DISCOLICHENES

py·re·no·my·ce·ta·les \pī,rē(,)nō,mīsə'tā(,)lēz\ [NL, fr. *pyren-* + *mycet-* + *-ales*] *syn of* PYRENOMYCETES

py·re·no·my·cete \pī'rēnō'mī,sēt, -¦rēnō,mī¦sēt\ *n* -s [NL *Pyrenomycetes*] **:** a fungus of the subclass Pyrenomycetes

py·re·no·my·ce·tes \=,==,='sēd·ēz\ *n pl*, *cap* [NL, fr. *pyren-* + *-mycetes*] *in some classifications* **:** a subclass of fungi (class Ascomycetes) including those that produce a typical perithecium and comprising the orders Sphaeriales, Perisporiales, Hypocreales, and Dothideales — **py·re·no·my·ce·tous** \=¦==¦=¦sēd·əs\ *adj*

py·re·no·peziza \pī¦rē(,)nō+\ *n*, *cap* [NL, fr. *pyren-* + *Peziza*] **:** a genus of fungi (family Mollisiaceae) that is similar to *Pseudopeziza* except in having dark-colored apothecia and that includes several parasites of economic plants

pyres *pl of* PYRE

pyret- *or* **pyreto-** *comb form* [Gk, fr. *pyretos* burning heat, fever, fr. *pyr* fire — more at FIRE] **:** fever ⟨*pyreto*genesis⟩ ⟨*pyret*etiology⟩

py·re·thrin \pī'rēthrən *also* -reth-\ *n* -s [ISV *pyrethr-* (fr. NL *Pyrethrum*) + *-in;* orig. formed as F *pyréthrine*] **:** either of two oily liquid esters $C_{21}H_{28}O_3$ and $C_{22}H_{28}O_5$ of pyrethrolone having high insecticidal properties and occurring esp. in pyrethrum flowers — called also respectively *pyrethrin I*, *pyrethrin II*

py·re·thro·lone \-thrə,lōn\ *n* -s [ISV *pyrethr*in + *-ol* + *-one*] **:** a viscous oily keto alcohol $C_{11}H_{14}O_2$ closely related to cinerolone and obtained by hydrolysis of the pyrethrins

py·re·thrum \pī'rēthrəm *also* -reth-\ *n* [NL, fr. L, pellitory, fr. Gk *pyrethron*, fr. *pyr* fire; fr. the spicy taste of the root] **1 a** *cap*, *in some esp former classifications* **:** a genus of composite plants with finely divided leaves that are now usu. included in the genus *Chrysanthemum* **b** -s **:** any of various chrysanthemums with finely divided and often aromatic leaves: as (1) **:** a chrysanthemum (as *C. coccineum* or *C. cinerariaefolium*) that is a source of insecticides (2) **:** any of several garden perennials that are derived from the Asiatic species (*C. coccineum*) and have white, pink, red, or rarely lilac flowers in late spring — called also *painted daisy* **2** -s **a** *or* **pyrethrum flowers :** an insecticide consisting of the dried powdered flowers of a Dalmatian pyrethrum (*Chrysanthemum cinerariaefolium*) or either of two Asiatic pyrethrums (*C. coccineum* and *C. marschallii*) — called also respectively *Dalmatian insect powder*, *Persian insect powder* **b** *or* **pyrethrum extract :** an extract of the powdered flowers containing pyrethrins and cinerins and used in insecticidal sprays

pyrethrum yellow *n* **:** a moderate yellow that is greener and deeper than colonial yellow, greener, lighter, and stronger than brass, and greener, stronger, and slightly lighter than mustard yellow — called also *golden-feather yellow*

py·ret·ic \(')pī¦red·ik\ *adj* [NL *pyreticus*, fr. Gk *pyretikos*, fr. *pyret-* + *-ikos* -ic] **:** of or relating to fever **:** FEBRILE

pyr·e·to·gen·ic \¦pirətō¦jenik, ¦pīr-; pī¦red·ə¦j-\ *also* **pyre·tog·e·nous** \¦pirə¦täjənəs, ¦pīr-\ *adj* [*pyret-* + *-genic* or *-genous*] **:** inducing fever

pyr·e·to·therapy \¦pirətō, ¦pīrətō, pī¦red·ə+\ *n* [ISV *pyret-* + *therapy*] **:** FEVER THERAPY

Py·rex \'pī,reks\ *trademark* — used for glass and glassware resistant to heat, chemicals, or electricity

py·rex·ia \pī'reksēə\ *n* -s [NL, fr. *pyrex-* (fr. Gk *pyressein* to be feverish, fr. *pyretos* fever) + L *-ia* -y] **:** elevation of body temperature to an abnormal level **:** FEVER — **py·rex·i·al** \(')pī¦reksēəl\ *adj* — **py·rex·ic** \-sik\ *adj*

py·rex·in \pī'reksən\ *n* -s [NL *pyrexia* + E *-in*] **:** a nitrogenous heat-stabile factor that is possibly a polypeptide, is found in inflammatory discharges, and may be responsible for the fever which accompanies inflammation — compare NECROSIN

pyr·ge·om·e·ter \,pī(ə)rjē'ämәd·ə(r), ,pi(-\ *n* [ISV *pyr-* + *ge-* + *-meter*] **:** an instrument for determining the radiation from the earth's surface into space ⟨the equipment of a modern observatory, including . . . ~*s* —*Science*⟩

pyr·go·cephalic \¦pər(,)gō+\ *adj* [F *pyrgocéphalie* pyrgocephaly (fr. Gk *pyrgos* tower + F *-céphalie* -cephaly) + E *-ic*] **:** having a skull with a high vertex — **pyr·go·ceph·a·ly** \,=='sefəlē\ *n* -ES

pyr·gus \'pərgəs\ *n*, *cap* [NL, fr. LL, tower, fr. Gk *pyrgos*, perh. of Gmc origin; akin to OHG *burg* fortified place — more at BOROUGH] **:** a widely distributed genus of skipper butterflies usu. having the wings largely checkered

pyr·heliometer \¦pī(ə)r, ¦pi(-+\ *n* [ISV *pyr-* + *heli-* + *-meter*] **:** an instrument for measuring the sun's total radiant energy as received at the earth in order to determine the solar constant

pyr·heliometric \"+\ *adj* [ISV *pyrheliometry* + *-ic*] **:** of or relating to pyrheliometry

pyr·heliometry \"+\ *n* [*pyrheliometer* + *-y*] **:** a branch of study dealing with the measurement of the heat of the sun's rays

Pyri·ben·za·mine \,pirə'benzə,mēn\ *trademark* — used for tripelennamine

pyr·i·bole \'pirə,bōl\ *n* -s [*pyr*oxene + amph*ibole*] **:** a constituent of a rock that is either pyroxene or amphibole or both

pyric \'pīrik, 'pir-\ *adj* [F *pyrique*, fr. *pyr-* + *-ique* -ic] **:** resulting from, induced by, or associated with burning ⟨a ~ ecological climax⟩

pyrid- *or* **pyrido-** *comb form* [fr. *pyridine*] **:** pyridine ⟨*pyr*idone⟩ ⟨*pyrido*-indole⟩

py·rid·azine \pī'ridə,zēn, ,pirə'da,z-, -zən\ *n* [ISV *pyrid-* + *azine*] **1 :** a liquid feeble heterocyclic base $C_4H_4N_2$; 1,2-diazine — called also *ortho-diazine* **2 :** a derivative of pyridazine

pyr·i·dine \'pirə,dēn, -dən\ *n* -s [*pyr-* + *-id* + *-ine*] **:** a toxic

structural formula for pyridine (three methods of representation, the hexagon without double bonds being acceptable only when it cannot be mistaken for piperidine)

water-soluble flammable liquid heterocyclic base C_5H_5N that has a disagreeable odor, that is obtained by distillation of bone oil or now usu. as a by-product of coking either by distillation of coal tar or by recovery from gas liquor, that is analogous to benzene in structure except that it contains a nitrogen atom and five carbon atoms in the ring, that is the parent of many naturally occurring organic compounds including alkaloids (as nicotine) and the vitamins nicotinamide and pyridoxine, and that is used chiefly as a solvent, as a denaturant for alcohol, and in the manufacture of pharmaceuticals (as antiseptics and antihistamine drugs) and waterproofing agents for textiles — compare PIPERIDINE, STRUCTURAL FORMULA

pyridine base *n* **:** any of several bases derived from pyridine and obtained with it as by-products of the coking process or made synthetically — compare COLLIDINE, LUTIDINE, METHYLETHYLPYRIDINE, PICOLINE

pyridine nucleotide *n* **:** a nucleotide characterized by a pyridine derivative as a nitrogen base; *esp* **:** a dinucleotide having nicotinamide as the pyridine base and adenine as the second base — compare DIPHOSPHOPYRIDINE NUCLEOTIDE, FLAVOPROTEIN, TRIPHOSPHOPYRIDINE NUCLEOTIDE

pyr·i·din·i·um \,pirə'dinēəm\ *n* -s [NL, fr. ISV *pyridine* + NL *-ium*] **:** a univalent ion $[C_5H_5NH]^+$ or radical C_5H_6N that is analogous to ammonium and is derived from pyridine

pyr·i·done \'pirə,dōn\ *n* -s [ISV *pyrid-* + *-one*] **:** any of several isomeric carbonyl compounds C_5H_5NO derived from pyridine: as **a :** the crystalline alpha isomer — called also *2-pyridone*, *2(1H)-pyridone* **b :** the crystalline gamma isomer — called also *4-pyridone*, *4(1H)-pyridone*

pyr·i·dox·al \,pirə'däksəl, -,sal\ *n* -s [ISV *pyridox*ine + *-al*] **:** a crystalline aldehyde $C_8H_9NO_3$ obtainable by oxidation of pyridoxine that is a member of the vitamin B_6 group and occurs in the form of a phosphate active as a coenzyme (as in decarboxylation and transamination); 3-hydroxy-5-(hydroxymethyl)-2-methyl-isonicotinaldehyde — compare CODECARBOXYLASE

pyr·i·dox·amine \,pirə'däksə,mēn, -mən\ *n* [ISV *pyridox*ine + *amine*] **:** a crystalline amine $C_8H_{12}N_2O_2$ obtainable from pyridoxine that is a member of the vitamin B_6 group and occurs in the form of a phosphate active as a coenzyme in transamination

pyr·i·dox·ic acid \¦pirə¦däksik-\ *n* [*pyridoxic* fr. *pyridox*ine + *-ic*] **:** a crystalline acid $C_8H_9NO_4$ isolated from urine and held to be formed by oxidation of pyridoxal as the major end product of vitamin B_6 metabolism — called also *4-pyridoxic acid*

pyr·i·dox·ine \,pirə'däk,sēn, -sən\ *also* **pyr·i·dox·in** \-sən\ *n* -s [*pyrid-* + *ox-* + *-in* or *-ine*] **:** a crystalline phenolic alcohol $C_8H_{11}NO_3$ derived from pyridine that is a member of the vitamin B_6 group convertible in the organism into pyridoxal and pyridoxamine, that occurs esp. in cereals but is usu. made synthetically, and that is administered chiefly in the form of its hydrochloride; 3-hydroxy-4,5-bis(hydroxymethyl)-2-methyl-pyridine; *broadly* **:** VITAMIN B_6

pyr·i·dyl \'pirə,dil\ *n* -s [ISV *pyrid-* + *-yl*] **:** any of three univalent radicals C_5H_4N derived from pyridine by removal of one hydrogen atom

pyr·i·form \'pirə,fȯrm\ *adj* [NL *pyriformis*] **:** having the form of a pear **:** PEAR-SHAPED

pyriform aperture *n* **:** the anterior opening of the nasal cavities in the skull

pyriformis *var of* PIRIFORMIS

pyriform lobe *or* **pyriform area** *n* **:** the lateral olfactory gyrus and the hippocampal convolution taken together

py·ril·amine \pī'rilə,mēn, -mən\ *n* [*pyril-* (contr. of *pyridyl*) + *amine*] **:** an oily liquid base $C_{17}H_{23}N_3O$ or its bitter crystalline maleate $C_{21}H_{27}N_3O_5$ used as an antihistamine drug in the treatment of various allergies

py·rim·i·dine \pī'rimə,dēn, -dən; 'pirəmə,dēn\ *n* -s [ISV, alter. of *pyridine;* prob. orig. formed as G *pyrimidin*] **1 :** a crystalline feeble heterocyclic base $C_4H_4N_2$ of penetrating odor that is usu. prepared indirectly from barbituric acid; 1,3-diazine — compare PURINE, STRUCTURAL FORMULA **2 :** a derivative of pyrimidine; *esp* **:** a base (as cytosine) that is a component of nucleosides and nucleotides

pyrimidine

py·rim·i·dyl \pī'rimədᵊl, 'pirəmə,dil\ *or* **py·rim·i·din·yl** \pī'rimə,dēnᵊl\ *n* -s [ISV *pyrimidi*ne + *-yl*] **:** any of three univalent radicals $C_4H_3N_2$ derived from pyrimidine by removal of one hydrogen atom

py·rit·a·ceous \¦pī,rīd·¦āshəs, ¦pirə¦tā-\ *adj* [*pyrite* + *-aceous*] **:** PYRITIC

py·rite \'pī,rīt\ *n* -s [L *pyrites*] **1** *obs* **:** PYRITES 1 **2 :** a common mineral that consists of iron disulfide FeS_2, has a pale brass-yellow color and brilliant metallic luster, crystallizes in isometric forms (as the cube and pyritohedron), and is burned in making sulfur dioxide and sulfuric acid (hardness 6–6.5, sp. gr. 4.95–5.10) — called also *fool's gold*, *iron pyrites*

py·rites \pə'rīd·(,)ēz, -ī(,)tēz *also* pī'r-; *also* ÷'pī,rīts\ *n*, *pl* **pyrites** \"\ [L, fr. Gk *pyritēs* of or in fire (in *pyritēs lithos* stone that strikes fire, pyrites), fr. *pyr* fire — more at FIRE] **1** *obs* **:** a stone that may be used for striking fire **2 :** any of various metallic-looking sulfides of which pyrite is the commonest — usu. used with a qualifying term indicating the component metal ⟨copper ~⟩ ⟨tin ~⟩

pyrite yellow *also* **pyrite green** *n* **:** a dark grayish to dark yellow that is slightly lighter than sulphine yellow or bister green

py·rit·ic \(')pī¦rid·ik\ *also* **py·rit·i·cal** \-d·əkəl\ *adj* [*pyrite* + *-ic* or *-ical*] **:** of, relating to, or resembling pyrites ⟨~ ores⟩

pyritic smelting *n* **:** a process of smelting pyritic ores without previous roasting and with little or no fuel by utilizing the heat resulting from the combustion of their high sulfur content

py·rit·if·er·ous \¦pī,rīd·¦if(ə)rəs\ *adj* [*pyrit*es + *-iferous*] **:** containing or producing pyrites

py·rit·iza·tion \ˌpīrˌīd·əˈzāshən\ *n* -s [*pyritize* + *-ation*] **:** development of pyrite in a solid rock
py·rit·ize \ˈpīˌrīd·ˌīz\ *vt* -ED/-ING/-S [ISV *pyrite* + *-ize*] **:** to convert into pyrite **:** introduce pyrite into ⟨*pyritized* plant remains⟩
py·ri·to·he·dral \pəˈrīd·əˈhēdrəl, (ˌ)pīˈr- *sometimes chiefly Brit* -hed-\ *adj* [NL *pyritohedron* + E *-al*] **:** of, relating to, or consisting of pyritohedrons
py·ri·to·he·dron \-drən *sometimes* -ˌdrän\ *n, pl* **pyritohedrons** *or* **pyritohedra** [NL, fr. *pyrito-* (fr. ISV *pyrite*) + *-hedron*] **:** a pentagonal dodecahedron that is a hemihedral form of the isometric system of crystalline symmetry common to pyrite

pyritohedron

¹py·rit·oid \ˈpīˌrīd·ˌȯid\ *adj* [ISV *pyrite* + *-oid*] **:** like pyrite
²pyritoid \"\ *n* -s [*pyrite* + *-oid*] **:** PYRITOHEDRON
py·ri·tous \pəˈrīd·əs, (ˈ)pīˈr-\ *adj* [*pyrite* + *-ous*] **:** PYRITIC
py·ro \ˈpī(ˌ)rō\ *n* -s [by shortening] **1 :** PYROCELLULOSE **2 :** PYROGALLOL — used esp. in photography **3 :** PYROMANIAC
pyro- — see PYR-
pyro *abbr* pyrotechnic; pyrotechnics
py·ro·aurite \ˌpīrōˈȯˌrīt\ *n* -s [Sw *pyroaurit*, fr. *pyr-* + L *aurum* gold + Sw *-it* -ite; fr. its resemblance to gold after being heated — more at ORIOLE] **:** a mineral $Mg_6Fe_2(OH)_{16}CO_3.4H_2O$ that is a hydrous basic carbonate of magnesium and iron
py·ro·belonite \ˌpī(ˌ)rō+\ *n* [*pyr-* + *belonite*] **:** a mineral $MnPb(VO_4)(OH)$ consisting of a basic lead manganese vanadate occurring in brilliant red needle-shaped crystals (hardness 3.5, sp. gr. 5.4)
py·ro·bitumen \ˌpī(ˌ)rō+\ *n* [*pyr-* + *bitumen*] **:** ASPHALT
py·ro·bituminous \"+\ *adj* [*pyr-* + *bituminous*] **:** yielding bituminous products on heating **:** PYROGENOUS
py·ro·borate \"+\ *n* [*pyr-* + *borate*] **:** TETRABORATE
py·ro·boric acid \"+ . . .-\ *n* [*pyroboric* fr. *pyr-* + *boric*] **:** TETRABORIC ACID
py·ro·catechin \"+\ *n* [ISV *pyr-* + *catechin*] **:** PYROCATECHOL
py·ro·catechol \"+\ *n* [ISV *pyr-* + *catechol*] **:** a crystalline phenol $C_6H_4(OH)_2$ obtained by pyrolysis of catechin, resins, lignins, and other natural substances but usu. made synthetically (as by alkaline fusion of *ortho*-chlorophenol or *ortho*-phenolsulfonic acid) and used chiefly as a photographic developer, as a developer in fur dyeing, as an intermediate in organic synthesis, and as an analytical reagent; *ortho*-dihydroxy-benzene — called also *catechol*
py·ro·cat·e·chu·ic acid \ˌpīrōˌkad·əˈchü\|ik-, -əˈshü\|, -əˈkyü\|\ *n* [*pyrocatechuic* fr. *pyr-* + *catechu* + *-ic*] **:** a crystalline acid $C_6H_3(OH)_2COOH$ derived from pyrocatechol; 2,3-dihydroxy-benzoic acid
py·ro·cellulose \ˌpī(ˌ)rō+\ *n* [*pyr-* + *cellulose*] **:** cellulose nitrate that is of lower degree of nitration than guncotton and that is used in smokeless powders
py·ro·chemical \"+\ *adj* [*pyr-* + *chemical*] **:** relating to or involving chemical activity at high temperatures ⟨a ~ decomposition product⟩ — **py·ro·chemically** \"+\ *adv*
py·ro·chlore \ˈpīrəˌklō(ə)r\ *n* -s [G *pyrochlor*, fr. *pyr-* + Gk *chlōros* greenish yellow — more at YELLOW] **:** a brown or dark reddish mineral $NaCaCb_2O_6F$ that is isomorphous with microlite and is an oxide and fluoride of sodium, calcium, and columbium
py·rochro·ite \ˌpīrəˈkrōˌīt, pīˈräkrəˌwīt\ *n* -s [Sw *pyrochroit*, fr. *pyr-* + Gk *chrōs* color + Sw *-it* -ite; fr. the fact that it becomes colored when heated — more at CHROMATIC] **:** a mineral $Mn(OH)_2$ that is a natural manganous hydroxide
py·ro·cinchonic acid \ˌpī(ˌ)rō+ . . .-\ *n* [*pyrocinchonic* ISV *pyr-* + *cinchonic*] **:** an unstable dicarboxylic acid $C_4H_6(COOH)_2$ obtained usu. in the form of its crystalline anhydride by pyrolysis of cinchonic acid; dimethyl-maleic acid
py·ro·clast \ˈpīrōˌklast\ *n* -s [*pyr-* + *-clast*] **:** a fragment of detrital volcanic material that has been expelled aerially from a vent
¹py·ro·clas·tic \ˌ==ˈklastik\ *adj* [*pyr-* + *-clastic*] **:** formed by fragmentation as a result of volcanic or igneous action ⟨~ rocks⟩
²pyroclastic \"\ *n* -s **:** a volcanic rock composed of pyroclasts
py·ro·coll \ˈpīrōˌkäl\ *n* -s [ISV *pyr-* + *-coll*] **:** a crystalline tricyclic inner amide $C_{10}H_6N_2O_2$ obtained by the distillation of gelatin, glue, or leather scrap or by the dehydration of pyrrole-carboxylic acid with acetic anhydride
py·ro·collodion \ˌpī(ˌ)rō+\ *n* [*pyr-* + *collodion*] **:** pyroxylin containing a high percentage of nitrogen
py·ro·condensation \"+\ *n* [*pyr-* + *condensation*] **:** chemical condensation brought about by heat
py·ro·conductivity \"+\ *n* [*pyr-* + *conductivity*] **:** electrical conductivity induced by application of heat
py·ro·cotton \"+\ *n* [*pyr-* + *cotton*] **:** cellulose nitrate containing about 12.6 percent nitrogen and used in smokeless powders — compare PYROCELLULOSE
py·ro·crystalline \"+\ *adj* [*pyr-* + *crystalline*] **:** crystallized from a molten magma
¹py·ro·electric \"+\ *adj* [ISV, back-formation fr. *pyroelectricity*] **:** of, relating to, or exhibiting pyroelectricity
²pyroelectric \"\ *n* **:** a pyroelectric substance
py·ro·electricity \ˌpī(ˌ)rō+\ *n* [ISV *pyr-* + *electricity*] **1 :** electrification produced on various crystals by change of temperature **2 :** a branch of science that deals with the phenomenon of pyroelectricity
py·ro·gallate \"+\ *n* [*pyrogallic* + *-ate*] **:** a salt or ether of pyrogallol
py·ro·gallic acid \"+...-\ *n* [*pyrogallic* ISV *pyr-* + *gallic*: orig. formed as F *pyrogallique*] **:** PYROGALLOL
py·ro·gal·lol \ˌpīrōˈgaˌlȯl, -ˌlōl\ *n* -s [ISV *pyrogallic* + *-ol*] **:** a poisonous bitter crystalline phenol $C_6H_3(OH)_3$ with weak acid properties that is obtained usu. by pyrolysis of gallic acid with water and is used chiefly as a photographic developer, in alkaline solution as an absorbent for oxygen in gas analysis, in making dyes and in dyeing, and in medicine in treating skin diseases; 1,2,3-trihydroxy-benzene
py·ro·gen \ˈpīrəjən, -ˌjen\ *n* -s [ISV *pyr-* + *-gen*] **1 a** *obs* **:** an element (as sulfur or phosphorus) characterized by great flammability **b :** a substance produced by the action of heat **2 :** a fever-producing substance (as various thermostable products of bacterial metabolism)
py·ro·ge·na·tion \ˌpīrəjəˈnāshən\ *n* -s [ISV *pyrogen* + *-ation*] **:** subjection to heat ⟨~ of formic acid⟩
py·ro·genesis \ˌpīrō+\ *n* [NL, fr. *pyr-* + L *genesis*] **1 :** the production of heat **2 :** production of some product by the action of heat
py·ro·genetic \ˌpī(ˌ)rō+\ *adj* [ISV *pyr-* + *-genetic*] **:** of, relating to, or produced by pyrogenesis — **py·ro·genetically** \"+\ *adv*
py·ro·gen·ic \ˌpīrōˈjenik\ *adj* [ISV *pyr-* + *-genic*] **1 :** producing or produced by heat **2 a :** of igneous origin ⟨~ strata⟩ **b :** formed by the action of magmatic heat **3 :** producing or due to fever
py·ro·ge·nic·i·ty \ˌpīrōjəˈnisəd·ē\ *n* -ES [*pyrogenic* + *-ity*] **:** the quality or state of being pyrogenic; *esp* **:** capacity to produce fever
py·rog·e·nous \(ˈ)pīˈräjənəs\ *adj* [*pyr-* + *-genous*] **:** PYROGENIC
py·ro·glazer \"+\ *n* [*pyr-* + *glazer*] **:** one that hand paints on glass with ceramic colors that are later fused on in a kiln
py·ro·gno·mic \ˌpīrəˈnōmik, -rəgˈn-, -ˈnäm-\ *adj* [*pyr-* + Gk *gnōmon* knower, discerner, index + E *-ic* — more at GNOMON] **:** readily becoming incandescent when heated due to rapid exothermic recrystallization — used of metamict minerals (as gadolinite)
pyr·og·nos·tic \ˌpīrəgˈnästik\ *adj* [ISV *pyr-* + *-gnostic*] **:** relating to or developed by the use of heat esp. as applied by a blowpipe
py·rog·nos·tics \ˌ==ˈstiks\ *n pl but sing or pl in constr* **:** the characteristics (as the degree of fusibility or the flame coloration) of a mineral observed by the use of the blowpipe
¹py·ro·graph \ˈpīrəˌgraf, -ˌrȧf\ *vb* [back-formation fr. *pyrography*] *vi* **:** to employ or engage in pyrography ~ *vt* **:** to decorate by pyrography
²pyrograph \"\ *n* **:** a production of pyrography
py·rog·ra·pher \pīˈrägrəfə(r)\ *n* -s **:** one that pyrographs
py·ro·graph·ic \ˌpīrəˈgrafik\ *adj* [*pyr-* + *-graphic*] **1 :** of, relating to, or produced by pyrography **2 :** marked by fire or burning
py·rog·ra·phy \pīˈrägrəfē\ *n* -ES [ISV *pyr-* + *-graphy*] **1 :** the art or process of producing designs or pictures (as on wood or leather) by burning or scorching with hot instruments **2 :** ornamentation or a piece of ornamentation produced by pyrography
py·ro·gra·vure \ˌpīrōgrəˈvyu̇(ə)r\ *n* [ISV *pyr-* + *gravure*; prob. orig. formed in F] **:** PYROGRAPHY
py·ro·la \ˈpīrələ\ *n* [NL, prob. fr. L *pyrum*, *pirum* pear + *-ola* -ole] **1** *cap* **:** a genus (the type of the family Pyrolaceae) of short-stemmed perennial herbs that have basal persistent leaves and racemes of white, pink, or purple pentamerous flowers containing 10 straight or declined stamens and that are natives of temperate or cool regions — see FALSE WINTERGREEN, SHINLEAF, WINTERGREEN 1 **2** -s **:** any plant of the genus *Pyrola*
py·ro·la·ce·ae \ˌpīrəˈlāsēˌē\ *n pl, cap* [NL, fr. *Pyrola*, type genus + *-aceae*] **:** a family that comprises mostly evergreen herbs (order Ericales) of temperate regions with pentamerous regular flowers succeeded by loculicidal capsules and that is sometimes included in Ericaceae — **py·ro·la·ceous** \ˌ==ˈlāshəs\ *adj*
py·rol·a·ter \pīˈräləd·ə(r)\ *n* -s [*pyr-* + *-later*] **:** a fire worshiper
py·rol·a·try \-lə·trē\ *n* -ES [*pyr-* + *-latry*] **:** FIRE WORSHIP
py·ro·lig·ne·ous \ˌpīrōˈlignēəs\ *adj* [F *pyroligneux*, fr. *pyr-* + *ligneux* woody, fr. L *lignosus*, fr. *lign-* + *-osus* -ose] **:** obtained by destructive distillation of wood ⟨~ liquor⟩ — compare PYROLIGNEOUS ACID
pyroligneous acid *n* **:** an acid reddish brown aqueous liquid of empyreumatic odor obtained by destructive distillation of hardwood and containing chiefly acetic acid, methanol, wood oils, and tars
py·ro·lig·nic \-nik\ *adj* [*pyr-* + *lign-* + *-ic*] **:** PYROLIGNEOUS
py·ro·lig·nite \ˌ==ˈ=ˌnīt\ *n* [F, fr. *pyroligneux* + *-ite*] **:** a crude acetate produced by treating pyroligneous acid with a metal or basic compound
pyrolignite of iron **:** IRON LIQUOR
py·ro·lig·nous \ˌ==ˈ=nəs\ *adj* [F *pyroligneux*] **:** PYROLIGNEOUS
py·ro·luminescence \ˌpī(ˌ)rō+\ *n* [*pyr-* + *luminescence*] **:** the characteristic spectral radiation (as produced by vaporized salts in a flame) of a gas or vapor excited by high temperature
py·ro·lu·site \ˌpīrəˈlüˌsīt\ *n* -s [G *pyrolusit*, fr. *pyr-* + Gk *lousis* washing (fr. *louein* to wash) + G *-it* -ite; fr. its use as glass soap — more at LYE] **:** a mineral MnO_2 that is of an iron-black or dark steel-gray color and metallic luster usu. soft native manganese dioxide and is the most important ore of manganese — see GLASS SOAP
py·rol·y·sis \pīˈräləsə̇s\ *n* [NL, fr. *pyr-* + *-lysis*] **:** chemical decomposition or other chemical change brought about by the action of heat regardless of the temperature involved — compare CARBONIZATION, CRACKING, DESTRUCTIVE DISTILLATION, THERMAL CRACKING
py·ro·lyt·ic \ˌpīrəˈlid·ik\ *adj* [*pyr-* + *-lytic*] **:** of, relating to, or produced by means of pyrolysis — **py·ro·lyt·i·cal·ly** \-d·ək(ə)lē\ *adv*
py·rol·y·zate \pīˈräləˌzāt, -ˌzət\ *n* -s [*pyrolyze* + *-ate*] **:** a product formed during pyrolysis
py·ro·lyze \ˈpīrəˌlīz\ *vt* -ED/-ING/-S [*pyr-* + *-lyze*] **:** to subject to pyrolysis
py·ro·magnetic \ˌpī(ˌ)rō+\ *adj* [*pyr-* + *magnetic*] **:** THERMOMAGNETIC 1
py·ro·man·cy \ˈpīrōˌman(t)sē\ *n* -ES [ME *piromancie*, fr. MF *pyromancie*, fr. LL *pyromantia*, fr. Gk *pyromanteia*, fr. *pyr* fire + *manteia* divination — more at FIRE, -MANCY] **:** divination by means of fire or flames
py·ro·mania \ˌpīrō+\ *n* [NL, fr. *pyr-* + *mania*] **:** an irresistible impulse to start fires — **py·ro·maniac** \"+\ *n* — **py·ro·maniacal** \ˌpī(ˌ)rō+\ *adj*
py·ro·meconic acid \ˌpī(ˌ)rō + . . .-\ *n* [*pyromeconic* ISV *pyr-* + *meconic* (*acid*); orig. formed as F *pyroméconique*] **:** a crystalline acid $C_5H_4O_3$ formed by heating meconic acid or comenic acid; 3-hydroxy-4-pyrone
py·ro·mellitic acid \"+. . . -\ *n* [*pyromellitic* ISV *pyr-* + *mellitic*] **:** a crystalline acid $C_6H_2(COOH)_4$ that is formed by the distilling of mellitic acid; 1,2,4,5-benzene-tetracarboxylic acid
py·ro·metallurgical \"+\ *adj* [*pyrometallurgy* + *-ical*] **:** of or relating to pyrometallurgy
py·ro·metallurgy \"+\ *n* [ISV *pyr-* + *metallurgy*] **:** chemical metallurgy that depends on heat action (as roasting and smelting)
py·ro·metamorphic \"+\ *adj* [*pyrometamorphism* + *-ic*] **:** of, relating to, or produced by pyrometamorphism ⟨~ changes in sedimentary rock⟩
py·ro·metamorphism \"+\ *n* [*pyr-* + *metamorphism*] **:** change produced in rocks by the action of heat but without the action of pressure or mineralizers — compare DYNAMOMETAMORPHISM
py·ro·metasomatic \"+\ *adj* [*pyr-* + *metasomatic*] **:** of, relating to, or involving high temperature metamorphism that results in important changes in chemical composition ⟨~ magnetite deposits⟩
py·rom·e·ter \pīˈräməd·ə(r)\ *n* [ISV *pyr-* + *-meter*] **:** an instrument for measuring temperatures (as beyond the range of thermometers) usu. by the increase of electric resistance in a metal when heated, by the generation of electric current by a thermocouple when acted upon by direct heat or focused radiation, or by the increase in intensity of light radiated by an incandescent body as its temperature increases — see OPTICAL PYROMETER, RADIATION PYROMETER
py·ro·met·ric \ˌpīrəˈme·trik\ *also* **py·ro·met·ri·cal** \-·trə̇kəl\ *adj* [ISV *pyrometry* + *-ic*; prob. orig. formed as F *pyrométrique*] **:** of or relating to pyrometry; *also* **:** determined by a pyrometer **:** used in the measurement of high temperatures — **py·ro·met·ri·cal·ly** \-ə̇k(ə)lē\ *adv*
pyrometric cone *n* **:** any of a series of small cones of different substances that soften and arch over successively as the temperature rises, that together form a scale of fusing points and that are used in finding approximately the temperature (as of a kiln) — called also *Seger cone*
py·rom·e·try \pīˈrämə·trē\ *n* -ES [ISV *pyr-* + *-metry*] **:** the techniques and methods of measuring high temperatures; *esp* **:** the art of using a pyrometer
py·ro·mor·phi·dae \ˌpīrəˈmȯrfəˌdē\ *n pl, cap* [NL, fr. *Pyromorpha*, type genus (fr. *pyr-* + *-morpha*) + *-idae*] **:** a family of day-flying moths with smoky or translucent wings that are sometimes marked with metallic colors
py·ro·mor·phite \-ˌfīt\ *n* -s [G *pyromorphit*, fr. *pyr-* + *morph-* + *-it* -ite; fr. the crystalline appearance it assumes from being heated] **:** a mineral $Pb_5(PO_4)_3Cl$ consisting of a lead chloride and phosphate isomorphous with mimetite and vanadinite and occurring in green, yellow, brown, gray, or white crystals or masses — called also *green lead ore*
py·ro·mor·phous \ˌ==ˈ=fəs\ *adj* [*pyr-* + *-morphous*] **:** crystallizing from a molten state
py·ro·motor \ˌpīrə+\ *n* [*pyr-* + *motor*] **:** a motor driven directly by heat or heat waves
py·ro·mucic acid \"+. . . -\ *n* [*pyromucic* ISV *pyr-* + *mucic* (*acid*); orig. formed as F *pyromucique*] **:** alpha-furoic acid
py·rone \ˈpīˌrōn\ *n* -s [ISV *pyr-* + *-one*] **1 :** either of two isomeric carbonyl compounds $C_5H_4O_2$ derived from pyran: **a :** an oily liquid delta-lactone; *2H*-pyran-2-one — called also *alpha-pyrone, 2-pyrone*; compare COUMALIN, COUMARIN **b :** a hygroscopic crystalline compound; *4H*-pyran-4-one — called also *gamma-pyrone, 4-pyrone*; compare CHROMONE; STRUCTURAL FORMULA **2 :** a derivative of either of the pyrones

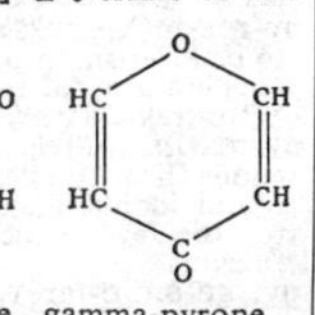

alpha-pyrone or 2-pyrone   gamma-pyrone or 4-pyrone

py·ro·ne·ma \ˌpīrəˈnēmə\ *n, cap* [NL, fr. *pyr-* + *-nema*] **:** a genus of saprophytic soil fungi (family Pezizaceae) that produce numerous small often bright pink apothecia which frequently form conspicuous masses on burned soil where brush heaps or logs have been fired
py·ro·nine \ˈpīrəˌnēn, -ˌnə̇n\ *n* -s [ISV *pyr-* + *-on* + *-ine*; orig. formed as G *pyronin*] **:** any of several basic xanthene dyes derived from diphenylmethane and used chiefly as biological stains
py·ro·ni·no·phil·ic \ˌpīrəˌnēnəˈfilik\ *adj* [*pyronine* + *-o-* + *-philic*] **:** staining selectively with pyronines
py·rope \ˈpīˌrōp\ *n* -s [ME *pirope*, fr. MF, fr. L *pyropus*, a red bronze, fr. Gk *pyrōpos*, lit., fiery-eyed, fr. *pyr-* + *ōp-*, *ōps* eye — more at EYE] **1** *obs* **:** a bright red gem (as a ruby or a carbuncle) **2 :** a magnesium-aluminum garnet that is deep red in color and is frequently used as a gem — compare CAPE RUBY
py·ro·pen \ˈpīrōˌpen\ *n* [*pyr-* + *pen*] **:** the heated stylus with which designs are burned in pyrography
py·roph·a·nite \pīˈräfəˌnīt\ *n* -s [G *pyrophanit*, fr. *pyr-* + *-phane* + *-it* -ite] **:** a mineral $MnTiO_3$ that is a manganese titanate isomorphous with geikielite and occurs in blood-red tabular rhombohedral crystals
py·roph·a·nous \(ˈ)pīˈräfənəs\ *adj* [*pyr-* + *-phane* + *-ous*] **:** becoming translucent or transparent when heated
py·ro·phile \ˈpīrōˌfīl\ *n* -s [*pyr-* + *-phile*] **:** one enthusiastic over fire or fireworks
py·roph·i·lous \(ˈ)pīˈräfələs\ *adj* [*pyr-* + *-philous*] **:** growing or thriving on burned or fired substrata ⟨~ fungi⟩ — compare PYRONEMA
py·ro·pho·bia \ˌpīrəˈfōbēə\ *n* [NL, fr. *pyr-* + *phobia*] **:** morbid dread of fire — **py·ro·phobic** \ˌ==ˈfōbik *also* -ˈfäb-\ *adj*
py·ro·phor·ic \ˌpīrəˈfȯrik\ *also* **py·roph·o·rous** \(ˈ)pīˈräfərəs\ *adj* [NL *pyrophorus* + E *-ic* or *-ous*] **:** igniting spontaneously ⟨finely divided ~ iron⟩
pyrophoric alloy *n* **:** an alloy (as ferrocerium) that has the property of emitting sparks when scratched or struck with steel and that is used in lighter flints
py·roph·o·rus \pīˈräfərəs\ *n* [NL, fr. Gk *pyrophoros* fire-bearing, fr. *pyr-* + *-phoros* -phorous] **1** *pl* **pyrophori :** any of several substances or mixtures (as a carbonized mixture of alum and sugar, or finely divided lead or iron) that ignite spontaneously on exposure to air **2** *cap* **:** a genus of large tropical American beetles (family Elateridae) bearing a pair of large luminous organs on the prothorax — see FIRE BEETLE
py·ro·phos·pha·tase \ˌpīrōˈfäsfəˌtās, -āz\ *n* [ISV *pyrophosphate* + *-ase*] **:** an enzyme that catalyzes the hydrolysis of a pyrophosphate to form orthophosphate — compare PHOSPHATASE
py·ro·phosphate \ˌpīrō+\ *n* [ISV *pyrophosphoric* (in *pyrophosphoric acid*) + *-ate*] **:** a salt or ester of pyrophosphoric acid — called also *diphosphate* — **py·ro·phosphatic** \"+\ *adj*
py·ro·phosphoric acid \"+. . . -\ *n* [*pyrophosphoric* ISV *pyr-* + *phosphoric*] **:** a crystalline acid $H_4P_2O_7$ that is formed when orthophosphoric acid is heated and is prepared in the form of salts by heating acid salts of orthophosphoric acid and that dissociates above its melting point into orthophosphoric acid and polyphosphoric acids — called also *diphosphoric acid*
py·ro·photography \ˌpī(ˌ)rō+\ *n* [*pyr-* + *photography*] **:** a process combining the use of photography and heat (as in producing fired-on pictures on porcelain)
py·ro·photometer \"+\ *n* [*pyr-* + *photometer*] **:** an optical pyrometer in which light from an incandescent body whose temperature is to be measured is passed through ruby glass and the red rays thus isolated are compared with those similarly received from a standard flame — compare PYROMETER
py·rophyl·lite \ˌpīrōˈfiˌlīt, pīˈräfə,l-\ *n* -s [G *pyrophyllit*, fr. *pyr-* + *phyll-* + *-it* -ite] **:** a mineral $AlSi_2O_5(OH)$ that is a usu. white or greenish hydrous aluminum silicate, resembles talc, and occurs in a foliated form or in compact masses — compare AGALMATOLITE
py·ro·phyte \ˈpīrōˌfīt\ *n* -s [*pyr-* + *-phyte*] **:** a woody plant with unusual resistance to fire because of exceptionally thick bark
py·ro·phy·tic \ˌ==ˈfid·ik\ *adj* [*pyrophyte* + *-ic*] **:** of, relating to, or made up of pyrophytes
pyropus *n, pl* **pyropi** [L, a red bronze — more at PYROPE] *obs* **:** PYROPE
py·ro·racemic acid \ˌpī(ˌ)rō + . . . -\ *n* [ISV *pyr-* + *racemic*] **:** PYRUVIC ACID
pyros *pl of* PYRO
py·ro·scope \ˈpīrəˌskōp\ *n* [*pyr-* + *-scope*] **:** any of various devices (as a pyrometric cone or an optical pyrometer) for determining the temperature of a furnace or kiln
py·ro·sis \pīˈrōsə̇s\ *n* -ES [NL, fr. Gk *pyrōsis* burning, inflammation, fr. *pyroun* to burn, fr. *pyr* fire — more at FIRE] **:** HEARTBURN
py·ros·ma·lite \pīˈräzməˌlīt\ *n* -s [G *pyrosmalit*, fr. *pyr-* + *osma-* (fr. Gk *osmē* odor) + *-lit* -lite; fr. the odor it gives off before the blowpipe — more at ODOR] **:** a mineral $(Mn,Fe)_4Si_3O_7(OH,Cl)_6$ consisting of a pale-brown, gray, or grayish green chiefly basic iron manganese silicate
¹py·ro·so·ma \ˌpīrəˈsōmə\ *n, cap* [NL, fr. *pyr-* + *-soma*] **:** a genus (coextensive with the family Pyrosomatidae of the order Ascidiacea) of chiefly tropical free-swimming brilliantly bioluminescent pelagic compound tunicates whose colony forms a hollow cylinder that is closed at one end and is often several feet long
²pyrosoma \"\ [NL, fr. *pyr-* + *-soma*] *syn of* BABESIA
py·ro·some \ˈ==ˌsōm\ *n* -s [NL *Pyrosoma*] **:** an ascidian of the genus *Pyrosoma*
py·ro·sphere \-ˌsfi(ə)r\ *n* [ISV *pyr-* + *sphere*] **1 :** the hot central portion of the earth **2 :** a hypothetical spherical zone of molten magma that is held to intervene between the crust of the earth and a solid nucleus and to supply lava to volcanoes
py·ro·stat \-ˌstat\ *n* -s [ISV *pyr-* + *-stat*] **1 :** any of various automatic devices that when exposed to heat, light, smoke, or some other manifestation of fire actuate a mechanism for giving a warning or for setting in operation a means of extinguishing such a fire — compare THERMOSTAT **2 :** THERMOSTAT; *esp* **:** one for use with high temperatures
py·ro·ste·gia \ˌpīrōˈstēj(ē)ə\ *n* -s [NL, fr. *pyr-* + *steg-* + *-ia*] **:** FLAME VINE
py·ro·stilp·nite \-tilp,nīt\ *n* -s [*pyr-* + Gk *stilpnos* glistening + *-ite* — more at STILBUM] **:** a mineral Ag_3SbS_3 that is a silver antimony sulfide polymorphous with pyrargyrite and occurs in tufts of hyacinth-red monoclinic crystals
py·ro·sulfate \ˌpī(ˌ)rō+\ *n* [ISV *pyrosulfuric* (in *pyrosulfuric acid*) + *-ate*] **:** a salt of pyrosulfuric acid — called also *disulfate*
py·ro·sulfite \"+\ *n* [ISV *pyr-* + *sulfite*] **:** METABISULFITE — used in the nomenclature adopted by the International Union of Pure and Applied Chemistry
py·ro·sulfuric acid \"+ . . .-\ *n* [ISV *pyr-* + *sulfuric*] **:** an unstable, crystalline acid $H_2S_2O_7$ that is usu. handled commercially as a thick oily fuming liquid, that is formed by the union of sulfur trioxide with sulfuric acid, that is a chief component of fuming sulfuric acid, and that is converted to sulfuric acid when mixed with water — called also *disulfuric acid*; compare OLEUM
py·ro·sulfuryl \"+\ *n* [ISV *pyrosulfuric* + *-yl*] **:** the bivalent radical, S_2O_5, of pyrosulfuric acid
py·ro·tartaric acid \"+ . . . -\ *n* [ISV *pyr-* + *tartaric*; orig. formed as F *pyrotartarique*] **:** a crystalline acid $HOOCCH_2CH(CH_3)COOH$ obtained by pyrolysis of tartaric acid or pyruvic acid and occurring in dextro, levo, and racemic forms; methyl-succinic acid
¹py·ro·tech·nic \ˌpīrəˈteknik, -rōˈt-, -nēk\ *also* **py·ro·tech·ni·cal** \-nə̇kəl, -nēk-\ *adj* [F *pyrotechnique* prob. fr. F *pyrotechnie*, fr. *pyrotechny* + *-ique* -ic; *pyrotechnical* fr. *pyrotechny* + *-ical*] **:** of or relating to pyrotechnics ⟨~ smokes⟩ — **py·ro·tech·ni·cal·ly** \-nə̇k(ə)lē, -nēk-, -li\ *adv*
²pyrotechnic \"\ *n* -s **1 pyrotechnics** *pl but sing or pl in constr* **:** the art of making or the manufacture and use of fireworks (as for display, military signaling, or illumination) **:** PYROTECHNY **2 pyrotechnics** *pl* **a :** materials (as fireworks, powders, and ammunition) for flares or signals **b :** a display of fireworks **3 :** a spectacular and usu. highly emotional display (as of oratory, rhetoric, anger, wit, or extreme virtuosity) ⟨pages of glittering ~ —Gamaliel Bradford⟩ — usu. used in pl.

py·ro·tech·ni·cian \\,==·ˈnishən\\ *n* [*pyrotechnic* + *-an*] : PYROTECHNIST

py·ro·tech·nist \\ˈ==ˈ=,nəst\\ *n* -s [*pyrotechny* + *-ist*] : one skilled in or given to pyrotechnics; *esp* : a manufacturer or an expert in the use and handling of fireworks

py·ro·tech·ny \\ˈ==,=nē, -ni\\ *n* -ES [MF *pyrotechnie*, fr. *pyr-* + Gk *technē* art, skill + MF *-ie* -y — more at TECHNICAL] **1** *archaic* : the use and application of fire in science and the arts **2** : PYROTECHNIC 1

py·ro·terebic acid \\ˌpī(,)rō + . . . -\\ *n* [ISV *pyr-* + *terebic*] : a liquid unsaturated acid $(CH_3)_2C{=}CHCH_2COOH$ obtained by pyrolysis of terebic acid; 4-methyl-3-penten-oic acid

py·ro·the·ria \\,pīrōˈthirēə\\ *n pl, cap* [NL, *pyr-* + *-theria*] : an order of Paenungulata or in some classifications a suborder of Ungulata comprising large So. American ungulates of Lower Tertiary age that have incisors like tusks and the cheek teeth all much alike and having two parallel transverse ridges

py·ro·toxin \\ˈpīrō+\\ *n* [ISV *pyr-* + *toxin*] : a toxin (as various bacterial endotoxins) that is capable of inducing fever

py·ro·tri·tar·ic acid \\ˈpīrōˈtrīˈtarik-\\ *also* **py·ro·tri·tar·tar·ic acid** *n* \\-ī,tärˈtarik-\\ [*pyrotritaric* ISV *pyr-* + *tri-* + *tartaric*; *pyrotritartaric* fr. *pyr-* + *tri-* + *tartaric*] : a crystalline acid $(C_6H_7O)COOH$ formed esp. by heating tartaric acid; 2,5-dimethyl-3-furoic acid

py·rox·ene \\pīˈräk,sēn, pəˈr-\\ *n* -s [F *pyroxène*, fr. *pyr-* + *-xène* -xene; prob. fr. the mistaken belief that it was alien to igneous rocks] **1** : a mineral of the pyroxene group usu. occurring in monoclinic short thick prismatic crystals or in square cross section or massive, often laminated, varying in color from white to dark green or black or rarely blue, and constituting a common constituent of igneous rocks (hardness 5–6, sp. gr. 3.2–3.6) **2** : a member of the pyroxene group

pyroxene group *n* : a group of silicate minerals closely related in crystal form and having the general formula $ABSi_2O_6$ where A represents usu. Ca or Na and B is usu. Mg, Fe, or Al that includes the orthorhombic species enstatite and hypersthene and several monoclinic species (as diopside, spodumene, jadeite, acmite, and augite)

py·rox·en·ic \\ˌpī,räkˈsenik\\ *adj* [ISV *pyroxene* + *-ic*] : relating to, containing, or composed of pyroxene

py·rox·e·nite \\pīˈräksə,nīt, pəˈr-\\ *n* -s [ISV *pyroxene* + *-ite*] : an igneous rock that is free from olivine, is composed essentially of pyroxene, and occurs in numerous varieties — **py·rox·e·nit·ic** \\(ˌ)=ˌ==ˈnidik\\ *adj*

py·rox·man·gite \\,pī,räkˈsman,gīt\\ *n* -s [ISV *pyroxene* + *mangan-* + *-ite*] : a rhodonite containing about 20 percent of manganese

py·roxy·lin \\pīˈräksələn, pəˈr-\\ *also* **py·roxy·line** \\", -,lēn\\ *n* -s [ISV *pyr-* + *xyl-* + *-in* or *-ine*; orig. formed as F *pyroxyline*] **1** : a substance that consists of lower-nitrated cellulose nitrate, usu. contains less than 12.5 percent nitrogen, is soluble in alcohol, a mixture of ether and alcohol, or other organic solvents, is flammable but less explosive than guncotton, and is used chiefly in making plastics (as celluloid), lacquers and other coatings, photographic films, and cements — called also *collodion cotton, soluble guncotton, soluble nitrocellulose* **2** : a product containing pyroxylin ⟨*pyroxylin*-coated fabric⟩

pyrrh- or **pyrrho-** *also* **pyrro-** *comb form* [Gk *pyrrh-*, *pyrrho-*, fr. *pyrrhos* red, tawny, fr. *pyr* fire — more at FIRE] : red : tawny ⟨*pyrrh*ite⟩ ⟨*pyrrho*tite⟩

[1]**pyr·rhic** \\ˈpirik, -rēk\\ *n* -s [L *pyrrhicha*, fr. Gk *pyrrhichē*] : an ancient Greek martial dance in quick time performed to the accompaniment of the flute

[2]**pyrrhic** \\"\\ *adj* [L *pyrrhichius*, fr. Gk *pyrrhichios*, fr. *pyrrhichē* pyrrhic dance] : of, belonging to, or constituting the pyrrhic dance

[3]**pyrrhic** \\"\\ *n* -s [L (*pes*) *pyrrhichius*, fr. Gk (*pous*) *pyrrhichios* pyrrhic foot] : a foot in prosody consisting of two short or unaccented syllables

[4]**pyrrhic** \\"\\ *adj* : of or relating to a pyrrhic : composed of pyrrhics ⟨~ verse⟩

[5]**pyrrhic** \\"\\ *adj, usu cap* [*Pyrrhus* †272 B.C. king of Epirus who sustained heavy losses in defeating the Romans at Asculum in Apulia in 279 B.C. (fr. L, fr. Gk *Pyrrhos*) + E *-ic*] : of, relating to, or resembling that of Pyrrhus

pyr·rhich·i·us \\pəˈrikēəs\\ *n* -ES [L] : [3]PYRRHIC

pyrrhic victory *n, usu cap P* [[5]*pyrrhic*] : a victory won at excessive cost ⟨would be a *Pyrrhic victory* sentencing the human race to ignorance, stagnation, and decadence —K.B.Clark⟩

pyr·rhite \\ˈpi,rīt\\ *n* -s [G *pyrrhit*, fr. *pyrrh-* + *-it* -ite] : PYROCHLORE

pyr·rhoc·o·rid \\pəˈräkərəd\\ *adj* [NL *Pyrrhocoridae*] : of or relating to the Pyrrhocoridae

[2]**pyrrhocorid** \\"\\ *n* -s : a bug of the family Pyrrhocoridae

pyr·rho·cor·i·dae \\,pirəˈkȯrə,dē\\ *n pl, cap* [NL, fr. *Pyrrhocoris*, type genus (fr. *pyrrh-* + Gk *koris* bedbug) + *-idae* — more at COREIDAE] : a family of moderately large often brightly colored bugs comprising the firebugs, having four-jointed beak and antennae and no ocelli, and sucking the juices of plants — compare COTTON STAINER, DYSDERCUS

[1]**pyr·rho·ni·an** \\pəˈrōnēən\\ *also* **pyr·rhon·ic** \\-ˈränik\\ *n* -s *usu cap* [*pyrrhonian* fr. L *pyrrhoneus*, n., pyrrhonian (fr. *pyrrhon-*, *Pyrrho fl* 4th cent. B.C. Greek philosopher) + E *-an*; *pyrrhonic* fr. L *pyrrhoneus* + E *-ic*] : PYRRHONIST

[2]**pyrrhonian** \\"\\ *also* **pyrrhonic** \\"\\ *adj, usu cap* [*pyrrhonian* fr. L *pyrrhoneus*, adj., pyrrhonian + E *-an*; *pyrrhonic* fr. L *pyrrhoneus* + E *-ic*] : of or relating to Pyrrho or Pyrrhonism : SKEPTICAL

pyr·rho·nism \\ˈpirə,nizəm\\ *n* -s *usu cap* [F *pyrrhonisme*, fr. *Pyrrhon* Pyrrho (fr. Gk *Pyrrhōn*) + *-isme* -ism] **1** : the doctrines of the founder of a school of skeptics in Greece (about 365–275 B.C.) who taught that all perceptions are of doubtful validity, that the external circumstances of life are therefore unimportant to the wise man, and that he should consequently always preserve tranquillity of mind **2** : skepticism esp. when total or radical

pyr·rho·nist \\ˈpirənəst\\ *n, usu cap* [L *pyrrhoneus* pyrrhonian (fr. *pyrrhon-*, *Pyrrho* 4th cent. B.C. Greek philosopher, fr. Gk *Pyrrhōn*) + E *-ist*] **1** : a follower of Pyrrho or an adherent of Pyrrhonism **2** : SKEPTIC

pyr·rho·tism \\ˈpirə,tizəm\\ *n* -s [Gk *pyrrhotēs* redness (fr. *pyrrhos* red) + E *-ism* — more at PYRRH-] : the condition or characteristic of having red hair

pyr·rho·tite \\-,tīt\\ *also* **pyr·rho·tine** \\-,tēn, -,tən\\ *n* -s [*pyrrhotite* alter. (influenced by *-ite*) of *pyrrhotine*; *pyrrhotine* fr. G *pyrrhotin*, fr. Gk *pyrrhotēs* redness + G *-in* -ine] : a bronze-colored mineral FeS of metallic luster consisting of ferrous sulfide usu. with a slight deficiency of iron, attracted by the magnet, and sometimes found in hexagonal crystals but usu. massive (hardness 3.5–4.5, sp.gr., 4.58–4.64) — called also *magnetic pyrites*

pyr·rhu·loxia \\ˈpir(y)ə+\\ *n* [NL, fr. *Pyrrhula*, genus of finches (fr. Gk *pyrrhoulas*, a red-colored bird, perh. the bullfinch, fr. *pyrrhos* red) + *Loxia*] **1** *cap* : a genus of large showy finches related to the cardinal, having short thick bills, a prominent crest, and gray and red plumage, and nesting through much of Mexico north to Texas **2** -s : any bird of the genus *Pyrrhuloxia*

pyrro- — see PYRRH-

pyrrol- or **pyrrolo-** *comb form* [fr. *pyrrole*] : pyrrole ⟨*pyrrol*idine⟩ ⟨*pyrrolo*pyridine⟩

pyr·role \\ˈpi,rōl, -,rȯl, pəˈr-\\ *n* -s [*pyrrh-* + *-ole*] **1** : a colorless toxic liquid heterocyclic compound C_4H_5N that contains four carbon atoms and one nitrogen atom in the ring, that has an odor suggestive of chloroform, that darkens in air and forms red polymers in the presence of acids, that is obtained by distillation of coal tar or bone oil or by synthesis (as by reaction of ammonia with furan over alumina), and that is the parent of many natural compounds (as the bile pigments, porphyrins, heme, chlorophyll, indigo, a few amino acids, and a few alkaloids) — compare INDOLE, STRUCTURAL FORMULA **2** : a derivative of pyrrole; *esp* : a homologue of pyrrole (as cryptopyrrole or hemopyrrole) —

pyrrole

pyr·rol·ic \\(ˈ)piˈrōlik, pəˈr-, -ˈräl-\\ *adj*

pyr·rol·idine \\pəˈrōlə,dēn, -ˈräl-, -,dən\\ *n* -s [ISV *pyrrol-* + *-idine*] : a flammable fuming liquid heterocyclic secondary amine C_4H_9N obtained from pyrrole by reduction and also prepared synthetically; *tetrahydro-pyrrole*

pyr·rol·idone \\-dōn\\ *n* -s [ISV *pyrrolidine* + *-one*] : a crystalline or liquid lactam C_4H_7NO made by a series of steps using acetylene, formaldehyde, and ammonia and used chiefly in making polyvinylpyrrolidone; 2-pyrrolidin-one — called also *2-pyrrolidone*

pyr·rol·idyl \\-(,)dil, -,dᵊl\\ *or* **pyr·rol·idin·yl** \\=ˌ==ˈdenᵊl\\ *n* -s [*pyrrolidine* + *-yl*] : any of three univalent radicals C_4H_8N derived from pyrrolidine by removal of one hydrogen atom

pyr·ro·line \\ˈpirə,lēn, -,lən\\ *n* -s [ISV *pyrrol-* + *-ine*] : either of two bases C_4H_7N intermediate between pyrrolidine and pyrrole; dihydro-pyrrole; *esp* : a fuming liquid obtained by reduction of pyrrole: 2,5-dihydro-pyrrole

pyr·roph·y·ta \\pəˈräfəd·ə\\ *n pl, cap* [NL, fr. *pyrrh-* + *-phyta*] : a division or other category of lower plants comprising yellowish-green to golden-brown algae that are mostly unicellular and biflagellate, that form starch, starchy compounds, or oil as food reserves, and that include the dinoflagellates and cryptomonads

pyr·ro·porphyrin \\ˈpi(,)rō+\\ *n* [ISV *pyrrh-* + *porphyrin*] : a dark red crystalline pigment $C_{32}H_{36}N_4O_2$ with a violet metallic luster that is the lower homologue of phylloporphyrin and that differs from most porphyrins in being a hepta-substituted derivative of porphin rather than an octa-substituted one

pyr·ryl \\ˈpirəl\\ *or* **pyr·ro·lyl** \\-rə,lil\\ *n* -s [ISV *pyrrole* + *-yl*] : any of three univalent radicals C_4H_4N derived from pyrrole by removal of one hydrogen atom

pyr·u·la \\ˈpir(y)ələ\\ [NL, fr. L *pyrum*, *pirum* pear + *-ula* -ule] *syn of* FICUS

pyr·u·lar·ia \\,==ˈla(a)rēə\\ *n, cap* [NL, prob. fr. L *pyrum*, *pirum* pear + *-ula* + NL *-aria*] : a small genus of chiefly Asiatic parasitic or half-parasitic shrubs (family Santalaceae) having alternate deciduous leaves, small green racemose apetalous flowers, and pear-shaped drupes with oily seeds — see RABBITWOOD

py·rus \\ˈpīrəs\\ *n, cap* [NL, fr. L *pyrus*, *pirus* pear-tree; akin to L *pyrum*, *pirum* pear — more at PEAR] : a genus of trees (family Rosaceae) native to the Old World that are distinguished by leaves which are mostly glabrous, hard and glossy at maturity, and involute in the bud but which have seven or all the flower stalks in each cluster arising from a stout central column, by styles usu. separate at the base, and by fruit with abundant grit cells — compare MALUS; see PEAR

pyruv- or **pyruvo-** *comb form* [ISV *pyruvic*] : pyruvic acid ⟨*pyruv*ate⟩ ⟨*pyruv*yl⟩

pyr·uv·aldehyde \\ˌpī,rüv, ˈpi,rüv, ˈpir,yüv+\\ *n* [*pyruv-* + *aldehyde*] : a yellow pungent volatile oil CH_3COCHO that polymerizes readily and is formed as an intermediate in the metabolism or fermentation of carbohydrates and lactic acid — called also *methylglyoxal, pyruvic aldehyde*

pyr·u·vate \\pīˈrü,vāt, pəˈrü-, pirˈyü-\\ *n* -s [*pyruv-* + *-ate*] : a salt or ester of pyruvic acid

pyr·u·vic acid \\(ˈ)=ˈ=vik-\\ *n* [*pyruvic* ISV *pyr-* + *uv-* (fr. L *uva* grape) + ISV *-ic* — more at UVULA] : a liquid keto acid CH_3COCO_2H that has an odor like acetic acid, that is obtained by the dry distillation of racemic or tartaric acid or by mild oxidation of lactic acid, and that is an important intermediate in metabolism and fermentation; acetyl-formic acid — see PHOSPHOPYRUVIC ACID

pyr·u·vo·yl \\=ˈ=vō,wil\\ *or* **pyr·u·vyl** \\-vəl\\ *n* -s [ISV *pyruv-* + *-yl*] : the univalent radical $CH_3COCO–$ of pyruvic acid

py·ryl·i·um \\pīˈrilēəm\\ *n* -s [NL, irreg. fr. ISV *pyran*] : a univalent ion $C_5H_5O^+$ of the oxonium type that is related to pyran

[1]**py·thag·o·re·an** \\pə,thagəˈrēən, (,)pī,th-, -thaig-\\ *n* -s *usu cap* [L *pythagoreus* Pythagorean (fr. Gk *pythagoreios*, fr. *Pythagoras*, 6th cent. B.C. Greek philosopher and mathematician) + E *-an*] **1** : a follower of Pythagoras **2** : a member of a school of philosophers and secret society named after Pythagoras and maintaining its organization in southern Italy until the middle of the 4th century B.C.

[2]**pythagorean** \\(ˈ)=ˈ==ˈ==\\ *adj, usu cap* : of or relating to the Greek philosopher Pythagoras, his philosophy, or the Pythagoreans

pythagorean comma *n, usu cap P* : DITONIC COMMA

py·thag·o·re·an·ism \\(,)=,==ˈə,nizəm\\ *n* -s *usu cap* [*pythagorean* + *-ism*] : the doctrines and theories of Pythagoras and the Pythagoreans who developed some basic principles of mathematics and astronomy, originated the doctrine of the harmony of the spheres, and believed in a theory of metempsychosis, the eternal recurrence of things, and a number mysticism

pythagorean scale *n, usu cap P* : a musical scale with its intervals regulated by mathematical ratios rather than by consonances

pythagorean semitone *n, usu cap P* : LIMMA 2

pythagorean theorem *n, usu cap P* : a theorem in geometry: the square of the length of the hypotenuse of a right triangle equals the sum of the squares of the lengths of the other two sides

pyth·a·gor·ic \\ˌpithəˈgȯrik\\ *also* **pyth·a·gor·i·cal** \\-rəkəl\\ *adj, usu cap* [L *pythagoricus*, fr. Gk *pythagorikos*, fr. *Pythagoras*, 6th cent. B.C. Greek philosopher and mathematician + Gk *-ikos* -ic] : PYTHAGOREAN

py·thag·o·ri·cian \\pə,thagəˈrishən, (,)pī,th-\\ *n* -s *usu cap* [*pythagoric* + *-an*] *archaic* : PYTHAGOREAN

py·thag·o·rism \\=ˈ==,rizəm\\ *n* -s *usu cap* [Gk *pythagorismos*, fr. *pythagorizein* to be a follower of Pythagoras] : PYTHAGOREANISM

py·thag·o·rist \\-,rəst\\ *n* -s *usu cap* [Gk *pythagoristēs*, fr. *pythagorizein* to be a follower of Pythagoras] : PYTHAGOREAN

py·thag·o·rize \\-,rīz\\ *vi* -ED/-ING/-S *usu cap* [Gk *pythagorizein* to be a follower of Pythagoras, fr. *Pythagoras*, 6th cent. B.C. Greek philosopher and mathematician + Gk *-izein* -ize] : to philosophize in the manner of the Pythagoreans

pyth·i·a·ce·ae \\,pithēˈāsē,ē\\ *n pl, cap* [NL, fr. *Pythium*, type genus + *-aceae*] : a family of fungi (order Peronosporales) having sporangia usu. borne successively and singly at the tips of branching sporangiophores which differ little if any from assimilative hyphae — see PHYTOPHTHORA, PYTHIUM — **pyth·i·a·ceous** \\=ˌ==ˈāshəs\\ *adj*

pyth·i·a·cys·tis \\,pithēəˈsistəs\\ *n, cap* [NL, fr. *pythia-* (fr. *Pythium*) + *-cystis*] *in former classifications* : a genus of fungi (family Pythiaceae) comprising a single species (*P. citrophthora*) that causes brown rot of citrus fruits and gummosis of citrus and other fruits and is now usu. included in *Phytophthora*

pyth·i·ad \\ˈpithē,ad\\ *n* -s *usu cap* [Gk *Pythia*, the Pythian games (fr. *Pythō* Pytho, early name of the town of Delphi in southern Greece where the Pythian games were held + Gk *-ia* -y) + E *-ad*] : the four-year period between celebrations of the Pythian games in ancient Greece

pyth·iam·bic \\,pithēˈambik, -,thīˈa-\\ *n* -s *usu cap* [NL *pythiambicus*, fr. L *pythius* pythian + *iambicus* iambic — more at IAMBIC] : an epodic distich in Greek and Latin prosody composed of a Pythian verse and an iambic dimeter or trimeter

[1]**pyth·i·an** \\ˈpithēən\\ *n* -s *usu cap* [L *pythius*, adj., pythian (fr. Gk *pythios*, fr. *Pythō* Pytho, Delphi) + E *-an*] **1** : a native or inhabitant of Delphi **2 a** : a priestess of Apollo at Delphi **b** : one who is phrenetic

[2]**pythian** \\"\\ *adj, usu cap* [L *pythius* pythian + E *-an*] **1 a** : of or relating to the ancient Greek god Apollo esp. as patron deity of Delphi **b** : being or relating to games celebrated at Delphi every four years in the third year of the Olympiad about the middle of August and forming one of the four great Panhellenic festivals **2** : like a Pythian priestess : PHRENETIC

pythian verse *n, usu cap P* : dactylic hexameter

pyth·ic \\ˈpithik\\ *adj, usu cap* [L *pythicus*, fr. Gk *pythikos*, fr. *Pythō* + Gk *-ikos* -ic] : PYTHIAN

pyth·i·um \\ˈpithēəm\\ *n* [NL, fr. Gk *pythein* to cause to rot + NL *-ium* — more at FOUL] **1** *cap* : a genus of destructive root-parasitic fungi (family Pythiaceae) having filamentous sporangia, smooth-walled spherical oogonia, and stalked antheridia and including forms (as *P. debaryanum*) that cause damping-off **2** -s : any fungus of the genus *Pythium* ⟨~ root necrosis⟩

pytho·gen·ic \\ˌpīthəˈjenik, ˈpith-\\ *adj* [*pytho-* (fr. Gk *pythein* to cause to rot) + *-genic*] : produced by or originating from decomposition or filth ⟨typhoid has been considered a ~ fever⟩

py·thon \\ˈpī,thän, -,thən\\ *n* [L *Python*, monstrous serpent that dwelt in the caves of Mount Parnassus near Delphi and that was killed there by Apollo, fr. Gk *Pythōn*] **1** -s : a large constricting snake (as a boa or anaconda) **2** *cap* [NL, fr. L *Python*] : a genus of large nonvenomous snakes of the family Boidae that includes the largest of recent snakes — see CARPET SNAKE, INDIAN PYTHON, RETICULATED PYTHON, ROCK PYTHON

pytho·ness \\ˈpīthənəs, ˈpith-\\ *n* -ES [ME *Phitonesse*, fr. MF *phitonise*, *pithonisse*, fr. LL *pythonissa*, fr. Gk *Pythōn* spirit of divination, fr. *Pythō* Delphi, where the Delphic oracle was located + LL *-issa* -ess] **1** : a woman believed to have a spirit of divination **2** : a priestess of Apollo held to have prophetic powers

py·thon·ic \\(ˈ)pīˈthänik, *in sense 1* " *or* pəˈth-\\ *also* **py·thon·i·cal** \\-nəkəl\\ *adj* [*pythonic* fr. LL *pythonicus*, fr. Gk *Pythōn* spirit of divination + L *-icus* -ic; *pythonical* fr. LL *pythonicus* + E *-al*] **1 a** : of, relating to, or like a Pythian priestess or other pythoness **b** : pretending to foretell events : ORACULAR **2** [*Python*, monstrous serpent killed by Apollo near Delphi (fr. L) + E *-ic*] **a** : of, relating to, or like a python **b** : HUGE, MONSTROUS

py·tho·nid \\ˈpīthənəd, -,nid\\ *n* -s [NL *Pythonidae*] : a snake of the family Pythonidae; *broadly* : PYTHON 1

py·thon·i·dae \\pīˈthänə,dē\\ *n pl, cap* [NL, fr. *Python*, type genus + *-idae*] *in some classifications* : a family comprising nonvenomous snakes closely related to the boas but having a supraorbital bone and usu. teeth on the premaxilla and the subcaudal scales mostly in two rows, including *Python* and closely related genera, and being now usu. treated as a subfamily of Boidae

py·tho·nine \\ˈpīthə,nīn\\ *adj* [NL *Python* + E *-ine*] : of or relating to the genus *Python* or the family Pythonidae

pytho·nism \\ˈpīthə,nizəm, ˈpith-\\ *n* -s [LL *python-*, *pytho* pythonic spirit (fr. Gk *Pythōn* spirit of divination) + E *-ism*] **1** : possession by or intercourse with a pythonic deity or spirit **2** : the art and practice of prophecy or divination

pytho·nis·sa \\,==ˈnisə\\ *n* -s *usu cap* [LL] *archaic* : PYTHONESS

pytho·nist \\ˈ==,nəst\\ *n* -s [LL *python-*, *pytho* pythonic spirit + E *-ist*] : a person who professes to prophesy through some divine or esoteric inspiration : SOOTHSAYER

py·tho·noid \\ˈpīthə,nȯid\\ *adj* [F *pythonoïde*, fr. *python* (fr. L *Python*, monstrous serpent killed by Apollo) + *-oïde* -oid] : like a python

[1]**py·thono·morph** \\pīˈthänə,mȯrf, ˈpīthən-\\ *or* **py·thono·mor·phic** \\(ˌ)=ˌ==ˈmȯrfik, ˈ=(,)==+\\ *also* **py·thono·mor·phous** \\-fəs\\ *adj* [*pythonomorph* fr. NL *Pythonomorpha*; *pythonomorphic*, *pythonomorphous* fr. NL *Pythonomorpha* + E *-ic* or *-ous*] : of or relating to the Pythonomorpha

[2]**pythonomorph** \\"\\ *n* -s : a pythonomorph reptile or fossil

py·thono·mor·pha \\,pī,thänəˈmȯrfə, ,pīthən-\\ *n pl, cap* [NL, fr. L *Python*, monstrous serpent killed by Apollo + NL *-morpha*] *in some classifications* : a suborder of Squamata or other group of large marine reptiles of the Cretaceous of No. America and Europe having a long snakelike scaly body, a head like that of a lizard with strong recurved teeth, and two pairs of paddle-shaped limbs

py·uria \\pīˈyu̇rēə\\ *n* -s [NL, fr. *py-* + *-uria*] : the presence of pus in the urine; *also* : a condition (as pyelonephritis) characterized by pus in the urine

[1]**pyx** \\ˈpiks\\ *n* -ES [ME *pyxe*, *pix*, fr. ML *pyxis*, fr. L, box, fr. Gk — more at BOX] **1** : the vessel, tabernacle, or container used ecclesiastically to hold the reserved sacrament on the altar or Holy Table or to carry the Eucharist to the sick **2** *also* **pix** \\"\\ **a** *or* **pyx chest** : a box used in the British mint as a place of deposit for sample coins reserved for testing of weight and fineness — see TRIAL OF THE PYX **b** : a similar box in the U.S. Mint **3** : a small chest or coffer : BOX

[2]**pyx** \\"\\ *also* **pix** \\"\\ *vt* -ED/-ING/-ES **1** : to put into or preserve or carry in a pyx **2** : to assay (a coin) at the trial of the pyx : test (a coin) for weight and fineness

pyx·id·an·thera \\,piksəˈdan(t)thərə\\ *n, cap* [NL, fr. L *pyxid-*, *pyxis* box + NL *-anthera*] : a monotypic genus of low evergreen shrubs (family Diapensiaceae) containing solely the pyxie

pyx·i·date \\ˈpiksə,dāt\\ *adj* [L *pyxid-*, *pyxis* box + E *-ate*] : resembling or constituting a pyxidium

pyx·id·i·um \\pikˈsidēəm\\ *n, pl* **pyxid·ia** \\-ēə\\ *or* **pyxidiums** [NL, fr. Gk *pyxidion*, dim. of *pyxis* box] **1** : a capsular fruit (as in the plantain) that dehisces around its circumference so that the upper portion falls off like a cap — compare CIRCUMSCISSILE **2** : CAPSULE 2b

pyx·ie *also* **pix·ie** *or* **pixy** \\ˈpiksē\\ *n, pl* **pyxies** *also* **pixies** [by shortening and alter. (influence of *-ie*) fr. NL *Pyxidanthera* (genus name of *Pyxidanthera barbulata*), fr. L *pyxid-*, *pyxis* box + NL *-anthera*] : a creeping evergreen shrub (*Pyxidanthera barbulata*) of the family Diapensiaceae that grows in the pine barrens of New Jersey and the Carolinas and has narrow imbricated leaves and mostly white early-blooming star-shaped flowers

pyx·is \\ˈpiksəs\\ *n, pl* **pyxi·des** \\-ksə,dēz\\ [L] **1** : ACETABULUM 2a **2** [ML, fr. L, box] **a** : an often cylindrical and ornately decorated covered container used in ancient Greece and Rome (as for the storage of salves and toiletries) **b** : PYX 1 **3** [NL, fr. L, box] **a** : PYXIDIUM 1 **b** : SCYPHUS 2

pyx–jury \\ˈ=,==\\ *n* [[1]*pyx*] : a committee of goldsmiths that makes the trial of the pyx

¹q \'kyü\ *n, pl* **q's** *or* **qs** *often cap, often attrib* **1 a :** the 17th letter of the English alphabet **b :** an instance of this letter printed, written, or otherwise represented **c :** a speech counterpart of orthographic *q* (as *q* in *quick, Iraq*) **2 :** a printer's type, a stamp, or some other instrument for reproducing the letter *q* **3 :** someone or something arbitrarily or conveniently designated *q* esp. as the 16th or when j is used for the 10th the 17th in order or class **4 :** something having the shape of the letter Q

²q \"\ *n, pl* **q's** *usu cap* [fr. initial letter of *quality factor*] **:** the ratio of the reactance to the resistance of an oscillatory circuit ⟨one of the primary factors in determining the degree of selectivity of a tuned circuit is the ~ —J.F.Rider & S.D. Uslan⟩

³q *abbr, often cap* **1** [L *quadrans*] farthing **2** [L *quaere*] inquire **3** quantity **4** quart **5** quarter; quarterly **6** quartermaster **7** quarto **8** quasi **9** queen **10** query **11** question **12** quetzal **13** quick **14** quintal **15** quire

⁴q *symbol, cap* **1** [fr. initial letter of *quality factor*] quality factor **2** [fr. initial letter of G *quelle* source] second source — used in biblical criticism to designate material belonging to a hypothetical written source used in addition to Mark and perhaps other sources in writing the Gospels of Matthew and Luke

qabbala *or* **qabbalah** *var of* CABALA

qad·a·rite *also* **kad·a·rite** \'kadə,rīt\ *n* -s [Ar *qadarīy* qadarite (fr. *qadar* fate, destiny, divine preordination) + E *-ite*] *usu cap* **:** a member of an early Muslim philosophical school asserting the doctrine of free will in opposition to the Jabarites

qa·di *also* **ca·di** *or* **ka·di** *or* **ka·dhi** \'kädē\ *or* **qa·zi** \'käzē\ *n* -s [Ar *qāḍī*] **:** a Muslim judge who interprets and administers the religious law of Islam — compare SHARI'A

qaid *var of* CAID

qaimaqam *or* **qaimmaqam** *var of* KAIMAKAM

qantar *var of* KANTAR

qaraqalpaq *usu cap, var of* KARAKALPAK

qar·ma·ti·an *or* **kar·ma·ti·an** \kär'mād·ēən\ *or* **kar·ma·thi·an** *also* **car·ma·thi·an** \-āthēən\ *n* -s *cap* [Hamdan *Qarmat*, 9th cent. Iraqi peasant who founded the sect + E *-an*] **:** a Muslim Shi'ite sect founded in the 9th century and flourishing during the middle ages as a communistic secret society that in time expanded to a small independent state on the Persian gulf from which its members raided neighboring lands

qash·qai *also* **quash·qai** *or* **qash·qai** \'käsh,kī\ *n, pl* **qashqai** *or* **qashqais** *usu cap* **1 :** a migratory Turkic-speaking people of the Zagros mountains situated east of the Bakhtiari **2 :** a member of the Qashqai people

qa·si·da *or* **ka·si·da** \kə'sēdə\ *n, pl* **qasida** *or* **kasida** [Ar *qaṣīdah*] **:** a laudatory, elegiac, or satiric poem in Arabic, Persian, or any of various related Oriental literatures

qat *var of* KAT

qat·a·ba·ni·an *also* **kat·a·ba·ni·an** \,kad·ə'bänēən\ *n* -s *usu cap* [*Qataban, Kataban*, ancient district of southern Arabia + E *-ian*] **1 :** a native or inhabitant of the ancient South Arabian kingdom of Qataban **2 :** the Sabaean language of the Qatabanians

qazaq *usu cap, var of* KAZAK

QB *abbr* **1** quarterback **2** Queen's Bench

q-boat \'=,=\ *n, usu cap Q* **:** an armed ship disguised as a merchant or fishing ship and used to decoy enemy submarines into gun range — called also *mystery ship*

QC *abbr* **1** Quartermaster Corps **2** Queen's Counsel

q-celtic \'=¦==\ *n, cap Q&C* **:** those Celtic languages in which the Indo-European labiovelars are found as velars **:** GOIDELIC

QD *abbr* **1** *often not cap* [L *quaque die*] every day **2** quarterdeck **3** *often not cap* [L *quater die*] four times a day

QDA *abbr, often not cap* quantity discount agreement

QE *abbr, often not cap* [L *quod est*] which is

QED *abbr* [L *quod erat demonstrandum*] which was to be demonstrated

QEF *abbr* [L *quod erat faciendum*] which was to be done

QEI *abbr* [L *quod erat inveniendum*] which was to be found out

qere *var of* KERE

qeri *var of* KERI

QF *abbr* quick-firing

q factor *n, usu cap Q* [*quality factor*] **:** ²Q

q fever *n, usu cap Q* [*q* fr. initial letter of *query*] **:** a disease somewhat like but much milder than typhus that is characterized by high fever, chills, and pains in the muscles and is commonly accompanied by an atypical pneumonia, that is caused by a microorganism (*Coxiella burnetii*) apparently widespread in ruminants and transmitted by raw milk, by contact, or by ticks, and that is widely distributed in No. America, Europe, and parts of Africa

QH *abbr* [L *quaque hora*] every hour

qib·la *or* **qib·lah** *also* **kib·la** *or* **kib·lah** \'kiblə\ *n* -s [Ar *qiblah*] **:** the direction of the Kaaba shrine in Mecca toward which all Muslims turn in ritual prayer

QID *abbr, often not cap* [L *quater in die*] four times a day

qinah *var of* KINAH

qin·tar \kin'tär\ *n, pl* **qintar** *or* **qintars** [Alb] **:** a monetary unit of Albania equal to $\frac{1}{100}$ lek — see MONEY table

qi·yas \kē'yäs\ *n* -ES [Ar *qiyās* analogy] **:** the principle of analogy applied in the interpretation of points of Muslim law not clearly covered in the Koran or sunna **:** analogical inference or deduction

ql *abbr* quintal

QL *abbr, often not cap* [L *quantum libet*] as much as you please

qlty *abbr* quality

QM *abbr* **1** quartermaster **2** *often not cap* [L *quo modo*] in what manner

QMC *abbr* Quartermaster Corps

q-meter \'=,==\ *n, usu cap Q* **:** an instrument for measuring the Q of an oscillatory circuit

QMG *abbr* quartermaster general

qmr *abbr* quartermaster

QMS *abbr* quartermaster sergeant

qn *abbr* **1** question **2** quotation

QN *abbr, often not cap* [L *quaque nocte*] every night

qoph *or* **koph** *also* **coph** \'kōf\ *n* -s [Heb *qōph*] **1 :** the 19th letter of the Hebrew alphabet — symbol ק; see ALPHABET table **2 :** the letter of the Phoenician or of any of various other Semitic alphabets corresponding to Hebrew qoph

qoran *usu cap, var of* KORAN

QP *abbr* **1** [L *quantum placet*] as much as you please **2** queen post

qq *abbr* questions

qq v *abbr* [L *quae vide*] which see

qr *abbr* **1** quarter **2** quire

qre *var of* KERE

q'ri *or* **qri** *var of* KERI

qrly *abbr* quarterly

qrs complex *n, usu cap Q&R&S* **:** the deflections in an electrocardiographic tracing that represent ventricular activity of the heart

qrtly *abbr* quarterly

QS *abbr* **1** *often not cap* [L *quantum sufficit*] as much as suffices **2** quarter section **3** quarter sessions

q's *or* **qs** *pl of* Q

q-ship \'=,=\ *n, usu cap Q* **:** Q-BOAT

q signal *n, usu cap Q* **:** any of various conventional code signals employed in radiotelegraphy that is a combination of three letters the first of which is Q (as QRS for "send slower", QSD for "your keying is bad")

qt \'kyü'tē\ *n* -s *often cap Q&T* [abbr. of *quiet*] **:** QUIET — usu. used in the phrase *on the qt* ⟨met several times on the ~⟩ ⟨has to visit him at his home on the ~ —Henry Miller⟩

qt *abbr* **1** quantity **2** quart

qtd *abbr* quartered

qtly *abbr* quarterly

qto *abbr* quarto

qtr *abbr* quarter; quarterly

qtrs *abbr* quarters

qty *abbr* quantity

qtz *abbr* quartz

qu *abbr* **1** quart; quarter; quarterly **2** quasi **3** query **4** question

¹qua \'kwā, 'kwä\ *prep* [L, fr. abl. sing. fem. of *qui* who — more at WHO] **:** in the character, role, or capacity of **:** AS ⟨his business ~ historian —*Modern Language Notes*⟩ ⟨the music ~ music . . . produces an impression of strength —Aaron Copland⟩ ⟨the renouncement of love ~ passion —Wilhelmine Delp⟩ ⟨belief that all men ~ men have certain essential rights —W.K.Frankena⟩ ⟨for art to use geometric forms, ~ geometric forms —Edgar Levy⟩

²qua \'kwä\ *var of* QUAW

³qua \'kwä, 'kwȯ\ *n* -s [imit.] **:** a European night heron

quabird \'=,=\ *n* [ᵌ*qua* + *bird*] **:** BLACK-CROWNED NIGHT HERON

¹quack \'kwak\ *vi* -ED/-ING/-S [imit.] **1 :** to make the characteristic cry of a duck **2 :** to make a noise resembling the cry of a duck

²quack \"\ *n* -s **1 :** the cry of the duck or a sound in imitation of it **2 :** a hoarse quacking noise ⟨the brisk ~ of the radio —Sinclair Lewis⟩

³quack \"\ *n* -s [short for *quacksalver*] **1 :** a pretender to medical skill **:** medical charlatan **:** ignorant or dishonest practitioner ⟨one of the most notorious cancer-cure ~*s* of the day —*Jour. Amer. Med. Assoc.*⟩ **2 :** one who professes skill or knowledge in any matter of which he knows little or nothing **:** CHARLATAN ⟨a ~, both as scientist and as historian —G.W. Johnson⟩ ⟨to distinguish between the expert and the ~ —Walter Moberly⟩

⁴quack \"\ *vb* -ED/-ING/-S *vi* **1 :** to make vain and loud pretensions esp. of medical ability **:** play the quack **2 :** to talk pretentiously without sound knowledge of the subject discussed ~ *vt* **:** to make extravagant claims for as a cure-all **:** advertise with fraudulent boasts

⁵quack \"\ *adj* **:** relating to or marked by boasting and unfounded pretension **:** used by quacks **:** pretending to cure diseases ⟨a ~ medicine⟩ ⟨a ~ doctor⟩ ⟨~ claims⟩ ⟨~ theology⟩ ⟨~ weather prophet⟩

quack·ery \'kwak(ə)rē, -ri\ *n* -ES **:** the practice, methods, or pretensions of a quack **:** CHARLATANRY ⟨religious ~⟩ ⟨political ~⟩ ⟨medical ~⟩ ⟨half-baked thinking which verges close to ~ —Lewis Mumford⟩

quack grass *also* **quack** *n* [*quack grass* alter. of *quick grass*; *quack* alter. of ⁵*quick*] **:** COUCH GRASS 1a

quack·ish \-kish, -kēsh\ *adj* **:** resembling a quack **:** boasting and fraudulent — **quack·ish·ly** *adv* — **quack·ish·ness** *n* -ES

quack·ism \-a,kizəm\ *n* -s **:** QUACKERY

¹quack·le \'kwakəl\ *vi* -ED/-ING/-S [imit.] *of a duck* **:** QUACK

²quackle \"\ *vb* -ED/-ING/-S [imit.] *dial Brit* **:** SUFFOCATE, CHOKE

quack·sal·ver \'kwak,salvə(r)\ *n* -s [obs. D *quacksalver* (now *kwakzalver*), fr. MD *quacsalver*, perh. alter. (influenced by MD *quacken, quaken* to quack, croak — of imit. origin — & *salven* to apply salve to, anoint) of *quicsilver* quicksilver; fr. the use of mercury in folk medicine — more at QUICKSILVER, SALVE] **:** CHARLATAN, QUACK

quacksalving *adj* [fr. *quacksalver*, after such pairs as E *goer: going*] **:** relating to, characteristic of, or like a quack **:** QUACKISH

quack·ster \'kwakstə(r)\ *n* -s [⁴*quack* + *-ster*] **:** QUACK

quacky \'kwakē\ *adj* -ER/-EST [³*quack* + *-y*] **:** QUACKISH

¹quad \'kwäd *sometimes* 'kwȯd\ *var of* QUOD

²quad \"\ *n* -s [by shortening] **:** QUADRANGLE

³quad \"\ *n* -s [short for ¹*quadrat*] **:** a block of type metal of the same belly-to-back size as the letters but not as high and ½, 1, 2, or 3 or more ems in width that is used in spacing and blank lines — compare SPACE

⁴quad \"\ *vb* **quadded; quadded; quadding; quads** *vt* **:** to fill out (as a typeset line) with quads; *also* **:** to blank out (a line) mechanically in machine composition by using a quadder — often used with *out* ~ *vi* **:** to become quadded ⟨short lines will automatically ~ —*Intertype Streamlined Composing Machines*⟩

⁵quad \"\ *adj* [short for ³*quadruple*] **1 :** being a size of paper four times as large as a specified size ⟨~ royal (40″ x 50″) is four times as large as royal (20″ x 25″)⟩ **2 :** QUADRUPLE ⟨~ cities⟩

⁶quad \"\ *n* -s [by shortening] **1 :** QUADRUPLET **2 :** a structural unit of four separately insulated wires twisted together used in cable construction **3 :** an assembly of four units having matched electrical characteristics (as varistors) **4 :** a group of four weapons (as machine guns) on one mount

quad *abbr* quadrant

quad·ded \-dəd\ *adj* [⁶*quad* + *-ed*] **:** having some wires arranged in quads ⟨a ~ cable⟩

quad·der \-ədə(r)\ *n* -s [⁴*quad* + *-er*] **:** a device in a composing machine that permits automatic blanking out of lines (as on each side of centered matter)

quad·dle \'kwäd'l, 'kwȯd'l\ *n* -s [imit.] *dial Eng* **:** GRUMBLER

qua·di \'kwä,dī\ *n pl, usu cap* [L] **:** an ancient Germanic people living between the headwaters of the Oder and the Danube — see HERMINONES

quadr- — see QUADRI-

qua·dra \'kwädrə\ *n, pl* **quad·rae** \-ä,drē\ [L, square, plinth, fillet; akin to L *quattuor* four] **1 :** the plinth of a pedestal, podium, or water table **2 :** FILLET, LISTEL **3 :** a square frame or border (as about a bas-relief)

¹quad·ra·ge·nar·i·an \,kwädrəjə'na(a)rēən\ *n* -s [L *quadragenarius* of forty, forty years old (fr. *quadrageni* forty each — fr. *quadraginta* forty — + *-arius* -ary) + E *-an*, n. suffix] **:** a person who is 40 or more and less than 50 years old

²quadragenarian \¦===¦===\ *adj* **:** 40 or between 40 and 50 years old

qua·dra·ge·nar·i·ous \-ēəs\ *adj* [L *quadragenarius*] **:** QUADRAGENARIAN

qua·drag·e·nary \(')kwä'drajə,nerē\ *adj* [L *quadragenarius*] **:** based on the number 40

quad·ra·ges·i·ma \,kwädrə'jesəmə, -jāzəmə *sometimes* ,kwȯd-\ *n* -s *usu cap* [LL, Lent, first Sunday in Lent, fr. L, fem. of *quadragesimus* fortieth, fr. *quadraginta* forty, fr. *quadra-* (akin to L *quattuor* four) + *-ginta* (akin to L *-ginti* in *viginti* twenty) — more at FOUR, VICENARY] **1** *or* **quadragesima sunday :** the first Sunday in Lent **2 :** the 40 days of Lent

quad·ra·ges·i·mal \¦==¦==məl\ *adj* [LL *quadragesimalis*, fr. *quadragesima* + L *-alis* -al] **1** *usu cap* **:** of, relating to, or used in Lent **:** LENTEN **2 :** consisting of 40 — used esp. of a fast (as the Lenten fast) consisting of or lasting for 40 days

quad·ra·ges·i·mo-oc·ta·vo \,kwädrə'jesəmō,äk'tā(,)vō\ *n* -s [L *quadragesimo octavo*, abl. of *quadragesimus octavus* forty-eighth, fr. *quadragesimus* fortieth + *octavus* eighth — more at OCTAVE] **:** FORTY-EIGHTMO — symbol *Fe;* see BOOK tables

quad·ran·gle \'kwä,draŋgəl, -raiŋ- *sometimes* 'kwȯ,-\ *n* -s [ME, fr. MF, fr. LL *quadrangulum, quadriangulum*, fr. L, neut. of *quadrangulus, quadriangulus*, fr. *quadri-* + *angulus* angle — more at ANGLE] **1 :** a plane figure having four angles and consequently four sides **:** any figure having four angles **2 a :** a square or quadrangular enclosure or court esp. when surrounded by buildings (as in some schools and colleges) **b :** the building or group of buildings enclosing a quadrangle **c :** a building or mass of buildings quadrangular in form **3 :** the tract of country represented by one of the atlas sheets published by the U. S. Geological Survey and measuring in densely populated regions 15′ in latitude by 15′ in longitude mapped on a scale of $\frac{1}{62,500}$ and elsewhere 30′ × 30′ mapped on a scale of $\frac{1}{125,000}$ or 1° × 1° on a scale of $\frac{1}{250,000}$; *also* **:** a sheet representing such a tract ⟨the determination of latitude and longitude is difficult without the possession of a U.S.G.S. ~ (for most small maps lack parallels and meridians) —*Chronica Botanica*⟩ **4** *often cap* **:** a rectangular area on the palm bounded by the lines of Head and Heart and usu. held by palmists to indicate a person's attitude toward others (as broad-mindedness or bigotry) ⟨a star in any portion of the ~ is an excellent sign —Louis Hamon⟩ — **in quadrangle :** placed one in each quarter of the field — used of four heraldic charges

quad·ran·gled \-ld\ *adj* [*quadrangle* + *-ed*] **1 :** QUADRANGULAR **2 :** enclosing or having a quadrangle

qua·dran·gu·lar \(')kwä'draŋgyələ(r), -raiŋ- *sometimes* (')kwȯ'-\ *adj* [LL *quadrangularis*, fr. *quadrangulum* quadrangle + L *-aris* -ar] **:** having four angles and consequently four sides **:** TETRAGONAL ⟨the interior structure was composed of a ~ skeleton of stout poles lashed together —*Amer. Anthropologist*⟩ — **qua·dran·gu·lar·ly** *adv*

quad·rans \'kwä,dranz\ *n, pl* **quadran·tes** \kwä'dran,tēz\ [L *quadrant-, quadrans*, lit., fourth part] **:** a bronze coin of the Roman republic worth ¼ of an as

¹quad·rant \'kwädrənt *sometimes* 'kwȯd-\ *n* -s [ME, fr. L *quadrant-, quadrans* fourth part, quarter; akin to L *quattuor* four — more at FOUR] **1 :** something shaped like a quarter-circle: as **a :** an instrument for measuring altitudes variously constructed and mounted for different specific uses (as in astronomy, surveying, gunnery) and consisting commonly of a graduated arc of 90° with an index or vernier and either plain or telescopic sights and usu. having a plumb line or spirit level for fixing the vertical or horizontal direction **b :** a device resembling a bell crank for converting the horizontal reciprocating motion of an engine piston rod into the vertical up-and-down movement of a pump rod **c :** a dial or an indexing sector of approximate quarter-circle range; *also* **:** a lever that moves over such a range **d :** a device on a spinning mule for controlling the winding of the yarn **2 a :** a quarter of a circle, an arc of 90°, or an arc subtending a right angle at the center **b :** the area bounded by a quadrant and two radii **3 a :** any of the four parts into which a plane is divided by rectangular coordinate axes lying in that plane **b :** any of the four more or less equal parts into which something is divided by two real or imaginary lines that intersect each other at right angles ⟨located in the upper left ~ of a page⟩ ⟨a building in the southeast ~ of the city⟩ ⟨most hurricanes . . . are not symmetrical — the winds are much stronger in some ~*s* —R.C.Gentry & R.H.Simpson⟩ **c :** a group comprising all the cells resulting from divisions of one of the first four blastomeres in spirally cleaving eggs with determinate cleavage **d :** any of four more or less equivalent segments into which an anatomic structure or surface may be divided by vertical and horizontal partitioning through its midpoint — used chiefly of the abdomen ⟨severe pain in the lower right ~⟩ **e :** the sector between the equisignal zones of a four-course aural radio range

quadrants 2

²quadrant *adj* [prob. alter. (influenced by ¹*quadrant*) of ¹*quadrate*] *obs* **:** SQUARE, QUADRATE

qua·dran·tal \(')kwä'drant'l\ *adj* [L *quadrantalis* containing the fourth part of a measure, fr. *quadrant-, quadrans* fourth part + *-alis* -al] **:** of or relating to a quadrant **:** included in or in the shape of a fourth part of a circle ⟨~ open-tiered stand —*Parke-Bernet Galleries Catalog*⟩

quadrantal correctors *n pl* **:** two spheres of iron attached to the port and starboard sides of the binnacle to correct the quadrantal deviation

quadrantal deviation *n* **:** the part of the compass deviation due to the transient magnetism induced in the horizontal soft iron of a ship by the horizontal component of the earth's magnetism

quadrantal error *n* **:** a directional error of a radio compass caused by reradiated fields created around the metallic parts of the airplane

quadrantal point *n* **:** INTERCARDINAL

quadrantal triangle *n* **:** a spherical triangle with one side equal to a quadrant

quadrant electrometer *n* **:** a sensitive electrometer consisting of a needle independently charged and suspended within a flat cylindrical metal box divided into four quadrants, those diametrically opposite being connected to each other and each pair being connected to one of two bodies whose potential difference is to be measured by means of the deflection of the needle toward one pair of quadrants through an angle approximately proportional to the difference of potential

quadrantes *pl of* QUADRANS

quadrant plate *n* **:** a slotted plate for carrying the change gears of a lathe in any desired position

quadrants *pl of* QUADRANT

¹quad·rat \'kwädrət\ *n* -s [alter. of ²*quadrate*] **1 a :** ³QUAD **b quadrats** *pl but sing in constr* **:** a game in which printer's quads are thrown like dice **2 :** a small usu. rectangular plot laid off (as in a forest, range, pasture, or cultivated field) for the study of vegetation or animals

²quadrat \"\ *vt* **quadratted; quadratted; quadratting; quadrats :** to lay out (a plot of land) in quadrats **:** divide into quadrats

¹qua·drate \'kwä,drāt, -ädrət *sometimes* 'kwȯ,-; *usu* -d·+V\ *adj* [ME, fr. L *quadratus*, past part. of *quadrare* to square, make square, fit; akin to L *quattuor* four — more at FOUR] **1 :** square or approximately square in form ⟨a roughened ~ area near the apex —L.F.Edwards⟩ ⟨the ~ masses of the rooftops —G.C.Vaillant⟩ **2** *obs* **:** SQUARE — used of numbers **3** *obs* **a :** SQUARED, BALANCED, CORRESPONDENT **b :** PERFECT, IDEAL **4 :** expanded into a square at the junction of the arms — used of a heraldic cross **5 :** being or relating to a bony or cartilaginous element of each side of the skull to which the lower jaw is articulated in most vertebrates below mammals

²quadrate \"\ *n* -s [ME, fr. L *quadratum*, fr. neut. of *quadratus*] **1 a :** SQUARE **b :** something more or less resembling a square (as a rectangular space or enclosure) **2 :** an object square or cubical in form or approximately so **3** *obs* **:** the aspect of two celestial bodies that are 90 degrees apart **4 :** a quadrate bone

³quadrate \-,drāt\ *vb* -ED/-ING/-S [L *quadratus*, past part. of *quadrare*] *vi* **:** SQUARE, AGREE, SUIT, CORRESPOND — usu. used with *with* ~ *vt* **1 :** to make square **:** divide into squares or cubes **2 :** to make accordant **:** cause to conform ⟨are all novels but an imperative that could ~ them would be a little astonishing —Bernard DeVoto⟩

quadrate lobe *or* **quadrate lobule** *n* **1 :** PRECUNEUS **2 :** a small lobe of the liver on the under surface of the right lobe to the left of the fissure for the gallbladder

¹quad·rat·ic \(')kwä¦drad·ik, -at|, |ēk *sometimes* (')kwȯ¦-\ *adj* [²*quadrate* + *-ic*] **1 :** of, relating to, or resembling a square **:** SQUARE **2 :** having terms of second degree as the highest ⟨a ~ equation is one in which the highest power of the unknown quantity is a square⟩ **3 :** TETRAGONAL ⟨~ system in crystallography⟩

²quadratic \"\ *n* -s **1 :** a quadratic polynomial or polynomial equation ⟨$3x^2+4x-1=0$ is a ~⟩ **2 qua·drat·ics** \kwä'drad·iks\ *pl but sing or pl in constr* **:** a branch of algebra treating of quadratic equations

qua·drat·i·cal \|əkəl\ *adj* [¹*quadratic* + *-al*] **:** QUADRATIC — **qua·drat·i·cal·ly** \|ək(ə)lē\ *adv*

quadratic formula *n* **:** a formula used to solve a quadratic equation in a single variable

quadratic mean *n* **:** the square root of the arithmetic mean of the squares of the quantities

¹qua·dra·to·jugal \kwä¦drād·ō+\ *adj* [¹*quadrate* + *-o-* + *jugal*] **1 :** of, relating to, or joining the quadrate and jugal bones **2 :** being a quadratojugal

²quadratojugal \"\ *n* **:** a small membrane bone that connects the quadrate and jugal bones on each side of the skull in many lower vertebrates

qua·dra·to·mandibular \"+\ *adj* [¹*quadrate* + *-o-* + *mandibular*] **:** relating to the quadrate bone and the lower jaw

quadrats *pl of* QUADRAT, *pres 3d sing of* QUADRAT

quadratted *past of* QUADRAT

quadratting *pres part of* QUADRAT

quad·ra·ture \'kwädrəchə(r), -rə,chü(ə)r, -,chüə *sometimes* 'kwȯd-\ *n* -s [L *quadratura* act of making square, fr. *quadratus* (past part. of *quadrare* to square) + *-ura* -ure — more at QUADRATE] **1** *obs* **:** square shape; *also* **:** something (as a place or region) square in shape **:** SQUARE, SQUARENESS **2 a :** the act or process of making square or of determining areas; *specif* **:** QUADRATURE OF THE CIRCLE **b :** the process of evaluating integrals **3 a :** a configuration in which two celestial bodies have a separation of 90 degrees ⟨the first quarter moon is in ~ to the sun⟩ **b :** either of two points on an orbit in a middle position between the syzygies **4 a :** a phase difference of one quarter cycle (as that between the currents in a two-phase power-distribution system) **b :** the angular distance between two points on an armature winding separated by one half the pole pitch or 90 electrical degrees

quadrature of the circle : a problem in mathematics that consists of finding the side of a square exactly equal in area to a given circular area and that has been shown to be impossible of solution by geometric methods limited to the use of ruler and compass alone

qua·dra·tus \kwä'drād·əs, -ātəs\ *n, pl* **quadra·ti** \-ād,ī, -ā,tī\ [NL, fr. L, past part. of *quadrare* to square] **:** any of several skeletal muscles more or less quadrangular in outline

quadrel *n* -s [It *quadrello,* fr. (assumed) VL *quadrellum* building stone — more at QUARREL] **:** a square block (as of brick, tile, plastic)

¹qua·dren·ni·al \(')kwä'dreneəl, -nyəl *sometimes* (')kwȯ'-\ *adj* [alter. of *quadriennial*] **1 :** comprising or lasting through four years ⟨a ~ period⟩ **2 :** occurring once in four years or at the end of every four years ⟨~ elections⟩

²quadrennial \"\ *n* -s **1 :** a quadrennial period ⟨a political organization . . . functions not by ~ but by decades and generations —W.A.White⟩ **2 :** a fourth anniversary or its celebration

quad·ren·ni·al·ly \-əlē, -li\ *adv* **:** every fourth year ⟨it is the election of the President that unites the scattered elements ~ —W.E.Binkley⟩

qua·dren·ni·um \kwä'dreneəm *sometimes* kwȯ'-\ *n, pl* **quadrenniums** \-ēəmz\ *or* **quadren·nia** \-ēə\ [alter. of *quadriennium*] **:** a period of four years

quadri- *or* **quadr-** *or* **quadru-** *comb form* [ME, fr. L; akin to L *quattuor* four — more at FOUR] **1 a :** four ⟨*quadri*lateral⟩ ⟨*quadr*ual⟩ **b :** square ⟨*quadr*ic⟩ **c :** TETRA- ⟨*quadri*basic⟩ **2 :** fourth ⟨*quadri*centennial⟩ **3 :** quadric ⟨*quadri*cone⟩

¹quad·ric \'kwädrik\ *adj* [ISV *quadr-* + *-ic*] **:** of or relating to the second degree — used where there are more than two variables (as in solid geometry)

²quadric \"\ *n* -s **1 :** a quantic of the second degree **2 :** a surface whose equation in Cartesian coordinates is of the second degree

quadric chain *or* **quadric crank chain** *n* **:** a chain consisting of four links joined by four turning pairs

quad·ri·centennial \¦kwädrə+\ *n* [*quadri-* + *centennial*] **:** a 400th anniversary or anniversary celebration

quad·ri·ceps \'kwädrə,seps\ *also* **quadriceps extensor** *or* **quadriceps fem·o·ris** \-'femərə̇s\ *n* -ES [NL *quadricipit-, quadriceps,* fr. *quadri-* + *-cipit-, -ceps* (as in *bicipit-, biceps* biceps)] **:** the great extensor muscle of the front of the thigh divided above into four parts which unite in a single tendon to enclose the patella as a sesamoid bone at the knee and insert as the patellar ligament into the tuberosity of the tibia

quad·ri·cip·i·tal \¦==¦sipəd·ᵊl\ *adj* [NL *quadricipit-, quadriceps* + E *-al*] **:** of, relating to, or being a quadriceps

quad·ri·color \'kwädrə+,-\ *adj* [ISV *quadri-* + *color*] **:** FOUR-COLOR

¹quad·ri·cy·cle \'kwädrə,sīkəl\ *n* [*quadri-* + *-cycle* (as in *tricycle*)] **1 :** a four-wheeled cycle or velocipede for pedal propulsion on roads or railroads **2 :** a motor vehicle with a live two-wheeled axle, a bicycle seat for the driver, and a four-wheeled forecarriage steered by handlebars

²quadricycle \"\ *adj* **:** four-wheeled ⟨a ~ landing gear⟩

quad·ri·en·ni·al \¦kwädrə¦eneəl\ *adj* [L *quadriennium* + E *-al*] **:** QUADRENNIAL

quad·ri·en·ni·um \,==¦eneəm\ *n, pl* **quadrienniums** \-ēəmz\ *or* **quadrien·nia** \-ēə\ [L, fr. *quadri-* + *-ennium* (fr. *annus* year) — more at ANNUAL] **:** QUADRENNIUM

quadriennium uti·le \-'yüd·ᵊl,ē\ *n* [ML or NL, lit., four-year period of equity] *Scots law* **:** the period of four years following attainment of majority within which the former minor or in case of his death his executor may act to avoid his contracts, gifts, or conveyances

quad·ri·fid \'kwädrə,fid\ *adj* [L *quadrifidus,* fr. *quadri-* + *-fidus* -fid] **:** divided into four parts ⟨a ~ petal⟩

quad·ri·filar \¦kwädrə+\ *adj* [*quadri-* + *filar*] **:** four-threaded **:** involving the use of four threads

quad·ri·form \'kwädrə,fȯrm\ *adj* [LL *quadriformis,* fr. L *quadri-* + *-formis* -form] **:** having a fourfold form or character

qua·dri·ga \kwä'drīgə\ *n, pl* **quadri·gae** \-ī,jē\ [L, back-formation fr. *quadrigae* (pl.) quadriga, contr. of *quadrijugae,* fem. pl. of *quadrijugus* of a team of four, fr. *quadri-* + *jugum* yoke, team — more at YOKE] **:** an ancient Roman car or chariot drawn by four horses abreast together with the horses drawing it; *sometimes* **:** the four horses without the chariot or the chariot alone

qua·drig·a·mist \kwä'drigəmə̇st\ *n* -s [*quadri-* + *-gamist* (as in *bigamist*)] **:** one who has married four times; *esp* **:** one who has four wives or four husbands at the same time

quad·ri·gem·i·nal bodies \¦kwädrə¦jemənᵊl-\ *or* **quad·ri·gem·i·nate bodies** \-mənə̇t-, -mə,nāt-\ *n pl* [*quadrigeminal bodies* fr. *quadrigeminal* (fr. L *quadrigeminus* fourfold — fr. *quadri-* + *geminus* twin — + E *-al*) + *bodies,* pl. of *body; quadrigeminate bodies* fr. *quadrigeminate* (fr. L *quadrigeminus* + E *-ate*) + *bodies;* both intended as trans. of NL *corpora quadragemina* — more at GEMINATE] **:** CORPORA QUADRIGEMINA

¹quad·ri·lat·er·al \¦kwädrə¦lad·ərəl, -atərəl, -a·trəl *sometimes* ¦kwȯd-\ *adj* [prob. fr. (assumed) NL *quadrilateralis,* fr. L *quadrilaterus* quadrilateral (fr. *quadri-* + *later-, latus* side) + *-alis* -al — more at LATERAL] **1 :** having four sides — used esp. of a plane figure **2 :** shared by four parties ⟨~ control by foreign powers⟩

²quadrilateral \"\ *n* -s **1 :** a plane figure of four sides and consequently four angles **:** a quadrangular figure **:** a plane figure formed by four lines — see COMPLETE QUADRILATERAL **2 :** something resembling or suggesting a quadrilateral; *specif* **:** an area defended by four fortresses supporting each other

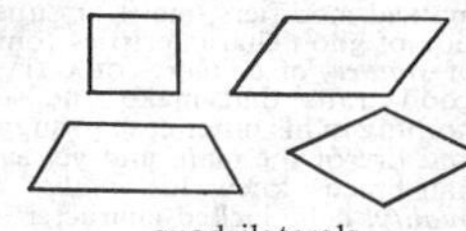

quadrilaterals

quad·ri·lingual \¦kwädrə+\ *adj* [*quadri-* + *lingual*] **1 :** using or made up of four languages ⟨a ~ inscription⟩ **2 :** speaking or having knowledge of four languages ⟨a ~ interpreter⟩ — **quad·ri·lin·gual·i·ty** \,kwädrə¦liŋ'gwaləd·ē\ *n* -ES

¹quad·ri·literal \¦kwädrə+\ *adj* [*quadri-* + *literal*] **:** consisting of four letters — used esp. of a Semitic root having four consonants instead of three

²quadriliteral \"\ *n* -s **:** a word of four letters; *specif* **:** a Semitic quadriliteral root

qua·dril·lage \kwä'drilij\ *n* -s [F, fr. *quadrille* lozenge, small square + *-age*] **:** a system of quadrille reference lines on a map ⟨overprinted a network of even kilometer squares upon their maps, in which ~ each line was numbered from a zero point in the southwest of the war zone —Erwin Raisz⟩

¹qua·drille \kwä'dril, k(w)ə'- *sometimes* kwȯ'-\ *n* -s [F, four-handed form of ombre, group of knights engaging in a carrousel] **:** a four-handed form of ombre popular in the 17th and 18th centuries

²quadrille \"\ *n* -s [F, group of knights engaging in a carrousel, troop of cavalry, fr. Sp *cuadrilla* troop, gang, group of horsemen at a tourney — more at CUADRILLA] **1 a :** one of four groups of knights engaging in a tournament or carrousel **b :** CARROUSEL 1a **2 a :** a square dance for four couples that is made up of five or six figures in various rhythms but chiefly in ⁶⁄₈ and ²⁄₄ time **b :** music for this dance **3 :** CUADRILLA

³quadrille \"\ *vi* -ED/-ING/-S **:** to dance a quadrille

⁴quadrille \"\ *adj* [F *quadrillé,* fr. *quadrille* lozenge, small square, group of knights engaging in a carrousel] **1 :** marked with squares or rectangles **:** having or consisting of thin lines crossing at right angles and usu. at equal intervals ⟨~ pattern⟩ ⟨a ~ design⟩ **2 :** crossing at right angles so as to form a quadrille pattern ⟨~ lines⟩ ⟨~ ruling⟩

⁵quadrille \"\ *n* -s **1 :** a quadrille pattern or ruling **2 :** QUADRILLE PAPER

quad·rilled \-ld\ *adj* [F *quadrillé* + E *-ed*] **:** QUADRILLE ⟨pages overlaid with faint gray ~ lines —Al Burns⟩

quadrille paper *n* **:** paper having quadrille ruling **:** GRAPH PAPER; *specif* **:** laid paper having quadrille watermarks and used esp. for postage stamps

¹qua·dril·lion \kwä'drilyən\ *n* -s [F, fr. MF, fr. *quadri-* + *-illion* (as in *million*)] — see NUMBER table

²quadrillion \"\ *adj* **:** being a quadrillion in number

¹qua·dril·lionth \-n(t)th\ *adj* **1 :** being number one quadrillion in a countable series — see NUMBER table **2 :** being one of a quadrillion equal parts into which anything is divisible

²quadrillionth \"\ *n* -s **:** one of a quadrillion equal parts of anything

qua·drip·a·rous \kwä'dripərəs\ *adj* [*quadri-* + *-parous*] **:** having given birth to four children

quad·ri·par·tite \¦kwädrə¦pär,tīt\ *adj* [ME, fr. L *quadripartitus,* fr. *quadri-* + *partitus,* past part. of *partire* to divide — more at PART] **1 :** consisting of or divided into four parts ⟨split which causes the chromosome pairs . . . to be actually ~ —C.H.Waddington⟩ **2 :** drawn up in four consecutive parts ⟨~ contract⟩ ⟨~ indenture⟩ **3 :** shared or participated in by four parties or persons ⟨~ government by foreign powers⟩ ⟨a ~ agreement⟩ ⟨~ supervision⟩ **4 :** being a vaulting in which the vault over each rectangle is divided into four parts — **quad·ri·par·tite·ly** *adv*

quad·ri·par·ti·tion \,kwädrəpär'tishən\ *n* [L *quadripartition-, quadripartitio,* fr. *quadripartitus* quadripartite + *-ion-, -io* -ion] **:** division into four parts

quad·ri·ple·gia \,kwädrə'plēj(ē)ə\ *n* -s [NL, fr. *quadri-* + *-plegia*] **:** paralysis of both arms and both legs — called also *tetraplegia*

quad·ri·ple·gic \-jik\ *n* -s [*quadriplegia* + *-ic*] **:** a person who is paralyzed in both arms and both legs

quadripole *var of* QUADRUPOLE

quad·ri·por·ti·cus \,kwädrə'pȯrd·əkəs\ *also* **quad·ri·por·ti·co** \-də,kō\ *n, pl* **quadriporticuses** [*quadriporticus* fr. LL, fr. L *quadri-* + *porticus* portico; *quadriportico* fr. It, fr. LL *quadriporticus* — more at PORCH] **:** a nearly square atrium surrounded by colonnaded porticoes

quad·ri·reme \'kwädrə,rēm\ *n* -s [L *quadriremis,* fr. *quadri-* + *-remis* (fr. *remus* oar) — more at REMI-] **:** a galley with four banks of oars

quad·ri·sect \-,sekt\ *vt* -ED/-ING/-S [*quadri-* + *-sect*] **:** to divide into four equal parts

quad·ri·syllabic \¦kwädrə+\ *adj* [ISV *quadri-* + *syllabic*] **:** having four syllables **:** of or relating to quadrisyllables

quad·ri·syllable \"+\ *n* [*quadri-* + *syllable*] **:** a word of four syllables

¹quad·ri·valent \"+\ *adj* [ISV *quadri-* + *valent*] **:** TETRAVALENT

²quadrivalent \"\ *n* -s **:** a tetravalent chromosome group

qua·driv·i·al \kwä'drivēəl\ *adj* [ML *quadrivialis,* fr. LL *quadrivium* + L *-alis* -al] **1 :** of or belonging to the quadrivium **2 :** having four ways or roads meeting in a point; *also* **:** leading in four directions

qua·driv·i·als \-lz\ *n pl* **:** the four liberal arts making up the quadrivium

qua·driv·i·um \-ēəm\ *n, pl* **quadriv·ia** \-ēə\ [LL, fr. L, crossroads, place where four roads meet, fr. *quadri-* + *via* way, road — more at VIA] **:** a group of studies in the Middle Ages consisting of arithmetic, music, geometry, and astronomy, constituting the higher division of the seven liberal arts, and forming the course for the three years of study between the B.A. and M.A. degrees — compare TRIVIUM

quad·ri·vol·tine \¦kwädrə¦vōl,tēn, -ltᵊn\ *adj* [*quadri-* + *-voltine* (as in *bivoltine*)] **:** producing four generations in one year — used of silkworms

qua·droon \(')kwä'drün *sometimes* (')kwȯ'-\ *n* -s [alter. (influenced by *quadri-*) of earlier *quarteron,* fr. Sp *cuarterón,* fr. *cuarto* fourth, fr. L *quartus;* akin to L *quattuor* four — more at FOUR] **1 :** the offspring of a mulatto and a white person **:** a person of one-quarter Negro ancestry **2 :** a person whose racial background resembles that of a quadroon; *esp* **:** one with a quarter aboriginal (as Indian) ancestry

quadru- — see QUADRI-

¹quad·ru·al \'kwädrəwəl\ *adj* [*quadri-* + *-al*] **:** being or relating to forms of pronouns or nouns denoting four (as in certain Austronesian languages) — compare TRIAL

²quadrual \"\ *n* -s **1 :** the quadrual number **2 :** a form denoting the quadrual number or a word in that form

quad·ru·la \'kwädrələ\ *n, cap* [NL, fr. LL, small square, fr. L *quadra* square + *-ula;* akin to L *quattuor* four] **:** a genus of freshwater mussels (family Unionidae) having a thick shell and often being approximately square in shape — see NIGGERHEAD

qua·dru·ma·na \kwä'drümənə\ *n pl* [NL, fr. *quadri-* + *-mana* (fr. L *manus* hand) — more at MANUAL] **:** primates excluding man considered as a group distinguished by hand-shaped feet — compare BIMANA — **qua·dru·ma·nal** \-nᵊl\ *adj* — **quad·ru·mane** \'kwädrə,mān\ *adj or n*

qua·dru·ma·nous \kwä'drümənəs\ *adj* [NL *Quadrumana* + E *-ous*] **1 :** having four hands **2 :** relating to the quadrumana

qua·drum·vir \kwä'drəmvə(r)\ *n* -s [back-formation fr. *quadrumvirate*] **:** a member of a quadrumvirate

qua·drum·vi·rate \-vərə̇t, -və,rāt\ *n* -s [*quadri-* + *-umvirate* (as in *triumvirate*)] **:** a group or association of four men

¹quad·ru·ped \'kwädrə,ped *sometimes* 'kwȯd-\ *n* -s [L *quadruped-, quadrupes,* fr. *quadruped-, quadrupes,* adj., having four feet, fr. *quadri-* + *ped-, pes* foot — more at FOOT] **:** an animal having four feet (as most mammals and many reptiles and amphibians) — usu. used of mammals

²quadruped \"\ *adj* [L *quadruped-, quadrupes*] **:** having four feet **:** QUADRUPEDAL — compare BIPED

quad·ru·pe·dal \(')kwä'drüpədᵊl, ¦kwädrə¦pedᵊl\ *adj* [ML *quadrupedalis,* fr. LL, having four metrical feet, fr. L *quadruped-, quadrupes* + *-alis* -al] **1 :** having four feet **:** using four limbs in walking **2 :** relating to a quadruped

quadrupl *abbr* quadruplicate

quad·ru·plane \'kwädrə,plān\ *n* [*quadri-* + *plane*] **:** an airplane with four main supporting surfaces one above another

¹quad·ru·ple \(')kwä'drüpəl *also* -rəp- *or* 'kwädrəp- *sometimes* (')kwȯ'- *or* 'kwȯdrəp-\ *vb* **quadrupled; quadrupled; quadrupling** \-p(ə)liŋ\ **quadruples** [ME (Sc) *quadruplen,* fr. L *quadruplare,* fr. *quadruplus* fourfold, quadruple] *vt* **:** to make four times as much, many, or great **~** *vi* **:** to become four times as much, many, or great

²quadruple \"\ *n* -s [MF, fr. *quadruple,* adj.] **1 :** a sum four times as great as another **:** a fourfold amount **:** the fourth multiple **2** *obs* **:** a coin worth four pistoles

³quadruple \"\ *adj* [MF or L; MF *quadruple,* fr. L *quadruplus,* fr. *quadri-* + *-plus* multiplied by — more at DOUBLE] **1 :** consisting of four **:** being four times as great or as many **:** FOURFOLD **2 :** taken by fours or in groups of four; *specif* **:** having four beats per measure ⟨~ time⟩ ⟨~ rhythm⟩

quadruple amputee *n* **:** a person who has lost all or part of both legs and both arms

quadruple counterpoint *n* **:** four-part counterpoint in which the parts are interchangeable without violating contrapuntal rules

quad·ru·ple·ness *n* -ES **:** the quality or state of being quadruple

quadruple point *n* **:** a point representing a set of conditions under which four phases of a physical-chemical system can exist in equilibrium

quadruple star *n* **:** four stars appearing as one

quad·rup·let \(')kwä'drəplə̇t, kwə'd-, -rüp-, 'kwäd- *sometimes* 'kwȧ,drəp- *or* (')kwȯd¦- *or* 'kwȯd-; *usu* -ə̇d-+V\ *n* -s [fr. *³quadruple,* after such pairs as E *double: doublet*] **1 a :** one of four children or offspring born at one birth **b quadruplets** *pl* **:** a group of four offspring born at one birth **2 :** a combination of four of a kind **3 :** a group of four musical notes to be performed in the time ordinarily given to three of the same kind **4 :** a bicycle for four riders

quadruplet 3

quadruple thread *n* **:** four equal threads any point of each of which at any right section is one quarter of a circumference in advance of the corresponding point of the next succeeding thread — compare DOUBLE THREAD

quad·ru·plex \'kwädrə,pleks\ *adj* [L *quadruplic-, quadruplex* fourfold, fr. *quadri-* + *-plic-, -plex* -fold — more at SIMPLE] **:** being or relating to a system of telegraphy by which two messages in each direction may be sent simultaneously over one wire

¹qua·dru·pli·cate \(')kwä'drüplə̇kə̇t, kwə'd-, -plēk- *sometimes* (')kwȯ'- *or* -lə,kāt, *usu* -ə̇d-+V\ *adj* [L *quadruplicatus,* past part. of *quadruplicare*] **1 :** made in four identical copies **:** FOURFOLD **2 :** FOURTH — used of one of a set of printed copies ⟨the duplicate and triplicate copies . . . transmitted to the court to which the petition is to be transferred, and the ~ copy transmitted to the district director —*U.S. Code*⟩

²qua·dru·pli·cate \-lə,kāt, *usu* -ād-+V\ *vt* -ED/-ING/-S [L *quadruplicatus,* past part. of *quadruplicare,* fr. *quadruplic-, quadruplex*] **:** to multiply by four **:** QUADRUPLE **:** reproduce thrice; *specif* **:** to make at one time an original and three carbon copies of

³qua·dru·pli·cate \-lə̇kə̇t, -lēkə̇t *sometimes* -lə,kāt, *usu* -ə̇d-+V\ *n* -s [¹*quadruplicate*] **1 :** a fourth thing like three others of the same kind **2 :** four copies all alike — used with *in* ⟨typed in ~⟩

qua·dru·pli·ca·tion \kwä,drüplə'kāshən\ *n* -s [LL *quadruplication-, quadruplicatio,* fr. L *quadruplicatus* (past part. of *quadruplicare*) + *-ion-, -io* -ion] **1 :** the act, process, or result of quadrupling **2** [ML *quadruplication-, quadruplicatio* (influenced in meaning by LL *replication-, replicatio* reply), fr. LL, act of quadrupling — more at REPLICATION] **:** a rebuttal pleading of the respondent or libelee corresponding to a common law rebutter with the original exception or answer having been followed by the replication or reply, duplication or triplication, and surrejoinder

quad·ru·plic·i·ty \,kwädrə'plisəd·ē\ *n* -ES [fr. ³*quadruple,* after E *simple: simplicity*] **:** the state of being quadruple

quad·ru·ply \'kwädrəplē\ *adv* **:** in a quadruple manner

quad·ru·pole *also* **quad·ri·pole** \'kwädrə,pōl\ *n* [ISV *quadri-* + *pole*] **:** a system composed of two electric dipoles of equal but oppositely directed electric moment

quads *pl of* QUAD, *pres 3d sing of* QUAD

quae·re \'kwirē\ *n* -s [L, imper. of *quaerere* to seek, ask] *archaic* **:** QUERY, QUESTION ⟨the great ~ is, when he will come again —Thomas Browne⟩

quae·si·tum \kwē'sīd·əm\ *n, pl* **quaesi·ta** \-d·ə\ [L, neut. of *quaesitus,* past part. of *quaerere* to seek, ask] **1 :** something sought for **:** END, OBJECTIVE ⟨our intuition that one of the ideas . . . is, at last, our ~ —William James⟩ **2 :** the true or actual value of a quantity as distinguished from one determined by empirical procedures (as of measurement) — compare ERROR 5a

quaes·tio \'kwīstē,ō\ *n, pl* **quaes·ti·o·nes** \,==¦ō,nās\ [L *quaestion-, quaestio* question, quaestio — more at QUESTION] **1 :** a criminal inquisition or trial under Roman law **2** *quaestiones pl* **:** the commissions for the trial of various offenses under Roman law or the proceedings before such commissions; *also* **:** criminal courts or tribunals

quaes·tor *or* **ques·tor** \'kwestə(r), 'kwēs-\ *n* -s [ME *questor,* fr. L *quaestor,* fr. *quaesitus, quaestus* (past part. of *quaerere* to seek, ask) + *-or*] **1 a :** any of various Roman officials in charge of public monies (as a treasurer of the state or paymaster of troops) **b :** a public judge or prosecutor in a criminal trial in early Rome **2** [ME *questor,* fr. ML, fr. L *quaestor*] **:** an agent of a pope or bishop appointed formerly as a public preacher, charged with the mission of collecting alms, and authorized to grant indulgences to those contributing **3** [modif. (influenced by L *quaestor*) of F *questeur,* fr. L *quaestor*] **:** QUESTEUR

quaes·to·ri·al \kwe'stȯrēəl, kwē'-, -tȯr-\ *adj* [L *quaestorius* quaestorial (fr. *quaestor* + *-ius* -ious) + E *-al*] **:** of or relating to a quaestor or a quaestorship

quaes·tor·ship \'kwestə(r),ship, 'kwēs-\ *n* **:** the office of quaestor

¹quaes·tu·ary \'kwes(h)chə,werē, 'kwēs-\ *adj* [MF *questuaire,* fr. LL *quaestuarius,* fr. L *quaestus* way of making money, trade, gain, profit (fr. *quaestus,* past part. of *quaerere* to seek, gain, ask) + *-arius* -ary] *archaic* **:** interested in or undertaken for monetary gain or profit ⟨this may be termed the ~ class, this being the end which they aim at —J.F.Ferrier⟩

²quaestuary *n* -ES [ML *quaestuarius,* fr. *quaestuarius,* adj., of the collection of alms, fr. LL *quaestuarius*] *obs* **:** QUAESTOR 2

¹quaff \'kwäf, 'kwaf, 'kwaa(ə)f, 'kwaif, 'kwȧf\ *vb* -ED/-ING/-S [origin unknown] *vi* **:** to drink freely or copiously; *specif* **:** to drink an intoxicating beverage in such a manner ⟨holding our glasses, we ~*ed,* and we sat down —Emily Hahn⟩ **~** *vt* **1 :** to drink (a beverage or liquid) freely or copiously ⟨was aghast to see citizens ~*ing* a brew as an eye-opener —Horace Sutton⟩ *specif* **:** to swallow (a drink) in large drafts ⟨I ~*ed* a cocktail without flinching —Oscar Wilde⟩ **2 :** to affect in a specified way by drinking ⟨~*ed* himself into drowsiness⟩

²quaff \"\ *n* -s **:** a drink quaffed ⟨each guest having taken a ~ of ale —G.R.Gissing⟩

quaff·er \-fə(r)\ *n* -s **:** one that quaffs

quaff·ing·ly *adv* [*quaffing* (pres. part. of ¹*quaff*) + *-ly*] **:** in a free, copious, or bibulous manner

¹quag \'kwag, 'kwaa(ə)g, 'kwäg, 'kwaig\ *n* -s [origin unknown] **:** MARSH, BOG, QUAGMIRE ⟨the feet of the horse that slopped through sandy ~*s* —Elizabeth M. Roberts⟩

²quag \"\ *vi* **quagged; quagged; quagging; quags** [prob. imit.] *archaic* **:** QUAKE, QUIVER, SHAKE

quag·ga \'kwagə\ *n, pl* **quaggas** *also* **quagga** [obs. Afrik *quagga* (now *kwagga*), prob. of Bantu origin; akin to Xhosa *i-qwara* something striped or speckled, Zulu *qwara*] **:** a wild ass (*Equus quagga*) of southern Africa related to the zebras but having its upper parts striped reddish brown, the posterior part plain grayish brown, and the belly and legs whitish, the ears smaller and the tail more heavily haired than in most asses and zebras

quag·gy \'kwagē, 'kwaagē, 'kwägē, 'kwaigē, -gi\ *adj* -ER/-EST [¹*quag* + *-y*] **1 :** having the characteristics of a quagmire **:** BOGGY, MARSHY **2 :** characterized by flabbiness **:** SOFT

¹quagmire \'kwag,mī(ə)r, 'kwaag-, 'kwäg-, 'kwaig-, -mīə\ *n* [¹*quag* + *mire*] **1 a :** soft wet miry land that shakes or yields under the foot ⟨the tamarack swamp . . . was too big and filled with bogs and ~*s* —Howard Troyer⟩ **b :** a usu. dry area of land converted into an expanse of soft wet ground by heavy rain or flooding ⟨a trampled ~ of mud under the never-ceasing downpour —G.R.Stewart⟩ ⟨rain had turned the prairie trails into ~*s* —Lyn Harrington⟩ **2 :** something flabby, soft, or yielding ⟨foggy ~*s* of fat and dropsy —Thomas Brown⟩ **3 :** a complex or precarious position where disengagement is difficult ⟨from a ~ of false nonsense to a firm island of reality —John Baker⟩ ⟨a ~ of perplexing problems —Fletcher Pratt⟩ ⟨sunk to the ears in a ~ of tedium and indifference —Claud Cockburn⟩ ⟨lost in ~*s* of negotiation⟩

²quagmire \"\ *vt* -ED/-ING/-S **:** to ensnare in or as if in a quagmire ⟨a man is never ~*d* till he stops —W.S.Landor⟩

quag·miry \-īrē\ *adj* -ER/-EST **:** resembling or consisting of a quagmire **:** QUAGGY ⟨a most hideous swamp, so thick with bushes and so ~ —John Winthrop⟩

¹qua·hog *also* **qua·haug** *or* **quo·hog** *or* **quo·haug** \'kwȯ,hȯg, 'k(w)ō,-, -,häg\ *n* -s *often attrib* [Narraganset *poquaûhock,* fr. *pohkeni* dark, closed + *hogki* shell] **1 :** a thick-shelled American clam (*Mercenaria mercenaria*) — called also *round clam* **2 :** a north Atlantic clam (*Cyprina islandica*) with a blackish brown periostracum — called also *black quahog*

²quahog *also* **quahaug** \"\ *vi* **quahogged** *also* **quahauged; quahogged** *also* **quahauged; quahogging** *also* **quahauging; quahogs** *also* **quahaugs :** to seek or dig quahogs

qua·hog·ger *or* **qua·haug·er** \-gə(r)\ *n* -s **:** one that digs, gathers, or drags for quahogs

quai \'kā\ *n* -s [F — more at QUAY] **:** QUAY; *esp* **:** one lying along the river Seine in Paris

quaich *or* **quaigh** \'kwāk\ *n, pl* **quaichs** *or* **quaiches** *or* **quaighs** [ScGael *cuach*] *chiefly Scot* **:** a small shallow vessel or drinking cup typically made of wood, pewter, or silver and having ears for use as handles

quaich

¹quail \'kwāl, *esp before pause or consonant* -āəl\ *n, pl* **quail** *or* **quails** [ME *quaile, quaille,* fr. MF *quaille,* fr. ML *quaccula,* of imit. origin] **1 a** (1) **:** a migratory gallinaceous game bird (*Coturnix coturnix* syn. *C. communis*) of Europe, Asia, and Africa that is about seven inches long and has the upper parts brown and black marked with buff, the throat black and white, the breast reddish buff, and the belly whitish (2) **:** any of various other birds of the genus *Coturnix* chiefly inhabiting eastern Asia, southern Africa, India, or Australia **b :** any of various small American game birds of the order Galliformes: as (1) **:** BOBWHITE (2) **:** any of various birds related to the bobwhite — often used in combination ⟨California ~⟩ ⟨mountain ~⟩ ⟨valley ~⟩ — see MASSENA QUAIL **c :** BUTTON QUAIL **2 a** *obs* **:** COURTESAN **b** *slang* **:** a young woman or girl; *specif* **:** one attending a coeducational institution **3 :** HAIR BROWN

²quail \"\ *vb* -ED/-ING/-S [ME *quailen*, fr. MF *quailler*, fr. L *coagulare* — more at COAGULATE] *vi* **1** *dial chiefly Eng* **:** CURDLE, COAGULATE **2** *chiefly dial* **a :** to waste away **:** WITHER, DECLINE ⟨length of time causeth man and beast to ~ —Thomas Howell⟩ **b :** to break down **:** give way **:** WITHER ⟨the religion . . . ~*ing* into abject superstition —H.H.Milman⟩ **3 :** to lose courage **:** become cowed or fearful **:** WEAKEN ⟨eminent men invariably ~*ed* before her —Bertrand Russell⟩ ⟨no wonder his enemies ~*ed* —Stringfellow Barr⟩ ⟨the strongest ~ before financial ruin —Samuel Butler †1902⟩ ~ *vt* **1** *obs* **:** to affect harmfully **:** SPOIL, WASTE, WITHER **2** *archaic* **:** to make fearful **:** COW, DAUNT ⟨as thunder ~*s* the inferior creatures —John Wilson †1854⟩ **syn** see RECOIL

³quail \"\ *dial Eng var of* COIL

quail·berry \ˈkwā(ə)l- — see BERRY\ *n* **:** WOLFBERRY 1

quail brush *n* **1 :** any of various mountain mahoganies of the western U. S. **2** *also* **quail bush :** a spiny shrub (*Atriplex lentiformis*) that has scurfy foliage and is found on the alkali plains of the southwestern U. S. and adjacent Mexico

quail call *or* **quail pipe** *n* [*quail call* fr. ¹*quail* + *call; quail pipe* fr. ME *quaile pipe*, fr. *quaile* quail + *pipe*] **:** a call or pipe imitating the characteristic note of a quail for the purpose of luring the birds into a net or within range

quail disease *n* **:** an ulcerative enteritis of quails, turkeys, or other birds

quail dove *n* **:** any of various tropical American pigeons of terrestrial habits of the genera *Geotrygon, Oreopeleia*, and *Starnoenas* several of which occur in the West Indies and on the Florida Keys

quail hawk *n* **1 :** BUSH HAWK **2 :** COOPER'S HAWK

quailhead \ˈ=,=\ *n* [so called fr. the similarity of its head markings to those of a quail] **:** LARK SPARROW

quail snipe *n* **1 :** DOWITCHER **2 :** SEED SNIPE

quaily \ˈkwālē\ *n* -ES [¹*quail* + -*y*] **:** UPLAND PLOVER

¹quaint \ˈkwānt\ *adj* -ER/-EST [ME *queinte, cointe*, fr. OF *cointe* expert, elegant, fr. L *cognitus*, past part. of *cognoscere* to become acquainted with, know — more at COGNITION] **1** *obs* **a :** marked as cunning, scheming, crafty, artful, or wily ⟨the ~ smooth rogue —Thomas Otway⟩ **b :** characterized by knowledge, skill, or learning; *esp* **:** skilled in the use of language ⟨how ~ an orator —Shak.⟩ **2 a :** characterized by cleverness or ingenuity **:** skillfully wrought or artfully contrived ⟨the arming of each joint, in every piece how neat and ~ —Michael Drayton⟩ ⟨~ with many a device in India ink —Herman Melville⟩ ⟨set in the close-grained wood were ~ devices —Amy Lowell⟩ **b :** marked by beauty or elegance of appearance **:** HANDSOME ⟨a body so fantastic, trim, and ~ in its deportment and attire —William Cowper⟩ ⟨the ~, powerful simplicity which sculptors sometimes had —Nathaniel Hawthorne⟩ **c :** marked by ingenuity or refinement of language ⟨a new thought or conceit dressed up in smooth ~ language —Richard Steele⟩ **3 a** (1) **:** unusual or different in character or appearance **:** ODD, STRANGE ⟨came forth a ~ and fearful sight —Sir Walter Scott⟩ ⟨my stroll was marked . . . by only one ~ happening —William Beebe⟩ (2) **:** so unusual or different as to be bizarre, eccentric, or incongruous ⟨the head terminating in the ~ duck bill which gives the animal its vernacular name —Bill Beatty⟩ ⟨this horse . . . with so many ~ points and characteristics —Johnston Forbes-Robertson⟩ **b :** uncommon, old-fashioned, or unfamiliar but often agreeable or attractive in character, appearance, or action **:** PICTURESQUE ⟨a vaulted roof supporting a ~ chimney, much admired —Aubrey Drury⟩ ⟨dresses with a ~ old-fashioned elegance —*Current Biog.*⟩ ⟨a ~ pronunciation of English words that delighted her listeners —C.B.Nordhoff & J.N.Hall⟩ ⟨to make our present knowledge seem incomplete and ~ —Alan Gregg⟩ **c :** affectedly or artificially unfamiliar, old-fashioned, or picturesque ⟨a tendency to be a little too ~ —Jerome Stone⟩ ⟨they appeal to tourists as ~ —C.K.Kluckhohn⟩ ⟨the summer folk . . . left the land to the ~ natives —W. G.O'Donnell⟩ **4** *obs* **:** overly discriminating or needlessly meticulous **:** FASTIDIOUS ⟨being too ~ and finical in his expression —Roger L'Estrange⟩ **5 :** highly incongruous, inappropriate, or illogical **:** NAIVE, UNREASONABLE — usu. used ironically ⟨out of a ~ sense of honesty —Paul Engle⟩ ⟨the ~ notion that a speaker should be heard as well as understood —H.F. & Katharine Pringle⟩ ⟨~ notion that it is a writer's business to write —J.K.Hutchens⟩ **syn** see STRANGE

²quaint \"\ *vb* [ME *coynten, quainten*, short for *acoynten, aquainten* to acquaint — more at ACQUAINT] *chiefly dial* **:** ACQUAINT

quaint·ish \-tish\ *adj* **:** marked somewhat by quaintness

quaint·ly *adv* [ME *queinteliche, queintely*, fr. *queinte* quaint + -*liche*, -*ly* -ly] **:** in a quaint manner

quaint·ness *n* -ES [ME *queyntnesse*, fr. *queynt, queinte* quaint + -*nes*, -*nesse* -ness] **:** the quality or state of being quaint

quais *pl of* QUAI

quait \ˈkwāt\ *dial var of* QUOIT

¹quake \ˈkwāk\ *vb* -ED/-ING/-S [ME *quaken*, fr. OE *cwacian*; akin to OE *cweccan* to shake, vibrate] *vi* **1 a :** to shake, vibrate, or tremble usu. from shock or convulsion ⟨boughs that ~*ed* at every breath —Sir Walter Scott⟩ ⟨ample bosom *quaked* mirthfully —Gerald Beaumont⟩ ⟨the earth *quaked* as if it had been struck a fantastic blow —Robert O'Brien⟩ **b :** to shake or shiver from the cold or other physical cause ⟨~ in the present winter's state, and wish that warmer days would come —Shak.⟩ ⟨with legs *quaking* —E.K.Kane⟩ **2 :** to tremble or shudder inwardly often in anticipation of difficulty or danger **:** QUAIL ⟨my heart did never ~, or courage faint —Christopher Marlowe⟩ ⟨it was a bold thing to say, and I *quaked* —Winston Churchill⟩ ~ *vt*, *obs* **:** to cause to quake ⟨humble and ~ us for our sins —Henry Greenwood⟩

²quake \"\ *n* -S [ME, fr. *quaken*, v.] **1 :** an instance of shaking or trembling **:** a tremulous agitation or convulsion **2 :** something that causes quaking; *esp* **:** EARTHQUAKE

quake grass *n* **1 :** QUAKING GRASS **2 :** COUCH GRASS 1a

quake ooze *n* **:** soft boggy ground **:** MARSH

quakeproof \ˈ=;=\ *adj* **:** able to withstand damage or destruction by an earthquake

¹quak·er \ˈkwākə(r)\ *n* -S *often attrib* [¹*quake* + -*er*] **1 :** one that quakes **2** *usu cap* **:** FRIEND 6 **3 a** (1) **:** an Australian night heron (*Nycticorax caledonicus*) (2) **:** the sooty albatross **b :** a grasshopper or locust of the genus *Oedipoda* **c** *or* **quaker moth :** any of several English noctuid moths (as *Graphiphora castanea*) **4** *often cap* **:** ART GRAY **5 :** QUAKER GUN **6** *or* **quaker aspen :** ASPEN **7** *cap* **:** PENNSYLVANIAN — used as a nickname **8 :** an immature or blighted coffee bean found in inferior grades of coffee — usu. used in pl.

²quaker \"\ *vi* [freq. of ¹*quake*] *dial Brit* **:** QUAKE

quakerbird \ˈ==,=\ *n* **:** SOOTY ALBATROSS

quaker blue *n, often cap Q* **:** a nearly neutral slightly bluish black that is lighter and slightly redder than lampblack

quaker bonnet *n, usu cap Q* **:** BLUET 1c(1)

quak·er·dom \ˈkwākə(r)dəm\ *n* -S *usu cap* **:** QUAKERISM

quaker drab *n, often cap Q* **:** a nearly neutral slightly purplish medium gray that is very slightly redder than frost gray

quak·er·ess \-kərə̇s\ *n* -ES *usu cap* **:** a female Quaker

quaker gray *n, often cap Q* **:** a light grayish olive color that is greener and paler than hemp, lighter than twine, and redder and darker than average citron gray — called also *acier, gray drab*

quaker green *n, often cap Q* **:** a moderate olive green that is yellower, stronger, and slightly lighter than forest green (sense 2), yellower, lighter, and stronger than cypress green, and stronger than Lincoln green

quaker gun *n, usu cap Q* [so called fr. the Friends' opposition to war] **:** a dummy piece of artillery that is usu. made of wood

quak·er·ish \-kərish\ *adj, usu cap* **:** similar to or having the characteristics of a Friend ⟨~ tidiness of her black dress and white collar —Ngaio Marsh⟩ ⟨~ notions —Frederick Chase⟩

quak·er·ism \-kə,rizəm\ *n* -S *usu cap* **:** the religious beliefs or practices of the Friends

quaker–ladies \ˈ==,==\ *n pl, often cap Q* **:** BLUETS

quak·er·ly *adj, usu cap* **:** of, relating to, or characteristic of a Friend **:** QUAKERISH ⟨~ meditation⟩

quaker meeting *n, usu cap Q* **1 :** a society or congregation of Friends **2 a :** a meeting of Friends for worship in which prolonged periods of silence often occur **b :** a social gathering marked by little or no conversation or by conversation with long pauses

quakes *pres 3d sing of* QUAKE, *pl of* QUAKE

quaketail \ˈ=,=\ *n* **:** YELLOW WAGTAIL

quak·i·ness \ˈkwākēnə̇s\ *n* -ES **:** the quality or state of being quaky

quak·ing \ˈkwākiŋ, -kēŋ\ *adj* [ME, fr. pres. part. of *quaken* to quake] **1 :** SHAKING, VIBRATING, TREMBLING **2** *usu cap* **:** QUAKERISH — **quak·ing·ly** *adv*

quaking aspen *also* **quaking ash** *or* **quaking asp** *n* **:** ASPEN

quaking bog *n* **:** a bog of forming peat that is wholly or partially floating and that shakes when walked on

quaking grass *n* **1 :** any of several grasses of the genus *Briza* having slender-stalked and pendulous ovate spikelets that quake and rattle in the wind **2 :** RATTLESNAKE GRASS

quaky \ˈkwākē\ *adj* -ER/-EST [¹*quake* + -*y*] **:** QUAKING, SHAKY, TREMULOUS

qual *abbr* **1** qualification; qualified; qualify **2** qualitative; quality

qua·le \ˈkwālē\ *n, pl* **qua·lia** \-ēə\ [L, neut. sing. of *qualis* of what kind — more at QUALITY] **1 a :** a quality that is an independent object ⟨establish . . . the vague form or ~ of spatiality —William James⟩ **b :** something that has a quality ⟨could never adjust ourselves to a universe in which we saw *qualia* or data but never objects —Campbell Crockett⟩ **2 :** a sense-datum or feeling having its own particular quality without meaning or external reference ⟨a ~ . . . such as, say, a certain shade of purple occurring in the presentation of a certain piece of cloth in a particular light —C.G.Hempel⟩

qual·i·fi·ca·tion \,kwäləfə̇ˈkāshən *sometimes* ,kwȯl-\ *n* -S [ML *qualification-, qualificatio*, fr. *qualificatus* (past part. of *qualificare* to qualify) + L -*ion-*, -*io* -ion — more at QUALIFY] **1 :** something that qualifies or restricts **:** LIMITATION, MODIFICATION ⟨~*s* amounting . . . to correctives —V.C.Aldrich⟩ ⟨the statement stands without ~⟩ **2 a** *obs* **:** distinctive character **:** NATURE ⟨the English tradesman . . . his ~ —Daniel Defoe⟩ **b** *archaic* **:** CHARACTERISTIC, TRAIT ⟨the ~*s* of the . . . nation —Joseph Addison⟩ **c** *archaic* **:** a specific capacity or attainment **:** ACCOMPLISHMENT ⟨every ~ is raised . . . to more than its true value —Jane Austen⟩ **3 a :** an endowment or acquirement that fits a person (as for an office) ⟨a person of outstanding ~*s* —*U. S. Code*⟩ ⟨physical ~*s* for pilots —H.G.Armstrong⟩ **b :** a condition precedent that must be complied with (as for the attainment of a privilege) ⟨residence ~*s* for membership —F.A.Ogg & P.O.Ray⟩

¹qual·i·fi·ca·tive \ˈkwäləfə̇,kād·iv\ *n* -S [ML *qualificatus* (past part. of *qualificare*) + E -*ive*, n. suffix] **:** a qualifying word ⟨~*s* . . . to describe the kinds of historical relationships —D.M.Taylor⟩

²qualificative \"\ *adj* [ML *qualificatus* (past part. of *qualificare*) + E -*ive*, adj. suffix] **:** QUALIFYING ⟨the ~ concords in four languages —Guy Atkins⟩

qual·i·fi·ca·tor \-d·ə(r)\ *n* -S [ML, fr. *qualificatus* (past part. of *qualificare*) + L -*or*] **:** an officer whose business it is to examine and prepare causes for trial in the ecclesiastical courts of the Roman Catholic Church

qual·i·fi·ca·tory \ˈkwäləfə̇kə,tōrē\ *adj* [ML *qualificatus* (past part. of *qualificare*) + E -*ory*] **:** QUALIFYING, LIMITING

qualified *adj* **1 a :** fitted (as by endowments or accomplishments) for a given purpose **:** COMPETENT, FIT ⟨~ to govern the country —G.B.Shaw⟩ ⟨poorly ~ officers —*Magazine Intelligence*⟩ **b :** having complied with the specific requirements or precedent conditions (as for an office or employment) **:** ELIGIBLE, CERTIFIED ⟨~ by age and residence to run for the office⟩ ⟨lacks two credits of being fully ~⟩ **2** *obs* **a :** having certain qualities; *esp* **:** possessed of good qualities **:** ACCOMPLISHED ⟨the fine ~ gentleman —Thomas Nash⟩ **b :** belonging to the aristocracy ⟨not ~ but . . . common and ordinary persons —Andrew Willet⟩ **3 :** limited or modified in some way ⟨properly ~ conclusions —W.J.Reilly⟩ ⟨the author's outlook . . . is one of ~ optimism —P.B.Sears⟩; *specif* **:** modified by the attachment of conditions ⟨a ~ acceptance of a bill of exchange⟩ **syn** see ABLE

qualified endorsement *n* **:** an endorsement passing title to a commercial paper but disclaiming liability of the indorser should the party primarily liable fail to pay when due

qualified fee *n* **:** a defeasible estate in fee that may come to an end (as for breach of a condition or on account of an executory limitation on a stated event); *specif* **:** a base or determinable fee simple — compare FEE SIMPLE CONDITIONAL

qual·i·fied·ly *adv* **:** in a qualified manner

qual·i·fied·ness *n* -ES **:** the quality or state of being qualified

qualified privilege *n* **:** a privilege that arises and is available in the law of libel and slander when there are facts justifying the statement written or spoken but that may not be available when the words are uttered with malice or without good faith — compare ABSOLUTE PRIVILEGE

qualified property *n* **1 :** ownership that is not absolute and complete **2 :** property the subject matter of which by nature is not permanent (as wild animals reduced to possession but not in captivity)

qual·i·fi·er \ˈkwälə,fī(ə)r, -īə *sometimes* ˈkwȯl-\ *n* -S **1 :** one that qualifies: as **a :** one that satisfies requirements or meets a specified standard (as of performance in an athletic contest) ⟨paced the ~*s* . . . in the trial heats —*N.Y. Times*⟩ **b :** a word (as an adjective or adverb) or word group that qualifies or restricts another word or word group ⟨resolved never to use a ~ again when . . . reviewing a book —Harvey Breit⟩ **2 :** QUALIFICATOR

qual·i·fy \-fī\ *vb* -ED/-ING/-ES [MF *qualifier*, fr. ML *qualificare*, fr. L *qualis* of what kind + -*ficare* -fy — more at QUALITY] *vt* **1 a :** to reduce from a general, undefined, or comprehensive to a particular or restricted form **:** MODIFY, LIMIT ⟨statements were explained and *qualified* in the author's lectures —H.O.Taylor⟩ **b :** to make less harsh or strict **:** MODERATE, SOFTEN ⟨time *qualifies* the spark and fire —Shak.⟩ ⟨the power to regulate commerce could not be cut down or *qualified* —O.W.Holmes †1935⟩ **c** *obs* **:** to maintain in proper condition **:** CONTROL **d :** to alter the strength or flavor of (a liquid) ⟨coffee *qualified* with cognac⟩ ⟨an infusion useful to ~ the rest —Havelock Ellis⟩ **e :** to limit or modify the meaning of (as a noun or verb or adjective) **2 :** to characterize by naming an attribute **:** DESCRIBE, DESIGNATE ⟨cannot ~ it as . . . either glad or sorry —T.S.Eliot⟩ **3 a :** to give the required qualities to **:** fit esp. for an office or privilege ⟨his skills ~ him for the job⟩ ⟨the cisterns ~ the farms for a Class A . . . rating —Don Cunnion⟩ **b** *obs* **:** to endow with qualities ⟨a mind excellently *qualified* —Robert Greene⟩ **c** (1) **:** to declare competent or adequate as meeting set standards **:** CERTIFY ⟨~ every candidate who can meet the requirements —H.G. Armstrong⟩ ⟨certificates . . . ~*ing* their meat —S.N.Behrman⟩ (2) **:** to invest (a person) with legal capacity **:** LICENSE *is* ⟨*qualified* to practice law in this state⟩ (3) **:** to give legal power to by administering an oath **:** swear in ⟨~ a jury⟩ ~ *vi* **1 :** to become fit (as for an employment) **:** become capable **:** measure up to or meet a set standard or requirement ⟨expects to ~ for the position⟩ ⟨*qualifies* as a complete man of letters —Selden Rodman⟩ ⟨approved land drainage *qualifies* for a government grant —F.D.Smith & Barbara Wilcox⟩ **2 :** to obtain legal or competent power or capacity by taking oath or giving bond or complying with the necessary forms or conditions ⟨*qualifies* by court order as an executor —R.B.Gehman⟩ ⟨have just *qualified* as barristers —*Brit. Book News*⟩ **3 a :** to exhibit in a game or sport a required degree of ability in one or more preliminary contests (as heats in a race or rounds in a golf tournament) **b :** to fire a score that makes one eligible for the award of a marksmanship badge **syn** see MODERATE, PREPARE

²qualify \"\ *n* -ES **:** a gambling game played with five dice usu. for merchandise or small cash prizes in which the caster tries in five rolls to amass as many as possible of as high a number as possible

qualifying *adj* **:** that qualifies — **qual·i·fy·ing·ly** *adv*

qualifying heat *or* **qualifying round** *or* **qualifying game** *n* **:** a preliminary contest (as in a race or tournament) the winner of which may enter the final contest

qual·i·ta·tive \ˈkwälə,tād·|iv, -āt|, |ēv *also* |əv *sometimes* ˈkwȯl-\ *adj* [LL *qualitativus*, fr. L *qualitat-, qualitas* + -*ivus* -ive] **:** of, relating to, or involving quality or kind ⟨~ change⟩ ⟨~ data⟩ — contrasted with *quantitative* — **qual·i·ta·tive·ly** \|əvlē, -li\ *adv*

qualitative analysis *n* **:** a branch of chemistry whose scope is to detect and characterize the elements or radicals in a pure substance or to identify the components of a mixture — compare ANALYSIS 4b

qualitative character *n* **:** a discrete heritable character that has transmitted well-defined limits and is in a simple alternate manner **:** a typical Mendelian character — compare QUANTITATIVE CHARACTER

qual·i·tied \ˈkwäləd·ēd, -ətēd *sometimes* ˈkwȯl-\ *adj* [¹*quality* + -*ed*] **:** having qualities **:** endowed with a quality ⟨he was well ~ —George Chapman⟩

¹qual·i·ty \-əd·ē, -ətē, -i\ *n* -ES [ME *qualite*, fr. OF *qualité*, fr. L *qualitat-, qualitas* (trans. of Gk *poiotēs*), fr. *qualis* of what kind + -*tat-*, -*tas* -ty; akin to L *qui* who — more at WHO] **1 a :** peculiar and essential character **:** NATURE, KIND ⟨differences in the ~ of the two temperaments —M.D.Howe⟩ ⟨self-interest and sympathy, opposite in ~ —John Dewey⟩ ⟨the ~ of mercy is not strained —Shak.⟩ ⟨the offender knew the nature and ~ of the act —B.N.Cardozo⟩ ⟨take on the ~ of animate life —H.V.Gregory⟩ **b :** a distinctive inherent feature **:** PROPERTY, VIRTUE ⟨the *qualities* of the circle⟩ ⟨has the . . . ~ that its color and spectrum fade out —Albert Szent-Györgyi⟩ ⟨herbs . . . and their true *qualities* —Shak.⟩ **c :** a character, position, or role usu. assumed temporarily **:** CAPACITY — usu. used in the phrases *in quality of, in the quality of* ⟨I make this inquiry in ~ of an antiquary —Thomas Gray⟩ ⟨in the ~ of reader and companion —Joseph Conrad⟩ **2 a** (1) **:** degree of excellence **:** GRADE, CALIBER ⟨decline in the ~ of students —H.L.Creek⟩ ⟨the ~ of the soil —J.M.Mogey⟩ ⟨manufactured in only one ~ —*Catalog of Plumbing Fixtures*⟩ ⟨the ~ of the . . . golfer's game —Judson Philips⟩ (2) **:** degree of conformance to a standard (as of a product or workmanship) **b** (1) **:** inherent or intrinsic excellence of character or type **:** superiority in kind ⟨merchandise of ~⟩ ⟨proclaimed the ~ of his wife —Compton Mackenzie⟩ ⟨colt with . . . plenty of ~ —G.F.T. Ryall⟩ (2) *of livestock* **:** refinement or excellence of appearance with close adherence to the standards of a breed (3) **:** fineness of texture (as of meat or plumage) (4) **:** the characteristics (as texture, marbling, color) of uncooked meat that influence tenderness and palatability **3 a :** social status **:** RANK ⟨your name, your ~ —Shak.⟩; *esp* **:** high social position ⟨a man of ~⟩ ⟨solicited a person of ~ for the appointment⟩ ⟨the colored people of ~ —Oscar Handlin⟩ **b :** persons of high social status **:** ARISTOCRACY ⟨companions . . . among the highest ~ in the land —*Fashion Digest*⟩ — usu. used with *the* ⟨flaunting themselves . . . as if they were the ~ —David Garnett⟩ **c** *obs* **:** a group of persons having distinctive character **:** FRATERNITY, PARTY, PROFESSION ⟨you are not of our ~ —Shak.⟩; *esp* **:** the acting profession ⟨players, I love yee, and your ~ —John Davies⟩ **4 a :** a special or distinguishing attribute **:** CHARACTERISTIC ⟨the boy has many fine *qualities*⟩ ⟨*qualities* of naïveté and inexperience —Peter Foster⟩ ⟨more than any other ~ . . . gregariousness —W.H.Whyte⟩ ⟨the man was much greater than the sum of his *qualities* —Willa Cather⟩; *esp* **:** a desirable trait **:** EXCELLENCE ⟨a man without *qualities* —Frederic Morton⟩ ⟨the defect as well as the *qualities* of its . . . origins —*Times Lit. Supp.*⟩ **b :** the character in a logical proposition of being affirmative or negative — see OPPOSITION 2a(2) **c :** the character of an estate as determined by the manner in which it is to be held or enjoyed **d** *archaic* **:** an acquired skill **:** ACCOMPLISHMENT ⟨she hath more *qualities* than a water spaniel —Shak.⟩ **5 a :** something that serves to identify a subject of perception or thought in the respect in which it is considered **b :** something from the possession of which a thing is such as it is **:** PREDICATE — see PRIMARY QUALITY, SECONDARY QUALITY, TERTIARY QUALITY **c** (1) **:** something that exists or can exist only as a qualification of something else (2) **:** an attribute that obtains only after a certain level has been reached and in a certain complex fitted to receive it ⟨in the theory of emergent evolution life and mind are *qualities*⟩ **6 :** manner of action — usu. used in the phrase *adverb of quality* **7 a :** vividness of hue **:** SATURATION CHROMA **b :** a property of a musical tone that distinguishes it from another tone having the same pitch and loudness and that is determined by the number and prominence of the overtones mixed with the fundamental — called also *timbre* **c :** the identifying character of a vowel sound determined chiefly by the resonance of the vocal chambers in uttering it **d :** the character of an X-ray beam that determines its penetrating power and is dependent upon its wavelength distribution **e :** the attribute of an elementary sensation that makes it different in kind and not simply in intensity, duration, or extent from any other sensation ⟨red, sweet, and cold are *qualities* of certain sensations⟩ **8 :** the ratio by weight of water vapor in wet steam to vapor and suspended liquid droplets together usu. expressed as a percentage

syn QUALITY, STATURE, and CALIBER are often interchangeable as indicating, when used in constructions without grammatical modifiers, merit or superiority because of a combination of good characteristics ⟨our candidate is a man of *quality*, of *stature*, of *caliber*⟩ QUALITY may stress inherent, enduring good traits that make one somewhat superior ⟨there was nothing in his outer case to suggest the fierceness and fortitude and fire of the man, and yet even the thick-blooded Mexican half-breeds knew his *quality* at once —Willa Cather⟩ ⟨had *quality*, if he lacked character —Ellen Glasgow⟩ ⟨as those of *quality* do, not as the vulgar —George Washington⟩ STATURE is likely to suggest height reached or development attained to and to connote considerations of prestige and eminence ⟨in time the expanding vitality attains its full *stature* —Ellen Glasgow⟩ ⟨men of *stature* and local prestige formed the personnel of these committees —C.G.Bowers⟩ Unlike QUALITY, STATURE is freely used with notions of increase or decrease ⟨probings in the realms of life and matter have seemed to diminish man's *stature* and to belittle his dignity —J.P. Marquand⟩ CALIBER may connote an unusual but measurable range, scope, breadth of intellectual capacity or of other ability ⟨it is true that, in the early years of George III's reign, there were Britons of the intellectual *caliber* of Hume and Gibbon who were avowed skeptics —G.M.Trevelyan⟩ ⟨in practically every country there is a decrease in the intellectual and moral *caliber* of those who carry the responsibility of public affairs —*Times Lit. Supp.*⟩

syn PROPERTY, CHARACTER, ATTRIBUTE, ACCIDENT: QUALITY is a general term applicable to any trait or characteristic; it is frequently used in relation to inherent traits not immediately apparent and ascertained only after experience or examination ⟨my intolerance is reserved for *qualities* and not for externals —A.C.Benson⟩ ⟨the persistent contemporariness that is a *quality* of all good art —Aldous Huxley⟩ ⟨there was only one *quality* in a woman that appealed to him — charm —John Galsworthy⟩ PROPERTY may refer to a peculiar or distinctive trait, often an essential or intrinsic one, which can be used to describe a species or type ⟨since ether is not material it has not any of the usual characteristics of matter — mass, rigidity, etc. — but it has quite definite *properties* of its own —A.S. Eddington⟩ ⟨weight is only an apparently invariable *property* of matter —Havelock Ellis⟩ CHARACTER may stress an identifying property ⟨hauynite and noselite show *characters* like sodalite, but they differ from it in containing the radical SO_4 in the place of chlorine —L.V.Pirsson⟩ ⟨deserves credit for having preserved the *character* and characteristics of his original —B.R.Redman⟩ ATTRIBUTE indicates a characteristic, often an essential concomitant, with which a person or thing has been endowed ⟨this Confederation had none of the *attributes* of sovereignty in legislative, executive, or judicial power —R.B.Taney⟩ ⟨the harder a writer tries to add beauty to clearness, the more surely does he feel himself to be held off from perfection by *attributes* of language which he did not make and cannot do away with —C.E.Montague⟩ ACCIDENT refers to an additional, concomitant trait, one nonessential and usu. noninherent in the thing under consideration

⟨certainly many mystics have been ascetic. But that has been the *accident* of their philosophy, and not the essence of their religion —Havelock Ellis⟩

2quality \"\ *adj* **1 :** of or relating to high society **:** ARISTOCRATIC ⟨~ folks⟩ ⟨bring ~ people to the wedding —Padraic Colum⟩ **2 :** of, relating to, or marked by good quality **:** EXCELLENT ⟨~ goods⟩ ⟨~ meat⟩ ⟨~ stocks⟩ ⟨~ leather⟩ ⟨this ~ revolution in . . . buying habits —*N.Y.Times*⟩ ⟨make it a ~ operation —Virgil Thomson⟩

quality control *n* **:** an aggregate of functions designed to insure adequate quality in manufactured products by initial critical study of engineering design, materials, processes, equipment, and workmanship followed by periodic inspection and analysis of the results of inspection to determine causes for defects and by removal of such causes

quality control chart *n* **:** a chart that gives the results of periodic sampling for rejects of a manufactured product and that is used in making decisions concerning the maintenance of product quality

quality factor *n* **1 :** QUALITY 8 **2 :** 2Q

qual·i·ty·less \'kwäləd·ēləs\ *adj* **:** lacking quality or qualities

quality magazine *n* **:** a periodical containing material designed to appeal esp. to readers of superior education or culture

quality point *or* **quality credit** *n* **:** one of the points or credits earned in a course according to a system by which the academic credit allotted to the course is multiplied by a factor that varies with the grade received ⟨an A in a 3-credit course gives the student 9 *quality points*⟩

qualm \'kwä|m, 'kwȧ| *also* 'kwȯ| *sometimes* |lm; *archaic* 'kwam\ *n* -s [origin unknown] **1 :** a usu. sudden attack of illness, faintness, or esp. nausea ⟨a jerk in the pit of his stomach caused him a severe internal ~ —G.B.Shaw⟩ **2 a :** a spasm of fear **:** a sudden misgiving or faintheartedness ⟨the memory gave him almost a ~ of terror —Anne D. Sedgwick⟩ ⟨had ~s about setting forth over the treacherous waters —V.G.Heiser⟩ **b :** a sudden access of disturbing sensation or emotion ⟨a little ~ of homesickness —C.S.Forester⟩ ⟨a ~ of tenderness shook his unstable heart —D.C.Peattie⟩ **3 :** a feeling of uneasiness about a point of conscience, honor, or propriety **:** COMPUNCTION ⟨their claims are formulated without any ~s of modesty —Herbert Read⟩ ⟨he could drop her without a ~ —Lester Atwell⟩ **syn** see SCRUPLE

qualm·ish \-mish, -mēsh\ *adj* **1 a :** having or tending to have qualms esp. of nausea **:** NAUSEATED ⟨my dear angel has been ~ of late —Tobias Smollett⟩ **b :** affected by scruples or compunction **:** SQUEAMISH ⟨~ . . . he refused to kill a spider —John Hersey⟩ **2 :** of, relating to, or likely to produce qualms ⟨a ~ . . . feeling in his stomach —Gladys Schmitt⟩ ⟨the ~ nightmare —J.G.Cozzens⟩ — **qualm·ish·ly** *adv* — **qualm·ish·ness** *n* -ES

qualmy \-mē\ *adj* -ER/-EST **:** QUALMISH

quamash *var of* CAMAS

qua·ma·sia \kwə'māzhēə, -āsēə\ *syn of* CAMASSIA

quam diu \(')kwäm'dē(,)ü\ *adv* [L, so long as] **:** so long as; *specif* **:** during good behavior — usu. used of the tenure of a judge

quam·o·clit \'kwamə,klit\ *n* [NL, perh. alter. of Nahuatl *cuauh-mochitl* camachile] **1** *cap* **:** a small genus of twining vines (family Convolvulaceae) of warm regions distinguished from *Ipomoea* by the salverform corolla and exserted stamens and style — see STAR IPOMOEA **2** -s **:** any plant of the genus *Quamoclit; esp* **:** CYPRESS VINE

quan·da·ry \'kwänd(ə)rē, -ri *sometimes* 'kwȯn-\ *n* -ES [origin unknown] **:** a state of perplexity or doubt **:** DILEMMA ⟨in a ~ as to where my road should lie —Clyde Higgs⟩ **syn** see PREDICAMENT

quan·dong *also* **quan·dang** *or* **quon·dong** \'kwän,däŋ\ *or* **quan·tong** \-n·,täŋ\ *n* -s [native name in Australia] **1 a :** a small or shrubby Australian tree (*Fusanus acuminatus* or *Elaeocarpus grandis*) of the family Santalaceae that has lanceolate leaves and small flowers in terminal panicles followed by round edible red drupes **b :** the fruit of the quandong tree — called also *native peach;* see QUANDONG NUT **2 :** BRISBANE QUANDONG

quandong nut *n* **:** the edible seed of the hard round pitted stone of the quandong

quan·dy \'kwändē\ *n* -ES [perh. imit.] *NewEng* **:** OLD-SQUAW

1quant \'kwant, 'kwänt\ *n* -s [ME *quante*] *dial Eng* **:** a punting pole with a flange near the end

2quant \'kwänt\ *n, pl* **quants** \-ts\ *or* **quan·ta** \-tə\ [ISV, by shortening] **:** QUANTUM 3 — used esp. in the phrase *light quant*

quant *abbr* quantitative

quanta *pl of* QUANTUM

quan·tal \'kwänt'l\ *adj* [L *quantus* how much + E *-al*] **1 :** of or relating to a quantum **2 :** being or relating to a sensitivity response marked by the presence or absence of a definite reaction ⟨an all-or-none response to a stimulus is ~⟩

1quan·tic \'kwäntik\ *n* -s [L *quantus* how much + E *-ic,* n. suffix] **:** a homogeneous polynomial in two or more variables

2quantic \"\ *adj* [ISV *quantum* + *-ic,* adj. suffix] **:** of or relating to a quantum

quan·ti·fi·abil·i·ty \,kwäntə,fīə'bilədē\ *n* **:** the quality or state of being quantifiable

quan·ti·fi·able \'==,fīəbəl, ,==='==\ *adj* **:** capable of being quantified

quan·ti·fi·ably \-blē\ *adv* **:** in a quantifiable manner

quan·ti·fi·ca·tion \,kwäntəfəkāshən\ *n* -s [fr. *quantify,* after E *qualify: qualification*] **1 a :** the operation of quantifying in logic: as (1) *Hamiltonism* **:** the process of making the quantity of a predicate explicit by prefixing it with *all* or *some* ⟨by ~ "all men are mortals" becomes "all men are some mortals"⟩ (2) **:** the operation in symbolic logic of forming a statement by prefixing a quantifier to a sentential function **b :** a statement formed by quantification **2 :** the introduction of the element of quantity; *specif* **:** the transformation of qualitative into quantitative data in scientific methodology ⟨a thermometer is used in the ~ of temperature⟩ — **quan·ti·fi·ca·tion·al** \;===;kāshən'l\ *adj* — **quan·ti·fi·ca·tion·al·ly** \-'lē\ *adv*

quan·ti·fi·er \'kwäntə,fī(ə)r\ *n* -s **1 :** a word (as a numeral) expressive of quantity ⟨*two, thirty, many,* and *much* are ~s⟩ **2 :** a prefix that binds the variables in a logical formula by specifying their quantity — see EXISTENTIAL OPERATOR, UNIVERSAL QUANTIFIER

quan·ti·fy \'kwäntə,fī *sometimes* 'kwȯn-\ *vt* -ED/-ING/-ES [ML *quantificare,* fr. L *quantus* how much + *-ficare* -fy — more at QUANTITY] **1 a :** to qualify (a term in a logical proposition) by indicating the logical quantity ⟨the word "all" *quantifies* "men" in the proposition "all men are mortal"⟩ **:** bind (a variable in a sentential function) by prefixing a quantifier **b :** to make (the logical quantity of a term) explicit (as by transforming "the Chinese are industrious" into "most Chinese are industrious") — compare QUANTIFICATION, QUANTIFIER **2 a :** to determine, express, or measure the quantity of **b :** to transform or translate from the qualitative into the quantitative

quan·tim·e·ter \kwän'timəd·ə(r)\ *n* [ISV *quantity* + *-meter*] **:** a device that is used to measure the quantity of X rays

quan·ti·tate \'kwän(t)ə,tāt *sometimes* 'kwȯn-\ *vt* -ED/-ING/-S [back-formation fr. *quantitative*] **:** to measure or estimate the quantity of **:** express in quantitative terms ⟨the doctor can . . . ~ the best formula for each infant —*Jour. Amer. Med. Assoc.*⟩ ⟨inability to ~ such a procedure —*Psychosomatic Medicine*⟩

quan·ti·ta·tion \,==='tāshən\ *n* -s [*quantitate* + *-ion*] **:** the act or process of quantitating ⟨a method used for ~ —*Chem. Abstracts*⟩

quan·ti·ta·tive \'==,tād·|iv, -āt|, |ēv *also* |əv\ *adj* [ML *quantitativus,* fr. L *quantitat-, quantitas* quantity + *-ivus* -ive] **1** *archaic* **:** having quantity (as mass, magnitude, extent in space, or duration in time) **2 :** of, relating to, or expressible in terms of quantity ⟨~ relation⟩ ⟨~ aspect⟩ ⟨export wheat without ~ limitation —*Sydney (Australia) Bull.*⟩ **3 :** of, relating to, or involving the measurement of quantity or amount — contrasted with *qualitative* ⟨dearth of ~ studies —W.O.Aydelotte⟩ **4 :** based upon quantity; *specif* **:** based upon temporal quantity or duration of sounds — used of a rhythmic system in which the base is some arrangement of elements distinguished as *long* and *short* (as in typical verse of the classical periods in Greek, Latin, Sanskrit, Arabic, and Persian); contrasted with *accentual;* compare QUANTITY 4a, SYLLABIC — **quan·ti·ta·tive·ly** \|əvlē, -li\ *adv* — **quan·ti·ta·tive·ness** \|ivnəs\ *n* -ES

quantitative analysis *n* **:** a branch of chemistry whose scope is to determine the amounts of elements or groups in a pure substance or to determine the percentage of components in a mixture — compare ANALYSIS 4b

quantitative character *n* **:** a heritable character that has indefinite limits and is transmitted as a continuous variation **:** a polygenic character — see QUANTITATIVE INHERITANCE; compare MULTIPLE FACTOR, QUALITATIVE CHARACTER

quantitative inheritance *n* **:** particulate inheritance of any quantitative character mediated by groups of multiple factors each allelic pair of which adds or subtracts a specific increment of the collectively controlled character (as height or skin color in man) so that each increment is essentially a qualitative character inherited in purely particulate fashion although the character as a whole appears to exhibit blending inheritance

quan·ti·tive \'kwän(t)əd·iv\ *adj* [by contr.] **:** QUANTITATIVE — **quan·ti·tive·ly** \-d·əvlē\ *adv*

1quan·ti·ty \'kwän(t)əd·ē, -ətē, -i *sometimes* 'kwȯn-\ *n* -ES [ME *quantite,* fr. OF *quantité,* fr. L *quantitat-, quantitas,* fr. *quantus* how much, how large + *-itat-, -itas* -ity; akin to L *quam* than, how, *quando* when, *qui* who — more at WHO] **1 a :** an indefinite amount or number ⟨a ~ of interesting information —Roy Lewis & Angus Maude⟩ ⟨a ~ of pleasure —I.V.Morris⟩ ⟨an impressive ~ of lawbooks —David Williamson⟩ **b :** a determinate or estimated amount ⟨the ~ of flour called for in the recipe⟩ ⟨measuring *quantities* of heat —K.K. Darrow⟩ **c :** total amount or number ⟨the ~ of shoes produced by the company⟩ ⟨the ~ of tone —Warwick Braithwaite⟩ ⟨the ~ of her devotion —Mark Van Doren⟩ **d** (1) **:** a great or very considerable amount or number **:** LOT, BULK ⟨a ~ of bright shawl . . . about her head —Charles Dickens⟩ ⟨bought a ~ of plants —Rachel Henning⟩ ⟨merchandise sold in ~⟩ (2) **quantities** *pl* **:** great amounts or numbers **:** SCADS ⟨~s of money⟩ ⟨~ of tan-backed girls —Edmund Wilson⟩ **e** *obs* **:** a small amount **:** MITE ⟨retaining but a ~ of life —Shak.⟩ **f** *obs* **:** relative amount **:** PROPORTION ⟨women's fear and love holds ~ —Shak.⟩ **2** *archaic* **:** a definite surface or extent in space ⟨grant of a sufficient ~ of . . . land —Edmund Burke⟩ **3 a :** the character of something that makes it possible to measure or number it or to determine that it is more or less than something else ⟨a matter of ~ of production rather than quality⟩ **b :** something that may be operated upon according to fixed mutually consistent mathematical laws — see MAGNITUDE 5 **4 a :** duration and intensity of sounds as distinct from their individual quality or phonemic character; *specif* **:** the relative length or brevity of sounds usu. indicated (as for Greek and Latin prosody) by a macron for the long, a breve for the short, and a combination of macron and breve for the common that may be either long or short **b** *archaic* **:** the relative length or duration of a musical tone **c :** the relative duration or time length of a speech sound or sound group **d :** the character of an estate as determined by its time of continuance or degree of interest (as in fee, for life, or for years) **5 a :** the extent in which a term in a given logical proposition is to be taken; *esp* **:** such extent as indicated by *all, some,* or *no* **b :** the character of a logical proposition as universal, particular, or singular **c :** the extension, intension, or information of a logical term **syn** see SUM

2quantity \"\ *adj* **:** of, relating to, or involving quantity ⟨~ basis⟩ ⟨~ production⟩

quantity of light : luminous energy that is the product of mean luminous flux by time ⟨*quantity of light* expressed in lumen-hours⟩

quantity surveyor *n* **:** one that estimates or measures building quantities

quantity theory *or* **quantity theory of money** *n* **:** a theory in economics: changes in the price level and the value of money vary with changes in the amount of money in circulation

quan·ti·za·tion \,kwäntə'zāshən, -än,tī'-\ *n* -s **:** the act or process of quantizing: as **a :** subdivision into quanta **b :** expression in terms of quantum theory

quan·tize \'kwän,tīz\ *vt* -ED/-ING/-S [*quantum* + *-ize*] **1 :** to express as multiples of a definite quantity **2 a :** to subdivide (as energy) into small finite increments **b :** to calculate or express (as the phenomena of radiation or photoelectric action) in terms of quantum mechanics **c :** to put into a definite quantum state ⟨a *quantized* molecule⟩

quantong *var of* QUANDONG

quants *pl of* QUANT

quan·tum \'kwäntəm *sometimes* 'kwȯn-\ *n, pl* **quan·ta** \-tə\ [L, neut. of *quantus* how much — more at QUANTITY] **1 a :** QUANTITY, AMOUNT ⟨the ~ of proof needed⟩ ⟨the ~ of damages to be assessed⟩ ⟨the tiny ~ of popular knowledge on any matter —John Buchan⟩ ⟨the ~ of the sin —Robert Burns⟩ **b :** a certain or an allotted amount **:** PORTION ⟨in almost all men . . . are *quanta* of love and tenderness —Levon West⟩ ⟨the Indian blood ~ of the population —D.P.Delorme⟩ **c :** gross quantity **:** AGGREGATE, BULK ⟨the total ~ of securities . . . that circulate in the economy —H.V.R.Iengar⟩ ⟨increase the ~ of material well-being —H.J.Laski⟩ **2** *obs* **:** something having quantity **:** BODY **3 a :** one of the very small increments or parcels into which many forms of energy are subdivided and which are always associated directly or indirectly with a frequency ν such that the quantum is equal to ν multiplied by Planck constant **b :** one of the small subdivisions of a quantized physical magnitude (as molecular spin, angular velocity, magnetic moment) — compare LIGHT QUANTUM, MAGNETON, PHONON, PHOTON

quantum efficiency *also* **quantum yield** *n* **:** the ratio of the number of photoelectrons released in a photoelectric process to the number of radiation quanta absorbed

quantum electrodynamics *n pl but usu sing in constr* **:** quantum mechanics applied to electrical interactions (as between nuclear particles)

quantum–equivalence law *n* **:** a principle of photoelectric action: when a quantum of radiation is involved in a photoelectric process its whole energy reappears in other forms since photoelectric processes do not absorb fractional quanta as do some other processes (as Compton effect)

quantum evolution *n* **:** comparatively rapid transition from one stable type of biological adaptation to another distinctly different type under the influence of some strong selection pressure

quantum jump *or* **quantum transition** *n* **:** an abrupt transition (as of an electron, an atom, or a molecule) from one discrete energy state to another with absorption or emission of a quantum of energy

quantum liquid *n* **:** HELIUM II

quantum–mechanical \;===;===\ *adj* **:** of or relating to quantum mechanics ⟨the *quantum-mechanical* theory of nuclear motion —*Physical Rev.*⟩

quantum mechanics *n pl but sing or pl in constr* **1 :** the mechanics of phenomena to which the quantum theory may be applied — called also *old quantum mechanics* **2 :** a general mathematical theory dealing with the interactions of matter and radiation in terms of observable quantities only (as the intensities and frequencies of spectral lines) — called also *new quantum mechanics;* compare ATOMIC THEORY, MATRIX MECHANICS, WAVE MECHANICS

quantum me·ru·it \-'merəwət\ *n* [L, as much as he deserved] **:** a count in a legal action grounded on a promise that the defendant would pay to the plaintiff for the plaintiff's work or labor as much as he should deserve

quantum number *n* **:** one of a set of integral or half-integral numbers used to define the magnitude of a quantity (as energy or angular momentum) that takes on only discrete values

quantum of action : PLANCK CONSTANT

quantum theory *n* **:** an extensive branch of physical theory based on Max Planck's concept of radiant energy subdivided into finite quanta and applied to a large number of processes involving transference or transformation of energy in an atomic or molecular scale — see QUANTUM 3

quantum unit of spin : a constant used as a unit of measurement for particle spin and equal to the Planck constant divided by 2π

quantum va·le·bant \-və'lē,bant\ *n* [L, as much as they were worth] **:** a count in a legal action of assumpsit to recover for goods sold or materials furnished as much as they were worth

qua·paw *also* **kwa·pa** \'kwȯ,pȯ\ *n, pl* **quapaw** *or* **quapaws** *usu cap* [Quapaw *Ugákhpa,* lit., downstream people] **1 a :** a Siouan people of the Arkansas river valley, Arkansas **b :** a member of such people **2 :** a dialect of Dhegiha

1qua·qua·ver·sal \,kwākwə;vərsəl\ *adj* [L *quaqua versus* turned in every direction (fr. *quaqua* wherever, in whatever direction, in every direction — fr. abl. fem. of *quisquis* whoever, every, redupl. of *quis* who — + *versus,* past part. of *vertere* to turn) + E *-al* — more at WHO, WORTH] **:** dipping from a center toward all points of the compass ⟨a ~ domal structure⟩ — used esp. of geological formations; opposed to *centroclinal;* contrasted with *partiversal;* compare DOME 7a — **qua·qua·ver·sal·ly** \-səlē\ *adv*

2quaquaversal \"\ *n* -s **:** a quaquaversal dome, ridge, or structure

quar *abbr* quarter; quarterly

quarantain *n* -s [F *quarantaine,* lit., period of forty days, fr. OF] *obs* **:** QUARANTINE

quar·an·tin·able \;kwȯrən;tēnəbəl, -wär-\ *adj* **1 :** liable to be quarantined **:** subject to quarantine ⟨a ~ immigrant⟩ **2 :** constituting grounds for quarantine **:** subjecting one to quarantine ⟨a ~ disease⟩

1quar·an·tine \'kwȯrən,tēn, -wär-, ,==';=\ *n* -s [in sense 1, fr. ML *quarentena,* fr. OF *quarantaine* period of forty days, fr. *quarante* forty, fr. L *quadraginta;* in other senses, fr. It *quarantina, quarantena* period of forty days, quarantine (of a ship), fr. MF *quarantaine* period of forty days, fr. OF — more at QUADRAGESIMA] **1 a :** the period often of 40 days during which a widow is permitted by law to remain in her deceased husband's principal home without being obliged to pay rent to the heirs **b :** a widow's right of quarantine **2 :** a period of 40 days **3 a :** a term (as of 40 days) during which a ship arriving in port and suspected of carrying serious contagious disease is forbidden all intercourse with the shore **b :** a regulation restraining a ship from intercourse with the shore while suspected of offering a threat of contagion **c :** a place where a ship is detained during quarantine **d :** a stoppage of travel, communication, or intercourse imposed as a precaution against contagion or infection or the spreading of plant or animal pests **4 :** a restraint or interdiction placed upon the transportation of animals, plants, or goods suspected of being carriers of disease or other pest **5 :** a place (as an isolation hospital) in which persons under quarantine are kept **6 :** a section of a prison or reformatory in which new arrivals are detained for examination and observation before being permitted to mingle with other prisoners **7 :** isolation enforced as a social or political penalty **:** SANCTION ⟨four South American countries refused to join a diplomatic ~ —R.W. Van Alstyne⟩ ⟨sheer vulgarity . . . is so blatant as to isolate itself and proclaim its own ~ —Louis Kronenberger⟩

2quarantine \"\ *vb* -ED/-ING/-S *vt* **1 :** to isolate as a precaution against contagious disease **:** detain in quarantine **2 :** to exclude by quarantine **3 :** to isolate or cut off from normal relations or intercourse as a social or political penalty or sanction ⟨brave words in regard to *quarantining* the aggressor —R.M.Lovett⟩ ~ *vi* **:** to establish or declare a quarantine

quarantine flag *n* **:** a yellow flag hoisted by all ships to request pratique on entering a harbor, by a ship to show that it has contagious or infectious disease aboard, or by a ship that has been quarantined — called also *yellow flag, yellow jack*

quarantine period *n* **:** a period of time that must elapse before those exposed to or attacked by a contagious disease can be considered as incapable respectively of developing or transmitting the disease

quar·an·tin·er \-ēnə(r)\ *n* -s **1 :** one that quarantines **2 :** one that is quarantined

quaranty *n* -ES [It *quarantia,* fr. *quaranta* forty, fr. L *quadraginta*] *obs* **:** a court of 40 magistrates in the Venetian republic

quare \'kwa(a)(ə)r, -we(ə)r, -wär\ *dial var of* 1QUEER

qua·re clau·sum fre·git \,kwärē,klau̇səm'frāgət\ *n* [L, why he broke the close] **:** a writ for land trespass

quare im·pe·dit \-'impədət\ *n* [L, why he hinders] *Eng law* **:** a writ by which a common-law action for deciding a disputed right of presentation to a benefice begins

quar·en·tene *like* 1QUARANTINE\ *n* -s [ML *quarentena,* fr. OF *quarantaine* period of forty days, set of forty — more at QUARANTINE] *archaic* **:** FURLONG, ROOD

qua·res·ma \kwä'rezmə\ *n* -s [Pg, lit., Lent, fr. LL *quadragesima* — more at QUADRAGESIMA] **:** BRAZILIAN SPIDERFLOWER

quark \'kwȯrk\ *vi* [imit.] *archaic* **:** CROAK

quarl *or* **quarle** \'kwȯrl, *esp before pause or consonant* -rəl\ *n* -s [alter. of 1*quarrel*] **:** a large brick or tile; *esp* **:** a curved firebrick used to support melting pots for zinc and retort covers

quarled \-ld\ *var of* QUARRELED

1quar·rel \'kwȯr(ə)l, -wär-\ *n* -s [ME, fr. OF *carrel, quarrel* square-headed arrow for an arbalest, building stone, fr. (assumed) VL *quadrellum,* fr. L *quadrum* square + *-ellum* -el; akin to L *quattuor* four — more at FOUR] **1 :** a square-headed bolt or arrow; *esp* **:** one for a crossbow or arbalest **2** [ME, square of glass, fr. MF, square of glass, building stone, fr. OF *carrel, quarrel* building stone] **:** a small quadrangular building member: as **a :** a square of glass esp. when set diagonally **b :** a small opening in window tracery of which the general form is nearly square **c :** a square or lozenge-shaped paving tile **3 :** a glazier's diamond **4 :** a stonecutter's chisel

quarrels 2a

2quarrel \"\ *n* -s [ME *querele,* fr. MF, complaint, fr. L *querela* fr. *queri* to complain — more at WHEEZE] **1 a :** a ground of complaint **:** an occasion for dislike or hostility **:** a cause of dispute or contest ⟨it is the apparent absence of this faith which is part of my ~ with those critics —J.D.Adams⟩ **b :** a conflict between antagonists **:** a moral or physical contest **:** DISPUTE, STRIFE ⟨so it would be prudent for both of us to agree now upon some compromise with each other, and not to push our postwar ~ to extremes —A.J.Toynbee⟩ **2 :** a cause or side in a dispute ⟨a just ~⟩ **3** *obs* **a :** an occasion to act **b :** AVERSION, DISLIKE **c :** QUARRELSOMENESS

syn WRANGLE, ALTERCATION, SQUABBLE, BICKERING, SPAT, TIFF: QUARREL usu. indicates a verbal contention with anger, hurt feeling, vexation, and recrimination ⟨she hated any kind of *quarrel* . . . she shuddered at raised voices and quailed before looks of hate —Jean Stafford⟩ WRANGLE may indicate noisy, insistent, discordant, futile disputation ⟨spent three hours in an inconclusive *wrangle* over what was to be included in the communiqué to the press —J.P.Lash⟩ ⟨pleaded against any changes that might produce a partisan *wrangle* —*N.Y. Times*⟩ ALTERCATION usu. indicates a determined verbal contention or dispute ⟨a rapid *altercation,* in which they fastened upon each other various strange epithets —Stephen Crane⟩ ⟨the fights and violent *altercations* which grew out of impassioned discussion of the day's doings —Herbert Asbury⟩ SQUABBLE may indicate a silly, puerile, wrangle over something petty ⟨*squabbles* with his fellow faddists —L.P.Smith⟩ BICKERING implies continuing irritable petulant verbal sparring ⟨the *bickering* and squabbles of the state parties —Gerald Priestland⟩ ⟨whose *bickerings* with her husband become tiresome —Leslie Rees⟩ SPAT may suggest a short lively dispute, perhaps over something trivial and perhaps ending quickly ⟨had short *spats* with Hughie when he came in unnecessarily drunk —Ruth Park⟩ TIFF refers to a trivial ill-humored dispute, often without consequence ⟨was just a passing *tiff* and that matters would speedily adjust themselves —P.G.Wodehouse⟩

3quarrel \"\ *vb* **quarreled** *or* **quarrelled; quarreled** *or* **quarrelled; quarreling** *or* **quarrelling; quarrels** [ME *querelen,* fr. *querele,* n.] *vi* **1 :** to find fault **:** CAVIL, COMPLAIN ⟨I have no compulsion to ~ with a society that has permitted me to work for what I believe —M.W.Straight⟩ **2 :** to contend or dispute actively **:** CLASH, STRIVE, STRUGGLE ⟨~*ed* frequently with his superiors —*London Calling*⟩ ~ *vt* **1** *obs* **:** to dispute or question the rightness or validity of **:** CHALLENGE **2** *Scot* **:** to find fault with **:** REBUKE **3** *obs* **:** to force by quarreling

4quarrel \"\ *n* -s [ME *quarelle,* alter. of *quarere, quarrere* — more at QUARRY (excavation)] *dial chiefly Eng* **:** a stone quarry

quar·reled *or* **quar·relled** *or* **quarled** \-r(ə)ld\ *adj* **:** made with or into quarrels (as a window)
quar·rel·er *or* **quar·rel·ler** \-r(ə)lə(r)\ *n* -s [alter. (influenced by *-er*) of ME *querelour*, fr. *querelen* to quarrel + *-our* -or] **:** one that quarrels
quarreling *or* **quarrelling** *adj* **1 :** engaged in a quarrel **2 :** QUARRELSOME — **quar·rel·ing·ly** *or* **quar·rel·ling·ly** *adv*
quarrelous *or* **quarrellous** *adj* [ME *querelous*, fr. MF, fr. LL *querelosus*, fr. L *querela* complaint + *-osus* -ose — more at QUARREL] **1** *obs* **:** QUERULOUS **2** *obs* **:** QUARRELSOME
quar·rel·some \ˈkwȯr(ə)lsəm, -wär-\ *adj* **:** apt or disposed to quarrel **:** CONTENTIOUS ⟨becoming more ~ as the campaign progressed⟩ **syn** see BELLIGERENT
quar·rel·some·ly *adv* **:** in a quarrelsome manner
quar·rel·some·ness *n* -ES **:** the quality or state of being quarrelsome
quar·ri·able *also* **quar·ry·able** \ˈkwȯrēəbəl, -wär-, -riə-\ *adj* **:** capable of being quarried
quar·ried \-rēd,-rid\ *adj* [fr. past part. of ⁴*quarry*] **1 :** dug from a stone quarry **2** [³*quarry* + *-ed*] **:** having stone quarries
quar·ri·er \-rēə(r), -riə-\ *n* -s [ME *quaryere*, fr. MF *quarrier*, fr. (assumed) OF *quare* + OF *-ier* -er] **:** one that quarries (as stone) **:** a quarry worker **:** QUARRYMAN
quar·ri·on \-rēən\ *n* -s [prob. native name in Australia] **:** COCKATIEL
¹**quar·ry** \ˈkwȯrē, -wär-, -ri\ *n* -ES [ME *querre*, *quirre* part of the entrails of a beast taken in hunting that is given to the hounds esp. by being placed on the beast's skin for them to eat, fr. MF *cuiree*, fr. OF, prob. alter. (influenced by *cuir* leather, skin, fr. L *corium*) of *coree* breast viscera, entrails, fr. LL *corata* (pl.), fr. L *cor* heart — more at HEART, CUIRASS] **1** *obs* **a :** a part of the entrails of a beast taken in hunting that is given to the hounds; *also* **:** a similar reward to a hawk that has killed a bird **b :** a heap of the game killed **2** *obs* **:** a heap of dead bodies (as on a battlefield) **3 a :** a game bird hunted with hawks **b :** the prey of any predatory bird or animal **c :** an animal, bird, or fish sought by a hunter or fisherman **:** the object of the chase **:** GAME **4 :** an object pursued or hunted ⟨city detectives kept the ~ under surveillance for weeks⟩ ⟨thinks of a woman as a ~ —Guy Fowler⟩ **5** *obs* **:** a falcon's attack or swoop on its prey **syn** see VICTIM
²**quarry** \"\ *vb* -ED/-ING/-ES *vt* **1** *obs* **:** to teach (a hawk) to seize quarry **2** *archaic* **:** to hunt down (a game animal) ~ *vi*, *obs* **:** to seize quarry — used with *on* or *upon*
³**quar·ry** \", *chiefly dial* -wer- *or* -war-\ *n* -ES [ME *quarey*, alter. of *quarere*, *quarrere*, fr. MF *quarrere*, *quarriere*, fr. OF, fr. (assumed) OF *quarre* squared stone (akin to OProv *cayre* squared stone), fr. L *quadrum* square — more at QUARREL (arrow)] **1 :** an open excavation usu. for obtaining building stone, slate, or limestone — compare ¹BANK, ⁴MINE, PIT **2 a :** a source from which material may be extracted **:** LODE ⟨other dramatists also found his books a workable ~ —*Times Lit. Supp.*⟩ **3 :** a large mass (as of stone or slate) fit for quarrying
⁴**quarry** \"\ *vb* -ED/-ING/-ES *vt* **1 :** to dig or take from or as if from a quarry ⟨had *quarried* limestone there for decades⟩ ⟨I have from time to time *quarried* out bits from the history of a special science to assist my exposition —J.B.Conant⟩ **2 :** to make a quarry in ⟨*quarried* the land industriously⟩ **3 :** to remove fragments of rock by impact (as in stream erosion) or by pressure and dragging (as in glacial erosion) **:** PLUCK ~ *vi* **:** to delve in or as if in a quarry ⟨never has to ~ to fill even the largest or most unusual order —*Amer. Guide Series: Vt.*⟩
⁵**quar·ry** \ˈkwȯr-, ˈkwär-\ *n* -ES [alter. of ¹*quarrel*] **1** *obs* **:** a square-headed bolt or arrow **2 a :** a diamond-shaped pane of glass **:** LOZENGE **b :** QUARRY TILE ⟨stood barefoot in front of him on the cold *quarries* —Mary Webb⟩ **c :** any of the four-sided units in a simple allover decorative pattern formed by two sets of straight lines intersecting at regular intervals; *also* **:** this pattern
⁶**quarry** \"\ *vt* -ED/-ING/-ES **:** to glaze or pave with quarries
quarry bed *n* **:** QUARRY FACE
quarry face *n* **:** the freshly split face of ashlar squared off for the joints only as it comes from the quarry and used esp. for massive work — distinguished from *rock face* — **quarry-faced** \ˌ=ˈ=\ *adj*
quarry-hawk \ˈ==,=\ *n* **:** MAKE-HAWK
quarrying *n* -s **:** the business, occupation, or act of extracting stone, marble, or slate from quarries
quarry light *n* **:** a diamond-shaped pane of glass designed to be set in leads
quar·ry·man \ˈ==mən\ *n*, *pl* **quarrymen :** one who quarries stone or performs other duties at a quarry **:** QUARRIER
quarrystone bond *n* **:** RUBBLEWORK
quarry tile *n* **:** machine-made unglazed tile
quarry water *n* **:** the moisture content of freshly quarried stone esp. if porous
¹**quart** \ˈkwȯr|t, -wō(ə)|, *usu* |d·+V\ *n* -s *often attrib* [ME, fr. MF *quarte*, fr. OF, fr. fem. of *quart*, adj., fourth, fr. L *quartus*; akin to L *quattuor* four — more at FOUR] **1 :** any of various units of capacity: as **a :** a British liquid or dry unit equal to ¼ imperial gallon or 69.355 cubic inches **b :** a U.S. liquid unit equal to ¼ gallon or 57.75 cubic inches **c :** a U.S. dry unit equal to ¹⁄₃₂ bushel or 67.200 cubic inches — see MEASURE table **2 a :** a vessel or measure having a capacity of one quart **b :** any of various units for bottled wine; *esp* **:** a unit for champagne containing 26 fluid ounces **3 a** [Sp *cuarto*, lit., fourth part, fr. *cuarto*, adj., fourth, fr. L *quartus*] **:** a token issued in 1802 or a coin struck in 1842 for Gibraltar equivalent to the Spanish ¼-real piece; *also* **:** a corresponding unit of value ⟨2-*quart* token⟩ ⟨½-*quart* coin⟩ **b** [F, lit., fourth part, fr. MF, fr. *quart*, adj., fourth, fr. OF, fr. L *quartus*] **:** a Swiss silver coin of the 16th and 17th centuries equal to three deniers
²**quart** \ˈkär|t, ˈkä|, *usu* |d·+V\ *n* -s [F *quarte* quart (in fencing), quart (in cards), fr. fem. of *quart*, adj., fourth] **1** *usu* **quarte** \"\ **:** a fencer's parry or guard position defending the upper inside left target in which the hand is at chest height with thumb up and fingernails to the left and the tip of the blade is directed at the opponent's eyes — compare PRIME **2 :** a sequence of four playing cards of the same suit

quart 2

³**quart** \"\ *vb* -ED/-ING/-S [F *quarter*, fr. *quarte*, n.] *archaic* **:** to assume or place in position for quart in fencing
quart- *comb form* [L, fr. *quartus*] **:** fourth ⟨*quartic*⟩
¹**quar·tan** \ˈkwȯrtᵊn, -wō(ə)t-\ *adj* [ME *quarteyne*, fr. OF *quartaine* (in the phrase *fievre quartaine* quartan fever), fr. L *quartana* (in the phrase *febris quartana* quartan fever), fem. of *quartanus* of the fourth, fr. *quartus* fourth + *-anus* -an] **:** occurring every fourth day reckoning inclusively; *specif* **:** recurring at approximately 72-hour intervals — used chiefly of malariae malaria ⟨~ chills and fever⟩; compare TERTIAN
²**quartan** \"\ *n* -s [ME *quarteyne*, fr. MF *quartaine*, fr. OF, fr. L *quartana*, fr. fem. of *quartanus* of the fourth] **:** an intermittent fever that recurs at approximately 72-hour intervals
quartan malaria *n* **:** MALARIAE MALARIA
quar·ta·tion \kwȯrˈtāshən\ *n* -s [*quart-* + *-ation*] **:** the alloying with silver of a button rich in gold in order to reduce the gold to such a proportion that the acid used in parting may act as desired
¹**quar·ter** *R* ˈkwȯr|d·ər, |tər *sometimes by r-dissimilation* -ō|; *-R* -ō(ə)|d·ə(r, |tə(r\ *n* -s [ME, fr. OF *quartier*, fr. L *quartarius*, fr. *quartus* fourth + *-arius* -ary — more at QUART] **1 :** one of four equal parts into which anything is divisible **:** a fourth part or portion ⟨a ~ of a pound⟩ **2 :** any of various units of capacity or weight equal to or derived from one fourth of some larger unit (as a hundredweight, imperial bushels, or a chaldron) **3 a :** any of various units of length or area equal to one fourth of some larger unit (as a yard) **b :** QUARTER SECTION **4 :** the fourth part of a measure of time: as **a :** one of a set of four 3-month divisions of a calendar or fiscal year **b :** a school or college term of about 12 weeks resulting when an academic year is divided into four parts one of which is taken up by the long summer vacation or used for summer school — compare SEMESTER 2 **c :** QUARTER HOUR 1 ⟨a ~ to six⟩ **5 a :** a coin worth a quarter of a dollar (as a U.S. or Canadian 25-cent piece) **b :** the sum of 25 cents **6 a :** one limb of a quadruped with the adjacent parts **:** one fourth part of the carcass of a slaughtered animal including a leg ⟨had a sack of flour and a ~ of a fine fat beef in his sleigh —Hamlin Garland⟩ — compare FIFTH QUARTER, FOREQUARTER, HINDQUARTER **b :** one of the four parts of a human body similarly divided (as in an execution for treason) **7 a :** the territory, region, or direction lying under any of the four divisions of the horizon conceived as corresponding to the cardinal points of the compass **b :** one of the four parts into which the horizon is divided or the cardinal point corresponding to it **c :** a compass point or direction other than the cardinal points ⟨the wind is in that ~⟩ **d** (1) **:** a person or group not definitely specified ⟨had his instructions from a very high ~⟩ (2) **:** a point, direction, or place not identified ⟨trade from that ~ is only a trickle —*Sydney (Australia) Bull.*⟩ ⟨procuring the release of a man in jail, by dropping a word in the right ~ —Peggy Durdin⟩ **8 a :** a district of a town or city devoted to a special purpose or activity, occupied by a particular group, or found notable for a conspicuous feature ⟨the market ~ of Paris⟩ ⟨the wholesale clothing ~ of New York⟩ ⟨a residential ~⟩ **b :** the inhabitants of such a quarter regarded as a group ⟨the ~ was aroused and indignant⟩ **9 a :** an assigned station or post; *esp* **:** the station assigned to a member of a ship's crew for a particular purpose — usu. used in pl. ⟨battle ~*s*⟩ ⟨collision ~*s*⟩ **b quarters** *pl* **:** an assembly of a ship's company for purposes of ceremony, drill, or emergency **c quarters** *pl* **:** living accommodations: as (1) **:** the living space of the crew aboard ship (2) **:** the lodgings of soldiers or sailors or their families (3) **:** the rooms, housing, or residence occupied by an individual, a family, or some other group ⟨bachelor ~*s*⟩ ⟨club ~*s*⟩ ⟨found ~*s* for his family⟩ **10 a :** the clemency of not putting to death a defeated enemy **:** FORBEARANCE, MERCY ⟨no ~ was asked or given; three women, two children, and a Negro servant survived —Oscar Handlin⟩ **b :** consideration shown to an opponent, antagonist, or fellow contestant by refraining from pressing advantages of superior strength or skill ⟨she had climbed trees and shot marbles and played ball with them, and neither expected nor received any ~ —Gertrude Schweitzer⟩ **11** *archaic* **a :** one of the four parts of a road marked out by horse tracks and wheel ruts **b :** the shoulder of a highway **12** *obs* **:** relations or attitude to another person — used esp. in the phrase *to keep good quarter with* **13** *archaic* **:** an upright wood framing member in a partition or wall **:** SCANTLING, STUD **14 a :** a fourth part of the moon's period — see MOON illustration **b :** QUADRATURE 3 **15 :** the side of a horse's hoof between the toe and the heel **16 a** (1) **:** any of the four parts into which a heraldic field is divided by horizontal and vertical lines through the fess point (2) **:** one of the parts into which a shield is divided by quartering — see GRAND QUARTER **b :** a bearing or charge occupying the first fourth part or thereabouts of a heraldic field — compare ¹CANTON 4 **17** *obs* **:** a garden bed or plot **18 :** the state of two machine parts that are exactly at right angles to one another or are spaced about a circle so as to subtend a right angle at the center of the circle ⟨the crankpin holes are out of ~⟩ **19 a :** the afterpart of a ship's side usu. corresponding in extent with the quarterdeck — see SHIP illustration **b :** the part of the yardarm outside of the slings **c** *archaic* **:** a fourth of a fathom **d** *or* **quarter point :** a fourth of the distance from one point of the compass to another reckoned as a fourth of 11°15′ or nearly 2°49′ **20 :** one side of the upper of a shoe or boot from heel to vamp — see SHOE illustration **21 a :** QUARTERBACK **b :** one of the four equal periods into which the playing time of some games (as football) is divided **:** one of the two subdivisions of a half ⟨romped to victory, scoring touchdowns in every ~⟩ **22 :** one teat together with the part of a cow's udder that it drains ⟨normal milk from all four ~*s*⟩ ⟨a three~ cow⟩
²**quarter** \"\ *vb* -ED/-ING/-S [ME *quarteren*, fr. *quarter*, n.] *vt* **1 a :** to divide into four equal or nearly equal parts **b :** to separate into either more or fewer than four parts ⟨~*ed* an orange⟩ **c :** to divide (a human body) into four parts **:** DISMEMBER ⟨the traitor was hanged and ~*ed*⟩ **2 :** to provide with lodging or shelter; *esp* **:** to assign (troops) to a lodging place — often used with *on* or *upon* ⟨~*ed* his men on the inhabitants⟩ **3 :** to pass back and forth across (an area) in many directions **:** cross and recross **:** search intensively ⟨the bombers had conducted a 300-mile search, ~*ing* and re-quartering the area —A.R.Griffin⟩ ⟨larger animals not only eat larger pieces of food, but also ~ more territory to find it —Orlando Park⟩ **4 a :** to arrange or bear (as different coats of arms) quarterly on one escutcheon **b :** to add (a coat of arms) to another or others on one escutcheon **:** arrange alternately and quarterly — often used with *with* **5 :** to adjust or locate (as cranks) at right angles in a machine **6 :** to groom (a horse) lightly ~ *vi* **1 :** to occupy a residence **:** LODGE ⟨the family ~*ed* in a big old house⟩ **2 :** to crisscross a district **:** range back and forth over an area like a dog in search of game ⟨our attack force had to ~ for them —Fletcher Pratt⟩ **3 :** to drive a vehicle so as to straddle the ruts in the road **4 :** to change from one quarter to another — used of the moon **5 a :** to strike or blow on a ship's quarter — used of the wind **b :** to sail with the wind on the quarter
³**quarter** \"\ *adj* [¹*quarter*] **1 :** consisting of or equal to a quarter **2 :** of or relating to the part in the mechanism of a clock or repeating watch governing the striking of the quarter hours — see QUARTER SNAIL **3 a :** placed at a right angle to another similar machine part ⟨a ~ crank⟩ **b :** having a branch at right angles to another ⟨a ~ crankshaft⟩ **4 :** of or relating to the quarter of a ship
quar·ter·age \-d·ərij, -tə-\ *n* -s [ME, fr. ¹*quarter* + *-age*] **1 :** a quarterly payment or allowance, tax, pension, or wage paid or received **2 a :** LODGING, SHELTER **b :** the provision of quarters (as for troops) or the cost of it
quarter ail *n* **:** ¹BLACKLEG 1
¹**quarterback** \ˈ==,=\ *n* **:** a backfield player in football who usu. lines up behind the center, calls the signals, and directs the offensive play of his team
²**quarterback** \"\ *vt* **1 :** to call the signals and direct the offensive play of (a football team) **2 :** to give executive direction to **:** issue orders to **:** BOSS ⟨~*ed* the original buying syndicate —*Time*⟩ ~ *vi* **:** to serve as quarterback ⟨~*ed* for his high school team⟩
quarterback sneak *n* **:** a quick or delayed run by a football quarterback inside the defensive guards or tackles
quarter belt *n* **:** a belt connecting pulleys whose axles are at right angles
quarter bend *n* **:** a bend changing direction 90 degrees (as in piping)
quarter bill *n* **:** a list specifying the stations to be taken by a ship's officers and crew in time of action or for given evolutions and the names of the men assigned to each — compare STATION BILL

quarter bend

quarter binding *n* **:** a book binding in which the material of the backbone (as leather) is different from that of the sides and extends upon the boards one quarter their width or less — compare FULL BINDING, HALF BINDING, THREE-QUARTER BINDING
quarter blanket *n* **:** a blanket used under a horse's harness to cover from the tail to beyond the saddle
quarter block *n* **:** a block fitted under the quarters of a yard on each side of the slings through which clew lines and sheets are rove
quarter blood *n* **:** a median grade of wool fineness — compare BLOOD 7, BRAID, ³FINE, HALF BLOOD
quarter boards *n pl* **:** boards raised above the bulwarks along a ship's quarter — called also *topgallant bulwarks*
quarter boat *n* **1 :** a boat hung on davits at a ship's quarter **2 :** a boat (as a houseboat) providing living quarters for a work crew
quarter boom *n* **:** a boat boom near the stern
quarter boot *n* **:** a boot for an overreaching horse's forefoot as a protection against injury by striking it with the hind foot
quarter-bound \ˌ=ˈ=\ *adj* **:** having a quarter binding — used of a book
quarter box *n* **:** a bearing housing with four adjustable brasses
quarter-breed \ˈ=,=\ *n* **:** a person with three grandparents of one and the fourth from another race; *specif* **:** a person one fourth American Indian and three fourths white
quarter butt *n* **:** a billiard cue that is shorter than the ordinary cue
quarter cask *n*, *archaic* **:** a cask that holds about ¼ of a hogshead
quarter-cleft \ˌ=ˈ=\ *adj*, *archaic* **:** QUARTERSAWED
quarter court *n*, *obs* **:** a court sitting every three months
quarter crack *n* **:** a sand crack usu. in a horse's forefoot
quarter-cut \ˌ=ˈ=\ *adj* **:** QUARTERSAWED
quarter day *n* [ME, fr. ¹*quarter* + *day*] **:** the day beginning a quarter of the year and often used as the date when a quarterly payment (as rent) falls due ⟨every *quarter day* Madame wept before the landlord —Philip O'Connor⟩
¹**quarterdeck** \ˈ==,=\ *n* **1 :** the afterpart of a ship's upper deck sometimes including the poop deck when raised and often reserved for officers and cabin passengers **2 :** a part of a deck on a naval vessel set aside for ceremonial and official use
²**quarterdeck** \"\ *vi* **:** to stride back and forth on or as if on a quarterdeck
quar·ter·deck·er \"ə(r)\ *n* [¹*quarterdeck* + *-er*] **1 :** a naval officer who cares more for regulations and etiquette than efficiency **2 :** SLIPPER LIMPET
quarter dollar *n* **:** a 25-cent piece
quarter eagle *n* **:** a $2.50 gold piece of the U.S. first issued in 1796 and last issued in 1929 — see EAGLE
quartered *adj* [fr. past part. of ²*quarter*] **1 :** divided into or containing heraldic quarters or quarterings **2 a :** divided into four equal parts, sections, or regions **:** cut into quarters **b :** QUARTERSAWED — used of lumber (as oak) **c :** cut in four successive layers from the same piece of wood and placed so that each piece forms one quarter of the whole surface thus producing a symmetrical pattern ⟨~ veneer⟩ **3 :** furnished with quarters **:** provided with shelter **:** LODGED, LOCATED
quar·ter·er \-d·ərə(r), -tə-\ *n* -s **:** one that quarters: as **a :** LODGER **b :** a clay target or live bird flying to a shooter's right or left
quarter evil *or* **quarter ill** *n* **:** BLACKLEG 1
quarter face *n* **:** a face turned away (as in a portrait) so that but one quarter is visible
quarter fast *n* **:** QUARTER ROPE
¹**quarterfinal** \ˌ==ˈ==\ *adj* **:** of or relating to the round in a sports contest just before the semifinal
²**quarterfinal** \"\ *n* **1 :** a quarterfinal match **2 quarterfinals** *pl* **:** a quarterfinal round
quar·ter·fi·nal·ist \"əst\ *n* **:** a contestant qualified for or participating in a quarterfinal
quarter gallery *n* **:** a balcony projecting from the quarter of a large sailing ship
quarter galley *n* **:** a small galley **:** a light sailing cruiser
quarter grabbing *n* [*grabbing* fr. gerund of *grab*] **:** an overreaching by a horse
quarter grain *n* **:** the grain of quartersawed wood (as oak)
quarter guard *n*, *Brit* **:** INTERIOR GUARD
quarter gunner *n*, *archaic* **:** GUNNER'S MATE
quarter hoop *n* **:** BULGE HOOP
quarter horse *n* [so called fr. its high speed for distances up to a quarter of a mile] **:** an alert cobby muscular horse developed on the ranges of the U.S. for great endurance under the saddle and now commonly recognized as a distinct breed — compare CUTTING HORSE
quarter hour *n* **1 a :** 15 minutes **b :** any of the quarter points of an hour ⟨listened apprehensively as the clock chimed successive *quarter hours*⟩ **2 :** an hour a week for an academic quarter devoted to class meetings — compare SEMESTER HOUR
¹**quartering** *n* -s [fr. gerund of ²*quarter*] **1 a :** the division of an escutcheon into four or more compartments showing coats of arms brought in by family alliances **b :** a quarter of an escutcheon or the coat of arms on it **2 a :** a dividing into quarters **:** a cutting or separation into four parts **b :** a division into some other number of parts **3 a :** the provision or assignment of quarters (as for soldiers) **b :** LODGING **4 a :** the use of quarters in building construction **b :** studding in place in a building **5 :** a ranging to and fro over an area **:** an intensive search or close coverage **:** CRISSCROSSING **6 :** the passing of the moon from one quarter to another **7 :** the adjustment (as of cranks or wrist pins) at right angles with each other **8 :** the sampling of crushed ore or other material by dividing it into quarters two of which are mixed and again quartered and repeating the operation until a sample of the desired size is obtained
²**quartering** \"\ *adj* [fr. pres. part. of ²*quarter*] **1 a :** coming from a point well abaft the beam of a ship but not directly astern — used of wind, waves, or any moving object ⟨the canoe danced and lurched over a ~ sea —C.S.Forester⟩ **b** (1) *archery* **:** oblique with reference to the target and the archer — used of the wind (2) **:** moving away diagonally to a shooter's right or left — used of a clay target or live game bird **c :** lying at right angles ⟨~ cranks of a locomotive⟩ **:** lying in planes forming a right angle with each other **2** [¹*quartering*] **:** of, relating to, or used in quartering
quartering machine *n* **:** a machine for simultaneously boring parallel holes (as the crankpin holes of locomotive driving wheels) so that the center line of one will be 90 degrees ahead of the center line of the other
quartering sea *n* **:** a sea striking a ship's quarter at an angle of about 45 degrees to its heading — compare FOLLOWING SEA, HEAD SEA
quartering wind *n* **:** a wind blowing obliquely to a specified direction (as of a ship's heading or of the shooting on a target range)
quarter iron *n* **1 :** a boom iron on the quarter of a yard **2 :** the iron band around the quarter of a sailing ship's yard to which the boom iron is screwed
quarter-jack \ˈ==,=\ *n* **:** a clock jack that strikes the quarter hours
quarter lift *n* **:** a lift running to the quarters of a sailing ship's yard or to the after but not extreme end of a boom
quarter light *n*, *Brit* **:** a side window in a closed carriage or automobile as distinguished from those in the doors
quarter line *n* **1 :** QUARTER ROPE **2 :** an extra hauling line fastened to the underside of a long seine
¹**quar·ter·ly** *R* ˈkwȯr|d·ərlē, |tər-, -li *sometimes by r-dissimilation* -ō|; *-R* -ōd·|əl-, -ōt|, |ᵊl-\ *adv* [ME, fr. ¹*quarter* + *-ly*, adv. suffix] **1 a :** in heraldic quarters or quarterings **:** in four or more divisions — used of an escutcheon **b :** in diagonally opposite quarters of an escutcheon ⟨two coats of arms borne ~⟩ **2 :** at three-month intervals **:** every quarter ⟨interest is compounded ~⟩
²**quarterly** \"\ *adj* [¹*quarter* + *-ly*, adj. suffix] **1 :** computed for or payable at three-month intervals ⟨a ~ insurance premium⟩ **:** recurring, issued, or spaced at three-month intervals ⟨a ~ meeting⟩ ⟨a ~ notice⟩ **2** *archaic* **:** moving in an oblique or quartering direction ⟨a ~ wind⟩ **3 :** divided into heraldic quarters or quarterings and specified by number if other than four ⟨~ of six⟩
³**quarterly** \"\ *n* -ES **:** a periodical that is published four times a year
quarterly court *n* **:** a county court held (as in Kentucky) every three months and having original and appellate jurisdiction in petty civil cases and in lesser crimes
quarterly meeting *n*, *usu cap Q&M* **1 :** an organizational unit of the Society of Friends usu. composed of several Monthly Meetings — compare YEARLY MEETING **2 :** a session of a Quarterly Meeting
quarterly quartered *adj* **1** *heraldry* **:** COUNTERQUARTERED **2** *heraldry* **:** quartered in the center and having each arm divided down the middle with the divisions of alternate tinctures — used of a saltire
quar·ter·man \ˈ==mən\ *n*, *pl* **quartermen :** a foreman in a shipbuilding yard who has charge of several groups of men doing the same kind of work
quartermaster \ˈ==,==\ *n* [ME *quarter maister*, fr. ¹*quarter* + *maister* master] **1 :** a petty officer who attends to a ship's helm, binnacle, and signals under the master or navigator

2 : a commissioned officer of the U. S. Army Quartermaster Corps **:** a commissioned officer whose duty is to provide clothing and subsistence for a body of troops

quartermaster general *n* **:** the U. S. Army major general commanding the Quartermaster Corps

quar·tern *R* ˈkwȯr|d·ərn, |tərn *sometimes by* r-*dissimilation* -ȯ|; -*R* -ȯ(ə)d·ən, -)tən, -tᵊn\ *n* -s [ME *quarteroun, quartron,* fr. OF *quarteron* fourth of a pound, fourth of a hundred, fr. *quartier* quarter — more at QUARTER] **1 :** a fourth part **:** QUARTER **2 :** a fourth of various units of measure (as of a pint, a gill, a peck, or a stone) **3 :** the fourth part of a sheet of paper **4** *Brit* **:** a loaf of bread weighing about four pounds

quarter nelson *n* **:** a wrestling hold gained when one wrestler kneeling beside a prone opponent places his far hand on the opponent's head and passes his near arm under the opponent's adjacent arm and grasps the wrist of his own far arm — compare FULL NELSON, HALF NELSON, THREE-QUARTER NELSON

quarter nettings *n pl* **:** hammock nettings along a ship's quarter rails

quarter note *n* **:** a musical note equal in time value to a fourth of a whole note or a half of a half note **:** CROTCHET

quarter notes

quarteron *or* **quarteroon** *archaic var of* QUADROON

quarterpace \ˈ==,=\ *n* **:** a staircase landing where the stair turns at a right angle — compare HALFPACE

quarter-phase *adj* **:** of or relating to a combination of two circuits energized by alternating electromotive forces that differ in phase by a quarter of a cycle or by 90 degrees **:** of or relating to a four-wire two-phase system or apparatus having the neutral points of the two phases at the same potential **:** TWO-PHASE

quarter pieces *n pl* **:** the timbers of a ship's quarters where they meet the stern

quarter-pierced \¦==¦=\ *adj, of a cross* **:** having the central square at the intersection of the arms cut out

quarter point *n* **:** QUARTER 19d

quarter post *n* **:** a post marking a corner of a quarter section of land

quarter race *n* **:** a quarter-mile race between two horses

quarter rack *n* **:** a rack regulating a clock's striking of the quarters

quarter rail *n* **:** a rail reaching from a ship's gangway to its stern — compare MONKEY RAIL

quarter rest *n* **:** a musical rest corresponding in time value to a quarter note

quarter rope *n* **:** a mooring rope from a ship's quarter

quarter round *n* **:** an ovolo presenting the profile of a quarter circle **:** ECHINUS

quarter run *n* **:** a contract providing for display of an advertising card in a fourth of the subway or trolley cars, railroad coaches, or buses in a district — compare FULL RUN, HALF RUN

quarters *pl of* QUARTER, *pres 3d sing of* QUARTER

quartersaw \ˈ==,=\ *vt* **:** to saw (a log) radially into quarters and then into boards or planks in which the annual rings are at or nearly at right angles to the wide face to secure lumber that will warp relatively little, will not be likely to check, and will show the grain advantageously — compare TANGENT-SAW

quarter screw *n* **:** any of the four regulating screws in a common kind of compensation watch or chronometer balance

quarter seal *n* **:** a seal that in shape and impression is a fourth part of the great seal of the nation

quarter section *n* **:** a fourth of a section **:** a piece of land 160 acres in area in a U. S. public-land survey

quarter sessions *n pl* [so called fr. its meeting quarterly] **1 a :** an English local court of record having original and appellate jurisdiction over petty crimes and less serious felonies and sometimes also over petty civil cases and local matters involving the public interest (as licenses and the repair of roads and bridges) and presided over usu. by two justices of the peace or by a magistrate or judge sitting with a jury in a county or by a recorder in a borough — compare PETTY SESSIONS **b :** a local Scottish court held quarterly by justices of the peace chiefly for review and appeal **c :** an intermediate court in parts of Australia (as New South Wales) having original and appellate criminal jurisdiction and consisting of a judge sitting with a jury **2 :** a local court with criminal jurisdiction and sometimes administrative functions (as the care of roads and bridges) in some states of the U.S. (as Pennsylvania)

quarter sling *n* **:** a sling supporting a yard at one of a ship's quarters

quarter snail *n* **:** the snail used in the quarter part of a clock or repeater

quarterstaff \ˈ==,=\ *n* **:** a long stout staff used as a weapon and wielded with one hand in the middle and the other between the middle and the end

quarter strap *n* **1 :** either of the straps leading from a cavalry saddle to the ring to which the cinch strap is made fast **2 :** a strap around a yard at a ship's quarter often supporting a ring or grommet

quarterstretch \ˈ==,=\ *n* [so called fr. its extent of about a quarter of a mile] **:** HOMESTRETCH

quarter timber *n* **:** either of the two main timbers in the stern of a sailing ship with the fashion piece forming the main framework of the counter

quarter tone *n* **1** *or* **quarter step a :** a musical interval of one half a half step **b :** a tone at such an interval **2 :** a coarse-screen cut made from an enlarged photograph of a proof from a fine-screen halftone

quarter-turn drive *n* **:** a belt drive between pulleys whose axes are at right angles

quartervine \ˈ==,=\ *n* [so called fr. the ease with which the stem can be divided into quarters] **:** CROSS VINE 1

quarter waiter *n, obs* **:** a gentleman usher on duty in the English court for three months of each year

quarter watch *n* **:** a watch including one half of a full watch or one fourth of the ship's crew

quarter-wave plate *n* **:** a crystal plate that changes the phase difference between the two components of polarized light traversing it by one-fourth cycle — compare HALF-WAVE PLATE

quarter-witted \¦==¦==\ *adj* **:** half as bright as a half-wit

quarter-yearly \¦==¦==\ *adv (or adj)* **:** at three-month intervals

quar·tet *or* **quar·tette** \(ˈ)kwȯr¦tet, -ȯ(ə)¦t-, *usu* -ed·+V\ *n* -s [alter. (influenced by *-et* or *-ette*) of *quartetto*] **1 a :** a musical composition or movement in four parts each performed by a single voice or instrument; *specif* **:** an instrumental piece in sonata form usu. for four stringed instruments ⟨composed a ~⟩ **b :** the group of four performers of such four-part music ⟨woodwind ~⟩ **c :** a performance of such a composition **2 :** a group consisting of four ⟨a ~ of articles —*Times Lit. Supp.*⟩ ⟨in some places no murder trial is complete without its pair or ~ of differing experts —Walter Goodman⟩ **3 :** any one of the four sets of micromeres cut off in spirally cleaving eggs with determinate cleavage in sequence from the four macromeres produced by the first two cleavage divisions

quartet table *n* **:** a nest of four small tables

quar·tet·to \=ˈted·(,)ō\ *n* -s [It, dim. of *quarto* fourth, fr. *quarto*, adj., fourth, fr. L *quartus;* akin to L *quattuor* four — more at FOUR] **:** QUARTET

1quar·tic \ˈkwȯrd·ik\ *n* -s [ISV *quart-* + *-ic*, n. suffix] **:** a quartic polynomial or equation

2quartic \"\ *adj* [*quart-* + *-ic*, adj. suffix] **:** of the fourth degree

quartic equation *n* **:** BIQUADRATIC EQUATION

1quar·tile \ˈkwȯr,tīl, -rd·ᵊl, -(,)til\ *n* -s [ML *quartilis*, adj., constituting or related to the aspect of two celestial bodies that are ninety degrees apart, fr. L *quartus* fourth + *-ilis* -ile (adj. suffix)] *archaic* **:** the aspect of two celestial bodies that are 90 degrees apart

2quartile \"\ *n* -s [ISV *quart-* + *-ile*, n. suffix] **:** any one of the three values that divide the items of a frequency distribution into four classes of one quarter each of the total number of items so that the values corresponding to the items in one class are less than the first quartile, those in a second class are greater than the first quartile and less than the second, those in a third class are greater than the second quartile and less than the third, those in a fourth class are greater than the third quartile

quartile deviation *n* **:** one half of the difference obtained by subtracting the first quartile from the third quartile in a frequency distribution

quarting *pres part of* QUART

quar·to \ˈkwȯr|d·(,)ō, -ȯ(ə)|, |(,)tō\ *n* -s [L, abl. of *quartus* fourth] **1 :** the size of a piece of paper cut four from a sheet; *also* **:** paper or a page of this size — abbr. *4to;* symbol *4°*; see BOOK tables **2 :** a book printed on quarto pages ⟨the volume is a ~, bound on the narrow side —Walter Millis⟩

quar·to·dec·i·man \,=(,)=ˈdesəmən\ *n* -s [LL *quartodecimanus*, fr. L *quartus decimus* fourteenth (fr. *quartus* fourth + *decimus* tenth) + *-anus* -an; akin to L *quattuor* four — more at FOUR, DIME] **1** *usu cap* **:** one of a group in the early church esp. in Asia Minor who during the 2d century and until the Nicene council in 325 observed Easter on the 14th of Nisan when the Jews slaughtered the Passover lamb no matter on what day of the week that date occurred **2 :** one of the Celtic Christians in the British Isles in the 7th century who followed a different mode of calculating the date of Easter from that used on the continent

quar·tole \ˈkwȯr,tōl\ *also* **quar·to·let** \¦kwȯrd·ᵊl¦et\ *n* -s [*quartole* ISV *quart-* + *-ole; quartolet* ISV *quartole* + *-et*] **:** QUADRUPLET 3

quart pot *n* [ME, fr. 1*quart* + *pot*] **:** a vessel holding a quart; *esp* **:** an Australian tin vessel used for cooking and as a drinking cup

quarts *pl of* QUART, *pres 3d sing of* QUART

quartz \ˈkwȯrts, -ȯ(ə)ts\ *n* -ES [G *quarz*, fr. MHG, perh. of Slav origin; akin to Czech *tvrdý* quartz, fr. *tvrdý*, adj., hard; akin to Gk *seira* cord, rope, Lith *tverti* to hold, contain] **1 :** a mineral SiO_2 consisting of a silicon dioxide that occurs in usu. colorless and transparent but sometimes yellow, brown, purple, or green hexagonal crystals, that occurs also in crystalline masses of vitreous luster and in cryptocrystalline massive forms, and that next to feldspar is the commonest mineral (hardness 7, sp. gr. of crystals 2.65–2.66) **2 :** gold or sometimes silver ore that is either broken or in place as distinguished from auriferous gravel

quartz battery *or* **quartz mill** *n* **:** STAMP MILL

quartz-crystal clock *or* **quartz clock** *n* **:** a clock in which the high uniform piezoelectric vibrations of a quartz crystal induced by current from a constant frequency generator are used to control the rate of a synchronous motor clock

quartz-diorite \ˈ=ˈ==,=\ *n* **:** diorite containing appreciable amounts of quartz

quartz flint *n* **:** POTTER'S FLINT

quartz glass *n* **:** VITREOUS SILICA

quartz·ic \-sik\ *adj* [ISV *quartz* + *-ic*] **:** QUARTZIFEROUS

quartz·if·er·ous \(ˈ)kwȯ(r)t¦sif(ə)rəs\ *adj* [*quartz* + *-iferous*] **:** bearing or containing quartz

quartz·ite \ˈkwȯrt,sīt\ *n* -s [ISV *quartz* + *-ite*] **:** a compact granular rock composed of quartz that is a metamorphosed sandstone in which the siliceous cement is often so blended with the quartz grains as to give the rock a nearly homogeneous texture

quartz·it·ic \(ˈ)=¦sid·ik\ *adj* **:** containing quartzite

quartz lamp *n* **:** a mercury-vapor lamp in a tube of quartz glass that transmits most of the ultraviolet radiation

quartz mining *n* **:** the mining of gold on veins or ore bodies in place as distinguished from surface digging or washing **:** underground mining in rock — compare PLACER MINING

quartz·oid \ˈkwȯrt,sȯid\ *n* -s **:** a crystal that is common with quartz and consists of a combination of the hexagonal prism and dipyramid

quartz·ose \-,sōs\ *or* **quartz·ous** \-səs\ *adj* [*quartzose* fr. *quartz* + *-ose; quartzous* prob. fr. F *quartzeux*, fr. *quartz* (fr. G *quarz*) + *-eux* -ous] **:** containing, consisting of, or resembling quartz

quartz plate *n* **:** a piece of quartz crystal cut in such a way as to be active piezoelectrically; *specif* **:** such a plate mounted with metal electrodes applied to its surfaces so that the combination is or resembles a condenser — compare PIEZOELECTRIC OSCILLATOR

quartz porphyry *n* **:** a porphyritic extrusive or dike rock in which quartz with more or less corroded crystals and orthoclase and usu. mica, amphibole, or pyroxene occur as phenocrysts in a groundmass that is felsophyric, granophyric, or vitrophyric

quartz sand *n* **:** a sand formed from quartz

quartz schist *n* **:** a metamorphosed schistose rock composed essentially of quartz often with some mica or tourmaline or both

quartz spectrograph *n* **:** a spectrograph having prisms and lenses of quartz and used for ultraviolet spectroscopy

quartz vein *n* **:** a vein filled with quartz either of igneous origin or deposited from solution

quartz wedge *n* **:** a piece of quartz cut in a thin wedge and used in the optical determination of minerals and in the study of polarized light

quartzy \-sē\ *adj* **:** QUARTZOSE

qua·ru·ba \kwəˈrübə\ *n* -s [prob. fr. Pg] **:** any of several trees of the genus *Vochysia*

1quas *var of* KVASS

2quas *pl of* QUA

1quash \ˈkwäsh *also* -ȯ-\ *vt* -ED/-ING/-ES [ME *quassen*, fr. MF *quasser, casser* to discharge, annul, partly fr. L *quassare* to shake, break into pieces and partly fr. LL *cassare* to annihilate, annul, fr. L *cassus* empty, void, without effect; L *cassus* akin to L *carēre* to be without — more at CASTE] *law* **:** to put an end to **:** make void **:** ABATE, ANNUL, OVERTHROW ⟨~ a writ⟩ ⟨~ a service⟩ ⟨~ an indictment⟩ ⟨amnesty decree to ~ or cut sentences of wide range of convicts —*N.Y.Times*⟩

2quash \"\ *vb* -ED/-ING/-ES [ME *quashen*, fr. MF *quasser, casser* to break, fr. L *quassare* to shake, break into pieces, fr. *quassus*, past part. of *quatere* to shake; akin to OE *hūdenian* to shake, MHG *hotzen* to set in motion, Icel *hossa* to bounce (a child) on one's knee, and perh. to Gk *passein* to sprinkle] *vt* **1 :** to beat down or in pieces **:** dash forcibly **:** SQUASH ⟨carts going by would ~ 'em —Lascelles Abercrombie⟩ **2 :** to suppress or extinguish summarily and completely **:** crush out **:** SUBDUE, QUELL ⟨~ a rebellion⟩ ~ *vi, obs* **:** to make a noise of splashing **syn** see CRUSH

quashqai *usu cap, var of* QASHQAI

quashy \ˈkwäshē\ *adj* -ER/-EST [2*quash* + *-y*] **:** MARSHY, SWAMPY, WET ⟨~ ground⟩

1qua·si \¦kwā,zī; *also* -äzē, -ā,sī, -äsē; *sometimes* -āzē, -ȯzē, -ȯsē; *or* -i *instead of* -ē\ *adv* [L, fr. *quam* than, how, as + *si* if — more at QUANTITY, SO] **1 :** as if **:** as it were **:** in a manner **:** in some sense or degree **:** SEEMINGLY, ALMOST ⟨the legatee was ~ an heir —O.W.Holmes †1935⟩ — usu. joined to second element with a hyphen ⟨a *quasi*-historical narrative⟩ ⟨*quasi*-universal literacy⟩ ⟨the *quasi*-diamond-shaped mouthpiece —William Yeomans⟩ ⟨served *quasi*-officially⟩ **2** \¦kwäzē, -i\ [It, fr. L] **:** in effect ⟨andante ~ allegro⟩ **:** APPROXIMATELY ⟨~ largo⟩ — used to qualify a musical direction

2quasi \"\ *adj* **1 :** having some resemblance (as in function, effect, or status) to a given thing **:** SEEMING, VIRTUAL ⟨a ~ argument⟩ ⟨its economic power gave it a position of ~ government —Fritz Tarnow⟩ ⟨in dance band orchestrations, the arranger develops into a ~ composer —Claude Lapham⟩ — often joined to second element with a hyphen ⟨a *quasi*-shawl⟩ ⟨*quasi*-republicanism⟩ **2 :** having a given legal status only by operation or construction of law and without reference to any intent of the party in interest (as the obligee or owner) ⟨~ crime⟩ ⟨a ~ trustee⟩ ⟨a ~ right⟩

quasi contract *n* **1 :** an obligation similar to that upon contract, enforced by action as upon contract, and imposed by law for reasons of justice and independently of the will of the person obliged — called also *contract quasi, implied contract* **2 :** an obligation imposed by law to prevent unjust enrichment of one at another's expense **:** RESTITUTION

quasi corporation *n* **:** a public or municipal body or organization (as a county) not specifically incorporated or vested with all the usual powers of a corporation but exercising certain corporate functions and rights in connection with public duties

quasi delict *n* [LL *quasi delictum*, fr. L *quasi* + *delictum* fault — more at DELICT] **1** *Roman law* **:** a wrong not arising out of a contract and implied and made actionable by praetorian edict though not previously recognized as a delictum **2** *civil & Scots law* **:** a wrong not arising out of a contract, implied under the circumstances, and made actionable as a matter of public policy rather than on account of any deliberately wrongful conduct or intention

quasi deposit *n* **:** a deposit or bailment implied in law from the circumstances whereby one coming into possession of another's personal property by chance or mistake is deemed to be a bailee in order to do justice between the parties and to prevent unjust enrichment **:** a constructive or quasi bailment

quasi easement *n* **:** APPARENT EASEMENT

quasi ex con·trac·tu \-,ekskən·ˈtrak(,)t(y)ü\ *adv (or adj)* [L] **:** as if from or by contract — compare QUASI CONTRACT

quasi in rem \-ənˈrem\ *adv (or adj)* [L, as if against a thing] **:** as if against a thing (as a right, status, property) ⟨proceedings and judgments are *quasi in rem* when they are in a court having no jurisdiction over the person of the defendant, not seeking to adjudicate a right, title, or status as against all in the world, but seeking to apply specific property within the power of the court insofar as that property is available in satisfaction of a personal action or claim against the defendant⟩ — compare IN PERSONAM, IN REM

quasi-judicial \¦=(,)=+\ *adj* **1 :** having a partly judicial character by possession of the right to hold hearings on and conduct investigations into disputed claims and alleged infractions of rules and regulations and to make decisions arrived at and enforced after the general manner of procedures in courts ⟨*quasi-judicial* bodies such as the National Labor Relations Board —*Atlantic*⟩ **2 :** essentially judicial in character but not within the judicial power or function nor belonging to the judiciary as constitutionally defined ⟨*quasi-judicial* functions⟩ ⟨some method of *quasi-judicial* review is desirable —*Harvard Law Rev.*⟩ — **quasi-judicially** \"+\ *adv*

quasi-legislative \"+\ *adj* **1 :** having a partly legislative character by possession of the right to make rules and regulations having the force of law ⟨the Interstate Commerce Commission is a *quasi-legislative* agency⟩ **2 :** essentially legislative in character but not within the legislative power or function or belonging to the legislative branch of government as constitutionally defined ⟨*quasi-legislative* powers⟩ ⟨*quasi-legislative* authority⟩

qua·si·mo·do \,kwäzəˈmō(,)dō, -äsə-\ *n* -s *usu cap* [L *quasi modo* as if just now; fr. part of the opening words of the introit for that day (based on 1 Pet 2:2), *quasi modo geniti infantes* as newborn babes] **:** LOW SUNDAY

quasi-optical *pronunc at* 1QUASI +\ *adj* **:** resembling light in character or behavior — used of ultrashort hertzian waves

quasi partner *n* **:** NOMINAL PARTNER

quasi-public \¦=(,)=+\ *adj* **:** essentially public (as in services rendered, functions performed, or source of income received) although under private ownership or control **:** affected with a public interest ⟨*quasi-public* enterprises like railroads⟩

quasi-pupillary substitution \"+...-\ *n, Roman law* **:** substitution of another heir upon the incapacity of an insane heir first named to take an inheritance

quasi rent *n* **:** revenue in excess of cost received from a service other than land use

quasi-reorganization \¦=(,)=+\ *n* **:** a corporate procedure whereby recapitalization is achieved by the elimination of the existing deficit and the establishment of a new earned surplus account for future earnings only and without resort to the legal formalities of a complete reorganization

quasi-tangent arc \"+...-\ *n* **:** CIRCUMZENITHAL ARC

quasi usufruct *n* **:** IMPERFECT USUFRUCT

quas·ky \ˈkwäskē\ *n* -ES [perh. irreg. fr. *oquassa*] **:** OQUASSA

quass *var of* KVASS

quas·sia \ˈkwäsh(ē)ə, -äsēə\ *n* [NL, fr. *Quassi*, 18th cent. Surinam Negro slave who discovered the medicinal value of Surinam quassia + NL *-ia*] **1** *cap* **:** a genus of shrubs or trees (family Simaroubaceae) having pinnate leaves with winged petioles and large racemose scarlet flowers **2** -s **:** a drug consisting of the heartwood of various tropical trees of the family Simaroubaceae used in medicine as a bitter tonic and as a remedy for roundworms in children, as an insecticide, and in brewing as a substitute for hops — see JAMAICA QUASSIA, SURINAM QUASSIA

quas·sin \ˈkwäsᵊn\ *n* -s [ISV *quass-* (fr. NL *Quassia*) + *-in*] **:** the bitter crystalline principle of quassia

1quat \ˈkwät, -at\ *vb* **quatted**; **quatted**; **quatting**; **quats** [ME *quaten*, fr. MF *quatir* to beat, fr. (assumed) *coactire* to press together — more at DECATING] *vt, dial chiefly Eng* **1 :** beat down **:** SQUASH **2 :** GLUT, SATIATE ~ *vi, chiefly dial* **:** SQUAT

2quat \"\ *adj* [ME, fr. past part. of *quaten*] *chiefly dial* **:** pressed close **:** SQUAT ⟨the rest lay so ~ and close that they could not be apprehended —John Bunyan⟩

3quat \"\ *Scot var of* QUIT

4quat \"\ *n* -s [origin unknown] **1** *dial chiefly Eng* **:** an eruption of the skin (as a pimple, boil, sty) **2** *chiefly dial* **:** UPSTART, WHIPPERSNAPPER

5quat *var of* KAT

quat *abbr* [L *quattuor*] four

qua·te·nus \ˈkwätənəs, -,ten-\ *prep* [L, how far, to what extent, fr. *qua* where, as, insofar as + *tenus* as far as, up to; akin to L *tendere* to stretch — more at QUA, THIN] **:** in the quality or capacity of **:** AS

quater- *comb form* [ISV, fr. L *quater* four times] **:** TETRA- — esp. in names of organic compounds to denote the quadrupling of a radical or molecule ⟨*quater*phenyl⟩ ⟨*quater*thiazole⟩

quater·centenary \¦kwäd·ə(r), -wād·-+\ *n* [L *quater* four times + E *centenary*] **:** a four-hundredth anniversary

1quater·nary \ˈkwäd·ər,nerē, kwäˈtərnərē\ *n* -ES [ME, fr. L *quaternarius*, adj., consisting of four each, fr. *quaterni* four each (fr. *quater* four times) + *-arius* -ary] **1 a :** a group of four **b :** a member of a fourth group **2** *usu cap* **:** the Quaternary period or system of rocks

2quaternary \"\ *adj* [L *quaternarius* consisting of four each] **1 :** consisting of four parts or components **:** by fours or in sets of four ⟨a ~ compound⟩ **2 a :** fourth in order **b** *usu cap* **:** of or relating to the geological period from the end of the Tertiary to the present time — see GEOLOGIC TIME table **3 :** characterized by replacement in the fourth degree: as **a :** united to four carbon atoms in organic radicals ⟨a ~ carbon atom⟩ **b :** consisting of or containing an atom (as nitrogen) united by four bonds to carbon atoms in organic radicals ⟨~ ammonium $[R_4N]^+$⟩ ⟨~ salts⟩

quaternary ammonium compound *also* **quaternary** *n* -ES **:** any of a large class of strong bases and their salts that may be regarded as compounds of ammonium in which all four hydrogen atoms are replaced by organic radicals and that in many cases are used as surface-active agents, as disinfectants and germicides, and as drugs — compare CATIONIC DETERGENT, METHONIUM

quaternary silver *n* **:** silver containing three alloying elements and used for coinage ⟨former British coinage of *quaternary silver* containing 50 percent silver, 40 percent copper, 5 percent nickel, and 5 percent zinc⟩

quater·nate \ˈkwäd·ər,nāt, kwäˈtərnət\ *adj* [prob. fr. (assumed) NL *quaternatus*, fr. L *quaterni* four each + *-atus* -ate] **:** composed of or arranged in sets of four ⟨~ leaves⟩

qua·ter·ni·on \kwəˈtərnēən, -wäˈt-\ *n* -s [ME *quaternioun*, fr. LL *quaternion-, quaternio*, fr. L *quaterni* four each (fr. *quater* four times) + *-ion-, -io* -ion; akin to L *quattuor* four — more at FOUR] **1 :** a set of four parts, things, or persons **:** TETRAD ⟨delivered him to four ~*s* of soldiers —Acts 12:4 (AV)⟩ ⟨the leading ~ of publishers —*Times Lit. Supp.*⟩ **2 a** (1) **:** *archaic* **:** a sheet of paper folded twice (2) **:** QUIRE 1a **b :** a sheet that is folded once to form two leaves or four pages and nested together with other sheets (as in ancient books) to form a section **3 :** a generalized complex number that is the sum of a real number and a vector and that depends on one real and three imaginary units the third of which is the product of the first two and also the negative of this product when the order of the factors is reversed so that multiplication over the field of quaternions is not commutative

qua·ter·ni·ty \kwäˈtərnəd·ē\ *n* -ES [LL *quaternitat-, quaternitas*, fr. L *quaterni* four each + *-itat-, -itas* -ity] **:** a union or group of four persons, things, or parts; *specif* **:** the union of four individuals in one godhead — compare TRINITY

quater·ni·za·tion \,kwäd·ə(r)nəˈzāshən, -wād·-, -,nīˈz-\ *n* -s **:** the process of quaternizing

qua·ter·nize \ˈ==ˌnīz\ *vt* -ED/-ING/-S [²*quaternary* + *-ize*] : to convert (as an amine) into a quaternary compound

qua·ter·phenyl \ˌ===+\ *n* [ISV *quater-* + *phenyl*] : any of several crystalline aromatic hydrocarbons $C_6H_5(C_6H_4)_2C_6H_5$ that contain a sequence of four benzene rings in the molecule; *esp* : the isomer whose central rings are attached at para positions and which is made by pyrolysis of biphenyl

quaters *var of* CATERS

qua·tor·zain \kəˈtȯrˌzān, kaˈt-, -ˌzᵊn; ˈkadərˌzān\ *n* -S [MF *quatorzaine* group of fourteen, fr. OF, period of fourteen days, fr. *quatorze* fourteen] : a poem of fourteen lines; *specif* : a poem resembling a sonnet but lacking strict sonnet structure

qua·torze \kəˈtō(ə)rz, kaˈt-\ *n* -S [F, lit., fourteen, fr. OF, fr. L *quattuordecim*, fr. *quattuor* four + *-decim* (fr. *decem* ten) — more at FOUR, TEN] : a set of 4 aces, kings, queens, jacks, or tens held in a hand at piquet and scoring 14 points

qua·train \ˈkwäˌtrān *also* =ˈ= *sometimes* ˈkwäˌtrən *or* kwəˈ-trān *or with* ō *for* ä\ *n* -S [F, fr. MF, fr. *quatre* four, fr. L *quattuor*] : a verse unit of four lines ⟨a ~ rhyming *abab*⟩

quatreble *n* -S [ME, fourfold amount, fr. *quatreble*, adj., quadruple, modif. (influenced by ME *treble*) of MF *quadruple*] *obs* : a musical voice part one octave higher than the mean

qua·tre·foil \ˈkad·ə(r)ˌfȯil, ˈka·trəˌf-\ *n* [ME *quaterfoil* set of four leaves, fr. MF *quatre* four + ME *-foil* (as in *trefoil*)] **1** : a conventionalized representation of a flower with four petals or of a leaf with four leaflets ⟨an allover pattern of tiny emerald green ~*s* —*Parke-Bernet Galleries Catalog*⟩; *specif* : a heraldic representation of a flower with four petals **2** : a figure enclosed by four joined foils; *specif* : a 4-lobed foliation in Gothic tracery — **qua·tre·foiled** \-ld\ *adj*

quatrefoils 2

quatrible *n* [alter. (influenced by obs. E *trible* treble, fr. ME) of ME *quatreble* fourfold amount — more at TREBLE] *obs* : a descant in fourths

quatroon *archaic var of* QUADROON

quats *pres 3d sing of* QUAT, *pl of* QUAT

quatted *past of* QUAT

quatting *pres part of* QUAT

quat·tri·no \kwäˈtrē(ˌ)nō\ *n, pl* **quattri·ni** \-nē\ [It, fr. *quattro* four] : an old coin of several of the Italian states

quat·tro·cen·tist \ˌkwä·trōˈchentəst\ *n, pl* **quattrocentists** *or* **quattrocenti·sti** \-ˌchenˈtē(ˌ)stē, -ˈtistē\ [It *quattrocentista*, fr. *quattrocento* + *-ista* -ist (fr. L)] **1** : an Italian of the quattrocento; *esp* : a poet or artist of this period **2** : a student of the art or literature of the quattrocento

quat·tro·cen·to \-ˈchen·(ˌ)tō\ *n, sometimes cap* [It, lit., four hundred (abbr. of fourteen hundred), fr. *quattro* four (fr. L *quattuor*) + *cento* hundred, fr. L *centum* — more at FOUR, HUNDRED] : the 15th century; *specif* : the 15th century period in Italian literature and art

quat·tuor·decillion \ˌkwäd·əˌwȯr, -äˌtw- +\ *n, often attrib* [L *quattuordecim* fourteen + E *-illion* (as in *million*)] — see NUMBER table

quat·uor \ˈkwädəˌwȯr, -äˌtw-\ *n* -S [F, fr. L *quattuor* four] : QUARTET

quauk \ˈkwak\ *Scot var of* QUAKE

¹**qua·ver** \ˈkwāvə(r)\ *vb* **quavered; quavered; quavering** \-v(ə)riŋ\ **quavers** [ME *quaveren*, freq. of *quaven* to tremble] *vi* **1** : TREMBLE, VIBRATE, SHAKE ⟨was ~*ing* inwardly with nervousness —Marcia Davenport⟩ **2** : to trill with the voice or on a musical instrument **3** : to utter sound in tremulous uncertain tones ⟨the full voice ~*ed* and broke —Zane Grey⟩ ~ *vt* : to utter with quavers; *esp* : to sing with trills or quavers ⟨eldest inhabitants . . . ~ out folk songs —Max Beerbohm⟩

²**quaver** \"\ *n* -S **1** : EIGHTH NOTE **2** : a trill in singing **3** : a tremulous uncertainty of tone (as in the voice due to emotion, old age)

qua·ver·ing·ly *adv* : in a quavering manner

qua·very \ˈkwāv(ə)rē, -ri\ *adj* [¹*quaver* + *-y*] : characterized by quavering : TREMBLING, UNSTEADY

quaw \ˈkwȯ\ *n* -S [origin unknown] *chiefly Scot* : QUAGMIRE

¹**quawk** \ˈkwȯk, -wäk\ *vi* [imit.] *chiefly dial* : CAW, SQUAWK

²**quawk** \ˈkwȯk\ *n* -S **1** : ²QUACK **2** : NIGHT HERON

¹**quay** \ˈkē, ˈk(w)ā\ *n* -S [alter. (influenced by F *quai* quay, fr. OF *cai*) of earlier *key*, fr. ME, fr. MF *cai*, fr. OF, of Celt origin; akin to Corn *kē* hedge, fence — more at HEDGE] : a stretch of paved and strengthened bank or a solid artificial landing place (as of stone) made along or parallel to the side of a navigable water for convenience in loading and unloading ships **syn** see WHARF

²**quay** \"\ *vt* -ED/-ING/-S : to furnish with a quay

quay·age \-ij, -ēj\ *n* -S [alter. (influenced by F *quayage*, fr. OF *caiage*) of earlier *keyage*, fr. ME, fr. MF *caiage*, fr. OF, fr. *cai* quay + *-age*] **1** : a charge for use of a quay : quay dues : WHARFAGE **2** : room on or for quays ⟨the total ~ of the port⟩ **3** : a system of quays ⟨reconstructed their harbor ~⟩

quayside \ˈ=ˌ=\ *n* : land bordering on or adjacent to a quay : the neighborhood of the quays ⟨the waterfront with its long, paved ~ —Steven Runciman⟩

queach \ˈkwēch\ *n* -ES [ME *queche*] *dial chiefly Eng* : THICKET

queachy \-chē, -chi\ *adj* [obs E, forming a dense growth, fr. *queach* + *-y*] *dial chiefly Eng* : BOGGY, MARSHY

queak \ˈkwēk\ *vb* -ED/-ING/-S [imit.] *dial* : SQUEAK

quean \ˈkwēn\ *n* -S [ME *quene*, *quen*, fr. OE *cwene* woman, female serf, prostitute; akin to OHG *quena* woman, wife, ON *kona*, Goth *qino* woman, wife, OE *cwēn* woman, wife, queen — more at QUEEN] **1** *also* **queen** \"\ : a disreputable woman; *specif* : PROSTITUTE ⟨a lively ~ who can dance, weep and love —*Time*⟩ **2 a** *chiefly Scot* : WOMAN; *esp* : one that is young or unmarried **b** *dial Brit* : a little girl

quean-cat \ˈ=ˌ=\ *n, dial Eng* : a female cat

queanish *adj, obs* : of, relating to, or resembling a quean

quea·si·ly \ˈkwēz(ə)lē, -li\ *adv* : in a queasy manner

quea·si·ness \-zēnəs, -zin-\ *n* -ES : the quality or state of being queasy

quea·sy *also* **quea·zy** \ˈkwēzē, -zi\ *adj* -ER/-EST [ME *coysy*, *qwesye*, *quasy*] **1** : full of doubt : UNSETTLED, HAZARDOUS ⟨last week's ~ market —*Time*⟩ ⟨the lightly rooted life upon one ~ planet —D.C.Peattie⟩ **2 a** : causing nausea : NAUSEATING ⟨~ motion of the waves⟩ ⟨a ~ mess upon the plate⟩ **b** : tending to be sick at the stomach : NAUSEATED **3 a** : causing qualms or uneasiness **b** (1) : easily disturbed : DELICATE, FASTIDIOUS, SQUEAMISH ⟨a ~ conscience⟩ (2) : experiencing a feeling of uneasiness : ill at ease ⟨how ~ we become in the presence of anyone who supposes that he has "charm," when he really has none —Clifford Bax⟩

¹**que·bec** \kwəˈbek, kwē- *sometimes* kāˈ-\ *adj, usu cap* [fr. *Quebec*, Canada] **1** : of or from Quebec, capital of the province of Quebec : of the kind or style prevalent in Quebec **2** : of or from the province of Quebec : of the kind or style prevalent in Quebec

²**quebec** \"\ *usu cap* [fr. *Quebec*, Canada] — a communications code word for the letter *q*

quebec deal *n, usu cap Q* : timber of any width and three inches or more in thickness — used esp. in the export trade

que·bec·er *or* **que·beck·er** \-kə(r)\ *n* -S *cap* [*Quebec*, Canada + E *-er*] : a native or resident of Quebec city or province, Canada

que·bec·ois *or* **qué·bec·ois** \ˌkäˌbeˈkwä\ *n, pl* **quebecois** *or* **québecois** \-(z)\ *cap* [F *Québecois*, fr. *Québec*, Canada] : QUEBECER

quebec standard deal *n, usu cap Q* : a deal board 3 inches by 11 inches by 12 feet

que·brach·a·mine \kāˈbrachəˌmēn, kəˈ-, -ˌmən\ *n* [ISV *quebracho* + *amine*] : a crystalline alkaloid $C_{19}H_{26}N_2$ obtained from aspidosperma

que·brach·ine \-chən\ *n* -S [ISV *quebracho* + *-ine*] : YOHIMBINE

que·brach·i·tol \-chəˌtȯl, -tōl\ *n* -S [ISV *quebracho* + *-ite* + *-ol*] : a sweet crystalline compound $C_6H_6(OH)_5(OCH_3)$ occurring esp. in quebracho bark and in the latex of hevea rubber; *levo*-inositol monomethyl ether

que·bra·cho \-(ˌ)chō\ *n* -S [AmerSp, alter. of *quiebracha*, *quiebrahacha*, fr. *quiebra* it breaks (3d sing. pres. indic. of *quebrar* to break, fr. L *crepare* to rattle, crack, creak) + *hacha* ax, fr. F *hache* — more at RAVEN, HASH] **1** : any of several tropical American trees with notably hard wood: as **a** : a tree (*Aspidosperma quebracho*) of Chile and Argentina that yields quebracho bark —called also *white quebracho* **b** : a tree (*Schinopsis lorentzii*) that is native to Argentina and is used as a source of tannin and in dyeing — called also *red quebracho* **c** : a So. American tree (*Iodina rhombifolia*) of the family Santalaceae used in tanning and dyeing **d** : any of several Central American and Mexican leguminous trees (as *Lysiloma divaricata*, *Caesalpinia platyloba*, *Pithecolobium arboreum*) **2** : the wood of a quebracho **3** : *or* **quebracho bark** : ASPIDOSPERMA 2

que·bra·da \kāˈbrädə\ *n* -S [Sp, fr. fem. of *quebrado*, past part. of *quebrar* to break — more at QUEBRACHO] **1** : RAVINE; *esp* : one that is normally dry or nearly dry but is filled by a torrent during a rain **2** : BROOK

quech·ua \ˈkechwə\ *also* **qui·chua** \ˈkēch-\ *or* **kech·ua** *or* **ki·chua** *n, pl* **quechua** *or* **quechuas** *usu cap* [Sp, fr. Quechua *kkechúwa* plunderer, despoiler, robber] **1 a** : a people of central Peru believed to be originally Aymara **b** : a member of such people **2** : a group of peoples constituting the dominant element of the Inca empire **3 a** : the language of the Quechua people that is also widely spoken by other Indian peoples of Peru, Bolivia, Ecuador, Chile, and Argentina **b** : a language family comprising the Quechua language

¹**quech·uan** *also* **qui·chuan** \-wən\ *n, pl* **quechuan** *or* **quechuans** *usu cap* [*Quechua* + *-an*] : QUECHUA

²**quechuan** *also* **quichuan** \"\ *adj, usu cap* : of or relating to the Quechua language family

queechy \ˈkwēchi\ *adj* [origin unknown] *dial Eng* : SICKLY, PUNY

queem \ˈkwēm\ *Scot var of* QUEME

¹**queen** \ˈkwēn\ *n* -S [ME *quen*, *quene*, fr. OE *cwēn* woman, wife, queen; akin to OS *quān* wife, ON *kvæn*, *kvān*, Goth *qens* wife, OIr *ben* woman, Gk *gynē*, Arm *kin*, Skt *jani*] **1 a** : the wife or widow of a king **b** : the wife or widow of a chief of a tribe (as of Indians) **2 a** : a woman who is the sovereign of a kingdom : a female monarch **b** : CHIEFTAINESS ⟨~ of the Iroquois⟩ ⟨gypsy ~⟩ **3 a** : a woman eminent in rank, power, or attractions ⟨a ~ in society⟩ ⟨movie ~⟩ **b** : a goddess or a thing personified as female and having supremacy in a specified realm ⟨Venus, ~ of love⟩ ⟨Paris, ~ of cities⟩ ⟨a new liner to join the ocean ~*s*⟩ **c** : a strikingly attractive girl or woman; *esp* : the winner of a beauty contest **4** : the most privileged piece in a set of chessmen having the power to move as either a rook or a bishop **5** : a playing card marked with a stylized figure of a queen and usu. the initial letter Q **6** : the fertile fully developed female of social bees, ants, and termites whose function in the colony is to lay eggs — compare SOLDIER, WORKER; see HONEYBEE illustration **7** : a mature female cat; *specif* : one kept for breeding **8** *slang* : HOMOSEXUAL — **to the queen's taste** : to the satisfaction of an extremely discriminating person

queen 4

²**queen** \"\ *vb* -ED/-ING/-S *vi* **1** : to act like a queen : behave in a queenly manner : put on airs ⟨~ it and makes with a production —Julian Halevy⟩ — usu. used with formulary *it* ⟨another woman ~*ing* it in the new penthouse —Helen Howe⟩ **2** : to reign as queen **3** : to become a queen in chess ~ *vt* **1** : to promote (a pawn) to a queen in chess **2** : to reign over as queen **3** : to make a queen of ⟨to ~ a woman⟩ **4** : to provide a queen for (as a hive of bees)

³**queen** \"\ *usu cap* [¹*queen*] — a communications code word for the letter *q*

⁴**queen** *var of* QUEAN

queen anne \-ˈan, -aa(ə)n\ *adj, usu cap Q&A* [after *Queen Anne* of England †1714] **1** : of, relating to, or having the characteristics of a style of furniture prevalent in England under Dutch influence esp. during the first half of the 18th century that is marked by extensive use of upholstery, marquetry, and Oriental fabrics, attention to comfort (as in shapes of chair backs), general use of walnut and of the cabriole, and the introduction of such pieces as the bureau bookcase and separate mirrors ⟨*Queen Anne* sofa⟩ ⟨*Queen Anne* stool⟩ **2 a** : of, relating to, or having the characteristics of a style of English building prevalent in the early 18th century characterized by modified classic ornament, generally unpretentious design, the use of red brickwork in which even relief ornament is carved, and general fitness for domestic architecture **b** : of, relating to, or characteristic of a style of wooden cottages developed in England and the U. S. during the last quarter of the 19th century

queen anne green *n, often cap Q&A* : TEA GREEN

queen anne's lace *n, pl* **queen anne's lace** *also* **queen anne's laces** *usu cap Q&A* [after *Queen Anne* of England] : WILD CARROT

queen bee *n* **1** : the fertile fully developed female of a social bee (as the honeybee) — compare QUEEN 6 **2** : a woman who dominates or leads a group (as in a social activity)

queen blue *or* **queen's blue** *n* : a moderate blue that is redder and duller than average copen, azurite blue, or Dresden blue and redder and less strong than bluebird

queen bolt *n* : a rod serving as a queen post in a roof truss

queen butterfly *also* **queen** *n* -S : a large brown white-spotted butterfly (*Danaus glippus*) of the warmer parts of America that is closely related to the monarch butterfly

queen cage *n* : a small container to hold a queen bee (as for shipment)

queen cell *n* : one of the large irregular thick-walled special cells usu. attached to the base of a brood comb in which the larvae of the queen bees are reared

queen closer *or* **queen closure** *n* : a closer that is less than half a brick; *specif* : a brick of full length and thickness but half width that is used at the end of a course next to the quoin header — compare KING CLOSER

queen conch *n* : a large yellowish conch (*Cassis madagascarensis*) with brown markings that is much used in cameo making; *also* : any of several other large conchs or helmet shells (as the king conch)

queen consort *n, pl* **queens consort** : the wife of a reigning king

queen crab *n* : a large edible crab (*Carpilius corallinus*) of the family Xanthidae that frequents shallow water from the Bahamas to Brazil and is usu. pale red marked with scarlet, white, and yellow

queen-cup \ˈ=ˌ=\ *n* : a perennial herb (*Clintonia uniflora*) of the Rocky Mountain region sometimes cultivated for its white flowers

queen·dom \ˈkwēndəm\ *n* -S **1** : the state or territory ruled by a queen **2** : the position of a queen

queen dowager *n* : the widow of a king

queen excluder *n* : a device usu. of perforated metal that shuts off the queen bee from some parts of a hive but permits the workers to pass

queen fern *n* : ROYAL FERN

queenfish \ˈ=ˌ=\ *n* : any of several marine fishes: as **a** : a common small California sciaenid fish (*Seriphus politus*) silvery blue above with the sides and belly silvery **b** : ³WAHOO **c** : any of several large carangid food and game fishes (genus *Chorinemus*) widespread in the tropical Indo-Pacific

queen·hood \ˈkwēnˌhu̇d\ *n* : the rank, dignity, or state of being of a queen

queen-in-council \ˈ==ˈ===\ *n, pl* **queens-in-council** *often cap Q&C* : KING-IN-COUNCIL — used when the British monarch is a queen

queen-in-parliament \ˈ==ˈ===\ *n, pl* **queens-in-parliament** *often cap Q&P* : KING-IN-PARLIAMENT — used when the British monarch is a queen

queen·ite \ˈkwēˌnīt\ *n* -S *usu cap* : one who supports or upholds a queen; *specif* : an adherent of Queen Isabella II of Spain against the Carlists

queen·less \ˈkwēnləs\ *adj* : lacking a queen

queen·let \-lət\ *n* -S : a petty queen

queenlike \ˈ=ˌ=\ *adj* : QUEENLY

queen lily *n* : a plant of the genus *Phaedranassa*

queen·li·ness \ˈkwēnlēnəs, -lin-\ *n* -ES : the quality or state of being queenly

¹**queen·ly** \-lē, -li\ *adj* -ER/-EST [¹*queen* + *-ly*] **1** : belonging to or befitting a queen ⟨clad in her ~ raiment —William Morris⟩ **2** : resembling a queen : MAJESTIC, REGAL, HAUGHTY ⟨the ~ poise of her head —Jack London⟩

²**queenly** \"\ *adv, often* -ER/-EST : in a queenly manner

queen mother *n* : a queen dowager who is mother of the reigning sovereign

queen of may *or* **queen of the may** *usu cap Q&M* : MAY QUEEN

queen of the meadow **1** : a meadowsweet (*Filipendula ulmaria*) **2** : any of several plants of the genus *Spiraea* **3** : MARSH MILKWEED

queen of the night : a tropical American climbing cactus (*Selenicereus grandiflorus*) with triangular branches that is often cultivated for its large showy night-blooming flowers

queen of the prairie : an American perennial herb (*Filipendula rubra*) with ample clusters of pale pink flowers

queen olive *n* : any of various olives grown esp. in the region of Seville, Spain, and having large oblong fruits with a small but long pit that are usu. cured green and are characterized by good keeping quality and delicate flavor

queen pigeon *n* : any of several crowned pigeons (as *Goura victoria*)

queenpin \ˈ=ˌ=\ *n, slang* : QUEEN BEE 2

queen post *n* : one of two vertical tie posts in a truss (as of a roof)

queen post truss *n* : QUEEN TRUSS

queen regent *n, pl* **queens regent** : a queen ruling in behalf of another or in her own right

queen regnant *n, pl* **queens regnant** : a queen reigning in her own right

queen posts

queenright \(ˈ)=ˈ=\ *adj, of a colony of bees* : having a queen in the hive

queen rod *n* : QUEEN BOLT

queenroot \ˈ=ˌ=\ *n* : QUEEN'S DELIGHT

¹**queens** *pl of* QUEEN, *pres 3d sing of* QUEEN

²**queens** \ˈkwēnz\ *adj, usu cap* [fr. *Queens* borough, New York, N.Y.] : of or from the borough of Queens, New York, N.Y. : of the kind or style prevalent in Queens

queen's arm *n* : MUSKET

queen's bench *n, usu cap Q&B* : COURT OF KING'S BENCH — used when the British monarch is a queen

queensberry rules *n pl, usu cap Q* : MARQUIS OF QUEENSBERRY RULES

queen's birthday *n, usu cap Q&B* : KING'S BIRTHDAY — used when the British monarch is a queen

queen's blue *var of* QUEEN BLUE

queen's champion *n, usu cap Q&C* : KING'S CHAMPION — used when the British monarch is a queen

queen's color *n, often cap Q&C* : KING'S COLOR — used when the British monarch is a queen

queen's counsel *n, usu cap Q&C* : KING'S COUNSEL — used when the British monarch is a queen

queen's crape myrtle *n* : a tree (*Lagerstroemia speciosa*) that is native to Asia, Australia, and the East Indies where it provides timber and that is used elsewhere as an ornamental for its large showy mauve to pink or purple flowers in large terminal clusters — see PYINMA

queen's-delight \ˈ==ˌ=\ *n, pl* **queen's-delights** : a perennial herb (*Stillingia sylvatica*) with a root that is used as an alterative and more recently shows promise as the source of a drying oil for paints and varnishes

queen's english *n, usu cap Q&E* : KING'S ENGLISH — used when the British monarch is a queen

queen's evidence *n, usu cap Q* : KING'S EVIDENCE — used when the British monarch is a queen

queen's fettle *n* : a monkshood (*Aconitum napellus*)

queen's-flower \(ˈ)=ˈ=\ *n, pl* **queen's-flowers** : QUEEN'S CRAPE MYRTLE

queen·ship \ˈkwēnˌship\ *n* **1** : QUEENHOOD **2** : QUEENLINESS

queens-in-council *pl of* QUEEN-IN-COUNCIL

queens-in-parliament *pl of* QUEEN-IN-PARLIAMENT

queens·land \ˈkwēnzˌland, -ˌlaa(ə)nd, -lənd\ *adj, usu cap* [fr. *Queensland* state, Australia] : of or from the state of Queensland, Australia : of the kind or style prevalent in Queensland

queensland beech *n, usu cap Q* **1** : an Australian timber tree (*Gmelina leichardtii*) with purplish white tubular flowers **2** : the hard heavy wood of the Queensland beech

queensland cherry *n, usu cap Q* **1** : an Australian shrub or small tree (*Antidesma dallachianum*) of the family Euphorbiaceae **2** : the red edible acid fruit of the Queensland cherry

queens·land·er \-də(r)\ *n* -S *cap* [*Queensland* state + E *-er*] : a native or inhabitant of the state of Queensland, Australia

queensland fruit fly *n, usu cap Q* : a trypetid fly (*Dacus tryoni*) that is a serious pest of fruits in New So. Wales

queensland grass-cloth plant *n, usu cap Q* : an Australian plant (*Pipturus argenteus*) whose fiber is used in making cloth

queensland hemp *n, usu cap Q* : an herb (*Sida rhombifolia*) of wide distribution in the tropics, that has a fine soft bast fiber superior to jute in strength, is used for forage and medicinally as a demulcent, and in some areas is an aggressive weed — called also *jellyleaf*

queensland hickory *n, usu cap Q* : an Australian evergreen tree (*Flindersia ifflaiana*) with yellow close-grained hard wood used typically for heavy construction and machine bearings — called also *Cairn's ash*

queensland kauri *n, usu cap Q* : any of various trees of the genus *Agathis*; *specif* : DUNDATHU PINE

queensland maple *n, usu cap Q* **1** : an Australian tree (*Flindersia brayleana*) **2** : the light-red wood of the Queensland maple that resembles mahogany

queensland nut *n, usu cap Q* **1** : MACADAMIA 2a **2** : MACADAMIA NUT

queensland silver wattle *n, usu cap Q* : a shrubby Australian wattle (*Acacia podalyriifolia*) with downy ash-colored or silvery phyllodes and globose golden yellow heads of flowers in axillary racemes

queensland trumpeter *n, usu cap Q* : a marine food fish (*Pomadasys hasta*) of the tropical Indo-Pacific

queensland walnut *n, usu cap Q* : AUSTRALIAN WALNUT

queen's mark *n, usu cap Q* : KING'S MARK — used when the British monarch is a queen

queen's metal *n* : an alloy somewhat resembling pewter or britannia metal and consisting essentially of tin with an admixture of antimony, zinc, and lead or copper

queen snake *n* : a harmless colubrid snake (*Natrix septemvittata*) of the central, eastern, and southern U. S.

queen's peace *n, sometimes cap Q&P* : KING'S PEACE — used when the British monarch is a queen

queen's proctor *n, usu cap Q&P* : KING'S PROCTOR — used when the British monarch is a queen

queen's regulations *n pl, usu cap Q&R* : KING'S REGULATIONS — used when the British monarch is a queen

queen's remembrancer *n, usu cap Q&R* : KING'S REMEMBRANCER — used when the British monarch is a queen

queen's-root \(ˈ)=ˈ=\ *n, pl* **queen's-roots** : QUEEN'S-DELIGHT

queen's scholar *n, usu cap Q&S* : a student in an English school or college who is supported by a foundation created by or under the auspices of a queen

queen's scout *n, usu cap Q&S* : KING'S SCOUT — used when the British monarch is a queen

queen's shilling *n* : KING'S SHILLING — used when the British monarch is a queen

queensware \ˈ=ˌ=\ *n* **1** : glazed English earthenware of a cream color **2** : cream-colored Wedgwood ware

queenswood \ˈ=ˌ=\ *n* : AUSTRALIAN WALNUT

queen's wreath *n* : PURPLE WREATH

queen's yellow *n* **1** : MIMOSA 3 **2** : CALOMEL

queen triggerfish *n* : a triggerfish (*Balistes vetula*) widely distributed in the tropical Atlantic and Indian oceans — called also *Bessy cerka*, *oldwench*, *oldwife*

queen truss *n* : a truss framed with queen posts

queen turtle *n* : an edible No. American soft-shelled turtle (*Trionyx mutica*)

[1]**queer** \'kwi(ə)r, -iə, *dial* -wa(a)|(ə)r, -we|, |ə, -wär, -wå(r\ *adj* -ER/-EST [origin unknown] **1 a :** differing in some odd way from what is usual or normal **:** STRANGE, CURIOUS, PECULIAR, UNEXPECTED ⟨deep fireplaces and ~ andirons —Austin Dobson⟩ ⟨spoke in a ~, kindly, foreign voice —Alan Tomkins⟩ ⟨~ bird rustlings and cries in the trees lull me to sleep —S.P.B.Mais⟩ **b** (1) **:** ECCENTRIC, UNCONVENTIONAL ⟨a likable but somewhat ~ folk —R.H.Shryock⟩ ⟨individuals who do not follow this routine are regarded as ~ —Ralph Linton⟩ ⟨looked like a gentleman, though he was as ~ a duck as you could meet —Mary McCarthy⟩ ⟨regarded him as a foreigner, and a ~ fish —Nevil Shute⟩ (2) **:** mildly insane **:** TOUCHED **c :** OBSESSED, HIPPED ⟨seems to be ~ for these early-morning conferences —Budd Schulberg⟩ ⟨~ on the subject of first editions⟩ ⟨~ about the circus⟩ **d** *slang* **:** sexually deviate **:** HOMOSEXUAL **2 a** *slang* **:** WORTHLESS, SPURIOUS, COUNTERFEIT ⟨~ money⟩ **b :** QUESTIONABLE, SUSPICIOUS ⟨a ~ transaction⟩ ⟨~ goings-on⟩ **3 :** not quite well **:** FAINT, GIDDY, QUEASY ⟨gave her a ~ sensation to think of standing in that room again —J.C.Powys⟩ **4** *Scot* **:** DROLL, AMUSING, COMICAL ⟨told his ~*est* stories —Robert Burns⟩ **syn** see STRANGE

[2]**queer** \"\ *adv* -ER/-EST **:** QUEERLY

[3]**queer** \"\ *vt* -ED/-ING/-S **1 :** to spoil the effect or success of **:** interfere with ⟨bad weather ~*ed* our plans⟩ **:** JEOPARDIZE, HARM, DISRUPT ⟨the old man may have ~*ed* his own promotion —J.A.Michener⟩ ⟨the spring lock had snapped, ~*ing* his exit —*Time*⟩ ⟨blurring of focus and muddled misdirection of attention: consequences of ~*ing* one discipline with the habits of another —F.R.Leavis⟩ **2 :** to put or get into an embarrassing or disadvantageous situation **:** put in a bad light ⟨~*ed* himself with the authorities by his lack of cooperation⟩ ⟨the giving of such perquisites, the exercise of such influence, ~*s* the profession —Virginia Woolf⟩ — **queer one's pitch** *or* **queer the pitch :** to spoil something planned, arranged, or attempted ⟨I answered rather cautiously so as not to *queer your pitch* —Stephen Haggard⟩

[4]**queer** \"\ *n* -S **1** *slang* **:** one that is queer; *esp* **:** a usu. male homosexual **2** *slang* **:** counterfeit money — usu. used with *the* ⟨jailed for passing the ~⟩

queer cuffin *n* **:** CHURL

queer·ish \-rish, -rēsh\ *adj* [[1]*queer* + *-ish*] **:** rather queer ⟨a ~ deal in imported crabmeat —*Pacific Fisherman*⟩ — **queer·ish·ly** *adv* — **queer·ish·ness** *n* -ES

queer·i·ty \-rəd·ē\ *n* -ES [[1]*queer* + *-ity*] *chiefly dial* **:** QUEERNESS

queer·ly *adv* **:** in a queer manner **:** ODDLY, STRANGELY ⟨a ~ inscribed stone —R.W.Murray⟩ ⟨behaved ~⟩ ⟨just inside the door stood a constable, looking ~ at home without his helmet —Ngaio Marsh⟩

queer·ness \-rnə̇s\ *n* -ES **1 :** the quality of being queer **:** ODDITY, ECCENTRICITY ⟨his actions for some weeks had given indication of ~ —S.H.Adams⟩ **2 :** a queer characteristic ⟨much liked despite his ~*es* —Mary Johnston⟩

queer street *n, usu cap Q&S* **:** an embarrassing situation or condition; *esp* **:** a condition marked by financial difficulties ⟨those commitments will put us in *Queer Street* next year —John Galsworthy⟩

queest \'kwēst\ *n* -S [ME *quyshte, quyste,* fr. OE *cūscote, cūcsceote*] **:** RINGDOVE

queet \'kwēt\ *n* -S [by alter.] *Scot* **:** [2]COOT

quekchi *usu cap, var of* KEKCHI

quelch \'kwelch, -lsh\ *vb* -ED/-ING/-ES [by alter.] *dial* **:** SQUELCH

que·lea \'kwēlēə\ *n* [NL, prob. fr. a native name in Africa] **1** *cap* **:** a genus of African weaverbirds **2** -S **:** any bird of the genus *Quelea; esp* **:** a red-billed bird (*Q. quelea*) often kept as a cage bird

que·li·te \kā'lēd·ē\ *n* -S [MexSp, fr. Nahuatl *quilitl* edible green] *Southwest* **:** any of various plants (as lamb's-quarters or purslane) cooked as greens **:** POTHERB

[1]**quell** \'kwel\ *vt* -ED/-ING/-S [ME *quellen,* fr. OE *cwellan;* akin to OS *quellian* to torture, kill, OHG *quellen* to torture, kill, ON *kvelja* to torment, torture; causative fr. the root of OE *cwelan* to die; akin to OE *cwalu* killing, murder, OHG *quelan* to suffer pain, *quāla* pain, torment, ON *kvöl* pain, torment, W *ballu* to die, Gk *dellithes* wasps, *belonē* sharp point, needle, Arm *kełem* I torment, OSlav *želja* pain] **1** *archaic* **:** KILL, SLAY ⟨never ~*ed* an enemy save in my just defense —Lord Byron⟩ **2 :** to put down **:** OVERPOWER, SUPPRESS, EXTINGUISH ⟨only step being taken to ~ the disturbances in the city —T.B.Costain⟩ ⟨emotions ~*ed* the conscious exercise of reason —H.O.Taylor⟩ **3 :** QUIET, ALLAY, PACIFY ⟨these generated fears must be ~*ed* —Henry Wallace⟩ ⟨curb our evil instincts and ~ our anguish —A.L.Guérard⟩ **syn** see CRUSH

[2]**quell** \"\ *n* -S [ME, fr. *quellen,* v.] *archaic* **:** KILLING, SLAUGHTER ⟨sooner than we would choose, bread will melt, water will burn, and the great ~ begin —W.H.Auden⟩; *also* **:** the power of quelling ⟨a sovereign ~ is in his waving hands —John Keats⟩

quell·able \-ləbəl\ *adj* **:** capable of being quelled ⟨a noise ~ only by maddened protest —F.A.Swinnerton⟩

quell·er \-ə(r)\ *n* -S [ME, fr. OE *cwellere* killer, fr. *cwellan* to kill + *-ere* -er — more at QUELL] **:** one that quells

quel·lung \'kwelәŋ\ *n* -S [G, lit., swelling, fr. *quellen* to well, gush, swell (fr. OHG *quellan*) + *-ung* -ing (fr. OHG *-unga, -ung*) — more at DEVIL] **:** swelling of the capsule of a microorganism after reaction with antibody ⟨~ phenomena⟩ ⟨~ reaction⟩

quel·que–chose \¦kelkə'shōz\ *n* -S [F *quelque chose,* lit., something, anything] **:** KICKSHAW

que·ma·de·ro \ˌkāmə'de(ˌ)rō\ *n* -S [Sp, fr. *quemado* (past part. of *quemar* to burn, fr. — assumed — VL *caimare,* alter. — perh. influenced by Gk *kaiein* to burn — of L *cremare* to burn up) + *-ero* -ary (fr. L *-arius*) — more at CAUSTIC, HEARTH] **:** a place of execution by burning

queme \'kwēm\ *adj* [ME, fr. OE gec*wēme;* akin to MD be*quame* pleasant, fitting, OHG bi*quāmi* fitting, suitable, ON *kvæmr* coming; derivative fr. the root of E *come*] **1** *dial chiefly Eng* **:** PLEASANT, AGREEABLE, COMFORTABLE **2** *dial chiefly Eng* **:** COMELY, ATTRACTIVE **3** *dial chiefly Eng* **:** HANDY

quem quaer·i·tis \¦kwem'kwerəd·ə̇s\ *n, usu cap 1st Q* [L, whom do you seek?] **:** an Easter introit trope derived from the account of the visit to Christ's tomb by the women, acted in the 10th century by ecclesiastics, and in its amplified dramatized form being the earliest known liturgical drama

que·na *also* **cue·na** \'kānə\ *n* -S [AmerSp *quena,* fr. Quechua *kkhína*] **:** a primitive vertical reed flute of the So. American Indians

[1]**quench** \'kwench\ *vb* -ED/-ING/-ES [ME *quenchen,* fr. (assumed) OE *cwencan* (as in *ācwencan* to quench, extinguish), causative fr. the root of (assumed) *cwincan* to become extinguished (as in *ācwincan* to vanish, be extinguished); akin to OFris *quinka* to vanish] *vt* **1 a :** to put out (as a fire or light) ⟨for three days after . . . the fire may not be ~*ed* —J.G. Frazer⟩ ⟨the signal among the palms was ~*ed* —William Beebe⟩ **b :** to put out the fire or light of (a source of heat or light) ⟨~ a fireplace⟩ ⟨~ a lamp⟩ **2 :** SUBDUE, OVERCOME ⟨~ hatred⟩ **3 :** DESTROY ⟨~ a rebellion⟩ ⟨the praise that ~*es* all desire to read the book —T.S.Eliot⟩ ⟨whose eagerness for culture was not ~*ed* by the toil of bringing up a family —C.A. Dinsmore⟩ **4 :** SLAKE, SATISFY ⟨~ a thirst⟩ **5 :** to cool (as heated steel) suddenly by immersion esp. in water or oil ⟨crushed ore melted and ~*ed* in cold water —C.L.Mantell⟩ **6 a :** SUPPRESS, INHIBIT ⟨~ luminescence⟩ ⟨~ a portion of a spectrum⟩ **b :** to arrest (as the discharge of an ion counter or the oscillation of an amplifier tube) by applying voltage ~ *vi* **1 :** to become extinguished **:** COOL ⟨the fire ~*es*⟩ **2 :** to become calm **:** SUBSIDE ⟨the bustle and the talking ~*ed* —W.B. Ready⟩ **syn** see CRUSH

[2]**quench** \"\ *n* -ES **:** the act of quenching or state of being quenched ⟨the sudden ~ of the white light —Saul Bellow⟩ ⟨the tube works without ~ and utilizes a gas that is 90 percent argon —*Scientific Monthly*⟩

quench·able \-chəbəl\ *adj* **:** capable of being quenched

quench·able·ness *n* -ES **:** the quality or state of being quenchable

quench aging *n* **:** aging of an alloy induced by rapid cooling from a high temperature

quenched gap *n* **:** a kind of spark gap used in radio transmitting apparatus and so designed as to extinguish the spark quickly after it starts thus opening the primary circuit and leaving the secondary circuit free to produce oscillating current

quench·er \-chə(r)\ *n* -S [ME *quenchere,* fr. *quenchen* to quench + *-ere* -er — more at QUENCH] **1 :** one that quenches **2 :** a satisfying drink

quench hardening *n* **:** hardening of a ferrous alloy induced by rapid cooling from a temperature above the transformation range

quenching bath *n* **:** water, oil, or other liquid in which heated metal is plunged for hardening

quench·less \-chlə̇s\ *adj* **:** UNQUENCHABLE ⟨her ~ defiance of the inquisition —*Time*⟩ ⟨quick wit and ~ curiosity —Max Lerner⟩ — **quench·less·ly** *adv* — **quench·less·ness** *n* -ES

quen·da \'kwendə\ *n* -S [native name in Australia] **:** a widely distributed Australian bandicoot (*Thylacis obesula*)

que·nelle \kə'nel\ *n* -S [F, fr. G *knödel* dumpling — more at KNÖDEL] **:** a ball or oval of forcemeat mixture cooked in boiling water or stock and served as a garnish or as a separate dish

que·nouille training \kə'nüy-\ *n* [*quenouille* fr. F, distaff, tree trained by quenouille training, fr. LL *conucla,* alter. of *colucula,* dim. of L *colus* distaff — more at COLULUS] **:** a method of training trees or shrubs in the shape of a cone or distaff by tying down the branches

quen·sel·ite \'kwen(t)sᵊlˌīt\ *n* -S [Sw *quenselit,* fr. Percy D. *Quensel b*1881 Swed. mineralogist + Sw *-it* -ite] **:** a mineral $PbMnO_2(OH)$ consisting of basic lead manganese oxide and occurring in black monoclinic crystals

quen·stedt·ite \'kwenˌsteˌtīt\ *n* -S [G *quenstedtit,* fr. Friedrich A. *Quenstedt* †1889 Ger. mineralogist + G *-it* -ite] **:** a mineral $Fe_2(SO_4)_3.10H_2O$ consisting of a hydrous ferric sulfate

que·ran·dí *or* **que·ren·dí** *also* **que·ren·dy** \ˌkārən'dē\ *n, pl* **querandí** *or* **querandís** *or* **querendí** *or* **querendís** *usu cap* [Sp *querandí, querendí,* fr. Guarani, fr. *quira* grease + *-ndi,* suffix denoting possession] **1 :** a people of uncertain linguistic affiliation on the right bank of the lower Plata and Paraná rivers **2 :** a member of the Querandí people

quer·ce·tag·e·tin \ˌkwərsə'tajətə̇n\ *n* -S [blend of *quercetin* and NL *Tagetes;* fr. its color's resembling that of quercetin] **:** a pale-yellow crystalline flavonol pigment $C_{15}H_4O_2(OH)_6$ obtained from African and French marigolds

quer·ce·tag·i·trin \-jə·trə̇n\ *n* -S [ISV *quercetag*etin + *-itrin* (as in *quercitrin*)] **:** a crystalline glucoside $C_{24}H_{20}O_{13}$ obtained from African marigolds that yields quercetagetin on hydrolysis

quer·ce·tin *also* **quer·ci·tin** \'kwərsətə̇n\ *n* -S [ISV *quercet-, quercit-* (fr. L *quercetum* oak forest, fr. *quercus* oak + *-etum*) + *-in* — more at FIR] **:** a yellow crystalline flavonol pigment $C_{15}H_5O_2(OH)_5$ occurring usu. in the form of glycosides (as quercitrin and rutin) in various plants and in the form of the dihydro derivative in Douglas fir

quer·ci·mer·i·trin \ˌ==ˈmerə·trə̇n\ *n* -S [ISV *quercimer-* (fr. *quercetin, quercitin* + Gk *meros* part) + *-itrin* (as in *quercitrin*) — more at MERIT] **:** a yellow crystalline glucoside $C_{21}H_{20}O_{12}$ occurring in cotton flowers and leaves and sunflowers and yielding quercetin and glucose on hydrolysis

quer·ci·tannin \¦==+\ *n* [L *quercus* oak + E *-i-* + *tannin*] **:** a tannin isolated from oak bark as a reddish white powder

quer·ci·tol \'kwərsəˌtȯl, -tōl\ *n* -S [ISV *quercit*in + *-ol*] **:** a sweet crystalline pentahydroxy cyclic alcohol $C_6H_7(OH)_5$ found in acorns and oak bark and in viburnums and other plants; deoxy-inositol

quer·ci·trin \'kwərsə·ˌtrin\ *n* -S [ISV *quercitr*on + *-in*] **:** a bitter pale yellow crystalline glycoside $C_{21}H_{20}O_{11}$ obtained esp. from quercitron bark and yielding quercetin and rhamnose on hydrolysis

quer·cit·ron \'kwərˌsi·trən, -ˌsə̇·t-, (ˌ)kwər'si·t-\ *n* -S [ISV, blend of NL *Quercus* and ISV *citron* (color)] **1 a** *or* **quercitron oak :** a black oak (*Quercus velutina*) **b :** the bark of this oak that is rich in tannin and yellow coloring matter and is used in tanning and dyeing **c :** a yellow dye consisting of finely divided quercitron bark — see DYE table I (under *Natural Yellow 10*), QUERCITRIN **2 :** ORPIMENT 2

quercitron lake *n* **:** YELLOW OCHER

quer·cus \'kwərkəs\ *n, cap* [NL, fr. L, oak — more at FIR] **:** a genus of hardwood often evergreen trees or shrubs (family Fagaceae) comprising the typical oaks and being widely distributed in the northern hemisphere but most abundant in temperate regions, having alternate linear to elliptical entire or variously lobed leaves, drooping staminate catkins, and pistillate flowers that are solitary in each involucre and succeeded in fruit by a characteristic acorn — see CORK OAK, LIVE OAK, WHITE OAK; LITHOCARPUS; compare FAGUS

que·re·cho \kə'rā(ˌ)chō\ *n, pl* **querecho** *or* **querechos** *usu cap* [Sp, of AmerInd origin] **:** an Apache esp. of the Jicarilla, Lipan, or Mescalero people

que·re·la \kwə'rēlə\ *n, pl* **quere·lae** \-ēˌlē\ [ML, fr. L, complaint — more at QUARREL] *civil & eccl law* **1 :** an action in a court **2 :** the bill of complaint in a court action

que·ren·cia \kā'rensyə\ *n* -S [Sp, fondness, haunt of an animal, favorite spot, querencia, fr. *querer* to want, like, love (fr. L *quaerere* to seek, gain, obtain, ask) + *-encia* -ence (fr. L *-entia*)] **:** an area in the arena taken by the bull for a defensive stand in a bullfight

[1]**que·rent** \'kwirənt\ *n* -S [L *quaerent-, quaerens,* pres. part. of *quaerere* to seek, ask] **:** INQUIRER; *specif* **:** one who consults an astrologer

[2]**querent** \"\ *n* -S [L *querent-, querens,* pres. part. of *queri* to complain — more at WHEEZE] *archaic* **:** COMPLAINANT, PLAINTIFF

quer·flö·te \'kwerˌflœd·ə, -flərd·ə\ *n* -S [G, fr. *quer* transverse, diagonal (fr. OHG *dwerah, twerh*) + *flöte* flute — more at THWART, BLOCKFLÖTE] **:** FLAUTO TRAVERSO 2

que·ri·da \kā'rēdə, ke'-\ *n* -S [Sp, fr. fem. of *querido,* past part. of *querer* to love — more at QUERENCIA] *chiefly Southwest* **:** a female sweetheart

que·ri·er \'kwirēə(r) *also* -wer-, -wēr-\ *n* -S **:** QUERIST

quer·i·ma·na \kwerə'mänə\ *also* **quer·i·man** \-'män\ *n* -S [D Creole (Surinam) *kweriman,* fr. Galibi *kweriman,* prob. fr. Tupi *curemá*] **:** a young mullet having only two anal spines rather than the three characteristic of the adult

quer·i·mo·ni·ous \¦kwerə¦mōnēəs\ *adj* [ML *querimoniosus,* fr. L *querimonia* complaint (fr. *queri* to complain) + *-osus* -ous — more at WHEEZE] **:** COMPLAINING, QUERULOUS — **quer·i·mo·ni·ous·ly** *adv* — **quer·i·mo·ni·ous·ness** *n* -ES

que·rist \'kwirə̇st *also* -wer-, -wēr-\ *n* -S [L *quaerere* to seek, ask + E *-ist*] **:** one who inquires **:** one who asks questions

querk \'kwərk, -wə̄k, -wəik\ *chiefly dial var of* QUIRK

querk·en \-kən\ *vt* -ED/-ING/-S [ME *querkenen;* akin to OFris *querka, quertza* to choke, MLG *querken,* ON *kyrkja, kvirkja;* denominatives fr. the root of ON *kverk* throat — more at GORGE] *dial chiefly Eng* **:** to cause to gasp **:** CHOKE

querl \'kwərl, *esp before pause or consonant* 'kwər·əl; 'kwə̄l, 'kwəil\ *chiefly Midland var of* CURL

quern \'kwərn, 'kwə̄n, 'kwəin\ *n* -S [ME, fr. OE *cweorn;* akin to OHG *quirn, quirna* hand mill, millstone, ON *kvern* hand mill, Goth *-qairnus* millstone, OIr *brāu* millstone, OSlav *žrŭny* mill, and prob. to Goth *kaurjos* (nom. pl.) heavy — more at GRIEVE] **1 :** a primitive mill for grinding grain consisting of two circular stones with the upper one being turned by hand **2 :** a small hand mill (as for grinding spices or nuts) **3 :** METATE

quernstone \'=ˌ=\ *n* [ME *quernston,* fr. OE *cweornstān,* fr. *cweorn* quern + *stān* stone — more at STONE] **:** MILLSTONE

quer·sprung \'kf|erˌshprůŋ, kə'v|, |ār-\ *n* -S [G, fr. *quer* transverse, diagonal + *sprung* jump, fr. OHG, fr. the stem of *springan* to jump — more at QUERFLÖTE, SPRING] **:** a maneuver for avoiding obstacles in skiing executed by turning at right angles in the air using one pole as a pivot

[1]**quer·u·lent** *also* **quer·u·lant** \'kwer(y)ələnt\ *adj* [*querulent* fr. *querulous* + *-ent* (as in *truculent*); *querulant* alter. of *querulent*] **:** abnormally given to suspicion and accusation **:** QUERULOUS

[2]**querulent** \"\ *n* -S **:** one that is querulent

quer·u·len·tial \¦==¦lenchəl\ *adj* **:** QUERULOUS

quer·u·list \'==ˌlə̇st\ *n* -S [*querul*ous + *-ist*] **:** COMPLAINER

quer·u·lous \-ləs\ *adj* [L *querulus,* fr. *queri* to complain — more at WHEEZE] **1 :** apt to find fault **:** disposed to murmur **:** habitually complaining ⟨~ disappointed old age —W.M. Thackeray⟩ ⟨the ~ boredom of a child that possesses too many toys —Lewis Mumford⟩ **2 :** expressing or suggestive of complaint **:** FRETFUL, WHINING ⟨somewhat ~ remarks about his own countrymen —*Geographical Jour.*⟩ ⟨sung in a subdued but ~ soprano —Nigel Dennis⟩ ⟨the ~ eyebrows, the thin peevish lips —D.B.W.Lewis⟩ **3 :** making a sound suggesting complaint ⟨one ~ rook —Charles Dickens⟩ ⟨the ~ sea —J.B.Cabell⟩ **syn** see IRRITABLE

quer·u·lous·ly *adv* **:** in a querulous manner **:** PEEVISHLY

quer·u·lous·ness *n* -ES **:** the quality or state of being querulous **:** PEEVISHNESS

[1]**que·ry** \'kwirē, -ri *also* -wer-, -wēr-\ *n* -ES [alter. of earlier *quere, quaere,* fr. L *quaere,* imper. of *quaerere* to seek, gain, obtain, ask] **1 :** QUESTION, INQUIRY ⟨my ~ as to the name of the pond —Frances H. Eliot⟩ ⟨to answer either ~ in detail would require an investigation beyond the scope of this appraisal —R.S.Thoman⟩ ⟨looking down in dazed and inarticulate ~ —Kay Boyle⟩ — sometimes used to introduce a question or a debatable proposition ⟨~, if this would be honorable⟩ **2 :** a question in the mind **:** DOUBT **3 a** *or* **query mark :** QUESTION MARK **b :** a notation (as ? or *qy*) written on a printer's proof to question the accuracy of something in the proof

[2]**query** \"\ *vt* -ED/-ING/-ES [alter. of earlier *quere,* fr. L *quaere,* imper. of *quaerere*] **1 :** to put as a question ⟨"can I buy two tickets?" he *queried*⟩ **2 :** to ask questions about esp. with an indication of doubt and with desire for a definite, clear, or certain statement or demonstration ⟨standard operating procedure would be to ~ the order —J.G.Cozzens⟩ **3 :** to ask questions of esp. with a certain formality or with desire for authoritative information ⟨*queried* some eminent authors for advice —*N.Y. Herald Tribune Bk. Rev.* **4 :** to mark with a query **syn** see ASK

que·ry·ing·ly *adv* **:** in a querying manner **:** INQUIRINGLY

que·ry·ist \-rēə̇st\ *n* -S **:** QUERIST

ques *abbr* question

que·sa·di·lla \ˌkāsə'dēyə\ *n* -S [Sp, dim. of *quesada* cheese turnover, fr. *queso* cheese (fr. L *caseus*) + *-ada* -ade (fr. LL *-ata*) — more at CHEESE] **:** a turnover made usu. with a cheese filling

quesal *var of* QUETZAL

[1]**que·si·ted** \kwē'sīd·ə̇d\ *adj* [L *quaesitus* (past part. of *quaerere* to seek, ask) + E *-ed*] *archaic* **:** sought or inquired about

[2]**quesited** \"\ *n* -S *in astrology* **:** a person or thing sought or inquired about

[1]**quest** \'kwest\ *n* -S [ME, fr. MF *queste,* fr. (assumed) VL *quaesta,* fr. L *quaesita, quaesta,* fem. of *quaesitus, quaestus* past part. of *quaerere* to seek, ask] **1 a** *chiefly dial* **:** an official inquiry **:** INQUEST **b :** a jury of inquest ⟨what lawful ~ have given their verdict up? —Shak.⟩ **c :** INVESTIGATION ⟨a long spiritual ~ into the entire Spanish past —Bohdan Chudoba⟩ ⟨limitations set to the child's sex ~ —*Structure & Meaning of Psychoanalysis*⟩ **2 a :** the action or an act or instance of seeking: (1) **:** EXPEDITION, PURSUIT, VENTURE ⟨the ~ for Neanderthal fossils —R.W.Murray⟩ ⟨all his work is a ~ for values —C.J.Rolo⟩ ⟨our united ~ of a just and lasting peace —D.D.Eisenhower⟩ (2) **:** a chivalrous enterprise in medieval romance usu. involving an adventurous journey **b** (1) *archaic* **:** a search (as by hounds) for game (2) *dial* **:** the baying of hounds in pursuit or barking on seeing game **3** *obs* **:** those who search or make inquiry ⟨hath sent about three several ~*s* to search you out —Shak.⟩ **4 :** collection of alms or donations esp. for religious uses — **in quest of** *prep* **:** in search of **:** SEEKING ⟨cast her eyes round the room *in quest of* some amusement —Jane Austen⟩ ⟨an expedition up the river *in quest of* fruit —Rachel Henning⟩

[2]**quest** \"\ *vb* -ED/-ING/-S [ME *questen,* fr. MF *quester,* fr. *queste*] *vi* **1** *of a dog* **a :** to search a trail (as of game) ⟨the dog after a little understood and ~*ed* —Robinson Jeffers⟩ **b :** to give tongue **:** BAY ⟨~*ing* like a hound on a broken trail —Rudyard Kipling⟩ **2 :** to make a search **:** go in pursuit **:** go on a quest **:** SEEK, ASK ⟨still ~*ing* for sultry love and high adventure —Henry Cavendish⟩ ⟨this indolence of the body while the soul is ~*ing* —H.S.Canby⟩ ⟨~*ing* ceaselessly for improvements —*Newsweek*⟩ ⟨giraffes come ~*ing* through the trees to take their turn to drink —Alan Moorehead⟩ ⟨things that die with their eyes open and ~*ing* —Ben Hecht⟩ **3 :** to seek alms esp. for religious uses ~ *vt* **1 :** to search for **:** EXAMINE, PURSUE ⟨hounds . . . should spread to ~ as individuals all the covert's fastnesses —E.G.W.W.Harrison⟩ ⟨baffled eyes ~*ing* more information —L.C.Douglas⟩ **2 :** to ask for **:** DEMAND ⟨~*ing* . . . your prayers —Augusta Gregory⟩

questant *n* -S *obs* **:** QUESTER

quest·er \'kwestə(r)\ *n* -S **:** one that quests ⟨a jester and a ~ and a bard —Louis MacNeice⟩ ⟨competent ~*s* who are hot on the trail —E.G.Lowry⟩

ques·teur \ke'stər(·)\ *n* -S [F, fr. L *quaestor* — more at QUAESTOR] **:** one of three members of either branch of the French parliament chosen as financial officers in charge of payment of senators or deputies and of expense accounts

questhouse \'=ˌ=\ *n, archaic* **:** a house for holding the inquests in a ward or parish

quest·ing·ly *adv* **:** in the manner of one that quests **:** INQUIRINGLY, SEARCHINGLY

[1]**ques·tion** \'kwes(h)chən, ÷-eshən\ *n* -S [ME *questioun,* fr. MF *question,* fr. L *quaestion-, quaestio,* fr. *quaesitus, quaestus* (past part. of *quaerere* to seek, ask) + *-ion-, -io* -ion] **1 a** (1) **:** an interrogative expression ⟨ask ~*s* about the candidates⟩ — see RHETORICAL QUESTION (2) **:** an interrogative sentence or clause (3) **:** an interrogative expression used to test knowledge (as in a written or oral examination) — compare [1]ANSWER 1b **b :** a subject or aspect that is in dispute, open for discussion, or to be inquired into **:** ISSUE ⟨the ~ whether or not the people of any time have ever considered their civilization with complete satisfaction —Virgil Jordan⟩ ⟨the ~ of whether some form of verse is a necessary condition of poetry —Alice Bensen⟩ ⟨the tariff ~⟩ ⟨raise the ~ of adequate financing⟩; *broadly* **:** PROBLEM, MATTER ⟨the ~ of how mankind will use the leisure —A.R.Sweezy⟩ ⟨the ~ of buying a car⟩ ⟨the ~*s* of where one lives and of the nature and quality of the common life in which one participates —N.M. Pusey⟩ ⟨composing is a ~ of paper and a pen full of ink —J.D.Cook⟩ **c** (1) **:** a subject or point of debate or a proposition being or to be voted on in a meeting (as of a legislative body) ⟨the ~ before the senate⟩ (2) **:** the bringing of such a subject or proposal to a vote ⟨loud cries for the ~⟩ ⟨put the matter to the ~⟩ — see PREVIOUS QUESTION **d :** the specific point at issue or under discussion ⟨a remark that was beside the ~⟩ **e :** something the correctness or existence of which is open to doubt ⟨no longer a ~ but an established fact⟩ ⟨an open ~ whether the addition is an improvement⟩ **2 a :** the action or an instance of asking **:** INQUIRY ⟨a long glance of sulky ~ —William Sansom⟩ ⟨this kind of division could not support very close ~ —T.S.Eliot⟩ **b :** examination with reference to a decisive result **:** INTERROGATION; *specif* **:** a judicial or official investigation **c :** torture as part of an examination ⟨he that was in ~ for the robbery —Shak.⟩ ⟨searched for something or put him to the ~ —C.B.Child⟩ **d** (1) **:** OBJECTION, DISPUTE ⟨obey without ~⟩ ⟨true beyond ~⟩ ⟨words that could without ~ be used —S.L.Payne⟩ ⟨one ~ remains unanswered⟩ (2) **:** room for doubt or objection ⟨no ~ about the official's honesty⟩ ⟨seemed little ~ that it would be able to count on government support —*Collier's Yr. Bk.*⟩ ⟨there is no ~ but that there will be a general rise in wages —E.A.Lahey⟩ (3) **:** possibility of or opportunity for a particular action **:** CHANCE — used in negative constructions ⟨there is no ~ of bypassing a statutory procedure —*Current History*⟩ ⟨there was no ~ of refusing to sit on any of these committees —Andrzej Panufnik⟩ ⟨no longer even any ~ of escape —John Farrelly⟩ — **in question 1 :** of such a nature or in such a position as to be subject to doubt **:** in dispute **:** at issue ⟨the dates are not *in question* —Herbert Read⟩ ⟨particularly *in question* were the federal security program, the granting of passports —*Annual Report: Amer. Civil Liberties Union*⟩ ⟨such interrogations put *in question* the very meaning of life —H.M.Parshley⟩ **2 :** being referred to or discussed **:** under consideration **:** CONCERNED, RELEVANT ⟨on the Sunday *in question* —Osbert Sitwell⟩ ⟨open at the page *in question* —Louis Auchincloss⟩ ⟨voice from behind the door of the room *in question* —

Edward Bok⟩ — **into question** *adv* **:** up for or subject to discussion in which doubt is cast — usu. used with *bring* or *call* or *come* ⟨bring several of the current beliefs of this sort *into question* —Ralph Linton⟩ ⟨only natural that all the former systems of classifying ancient as well as more recent fossil men should be brought *into question* —R.W.Murray⟩ — **out of question** *archaic* **:** UNQUESTIONABLY ⟨*out of question*, 'tis Maria's hand —Shak.⟩ — **out of the question 1 :** alien to the question or subject being discussed **2 :** not worthy of consideration **:** not to be thought of ⟨such a course is *out of the question*⟩ **3 :** IMPOSSIBLE ⟨sleep during this interval was *out of the question* —T.L.Peacock⟩

²question \"\ *vb* **questioned; questioned; questioning** \-es(h)chəniŋ, ÷ -esh(ə)n-\ **questions** [MF *questionner*, fr. *question*, n. — more at ¹QUESTION] *vt* **1 :** to ask a question of or about ⟨~*ed* the Indians as to the river's name —*Amer. Guide Series: Minn.*⟩ ⟨~ the absence of a club member⟩ **2 a :** to subject to judicial or police examination ⟨~ a suspect⟩ **b :** to call to account **:** ACCUSE, CHARGE **3 a** (1) **:** to express doubt about **:** demonstrate lack of conviction about **:** CHALLENGE, DISPUTE ⟨the honesty of these writers is unimpeachable, however much their competency may be ~*ed* —Edward Clodd⟩ (2) **:** to feel doubts about **:** DOUBT ⟨~*ed* her wisdom in staying on the farm —E.T.Thurston⟩ **b :** to subject to analysis **:** EXAMINE, RESEARCH, PONDER, CONSIDER ⟨Babylonian sages who ~*ed* the stars in their efforts to measure time —W.K.Ferguson⟩ ⟨no more accustomed to ~ language itself than to ~ the weather —Stuart Chase⟩ ~ *vi* **1 :** to ask questions **:** INQUIRE **2** *obs* **:** TALK, CONVERSE, ARGUE **syn** see ASK

ques·tion·able \-es(h)chənəbəl, ÷ -esh(ə)n-\ *adj* **1** *obs* **:** admitting of being questioned **:** inviting or seeming to invite inquiry **2** *obs* **:** liable or amenable to judicial inquiry or action **3 :** affording reason for being doubted, questioned, or challenged **:** not certain or exact **:** not acceptable immediately or without examination **:** PROBLEMATICAL, UNCERTAIN, UNSAFE ⟨the illustration is ~ but the notion implied may be sound —Samuel Alexander⟩ ⟨canners had taken in any ~ type of fruit at top prices —*Farmer's Weekly (So. Africa)*⟩ ⟨a highly ~ exercise of executive authority —A.F.Westin⟩ ⟨a general storm area . . . making even a daylight flight a ~ venture —C.A. Lindbergh †1974⟩ **4 :** attended by well-grounded suspicions of being immoral, crude, false, or unsound **:** DUBIOUS ⟨the propriety . . . was at least ~ —G.B.Shaw⟩ ⟨the habit of living in ~ neighborhoods —M.D.Geismar⟩ ⟨a ~ insurance broker —Milton Silverman⟩ **syn** see DOUBTFUL

ques·tion·able·ness \-bəlnəs\ *n* -ES **:** the state of being questionable

ques·tion·ably \-blē, -bli\ *adv* **:** in a questionable manner **:** DOUBTFULLY, DUBIOUSLY, SUSPICIOUSLY ⟨estates her husband had ~ acquired —*Brit. Book News*⟩

¹ques·tion·ary \'kwes(h)chə,nerē\ *n* -ES [¹*question* + *-ary* (n. suffix)] **:** a collection of questions; *esp* **:** QUESTIONNAIRE ⟨a ~ circulated two years ago to about 5000 laboratories —*Lancet*⟩ ⟨~ containing 102 phrases and locutions —Wallace Rice⟩

²questionary \"\ *adj* [¹*question* + *-ary* (adj. suffix)] **:** put in the form of a question **:** asking or involving questions

¹question–begging \'≈≈,≈≈\ *adj* **:** that involves the fallacy of petitio principii **:** that involves an assumption of something whose truth may be questioned ⟨*question-begging* arguments⟩ ⟨*question-begging* epithets⟩ — compare BEG *vt* 3b

²question–begging \"\ *n* -S **:** something that involves an assumption whose truth may be questioned ⟨most of us may think this *question-begging* —*Manchester Guardian Weekly*⟩

ques·tion·ee \,≈≈'ē\ *n* -S **:** one that is questioned

ques·tion·er \'kwes(h)chənə(r), ÷ 'kwesh(ə)n-\ *n* -S **:** one that questions

¹questioning *n* -S [fr. gerund of ²*question*] **:** the asking of questions **:** examination by question **:** INTERROGATION ⟨an age of disillusion, of doubt and ~ —Jawaharlal Nehru⟩ ⟨our ~s lose some of their point —Jacob Kohn⟩ ⟨~s of suspects⟩

²questioning *adj* [fr. pres. part. of ²*question*] **1 :** expressing or implying a question ⟨a ~ look⟩ **2 :** INQUIRING, INQUISITIVE ⟨a keen ~ mind —C.I.Glicksberg⟩

ques·tion·ing·ly *adv* **:** in a questioning manner ⟨looked ~ at the doctor —G.G.Carter⟩

ques·tion·ist \-nəst\ *n* -S **1 a :** one that questions esp. intensively or habitually **b** *obs* **:** SCHOOLMAN 1 **2** *archaic* **:** a candidate for the bachelor's degree in certain British universities during the last term before final examinations

¹ques·tion·less \'≈≈ləs\ *adj* [¹*question* + *-less*] **1 :** not to be questioned **:** INDUBITABLE ⟨remained always its born and ~ master —J.R.Lowell⟩ **2 :** UNQUESTIONING ⟨clear mind and ~ faith —Lew Wallace⟩

²questionless \"\ *adv, archaic* **:** UNQUESTIONABLY, UNDOUBTEDLY ⟨can ~ write a good hand —George Eliot⟩

ques·tion·less·ly *adv* **:** in a questionless manner

question mark *n* **1 :** the mark ? used in writing and printing at the conclusion of a sentence to indicate a direct question or usu. in parenthesis after a particular to indicate conjecture or uncertainty or by editors and proofreaders to indicate a queried detail **2 :** something unknown, unknowable, or uncertain ⟨the future of the controversial movie . . . will remain a *question mark* at least until today —*Springfield (Mass.) Union*⟩ **3 :** VIOLET TIP

¹ques·tion·naire *also* **ques·tion·aire** \,kwes(h)chə'na(a)-](ə)r, -ne(,]ə\ *n* -S [F *questionnaire*, fr. *questionner* to question + *-aire* -ary — more at QUESTION] **1 :** a set of questions for obtaining statistically useful or personal information from an individual ⟨devise a special ~ on children's reading habits⟩ ⟨a telephone ~ addressed to six authors —J.K.Hutchens⟩ **2 :** a written or printed questionnaire often with spaces for answers **3 :** a survey made by the use of a questionnaire ⟨tabulate the results of a ~⟩

²questionnaire \"\ *vt* -ED/-ING/-S **:** to send a questionnaire to or obtain information from by means of a questionnaire ⟨has begun to ~ scientifically trained men —*Textile World*⟩

question of fact : FACT IN ISSUE

question of law : ISSUE OF LAW

question of privilege : a question that concerns the rights or privileges of a legislative body or of any of its members

question time *n* **:** a period in a session of a British parliamentary body during which members may put to a minister questions on matters concerning his department ⟨*question time* . . . is one of parliament's most valuable institutions —*Brit. Parliament*⟩

quest·man \'≈mən\ *n, pl* **questmen** [ME, fr. *quest* + *man*] *archaic* **:** one legally empowered to solicit alms; *specif* **:** SIDESMAN 1

questor *var of* QUAESTOR

questrist *n* -S [*quester* + *-ist*] *obs* **:** SEEKER, PURSUER ⟨his knights, hot ~s after him —Shak.⟩

quests *pl of* QUEST, *pres 3d sing of* QUEST

quet \'kwet\ *n* -S [origin unknown] *dial Eng* **:** the common guillemot

quetch \'kwech\ *vi* -ED/-ING/-ES [ME *quecchen*, *quicchen*, fr. OE *cweccan* to shake, shake off, move, vibrate — more at QUAKE] **1** *chiefly dial* **:** TWITCH, STIR ⟨~*ing* with pain⟩ **2 :** to break silence **:** utter a sound

quête \'ket\ *n* -S [F, search, quest, collection, fr. OF *queste* — more at QUEST] **:** a collection of money (as for use as a payment to street musicians or strolling players)

¹quetsch \'kwech, 'kve-\ *n* -ES [G, fr. G dial. (Alsace) *quetsch*, *quetsche* plum, fr. a F dial. word akin to OF *davoisne* damson plum, fr. (assumed) VL *damascena*, fr. pl. of L (*prunum*) *Damascenum* — more at DAMSON] **:** a dry white Alsatian brandy distilled from fermented plum juice

²quetsch \"\ *n* -ES [G *quetsche* press, roller, fr. *quetschen* to squeeze, crush, flatten, fr. MHG *quetzen*, *quetschen* to strike, squeeze, crush; akin to MLG *quetsen*, *quessen* to strike against, MD *quetsen*, *quetschen* to injure, wound, break up] **1 :** a vat equipped with rollers for applying chemical solutions or sizing to yarn or cloth and used esp. in the slashing process **2 :** one of the rollers in a quetsch

quet·ta \'kwed·ə\ *adj, usu cap* [fr. *Quetta*, town in Baluchistan, Pakistan] **:** of or belonging to a culture of northern Baluchistan of about the fourth millennium B.C. characterized by pottery decorated in geometric designs with purplish brown or black paint on a buff ground or occas. black on a gray ground

quet·zal \ket'säl, -sal\ *also* **que·zal** *or* **que·sal** \kā's-\ *n, pl* **quetzals** \-lz\ *or* **quetza·les** \-(,)lās\ [AmerSp, fr. Nahuatl *quetzalli* large brilliant tail feather] **1** *also* **quetzal bird :** a large Central American trogon (*Pharomachrus mocinno*) having a compressed crest, brilliant plumage with the upperparts and throat iridescent greenish and the underparts crimson, and in the male upper tail coverts often exceeding two feet in length **2** *pl usu* **quetzales a :** the basic monetary unit of Guatemala — see MONEY table **b :** a silver coin representing one quetzal **c :** a note representing one quetzal **3** *quetzales pl but often sing in constr, or* **quetzal dance :** a men's longways dance of the Mexican Totonacs dedicated in pre-Columbian times to the quetzal bird as sun symbol and still suggesting the sun with huge disk headdresses

¹queue \'kyü\ *n* -S [MF, fr. OF *coe*, *coue* — more at COWARD] **1 :** a taillike braid of natural or artificial hair usu. worn hanging at the back of the head and sometimes as part of a wig or as an addition to a hat **2 :** a line esp. of persons or vehicles ⟨most of us in the customs ~ —Nancy Debenham⟩ ⟨pedicabs wait for custom . . . in great dead ~*s* —G.S.Gale⟩ ⟨gave up places in the production ~ —*Sperryscope*⟩ **3 :** a metal piece attached to the side of the breastplate of a suit of armor and used as a rest for the butt of a lance **4 :** the tailpiece of a violin or other stringed instrument **5 :** the tail of a musical note

queue 1

²queue \"\ *vb* **queued; queued; queuing** *or* **queueing; queues** *vt* **:** to arrange or form in a queue ~ *vi* **:** to line up or wait in a queue ⟨the everlasting *queuing* for whatever food was available —J.G.Winant⟩ ⟨the salmon ~*s* to jump the weir —Edward Hyams⟩ — often used with *up* ⟨you had to ~ up at the bus stop —Joseph Wechsberg⟩

queu·er \-ü(ə)r, -üə\ *n* -S **:** one that queues ⟨~*s* were hoping for standing room —*Time*⟩

que·venne's iron \kə'venz-\ *n, usu cap Q* [after Theodore *Quevenne*, 19th cent. Fr. pharmacist] **:** REDUCED IRON

quey \'kwā\ *n* -S [ME *quy*, *quee*, of Scand origin; akin to Dan *kvie* heifer, Sw & Norw *kviga*, ON *kvīga*; prob. akin to ON *kȳr* cow — more at COW] *dial Brit* **:** HEIFER

queyn \'kwān\ *Scot var of* QUEAN

que·zon city \'kā,sōn-\ *adj, usu cap Q&C* [fr. *Quezon City*, Philippines] **:** of or from Quezon City, capital of the Philippines **:** of the kind or style prevalent in Quezon City

quia·quia \,kēə'kēə\ *n* -S [AmerSp *quiaquia*, prob. fr. *quiaquia*, a kind of rattle made from a tortoise shell, of imit. origin] **:** ROUND SCAD

¹quib·ble \'kwibəl\ *n* -S [prob. dim. of obs. *quib* quibble, perh. fr. L *quibus*, dat. & abl. pl. of *qui* who, which (often used in legal documents) — more at WHO] **1** *archaic* **:** PUN **2 a** (1) **:** something (as a line of reasoning adopted, an objection made, a distinction drawn, a point advanced) that evades, shifts from, or obscures the real point at issue in some discussion or argument by reason of centering on what is relatively unimportant and often petty or totally irrelevant and that is marked typically by hedging or equivocation ⟨produces more ~*s* and qualifications than it does direct answers —S.L.Payne⟩ (2) **:** a minor objection or piece of criticism arising typically from an exaggerated tendency to find fault ⟨had a few ~*s* about the quality of the performance⟩ **b :** argumentation, protestation, or criticism marked by or consisting of quibbles ⟨in discussing this situation there is no room for ~ —W.H.Camp⟩ ⟨a procedure that is open to ~⟩

²quibble \"\ *vb* **quibbled; quibbled; quibbling** \-b(ə)liŋ\ **quibbles** *vi* **1** *archaic* **:** PUN **2 a** (1) **:** to make use of, indulge in, or resort to quibbles ⟨had no desire to ~ when decisive action was called for⟩ (2) **:** to object to something or criticize something on minor grounds that typically reflect an exaggerated tendency to find fault **:** CAVIL, CARP ⟨was a peevish critic, always ready to ~⟩ **b :** to indulge in argumentation, protestation, or criticism marked by or consisting of quibbles **:** BICKER ⟨the usual *quibbling* over what should be included in the humanities —W.H.Whyte⟩ ~ *vt* **:** to subject to quibbles ⟨aren't inclined to ~ the point —S.E.Hyman⟩

quib·bler \-b(ə)lə(r)\ *n* -S **:** one that quibbles

¹quibbling *n* -S [fr. gerund of ²*quibble*] **1 :** the action of one that quibbles **2 :** an instance of quibbling ⟨theological ~*s* —Corra Harris⟩

²quibbling *adj* [fr. pres. part. of ²*quibble*] **:** marked by or consisting of quibbles **:** CARPING, CAVILING ⟨had no patience with ~ criticism⟩ — **quib·bling·ly** *adv*

qui·ca \'kēkə\ *n* -S [Pg *cuíca*, fr. Tupi] **:** FOUR-EYED OPOSSUM

¹qui·che \(')kē'chā\ *n, pl* **quiche** *or* **quiches** *usu cap* [Sp *quiché*, of AmerInd origin] **1 a :** an Indian people of south central Guatemala **b :** a member of such people **2 :** the Mayan language of the Quiche people

²quiche \'kēsh\ *n* -S [F, fr. G dial. (Lorraine) *küche*, dim. of *kuche*, *kuchen* cake, fr. OHG *kuocho* — more at CAKE] **:** a baked custard pie usu. having an added savory ingredient (as chopped ham, seafood, or vegetables)

qui·choid \'kē,chȯid\ *n* -S *usu cap* [¹*Quiche* + *-oid*] **:** a linguistic subdivision of the Mayan of Guatemala, El Salvador, and Mexico

quichua *usu cap, var of* QUECHUA

quichuan *usu cap, var of* QUECHUAN

¹quick \'kwik\ *adj, usu* -ER/-EST [ME *quik*, *quike*, fr. OE *cwic*, *cwicu*; akin to OFris & OS *quik* alive, OHG *quec*, ON *kvikr*, Goth *qiwai* (nom. pl.), L *vivus* alive, *vivere* to live, Gk *zōē* life, *bios* mode of life, Lith *gyvas* living, Skt *jīva*] **1 a** *archaic* **:** marked by the presence of life **:** not dead **:** LIVING, ALIVE, ANIMATE ⟨shall judge the ~ and the dead —2 Tim 4:1 (AV)⟩ **b** *archaic* **:** arrived at a stage of pregnancy at which the motion of the fetus is perceptible ⟨women . . . ~ with child —Oliver Goldsmith⟩ **c** *chiefly Brit* **:** formed of living plants ⟨a ~ hedge⟩ **2 :** that moves, functions, or is accomplished or obtained swiftly and with vigor, energy, and promptness or that is capable of so moving or functioning or of being so accomplished or obtained **:** RAPID, SPEEDY: as **a** (1) **:** fast in understanding, thinking, or learning **:** speedy in mental processes **:** mentally agile **:** mentally nimble ⟨a ~ mind⟩ ⟨~ thinking⟩ ⟨~ students⟩ (2) **:** reacting to stimuli with speed and keen sensitivity **:** delicate and sharp in perception ⟨a ~ sense of the tactful thing to do⟩ ⟨a ~ eye for beauty⟩ (3) **:** aroused immediately and intensely ⟨~ resentment⟩ ⟨a ~ temper⟩ **b** (1) **:** fast in development or occurrence ⟨a ~ succession of events⟩ (2) **:** done or taking place with rapidity **:** done or taking place within only a small interval of time ⟨gave her a ~ kiss⟩ ⟨a ~ finish to the race⟩ ⟨gave them a ~ look⟩; *esp* **:** begun and ended in an instant ⟨a ~ flash of lightning⟩ (3) **:** rapidly often almost instantaneously accomplished or achieved ⟨a ~ profit⟩ ⟨a ~ victory⟩ (4) **:** consumed rapidly or hurriedly ⟨had a ~ bite to eat⟩; *esp* **:** swallowed rapidly or hurriedly ⟨had a ~ drink at the bar⟩ **c** (1) **:** marked by speed, readiness, or promptness of action ⟨did a ~ job⟩ ⟨finished it with ~ efficiency⟩ (2) **:** marked by speed, readiness, or promptness of physical movement ⟨walked with ~ steps⟩ **d** (1) **:** inclined to hastiness of action or treatment **:** OVERHASTY ⟨must not be too ~ in the experiment⟩ (2) **:** inclined to impatience or anger **:** easily aroused to impatience or anger ⟨was too ~ with her students⟩ **3** *archaic* **a :** not stagnant **:** RUNNING, FLOWING ⟨gently winding valleys, with clear, ~ water —Walter Pater⟩ ⟨sweet and ~ stream —John Evelyn⟩ **b :** extremely soft and mobile from being mixed with water so as to tend to suck down an object touching the surface ⟨the patch of ~ ground —P.H.Emerson⟩ ⟨~ mud⟩ **4 a** (1) *archaic* **:** burning with intense heat **:** FIERY ⟨the ~ flames —P.B. Shelley⟩ **:** GLOWING ⟨a ~ coal —George Herbert⟩ (2) *obs* **:** rapidly combustible ⟨~ sulfur —Edmund Spenser⟩ **b** *of soil* **:** readily absorbing heat by reason of being highly porous in composition **5** *obs* **:** full of activity **:** BUSY, BRISK ⟨the markets were very ~ —Henry Best⟩ **6** *obs* **a :** bitingly sharp in taste or odor **:** PUNGENT **b :** stingingly severe **:** CAUSTIC **7 :** turning, curving, or bending at a sharp angle ⟨a ~ turn in the road⟩ **8 :** IMBUED, FILLED, CHARGED, INSTINCT ⟨a speech ~ with passion⟩

syn PROMPT, READY, APT: QUICK describes ability to respond instantly or rapidly, often an ability native rather than acquired, or a marked capacity for speedy perception or learning ⟨examined the hall and the men who passed, with the same *quick*, sharp cunning with which he had examined the street —Liam O'Flaherty⟩ ⟨a *quick* and brilliant student . . . was elected to Phi Beta Kappa and was the valedictorian of his graduating class —*Current Biog.*⟩ PROMPT may apply to speedy response, often due to training, discipline, preparation, or extreme willingness to serve, sometimes servilely ⟨*prompt* to spring forward when anything was wanted —R.L.Stevenson⟩ ⟨like a competent man of affairs, he was *prompt* in meeting engagements —V.L.Parrington⟩ ⟨a people, gentle, submissive, *prompt* to obey, and accustomed . . . to the inexorable demands of tyranny —Agnes Repplier⟩ READY may suggest speed in response or compliance coupled with willingness, vigilance, impetus, skill, or facility ⟨the young lady proved to be as *ready* as the squire, and the preliminaries [of the marriage] were arranged in little more than five minutes —T.L. Peacock⟩ ⟨their *ready* guns begin to bark —E.L.Beach⟩ ⟨not a *ready* speaker, and so . . . he had written out what he had to say —H.E.Scudder⟩ APT may focus attention on the fact of possession of qualities, such as intelligence or talent, facilitating speedy response ⟨have proved themselves not only *apt* pupils, but in many cases . . . have outstripped their teachers —D.C.Buchanan⟩ ⟨to become *apt* in argument —C.T.Copeland⟩ **syn** see in addition FAST

²quick \"\ *adv, usu* -ER/-EST [ME *quik*, fr. *quik*, adj.] **:** QUICKLY

³quick \"\ *n* -S [ME *quik*, *quike*, fr. OE *cwic*, *cwicu*, fr. *cwic*, *cwicu*, adj.] **1** *obs* **:** a living thing **2** *chiefly Brit* **:** QUICKSET 1 **3** [prob. of Scand origin; akin to ON *kvikva*, *kvika* quick (of the flesh), fr. *kvikr* alive — more at ¹QUICK] **a :** a raw painfully sensitive spot or area of exposed flesh: as (1) **:** the extremely sensitive flesh underlying a fingernail or toenail (2) **:** the extremely sensitive flesh underlying a corn, bunion, or callus (3) **:** the extremely sensitive part of a sore or wound (4) **:** the sensitive layers of tissue underlying the epidermis **b :** the inmost sensibilities of an individual ⟨felt hurt to the ~ by their remark⟩ **c :** the very center of something **:** the vital essence **:** HEART ⟨the ~ of the matter⟩ **4** *archaic* **:** LIFE 12 **5 :** QUICKSILVER **6 :** QUICKIE

⁴quick \"\ *vb* -ED/-ING/-S [ME *quiken*, fr. OE *cwician*, fr. *cwic*, *cwicu*, adj.] *archaic* **:** QUICKEN

⁵quick \"\ *n* -S [ME (northern dial.) *quike*, prob. of Scand origin; akin to Sw dial. *kvicka*, *kveka*, couch grass, Norw dial. *kvika* — more at QUITCH] **:** COUCH GRASS 1a

quick assets *n pl* **:** cash, accounts receivable, and other current assets excluding inventories

quick bead *n* **:** a bead that is flush with the surface of a molding — compare COCK BEAD

quickbeam \'≈,≈\ *n* [fr. (assumed) ME *quikbeem*, fr. OE *cwicbēam*, fr. *cwic* alive + *bēam* tree — more at QUICK, BEAM] **:** ROWAN TREE 1

quick bread *n* **:** a bread (as corn bread, muffins, biscuits) made with a leavening agent (as baking powder, soda) that permits immediate baking of the dough or batter mixture

quick–break \(')≈;≈\ *adj* **:** designed to break an electric circuit automatically and quickly esp. so as to shorten arcing and burning ⟨a *quick-break* switch⟩

quick–change \(')≈;≈\ *adj* **:** that changes quickly or that is adapted to changing or being changed quickly (as from one function to another) ⟨a *quick-change* tool part⟩

quick–change artist *n* **:** an individual adroit at quickly switching from one thing to another; *esp* **:** a performer skilled at quickly changing costume and makeup

quick decline *n* **:** a disease of grafted citrus trees with bitter orange rootstocks that is identical with or closely related to tristeza in cause and symptoms

¹quick·en \'kwikən\ *vb* **quickened; quickened; quickening** \-k(ə)niŋ\ **quickens** [ME *quickenen*, fr. *quik*, *quike* quick + *-nen* -en — more at QUICK] *vt* **1 a :** to make alive **:** REVIVE ⟨warm spring days that ~ the earth⟩ **b :** to cause to be enlivened **:** AROUSE, STIMULATE, EXCITE ⟨~*ing* their interest with vivid details⟩ **2** *archaic* **a :** KINDLE **b :** to cause to burn more brightly or more intensely **3 :** to make rapid or more rapid **:** HASTEN, ACCELERATE ⟨~*ed* her steps⟩ **4 a :** to make (a curve) sharper **b :** to make (a slope) steeper **5 :** to treat (articles to be plated) with a quickening liquid ~ *vi* **1 :** to quicken something **2 :** to come to life **:** become alive **:** become charged with life ⟨seed that ~*s* and becomes ripe grain⟩ **3 :** to reach the stage of gestation at which motion of the fetus is first begun or felt **4 :** to shine brightly or more brightly ⟨watched the dawn ~*ing* in the East⟩ **5 :** to become rapid or more rapid ⟨her pulse ~*ed* at the sight⟩

syn QUICKEN, ANIMATE, ENLIVEN, VIVIFY mean, in common, to make alive or lively. QUICKEN chiefly stresses the renewal of suspended life or growth or the arousing to full activity, usu. suddenly ⟨its characters never *quicken* with the life one feels lurks somewhere within them —Jerome Stone⟩ ⟨grand aspirations which *quicken* the energies of men —M.R.Cohen⟩ ⟨he felt his own blood *quicken* —Elyne Mitchell⟩ ANIMATE emphasizes the imparting of motion and activity, esp. lifelike, to something mechanical or artificial ⟨all living creatures, human and animal, are *animated* by souls or spirits —Frederica de Laguna⟩ ⟨almost every gathering is *animated* by spontaneous folk dancing —*Amer. Guide Series: Mich.*⟩ ⟨a child's *animated* doll⟩ ENLIVEN suggests a stimulus that kindles, exalts, or brightens something usu. dulled, depressed, or torpid ⟨*enliven* the meal by a few foolish jokes —Ellen Glasgow⟩ ⟨the crowded chapel was *enlivened* with bright colors —Josephine Y. Case⟩ ⟨a barrel of home brew on a sledge to *enliven* the occasion —Roderick Finlayson⟩ VIVIFY suggests the renewal of vitality, a freshening or energizing ⟨the room was dead. The essence that had *vivified* it was gone —O.Henry⟩ ⟨the vital force which was *vivifying* the nation at the expense of an occasional lapse from good taste —Agnes Repplier⟩ **syn** see in addition PROVOKE, SPEED

²quicken \"\ *or* **quicken tree** *n* -S [ME (northern dial.) *quikentre*, fr. *quik*, *quike* alive, quick + *tre* tree — more at QUICK, TREE] **:** ROWAN TREE 1

¹quickening *adj* [ME, fr. pres. part. of *quickenen* to quicken — more at QUICKEN] **:** that quickens ⟨as ~ as the ideas . . . that had followed in the wake of the French Revolution —Donald Davidson⟩

²quickening *n* -S [ME, fr. gerund of *quickenen* to quicken] **:** the first motion of a fetus in the uterus felt by the mother usu. somewhat before the middle of the period of gestation

quickening liquid *n* **:** a solution of a salt of mercury in which articles to be plated with silver are plunged before being put into the silver bath

quicker *comparative of* QUICK

quickest *superlative of* QUICK

quick fire *n* **:** the firing of shots in rapid succession; *esp* **:** marksmanship fire employed when bobbing targets are specified

quick–fire \(')≈;≈\ *or* **quick–firing** \(')≈;≈≈\ *adj* **:** firing or adapted for firing in rapid succession ⟨a *quick-fire* rifle⟩

quick–firer \(')≈;≈≈\ *n* -S **:** a quick-fire gun

¹quick–freeze \'≈;≈\ *vb* [²*quick* + *freeze*] *vt* **:** to freeze (food) so rapidly for preservation that ice crystals formed are too small to impair seriously the composition of the cells and consequently natural juices and flavor are preserved ~ *vi* **1 :** to quick-freeze something **2 :** to become quick-frozen

²quick–freeze \"\ *also* **quick–freezer** \'≈;≈≈\ *n* **:** FREEZER 1d(1)

quick grass *n* **:** COUCH GRASS 1a

quick·hatch \'kwik,hach\ *n* -ES [of Algonquian origin; akin to Cree *kwīkkwâhâketsh*, *kīkkwâhakes* wolverine, Ojibwa *gwīngwâage*, Algonquian Montagnais *karkajou*; derivatives fr. a stem represented by Cree *kwīkkw*, *kīkkw* to graze (with a shot)] **:** WOLVERINE

quick·ie *also* **quicky** \'kwikē, -ki\ *n, pl* **quickies** [¹*quick* + *-ie*, *-y*] **:** something done or made in a hurry: as **a** (1) **:** a hurriedly and cheaply produced motion picture or play (2) **:** a book or other publication hurriedly written and published **b :** a hurriedly planned and executed program (as of studies) **c :** a hurried trip or other activity **d :** a sudden often unauthorized brief strike of workers **e :** QUICK ONE

quick–in–the–hand \≈≈≈'≈\ *n* **:** JEWELWEED b

quicklier *archaic comparative of* QUICKLY

quickliest *archaic superlative of* QUICKLY

quicklime \'≈,≈\ *n* **:** the first solid product obtained by calcining limestone **:** ¹LIME 2a

quick–lunch \'≈;≈\ *n* **:** an eating establishment (as a lunch stand, sandwich shop) specializing in light quickly prepared dishes

quick·ly \ˈkwiklē, -li\ *adv* [ME *quikly*, fr. *quik*, *quike* quick + *-ly* — more at QUICK] **1** : in a quick manner: as **a** : RAPIDLY, SPEEDILY ⟨had got rich ~ —J.D.Hart⟩ **b** : without delay : SOON ⟨said she would hear from him ~⟩ **2** *archaic* : in a sensitively responsive manner : with sensitivity ⟨the language was still too rich and stiff to turn and twist ~ and freely upon half a sheet of notepaper —Virginia Woolf⟩

quick march *n* : a march in quick time

quick match *n* : a wick of cotton impregnated with a flammable mixture (as a paste of black powder and starch) that is used in lighting and carrying fire from one part to another in fireworks and flares

quick·ness \ˈkwiknəs\ *n* -ES [ME *quiknesse*, fr. *quik*, *quike* quick + *-nesse* -ness] : the quality or state of being quick

quick one *n* : a usu. alcoholic drink hurriedly tossed off

quick oven *n* : HOT OVEN

quick return *n* : a device used in a machine tool to cause the return stroke (as of a reciprocating tool) to be faster than the cutting stroke

quicks *pl of* QUICK, *pres 3d sing of* QUICK

quicksand \ˈ=,=\ *n*, *often attrib* [ME *qwykkesand*, fr. *quik*, *quike* quick + *sand* — more at QUICK, SAND] **1 a** (1) : a bed of sand which is usu. saturated with upward flowing water and made up of smooth rounded grains with little tendency to mutual adherence and in which the admixture of smooth grains and water constitutes a soft highly mobile shifting mass that yields easily to pressure and that tends to suck down and engulf objects resting on its surface (2) : an area marked by the presence of one or more such beds **b** : sand of the kind found in such a bed **2** : something treacherously shifting and mobile that tends to entrap and destroy ⟨the ~s of human existence —Dorothy C. Fisher⟩ — **quicksandy** \(ˈ)=¦==\ *adj*

quickset \ˈ=,=\ *n* [ME *quyksette*, fr. *quyk*, *quik* quick + *sette*, *set* set — more at QUICK, SET] **1 a** : living slips or cuttings of a plant set in the ground to grow; *esp* : slips or cuttings (as of hawthorn) used for a hedge ⟨enclosed the ground with a single row of ~ —Robert Southey⟩ **b** : a single slip or cutting of a plant ⟨when a ~ of a vine is planted in a vineyard —Philemon Holland⟩ **2** *chiefly Brit* : QUICKSET HEDGE

quick-set \"\ *n* [²*quick* + *set*, past part. of *set*] : a quick-setting material

quickset hedge *n*, *chiefly Brit* : a hedge or thicket planted for ornamentation or as a boundary marker and typically made up of English hawthorn

quick-setting \(ˈ)=¦==\ *adj* : that is made so as to set more quickly than is usual ⟨*quick-setting* concrete⟩

quick-sighted \(ˈ)=¦==\ *adj* : marked by keen quickly responsive sight ⟨*quick-sighted* as a cat⟩ or sharp quickly responsive discernment ⟨*quick-sighted* into the faults of the time —Leonard Bacon⟩ : quick to see or discern : SHARP-SIGHTED — **quick-sight·ed·ness** *n* -ES

¹quicksilver \ˈ=,==\ *n* [ME *quiksilver*, fr. OE *cwicseolfor*, fr. *cwic* alive + *seolfor* silver; trans. of L *argentum vivum* like MD *quicsilver* quicksilver, OHG *quecsilbar* — more at QUICK, SILVER] **1** : MERCURY 1a **2** : something resembling or suggestive of quicksilver : something mercurial

²quicksilver \"\ *adj* : resembling or suggestive of quicksilver : MERCURIAL

³quicksilver \"\ *vt* : to overlay with or as if with quicksilver; *esp* : to coat (glass) with an amalgam of quicksilver and tin in making mirrors

quicksilvering ˈ=,=(=)=\ *n* : the amalgam that forms the reflecting surface of some mirrors

quicksilver rock *n* : an altered serpentine consisting mainly of dark opal and chalcedony and commonly associated with the ore in mercury deposits in serpentine

quicksilver vermilion *n* : VERMILION 1a

quicksilver water *n* : a solution of mercury nitrate used in gilding

quicksilver weed *n* : EARLY MEADOW RUE

quicksilvery \ˈ=¦=(=)=\ *adj* : resembling or suggestive of quicksilver : MERCURIAL

quickstep \ˈ=,=\ *n* **1** : a spirited march tune; *esp* : a spirited march tune designed to accompany a military march in quick time **2** : a combination of short rapid dance steps

quick stick *also* **quick sticks** *adv*, *archaic* : QUICKLY

quick study *n* : one that can speedily learn the essentials of something to be done; *esp* : a performer (as an actor, musician) with a gift for learning with remarkable speed new material (as lines, stage business, scores)

quick-tempered \(ˈ)=¦==\ *adj* : easily aroused to anger : IRASCIBLE

quickthorn \ˈ=,=\ *n* : the common European hawthorn (*Crataegus oxyacantha*)

quick time *n* : a rate of marching in which 120 steps each 30 inches in length are taken in one minute

quick trick *n* : HONOR TRICK

quickwater \ˈ=,==\ *n* **1** : QUICKSILVER WATER **2 a** : the part of a stream that has a strong current **b** : an artificial current or bubbling patch of water just astern of a moving boat

quick-witted \(ˈ)=¦==\ *adj* : quick in perception and understanding : mentally nimble and wide-awake : brightly alert : SHARP ⟨a *quick-witted* opponent⟩ ⟨a *quick-witted* answer⟩ ⟨saved an embarrassing situation with *quick-witted* tact⟩ **syn** see INTELLIGENT

quick-wit·ted·ly *adv* : in a quick-witted manner

quick-wit·ted·ness \-nəs\ *n* -ES : the quality or state of being quick-witted

quickwork \ˈ=,=\ *n*, *archaic* : one of several sections of planking or plating in the upper or sometimes the lower part of a ship's hull

quicky *var of* QUICKIE

¹quid \ˈkwid\ *n* -S [L, what, anything, something, neut. of *quis* who, anyone — more at WHO] **1** : QUIDDITY **2** [L (as in *quid pro quo*)] : something given or received for something else ⟨bilateral deals that would ensure us a large ~ for every single quo —W.L.Thorp⟩

²quid \"\ *n*, *pl* **quid** *also* **quids** [origin unknown] *slang Brit* : POUND STERLING, SOVEREIGN

³quid \"\ *n* -S [E dial., cud, fr. ME *quide*, fr. OE *cwidu* — more at CUD] : a cut or wad of something to be chewed but not swallowed; *esp* : a cut of chewing tobacco

⁴quid \"\ *vi* **quidded**; **quidded**; **quidding**; **quids** *of a horse* : to drop chewed food from the mouth

quiddany *n* -ES [modif. of obs. F *codignat* (now *cotignat*), fr. MF, fr. OProv *coudonat*, *codonhat*, fr. *codon* quince, fr. L *cotoneum* — more at QUINCE] *obs* : a jelly or syrup made from fruit (as quinces)

quid·da·tive *also* **quid·di·tive** \ˈkwidəd·iv\ *adj* [*quiddative* irreg. fr. *quiddity* + *-ative*; *quidditive* fr. *quiddity* + *-ive*] : QUIDDITATIVE

quid·der *or* **quid·dor** \ˈkwidə(r)\ *n* -S [⁴*quid* + *-er* or *-or*] : a horse that quids

quid·dit \ˈkwidət, *usu* -əd.+V\ *n* -S [ML *quidditas*, *quiditas*] *archaic* : a quibbling subtlety

quid·di·tas \ˈkwidə,tas\ *n*, *pl* **quid·di·ta·tes** \,==ˈtād·(,)ēz, -ä,tēz\ [ML] : QUIDDITY 1a

quid·di·ta·tive \ˈ===,tād·iv\ *adj* [*quiddity* + *-ative*] : of, relating to, or constituting the essential nature of something

quid·di·ty \ˈkwidəd·ē, -ətē, -i\ *n* -ES [ML *quidditas* essence, fr. L *quid* what, anything + *-itas* -ity — more at QUID] **1 a** (1) : a quibbling subtlety : a trifling point : QUIBBLE (2) : an inclination to quibble **b** : an odd little feature : ECCENTRICITY ⟨his own personality, with all its quirks and *quiddities* —Clifton Fadiman⟩ **2** : the essential nature or ultimate form of something : what makes something to be the type of thing that it is — compare HAECCEITY

¹quid·dle \ˈkwidᵊl\ *vb* **quiddled**; **quiddled**; **quiddling** \-d(ᵊ)liŋ\ **quiddles** [prob. blend of *quiddity* and *fiddle* or *twiddle*] *chiefly dial* : DAWDLE, TRIFLE

²quiddle \"\ *n* -S *chiefly dial* : a fussy or fastidious person

quid·nunc \ˈkwid,nəŋk\ *n* -S [L *quid nunc* what now?] : one that is avidly curious and given to speculating esp. about ephemeral or petty things : an inquisitive usu. small-minded individual : NEWSMONGER, BUSYBODY, GOSSIP

quid pro quo \¦kwid,prō¦kwō\ *n*, *pl* **quid pro quos** *or* **quids pro quos** *also* **quids pro quo** [L, something for something (else)] : something given or received for something else ⟨would be folly to grant that increase without insisting on some *quid pro quo* —*Newsweek*⟩

quie·bra·cha \kyāˈbrächə\ *or* **quie·bra·ha·cha** \,=,brä-ˈhächə\ *n* -S [AmerSp — more at QUEBRACHO] : QUEBRACHO

qui·esce \kwīˈes, kwēˈ-\ *vi* -ED/-ING/-S [L *quiescere* to be quiet — more at QUIET] : to become quiet, calm, or silent

qui·es·cence \kwīˈesᵊn(t)s, kwēˈ-\ *n* -S [LL *quiescentia*, fr. L *quiescent-*, *quiescens* + *-ia*] : the quality or state of being quiescent

qui·es·cen·cy \-ᵊnsē\ *n* -ES [LL *quiescentia*] : QUIESCENCE

¹qui·es·cent \-nt\ *adj* [L *quiescent-*, *quiescens*, pres. part. of *quiescere* to be quiet — more at QUIET] **1 a** : marked by a state of inactivity or repose : tranquilly at rest : MOTIONLESS, QUIET ⟨the ~ melancholy of the town —Arnold Bennett⟩ **b** (1) : ARRESTED ⟨~ tuberculosis⟩ (2) : causing no symptoms ⟨~ gallstones⟩ **2** *of a letter* : not pronounced : SILENT — compare MOVABLE **syn** see LATENT

²quiescent \"\ *n* -S : a silent letter (as in Hebrew)

qui·es·cent·ly *adv* : in a quiescent manner

¹qui·et \ˈkwīət, *usu* -əd.+V\ *n* -S [ME, fr. L *quiet-*, *quies* rest, quiet — more at WHILE] : the quality or state of being quiet : TRANQUILLITY, REPOSE, STILLNESS — often used as a command — **at quiet** : at rest ⟨began . . . to grow more *at quiet* with himself —R.L.Stevenson⟩ — **on the quiet** *adv* (*or adj*) : in a secret or underhand manner ⟨bought the goods *on the quiet*⟩

²quiet \"\ *adj*, *usu* -ER/-EST [ME, fr. MF *quiet*, *quiete*, fr. L *quietus*, fr. past part. of *quiescere* to be quiet, fr. *quies* rest, quiet] **1 a** (1) : marked by little or no motion or agitation : making little stir : CALM ⟨the ~ waters of a lagoon⟩ (2) : marked by little or no activity ⟨during the morning, business was ~⟩ : not moving about : INACTIVE ⟨a ~ throng of onlookers⟩ **b** : causing no trouble or disturbance : not turbulent : GENTLE ⟨a ~, peace-loving people⟩ **c** (1) : not excited, anxious, or wrought up : SETTLED ⟨leading a ~ life⟩ ⟨went about her work with ~ efficiency⟩ (2) : not disturbed, bothered, or annoyed : not interfered or meddled with ⟨decided to do a little ~ reading⟩ : enjoyed in peace and relaxation ⟨a ~ cup of tea⟩ (3) : free of strife, bustle, and commotion : PLACID ⟨a ~ countryside⟩ **2 a** (1) : making no noise or uproar : acting, moving, or resting in silence ⟨the class was ~ and listened intently⟩ (2) : free from noise or uproar : SILENT, STILL, HUSHED ⟨the room was dark and ~⟩ **b** : not marked by extremes : not such as to attract undue attention : not showy or obtrusive ⟨clothes that were in ~ good taste⟩ **3** : RETIRED, SECLUDED ⟨a ~ nook⟩ **4** *of a volcanic eruption* : marked by the extrusion of lava without violent explosions

³quiet \"\ *adv*, *usu* -ER/-EST : QUIETLY

⁴quiet \"\ *vb* -ED/-ING/-S [LL *quietare* to set free, calm, fr. L *quietus* quiet — more at ²QUIET] *vt* **1** : to cause to be quiet : PACIFY, CALM ⟨had no trouble in ~*ing* the crowd⟩ **2** : to put at rest by freeing the fact of ownership from dispute or question — usu. used in the phrase *to quiet title* ~ *vi* : to become quiet — usu. used with *down* ⟨had been excited but soon ~*ed* down⟩ **syn** see CALM

quiet day *n* : a day set apart in the Anglican church for special devotions, meditations, and instructions

qui·et·en \ˈkwīətᵊn, -ətᵊn\ *vb* **quietened**; **quietened**; **quietening** \-t(ᵊ)niŋ\ **quietens** [²*quiet* + *-en*] *chiefly Brit* : QUIET **syn** see CALM

qui·et·ism \ˈkwīə,tizəm\ *n* -S [It *quietismo*, fr. *quieto* quiet (fr. L *quietus*) + *-ismo* -ism — more at QUIET] **1 a** : a 17th century Christian mysticism that stressed passive self-annihilation through religious meditation and complete absorption in the contemplation of God and ethical antinomianism based on the view that in the state of perfect surrender the soul is indifferent to the demands of sense, desire, virtue, or morality **b** : a nonactivistic mysticism stressing passive contemplation, concentration on the interior life, and nonparticipation in affairs of the world **2** : a state of calmness or passivity

¹qui·et·ist \-əd·əst\ *n* -S [It *quietista*, fr. *quieto* + *-ista* -ist] : one that advocates or practices quietism

²quietist \"\ *or* **qui·et·is·tic** \¦==ˈtistik\ *adj* : of, relating to, or typical of quietists or quietism

qui·e·tive \ˈkwīəd·iv\ *n* -S [⁴*quiet* + *-ive*] : something that has a tranquilizing effect : SEDATIVE ⟨~*s* rather than incentives will be in demand —Helmut Kuhn⟩

qui·et·ly *adv* : in a quiet manner

qui·et·ness *n* -ES [ME *quietnes*, fr. *quiet* + *-nes* -ness] : the quality or state of being quiet : TRANQUILLITY, REPOSE, STILLNESS

qui·et·some \ˈkwīətsəm\ *adj* [²*quiet* + *-some*] *archaic* : TRANQUIL

quiet-spoken \¦==¦==\ *adj* : marked by or using quiet speech ⟨a *quiet-spoken* young woman —Ethel Wilson⟩

qui·e·tude \ˈkwīə,tüd, -ə,tyüd\ *n* -S [MF, fr. ML *quietudo*, fr. L *quietus* quiet — more at QUIET] : QUIETNESS

qui·e·tus \kwīˈēd·əs, -ētəs\ *n* -ES [ME *quietus* (*est*), fr. ML, (he is) discharged, acquitted] **1 a** : final discharge or acquittance (as from debt or obligation) : final settlement : EXTINCTION ⟨obtained a ~ of the sum owed⟩ **b** *archaic* : discharge from office or duty **c** : RELEASE; *specif* : a proceeding in a probate court whereby an administrator obtains a full discharge **2** : removal from or extinction of activity; *esp* : DEATH ⟨met their ~ without protest⟩ **3** : something that produces a cessation of activity : something that quiets or represses ⟨this disaster . . . had the effect of a ~ —Susan E. Ferrier⟩ **4** : a period of inactivity ⟨the long ~ of thirty years —C.R.Anderson⟩

¹quiff \ˈkwif\ *n* -S [alter. of *whiff*] **1** : a puff of tobacco smoke **2** : a puff of air

²quiff \"\ *n* -S [origin unknown] *Brit* : a prominent forelock of hair

³quiff \"\ *n*, *pl* **quiff** *also* **quiffs** [origin unknown] *slang* : GIRL, FEMALE

qui·i·na \kwēˈīnə\ *n*, *cap* [NL] : a genus (the type of the family Quiinaceae) of tropical American shrubs and trees

qui·i·na·ce·ae \,kwēəˈnāsē,ē\ *n pl*, *cap* [NL, fr. *Quiina*, type genus + *-aceae*] : a family of tropical American shrubs and trees (order Parietales) with opposite coriaceous leaves, small verticillate flowers in terminal spikes or racemes, and baccate one-seeded fruit

qui·la \ˈkēlə\ *n* -S [AmerSp, fr. Araucan *cula*] : a grass (*Chusquea quila*) of the southern part of So. America that resembles bamboo, is used as forage, and has a fiber used in making paper

quile \ˈkwī(ə)l\ *dial var of* ⁴COIL

quil·e·ute *or* **quil·la·yute** \¦kwilə¦yüt\ *n*, *pl* **quileute** *or* **quileutes** *or* **quillayute** *or* **quillayutes** *usu cap* **1 a** : a Chemakuan people of the western part of the state of Washington **b** : a member of such people **2** : the language of the Quileute people

¹quill \ˈkwil\ *n* -S [ME *quil*; akin to MHG *kil* quill (feather), LG *quiele*] **1 a** (1) : a bobbin, spool, or spindle on which filling yarn is wound before insertion into a shuttle in the process of weaving (2) : a hollow shaft often surrounding another shaft and used in various mechanical devices **b** (1) : a hollow stem (as a reed) used for producing musical tones (2) : PANPIPE (3) : WHISTLE **c** : a roll of dried bark ⟨a ~ of cinnamon⟩ **2 a** (1) : the hollow horny barrel of a feather (2) : a bird's feather; *esp* : one of the large stiff feathers of a bird's wing or tail **b** : one of the hollow sharp spines of a porcupine or hedgehog **3** : one of various articles made from or resembling the quill of a feather: as **a** : a pen for writing **b** : a plectrum for plucking the strings of a harpsichord, lute, or similar instrument **c** : TOOTHPICK **d** : QUILL FLY **4** : a float for a fishline **5** : something in its truest, purest, or best state : the real thing : MCCOY — usu. used with *pure* ⟨fine old liquor that was the pure ~⟩

²quill \"\ *vt* -ED/-ING/-S **1 a** : to remove quills from **b** : to pierce with or as if with quills **2 a** : to wind (thread or yarn) on a quill **b** : to make a series of small rounded ridges in (cloth)

quil·la·cin·ga \,kwiləˈsiŋgə\ *n*, *pl* **quillacinga** *or* **quillacingas** *usu cap* [Sp, of AmerInd origin] **1 a** : a people of southwestern Colombia and northern Ecuador **b** : a member of such people **2** : the language of the Quillacinga people

qui·llai \kēˈ(y)ī\ *or* **qui·llaia** *or* **qui·llia** \-ˈīə\ *n* -S [AmerSp *quillai*, *quillay*, fr. Mapuche] : SOAPBARK

quil·la·ic acid \kwəˈlāik-\ *n* [*quillai* + *-ic*] : a poisonous crystalline triterpenoid sapogenin $C_{30}H_{46}O_5$ obtained by hydrolysis of the saponin from soapbark

quil·la·ja \kwiˈlāyə, -jə\ *n*, *cap* [NL, fr. AmerSp *quillai*, *quillay*] : a genus of trees (family Rosaceae) native to Brazil, Peru, and Chile and distinguished by their saponaceous bark — see SOAPBARK

quillback \ˈ=,=\ *or* **quillback carpsucker** *n*, *pl* **quillback** *or* **quillbacks** **1** : a small carpsucker (*Carpiodes velifer*) that has the dorsal fin distinguished by a very long first ray and that is widely distributed esp. in larger streams of central and eastern No. America **2** : any of several fishes related to the quillback; *esp* : the common carpsucker (*Carpiodes carpio*)

quill bark *n* : a roll of dried cinchona bark

quill bit *n* : a long pod bit

quill drive *n* : a drive used on electric locomotives in which the motors are mounted on a nonrotatable quill that surrounds the axle of the driving wheels and which transmits power to the wheels by means of pins on the armature structure that engage the spokes of the driving wheels

quill-driver \ˈ=,==\ *n* : one that works with a pen : WRITER, CLERK

quilled *adj* **1** : that has the shape of a quill: as **a** (1) : rolled into the form of a quill ⟨~ cinchona bark⟩ (2) : fluted into rounded folds ⟨~ cloth⟩ **b** : having nearly tubular corollas or florets ⟨the ~ flowers of the cactus dahlia⟩ **2** : that is furnished with a quill ⟨the ~ jack of a harpsichord⟩

quill embroidery *n* : QUILLWORK

quill·er \ˈkwilə(r)\ *n* -S [¹*quill* + *-er*] **1** : a machine used in transferring yarn from spools and cones to quills **2** : the operator of a quiller

¹quil·let \ˈkwilət, *usu* -əd.+V\ *n* -S [origin unknown] *chiefly dial* : a small tract of land

²quillet \"\ *n* -S [prob. short for obs. *quillity*, alter. of *quiddity*] *archaic* : a subtle distinction : QUIBBLE

³quill·et \"\ *n* -S [¹*quill* + *-et*] *archaic* : a small tube (as of paper)

quill fern *n* : MARSH FERN 1

quillfish \ˈ=,=\ *n* : any of various small very slender blennies of the north Pacific of the family Ptilichthyidae

quill fly *n* : an artificial angling fly with a quill body

quill gear *n* : an arrangement consisting of a gear wheel made integral with a hollow spindle or shaft; *esp* : a hollow shaft with a gear wheel on each end used in the back gear of a lathe or other machine tool

quilling *n* -S [in sense 1, fr. gerund of ²*quill*; in sense 2, fr. ¹*quill* + *-ing*] **1** : the process of quilling yarn or cloth **2** : a strip of quilled cloth

quill mite *n* : a mite (*Syringophilus bipectinatus*) that lives in the shafts of the primary wing feathers of poultry

quil·lon \kēyōⁿ\ *n* -S [F, fr. MF, dim. of *quille* bowling pin, fr. MHG *kegel*, fr. OHG *kegil* stake, club — more at KEG] : an arm of the cross guard of a sword

quill pig *n* : PORCUPINE

quills *pl of* QUILL, *pres 3d sing of* QUILL

quilltail \ˈ=,=\ *or* **quilltail coot** *n* : RUDDY DUCK

quillwork \ˈ=,=\ *n* : ornamentation of skins, bark, or fabrics by overlaying with porcupine or bird quills

quillwort \ˈ=,=\ *n* **1** : a plant of the genus *Isoetes* **2** : MARSH MILKWEED

¹quilt \ˈkwilt\ *n* -S [ME *cowete*, *quilte*, fr. OF *coilte*, *cuilte*, *coute* quilt, mattress, fr. L *culcita* mattress, bed, cushion; perh. akin to Skt *kūrca* beard, bunch, bundle of grain] **1 a** *obs* : MATTRESS **b** : a bed covering made of two layers of cloth of which the top one is usu. pieced or appliquéd and having a filling of wool, cotton, or down held in place by stitched designs or tufts worked through all thicknesses **c** : a bedspread with a woven design resembling quilting **d** : a design or figure formed by quilting **2 a** : a piece of thick padding resembling a quilt and usu. used as a protective covering; *esp* : a pad formerly worn under or in place of armor **b** *obs* : POULTICE **c** : a heat-insulating material consisting of fibrous materials matted together and stitched or quilted between two layers of heavy paper **3** : the core of a cricket ball or of a field-hockey ball

²quilt \"\ *vb* -ED/-ING/-S *vt* **1 a** : to fill, pad, or line with material like that used in quilts ⟨a helmet whose interior had been ~*ed*⟩ **b** (1) : to stitch, sew, or cover with lines or patterns like those used in quilts ⟨~*ed* the surface with a scroll pattern⟩ (2) : to stitch (designs) through layers of cloth **c** : to bind up or cover with interlacings (as of cord) ⟨a short pipe ~*ed* over with string —Charles Dickens⟩ **d** : to fasten or sew up between two pieces of material ⟨~*ed* money in his belt⟩ **2 a** : to make (a quilt) by stitching or usu. by sewing together two layers of cloth with some padding between them **b** : to make (a garment) in quilted work **3** : to compile (as a book) by piecing together items or scraps from various sources : do in a patchwork way ⟨~*ed* together a collection of verse⟩ **4** *chiefly dial* : to strike repeatedly : THRASH ~ *vi*, **1** : to make quilts **2** : to do quilted work

³quilt \"\ *vb* -ED/-ING/-S [origin unknown] *dial Eng* : GULP, SWALLOW

quilted *adj* **1** : furnished with a quilt **2** : resembling a quilt in design ⟨embossed cottons with ~ effect —*Women's Wear Daily*⟩ **3** : padded like a quilt

quilted maple *n* : OREGON MAPLE

quilt·er \ˈkwiltə(r)\ *n* -S **1** : one that quilts **2** : a sewing machine attachment for quilting

quilting *n* -S **1** : the process of quilting **2 a** : material that is quilted or that is used for making quilts or for doing other quilted work **b** : stitching usu. worked in designs that holds two or more layers of cloth together **c** : a covering made of sennit **3** : QUILTING PARTY

quilting party *or* **quilting bee** *n* : a social gathering of women at which they work together at making quilts or doing other quilted work

quim·baya \kimˈbīə\ *n*, *pl* **quimbaya** *or* **quimbayas** *usu cap* **1 a** : an extinct people of western Colombia **b** : a member of such people **2** : a language of the Quimbaya people that is probably Cariban

quim·per \(ˈ)kaⁿ¦pe(ə)r, -amˌp-\ *n* -S *often cap* [*Quimper ware*] : a grayish blue that is redder, lighter, and slightly stronger than electric, greener and stronger than copenhagen or old china, and redder, stronger, and slightly lighter than Gobelin

quimper ware *n*, *usu cap Q* [fr. *Quimper*, France, where it is produced] : a French glazed earthenware decorated in bright colors with marine subjects, peasant figures, or floral patterns

quin \ˈkwin\ *n* -S [by shortening] : QUINTUPLET

quin- *or* **quino-** *comb form* [Sp *quina* cinchona bark — more at QUININE] **1** : quina : cinchona bark ⟨*quino*tannic⟩ ⟨*quino*line⟩ ⟨*quin*ine⟩ **2** : quinic acid ⟨*quin*ate⟩ **3** : quinoline ⟨*quino*cyanine⟩ **4** : quinone ⟨*quin*itol⟩ ⟨*quin*oid⟩

qui·na \ˈkēnə\ *n* -S [Sp] : CINCHONA

quin·a·crine \ˈkwinə,krēn, -,krən\ *also* **chin·a·crin** *or* **chin·a·crine** \ˈkin-\ *n* -S [*quinacrine*, fr. *quin-* + *acridine*; *chinacrin*, *chinacrine*, fr. *Chinacrin*, a trademark] : an antimalarial drug derived from acridine and used chiefly in the form of its bitter yellow crystalline dihydrochloride $C_{23}H_{30}ClN_3O.2HCl.2H_2O$

quin·al·dic acid \(ˈ)kwi¦naldik-\ *or* **quin·al·din·ic acid** \¦kwi,nal¦dinik-\ *n* [ISV *quinaldine* + *-ic*] : a crystalline acid C_9H_6NCOOH obtained esp. by oxidation of quinaldine and used in chemical analysis; 2-quinoline-carboxylic acid

quin·al·dine \kwiˈnal,dēn, -dᵊn\ *n* [ISV *quin-* + *ald-* + *-ine*] : an oily liquid base $CH_3C_9H_6N$ of a slightly pungent odor obtained by condensation of acetaldehyde and aniline and occurring also in coal tar that is used chiefly in the manufacture of dyes and pharmaceuticals; 2-methyl-quinoline

quin·al·din·i·um \,kwi,nalˈdinēəm\ *n* -S [NL, fr. ISV *quinaldine* + NL *-ium*] : a univalent ion $[C_{10}H_9NH]^+$ that is analogous to ammonium and is derived from quinaldine

quin·alizarin \¦kwin+\ *n* [ISV *quin-* + *alizarin*] : a red crystalline compound $C_{14}H_4O_2(OH)_4$ with green metallic luster used chiefly in chemical analysis; 1,2,5,8-tetrahydroxy-anthraquinone

quin·a·mine \ˈkwinə,mēn, -mən\ *n* [ISV *quin-* + *amine*] : a crystalline alkaloid $C_{19}H_{24}N_2O_2$ in various cinchona barks

qui·naph·thol \(ˈ)kwi+\ *n* [blend of *quin-* and *naphthol*] : CHINAPHTHOL

qui·nar·i·us \kwiˈna(a)rēəs\ *n*, *pl* **quinar·ii** \-ē,ī\ [L, fr. *quinarius*, adj., quinary] **1** : a Roman silver coin issued occasionally from the 3d century B.C. and equivalent to ½ denarius **2** : a gold ½-aureus piece of imperial Rome

¹qui·na·ry \ˈkwīnərē, -win-\ *adj* [L *quinarius*, fr. *quini* five apiece + *-arius* -ary; akin to *quinque* five — more at FIVE] **1 :** consisting of five **:** arranged by fives **:** QUINTUPLE ⟨the ~ system is based on counting the fingers of one hand —H.J. Spinden⟩ **2 :** of the fifth order or rank

²quinary \"\ *n* -ES **:** a quinary group or system

¹qui·nate \ˈkwī,nāt\ *adj* [L *quini* five apiece + E *-ate*] **:** arranged in or composed of sets of five — used esp. of compound leaves with five leaflets

²quinate \", ˈkwi,n-\ *n* -S [ISV *quin-* + *-ate*] **:** a salt or ester of quinic acid

qui·nault *or* **qui·naielt** \kwəˈnȯlt\ *n, pl* **quinault** *or* **quinaults** *or* **quinaielt** *or* **quinaielts** *usu cap* **1 a :** a Salishan people of the valley of the Quinault river and contiguous Pacific coast, Washington **b :** a member of such people **2 :** the language of the Quinault people

quin·az·o·line \kwəˈnazə,lēn, -ˌlən\ *n* -S [ISV *quin-* + *azole* + *-ine*; orig. formed as G *chinazolin*] **:** a yellow crystalline compound $C_8H_6N_2$ with an odor like that of naphthalene regarded as derived from quinoline by substitution of a nitrogen atom for a methylidyne group in the 3-position; *also* **:** a derivative of this compound

quince \ˈkwin(t)s\ *n* -S [ME *quynce*, pl., quinces, fr. *quyn*, *coyn* quince, fr. MF *coin, cooin*, fr. L *cotoneum, cydoneum, cydonia, cydoneum (malum)*, fr. Gk *kydōnion*, prob. fr. neut. of *kydōnios* Cydonian, fr. *Kydōnia* Cydonia, ancient city on the north coast of Crete] **1 :** the fruit of a widely cultivated central Asiatic tree (*Cydonia oblonga*) somewhat resembling a large yellow apple, differing in having many seeds in each carpel and a hard acid flesh that is used for marmalade, jelly, and preserves, and producing seeds that are covered with a mucilaginous material which is used in making a mucilage and in the preparation of toilet lotions **2 :** the tree that bears quinces and is often used as a dwarfing stock for the pear — see CHAENOMELES, FLOWERING QUINCE

quince curculio *n* **:** a small gray and yellow curculio (*Conotrachelus crataegi*) whose larva burrows in quinces

¹quin·centenary \(ˈ)kwin+\ *n* [L *quinque* five + E *centenary*] **:** a 500th anniversary or its celebration

²quincentenary \"\ *adj* **:** of or relating to a 500th anniversary

quin·centennial \ˌkwin+\ *adj or n* [L *quinque* five + *centennial*] **:** QUINCENTENARY

quince yellow *n* **:** a moderate yellow that is greener and darker than colonial yellow, greener and stronger than mustard yellow, and greener, lighter, and stronger than brass — called also *capucine, copper yellow*

quinc·ke tube \ˈkwiŋkə-, ˈkv-\ *n, usu cap Q* [after Georg H. *Quincke* †1924 Ger. physicist] **:** a glass tube sounded like a bottle by blowing across its mouth and used for obtaining high notes in experiments on difference tones

quin·cun·cial \(ˈ)kwinˈkənchəl\ *or* **quin·cunx·ial** \-əŋ(k)-sēəl\ *adj* [*quincuncial* fr. L *quincuncialis*, fr. *quincunc-, quincunx* + *-alis* -al; *quincunxial* fr. L *quincunx* + E *-al*] **1 :** relating to, consisting of, or arranged in a quincunx or quincunxes **2 a :** having the members so imbricated that two are exterior, two are interior, and the other has one edge exterior and one interior — used of a pentamerous calyx or corolla ⟨~ estivation⟩ **b :** PENTASTICHOUS — **quin·cun·cial·ly** \-chəlē\ *adv*

quin·cunx \ˈkwin,kəŋ(k)s\ *n* -ES [L, lit., five twelfths, fr. *quinque-* + *uncia* twelfth part, ounce — more at OUNCE] **1 :** an arrangement of five things with one at each corner and one in the middle of a square **2 a :** an arrangement of plants (as trees) with one at each corner and one at the center of a square or rectangle **b :** a planting in the form of a series of squares or rectangles with a plant at the center of each **3 :** a quincuncial arrangement of the parts of a flower in estivation

quincunx 2b

quin·decagon \(ˈ)kwin+\ *n* [L *quindecim* fifteen + E *-agon* (as in *heptagon*)] **:** a usu. plane polygon with 15 angles and 15 sides

quin·deca·syllabic \(ˌ)kwin+ˈdekə+\ *adj* [*quindeca-*, modif. (influenced by *deca-*) of L *quindecim* fifteen + E *syllabic*] **:** having 15 syllables

quin·decemvir \ˌkwin+\ *n* [L *quindecimvir*, fr. *quindecim* fifteen + *vir* man — more at VIRILE] **:** one of a commission, council, or ruling body of 15; *specif* **:** a member of a college of priests in ancient Rome having charge of the sibylline books

quin·decemvirate \"+\ *n* [*quindecemvir* + *-ate*] **1 :** the office or government of quindecemvirs **2 :** a body of quindecemvirs

quin·decillion \"+\ *n, often attrib* [L *quinque* five + E *decillion*] — see NUMBER table

quin·de·cim \ˈkwində,sim\ *n* -S [ME *quindesin, quindecime*, fr. LL *quindecima*, fem. of *quindecimus* fifteenth, fr. L *quindecim* fifteen, fr. *quinque-* + *decem* ten — more at TEN] **1** *obs* **:** a tax of one fifteenth **2 :** QUINDENE

quin·dec·i·ma \kwinˈdesəmə\ *n* -S [ML, fr. LL, fem. of *quindecimus*] **1 :** FIFTEENTH 4b **2 :** a pipe-organ stop whose tones are two octaves above the notes

quin·dene \ˈkwin,dēn\ *n* -S [ML *quindena*, fr. fem. of L *quindeni* fifteen each, fr. *quini* five each + *deni* ten by ten, ten each — more at QUINARY, DENIER] **:** the 15th or in modern reckoning 14th day after a church festival

quine \ˈkwēn\ *Scot var of* QUEAN

-quine \ˌkwēn, ˌkwən\ *n comb form* -S [fr. *quinoline*] **:** quinoline ⟨prima*quine*⟩ ⟨penta*quine*⟩

qui·ne·tum \kwīˈnēd·əm, kwəˈn-\ *n* -S [*quin-* + L *-etum* (n. suffix denoting a garden or group of plants)] **:** a mixture of the alkaloids in varying proportions as they occur naturally in the bark of red cinchona used as an antiperiodic

quin·gen·ten·a·ry \ˌkwin,jenˈtenərē, kwinˈsentˀn,erē\ *n* -ES [L *quingenti* five hundred (alter. of *quincenti*, fr. *quinque-* + *centum* hundred) + *-enary* (as in *centenary*) — more at HUNDRED] **:** QUINCENTENARY

quin·hy·drone \kwinˈhī,drōn, ˈ=,==\ *n* -S [ISV *quin-* + *hydro*quinone] **1 :** a green crystalline compound $C_6H_4O_2.C_6H_4(OH)_2$ with metallic luster formed by combination of equimolecular amounts of *para*-quinone and hydroquinone or in the oxidation of hydroquinone or the reduction of quinone **2 :** any of a class of highly colored compounds similar to quinhydrone

quinhydrone electrode *n* **:** an electrode consisting of a platinum wire in a solution containing quinhydrone used to determine hydrogen-ion concentration

quinible *n* -S [ME, fr. L *quini* five each, five + ME *-ible* (as in *trible* treble) — more at TREBLE] **1** *obs* **:** a musical descant in fifths **2** *obs* **:** a voice part one octave higher than the treble

quinic acid \ˈkwi|nik-, ˈkwī|\ *n* [*quinic* fr. *quin-* + *-ic*] **1 :** a crystalline acid $C_6H_7(OH)_4COOH$ obtained from cinchona bark, coffee beans, and other plant products and synthetically by hydrolysis of chlorogenic acid; 1,3,4,5- tetrahydroxy-cyclohexane-carboxylic acid **2 :** QUINIINIC ACID

qui·ni·cine \ˈkwinə,sēn, -sən\ *n* -S [ISV *quinic* (in *quinic acid*) + *-ine*; orig. formed in F] **:** a bitter poisonous reddish yellow amorphous alkaloid $C_{20}H_{24}N_2O_2$ isomeric with quinine and obtained from cinchona bark or by heating a salt of quinine — called also *quinotoxine*

qui·ni·dine \ˈkwinə,dēn, -ˌdən\ *also* **chin·i·dine** \ˈki-\ *n* -S [ISV *quin-* or *chin-* + *-idine*; prob. orig. formed as F *quinidine*] **:** a crystalline dextrorotatory alkaloid $C_{20}H_{24}N_2O_2$ stereoisomeric with quinine found in some species of cinchona and used sometimes in place of quinine but chiefly in the form of its sulfate in the treatment of auricular fibrillation

qui·nie·la \kēnˈyelə\ *or* **qui·nel·la** \-ēˈnelə\ *n* -S [AmerSp *quiniela*, a game of chance, quiniela] **1 :** a betting pool in which the bettor selects the contestants to finish in first and second place but need not designate their order of finish **2 :** a wager in a quiniela

qui·nine \ˈkwī,nīn *also* ˈkwi,nīn *or* kwəˈnīn *sometimes* kwəˈnēn *or* ˈkwi,nēn *or* kəˈnēn *or* ˈkwinən; *Brit usu* kwəˈnēn\ *n* -S [Sp *quina* cinchona bark (short for *quinaquina, quinquina*, fr. Quechua, perh. modif. of NL *Cinchona*) + E *-ine* — more at CINCHONA] **1 :** a bitter efflorescent crystalline levorotatory alkaloid $C_{20}H_{24}N_2O_2$ obtained from cinchona bark that is a diacid base forming two series of salts and is derived from methoxy-quinoline and quinuclidine and that is used in medicine esp. in the form of salts **2 :** any of the salts of quinine (as the hydrochlorides or sulfates) used as a febrifuge, antimalarial, antiperiodic, and bitter tonic

quinine bush *n* **1 :** a western American shrub of the genus *Garrya; esp* **:** BEAR BRUSH **2 :** CLIFF ROSE 2 **3** *Austral* **:** BITTERBARK 1a(1)

quinine cherry *n* **:** BITTER CHERRY

quinine flower *n* **:** a bitter herb (*Sabbatia elliottii*) of the southern U. S. that has star-shaped white flowers and is said to possess antiperiodic properties and to have been used as a substitute for quinine

quinine tree *n* **1 :** HORSERADISH TREE **2 :** HOP TREE **3 :** NATIVE QUINCE

quinine water *n* **:** a carbonated beverage flavored with a small amount of quinine, lemon, and lime

qui·nin·ic acid \(ˈ)kwī|ninik, kwəˈ|\ *n* [*quininic* ISV *quinine* + *-ic*] **:** a yellowish crystalline acid $CH_3OC_9H_5NCOOH$ obtained by oxidation of quinine or quinidine; 6-methoxycinchoninic acid

quin·i·tol \ˈkwinə,tȯl, -tōl\ *n* -S [*quin-* + *-itol*] **:** a crystalline cyclic glycol $C_6H_{10}(OH)_2$ obtained by reduction of hydroquinone in cis and trans forms having a sweet taste with a bitter aftertaste; 1,4-cyclohexane-diol

qui·niz·a·rin \kwəˈnizərən\ *n* -S [ISV *quin-* + *alizarin*] **:** a red crystalline compound $C_{14}H_6O_2(OH)_2$ isomeric with alizarin made from phthalic anhydride and either hydroquinone or *para*-chlorophenol and used as a dye intermediate and organic pigment; 1,4-dihydroxy-anthraquinone — see DYE table I (under *Pigment Violet 12*)

quink \ˈkwiŋk\ *or* **quink goose** *n* -S [imit.] **:** BRANT

quin·nat salmon \ˈkwinat-\ *also* **quinnat** *n* -S [*quinnat* fr. Interior Salish *t'kwinnat*] **:** KING SALMON

quin·ni·pi·ac \ˈkwinəpē,ak, ˌ===ˈ=\ *n, pl* **quinnipiac** *or* **quinnipiacs** *usu cap* **1 a :** an extinct Algonquian people of central Connecticut **b :** a member of such people **2 :** the Algonquian language of the Quinnipiac people

quino- — see QUIN-

qui·noa \kēˈnōə\ *or* **qui·nua** \ˈkēn,wä\ *n* -S [Sp, fr. Quechua *quinua*] **1 :** a pigweed (*Chenopodium quinoa*) of the high Andes of So. America **2 :** the seeds of the quinoa plant that are ground for food and widely used as a cereal in Peru

quino·cyanine \ˌkwi(ˌ)nō+\ *n* [*quin-* + *cyanine*] **:** a simple cyanine dye containing two quinoline rings

¹quinoid \ˈkwi,nȯid\ *var of* QUINONOID

²quinoid \"\ *n* -S **:** a quinonoid compound — **qui·noi·dal** \(ˈ)kwiˈnȯidˀl\ *adj*

qui·noi·dine \kwəˈnȯi,dēn, -ˌdˀn\ *or* **qui·noi·din** \-ˌdˀn\ *n* -S [ISV *quin-* + *-oid* + *-ine* or *-in*] **:** a bitter brownish resinous mixture often molded into sticks of amorphous alkaloids obtained as a by-product in the extraction of cinchona bark for crystalline alkaloids and formerly used as a substitute for quinine

quin·ol \ˈkwi,nȯl, -nōl\ *n* -S [*quin-* + *-ol*] **:** HYDROQUINONE

quinolin- *or* **quinolino-** *comb form* [ISV *quinoline*] **:** quinoline **:** quinolinic acid ⟨*quinolin*ic⟩ ⟨*quinolino*nitrile⟩

quin·o·line \ˈkwinˀl,ēn, -ˀlən\ *also* **chin·o·line** \ˈkin-\ *n* -S [ISV *quin-* or *chin-* + *-ol* + *-ine*] **1 :** a pungent oily nitrogenous base C_9H_7N that is obtained usu. by the distillation of coal tar or by synthesis from aniline, that is oxidized to quinolinic acid and nicotinic acid, and that is the parent compound of many alkaloids (as quinine), antimalarial drugs, amebicides, and dyes — compare ISOQUINOLINE, SKRAUP SYNTHESIS, STRUCTURAL FORMULA **2 :** a derivative of quinoline

quinoline

quinoline blue *n* **:** CYANINE 3

quinoline dye *n* **:** any of a small class of dyes derived from quinoline — see DYE table I

quinoline yellow *n, often cap Q&Y* **:** any of several quinoline dyes — see DYE table I (under *Acid Yellow 2* and *3*, *Direct Yellow 5*, and *Solvent Yellow 33*)

quin·o·lin·ic acid \ˌkwinˀlˈinik-\ *n* [*quinolinic* fr. *quinolin-* + *-ic*] **:** a crystalline acid $C_5H_3N(COOH)_2$ made by oxidizing quinoline and yielding nicotinic acid when heated; 2,3-pyridine-dicarboxylic acid

quin·o·lin·i·um \ˌkwinˀlˈinēəm\ *n* -S [NL, fr. *quinolin-* + *-ium*] **:** a univalent ion $[C_9H_7NH]^+$ that is analogous to ammonium and is derived from quinoline

quin·o·lin·ol \ˈkwinˀlə,nȯl, -,nōl\ *n* -S [*quinolin-* + *-ol*] **:** HYDROXYQUINOLINE

quin·o·lin·yl \-,nil\ *n* -S [*quinolin-* + *-yl*] **1 :** the bivalent radical $C_5H_3N(CO-)_2$ of quinolinic acid **2 :** QUINOLYL

qui·nol·o·gist \kwīˈnäləjəst, kwəˈn-\ *n* -S [ISV *quinology* + *-ist*] **:** a specialist in quinology

qui·nol·o·gy \-jē\ *n* -ES [ISV *quin-* + *-logy*] **:** the science dealing with the cultivation, chemistry, and medicinal use of the cinchonas

quin·o·lyl \ˈkwinˀl,il\ *n* -S [ISV *quinoline* + *-yl*] **:** any of seven univalent radicals C_9H_6N derived from quinoline by removal of one hydrogen atom

qui·none \kwəˈnōn, ˈkwi,nōn\ *also* **chi·none** \kəˈ-, ˈkwi,-\ *n* -S [ISV *quin-* or *chin-* + *-one*; orig. formed as G *chinon*] **1 :** either of two isomeric cyclic crystalline compounds $C_6H_4O_2$ that are diketo derivatives of dihydro-benzene: **a :** the pungent yellow para isomer obtained by oxidation of quinic acid or hydroquinone but usu. made by oxidation of aniline (as in the manufacture of hydroquinone) and used chiefly as an oxidizing agent — called also *benzoquinone, para-benzoquinone, p-benzoquinone, para-quinone, p-quinone;* compare QUINHYDRONE, STRUCTURAL FORMULA **b :** the red or colorless ortho isomer made by oxidation of pyrocatechol — called also *ortho-benzoquinone, o-benzoquinone, ortho-quinone, o-quinone* **2 :** any of various compounds containing quinone structures that are usu. yellow to orange (as in the para isomers) and orange to red (as in the ortho isomers) — compare ANTHRAQUINONE, NAPHTHOQUINONE

para isomer ortho isomer

quinone 1

quinone di·imine \-ˈdīə,mēn\ *n* [*diimine* fr. *di-* + *imine*] **1 :** a colorless crystalline compound $HN{=}C_6H_4{=}NH$ regarded as derived from quinone (sense 1a) by replacement of both oxygen atoms by imino groups but made by oxidation of *para*-phenylenediamine — called also *p-benzoquinone diimine, p-quinone diimine* **2 :** a compound derived from a quinone by replacement of both oxygen atoms by imino groups

quinone imine *or* **qui·non·imine** \kwəˈnōnə,mēn, -ˌmən\ *n* [ISV *quinone* + *imine*] **1 :** a colorless crystalline compound $O{=}C_6H_4{=}NH$ regarded as derived from quinone (sense 1a) by replacement of one oxygen atom by the imino group but made by oxidation of *para*-aminophenol — called also *p-benzoquinone imine, p-quinonimine* **2 :** a compound derived from a quinone by replacement of one or both oxygen atoms by the imino group

quinone oxime *n* **:** an oxime of a quinone; *esp* **:** the monoxime $O{=}C_6H_4{=}NOH$ of quinone (sense 1a) that is tautomeric with the para isomer of nitrosophenol

qui·non·iza·tion \kwə,nōnəˈzāshən, ˌkwi,nō-\ *n* -S [*quinonize* + *-ation*] **:** the formation of a quinone

qui·non·ize \kwəˈnō,nīz, ˈkwi,nō-\ *vt* -ED/-ING/-S *see -ize in Explan Notes* [*quinone* + *-ize*] **:** to cause to form a quinone

qui·no·noid \kwəˈnō,nȯid, ˈkwinə,nȯid\ *or* **quin·oid** \ˈkwi,nȯid\ *adj* [*quinonoid* fr. *quinone* + *-oid; quinoid* ISV *quin-* + *-oid*] **:** resembling quinone; *esp* **:** having a structure characterized by a benzene nucleus containing two instead of three double bonds within the nucleus and two external double bonds attached to the nucleus either at ortho or para positions (as in the two carbonyl groups of quinones) ⟨anthraquinone and related ~ dyes⟩

qui·no·nyl \kwəˈnōnˀl, ˈkwinə,nil\ *n* -S [*quinone* + *-yl*] **:** the univalent radical $C_6H_3O_2$ derived from quinone by removal of one hydrogen atom

quin·o·phan \ˈkwinə,fan\ *n* -S [*quin-* + *-phan* (irreg. fr. *phenyl*)] **:** CINCHOPHEN

quino·tannic acid \ˌkwinə+...-\ *n* [*quinotannic* ISV *quin-* + *tannic*] **:** a light yellow tannin found in cinchona bark

quino·toxine \ˌkwinō+\ *n* [ISV *quin-* + *toxine*] **:** QUINICINE

qui·no·va·tannic acid \kwəˈnōvə+...-\ *n* [ISV *quinova-* (fr. *quinovic*) + *tannic*] **:** a tannin obtained from the bark of a cinchona

qui·no·vic acid \kwəˈnōvik-\ *also* **quin·o·va·ic acid** \ˌkwinə-ˈvāik-\ *or* **chi·no·vic acid** \kəˈnōvik-\ *n* [ISV *quinov-, quinova-, chinov-* (contr. of NL *quina nova, china nova*, tree whose bark yields quinovin, fr. *quina, china* + *nova*, fem. of L *novus* new) + *-ic;* orig. formed as F *kinovique* — more at NEW] **:** a crystalline triterpene acid $C_{30}H_{46}O_5$ obtained by hydrolysis of quinovin

qui·no·vin \kwəˈnōvən\ *also* **chi·no·vin** \kəˈn-\ *n* -S [ISV *quinovic* (in *quinovic acid*) + *-in*] **:** a bitter crystalline glycoside found in cinchona and other barks

qui·no·vose *also* **chi·no·vose** \-vōs *also* -vōz\ *n* -S [*quinovin* + *-ose*] **:** a deoxy-hexose sugar $CH_3(CHOH)_4CHO$ formed by hydrolysis of quinovin; 6-deoxy-D-glucose

qui·nox·a·line \kwəˈnäksə,lēn, -ˌlən\ *also* **qui·nox·a·lin** \-ˌlən\ *n* -S [ISV *quin-* + *glyoxal* + *-ine* or *-in*] **1 :** a crystalline feebly basic compound $C_8H_6N_2$ made by condensing *ortho* phenylenediamine with glyoxal and regarded as derived from quinoline by substitution of a nitrogen atom for a methylidyne group in the 4-position **2 :** a derivative of quinoxaline

¹quin·qua·ge·nar·i·an \ˌkwinkwəjəˈna(a)rēən, (ˌ)kwinˌkwäj-\ *adj* [L *quinquagenarius* of fifty, fifty years old (fr. *quinquageni* fifty each — fr. *quinquaginta* fifty — + *-arius* -ary) + E *-an*] **:** fifty years old **:** characteristic of a person of such an age

²quinquagenarian \"\ *n* -S **:** a quinquagenarian person

¹quin·quag·e·nary \kwinˈkwäjə,nerē\ *n* -ES [L *quinquagenarius*] **:** a fiftieth anniversary

²quinquagenary \"\ *adj* [L *quinquagenarius*] **:** QUINQUAGENARIAN

quin·qua·ges·i·ma \ˌkwinkwəˈjesəmə, -jāzəmə\ *n* -S *usu cap* [ML, fr. L, fiftieth, fr. *quinquaginta* fifty, fr. *quinqua-* (akin to L *quinque* five) + *-ginta* (akin to L *-ginti* in *viginti* twenty) — more at FIVE, VICENARY] **1** *obs* **:** the period extending from the Sunday before Lent to Easter Sunday or the first week of this period **2 :** the Sunday before Lent or the seventh before Easter in the church year observed by various branches of the Christian Church — called also *Quinquagesima Sunday, Shrove Sunday*

quin·qua·ges·i·mal \ˌ==ˈ==məl\ *adj* [ML *quinquagesima* + E *-al*] **:** occurring in a season of fifty days **:** consisting of fifty days ⟨the ~ period between Easter and Pentecost⟩

quin·quan·gle \ˈkwin,kwaŋgəl\ *n* -S [LL *quinquangulus* five-cornered, fr. L *quinque-* + *angulus* corner, angle — more at ANGLE] *archaic* **:** PENTAGON

quin·quan·gu·lar \(ˈ)kwinˈkwaŋgyələ(r)\ *adj* [LL *quinquangulus* + E *-ar*] *archaic* **:** PENTAGONAL

quin·quar·tic·u·lar \ˌkwin,kwärˈtikyələ(r)\ *adj* [NL *quinquarticularis*, fr. L *quinque-* + *articulus* joint, division of a discourse, article + *-aris* -ar — more at ARTICLE] **:** relating to five articles or points ⟨~ dispute between Arminians and Calvinists⟩

quinque- *or* **quinqu-** *comb form* [L, fr. *quinque* five — more at FIVE] **1 :** five ⟨*quinque*capsular⟩ ⟨*quinque*lateral⟩ **2 :** into five parts ⟨*quinque*section⟩

quin·que·foliolate \ˌkwinkwə+\ *adj* [*quinque-* + *foliole* + *-ate*] **:** having five leaflets

¹quin·que·literal *or* **quin·qui·literal** \ˌkwinkwə+\ *adj* [*quinque-* + *literal*] **:** consisting of five letters or consonants — used esp. of Hebrew roots

²quinqueliteral *or* **quinquiliteral** \"\ *n* **:** a quinqueliteral character

quin·quen·a·ry \(ˈ)kwinˈkwenərē, ˈkwinkwə,nerē\ *adj* [*quinque-* + *-nary* (as in *quinary*)] **:** QUINARY

quin·quen·na·lia \ˌkwinkwəˈnālēə\ *n pl* [L, neut. pl. of *quinquennalis*, fr. *quinquennium* period of five years + *-alis* -al] **:** public games celebrated in ancient Rome every five years

quin·quen·ni·ad \kwinˈkwenē,ad\ *n* -S [L *quinquennium* + E *-ad*] **:** QUINQUENNIUM

¹quin·quen·nial \(ˈ)kwinˈkwenēəl, -enyəl\ *adj* [ME *quinqueniale*, fr. MF *quinquennial*, fr. L *quinquennium* period of five years (fr. *quinque-* + *-ennium*, fr. *annus* year) + MF *-al* — more at ANNUAL] **1 :** occurring once in five years ⟨~ enumeration⟩ **:** occurring at the end of every five years **2 :** lasting five years ⟨a ~ grant⟩ ⟨has a place in the ~ and annual economic plans of the country —J.P.M.Somerville⟩

²quinquennial \"\ *n* -S **:** a quinquennial term or office

quin·quen·nial·ly \-əlē, -əli\ *adv* **:** every five years

quin·quen·ni·um \kwinˈkwenēəm\ *n, pl* **quinquenniums** \-ēəmz\ *or* **quin·quen·nia** \-ēə\ [L] **:** a period of five years

quin·que·reme *also* **quin·qui·reme** \ˈkwinkwə,rēm\ *n* -S [MF, fr. L *quinqueremis*, lit., having five banks of oars, fr. *quinque-* + *remus* oar — more at ROW] **:** an ancient galley propelled by five banks of oars

quin·que·valent *also* **quin·qui·valent** \ˌkwinkwə+\ *adj* [*quinque-* + *valent;* trans. of G *fünfwertig*] **:** PENTAVALENT

quin·que·vir \ˈkwinkwə,vi(ə)r\ *n, pl* **quinquevirs** \-rz\ *or* **quin·quev·i·ri** \kwinˈkwevə,rī\ [L, fr. *quinque-* + *vir* man — more at VIRILE] **:** one of a commission, council, or ruling body of five (as in ancient Rome)

quin·quev·i·rate \kwinˈkwevərət, -ˌrāt\ *n* -S [L *quinqueviratus*, fr. *quinquevir* + *-atus* -ate] **1 :** the office or government of quinquevirs **2 :** a body of quinquevirs

quin·que vo·ces \ˌkwiŋ(ˌ)kwāˈwō,kās\ *n pl* [L, five words] **:** the five predicables of traditional logic

quin·qui·na \kinˈkēnə\ *n* -S [Sp — more at QUININE] *archaic* **:** CINCHONA

quins *pl of* QUIN

quin·sied \ˈkwinz|ēd, |id *sometimes* -n(t)s|\ *adj* **:** affected with quinsy

quin·sy \|ē, |i\ *n* -ES [ME *quinsie, quinesie* inflammation of the throat, modif. of MF *quinancie*, fr. LL *cynanche*, fr. Gk *kynanchē* sore throat, dog's quinsy, fr. *kyōn* dog + *anchein* to strangle — more at HOUND, ANGER] **:** PERITONSILLAR ABSCESS

quinsyberry \ˈ==- — *see* BERRY\ *n* **1 :** an Old World black currant (*Ribes nigrum*) that yields a jelly used esp. formerly as a remedy for quinsy **2 :** NORTHERN BLACK CURRANT

¹quint \ˈk(w)int, ˈkant, ˈkaⁿt\ *n* -S [in sense 1, fr. MF, lit., fifth, fr. L *quintus;* in other senses, fr. F *quinte*, fem. of *quint* fifth, fr. MF; akin to L *quinque* five — more at FIVE] **1** *or* **quinte** \"\ *archaic* **:** a tax of one fifth **2 :** a sequence of 5 playing cards of the same suit ⟨a ~ in piquet⟩ **3** *or* **quinte** **a :** the musical interval of a fifth **b :** a pipe-organ stop giving tones a fifth higher than the normal pitch of the digitals **c :** the smallest of the three kinds of viola da braccio **d :** the E string of a violin **e :** QUINTON

²quint \ˈkwint\ *n* -S [by shortening] **:** QUINTUPLET

³quint \"\ *n* -S [by shortening] **:** QUINTET 2c

quint *abbr* **1** quintuple **2** [L *quintus*] fifth

quint- *or* **quinti-** *comb form* [ME, fr. MF, fr. L, fr. *quintus;* akin to L *quinque* five — more at FIVE] **1 :** fifth ⟨*quint*illion⟩ **2 :** QUINQUE- ⟨*quinti*ped⟩ **3 :** a (specified) musical instrument having its pitch a fifth above the normal

quin·ta \ˈkintə, ˈkēn-\ *n* -S [Sp & Pg, quinta, ranch, farm rented at one fifth of its income, fr. L, fem. of *quintus* fifth] **:** a country or suburban house with a garden, vineyard, or orchard **:** ESTATE, VILLA

quin·ta·de·na \ˌkwintəˈdēnə\ *also* **quin·ta·dene** \ˈ==,dēn\ *n* -S [NL *quintadena*, prob. fr. L *quintus* fifth + NL *-dena* twelfth (fr. L *duodeni* twelve each); fr. its sounding of the twelfth, or fifth of the second octave — more at DUODENARY] **:** a pipe-organ stop of narrow covered metal or wood pipes giving with its own fundamental a pronounced harmonic fifth in the second octave above and of 4-foot, 8-foot, or 16-foot pitch

1quin·tain \ˈkwintᵊn\ *n* -s [ME *quintaine*, fr. MF, fr. L *quintana* street in a Roman camp separating the fifth maniple from the sixth where military exercises were performed, fr. fem. of *quintanus* fifth in rank, fr. *quintus* fifth + *-anus* -an] **1 :** an object to be tilted at; *esp* **:** a post with a crosspiece having at one end a broad board and at the other end a sandbag used esp. in the middle ages in a sport the object of which was to strike the board with a lance while riding under and to get past without being hit by the sandbag **2 :** the sport of tilting at a quintain

2quintain *n* -s [*quinti-* + *-ain* (as in *quatrain*)] *obs* **:** a five-line stanza

quin·tal \ˈkwintᵊl\ *n* -s [ME, hundredweight, metric weight of 100 kilograms, fr. MF, fr. ML *quintale*, fr. Ar *qinṭār* — more at KANTAR] **1 :** any of various units of weight used esp. in Latin American and Mediterranean countries and equal to from 100 to about 130 pounds **:** HUNDREDWEIGHT **2 :** a metric unit equal to 100 kilograms — see METRIC SYSTEM table

quin·tan \ˈkwintᵊn, -tən\ *adj* [L *quintanus*, fr. *quintus* fifth + *-anus* -an] **:** occurring as the fifth after four others; *also* **:** occurring every fifth day reckoning inclusively ⟨a ~ fever⟩

quin·tant \-nt²nt,-ntənt\ *n* -s [*quint-* + *-ant* (as in *quadrant*)] **:** a portable instrument similar to a sextant but with an arc of 72 degrees and capable of measuring angles of twice that

quin·ta·to \kwin·ˈtäd·(ˌ)ō\ *n* -s [alter. of *quintaton*] **:** QUINTADENA

quin·ta·ton \ˈkwintə,ˌtōn, ˌ==ˈ=\ *also* **quin·ta·ten** \ˌten\ *n* -s [*quintaton* fr. G, modif. (influenced by *ton* tone, fr. MHG *tōn*, fr. L *tonus*) of NL *quintadena*; *quintaten* prob. modif. of G *quintaton* — more at TONE] **:** QUINTADENA

quinte \ˈkant, ˈkaⁿt\ *n* -s [F, fr. L *quinta*, fem. of *quintus* fifth; akin to L *quinque* five; fr. its being the fifth of the eight parrying positions — more at FIVE] **1 :** a parry with a foil or épée that defends the lower inside target with the hand to the left at waist height in a position of pronation with the tip of the blade higher than the hand — compare SEPTIME **2 :** a parry with a saber that protects the head with the hand and forearm raised above the head and the hand held to the right in a position of pronation with the point of the blade to the left and higher than the hand

quin·ter·ni·on \kwin·ˈtərnēən\ *n* -s [*quint-* + *-ernion* (as in *quaternion*)] **:** five sheets of paper combined into a set or section

1quin·tes·sence \kwin·ˈtesᵊn(t)s *archaic* ˈkwintəsən-\ *n* [ME, fr. MF *quinte essence*, fr. ML *quinta essentia* (trans. of Gk *pemptē ousia*), fr. L *quinta* (fem. of *quintus* fifth) + *essentia* essence — more at ESSENCE] **1 a :** the fifth or last and highest substance in ancient and medieval philosophy above fire, air, water, and earth that permeates all nature and is the constituent matter of the celestial bodies **:** ETHER 1b **b** *old chem* **:** an alcoholic tincture obtained by extraction **2 :** the essence of an esp. immaterial thing in its purest and most concentrated form **:** the most perfect or rarest distillation or extract ⟨the ~ of music is, after all, melody —Winthrop Sargeant⟩ ⟨gets his articles down to digests and his digests down to ~*s* in single paragraphs or sentences —F.L.Mott⟩ **3 :** the most typical example or representative **:** the consummate instance (as of a quality or class) ⟨the ~ of pride⟩ ⟨the ~ of all the heroines of fiction —*Saturday Rev.*⟩

2quintessence \"\ *vt* -ED/-ING/-S **:** QUINTESSENTIALIZE ⟨love *quintessenced* and alembicated till it hardly knows itself — Gamaliel Bradford⟩

1quin·tes·sen·tial \ˌkwintəˈsenchəl\ *adj* [fr. *1quintessence*, after E *essence: essential*] **:** being a quintessence **:** purest of its kind **:** TYPICAL ⟨~ extract of mediocrity —George Eliot⟩ ⟨the task of defining primary or ~ literary value —C.W.Shumaker⟩ ⟨not aristocrats, but ~ proletarians —M.S.Dworkin⟩ — **quin·tes·sen·ti·al·i·ty** \ˌ==ˌ=chēˈaləd·ē\ *n* — **quin·tes·sen·tial·ly** \ˌ==ˈsench(ə)lē\ *adv*

2quintessential \"\ *n* **:** a quintessential element — usu. used in pl. ⟨compendium of the essentials and the ~*s* of originality — J.L.Lowes⟩ ⟨compress the ~*s* of the metropolis's metabolism into a book —Cleveland Rodgers⟩

quin·tes·sen·tial·ize \ˌ==ˈsenchə,līz\ *vt* [*quintessential* + *-ize*] **1 :** to distill or extract as a quintessence **2 :** to extract the quintessence of

quin·tet *also* **quin·tette** \(ˈ)kwin·ˈtet, *usu* -ed·+V\ *n* -s [*quintet* fr. It *quintetto*, dim. of *quinto* fifth, fr. *quinto*, adj., fifth, fr. L *quintus*; *quintette* fr. F, fr. It *quintetto*] **1 :** a musical composition or movement for five singers or five instrumentalists with or without accompaniment **2 a :** a group of five persons who sing or play five-part music **b :** any group or set of five ⟨a ~ of names seldom found in isolation — *Irish Statesman*⟩ ⟨took a rough bearing and led the surviving ~ across the hard flat ground —Fred Majdalany⟩ ⟨as the ~ came up the sidewalk —Peggy Bennett⟩ **c :** a male basketball team **3 :** a game similar to tenpins except that only five pins arranged triangularly are used

quin·tet·to \kwin·ˈted·(ˌ)ō\ *n* -s [It] **:** QUINTET ⟨this amiable and enlightened ~ —T.L.Peacock⟩

quinti- — see QUINT-

1quin·tic \ˈkwintik\ *adj* [*quint-* + *-ic*] **1 :** of the fifth degree **2 :** having five links ⟨a ~ chain⟩

2quintic \"\ *n* -s **:** a polynomial or polynomial equation of the fifth degree

quin·tile \ˈkwin·ˌtīl, -ntᵊl, -n(ˌ)tīl\ *n* -s [*quint-* + *-ile*] **1** *obs* **:** the aspect of planets when separated a fifth part of a circle or 72 degrees **2 :** any of the four values that divide the items of a frequency distribution into five classes each containing one fifth of the total number of items such that the values corresponding to the items in one class are less than the first quintile, those in a second class are greater than the first quintile and less than the second quintile, and so on throughout

quin·til·lian \kwin·ˈtilyən\ *n* -s *usu cap* [*Quintilla*, believed to be a prophetess of the sect + E *-ian*] **:** one of a party of Montanists of the 2d century A.D.

1quin·til·lion \kwin·ˈtilyən\ *n* -s [*quint-* + *-illion* (as in *million*)] — see NUMBER table

2quintillion \"\ *adj* **:** being a quintillion in number

1quin·til·lionth \(ˈ)ˌ=ˈ=yən(t)th\ *adj* **1 :** being number one quintillion in a countable series — see NUMBER table **2 :** being one of a quintillion equal parts into which anything is divided

2quintillionth \"\ *n, pl* **quintillionths** \-yən(t)s, -n(t)ths\ **:** one of a quintillion equal parts of anything

quin·tin·ia \kwin·ˈtinēə, kan-·\ *n, cap* [NL, after Jean de la *Quintinie* †1688 Fr. botanist] **:** a small genus of New Zealand and in some classifications Philippine shrubs and trees (family Saxifragaceae) with alternate leaves and axillary or terminal racemes of white or lilac flowers — see KUMARAHOU b, OPOSSUM WOOD

quin·tole \ˈkwin·ˌtōl\ *or* **quin·to·let** \ˌkwintᵊlˈet\ *n* -s [*quintole* fr. *quint-* + *-ole* (dim. suffix); *quintolet* fr. *quintole* + *-et*] **:** QUINTUPLET 3

quin·ton \kaⁿˈtōⁿ\ *n, pl* **quintons** \-(z)\ [F, fr. *quint* fifth, fr. MF — more at QUINT] **:** a five-stringed violin tuned g, d′, a′, d″, g″

quin·troon \(ˈ)kwin·ˈtrün\ *n* -s [Sp *quinterón*, fr. *quinto* fifth, fr. L *quintus*] **:** the offspring of an octoroon and a white

quints *pl of* QUINT

1quin·tu·ple \(ˈ)kwin·ˈt(y)üpəl *also* -təp- *or* ˈkwin‿təp-\ *adj* [MF, fr. LL *quintuplic-, quintuplex*, fr. L *quintus* fifth (akin to L *quinque* five) + *-plic-, -plex* -fold — more at FIVE, SINGLE] **1 a :** consisting of five **:** being five times as great or as many **:** FIVEFOLD **b :** taken by fives or in groups of five **2 :** having five beats — used of a musical measure

2quintuple \"\ *n* -s **:** a sum five times as great as another **:** a fivefold amount **:** the fifth multiple

3quintuple \"\ *vb* **quintupled; quintupled; quintupling** \-p(ə)liŋ\ **quintuples** *vt* **:** to make five times as much or as many ~ *vi* **:** to become five times as much or as many

quintuple point *n* **:** a point representing a set of conditions under which five phases of a physical-chemical system can exist in equilibrium

quin·tu·plet \(ˈ)kwin·ˈtəplət, -ˈt(y)üp- *sometimes* -n‿təp-; *usu* -əd·+V\ *n* -s [*1quintuple* + *-et*] **1 :** a combination of five of a kind **2 a :** one of five children or offspring born at one birth **b quintuplets** *pl* **:** a group of five such offspring **3 :** a group of five musical notes to be played or sung in the time of four of the same value

1quin·tu·pli·cate \(ˈ)kwin·ˈtüplə̇kə̇t, -lēk- *sometimes* -lə-, ˌkā|; *usu* |d·+V\ *adj* [L *quintuplicatus*, past part. of *quintuplicare* to quintuplicate, fr. *quintuplic-, quintuplex* quintuple] **:** made in five identical copies **:** FIVEFOLD

2quintuplicate \"\ *n* -s **1 :** a fifth thing like four others of the same kind **2 :** five copies all alike — used with *in* ⟨typed in ~⟩

3quin·tu·pli·cate \-lə,kāt, *usu* -ād·+V\ *vt* -ED/-ING/-S **:** to multiply by five **:** QUINTUPLE **:** reproduce four times; *specif* **:** to make at one time an original and four carbon copies of

quin·tu·ply \(ˈ)kwin·ˈt(y)üplē, -li *also* -təp- *or* ˈkwin‿təp-\ *adv* **:** in a quintuple manner **:** in fivefold quantity

quin·tus \ˈkwintəs\ *n* -ES [ML, fr. L, fifth] **:** a fifth voice or part in medieval music

quinua *var of* QUINOA

qui·nu·cli·dine \kwə̇ˈnüklə,dēn, -ˌdə̇n\ *n* -s [*quinine* + *nucl-* (fr. *nucle-*) + *-idine*] **:** a crystalline bicyclic base $C_7H_{13}N$ of which quinine and related alkaloids are derivatives

quin·yie \ˈkwin(y)ē\ *n* -s [alter. of *cunyie* coin, corner, fr. ME *cunye* — more at CUNYIE] **1** *Scot* **:** COIN **2** *Scot* **:** CORNER

quin·zaine \(ˈ)kaⁿˈzān, (ˈ)kanˈ-\ *n* -s [F, fr. MF, fr. *quinze* fifteen, fr. L *quindecim* — more at QUINDECIM] **:** a period of 15 days; *specif* **:** an ecclesiastical period comprising a feast day and the fortnight after or (as at Easter) the week before and the week after

quin·zième \(ˈ)kaⁿˈzyem, (ˈ)kanz-\ *n* -s [ME *quinsime*, fr. MF *quinzime* fifteenth, fr. *quinze* fifteen] *archaic* **:** a tax of a fifteenth

1quip \ˈkwip\ *n* -s [earlier *quippy*, perh. fr. L *quippe* indeed, to be sure (often ironical), fr. *quid* what, anything, something — more at QUID] **1 a :** a clever usu. taunting remark **:** GIBE ⟨a political candidate getting off ~*s* at his rival's expense⟩ **b :** a witty or funny observation or response usu. made on the spur of the moment ⟨the ~*s* and puns of poor comedians⟩ **2 :** QUIBBLE, EQUIVOCATION **3 :** something strange, droll, curious, or eccentric **:** ODDITY **syn** see JOKE

2quip \"\ *vb* **quipped; quipped; quipping; quips** *vi* **:** to make quips **:** GIBE — often used with *at* ⟨*quipping* at people making critical remarks⟩ ~ *vt* **:** to jest or gibe at **:** assail with quips

quip·per \-pə(r)\ *n* -s **:** one that quips

quip·pish \-pish\ *adj* [*quip* + *-ish*] **:** witty or taunting esp. in response — **quippish·ness** *n* -ES

quip·ster \-pstə(r)\ *n* -s [*quip* + *-ster*] **:** a person adept in making quips

qui·pu \ˈkē(ˌ)pü\ *also* **qui·po** \-pō\ *n* -s [Sp *quipo*, fr. Quechua *quipu*] **:** a contrivance consisting of a main cord with smaller varicolored cords attached and knotted and employed by the ancient Peruvians for calculating and record keeping (as of important facts and events)

qui·ra \ˈkērə\ *n* -s [AmerSp] **1 :** any of several tropical American trees constituting a genus (*Platymiscium*) of the family Leguminosae, having pinnate leaves and yellow flowers, and including several (as *P. polystachyum* and *P. pinnatum*) that yield economically important timber **2 :** the reddish brown heavy wood of a quira — see PANAMA REDWOOD

1quire \ˈkwī(ə)r, -īə\ *n* -s [ME *quair*, fr. MF *quaer*, fr. (assumed) VL *quadernum*, alter. (influenced by L *quadrum* square) of L *quaterni* set of four, four each, fr. *quater* four times; akin to L *quattuor* four — more at FOUR] **1 a :** four sheets (as of paper) folded together into eight leaves **b :** a set of folded sheets (as of a book) fitting one within another **2 :** a collection of 24 or sometimes 25 sheets of paper of the same size and quality either not folded or having a single fold — compare REAM **3** *obs* **:** a small book or pamphlet that makes up or could make up a quire **:** a work (as a poem or essay) that is or might be contained in a quire — **in quires :** in sheets **:** UNBOUND ⟨a book *in quires*⟩

2quire \"\ *vt* -ED/-ING/-S **:** to make or divide into quires or so that folded sheets may be placed one within another ⟨~ sheets for a catalog⟩; *also* **:** to fold (paper) in half when packing in reams

3quire *var of* CHOIR

quirewise \ˈ=,=\ *adv* [*quire* + *wise*] **:** in quires so as to allow one sheet to be fitted within another ⟨print a pamphlet ~⟩

quir·is·ter \ˈkwirəstə(r)\ *n* -s [ME *querister* — more at CHORISTER] **:** CHORISTER

quir·i·tar·i·an \ˌkwirəˈterēən\ *adj* [ML *quiritarius* of Roman civil law (fr. L *Quirit-, Quiris* Roman citizen — prob. fr. (assumed) OL *coviriom* assemblage of citizens, fr. L *co-* + *-virius*, fr. *vir* man — + *-arius* -ary) + E *-an* — more at VIRILE] **1 :** of, relating to, or constituting the old law of Rome as distinguished from the law introduced by the praetor on equitable principles **2 :** conforming to or enforced by the quiritarian law **:** legal as opposed to equitable or beneficial

quir·i·tary \ˈkwirə,terē\ *adj* [ML *quiritarius*] **:** QUIRITARIAN

1quirk \ˈkwərk, -wə̄k, -wəik\ *n* -s [origin unknown] **1 :** a triangular shaped area: as **a** (1) *dial Eng* **:** a hosiery clock (2) **:** a small gusset set in at the base of a thumb or the fingers of a glove **b :** a diamond-shaped windowpane **2 :** an abrupt turn, twist, or curve or other deviation from a regular course or pattern **:** BEND, CROOK: as **a** (1) **:** a turn of a pen in writing **:** FLOURISH (2) *obs* **:** a sudden whimsical turn or phrase in music **b** (1) **:** a clever retort **:** CONCEIT, QUIP (2) **:** a clever or cunning evasion **:** SUBTERFUGE, QUIBBLE **c :** a peculiarity of action, behavior, or bearing **:** MANNERISM **3** *obs* **:** a sudden fit **:** short paroxysm **4 a :** a small channel or groove separating a bead or other molding from the adjoining members — see QUIRK MOLDING **b :** the bead or fillet of a grooving plane in woodworking

2quirk \"\ *vb* -ED/-ING/-S *vt* **1 :** to subject to quirks or quips **2 :** to give a quirk to ⟨holding her skirts with ~*ed* fingers —Rosamond Lehmann⟩ ⟨a peculiarly ~*ed* mouth⟩; *specif* **:** to fashion (as molding) with quirks **3 :** to strike with a sharp sudden jerk of a whip ⟨the coachman lets fly his whip and ~*s* his off-wheeler on the thigh —Amy Lowell⟩ ~ *vi* **:** to make or exhibit a quirk ⟨Annie's mouth ~*ed* a little —G.W.Brace⟩; *specif* **:** to speak or act with a quirk of manner

quirk bead *or* **quirked bead** *n* **:** a bead and groove at the edge of a board or panel — compare COCK BEAD, RETURN-COCKED BEAD; see BEAD illustration

quirk·i·ly \-kəlē\ *adv* **:** in a quirky manner ⟨a ~ entertaining way⟩ ⟨a ~ humorous personality⟩

quirk·i·ness \-kēnə̇s\ *n* -ES **:** the quality or state of being quirky

quirk molding *n* **:** a molding distinctly set off by quirks

quirky \-kē\ *adj* -ER/-EST **1 :** full of quirks **:** TRICKY ⟨a ~ lawyer⟩ **2 :** having, exhibiting, or suggesting sharp or unexpected turns, features, or qualities ⟨the inns of New England, indeed, have a ~ character all their own —B.M.Bowie⟩ ⟨~ and individualistic music —Irving Kolodin⟩

quirk molding

quirl \ˈkwər(·ə)l\ *chiefly Midland var of* CURL

quir·quin·cho \kirˈkin(ˌ)chō\ *n* -s [AmerSp, fr. Quechua *quirquinchu* armadillo] **1 :** PICHI **2 :** PELUDO

1quirt \ˈkwər|t, -wə̄|, -wəi|, *usu* |d·+V\ *n* -s [MexSp *cuarta* quirt, whip, prob. fr. *cuarta* lead mule, lead mule of a four-mule team, fr. Sp, fem. of *cuarto* fourth, fr. L *quartus* — more at QUART] **:** a riding whip used esp. in the western U.S. and consisting of a short handle (as of wood or leather) to which is attached a rawhide lash

2quirt \"\ *vt* -ED/-ING/-S **:** to strike, coerce, or drive with or as if with a quirt

quis \ˈkwis\ *n* -ES [perh. fr. L, who] **:** a European woodcock

qui·sle \ˈkwizəl\ *vi* -ED/-ING/-S [back-formation fr. *quisling*] **:** to serve or act as a quisling

quis·ler \-z(ə)lə(r)\ *n* -s [*quisle* + *-er*] **:** QUISLING

quis·ling \ˈkwizliŋ, -lēŋ\ *n* -s [after Vidkun *Quisling* †1945 Norw. politician] **:** a traitorous national who aids the invader of his country and often serves as chief agent or puppet governor

quis·ling·ism \-ŋ,izəm\ *n* -s [*quisling* + *-ism*] **:** TREASON; *esp* **:** the betrayal by a national of his own country followed by his enjoyment of high position under the protection of the alien occupying power

quirt

quis·qual·is \kwə̇sˈkwāləs\ *n, cap* [NL, fr. L *quis* who + *qualis* of what kind — more at WHO, QUALITY] **:** a small genus of tropical Asiatic, Indo-Malayan, and African woody vines (family Combretaceae) having red or orange spicate flowers with a superior calyx whose limb is deciduous from the long tube and a fruit possessed of five wings — see RANGOON CREEPER

quis·que·ite \ˈkiskə,īt\ *n* -s [*Quisque*, district near Mina Ragra, Pasco, Peru, its locality + E *-ite*] **:** a brittle black lustrous substance mostly composed of sulfur and carbon and accompanying the vanadium ores of Peru **:** sulfurous asphaltum

qui·sutsch \ˈkē,səch\ *n* -ES [native name in Kamchatka and Alaska] **:** SILVER SALMON

1quit \ˈkwit, *usu* -id·+V\ *adj* [ME *quit, quite*, fr. OF *quite*] **1 :** released from obligation, charge, or penalty **:** ABSOLVED, ACQUITTED; *esp* **:** FREE ⟨~ of unnecessary fears⟩ **2** *obs* **:** DESTITUTE, BEREFT — used with *of* **3** *obs* **:** QUITS

2quit \"\ *vb* **quit** *also* **quitted; quit** *also* **quitted; quitting; quits** [ME *quiten, quitten*, fr. MF *quiter, quitter*, fr. OF, fr. *quite* free of, released, calm, fr. L *quietus* calm, quiet — more at QUIET] *vt* **1 :** to set free **:** RELIEVE, RELEASE ⟨~ me of fear⟩ **2 :** to pay up **:** DISCHARGE ⟨may fairly ~ the debt —William Cowper⟩ **3 :** CONDUCT, ACQUIT ⟨youths ~ themselves like men⟩ **4 :** to leave or leave off from: as **a :** to depart from or out of ⟨as soon as she *quitted* the room he returned to it —W.H. Hudson †1922⟩ ⟨*quitted* Cambridge . . . before being formally ejected —Douglas Bush⟩ **b :** to leave esp. peremptorily the company of ⟨the hero *quitted* him with some contempt —George Meredith⟩ **c :** to give over (as a way of thought, acting, or living) **:** RELINQUISH, ABANDON, FORSAKE ⟨a tribe that *quitted* the plains for the mountains⟩ **d :** to terminate (as an action, activity, or employment) esp. with finality **:** LEAVE ⟨~ a job⟩ ~ *vi* **1 :** to leave off or cease normal, expected, or necessary action ⟨the engine coughed, sputtered, and ~⟩ **2 :** to give up employment **:** stop working **:** LEAVE ⟨a worker *quitting* because of poor pay⟩ **3 :** to give up **:** admit defeat **:** stop struggling, fighting, or contending ⟨despairing creatures who have ~ on life —*Time*⟩ **syn** see BEHAVE, GO, STOP

3quit \"\ *n* -s **1 :** the act or action of quitting ⟨a factory with many ~*s* per year among its workers⟩ **2 :** tendency to quit ⟨a fighter with little ~ in him⟩

4quit \"\ *n* -s [prob. imit.] **:** any of various small passerine birds chiefly of the West Indies (as banana quit and grassquit)

qui tam \ˈkwīˈtam\ *or* **qui tam action** *n* -s [LL, lit., who as much, who as well; fr. the first words of the clause referring to the plaintiff as one who sues as much for the state as for himself] **:** an action to recover a penalty under a statute that gives part of the penalty to the one bringing the action and the rest to the state or a public body — compare POPULAR ACTION

quitch \ˈkwich\ *or* **quitch grass** *n* -ES [fr. (assumed) ME *quicche*, fr. OE *cwice*; akin to MD *queke* couch grass, OHG *quecca*, Sw dial. *kvicka, kveka*, Norw dial. *kvika*; all fr. a prehistoric Gmc word derived fr. the adj. represented by OE *cwic* alive — more at QUICK] **:** COUCH GRASS 1a

1quitclaim *vt* [ME *quite-claimen*, fr. MF *quiteclamer*, lit., to declare free, fr. OF, fr. *quite* free, free of + *clamer* to declare, claim — more at CLAIM] **1** *obs* **:** ACQUIT **2 :** to release or relinquish a legal claim to; *esp* **:** to release a claim to or convey by a quitclaim deed

2quit·claim \ˈkwit,klām\ *n* [ME *quite-claim*, fr. MF *quiteclame*, fr. *quiteclamer* to quitclaim] **:** a release of a claim **:** a deed of release; *specif* **:** a legal instrument by which some right, title, interest, or claim by one person in or to an estate held by himself or another is released to another and which is sometimes used as a simple but effective conveyance for making a grant of lands whether by way of release or as an original conveyance

1quite \ˈkwīt, *usu* -īd·+V\ *adv* [ME, fr. *quite, quit*, adj., released, free — more at QUIT] **1 :** COMPLETELY, WHOLLY, TOTALLY ⟨work not ~ done⟩ ⟨~ mistaken⟩ ⟨not ~ master of himself⟩ **2 :** to an extreme **:** POSITIVELY ⟨~ the rage⟩ ⟨~ drunk⟩ ⟨~ so⟩ **3 :** to a considerable extent **:** PRETTY, RATHER ⟨~ near⟩ ⟨~ ill⟩ ⟨~ rich⟩

2qui·te \ˈkē(ˌ)tā\ *n* -s [Sp, lit., act of taking away, fr. *quitar* to take away, release, prob. fr. LL *quietare* to set free, calm — more at QUIET] **:** a series of passes made by a matador with his cape to draw the bull away from a horse or fallen picador

quitely *adv* [ME, fr. *quit, quite*, adj., free + *-ly*] *obs* **:** ENTIRELY, QUITE

qui·to \ˈkē(ˌ)tō\ *adj, usu cap* [fr. *Quito*, Ecuador] **:** of or from Quito, the capital of Ecuador **:** of the kind or style prevalent in Quito

quit·rent \ˈkwit·,rent\ *n* [ME *quiterent*, fr. *quite, quit* free + *rent*] **:** a fixed rent usu. small in amount and payable by a freeholder or copyholder to his feudal superior in commutation of services; *specif* **:** a fixed rent due from a socage tenant

1quits \ˈkwits\ *adj* [ME, released from liability, prob. fr. ML *quittus* quit, free, fr. *quietus* free, calm, fr. L, calm, quiet — more at QUIET] **1** *obs* **:** released or cleared from liability **2 :** even or equal with another or each other by repayment of an obligation or by requital (as of a favor or injury)

2quits \"\ *n pl* **:** RECOMPENSE, RETALIATION

3quits *pres 3d sing of* QUIT, *pl of* QUIT

quittal *n* -s [*2quit* + *-al*] *obs* **:** REQUITAL; *also* **:** ACQUITTAL

1quit·tance \ˈkwitᵊn(t)s\ *n* -s [ME *quitance, quetaunce*, fr. OF *quittance*, fr. *quitter* to release, quit + *-ance* — more at QUIT] **1 a :** the act of freeing or releasing; *specif* **:** discharge from a debt or an obligation **b :** a document evidencing quittance **2 :** RECOMPENSE, REQUITAL ⟨money received in ~ of wrongs⟩

2quittance *vt, obs* **:** REPAY, REQUITE; *also* **:** to give up

quitted *past of* QUIT

quitted trick *n* **:** a trick in card games after all of the cards composing it have been irrevocably played and it has been stacked with the cards in it facedown

1quitter *n* -s [ME *quittere, quiture* pus, quittor] **1** *obs* **:** matter discharged from a sore **:** PUS **2** *obs* **:** slag from tin smelting

2quit·ter \ˈkwid·ə(r), -itə-\ *n* -s [*2quit* + *-er*] **1 :** one that quits a task, danger, or trial **:** COWARD **2 :** a young male fur seal making its first entrance upon the breeding grounds from which it may easily be driven by old bulls already established

quitting *pres part of* QUIT

quit·tor \ˈkwid·ə(r), -itə-\ *n* -s [ME *quittere, quiture* pus, quittor, prob. fr. OF *quiture, cuiture* act of boiling, act of cooking, fr. L *coctura*, fr. *coctus* (past part. of *coquere* to cook, boil) + *-ura* -ure — more at COOK] **:** a purulent inflammation (as a necrobacillosis) of the feet of horses and other solidungulates occurring chiefly in a cartilaginous form characterized by a chronic persistent inflammation of the lateral cartilage of the foot leading to suppuration and the formation of one or more fistulous openings above the coronet and causing marked lameness or a cutaneous form characterized by an inflammation of the soft tissues just above the hoof involving suppuration and sloughing of the skin before healing

1quiv·er \ˈkwivə(r)\ *adj* [ME *quiver, cwiver*, fr. (assumed) OE *cwifer*] *archaic* **:** FAST-MOVING, AGILE, LIVELY

2quiver \"\ *n* -s [ME, fr. AF *quiveir*, fr. OF *quivre, cuevre*, of Gmc origin; akin to the root of E *1cocker*] **1 :** a case for carrying arrows; *also* **:** the arrows in a quiver **2 :** a container capable of holding a set or number of units; *also* **:** a large group or array

3quiver \"\ *vb* **quivered; quivered; quivering** \-v(ə)riŋ\ **quivers** [ME *quiveren*, prob. fr. *1quiver*] *vi* **:** to shake or move with slight tremulous motion **:** TREMBLE ⟨~*ing* branches⟩ ~ *vt* **:** to cause to quiver

quiver 1

4quiver \"\ *n* -s **1 a :** the act or action of quivering **:** TREMOR ⟨the ~ of a leaf⟩ ⟨a ~ of excitement⟩ **b :** QUAVER ⟨a slight ~ in his voice —Carleton Beals⟩ **2 :** a sudden radiance **:** FLASH ⟨a ~ of lightning⟩

5quiver \"\ *vi* -ED/-ING/-S [*2quiver*] **:** to come to rest — used of an arrow ⟨the arrow ~*s* in a tree⟩

quiv·ered \-və(r)d\ *adj* **1 :** equipped with or carrying a quiver ⟨the ~ warriors of antiquity⟩ **2** [fr. past part. of *5quiver*] **:** sheathed in or as if in a quiver ⟨whose quills stand ~ —Alexander Pope⟩

quiv·er·er \-vərə(r)\ *n* -s : one that quivers
quiv·er·ful \'kwivə(r),fu̇l\ *n, pl* **quiverfuls** *or* **quiversful** [²*quiver* + *-ful*] **1** : as many as a quiver will hold ⟨a ~ of arrows⟩ **2** : a good number : LOT ⟨a ~ of children⟩
quivering *adj* : TREMBLING, QUAKING ⟨~ leaves⟩
quiv·er·ing·ly *adv* : in a quivering manner
quiverleaf \'==,=\ *n* [³*quiver* + *leaf;* fr. its tremulousness] : ASPEN; *esp* : AMERICAN ASPEN
quiv·er·ness \-)nəs\ *n* -ES : the quality or state of being shaky or atremble
quiver tree *n* [trans. of Afrik *kokerboom;* fr. its hollowed stems being used by natives for arrow quivers] : a tall much-branched southern African aloe (*Aloe dichotoma*)
quiv·ery \'kwiv(ə)rē, -ri\ *adj* : that quivers : TREMBLING
qui vive \kē'vēv\ *n* [F, lit., long live who? (i.e., whom do you favor?); fr. the challenge of a French sentry or patrol] **1** : CHALLENGE 3c **2** : ALERT, LOOKOUT — used in the phrase *on the qui vive* ⟨on the *qui vive* for errors⟩
quix·ote \'kwiksət, -,sōt\ *n* -s *often cap* [after Don *Quixote* de la Mancha, chivalrous hero of the satiric novel *Don Quixote de la Mancha* (1605, 1615) by Miguel de Cervantes Saavedra †1616 Span. novelist] : a quixotic person
quix·ot·ic \(')kwik¦säd·ik, -ät\, ¦ēk\ *also* **quix·ot·i·cal** \¦əkəl, ¦ēk\ *adj* [*quixote* + *-ic* or *-ical*] : idealistic and utterly impractical; *esp* : marked by rash lofty romantic ideas or chivalrous action doomed to fail ⟨~ as a restoration of medieval knighthood —M.R.Cohen⟩ **syn** see IMAGINARY
quix·ot·i·cal·ly \¦ək(ə)lē, ¦ēk-, -li\ *adv* : in a quixotic manner
quix·o·tism \'kwiksə,tizəm\ *n* -s [*quixote* + *-ism*] : quixotic action or thought; *also* : an example of such action or thought
quix·o·tize \-,tīz\ *vb* -ED/-ING/-S [*quixote* + *-ize*] : to make or to be quixotic
quix·o·try \'kwiksətrē\ *n* -ES [*quixote* + *-ry*] : QUIXOTISM
¹**quiz** \'kwiz\ *n, pl* **quizzes** [origin unknown] **1 a** : an odd or eccentric person **b** : a person who ridicules or mocks ⟨she was a light-hearted girl, and a born ~ —George Dangerfield⟩ **2** : PRACTICAL JOKE; *also* : a jesting or joking piece (as of prose or conversation) ⟨a novel that was a ~ upon the silly romances of the day⟩ **3** : the act or action of quizzing; *specif* : a short oral or written test often taken without special preparation
²**quiz** \"\ *n, pl* **quizzes** : BANDALORE
³**quiz** \"\ *vb* **quizzed; quizzed; quizzing; quizzes** *vt* **1** : to ridicule wittily : MOCK ⟨when they see you standing up with somebody else, they will ~ me famously —Jane Austen⟩ **2** : to peer at esp. mockingly **3** : to give a quiz to ⟨~ a class⟩ **4** : to question seriously, soberly, or methodically ⟨~ murder suspects⟩ ~ *vi* : to conduct or give a quiz **syn** see ASK
quiz·ee *also* **quiz·zee** \(')kwi¦zē\ *n* -s : a person who is quizzed; *esp* : a participant in a quiz game ⟨intelligent questions directed at carefully selected ~s —W.V.T.Clark⟩
quiz game *n* : a form of entertainment often used on radio or television in which the members of a panel compete in answering questions
quiz kid *n* : a prematurely intelligent or knowing child
quizmaster \'=,==\ *n* : one who puts the questions to the contestants in a quiz game
quiz program *or* **quiz show** *n* : a quiz game presented on radio or television
quiz·zer \'kwizə(r)\ *n* -s : one that quizzes; *also* : a quiz game, program, or show
quiz·zi·cal \'kwizəkəl, -zēk-\ *adj* [¹*quiz* + *-ical*] **1 a** : slightly and amusingly eccentric : ODD ⟨a ~ old man⟩ **b** : WHIMSICAL ⟨~ understatement⟩ **2** : marked or characterized by mockery or banter ⟨a ~ smile⟩ **3** : QUESTIONING, CURIOUS ⟨a ~ look⟩
quiz·zi·cal·i·ty \,kwizə'kaləd·ē\ *n* -ES : QUIZZICALNESS ⟨~ mixed with slow amiable shrewdness —R.P.Warren⟩
quiz·zi·cal·ly \'kwizək(ə)lē, -zēk-, -li\ *adv* : in a quizzical manner ⟨sitting with her . . . head ~ tilted —John Updike⟩
quiz·zi·cal·ness \-kəlnəs\ *n* -ES : the quality or state of being quizzical ⟨the ~ of a policeman's stare⟩
quizzing glass *n* : a small eyeglass (as a monocle with a handle)
qung *also* **kung** \'ku̇ŋ\ *n, pl* **qung** *or* **qungs** *usu cap* **1** : a southern African people of the Omatako river **2** : a member of the Qung people
¹**quo** \'kwō\ *var of* QUOTH
²**quo** \"\ *n* -s [L *quid pro quo*] : something received or given for something else ⟨the exchange of quids for ~s out of the public's sight and hearing —R.H.Rovere⟩
quoc–ngu \¦kwäk³n¦gü, 'kwäk¦nü\ *n* -s [Vietnamese *kuăk ŋü*, lit., national language] : a writing system based on the Roman alphabet with additional letters and diacritics and used for the Vietnamese language

quizzing glass

¹**quod** \'kwōd\ *var of* QUOTH
²**quod** \'kwäd\ *n* -s [origin unknown] *slang Brit* : PRISON
³**quod** \"\ *vt* **quodded; quodded; quodding; quods** *slang Brit* : to put in prison
quod com·pu·tet \kwäd'kämpyə,tet\ *n* [LL, lit., that he account] : a legal judgment ordering a defendant to account
quod·dy \'kwädē\ *also* **quoddy boat** *n* -ES [fr. Passama*quoddy* Bay, inlet between New Brunswick, Canada, and Maine] : an open sloop-rigged sailboat once used esp. for fishing along the Maine coast
quod·li·bet \'kwädlə,bet\ *n* -s [ME, fr. ML *quodlibetum*, fr. L *quod libet* what you will, as you please, fr. *quod* (neut. of *qui* who) + *libet* it pleases, fr. *libēre* to please — more at WHO, LOVE] **1 a** : a subtle or debatable point; *esp* : a theological or scholastic question proposed for argument or disputation **b** : a scholastic or theological debate over such a question **2 a** : a humorous musical medley or fantasia **b** : a whimsical harmonic combination of melodies
quod·li·bet·ic \¦==¦bed·ik\ *also* **quod·li·bet·i·cal** \-d·əkəl\ *adj* [*quodlibet* + *-ic* or *-ical*] : consisting of or of the nature of a quodlibet : purely academic; *also* : characterized by or fond of academic discussion — **quod·li·bet·i·cal·ly** \-d·ək(ə)lē\ *adv*
quohog *or* **quohaug** *var of* QUAHOG
quoil \'kwȯi(ə)l\ *dial var of* COIL
¹**quoin** \'k(w)ȯin\ *or* **coign** \'kȯin\ *n* -s [alter. of *coin*] **1** : ANGLE, CORNER **2** : any of various wedges: as **a** : a beveled wooden block or a mechanically expandable metal device used by printers to lock up a form within a chase or to secure type on a galley **b** : a wedge used on ships to keep casks from rolling or to raise or depress the muzzles of guns **c** : the keystone or a voussoir of an arch **3** : one of the stone, brick, or wood members forming the exterior angle or corner at the juncture of two walls or planes which are distinguished from the adjoining surfaces or the units which form them by material, texture, color, size, or projection **4** : LOZENGE 2d(1)

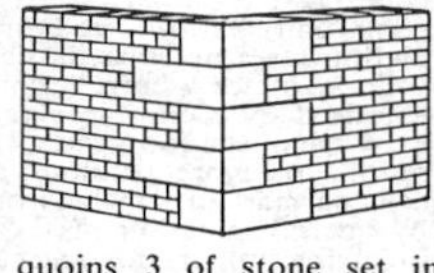
quoins 3 of stone set in brickwork

²**quoin** \"\ *or* **coign** \"\ *vt* -ED/-ING/-S **1** : to place quoins in (a form) in printing (as between the chase and imposed matter) preparatory to locking up — often used with *up* **2** : to provide with quoins or distinctive corners ⟨~*ed* walls⟩
quoin·ing \-niŋ\ *n* -s : the architectural members which form a distinctive corner at the juncture of two walls or planes
quoin post *n* : a corner post; *specif* : the vertical member at the hinged end of a gate in a navigation lock
¹**quoit** \'kwā¦t, 'k(w)ȯi¦, *usu* ¦d·+V; *chiefly dial* 'kwāk\ *n* -s [ME *coite*, perh. fr. MF *coite, coute* quilt, mattress — more at QUILT] **1** : a flattened ring of iron or circle of rope used in a throwing game **2 quoits** *pl but sing in constr* : a game played with quoits that are thrown from a mark toward a pin in an attempt to ring the pin or to come as near to it as possible **3** : the stone cover of a cromlech or cist; *also* : CROMLECH, CIST
²**quoit** \"\ *vb* -ED/-ING/-S [ME *coiten*, fr. *coite* quoit] *vi* : to play quoits ~ *vt* : to throw like a quoit ⟨~ a hat across a room⟩
quoit·er *pronunc at* ¹QUOIT +ə(r)\ *n* -s [ME *coiter*, fr. *coiten* + *-er*] : one who plays quoits

quoits 1

quok·ka \'kwäkə\ *n* -s [native name in Australia] : a stocky Australian pademelon (*Setonix brachyurus*) with a short tail — called also *short-tailed wallaby*
quo·mi·nus \'kwōmənəs\ *n* [L, whereby the less, that not; fr. the clause in the writ alluding to the plaintiff's diminished ability to pay his crown debts] **1** : a writ under old English law for preventing waste of a wood by one having housebote and haybote therein **2** : a writ formerly used to found jurisdiction in the Exchequer Court alleging the plaintiff's diminished ability to pay his crown debts
quo·mo·do \'kwōmə,dō\ *n* -s [L, in what manner, how, fr. *quo* (abl. of *qui* who, what) + *modo*, abl. of *modus* manner — more at METE] : MEANS, MANNER ⟨the ~ with which to pay off debts⟩
quon·dam \'kwändəm, -,dam\ *adj* [L, at one time, formerly, fr. *quom, cum* when (akin to L *qui* who) + *-dam* (akin to L *de* from, down, away) — more at WHO, DE-] : having been formerly : FORMER, SOMETIME ⟨a ~ friend⟩
quondong *var of* QUANDONG
quonk \'kwäŋk\ *or* **quonk·ing** \-ŋkiŋ\ *n* -s [imit.] : noise (as from conversation) that disturbs or disrupts a television or radio program because of its proximity to the microphones or cameras
Quon·set \'kwän(t)sət- *also* -wȯn- *or* -nzət-\ *trademark* — used for a prefabricated shelter set on a foundation of bolted steel trusses and built of a semicircular arching roof of corrugated metal insulated inside with wood fiber
quop \'kwäp\ *vi* [earlier *quap*, fr. ME *quappen*] *chiefly dial* : THROB
quor·a·te·an \,kwȯrə'tēən\ *n* -s *usu cap* [Yurok *Quoratem*, area near Salmon River, Idaho + E *-an*] : a language family of the Hokan stock in California comprising Karok
quo·rum \'kwōrəm, -wȯr-\ *n* -s [ME, fr. L, of whom, gen. pl. of *qui* who; fr. the wording of the commission once issued to justices of the peace in England — more at WHO] **1** : a select number of English justices of the peace formerly required to be present at sessions to constitute a lawful bench ⟨justices of the ~⟩ **2** : a select group ⟨the deepest sot among the topers of the ~ —T.H.Green⟩ **3** : the number of the members of an organized body of persons (as a legislature, court, or board of directors) that when duly assembled is legally competent to transact business in the absence of the other members : a usu. specified number of members (as an absolute majority) in the absence of which an organized body cannot act legally **4** : a general council or local section of those having the same office in the Mormon priesthood
quorum call *n* : the action of calling off a list of names (as of the members of a legislature) to determine whether a quorum is present
quos *pl of* QUO
quot *abbr* quotation; quoted
¹**quo·ta** \'kwōd·ə, -ōtə\ *n* -s [ML, fr. fem. of L *quotus* of what number, how many — more at QUOTE] **1** : a proportional part : SHARE; *esp* : the share or proportion assigned to each in a division or to each member of a body ⟨the ~ of troops required for an area⟩ **2** : the share or proportion received, granted, or necessary to a person as being one of a certain number entitled to a part; *specif* : the smallest number of votes in proportional political representation required for election and sometimes determined by dividing the total number of votes cast by one more than the number of seats to be filled and rounding off to the next higher full number **3** : the number of immigrants allowed to enter a country in a particular year and sometimes determined by the proportionate numbers of foreign-born groups in a given census **4** : a fixed number or percentage of minority group members who may be admitted into some activity or institution ⟨gradual desegregation by ~⟩
²**quota** \"\ *vt* -ED/-ING/-S : to divide or fix by quotas ⟨an institution with a ~*ed* admission policy⟩ : assign a quota to
quot·abil·i·ty \,kwōd·ə'biləd·ē, -ōtə-, -lətē, *-i also* ÷,kō-\ *n* [*quotable* + *-ity*] : the quality or state of being quotable
quot·able \'== bəl\ *adj* [¹*quote* + *-able*] **1** : capable of being quoted; *esp* : effective for or adapted to quotation ⟨a ~ phrase⟩ ⟨a ~ author⟩ **2** : fit to be repeated or published ⟨what was said was funny but not ~⟩
quot·able·ness *n* -ES [*quotable* + *-ness*] : QUOTABILITY
quota immigrant *n* : an immigrant subject to the quota restrictions imposed by various U. S. immigration laws
quo·ta·tion \kwō'tāshən *also* ÷kō- *sometimes chiefly Brit* kwə't-\ *n* -s [ML *quotation-, quotatio-* numeration, numbering of references, division by numbers, fr. *quotare* to divide by numbers, mark the number of + *-ion-, -io* -ion] **1** *obs* : a marginal reference or note in a book **2 a** : something that is quoted; *esp* : a passage referred to, repeated, or adduced esp. as evidence or illustration **b** : a striking, distinctive, or popular passage suitable for quoting ⟨a book of ~s⟩ **3** : the act or process of quoting ⟨his ~ of prices⟩; *esp* : the naming or publishing of current bids and offers or current prices of securities or commodities; *also* : the bids, offers, or prices so named or published **4 a** : QUOTATION FURNITURE **b** : QUOTATION QUAD **5** : QUOTATION MARK
quo·ta·tion·al \-āshən³l,-āshnəl\ *adj* : of the nature of a quotation : indicating quotation — **quo·ta·tion·al·ly** \-³lē, -əlē\ *adv*
quotation board *n* : a large board (as in a broker's office) on which are posted the current prices of stocks, bonds, or commodities on the several exchanges
quotation furniture *n* [prob. so called fr. its being used orig. to fill between marginal notes] : metal printing furniture cast hollow with the bottom side open which closely resembles quotation quads and whose dimensions are usu. given in picas
quotation mark *n* : one of a pair of punctuation marks " ", ' ', » «, or ‚ ' used to indicate the beginning and the end of a quotation in which the exact phraseology of another or of a text is directly cited — usu. used to enclose the titles of poems, paintings, lectures, articles, and parts of books and sometimes used to enclose technical terms expected to be unfamiliar to the reader, words used in an unusual, ironical, or eye-catching sense, or words (as slang expressions) for which a writer offers a slight apology
quotation noun *or* **quotation word** *n* : HYPOSTASIS 7b
quotation quad *n* : a hollow printing quad with the bottom side open whose dimensions are usu. given in points
¹**quote** \'kwōt *also* ÷'kō-; *usu* -ōd·+V\ *vb* -ED/-ING/-S [ML *quotare* to divide into chapters by numbers, mark references by numbers, mark the number of, fr. L *quotus* of what number, how many, fr. *quot* how many, as many as; akin to L *quis* who — more at WHO] *vt* **1 a** : to speak or write (a passage) from another's work verbatim and with due acknowledgment or with the supposition that the fact of unoriginality will be apparent ⟨*quoting* an epigram from the poem⟩ **b** : to speak or write a passage from esp. in substantiation, illustration, or adornment ⟨~ the Bible⟩ **2** : to adduce (material) in illustration ⟨~ instances⟩ ⟨~ cases⟩ **3 obs a** : to give a reference to : supply a source for **b** : to write down or record **c** : NOTICE, MARK **4 a** (1) : to name the current price of (a commodity, stock, or bond) (2) : to name (the current price) of a commodity, stock, or bond **b** : to give (the current bid and asked prices) for a commodity, stock, or bond **5** : to set off (as a written or printed passage) by quotation marks
syn CITE, REPEAT: QUOTE usu. involves a use of another's words, commonly with faithful exactness or an attempt at it, for some special effect like adornment, illustration, close examination ⟨I will *quote* a passage which is unfamiliar enough to be regarded with fresh attention —T.S.Eliot⟩ CITE is likely to stress the idea of adducing, bringing forward, or mentioning for a particular reason, like substantiation or proof, with or without the idea of uttering another's words ⟨the critic *cited* in the opening of this chapter —F.R.Leavis⟩ REPEAT stresses the fact of a saying or writing over again of someone else's words; it may suggest lack of the dignified reasons for the procedure attached to QUOTE and CITE ⟨unrealistic to go on *repeating* phrases about the connection of industry with personal independence —John Dewey⟩
²**quote** \"\ *n* -s **1** : QUOTATION **2** : QUOTATION MARK — often used orally to indicate the beginning of a direct quotation
quoted *past of* QUOTE
quoted price *n* [*quoted* fr. past part. of ¹*quote*] : the bid and offered prices of a security on a stock exchange at a given time
quot·ee \(')k(w)ōd·¦ē, -ō¦tē\ *n* -s [*quote* + *-ee*] : one who is quoted
quote mark *n* : QUOTATION MARK
quot·er \'k(w)ōd·ə(r), -ōtə-\ *n* -s [*quote* + *-er*] : one that quotes; *specif* : a clerk who keeps a record of insurance policy dividends and figures the interest due on them
quotes *pres 3d sing of* QUOTE
quoth \'kwōth\ *vb past* [ME, past of *quethen* to say, fr. OE *cwethan, cwæthan;* akin to OHG *quethan, quedan* to say, ON *kvetha*, Goth *qithan*] *archaic* : SAID — used chiefly in the first and third persons with a postpositive subject
quotha \'kwōthə\ *interj* [alter. of *quoth he*] *archaic* — used to express surprise, contempt, or assertive self-affirmation
quotid *abbr* [L *quotidie*] every day
¹**quo·tid·i·an** \kwō'tidēən\ *adj* [ME *cotidian*, fr. MF, fr. L *cotidianus, quotidianus*, fr. *cotidie, quotidie* each day, daily (fr. *quot* as many as, how many + *dies* day) + *-anus* -an — more at QUOTE, DEITY] **1** : occurring every day ⟨~ fever⟩ **2** : belonging to everyday ⟨~ routine⟩ **3** : COMMONPLACE, ORDINARY ⟨~ drabness⟩
²**quotidian** \"\ *n* -s [ME *cotidian*, fr. *cotidian*, adj.] : something that occurs each day (as an intermittent fever)
quo·tient \'kwōshənt\ *n* -s [ME *quocient*, modif. (influenced by *-ent*, n. suffix) of L *quoties, quotiens* how many times, how often, as often as (taken as a pres. part. stem in *-ent-*), fr. *quot* how many, as many as; akin to L *quis* who — more at WHO] **1** : the number resulting from the division of one number by another : the result of a process inverse to multiplication : the quantity such that the product of it and the divisor equals the dividend or such that the product of it and the divisor plus the remainder equals the dividend **2** : the numerical ratio usu. multiplied by 100 between a test score and a measurement on which that score might be expected largely to depend **3** : PROPORTION, QUOTA
quotient verdict *n* : a verdict in a legal action for damages wherein the amount assessed by the jury is reached by determining an average of the amounts suggested by each member of the jury
quoting *pres part of* QUOTE
quot·li·bet \'kwätlə,bet\ *n* -s [by alter.] : QUODLIBET 2
quo·tum \'kwōd·əm\ *n* -s [L, neut. of *quotus* of what number — more at QUOTE] : PROPORTION, PART
quo war·ran·to \,kwōwə'rän·(,)tō, -ran-\ *n* [ML, by what warrant] **1 a** : an English writ of right formerly issued on behalf of the crown requiring a person to show by what authority he exercises his office, franchise, or liberty **b** : the entire pleadings that such a writ calls forth or the action or proceeding itself **2 a** : a legal proceeding that is brought by the state, sovereign, or public officer, has a purpose similar to that of the ancient writ of quo warranto, is usu. criminal in form and sometimes authorizes the imposition of a fine but is essentially civil in nature and seeks to correct often at the relation or on the complaint of a private person a usurpation, misuser, or nonuser of a public office or corporate or public franchise, and may result in judgments of ouster against individuals and of ouster and seizure against corporations **b** : the pleadings in such a proceeding
quoz \'kwäz\ *n* -ES [prob. alter. of *quiz*] *archaic* : something queer or absurd
qu·raish *or* **qu·raysh** *or* **ko·reish** \kə'rīsh\ *n, pl* **quraish** *or* **quraishes** *or* **quraysh** *or* **qurayshes** *or* **koreish** *or* **koreishes** *usu cap* [Ar *Quraish*] **1** : an Arab people of which Muhammad was a member and which from the 5th century was distinguished by a religious preeminence associated with its hereditary provision of the pre-Islamic custodians of the Kaaba at Mecca **2** : a member of the Quraish people
qu·raish·ite *or* **qu·raysh·ite** *also* **ko·reish·ite** \-ī,shīt\ *n* -s *usu cap* : a member of the Quraish people
qur'an *or* **quran** *usu cap, var of* KORAN
qursh \'ku̇(ə)rsh\ *or* **qu·rush** \'ku̇rəsh\ *n, pl* **qursh** *or* **qurshes** *or* **qurush** *or* **qurushes** [Ar *qirsh* (pl. *qurūsh*)] **1** : a monetary unit of Saudi Arabia equal to 1/20 riyal **2** : a coin representing one qursh
qutb \'ku̇d·əb\ *n* -s [Ar *quṭb*] *usu cap* : an Islamic saint who has attained the highest degree of sanctity and has become within some areas of Islamic mysticism responsible for the invisible government of the world
QV *in sense 2* 'kyü'vē *or* '(h)wich'sē\ *abbr, often not cap* **1** [L *quantum vis*] as much as you will **2** [L *quod vide*] which see
q–value \'=,=(,)=\ *n, usu cap Q* : ²Q
q wedge *n* -s *usu cap Q* : QUARTZ WEDGE
qy *abbr* query
qyrghyz *usu cap, var of* KIRGHIZ
qz *abbr* quartz

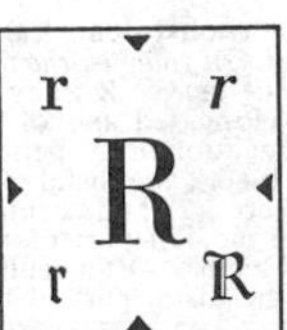

¹r \'är, 'å\ *n, pl* **r's** *or* **rs** \'ärz, 'åz\ *often cap, often attrib* **1 a :** the 18th letter of the English alphabet **b :** an instance of this letter printed, written, or otherwise represented **c :** a speech counterpart of orthographic *r* (as *r* in *run, fry, arid, far-off*, Spanish *para, rey*, French *rire*, or German *rohr*) **2 :** a printer's type, a stamp, or some other instrument for reproducing the letter *r* **3 :** someone or something arbitrarily or conveniently designated *r* esp. as the 17th or when j is used for the 10th the 18th in order or class **4 :** something having the shape of the letter R **5** *cap* **:** one of the three R's ⟨controversy over the first *R*⟩

²r *abbr, often cap* **1** rabbi **2** racemic **3** radical **4** radio **5** radius **6** railroad; railway **7** rain **8** range **9** rank **10** rare; rarity **11** ratio **12** real **13** rear **14** Reaumur **15** received **16** recipe **17** reconnaissance **18** recto **19** rector **20** red; reddish **21** refraction **22** refrigerator **23** [L] regina **24** registered **25** regulating **26** reigned **27** republic; republican **28** reserves **29** reside; residence; resident **30** resistance; resistor **31** respiration **32** respond; response **33** [F *retarder*] slow **34** retired **35** retree **36** returning **37** [L] rex **38** rifle **39** right **40** ring **41** riser **42** rises **43** river **44** road **45** rod **46** roentgen **47** roman **48** rood **49** rook **50** rotor **51** rough **52** route **53** royal **54** rubber **55** ruble **56** rule **57** run **58** runic **59** rupee

³r *symbol* **1** correlation coefficient **2** *cap* gas constant **3** *cap* radical — used esp. of a univalent hydrocarbon radical (as alkyl); compare GENERAL FORMULA **4** *cap* recipe — often ℞ **5** *cap* registered trademark — often enclosed in a circle **6** *cap* Reynolds number **7** *cap* Rydberg constant **8 a** *cap* a relation in a logical or mathematical proposition **b** a proposition in a logical operation

RA *abbr* **1** radioactive **2** rate of application **3** rear admiral **4** reduction of area **5** refer to acceptor **6** regular army **7** [L *reverendus admodum*] very reverend **8** right ascension

Ra *symbol* radium

¹raad \'räd\ *n, pl* **ra·den** \-dᵊn\ [D, lit., counsel, council; akin to OE *rǣd* advice, counsel, council — more at READ] **:** a legislative assembly in one of the Boer republics of So. Africa before the establishment of British administration — compare HEEMRAAD, VOLKSRAAD

²ra·ad \rə'äd, 'räd\ *n* -s [Ar *ra"ād*, lit., threatener, striker] **:** ELECTRIC CATFISH

raad·zaal \'räd,zäl\ *n, pl* **raad·za·len** \-lən\ [D *raad* + *zaal* hall, fr. MD *sale* — more at SALOON] **:** the assembly hall of a raad ⟨left the ~ in a rage —Manfred Nathan⟩

raan \'rän\ *n* -s [origin unknown] *chiefly Scot* **:** BROWN HEART 2b

rab \'rab\ *n* -s [F *rabot*] **:** a beater for mixing hair with mortar

ra·ban·na \rə'banə\ *n* -s [Malagasy *rebana*] **:** a coarse matting handwoven from raffia fibers in Madagascar

¹ra·bat \'rabē, rə'bat\ *n* -s [MF, turndown collar, rabat, fr. *rabattre* to turn back down, to reduce — more at REBATE] **:** a short cloth breast piece fitted to a Roman collar and worn chiefly by Roman Catholic and Anglican clergymen — called also *rabbi*

rabat

²rab·at \'rabət\ *n* -s [F, fr. MF *rabattre* to reduce] **:** a polishing material made from imperfectly fired potter's clay

³ra·bat \rə'bät\ *adj, usu cap* [fr. *Rabat*, capital of Morocco] **:** of or from Rabat, the capital of Morocco **:** of the kind or style prevalent in Rabat

ra·ba·to \rə'bä|d·(,)ō, -bā|, |(,)tō\ *n* -s [modif. of MF *rabat* — more at RABAT] **1 :** a wide lace-edged collar of the early 17th century worn turned down to lie across the shoulders or stiffened to stand high at the back and often open in front **2 :** a stiff support (as of wire) for a ruff or standing collar of the early 17th century

rabb *abbr* rabbinic

rab·ban \'rabən, rə'bän\ *n, pl* **rabba·nim** \rə'bänəm, ,räbə'nēm\ [Heb *rabbān*, fr. Aram] **:** TEACHER, MASTER — used as a Jewish title of honor higher than *rabbi* and given to heads of the Sanhedrin

¹rab·bet \'rabət, *usu* -əd·+V\ *also* **re·bate** \(')rē¦bāt, 'rabət, *usu* -d·+V\ *n* -s [ME *rabet*, fr. MF *rabat* act of beating down, fr. OF *rabattre* to beat down, reduce — more at REBATE] **1 a :** a channel, groove, or recess cut out of the edge or face of any body; *esp* **:** one intended to receive another member (as a panel) so as to break or cover the joint or more easily to hold the members in place **b :** strips of material joined to the trim of a structure or to a member received by the structure (as to serve as a stop for a door or to make dustproof) **2 a :** RABBET JOINT **b :** RABBET PLANE

²rabbet \"\ *vb* -ED/-ING/-S [ME *rabeten*, fr. *rabet*, n.] *vt* **1 :** to cut a rabbet in **:** furnish with a rabbet **2 :** to unite the edges of (as boards) in a rabbet joint ~ *vi* **:** to be joined by means of a rabbet

rabbeted lock *n* [fr. past part. of ²*rabbet*] **:** a lock whose front conforms to a rabbet on the edge of a door

rab·bet·er \-bəd·ə(r)\ *n* -s [²*rabbet* + *-er*] **:** one that rabbets; *esp* **:** an operator of a sticker for grooving wooden door or window parts for the inset of glass or panels

rabbet joint *n* [¹*rabbet*] **:** a joint formed by fitting together rabbeted boards or timbers — see MITER JOINT illustration

rabbet plane *n* **:** an openside plane with the plane iron extending to the outer edge of the open side to permit planing of sharp corners and grooves

rabbet joint

¹rab·bi \'ra,bī\ *n* -s [LL, fr. Gk *rhabbi*, fr. Heb *rabbī* my master, fr. *rabh* great one, master + *-ī* my] **1 :** MASTER, TEACHER — used by Jews as a term of address ⟨they said to him, "*Rabbi*, when did you come here" —Jn 6:25 (RSV)⟩ **2 a :** a Jew qualified by study of the Jewish civil and religious law forming esp. the halakah to expound and apply it (as by deciding legal questions on request or filling an administrative or judicial office) ⟨naturally the ~s or their disciples who were members of the congregation or . . . visitors were preferred as preachers because of their greater fitness —G.F.Moore⟩ **b** *often cap* **:** one of the scholars who developed the Talmudic basis of orthodox Judaism during the first centuries of the Christian era — see AMORA, SABORA, TANNA; compare SCRIBE **3 :** a Jew of modern times trained and ordained by another rabbi or group of rabbis (as the faculty of a theological school) for professional religious leadership; *specif* **:** one acting as the official leader of a Jewish congregation and performing various duties (as preaching, officiating at weddings and funerals)

²rab·bi \'rabē\ *n* -s [alter. of ¹*rabat*] **:** ¹RABAT

rab·bin \'rabən\ *n* -s [F, perh. fr. Aram *rabbīn*, pl. of *rab* master; akin to Heb *rabh* master] **:** RABBI 2

rab·bin·ate \'rabənət, -bə,nāt\ *n* -s [*rabbin* + *-ate*] **1 :** the office or tenure of office of a rabbi ⟨studying for the ~⟩ ⟨during his ~⟩ **2 :** a group of rabbis ⟨the American ~⟩

¹rab·bin·ic \rə'binik, ra'-, -nēk\ *or* **rab·bin·i·cal** \-nəkəl, -nēk-\ *adj* [*rabbin* + *-ic, -ical*] **1 a :** of or relating to rabbis or their writings ⟨the Catholic interracial council and the *rabbinical* association have issued statements —*Christian Century*⟩ **b** *usu cap* **:** of or relating to the rabbis of the Talmudic periods ⟨the *Rabbinic* period⟩ ⟨*Rabbinic* Judaism⟩ **2 :** characterized by preoccupation with minute analysis or hypothetical casuistry ⟨the textual criticism . . . concentrates its *Rabbinical* attention on details of prosody and grammar that have no value and no meaning in themselves —*Times Lit. Supp.*⟩ **3 :** of or preparing for the rabbinate ⟨train rabbis and *rabbinical* students in psychiatry —*Current Biog.*⟩ **4 :** comprising or belonging to any of several sets of Hebrew characters simpler than the square Hebrew letters ⟨commentaries printed in ~ type⟩ — **rab·bin·i·cal·ly** \-nək(ə)lē, -nēk-, -li\ *adv*

²rabbinic \"\ *n* -s *usu cap* **:** RABBINIC HEBREW

rabbinical literature *n* **:** the literature of Hebrew theology and philosophy including the Talmud and its exegesis

rabbinic hebrew *n, usu cap R&H* **:** Hebrew as used by the rabbis particularly in the medieval period

rab·bin·ics \-ks\ *n pl but sing or pl in constr, sometimes cap* [*rabbin* + *-ics*] **:** the study of rabbinical literature

rab·bin·ism \'rabə,nizəm\ *n* -s [*rabbin* + *-ism*] **1 :** a rabbinic expression or phraseology **:** a peculiarity of the language of the rabbis **2 :** the teachings and traditions of the rabbis **3 :** the quality or state of being rabbinic in analysis or casuistry

rab·bin·ite \'rabə,nīt\ *or* **rab·bin·ist** \-ənəst\ *or* **rab·ban·ite** \-ə,nīt\ *or* **rab·ban·ist** \-ənəst\ *n* -s *usu cap* [*rabbin* or *rabban* + *-ite* or *-ist*] **:** a Jew adhering to the Talmud and the traditions of the rabbis in opposition to the Karaites — **rab·bin·it·ic** \¦rabə¦nid·ik\ *or* **rab·bin·is·tic** \-nistik\ *adj, usu cap*

¹rab·bit \'rabət, *usu* -əd·+V\ *n* -s *see sense 1, often attrib* [ME *rabet*, prob. fr. Walloon *robett, robete*, fr. MD *robbe* rabbit + Walloon *-ett, -ete* -et] **1** *pl also* **rabbit a :** a small grayish brown mammal (*Oryctolagus cuniculus*) that differs from the related hares in its burrowing habits and in having the young born naked and helpless, is native to southern Europe and northern Africa but has been introduced into various other regions where it is often a pest because of its rapid reproduction, and has developed under domestication many varieties differing from the wild form in size, conformation, and coloring and variously adapted to the production of meat and fur or for pet and show stock **b :** any of various hares — often used in combination ⟨jack*rabbit*⟩ **c :** the fur of the rabbit often processed and dyed to imitate other furs **2** *Brit* **:** a weak player (as in tennis); *specif* **:** a cricketer who is not a good batsman **3 :** WELSH RABBIT **4 :** BROCCOLI BROWN **5 a :** a figure of a rabbit sped mechanically along the edge of a dog track as an object of pursuit **b :** a small container usu. moved pneumatically for transferring radioactive samples in an atomic-energy plant or laboratory

²rabbit \"\ *vi* -ED/-ING/-S **:** to hunt rabbits

³rabbit \"\ *vt* -ED/-ING/-S [perh. alter. of ³*rat*] **:** CONFOUND, DRAT — used as an expletive

rabbit ball *n* **:** a baseball held to be lively

rabbit bandicoot *n* **:** a bandicoot of the genus *Thylacomys; esp* **:** a long-eared bandicoot (*T. lagotis*)

rab·bit·berry \'rabət- — *see* BERRY\ *n* [*rabbit* + *berry*] **:** BUFFALO BERRY

rabbit brush *also* **rabbit bush** *n* **1 :** any of various plants of the genus *Chrysothamnus; esp* **:** a common shrub (*C. graveolens*) of western No. America that covers vast areas affording a retreat for jackrabbits **2 :** RABBITWEED

rabbit cat *n* **1 a :** ABYSSINIAN CAT **b :** MANX CAT **2 :** a reputed hybrid between cat and rabbit

rabbit-ear \'=ˌ=ˌ=\ *n* **1 :** TOADFLAX **2** *also* **rabbit ears cactus :** a cactus (*Opuntia microdasys*) with erect much branched flat branches covered with prominent bristles

rabbit-ear faucet *n* **:** a self-closing faucet opened by squeezing together two small handles

rabbit-ear faucet

rabbit ear mite *n* **:** a mite that is a variety of the scab mite and attacks the ear of rabbits

rabbit ears *n pl but sing in constr* **:** a condition in a sports player of sensitive awareness to criticism

rab·bit·er \'rabəd·ə(r)\ *n* -s [²*rabbit* + *-er*] **:** one that rabbits; *specif* **:** one who traps or destroys rabbits as a means of livelihood ⟨the official ~ of an Australian sheep station⟩

rabbiteye \'=ˌ=ˌ=\ *or* **rabbiteye blueberry** *n* [*rabbit* + *eye*] **:** a blueberry (*Vaccinium ashei*) native to the southeastern U.S. and grown commercially esp. for the canning industry

rabbit fever *n* **:** TULAREMIA

rabbitfish \'=ˌ=ˌ=\ *n* [*rabbit* + *fish*; fr. the rabbitlike nose] **1 :** a chimaera (*Chimaera monstrosa*) having a long tail and occurring in deep waters of the Atlantic ocean **2 a :** GLOBEFISH **b :** a slender elongated steel-blue marine food fish (*Promethichthys prometheus*) related to the escolar and widely distributed in warm regions **c** *southern Africa* **:** any of several small slimy-skinned compressed fishes of the genus *Siganus* — compare SIGANIDAE

rabbit flea *n* **:** any of several fleas (esp. *Hoplopsyllus affinis*) that attack rabbits

rabbit flower *n* **1 :** TOADFLAX **2 :** FOXGLOVE 1

rabbit-foot \'=ˌ=ˌ=\ *or* **rabbit's foot** *n* **:** the hind foot of a rabbit carried as a good-luck piece

rabbit-foot clover *also* **rabbit foot** *n* **:** a European clover (*Trifolium arvense*) naturalized in the U. S. having soft and hairy flower heads that resemble rabbits' paws — called also *old-field clover*

rabbit-foot grass *or* **rabbit's foot** *n* **:** an Old World annual weedy grass (*Polypogon monspeliensis*) common in California and having bristly greenish yellow spikes

rabbit-hunting \'=ˌ=ˌ=\ *n* **:** examination of undealt cards by a poker player who has dropped to see what he would have received if he had stayed in

rabbitlike \'=ˌ=ˌ=\ *adj* [*rabbit* + *like*] **:** resembling a rabbit or that of a rabbit ⟨~ ears⟩

rabbit louse *n* **:** a common louse (*Haemodipsus ventricosus*) that infests rabbits and hares in Europe and No. America and is one of the carriers of tularemia

rabbit-meat \'=ˌ=ˌ=\ *n* **:** RED ARCHANGEL

rabbit moth *n* **:** a moth (*Megalopyge opercularis*) of the southern Atlantic states the larva of which feeds on the orange and other trees and bears stinging spines

rabbit-mouthed \¦=ˌ=¦=\ *also* **rabbitmouth** \'=ˌ=ˌ=\ *adj* **:** HARE-LIPPED

rabbit pea *also* **rabbit's pea** *n* **:** CATGUT 3

¹rabbit punch *n* [fr. the manner in which a rabbit is stunned prior to being killed and butchered] **:** a short chopping blow delivered to the back of the neck or the base of the skull with the edge of the hand opposite the thumb

²rabbit punch *vt* **:** to strike with a rabbit punch

rabbit rat *n* **1 :** a small Australian rodent (*Conilurus albipes*) **2 :** RABBIT BANDICOOT

rab·bit·ry \'rabətrē\ *n* -ES [*rabbit* + *-ry*] **:** a place where domestic rabbits are kept; *also* **:** a rabbit-raising enterprise

rabbits *pl of* RABBIT, *pres 3d sing of* RABBIT

rabbit's-ear \'=ˌ=ˌ=\ *n, pl* **rabbit's-ears :** HARE'S-EAR 1

rabbit's-foot fern *n* **:** SERPENT FERN

rabbit's-mouth \'=ˌ=ˌ=\ *n, pl* **rabbit's-mouths :** SNAPDRAGON

rabbit squirrel *n* **:** MOUNTAIN VIZCACHA

rabbit's-root \'=ˌ=ˌ=\ *n, pl* **rabbit's-roots :** WILD SARSAPARILLA 1

rabbit stick *n* **:** a flat curved club resembling a boomerang and used by the Hopi Indians in hunting small game

rabbit syphilis *n* **:** a venereal disease of rabbits that is caused by a spirochete (*Treponema cuniculi*) resembling that of human syphilis but infective only for the rabbit and is marked by superficial nodule formation and ulceration with edematous swelling of surrounding tissues esp. about the external genitalia — called also *vent disease*

rabbit-tail grass *n* **:** HARE'S-TAIL GRASS

rabbit thorn *n* **:** a rough thorny shrub (*Lycium pallidum*) of the desert regions of the southwestern U.S. having numerous zigzag branches, bell shaped white or lavender flowers, and globose greenish fruit

rabbit tick *n* **:** a tick (*Haemaphysalis leporis-palustris*) common throughout America and living chiefly on rabbits and birds

rabbit tobacco *n, Midland* **:** a balsamweed (*Gnaphalium obtusifolium*) sometimes used for smoking

rabbit vine *n* **:** GROUNDNUT 2a

rabbit warren *n* **:** WARREN 3

rabbitweed \'=ˌ=ˌ=\ *n* [*rabbit* + *weed*] **:** a stiff woody herb (*Gutierrezia sarothrae*) of the central and southwestern U.S. with paniculate heads of small yellow flowers

rabbitwood \'=ˌ=ˌ=\ *n* [*rabbit* + *wood*] **:** a shrub (*Pyrularia pubera*) that is parasitic on the roots of the hemlock and has greenish racemose flowers and pulpy drupaceous fruits — see BUFFALO NUT

rab·bity \'rabəd·ē\ *adj* [*rabbit* + *-y*] **1 :** overrun with rabbits ⟨a ~ region⟩ **2 :** resembling (as in appearance) a rabbit or that of a rabbit ⟨~ teeth⟩ **3 :** TIMID, SHY ⟨a ~ little clerk⟩

¹rab·ble \'rabəl\ *n* -s [ME *rabel*; perh. akin to ⁴*rabble*] **1 :** a pack, string, or swarm of animals or insects ⟨great ~s of rats roamed the streets —Elizabeth Enright⟩ **2 a** *dial chiefly Eng* **:** a confused or meaningless string of words **:** RIGMAROLE **b :** a heterogeneous, disorganized, or confused collection of things ⟨giant trees under whose dense canopy the alien and tangled ~ of the jungle does not thrive —P.B.Sears⟩ **3 a :** a disorganized or disorderly crowd of people ⟨a mere ~ of field hands pretending to be soldiers —Kenneth Roberts⟩ **:** MOB ⟨besieged by a ~ of small children —Sacheverell Sitwell⟩ **b :** a group, class, or body regarded with contempt ⟨a ~ of nobility . . . conspires to mount a gruesome charade —*Time*⟩ **c :** the lowest class of people ⟨in the Civil War, the ~ made common cause with the . . . nobility against the middle classes —Roy Lewis & Angus Maude⟩ **:** persons of the lowest class ⟨the London ~, chimney sweepers, watermen, costermongers, thieves —E.G.Johnson⟩

²rabble \"\ *adj* **1 :** of, relating to, or forming a rabble ⟨those were the enemy, a ~ crew —S.L.Gwynn⟩ **2 :** resembling or suited to a rabble ⟨to burn the jails . . . was a good ~ trick —Samuel Johnson⟩

³rabble \"\ *vt* **rabbled; rabbled; rabbling** \-b(ə)liŋ\ **rabbles 1 :** to insult or assault by a mob **:** MOB **2 :** to mob and drive out ⟨members of the Scottish Episcopalian clergy were often ~*ed* during the English Revolution⟩

⁴rabble \"\ *vb* -ED/-ING/-S [ME *rablen*; akin to D *rabbelen* to chatter, rattle, LG *rabbeln*] *dial chiefly Brit* **:** BABBLE

⁵rabble \"\ *n* -s [F *râble* fire shovel, fr. MF *roable*, fr. ML *rotabulum*, fr. L *rutabulum*, fr. *rutus*, past part. of *ruere* to dig up, rake up — more at RUG] **1** *obs* **:** a charcoal burner's shovel **2 a :** an iron bar with the end bent for use like a rake used in puddling iron **b :** any similar device (as a rotating arm with a scraper) for skimming the bath in a melting or refining furnace or for stirring the ore in a roasting furnace by hand or mechanically

rabbles 2b

⁶rabble \"\ *vt* -ED/-ING/-S **:** to stir, skim, or gather with a rabble

rab·ble·ment \-lmənt\ *n* -s [¹*rabble* + *-ment*] **1 :** RABBLE **2 :** DISTURBANCE, TUMULT

¹rab·bler \'rab(ə)lə(r)\ *n* -s [³*rabble* + *-er*] **:** one that rabbles another or is part of a rabble

²rabbler \"\ *n* -s [⁶*rabble* + *-er*] **1 :** a workman who uses a rabble **2 :** an instrument for rabbling

rabble-rouse \'=ˌ=ˌ=\ *vi* [back-formation fr. *rabble-rouser*] **:** to stir up public sentiment by emotionalism **:** AGITATE ⟨ashamed of indignation, ashamed to *rabble-rouse* —T.J.Haas⟩

rabble-rouser \'=ˌ=ˌ=\ *n* [¹*rabble*] **:** one who stirs up the masses of the people (as to hatred or violence) **:** DEMAGOGUE

rab·bo·ni \rə'bō,nī, -ōnē\ *n* [Aram *rabbōnī* my master, teacher, fr. *rabbān* master + *-ī* my; akin to Heb *rabh* master] **:** MASTER, TEACHER — used as a Jewish title of respect applied esp. to spiritual instructors and learned persons

rab·e·lai·si·an \¦rabə¦lāzēən, -zhən\ *adj, usu cap* [François *Rabelais* †1553 French humorist + E *-ian*] **1 :** of, relating to, or characteristic of Rabelais or his works **2 :** marked by or manifesting a gross robust humor, an extravagance of caricature, or a bold naturalism similar to that distinguishing the satire of Rabelais

rab·fak *or* **rab·fac** \'rab,fak\ *n* -s [Russ *rabfak*, fr. *rabochiĭ fakul'tet*, fr. *rabochiĭ* of labor (fr. *rabota* labor, work) + *fakul'tet* faculty, college, fr. G *fakultät*, fr. ML *facultat-, facultas*; akin to OHG *arbeit, arabeit* need, work, Goth *arbaiths* distress, need, L *orbus* bereft — more at ORPHAN, FACULTY] **:** a Soviet school giving preliminary university training to workers

¹ra·bi \'rəbē\ *n* -s *usu cap* [Ar *rabī'* spring] **:** one of two months called Rabi I and Rabi II of the Muhammadan year — see MONTH table

²rabi \"\ *adj* [Urdu *rabī* spring crop, fr. Ar *rabī'* spring] **:** of, relating to, or constituting India's spring and major crop that includes wheat, barley, millet, peas, and mustard and is planted in autumn — compare KHARIF

rab·ic \'rabik\ *adj* [ISV *rab*ies + *-ic*] **:** of or relating to rabies ⟨~ virus⟩ ⟨~ symptoms⟩

rab·id \'rabəd\ *adj* [L *rabidus* raving, mad, fr. *rabere* to rave — more at RAGE] **1 a :** extremely violent **:** FURIOUS, RAGING ⟨was made . . . ~ by the gout —Charles Dickens⟩ **:** VIRULENT ⟨a country . . . that may again be tempted by ~ nationalism —*New Republic*⟩ **b :** having some feeling, interest, or view in a violent degree **:** going to extreme or unreasonable lengths in expressing or pursuing a feeling or opinion ⟨a ~ baseball fan⟩ ⟨~ on the subject of capital punishment⟩ ⟨~ for their candidate⟩ ⟨~ in his hatred of his rival⟩ **2 :** affected with rabies ⟨a ~ fox⟩ — **ra·bid·i·ty** \rə'bidəd·ē\ *n* -ES — **rab·id·ly** *adv* — **rab·id·ness** *n* -ES

ra·bies \'rā|bēz *sometimes* 'ra| *or* |,b-\ *n, pl* **rabies** [NL, fr. L, rage, madness, fr. *rabere* to rave] **:** an acute virus disease of warm-blooded animals that attacks chiefly the nervous system, is uniformly fatal when untreated, and is transmitted with infected saliva usu. through the bite of a rabid animal — see DUMB RABIES, FURIOUS RABIES, PASTEUR TREATMENT

ra·bi·form \'rābə,fȯrm\ *adj* [NL *rabies* + E *-form*] **:** resembling or characteristic of rabies ⟨~ symptoms⟩

rab·i·net \'rabə,net\ *n* -s [alter. of *robinet*] **:** a small piece of ordnance used in the 16th, 17th, and 18th centuries

rabious *adj* [L *rabiosus*, fr. *rabies* + *-osus* -ous] *obs* **:** FIERCE, RABID

ra·bi·ru·bia \,räbə'rübēə\ *n* -s [AmerSp *rabirrubia*, fr. Sp *rabo* tail (fr. L *rapum* turnip, knob formed by a tree root) + *rubia*, fem. of *rubio* yellow, fr. L *rubr-, ruber* red — more at RAPE, RED] **:** YELLOWTAIL e

rabs *pl of* RAB

rab·u·lis·tic \¦rabyə¦listik\ *adj* [L *rabula* brawling advocate (prob. of Etruscan origin) + E *-istic*] **:** characterized by railing or pettifoggery

raccommode *vt* -ED/-ING/-S [F *raccommoder*, fr. *re-* + *accommoder* to adapt, fr. L *accommodare* — more at ACCOMMODATE] *obs* **:** to set right

rac·coon *also* **ra·coon** \(')ra¦kün *sometimes* rə'-\ *n, pl* **raccoon** *or* **raccoons** *also* **racoon** *or* **racoons** [*ärähkun* (in some Algonquian language of Virginia), fr. *ärähkunēm* he scratches with his hands] **1 a :** a nearly omnivorous nocturnal mammal (*Procyon lotor*) related to but much smaller than the bear that inhabits most of No. America, lives largely in trees, and is chiefly gray with black and white facial markings, a bushy ringed tail, and coarse fur much used in furriery **b :** CRAB-EATING RACCOON **2 :** any of various animals somewhat similar to or related to the raccoon: as **a :** CACOMISTLE **b :** PANDA

rac·coon·berry \(')=¦=- — *see* BERRY\ *n* [*raccoon* + *berry*] **:** MAYAPPLE 2

raccoon dog *n* **:** a small short-muzzled canid (*Nyctereutes procyonides*) having dark facial markings like those of the raccoon, short legs, and a short bushy tail and being widely distributed in eastern Asia and Japan and reputedly bred as a furbearer in Russia

raccoon family *n* **:** PROCYONIDAE

raccoon fox *n* **:** CACOMISTLE

raccoon grape *n* **1 :** FOX GRAPE **2 :** a climbing or erect shrub (*Ampelopsis cordata*) chiefly of the southeastern U. S.

raccoon oyster *n* **:** COON OYSTER

raccoon perch *n* **:** YELLOW PERCH

rac·croc stitch \ra'krō+\ *n* [F *raccrocher* to hook up again, fr. *re-* + *accrocher* to hook up, attach, get hold of, fr. MF *acrochier* — more at ACCROACH] **:** an invisible stitch for joining lace or net

¹race \'rās\ *n* -s [ME *ras, rase*, fr. ON *rās*; akin to OE *rǣs* rush, running leap, MLG *rās* strong current, MHG *rasen* to storm, rage, L *rorarii* skirmishers, Gk *erōē* rush, impetus] **1** *chiefly Scot* **:** the act of rushing onward **:** RUN **2 a :** a strong or rapid current of water that flows through a narrow channel **b :** a heavy or choppy sea; *esp* **:** one produced by the meeting of two tides **c :** a watercourse (as a brook or run) used or made for an industrial purpose (as for mining or for turning the waterwheel of a mill) **d :** the current flowing in such a course **3 a :** a set course (as of the sun) or duration of time **:** PERIOD **b :** the course of life **:** CAREER **4 a :** a running in competition **:** a contest of speed (as in running, riding, sailing) **b races** *pl* **:** a meeting for contests in the running esp. of horses ⟨attended the ~*s*⟩ — compare HANDICAP, PURSE RACE, STAKE RACE, SWEEPSTAKE **c :** a contest involving progress toward a goal (as election to public office or a winning total of games in a season's play) ⟨three-cornered ~ for governor⟩ ⟨finished second in the professional hockey league ~⟩ **5 :** a fenced lane or passageway; *specif, Austral* **:** a passageway in a sheep drafting yard **6 :** a track or channel in which something rolls or slides: as **a :** a slide on the lay of a loom for a shuttle **b :** a groove for the balls in a ball bearing or rollers in a roller bearing — see ROLLER BEARING illustration **c :** a groove in a pulley in which a rope runs **7 :** SLIPSTREAM

²race \"\ *vb* -ED/-ING/-S *vi* **1 :** to run or engage in a race **:** compete in speed ⟨eight horses will ~ for the cup⟩ **2 :** to go, move, or run at top speed or out of control esp. through urgency, compulsion, or zest ⟨we'll move out . . . and send the rebels *racing* for safety —Kenneth Roberts⟩ ⟨his mind *raced* ahead to guess the full import of the message —Gordon Merrick⟩ **3 :** to run too fast under a diminished load ⟨the propeller *raced* wildly as the stern rose⟩ ~ *vt* **1 :** to engage in a race with **:** contest with in speed ⟨offered to ~ him to the big tree⟩ **2 a :** to enter in a race **:** cause to contend in a race ⟨~ a maiden horse against a winner⟩ **b :** to race against ⟨*racing* the clock⟩ **c :** to drive at high speed ⟨*raced* his car across the desert⟩ **d :** transport or propel at maximum speed and haste ⟨fast-sailing ships . . . built expressly to ~ tea from China —*Brit. Bk. Centre*⟩ **3 :** to speed (as an engine or motor) without a working load or in disengagement from the transmission **syn** see RUN

³race \"\ *vb* [ME *racen*, short for *aracen*, fr. ONF *aracier*, modif. (influenced by OF *a-* off, away — fr. L *ab*) of L *eradicare* to pluck out by the roots — more at OF, ERADICATE] *obs* **:** TEAR, PLUCK, SNATCH

⁴race \"\ *n, dial chiefly Eng* **:** PLUCK 2a

⁵race \"\ *vt* -ED/-ING/-S [ME *racen*, alter. of *rasen* to rase] **1 :** to cut, scratch, or score with a sharp point **2** *obs* **:** ERASE

⁶race \"\ *n* -S **:** a shallow cut **:** SCRATCH, SLASH

⁷race \"\ *n* -S [MF, generation, family, fr. It *razza*] **1 a** *obs* **:** GENERATION **b** *obs* **:** the act of breeding or producing offspring ⟨male he created thee, but thy consort female for ~ —John Milton⟩ **c :** a breeding stock of animals ⟨~ of mares⟩ **2 a :** the descendants of a common ancestor **:** a family, tribe, people, or nation belonging to the same stock ⟨the impoverished scion of a noble ~⟩ **b :** a class or kind of individuals with common characteristics, interests, appearance, or habits as if derived from a common ancestor ⟨the ~ of doctors⟩ ⟨the whole ~ of mankind —Shak.⟩ ⟨the Anglo-Saxon ~⟩ ⟨the Jewish ~⟩ **3 :** any of various infraspecific taxonomic groups: as **a :** MICROSPECIES **b :** SUBSPECIES **c :** a permanent or fixed variety **d :** BREED **e :** PHYSIOLOGIC RACE **f :** a division of mankind possessing traits that are transmissible by descent and sufficient to characterize it as a distinct human type ⟨Caucasian ~⟩ ⟨Mongoloid ~⟩ **4** *obs* **:** inherited temperament or disposition ⟨now I give my sensual ~ the rein —Shak.⟩ **5 a :** distinctive flavor, taste, or strength (as of wine) **:** the quality indicating origin or kind **b** *archaic* **:** RACINESS

syn RACE, NATION, and PEOPLE, even though in technical use they are commonly differentiated, are often used popularly and interchangeably to designate one of a number of great divisions of mankind, each made up of an aggregate of persons who are thought of, or think of themselves, as comprising a distinct unit. In technical discriminations, all more or less controversial and often lending themselves to great popular misunderstanding or misuse, RACE is anthropological and ethnological in force, usu. implying a distinct physical type with certain unchanging characteristics, as a particular color of skin or shape of skull ⟨the Caucasian *race*⟩ ⟨the Malay *race*⟩ ⟨the Ethiopian *race*⟩ although sometimes, and most controversially, other presumed common factors are chosen, as place of origin ⟨the Nordic *race*⟩ or common root language ⟨the Aryan *race*⟩. In popular use RACE can apply to any more or less clearly defined group thought of as a unit usu. because of a common or presumed common past ⟨the Anglo-Saxon *race*⟩ ⟨the Celtic *race*⟩ ⟨the Hebrew *race*⟩ NATION, primarily political in force, usu. designates the citizenry as a whole of a sovereign state and implies a certain homogeneity because of common laws, institutions, customs, or loyalty ⟨the British *nation*⟩ ⟨the French *nation*⟩ ⟨the house must have been built before this country was a *nation* —Allen Tate⟩ ⟨what is a *nation?* A group of human beings recognizing a common history and a common culture, yearning for a common destiny, assuming common habits, and generally attached to a specific piece of the earth's surface —David Bernstein⟩ Sometimes it is opposed to *state* ⟨a state is accidental; it can be made or unmade; but a *nation* is something real which can be neither made nor destroyed —J.R.Green⟩ and often not clearly distinguishable from RACE in comprising any large group crossing national boundaries and with something significantly in common ⟨the children of the world are one *nation;* the very old, another —Jan Struther⟩ ⟨for the two *nations* that alone inhabit the earth, the rich and the poor —Edith Sitwell⟩ ⟨the Gypsy *nation*⟩ PEOPLE, sometimes interchangeable with NATION though stressing a cultural or social rather than a national unity, can apply to a body of persons, as a whole or as individuals, who show a consciousness of solidarity or common characteristics not wholly comprised by RACE or NATION, suggesting a common culture or common interests or ideals and a sense of kinship ⟨the Mexican *people* —Virginia Prewett⟩ ⟨the British and American *peoples* —Sir Winston Churchill⟩ ⟨we, the *people* of the United States —*U. S. Constitution*⟩ ⟨we, the *peoples* of the United Nations —*U. N. Charter*⟩ ⟨a new government, which, for certain purposes, would make the people of the several states one *people* —R.B.Taney⟩ **syn** see in addition VARIETY

⁸race \"\ *n* -S [origin unknown] **:** an elongate white mark on the face of a horse or dog

⁹race \"\ *n* -S [MF *rais* root, fr. L *radic-, radix* — more at ROOT] **:** a root of ginger

¹⁰race \"\ *adj* [F *ras* shaven, flat, fr. L *rasus*, past part. of *radere* to scrape — more at RAT] *of a ship* **:** designed to lie low in the water

raceabout \'=,=,=\ *n* -S [²*race* + *about*] **1 :** a small sloop usu. having a keel and derived from the knockabout but having finer lines and carrying more sail **2 :** a roadster with body lines simulating those of a racing car

race-baiter \'=,=,=\ *n* **:** one who baits a racial group

race-baiting \'=,=,=\ *n* [⁷*race* + *baiting*] **:** the making of malicious attacks (as through taunts and insinuations) upon the members of a racial group

race board *n* **:** RACE 6a

racecourse \'=,=\ *n* [¹*race* + *course*] **1 :** a course for racing; *esp* **:** a turf course for steeplechase or cross-country racing **2 :** RACEWAY 1

raced *past of* RACE

race ginger *n* [⁹*race*] **:** GINGERROOT

race glass *n* [¹*race*] **:** a field glass for use at races

racegoer \'=,=,=\ *n* **:** one who goes regularly to horse races

racehorse \'=,=\ *n* [¹*race* + *horse*] **1 :** a horse bred and trained for racing esp. under saddle — compare HARNESS HORSE, THOROUGHBRED **2 :** STEAMER DUCK

racehorse grass *n* **:** JOHNSON GRASS

racehorse keno *n* **:** a lottery game in which each player may select 10 numbers out of 80 and wins if his 10 numbers are among 20 numbers drawn at random

race knife *n* [⁵*race*] **:** a cutting tool with a blade hooked at the tip used for marking outlines on boards or metal

raceline \'=,=\ *n* [¹*race* + *line*] **:** an artificial channel for conveying water

rac·e·mase \'rasə,mās\ *n* -S [*racemic* + *-ase*] **:** any of various enzymes that catalyze racemizations and occur esp. in bacteria ⟨alanine ~⟩

rac·e·mate \-āt\ *n* -S [ISV *racemic* + *-ate*] **1 :** a salt or ester of racemic acid **2 :** a racemic compound or mixture

racemation *n* -S [LL *racemation-, racematio*, fr. L *racematus* (past part. of *racemari* to glean, fr. *racemus* cluster of grapes) + *-ion-, -io* -ion] **1** *obs* **:** the gathering or gleaning of grapes **2** *obs* **:** CLUSTER

ra·ceme \rā'sēm, rə'-\ *n* -S [L *racemus* cluster of grapes or berries] **1 :** an inflorescence (as in the currant and lily-of-the-valley) in which the flowers are borne on stalks of about equal length along an elongated axis that continues to grow during flowering and open in succession from below — compare CYME, CORYMB; see INFLORESCENCE illustration **2 :** something (as a synaptic nerve ending) that resembles a racemose inflorescence

ra·cemed \-md\ *adj* [*raceme* + *-ed*] **:** bearing or forming a raceme

race meeting *n* [¹*race*] *chiefly Brit* **:** a number of horse races held at a particular track on the same day or on several successive days

race memory *n* [⁷*race*] **:** the body of experiences, beliefs, and general recollections transmitted from one generation of mankind or of a race to another **:** racial tradition

ra·ce·mic \rā'sēmik, rə'-, -sem-, -mēk\ *adj* [F *racémique*, fr. L *racemus* + F *-ique* -ic] **1 :** relating to or derived from racemic acid **2 :** of, relating to, or constituting a compound or mixture that is composed of equal amounts of dextrorotatory and levorotatory forms of the same compound and hence is optically inactive toward polarized light — compare DL-, MES-

racemic acid *n* **:** optically inactive tartaric acid that consists of equal parts of *dextro-* and *levo-* tartaric acids into which it can be separated, is often found with *dextro*-tartaric acid in the juice of grapes, and is formed by oxidation of mannitol or dulcitol and in other ways

rac·e·mif·er·ous \ˌrasə'mif(ə)rəs\ *adj* [L *racemifer* bearing clusters, fr. *racemus* + *-fer* -ferous] **:** bearing racemes

ra·ce·mi·form \rā'sēmə,fȯrm\ *adj* [ISV *raceme* + *-iform*] **:** having the form of a raceme

rac·e·mism \'rasə,mizəm\ *n* -S [*racemic* + *-ism*] **:** the quality or state of being racemic

race·mi·za·tion \ˌrasəmə'zāshən; rā,sēm-, rə,s-\ *n* -S [*racemize* + *-ation*] **:** the action or process of changing from an optically active compound into a racemic compound or mixture — opposed to *resolution*

rac·e·mize \'rasə,mīz, rā'sē,-, rə'sē,-\ *vb* -ED/-ING/-S [ISV *racemic* + *-ize*] *vt* **:** to subject to racemization ~ *vi* **:** to undergo racemization

rac·e·mose \'rasə,mōs\ *adj* [L *racemosus* full of clusters, fr. *racemus* + *-osus* -ose] **1 :** relating to, occurring in the form of, or resembling a raceme ⟨a ~ inflorescence⟩ **2** *of a gland* **:** compound with freely branching ducts that end in acini so that the whole somewhat resembles a compact cluster of grapes ⟨the pancreas and salivary glands are ~ glands⟩ — **rac·e·mose·ly** *adv*

rac·e·mous \-səməs\ *adj* [L *racemosus*] **:** RACEMOSE — **rac·e·mous·ly** *adv*

race of the propeller [¹*race*] **:** SLIPSTREAM

rac·e·phed·rine \ˌrasə'fedrən\ *n* [*racemic* + *ephedrine*] **:** synthetic racemic ephedrine

race plate *n* **1 :** RACE 6a **2 :** TRAVERSE CIRCLE

race prejudice *n* [⁷*race*] **:** prejudice against or hostility toward people of another race or color or of an alien culture

race problem *n* **:** a political or social problem that arises out of a mixture of or conflict between races in a country or region

race psychology *n* **1 :** FOLK PSYCHOLOGY **2 :** COMPARATIVE PSYCHOLOGY 2

rac·er \'rāsə(r)\ *n* -S [²*race* + *-er*] **1 :** one that races **:** something designed or adapted chiefly or solely for speed or used for racing **2 :** RACING CRAB **3 :** any of various snakes of the genera *Coluber* and *Mastigophis:* as **a :** BLACK RACER **b :** BLUE RACER **4 :** a poor, thin, or spent fish **5 :** a fast running part in a machine **6 a :** TRAVERSE CIRCLE **b :** a turntable to which the chassis of a coast artillery gun is secured and used in traversing the gun **7 :** RACING SKATE

race riot *n* [⁷*race*] **:** a riot animated by racial dissensions or hatreds; *specif* **:** such a conflict between whites and Negroes

race rotation *n* [¹*race*] **:** the rotary motion given to the slipstream by the action of the propeller

race runner *n* **:** a No. American lizard (*Cnemidophorus sexlineatus*) noted for swiftness of movement — called also *sand lizard, striped lizard*

races *pl of* RACE, *pres 3d sing of* RACE

race suicide *n* [⁷*race*] **:** the gradual extinction of a people or racial strain through a tendency to restrict voluntarily the rate of reproduction

racetrack \'=,=\ *n* [¹*race* + *track*] **:** a usu. oval course over which races are run; *esp* **:** a dirt track for flat or harness races

racetrack: diagram of a regulation mile track (R=radius)

raceway \'=,=\ *n* [¹*race* + *way*] **1 a :** a canal for a current of water (as a millrace or a mining race) **b :** FISHWAY **2 :** a channel designed for loosely holding electrical wires or cables in buildings **3 :** RACE 6b **4 :** a track for harness racing

race-wide \'=,=\ *adj* [⁷*race* + *wide*] **:** extending or existing throughout a race

rach *or* **rache** \'rach\ *n, pl* **raches** [ME *racche, ratche*, fr. OE *ræcc;* akin to ON *rakki* dog] *dial chiefly Brit* **:** a dog that hunts by scent **:** HOUND

ra·chel \rə'shel\ *n* -S [after Mlle. *Rachel* (Élisa Félix) †1858 Fr. actress] **:** a tannish face powder with pink undertones

rachet *var of* RATCHET

rachi- *or* **rachio-** *also* **rhachi-** *or* **rhachio-** *comb form* [Gk *rhachi-*, fr. *rhachis* lower part of the back, spine, backbone; akin to Gk *rhachos* thorn hedge, MIr *fracc* needle, Lith *ražas* stubble, tine of a fork]**:** spine **:** spinal **:** spinal and ⟨*rachicentesis*⟩ ⟨*rachiodont*⟩ ⟨*rachiometer*⟩

ra·chi·al \'rākēəl\ *or* **ra·chid·i·al** \rə'kidēəl\ *adj* [*rachial* fr. *rachi-* + *-al; rachidial* fr. NL *rachid-, rachis* + E *-ial*] **:** RACHIDIAN

ra·chi·a·nec·tes \ˌrākēə'nek,tēz\ *syn of* RHACHIANECTES

ra·chi·centesis \ˌrākē+\ *n* [NL, fr. *rachi-* + *centesis*] **:** LUMBAR PUNCTURE

rachides *pl of* RACHIS

-ra·chid·ia \rə'kidēə\ *n comb form* -S [NL, fr. *rachid-, rachis* + *-ia*] **:** condition of the spine ⟨*atelorachidia*⟩

ra·chid·i·an \-ēən\ *adj* [F *rachidien*, fr. NL *rachid-, rachis* + F *-ien* -ian] **:** of or relating to a rachis; *sometimes* **:** SPINAL ⟨~ nerves⟩

ra·chi·form \'rākə,fȯrm\ *adj* [*rachi-* + *-form*] **:** having the form of a rachis

ra·chi·glos·sa \ˌrākē'gläsə\ *n pl, cap* [NL, fr. *rachi-* + *-glossa*] **:** a division of Stenoglossa (order Pectinibranchia) comprising marine mostly carnivorous gastropods having typically a long retractile proboscis, a distinct siphon, and the radula with three or one longitudinal series of teeth of which each may bear many cusps and including many of the large ornamental shells (as the miter shells, murices, olive shells, volutes, and whelks) — **ra·chi·glos·sate** \ˌ=='glä,sāt\ *adj or n*

ra·chil·la \rə'kilə\ *n, pl* **rachil·lae** \-i,lē\ [NL, dim. of *rachis*] **:** a small or secondary rachis; *specif* **:** the axis of a spikelet of a grass or sedge

rachio- — see RACHI-

ra·chi·o·dont \'rākēə,dänt\ *adj* [*rachi-* + *-odont*] **:** having gular teeth consisting of modified ventral vertebral spines ⟨~ egg-eating snake⟩

ra·chi·om·e·ter \ˌrākē'ämәd-ә(r)\ *n* [*rachi-* + *-meter*] **:** an instrument for measuring spinal curvatures

ra·chi·on \'rākēən\ *n* -S [NL, fr. Gk *rhachia* surf, rocky shore, reef, fr. *rhachis* spine, ridge — more at RACHI-] **:** the marginal line of a lake at which maximum wave action and undertow turmoil occur

ra·chis \'rākəs\ *n, pl* **rachises** \-səz\ *or* **rach·i·des** \'rakə,dēz, 'rāk-\ [NL *rachid-, rachis*, modif. of Gk *rhachi-, rhachis* — more at RACHI-] **1 :** VERTEBRAL COLUMN, SPINE **2 :** any of various axial structures: as **a** (1) **:** the elongated axis of an inflorescence (2) **:** the extension or prolongation of the petiole bearing the leaflets of a compound leaf **b** (1) **:** the distal part of the shaft of a feather that bears the web (2) **:** the central cord in the stem of a crinoid (3) **:** the median part of the radula of a mollusk that bears the central teeth (4) **:** a central cord of the ovary of nematodes (5) **:** the distal part of the shaft of a sea pen or similar organism

ra·chis·chi·sis \rə'kiskəsəs\ *n, pl* **rachischi·ses** \-kə,sēz\ [NL, fr. *rachi-* + *-schisis*] **:** cleft spine **:** congenital failure of union of the paired vertebral arches **:** SPINA BIFIDA

ra·chit·ic \rə'kid·|ik, -it|, |ēk\ *adj* [NL *rachitis* + E *-ic*] **1 :** of, relating to, or affected by rickets **2 :** resembling or suggesting the condition of one suffering from rickets **:** RICKETY ⟨natives with over-valued ~ currencies —*Time*⟩ ⟨a tall, narrow-shouldered and ~ house in a little obscure square —Aldous Huxley⟩

rachitic rosary *n* [so called fr. its resemblance to a string of beads] **:** BEADING f

ra·chi·tis *also* **rha·chi·tis** \rə'kīd·əs, -ītəs\ *n, pl* **ra·chit·i·des** \-kid·ə,dēz\ [NL, fr. Gk *rhachitis* disease of the spine, fr. *rhachis* + *-itis*] **:** RICKETS

rach·i·to·gen·ic \ˌrakəd·ō¦jenik\ *adj* [*rachit-* (fr. NL *rachitis*) + *-o-* + *-genic*] **:** leading or tending to the development of rickets ⟨a ~ diet⟩

ra·chit·o·mi \rə'kid·ə,mī\ [NL, pl. of *rachitomus* rhachitomous] *syn of* RHACHITOMI

rachitomous *var of* RHACHITOMOUS

rachy·cen·tron \ˌrakē'sen,trän\ *n, cap* [NL, irreg. fr. *rachi-* + Gk *kentron* sharp point — more at CENTER] **:** a genus (coextensive with the family Rachycentridae) of pelagic marine percoid fishes comprising solely the cobia

ra·cial \'rāshəl\ *adj* [⁷*race* + *-ial*] **1 :** of, relating to, or based on a race ⟨~ evolution⟩ ⟨~ traits⟩ ⟨~ group⟩ ⟨~ segregation⟩ **2 :** existing or occurring between races ⟨~ conflict⟩ ⟨~ differences⟩ — **ra·cial·ly** \-shəlē, -li\ *adv*

ra·cial·ism \-shə,lizəm\ *n* -S [*racial* + *-ism*] **1 :** racial prejudice or discrimination **:** race hatred **2 :** RACISM

ra·cial·ist \-ˌləst\ *n* -S [*racial* + *-ist*] **1 :** one animated by or practicing racialism **2 :** one who advocates or believes in racism

ra·cial·is·tic \ˌrāshə¦listik, -tēk\ *adj* [*racial* + *-istic*] **:** of, relating to, or based on racialism ⟨~ hysteria⟩ ⟨~ vices⟩

ra·ci·al·i·ty \ˌrāshē'alәd·ē\ *n* -ES [*racial* + *-ity*] **:** racial quality

ra·cial·iza·tion \ˌrāshәlә'zāshәn\ *n* -S [*racial* + *-ization*] **:** the act or process of imbuing a person with a consciousness of race distinctions or of giving a racial character to something or making it serve racist ends

ra·cial·ize \'rāshә,līz\ *vt* -ED/-ING/-S [back-formation fr. *racialization*] **:** to subject to racialization ⟨to ~ science and art⟩

racial unconscious *n* **:** COLLECTIVE UNCONSCIOUS

ra·ci·a·tion \ˌrāshē'āshәn\ *n* -S [irreg. (influenced by *speciation*) fr. ⁷*race* + *-ation*] **:** differentiation of local infraspecific groups within a population through continued selection for ecologically useful variations under conditions of at least partial isolation — compare SPECIATION

r acid *n, usu cap R* **:** a crystalline sulfonic acid $HOC_{10}H_5\text{-}(SO_3H)_2$ derived from beta naphthol and used as a dye intermediate; 2-naphthol-3,6-disulfonic acid

racier *comparative of* RACY

raciest *superlative of* RACY

rac·i·ly \'rāsәlē, -li\ *adv* [¹*racy* + *-ly*] **:** in a racy manner **:** with raciness ⟨his work, which includes . . . beer and cider jugs and mugs . . . has a ~ native character, without any affectation —Charles Marriott⟩ ⟨~ vernacular in speech⟩

rac·i·ness \-sēnәs, -sin-\ *n* -ES [¹*racy* + *-ness*] **:** the quality of being racy **:** EARTHINESS ⟨with a more polite, standardized speech a lot of the ~ has departed from the London streets —H.V.Morton⟩ ⟨an idiomatic ~ of speech, expressing a strong vitality —F.R.Leavis⟩

¹racing *n* -S [fr. gerund of ²*race*] **1 :** the sport or profession of engaging in or holding races **2 :** horse races as a sport or a business

²racing *adj* **:** relating to or used in racing ⟨~ boat⟩ ⟨~ clothes⟩ ⟨~ club⟩ ⟨~ swimming stroke⟩

racing colors *n pl* **:** the registered colors of a jockey's cap and jacket designating the horse's owner

racing crab *n* [fr. pres. part. of ²*race*] **:** any of several swift-running crabs of the family Ocypodidae

racing form *n* [²*racing*] **:** an information sheet giving pertinent data about horse races including entries, post positions, jockeys, probable odds, and past records of horses

racing glass *n* **:** RACE GLASS

racing iron *n* [fr. gerund of ⁵*race*] **:** an iron or a steel bar for racing grindstones

racing plate *n* [²*racing*] **:** a very light horseshoe used for racehorses

racing-sheet \'==,=\ *n* **:** RACING FORM

racing skate *n* **:** a skate with a long blade projecting beyond the toe and heel of the shoe and with a thin steel tube brazed to the blade for added strength — called also *racer*

racing skate

ra·ci·ol·o·gy \ˌrāsē'älәjē\ *n* -ES [irreg. fr. *race* + *-o-* + *logy*] **:** the study of human races

rac·ism \'rā,sizәm\ *n* -S [prob. fr. F *racisme*, fr. *race* + *-isme* -ism] **1 :** the assumption that psychocultural traits and capacities are determined by biological race and that races differ decisively from one another which is usu. coupled with a belief in the inherent superiority of a particular race and its right to domination over others **2 a :** a doctrine or political program based on the assumption of racism and designed to execute its principles **b :** a political or social system founded on racism **3 :** RACIALISM 1

¹rac·ist \'rāsәst\ *n* -S [prob. fr. F *raciste*, fr. *race* + *-iste* -ist] **:** one who advocates or believes in racism

²racist \"\ *adj* **1 :** of, relating to, or based on racism ⟨~ ideas⟩ **2 :** advocating or practicing racism ⟨a ~ leader⟩

¹rack \'rak\ *n* -S [ME *rac, rak;* prob. of Scand origin; akin to Norw & Sw dial. *rak* wreck, wreckage; akin to OE *wrecan* to drive — more at WREAK] **1 a** *obs* **:** shock of meeting **:** RUSH, CHARGE **b** *obs* **:** a sound as of a collision **:** CRASH **2 a :** a wind-driven mass of high often broken clouds **b** *obs* **:** a driving mist or fog

²rack \"\ *vi* -ED/-ING/-S **:** to fly or scud in high wind

³rack \"\ *n* -S [ME *rekke, racke*, prob. fr. MD *rec* framework; akin to OE *reccan* to stretch, OHG *recchen*, ON *rekja* to spread out, Goth *ufrakjan* to stretch out, Gk *oregein* — more at RIGHT] **1** *dial chiefly Eng* **:** a bar or a set of bars esp. for supporting a roasting spit **2 :** a framework for holding fodder for livestock usu. with upright partitions so placed as to leave room only for one animal's head between them **3 a :** an instrument of torture formerly much used in Europe and consisting of a frame having rollers at each end to which the limbs are fastened and between which the body is stretched **b :** a framework for stretching leather to a certain specified pull used for purposes of official measurement of the area and thickness of skins and hides **c :** an instrument for bending a crossbow **4 a :** a cause of anguish or pain or the resulting suffering ⟨the ~ of gout⟩ **b :** RACK RENT **c :** a straining or wrenching ⟨a tree twisted by the ~ of storms⟩ **5 :** a framework, stand, or grating on or in which articles are placed (as for keeping or for display) ⟨clothes ~⟩ ⟨cake ~⟩ ⟨bottle ~⟩: as **a :** a frame fitted to a wagon or truck for carrying hay, straw, grain, tobacco on the stalk, or other bulky loads **b :** a series of bins or compartments into which items may be sorted ⟨mail ~⟩ **c :** any compartmented container for holding type cases, galleys, forms, leads, or furniture **d :** a stationary inclined

rack 8a and pinion

frame or table on which ores are washed **6 :** a frame placed in a stream to stop the passage of fish and floating or suspended matter **7** *or* **rack block :** a piece or frame of wood having several sheaves through which the running rigging of a ship passes **8 a :** a bar with teeth on one face for gearing with those of a pinion, bevel wheel, or worm gear **b :** a notched bar used as a ratchet to engage with a pawl, click, or detent **c :** a sector-gear pivoted to contact a snail and regulate the number of hammer blows in a striking clock or repeater watch **9 :** a support with springs to offset vibration on which the camera and the subject are fastened in process photography; *also* **:** a support for holding several films or plates during processing **10 :** a pair of antlers **11 :** a wooden triangular frame used to set up the balls for the opening shot in pool games; *also* **:** the balls as set up when the triangle has been removed — **at rack and manger** *archaic* **:** in abundance **:** in an extravagant fashion ⟨living *at rack and manger* —Thomas Carlyle⟩ — **on the rack** *adv* (*or adj*) **:** under great mental or emotional stress **:** in acute anxiety or uncertainty — **to rack and manger** *archaic* **:** to waste and destruction **:** to wrack and ruin ⟨the moment my back is turned everything goes *to rack and manger* —Henry Fielding⟩

4**rack** \"\ *vb* -ED/-ING/-S [partly fr. ME *rakken,* prob. fr. MD *recken* to stretch (akin to OE *reccan* to stretch); partly fr. 3*rack*] *vt* **1 :** to torture on the rack **:** inflict pain or punishment by pulling or straining **2 a :** to afflict with torture, pain, or anguish comparable to that suffered on a rack ⟨her heart went out to this ~*ed* girl —Adria Langley⟩ ⟨~*ed* with jealousy⟩ **b :** to afflict and agitate very much with or as if with trouble, stress, anxiety, doubt, unpleasant emotion, or illness ⟨the Greco-Roman world had been ~*ed* by revolutions —A.J.Toynbee⟩ ⟨was obviously ~*ing* his brains as his answer . . . disclosed —Robert Grant †1940⟩ **3 a :** to stretch, strain, or extend violently **b :** to twist the meaning of **:** pervert the sense of **c :** to raise (rents) oppressively **d :** to harass or oppress with high rents, exactions, or extortions **4** *chiefly Brit* **a :** to supply a rack with feed for (as a horse) — used with *up* **b :** to fasten (an animal) in place at the rack **5 :** to work, stretch, or treat (material) on a rack ⟨~ leather⟩ ⟨~ rubber⟩ ⟨~ ore⟩ **6 :** to work by a rack and pinion or worm so as to extend or contract ⟨~ a camera⟩ **7 :** to seize (as parallel ropes of a tackle) together so as to prevent running through the block **8 :** to place (as pool balls) in a rack — often used with *up* ~ *vi* **1 a :** to become forced out of shape or out of plumb **b :** to sway together from side to side of their proper position relative to the keel — used of a ship's sides **2** *Scot* **:** to undergo straining or stretching **:** lengthen or give under tension **syn** see AFFLICT

5**rack** \"\ *vt* -ED/-ING/-S [ME *rakken* fr. OProv *arraca,* fr. *raca* stems and husks of grapes after pressing] **1 :** to draw off (as wine) from the lees or sediment into new casks — used often with *off* **2 :** to fill (trade casks) with ale or stout

6**rack** \"\ *vi* -ED/-ING/-S [prob. alter. of 1*rock*] *of a horse* **:** to use either gait called a rack

7**rack** \"\ *n* -S **:** either of two gaits of a horse: **a :** PACE 5b **b :** a fast showy usu. artificial four-beat gait in which the feet leave the ground in the same sequence as in the walk but faster and with higher action — called also *single-foot*

8**rack** \"\ *n* -S [perh. fr. 3*rack*] **1 a :** the neck and spine of a forequarter of veal, pork, or esp. mutton **b :** the rib section of a foresaddle of lamb used for chops and roasts — see HOTEL RACK; LAMB illustration **2 :** the side planking or side buffer of a ferry slip **3 :** RACKABONES

9**rack** \"\ *var of* WRACK

10**rack** \"\ *n* -S [by shortening] **:** ARRACK

11**rack** \"\ *n* -S [perh. alter. of 4*rake*] *dial* **:** the path or track made by a moving object or animal — **by rack of eye** *dial Eng* **:** by gauging with the eye alone ⟨working *by rack of eye*⟩

12**rack** \"\ *dial Brit var of* RECK

13**rack** \"\ *n* -S [origin unknown] **:** a nearly full-grown young rabbit; *also* **:** its skin

rack·a·bones \ˈrakə,bōnz\ *n pl but sing in constr* [alter. of *rack of bones*] **:** a very lean person or animal; *esp* **:** a lean horse

rack·an \ˈrakən\ *also* **reck·an** \ˈrekən\ *n* -S [ME *racand,* fr. OE *racente;* akin to OHG *rahchinza* chain, ON *rekendi*] **1** *obs* **:** CHAIN, FETTER **2** *dial chiefly Eng* **:** a hook for hanging pots over a fire

rack-and-lever jack \ˈ⸗⸗ˈ⸗⸗-\ *n* [3*rack*] **:** RATCHET JACK

rack-and-pinion press \ˈ⸗⸗ˈ⸗⸗-\ *n* **:** a punch press in which the pressure is applied to the slide by a rack-and-pinion mechanism

rack-and-pinion railway *n* **:** RACK RAILWAY

rack and snail *n* [3*rack*] **:** a mechanical arrangement in striking timepieces that allows the hands to be advanced to correct time without waiting for the striking to run through — compare 3RACK 8c

rack back *vt* [4*rack*] *slang* **:** REPRIMAND

rack bar *n* [3*rack*] **1 :** 3RACK 8a **2 :** a stick of wood used to bouse taut a rope binding something together

rack block *n* **:** 3RACK 7

rack body *n* **:** a truck body with latticed sides

rack car *n* **:** a freight car having end racks but no sides and used primarily for hauling pulpwood loaded crosswise on the car

racked *past of* RACK

racked rubber *n* [fr. past part. of 4*rack*] **:** rubber stretched to a much elongated thin strip that contracts only partially when warmed

rack·er \ˈrakə(r)\ *n* -S [4*rack* + -*er*] **:** one that racks: as **a :** a worker who puts articles on racks, as for drying, cooling, storage, transportation, or further processing — called also *rackman* **b :** a worker who lays out on a rack the sections of a chain of pocketed springs for an innerspring mattress and sews them together **c :** one who racks pool balls

1**rack·et** *also* **rac·quet** \ˈrakət, *usu* -əd·+V\ *n* -S [MF *raquette,* fr. Ar *rāḥah* palm of the hand] **1 a :** a light bat consisting of a catgut, nylon, or formerly, cord netting stretched in a somewhat oval open frame with handle attached used for striking the ball in tennis and in similar games **b :** a small round paddle with a squat handle used in table tennis **2** *usu* **racquets** *pl but sing in constr* **:** a game for two or four played with ball and racket on a four-walled court — compare SQUASH RACQUETS **3 a :** SNOWSHOE **b :** a broad wooden shoe for a man or horse for walking on soft ground

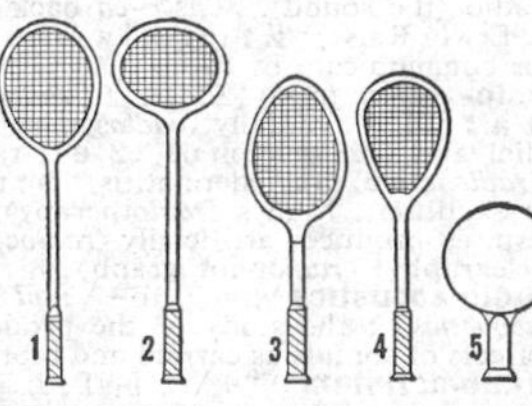

rackets 1: *1* badminton, *2* racquets, *3* tennis, *4* court tennis, *5* table tennis

2**racket** \"\ *vt* -ED/-ING/-S *obs* **:** to strike with or as if with a racket **:** BANDY

3**racket** \"\ *n* -S [prob. of imit. origin] **1 a :** confused clattering noise ⟨the ~ of the lunchroom⟩ ⟨~ of a street repair gang⟩ **b :** noisy, disturbing, or objectionable talk or activity **:** CLAMOR ⟨made such a ~ that she couldn't nap⟩ ⟨the dogs set up a terrific ~⟩ **2 a :** social whirl or excitement **:** REVELING, MERRYMAKING **b :** a large noisy party ⟨used to give at least one ~ a year⟩ **c :** the strain of exciting or trying experiences or ordeals — used with *the* ⟨getting too old to stand the ~⟩ **3 a :** a fraudulent scheme, enterprise, or activity ⟨to him everything was a ~ —God, education, radio, marriage, children, Communism, astronomy . . . osteopathy, Hollywood —*Time*⟩ ⟨sees through pompous ~ of the publicity campaign —Hans Meyerhoff⟩ ⟨fashion is a ~ to sell clothes —*New Yorker*⟩ **b :** a usu. illegitimate enterprise or activity that is made workable by coercion, bribery, or intimidation ⟨narcotics ~⟩ ⟨numbers ~⟩ ⟨officials consorting with mobsters, protecting the ~*s* and getting in return a share of the take —*N.Y.Times*⟩ **c :** a system of obtaining money or other advantage illegally, fraudulently, or undeservedly usu. with the outward consent of the victims ⟨the fortune-telling ~⟩ **d :** an easy and lucrative means of livelihood **e** *slang* **:** OCCUPATION, BUSINESS **syn** see DIN

4**racket** \"\ *vi* -ED/-ING/-S **1 :** to engage in active social life or pleasure seeking — used usu. with *about* or *around* ⟨woman of the type often referred to as "gallant" mostly because she's done more than her share of ~*ing* around —*New Yorker*⟩ ⟨~*ed* round in my car, had no aim or ambition —G.W.Brace⟩ **2 :** to move with or make a racket ⟨~*ing* along in bus or train —K.W.Slifer⟩ ⟨a machine gun would start ~*ing* in the jungle —Norman Mailer⟩

1**rack·e·teer** \,rakəˈti(ə)r, -iə\ *n* -S [3*racket* + -*eer*] **:** one who extorts money or advantages by threats of violence or by blackmail or by threatened or actual unlawful interference with business or employment **:** one who engages in a racket

2**racketeer** \"\ *vb* -ED/-ING/-S *vi* **:** to carry on a racket **:** use fraud or intimidation in extorting money or commercial or political advantage ~ *vt* **:** to practice extortion on ⟨these peddlers are frequently ~*ed* by gangsters —D.W.Maurer⟩

1**rack·et·er** \ˈrakəd·ə(r)\ *n* -S [1*racket* + -*er*] **:** one who uses a racket: as **a :** one who plays tennis, squash, badminton **b :** one who uses snowshoes

2**racketer** \"\ *n* -S [3*racket* + -*er*] **1 :** one who makes a racket or noisy disturbance **2** *obs* **:** RACKETEER, SWINDLER

racketlike \ˈ⸗⸗,⸗\ *adj* [1*racket* + -*like*] **:** resembling a racket; *specif* **:** having or consisting of a flat expanded rounded part at the end of a straight shaft ⟨a ~ feather⟩

rack·et·ry \ˈrakətrē\ *n* -ES [3*racket* + -*ry*] **:** RACKET, UPROAR, EXCITEMENT

racket store *n* [prob. fr. 3*racket*] *chiefly Midland* **:** VARIETY STORE

rack·ett \ˈrakət\ *n* -S [G] **:** an obsolete bass instrument of the oboe family having its tube bent upon itself in short lengths that are enclosed in a cylinder — called also *sausage bassoon*

rackettail \ˈ⸗⸗,⸗\ *also* **racket-tailed hummingbird** \ˈ⸗⸗,⸗-\ *n* [1*racket* + *tail*] **:** any of several hummingbirds of the genera *Ocreatus* and *Discosura* having two of the tail feathers very long and racket-shaped

racket wheel *n* [by alter.] **:** RATCHET WHEEL

rack·ety *also* **rack·et·ty** \ˈrakəd·ē, -ətē, -i\ *adj, sometimes* -ER/-EST [3*racket* + -*y*] **1 :** NOISY ⟨~ streetcar⟩ **:** EXCITING **2 :** addicted to or characterized by racketing or reveling **:** GAY, DISSIPATED, ROWDY, RAFFISH ⟨rather ~ but class-conscious world of sport —*Times Lit. Supp.*⟩ **3 :** RICKETY ⟨his memory was even more ~ —E.C.Wagenknecht⟩

rack·ful \ˈrak,fu̇l\ *n* -S [3*rack* + -*ful*] **:** the quantity contained in a rack ⟨~*s* of highly elaborate gowns —*New Yorker*⟩

rack·ing \ˈrakiŋ\ *n* -S [4*rack* + -*ing*] **1 :** the setting back slightly of the end of each course of brick or stone as it is laid near the junction with another wall so that each course is shorter than the one below **2 :** spun yarn or other seizing used in racking ropes **3 :** the motion of a knitting machine that controls the needle position for dropping, transferring, or changing stitches

racking 1

rack·ing·ly *adv* [*racking* (pres. part. of 4*rack*) + -*ly*] **:** in a racking manner **:** so as to shake or strain

1**rack·le** \ˈrakəl\ *adj* [ME *rakel, rakil*] *chiefly Scot* **:** IMPETUOUS, HEADSTRONG — **rack·le·ness** *n* -ES *obs*

2**rackle** \"\ *vb* -ED/-ING/-S [imit.] *dial Brit* **:** RATTLE

rack·less \ˈrakləs\ *dial var of* RECKLESS

rack·man \ˈrakmən\ *n, pl* **rackmen** [3*rack* + *man*] **1 :** a power plant or mill worker who cleans the racks that screen fish, weeds, and other foreign matter from river water before it enters machines **2 :** one who working from a raised loading rack fills tank cars, trucks, or ships with petroleum products **3 :** a worker who places starting blanks between anodes in electrolysis tanks before the deposition of copper starting sheets on the blanks **4 :** RACKER a

rack-o'-bones \ˈrakə,bōnz\ *n pl but sing in constr* **:** RACKABONES

rack punch *n* [3*rack*] **:** MULTIPLE-DIE PRESS

rack rail *n* **:** COGRAIL

rack railway *or* **rack railroad** *n* **:** a railway having between its rails a rack that meshes with a gear wheel or pinion of the locomotive for climbing grades too steep for traction through ordinary adhesion of the wheels to the rail

rack rent *n* [4*rack*] **:** a rent equal or nearly equal to the full annual value of the property **:** an excessive or unreasonably high rent

rack-rent \ˈ⸗,⸗\ *vt* **:** to subject (as a farm or a tenant) to rack rent

rack-renter \ˈ⸗ˈ⸗⸗\ *n* **1 :** one who pays rack rent **2 :** one who exacts rack rent

racks *pl of* RACK, *pres 3d sing of* RACK

rack up *vt* [4*rack*] **:** ACHIEVE, SCORE ⟨*racked* 30 points *up* in the first half⟩ ⟨*racked up* his fourth straight victory of the season⟩

rackway \ˈ⸗,⸗\ *n* [3*rack* + *way*] **:** RACK RAILWAY

rack wheel *n* **:** GEAR WHEEL

rackwork \ˈ⸗,⸗\ *n* **:** a mechanism (as a rack and pinion) having a rack

ra·con \ˈrā,kän, -ākən\ *n* -S [*radar* + *beacon*] **:** a radar beacon that sends out a coded signal in response to the proper radar signal received from a ship or aircraft and thus enables the navigator to identify the beacon as well as to determine his own range and bearing from it

rac·on·teur *R* ,ra,känˈtər, -akən-, +V -ˈtər-; -*R* -ˈtə̄, + *vowel in a word following without pause* -ˈtər- *or* -ˈtə̄ *also* -ˈtər\ *n* -S [F, fr. MF, fr. *raconter* to tell (fr. OF, fr. *re-* + *aconter* to tell, count) + -*eur* — more at ACCOUNT] **:** one who excels in telling anecdotes **:** STORYTELLER

rac·on·teuse \-ˈtərz, -ˈtə̄z, -ˈtüz, -ˈtəz\ *n* -S [F, fem. of *raconteur*] **:** a female raconteur

racoon *var of* RACCOON

1**ra·co·vi·an** \rəˈkōvēən\ *adj, usu cap* [*Raków,* village in southeast Poland + E -*ian*] **:** of or relating to Raków or to the Polish Socinians whose intellectual center in the 17th century was Raków

2**racovian** \"\ *n* -S *usu cap* **:** a Polish Socinian

1**racquet** *var of* 1RACKET

2**rac·quet** \ˈrakət\ *n* -S **:** GAZELLE 2

1**racy** \ˈrāsē, -si\ *adj* -ER/-EST [7*race* + -*y*] **1 :** having the distinctive or characteristic flavor, quality, or excellence of a race or kind **:** manifesting the quality of a thing in its native, original, genuine, or most characteristic form or state **:** NATURAL, UNSPOILED, FRESH ⟨~ morsels of the vernacular —Walter Pater⟩ **2 a :** full of life, zest, or vigor **:** LIVELY, SPIRITED **b :** PIQUANT, PUNGENT, EXHILARATING ⟨written with energy and with ~ humor —H.S.Commager⟩ **c :** RISQUÉ, SUGGESTIVE ⟨~ anecdotes⟩ **syn** see PUNGENT

2**racy** \"\ *adj* -ER/-EST [partly fr. 1*racy;* partly fr. 2*race* + -*y*] **1 :** having a build fitted for racing **2** *of an animal* **:** long-bodied and lean

1**rad** \ˈrad\ *adj* [ME, fr. OE *hræd* — more at RATHE] *dial* **:** QUICK, READY, EAGER; *also* **:** ELATED, EXHILARATED

2**rad** \"\ *adj* [ME, of Scand origin; akin to ON *hræddr* afraid, *hræða* fear, *hrathr* quick, rash — more at RATHE] *Scot* **:** AFRAID

3**rad** \"\ *n* -S [short for *radiation*] **:** a unit of absorbed dose of ionizing radiation equal to an energy of 100 ergs per gram of irradiated material

rad *abbr* **1** radial **2** radian **3** radiant **4** radiator **5** radical **6** radio **7** radium **8** radius **9** [L *radix*] root

ra·dar \ˈrā,där, -dȧ(r\ *n* -S *often attrib* [radio detecting and ranging] **:** a radio device or system for locating an object by means of emitting radio signals usu. in the form of pulses of an ultrahigh frequency and observing and analyzing the minute signals reflected from the object and received at or near the point of transmission in such a way that range, bearing, and other characteristics of the object may be determined

radar beacon *n* **:** a radar transmitter that upon receiving a radar signal emits a signal which reinforces the normal reflected signal or which introduces a code into the reflected signal for identification purposes

ra·dar·man \-mən, -,man\ *n, pl* **radarmen :** an operator of a radar device

ra·dar·scope \-,skōp, -,də(r)-\ *n* [*radar* + oscillo*scope*] **:** an oscilloscope having a cathode-ray tube whose fluorescent end serves as the visual indicator in a radar receiver — called also *scope*

1**rad·dle** \ˈradᵊl\ *n* -S [prob. alter. of 1*ruddle*] **:** RED OCHER; *also* **:** other coloring matter used for marking animals

2**raddle** \"\ *vt* -ED/-ING/-S **1 :** to mark or paint with or as if with raddle **:** color highly with rouge **:** RUDDLE ⟨people who never *raddled* their faces with greasepaint —*Times Lit. Supp.*⟩ ⟨a *raddled* barmaid —Janet Tobitt⟩ ⟨*raddled* tile floor —Flora Thompson⟩ ⟨*raddled* with the paint of pokeberry juice —Ellen Glasgow⟩ **2** *Austral* **:** to mark the brisket of a ram with raddle to identify the ewes he serves **3 :** PIT, SCAR ⟨when they kept to the open sea . . . his broadsides *raddled* them —*Time*⟩ ⟨poverty-haunted, crime-*raddled* neighborhood —Edmund Fuller⟩

3**raddle** \"\ *n* -S [MF *rudelle, redelle* stout pole, rail of a cart, prob. fr. MHG *reitel*] **1** *chiefly dial* **:** a long supple stick, rod, or branch often interwoven with others in making a hedge or fence or plastered with clay to make a wall **2** *chiefly dial* **:** a structure made with raddles **3 :** a bar usu. of wood having pegs between which warp yarns are guided while being wound on the beam

4**raddle** \"\ *vt* -ED/-ING/-S **1 :** to twist together **:** make by interlacing **:** INTERWEAVE **2 :** to regulate by means of a raddle

5**raddle** \"\ *vt* [perh. fr. 3*raddle*] *Scot* **:** BEAT, THRASH

rad·dled \-ᵊld\ *adj* [origin unknown] **1 :** CONFUSED, BEFUDDLED ⟨if you'd been as ~ as I was last night —Norman Douglas⟩ ⟨a ~ old man⟩ **2 :** WORN, BROKEN, BROKEN-DOWN ⟨factories lay like ~ skeletons —*Time*⟩ ⟨that ~ but still noble face —Esther Forbes⟩ ⟨battered trumpets . . . ~ radios —*New Yorker*⟩ ⟨the mouth was firm . . . in the loose, ~ flesh about it —Eric Ambler⟩

rad·dle·man \-ᵊlmən\ *n, pl* **raddlemen** [1*raddle* + *man*] **:** RUDDLEMAN

rade [ME, fr. OE *rād*] *chiefly dial past of* RIDE

raden *pl of* RAAD

ra·di·a·bil·i·ty \,rādēəˈbiləd·ē\ *n* [*radia*tion + -*ability*] **:** the capability of transmitting radiation esp. X rays ⟨the ~ is altered by differences in thickness of the bone —K.H.Thoma⟩

ra·di·ac \ˈrādē,ak\ *n* -S [*radi*oactivity *d*etection *i*dentification *a*nd *c*omputation] **:** the act or process of detecting, identifying, and measuring the nuclear radiation at a given place

1**ra·di·al** \ˈrādēəl\ *adj* [ML *radialis,* fr. L *radius* ray, beam + -*alis* -al — more at RAY] **1 :** issuing in rays **:** relating to rays of light ⟨intense ~ heat is applied —*Chem. Abstracts*⟩ **2 a :** arranged or having parts arranged like rays ⟨~ blades in a blower⟩ ⟨most cities show a ~ pattern of main highways leading outward from their center —C.L.White & G.T. Renner⟩ ⟨young dome mountains and volcanoes have ~ drainage lines —A.K.Lobeck⟩ ⟨~ seating in an auditorium⟩ **b :** being an architectural plan in which the disposition is radial as distinguished from longitudinal ⟨~ plan of a church⟩ **3 a :** relating to or placed like a radius ⟨~ blocks for chimney-construction —L.A.Harding⟩ **:** moving or taking place along a radius **:** having the direction of a radius ⟨~ acceleration⟩ ⟨~ velocity⟩ **b :** characterized by divergence from or as if from a center **4 a :** of, relating to, or adjacent to a bodily radius (as the bone of the forearm or the ray of a starfish) **b :** being any of various plates of a crinoid that lie between the basal and brachial plates **5 a :** developing uniformly around a central axis — opposed to *dorsiventral* **b :** relating to a ray or ray flower **c :** having the xylem and phloem lying on alternate radii of the axis usu. separated by nonvascular tissue ⟨a ~ actinostele⟩

2**radial** \"\ *n* -S **1 a :** radial part: as (1) **:** a bar at right angles to a curved part (as in an arch) (2) **:** the radial arm or quadrant on which the change wheels are secured in a screw-cutting lathe **b :** any of a system of radial lines **:** RAY; *specif* **:** a line of position radiating from a radio navigational aid transmitter **2 a :** a body part (as an artery, nerve, or plate) lying near or following the course of the radius; *sometimes* **:** RADIALE **b :** HYPERCORACOID **3 :** RADIAL ENGINE

radial arm *n* **:** a device for controlling the direction of a pipeline when the angle is less than 30 degrees

radial artery *n* **:** the smaller of the two branches into which the brachial artery divides just below the bend of the elbow and which passes along the radial side of the forearm to the wrist then winds backward around the outer side of the carpus and enters the palm between the first and second metacarpal bones to form the deep palmar arch — see PULSE

radial bearing *n* **:** a ball bearing in which the direction of action of the load transmitted is radial to the axis of the shaft

radial brick *n* **:** brick with tapering sides to form a circular wall (as of a chimney or tower)

radial canal *n* **1 :** one of the numerous minute canals lined with choanocytes which radiate from the paragastric cavity in some sponges and end just below the surface of the sponge **2 :** one of the canals extending through the substance of the umbrella from the gastric cavity to the marginal circular canal in jellyfishes **3 :** a tube extending outward along each ambulacral area from the circumoral canal in most echinoderms

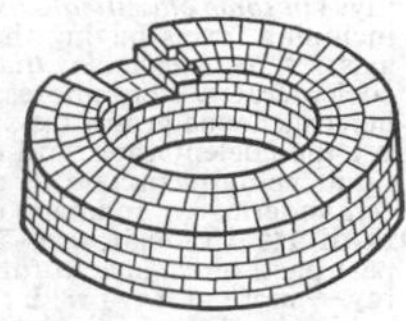
radial brick used in chimney construction

radial drill *n* **:** a drilling machine with the drill spindle in a toolhead and saddle that are movable along a projecting arm which itself can be rotated about a vertical column

ra·di·ale \,rādēˈa(,)lē, -ˈā(-, -ˈä(-\ *n, pl* **radi·alia** \-lēə\ [NL, fr. ML, neut. sing. of *radialis* radial] **1 a :** a bone or cartilage of the carpus that articulates with the radius; *specif* **:** the navicular in man **b :** a bone in the carpus of a bird made up of the radiale fused with either the intermediure or the centrale **2 :** a radial plate of a crinoid **3 :** a bone or cartilage distal to the basale and directly supporting a ray in a fish's fin; *also* **:** ACTINOST

radial engine *n* **:** a usu. internal-combustion engine having cylinders arranged radially like the spokes of a wheel; *specif* **:** such an engine in which the cylinders are stationary and the crankshaft revolves — see ROTARY ENGINE

radial-flow \ˈ⸗⸗⸗ˈ⸗\ *adj* **:** having the working fluid flowing mainly along the radii of rotation ⟨a *radial-flow* turbine⟩ — compare AXIAL-FLOW

radial gate *n* **:** a device used for controlling the flow of water over spillways or into canals by having the upstream face curved in the form of an arc the center of which is at the center of the gate hinge — called also *tainter gate*

radial head *n* **:** a rounded eminence by which the humerus articulates with the radius

ra·di·al·ly \ˈrādēəlē, -li\ *adv* **:** in a radial manner

radial nerve *n* **:** a large nerve that arises from the posterior cord of the brachial plexus and passes spirally down the humerus to the front of the lateral epicondyle where it divides into a superficial branch distributed to the skin of the back of the hand and arm and a deep branch to the underlying extensor muscles

radial quantum number *n* **:** an integer associated with the radial component of the momentum of an atomic electron in one of its possible stationary states — compare AZIMUTHAL QUANTUM NUMBER, PRINCIPAL QUANTUM NUMBER

radial saw *n* **:** a circular saw in which the saw wheel is suspended from a traverse head in turn suspended from a rotatable arm

radial sector *n* **:** a vein in the wings of most insects that usu. arises from the radius

radial shield *n* **:** one of a pair of plates situated on the disk at the base of each ray of an ophiuran

radial symmetry *n* **:** the condition of having similar parts regularly arranged about a central axis (as in a starfish)

radial vein *n* **1 :** a superficial vein ascending along the radial side of the forearm and uniting with the median cephalic vein to form the cephalic vein **2 :** a vein accompanying a radial artery

radial velocity *n* **1 :** the component of velocity of a particle in the direction of its radius vector **2** *or* **radial motion :** the velocity of relative approach or recession of an observer and a celestial body or other sources of radiation in the line connecting the two **:** speed in the line of sight

ra·di·an \'rādēən\ *n* -s [*radi*us + *-an*] **:** a unit of plane angular measurement equal to the angle at the center of a circle subtended by an arc equal in length to the radius ⟨since the circumference of a circle is equal to 2π times its radius, the number of ~*s* in an angle of 360 degrees or in a complete turn is 2π, so that 1 ~ equals about 57.29 degrees⟩

ra·di·ance \'rādēən(t)s\ *also* **ra·di·an·cy** \-nsē, -nsi\ *n, pl* **radiances** *or* **radiancies** [*radiance* fr. 1*radiant*, after such pairs as E *attendant: attendance; radiancy* fr. 1*radiant* + *-cy*] **1 :** the quality or state of being radiant **:** vivid brightness **:** SPLENDOR ⟨the sun touched the tops of the still trees, and poured its ~ over the hill —Charles Dickens⟩ ⟨light up the family story with the ~ of great events —E.E.Morison⟩ ⟨in the ~ of that old summer —Ellen Glasgow⟩ ⟨pulling a cap over the ~ of her hair —C.B.Kelland⟩ **2 :** the flux density of radiant energy per unit solid angle and per unit projected area of radiating surface **3 :** a deep pink that is bluer, lighter, and stronger than average coral (sense 3b), deeper than fiesta, and yellower and deeper than begonia **4 :** GLORY ⟨a figure of the Virgin Mary with the child standing on a crescent and surrounded by a ~ —W. de G. Birch⟩

1**ra·di·ant** \-nt\ *adj* [ME, fr. L *radiant-, radians*, pres. part. of *radiare* to emit rays, radiate — more at RADIATE] **1 a :** radiating rays of light **:** emitting or reflecting beams of light **b :** radiating or diffusing splendor, glory, or a similar quality **:** vividly bright and shining **:** GLOWING, BRILLIANT ⟨~ as a double dawn in sky and water —Elinor Wylie⟩ ⟨his hands are ~ with rings — diamonds and sapphires —Truman Capote⟩ ⟨the fields . . . were ~ with early summer —Nancy Hale⟩ ⟨the ~ images of religion and of art as well as of science —Havelock Ellis⟩ **2 :** RAYONNANT 1 **3 :** marked by or expressive of joy, pleasure, love, confidence, or happiness **:** seeming to radiate some quality esp. good ⟨~, like a schoolboy who has received an unexpectedly large tip —Christopher Isherwood⟩ ⟨one of the most ~ lyrics in the language —W.Y.Tindall⟩ ⟨gray eyes full of a ~ curiosity —Scott Fitzgerald⟩ ⟨~ with idealism —V.L.Parrington⟩ **4 a :** emitted or transmitted by radiation **b :** emitting or relating to radiant heat ⟨~ lamp⟩ ⟨a ~ type radiator⟩ ⟨a ~ baseboard⟩ **5 :** of or relating to a biological radiant or biological radiation **syn** see BRIGHT

2**radiant** \"\ *n* -s **:** something that radiates: as **a :** the point in the heavens at which the visible paths of meteors appear to meet when traced backward or whence they appear to radiate although in reality the paths of the meteors are parallel **b :** a straight line proceeding from a given point or fixed pole about which it is conceived to revolve **c :** a point or object from which light emanates **d :** the part of a gas or electric heater that becomes incandescent and emits radiant heat **e :** an organism or group of organisms (as a species) that has reached its present geographical location as the result of a dispersal from a primary place of origin — compare RADIATION

radiant energy *n* **:** energy traveling as a wave motion; *specif* **:** the energy of electromagnetic waves (as radio waves, infrared rays, visible light, ultraviolet rays, X rays, and gamma rays) — compare LUMINOUS ENERGY

radiant flux *n* **:** the rate of emission of radiant energy or of its transmission through a specified region usu. expressed in watts — compare LUMINOUS FLUX

radiant-flux density *n* **:** the radiant energy in a beam of electromagnetic, thermal, or acoustic radiation passing through a unit normal section per unit time — called also *intensity of radiation*

radiant glass *n* **:** glass that is usu. in panels and contains radiant heating elements

radiant heat *n* **:** heat transmitted by radiation as contrasted with that transmitted by conduction or convection ⟨electrical ceiling cables that provide invisible *radiant heat* from above — just like the sun —*Sweet's Catalog Service*⟩

radiant heater *n* **:** a heating unit emitting radiant energy; *esp* **:** such a heater in which a refractory is heated to incandescence by a gas flame

radiant heating *n* **:** PANEL HEATING

radiant intensity *n* **:** the radiant energy that is emitted by a source per unit time per unit solid angle in a given direction under conditions that the source may be considered as sensibly a point source and that is measured in units of watts per steradian

ra·di·ant·ly *adv* **:** in a radiant manner ⟨the bride smiled ~⟩

radiant point *n* **:** RADIANT b

radiant yellow *n* **:** CADMIUM YELLOW

ra·di·a·ta \,rādē'äd·ə, -'ād·ə\ *n pl, cap* [NL, fr. L, neut. pl. of *radiatus* furnished with rays, fr. past part. of *radiare* to emit rays] *in some classifications* **:** a major category of invertebrates including forms having the parts arranged radially about an axis: **a** *in former classifications* **:** all the radiate animals (as coelenterates, ctenophores, and echinoderms) together with a heterogeneous group (as sponges, bryozoans, and flatworms) **b :** the coelenterates and ctenophores which are regarded as fundamentally radiate in contrast to the secondarily radiate echinoderms — compare BILATERIA, DIPLEURULA

1**ra·di·ate** \'rādē,āt, *usu* -ād·+V\ *vb* -ED/-ING/-S [L *radiatus*, past part. of *radiare* to furnish with rays, emit rays, fr. *radius* ray — more at RAY] *vi* **1 :** to send out rays of or as if of light **:** shine brightly ⟨in the last white-hot phase of its collapse, the sun would begin to ~ as a star —F.L.Whipple⟩ ⟨a *radiating* focus of goodwill —R.L.Stevenson⟩ **2 :** to issue in rays or as if in rays **:** move, traverse, emanate or be sent out from a focal point ⟨light ~*s*⟩ ⟨heat ~*s*⟩ ⟨influences *radiating* from Paris —H.O.Taylor⟩ ⟨the system of patronage . . . provided a fixed center from which their work could ~ over society —C.D. Lewis⟩ **3 :** to proceed or be arranged in a direct line from or toward a center in the manner of a radius ⟨the web of little wrinkles that *radiated* from the corners of her eyes —Hamilton Basso⟩ ⟨streets *radiating* from a square⟩ **4 :** to evolve by radiation ⟨remarkably endowed creatures . . . *radiated* with amazing rapidity into a diversity of forms —L.C.Eiseley⟩ ~ *vt* **1 :** to send out in or as if in rays ⟨the sun ~*s* light and heat⟩ ⟨his blithe, buoyant personality *radiated* joy of life and goodwill —F.H.Garrison⟩ ⟨seems to ~ power and vitality —James Hewitt⟩ ⟨include . . . a man *radiating* peace, joy and wisdom —Henry Miller⟩ **2 :** IRRADIATE **3 :** to spread abroad or around as if from a center **:** DISSEMINATE, DIFFUSE ⟨each center would then ~ influence until proper methods in science should gradually spread throughout the educational system —D.S. & Jessie K. Jordan⟩ **4 :** to broadcast by radio or television ⟨to ~ a program⟩ **syn** see SPREAD

2**ra·di·ate** \-ēə̇\|t, -ē,ā\|, *usu* \|d·+V\ *adj* [L *radiatus* furnished with rays, fr. past part. of *radiare* to furnish with rays, emit rays] **:** having rays or radial parts **:** RADIATED, RADIAL: as **a :** having ray flowers — used of the head in many plants of the family Compositae; compare DISCOID 2 **b** (1) **:** characterized by radial symmetry ⟨a ~ structure in an animal⟩ (2) **:** relating to the Radiata **c :** RADIAL 2b

3**radiate** \"\ *n* -s [NL *Radiata*] **:** one of the Radiata

radiated *adj* [fr. past part. of 1*radiate*] **1 :** emitted in rays or direct lines **2 :** formed of or arranged like rays or radii **:** having radial parts or markings ⟨a ~ group of crystals⟩ ⟨oriental crowns, the points alternately ~ —*Burke's Peerage*⟩ **3 :** exposed to radiation; *specif* **:** treated with X rays or radium ⟨~ body parts⟩

ra·di·ate·ly *adv* **:** in a radiate manner ⟨a ~ ribbed sea shell⟩

ra·di·ate·ness *n* -ES **:** the quality or state of being radiate ⟨the ~ in a starfish⟩

ra·di·a·tion \,rādē'āshən\ *n* -s [L *radiation-, radiatio*, fr. *radiatus* (past part. of *radiare* to radiate) + *-ion-, -io* -ion] **1 a :** the act or process of radiating ⟨with ~ of the pain there may be tenderness over the sciatic nerve —J.A.Key⟩ ⟨~ of a radio program⟩ ⟨the ~ of their world-conquering culture —*Harper's*⟩ ⟨his smile . . . is a ~ of light —*Saturday Rev.*⟩ **b :** the process of emitting radiant energy in the form of waves or particles ⟨~ is easily distinguished from other forms of heat transfer . . . by its speed of propagation which equals that of light, and by the fact that no intervening medium is required for its transmission —J.G.Charney⟩; *also* **:** the combined processes of emission, transmission, and absorption of radiant energy **2 a :** something that is radiated ⟨the real apostolic ~ which goes out from a contemplative monastery springs from the interior purity of the monks' own souls —Thomas Merton⟩ ⟨believe in the presence of ~*s* which stream to earth from mysterious realms beyond —Edward Sapir⟩ **b :** energy radiated in the form of waves or particles (as sound waves, electromagnetic waves, and corpuscular emissions that include alpha rays, beta rays, and neutrons released in atomic nuclear changes as well as cosmic rays) ⟨the essential identity of light, heat, and other electromagnetic ~ —D.L.Harms⟩ ⟨an antenna in free space . . . sends out ~ in all directions —J.C.Slater⟩ **3 :** radial arrangement; *also* **:** a radial thing or part **4 a :** biological evolution in a group of organisms that is characterized by spreading into different environments and by divergence of structure ⟨adaptive ~ in which new species arise better fitted to live under new conditions than in the ancestral habitat⟩ **b :** the totality of new species, varieties, or other groups produced by radiation **5 :** a method of surveying in which the field is triangulated by lines radiating from a central point **6 :** a tract of nerve fibers within the brain; *esp* **:** one concerned with the distribution of impulses arising from sensory stimuli to the relevant coordinating centers and nuclei **7 :** a device for radiating heat

ra·di·a·tion·al \¦==¦āshənᵊl, -shnəl\ *adj* **:** of or relating to radiation

radiation belt *n* **:** VAN ALLEN RADIATION BELT

radiation chemistry *n* **:** chemistry that deals with the chemical effects of nuclear and other radiations on matter

radiation field *n* **:** a region traversed by radiation of any kind

radiation fog *n* **:** an evening fog over damp grounds or valleys resulting from cooling by radiation

radiation pressure *n* **:** the pressure exerted by light or other electromagnetic radiation upon matter in its path or the pressure due to the incidence of acoustic energy

radiation pyrometer *n* **:** a pyrometer that measures the intensity of radiation from a body having an extremely high temperature

radiation resistance *n* **:** the component of antenna resistance that accounts for the power radiated into space and is equal in ohms to the radiated power in watts divided by the square of the effective current in amperes at the point of power supply

radiation sickness *also* **radiation syndrome** *n* **:** sickness resulting from exposure to radiation (as in radiotherapy or the explosion of an atom bomb) commonly marked by fatigue, nausea, vomiting, loss of teeth and hair, and in more severe cases by damage to blood-forming tissue with decrease in red and white blood cells and with bleeding

radiation therapy *n* **:** RADIOTHERAPY

ra·di·a·tive \'rādē,ād·iv\ *adj* [*radiat*ion + *-ive*] **:** of, relating to, giving rise to, or exhibiting radiation

ra·di·a·tor \-ād·ə(r), -ātə- *sometimes chiefly dial* 'rad-\ *n* -s [1*radiate* + *-or*] **:** one that radiates something (as heat, light, or sound): as **a :** any of various devices (as a nest of pipes containing circulating steam or hot water for heating a room, a system of rings on a gun barrel for cooling it, or a nest of tubes with large radiating surface for cooling circulating water) for heating external objects or for cooling an internal substance by radiation **b** (1) **:** TRANSMITTER a (2) **:** TRANSMITTER b (3) **:** a transmitting antenna **c :** a radioactive substance

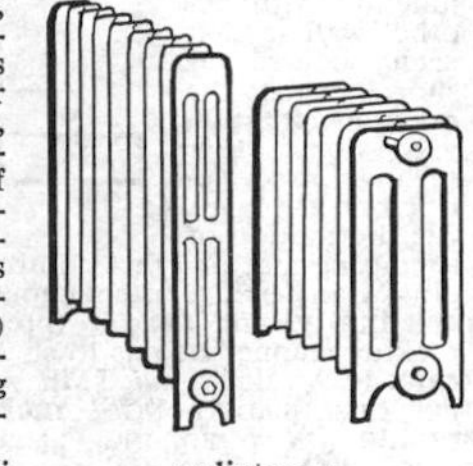

radiators a

ra·di·a·to·ry \'rādēə,tōrē\ *adj* [1*radiate* + *-ory*] **1 :** RADIATING **2 :** of or relating to radiation

1**rad·i·cal** \'radə̇kəl, -dēk-\ *adj* [ME, fr. LL *radicalis*, fr. L *radic-, radix* root + *-alis* -al — more at ROOT] **1 :** of or relating to the root **:** proceeding directly from the root: as **a** (1) **:** of or proceeding from the root of a plant ⟨~ tubers⟩ (2) **:** proceeding from the base of a stem, from a rootlike stem, or from a stem that does not rise above the ground ⟨~ leaves⟩ — compare CAULINE **b :** of, relating to, or constituting a linguistic root ⟨a ~ verb form⟩ **c :** of or relating to the root of a nativity or an election in astrology **d :** of or relating to a mathematical root **e :** designed to remove the root of a disease or all diseased tissue ⟨~ surgery⟩ — compare CONSERVATIVE **2 :** of or relating to the root or origin **:** ORIGINAL **:** FUNDAMENTAL **:** INHERENT ⟨differences that may be ascribed to ~ peculiarities of mind —Robert Bridges †1930⟩ ⟨the ~ trouble is that man is by nature a liar —Henry Adams⟩ ⟨~ differences in English and Navaho language structure —J.B.Carroll⟩ ⟨her ~ unfitness for an ascetic regimen —George Santayana⟩ ⟨reacting against the ~ faults of man and society —C.W.Hendel⟩ **3 a :** marked by a considerable departure from the usual or traditional **:** EXTREME, THOROUGHGOING, DRASTIC ⟨the most ~ proposals have called for the abandonment of the bicameral system —A.N.Holcombe⟩ ⟨to seek education for women at a time when the idea was considered a dangerously ~ doctrine —*Current Biog.*⟩ ⟨the ~ music written between 1910 and 1930 —*New Republic*⟩ **b :** tending or disposed to make extreme changes in existing views, habits, conditions, or institutions ⟨observation will reveal many people who are ~ in politics and conservative in religion —D.D.McKean⟩ ⟨the truly ~ party, the party of the destroyers of traditional values —*New Republic*⟩ **c :** of, relating to, or constituting a political group associated with views, practices, and policies of extreme change: as (1) *usu cap* **:** of, relating to, or constituted by the British radicals of the 19th century (2) *usu cap* **:** of, relating to, or constituted by the Radical Republicans **syn** see LIBERAL

2**radical** \"\ *n* -s **1 a :** a root part ⟨some ~ of our being which is persistent —H.B.Alexander⟩ **b :** basic principle **:** BASIS, FOUNDATION, SUPPORT **2 a :** an uncompounded word or element without prefix, infix, suffix, or inflectional ending **:** ROOT **b :** a sound or letter belonging to a radical; *esp* **:** an original unchanged initial consonantal sound in Celtic languages or one of the three original consonants forming the triliteral roots in Semitic languages **c :** one of 214 Chinese characters that represent categories of sense and are combined with phonetics to form phonograms whose meaning they suggest **3 a :** a radical expression in mathematics ⟨the expression $\sqrt[n]{a}$ is called a ~ of order *n* —R.S.Underwood & F.W.Sparks⟩ **b :** RADICAL SIGN **4 :** one that is radical: as **a :** one that advocates a decided and often extreme change from existing, usual, or traditional views, habits, conditions, or methods ⟨a literary ~ at heart, he was fighting . . . for a reevaluation of values —R.E.Spiller⟩ ⟨regarded as something of a ~ in anthropological circles . . . when he proposed that Neanderthal man might be classified as *Homo sapiens* —R.W. Murray⟩ ⟨the young ~*s* . . . who met regularly to discuss the new musical theories —Edward Sackville-West & Desmond Shawe-Taylor⟩ **b :** one that advocates radical and sweeping changes in laws, institutions, and methods of government with the least delay: as (1) **:** a member of the extreme wing of the British Liberal party in the 19th century (2) **:** a member of a group in the North favoring extreme measures against the South during the Civil War (3) **:** a member of a group in the North favoring a policy of reconstruction in the South after the Civil War **5** [F, fr. *radical*, adj., fr. LL *radicalis*] **:** a fundamental constituent of a chemical compound: **a** *according to Lavoisier* **:** the part of an acid that does not contain oxygen and that in combination with the acidifying principle oxygen constitutes the acid **b :** a single replaceable atom of the reactive atomic form of an element **c :** a group of atoms that is replaceable by a single atom or that is capable of remaining unchanged during a series of reactions, that need not be isolable (as acetyl, tertiary butyl, methylene, cyanogen, hydroxyl) but that sometimes is isolable, or that may show a definite transitory existence in the course of a reaction

radical axis *n* **1 :** a straight line that is the locus of points from which tangents drawn to two given circles are equal **2 :** a straight line common to the three radical planes of three given spheres taken in pairs

radical center *n* **:** a point from which tangents drawn to three given circles or four spheres are equal

radical empiricism *n* **:** an epistemological theory excluding from its formulations any elements not derived from experience and considering relations to be experienceable

radical expression *n* **:** a mathematical expression involving radical signs

rad·i·cal·ism \-kə,lizəm\ *n* -s **1 :** the quality or state of being radical **2 a :** the doctrines or principles of radicals **b :** a radical movement **3 :** the will or the effort to uproot and reform that which is established

rad·i·cal·i·ty \,radə'kaləd·ē\ *n* -ES **1 :** the quality or state of being fundamental **2 :** RADICALISM

rad·i·cal·iza·tion \,radə̇kələ̇'zāshən, -dēk-, -,lī'z-\ *n* -s [*radicalize* + *-ation*] **:** the act or process of radicalizing or the condition of being radicalized

rad·i·cal·ize \'===,līz\ *vt* -ED/-ING/-S **:** to make radical esp. in politics

rad·i·cal·ly \'radə̇k(ə)lē, -dēk-, -li\ *adv* **1 :** as regards root or source **:** in origin or essence **:** NATURALLY ⟨the Romance languages are ~ from the Latin vernacular⟩ **2 :** in a radical manner **:** in a thoroughgoing or extreme manner **:** FUNDAMENTALLY ⟨follows the same route at periodical intervals, unless ~ disturbed —*How to Catch More Fur*⟩ ⟨a civilization ~ different from our own⟩ ⟨the destroyers zigzagged ~ —Walter Karig & Welbourn Kelley⟩

rad·i·cal·ness \-kəlnə̇s\ *n* -ES **:** the quality or state of being radical

radical plane *n* **:** a plane that is the locus of points from which tangents drawn to two given spheres are equal

radical republican *n, usu cap both Rs* **:** a Republican favoring drastic and usu. repressive measures against the southern states in the period following the Civil War

radical sign *n* **:** the sign √ placed before an expression to denote that the square root is to be extracted (as $\sqrt{a}$, $\sqrt{a+b}$, $\sqrt{2}$) or that some other root is to be extracted when a corresponding index (as ^{3} to indicate a cube root) is placed over the sign

rad·i·cand \'radə,kand, ,=='=\ *n* -s [L *radicandum*, neut. of *radicandus*, gerundive of *radicare, radicari* to take root] **:** the quantity under a radical sign

1**rad·i·cate** \'radə,kāt\ *vb* -ED/-ING/-S [ME *radicaten*, fr. L *radicatus*, past part. of *radicare, radicari* to take root, fr. *radic-, radix* root — more at ROOT] *vt* **1 :** to cause to take root **:** plant deeply and firmly **2 :** to fix or establish firmly ⟨the missionary function of the Church is *radicated* in . . . God's Providence —J.D.Hassett⟩ ~ *vi, obs* **:** to take root

2**radicate** *adj* [L *radicatus*, past part. of *radicare, radicari* to take root] *obs* **:** RADICATED

rad·i·ca·tion \,radə'kāshən\ *n* -s [ML *radication-, radicatio*, fr. L *radicatus*, past part. + *-ion-, -io* -ion] *archaic* **:** the process or condition of radicating **:** a taking root

radices *pl of* RADIX

rad·i·cic·o·lous \¦radə¦sikələs\ *adj* [ISV *radici-* (fr. L *radic-, radix* root + *-i-*) + *-colous*] **:** living on or in roots ⟨~ flora⟩

rad·i·cle \'radə̇kəl, -dēk-\ *n* -s [L *radicula* little root, dim. of *radic-, radix* root] **1 a :** the lower portion of the axis of a plant embryo or seedling; *specif* **:** its extremity or root portion **b :** the hypocotyl and the root **:** HYPOCOTYL **2 :** the rootlike beginning of an anatomical vessel or part ⟨the ~ of a lacteal in a villus of the intestine⟩ ⟨the ~ of a lung⟩ **3** [by alter.] **:** RADICAL ⟨a chemical ~⟩

ra·dic·o·la \rə'dikələ, ra'-,rā'-\ *n, pl* **radico·lae** \-,lē, -,lī\ [NL, fr. L *radic-, radix* root + NL *-cola*] **:** the stage or an individual of a phylloxeran that attacks roots

ra·dic·o·lous \(')ra¦dikələs, (')rā¦-\ *adj* [by contr.] **:** RADICICOLOUS

ra·dic·u·la \='=kyələ\ [NL, fr. L, little root, dim. of *radic-, radix* root] *syn of* NASTURTIUM

ra·dic·u·lar \(')=¦==lə(r)\ *adj* [ISV *radicul-* (fr. L *radicula* little root) + *-ar*] **1 :** of or relating to the radicle or the root of a plant **2 :** of, relating to, or involving a nerve root ⟨~ lesions are typically responsible for severe sciatic pain⟩

ra·dic·u·lec·to·my \rə,dikyə'lektəmē, (,)ra,-, (,)rā,-\ *n* -ES [L *radicula* little root + E *-ectomy*] **:** RHIZOTOMY

ra·dic·u·li·tis \-līd·ə̇s\ *n* -ES [NL, fr. L *radicula* little root + NL *-itis*] **:** inflammation of a nerve root

ra·dic·u·lose \(')ra¦dikyə,lōs, (')rā¦-\ *adj* [ISV *radicul-* (fr. L *radicula* small root, dim. of *radic-, radix* root) + *-ose* — more at ROOT] **:** producing numerous rootlets

ra·dif·er·ous \(')rā¦dif(ə)rəs\ *adj* [ISV *radi*um + *-ferous*] **:** containing radium

radii *pl of* RADIUS

1**ra·dio** \'rādē,ō *sometimes esp formerly* 'rad-\ *n* -s [short for *radiotelegraphy*] **1 a :** the transmission and reception of electric impulses or signals by means of electromagnetic waves without a connecting wire ⟨~ includes wireless, television, and radar⟩ **b :** the use of these waves for the wireless transmission of electromagnetic impulses into which sound is converted — often distinguished from *television* **2 :** a radio message **:** RADIOGRAM **3 :** a radio receiving set **4 a :** a radio sending station **b :** a radio broadcasting organization ⟨a national ~⟩ **c :** the radio broadcasting industry ⟨became the youngest announcer in ~ —*Current Biog.*⟩ **d :** radio as a medium of communication ⟨jurisdiction over press, ~, and film —*Current Biog.*⟩

2**radio** \"\ *adj* **1 :** of, relating to, employing, or operated by radiant energy esp. of electromagnetic waves **:** relating to or employed in radiotelegraphy or radiotelephony or other applications of radio waves ⟨~ communication⟩ **2 :** of or relating to electric currents or phenomena of frequencies between about 15,000 and $(10)^{11}$ per second **3 a :** of, relating to, or used in radio or a radio set ⟨~ transformer⟩ ⟨~ dial⟩ **b :** specializing in radio or employed in or associated with the radio industry ⟨~ engineer⟩ **c** (1) **:** transmitted by radio ⟨~ message⟩ ⟨~ concert⟩ (2) **:** making or participating in radio broadcasts ⟨~ announcer⟩ ⟨~ commentator⟩ ⟨~ entertainers⟩ **d :** controlled or directed by radio

3**radio** \"\ *vb* -ED/-ING/-S *vt* **1 :** to send or communicate by radio ⟨the sound . . . is ~*ed* back automatically to the ship —Erwin Raisz⟩ **2 :** to send a radio message to ~ *vi* **:** to send or communicate by radio

radio- *comb form* [F, fr. L *radius* ray — more at RAY] **1 a :** radial **:** radially ⟨*radio*symmetrical⟩ ⟨*radio*litic⟩ **b :** radial and ⟨*radio*bicipital⟩ **2 a :** radiant energy **:** radiation ⟨*radio*active⟩ ⟨*radio*dermatitis⟩ **b :** radioactive ⟨*radio*element⟩ **c :** radium **:** X rays ⟨*radio*therapy⟩ **d :** radioactive isotope esp. as produced artificially ⟨*radio*carbon⟩ **e :** radio ⟨*radio*telegraphy⟩ ⟨*radio*photograph⟩

ra·dio·acoustics \¦rādē(,)ō+\ *n pl but sing in constr* [*radio-* + *acoustics*] **:** the study of the production, transmission, and effects of sounds as carried and reproduced by radio

ra·dio·actinium \"+\ *n* [NL, fr. *radio-* + *actinium*] **:** the radioactive isotope of thorium of mass number 227 formed by disintegration of actinium — symbol *RdAc* or Th^{227}; — see ACTINIUM SERIES

ra·dio·activate \"+\ *vt* [*radioactive* + *-ate*] **:** to make radioactive

ra·dio·active \"+\ *adj* [ISV *radio-* + *active*] **:** of, relating to, caused by, or exhibiting radioactivity ⟨~ element⟩ ⟨~ decay⟩ ⟨~ isotope⟩

radioactive chain *n* **:** RADIOACTIVE SERIES

radioactive constant *n* **:** a constant of radioactivity represented by λ in the equation $I_t = I_o e^{-\lambda}$, where I_o is initial activity, I_t activity after time *t*, and *e* the natural logarithmic base

radioactive equilibrium *n* **:** the condition in which a radioactive species and its successive radioactive products have attained such relative proportions that they all disintegrate at the same numerical rate and therefore maintain their proportions constant

ra·dio·actively \"+\ *adv* **:** in a radioactive manner

radioactive series *n* **:** a series of elements that are formed by disintegration of a long-lived parent (as actinium, thorium, or uranium) through the successive loss of alpha or beta particles sometimes by alternative routes and that are all radioactive except the end products which are stable isotopes of lead or bismuth — compare NEPTUNIUM SERIES

ra·dio·activity \,rādē,ō+\ *n* [ISV *radio-* + *activity*] **:** the emission of radiant energy **:** the property, possessed by some elements (as radium, uranium, thorium, and their products) whether free or combined of spontaneously emitting alpha or beta rays and sometimes also gamma rays by the disintegration of the nuclei of atoms

radio altimeter *n* **:** an altimeter utilizing the lag between the time of transmission of a radio wave from an airplane and the time of reception of the same wave after reflection from the ground

ra·dio·assay \ˈrādē(ˌ)ō+\ *n* [*radio-* + *assay*] **:** an assay (as of ore) based on examination of the sample in terms of radiation components

radio astronomer *n* **:** a specialist in radio astronomy

radio astronomy *n* **:** a branch of astronomy dealing with electromagnetic radiations of radio frequency received from outside of the earth's atmosphere (as from the sun, a star, or a galaxy) or with investigations of celestial bodies (as meteors or the moon) by means of radar waves

ra·dio·au·to·gram \ˌrādē(ˌ)ōˈȯd·ə,gram\ *n* [*radio-* + *auto-gram*] **:** AUTORADIOGRAPH

[1]**ra·dio·autograph** \ˌrādē(ˌ)ō+\ *n* [*radio-* + *autograph*] **:** AUTORADIOGRAPH — **ra·dio·autographic** \"+\ *adj* — **ra·dio·autography** \"+\ *n*

[2]**radioautograph** \"\ *vt* **:** to make an autoradiograph of

radio balloon *n* **:** a small unmanned sounding balloon carrying diminutive radio sets for transmitting meteorological recordings to ground observers or for measuring cosmic rays in the stratosphere

radio beacon *n* **:** a radio transmitting station that transmits special radio signals for use (as on a landing field or ship) in determining the direction or position of those receiving them

radio beam *n* **:** BEAM 2e

radio bearing *n* **:** the angle between the observed direction of incoming radio waves and a fixed line (as the axis of a ship)

ra·dio·biological *or* **ra·dio·biologic** \ˈrādē(ˌ)ō+\ *adj* [*radiobiology* + *-ical* or *-ic*] **:** relating to, produced by, or employing radiobiology — **ra·dio·biologically** \"+\ *adv*

ra·dio·biologist \"+\ *n* [*radiobiology* + *-ist*] **:** a specialist in radiobiology

ra·dio·biology \"+\ *n* [*radio-* + *biology*] **:** a branch of biology dealing with the interaction of biological systems and radiant energy or radioactive materials

ra·dio·broadcast \"+\ *vt* [*radio-* + *broadcast*] **:** BROADCAST 3 — **ra·dio·broadcaster** \"+\ *n*

radio car *n* **:** an automobile (as a police car) equipped with radio for communication

ra·dio·carbon \"+\ *n* [ISV *radio-* + *carbon*] **:** radioactive carbon; *esp* **:** CARBON 14

ra·dio·cast \ˈrādēō+,-\ *vt* [*radio-* + broad*cast*] **:** BROADCAST 3 — **ra·dio·caster** \"+,-\ *n*

ra·dio·chemical \ˈrādē(ˌ)ō+\ *adj* [*radio-* + *chemical*] **:** of, relating to, or using the methods of radiochemistry

ra·dio·chemist \"+\ *n* [back-formation fr. *radiochemistry*] **:** a specialist in radiochemistry

ra·dio·chemistry \"+\ *n* [*radio-* + *chemistry*] **1 :** the chemistry of radioactive substances and phenomena including tracer studies — called also *nuclear chemistry* **2 :** RADIATION CHEMISTRY

ra·dio·cobalt \"+\ *n* [*radio-* + *cobalt*] **:** radioactive cobalt; *esp* **:** COBALT 60

ra·dio·colloid \"+\ *n* [*radio-* + *colloid*] **:** a colloidal aggregate consisting of or containing a radioactive element — **ra·dio·colloidal** \"+\ *adj*

radio compass *n* **:** a direction finder used in navigation

radio control *n* **:** control of mechanisms other than signaling apparatus at a distance by radio waves

radio-control \ˈrādē(ˌ)ō+\ *vt* [*radio control*] **:** to operate by radio control ⟨*radio-controlled* airplane⟩

ra·dio·dermatitis \"+\ *n* [NL, fr. *radio-* + *dermatitis*] **:** dermatitis resulting from overexposure to sources of radiant energy (as X rays or radium)

ra·dio·detector \"+\ *n* [*radio-* + *detector*] **:** DETECTOR e

radio direction finder *n* **:** DIRECTION FINDER

ra·di·odon·tia \ˌrādēōˈdänch(ē)ə\ *n* -s [NL, fr. *radio-* + *-odontia*] **:** the making and interpreting of radiographs of teeth and related adjacent structures — **ra·di·odon·tic** \ˈrādēōˈdäntik\ *adj* — **ra·di·odon·tist** \ˌrādēōˈdäntəst\ *n* -s

radioed *past of* RADIO

radio electrician *n* **:** a warrant officer (as in the U.S. Navy) whose specialty is supervision of the maintenance and operation of radio and other electronic equipment

ra·dio·element \ˈrādē(ˌ)ō+\ *n* [ISV *radio-* + *element*] **:** a radioactive element whether formed naturally or produced artificially — compare RADIOISOTOPE

radio engineering *n* **:** a branch of electrical engineering concerned with the construction, operation, and maintenance of radio equipment

radio field intensity *or* **radio field strength** *n* **:** the electromagnetic field intensity consisting of an electric and a magnetic field intensity produced by a radio wave and commonly expressed in millivolts per meter or microvolts per meter

radio fix *n* **1 :** the location of a radio transmitter by means of direction-finding equipment **2 :** a fix obtained by radio

radio frequency *n* **:** an electromagnetic wave frequency intermediate between audio frequencies and infrared frequencies used in radio and television transmission

RADIO FREQUENCIES

CLASS	ABBREVIATION	RANGE
extremely low frequency	ELF	30 to 300 hertz
voice frequency	VF	300 to 3000 hertz
very low frequency	VLF	3 to 30 kilohertz
low frequency	LF	30 to 300 kilohertz
medium frequency	MF	300 to 3000 kilohertz
high frequency	HF	3 to 30 megahertz
very high frequency	VHF	30 to 300 megahertz
ultrahigh frequency	UHF	300 to 3000 megahertz
superhigh frequency	SHF	3 to 30 gigahertz
extremely high frequency	EHF	30 to 300 gigahertz

radio-frequency \ˈ==(ˌ)=ˈ===\ *adj* [*radio frequency*] **:** operating at radio frequency **:** using or having a radio frequency ⟨*radio-frequency* heating⟩

radio-frequency amplification *n* **:** amplification of current of radio frequency that in receiving sets is in the stages preceding the detector

ra·dio·genetics \ˈrādē(ˌ)ō+\ *n pl but sing or pl in constr* [*radio-* + *genetics*] **:** a division of radiobiology dealing with genetic systems

ra·dio·gen·ic \ˈrādēōˈjenik\ *adj* [*radio-* + *-genic*] **1 :** produced by radioactivity ⟨~ lead⟩ **2 :** eminently suitable for broadcast by radio — **ra·dio·gen·i·cal·ly** \-nək(ə)lē\ *adv*

ra·dio·goniometer \ˈrādē(ˌ)ō+\ *n* [ISV *radio-* + *goniometer*] **:** DIRECTION FINDER

ra·dio·goniometric \"+\ *adj* [*radiogoniometry* + *-ic*] **:** relating to, using, or determined by radiogoniometry

ra·dio·goniometry \"+\ *n* [ISV *radio-* + *goniometry*] **:** the art or science of measuring the direction from which radio waves come

ra·dio·gram \ˈrādēə,gram, -ēō,-, -raa(ə)m\ *n* [*radio-* + *-gram*] **1 :** RADIOGRAPH **2 :** a message transmitted by radiotelegraphy **3** *or* **ra·dio·gramophone** \ˈrādē(ˌ)ō+\ [*radiogram* short for *radiogramophone; radiogramophone* fr. *radio-* + *gramophone*] *Brit* **:** a combined radio receiver and record player

[1]**ra·dio·graph** \ˈrādēə,graf, -ēō,-, -gräf\ *n* [*radio-* + *-graph*] **:** a picture produced upon a sensitive surface (as of a photographic film) by a form of radiation other than light; *specif* **:** an X-ray or gamma ray photograph

[2]**radiograph** \"\ *vt* **:** to make a radiograph of

[3]**radiograph** \"\ *vt* [*radio-* + *telegraph*] **:** to send (a person) a radiogram

ra·di·og·ra·pher \ˌrādēˈägrəfə(r)\ *n* -s [[2]*radiograph* + *-er*] **:** one who radiographs; *specif* **:** an X-ray technician

ra·dio·graph·ic \ˌrādēəˈgrafik, -ēō-\ *adj* [ISV *radiography* + *-ic*] **:** of or relating to radiography; *specif* **:** of or relating to the process that depends on the differential absorption of rays transmitted through heterogeneous media — **ra·dio·graph·i·cal·ly** \-fək(ə)lē\ *adv*

ra·di·og·ra·phy \ˌrādēˈägrəfē\ *n* -ES [ISV [1]*radiograph* + *-y*] **:** the art, act, or process of making radiographs

ra·dio·halo \ˈrādē(ˌ)ō+\ *n* [*radio-* + *halo*] **:** a halo usu. of microscopic dimensions in a mineral or a rock produced by radioactive emanations from an included small grain of some other mineral

ra·dio·humeral bursitis \"+ . . . -\ *n* [*radiohumeral* fr. *radio-* + *humeral*] **:** TENNIS ELBOW

radiohumeral index *n* **:** the ratio of the length of the radius of the human arm to the length of the humerus multiplied by 100

radioing *pres part of* RADIO

ra·dio·iodide \"+\ *n* [*radio-* + *iodide*] **:** an iodide containing radioactive iodine

ra·dio·iodine \ˈrādē(ˌ)ō+\ *n* [*radio-* + *iodine*] **:** radioactive iodine; *esp* **:** IODINE 131

ra·dio·iron \"+\ *n* [*radio-* + *iron*] **:** radioactive iron; *esp* **:** a heavy isotope having the mass number 59 produced in nuclear reactors or cyclotrons and used chiefly in biochemical and metallurgical tracer studies

ra·dio·isotope \"+\ *n* [ISV *radio-* + *isotope*] **:** a radioactive isotope — compare RADIOELEMENT

radio knife *n* **:** a needlelike surgical instrument using high-frequency oscillations in the form of a tiny electric arc at the point for cutting through or cutting away tissue and at the same time sterilizing the edges of the wound and sealing cut blood vessels

ra·di·o·lar·ia \ˌrādēōˈla(a)rēə\ *n pl, cap* [NL, fr. LL *radiolus* small sunbeam (dim. of L *radius* ray, beam) + NL *-aria* — more at RAY] **:** a large order of rhizopods having protoplasm that is divided into an inner nucleated portion enclosed in a perforated membrane of chitinous material and an outer vacuolated portion from which radiate threadlike pseudopodia, usu. a horny or siliceous skeleton composed of spicules that may unite to form a basket-shaped structure, and numerous symbiotic unicellular yellow algae scattered in the protoplasm — compare ZOOXANTHELLA

[1]**ra·di·o·lar·i·an** \ˈ===ˈ=rēən\ *adj* [NL *Radiolaria* + E *-an*, adj. suffix] **:** of or relating to the Radiolaria

[2]**radiolarian** \"\ *n* -s [NL *Radiolaria* + E *-an*, n. suffix] **:** a rhizopod of the order Radiolaria

radiolarian ooze *n* **:** siliceous mud of the bottom of deep seas composed largely of skeletal remains of radiolarians

ra·di·o·lar·ite \ˌ===ˈ=,rīt\ *n* -s [ISV *radiolar-* (fr. NL *Radiolaria*) + *-ite*] **1 :** a fossil radiolarian shell **2 :** a sediment or earth composed of the skeletal remains of radiolaria

ra·dio·lead \ˈrādēōˈled\ *n* [*radio-* + *lead*] **:** lead formed in the disintegration of radium (as in the uranium series); *esp* **:** a radioactive isotope of lead

radio link *n* **:** a radiophone circuit connecting two fixed points (as interconnections with sections of ordinary wire circuit)

[1]**ra·di·o·lite** \ˈrādēō,līt\ *n* -s [NL *Radiolites*] **:** a fossil of the genus *Radiolites* or family Radiolitidae

[2]**radiolite** \"\ *n* -s [G *radiolith*, fr. *radio-* + *-lith* -lite] **:** a spherulite made up of radiating needles

ra·di·o·li·tes \ˌrādēōˈlīd·(ˌ)ēz\ *n, cap* [NL, fr. LL *radiolus* small sunbeam + NL *-ites*] **:** a genus (the type of the family Radiolitidae) of Cretaceous lamellibranchs with the lower valve conical and the upper nearly flat

ra·di·o·lit·ic \ˈrādēōˈlid·ik\ *adj* [ISV *radio-* + *-litic*] **:** of or relating to a texture of igneous rock that is not truly spherulitic but that shows only sectors of spherulites or radial fanlike groupings of needles

[1]**ra·di·o·litid** \-līd·əd, -lid-\ *adj* [NL *Radiolitidae*, family of lamellibranchs, fr. *Radiolites* + *-idae*] **:** of or relating to the genus *Radiolites* or the family Radiolitidae

[2]**radiolitid** \"\ *n* -s **:** a radiolitid lamellibranch or fossil

ra·dio·location \ˈrādē(ˌ)ō+\ *n* [*radio-* + *location*] **:** the method or process of detecting the position and course of distant objects by radar

ra·dio·locator \"+\ *n* [*radio-* + *locator*] **:** RADAR — used by the British before official adoption of *radar*

ra·dio·log·i·cal \ˈrādēəˈläjəkəl\ *or* **ra·dio·log·ic** \-jik\ *adj* [*radiological* fr. *radiology* + *-ical; radiologic* ISV *radiology* + *-ic*] **1 :** of or relating to radiology ⟨~ treatment⟩ **2 :** of or relating to esp. nuclear radiation ⟨~ physics⟩; *specif* **:** producing or capable of producing casualties by nuclear radiation ⟨~ warfare⟩ ⟨~ hazards⟩ — **radiologically** *adv*

ra·di·ol·o·gist \ˌrādēˈäləjəst\ *n* -s [ISV *radiology* + *-ist*] **:** a specialist in the use of radiant energy (as X rays or radium) in the diagnosis and treatment of disease

ra·di·ol·o·gy \-jē\ *n* -ES [*radio-* + *-logy*] **:** the science of radioactive substances, X rays, and other high-energy radiations; *specif* **:** the use of sources of radiant energy (as X rays and radium) in the diagnosis and treatment of disease

ra·dio·lucence \ˈrādē(ˌ)ōˈlüsᵊn(t)s\ *or* **ra·dio·lu·cen·cy** \-nsē\ *n, pl* **radiolucences** *or* **radiolucencies** [*radiolucence* fr. *radiolucent*, after such pairs as E *different: difference; radiolucency* fr. *radiolucent* + *-cy*] **:** the quality or state of being radiolucent

ra·dio·lu·cent \-nt\ *adj* [*radio-* + *lucent*] **:** partly or wholly permeable to X rays or other forms of radiation ⟨~ tissues⟩ ⟨~ areas⟩ — contrasted with *radiopaque*

ra·dio·luminescence \ˈrādē(ˌ)ō+\ *n* [ISV *radio-* + *luminescence*] **1 :** luminescence excited by impact of radioactive particles **2 :** luminescence excited by either electromagnetic or corpuscular radiation — **ra·dio·luminescent** \"+\ *adj*

ra·di·ol·y·sis \ˌrādēˈäləsəs\ *n, pl* **radioly·ses** \-lə,sēz\ [NL, fr. *radio-* + *-lysis*] **:** chemical decomposition by the action of radiation — compare PHOTOLYSIS

ra·dio·man \ˈrādē,ō,man\ *n, pl* **radiomen** [[1]*radio* + *man*] **1 :** a radio operator or technician **2 :** an employee of an electric company who locates the sources of trouble in defective power lines or equipment by means of a radio-equipped car

radio marker *n* **:** a radio transmitter of low power emitting a characteristic signal to indicate course positions with respect to a landing field or an airway — compare FAN MARKER

ra·dio·metallography \ˈrādē(ˌ)ō+\ *n* [*radio-* + *metallography*] **:** the determination of the structure of metal by means of X rays **:** the study of metals and alloys by X rays

radio meteor *n* **:** a meteor detected by the methods of radio astronomy (as by the reflection of radio waves from the ionized path it leaves in the upper atmosphere)

ra·dio·meteorograph \ˈrādē(ˌ)ō+\ *n* [*radio-* + *meteorograph*] **:** RADIOSONDE — **ra·dio·meteorography** \"+\ *n*

ra·di·om·e·ter \ˌrādēˈämədə(r)\ *n* [*radio-* + *-meter*] **:** an instrument for detecting and measuring the intensity of electromagnetic or acoustic radiation

radiometer

ra·dio·met·ric \ˈrādēōˈme·trik\ *adj* [ISV *radio-* + *-metric*] **1 :** relating to, using, or measured by the radiometer ⟨~ analysis⟩ ⟨~ data⟩ **2 :** of or relating to the measurement of geologic time by means of the rate of disintegration of radioactive elements — **ra·dio·met·ri·cal·ly** \-rək(ə)lē\ *adv*

radiometric magnitude *n* **:** the magnitude of a star as determined by the radiometer or a similar instrument

ra·di·om·e·try \ˌrādēˈämə·trē\ *n* -ES [ISV *radio-* + *-metry*] **:** the use of the radiometer **:** the measurement of radiation

ra·dio·micrometer \ˈrādē(ˌ)ō+\ *n* [ISV *radio-* + *micrometer*] **:** an exceedingly sensitive thermoelectric radiometer consisting of a D'Arsonval galvanometer with suspended coil replaced by a short-circuited thermocouple forming a loop

ra·dio·mimetic \"+\ *adj* [ISV *radio-* + *mimetic*] **:** producing esp. biological effects similar to those produced by radiation

radio navigation *n* **:** the process of conducting an airplane or ship from one point to another by means of radio aids (as beacons, direction finders, or radioed bearings)

ra·dio·necrosis \"+\ *n* [NL, fr. *radio-* + *necrosis*] **:** ulceration or destruction of tissue resulting from irradiation

ra·dio·necrotic \"+\ *adj* **:** of or relating to radionecrosis

ra·di·on·ic \ˈrādēˈänik\ *adj* [*radio-* + electr*onic*] **:** ELECTRONIC

ra·di·on·ics \ˌrādēˈäniks\ *n pl but sing in constr* [*radio-* + electr*onics*] **:** ELECTRONICS

ra·dio·nuclide \ˈrādē(ˌ)ō+\ *n* [*radio-* + *nuclide*] **:** a radioactive nuclide

radio observatory *n* **:** an observatory concerned esp. with radio astronomy

ra·di·opacity \ˌrādē+\ *n* [*radio-* + *opacity*] **:** the quality or state of being radiopaque

ra·di·opaque \ˈrādē+\ *adj* [*radio-* + *opaque*] **:** being opaque to X rays or other forms of radiation **:** not transmitting radiant energy ⟨barium sulfate is ~⟩ — contrasted with *radiolucent*

ra·dio·phare \ˈrādēə+,-\ *n* [*radio-* + *phare*] **:** a radiotelegraphic station used for determining the position of ships

ra·dio·phone \ˈrādēə,fōn\ *n* [*radio-* + *-phone*] **1 :** an apparatus (as the photophone) for the production of sound by the action of radiant energy **2 a :** a transmitting set for radiotelephony **b :** a receiving set for radiotelephony

ra·dio·phosphorus \ˈrādē(ˌ)ō+\ *n* [NL, fr. *radio-* + *phosphorus*] **:** radioactive phosphorus; *esp* **:** PHOSPHORUS 32

ra·dio·photo \"+\ *vt* [*radiophoto*, n.] **:** to send (a picture) by radio

ra·dio·photograph *or* **ra·dio·photo** \"+\ *n* [*radio-* + *photograph* or *photo*] **:** a picture transmitted by radio

radio proximity fuse *n* **:** PROXIMITY FUSE

radio range *n* **:** a radio facility providing means for aiding in the navigation of airplanes

radio range beacon *n* **:** a radio beacon that transmits in such a way as to mark out a fixed straight line (as for directing the course of airplanes to or from a landing field)

radio range station *n* **:** a radio transmitter that provides the signals used in a radio range

radio receiver *n* **:** a radio receiving set

radio relay *n* **:** a radio station that receives and retransmits a signal

ra·dio·resistant \ˈrādē(ˌ)ō+\ *adj* [ISV *radio-* + *resistant*] **:** resistant to the effects of radiant energy — used esp. of cells (as cancer cells) that are not destroyed by radiation; compare RADIOSENSITIVE

radios *pl of* RADIO, *pres 3d sing of* RADIO

ra·dio·scope \ˈrādēə,skōp\ *n* [*radio-* + *-scope*] **1 :** a device for detecting the presence of a radioactive substance **2 :** FLUOROSCOPE

ra·dio·scop·ic \ˈrādēəˈskäpik\ *or* **ra·dio·scop·i·cal** \-pəkəl\ *adj* [*radioscopic* ISV *radioscopy* + *-ic; radioscopical* fr. *radioscopy* + *-ical*] **:** of or relating to radioscopy — **ra·dio·scop·i·cal·ly** \-pək(ə)lē\ *adv*

ra·di·os·co·py \ˌrādēˈäskəpē\ *n* -ES [ISV *radio-* + *-scopy*] **:** direct observation of objects opaque to light by means of some other form of radiant energy (as X rays)

ra·dio·sensitive \ˈrādē(ˌ)ō+\ *adj* [*radio-* + *sensitive*] **:** sensitive to the effects of radiant energy — used of cells (as cancer cells) that can be destroyed by radiation; compare RADIORESISTANT — **ra·dio·sensitivity** \"+\ *n*

radio set *n* **1 :** a radio receiving set **2 :** a radio transmitting set

radio silence *n* **:** a condition that exists when radios are not transmitting; *also* **:** the period of time during which this condition exists

ra·dio·sodium \ˈrādē(ˌ)ō+\ *n* [NL, fr. *radio-* + *sodium*] **:** radioactive sodium; *esp* **:** a heavy isotope having the mass number 24, produced in nuclear reactors, and used in the form of a salt (as sodium chloride) chiefly in biochemical tracer studies

ra·dio·sonde \ˈrādēō+,-\ *n* -s [ISV *radio-* + *sonde*] **:** a miniature radio transmitter with instruments that is carried aloft (as by an unmanned balloon) for broadcasting by means of precise tone signals or other suitable method the humidity, temperature, and pressure every few seconds

radio source *n* **:** a region of the sky exclusive of the sun and members of the solar system from which microwave energy is received

radio spectrum *n* **1 :** the region of the electromagnetic spectrum usu. including frequencies below thirty thousand megacycles in which radio or radar transmission and detection techniques may be used **2 :** the molecular absorption spectrum of a substance in the radio-spectrum region

radio star *n* **:** a radio source of very small dimensions and relatively strong radiation and sometimes identified with certain small nebulosities and galaxies

ra·dio·strontium \ˈrādē(ˌ)ō+\ *n* [NL, fr. *radio-* + *strontium*] **:** radioactive strontium; *esp* **:** STRONTIUM 90

radio sun *n* **:** the sun as observed in the radio region of the spectrum

ra·dio·surgery \ˈrādē(ˌ)ō+\ *n* [*radio-* + *surgery*] **:** surgery by means of the radio knife

ra·dio·symmetrical \"+\ *adj* [*radio-* + *symmetrical*] **:** radially symmetrical; *specif* **:** ACTINOMORPHIC — compare MONOSYMMETRICAL

ra·dio·technology \"+\ *n* [*radio-* + *technology*] **1 :** the technology of radio **2 :** the application of X rays to industrial problems **3 :** the application of any form of radiation to industrial problems

ra·dio·telegram \"+\ *n* [ISV *radio-* + *telegram*] **1 :** RADIOGRAM 2 **2 :** a message transmitted by radiotelegraphy to or from a ship or other mobile station

[1]**ra·dio·telegraph** *also* **ra·dio·telegraphy** \"+\ *n* [ISV *radio-* + *telegraph* or *telegraphy*] **:** telegraphy carried on by the aid of radio waves and without connecting wires

[2]**radiotelegraph** \"\ *vt* **:** to send (a message) by radiotelegraphy

ra·dio·telegraphic \ˈrādē(ˌ)ō+\ *adj* [*radiotelegraphy* + *-ic*] **:** of, relating to, or transmitted by means of radiotelegraphy

ra·dio·telegraphist \"+\ *n* [ISV [1]*radiotelegraph* + *-ist*] **:** one licensed to operate radiotelegraph equipment

ra·dio·telephone \"+\ *n* [ISV *radio-* + *telephone*] **:** RADIOPHONE 2

ra·dio·telephony \"+\ *n* [ISV *radio-* + *telephony*] **:** telephony carried on by the aid of radio waves without connecting wires

radio telescope *n* **:** a radio receiver-antenna combination used for observations in radio astronomy

ra·dio·therapeutic \"+\ *adj* [*radio-* + *therapeutic*] **:** of or relating to radiotherapy — **ra·dio·therapeutically** \"+\ *adv*

ra·dio·therapeutics \"+\ *n pl but sing in constr* [*radio-* + *therapeutics*] **:** RADIOTHERAPY

ra·dio·therapeutist \"+\ *n* [*radio-* + *therapeutist*] **:** RADIOTHERAPIST

ra·dio·therapist \"+\ *n* [*radiotherapy* + *-ist*] **:** a specialist in radiotherapy

ra·dio·therapy \"+\ *n* [ISV *radio-* + *therapy*] **:** treatment of disease by means of X rays or radioactive substances (as radium)

ra·dio·ther·mics \ˌrādēōˈthərmiks\ *n pl but sing in constr* [*radiothermy* + *-ics*] **:** the science of heat generation by radio-frequency currents or by radio waves

ra·dio·ther·my \ˈ===,mē\ *n* -ES [*radio-* + *-thermy*] **:** diathermy by means of a shortwave radio machine

ra·dio·thorium \ˈrādē(ˌ)ō+\ *n* [NL, fr. *radio-* + *thorium*] **:** the radioactive isotope of thorium of mass number 228 formed from mesothorium 2 — symbol *RdTh* or Th^{228}; see THORIUM SERIES

ra·dio·toxicity \"+\ *n* [*radio-* + *toxicity*] **:** the toxicity of radioactive substances

ra·dio·tracer \"+\ *n* [*radio-* + *tracer*] **:** a radioactive tracer

radio transmitter *n* **:** a radio transmitting set

ra·dio·tri·cian \ˌrādēōˈtrishən\ *n* -s [*radio-* + elec*trician*] **:** one who specializes in radio work

ra·dio·trop·ic \ˈrādēōˈträpik\ *adj* [*radio-* + *-tropic*] **:** of, relating to, or characterized by radiotropism

ra·di·ot·ro·pism \ˌrādēˈä·trə,pizəm\ *n* [*radio-* + *tropism*] **:** a tropism in which some form of radiation is the orienting factor

radio tube *n* **:** a vacuum tube for radio

radious *adj* [L *radiosus*, fr. *radius* ray + *-osus* -ous — more at RAY] *obs* **:** RADIANT, RADIATING

ra·dio·vi·sion \ˈrādēōˈvizhən\ *n* [*radio-* + tele*vision*] **:** television carried on by radio waves without connecting wires

radio wave *n* **:** an electromagnetic wave having radio frequency

rad·ish \ˈradish, ÷ˈred-\ *n* -ES [ME, alter. of OE *rædic*, fr. L *radic-*, *radix* root, edible root, radish — more at ROOT]

1 : the pungent fleshy root of a plant (*Raphanus sativus*) eaten raw as a relish **2 :** the plant that produces radish roots

radish tree *n* **:** an Australian shrub or small tree (*Codonocarpus cotinifolius*) of the family Phytolaccaceae with pale glaucous foliage and small unisexual flowers in racemes

¹ra·di·um \'rādēəm\ *n* -s [NL, fr. L *radius* ray, beam + NL *-ium* — more at RAY] **:** an intensely radioactive shining white metallic element of the alkaline-earth group that resembles barium chemically, that occurs in combination in minute quantities in pitchblende, carnotite, and other uranium minerals principally as the isotope of mass number 226 formed from uranium 238, having a half-life of 1620 years, and emitting alpha particles and gamma rays to form radon, and that is used chiefly in luminous materials (as paint made by admixture with zinc sulfide or other phosphor), in medicine esp. in the treatment of cancer, and in radiography — symbol *Ra;* see ACTINIUM SERIES, ELEMENT table, THORIUM SERIES, URANIUM SERIES

²radium \"\ *n* -s [fr. *Radium*, a trademark] **:** a smooth lustrous supple fabric made of silk or rayon in plain weave and used esp. for women's clothing and curtains

radium clock *n* **:** an electroscope alternately charged by the accumulation of alpha particles from radium in a closed tube and discharged by automatic grounding at regular intervals

radium dial *n* **:** a clock, watch, or instrument dial having figures coated with luminous paint

radium emanation *n* **:** RADON 1

ra·di·um·ize \'rādēə,mīz\ *vt* -ED/-ING/-S *see -ize in Explan Notes* [¹*radium* + *-ize*] **:** to subject to the action of radium ⟨the green effect in *radiumized* diamonds —*Time*⟩

radium needle *n* **:** a hollow radium-containing device shaped like a needle and used esp. in medical treatment

radium pack *n* **:** radium in a pack for therapeutic application

radium series *n* **:** URANIUM SERIES

radium therapy *n* **:** RADIOTHERAPY

radium vermilion *n* **:** a red lead that is coated with an organic color

¹ra·di·us \'rādēəs\ *n, pl* **ra·dii** \-ē,ī\ *also* **radiuses** [L, radius, ray, rod, spoke — more at RAY] **1 a :** the preaxial bone of the human forearm or of the corresponding part of the forelimb of vertebrates above fishes that in man is movably articulated with the ulna at both ends so as to admit of partial rotation about that bone, that bears on its inner anterior aspect near the head a prominence for the insertion of the biceps tendon, and that has the lower end broadened for articulation with the proximal bones of the carpus so that rotation of the radius involves also that of the hand — compare PRONATION, SUPINATION **b :** HYPERCORACOID **c :** HYPOCORACOID **2 :** a line segment extending from the center of a circle or sphere to the curve or surface **3 :** one of a number of rods, bars, or lines extending usu. in a single plane out from a center or hub ⟨*radii* of a wheel⟩ **4 a :** the distance of a radius ⟨a ~ of 10 miles from home⟩ ⟨truck with a short turning ~⟩ **b :** the circular area implicated by a stated radius ⟨40 inland lakes within a ~ of 20 miles —*Amer. Guide Series: Mich.*⟩ **c :** a bounded or circumscribed area **:** a limited range ⟨at the limit of the operating ~ of any fleet from Europe —S.L.A.Marshall⟩ **d :** a range of operation, activity, influence, concern, or knowledge ⟨a modern hospital that serves a wide ~ —*Amer. Guide Series: Vt.*⟩ ⟨the ~ of action of an airplane⟩ ⟨all who had come within the ~ of his kind if somewhat stern influence —F.S.Betten⟩ **5 :** a part analogous to the radius of a circle **:** a radial part (as the movable limb of a sextant or other angle-measuring instrument or a wheel spoke) **6 :** the distance from a center line or point to an axis of rotation **:** THROW, ECCENTRICITY **7 a :** an imaginary radial plane dividing the body of a radially symmetrical animal into similar parts — compare ADRADIUS, INTERRADIUS, PERRADIUS **b :** any of five radiating ossicles in the Aristotle's lantern of a sea urchin **c :** a main vein in the wing of an insect **:** the third and usu. largest vein of an insect's wing — see RADIAL SECTOR **d :** one of the grooves extending from the focus of a fish scale toward the margin **8 :** a rounded part (as an edge or fillet) produced by radiusing ⟨put a $\frac{1}{64}$ inch ~ on the cutting tip of this lathe tool⟩ **syn** see RANGE

²radius \"\ *vt* -ED/-ING/-ES **:** to cut (as a fillet or rounded-off edge) on an arc of a circle ⟨faceted and ~*ed* tool edges —Paul Grodzinski⟩ ⟨chamfering or ~*ing* of the bearings —*Aero Products*⟩

radius bar *n* **:** RADIUS ROD

radius clause *n* **:** a clause in an agreement with an employer by which a trainee engages not to seek employment with another company for a stated period

radius gage *n* **:** a gage for determining the curvature of internal and external fillets

radius of curvature : the reciprocal of the curvature of a curve

radius gage

radius of gyration : the radius of a cylindrical surface coaxial with the axis of rotation of a body such that if the entire mass of the body were concentrated in that surface the moment of inertia and energy of rotation would be unchanged ⟨the *radius of gyration* equals the square root of the quotient of the moment of inertia of the body divided by its mass⟩

radius of torsion : the reciprocal of the torsion of a space curve

radius rod *n* **:** a bar for preserving an invariable distance between two pieces of a mechanism and permitting one to move around the other as a fixed point

radius vector *n, pl* **radii vec·to·res** \-,vek'tōr(,)ēz\ **1 :** a straight line segment or its length from a fixed point, pole, or center to a variable point **:** the linear polar coordinate of a variable point **2 :** a straight line joining the center of an attracting body (as the sun) with that of a body (as a planet or comet) describing an orbit around it

ra·dix \'rādiks\ *n, pl* **radi·ces** \'radə,sēz, 'rād- *or* **radixes** \'rādiksəz\ [L, root — more at ROOT] **1 :** BASE 6d ⟨10 is the ~ of the common system of logarithms⟩ **2** *obs* **:** ROOT 4a **3 :** the primary source **:** the originating cause **4** *archaic* **:** ETYMON, ROOT 6 **5 :** the root of a plant **6 :** RADICLE 2; *esp* **:** a root of a cranial or spinal nerve

radix gra·mi·nis \-'gramənəs\ *n* [L, root of grass] **:** the rootstock of a couch grass (*Agropyron repens*) formerly used as a diuretic and aperient

rad·knight \'rad,nīt\ *n* [OE *rādcniht*, lit., riding knight, fr. *rād* riding + *cniht* military follower — more at ROAD, KNIGHT] **:** one of a class of feudal tenants in some parts of England holding on condition of doing service on horseback besides other services (as plowing) — called also *radman;* compare ESQUIRE

radm *abbr, often cap R&A & sometimes cap D & M* rear admiral

rad·man \-,mən\ *n, pl* **radmen** [(assumed) OE *rādman*, fr. OE *rād* riding + *man* — more at MAN] **:** RADKNIGHT

rad·nor·shire \'radnər,shi(ə)r, -,shər\ *or* **rad·nor** \-nər, -,nȯ(ə)r\ *adj, usu cap* [fr. *Radnorshire* or *Radnor*, county in Wales] **:** of or from the county of Radnor, Wales **:** of the kind or style prevalent in Radnor

ra·dome \'rā,dōm\ *n* [*radar dome*] **:** a usu. dome-shaped plastic housing used (as on the exterior surfaces of an airplane) to shelter the antenna assembly of a radar set

ra·don \'rā,dän\ *n* -s [NL, fr. *rad-* (fr. *radium*) + *-on*] **1 a :** heavy radioactive gaseous element of the group of inert gases formed by disintegration of radium and used similarly to radium in medicine — symbol *Rn;* called also *radium emanation;* see ELEMENT table, URANIUM SERIES **2 :** an isotope of radon: as **a :** ACTINON **b :** THORON

radon seed *n* **:** radon packed in a container for local application in cancer — compare SEED 4b

ra·doph·o·lus \rə'däfələs\ *n, cap* [NL] **:** a genus of chiefly tropical plant-parasitic nematodes (family Tylenchidae) including pests of the roots of sugarcane, rice, and other economically important plants

rads *pl of* RAD

rad·u·la \'rajələ\ *n, pl* **radu·lae** \-,lē, -,lī\ [NL, fr. L, scraper, fr. *radere* to scrape — more at RAT] **:** a chitinous band in nearly all mollusks except bivalves that bears numerous usu. very minute teeth on its dorsal surface and slides backward and forward by special muscles over a more or less protrusible prominence on the floor of the mouth and serves to tear up the food and draw it into the mouth — see ODONTOPHORE — **rad·u·lar** \-lə(r)\ *adj*

radular sac *n* **:** the posterior extension of the radula forming a narrow curved pouch opening on the floor of the mouth

rad·u·late \-lət, -,lāt\ *adj* [NL *radula* + E *-ate*] **:** having a radula

radu·li·form \rə'd(y)ülə,fȯrm, 'rajəl-\ *adj* [L *radula* scraper + E *-iform*] **:** like a rasp **:** CARDIFORM

rad·zi·mir \'radzə,mi(ə)r\ *n* -s [prob. modif. of F *ras de Saint-Maur* short-napped cloth of Saint Maur] **1** *archaic* **:** a silk fabric usu. black for mourning clothes **2 :** a firm silk or rayon fabric for women's clothing often made with lengthwise ribs or a broken twill weave

raetam *var of* RETEM

raeto-romance *var of* RHAETO-ROMANCE

ra·fale \rə'fal\ *n* -s [F, lit., squall, gust of wind, prob. fr. MF *rafle, raffe* act of snatching — more at RAFFLE] **:** a burst of artillery fire consisting of several rounds discharged as rapidly as possible from each gun of a battery

¹raff \'raf, 'raa(ə)f, 'raif\ *n* -s [ME *raf*, perh. fr. MF *raffe, rafle* act of snatching, sweeping — more at RAFFLE] **1** *dial Brit* **a :** HODGEPODGE, JUMBLE **b :** RUBBISH, TRASH **2 a :** RIFFRAFF **b :** a coarse disreputable person

²raff \'raf\ *n* -s [G dial. *raf, raffe;* akin to ON *raptr* rafter — more at RAFTER] *dial Eng* **:** LUMBER

raffaelesque *usu cap, var of* RAPHAELESQUE

raffe \'raf\ *or* **raf·fee** \ra'fē\ *n* -s [origin unknown] **:** a usu. triangular topsail set above a square lower sail

raffe

raf·fia \'rafēə, -fyə\ *n* -s [Malagasy *rafia, raofia, rofia*] **1 :** the fiber of the raffia palm of Madagascar used for tying plants and making articles (as baskets or hats) **2 :** RAFFIA PALM

raffia palm *n* **1 :** a pinnate-leaved palm (*Raphia ruffia*) native to Madagascar that is of considerable economic importance on account of the strong fiber obtained from its leafstalks — see RAFFIA 1 **2 :** JUPATI

raffia wax *n* **:** a hard light-brown wax obtained as a by-product from the leaves of the raffia palm or similar palms native to tropical Africa and So. America

raf·fi·nase \'rafə,nās\ *n* -s [ISV *raffin-* (fr. *raffinose*) + *-ase*] **:** an enzyme that catalyzes the hydrolysis of raffinose and occurs in various molds (as *Aspergillus niger*) and yeasts

raf·fi·nate \-āt\ *n* -s [F *raffiner* to refine (fr. *re-* + *affiner* to make fine) + ISV *-ate* — more at AFFINE] **:** a liquid product resulting from extraction of a liquid with a solvent; *also* **:** the less soluble residue that remains after extraction (as in refining lubricating oil)

raff·ing \'rafən, -fiŋ\ *adj* [origin unknown] *Scot* **:** RIP-ROARING

raf·fi·nose \'rafə,nōs\ *n* -s [F, fr. *raffiner* to refine + *-ose* — more at RAFFINATE] **:** a crystalline slightly sweet nonreducing trisaccharide sugar $C_{18}H_{32}O_{16}$ that is obtained by aqueous extraction of cottonseed meal but also found in small quantities in sugar beet, eucalyptus manna, and many cereals and that yields on hydrolysis D-fructose and melibiose

raff·ish \'rafish, 'raaf-, 'raif-, -fēsh\ *adj* [¹*raff* + *-ish*] **1 :** marked by or suggestive of flashy vulgarity, crudeness, or rowdiness **:** TAWDRY, UNKEMPT ⟨a *raffish*-looking old man with stringy gray hair, angry eyes, wrinkled stockings —Kenneth Roberts⟩ ⟨a district of ~ lodging houses —T.W.Duncan⟩ ⟨the ~ locutions of their dialogue —*Times Lit. Supp.*⟩ **2 :** marked by a careless or carefree unconventionality or disreputableness **:** DEVIL-MAY-CARE, RAKISH ⟨a cocktail party given by some . . . ~ bachelors —Crary Moore⟩ ⟨sported a ~ handlebar moustache —Anthony West⟩ — **raff·ish·ly** *adv* — **raff·ish·ness** *n* -ES

¹raf·fle \'rafəl\ *n* -s [ME *rafle*, fr. MF] **1 a :** a game with three dice in which the winner of the stakes is the player who throws all three alike or the highest pair if no triplet is thrown **b :** any three of a kind in chuck-a-luck with the banker taking all bets not on triplets **2 :** a lottery in which each participant buys a ticket for an article put up as a prize with the winner being determined by a random drawing ⟨selling tickets for a ~ on a new car⟩

²raffle \"\ *vb* **raffled; raffled; raffling** \-f(ə)liŋ\ **raffles** *vi* **:** to engage in a raffle ⟨~ for a watch⟩ ~ *vt* **:** to dispose of by means of a raffle — used often with *off* ⟨*raffled off* a sewing machine at the bazaar⟩

³raffle \"\ *n* -s [prob. fr. F *rafle* act of snatching, sweeping, fr. MF *rafle, raffe*, fr. MHG *raffen* to snatch; akin to OE *hreppan* to touch, ON *hreppa* to catch, receive, OE *hearpe* harp — more at HARP] **1 :** RABBLE, RIFFRAFF **2 :** REFUSE, RUBBISH; *specif* **:** a jumble or tangle of nautical material (as cordage or spars) ⟨her decks forward covered with ~ —W.C.Russell⟩

⁴raffle \"\ *vt* -ED/-ING/-S [prob. alter. of ¹*ruffle*] **:** SERRATE ⟨~ a leaf⟩

⁵raf·fle \"\ *vt* -ED/-ING/-S [alter. of ¹*ravel*] *dial Brit* **:** ENTANGLE

raf·fles \'rafəlz\ *n* -ES *often cap* [fr. *Raffles*, hero of the story *The Amateur Cracksman* (1899) by E. W. Hornung †1921 Eng. novelist] **:** an amateur or gentleman burglar

raf·fle·sia \rə'flēzh(ē)ə, ra'-, -zēə\ *n* [NL, fr. Sir Stamford *Raffles* †1826 Eng. colonial administrator + NL *-ia*] **1** *cap* **:** a genus (the type of the family Rafflesiaceae) of Malaysian stemless leafless plants having huge dioecious apetalous flowers that grow parasitically on the stems and roots of various plants of the genus *Cissus*, have a calyx of five spreading fleshy lobes, and usu. exhale an odor like that of carrion **2** -s **:** any plant of the genus *Rafflesia*

raf·fle·si·a·ce·ae \rə,flēz(h)ē'āsē,ē, ra,-\ *n pl, cap* [NL, fr. *Rafflesia*, type genus + *-aceae*] **:** a family of endotrophic parasitic plants (order Aristolochiales) found chiefly in warm regions of the Old World and sometimes in Mexico that lack stems, have imbricated scales in place of leaves, and have apetalous flowers emerging from the host and having five to ten calyx lobes — **raf·fle·si·a·ceous** \¦=¦==¦āshəs\ *adj*

raff·man \'rafmən\ *n, pl* **raffmen** [alter. of *raftman*] **:** ³RAFTER

raffs *pl of* RAFF

ra·fraî·chis·soir \rə,freshə'swär\ *n* -s [F, wine cooler, fr. *rafraîchiss-* (stem of *rafraîchir* to refresh, cool, fr. *re-* + *a-* ad- + *frais* fresh, cool, fr. OF *freis*) + *-oir* -ory — more at FRESH] **:** a small table or stand having a marble top with wells sunk into it esp. for containing plants or flowers

¹raft *archaic past of* REAVE

²raft \'raft, 'raa(ə)ft, 'raift, 'räft\ *n* -s [ME *rafte*, fr. ON *raptr* rafter — more at RAFTER] **1** *archaic* **:** RAFTER, SPAR **2 a :** a collection of usu. logs or timber fastened together for transportation by floating ⟨great ~*s* of logs . . . for the English market —*Amer. Guide Series: Vt.*⟩ **b :** a flat structure for support or conveyance (as of people or cargo) on a body of water ⟨floating down the river on a ~⟩ ⟨rubber ~*s* filled with men —K.M.Dodson⟩ **c :** a floating platform; *esp* **:** one used by swimmers **:** FLOAT 4c(1) ⟨in the park pool swimming out to the ~ —Donald Windham⟩ **d :** a rubber lifesaving apparatus that is inflated for use usu. in emergency landings of airplanes on water ⟨the ~ resembled an overlarge bedroll —E.K.Gann⟩ ⟨get out fast and inflate the ~ —Howard Hunt⟩ **3 a :** a mass of floating logs, driftwood, or debris that impedes or blocks navigation of a watercourse ⟨the ~ covered the stream from shore to shore —*Amer. Guide Series: Ark.*⟩ **b :** a floating cohesive mass (as of seaweed or insect eggs) **c :** an aggregation of waterfowl (as ducks) resting on the water ⟨estuaries . . . where ~*s* of wildfowl lie offshore —N.C. Stevenson⟩ **4 :** MAT 3d ⟨~ foundation⟩ ⟨~ construction⟩

³raft \"\ *vb* -ED/-ING/-S *vt* **1 a :** to transport (as logs or timber) in the form of a raft by floating ⟨~*ed* his logs down the lakes —*Amer. Guide Series: Mich.*⟩ **b :** to convey (as people or cargo) on or by means of a raft ⟨~*ed* them across the stream⟩ ⟨freight ~*ed* down the river —*Amer. Guide Series: La.*⟩ **2 :** to make into a raft ⟨~ the logs at hand⟩ **3 :** to go along or across (a watercourse) on a raft ⟨~ a river⟩ **4 :** to transport (land-derived debris, boulders, or silt) embedded in floating ice or in masses of floating organic material (as seaweed) to places not reached by the currents of rivers, lakes, or seas ~ *vi* **1 :** to manage a raft **:** travel by raft ⟨~*ing* across rivers —Jack Kelsey⟩ **2 :** RAFTER

⁴raft \"\ *n* -s [alter. (influenced by ²*raft* mass of logs) of ¹*raff*] **1 :** a large and often motley collection (as of people or things) **:** a great amount or number **:** LOT, SLEW ⟨a ~ of shiftless brothers and sisters —W.L.Gresham⟩ ⟨had a ~ of patients —Carson McCullers⟩ ⟨assembled a ~ of facts and figures —*New Yorker*⟩ ⟨sold a ~ of bathtubs —*advt*⟩

raft dog *n* [²*raft*] **:** an iron bar with bent-down sharpened ends that fastens together the logs forming a raft — compare DOG 3a

raft duck *n* [²*raft;* fr. its swimming in dense flocks] **1 :** SCAUP DUCK **2 :** REDHEAD 2b

¹raf·ter \'raftə(r), 'raaf-, 'raif-, 'räf-\ *n* -s [ME, fr. OE *ræfter;* akin to MLG *rafter, rachter* rafter, ON *raptr*] **1 :** one of the often sloping beams that support a roof — compare HIP RAFTER, JACK RAFTER, VALLEY RAFTER; see ROOF illustration **2** *or* **rafter bird :** SPOTTED FLYCATCHER

²rafter \"\ *vb* -ED/-ING/-S *vt* **1 :** to furnish (as a house) with rafters **2** *dial Eng* **:** to plow so as to turn the grass side of each furrow upon an unplowed ridge **:** RIDGE 2a ~ *vi* **:** to override and underrun one another — used of pieces of ice under pressure

³raft·er \"\ *n* -s [³*raft* + *-er*] **:** one who by walking on floating logs or booms or working from a boat maneuvers logs into position and binds them into rafts that can be towed to a mill — called also *boom man, raffman, raftsman*

⁴rafter \"\ *n* -s [⁴*raft* + *-er*] **:** FLOCK — used esp. of turkeys

rafter dam *n* [¹*rafter*] **:** a dam formed by long horizontal timbers set at an angle to the banks and meeting in the center of the stream like the rafters of a roof principal

rafting auger *n* [fr. gerund of ³*raft*] **:** an auger turned by a bar placed through an eye in the end of the shank and used for boring large and deep holes in heavy timbers

raft port *n* [²*raft*] **:** a large square port forward or aft in a ship for loading or unloading bulky material (as timber)

rafts·man \'raftsmən\ *also* **raft·man** \-tm-\ *n, pl* **raftsmen** *also* **raftmen** [²*raft*] **1 :** one who engages in rafting ⟨intrepid *raftsmen* crossing the Pacific⟩ **2 :** ³RAFTER

raf·ty \'rafti\ *adj* [origin unknown] **1** *dial Eng* **:** DAMP, RAW — used of weather **2** *dial Eng* **a :** MUSTY, FUSTY **1 b :** RANCID — used of bacon

¹rag \'rag, 'raa(ə)g, 'raig\ *n* -s [ME *ragge*, fr. (assumed) OE *ragg* (whence OE *raggig* raggy), fr. ON *rögg* tuft, shagginess — more at RUG] **1 a :** a waste piece of cloth torn or cut off (as from a fabric or garment) **:** TATTER **b rags** *pl* **:** remnants of used or unused cloth and discarded clothing **c rags** *pl* **:** CLOTHES ⟨sumptuous ~*s* . . . cover her emaciated body —Otis Fellows⟩ ⟨his neat black suit . . . among the colored ~*s* of the other passengers —Dan Jacobson⟩; *esp* **:** poor or ragged clothing — often used in the phrase *in rags* ⟨accosted by a beggar in ~*s*⟩ **d :** a small cloth; *esp* **:** one devoted to a particular use — usu. used in combination ⟨wash*rag*⟩ ⟨dish*rag*⟩ **2 a :** an unevenly shaped or torn fragment **:** SHRED ⟨~*s* of meat⟩ ⟨a ~ of cloud⟩ ⟨~*s* of land⟩ ⟨~*s* of bark⟩ **b :** SCRAP, REMNANT ⟨still clinging . . . to some ~ of honor —R.L. Stevenson⟩ ⟨tearing their arguments to ~*s*⟩ ⟨not a ~ of legality⟩ ⟨not a ~ of evidence against him⟩ **3 :** something resembling a rag in appearance: as **a :** SAIL ⟨a clipper with every ~ set —J.R.Lowell⟩ **b :** the stringy axis and the white fibrous membrane investing the pulp and sectional divisions of a citrus fruit **c :** something without strength or stamina ⟨kept . . . on the jump and left her a ~ —W.D.Steele⟩ **4 :** something resembling a rag in low worth or repute: as **a :** a person held in low esteem ⟨washed-out ~ he'd been dragging to dances —Martin Dibner⟩ **b :** depreciated paper money **c :** a low or worthless playing card **5 a :** a ragged edge; *specif* **:** one left by a cutting tool in metalworking **b :** a fin or burr on cast metal **6 :** NEWSPAPER, PERIODICAL

²rag \"\ *n* -s [origin unknown] **1 :** any of various hard rocks (as a quartzose mica schist used for whetstones or a hard limestone used in building) ⟨coral ~⟩ ⟨walls of yellowish, gravelly ~ —F.D.Ommanney⟩ **2 :** a large roofing slate left rough on one side

³rag \"\ *vb* **ragged** \-gd\; **ragged; ragging; rags** [origin unknown] *vt* **1 :** to rail at **:** SCOLD ⟨*ragging* the government —J.A. Michener⟩ ⟨*ragging* a waiter because the toast was cold —Leonard Merrick⟩ **2 a :** to persecute in petty ways **:** TORMENT, ANNOY ⟨gave my form a punishment for *ragging* him —R.G.G.Price⟩ **b :** to make fun of or find fault with good-naturedly **:** TEASE, CHAFF ⟨*ragged* each other about that all day long —F.M.Ford⟩ ~ *vi, chiefly Brit* **:** to engage in horseplay (as in a school dormitory) ⟨~ in the corridors at night —Cyril Connolly⟩

⁴rag \"\ *n* -s **1** *chiefly Brit* **a :** an outbreak of boisterous and usu. mischievous merrymaking (as of students in the streets after a football match) **:** a student riot **b :** a traditional student revel at British universities marked by playful disorder, comic pageantry, and mockery of the authorities **2** *chiefly Brit* **:** PRANK, HOAX ⟨~*s* and japes —Thomas Wood †1950⟩ ⟨quite serious . . . no ~ —E.F.Benson⟩

⁵rag \"\ *vt* **ragged; ragged; ragging; rags** [origin unknown] **1 :** to break (ore) into lumps for sorting **2 :** to cut or dress roughly (as a grindstone)

⁶rag \"\ *n* -s [by shortening] **1 :** RAGTIME **2 :** a dance in ragtime

⁷rag \"\ *vb* **ragged; ragged; ragging; rags** *vt* **:** to play (a musical composition) in ragtime ~ *vi* **:** to dance to ragtime music

ra·ga \'rägə\ *n* -s [Skt *rāga*, lit., color, musical tone; akin to Skt *rajyati* it is dyed, Gk *rhezein* to dye] **1 :** one of the ancient traditional melodic patterns of Hindu music **2 :** an improvisation on the notes of a traditional raga

rag·a·bash \'ragə,bash\ *also* **rag·a·brash** \-brash\ *n* -ES [prob. fr. ¹*rag* + *-abash, -abrash*, of unknown origin] *dial Brit* **:** RIFFRAFF

rag·a·muf·fin \'ragə,məfən\ *n* -s [fr. *Ragamoffyn*, name of a demon in *Piers Plowman* (1393), attributed to William Langland †1400? Eng. poet] **1 :** a ragged dirty man or boy ⟨friendly . . . little ~, full of impulsive energies —Peggy Bennett⟩; *esp* **:** a disreputably tattered person ⟨have led my ~*s* where they are peppered —Shak.⟩ ⟨a ~ brigade of women and children and dogs —*Scribner's*⟩ **2 :** a child in masquerade costume (as for Halloween) ⟨~*s* ringing doorbells⟩

rag-and-bone man \,==ˈ=-\ *n, chiefly Brit* **:** a usu. itinerant dealer in things of small value (as secondhand clothes and old newspapers) **:** OLD-CLOTHESMAN

rag baby *n* **:** RAG DOLL 1 ⟨looked like an adorable old *rag baby* —W.A.White⟩

ragbag \'=,=\ *n* [¹*rag* + *bag*] **1 :** a bag in which scraps or worn-out pieces of cloth are kept for future use or disposal ⟨~ of ends and tufts of brocade —R.W.Emerson⟩ **2 :** a heterogeneous collection of usu. trivial or useless objects ⟨a ~ of prejudices —J.R.Newman⟩

rag bolt *n* **1 :** a joining piece with a barbed shank hindering withdrawal when driven into wood — called also *barb bolt* **2 :** JAG BOLT

rag doll *n* **1 :** a stuffed and usu. painted cloth doll **2 :** a device for testing the germination of seed consisting of a strip of cloth that has numbered squares on which the seeds are placed and that is rolled into a bundle and kept moist during the test; *also* **:** a modification of this device used for inoculation of seed by disease organisms (as for tests of disease resistance)

¹rage \'rāj\ *n* -s [ME, fr. MF, fr. LL *rabia*, fr. L *rabies* rage, madness, fr. *rabere* to rave, be mad; akin to Skt *rabhas* violence, impetuosity] **1 a :** violent and uncontrolled anger often accompanied with raving **:** FURY ⟨overcome with a mighty ~⟩ ⟨out of this helplessness and ~ comes the will to endure —Leon Edel⟩ **b :** a fit of violent wrath ⟨fell into an appalling ~ and started out to destroy everything in sight —T.R.Ybarra⟩ **c** *archaic* **:** INSANITY ⟨mighty omens which presage the loss of reason and conclude in ~ —John Dryden⟩ **2 a :** violent action of the elements (as wind or sea) ⟨river hurled itself in thundering lacy-white ~ against jagged boulders —F.V.W.Mason⟩ **b :** a furious storm **:** TEMPEST ⟨a ~ on the bar kept seaside dwellers indoors⟩ **3 a :** extreme force of feeling **:** PASSION, FRENZY ⟨a ~ for order⟩ ⟨a ~ for power⟩ ⟨a ~ to live⟩ ⟨convulsed with a ~ of grief —Nathaniel Hawthorne⟩ ⟨the old man is in a ~ of excitement —Clemence Dane⟩ **b :** a state or feeling of exalted fervor (as of enthusiasm or inspiration) ⟨chill penury repressed their noble ~ —Thomas Gray⟩ ⟨that sacred ~ . . . we associate with the great novels on social issues —*New Republic*⟩ **4 :** something eagerly and usu. excessively sought after or pursued **:** CRAZE, VOGUE ⟨the current ~ for . . . how-to-do-it material —W.I.Nichols⟩ — often used in the phrase *all the rage* ⟨a period when cures and taking the waters were all the ~ —Peter Forster⟩ **syn** see ANGER, FASHION

[2]rage \"\ *vi* -ED/-ING/-S [ME *ragen,* fr. OF *ragier,* fr. *rage* anger] **1 :** to be in a rage **:** be furious **:** RAVE ⟨a person who everlastingly ~*s* —H.A.Overstreet⟩ — usu. used with *over, at,* or *against* ⟨*raging* over the waste of her small capital —*Amer. Guide Series: Tenn.*⟩ ⟨*raged* at him for his carelessness⟩ ⟨~ at the imposed weight —Arnold Bennett⟩ **2 a :** to become stirred up violently **:** be in a tumult ⟨the storm still *raging* outside —W.H.Hudson †1922⟩ ⟨the wind might ~ unbridled —C.G.D. Roberts⟩ **b :** to move wildly or turbulently **:** go on a rampage ⟨sent his brother *raging* after women —G.K.Chesterton⟩ ⟨the winds of doctrine . . . ~ through the land —V.L.Parrington⟩ ⟨rivers ~ through fertile bottom lands —*Amer. Guide Series: N. C.*⟩ **3 a :** to be intense or overwhelming **b :** to prevail uncontrollably **:** spread with destructive effect ⟨yellow fever was *raging* —W.P.Webb⟩ ⟨for two weeks . . . the controversy *raged* —A.L.Funk⟩ ⟨the fallacies . . . which ~ in the world —H.L.Mencken⟩

rage·ful \-jfəl\ *adj* **:** full of rage **:** FURIOUS

rag engine *n* **:** a beater used in converting rags into pulp

ra·geous \'rājəs\ *adj* [ME, fr. MF *rageux,* fr. *rage* anger + *-eux* -ous — more at RAGE] *dial chiefly Eng* **:** ENRAGED, FURIOUS

rag fair *n* **:** a street market where old or secondhand clothing is sold

rag felt *n* **:** a heavy paper that is made from rags impregnated with asphalt and is used for roofing and shingles

ragfish \'=,=\ *n* [[1]*rag* + *fish*] **:** a marine fish of the family Icosteidae remarkable for the soft skeleton

rag·ged \'ragəd\ *adj, sometimes* -ER/-EST [ME, fr. *ragge* rag + *-ed*] **1 :** roughly unkempt **:** SHAGGY ⟨~ sheep —John Dryden⟩ ⟨~ rust-colored hair —Willa Cather⟩ **2 a :** having an irregular edge or broken outline **:** having sharp indentations, notches, or projections **:** JAGGED ⟨a ~ wound⟩ ⟨a ~ . . . shoreline —*Amer. Guide Series: Va.*⟩ ⟨a ~ edge of corrugated iron —B.J.Haimes⟩ ⟨almost choked . . . on a ~ bone —D.C.Allen⟩ **b :** RAGULY **c :** not flush **:** not justified **:** UNEVEN — used of the ends of lines of text in printing ⟨set left-hand margins flush, right-hand margins ~⟩ **3 a :** torn or worn to tatters **:** having the texture broken **:** TATTERED, FRAYED ⟨a ~ flag⟩ ⟨a ~ sail⟩ ⟨discarded and ~ garments —Jack London⟩ **b :** almost exhausted from stress and strain **:** worn out ⟨drove us ~ with questions that revealed the most fantastically confused sources of information —Verna C. Millan⟩ — compare RUN RAGGED **4 :** wearing tattered clothes ⟨men ~ as the tramps, but going back to cold houses —Josephine Johnson⟩ **5 a :** irregularly strung out **:** STRAGGLY ⟨a ~ grove of palms —T.E. Lawrence⟩ **b :** executed or performed in an irregular, uneven, or uncoordinated manner **:** UNPOLISHED ⟨a rambling, ~ . . . book —*Times Lit. Supp.*⟩ ⟨send up a ~ cheer —Arnold Hill⟩ ⟨~ play on defense —*N.Y.Times*⟩ **c** *of a sound* **:** HARSH, DISSONANT ⟨a voice ~ with anxiety —Alan Sullivan⟩ ⟨the engine sounded ~ —H.H.Arnold & I.C.Eaker⟩ — **on the ragged edge :** in a state of anxiety or foreboding **:** on the verge of something dreaded ⟨a year lived *on the ragged edge* —Harlan Cleveland⟩ ⟨*on the ragged edge* of want —F.L.Allen⟩

ragged cup *n* **:** CUP PLANT

ragged fringed orchid *n* **:** RAGGED ORCHIS

ragged jack *n* **:** RAGGED ROBIN

ragged jacket *n* **:** a harp seal during its first molt

ragged lady *n* **1 :** SCARLET GAURA **2 :** LOVE-IN-A-MIST 1

rag·ged·ly *adv* **:** in a ragged manner: as **a :** ROUGHLY, SHAGGILY ⟨a white beard, ~ cut —Charles Dickens⟩ **b :** IRREGULARLY, STRAGGLINGLY ⟨the line of volunteers crawled forward ~ —Marjory S. Douglas⟩ ⟨stone walls trail ~ through the woods —*Amer. Guide Series: Vt.*⟩ **c :** without coordination **:** UNEVENLY ⟨a band struck up ~ —Lawrence Durrell⟩

rag·ged·ness *n* -ES **:** the quality or state of being ragged

ragged orchis *or* **ragged orchid** *n* **:** a fringed orchid (*Habenaria lacera*) of the eastern U. S. having a greenish flower with the lip deeply lacerate — called also *green fringed orchis*

ragged robin *n* **:** a perennial herb (*Lychnis floscuculi*) cultivated for its pink flowers with petals cut into narrow lobes

ragged sailor *n* **1 :** CORNFLOWER 1b **2 :** PRINCE'S-FEATHER 2 **3 :** a moderate purplish blue that is lighter and stronger than marine blue, bluer and less strong than average cornflower, and bluer, lighter, and stronger than gentian blue

ragged school *n* **:** a free school for destitute English children

ragged staff *n* [ME *ragged staffe,* fr. *ragged* + *staffe* staff] **:** a staff with knobs on each side

ragged-tooth shark \'==,=-\ *n* **:** a medium-sized grayish sand shark (*Carcharias taurus*) widely distributed in warm seas and in some regions regarded as a dangerous man-eater

rag·gedy \'ragədē, -di\ *adj* [*ragged* + *-y*] **:** marked by or tending to raggedness **:** somewhat ragged ⟨a ~ man⟩ ⟨~ hair⟩ ⟨you look starved and ~ —Saul Bellow⟩ ⟨making ~ yellow and black patterns —Richard Llewellyn⟩ ⟨~ carnival tune —Truman Capote⟩

rag·ger \'ragə(r)\ *n* -S [[1]*rag* + *-er*] **:** an engine-lathe operator who rough-turns hardened steel rolls

rag·gety \'ragədē\ *adj* [alter. of *raggedy*] *dial* **:** RAGGED

ragging *n* -S [fr. gerund of [5]*rag*] **1 :** grains of heavy material placed on the sieve of a jig to form an artificial bed in ore dressing **2 :** the act or process of breaking lumps of ore with a heavy sledge

[1]rag·gle \'ragəl\ *vt* -ED/-ING/-S [origin unknown] **:** to cut a raggle in (stone)

[2]raggle \"\ *n* -S **1 :** a groove cut in masonry; *esp* **:** one that receives the upper edge of a flashing above a roof **2 :** a manufactured building unit provided with a groove into which metal flashing can be fitted

rag·gle-tag·gle \ˌragəlˈtagəl\ *adj* [irreg. fr. *ragtag*] **:** MOTLEY ⟨*raggle-taggle* gypsies⟩ ⟨a forlorn, *raggle-taggle* show —Edwin Corle⟩

[1]rag·gy \'ragē\ *adj* -ER/-EST [ME, fr. OE *raggig,* fr. (assumed) *ragg* rag + *-ig* -y — more at RAG] **:** RAGGED, ROUGH

[2]raggy \"\ *adj* -ER/-EST [[6]*rag* + *-y*] **:** of, relating to, or marked by ragtime ⟨the ~ early brass band jazz —Rudi Blesh⟩

ra·gi *also* **rag·gee** *or* **rag·gi** *or* **rag·gy** \'ragē\ *n* -S [Hindi *rāgī*] **:** an East Indian cereal grass (*Eleusine coracana*) from whose seeds is ground a somewhat bitter flour that is a staple food in the Orient — called also *finger millet, korakan*

raging *adj* [fr. pres. part. of [2]*rage*] **1 :** that rages **2 :** causing great pain or distress ⟨troubled with a ~ tooth —Shak.⟩ **3 :** VIOLENT, WILD ⟨the ~ passion of the victors —Laurence Binyon⟩ **4 :** EXTRAORDINARY, TREMENDOUS ⟨a ~ beauty —William Plomer⟩ ⟨a ~ success —Leslie Rees⟩ — **rag·ing·ly** *adv*

rag·lan \'raglən\ *n* -S [after F.J.H.Somerset, Baron *Raglan* †1855 Brit. field marshal] **:** any of various loose overcoats with raglan sleeves

raglan sleeve *n* [*raglan* + *sleeve*] **:** a sleeve extending to the neckline and so having slanted seams from the underarm to the neck in front and back

rag·let \'raglət\ *n* -S [origin unknown] **:** RAGGLE 1

rag·man \'=,man, -,maa(ə)n, -,mən\ *n, pl* **ragmen** [[1]*rag* + *man*] **:** a man who collects or deals in rags and refuse

rag·man roll \'ragmən-\ *or* **ragman's roll** *n* [ME *Ragmane rolle,* roll used in a medieval game and containing verses describing various characters, fr. AF *Ragemon le bon,* lit., Ragemon the good (fr. the name of one of the characters serving as title of the verses) + ME *rolle* roll] **1** *obs* **:** a long list (as on a scroll or document) **:** CATALOG ⟨the whole *ragman roll* of fasting days —Thomas Nash⟩ **2 :** a series of rolls of deeds on parchment in which the Scottish nobility and gentry subscribed allegiance to Edward I of England in 1291 and esp. in 1296 during Edward's progress through Scotland and at the parliament of Berwick — usu. used in pl.

raglan sleeve

rag·mat·i·cal \(')rag'mad·əkəl\ *adj* [origin unknown] *archaic* **:** TURBULENT, RIOTOUS ⟨~ fellow —Tobias Smollett⟩

ra·gout \ra'gü\ *n* -S [F *ragoût,* fr. *ragoûter* to revive the taste, fr. *re-* + *a-* ad- + *goût* taste, fr. L *gustus;* akin to L *gustare* to taste — more at CHOOSE] **:** meat and vegetables well seasoned and cooked in a thick rich usu. brown sauce

rag paper *n* **:** a paper made wholly or partly from rags

ragpicker \'=,==\ *n* **:** one that picks up rags and refuse (as from rubbish cans or public dumps) as a means of livelihood

ragpicker's disease *or* **ragsorter's disease** *n* **:** pulmonary anthrax caused by inhalation of spores of the anthrax bacillus from contaminated wool or other hair

rag rug *n* **:** a hand-woven or machine-woven rug made with a heavy cotton warp and a filling of rags torn into strips whose ends are tied or sewed together

rags *pl of* RAG, *pres 3d sing of* RAG

ragshag \'=,=\ *n* -S [[1]*rag* + *shag*] **:** a person in ragged or masquerade dress ⟨a ~ parade⟩

ragsorter \'=,==\ *n* **:** one that sorts and prepares rags and old clothing for new uses (as in papermaking)

ragstone \'=,=\ *n* [[2]*rag*] **:** any of various hard rocks **:** RAG

ragtag \'=,=\ *n* [[1]*rag* + *tag*] **:** a motley crowd ⟨a ~ of admiring youngsters at his heels —Paul Gallico⟩

rag, tag, and bobtail *or* **ragtag and bobtail** *n* **:** RABBLE, RIFFRAFF ⟨the *rag, tag, and bobtail* of the city —Kenneth Roberts⟩ ⟨a *ragtag and bobtail* army —F.V.W.Mason⟩

rag·time \'rag,tīm\ *n* [prob. fr. *ragged* + *time*] **1 :** rhythm characterized by strong syncopation in the melody with a regularly accented accompaniment **2 :** music having ragtime rhythm

rag·tim·er \-mə(r)\ *n* [*ragtime* + *-er*] **:** a person who composes or plays ragtime ⟨the first . . . ~*s* were piano syncopators of decided originality —Wilder Hobson⟩

rag·timey \-mē\ *adj* **:** of, relating to, or like ragtime

rag·u·ly \'ragyəlē\ *also* **rag·u·lé** \ˌragyəˌlā\ *adj* [perh. fr. [1]*rag* + *-uly, -ulé* (as in *nebuly, nebulé*)] **:** notched in regular oblique breaks — used of a heraldic line of partition or charge (as a cross or saltier)

ragweed \'=,=\ *n* [[1]*rag* + *weed;* fr. the ragged shape of the leaves] **1 :** TANSY RAGWORT **2 :** any of various chiefly No. American weedy herbaceous plants that constitute the genus *Ambrosia* and produce highly allergenic pollen responsible for much hay fever and asthma: as **a :** an annual weed (*A. artemisiifolia*) with finely divided foliage that is common on open or cultivated ground in much of No. America and is introduced elsewhere by accident **b :** GREAT RAGWEED **c :** an annual to perennial highly variable weed (*A. psilostachya*) chiefly of dry barren lands of the southwestern U. S. and Mexico **3 :** FRANSERIA 2

ragweed family *n* **:** AMBROSIACEAE

rag wheel *n* **1 :** SPROCKET WHEEL **2 :** a polishing wheel made of disks of cloth clamped together

ragwork *n* **:** rubblework of thin small stones

rag worm *n* **:** any of various aquatic worms used as bait

ragwort \'=,=\ *n* [ME, fr. *ragge* rag + *wort;* fr. the ragged shape of its leaves] **:** any of several herbs of the genus *Senecio; esp* **:** TANSY RAGWORT — see GOLDEN RAGWORT, PURPLE RAGWORT

[1]rah \'rä, 'rȯ\ *interj* [short for *hurrah*] — used esp. in a cheer and usu. reduplicated to express joy, approbation, or encouragement

[2]rah \"\ *n* -S **:** HURRAH

[3]rah \"\ *vi* -ED/-ING/-S **:** HURRAH

ra·han·wein \ˌrähən'wēn\ *n, pl* **rahanwein** *or* **rahanweins** *usu cap* **:** one of a group of peoples in Somaliland characterized esp. by a strong Negroid mixture

rah·dar \'rä,där, =ˈ=\ *n* -S [Hindi *rāhdār,* fr. Per] *India* **:** a keeper of a toll road

[1]rah-rah \'=,=\ *adj* [fr. redupl. of [1]*rah*] **1 :** given to cheering (as at games) **:** demonstrative in the expression of college spirit ⟨the pennant-waving, *rah-rah* boy —*Badger Report*⟩ **2 :** relating to the boisterous or enthusiastic expression of college spirit ⟨typical college *rah-rah* activities —Clyde Kennedy⟩

[2]rah-rah \"\ *vi* -ED/-ING/-S **:** HURRAH

ra·ia \'rā(y)ə\ [NL, fr. L, ray] *syn of* RAJA

ra·iae \'rā,(y)ē\ [NL, fr. L, pl. of *raia* ray] *syn of* BATOIDEI

[1]raid \'rād\ *n* -S [Sc dial., fr. OE *rād* ride, raid — more at ROAD] **1 a :** a hostile or predatory incursion by mounted men ⟨a border ~⟩ **b :** a sudden and rapid invasion or military operation esp. on a small scale **:** FORAY, INROAD ⟨a ~ specifically designed to capture one or more prisoners —*Combat Forces Jour.*⟩; *specif* **:** a surprise attack made usu. by a small force (as of airplanes, fast naval craft, or ground or amphibious forces) and with no intention of holding the territory or area invaded — compare AIR RAID **c :** an attack upon enemy or neutral merchant ships in shipping lanes **2 a :** a brief expedition or hurried movement into a place or situation outside one's usual sphere esp. for the purpose of obtaining something ⟨a ~ upon the neighborhood shops⟩ **b :** a sudden attack or invasion by officers of the law (as for the purpose of making arrests or seizing illicit stores) ⟨a ~ upon a gambling house⟩ **c :** a venture by wild animals or birds onto cultivated land esp. for food ⟨on its early morning ~*s* on the peas in adjacent gardens —*Brit. Birds in Colour*⟩ ⟨~*s* by baboons⟩ **d :** a daring or unorthodox operation against a competitor or rival (as to gain recruits or exert pressure) ⟨signed many baseball stars in a ~ of the major leagues⟩; *specif* **:** an effort by one union to win as members workers already belonging to another union **3 :** the act of mulcting esp. public money (as by graft or pork-barrel appropriations) ⟨forestall a ~ on the treasury⟩ **4 :** an attempt by professional operators to depress prices of stocks by concerted selling

[2]raid \"\ *vb* -ED/-ING/-S *vt* **:** to make a raid upon or into ⟨amassed their cattle and horses by ~*ing* the herds of other clans —*Current Biog.*⟩ ⟨rear-area units ~*ed* of their physically fit —*Time*⟩ ⟨the sinking fund was ~*ed* year after year for ever-increasing amounts —J.H.Plumb⟩ ⟨when the barn owl ~*s* sparrow roosts —W.H.Dowdeswell⟩ ⟨~ the icebox⟩ ~ *vi* **:** to conduct or take part in a raid **:** MARAUD ⟨300 Indians were sent . . . to ~ on the settlers —Louise Koier⟩ ⟨~*ing* parties crossed the border repeatedly⟩

raid·er \'rādə(r)\ *n* -S **1 :** one that raids **:** one that leads or participates in a raid **2 :** a fast unarmored lightly armed ship designed to capture or destroy merchant shipping — called also *commerce raider* **3 :** an airplane engaged in raiding ⟨most of the ~*s* were two-engined fighter-bombers —*Newsweek*⟩ **4 :** a member of a battalion (as of U. S. Marines) specially trained for close-range fighting — compare COMMANDO, RANGER

raie ul·time \ˌrā,ül'tēm\ *n, pl* **raies ultimes** \"\ [F, lit., ultimate line] **:** one of the observed lines of the spectrum of an element which are the last to disappear as the quantity of the element is decreased — called also *ultimate line*

ra·ii·dae \'rā(y)ə,dē\ [NL *Raia,* type genus + *-idae*] *syn of* RAJIDAE

[1]raik \'rāk\ *vi* [ME *raiken* to go, stroll, wander, fr. ON *reika*] *archaic* **:** [3]RAKE

[2]raik \"\ *n* -S [ME, act of going, wandering, ground over which animals move, fr. ON *reik,* act of wandering] *archaic* **:** [4]RAKE

[1]rail \'rāl, *esp before pause or consonant* 'rāəl\ *n* -S [ME *reil,* fr. OE *hrægl* garment, cloak; akin to OFris *hreil* garment, OHG *hregil*] **1** *archaic* **:** a loose garment worn in varying style esp. by women since the early medieval period **2** *obs* **:** a neckerchief for women

[2]rail \"\ *n* -S [ME *raile,* fr. MF *reille* ruler, bar, fr. L *regula* straight piece of wood, ruler, fr. *regere* to keep straight, direct, rule — more at RIGHT] **1 a :** a bar usu. of timber or metal extending from one post or support to another as a guard or barrier (as in a fence, balustrade, or staircase); *specif* **:** one made by splitting a small log and used esp. in making rail fences — compare RIDER 6a **b :** a horizontal structural member in a frame or paneling (as in furniture, woodwork, or stage flats) — compare NEWEL, STILE; see DOOR illustration **c :** a long piece of wood or other material serving as a structural member or support (as in a piano action or an automobile frame) ⟨curtain ~⟩ ⟨the side ~*s* of a ladder⟩ ⟨the brass ~ in a saloon⟩ **2 a :** a construction of bars and posts **:** FENCE, RAILING **b** (1) **:** the stout narrow plank that forms the top of the bulwarks of a ship (2) **:** a light structure of wood or metal serving as a guard at the outer extremity of a deck — often used in combination ⟨poop ~⟩ ⟨forecastle ~⟩ — see SHIP illustration (3) **:** a section of planking with holes for belaying pins (as around a mast or across the shrouds) — see FIFE RAIL; compare PINRAIL **c :** a fence bounding a racetrack ⟨the inner ~⟩ ⟨the outer ~⟩ **3 a :** a bar orig. of wood but now usu. of rolled steel forming a track for vehicles whose wheels run in a depression in the bar (as in street railways) or on the top of the bar ⟨piers carry the overhead crane ~*s* —*Architectural Rev.*⟩ — compare BULLHEADED 3b, FLANGE RAIL, T RAIL **b** (1) **:** railroad rails in bulk ⟨trend toward the use of heavier ~ —*Yrbk. of Railroad Information*⟩ (2) **:** a continuous line of railroad rails ⟨boys walking on the ~⟩ ⟨lay ~⟩ (3) **:** TRACK ⟨the meanest stretch of ~ ever spiked —A.W.Somerville⟩ — usu. used in pl. ⟨a sleek and shining streamliner hurrying along the ~*s* —*Stories Behind the Pictures*⟩ ⟨network of ~*s* sharply divides the industrial section —*Amer. Guide Series: Texas*⟩ **c :** RAILROAD ⟨travel or ship by ~⟩ ⟨the ~*s* want more liberal treatment as to tax write-offs for depreciation —*Sat. Eve. Post*⟩ ⟨the terminal of the central ~ —Irene S. van Dongen⟩ **4 rails** *pl* **:** stocks or bonds of railroad companies **5** *slang* **:** a railroad employee **6 :** CARRIAGE RAIL **7 :** the cushioned rim around the bed of a billiard, pool, or crap table — **on the rails 1 :** progressing satisfactorily or rapidly **:** well under way ⟨got the joint European defense effort *on the rails* —*Christian Science Monitor*⟩ **2 :** on the proper course ⟨weak men would apparently take to crime who had previously been kept *on the rails* by a certain balance existing in society —Herbert Butterfield⟩ — **over the rail** *adv* **:** over the side of a ship ⟨paused a second and then went *over the rail* —L.M.Uris⟩

[3]rail \"\ *vt* -ED/-ING/-S [ME *railen,* fr. *raile* rail] **1 :** to provide with rails or a railing **:** FENCE ⟨being ~*ed* away solicitously from small precipices —Elizabeth Bowen⟩ — often used with *in* or *off* ⟨~ in a space⟩ **2** *chiefly Brit* **:** to transport by railroad ⟨apricots and plums, ~*ed* in large containers —*Farmer's Weekly (So. Africa)*⟩

[4]rail \"\ *adj* **:** of or relating to railroads ⟨~ connections for various points⟩

[5]rail \"\ *n, pl* **rail** *or* **rails** [ME *rale, raile,* fr. MF *raale*] **:** any of numerous precocial wading birds structurally related to the cranes but of small or medium size having short rounded wings, a short tail, and usu. very long toes that enable them to run on the soft mud of swamps and constituting a distinct subfamily of Rallidae; *broadly* **:** a bird of the family Rallidae — see BLACK RAIL, CLAPPER RAIL, CORNCRAKE, KING RAIL, SORA, WATER RAIL

[6]rail \"\ *vb* -ED/-ING/-S [ME *railen,* fr. MF *railler* to ridicule, mock, fr. OProv *ralhar* to babble, joke, fr. (assumed) VL *ragulare* to bray, fr. LL *ragere* to neigh] *vi* **1 :** to revile or scold in harsh, insolent, or vituperative language **:** utter reproaches, abuse, or angry complaints **:** RANT ⟨listened to herself ~ on —Clae Waltham⟩ ⟨cursed and ~*ed,* and finally declared he was going to trail the raiders —Zane Grey⟩ ⟨went abroad to ~ at the insecurity and poverty —Edmund Wilson⟩ ⟨made their listeners aware of the very things they were ~*ing* against —J.G.Harrison⟩ **2** *obs* **:** SCOFF, JEST, BANTER ~ *vt, archaic* **:** to move, effect, or influence by railing ⟨noble natures . . . are not ~*ed* into vice —Sir Thomas Browne⟩ **syn** see SCOLD

[7]rail \"\ *n* -S **:** RAILING, TAUNTING, SCOLDING

rail·age \'rālij\ *n* -S [[3]*rail* + *-age*] *Brit* **:** railroad transportation **:** the charge for conveyance by rail

rail anchor *n* [[2]*rail*] **:** a device to help maintain the proper line and gage of track by resisting the longitudinal movement of rails under traffic and maintaining proper expansion allowance at joint gaps for temperature changes

railbed \'=,=\ *n* **:** the roadbed of a railroad track ⟨crossed a ~ buried in the snow —Wright Morris⟩

railbird \'=,=\ *n* [[5]*rail* + *bird*] **1 :** RAIL; *esp* **:** SORA **2** [[2]*rail* + *bird*] **:** a racing enthusiast who sits on or near the track rail to watch a race or workout

rail bond *n* [[2]*rail*] **:** an electric jumper around a joint in the rails of a track to insure continuity of conductivity for signal currents

rail bus *n* **:** a passenger car with an automotive engine for operation on rails

railcar \'=,=\ *n* **:** a self-propelled railroad car carrying passengers, baggage, mail, goods, or combinations of these — compare RAIL DIESEL CAR

rail carrier *n* **:** a company whose business is transporting persons or goods or both by railroad

rail chair *n* **:** CHAIR 5a

rail clamp *n* **:** a device for clamping on rails to prevent or halt the movement of railroad cars past a given point (as at platforms or on stub tracks)

rail clip *n* **1 :** a metal plate projecting over the base of a rail for bolting the rail to its support **2 :** an anchor for fastening the rear of a derrick car or a crane to the rails of a track to keep the crane from tipping while lifting a heavy load **3 :** a metal support bolted or clamped to a rail for carrying a detector bar

rail creep *n* **:** the longitudinal movement of rail produced by the passage of trains over it

rail diesel car *n* **:** a self-propelled railroad car powered by a diesel engine and capable of operating as a single unit or in combination with other rail diesel cars as a train — abbr. *RDC;* compare RAILCAR

railed *past of* RAIL

rail·er \'rālə(r)\ *n* -S [[6]*rail* + *-er*] **:** one that rails **:** REVILER

railfan \'=,=\ *n* [[2]*rail* + *fan*] **:** one whose hobby is railroads or model railroads **:** a railroad enthusiast

rail fence *n* [[2]*rail*] **:** a fence of posts and usu. split rails — compare WORM FENCE

rail-fence cipher *n* **:** a zigzag transposition method in which alternate letters of the plaintext are juxtaposed (as in the encipherment $^{b}{}_{r}{}^{i}{}_{g}{}^{e}$=bigrde)

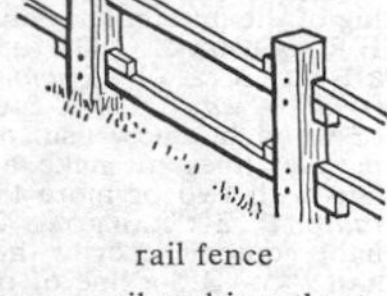

rail fence

rail fork *n* **:** a bar with a forked end for turning railroad rails

rail guard *n* **:** a vertical metal device attached to the front of a locomotive ahead of either front wheel to clear the rail of obstructions

railhead \'=,=\ *n* **1 a** (1) **:** a point on a railroad at which traffic may originate or terminate (2) **:** a point on a railroad in a theater of operations at which supplies for troops are unloaded for distribution and forwarding **b :** the end of a railroad line (as of one under construction) **2 :** the top portion of the rail that carries the wheels of rolling stock

[1]railing *n* -S [fr. gerund of [3]*rail*] **1 :** a barrier (as a fence or balustrade) consisting of a rail and supports **2 :** RAILS; *also* **:** material for making rails **3 :** a strip of wood covering the exposed ends or edges of a board or piece of plywood

[2]railing *n* -S [fr. gerund of [6]*rail*] **:** INVECTIVE, RANTING ⟨his self-pity and his ~*s* at fate —*Times Lit. Supp.*⟩

[3]railing *n* -S [fr. gerund of [3]*rail*] *Brit* **:** a shipment by rail ⟨potato ~*s* were well maintained —*Farmer's Weekly (So. Africa)*⟩

rail·ing·ly *adv* [[2]*railing* + *-ly*] **:** in a railing manner

rail·lery \'rālərē, -ri\ *n* -ES [F *raillerie,* fr. MF *railler* to rail + *-erie* -ery — more at RAIL] **1 :** good-natured ridicule **:** pleasantry touched with satire **:** BANTER, CHAFFING, MOCKERY ⟨mistaking bustle for style, ~ for badinage, and noise for gaiety —Benjamin Disraeli⟩ ⟨know when delicate ~ was properly called for —Jane Austen⟩ ⟨actually refers to you without fury, even with ~ —G.B.Shaw⟩ **2 :** an instance of good-natured ridicule **:** JEST

rail·less \'rālləs\ *adj* [[2]*rail* + *-less*] **:** being without rails or railing **:** UNRAILED ⟨~ trolley⟩ ⟨sit on the ~ porch —James Jones⟩ ⟨a thousand ~ miles —T.H.White b. 1915⟩

rail·leur \ra'yər\ *n* -S [F, fr. MF *railler* + *-eur* -or] **:** one given to raillery

rail·lie·ti·na \ˌrālyəˈtīnə\ *n, cap* [NL, fr. A. *Railliet,* 19th cent. Fr. biologist + NL *-ina*] **:** a large genus of armed tapeworms (family Davaineidae) having the adults parasitic in birds, rodents, or rarely man and the larvae in various insects

raillike \'=,=\ *adj* **:** resembling a rail

rail lugger *n* [perh. alter. of *rail hugger,* fr. [2]*rail* + *hugger*] *slang* **:** a horse or dog that bears toward or runs close to the inside rail in a race

rail·ly \'rālē\ *vb* [F *railler*, fr. MF — more at RAIL] *vt, archaic* **:** JEST, MOCK ~ *vi, archaic* **:** RALLY, RIDICULE

rail·man \'⸗mən\ *n, pl* **railmen** **1 :** a cable hand **2 :** a dock worker who signals from the ship's rail during loading and unloading **3 :** one employed on a railroad

rail-motor \'⸗'⸗⸗\ *adj* **:** relating to service or rates involving transportation partly by railroad and partly by highway vehicle

¹**rail·road** \'rā(ə)l,rōd *sometimes* 'raů,- *or* 'reů,-\ *n, often attrib* [²*rail* + *road*] **1 :** RAILWAY 1, 3 **2 a :** a permanent road having a line of rails fixed to ties and laid to gage usu. on a leveled or graded ballasted roadbed and providing a track for freight cars, passenger cars, and other rolling stock designed to be drawn by locomotives or sometimes propelled by self-contained motors — see ELEVATED RAILROAD, LIGHT RAILWAY; compare TRAMWAY **b :** such a road together with all the lands, buildings, rolling stock, franchises, and other assets relating thereto and constituting a single property **:** a railroad company ⟨~ shares⟩ **3 railroads** *pl* **:** the securities of railroad transportation companies **4 :** a split in bowling in which there is a greater than one-pin distance between the pins left standing making it necessary to hit one pin on the side to slide it across the intervening space to hit another pin in order to make a spare ⟨6-7-10 ~⟩ ⟨8-10 ~⟩

²**railroad** \"\ *vt* **1 :** to build railroads in ⟨~ a country⟩ **2 :** to transport by railroad **3 a :** to send or put through in great haste or without due consideration (as for private benefit) ⟨~ the measure through the legislature⟩ **b** (1) **:** to send (type matter) to press before reading and correction (2) **:** to send (copy) to the composing room without careful editing **4 :** to convict and send esp. to prison with undue haste and usu. by the use of false charges or insufficient evidence **:** FRAME ⟨a convicted person who claims to have been ~*ed* by evidence that was improperly procured —O.K.Fraenkel⟩ ⟨being ~*ed* into a booby hatch —Sidney Howard⟩ ⟨~*ed* two radicals to death —Lawrence Elliott⟩ ~ *vi* **1 :** to become employed on a railroad **2 :** to travel by rail **3 :** to build a railroad ⟨this new, raw land was well worth ~*ing* into —*Amer. Guide Series: Wash.*⟩

³**railroad** \"\ *adj, of a card game* **:** adapted for play by commuters on railroads with the rules of the game modified to produce quick decisions ⟨~ bridge⟩ ⟨~ euchre⟩

railroad board *n* **:** a coated or uncoated board used for show-cards, tickets, car signs, and tags

railroad bridge *n* **:** a bridge constructed for the exclusive or chief purpose of carrying railroad traffic

railroad car *n* **:** CAR 1c

railroad engineer *n* **:** RAILWAY ENGINEER

railroad engineering *n* **:** RAILWAY ENGINEERING

rail·road·er \-də(r)\ *n* -s [¹*railroad* + *-er*] **:** a railroad employee or official

railroad flat *or* **railroad apartment** *n* **:** an apartment in a substandard building having a series of narrow rooms arranged in line usu. with each room forming the corridor to the next and with only the front and rear rooms having windows

railroad furniture *n* **:** metal printing furniture that resembles railroad rails in shape and is used mostly to fill gutters

rail·road·i·ana \,rāl,rōdē'anə\ *n pl* [¹*railroad* + *-ana*] **1 :** literature of or relating to railroads **2 :** the history or lore of railroads

railroading *n* [fr. gerund of ²*railroad*] **:** construction or operation of a railroad line **:** the business of managing a railroad or of working as an employee of a railroad

railroad jack *n* **1 :** a portable jack used for heavy lifting **2 a :** a 4-screw or 6-screw hoist operated by electric motors for lifting locomotives off their wheels while they are undergoing repairs **b :** a hydraulic lift device operated either by hand lever or motor

railroad man *n* **:** RAILROADER

railroad manila *n* **:** a cheap yellow writing paper containing groundwood and used for school writing tablets, sales books, and order blanks

railroad sickness *n* **:** a disease of cattle resembling milk fever presumably due to comparable metabolic imbalance and occurring esp. in cows in advanced pregnancy and in fat cows or steers during or after a long drive or journey by rail or truck — compare GRASS TETANY

railroad spike *n* **:** a hook-headed spike for securing the rails of a railroad to the ties

railroad station *n* **:** a building containing accommodations for railroad passengers or freight — called also *depot*

railroad vine *n* **:** a creeping or climbing vine (*Ipomea pes-capri*) of the coastal sand dunes from Florida to Texas having flowers with a purple corolla limb and suborbicular leaves with an apical notch

railroad worm *n* **1 :** APPLE MAGGOT **2 :** the larva or wingless female of any of several So. American beetles (genus *Phrixothrix*) of the family Cantharidae

rails *pl of* RAIL, *pres 3d sing of* RAIL

railside \'⸗,⸗\ *adj* [²*rail* + *side*] **:** situated beside a railroad track or right of way

rail-splitter \'⸗,⸗⸗\ *n* **:** one that makes logs into fence rails

railroad spike

rail sweep *n* **:** a device on the front of a railcar for brushing easily removable obstructions from the surface of the railhead

rail tongs *n pl* **:** tongs used by trackmen for lifting rails

rail train *n* **:** a train of rolls in a rolling mill for making railroad rails

rail-water \'⸗'⸗⸗\ *adj* **:** of or relating to transportation rates or service partly by railroad and partly by inland waterway or ocean transport esp. by through bill of lading ⟨the narrowing of the differential between all-rail and *rail-water* routes —E.R.Johnson & G.G.Huebner⟩

rail·way \'rā(ə)l,wā *sometimes* 'raů,- *or* 'reů,-\ *n, often attrib* [²*rail* + *way*] **1 :** a runway or track formed of rails orig. of wood but now usu. of steel laid end to end usu. in two parallel lines to make a permanent way for cars **:** a way laid with two or more tracks in such manner — called also *railroad* **2 :** RAILROAD 2; *often* **:** a railroad operating with light equipment or within a small area — compare STREET RAILWAY **3 :** a line of track providing a runway for wheels ⟨a cash or parcel ~ in a department store⟩ ⟨the ~ of a traveling crane⟩

rail·way·ac \-wā,ak\ *n* -s [*railway* + maniac] *Brit* **:** RAILFAN

railway artillery *n* **:** artillery mounted on and fired from artillery cars

railway bridge *n* **:** RAILROAD BRIDGE

railway engineer *n* **:** an engineer whose training or occupation is in railway engineering

railway engineering *n* **:** a branch of civil engineering dealing with the location, construction, and maintenance of railroads

rail·way·less \-wāləs\ *adj* **:** lacking railways ⟨the all but roadless, ~ deserts —Joseph Wechsberg⟩

railway letter *n, Brit* **:** a letter carried on a railway or ship by the railway service instead of by the postal service and received by the railway from the sender and delivered by the railway to the addressee either directly at a railway station or through a post office

railway mail car *n* **:** a railroad car carrying mail that is sorted in transit — compare POSTAL STORAGE CAR

railway mail clerk *n* **:** one who sorts and classifies mail in a railway mail car

rail·way·man \'⸗⸗,man, -,maa(ə)n, -,mən\ *n, pl* **railwaymen** [*railway* + *man*] **:** RAILROADER

railway post office *n* **:** RAILWAY MAIL CAR

railway station *n* **:** RAILROAD STATION

¹**rai·ment** \'rāmənt\ *n* -s [ME *rayment*, short for *arrayment, arayment*] **1 :** CLOTHING, VESTURE, GARMENTS ⟨if these strangers were of important air and costly ~ —Brian O'Nolan⟩ ⟨had no change of ~ —John Buchan⟩ ⟨bore necessities of life, such as food and ~ and shelter —*New Yorker*⟩ **2** *obs* **:** an article of dress

²**raiment** \"\ *vt* -ED/-ING/-S **:** CLOTHE, GARB, APPAREL ⟨was ~*ed* in silks⟩

rai·ment·less \-tləs\ *adj* **:** lacking raiment

¹**rain** \'rān\ *n* -s *often attrib* [ME *reyn*, fr. OE *regn, rēn;* akin to OHG *regan* rain, ON *regn*, Goth *rign*, and perh. to ON *raki* dampness, L *rigare* to water] **1 a :** water falling in drops condensed from vapor in the atmosphere — compare DRIZZLE, MIST **b :** the descent of water in drops esp. from the clouds **c :** water that has fallen as rain **:** RAINWATER ⟨the ~ on the door log had turned to ice —Conrad Richter⟩ **2 a :** a fall of rain esp. heavier or of longer duration than a shower **:** RAINSTORM ⟨the roads . . . can be used in summer only and then if there are no unusual ~s —W.E.Rudolph⟩ ⟨spring ~s⟩ **b rains** *pl* **:** the rainy season (as in India) **3 :** rainy weather ⟨a week of ~⟩ **4 a :** a falling or driving of numerous particles or bodies ⟨a ~ of petals⟩ ⟨a ~ of soot⟩ ⟨warships maintained a steady ~ of fire —H.L.Merillat⟩; *also* **:** multitudinous onset ⟨a ~ of protests⟩ ⟨a ~ of abuse⟩ **b :** falling or driven particles ⟨an average pollen ~ for a locality —S.A.Cain⟩ **5 :** a scratch or marking running lengthwise of a motion picture film that on projection appears as a vertical streak **6 rains** *pl* **:** regions of calms and heavy rainfalls ⟨the ~s of the north Atlantic⟩

²**rain** \"\ *vb* -ED/-ING/-S [ME *reynen*, fr. OE *regnian;* akin to OHG *reganōn* to rain, ON *regna*, Goth *rignjan;* all fr. a prehistoric Gmc verb derived fr. the ancestor of OE *regn* rain] *vi* **1 :** to fall as water in drops from the clouds ⟨care must be taken that such materials are dry and not ~*ed* on —*Bull. of Amer. Inst. of Architects*⟩ — often used with *it* ⟨it may ~⟩ ⟨it is ~*ing* in at the window⟩ **2 :** to send down rain ⟨caused the clouds to ~ —Norman Douglas⟩ **3 a :** to fall or drop like rain ⟨bombs, grapeshot, and cannonballs ~*ed* upon the defenseless town —*Amer. Guide Series: Maine*⟩ **b :** to occur in a multitudinous onset ⟨conflicting thoughts ~ thick and fast —*Saturday Rev.*⟩ **4 :** to be in a form or arrangement suggestive of falling rain ⟨gray hair ~*ing* down over his eyebrows —Anna Ortese⟩ ⟨trunks whose lower boughs were out of sight among the ~*ing* aerial roots as fine as hairs —D.C.Peattie⟩ ~ *vt* **1 :** to pour from or as if from the clouds **:** shower down ⟨behold, I will ~ bread from heaven for you —Exod 16:4 (RSV)⟩ ⟨petals are ~*ed* down upon them from windows and balconies —John Kobler⟩ **2 :** to bestow profusely or abundantly **:** yield or shed copiously ⟨more blows were ~*ed* on him —T.B.Costain⟩ ⟨~ favors⟩

rain area *n* **1 :** the area indicated on a weather map over which rain fell within a period of time **2 :** the area over which rain is falling **3 :** the most rainy portion of a cyclonic storm

rainband \'⸗,⸗\ *n* **:** a dark band in the yellow portion of the solar spectrum near the sodium lines caused by watery vapor in the atmosphere and therefore sometimes used in weather predictions

rain barrel *n* **:** a barrel of or for rain water; *esp* **:** a barrel placed so as to catch water from eaves

rain beetle *n* **:** any of several black hairy beetles (genus *Pleocoma*) related to the scarab beetles

rain belt *n* **:** a region of relatively heavy rainfall

rain·belt·er \'rān,beltə(r)\ *n* -s [*rain belt* + *-er*] *West* **:** a new settler who takes up farming in a semiarid region during a rainy season

rainbird \'⸗,⸗\ *n* **:** any of numerous birds chiefly of the family Cuculidae whose cries are popularly believed to augur rain: as **a :** RAIN CROW **b :** a West Indian lizard cuckoo (*Saurothera vetula*) **c :** a koel (*Eudynamys scolopacea*) of India **d :** a So. American cuckoo of the genus *Piaya* **e** *dial Eng* **:** GREEN WOODPECKER

rain boot *n* **:** an ankle-high overshoe of rubber or plastic for wear in rain and mud

¹**rain·bow** \'rān,bō\ *n* [ME *reinbowe*, fr. OE *rēnboga;* akin to OHG *reginbogo* rainbow, ON *regnbogi;* all fr. a prehistoric WGmc-NGmc compound whose first constituent is represented by OE *regn, rēn* rain and whose second constituent is represented by OE *boga* bow — more at RAIN, BOW] **1 a :** a circle or from the usual viewpoint an arc of a circle exhibiting in concentric bands the several colors of the spectrum and formed opposite the sun by the refraction and reflection of the sun's rays in drops of rain — see PRIMARY RAINBOW, SECONDARY RAINBOW **b :** a phenomenon similar to a rainbow in formation and appearance — see FOGBOW, MOONBOW, WHITE RAINBOW **2 a :** an arrangement of the colors of the spectrum **:** a multicolored or glittering array ⟨horizontal stripes in a ~ of colors —*New Yorker*⟩ ⟨silken cloak and a ~ of medals —E.T.Gilliard⟩ **b :** a wide assortment **:** a broad or complete range **:** GAMUT ⟨party was a catchall large enough to hold a ~ of opinions —E.O.Hauser⟩ **3 a :** ILLUSION, WILL-O'-THE-WISP ⟨families chasing the ~ of better fortune ever westward —Dixon Wecter⟩ ⟨proof that the early owners were not following a ~ —Allan Forbes & R.M.Eastman⟩ **b :** attainment of success or fortune **4 :** any of several brilliantly colored fork-tailed Andean hummingbirds of the genus *Coeligena* **5 :** RAINBOW TROUT

²**rainbow** \"\ *adj* **:** having the colors of the rainbow **:** MULTICOLORED ⟨shining robes, and wonderful ~ wings —Mark Twain⟩ ⟨~ effect⟩

³**rainbow** \"\ *vt* -ED/-ING/-S **:** to produce rainbows on **:** cause to be like a rainbow (as in coloring or form) **:** span as or like a rainbow ⟨~*ed* mists of the mountains —Frank Yerby⟩ ⟨under the ~*ed* prisms of the great chandelier —Winston Churchill⟩ ~ *vi* **:** to appear like a rainbow (as in coloring or in arrangement of colors ⟨stripes of color ~*ing* along Varadero Beach —Budd Schulberg⟩

rainbow bird *n* **:** an Australian bee-eater (*Merops ornatus*)

rainbow boa *n* **:** a moderate-sized iridescent boa (*Epicrates cenchris*) of the American tropics

rainbow cactus *n* **:** a stout cylindric cactus (*Echinocereus rigidissimus*) of the southwestern U.S. and adjacent Mexico with spines partly red and partly white, showy red flowers, and edible red fruit

rainbow chaser *n* **:** VISIONARY

rainbow-colored \'⸗,⸗'⸗⸗\ *adj* **:** exhibiting the colors of the spectrum **:** MULTICOLORED

rainbow darter *n* **:** a bright-colored darter (*Poecilichthys caeruleus*) of the Mississippi drainage and north and east into Ontario and New York

rainbow drops *n pl but sing or pl in constr* **:** a plant of the genus *Viscaria*

rainbow duck *n* **:** WOOD DUCK 1

rainbow fish *n* **1 :** any of numerous brilliantly colored wrasses and parrot fishes of tropical seas **2 :** GUPPY **3 :** a small brilliantly striped Australian freshwater silversides (*Melanotaenia nigrans*) sometimes kept in the tropical aquarium

rainbow herring *n* **:** a brilliantly colored smelt (*Osmerus dentex*) of the Bering sea region

rainbow moss *n* **:** a Chinese club moss (*Selaginella uncinata*) cultivated for its feathery blue-green foliage

rainbow parrot fish *n* **:** a large variably colored heavy-bodied parrotfish (*Pseudoscarus guacamaia*) of the tropical western Atlantic that is esp. common about Bermuda and may attain a length of four feet

rainbow perch *n* **:** a small surf fish (*Hypsurus caryi*) of the Pacific coast of No. America that is brilliantly striped in red, orange, and light blue and is of some importance as a market fish; *also* **:** a similar but larger and duller fish (*Taeniotoca lateralis*) of the same region

rainbow pink *n* **:** CHINA PINK

rainbow rock cress *n* **:** a plant of the genus *Aubrietia*

rainbow roof *n* **:** a pitched roof whose slopes are slightly convex giving it a delicately rounded appearance

rainbow runner *n* **:** a large brilliantly marked blue and yellow carangid food and sport fish (*Elagatis bipinnulatus*) nearly cosmopolitan in warm seas

rainbow serpent *n* **:** a widely recognized serpent deity of contemporary primitive societies symbolized by the rainbow which is mythically interpreted as a great snake

rainbow roof

rainbow shower *n* **:** a showy hybrid ornamental tree (*Cassia javanica* x *C. fistula*) developed in Hawaii and having flowers that range in color from cream to orange and red

rainbow snake *n* **:** a shy burrowing No. American colubrid snake (*Abastor erythrogrammus*) that is brightly colored in red, blue, and yellow — called also *hoop snake*

rainbow trout *n* **:** a large stout-bodied and sometimes anadromous trout (*Salmo gairdnerii*) of still and flowing waters of the Pacific coast of No. America from southern California to Alaska that has a large head and small mouth, that in the typical freshwater form is greenish above and white on the belly with a pink, red, or lavender stripe more or less developed along each side of the body and usu. profusely sprinkled with black dots, and that is highly esteemed as a sport and food fish although in parts of Alaska considered a pest because of its destruction of salmon eggs — see STEELHEAD

rainbowweed \'⸗,⸗,⸗\ *n* [*rainbow* + *weed*] **:** PURPLE LOOSESTRIFE

rain·bowy \'rān,bōē\ *adj* **:** like a rainbow

rain cape *n* **:** a cape of waterproof or water-resistant material for wear in the rain

rain check *n* **1 :** the stub of a ticket (as to a baseball game) retained by the spectator and good for admission to a later performance if the scheduled performance is interrupted during its early part (as, in baseball usu. before 4½ innings are over) by rain or bad weather **2 :** an extension of the offer of a favor or privilege until a more appropriate or convenient time ⟨decided to pass up the invitation for the moment, but told him we wanted a *rain check* for transportation across with the last officers who would leave the city —R.A.Gunnison⟩ ⟨who smiles, confers a *rain check* to an untoward hour —Marsden Hartley⟩ — often used with *take* or *give* ⟨take a *rain check* on that dinner⟩

rain cloud *n* **:** a cloud (as a nimbus) bringing rain

raincoat \'⸗,⸗\ *n* **:** a coat of waterproof or water-resistant material for wear in the rain

rain crow *n* **1 :** the black-billed or the yellow-billed cuckoo **2** *or* **rain dove :** MOURNING DOVE

rain dance *n* **:** a dance forming part of a ritual for invoking rain (as the ancient hula of Hawaii and the surviving corn dances of American Indians)

rain doctor *n* **:** a priest or sorcerer among nonliterate peoples who employs magic rituals and incantations for the purpose of producing rain

raindrop \'⸗,⸗\ *n* [ME *reindrope*, fr. OE *rēndropa*, fr. *regn, rēn* rain + *dropa* drop] **:** a drop of rain ⟨the ~s were falling more thickly —J.C.Lincoln⟩

rained *past of* RAIN

rai·nette green \rā'net-\ *n* [F *rainette* tree frog, dim. of *raine* frog, fr. L *rana*, prob. of imit. origin] **:** a moderate yellow green that is paler than average moss green and yellower and duller than average pea green or apple green (sense 1)

rain·ey's corpuscle \'rānēz-\ *n, usu cap R* [after George *Rainey* †1884 Eng. anatomist] **:** the crescent-shaped spore of a sarcosporidian

rainfall \'⸗,⸗\ *n* **1 :** a fall of rain ⟨there was another ~ that night —Dan Wickenden⟩ **2 a :** the water or amount of water that falls in rain usu. measured by the depth in inches ⟨~ increases steadily from the desert margin toward the south —P.E.James⟩ **b :** an amount of precipitation esp. during a given time ⟨having a ~, including snowfall, of from sixty to eighty inches —*Economic Geology*⟩

rain forest *n* **1 :** a tropical woodland that has an annual rainfall of at least 100 inches and often much more, is typical of but not wholly restricted to certain lowland areas, is characterized by lofty broad-leaved evergreen trees forming a continuous canopy, lianas, and herbaceous and woody epiphytes and by nearly complete absence of low-growing or understory ground-rooted plants — called also *tropical rain forest* **2 :** TEMPERATE RAIN FOREST

rainfowl \'⸗,⸗\ *n* [ME *reynfowle*, fr. *reyn* rain + *fowle, foul* fowl] **1 :** CHANNELBILL **2** *dial Eng* **:** GREEN WOODPECKER

rainfrog \'⸗,⸗\ *n, chiefly South & Midland* **:** a small green frog

rain·ful \'rānfəl\ *adj* **:** full of rain **:** RAINY ⟨nearing the base of the clouds . . . I felt . . . a faint distaste for climbing into their cold, ~ interior —J.L.Rhys⟩

rain gage *n* **:** an instrument for measuring the quantity of precipitation that falls at a given place and time

rain glass *n* **:** BAROMETER

rainier *comparative of* RAINY

rainiest *superlative of* RAINY

rain·i·ly \'rānəlē\ *adv* **:** in a rainy manner

rain·i·ness \-nēnəs\ *n* -ES **:** the quality or state of being rainy

raining *pres part of* RAIN

rain insurance *n* **:** insurance against loss from cancellation of a scheduled event because of rain

rain leader *or* **rain pipe** *n* **:** DOWNSPOUT

rain·less \'rānləs\ *adj* **:** lacking rain **:** lacking precipitation ⟨a ~ month⟩ — **rain·less·ness** *n* -ES

rain lily *n* **:** any of several plants of the southwestern U.S. that frequently flower after rain: as **a :** EVENING STAR; *also* **:** a related plant (*Cooperia pedunculata*) **b :** ATAMASCO LILY

rainmaker \'⸗,⸗⸗\ *n* **:** one that seeks to produce rain: as **a :** an American Indian medicine man who uses incantations and magic rituals for the purpose of producing rain **b :** a person who attempts rainmaking

rainmaking \'⸗,⸗⸗\ *n* **:** the act or process of attempting by some scientific or other artificial means to produce rain or to make rain fall earlier or in greater amounts than it would fall naturally

rain or shine **1 :** whatever the weather may be **:** without fail ⟨the auction will be held *rain or shine*⟩ **2 :** whatever the circumstances ⟨always cheerful, *rain or shine*⟩

rain out *vt* **:** to interrupt or prevent by rain ⟨the afternoon's game was *rained out* —Mary Deasy⟩ ⟨educational and social events in this area have been *rained out* right and left —*Springfield (Mass.) Daily News*⟩

rain pie *n, Brit* **:** GREEN WOODPECKER

rainpool \'⸗,⸗\ *n* **:** a pool of water formed in the rainy season or after a rain ⟨moringa trees in blossom grew by a great ~ —G.W.Murray⟩

rain print *n* **:** a small shallow depression formed by the impact of a raindrop in fine sand, mud, or clay and sometimes preserved on the bedding planes of sedimentary rocks

¹**rainproof** \'⸗'⸗\ *adj* [¹*rain* + *proof*] **:** impervious to rain ⟨a ~ bag⟩ — compare SHOWERPROOF, WATERPROOF

²**rainproof** \"\ *n* **:** a rainproof coat or cape

³**rainproof** \"\ *vt* **:** to make rainproof — **rain·proof·er** \'rān,prüfə(r)\ *n*

rain quail *n* **:** a migratory Indian quail (*Coturnix coromandelica*)

rain rot *n* **:** a severe weeping dermatitis accompanied by swelling of the skin and loss of wool occurring in heavy-wooled sheep exposed to rain for prolonged periods — called also *fat scab, wool rot*

rains *pl of* RAIN, *pres 3d sing of* RAIN

rain shadow *n* **:** a region of reduced rainfall to the lee of high mountains

rainspout \'⸗,⸗\ *n* **:** WATERSPOUT

rainsquall \'⸗,⸗\ *n* **:** a squall accompanied by rain ⟨a thick ~ passed over the two boats —Joseph Conrad⟩ ⟨a black ~ makes up from windward —S.E.Morison⟩

rainstone \'⸗,⸗\ *n* **:** a stone used in rainmaking magic

rainstorm \'⸗,⸗\ *n* **:** a storm of or with rain

raintight \'⸗'⸗\ *adj* **:** so tight as to exclude rain ⟨an aluminum ~ window⟩

rain toad *n* **:** a tree toad (*Hyla versicolor*) whose call is popularly supposed to predict rain

rain tree *n* [so called fr. the belief that it exudes water from its leaflets] **:** an ornamental tropical American tree (*Pithecolobium saman*) having bipinnate leaves, globose clusters of flowers with crimson stamens, and sweet-pulp pods eaten by cattle

rainwash \'⸗,⸗\ *n* **1 :** the washing away of material by rain ⟨some solid material is carried into streams by ~ —C.A.Cotton⟩ **2 :** material washed away by rain ⟨eventually the ~ is swept into rills and streams —Arthur Holmes⟩

rainwater \'⸗,⸗⸗\ *n* [ME, fr. OE *rēnwæter*, fr. *regn, rēn* rain + *wæter* water] **:** water fallen as rain that has not had an opportunity to collect soluble matter from the soil and is therefore quite soft — compare SPRINGWATER

rainwater fish *n* **:** a very small American killifish (*Lucania parva* or a related species) living in swamps and brackish water along the eastern and southern Atlantic coast and being of considerable value as a destroyer of mosquito larvae

rainwater head *n* : LEADER HEAD

rainwear \'ˌ=,=\ *n* : waterproof or water-resistant clothing (as a raincoat) for bad weather wear

rainworm \'=,=\ *n* [prob. trans. of G *regenwurm;* fr. its habit of appearing above ground esp. during a heavy rain] **1** : EARTHWORM **2** : an adult mermithid worm

rainy \'rānē, -ni\ *adj* -ER/-EST [ME *reyny,* fr. *reyn* rain + *-y*] **1** : abounding with or characterized by rain : WET, SHOWERY ⟨~ weather⟩ ⟨a ~ spell⟩ ⟨~ regions⟩ **2** : being a time when much rain falls ⟨the ~ season in a tropical land⟩ **3** : bringing rain ⟨~ winds⟩ ⟨~ clouds⟩ **4** : affected by rain : like rain ⟨very dark by contrast even with the subdued, ~ light of the woods —H.M.Rideout⟩

rainy day *n* : a period of want or need ⟨imperative that a couple should so live as to set something aside for a *rainy day* —*Saturday Rev.*⟩

¹ra·ioid \'rā,(y)ȯid\ *adj* [L *raia* ray + E *-oid*] : resembling or related to a ray : BATOID ⟨a ~ fish⟩

²raioid \"\ *n* -s : ¹RAY

rai·on \rī'ōn\ *n* -s [Russ *raĭon,* district, province, fr. F *rayon* honeycomb, department of a store, fr. OF *ree, raie* honeycomb, of Gmc origin; akin to OHG *rāza* honeycomb, MD *rāte,* and perh. to L *cratis* wickerwork, hurdle — more at HURDLE] : a political subdivision in the U.S.S.R. comparable to the U.S. county : DISTRICT

¹rais *or* **reis** \'rīs\ *n, pl* **rais** *or* **reis** [F *reis,* fr. Ar *ra'īs* chief, fr. *ra's* head] **1** : a Muslim ship's captain **2** : a Muslim chief or ruler

²rais \"\ *n pl, usu cap* : a Mongoloid people of Nepal who speak Kiranti

rais·able *also* **raise·able** \'rāzəbəl\ *adj* [¹*raise* + *-able*] : capable of being raised ⟨some questions . . . are not . . . ~ in an action between parties —James Bryce⟩

¹raise \'rāz\ *vb* -ED/-ING/-S [ME *reisen, raisen,* fr. ON *reisa* to raise, cause to rise — more at REAR] *vt* **1 a** : to lift or restore to or set in an erect position : set upright : cause or help to stand ⟨caught the fallen child's hand and *raised* her up⟩ **b** *archaic* : to rouse from bed or from sleep : BESTIR : WAKEN **c** : to rouse (a game bird or mammal) for a hunter's pursuit : FLUSH **d** : to rouse or incite to action or effort : summon to resist or repel injury : call to war, struggle, or conflict ⟨~ the countryside at the threat of invasion⟩ **e** : to impart strength, courage, or cheer to (the mind or heart) : ENCOURAGE, INSPIRIT **f** (1) : to bring up (as a familiar spirit or the spirit of one departed) from a lower world : evoke or summon from the world of spirits (2) : to bring back from the dead : restore to life : RESURRECT ⟨why is it thought incredible by any of you that God ~s the dead —Acts 26:8 (RSV)⟩ **g** *chiefly Scot* : to make (one) angry or excited **2 a** : to put up (a building) : ERECT, CONSTRUCT ⟨those arts which were destined to ~ our Gothic cathedrals —G.G.Coulton⟩ **b** *obs* : to draw (a mathematical figure) on a given base **3 a** *archaic* : to bring (children) into existence : BEGET **b** : to give (children) a parent's fostering care : bring up : NURTURE, REAR **c** : to breed and care for (animals) to maturity ⟨*raised* dogs as a hobby⟩ **d** : to practice the cultivation of (plants or crops) : GROW, PRODUCE ⟨*raised* great acreages of wheat⟩ **4 a** : to bring into being : cause to arise or appear ⟨I will ~ up for them a prophet —Deut 18:18 (RSV)⟩ **b** : to bring about : stir up : set in motion ⟨*raised* a storm over his fancied injustices⟩ ⟨*raised* prejudices difficult to dispel⟩ **5 a** : to utter loudly or vehemently ⟨*raised* a hue and cry⟩ ⟨*raised* the alarm throughout the district⟩ ⟨*raised* the shout of victory⟩ **b** : VOICE ⟨he *raised* a sigh so piteous and profound as it did seem to shatter all his bulk —Shak.⟩ **c** : to strike up : SING ⟨*raised* a song of sheer jubilation⟩ **d** : to make (the voice) heard ⟨voices were *raised* widely in opposition⟩ **6 a** : to promote or advance (one) to some dignity, office, or rank : EXALT, HONOR ⟨was *raised* to a baronetcy for his services to the nation —*Current Biog.*⟩ ⟨was *raised* to the priesthood —R.J.Purcell⟩ **b** : to elevate the moral or mental state of : UPLIFT ⟨detected the law of gravitation, and in so doing, *raised* his power of thought—ours with it—above the mere multitudinousness and opacity of separate things —H.A. Overstreet⟩ **c** : to lift higher : draw up : cause to rise : ELEVATE ⟨*raised* a fist to strike⟩ ⟨*raised* the flag each morning outside the barracks⟩ ⟨*raised* the general standard of living⟩ **7 a** : to cause the beginning of : touch off : START ⟨*raised* a smile even from his friends —*Times Lit. Supp.*⟩ **b** : INSTITUTE, CREATE, ESTABLISH **8** : to bring together : COLLECT, GATHER, LEVY ⟨the government *raised* large sums for highway construction by a tax on gasoline sales⟩ ⟨the budget . . . is *raised* by registration fees, ticket sales, and grants —Hartzell Spence⟩ ⟨difficult to ~ enough money to pay for campaign expenses⟩ ⟨*raised* a company of minutemen from his county —E.K. Alden⟩ **9** : to lift (a siege or blockade) by withdrawing the besieging troops or by forcing the besieging troops to withdraw **10** : to cause to ascend (as dust or smoke) **11 a** : to cause to increase in height, level, bulk, size, amount, or value ⟨heavy rains *raised* the river stage⟩ ⟨*raised* the price to retailers a cent a gallon⟩ **b** : to make light and spongy (as bread by leavening with yeast) or thicker (as hides by steeping in a fermenting liquor) **c** : to multiply (a quantity) by itself a specified number of times — compare CUBE, POWER, SQUARE **d** : to lift to a higher degree according to some scale ⟨~ the temperature⟩ ⟨*raised* the instrument's pitch⟩ **e** : to make keener : HEIGHTEN, INTENSIFY, SHARPEN ⟨~s ordinary joys to an agonized ecstatic pitch⟩ **f** : to make hotter, brighter, or faster ⟨~ the metal to white heat⟩ ⟨*raised* his pulse to a drumbeat⟩ **g** : to bring up the nap of (cloth) with teasels or wire cards **12 a** : to come in view of : SIGHT ⟨they *raised* the islands after two hours of hard running —Arthur Mayse⟩ **b** : to cause (an object) to appear above the horizon or to seem to grow higher by coming nearer at sea — compare LAY, SETTLE **13** *obs* : OBTAIN, WIN **14** : to bring up for consideration : introduce into discussion : offer as an objection, a problem, or a significant point ⟨all these new views of the world *raised* problems for scholars as well as statesmen —R.W. Southern⟩ ⟨~s the moral question —E.M.Woolf⟩ ⟨~s the issue of the failure to distinguish between normal and abnormal —Abram Kardiner⟩ **15** : to cause to come up (as mucus from the lungs or gas from the stomach) **16** : to add fraudulently to the face value of (a bank check or other negotiable paper) by altering the writing, figures, or printing in which the sum payable is shown **17 a** (1) : to increase (a poker bet or pot) by a specified amount (2) : to bet more than (a previous bettor) — compare CALL **b** : to make a higher bridge bid in (a partner's suit) **18** : to move (a curling stone) ahead in the line of direction by a hit from behind with another stone **19** : to form (hollow ware) from a flat sheet of metal by alternately hammering and annealing **20 a** : to elevate (a part of the tongue) closer to the palate in uttering a vowel **b** : to utter (a vowel) with the tongue in a higher position **21** : to establish radio communication with : elicit a response from (a station being called) ⟨next time you ~ the ship, tell them I'm on my way —K.M.Dodson⟩ ~ *vi* **1** *dial* : RISE, ARISE **2 a** : to make a poker bet that increases the stake **b** : to make a higher bridge bid in a partner's suit **3** : to drive a raise in a mine **syn** see BUILD, LIFT

²raise \"\ *n* -s **1** : an act or method of raising : a lifting up : ELEVATION ⟨firemen are taught ~s of several kinds to get their ladders up⟩ **2** : a rising stretch of road : an upward grade : RISE **3** : an increase in amount ⟨opposed the administration's request for a ~ in the national debt limit —*New Republic*⟩: as **a** : an increase in wages or salary ⟨braced the boss for a ~⟩ **b** (1) : the act of increasing a bet (2) : the amount of such increase **4** : a vertical or inclined opening or passageway driven to connect one mine working place with another at a higher level — called also *rise, riser* **5** : the spinning of a curling stone toward a target circle

³raise \"\ *n* -s [ME *rase,* fr. OE *rǣs*] *dial Eng* : CAIRN, MOUND — used esp. in place names

raiseable *var of* RAISABLE

raised *adj* [fr. past part. of ¹*raise*] **1 a** : having a pattern or design in relief ⟨~ metalwork⟩ ⟨~ needlework⟩ ⟨~ textiles⟩ ⟨~ braille lettering⟩ **b** : NAPPED ⟨a ~ fabric⟩ **2** : leavened with yeast rather than with baking powder or soda ⟨~ doughnuts⟩

raised band *n* : a ridge across the backbone of a hand-sewn book produced when the cords or bands are not sawed in; *also* : a similar ridge raised on a machine-sewn book by applying a heated die — compare SUNKEN CORD

raised bands

raised beach *n* : a beach formed by a sea or lake and subsequently elevated above high-water level either by local crustal movements or by lowering of sea level

raised cottage *n* : a cottage built on stilts (as brick piers) for protection against flood waters

raised initial *n* : a cockup initial

raised point *n* : needlepoint lace chiefly of Venetian origin with padded floral designs in high relief — called also *gros point*

raised printing *n* : printing in which the letters or image are raised above the surface of the paper (as by embossing)

raised table *n* : a raised or projecting member of a flat architectural or sculptural surface that is large in proportion to the projection

raise·man \'=mən\ *n, pl* **raisemen** [²*raise* + *man*] : a miner who works in a raise

rais·er \'rāzə(r)\ *n* -s [ME, fr. *raisen* to raise + *-er*] **1** : one that raises ⟨a sheep ~⟩ ⟨a cotton ~⟩ ⟨a fund ~⟩ ⟨a check ~⟩ **2** : LETTERER d **3** : PROOFER 2 **4** : one that sets up the staves for barrels, shapes the barrels, and drives on the forming hoops

raises *pres 3d sing of* RAISE, *pl of* RAISE

¹rai·sin \'rāz°n\ *n* -s *often attrib* [ME *raisin, reisin,* fr. MF, grape, fr. L *racemus* cluster of grapes or berries, of non-IE origin; akin to the source of Gk *rhag-, rhax* berry, grape] **1** : any of various grapes dried in the sun or by artificial heat, containing a high sugar percentage, and having a flavor quite different from that of the fresh grape **2** : a dark purplish red that is bluer and duller than pansy purple, bluer and lighter than dahlia purple (sense 1), bluer and paler than Bokhara, and bluer and less strong than redgrape

²raisin \"\ *vi* -ED/-ING/-S *of grapes* : to dry on the vine and take on an appearance like that of raisins

raisin black *n* : a dark grayish purple that is redder than average purple wine and redder and stronger than old lavender (sense 2)

rai·si·né \,rāzə'nā\ *n* -s [F, fr. *raisin* grape] : a preserve esp. of pears with quinces or of grapes with quinces cooked slowly in sweet wine or cider

rais·ing \'rāziŋ, -zēŋ\ *n* -s [ME, fr. gerund of *raisen* to raise] **1** : the act or process of lifting : ELEVATION ⟨attempted idly to guess what that ~ of her finger had meant⟩ **2** : a party or bee for raising the frame of a building ⟨came the day of the ~ . . . all the men from the village and the near farms gathered to help make a home for the newcomers —Irving Bacheller⟩ **3 a** : the fostering care of parents for children : NURTURE, UPBRINGING **b** : the breeding and care of animals ⟨turkey ~⟩ ⟨cattle ~⟩ **c** : the growing of plants : CULTIVATION ⟨wheat ~⟩ **4** : the driving of a raise in a mine

raising hammer *n* : a hammer with a rounded face used in raising sheet metal

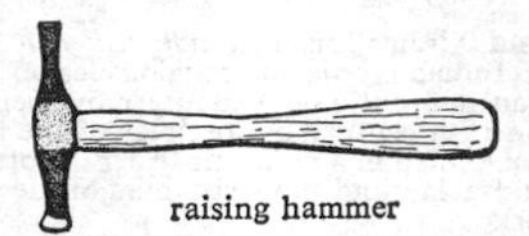

raising hammer

raising plate *n* : PLATE 5a(1)

raisin grape *n* : a grape grown primarily for making raisins

raisin moth *n* : a phycitid moth (*Cadra figulilella*) the larva of which attacks dried fruits and cereal products

raisin purple *n* : a dark reddish purple that is redder and less strong than patriarch or amaranth

raisin-seed oil *n* : GRAPE-SEED OIL

raisin tree *n* : RED CURRANT 1a(1)

raisin wine *n* : a usu. inferior wine made by the fermentation of an infusion of raisins

rai·siny \'rāz°nē\ *adj* : containing or resembling raisins

rai·son d'être \,rā,zōn'det(rə), -zōⁿ-, -zän'-, -tr(°)\ *n, pl* **raisons d'être** [F] : reason or justification for existence

rais·ty \'rāstē\ *var of* REASTY

raith \'rāth\ *n* -s [ScGael *rāith*] *Scot* : a quarter of a year

rai·vel \'rāvəl\ *chiefly Scot var of* RAVEL

raiyat *var of* RYOT

raiyatwari *var of* RYOTWAR

raj \'räj\ *n* -ES [Hindi *rāj,* fr. Skt *rājya,* fr. *rājati* he rules; akin to Skt *rājan* king] : REIGN, RULE

¹ra·ja *or* **ra·jah** \'räjə\ *n* -s *often cap* [Hindi *rājā,* fr. Skt *rājan* — more at ROYAL] **1 a** : an Indian prince or king **b** : a petty chief or dignitary **c** : the bearer of a title of nobility among the Hindus **2** : a Malay prince, ruler, or chief

²ra·ja \'räjə\ *n, cap* [NL, fr. L *raia* ray] : a genus (the type of the family Rajidae) of skates with the body angular in outline

ra·jab \rə'jab\ *n* -s *usu cap* [Ar] : the seventh month of the Muhammadan year — see MONTH table

ra·jah \'räjə\ *n* -s [fr. *Rajah,* a trademark] : a silk clothing fabric with a rough surface somewhat similar to pongee

rajah rat *n* [NL *rajah* (specific epithet of *Rattus rajah*), fr. E *rajah*] : a reddish often spiny rat (*Rattus rajah*) occurring in numerous races that are widely distributed in southeastern Asia and the East Indies

ra·jas \'rəjəs\ *n* -ES [Skt, lit., darkness, dust; akin to ON *røkkr* darkness, Goth *riqis,* Gk *erebos*] : the extension or passion that constitutes one of the three gunas of Sankhya philosophy — compare SATTVA, TAMAS

ra·ja·ship *or* **ra·jah·ship** \'räjə,ship\ *n* : the dominion or the rank of a raja

ra·ja·stha·ni \,räjə'stänē\ *n* -s *usu cap* [Hindi *Rājasthān* Rajputana, region of northwest Indian Union] : the Indic colloquial language of Rajasthan — compare HINDI

raja-yoga \'==¦==\ *n* [Skt *rājayoga,* fr. *rājan* king + *yoga* — more at YOGA] : a yoga discipline that consists of eight stages leading to self-realization and liberation — compare ASANA, DHYANA, SAMADHI; HATHA-YOGA, JNANA-YOGA, KARMA-YOGA

raj·ban·si \räj'bən(t)sē\ *n* -s [Hindi *rājbāsī* of royal race, fr. Skt *rājan* king + *vaṁśa* lineage] : a member of an extensive Koch caste of Assam and Bengal

raj·i·dae \'rajə,dē\ *n pl, cap* [NL, fr. ²*Raja,* type genus + *-idae*] : a family of elasmobranch fishes consisting of the skates

raj·ma·hal creeper \'räjmə¦häl-\ *n, usu cap R* [fr. *Rajmahal* Hills, Bihar prov., India] : a woody vine (*Marsdenia tenacissima*) the stems of which yield a fiber — see RAJMAHAL HEMP

rajmahal hemp *n, usu cap R* : a strong silky fiber derived from the stems of the Rajmahal creeper and used in India for bowstrings and cordage

raj·pra·mukh \'räjprə,mu̇k\ *n* -s [Hindi *rājpramukh,* fr. Skt *rājapramukha,* fr. *rājan* king + *pramukha* chief, fr. *pra-* before + *mukha* face, mouth — more at FOR] : the constitutional head of a state of India formed from several former princely states who is elected by a council of rulers

raj·put *or* **raj·poot** \'räj,püt, -pu̇t\ *n* -s *usu cap* [Hindi *rājpūt,* fr. Skt *rājaputra* king's son, fr. *rājan* king + *putra* son — more at FEW] : a member of a dominant military caste of Kshatriya rank and Indo-Aryan race numerous in northern India

ra·k'a *or* **ra·k'ah** \'rəkə\ *n* -s [Ar *rak'ah*] : a fixed series of ritual movements and formulas (as bowings and recitations) repeated in the daily prayers of Muslims

¹rake \'rāk\ *n* -s [ME, fr. OE *raca, racu;* akin to OHG *rehho* rake, ON *reka* spade, shovel, Goth *rikan* to heap up, collect, and perh. to Gk *oregein* to stretch out — more at RIGHT] **1 a** : a hand tool consisting usu. of a bar with projecting prongs that is set transversely at the end of a long handle and used for gathering grass, leaves, or other material or for loosening or smoothing the surface of the ground **b** : a machine rake for gathering hay — compare DUMP RAKE, SIDE-DELIVERY RAKE **2** : any of various implements resembling a rake or a hoe (as for mixing plaster or scraping hides) **3 a** : a small steel tool formerly used by hand binders to scratch the backs of books during forwarding permitting glue to permeate deeper and so strengthening the binding **b** : a wire-toothed wooden tool similar to a lawn rake used to make patterns in a bookbinder's marbling vat **4** : a device for studying pressure distribution in a flow field by means of tubes arranged like rake teeth and connected with pressure-indicating devices

rakes 1a

²rake \"\ *vb* -ED/-ING/-S [ME *raken,* fr. ¹*rake*] *vt* **1 a** : to collect, gather, or separate with or as if with a rake ⟨*raked* the grass from the lawn after mowing⟩ ⟨*raked* the stuff into separate piles⟩ **b** : to stir up, loosen, or make even or smooth with or as if with a rake ⟨*raked* the soil level after spading and seeding⟩ ⟨*raked* the fire and added coal⟩ **c** : to clean or purify as if by raking ⟨~ a fatty oil⟩ **2** *obs* : to cover over or bury by or as if by raking **3** : to bank (a fire) with cinders **4** : to remove obstructing excrement from the rectum of (a costive horse) with the hand : BACK-RAKE **5** : to gain (wealth or possessions) rapidly or in abundance — usu. used with *in* ⟨had *raked* the cash in night after night for years at a small strategically placed stand⟩ **6 a** : to scrape or scratch as if with a rake : pass over lightly : RUB, TOUCH ⟨like clouds that ~ the mountain summits —William Wordsworth⟩ ⟨the blade *raked* the other's cheek⟩ **b** : to censure severely : attack verbally : administer a dressing down to — often used with *over* **7 a** : to search through : SCOUR, RANSACK ⟨the statesman ~s the town to find a plot —Jonathan Swift⟩ **b** : to dig out and present (as unfavorable evidence) — usu. used with *up* ⟨*raked* up long buried scandal to discredit his enemy⟩ **8 a** : to fire in a direction with the length of : ENFILADE ⟨blockhouses at opposite corners enabled watchers to ~ the walls with rifle fire —*Amer. Guide Series: Tenn.*⟩ ⟨*raked* each wave of advancing troops with gunfire⟩ **b** : to sweep (a length or area) with gunfire, shells, or bombs ⟨*raked* the area with a dive-bombing and strafing attack —Merle Miller⟩ **9** *of a falcon* : to attack while flying **10** : to glance over rapidly : SCAN, SURVEY ⟨a three-decker pulpit from which the preacher can ~ his congregation from end to end —Charles Gordon⟩ ⟨*raked* the leaden sky with his binoculars —J.E.Macdonnell⟩ **11** : to scrape off (loose mortar) preparatory to pointing : remove (green mortar) to a uniform depth from the face of a wall — often used with *out* ~ *vi* : to do a task with or as if with a rake : COLLECT, SCRAPE, SEARCH — **rake over the coals** : to censure severely : REPRIMAND, SCOLD ⟨was *raked over the coals* for his habitual lateness⟩

³rake \"\ *vi* -ED/-ING/-S [ME *raken,* fr. OE *racian*] **1** *chiefly dial* : to move forward esp. swiftly : run rapidly **2** *chiefly dial* : ROAM, ROVE **3** *of a hawk* : to fly after game — **rake out** *or* **rake off** *or* **rake away** *falconry* : to fly wide of the quarry

⁴rake \"\ *n* -s [ME *rake,* fr. ON *rāk* streak, stripe; akin to ON *reka* to drive — more at WREAK] **1** *dial Eng* **a** : WAY, PATH; *esp* : a cattle path **b** : pasture land **2** *dial Eng* **a** : a trip esp. for bringing something back : GO **b** : as much as can be carried in one trip : LOAD **3** *chiefly Scot* : GASH VEIN

⁵rake \"\ *vb* -ED/-ING/-S [origin unknown] *vi* : to incline from the perpendicular ⟨the roof of the dwelling *raked* sharply —Willard Robertson⟩ ~ *vt* : to cause to incline from the perpendicular

⁶rake \"\ *n* -s **1 a** : inclination from the perpendicular (as of a mast or funnel); *esp* : the overhang of a ship's bow or stern **b** : the slope of a ship's sternpost or of the forepart of the rudder **2** : inclination from the horizontal (as of a stage or auditorium floor) **3** : the angle between the top cutting surface of a cutting tool (as on a lathe) and a plane which is perpendicular to the surface of the work and to the direction of motion of the tool with respect to the work — compare CUTTING ANGLE, SIDE RAKE **4** : PLUNGE 4 **5** : an inclined edge of a building ⟨the ~ of a cornice⟩ ⟨the ~ of a gable⟩ **6** : the angle between a wing-tip edge that is sensibly straight in planform and the plane of symmetry of an airplane

⁷rake \"\ *n* -s [short for ²*rakehell*] : a dissolute or licentious man or woman : LIBERTINE ⟨turned his attention to the pleasures of this life and a more perfect ~ has seldom existed —Nancy Mitford⟩

⁸rake \"\ *vi* -ED/-ING/-S : to act the rake : lead a dissolute or licentious life ⟨swear and rant and ~ . . . with the best of them —George Farquhar⟩

rake angle *n* : ⁶RAKE 3

raked *adj* [fr. past part. of ⁵*rake*] : slanted from the perpendicular or horizontal : INCLINED ⟨drop-leaf table . . . ~ square tapering legs —*Parke-Bernet Galleries Catalog*⟩

raked joint *n* [fr. past part. of ²*rake*] : a masonry joint from which the mortar is raked out to a specified depth while still green — see JOINT illustration

¹rake·hell \'rāk,hel\ *or* **rake·helly** \-lē\ *adj* [*rakehell* perh. alter. (influenced by the phrase *to rake hell*) of earlier *rackle* rash, impetuous, headstrong, fr. ME *rakel, rakil; rakehelly* fr. ²*rakehell* + *-y*] : of, relating to, or characteristic of a rakehell : DISSOLUTE, LICENTIOUS, RASCALLY ⟨ready to abjure the ~ life —Lee Rogow⟩ ⟨~ amours⟩

²rakehell \"\ *n* : a dissolute or profligate person : LIBERTINE, RAKE, RASCAL ⟨the favorite resort of the courtesans and the ~s —W.S.Clark⟩

rake·hell·ish \-lish\ *adj* : RAKEHELL

rake·man \'=mən\ *n, pl* **rakemen** [¹*rake* + *man*] : a rackman who uses a rake

rake–off \'=,=\ *n* -s [²*rake* + *off;* fr. the use of a rake by a croupier to collect the operator's profits in a gambling casino] : a percentage or cut (as of winnings, profits, or loot) taken or retained by an operator or enterpriser or by a gang boss ⟨take kindly to organized oppressions of industries, to the collection of *rake-offs* —*Harper's*⟩ ⟨a big private *rake-off* on government purchases —*Atlantic*⟩ ⟨gamblers . . . get their share of the *rake-off* —Lewis Mumford⟩

rak·er \'rākə(r)\ *n* -s [²*rake* + *-er*] **1** : one that rakes: as **a** : one that gathers clams with a rake **b** : one that rakes dead leaves and other debris from around turpentine trees to lessen fire hazards **c** : ¹GUMMER 1 **d** : an iron bar with pointed steel ends bent at right angles in opposite directions that is used for raking out old mortar in walls before pointing **e** : a raft dog similarly shaped **f** : one of a number of short teeth with deep gullet and considerable rake that are interspersed among the other teeth in some saws to clean out the kerf **2** [⁵*rake* + *-er*] : any of a number of shores except the bottom innermost one that prop up a wall **3** : GILL RAKER

raker tooth *n* : an unset sawtooth that cleans out the bottom of a cut

rak·ery \'rāk(ə)rē\ *n* -ES [⁷*rake* + *-ery*] *archaic* : DEBAUCHERY, LEWDNESS

rakes *pl of* RAKE, *pres 3d sing of* RAKE

rakeshame \'=,=\ *n* [²*rake* + *shame*] *archaic* : a base or degraded person

rake's progress *n* [fr. *The Rake's Progress* (1735), series of engravings by William Hogarth †1764 Eng. artist] : a reckless course : a steady deterioration ⟨while a painful policy of deflation is being pursued in some countries, the inflationary *rake's progress* is going merrily on —*Irish Statesman*⟩

rake·steel *or* **rake·stele** \'rāk,stēl\ *n* [¹*rake* + *stele* (handle)] *dial chiefly Eng* : a rake handle

rake vein *n* [⁴*rake*] *chiefly Scot* : GASH VEIN

ra·ki \rə'kē, 'rakē, 'räkē\ *n* -s [Turk] : a Turkish liqueur distilled usu. from fermented raisins but occas. from figs or dates and flavored with aniseed

ra·ki·ja *or* **ra·kia** \'räkē(y)ə\ *n* -s [Serbo-Croatian *rakija*] : a brandy made in Yugoslavia

¹raking *n* -s [fr. gerund of ²*rake*] **1** : a raked area **2** : the stuff gathered with a rake

²raking *n* -s [fr. gerund of ⁸*rake*] : dissolute conduct : LICENTIOUSNESS

³raking *adj* [fr. pres. part. of ⁸*rake*] : DISSOLUTE

⁴raking *adj* [fr. pres. part. of ⁵*rake*] : inclined from the perpendicular or horizontal ⟨shadows and markings revealed in the ~ light of dawn or sunset —C.M.Lerici⟩

5**raking** *adj* [fr. pres. part. of 3*rake*] **:** SPEEDY, SWIFT ⟨a fellow with . . . a powerful ~ stride —John Buchan⟩

raking bond *n* [4*raking*] **1 :** DIAGONAL BOND **2 :** HERRINGBONE BOND

raking cornice *n* **:** a cornice that follows the slope of a gable or pediment

raking course *n* **:** a course of bricks laid diagonally between the face courses in a thick wall to strengthen it

raking light *n* **:** a bright light directed at a painting from the side to show up details of painting technique

rak·ing·ly *adv* **:** in a raking manner **:** OBLIQUELY

raking molding *n* **:** a slanted molding (as in a pediment)

raking piece *n* **:** a peaked or sloping piece of theatrical scenery

raking shore *n* **:** RAKER 2

raking shot *n* **:** a shot fired (as at game) from an acute angle

1**rak·ish** \ˈrākish, -kēsh\ *adj* [7*rake* + *-ish*] **:** of or relating to a rake **:** LICENTIOUS, WANTON ⟨he combined the studies and the ~ life —P.E.More⟩

2**rakish** \"\ *adj* [prob. fr. 5*rake* + *-ish;* fr. the raking masts of pirate ships] **1 :** having a smart stylish appearance suggestive of speed ⟨a ~ ship⟩ ⟨in his battered, ~ roadster —MacKinlay Kantor⟩ **2 :** negligent of convention or strict formality **:** CARELESS, JAUNTY, SPORTY ⟨the languid ~ habit of wearing a hat indoors at his desk —*Amer. Guide Series: N. C.*⟩

rak·ish·ly *adv* **:** in a rakish manner

rak·ish·ness *n* -ES **:** the quality or state of being rakish

rak·sha·sa \ˈrȧkshəsə\ *n* -S [Skt *rākṣasa,* fr. *rakṣas,* lit., injury; akin to Gk *erechthein* to rend, break] **:** a demon or evil spirit of Hindu mythology

ra·ku ware \ˈrä(ˌ)kü-\ *n* [Jap *raku* enjoyment; fr. the engraving of this word on the gold seal with which the original ware was stamped] **:** a soft low-fired, lead-glazed, and often hand-modeled Japanese pottery used since the 16th century esp. for teabowls

rale \ˈral, ˈräl, ˈrȧl\ *n* -S [F *râle,* fr. *râler* to make a rattling sound in the throat] **:** an abnormal sound heard accompanying the normal respiratory sounds on auscultation of the chest ⟨the ~*s* produced when air passes through mucus-clogged bronchioles⟩ — compare RHONCHUS

ra·leigh \ˈrólē, ˈrälē, -li\ *adj, usu cap* [fr. *Raleigh,* capital of No. Carolina] **:** of or from Raleigh, the capital of No. Carolina ⟨a *Raleigh* club⟩ **:** of the kind or style prevalent in Raleigh

1**ral·len·tan·do** \ˌrälən¦tän(ˌ)dō, ¦ralən¦tan-\ *adv (or adj)* [It, lit., slowing down, verbal of *rallentare* to relax, slow down again, fr. *r-* re- + *allentare* to slow down, fr. LL, fr. L *al-* ad- + *lentus* pliant, tough, slow — more at LITHE] **:** with a gradual decrease or slackening in tempo **:** RITARDANDO — used as a direction in music

2**rallentando** \"\ *n* -S **1 :** a gradually slackening musical tempo **2 :** a musical passage or movement gradually decreasing in tempo

ral·len·ta·to \ˌrälən¦täd·(ˌ)ō\ *adv (or adj)* [It *rallentato,* past part. of *rallentare*] **:** RALLENTANDO — used as a direction in music

rallery *n* -ES [modif. of F *raillerie* raillery] **1** *obs* **:** RAILLERY **2** *obs* **:** a playful act

ral·li cart \ˈralē-\ *n, often cap R* [fr. *Ralli,* name of its first purchaser] **:** a light two-wheeled horse-drawn cart for four persons having the body brought rather low by shafts fastened within rather than below it — compare DOGCART, GOVERNESS CART

ral·li·dae \ˈraləˌdē\ *n pl, cap* [NL, fr. *Rallus,* type genus + *-idae*] **:** a family of gruiform birds consisting of the rails, crakes, wekas, coots, gallinules, and related forms

ral·li·er \ˈralēə(r)\ *n* -S **:** one that rallies

ral·li·form \ˈraləˌfȯrm\ *adj* [ML *rallus* rail + E *-iform* — more at RALLUS] **:** resembling or related to the rails

ral·line \ˈraˌlīn\ *adj* [ML *rallus* rail + E *-ine*] **:** of, relating to, or resembling the rails

rallo *abbr* rallentando

ral·lus \ˈraləs\ *n, cap* [NL, fr. ML *rallus* rail, fr. MF *raale*] **:** the type genus of Rallidae comprising slender-billed rails (as the European water rail, the clapper rail, and the king rail)

1**ral·ly** \ˈralē, -li\ *vb* -ED/-ING/-ES [F *rallier,* fr. OF *ralier,* fr. *re-* + *alier* to unite — more at ALLY] *vt* **1 a :** to muster, call up, or summon for a common purpose ⟨they knew well that he would ~ his friends and pursue them —H.E.Scudder⟩ **b :** to recall (a scattered force or group) to order or unity **:** REGATHER, REUNITE ⟨would permit the chancellor to ~ the drifting and disillusioned voters once more around the . . . banner —F.E. Hirsch⟩ **2 a :** to stir up (a power of mind or body) **:** COLLECT ⟨*rallied* his tired wits to face this fresh problem⟩ ⟨*rallied* his energies and struck again⟩ **b :** to rouse (one) from depression or weakness **:** restore the spirits or courage of ⟨felt she had to be salty to ~ him⟩ **3 :** to strengthen the price of (as securities) after a decline **:** cause to rise in price ⟨the news *rallied* an unsteady market⟩ **4 :** to haul or let run (a sail) sharply in a specified direction ~ *vi* **1 :** to reunite so as to renew an effort (as a battle) **:** recoup forces **:** REASSEMBLE ⟨the soldiers . . . *rallied* at the top of a high hill —O.G.Libby⟩ **2 :** to unite as supporters or followers **:** join in a common cause ⟨upwards of 700 people *rallied* to him —G.H.Genzmer⟩ **3 a :** to collect one's vital powers **:** RECUPERATE, REVIVE ⟨*rallied* after months of prostration from grief and shock⟩ **b :** to rebound in price ⟨stocks *rallied* after brief uncertainty⟩ **c :** to regain offensive strength **:** recapture initiative **:** come back — used esp. of an athletic contestant or team **4 a :** to engage in a court rally **b :** to practice or warm up by exchanging shots (as in tennis) with an opponent **syn** see STIR

2**rally** \"\ *n* -ES **1 a :** a recouping or reuniting of forces: as (1) **:** a mustering together of scattered forces to renew an effort or contest (2) **:** a summoning up of strength or courage after weakness, sickness, or dejection **b :** a recovery of price after a decline ⟨a sharp ~ lent buoyancy to the market before closing⟩ **2 :** a mass meeting intended to arouse group enthusiasm or support (as for a political candidate or a school team) **3 :** a series of strokes that are interchanged between players (as in tennis) before a point is won **4** *also* **ral·lye** \"\ -S **:** a competitive long-distance automobile run esp. of sport cars over public roads and under ordinary traffic rules with the object of maintaining a specified exact average speed between checkpoints over a route unknown to the participants until the start of the run

3**rally** \"\ *vb* -ED/-ING/-ES [F *railler,* fr. MF — more at RAIL] *vt* **:** to attack with raillery **:** BANTER, RIDICULE ⟨*rallied* him on his overweening pretensions⟩ ~ *vi, archaic* **:** to indulge in raillery, pleasantry, or derision **syn** see RIDICULE

rallying cry *n* [fr. gerund of 1*rally*] **:** SLOGAN

ral·ly·ing·ly *adv* [*rallying* (fr. pres. part. of 3*rally*) + *-ly*] **:** BANTERINGLY

rallying point *n* [fr. gerund of 1*rally*] **:** a point, place, or principle at or upon which scattered forces unite or opposing groups come together

ral·ston·ite \ˈrȯlztəˌnīt, -lst-\ *n* -S [J. Grier *Ralston,* 19th cent. Am. clergyman + E *-ite*] **:** a mineral $NaMgAl_5F_{12}(OH)_6.3H_2O$ consisting of a hydrous basic fluoride of aluminum, sodium, and magnesium in octahedral crystals

1**ram** \ˈram, ˈraa(ə)m\ *n* -S [ME, fr. OE *ramm;* akin to MLG, MD, & OHG *ram,* and prob. to ON *rammr, ramr* strong, bitter, sharp, OIr *remor* thick, fat, OSlav *ramĕnŭ* violent] **1 a :** a male sheep **b** *southern Africa* (1) **:** a male goat (2) **:** the male of any of numerous small antelopes **:** BUCK **2 a** (1) **:** BATTERING RAM (2) **:** something resembling or used as a battering ram **b** (1) **:** a warship fitted with a heavy steel or iron beak at the prow for piercing or cutting an enemy's ship (2) **:** the prow of a ship fitted with such a beak **3 :** any of various guided pieces for exerting considerable pressure or for driving or forcing something by impact: as **a :** the plunger of a hydrostatic press, hydraulic elevator, or force pump **b :** the reciprocating arm or piece carrying the tool head in a shaping or a slotting machine **c :** the weight which strikes the blow esp. in a pile driver or steam hammer **4 :** HYDRAULIC RAM **5 :** RAM EFFECT

2**ram** \"\ *vb* **rammed; rammed; ramming; rams** [ME *rammen,* prob. fr. *ram,* n.] *vi* **1 :** to pound earth in order to make it hard and solid **2 :** to strike with violence **:** CRASH ⟨three perished when their auto *rammed* into a tree —*Pasadena (Calif.) Independent*⟩ **3 :** to move with extreme rapidity and force ⟨a passenger train *ramming* past in the final heat of its run from Chicago —H.L.Davis⟩ **4 :** to produce a ram effect upon air ~ *vt* **1 a :** to force down usu. by driving, pressing, or pushing ⟨~ fence posts into the ground⟩ ⟨*rammed* his hat over his ears⟩ ⟨~ the mix little by little into the mold with a mallet —F.H.Norton⟩ **b :** to make compact (as earth) esp. by pounding or stamping ⟨*rammed* earth construction is not new —*New Republic*⟩ **2 :** to stop up **:** block to prevent passage ⟨*rammed* the mouse hole with a tin can⟩ **3 a :** to press or push in the contents of **:** fill firmly ⟨*rammed* his pipe with his finger⟩ **b** (1) **:** to force ammunition into (a gun) (2) **:** to force (as ammunition) into a gun **c :** to force recognition of (as a point of view) — usu. used with *home* ⟨he despaired of his ability to ~ home the reality of the beauty of the Church —Bruce Marshall⟩ ⟨~*s* home the pure and shrieking insanity of war —Clifton Fadiman⟩ **4 :** to thrust into **:** press closely and tightly together ⟨*rammed* the clothes into a packing case⟩ ⟨his hands were *rammed* hard in his pants' pockets —E.V. Roberts⟩ ⟨great slices of meat onto his fork and *ramming* them into his mouth —Bruce Marshall⟩ **5 :** to fill up **:** CRAM ⟨the closet was *rammed* with the children's toys⟩ **6 :** to butt or strike against violently **:** drive against or through **:** crash into ⟨side-swiped one parked machine then *rammed* the rear of another —*Springfield (Mass.) Daily News*⟩ **7 :** to drive forcefully and with extreme rapidity ⟨was *ramming* his airplane across the U. S. at eight miles a minute —Horace Sutton⟩ **syn** see PACK — **ram down one's throat :** to force (one) to accept ⟨there is no attempt to *ram* . . . ideas *down* other people's *throats* —T.O.Beachcroft⟩

3**ram** \ˈram\ *adj* [of Scand origin; akin to Sw dial. *ram* strong-smelling, strong or unpleasant to the taste, Dan dial., strong, biting, ON *rammr, ramr* strong, bitter, sharp — more at 1RAM] *dial Eng* **:** RANCID

ra·ma \ˈrämə\ *n, pl* **rama** *or* **ramas** *usu cap* [Sp, of AmerInd origin] **1 a :** a Chibchan people of southeastern Nicaragua **b :** a member of such people **2 :** the language of the Rama people

ramack *var of* RAMMACK

ra·ma·da \rəˈmädə, -madə\ *n* -S [Sp, fr. *rama* branch (alter. of *ramo,* fr. L *ramus*) + *-ada* (fr. L *-ata* -ate) — more at RAMIFY] **1 :** a structure resembling a pergola **:** ARBOR **2 :** an open porch

ram·a·dan \ˌramə¦dän\ *or* **ram·a·zan** \-ˈzän\ *also* **ram·a·dhan** \-ˈdän\ *n* -S *usu cap* [Ar *Ramaḍān*] **1 :** the 9th month of the Muhammadan year observed as a sacred month on each day of which strict fasting is practiced from dawn to sunset — see MONTH table **2 :** the fasting observed in Ramadan

1**ramage** *adj* [ME, fr. OF, living in the branches of trees, wild, fr. *ram, raim* branch (fr. L *ramus*) + *-age* (as in *salvage* savage) — more at RAMIFY] *obs* **:** UNTAMED, WILD

2**ram·age** \ˈramij\ *n* -S [F, fr. OF, fr. *ram, raim* branch + *-age*] **1 :** the boughs or branches of a tree **2 :** the cry of birds ⟨grew from the ~ of birds to the hurry of wind —Hugh McCrae⟩ **3 :** a genealogical tree of a segmentary unilateral descent group

ramage hawk *n* **:** 1BRANCHER

ra·ma·ism \ˈräməˌizəm\ *n* -S *usu cap* [*Rama,* Hindu epic hero (fr. Skt *Rāma*) + E *-ism*] **:** the worship of the Hindu epic hero Rama as an incarnation of the god Vishnu

ra·ma·ite \-ˌīt\ *n* -S *usu cap* [*Rama* + E *-ite*] **:** one who worships Rama

ra·ma·krish·na \ˌrämə¦krishnə\ *adj, usu cap* [after *Ramakrishna* †1886 Indian mystic and religious leader] **:** of, relating to, or being an international Vedanta movement founded at the end of the 19th century by disciples of the mystic Ramakrishna and embodied in a monastic order devoted to spiritual cultivation and a lay and monastic mission devoted to philanthropic work

ra·mal \ˈrāməl\ *adj* [NL *ramus* + E *-al*] **:** of or relating to a ramus

ra·ma·li·na \ˌraməˈlīnə\ *n, cap* [NL, fr. L *ramale* twigs, brushwood (fr. *ramus* branch + *-ale,* neut. of *-alis* -al) + NL *-ina* — more at RAMIFY] **:** a genus of fruticose lichens (family Usneaceae) that have a thallus with flattened usu. tufted lobes which are more or less dichotomously branched and that include several (as *R. fraxinea*) which are sources of dyes or perfume

ra·man \ˈrämən\ *adj, usu cap* [*Rama,* Hindu epic hero + E *-an*] **:** of or relating to Rama

ram·a·nas rose \ˈramənəs-\ *n* [perh. fr. Jap *ramman* blooming profusely] **:** a red-flowered cultivated rose that is a variety of the Japan rose

ra·man effect \ˈrämən-\ *n, usu cap R* [after Sir Chandrasekhara V. *Raman* *b*1888 Indian physicist] **:** a change in frequency undergone by a portion of the light that has been scattered in passage through a transparent liquid, solid, or gas whose characteristics determine the amount of change

raman spectrum *n, usu cap R* **:** the characteristic array of frequencies of light that are observed when a fixed single frequency of light is scattered by a pure substance — compare RAMAN EFFECT

ra·ma·pi·the·cus \ˌräməpəˈthēkəs, -məˈpithəkəs\ *n, cap* [NL, fr. *Rama,* Hindu epic hero + *-pithecus*] **:** a genus of Upper Pliocene Indian apes related to those of the genus *Dryopithecus* but exhibiting almost human dentition and dental arch

ra·mark \ˈrāˌmärk\ *n* -S [*radar marker*] **:** a continuously transmitting radar beacon that provides bearing information for ships and airplanes

ramass *vt* -ED/-ING/-S [MF *ramasser,* fr. *re-* + *amasser* to amass — more at AMASS] *obs* **:** to collect together **:** GATHER

ra·mate \ˈrāˌmāt\ *adj* [L *ramus* branch + E *-ate* — more at RAMIFY] **:** characterized by the presence of branches **:** BRANCHED

ram·bla \ˈrämblə\ *n* -S [Sp, fr. Ar *ramlah*] **1 :** a dry ravine ⟨in the adjoining ~ the birds assemble in their hundreds —*Manchester Guardian Weekly*⟩ **2 :** a very broad street

1**ram·ble** \ˈrambəl, -aam-\ *vb* **rambled; rambled; rambling** \-b(ə)liŋ\ **rambles** [perh. alter. of *romble,* fr. ME *romblen,* freq. of *romen* to roam — more at ROAM] *vi* **1 a :** to move usu. by walking from place to place without conscious aim or goal **:** stroll here and there **:** ROVE, WANDER ⟨*rambling* till suppertime through the orderly avenues between the lines of English walnut trees —Jean Stafford⟩ ⟨to ~ through the country and to talk about books —J.P.Marquand⟩ **b :** to explore without any particular purpose ⟨most students *rambled* around among a lot of different subjects —Sloan Wilson⟩ **2 :** to talk or write in a desultory fashion ⟨this essay ~*s* a great deal, darting . . . from point to point —*Saturday Rev.*⟩ ⟨great temptation . . . to ~ on interminably in praise of the delights of sailing —E.J. Schoettle⟩ **3 a :** to grow at random ⟨roses that ~ over our summer house —Nora Waln⟩ **b :** to extend or stretch seemingly without design or plan ⟨a little tame wood which *rambled* up from the village —Audrey Barker⟩ ⟨roads and drives ~ past great estates —*Amer. Guide Series: N. C.*⟩ ~ *vt* **:** to wander over **:** ROAM ⟨*rambling* the streets of London —Virginia Woolf⟩ ⟨*rambling* the woods with his father on quiet Sunday afternoons⟩

2**ramble** \"\ *n* -S **1 :** the act of rambling **:** a walk taken without a specific aim or goal **:** leisurely excursion for pleasure ⟨in my ~*s* about the city —John Reed⟩ **2 :** an informal discursive piece of writing ⟨contain in this short ~ give a simple and sincere account of my own life —E.B.White⟩

ram·bler \-b(ə)lə(r)\ *n* -S **1 :** one that rambles ⟨still time to save this ancient hunting ground of Norman kings for the woodland ~ —S.P.B.Mais⟩ **2** *or* **rambler rose :** any of various climbing roses with rather small often double flowers in large clusters: as **a :** CRIMSON RAMBLER **b :** any of several yellow-flowered or white-flowered relatives of the crimson rambler **3 :** RANCH HOUSE

rambler rose *n* **:** a deep pink to moderate purplish red that is yellower and less strong than peachblossom (sense 2)

rambling *adj* **1 :** moving about from one place to another **:** wandering without purpose ⟨envied the ~ deer⟩ **2 :** straying from subject to subject **:** often incoherent **:** MEANDERING ⟨~ quality of the average medieval tale —G.C.Sellery⟩ ⟨talked . . . in his smiling ~ way —Hugh Walpole⟩ ⟨talked in a ~ excited manner about her marriage —Ellen Glasgow⟩ **3 :** stretching or spreading irregularly without or as if without plan ⟨a ~ dispersed series of streamlets flowing erratically —L.C.Eiseley⟩ ⟨the ridges along the valley climb into low ~ mountains —*Amer. Guide Series: Vt.*⟩ **4 :** informally designed **:** LARGE, SPRAWLING ⟨a ~ old manor house —James Stern⟩ ⟨lovely old Saxon church and ~ vicarage —Sam Pollock⟩

ram·bling·ly *adv* **:** in a rambling manner

ram·bong \ramˈbäŋ\ *n* -S [Atjehnese] **:** a rubber plant (*Ficus elastica*)

rambong rubber *or* **rambong** *n* -S **:** rubber obtained from the rambong

ram·bouil·let \ˌrambə¦lā, räⁿbüyeˈ\ *n* [fr. *Rambouillet,* Dept. Seine-et-Oise, France] **1** *usu cap* **:** a French breed of large sturdy plain-bodied sheep developed by selection for both mutton and wool production from Spanish merino sheep **2** -S *often cap* **:** an animal of the Rambouillet breed

ram bow *n* **:** a strongly built extension below water of the bow of a ship for the purpose of piercing the hull of an enemy

ram·bunc·tious \(ˈ)ram¦bəŋ(k)shəs, (ˈ)raam-\ *adj* [prob. alter. of *rumbustious*] **1 :** outrageously flamboyant in behavior **:** excessively exuberant **:** WILD, UNCONTROLLABLE, UNRULY ⟨ever since she got out of college she's been too ~ to live with —Sinclair Lewis⟩ **2 :** difficult to manage or bring under control **:** UNTAMED ⟨the ~ region on which this young man was to have so much influence —S.H.Holbrook⟩

ram·bunc·tious·ly *adv* **:** in a rambunctious manner ⟨heard him shout ~ from the front door as he entered⟩

ram·bunc·tious·ness *n* -ES **:** the quality or state of being rambunctious ⟨the traditional ~ of the fraternities —*Time*⟩

ram·bu·tan \ramˈbütᵊn\ *or* **ram·bo·tan** *or* **ram·boe·tan** *or* **ram·bou·tan** \ˈrambəˌtan\ *also* **ram·bus·tan** \-bəˌstan\ *n* -S [Malay *rambutan,* fr. *rambut* hair; fr. the hairy integument of the fruit] **1 :** a bright red oval Malayan fruit that has a pleasant acid pulp and is covered with long soft spines **2 :** a tree (*Nephelium lappaceum*) that is closely related to the litchi and bears fruits which are rambutans

ram cat *n* **:** a male cat

ram·dohr·ite \ˈrämˌdōˌrīt\ *n* -S [G *ramdohrit,* fr. Paul *Ramdohr* *b*1890 Ger. mineralogist + G *-it* -ite] **:** a mineral $Pb_3Ag_2Sb_6S_{13}$ consisting of a rare compound of lead, silver, antimony, and sulfur

ra·me·an \ˈrāmēən\ *adj, usu cap* [Petrus *Ramus* + E *-ean* — more at RAMISM] **:** RAMIST

ramee *var of* RAMIE

ram effect *n* -S **:** the compressing effect obtained by locating the entrance to an air-intake duct in an airplane in the air stream in such a manner as to take advantage of the relative velocity between the air intake and the air stream by increasing the static pressure in the system to aid in compressing the charge air or to maintain the flow of air through a cooling system

ram·e·kin *or* **ram·e·quin** \ˈraməkən\ *n* -S [F *ramequin,* fr. LG *ramken,* dim. of *ram* cream, fr. MLG *rōm, rōme* — more at REAM] **1 :** a preparation of cheese usu. with bread crumbs, puff paste, or eggs baked in a mold or shell **2 :** an individual baking dish in which food is baked and served ⟨oysters in ~*s*⟩

ram·el·lose \ˈraməˌlōs\ *adj* [L *ramus* branch + *-ellus,* dim. suffix + E *-ose*] **:** bearing little branches

ra·ment \ˈrāmənt\ *n* -S [NL *ramentum*] **:** RAMENTUM 2

ram·en·ta·ceous \ˌramən¦tāshəs\ *or* **ra·men·tal** \rəˈmentᵊl\ *adj* [NL *ramentum* + E *-aceous* or *-al*] **:** covered with, consisting of, or resembling ramenta

ram·en·tif·er·ous \ˌramən¦tif(ə)rəs\ *adj* [NL *ramentum* + E *-iferous*] **:** bearing ramenta

ra·men·tum \rəˈmentəm\ *n, pl* **ramen·ta** \-tə\ [L, fr. *radere* to scratch, scrape + *-mentum* -ment — more at RAT] **1 :** something scraped off **:** a minute particle **:** SHAVING **2** [NL, fr. L] **a :** any of the thin brownish often fringed or laciniate scales that are borne upon the leaves or young shoots of many ferns and that consist of a single layer of cells **b :** the armor of a fossil cycad stump that suggests in appearance the ramenta of existing ferns

ra·me·ous \ˈrāmēəs\ *adj* [L *rameus,* fr. *ramus* branch — more at RAMIFY] **:** RAMAL

rames \ˈrāmz\ *n pl* [fr. pl. of ME *rame* skeleton, prob. fr. MD *raem, rame* frame; akin to MLG *rame* frame, OHG *rama* pillar, support, weaver's frame, OE *rima* rim — more at RIM] *dial chiefly Eng* **:** BONES, SKELETON ⟨'tis said I be only the ~ of a man —Thomas Hardy⟩

ram·e·se·um \ˌraməˈsēəm\ *n* -S *usu cap* [*Rameses* (*Ramses*) + E *-eum* (as in *museum*)] **:** a temple erected by or in honor of a Ramesside king; *specif* **:** a temple erected in honor of Ramses II at Thebes in Egypt

1**ram·es·side** \ˈraməˌsīd, -ˌsəd\ *also* **ram·es·sid** \-ˌsəd\ *adj, usu cap* [irreg. (influence of the Gk form *Rhamessēs*) fr. *Rameses* (*Ramses*), the name of 12 kings of ancient Egypt that reigned intermittently fr. *ab*1315–1090 B.C. + E *-ide, -id*] **:** of or relating to the kings of ancient Egypt named Ramses; *esp* **:** of or relating to the kings of the XXth dynasty founded by Ramses III about 1200 B.C.

2**ramesside** \"\ *also* **ramessid** \"\ *n* -S *usu cap* **:** a king of the XXth Egyptian dynasty

ra·met \ˈrāmət\ *n* -S [L *ramus* branch + E *-et* — more at RAMIFY] **:** a plant that is an independent member of a clone — compare ORTET

ram·fee·zled \ramˈfēzəld\ *adj* [origin unknown] *Scot* **:** worn out **:** EXHAUSTED

ramhead *n* **1** *obs* **:** a stupid or dull-witted person **:** BLOCKHEAD **2** *obs* **:** an arm or hook of a crane

rami *pl of* RAMUS

ram·i·corn \ˈraməˌkȯrn\ *adj* [L *ramus* branch + E *-i-* + *-corn* — more at RAMIFY] **:** having branched antennae

ram·ie *or* **ram·ee** \ˈramē, ˈrāmē\ *n* -S [Malay *rami*] **1 :** a tall perennial herb of eastern Asia (*Boehmeria nivea*) having dark green rather thick broad leaves that are white and woolly on the undersurface and being commercially cultivated in China, Japan, the Philippines, and more recently the southern U.S. for its fiber **2 a :** the strong lustrous bast fiber of ramie capable of being spun or woven **b :** any of the various strong smooth lustrous fabrics of ramie often similar to linen or silk made in various weights usu. for underwear, household linens, upholstery, or curtains

ramie hemp *n* **:** RAMIE 2a

ram·i·fi·ca·tion \ˌraməfəˈkāshən\ *n* -S [F, fr. MF, fr. ML *ramificatus* (past part. of *ramificare*) + MF *-ion*] **1 :** the act or process of branching; *specif* **:** the mode of arrangement of branches **2 a :** a branch or offshoot from a main stock or channel ⟨the ~ of an artery⟩ **b :** the resulting branched structure ⟨make visible the whole ~ of the dendrite⟩ **3 :** something that springs from another in the manner of a branch **:** OUTGROWTH, SUBDIVISION **:** an extension of a basically simple idea, plan, or problem **:** a resulting development **:** CONSEQUENCE ⟨a university whose daily life abounds with events of far-reaching ~*s* —T.D.Durrance⟩ ⟨his banking house had ~*s* throughout Europe —R.A.Hall b.1911⟩ ⟨his mind brooded on the ~*s* of clans and tartans —W.B.Yeats⟩

ram·i·form pit \ˈraməˌfȯrm-\ *n* [L *ramus* branch + E *-iform*] **:** a branched pit formed by the coalescence of the cavities of two or more simple pits (as in the walls of brachysclereids)

ram·i·fy \ˈraməˌfī\ *vb* -ED/-ING/-ES [MF *ramifier,* fr. ML *ramificare,* fr. L *ramus* branch + *-ificare* -ify; akin to L *radix* root — more at ROOT] *vt* **1 :** to cause to branch **:** spread out **2 :** to separate into divisions or ramifications ~ *vi* **1 :** to split up into branches or constituent parts **2 :** to send forth branches, outgrowths, shoots, or extensions resembling them ⟨closely spaced veinlets of quartz . . . ~ in all directions —A.M.Bateman⟩ **3 :** to extend by means of branches or divisions ⟨a long-range industrial research program . . . should ~ into the field of substitute materials —W. H.Camp⟩ **syn** see BRANCH

ram·il·lie *or* **ram·i·lie** \ˈraməlē\ *also* **ram·il·lies** *or* **ram·i·lies** \-ēz\ *n, pl* **ramillies** *or* **ramilies** *sometimes cap* [fr. *Ramillies,* Belgium, in commemoration of a battle in 1706 when the British defeated the French] **:** an 18th century wig with a long plait in back that is tied top and bottom with bows

ramillie

ra·mism \ˈrāˌmizəm\ *n* -S *usu cap* [F *ramisme,* fr. Petrus *Ramus* (Pierre de La Ramée) †1572 Fr. philosopher and mathematician + F

-isme -ism] **:** the doctrines of Petrus Ramus who opposed scholasticism and advocated Calvinism as well as a logic more informal than Aristotelian and designed to be amalgamated with rhetoric

1**ra·mist** \ˈrāməst\ *n* -s *usu cap* [F *ramiste*, fr. P. *Ramus* + F *-iste* -ist] **:** an advocate of Ramism

2**ramist** \"\ *or* **ra·mis·tic** \rəˈmistik\ *adj, usu cap* **:** of or relating to Petrus Ramus or to Ramism

ramjet engine \ˈ=,=-\ *or* **ramjet** *n* [2*ram* + *jet*] **:** a jet engine having in its forward end a continuous inlet of air so that there is a compressing effect produced on the air taken in while the engine is in motion with the compressed air that enters the combustion chamber and the constant burning of the fuel resulting in a continuous jet of hot gases

ram·ko·ka·mek·ra \ramˈkōkə,mekrə\ *n, pl* **ramkokamekra** *or* **ramkokamekras** *usu cap* **1 a :** a Ge people of northeastern Brazil **b :** a member of such people **2 :** the language of the Ramkokamekra people

ram leather *n* **:** CUP LEATHER

ramline \ˈ=,=\ *n* **:** a line used to mark a straight middle line (as on a spar or mast)

ram·mack *also* **ram·ack** \ˈramək\ *vi* -ED/-ING/-S [origin unknown] *dial* **:** to rush around

rammed *past of* RAM

ram·mel \ˈraməl\ *n* -s [ME *ramell, ramail*, fr. MF *ramaille*, fr. *ram, rame, raim* branch — more at RAMAGE] **1** *dial chiefly Eng* **:** UNDERBRUSH **2** *dial chiefly Eng* **:** TRASH **3** *dial chiefly Eng* **:** hard barren soil

ram·mels·berg·ite \ˈraməlz,bər,gīt\ *n* -s [Karl F. *Rammelsberg* †1899 Ger. mineralogist + E *-ite*] **:** a mineral $NiAs_2$ consisting of a native nickel diarsenide related to loellingite and polymorphous with pararammelsbergite

ram·mer \ˈramə(r)\ *n* -s [ME, fr. *rammen* to ram + *-er* — more at RAM] **:** one that rams: as **a :** an instrument for driving something (as stones, piles, earth) with force **b :** a rod made chiefly of wood and operated by hand or entirely of metal and operated by power that is used for ramming home the projectile or the charge of a gun **c :** a worker who compacts sand around mold patterns

ramming *pres part of* RAM

ramming effect *or* **ramming** *n* -s **:** RAM EFFECT

ram·mish \ˈramish\ *adj* [ME *rammissh*, fr. 1*ram* + *-issh*, -ish] **1 :** resembling a ram **2** *chiefly dial* **:** rank in smell or taste

ram·mish·ness *n* -ES **:** the quality or state of being rammish

ram·my \-mē\ *adj* -ER/-EST [1*ram* + *-y*] **:** RAMMISH

ra·mon \rəˈmōn\ *n* -s [AmerSp *ramón*, fr. Sp, browse, aug. of *ramo* branch, twig — more at RAMADA] **:** BREADNUT 1

ra·mo·na \rəˈmōnə\ [NL, prob. after *Ramona*, heroine of a novel (1884) of the same name by Helen Hunt Jackson †1885 Am. writer] *syn of* AUDIBERTIA

ra·mo·neur \,raməˈnər\ *n* -s [F, fr. MF, fr. *ramoner* to sweep (fr. OF, fr. *ramon* broom, dim. of *ram, raim* branch) + *-eur* -or — more at RAMAGE] *Brit* **:** CHIMNEY SWEEP

ra·mont·chi \rəˈmänchē\ *n* -s [origin unknown] **:** GOVERNOR'S PLUM

ramoosi *usu cap, var of* RAMUSI

ra·mose \ˈrā,mōs, rəˈmōs\ *adj* [L *ramosus*, fr. *ramus* branch + *-osus* -ose — more at RAMIFY] **:** consisting of or having branches or lateral divisions **:** BRANCHED — **ra·mose·ly** *adv* — **ra·mos·i·ty** \rəˈmäsəd-ē\ *n* -ES

ra·mos gin fizz *also* **ra·mos fizz** \ˈrāməs-\ *n, usu cap R* [after Henry Charles *Ramos*, 19th–20th cent. Am. bartender] **:** a mixed drink consisting of gin, cream, white of egg, lemon and lime juice, sugar, and orange-flower water shaken vigorously, strained, and served often with the addition of a little soda water in a tall glass

ra·mous \ˈrāməs\ *adj* [L *ramosus*] **1 :** RAMOSE **2 :** of, relating to, or resembling branches

1**ramp** \ˈramp, ˈraa(ə)mp, ˈraimp\ *vb* -ED/-ING/-S [ME *rampen*, fr. OF *ramper*, to climb, crawl, rear, of Gmc origin; akin to MD & MLG *ramp* cramp, MHG *rampf* cramp, OHG *rimpfan* to wrinkle — more at RUMPLE] *vi* **1 a :** to be rampant or in the posture of a beast rampant in heraldry **b** (1) **:** to stand or advance with forelegs or with arms raised as if in menace, anger, or excitement (2) **:** to move or act furiously **:** RAGE, STORM ⟨would ~ and rage and hop about like a veritable Sioux —Norman Douglas⟩ **c** *chiefly dial* **:** to rush about esp. in a boisterous excited manner **2 :** to crawl or move along the ground ⟨a boa does not ~ about the jungle —*Current History*⟩ **3 a** (1) **:** CLIMB (2) **:** to creep up — used esp. of plants ⟨grew here as roses should be allowed to grow — untamed . . . ~*ing* over the rocks —Douglas Carruthers⟩ **b** *chiefly dial* **:** to grow rapidly **4 :** to rise or fall to a higher or lower level ~ *vt* **1 :** to bend so as to fit to a ramp (as in a stair rail) ⟨gracefully ~*ed* mahogany handrail —H.S.Morrison⟩ **2 :** to furnish with a ramp ⟨the auditorium was ~*ed* to better visual efficiency —Al Hine⟩

2**ramp** \"\ *n* -s **:** the act of ramping; *esp* **:** a rearing or advancing in a threatening or warlike posture ⟨in the roar and the ~ of the southern gale —Hamlin Garland⟩

3**ramp** \"\ *n* -s [F *rampe*, fr. *ramper*] **1 a :** the perpendicular distance between the springing lines of a rampant arch **b :** a sloping member other than a purely constructional one (as a continuous parapet to a staircase) **2 :** a short bend, slope, or curve usu. in the vertical plane where a handrail or coping changes its direction; *esp* **:** a vertical curve in a handrail, concave, or top **:** EASING **3 :** a sloping way: as **a :** a sloping floor or walk leading from one level to another — see BASTION illustration **b :** a platform and incline from which logs are loaded **c :** an inclined roadway connecting two thoroughfares (as in an interchange) or serving as a means of access to or exit from a bridge, a tunnel, or a parking area ⟨inclined ~*s* at each end of the pontoon bridge —C.R.Ege⟩ **4 :** a contrivance (as of blocks or wedges of wood) laid parallel in a roadway for passing traffic over lines of hose **5 a :** APRON 8c(1) **b :** the stairway by which passengers enter the main door of an airplane **6 :** a wedge-shaped block forming a base for a front sight of a firearm **7 a :** a thrust fault having a relatively high angle of dip **b :** RAMP VALLEY **c :** an accumulation of snow forming an inclined plane between land or land ice and sea or shelf ice

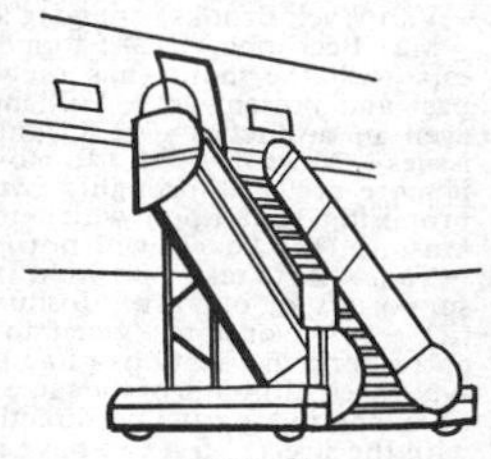
ramp 5b

4**ramp** \"\ *n* -s [ME *rampe*, perh. fr. *rampen* to ramp, rage — more at 1RAMP] **:** a bold woman

5**ramp** \"\ *n* -s [in sense 1, by shortening; in sense 2, back-formation fr. *ramps*, alter. of *rams*, fr. ME, fr. OE *hramsa* — more at RAMSON] **1 :** RAMPION **2 :** any of several plants of the genus *Allium*; *esp* **:** RAMSON

6**ramp** \ˈramp\ *vt* -ED/-ING/-S [origin unknown] **1** *Brit* **:** ROB **2** *Brit* **:** to swindle from

7**ramp** \"\ *n* -s *Brit* **:** a confidence game **:** HOAX, SWINDLE ⟨the whole thing was a moneymaking ~ —Nicholas Monsarrat⟩

1**ram·page** \(ˈ)ramˈpāj, (ˈ)raam- *sometimes* -ˈpij *or* -ˈpej\ *vb* -ED/-ING/-S [fr. Sc, prob. irreg. fr. 1*ramp*] *vi* **:** to go on a rampage **:** act, rush, or storm wildly or excitedly ⟨go *rampaging* over the western prairies —Elinor Wylie⟩ ~ *vt* **:** to rush or storm in or about ⟨the peculiarly stirring timbres of thin brass . . . which can ~ a man's soul —Whitney Balliett⟩

2**ram·page** \ˈ=,pāj *sometimes* -,pij *or* -,pej\ *n* -s **:** violent, riotous, or reckless action or behavior **:** a state of being turbulently active, wildly agitated, or destructive ⟨the river going on a ~ —N.M.Clark⟩ ⟨~ of wanton killings —Vicki Baum⟩

ram·pa·geous *also* **ram·pa·gious** \(ˈ)ramˈpājəs, (ˈ)raam-\ *adj* **:** displaying violence or recklessness **:** often destructive **:** being out of control **:** UNRULY ⟨seamen who are wild and ~ —Kenneth Roberts⟩ ⟨vegetation is startlingly — almost overwhelmingly ~ —Hamilton Basso⟩

ram·pa·geous·ly *adv* **:** in a rampageous manner ⟨the lobsters . . . were ~ lively when they reached me —*New Yorker*⟩

ram·pa·geous·ness *n* -ES **:** the quality or state of being rampageous ⟨his ~ on finding himself in a frontier township after months of hard and dangerous work —*Times Lit. Supp.*⟩

rampaging *adj* **:** wildly storming **:** TURBULENT, VIOLENT ⟨safe from the ~ surf —*Springfield (Mass.) Union*⟩ ⟨~ self-pity —David Driscoll⟩

ram·pal·lian *also* **ram·pal·lion** \ramˈpalyən\ *n* -s [origin unknown] **:** a good-for-nothing scoundrel **:** WRETCH

ram·pan·cy \ˈrampənsē\ *n* -ES **:** the quality or state of being rampant **:** excessive exuberance **:** EXTRAVAGANCE

ram·pant \ˈrampənt, ˈraam- *also* -m,pant *or* -m,paa(ə)nt\ *adj* [ME *rampaunt*, fr. MF *rampant*, pres. part. of *ramper* to climb, crawl, rear — more at RAMP] **1 a :** rearing upon the hind legs with forelegs or forepaws extended **b** *of a heraldic beast* **:** reared up, standing on one hind foot with one foreleg raised above the other, and seen in profile **2 :** characterized by fierceness or high spirits ⟨below was the bull, ~, slobbering froth —Francis Birtles⟩ ⟨the long crow of a ~ cock —William Sansom⟩ **3 :** marked by the absence of check or restraint **:** UNBRIDLED ⟨the crime wave ~ here in recent months —T.W. Arnold⟩ ⟨rumor ran ~ . . . the other day —Harvey Breit⟩ **4 :** threatening or extravagant in action, bearing, or manner **:** displaying aggression or violence ⟨her wrath, feral and ~, utterly possessed her —W.H.Wright⟩ **5 :** having one impost or abutment higher than the other ⟨a ~ arch⟩ **6 a :** extremely profuse in growth **:** RANK ⟨~ beds of yellow flowers on the lawn —Janet Flanner⟩ **b :** used extravagantly **:** very much in evidence ⟨pleats . . . are ~ in skirts for daytime —Lois Long⟩

ram·pant·ly *adv* **:** in a rampant manner

1**ram·part** \ˈram,pärt, ˈraam-, -pət, -mpə(r)t, *usu* -d·+V\ *n* -s [MF *rampart, rempart*, fr. *ramparer, remparer* to fortify, strengthen, fr. *re-* + *emparer* to defend, protect, seize, fr. OProv *antparar, amparar*, fr. (assumed) VL *anteparare* — more at AMPARO] **1 :** a broad embankment or mound of earth raised as a fortification about a place and usu. surmounted by a parapet **2 :** something that fortifies, defends, or secures against attack or intrusion **:** a protective barrier **:** BULWARK ⟨our villages . . . are often surrounded by these great ~*s* of trees —Anne D. Sedgwick⟩ ⟨the great ~ of mountains loomed before them⟩ **3 :** a ridge like a wall of unconsolidated rock fragments, earth, or other debris: as **a :** ice pushed up along a lakeshore **b :** snow at the foot of a talus slope **c :** a shingle ridge formed along a beach by strong waves and currents

2**rampart** \"\ *vt* -ED/-ING/-S **:** to surround or protect with or as if with a rampart ⟨glittering dells proudly ~*ed* with rocks —S.T.Coleridge⟩

ramped *past of* RAMP

ram·per \ˈrampə(r)\ *n* -s [by alter.] *dial* **:** LAMPREY

ram·phas·ti·dae \ramˈfastə,dē\ *n pl, cap* [NL, fr. *Ramphastos*, type genus + *-idae*] **:** a family of birds (order Piciformes) consisting of the toucans

ram·phas·ti·des \-ēz\ *n pl, cap* [NL, fr. *Ramphastos* + *-ides*] *in some esp. former classifications* **:** a suborder of birds coextensive with the family Ramphastidae

ram·phas·tos \-ˈfa,stäs\ *n, cap* [NL, irreg. fr. Gk *rhamphos* curved beak + *astos* citizen, fr. *asty* city; akin to Skt *vasati* he remains, dwells — more at RHAMPH-, WAS] **:** a genus (the type of the family Ramphastidae) comprising various typical toucans

ramphoid *var of* RHAMPHOID

ram·pick \ˈram,pik\ *dial var of* RAMPIKE

ram·pike \-,pīk\ *n* [origin unknown] **:** a dead tree **:** a pointed stump or partly-burned tree **:** a tree broken off by the wind leaving a splintered end to the trunk

ramping *pres part of* RAMP

ram·pi·on \ˈrampēən\ *n* -s [prob. modif. of MF *raiponce*, fr. OIt *raponzo*, prob. fr. *rapa, rapo* turnip, fr. L *rapa, rapum* rape, turnip — more at RAPE] **:** a European bellflower (*Campanula rapunculus*) having an edible tuberous root used with the leaves as a salad

1**ram·pire** \ˈram,pī(ə)r\ *n* -s [MF *rampar, rempart, rampart* — more at RAMPART] **:** RAMPART

2**rampire** \"\ *vt* -ED/-ING/-S [MF *remparer, ramparer* — more at RAMPART] *archaic* **:** to fortify, strengthen, secure, or enclose with or as if with a rampart

ramp·man \ˈrampmən\ *n, pl* **rampmen** [3*ramp* + *man*] **:** a sawmill worker who unloads logs from truck or conveyor to deck

ram pressure *n* **:** the difference between the observed scoop pressure in the inlet air system of an airplane engine and the atmospheric pressure

ramps *pl of* RAMP, *pres 3d sing of* RAMP

ram·pur \ˈräm,pu̇(ə)r\ *adj, usu cap* [fr. *Rampur*, India] **:** of or from the city of Rampur, India **:** of the kind or style prevalent in Rampur

ramp valley *n* [3*ramp*] **:** a fault trough bounded laterally by faults that dip away from the valley axis and underlaid by a depressed block that is supposed to have been forced down by lateral pressure

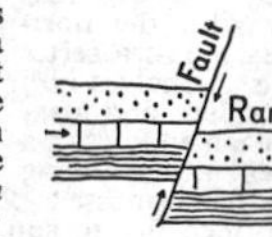

ramrace \ˈ=,=\ *n* [1*ram* (animal) + *race*] *chiefly Scot* **:** a headlong rush **:** a short hard run

ram rocket [2*ram*] *n* **:** a rocket propelled by a ramjet engine

1**ramrod** \ˈ=,=\ *n* [2*ram* + *rod*] **1 :** a rod used in ramming home the charge in a muzzle-loading firearm **2 :** a strict disciplinarian; *esp* **:** the foreman of a ranch

2**ramrod** \"\ *vt* **:** to exert discipline and authority on ⟨he was *ramrodding* the whole outfit⟩

3**ramrod** \"\ *adj* **:** very straight and unbending **:** characterized by rigidity, severity, or stiffness **:** INFLEXIBLE ⟨in awe of the ~ characteristics of the elders —J.H.Raleigh⟩ ⟨the ~ rote of a Prussian drillmaster —Al Hine⟩

1**rams** *pl of* RAM, *pres 3d sing of* RAM

2**rams** \ˈrämz\ *n* -ES [G *rams, rammes, ramsch*, rams, ramsch — more at RAMSCH] **:** a card game similar to loo

ram·sack \ˈram,sak\ *dial var of* RANSACK

ram·say·ite \ˈramzē,īt\ *n* -s [Sir Andrew C. *Ramsay* †1891 Brit. geologist + E *-ite*] **:** a mineral $Na_2Ti_2Si_2O_9$ consisting of a silicate of titanium and sodium

rams·bot·tom safety valve \ˈramz,bäd·əm-\ *n, usu cap R* [after John *Ramsbottom*, 19th cent. Brit. mechanical engineer] **:** a safety valve used esp. on locomotives in which two valves are pressed down by a single spring attached to a crosspiece prolonged to form a hand lever by which the valves may be eased up to test their adjustment

ramsch \ˈräm(p)sh\ *n* -ES [G, fr. F dial. *ramser* to collect, ramass, alter. of *ramasser* — more at RAMASS] **:** a game in which the jacks alone are trumps and the object is to lose tricks

ram schooner *n* **:** a schooner with pole masts but no topmasts

rams·dell·ite \ˈramz,de,līt\ *n* -s [Lewis S. *Ramsdell* b1895 Am. mineralogist + E *-ite*] **:** a mineral consisting of manganese dioxide that is polymorphous with pyrolusite

rams·den eyepiece \ˈramzdən-\ *n, usu cap R* [after Jesse *Ramsden* †1800 Eng. instrument maker] **:** a nearly achromatic optical system of two lenses used as a magnifying glass or as an eyepiece in transits or telescopes fitted with micrometer wires **:** a positive eyepiece

1**ram·shackle** \ˈram,shakəl, ˈraam-\ *adj* [short for earlier *ramshackled*, alter. of *ransackled*, fr. past part. of obs. *ransackle* to ransack, freq. of *ransack*] **1 :** appearing as if ready to collapse **:** DILAPIDATED, RICKETY ⟨once imposing though now ~ roof —Ellen Glasgow⟩ ⟨mounted on a ~ horse —W.F. Starkie⟩ ⟨a dirty ~ pier —George Santayana⟩ **2 :** having little moral sense **:** DISSIPATED, UNRULY ⟨worrying about the ~ morality of . . . adolescents —John McCarten⟩ ⟨I may be getting ~ —H.G.Wells⟩ **3 :** carelessly or loosely constructed ⟨the plot is innocent and ~ —Wolcott Gibbs⟩ ⟨the book is a ~ affair —J.A.Michener⟩

2**ramshackle** \"\ *n* **:** a ramshackle thing ⟨here in the faded ~ —Carl Sandburg⟩

ram·shack·le·ness *n* -ES **:** the quality or state of being ramshackle

ram·shack·ly \-klē\ *adj* [1*ramshackle* + *-y*] **:** RAMSHACKLE ⟨~ booths displaying souvenirs —Joseph Mitchell⟩

ram's-head \ˈ=,=\ *also* **ram's-head lady's slipper** *n, pl* **ram's-heads :** an orchid (*Cypripedium arietinum*) of northern No. America having a brownish green flower with a red-and-white veiny lip suggestive of a ram's head

ram's head *n* **:** a carved or sculptured decoration found in Greek and Roman art and revived as a decorative motive esp. in 18th century furniture

ram's horn *n* **1 :** a box with holes in the sides in which fish are washed **2 a :** a cat's claw (*Acacia greggii*) **b :** UNICORN PLANT **3 :** a crane attachment consisting of two hooks forged into one in a manner suggesting the shape of a ram's horns **4 :** SHOFAR

ram's horn 3

ramshorn \ˈ=,=\ *also* **ramshorn snail** *n* **:** a snail of the genus *Planorbis* often used as a scavenger in aquariums

ramshorn crab *n* **:** a small Australian spider crab (*Noxia aries*) with divergent rostral spines and very slender legs

ram·son \ˈramzən, -msən\ *n* -s [ME *ramsyn*, fr. OE *hramsan*, pl. of *hramsa*; akin to MLG *ramese, remese* ramson, OHG *ramusia*, Sw, Dan & Norw *rams* ramson, MIr *crim* garlic, Gk *kremyon, kromyon*, a kind of onion, Lith *kermušė* wild garlic] **1 :** a broad-leaved garlic (*Allium ursinum*) common in European gardens **2 :** the bulbous root of the ramson used esp. in salads — used chiefly in pl.

1**ram·stam** \ˈram,stam\ *adj* [prob. by redupl. & alter. fr. 1*ram*] *Scot* **:** HEADSTRONG, RECKLESS

2**ramstam** \"\ *adv, Scot* **:** HEADLONG

ramstead *var of* RANSTEAD

ram through *vt* **:** to force the passage or acceptance of usu. over considerable opposition ⟨*rammed through* his law —*Time*⟩ ⟨*rammed through* the bitterly opposed nomination —*New Republic*⟩ ⟨legislation *rammed through* by a bare majority of left-wing fellow travelers —T.R.Ybarra⟩

ram·til \ˈram,til\ *n* -s [Hindi *rāmtil*, fr. Skt *Rāma* Rama, Hindu epic hero + *tila* sesamum] **:** a tropical African herb (*Guizotia abyssinica*) of the family Compositae widely cultivated in India for its seeds — see NIGER SEED

ram·u·lar \ˈramyələ(r)\ *adj* [L *ramulus* small branch + E *-ar* — more at RAMULUS] **:** of or relating to a branch ⟨~ trace⟩

ram·u·lar·ia \,ramyəˈla(a)rēə\ *n, cap* [NL, fr. L *ramulus* + NL *-aria*] **:** a genus of imperfect fungi (family Moniliaceae) having oblong to cylindrical hyaline septate conidia often borne in chains

ram·u·lif·er·ous \ˈ;ramyəˈlif(ə)rəs\ *adj* [*ramulus* + *-iferous*] **:** bearing ramuli

ram·u·lose \ˈ==,lōs\ *or* **ram·u·lous** \-ləs\ *adj* [L *ramulosus*, fr. *ramulus* + *-osus* -ose, -ous] **:** having many small branches

ram·u·lus \-ləs\ *n, pl* **ramu·li** \-yə,lī\ [L, dim. of *ramus* branch] **:** a small branch **:** BRANCHLET

ra·mus \ˈrāməs\ *n, pl* **ra·mi** \-ā,mī\ [NL, fr. L, branch of a tree — more at RAMIFY] **:** a projecting part or elongated process **:** RAMIFICATION: as **a :** the posterior more or less vertical part of the lower jaw on each side which articulates with the skull; *also* **:** the entire right or left half of the jaw — used when the jaw has no plainly distinguishable vertical part **b :** one of the branches of the pubis or ischium **c :** either of the two branches of the incus in the mastax of a rotifer **d :** a branch of a nerve ⟨the dorsal and ventral *rami* of the spinal nerve roots⟩ — compare RAMUS COMMUNICANS **e :** a barb of a feather

ramus com·mu·ni·cans \-kəˈmyünə,kanz\ *n, pl* **rami com·mu·ni·can·tes** \-=,==ˈkan-,tēz\ [NL, communicating ramus] **:** one of the bundles of nerve fibers connecting a sympathetic ganglion with a spinal nerve and being divided into white rami communicantes consisting of preganglionic fibers and gray rami communicantes of postganglionic fibers

ra·mus·cule \rəˈmə,skyül\ *n* -s [NL *ramus* + L *-culus*, dim. suffix] **:** a small ramus

ra·mu·si \rəˈmüsē\ *also* **ra·moo·sii** \-ē,ē\ *n, pl* **ramusi** *or* **ramusis** *also* **ramoosii** *or* **ramoosiis** *usu cap* **:** one of a pre-Aryan people in northwestern India

1**ran** [ME, fr. OE & ON *rann*] *past of* RUN

2**ran** \ˈran\ *n* -s [origin unknown] **:** a hank of twine

1**ra·na** \ˈränə\ *n* -s [Hindi *rānā*, fr. Skt *rājan* — more at RICH] **:** an Indian prince ⟨the ~ of Koti . . . rode in a sedan chair, as befitted the ruler of the Indian state —*Time*⟩

2**ra·na** \ˈrānə\ *n, cap* [NL, fr. L, frog, prob. of imit. origin] **:** a nearly cosmopolitan genus of frogs that is the type of the family Ranidae

ra·na·les \rəˈnā(,)lēz\ *n pl, cap* [NL, irreg. fr. *Ranunculus* + *-ales*] **:** a large order of dicotyledonous herbs, shrubs, and trees including the Ranunculaceae, Berberidaceae, Magnoliaceae, Annonaceae, and Lauraceae and being distinguished in general by flowers with spirally arranged parts, numerous stamens, and an apocarpous gynoecium

ra·na·li·an \rəˈnālēən\ *also* **ra·nal** \ˈrānᵊl\ *adj* [*ranalian* fr. NL *Ranales* + E *-ian*; *ranal* fr. NL *Ranales*] **:** relating to or belonging to the order Ranales

ran·a·tra \ˈranə·trə\ *n, cap* [NL] **:** a genus of elongate very slender bugs (family Nepidae) with long slender legs the first pair of which is fitted for seizing prey in the manner of a mantis

rancel *vi* **rancelled; rancelled; rancelling; rancels** [of Scand origin; akin to Icel *reynsla* experience, trial & Norw *røynsla* experience, fr. ON *reyna* to experience, examine, search, causative-denominative *raun* attempt, trial, experience; akin to Gk *ereunan* to seek, search for, *ereuna* inquiry, search] *obs Scot* **:** to search thoroughly **:** RANSACK

ran·cel·man \ˈran(t)sᵊlmən\ *n, pl* **rancelmen** *Scot* **:** a constable with the duty of searching for stolen or missing goods

ranc·er \ˈran(t)sə(r)\ *n* -s [prob. fr. Sc *rance, ranse* bar, stick (perh. fr. F dial. *rance* bar, peg, rung, fr. L *ramic-, ramex* staff, fr. L *ramus* branch) + *-er* — more at RAMIFY] **:** REAMER

1**ranch** \ˈranch, ˈraa(ə)nch, ˈrainch, ˈrånch\ *vt* -ED/-ING/-ES [ME *ranschen, ranchen*, alter. of *rasen, racen* — more at RASE] *archaic* **:** SCRATCH, TEAR

2**ranch** \"\ *n* -ES [MexSp *rancho* small ranch, fr. Sp, camp, temporary habitation, hut & Sp dial. (Andalusia), small farm, fr. OSp *ranchar(se), ranchear(se)* to take up quarters, be billeted, fr. MF *(se) ranger* to take up a position, be quartered, fr. *ranger* to set in a row, place, station — more at RANGE] **1 :** an establishment for the grazing and rearing of horses, cattle, or sheep that usu. includes the buildings occupied by the owner and employees with the adjacent barns and corrals **2 :** a farm of any size usu. devoted to the raising of one particular specialty ⟨poultry ~⟩ ⟨wheat ~⟩ ⟨mink ~⟩ **3 :** DUDE RANCH

3**ranch** \"\ *vb* -ED/-ING/-ES *vi* **:** to live or work on a ranch **:** engage in the business of a rancher ~ *vt* **1 :** to work as a rancher on ⟨settlers who ~ the dry uplands —Elspeth Huxley⟩ **2 :** to raise on a ranch ⟨~*es* cattle —*Time*⟩ **3 :** to breed and care for (fur-bearing animals) on or as if on a ranch; *esp* **:** to care for animals belonging to another on shares or for a fee ⟨do not offer to ~ animals for the purchaser for an indefinite period of time —*Nat'l Fur News*⟩

4**ranch** \"\ *adj, of furs* **:** coming from animals bred and raised in captivity — compare WILD

ranche \ˈranch\ *n* -s [F, bar, peg, rung, fr. a dial. word (Normandy or Picardy) derived fr. L *ramic-, ramex* staff — more at RANCER] **:** a stroke in pin pool that leaves only the center pin standing and thereby wins the game

ranch·er \ˈranchə(r), ˈraan-, ˈrain-, ˈrȧn-\ *n* -s [MexSp *ranchero*, fr. *rancho* small ranch + *-ero* -er — more at RANCH] **1 :** one who owns, operates, or is employed on a ranch — called also *ranchero, ranchman* **2 :** one who ranches a particular kind of animal ⟨a mink ~⟩ ⟨wise ~*s* . . . naturally look for . . . qualities in selecting their fox and mink feed —*Amer. Fur Breeder*⟩

ran·che·ria \,ranchəˈrēə\ *n* -s [MexSp *rancheria*, fr. *ranchero* + Sp *-ia* -y (fr. L *-ia*)] **1 :** a dwelling place of a ranchero **2 :** a small settlement often consisting of huts occupied esp. by Amerindians or Mexicans ⟨it was among these ~*s* . . . that the missions found their most fertile field for labor —F.M. & Marie Keesing⟩

ran·che·ro \ranˈche(,)rō, raan-\ *n* -s [MexSp] **:** RANCHER

ranch house *n* **1 :** the main dwelling house on a ranch **2 :** a one-story dwelling typically having an open plan and a low-pitched roof

ranch house 2

ranch·land \'‹,›‹\ *n* **:** land suitable for ranching
ranch·man \'‹man\ *n, pl* **ranch·men :** RANCHER
ranch mink *n* **:** mink scientifically bred and raised for fur production
ran·cho \'ran(,)chō, 'raan-, 'rän-\ *n* -s [MexSp, small ranch — more at RANCH] **:** RANCH
ranchwoman \'‹,‹‹\ *n, pl* **ranchwomen :** a woman who operates or lives on a ranch
ran·cid \'ran(t)sə̇d, 'raan-, 'rain-\ *adj* [L *rancidus*, fr. *rancēre* to be rancid, stink] **1 :** having a rank smell or taste usu. from chemical change or decomposition **:** affecting the senses disagreeably or unpleasantly ⟨~ butter⟩ ⟨the wet ~ smells of a basement —Ben Hecht⟩ **2 :** showing an obnoxious quality **:** ODIOUS, ROTTEN ⟨a ~ little psychopath who murdered a number of people —Bernard De Voto⟩ — **ran·cid·ly** *adv* — **ran·cid·ness** *n* -ES
ran·cid·i·fi·ca·tion \ran,sidəfə'kāshən\ *n* -s **:** the chemical change that produces rancidity
ran·cid·i·fy \ran'sidə,fī\ *vb* -ED/-ING/-ES [*rancid* + *-ify*] *vt* **:** to make rancid ~ *vi* **:** to become rancid
ran·cid·i·ty \ran'sidəd-ē, raan-, -ətē, -i\ *n* -ES **:** the quality or state of being rancid **:** a rancid odor or flavor
ran·cio \'rän(t)sē,ō\ *adj* [Sp, rancid, stale, old, rancio, fr. L *rancidus* rancid — more at RANCID] **:** of, relating to, or constituting the nutty flavor peculiar to some fortified wines (as sherry and Madeira)
ran·cor \'raŋkə(r), 'raiŋ-\ *n* -s *see -or in Explan Notes* [ME *rancour*, fr. MF *ranceur*, fr. LL *rancor* rancidity, grudge, rancor, fr. L *rancēre* to be rancid, stink + *-or*] **:** vehement hatred or ill will **:** intense malignity or spite **:** deep-seated enmity **:** inveterate malevolence ⟨hopelessly involved . . . in the political ~s of the times —E.M.Coulter⟩ **syn** see ENMITY
ran·cored \-(r)d\ *adj* **:** infected by rancor **:** made rancorous ⟨voice, ~ by a deep-seated . . . malignity —Beatrice Levin⟩
ran·cor·ous \-k(ə)rəs\ *adj* **:** full of rancor **:** evincing or caused by rancor **:** deeply malevolent **:** MALIGNANT ⟨preserve . . . from ~ envy of the rich —Aldous Huxley⟩ ⟨a ~ man, as petty and cruel as he was dictatorial —C.H.Grandgent⟩ — **ran·cor·ous·ly** *adv*
¹rand \'rand\ *n* -s [ME, fr. OE *rand, rond;* akin to MD & MLG *rant* edge, rim, OHG edging, rim of a shield, shield, ON *rönd* rim, shield, OE *rima* rim — more at RIM] **1** *dial chiefly Eng* **:** an unplowed edge of a field **:** BORDER **2** *dial* **:** the coarse grass growing on the edge **3** *Africa* **:** a long low stony ridge **4 :** a beveled U-shaped strip usu. of leather put on a shoe before the lifts of the heel **5 :** a course of simple weaving in basketmaking with one osier rod at a time often of thin material used to fill in — see BASKET illustration
²rand \"\ *vt* -ED/-ING/-S **1 :** to cut into rands or strips **2 :** to fit with rands (as in the manufacture of shoes)
ran·dall grass \'randᵊl-\ *n* [fr. the name *Randall*] **1 :** MEADOW FESCUE **2 :** PERENNIAL RYEGRASS
ran·dall·ite \'randᵊl,īt\ *n* -s *usu cap* [Benjamin *Randall* †1808 Am. religious leader + E *-ite*] **:** one of a group of Freewill Baptists organized in the northern part of the U. S. in 1787
¹ran·dan \'ran,dan, ‹'‹\ *n* -s [origin unknown] *dial* **:** boisterous noisy conduct **:** RAMPAGE, SPREE
²randan \"\ *n* -s [origin unknown] **1 :** a boat propelled by three rowers of whom the middle rower pulls two short oars while bow and stroke pull one oar each **2 :** the style used to row a randan
ran·dan·nite \ran'da,nīt\ *n* -s [modif. of F *randanite*, fr. *Randan*, Dept. Puy-de-Dôme, France + F *-ite*] **1 :** a variety of diatomaceous earth **2 :** an earthy form of opal
R and C *abbr* rail and canal
R and CC *abbr* riot and civil commotion
¹ran·dem \'randəm\ *adv* [prob. blend of ²*random* and *tandem*] **:** with three horses harnessed to a vehicle one behind another
²randem \"\ *n* -s **:** a team or vehicle driven randem
rand·er \'randə(r)\ *n* -s **:** a worker who trims or bevels the edges of shoe soles or welts
ran·dia \'randēə\ *n, cap* [NL, fr. Isaac *Rand* †1743 Eng. botanist + NL *-ia*] **:** a large genus of tropical shrubs and trees (family Rubiaceae) having white or yellow solitary or clustered flowers and a many-seeded berry — see BOX BRIER
randie *chiefly Scot var of* ¹RANDY
randies *pl of* RANDY
rand·ing \'randiŋ\ *n* -s **1 a :** the act of making a rand **b :** the material for making a rand **2 :** the act or process of making and applying rands for shoes
rand·kluft \'ränt,klüft\ *n* -s [G, fr. *rand* rim (fr. OHG *rant*) + *kluft* crevice, fr. OHG, gap, tongs — more at RAND, CLEFT] **:** a chasm formed when ice recedes from a mountainside or breaks away from stationary ice
R and L *abbr* rail and lake
ran·dle tree \'randᵊl-\ *var of* RANNEL TREE
R and O *abbr* rail and ocean
¹ran·dom \'randəm, 'raan-\ *n* -s [ME *randoun, raundon, random*, fr. MF *randon* (as in *de randon, a randon* with impetuosity), fr. OF, fr. *randir* to run, gallop, of Gmc origin; akin to G dial. (Bavarian & Alemannic) *rand* run, running, fr. stem of OHG *rinnan* to run — more at RUN] **1** *obs* **:** FORCE, IMPETUOSITY **2 :** a haphazard course **:** chance progress **3** *obs* **a :** the range of a gun or projectile **b :** the elevation given to a gun **4 :** ³BANK 3b — **at random** *adv* **1 :** without definite aim, direction, rule, or method **:** with no specific goal or purpose in view ⟨upon the table soiled dishes were piled *at random* —William Faulkner⟩ ⟨worn cow paths led through *at random* —Christopher Rand⟩ **2** *obs* **:** without restraint or attention **:** at liberty ⟨to be left *at random*⟩
²random \"\ *adv* **:** in a random manner **:** at random — usu. used in combination ⟨*random*-jointed⟩
³random \"\ *adj* **1 :** lacking or seeming to lack a regular plan, purpose, or pattern ⟨~ thoughts laid hold of him —George Meredith⟩ ⟨a ~ assortment of vases, ivory elephants and other . . . ornaments —Robert Shaplen⟩ ⟨~ brick and timber panels —*Amer. Guide Series: Conn.*⟩ ⟨~ widths⟩ **2 a :** marked by absence of bias **:** chosen at random ⟨a true ~ sample of the whole list —Daniel Melcher & Nancy Larrick⟩ ⟨placing a finger on a ~ passage —Charlton Laird⟩ **b :** involving or resulting from randomization **c :** having the same probability of occurring as every other member of a set ⟨~ numbers⟩
syn HAPHAZARD, HIT-OR-MISS, DESULTORY, CHANCE, CHANCY, CASUAL, HAPPY-GO-LUCKY: RANDOM stresses lack of definite aim, fixed goal, regular procedure, or predictable incidence ⟨a *random* collection of literary and archeological odds and ends —Aldous Huxley⟩ ⟨the clerks become tired and bored and start making *random* mistakes —Martin Gardner⟩ ⟨a kitten's *random* play with a spool or ball⟩ That which is HAPHAZARD is done according to chance or whim without regularity or order and with careless disregard for ultimate fitness or efficiency. HIT-OR-MISS further stresses lack of aim, care, plan, or system ⟨all his shop training had given him a profound prejudice against inexact work, experimental work, *hit-or-miss* work —C.S.Forester⟩ DESULTORY stresses lack of regularity or steadiness and suggests an erratic performance marked by false starts, lapses, breaks, shifts, or inconsistencies ⟨medieval warfare was often of the nature of a mild adventure . . . the fighting was generally sporadic and *desultory* —Edwin Benson⟩ ⟨a little Latin and Greek and much outdoor life, with a *desultory* education got from vagrant books —V.L. Parrington⟩ CHANCE stresses complete lack of design, intent, plan, or prearrangement ⟨he had never before given Cuba, under Spanish rule, a thought, but at a *chance* sentence it dominated him completely —Joseph Hergesheimer⟩ It suggests lack of plan, reason, forethought in connection with persons encountered or objects found or discovered in various places ⟨his temper grew uncertain and he found it increasingly difficult to welcome *chance* visitors with his usual affability —Robert Graves⟩ ⟨snatching a *chance* piece of billiard chalk from his pocket, he ran it across the hall floor —G.K.Chesterton⟩ In reference to things and situations CHANCY suggests uncertainty of outcome through dependence on chance and hence implies risk or hazard ⟨despite recent advances in geophysics, oil drilling is still a *chancy* business —H.T.Kane⟩ CASUAL suggests lack of intentness or purpose ⟨his jottings are by no means *casual* —*Listener*⟩ HAPPY-GO-LUCKY suggests carefree, insouciant lack of forethought or plan or cheerful, indifferent acceptance of what ensues ⟨a funny little *happy-go-lucky*, native-managed railway —Rudyard Kipling⟩ ⟨the old *happy-go-lucky* methods of production —Bernard Pares⟩
random bond *n* **:** a bond in stonemasonry in which the stones are laid at random and not in regular courses
random error *n* **:** a statistical error that is wholly due to chance and does not recur — opposed to *systematic error*
ran·dom·iza·tion \,randəmə'zāshən\ *n* -s **1 :** controlled distribution usu. of given tests, factors, samplings, treatments, or units so as to simulate a random or chance distribution and yield unbiased data from which a generalized conclusion can be drawn **2 :** a random process used in a statistical experiment to reduce or eliminate interference by variables other than those being studied
ran·dom·ize \'randə,mīz\ *vt* -ED/-ING/-S [³*random* + *-ize*] **:** to distribute by or use randomization on
randomized block *n* **:** an experimental design (as in horticulture) in which different treatments are distributed in random order within a block or plot
random line *also* **random traverse** *n* **:** a trial surveying line avoiding obstacles between stations
ran·dom·ly *adv* **:** in a random manner
ran·dom·ness *n* -ES **:** the quality or state of being random
random noise *n* **:** a usu. electric or acoustic signal that consists of equal amounts of all frequencies
random variable *n* **:** a variable that is itself a function of the result of a statistical experiment in which each outcome has a definite probability of occurrence ⟨the number of spots showing if two dice are thrown is a *random variable*⟩ — called also *variate*
random walk *n* **:** a process (as Brownian movement or genetic drift) consisting of a sequence of steps (as movements or changes in gene frequency) each of whose characteristics (as magnitude and direction) are determined by chance
¹ran·dori \rän'dōrē\ *n* -s [Jap, lit., free practice] **:** free practice between two judo students
²randori \"\ *vi* -ED/-ING/-S **:** to practice judo informally
R and R *abbr* **1** rest and recreation; rest and recuperation; rest and rehabilitation **2** rock 'n' roll
rands *pl of* RAND, *pres 3d sing of* RAND
R and W *abbr* rail and water
¹ran·dy \'randē, -di\ *adj* [prob. fr. obs. E *rand* to rant, rave (fr. obs. D *randen, ranten*) + E *-y*] **1** *chiefly Scot* **:** having a coarse manner **:** loud-spoken **2 :** LUSTFUL, LECHEROUS
²randy \"\ *n* -ES **1** *chiefly Scot* **:** a rough-mannered beggar **2** *chiefly Scot* **:** a scolding or dissolute woman
³randy \"\ *n* -ES *dial Brit* **:** a noisy festivity **:** CAROUSAL ⟨the next ~ we come to . . . is to be a wedding —Mary Webb⟩ ⟨a rattling good ~ with fiddles and bass viols —Thomas Hardy⟩
ranee *var of* RANI
ra·nel·la \rə'nelə\ *n* [NL, fr. L *rana* frog + NL *-ella* — more at RANA] **1** *cap* **:** a genus of marine snails related to *Triton* having a thick shell usu. with two lateral varices continuous over all the whorls **2** -s **:** any snail of the genus *Ranella*
ra·ney nickel \'rānē-\ *n, usu cap R* [after Murray *Raney* †1966 Am. engineer and manufacturer] **:** a finely divided nickel in the form of a pyrophoric powder or crystals or a suspension (as in alcohol) that is prepared from an alloy of equal parts of nickel and aluminum by dissolving the aluminum in warm sodium hydroxide solution and rinsing thoroughly and that is used as a catalyst for the hydrogenation of various organic compounds
rang [ME, alter. (prob. influenced by ¹*sang*) of *ringde*, fr. OE *hringde*] *past of* RING
ranga·ti·ra \,räŋə'tirə\ *n* -s [Maori] **1 :** a Maori chief **:** a Maori of rank, authority, or distinction **2** *NewZeal* **:** a leading citizen **:** MAGISTRATE
rang·doo·dles \'raŋ,düdᵊlz\ *n pl* [prob. alter. of *roodles*] **:** roodles in draw poker
¹range \'rānj\ *n* -s *often attrib* [ME, fr. MF, fr. OF *renge*, fr. *renc, reng* line, place, row — more at RANK] **1 a :** a row or rank usu. of people or animals ⟨the first ~ of soldiers⟩ ⟨pupils in a ~⟩ **b :** a series of things in a line: as (1) **:** a line of buildings or sections of a building ⟨in a ~ of buildings near the house was a dairy and meat store —H.V.Morton⟩ ⟨a big nursery over which was a ~ of attics —David Garnett⟩ (2) **:** a row or course of masonry with the horizontal joints continuous (3) **:** a series of double-faced sections of shelves in a stack abutting one another and usu. terminating in aisles at each end (4) **:** a greenhouse establishment often having several houses that may be connected **2 a :** a grate let down when required over an open fire to support cooking utensils **b :** a cooking apparatus enclosing controlled heat (as from wood, coal, gas, electricity) and having a flat top with solid plates or open racks to hold utensils over flames or coils and an oven and sometimes also a storage space for utensils or a second oven **3 a :** something that may be ranged over **:** place or room for excursion **b :** an open region over which cattle, sheep, or other livestock may roam and feed **:** pasturage esp. when unenclosed ⟨low-lying valley bottoms . . . providing meager amounts of winter ~ —T.R.Weir⟩ **c :** the region throughout which a kind of organism or ecological community naturally lives or occurs ⟨the elk ~ in the Rocky mountain area —T.W.Daniels⟩ ⟨this snail thrived and spread . . ., its ~ being directly increased —Joyce Allan⟩ **4 a :** the act of ranging about or of roving **:** EXCURSION, RAMBLE ⟨taking the dogs for a ~⟩ **b :** freedom to range **:** opportunity to roam about ⟨giving the horses free ~⟩ **5 a** (1) **:** the horizontal distance to which a shot or other projectile is or may be propelled ⟨the gun has a ~ of six miles⟩ (2) **:** the horizontal distance of the target or thing aimed at from a weapon (3) **:** a place where shooting (as with bows, guns, or missiles) is practiced **b :** the maximum distance an airplane or other vehicle (as a tank) can travel without refueling — compare RADIUS 4d **c :** the average distance radioactive or other projected particles of a given type will penetrate a given medium before their velocity is reduced to less than a detectable value **6 :** an aggregate of individuals in one order **:** a social class ⟨in the lower ~s of the council —F.M.Stenton⟩ ⟨at the lowest ~ the family, at the uppermost the state —B.N.Cardozo⟩ **7 a :** a large cleat in the waist of a sailing ship for handling lines **b :** a length of slack cable ranged along the deck preparatory to letting go the anchor **8 a :** the space or extent included, covered, or used ⟨a faith worldwide in its ~ and power —Norman Goodall⟩ **b :** a field of operation **:** an area actively occupied or used ⟨lanterns at night to attract fish within ~ of net or spear —*Lamp*⟩ **c :** the scope or span usu. of activity, experience, or knowledge ⟨a technical vocabulary a little outside my ~ —Wolcott Gibbs⟩ **d :** COMPASS 1d **9 :** a direction line **:** DIRECTION ⟨the buoys in ~ with the pier⟩ **10 a** (1) **:** a series or chain of mountain peaks considered as forming one connected system **:** a ridge of mountains ⟨from the summit they could see ~ after ~ of mountains⟩ (2) **:** mountainous country — often used in pl. **b :** a mineral belt; *esp* **:** an iron-bearing formation **11 a :** a sequence, series, or scale between limits ⟨a wide ~ of patterns⟩ ⟨a ~ of possible solutions —W.S.Campbell⟩ **b :** the limits of a series **:** the distance or extent between possible extremes ⟨spring tides . . . have a greater ~ —C.F.Chapman⟩ **12 a** (1) **:** a strip of leather cut from a butt or hide (2) **:** the lie or line of the upper edge of the counter in a top boot (3) **:** the cutting of a butt or side of sole leather into strips **b :** a part of a hide **13 :** one of the north-south rows of townships in a U. S. public-land survey that are numbered east and west from the principal meridian of the survey **14 a :** a set of points lying on a line (as on the axis of an independent variable at which a function is defined) **b :** the difference between the least and greatest values of the attribute or variable of a frequency distribution **15 :** the class of admissible values of a variable **16 :** a gage for determining the thickness of glass **17 :** a group of shipping ports within an area for which the same rates are charged **18 :** RADIO RANGE

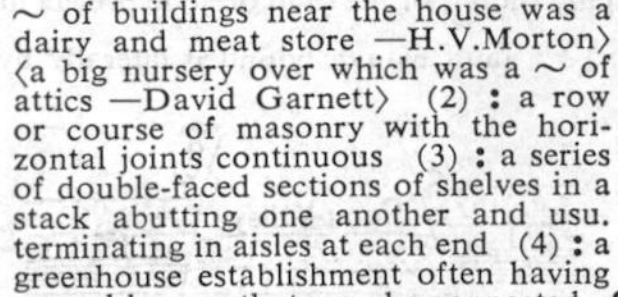

range 2b

syn GAMUT, REACH, RADIUS, COMPASS, SWEEP, SCOPE, ORBIT, HORIZON, KEN, PURVIEW: RANGE is the general term indicating the extent of one's perception or the extent of powers, capacities, or possibilities ⟨safe, well out of the *range* of the pursuers⟩ ⟨a beautiful voice with a wide *range* between the high and the low tones —Havelock Ellis⟩ ⟨a creative writer can do his best only with what lies within the *range* and character of his deepest sympathies —Willa Cather⟩ ⟨the whole *range* of Greek political life —G.L.Dickinson⟩ GAMUT suggests a graduated series running from one possible extreme to another ⟨types of light each occupying its particular place in that far-reaching roster or *gamut* which is called the spectrum —K.K.Darrow⟩ REACH suggests an extent of perception, knowledge, ability, or activity attained to or experienced by or as if by stretching out ⟨moving step by step toward the widest generalizations within his *reach* —L.J.Henderson⟩ ⟨out of *reach* of the first invading forces⟩ ⟨anything like sustained reasoning was beyond his *reach* —Leslie Stephen⟩ RADIUS suggests an area, usu. circular, of activity, implied by a known or determined center ⟨the town's history has been the history of coal; within a *radius* of five miles are twelve large mines —*Amer. Guide Series: Pa.*⟩ COMPASS indicates an extent, sometimes more limited than that suggested by RANGE, of perception, knowledge, or activity; it is likely to connote a bounding circumference ⟨the powers expressly granted to the government . . . are to be contracted . . . into the narrowest possible *compass* —John Marshall⟩ ⟨here we get in very small *compass* . . . as many different reminders of the continuity of the country . . . as you will find anywhere —S.P.B.Mais⟩ SWEEP suggests extent, often circular or arc-shaped, of motion or activity, which latter notion it more strongly suggests than the preceding terms ⟨the boldness and *sweep* of Webster's original scheme appear plainly —Kemp Malone⟩ ⟨in the *sweep* of their universal robbery, they showed at least no discrimination between native and foreign victims —Osbert Sitwell⟩ SCOPE is applicable to an area of activity, an area predetermined and limited, but an area of free choice within the set limits ⟨its *scope* was widened by the legislature to include other departments —*Amer. Guide Series: Texas*⟩ ⟨the infinite *scope* for personal initiative in business —G.B.Shaw⟩ ORBIT suggests a range of activity or influence, often circumscribed and bounded, within which forces work toward accustoming, integrating, absorbing ⟨communities . . . outside the *orbit* of modernity —Walter Lippmann⟩ ⟨the war as a gigantic cosmic drama, embracing every quarter of the globe and the whole *orbit* of man's life —John Buchan⟩ HORIZON suggests an area, perhaps arc-shaped or semicircular, of knowledge, interest, perception; it may suggest the new or the potential or envisioned ⟨science has provided a new frontier with unlimited *horizons* —A.H.Compton⟩ ⟨possibilities he hadn't known were upon its *horizon* —Mary Austin⟩ KEN indicates range of perception or cognizance ⟨they seemed trivial at the time they came into his *ken* —W.A.White⟩ ⟨the bulk of his known reading, until the great Italians swam into his *ken*, was French —J.L.Lowes⟩ PURVIEW may indicate either range of perception or knowledge or range of authority or competence ⟨the inclusion of dependent areas within the *purview* of Point Four —Rupert Emerson⟩ ⟨the problem of ethnic variation falls very definitely within the *purview* of the student of the social life of man —M.F.A.Montagu⟩
²range \"\ *vb* -ED/-ING/-S [ME *raungen, rangen*, fr. MF *ranger* to set in a row, place, station, fr. OF *rengier*, fr. *renc, reng* line, place, row — more at RANK] *vt* **1 a :** to set in a row **:** place in a regular line **:** dispose in the proper order ⟨half a dozen straight-backed chairs are *ranged* in front of the desk —Philip Hamburger⟩ ⟨the women, *ranged* along the north side, wore their usual dress —Oliver LaFarge⟩ **b :** to place among others in a given position or situation ⟨*ranged* himself with the reform movement —Charles Moore⟩ ⟨came and *ranged* yourself beside me —T.B.Costain⟩ **2 a :** to rove over or through **:** ROAM ⟨took his fine new rifle and *ranged* the woods —S.H.Holbrook⟩ **b :** to cause to pass over ⟨*ranged* his eyes over the scene before him⟩ **3 :** to dispose in a classified or systematic order **:** place in a class, rank, or category ⟨~ plants in genera⟩ **4 :** to sail or pass along or about usu. in a direction parallel to or near ⟨had been out the night before, *ranging* the enemy coast —Irwin Shaw⟩ **5 :** to arrange (an anchor cable) on deck **6** *chiefly Brit* **:** ALIGN; *specif* **:** to place (a line of type) so that one end is flush with the end of a preceding or following line **7 :** to graze or pasture (livestock) on or as if on a range ⟨on the uplands thousands of head of cattle are *ranged* each year —*Spokane (Wash.) Spokesman-Rev.*⟩ **8 :** to determine the elevation necessary for (a gun) to propel a projectile to a given distance **:** give (a gun) such elevation ~ *vi* **1 a** (1) **:** to roam here and there **:** rove at large ⟨the custom . . . to ~ through the town on the last night of carnival —P.L.Fermor⟩ ⟨*ranged* like a grey moose . . . guiding himself by the sun —Van Wyck Brooks⟩ ⟨*ranging* around remote parts of England —Max Beerbohm⟩ (2) **:** to move out or about freely **:** survey esp. with the mind ⟨has *ranged* among the masterpieces of past and present art —William Barrett⟩ ⟨talk *ranged* widely, even in aesthetics —H.S.Canby⟩ ⟨likes to ~ over current issues —*Newsweek*⟩ **b :** to move over an area so as to explore it more or less thoroughly ⟨*ranging* about in search of some promising spot upon which to pitch the . . . tent —F.V.W. Mason⟩ ⟨the beagle will not ~ too far afield of the hunter —*Time*⟩ **2 :** to take a position ⟨*ranged* with the great pillars and supporters of our art —Joshua Reynolds⟩ **3** *archaic* **:** to be fickle or inconstant ⟨given to ~ —Lord Byron⟩ **4 a :** to correspond in direction or line **b** *chiefly Brit* **:** ALIGN ⟨these two type faces, although of the same size, do not ~ well⟩ **c :** to have or extend in a particular direction **:** run in a line ⟨the fence ~s with the street⟩ **5 a :** to have a range **:** be capable of projecting or to admit of being projected ⟨the gun ~s over three miles⟩ ⟨the shot *ranged* along a four mile course⟩ **b :** to obtain the range of an object by firing alternately over and short of it altering the elevation after each shot until a hit is made **6 :** to change or differ within limits ⟨its products ~ from carpet tacks to pig iron —*Amer. Guide Series: N. Y.*⟩ ⟨discounts ~ from 20% to 40% —Nathan Kelne⟩ **7** *of an organism* **:** to live or occur in or be native to an indicated district or region ⟨the hardy ring-necked pheasant . . . ~s over all but the most northern areas —*Amer. Guide Series: Minn.*⟩ **8 :** to obtain the range of an object by means of a range finder
range angle *n* **:** the angle formed between a vertical line and the line of sight to an aiming point at the instant of release of an aerial bomb — called also *dropping angle, sighting angle*
range bracket *n* **:** BRACKET 5a(1)
range-bred \'‹;‹\ *adj* **:** bred and reared on the range **:** accustomed to the open country
range crane fly *n* **:** a grayish brown crane fly (*Tipula simplex*) with a wingless female and a pale brown burrowing larva that emerges from the ground at night or on dull days to feed on green vegetation and is sometimes very destructive to grasslands and grain crops in the southwestern U. S.
ranged *adj* [fr. past part. of ²*range*] **:** arranged in line, in ranks, or according to a system ⟨a kitchen gleaming with ~ coppers —Anne D. Sedgwick⟩ ⟨the hierarchically ~ members of the staff —Lyman Bryson⟩
ranged rubble *n* **:** masonry in which the quarry stones are roughly dressed to an almost uniform height
range finder *n* **1 :** an instrument used to determine the distance of an object and usu. constructed to give a rapid mechanical solution of a triangle having the target at its apex and the range finder at one corner of its base **2 :** TACHYMETER **3 :** a camera attachment for measuring by optical means the distance between the camera and an object
range-finding \'‹,‹‹\ *n* **1 :** the determination of the range to a target by adjusting fire on it **2 :** the determination of a range by means of a range finder at which to start adjustment on a target
rangeland \'‹,‹\ *n* **:** land used or suitable for range ⟨scrub-covered ~s⟩
range·ley lake trout \'rānjlē-\ *n, usu cap R* [fr. *Rangeley lakes*, chain of lakes in western Maine] **:** OQUASSA

range light *n* **1 :** either of two or more lights on shore placed to guide a ship by keeping it in line (as through a channel) **2 a range lights** *pl* **:** two white lights in the same vertical plane as the keel with one at least fifteen feet higher than and horizontally distant from the other that may be carried by a steamer under way to indicate her course **b :** the after of these two lights
range masonry *n* **:** RANGEWORK
range of accommodation : the range through which accommodation is able so to adjust the optical system of the eye that an image falls in sharp focus on the retina **:** the distance between the near point and the far point of the eye
range officer *n* **:** one who is in charge of a firearms range and of firing on the range
range oil *n* **:** a high-boiling petroleum distillate for burning in the wick of an oil-burning kitchen range; *esp* **:** the least volatile portion of the kerosine fraction
range paralysis *n* **:** NEUROLYMPHOMATOSIS
range pole *also* **ranging pole** *n* **:** a straight pole or rod sometimes jointed, usu. painted in one-foot bands of alternate colors of red and white, and used for sighting points and lines in surveying — called also *flagpole*
rang·er \ˈrānjə(r)\ *n* -s [ME *raunger*, fr. *raungen, rangen* to range + *-er* — more at RANGE] **1 a :** the keeper of a British royal park or forest; *esp* **:** a royal officer formerly appointed to walk through the forest, recover beasts that had strayed, watch the deer, and prevent trespasses **b :** FOREST RANGER **2** *archaic* **:** one who wanders **:** ROVER **3 :** an animal that ranges: as **a :** a dog that covers the course fully in search of game **b :** HARBOR SEAL **c :** a meat animal marketed directly from the range without being fattened on grain **4 a :** one usu. of a body of troops or organized armed men who range over a region for its protection **b :** an officer of a county who is responsible for taking charge of and protecting an area against stray animals **c :** a soldier specially trained in close-range fighting and raiding tactics — compare COMMANDO **5 :** a senior member of the Girl Guide movement in Britain, Canada, and various other countries — compare SENIOR GIRL SCOUT
range rake *n* **:** a device that is used in harbor-defense gunnery for determining the range deviations of shots from a target and that consists essentially of two arms in the form of a T along whose cross member pegs are placed at regular intervals
rang·er·ship \-(r),ship\ *n* **:** the position of ranger of a park or forest
ranges *pl of* RANGE, *pres 3d sing of* RANGE
range shelter *n* **:** a small open usu. movable shelter for growing fowls on range
range table *n* **:** a large table made up of a set of identical small tables placed side by side
rang·ette \(ˈ)rān¦jet\ *n* -s [¹*range* + *-ette*] **:** a portable cooking apparatus consisting of a top with one or more burners for gas or electricity but having no oven; *also* **:** a very small range with an oven

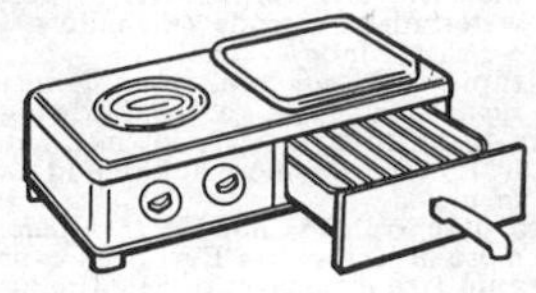
rangette (electric)

rangework \ˈ=,=\ *n* **:** ashlar laid in horizontal courses of even height **:** COURSED ASHLAR — called also *range masonry;* compare BROKEN ASHLAR
ran·gi·fer \ˈranjəfə(r)\ *n, cap* [NL, fr. ML, reindeer, prob. modif. of MF *rangier*, fr. ON *hreindýri* — more at REINDEER] **:** a genus consisting of the domestic and wild reindeer and caribous
ran·gif·er·ine \ranˈjifə,rīn\ *adj* [NL *Rangifer* + E *-ine*] **:** of or relating to the genus *Rangifer*
rang·i·ness \ˈrānjēnə̇s\ *n* -ES **:** the quality or state of being rangy ⟨the dark blue jacket . . . was much too skimpy for a man of his ~ —Alan Masters⟩ ⟨a ~, a freewheeling robustness, an engaging lustiness of style and expression here —V.P.Hass⟩
ranging *pres part of* RANGE
ranging bond *n* **:** a chain bond formed by strips of wood projecting slightly from the face to provide a nailing surface
ran·gi·o·ra \,raŋgēˈōrə\ *n* -s [Maori] **:** a New Zealand shrub or small tree (*Brachyglottis repanda*) of the family Compositae having stout branches and lower leaf surfaces densely covered with white tomentum and small heads of flowers crowded in terminal clusters
rang·khol \rǎŋˈkōl\ *n* -s *usu cap* **:** one of a Kuki people of eastern Assam
ran·gle \ˈraŋgəl\ *n* -s [origin unknown] **:** bits of gravel fed to hawks
¹ran·goon \(ˈ)ran¦gün, -aŋ¦-\ *adj, usu cap* [fr. *Rangoon*, Burma] **:** of or from Rangoon, the capital of Burma **:** of the kind or style prevalent in Rangoon
²rangoon \"\ *n* -s *often cap* **:** SHERRY 2
rangoon creeper *n, usu cap R* **:** a woody vine (*Quisqualis indica*) that is native to Burma, Malaysia, and the Pacific islands and that is grown in tropical regions for its showy flowers
rang·pur \ˈraŋ,pu̇(ə)r, =ˈ=\ *or* **rangpur lime** *n* -s [fr. *Rangpur*, town and region in East Bengal, Pakistan] **:** any of various mandarin oranges with sour highly acid fruits
rangy *also* **rangey** \ˈrānjē, -ji\ *adj, sometimes* **rangier;** *sometimes* **rangiest** [¹*range* & ²*range* + *-y*] **1 :** having room for ranging **:** OPEN, SPACIOUS ⟨our vast, unpeopled, ~ country —E.A.Weeks⟩ **2 :** having ranges **:** MOUNTAINOUS **3 :** inclined, able, or apt to range or rove about often for considerable distances **4** *of an animal* **a :** of large proportions **:** being long-limbed and long-bodied ⟨big ~ cattle, strong enough to climb over the hills to market —Russell Lord⟩ **b :** giving an appearance of slenderness ⟨a horse to be fast must be long and ~ —C.W.Gay⟩ — compare COBBY, CHUFFY **5** *of a person* **:** being long-legged and slender ⟨~ kilted soldiers stalking along the streets —A.W.Long⟩ **6 :** having great range or scope ⟨these ~ considerations rise immediately out of reading —Richard Sullivan⟩
ra·ni *or* **ra·nee** \(ˈ)räˈnē\ *n* -s [Hindi *rānī*, fr. Skt *rājñī*, fem. of *rājan* king — more at ROYAL] **:** a Hindu queen **:** a rajah's wife **:** a reigning Indian princess
rani- *comb form* [L *rana* — more at RANA] **:** frog ⟨*raniform*⟩
¹ran·id \ˈranə̇d\ *adj* [NL *Ranidae*] **:** of or relating to the Ranidae
²ranid \"\ *n* -s **:** a frog of the family Ranidae
ran·i·dae \ˈranə,dē\ *n pl, cap* [NL, fr. *Rana*, type genus + *-idae*] **:** a large family of frogs (suborder Diplasiocoela) distinguished by slightly dilated transverse sacral processes and comprising the typical frogs — see RANA
ra·ni·khet disease \ˈränə,ket-\ *n, usu cap R* [fr. *Ranikhet*, town in northern India] **:** NEWCASTLE DISEASE
ra·ni·na \rəˈnīnə\ *n, cap* [NL, fr. L *rana* frog + NL *-ina* — more at RANA] **:** the type genus of Raninidae comprising typical frog crabs — **ra·nin·i·an** \-ˈninēən\ *adj or n*
ra·nine \ˈrā,nīn\ *adj* [L *rana* frog + E *-ine*] **1 :** of or relating to frogs **2 :** of or relating to the region beneath the tip of the tongue; *specif* **:** constituting the branch of the lingual artery supplying this region or the corresponding vein which is a tributary of the facial vein
ranine artery *n* **:** the terminal part of the lingual artery supplying the tip of the tongue
ra·nin·i·dae \rəˈninə,dē\ *n pl, cap* [NL, fr. *Ranina*, type genus + *-idae*] **:** a family of atypical elongated crabs (tribe Brachyura) that have existed since at least Cretaceous time and comprise the frog crabs
¹rank \ˈraŋk, ˈraiŋk\ *adj, often* -ER/-EST [ME, fr. OE *ranc* overbearing, strong, brave, mature, ostentatious; akin to MD & MLG *ranc* tall and thin, slender, ON *rakkr* straight, slender, bold, OE *riht* right — more at RIGHT] **1** *chiefly dial* **a :** STRONG, MIGHTY, POWERFUL **b :** HEADLONG, VIOLENT **2 a :** luxuriant or vigorous in growth **:** grown to immoderate height **:** grown coarse ⟨~ weeds⟩ ⟨seven ears of corn came up upon one stalk, ~ and good —Gen 41:5 (AV)⟩ ⟨among the forms of ~ plant life common in the hot humidity . . . were great tree ferns —R.W.Murray⟩ **b :** covered with a vigorous growth esp. of vegetation **:** producing luxuriantly **:** excessively rich and fertile ⟨its garden was . . . ~, too thickly crowded with trees and bushes and plants —Rebecca West⟩ **3 :** offensively gross or coarse **:** INDECENT, FOUL ⟨objected to his ~ language⟩ **4** *obs* **:** grown too large **:** GROSS, SWOLLEN **5** *chiefly dial* **a :** crowded together **b :** NUMEROUS **6 a :** conspicuously or shockingly poor, stupid, or wrong ⟨must lecture him on his ~ disloyalty —David Walden⟩ **b :** COMPLETE — used as an intensive ⟨that is . . . the opinion of a ~ outsider —G.W.Johnson⟩ ⟨most of the actors were not big names, but ~ beginners —Dean Jennings⟩ **7** *archaic* **a :** filled with lust **b :** RUTTISH ⟨the ewes, being ~, in the end of autumn turned to the rams —Shak.⟩ **8 :** offending with or as if with a strong rancid odor or taste **:** having a heavy offensive smell ⟨wreathed in smoke from a ~ cigar —Ralph Watson⟩ ⟨the heat seemed to purify the ~ air —Willa Cather⟩ **9 :** marked by putridity **:** CORRUPT, FESTERING ⟨the ~ wounds of the dying men⟩ **10 :** unreasonably high in amount **:** EXCESSIVE ⟨a ~ modus⟩ ⟨a ~ rate of interest⟩ **11 :** projecting to an unusual extent beyond a surface **syn** see FLAGRANT

RANKS OF THE UNITED STATES ARMED FORCES

ARMY	MARINES	NAVY	AIR FORCE	COAST GUARD
general of the army		fleet admiral	general of the air force	
general	general	admiral	general	admiral *or* commandant
lieutenant general	lieutenant general	vice admiral	lieutenant general	vice admiral
major general	major general	rear admiral	major general	rear admiral
brigadier general	brigadier general	commodore	brigadier general	commodore
colonel	colonel	captain	colonel	captain
lieutenant colonel	lieutenant colonel	commander	lieutenant colonel	commander
major	major	lieutenant commander	major	lieutenant commander
captain	captain	lieutenant	captain	lieutenant
first lieutenant	first lieutenant	lieutenant, j.g.	first lieutenant	lieutenant, j.g.
second lieutenant	second lieutenant	ensign	second lieutenant	ensign
chief warrant officer, W-4	chief warrant officer, W-4	chief warrant officer, W-4	chief warrant officer, W-4	chief warrant officer, W-4
chief warrant officer, W-3	chief warrant officer, W-3	warrant officer, W-3	chief warrant officer, W-3	warrant officer, W-3
chief warrant officer, W-2	chief warrant officer, W-2	warrant officer, W-2	chief warrant officer, W-2	warrant officer, W-2
warrant officer, W-1	warrant officer, W-1	warrant officer, W-1	warrant officer, W-1	warrant officer, W-1
sergeant major of the army	sergeant major of the marine corps	master chief petty officer of the navy	chief master sergeant of the air force	master chief petty officer of the coast guard
command sergeant major	sergeant major *or* master gunnery sergeant	master chief petty officer	chief master sergeant	master chief petty officer
first sergeant *or* master sergeant	first sergeant *or* master sergeant	senior chief petty officer	senior master sergeant	senior chief petty officer
platoon sergeant *or* sergeant first class *or* specialist 7	gunnery sergeant	chief petty officer	master sergeant	chief petty officer
staff sergeant *or* specialist 6	staff sergeant	petty officer first class	technical sergeant	petty officer first class
sergeant *or* specialist 5	sergeant	petty officer second class	staff sergeant	petty officer second class
corporal *or* specialist 4	corporal	petty officer third class	sergeant	petty officer third class
private first class	lance corporal	seaman	airman first class	seaman
private, E-2	private first class	seaman apprentice	airman	seaman apprentice
private, E-1	private	seaman recruit	airman basic	seaman recruit

²rank \"\ *adv* **:** RANKLY
³rank \"\ *n* -s [MF *renc, ranc, reng, rang* line, place, row, rank, of Gmc origin; akin to OHG *hring* ring, circle, circle of warriors, meeting — more at RING] **1 a :** a straight row or line **:** RANGE, SERIES ⟨a ~ of marble pillars —Sax Rohmer⟩ ⟨~s of parcel lockers —Lewis Mumford⟩ ⟨great pines, whose ~s climbed to the mountaintops —Agnes M. Cleaveland⟩ **b :** a series or set of organ pipes of the same construction and quality having one pipe for each digital **c** *Brit* **:** STAND 6 ⟨a taxi at the ~ just at the end of the street —Katherine Mansfield⟩ **2 :** a row of people ⟨the men and women . . . were standing in two separate ~s —Ivor Jones⟩ **3 :** an orderly arrangement **:** ARRAY, FORMATION ⟨the company break ~s —Lafcadio Hearn⟩ **4 a :** a line of soldiers ranged side by side in close order ⟨armored ~s of men-at-arms —John Reed⟩ — compare FILE **b ranks** *pl* **:** ARMED FORCES **:** ARMY **c ranks** *pl* **:** the body of enlisted men ⟨he rose from the ~s⟩ **5 :** an aggregate of individuals classed together **:** a division of the social order — usu. used in pl. ⟨excluded from the ~s of organized labor —Oscar Handlin⟩ ⟨would consider any opportunity . . . provided it is in your executive ~s —*Phoenix Flame*⟩ ⟨keep the ~s of fire fighters thin —Richard Ginder⟩ **6 :** a row of squares extending horizontally across a chessboard ⟨each player's pieces are placed on his first ~ and his pawns on his second ~⟩ **7 a :** a position or order in relation to others in a group **:** relative standing ⟨occupied a particularly high ~ among the dramas —Matthew Arnold⟩ ⟨declining to consider him a novelist of the first ~ —Granville Hicks⟩ **b :** a degree or position of dignity, eminence, or excellence **:** DISTINCTION ⟨soon took ~ as a leading attorney —J.D.Hicks⟩ **c :** high social position or standing ⟨many of the institutions . . . maintained and emphasized the privileges of ~ —Abram Kardiner⟩ ⟨his distinction lay in office, not in ~ —John Buchan⟩ **d :** a faculty position usu. in an institution of higher learning ⟨visiting lecturer in psychology . . . with ~ of full professor —W.H.Hale⟩ **8 :** a grade of official standing: as **a :** a grade in the armed forces **b :** a title of nobility **c :** a diplomatic or high government position ⟨appointed with the ~ of ambassador⟩ ⟨office of cabinet ~⟩ **9 a :** the standing of words in their mutual relations as qualified and qualifying terms **b :** the functioning of a word, word group, or clause as substantive, adjective, or adverb **10 :** the order according to some statistical characteristic **11 :** one of the classes or varieties of coal arranged in a series extending from lignite through bituminous to anthracite that indicates its thermal properties
⁴rank \"\ *vb* -ED/-ING/-s *vt* **1 :** to arrange usu. in lines **:** draw up in a regular formation ⟨gazed lazily out a window above the ~ed heads —William Faulkner⟩ ⟨the battalion, perfectly ~ed, listened to the citation⟩ **2 :** to arrange in a row or pattern **:** place in order ⟨the hills ~ed with apple trees —John Dos Passos⟩ ⟨the ranch and chuck wagons were ~ed out of the weather —Luke Short⟩ ⟨carefully ~ed the little figurines along the mantlepiece⟩ **3 :** to determine the relative position or merit of **:** CLASSIFY, IDENTIFY, RATE ⟨seldom given to ~ing the concerns of others as high as his own —M.C.Bauer⟩ ⟨were asked to ~ the instructor —W.C.Allee⟩ ⟨a population of 205,000 ~s the city third —Howell Walker⟩ **4 :** to place properly or in order of priority among the claimants upon a bankrupt estate according to Scots law **5 :** to take precedence of **:** OUTRANK ⟨the chairman ~s all other officers —A.J.Liebling⟩ ⟨did not know who ~ed whom in the new . . . setup —*Newsweek*⟩ **6** *Scot* **:** to get ready — usu. used with *out* ~ *vi* **1 :** to form or move in ranks **:** take a place in a rank **2 :** to become ranged in order or graded esp. according to rank or merit **:** have a place or grade in an ascending series ⟨English ~s as the most important and essential subject in the curriculum of our public schools —*Education Digest*⟩ ⟨the artisan . . . ~s no doubt lower than the professional man —G.L.Dickinson⟩ ⟨the profession of religion . . . ~s above all the other professions —Virginia Woolf⟩ **3 :** to have a place among the list of claims or claimants upon a bankrupt estate **4 :** to have the highest rank **:** be senior **:** be supremely eminent ⟨ordered by the ~ing head of the provincial government —Marjory S. Douglas⟩
rank and file *n* **1 :** the enlisted men of an armed force (as privates and corporals) whose normal position is in the ranks of a formation ⟨most of their *rank and file* . . . had heavy shields bound with iron and a long cutting sword —Tom Wintringham⟩ **2 a :** the individuals who constitute the body of an organization, society, or nation ⟨the *rank and file* was made up of brawling adventure lovers —Julian Dana⟩ ⟨the inner circle of leaders had forced the program, rather than the *rank and file* —F.L.Paxson⟩ ⟨bring the government . . . into more intimate relations with the *rank and file* —F.A.Ogg & Harold Zink⟩ **b :** the general membership of a union ⟨when irresponsible labor leaders . . . entice away the *rank and file* from the responsible leaders —A.M.Schlesinger b.1917⟩
rank-and-filer \ˈ==ˈfilə(r)\ *n* [*rank and file* + *-er*] **:** one that belongs to the rank and file ⟨still basically a *rank-and-filer* —C.Y.Harrison⟩
rank badge *n* **:** one of the Girl Scout badges designating rank (as for first class, second class)
rank correlation *n* **:** a measure of correlation depending on rank
rank-difference coefficient of correlation : the correlation coefficient applied to the rank numbers of two sets of variables

rank badge, second class

¹ranker *comparative of* RANK
²rank·er \ˈraŋkə(r)\ *n* -s [in sense 1, fr. ⁴*rank* + *-er;* in sense 2, fr. ³*rank* + *-er*] **1 :** one that ranks or draws up in line **2 :** one who serves in the ranks of the armed forces; *esp* **:** a commissioned officer promoted from the ranks
rankest *superlative of* RANK
ran·ket \ˈraŋkə̇t\ *n* -s [G *rackett, rankett*] **1 :** RACKETT **2 :** a reed organ pipe of 16-foot or 8-foot pitch producing a smothered tone
rank indigo *n* **:** indigo derived from the leaves of an East Indian woody vine (*Marsdenia tinctoria*)
ran·kine \ˈraŋkə̇n\ *adj, usu cap* [after William J. M. *Rankine* †1872 Scot. engineer and physicist] **:** being, according to, or relating to an absolute-temperature scale on which the unit of measurement equals a Fahrenheit degree and according to which the freezing point of water is 491.67° and the boiling point 671.67°
rankine cycle *n, usu cap R* **:** an ideal reversible heat-engine cycle approximated by the operating cycle of an actual steam engine
ranking bar *n* **:** a handbarrow used by lumbermen
ranking jumper *n* **:** an all-wood sled used by lumbermen for hauling tanbark
ranking member *n* **1 :** the congressional member next to the chairman in order of seniority **2 :** the senior in rank or service who becomes chairman of a committee or court-martial
ran·kin·ite \ˈraŋkə̇,nīt\ *n* -s [George A. *Rankin* †1963 Am. chemist + E *-ite*] **:** a mineral $Ca_3Si_2O_7$ consisting of a rare calcium silicate
¹ran·kle \ˈraŋkəl, ˈraiŋ-\ *vb* **rankled; rankled; rankling** \-k(ə)liŋ\ **rankles** [ME *ranclen*, fr. MF *rancler*, fr. OF *draoncler, raoncler, rancler*, fr. *draoncle, drancle, raoncle, rancle* festering sore, fr. ML *dracunculus*, fr. L, small serpent, dim. of *draco* serpent, dragon — more at DRAGON] *vi* **1 a :** to become inflamed or infected **:** FESTER **b** *obs* **:** to inflict a painful wound **2 a :** to produce or continue to produce an effect resembling a festering sore ⟨much hatred still ~s —H.L. Matthews⟩ **b :** to continue to cause anger, irritation, or bitter often malignant feelings ⟨this escapade *rankled* longer in his mind —Leonard Bacon⟩ ⟨has long *rankled* as an act of injustice —Clement Attlee⟩ **3 :** to become inflamed with anger **:** chafe in vexation ⟨the prophets . . . who ~ under defeat —J.G.Fletcher⟩ ~ *vt* **1 :** to cause to fester **2 :** to cause irritation or bitter feelings in **:** make angry **:** INFLAME ⟨paying . . . above the market price which *rankled* him —J.H.Wheelwright⟩
²rankle \"\ *n* -s **:** an emotion that rankles
rankling *adj* **:** festering within the mind **:** producing angry often malignant feelings **:** insidiously irritating or annoying ⟨a ~ word —R.M.Coates⟩ ⟨dull ~ anger —Rudyard Kipling⟩ ⟨a ~ sentiment of injustice —A.L.Guérard⟩ — **rank·ling·ly** *adv*
rank·ly *adv* [ME, fr. OE *ranclīce* boldly, ostentatiously, fr. *ranc* overbearing, strong, brave + *-līce* -ly — more at RANK] **:** in a rank manner
rank·ness *n* -ES [ME *ranknesse*, fr. *rank* + *-nesse* -ness] **:** the quality or state of being rank
rank of a determinant : the rank of the matrix of the determinant
rank of a matrix : the order of the nonzero determinant of highest order that may be formed from the elements of a matrix by selecting arbitrarily an equal number of rows and columns from it
rank order *n* **:** arrangement according to rank
ranks *pl of* RANK, *pres 3d sing of* RANK
rann \ˈran\ *n* -s [IrGael] *Irish* **:** a stanza esp. of a song ⟨known . . . for his stinging ~s —Padraic Colum⟩
ran·nel tree \ˈranᵊl-\ *or* **rannel bean** *n* [*rannel* prob. of Scand origin; akin to Norw dial. *randatre* rannel tree, fr. *rand* edge, space above a fireplace (fr. ON *rand-, rönd* rim, shield) — more at RAND] *dial Brit* **:** a bar to support pothooks over an open fireplace
¹ran·ny \ˈranī\ *n* -ES [prob. modif. of L *araneus* (*mus*), fr. *araneus* of a spider (fr. *aranea* spider) + *mus* mouse — more at ARACHN-] *dial Eng* **:** SHREW 1
²ran·ny \ˈranē\ *n* -ES [origin unknown] **:** a poor quality calf of mongrel breeding
rans *pl of* RAN
¹ran·sack \ˈran¦sak, ˈraan-\ *vt* -ED/-ING/-s [ME *ransaken*, fr. ON *rannsaka*, fr. *rann* house + *-saka* (akin to ON *sækja* to seek) — more at REST, SEEK] **1 :** to look very thoroughly and zealously through **:** search often forcefully or roughly **:** RUMMAGE ⟨~ed the kitchen for candles —Dorothy Sayers⟩ **2 :** to subject to close investigation or study **:** examine critically and carefully ⟨with the true persistence of a scholar has ~ed all the authorities —T.G.Bergin⟩ ⟨~ed literature and the dictionary for the unusual word —J.G.Southworth⟩ **3 :** to remove wealth or valuables from **:** PLUNDER ⟨~ed the premises⟩ **syn** see SEEK
²ransack \"\ *n* -s *archaic* **:** the act of ransacking
ran·sack·er \-kə(r)\ *n* -s **:** one that ransacks
ran·sack·le \ˈran,sakəl\ *vt* -ED/-ING/-s [freq. of *ransack*] *archaic* **:** RANSACK
ransel *var of* RANCEL
¹ran·som \ˈran(t)səm, ˈraan-, ˈrain-\ *n* -s [ME *raunsoun, ransoun*, fr. OF *reançon, rançon*, fr. L *redemption-, redemptio* redemption, ransom — more at REDEMPTION] **1 :** the money, price, or consideration paid or demanded for the redemption

of a captured person : a payment that releases from captivity **2** : the act of ransoming : the redeeming or releasing of a captive by a payment esp. of money **3** : something paid in medieval times for the pardon of an offense in lieu of corporal punishment : FINE

²ransom \"\ *vt* -ED/-ING/-S [ME *raunsounen, ransounen,* fr. OF *reançonner, rançonner,* fr. *reançon, rançon,* n.] **1** : to deliver esp. from sin or its penalty ⟨He lives, triumphant o'er the grave, . . . my ~*ed* soul to keep and save —Charles Wesley⟩ **2** *archaic* : to atone for : EXPIATE **3** : to redeem usu. from captivity, slavery, or punishment by paying a price : buy out of bondage ⟨an escaped slave . . . he was ~*ed* by two Englishwomen —*Amer. Guide Series: Md.*⟩ **4** : to exact a ransom for or from : hold or offer for ransom : oppress by exacting ransoms or fines **syn** see RESCUE

ran·som·able \-məbəl\ *adj* : capable of being ransomed ⟨during the Crusades . . . the search for ~ prisoners became so intense —*N.Y.Times*⟩

ransom bill *also* **ransom bond** *n* : a contract valid by the law of nations given in time of war for the ransom of property esp. when captured at sea and a safe-conduct for it to a friendly destination

ran·som·er \-mə(r)\ *n* -s : one that ransoms or redeems; *specif* : a hostage for the ransom of a captured vessel under a ransom bill

ran·som·ite \ˈran(t)sə,mīt\ *n* -s [Frederick L. *Ransome* †1935 Am. mining geologist + E *-ite*] : a mineral $Cu(Fe,Al)_2(SO_4)_4.7H_2O$ consisting of hydrous sulfate of copper, iron, and aluminum

ran·som·less \ˈran(t)səmləs\ *adj* : free from or lacking ransom

ransom theory *n* : a patristic theory of the atonement: on the cross Christ gave his finite soul as a ransom to the devil for the souls of sinful humanity over which he had acquired rights by the fall; hell could not hold a soul without sin; and in the resurrection divine love triumphed once and for all over sin and death — compare SATISFACTION THEORY

ran·stead \ˈran,sted\ *or* **ram·stead** \-am,-\ *n* -s [prob. after *Ranstead,* 18th cent. American born in Wales] : an erect perennial Old World toadflax (*Linaria vulgaris*) that bears racemes of pale yellow to citron yellow flowers with coppery markings and is naturalized in No. America where it is sometimes a troublesome weed

¹rant \ˈrant, -aa(ə)nt,-aint\ *vb* -ED/-ING/-S [obs. D *ranten, randen*] *vi* **1** *archaic* : to have a noisy good time with dancing, singing, and drinking : CAROUSE, REVEL **2** : to talk noisily, excitedly, often extravagantly : declaim in bombastic fashion ⟨~ and rave in loud voices —Priscilla Hughes⟩ **3** : to scold vehemently : be in a rage : RAIL ⟨~*ed* at the boy who paid no attention⟩ ~ *vt* : to speak in an extravagant grandiose fashion : declaim noisily ⟨the actor who ~*s* Shakespeare —H.E. Clurman⟩

²rant \"\ *n* -s **1 a** : ostentatious speech or utterance : discourse that is often wildly excessive and unrestrained ⟨going to yell out the customary ~ which he kept for big occasions —Bruce Marshall⟩ ⟨the depth of feeling without ~ —Walter Hampden⟩ **b** : extravagant often flowery language or sentiment usu. empty of meaning ⟨sometimes mere ~, the book has genuine depths —Edgar Johnson⟩ **2** *dial Brit* **a** : a rousing good time : SPREE **b** : a gay song or dance tune **3** : the act of ranting : a ranting state **syn** see BOMBAST

ran-tan \ˈran·,tan\ *n* -s [imit.] **1** : a knocking, banging, or pounding noise ⟨no rest for Niagara, but perpetual ~ on those limestone rocks —H.D.Thoreau⟩ **2** : riotous conduct : SPREE

ran·tan·ker·ous \(ˈ)ran·¦taŋk(ə)rəs, -aan·¦taŋ-\ *adj* [by alter.] : CANTANKEROUS

rant·er \ˈrantə(r), -aan-,-ain-\ *n* -s **1** : one that rants; *esp* : a noisy bombastic speaker **2** *usu cap* **a** : a member of a 17th century pantheistic, antinomian, and highly individualistic religious group in England **b** : a member of the Primitive Methodists who seceded from the Wesleyan Methodists as being deficient in fervor and zeal — usu. used in derision and in allusion to the loud tones of their preaching and responses

ranter-go-round \ˈ≈≈(,)≈,≈\ *n* : a round game in which each player is dealt a card face down which in some circumstances he may pass to the player on his left for exchange, the object being to win the pool by showing the lowest card at the table

rant·er·ism \-tə,rizəm\ *n* -s *usu cap* : the practice or tenets of the Ranters

rant·ing·ly *adv* [fr. *ranting,* pres. part. of *rant* + *-ly*] : in a ranting manner

¹rant·i·pole \-tē,pōl -tə,-\ *n* -s [prob. fr. *ranty* + *pole,* alter. of *poll* (head)] : a wild reckless sometimes quarrelsome person

²rantipole \"\ *adj* : characterized by a wild unruly manner or attitude : RAKISH ⟨~ laughter —J.B.Cabell⟩

³rantipole \"\ *vi* -ED/-ING/-S : to act like a rantipole

rant·ism \-n·,tizəm\ *n* -s *usu cap, obs* : RANTERISM

ran·tree \ˈrän·(,)trē\ *Scot var of* ROWAN TREE

ran·tum-scan·tum \¦rantəm¦skantəm\ *adj* [irreg. fr. ¹*rant*] : CARELESS, DISORDERLY

ranty \ˈranti\ *adj* [¹*rant* + *-y*] *dial Brit* : EXCITED, RIOTOUS

ran·u·la \ˈranyələ\ *n* -s [NL, fr. L, little frog, little swelling on the tongue of cattle, dim. of *rana* frog — more at RANA] : a cyst formed under the tongue by obstruction of the duct of a sublingual or submaxillary gland or any mucous gland

ra·nun·cu·la·ce·ae \rə,nəŋkyəˈlāsē,ē\ *n pl, cap* [NL, fr. *Ranunculus,* type genus + *-aceae*] : a large family of plants (order Ranales) distinguished by colorless acrid juice, usu. alternate leaves, and regular or irregular polypetalous or apetalous flowers with hypogynous stamens — see RANUNCULUS

ra·nun·cu·la·ceous \≈¦≈≈¦lāshəs\ *adj* [NL *Ranunculaceae* + E *-ous*] : of or relating to the Ranunculaceae

ra·nun·cu·la·les \≈,≈≈ˈlā(,)lēz\ [NL, fr. *Ranunculus* + *-ales*] *syn of* RANALES

ra·nun·cu·lus \≈ˈ≈≈ləs\ *n* [NL, fr. L, any of several species of Ranunculus, lit., small frog, dim. of *rana* frog] **1** *cap* : a large and widely distributed genus (the type of the family Ranunculaceae) of herbs that have simple or variously lobed leaves and mostly yellow flowers with five deciduous sepals and five nectariferous petals followed by numerous flattened achenes borne in a head or spike — see BUTTERCUP **2** *pl* **ranunculus·es** \-ləsəz\ *or* **ranuncu·li** \-,lī\ : any plant of the genus *Ranunculus*

ran·vier's node \(ˈ)ränⁿvyāz-\ *n, usu cap R* : NODE OF RANVIER

ran·za·nia \ranˈzānēə, -nyə\ *n, cap* [NL, fr. C. A. *Ranzani* †1841 Ital. naturalist + NL *-ia*] : a genus of marine sunfishes (family Molidae) with slightly elongated bodies

ranz des vaches \räⁿ(s)dāväsh\ *n* [F dial. (Switzerland), lit., rows of cows; prob. intended as trans. (influence of G *reihen* rows) of G dial. (Switzerland) *kuhreihen, kuhreigen*] : a melody sung by Swiss herdsmen or played on the alpenhorn to call cattle

ra·ob \ˈrā,äb\ *n* -s *often cap* [*ra*diosonde *ob*servation] : a meteorological observation made by means of a radiosonde

ra·ou·lia \räˈülēə\ *n* [NL, fr. Étienne F. L. *Raoul* †1852 French surgeon + NL *-ia*] **1** *cap* : a genus of large white hoary caespitose cushion plants (family Compositae) that are natives chiefly of New Zealand uplands and have small solitary flower heads resembling those of *Helichrysum* — see SHEEP PLANT **2** -s : any plant of the genus *Raoulia*

ra·oult's law \räˈülz-\ *n, usu cap R* [after François M. *Raoult* †1901 French chemist] : a law in physical chemistry: the fraction by which the vapor pressure of a liquid is lowered when a small amount of a substance that is nonvolatile, not dissociable, and usu. not a high polymer is dissolved in it is equal to the mole fraction of the solute — compare IDEAL SOLUTION

raoult's method *n, usu cap R* [after F. M. *Raoult*] : a method of determining the molecular weight of a dissolved substance by the extent to which it depresses the freezing point of the solvent

RAP *abbr* **1** regimental aid post **2** rupees, annas, pies

¹rap \ˈrap\ *n* -s [ME *rappe,* prob. of imit. origin] **1 a** : a quick sharp blow ⟨got a ~ on the knuckles from the teacher's stick⟩ **b** : a sharp knock ⟨heard a ~ on the door⟩ **2 a** : a sharp rebuke ⟨got a hard ~ from his boss for the blunder⟩ **b** : an adverse criticism ⟨annoyed by her ~*s* at his slowness⟩ **3 a (1)** : the legal responsibility for and consequences of a criminal act ⟨accused of trying to take the ~ for his fellow officers —*Springfield (Mass.) Union*⟩ **(2)** : a criminal charge ⟨in court to face a forgery ~⟩ **(3)** : a prison sentence ⟨sent up for a 30 year ~⟩ **b** : the blame for or adverse consequences of an action ⟨scapegoats . . . who took the ~ and kept their mouths shut —Percy Winner⟩ **4** *slang* : an identification of one charged with a crime

²rap \"\ *vb* **rapped; rapped; rapping; raps** [ME *rappen,* prob. of imit. origin] *vt* **1** : to strike with a quick smart blow ⟨~ struggling rioters with nightsticks⟩ ⟨*rapped* a double off the left-field wall —W.G.Smith⟩ : strike a rap with ⟨~*s* his pipe on the ashtray⟩ **2** : to utter suddenly and forcibly — usu. used with *out* ⟨~*s* out a series of curt commands⟩ **3** *slang* : to swear or testify to esp. falsely **4 a** : to cause to be or come by rapping ⟨~ the occupants awake⟩ ⟨~ the meeting to order⟩ **b** : to communicate (a message) by knocks ⟨says the spirit ~*s* out an answer to the medium's question⟩ **5** : to censure severely : criticize sharply ⟨criticism . . . *rapping* the pretensions of semi-intellectuals —B.R.Redman⟩ **6** *slang* : to arrest, hold, or sentence on a criminal charge ⟨had been . . . *rapped* with one-to-ten years at the state reformatory —Bunque Mooney⟩ ~ *vi* **1** : to strike a person or thing with a quick sharp blow or succession of blows ⟨~*s* on wood for good luck⟩ **2** : to make a short sharp sound or a succession of such sounds ⟨clatter of hoofs *rapped* sharply from the walls —Zane Grey⟩

³rap \"\ *vt* **rapped** *also* **rapt; rapped** *also* **rapt; rapping; raps** [back-formation fr. ¹*rapt*] **1** *obs* : to snatch and steal : GRAB **2 a** : to snatch away : to seize and hurry off **b** : to carry upward (as by supernatural force) ⟨it *rapt* us from red gulphs of war —P.B.Shelley⟩ **3** : to transport out of oneself : affect with ecstasy or rapture — **rap and rend 1** : to seize and steal **2** : to get together by fair means or foul : procure at any cost ⟨make and mend, or *rap and rend,* for me —Robert Browning⟩

⁴rap \"\ *n* -s [perh. fr. ¹*rap*] **1 a** : a counterfeit halfpenny in circulation in Ireland early in the 18th century **b** : a coin of trifling value **2** : the least bit ⟨don't care a ~⟩

ra·pa·cious \rəˈpāshəs\ *adj* [L *rapac-, rapax* rapacious, (fr. *rapere* to seize and carry off, snatch away) + *-ious* — more at RAPID] **1** : excessively grasping or covetous : given to seizing or extorting what is coveted ⟨~ invaders⟩ **2** : subsisting on prey : PREDACIOUS ⟨the ~ wolf⟩ **3** : RAVENOUS ⟨a ~ appetite⟩ **syn** see VORACIOUS

ra·pa·cious·ly *adv* : in a rapacious manner

ra·pa·cious·ness *n* -ES : the quality or state of being rapacious

ra·pac·i·ty \rəˈpasəd·ē, -paas-, -sətē, -i\ *n* -ES [MF *rapacité,* fr. L *rapacitat-, rapacitas,* fr. *rapac-, rapax* rapacious + *-itat-, -itas* -ity — more at RAPACIOUS] **1** : RAPACIOUSNESS **2** : a rapacious act or appetite **syn** see CUPIDITY

ra·pa·ki·vi \¦räpə¦kēvē\ *n* -s [Finn, fr. *rapa* dregs, mud, gravel + *kivi* stone, rock] : a coarse red granite quarried in Finland having curious ovoid ringed feldspars composed of central cores of orthoclase surrounded by a shell of oligoclase and being much used for building in northern Russia

rap·a·nea \,rapəˈnēə\ *n, cap* [NL] : a genus of chiefly tropical trees or shrubs (family Theophrastaceae) having mostly shining leathery leaves and small white flowers with stamens adnate to the corolla lobes

ra·pa·te·a·ce·ae \rə,pād·ēˈāsē,ē\ *n pl, cap* [NL, fr. *Rapatea,* type genus (prob. fr. a native name in Guiana) + *-aceae*] : a family of So. American herbs (order Xyridales) somewhat resembling members of the family Juncaceae and having a greenish perianth in two series, six anthers, and numerous capitate flowers subtended by two foliaceous bracts — **ra·pa·te·a·ceous** \≈¦≈≈¦āshəs\ *adj*

¹rape \ˈrāp\ *n* -s [ME, fr. OE *rāp,* lit., rope; prob. fr. such districts being marked out by stakes and ropes — more at ROPE] : one of six divisions of the county of Sussex, England, intermediate between a hundred and a shire

²rape \"\ *n* -s [ME, fr. L *rapa, rapum* turnip, rape; akin to MD *roeve* turnip, rape, MLG *röve,* OHG *rāba & ruoba, ruoppa* turnip, rape, ON *rōfa* hard part of a tail, Gk *rhapys, rhaphys* turnip, Lith *ropė*] **1** *obs* : TURNIP **2** : an annual herb (*Brassica napus*) of European origin but known only as a cultigen that differs from the cabbage in its deeply lobed leaves which are not hairy like those of the turnip and is widely grown in the Old World as a forage crop for sheep and in the U. S. chiefly as a forage crop for hogs and sheep, as a cover crop in orchards, or for its seeds which yield rape oil and are a food for birds

³rape \"\ *vt* -ED/-ING/-S [ME *rapen,* fr. L *rapere* — more at RAPID] **1** *archaic* : to seize and take away by force : PLUNDER, DESPOIL **2** : to commit rape upon **3** *archaic* : to make rapt (as with delight) : TRANSPORT

⁴rape \"\ *n* -s [ME, fr. *rapen*] **1** : the act or an instance of robbing or despoiling : violent seizure ⟨the ~ of the city by the invading soldiers⟩ ⟨the ~ of the region's forests⟩ **2** : the act of carrying away a person by force ⟨the ~ of the Sabine women⟩ **3 a** : illicit sexual intercourse without the consent of the woman and effected by force, duress, intimidation, or deception as to the nature of the act — see STATUTORY RAPE **b** : sexual aggression other than by a man toward a woman **4** : an outrageous violation (as of a fundamental principle or institution) ⟨trials that have been criticized as a ~ of justice —Hal Foust⟩ ⟨a judicial ~ of the Constitution —H.E.Talmadge⟩

⁵rape \"\ *n* -s [F *râpe* grape stalk, prob. of Gmc origin; akin to OHG *raspōn* to scrape together, collect — more at RASP] **1** : the pomace of grapes left after expression of the juice or must and used for filtering (as in vinegar making) — often used in pl. **2** : a filter consisting of a large cask with a false bottom and containing rape or some other filtering material

⁶rape \"\ *dial var of* ROPE

rape butterfly *n* [²*rape*] : a cabbage butterfly (*Pieris napi*) occurring in Europe and No. America

rape cake *n* [²*rape*] : the residue from rapeseed that remains after the oil is expressed and is used as cattle feed or ground to rapeseed meal

rap·ee \(ˈ)rā¦pē\ *n* -s [³*rape* + *-ee*] : the victim of a rape

rape oil *n* [²*rape*] : a light yellow to brown fatty nondrying or semidrying oil obtained from rapeseed and turnip seed and used chiefly as a lubricant, illuminant, and food — compare COLZA OIL

rap·er \ˈrāpə(r)\ *n* -s [³*rape* + *-er*] : one that rapes : RAPIST

rapeseed \ˈ≈,≈\ *n* [²*rape* + *seed*] : the seed of rape

rapeseed meal *n* : ground rape cake

¹rap full *adj* [prob. fr. ³*rap*] **1** : sailing with sails filled and almost close-hauled **2** *of sails* : being full and drawing steadily

²rap full *n* : a state of having the sails full of wind ⟨with a *rap full* she would heel more —H.A.Calahan⟩

raph·a·el·esque *or* **raf·fa·el·esque** \¦rafēə¦lesk, ¦rāf-\ *adj, usu cap* [*Raphael* or *Raffael* (*Raffaello Santi* or *Sanzio*) †1520 Ital. painter + E *-esque*] : done in or resembling the style of the painter Raphael

raph·a·el·ism \ˈ≈≈ə,lizəm\ *n* -s *usu cap* [*Raphael* + E *-ism*] : the artistic principles, method, or style of the painter Raphael

¹raph·a·el·ite \-,līt\ *n* -s *usu cap* [*Raphael* + E *-ite*] : one who advocates or adopts Raphaelism

²raphaelite \"\ *n* -s : VANADIFEROUS ASPHALTUM

raph·a·nus \ˈrafənəs\ *n, cap* [NL, fr. L, radish, fr. Gk *raphanos;* akin to Gk *rhapys, rhaphys* turnip — more at RAPE] : a genus of Eurasian herbs (family Cruciferae) characterized by the torulose pods containing globose seeds in a single row — see JOINTED CHARLOCK, RADISH

ra·phe *or* **rha·phe** \ˈrāfē\ *n* -s [NL, fr. Gk *rhaphē* seam, suture of the skull, fr. *rhaptein* to sew together, stitch — more at WRAP] **1** : the seamlike union of the two lateral halves of a part or organ (as of the tongue, perineum, scrotum) having externally a ridge or furrow, and internally often a fibrous connective tissue septum **2 a** : the part of the funiculus of an anatropous ovule adnate to the integument, forming a ridge along the body of the ovule, and providing a diagnostic character in various seeds (as those of *Sarracenia*) **b** : the median line or slit of a valve of a diatom **c** : the suture between the two mericarps of the fruit of an umbelliferous plant

ra·phia \ˈrāfēə\ *n* [NL, fr. E *raffia*] **1** *cap* : a genus of pinnate-leaved palms native to Africa and So. America with short stout trunks, very large spiny leaves, spicate inflorescences often six feet in length, and spongy fruit containing a single hard seed — see JUPATI, RAFFIA PALM **2** -s : RAFFIA 1

raphia wax *n* : RAFFIA WAX

raph·i·dae \ˈrafə,dē\ *n pl, cap* [NL, fr. *Raphus,* type genus + *-idae*] : a family of extinct flightless birds (order Columbiformes) related to the pigeons and comprising the dodos and solitaires

ra·phide \ˈrāfəd, -,fīd\ *n* -s [back-formation fr. *raphides,* pl., fr. NL, irreg. fr. Gk *rhaphid-, rhaphis* needle, fr. *rhaptein* to sew together — more at WRAP] : one of the needle-shaped crystals irritating to mucous membrane and usu. consisting of calcium oxalate that occur in bundles or sheaflike groups as metabolic by-products of plant cells, are found most abundantly in stems, leaves, and roots of herbs and in the bark of trees, and are discharged when moistened — see CRYSTAL SAND

¹ra·phid·i·an \rəˈfidēən\ *or* **ra·phid·i·id** \rəˈfidēəd\ *adj* [*raphidian* fr. NL *Raphidium* + E *-an; raphidiid* fr. NL *Raphidiidae*] : of or relating to the Raphidiidae

²raphidian \"\ *or* **raphidiid** \"\ *n* -s : an insect of the family Raphidiidae

raph·i·dif·er·ous \¦rafə¦dif(ə)rəs\ *adj* [*raphide* + *-iferous*] : bearing or containing raphides

raph·i·di·idae \,≈≈ˈdīə,dē\ *n pl, cap* [NL, fr. *Raphidium,* type genus (irreg. fr. Gk *rhaphid-, rhaphis* needle + NL *-ium*) + *-idae* — more at RAPHIDE] : a family of predatory insects (suborder Raphidiodea) remarkable for their long prothorax and elongate setiform ovipositor

ra·phid·i·o·dea \rə,fidēˈōdēə\ *n pl, cap* [NL, fr. *Raphidium* + *-odea*] : a small suborder of Neuroptera that comprises the snake flies, includes the family Raphidiidae and a few related insects, and is often considered an independent order or replaced by Megaloptera

raph·i·ol·e·pis \,rafēˈäləpəs\ *n, cap* [NL, irreg. fr. Gk *rhaphis* needle + NL *-o-* + *-lepis*] : a small genus of ornamental Asiatic shrubs (family Rosaceae) grown for their evergreen, glossy, alternate leaves and rather showy white or pink flowers in racemes or panicles — see INDIAN HAWTHORN, JAPANESE HAWTHORN

ra·phus \ˈrāfəs\ *n, cap* [NL] : the type genus of Raphidae — see DODO

¹rap·id \ˈrapəd\ *adj, often* **rapider;** *often* **rapidest** [L *rapidus* seizing, tearing, hurrying, rapid, fr. *rapere* to seize, rob, kidnap, ravish; akin to OE *refsan, repsan* to reprove, blame, OS *respian* to reprove, OHG *refsen* to punish, ON *refsa* to punish, Gk *ereptesthai* to feed on, Lith *aprėpti* to seize; basic meaning: to seize, grasp] **1** : marked by a notably high rate of motion, activity, succession, or occurrence : requiring notably little time : not slow or retarded ⟨a ~ stream⟩ ⟨a ~ train⟩ ⟨a ~ journey⟩ ⟨~ movement⟩ ⟨racquets, most delightfully ~ of games —H.W.Nevinson⟩ **2** : marked by abrupt action or decision without delay or hesitation ⟨a train of thought made ~ by the stimulus of cupidity —George Eliot⟩ ⟨the ~ assurance of one who needs not to inquire about tastes and appetites —Arnold Bennett⟩ **3** : permissive of or conducive to action in less than normal or ordinary time ⟨~ growth⟩ **4** : FAST 5d **syn** see FAST

²rapid \"\ *n, pl* **rapids** *but sing or pl in constr* : a part of a river where the current moves with great swiftness and where the surface is usu. broken by obstructions but has no actual waterfall or cascade ⟨a shallow ~ —P.B.Shelley⟩ ⟨shoot the ~*s* in a canoe⟩

³rapid \"\ *adv* : RAPIDLY — usu. used in combination ⟨a *rapid*-firing gun⟩ ⟨a *rapid*-flowing stream⟩

ra·pi·da·men·te \,räpēdäˈmen·(,)tā\ *adv* [It, fr. *rapido* rapid, fr. L *rapidus* — more at RAPID] : RAPIDLY — used as a direction in music

ra·pide \raˈpēd\ *n* -s [F, fr. *rapide,* adj., rapid, fr. L *rapidus* — more at RAPID] : a European express train

rapid fire *n* : a class of rifle fire in which a time limit is set for completing the required number of shots

rapid-fire \¦≈≈¦≈\ *adj* [*rapid fire*] **1** : firing or adapted for firing shots in rapid succession **2** : proceeding with or characterized by rapidity, liveliness, or sharpness ⟨a *rapid-fire* cross-examination⟩

rapid-fire gun *n* : CASE GUN

rapid-fire mount *n* : a mount permitting easy and quick elevation or depression and training of a gun and fitted with a device for taking up the recoil

ra·pid·i·ty \rəˈpidəd·ē, raˈ-, -dətē, -i\ *n* -ES [L *rapiditas,* fr. *rapidus* rapid + *-itas* -ity — more at RAPID] : the quality or state of being rapid : SWIFTNESS, CELERITY, VELOCITY ⟨the ~ of a current⟩

rap·id·ly *adv* : in a rapid manner : at a rapid rate

rap·id·ness *n* -ES : the quality or state of being rapid : RAPIDITY

ra·pi·do \ˈräpē,dō\ *n* -s [It (fr. *rapido,* adj., rapid, fr. L *rapidus*) & Sp *rápido,* fr. *rápido,* adj., rapid, fr. L *rapidus* — more at RAPID] : an express train of Italy, Spain, or Latin America

rapid plant bug *n* : a No. American mirid bug (*Adelphocoris rapidus*) that is a serious pest on cotton, alfalfa, and other crops

rapid transit *n* **1** : local passenger transportation in or near cities by methods of conveyance (as subway, elevated railway) more rapid than the ordinary ones **2** : chess play with a limit of a few (as ten) seconds per move — called also *lightning chess*

ra·pier \ˈrāpēə(r), -pyə(r)\ *n* -s [MF (*espee*) *rapiere*] : a straight two-edged sword esp. of the 16th and 17th centuries with a narrow pointed blade used chiefly for thrusting and heavier than the 18th century smallsword

rapier

rap·ine \ˈrapən\ *n* -s [ME *rapyne,* fr. L *rapina,* fr. *rapere* to seize, rob, kidnap, ravish + *-ina* (fr. fem. of *-inus* -ine) — more at RAPID] : the seizing and carrying away of things by force : SPOLIATION, PILLAGE, PLUNDER

raping *pres part of* RAPE

rap·ist \ˈrāpəst\ *n* -s [⁴*rape* + *-ist*] : one who commits rape

¹rap·loch \ˈrapləḵ\ *adj* [origin unknown] *Scot* : COARSE, ROUGH

²raploch \"\ *n* -s *Scot* : homespun woolen cloth

rap·pa·ree \,rapəˈrē\ *n* -s [IrGael *rāpaire, ropaire* short pike, rapparee] **1** : an Irish irregular soldier or freebooter esp. of the 17th century **2** : PLUNDERER, VAGABOND

rapped *past of* RAP

rap·pee \raˈpē\ *n* -s [F (*tabac*) *râpé,* lit., grated tobacco, fr. *tabac* tobacco + *râpé,* past part. of *râper* to grate, fr. (assumed) MF *rasper* — more at RASP] : a moist pungent snuff made from dark rank tobacco leaves

¹rap·pel \raˈpel, rəˈ-\ *n* -s [F, lit., recall, summons, fr. OF *rapel,* fr. *rapeler* to call again, recall, summon, fr. *re-* + *apeler* to summon, appeal, accuse — more at APPEAL] **1** *archaic* : the drum call to arms **2** : descent of a precipitous cliff by means of a double rope passed under one thigh, diagonally across the body, and over the opposite shoulder

²rappel \"\ *vi* **rappelled; rappelled; rappelling; rappels** : to make a rappel ⟨*rappelling* down a cliff⟩

rap·pen \ˈräpən\ *n, pl* **rappen** [G, fr. *rappe, rappen* raven, crow, black horse (with jocular reference to the eagle on the first rappen), fr. MHG *rappe;* akin to OHG *hraban* raven — more at RAVEN] : a small Swiss coin; *specif* : the Swiss centime

¹rap·per \ˈrapə(r)\ *n* -s [²*rap* + *-er*] **1** : one that raps; *specif* : the knocker of a door **2 a** *archaic* : a whopping oath or curse ⟨if you can swear such ~*s* —John Dryden⟩ **b** *dial* : a barefaced lie

²rapper \"\ *n* -s [prob. by folk etymology fr. *rapier*] : a short flat flexible steel sword made with a handle at each end and used in English folk dancing

rapping *pres part of* RAP

rap·pi·ni \raˈpēnē\ *n pl* [It *rapini,* pl. of *rapino* small turnip, dim. of *rapo* turnip, fr. L *rapum* turnip, rape — more at RAPE] : small turnip plants pulled from the soil prior to the development of the fleshy root and marketed in bunches or in bulk for use as greens

rapp·ist \ˈrapəst\ *or* **rapp·ite** \-,pīt\ *n* -s *usu cap* [George (Johann Georg) *Rapp* †1847 Am. religious leader born in Germany + E *-ist* or *-ite*] : HARMONITE

rap poker *n* : KNOCK POKER

rap·port \raˈpō(ə)r, rəˈ-, -ó(ə)r, -ōə, -ó(ə) *sometimes* "+t *or* (*before a vowel*) d·\ *n* -s [F, relation, connection, ratio, rapport, fr. *rapporter* to bring back, yield, produce, refer, ascribe, report, fr. OF *raporter* to bring back, fr. *re-* + *aporter* to bring — more at APPORT] **1** : RELATION; *esp* : relation characterized by harmony, conformity, accord, or affinity ⟨bring one into closer ~ with his environment⟩ — compare

EN RAPPORT **2** : confidence of a subject in the operator (as in hypnotism, psychotherapy, mental testing) with willingness to cooperate

rap·por·tage \ˌra,pȯrˈtäzh\ *n* -s [F, fr. *rapporter* + *-age*] : REPORTAGE 2

rap·por·teur \-ˈtər(·)\ *n* -s [F, fr. *rapporter* + *-eur* -or] : an official charged with drawing up and presenting reports (as from a parliamentary commission to the main body)

rap·proche·ment \ˌra,prōshˈmä^{n} *also* ˌrä,- *or* ˌrȧ,- *or* -rōsh- *or* ==ˈ=,= *sometimes* -mänt; *sometimes* raˈ=,= *or* raˈ=ˈ=\ *n* -s [F, fr. *rapprocher* to bring together (fr. MF, fr. *re-* + *approcher* to approach, bring near, fr. OF *aprochier*) + *-ment* — more at APPROACH] : the act or fact of coming or being drawn near or together : establishment or a state of cordial relations ⟨the gradual ~ between the papacy and Austria —Wilfrid Ward⟩

raps *pl of* RAP, *pres 3d sing of* RAP

rap·scal·lion \rapˈskalyən\ *n* -s [alter. of *rascallion*] : RASCAL, NE'ER-DO-WELL **syn** see VILLAIN

rap·scal·lion·ly *adj* : good for nothing : RASCALLY

rap·son's slide \ˈrapsənz-\ *n, usu cap R* [fr. the name *Rapson*] : a device that consists of a crosshead capable of moving in fixed guides and having a pivoted block with a hole in it through which passes a lever hinged at a fixed point outside and that is used as a differential gear for a ship's rudder

^{1}rapt \ˈrapt\ *adj* [ME, fr. L *raptus*, past part. of *rapere* to seize, rob, kidnap, ravish — more at RAPID] **1** : lifted (as by supernatural force) and carried up or away : transported in spirit or to another place ⟨~ into future times, the bard began —Alexander Pope⟩ **2** : transported with emotion (as love, delight) : ENRAPTURED ⟨the ~ exaltation of the devotee —J.A. Symonds⟩ **3** : wholly absorbed or engrossed (as in feeling, meditation, or special interests) ⟨~ in secret studies —Shak.⟩ **4** *obs* : ABDUCTED, RAPED — **rapt·ly** *adv* — **rapt·ness** *n* -ES

^{2}rapt \"\ *n* -s [L *raptus* action of seizing, robbing, kidnapping, or ravishing, fr. *raptus*, past part. of *rapere*] : a violent or sudden transporting; *also* : an ecstatic state : RAPTURE

^{3}rapt *vt* -ED/-ING/-s [L *raptus*, past part.] *obs* : to carry away by force : TRANSPORT, RAVISH

^{4}rapt *past of* RAP

rap·ta·to·ri·al \ˌraptəˈtōrēəl, -tȯr-\ *adj* [alter. (influenced by L *raptatus*, past part. of *raptare* to seize and carry off, ravage, plunder, fr. *raptus*, past part. of *rapere*) of *raptorial*] : PREDACIOUS

rap·tor \ˈraptər, -,tȯ(ə)r\ *n* -s [L, one that robs, plunders, kidnaps, or ravishes, fr. *raptus* (past part. of *rapere* to seize, rob, kidnap, ravish) + *-or* — more at RAPID] **1** *obs* : one that rapes **2** *also* **rap·tore** \-,tō(ə)r\ [NL *Raptores*] : a bird of the order Raptores : bird of prey

^{1}rap·to·res \rapˈtōr(,)ēz\ *n pl, cap* [NL, fr. L, pl. of *raptor*] *in former classifications* : an order of birds comprising Falconiformes and Strigiformes of current usage and including all the birds of prey

^{2}raptores \"\ [NL, fr. L, pl. of *raptor*] *syn of* FALCONIFORMES

rap·to·ri·al \(ˈ)rapˈtōrēəl, -tȯr-\ *adj* [*raptor* + *-ial*] **1** : living on prey **2** : adapted to seize prey **3** : of or relating to the Raptores

^{1}rap·ture \ˈrapchə(r)\ *n* -s [L *raptus* (past part. of *rapere*) + E *-ure*] **1** *archaic* **a** : the act of seizing and carrying off with force : forcible capture : ABDUCTION **b** : RAPE 3a **2** *archaic* : the act of carrying or being carried along : force of onward movement **3 a** : a carrying of a person to heaven **b** : Christ's raising up of his true church and its members to a realm above the earth where the whole company will enjoy celestial bliss with its Lord **4 a** : the state of being carried out of oneself : spiritual or emotional ecstasy : possession by an overwhelming emotion (as joy, love) **b** : an experience of this sort ⟨the ~s of the deep hazardous to divers are caused by nitrogen narcosis⟩ **5** : a spasm or fit of emotion : PAROXYSM **6** : an expression or manifestation of ecstasy or passionate feeling : RHAPSODY **7** : a mystical phenomenon in which the soul is borne out of itself and exalted to a knowledge of divine things **syn** see ECSTASY

^{2}rapture \"\ *vt* -ED/-ING/-s : to transport with rapture (as of joy) : ENRAPTURE

rap·ture·less \ˈchə(r)ləs\ *adj* : feeling or expressing no rapture

rap·tur·ize \-chə,rīz\ *vi* -ED/-ING/-s [^{1}*rapture* + *-ize*] : to indulge in rapture

rap·tur·ous \-chərəs\ *adj* : feeling, expressing, or marked by rapture : ECSTATIC ⟨~ crowds⟩ ⟨~ applause⟩ ⟨a ~ moment⟩ — **rap·tur·ous·ly** *adv* — **rap·tur·ous·ness** *n* -ES

rap·tus \ˈraptəs\ *n* -ES [NL, fr. L, action of seizing, fr. *raptus*, past part. of *rapere*] **1** : a state of spiritual rapture marked by anesthesia **2** : a state of intense mental or emotional excitement ⟨the unpredictable ~ of the poet⟩ **3** : a pathological paroxysm of activity giving vent to impulse or tension (as in an act of violence)

raquet organ *n* : one of a series of racket-shaped or T-shaped structures found on the last pair of legs of a solpugid and regarded as sense organs

rara avis \ˌra(a)rəˈāvəs, ˌrärəˈäwəs\ *n, pl* **rara avises** \-əsəz\ *or* **ra·rae aves** \ˌrä,rīˈä,wās\ [L, rare bird] : a rare person or thing : RARITY ⟨that *rara avis* of politics, a disinterested man —*Atlantic*⟩

^{1}rare \ˈra(a)(ə)r, ˈre|, |ə\ *adj* **rarer; rarest** [alter. (influenced by ^{2}*rare*) of earlier *rere*, fr. ME, fr. OE *hrēre* boiled lightly; akin to OE & OS *hrōr* busy, active, strong, OE *hrēran* to stir — more at CRATER] : cooked to a slight degree ⟨a ~ roast beef⟩

^{2}rare \"\ *adj* **rarer; rarest** [ME, fr. L *rarus*; perh. akin to L *rete* net — more at RETINA] **1** : characterized by wide separation of component particles : THIN ⟨the ~ air of the mountain top⟩ — compare DENSE **2 a** : marked by unusual quality, merit, appeal, or capacity to please : DISTINCTIVE, EXCELLENT ⟨what is so ~ as a day in June —J.R.Lowell⟩ **b** : superlative or extreme in its kind : FINE, GREAT, REAL ⟨he'll make a ~ fuss —Eden Phillpots⟩ **3** : seldom occurring or appearing : widely separated in space or time : few and far between : UNUSUAL, UNCOMMON, INFREQUENT ⟨~ patches of green in the desert —Emma Hawkridge⟩ ⟨in back country where automobiles from other parts are ~ —Cornelius Weygandt⟩; *specif* : belonging to a small group or class ⟨argon is a ~ gas⟩ **4** : valued for its scarcity or exceptional character ⟨a ~ book⟩ **syn** see CHOICE, THIN

^{3}rare \"\ *adj & adv* [prob. alter. of *rathe*] *chiefly dial* : EARLY

^{4}rare \"\ *chiefly dial var of* REAR

^{5}rare \"\ *chiefly dial var of* ROAR

rare bird *n* [trans. of L *rara avis*] : RARA AVIS

rare·bit \ˈra(a)(ə)rbət, ˈre|, |əb-, *usu* -əd·+V\ *n* -s [(*Welsh*) *rarebit*] : WELSH RABBIT

rare earth *n* **1** : any of a group of very similar oxides of metals or a mixture of such oxides that occur together often associated with thorium in widely distributed but relatively scarce minerals (as monazite, bastnaesite, xenotime, gadolinite) and that are separated only with difficulty (as by fractional crystallization or by ion exchange) **2** *or* **rare-earth element** *or* **rare-earth metal** : any of the series of metallic elements whose oxides are the rare earths, which include the fourteen elements following lanthanum through lutetium with atomic numbers 58 through 71, usu. lanthanum itself, and according to some yttrium and even scandium, which are chiefly trivalent, and which except for lanthanum, lutetium, yttrium, and scandium form paramagnetic salts in many cases colored — symbol *RE*; compare CERIUM METAL, LANTHANIDE, PERIODIC TABLE, YTTRIUM METAL; ELEMENT table

rar·ee-show \ˈra(a)rē-, ˈrerē-\ *n* [^{2}*rare* + *-ee*] **1** : a show carried about in a box : PEEP SHOW **2** : a cheap street show : CARNIVAL

rar·e·fac·tion \ˌra(a)rəˈfakshən, ˌrer-\ *n* -s [F or ML; F *raréfaction*, fr. MF *rarefaction*, fr. ML *rarefaction-, rarefactio*, fr. L *rarefactus* (past part. of *rarefacere* to rarefy) + *-ion-, -io* -ion — more at RAREFY] **1** : the act or process of rarefying **2** : the quality or state of being rarefied ⟨~ of bone⟩ **3** : a state or region of minimum pressure in a medium traversed by compression waves (as sound waves) — compare CONDENSATION 4b — **rar·e·fac·tion·al** \-shən^{ə}l, -shnəl\ *adj*

rar·e·fac·tive \-ktiv\ *adj* [prob. fr. F *raréfactif*, fr. MF *rarefactif*, fr. L *rarefactus* + MF *-if* -ive] : producing or marked by rarefaction

rar·e·fi·able \ˌra(a)rəˈfīəbəl, ˌrer-\ *adj* : capable of being rarefied

rarefied *adj* [fr. past part. of *rarefy*] **1** : of, belonging to, or interesting to a select group : ESOTERIC, ABSTRUSE ⟨the ~ realm of first editions —John Mason Brown⟩ ⟨~ aristocrats⟩ **2** : very high ⟨former colonels and majors, newly promoted to ~ rank —*Newsweek*⟩

rar·e·fi·er \ˈ==,fī(ə)r\ *n* -s : one that rarefies

rar·e·fy *also* **rar·i·fy** \-rə,fī\ *vb* -ED/-ING/-ES [*rarefy* fr. ME *rarefien*, fr. MF *rarefier*, modif. (influenced by *-fier* -fy) of L *rarefacere*, irreg. fr. *rarus* + *facere* to make, do; *rarify* fr. ME *rarifien*, fr. ML *rarificare*, fr. L *rarus* + *-ificare* -ify — more at RARE, DO] *vt* **1** : to make rare, thin, porous, or less dense : expand or enlarge without adding any new portion of matter to — opposed to *condense* ⟨the expansive power of moisture *rarified* by heat —T.B.Macaulay⟩ **2** : to make more spiritual, refined, tenuous, or abstruse ⟨their wits are refined and *rarefied* —Ben Jonson⟩ ~ *vi* : to become less dense or gross : become rare **syn** see THIN

rarefying osteitis *n* : OSTEOPOROSIS

rare gas *n* : INERT GAS 2

rare·ly *adv* **1** *obs* : not thickly, not densely, not compactly **2** : not often : SELDOM ⟨sometimes it is of clay, ~ of gold, most commonly of porcelain —Lafcadio Hearn⟩ **3** : with rare skill : BEAUTIFULLY, EXCELLENTLY ⟨played so ~ on the flageolet —Sir Walter Scott⟩ **4** : in an exceptional degree : EXTREMELY, UNUSUALLY ⟨she was ~ beautiful⟩

rare·ness *n* -ES : the quality or state of being rare : RARITY

rarer *comparative of* RARE

^{1}rareripe \(ˈ)=ˈ=\ *adj* [^{3}*rare* + *ripe*] : early ripe : ripe before others or earlier than usual

^{2}rareripe \"\ *n* -s **1** : an early ripening fruit or vegetable **2** *dial* : GREEN ONION

rarest *superlative of* RARE

raring *adj* [fr. pres. part. of ^{4}*rare*] : full of enthusiasm or eagerness — usu. used with an infinitive ⟨all set and ~ to go⟩

rar·i·o·ra \ˌra(a)rēˈōrə\ *n pl* [NL, fr. L, neut. pl. of *rarior*, comp. of *rarus* rare — more at RARE] : rare collectors' items (as books) ⟨a place in ~ —A.E.Norman⟩

rar·ish \ˈra(a)rish, ˈrer-\ *adj* [^{1}*rare* + *-ish*] : somewhat rare

rar·i·ty \ˈra(a)rəd·ē, ˈrer-, -rətē, -i\ *n* -ES [L *raritas*, fr. *rarus* rare + *-itas* -ity — more at RARE] **1 a** : the quality or state of being rare ⟨relish the ~ of his wit⟩ **b** : the fact of being rare : INFREQUENCY, SCARCITY ⟨occurs only twice or three times, or with extreme ~ —Joshua Whatmough⟩ **2** : something rare

^{1}ra·ro·i·an \ˌrärəˈwēən\ *adj, usu cap* [*Raroia*, island in the Tuamotu archipelago in the southern Pacific + E *-an*] : of or relating to the island of Raroia

^{2}raroian \"\ *n* -s *cap* : a native or inhabitant of Raroia Island

^{1}rar·o·ton·gan \ˌrarəˈtäŋgən\ *adj, usu cap* [*Rarotonga*, chief island of the Cook islands in the southern Pacific + E *-an*] : of or relating to the island or language of Rarotonga

^{2}rarotongan \"\ *n* -s *cap* **1** : a native or inhabitant of Rarotonga **2** : the Polynesian language of the Rarotongan people

^{1}ras \ˈräs\ *n* -ES [Ar *ra's* lit., head] **1** : CAPE, HEADLAND **2** : an Ethiopian prince or feudal overlord; *also* : the ruler of an Ethiopian province **3** : a local Italian Fascist boss orig. acting as a despot in his area

^{2}ras \ˈrəs, ˈräs\ *also* **ra·sa** \-sə\ *n, pl* **rasas** [native name in India] : a Manipuri dance drama enacting the legend of the deity Krishna and his consort Radha

ras·a·ma·la \ˌrasəˈmälə\ *n* -s [Malay (*kayu*) *raksamala*, (*kayu*) *ra'samala*, fr. *kayu* tree + *raksamala*, *ra'samala*, a kind of fragrance, fr. Skt *surasa* sweet + *mālā* garland] : a southern Asiatic timber tree (*Altingia excelsa*) of the family Hamamelidaceae yielding a fragrant resin

ras·bo·ra \razˈbōrə, ˈrazbərə\ *n* [NL, fr. a native name in the East Indies] **1** *cap* : a genus of tiny brilliantly colored freshwater fishes (family Cyprinidae) of which several forms are often kept in the tropical aquarium **2** -s : any fish of the genus *Rasbora*

ras·ca·cio \räˈskä(,)syō\ *n* -s [Sp *rascacio*, *rescacio*, fr. Prov *rascasso*, fr. fem. of *rascàs* mangy, rough, wrinkled, fr. *rasco* ringworm, fr. *rascà* to scratch, scrape, fr. (assumed) VL *rasicare* — more at RASH] **1** : a variegated spinose scorpion fish (*Scorpaena plumieri*) of the western Atlantic from Cape Cod to Brazil **2** : any of various scorpion fishes

^{1}ras·cal \ˈraskəl, ˈraas-, *chiefly Brit* ˈrȧs-\ *n* -s [ME *rascaile*, *rascaille*, prob. fr. ONF *rasque* mud, ordure] **1 a** *obs* : the lowest class of an army or populace : RABBLE **b** *archaic* : a member of the rabble ⟨he was rich and I was still a ~ —Robert Frost⟩ **2** *obs* **a** : the inferior and ill-conditioned animals in a herd of deer **b** : a deer of this kind **3 a** : a mean, unprincipled, or dishonest person : ROGUE ⟨believed that dishonesty in public office . . . was more dangerous than incompetence, and he rode past the blatherskites to get at the ~s —James Thurber⟩ **b** : a person often of a pleasingly mischievous nature ⟨nostalgic sketches of many lovable ~s —*Linguaphone Mag.*⟩ ⟨the Yankee . . . was already established as a comic ~ —Bergen Evans⟩ **syn** see VILLAIN

^{2}rascal \"\ *adj* [ME *rascayl*, fr. *rascaile*, *rascaille*, n.] : of, forming, or befitting the rabble : LOW, MEAN, BASE ⟨~ fiddler —Shak.⟩ ⟨the ~ many —Edmund Spenser⟩ ⟨a battered ~ guard —Vachel Lindsay⟩

ras·cal·dom \-dəm\ *n* -s : the whole body of rascals

ras·cal·i·ty \raˈskaləd·ē, -lətē, -i, *chiefly Brit* rȧˈ-\ *n* -ES **1** : the rascals forming a group or class : RABBLE **2 a** : the character or actions of a rascal : KNAVERY ⟨more evidence of ~ and selfishness than disinterested benevolence —Daniel Aaron⟩ **b** : a rascally act ⟨political *rascalities*⟩

ras·cal·lion \raˈskalyən\ *n* -s [^{1}*rascal* + *-ion* (as in *cullion*)] : RAPSCALLION

^{1}ras·cal·ly \ˈrask(ə)lē, ˈraas-, -li, *chiefly Brit* ˈrȧs-\ *adj* [^{1}*rascal* + *-ly*] **1** *obs* : of or relating to the rabble **2** : of or characteristic of a rascal : meanly tricky or dishonest : MEAN, BASE, WORTHLESS ⟨notorious for their quarrelsome and ~ proclivities —Jack London⟩ ⟨our ~ porter is fallen fast asleep —Jonathan Swift⟩

^{2}rascally \"\ *adv* : in a rascally fashion

ras·cal·ry \-kəlrē, -ri\ *n* -ES : RASCALITY

ras·casse \raˈskas\ *n* -s [F, fr. Prov *rascasso* rascacio — more at RASCACIO] : RASCACIO 2

ra·sce·ta \raˈsēd·ə\ *n pl* [ML *raseta*, fr. Ar *rāḥah* palm of the hand] : transverse creases of the skin on the palmar surface of the wrist

ras·cette \raˈset\ *n* -s [F, fr. ML *raseta*] : a line crossing the wrist below the palm of the hand that is sometimes held by palmists to provide additional indication of a strong or weak constitution — called also *bracelet*; see PALMISTRY illustration

ra·schel knitting \(ˈ)räˈshel-\ *n* [fr. *Raschel* (*machine*), a kind of loom, fr. G *Raschelmaschine*, after *Rachel* (Elisa R. Félix) †1858 Fr. actress] : warp knitting resembling tricot but usu. coarser and with openwork patterns

ra·schig ring \ˈräshəg-\ *n, usu cap 1st R* [fr. the name *Raschig*] : a small hollow cylinder having a length about equal to the diameter, made usu. of metal, carbon, or ceramic material, and used as packing material for chemical towers

^{1}rase *vt* [ME *rasen*, alter. of *racen* — more at ^{3}RACE] *obs* : PLUCK, PULL, SNATCH

^{2}rase \ˈrāz\ *vb* -ED/-ING/-s [ME *rasen*, fr. MF *raser*, fr. (assumed) VL *rasare*, fr. L *rasus*, past part. of *radere* to scrape, shave — more at RAT] *vt* **1 a** *obs* : to slash, tear, or scratch with something sharp **b** : to form by carving or engraving : INCISE **2 a** : to rub, scrape, or scratch out or off : ERASE **b** *obs* : alter by erasing **3** : RAZE 1 ~ *vi* : to make an incised mark

rased *adj, heraldry* : ERASED

ras·er \ˈrāzə(r)\ *n* -s : one that rases

ras·ga·do \räsˈgä(,)dō\ *n* -s [Sp, lit., tear, rip, fr. past part. of *rasgar* to tear, rip, alter. (influenced by *rascar* to scratch, fr. — assumed — VL *rasicare*) of *resgar*, fr. L *resecare* to cut loose, cut off, fr. *re-* + *secare* to cut — more at RASH, SAW] : the arpeggio effect produced by sweeping the strings with the thumb in guitar playing

^{1}rash \ˈrash, -aa(ə)sh, -aish\ *adj* -ER/-EST [ME (northern dial.) *rasch* active, quick, eager, prob. fr. MD or MLG; akin to OHG *rasc* fast, hurried, strong, clever, ON *röskr* brave, vigorous, and perh. to OE *ræd*, *ræth* quick, OHG *rado* quickly, Goth *rathizo* easier] **1** *chiefly dial* : full of life and vigor : ENERGETIC **2** : characterized by or proceeding from lack of deliberation or caution : acting, done, or expressed with undue haste or disregard for consequences : imprudently involving or incurring risk : PRECIPITATE ⟨in Elizabethan drama the critic is ~ who will assert boldly that any play is by a single hand —T.S.Eliot⟩ ⟨given to ~ generalization from inadequate data —V.L.Parrington⟩ ⟨do something ~ that he will forever repent —George Meredith⟩ **3** *obs* : working quickly and strongly : quickly effective ⟨do this . . . with no ~ potion but with a lingering dram —Shak.⟩ **4** *obs* : PRESSING, URGENT ⟨my matter is so ~ —Shak.⟩ **syn** see ADVENTUROUS

^{2}rash \"\ *adv* [ME (northern dial.) *rasshe* swiftly, vigorously, fr. *rasch*, adj.] *archaic* : RASHLY

^{3}rash \"\ *n* -ES [modif. of MF *ras*, fr. OIt *raso*, fr. *raso*, adj., smooth, fr. L *rasus*, past part. of *radere* to scrape, shave — more at RAT] : an English clothing fabric of the 16th, 17th, and 18th centuries made of silk or wool or silk and wool

^{4}rash \"\ *n* -ES [obs. F *rache* scurf, fr. OF *rasche*, *rache*, fr. OF *raschier* to scratch (attested only in the meaning "to spit"), fr. (assumed) VL *rasicare*, fr. L *rasus*, past part. of *radere* to scrape, shave — more at RAT] **1 a** : an eruption on the body typically with little or no elevation : EXANTHEM **b** : a large number of instances or manifestations in the same period ⟨the ~ of archaeological forgeries that had broken out all over town —John Kobler⟩ ⟨fiesta week is also a ~ of lavish parties —Ray Duncan⟩ **2** : coal so mixed with waste as to be unsalable : dirty coal

^{5}rash \"\ *dial var of* RUSH

^{1}rash·er \ˈrashə(r), ˈraash-, ˈraish-\ *n* -s [perh. fr. obs. *rash* to cut, slash (fr. ME *rashen*, prob. alter. of *rasen*) + *-er* — more at RASE] : a thin slice of bacon or ham broiled or fried; *also* : a portion (as of bacon) consisting of several slices ⟨eggs with a ~ of bacon⟩

^{2}rasher \"\ *n* -s [perh. modif. of Sp *rescacio*, *rascacio* rascacis — more at RASCACIO] : a large brick-red or vermilion rockfish (*Sebastodes miniatus*) of the Pacific coast from Vancouver Island to southern California

rash·ing \-shiŋ, -shēŋ\ *n* -s [perh. fr. E dial. *rash* brittle + *-ing* — more at ^{1}RASH] : soft flaky rock or clay immediately beneath a coal seam that is readily mixed with the coal in mining

rash·ly *adv* : in a rash manner

rash·ness *n* -ES : the quality or state of being rash

rasing *pres part of* RASE

rasing iron *n* : a caulker's tool for cleaning out seams before recaulking — compare RAVEHOOK

ras·kol·nik \rəˈskȯlnik\ *n, pl* **raskolniks** \-ks\ *or* **raskol·ni·ki** \-nəkē\ *usu cap* [Russ *raskol'nik*, fr. *raskol* schism (fr. *raz-*, prefix denoting separation — fr. OSlav — + *-kol*, fr. *kolot'* to separate, divide) + *-nik*, n. suffix denoting a person engaged in or connected with something specified; akin to Lith *kalti* to beat, forge — more at HALT (lame)] : a dissenter from the Russian Orthodox Church and member of one of the several groups (as the Doukhobors, Khlysty) developing from the schism of the 17th century in protest against liturgical reforms — called also *Old Believer, Old Ritualist*

rason *var of* RHASON

rasophore *var of* RHASOPHORE

ra·so·res \rəˈsōr(,)ēz\ *n pl, cap* [NL, fr. LL, pl. of *rasor* one that scrapes, fr. L *rasus* (past part. of *radere* to scrape, shave) + *-or* — more at RAT] *in former classifications* : an order of birds comprising the Gallinae and the Columbae or coextensive with Gallinae

ra·so·ri·al \-ˈsōrēəl, -sȯr-\ *adj* [NL *Rasores* + E *-ial*] **1** *of a bird* : habitually scratching the ground in search of food **2** : of or relating to the Rasores : GALLINACEOUS

ra·sor·ite \ˈrāzə,rīt\ *n* -s [C. M. *Rasor*, 20th cent. Am. engineer + E *-ite*] : KERNITE

^{1}rasp \ˈrasp, -aa(ə)-, -ai-, -ȧ-\ *vb* -ED/-ING/-s [ME *raspen*, fr. (assumed) MF *rasper* (whence *raper*), of Gmc origin; akin to OHG *raspōn* to scrape together, collect; akin to OE *gehrespan* to tear, OFris *hrespa* to tear, OHG *hrespan* to pluck, and perh. to OE *hreppan* to touch — more at RAFFLE] *vt* **1** : to rub or grate with something rough or harsh ⟨a cataract that ~s away the rock⟩; *specif* : to abrade with a rasp ⟨~ off any irregularities or sharp corners⟩ **2** : to grate harshly upon : serve as an irritant to ⟨some sounds ~ the ear⟩ ⟨remarks that ~ the nerves⟩ **3** : to utter in an irritated or grating tone ⟨~ out a denial⟩ ~ *vi* **1** : to grate or scrape something **2** : to produce or move while producing a grating sound ⟨the chalk ~*ed* across the blackboard⟩

^{2}rasp \"\ *n* -s [MF *raspe*, fr. OF, fr. (assumed) *rasper*] **1 a** : a coarse file on which the cutting prominences are distinct points raised by the oblique stroke of a sharp punch instead of lines raised by a chisel (as on the true file) — called also *rasp-cut file* **2** : a machine or contrivance used for rasping or grating **3** : an act or effect of rasping : a rasping sound, sensation, or effect ⟨the ~ of a cricket⟩; *specif* : an unpleasant quality imparted to the voice by excessive tightness of the muscles of the larynx and pharynx ⟨some voices have the hail= fellow ~ of the western plains —R.M.Hodesh⟩ **4 a** : a roughened surface (as in the stridulating organ of an insect) **b** : TOOTH, DENTICLE ⟨lamprey eels . . . with row upon row of horny ~s in place of teeth —Robert Kane⟩

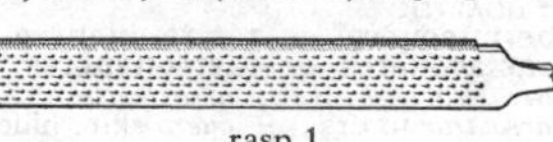

rasp 1

^{3}rasp \"\ *n* -s [short for earlier *raspis*, of unknown origin] *chiefly dial* : RASPBERRY

ras·pa \ˈräspə\ *n* -s [MexSp, fr. Sp *raspar* to scrape, of Gmc origin; akin to OHG *raspōn* to scrape together, collect — more at RASP] : a modern Mexican couple dance consisting of an alternate shuffling of the feet forward and backward and ending with a polka pivot

ras·pa·dor \ˌräspəˈdō(ə)r\ *n* -s [Sp, fr. *raspado* (past part. of *raspar* to scrape) + *-or*] : a crude machine for decorticating or scraping fiber of henequen or sisal

ras·pa·to·ry \ˈraspə,tōrē\ *n* -ES [ML *raspatorium*, fr. *raspatus* (past part. of *raspare* to rasp, of Gmc origin; akin to OHG *raspōn* to scrape together, collect) + L *-orium* -ory — more at RASP] : a file or rasp used (as for scraping bone) in surgery

rasp-bar cylinder \ˈ=,=-\ *n* : a thresher or combine cylinder with coarse rasps instead of teeth bolted to the cylinder bars

rasp·ber·ry \ˈra|z,berē, ˈrȧ|, -,b(ə)rē, -ri *sometimes* |s(,)b- — *see* BERRY\ *n* [^{3}*rasp* + *berry*] **1 a** : any of various usu. black or red sweet juicy edible berries that technically are aggregate fruits consisting of numerous small drupes crowded upon a fleshy receptacle from which they are easily separated when ripe and that are usu. rounder and smaller than the closely related blackberries **b** : any of various plants of the genus *Rubus* that bear raspberries and include various cultivated forms derived chiefly from a common European raspberry (*Rubus idaeus*), an American red raspberry (*R. strigosus*), and the blackcap **2 a** : a variable color averaging a dark purplish red that is bluer and paler than pansy purple, lighter and stronger than raisin, and bluer, lighter, and stronger than Bokhara or dahlia purple (sense 1) **b** : a dark red that is bluer, lighter, and stronger than average garnet or average wine and bluer and paler than cranberry **3 a** : a sound of contempt or derision made by trilling the extended tongue between the protruded lips **b** : something resembling a raspberry in expressing dislike, disapproval, or derision

raspberry beetle *n* : a small brownish beetle (*Byturus unicolor*) whose adults feed on the buds and whose larvae feed on the fruits of raspberries

raspberry bug *n* : a very small nearly black negro bug (*Corimelaena pulicaria*) that infests the raspberry, strawberry, and blackberry giving them a very disagreeable flavor

raspberry cane borer *n* : a slender black and yellow longicorn beetle (*Oberea bimaculata*) having a larva that is a borer in the canes of raspberries, blackberries, and sometimes roses

raspberry cane maggot *n* : the larva of a small fly (*Pegomya rubivora*) of the family Anthomyiidae that mines in the shoots of the raspberry and blackberry

raspberry curl *n* : LEAF CURL c

raspberry fruit worm *n* : the larva of either of two dermestid beetles (*Byturus bakeri* or *B. rubi*) that bores into the fruit of raspberries

raspberry glacé *n* : a grayish purplish red that is redder, lighter, and stronger than average rose plum or Aztec maroon and redder and deeper than tourmaline pink

raspberry jamwood *n* **:** the very hard lustrous wood of an Australian tree (*Acacia acuminata*) having a fragrance suggestive of raspberry jam

rasp·ber·ry·like \-,līk\ *adj* **:** resembling the raspberry

raspberry mosaic *n* **:** any of several virus diseases affecting raspberries and sometimes other cane fruits and causing leaf mottling and yellowing

raspberry red *n* **:** a moderate red that is yellower and lighter than cerise, claret (sense 3a), Harvard crimson (sense 1), or Turkey red and yellower, lighter, and very slightly less strong than average strawberry (sense 2a) — called also *jacqueminot*

raspberry root borer *n* **:** the larva of a large clearwing moth (*Bembecia marginata*) of the family Aegeriidae that bores in the roots and canes of the raspberry and blackberry

raspberry root rot *n* **:** a very destructive rot of the crowns of raspberry bushes in Australia and New Zealand caused by an agaric (*Hypholoma fasciculare*)

raspberry rose *n* **:** a variable color averaging a moderate purplish red that is bluer and deeper than average rose, redder and deeper than violine pink, paler and slightly redder than magenta rose, and bluer and paler than fuchsia rose

raspberry sawfly *n* **:** a small black sawfly (*Monophadnoides geniculatus*) with reddish abdomen the spiny greenish larva of which eats the leaves of the raspberry and blackberry

raspberry streak *n* **:** BLUESTEM 2b

raspberry wine *n* **:** a dark purplish red that is bluer and duller than redgrape or pansy purple, darker and slightly bluer than raisin, and bluer and paler than Bokhara

raspberry yellows *n pl but sing or pl in constr* **:** RASPBERRY MOSAIC

rasp–cut file \'=,=-\ *n* **:** RASP

rasped *adj* **1** *of a book cover* **:** having the sharp angles removed but not beveled **2** *of a book edge* **:** uncut but roughened with a coarse rasp to imitate a deckle edge

rasp·er \'raspə(r), -aa(ə)-,-ai-,-á-\ *n* -s **:** one that rasps: as **a :** an instrument or machine for rasping (as a file for removing the black surface from a burnt loaf of bread, a grater for beetroot or potatoes, a sawmill for reducing dyewoods to powder) **b :** one that smooths something (as of metal or wood) with a rasp **c :** a rasping fence

rasp house *n* **:** a house of correction formerly in use (as in Holland, Germany) whose prisoners rasped wood to powder for dyeing

¹**rasping** *n* -s [fr. gerund of ¹*rasp*] **:** a particle or piece separated by rasping ⟨~*s* of logwood⟩

²**rasping** *adj* [fr. pres. part. of ¹*rasp*] **1 :** GRATING, HARSH, IRRITATING ⟨a ~ sound⟩ ⟨a ~ smell⟩ ⟨~ inconveniences⟩ **2** *hunting* **a :** high or difficult to leap ⟨a ~ ditch⟩ ⟨a ~ fence⟩ **b :** very fast ⟨a ~ pace⟩ — **rasp·ing·ly** *adv* — **rasp·ing·ness** *n* -ES

rasp·ish \-pish, -pēsh\ *adj* [¹*rasp* + *-ish*] **:** IRRITABLE, RASPING

rasp·ite \'ra,spīt, 'rä,-\ *n* -s [G *raspit*, fr. Charles *Rasp*, 19th cent. Australian prospector + G *-it* -ite] **:** a mineral $PbWO_4$ consisting of lead tungstate occurring in yellow monoclinic crystals (hardness 2.5)

rasp leaf *n* [²*rasp*] **:** a virus disease of cherry characterized by the development of elongated outgrowths from the lower leaf surfaces and depressed lighter green areas on the upper leaf surfaces

rasps *pres 3d sing of* RASP, *pl of* RASP

raspy \'raspē, -aa(ə)-,-ai-,-á-, -pi\ *adj* -ER/-EST [¹*rasp* + *-y*] **1 a :** resembling the sound made by a rasp **:** GRATING, HARSH ⟨talks with a ~ New England twang —*New Yorker*⟩ **b :** having a rough texture ⟨pulled the ~ army blanket about my shoulders —Herbert Gold⟩ **2 :** RASPISH, IRRITABLE ⟨they were all ~ from lack of sleep —Ira Wolfert⟩

rasse \'rasə, 'ras\ *n* -s [Jav *rasé*] **:** a grizzled black-marked semiarboreal civet (*Viverricula malaccensis* or *V. indica*) that is related to but is smaller than the common civet, is native to China and the East Indies, and furnishes a perfume prized by the Javanese — called also *lesser civet*

ras·sen·kreis \'räsᵊn,krīs\ *n, pl* **rassenkrei·se** \-īzə\ *usu cap* [G, fr. *rasse* race + *kreis* circle, cycle] **:** a polytypic species esp. when exhibiting a pattern of geographical replacement of one type by another

ras sham·ra \'räs'shamrə\ *adj, usu cap R & S* [fr. *Ras Shamra*, Syria] **1 :** of or from the village of Ras Shamra, Syria, site of the ancient city of Ugarit **2 :** of or being the alphabetical cuneiform script of Ugaritic discovered on a collection of clay tablets excavated at Ras Shamra between 1929 and 1936 **:** UGARITIC

ras·ta·couère *or* **ras·ta·quouère** \,rastə'kwe(ə)r\ *n, pl* **rastacouères** *or* **rastaquouères** \-(z)\ [F, fr. AmerSp *arrastracuero*, fr. Sp *arrastra* he drags (3d sing. pres. ind. of *arrastrar* to drag) + *cuero* skin, hide, fr. L *corium* — more at ARRASTRA, CUIRASS] **:** a foreign parvenu

ra·stel·lus \rə'steləs\ *n* -ES [NL, fr. L, small rake, mattock, dim. of *rastrum* rake, mattock] **:** a toothed structure like a rake on the basal segment of the chelicera of many burrowing spiders that is of use in digging

ras·ter \'rastə(r)\ *n* -s [G, fr. L *raster, rastrum* rake, mattock, fr. *radere* to scrape, rake, shave — more at RAT] **:** the area upon which the image is reproduced in the cathode-ray tube of a television set

ras·tik *or* **ras·tick** \'rastək\ *n* -s [Turk *rastik*, fr. Per *rāsukht*] **:** any of various hair dyes: as **a :** a paste made formerly from nutgalls roasted with copper and iron filings and oil **b :** a mixture containing pyrogallol and a metallic salt (as ferrous sulfate)

ra·sure \'rāzhə(r)\ *n* -s [MF, fr. L *rasura*, fr. *rasus* (past part. of *radere* to scrape, shave) + *-ura* -ure — more at RAT] **:** the act of rasing, scraping, or erasing **:** ERASURE, OBLITERATION

¹**rat** \'rat, *usu* -ad·+V\ *n* -s [ME, fr. OE *ræt*; akin to OS *ratta* rat, MLG *rotte*, MD *ratte*, OHG *ratta, rato, ratza* rat, *rāzi* wild, sharp to the taste, L *rodere* to gnaw, *radere* to scrape, shave, W *rhathell* rasp; basic meaning: to scrape, gnaw] **1 a :** any of numerous rodents (family Muridae) of *Rattus* and related genera that differ from the murid mice by their usu. considerably larger size and by features of the teeth and other structures and that include forms (as the brown rat, the black rat, and the roof rat) which live in and about human habitations and in ships, have become naturalized by commerce in most parts of the world, and are destructive pests consuming or destroying vast quantities of food and other goods and acting as vectors of various diseases (as bubonic plague) **b :** any of various other rodents of similar size and appearance — used often in combination ⟨musk*rat*⟩ ⟨spiny ~⟩ **2 a :** one who deserts his party, friends, or associates (as in adversity or for selfish ends) **b** (1) **:** a printer who works for less than the established or prevailing rate of pay (2) **:** SCAB 4b **c :** a despicable or contemptible person **:** LOUSE, HEEL ⟨hoodlums, shysters, and assorted ~*s* —Stanley Walker⟩; *esp* **:** INFORMER 3, STOOL PIGEON **3 :** a pad with tapering ends over which a woman's hair is arranged for an illusion of greater quantity **4 :** an olive gray that is deeper and slightly greener than the color mouse, deeper than nutria, and redder and deeper than stone gray

²**rat** \"\ *vb* **ratted; ratted; ratting; rats** *vi* **1 :** to desert one's party or associates for personal advantage ⟨incurring the reproach of having *ratted*, solely by his inability to follow the friends of his early days —Thomas De Quincey⟩ **2 :** to catch rats; *esp* **:** to hunt rats with a dog **3 :** to work as a rat **:** SCAB; *specif* **:** to work as a printer for less than the established or customary rate of pay **4 :** to act as an informer or stool pigeon **:** SQUEAL ⟨*ratting* on the men they live with —J.M. Murtagh & Sara Harris⟩ ~ *vt* **1 :** to employ scabs or strikebreakers in (an industry) **2 :** to give (hair) the effect of greater quantity by use of a rat or style of combing — **rat on :** to go back on (as an agreement or statement) **:** welsh on **:** RECANT ⟨*ratted on* her debts —Ellery Sedgwick⟩ ⟨*ratting on* a private confession written to him fourteen years ago —William Empson⟩

³**rat** \"\ *vt* **ratted; ratted; ratting; rats** [prob. euphemism for ¹*rot*] **:** DAMN, CONFOUND, DRAT — used as a mild oath ⟨~ me if it was not a meritorious action —Henry Fielding⟩

ra·ta \'räd·ə\ *n* -s [Maori] **1 :** a tree of the genus *Metrosideros*; *esp* **:** either of two New Zealand timber trees (*M. robusta* and *M. lucida*) **2 :** the hard dark red wood of a rata tree used by the Maoris for paddles and war clubs **3 :** POLYNESIAN CHESTNUT

rat·abil·i·ty *or* **rate·abil·i·ty** \,rād·ə'biləd·ē, ,rātə'-, -lətē, -i\ *n* **:** the quality or state of being ratable

rat·able *or* **rate·able** \'==bəl\ *adj* [¹*rate* + *-able*] **1 :** capable of being rated or estimated ⟨~ taking of gas —W.F.Cloud⟩ **2 :** made or reckoned according to a proportionate rate **:** PROPORTIONAL ⟨a ~ distribution of an estate⟩ **3** *Brit* **:** TAXABLE ⟨the ~ value of property⟩ ⟨the analysis of ~ values —*Country Life*⟩

rat·ably *or* **rate·ably** \-blē, -bli\ *adv* **:** in a ratable manner **:** PROPORTIONATELY ⟨distribute the net proceeds . . . among the shareholders ~ —T.J.Grayson⟩

rat·a·fia \,rad·ə'fēə\ *n* -s [F] **1 :** a liqueur made by infusion and usu. not distilled, flavored with plum, peach, and apricot kernels and bitter almonds, and supplied with a base of brandy and fruit juices **2 :** a small sweet biscuit made from almond paste

ratama *var of* RETAMA

ratan *var of* RATTAN

ra·ta·na church \rə'tänə-\ *n, cap R&C* [after Wiremu Tahupotiki *Ratana*, 20th cent. New Zealand religious leader] **:** a Christian sect organized in New Zealand about 1925 that emphasizes faith healing and the agency of angels

rat·a·plan \,rad·ə'plan, -aa(ə)n\ *n* -s [F, of imit. origin] **:** the iterative sound of beating (as from a drum or the hoofs of a galloping horse) ⟨the ~ of machine guns —H.W.Baldwin⟩

rat–a–tat \,rad·ə¦tat, -atə¦-, *usu* -tad·+V\ *or* **rat–a–tat–tat** \¦==,=¦=\ *n* -s [imit.] **:** a sound of sharp, repeated knocking or tapping ⟨a peremptory *rat-a-tat* on the door⟩

ra·ta·touille \râtàtüy\ *n* -s [F, fr. *touiller* to stir, fr. L *tudiculare*, fr. *tudes* hammer, fr. the root of *tundere* to beat — more at STUTTER] **:** a stew made of eggplant, tomatoes, green peppers, squash, and sometimes meat and seasoned with garlic and other condiments

ratbag \'=,=\ *n, Austral* **:** an odd or disagreeable person

rat bandicoot *n* **:** any of numerous small ratlike bandicoots that are related to the rabbit bandicoots but have shorter ears and hindlegs

rat–bite fever \'=,=-\ *n* **:** either of two febrile diseases of man commonly transmitted by the bite of a rat or other animal vector: **a :** a septicemia marked by irregular relapsing fever, rashes, muscular pain and arthritis, and great weakness and caused by a microorganism (*Streptobacillus moniliformis* or *Haverhillia multiformis*) that is included among the typical bacteria or regarded as an actinomycete **b :** a disease that is marked by sharp elevation of temperature, swelling of lymph glands, eruption, recurrent inflammation of the bite wound, and muscular pains in the part where the bite wound occurred and that is caused by a bacterium (*Spirillum minus*) — called also *sodoku*

ratcatcher \'=,==\ *n* **1 :** a person or animal employed in exterminating rats **2** *chiefly Brit* **:** informal hunting dress; *esp* **:** a tweed jacket with tan breeches

¹**ratch** *var of* RACH

²**ratch** \'rach\ *n* -ES [origin unknown] *chiefly dial* **:** a blaze on an animal's face

³**ratch** \"\ *vi* -ED/-ING/-ES [back-formation fr. *raught*, after E *caught: catch*] *chiefly dial* **:** STRETCH, REND

⁴**ratch** \"\ *n* -ES **:** the distance between nip of back and front drafting rolls in spinning

⁵**ratch** \"\ *n* -ES [G *ratsche, rätsche* clapper, rattle, ratchet, fr. *ratschen, rätschen* to rattle, fr. MHG *ratzen;* akin to MHG *razzeln* to rattle — more at RATTLE] **1 :** RATCHET 1 **2 :** a notched bar with which a pawl or click works to prevent reversal of motion

⁶**ratch** \"\ *vt* -ED/-ING/-ES **1 :** to cut gear teeth on (a wheel) **2 :** to turn (as a tool) by or as if by a ratchet and pawl

rat cheese *also* **rat–trap cheese** *n* **:** STORE CHEESE

¹**ratch·et** *or* **rach·et** \'rachət, *usu* -əd·+V\ *n* -s [alter. (influenced by ⁵*ratch*) of earlier *rochet*, fr. F, alter. of MF *rocquet* head of a lance, of Gmc origin; akin to OHG *rocko, roccho* distaff — more at ROCK (distaff)] **1 :** a pawl, click, or detent for holding or propelling a ratchet wheel **2 :** a mechanism that consists of a bar or wheel having inclined teeth into which a pawl drops so that motion can be imparted to the wheel or bar or can be governed or prevented and that is used in a hand tool (as a carpenter's brace or screwdriver) to allow effective motion in one direction only; *specif* **:** a mechanism on a typewriter roll for governing the vertical spacing of the lines **3 :** a tool with a toothed blade used to turn the toothed wheels that clamp and release patent blocks or bases in printing

²**ratchet** \"\ *vb* **ratchetted; ratchetted; ratchetting; ratchets** *vi* **:** to move or operate by a ratchet ~ *vt* **:** to furnish (as a machine or tool) with a ratchet

ratchet brace *n* **1 :** a carpenter's bitbrace that has a ratchet-driven chuck and is used in close quarters where complete revolutions of the handle are impossible **2 :** a lever that has a ratchet-driven chuck at one end and is used for drilling holes in metal by hand

ratchet coupling *n* **:** a shaft coupling having a ratchet and pawl or a similar device whereby the driven member may be turned in one direction only by the driving member and may also overrun the driving member

ratchet crank *n* **:** a crank mounted on but not keyed to a shaft which it moves intermittently through a ratchet wheel and pawl

ratchet drill *n* **:** a hand drill in which the drill holder is revolved intermittently by a lever through a ratchet wheel and pawl

ratchet jack *n* **:** a jack raised or lowered by means of a pawl and ratchet

ratchet screwdriver *n* **:** a screwdriver that is operated by the reciprocating motion of the handle and that usu. has a removable screwdriver bit

ratchet stop *n* **:** a device for limiting the motion of machinery in one direction that consists of a ratchet wheel or bar and a pawl which acts as a positive stop or controls the motion through a friction brake

ratchet thread *n* **:** BUTTRESS THREAD

ratchet tooth *n* **:** a gear tooth one side of which is radial and the other inclined so that a pawl will catch on the former and slide over the latter

ratchet wheel *n* **1 :** a notched or toothed wheel either held in position or turned by an engaging detent, pawl, or click **2 :** the retaining wheel over the mainspring arbor of a timepiece

ratchet wrench *n* **:** a wrench in which torque is applied in one direction only by means of a ratchet

ratch·ety \'rachəd·ē, -chətē, -i\ *adj* **:** resembling the operation of a ratchet **:** JERKY, IRREGULAR, CREAKY

rat chinchilla *n* **:** ABROCOME

ratching *n* -s [fr. gerund of ³*ratch*] **:** extra draft due to excess speed of the mule carriage over the roller delivery in spinning

rat–claw foot \'=,=-\ *n* **:** a claw-and-ball foot on a piece of furniture having the claws very sharp and thin

ratchet wheel: *1* wheel, *2* reciprocating lever, *3* click, pawl, or ratchet for communicating motion, *4* pawl for preventing backward motion

¹**rate** \'rāt, *usu* -ād·+V\ *vb* -ED/-ING/-S [ME *raten*, perh. of Scand origin; akin to Sw *rata* to find fault, blame, despise, ON *hrata* to fall, stagger — more at CARDINAL] *vt* **1 :** to rebuke (as a person or a hunting dog) angrily or violently **:** SCOLD, UPBRAID ⟨shall have you soundly *rated* and dismissed —Rex Ingamells⟩ ⟨the proper words for *rating* foxhounds —C.E. Hare⟩ **2** *obs* **:** to drive away (a person or dog) by scolding ⟨*rated* mine uncle from the council board —Shak.⟩ ~ *vi* **:** to voice angry reprimands — usu. used with *at* ⟨like her none the less for *rating* at her —Alfred Tennyson⟩ **syn** see SCOLD

²**rate** \"\ *n* -s [ME, fr. MF, fr. ML *rata*, fr. L (*pro*) *rata* (*parte*) according to a fixed proportion, fr. *pro* for, according to + *rata* calculated, fixed (fem. of *ratus*, fr. past part. of *reri* to reckon, calculate) + *parte*, abl. of *pars* part — more at REASON] **1 a :** reckoned value **:** VALUATION ⟨stones whose ~*s* are . . . as fancy values them —Shak.⟩ ⟨appraised him at a low ~⟩ **b** *obs* **:** ESTIMATION ⟨wise men . . . in the ordinary ~ and esteem of the world —Daniel Defoe⟩ **2** *obs* **:** a fixed or established portion or measure **:** QUANTITY ⟨brought every man his present . . . a ~ year by year —2 Chron 9:24 (AV)⟩ **3 a :** a fixed relation (as of quantity, amount, or degree) between two things **:** RATIO ⟨~ of exchange⟩ **b :** a charge, payment, or price fixed according to a ratio, scale, or standard ⟨hotel ~*s*⟩ ⟨the publisher's usual ~ for short stories⟩ ⟨drapery fabrics bought at the ~ of a dollar a yard⟩ ⟨sold at cut ~*s*⟩: as (1) **:** a charge per unit of a public-service commodity (as electricity, gas, water) ⟨an electric ~ of 7 cents per kilowatt-hour⟩ (2) **:** a price or charge per unit of freight or passenger service (as cents per hundred pounds or dollars per ton, per car, per passenger-mile); *specif* **:** a common carrier charge shown on an official published tariff on file with a governmental regulatory agency (3) **:** the price charged an advertiser per unit of publication space or of radio or television time (4) **:** a unit charge or ratio used by the government for assessing taxes on property (5) *Brit* **:** a local tax — usu. used in pl. ⟨parish ~*s*⟩ **4 a :** quantity, amount, or degree of something measured per unit of something else (as time) ⟨at the ~ of 60 miles an hour⟩ ⟨a birth ~ of 40 per thousand of population⟩ ⟨~ of progress over the past century⟩ ⟨the ~ of corporate profits⟩ ⟨~ of depreciation⟩ **b :** amount of payment or charge based on some other amount ⟨~ of interest per annum⟩ ⟨~ of commission per bond sold⟩: as (1) **:** the wage paid on an incentive or time basis for a particular job (2) **:** the amount of premium per unit of insurance or exposure **5 a** *archaic* **:** relative behavior or manner **:** STYLE, FASHION — usu. used with *after* ⟨I proceed much after the old ~ —William Cowper⟩ **b :** relative condition or quality **:** RANK, KIND ⟨I am a spirit of no common ~ —Shak.⟩ **6 a :** the order or class to which a warship belongs determined according to a specified criterion (as size or armament) ⟨a ship of the first ~⟩ **b :** the class of a merchant ship for marine insurance determined by its relative safety as a risk (as A 1, A 2) **c :** the relative standing or grade of a sailor; *specif* **:** the rank of an enlisted man (as in the U. S. Navy) within a specified rating ⟨the ~ of radarman third class⟩ **7 :** the gain or loss in the running of a timepiece within a specified unit of time ⟨daily ~⟩ ⟨hourly ~⟩ — **at any rate** *adv* **1** *obs* **:** at any price **2 :** in any case **:** at least ⟨art . . . perhaps immature but *at any rate* virile —Alan McCulloch⟩ — **at this rate** *or* **at that rate** *adv* **:** under such conditions **:** this being so ⟨*at this rate*, he won't be elected⟩

³**rate** \"\ *vb* -ED/-ING/-S [ME *raten*, fr. *rate*, n.] *vt* **1** *obs* **:** to allot (a share) to ⟨had not *rated* him his part —Shak.⟩ **2 :** CONSIDER, REGARD ⟨*rated* an excellent golfer⟩ ⟨*rated* the highest office in the state⟩ **3 a :** to set an estimate on **:** APPRAISE, VALUE ⟨copper is *rated* . . . above its real value —Adam Smith⟩ ⟨buyers . . . ~ black broadcloth high for fall —*Women's Wear Daily*⟩ **b** *chiefly Brit* **:** to assess the value of (property) for taxing purposes **c** *archaic* **:** to calculate the total ⟨then must we ~ the cost —Shak.⟩ **d :** to determine or assign the relative rank or class of (as a ship or a seaman) **e :** to evaluate with reference to specific traits or given standards **:** GRADE ⟨~ the way the . . . companies treat their dealers —S.L.Payne⟩ ⟨each job was *rated* on a five-point scale —Mildred Mitchell⟩ **f :** to estimate the normal capacity or power of ⟨current flowing at the *rated* capacity —*Cannon Catalog*⟩ ⟨flooring system is *rated* to withstand a . . . fire and water test —*Amer. Builder*⟩ **4 :** to fix the amount of premium to be charged per unit of insurance or exposure on (a particular risk) **5 a :** to adjust (a timepiece) to a given rate of going (as by altering the effective length of the pendulum) **:** REGULATE **b :** to find the gain or loss of (a timepiece) in a given unit of time **c :** to pace or restrain (as a horse or oneself) in a race in order to conserve energy for the finish ⟨*rated* the 4-year-old . . . colt perfectly —F.M.Blunk⟩ **6 :** to have a right to **:** DESERVE ⟨most . . . do not ~ so much remembrance —*Harper's*⟩ ⟨sufficient appeal to ~ a network show —Charles Miller⟩ ~ *vi* **:** to be of consequence **:** RANK, COUNT ⟨human ingenuity was to ~ . . . as a vital national resource —*Steelways*⟩; *specif* **:** to enjoy a status of special privilege or consideration ⟨I never did ~ with him —Bess A. Garner⟩ **syn** see DESERVE, ESTIMATE

⁴**rate** \"\ *dial Eng var of* RET

rateable *var of* RATABLE

rate base *n* **:** the valuation of a property that is used by a commission or court to determine the reasonableness of rates or taxes on it

rate basis *n* **:** the combination of factors that constitute the formula used in making a rate

rate bill *n* **:** a school fee collected from each pupil by American schools in the 18th and early 19th centuries

rate–buster \'=,==\ *n* **:** a pieceworker who produces to the utmost of his ability despite opposition by his fellows who fear that his high earnings may cause a reduction in the piece rate

rated horsepower *n* **:** the maximum power an airplane engine can develop without failure when operated continuously or for a specified long period under specified conditions

rated load *n* **:** the load a machine is designed to carry as usu. stated on the nameplate in appropriate power units (as of horsepower for motors and engines or of kilovolt amperes for alternating-current generators)

rate–gene \'=,=\ *n* **:** a gene controlling the speed at which a developmental process occurs and therefore indirectly the relative effectiveness of that process in competition with various others occurring at the same time

ra·tel \'rād·ᵊl, 'räd-\ *n* -s [Afrik, lit., rattle, fr. MD *ratele, ratel;* fr. its cry — more at RATTLE] **:** any of several powerful nocturnal carnivorous mammals of the genus *Mellivora* resembling the badger and having the pelt ashy gray above and black beneath (as the southern African *M. capensis* and the Indian *M. indica*)

rate meter *n* **:** an instrument that indicates the counting rate of an electronic counter — compare ²COUNTER e

rate–of–climb indicator *n* **:** a standard flight instrument that indicates the rate of ascent or descent of an airplane

rate of exchange : the amount of one currency that will buy a given amount of another

rate of interest : the percentage usu. on an annual basis that is paid by the borrower to the lender for a loan of money — compare INTEREST 3a

rate of return : the ratio of net railway operating income to the value of the property in common carrier use including allowance for working capital

rate–of–rise thermostat \¦=¦=-\ *n* **:** a thermostat that operates when the rate of increase of temperature exceeds a predetermined amount

ratepayer \'=,==\ *n, Brit* **:** TAXPAYER

rat·er \'rād·ə(r), -ātə-\ *n* -s [³*rate* + *-er*] **1 :** one that rates **:** a person who scores, estimates, or determines a rating (as of examination papers, merit of employees, or premium on property insurance) **2 :** a person or thing (as a ship) of a certain rating or class — usu. used in combination ⟨a first-*rater*⟩

rate range *n* **:** a series of rates of pay for the same job running from a stated minimum to a stated maximum

rates *pres 3d sing of* RATE, *pl of* RATE

rate setter *n* **:** a person charged with determining the proper rate of pay for a job esp. on an incentive rate basis

rate up *vt* **:** to class with risks paying a higher rate of premium in order to offset additional risk

ratfish \'=,=\ *n* **:** ²CHIMAERA 2; *esp* **:** a silvery iridescent white-spotted chimaera (*Hydrolagus colliei*) of cold deep waters of the Pacific coast of No. America

rat flea *n* **:** any of various fleas that occur on rats; *esp* **:** either of two fleas (*Nosopsyllus fasciatus* and *Xenopsylla cheopis*) that are carriers of bubonic plague

rat goose *n* **:** BRANT

rat guard *n* **:** one of the circular sheet metal shields fastened to the mooring lines of a vessel to prevent rats from boarding or leaving it

rath \'räth, 'rä\ *n* -s [IrGael *rāth*] **:** a usu. circular earthwork serving as stronghold and residence of an ancient Irish chief ⟨fairy denizens of ~ and hill —O.S.J.Gogarty⟩

rat hare *n* **:** PIKA

¹**rathe** \'rāth, 'rath\ *adv* [ME, rapidly, fr. OE *hrathe, hræthe;* akin to MD *rade* rapidly, OHG *rado;* derivative fr. the stem of OE *hræd* rapid, fast] *chiefly dial* **:** early in the day, season, or period ⟨~ she rose —Alfred Tennyson⟩

²**rathe** \"\ *or* **rath** \'rath\ *adj* [ME, quick, rapid, fast, fr. OE *hræth*, alter. (influenced by *hrathe, hræthe*, adv.) of *hræd;* akin to MD & MLG *rat* quick, rapid, fast, OHG *hrad, rad*, ON *hrathr*, and perh. MIr *crothaim* I shake, Lith *kresti* to shake] *chiefly dial* **:** early in the day, the season, or year **:** done, com-

ing, or ready before others of its class or before the usual time or season; *specif* **:** early-blooming or early-bearing ⟨bring the ~ primrose that forsaken dies —John Milton⟩ ⟨the ~ wheat —W.E.Henley⟩ — **rathe·ness** *n* -ES

¹rath·er \'rathə(r), ÷'rəth- *also* 'räth- *or* 'reth- *or* 'räth-\ *adv* [ME, fr. OE *hrathor*, comp. of *hrathe*, *hræthe* rapidly, quickly] **1** *dial chiefly Eng* **:** more quickly **:** EARLIER, BEFORE **2 :** with better reason or more propriety ⟨pity ~ than despise —Shak.⟩ **3 :** more readily or willingly **:** PREFERABLY ⟨my soul chooseth . . . death ~ than my life —Job 7:15 (AV)⟩ ⟨would ~ starve than pick the garbage dump —Erskine Caldwell⟩ — often used as an interjection to express decided affirmation ⟨"Do you smoke?" "*Rather!*" —J.D.Beresford⟩ **4 :** more properly or truly **:** more correctly speaking ⟨~ like a dream than an assurance —Shak.⟩ ⟨their inspiration or, ~, their idol⟩ **5 :** to the contrary **:** INSTEAD ⟨was no better but ~ grew worse —Mk 5:26 (RSV)⟩ ⟨no longer a traveler's nightmare, ~ his joy —Wyn Roberts⟩ **6 :** in some degree **:** SOMEWHAT, QUITE ⟨it's ~ cold⟩ ⟨a ~ unusual gesture⟩ ⟨a boring play⟩ ⟨shaped ~ like an onion⟩ ⟨~ on the childish side⟩ ⟨cost ten thousand or ~ more⟩ ⟨~ doubted the truth of the remark⟩ — **the rather 1** *obs* **:** the more quickly **:** the sooner ⟨asleep (whereto *the rather* shall his day's hard journey soundly invite him) —Shak.⟩ **2 :** the more so **:** all the more **:** ESPECIALLY ⟨you are come to me in happy time *the rather* for I have some sport in hand —Shak.⟩ ⟨*all the rather*⟩

²rather \"\ *verbal auxiliary* **:** prefer to — not often in formal use ⟨I ~ sleep than eat⟩

¹ratheripe \(')=¦=\ *also* **rathripe** \(')=¦=\ *adj* [¹*rathe* + *ripe*] *chiefly dial* **:** RARERIPE, PRECOCIOUS

²ratheripe \"\ *n, chiefly dial* **:** RARERIPE

rath·er·ish *pronunc at* RATHER + ish\ *adv* [¹*rather* + *-ish*] **:** SOMEWHAT, FAIRLY ⟨a ~ handsome fellow⟩

rath·er·ly *adv* [¹*rather* + *-ly*] *dial Brit* **:** RATHER, SOMEWHAT ⟨his deep voice that was like a mellow bell and trembled ~ —Hall Caine⟩

rath·ite \'rä,tīt, -,thīt\ *n* -S [G *rathit*, fr. G. vom Rath †1888 Ger. mineralogist + G *-it* -ite] **:** a mineral $Pb_{13}As_{18}S_{40}$ consisting of a lead arsenic sulfide occurring in dark gray metallic orthorhombic crystals (hardness 3, sp. gr. 5.4)

rath·ke's pouch \'rätkəz-\ *also* **rathke's pocket** *n, usu cap R* [after Martin H. *Rathke* †1860 Ger. anatomist] **:** a pouch of ectoderm that grows out from the upper surface of the embryonic stomodaeum and gives rise to the anterior lobe of the pituitary body

rathole \'=,=\ *n* **1 a :** a rat's burrow **b :** a hole gnawed by a rat **2 a :** a narrow opening, tunnel, or passageway **b :** a cramped space (as for storage or living quarters); *esp* **:** one that is oppressive or filthy ⟨cooped up in a ~ like this —Jack Ward⟩ **3 :** a seemingly bottomless or unfillable hole ⟨his last pile of money . . . went down the ~ when he tried to save an old friend from bankruptcy —Stanley Walker⟩

raths·kel·ler \'rät,skelə(r), 'rat,s-, 'rát,s-, 'rath,s-, 'raath-\ *n* -S [G *ratskeller* (formerly spelled *rathskeller*) restaurant in the basement of a town hall, fr. *rat* council (fr. MHG *rāt* advice, supply, council, fr. OHG, advice, supply) + *keller* cellar, basement, fr. OHG *kellāri*, fr. L *cellarium* — more at READ, CELLAR] **:** a restaurant located usu. below the street level and patterned after the cellar or basement of a German city hall where beer or wine is sold

ra·tib·i·da \rə'tibədə\ *n, cap* [NL] **:** a genus of perennial No. American composite herbs that are sometimes cultivated for their showy flower heads

rat·i·cide \'rad·ə,sīd\ *n* -S [¹*rat* + *-i-* + *-cide*] **:** a substance (as red squill) for killing rats

rat·i·fi·ca·tion \,rad·əfə'kāshən, -atə-\ *n* -S [ME, fr. MF or ML; MF, fr. ML *ratification-*, *ratificatio*, fr. *ratificatus* (past part. of *ratificare* to ratify) + L *-ion-*, *-io* -ion — more at RATIFY] **:** the act or process of ratifying **:** CONFIRMATION, SANCTION ⟨proposed . . . ~ of treaties by a simple majority of both houses of Congress —Vera M. Dean⟩

rat·i·fi·ca·tion·ist \-sh(ə)nəst\ *n* -S **:** an advocate of ratification (as of a treaty or contract)

rat·i·fi·er \'==,fī(ə)r\ *n* -S **:** one that ratifies

rat·i·fy \'rad·ə,fī, -atə-\ *vt* -ED/-ING/-ES [ME *ratifien*, fr. MF *ratifier*, fr. ML *ratificare*, fr. L *ratus* calculated, fixed, determined + *-ificare* -ify — more at RATE] **1 :** to approve and sanction esp. formally (as the act of an agent or servant) **:** make (as a treaty) valid or legally operative **:** CONFIRM ⟨~ the nomination⟩ ⟨~ the contract⟩ ⟨can by . . . refusal to ~ the adopted amendment prevent its coming into force —Herbert Weinschel⟩ ⟨~*ing* his precocious habit of smoking —Arnold Bennett⟩ **2 :** to confirm the truth of **:** VERIFY ⟨time had *ratified* the soundness of the idea⟩ ⟨merely ~*ing* a tradition —E.R. Bentley⟩

rat·i·ha·bi·tion \,rad·ēhə'bishən\ *n* -S [LL *ratihabition-*, *ratihabitio*, fr. L *ratus* fixed, determined + LL *habition-*, *habitio* act of having, fr. L *habitus* (past part. of *habēre* to move) + *-ion-*, *-io* -ion — more at RATE, GIVE] **:** RATIFICATION, SANCTION

ra·ti·né \,ratᵊn¦ā\ *or* **ra·tine** \", ra'tēn\ *n* -S [F *ratiné*, fr. past part. of *ratiner* to frieze, fr. *ratine* ratteen] **1** *also* **ratiné yarn :** a nubby ply yarn of various fibers made by twisting under tension a thick and a thin yarn **2 :** a rough bulky fabric often of cotton but also of other fibers that is usu. woven loosely in plain weave from ratiné yarns and is used for dresses, suits, and coats — called also *sponge cloth*

¹rating *n* -S [fr. gerund of ¹*rate*] **:** SCOLDING, REBUKE ⟨gave him a severe ~⟩

²rating *n* -S [fr. gerund of ³*rate*] **1 :** a classification according to grade **:** RANK: as **a :** the relative standing of a sailor in a ship's company ⟨had the ~ of boatswain's mate⟩ **b :** an assignment in an occupational group (as in the U.S. Navy) within which a petty officer holds a rate ⟨a petty officer with a ~ of radarman⟩ **c :** a specialist classification in the armed forces (as pilot, parachutist, gunner) **2** *chiefly Brit* **:** a naval enlisted man ⟨two officers and ten ~*s* aboard each vessel —*Manchester Guardian Weekly*⟩ **3 a :** a relative estimate or evaluation (as of status, achievement, or appeal) **:** STANDING, MARK ⟨his ~ was high⟩ ⟨the good academic ~ of the school⟩ ⟨a high ~ for honesty in government —J.A.Morris b. 1904⟩ ⟨had the highest ~ in the examination⟩ **b :** an estimate of the credit and responsibility of an individual or business concern **c :** estimation of an individual's traits and qualities (as interests, abilities, attitudes, or personality) by his indicated preferences on a scale of items **d :** an estimate of the percentage of the public listening to or viewing a particular radio or television program ⟨was Mr. Television himself . . . had a ~ of twenty-eight —Pete Martin⟩ **4 :** a stated operating limit of a machine expressible in power units (as in horsepower of a motor, kilowatts of a direct-current generator, or kilovolt amperes of an alternator) or in characteristics (as speed, voltage, or frequency) — compare DUTY 5b

rating badge *n* **:** a distinctive mark of a petty officer (as in the U.S. Navy) that consists of an eagle, one, two, or three chevrons, an arc for a chief, and a specialty mark and that is worn between shoulder and elbow formerly on the right by members of the seaman branch and on the left by others but from 1948 on the left by all branches

rating badge of a chief radioman

rating flume *n* **:** a flume of known capacities at different depths and velocities that is used for the measurement of large flows of irrigation water

rating nut *n* **:** a milled nut under a pendulum bob for varying the effective pendulum length in rating a clock

ra·tio \'rā,shō, -,shē,ō\ *n* -S [L, reason, computation, reasoning — more at REASON] **1 a :** the real ground or nature of a thing esp. as determined by its relation to other things **:** RATIONALE — compare PYTHAGOREANISM, REASON **b :** the understanding or reason in Scholasticism that has the capacity to think discursively and make abstractions — compare INTELLECT **2 a :** the quotient of one quantity divided by another **b :** the fixed or approximate relation of one thing to another or between two or more things (as in number, quantity, or degree) **:** RATE, PROPORTION ⟨the ~ between births and deaths⟩ ⟨the 10:1 student-teacher ~ of the school⟩ ⟨the ~ between stock prices, earnings, and dividends —*Time*⟩ ⟨combining . . . in such ~ understanding of technics and of human rights —Roger Burlingame⟩; *specif* **:** specified proportion of ingredients (as in plant foods or fertilizers) ⟨tomatoes were grown outdoors with . . . use of widely different nutrient ~*s* —*Experiment Station Record*⟩ **c :** the expression of the relative values of gold and silver as determined by the currency laws of a country — called also *coinage ratio* **3** *archaic* **:** RATION, PORTION ⟨furnished the . . invaders with a ~ of biscuit and wine —Archibald Duncan⟩

ratio arm *n* **:** a branch of an electrical bridge circuit — compare WHEATSTONE BRIDGE

ratio chart *n* **:** a chart employing the Cartesian coordinate system in which the points on a curve are determined by measuring time as the independent variable along one axis and the logarithms of the values of the corresponding dependent variables along the other

rati·oci·nate \,rad·ē'ōsᵊn,āt, -ashē-,-atē-, -ē'äs-, *usu* -ād·+V\ *vi* -ED/-ING/-S [L *ratiocinatus*, past part. of *ratiocinari* to reckon, deliberate, consider, fr. *ratio* reason, computation, reasoning] **:** to reason discursively or according to a logical process

rati·oci·na·tion \,==,=='āshən\ *n* -S [MF or L; MF, fr. L *ratiocination-*, *ratiocinatio*, fr. *ratiocinatus* + *-ion-*, *-io* -ion] **1 a :** the process of exact thinking **:** REASONING ⟨pure ~, where the intellect works cold and aloof in dry light —J.L.Lowes⟩ **b :** a specific train of thought or piece of reasoning ⟨~*s* on conscience and conventional morality —M.S.Day⟩ **2** *archaic* **a :** the faculty of reason **b :** the habit of reasoning

rati·oci·na·tive \,==,=,ād·iv\ *adj* [L *ratiocinativus*, fr. *ratiocinatus* + *-ivus* -ive] **1 :** of or relating to ratiocination ⟨~ powers⟩ ⟨stimulate one's ~ faculties —Max Beerbohm⟩ **2 :** marked by or devoted to ratiocination ⟨assume a dogmatic rather than a ~ attitude —*Scientific Monthly*⟩ ⟨our educational system . . . not basically ~ —C.W.Shumaker⟩

rati·oci·na·tor \-,ād·ə(r)\ *n* -S [L, fr. *ratiocinatus* + *-or*] **:** REASONER

rati·oci·na·to·ry \-sᵊnə,tōrē, -ōrē, -ri\ *adj* **:** RATIOCINATIVE

ra·tio cog·no·scen·di \'räd·ē,ō,kōgnə'sken(,)dē\ *n, pl* **rati·o·nes cognoscendi** \,räd·ē'ō(,)nā,skōg-\ [L] **:** the ground of knowledge **:** something through or by means of which a thing is known

ratio de·ci·den·di \-,desə'den(,)dē\ *n, pl* **rationes decidendi** [L] **:** the reason or ground for a judicial decision

ratio es·sen·di \-e'sen(,)dē\ *n, pl* **rationes essendi** [ML] **:** the cause or ground of the existence of a thing

ra·ti·om·e·ter \,rāshē'ämədə(r)\ *n* [*ratio* + *-meter*] **:** a device for making a succession of photographic exposures to obtain the filter ratios of color-sensitive materials under given conditions of work

ratiomotor \'=(=),=,==\ *n* **:** a motor integral with a speed-reducing gear

¹ra·tion \'rashən, 'rāsh-\ *n* -S [F, fr. L *ration-*, *ratio* reason, computation, reasoning — more at REASON] **1** *archaic* **:** RATIO **2 a :** the food allowance of one person or one animal for one day; *specif* **:** a fixed daily food allowance provided for the subsistence of a soldier or sailor — compare FIELD RATION, K RATION **b rations** *pl* **:** FOOD, PROVISIONS ⟨cooked two days' ~*s* —G.R.Stewart⟩ ⟨issued ~*s* to the needy —*Amer. Guide Series: Fla.*⟩ **3 :** a share esp. as determined by supply **:** allotted or permitted amount ⟨a reduction of the wartime meat ~⟩ ⟨saved up their gas ~ to go on a short motor trip —MacKinlay Kantor⟩ ⟨pouring the whiskey, a neat two fingers, obviously a ~ —Margery Allingham⟩

²ration \"\ *vt* **rationed; rationed; rationing** \-sh(ə)niŋ\ **rations 1 :** to supply with rations **:** put on rations ⟨~ the inhabitants of a besieged city⟩ ⟨the Food Administration did not ~ the people —Will Irwin⟩ **2 a :** to distribute as rations **:** allot in rations ⟨~ sugar during the emergency⟩ ⟨~*ed* out beef, pork, and flour, often to hundreds —*Amer. Guide Series: Minn.*⟩ **b :** to distribute or divide (as commodities in short supply) in an equitable manner or so as to achieve a particular object (as maximum production of particular items) — compare DIRECT CONTROL **c :** to use or indulge in sparingly ⟨an official communiqué in which words were strictly ~*ed* —*Time*⟩ **syn** see APPORTION

¹ra·tio·nal \'rashənᵊl, -shnəl, 'raash-, 'raish-\ *adj* [ME *racional*, fr. L *rationalis*, fr. *ration-*, *ratio* reason, computation, reasoning + *-alis* -al] **1 :** having reason or understanding **:** REASONING ⟨~ creature⟩ ⟨a ~ being⟩ ⟨embryo had a vegetable life, then an animal life, and finally a ~ life —S.F.Mason⟩ **2 a :** of, relating to, or based upon reason ⟨provide a literary as well as a ~ education —G.K.Chalmers⟩ ⟨~ analysis of the problem —R.C.Doty⟩ **b :** using medical treatments based on reason or general principles — used esp. of an ancient school of physicians; opposed to *empirical* **3 :** involving only multiplication, division, addition, and subtraction and only a finite number of times **:** not involving a surd or indicated but not extractable root ⟨3 and 2+⅗ are ~ expressions⟩ **4 a :** agreeable to reason **:** INTELLIGENT, SENSIBLE ⟨gives a quite ~ explanation of the passage —*Modern Language Notes*⟩ ⟨a ~ . . . world trade policy —*Nation's Business*⟩ ⟨the advantages of a ~ orthography —C.H.Grandgent⟩ **b :** RATIONALISTIC **5 :** capable of being measured in terms of the mora in Greek and Latin prosody **:** having the normal ratio between arsis and thesis

syn REASONABLE: RATIONAL usu. implies a latent or active power to make logical inferences and draw conclusions that enable one to understand the world about him and relate such knowledge to the attainment of ends, often, in this use, opposed to *emotional* or *animal;* in application to policies, projects, or acts, RATIONAL implies satisfactory to the reason or chiefly actuated by reason ⟨the triumph of the *rational* over the emotional side of man⟩ ⟨his was a mind so purely *rational* that it had long since demanded and received absolute divorce from his naturally impetuous heart —Elinor Wylie⟩ ⟨the *rational*, the intelligent, the orderly processes of behavior —Lewis Mumford⟩ ⟨we may seek to change another person's convictions in a *rational* manner either by bringing to his notice evidence that he did not previously know about or by inducing in him a process of *rational* inference —R.H.Thouless⟩ REASONABLE usu. carries a much weaker implication of the power to reason in general or of guidance by conclusions drawn by the reasoning power, rather applying to actions or decisions or choices that are practical, sensible, just, or fair ⟨the longing to achieve is more emotional than *reasonable* —H.S.Canby⟩ ⟨no English author has given an ampler and more *reasonable* interpretation of life —W.S.Maugham⟩ ⟨the amount of uncompleted work is relatively small and can be completed within a *reasonable* period of time —*Loyola Univ. Bull.*⟩ ⟨the heifers and cows may be expected to give a *reasonable* milk yield —Allan Fraser⟩ ⟨contributions must be *reasonable* in amount —C.M.Winslow⟩

²rational \"\ *n* -S **:** something rational: as **a** *archaic* **:** a rational creature; *esp* **:** a human being ⟨not as ~*s*, but as animals —Thomas Paine⟩ **b :** a rational expression in mathematics ⟨consider the set of all ~*s*, excluding zero —Harry Lass⟩ **c :** RATIONALE ⟨the decided shift in production ~ —*Dun's Rev.*⟩

ra·tio·nale \¦rashə¦nal *sometimes* -näl *or* -nál *or* ,=='=ē *or* ,=='nälē *or* -li\ *n* -S [L, neut. of *rationalis* rational — more at RATIONAL] **1 :** an explanation or exposition of controlling principles (as of an opinion, belief, practice, or phenomenon) ⟨the ~ of the decision in the case —J.D.Johnson⟩ ⟨the most popular ~ of religious behavior —J.D.Hart⟩ ⟨a ~ of present practice in probation and parole —*Columbia Univ. Press Books*⟩ ⟨a ~ of retail prices —C.G.Burke⟩ **2 :** the underlying reason **:** rational basis **:** JUSTIFICATION, GROUND ⟨the ~ of the law —Walter Adams⟩ ⟨a plausible . . . ~ for conformity —W.H.Whyte⟩ ⟨no ~ underlying the new therapeutic approach can be offered at this early stage —*Jour. Amer. Med. Assoc.*⟩

rational fraction *n* **:** a fraction of which both numerator and denominator are rational numbers or are polynomials

rational function *n* **1 :** POLYNOMIAL **2 :** the quotient of two polynomials

rational horizon *n* **:** HORIZON 1b(1), 1b(2)

ra·tio·nal·ism \'rashənᵊl,izəm, -shnə,li-, 'raash-, 'raish-\ *n* -S **1 :** reliance on reason as the basis for establishment of religious truth ⟨outbreaks of ~ . . . manifested themselves in heretical movements —S.H.Cross⟩ **2 a :** a theory that reason is in itself a source of knowledge superior to and independent of sense perceptions — contrasted with *sensationalism* **b :** a theory that philosophical knowledge may be arrived at by deduction from a priori concepts or necessary ideas **:** APRIORISM — compare INTUITIONISM; contrasted with *empiricism* **c :** elaboration and development of theories (as in pure mathematics) by reasoning alone without testing them by experience **d :** a view that an appeal to reason and experience rather than to the nonrational (as emotion, intuition, faith, revelation, or authority) is to be employed as the fundamental criterion in the solution of problems **3 :** the technical and practical approach to architectural design as opposed to the traditional **:** FUNCTIONALISM

¹ra·tio·nal·ist \-shənᵊləst, -shnəl-\ *n* -S [¹*rational* + *-ist*] **:** an advocate of rationalism

²rationalist \"\ *adj* **:** RATIONALISTIC ⟨ruthless suppression of ~ opinion —Kingsley Martin⟩

ra·tio·nal·is·tic \¦rashənᵊl¦istik, -shnə¦l-, 'raash-, ¦raish-, -tēk\ *adj* **1 :** of, relating to, or in accordance with the principles of rationalism ⟨~ philosophies⟩ ⟨a ~ theory⟩ ⟨all ~ argument from axiomatic principles —J.H.Randall⟩ **2 :** marked by or having a tendency toward rationalism ⟨~ liberalism⟩ ⟨the possibility of viewing thinkers as predominantly either ~ or mystic —M.R.Cohen⟩ — **ra·tio·nal·is·ti·cal·ly** \-tək(ə)lē, -tēk-, -li\ *adv*

ra·tio·nal·i·ty \,rashə'naləd·ē, ,raash-, ,raish-, -lətē, -i\ *n* -ES [LL *rationalitas*, fr. L *rationalis* rational + *-itas* -ity — more at RATIONAL] **1 :** the quality or state of being rational ⟨man's ~ is not a higher faculty . . . imposed upon his animal nature —Grace De Laguna⟩ **2 :** acceptability to reason **:** REASONABLENESS ⟨gives a ~ . . . and a justification to the universe —J.W.Krutch⟩ ⟨the social ~ that . . . alone can save us —A.L. Locke⟩ **3 :** something (as an opinion, belief, or practice) that is rational — usu. used in pl ⟨a race . . . between the *rationalities* of technology and the irrationalities of style —Lewis Mumford⟩

ra·tio·nal·iza·tion \,rashənᵊlə'zāshən, -shnələ-, ,raash-, ,raish-, -ᵊl,ī'-, -nə,lī'-\ *n* -S **:** the act, process, or result of rationalizing: as **a :** substitution of a rational for a supernatural explanation ⟨by giving the Bible a poetic . . . interpretation . . . in short, by ~ —*Humanist*⟩ **b :** an account or ordering in conformity with reason or rational principles ⟨offering this ~ of a people —Kay Boyle⟩ ⟨a ~ of . . . customs procedures —*N. Y. Times*⟩ ⟨this process of ~ in . . . biological thinking —P.S.Hudson⟩ **c :** the organization of a business or industry upon scientific principles of management and simplified procedures to obtain greater efficiency of operation **d :** the provision of plausible reasons to explain to oneself or others behavior for which one's real motives are different and unknown or unconscious ⟨the reasons most commonly given for anti-Semitism . . . are ~*s* of prejudices —*Harper's*⟩

ra·tio·nal·ize \'rashənᵊl,īz, -shnə,līz, 'raash-, 'raish-\ *vb* -ED/-ING/-S [¹*rational* + *-ize*] *vt* **1 :** to free (a mathematical equation) from irrational expressions **2 a :** to make conformable (as an attitude or belief) with rational principles **:** give a rational explanation of ⟨~ one's attitude to life⟩ ⟨chauvinists ~ race prejudice⟩ ⟨labored . . . to ~ history into a science —H.S.Commager⟩ **b :** to substitute a natural for a supernatural explanation of ⟨~ the Greek myths⟩ — often used with *away* ⟨~ away all miracles⟩ **3 :** to attribute (one's actions) to rational and creditable motives without adequate analysis of the true and esp. unconscious motives ⟨easy for men of principle to ~ lapses from high standards where the cause seems to them good —J.A.R.Pimlott⟩ **4 :** to apply the principles of scientific management to (a factory, industrial process, or industry) ⟨*rationalizing* the supply lines so as to eliminate duplicate hauling —*Fortune*⟩ ~ *vi* **:** to provide plausible but untrue reasons or motives for a course of conduct ⟨urged him to stop *rationalizing* and admit he acted selfishly⟩ **syn** see EXPLAIN

ra·tio·nal·ly \-nᵊlē, -nəlē, -li\ *adv* **:** in a rational manner: as **a :** in accordance with reason **:** REASONABLY, SENSIBLY ⟨conditions . . . required for living ~ —Herbert Read⟩ **b :** with respect to reason ⟨training and direction would make them . . . ~ competent beings —G.P.Musselman⟩

ra·tio·nal·ness *n* -ES **:** RATIONALITY 1

rational number *n* **:** an integer or the quotient of two integers (as ⅔)

rationals *pl of* RATIONAL

rational soul *n* **:** the soul that in the scholastic tradition has independent existence apart from the body and that is the characteristic animating principle of human life as distinguished from animal or vegetable life — compare ANIMAL SOUL, VEGETABLE SOUL

rationed *past of* RATION

ra·ti·o·ne do·mi·ci·lii \,räd·ē'ō(,)nā,dōmə'kilē,ē\ *adv* [L] **:** by reason of domicile

ratione rei si·tae \-,rā,ē'si,tī\ *adv* [L] **:** by reason of the situs of the thing

rationes cognoscendi *pl of* RATIO COGNOSCENDI

rationes decidendi *pl of* RATIO DECIDENDI

rationes essendi *pl of* RATIO ESSENDI

rationing *n* -S [fr. gerund of ²*ration*] **:** the act or process of distributing commodities as rations ⟨~ device⟩ ⟨~ system⟩ ⟨moved promptly to eliminate ~ on gasoline, fuel oil —H.S. Truman⟩

rations *pl of* RATION, *pres 3d sing of* RATION

ratio of a geometric progression : the constant quantity by which each term in a geometric progression is multiplied to produce the succeeding one

ratio of expansion : the ratio of the volume of steam in an engine cylinder or turbine when the piston is at the end of the stroke to the volume at cut-off

ratio of similitude : the ratio between any two corresponding linear extents (as line segments) in two similar figures

ratios *pl of* RATIO

ra·ti·tae \rə'tīd·,ē\ *n pl, cap* [NL, fr. L, fem. pl. of *ratitus* marked with the figure of a raft, fr. *ratis* raft; perh. akin to L *rete* net — more at RETINA] *in some classifications* **:** a superordinal group of birds comprising forms with small or rudimentary wings, no pygostyle, and no keel to the breastbone that are nonetheless evidently descended from birds with the power of flight, including the ostriches, rheas, cassowaries and emus, elephant birds, moas, and kiwis, and usu. constituting a primary subdivision of the subclass Neornithes

¹rat·ite \'ra,tīt\ *adj* [NL *Ratitae*] **1 :** having a flat unkeeled breastbone — compare CARINATE **2 :** of or relating to the Ratitae

²ratite \"\ *n* -S **:** a bird with a flat breastbone **:** one of the Ratitae

rat·i·tous \'rad·əd·əs\ *adj* [NL *Ratitae* + E *-ous*] **:** RATITE

rat kangaroo *n* **:** any of various small Australian and Tasmanian kangaroos of *Bettongia*, *Potorous*, and closely related genera that are no larger than a rabbit and have persistent canine teeth and a long and often prehensile tail

ratlike \'=,=\ *adj* **1 :** of, relating to, or characteristic of a rat ⟨a ~ tail⟩ **2 :** resembling a rat in appearance or behavior ⟨a ~ slippery little man with sharp features and small beady eyes⟩

rat·line *also* **rat·lin** *or* **rat·ling** \'ratlən\ *n* -S [origin unknown] **1** *or* **ratline stuff :** small, usu. 3-stranded, tarred rope used for cross ropes on ship's shrouds **2 :** one of the small transverse ropes attached to the shrouds of a ship and forming the steps of a rope ladder — see SHIP illustration

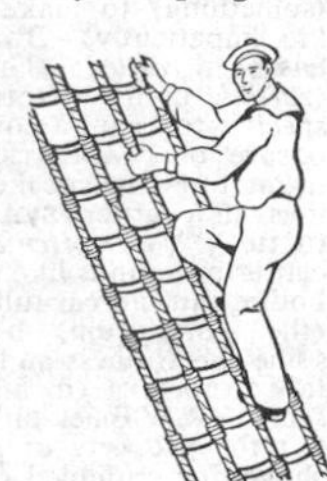

ratlines and shrouds

rat louse *n* **:** a sucking louse (*Polyplax spinulosa*) that is a widely distributed parasite of rats

rat mite *n* **:** a widely distributed mite (*Bdellonyssus bacoti*) formerly limited to warm regions but rapidly spreading into more temperate areas that sometimes causes severe dermatitis in man and is a vector of epidemic typhus particularly in the Orient

rat mole *n* **:** MOLE RAT

RATO \'räd·(,)ō\ *abbr, often not cap* **:** rocket-assisted takeoff

¹ra·toon \ra'tün\ *n* -S [Sp *retoño* sprout, shoot, fr. *retoñar* to sprout, shoot a second time, fr. *re-* + *otoñar* to grow in the autumn, fr. *otoño* autumn, fr. L *autumnus*] **1 :** a stalk or shoot arising from the root or crown of a perennial plant:

as **a** : a sugarcane sucker arising from the base of a harvested plant **b** : one of the suckers arising below the developing pineapple fruit and used to produce a second crop **c** : a shoot of the third generation after planting of a banana plant **d** : Jamaica ginger of inferior quality consisting of small fibrous offsets of the rhizome **2** *or* **ratoon crop** : a crop (as of cotton or pineapples) produced by or on ratoon growth

2ratoon \"\ *vb* -ED/-ING/-S [Sp *retoñar*] *vi* : to sprout or spring up from the root ⟨some cottons ~ freely⟩ ⟨sugarcane ~*ing* from the root of the previous year's planting⟩ ~ *vt* : to grow or produce (a crop) from or on ratoons ⟨~ a pineapple field⟩

ra·toon·er \-nə(r)\ *n* -S : a plant that propagates by ratooning

rato unit *n* : JATO UNIT

rat-poison plant \ˈ=ˌ==-\ *n* : SCARLET HAMELIA

1ratproof \ˈ=ˌ=\ *adj* [¹*rat* + *proof*] : proof against rats ⟨~ construction⟩ ⟨a ~ warehouse⟩

2ratproof \"\ *vt* : to make (as a building or ship) secure against the entry of rats

rat race *n* : a violent, confused, and usu. competitive activity or rush; *esp* : one that is meaningless or profitless : VICIOUS CIRCLE ⟨life was a *rat race* . . . no time for gracious living or warm family feeling —Frances G. Patton⟩ ⟨caught in the *rat race*, they may still work hard —Henry Hazlitt⟩

rat rhyme *n* **1** *chiefly Scot* : a scrap of nonsense or doggerel verse **2** *chiefly Scot* : RIGMAROLE

1rats *pl of* RAT, *pres 3d sing of* RAT

2rats \ˈrats\ *interj* [fr. pl. of ¹*rat*] — used to express disappointment, disgust, or scoffing incredulity

ratsbane \ˈ=ˌ=\ *n* -S **1** : ARSENIC TRIOXIDE **2** : any of various plants that are or are supposed to be poisonous to rats: as **a** : a West African shrub (*Dichapetalum toxicarium*) with extremely poisonous seeds — called also *African ratsbane* **b** : a No. American rattlesnake plantain (*Goodyera pubescens*) **c** : SPOTTED WINTERGREEN **d** : CHERVIL 1

rat snake *n* : any of numerous rat-eating colubrid snakes: as **a** : any member of a common Indian genus (*Ptyas*) of snakes that enter buildings in pursuit of their prey **b** : any member of a No. American genus (*Elaphe*) of large constricting snakes that include the widely known pilot black snake and the chicken snake

rat's-tail fescue \ˈ=ˌ=-\ *n* : RATTAIL FESCUE

rat-stripper \ˈ=ˌ==\ *n* : MOUNTAIN LOVER 1

1rattail \ˈ=ˌ=\ *n* [¹*rat* + *tail*] : something suggestive of a rat's tail: as **a** (1) : a horse's tail having little or no hair (2) : a horse with such a tail (3) : MULE **b** (1) *also* **rattail fish** *or* **rattail grenadier** : GRENADIER 2 (2) : ²CHIMAERA **c** (1) : any of several plants (as a plantain or various grasses) having elongated terete spikes (2) : any of several grasses having slender cylindrical flower spikes

2rattail \"\ *adj* : round, slender, and tapering : resembling a rat's tail

rattail cactus *n* : a commonly cultivated tropical American cactus (*Aporocactus flagelliformis*) having slender creeping stems and very showy crimson flowers three inches long that bloom for several days

rat-tailed \(ˈ)=ˈ=\ *adj* : having a long tapering tail like that of a rat ⟨a *rat-tailed* horse⟩

rat-tailed larva *or* **rat-tailed maggot** *n* : the larva of a syrphid fly of *Eristalis* or related genera that is remarkable for the long telescopic tubular tail with spiracles at the tip through which air is brought down from above the mud or putrefying matter in which the larva lives

rat-tailed radish *n* : a radish (*Raphanus sativus caudatus* or *R. caudatus*) that has an inedible root and is grown for its long slender edible pods

rat-tailed serpent *n* : FER-DE-LANCE

rat-tailed shrew *n* : MUSK SHREW 1

rattail fescue *n* : a slender European grass (*Festuca myuros*) naturalized as a weed in the eastern U. S.

rattail file *n* : a small round file

rattail hinge \ˈ=ˌ=-\ *n* : a pintle type hinge in which the pin is extended so that it can be fastened to the casing of a door

rattail spoon *n* : a form of spoon developed in the later 17th century with a thin pointed tongue on the bottom of the bowl to reinforce the joint of bowl and handle

rattail hinge

1rat·tan *also* **ra·tan** \raˈtan, rəˈ-, -aa(ə)n, ˈraˌt-\ *or* **rattan palm** *or* **ro·tan** \rəˈt-\ *n* -S [Malay *rotan*] **1** : any of several climbing palms (esp. of the genera *Calamus* and *Daemonorops*) remarkable for the great length attained by their stems **2** : a portion of the very tough stem of a rattan palm used esp. for walking sticks, wickerwork, chairs, seats of chairs, cords, and cordage — see CALAMUS 4, MALACCA CANE **3** : a rattan cane or switch ⟨whipping on the open hand with a thin ~ —R.M.Lovett⟩

2rat·tan \raˈtan, rəˈ-, -aa(ə)n\ *vt* **rattaned** *or* **rattanned**; **rattaned** *or* **rattanned**; **rattaning** *or* **rattanning**; **rattans** **1** : to provide or strengthen with rattan **2** : to punish by striking with a rattan ⟨the schoolmaster ~*ing* a young culprit⟩

3rat·tan *or* **rat·ten** \ˈratᵊn\ *var of* RATTON

rattan vine *n* : SUPPLEJACK 1a

rat-tat \(ˈ)ra(t)ˌtat, *usu* -tad·+V\ *also* **rat-tat-tat** \ˌrad·əˈtat, *usu* -tad·+V\ *or* **rat·tat·too** \ˌ==ˈtü\ *n* -S [imit.] : RAT-A-TAT

ratted *past of* RAT

rat·teen \raˈtēn\ *n* -S [F *ratine*] *archaic* : any of various coarse woolen fabrics (as frieze, baize, drugget)

rat·ter \ˈrad·ə(r), -atə-\ *n* -S [¹*rat* + *-er*] : RATCATCHER; *specif* : a rat-catching dog or cat

ratti *var of* RUTTEE

rattier *comparative of* RATTY

rattiest *superlative of* RATTY

ratting *pres part of* RAT

rat·tish \ˈrad·ish, -atish, -ēsh\ *adj* [¹*rat* + *-ish*] : resembling or having the characteristics of a rat ⟨a fellow with a ~ look⟩

1rat·tle \ˈrad·ᵊl, -atᵊl\ *vb* **rattled**; **rattled**; **rattling** \-d·ᵊliŋ, -t(ᵊ)l-\ **rattles** [ME *ratelen*; akin to OE *hratele*, a plant, MD *ratelen* to rattle, *ratele*, *ratel* rattle, MHG *razzeln*, *razzen* to rage, rattle, ON *hrata* to fall, stagger — more at CARDINAL] *vi* **1** : to make, cause, or emit a rapid succession of short sharp noises or of similarly discontinuous sounds (as through shaking or recurrent collisions of hard bodies) : CLATTER ⟨the windows ~ in the wind⟩ ⟨a diamondback rattlesnake . . . slow to coil or ~ unless angered —Marjory S. Douglas⟩ **2** : to make a rattle in the throat **3** : to chatter incessantly and aimlessly ⟨she *rattled* on for an hour⟩ ⟨walked over the grounds . . . *rattling*, chatting —George Meredith⟩ **4** : to move or proceed with a clatter or rattle : drive or ride clatteringly ⟨a wagon *rattling* through the streets⟩ ⟨we *rattled* along briskly⟩ ~ *vt* **1** : to say, perform, or affect in a brisk lively fashion esp. with a rattle or clatter ⟨the gale *rattled* the tiles from the roof⟩ — often used with *off* ⟨guides . . . ~ off the history of atomic energy —Daniel Lang⟩ **2** : to cause (something) to make a rattling sound ⟨*rattling* their mess kits impatiently⟩ **3** *archaic* : to rail at : SCOLD ⟨for this he has been *rattled* —Thomas Gray⟩ **4** : to shake up : ROUSE ⟨*rattling* us up at this hour of the night —Walter Macken⟩; *specif* : to beat (a cover) for game **5** : to disturb the composure of : AGITATE, DISCONCERT ⟨~ a player⟩ ⟨hecklers trying to ~ the speaker⟩ **6** : to test or tumble (as metal castings) in a rattler **syn** see EMBARRASS

2rattle \"\ *n* -S *often attrib* **1 a** : a rapid succession of sharp clattering sounds like those made by repeated collision of hard bodies ⟨an old car full of knocks and ~*s*⟩ ⟨the ~ of musketry⟩ ⟨the ~ of a drum⟩ **b** : RACKET ⟨cannot bear a place without some cheerfulness and ~ —Samuel Johnson⟩ **c** : noisy rapid talk : CHATTER ⟨in a good deal of ~ . . . a grain or two of sense —R.W.Emerson⟩ ⟨a light ~ of small talk —E.G.Lowry⟩ **d** : the property of paper that causes it to be noisy when shaken or crumpled ⟨starch . . . imparts snap and ~ to the sheet —F.H.Norris⟩ **2 a** : a child's toy that rattles when shaken and that consists usu. of a case containing loose pellets **b** : a noisemaker with a tongue that plays on the teeth of a ratchet wheel when revolved formerly used by watchmen and now by merrymakers — called also *watchman's rattle* **c** : a dance instrument (as a receptacle with noise-making contents or a stick with clashing objects) that is rhythmically shaken during various dances (as of American Indians) : IDIOPHONE **d** : a tiresome or frivolous chatterer : senseless talker ⟨from the point of view of an artless, affectionate ~ —Mary Bailey⟩ **3 a** : a plant of the genus *Rhinanthus*; *esp* : an annual herb (*R. crista-galli*) of the north temperate zone with showy yellow purple-spotted flowers that is partially parasitic on grasses and other plants and that has seeds which rattle in the inflated capsule when ripe — called also *yellow rattle* **b** : a European lousewort (*Pedicularis palustris*) — called also *red rattle* **4 a** : the sound-producing organ on a rattlesnake's tail **b** : one of the constituent segments of this organ **5** : the noise in the throat caused by air passing through mucus; *specif* : that heard at the approach of death — compare RALE **6** : a movement of brushing forward and striking back with the ball of the foot in dancing

3rattle \"\ *vt* **rattled**; **rattled**; **rattling** \-d·ᵊliŋ, -t(ᵊ)l-\ **rattles** [back-formation fr. ²*rattling*] : to furnish (a ship's shrouds) with ratlines : fasten ratlines on — often used with *down* ⟨~ down the rigging⟩

rattle about *vi* : to rattle around

rattle around *vi* : to have or give the impression of being tumbled about (as by living in too spacious quarters or holding a post one cannot fill) ⟨gave him a suite of offices to *rattle around* in but nothing to do⟩

rattlebag \ˈ=ˌ=\ *n* **1** : a rattle in the form of a bag **2 a** *usu* **rattlebags** *pl but sing or pl in constr* : BLADDER CAMPION 1 **b** : RATTLE 3a

rattlebones \ˈ==ˌ=\ *n pl* **1** : ¹BONE 5a **2** *usu sing in constr* : a lean and bony person or animal

rattlebox \ˈ==ˌ=\ *n* **1** : a rattle in the shape of a box **2 a** : RATTLE 3a **b** : a plant of the genus *Crotalaria*; *esp* : an American annual herb (*C. sagittalis*) the ripe seeds of which rattle in the inflated pod **c** : SILVER BELL **d** : BLADDER CAMPION 1 **e** : SEEDBOX 2

rattlebrain \ˈ==ˌ=\ *n* : a rattlebrained person : an empty-headed chatterer

rattlebrained \ˈ=ˈ=\ *adj* : marked by giddiness : EMPTY-HEADED ⟨a ~ youngster —Sinclair Lewis⟩ ⟨his ~ . . . crackpot ideas —Ellen Glasgow⟩

rattlebush \ˈ==ˌ=\ *n* **1** : a rattlebox (*Crotalaria sagittalis*) **2** : INDIGO BROOM

rattlehead \ˈ==ˌ=\ *n* : RATTLEBRAIN ⟨his idea of a mighty pretty girl was a ~ —W.A.White⟩

rattleheaded \ˈ==ˈ==\ *adj* : RATTLEBRAINED

rattlemouse *n*, *obs* : ³BAT

rattlepate \ˈ==ˌ=\ *n* : RATTLEBRAIN

rattlepated \ˈ==ˈ==\ *adj* : RATTLEBRAINED ⟨how ~ I am! I've forgotten what I came for —Glenway Wescott⟩

rattlepod \ˈ==ˌ=\ *n* : SEEDBOX 2

rat·tler \ˈratlə(r), -adᵊl-, -atᵊl-\ *n* -S [ME *rateler*, fr. *ratelen* to rattle + *-er* — more at RATTLE] **1** : one that rattles: as **a** : RATTLE 2b **b** : a vehicle (as an automobile, trolley car, or railway car) that rattles; *specif* : a freight train ⟨grab fast ~*s* for the West —Thomas Wolfe⟩ **2** : something extraordinarily good of its kind : a fine specimen (as of a horse, storm, blow, game, or book) ⟨a ~ of a storm⟩ **3 a** : RATTLESNAKE **b** : RATTLE 4 — usu. used in pl. ⟨a rattlesnake rattling his ~*s* —Ernest Hemingway⟩ **4 a** : a revolving drum in which paving bricks are rotated with a charge of cast iron to test their abrasive resistance **b** : a device for shaking out the cores from small castings : TUMBLING BARREL **c** : a device for finishing materials (as metal, concrete blocks, or bricks) consisting of a closed receptacle in which the material to be finished is shaken up with blocks of metal or abrasive **5** : RATTLEBRAIN

rattleroot \ˈ==ˌ=\ *n* : a bugbane (*Cimicifuga racemosa*)

rattlertree \ˈ==ˌ=\ *n* : WHITE POPLAR 1a

rattles *pres 3d sing of* RATTLE, *pl of* RATTLE

rattlesnake \ˈ==ˌ=\ *n* : any of numerous New World pit vipers that have a series of horny interlocking joints at the end of the tail which make a sharp rattling sound when vibrated, that comprise two genera of which one (*Sistrurus*) contains small snakes (as the massasaugas and ground rattlesnakes) having the head covered with symmetrical plates and the other (*Crotalus*) contains usu. larger snakes that have scales instead of headplates, are rather thick-bodied, large-headed snakes of sluggish disposition which seldom bite unless startled or pursuing prey, and occur across most of America from southern Canada to Argentina — see CANEBRAKE RATTLER, DIAMONDBACK RATTLESNAKE, PRAIRIE RATTLESNAKE, SIDEWINDER, TIMBER RATTLESNAKE, WESTERN DIAMOND RATTLESNAKE

rattlesnake-bite \ˈ==ˌ=ˌ=\ *n* : TALL MEADOW RUE

rattlesnake fern *n* **1** : any of several American grape ferns (esp. *Botrychium virginianum*) with clustered sporangia resembling a snake's rattles **2** : CHAIN FERN

rattlesnake flag *n* : any of several flags bearing a rattlesnake and usu. the motto "Don't Tread On Me" in use by the colonies at the outbreak of the American Revolution

rattlesnake grass *n* : a showy American grass (*Glyceria canadensis*) with an ample panicle of rather large ovate spikelets whose shape suggests a snake's rattle

rattlesnake herb *n* : BANEBERRY

rattlesnake master *or* **rattlesnake's master** *n* : any of various plants held to cure the bite of a rattlesnake: as **a** : any of various button snakeroots of the genera *Liatris* or *Eryngium* **b** : FALSE ALOE 1

rattlesnake pilot *n* : COPPERHEAD 1a

rattlesnake plantain *n* : an orchid of the genus *Goodyera*

rattlesnake root *n* : any of various plants formerly believed to be distasteful to rattlesnakes or effective against their venom: as **a** : a lion's foot of the genus *Prenanthes* — called also *cankerweed*; compare GALL OF THE EARTH **b** : SENEGA ROOT 1 **c** : a bugbane (*Cimicifuga racemosa*)

rattlesnake violet *n* : DOGTOOTH VIOLET

rattlesnake weed *n* **1** : a hawkweed (*Hieracium venosum*) with purple-veined leaves **2** : BUTTON SNAKEROOT **3** : a weedy herb (*Daucus pusillus*) of the western U.S. having short involucral bracts and bristly fruit — called also *bristly carrot* **4** : RATTLEBOX 2b **5** : RATTLESNAKE PLANTAIN

rattle-top \ˈ==ˌ=\ *n* : a bugbane (*Cimicifuga racemosa*)

1rattletrap \ˈ==ˌ=\ *n* [*rattle* + *trap*] **1** : a small showy article of little value : GEWGAW, KNICKKNACK — usu. used in pl. ⟨a mantelpiece covered with ~*s*⟩ **2** : something rattling or rickety (as a vehicle) ⟨my car . . . an old ~ —Ida A.R.Wylie⟩ ⟨~ of a typewriter —J.G.Jones⟩

2rattletrap \"\ *adj* : RAMSHACKLE, RICKETY ⟨a ~ car⟩ ⟨the ~ desk in the lobby —Donald Windham⟩

rat·tle·ty-bang \ˌrad·ᵊldēˌ=\ *n* [irreg. fr. ¹*rattle* + *bang*] : a loud rattling and banging sound ⟨the ~ in the barn had . . . ceased —G.A.Chamberlain⟩

rattleweed \ˈ==ˌ=\ *n* [²*rattle* + *weed*] **1** : any of various leguminous plants esp. of the genera *Astragalus*, *Phaca*, and *Oxytropis* **2** : BLADDER CAMPION 1 **3** : BUGBANE **4** : RATTLEBOX 2b

1rattling *adj* [ME *rateling*, fr. pres. part. of *ratelen* to rattle — more at RATTLE] **1** : that rattles ⟨a ~ cough⟩ ⟨the harness . . . thrown with a ~ crash on the floor —Sherwood Anderson⟩ **2** : marked by liveliness and quickness (as in speech or action) : BRISK, SPRIGHTLY ⟨a ~ breeze⟩ ⟨move at a ~ pace⟩ ⟨her energy . . . and ~ independent tongue —Mary McCarthy⟩ **3** : extraordinarily good : SPLENDID ⟨played a ~ game —*Sunday Independent* (*Dublin*)⟩ ⟨bought ~ outfits —O.Henry⟩ — **rat·tling·ly** *adv*

2rattling *adv* : EXTREMELY ⟨a ~ good story⟩

3rattling *var of* RATLINE

rat·tly \ˈrad·ᵊlē, -at(ᵊ)lē, -li\ *adj* [¹*rattle* + *-y*] : having a tendency to rattle : making a rattling sound ⟨a little boy . . . with his ~ red wagon —Florence Butler⟩

1rat·ton \ˈratᵊn\ *n* -S [ME *ratoun*, fr. MF *raton* small rat, fr. OF, dim. of *rat*, prob. of Gmc origin; akin to OS *ratta* rat — more at RAT] *chiefly dial* : RAT

2ratton *also* **rattoon** *var of* RATOON

rattrap \ˈ=ˌ=\ *n* **1** : a trap for rats **2** : a dirty ramshackle structure ⟨~ that passed for a jail —Pat Brennan⟩ **3** : a situation of hopeless doom ⟨troops surrounded and caught in a ~ with the river at their backs⟩

rat-trap cheese *var of* RAT CHEESE

rattrap pedal *n* : a pedal (as for a bicycle or tricycle) made with toothed edges in order to prevent slipping of the shoe

rat·tus \ˈrad·əs\ *n*, *cap* [NL, fr. E ¹*rat*] : a genus of rodents (family Muridae) that comprises the common rats and is distinguished from the closely related *Mus* by bevel-edged upper incisors and comparatively large second and third molars

rat·ty \ˈrad·ē, -atē, -i\ *adj* -ER/-EST [¹*rat* + *-y*] **1 a** : infested with rats ⟨live on one floor of a ~ tenement —Joseph Mitchell⟩ **b** : rat-eaten in appearance : SHABBY, UNKEMPT ⟨~ and ragged —P.H.Lowrey⟩ ⟨a ~ brown overcoat —John Lardner⟩ ⟨a long ~ moustache —Eve Langley⟩ **c** : of, relating to, or characteristic of a rat ⟨like a terrier who smells something . . . ~ —E.F.Benson⟩ ⟨said in his ~ voice —Floyd Dell⟩ **2 a** : having a low, despicable, or treacherous character : MEANSPIRITED ⟨mean as a snake . . . forever taking up with ~ people —Frances G. Patton⟩ **b** : having an irritable or irascible disposition : ILL-TEMPERED, NASTY ⟨that ~ genius whose words . . . were thunder and lightning —Geoffrey Grigson⟩

ra·tu·fa \rəˈtüfə, rəˈtyü-\ *n*, *cap* [NL] : a genus of rodents (family Sciuridae) comprising the Asiatic giant squirrels

rat unit *n* : a bioassay unit consisting of the amount of a material (as a vitamin) that under standardized conditions is just sufficient to produce a specified response in all or a designated proportion of a group of experimental rats

rat·wa \ˈratwə\ *n* -S [Nepali *ratuwā*] : a muntjac (*Muntiacus muntjak*)

rau·cid \ˈrȯsəd\ *adj* [L *raucus* + E *-id* (as in *rancid*)] : RAUCOUS

rau·ci·ty \-səd·ē, -ətē, -i\ *n* -ES [L *raucitas*, fr. *raucus* hoarse + *-itas* -ity] : the quality or state of being raucous

rau·cle \ˈrákəl\ *Scot var of* RACKLE

rau·cous \ˈrȯkəs\ *adj* [L *raucus* hoarse; akin to L *ravus* hoarse — more at RUMOR] **1** : disagreeably harsh or strident : HOARSE ⟨a ~ voice⟩ **2** : boisterously disorderly **syn** see LOUD

rau·cous·ly *adv* : in a raucous manner

rau·cous·ness *n* -ES : the quality or state of being raucous

raught [ME *raughte* (past), *raught* (past part.), fr. OE *rǣhte* (past), *gerǣht* (past part.) — more at REACH] *dial chiefly Brit past of* REACH

1rauk \ˈrȯk\ *vb* -ED/-ING/-S [prob. alter. of ²*rake*] **1** *dial Brit* : SCRATCH **2** *dial Eng* : POKE, STIR

2rauk *var of* ROKE

rau·li \(ˈ)raůˈlē\ *also* **rauli beech** *n* -S [AmerSp *rauli*, *reuli*, fr. Mapuche *ruylin*, *ruili*] : a large Chilean timber tree (*Nothofagus procera*) yielding a coarse lumber that is used esp. for cooperage

raun \ˈrȯn\ *n* -S [ME *rawne*, of Scand origin; akin to ON *hrogn* roe — more at ROE] : ROE, SPAWN; *also* : a female fish (as a herring or salmon)

raunchy \ˈrȯnchē, ˈrȧu-, ˈrän-, -chi\ *adj*, *sometimes* -ER/-EST [origin unknown] : falling below a usual or normal standard: as **a** : SLOVENLY, UNKEMPT ⟨refuses to serve such ~ people as motorcyclists —*Newsweek*⟩ **b** : LEWD, VULGAR ⟨merry musings of that ~ old Wife of Bath —A.H.Weiler⟩

raunge *obs var of* RANGE

rau·po \ˈraů(ˌ)pō\ *n* -S [*Maori*] : a common cattail (*Typha angustifolia*) used esp. in New Zealand for thatching

rau·ra·ci *also* **rau·ri·ci** \ˈrȯrəˌsī\ *n pl*, *usu cap* [L] : an ancient people of Gaul west of the Rhine and near Basel

rau·ri·ki \ˈraůrə(ˌ)kē\ *n* -S [Maori, fr. *rau* leaf + *riki* small] *NewZeal* : SOW THISTLE

rausch·pfei·fe \ˈraůsh,(p)fīfə\ *n* -S [G, fr *rausch* reed + *pfeife* pipe] : a 2-rank mixture stop in a pipe organ speaking at 2 and 1⅓ foot pitches

rausch·quin·te \-ˌkuintə\ *n* -S [G, fr. *rausch* reed + *quinte* fifth (in music)] : a 2-rank mixture stop in a pipe organ speaking at 2⅔ and 2 foot pitches

rau·vite \ˈrȯˌvīt, ˈraůˌv-\ *n* -S [fr. the symbols *Ra* + *U* + *V* + E *-ite*] : a mineral $CaU_2V_{12}O_{36}.20H_2O$ that is a hydrous oxide of calcium, uranium, and vanadium

rau·wol·fia \raůˈwůlfēə, rȯˈw-, -wȯl-\ *n* [NL, fr. Leonhard *Rauwolf* †1596 Ger. botanist + NL *-ia*] **1 a** *cap* : a large pantropical genus of somewhat poisonous trees and shrubs (family Apocynaceae) having verticillate leaves and small cymose flowers with a salver-shaped corolla and bicarpellary ovary and yielding emetic and purgative substances and in the case of an Indian form (*R. serpentina*) an alkaloidal root extract used in the treatment of hypertension and some mental disorders **b** -S : any plant of the genus *Rauwolfia* **2** -S : the medicinal extract that is obtained from the root of the Indian rauwolfia

1rav·age \ˈravij, -vēj\ *n* -S [F, fr. MF, fr. *ravir* to ravish + *-age* — more at RAVISH] **1** : an act or operation of ravaging : a violently destructive action or agency ⟨complete a victory with ~⟩ ⟨secure from ~ by fire⟩ **2** : havoc or damage resulting from ravaging : violently destructive effect : RUIN, DEVASTATION ⟨repair the ~ wrought by war⟩ ⟨the ~ of time⟩

2ravage \", *esp in pres part* -vəj\ *vb* -ED/-ING/-S [F *ravager*, fr. MF, fr. *ravage*] *vt* : to lay waste to : subject to depredations : work havoc or devastation upon : PLUNDER ~ *vi* : to commit ravages — **rav·ag·er** \-jə(r)\ *n* -S

syn DEVASTATE, WASTE, SACK, PILLAGE, DESPOIL, SPOLIATE: RAVAGE implies violent severe depredation, wasting, and destruction, often cumulative, so that restoration is impossible or unlikely ⟨a forest area *ravaged* by fire⟩ ⟨four major disasters had *ravaged* the country in the interval; the great smallpox epidemic, the great rinderpest outbreak, an intense drought with consequent famine and a devastating locust invasion —L.S.B.Leakey⟩ ⟨the cities of the Main were *ravaged*, citizens were tortured, robbed, murdered, women were ravished, churches looted while the bells tolled horror —Marjory S. Douglas⟩ DEVASTATE may stress the ruin and desolation ensuing from ravaging, demolishing, burning, and eradicating ⟨*devastating* conflicts such as those which destroyed Greek, Roman, and Saracen civilization, which drenched Europe in blood —M.R.Cohen⟩ ⟨the city was a *devastated* waste of smoldering embers: seventeen thousand four hundred and fifty people were homeless —*Amer. Guide Series: Mass.*⟩ ⟨if an atom or hydrogen bomb should be dropped on an American city, the *devastated* community would not be expected to confront the emergency unaided —Felix Morley⟩ WASTE, often a close synonym for DEVASTATE, may on the other hand apply to situations in which damage and desolation are accomplished more slowly and less dramatically and definitively ⟨with four legions, seized their cattle, *wasted* their country —J.A.Froude⟩ ⟨his fingers *wasted* by illness —Winston Churchill⟩ SACK may apply to the acts of a victorious invader in stripping a captured area of everything of value; it may suggest large-scale or complete burglarizing and looting ⟨the retreating Federals *sacked* and burned as they went, leaving scarcely a cabin in their wake —*Amer. Guide Series: La.*⟩ ⟨after De Soto helped Pizarro *sack* Peru —*Amer. Guide Series: Fla.*⟩ ⟨summer cottages *sacked* by the gang⟩ PILLAGE, often interchangeable with SACK, may suggest somewhat less ruthless and general devastation and slightly more selectivity in plundering ⟨their goods and chattels are *pillaged*, or filched for worthless money —Sir Winston Churchill⟩ DESPOIL usu. applies to the ransacking, looting, or expropriation of valuables, often of a particular building or specific place ⟨the same Roman raid that had *despoiled* his home and enslaved him at twenty had likewise brought disaster to their neighbors —L.C. Douglas⟩ SPOLIATE is a legalistic synonym for DESPOIL, often applicable to destruction visited on a neutral, noncombatant, or victim of piracy ⟨from the ages, from the barbarians, the land has been burnt and *spoliated* —Richard Llewellyn⟩

1rave \ˈrāv\ *vb* -ED/-ING/-S [ME *raven*, prob. fr. MF *resver*, *raver*, *rever* to wander, be delirious] *vi* **1 a** *obs* : to be or seem to be mad or delirious **b** : to talk irrationally in or as if in delirium **c** : to declaim wildly, passionately, or boisterously ⟨in vain may heroes fight, and patriots ~ —Alexander Pope⟩ **2** : to move or advance with violence or in wild agitation : STORM, RAGE — used esp. of a natural phenomenon ⟨'tis dark: the iced gusts still ~ and beat —John Keats⟩ **3** : to be unduly loud or rapturous in one's praise : talk with excessive enthusiasm ⟨~ about her beauty⟩ ⟨*raved* over the baby⟩ ~ *vt* : to utter in madness or frenzy : pour forth wildly

2rave \"\ *n* -S *often attrib* **1** : an act or instance of raving **2 a** : INFATUATION, CRUSH **b** : an extravagantly commendatory critique : BLURB; *esp* : an excessively favorable dramatic criticism ⟨~ reviews of the new show⟩

3rave \"\ *n* -S [alter. of *rathe*, fr. ME] : one of the upper side pieces of the frame of the body of a wagon or sleigh

ravehook \'=,=\ *n* [prob. fr. obs. *rave* to pull (fr. ME *raven*) + *hook*] **:** a hooked tool for enlarging or clearing seams (as of a boat) to receive oakum or other caulking material

ravehook

1rav·el \'ravəl\ *vb* **raveled** *or* **ravelled; raveled** *or* **ravelled; raveling** *or* **ravelling** \-v(ə)liŋ\ **ravels** [D *rafelen*, fr. *rafel* loose thread; akin to OHG *ravo, rāvo* beam, rafter, OE *ræfter* — more at RAFTER] *vt* **1 a :** to let fall into a tangled mass (as the threads of a fabric after pulling it apart) **b :** to make intricate **:** ENTANGLE, INVOLVE **2 :** to separate or undo the texture of **:** UNRAVEL, UNTWIST, UNWIND, UNWEAVE — often used with *out* or sometimes with *off* **3 :** to undo the intricacies of **:** make plain ~ *vi* **1** *obs* **a :** to become entangled or confused **b :** to make investigation or search **2 :** to become untwisted, unwoven, or unwound **:** FRAY; *also* **:** to become disentangled **:** become cleared of intricacy — often used with *out* **3 :** to crumble or break up — used of the surface of a roadway when the road metal is no longer bonded and loose pieces are scattered about **4 :** to fracture and partly cave **:** SLOUGH — used of ground about a mining drill hole

2ravel \"\ *n* -S **:** an act or result of raveling: as **a :** something (as a mass or situation) that is tangled **:** SNARL **b :** something raveled out, torn, or frayed **:** a loose thread **:** RAVELING

3ra·vel \'rāvəl\ *n* -S [origin unknown] *Scot* **:** RAILING ⟨a wooden stair ~⟩

4rav·el \'ravəl\ *n* -S [3*rave* + -*el*] **:** RADDLE 3

rav·el·er *or* **rav·el·ler** \-v(ə)lə(r)\ *n* -S **:** one that ravels

rave·lin \'ravlən\ *n* -S [MF, fr. OIt *ravellino*, alter. of *rivellino*, dim. of *riva* bank, fr. L *ripa* — more at RIVE] **:** a detached work formerly used in fortifications and consisting of two embankments forming a salient angle in front of the curtain of the fortified position

rav·el·ing *or* **rav·el·ling** \'rav(ə)liŋ, -lən\ *n* -S **:** something that is raveled out; *esp* **:** a thread that is detached from a fabric

rav·el·ly \-v(ə)lē, -li\ *adj* **:** raveled or likely to ravel

rav·el·ment \'ravəlmənt\ *n* -S **:** RAVEL, TANGLE

1ra·ven \'rāvən\ *n* -S [ME *raven, reven*, fr. OE *hræfn*; akin to MD & MLG *raven*, OHG *hraban*, ON *hrafn*, L *corvus* raven, *cornix* crow, *crepare* to crack, creak, break, Gk *korax* raven, and perh. to Skt *kṛpate* he laments, implores] **1 a :** a large glossy-black bird (*Corvus corax*) that is widely distributed in northern parts of the northern hemisphere but now largely extinct in the eastern U. S., occurs in many local races, is omnivorous and somewhat predacious and noted for intelligent and mischievous behavior, and differs from the closely related common crow chiefly in its greater size and in having the feathers of the throat narrow and pointed **b :** any of several other usu. large and glossy-black birds of the genus *Corvus* or family Corvidae; *esp* **:** a somewhat predacious Australian bird (*C. coronoides*) — called also *Australian raven* **2 :** a figure of a raven (as on a standard or coat of arms)

2raven \"\ *adj* **:** of the color or glossy sheen of the raven **:** of the color raven black ⟨~ curls⟩ ⟨~ darkness⟩

3raven *var of* RAVIN

4rav·en *also* **rav·in** \'ravən\ *vb* **ravened; ravened; ravening** \-v(ə)niŋ\ **ravens** [MF *raviner* to rush forward, take by force, ravish, fr. *ravine* rapine, impetuosity, rush — more at RAVINE] *vt* **1** *obs* **:** to obtain or seize by violence **2 :** to devour eagerly or greedily **:** consume wholly ⟨like rats that ~ down their proper bane —Shak.⟩ ~ *vi* **:** to prey or plunder with rapacity **:** prowl after or devour prey **:** feed greedily **:** be or become ravenous or consuming ⟨shall ~ as a wolf —Gen 49:27 (AV)⟩

rav·e·na·la \,ravə'nālə\ *n* [NL, fr a native name in Madagascar] **1** *cap* **:** a genus of tropical woody plants (family Musaceae) having tall trunks, oblong distichous very long-stalked leaves, and large flowers with three sepals and three petals followed by woody 3-valved capsules — see TRAVELER'S-TREE **2** -S **:** any plant of the genus *Ravenala*

raven black *n* **:** a black approximating to violet in hue

raven cockatoo *n* **:** a black cockatoo of the genus *Calyptorhynchus*

rav·e·nel·ia \,ravə'nēlēə, -lyə\ *n, cap* [NL, fr. Henry W. Ravenel †1887 Am. botanist + NL -*ia*] **:** a genus of rust fungi (family Pucciniaceae) having the teliospores united into a head on a compound pedicel and being mostly parasites of leguminous plants

rav·en·er \'rav(ə)nə(r)\ *n* -S [ME *ravaynour, ravener*, fr. MF *ravineor*, fr. *raviner* to rush forward, take by force, ravish + -*eor* -or — more at RAVEN] **1 :** one that ravens, plunders, or ravishes **:** ROBBER, RAVISHER **2 :** a ravenous person or animal **:** GLUTTON

raven gray *n* **:** a dark gray approximating to violet in hue

1ravening *adj* [fr. pres. part. of 4*raven*] **1 :** greedily devouring **:** RAPACIOUS, PREYING **2 :** MAD, RABID **syn** see VORACIOUS

2ravening *n* -S [fr. gerund of 4*raven*] **1 :** RAVIN **2** *obs* **:** RABIES

ra·ven·ling \'rāvənliŋ, -lēŋ\ *n* -S [1*raven* + -*ling*] **:** a young raven

ra·ven·na grass \rə'venə-\ *n, usu cap R* [fr. *Ravenna*, province and commune in northern Italy] **:** a grass (*Erianthus ravennae*) that is often cultivated for its long white-ribbed leaves and large plumes resembling those of pampas grass — called also *plume grass, wool grass*

rav·en·ous \'rav(ə)nəs\ *adj* [ME *rauynous* rushing, impetuous, rapacious, fr. MF *ravineus*, fr. *raviner* + -*eus* -ous] **1 :** RAPACIOUS; *esp* **:** devouring with voracious eagerness ⟨nations ~ as wolves⟩ **2 :** urgently eager for food **:** craving for satisfaction or gratification ⟨~ appetite⟩ ⟨a ~ boy⟩ ⟨this ~ desire⟩ **syn** see VORACIOUS

rav·en·ous·ly *adv* **:** in a ravenous manner **:** to a ravenous degree ⟨~ hungry⟩

rav·en·ous·ness *n* -ES **:** the quality or state of being ravenous

ra·ven·ry \'rāvənrē\ *n* -ES [1*raven* + -*ry*] **:** a place where ravens nest

ravens *pl of* RAVEN, *pres 3d sing of* RAVEN

rav·en·sa·ra \,ravən'sārə\ *n, cap* [NL, fr. Malagasy *ravendsara, ravin'tsara*, a tree of the genus Ravensara, lit., good leaf] **:** a genus of Madagascan trees (family Lauraceae) having trimerous flowers and lobed seeds — see CLOVE NUTMEG

rav·er \'rāvə(r)\ *n* -S [ME, fr. *raven* to rave + -*er* — more at RAVE] **:** one that raves

rav·ery \-v(ə)rē\ *n* -ES [ME *ravery*, fr. MF *resverie, reverie, raverie* — more at REVERIE] **:** a fit of madness or passion **:** RAVING, DELIRIUM

raves *pres 3d sing of* RAVE, *pl of* RAVE

ra·vi·gote \rávēgót\ *n* -S [F, fr. *ravigoter* to revive, refresh, alter. of *ravigorer*, fr. MF, fr. *ra-* (fr. L *re-*) + *vigueur* vigor — more at VIGOR] **:** a sauce or dressing colored green with spinach puree and seasoned with vinegar and a mixture of herbs (as chervil, tarragon, chives, capers)

1rav·in *also* **rav·en** \'ravən\ *n* -S [ME *ravin, ravine*, fr. MF *ravine* — more at RAVINE] **1 :** RAPINE, RAPACITY **2 a :** an act or habit of preying or devouring **:** PREDACITY, PREDATISM **b :** something seized or devoured as prey ⟨red in tooth and claw with ~ —Alfred Tennyson⟩

2ravin *adj* [ME, fr. *ravin, ravine*, n.] *obs* **:** RAVENOUS

3ravin *var of* RAVEN

ra·vi·nat·ed \'ravə,nād·əd\ *adj* [2*ravine* + -*ate* + -*ed*] **:** having or broken by ravines ⟨~ hills⟩

1ra·vine \rə'vēn\ *n* -S [F, mountain torrent, ravine, fr. OF, rapine, rush, impetuosity, rush of water, fr. L *rapina* rapine — more at RAPINE] **:** a small narrow steep-sided valley that is larger than a gully and smaller than a canyon and is usu. worn down by running water **:** GORGE, GULCH

2ravine \"\ *vt* -ED/-ING/-S **:** to mark or score with or as if with ravines ⟨a badly *ravined* road⟩

rav·ined \'ravənd\ *adj* [1*ravin* + -*ed*] *obs* **:** RAVENOUS

ravine deer *or* **ravine buck** *n* **:** FOUR-HORNED ANTELOPE

ra·viney \rə'vēnē\ *adj* [2*ravine* + -*y*] **:** full of or marked by ravines

1rav·ing \'rāviŋ, -vēŋ\ *n* -S [ME, fr. gerund of *raven* to rave — more at RAVE] **:** irrational, incoherent, wild, or extravagant utterance or declamation; *also* **:** an utterance of such character — usu. used in pl.

2raving *adj* [ME, fr. pres. part. of *raven* to rave] **1 :** talking wildly or irrationally ⟨a ~ lunatic⟩ **2 :** worth raving about **:** notable of its kind **:** SUPERLATIVE ⟨a ~ beauty⟩

3raving *or* **ravingly** *adv* **:** in a raving manner **:** to such a degree as to cause or deserve raving ⟨~ mad⟩

rav·i·o·li \,ravē'ōlē, -li\ *n* -S [It *raviuoli, ravioli*, fr. It dial. (southern Italy), pl. of *raviuolo, raviolo*, lit., little turnip, dim. of *rava* turnip, fr. L *rapa* — more at RAPE] **:** alimentary paste made in little shells or cases and stuffed (as with cheese, spinach, or meat)

rav·ish \'ravish, -vēsh, *esp in pres part* -vəsh\ *vb* -ED/-ING/-ES [ME *ravisshen*, fr. MF *raviss-*, extended stem of *ravir*, fr. (assumed) VL *rapire*, alter. of L *rapere* to seize, rob, kidnap, ravish — more at RAPID] *vt* **1 a :** to seize and carry away by violence **:** snatch by force ⟨this hand shall ~ thy pretended right —John Dryden⟩ **b** (1) **:** to remove from one place or state to another (as from earth to heaven); *esp* **:** to transport spiritually (2) **:** to transport with emotion and esp. with joy or delight ⟨~*ed* by Rome's beauty⟩ **c** (1) *obs* **:** to carry (a woman) away forcibly or unlawfully **:** ABDUCT (2) **:** to commit rape upon (a woman) **:** VIOLATE **2 :** PLUNDER, ROB, DESPOIL **3** *obs* **a :** to alter in state, belief, or other quality — used with *from* or *to* **b :** CORRUPT ~ *vi* **:** to transport one with emotion

rav·ished·ly \-shtlē\ *adv* **:** in a ravished manner **:** as if ravished

rav·ish·er \-shə(r)\ *n* -S [ME *ravissher*, fr. *ravisshen* + -*er*] **:** one that ravishes

rav·ish·ing \'ravishiŋ, -vēsh-\ *adj* [ME *ravisshing*, fr. pres. part. of *ravisshen*] **:** outstandingly attractive, pleasing, or striking — **rav·ish·ing·ly** *adv*

rav·ish·ment \-mənt\ *n* -S [MF *ravissement*, fr. *raviss-* (stem of *ravir*) + -*ment*] **1 :** an act or the means or effect of ravishing **2 :** the condition of being ravished; *usu* **:** TRANSPORT, RAPTURE, ECSTASY

rav·i·son \'ravəsən\ *n* -S [F, modif. (influenced by *rave* turnip, rape, fr. L *rapa*) of G dial. *rübesan*, fr. G *rübe* rape (fr. OHG *ruoba*) + G dial. *san* seed, fr. OHG *sāmo*; akin to OS *sāmo* seed, OHG *sājen* to sow — more at RAPE, SOW] **:** rapeseed of an inferior quality

ravison oil *n* **:** a fatty oil similar to rape oil obtained from ravison in the Black sea region

1raw \'rȯ\ *adj* -ER/-EST [ME, fr. OE *hrēaw, hrǣw*; akin to OHG *hrō* raw, ON *hrār* raw, L *cruor* blood, *crudus* raw, Gk *kreas* flesh, Skt *kravis* raw flesh] **1 :** not subjected to heat in the course of preparation as food **:** not cooked ⟨lived on ~ grains and fruits⟩ ⟨a ~ egg⟩ ⟨likes his steak nearly ~⟩ **2 a :** being in or nearly in the natural state **:** little changed by art or technical processes **:** UNWROUGHT, UNPROCESSED, CRUDE 1 ⟨~ textile fibers⟩ ⟨~ starch⟩ ⟨~ linseed oil⟩; *also* **:** not diluted or blended ⟨~ spirits⟩ **b :** unprepared or imperfectly prepared for use or enjoyment **:** lacking a normal or usual finish **:** UNDRESSED ⟨left the edges ~⟩ ⟨~ wooden shacks⟩ **c :** not presented in polished and finished form **:** UNDIGESTED, UNCORRECTED, UNEDITED ⟨a ~ draft of a thesis⟩ ⟨~ statistics⟩ **d :** lacking the usual guard **:** UNBOUND ⟨a shoe with ~ eyelets⟩ ⟨a ~ buttonhole⟩ **e :** UNCULTIVATED, UNIMPROVED ⟨~ land awaiting the builder⟩ **f** *of photographic film* **:** UNEXPOSED **3 a** (1) **:** having the skin removed so that the underlying tissues are exposed **:** severely chafed or galled ⟨a ~ wound⟩ (2) **:** sore from or as if from being galled ⟨a ~ irritated throat⟩ (3) **:** looking as if galled **:** RAWBONED **b :** lacking a natural covering ⟨a ~ eroded slope⟩ **c :** lacking clothing **:** NAKED ⟨liked to swim ~⟩ **4 a :** lacking in experience or understanding **:** serving in a new and unfamiliar role **:** untrained and unskilled and of problematical worth **:** GREEN ⟨a civilizing influence for me as for other ~ youths —R.M. Lovett⟩ ⟨~ servant girls⟩: as (1) *obs* **:** UNRIPE, IMMATURE (2) **:** new to military life ⟨an army of ~ recruits⟩ **b :** lacking in amenities and refinements since newly developed, occupied, or established and elemental, direct, primitive, and unrestrained ⟨in the West of the ~ and exciting days before the coming of the automobile —Seth Agnew⟩ ⟨creating a new world in a ~ continental mass⟩ **c :** starkly new and entirely unmellowed ⟨endless new buildings, ~ and just finished —*New Yorker*⟩ **d** (1) **:** lacking in refinement or graciousness **:** deficient in savoir faire or elegance **:** CRUDE 5 (2) *slang* **:** COARSE, INDELICATE, VULGAR ⟨a ~ remark⟩ **5 :** disagreeably damp or cold **:** chilly and disagreeable **:** BLEAK ⟨a ~ wind⟩ ⟨~ winter days⟩ **6** *of a ceramic glaze mixture* **:** having no soluble ingredients and not requiring fritting **syn** see RUDE

2raw \"\ *vt* -ED/-ING/-S [ME *rawen*, fr. *raw*, adj.] **:** to cause to become raw

3raw \"\ *n* -S **1 :** a raw, sore, or galled place **:** a sensitive spot **2 :** someone or something raw, uncultivated, or unprocessed — usu. used in pl. of commercial products (as sugar or oysters) ⟨bought 100 tons of ~*s*⟩ — **in the raw :** in the natural or crude state **:** with the true nature or character exposed **:** NAKED ⟨life *in the raw*⟩ ⟨always slept *in the raw*⟩

4raw \"\ *chiefly Scot var of* ROW

ra·wal·pin·di \,rȯwəl'pindē\ *adj, usu cap* [fr. *Rawalpindi*, Pakistan] **:** of or from the city of Rawalpindi, Pakistan **:** of the kind or style prevalent in Rawalpindi

rawbone \(')=;=\ *adj, archaic* **:** RAWBONED

rawboned \(')=;=\ *adj* **:** having little flesh **:** gaunt to such a degree that the prominent bones seem to press on the skin **syn** see LEAN

rawbones \'=,=\ *n pl but sing or pl in constr* **:** a rawboned individual **:** SKELETON

raw deal *n* **:** unfair treatment **:** an act of injustice ⟨the boss gave him a *raw deal*⟩

raw edge *n* **:** an unfinished, rough, or undecorated edge (as at the top of a piece of hollow ware or at the margin of a piece of textile) — compare SELVAGE

raw file *n* **:** a file of uncoordinated and unevaluated data (as on a person or project)

rawhead \'=,=\ *n* **:** HOBGOBLIN, SPECTER — see BLOODYBONES

1rawhide \'=,=\ *n* [1*raw* + *hide*] **1 :** untanned cattle skin that is made into leather by dehairing, liming, stuffing, and other processes **2 :** a whip of untanned hide that is twisted, braided, or rolled

2rawhide \"\ *vt* **1 :** to whip or drive with or as if with a rawhide **2 :** to carry (as ore) in a hide sack

raw·hid·er \-də(r)\ *n* **1 :** one that rawhides: as **a :** a miner who rawhides ore; *broadly* **:** a small-scale miner **:** PROSPECTOR **b :** a harsh taskmaster (as a domineering executive) **2 :** a user of rawhide: as **a :** a border pioneer of the southwestern U.S. **b :** one that puts a protective leather covering on wooden artificial limbs

ra·win \'rā(,)win\ *n* -S [*radar* + *wind*] **:** a wind sounding of the atmosphere made by tracking a balloon with radar

ra·win·sonde \-,sänd\ *n* -S [*rawin* + *radiosonde*] **:** a radiosonde that is tracked by a radio direction-finding device to determine the velocity of winds aloft

raw·ish \'rȯish, -ēsh\ *adj* [1*raw* + -*ish*] **:** somewhat raw — **raw·ish·ness** *n* -ES

Rawl \'rȯl\ *trademark* — used for a fiber expansion insert used to fasten screws in masonry

raw·ly *adv* **:** in a raw manner **:** so as to be raw

raw material *n* **:** material available, suitable, or required for manufacture, development, training, or other finishing process but not yet so used

raw milk *n* **:** milk that has not been pasteurized

rawn \'rȯn\ *dial Eng var of* ROWEN

raw·ness *n* -ES [ME *rawnesse*, fr. *raw* + -*nesse* -ness] **:** the quality or state of being raw

raw oil *n* **:** untreated oil; *specif* **:** linseed oil that has not been heated or treated with driers

raw-pack method \'=;=-\ *n* **:** COLD-PACK METHOD 1

raw score *n* **:** an individual's actual achievement (as on a test) usu. expressed numerically and uncorrected for relative position (as in regard to age) in the reference population

raw sienna *n* **1 :** sienna that has not been calcined — compare BURNT SIENNA 1 **2 :** a brownish orange to light brown that is yellower than sorrel or tawny and yellower and darker than caramel — called also *Italian earth, Italian ocher, Mexican red, terra sienna*

raw silk *n* **1 :** reeled silk before the gum is removed **2 :** a woven or knitted fabric of spun silk

raw stock *n* **1 :** BODY PAPER **2 :** raw film

raw sugar *n* **:** the product of sugar manufacture before refining that consists of pale yellow to brown sugar crystals covered with a film of syrup

raw umber *n* **1 :** umber that has not been calcined — compare BURNT UMBER 1 **2 :** a moderate to dark yellowish brown — called also *Cyprus earth, partridge, Roman umber, Sicilian umber, Turkey umber, umber*

raw water *n* **1 :** water that has not been purified ⟨for *raw water*, there's the Mississippi river at your factory door —*Time*⟩ **2 :** water that has not been distilled (as for use in making ice)

rax \'raks\ *vb* [ME (northern dial.) *raxen*, fr. OE *raxan*; akin to OE *reccan* to stretch — more at RACK] *vi, chiefly Scot* **:** to stretch oneself (as on awaking); *also* **:** to become longer **:** ELONGATE ~ *vt, chiefly Scot* **:** to stretch or strain (oneself) toward or after; *also* **:** PASS, HAND

1ray \'rā\ *n* -S [ME *raye*, fr. MF *raie*, fr. L *raia*] **:** any of numerous elasmobranch fishes of the order Hypotremata and esp. of the suborder Batoidea having the body dorsoventrally flattened often to an extreme degree with the mouth and gill clefts on the lower and the eyes on the upper surface, the pectoral fins usu. enormously developed and continuous along the margin of the head and body, the pelvic fins of moderate size, the anal fin absent, and typically a slender whiplike caudal process often with venomous spines, being adapted for life on the sea bottom, and feeding chiefly on mollusks which they crush with blunt flattened pavement teeth; *sometimes* **:** any of the typical rays as distinguished from the skates and the more sharklike members of the order — see ELECTRIC RAY, GUITARFISH, STINGRAY; compare SAWFISH

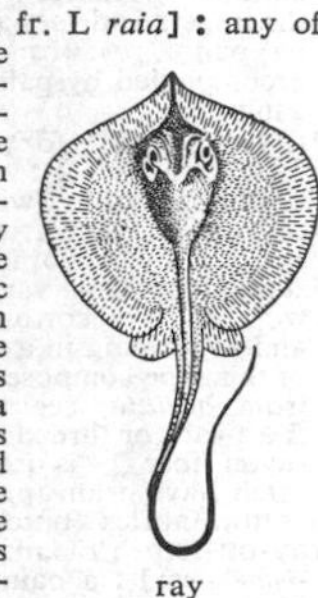

ray

2ray \"\ *n* -S [ME, fr. MF *rai*, fr. L *radius* staff, rod, spoke, radius, ray, beam; perh. akin to L *radix* root — more at ROOT] **1 a :** one of the lines of light that appear to radiate from a bright or luminous object **b :** a beam of light or other radiant energy of small cross section or infinitesimal cross section **c :** a geometrical line normal to the wave front in which radiation (as heat or light) is propagated **d :** a stream of material particles all traveling in the same line (as in radioactive phenomena); *also* **:** a single particle of such a stream ⟨an alpha ~⟩ **e :** a specific or limited portion of the total radiation ⟨the red ~⟩ **2** *obs* **:** a glance of the eye **:** SIGHT, VISION, PERCEPTION — see VISUAL RAY **3 a :** light cast by or in a ray or rays **:** RADIANCE ⟨glimmering by the lantern's dim ~⟩ **b :** moral or intellectual light or a gleam of such light **4 :** a thin line suggesting a ray: **a :** any of a group of lines or processes diverging from a common center like the radii of a circle **b :** any of a system of lines passing through a point and regarded as extending indefinitely in both directions **:** HALF LINE **c :** any of the bright whitish lines seen on the moon near full and appearing to radiate from lunar craters **5 :** any of various parts or structures (as of organisms) that are felt to resemble rays of light: as **a** (1) **:** any of the nearly parallel or somewhat divergent bony or cartilaginous or horny rods that extend and support the membrane in the fin of a fish and are ordinarily slender bony rods supported at their bases by parts of the internal skeleton and usu. transversely segmented into many short segments near their outer end which is often also longitudinally cleft so that the ray is soft and flexible but are stiff and unsegmented forming definite spines (2) **:** any of the radiating divisions of the body of an echinoderm with all its included parts; *also* **:** an arm of a crinoid or starfish (3) **:** any of the longitudinal veins of an insect's wing **b** (1) **:** RAY FLOWER (2) **:** a branch or flower stalk of an umbel (3) **:** a radially oriented band of parenchymatous tissue in the stele of a vascular plant usu functioning as a storage tissue and in the radial transport of nutrients — see MEDULLARY RAY, VASCULAR RAY **6 :** a representation of a ray of light **:** a bright strip, bar, or band **7 :** a small or unsubstantial amount **:** PARTICLE, TRACE ⟨saw the merest ~ of hope⟩

3ray \"\ *vb* -ED/-ING/-S *vi* **1 :** to shine or shine out with or as if with rays **:** emit rays; *also* **:** to issue as rays **2 :** to issue or extend like the radii of a circle **:** RADIATE ⟨the little town ~*ed* out into leafy lanes —Anne D. Sedgwick⟩ ~ *vt* **1 :** to send forth or emit in rays ⟨eyes that ~ out intelligence —Thomas Carlyle⟩ **2 :** to furnish or mark with rays, radiating lines, or stripes **3 a :** to brighten or illuminate (as one's face or darkness) with rays of light **b :** to expose to rays (as X rays, radiations from radium, or ultraviolet light) **:** IRRADIATE

4ray \"\ *n* -S [ME *raye*, fr. AF (*drap de*) *raye*, lit., striped cloth; *raye* fr. OF *raie, roie* stripe, furrow, of Celt origin; akin to Gaulish *rica* furrow, W *rhych*; akin to OE *furh* furrow — more at FURROW] **:** a striped woolen cloth used from the 13th to the 16th centuries

5ray \"\ *vt* -ED/-ING/-S [ME *rayen*, short for *arayen, arrayen* — more at ARRAY] **1** *obs* **:** to form in order or array **:** EQUIP, ARRANGE; *also* **:** to deal with or dispose of **2** *dial chiefly Eng* **:** ARRAY, DRESS **3** *obs* **:** to make dirty **:** SOIL

6ray *n* -S [ME, short for *aray, array* — more at ARRAY] **1** *obs* **:** ARRAY, ORDER, ARRANGEMENT; *also* **:** a line or rank (as of soldiers) **2** *obs* **:** DRESS, RAIMENT

7ray \'rā\ *chiefly Scot var of* RYE

8ray \"\ *var of* RE

ra·ya *or* **ra·yah** \'rīə\ *n* -S [Turk *rāiyye*, fr. Ar *ra'īyah* flock, herd] **:** a subject Christian peasant under the Ottoman empire

ray blight *n* **:** a disease of chrysanthemums caused by a fungus (esp. *Ascochyta chrysanthemi*) that produces a rapid blighting of the ray flowers and often also blind or one-sided flower heads

rayed *adj* **1 :** having rays — often used in combination ⟨spiny-*rayed* fishes⟩ **2 :** having ray flowers

ray·er \'rāə(r)\ *n* -S [3*ray* + -*er*] **:** one that gives a swirl or radial finish to watch parts on a specially adjusted lathe

ray filter *n* **:** COLOR FILTER

ray flower *or* **ray floret** *n* **1 :** one of the flowers with strap-shaped corolla occupying the margin of the head in composite plants that also have disk flowers (as aster, goldenrod, daisy, and sunflower) or making up the entire head when disk flowers are lacking (as in chicory) — see COMPOSITE illustration **2 :** one of the usu. larger flowers at the margin of the umbel in some plants of the family Umbelliferae

ray fungus *n* **:** ACTINOMYCETE

ray grass *n* **:** PERENNIAL RYEGRASS

ray gun *n* **:** a hypothetical future weapon releasing deadly or stunning rays of unknown nature

ray initial *n* **:** a cell in the cambium that gives rise to cells of the rays [sense 5b (3)] — compare FUSIFORM INITIAL

ray·leigh disk \'rālē-, -li-\ *n, usu cap R* [after Baron John W. S. *Rayleigh* †1919 Eng. physicist] **:** a thin circular disk of mica or aluminum that when suspended in a beam of sound tends to set itself at right angles to the direction of propagation and by the angle assumed gives a measure of the sound intensity

rayleigh equation *n, usu cap R* [after Baron John W. S. *Rayleigh*] **:** an equation expressing the proportions in which red and green must be mixed to appear to match a given yellow in a test for anomalous color vision

rayleigh–jeans law \-'jēnz-\ *n, usu cap R&J* [after Baron J. W. S. *Rayleigh* and Sir James Hapwood *Jeans* †1946 Eng. physicist] **:** an approximation in respect to thermal radiation: the emissive power of a blackbody at absolute temperature T and at a given wavelength λ is directly proportional to T and inversely proportional to λ^4 — compare PLANCK RADIATION LAW

rayleigh scattering *n, usu cap R* [after Baron John W. S. *Rayleigh*] **:** scattering of light by particles small enough to render the effect selective so that different colors are deflected through different angles — compare TYNDALL EFFECT

rayleigh wave *n, usu cap R* [after Baron John W. S. *Rayleigh*] **:** an elastic wave confined to the surface layers of a solid medium; *specif* **:** an elastic wave traveling along the surface of the earth with the plane of vibration coincident with the plane of propagation that is observed esp. in seismic disturbances

ray·less \ˈrāləs\ *adj* **:** having no rays: as **a :** DARK, BLIND **b :** having no raylike parts; *specif* **:** lacking ray flowers **c :** emitting no rays ⟨a ~ sun⟩ **d :** admitting no rays ⟨in ~ caverns dim —Lewis Morris⟩
rayless chamomile *n* **:** PINEAPPLE WEED
rayless goldenrod *n* **:** any of several plants of *Haplopappus* and related genera some of which (esp. *H. heterophyllus* and *H. fruticosus*) produce trembles in cattle — see CHRYSOTHAMNUS
ray·less·ness *n* -ES **:** the quality or state of being rayless
ray·let \ˈrālət\ *n* -S **:** a small ray
raylike \ˈ=,=\ *adj* **:** resembling a ray esp. in having a slender elongated tapering form
ray–liver oil *n* [ˡ*ray*] **:** a fish-liver oil from rays
ray·naud's disease \(ˈ)rā¦nōz-\ *n, usu cap R* [after Maurice *Raynaud* †1881 French physician] **:** a vascular disorder marked by recurrent spasm of the capillaries and esp. those of the fingers and toes and during exposure to cold, characterized by pallor, cyanosis and redness in succession, commonly accompanied by pain, and in severe cases progressing to local gangrene
ˡrayon \(ˈ)rā¦(y)ōⁿ\ *n* -S [MF, fr. *rai* ray — more at RAY] **1 :** RAY, BEAM **2 :** RADIUS ⟨the ~ of a cannon's fire⟩ **3 :** a postal district in Switzerland
²ray·on \ˈrā,än\ *n* -S *often attrib* [irreg. fr. ²*ray*] **1 a :** a fine smooth hygroscopic textile fiber made in filament and staple form from various solutions of modified cellulose (as of wood pulp or cotton linters) by extruding through spinnerets and solidifying in a chemical bath or in warm air **b :** a fiber of this type composed of regenerated cellulose — distinguished from *acetate;* see CUPRAMMONIUM RAYON, VISCOSE RAYON **2 a :** yarn or thread made from continuous or staple lengths of rayon fiber ⟨~ is used in tire cords⟩ **b :** fabric made of rayon often having an appearance similar to that of silk, linen, or cotton fabrics ⟨butcher linen is a ~⟩ — see SPUN RAYON
ray·on·ism \ˈrāə,nizəm\ *n* -S [F *rayonisme,* fr. *rayon* ray + *-isme* -ism] **:** a painting style initiated in Russia in 1911 by Michael Larionov in which natural appearances are depicted as semiabstractions of radiating rays of light
ray·on·nant \ˈrāənənt\ *adj* [F, fr. pres. part. of *rayonner* to radiate, fr. MF, fr. *rayon* ray — more at RAYON] **1 :** depicted with rays darting forth — used esp. in heraldry ⟨a sun ~⟩ **2 :** characterized by the use of radiating lines (as in window tracery) — used of a French Gothic architectural style of the 14th century
ray parenchyma *n* [²*ray*] **:** the horizontal and usu. radially arranged parenchyma that constitutes all or most of a plant ray — compare PHLOEM PARENCHYMA, WOOD PARENCHYMA
rays *pl of* RAY, *pres 3d sing of* RAY
ray's woodsia \ˈrāz-\ *n, usu cap R* [fr. the name *Ray*] **:** RUSTY WOODSIA
ray tracheid *n* [²*ray*] **:** any of various chiefly marginal tracheids in the vascular rays of some gymnosperms that have bordered pits and lack living contents but resemble typical ray cells in position and shape
ˡraze \ˈrāz\ *vt* -ED/-ING/-S [alter. of *rase*] **1 :** to overthrow from the foundation **:** lay level with the ground **:** DESTROY **2 a :** to scrape, cut, or shave off **b** *obs* **:** ERASE, EFFACE, OBLITERATE **3 a** *archaic* **:** CUT, SCRATCH **b** *archaic* **:** to scrape, graze, or wound slightly **syn** see DESTROY
²raze \"\ *n* -S *obs* **:** an act or the result of razing **:** CUT, SCRAPE
ˡra·zee \rāˈzē\ *n* -S [F (*vaisseau*) *rasé,* fr. *vaisseau* ship + *rasé,* past part. of *raser* to raze, raze — more at RASE] **1 :** a wooden ship having its upper deck cut away and thus reduced to the next lower rate or to an intermediate class (as a seventy-four cut down to a frigate) **2 :** something (as a chest) subjected to razeeing
²razee \"\ *vt* **razeed; razeed; razeeing; razees 1 :** to convert (a ship) to a razee **2 :** to make less, prune, or abridge by or as if by cutting off or retrenching parts ⟨men *razeed* by poverty⟩
raz·er \ˈrāzə(r)\ *n* -S **:** one that razes
razmataz *var of* RAZZMATAZZ
ra·zon \ˈrā,zän-\ *or* **razon bomb** *n* -S [blend of *range* and *azon* bomb] **:** an aerial bomb that can be guided to the right or left and controlled in range by radio means — compare AZON
ˡra·zor \ˈrāzə(r)\ *n* -S *often attrib* [ME *rasour,* fr. OF *raseor,* fr. *raser* to rase, shave + *-eor* -or — more at RASE] **1 :** a keen-edged cutting instrument made with the cutting blade and handle in one (as a straight razor) or with the cutting blade inserted into a holder (as a safety razor or electric razor) and used chiefly for shaving or cutting the hair **2 :** RAZOR CLAM **3 :** OCKHAM'S RAZOR

razors: *1* straight, *2* safety

²razor \"\ *vt* -ED/-ING/-S **:** to shave or cut with or as if with a razor ⟨a closely ~*ed* beard⟩
ra·zor·able \-rəbəl\ *adj* [²*razor* + *-able*] *obs* **:** ready or suitable for shaving
razorback \ˈ==,=\ *n* **1 :** RORQUAL **2** *or* **razorback hog** *or* **razor-backed hog :** a thin-bodied long-legged hog chiefly of the southeastern U.S. that is the half-wild mongrel descendant of improved breeds **3 :** a sharp narrow back or ridge (as of a range of hills) ⟨ridges and ~*s* rise precipitously from deep valleys —Lowell Thomas⟩ **4 :** a laborer who loads and unloads the cars of a traveling circus **:** ROUSTABOUT ⟨the audience at rehearsal included all the . . . ~*s* —T.W.Duncan⟩
razorback buffalo fish *n* **:** SMALLMOUTH BUFFALO
razor–backed \¦==¦=\ *or* **razorback** \¦==¦=\ *adj* **:** having a sharp narrow back ⟨a *razor-backed* horse⟩
razorback sucker *n* **:** HUMPBACK SUCKER
razorbill \ˈ==,=\ *n* **1** *or* **razor–billed auk :** an auk (*Alca torda*) of the American and European coasts and islands of the northern No. Atlantic that is about 16 inches long with the plumage black above and white below and has a compressed sharp-edged black bill crossed by a white band **2 :** SKIMMER 3
razor–billed \¦==¦=\ *or* **razorbill** \¦==¦=\ *adj* **:** having a razor-shaped bill
razor–billed curassow *n* **:** any of several So. American curassows of the genus *Mitu* having a short laterally compressed bill with a knob on the culmen
razor clam *n* **:** any of numerous marine bivalve mollusks (family Solenidae) having a long narrow curved thin shell
razor–edge \ˈ==,=\ *n* **:** an edge comparable to a razor's edge (as in fineness, sharpness, hazardous possibilities) ⟨an appetite whetted to a ~⟩
razor fish *n* **1 a :** any of several small wrasses (genus *Xyrichthys*); *esp* **:** a fish (*X. psittacus*) marked with bright red and blue and found esp. in the Mediterranean and West Indies **b** *southern Africa* **:** a common heavily armored shrimpfish (*Aeoliscus punctulatus*) that is found in the Indian ocean **2 :** RAZOR CLAM
razor grass *n* **:** a West Indian climbing sedge (*Scleria scindens*) with very rough triangular stems and leaves
razor–grinder \ˈ==,==\ *n, Brit* **:** GOATSUCKER
ra·zor·less \ˈ==ləs\ *adj* **:** lacking a razor
razor saw *n* **:** a narrow saw used in excavating limestone
razor–sharp \¦==¦=\ *adj* **:** very sharp **:** notably keen ⟨a *razor-sharp* wit⟩
razor shell *n* **1 :** RAZOR CLAM; *also* **:** its shell **2 :** PEN SHELL
razor stone *n* **:** NOVACULITE
razor strop *n* **:** STROP b
ˡrazz \ˈraz, -aa(ə)z\ *n* -ES [short for *razzberry,* alter. of *raspberry*] *slang* **:** RASPBERRY 3
²razz \"\ *vt* -ED/-ING/-ES **:** to tease and banter at **:** RIDICULE ⟨~*ed* me over my friend⟩ ⟨the fans who sit in the bleachers and ~ the visiting outfielders⟩
raz·zia \ˈrazēə\ *n* -S [F, fr. colloq. Ar *ghazyah* (Ar *ghazwah, ghazāh*)] **:** a plundering and destructive incursion **:** FORAY, RAID
raz·zle \ˈrazəl\ *n* -S [by shortening] **:** RAZZLE-DAZZLE 1
razzle–dazzle \¦==¦==\ *n* [irreg. redupl. of *dazzle*] **1 :** a state of confusion, hilarity, or disorder; *esp* **:** SPREE **2 :** something that induces or is intended to induce a state of confusion: as **a :** a swiftly revolving undulating carrousel without seats **b :** complex maneuvers (as in a competitive sport) designed to confuse the opponent ⟨complaining about the lack of much *razzle-dazzle* in modern football⟩ **c :** a loud, fast-moving, and often cheap atmosphere or exhibition ⟨the *razzle-dazzle* of the circus⟩ ⟨a sideshow of dancing girls and other *razzle-dazzle* —*Time*⟩
razz·ma·tazz *also* **raz·ma·taz** \¦razmə¦taz, ¦raaz-, -taa(ə)z\ *n* -ES [by alter.] **:** RAZZLE-DAZZLE
rb *abbr* ruble
RB *abbr* **1** rifle brigade **2** right back **3** right fullback
Rb *symbol* rubidium
RBC *abbr* red blood cells; red blood count
RBH *abbr* regimental beachhead
RBI *abbr or n* -S **:** a run batted in
rbl *abbr* ruble
RC \ˈär¦sē\ *abbr or n* -S Roman Catholic
RC *abbr* **1** recruiting center **2** rehabilitation center **3** reinforced concrete **4** relief claim **5** release clause **6** remote control **7** reply coupon **8** *often not cap* resistance-capacitance **9** right center
rcd *abbr* **1** received **2** record
RCG *abbr, often not cap* reverberation-controlled gain
RCL *abbr* ruling case law
RCM *abbr* **1** radar countermeasure **2** regimental court-martial
rcn *abbr* reconnaissance
r color *n* **:** an acoustic effect of a simultaneously articulated \r\ imparted to a vowel by retroflexion or bunching of the tongue — **r–colored** \ˈ=,==\ *adj*
rcpt *abbr* receipt
rct *abbr* **1** receipt **2** recruit
RCT *abbr* regimental combat team
rctg *abbr* recruiting
rcvr *abbr* receiver
rd *abbr* **1** red **2** reduce; reduced; reduction **3** road **4** rod **5** rood **6** round **7** rutherford
-rd *symbol* — used after the figure 3 to indicate the ordinal number *third* or any ordinal number ending with *third* ⟨June 3rd⟩ ⟨43rd St.⟩; compare -D, -ND
RD *abbr* **1** reaction of degeneration **2** refer to drawer **3** regional director **4** right defense **5** *often not cap* rix dollar **6** *often not cap* running days **7** rural dean **8** rural delivery **9** rural district
RDA *abbr, often not cap* recommended dietary allowance
RdAc *symbol* radioactinium
RDC *abbr* **1** rail diesel car **2** running-down clause **3** rural district council
RDF *abbr* radio direction finder
rdg *abbr* **1** reading **2** reducing **3** ridge
rdm *abbr* **1** radarman **2** random
rdo *abbr* radio
RdTh *symbol* radiothorium
rdv *abbr* rendezvous
RDX \¦är(,)dē¦eks\ *n* -ES [code name, prob. fr. *R*esearch *D*epartment *ex*plosive] **:** CYCLONITE
RDY *abbr* royal dockyard
ˡre *or* **ray** \ˈrā\ *n* -S [ML *re,* fr. L *re*sonare to resound, a word sung to this note in a medieval hymn to St. John the Baptist] **1 :** the second tone of the diatonic scale in solmization **2 :** the tone *D* in the fixed-do system
²re \ˈrā, ˈrē\ *prep* [L, abl of *res* thing, affair, matter — more at REAL] **:** with regard to **:** REGARDING **:** in the matter of **:** on the subject of **:** CONCERNING **:** IN RE ⟨their remarks ~ the new building were most interesting⟩ ⟨~ your letter of last month⟩
re- *prefix* [ME, fr OF, fr L *re-, red-*] **1 :** again **:** anew ⟨*re*do⟩ ⟨*re*tell⟩ — usu. joined to the second element by a hyphen when (1) the word (as *re-create*) would otherwise be confused with another word (as *recreate*) of different meaning, or (2) the word (as *re-recover*) has a second element beginning with *re-,* or (3) the second element begins with a capital letter (as *re-Christianization*) **2 :** back **:** backward ⟨*re*call⟩
re *abbr* **1** reference **2** rupee
RE *abbr* **1** rate of exchange **2** real estate **3** red edges **4** repayable to either **5** *often not cap* reticuloendothelial **6** right end **7** right eye **8** right excellent **9** rural electrification
RE *symbol* rare earth (sense 2)
Re *symbol* rhenium
're \(ə)r, ə\ *vb* [by contr.] **:** ARE ⟨what'*re* you doing⟩ ⟨these '*re* right⟩
rea *var of* REUS
re·able \(ˈ)rē+\ *vt* -ED/-ING/-S [*re-* + *able*] *chiefly Brit* **:** REHABILITATE — **re·able·ment** \(ˈ)rēābəlmənt\ *n* -S
re·absorb \¦rē+\ *vb* [*re-* + *absorb*] *vt* **:** to absorb again; RESORB 2 ~ *vi* **:** RESORB
re·absorption \"+\ *n* [*re-* + *absorption*] **:** the act, process, or condition of absorbing again or of being absorbed again
re·accept \"+\ *vt* [*re-* + *accept*] **:** to accept again — **re·acceptance** \"+\ *n*
re·access \(¦)rē+\ *n* [*re-* + *access*] **:** renewed access **:** RETURN ⟨a ~ of fever⟩
re·accession \¦rē+\ *n* [*re-* + *accession*] **:** renewed accession ⟨~ to power⟩
re·acclimatization \"+\ *n* [*re-* + *acclimatization*] **:** the act or process of reacclimatizing or condition of being reacclimatized ⟨the patient's ~ to society —*Digest of Neurology & Psychiatry*⟩
re·acclimatize \"+\ *vt* [*re-* + *acclimatize*] **:** to acclimatize again ⟨~ their children and themselves to the different rhythms of urban life —*N. Y. Times*⟩
re·accommodate \¦rē+\ *vt* [*re-* + *accommodate*] **:** to accommodate again
re·accommodation \"+\ *n* [*re-* + *accommodation*] **:** renewed accommodation
re·accounting \"+\ *n* [*re-* + *accounting*] **:** retroactive accounting
re·accredit \"+\ *vt* [*re-* + *accredit*] **:** to accredit again ⟨~ their envoys —*N. Y. Times*⟩
re·accreditation \"+\ *n* [*re-* + *accreditation*] **:** renewed accreditation
re·acetylation \"+\ *n* [*re-* + *acetylation*] **:** renewed acetylation
ˡreach \ˈrēch\ *vb* **reached** \ˈrēcht\ *or dial* **retch** \ˈrech\ *or dial chiefly Brit* **raught** \ˈrȯ(k)t\ *or dial chiefly Brit* **rought** \"\ **reached** *or dial chiefly Brit* **raught** *or dial chiefly Brit* **rought; reaching; reaches** [ME *rechen* (past *raughte, rechede,* past part. *raught, yraught, reched, yreched*), fr. OE *rǣcan* (past *rǣhte,* past part. *gerǣht*); akin to OHG *reichen* to reach, ON *reik* parting of the hair, Lith *rāižytis* to stretch oneself repeatedly] *vt* **1 a** (1) **:** to stretch out **:** EXTEND ⟨~*ed* out his hand to her⟩ (2) **:** to put forth ⟨a tree that ~*es* its branches over the wall⟩ **b :** THRUST ⟨~*ed* his sword up and touched the mark⟩ **c** *archaic* (1) **:** to strike, hit, or touch with a weapon (2) **:** to aim or deliver (a blow) by stretching out the hand **:** DEAL ⟨a sudden punch which he ~*ed* at the nose of his lordship —Henry Brooke⟩ **2 a** *obs* **:** to get possession of esp. by or as if by seizing and making off with ⟨the hand of death hath *raught* him —Shak.⟩ **b** (1) **:** to succeed in touching or grasping by or as if by stretching out the hand or some other part of the body or some other object ⟨the shelf was too high for the little boy to ~ it⟩ ⟨probed about in the darkness with his foot and at last ~*ed* the bottom step⟩ ⟨could not ~ the bullet with the probe⟩ (2) *archaic* **:** SNATCH (3) **:** to pick up and draw toward one **:** TAKE ⟨~*ed* a cup from the shelf⟩ ⟨~*ed* down his hat⟩ **c** (1) **:** to stretch out as far as **:** extend to ⟨by evening the shadow of the tree ~*ed* the wall⟩ (2) **:** to arrive at **:** get up to or as far as **:** come to ⟨can ~ the gate by following this path⟩ ⟨your letter has ~*ed* me⟩ ⟨her voice was not strong enough to ~ everyone in the auditorium⟩ ⟨has ~*ed* middle age⟩ **:** go as far as ⟨has ~*ed* a new height of absurdity⟩ ⟨a book that has now ~*ed* its third edition⟩ **:** ATTAIN ⟨spent his whole life trying to ~ happiness⟩ ⟨think we can ~ an understanding by further discussion⟩ (3) **:** to penetrate to ⟨a telescope that ~*es* remote points in space⟩ ⟨the news ~*ed* every part of the world⟩ (4) **:** to succeed in getting or obtaining **:** ACQUIRE ⟨~*ing* a profound knowledge of the subject⟩ **d** (1) **:** to stretch out to and affect **:** COVER, EMBRACE ⟨a situation that the law certainly ~*es*⟩ (2) **:** to get into contact with (as intellectually or emotionally) and so influence ⟨was not sure how she could ~ a person with a background like that⟩ **:** make an impression on (3) **:** to get in touch with (as by correspondence, publication) **:** communicate with ⟨~*ed* him by phone at the office⟩ ⟨you can ~ me by addressing your letters to New York⟩ ⟨could ~ a vast audience with such a magazine⟩ **3** *dial chiefly Eng* **:** to cause (as a piece of leather) to be stretched **4 :** to take hold of and give **:** PASS **:** hand over ⟨~ me the catsup⟩ **5** *archaic* **:** to succeed in understanding **:** COMPREHEND ⟨some double sense that I ~ not —P.B.Shelley⟩ **~** *vi* **1 a :** to make a stretch (as in proceeding to grasp, touch, strike) in some direction with or as if with one's hand or some other part of the body **:** stretch out ⟨~*ed* for some money⟩ ⟨stood on tiptoe and ~*ed* toward the book on the top shelf⟩ ⟨~*ed* for the stone with his foot⟩ **b** (1) **:** to make a stretch of a particular length or extent ⟨does not dare to ~ after fame⟩ (2) **:** to strain after something **:** make efforts ⟨~*ing* above our nature does no good —John Dryden⟩ **2 a :** to undergo continuous extension **:** become drawn out **:** PROJECT, EXTEND ⟨his land ~*es* to the river⟩ ⟨power that ~*es* to every corner of the country⟩ **b :** to get up to or as far as something **:** arrive at something **:** come to something **:** PENETRATE, CARRY ⟨the forest stretched as far as the eye could ~⟩ **3** *dial chiefly Eng* **:** to become stretched **:** undergo stretching **4 :** to sail on a reach

syn GAIN, COMPASS, ACHIEVE, ATTAIN: REACH may be used in reference to any goal, point, or end arrived at ⟨our team *reached* the finals⟩ ⟨the wheat crop *reached* 500,000 tons⟩ ⟨the automobile *reached* a speed of 120 miles per hour⟩ ⟨the life boat *reached* land in the morning⟩ ⟨Pictured Rocks, where the coloration *reaches* its greatest intensity —*Amer. Guide Series: Mich.*⟩ GAIN often but not always implies coming to a desired goal, vantage point, or advantage through effort or struggle ⟨to *gain* the championship⟩ ⟨*gaining* the presidency⟩ ⟨*gaining* distinction by his research⟩ ⟨*gaining* prestige⟩ ⟨*gaining* success in his field⟩ ⟨he *gained* the confidence of the mountain people by his understanding and sympathetic approach —F.T. Persons⟩ COMPASS may suggest gaining an end as by skillful resolution, crafty encirclement, circumvention, or extension ⟨*compassing* almost equally with verse man's thought however sublime, his emotion however profound —A.T.Quiller-Couch⟩ ⟨he certainly managed to *compass* the hardest thing that a man who has drunk heavily can do. He took his peg and wine at dinner; but he never drank alone, and never let what he drank have the least hold on him —Rudyard Kipling⟩ ACHIEVE may imply skill, courage, persistence, or endurance in struggle or quest ⟨in twenty-five years of unremitting toil, he had *achieved* a distinguished position —R.J.Wickenden⟩ ⟨man will want consciously and desperately to *achieve* the consolation and create the beauty we have always called literature —C.F. Strauch⟩ ATTAIN sometimes suggests a reaching to the extreme, the difficult, the unusual ⟨an object, in its own nature so really and undeniably good, as to be the compensation of a great deal of thought in the *compassing,* and a great deal of trouble in the *attaining* —J.H.Newman⟩ ⟨men had *attained* the stratosphere —Waldemar Kaempffert⟩ ⟨its refinement of detail and subtle proportions, which *attain* an almost monumental quality —*Amer. Guide Series: Maine*⟩

²reach \"\ *n* -ES **1 a** (1) **:** the action or an act of reaching ⟨made a ~ for the nearest one⟩ (2) **:** a single movement **:** an individual part of a progression or journey ⟨arriving at the post after three ~*es*⟩ **b** (1) **:** the particular distance or extent of reaching ⟨if the shelf is lowered, a long ~ won't be necessary⟩ (2) **:** the particular distance over which or the extent to which one can reach ⟨has a remarkable ~⟩ ⟨this is within your ~⟩ **c :** power of comprehension or range of knowledge or thought ⟨a mind of vast ~⟩ **2 a :** a continuous unbroken stretch or expanse: as (1) **:** an extended portion of water or land (2) **:** a straight portion of a stream or river (3) **:** a level stretch of water between locks in a canal (4) **:** an arm of the sea extending up into the land (5) **:** PROMONTORY **b :** a limited distance **:** a measured part ⟨the narrow stairwell turned back upon itself in a succession of niggard ~*es* —William Faulkner⟩ **3** *obs* **:** DESIGN, SCHEME, PLAN **4 a :** a bearing shaft or a coupling pole; *esp* **:** the pole or rod joining the hind axle to the forward bolster of a wagon **b :** the sum of the hoist and the minimum distance between the hooks of a pulley tackle **c :** the length of the threaded portion of a bolt or spark plug **5 :** the tack sailed by a ship with the wind coming just forward of the beam or with the wind directly abeam or abaft the beam **syn** see RANGE
³reach \"\ *vb* -ED/-ING/-ES [prob. fr. (assumed) ME *rechen,* fr. OE *hrǣcan;* akin to OE *hrāca* phlegm from the throat, ON *hrāki* spittle, *hrækja* to hawk, spit, Lith *krēgéti* to grunt, L *crepare* to crack, creak, break — more at RAVEN] **1** *dial chiefly Eng* **a :** SPIT **b :** HAWK **2** *dial chiefly Eng* **a :** VOMIT **b :** RETCH
reach·able \-chəbəl\ *adj* **:** capable of being reached ⟨all these cities are ~ in a few hours —*N. Y. Times*⟩
reached *past of* REACH
reach·er \ˈrēchə(r)\ *n* -S [ˡ*reach* + *-er*] **:** HANDER-IN
reacher–in \¦==¦=\ *n, pl* **reacher–ins** *also* **reachers–in** [fr. the phrase *reach in* + *-er*] **:** HANDER-IN
reaches *pres 3d sing of* REACH, *pl of* REACH
ˡreaching *n* -S [ME *rechynge,* fr. OE *rǣcing,* fr. *rǣcan* to reach + *-ing* (suffix forming nouns from verbs)] **:** the action of one that reaches for something or an instance of grasping or seeking to grasp ⟨incomplete, abstracted ~*s* for the meaning of things —Walter Lippmann⟩
²reaching *adj* [fr. pres. part. of ˡ*reach*] **:** that reaches out, forward, or into something; *esp* **:** deeply penetrating ⟨the views of the lord deputy, somewhat more ~ than their own, startled them —Robert Browning⟩
reaching jib *or* **reaching sail** *n* **:** BALLOON SAIL
reaching post *n* **:** the post at the lower end of a rope walk
reach·less \ˈrēchləs\ *adj* **:** that cannot be reached **:** not within reach ⟨~ heights⟩
reach–me–down \ˈ=,=,=\ *adj or n, chiefly Brit* **:** HAND-ME-DOWN
reach rod *n* **:** a rod with a double eye at each end for communicating the motion of the reversing lever of a link motion to the lifting shaft
reachy \ˈrēchē\ *adj* -ER/-EST [²*reach* + *-y*] **1 :** marked by notable extension ⟨a long, ~ trot —C.W.Gay⟩ **2 :** marked by notable length of neck and body ⟨~ poultry⟩
re·acknowledge \¦rē+\ *vt* [*re-* + *acknowledge*] **:** to acknowledge again
re·acquaint \"+\ *vt* [*re-* + *acquaint*] **:** to make acquainted again
re·acquire \"+\ *vt* [*re-* + *acquire*] **:** to acquire again
re·acquisition \(¦)rē+\ *n* [*re-* + *acquisition*] **:** renewed acquisition
re·act \rē+\ *vb* -ED/-ING/-S [NL *reactus,* past part. of *reagere,* fr. L *re-* + *agere* to drive, act — more at AGENT] *vi* **1 :** to exert a reciprocal or counteracting force or influence — often used with *on* or *upon* ⟨exhausting work must ~ on human character —Samuel Van Valkenburg & Ellsworth Huntington⟩ **2 :** to respond in a particular way to a particular treatment, situation, or other stimulus ⟨~*ed* with instinctive indignation —J.P.Frank⟩ — often used with *to* ⟨was not sure how the patient would ~ to the drug⟩ **3 :** to act in opposition to some force or influence — usu. used with *against* ⟨~*ed* against the threat of dictatorship —*New School for Social Research Bull.*⟩ ⟨~*ing* against mass ideologies —Henry Hewes⟩ **4 :** to move in or tend toward a reverse direction **:** return to or toward a prior condition ⟨public opinion wavered briefly but soon ~*ed* in his favor⟩ ⟨stock prices ~*ed* strongly after a brief drop⟩ **5 :** to undergo chemical reaction **~** *vt* **:** to cause to react; *specif* **:** to bring about a chemical reaction in ⟨produces ethyl chloride by ~*ing* chlorine with waste —*Lamp*⟩ **syn** see ACT
re–act \(ˈ)rē+\ *vt* [*re-* + *act*] **:** to act or perform a second time ⟨in his imagination he *re-acted* the scene —Aldous Huxley⟩
re·ac·tance \rēˈaktən(t)s\ *n* -S [ISV *react* + *-ance*] **1 :** the part of the impedance of an alternating-current circuit that is due either to capacitance or inductance or to both and that is expressed in ohms **2 :** ACOUSTIC REACTANCE
reactance coil *n* **:** REACTOR 3
reactance drop *n* **:** the voltage drop in a circuit due to the current traversing the reactance
reactance tube *n* **:** an electron tube that by a variation of its operating voltage can give the effect of a variation of reactance across its electrodes or across a network connected to its electrodes

1re·ac·tant \-nt\ *n* -s [*react* + *-ant*, n. suffix] **1 :** a chemically reacting substance **2 :** an initial factor in a chemical reaction — opposed to *resultant*

2reactant \"\ *adj* [*react* + *-ant*, adj. suffix] **1 :** of, relating to, or marked by reactance **2** [*1reactant*] **:** of or relating to a reactant

re·action \rē+\ *n* -s [NL *reaction-, reactio*, fr. *reactus* (past part. of *reagere* to react) + L *-ion-, -io* -ion — more at REACT] **1 a :** exertion of reciprocal or counteracting force or influence ⟨the ~ between an individual and his environment⟩ **b :** action in opposition to some force or influence ⟨~ against dictatorship⟩ **c :** movement in or tendency toward a reverse direction **:** return to a prior condition ⟨a strong ~ in stock prices⟩ **d :** a tendency toward or movement in support of a former esp. outmoded or repressive political or social condition, policy, or form of government ⟨mixture of sober conservatism, timid standpattism, and angry ~ —Clinton Rossiter⟩ **2 a :** a particular response to a particular treatment, situation, or other stimulus ⟨watched her ~ to the news⟩ **b :** bodily response to or activity aroused by a stimulus: (1) **:** motor response (as muscular movement or secretion) to stimulation (2) **:** the whole sensorimotor process comprising intellectual and emotional elements as well as pure motor response **:** total response of an organism to a stimulus **c** (1) **:** an action induced by vital resistance to some other action ⟨inflammatory ~ to bacterial infection⟩; *esp* **:** the specific result (as hemolysis, local inflammation, or a rise in bodily temperature) characteristically evoked in cells or tissues or in vitro by a foreign substance and used in various serological tests to determine specific sensitivities or the presence of particular infection ⟨the tuberculin ~⟩ ⟨the precipitin ~⟩ ⟨allergic ~*s*⟩ (2) **:** depression or exhaustion of vital force consequent on overexertion or overstimulation (3) **:** heightened activity and overaction succeeding depression or shock (4) **:** a psychosis, psychoneurosis, or other mental or emotional disorder forming an individual's response to his life situation ⟨an anxiety ~⟩ ⟨a schizophrenic ~⟩ **3 :** the force that a body subjected to the action of a force from another body exerts in the opposite direction **4 a** (1) **:** chemical transformation or change **:** the reversible or irreversible interaction of molecules, atoms, ions, or radicals to form one or more new substances ⟨the ~ of acid with base⟩ ⟨the ~ of hydrogen with oxygen gives water⟩ ⟨endothermic and exothermic ~*s*⟩ — see EQUATION 2b, ORDER OF A REACTION; compare CATALYSIS, DECOMPOSITION, POLYMERIZATION, SUBSTITUTION, SYNTHESIS (2) **:** the state resulting from such a reaction ⟨an alkaline ~⟩ **b :** a process involving change in atomic nuclei (as the disintegration of uranium 239 into neptunium and an electron or the union of heavy-hydrogen nuclei to form helium nuclei) — called also *nuclear reaction;* compare CHAIN REACTION, FISSION, FUSION, SPALLATION **5 :** the effect of organisms upon their habitat — compare COACTION **6 :** the degree of acidity or alkalinity of soil

re·ac·tion·al \rē'akshənᵊl, -kshnəl\ *adj* [ISV *reaction* + *-al*] **:** of, relating to, or marked by reaction ⟨a ~ rise in temperature⟩ — **re·ac·tion·al·ly** \-ᵊlē, -əlē\ *adv*

re·ac·tion·ar·i·ness \rē'akshə,nerēnəs, -rin-, ˌ=ˌ==ˈ===\ *n* -ES **:** REACTIONISM

re·ac·tion·arism \=ˈ==_nə,rizəm\ *n* -s [*1reactionary* + *-ism*] **:** REACTIONISM

re·ac·tion·arist \-_rəst\ *n* -s [*1reactionary* + *-ist*] **:** REACTIONARY

1re·ac·tion·ary \rē'akshə,nerē, -eri\ *adj* [F *réactionnaire*, fr. *réaction* reaction (fr. NL *reaction-, reactio*) + *-aire* -ary] **:** relating to, marked by, or favoring reaction (as toward a former political order) **syn** see CONSERVATIVE

2reactionary \"\ *n* -ES **:** one that is reactionary

re·ac·tion·ary·ism \-,izəm\ *n* -s [*1reactionary* + *-ism*] **:** the quality or state of being reactionary **:** REACTIONISM

reaction engine *n* **:** an engine that develops thrust by expelling a jet of fluid or a stream of particles

reaction formation *n* **:** an attitude, trait, or behavioral tendency that substitutes for or conceals a diametrically opposed repressed impulse

re·ac·tion·ism \-shə,nizəm\ *n* -s [*reaction* + *-ism*] **:** the quality or state of being reactionary

1re·ac·tion·ist \-sh(ə)nəst\ *n* -s [*reaction* + *-ist*] **:** REACTIONARY

2reactionist \"\ *adj* **:** REACTIONARY

reaction kinetics *n pl but sing or pl in constr* **:** a branch of chemistry that deals with the rate of chemical reactions, with factors influencing such rates, and with applications of rate studies to elucidate the mechanism of reactions — compare ORDER OF A REACTION

reaction motor *n* **:** REACTION ENGINE

reaction propulsion *n* **:** propulsion produced by a reaction engine

reaction rim *also* **reaction border** *n* **:** a zone of one or more species of mineral surrounding a larger crystal of another kind and representing reaction between a solidified mineral and the surrounding liquid magma — compare RESORPTION BORDER

reaction ring *n* **:** a heavy internal cast-iron flange set in cement and used to resist the thrust of the jacks when sinking a shaft by a process in which a continuous casing is forced downward as the excavation progresses

reactions *pl of* REACTION

reaction time *n* **:** the time elapsing between the beginning of the application of a stimulus and the beginning of an organism's reaction to it — compare LATENT PERIOD, PRESENTATION TIME

reaction turbine *n* **:** a turbine with rotating blades curved and arranged so as to develop torque from gradual decrease of steam pressure from inlet to exhaust — compare IMPULSE TURBINE

reaction type *n* **:** PHENOTYPE

reaction wood *n* **:** wood (as compression wood, tension wood) that develops abnormally by reason of varying factors (as atypical gravitational pull)

re·activate \(')rē+\ *vb* [*re-* + *activate*] *vt* **:** to activate again **:** cause to be again active or more active **:** restore to a state of activity or greater activity **:** make again operational and effective **:** REVIVE, REVIVIFY: as **a** (1) **:** to restore (as a military unit) to an active state (as from a state of disorganization or deactivation) (2) **:** to cause (as an industrial plant, a society, a program, a commission) to function again after a suspension of activity ⟨*reactivated* the factory as soon as the strike was over⟩ **b :** to cause (as a repressed complex) to reappear in consciousness or behavior ⟨persecution feelings *reactivated* by new social failures⟩ **c :** to cause (a quiescent disease) to become active again in an individual ⟨tuberculosis that was *reactivated* by fatigue⟩ **d :** to restore complement to (an inactivated serum) by addition of fresh normal serum **e :** to restore ability of (an electron tube) to emit electrons copiously from a cathode **f :** to make (as a catalyst or an adsorbent) active again **~** *vi* **:** to become active again

re·activation \(ˌ)rē+\ *n* [*reactivate* + *-ion*] **:** the act or process of reactivating or condition of being reactivated

re·activator \(')rē+\ *n* [*reactivate* + *-or*] **:** one that reactivates: as **a :** a substance that restores the reactivity of another substance **b :** ACTIFIER

re·active \rē+\ *adj* [prob. fr. (assumed) NL *reactivus*, fr. NL *reactus* (past part. of *reagere* to react) + L *-ivus* -ive — more at REACT] **1 a :** of, relating to, or marked by reaction ⟨~ symptoms⟩ ⟨a ~ process⟩ **b :** of, relating to, or marked by reactance **2 a :** readily responsive to stimulus ⟨the skin of the geriatric is less ~ than that of younger persons —Louis Tuft⟩ **b :** occurring as a result of stress or emotional upset ⟨~ depression⟩ — **re·actively** \"+\ *adv* — **re·activeness** \"+\ *n*

reactive coil *n* **:** REACTOR 3

reactive component *n* **1 :** the component of an alternating current that has a phase difference of 90° with the electromotive force **2 :** the component of the voltage across the circuit that is in quadrature with the current and that produces no power in an alternating current circuit — called also *wattless component*

reactive factor *n* **:** a factor that is constituted by the ratio of the reactive volt-amperes to the apparent power in an alternating-current circuit and that is equal to the sine of the angular phase difference between voltage and current

reactive load *n* **:** a load which is carried by an alternating current generating station or system in which the current and voltage are out of phase and which is measured in volt-amperes or kilovolt-amperes

reactive power *n* **:** REACTIVE VOLT-AMPERES

reactive volt-amperes *n pl* **:** the product of the effective voltage and effective current in an alternating-current circuit and the sine of the angular phase difference between them

re·activity \(,)rē+\ *n* [ISV *reactive* + *-ity*] **1 :** the quality or state of being reactive **2 :** the rate of nuclear disintegration in a reactor

re·ac·to·log·i·cal \rē¦aktə¦läjəkəl\ *adj* **:** of or relating to reactology

re·ac·tol·o·gist \(,)rē,ak'tälə̇jəst\ *n* -s **:** a specialist in reactology

re·ac·tol·o·gy \-jē\ *n* -ES [*reaction* + *-o-* + *-logy*] **:** the scientific study of psychological reactions — compare REFLEXOLOGY

re·actor \rē+\ *n* -s [ISV *react* + *-or*] **1 :** one that reacts: as **a :** a chemical reagent **b** (1) **:** the subject reacting to a stimulus in a psychological experiment (2) **:** the subject reacting positively to a foreign substance (as in a test for disease) ⟨tuberculous cattle are ~*s* to tuberculin⟩ **2 :** an organism that produces reaction in its environment **3 :** a coil, winding, or conductor of small resistance and large inductance used in an alternating-current circuit to impede or throttle the current or to change its phase **4 a :** a piece of equipment in which a chemical reaction is carried out esp. on an industrial scale ⟨batch and continuous ~*s*⟩ **b :** an apparatus in which a chain reaction of fissionable material is initiated and controlled (as for generation of heat for power or for production of plutonium from uranium) — called also *atomic furnace, atomic pile, nuclear reactor, pile*

re·actualization \(ˌ)rē+\ *n* **:** the act of reactualizing or condition of being reactualized

re·actualize \(')rē+\ *vt* [*re-* + *actualize*] **:** to actualize again

re·actuate \"+\ *vt* [*re-* + *actuate*] **:** to actuate again

1read \'rēd\ *vb* **read** \'red\ **read** \"\ **reading** \'rēdiŋ, -dēŋ\ **reads** \'rēdz\ [ME *reden* to read, advise, interpret, govern, fr. OE *rǣdan;* akin to OE *rǣd* advice, counsel, council, OHG *rātan* to advise, *rāt* advice, supply, ON *rātha* to advise, interpret, govern, *rāth* advice, management, Goth ga*redan* to take into consideration, Skt *rādhnoti, rādhyati* he succeeds, prepares, accomplishes, Gk *arariskein* to fit — more at ARM] *vt* **1 a** (1) **:** to look at or otherwise scan (as letters or other symbols representing words or sentences) with mental formulation of the words or sentences represented ⟨~*ing* books⟩ ⟨~*ing* inscriptions⟩ (2) **:** to study the movements of (as lips) or the formation of (as smoke signals) or the manipulation of (as signaling flags) with mental formulation of the communication expressed ⟨can ~ lips⟩ (3) **:** to form with the lips or utter aloud (such mental formulations) ⟨~ the text clearly⟩ (4) **:** to understand the meaning and grasp the full sense of (such mental formulations) either with or without vocal reproduction ⟨students that can really ~ the classics⟩ **b** (1) **:** to see or find in printed or written form or in some similar form ⟨~ that the marriage would take place soon⟩ (2) **:** to learn from what one has seen or found in such form ⟨had ~ that the mineral was rare⟩ **c :** to deliver aloud by or as if by reading: as (1) **:** to cause another to become acquainted with the contents of (as something written or printed) ⟨please ~ me the letter⟩ ⟨~ them a story⟩ (2) *obs* **:** to give instruction in ⟨~ Euclid to some of his disciples —John Davies †1693⟩ (3) **:** to submit (a proposed measure) to a legislative assembly by reading all or part of (4) **:** to speak the lines of (as a character in a play) or deliver the text of (as a selection by a particular writer) and interpret (as by intonation, gesture) ⟨~*s* the part with conviction⟩ ⟨~*s* Shakespeare with moving simplicity⟩ **d** (1) **:** to go over or become acquainted with or get through the contents of (as a book, magazine, newspaper, letter) by reading **:** PERUSE ⟨~*ing* the evening newspapers⟩ ⟨haven't yet ~ the novel⟩ (2) **:** to make a special study of (as by reading books and attending lectures) **:** apply oneself to the study of by following an organized course in ⟨~ law but later chose journalism —E.E.Allen⟩ **e :** to read books or other printed or written material in (a particular language) ⟨is learning to ~ Danish⟩; *esp* **:** to have such knowledge of (a particular language) as to be able to read with full understanding ⟨~*s* German, French, and Italian⟩ ⟨~*s* Spanish but can't speak it⟩ **f :** to observe and note the indications of (as a thermometer or other graduated instrument) ⟨is ~*ing* the meter⟩ **g** (1) **:** to check or edit (copy) to be set in type (2) **:** to check (proof) for discrepancies between proof and copy **h** (1) **:** to receive (a message) over a communication system (2) **:** to be able to understand (as a transmitted message) ⟨~ you loud and clear⟩ (3) **:** COMPREHEND, JUDGE ⟨sister . . . I ~ you all wrong —C.B.Kelland⟩ **i** *of a computer* **:** to scan and register or reproduce: (1) **:** to transfer (data fed in) to an internal medium (as magnetic tape, cards) for storage or computation (2) **:** to transfer (stored or computed data) to an external reproducing medium **2 a :** to study and advance an interpretation of the meaning or significance of (as a riddle, dream, omen, the palms of the hands) **b :** to make known (as the future) beforehand **:** FORETELL, PREDICT, FORESEE ⟨says she can ~ your fortune⟩ **3 a** (1) **:** to find revealed (as in the face or look of a person) ⟨~ dismay in her countenance⟩ (2) **:** to penetrate into (as the thoughts, mind of another) ⟨claims he can ~ your thoughts⟩ **b :** to learn the nature of (as another's character, feelings) by close observation of outward signs ⟨~ him like a book⟩ **4 a :** to attribute a particular meaning or interpretation to (something read) **:** take in a particular way **:** put a particular construction on **:** infer as being meant ⟨asked him how he ~ the passage⟩ **b :** to adopt a particular view of under a particular aspect or insight ⟨can ~ the situation in two ways⟩ **c :** to cause (as a particular often wrong idea) to be introduced into something being read or considered ⟨~*ing* false implications into the book⟩ **5 a :** to have or give (as a particular form of a word, phrase, or similar element) in a particular passage, text, or version ⟨in this copy the text ~*s hurry* rather than *harry*⟩ **b :** to cause (such an element) to be substituted in a particular passage, text, or version ⟨told him to ~ *hurry* for *harry*⟩ **6 :** to record and show **:** INDICATE ⟨the thermometer ~*s* zero⟩ **7 a :** to transfer (a pattern) in jacquard weaving to a set of cards by the perforation of each card with a punch **b :** to set up (a loom) for such a patterned fabric **8 :** to interpret and perform (a musical passage or composition) ⟨~*s* Bach with astonishing insight⟩ **~** *vi* **1 a :** to read something ⟨looks as though he's ~*ing*⟩ **b :** to apply oneself or devote oneself to reading books or other printed or written material ⟨likes to ~⟩ **c** (1) **:** to learn something by reading books or other printed or written material ⟨is ~*ing* up on space rockets⟩ (2) **:** to devote oneself to the special study of something (as by reading books and attending lectures) ⟨~ in classics and passed the honors examination —*Current Biog.*⟩ **2 a** (1) **:** to give a particular meaning, piece of information, or instruction when read ⟨the book ~*s* in only one unmistakable way⟩ (2) **:** to produce a particular impression when read ⟨was not sure how the letter would ~ to her⟩ **b** (1) **:** to have particular qualities (as of style, organization) that affect comprehension or enjoyment ⟨a book that ~*s* well⟩ (2) **:** to have particular qualities that favor comprehension and enjoyment ⟨gifted at writing magazine articles that ~⟩ **3 :** to consist of or be drawn up in certain words, phrases, or other similar elements ⟨a passage that ~*s* differently in the older versions⟩ — **read a lecture** *also* **read a lesson :** to reprimand severely — **read the riot act 1 :** to order (as a mob) to disperse **2 a :** to issue a peremptory order or warning to cease doing something **b :** to protest vehemently **:** express great objection **c :** to reprimand severely

2read \'rēd\ *n* -s **:** an act or period of reading ⟨thought I would have a ~ in it presently —Rose Macaulay⟩

3read *or* **reed** \'rēd\ *n* -s [ME *rede*, fr. OE *rēada*] **:** ABOMASUM

4read \'red\ *adj* [fr. past part. of *1read*] **:** instructed by or informed through reading **:** LEARNED ⟨far better ~ than most —B.J.Hendrick⟩ ⟨is widely ~ in contemporary literature⟩

read·abil·i·ty \,rēdə'biləd·ē\ *n* **:** the quality or state of being readable ⟨traces our history with skill and ~ —R.L.Duffus⟩ ⟨the physical ~ of the book is poor because of its heavy, close typography —Robert Halsband⟩ ⟨testing the ~ of prose by measuring the length of sentences —F.L.Mott⟩ ⟨improvement in the ~ of newspaper writing —Bruce Westley⟩

read·able \'rēdəbəl\ *adj* **1 :** that can be read with ease: **a :** LEGIBLE ⟨~ handwriting⟩ **b :** pleasing, interesting, or offering no great difficulty to the reader ⟨a ~ novel⟩ ⟨a ~ treatise on physics⟩ **c** *of a map* **:** clear in detail and the significance of symbols **2 :** that can be read throughout ⟨a novel, ~ at a sitting⟩

read·able·ness *n* -ES **:** READABILITY

read·ably \-blē\ *adv* **:** in a readable manner **:** in such a way as to be readable

re·adapt \ˌrē+\ *vb* [*re-* + *adapt*] *vt* **:** to adapt again **~** *vi* **:** to become adapted again

re·adaptability \"+\ *n* **:** the quality or state of being readaptable

re·adaptable \"+\ *adj* **:** capable of being adapted again

re·adaptation \(ˌ)rē+\ *n* **:** renewed adaptation

re·address \"+\ *vt* [*re-* + *address*] **:** to address again; *esp* **:** to put a new address on ⟨~*ed* and forwarded the letter⟩

read·er \'rēdə(r)\ *n* -s [ME *redere*, fr. OE *rǣdere*, fr. *rǣdan* to read + *-ere* -er] **1 :** one that reads: as **a** (1) **:** one that is able to read ⟨a slow ~⟩ ⟨a good ~⟩ (2) **:** one that applies himself to reading ⟨a room set aside for ~*s*⟩ (3) **:** one devoted to reading **:** one fond of reading ⟨is a great ~⟩ **b :** one that is appointed to read to others: as (1) **:** one appointed to read aloud during meals (as in a monastery or convent) (2) **:** LECTOR 1 (3) **:** one chosen to read aloud selected material in a Christian Science church or society **c** (1) **:** PROOFREADER (2) **:** one that reads and evaluates manuscripts (as for possible publication or for use as material in producing a motion picture or play) (3) **:** one that reads esp. newspapers and other periodical literature and indicates items to be marked, copied, abstracted, or clipped as having special interest or value to some individual or group **d :** one that reads and records the indications of meters or similar gauges (as for a public utilities company) **e :** one that assists a professor or other teacher by reading and marking the papers of students enrolled in a class **2** *Brit* **:** one who reads lectures or expounds subjects to students: **a :** a lecturer on law in the Inns of Court — used as an honorary title **b :** a university teacher chosen as a specialist in a particular field and ranking lower than a professor **3 a :** READING GLASS **b :** a device for projecting a readable image of a transparency on a self-contained or separate screen **c :** a unit (as of a computer) that scans material recorded (as on punched cards, magnetic tape) for storage or computation **4 a :** a book for instruction and practice in reading ⟨a third-grade ~⟩ **b :** a book containing selections for reading esp. for beginners in a subject ⟨a citizenship ~⟩ ⟨a French ~⟩ **c :** ANTHOLOGY ⟨a G.B. Shaw ~⟩ **5 a :** READING NOTICE **b :** a card (as in a window display) that carries a sale price, caption, or similar information **6 :** a playing card marked on the back so that it can be identified (as by a gambler, conjurer) — compare STAMP **7 :** a worker who records a textile design (as in string or in numbers) that he reads from a card

read·er·ship \-,ship\ *n* **1 a :** the quality or state of being a reader ⟨subscribers and purchasers on most levels of ~ —F.L.Mott⟩ **b :** the office, position, or profession of being a reader; *esp, Brit* **:** the position of a university teacher ranking lower than a professor ⟨there are new chairs and ~*s* in almost every British university —M.M.Postan⟩ **2 a :** the total mass of individuals actually reading or estimated to read something (as a book, magazine, newspaper, advertisement) ⟨increasing the ~ of a magazine⟩ — distinguished from *circulation* 5 **b :** a particular class of readers ⟨will appeal to an intelligent ~⟩

re·adhere \ˌrē+\ *vi* [*re-* + *adhere*] **:** to adhere again

re·adhesion \"+\ *n* [*re-* + *adhesion*] **:** the action of readhering

readied *past of* READY

readies *pres 3d sing of* READY, *pl of* READY

readier *comparative of* READY

readiest *superlative of* READY

read·i·ly \'redᵊlē, -ᵊli, -dl-, -dəl-\ *adv* [ME *redily*, fr. *redy* ready + *-ly*] **:** in a ready manner **:** with readiness: as **a :** with prompt willingness **:** without hesitating, quibbling, or delaying **:** with alacrity **:** WILLINGLY ⟨~ accepted my help —Nora Waln⟩ **b :** with fairly quick efficiency **:** without needless loss of time **:** reasonably fast **:** SPEEDILY ⟨information can when needed be ~ acquired by consulting appropriate books —J.B.Conant⟩ **c :** with a fair degree of ease **:** without much difficulty **:** with facility **:** EASILY ⟨ideas that a layman could ~ understand if plainly expressed —E.S.McCartney⟩

read in *vt* **:** to cause (oneself) to enter formally upon a new benefice in the Church of England after appointment by public reading of a set of accepted doctrinal statements and by assenting to the statements **~** *vi* **:** to enter formally upon a new benefice in the Church of England by reading oneself in

read·i·ness \'redēnəs, -din-\ *n* -ES [ME *redinesse*, fr. *redy* ready + *-nesse* -ness] **:** the quality or state of being ready: as **a :** prompt willingness **:** ALACRITY ⟨~ to welcome more co-operative relations —*Current Biog.*⟩ ⟨~ to continue discussions —*Wall Street Jour.*⟩ **b :** fairly quick efficiency **:** reasonable speed ⟨acquired ~ and accuracy in writing —J.S. Reeves⟩ **c :** EASE, FACILITY ⟨a happy ~ of conversation —Jane Austen⟩ **d :** a state of preparation ⟨putting them in ~ —H.E.Scudder⟩ ⟨gauging the child's ~ to begin reading⟩

1read·ing \'rēdiŋ, -dēŋ\ *n* -s [ME *redinge*, fr. OE *rǣding*, fr. *rǣdan* to read + *-ing* (suffix forming nouns from verbs)] **1 a :** material designed to be read **:** matter for reading ⟨chose the ~ for the great books course⟩; *esp* **:** a particular selection of such material designed to be read at one time or as a unit ⟨~*s* from contemporary fiction⟩ **b** (1) **:** the material read (as in a particular field) by an individual ⟨were discriminating in their ~⟩ ⟨thought he had seen the word somewhere in his ~⟩ (2) **:** the extent to which an individual has read ⟨a person of vast ~⟩ **2 a :** the particular form (as a variation in spelling, style, syntax, choice of vocabulary) used in a particular edition or other source of material designed to be read **:** a particular version ⟨found an interesting ~ of the same passage in one of the older manuscripts⟩ ⟨the generally accepted ~⟩ **b :** an indication of particular data made by an instrument ⟨examined the ~ of the thermometer⟩ **3 a :** a particular interpretation of something observed, studied, or experienced ⟨new ~*s* of the history —James Martineau⟩ **b :** a particular performance and interpretation of something (as the lines of a play, the score of a musical composition) ⟨a sensitive ~ of the principal role⟩ ⟨a knowledgeable ~ of the symphony⟩

2reading \"\ *adj* **1 :** of or relating to reading ⟨a ~ list⟩ or readers ⟨formed a small ~ group⟩ **2 a :** designed or used for reading ⟨a ~ lamp⟩ ⟨a ~ desk⟩ **b :** set aside for reading ⟨a ~ room⟩

3read·ing \'rediŋ, -dēŋ\ *adj, usu cap* [fr. *Reading*, county borough in southern England] **1 :** of or from the county borough of Reading, England **:** of the kind or style prevalent in Reading **2** [fr. *Reading*, city in southeast Pennsylvania] **:** of or from the city of Reading, Pa. **:** of the kind or style prevalent in Reading

reading chair *n* **:** a chair with a narrow back, high short arms, a small slanted shelf attached to the top of the back, and a seat designed for straddling and for permitting one to sit facing the shelf

reading chair

reading clerk *n* **:** a clerk in a legislative assembly whose principal duty is the reading of bills or other formal documents to the assembly

reading desk *n* **:** a desk with a sloping top used to support a book in a convenient position for a reader standing before it

reading glass *n* **:** a large magnifying lens that is usu. attached to a handle and that is used to facilitate reading (as of fine print) or examination (as of map details)

reading man *n* **:** one who by choice does much reading; *esp, chiefly Brit* **:** a university student devoted often excessively to reading and study

reading matter *n* **:** the regular contents (as news, features) of a newspaper or other periodical exclusive of the advertising

reading notice *n* **:** an advertisement in a newspaper or other periodical that is set up to have the appearance of regular reading matter but is usu. labeled inconspicuously and in fine print as an advertisement

re·adjourn \ˌrē+\ *vb* [F *réajourner*, fr. MF *reajourner*, fr. *re-* + *ajourner* to adjourn] *vt* **:** to adjourn again ~ *vi* **:** to become adjourned again

re·adjust \"+\ *vb* [*re-* + *adjust*] *vt* **:** to adjust again; *esp* **:** to modify (the terms of a corporation's debts and sometimes preferred stocks) by voluntary action so as to meet new conditions and take advantage of new opportunities ~ *vi* **:** to become readjusted

re·adjustable \"+\ *adj* **:** capable of being readjusted

re·adjustment \"+\ *n* **:** the act of readjusting or state of being readjusted

re·administer \"+\ *vt* [*re-* + *administer*] **:** to administer again

re·admission \"+\ *n* [*re-* + *admission*] **:** the act of readmitting

re·admit \"+\ *vt* [*re-* + *admit*] **:** to admit again

re·admittance \"+\ *n* **:** READMISSION

re·adopt \"+\ *vt* [*re-* + *adopt*] **:** to adopt again

re·adoption \"+\ *n* [*re-* + *adoption*] **:** the act or process of readopting or state of being readopted

re·adorn \"+\ *vt* [*re-* + *adorn*] **:** to adorn again

read out *vt* **1 :** to read aloud **2 :** to expel (as from a political party or other organization) by or as if by a public reading of notice of dismissal ⟨threatened to have him *read out* of the party⟩

readout \ˈ=ˌ=\ *n* -s [*read out*] **1 :** the act of reading out **2 :** a device that displays in digits data computed or registered

reads *pres 3d sing of* READ, *pl of* READ

¹**re·advance** \(ˈ)rē+\ *vb* [*re-* + *advance*] *vt* **:** to advance again ~ *vi* **1 :** to go forward again **2** *of a glacier* **:** to advance again after having retreated from a position occupied in an earlier advance

²**readvance** \"\ *n* -s **:** the action of readvancing

re·advent \"+\ *n* [*re-* + *advent*] **:** a renewed advent

¹**ready** \ˈredē, -di\ *adj, usu* -ER/-EST [ME *redy*; akin to OE *rǣde* ready, OHG *reiti*, ON *greithr* ready, Goth *garaiths* ordered, Gk *arariskein* to fit — more at ARM] **1 a** (1) **:** prepared for something about to be done or experienced ⟨are ~ to see their father⟩ ⟨is ~ to hear the news⟩ (2) **:** prepared for immediate movement or action ⟨the troops are ~ to march⟩ **b :** equipped or supplied with what is needed for some action or event ⟨are ~ for the trip⟩ **c :** fitted, arranged, or placed for immediate use ⟨a room is now ~ for you⟩ ⟨dinner is ~⟩ **2 a** (1) **:** prepared in mind or disposition so as to be willing and not reluctant **:** not hesitant **:** INCLINED, DISPOSED ⟨are ~ to die for their country⟩ (2) **:** brought into or being in such a state as to be likely to do something indicated **:** immediately liable **:** on the verge of something ⟨seemed ~ to cry⟩ ⟨the house looks as though it's ~ to fall down⟩ **b :** spontaneously prompt **:** not slow ⟨always has a ~ answer for any difficulty that may arise⟩ ⟨with a ~ smile on her lips⟩ **3 :** quick in some indicated action or perception in such a way as to be notably dexterous, adroit, or skilled ⟨a ~ wit⟩ ⟨a ~ worker⟩ **4 :** that is immediately available or at hand **:** that can be had or used at once ⟨~ assets⟩ ⟨~ cash⟩ ⟨had a gun ~⟩ **syn** see QUICK

²**ready** \"\ *adv, usu* -ER/-EST [ME *redy*, fr. *redy*, adj.] *archaic* **:** READILY

³**ready** \"\ *vt* -ED/-ING/-ES [ME *redien*, fr. *redy*, adj.] **:** to cause to be ready **:** PREPARE ⟨~*ing* themselves for battle⟩ **syn** see PREPARE

⁴**ready** \"\ *n* -ES [¹*ready*] **1 :** money on hand **:** ready cash ⟨was well supplied with the ~⟩ **2 :** the state of being ready; *esp* **:** preparation of a gun (as by loading, cocking, and holding in readiness) for immediate aiming and firing ⟨had their rifles at the ~⟩ **3 :** a left-handed strand formed by twisting together a number of right-handed yarns of which three go to form a plain-laid rope

ready box *n* **:** a box placed near a gun (as on a ship) to hold ammunition kept ready for immediate use

¹**ready-made** \ˌ==ˈ=\ *adj* **1 a :** made and finished in such a way as to be ready for immediate sale or use with few or no alterations **:** ready for general sale or use rather than prepared according to individual specifications ⟨a *ready-made* suit⟩ — opposed to *made-to-order* **b :** of, relating to, or dealing in what is ready-made ⟨a *ready-made* clothier⟩ **2 :** lacking individual distinctiveness **:** not original **:** COMMONPLACE, STOCK ⟨a banal play full of *ready-made* situations⟩

²**ready-made** \"\ *n, pl* **ready-mades** *or* **ready-made :** something that is ready-made

¹**ready-mix** \ˈ==ˌ=\ *n* [¹*ready* + *mix*] **:** a combination of ingredients commercially mixed and prepared so as to be sold or delivered in a form requiring the addition of few or no further ingredients before use: as **a :** MIX 2a **b :** a concrete or mortar manufactured for sale or delivery in a plastic state **c :** a paint mixed and ready for use

²**ready-mix** \"\ *or* **ready-mixed** \ˈ==ˌ=\ *adj* [*ready-mix* fr. ¹*ready-mix*; *ready-mixed* fr. ¹*ready* + *mixed*] **:** consisting of a ready-mix ⟨*ready-mixed* concrete⟩

ready money *n* [ME *redy monay*] **:** money on hand or quickly available; *esp* **:** money held ready for payment or actually paid at the time of a transaction

readyprint \ˈ==ˌ=\ *n* **:** newsprint sold in newspaper-size sheets on the inside pages of which feature material and advertisements have already been printed at the time of sale

ready reckoner *n* **:** RECKONER 2

ready room *n* **:** a room or compartment (as of an aircraft carrier) in which plane pilots are briefed and in which they await takeoff orders

¹**ready-to-wear** *also* **ready-for-wear** \ˌ===ˈ=\ *adj* **:** READY-MADE ⟨*ready-to-wear* clothing⟩

²**ready-to-wear** \"\ *n, pl* **ready-to-wears** *or* **ready-to-wear :** something ready-made; *esp* **:** a ready-made garment or suit

ready-witted \ˌ==ˈ==\ *adj* **:** quick in intelligence and perception **:** SHARP

reae *pl of* REA

re·aeration \(ˌ)rē+\ *n* [*re-* + *aeration*] **:** renewed aeration

re·affirm \ˌrē+\ *vt* [*re-* + *affirm*] **:** to affirm again esp. so as to strengthen or confirm ⟨~*ed* certain fundamental principles —Vera M. Dean⟩

re·affirmance \"+\ *n* [*re-* + *affirmance*] **:** REAFFIRMATION

re·affirmation \(ˌ)rē+\ *n* **:** the act of reaffirming or condition of being reaffirmed

re·afforest \ˌrē+\ *vt* [*re-* + *afforest*] *chiefly Brit* **:** REFOREST

re·afforestation \(ˌ)rē+\ *n, chiefly Brit* **:** REFORESTATION

re·agency \rē+\ *n* [fr. *react*, after E *act*: *agency*] **:** reactive power or operation

re·agent \"+\ *n* [NL *reagent-*, *reagens*, pres. part. of *reagere* to react — more at REACT] **1 :** a substance used for various purposes (as in detecting, examining, or measuring other substances, in preparing material, in developing photographs) because it takes part in one or more chemical reactions or biological processes **2 :** the subject of a psychological experiment; *esp* **:** one who reacts to a stimulus

re·agin \rēˈājən\ *n* -s [ISV *reagent* + *-in*] **1 :** a substance in the blood of persons with syphilis that is sometimes held to be an antibody and is responsible for positive Wassermann, Kahn, or other serological reactions for syphilis **2 :** an antibody in the blood of individuals with atopic allergy that does not react visibly in vitro but possesses the power of passively sensitizing the skin of normal individuals — **re·agin·ic** \ˌrēəˈjinik\ *adj* — **re·agin·i·cal·ly** \-nək(ə)lē\ *adv*

reaks \ˈrēks\ *n pl* [origin unknown] *chiefly Scot* **:** PRANKS

¹**re·al** \ˈrē(ə)l, ˈriəl *sometimes* ˈril\ *adj, often* -ER/-EST [ME, real, actual, of or relating to things (in law), fr. MF, fr. ML & LL; ML *realis* of or relating to things (in law), fr. LL, real, actual, fr. L *res* thing, fact + *-alis* -al; akin to Skt *rai* wealth, property] **1** *law* **a :** of or relating to things themselves or to a jus in rem ⟨a ~ right⟩ ⟨~ privileges⟩ — opposed to *personal* **b** *of a contract in Roman & civil law* **:** existing, made, or accompanied by delivery of the object concerned — opposed to *consensual* **c :** of or relating to things (as lands, tenements) that are fixed, permanent, or immovable; *specif* **:** of or relating to real estate ⟨~ property⟩ **2 a :** that is precisely what its name implies **:** not merely so called **:** truly possessing the essence of what it is called: as (1) **:** AUTHENTIC, GENUINE ⟨was made of ~ gold⟩ (2) **:** not merely apparent **:** ACTUAL, TRUE ⟨discovered the ~ reason⟩ (3) **:** not artificial or counterfeit ⟨a bouquet of ~ flowers⟩ **:** NATURAL (4) **:** not illusory **:** INDUBITABLE, UNQUESTIONABLE ⟨at last found ~ happiness⟩ (5) **:** free from affectation or pretense ⟨had a ~ interest in what was happening⟩ ⟨is a ~ friend⟩ **b :** actually existing, occurring, or present in fact **:** corresponding to actuality ⟨a story from ~ life⟩ **c** (1) **:** having an objective independent existence ⟨could hardly believe that what she saw was ~ and not a hallucination⟩ (2) **:** relating to, based on, or concerned with individual objectively existent things in the physical world ⟨~ propositions —J.H.Newman⟩ **d** (1) **:** that is neither derivative nor dependent **:** necessarily existent **:** not contingent **:** ABSOLUTE ⟨the concept of a ~ being as opposed to an accidental being⟩ (2) **:** that is fundamental, intrinsic, and ultimate **:** not nominal or relative ⟨~ essences —J.S.Mill⟩ **e** (1) **:** belonging to the set of real numbers ⟨the ~ roots of an equation⟩ (2) **:** concerned with or containing real numbers ⟨~ analysis⟩ **f :** not merely verbal or formal **:** SIGNIFICANT ⟨a ~ statement⟩ **g** *of a name* **:** not assumed by oneself nor applied to oneself by others in place of one's original name ⟨refused to give her ~ name⟩ **h** *of wages or income* **:** measured by actual purchasing power **3 :** exact as regards repetition of musical intervals in transposition ⟨a ~ fugue⟩ — compare TONAL **4** *of lace* **:** HANDMADE 1

syn ACTUAL, TRUE: these words are here considered only in their general uses and not in uses philosophical, aesthetic, or critical. So considered, they are often interchangeable. REAL may stress genuineness, especially identity or correspondence between appearance and essence ⟨a *real* diamond⟩ ⟨*real* people who had actually lived around here and who had been part of some *real* event —Dorothy Barclay⟩ ⟨the difference between *real* and sham enjoyment —G.B.Shaw⟩ ⟨*real* intelligence must recognize its own limitations —M.R.Cohen⟩ ACTUAL stresses the fact of existence, of fidelity to the existent, as opposed to the nonexistent, hypothetical, abstract, or conjectural ⟨the possible way — I am far from asserting it was the *actual* way —Havelock Ellis⟩ ⟨a cultural — perhaps, for some, impossible — ideal and not the *actual* pattern of behavior, even in our own society —Weston La Barre⟩ ⟨most men are potential autocrats, the strong and capable may become *actual* autocrats —V.L. Parrington⟩ TRUE states or implies conformity to the real or actual, esp. as indicating or implying a standard, norm, or type ⟨a *true* poet —A.T.Quiller-Couch⟩ ⟨in the seventh and eighth centuries there were no *true* kings of England —Kemp Malone⟩ ⟨of the three waterways surrounding Manhattan, only the Hudson River is a *true* river —*Amer. Guide Series: N.Y.City*⟩

²**real** \"\ *n* -s **:** something real: **a :** a particular reality; *esp* **:** a mathematical real quantity **b :** reality in general — used with *the* ⟨the ~ as contrasted with what is ideal⟩

³**real** \"\ *adv* **:** VERY ⟨was ~ glad to see her⟩ — not often in formal use

⁴**re·al** \rāˈäl, rēˈ-\ *n, pl* **reals** \-lz\ *or* **re·ales** \rāˈä(ˌ)lās\ *or* **reis** \ˈrās(h), -āz\ *see numbered senses* [Sp, fr. *real*, adj., royal, fr. L *regalis* — more at ROYAL] **1** *or* **ri·al** \rēˈ-\ *pl* **reals** *or* **reales** *or* **rials** *or* **ri·a·les** **a :** a former basic monetary unit of Spain and Spanish-America **b :** an old silver coin representing one real **2** *pl* **reals** *or* **reis** [Pg, fr. *real*, adj., royal, fr. L *regalis*] **a :** a Portuguese monetary unit before 1911 which became so depreciated that it was usu. quoted in milreis **b :** a monetary unit of Brazil before 1942

real account *n* **:** any one of the asset, liability, or net worth accounts — compare MIXED ACCOUNT, NOMINAL ACCOUNT

real action *n* **1 :** a local legal action founded on seisin or possession in which title is placed in issue and which aims at establishing title to a particular piece or part of real estate and at recovering the piece or part of real estate — compare LOCAL ACTION, PERSONAL ACTION, TRANSITORY ACTION **2** *Roman & civil law* **:** an action which aims at recovering a movable or immovable subject of property or at establishing a property interest therein

real attribute *n, logic* **:** an attribute inherent in the substance of the thing rather than merely involved in the thought of it

real burden *n, Scots law* **:** a duty of the grantee or owner of specific land to pay the grantor or another at stated times a fixed sum of money that is charged upon the land and its succeeding owners and that is apparent from the public record of the grant

real cost *n* **:** cost as measured by the physical labor and materials consumed in production

real covenant *n* **:** a legal covenant affecting real property or requiring its conveyance; *esp* **:** a covenant that runs with the land — compare PERSONAL COVENANT

real definition *n* **:** a statement of the nature or essence of a thing — contrasted with *nominal definition*

realer *comparative of* REAL

real essence *n, Lockeanism* **:** the objectively real resemblance of constitution that may underlie a group of individuals to which a general name has been given — contrasted with *nominal essence*

realest *superlative of* REAL

real estate *n* **1 :** lands, tenements, or hereditaments that on the owner's death pass to his heir or devisee rather than to his administrator or executor **2 a** (1) **:** land and its permanently affixed buildings or other structures together with its improvements and its natural assets (as minerals, crops, waters) and with the inclusion of corporeal rights or incorporeal rights that follow ownership of the land and with the interests in such rights (2) **:** a freehold estate either in possession or in remainder in such real estate **b** *in some statutes* **:** leasehold estates, ordinary personalty, or equitable interests

real fallacy *n* **:** MATERIAL FALLACY

re·al·gar \rēˈalˌgär, -gər\ *n* -s [ME, fr. ML, fr. Catal, fr. Ar *rahj al-ghār* powder of the mine] **:** an orange-red mineral As_4S_4 or AsS that consists of arsenic sulfide and that occurs in monoclinic crystals or in granular or compact form, has a resinous luster, and burns with a bluish flame giving off arsenical and sulfurous fumes while burning (hardness 1.5–2, sp. gr. 3.56) — see ARSENIC DISULFIDE

realgar orange *n* **:** DUTCH ORANGE

realgar yellow *n* **:** ORPIMENT 2

re·al·gym·na·si·um \rāˈäl(ˌ)gimˈnäzēəm\ *n, pl* **realgymnasiums** \-ēəmz\ *or* **realgymna·sia** \-ēə\ [G, fr. *real* objective, practical (fr. LL *realis* real, actual) + *gymnasium*] **:** a German secondary school that prepares students for the university, that offers Latin but no Greek, and that typically emphasizes sciences and modern languages — compare GYMNASIUM

re·a·lia \rēˈālēə, -rāˈäl-\ *n pl* [LL, neut. pl. of *realis* real, actual] **1** *philos* **:** real things **:** REALITIES **2 :** objects or activities used by a teacher to relate classroom teaching to real life; *esp* **:** things (as costumes, tools, objects of worship) relating to the daily living of peoples studied in geography or language classes

real idealism *n* **:** IDEAL REALISM

re·align *also* **re·aline** \ˌrē+\ *vt* [*re-* + *align, aline*] **:** to align again; *esp* **:** to make new divisions or groupings of according to other lines of cleavage ⟨~ American political parties⟩

re·aligner *also* **re·aliner** \"+\ *n* **:** one that realigns

re·alignment *also* **re·alinement** \"+\ *n* [*re-* + *alignment, alinement*] **:** the act of realigning or condition of being realigned

real image *n* **:** an optical image formed of real foci

real injury *n* **1** *civil & Scots law* **:** an intentional injury inflicted by an unlawful act and affecting the person, honor, or dignity of another **2** *Scots law* **:** misappropriation of another's coat of arms

re·al·ise *like* REALIZE\ *chiefly Brit var of* REALIZE

re·al·ism \ˈrēəˌlizəm, ˈriə- *also* ˈrēˌl- *sometimes* ˈriˌl-\ *n* -s [G *realismus* philosophical realism, fr. LL *realis* real, actual + G *-ismus* -ism — more at REAL] **1 :** preoccupation with fact or reality **:** objective procedure not influenced by idealism, speculation, or sentimentalism **:** disposition to think and act objectively and unemotionally and to reject what is impractical or visionary **2 a :** a doctrine in philosophy that universals exist outside the mind **:** the conception that what a general or abstract term names is an independent and unitary reality or essence: (1) **:** the doctrine that universals exist prior to things — called also *Platonic realism* (2) **:** the doctrine that universals exist in things — called also *Aristotelian realism* **b :** the philosophical conception that objects of sense perception or sometimes of cognition in general are real in their own right and exist independently of their being known or related to mind — called also *epistemological realism*; compare IDEALISM, PHENOMENALISM **c :** a doctrine or theory in sociology that holds that a human collectivity, group, or institution has a reality apart from the individual members comprising it — contrasted with *nominalism* **3 a :** the theory or practice in art and literature of fidelity to nature or to real life and to accurate representation without idealization of the most typical views, details, and surroundings of the subject ⟨photographic ~ or naturalism in the realm of art —John Somerville⟩ — opposed to *idealism* **b :** excessive minuteness of detail or preoccupation with trivial, sordid, or squalid subjects in art and literature ⟨a fearless ~ that exploited until then forbidden subject matter —J.W.Aldridge⟩ **4 :** a conception of the science of law and of the administration of justice that sees significance in the unique elements of particular cases, judges rules by their consequences, and emphasizes the nonlogical and irrational factors in decision

¹**re·al·ist** \-ləst\ *n* -s [F *réaliste*, fr. MF *realiste*, fr. *real* real, actual + *-iste* -ist — more at REAL] **:** an adherent or advocate of realism **:** one that is influenced by or acts in accordance with the principles of realism

²**realist** \"\ *adj* **:** of or relating to realists or realism **:** REALISTIC

re·al·is·tic \ˌrēəˈlistik, ˌriə-, -tēk\ *adj* **1 a :** of, relating to, or marked by literary or artistic realism ⟨a ~ novel⟩ ⟨~ portraiture⟩ **b :** advocating or characterized by philosophical or juristic realism ⟨a ~ system of thought⟩ ⟨~ jurisprudence⟩ **2 :** facing reality squarely **:** not impractical or visionary ⟨a ~ view of the possibilities⟩ — **re·al·is·ti·cal·ly** \-tək(ə)lē, -tēk-, -li\ *adv*

re·al·i·ty \rēˈalədē, -lətē, -i\ *n* -ES [ML *realitat-, realitas*, fr. LL *realis* real, actual + L *-itat-, -itas* -ity] **1 :** the quality or state of being real ⟨remove the vagueness from history and give it ~ —G.W.Curtis⟩ ⟨doubted the ~ of what was alleged⟩ **2 a** (1) **:** something that is real ⟨the *realities* of life⟩ ⟨what was his dream is now a ~⟩ (2) **:** the aggregate of real things ⟨trying to escape from ~⟩ **b** (1) **:** the actual nature or constitution of something ⟨had read about love but was amazed by its ~⟩ (2) **:** the actual state of things ⟨had evaded the issue but at last told her of the ~⟩ **c** (1) **:** what actually exists **:** what has objective existence **:** what is not a mere idea **:** what is not imaginary, fictitious, or pretended (2) **:** what exists necessarily **:** what is neither derivative nor dependent **3** *obs* **:** sincere devotion or loyalty to some individual — **in reality** *adv* **:** in actual fact

reality principle *n* **:** the tendency for man to defer immediate instinctual gratification so as to achieve longer-range goals or so as to meet the demands of physical environment, reference group, or other form of external pressure — compare PLEASURE PRINCIPLE

reality testing *n* **:** a function of the ego in which acts are explored and their outcomes determined so that the individual will be aware of these consequences when the stimulus to act in a given fashion recurs

re·al·iz·abil·i·ty \ˌrēəˌlīzəˈbilədē, ˌriə-, -lətē, -i\ *n* **:** the quality or state of being realizable

re·al·iz·able \ˈ==ˌ=zəbəl, ˌ=='===\ *adj* [F *réalisable*, fr. *réaliser* to realize + *-able*] **:** capable of being realized

re·al·iz·ably \-blē, -bli\ *adv* **:** in a realizable manner

re·al·iza·tion \ˌrē(ə)ləˈzāshən, ˌriəl-, -ˌlīˈz- *sometimes* ˌri(ˌ)l-\ *n* -s [F *réalisation*, fr. MF *realisation*, fr. *realiser* to realize + *-ation*] **1 a :** the action of realizing or condition of being realized **b** *philos* **:** the act or process of becoming real **2 :** something realized

realization and liquidation account *n* **:** an account or statement used in settling or winding up a business or estate to show the results of the disposition of assets and the liquidation of the debts

re·al·ize \ˈrēəˌlīz, ˈriəˌl- *also* ˈrēˌl- *sometimes* ˈriˌl-\ *vb* -ED/-ING/-S *see -ize in Explan Notes* [F *réaliser*, fr. MF *realiser*, fr. *real* real, actual + *-iser* -ize — more at REAL] *vt* **1 a** (1) **:** to make real **:** change from what is imaginary or fictitious into what is actual **:** bring into concrete existence **:** ACCOMPLISH ⟨*realizing* a long-cherished wish⟩ ⟨*realized* the project at last⟩ (2) **:** to bring from potentiality into actuality **:** ACTUALIZE **b** (1) **:** to cause to seem real **:** make appear real ⟨a stage set that *realized* the atmosphere of a colonial town perfectly⟩ (2) **:** to present or bring before the mind with vividness and clarity ⟨a picture that recalled to her and *realized* scenes of her early childhood⟩ **2 a** (1) **:** to convert into actual money ⟨*realized* assets⟩ (2) **:** to bring by sale or investment ⟨*realized* a good price on the sale of his house⟩ **b :** to acquire as an actual possession **:** obtain as the result of plans and efforts **:** GAIN ⟨*realized* a large profit on the deal⟩ **3 :** to conceive vividly as real **:** be fully aware of **:** understand clearly ⟨*realized* the risk he was taking⟩ ⟨*realized* that everything depended on the move⟩ ⟨hardly *realized* what was happening⟩ **4 :** to write out or play at sight on a keyboard instrument the full harmony as indicated by a figured bass with or without elaborate ornamentation ~ *vi* **1 :** to convert an intangible right or property into real property **2 :** to convert tangible property into money **syn** see THINK

re·al·iz·er *pronunc at* REALIZE +ə(r)\ *n* -s **:** one that realizes

realizing *adj* **:** marked by keen awareness (as of the meaning or implications of something) ⟨a more ~ sense . . . of the true meaning of German conquest —B.K.Sandwell⟩ — **re·al·iz·ing·ly** *adv*

re·allege \ˌrē+\ *vt* [*re-* + *allege*] **:** to allege again

re·alliance \"+\ *n* [*re-* + *alliance*] **:** renewed alliance

re·allocate \(ˈ)rē+\ *vt* [*re-* + *allocate*] **:** to allocate again

re·allocation \(ˌ)rē+\ *n* [*re-* + *allocation*] **:** the act of reallocating or state of being reallocated

re·allot \ˌrē+\ *vt* [*re-* + *allot*] **:** to allot again

re·allotment \"+\ *n* **:** renewed allotment

re·al·ly \ˈrē(ə)lē, ˈri(ə)-, -li\ *adv* [ME *rialliche*, fr. *rial, real* real, actual + *-liche* -ly] **1 a :** in actual fact **:** in reality **:** ACTUALLY ⟨didn't ~ mean what she said⟩ ⟨was ~ the best thing that we did⟩ **b :** UNQUESTIONABLY, TRULY ⟨was a ~ beautiful morning⟩ **2 :** INDEED ⟨well ~, you needn't have said that⟩

re·ally \(ˈ)rē+\ *vt* [ME *realyen* to rally, fr. MF *realier*, *ralier* — more at RALLY] **:** to ally again

realm \ˈrelm, ˈreům\ *n* -s [ME *realme, reaume*, fr. OF *reialme, realme, reaume*, modif. (influenced by OF *reial* royal, fr. L *regalis*) of L *regimen* rule, government — more at REGIMEN, ROYAL] **1 :** KINGDOM **2 a :** REGION, TERRITORY ⟨seized power throughout the whole ~⟩ **b :** SPHERE, DOMAIN, RANGE ⟨within the ~ of possibility⟩ **3 :** any of several major biogeographic divisions: as **a :** a primary marine faunal division **b :** a primary terrestrial division consisting of one or more regions **c :** a division coordinate with a biogeographic region

re·al·ness *n* -ES **:** the quality or state of being real **:** REALITY ⟨began to feel a ~ in life again —Adria Langley⟩

real number *n* **:** a number in which there is no imaginary part

real party in interest 1 : the party entitled to the benefits or proceeds of a cause of action (as an assignee or subrogee) as distinguished from the person ordinarily entitled to maintain the action **2 :** the party primarily responsible for a liability or obligation

re·al·po·li·tik \rāˈälˌpōlēˌtēk\ *n* -s [G, fr. *real* objective, practical (fr. LL *realis* real, actual) + *politik* politics, fr. F *politique*, fr. LL *politice*, fr. Gk *politikē*, fr. fem. of *politikos* political — more at POLITIC] **:** practical politics **:** politics based on practical and material factors, on political realities, or on the realities of national interest and power esp. as distinguished from theoretical, ethical, or moralistic objectives **:** politics considered as an end in itself rather than as a means to objectives — compare MACHTPOLITIK, POWER POLITICS

re·al·po·li·ti·ker \-ˌpōˈlēdəkə(r)\ *n* -s [G, fr. *real* + *politiker* politician, fr. *politik* + *-er*] **:** one that believes in, advocates, or practices realpolitik

real presence *n, often cap R&P* **:** the doctrine that Christ is actually present in the Eucharist ⟨Roman Catholic, Lutheran, and Anglican interpretations of *real presence*⟩ — compare CONSUBSTANTIATION, TRANSUBSTANTIATION

real representative *n* **:** the representative (as the heir, devisee, or sometimes an executor or administrator) for a deceased person with regard to the person's real estate

reals *pl of* REAL

re·al·schu·le \rāˈälˌshülə\ *n, pl* **realschu·len** \-lən\ [G, fr. *real* objective, practical (fr. LL *realis* real, actual) + *schule* school, fr. OHG *scuola*, fr. L *schola* — more at REAL, SCHOOL] **:** a German secondary school that includes in its curriculum modern languages, mathematics, science, practical arts, and commercial subjects and that teaches no classics and is not designed to prepare students for the university — compare GYMNASIUM

real servitude *n, civil law* **:** a praedial servitude or right over one tract of real estate in favor of another

real subject *n* **:** LOGICAL SUBJECT

re·alter \(ˈ)rē+\ *vt* [*re-* + *alter*] **:** to alter again

Re·al·tor \ˈrē(ə)ltər, ˈrēəl-, -ˌtȯ(ə)r *sometimes* rēˈal(ˌ)- *or substand* rēˈalədər *or* ˈrēlədər\ *collective mark* — used for a real estate agent who is a member of the National Association of Realtors

real treaty *n* **:** a treaty relating only to the subject matter of a compact — compare PERSONAL TREATY

re·al·ty \ˈrē(ə)ltē, ˈrēəl-, -ti\ *n* -ES [*1real* + *-ty*] **:** REAL ESTATE

real variable *n* **1 :** a mathematical variable whose values are real **2 :** FREE VARIABLE

real yellow wood *n* **:** any of certain podocarps of the southern part of Africa; *esp* **:** a large tree (*Podocarpus latifolius*) of the southern part of Africa

1ream \ˈrēm, ˈrām\ *n* -S [ME *rem* cream, froth, fr. OE *rēam* cream; akin to MLG *rōm*, *rōme* cream, MHG *roum*, Icel *rjōmi* cream, Av *raoγna-* butter] **1** *dial chiefly Brit* **:** CREAM **2** *dial chiefly Brit* **:** froth or foam on top of a liquid

2ream \"\ *vb* -ED/-ING/-S [ME *remen*, fr. *rem*, n.] *vi, dial chiefly Brit* **:** FROTH, FOAM ~ *vt, dial chiefly Brit* **:** to skim cream or foam from

3ream \"\ *vb* -ED/-ING/-S [ME *remen*, perh. fr. OE *-rǣman* to raise (in *ārǣman* to raise) — more at ROAM] *dial chiefly Eng* **:** STRETCH

4ream \ˈrēm\ *n* -S [ME *rem*, *reme*, fr. MF *raime*, fr. Ar *rizmah*, lit., bundle] **1 :** a quantity of paper in lots that vary in the number of sheets included: **a :** a lot of 480 sheets of paper **:** 20 quires **b :** a lot of 472 sheets of drawing paper or handmade paper **c :** 500 sheets of book paper or of newsprint **d :** PRINTER'S REAM **2 :** a great amount (as of something printed) — usu. used in pl. ⟨wrote ~*s* on the subject⟩

5ream \"\ *vt* -ED/-ING/-S [perh. fr. (assumed) ME (dial.) *remen* to open up, clear, fr. OE (dial.) *rēman* to open up, clear, extend; akin to OE *rȳman* to open up, clear, extend, OHG *rūmen* to vacate, make room, ON *rȳma*; causative fr. the root of OE *rūm* spacious — more at ROOM] **1 a :** to widen the opening of (a hole) **:** bevel out **:** COUNTERSINK **b :** to enlarge or dress out (a hole) with a reamer **:** enlarge the bore of (as a gun) in this way **c :** to remove (a defective part) by reaming — often used with *out* **2 :** to open (the seams of a ship's planking) for the purpose of caulking them **3 a :** to press out (fruit juice) with a reamer **b :** to press out the juice of (as an orange or similar fruit) with a reamer **4 :** CHEAT, VICTIMIZE ⟨in the capacity of storekeepers or handymen, cheerfully ~ them at every opportunity —A.C.Spectorsky⟩

ream·age \ˈrēmij\ *n* -S **:** the number of reams in a lot of paper

re·amend \ˌrē+\ *vt* [*re-* + *amend*] **:** to amend again

1ream·er \ˈrēmə(r)\ *n* -S [*5ream* + *-er*] **:** one that reams: as **a** (1) **:** a rotating finishing tool with straight or spiral cutting edges used to enlarge or shape a hole (2) **:** a drilling tool for enlarging a bored well or for making the borehole circular when the drill has failed to do so (3) **:** a chisel for cutting two V-shaped grooves from a round blasthole in the line of the desired rift (4) **:** an instrument used in dentistry to enlarge a hole in a tooth preparatory to filling the hole **b :** a fruit squeezer with a ridged and pointed dome projecting from the hollowed center of a plate **c :** a worker who enlarges or shapes holes or smooths a bore with a reamer

reamers a(1)

2reamer \"\ *vt* -ED/-ING/-S **:** to use a reamer on

re·amination \(ˌ)rē+\ *n* [*re-* + *amination*] **:** TRANSAMINATION

reaming *n* -S [fr. gerund of *5ream*] **:** SCORING

ream out *vt* [*5ream*] *slang* **:** to reprimand severely

re·amputation \(ˌ)rē+\ *n* [*re-* + *amputation*] **:** the second of two amputations performed upon the same member

re·analysis \ˌrē+\ *n* [*re-* + *analysis*] **:** renewed analysis

re·analyze \(ˈ)rē+\ *vt* [*re-* + *analyze*] **:** to analyze again

re·anchor \"+\ *vb* [*re-* + *anchor*] *vt* **:** to anchor again ~ *vi* **:** to become anchored again

1re·animate \"+\ *vb* [*re-* + *animate*, v.] *vt* **:** to animate again ~ *vi* **:** to become reanimated

2re·animate \"+\ *adj* [*re-* + *animate*, adj.] **:** REANIMATED

re·animation \(ˌ)rē+\ *n* **:** the action of reanimating or state of being reanimated

re·anneal \ˌrē+\ *vt* [*re-* + *anneal*] **:** to anneal again

re·annex \(ˌ)rē+\ *vt* [ME *reannexen*, fr. MF *reannexer*, fr. *re-* + *annexer* to annex] **:** to annex again

re·annexation \"+\ *n* **:** the act of reannexing or state of being reannexed

1reap \ˈrēp\ *vb* -ED/-ING/-S [ME *repen*, *ripen*, fr. OE *reopan*, *rīpan*; akin to MD *repen*, *reipen* to hackle, card, Norw *ripa* to scratch, OE *rāw* row — more at ROW] *vt* **1 a** (1) **:** to cut (as grain) with a sickle, scythe, or reaping machine ⟨~*ed* the rye in that part of the field⟩ (2) **:** to clear (as a field) of a crop by so cutting **b :** to gather or obtain by so cutting; *esp* **:** HARVEST ⟨has ~*ed* all his crops⟩ **2 :** to gather, obtain, or win as the fulfillment, reward, or other recompense of effort, labor, or some other action ⟨~ lasting benefits⟩ ~ *vi* **:** to reap something **:** gather a harvest **:** gain or receive a return or requital ⟨they that sow in tears shall ~ in joy —Ps 126:5 (AV)⟩

syn REAP, GLEAN, GATHER, GARNER, and HARVEST may mean, in common, to do the work or a given part of the work of collecting ripened crops. REAP applies to the cutting down and usu. collecting of ripened grain; in extension, it may suggest a return or requital ⟨*reap* early wheat for market⟩ ⟨the lucky artisan producing something they could use would *reap* a fortune —R.A.Billington⟩ GLEAN applies to the stripping of a field or vine that has already been gone over once, extending in meaning to any picking up of valuable bits from here and there, esp. what has been left or missed ⟨*glean* in the fields after the reapers have gone⟩ ⟨assembled a multitude of facts *gleaned* from many and varied sources —*Amer. Guide Series: Wash.*⟩ ⟨she had *gleaned* all the information the library contained —Robertson Davies⟩ ⟨data *gleaned* from the questionnaire —Estelle C. Terry⟩ GATHER, the most general of these, applies to the collecting or bringing together of all the produce of the farm, plantation, or garden; in extension, it can apply to any similar amassing or accumulating ⟨the fruit is *gathered* in late July and August —*Amer. Guide Series: Tenn.*⟩ ⟨workers who *gathered* rubber —P.E.James⟩ ⟨she had traveled by safari to *gather* her material —*Current Biog.*⟩ ⟨the multitude of pitfalls in the *gathering*, writing, and processing of the news —F.L.Mott⟩ ⟨mail is *gathered* and distributed by electrically operated conveyors —*Amer. Guide Series: Minn.*⟩ GARNER implies the storing of produce, esp. grain; in extension, it can apply to any laying away as of a store ⟨more harvest than one man can *garner* —Pearl Buck⟩ ⟨a skilled picker may *garner* 100 quarts —*Amer. Guide Series: Ark.*⟩ ⟨wisdom *garnered* through the years —W.F.Hambly⟩ ⟨these short pieces *garnered* from a magazine catering to the masculine taste —Lisle Bell⟩ HARVEST, the general term, may imply any or all of these processes, extending in meaning to apply to any gathering together or husbanding ⟨the *harvesting* of cranberries —E.B.Garside⟩ ⟨the *harvesting* of shellfish —*Amer. Guide Series: Conn.*⟩ ⟨busy *harvesting* your crop of furs —*Nat'l Fur News*⟩ ⟨he had sown pain and *harvested* regret —Maurice Samuel⟩

2reap \", ˈrip\ *n* -S [ME *repe*, fr. OE *reopa*; akin to OE *reopan*, *rīpan*, v.] *dial chiefly Eng* **:** a handful or unbound sheaf of grain

3reap \"\ *vt* -ED/-ING/-S [alter. of *rip*] *chiefly dial* **:** to bring (as a subject, a person) into conversation — often used with *up*

4reap \"\ *dial Eng var of* ROPE

reap·er \ˈrēpə(r)\ *n* -S [ME *repere*, fr. OE *rīpere*, fr. *reopan*, *rīpan* to reap + *-ere* -er] **:** one that reaps: as **a :** HARVESTER **b :** a machine that cuts a crop and drops it in unbound gavels

reaper-binder \ˈ==ˌ==\ *n* **:** BINDER 4b

reaper-thresher \ˈ==ˌ==\ *n* **:** COMBINE 3

reaping *pres part of* REAP

reaping hook *or* **reap hook** *n* **:** a hand implement with a hook-shaped blade used in reaping **:** SICKLE

reaping machine *n* **:** a machine used in reaping grain and typically equipped with a raking device that bends the grain against the cutter bar with power taken from a ground wheel — compare BINDER 4b, COMBINE 3

re·apparel \ˌrē+\ *vt* [*re-* + *apparel*] **:** to apparel again

re·apparition \(ˌ)rē+\ *n* [*re-* + *apparition*] **:** REAPPEARANCE

re·appeal \ˌrē+\ *vb* [*re-* + *appeal*] *vt* **:** to appeal again ~ *vi* **1 :** to resort to a further appeal **2 :** to arouse again a particular interest or attraction

re·appear \"+\ *vi* [*re-* + *appear*] **:** to appear again

re·appearance \"+\ *n* **:** the act of reappearing **:** a second or fresh appearance

re·application \(ˌ)rē+\ *n* [*re-* + *application*] **:** a second or fresh application

re·applier \ˌrē+\ *n* **:** one that reapplies

re·apply \"+\ *vb* [*re-* + *apply*] *vt* **:** to apply again ~ *vi* **:** to engage in or undergo reapplication

re·appoint \"+\ *vt* [*re-* + *appoint*] **:** to appoint again

re·appointment \"+\ *n* **:** a second or fresh appointment

re·apportion \"+\ *vt* [*re-* + *apportion*] **:** to apportion again

re·apportionment \"+\ *n* **:** the act of reapportioning or state of being reapportioned

re·appraisal \"+\ *n* [*re-* + *appraisal*] **:** a second or fresh appraisal **:** REVALUATION ⟨if reforms do emerge from whatever agonizing ~ is now to be attempted —H.S.Commager⟩

re·appraise \"\ *vt* [*re-* + *appraise*] **:** to appraise again **:** make a new valuation of **:** REVALUATE

re·appraisement \"+\ *n* **:** REAPPRAISAL

re·apprehend \(ˌ)rē+\ *vt* [*re-* + *apprehend*] **:** to apprehend again

re·approach \ˌrē+\ *vt* [*re-* + *approach*] **:** to approach again

re·appropriate \"+\ *vt* [*re-* + *appropriate*] **:** to appropriate again

re·appropriation \"+\ *n* **:** the act of reappropriating

reaps *pres 3d sing of* REAP, *pl of* REAP

reaptd *abbr* reappointed

1rear \ˈri(ə)r, -iə\ *vb* -ED/-ING/-S [ME *reren*, fr. OE *rǣran*; akin to OHG *rēren* to cause to fall, ON *reisa* to raise, Goth *urraisjan* to arouse, raise, lift up; causative fr. the root of OE *rīsan* to rise — more at RISE] *vt* **1 a :** to erect by building **:** CONSTRUCT ⟨~*ed* a huge pagan temple⟩ **b** *obs* **:** to bring into being **:** PRODUCE, ORIGINATE **2 a** (1) **:** to lift up to an erect position **:** set up on end **:** raise upright ⟨~*ed* a flagpole in front of the building⟩ ⟨~*ing* heavy marble columns⟩ (2) **:** to lift upward esp. so as to hold aloft or so as to cause to project far upward **:** ELEVATE, RAISE ⟨a castle that ~*s* its towers into the sky⟩ **b** *dial chiefly Eng* (1) **:** to rouse from bed or sleep (2) **:** to drive (game) from cover **c** *dial chiefly Eng* **:** to stir up to action **:** AROUSE **3 a** (1) **:** to breed and raise (an animal) for use or market (2) **:** to bring up (a person) by fostering, nourishing, and instructing ⟨was ~*ed* in a fine family⟩ **b :** to cause (as plants, produce) to grow **4 :** to cause (a horse) to rise up on the hind legs ~ *vi* **1 a :** to rise up to an erect position **:** rise high **:** TOWER ⟨a steeple ~*ing* far into the sky⟩ **b** *of a horse* **:** to rise up on the hind legs **2** *dial* **:** to come into sight **:** APPEAR **syn** see BUILD, LIFT

2rear *vt* -ED/-ING/-S [ME *reren*, of unknown origin] *obs* **:** to slice up (as a roasted fowl) **:** CARVE

3rear \ˈri(ə)r, -iə\ *dial var of* 1RARE

4rear \"\ *n* -S [prob. fr. *rear* (in such terms as *rear guard*)] **1 :** the back part of something **:** hindmost part: as **a :** the unit (as of an army) or area farthest from the enemy **b :** the part of something that is located opposite to its front ⟨the ~ of a store⟩ ⟨the ~ of a house⟩ ⟨the ~ of a bookcase⟩ **c :** BUTTOCKS ⟨got kicked in the ~⟩ **2 :** the space or position behind or at the back ⟨moved to the ~⟩

5rear \"\ *adj* **:** being at the back or in the hindmost part **:** HINDMOST ⟨the ~ rank of a company⟩

6rear \"\ *adv* **:** toward or from the rear — used chiefly in combination ⟨a *rear*-driven car⟩

rear admiral *n* **:** a commissioned naval officer ranking just below a vice admiral and above a captain — abbr. *Rear Adm*, *R.A.*

rear arch *also* **rere-arch** \ˈri(ə)rˌärch\ *n* **:** an inner arch of an opening (as for a door or window) that differs in size or form from the external arch of the opening

rear commodore *n* **:** an officer of a yacht club who ranks lower than a vice-commodore

rear echelon *n* **:** an element of a military headquarters or unit located at a considerable distance from the front and concerned esp. with administrative and supply duties — compare FORWARD ECHELON

rear end *n* **1 :** the back part, division, or section of something ⟨crashed into the *rear end* of the train⟩ **2 :** BUTTOCKS

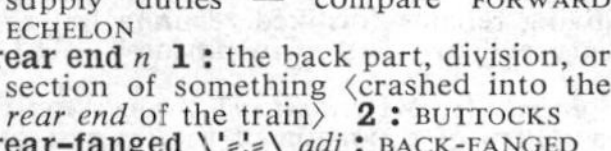

rear arch

rear-fanged \ˈ=ˌ=\ *adj* **:** BACK-FANGED

rear guard *n* [ME *reregarde*, fr. MF, fr. OF *reregarde*, *rereguarde*, fr. *rere*, *riere* backward, behind (fr. L *retro*) + *garde*, *guarde* guard — more at RETRO-, GUARD] **:** a military detachment detailed to bring up and protect the rear of a main body or force

rearguard action *n* **1 :** a defensive or delaying fight engaged in by a rear guard (as in covering the retreat of an army or the evacuation of a besieged garrison) **2 :** an effort put forth by means of preventive or delaying measures or tactics and usu. against great odds in defense of a threatened existing order or situation or in opposition to a proposed new departure ⟨to be something of a brake, to perform a *rearguard action*, if you will, on inflationary trends —D.V.Brown⟩ ⟨dissipate their influence in relatively ineffective *rearguard actions* designed to prevent particular regulatory measures —H.R.Bowen⟩

re·argue \(ˈ)rē+\ *vt* [*re-* + *argue*] **:** to argue again

re·argument \"+\ *n* **:** a second or fresh argument

rearhorse \ˈ=ˌ=\ *n* [*1rear* + *horse*; fr. the way it rears up when disturbed] **:** MANTIS

re·arise \ˌrē+\ *vi* [*re-* + *arise*] **:** to arise again

re·arm \(ˈ)rē+\ *vb* [*re-* + *arm*] *vt* **:** to arm again: as **a :** to equip (as a disarmed nation) with military materiel **b :** to equip with new or better weapons ~ *vi* **:** to become armed again

re·armament \"+\ *n* [*re-* + *armament*] **:** the act of rearming or state of being rearmed

rear·most \ˈri(ə)rˌmōst, -iə,m-\ *adj* **:** farthest in the rear **:** LAST

rearmouse *var of* REREMOUSE

re·arousal \ˌrē+\ *n* **:** a second or fresh arousal

re·arouse \"+\ *vt* [*re-* + *arouse*] **:** to arouse again

rear projection *n* **:** the projection of a motion or still picture upon a large translucent screen from the rear to serve as a background for performances of motion-picture actors being photographed in front of the screen

re·arrange \ˌrē+\ *vb* [*re-* + *arrange*] *vt* **:** to arrange again ~ *vi* **:** to undergo chemical rearrangement

re·arrangement \"+\ *n* **1 :** the act of rearranging or state of being rearranged **2 :** a shifting of the atoms or groups in the molecule of a compound to form an isomeric compound **:** ISOMERIZATION

re·arranger \"+\ *n* **:** one that rearranges

re·array \"+\ *vt* [*re-* + *array*] **:** to array again

1re·arrest \"+\ *vt* [*re-* + *arrest*] **:** to arrest again

2re·arrest \"+\ *n* **:** a second or fresh arrest

rears *pres 3d sing of* REAR, *pl of* REAR

rear sight *n* **:** the sight nearest the breech of a firearm

rear vassal *n* [trans. of F *arrière-vassal*] **:** a vassal's vassal

1rear vault *n* [*5rear* + *vault* (arched structure); trans. of F *arrière-voussure*] **:** a rear arch used where a wall is very thick and the window recess becomes a vaulted area

2rear vault *n* [*5rear* + *vault* (leap)] **:** a vault in which the body is raised sideward to either right or left and then rotated a quarter turn outward so that the back of the body passes over the apparatus used

rearview mirror \ˈ=ˌ=-\ *or* **rear-vision mirror** \ˈ=ˌ==-\ *n* **:** a mirror (as in an automobile) designed to give a view of the area behind a vehicle

1rear·ward \ˈri(ə)rˌwȯrd, -iə,wȯ(ə)d\ *n* -S [ME *rerewarde*, fr. AF; akin to OF *reregarde*, *rereguarde* rear guard — more at REAR GUARD] **:** REAR; *esp* **:** the rear division of an army or fleet

2rear·ward \-ˌwə(r)d\ *adj* [*4rear* + *-ward*, adj. suffix] **1 :** located at, near, or toward the rear ⟨the ~ section of the store⟩ **2 :** directed toward the rear **:** BACKWARD ⟨bumping it shut with a ~ motion —Gertrude Schweitzer⟩ — **rear·ward·ness** *n* -ES

3rearward \"\ *also* **rear·wards** \-dz\ *adv* [*4rear* + *-ward*, *wards*, adv. suffix] **:** at, near, or toward the rear **:** BACKWARD ⟨gazing ~ out the window —*Monsanto Mag.*⟩ ⟨lobbed the football ~ to one of the halfbacks⟩

rear·ward·ly *adv* [*2rearward* + *-ly*] **:** REARWARD

re·ascend \ˌrē+\ *vb* [ME *reascenden*, fr. *re-* + *ascenden* to ascend] *vt* **:** to ascend (as stairs) again ~ *vi* **:** to go up again

re·ascendancy \"+\ *n* [*reascendant* + *-cy*] **:** renewed ascendancy

re·ascendant \"+\ *adj* [*re-* + *ascendant*] **:** again ascendant

re·ascension \"+\ *n* [*re-* + *ascension*] **:** a second ascension

re·ascent \"+\ *n* [*re-* + *ascent*] **:** a second or fresh ascent

re·ascertain \(ˌ)rē+\ *vt* [*re-* + *ascertain*] **:** to ascertain again

re·ascertainment \"+\ *n* **:** the act of reascertaining

re·ask \(ˈ)rē+\ *vb* [*re-* + *ask*] *vt* **:** to ask again ~ *vi* **:** to make a new inquiry or petition

1reas·on \ˈrēzᵊn\ *n* -S [alter. of ME *rasen*, fr. OE *ræsn*; akin to Goth *razn* house — more at RANSACK] **:** a horizontal timber over a row of posts or puncheons supporting a hove

2rea·son \ˈrēzᵊn\ *n* -S [ME *resoun*, fr. OF *raison*, fr. L *ration-*, *ratio* reason, computation, reasoning; akin to OFris *rethe* speech, proof, OHG *redia* account, Goth *rathjo* account, number, *garathjan* to count, L *reri* to calculate, believe, think, Gk *arariskein* to fit — more at ARM] **1 a :** an expression or statement offered as an explanation of a belief or assertion or as a justification of an act or procedure ⟨gave ~*s* that were quite satisfactory⟩ **b :** a consideration, motive, or judgment inducing or confirming a belief, influencing the will, or leading to an action or course of action **:** a rational ground or motive ⟨will mention a ~ for this situation⟩ ⟨the ~ that this is so should now be clear⟩ ⟨a good ~ to act as you do⟩ ⟨does not know the ~ why⟩ **c :** a sufficient ground of explanation or of logical defense; *esp* **:** a general principle, law, or warranted presumption that supports a conclusion, explains a fact, or validates a course of conduct ⟨brilliantly outlined the ~*s* that supported his client's action⟩ **d :** the thing that makes some fact intelligible **:** CAUSE ⟨the ~ for the tides lies in the gravitational pull of the moon and the sun⟩ **e :** a sane or sound view or consideration ⟨that's a ~ that you should keep in mind⟩ **2 a** (1) **:** the power of comprehending, inferring, or thinking esp. in orderly, sensible, rational ways ⟨was afraid that his ~ might be deranged⟩ ⟨must use ~ to solve this problem⟩ **:** the ability to trace out the implications of a combination of facts or suppositions ⟨a ~ that is far beyond her years⟩ (2) **:** proper exercise of the intellective faculty in accordance with right judgment **:** right use of the mind **:** right thinking ⟨attempted to bring her to ~⟩ (3) **:** a sane or sound mind marked by the right use of the intellective faculty **:** reasonableness and sanity of the mind ⟨was afraid she would lose her ~⟩ **b** (1) **:** a distinct cognitive faculty coordinate with perception and understanding **:** human intelligence or intellect (2) **:** the sum of the intellectual powers (3) **:** universal or general rationality of all minds viewed as a whole (4) **:** mind or intelligence viewed as a rational soul pervading the whole of nature or of the universe **c :** NOUS, NOESIS ⟨a transcendent ideal that only ~ beyond experience can conceive —John Dewey⟩ **d** *Aristotelianism* (1) **:** the function of the soul that is pure actuality, operates on the material furnished by passive reason, is immaterial and imperishable, and enjoys impersonal immortality — called also *active reason*, *creative reason* (2) **:** the function of the soul which operates with sensuous images and in which concepts are merely potential so that they need to be formed by active reason — called also *passive reason* (3) **:** PRACTICAL REASON **e** *Scholasticism* (1) **:** INTELLECT (2) **:** RATIO **f** *Kantianism & German idealism* **:** the highest faculty of the mind esp. when conceived of as the faculty of framing general conceptions or of directly apprehending universals — distinguished from *understanding* **3** *logic* **:** PREMISE; *esp* **:** MINOR PREMISE **4 a** *archaic* **:** equitable or honorable treatment that affords satisfaction and that is prompted by the demands of either propriety or justice **b** *archaic* **:** a formal accounting **c** *obs* **:** a reasonable amount or degree

syn REASON, GROUND, ARGUMENT, PROOF can mean, in common, a point or set of related points offered or offerable in support of something disputed. REASON can indicate any motive, consideration, or inducement offered in explanation or defense of a practice, action, opinion, or belief ⟨the family side of the house is used for cooking, and for this *reason* visitors are invited to sit at the other end —Wilfred Thesiger⟩ ⟨for various *reasons*, the times and his own health included —J.C.Archer⟩ ⟨present illogical but forceful *reasons* for refusing an invitation⟩ GROUND and GROUNDS are often used interchangeably with REASON and REASONS but tend to apply to evidence, facts, data, reasoning used in defense rather than to motives or considerations, often suggesting a more solid support than REASON ⟨a *ground* for apprehension that is not unjustified —D.W. Brogan⟩ ⟨belittles the effectiveness of several provisions on the *ground* they are not new —*Wall Street Jour.*⟩ ⟨the future as we see it offers no *grounds* for easy optimism —*Current Biog.*⟩ ⟨objects to the statement on *grounds* that it reflects upon him personally —*Monsanto Mag.*⟩ ARGUMENT stresses the intent to convince or persuade, implying the use of evidence or reasoning in support of a contention or enhancement of the persuasive effect ⟨hear the *arguments* for and against pacifism⟩ ⟨a good *argument* can be made for the position that economic integration is very difficult if it is tackled on its own side alone —Dean Acheson⟩ ⟨this book is an inquiry into the proper limitations upon freedom of speech, and is in no way an *argument* that any one should be allowed to say whatever he wants anywhere and at any time —Zechariah Chafee⟩ ⟨one of the commonest of all evasions; the *argument* which is not an argument but an appeal to the emotions —Virginia Woolf⟩ ⟨the best *argument* against vegetarianism is the Eskimos —Rudolf Flesch & A.H.Lass⟩ PROOF implies conclusive logical demonstration but has come to mean any piece of evidence (as a fact or document), any testimony or argument that evokes a feeling of certainty in those who are to be convinced ⟨Euclid, the author of the Elements, who gave irrefutable *proofs* of the looser demonstrations of his predecessors —Benjamin Farrington⟩ ⟨that he did not break under the terrible strain seems *proof* enough that he was sent by Providence to lead America to freedom —F.V.W.Mason⟩ ⟨laughter is supposed to be our affair and optimism a *proof* of our youth and our resilience —John Mason Brown⟩ ⟨left the house with a ton of conjecture, though without a grain of *proof* —Thomas Hardy⟩

syn UNDERSTANDING, INTUITION: REASON centers attention on the faculty for order, sense, and rationality in thought, inference, and conclusion about perceptions ⟨the maintenance of *reason* — the establishment of criteria, by which ideas are tested empirically and in logic —Dorothy Thompson⟩ ⟨*reason* is logic; its principle is consistency; it requires that conclusions shall contain nothing not already given in their premises —H.M. Kallen⟩ UNDERSTANDING may sometimes widen the scope of REASON to include both most thought processes leading to comprehension and also the resultant state of knowledge ⟨*understanding* is the entire power of perceiving and conceiving, exclusive of the sensibility; the power of dealing with the impressions of sense, and composing them into wholes —S.T. Coleridge⟩ ⟨philosophy is said to begin in wonder and end in *understanding* —John Dewey⟩ INTUITION stresses quick knowledge or comprehension without orderly reason, thought, or cogitation ⟨all this . . . I saw, not discursively, or by effort, or by succession, but by one flash of horrid simultaneous *intuition* —Thomas De Quincey⟩ ⟨do we not really trust these faint lights of *intuition*, because they are lights, more than *reason*, which is often too slow a councillor? —G.W.Russell⟩ Used in connection with 19th century literary and philosophic notions, UNDERSTANDING often suggests the cold analytical order usually associated with REASON and REASON in turn suggests the spontaneity of INTUITION ⟨the *understanding* was the faculty that observed, inferred, argued, drew conclusions . . . the cold, external, practical notion of life . . . . The *reason* was the faculty of intuition, warm, perceptive, immediate that represented the mind of young New England —Van Wyck Brooks⟩ **syn** see in addition CAUSE

— **in reason** *adv* **:** with reason **:** JUSTIFIABLY, RIGHTLY ⟨cannot *in reason* doubt that this must be done⟩ — **within reason** *adv* **:** within reasonable limits ⟨drinks and relaxes *within reason*⟩ — **with reason** *adv* **:** with good cause **:** JUSTIFIABLY ⟨have chosen to do so *with reason*⟩

³**reason** \"\ *vb* **reasoned; reasoned; reasoning** \-z(ᵊ)niŋ\ **reasons** [ME *resonen*, fr. MF *raisonner* to discuss, reason, fr. OF, fr. *raison*, n. — more at ²REASON] *vi* **1 :** to use the faculty of reason so as to arrive at conclusions **:** THINK ⟨is able to ~ brilliantly⟩ **2 a** *obs* **:** to take part in a conversation, discussion, or argument with another **b :** to talk or discourse persuasively with another so as to influence, modify, or change the other's actions or opinions ⟨is someone you simply can't ~ with⟩ ~ *vt* **1** *archaic* **a :** DISCUSS, ARGUE ⟨am in no humor to ~ that point —Maria Edgeworth⟩ **b** (1) **:** to analyze by the use of reason (as in critically examining or in seeking out inferences or conclusions) (2) **:** to justify or support with reasons ⟨this boy . . . does ~ our petition —Shak.⟩ **2 :** to persuade, influence, or otherwise prevail on by the use of reason ⟨~*ed* myself out of the instincts and rules by which one mostly surrounds oneself —W.B.Yeats⟩ ⟨~*ed* her into believing what he said⟩ **3 :** to discover, formulate, or conclude by the use of reason — usu. used with *out* ⟨~ out a plan⟩ ⟨the steadiness of a ~*ed* conviction —A.L.Guérard⟩ **syn** see THINK

rea·son·abil·i·ty \ˌrēz(ᵊ)nəˈbiləd·ē\ *n* **:** the quality or state of being reasonable **:** REASONABLENESS

¹**rea·son·able** \ˈrēz(ᵊ)nəbəl\ *adj* [ME *resonable*, fr. OF *raisonable*, fr. L *rationabilis*, fr. *ration-, ratio* reason + *-abilis* -able — more at REASON] **1 a :** being in agreement with right thinking or right judgment **:** not conflicting with reason **:** not absurd **:** not ridiculous ⟨a ~ conviction⟩ ⟨a ~ theory⟩ **b :** being or remaining within the bounds of reason **:** not extreme **:** not excessive ⟨a ~ request⟩ ⟨a ~ hope of succeeding⟩ ⟨spent a ~ amount of time in relaxation⟩ ⟨is of a ~ size⟩ **c :** MODERATE: as (1) **:** not demanding too much ⟨a ~ boss⟩ (2) **:** not expensive ⟨fresh vegetables are now ~⟩ (3) **:** that allows a fair profit ⟨sold the material at a ~ rate⟩ **2 a :** having the faculty of reason **:** RATIONAL ⟨a ~ being⟩ **b :** possessing good sound judgment **:** well balanced **:** SENSIBLE ⟨can rely on the judgment of a ~ man⟩ **syn** see RATIONAL

²**reasonable** \"\ *adv* [ME *resonable*, fr. *resonable*, adj.] *chiefly dial* **:** REASONABLY ⟨can do it ~ well⟩

reasonable care *n* **:** DUE CARE

reasonable doubt *n* **:** solid doubt about the actual guilt of a defendant that arises or remains after careful and impartial examination of all evidence

rea·son·able·ness *n* -ES **:** the quality or state of being reasonable **:** REASONABILITY

reasonable part *n* **:** the portion of his estate that a decedent could not under Old English law will away from his widow and children — compare DEAD'S PART, JUS RELICTAE, LEGITIM

rea·son·ably \-blē, -bli\ *adv* [ME *resonably*, fr. *resonable*, adj. + *-ly*] **1 :** in a reasonable manner ⟨acted quite ~⟩ **2 :** to a fairly sufficient extent ⟨a book that is ~ good⟩

reasoned *adj* **1 :** based on or marked by reasoning ⟨material for a ~ verdict —John Buchan⟩ **2 :** provided with or marked by the detailed listing or mention of reasons ⟨by means of a ~ amendment —T.E.May⟩

rea·son·er \ˈrēz(ᵊ)nə(r)\ *n* -S **:** one that reasons

reasoning *n* -S [ME *resoninge*, fr. gerund of *resonen* to reason] **1 :** the use of reason; *esp* **:** the drawing of inferences or conclusions through the use of reason — compare APPREHENSION **2 :** a particular instance of the use of reason; *esp* **:** a particular argument ⟨seems to me that this ~ is altogether sound⟩

rea·son·less \ˈrēzᵊnləs\ *adj* [ME *resonles*, fr. *reson*, *resoun* reason + *-les* -less] **1 a :** not having the faculty of reason ⟨a ~ brute⟩ **b :** not marked by the use of reason **:** devoid of common sense **:** SENSELESS ⟨a ~ hostility⟩ **2 :** not based on or supported by reasons ⟨an apparently arbitrary and ~ change⟩ — **rea·son·less·ly** *adv* — **rea·son·less·ness** *n* -ES

reason of state [trans. of F *raison d'état*] **:** a motive for governmental action based on alleged needs or requirements of a political state regardless of possible transgressions of the rights or the moral codes of individual persons

reasons *pl of* REASON, *pres 3d sing of* REASON

re·assail \ˌrē+\ *vt* [*re-* + *assail*] **:** to assail again

re·assault \"+\ *vt* [*re-* + *assault*] **:** to assault again

re·assay \"+\ *vb* [*re-* + *assay*] *vi* **:** to make a new attempt ~ *vt* **:** to assay again

re·assemblage \"+\ *n* [*re-* + *assemblage*] **:** a new assemblage

re·assemble \"+\ *vb* [*re-* + *assemble*] *vt* **:** to bring or put together again ~ *vi* **:** to come together again

re·assembly \"+\ *n* [*re-* + *assembly*] **:** a second or fresh assembly

re·assent \"+\ *vi* [*re-* + *assent*] **:** to assent again

re·assert \"+\ *vt* [*re-* + *assert*] **:** to assert again

re·assertion \"+\ *n* **:** a second or fresh assertion

re·assertor \"+\ *n* **:** one that reasserts

re·assess \"+\ *vt* [*re-* + *assess*] **:** to assess again

re·assessment \"+\ *n* [*re-* + *assessment*] **:** a second or fresh assessment

re·assign \"+\ *vt* [*re-* + *assign*] **:** to assign again

re·assignment \"+\ *n* **:** the act of reassigning or state of being reassigned

re·associate \ˌrē+\ *vb* [*re-* + *associate*] *vt* **:** to bring into association again ~ *vi* **:** to become reassociated

re·association \"+\ *n* **1 :** the act of reassociating or state of being reassociated **2 :** the restoration of lost memories and behavior patterns — opposed to *dissociation*

re·associative \"+\ *adj* **:** of, relating to, or marked by reassociation

re·assort \"+\ *vb* [*re-* + *assort*] *vt* **:** to assort again ~ *vi* **:** to become assorted again **:** separate anew ⟨the genes ~ during meiosis⟩

re·assortment \"+\ *n* **:** the action of reassorting or state of being reassorted

re·assume \"+\ *vt* [ML *reassumere*, fr. L *re-* + *assumere* to assume] **:** to assume again **:** take up once more **:** adopt again ⟨*reassumed* the place she had held before⟩

re·assumption \"+\ *n* [*re-* + *assumption*] **:** the act of reassuming or state of being reassumed

re·assurance \"+\ *n* **1 :** the action of reassuring or state of being reassured ⟨a timid man in constant need of ~⟩ **2 :** REINSURANCE

re·assure \"+\ *vt* [*re-* + *assure*] **1 :** to assure anew **2 :** REINSURE — **re·assurement** \"+\ *n* -S — **re·assurer** \"+\ *n*

reassured *adj* **1 :** having confidence restored **:** freed from fear or anxiety **2 a :** having renewed insurance **b :** having insurance covered by being placed with another insurance company

re·assuredly \"+\ *adv* **:** by way of reassurance

reassuring *adj* **:** restoring or intended to restore confidence ⟨a very ~ remark⟩ — **re·as·sur·ing·ly** *adv*

reas·ti·ness \ˈrēstinəs, ˈrās-,ˈras-\ *n* -ES *dial chiefly Eng* **:** RANCIDITY

reas·ty \-ti\ *adj* -ER/-EST [ME *resty*, fr. OF *resté* left over, past part. of *rester* to remain — more at REST] *dial chiefly Eng* **:** RANCID

re·ata \rēˈad·ə, -ˈä-\ *n* -S [AmerSp, lariat, lasso — more at LARIAT] **:** LARIAT

re·attach \ˌrē+\ *vb* [*re-* + *attach*] *vi* **:** to become attached anew ⟨the parasite ~*es* to the host⟩ ~ *vt* **:** to attach again

re·attachment \"+\ *n* [*re-* + *attachment*] **:** the act of reattaching or state of being reattached

re·attack \"+\ *vb* [*re-* + *attack*] *vt* **:** to attack again ~ *vi* **:** to make a new attack

re·attain \"+\ *vt* [*re-* + *attain*] **:** to attain again

re·attainment \"+\ *n* **:** the act of reattaining or state of being reattained

¹**re·attempt** \"+\ *vb* [*re-* + *attempt*] *vt* **:** to attempt again ~ *vi* **:** to make a new attempt

²**reattempt** \"\ *n* **:** a new attempt

re·attire \ˌrē+\ *vt* [*re-* + *attire*] **:** to attire again

re·auction \(ˈ)rē+\ *vt* [*re-* + *auction*] **:** to auction again

re·audit \(ˈ)rē+\ *vt* [*re-* + *audit*] **:** to audit again

re·audition \ˌrē+\ *vt* [*re-* + *audition*] **:** to audition again

re·au·mur \ˌrāōˈmyu̇(ə)r, -āə̇m-, -ˌmər\ *adj, usu cap* [after René Antoine Ferchault de *Réaumur* †1757 Fr. physicist who formulated the Reaumur scale] **:** relating or conforming to a thermometric scale on which under standard atmospheric pressure the boiling point of water is at 80 degrees above the zero of the scale and the freezing point is at zero — abbr. *R*

re·authenticate \ˌrē+\ *vt* [*re-* + *authenticate*] **:** to authenticate again

re·authentication \"+\ *n* [*re-* + *authentication*] **:** the act of reauthenticating or state of being reauthenticated

re·authorize \(ˈ)rē+\ *vt* [*re-* + *authorize*] **:** to authorize again

¹**reave** \ˈrēv\ *vb* **reaved** \-vd\ *or* **reft** \ˈreft\ *or archaic* **raft** \ˈraft\ **reaved** *or* **reft** *or archaic* **raft; reaving; reaves** [ME *reven*, fr. OE *rēafian*; akin to OHG *roubōn* to rob, ON *raufa* to break up, open, Goth *biraubon* to rob, strip, L *rumpere* to break, burst, Skt *ropayati* he breaks off, ON *rögg* tuft, shagginess — more at RUG] *vi, archaic* **:** to take something away by or as if by stealth or force **:** PILLAGE, PLUNDER, ROB ~ *vt, archaic* **:** to take away by or as if by stealth or force: as **a :** ROB, DESPOIL ⟨of what enjoyments thou hast *reft* us —Robert Burns⟩ **b** (1) **:** to deprive one of ⟨~ his life —Edmund Spenser⟩ (2) **:** SEIZE ⟨thy father . . . *reft* from my dead lord a field with violence —Alfred Tennyson⟩ **c :** to carry or tear away **:** REMOVE ⟨who hath *reft* . . . my dearest pledge —John Milton⟩

²**reave** \"\ *vb* **reaved** \-vd\ *or* **reft** \ˈreft\ **reaved** *or* **reft; reaving; reaves** [ME *reven*, prob. modif. (influenced by ME *reven* to take away by or as if by stealth or force, rob, despoil) of ON *rīfa* to rive, tear — more at RIVE] *archaic* **:** BURST, TEAR, SPLIT

rea·vel \ˈrāvəl\ *chiefly Scot var of* RAVEL

reav·er *or* **riev·er** \ˈrēvə(r)\ *n* -S [ME *revere*, fr. OE *rēafere*, fr. *rēafian* to take away by or as if by stealth or force, rob, despoil + *-ere* -er] **:** one that takes away by or as if by stealth or force

re·awake \ˌrē+\ *vb* [*re-* + *awake*] *vt* **:** to awake again ~ *vi* **:** to become reawaked

re·awaken \"+\ *vb* [*re-* + *awaken*] *vt* **:** to awaken again ~ *vi* **:** to become reawakened

re·awakenment \"+\ *n* **:** the act of reawakening or state of being reawakened

re·aware \"+\ *adj* [*re-* + *aware*] **:** again aware **:** freshly aware

¹**reb** \ˈreb\ *n* -S [short for *rebel*] **:** JOHNNY REB

²**reb** \"\ *n* -S *usu cap* [Yiddish, fr. Heb *rabbī* my master, rabbi — more at RABBI] **:** RABBI, MISTER — used as a complimentary title

re·bab \rəˈbäb\ *n* -S [Ar *rebāb*] **:** a medieval Arabic bowed musical instrument having from one to three strings, shaped typically like a small lute, and now used in gamelan orchestras

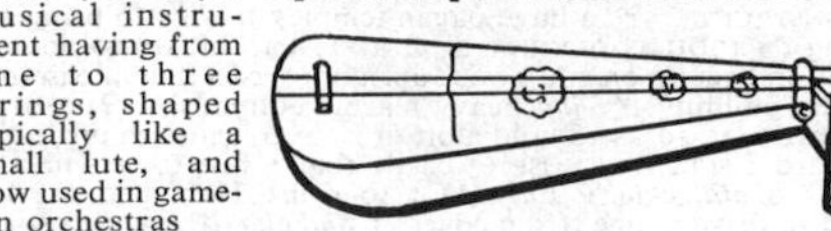
rebab

re·back \(ˈ)rē+\ *vt* [*re-* + *back*] **1 :** to reshape the backbone of (a book) after casing or covering **2 a :** to add a new backbone to (a book) without entirely rebinding **b :** to support the backbone of (a book) with new material

re·banking \"+\ *n* [*re-* + *banking*, fr. gerund of ²*bank*] **:** a malfunction in a watch caused by excessive balance motion that makes the roller jewel strike outside the fork horns and renders the escapement inoperative — distinguished from *overbanking*

re·baptism \"+\ *n* [*re-* + *baptism*] **:** a second baptism

re·baptismal \(ˌ)rē+\ *adj* [*rebaptism* + *-al*] **:** of or relating to a second baptism

re·baptize \"+\ *vt* [LL *rebaptizare*, fr. *re-* + *baptizare* to baptize] **:** to baptize again or a second time; *also* **:** to name or christen again

re·baptizer \"+\ *n* **:** one that rebaptizes

re·bar·ba·tive \rēˈbärbəd·iv, -bȧb-\ *adj* [F *rébarbatif*, fr. MF *rebarber* to be repellent (fr. *re-* + *barbe* beard, fr. L *barba*) + *-atif* -ative — more at BEARD] **:** serving or tending to repel or irritate **:** CRABBED, REPELLENT ⟨the impression given by these letters is not so much ~ as infinitely pathetic —*New Statesman & Nation*⟩

¹**re·bate** \ˈrēˌbāt, ₌ˈ₌, *usu* -ād·+V\ *vb* -ED/-ING/-S [ME *rebaten*, fr. MF *rabattre* to beat down again, turn back down, reduce, fr. OF, fr. *re-* + *abattre* to beat down, fr. *a-* (fr. L *ad-*) + *battre* to beat, fr. L *battuere*, *battere* — more at BAT] *vt* **1 :** to reduce the force, effect, intensity, or activity of **:** DIMINISH, LESSEN **2 :** to reduce the sharpness or edge of **:** make dull **:** BLUNT ⟨~ and blunt his natural edge —Shak.⟩ **3** *heraldry* **:** to remove a part of (a charge) **b :** to remove part of a charge from (an escutcheon) **4 a :** to make a rebate of ⟨*rebated* over a hundred dollars in interest⟩ **b :** to give a rebate to ⟨secretly *rebated* a few large shippers of freight⟩ ~ *vi* **:** to give or make a practice of giving rebates ⟨disliked *rebating* but accepted it as a necessary evil to . . . stay in business —D.L. Kemmerer⟩

²**rebate** \"\ *n* -S [F *rabat*, fr. MF *rabattre*] **:** ABATEMENT, REPAYMENT: as **a :** a return of a portion of the interest on a loan for payment of the loan before its due date **b :** a retroactive abatement, credit, discount, or refund (as from a wholesaler to a retailer) usu. as consideration for a specified volume of business **c :** a portion of an insurance premium returned directly or indirectly to the policyholder by an agent or broker from commissions received either as an inducement to purchase insurance or to gain a competitive advantage over another agent or broker in selling insurance

³**rebate** *var of* RABBET

re·bate·ment \rēˈbātmənt\ *n* -S [MF, fr. *rebatre* to reduce (fr. OF, fr. *re-* + *battre*, *batre* to beat) + *-ment* — more at REBATE] **:** ABATEMENT 2

re·bat·er \ˈrēˌbād·ə(r), ₌ˈ₌₌\ *n* -S **:** one that rebates

re·ba·to \rəˈbäd·(ˌ)ō\ *n* -S [modif. of MF *rabat* — more at RABAT] **:** RABATO

reb·be \ˈrebə\ *n* -S [Yiddish, fr. Heb *rabbī* rabbi] **1 :** a teacher of Hebrew esp. in a heder **2 :** a rabbi or Jewish spiritual leader esp. of the Hasidic sect

re·betz·in *or* **reb·bitz·in** \-bətsən\ *n* -S [Yiddish, fem. of *rebbe*] **:** the wife of a rabbi

re·beamer \(ˈ)rē+\ *n* [*re-* + ¹*beam* + *-er*] **:** a textile worker who winds cloth and yarn from one beam to another

re·bec *or* **re·beck** \ˈrēˌbek\ *n* -S [MF *rebec*, alter. (perh. influenced by *bec* beak) of OF *rebebe*, fr. OProv *rebeb*, fr. Ar *rebāb* rebab — more at BEAK] **:** a bowed musical instrument derived from the rebab and having a pear-shaped body, a slender neck, and usu. three strings ⟨the jocund ~*s* sound —John Milton⟩

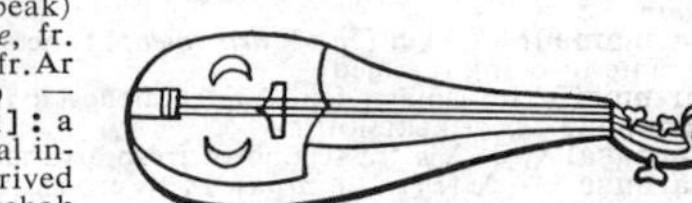
rebec

¹**reb·el** \ˈrebəl\ *adj* [ME, fr. OF *rebelle*, fr. L *rebellis*, fr. *re-* + *bellum* war, fr. OL *duellum* — more at DUEL] **1 a :** opposing or taking arms against the government or ruler of a country ⟨the ~ general⟩ ⟨the ~ lord⟩ ⟨his ~ son⟩ **b :** of, relating to, or belonging to rebels ⟨the ~ army⟩ ⟨the ~ camp⟩ **2 :** DISOBEDIENT, REBELLIOUS ⟨fonder of alliterative rhythm, and more ~ to strict metrical ways —George Saintsbury⟩

²**rebel** \"\ *n* -S [ME, fr. MF *rebelle*, fr. OF *rebelle*, adj.] **1 :** one who opposes authority or restraint **:** one who breaks with established custom or tradition ⟨a ~ against the conventions of education —Allen Johnson⟩ ⟨a ~ priding himself on his unorthodoxy —Anthony West⟩ **2 :** one who participates in a rebellion ⟨forsook peaceful methods of reform and became a real ~ —*Amer. Guide Series: R. I.*⟩ ⟨cities that were faithful have gone under to ~*s* —Gilbert Parker⟩

³**re·bel** \rəˈbel, rēˈ-\ *vi* **rebelled; rebelled; rebelling; rebels** [ME *rebellen*, fr. MF *rebeller*, fr. L *rebellare* to make war again, rebel, fr. *re-* + *bellare* to make war, fr. *bellum* war] **1 a :** to oppose or disobey one in authority or control ⟨*rebelled* against the leaders of his party and voted with the opposition⟩ **b :** to renounce and resist by force the authority of the ruler or government to which one owes allegiance ⟨*rebelled* and raised an army to overthrow the king⟩ ⟨*rebelled* against the national government and declared their autonomy⟩ **2 a :** to put up a fight **:** show opposition ⟨*rebelled* against the industrialized urban life about him —W.P.Clancy⟩ ⟨*rebelled* at the routine of a clerk's work —J.E.Ferris⟩ **b :** to feel or exhibit anger or revulsion ⟨*rebelled* at the injustice of his situation and cursed his fate⟩ ⟨his senses *rebelled* at the sights and smells of the town⟩

reb·el·dom \ˈrebəldəm\ *n* -S [²*rebel* + *-dom*] **:** an area controlled by rebels

re·bel·ler \rəˈbelə(r), rēˈ-\ *n* -S [ME, fr. *rebellen* to rebel + *-er*] **:** REBEL

re·bel·lion \-lyən\ *n* -S [ME, fr. MF, fr. L *rebellion-, rebellio*, fr. *rebellare* to rebel + *-ion-, -io* -ion] **1 :** open opposition to a person or thing in a position of authority or dominance ⟨continuing the ~ started by the beboppers —Whitney Balliett⟩ ⟨a moral ~ against the oppression of everyday pettiness and misery —A.H.Pekelis⟩ **2 a :** open defiance of or armed resistance to the authority of an established government ⟨gross ~ and detested treason —Shak.⟩ **b** *often cap* **:** an instance of such defiance or resistance ⟨a taxpayers' ~⟩ ⟨the Great *Rebellion*⟩ ⟨the Whiskey *Rebellion*⟩ **3** *Scots law* **:** disobedience of a legal command or summons resulting in actual outlawry or later in certain penalties

syn REVOLUTION, UPRISING, REVOLT, INSURRECTION, MUTINY, PUTSCH: REBELLION commonly indicates open armed resistance to government of such strength as to constitute a formidable problem to the authorities ⟨the term *rebellion* is applied to an insurrection of large extent, and is usu. a war between the legitimate government of a country and portions or provinces of the same who seek to throw off their allegiance to it and set up a government of their own —*Instructions for Govt. of U. S. Armies*⟩ REVOLUTION usu. applies to a successful rebellion accomplishing the overthrow of a government or the permanent nullifying of its sovereign authority in the territory in question, sometimes with concomitant sweeping economic and social changes ⟨distinguish between *revolutions* affecting a change in a whole way of life, including religion, economics, and manners, as well as politics, and *revolutions* changing the form of government —C.J.Friedrich⟩ UPRISING may refer to a localized rebellion that flares into sudden, spontaneous, militant activity designed to overthrow authority ⟨an Indian *uprising* drove him and his family from home, but on its suppression they returned —W.J.Ghent⟩ ⟨an *uprising* now viewed as the real beginning of Ireland's "War of Independence" —*Current Biog.*⟩ REVOLT may apply to a rebellion or uprising against legitimate authority by those owing it allegiance but refusing to accept its dictates ⟨a premature *revolt*, of some 200 native soldiers . . . had resulted in the deaths of their officers and in lusty shouts for independence —C.A.Buss⟩ INSURRECTION may suggest more truculent intransigeance and surging activity and less organized purpose than REVOLT ⟨the new government was harassed by internal controversies and by assassinations, disorders, and *insurrections* —*Collier's Yr. Bk.*⟩ MUTINY applies to a determined localized insurrection and insubordination against maritime, naval, or military authority ⟨*mutiny* imports collective insubordination and necessarily includes some combination of two or more persons in resisting lawful military authority —*U. S. Manual for Courts-Martial*⟩ PUTSCH suggests a revolt, turbulent demonstration, or planned attempt at a coup to seize a governmental administration ⟨a *putsch* to take control of the government —A.L.Funk⟩

re·bel·lious \-yəs\ *adj* [ME, fr. ML *rebelliosus*, fr. L *rebellio* rebellion + *-osus* -ous] **1 a :** given to or engaged in rebellion against constituted authority ⟨~ troops⟩ ⟨a ~ politician⟩ ⟨a ~ student⟩ **b :** of, relating to, or characteristic of a rebel or rebellion ⟨~ actions⟩ ⟨~ speeches⟩ ⟨~ times⟩ **c :** resisting control **:** hostile to authority or tradition ⟨the early twentieth century was increasingly raucous, ~, and ribald —H.F. Mooney⟩ **2 :** resisting treatment or management **:** REFRACTORY, UNYIELDING ⟨eczema of long standing or which is ~ to treatment —H.G.Armstrong⟩ ⟨bend his head and crash with his full weight into ~ circumstances —Francis Hackett⟩ **syn** see INSUBORDINATE

re·bel·lious·ly *adv* **:** in a rebellious manner

re·bel·lious·ness *n* -ES **:** the quality or state of being rebellious

reb·el·ly \ˈrebəlē\ *adj* [²*rebel* + *-y*] **:** REBELLIOUS ⟨the ~ spirit of the century —Sean O'Faolain⟩

rebels *pl of* REBEL, *pres 3d sing of* REBEL

rebel yell *n* **:** a prolonged high-pitched yell traditionally given by Confederate soldiers in the U. S. Civil War

¹**re·bid** \(ˈ)rē+\ *vb* [*re-* + *bid*] *vt* **:** to bid (one's previously bid suit) again in bridge ~ *vi* **:** to bid again in the auction of a bridge deal

²**re·bid** \ˈrē+ˌ₌\ *n* **:** a bid by a bridge player who has previously bid

re·biddable \(ˈ)rē+\ *adj* **:** capable of being rebid **:** long or strong enough to warrant a rebid even if not supported by one's partner ⟨a ~ suit⟩

re·billing \"+\ *n* [*re-* + *billing*] **:** the issuing of a new waybill at a junction point

¹**re·bind** \"+\ *vt* [*re-* + *bind*] **:** to bind anew or again; *esp* **:** to put a new binding on (a book)

²**re·bind** \ˈrē+ˌ₌\ *n* **:** a rebound book

re·birth \(ˈ)rē+\ *n* [*re-* + *birth*] **1 a :** a new or second birth **:** METEMPSYCHOSIS ⟨the individual continues his pilgrimage through various ~*s* —R.N.Dandekar⟩ **b :** spiritual regeneration ⟨a bench in the front of the church to which all sinners and those in the struggle of ~ were invited —J.C.Brauer⟩ ⟨a novel of death and ~ — of a spiritual purging and regeneration —M.D.Geismar⟩ **2 :** RENAISSANCE, REVIVAL ⟨the greatest achievement of modern science has been the ~ of the historical sense —Benjamin Farrington⟩ ⟨the ~ of the nationalist movement —M.S.Handler⟩

re·blo·chon \ˌrebləˈshōⁿ\ *n* -S [F] **:** a soft French whole-milk cheese of delicate flavor

reb·o·ant \ˈrebəwənt\ *adj* [L *reboant-, reboans*, pres. part. of *reboare* to resound, fr. *re-* + *boare* to cry aloud, roar, fr. Gk *boan* to cry aloud, shout, of imit. origin] **:** REVERBERATING ⟨gave out a joyous howl, ~ with the sounds of conquest —Adria Langley⟩

reb·o·a·tion \-əˈwāshən\ *n* -S [L *reboatus* (past part. of *reboare*) + E *-ion*] **:** a loud reverberation ⟨the deep-mouthed ~ of a ship's horn seems to have lost itself in the fog —*Atlantic*⟩

re·boil \(ˈ)rē+\ *vt* [ME *reboilen*, fr. MF *rebouillir*, fr. *re-* + *bouillir*, *boillir* to boil] **:** to boil again; *specif* **:** to boil (as distilled water) again in order to remove occluded air and gases

re·boil·er \"+ə(r)\ *n* [*reboil* + *-er*] **:** a piece of equipment (as one with steam coils) for supplying additional heat esp. to the lower part of a fractionating column

re·boise \rəˈbȯiz, rəbˈwäz\ *vt* -ED/-ING/-S [F *reboiser*, fr. *re-* + *bois* wood, forest — more at BOISERIE] **:** REFOREST — **re·boise·ment** \-mənt\ *n* -S

re·bo·le·ra \ˌrebəˈlerə\ *n* -S [Sp] **:** a pass ending a series of veronicas in bullfighting in which one end of the cape is released and swung in a graceful arc around the bullfighter's waist

re·bop \ˈrēˌbäp\ *n* [imit.] **:** ³BOP

re·born \(ˈ)rē+\ *adj* [*re-* + *born*] **:** born again **:** having or experiencing a rebirth **:** REGENERATED, REVIVED ⟨thus men could be ~ and become sons of God —K.S.Latourette⟩ ⟨old states were ~ and new ones created —Samuel Van Valkenburg & Ellsworth Huntington⟩

rebosa *or* **reboso** *var of* REBOZO

re·bo·te \rəˈbōd·ē\ *n* -S [Sp, bounce, rebound, fr. *rebotar* to rebound, fr. *re-* + *botar* to hurl, thrust, fr. OF *boter* to butt — more at BUTT] **1 :** the rear wall of a jai alai court **2 :** a shot played off the rebote

re·bou·lia \rēˈbülēə\ *n, cap* [NL, fr. H. P. I. *Reboul* †1839 French naturalist + NL *-ia*] **:** a genus of liverworts (family Marchantiaceae) that are widely distributed on rocks and soil and are distinguished by a conspicuous pseudoperianth split into fringy lanceolate lobes

¹**re·bound** \(ˈ)rē+\ *vb* [ME *rebounden*, fr. MF *rebondir*, fr. OF, fr. *re-* + *bondir* to bound — more at BOUND] *vi* **1 a :** to spring back on collision or impact with another body ⟨a lattice or diffraction grating from which the electrons would ~ —*Current Biog.*⟩ **b :** to recover from or react to a setback or frustration ⟨~*ed* less quickly from disappointment —Ellen Glasgow⟩ ⟨was supposed to fall in love with someone else quickly . . . but she herself had ~*ed* differently —G.R.Stewart⟩ **2 :** to bound back as if upon impact **:** LEAP, SPRING ⟨released

from the downward pull, the submerged crustal material would ~ upward —A.E.Benfield⟩ **3 :** REECHO ⟨such a resounding whack that the echoes ~*ed* from the mountains forty miles away —Darrell Berrigan⟩ **~** *vt* **1 :** to cause to spring back **:** RETURN **2 :** to make resound **:** REECHO

syn REVERBERATE, RECOIL, RESILE, REPERCUSS: REBOUND indicates a resilient springing, bouncing, or hurtling back after or as if after some collision, impact, or other forcible contact ⟨a ball *rebounding* from the wall⟩ ⟨literature is *rebounding* again from the scientific-classical pole to the poetic-romantic one —Edmund Wilson⟩ REVERBERATE is used of waves or rays that bound back or are forced back, reflected, or deflected; it is most typically used of sound and suggests loud reechoing ⟨the explosion *reverberated* between a series of low ridges, sounding like some giant's bowling ball —F.V.W.Mason⟩ ⟨its acoustics are magnificent: the merest mumble *reverberates* like the solemn voice of judgment —Green Peyton⟩ ⟨she presents even simple subjects with a perceptiveness that makes them *reverberate* in the mind —Babette Deutsch⟩ RECOIL applies to a springing or flying back, commonly in consequence of a release of pressure or stretching, to or against a point of origin, or in retreat, receding, or shrinking in apprehension or revulsion ⟨a spring *recoiling* to its natural position⟩ ⟨military commentators *recoiled* from the spectacle as if it were too loathsome for remark —S.L.A.Marshall⟩ RESILE may apply to a resilient but not abrupt drawing back to a former position ⟨the rubber attachments *resiling* at the normal temperatures⟩ ⟨apprehensive about the agreement and trying to *resile* to his former unattached position⟩ REPERCUSS, now notably less common than the noun *repercussion*, implies the return of something moving ahead with or as if with great force back to or toward the starting point ⟨sickness produces an abnormally sensitive emotional state in almost everyone, and in many cases the emotional state *repercusses*, as it were, on the organic disease —F.W.Peabody⟩

²rebound \"\ *n* **1 a :** the action of rebounding **:** a springing back after impact or the sudden release of pressure **:** RECOIL, RESILIENCE ⟨the reflection of light was just a ~ of the light particles from an elastic surface —S.F.Mason⟩ ⟨the origin of nationalism in Asia was in the nature of a ~ from the European imperialism of the last century —B.R.Sen⟩ **b :** an upward leap or movement **:** RECOVERY ⟨strength in selected issues . . . ushered in a sharp ~ in prices —J.G.Forrest⟩ **2 :** something that is reverberated **:** ECHO ⟨such ~*s* our inward ear catches sometimes from afar —William Wordsworth⟩ **3 a :** a basketball or hockey puck that rebounds (as from a backboard or sideboard) ⟨grabbed the ~ and sank a basket⟩ **b :** an instance of securing possession of a rebounding basketball ⟨leads the league in ~*s*⟩ **4 :** an immediate and spontaneous reaction to a setback, frustration, or intellectual or emotional crisis ⟨is also on the ~, not from ennui but from a dead lover —*Time*⟩ ⟨caught the middle class on the ~, and received perhaps a million votes which in subsequent elections it failed to hold —*Times Lit. Supp.*⟩

rebound clip *n* **:** a clip surrounding the back and one or two other leaves of a leaf spring and usu. rigidly fastened to the shortest to distribute the load during rebounds

re·bounder \"+\ *n* [*²rebound* + *-er*] **:** a basketball player skilled at getting possession of rebounds ⟨the top ~ on the team⟩

re·bo·zo \rā'bō(,)sō, rə'-\ *also* **re·bo·sa** \-,sə\ *or* **re·bo·so** \-(,)sō\ *or* **ri·bo·so** \rə'-\ *n* -S [Sp *rebozo* shawl, fr. *rebozar* to muffle, fr. *re-* + *bozo* mouth, lips, fr. (assumed) VL *bucceum*, fr. L *bucca* cheek — more at POCK] **:** a long scarf made of any of various plain or embroidered fabrics often fringed on the ends and worn chiefly by Mexican women ⟨all decently shawled in long black ~*s* —Gertrude Diamant⟩

re·breather \(')rē+\ *n* [*re-* + *breathe* + *-er*] **:** an apparatus with face mask and gas supply forming a closed system from which one can breathe as long as the concentrations of oxygen and carbon dioxide remain within tolerable limits

¹re·broadcast \"+\ *vt* [*re-* + *broadcast*] **1 :** to broadcast simultaneously (a radio or television program or signals being received from another source) **2 :** to repeat (a radio or television broadcast) at a later time usu. by transcription

²rebroadcast \"\ *n* **:** something that is broadcast again; *specif* **:** a usu. transcribed repetition of a radio or television program

rebs *pl of* REB

¹re·buff \rə'bəf, rē'-\ *vt* -ED/-ING/-S [MF *rebuffer*, fr. It *ribuffare*, to reprimand, fr. *ribuffo* reprimand] **1 :** to refuse or repulse without ceremony **:** give a sharp check to **:** SNUB ⟨mix only with the right people and ~ invitations from those we didn't like —H.E.Salisbury⟩ **2 :** to drive or beat back ⟨thunder and drenching flood ~ the winds —Robert Bridges †1930⟩ ⟨~*ed* the enemy attack⟩

²rebuff \", 'rē,-\ *n* -S [MF *rebuffe*, fr. It *ribuffo* reprimand] **1 :** an abrupt or unceremonious rejection of an offer or advance **:** SNUB ⟨the task was uncongenial to one sensitive to ~*s*, but he succeeded in raising the outside amount necessary —H.K.Rowe⟩ **2 :** a sharp setback **:** REPULSE ⟨four costly ~*s* of a tiny outpost detachment —F.V.W.Mason⟩ ⟨the reader who picks it up as casually as he would a common novel is headed for a ~ that will set him back upon his heels —B.R. Redman⟩

¹re·build \(')rē+\ *vb* [*re-* + *build*] *vt* **1 a :** to make extensive repairs to including the replacement of missing or defective parts **:** RECONSTRUCT ⟨~ a vacuum cleaner⟩ **b :** to restore to a previous state or condition **:** RE-CREATE ⟨was struggling to ~ values for stockholders —L.M.Hughes⟩ ⟨~ inventories⟩ ⟨~ grazing resources⟩ **2 :** to make extensive changes in **:** REMODEL ⟨individuals should ~ their lives, so that social morality as a whole may be strengthened —D.R.Weimer⟩ **~** *vi* **:** to build again or anew ⟨bought the house with the intention of ~*ing*⟩ **syn** see MEND

²re·build \'rē+,-\ *n* **:** something that is rebuilt ⟨many soldiers prefer the ~*s*, because they are pliable and easier on the feet —*Newsweek*⟩

re·builder \(')=+\ *n* **:** one that rebuilds

re·built \"+\ *adj* [fr. past part. of *¹rebuild*] **:** disassembled and reconstructed with the addition of new parts ⟨a ~ typewriter⟩

re·buk·able \rə'byükəbəl, rē'-\ *adj* [*¹rebuke* + *-able*] **:** meriting rebuke ⟨~ and worthy shameful check —Shak.⟩

¹re·buke \-'byük\ *vt* -ED/-ING/-S [ME *rebuken*, fr. ONF *rebuker*, fr. *re-* + *-buker* (perh. fr. MHG *būsch* cudgel) — more at BOAST] **1 a :** to criticize sharply **:** censure severely **:** REPRIMAND ⟨their children where they could be watched and *rebuked* if they became restless —J.H.Cutler⟩ ⟨*rebuked* abuse of the uniform for commercial purposes —Dixon Wecter⟩ **b :** to serve as a rebuke to ⟨his industry ~*s* me⟩ **2 :** to turn back or keep down **:** CHECK, REPULSE ⟨whose courtiers vowed he could ~ the waves —Thomas Wood †1950⟩ ⟨the mountaineering willow, sharply *rebuked* by drying winds, rises no higher than an inch —Andrew Young⟩ **syn** see REPROVE

²rebuke \"\ *n* -S [ME, fr. *rebuken* to rebuke] **:** an expression of strong disapproval **:** REPRIMAND, REPROOF ⟨clambering on the divan with muddy shoes brought sharp parental ~ —Lucius Garvin⟩ ⟨dreading a ~ . . . by venturing to dance —Jane Austen⟩

re·buke·ful \-fəl\ *adj* [*²rebuke* + *-ful*] **:** serving to or disposed to rebuke — **re·buke·ful·ly** \-fəlē\ *adv*

re·buk·er \-kə(r)\ *n* -S [ME, fr. *rebuken* to rebuke + *-er*] **:** one that rebukes ⟨able to recall that no one was more mischievous than their ~ in his own youth —A.D.Rees⟩

re·buk·ing·ly *adv* [*rebuking* (pres. part. of *¹rebuke*) + *-ly*] **:** in a rebuking manner

re·burial \(')rē+\ *n* [*re-* + *burial*] **:** an act or instance of reburying

re·bury \"+\ *vt* [*re-* + *bury*] **:** to bury again

¹re·bus \'rēbəs\ *n* -ES [L, by things (abl. pl. of *res* thing) — more at REAL] **1 :** a representation of words or syllables by pictures of objects or by symbols whose names resemble the intended words or syllables in sound; *also* **:** a riddle made up wholly or in part of such pictures or symbols ⟨*ICURYY4 me* is a ~ for *I see you are too wise for me*⟩ **2 :** a badge that suggests the name of the person to whom it belongs — compare CANTING 2

²rebus \"\ *vt* **rebused; rebused; rebusing; rebuses :** to mark with or indicate by a rebus ⟨Abbot Islip's . . . name is ~*ed* as an eye and the slip of a tree with the hand apparently of a slipping man hanging to it —Edward Clodd⟩

rebus sic stan·ti·bus \-(,)sik'stantəbəs\ *adv* [NL, lit., things continuing thus] **:** so long as conditions have not substantially changed ⟨a doctrine in international law that treaties are binding only *rebus sic stantibus*⟩

re·but \rə'bət, rē'-, *usu* -əd·+V\ *vb* **rebutted; rebutted; rebutting; rebuts** [ME *rebuten*, fr. OF *reboter*, fr. *re-* + *boter* to butt, thrust — more at BUTT] *vt* **1 a :** to drive or beat back **:** REPULSE ⟨this mare . . . took no interest in the horse and . . . she did not ~ him either —Henry Wynmalen⟩ **b :** to check the advance or influence of **:** REPEL ⟨luckily a few pictures in the house to ~ a despairing mood —Sacheverell Sitwell⟩ **2 a :** to contradict, meet, or oppose by formal legal argument, plea, or countervailing proof ⟨where evidence is offered to ~ presumption against suicide, presumption disappears —*Detroit Law Jour.*⟩ **b :** to expose the falsity of **:** CONTRADICT, REFUTE ⟨~ my contention that something cannot be done by doing it —F.H.Cleobury⟩ ⟨in her first sentence she ~*s* the long-accepted dictum that Africa is a continent without a history —D.H.Jones⟩ **~** *vi* **:** to make or put in an answer or counter proof (as to a plaintiff's surrejoinder) **:** make a rebuttal **syn** see DISPROVE

re·bute \rə'büt, -bət, -byüt\ *n* -S [ME, fr. *rebuten* to rebut] *Scot* **:** REBUFF

re·but·ment \rə'bətmənt, rē'-\ *n* -S [*¹rebut* + *-ment*] **:** REBUTTAL

re·but·table \-bəd·əbəl\ *adj* **:** capable of being rebutted

rebuttable presumption *n* **:** a presumption that may be rebutted by other legal evidence — compare PRESUMPTION OF LAW

re·but·tal \rə'bəd·ᵊl, rē'-, -ətᵊl\ *n* -S [*¹rebut* + *-al*] **:** the act of rebutting; *specif* **:** the giving of evidence in a legal suit to destroy the effect of evidence introduced by the other side in the same suit

¹re·but·ter \-əd·ə(r), -ətə-\ *n* -S [AF *rebuter*, fr. OF *reboter*, *rebouter* to rebut] **:** the answer of a defendant in matter of fact to a plaintiff's surrejoinder

²rebutter \"\ *n* -S [*¹rebut* + *-er*] **:** something that rebuts or refutes **:** REFUTATION

rec \'rek\ *adj* [by shortening] **:** RECREATION ⟨~ hall⟩ ⟨~ activities⟩

rec *abbr* **1** receipt **2** receive; receiver **3** receptacle **4** reception **5** recipe **6** reclamation **7** recommended **8** record; recorded; recorder; recording **9** recovery

re·cal·ci·trance \rə'kalsətrən(t)s, rē'-\ *or* **re·cal·ci·tran·cy** \-nsē, -si\ *n, pl* **recalcitrances** *or* **recalcitrancies** [*recalcitrance* fr. *recalcitrant*, after such pairs as E *obedient: obedience; recalcitrancy* fr. *recalcitrant* + *-cy*] **:** the state of being recalcitrant **:** obstinate noncompliance **:** stubborn opposition ⟨in the best reformed society elements of selfish ~ will remain —J.A.Hobson⟩ ⟨a wayward, contrary, ungovernable element in human nature — an element akin to the ~ of our cousins the camel, mule, and goat —A.J.Toynbee⟩

¹re·cal·ci·trant \-nt\ *adj* [LL *recalcitrant-*, *recalcitrans*, fr. pres. part. of *recalcitrare* to be stubbornly disobedient, fr. L, to kick back, fr. *re-* + *calcitrare* to kick, fr. *calc-*, *calx* heel — more at CALK] **1 :** obstinately defiant of authority or restraint **:** stubbornly disobedient ⟨~ and dangerous heretics and obstructionists —G.L.Kline⟩ ⟨a ~ child⟩ ⟨call forth the forces of the Union to coerce ~ states —S.E.Morison & H.S.Commager⟩ **2 a :** difficult or impossible to handle or operate **:** UNMANAGEABLE ⟨the materials in these fields are more complex and more ~ than the simpler and more readily measurable phenomena of the languages —Mortimer Graves⟩ ⟨the car had a ~ gearshift lever —M.M.Musselman⟩ **b :** not responsive to treatment ⟨many of these patients were suffering from ~ forms of the disease —*Jour. Amer. Med. Assoc.*⟩ **c :** RESISTANT — usu. used with *to* ⟨this subject is ~ both to observation and to experiment —G.G.Simpson⟩ ⟨nothing perhaps is more ~ to logical systematization than local custom —G.H.Sabine⟩ **syn** see UNRULY

²recalcitrant \"\ *n* -S **:** one who is recalcitrant

re·cal·ci·trate \-sə,trāt, *usu* -ād·+V\ *vi* -ED/-ING/-S [L *recalcitratus*, past part. of *recalcitrare* to kick back] **1 :** to kick back **2 :** to protest or resist vigorously **:** show stubborn opposition

re·cal·ci·tra·tion \=,==ˈtrāshən\ *n* -S [*recalcitrate* + *-ion*] **:** a kicking back or against something **:** OPPOSITION, REPUGNANCE, REFRACTORINESS

re·calculate \(')rē+\ *vt* [*re-* + *calculate*] **:** to calculate or estimate again esp. in order to discover the source of an error or formulate new conclusions ⟨*recalculated* their data and tried to explain the unexpected force of the big blast —*Time*⟩ ⟨requires that the United States ~ our own risks and reconsider the possible alternatives —Herbert Hoover⟩

re·calculation \¦rē+\ *n* **:** an act or process of recalculating

re·ca·les·cence \,rēkə'lesᵊn(t)s\ *n* -S [L *recalescere* to grow warm again (fr. *re-* + *calescere* to grow warm, incho. of *calēre* to be warm) + E *-ence* — more at LEE] **:** the increase in temperature when the rate of heat liberation during transformation exceeds the rate of heat dissipation while cooling metal through a transformation range — compare DECALESCENCE

re·ca·les·cent \¦==ˈlesᵊnt\ *adj* [prob. back-formation fr. *recalescence*] **:** of, relating to, or marked by recalescence

¹re·call \rə'kȯl, rē'-\ *vt* [*re-* + *call*] **1 a :** to call back **:** summon or cause to return ⟨was ~*ed* from abroad to report to the government⟩ ⟨was ~*ed* to active service⟩ ⟨other automotive divisions will ~ their hourly workers —*Sacramento (Calif.) Bee*⟩ ⟨is thought that his soul has quitted his body and must be ~*ed* —J.G.Frazer⟩ **b :** to call or bring back the thought or memory of ⟨the sight of the streets thronged with buyers . . . ~*ed* to me the purpose of my journey —James Joyce⟩ ⟨knowledge of an event or fact which the sign ~*s* —Edward Clodd⟩ **c :** to remind one of **:** exhibit a resemblance to ⟨look with suspicion upon anything that might savor of economic exploitation or ~ old imperialist ideas —Arthur Rucker⟩ ⟨the rectangular, four-story mass of unusually high proportions ~*s* numerous courthouse designs of the period —*Amer. Guide Series: N.Y.*⟩ **d :** RECOLLECT ⟨seem always to ~ him in his brown velvet smock —Osbert Sitwell⟩ ⟨~*ing* the emotions and events and spectacles which have come to a man with the years —P.E.More⟩ **2 :** to annul by taking back ⟨past sentence may not be ~*ed* —Shak.⟩ **3 :** to cause to exist again **:** RESTORE ⟨beauty . . . whose season was, and cannot be ~*ed* —William Wordsworth⟩ **4 :** to bring back to consciousness or awareness **:** REVIVE ⟨trying to ~ her stunned senses —George Meredith⟩ ⟨stared and ~*ed* himself and was ashamed —Pearl Buck⟩ **syn** see REMEMBER, REVOKE

²re·call \'rē,kȯl, rə'k-, rē'k-\ *n* **1 a :** the act or an instance of calling back **:** a summons to return from or to a position, situation, or place ⟨the ~ of an ambassador from his post⟩ ⟨the ~ of a reserve officer to active duty⟩ ⟨announced the ~ of 500 workers after a 2-week layoff⟩ **b** (1) **:** a signal (as a bugle call) summoning soldiers back (as to ranks or camp) or indicating the end of a drill or work period (2) **:** a signal calling a boat back to a ship **c :** the right or procedure by which a legislative, judicial, or executive official may be removed from office before the end of his term by a vote of the people to be taken on the filing of a petition signed by a required number (as 25 percent) of qualified voters ⟨nearly one third of the states allow the ~ to be used by all cities —J.E. Pate⟩ ⟨~ election⟩ **2 :** remembrance of what has been previously learned or experienced **:** REPRODUCTION, REVIVAL — compare RECOGNITION ⟨mere ~ of past memories without integrating them in terms of current reality is ineffective —M.H.Erickson⟩ ⟨could remember strange streets, bays, oceans, harbors, countrysides with almost total visual ~ —Henry Wallace⟩ **3 :** the act of revoking or the possibility of being revoked ⟨the war is completed — the price is paid — the title is settled beyond ~ —Walt Whitman⟩ ⟨this is a matter past ~ —Robert Browning⟩

re·call·able \rə'kȯləbəl\ *adj* **:** capable of being recalled

recall dose *n* **:** BOOSTER 10a

re·call·ment \-lmənt\ *n* -S [*¹recall* + *-ment*] **:** RECALL

ré·ca·mier \,rākə'myā\ *n* -S *often cap* [after Mme. J. F. J. A. *Récamier* †1849 Fr. society beauty and wit] **:** a moderate pink to strong yellowish pink

re·cant \rə'kant, rē'-, -kaa(ə)nt\ *vb* -ED/-ING/-S [L *recantare*, fr. *re-* + *cantare* to sing — more at CHANT] *vt* **1 a :** to withdraw or repudiate (a statement or belief) formally and publicly ⟨~ all opinions which differed from those proclaimed by the central leadership —P.E.Mosely⟩ **b :** to make renunciation of (a course of action) ⟨didn't show up . . . to ~ his sins —*Time*⟩ **2 :** RETRACT, REVOKE ⟨do this or else I do ~ the pardon —Shak.⟩ **~** *vi* **:** to take back or disavow an opinion, declaration, or course of action **:** make an open confession of error ⟨never hesitates to ~ whenever the progress of his thinking has brought about what he considers an improvement upon his former views —André Martinet⟩ **syn** see ABJURE

re·can·ta·tion \,rē,kan-'tāshən, -kaan-\ *n* -S [*recant* + *-ation*] **:** the act or an instance of recanting **:** public confession of error **:** RETRACTION ⟨~*s* among those who had opposed him —Waldemar Kaempffert⟩

re·cant·er \rə'kantə(r)\ *n* -S **:** one that recants

¹re·cap \(')rē¦kap\ *vt* [*re-* + *cap*] **1 :** to cap again **:** put a new cap on **2 :** to cement, mold, and vulcanize a strip of camelback upon the buffed and roughened surface of the tread of (a worn pneumatic tire) — distinguished from *retread*

²recap \'rē,kap\ *n* **:** a recapped tire

³recap \"\ *vt* [by shortening] **:** RECAPITULATE

⁴recap \"\ *n* [by shortening] **:** RECAPITULATION

re·cap·i·tal·iza·tion \¦rē,kapəd·ᵊlə¦zāshən\ *n* [*recapitalize* + *-ation*] **:** a revision of the capital structure of a corporation commonly effected by amendment of the charter or merger with a subsidiary

re·capitalize \(')rē+\ *vt* [*re-* + *capitalize*] **:** to capitalize again **:** change the capital structure of

re·ca·pit·u·late \,rēkə'pichə,lāt, *usu* -ād·+V\ *vb* [LL *recapitulatus*, past part. of *recapitulare* to sum up, restate by heads, fr. L *re-* + LL *capitulare* (fr. *capitulum* division of a book, heading) — more at CHAPTER] *vt* **1 a :** to repeat the principal points of **:** restate briefly **:** give a summary of ⟨~ . . . the whole situation as I see it —J.C.Powys⟩ ⟨a host of writers have attempted to define addiction and there is no point in *recapitulating* here the history of those attempts —D.W. Maurer & V.H.Vogel⟩ **b :** to repeat the principal stages or phases of ⟨adopted the theory that the child ~*s* primitive experience —H.J.Muller⟩ ⟨the individual organism ~*s* the history of its race —S.F.Mason⟩ **2 :** UNITE ⟨to ~ ourselves, to assemble and muster ourselves —John Donne⟩ **~** *vi* **:** to sum up **:** go back over an argument or discussion ⟨now that I ~ he was correct with less than one percent error —*New Republic*⟩

re·ca·pit·u·la·tion \,==,==ˈlāshən\ *n* [ME *recapitulacion*, fr. MF or LL; MF *recapitulation*, fr. LL *recapitulation-*, *recapitulatio*, fr. *recapitulatus* + *-ion-*, *-io* -ion] **1 a :** the act of recapitulating **:** a summing up ⟨the third and very important contribution to a successful daytime serial is the announcer's ~ of what went on yesterday —Goodman Ace⟩ **b :** the process by which according to Irenaeus the Logos passed through all phases of human experience thus reversing the evil caused by sin and winning complete salvation for man **2 :** the supposed repetition in the development of the individual of its phylogenetic history — see RECAPITULATION THEORY **3 :** the third section of a musical movement in sonata form consisting of a usu. modified repetition of the exposition and typically followed by a coda

re·ca·pit·u·la·tion·ist \-sh(ə)nəst\ *n* -S **:** one who accepts the recapitulation theory

recapitulation theory *n* **:** a theory in biology: an organism passes through successive stages resembling the series of ancestral types from which it has descended so that the ontogeny of the individual is a recapitulation of the phylogeny of its group — compare BIOGENESIS 2, PALINGENESIS, VON BAER'S LAW

re·ca·pit·u·la·tive \,==ˈpichə,lād·|iv, -āt|, |ēv *also* |əv\ *adj* [*recapitulate* + *-ive*] **:** of, relating to, or characterized by recapitulation — **re·ca·pit·u·la·tive·ly** \|əvlē\ *adv*

re·ca·pit·u·la·to·ry \,==ˈpichələ,tōrē, -tȯr-, -ri\ *adj* [*recapitulate* + *-ory*] **:** of, relating to, or marked by recapitulation ⟨the apparent ~ relationship between growth stages and adults —G.F.Elliott⟩

re·cap·pa·ble \(')rē¦kapəbəl\ *adj* [*³recap* + *-able*] **:** capable of being recapped

re·cap·per \-pə(r)\ *n* **:** one that recaps

re·cap·tion \rə'kapshən\ *n* [*re-* + L *caption-*, *captio* act of taking, seizing — more at CAPTION] **:** the act of retaking; *specif* **:** the peaceable retaking of one's own goods, chattels, wife, or children from one who has taken and wrongfully detains them

re·cap·tor \-ptə(r)\ *n* [*re-* + L *captus* (past part. of *capere* to take, capture) + E *-or* — more at HEAVE] **1 :** one that recaptures; *specif* **:** one that takes a prize at sea that had been previously taken **2 :** one that recovers (something) by recaption

¹re·capture \(')rē+\ *n* [*re-* + *capture*, n.] **1 a** (1) **:** the act of retaking or the fact of being retaken **:** RECOVERY ⟨the ~ of three fourths of the lake shore, which had fallen completely into private ownership —Harland Bartholomew⟩ ⟨the development of new markets and ~ of former markets —W.M. Blair⟩ (2) **:** the retaking of a prize or goods usu. thereby under international law devesting the property acquired in captured booty or prize — compare POSTLIMINIUM **b :** a governmental seizure under law of earnings or profits beyond a fixed amount **c :** a capture that completes an even exchange in chess **2 :** something that is captured again

²recapture \"\ *vt* [*re-* + *capture*, vb.] **1 a :** to capture again ⟨*recaptured* the hill they had lost the day before⟩ ⟨informal history that ~*s* much of the flavor of a composite society —W.H.Stephenson⟩ **b :** to experience again **:** RECOVER ⟨by no effort of the imagination could she ~ the ecstasy —Ellen Glasgow⟩ ⟨~ the past⟩ **2 :** to take by law or through negotiations under law ⟨a portion of earnings or profits above a fixed amount⟩ — **re·cap·tur·er** \"+ə(r)\ *n* -S

re·carbonize \"+\ *vt* [*re-* + *carbonize*] **:** to carbonize again

re·carburization \(¦)rē+\ *n* **:** the process of recarburizing

re·carburize \(')rē+\ *vt* [*re-* + *carburize*] **:** to carburize again

re·car·bu·riz·er \(')rē¦kärbyə,rīzə(r)\ *n* [*recarburize* + *-er*] **:** a recarburizing agent (as spiegeleisen or anthracite coal)

re·case \(')rē+\ *vt* [*re-* + *case*] **:** to put the original or another cover on (a book separated from its cover) without changing the construction of the leaves

¹re·cast \(')rē'kast, -kaa(ə)st, -kaist, -kȧst\ *vb* [*re-* + *cast*] *vt* **1 :** to throw again; *esp* **:** to make a second cast of (a fishline) **2 a :** to put into a mold again **:** REMOLD ⟨many hypothetical questions can be ~ into a factual mold —S.L.Payne⟩ **b :** to give a different form or quality to **:** REFASHION, REMODEL ⟨we have only to alter slightly, not to ~, the standards by which we have judged —Virginia Woolf⟩ ⟨all our notions of relative velocity must be ~ —A.N.Whitehead⟩ ⟨~ the poem⟩ **3 :** to compute again **:** RECALCULATE ⟨descended to the store cellars, ~*ing* the inventory of their supplies —A.J.Cronin⟩ **4 :** to provide a new set of performers for ⟨the opera has been almost completely ~⟩ **~** *vi* **:** to cast again; *esp* **:** to make a second cast in fishing — **re·cast·er** \-tə(r)\ *n*

²recast \'=,=\ *n* **1 :** the act or an instance of recasting **2 :** a product of recasting **:** a new form of something

rec·ce \'rekē\ *also* **rec·co** \-e(,)kō\ *or* **rec·cy** \-ekē\ *n, pl* **recces** *also* **reccos** *or* **reccies** [by shortening and alter.] **:** RECONNAISSANCE ⟨rain . . . prevented a plane ~ of the blocked river —*Jour. of the Royal Central Asian Society*⟩

recd *abbr* received

¹re·cede \rə'sēd, rē'-\ *vi* [L *recedere* to go back, withdraw, fr. *re-* + *cedere* to go — more at CEDE] **1** *archaic* **:** DIFFER, VARY — usu. used with *from* **2 :** to go away **:** DEPART ⟨watched the August days ~ —Francis Russell⟩ ⟨had drooped in his chair after dinner, and the accumulation of ninety years had *receded* abruptly into history —Victoria Sackville-West⟩ **3 a :** to move back or away **:** fall or draw back to a more distant line or position **:** WITHDRAW ⟨the tide, having risen to its highest, was *receding* —Arnold Bennett⟩ ⟨a hairline *receding* almost visibly —Leslie Waller⟩ ⟨far too self-willed to ~ from a position —Thomas Hardy⟩ **b** (1) **:** to extend farther back **:** lie more remote ⟨south of the town the river not only spreads out, but the hills ~ —Sherwood Anderson⟩ (2) **:** to slant backward ⟨a *receding* forehead⟩ **4 a :** to withdraw wholly (as from an agreement or promise) ⟨once he had given his word, he could not ~⟩ ⟨*receded* from the bargain he had made⟩ **b :** to deviate in some degree (as from a principle, belief, position) ⟨a height of devotion to human liberties from which she has never *receded* —F.A.Ogg & Harold Zink⟩ ⟨define a position from which he never *receded* —Stanislaus Joyce⟩ **c :** to withdraw opposition to an amendment passed by the other house of a bicameral legislature **5 a :** to grow less **:** CONTRACT, DIMINISH, SHRINK ⟨some feared that employment might ~ to as few as 14,000 employees —*N.Y. Times*⟩ ⟨colleges will ~ in their public importance —R.W.Emerson⟩ **b :** to fall to a lower level **:** DECLINE ⟨demand in general eased and prices *receded* for practically all types of skins —*Farmer's Weekly (So. Africa)*⟩ **6** *of a color* **:** to seem to go away from the viewer ⟨light colors ~⟩ — contrasted with *advance*

syn RETREAT, RETROGRADE, RETRACT, BACK: RECEDE is applied to withdrawing or going backward, sometimes slowly and gradually, from some fixed or definite forward or high point or position ⟨the flood waters *receded*⟩ ⟨the frontier soon *receded* before the ax and plow —*Amer. Guide Series: Texas*⟩ ⟨west coast lay opinion *receded* somewhat from its previous intransigent attitude —*Americana Annual*⟩ RETREAT often applies to a drawing back or withdrawing induced by uncertainty, danger, fear, or superior opposing force or other agency exciting pressure ⟨the outnumbered troops *retreated* before the enemy⟩ ⟨have been forced to *retreat*, for the earliest tabulations produced patterns too complex to be handled or understood —W.O.Aydelotte⟩ ⟨educational theory and practice have *retreated* into cultural parochialism —Douglas Bush⟩ RETROGRADE applies to movement backward in contrast to expected forward movement, to reversion or going backward rather than progressing ⟨where one man advances, hundreds *retrograde* —T.L.Peacock⟩ ⟨he had progressed, and he could never, by any possibility, afford to *retrograde* —P.B.Kyne⟩ RETRACT indicates a drawing backward or inward from an outer, exposed, prominent, or more apparent position ⟨a cat *retracting* its claws⟩ ⟨*retracted* the platoons on the left flank⟩ BACK may refer to any backward or reversed motion or, esp. with *down*, to a receding or retreating ⟨*back* a car⟩ ⟨water *backing* up in the pipes⟩ ⟨*back* down and accept defeat⟩

2re·cede \(ˈ)rē+\ *vt* [*re-* + *cede*] **:** to cede back **:** grant or yield again to a former possessor

re·ced·ence \rəˈsēdᵊn(t)s\ *n* -S [1*recede* + *-ence*] **:** RECESSION

re·ced·er \rəˈsēdə(r)\ *n* -S **:** one that recedes; *specif* **:** a device in a sawmill for making the knees of the headblocks recede a sufficient distance to take on another log when the last board of the previous log has dropped

receding color *n* **:** any of various colors (as greens, blues, violets, and their variations) that tend to appear farther from the eye than other colors lying in the same plane

1re·ceipt \rəˈsēt, rēˈ-, *usu* -sēd·+V\ *n* -S [ME *receite*, fr. ONF, fr. ML *recepta* (sing.), prob. fr. L *recepta*, neut. pl. of *receptus*, past part. of *recipere* to receive, take] **1 a :** RECIPE ⟨a very special kind of mince pie she had been trying a new ~ on —Esther Forbes⟩ ⟨a perfect man, as the baronet trusted to make this one son of his, after a ~ of his own —George Meredith⟩ **b :** something that serves as a cure or remedy ⟨the newest ~ for avoiding calumny —R.B.Sheridan⟩ **2 a** *obs* **:** a place for receiving or storing something **:** RECEPTACLE **b :** a place at which money is officially received **:** a revenue office esp. formerly in England ⟨a man . . . sitting at the ~ of custom —Mt 9:9 (AV)⟩ **3 :** the act or process of receiving ⟨in ~ of a salary which he had earned —O.S.J.Gogarty⟩ ⟨ports equipped for the ~ of large vessels —L.D.Stamp⟩ **4 :** something (as food, goods, money) that is received — usu. used in pl. ⟨ranks about tenth in the United States in volume of fresh fruit and vegetable ~*s* —*Calif. Agric. Bull.*⟩ ⟨improve the harbor to accommodate larger raw material ~*s* —*Steel Facts*⟩ ⟨took the day's ~*s* to the bank's night depository —J.C. Furnas⟩ **5 :** a writing acknowledging the taking or receiving of goods or money delivered or paid ⟨could offer only poor paper money or ~*s* to pay for it —F.V.W.Mason⟩ ⟨paid the bill in cash and was given a ~⟩

2receipt \"\ *vb* -ED/-ING/-S *vt* **1 :** to give a receipt for or acknowledge the receipt of ⟨the radio officer ~*ed* the message and took a copy of it up to the bridge —R.F.Mirvish⟩ **2 :** to mark paid ⟨had paid by check, and the ~*ed* bill had been returned to him on the following day —F.W.Crofts⟩ ~ *vi* **:** to give a receipt — used with *for* ⟨an officer of the receiving side would ~ for each lot —*Newsweek*⟩

receipt book *n* **1 :** a book containing recipes **2 :** a book containing forms to be used in giving receipts for payment of money

re·ceipt·or \-sēd·ə(r)\ *n* -S [2*receipt* + *-or*] **:** one that receipts for property taken by a sheriff and agrees to return it upon demand

re·ceiv·abil·i·ty \rəˌsēvəˈbiləd·ē\ *n* **:** the quality or state of being receivable

re·ceiv·able \rəˈsēvəbəl, rēˈ-\ *adj* [*receive* + *-able*] **1 :** capable of being received ⟨a broadcast ~ over a wide area⟩; *specif* **:** legally admissible or acceptable ⟨~ testimony⟩ ⟨~ evidence⟩ ⟨~ certificates⟩ **2 :** subject to a call or claim for payment ⟨accounts ~⟩ ⟨notes ~⟩

re·ceiv·ables \-lz\ *n pl* **:** accounts, accepted bills, or notes created in the course of business that are due from others or will become due at an assignable date ⟨retail department stores, where the ~ are high in volume —R.M.Trueblood & R.M.Cyert⟩

re·ceiv·al \rəˈsēvəl\ *n* -S [*receive* + *-al*] **:** RECEIPT 3

re·ceive \rəˈsēv, rēˈ-\ *vb* -ED/-ING/-S [ME *receiven*, fr. ONF *receivre*, fr. L *recipere* to take back, take, accept, receive, fr. *re-* + *-cipere* (fr. *capere* to take) — more at HEAVE] *vt* **1 a** (1) **:** to take possession or delivery of ⟨~ a gift⟩ ⟨~ a letter⟩ (2) **:** to knowingly accept (stolen goods) ⟨suspected of *receiving* the stolen jewels⟩ **b :** to give attention to **:** listen to ⟨~ his confession⟩ ⟨refused to ~ advice from his friends⟩ **2 a :** to take in **:** act as a receptacle or container for ⟨a great interior lake *received* this young giant among rivers —Tom Marvel⟩ **b :** to take in through the mind or senses ⟨any young, active mind that was ready to ~ ideas —M.R.Cohen⟩ ⟨at an age when he was most ready to ~ new impressions⟩ **c :** CONTAIN, HOLD ⟨too small to ~ the burnt offering —1 Kings 8:64 (RSV)⟩ **3 a :** to give accommodation, protection, or refuge to **:** HARBOR ⟨go back to a husband who was still ready to ~ her —*Atlantic*⟩ **b** *of a female mammal* **:** ACCEPT 8 **4 a :** to admit or accept in some character or capacity ⟨*received* him as a colleague⟩ ⟨would not ~ her as his son's wife⟩ **b :** to admit to a place, faith, group, or condition ⟨they were *received* both at the tribal fire and at the trading post —*Amer. Guide Series: Minn.*⟩ ⟨having shortly before abandoned his skepticism and been *received* into the Catholic faith —H.W. H.Knott⟩ **5 a :** to welcome on arrival **:** GREET ⟨the small lady who *received* them at his house —William Black⟩ **b :** to give a formal and official welcome to ⟨shall ~ ambassadors and other public ministers —*U. S. Constitution*⟩ **c :** to greet or react to in a specified manner ⟨began his first concert tour, on which he was well *received* —*Current Biog.*⟩ ⟨the academic world *received* it with hostility —Max Lerner⟩ **6 a :** to acquiesce in or submit to **:** endure willingly ⟨couldn't unquestioningly ~ acceptance by these white patients —F.A.Perry⟩ **b :** to support the weight or pressure of **:** BEAR ⟨~*s* the weight of the world on his shoulders⟩ **c :** to take (a mark or impression) from the weight or pressure of something ⟨the ground was too hard to ~ a footprint⟩ ⟨his tenderer cheek ~*s* her soft hand's print —Shak.⟩ **d :** to undergo the impact of or interrupt the course of **:** CATCH, INTERCEPT ⟨get their full share of light, *receiving* the cooler level rays of the rising and setting sun —Andrew Young⟩ ⟨available to ~ the discharge of such emotions —R.M.Weaver⟩ **7 a :** to come into possession of **:** ACQUIRE ⟨*received* his early education in the public schools⟩ ⟨*received* his medical training abroad⟩ **b :** to meet with **:** EXPERIENCE ⟨a book that has never *received* the attention it deserves⟩ ⟨has *received* love and understanding from those around him⟩ **c :** to be exposed or subjected to **:** SUFFER ⟨*received* the royal displeasure on one occasion —Harvey Graham⟩ **d :** to be hurt or damaged by (a specified blow or injury) ⟨*received* a mortal wound⟩ ⟨*received* a broken nose⟩ **e :** to be placed under the burden, charge, or constraint of **:** be made subject to ⟨*received* a heavy sentence from the judge⟩ ⟨*received* written orders from the commanding general⟩ ⟨*received* a subpoena⟩ **8 a :** to partake of (the eucharistic sacrament) **b :** to take in at the mouth ⟨for fear of opening my lips and *receiving* the bad air —Shak.⟩ ⟨~ nourishment⟩ **9 a :** to accept as true or valid **:** recognize as authoritative **:** BELIEVE ⟨attacked *received* theological and philosophical opinion on the nature of the universe —*Brit. Book News*⟩ ⟨the material theory of heat, the idea of caloric, which was generally *received* until the 1850's —S.F.Mason⟩ **b :** to admit as evidence ⟨no objection to the ice pick being *received* in evidence —Erle Stanley Gardner⟩ ~ *vi* **1 :** to be a recipient ⟨more blessed to give than to ~ —Acts 20:35 (AV)⟩ **2 :** to take the eucharistic sacrament **:** take Communion **3 :** to be at home to visitors ⟨she ~*s* on Tuesdays⟩ **4 :** to catch pitched balls in a baseball game ⟨worked hard on his *receiving* —Lou Boudreau⟩ **5 :** to convert incoming radio waves into perceptible signals

syn ACCEPT, ADMIT, TAKE: although RECEIVE can sometimes suggest a positive welcoming or recognition ⟨*receive* the group with open arms⟩ ⟨the work has been *received* with enthusiasm —*Current Biog.*⟩ it usu. implies that something comes or is allowed to come into one's presence, possession, group, consciousness, or substance while one is passive ⟨*receive* military instruction⟩ ⟨*receive* a gift⟩ ⟨be *received* into the church⟩ ACCEPT adds to this the notion of positive acquiescence or consent even though tacit ⟨*accept* a gift⟩ ⟨*accept* an appointment⟩ ⟨*accept* an apology⟩ ⟨*accept* a new member into a club⟩ ADMIT suggests permission given or sufferance granted to come or enter ⟨*admit* an ambassador into one's presence⟩ ⟨*admit* new members into a club⟩ ⟨a door wide enough to *admit* a small car⟩ TAKE carries the notion of accepting or, more commonly, of making no positive protest against receiving, often of almost welcoming on principle, something offered, conferred, or inflicted ⟨*take* a plate when it is passed to you⟩ ⟨*take* advice in good spirit⟩ ⟨*take* a good deal of punishment before protesting⟩

received pronunciation *n, usu cap R & P* **:** the pronunciation of Received Standard

received standard *n, usu cap R&S* **:** the form of English spoken at the English public schools, at the universities of Oxford and Cambridge, at the English court, and by many educated Englishmen elsewhere

re·ceiv·er \-və(r)\ *n* -S [ME *receyvour*, *receivere*, fr. (assumed) ONF *receivour*, fr. *receivre* to receive + *-our* -er] **1 :** one that receives ⟨the sense of touch, not ordinarily a ~ of information originating at a distance —F.A.Geldard⟩ ⟨threw a long forward pass into the arms of a waiting ~⟩ **2 :** one that receives on behalf of others: as **a :** a person appointed to receive money due **:** TREASURER **b** (1) **:** a person appointed usu. by a court of equity jurisdiction to receive and conserve property that is the subject of litigation, to administer it under the supervision of the court as its agent, and to apply, manage, and dispose of it in accordance with the orders and decrees of the court until the final determination of the litigation (2) **:** a person appointed under a statute by an administrative public officer to wind up the affairs of a business (as a bank, railroad, or insurance company) involving a public interest in case of dissolution or insolvency or to manage under the direction of a court a corporation financially embarrassed during a period of reorganization in an effort to avoid bankruptcy (3) **:** a person appointed by a court under British statute to receive the income of those incompetent to manage their affairs (4) **:** a person appointed by a court under British statute to conserve the property of an alleged bankrupt until it can be determined whether he is a bankrupt (5) **:** a person appointed under British statute by a mortgagee or other holder of security in accordance with the terms of the mortgage or security agreement to take possession of the security and apply it in satisfaction of the indebtedness in accordance with the statute and agreement **3 :** one who knowingly takes or buys stolen goods from a thief **:** FENCE 4a **4 :** something that acts as a receptacle or container: as **a :** the bell jar of an air pump **b :** a vessel used to store a product (as steam or air) for later use **c** (1) **:** the metal frame in which the action of a firearm is fitted and to which the breech end of the barrel is attached (2) **:** the main body of the lock in a breech mechanism **d** (1) **:** a vessel or tube for use esp. with a condenser or retort to collect and sometimes to condense the product of distillation (2) **:** a vessel to receive and contain gases **5 :** one that receives electric currents or waves: as **a :** RECEIVING SET **b :** the portion of a telegraphic or telephonic apparatus by which the electric currents or waves are converted into visible or audible signals

receiver general *n, pl* **receivers general** [ME *receyvour general*, fr. *receyvour* receiver + *general*, adj.] **:** a public officer in general charge of receipts ⟨*receiver general* of Massachusetts⟩

receiver ring *n* **:** the threaded ringlike portion of the forward end of the receiver of a rifle into which the breech end of the barrel is fitted

receiver's certificate *n* **:** a promise to repay to a lender a definite sum loaned and an acknowledgment thereof made by a receiver under order of court to obtain funds for the preservation of the assets held by him (as for operating a railroad) and often made by the court a first lien upon the receivership assets

re·ceiv·er·ship \-(r),ship\ *n* [ME *receyvourship*, fr. *receyvour* + *-ship*] **1 :** the office or function of a receiver appointed by a court or under a statute **2 :** the state or condition of being in the hands of a receiver ⟨put a corporation into ~⟩

receives *pres 3d sing of* RECEIVE

receiving *pres part of* RECEIVE

receiving barn *n* **:** a supervised barn into which racehorses are checked several hours before saddling to prevent their being doped

receiving blanket *n* **:** a small lightweight blanket used to wrap an infant (as after bathing)

receiving clerk *n* **:** one who takes charge of the receipt of goods shipped to a business concern

receiving gauge *n* **:** a gauge that has an inside measuring surface for testing the size and contour of a male part

receiving order *n, Brit* **:** an order made by a bankruptcy court appointing a receiver for a bankrupt's estate

receiving set *n* **:** an apparatus for receiving radio or television signals and broadcasts

receiving ship *n* **:** a usu. obsolete or unseaworthy ship moored at a navy yard and used for new recruits or men in transit between stations

receiving yard *n* **:** a railroad yard where freight trains are received — compare CLASSIFICATION YARD, DEPARTURE TRACK

re·cen·cy \ˈrēsᵊnsē, -nsi\ *n* -ES [fr. *recent* + *-cy*] **:** the quality or state of being recent ⟨the eagerness of the people for ~ in their news —F.L.Mott⟩

re·cense \rəˈsen(t)s, rēˈ-\ *vt* -ED/-ING/-S [L *recensēre* to review, revise] **:** to make a recension of

re·cen·sion \-nchən\ *n* -S [L *recension-*, *recensio*, fr. *recensēre* to review, revise (fr. *re-* + *censēre* to assess, tax, estimate) + *-ion-*, *-io* -ion — more at CENSOR] **1 :** REVIEW, SURVEY ⟨some 30 pages are devoted in each issue to a review of reviews on philosophy and theology . . . this ~ may prove of special use —*Times Lit. Supp.*⟩ **2 a :** a revising of a text (as of an ancient author) by an editor; *esp* **:** critical revision with intent to establish a definitive text ⟨did pioneer work in the ~ of newly discovered manuscripts⟩ **b :** a version of a text established by critical revision ⟨has come down to us in various ~*s* —R.L. Ramsay⟩ **3 :** a revised form of something ⟨started a vogue for sophisticated ~*s* of ancient myths —Paul Pickrel⟩

re·cent \ˈrēsᵊnt\ *adj, sometimes* -ER/-EST [MF or L; MF *recent*, fr. L *recent-*, *recens* fresh, recent; akin to Gk *kainos* new, Skt *kanīna* young] **1 a :** of or belonging to the present period or the very near past ⟨~ alumni⟩ ⟨~ leaders⟩ ⟨the ~ election⟩ ⟨the ~ storm⟩ **b :** having lately come into existence **:** just made or formed **:** NEW ⟨~ buds on the peach trees⟩ ⟨pride ourselves on our ~ transcontinental highways —R.W.Murray⟩ ⟨almost before the ~ ink is dry —John Keats⟩ **c :** newly arrived ⟨~ from the roar of foreign foam —A.C.Swinburne⟩ **2 :** of or belonging to a period of time relatively near **:** not remote ⟨in more ~ times the Romans formed a great camp here —J.K.Jerome⟩ ⟨is only of ~ origin, and was wholly unknown in old times —Herman Melville⟩ **3** *usu cap* **:** of or relating to the present or existing epoch which is dated from the close of the Pleistocene **:** DILUVIAL 3, HOLOCENE — see GEOLOGIC TIME table — **re·cent·ly** *adv* — **re·cent·ness** *n* -ES

re·cept \ˈrē,sept\ *n* -S [*re-* + *-cept* (as in *concept*, *percept*)] **:** a mental image or idea formed by repeated exposure to a particular stimulus or class of stimuli

re·cep·ta·cle \rəˈseptəkəl, rēˈ-, -tēk-\ *n* -S [L *receptaculum*, fr. *receptare* (iterative of *recipere* to receive) + *-culum*, suffix denoting an instrument — more at RECEIVE] **1 :** one that receives and contains something **:** CONTAINER, REPOSITORY ⟨a metal ~ to catch the sap —Hamilton Basso⟩ ⟨the poet's mind is in fact a ~ for seizing and storing up numberless feelings —T.S.Eliot⟩ **2 :** a place of shelter ⟨palatial gloomy chambers for parade . . . never constructed as ~*s* —Robert Browning⟩ **3 a :** an intercellular cavity containing oil, resin, or other secretion products **b :** the end of the flower stalk upon which the floral organs are borne and which is often somewhat enlarged (as in the composites) — called also *torus* **c :** an organized often stalked structure in a cryptogamous plant containing reproductive bodies **:** a modified branch bearing sporangia: as (1) **:** a swollen tip of a thallus branch of a seaweed (as of the genus *Fucus*) (2) **:** any of various envelopes or structures supporting the fructification of a fungus (3) **:** an umbrella-shaped outgrowth of the thallus of various liverworts (as of the genus *Marchantia*) that bears the sex organs **:** CUPULE (4) **:** PLACENTA 2b **4 :** a permanently mounted female electrical fitting that contains the live parts of the circuit

re·cep·tac·u·lar \ˌrē,sepˌtakyələ(r)\ *adj* [NL *receptaculum* + E *-ar*] **:** of, relating to, or developing from the receptacle of a plant

re·cep·ta·cu·li·da \rə,septəˈkyüləda\ *n pl, cap* [NL, fr. *receptaculum* + *-ida*] **:** a class of calcareous fossils of uncertain systematic relations — see RECEPTACULITIDAE

re·cep·tac·u·li·tes \,rēsep,takyəˈlīd·(,)ēz\ *n, cap* [NL, fr. *receptaculum* + *-ites*] **:** a genus (the type of the family Receptaculitidae) of Ordovician and Devonian calcareous fossils consisting of closely spaced plates or pillars that form a globose or discoidal mass — see SUNFLOWER CORAL

re·cep·tac·u·li·tid \-d·əd\ *n* -S [NL *Receptaculidae*] **:** a fossil of the family Receptaculitidae

re·cep·tac·u·lit·i·dae \,==,==ˈlid·ə,dē\ *n pl, cap* [NL, fr. *Receptaculites*, type genus + *-idae*] **:** a family of calcareous fossils sometimes placed in the Hyalospongiae but usu. set apart as the class Receptaculida — see RECEPTACULITES

re·cep·tac·u·lum \,rē,sepˈtakyələm\ *n, pl* **receptacu·la** \-lə\ [NL, fr. L — more at RECEPTACLE] **:** RECEPTACLE 3

receptaculum chy·li \-ˈkī,lī\ *n* [NL, lit., receptacle of the chyle] **:** CISTERNA CHYLI

re·cep·ti·bil·i·ty \rə,septəˈbiləd·ē\ *n* -ES **:** the quality or state of being receptible

re·cep·ti·ble \rəˈseptəbəl, rēˈ-\ *adj* [LL *receptibilis* recoverable, fr. L *receptus* + *-ibilis* -ible] **:** capable of receiving or of being received

re·cep·tion \rəˈsepshən, rēˈ-\ *n* -S [ME *recepcion*, fr. MF or L; MF *reception*, fr. L *reception-*, *receptio*, fr. *receptus* (past part. of *recipere* to take back, receive) + *-ion-*, *-io* -ion — more at RECEIVE] **1 :** the act or action of receiving in place or position ⟨the native soil . . . is boxed out for the ~ of the pavement —John Kemp⟩ ⟨clearing away a space at the top for the ~ of a small piece of butter —T.L.Peacock⟩ **2 :** the act or action of taking possession or getting **:** RECEIPT ⟨the ~ of significant amounts of American capital —A.B.Lans⟩ **3 a :** the act or action of taking in or giving shelter to **:** HARBORING ⟨make ready for the ~ of ten thousand sheep —Rachel Henning⟩ ⟨the ~ of outlaws —F.M.Stenton⟩ **b :** the state or fact of being admitted or given shelter **:** ADMISSION ⟨my ~ into grace —John Milton⟩ ⟨his ~ into the church⟩ **4 a :** REACTION, RESPONSE ⟨met with an unfriendly ~ from the critics⟩ ⟨the play received a mixed ~⟩ **b :** the act or action of giving assent, approval, or recognition ⟨a world ready for the ~ of new ideas⟩ ⟨~ of a point of view other than their own —J.D.Adams⟩ **5 a :** the act of greeting or welcoming ⟨gave a cordial ~ to her guest⟩ ⟨received an enthusiastic ~ from the crowds lining the streets⟩ **b :** a social gathering often for the purpose of extending a ceremonious or formal welcome ⟨an afternoon ~ for the new members of the staff⟩ **6 a :** mental apprehension ⟨has very weak powers of ~ and is slow to understand anything⟩ **b :** the process by which a stimulus affects a sensory end organ by means of real but usu. minute and transitory physical or chemical alteration of the end organ **7 :** the receiving of a radio or television broadcast ⟨a fringe area where ~ is poor⟩

reception center *n* **:** a place where persons (as agricultural workers or military recruits) are assembled and processed

re·cep·tion·ism \-shə,nizəm\ *n* -S [*reception* + *-ism*] **:** the view that in the Communion the bread and wine remain as such but that with them the faithful communicant receives the body and blood of Christ

re·cep·tion·ist \-shənəst\ *n* -S [*reception* + *-ist*] **1 :** one who believes in the doctrine of receptionism **2 :** one who is employed in a business or professional establishment to greet and help visitors, business callers, or patients

reception room *n* **:** a room for the formal reception of visitors (as in a place of business or an institution)

re·cep·tive \rəˈseptiv, rēˈ-, -tēv *also* -təv\ *adj* [ML *receptivus*, fr. L *receptus* (past part. of *recipere* to take back, receive) + L *-ivus* -ive — more at RECEIVE] **1 a :** able or inclined to receive; *specif* **:** open to ideas, impressions, or suggestions ⟨incredulous where they should be ~ —Bertrand Russell⟩ ⟨made ~ by education at its best —E.T.Cone⟩ **b :** characterized by passive dependency and a need to receive or accept **2 a** *of a sensory end organ* **:** fit to receive and transmit stimuli **b :** of or relating to sense organs or the reception of stimuli **:** SENSORY **3** *of a female mammal* **:** willing to accept a male — **re·cep·tive·ly** \-təvlē, -li\ *adv* — **re·cep·tive·ness** \-tivnəs, -tēv- *also* -təv-\ *n* -ES

receptive hypha *n* **:** a haploid hyphal thread that develops from an aecial primordium in many heterothallic rust fungi, that protrudes from a pycnium, and that is joined by a pycniospore to establish a diploid mycelium prior to aeciospore formation

receptive spot *n* **:** the colorless spot in an egg or oosphere at which a male gamete or sperm enters

re·cep·tiv·i·ty \(,)rē,sepˈtivəd·ē, rə,s-, -ətē, -i\ *n* -ES [*receptive* + *-ity*] **:** the quality or state of being receptive; *specif* **:** the power or capacity of receiving impressions **:** SENSIBILITY ⟨her active intellectual ~ —Havelock Ellis⟩ ⟨heighten the spectator's ~ to the theme —Michael Kitson⟩

re·cep·tor \rəˈseptə(r), rēˈ-\ *n* -S [ME *receptour*, fr. MF, fr. L *receptor*, fr. *receptus* (past part. of *recipere* to receive) + *-or*] **1 :** one that receives: as **a :** a part of the body (as a cell, group of cells, complex organ) that is esp. sensitive to alteration of some environmental factor (as light or sound waves, temperature, pressure), that undergoes specific stimulation when exposed to such alteration, and that transmits impulses arising from such stimulation to the central nervous system **:** SENSE ORGAN — distinguished from *effector* **b :** a body or surface sensitive to radiation **:** a surface illuminated in making a color test **c :** STOCK 5b(1) **d :** the part of a stall shower that receives and drains away the water **2 :** the chemical groups or groupings of an antigen or hapten that combine specifically with the corresponding groups of antibody **:** chemical groups of a cell that combine esp. with antibodies or viruses

recepts *pl of* RECEPT

re·cep·tu·al \rəˈsepchəwəl\ *adj* [fr *recept*, after such pairs as E *concept: conceptual*] **:** of or relating to recepts — **re·cep·tu·al·ly** \-wəlē\ *adv*

re·cer·ce·lée \rəˌsərsəˌlā\ *adj* [obs. F, fr. OF, fem. of past part. of *recerceler* to curl back, fr. OF *re-* + *cerceler* to circle, curl, fr. *cercle*, *cercel* circle — more at CIRCLE] *of a cross* **:** having the ends of the arms divided and curled back on each side like rams' horns — compare MOLINE

1re·cess \ˈrē,ses, rəˈses, rēˈses\ *n* -ES [L *recessus*, fr. *recessus*, past part. of *recedere* to withdraw, recede — more at RECEDE] **1 :** the action of receding **:** RECESSION ⟨the ~ of the tides⟩ **2 a** (1) **:** a hidden or retired place ⟨the ~*es* of the echoing mountains —John Muir †1914⟩ ⟨took from some ~ in his crumpled clothing a copper coin —Pearl Buck⟩ (2) **:** an inner or concealed part of something ⟨sought to lay bare the ~*es* of the soul —R.W.Southern⟩ ⟨explore the hidden ~*es* of the mind —C.B.Tinker⟩ ⟨illuminating the ~*es* of American politics —*Times Lit. Supp.*⟩ **b :** a secret hiding place or retreat ⟨there I lay close covered o'er in my ~ —Robert Browning⟩ **3 a :** an indentation in a straight line or in a surface bounded by a line conceived of as straight **:** CLEFT ⟨a large ~ in the steep, rocky bank —*Amer. Guide Series: Maine*⟩ **b :** ALCOVE ⟨lazily reading in an armchair in the pleasant ~ where the books are —Rachel Henning⟩ **c** : a cleft in a living body : SINUS **4 a** : a suspension of business or procedure (as of a legislative body, court, school) for a comparatively short time : a usu. brief vacation period ⟨most members of Congress took advantage of the Easter ~ to go back to their home districts —*Springfield (Mass.) Union*⟩ ⟨the justices adjourned for their summer ~ —*N.Y.Times*⟩ ⟨~ from December 21 to January 4 inclusive —*Official Register of Harvard Univ.*⟩ **b** : a period lasting from 10 minutes to an hour that intervenes between the class or study periods of a school day and is used for rest, play, or lunch **5** [ML *recessus*, fr. L, act of receding, going away; fr. the practice of writing up the decrees before the members of the diet departed] : a decree or ordinance of a diet of the Holy Roman Empire or the Hanseatic League ⟨the Frankfort ~⟩

2**recess** \"\ *vb* -ED/-ING/-ES *vt* **1** : to put into a recess : conceal or seclude in a recess : set back ⟨~*ed* lighting fixtures⟩ ⟨in the school auditorium are four ~*ed* mural panels —*Amer. Guide Series: Mich.*⟩ **2** : to make a recess in ⟨~*ed* type⟩ **3** : to interrupt the course or sitting of for a comparatively short period ⟨~*ed* contract negotiations until this week —*Newsweek*⟩ ⟨can ~ the Senate when its work is done —*Time*⟩ ~ *vi* : to take a recess ⟨the court will now ~ for lunch⟩

recess appointment *n* : an appointment made by a president of the U.S. under his constitutional powers to fill vacancies when the Senate is not in session subject to later confirmation by the Senate

recess bed *n* : a bed so constructed that it may be folded and stood or hung vertically in a recess or closet when not in use — compare DOOR BED

recessed arch *n* [fr. past part. of 2*recess*] : an arch set within another to correspond with splayed jambs of a doorway

recess engraving *n* [1*recess*] : intaglio engraving

re·cess·er \-sə(r)\ *n* -s : one that recesses; *specif* : a worker who recesses watch dials to make track for the second hand

1**re·ces·sion** \rə'seshən, rē'-\ *n* -s [L *recession-, recessio*, fr. *recessus* (past part. of *recedere* to recede) + *-ion-, -io* -ion — more at RECEDE] **1 a** : the act or action of receding : RETREAT ⟨the shy ~ of a votary of love taking the veil —Rebecca West⟩ ⟨the ~ of optimism —R.H.Bainton⟩ **b** : the appearance or effect of receding ⟨flatten his figures by reducing their rounds and ~*s* to roughly the same plane —R.M.Coates⟩ **c** : a return procession (as of clergy and choir after a service) **2** : the receding or diminishing of a natural feature or the process by which such movement occurs: as **a** : the upstream retreat of a waterfall **b** : the retreat of an eroded escarpment **c** : the melting back of a glacier **d** : the landward movement of a shoreline undergoing erosion **e** : the withdrawal of a body of water exposing formerly submerged areas to the air **3** : a period of reduced general economic activity marked by a decline in employment, profits, production, and sales that is not as severe or as prolonged as a depression

2**re·cession** \(')rē+\ *n* [*re-* + *cession*] : the act of ceding back : RESTORATION ⟨the ~ of conquered territory⟩

1**re·ces·sion·al** \rə'seshən°l, rē'-, -shnəl\ *adj* [*recession* + *-al*] : of or relating to a retirement or withdrawal

2**recessional** \"\ *n* -s **1** : RECESSIONAL HYMN **2** : a musical piece played at the end of a play, performance, or service while the audience or congregation is leaving

recessional hymn *n* [1*recessional*] : a hymn sung during the recession of the clergy and choir from the chancel to the robing room

recessional moraine *n* : a moraine left by a glacier during a temporary halt in the retreat of the ice

re·ces·sion·ary \rə'seshə,nerē\ *adj* [*recession* + *-ary*] : RECESSIVE

1**re·ces·sive** \rə'sesiv, rē'-, -sēv *also* -səv\ *adj* [L *recessus* (past part. of *recedere* to recede) + E *-ive*] **1 a** : tending to go back : RECEDING ⟨the mental apparatus of a considerable percentage of the population tends to be disorganized, becoming ~ —P.A. Sorokin⟩ **b** : RETIRING, WITHDRAWN ⟨a lonely ~ savant who could hardly bear to raise his voice in the classroom —*Harper's*⟩ **2** *of an allele* : being subordinate to a contrasting allele in manifestation — opposed to *dominant*; compare MENDEL'S LAW — **re·ces·sive·ly** \-səvlē\ *adv* — **re·ces·sive·ness** \-sivnəs\ *n* -ES

2**recessive** \"\ *n* -s **1** : a recessive character or factor **2** : an organism possessing one or more recessive characters

recessive accent *n* : an accent typically falling on the first syllable of a word (as in English words of Old English origin) or as far from the end of a word as the accentual habits of the language permit (as in Latin or in some classes of Greek words)

recess-print \'=,=\ *vt* [1*recess* + *print*] : to print by an intaglio-engraved die or plate ⟨a *recess-printed* stamp⟩

re·ces·sus \rə'sesəs\ *n* -ES [NL, fr. L, recession, retired place — more at RECESS] : 1RECESS 3c

rech·ab·ite \'rekə,bīt\ *n* -s *usu cap* [LL *Rechabitae* (pl.), fr. Heb *Rēkhābh* Rechab, ancestor of the family (Jer 35:2) + L *-ita* -ite] **1** : a member of a family group in ancient Israel that lived in tents rather than in houses and abstained from drinking wine **2** : an abstainer from intoxicating drinks; *esp* : a member of a benefit society founded in England in 1835 and dedicated to total abstinence **3** : one who lives in tents

rech·a·bit·ism \-,bīd,izəm, -ī,tiz-\ *n* -s *usu cap* : the practice of a Rechabite

re·channel \(')rē+\ *vt* [*re-* + *channel*] : to direct into a different channel ⟨the impact of such persons . . . diverts or ~*s* the tide of history —A.B.Miller⟩

1**re·charge** \"+\ *vb* [*re-* + *charge*] *vi* : to make a new attack ⟨the bull *recharged* as the pase natural finished —Ernest Hemingway⟩ ~ *vt* : to charge again : put a new charge in ⟨~ a battery⟩ ⟨refreshes and ~*s* your morals, remodels and revivifies your intellect —R.P.Blackmur⟩

2**recharge** \"\ *n* **1** : the act of recharging ⟨raise basin water levels above sea levels by direct ~ —F.B.Laverty⟩ **2** : a new load ⟨clean off a small area next to the hot coals and cover it with a small ~ of nut coal —*Newsweek*⟩

1**ré·chauf·fé** \'rā(,)shō¦fā\ *n* -s [F, fr. *réchauffé* warmed over] **1** : a dish of food that has been warmed over ⟨a ~ of lamb⟩ **2** : something that is served up again : REHASH ⟨the crudest, clumsiest ~ of an old dreary melodrama —*Sydney (Australia) Bull.*⟩

2**réchauffé** \"\ *adj* [F, past part. of *réchauffer* to warm again, fr. *ré-* re- + *chauffer* to warm, fr. MF *chaufer* — more at CHAFE] **1** : warmed over ⟨chicken ~⟩ **2** : worked over : REHASHED ⟨two hundred pages of reasonably fresh material and six hundred that are merely ~ —*Nation*⟩

re·cheat \rə'chēt\ *also* **re·chate** \-chāt\ *n* -s [ME *rechate*, fr. *rechaten* to blow the recheat, fr. MF *rachater, racheter* to assemble, rally, fr. *re-* + *achater, acheter* to acquire, fr. (assumed) VL *accaptare*, fr. L *ac-* + *captare* to seek to obtain, intens. of *capere* to take, receive — more at HEAVE] : a hunting call sounded on a horn to assemble the hounds

re·check \(')rē+\ *vb* [*re-* + *check*] : to check again

re·cher·ché *also* **re·cher·che** \rə¦sher¦shā\ *adj* [F, fr. past part. of *rechercher* to seek out — more at RESEARCH] **1 a** : sought out with care ⟨the exhibition consists of a ~ choice of the finest productions of their archaic arts ever discovered —Janet Flanner⟩ **b** : EXOTIC, RARE ⟨feel cheated of the ~ experiences we have come to expect —*New Republic*⟩ ⟨discusses all manner of words — common, ~, and slang —*New Yorker*⟩ **c** : FARFETCHED, PRECIOUS ⟨his inner monologues and their ~ highbrow references —Anthony Green⟩ **2** : lavishly elegant and refined : CHOICE, EXQUISITE ⟨we are not accustomed to seeing this type of book in such a ~ format —F.O.Brenner⟩ **syn** see CHOICE

re·chew \(')rē+\ *vb* [*re-* + *chew*] : to chew again

re·christen \(')rē+\ *vt* [*re-* + *christen*] : to christen again : change the name of ⟨the Curb finally acknowledged the fact that it was no longer on the sidewalk and ~*ed* itself the American Stock Exchange —John Brooks⟩

re·ci·bien·do \,rāsē¦byen(,)dō\ *adv* [Sp, lit., receiving, fr. L *recipiendum*, gerund of *recipere* to receive — more at RECEIVE] *of a bullfighter* : in a stance with feet motionless to receive the bull's charge

re·cid·i·vate \rə'sidə,vāt, rē'-, *usu* -ād.+V\ *vi* -ED/-ING/-S [ML *recidivatus*, past part. of *recidivare* to fall back, relapse, fr. L *recidivus* falling back, recurring — more at RECIDIVOUS] : to fall back : RELAPSE ⟨those who ~ are characteristically minor offenders —P.W.Tappan⟩

re·cid·i·va·tion \=,=='vāshən\ *n* -s [ML *recidivation-, recidivatio*, fr. *recidivatus* + *-ion-, -io* -ion] : RECIDIVISM

re·cid·i·vism \='==,vizəm\ *n* -s [fr. *recidivist*, after such pairs as E *purist: purism*] : a tendency to relapse into a previous condition or mode of behavior ⟨a study of ~ in mental patients⟩; *specif* : repeated relapse into criminal or delinquent habits ⟨unemployment of discharged prisoners is at the root of much of the ~ that is overcrowding the prisons —*Survey Midmonthly*⟩

re·cid·i·vist \-,vəst\ *n* -s [F *récidiviste*, fr. *récidiver* to recidivate (fr. ML *recidivare*) + *-iste* -ist] : one who relapses or has suffered a relapse ⟨some of the patients admitted are new cases, others are ~*s*⟩; *specif* : one who persists in crime : an habitual criminal : REPEATER ⟨the casual offender expiates his offense in the company of defectives and ~*s* —B.N.Cardozo⟩

re·cid·i·vous \-vəs\ *adj* [L *recidivus*, fr. *recidere* to fall back, recur (fr. *re-* + *cadere* to fall) + *-ivus* -ive — more at CHANCE] : tending to relapse or having relapsed

re·ci·fe \rə'sēfə\ *adj, usu cap* [fr. *Recife*, city of eastern Brazil] : of or from the city of Recife, Brazil : of the kind or style prevalent in Recife

recip *abbr* reciprocal; reciprocate; reciprocity

rec·i·pe \'resə(,)pē\ *n* -s [L, take, imper. of *recipere* to take, receive — more at RECEIVE] **1** : a formula for compounding a medicine or remedy : PRESCRIPTION ⟨some of his ~*s* are printed in pharmacopoeias of today —Norman Douglas⟩ **2 a** : a set of instructions for making something; *esp* : a formula for compounding something from various ingredients ⟨many hundreds of different ~*s* are used in making steel, and each ingredient is measured to a fraction of one percent —*Hot-Metal Magic*⟩ **b** : a formula for cooking or preparing something to be eaten or drunk : a list of ingredients and a statement of the procedure to be followed in making an item of food or drink ⟨a ~ for salad dressing⟩ ⟨a ~ for a new cocktail⟩ **3** : a method or procedure for doing or attaining something ⟨attempts to extract from science the ~ for all human activities —Peggy Erskine⟩ ⟨presents a four-page ~ for organizing and conducting a meeting —W.A.L.Johnson⟩ ⟨a ~ for success⟩ ⟨reading good books . . . is the ~ for those who would learn to read —M.J.Adler⟩

1**re·cipher** \(')rē+\ *vt* [*re-* + *cipher*] : to encipher (a message in code) for added security

2**recipher** \"\ *n* : a reciphered message

re·cip·i·ence \rə'sipēən(t)s, rē'-\ *or* **re·cip·i·en·cy** \-nsē, -si\ *n, pl* **recipiences** *or* **recipiencies** [*recipience* fr. 1*recipient*, after such pairs as E *benevolent: benevolence*; *recipiency* fr. 1*recipient* + *-cy*] : RECEPTIVITY

1**re·cip·i·ent** \-nt\ *adj* [L *recipient-, recipiens*, pres. part. of *recipere* to receive — more at RECEIVE] : serving to receive or capable of receiving ⟨elements of the invading and ~ cultures have been blended —G.R.Willey⟩

2**recipient** \"\ *n* -s : one that receives : RECEIVER ⟨two choices open to the unfortunate ~ of homemade cookies —J.P. O'Neill⟩ ⟨the ~ of honorary degrees —*Current Biog.*⟩

1**re·cip·ro·cal** \rə'siprəkəl, rē'-\ *adj* [L *reciprocus* returning the same way, alternating (fr. — assumed — *recus* backward — fr. *re-* — + — assumed — *procus* forward, fr. *pro-* 1pro-) + E *-al*] **1 a** : inversely related : OPPOSITE ⟨each flexor muscle which contracts has its ~ extensor muscle which operates in the reverse direction —A.E.Wier⟩ **b** : of, constituting, or resulting from paired crosses in which the form that supplies the male parent of the first cross supplies the female parent of the second cross and vice versa ⟨a cross between a black Leghorn male and a white Leghorn female and one between a white Leghorn male and a black Leghorn female are ~ crosses⟩ **2 a** : mutually existing : shared, felt, or shown by both sides ⟨two congenial spirits united . . . by mutual confidence and ~ virtues —T.L.Peacock⟩ ⟨~ love⟩ ⟨~ understanding⟩ **b** : expressive of mutual action or relationship — used of verbs and esp. of compound pronouns; compare RECIPROCAL PRONOUNS **3** : serving to reciprocate : consisting of or functioning as a return in kind ⟨an unselfish friend who helped him without expecting any ~ benefit⟩ **4 a** : corresponding to each other : being equivalent or complementary ⟨agreed to extend ~ privileges to each other's citizens⟩ ⟨~ cultural missions⟩ ⟨the public and private systems engage in ~ services —Albert Lepawsky⟩ **b** : marked by or based upon reciprocity ⟨~ trade agreements⟩

syn MUTUAL, COMMON: RECIPROCAL describes an equivalence, balance, equal counteraction, equal return, or equal sharing ⟨not a mere cooperation of distinct forces, but an extremely powerful *reciprocal* action, each in turn firing the other and fired by it —C.E.Montague⟩ ⟨the connection between law and political theory has not been one-sided; it has been completely *reciprocal* —Huntington Cairns⟩ MUTUAL is likely to apply to feelings or actions shared by two, indicating either an accompanying reciprocity, equality, or intereaction or simply stressing the fact of a common experience or emotion ⟨a devoted attachment and *mutual* admiration between aunt and niece —George Eliot⟩ ⟨*mutual* obligation — on the part of the lord to protect his vassal against the violence of others, and on the vassal's part to make good the homage pledged by him —H.O. Taylor⟩ ⟨sometimes mingles poetry and propaganda to their *mutual* disaster —J.L.Lowes⟩ COMMON conveys no suggestion of reciprocity between two parties or agencies; instead it indicates the fact of joint participation or possession among any number ⟨death and other incidents of our *common* fate —M.R. Cohen⟩ ⟨generally agreed that all men belong to the same species, that all were probably derived from the same ancestral stock, and that all share in a *common* patrimony —M.F.A. Montagu⟩ ⟨looked at each other for one instant, as if each had in mind those few moments during which a certain moonlit scene was *common* to both —Thomas Hardy⟩

2**reciprocal** \"\ *n* -s **1** : something that reciprocates or has a reciprocal relationship to something else; *esp* : a reciprocal term, expression, or concept ⟨freedom — or its ~, the control of human behavior —B.F.Skinner⟩ ⟨corruption is a ~ to generation —Francis Bacon⟩ **2** : a number that when multiplied by a given number gives one ⟨$4/3$ is the ~ of $3/4$⟩ ⟨$1/9$ is the ~ of 9⟩ **3** : RECIPROCAL EXCHANGE

reciprocal alphabet *n* : a substitution alphabet in which cipher and plaintext equivalents are reciprocal (as when $A_p = X_c$ and $X_p = A_c$)

reciprocal demand *n* : the demand of two persons or communities for one another's products

reciprocal diagram *n* : the force diagram for a framed structure — see BOW'S NOTATION

reciprocal exchange *n* : an unincorporated association of companies or individuals set up to permit its members to take out reciprocal insurance

reciprocal insurance *n* : a plan of insurance by which each member of a reciprocal exchange acting through an attorney-in-fact becomes an insurer of and is insured by every other member — called also *interinsurance*

re·cip·ro·cal·i·ty \=,=='kaləd·ē, -lətē, -i\ *n* -ES [1*reciprocal* + *-ity*] : RECIPROCITY

re·cip·ro·cal·ly \='==k(ə)lē, -li\ *adv* [1*reciprocal* + *-ly*] **1** : INVERSELY ⟨wavelength and frequency are, of course, related ~ —F.A.Geldard⟩ **2** : MUTUALLY ⟨the ultimate goals of the various negotiators are not ~ exclusive —W.R.Frye⟩ **3** : in return ⟨he trusted his friend and his friend ~ trusted him⟩ **4** : CONVERSELY

reciprocally proportional *adj* : INVERSELY PROPORTIONAL

reciprocal pronoun *n* : a pronoun (as *each other*) that is used to denote a mutual action or cross relationship between the members comprised in a plural subject (as in *A and B like each other*; that is, *A likes B and B likes A*)

reciprocal quantities *n pl* : two quantities whose product is 1

reciprocal ratio *n* : INVERSE RATIO

reciprocal switching *n* : an interchange of inbound and outbound carload freight among railroads in which the cars are switched by one railroad to or from the siding of another under a regular switching charge that is usu. absorbed by the carrier receiving the line-haul

reciprocal translocation *n* : exchange of parts between nonhomologous chromosomes

reciprocal wills *n pl* : MUTUAL WILLS

re·cip·ro·cate \rə'siprə,kāt, rē'-, *usu* -ād.+V\ *vb* -ED/-ING/-S [L *reciprocatus*, past part. of *reciprocare* to move back and forth, to reciprocate, fr. *reciprocus* alternating — more at RECIPROCAL] *vt* **1** : to give and take reciprocally : exchange mutually : INTERCHANGE ⟨the two countries *reciprocated* pledges of friendship⟩ **2** : to cause to move in alternate directions **3** : to return in kind or degree : respond in like measure to : REPAY ⟨~ the compliments just paid them —J.G.Cozzens⟩ ⟨is peevish and sensitive when his advances are not *reciprocated* —G.B.Shaw⟩ ~ *vi* **1** : to make a return for something done, given, or said ⟨hope in a few days to ~ for your verses by sending you a few remarks —O.W.Holmes †1935⟩ **2** : to move forward and backward alternately usu. in a straight line ⟨a tiny knife *reciprocating* rapidly up and down —J.V.A.Long⟩ **3** : to be equivalent or correspondent

syn RECIPROCATE, RETALIATE, REQUITE, and RETURN can mean to give back usu. in kind or in quantity. RECIPROCATE can imply a mutual, equivalent or roughly equivalent, exchange or a paying back of what one has received ⟨the love of Lavinia for the hero, most correctly *reciprocated* by him —H.O.Taylor⟩ ⟨touched his friend's glass lightly and *reciprocated* the former toast —James Joyce⟩ ⟨a man for whom he has an intense and growing dislike, which the other *reciprocated* —*Times Lit. Supp.*⟩ ⟨bringing their rude gifts of mussels and wild seeds, which were always *reciprocated* with beads and some of our food —Francisco Palou⟩ RETALIATE usu. implies a paying back in exact kind, often vengefully ⟨considers the possibility of revenge, of *retaliating* on those who have injured him —J.W. Krutch⟩ ⟨our need to protect ourselves from military attack and to *retaliate* in case an enemy dared to attack us —Mary Gregoire⟩ ⟨*retaliate*, blow for blow⟩ REQUITE can imply simply a paying back usu. reciprocally, but also often implies a paying back according to what one considers the merits of the case ⟨*requite* a friend's love⟩ ⟨face every danger rather than *requite* with ingratitude and treachery the devoted attachment of the Western peasantry —T.B.Macaulay⟩ ⟨hospitality should be *requited* in kind —Agnes M. Miall⟩ ⟨*requited* their hospitality by robbing them of much of their supplies —*Amer. Guide Series: Maine*⟩ RETURN usu. implies only a giving back in return ⟨*return* a social call⟩ ⟨*return* good for evil⟩

reciprocating *adj* [fr. pres. part. of *reciprocate*] **1** : characterized by alternation in movement : moving to-and-fro ⟨a ~ piston⟩ **2** : having parts characterized by alternation in movement; *specif* : having a reciprocating piston ⟨a ~ engine⟩

reciprocating conveyor *n* : a vibrating trough conveyor

reciprocating drill *n* : PISTON DRILL

reciprocating proposition *n* : a proposition in logic that asserts an interchangeable relationship between subject and predicate

re·cip·ro·ca·tion \rə,siprə'kāshən, rē'-\ *n* -s [L *reciprocation-, reciprocatio*, fr. *reciprocatus* (past part. of *reciprocare* to reciprocate) + *-ion-, -io* -ion] **1 a** : a mutual exchange ⟨the ~ of courtesies between the two families⟩ **b** : a return in kind or of like value ⟨the ~ of hatreds must produce a greater hatred —Stuart Hampshire⟩ **2** *archaic* : the quality or state of being harmonious : CORRESPONDENCE **3** : an alternating motion, action, or succession : ALTERNATION ⟨the reciprocating action continues with the dropper in action lowering two needles at each ~ —W.E.Shinn⟩

re·cip·ro·ca·tive \='==,kād·iv, -,kəd·-\ *adj* [*reciprocate* + *-ive*] : characterized by reciprocation or serving to reciprocate

re·cip·ro·ca·tor \-,kād·ə(r)\ *n* -s [*reciprocate* + *-or*] : one that reciprocates

re·cip·ro·ca·to·ry \-,kə,tōrē, -tȯr-, -ri, *chiefly Brit* =¦==¦kātəri *or* -ā·tri\ *adj* [*reciprocate* + *-ory*] : RECIPROCATING

rec·i·proc·i·ty \,resə'präsəd·ē, -sətē, -i\ *n* -ES [L *reciprocus* reciprocal + E *-ity*] **1** : the quality or state of being reciprocal : mutual dependence, action, or influence : GIVE-AND-TAKE, MUTUALITY ⟨a deep ~ of sympathy and strength between lovers —Mary Webb⟩ ⟨a ~ of influence between a writer and his public —*College English*⟩ **2 a** : a mutual exchange of trade or other concessions or privileges (as reduction of tariff rates and liberalization of quota and exchange restrictions) between two countries **b** : a mutual exchange of courtesies between two states or institutions; *specif* : a recognition by each state or institution of the validity of licenses or privileges granted by the other to its citizens or members

reciprocity law *n* : a statement in photography: a constant density is obtained on a photographic material if the product of the intensity of light and the time for which it acts is a constant

re·circulate \(')rē+\ *vt* [*re-* + *circulate*] : to circulate again

re·ci·sion \rə'sizhən, rē'-\ *n* -s [MF, alter. (influenced by *recision* act of cutting back, fr. L *recision-, recisio*, fr. *recisus* — past part. of *recidere* to cut back, lop off, fr. *re-* + *caedere* to cut — + *-ion-, -io* -ion) of *rescision*, fr. L *rescission-, rescissio* — more at CONCISE, RESCISSION] : the act or action of rescinding : CANCELLATION ⟨no criticism or ~ of its doctrinal contents was expressed or implied by such withdrawal —Theodore Graebner⟩

ré·cit \rā'sē\ *n* -s [F, narrative, account, fr. MF *reciter* to narrate, tell — more at RECITE] : a brief novel usu. with a simple narrative line

recit *abbr* recitative

re·cit·al \rə'sīd·°l, rē'-, -sīt°l\ *n* -s [*recite* + *-al*] **1** : the formal statement or setting forth of some relevant matter of fact in a deed or legal document (as to explain the reasons for a transaction, to evidence the existence of facts, or to introduce a positive allegation in pleading) **2 a** : a particularized account : ENUMERATION ⟨too much a ~ of details —H.S.Ellis⟩ **b** : something that is told or related : DISCOURSE, STORY ⟨listened to this ~ with a mixture of awe and skepticism —Hallam Tennyson⟩ **3 a** : a reading or repetition from memory of some piece of writing ⟨gave a ~ of his own poems before a large and attentive audience⟩ **b** (1) : a homogeneous program of vocal or instrumental music usu. by a single performer or by a soloist with an accompanist ⟨a piano ~⟩ ⟨a song ~⟩ — distinguished from *concert* (2) : an exhibition concert given by music pupils **c** (1) : a public performance given by a dancer (2) : a dance concert; *esp* : an exhibition concert given by dance pupils

re·cit·al·ist \-°ləst\ *n* -s [*recital* + *-ist*] : one who gives recitals ⟨a lieder ~ —Abraham Veinus⟩

re·ci·tan·do \,rāchē'tän·(,)dō\ *adv (or adj)* [It, fr. L *recitandum*, gerund of *recitare* to recite] : in reciting style : DECLAMATORY — used as a direction in music

rec·i·ta·tif \¦res(ə)tə¦tēf\ *n* -s [F, fr. It *recitativo*] : RECITATIVE

rec·i·ta·tion \,resə'tāshən\ *n* -s [MF or L; MF *recitation*, fr. L *recitation-, recitatio*, fr. *recitatus* (past part. of *recitare* to recite) + *-ion-, -io* -ion] **1** : the act of enumeration : DETAILING ⟨explanation in this type of philosophy consists of a ~ of relevant events —L.A.White⟩ **2** : the act or an instance of reading or repeating aloud esp. before an audience ⟨a ~ of the rosary at 8 P.M. Sunday —*Springfield (Mass.) Daily News*⟩ ⟨the program consisted usually of a serious play, followed by songs, ~*s*, tableaux —*Amer. Guide Series: Ind.*⟩ **3 a** : a school exercise in which students in a class or course reply orally to questions on subject matter previously taught or assigned ⟨poor ~*s* in history⟩ **b** : a regularly scheduled class period or course session ⟨only ten ~*s* a week⟩

rec·i·ta·tion·ist \-sh(ə)nəst\ *n* -s [*recitation* + *-ist*] : ELOCUTIONIST

1**rec·i·ta·tive** \¦res(ə)tə¦tēv\ *adj* [It *recitativo*, n.] : of, relating to, or having the characteristics of recitative — distinguished from *ariose*

2**recitative** \"\ *n* -s [It *recitativo*, fr. *recitare* to recite (fr. L) + *-ivo* -ive] **1 a** : a vocal passage, part, or performance in which a singer delivers a narrative text (as in opera or oratorio) in a declamatory and rhetorical manner and which is characterized by freedom from strict form in its tonal and metrical structure and by speechlike recitation instead of flowing melody **b** : a composition intended to be sung as a recitative — compare ARIA **c** : a passage of instrumental music in the style of a recitative **2** : RECITATION ⟨a long, leisurely ~ about curates at teas —Anne Fremantle⟩

rec·i·ta·ti·vo \,resəd·ə'tē(,)vō\ *n, pl* **recitati·vi** \-(,)vē\ *or* **recitativos** [It] : RECITATIVE

re·cite \rə'sīt, rē'-, *usu* -īd.+V\ *vb* [ME *reciten*, fr. MF or L; MF *reciter* to narrate, recite, fr. L *recitare* to read aloud, repeat from memory, recite, fr. *re-* + *citare* to call, cite — more at CITE] *vt* **1** : to state formally in a deed or legal document ⟨all representations and agreements required by this section shall be *recited* in the instrument of transfer —*U. S. Code*⟩ **2** : to repeat from memory or read aloud esp. before an audience ⟨still sing the folksongs and ~ the charms of their childhood

—Amer. Guide Series: Minn.) ⟨*recited* ballads in public —W.P. Eaton⟩ ⟨*recited* his poems from manuscript⟩ **3 a :** to give a detailed narration of : relate in full ⟨the other gabblers who ~ dull anecdotes, in fullest detail, of relatives and friends unknown to the hearer —Sophie Kerr⟩ **b :** to list in detail : set out : ENUMERATE ⟨*recited* with indignation . . . a catalog of illegalities and atrocities —F.L.Paxson⟩ **4 :** to repeat or answer questions about (a school assignment or lesson) ⟨could only ~ what they had copied from the blackboard —*Americas*⟩ **~ vi 1 :** to repeat or read aloud esp. before an audience something memorized or prepared ⟨who ~*s* aloud with a dramatic art that she has made her own —H.V.Gregory⟩ **2 :** to reply to a teacher's question on a lesson or assignment ⟨the teacher called on him to ~⟩ **syn** see RELATE

re·cit·er \-d·ə(r), -tə-\ *n* **:** one that recites

reciting note *n* [fr. *reciting*, gerund of *recite*] **:** a musical note on which a varying number of syllables are uttered in chanting as distinguished from a note that receives but one syllable

¹reck \ˈrek\ *vb* -ED/-ING/-S [ME *recchen, recken* to be concerned, take heed, fr. OE *reccan, rēcan;* akin to OHG *ruohhen* to take heed, ON *rækja*] *vi* **1 a :** to be apprehensive or fearful — usu. used with *of* ⟨little ~*ing* of the dangers I was running —Claud Cockburn⟩ **b :** to take heed or thought : take account : be aware : CONSIDER, DEEM — usu. used with *of* ⟨the language ~*ed* of their decrees as little as the advancing ocean did of those of Canute —R.C.Trench⟩ ⟨content with the plaudits of the hour, and ~*ing* little of the morrow —B.N. Cardozo⟩ **c :** to become concerned : CARE ⟨little we ~*ed* . . . we had a holiday spirit —Stephen Graham⟩ **2 :** to be of account or interest : MATTER ⟨it ~*s* little to think of that now . . . what he has done cannot be effaced —R.A.T.G.Cecil⟩ **~ vt 1 :** to care for : take account of : REGARD ⟨lay in a bed of musk and tenderness, nor ~*ed* no risk —Henry Treece⟩ **2 :** to matter to : CONCERN ⟨what ~*s* it them —John Milton⟩

²reck \"\ *chiefly dial var of* RICK

reckan *var of* RACKAN

reck·less \ˈrekləs\ *adj* [ME *recheles, reckeles*, fr. OE *recceleās, rēceleās*, fr. (assumed) *recce, rēce* care, heed (akin to *reccan, rēcan* to give heed) + *-leās* -less — more at RECK] **1 a :** lacking in caution : deliberately courting danger : FOOLHARDY, RASH ⟨brave and daring but never foolishly ~ —J.L.Hodson⟩ ⟨a band of brigands, outlawed by government, strong in discipline, furious from penury, ~ by habit —J.L.Motley⟩ **b :** CARELESS, NEGLECTFUL, THOUGHTLESS — often used with *of* ⟨lives on his nervous energy, ~ of consequences —Rose Macaulay⟩ **2 a :** marked by a lack of caution : HEEDLESS, RASH ⟨gold in the men's purses meant heavy drinking and ~ gambling —Robert Graves⟩ ⟨~ audacity came to be considered courage —Derek Patmore⟩ **b :** marked by a lack of foresight or consideration : IMPROVIDENT, NEGLIGENT ⟨devastated by forest fires and ~ lumbering —*Amer. Guide Series: Pa.*⟩ ⟨replace the ~ mining habits of the earlier period with a thrifty and conservative use of the natural environment —Lewis Mumford⟩ **c :** IRRESPONSIBLE, WILD ⟨~ in its charges⟩ ⟨a check on ~ generalizations and the vagaries of impressionism —C.I.Glicksberg⟩ **syn** see ADVENTUROUS

reckless driving *n* **:** driving that evidences a deliberate or culpably negligent disregard of life and property and creates an unreasonable risk of harm to others

reck·less·ly *adv* [ME *recchelesly*, fr. OE *recceleāslīce*, fr. *recceleās* reckless + *-līce* -ly] **:** in a reckless manner

reck·less·ness *n* -ES [ME *rechelesnes*, fr. OE *rēceleāsnes*, fr. *rēceleās* reckless + *-nes* -ness] **:** the quality or state of being reckless

reck·ling \ˈreklən, -liŋ\ *n* -S [origin unknown] **1** *dial Eng* **:** the weakest or smallest one of a litter, brood, or family : RUNT **2** *dial Eng* **:** WEAKLING

reck·ling·hausen \ˈrekliŋˌhau̇zən\ *adj, usu cap* [fr. *Recklinghausen*, city of northwest Germany] **:** of or from the city of Recklinghausen, Germany **:** of the kind or style prevalent in Recklinghausen

recklinghausen's disease *n, usu cap R* [after F. D. von *Recklinghausen* †1910 Ger. pathologist] **:** NEUROFIBROMATOSIS

reck·on \ˈrekən\ *vb* **reckoned; reckoned; reckoning** \-k(ə)niŋ\ **reckons** [ME *rekenen, rikenen*, fr. OE *-recenian* (as in *gerecenian* to recount, narrate); akin to MD *rekenen* to reckon, OHG *rehhanōn*, OE *reccan* to give heed — more at RECK] *vt* **1 :** to go over one by one : ENUMERATE — used with *up* or *over* ⟨would need several pages merely to ~ up the names⟩ ⟨~*ing* her wrongs over vividly —George Meredith⟩ **2 a :** COUNT ⟨I have not art to ~ my groans —Shak.⟩ **b :** to arrive at or estimate by calculation : COMPUTE ⟨in ~*ing* the height, allow for a thick mat or excelsior cushion underfoot —Emily Holt⟩ ⟨stood gazing about, trying to ~ the size of the cave —Willa Cather⟩ **c :** to calculate or determine by reference to a fixed point or basis ⟨the existence of the U. S. is ~*ed* from the Declaration of Independence⟩ ⟨the society is matrilineal and all blood relations and personal loyalties are ~*ed* on the blood ties —Abram Kardiner⟩ **3 a :** to regard or think of as : ACCOUNT, CONSIDER ⟨the artist is ~*ed* a freak —Clive Bell⟩ ⟨taught men to ~ virtue of more moment than security —W.F. Hambly⟩ **b :** to include as part of a total or classification : CLASS, PLACE ⟨has commonly been ~*ed* an American philosopher —*Americana Annual*⟩ ⟨many anthropologists have accordingly ~*ed* them as an early Caucasoid offshoot —A.L. Kroeber⟩ **c :** ATTRIBUTE, ASSIGN — used with *to* ⟨despite his astonishing anticipations of the painting of the end of the nineteenth century, it seems better to ~ him to the old school —F.J.Mather⟩ **d :** to evaluate the character or worth of : SUM — used with *up* ⟨sitting opposite the boys in church, and ~*ing* them up with her keen eyes —Samuel Butler †1902⟩ **4 a :** to conclude on the basis of a calculation or estimation ⟨~ that we lost a fifth of the oats through sprouting —*Country Life*⟩ ⟨~*s* that his phone rings on an average three times a day —*N. Y. Herald Tribune*⟩ **b** *chiefly dial* **:** to be of the impression or opinion that : SUPPOSE, THINK ⟨been doing this work for six years and we ~ we know something about it —C.D. Lewis⟩ **~ vi 1 :** to settle accounts or claims — usu. used with *with* ⟨after a long time the lord of those servants cometh, and ~*eth* with them —Mt 25:19 (AV)⟩ **2 :** to make a calculation : COMPUTE ⟨seemed to ~ in her mind —H.G.Wells⟩ ⟨~*ed*, and put his money on his newfound fellow clerk —Winston Churchill⟩ **3** *chiefly dial* **a :** EXPECT, INTEND **b :** CLAIM, PRETEND **4 a :** ESTIMATE, JUDGE ⟨thoroughly nice people, as the world ~*s* —Mary Ross⟩ **b** *chiefly dial* **:** SUPPOSE, THINK ⟨it's faith, I ~, that's kept her goin' —Ellen Glasgow⟩ **5 :** to place reliance : COUNT, DEPEND — used with *on* or *upon* ⟨~ on your promise to aid me —George Meredith⟩ ⟨do not ~ upon it with certainty —Rachel Henning⟩ **syn** see CALCULATE, CONSIDER, RELY — **reckon with :** to take into account ⟨it had to *reckon with* a challenging current of popular contradiction —Herbert Feis⟩ ⟨a man to be *reckoned with*⟩ — **reckon without :** to leave out of account : IGNORE ⟨*reckoned without* chemistry and man's ingenuity when he predicted that man sooner or later faced starvation —*Monsanto Mag.*⟩

reck·on·able \-k(ə)nəbəl\ *adj* **:** capable of being reckoned ⟨an occupation which seemed to them idleness because it made no ~ profits —H.S.Canby⟩

reck·on·er \-k(ə)nə(r)\ *n* -S [ME *rikenere*, fr. *rikenen* to reckon + *-ere* -er] **1 :** one that reckons **2 :** an aid to reckoning; *esp* **:** a book of tables — called also *ready reckoner*

reck·on·ing \-k(ə)niŋ, -neŋ\ *n* -S [ME *rekening*, fr. gerund of *rekenen* to reckon] **1 a :** the act or an instance of computing or calculating ⟨the ~*s* of local, solar, and sidereal time —*Times Lit. Supp.*⟩ **b :** a method of calculating ⟨a need felt for a more precise time ~ —A.L.Kroeber⟩ **c :** a calculation or statement of money owed : ACCOUNT, BILL ⟨an old beggar who could not pay his ~ —Virginia Woolf⟩ **d :** the result of a process of calculating : COMPUTATION ⟨more than 10 percent off in his ~⟩ ⟨experiments verified the correctness of his ~⟩ **e** (1) **:** the calculation of a ship's position from astronomical observations or from dead reckoning; *also* **:** dead reckoning as opposed to observation (2) **:** the position of a ship determined by reckoning **2 :** the act or an instance of settling accounts ⟨would demonstrate their loyalty by postponing a ~ of their grievances —Oscar Handlin⟩ **3 :** the act of accounting for one's conduct or the fact of being called to account ⟨if the cause be not good, the king himself hath a heavy ~ to make —Shak.⟩ ⟨a time of ~⟩ ⟨a bitter ~⟩ — see DAY OF RECKONING **4 :** the act or an instance of judging : a summing up : APPRAISAL ⟨when the final ~ of this composer's complete works is made —Arthur Berger⟩ ⟨its people have lived under the system for more than a generation . . . a ~ can now be taken —Nathaniel Peffer⟩

recks *pres 3d sing of* RECK

¹re·claim \rəˈklām, rēˈ-\ *vb* [ME *reclamen, reclaimen*, fr. OF *reclamer* to appeal to, call back, fr. L *reclamare* to cry out against, call for, fr. *re-* + *clamare* to cry out, call — more at CLAIM] *vt* **1** *obs* **:** to call back (as a hawk to the wrist) : RECALL **2 a :** to recall from wrong or improper conduct : amend the behavior or character of : REFORM ⟨~*ed* him from a life of drunkenness⟩ ⟨~ the wicked⟩ **b :** to make obedient : SUBDUE, TAME ⟨my heart is wondrous light, since this same wayward girl is so ~*ed* —Shak.⟩ **3 a :** to rescue from an undesirable or unhealthy state : bring to a state of literacy, culture, or health ⟨an effort to ~ the illiterates who would otherwise be excellent material for the armed forces —*Amer. Library Assoc. Bull.*⟩ ⟨work done in ~*ing* diseased and debilitated horses —Charles Murray⟩ **b :** to rescue from a wild or uncultivated state : make fit for cultivation or use ⟨filled in valleys, diverted creeks and ~*ed* swamps —G.R.Gilbert⟩ ⟨the most arid area in the country ~*ed* from the desert by irrigation —*Amer. Guide Series: Calif.*⟩ **4 a :** to obtain from a waste product or by-product : RECOVER ⟨~ wool fibers from textile wastes⟩ **b :** to recover the useful material from ⟨~ scraps⟩ **~ vi 1 :** to cry out : OBJECT, PROTEST ⟨his opponents loudly ~*ed* against his attempt to shut off debate⟩ **2** *Scots law* **:** to appeal from a judgment of the lord ordinary of the Court of Session to the Inner House **3 :** to demand surrender of a person or thing belonging to one state and found to be irregularly under the control of another state or its citizens **syn** see RESCUE

²reclaim \"\ *n* [ME, fr. OF, appeal, recall, fr. *reclamer*] **1 :** a reclaiming or state of being reclaimed ⟨past hope of all ~ —Ben Jonson⟩ **2 :** something that is reclaimed; *esp* **:** RECLAIMED RUBBER

re–claim \(ˈ)rē+\ *vt* [*re-* + *claim*] **1 :** to claim back : demand the return of as a right : attempt to recover possession of ⟨returned from the war and *re-claimed* his factory job —J.N. Bell⟩ **2 :** to regain possession of ⟨the tall young pines which slowly but surely are *re-claiming* the land a former generation toiled to clear —Corey Ford⟩

re·claim·able \-məbəl\ *adj* **:** capable of being reclaimed

re·claim·ant \-mənt\ *n* -S [ˈ*reclaim* + *-ant* (n)] **:** one who reclaims

reclaimed rubber *n* **:** rubber recovered from vulcanized scrap rubber (as by grinding old tires and treating with alkali, oils, and plasticizers), often mixed with crude rubber for compounding, and used chiefly in mechanical rubber goods

re·claim·er \-mə(r)\ *n* **:** one that reclaims ⟨oil ~*s* are used to clarify used lubricants⟩; *esp* **:** WARMER 1b

rec·la·ma·tion \ˌrekləˈmāshən\ *n* -S [MF, fr. L *reclamation-, reclamatio*, fr. *reclamatus* (past part. of *reclamare* to cry out against) + *-ion-, -io* -ion — more at RECLAIM] **1 :** the act of making a claim or protest ⟨~*s* of disappointed investors —R.E.Cameron⟩ **2 :** the act or process of reforming or rehabilitating ⟨an agency devoted to the ~ of delinquents⟩ ⟨its ministry of ~ to down-and-out men —Sidney Lovett⟩ **3 :** the act or process of restoring to cultivation or use ⟨land ~⟩ ⟨a large-scale ~ project⟩

reclamation disease *n* **:** a copper-deficiency disease of many crops and esp. of cereals occurring chiefly on newly reclaimed peat land and characterized by chlorotic leaf tips and failure to set seed

reclamation district *n* **:** a district created by legislation for the purpose of reclaiming swamp, marshy, or desert lands and making them suitable for cultivation and usu. given the power to levy assessments or issue bonds

ré·clame \rāˈklām\ *n* -S [F, advertising, publicity, fr. *réclamer* to claim, appeal, fr. OF *reclamer* to appeal, call back — more at RECLAIM] **1 :** public attention or acclaim not necessarily based on or proportionate to real value or achievement : PUBLICITY, VOGUE ⟨wrote pungent articles which enjoyed immense ~ —F.A.Swinnerton⟩ **2 :** a gift or passion for publicity : SHOWMANSHIP ⟨his energy, his experimental verve, his ~ —Herbert Read⟩ ⟨that innocent ~ of his, that irresistible passion for the limelight —Van Wyck Brooks⟩

re·classification \(ˌ)rē+\ *n* [*re-* + *classification*] **:** the act, the result, or a method of reclassifying

re·classify \(ˈ)rē+\ *vt* [*re-* + *classify*] **1 :** to group or segregate into classes again on a new basis : RE-SORT **2 :** to move from one class, classification, or category to another : REASSIGN

re·clean \(ˈ)rē+\ *vt* [*re-* + *clean*] **:** to clean again

re·clin·able \rəˈklīnəbəl, rēˈ-\ *adj* **:** able to be reclined

rec·li·nate \ˈrekləˌnāt, -nət\ *also* **rec·li·nat·ed** \-ˌnād·əd\ *adj* [L *reclinatus*, past part. of *reclinare* to recline] **:** bent downward so that the apex is below the base — used esp. of a stem or leaf

rec·li·na·tion \ˌ≈≈ˈnāshən\ *n* -S [LL *reclination-, reclinatio*, fr. L *reclinatus* + *-ion-, -io*, -ion] **:** the act of reclining or the state of being reclined

re·cline \rəˈklīn, rēˈ-\ *vb* -ED/-ING/-S [ME *reclinen*, fr. MF or L; MF *recliner*, fr. L *reclinare*, fr. *re-* + *clinare* to bend, lean — more at LEAN] *vt* **:** to cause or permit to incline backward : place in a recumbent position : LEAN, REST ⟨~*s* her head on a pillow⟩ ⟨*reclined* the seat a little —Henry LaCossitt⟩ **~ vi 1 :** to lean or incline backward ⟨was *reclining* against the mantelpiece in a strained counterfeit of perfect ease —Scott Fitzgerald⟩ **2 :** to lie in a recumbent position — usu. used with *on* ⟨on a sofa with two cylindrical pillows *reclined* a . . . pretty woman —Thomas Hardy⟩

reclined *adj* [fr. past part. of *recline*] **:** in a reclining position; *specif* **:** RECLINATE

re·clin·er \-nə(r)\ *n* -S **:** one that reclines; *specif* **:** a reclining dial or plane

reclining *adj* [fr. pres. part. of *recline*] **1 a :** bending or curving gradually back from the perpendicular **b :** RECUMBENT **2** [fr. gerund of *recline*] **:** suitable for reclining in ⟨a ~ chair⟩

reclining-chair car *n* **:** CHAIR CAR 1

re·closer \(ˈ)rē+\ *n* [*re-* + *closer*] **:** a switch or circuit breaker that establishes an electrical circuit again manually, remotely, or automatically after an interruption of service

re·closure \"+\ *n* [*re-* + *closure*] **:** establishment of an interrupted electrical circuit again by the closing of a switch or circuit breaker

¹rec·luse \ˈreˌklüs, -rəˈk-, rēˈk-, -üz\ *adj* [ME *reclus, recluse*, fr. OF *reclus*, lit., shut up, fr. LL *reclusus*, past part. of *recludere* to shut up, fr. L *re-* + *claudere* to shut, close — more at CLOSE] **1 a :** removed from society : shut up : CLOISTERED ⟨wondered who the ~ reader previously occupying the house could have been —F.N.Souza⟩ **b :** avoiding others : SOLITARY ⟨this bird . . . is shy and ~, affecting remote marshes —John Burroughs⟩ **2 :** characterized by solitariness or retirement from society ⟨a ~ existence⟩ **3 :** REMOTE, SECLUDED ⟨a barren and ~ region⟩ — **rec·luse·ly** *adv* — **rec·luse·ness** *n* -ES

²recluse \"\ *n* -S [ME *reclus, recluse*, fr. MF *reclus, fr. reclus* shut up] **1 :** a person who lives in seclusion; *specif* **:** INCLUSE **2 :** one who leads a retired or solitary life ⟨the quiet doings of an old would-be ~ —O.W.Holmes †1935⟩

³recluse *vt* -ED/-ING/-S [ME *reclusen*, fr. LL *reclusus*, past part. of *recludere*] *obs* **:** to shut up : SECLUDE

re·clu·sion \rəˈklüzhən, rēˈ-\ *n* -S [ME, fr. ML *reclusion-, reclusio*, fr. LL *reclusus* + L *-ion-, -io* -ion] **:** the state of being shut up or removed from society

re·clu·sive \rəˈklüs|iv, ˈrē,k-, |ēv *also* -üz| *or* |əv\ *adj* [³*recluse* + *-ive*] **1 :** marked by seclusion or retirement : SOLITARY ⟨a vast difference between an acceptable social attitude and an asocial or ~ attitude —A.T.Weaver⟩ ⟨sit under the ~ calm of the acacia tree —H.E.Bates⟩ **2 :** seeking solitude : retiring from society ⟨said to be broken down in health and mind, to be ~, melancholy —Joyce Cary⟩

recm *abbr* recommend; recommended

re·coal \(ˈ)rē+\ *vb* [*re-* + *coal*] *vt* **:** to load with a fresh supply of coal ⟨~*ing* a ship⟩ **~ vi :** to take on a fresh supply of coal ⟨traveled without ~*ing*⟩

re·coat \"+\ *vt* [*re-* + *coat*] **:** to coat again

re·coat·a·bil·i·ty \(ˌ)≈ˌkōd·əˈbiləd·ē\ *n* [*recoat* + *-ability*] **:** a quality in a paint that makes the paint esp. adapted to being applied in a coat over which one or more additional coats can be satisfactorily applied

re·cock \(ˈ)rē+\ *vb* [*re-* + *cock*] *vt* **:** to cock again ⟨~*ed* the gun⟩ **~ vi :** to cock a firearm again

recoct *vt* -ED/-ING/-S [L *recoctus*, past part. of *recoquere* to cook again, fr. *re-* + *coquere* to cook — more at COOK] *obs* **:** to cook or boil a second time

re·code \(ˈ)rē+\ *vt* **:** to code again

re·codification \(ˌ)rē+\ *n* [fr. *recodify*, after E *codify: codification*] **:** the action of recodifying or state of being recodified

re·codify \(ˈ)rē+\ *vt* [*re-* + *codify*] **:** to codify again

re·cogitate \(ˈ)rē+\ *vi* [L *recogitatus*, past part. of *recogitare* to think over again, fr. *re-* + *cogitare* to cogitate] **:** to think over again

rec·og·ni·tion \ˌrekəgˈnishən, -kēg'n- *sometimes* -kəˈ-\ *n* -S [L *recognition-, recognitio*, fr. *recognitus* (past part. of *recognoscere* to recognize, examine, investigate) + *-ion-, -io*, -ion — more at RECOGNIZE] **1 :** the action of recognizing or state of being recognized: as **a :** formal acknowledgment (as of a fact or claim): (1) **:** an expression of reception of the sovereign by the people at a coronation (2) **:** a formal acknowledgment of the de facto existence of a government of a country or of the independence of an insurgent or rebelling community or province that allows the establishment of relations but does not imply the de jure acknowledgment of the government recognized (3) **:** formal acknowledgment of a union by an employer in its capacity as the official representative of or bargaining agent for an employee group or bargaining unit **b :** acceptance of an individual as being entitled to consideration or attention ⟨~ by the chair of one rising to speak in a meeting⟩ **c :** acknowledgment of something done or given esp. by making some return ⟨a gift in ~ of a service⟩ **d :** perception of identity as already known in fact or by description ⟨~ of a former friend⟩ ⟨~ of a genuine diamond⟩ ⟨escaped ~⟩ **e :** discernment of the character, status, or class of something ⟨~ of a principle involved⟩ **f :** the form of memory that consists in knowing or feeling that a present object has been met before — compare RECALL **g :** an incident or solution of plot in tragedy in which the main character recognizes his own or some other character's true identity or discovers the true nature of his own situation **h :** identification of friendly and enemy planes and ships **2 :** special notice or attention ⟨a writer who has received much ~⟩ **3 a :** a form of inquest by jury existing under the early Norman kings **b** *Scots law* **:** the act of a feudal superior in recognoscing lands from a tenant esp. for unauthorized alienation

re–cognition \ˌrē+\ *n* [*re-* + *cognition*] **:** a second cognition : a knowing usu. without conscious identification of something that has been known before — **re–cognitional** \"+\ *adj*

recognition mark *n* **:** a distinctive usu. conspicuous marking of an animal (as the white tail of an antelope) supposed to serve as a signal to other animals of the same kind

recognition panel *n* **:** a distinctively colored piece of cloth used to mark the position of friendly ground forces and serving as a visual aid to pilots coming in to fire on nearby enemy troops or to drop supplies or reinforcements

re·cog·ni·tive \rəˈkägnəd·iv\ *adj* [L *recognitus* (past part. of *recognoscere* to recognize) + E *-ive*] **:** of, relating to, or marked by recognition

re·cog·ni·tor \-nəd·ə(r)\ *n* -S [ML, fr. L *recognitus* (past part. of *recognoscere* to know again, examine, investigate) + *-or* — more at RECOGNIZE] **:** one of a jury impaneled on an assize to hold a recognition in England in the period following the Norman Conquest

re·cog·ni·to·ry \-nəˌtōrē\ *adj* [L *recognitus* + E *-ory*] **:** of, relating to, or marked by recognition

rec·og·niz·abil·i·ty \ˌrekəgˌnīzəˈbiləd·ē, -kēg,n- *sometimes* -kə,n- *or* -ləté, -i\ *n* **:** the quality or state of being recognizable

rec·og·niz·able \ˈ≈≈ˌnīzəbəl, ˌ≈≈ˈ≈≈≈\ *adj* **:** capable of being recognized

rec·og·niz·ably \-blē, -bli\ *adv* **:** in a recognizable manner

re·cog·ni·zance \rəˈkägnəzən(t)s, rēˈ- *sometimes* -ˈkänə-\ *n* -S [alter. (influenced by *recognize*) of ME *reconissaunce*, fr. MF *reconoissance* recognition, fr. *reconois-* (stem of *reconoistre* to recognize) + *-ance*] **1 a** (1) **:** an obligation of record entered into before a court of record or before a magistrate duly authorized that makes the performance of some act (as appearing in court, keeping the peace, paying a debt) the condition of nonforfeiture and that is witnessed by the record only — compare BOND 5a(1) (2) **:** the sum liable to forfeiture upon such an obligation **b :** a simple personal obligation or undertaking entered into before a magistrate and having no money penalty attached ⟨on his own ~⟩ **2** *archaic* **:** RECOGNITION **3** *archaic* **:** TOKEN, PLEDGE

re·cog·ni·zant \-zənt\ *adj* [*recognize* + *-ant*] *archaic* **:** recognizing or acknowledging something — usu. used with *of*

re–cognize \(ˈ)rē+\ *vt* [*re-* + *cognize*] **:** to cognize again

rec·og·nize \ˈrekəgˌnīz, -kēg,n- *also* ÷ -kə,n-\ *vb* -ED/-ING/-S *see -ize in Explan Notes* [modif. (influenced by L *recognoscere* & E *-ize*) of MF *reconoiss-* (stem of *reconoistre*, fr. L *recognoscere* to know again, recognize, examine, investigate, fr. *re-* + *cognoscere* to know) — more at COGNITION] *vt* **1** *obs* **a :** to admit the fact, truth, or validity of **b :** REVISE, CORRECT **2 a :** to recall knowledge of : make out as or perceive to be something previously known ⟨*recognized* her long lost brother⟩ ⟨*recognized* the word when they heard it again⟩ ⟨*recognized* something familiar about the place⟩ **b :** to perceive clearly : be fully aware of : REALIZE ⟨*recognized* that this sort of thing had to stop sometime⟩ **3 :** to acknowledge formally: as **a :** to admit as being of a particular status ⟨*recognized* as the legitimate representative⟩ ⟨*recognized* him as king⟩ **b :** to admit as being one entitled to be heard (as in a meeting) : give the floor to **c** (1) **:** to acknowledge the de facto existence of (as a government in a state) (2) **:** to acknowledge the independence of (as a community or body that has thrown off the sovereignty of a state to which it was subject) and treat as independent or as otherwise effective **4 :** to acknowledge in some definite way : take notice of: as **a :** to acknowledge with a show of approval or appreciation ⟨*recognizing* with gratitude what had been done⟩ **b :** to acknowledge acquaintance with ⟨refused to ~ him when he walked into the room⟩ **c :** to admit the fact or existence of ⟨*recognized* the obligation⟩ **5 :** to bind by a recognizance **~ vi :** to enter into an obligation of record before a tribunal

rec·og·nized·ly \ˌ≈≈ˈnīz(ə)dlē, -li\ *adv* [*recognized* (fr. past part. of *recognize*) + *-ly*] **:** in a way that is recognized or acknowledged or that allows or compels recognition : ADMITTEDLY ⟨is ~ superior in this sort of work⟩

re·cog·ni·zee \rəˌkä(g)nəˈzē\ *n* -S [*recognize* + *-ee*] **:** the person in whose favor a recognizance is made

rec·og·niz·er \ˈrekəgˌnīzə(r), -kēg,n- *sometimes* -kə,n-\ *n* -S [*recognize* + *-er*] **:** one that recognizes

rec·og·niz·ing·ly *adv* [*recognizing* (pres. part. of *recognize*) + *-ly*] **:** with recognition ⟨looked at him ~⟩

re·cog·ni·zor \rəˌkä(g)nəˈzó(ə)r\ *n* -S [*recognize* + *-or*] **:** one that enters into a recognizance

re·cog·nosce \ˌrēˌkägˈnäs\ *vb* -ED/-ING/-S [L *recognoscere* to recognize] *vt, Scots law* **:** to resume the possession of (lands granted to a tenant) esp. for unauthorized alienation **~ vi,** *Scots law, of lands* **:** to return to the superior by recognition

¹re·coil \rəˈkȯil, rēˈ-, *esp before pause or consonant* -ȯiəl\ *vb* -ED/-ING/-S [ME *reculen, recoilen*, fr. OF *reculer*, fr. *re-* + *cul* backside, fr. L *culus* — more at CULET] *vt, obs* **:** to force back : cause to retreat or withdraw **~ vi 1 a :** to fall or draw back under the impact of force or pressure : undergo a forcing backward ⟨the troops ~*ed* before the savage onslaught of the enemy⟩; *esp* **:** to reel back ⟨~*ed* under the heavy blows⟩ **b :** to shrink back esp. with a sudden movement (as in horror, fear, disgust) : move suddenly backward or away ⟨opened the door and ~*ed* in terror⟩ **2** *archaic* **:** to withdraw oneself (as into solitude) : go away or apart : RETIRE ⟨~*ed* into the wilderness —William Wordsworth⟩ **3 a :** to spring back : REBOUND: as (1) **:** to fly back (as of a released spring) into an uncompressed position (2) **:** to kick back (as of a gun being fired) **b :** to return suddenly to or as if to a source or starting point ⟨their hatred ~*ed* on themselves⟩ **4** *obs* **:** DEGENERATE

syn SHRINK, FLINCH, WINCE, BLENCH, QUAIL: RECOIL may indicate a drawing back, starting back, or swerving backward through fear, shock, or disgust; it may indicate an inner drawing back with emotion ⟨she makes a gesture as if to touch him.

He *recoils* impatiently —G.B.Shaw⟩ ⟨he had so great a dread of snakes that he instinctively *recoiled* at the sight of one —T.B.Costain⟩ SHRINK indicates an instinctive recoil through sensitiveness, scrupulousness, or cowardice ⟨when it came to telling the truth about himself he *shrank* from the task with all the horror of a well-bred English gentleman —Virginia Woolf⟩ ⟨a nervous avoidance of crowds, a *shrinking* from any change in her secluded manner of living —Ellen Glasgow⟩ ⟨to *shrink* from responsibility is to invite social and economic insecurity —H.G.Armstrong⟩ FLINCH involves a recoiling, retreating, or evading when one cannot muster up resolution to face the frightening, painful, or revolting ⟨all retreat was cut off, and he looked his fate in the face without *flinching* —John Burroughs⟩ ⟨he raised the head that lay in the dust with cautious strength, fearing that any touch might only be so much more needless pain. But there was no appearance of *flinching* —W.F.De Morgan⟩ ⟨did not *flinch* from the contemplation of the violent aggression —J.H.Plumb⟩ WINCE applies to an involuntary starting back or away caused by sensitiveness, dread, fear, or pain ⟨to bring a beaten and degraded look into a man's face, rend manhood out of him in fear, is a sight that makes decent men *wince* in pain; for it is an outrage on the decency of life, an offense to natural religion, a violation of the human sanctities —G.D.Brown⟩ ⟨her eyes *winced* for a moment as if she had become suddenly afraid —Liam O'Flaherty⟩ ⟨he *winced* as though she had uttered blasphemy —W.J.Locke⟩ BLENCH may refer especially to fainthearted fearful flinching ⟨she had not been prepared for an attack in flank, and *blenched* before it —Maurice Hewlett⟩ ⟨though his death seemed near he did not *blench* —John Masefield⟩ QUAIL implies cowering and shrinking in fright, consternation, or defeated dejection ⟨despite his professions of sanity and reason, had an inexplicable, invincible horror of death; he *quailed* at the mere mention of the black phantom —Norman Douglas⟩ ⟨I am never known to *quail* at the fury of a gale —W.S.Gilbert⟩ **syn** see in addition REBOUND

²recoil \", 'ˌ=\ *n* -s **1 a :** the action of recoiling; *esp* **:** the kickback of a gun upon being fired **b :** the action of having recoiled; *specif* **:** REACTION ⟨the ~ from formalism is skepticism —F.W.Robertson⟩ **2 :** the extent to which something (as a gun, spring) recoils

re-coil \(ˈ)rē+\ *vb* [*re-* + *coil*] *vt* **:** to coil again ~ *vi* **:** to become coiled again

recoil click *n* **:** a pawl in a timepiece that recoils slightly after each winding and that is designed to prevent excessively tight coiling of the mainspring

recoil cylinder *n* **:** a fixed cylinder into which a piston attached to a gun that is to be fired is forced by the recoil of the gun on firing and which is so designed (as by the use of a hydraulic system or pneumatic system) as to lessen or altogether check the recoil or counterrecoil of the gun

recoil escapement *n* **:** ANCHOR ESCAPEMENT

re·coil·less \-lləs\ *adj* [²*recoil* + *-less*] **:** having a minimum of recoil ⟨a ~ gun⟩

re·coil·ment \-lmənt\ *n* -s [¹*recoil* + *-ment*] *archaic* **:** RECOIL

recoil-operated \(ˈ)=ˌ=ˈ==ˌ==\ *adj* [²*recoil* + *operated*, past part. of *operate*] *of a firearm* **:** having an action that functions by the movement of parts in recoil

recoil pad *n* **:** a soft rubber pad fitted to the butt of a rifle or shotgun for absorbing part of the shock of recoil

recoil spring *n* **:** a spring used to cushion the shock of a recoiling gun or other mechanism

re·coin \(ˈ)rē+\ *vt* [*re-* + *coin*] **:** to coin again; *specif* **:** to melt down (old or worn coin) and make into new coin

re·coinage \"+\ *n* [*re-* + *coinage*] **1 :** the action or process of recoining **2 :** coinage produced by recoining

re-collect \ˌrē+\ *vb* [partly fr. L *recollectus*, past part. of *recolligere* to gather again, fr. *re-* + *colligere* to collect; partly fr. *re-* + *collect* — more at COLLECT] *vt* **1 a :** to gather together again ⟨*re-collecting* the frightened chicks⟩ **b :** to get back again **:** RECOVER ⟨*re-collected* his courage⟩ **c :** to pull (oneself) together **:** recover control over (oneself) **:** COMPOSE ⟨was briefly flurried but then *re-collected* herself⟩ **2** *obs* **:** RECALL ⟨can also ~ you from . . . desperation —John Donne⟩ ~ *vi* **:** REASSEMBLE ⟨found the people gradually *re-collecting* in the town square⟩

rec·ol·lect \ˌrekəˈlekt\ *vb* -ED/-ING/-S [ML *recollectus*, fr. past part. of *recolligere* to recall to mind, fr. L, to gather again] *vt* **1 a :** to recall the knowledge of **:** call to mind ⟨~*ed* having seen her somewhere⟩ **b :** to recall something forgotten to (oneself) ⟨~*ed* himself just in time and addressed her by name⟩ **2 :** to cause (as oneself, one's mind) to be absorbed in thought, meditation, or contemplation ⟨could not ~ herself in church⟩ ~ *vi* **:** to call something to mind **:** remember something **:** have a recollection **syn** see REMEMBER

recollected *adj* [fr. past part. of *recollect*] **1 :** COMPOSED, CALM ⟨not sufficiently ~ to discuss the matter⟩ ⟨cool and ~ at all times⟩ **2 :** marked by or given to recollection ⟨a ~ nun⟩ **3 :** recalled to memory ⟨~ happiness⟩ — **rec·ol·lect·ed·ly** *adv* — **rec·ol·lect·ed·ness** *n* -ES

re-collection \ˌrē+\ *n* [*re-collect* + *-ion*] **:** the action of re-collecting **:** a gathering together again

rec·ol·lec·tion \ˌrekəˈlekshən\ *n* -S [F *récollection*, fr. ML *recollection-, recollectio*, fr. *recollectus* (past part. of *recolligere* to recollect) + L *-ion-, -io* -ion] **1 :** quiet tranquillity of mind and self-possession; *esp* **:** religious composure **2 a** (1) **:** the action of recalling to the mind **:** REMEMBRANCE (2) **:** the power of recalling to the mind **:** MEMORY **b :** what is recalled to the mind ⟨happy ~*s*⟩ **syn** see MEMORY

rec·ol·lec·tive \ˌrekəˈlektiv\ *adj* [*recollect* + *-ive*] **1 :** of or relating to recollection **:** RECOLLECTED **2 :** having the power of recollecting — **rec·ol·lec·tive·ly** \-tə̇vlē\ *adv* — **rec·ol·lec·tive·ness** \-tivnə̇s\ *n* -ES

rec·ol·let \ˌrekəˌlet, rāköˈlā\ *n* -S [CanF *récollet*, fr. F, member of a branch of the Franciscan order, fr. ML *recollectus*, lit., recollected, fr. past part. of *recolligere* to recollect; fr. the resemblance of the bird's crest to the friar's hood] **:** CEDAR WAXWING

re·colonization \(ˌ)rē+\ *n* [*recolonize* + *-ation*] **:** the action of recolonizing or state of being recolonized

re·colonize \(ˈ)rē+\ *vt* [*re-* + *colonize*] **:** to colonize again

re·color \(ˈ)rē+\ *vt* [*re-* + *color*] **:** to color again

re·comb \(ˈ)rē+\ *vt* [*re-* + *comb*] **:** to comb again

re·com·bi·nant \rēˈkämbənənt\ *n* -S [*recombination* + *-ant*] *biol* **:** an individual exhibiting recombination

re·combination \(ˌ)rē+\ *n* [*re-* + *combination*] **1 a :** the formation of new combinations of genes in fertilization **b :** the formation of new combinations of linked genes (as by crossing over) resulting in new heritable characters or new combinations of such characters **2 :** the union of a positive and a negative ion to form a neutral atom or molecule — **re·combinational** \"+\ *adj*

re·combine \ˌrē+\ *vb* [*re-* + *combine*] **:** to combine again

recombined milk *n* [*re-* + *combined*] **:** milk made by combining cream, butterfat, or milk fat and water with nonfat dry milk solids — compare RECONSTITUTED MILK

re·comfort \rə̇+\ *vt* [ME *recomforten*, fr. MF *reconforter*, fr. OF, fr. *re-* + *conforter* to comfort] **1** *archaic* **:** COMFORT, CONSOLE **2** *archaic* **:** REFRESH, STRENGTHEN

re·commence \ˌrē+\ *vb* [ME *recommencen*, fr. MF *recommencer*, fr. OF, fr. *re-* + *commencer* to commence] *vi* **:** to undergo a new beginning **:** start up again **:** commence again ~ *vt* **:** to cause to begin again **:** RENEW

re·commencement \"+\ *n* [*re-* + *commencement*] **:** a second or fresh commencement

re·com·menc·er \-(t)sə(r)\ *n* [*recommence* + *-er*] **:** one that recommences

¹rec·om·mend \ˌrekəˈmend, ˈ==ˌ=\ *vb* -ED/-ING/-S [ME *recommenden*, fr. ML *recommendare*, fr. L *re-* + *commendare* to commend] *vt* **1 a** *obs* **:** PRAISE **b** (1) **:** to mention or introduce as being worthy of acceptance, use, or trial ⟨~*ed* the medicine⟩ (2) **:** to make a commendatory statement about as being fit or worthy (as for a job) ⟨~*ed* him highly⟩ (3) **:** to bring forward as being fit or worthy **:** present with approval **:** indicate as being one's choice for something or as otherwise having one's approval or support **:** offer or suggest as favored by oneself ⟨~*ed* several people to the governor for appointment⟩ ⟨~*ed* the book for leisure reading⟩ ⟨asked the waitress which item she would ~⟩ **2 :** ENTRUST, COMMIT, CONSIGN ⟨~*ed* them with confidence to her care⟩ ⟨~*ed* his soul to God⟩ ⟨~*ed* the case to the courts —Irving Brant⟩ **3 :** to make acceptable **:** attract favor to ⟨had other points to ~ it —Archibald Marshall⟩ **4 :** ADVISE, COUNSEL ⟨asked him what he would ~ doing⟩ ~ *vi* **:** to recommend something **:** make a recommendation ⟨a committee with power only to ~⟩

²recommend \"\ *n* -S *chiefly Brit* **:** RECOMMENDATION ⟨would get you a ~ —D.H.Lawrence⟩

rec·om·mend·able \-dəbəl\ *adj* [ME, fr. *recommenden* + *-able*] **1 :** that can be recommended **:** deserving recommendation ⟨a highly ~ novel⟩ **2 :** that is to be advised **:** PRUDENT, ADVISABLE ⟨it is ~ to keep apart large and small minorities —Yakov Malkiel⟩

rec·om·men·da·tion \ˌrekəmənˈdāshən, -ˌmenˈ-\ *n* -S [ME *recommendacion*, fr. ML *recommendation-, recommendatio*, fr. *recommendatus* (past part. of *recommendare* to recommend) + *-ion-, -io* -ion] **1 :** the action of recommending or condition of having been recommended **2 a :** a letter or some similar piece of writing indicating commendation ⟨had several good ~*s* with him when he applied for the job⟩ **b :** a statement expressing commendation ⟨could not get a ~ from him⟩ or giving advice or counsel ⟨followed his ~*s*⟩ **3 :** something that makes acceptable or pleasing ⟨a personality like that is already a big ~⟩

rec·om·mend·a·to·ry \ˌ==ˈmendəˌtōrē, -tȯr-, -ri\ *adj* [ML *recommendatus* + E *-ory*] **1 :** serving to commend or to attract favorable attention ⟨a ~ letter⟩ ⟨~ features⟩ **2 :** made or being in the form of a recommendation **:** ADVISORY ⟨~ legislation⟩

¹re·commission \ˌrē+\ *vt* [*re-* + *commission*] **:** to commission again

²recommission \"\ *n* **1 :** the action of recommissioning or state of being recommissioned **2 :** RECOMMITMENT

re·commit \"+\ *vt* [*re-* + *commit*] **1 a :** to refer (as a bill) again to a committee ⟨voted to ~ the bill for further study —*N.Y. Times*⟩ **b :** to entrust or consign again ⟨was *recommitted* into her keeping⟩ **2 :** to commit (as an offense, error) again ⟨*recommitted* the same offense⟩

re·commitment \"+\ *also* **re·committal** \"+\ *n* [*recommit* + *-ment, -al*] **:** the action of recommitting or state of being recommitted

re·communicate \"+\ *vb* [*re-* + *communicate*] *vt* **:** to communicate again ~ *vi* **:** to enter into communication again **:** hold fresh or further communication

re·compare \"+\ *vt* [*re-* + *compare*] **:** to compare again

re·comparison \"+\ *n* [*re-* + *comparison*] **:** a second or fresh comparison

rec·om·pence \ˈrekəmˌpen(t)s\ *archaic var of* RECOMPENSE

rec·om·pen·sa·ble \ˈ==ˌpen(t)səbəl\ *adj* [¹*recompense* + *-able*] **:** capable of being recompensed

re·compensation \(ˌ)rē+\ *n* [ME *recompensacion*, fr. MF, fr. LL *recompensation-, recompensatio*, fr. *recompensatus* (past part. of *recompensare* to recompense) + *-ion-, -io* -ion] **1** *obs* **:** RECOMPENSE **2** *Scots law* **:** a plaintiff's plea of a counterclaim made to meet a defendant's counterclaim in an action for debt

¹rec·om·pense \ˈrekəmˌpen(t)s\ *vb* -ED/-ING/-S [ME *recompensen*, fr. MF *recompenser*, fr. LL *recompensare*, fr. L *re-* + *compensare* to compensate] *vt* **1 a :** to give compensation to **:** REQUITE, REMUNERATE, COMPENSATE ⟨*recompensed* him for his losses⟩ ⟨were *recompensed* for our efforts⟩ **b :** to give an equivalent for **:** make up for by or as if by atoning for or requiting **:** pay for ⟨agreed to ~ all losses⟩ ⟨a pleasure that *recompensed* our trouble⟩ **2 :** to return in kind **:** reciprocate by or as if by rewarding or avenging **:** pay back ⟨*recompensed* the deed —William Cowper⟩ ~ *vi* **:** to repay something **:** make amends **:** make requital **syn** see PAY

²recompense \"\ *n* -S [ME, fr. MF, fr. *recompenser* to recompense] **1 :** the action or fact of recompensing **2 a :** an equivalent or a return for something done, suffered, or given **:** a repayment made (as by way of satisfaction, restitution, retribution) **:** COMPENSATION ⟨offered in ~ for his injuries⟩

rec·om·pens·er \-n(t)sə(r)\ *n* -S **:** one that recompenses

rec·om·pen·sive \-siv\ *adj* [¹*recompense* + *-ive*] **:** that recompenses

re·compete \ˌrē+\ *vi* [*re-* + *compete*] **:** to compete again

re·compile \"+\ *vt* [*re-* + *compile*] **:** to compile again

re·complete \"+\ *vt* [*re-* + *complete*] **:** to make complete again

re·completion \"+\ *n* [*recomplete* + *-ion*] **:** the action of recompleting or state of being recompleted

re·complicate \(ˈ)rē+\ *vt* [*re-* + *complicate*] **:** to complicate again

re·complication \(ˌ)rē+\ *n* [*recomplicate* + *-ion*] **:** the action of recomplicating or state of being recomplicated

re·comply \ˌrē+\ *vi* [*re-* + *comply*] **:** to comply again

re·compose \"+\ *vb* [*re-* + *compose*] *vt* **1 :** to compose again **:** form anew **:** RECOMBINE, REARRANGE ⟨shifting colors that constantly ~ themselves⟩ **2 :** to restore to composure ⟨*recomposed* his spirits⟩ ~ *vi* **:** to become recomposed

re·composition \(ˌ)rē+\ *n* [fr. *recompose*, after E *compose: composition*] **:** the action of recomposing or state of being recomposed

re·compound \ˌrē+\ *vt* [*re-* + *compound*] **:** to compound again

re·compress \"+\ *vt* [*re-* + *compress*] **:** to compress again **:** subject again to compression

re·compression \"+\ *n* [*recompress* + *-ion*] **:** the action of recompressing or state of being recompressed

re·computation \(ˌ)rē+\ *n* [*recompute* + *-ation*] **:** the action of recomputing or state of being recomputed

re·compute \ˌrē+\ *vt* [*re-* + *compute*] **:** to compute again

re·con \rə̇ˈkän, rēˈ-\ *n* -S [by shortening] **:** RECONNAISSANCE

re·conceive \ˌrē+\ *vt* [*re-* + *conceive*] **:** to conceive again

re·concentrate \(ˈ)rē+\ *vb* [*re-* + *concentrate*] *vt* **:** to concentrate again **:** subject again to reconcentration ~ *vi* **:** to become reconcentrated

re·concentration \(ˌ)rē+\ *n* [*reconcentrate* + *-ion*] **:** the action of reconcentrating or state of being reconcentrated; *esp* **:** the action or policy of concentrating the rural population in or about towns for convenience in political or military administration (as in Cuba during the revolution of 1895–98)

re·conception \ˌrē+\ *n* [*re-* + *conception*] **:** the action of reconceiving or state of being reconceived

re·conceptualization \"+\ *n* [*re-* + *conceptualization*] **:** a second or fresh conceptualization

re·conceptualize \"+\ *vt* [*re-* + *conceptualize*] **:** to conceptualize again

rec·on·cil·abil·i·ty \ˌrekənˌsīləˈbilədē, -lətē, -i\ *n* **:** the quality or state of being reconcilable

rec·on·cil·able \ˈrekənˌsīləbəl, ˌ==ˈ===\ *adj* **:** capable of being reconciled — **rec·on·cil·able·ness** *n* -ES

rec·on·cil·ably \-blē, -bli\ *adv* **:** in a reconcilable manner

rec·on·cile \ˈrekənˌsīl, ˌ==ˈ=\ *vb* -ED/-ING/-S [ME *reconcilen*, fr. MF or L; MF *reconcilier*, fr. L *reconciliare*, fr. *re-* + *conciliare* to conciliate] *vt* **1 a** (1) **:** to restore to friendship, compatibility, or harmony ⟨*reconciled* the two quarreling factions⟩ (2) **:** to restore (one under ecclesiastical interdict or excommunication) to communion (3) **:** to restore (as a desecrated church or cemetery) to sacred use esp. by reconsecration **b :** ADJUST, SETTLE ⟨*reconciling* differences⟩ **2 a :** to make consistent or congruous **:** HARMONIZE ⟨*reconciled* their ideals with practical reality⟩ **b :** to obtain agreement between (two financial records) by accounting for all outstanding items ⟨~ a checkbook with a bank statement⟩ **3 :** to cause to submit to or accept **:** bring into acquiescence with ⟨*reconciled* to hardship⟩ ~ *vi* **:** to become reconciled **syn** see ADAPT

rec·on·cile·less \ˈ==ˌsīlləs\ *adj* [*reconcile* + *-less*] *archaic* **:** IRRECONCILABLE

rec·on·cile·ment \-lmənt\ *n* -S [*reconcile* + *-ment*] **:** RECONCILIATION

rec·on·cil·er *also* **rec·on·ci·lor** \ˈrekənˌsīlə(r)\ *n* -S [*reconcile* + *-er, -or*] **:** one that reconciles

rec·on·cil·i·ate \ˌrekənˈsilēˌāt\ *vt* [L *reconciliatus*, past part. of *reconciliare* to reconcile] **:** RECONCILE

rec·on·cil·i·a·tion \ˌ==ˌ==ˈāshən\ *n* -S [ME *reconciliacion*, fr. MF or L; MF *reconciliation*, fr. L *reconciliation-, reconciliatio*, fr. *reconciliatus* + *-ion-, -io* -ion] **:** the action of reconciling or state of being reconciled

rec·on·cil·i·a·tor \ˈ==ˌ==ˌād·ə(r)\ *n* -S [L, fr. *reconciliatus* + *-or*] **:** RECONCILER

rec·on·cil·ia·to·ry \ˌ==ˈsilyəˌtōrē, -lēə-, -tȯr-, -ri\ *adj* [L *reconciliatus* + E *-ory*] **:** serving or tending to reconcile

reconciling *adj* [fr. pres. part. of *reconcile*] **:** that reconciles — **rec·on·cil·ing·ly** *adv*

re·condemn \ˌrē+\ *vt* [*re-* + *condemn*] **:** to condemn again

re·condemnation \(ˌ)rē+\ *n* [*recondemn* + *-ation*] **:** the action of recondemning or state of being recondemned

re·condensation \"+\ *n* [*recondense* + *-ation*] **:** the action of recondensing or state of being recondensed

re·condense \ˌrē+\ *vb* [*re-* + *condense*] *vt* **:** to condense again ~ *vi* **:** to become condensed again

recon·dite \ˈrekənˌdīt, rə̇ˈkän-, rēˈk-, *usu* -īd.+V\ *adj* [L *reconditus*, fr. past part. of *recondere* to put up again, lay up, conceal, fr. *re-* + *condere* to bring together, store up — more at CONDITE] **1** *archaic* **:** hidden away or otherwise concealed so as not to be seen ⟨produced some ~ flasks of wine —T.L.Peacock⟩ **2 a :** very difficult to understand and beyond the reach of ordinary comprehension and knowledge **:** DEEP ⟨found the subject somewhat too ~⟩ **b** (1) **:** consisting of, relating to, or dealing with what is uncommon, abstruse, or profound ⟨spent his life in ~ studies⟩ (2) **:** unknown or little known except to a specialist ⟨the ~ literature of ancient India⟩ **c :** OBSCURE ⟨~ mysteries⟩

recon·dite·ly *adv* **:** in a recondite manner

recon·dite·ness *n* -ES **:** the quality or state of being recondite

re·condition \ˌrē+\ *vt* [*re-* + *condition*] **1 :** to restore to a good condition (as by repairing, replacing parts, beautifying) ⟨a ~*ed* car⟩ **2 :** REFORM ⟨~*ing* her emotional attitudes⟩

re·conduct \ˌrē+\ *vt* [L *reconductus*, past part. of *reconducere* to lead back, fr. *re-* + *conducere* to conduct] **:** to conduct back

re·conduction \"+\ *n* [*reconduct* + *-ion*] **1 :** the action of reconducting or state of being reconducted **2** [F *réconduction*, fr. L *reconductus* (past. part. of *reconducere* to lead back, lease again, fr. *re-* + *conducere* to conduct, hire, lease) + F *-ion*] *civil law* **:** a renewal of a lease **:** RELOCATION

re·confer \"+\ *vt* [*re-* + *confer*] **:** to confer again

re·confess \"+\ *vb* [*re-* + *confess*] *vt* **:** to confess again ~ *vi* **:** to make another or a new confession

re·confide \"+\ *vt* [*re-* + *confide*] **:** to confide again

re·confine \"+\ *vt* [*re-* + *confine*] **:** to confine again

re·confirm \"+\ *vt* [*re-* + *confirm*] **:** to confirm again; *esp* **:** to confirm again the reservation of (a seat on a particular plane flight)

re·confirmation \(ˌ)rē+\ *n* [*reconfirm* + *-ation*] **:** the action of reconfirming or state of being reconfirmed

re·confiscate \(ˈ)rē+\ *vt* [*re-* + *confiscate*] **:** to confiscate again

re·confiscation \(ˌ)rē+\ *n* [*reconfiscate* + *-ion*] **:** the action of reconfiscating or state of being reconfiscated

re·congeal \ˌrē+\ *vb* [*re-* + *congeal*] **:** to congeal again

re·con·nais·sance *also* **re·con·nois·sance** \rēˈkänəzən(t)s, rə̇ˈ-, -əsən-\ *n* -S *often attrib* [F *reconnaissance* recognition, exploration, fr. obs. *reconoissance*, fr. MF *reconoissance* — more at RECOGNIZANCE] **1 :** an exploratory or preliminary survey, inspection, or examination made to gain information: as **a :** an exploratory military survey (as by aircraft or by the probes of small land units) of enemy territory and of enemy installations, movements, activities, and strength **b :** aerial photographing of activity (as shipping) or installations in friendly, enemy, or neutral areas **c** (1) **:** an engineering survey of a region (as in preparing for triangulation of the region) designed esp. to yield information about its general natural features (2) **:** a geological survey of a region **2** *or* **reconnaissance car :** a fast military car used for reconnaissance and typically provided with light armor, machine guns, and a two-way radio

reconnaissance in force : an attack by a large force for the purpose of discovering the position and strength of an enemy

re·connect \ˌrē+\ *vt* [*re-* + *connect*] **:** to connect again

¹recon·noi·ter *also* **recon·noi·tre** \ˌrekəˈnȯid·ə(r), ˌrēk-, -ȯitə-\ *vb* **reconnoitered** *also* **reconnoitred; reconnoitered** *also* **reconnoitred; reconnoitering** *also* **reconnoitring** \-ȯid·əriŋ, -ȯi·triŋ\ **reconnoiters** *also* **reconnoitres** [obs. F *reconnoître*, to recognize, examine, explore, fr. MF *reconoistre* — more at RECOGNIZE] *vt* **1 :** to make an exploratory or preliminary survey, inspection, or examination of **:** make a reconnaissance of ⟨~*ing* enemy territory⟩ **2** *obs* **:** RECALL, REMEMBER ~ *vi* **:** to make a reconnaissance

²reconnoiter *also* **reconnoitre** \"\ *n* -S **:** RECONNAISSANCE

recon·noi·ter·er \-ȯid·ərə(r), -ȯi·trə-\ *also* **recon·noi·trer** \-·trə(r)\ *n* -S **:** one that reconnoiters

recon·noi·ter·ing·ly *adv* [*reconnoitering* (pres. part. of ¹*reconnoiter*) + *-ly*] **:** in such a way as to reconnoiter

re·conquer \(ˈ)rē+\ *vt* [*re-* + *conquer*] **:** to conquer again; *esp* **:** recover by conquest

re·conquest \"+\ *n* [*re-* + *conquest*] **:** a second or new conquest of something previously conquered; *esp* **:** recovery of something by conquest

re·consecrate \(ˈ)rē+\ *vt* [*re-* + *consecrate*] **:** to consecrate again

re·consecration \(ˌ)rē+\ *n* [*reconsecrate* + *-ion*] **:** the action of reconsecrating or state of being reconsecrated

re·consider \ˌrē+\ *vb* [*re-* + *consider*] *vt* **:** to consider again: as **a :** to think over, discuss, or debate (as a plan, decision) esp. with a view to changing or reversing ⟨an opportunity to ~ my decision, so painfully arrived at —R.M.Lovett⟩ **b :** to take up again (as a motion or vote previously acted on) in a meeting (as a legislative assembly) ⟨asked the house to ~ the measure⟩ ~ *vi* **:** to consider something again **:** engage in reconsideration ⟨asked him to ~ before taking such a step⟩

re·consideration \"+\ *n* [*reconsider* + *-ation*] **:** the action of reconsidering or state of being reconsidered

re·consign \"+\ *vt* [*re-* + *consign*] **:** to consign again or anew

re·consignment \"+\ *n* [*reconsign* + *-ment*] **:** the action of reconsigning or state of being reconsigned; *esp* **:** a change (as in consignee, destination, route) in the original billing of goods in transit

re·console \"+\ *vt* [*re-* + *console*] **:** to console again

re·consolidate \"+\ *vb* [*re-* + *consolidate*] *vt* **:** to consolidate again ~ *vi* **:** to become reconsolidated

re·consolidation \"+\ *n* [*re-* + *consolidation*] **:** the action of reconsolidating or state of being reconsolidated **:** a second or fresh consolidation

¹re·constituent \"+\ *adj* [*re-* + *constituent*] **:** that reconstitutes; *esp* **:** serving to build up new tissue to replace that wasted by disease or other factors ⟨a ~ tonic⟩

²reconstituent \"\ *n* **:** something that is reconstituent

re·constitute \(ˈ)rē+\ *vt* [*re-* + *constitute*] **1 :** to build up again by putting back together the original parts or elements **:** RECONSTRUCT, RE-FORM ⟨~ a fragmentary text⟩; *esp* **:** to restore the constitution of (as a concentrated juice) by adding water **2 :** to build up again in a somewhat new or different form **:** REORGANIZE ⟨~ a bankrupt company⟩ ⟨~ an armored division⟩

reconstituted milk *n* [fr. past part. of *reconstitute*] **:** milk reconstituted by combining dry whole milk solids with the appropriate amount of water; *also* **:** milk made by adding water to evaporated milk —compare RECOMBINED MILK

re·constitution \(ˌ)rē+\ *n* [*re-* + *constitution*] **1 :** the action of reconstituting or state of being reconstituted **2 :** regeneration of an organic form by reorganization of existent tissue without blastema formation

re·construct \ˌrē+\ *vt* [*re-* + *construct*] **:** to construct again: as **a** (1) **:** to build again **:** REBUILD ⟨~*ing* destroyed railroads⟩ (2) **:** to make over **:** REPAIR ⟨~*ed* the highways that needed it⟩ **b :** to subject (an organ or part of the body) to surgery so as to correct a defect in or to reform **c** (1) **:** RECONSTITUTE ⟨~*ed* lemon juice⟩ (2) **:** REORGANIZE, REESTABLISH ⟨~*ing* society during the postwar period⟩ (3) **:** REHABILITATE ⟨~*ing* a twisted personality⟩ **d** (1) **:** to put together again **:** REASSEMBLE ⟨~*ing* a ruined pagan temple⟩ (2) **:** to restore or mount (a sheet of postage stamps) in the original form or in a replica of the original form (3) **:** to form (as a gem) by fusing together particles derived from one or more natural stones of the kind desired ⟨a ~*ed* ruby⟩ **e :** to build up again mentally (as from available evidence) **:** form a concept of **:** REEVOKE, RE-CREATE ⟨~*ing* the culture of a lost civilization⟩ **f :** to win over, make conform, or reconcile to a new or different order ⟨refuses to be ~*ed* by events —Carl Van Doren⟩

re·constructible \"+\ *adj* : capable of being reconstructed
re·construction \"+\ *n* [*re-* + *construction*] **1 a** : the action of reconstructing or state of being reconstructed **b** *often cap* : the reorganization and reestablishment in the Union during a period (1867–1877) following the American Civil War of those states that had seceded **2** : something reconstructed: as **a** : a model or replica of something **b** : something reassembled (as from parts) into its original form or appearance
re·constructional \"+\ *adj* [*reconstruction* + *-al*] : of or relating to reconstruction
re·con·struc·tion·ary \ˌrēkənˈstrəkshəˌnerē, -kənˈstr-\ *adj* [*reconstruction* + *-ary*] : RECONSTRUCTIONAL
re·constructionism \ˌrē+\ *n* [*reconstruction* + *-ism*] : adherence to or advocacy of reconstruction; *specif, often cap* : a movement in 20th century American Judaism influenced by Conservative Judaism and by pragmatism that advocates a creative adjustment of Jewish life to contemporary conditions by stressing the cultivation of traditions and folkways shared by all Jews as a basis for reconstructing historic Judaism into a religious civilization that would transcend denominationalism and ensure the unity and survival of the Jewish people
re·constructionist \"+\ *n* [*reconstruction* + *-ist*] **1** : an adherent or advocate of reconstruction **2** *often cap* : an adherent or advocate of reconstructionism
re·constructive \"+\ *adj* [*reconstruct* + *-ive*] : relating to, marked by, or aimed at reconstruction ⟨~ penology⟩ — **re·constructively** \"+\ *adv*
reconstructive surgery *n* : surgery that aims at restoring function or normal appearance by remaking defective organs or parts ⟨*reconstructive surgery* of the femoral head⟩
re·constructor \"+\ *n* [*reconstruct* + *-or*] : one that reconstructs
re·construe \"+\ *vt* [*re-* + *construe*] : to construe again
re·consult \"+\ *vb* [*re-* + *consult*] *vt* : to consult again ~ *vi* : to engage in a second or fresh consultation
re·consultation \(ˌ)rē+\ *n* [*re-* + *consultation*] : a second or fresh consultation
re·contact \(ˈ)rē+\ *vt* [*re-* + *contact*] : to contact again
re·contaminate \ˌrē+\ *vt* [*re-* + *contaminate*] : to contaminate again
re·contamination \"+\ *n* [*recontaminate* + *-ion*] : the action of recontaminating or state of being recontaminated
re·contemplate \(ˈ)rē+\ *vt* [*re-* + *contemplate*] : to contemplate again
re·contemplation \(ˌ)rē+\ *n* [*recontemplate* + *-ion*] : the action of recontemplating or state of being recontemplated
re·continue \ˌrē+\ *vb* [*re-* + *continue*] *vt* : to continue again ~ *vi* : to proceed again
¹re·contract \(ˈ)rē+, ˌrē+\ *vb* [*re-* + *contract*, v.] *vt* : to contract again ~ *vi* **1** : to make a new contract **2** : to undergo a new contraction
²re·contract \(ˈ) rē+\ *n* [*re-* + *contract*, n.] : a new contract
re·contraction \ˌrē+\ *n* [*re-* + *contraction*] : a new contraction
¹re·control \"+\ *vt* [*re-* + *control*] : to subject (as prices, rents) to new control
²recontrol \"\ *n* : the action of recontrolling or state of being recontrolled
re·convalesce \(ˌ)rē+\ *vi* [*re-* + *convalesce*] : to undergo reconvalescence
re·convalescence \"+\ *n* [*re-* + *convalescence*] **1** : renewed convalescence **2** : complete convalescence
re·convalescent \"+\ *adj* [*re-* + *convalescent*] : of or relating to reconvalescence
re·convene \ˌrē+\ *vb* [*re-* + *convene*] *vi* : to convene again : assemble once more in a meeting ~ *vt* : to cause to convene again
re·convention \"+\ *n* [MF, fr. *re-* + *convention* agreement between two parties — more at CONVENTION] : a cross action by a defendant against a plaintiff before the same judge : COUNTERCLAIM
re·converge \"+\ *vi* [*re-* + *converge*] : to converge again
re·conversion \"+\ *n* [*re-* + *conversion*] **1** : a second or fresh conversion **2** : conversion back to a previous state: as **a** : change back to a previous state of belief or other conviction **b** : change back to a previous complex of qualities **c** : change (as of industry) from a wartime basis to a peacetime basis
re·convert \"+\ *vb* [*re-* + *convert*] *vt* : to cause to undergo reconversion : cause to change back ~ *vi* : to undergo reconversion : become changed back
re·convertible \"+\ *adj* [*reconvert* + *-ible*] : capable of being reconverted
re·convey \"+\ *vt* [*re-* + *convey*] **1** : to convey back (as to a previous place or position) **2** : to restore (as an estate) to a previous owner
re·conveyance \"+\ *n* [*reconvey* + *-ance*] : the action of reconveying or state of being reconveyed
re·convict \"+\ *vt* [*re-* + *convict*] : to convict again
re·conviction \"+\ *n* [*re-* + *conviction*] : a second or fresh conviction
re·convince \"+\ *vt* [*re-* + *convince*] : to convince again
re·convocation \(ˌ)rē+\ *n* [*re-* + *convocation*] : the action of reconvoking or state of being reconvoked
re·convoke \ˌrē+\ *vt* [*re-* + *convoke*] : to convoke again
re·cook \(ˈ)rē+\ *vt* [*re-* + *cook*] : to cook again
re·cool \"+\ *vt* [*re-* + *cool*] : to cool again
re·cooper \"+\ *vt* [*re-* + *cooper*] : to repair faults in (as barrels, casks, crates)
re·copper \"+\ *vt* [*re-* + *copper*] : to copper again
re·copy \"+\ *vt* [*re-* + *copy*] : to copy again
¹re·cord \rəˈkȯ(ə)rd, rēˈ-, -ȯ(ə)d\ *vb* -ED/-ING/-S [ME *recorden* to recall, recite, set down in writing, fr. OF *recorder*, fr. L *recordari* to call to mind, remember, fr. *re-* + *cord-, cor* heart, mind — more at HEART] *vt* **1 a** *obs* : RECALL, REMEMBER **b** *archaic* : SING, WARBLE ⟨hear the lark ~ her hymns —Edward Fairfax⟩ **2 a** (1) : to set down in writing : make a written account or note of : furnish written evidence of : put into written form ⟨a people that carefully ~*ed* their history⟩ ⟨~*ed* her impressions in a series of books⟩ ⟨~*ed* the sounds heard in phonetic symbols⟩ (2) : to make or have made an authentic official copy of (as a deed, mortgage, lease) and deposit or have deposited esp. as in an office designated by law (3) : to cause to be noted officially in or as if in writing ⟨~*ing* and tallying the votes⟩ ⟨~*ed* the proceedings of the court⟩ **b** (1) : to make an objective lasting indication of in some mechanical or automatic way : register permanently by mechanical means ⟨studied the intensity of the earthquake as it had been ~*ed* by the seismograph⟩ (2) *of an instrument* : to point out (data) at a particular time or under particular circumstances on or as if on a scale : show in this way ⟨noticed that at that moment the thermometer ~*ed* 90°⟩ **c** : to give evidence of ⟨the extent of the explosion is ~*ed* on the charred tree trunks of the surrounding area⟩ **3 a** : to cause (sound, visual images) to be transferred to and registered on something (as a phonograph disc, magnetic tape) by mechanical usu. electronic means in such a way that the thing so transferred and registered can (as by the use of a phonograph, tape recorder) be subsequently reproduced **b** : to register in this way a performance of (as an orchestra, singer, actor) or rendition or playing of (as a piece of music, an instrument) ~ *vi* **1 a** : to record something ⟨spent the whole day ~*ing*⟩ **b** : to admit of being recorded ⟨a voice that ~*s* beautifully⟩ **2** *archaic* : SING, WARBLE
²rec·ord \ˈrekə(r)d, -ˌkȯ(ə)d\ *n* -S [ME, fr. MF, fr. *recorder* to record] **1 a** : the state or fact of being recorded **b** : something (as a monument) on which a record has been made **c** (1) : evidence, knowledge, or information remaining in permanent form (as a relic, inscription, document) ⟨the ~ of an extinct people⟩ (2) : an account in writing or print (as in a document) or in some other permanent form (as on a monument) intended to perpetuate a knowledge of acts or events **2** : something that serves to record: as **a** (1) : a piece of writing that recounts or attests to something ⟨a ~ of the early history of a nation⟩ (2) : an official contemporaneous document recording the acts of some public body or public officer ⟨a ~ of city ordinances⟩ (3) : an authentic official copy of a document entered in a book or deposited in the keeping of some officer designated by law — compare CONVEYANCE 2b (4) : an official contemporaneous memorandum stating the proceedings of a court of justice (5) : an official copy of the legal papers used in a case and of memoranda of the proceedings of the court **b** : something that is known or can be learned or has been recorded: as (1) : an officially or sometimes nonofficially attested top performance or achievement (as in a competitive sport) ⟨a high jump that broke the ~⟩ (2) : cumulative data usu. consisting of written systematically arranged notes relating to an individual's or group's activities, abilities, accomplishments, or physical or moral qualities in a particular area (as school, business) ⟨a child with a good school ~⟩ ⟨carefully kept health ~*s*⟩ (3) : a body of known, recorded, or available facts about something : the sum of something done or achieved or the body of data known, recorded, or available about something ⟨looked at the ~ of the candidate⟩ ⟨had a long criminal ~⟩ ⟨a brilliant ~ as an executive⟩ **3** : something to which sound has been transferred by mechanical usu. electronic means and so registered as to be capable of subsequent reproduction by a specially designed instrument; *specif* : a disc with a spiral groove carrying recorded sound — **off the record** *adv* (*or adj*) : not for quotation (as by the press) or publication as something official or authoritative ⟨spoke *off the record*⟩ ⟨my remarks are *off the record*⟩ — **of record 1** : appearing on the record of a court in connection with a particular case, judgment, or other proceeding ⟨the attorney *of record*⟩ **2** : documented or otherwise attested ⟨a reversal of opinion that is *of record*⟩ — **on record** *adv* **1** : in the position of having publicly declared oneself ⟨go *on record* as opposing tax increases⟩ **2** : in the status of being known, published, or documented ⟨the judge's opinion is *on record*⟩
³record \"\ *adj* : of, relating to, or consisting of something (as a performance, occurrence, condition) that goes beyond or is extraordinary among others of its kind ⟨a ~ run⟩ ⟨~ prices⟩ ⟨~ heat⟩
re·cord·able \rəˈkȯ(ə)rdəbəl, rēˈ-, -ȯ(ə)d-\ *adj* : suitable for recording or capable of being recorded ⟨~ music⟩ ⟨~ underground explosions⟩ ⟨~ aspects of African life —*Geog. Jour.*⟩
record agent *n* [²*record*] : RECORDING AGENT
re·cord·ant \rəˈkȯrdᵊnt, -ȯ(ə)d-\ *adj* [¹*record* + *-ant*] *archaic* : RECORDATIVE
rec·or·da·tion \ˌrekə(r)ˈdāshən\ *n* -S [ME *recordacion*, fr. MF or L; MF *recordation*, fr. L *recordation-, recordatio*, fr. *recordatus* (past part. of *recordari* to remember) + *-ion-, -io* -ion — more at RECORD] **1** *obs* : REMEMBRANCE, RECOLLECTION **2** : the action or process of setting down in writing a record (as of transactions, data, events) ⟨~ of property acquired⟩ ⟨careful fieldwork, with meticulous ~ —E.K.Reed⟩ ⟨~ of past events —*Atlantic*⟩
re·cor·da·tive \rəˈkȯrdədiv\ *adj* [MF *recordatif*, fr. LL *recordativus*, fr. L *recordatus* + *-ivus* -ive] *archaic* : bearing or containing a record : evoking a memory or reminiscence of something : COMMEMORATIVE
record-breaking \ˈ==ˌ==\ *adj* [²*record* + *breaking*, pres. part. of *break*] : that surpasses some previously established record ⟨a *record-breaking* high jump⟩ ⟨*record-breaking* production⟩ ⟨a *record-breaking* crowd⟩
record changer *n* : a phonograph attachment that automatically places in position and plays successively each one of a stack of records
re·cord·er \rəˈkȯrdər, rēˈ-, -ȯ(ə)də\ *n* -S [ME, partly fr. *recorden* to record + *-er*, partly fr. AF *recordour* a magistrate, fr. *recorder* to record (fr. L *recordari*) + *-our* -or] **1** : one that records: as **a** (1) : one whose official duty it is to make a record of writings or transactions (2) : a surveying party's noteman (3) : one that inspects and records the progress of construction work **b** : a machine, instrument, or device that records (as sound, visual images) for subsequent reproduction **2 a** : the chief judicial magistrate of some British cities and boroughs having now only criminal jurisdiction **b** : a judge with criminal jurisdiction of first instance and sometimes also a magistrate's civil jurisdiction in a municipality **3 a** : a fipple flute with eight finger holes — called also *English flute* **b** : a pipe-organ stop similar in tone quality to the recorder : BLOCKFLÖTE 2

recorder 3a

re·cord·er·ship \-ˌship\ *n* [*recorder* + *-ship*] : the office or term of office of a recorder
recording *n* -S [fr. gerund of ¹*record*] **1 a** : the process of recording something esp. sound ⟨the ~ took place at the studio⟩ **b** : a period or session of recording something ⟨said several ~*s* would be necessary⟩ **2 a** : what is recorded (as on a phonograph record, magnetic tape) ⟨analyzed the ~⟩ **b** : a phonograph record, magnetic tape, or some other thing (as film, wire, one of the perforated rolls played by a player piano) on which sound or visual images have been recorded for subsequent reproduction ⟨has a collection of unusual ~*s*⟩
recording agent *n* [fr. pres. part. of ¹*record*] : a local insurance agent empowered to commit the companies represented and to issue policies in their behalf
recording head *also* **record head** *n* : a device used in the recording of sound for transforming electrical energy into a magnetic record or into a groove undulation on a disc
recording meter *n* : an instrument usu. driven by clockwork and containing a chart upon which a record of variations (as in current, pressure) is made
re·cord·ist \rəˈkȯrdəst, rēˈ-, -ȯ(ə)d-\ *n* -S [¹*record* + *-ist*] : one who records (as sound on film)
rec·ord·less \ˈrekə(r)dləs\ *adj* [²*record* + *-less*] : lacking a recorded history ⟨the student of ~ primitive peoples —Margaret Hodgen⟩
record-of-performance *also* **record-of-production** \ˈ====ˈ==\ *adj* **1** : based on or used for determining the relative productivity of a domestic animal under standardized conditions ⟨*record-of-performance* tests⟩ ⟨a *record-of-performance* rating⟩ **2** : attaining an acceptable level of productivity on a record-of-performance test ⟨a *record-of-production* sire⟩ ⟨*record-of-performance* hens⟩
record player *n* [²*record*] : an instrument for reproducing the recorded sound of a phonograph record; *esp* : such an instrument using an electric pickup whose output is fed into one or more audio amplifiers and loudspeakers
records *pres 3d sing of* RECORD, *pl of* RECORD
re·cork \(ˈ)rē+\ *vt* [*re-* + *cork*] : to cork again
re·correct \ˌrē+\ *vt* [*re-* + *correct*] : to correct again
re·corrupt \"+\ *vt* [*re-* + *corrupt*] : to corrupt again
re·cor·te \rāˈkȯrˌdā\ *n* -S [Sp, fr. *recortar* to cut off, trim, fr. *re-* + *cortar* to cut — more at CORTADERIA] : a cape movement executed after a series of Veronicas to cut short a bull's charge, turn him, and place him for the picadors
¹re·count \rəˈkau̇nt, rēˈ-\ *vt* [ME *recounten*, fr. MF *reconter*, fr. *re-* + *conter* to count, relate — more at COUNT] **1** : to give a detailed account of : tell the particulars of : NARRATE ⟨~*s* his adventures with admirable restraint —Lynn Groh⟩ **2** : to go over, call to mind, or mention one by one ⟨~*ing* all their victories⟩ **3** *obs* : REGARD, CONSIDER **syn** see RELATE
²re·count \(ˈ)rē+\ *vb* [*re-* + *count*, v.] *vt* : to count over again ~ *vi* : to make a new count
³recount \"\ *n* [*re-* + *count*, n.] : a second or fresh count ⟨a of election votes⟩
re·count·al \rəˈkau̇ntᵊl, rēˈ-\ *n* -S [¹*recount* + *-al*] : a detailed account : NARRATION, RECITAL
re·coup \(ˈ)rēˈküp, rəˈ-\ *vb* -ED/-ING/-S [F *recouper* to cut back, fr. OF, fr. *re-* + *couper* to cut — more at COPE] *vt* **1** *law* : to keep back rightfully a part of so as to diminish a sum due : DEDUCT; *specif* : to abate or reduce (a claim sued on) by setting up in defense some act or fact growing out of the matters constituting the cause or ground of the action brought **2 a** : to make good (as expenses, losses) ⟨this is largely ~*ed* to states from taxes —John Kemp⟩ : make up for ⟨~*ed* their losses⟩ **b** : to compensate (as oneself) for something (as expenses, losses) : REIMBURSE, INDEMNIFY ⟨in order to ~ himself for this outlay —G.G.Coulton⟩ **3** : to get back : REGAIN ⟨an attempt to ~ his fortunes —W.J.Ghent⟩ ⟨try to ~ their strength —Gordon Harrison⟩ ⟨so as to ~ without interruption the hour of sleep they had lost —*N.Y. Times*⟩ ~ *vi* : to regain, make good, or make up for something lost ⟨needed time to ~⟩ **syn** see RECOVER
re·couple \(ˈ)rē+\ *vt* [*re-* + *couple* (v.)] : to couple again
re·coup·ment \rēˈküpmənt, rəˈ-\ *n* -S [*recoup* + *-ment*] **1** : the action of recouping or state of being recouped **2** : something recouped — compare COUNTERCLAIM, SETOFF
¹re·course \ˈrēˌkō(ə)rs, -ō(ə)rs, -ōəs, -ō(ə)s, =ˈ=\ *n* [ME *recours*, fr. MF, fr. LL *recursus*, fr. L, act of running back, fr. *recursus*, past part. of *recurrere* to run back — more at RECUR] **1 a** : a turning to someone or something in search of help, support, protection, or safety ⟨had ~ to his brother⟩ ⟨does not hesitate to have ~ to religion —J.G.Frazer⟩ ⟨handle their own difficulties without ~ to outside help —G.P.Wibberley⟩ **b** : someone or something that can be turned to for help, support, protection, or safety : a source of help or strength : RESORT ⟨was afraid no ~ was left⟩ **2** *obs* **a** : a movement or flow in one direction or another **b** : a periodical recurrence of something **c** : repeated visiting : habitual resort **d** : admittance to someone or something : ACCESS **3** : the right to demand payment; *specif* : the right to demand payment from the one that makes out or endorses a negotiable instrument (as a check) — used chiefly in the phrase *without recourse* placed after the endorsement of a negotiable instrument to protect the endorser from liability to the endorsee and subsequent holders
²recourse *vi, obs* : to have recourse : RESORT
¹re·cov·er \rəˈkəvə(r), rēˈ-\ *vb* **recovered; recovered; recovering** \-v(ə)riŋ\ **recovers** [ME *recoveren*, fr. MF *recoverer*, fr. L *recuperare*; akin to L *recipere* to take back, receive — more at RECEIVE] *vt* **1** : to get or win back ⟨sat down to ~ his breath⟩ ⟨died without ~*ing* consciousness⟩ ⟨answered as soon as he could ~ his voice⟩ ⟨~ the pioneering spirit of their ancestors⟩ **2** *archaic* : to get well from (as an injury, a sickness) **3 a** : to bring (oneself) back to normal balance or self-possession ⟨stumbled and ~*ed* himself⟩ **b** *archaic* : RESCUE, DELIVER ⟨that they may ~ themselves out of the snare of the devil —2 Tim 2:26 (AV)⟩ **4 a** : to make good the loss, injury, or cost of : make up for ⟨~ increased costs through higher prices⟩ ⟨hoped to ~ his gambling losses with a big coup⟩ **b** : to gain by legal process ⟨~ damages and costs in a libel suit⟩ ⟨~ title to a disputed property⟩ ⟨~ judgment against a defendant⟩ **5** *archaic* : to gain by motion or effort : REACH **6** *archaic* : RESTORE, CURE, HEAL ⟨from death to life thou might'st him yet ~ —Michael Drayton⟩ ⟨she hath ~*ed* the king and undone me —Shak.⟩ **7** : to find again ⟨~ a lost scent⟩ ⟨~ the trail of a fugitive⟩ **8 a** : to obtain from an ore, a waste product, or a by-product ⟨~ gold from ore with cyanide⟩ **b** : to save from loss and restore to usefulness : RECLAIM ⟨~ land from the sea⟩ **c** : to bring out or bring to light after neglect, burial, obscurity ⟨~ the lost secrets of ancient glassblowers⟩ ⟨~ the key of a cryptographic message⟩ ⟨~ petroleum from deep deposits⟩ ~ *vi* **1 a** : to regain health after sickness : become well ⟨~*ing* from a bout of pneumonia⟩ ⟨patients on the southern side of a hospital ~ faster than those on the northern side —Herbert Spencer⟩ **b** : to regain a former or normal state (as of vigor, self-control, consciousness) ⟨when she had ~*ed* from the first shock of the news⟩ ⟨the cotton industry was ~*ing* after a slump during the war⟩ **2** : to regain a position of guard or readiness ⟨~ after a lunge in fencing⟩ ⟨~ for the next rowing stroke⟩ **3** : to obtain a final judgment in one's favor : to succeed in a lawsuit or proceeding **4** *obs* : to make one's way back : RETURN

syn RECOVER, REGAIN, RETRIEVE, RECOUP, and RECRUIT can mean to get back what has been let go or lost. RECOVER, the most comprehensive, can apply to anything lost and got back in any way ⟨*recover* a lost wallet⟩ ⟨*recover* one's sanity⟩ ⟨*recover* one's balance⟩ ⟨*recover* one's position in a firm⟩ REGAIN, often interchangeable with RECOVER, implies more strongly a winning back ⟨*regain* one's health⟩ ⟨*regain* one's liberty after a long imprisonment⟩ ⟨*regain* one's rights as a citizen⟩ ⟨*regain* popularity⟩ RETRIEVE implies a recovering or regaining after some effort ⟨*retrieve* a lost fortune⟩ ⟨*retrieve* one's position lost through ill fortune⟩ although the verb can have as its object such a word as *loss, error, failure*, or *disaster*, with which it then implies a reparation or a setting right ⟨*retrieve* an error in addition⟩ ⟨*retrieve* a bad financial disaster by careful investment⟩ RECOUP, a legal term implying a fair deduction as of part of a claim of a successful plaintiff in a law suit, in common use implies recovery or retrieval, usu. in equivalent rather than identical form, of something lost ⟨*recoup* gambling losses by more careful play⟩ ⟨*recoup* by some good hard work the money lost in bad investments⟩ RECRUIT in this context can imply a regaining, by fresh additions or a replenishment of the supply, of what has been lost ⟨*recruit* a new battalion for the foot army⟩ ⟨the present difficulty of *recruiting* staff in the accountancy profession —*Accountancy*⟩ ⟨I fed and watered my horse and *recruited* my own energies with roast beef —W. H. Hudson †1922⟩ In extension it has come to apply to any acquiring as of members or a supply ⟨a fair-sized audience can be *recruited* —Sidney Kaufman⟩ ⟨hundreds of thousands of Americans who had never worked before . . . were *recruited* for war production —Dorothy Jones⟩ ⟨*recruit* a staff for a new restaurant⟩
²recover \"\ *n* -S [ME *recovere*, fr. MF *recovre*, fr. *recoverer* to recover] : RECOVERY 3
re-cover \(ˈ)rē+\ *vt* [ME *recoveren*, fr. *re-* + *coveren* to cover] : to cover again : provide with a new covering ⟨*re-cover* an upholstered couch⟩ ⟨*re-cover* a lampshade⟩
re·cov·er·able \rəˈkəv(ə)rəbəl, rēˈ-\ *adj* [ME, fr. *recoveren* to recover + *-able*] : capable of being recovered ⟨~ truth of a past event⟩ or of recovering ⟨~ action at law⟩ — **re·cov·er·able·ness** *n* -ES
re·cov·er·ance \-v(ə)rən(t)s\ *n* -ES [ME, fr. MF *recovrance*, fr. OF, fr. *recoverer* to recover + *-ance*] *archaic* : RECOVERY
recovered *adj* [ME, fr. past part. of *recoveren* to recover] : no longer sick : CURED, WELL ⟨when the ~ patient tries to remember what occurred during his delirium —Norman Cameron⟩ ⟨appears to be entirely ~⟩
re·cov·er·ee \rəˌkəvəˈrē, rēˌk-\ *n* -S [¹*recover* + *-ee*] : the person against whom a judgment is obtained in common recovery
re·cov·er·er \rəˈkəv(ə)rə(r), rēˈ-\ *n* -S [ME, fr. *recoveren* to recover + *-er*] : one that recovers
recovering *pres part of* RECOVER
re·cov·er·or \rəˈkəvəˌrȯ(ə)r, rēˈ-, -rȯə, =ˈ==ˌrə(r)\ *n* -S [¹*recover* + *-or*] : the demandant in a common recovery after judgment in his favor
recovers *pres 3d sing of* RECOVER, *pl of* RECOVER
re·cov·ery \rəˈkəv(ə)rē, rēˈ-, -ri\ *n* -ES [ME, perh. fr. MF *recovree*, fr. *recoverer* to recover + *-ee* -y] **1** *obs* : means of restoration : CURE, REMEDY **2 a** : the obtaining in a suit at law of a right to something by a verdict, decree, or judgment of court **b** : COMMON RECOVERY **3 a** : the action of regaining an upright position after curtseying **b** : a movement sequence in dance technique for rising after a fall **c** : the action of regaining the position of guard after making an attack in fencing or sparring **d** : the action following the completion of a rowing stroke in which the blade is raised and feathered and readied for the next stroke **e** : a golf stroke played from the rough or a trap to the green or fairway **4** : the act of regaining or returning toward a normal or usual state ⟨~ from a heart attack⟩ ⟨~ from childbirth⟩ ⟨~ in the bond market⟩ **5** : a period of economic upturn following a depression **6 a** : the recovering of useful material from spent products or waste ⟨~ of solvents used for dry cleaning⟩ ⟨~ of aluminum from loose scrap⟩ **b** : the amount of metal or valuable substance obtained in a process of ore treatment expressed sometimes as a percentage of the metal orig. in the ore **7** : removal of residual stress from cold worked metal by low-temperature annealing
recovery furnace *n* : ¹SMELTER
recovery oven *n* : BY-PRODUCT OVEN
recovery room *n* : a hospital room which is equipped with apparatus for meeting postoperative emergencies and in which surgical patients are kept during the immediate postoperative period for care and recovery from anesthesia
recp *abbr* reception
recpst *abbr* receptionist
recpt *abbr* receipt
recr *abbr* receiver
re·crat·er \(ˈ)rēˈkrātə(r)\ *n* -S [*re-* + *crate* + *-er*] *Brit* : a machine for loading bottles or cans into shipping cases — compare DECRATER

rec·re·ance \'rekrēən(t)s\ *n* -s [fr. ¹*recreant*, after such pairs as E *assistant: assistance*] : RECREANCY

rec·re·an·cy \-nsē, -si\ *n* -ES [¹*recreant* + *-cy*] : the quality or state of being recreant : shameful cowardice : PERFIDY

¹rec·re·ant \-nt\ *adj* [ME, fr. MF, fr. pres. part. of *recroire* to renounce one's cause in a trial by battle, to surrender, fr. OF, fr. *re-* + *croire* to believe, fr. L *credere* — more at CREED] **1 :** crying for mercy esp. in the trial of battle : yielding in a cowardly manner : CRAVEN **2 :** unfaithful to one's duty or allegiance : APOSTATE, FALSE ⟨those responsible for teaching the common folk were ~ to their task —I.M.Price⟩ **syn** see COWARDLY

²recreant \"\ *n* -s [ME, fr. MF, fr. *recreant*, adj.] **1 :** one that yields cravenly in combat : a cowardly wretch **2 :** one that is unfaithful : BETRAYER, DESERTER

rec·re·ate \'rekrē,āt, *usu* -ād·+V\ *vb* [L *recreatus*, past part. of *recreare* to create anew, restore, refresh, fr. *re-* + *creare* to create] *vt* **1 a :** to cheer by giving consolation or encouragement **b :** to renew or enliven (as the spirits) through the influence of pleasant surroundings **2 :** to refresh after wearying toil or anxiety usu. by change or diversion ⟨might not choose to ~ themselves on a scenic railway —*Blackwood's*⟩ ⟨I charge you not to hunt or ~ yourselves on that sacred day —R.S.Monahan⟩ **3 :** to give fresh life to : restore the strength of : REVIVE ⟨my soul stood at that gate to ~ itself with bliss —A.T.Quiller-Couch⟩ ~ *vi* : to take recreation ⟨all nuns of the same community dress alike, eat alike, and ~ alike —Sister Marian Elizabeth⟩ **syn** see AMUSE

re-create \¦rē+\ *vt* [*re-* + *create*] : to create again ⟨*re-create* the boom of the old frontier on a small scale —W.P.Webb⟩ : form anew esp. in the imagination : recollect and reform in the mind ⟨his mind, which *re-creates* the cosmos out of a grain of sand —L.J.Halle⟩

¹rec·re·a·tion \,rekrē'āshən\ *n* -s [ME *recreacion*, fr. MF *recreation*, fr. L *recreation-*, *recreatio* restoral to health, fr. *recreatus* (past part. of *recreare* to restore, refresh) + *-ion-*, *-io* -ion] **1 a :** the act of recreating or the state of being recreated : refreshment of the strength and spirits after toil : DIVERSION, PLAY ⟨to sit in the sun . . . is one of my country ~s —L.P.Smith⟩ ⟨obvious that there is little time for ~ —J.M.Mogey⟩ ⟨I . . . consider intervals of ~ and amusement as desirable for everybody —Jane Austen⟩ **b :** a means of getting diversion or entertainment ⟨his ~ is gardening —*Current Biog.*⟩ **2** *obs* : one that provides recreation or amusement ⟨if I do not gull him . . . and make him a common ~ —Shak.⟩

²recreation \"\ *adj* : RECREATIONAL; *esp* : equipped so as to provide diversions or amusements ⟨has introduced winter ~ facilities —*Amer. Guide Series: Pa.*⟩

re-creation \¦rē+\ *n* [*re-* + *creation*] : the act of creating over again : RENEWAL ⟨our watchful care for their interests, for the *re-creation* of their industries —Ernest Bevin⟩ ⟨not merely playacting but the *re-creation* of a great story —R.M. Hodesh⟩

rec·re·a·tion·al \¦rekrē¦āshənᵊl, -shnəl\ *adj* : of or relating to recreation ⟨a ~ area with cinder track, tennis courts, and practice fields —*Amer. Guide Series: Oreg.*⟩ ⟨reading matter which is at once ~ and mentally activating —A.C.Ward⟩

recreational therapist *n* : one trained in or engaged in the practice of recreational therapy

recreational therapy *n* : therapy by means of recreational activities engaged in by the patient — compare OCCUPATIONAL THERAPY

rec·re·a·tion·ist \,rekrē'āsh(ə)nəst\ *n* -s [*recreation* + *-ist*] : one who takes or seeks recreation esp. in the open

recreation room *n* **1 :** a room (as a playroom or rumpus room) furnished and reserved for relaxation and recreation **2 :** a public room (as in a hospital) for recreational and social activities

rec·re·a·tive \'rekrē,ād·iv, -ātiv, -ēv *also* -əv\ *adj* [*recreate* + *-ive*] : tending to recreate : giving pleasure and enjoyment : DIVERTING ⟨some activities are ~ and amusing because of their contrast with work —John Dewey⟩

re-creative \¦rē+\ *adj* [*re-create* + *-ive*] : able to create again ⟨constantly grew in insight and *re-creative* power —C.M.Smith⟩

re-creator \"+\ *n* [*re-create* + *-or*] : one that creates again ⟨known as the *re-creator* of the Hebrew language —*Springfield (Mass.) Union*⟩

rec·re·a·tor \'rekrē,ād·ə(r), -ātə-\ *n* -s [*recreate* + *-or*] : one that recreates ⟨from the standpoint of the ~, most recreation is intensely purposeful —George Hjelte⟩

rec·re·a·to·ry \-ēə,tōrē, -tȯr-, -ri\ *adj* [*recreate* + *-ory*] : RECREATIONAL ⟨the students return to their fourth-grade room for . . . ~ reading —Roul Tunley⟩

re·credential \¦rē+\ *n* [*re-* + *credential*] : a letter of appreciation given to a diplomatic envoy on his permanently leaving a post by the head of the state to which he has been accredited — compare LETTER OF CREDENCE

rec·re·ment \'rekrəmənt\ *n* -s [MF or L; MF *recrement*, fr. L *recrementum*, fr. *re-* + *cre-* (stem of *cernere* to separate, sift) + *-mentum* -ment — more at CERTAIN] : superfluous matter separated from that which is useful : DROSS, SCORIA ⟨the ~ of ore⟩

rec·re·men·ti·tious \¦==mən¦tishəs, -,men-\ *adj* [*recrement* + *-itious*] : of, relating to, consisting of, or of the nature of recrement or dross : SUPERFLUOUS

re·crim·i·nate \rə'krimə,nāt, rē'-, *usu* -ād·+V\ *vb* [ML *recriminatus*, past part. of *recriminare*, fr. L *re-* + *criminare*, *criminari* to accuse — more at CRIMINATE] *vi* : to make a counter accusation : charge back a fault or crime upon an accuser ⟨in the moment's mortification however, I *recriminated* —W.J.Locke⟩ ~ *vt* **1 :** to make a charge against (an accuser) in return **2 :** to return (as a charge) in bitter retort ⟨*recriminated*, "You've made the same mistake yourself"⟩

re·crim·i·na·tion \=,==′nāshən\ *n* [ML *recrimination-*, *recriminatio*, fr. *recriminatus* (past part. of *recriminare* to recriminate) + *-ion-*, *-io* -ion] **1 :** the act of recriminating : an accusation brought by the accused against the accuser : a counter accusation ⟨work so often demands . . . that we refrain from ~s that won't mend the situation —Alan Gregg⟩ **2 :** a counter accusation barring a divorce esp. where the plaintiff is also guilty of conduct constituting cause for divorce

re·crim·i·na·tive \=′krimə,nā|d·|iv, -m(ə)nə|, |t|, |ēv *also* |əv\ *adj* [*recriminate* + *-ive*] : RECRIMINATORY

re·crim·i·na·tor \-,nād·ə(r)\ *n* [*recriminate* + *-or*] : one that recriminates

re·crim·i·na·to·ry \-nə,tōrē, -tȯr-, -ri\ *adj* [*recriminate* + *-ory*] : having the character or nature of recrimination : RECRIMINATING ⟨a ~ defence⟩ ⟨approval of the tense ~ speeches was expressed —Jean Lyon⟩

re·cross \(')rē+\ *vb* [*re-* + *cross*] *vi* : to cross again ⟨his legs crossing, uncrossing, ~*ing* —A.T.Quiller-Couch⟩ ~ *vt* : to traverse again ⟨watching the man in overalls ~ the floor —William Faulkner⟩

re·cru·desce \,rēkrü'des\ *vi* -ED/-ING/-S [L *recrudescere* — more at RECRUDESCENT] : to become recrudescent : break out again : renew activity ⟨the general influence . . . which is likely every now and then to ~ in his absence —Edmund Gurney⟩

re·cru·des·cence \-sᵊn(t)s\ *n* -s [L *recrudescere* + E *-ence*] : the state of being recrudescent: as **a :** a return or revival (as of an undesirable condition or ill-advised idea) after a period of abatement or inactivity : RENEWAL ⟨a marked ~ of nationalist slogans and propaganda —E.J.Salter⟩ ⟨confident of its ability to handle any ~ of aggression from neighboring states —John Hersey⟩ **b :** increased severity of a disease after a remission, or recurrence after a brief intermission — compare RELAPSE

re·cru·des·cen·cy \-nsē, -si\ *n* -ES [L *recrudescere* + E *-ency*] : RECRUDESCENCE

re·cru·des·cent \¦==′desᵊnt\ *adj* [L *recrudescent-*, *recrudescens*, pres. part. of *recrudescere* to become raw again, fr. *re-* + *crudescere* to become hard or raw, fr. *crudus* raw — more at RAW] : breaking out again : renewing disease or dangerous activity after abatement, suppression, or cessation ⟨a ~ typhus⟩ ⟨a ~ discontent among the factory workers⟩

¹re·cruit \rə'krüt, rē'- *also* 'rē,-, *usu* -üd·+V\ *n* -s [F *recrute*, *recrue*, lit., regrowth, fresh growth, fr. *recru*, past part. of *recroître* to grow up again, fr. L *recrescere*, fr. *re-* + *crescere* to grow — more at CRESCENT] **1 a :** a renewal of strength : a return to a previously satisfactory condition **b :** a means of recovery **2 a** *obs* : a number of people added to or replacing a group **b :** a fresh or additional supply **3 a** *obs* : a newly raised or additional body of soldiery **b** *obs* : a strengthening or increase of an army by reinforcements or new levies **4 a** (1) : a fresh levy : REINFORCEMENTS —usu. used in pl. (2) : a newly enlisted or drafted member of the armed services; *specif* : an enlistee or draftee of the lowest grade in the army **b :** a newcomer to a field of activity ⟨accommodate more ~s on farms —*Atlantic*⟩ ⟨find among these men good ~s for our faculties —F.N.Robinson⟩

²recruit \"\ *vb* -ED/-ING/-S [F *recruter*, fr. *recrute*, *recrue* recruit] *vt* **1 a** (1) : to strengthen or supply (as an army, a military organization) with fresh or additional members : to reinforce, fill up, or make up by enlistment of personnel : MUSTER, RAISE ⟨when a nation must suddenly ~ a maximal armed force —Leonard Carmichael⟩ ⟨~ a regiment⟩ (2) : to enlist as a member of an armed service ⟨~*ed* 300 men in two days⟩ **b :** to increase or maintain the number of : build up : fill up ⟨America having ~*ed* her population largely from foreign immigrants —Katharine E. Caffrey⟩ ⟨the party was ~*ed* chiefly from among the farmers⟩ **c :** to hire or otherwise obtain to perform services (as on a work force or for an organization) : secure the services of ⟨came to look for her husband who was ~*ed* for the mines —Alan Paton⟩ ⟨our big job was to ~ youths for future teachers —*Education Digest*⟩ ⟨busy ~*ing* volunteer social workers⟩ **2 :** to provide with what is needed (as with fresh supplies, material, efforts) to correct or prevent depletion, exhaustion, or waste : add to : REPAIR, REPLENISH ⟨it was from gifts bestowed upon him . . . that he ~*ed* his finances —Charles Dickens⟩ **3 :** to restore the vigor or health of : invigorate anew ⟨detach him . . . till he ~s his strength —Walt Whitman⟩ ⟨come down here . . . to ~ yourself after an excess of work —G.B.Shaw⟩ ~ *vi* **1 a :** to raise or enlist or attempt to raise or enlist new soldiers ⟨both armies ~*ed* easily⟩ ⟨the army is not ~*ing* at present⟩ **b :** to raise or seek to raise new supplies of men for service and work forces **2 :** to recover what has been lost or spent (as strength or health) : RECUPERATE **syn** see RECOVER

re·cruit·al \rə'krüd·ᵊl, rē'-, -üt°nl\ *n* -s [²*recruit* + *-al*] : a new supply

re·cruit·er \-üd·ə(r), -tə(r)\ *n* -s [²*recruit* + *-er*] **1 :** an extra member of the British parliament chosen to increase the number esp. during an emergency (as the Civil War) **2 :** one that recruits ⟨a navy ~⟩ ⟨~s from 600 companies are on the nation's college and university campuses —*Fortune*⟩

¹recruiting *adj* [fr. pres. part. of ²*recruit*] : having military or personnel recruiting as a duty or purpose ⟨a ~ officer⟩ ⟨we have encountered high-powered ~ programs —R.S.Bogue⟩ ⟨the employment department is in a position to begin its ~ activities —*Labor Problems in America*⟩

²recruiting *n* -s [fr. gerund of ²*recruit*] : the raising of recruits (as for the armed forces, a labor force, a volunteer agency)

recruiting ground *n* [²*recruiting*] : a place for obtaining, enlisting, or supplying recruits : a source of supply ⟨the *recruiting ground* for young politicians —Lytton Strachey⟩

re·cruit·ment \rə'krütmənt, rē'-\ *n* -s [²*recruit* + *-ment*] **1 :** REINFORCEMENT ⟨would guarantee the ~ of this group from the most promising young men of the land —J.B.Conant⟩ **2 :** the act or process of recruiting: as **a :** the recruiting of men for an army **b :** an act of offering inducement to qualified personnel to enter a particular job or profession ⟨a ~ of teachers which shall bring to the profession . . . men and women of right minds —K.I.Brown⟩ **3 :** an increment to a natural population (as that resulting from increased survival over a period of time) **4 :** the increase in intensity of a reflex when the initiating stimulus is prolonged without alteration of intensity due to the activation of increasing numbers of motoneurons — compare FACILITATION **5 :** an abnormally rapid increase in the sensation of loudness with increasing sound intensity that occurs in deafness of neural origin and esp. in neural deafness of the aged in which soft sounds may be completely inaudible while louder sounds are distressingly loud

re·crusher \(')rē+\ *n* [*re-* + *crusher*] : a rock crusher for producing fine aggregate for concrete by crushing again material which has already been crushed

re·crystallization \(¦)rē+\ *n* [*recrystallize* + *-ation*] : the act or process of recrystallizing: as **a :** replacement of the distorted grain structure of a cold-worked metal by a new strain-free grain structure during annealing **b :** the regeneration of rock fabric producing coarser texture and eliminating impurities ⟨limestone transformed by ~ to marble⟩

recrystallize *vb* [*re-* + *crystallize*] *vt* : to crystallize again or repeatedly ~ *vi* : to become crystallized again

rect *abbr* **1** receipt **2** rectangle **3** rectified; rectifier **4** rector; rectory

¹rect- *or* **recti-** *comb form* [L *rectus* — more at RIGHT] : straight, right ⟨*recti*lineal⟩ ⟨*rect*angular⟩

²rect- *or* **recto-** *comb form* [NL *rectum*] **1 :** rectum ⟨*recto*cele⟩ **2 :** rectal and ⟨*recto*abdominal⟩

recta *pl of* RECTUM

rec·tag·o·nal \(')rek¦tagənᵊl, -taig-\ *adj* [irreg. fr. ¹*rect-* + *-gon* + *-al*] : RECTANGULAR

rec·tal \'rektᵊl\ *adj* [²*rect-* + *-al*] : of, relating to, affecting, or located near the rectum — **rec·tal·ly** \-tᵊlē, -li\ *adv*

rectal valve *n* : any of three or four crescentic folds projecting into the cavity of the rectum

rect·an·gle \'rek,taŋgəl, -taiŋ-\ *n* [ML *rectangulus* having a right angle, fr. L *rectus* right + *angulus* angle — more at RIGHT, ANGLE] : a parallelogram all of whose angles are right angles; *esp* : one with adjacent sides of unequal length — see AREA table

rectangles

rect·an·gled \-gəld\ *adj* [*rectangle* + *-ed*] : RECTANGULAR

rect·an·gu·lar \(')rek¦taŋgyələ(r), -taiŋ-\ *adj* [ML *rectangulus* having a right angle + E *-ar*] **1 :** having a flat surface shaped like a rectangle **2 a :** crossing, lying, or meeting at a right angle ⟨~ axes⟩ **b :** having edges, surfaces, or faces that meet at right angles : having faces or surfaces shaped like rectangles ⟨~ parallelepipeds⟩ ⟨~ blocks⟩

rectangular coordinate *n* : either of two Cartesian coordinates which have two or three dimensions and in which the axes are mutually at right angles

rectangular drainage pattern *n* : the drainage pattern of streams that make many right-angle bends

rectangular hyperbola *n* : EQUILATERAL HYPERBOLA

rect·an·gu·lar·i·ty \(')rek¦taŋgyə'larəd·ē, -taiŋ-, -ləte, -i *also* -ler-\ *n* -ES [*rectangular* + *-ity*] : the quality or state of being rectangular : rigidity of form

rect·an·gu·lar·ly *adv* : in a rectangular manner

rectangular parallelepiped *n* : a parallelepiped whose dihedral angles are right angles

rect·an·gu·lom·e·ter \(')=¦==′lämәd·ə(r)\ *n* [*rectangular* + *-o-* + *-meter*] : an instrument used for testing right angles

recti *pl of* RECTUS

recti- — see RECT-

rec·ti·fi·abil·i·ty \¦rektə,fīə'biləd·ē, -ətē, -i\ *n* -ES : the property of being rectifiable

rec·ti·fi·able \'rektə,fīəbəl, ,==′===\ *adj* : capable of being rectified; *esp* : having finite length ⟨a ~ curve⟩

rec·ti·fi·ca·tion \,==fə'kāshən\ *n* -s [LL *rectification-*, *rectificatio*, fr. *rectificatus* (past part. of *rectificare* to rectify) + *-ion-*, *-io* -ion] **1 :** the act or process of making or setting right (as by correcting an error or amending a fault) ⟨mistakes needing ~⟩ ⟨interpreted this to mean the ~ of its own grievances —Harry Hansen⟩ **2 :** the determination of a straight line equal in length to a portion of a curve : the determination of the length of a given curve or of a portion of it **3 :** the conversion of alternating to direct current **4 :** a new alignment to correct a deviation (as of a river channel or bank) **5 :** a procedure for correcting the distortions in perspective caused by the tilt of a camera during exposure by printing the negative with a compensating tilt so that vertical and horizontal lines in the reproduction have the same appearance as in the original scene **6 :** a process by which distilled spirits are blended together or substantially changed by the addition usu. of spirits, flavoring, or coloring material — **rectification of a globe** : the adjustment of a globe (as for latitude) preparatory to solution of a proposed problem

rec·ti·fi·ca·tor \'rektəfə,kād·ə(r)\ *n* -s [LL *rectificatus* + E *-or*] : RECTIFIER

rectified *adj* [fr. past part. of *rectify*] : having unusual color markings : showing variegation caused by a virus — used of flowers esp. tulips

rectified spirit *n* : alcohol purified or concentrated by redistillation

rec·ti·fi·er \'rektə,fī(ə)r, -īə\ *n* -s **1 :** one that rectifies **2 a :** one who blends different whiskeys or who mixes whiskey with distilled water and alcohol to obtain a desired proof **b :** a part of a distilling apparatus in which the more volatile portions are separated by evaporation and condensation; *esp* : COLUMN 3d **3 :** a device (as a vacuum tube) for converting alternating current into direct current **4 :** a part of a gas refrigerating apparatus in which the water vapor is condensed from the ammonia vapor

rectifier instrument *n* : an instrument used for measuring alternating currents and consisting of a rectifier in conjunction with a direct-current meter whose reading gives the value of the rectified alternating current

rec·ti·fy \'rektə,fī\ *vt* -ED/-ING/-S [ME *rectifien*, fr. MF *rectifier*, fr. ML *rectificare*, fr. L *rectus* straight, right + *-ificare* -ify — more at RIGHT] **1 a :** to make or set right (as a faulty position or state) : REMEDY ⟨a situation that can be *rectified* only by . . . evidence with which we can relate the past to the present —A.H.Shroeder⟩ **b :** to make good (as a mistake or omission) : AMEND ⟨and would do your best to ~ the mischief —George Meredith⟩ ⟨mistakes can be *rectified* by care and industry —Bertrand Russell⟩ **2 a :** to restore to a healthy state ⟨set about cutting down the contracted hoofs and ~*ing* the horny pad —Gerald Beaumont⟩ **b :** to restore to a condition previously considered desirable ⟨the increase would not ~ unbalanced world trade —*Time*⟩ **3 a :** to reform from erroneous or evil ways ⟨must ~ his life if he would be saved⟩ **b** *obs* : to free from mistaken ideas or errors ⟨a man has frequent opportunities of . . . ~*ing* the prejudiced —Joseph Addison⟩ **4 :** to purify esp. by repeated or fractional distillation sometimes with the addition of flavoring substances **5 :** to correct by removing errors or mistakes ⟨it is important to ~ the opinion —Curt Stern⟩ ⟨compile a better set of astronomical tables, ~ the calendar —H.J.J.Winter⟩ **6 a :** to set right by adjustment or calculation **b :** to determine the length of (an arc of a curve) **7 :** to bring into line : STRAIGHTEN ⟨~*ing* the guttering after that gale —Adrian Bell⟩ **8 :** to make (an alternating current) unidirectional **syn** see CORRECT

rec·ti·grade \-,grād\ *adj* [¹*rect-* + *-grade*] : moving or proceeding in a straight line or course

rec·ti·lineal \¦rektə+\ *adj* [LL *rectilineus* + E *-al*] : RECTILINEAR

rec·ti·linear \"+\ *adj* [LL *rectilineus* (fr. L *rectus* straight + *linea* line) + E *-ar* — more at RIGHT, LINE] **1 :** moving in a straight line : having an undeviating direction : forming a straight line **2 a :** characterized by straight lines **b :** lying in a straight line : formed or bounded by straight lines **3 :** PERPENDICULAR 5 — **rec·ti·linearly** \"+\ *adv*

rectilinear coordinate *n* : RECTANGULAR COORDINATE

rectilinear lens *n* : a lens specially corrected for distortion so that straight lines are reproduced accurately even on the margins of the pictures

rectilinear motion *n* : a linear motion in which the direction of the velocity remains constant and the path is a straight line

rec·tion \'rekshən\ *n* -s [L *rection-*, *rectio*, fr. *rectus* (past part. of *regere* to rule) + *-ion-*, *-io* -ion — more at RIGHT] : GOVERNMENT 5a

rec·ti·pe·tal·i·ty \,rektəpə'taləd·ē\ *n* -ES [¹*rect-* + *-petal* + *-ity*] : the tendency of growing plant organs to grow in a straight line

rec·ti·rostral \¦rektə+\ *adj* [*rect-* + L *rostrum* beak + E *-al* — more at ROSTRUM] : having a straight beak

rec·ti·tude \'rektə,tüd, -ə-,tyüd\ *n* -s [ME, fr. MF, fr. LL *rectitudin-*, *rectitudo*, fr. L *rectus* straight, right + *-i-* + *-tudin-*, *-tudo* -tude — more at RIGHT] **1 a :** the quality or state of being straight : STRAIGHTNESS ⟨the young pines bent by the snow . . . regain their natural ~ —Van Wyck Brooks⟩ **b :** a straight line **2 :** strict observance of standards of integrity and honesty : adherence to a high moral code : intrepid virtue : RIGHTEOUSNESS ⟨the absolute truth of his speech and the ~ of his behavior —R.W.Emerson⟩ **3 :** correctness of judgment or procedure esp. in the field of intellectual or artistic activity ⟨was . . . convinced of the ~ of his musical ideas —Charles O'Connell⟩

rec·ti·tu·di·nous \¦==¦tüdənəs, -¦tyü-\ *adj* [LL *rectitudin-*, *rectitudo* rectitude + E *-ous*] : piously self-righteous — **rec·ti·tu·di·nous·ly** *adv*

¹rec·to \'rek(,)tō\ *n* -s [ML (*breve de*) *recto*] : WRIT OF RIGHT

²recto \"\ *n* -s [NL *recto* (*folio*), the page being straight, i.e. unturned] **1 :** the side of a leaf (as of a manuscript) that is to be read first — contrasted with *verso* **2 :** a right-hand page (as of a book) usu. carrying an odd page number **3 :** the front cover esp. the outside front cover of a book; *also* : the corresponding part of a book jacket

recto- — see RECT-

rec·to·cele \'rektə,sēl\ *n* -s [ISV ²*rect-* + *-cele*] : a bulging of the rectum into the vagina

rec·to·coccygeus \¦rektō+\ *n* [NL, fr. ²*rect-* + *coccyg-*, *coccyx* coccyx + L *-eus* -eous] : a band of smooth muscle extending from the coccyx to the posterior wall of the rectum and serving to retract and elevate the rectum

rec·tor \'rektə(r)\ *n* -s [L, fr. *rectus* (past part. of *regere* to rule, govern) + *-or*; in senses 3 & 4, fr. ML *rector* ecclesiastical director, parish priest, director of a university, fr. L, governor, ruler — more at RIGHT] **1** *obs* **a :** a governor or ruler usu. of a country **b** *cap* : God as ruler of the world **2 :** one that directs : LEADER **3 a :** a clergyman of the Church of England who has the charge and care of a parish and owns the tithes from it : the clergyman of a parish where the tithes are not impropriate **b :** a clergyman of the Protestant Episcopal Church elected by the vestrymen who is the spiritual head and legally the presiding officer of a parish **c** *Roman Catholicism* : the head priest of a church or other religious institution **4 :** the head of a university, school, or other teaching institution: as **a :** LORD RECTOR **b :** the master of a college at some English universities **c :** the head of one of the 17 departments into which the French educational system is divided **d :** the head of a German elementary or secondary school

rec·tor·al \-,t(ə)rəl\ *adj* [*rector* + *-al*] : RECTORIAL; *specif* : of or relating to God as governor or ruler of men

rec·tor·ate \-t(ə)rət, *usu* -əd·+V\ *n* -s [ML *rectoratus*, fr. L *rector* + *-atus* -ate] : the office, rank, station, or term of a rector

rec·tor·ess \-rəs\ *n* -ES [*rector* + *-ess*] : the wife of a rector

rec·to·ri·al \(')rek¦tōrēəl, -tȯr-\ *adj* [*rector* + *-ial*] : of or relating to a rector, a rectory, or a rectorate

rec·tor·ship \'rektə(r),ship\ *n* [*rector* + *-ship*] **1 :** the office of a governor or ruler **2 :** the office of rector esp. of a university or of a parish

rec·to·ry \'rekt(ə)rē, -ri\ *n* -ES [MF or ML; MF *rectorie*, fr. ML *rectoria* office of a governor, fr. fem. of *rectorius* of a governor, fr. L *rector* governor, rector] **1 a :** a benefice held by a rector : the province of a rector : a parish church, parsonage, or spiritual living with all its rights, tithes, and glebes **b :** a rector's residence : PARSONAGE **2** *obs* : RECTORSHIP

rec·to·scope \'rektə,skōp\ *n* [ISV *rect-* + *-scope*] : PROCTOSCOPE

rec·to·sigmoid \¦rek(,)tō+\ *n* [*rect-* + *sigmoid*] : the distal part of the sigmoid flexure and the proximal part of the rectum

rec·to·sigmoidoscope \"+\ *n* [*rectosigmoid* + *-o-* + *-scope*] : SIGMOIDOSCOPE — **rec·to·sigmoidoscopic** \"+\ *adj* — **rec·to·sigmoidoscopy** \"+\ *n* -ES

rec·to·vesical fascia \"+-\ *n* [*rect-* + L *vesica* bladder + E *-al* — more at VENTER] : a membrane derived from the pelvic fascia and investing the rectum, bladder, and adjacent parts

rectress *n* -ES [*rector* + *-ess*] *obs* **:** a woman that rules

rec·trix \ˈrektriks\ *n, pl* **rectri·ces** \rekˈtrī(ˌ)sēz\ [L, fem. of *rector* — more at RECTOR] **1 :** RECTRESS **2** [NL, fr. L] **:** any of the quill feathers of the tail of a bird that are important in controlling the direction of flight — usu. used in pl.

rects *pl of* RECT

rec·tum \ˈrektəm\ *n, pl* **rectums** \-mz\ *or* **rec·ta** \-tə\ [NL, fr. *rectum intestinum*, lit., straight intestine] **:** the terminal part of the intestine being in man the part of the large intestine of somewhat variable length but usu. about eight inches from the sigmoid flexure to the anus

rec·tus \ˈrektəs\ *n, pl* **rec·ti** \-ˌtī\ [NL, fr. *rectus musculus*, lit., straight muscle] **1 :** any of several straight muscles (as the rectus abdominis or the rectus femoris) **2** *or* **rectus ocu·li** \-ˈäkyəˌlī\ [NL, lit., rectus of the eye] **:** any of four muscles of the eyeball that arise from the borders of the optic foramen and running forward are inserted into the sclerotic coat of the eyeball and that are distinguished according to position as the superior, inferior, lateral (or external), and medial (or internal) recti

rectus ab·do·mi·nis \-abˈdämənəs\ *n* [NL, lit., rectus of the abdomen] **:** a long flat muscle on either side of the linea alba extending along the whole length of the front of the abdomen, arising from the pubic crest and symphysis, and being inserted into the cartilages of the fifth, sixth, and seventh ribs

rectus fe·mo·ris \-femərəs\ *n* [NL, lit., rectus of the thigh] **:** a division of the quadriceps muscle lying in the anterior middle region of the thigh, arising from the ilium by two heads, and inserted into the tuberosity of the tibia by a narrow flattened tendon

rectus in cu·ria \-inˈkyu̇rēə\ *adj (or adv)* [NL] **:** upright in the court **:** free from charge or impeachment **:** competent to participate in litigation and entitled to the benefit of law — see LEGALIS HOMO

re·cuay \rāˈkwī\ *adj, usu cap* [fr. *Recuay*, town in northern Peru] **:** of or belonging to a cultural period in northern Peru characterized by houses of two or three stories below ground, stone carving of felines in high relief and seated figures in the round, and pottery in a great variety of shapes

recule *obs var of* RECOIL

re·cumb \rəˈkəm\ *vi* -ED/-ING/-S [L *recumbere* — more at RECUMBENT] **:** LEAN, RECLINE

re·cum·bence \rəˈkəmbən(t)s, rēˈ-\ *n* -S [fr. L *recumbent-, recumbens* recumbent, after such pairs as L *excellent-, excellens* excellent: E *excellence*] **:** RECUMBENCY

re·cum·ben·cy \-nsē, -si\ *n* -ES [L *recumbent-, recumbens* + E *-cy*] **1 :** the state of leaning, resting, or reclining **:** a recumbent position **:** REPOSE **2 :** a reliance or dependence upon something

¹re·cum·bent \-nt\ *n* -S [L *recumbent-, recumbens*, pres. part. of *recumbere*] **:** one that is recumbent

²recumbent \"\ *adj* [L *recumbent-, recumbens*, pres. part. of *recumbere* to lie back, lie down, recline, fr. *re-* + *-cumbere* to lie down (akin to L *cubare* to lie down) — more at HIP] **1 a :** suggestive of repose **:** LEANING, RESTING ⟨comfortably ~ against a fallen tree⟩ **b :** having a horizontal position **:** lying down ⟨the horse who was now ~ with one of my legs under him —Siegfried Sassoon⟩ ⟨the pulse may be as rapid in the ~ as in the standing posture —F.A.Faught⟩ **c :** representing a person lying down **2** *biol* **:** of or relating to structures which tend to rest upon the surface from which they extend **syn** see PRONE

recumbent anticline *n* **:** an overturned anticline having its axial plane more nearly horizontal than vertical

re·cum·ben·ti·bus \ˌrekəmˈbentəbəs\ *n* -ES [ME, fr. L *recumbent-, recumbens* + *-ibus*, dat. or abl. pl. ending] **:** a knockdown blow ⟨the advantage of inflicting upon an assailant a ~ —J.R.Newman⟩

re·cu·per·a·bil·i·ty \rəˌk(y)üp(ə)rəˈbiləd·ē\ *n* [L *recuperare* + E *-ability*] **:** the power of recuperation

re·cu·per·ate \rəˈk(y)üpəˌrāt, rēˈ-, *usu* -ād·+V\ *vb* -ED/-ING/-S [L *recuperatus*, past part. of *recuperare* to recover — more at RECOVER] *vt* **:** to get back **:** RECOVER, REGAIN ⟨*recuperating* health and strength after pneumonia⟩ ~ *vi* **1 :** to recover health or strength **:** CONVALESCE ⟨the animals . . . would not ~ until they got water —Willa Cather⟩ **2 :** to recover from pecuniary loss

re·cu·per·a·tion \⸗ˌ⸗pəˈrāshən\ *n* -S [L *recuperation-, recuperatio*, fr. *recuperatus* + *-ion-, -io* -ion] **1 :** recovery esp. of something lost; *specif* **:** restoration to health or strength **2** *biol* **:** reappearance of the property of competence at a late stage of development (as in blastema formation) **3 :** the heating of incoming gases in a furnace by passing them through flues adjacent to the exhaust flues ⟨in ~ some of the heat from the flue gases is transferred to the air supply⟩

re·cu·per·a·tive \rəˈk(y)üpəˌrād·|iv, -p(ə)rə|, |t|, |ēv *also* |əv\ *adj* [LL *recuperativus* recoverable, fr. *recuperatus* + L *-ivus* -ive] **1 :** of or relating to recuperation **:** tending to recovery **:** RESTORATIVE **:** having the power of recuperating ⟨~ powers⟩ ⟨strongly ~ remedies⟩ **2 :** having a recuperator ⟨a ~ furnace⟩ — **re·cu·per·a·tive·ness** *n* -ES

re·cu·per·a·tor \-ˌrād·ə(r)\ *n* -S *see sense 2* [L, lit., recoverer, fr. *recuperatus* + *-or*] **1 :** one that recuperates **2** *also pl* **recuperato·res** \⸗ˌ⸗pərəˈtōr(ˌ)ēz\ **:** a judge in ancient Rome orig. appointed to hear cases involving foreigners **3 :** REGENERATOR 4 **4 :** a device for returning a gun into the firing position after recoil

re·cu·per·a·to·ry \rəˈk(y)üp(ə)rəˌtōrē, rēˈ-, -tōr-, -ri\ *adj* [L *recuperatorius*, fr. *recuperatus* + *-orius* -ory] **:** of or relating to recuperation or a recuperator

re·cur \R rəˈkər, rēˈ-, + V -kər-; -R -kə̄, + *suffixal vowel* -kər- *also* -kə̄r, + *vowel in a word following without pause* -kər· *or* -kə̄ *also* -kər\ *vi* **recurred; recurred; recurring; recurs** [ME *recurren*, fr. L *recurrere* to run back, return, fr. *re-* + *currere* to run — more at CURRENT] **1 :** to return to a place or status ⟨may elect to ~ to his nationality of parentage —W.E.Hall⟩ **2 :** to have recourse **:** go for help **:** RESORT ⟨the dire necessity of *recurring* to arms in the face of . . . stubborn and stupid refusal to govern otherwise —Salvador de Madariaga⟩ **3 :** to go back in thought or discourse ⟨in his conversations here he *recurred* to the plan he had outlined —C.G.Bowers⟩ **4 :** to come up again for consideration **:** confront one again ⟨a problem which has *recurred* to this day —G.G.Weigend⟩ ⟨knew the difficulties would only ~⟩ **5 :** to come again to mind **:** return vividly to the memory ⟨he had forgotten it . . . but it *recurred* to him now —Archibald Marshall⟩ **6 :** to happen, take place, or appear again **:** occur again usu. after a stated interval or according to some regular rule ⟨would the occasion ever ~ —Van Wyck Brooks⟩ ⟨by the light of each *recurring* full moon —G.W.Johnson⟩ **7 :** to repeat itself usu. indefinitely in fixed periods of figures (as of a decimal)

recure *vt* [ME *recuren*, fr. L *recurare*, fr. *re-* + *curare* to take care of, heal — more at CURE] **1 a** *obs* **:** to restore to health **:** CURE **b** *obs* **:** to bring back to a better state or condition **2 a** *obs* **:** to make whole **:** HEAL ⟨thy death's wound which he who comes thy Savior shall ~ —John Milton⟩ **b** *obs* **:** to provide a remedy for **:** REPAIR **3** [ME *recuren*, alter. (influenced by *recuren* to restore to health) of *recouren*, contr. of *recoveren* to recover] *obs* **:** to get back **:** RECOVER

re·cur·rence \rəˈkər·ən(t)s, rēˈ- *also* -kə̄rə-\ *n* -S [*recur* + *-ence*] **1 :** a periodic or frequent returning **:** REAPPEARANCE ⟨~*s* of faith and resignation and simple joy —James Joyce⟩ **2 :** RECOURSE, RESORT ⟨the treaty should eliminate further ~ to armed action⟩ **3 :** the act or fact of recurring **:** the state of being recurrent ⟨the main ~*s* of life are too insistent to escape . . . notice —A.N.Whitehead⟩ **4** *bot* **:** repetition of the same type **5 a :** return of symptoms of a disease after a remission **b :** reappearance of a tumor after previous removal

recurrence formula *n* **:** a formula expressing any term of a sequence or series after a stated term as a function of preceding terms

re·cur·rent \-nt\ *adj* [L *recurrent-, recurrens*, pres. part. of *recurrere* to run back, recur — more at RECUR] **1 a :** running or turning back in a direction opposite to its former course — used of various nerves and branches of vessels in the arms and legs ⟨the radial ~ artery⟩ ⟨the ~ laryngeal nerve⟩ **b** *of a veinlet* **:** returning toward the main rib **2 :** returning from time to time **:** appearing or coming periodically **:** happening again and again ⟨food is the urgent and ~ need of individuals and of society —Ellen Semple⟩ ⟨investigate the ~ . . . strike situation —*Current Biog.*⟩ ⟨an endlessly ~ set of problems —I.A.Richards⟩ **3 :** reappearing at other than the first geologic horizon ⟨a ~ fauna⟩

recurrent fever *n* **:** RELAPSING FEVER

re·cur·rent·ly *adv* **:** in a recurrent manner ⟨the problem has been around ~ for a long time —*Time*⟩

recurrent nova *n* **:** a variable star that at intervals usu. of several decades undergoes outbursts similar to that of a nova and declines in brightness

recurring *adj* [fr. pres. part. of *recur*] **:** coming or happening again ⟨a ~ need for solitude and silence —Havelock Ellis⟩ — **re·cur·ring·ly** *adv*

recurring decimal *n* **:** a repeating decimal

re·cur·sion \rəˈkər|zhən, rēˈ-, -kə̄|, -kəi|, *chiefly Brit* |shən\ *n* -S [LL *recursion-, recursio*, fr. *recursus* (past part. of *recurrere* to run back, return) + *-ion-, -io* -ion — more at RECUR] **:** RETURN

re·cur·sive definition \rəˈkər|s|iv, rē-, (ˈ)rē|ˈ|k-, -kə̄|, -kəi|, |z|, |ēv *also* |əv-\ *n* [²*recursion* + *-ive*] **:** a definition of a function permitting values of the function to be calculated systematically in a finite number of steps; *esp* **:** a mathematical definition in which the first case is given and the nth case is defined in terms of one or more previous cases and esp. the immediately preceding one ⟨a ~ of the factorial is given by 0! = 1 and (n + 1)! = (n + 1) · n!⟩

¹re·cur·vate \rəˈkərˌvāt, ˈrēkərˌ-\ *vb* -ED/-ING/-S [L *recurvatus*, past part. of *recurvare*, fr. *re-* + *curvare* to curve — more at CURVE] *vt* **:** to cause to bend backwards ~ *vi* **:** to curve back — **re·curvation** \ˌrē+\ *n*

²re·cur·vate \rəˈkərˌvāt, (ˈ)rē¦kərvət\ *adj* [L *recurvatus*] **:** RECURVED

re·curved \(ˈ)rē+\ *adj* [*re-* + *curved*] **:** curved backward or inward — compare DECURVED

re·cur·vi·rostra \rəˌkərvəˈrästrə\ *n, cap* [NL, fr. L *recurvus* curved back (fr. *re-* + *curvus* curved) + *-i-* + *rostrum* beak — more at CROWN, ROSTRUM] **:** a genus (the type of the family Recurvirostridae) of birds consisting of the avocets

re·cur·vi·rostral \⸗ˌ⸗⸗+\ *adj* [L *recurvus* + *-i-* + *rostrum* + E *-al*] **:** having the beak bent upward

recu·sance \ˈrekyəzən(t)s, rəˈkyüzᵊn(t)s\ *n* -S [fr. *recusant*, after such pairs as E *assistant: assistance*] **:** RECUSANCY

recu·san·cy \-nsē, -si\ *n* -ES [*recusant* + *-cy*] **1 :** the quality or state of being recusant **:** refusal to accept or obey constituted authority **:** NONCONFORMITY ⟨for there is in her . . . a ~, a stubborn antipathy to the disciplining —R.B.Heilman⟩ **2 :** the refusal esp. of Roman Catholics to attend the services of the Church of England constituting a statutory offense punishable by fines and disabilities until the late 18th century

¹recu·sant \-nt\ *n* -S [L *recusant-, recusans*, pres. part. of *recusare* to object to, refuse, fr. *re-* + *-cusare* (fr. *causari* to give a reason, plead, fr. *causa* cause, reason) — more at CAUSE] **1 a :** a person (as a Roman Catholic) refusing to attend the services of the Church of England **b :** one that dissents **:** NONCONFORMIST ⟨a secular ~ who favored what he called the liberal divinities of Greece —R.L.Cook⟩ **2 :** one who refuses to comply with some regulation or to conform to some general practice or opinion

²recusant \"\ *adj* [L *recusant-, recusans* refusing] **1 :** refusing to attend the services of the Church of England **2 :** refusing to submit to authority **:** DISSENTIENT ⟨the ~ electors returned . . . and cooperated in electing a new Senate —Mary W. Williams⟩

rec·u·sa·tion \ˌrekyəˈzāshən\ *n* -S [MF or L; MF *recusation*, fr. L *recusation-, recusatio* refusal, fr. *recusatus* (past part. of *recusare* to refuse) + *-ion-, -io* -ion] *civil & canon law* **:** REFUSAL, OBJECTION, EXCEPTION; *esp* **:** a plea challenging a judge for alleged interest, partiality, or other incompetency

re·cu·sa·tor \rəˈkyüzəd·ə(r)\ *n* -S [L *recusatus* + E *-or*] *Scots law* **:** a recusation to a judge

re·cuse \rəˈkyüz\ *vt* -ED/-ING/-S [ME *recusen*, fr. MF *recuser*, fr. L *recusare* to refuse — more at RECUSANT] *civil and canon law* **:** REFUSE, REJECT: as **a :** to challenge or except to (a judge) as interested or otherwise incompetent **b :** to disqualify (oneself) as judge in a particular case

re·cut \(ˈ)rē+\ *vt* [*re-* + *cut* (v)] **:** to cut again

¹re·cycle \(ˈ)rē+\ *vt* [*re-* + *cycle*] **:** to pass again through a cycle of changes or treatment ⟨an industrial plant . . . ~*s* cooling water through cooling towers as many as 50 times —J.R. Whitaker & E.A.Ackerman⟩; *esp* **:** to feed back continuously in a laboratory or industrial operation or process for further treatment

²recycle \"\ *n* **:** a fraction of a product that is recycled

¹red \ˈred\ *adj* **redder; reddest** [ME *read, reed, red*, fr. OE *rēad*; akin to OE *rēod* red, OHG *rōt*, ON *rauthr* & *rjōthr*, Goth *rauths*, L *ruber* & *rufus*, Gk *erythros* red, Skt *rohita* red, reddish, *rudhira* red, bloody] **1 a :** of the color red ⟨~ rose⟩ ⟨as ~ as a ruby⟩ **b :** lit by or as if by fire ⟨no matter how scarlet the sunset, those ~ hills never became vermilion —Willa Cather⟩ **2 a** (1) **:** dyed with red ⟨the ~ hat of a cardinal⟩ (2) **:** producing a red color ⟨logwood used for ~ dyes⟩ **b :** having red as a distinguishing color ⟨captain of the ~ team⟩ **3 a** (1) **:** flushed esp. with anger or embarrassment ⟨plain from his ~ face that the insult had struck home⟩ ⟨turned uncomfortably ~ when called upon to speak⟩ (2) **:** RUDDY, FLORID ⟨the large ~ health that uncivilized women admire —Walter Bagehot⟩ (3) **:** of a coppery hue ⟨~ skin of the American Indian⟩ **b** *of the eyes* (1) **:** naturally red (2) **:** reddened by inflammation **:** BLOODSHOT ⟨eyes ~ from weeping⟩ **c** *of hair or the coat of an animal* **:** being somewhere in the color range between carrot red and russet or bay ⟨a flaming thatch of ~ hair⟩ ⟨~ setter⟩ ⟨~ roan⟩ **d :** tinged with red **:** REDDISH ⟨flat sandy country . . . the ~ heart of Australia —Myrtle R. White⟩ **4 a :** stained or covered with blood ⟨waving our ~ weapons o'er our heads —Shak.⟩ **b :** full of or colored with blood ⟨good ~ beef⟩ **5 :** heated to redness **:** GLOWING ⟨~ slag from a blast furnace⟩ ⟨~ lava flowing from a volcano⟩ **6 a :** characterized by wrath or violence **:** CHOLERIC, BLOODY ⟨convulsed with ~ rage —Hudson Strode⟩ ⟨the ~ rules of tooth and claw —P.B.Sears⟩ **b :** of an extreme or profligate nature **:** FLAGRANT, WANTON ⟨the ~ waste of his youth —Thomas Wolfe⟩ ⟨is she really so . . . ~ as she is painted —W.J.Locke⟩ **7** [fr. the flag used by revolutionaries] **a :** inciting or endorsing sweeping social or political reform esp. by the use of force **:** REVOLUTIONARY, RADICAL — compare WHITE 8 **b** *often cap* **:** COMMUNIST ⟨fighting ~ guerrillas in the Malayan forests —J.M.Flagler⟩ **c** *often cap* **:** of or relating to the U.S.S.R. or its allies or satellites **:** lying within or emanating from the Soviet orbit ⟨each *Red* worker must be politically educated . . . in Marxist-Leninist terms —O.O.Trullinger⟩ ⟨building up the German ~ army —R.E.M.Morris⟩ ⟨Kremlin is pouring a torrent of ~ books and newspapers into India —F.C.Laubach⟩ **8** [so called fr. the bookkeeping practice of entering debit items in red ink] **:** failing to show a profit ⟨haven't had a ~ month in the past year —R.J.Schrick⟩

²red \"\ *n* -S [ME *read, reed, red*, fr. *read, reed, red*, adj.] **1 a :** a color whose hue resembles that of blood or of the ruby or is that of the long-wave extreme of the visible spectrum **b :** the one of the four psychologically primary hues that is evoked in the normal observer under normal conditions by radiant energy from the long-wave extreme of the visible spectrum combined with a very small amount of radiant energy from the shortwave extreme **c :** one of the six psychologically primary object colors **2 a :** red clothing or cloth ⟨lady in ~⟩ **b :** one that uses red as a distinguishing color; *specif* **:** a member of an athletic team having red insignia ⟨Cincinnati *Reds*⟩ **3 a :** one that is of a red or reddish color: as (1) **:** RED WINE ⟨killed another bottle of California ~ —A.R.Foff⟩ (2) **:** RED CENT ⟨not another cent to waste, not another . . . ~ —P.E. Green⟩ (3) **:** the red ball in billiards (4) **:** an animal with a reddish coat ⟨pressed his pony, a small, nervous ~ —W.V.T. Clark⟩ **b :** an American Indian **:** REDSKIN ⟨risking himself on a wearied horse in a country alive with ~*s* —S.H.Adams⟩ **4 a :** a pigment or dye that colors red ⟨~ can be made from the cochineal insect —Helen Coates⟩; *specif* **:** ROUGE ⟨plenty of powder, and a little ~ too —Willa Cather⟩ **b :** a shade or tint of red ⟨the ~*s* in the petrified woods of Arizona —*Buick Mag.*⟩ **c :** an incandescent glow ⟨the ~ of his cigar like a small, fiery flower between his fingers —Josephine Johnson⟩ **d reds** *pl* **:** insoluble red substances yielded by vegetable tanning materials (as phlobaphenes) and deposited on the surface of the leather **5 a :** one who advocates or is thought to advocate or endorse the violent overthrow of an existing social or political order **:** SUBVERSIVE, REVOLUTIONARY ⟨leftists called themselves liberals, and their opponents called them ~*s* —Upton Sinclair⟩ ⟨rank-and-file German Social Democrats, whom they classify as ~*s* —*Atlantic*⟩ — compare ¹⁰PINK 3, RED REPUBLICAN **b** *usu cap* **:** COMMUNIST ⟨in Kremlin protocol he now takes precedence . . . over all European satellite *Reds* —E.P. Snow⟩ ⟨*Reds* reject . . . all hope of real reforms without a revolution —Jacob Spolansky⟩ **c :** COMMUNISM, RADICALISM ⟨lesser forms of internationalism . . . have a distinctly lighter tinge of ~ —*New Freeman*⟩ **6 a :** the red circle of an archery target that is next to the gold **b :** a shot that hits such a circle **7** [so called fr. the bookkeeping practice of entering debit items in red ink] **:** the condition of showing a loss — usu. used with *the* ⟨a moneymaking scheme for getting the organization out of the ~⟩; opposed to *black* **8 :** RED ALERT

³red \"\ *vb* **redded; redded; redding; reds** [ME *readen*, fr. *read, reed, red*, adj.] *chiefly dial* **:** REDDEN

red *abbr* **1** redactor **2** reduce; reduced; reducer; reducing **3** reduction

re·dact \rəˈdakt, rēˈ-\ *vt* -ED/-ING/-S [L *redactus*, past part. of *redigere* to drive, lead, or bring back, get together, collect, arrange, reduce, fr. *red-* re- + *-igere* (fr. *agere* to drive, lead, act, do) — more at AGENT] **1** *obs* **:** to lower in condition or quality **:** REDUCE ⟨being a little prodigal in his spending, ~*ed* his estate to a weak point —Robert Monro⟩ **2** [back-formation fr. *redaction*] **a :** to put in writing **:** make a draft of **:** COMPOSE, FRAME ⟨council of ministers . . . engaged in ~*ing* the two proclamations —W.G.Clark⟩ **b :** to select or adapt for publication **:** EDIT, REVISE ⟨historical accounts ~*ed* for the modern reader⟩

re·dac·tion \-kshən\ *n* -S [F *rédaction*, fr. LL *redaction-, redactio* action of bringing back, gathering together, reduction, fr. L *redactus* + *-ion-, -io* -ion] **1 a :** an act or instance of preparing for publication **:** EXPOSITION, REVISION ⟨deciding that your search for material is completed, you turn to its ~ —André Morize⟩ **b :** an act or instance of putting into a different written form **:** ADAPTATION, TRANSLATION ⟨a novel which seems as though it were the ~ of a play —W.T.Scott⟩ ⟨English ~*s* of earlier French romances⟩ **2 :** a work that has been redacted **:** EDITION, VERSION ⟨it may be expedient to edit the various ~*s* separately —L.P.G.Peckham⟩ — **re·dac·tion·al** \-nᵊl\ *adj*

re·dac·tor \-ktə(r)\ *n* -S [G & F; G *redakteur*, fr. F *rédacteur*, fr. L *redactus* + F *-eur* -or] **:** one that redacts; *esp* **:** EDITOR

red admiral *n* **:** a showy butterfly (*Vanessa atalanta*) common in both Europe and America having the front wings crossed by a broad orange-red band and larvae that feed on nettles — compare WHITE ADMIRAL

red alder *n* **1 :** an alder (*Alnus rubra*) of the Pacific coast of No. America **2 :** the hard red wood of the red alder tree much used for furniture

red-alder family *n* **:** CUNONIACEAE

red alert *n* **:** the final stage of alert in which attack by enemy aircraft appears to be imminent; *also* **:** the signal for this ⟨at the sound of the *red alert* pedestrians must take shelter⟩ — compare BLUE ALERT, WHITE ALERT, YELLOW ALERT

red alga *n* **:** an alga (division Rhodophyta) having predominantly red pigmentation

red alpine campion *n* **:** ALPINE CAMPION

red amaranth *n* **1 :** THORNY AMARANTH **2 :** PRINCE'S-FEATHER 1

re·dan \rəˈdan\ *n* -S [F, alter. of *redent*, fr. *re-* + *dent* tooth, fr. L *dent-, dens* — more at TOOTH] **:** a fortification having two parapets forming a salient angle, an unfortified entrance usu. protected by its location (as on the bank of a stream, at the head of a bridge, or in advance of a strong line), and often a connection (as by curtains) with other such fortifications as a simple form of fieldwork

red ant *n* **:** any of various reddish ants: as **a :** PHARAOH ANT **b :** the sanguinary ant or any of several rather large closely related ants of Europe and America that make hills in open ground

red antimony *n* **:** KERMESITE

red ape *n* **:** ORANGUTAN

red archangel *n* **:** a Eurasian annual weedy herb (*Lamium purpureum*) naturalized in No. America and having purplish red flowers in axillary clusters — called also *red dead nettle*

re·dar·gue \rəˈdärˌgyü\ *vt* -ED/-ING/-S [ME *redarguen*, fr. L *redarguere*, fr. *red-* re- + *arguere* to accuse, assert, make clear — more at ARGUE] *archaic* **:** to confute by argument **:** DISPROVE

red·ar·gu·tion \ˌredärˈgyüshən\ *n* -S [MF, fr. LL *redargution-, redargutio*, fr. L *redargutus* (past part. of *redarguere*) + *-ion-, -io* -ion] *archaic* **:** REFUTATION

red arsenic *n* **:** REALGAR

red arsenic glass *n* **:** ARSENIC DISULFIDE

red ash *n* **1 a :** an American ash (*Fraxinus pennsylvanica*) with densely velvety tomentose branchlets and petioles and lower leaf surfaces pubescent — called also *downy ash;* see GREEN ASH **b :** an Australian tree (*Alphitonia excelsa*) of the family Rhamnaceae with hard wood **c :** an Australian tree (*Orites excelsa*) of the family Proteaceae **2 :** the wood of a red ash tree

redback \ˈ⸗ˌ⸗\ *n* **1 :** a non-interest-bearing treasury note issued in 1838 by the Republic of Texas **2 :** RED-BACKED SANDPIPER

red-backed cutworm \ˈ⸗ˌ⸗-\ *n* **:** a cutworm that is the larva of a noctuid moth (*Euxoa ochrogaster*), that is a serious pest on wheat, barley, rye, sugar beets and other plants in Canada and northern U. S., and that feeds both above and below ground

red-backed lemming *n* **:** GRAY LEMMING

red-backed mouse *n* **:** any of many small short-tailed voles of the genus *Clethrionomys* of northern and mountainous parts of Europe, Asia, and America

red-backed parrot *n* **:** a small long-tailed green parrot (*Psephotus haematonotus*) of New So. Wales, Victoria, and So. Australia having a red patch on the lower portion of the back — called also *grassie;* compare GRASS PARROT

red-backed saki *n* **:** an active untamable rufous-tinged So. American monkey (*Pithecia chiropotes*) — compare SAKI

red-backed salamander *n* **:** a common salamander (*Plethodon cinereus*) of eastern No. America; *also* **:** a related salamander (*P. vehiculum*) of the Pacific coast

red-backed sandpiper *n* **:** a widely distributed rather small sandpiper (*Erolia alpina*) that is typically cinnamon to rusty brown above, often variously streaked or marked with black (as on the abdomen), and largely white below, has a long and downcurved bill, breeds in northern or arctic regions, and winters chiefly in the southern U.S. and around the Mediterranean — called also *dunlin*

red-backed shrike *n* **:** a European shrike (*Lanius collurio*)

redback spider *n* **:** a theridiid spider (*Latrodectus hasselti*) that is closely related to the American black widow and prob. identical with the katipo, has a venom which produces neurotoxic symptoms in man, and occurs in Australia, New Zealand, and the major islands of the East Indies — called also *red-streaked spider*

red bag *n* **:** prolapse and eversion of the vagina esp. in a ewe

red-bait \ˈredˌbāt\ *vb, often cap R* [back-formation fr. *red-baiter* & *red-baiting*, n.] *vi* **:** to engage in red-baiting ⟨indignantly pointed out that he had never *Red-baited* in his life —W.E.Shelton⟩ ~ *vt* **:** to subject to red-baiting ⟨you will be *red-baited* almost beyond endurance —Henry Wallace⟩

red-baiter \ˈ⸗ˌ⸗⸗\ *n, often cap R* [²*red* + *baiter*] **:** one that red-baits ⟨do not intend to let the smear tactics of professional *red-baiters* produce in me a silly timidity in saying what I think to be the truth —*Nation's Schools*⟩

red-baiting \ˈ⸗ˌ⸗⸗\ *n, often cap R* [²*red* + *baiting*] **:** the act of baiting or harassing as a red often in a malicious or irresponsible manner ⟨the increase of *red-baiting* within the country in order to stifle even liberal dissent —Joseph Barnes⟩

¹red ball *adj* [so called fr. the red mark painted on freight cars requiring expeditious movement] **:** having top priority **:** URGENT — used of freight or a carrier moving top priority freight ⟨*red ball* train⟩ ⟨*red ball* express⟩

²red ball *n* **:** HOTSHOT 1a

red-banded leaf roller \ˈ⸗ˌ⸗⸗-\ *n* **:** a leaf roller that is the larva of a small grayish brown moth (*Argyrotaenia velutinana*) and that has become a serious orchard pest in the northeastern U.S.

red–banded thrips *n* **:** a chiefly tropical thrips (*Selenothrips rubrocinctus*) that is extremely destructive to cacao and in Florida is sometimes a pest of avocado and mango — called also *cacao thrips*

red baneberry *n* **:** a No. American perennial herb (*Actaea rubra*) with ternately compound leaves, small white flowers in terminal racemes, and bright red oval berries — called also *redberry*

red bark *n* **:** a reddish bark obtained from a cinchona tree (*Cinchona succirubra*) and its hybrids containing quinine and used esp. in the manufacture of a bitter tonic — compare CINCHONA 3

red bartsia *n* **:** a European annual herb (*Odontites serotina*) of the family Scrophulariaceae that is naturalized in northeastern No. America, and that has oblong-lanceolate remotely serrate leaves and rose-red flowers in elongated spikes

red bass *n* **1 :** CHANNEL BASS **2** *Austral* **:** any of several snappers (family Lutjanidae); *esp* **:** a common food fish (*Lutjanus coatesi*) of tropical coral reefs and kelp beds

red bat *n* **:** a brick red to rusty red No. American bat of the genus *Lasiurus* (*L. borealis*) that has the upper surface of the membrane between the hind limbs densely hairy

red bay *n* **:** a small tree (*Persea borbonia*) of the southern U. S. having dark red heartwood

red bean *n* **:** an Australian tree (*Dysoxylum muelleri*) of the family Meliaceae whose timber resembles rosewood — called also *pencil cedar*

red bear *n* **:** a heavily furred often reddish bear (*Ursus arctos isabellinus*) of the Himalayan mountains

red bearberry *n* **:** BEARBERRY 1

red beds *n pl* **:** sedimentary strata predominantly red in color and composed largely of sandstone and shale

red beech *n* **1 :** AMERICAN BEECH **2 :** an Australian timber tree (*Tarrietia trifoliolata*) of the family Sterculiaceae **3 :** RED BIRCH 3

red bell *n* **:** a columbine (*Aquilegia canadensis*)

red–bellied snake \ˈ=,==-\ *n* **1 :** any of several American colubrid snakes with coral or reddish ventral surfaces: as **a :** WESTERN RING-NECKED SNAKE **b :** a woodland snake (*Storeria occipitomaculata*) of the Mississippi valley and southeast to Florida **2 :** an Australian elapid snake (*Pseudelaps squamulosus*) that is brown or blackish above and salmon-red below and is venomous but not dangerous to man

red–bellied snipe *n* **:** DOWITCHER

red–bellied squirrel *n* **:** any of numerous arboreal squirrels (genus *Callosciurus*) of southeastern Asia; *esp* **:** a squirrel (*C. erythraeus*) having reddish underparts and a greenish gray or reddish back more or less marked with black

red–bellied terrapin *or* **red–bellied turtle** *n* **:** a terrapin (*Pseudemys rubriventris*) of the tributaries of Chesapeake Bay having more or less red on the plastron and carapace and reaching a length of about 18 inches — called also *redbelly, red fender*

red–bellied woodpecker *n* **:** a woodpecker (*Melanerpes carolinus* or *Centurus carolinus*) of the eastern U. S. having a scarlet head and nape, barred black-and-white back, and grayish underparts tinged with red

redbelly \ˈ=,==\ *n* **1 a :** a pumpkinseed (*Lepomis gibbosus*) **b :** a European char (*Salvelinus salvelinus*) **c :** RED GROUPER **2 :** RED-BELLIED TERRAPIN

redbelly dace *or* **red–bellied dace** *n* **:** either of two small No. American cyprinid fishes (*Phoxinus eos* and *P. erythrogaster*) that are widely but irregularly distributed from the Hudson Bay drainage to New Brunswick and southward and westward to New Mexico, are dusky greenish black above with a creamy or pale yellow stripe along each side bounded by narrower black stripes, the belly deep red and the fins golden more-or-less marked with black and red, and esteemed in Europe as aquarium fishes

red benjamin *n* **:** a birthroot (*Trillium erectum*)

red–berried elder \ˈ=,==-\ *n* **:** a common No. American shrub (*Sambucus pubens*) with pointed cymes of small whitish flowers and bright scarlet fruit

red·berry \ˈred- — *see* BERRY\ *n* **1 :** any of several Australian shrubs of the genus *Rhagodia* having red berries **2 a :** RED BANEBERRY **b :** a ginseng (*Panax quinquefolium*) of No. America **c :** a spiny evergreen California shrub (*Rhamnus crocea*) with minute flowers and bright red berries

redberry disease *n* **:** a disease of blackberries caused by a gall mite (*Aceria essigi* syn. *Eriophyes essigi*) that feeds on the young fruit and causes it to become hard and bright red

red betty *n* [*betty* fr. the name *Betty*] **:** CARDINAL FLOWER

redbill \ˈ=,=\ *n* **1 :** an oyster catcher (*Haematopus unicolor*) of New Zealand **2 :** the common black-and-white long-tailed whydah (*Vidua macroura*) of Africa **3 :** an African waxbill (*Estrilda astrild*)

red–billed mud hen \ˈ=,=-\ *n* **:** FLORIDA GALLINULE

red–billed pigeon *n* **:** a large pigeon (*Columba flavirostris*) that occurs from extreme southern Texas southward into Nicaragua, is highly esteemed as a game bird, has much reddish purple on head, breast, and lesser wing coverts, grayish brown greater coverts and remiges, and the rest of the body bluish gray, and is distinguished by a reddish bill tipped with bright yellow — called also *blue rock*

red–billed teal *n* **:** a southern African duck (*Anas erythrorhyncha*)

red–billed tropic bird *n* **:** a tropic bird (*Phaëton aethereus*)

red birch *n* **1 :** RIVER BIRCH 1 **2 :** the heartwood lumber of the yellow birch (*Betula lutea*) and of the sweet birch (*Betula lenta*) **3 a :** a valuable New Zealand timber tree (*Nothofagus fusca*) — called also *clinker beech, red beech* **b :** the hard wood of this tree

redbird \ˈ=,=\ *n* **1 :** CARDINAL **2 a :** SUMMER TANAGER **b :** SCARLET TANAGER **3 :** the European bullfinch

redbird cactus *or* **redbird flower** *n* **:** a jewbush (*Pedilanthus tithymaloides*)

red bird of paradise : a bird of paradise (*Uranornis rubra*) with red lateral plumes in the male

red bird's–eye *n* **1 :** HERB ROBERT **2 :** RED CAMPION

red–blind \ˈ=,=\ *adj* **:** affected with red blindness

red blindness *n* **:** color blindness in which red is not perceived as such **:** PROTANOPIA

red blood cell *or* **red blood corpuscle** *n* **:** one of the cells responsible for the red color of vertebrate blood **:** ERYTHROCYTE

red–blooded \ˈ=,==\ *adj* **:** full of spirit and vigor **:** LUSTY, ENERGETIC ⟨a *red-blooded* American⟩ ⟨a *red-blooded* adventure story⟩

red blotch *n* **:** ADUSTIOSIS

red board *n* **:** a railroad stop signal — called also *red eye*

red body *n* **:** a mass of capillaries on the inner wall of the air bladder of various teleost fishes thought to control the diffusion and absorption of the gases contained in the air bladder

red bole *n* **:** BOLE 3

red bone *n, usu cap R&B* **1 :** one of a group of people of mixed white, Indian, and Negro ancestry esp. in Louisiana — often used disparagingly **2 :** CROATAN

redbone \ˈ=,=\ *n* **:** a moderate-sized speedy dark red or red and tan American hound used esp. for hunting coon and sometimes considered a distinct breed

red book *n, usu cap R&B* **:** an official British register bound in red; *esp* **:** a 19th century British peerage or court guide

red box *n* **1 :** any of several Australian eucalypts; *esp* **:** a gum tree (*Eucalyptus polyanthemos*) **2 :** an Australian timber tree (*Tristania conferta*)

red brass *n* **1 :** brass having a reddish tint due to a high copper content **:** GUINEA GOLD **2 :** COMPOSITION METAL

redbreast \ˈ=,=\ *n* [ME *redbrest,* fr. ¹*red* + *brest* breast] **1 a :** ROBIN **b :** ³KNOT **2** *or* **red–breasted bream :** a sunfish (*Lepomis auritus*) of the eastern and southern U. S. having the belly largely orange-red

red–breasted goose \ˈ=,==-\ *n* **:** a Siberian goose (*Branta ruficollis*) that is chiefly black-and-white with a chestnut breast

red–breasted merganser *n* **:** a widely distributed merganser (*Mergus serrator*) of Europe and America having in the male a reddish breast band separated from the green head by a conspicuous white collar

red–breasted nuthatch *n* **:** a nuthatch (*Sitta canadensis*) of coniferous forests having the upper parts bluish gray and black and the underparts white and reddish

red–breasted rail *n* **:** VIRGINIA RAIL

red–breasted sandpiper *or* **red–breasted plover** *n* **:** ³KNOT

red–breasted sapsucker *n* **:** a sapsucker (*Sphyrapicus varius ruber*) of western No. America

red–breasted snipe *n* **:** DOWITCHER

red–brown butt rot *n* **:** a destructive butt and root rot of various conifers caused by a pore fungus (*Polyporus schweinitzii*)

red–brown rot *n* **:** a fungous decay of conifers and various deciduous plants caused by a pore fungus (*Fomes pinicola*)

redbrush \ˈ=,=\ *n* **:** either of two No. American cornels with red or reddish purple twigs: **a :** SILKY CORNEL **b :** RED OSIER 2

red bryony *n* **:** a bryony (*Bryonia dioica*)

redbuck \ˈ=,=\ *n, pl* **redbuck** *or* **redbucks :** IMPALA

red buckeye *n* **:** a shrubby buckeye (*Aesculus pavia*) of the southern U. S.

redbud \ˈ=,=\ *n* **:** an American tree of the genus *Cercis; esp* **:** a tree (*C. canadensis*) of eastern No. America that resembles but is usu. smaller than the common Eurasian Judas tree and has pale rosy pink or occasionally white flowers appearing before the leaves expand

red buffalo *n* **:** a small reddish tropical African buffalo that constitutes a race (*Bubalus caffer nana*) of the Cape buffalo

red bug *n* **:** any of various red insects: as **a** *South & Midland* **:** CHIGGER 2 **b :** any of several red mirid bugs that live on apple trees **c :** COTTON STAINER

red campion *n* **:** a biennial European catchfly (*Lychnis dioica*) having red or pink flowers — called also *red bird's-eye*

redcap \ˈ=,=\ *n* **1 :** one that wears a red cap: as **a :** a baggage porter at a transportation terminal (as a railroad station) **b** *Brit* **:** MILITARY POLICEMAN **2** *dial Eng* **:** GOLDFINCH 1 **3** *usu cap* **a :** an old English breed of medium-sized domestic fowls resembling Old English Game fowls but distinguished by a very large full rose comb **b :** a bird of this breed

red carabeen *also* **red carrobean** *n* **:** any of several Australian trees; *specif* **:** a large tree (*Geissois bentanii*) of the family Cunoniaceae having reddish brown hard heavy wood that is used in flooring and paneling

red cardinal *n* **:** CARDINAL FLOWER

red carp *n* **:** GOLDFISH 1a

red–carpet \ˈ=,==\ *adj* [so called fr. the traditional laying down of a red carpet for important guests to walk upon] **:** marked by the formal ceremonial courtesy accorded persons of rank or importance ⟨the *red-carpet* treatment given visiting dignitaries⟩

red cedar *n* **1 a :** an American juniper (*Juniperus virginiana*) found commonly east of the Rocky mountains and having dark green closely imbricated needle-shaped leaves — called also *eastern red cedar;* see TREE illustration **b :** the fragrant close-grained red wood of this tree **c :** any of several related trees of the genus *Juniperus* **2 a :** CANOE CEDAR **b :** the strong durable wood of this tree **c :** INCENSE CEDAR **d :** SPANISH CEDAR **3** *Austral* **a :** TOON **b :** FLINDOSA

red cell *or* **red corpuscle** *n* **:** a red blood cell **:** ERYTHROCYTE

red cent *n* **1 :** CENT 1b; *specif* **:** a large copper U.S. cent of the series coined 1793-1857 **2 :** a trivial amount **:** PENNY, WHIT

red chalk *n* **:** BOLE 3

red char *n* **:** a common European char (*Salvelinus alpinus*)

red charcoal *n* **:** a substance intermediate between wood and ordinary charcoal made by heating wood to about 300° C

red chickweed *n* **:** SCARLET PIMPERNEL

red chokeberry *n* **:** a common swamp shrub (*Aronia arbutifolia*) of the eastern U. S. with terminal cymes of pearly white flowers and bright red long-persistent fruit

red clay *n* **1 :** clay that usu. owes its reddish color to oxide of iron **2 :** a slowly accumulating abysmal deposit covering some 55,000,000 square miles of the deepest parts of the ocean bottom and consisting of the insoluble residual material of volcanic and meteoritic or cosmic dust mingled with nodules of manganese oxide, crystals of the zeolite phillipsite, sharks' teeth, the siliceous tests of Radiolaria, and other resistant organic debris

red clover *n* **:** a Eurasian clover (*Trifolium pratense*) naturalized in America, cultivated as a hay, forage, and cover crop, and having globose heads of reddish purple flowers

red cluster pepper *n* **:** a rather small compact pepper (*Capsicum frutescens fasciculatum*) that has narrow clustered leaves and is sometimes cultivated for its slender elongated brilliant red and extremely pungent fruits

redcoat \ˈ=,=\ *n, often cap* **:** a member of the British armed forces in America during the Revolutionary War

red coat *n* **:** BEDBUG 1a

red coati *n* **:** a coati (*Nasua rufa*) of So. America

red cobalt *n* **:** ERYTHRITE

red cock *n* **:** the male of the red grouse

red cod *n* **1 :** a gadid food fish (*Physiculus bachus*) of Australia and New Zealand that is reddish gray above and pink beneath but quickly becomes red when removed from the water **2 :** RED ROCK COD

red coffee borer *n* **:** TEA BORER

red copper ore *n* **:** CUPRITE

red coral *n* **:** an alcyonarian (*Corallium nobile* syn. *C. rubrum*) of the Mediterranean and adjacent parts of the Atlantic that forms branching shrubby colonies sometimes about a foot high and has in the axis of the stems and branches a hard stony skeleton of a delicate red or pink color used for ornaments and jewelry; *also* **:** a related coral of the Indian ocean

red core *n, chiefly Brit* **:** RED STELE

red cotton bug *n* **:** a pyrrhocorid bug (*Dysdercus cingulatus*) that causes great damage to cotton in parts of Asia

red cotton tree *n* **:** a tree (*Bombax malabaricum*) of India having striking red fleshy flowers borne while the leaves are off the tree

red count *n* **:** a blood count of the red blood cells

red crab *n* **:** a dark red edible crab (*Cancer productus*) widely distributed in shallow water from Alaska to Mexico

red crescent *adj, usu cap R&C* **:** of or relating to the Muslim equivalent of the International Red Cross

red–crested pochard \ˈ=,==-\ *n* **:** an Old World duck (*Netta rufina*) having in the male a chestnut head with a large crest, a red bill and feet, and a white speculum

¹**red cross** *n, usu cap R&C* **:** a red Greek cross on a white ground adopted by the Geneva convention of 1864 as the emblem to identify noncombat installations, vehicles, and personnel ministering to the sick and wounded in war and now used as the emblem of the International Red Cross and its affiliates not only in war but in disaster relief and other humanitarian services — called also *Geneva cross*

²**red cross** *adj, usu cap R&C* [fr. the *Red Cross,* an international humanitarian organization] **:** of or relating to the International Red Cross or its affiliates — compare RED CRESCENT

red crossbill *n* **:** a common crossbill (*Loxia curvirostra*) of the northern hemisphere being in the male crimson with dark brown wings and tail

red crowberry *n* **1 :** a low heathlike subantarctic shrub (*Empetrum rubrum*) bearing red berries and forming a main constituent of peat deposits in some areas **2 :** the edible red berry of red crowberry

red curlew *n* **1 :** SCARLET IBIS **2 :** MARBLED GODWIT

red currant *n* **1 a :** any of various red-fruited currants: as (1) **:** any of numerous cultivated currants derived from either of two natural species (*Ribes sativum* and *R. rubrum*) (2) **:** WILD RED CURRANT 1 **b :** WILD RED CURRANT 2 **2 :** GOYA

red cypress *n* **1 :** a bald cypress (*Taxodium distichum*) **2 :** the wood of bald cypress

¹**redd** \ˈred\ *vt* [ME *redden,* fr. OE *hreddan;* akin to OFris *hredda* to save, OS *riddian,* OHG *hretten, retten* to save, free, and prob. to OE *hræd* quick, rapid, fast — more at RATHE] *chiefly dial* **:** to make free (as from trouble or from another person) **:** DELIVER, RESCUE

²**redd** \"\ *vb* **redded** *or* **redd; redded** *or* **redd; redding; redds** [ME *redden,* prob. alter. (influenced by *redden* to save, free) of *ridden* to rid — more at RID] *vt* **1** *archaic* **a :** to clear (a passage) out **:** OPEN, UNBLOCK **b :** UNRAVEL, DISENTANGLE **c :** to take (as combatants) apart **d :** to put an end to (a controversy) **:** compose (a difference) **2** *chiefly dial* **a :** to set in order **:** clear of debris **:** NEATEN, SMARTEN — usu. used with *up* or *out* ⟨~ up the bedrooms, get fresh flowers, dust —Jessamyn West⟩ ⟨~ out the cabin —Conrad Richter⟩ **b :** to straighten out **:** ARRANGE, SETTLE — usu. used with *up* ⟨~ up the affairs of Europe —John Buchan⟩ **3** *Midland* **:** COMB ⟨~ the hair⟩ ~ *vi, chiefly dial* **:** to make things tidy — usu. used with *up* ⟨stay and ~ up . . . I want to leave things nice —B.A.Williams⟩

³**redd** \"\ *n* -S [ME *red,* fr. *redden,* v.] **1** *chiefly Scot* **:** an act of redding **2** *chiefly Scot* **:** LITTER, REFUSE

⁴**redd** \"\ *adj* [fr. past part. of ²*redd*] *chiefly Scot* **:** cleared for a new occupant ⟨leaves my premises void and ~ —Sir Walter Scott⟩

⁵**redd** \"\ *n* -S [origin unknown] **1 :** the spawn of a fish **2 :** the spawning ground or nest of various fishes (as the salmon and trout)

red dagga *n* **:** ¹DAGGA 2

red daisy *n* **:** ORANGE HAWKWEED

red dane *or* **red danish** *n* **1** *usu cap R&D* **:** a Danish breed of highly productive usu. solid red dairy cattle that are very popular in northern Europe **2** *often cap R & usu cap D* **:** an animal of the Red Dane breed

red dead nettle *n* **:** RED ARCHANGEL

red deal *n* **:** the wood of Scotch pine

redded *past of* RED

red deer *n* **1 :** the common stag (*Cervus elaphus*) of temperate Europe and Asia similar to but smaller than the wapiti **2 :** the Virginia deer in its summer coat

red·den \ˈredᵊn\ *vb* **reddened; reddened; reddening** \-d(ᵊ)niŋ\ **reddens** [¹*red* + *-en*] *vt* **:** to make red or reddish ⟨blood ~*s* the bandage⟩ ~ *vi* **1 :** to become suffused with red **:** BLUSH ⟨the lawyer's face ~*s* with annoyance —Stuart Chase⟩ **2 :** to turn red or reddish in color ⟨the long sunlight ~*ed* slowly in the little room —Mary Deasy⟩

red·den·do \rəˈden(,)dō, reˈ-\ *n* -S [L, abl. of *reddendum;* fr. its being the first word in such clauses] *Scots law* **1 :** a clause in a charter specifying the particular duty or service due from a vassal to his superior **2 :** the duty specified in a reddendo

red·den·dum \-ndəm\ *n, pl* **redden·da** \-ndə\ [L, neut. of *reddendus,* gerundive of *reddere* to give back, hand over, yield, grant — more at RENDER] **:** a clause in a deed usu. following the tenendum by which some new thing (as rent) is reserved out of what had been granted before

redder *comparative of* RED

red desert soil *n* **:** any of a group of zonal soils of warm-temperate and tropical deserts that have light reddish brown friable soil over a reddish brown or dull red heavy horizon which grades into an accumulation of calcium carbonate and that supports more or less scanty desert-shrub vegetation

reddest *superlative of* RED

red·di \ˈredē\ *n, pl* **reddi** *or* **reddis** *usu cap* **1 :** a Munda-speaking migratory agricultural people of central India situated along the Godavari river in southeast Hyderabad, representing an ancient pre-Dravidian agricultural group of the Deccan plateau **2 :** a member of the Reddi people

red diarrhea *or* **red dysentery** *n* **:** bloody diarrhea of calves; *esp* **:** coccidiosis caused by a microscopic animal parasite of the genus *Eimeria* (*E. zurnii*)

red·ding \ˈrediŋ\ *n* -S [ME *reding,* fr. *read, reed, red* red + *-ing* — more at RED] *chiefly dial* **:** RED OCHER 1

red·ding·ite \ˈrediŋ,īt\ *n* -S [*Redding,* Conn. + E *-ite*] **:** a mineral $Mn_3(PO_4)_2.3H_2O$ consisting of a pinkish or yellowish white orthorhombic hydrous manganese phosphate isomorphous with phosphoferrite

red·dish \ˈredish, -dēsh\ *adj* [ME *redische,* fr. *read, reed, red* red + *-ische, -ish* -ish] **:** tinged with red

reddish–brown lateritic soil *n* **:** any of a group of zonal soils developed under humid tropical forest vegetation that have granular dark reddish brown surface soils underlain by reddish friable clay B-horizons and red reticulately mottled lateritic parent material

reddish chestnut soil *n* **:** any of a group of zonal soils developed under mixed grass with some shrubs in a warm-temperate semiarid climate that have dark brown surface soils tinted pinkish or reddish and up to 2 feet thick underlain by heavier reddish brown soil on grayish or pinkish lime accumulations

reddish egret *n* **:** a medium-sized heron (*Dichromanassa rufescens*) of Central America, the Gulf states, and the West Indies that is usu. slate colored with rufous head and neck and black legs but has forms in which the entire plumage is white

red·dish·ness *n* -ES **:** the quality or state of being reddish

reddish prairie soil *n* **:** any of a group of zonal soils developed under tall grass in a warm-temperate humid to subhumid climate that have dark reddish brown somewhat acid surface soils which grade to the parent material through slightly heavier reddish soils

red·di·tion \rəˈdishən\ *n* -S [ME *reddicion,* fr. MF *reddition* act of rendering, fr. LL *reddition-, redditio,* fr. L *redditus* (past part. of *reddere* to give back, hand over, yield, grant) + *-ion-, -io* -ion — more at RENDER] **1** *archaic* **:** RESTITUTION, SURRENDER **2** *obs* **a :** ELUCIDATION **b :** the application of a comparison **c :** the clause that contains such application

reddle *var of* RUDDLE

red·dock \ˈredək\ *dial Eng var of* RUDDOCK 1

red dog *n* **1** [so called fr. the red ink endorsement] **:** unreliable paper money issued by wildcat banks in the U.S. prior to the establishment of the national banking system **2** [so called fr. the fact that such flour was once packed in bags with a red dog on the front] **:** the lowest grade of flour; *specif* **:** a dark flour containing aleurone, little wheat flour, and bran particles obtained as a by-product of flour milling and used as an animal feed **3 :** a card game in which each player contributes to a pool and then in turn bets that he holds in his hand a card of the same suit and of higher rank than the top card of the stock — called also *high-card pool* **4 :** DHOLE **5 :** reddish ashes derived from burning piles of rejected coal and used esp. for paving in mine areas **6 :** a rush by the linebackers on the passer in football

red–dog \ˈ=,=\ *vb* [fr. the noun phrase *red dog*] *vt* **:** to rush (the passer) in football ~ *vi* **:** to rush the passer in football

red dogwood *n* **1 :** a common and often cultivated European shrub (*Cornus sanguinea*) with white flowers in dense cymes and bright red twigs **2 :** RED OSIER 2

red drum *n* **:** CHANNEL BASS

redds *pres 3d sing of* REDD, *pl of* REDD

redd–up \ˈ=,=\ *adj* [fr. past part. of *redd up*] *chiefly dial* **:** redded up **:** TIDIED

red duster *n* **:** RED ENSIGN

red dwarf *n* **:** a star at the lower end of the main sequence in the spectrum-luminosity diagram having low surface temperature and small intrinsic luminosity, mass, and size

¹**rede** \ˈrēd\ *vt* [ME *reden* to read, advise, interpret, govern, guess — more at READ] **1** *dial Brit* **a :** to arrive at by conjecture **:** GUESS, SURMISE **b :** PREDICT **2** *dial* **:** to give counsel to **:** ADVISE, WARN ⟨I ~ you not to stay here when I am gone —J.H.Wheelwright⟩ **3** *dial* **:** to put a construction upon **:** INTERPRET, EXPLAIN ⟨found the riddle . . . not possible to ~ —C.G.Harper⟩

²**rede** \"\ *n* -S [ME *reed, red, rede,* fr. OE *rǣd* advice, counsel, council — more at READ] **1** *chiefly Brit* **:** COUNSEL, ADVICE ⟨my ~ is this, that we to gain . . . bliss, risk dying —William Morris⟩ **2** *archaic* **a :** an explanatory statement or interpretation **:** ACCOUNT, STORY ⟨read your ~ to me then boldly —Richard Brathwaite⟩ **b :** a proverbial saying **:** ADAGE, MAXIM

redear \ˈ=,=\ *also* **redear sunfish** *n* -S **:** a common sunfish (*Lepomis microlophus*) of the southern and eastern U.S. resembling the bluegill but somewhat darker above and paler beneath and with the back part of the gill cover bright orange-red — called also *shellcracker*

red earth *n* **:** hard red deep clays of tropical climates that are usu. leached and low in combined silica

re·decorate \(ˈ)rē+\ *vb* [*re-* + *decorate*] *vt* **:** to freshen or change in appearance **:** REFURBISH, RENOVATE; *esp* **:** to paint or paper (as the interior of a building) ~ *vi* **:** to freshen or change a decorative scheme; *esp* **:** to paint or paper walls and woodwork ⟨under the terms of the lease, the landlord is required to ~ every three years⟩

re·decoration \(ˈ)rē+\ *n* **:** an act or instance of redecorating

re·decussate \(ˈ)rē, ¦rē+\ *vi* [*re-* + *decussate*] *of nerve fibers* **:** to cross again

re·dedicate \(ˈ)rē+\ *vt* [*re-* + *dedicate*] **:** to dedicate again ⟨repair and ~ a gutted church⟩

re·dedication \(ˈ)rē+\ *n* **:** an act or instance of rededicating

re·deem \rə'dēm, rē'-\ *vb* -ED/-ING/-S [ME *redemen*, modif. (perh. influenced by *demen* to judge, deem) of MF *redimer*, fr. L *redimere*, fr. *red-* re- + *-imere* (fr. *emere* to take, buy, acquire); akin to OIr *arfoem* to take, Lith *imti* to take, OSlav *imǫ* I take away, Hitt *u-emijami* I grasp, find] *vt* **1 a :** to buy back : REPURCHASE ⟨if a man sell a dwelling house in a walled city, then he may ~ it within a whole year after —Lev 25:29 (RSV)⟩ **b :** to get or win back ⟨~*ed* his championship status by winning the return bout⟩ **2 a :** to liberate (as from slavery or captivity) by paying a price : RANSOM ⟨a parley to decide the terms for ~*ing* captured warriors⟩ **b** (1) **:** to free by force : LIBERATE ⟨the ~*ed* land of France —*N.Y. Times*⟩ (2) **:** to extricate from or help to surmount (a detrimental influence or circumstance) ⟨~*s* life from futility and meaninglessness —J.H.Hallowell⟩ **c :** to release from blame or debt : CLEAR, JUSTIFY ⟨a yearly tribute . . . ~*ed* the borough from all claims —E.A.Freeman⟩ ⟨eager . . . to ~ himself by furthering the national interest —Oscar Handlin⟩ **d** [modif. of LL *redimere*, fr. L] **:** to absolve from the bondage of sin ⟨Christ hath ~*ed* us from the curse of the law —Gal 3:13 (AV)⟩ ⟨God has demonstrated His love for human souls by ~*ing* them through a supreme act of self-sacrifice —A.J. Toynbee⟩ **e :** to change from worse to better : PURIFY, REFORM ⟨our civilization cannot survive materially unless it be ~*ed* spiritually —Woodrow Wilson⟩ ⟨your auditors are hardened sinners, not easily ~*ed* —B.N.Cardozo⟩ **f :** to put back into proper condition : REPAIR, RESTORE ⟨~*ing* cocoa plantations which have been neglected in recent years —*N.Y. Times*⟩ **g** *archaic* **:** to recover from a state of submersion : RECLAIM ⟨considerable spaces were ~*ed* from the original ocean and converted into dry land —Charles Lyell⟩ **3 a :** to repossess upon fulfillment of an obligation; *specif* **:** to free (property) from a lien or encumbrance and regain absolute title by payment of an amount secured thereby or by performing the condition securing the same **b** (1) **:** to remove the obligation of by payment ⟨the U. S. Treasury ~*s* war bonds upon demand⟩ (2) **:** to convert into something of value ⟨people who always ~ trading stamps⟩ **c** (1) **:** to make good (a promise or pledge) : FULFILL ⟨graver peril arose, and Washington ~*ed* his promise to stand by the army —H.E.Scudder⟩ (2) **:** to convert into actuality : REALIZE ⟨looked to the north with a childlike trust which . . . has not been ~*ed* by the event —W.L.Sperry⟩ **4 a :** to atone for or cleanse : EXPIATE, PURGE ⟨~ an error⟩ ⟨a tireless attempt to make the twentieth century ~ this tragedy of the nineteenth —Anne Fremantle⟩ ⟨~ themselves by means of frank confessions —Q.K.Y. Huang⟩ **b** (1) **:** to cancel out the detrimental effect of : make up for : COMPENSATE, OFFSET ⟨a plain pale face ~*ed* by very beautiful eyes —Elizabeth Goudge⟩ ⟨style and malicious epigram . . . ~ much that is tedious —L.O.Coxe⟩ (2) **:** to make worth while : give merit to : RETRIEVE ⟨a resynthesis . . . might ~ the whole undertaking —R.M.Weaver⟩ **c** *obs* **:** to be accepted in exchange for ⟨would some part of my young years might but ~ the passage of your age —Shak.⟩ **5 :** to make profitable use of (time) ⟨worked . . . with indefatigable energy, ~*ing* the time —J.F.Clarke⟩ ~ *vi* **1 :** DELIVER, SAVE ⟨is my hand shortened, that it cannot ~ —Isa 50:2 (RSV)⟩ **2 :** to buy back property : regain title by purchase ⟨rights . . . must be exercised within forty years from the time at which the proprietor is allowed to ~ —William Bell⟩ **syn** see RESCUE

re·deem·abil·i·ty \rə͵dēmə'biləd·ē\ *n* **:** capability of being redeemed

re·deem·able \rə'dēməbəl, rē'-\ *adj* **:** capable of being redeemed: as **a :** recoverable upon payment of a price or fulfillment of a condition ⟨~ goods in a pawn shop⟩ **b :** convertible into cash at the request of the holder ⟨~ stocks and bonds⟩ **c :** susceptible to improvement or reform or esp. to spiritual redemption ⟨~ sinner⟩ — **re·deem·ably** \-blē\ *adv*

re·deem·er \-mə(r)\ *n* -S [ME *redemer*, fr. *redemen* to redeem + *-er* — more at REDEEM] **:** one that redeems ⟨has been called the ~ of his people⟩

redeeming *adj* **:** serving to offset or compensate for a defect ⟨a cynical man with a ~ sense of humor⟩ ⟨the ~ feature of the plan is its simplicity⟩

re·deem·less \-mləs\ *adj, archaic* **:** admitting of no improvement or recovery ⟨change his pleasure into wretched and ~ misery —Henry Chettle⟩

re·define \¦rē+\ *vt* [*re-* + *define*] **:** to define (a concept) again; *esp* **:** REFORMULATE ⟨business men must ~, liberalize capitalism —*Magazine Intelligence*⟩ ⟨to deal with the problem effectively, we must ~ our terms⟩

re·definition \(¦)rē+\ *n* [*re-* + *definition*] **:** an act or instance of redefining ⟨asking for . . . a ~ of the objectives of the liberal college —B.F.Wright⟩ ⟨such terms as *liberal* call for periodic ~⟩

red eft *n* **:** a brick red terrestrial form of a common No. American newt (*Triturus viridescens*)

red elder *n* **:** CRANBERRY TREE

re·deliver \¦rē+\ *vt* [*re-* + *deliver*] **1** *archaic* **a :** to give back : RETURN **b :** to set free : LIBERATE **2 a** *obs* **:** to report the answer of ⟨shall I ~ you e'en so —Shak.⟩ **b** *archaic* **:** to utter again : REPEAT

re·delivery \"+\ *n* **:** an act or instance of redelivering; *esp* **:** RESTITUTION

red elm *n* **1 :** any of several American elms having reddish wood: as **a :** SLIPPERY ELM **b :** WINGED ELM **c :** SEPTEMBER ELM **2 :** the wood of a red elm tree

red els \-'elz\ *n, pl* **red elses** [part trans. of Afrik *rooie-els*, fr. *rooie* red + *els* alder, fr. MHG *else*; akin to OHG *elira*, *erila* alder — more at ALDER] **:** a southern African shrub or small tree (*Cunonia capensis*) having bark that yields tannin

re·demand \¦rē+\ *vt* [*re-* + *demand*] **:** to demand again — **re·de·mand·able** \"+əbəl\ *adj*

re·demp·ti·ble \rə'dem(p)təbəl\ *adj* [*redemption* + *-ible*] **:** REDEEMABLE

re·demp·tion \rə'dem(p)shən, rē'-\ *n* -S [ME *redempcioun*, fr. MF *redemption*, fr. LL & L; LL *redemption-*, *redemptio* redemption from sin, fr. L, act of buying back or redeeming, ransom, fr. *redemptus* (past part. of *redimere* to redeem) + *-ion-*, *-io* -ion — more at REDEEM] **1 a :** deliverance from the bondage of sin : spiritual salvation ⟨man's damnation and God's ~ —J.C.Brauer⟩ **b :** expiation of guilt or wrong : EXONERATION, ATONEMENT ⟨disgrace . . . from which there could never be ~ —Thomas Wolfe⟩ **2 a :** emancipation or liberation through payment of a price : RANSOM ⟨modes of ~ and manumission —*Notes & Queries on Anthropology*⟩ **b :** PIDYON HABEN **3 a :** an act or instance of repairing or restoring : RECLAMATION ⟨the ~ of chronically polluted areas —R.M.Paul⟩ **b :** an act or instance of bettering : IMPROVEMENT ⟨the ~ of society through science —Mary Austin⟩; *esp* **:** REFORM ⟨the defective or recidivist, whose ~ is hopeless —B.N.Cardozo⟩ **c :** release from a detrimental influence or circumstance ⟨the aim of life is ~ from the wheel of rebirth —F.B.Artz⟩ **4 a :** the removal of an obligation by payment ⟨~ of a promissory note⟩ ⟨~ of the unused portion of a railroad ticket⟩ **b :** the regaining of property by satisfaction of an obligation; *specif* **:** the process of regaining absolute legal title by annulling a defeasible title — **re·demp·tion·al** \-shən°l\ *adj*

re·demp·tion·er \-nə(r)\ *n* -S **1 :** an emigrant from Europe to America in the 18th and 19th centuries obtaining passage by becoming an indentured servant at the disposal of the shipowner or master for a specified length of time **2 :** one redeeming himself or his property (as from servitude or debt)

re·demp·tion·ist \-nəst\ *n* -S *cap* **:** TRINITARIAN 1

re·demp·tive \-(p)tiv, -tēv *also* -təv\ *adj* [*redemption* + *-ive*] **:** of, relating to, or bringing about redemption ⟨a detailed ~ theory about life —E.K.Brown⟩ ⟨the ~ love of the Gospels —W.B.Stein⟩

re·demp·tor \-tə(r)\ *n* -S [ME *redemptour*, fr. LL *redemptor*, fr. L, contractor, fr. *redemptus* (past part. of *redimere* to redeem, contract) + *-or* — more at REDEEM] **:** REDEEMER

re·demp·to·ri·al \¦rē¦dem(p)¦tōrēəl\ *adj* [*redemptor* + *-al*] **:** REDEMPTIVE

re·demp·tor·ist \rə'dem(p)tərəst, rē'-\ *n* -S *cap* [F *rédemptoriste*, fr. LL *redemptor* + F *-iste* -ist] **:** a member of the Roman Catholic Congregation of the Most Holy Redeemer founded in Naples in 1732 by St. Alphonsus Liguori and devoted to preaching to the poor

re·demp·to·ry \-tə-, -ri\ *adj* [*redemption* + *-ory*] **:** REDEMPTIVE

re·demp·tress \-trəs\ *n* -ES [*redemptor* + *-ess*] **:** REDEMPTRIX

re·demp·trix \-riks\ *n, pl* **redemptri·ces** \-rə͵sēz\ [LL, fem. of *redemptor*] **:** a female redeemer

red ensign *n* **:** an ensign with a red field borne by British merchantmen — called also *red duster*

re·deploy \¦rē+\ *vb* [*re-* + *deploy*] *vt* **:** to transfer (military forces or equipment) from one area or fighting front to another ⟨forces which recently attacked the Allied beachhead . . . have now been ~*ed* to the southwest —*Army-Navy-Air Force Jour.*⟩ ⟨the first plane to be ~*ed* —*N.Y. Times*⟩ ~ *vi* **:** to carry out a redeployment ⟨aiding the Army to ~ —H.S. Truman⟩

re·de·ploy·ment \"+mənt\ *n* **:** a relocation or reassignment of men or equipment ⟨~ of United States forces from western Europe to the Far East —E.L.Erickson⟩ ⟨large-scale ~ of labor —Thomas Balogh⟩ ⟨the Soviet Union's mammoth ~ of industry into the Ural Mountains —*Newsweek*⟩

¹re·deposit \¦rē+\ *vt* [*re-* + *deposit*] **:** to deposit again ⟨~*ed* interest⟩ ⟨manganese ore . . . dissolved and ~*ed* in the form of concretions —*Jour. of Geol.*⟩

²redeposit \"\ *n* **:** something that is deposited again ⟨the ~ is made up of the exact amount refunded —*Your Retirement System*⟩

re·deposition \(¦)rē+\ *n* [*re-* + *deposition*] **:** formation into a new accumulation ⟨clearly a product of solution and ~ in a highly porous rock —*Jour. of Geol.*⟩

redes *pl of* REDE

re·descend \¦rē+\ *vb* [*re-* + *descend*] **:** to descend again

¹re·design \"+\ *vt* [*re-* + *design*] **:** to revise in appearance, function, or content ⟨~ a tool⟩ ⟨~ a curriculum⟩

²redesign \"\ *n* **:** a revision or act of revising in design ⟨a ~ of the existing product label —*Modern Packaging*⟩ ⟨called in . . . to go over the blueprints and advise in the ~ and rebuilding of the fireplaces —*New Yorker*⟩

re·determination \¦rē+\ *n* **:** an act or instance of fixing again or confirming ⟨administrative procedures . . . in the ~ of prices —*Jour. of Accountancy*⟩ ⟨undertook the ~ of the atomic weights —William Ramsay⟩

re·determine \"+\ *vt* [*re-* + *determine*] **:** to fix again : REESTABLISH, CONFIRM ⟨~ the orbit of a comet⟩ ⟨~ the boiling point of liquid hydrogen⟩

re·develop \"+\ *vt* [*re-* + *develop*] **1 :** to develop again : REDESIGN, REBUILD ⟨~ a slum area⟩ **2 a :** to reverse the tones of (a photographic image) — compare REVERSAL 2 **b :** to make (a developed image) more intense **c :** to tone (a developed image) by bleaching and sulfiding — **re·de·vel·op·er** \"+ə(r)\ *n*

re·de·vel·op·ment \"+mənt\ *n* **:** the act or process of redeveloping; *esp* **:** the renovation of a blighted area ⟨urban ~⟩

redevelopment company *n* **:** a public or private body corporate organized to encourage the economic development of a particular area by loaning capital to business enterprises willing to locate in that area or by leasing or selling real estate owned by it to such enterprises

redeye \'=͵=\ *n* **1 :** any of several fishes with more or less reddish eyes: as **a :** RUDD **b :** ROCK BASS 1 **c** (1) **:** SMALLMOUTH BLACK BASS (2) **:** REDEYE BLACK BASS **d :** WARMOUTH **2 :** COPPERHEAD 1a

red-eye \'=͵=\ *n* **1 :** cheap whiskey **2 a :** RED-EYED VIREO **b :** a large black Australian cicada (*Psaltoda moerens*)

red eye *n* **:** RED BOARD

redeye black bass *n* **:** a black bass (*Micropterus coosae*) of the southeastern U.S. in most respects resembling a smallmouth black bass but usu. considered a distinct species — called also *redeye*

red-eyed \'=¦=\ *adj* **1 a :** having red eyes **b :** having a red ring around the eye **2 :** having the eyes reddened or inflamed (as from weeping)

red-eyed pochard *n* **:** a pochard (*Aythya ferina*) — called also *redhead*

red-eyed vireo *n* **:** a common vireo (*Vireo olivaceus*) of northeastern No. America having a grayish green back, white underparts, and the iris red — called also *red-eye*

redeye gravy *n* **:** gravy made by adding water or coffee to drippings rendered from panbroiled ham steak

red-faced \'=¦=\ *adj* **:** having a red face; *esp* **:** flushed with anger or embarrassment — **red-fac·ed·ly** \(')=¦fāsədlē, -stl-, -li\ *adv*

red factor *n* **:** a canary carrying some proportion of black-hooded red siskin blood and used in breeding to increase reddish tones in the plumage of the offspring

red feather *adj, usu cap R&F* [so called fr. the red feather symbolic of the United Fund, a charitable organization in the U.S.] **:** of, relating to, or supported by contributions to a community chest ⟨*Red Feather* agency⟩

red feed *n* **:** small red marine surface-swimming copepod crustaceans that are a leading food of some commercial fishes — called also *red seed*

red fender *n* **:** RED-BELLIED TERRAPIN

red fescue *n* **:** a perennial pasture and turf grass (*Festuca rubra*) of Europe and America with creeping rootstocks, erect culms, and reddish spikelets

red fever *n* **:** SWINE ERYSIPELAS

red-figure \'=¦==\ *or* **red-figured** \'=¦==\ *adj* **:** of, relating to, or constituting a style of ceramic painting developed in Athens at the end of the 6th century B.C. in which the outer surfaces of the ware are covered in black except for the decorative figures and other elements which show as exposed areas of the red body clay and which are drawn chiefly from mythology in a style distinguished by convincing representation and graceful line ⟨*red-figure* vase⟩ ⟨*red-figure* ware⟩ — compare BLACK-FIGURE, POLYCHROME

redfin \'=͵=\ *n* **:** any of various fishes with more or less red fins: as **a :** the common shiner (*Notropis cornutus*) the male of which has bright red fins in the breeding season **b** *also* **redfin shiner :** a similar and closely related fish (*N. umbratilis*) esp. abundant in sluggish prairie streams of central No. America **c :** REDHORSE

redfin pickerel *n* **:** a small but gamy pickerel (*Esox americanus*) of the Atlantic coastal states that is dusky green with curved black bars on the sides — called also *barred pickerel*

red fir *n* **1 a :** any of several western American firs of the genus *Abies*: as (1) **:** NOBLE FIR (2) **:** CALIFORNIA RED FIR (3) **:** AMABILIS FIR **b :** the wood of a red fir tree **2 :** DOUGLAS FIR **3 :** NORWAY SPRUCE **4 :** SCOTCH PINE

red fire *n* **:** a composition usu. containing a strontium or lithium salt that burns with a bright red light for use in pyrotechny and signaling

redfish \'=͵=\ *n, pl* **redfish** *or* **redfishes :** any of various more or less reddish fishes: as **a** (1) **:** BLUEBACK SALMON (2) *Brit* **:** the male salmon in spawning condition **b :** ROSEFISH **c :** a sheepshead (*Pimelometopon pulcher*) **d :** CHANNEL BASS **e :** a red phase of the coney (*Cephalopholis fulvus*)

red flannel hash *n* **:** hash made from corned beef, beets, potatoes, and other leftover vegetables and turned red according to the quantity of beets

red flannels *n pl* **:** winter underwear; *esp* **:** red long johns

red flour beetle *n* **:** a reddish brown beetle (*Tribolium castaneum*) that feeds on grain, cereals, stored fruits and other products

red-footed booby \'=͵==-\ *also* **redfoot** \'=͵=\ *n, pl* **red-footed boobies** *also* **redfoots :** a booby (*Sula piscator*) of the coasts of Central America and southern No. America

red-footed falcon *n* **:** a small chiefly lead-colored European falcon (*Falco vespertinus*) with bright reddish orange bill, eye patches and legs — called also *red-legged falcon*

red for lake *n, usu cap R&L* **:** LAKE RED

red fox *n* **:** a fox with bright orange red to dusky reddish brown fur that is usu. considered to constitute a single circumpolar species (*Vulpes vulpes*) with several subspecies and that exhibits a marked tendency to deviation from the typical coloring — see BLACK FOX, CROSS FOX, SILVER FOX

red giant *n* **:** a star that has low surface temperature and a diameter that is large relative to the sun

red ginger *n* **:** an ornamental ginger (*Alpinia purpurata*) native to islands of the western Pacific

red gland *n* **:** a red body covered with glandular epithelium in the air bladder of various teleost fishes

red goatfish *n* **:** a small usu. brilliant but highly variable red mullet (*Upeneus maculatus*) of the tropical western Atlantic and the West Indies

red goosefoot *n* **:** a common Eurasian annual weed (*Chenopodium rubrum*) naturalized in No. America — called also *French spinach*

red grain beetle *n* **:** SQUARE-NECKED GRAIN BEETLE

redgrape \'=͵=\ *n* **:** a dark purplish red that is bluer and duller than pansy purple, redder and stronger than raisin, bluer, lighter, and stronger than Bokhara, and bluer and deeper than Indian purple

red grape *n* **:** MISSOURI GRAPE

red grass *n* **:** a southern African grass (*Themeda triandra*) used for pasture and forage — called also *red oat*

red-green blindness \'=¦=-\ *n* **:** dichromatism in which the spectrum is seen in tones of yellow and blue — see DALTONISM, DEUTERANOPIA, PROTANOPIA

red groper *n* **:** a groper (sense 2) of the red color phase

red grouper *n* **:** a common marine food fish (*Epinephelus morio*) of the Atlantic coast from Virginia southward reaching a length of three feet and with age acquiring a flesh-red color — called also *negre, red snapper*; compare SNAPPER 3b

red grouse *n* **:** a ptarmigan (*Lagopus scoticus*) of the British Isles, closely related to the willow ptarmigan but not turning white in winter as related birds do — called also *moorbird, moorfowl, moor game*

¹red gum *n* [by folk etymology fr. *redgound*, fr. ME *red-gownd*, fr. *read, reed, red* red + *gound, gownd* pus, fr. OE *gund* — more at RED, GROUNDSEL] **:** STROPHULUS

²red gum *n* [¹*red* + *gum*] **1 a** (1) **:** any of several Australian trees of the genus *Eucalyptus* (esp. *E. camaldulensis, E. amygdalina*, and *E. calophylla*) (2) **:** the timber of one of these trees **b :** EUCALYPTUS GUM **c :** red acaroid resin **2 :** SWEET GUM 1

red gurnard *n* **1 :** a European gurnard (*Trigla cuculus*) that is chiefly red in color **2 :** an Australian fish (*Chelidonichthys kumu*) that is related to the European red gurnard

red hand *n, usu cap R&H* **:** a heraldic hand that is erect, open, and couped at the wrist — called also *Badge of Ulster*

red-handed \'=¦==\ *adv* (*or adj*) [so called fr. the idea of a murderer caught with the blood of his victim on his hands] **:** in the act of committing or exhibiting evidence of having committed a crime or misdeed : with the mainour ⟨surprised the murderer *red-handed* in the study —Erle Stanley Gardner⟩ ⟨caught *red-handed* with a hand in the cookie jar⟩ ⟨have a preacher catch us *red-handed* in the act of sinning —Frederick Way⟩

red-hard \'=¦=\ *adj* **:** hard when red-hot — used esp. of high-speed steel — **red-hard·ness** *n*

red-harden \'=¦==\ *vt* **:** to make (metal) red-hard

red hare *n* **:** ROCK HARE

red hartebeest *n* **:** CAPE HARTEBEEST

red hat *n* **:** CARDINAL'S HAT

red haw *n* **:** any of several American hawthorns: as **a :** a spiny shrub or small tree (*Crataegus coccinea*) **b :** a red-fruited hawthorn (*C. mollis*) with foliage and inflorescence copiously tomentose — called also *downy haw*

red hawk *n* **:** a hawk in its first year

redhead \'=͵=\ *n* **1 a :** a person having red hair **b :** a member of a group distinguished by red headgear **c** *usu cap* **:** KIZILBASH 3 **2 a :** RED-EYED POCHARD **b :** an American duck (*Aythya americana*) that is similar to the European pochard and highly esteemed as a game bird and that is also related to the canvasback but has in the male a brighter rufous head and a shorter bill **3 a :** REDHEADED WOODPECKER **b :** HOUSE FINCH

redheaded \'=¦==\ *adj* **1 :** having red hair or a red head **2 a :** EXCITABLE, IMPETUOUS **b :** HOT-TEMPERED — **red·head·ed·ly** *adv*

redheaded fungus *also* **redheaded scale fungus** *n* **:** any of various ascomycetous fungi (genus *Sphaerostilbe*) that are parasitic on scale insects; *esp* **:** a fungus (*S. aurantiicola*)

redheaded linnet *n* **:** HOUSE FINCH

redheaded lizard *n* **:** BLUE-TAILED SKINK

red·head·ed·ness *n* -ES **1 :** the quality or state of having red hair or a red head ⟨~ runs in the family⟩ **2 :** the quality or state of being excitable : IMPETUOSITY, TEMPER

red-headed pine sawfly *n* **:** a sawfly (*Neodiprion lecontei*) that feeds in the larval stage on various pines in the eastern U.S.

redheaded woodpecker *n* **:** a rather large woodpecker (*Melanerpes erythrocephalus*) widely but irregularly distributed in No. America having in the adult white underparts and wing patches with back, tail, and the rest of the wings black and a red head and neck — called also *redhead*

redhead-grass \'=͵=͵=\ *n* **:** a very common submerged pondweed (*Potamogeton perfoliatus*) with broad clasping or perfoliate leaves and a terminal spike of greenish apetalous flowers

red heart *n* **:** incipient decay in lumber indicated by a dark red discoloration not found in sound wood; *specif* **:** RED ROT 2b

redheart \'=͵=\ *n* **:** a California straggling shrub or small tree (*Ceanothus spinosus*) having dark red wood and blue-gray to white flowers and being used as an ornamental

redheart hickory *n* **:** SHAGBARK HICKORY

red heat *n* **:** a temperature at which a substance glows red

red heath *n* **1 :** a heather (*Calluna vulgaris*) **2 :** a New Zealand shrub (*Dracophyllum recurvum*) of the family Epacridaceae resembling a heath and having small red flowers **3** *or* **red heather :** either of two low growing alpine heaths (*Phyllodoce empetriformis* and *P. bremeri*) having rose-colored flowers

red hematite *n* **:** HEMATITE

red herring *n* [ME] **1 :** a herring cured by heavy salting and slow smoking to a dark brown color — compare ²KIPPER; see *neither fish nor fowl* at ¹FISH **2** [so called fr. the traditional practice of dragging a red herring across a trail to destroy the scent] **:** a diversion intended to distract attention from the real issue ⟨there are many false issues, straw men, and red herrings —H.W.Baldwin⟩ ⟨the nominal subject of imaginative art . . . is nearly always a *red herring* —*Times Lit. Supp.*⟩ **3 :** a preliminary prospectus for a new security with a warning notice in red on each page that sale will begin only when the registration statement is effective ⟨a *red herring* . . . is sent to the dealers for their information —B.E.Shultz⟩

red·hi·bi·tion \͵red(h)ə'bishən\ *n* -S [F *rédhibition*, fr. L *redhibition-*, *redhibitio*, fr. *redhibitus* (past part. of *redhibēre* to take back, give back, fr. *red-* re- + *-hibēre*, fr. *habēre* to hold, have) + *-ion-*, *-io* -ion — more at GIVE] *civil law* **:** an annulment of the sale of an article and return of it to the seller because of some material defect

red·hib·i·to·ry \red'hibə͵tōrē\ *adj* **:** of or relating to redhibition

red hickory *n* **1 :** MOCKERNUT **2 :** a pignut (*Carya glabra*)

red hind *n* **1 :** a grouper (*Epinephelus guttatus*) ranging from the Carolinas to Brazil having red spots, being variably colored but usu. light gray, tannish yellow, or whitish, and being important as a food fish in Cuba — called also *cabrilla* **2 :** GRAYSBY

red honeysuckle *n* **:** an Australian shrub (*Banksia serrata*) often cultivated for its beautiful rusty foliage and thick spikes of red flowers

redhorse \'=͵=\ *or* **redhorse sucker** *n* **1 :** any of numerous large suckers of the genera *Moxostoma* and *Placopharynx* of No. American rivers and lakes having in the male red fins esp. in the breeding season — called also *redfin* **2 :** CHANNEL BASS

red horse chestnut *n* **:** a much cultivated ornamental tree (*Aesculus carnea*) of hybrid origin resembling the common horse chestnut but having red flowers

¹red-hot \'=¦=\ *adj* [¹*red* + *hot*] **1 :** glowing red with heat ⟨*red-hot* iron⟩ **2 a :** exhibiting or characterized by intense emotion : BURNING, FURIOUS ⟨*red-hot* abolitionist⟩ ⟨*red-hot* political campaign⟩ ⟨*red-hot* passion⟩ **b :** full of scandal : JUICY, TORRID ⟨*red-hot* story of a love affair⟩ **c** (1) **:** full of energy or enthusiasm : VIGOROUS, PEPPY ⟨*red-hot* line drive⟩ ⟨*red-hot* jazz band⟩ (2) : arousing enthusiasm : currently extolled ⟨a *red-hot* favorite to win the derby⟩ **3** : of or relating to the immediate present : up-to-the-minute : FRESH, RECENT ⟨*red-hot* news⟩ ⟨*red-hot* data⟩

²red–hot \ˈ=,=\ *n* **1** : one that exhibits intense emotion or partisanship **2 a** : HOT DOG **b** : a small red candy strongly flavored with cinnamon

red hot cattail *n* : CHENILLE

red–hot poker *n* : POKER PLANT

red–humped caterpillar \ˈ=,=-\ *n* : a variably but predominantly black and yellow striped gregarious caterpillar with the head and dorsally humped fourth body segment bright red that is the larva of a notodontid moth (*Schizura concinna*) and is an important pest on various deciduous trees in No. America

re·dia \ˈrēdēə\ *n, pl* **redi·ae** \-dē,ē\ [NL, fr. Francesco *Redi* †1698? Ital. naturalist + NL *-ia*] : a larva produced within the sporocyst of many trematodes that in turn either produces another generation of rediae or develops into a cercaria — compare ¹FLUKE 2 — **re·di·al** \-dēəl\ *adj*

redid *past of* REDO

re·differentiation \(ˌ)rē+\ *n* [*re-* + *differentiation*] : the act, process, or result of developing additional new characteristics

re·diffusion \"+\ *n* [*re-* + *diffusion*] *chiefly Brit* : an act or instance of broadcasting or rebroadcasting a radio or television program

re·digest \"+\ *vt* [*re-* + *digest*] : to digest again — **re·digestion** \"+\ *n*

red indian *n* **1** *usu cap R & I* : AMERICAN INDIAN **2** *usu cap I* : an Indian paintbrush (*Castilleja coccinea*)

red indian paint *n, usu cap I* : BLOODROOT 1

red·in·gote \ˈrediŋ,gōt\ *n* -s [F, modif. of E *riding coat*] : a fitted outer garment: as **a** (1) : a double-breasted coat with wide flat cuffs and collar worn by men in the 18th century (2) : a late 19th century chesterfield **b** (1) : a woman's lightweight coat usu. cut in princess style, belted, and open at the front to show the skirt of the dress (2) : a coatdress with a front gore of a contrasting material

redingote b(2)

red·ing·ton·ite \ˈrediŋtə,nīt\ *n* -s [*Redington* mercury mine, Napa county, Calif. + E *-ite*] : a mineral approximately$(Fe,Mg,Ni)(Cr,Al)_2(SO_4)_4.22H_2O$ consisting of a hydrous sulfate of iron, magnesium, nickel, chromium, and aluminum that is possibly a chromium halotrichite

red ink *n* **1** : red-colored ink used esp. in financial statements to indicate a loss **2 a** : a business loss : DEFICIT **b** : the condition of showing a loss ⟨the company was going into *red ink*⟩

red–ink \ˈ=ˈ=\ *vt* [*red ink*] : to mark with or print in red ink

red inkberry *or* **red–ink plant** *n* : POKEWEED

¹re·din·te·grate \rəˈdintə,grāt, rē'-, re'-\ *vt* [ME *redintegraten*, fr. L *redintegratus*, past part. of *redintegrare*, fr. *red-* re- + *integrare* to make complete — more at INTEGRATE] **1** *archaic* : to put back together : REPAIR, REUNITE **2** *archaic* : to restore to integrity or soundness : REESTABLISH, REINSTATE

²redintegrate \"\ *adj* [L *redintegratus*, past part.] *archaic* : REDINTEGRATED

re·din·te·gra·tion \=,==ˈgrāshən\ *n* -s [ME *redyntegracyon*, fr. L *redintegration-, redintegratio*, fr. *redintegratus* + *-ion-, -io* -ion] **1** *archaic* : restoration to a former state **2 a** : revival of the whole of a previous mental state when a phase of it recurs **b** : arousal of any response by a part of the complex of stimuli that orig. aroused that response

re·din·te·gra·tive \=ˈ==,grād·iv\ *adj* : of or relating to redintegration

re·dip \(ˈ)rēˈdip\ *vb* [*re-* + *dip*] : to dip again

re·dip·per \-pə(r)\ *n* : one that redips; *esp* : a worker who gives tin plate a protective coating by dipping it into a terne= mixture bath as it comes from the tinning machine

re·direct \ˌrē+\ *vt* [*re-* + *direct*, v.] **1 a** : to change the course of : channel in a new direction ⟨the policeman ~s him⟩ ⟨~*ing* attitudes . . . toward acceptable life standards —M.E. Alexander⟩ ⟨in an emergency ~ the scientist from basic research to applied research —M.H.Trytten⟩ **b** : READDRESS ⟨~*ed* the letter⟩ **2** : to change the direction of (as a flux) in a definite manner — **re·directive** \"+\ *adj*

redirect examination *n* [*re-* + *direct*, adj.] : the examination of a witness by the party calling him after the cross-examination to clarify matters brought out on the cross-examination

re·direction \"+\ *n* : an act or instance of redirecting

red ironbark *n* : any of several Australian eucalypts (as *Eucalyptus sideroxylon*) with white to pink or red flowers — called also *mugga*

red iron ore *n* : HEMATITE

red ironwood *n* **1** : a small tree (*Reynosia septentrionalis*) of the family Rhamnaceae of the Bahamas and southern Florida with persistent usu. opposite leaves and an edible drupe — called also *Darling plum* **2** : a closely related Cuban tree (*Reynosia latifolia*)

¹re·dis·count \(ˈ)rēˈdi,skaunt *also* ˌrēdə'ˌs-\ *vt* [*re-* + *discount* (v.)] : to discount again (as commercial paper) ⟨a Federal Reserve Bank may also ~ any bill drawn by a bank —Alexander Wall⟩ — **re·dis·count·able** \-təbəl\ *adj*

²rediscount \"\ *n* [*re-* + *discount* (n.)] : the act or process of rediscounting or the negotiable paper involved in such a transaction

rediscount rate *n* : the discount rate charged by Federal Reserve banks for rediscounting commercial paper for member banks or making secured advances to them on their own notes

re·discover \ˌrē+\ *vt* [*re-* + *discover*] **1 a** : to find again ⟨~*ed* the island of Madeira —H.W. Van Loon⟩ **b** : to arrive at independently or try to recapture by analysis (a technique or concept already discovered or once employed) ⟨~*ing* the methods of the Greek sculptors —Herbert Read⟩ **2 a** : to bring to light again ⟨the original Hittites, recently ~*ed* by excavation and decipherment —*advt*⟩ **b** : to take new interest in or create fresh appreciation for (one fallen into low esteem) ⟨Americans . . . have ~*ed* their frontier painters —Bernard Smith⟩ **c** : to make new use of (a neglected asset) ⟨~*ed* the Slavonic sources of their culture —Oscar Handlin⟩ — **re·discovery** \"+\ *n*

re·dispose \"+\ *vt* [*re-* + *dispose*] : REDEPLOY — **re·disposition** \(ˌ)rē+\ *n*

re·disseise *or* **re·disseize** \(ˌ)rē+\ *vt* [*re-* + *disseise* or *disseize*] : to disseise anew — **re·disseisor** *or* **re·disseizor** \"+\ *n*

re·disseisin *or* **re·disseizin** \"+\ *n* [*re-* + *disseisin* or *disseizin*] : a disseisin by one previously adjudged to have disseised the same person of the same estate

re·dissoluble \ˌrē+\ *adj* [*re-* + *dissoluble*] : capable of dissolving or being dissolved more than once

re·dissolution \(ˌ)rē+\ *n* [*re-* + *dissolution*] : an act or process of dissolving again

re·dissolve \ˌrē+\ *vb* [*re-* + *dissolve*] *vt* **1** : to cause to dissolve again **2** : to disperse again ~ *vi* : to dissolve again

re·distill \"+\ *vt* [*re-* + *distill*] : to distill again or repeatedly — **re·distillation** \(ˌ)rē+\ *n*

re·distribute \ˌrē+\ *vt* [*re-* + *distribute*] **1** : to alter the distribution of : apportion again : REALLOCATE, REASSIGN ⟨~ land⟩ ⟨~ income⟩ **2** : to spread to other areas : DISSEMINATE ⟨mountains turn . . . the upper air currents and ~ their moisture —*Amer. Guide Series: Tenn.*⟩ — **re·distribution** \(ˌ)rē+\ *n*

re·distributive \ˌrē+\ *adj* : tending to redistribute ⟨public finance is ~ when it makes real incomes less unequal by manipulating taxes —K.E.Knorr⟩

re·district \(ˈ)rē+\ *vt* [*re-* + *district*] : to organize into new territorial esp. political divisions

red·i·vi·vus \ˌredəˈvīvəs\ *adj* [LL (influenced in meaning by L *vivere* to live), fr. L, renovated, restored, perh. fr. *reduvia, redivia* hangnail, exuviae (fr. *red-* re- + *-uvia, -ivia*, fr. *-uere* to put on) + *-ivus* -ive — more at QUICK, EXUVIAE] : brought back to life : living again : REBORN ⟨a case of the phoenix ~ —*Fortune*⟩

red ivory *n* : a southern African buckthorn (*Rhamnus zeheri*) with hard heavy even grained wood esp. suitable for decorative work and turnery

re·djang *also* **re·jang** \rāˈzhaŋ\ *n, pl* **redjang** *or* **redjangs** *usu cap* [native name in southern Sumatra] **1** : an Indonesian people of southern Sumatra **2** : a member of the Redjang people

red jasmine *or* **red jessamine** *n* **1** : a frangipani (*Plumeria rubra*) widely cultivated in warm regions for its very large leaves and large terminal cymes of pink, red, or purple richly fragrant flowers **2** : CYPRESS VINE

red–jointed fiddler crab \ˈ=,==-\ *n* : a brackish marsh fiddler crab (*Uca minax*) of the eastern coast of No. America

red juniper *n* : RED CEDAR

red kangaroo *n* : a large kangaroo (*Macropus rufus*) of the plains and tablelands of So. Australia — compare BLUE DOE

red kauri *n* **1** : KAURI 1 **2** : a tree (*Agathis lanceolata*) of New Zealand having glossy leaves and scaly reddish brown bark

red lac *n* : JAPANESE WAX TREE

red larch *n* : a tamarack (*Larix laricina*)

red larkspur *n* : a perennial herb (*Delphinium nudicaule*) of the Pacific coast often cultivated for its reddish yellow flowers

red–lattice \ˈ=ˈ==\ *adj* [so called fr. the red latticework formerly common in windows of alehouses] *obs* : of or relating to an alehouse ⟨your *red-lattice* phrases —Shak.⟩

red lauan *n* **1 a** : a valuable Philippine timber tree (*Shorea teysmanniana* **b** : the hard heavy red wood of the red lauan tree often sold as Philippine mahogany **2** : TANGUILE

red laurel *n* : CATAWBA RHODODENDRON

red laver *n* : any of several common purple seaweeds of the genus *Porphyra* (esp. *P. laciniata* and *P. vulgaris*) the fronds of which are eaten in Europe either stewed or pickled

red lead *n* **1** : an orange-red to brick-red lead oxide Pb_3O_4 that is prepared by heating lead monoxide in the presence of air, that when produced commercially may contain litharge and other impurities, and that is used chiefly in storage= battery plates, in glass and ceramics, and as a paint pigment (as for protecting metals from corrosion) — called also *minium* **2** : FIERY RED **3** *slang* : CATSUP

red–lead \ˈredˈled\ *vt* [*red lead*] : to paint with red lead

red–lead·er \-də(r)\ *n* [*red-lead* + *-er*] : a worker who paints exposed metal surfaces with red lead

red lead ore *n* : CROCOITE

red–lead putty *n* : a mixture of red and white lead and boiled linseed oil used as a lute in pipe fitting

red leaf *n* **1** : a smartweed (*Polygonum hydropiper*) **2** : any of several plant diseases characterized by reddening of the foliage: as **a** : a nonparasitic disease of oats of uncertain cause **b** : a disease of the pear and grape caused by nutritional disturbances producing dark red or purplish red discoloration of the leaves **3** : a high grade of Burley tobacco comprised of leaves from near the top of the stalk

red leaf blight *n* : a disease of cotton characterized by red or reddish brown foliage and reduced vigor and believed to be related to a shortage of potash

red leaf spot *n* : a disease of the cranberry caused by a fungus (*Exobasidium vaccinii*)

redleg \ˈ=,=\ *n* **1 a** : REDSHANK **b** : TURNSTONE **c** : RED= LEGGED PARTRIDGE **d** *Wales* : PURPLE SANDPIPER **2** : a bacterial disease of frogs that is esp. destructive when numbers of them are kept together **3 a** *usu cap* [so called fr. the red leggings worn] : a guerrilla raider of pro-secessionist territory esp. in Missouri during the Civil War — compare BUSHWHACKER c **b** *often cap* [so called fr. the red piping formerly worn on the legs by U. S. artillerymen] : ARTILLERYMAN

red–legged crow \ˈ=,=(=)-\ *n* : CHOUGH

red–legged earth mite *n* : a mite (*Halotydeus destructor*) that is an important pest of clover and other crops in parts of Australia

red–legged falcon *n* : RED-FOOTED FALCON

red–legged grasshopper *also* **red–legged locust** *n* : a very widely distributed and sometimes highly destructive small No. American grasshopper (*Melanoplus femurrubrum*) with red hind legs

red–legged ham beetle *n* : a small cosmopolitan bluish green iridescent beetle (*Necrobia rufipes*) with the legs and the bases of the antennae reddish that feeds on animal products and cereal grains and that is often a pest around warehouses and ships

red–legged kittiwake *n* : a kittiwake (*Rissa brevirostris*) of the north Pacific having red legs and a red bill — compare PACIFIC KITTIWAKE

red–legged partridge *n* **1** : a common western European partridge (*Alectoris rufa*) having bright red legs and bill **2** : a partridge of the genus *Alectoris* having distinctly red legs — called also *redleg*

red–legged plover *n* : TURNSTONE

red–legged snipe *n* : REDSHANK

red–letter \ˈ=ˈ==\ *adj* **1** : employing red letters to call attention to something of special significance ⟨*red-letter* Bible⟩ **2** [so called fr. the practice of marking holy days in red letters in church calendars] : of special significance : HAPPY, MEMORABLE ⟨*red-letter* day⟩ ⟨the testimonial dinner was a *red-letter* occasion⟩

red light *n* **1 a** : a warning signal ⟨four times the *red light* on the instrument board blinked —*Time*⟩; *esp* : a red traffic signal ⟨at a *red light* a snarl of traffic waited —Thomas Savage⟩ **b** : a cautionary sign : DETERRENT ⟨the bill is a *red light* to labor, warning of what may lie ahead —*New Republic*⟩ **2** : a game in which players run toward a goal while the player who is it with his back to them counts ten and whips around on the phrase "red light" when any player he catches in motion must return to the starting line

red–light district *n* [so called fr. the traditional practice of employing red lights to indicate houses of prostitution] : a district in which houses of prostitution are frequent

red lily *n* **1 a** : WOOD LILY 1 **b** : WESTERN RED LILY **c** : SOUTHERN RED LILY **2** *West Indies* : BARBADOS LILY

redline \ˈ=,=\ *vt* **1** : to cross off (an item) from a list (as a military payroll); *also* : to cross off or remove the name of from a roll or roster **2 a** : GROUND ⟨~ an airplane⟩ **b** : to indicate the maximum safe speed of (an airplane)

red liquor *n* **1 a** : the mother liquor left in the evaporation of the solution obtained by leaching black ash in the Leblanc process **b** : the mother liquor obtained in the recrystallization of tartar **2** *also* **red mordant** : a solution consisting essentially of an aluminum acetate used in making red color lakes and as a mordant esp. in dyeing red

red lobelia *n* : CARDINAL FLOWER

red locust *n* **1** : an African insect (*Nomadacris septemfasciata*) that often forms migratory swarms in southern Africa **2 a** : LOCUST 3 a (2) **b** : CLAMMY LOCUST

red louse *n* **1** : CHIGGER **2** : a small reddish biting louse (*Bovicola bovis*) that infests the skin of cattle feeding chiefly on hair and skin debris — compare BLUE LOUSE

red·ly *adv* : in a red manner : with red color : FLAMINGLY, RUDDILY ⟨the forge belched ~ at the sky —Adria Langley⟩

red maggot *n* : the larva of the wheat midge

red mahogany *n* **1 a** (1) : an Australian eucalypt (*Eucalyptus resinifera*) that yields a dark-colored kino (2) : the hard deep red commercially valuable wood of this tree **b** : an African mahogany (*Khaya nyasica*) **2** : a variable color averaging a dark reddish brown

red maids *n pl but sing or pl in constr* : an annual branching herb (*Calandrinia menziesii*) of the Pacific coast of No. America cultivated for its crimson flowers

red man *n* **1** : AMERICAN INDIAN **2** *usu cap R & M* : a member of one of the major benevolent and fraternal orders

red manganese oxide *n* : MANGANESE TETROXIDE

red mange *n* : DEMODECTIC MANGE

red mangrove *n* **1 a** : a true mangrove having red wood; *esp* : an African tree (*Rhizophora mangle*) **b** : the wood of the African red mangrove tree **2** : any of several trees of the genus *Bruguiera* (family Rhizophoraceae) of Australia and Polynesia **3** : LOOKING-GLASS PLANT

redman's orchard \ˈ=,=-\ *n, West* : a grove or stand of a piñon (*Pinus monophylla*)

red maple *n* : any of several American maples distinguished by crimson flowers produced before the leaves in very early spring; *esp* : a common tree (*Acer rubrum*) of the eastern and central U.S. that grows chiefly on moist soils, has reddish twigs and somewhat pubescent leaves, and yields a lighter and softer wood than the sugar maple — called also *swamp maple*

red marrow *n* : MARROW 1 a (2)

red mass *n. often cap R & M* : a votive mass of the Holy Spirit celebrated in red vestments esp. at the opening of courts and congresses

red meat *n* **1** : meat (as beef or lamb) that in its raw and uncured state is distinctly red **2** : meat from one of the larger domestic mammals as distinguished from poultry or fish

red mite *n* : any of several mites having a red color: as **a** : CHIGGER **b** : EUROPEAN RED MITE **c** : CHICKEN MITE **d** *Austral* : CLOVER MITE

red mombin *n* : SPANISH PLUM

red monkey *n* **1** : the patas or a related monkey **2** : TOQUE MACAQUE

redmouth \ˈ=,=\ *n* **1** : any of several grunts having the inside of the mouth red or pink **2** : a common buffalo fish (*Ictiobus cyprinella*)

redmouthed buffalo fish \ˈ=,=-\ *n* : REDMOUTH 2

red–mouthed grunt \ˈ=,=-\ *or* **redmouth grunt** *n* : REDMOUTH

red mud *n* **1** : a marine offshore deposit deriving its yellow= brown to red-brown color from iron oxide ⟨*red mud* . . . is most prevalent in the Yellow sea and off the coasts of Brazil —F.C.Lane⟩ — compare BLUE MUD **2** : a residue high in iron oxide resulting from purification of alumina in the Bayer process

red mulberry *n* **1** : a No. American forest tree (*Morus rubra*) with soft weak but durable wood — called also *black mulberry* **2** : the dark purple edible fruit of the red mulberry tree

red mullet *n* **1** : a mullet of the family Mullidae — distinguished from *gray mullet* **2** : a redhorse (*Moxostoma macrolepidotum*) of the streams of the eastern U.S. from Delaware to No. Carolina

red mustard *n* : BLACK MUSTARD

redneck \ˈ=,=\ *n* : a white member of the Southern rural laboring class — usu. used disparagingly

red–necked cane borer \ˈ=,=-\ *n* : the larva of a buprestid beetle (*Agrilus ruficollis*) that bores into the canes of raspberry and blackberry producing swellings or galls

red–necked gazelle *n* : ADDRA

red–necked grebe *n* : a large stocky Holarctic grebe (*Podiceps grisegena*) with a light throat contrasting with a dark neck

red–necked nightjar *n* : a nightjar (*Caprimulgus ruficollis*) of southwestern Europe and northern Africa

red–necked phalarope *n* : NORTHERN PHALAROPE

red·ness \ˈrednəs\ *n* -ES [ME *rednesse*, fr. *read, reed, red* red + *-nesse* -ness — more at RED] : the quality or state of being red or red-hot

red node *n* : a virus disease of beans characterized by reddish discoloration at the nodes

red nucleus *n* : a nucleus of gray matter in the tegmentum of the midbrain on each side of the middle line that receives fibers from the cerebellum of the opposite side by way of the superior cerebellar peduncle and gives rise to fibers of the rubrospinal tract of the opposite side

¹re·do \(ˈ)rē+\ *vt* [*re-* + *do*] **1 a** : to execute again : do over : REPRODUCE, RESTYLE **b** : REDACT ⟨Broadway successes *redone* on radio or television —J.C.Bushman⟩ **2** : REDECORATE ⟨~ the kitchen in yellow⟩

²re·do \ˈrē,dü\ *n* -s **1** : REPETITION, RESTYLING ⟨no pleasanter prospect than a ~ of our South American trek —D.B.Shields⟩ **2** : REDACTION

red oak *n* **1** : any of numerous American oaks having four stamens in each floret, acorns that require two years to mature and that have the inner surface of the shell lined with woolly hairs, the acorn cap covered with thin scales, and leaf veins that usu. run beyond the margin of the leaf to form bristles: as **a** : a large symmetrical oak (*Quercus borealis* or *Q. rubra*) that has large leaves with triangular spiny tipped lobes and medium-weight coarse-grained wood less durable than white oak and that is widely distributed in eastern No. America with the exception of the southern coastal region and piedmont — called also *northern red oak* **b** : a large round-topped oak (*Q. falcata* or *Q. rubra*) that has thin leaves with deeply sinuate lobes and wood similar to the northern red oak and that is widely distributed in eastern No. America from New Jersey to Illinois and southward — called also *southern red oak, Spanish oak, turkey oak* **2** : the wood of red oak

red oat *n* **1** : an oat (*Avena byzantina*) with red hulls esp. adapted to warm climates **2** : RED GRASS

¹red ocher *n* [ˈ*red* + *ocher*] **1** : a red earthy and often impure hematite used as a pigment **2** : BOLE 3

²red ocher *adj, usu cap R&O* : of or relating to a phase of the Woodland pattern characterized by beautifully made leaf-shaped projectile points, crude pottery, copper implements, and burials covered with red ocher

red oil *n* **1** : any of various oils that are red often because they are impure: as **a** : commercial oleic acid containing other fatty acids (as linoleic, palmitic, or stearic acid) **b** : a domestic remedy for bruises made by macerating the tops of the common St.-John's-wort in olive oil **2** : a lubricating oil produced from petroleum in various ways

red·o·lence \ˈredᵊlən(t)s\ *n* -s [ME, fr. MF, fr. *redolent*] : the quality or state of being redolent : SCENT, AROMA **syn** see FRAGRANCE

red·o·lent \-nt\ *adj* [ME, fr. MF, fr. L *redolent-, redolens*, pres. part. of *redolere* to emit a scent, smell like, fr. *red-* re- + *olēre* to smell — more at ODOR] **1 a** : exuding fragrance : AROMATIC ⟨the pinewoods were more ~ —Jean Stafford⟩ **b** : RICH, DISTINCTIVE — used of an odor ⟨the ancient ~ odor of plowed land —Norman Mailer⟩ **2 a** : full of fragrance : SCENTED, SMELLING — used with *of* or *with* ⟨a corridor ~ of floor wax —Joseph Wechsberg⟩ ⟨~ with home-grown apples —*Nat'l Geographic*⟩ ⟨air . . . ~ with the fumes of beer and whiskey —Herbert Asbury⟩ **b** : conveying an aura : tending to suggest : EVOCATIVE, REMINISCENT ⟨cannot forbear to close on this ~ literary note —Wilder Hobson⟩ — usu. used with *of* or *with* ⟨every page here is ~ of . . . fine scholarship —Walter Pach⟩ ⟨a perfect day . . . ~ with the charm of late autumn —Gerald Beaumont⟩ ⟨conversation . . . ~ with profanity —P.A.Rollins⟩

red·o·lent·ly *adv* : in a redolent manner

re·domesticate \ˌrē+\ *vt* [*re-* + *domesticate*] : to domesticate again

re·don·di·lla \ˌrädōnˈdēlyə\ *n* -s [Sp, dim. of *redonda* district, province, pastureland, fr. fem. of *redondo* round, fr. L *rotundus* — more at ROUND] : a Spanish verse form consisting of a quatrain of octosyllabic lines with varying rhyme scheme

re·doppe \rəˈdäp\ *n* -s [F, fr. It *raddoppio*, lit., redoubling, fr. *raddoppiare* to double, redouble, fr. *rad-* (fr. *re-* — fr. L *re-* — + *ad-*, fr. L) + *doppiare* to double, fr. L *duplare* — more at DOUBLE] : a show-ring movement in which a horse gallops in circles whose diameter never exceeds ten feet

red orache *n* : an annual weed (*Atriplex rosea*) native to the Old World but established in parts of No. America and having fruiting bracteoles with dark veinlets — called also *red scale*

red orpiment *n* : REALGAR

redos *pl of* REDO

red osier *n* **1** : any of several willows with reddish twigs that are used for basketry; *esp* : PURPLE WILLOW **2** *also* **red osier dogwood** : a common No. American shrub (*Cornus stolonifera*) with reddish purple twigs, white flowers, and globose blue or whitish fruit — called also *kinnikinnick, redbrush, red dogwood* **3** : SILKY CORNEL

re·double \(ˈ)rē+\ *vb* [*re-* + *double*, v.] *vt* **1** : to make twice as great in size or amount : renew more vigorously : DOUBLE, INTENSIFY ⟨*redoubled* attacks⟩ ⟨the German radio *redoubled* its frenzied screaming —S.L.A.Marshall⟩ **2 a** *obs* : to echo back ⟨their moans the vales *redoubled* —John Milton⟩ **b** *archaic* : to repeat a second time : DUPLICATE

⟨the negative . . . should be once expressed in a simple sentence; but we generally find it *redoubled* in old English —John Stoddart⟩ ~ *vi* **1 :** to become twice as great or greatly intensified ⟨the wails *redoubled* —Josephine Pinckney⟩ **2** *archaic* **:** RESOUND ⟨peal upon peal *redoubling* all around —William Cowper⟩ **3 :** to double again ⟨the noise doubles and *redoubles*⟩ ⟨the mountain path doubles and *redoubles* upon itself⟩ **4 :** to double an opponent's double in bridge

²redouble \"\ *n* **1 :** an act or instance of redoubling; *specif* **:** a bridge call permissible only when the last previous call other than a pass was a double by an opponent and having the effect of doubling the scoring values established by the double for tricks and penalties — compare AUCTION BRIDGE, CONTRACT BRIDGE **2 :** any attack excepting the straight thrust made when a fencing opponent closes the original line of attack but does not riposte

re·dou·ble·ment \"+mənt\ *n* [F, fr. MF, fr. *redoubler* to redouble (fr. *re-* + *doubler* to double) + *-ment* — more at DOUBLE] *archaic* **:** an act or instance of redoubling

¹re·doubt \rə'daủt, rē'-, *usu* -aủd.+V\ *vt* [ME *redouten*, fr. MF *redouter*, fr. *re-* + *douter* to doubt, fear — more at DOUBT] *archaic* **:** to regard with awe or dismay **:** DREAD, FEAR

²redoubt \"\ *n* [F *redoute*, fr. It *ridotto*, fr. ML *reductus* secret place, fr. L, withdrawn, fr. past part. of *reducere* to lead or bring back, withdraw — more at REDUCE] **1 a** *obs* **:** a small separate work inside a fortification — compare RAVELIN **b :** a small usu. temporary enclosed defensive work used esp. in fortifying a hilltop or pass ⟨saw that Bunker Hill had been crowned in the night by a strong ~ —Mabel Swan⟩ **c :** a defended position or protective barrier ⟨encircling the Ruhr and reducing the south German ~ —W.H.Hale⟩ ⟨surrounded by a ~ of lawbooks —R.L.Neuberger⟩ **2 :** a secure retreat **:** STRONGHOLD ⟨the missionary's final ~, faith —Jerome Ellison⟩

re·doubt·able \-aủd·əbəl, -aủtəb-\ *adj* [ME *redoutable*, fr. MF, fr. *redouter* + *-able*] **1 a :** causing fear or alarm **:** FORMIDABLE ⟨a tougher and more ~ adversary than the heel-clicking, jackbooted fanatic —G.H.Johnston⟩ ⟨~ gains made by the Communist Party —Max Ascoli⟩ **b :** inspiring awe or reverence **:** AUGUST, EMINENT ⟨that ~ scholar of Spain's golden age —Carol Bache⟩ **2 :** DOUGHTY, ILLUSTRIOUS ⟨a nimble-witted . . . guest, as ~ with a clue as he is at a press conference —*N.Y. Herald Tribune*⟩ ⟨born . . . of the ~ flour-milling family —*New Yorker*⟩

re·doubt·ably \-blē, -li\ *adv* **:** in a redoubtable manner

re·doubt·ed \-aủd·əd\ *adj* [ME, fr. past part. of *redouten*, *redoubten* to redoubt — more at REDOUBT] *archaic* **:** REDOUBTABLE

re·dound \rə'daủnd, rē'-\ *vi* -ED/-ING/-S [ME *redounden*, fr. MF *redonder*, fr. L *redundare* to overflow, be in excess, fr. *red-* re- + *undare* to overflow, fr. *unda* wave — more at WATER] **1** *archaic* **a :** to become swollen **:** surge up **:** BILLOW ⟨waves *~ing* roar —Alexander Pope⟩ **b :** to be excessive in quantity **:** PREDOMINATE, OVERFLOW ⟨for every dram of honey therein found, a pound of gall doth over it ~ —Edmund Spenser⟩ **2 a :** to have an effect for good or ill **:** CONDUCE ⟨their efforts . . . will ~ to the general good —Lucius Garvin⟩ **b :** to be a contributing factor to repute ⟨will always ~ to his honor and self-sacrifice —Aidan Mulloy⟩ ⟨what he does *~s* to the credit of geology —K.K.Darrow⟩ **3 a :** to become transferred or added **:** ACCRUE ⟨every value he creates ultimately *~s* to himself, his neighbor and his country —A.R.Williams⟩ **b** *obs* **:** to issue forth ⟨sacred lore . . . from her sweet lips did ~ —Edmund Spenser⟩ **4 :** to become deflected backward **:** REBOUND, REFLECT ⟨the child's behavior *~s* on the mother⟩

red out *vi* **:** to experience a redout — compare BLACK OUT, GRAY OUT

redout \'⸗,⸗\ *n* -S [*red out*] **:** a condition in which blood is driven to the head as a result of centripetal acceleration that causes severe headache and reddening of the field of vision — compare BLACKOUT, GRAYOUT

red·o·wa \'redəwə, -dəvə\ *n* -S [F & G; F *rédowa*, fr. G *redowa*, fr. Czech *rejdovák*, fr. *rejdovati* to steer around, drive, whirl around] **:** either of two popular Bohemian ballroom dances of the 19th century: **a :** a dance in triple time resembling a waltz **b :** a dance in ¾ time resembling a polka

red owl *n* **:** an American screech owl in its red phase

re·dox \'rē,däks\ *adj* [*red*uction + *ox*idation] **:** of or relating to oxidation-reduction

red oxide *also* **red oxide of iron** *n* **:** ferric oxide esp. when used as a pigment

red oxide of zinc : ZINCITE

redox potential *n* **:** OXIDATION-REDUCTION POTENTIAL

red–pencil \'⸗'⸗⸗\ *vt* **:** to censor, correct, or revise with or as if with a red pencil ⟨much of the truth about the . . . peace talks has been *red-penciled* —R.C.Miller⟩ ⟨*red-penciling* the program down to this figure —*Newsweek*⟩ — compare BLUE-PENCIL

red pepper *n* **:** CAYENNE PEPPER; *esp* **:** a pepper fruit that is red at maturity

red perch *n* **:** YELLOW PERCH

red periwinkle *n* **:** ¹PERIWINKLE 1c

red phalarope *n* **:** a phalarope (*Phalaropus fulicarius*) breeding in the arctic regions of the Old and New Worlds and often occurring in large flocks far out at sea

red phosphorus *n* **:** the element phosphorus in its red allotropic form

red pimpernel *n* **:** SCARLET PIMPERNEL

red pine *n* **1 a :** a No. American pine (*Pinus resinosa*) having reddish bark **b :** the hard but not durable wood of the No. American red pine tree consisting chiefly of sapwood — called also *Canadian red pine* **c :** PONDEROSA PINE **d :** DOUGLAS FIR **2 a :** an Australian cypress pine (*Callitris calcarata*) **b :** the timber of the Australian cypress pine **3 a :** RIMU **b :** a black pine (*Podocarpus spicata*) of New Zealand

red plum *n* **1 :** a red-fruited plum; *specif* **:** either of two American wild plums (*Prunus americana* and *P. nigra*) **2 :** a variable color averaging a dark purplish red that is bluer and duller than pansy purple or raisin, bluer and paler than Bokhara or dahlia purple (sense 1), and bluer and less strong than redgrape

red podzolic soil *n* **:** any of a group of zonal soils developed in a warm-temperate moist climate under deciduous or mixed forests that have thin organic and organic-mineral layers overlying a yellowish brown leached layer resting on an illuvial red horizon — called also *red soil*

redpole \'⸗,⸗\ *n* [by folk etymology] **:** REDPOLL 1

redpoll \'⸗,⸗\ *n* **1** *or* **redpoll linnet :** any of several small finches (genus *Carduelis* or *Acanthis*) of northern Europe, Asia, and America which are similar in size and habits to the siskins and in which the males usu. have a red or rosy crown and streaked back and sides: as **a :** a common bird (*C. flammea*) distinguished by a rosy breast and rump — compare HORNEMANN'S REDPOLL **b :** LINNET 1 **2** *also* **redpoll warbler :** a palm warbler (*Dendroica palmarum*) — compare YELLOW PALM WARBLER

red poll *also* **red polled** *n* **1** *usu cap R&P* **:** a British breed of large hornless fast-growing long-lived dual-purpose cattle that are red with a little white on switch and belly **2** *often cap R&P* **:** an animal of the Red Poll breed

red pop *n*, *South* **:** the male painted bunting (*Passerina ciris*)

red poppy *n* **:** CORN POPPY

red porgy *n* **:** PORGY 1a

red precipitate *n* **:** red mercuric oxide

red prussiate of potash : POTASSIUM FERRICYANIDE

red puccoon *n* **:** BLOODROOT 1

red quebracho *n* **:** QUEBRACHO 1b

¹re·draft \(')rē+\ *n* [*re-* + *draft*, n.] **1 :** a draft on the maker or endorsers of a bill of exchange dishonored by the drawee for the amount of the bill and the protest fee and other charges **2 :** a modified draft **:** REVISION

²redraft \"\ *vt* [*re-* + *draft*, v.] **:** to prepare a revised copy or a new version of

red rag *n* [so called fr. the tradition that a red rag incites a bull to rage] **:** something that incites to anger or vexation ⟨the jibe was a *red rag* goading him to violence⟩

red raspberry *n* **1 :** a raspberry plant with red fruit: as **a :** a European bramble (*Rubus idaeus*) with red or sometimes yellow fruit **b :** a No. American bramble (*R. strigosus*) with red fruit **c :** any of various cultivated raspberry plants that have red fruit and have been derived from the European or American red raspberry by selection or breeding **2 :** the fruit of a red raspberry

red rat snake *n* **:** CORN SNAKE

red rattle *n* **:** RATTLE 3b

red rattlesnake *n* **:** a reddish diamondback rattlesnake (*Crotalus ruber*) of the extreme southwestern U.S. and adjacent Mexico

re·draw \(')rē+\ *vb* [*re-* + *draw*] *vi* **:** to issue a new bill of exchange to cover a protested one ~ *vt* **1 :** to draw again **2 :** to take out or select by lot again **3 :** to delineate again or in another way **4 :** REVISE **5 :** to extrude or shape again **6 :** REWIND

re·draw·er \"+(ə)r\ *n* **:** one that redraws; *specif* **:** WINDER

red republican *n* **1** *usu cap both Rs* **:** an extreme Republican of the French Revolution **2 :** an extreme radical in political reform — compare RED 5a

¹re·dress \rə'dres, rē'-\ *vt* [ME *redressen*, fr. MF *redresser*, fr. OF *redrecier*, fr. *re-* + *drecier* to make straight — more at DRESS] **1** *obs* **a :** to make vertical again ⟨~ a leaning wall —Earl of Shaftesbury †1713⟩ **b :** to put back into good condition physically or spiritually **:** REPAIR ⟨rise God . . . this wicked earth ~ —John Milton⟩ **2 a** (1) **:** to set (a wrong) right **:** REMEDY ⟨looked to charity, not to legislation, to ~ social wrongs —W.R.Inge⟩ (2) **:** to make up for **:** COMPENSATE ⟨what they lacked in apparatus they *~ed* in understanding —C.F.Mullett⟩ **b :** to remove the cause of (a grievance or complaint) ⟨had not the slightest intention of listening to the grievances of the colonies with a desire to ~ them —H.E. Scudder⟩ ⟨committee has *~ed* these medievalisms and submitted its draft bill —Harvey Breit⟩ **c :** to exact reparation for **:** AVENGE ⟨must such wrongs either be ignored or *~ed* in hot blood —R.H.Jackson⟩ **3** *archaic* **a :** to requite (a person) for a wrong or loss **b :** HEAL **4 a :** to eliminate the faults of **:** impart renewed stability to **:** RECTIFY ⟨divided about how to ~ the economy —*New Statesman & Nation*⟩ **b :** to neutralize the effect of **:** COUNTERACT, OFFSET ⟨another broadcast may ~ whatever imbalances the first creates —Gilbert Seldes⟩ **c :** to return (an airplane) to normal flying position **:** flatten out **syn** see CORRECT

²re·dress \", 'rē,dres\ *n* -ES [ME *redresse*, fr. AF *redresse*, *redresce*, fr. OF *redrecier*] **1 a :** relief from distress ⟨suicide . . . is a common method of seeking ~ —K.E.Read⟩ **b** *obs* **:** removal of faults **:** REFORMATION, IMPROVEMENT ⟨too long have we driven off the applying of our ~ —Joseph Hall⟩ **c :** the means or possibility of seeking a remedy ⟨there is no ~ whatever, since the accused may not be tried twice for the same offense —Curtis Bok⟩ **2 :** compensation for a wrong or loss **:** REPARATION ⟨discharged officials could seek . . . ~ by appeal —*New Statesman & Nation*⟩ **3 a :** an act or instance of redressing ⟨petition the government for a ~ of grievances —*U.S. Constitution*⟩ **b :** CORRECTION, RETRIBUTION ⟨the pedestrian can walk dangerously without the slightest fear of ~ —*Brit. Automobile Racing Club Gazette*⟩

³re–dress \(')rē+\ *vt* [*re-* + *dress*] **:** to dress again; *esp* **:** to put through a finishing process again ⟨~ leather before dyeing⟩ ⟨~ tools that show signs of wear⟩

re·dress·er \rə'dresə(r)\ *n* [ME *redressere*, fr. *redressen* + *-ere* -er] **:** one that redresses

re·dress·ment \-smənt\ *n* -S **:** REDRESS

red ribbon *n* **:** a red ribbon usu. with appropriate words or markings awarded the second-place winner in a competition

red rice *n* **1 :** a Chinese vegetable dye used in food products — called also *ang-khak* **2 :** a wild rice (*Oryza rufipogon*) with a red husk and pinkish white seed that is considered an objectionable weed in the rice fields of the southern U.S. but that has grain which is comparable to common rice in nutritive value

re·dri·er \(')rē,drī(ə)r\ *n* [*redry* + *-er*] **:** a device for drying panels of plywood after they are glued

red ring *n* **:** a disease of tomatoes caused by a plant bug (*Cyrtopeltis varians*) and characterized by reddish brown marks around the stems and petioles

red ring disease *n* **:** a disease of the coconut palm caused by an eelworm (*Aphelenchoides cocophilus*) in which a cross section of the trunk shows a red ring

red river hog *n* **:** PAINTED PIG

red river maple *n*, *usu cap both Rs* [fr. the *Red river* in Kentucky or the *Red river* in Tennessee] **:** BOX ELDER

red–roan \'⸗'⸗\ *adj* **:** of a roan color produced by mingling of bay and white hairs

red robin *n* **1 :** SCARLET TANAGER **2** *dial Eng* **:** HERB ROBERT **3 :** INDIA RED

red rock *n* **:** RED BEDS

red rock cod *n* **1 :** any of numerous pinkish or red rockfishes (genus *Sebastodes*) of considerable importance as market fishes along the Pacific coast of No. America — called also *red cod* **2 :** a fish (*Scorpaena cruenta*) of southern Australia, Tasmania, and New Zealand related to the American red rock cods

red rockfish *n* **1 :** a large rockfish (*Sebastodes ruberrimus*) of the Pacific coast of No. America that is crimson above fading to yellowish pink on the sides and is a highly esteemed food fish — called also *red snapper* **2 :** a red color phase of a large common grouper (*Mycteroperca venenosa* or *Trisotropis venenosa*) of the tropical western Atlantic and the West Indies — called also *rock grouper*

red rock trout *n* **:** a greenling (*Hexagrammos superciliosus*)

red rod *n* **:** SILKY CORNEL

red roe *n* **:** CORAL 3a

red roman *n* **:** ROMAN 6

red roncador *n* **1 :** BLACK CROAKER **2 :** SPOTFIN CROAKER

redroot \'⸗,⸗\ *n* **1 :** a perennial herb (*Lachnanthes tinctoria*) of the eastern U.S. having sword-shaped leaves, cymose woolly flowers, and a red root that is sometimes used as the source of a dye **2 :** a plant of the genus *Ceanothus*; *esp* **:** NEW JERSEY TEA **3 :** BLOODROOT 1 **4 :** a gromwell (*Lithospermum officinale*) **5 :** ALKANET 1a **6** *or* **redroot pigweed :** PIGWEED a **7 :** a West Indian and Central American shrub (*Morinda roioc*) with white flowers **8 :** PINKROOT

red rot *n* **1 :** a common sundew (*Drosera rotundifolia*) **2 a :** either of two diseases of sugarcane: (1) **:** a destructive disease caused by a fungus (*Physalospora tucumanensis*) characterized by red patches within the canes and found also on sorgo (2) **:** a rot of the leaf sheaths caused by a fungus (*Sclerotium rolfsii*) **b :** a wood decay of various conifers and deciduous trees caused by various pore fungi — called also *red heart* **c :** ADUSTIOSIS

red rover *n* **:** a game in which two teams line up facing each other, a challenged player rushes the opposition's line in an effort to break through their joined hands, and upon failure to do so becomes one of their number

red rust *n* **1 a :** the uredinial stage of a rust (as of a cereal grass) **b :** the diseased condition produced by such fungi **2 :** an infestation of plants by red spiders **3 a :** a disease of the leaves or twigs of tropical or subtropical plants (as tea and citrus) characterized by a rusty appearance and caused by a parasitic green alga (*Cephaleuros virescens*) of the family Trentepohliaceae — called also *algal disease* **b :** the alga producing red rust of tea

re·dry \(')rē+\ *vt* [*re-* + dry] **:** to dry again after restoring water or moisture

reds *pl of* RED, *pres 3d sing of* RED

red sable *n* **:** KOLINSKY 1b

red sage *n* **1 :** a tropical shrub (*Lantana camara*) with flat clusters of small tubular flowers that open yellow or pink but change to scarlet or orange — called also *wild sage* **2 :** any of various plants of the genus *Kochia* (esp. *K. americana*)

red salamander *n* **1 :** any of several salamanders (genus *Pseudotriton*) of the eastern U.S. exclusive of New England **2 :** a Pacific coast salamander (*Ensatina escholtzii escholtzii*) related to the eastern red salamander

red salmon *n* **:** SOCKEYE

red sandalwood *n* **1 a** *or* **red sanders** *or* **red sanderswood** *or* **red saunders :** a tree (*Pterocarpus santalinus*) of India and the East Indies **b :** the hard durable fragrant timber of this tree that is much prized for cabinetwork — called also *ruby wood* **c :** the dark red heartwood of red sandalwood used as a dyewood and for coloring tinctures and other liquid preparations **2 :** an East Indian tree (*Adenanthera pavonina*) much cultivated for ornament — called also *bead tree, Barbados pride, coralwood;* see CIRCASSIAN SEED

red sandpiper *n* **:** the knot in summer plumage

red scale *n* **1 :** a red or reddish scale: as **a :** CALIFORNIA RED SCALE **b :** FLORIDA RED SCALE **2 :** RED ORACHE

red seaweed *n* **:** RED ALGA; *specif* **:** a red alga of the genus *Polysiphonia*

red seed *n* **:** RED FEED

red–seeded dandelion \'⸗,⸗⸗-\ *n* **:** a European perennial dandelion (*Taraxacum laevigatum*) naturalized in No. America and having narrow leaf lobes and sulphur yellow flowers

red–shafted \'⸗'⸗⸗\ *adj* **:** having the shaft of the quills red

red–shafted flicker *n* **:** a flicker (*Colaptes caper collaris*) of the western U.S. differing from the common eastern flicker in lacking the red nape patch and in having the undersurface of the wings and tail reddish and in the male a red stripe on the side of the throat

redshank \'⸗,⸗\ *n* **1 :** a common Old World limicoline bird (*Tringa totanus*) having the legs and feet pale red — called also *redleg, red-legged snipe;* compare SPOTTED REDSHANK **2 :** a Celtic inhabitant of the Scottish Highlands or of Ireland; *esp* **:** HIGHLANDER — often used disparagingly **3 a :** REDROOT 2 **b :** any of various persicaries with red stem bases (as *Polygonum persicaria* and *P. hydropiper*)

red shift *n* **:** a displacement of a spectrum toward longer wavelengths: as **a :** such a displacement in the spectrum of a celestial body usu. caused by the Doppler shift that results from a recession relative to the observer **b :** a shift in the spectrum of galaxies outside the local group that is interpreted as a Doppler shift, increases in proportion to distance, and constitutes evidence for belief in the expanding universe

redshirt \'⸗,⸗\ *n* **:** a member of an organization having a red shirt as a distinctive part of its dress or uniform; *esp* **:** a member of the revolutionary forces of Giuseppe Garibaldi

red–short \'⸗,⸗\ *adj* [by folk etymology fr. Sw *rödskört*, neut. of *rödskör*, fr. *röd* red (fr. OSw *röther*) + *skör* brittle, fr. OSw *skör, skyr;* akin to ON *rauthr* red and ON *skera* to cut — more at RED, SHEAR] *of metal* **:** brittle when red-hot — compare COLD-SHORT, HOT-SHORT

red–short·ness *n* **:** the quality or state of being red-short

red–shouldered hawk \'⸗,⸗⸗-\ *n* **:** a common hawk (*Buteo lineatus*) of eastern No. America that is slightly smaller than the red-tailed hawk and has reddish rufous lesser wing coverts in the adult — called also *hen hawk*

red shrew *n* **:** a musk shrew (*Crocidura flavescens*)

red shrimp *n* **:** BRAZILIAN SHRIMP

redside dace \'⸗,⸗-\ *also* **red–sided dace** \'⸗,⸗⸗-\ *n* **:** a small freshwater cyprinid fish (*Clinostomus elongatus*) of central and eastern No. America having in the male in the breeding season a red band along each side

red silk cotton *n* **:** SIMAL

red silky oak *n* **:** a beefwood (*Stenocarpus salignus*)

red silver fir *n* **:** AMABILIS FIR

red silver ore *n* **1 :** PYRARGYRITE **2 :** PROUSTITE

red sindhi *n* **1** *usu cap R&S* **:** an Indian breed of rather small red humped dairy cattle extensively used for crossbreeding with European stock in tropical areas **2** *often cap R&S* **:** an animal of the Red Sindhi breed

red siskin *n* **:** a finch (*Carduelis cucullata*) of northern So. America that is scarlet with black head, wings, and tail, is often kept as a cage bird, and is the wild parent of the red factor canary

redskin \'⸗,⸗\ *n* **:** a No. American Indian — usu. taken to be offensive

red snapper *n* **:** any of various reddish fishes: as **a :** any of several snappers; *esp* **:** a large chiefly rose-red form (*Lutjanus aya*) that ranges from Long Island to Brazil, is abundant in the Gulf of Mexico and on banks off the Florida coast, and is an important food fish **b** (1) **:** RED ROCKFISH (2) **:** RASHER **c :** RED GROUPER **d** *Austral* **:** a fish of the family Berycidae; *esp* **:** a silvery blood-red fish (*Trachichthodes girardi*) much prized as a food fish

red snow *n* **1 :** snow colored by various airborne dusts or by the growth of various algae (as the flagellate *Chlamydomonas nivalis*) that contain red pigment and live in the upper layer of snow in arctic and alpine regions **2 :** an alga causing red snow

red soil *n* **:** RED PODZOLIC SOIL

red sorrel *n* **1 :** ROSELLE **2 :** SHEEP SORREL

red spider *also* **red spider mite** *n* **:** any of the small web-spinning mites of the family Tetranychidae that are pests attacking forage and crop plants and in some areas seriously damaging fruit trees by piercing the leaves with their mouthparts and draining out the cellular material near the puncture

red spider crab *n* **:** CORAL CRAB 1

red spirit *n* **:** a tin spirit used in dyeing red

red–spotted purple \'⸗,⸗⸗-\ *n* **:** a butterfly with red spots on the underwing surfaces that constitutes a variety of and generally resembles the banded purple

red spruce *n* **:** a coniferous tree (*Picea rubens*) of eastern No. America having deeply furrowed brown or purplish bark and in two rows short-stalked blunt dark green needles which are lighter beneath and being the chief lumber spruce of the area and important as a source of pulp wood — called also *eastern spruce, yellow spruce*

red squill *n* **1 :** a European squill (*Urginea maritima*) of the form with a reddish brown bulb — compare WHITE SQUILL **2 :** a rat poison derived from the bulb of red squill

red squirrel *n* **1 :** a common and widely distributed No. American squirrel (*Tamiasciurus hudsonicus* or *Sciurus hudsonicus*) much smaller than the gray squirrel and having the upper parts chiefly red — called also *chickaree, mountain boomer* **2 :** the native English squirrel (*Sciurus vulgaris leucourus* or *S. leucourus*)

red stain *n* **:** a reddish discoloration of the wood of trees esp. as caused in jack pine by fungi of the genera *Fornes* and *Stereum*

red–stalk aster *n* **:** COCASH

red star *n* **:** a star of spectral type M, N, R, or S having a very low surface temperature and a red color

redstart \'⸗,⸗\ *n* [¹*red* + obs. E *start* tail, fr. ME *stert* — more at START] **1 :** a small European singing bird (*Phoenicurus phoenicurus*) related to the redbreast, bluethroat, and nightingale and having a white forehead, black face and throat, and bright chestnut breast and tail — called also *redtail;* compare AMERICAN REDSTART **2 :** any of various Asiatic or European birds of the genus *Phoenicurus* (as the black redstart *P. ochruros* syn. *P. titys* of Europe)

red steenbras *n* **:** a southern African fish (*Dentex rupestris*) resembling a snapper and reaching a weight of 50 to 60 pounds — compare WHITE STEENBRAS

red stele *n* **:** a fatal root-rotting disease of strawberries caused by a fungus (*Phytophthora fragariae*) and characterized by dwarfing and sudden wilting of the plants and by reddening of the steles of affected roots — called also *red core*

red–stem filaree *also* **red–stemmed filaree** \'⸗,⸗-\ *n* **:** ALFILARIA

red stopper *n* **:** a small tree (*Eugenia rhombea*) of southern Florida and the West Indies having white flowers and orange or blackish fruit

red–streaked spider \'⸗,⸗-\ *or* **red striped spider** *n* **:** RED-BACK SPIDER

red stringybark *n* **:** an Australian tree (*Eucalyptus macrorrhyncha*) with light brown moderately hard wood

red stripe *n* **:** any of several diseases of plants marked by reddish stripes or streaks: as **a :** a decay of timber caused by a pore fungus (*Polyporus vaporarius*) and characterized by red or brown streaks **b :** a disease of sugarcane caused by a bacterium (*Xanthomonas rubrilineans*) and characterized by long narrow dark red streaks on the leaves of young plants and later invasion of the vascular system with occasional top rotting

red stuff *n* **:** a polishing agent consisting of rouge or crocus

red stumpnose *n* **:** a southern African sea bream (*Chrysoblephus gibbiceps*) — compare WHITE STUMPNOSE

red sumac *n* **:** SMOOTH SUMAC

red sunflower *n* **:** PURPLE CONEFLOWER

red suture *n* **:** a virus disease of peaches marked by a premature reddish coloration that is evident first in the suture

redtab \'⸗,⸗\ *n* [so called fr. the red tabs on the collar] **:** a high-ranking officer in the British army

red tai *n* **:** a brilliant crimson Pacific porgy (*Pagrus major* or *Chrysophrys major*) that is a favorite food fish of Japan and is commonly figured as a symbol of the Japanese fish god

redtail \'⸗,⸗\ *n* **1 a :** RED-TAILED HAWK **b :** REDSTART 1 **2 :** BRAZILIAN SHRIMP

red-tailed hawk \'⸗,⸗-\ *n* **:** a widely distributed New World buteonine hawk (*Buteo jamaicencis*); *esp* **:** a common rodent-eating hawk (*Buteo jamaicensis borealis*) of eastern No. America that is mottled dusky above and white tinged with buff and streaked dusky below and has a rather short typically rufous tail — called also *redtail;* see HARLAN'S HAWK, KRIDER'S HAWK

red-tailed tropic bird *n* **:** a tropic bird (*Phaëton rubricauda*)

red tail snapper *n* **:** LANE SNAPPER

red tape *n* [so called fr. the red tape formerly used to tie up legal documents in England] **:** bureaucratic procedure esp. as characterized by mechanical adherence to regulations, needless duplication of records, and the compilation of an excessive amount of extraneous information resulting in prolonged delay or inaction

red-tape·ism *or* **red-tap·ism** \'red'tā,pizəm\ *n* -s **:** insistence on or preoccupation with red tape

red tassel flower *n* **:** a prairie clover (*Petalostemon purpureus*) of central No. America with linear leaflets and purplish flowers

red thread *n* **:** a disease of turf grasses caused by a fungus (*Cortecium fuciforme*) and characterized esp. by reddish stromata on or in the pinkish web of hyphal threads

red three-awn *n* **:** a needlegrass (*Aristida longiseta*)

redthroat \'⸗,⸗\ *n* **:** a small Australian singing bird (*Pyrrholaemus brunneus*) having the upper parts brown and the center of the throat rufous

red-throated loon *or* **red-throated diver** \'⸗,⸗⸗-\ *n* **:** a small loon (*Gavia stellata*) with a thin and uptilted bill and a reddish throat patch

redthroat trout *n* **:** CUTTHROAT TROUT

red tick *n* **:** a common African tick (*Rhipicephalus evertsi*) that transmits various protozoan and spirochete diseases to cattle

red tide *n* **:** seawater discolored by the presence of large numbers of dinoflagellates (esp. of the genera *Peridinium* and *Gymnodinium*) in a density fatal to many forms of marine life — called also *red water*

red tiercel *n* **:** an immature male peregrine falcon

red titi *n* **:** LEATHERWOOD 1b

red tobacco *n* **:** leaves of air-cured or flue-cured tobacco having a reddish color

red-toothed shrew \'⸗,⸗-\ *n* **:** a shrew of the genus *Sorex* — compare WHITE-TOOTHED SHREW

redtop \'⸗,⸗\ *also* **redtop grass** *n* **1 :** any of various grasses of the genus *Agrostis; esp* **:** an important pasture forage and lawn grass (*A. alba*) of eastern No. America having reddish panicles — called also *bonnet grass* **2 :** BLUEJOINT 1 **3 :** NATAL GRASS

red tourlourou *n* -s **:** BLACK CRAB

red tree mouse *n* **:** a large lemming mouse (*Phenacomys longicaudus*) of a bright reddish cinnamon color with a long hairy black tail and whitish underparts

red trillium *n* **:** any of several wake-robins of the genus *Trillium* with red or dark purple flowers (esp. *T. sessile* and *T. erectum*)

red truffle *n* **:** a hard-skinned puffball (*Melanogaster variegatus*)

red tulip oak *n* **:** an Australian tree (*Tarrietia argyrodendron*) of the family Sterculiaceae with variegated pink to reddish brown wood

red turnip beetle *n* **:** a leaf beetle (*Entomoscelis americana*) that does severe damage to cruciferous garden crops in western No. America

red turpentine beetle *n* **:** a rather large reddish bark beetle (*Dendroctonus valens*) that attacks the basal part of various pines throughout most of No. America

re·duce \rə̇'d(y)üs, rē'-\ *vb* -ED/-ING/-S [ME *reducen* to lead back, bring back, draw together, fr. L *reducere*, fr. *re-* + *ducere* to lead — more at TOW] *vt* **1 a :** to draw together or cause to converge **:** CONDENSE, CONSOLIDATE ⟨for the sake of brevity I ~ all their questions to one —Arnold Isenberg⟩ ⟨all springs ~ their currents to my eyes —Shak.⟩ **b** (1) **:** to diminish in size, amount, extent, or number **:** make smaller **:** LESSEN, SHRINK ⟨the highway, here *reduced* to a street —G.R. Stewart⟩ ⟨~ excise rates on automobiles —*Wall Street Jour.*⟩ ⟨abolition of aggressive weapons would . . . ~ the likelihood of aggressive war —R.L.Buell⟩ ⟨a safety campaign to ~ forest fires⟩ ⟨a diet to ~ weight⟩ (2) **:** to decrease the volume and concentrate the flavor of (as a gravy) by boiling off excess liquid (3) **:** to concentrate or decrease the volume of (as crude petroleum) by removing light hydrocarbons by distillation ⟨the residue or topped crude oil is further *reduced* —W.L.Nelson & A.P.Buthod⟩ **c :** to narrow down **:** CONFINE, LIMIT, RESTRICT ⟨when we know more about the capacities of man, we do not ~ them, but expand them —A.H.Compton⟩ ⟨the Indians were *reduced* to a small fragment of their former domain —E.M.Coulter⟩ **d :** to make shorter or divest of nonessentials **:** ABRIDGE, CURTAIL ⟨great body of religious lyrics . . . skillfully *reduced* and edited —H.S.Bennett⟩ ⟨double ax-head occurring among the hieroglyphic forms *reduced* to a linear outline —Edward Clodd⟩ **2** *archaic* **a :** to lead back **:** cause to return ⟨~ the Protestants within the pale of the Romish Church —Nicholas Tindal⟩ **b :** to restore to righteousness **:** SAVE ⟨if any of these erring men may be *reduced*, I have my end —John Milton⟩ **3 a** *obs* **:** REDIRECT ⟨with these words ~ they thoughts that roam —William Austin⟩ **b** *obs* **:** to bring back ⟨~, replant our bishop president —Edward Dering⟩ **c :** to bring to a specified state or condition by guidance or leadership ⟨his task was to ~ to order the economic and political chaos following war —W.L.Fleming⟩ **4** *archaic* **a :** to cause to recur ⟨traitors . . . that would ~ these bloody days again —Shak.⟩ **b :** to restore to a former condition ⟨~ them to their former shape —Jonathan Swift⟩ **5 a** (1) **:** to force to capitulate **:** bring under control **:** SUBDUE, SUBJUGATE ⟨after a long siege he *reduced* Alexandria —*Encyc. Americana*⟩ ⟨a pioneer . . . *reducing* the savage wilderness for civilization —D.B.Davis⟩ ⟨about thirty years ago the aboriginal tribes of the interior were *reduced* —E.P.Hanson⟩ (2) **:** to wipe out (an enemy position) **:** ELIMINATE, DEMOLISH ⟨~ a salient⟩ ⟨~ a machine gun nest⟩ **b :** to make captive or hand over ⟨helped ~ the New Amsterdam Dutch to English control —R.P.Stearns⟩ **c** (1) **:** to put under obligation **:** MAKE, COMPEL ⟨one passage so painful that he was *reduced* to explain it by the arts of . . . wizards —G.G.Coulton⟩ (2) **:** to force to resort ⟨were *reduced* to the knee holds and body clings detested by all mountaineers —D.L.Busk⟩ (3) **:** to cause to succumb ⟨a scene that had *reduced* his wife to tears —Scott Fitzgerald⟩ ⟨his exaggerated stories had *reduced* the patrons to openmouthed credulity —*Amer. Guide Series: Pa.*⟩ **d** *obs* **:** to make more temperate **:** OVERCOME ⟨it was necessary . . . their tempers be *reduced* by my kindness —Daniel Defoe⟩ **e :** to cause to revert to one's possession by exercising a legal claim **6 a :** to assign to or describe in terms of some fundamental classification ⟨attempt to ~ life, mind, and spirit to the quantitative categories of physics, chemistry, and mathematics —W.R.Inge⟩ **b :** to bring to a systematic form or character — used with *to* ⟨system of nature, which it is the business of science to study and ~ to laws —C.H.Whiteley⟩ **c :** to endow with a definite shape ⟨the idea . . . was *reduced* to exact form —Graham Wallas⟩ **d :** to transfer to or as if to paper — used with *to* ⟨~ to writing his notions regarding the ideal bird dog —W.F.Brown b.1903⟩ **7 a :** to put back (as a herniated mass) into place **b :** to restore (as elevated blood pressure) to a normal condition **c :** to set (as a fracture) by restoring misplaced parts to a normal position **8 a** *chiefly Scots law* **:** RESCIND, ANNUL **b :** to lower in grade or rank **:** DEMOTE ⟨*reduced* from cruiser command to an inconspicuous post in the merchant marine because of . . . political differences —Lee Rogow⟩ **9 a :** to lower in condition or status **:** DEBASE, DOWNGRADE ⟨at storekeeping he was a failure, and . . . was soon *reduced* to poverty —H.E. Starr⟩ ⟨an old Crusader . . . *reduced* to menial work —T.B. Costain⟩ ⟨historical reporting . . . ~*s* the novel to a news supplement —Allen Tate⟩ **b :** to be driven by poverty or deficiency ⟨*reduced* to going about the . . . villages soliciting alms —J.G.Frazer⟩ ⟨radicals . . . who used to speak of Russia as a land of hope are now *reduced* to saying that it is no worse than any other country —Zechariah Chafee⟩ **c :** to make physically weak ⟨my father was so *reduced*, that I . . . made a bed for him on the deck —Charles Dickens⟩ **d :** to diminish in strength or density ⟨rising sun quickly *reduced* the fog⟩: as (1) **:** to dilute (as a paint) with a thinner (2) **:** to extend (as a pigment) with an inert extender or pigment (3) **:** to make (a photographic negative) less dense **e :** to diminish in value ⟨stocks have been *reduced* to a low level —*Collier's Yr. Bk.*⟩ **10 a** (1) **:** to change the denominations of without changing the value ⟨~ days and hours to minutes⟩ (2) **:** to change the form of (an arithmetical expression) without changing the value ⟨~ fractions to a common denominator⟩ (3) **:** to construct a geometrical figure similar to but smaller than (a given figure) **b :** to transpose from one form into another **:** CONVERT, TRANSLATE ⟨given . . . credit for *reducing* time to space —N.E.Nelson⟩ ⟨~ disputes about ideas and values to factual, sociological terms —Cushing Strout⟩ ⟨~ government regulations to plain language⟩ **c** (1) **:** to change (an expression) from a form that is given to another that is equivalent but considered to be more fundamental or important ⟨*reducing* all sentential connectives to the stroke function⟩ (2) **:** to change (a syllogism) to a mood in the first figure **11 a :** to break down (as by crushing, grinding, or burning) **:** cause to disintegrate **:** PULVERIZE ⟨breaker rolls . . . ~ the wheat kernels to middlings —*Amer. Guide Series: Minn.*⟩ ⟨tree stumps left on a clearing . . . are *reduced* by swarms of ants —C.D.Forde⟩ ⟨a recent earthquake *reduced* the cathedral of Cuzco almost to a heap of rubble —Angélica Mendoza⟩ **b** *archaic* **:** to cause (a military unit) to disperse **:** DISBAND **c :** to separate into commercially usable elements ⟨~ trees to lumber⟩ ⟨~ pilchards into oil and meal⟩ **d :** to treat (garbage) so as to recover grease and other products **12 a :** to bring to the metallic state by removal of nonmetallic elements ⟨iron ores are *reduced* to metallic iron⟩ ⟨metals are *reduced* from their ores⟩ — compare SMELT **b :** DEOXIDIZE ⟨~ anthraquinone to anthracene⟩ **c :** to combine with or subject to the action of hydrogen **:** HYDROGENATE ⟨acetaldehyde is *reduced* to alcohol in the final step of alcoholic fermentation⟩ **d :** to change (a compound) by decreasing the proportion of the electronegative part ⟨~ mercuric chloride to mercurous chloride⟩ **:** change (an element or ion) from a higher to a lower oxidation state ⟨in electrolysis, ferric ions are *reduced* to ferrous ions at the cathode —Farrington Daniels & R.A.Alberty⟩ **:** add one or more electrons to (an atom or ion or molecule) ⟨~ ionic copper to metallic copper⟩ — opposed to *oxidize* **13 :** to transform to actuality ⟨faces the task of *reducing* theory to a course of instruction —J.R. Butler⟩ **14 a** (1) **:** to use an unstressed vowel (as \ə\) or no vowel at all instead of (a stressed vowel) (2) **:** to make such alteration in (a syllable) **b :** to cause the loss of a member from (a series of consonants or vowels) ~ *vi* **1 a :** to become diminished or lessened; *esp* **:** to lose weight by dieting ⟨no more, thanks, I'm *reducing*⟩ **b :** to become concentrated ⟨let the stock ~, strain . . . and keep hot —Roger Angell⟩ **c :** to undergo meiosis **d :** to become consolidated ⟨the number 53, which is composed of 5 and 3, *reduces* to the primate number 8 —W.B.Gibson⟩ **2 :** to become converted or equated ⟨romanticism and classicism . . . ~ in the end to differences of psychological type —Herbert Read⟩ **3 :** to become weakened or diluted ⟨poster paints ~ with water⟩ **4 :** to undergo processing esp. for commercial purposes ⟨canneries send a stink of *reducing* fish into the air —John Steinbeck⟩ **syn** see CONQUER, DECREASE

re·duce·able \-səbəl\ *adj, archaic* **:** REDUCIBLE

re·duced \-st\ *adj* **1 a :** made smaller ⟨a ~ illustration⟩ **b :** imperfect in form or function or lacking parts **:** DWARFED, VESTIGIAL **2 :** WEAKENED, IMPOVERISHED ⟨his poor ~ body —Charles Dickens⟩

reduced hematin *n* **:** HEME 1

reduced iron *n* **:** finely divided iron prepared by a chemical process (as by heating ferric oxide at a dull red heat in hydrogen) and used as a tonic

reduced oil *n* **:** petroleum freed from volatile and suspended matter

reduced rate contribution clause *n* **:** AVERAGE CLAUSE 1

reducement *n* -s **1** *obs* **:** restoration to righteousness **2** *obs* **:** SUBJUGATION **3** *obs* **:** DIMINUTION

re·duc·er \-sə(r)\ *n* -s **1 :** one that reduces **2 a :** one that condenses or consolidates **b :** one that makes smaller or less: as (1) **:** REDUCING COUPLING (2) **:** REDUCING VALVE (3) **:** a hydraulic device that lowers pressure and increases movement used to transmit the load from the hydraulic support of the lower shackle to the lever weighing apparatus in some kinds of heavy testing machines (4) **:** SHELL REDUCER **3 :** one that weakens or dilutes: as **a :** REDUCING AGENT; *specif* **:** one used in photographic development **b :** a chemical solution for reducing the density of a silver image in photography **c :** a paint thinner **d :** a vessel or apparatus in which chemical reduction is carried out **:** REDUCTOR **e :** a worker who adds thinners to paint or varnish to obtain the proper consistency **4 :** one that processes esp. for commercial use ⟨a ~ of iron ore⟩

reducer sleeve *n* **:** TAPER REDUCER SLEEVE

reduces *pres 3d sing of* REDUCE

re·duc·ibil·i·ty \rə̇,d(y)üsə'bilәd·ē, rē,-, -lətē, -i\ *n* -ES **:** the quality or state of being reducible

re·duc·ible \rə̇'d(y)üsəbəl, rē'-\ *adj* [*reduce* + *-ible*] **:** capable of being reduced ⟨~ to a set of principles of human nature —Edmund Wilson⟩

reducible polynomial *n* **:** a polynomial expressible as the product of two or more polynomials of lower degree

re·duc·ibly \-blē, -li\ *adv* **:** in a reducible manner

[1]**re·duc·ing** \-siŋ, -sēŋ\ *n* -s [ME, fr. gerund of *reducen* to reduce — more at REDUCE] **:** REDUCTION

[2]**reducing** \"\ *adj* [fr. pres. part. of *reduce*] **:** causing or facilitating reduction

reducing agent *n* **:** a substance that reduces; *esp* **:** a substance (as hydrogen, sodium, or hydroquinone) that donates electrons or a share in its electrons to another substance — called also *reducer*, *reductant;* compare OXIDIZING AGENT

reducing coupling *n* **:** a coupling for joining a pipe to another of smaller diameter

reducing flame *n* **:** a flame or part of a flame (as the inner cone of a gas flame) having partially burned gas and being capable of extracting oxygen from various metallic oxides placed within it

reducing furnace *n* **:** a furnace for reducing ores

reducing glass *n* **:** a diverging lens or convex mirror giving a virtual image of reduced size of an object

reducing press *n* **:** a punch press for redrawing metal articles (as cartridge shells)

reducing sugar *n* **:** a sugar that is capable of reducing a mild oxidizing agent (as Fehling solution) ⟨glucose, maltose, and lactose are *reducing sugars* but sucrose and methyl glucoside are not⟩ — compare BENEDICT'S TEST

reducing turbine *n* **:** a steam turbine that is used as a reducing valve to perform useful work in the process of pressure reduction

reducing valve *n* **:** an automatic valve that reduces pressure (as of steam entering a pipe from a boiler)

re·duct \rə̇'dəkt\ *vt* -ED/-ING/-S [L *reductus*, past part. of *reducere* — more at REDUCE] **1 :** REDUCE **2** *dial* **:** DEDUCT ⟨you can ~ it from my wages —A.E.Coppard⟩

re·duc·tant \rə̇'dəktənt\ *n* -s [*reduction* + *-ant*] **:** REDUCING AGENT — compare OXIDANT

re·duc·tase \-k,tās, -āz\ *n* -s [*reduction* + *-ase*] **:** an enzyme that catalyzes reduction — compare DEHYDROGENASE

reductase test *n* **:** a test for the bacterial content esp. of milk and milk products in which methylene blue is added and the time determined for decolorization of the dye by the reducing action of the bacteria

re·duc·tic acid \-ktik-\ *n* [*reduction* + *-ic*] **:** a crystalline enolic ketone $C_5H_6O_3$ that has properties both of an acid and a strong reducing agent in alkaline solution and is formed by the action of dilute sulfuric acid on various carbohydrates at high temperature or synthetically from cyclopentanone; 2,-3-dihydroxy-2-cyclopenten-one

re·duc·tio \rə̇'dəkshē,ō, rē'-; rā'du̇ktē,ō\ *n, pl* **reducti·o·nes** \⸗,⸗⸗'ō,nēz; ⸗,⸗⸗'ō,nās\ [LL — more at REDUCTION] **:** an act or process of reducing — used as the first term in phrases relating to disproof of a proposition by arguing it to an obviously false conclusion ⟨~ ad impossibile⟩; compare AD ABSURDUM

re·duc·tion \rə̇'dəkshən, rē'-\ *n* -s [ME *reduccion*, fr. MF *reduction*, fr. LL & L; LL *reduction-*, *reductio* reduction (in a syllogism), fr. L, action of leading or bringing back, restoration, fr. *reductus* (past part. of *reducere* to lead back, bring back, draw together) + *-ion-*, *-io* -ion — more at REDUCE] **1** *obs* **:** REDEMPTION, RESTORATION ⟨~ of the soul —Theophilus Gale⟩ ⟨~ of Christ from the dead —John Owen⟩ **2 a** (1) **:** domination by force **:** CONQUEST, SUBJUGATION (2) **:** elimination of a defended enemy position **b** (1) **:** the act or process of resettlement (as by Spanish missionaries) of So. American Indians in villages or compounds for purposes of acculturation or control (2) **:** a village or compound so established **3 a** (1) **:** the conversion of numbers into units of the same denomination (2) **:** the reducing of an algebraic equation to its simplest terms (3) **:** the determination of the true position of a celestial object by correcting observational data for known errors (4) **:** the substitution for a meteorological reading of a value computed from it so as to bring all to a common basis (as pressures to sea level values) **b :** an act or instance of reproducing in a smaller size ⟨~*s* — scaled down from life size —J.C.Furnas⟩ **4 a :** the act or process of reducing a syllogistic argument to the first figure — compare DIRECT REDUCTION, INDIRECT REDUCTION **b** (1) **:** the classification or description (as of a set of terms or phenomena) in terms of what are regarded as simpler or more fundamental concepts ⟨~ of the complex problems of intergroup relations to attitude formation —J.R.Kantor⟩; *specif* **:** the process of explaining the terms of a science on the basis of and deducing its laws from those of another ⟨the ~ of chemical to physical laws —C.H.Whiteley⟩ (2) **:** analysis of a psychological motive into its instinctive elements **c :** the act or process of investing with definite form ⟨behavioral responses which are in process of ~ to habitual terms —Ralph Linton⟩ ⟨the ~ of generalization to particular fact —Jonathan Daniels⟩ **5 :** the replacement or realignment of a body part in normal position or restoration of a bodily condition to normal **6 a :** the process of reducing by chemical or electrochemical means ⟨the ~, or deoxidation, of the iron ore is brought about by carbon monoxide produced by the combustion of the coke —J.H.Bateman⟩ ⟨the photographic process depends upon . . . the ~ of silver ion to metallic silver by a developing solution —C.E.K.Mees⟩ **b :** treatment under reducing conditions by exclusion of air to a point below that needed for complete combustion of fuel gases (as in a pottery kiln) ⟨~ produces various color effects in pottery⟩ **7 a** (1) **:** a decrease in size, amount, extent, or number **:** DIMINUTION; *specif* **:** the psychological diminishment of emotion through activity or adjustment (2) **:** SUBTRACTION ⟨arrangements can be made for premiums to be paid by ~ from salary —*Irish Digest*⟩ **b :** MEIOSIS; *specif* **:** production of the gametic chromosome number in the first meiotic division **c :** limitation in scope **:** RESTRICTION ⟨whether the ~ of *existence* to *human existence* does not seriously . . . restrict the domain of philosophy —J.E. Smith⟩ **8 a :** demotion in rank **b :** lowering in condition or status **:** DEGRADATION ⟨~ of living to an animal business of . . . survival —Fred Majdalany⟩ ⟨~ to absurdity is a common device by which teachers demonstrate the essential fallacy of a proposal —Alexander Laing⟩ **9 a :** transformation into objective form or reality ⟨~ of a novel to words on paper⟩ ⟨~ of the device to practice —Ruth Riddell⟩ **b :** transformation into a new or different form **:** ADAPTATION, TRANSLATION ⟨~ of a metaphor⟩ ⟨every art involves a system of ~ —Stuart Gilbert⟩ **c :** a musical arrangement; *esp* **:** a piano score or part arranged or reduced from an orchestral score **10 :** an act or instance of breaking down **:** DISINTEGRATION, PROCESSING ⟨~ of land surfaces . . . to low plains —O.D. Von Engeln⟩ ⟨~ of . . . pine by lumbering, turpentining, and fire —*Amer. Guide Series: N.C.*⟩ ⟨~ of fish and fish waste to . . . oil —*Commercial Fisheries Rev.*⟩; *specif* **:** the gradual crushing of grain in milling by passing it repeatedly through break rolls **11 :** an act or instance of reducing phonetically

re·duc·tion·al \-nᵊl\ *adj* **:** of, relating to, or characterized by reduction

reduction crusher *n* **:** a crusher for reducing particle sizes of coal, rock, or ore

reduction division *n* **:** the first meiotic division

reduction gear *n* **:** a pair or combination of gears to reduce the input speed (as of a marine turbine) to a lower output speed (as of a ship's propeller)

reduction-improbation \⸗'⸗⸗,⸗⸗'⸗⸗\ *n, Scots law* **:** a rescissory action for setting aside a writing or a part of it in which the summons provides that if the document is not produced it will be judged false or forged

re·duc·tion·ism \rə̇'dəkshə,nizəm, rē'-\ *n* -s **:** a procedure or theory of reducing complex data or phenomena to simple terms; *esp* **:** OVERSIMPLIFICATION ⟨materialism and idealism have been criticized as ~*s*⟩ ⟨the phenomenalistic ~ according to which statements about objects or the physical world can be translated into statements about sense-data or immediate experience⟩

re·duc·tion·ist \-_nə̇st\ *n* -s **:** an advocate of reduction or reductionism

re·duc·tion·is·tic \⸗¦⸗⸗¦nistik\ *adj* **:** REDUCTIVE

reduction potential *n* **:** the potential at which reduction occurs at the cathode in an electrochemical cell — compare OXIDATION-REDUCTION POTENTIAL

reduction roll *n* **:** a roller for decreasing the thickness of ductile material

[1]**re·duc·tive** \rə̇'dəktiv, rē'-, -tēv *also* -təv\ *adj* [*reduction* + *-ive*] **1 :** of, relating to, characterized by, or causing diminution or curtailment **:** REDUCING ⟨their views of life were . . . ~ and depreciatory —R.H.Rovere⟩; *esp* **:** of or relating to psychological reduction (as of emotional tension) **2 :** of, relating to, or advocating analytical reduction or reductionism **:** REDUCTIONISTIC ⟨the attempt to squeeze these data, with all their variegated content, into the limited perspectives of one science . . . must always lead to ~ distortion —J.D.Wild⟩ **3 :** of or relating to conversion or processing into another form — **re·duc·tive·ly** \-tə̇vlē\ *adv*

[2]**reductive** \"\ *n* -s **:** a reductive agent

re·duc·tone \-k,tōn\ *n* -s [*reduction* + *-one*] **:** any of a class of reducing enediol aldehydes or ketones $RC(OH)=C(OH)COR$; *esp* **:** a crystalline osone $HOCH_2COCHO$ or a tautomer [as $HOCH=C(OH)CHO$] that is a strong reducing agent in alkaline solution and is obtained from glucose by alkaline degradation or from dihydroxy-acetone by oxidation; hydroxy-pyruvaldehyde ⟨ascorbic acids . . . may be considered as ~*s* —W.W.Pigman & R.M.Goepp †1946⟩

re·duc·tor \-ktə(r)\ *n* -s [*reduction* + *-or*] **:** an apparatus for carrying out chemical reduction (as of a ferric salt to a ferrous salt) — compare JONES REDUCTOR

re·duc·to·ri·al \¦rē,dək¦tōrēəl\ *adj* **:** REDUCTIVE

reducts *pres 3d sing of* REDUCT

re·dun·ca \rə̇'dəŋkə\ *n, cap* [NL, fr. L, fem. of *reduncus* bent backward, fr. *red-* re- + *uncus* bent, curved; akin to L *uncus* hook — more at ANGLE] **:** a genus of antelopes consisting of the reedbucks — **re·dun·cine** \-dən(t),sīn\ *adj*

re·dun·dan·cy \rə̇'dəndənsē, rē'-, -si\ *also* **re·dun·dance** \-n(t)s\ *n, pl* **redundancies** *also* **redundances** [L *redundantia*, fr. *redundant-*, *redundans* + *-ia* -y] **1 :** the quality or state of being redundant **:** SUPERFLUITY ⟨dread of economic ~ that drove terrified mill hands to wreck Arkwright's spinning jenny —*Times Lit. Supp.*⟩ **2 a :** a lavish or excessive supply **:** PROFUSION, OVERABUNDANCE ⟨a ~ of jewelry and a scarcity of clothing —Alan Moorehead⟩ ⟨a magnificent ~ of beard —Elinor Wylie⟩ **b :** a nonessential appendage **c :** surplusage in a legal pleading **3 a :** superfluous repetition or verbosity **:** PROLIXITY, TAUTOLOGY ⟨the . . . florid ~ of Italian prose —Havelock Ellis⟩ **b :** an act or instance of needless repetition ⟨*redundancies* result . . . when the writer fails to perceive the scope of a word —Bruce Westley⟩ **4 :** the part of a communication that can be eliminated without loss of essential information; *specif* **:** the number arrived at by subtracting from one the ratio of the actual information content of a communication to the maximum information content and expressed as a percentage

re·dun·dant \-nt\ *adj* [L *redundant-*, *redundans*, pres. part.

of *redundare* to overflow, be in excess — more at REDOUND] **1 a :** exceeding what is necessary or normal **:** SUPERFLUOUS, SURPLUS ⟨older areas, plants and occupations are becoming ~ and obsolete —Solomon Barkin⟩ ⟨so many books on heraldry . . . that yet another might be thought ~ —*Times Lit. Supp.*⟩ ⟨a ~ secretion of bile⟩; *specif* **:** PLEONASTIC ⟨at the risk of being ~, I return to my original proposition —J.B.Conant⟩ **b :** characterized by or containing an excess ⟨the skin . . . was ~ and lay too loosely on her fingers —Jean Stafford⟩; *specif* **:** IMMATERIAL 3b ⟨the court may order stricken from any pleading . . . any ~, immaterial, impertinent, or scandalous matter —*U.S. Code*⟩ **2 :** characterized by abundance **:** PROFUSE, LAVISH ⟨skirts became somewhat shorter and less ~ —G.M. Trevelyan⟩ **3 :** expanding beyond ordinary bounds **:** SWELLING, OVERFLOWING ⟨a gradual spilling over of the ~ population —Ellen Semple⟩ **syn** see WORDY

re·dun·dant·ly *adv* **:** in a redundant manner

redundant member *n* **:** a member in a framed structure that is not actually necessary for support

redundant verb *n* **:** a verb that has alternative forms (as for the past tense)

¹re·du·pli·cate \(ˈ)rē¦d(y)üplə,kāt, rə̇ˈd-, *usu* -ād.+V\ *vt* [LL *reduplicatus*, past part. of *reduplicare*, fr. L *re-* + *duplicare* to double — more at DUPLICATE] **1 :** to make or perform again **:** COPY, REITERATE ⟨mechanism . . . capable of being *reduplicated* almost without limit —George Iles⟩ ⟨*reduplicating* oaths on different altars —H.C.Lea⟩ **2 :** to repeat all or part of (a radical word element) **:** form (a word) by reduplication

²re·du·pli·cate \-lə̇kə̇t, -lə,kāt, *usu* -d.+V\ *adj* [LL *reduplicatus*, past part.] **1 :** REDUPLICATED **2 :** valvate with the margins curved outwardly

re·du·pli·cat·ed \-lə,kād.ə̇d\ *adj* **1** *archaic* **:** DOUBLED, REITERATED **2 :** having radical elements repeated **:** formed by reduplication

re·du·pli·ca·tion \(ˌ)rē,d(y)üpləˈkāshən, rə̇,-\ *n* [LL *reduplication-, reduplicatio*, fr. *reduplicatus* + L *-ion-, -io* -ion] **1 :** an act or instance of doubling or reiterating **:** DUPLICATION, REPLICA **2 a :** repetition of a radical element or a part of it occurring usu. at the beginning of a word, often accompanied by change of the radical vowel, found in many languages, and in some Indo-European languages being grammatically functional esp. in the formation of the perfect and present tenses (as in Sanskrit *dadāmi* "I give", Sanskrit *dadarśa* "I have seen", Latin *poposci* "I have demanded", Gothic *lailot* "I have let") **b (1) :** a word or form produced by reduplication **(2) :** the repeated element in such a word or form (as *po-* in Latin *poposci*) **3 :** ANADIPLOSIS

¹re·du·pli·ca·tive \(ˈ)rē¦d(y)üplə,kād.iv, rə̇ˈd-\ *adj* [*reduplicate* + *-ive*] **:** of, relating to, or formed by reduplication

²reduplicative \"\ *n* -s **:** ITERATIVE

re·du·pli·ca·ture \-lə̇kə,chu̇(ə)r\ *n* -s **:** a part folded back on itself

¹re·du·vi·id \rə̇ˈd(y)üvēə̇d\ *adj* [NL *Reduviidae*] **:** of or relating to the Reduviidae

²reduviid \"\ *n* -s **:** a bug of the family Reduviidae

re·du·vi·idae \,rejəˈvīə,dē\ *n pl, cap* [NL, fr. *Reduvius*, type genus + *-idae*] **:** a very large and widely distributed family of bloodsucking hemipterous insects comprising the assassin bugs and having a short 3-jointed proboscis that is curved back under the head when at rest and 3-jointed tarsi — see TRIATOMA

re·du·vi·us \rə̇ˈd(y)üvēəs\ *n, cap* [NL, fr. L *reduvia, redivia* hangnail, exuviae — more at REDIVIVUS] **:** the type genus of Reduviidae

red valerian *n* **:** a European herb (*Centranthus ruber*) with small crimson or white spurred flowers — called also *French honeysuckle*

red vitriol *n* **1 :** BIEBERITE **2 :** COLCOTHAR

red·ward \ˈredwə(r)d\ *adv (or adj)* **:** toward the red end of the spectrum

¹redware \ˈ=,=\ *n* [¹*red* + *ware* (seaweed)] **:** a large brown edible seaweed (*Laminaria digitata*)

²redware \"\ *n* [¹*red* + *ware* (pottery)] **:** any of various claywares made from clays rich in iron oxide: as **a :** coarse low-firing red pottery (as of various primitive cultures or of the Pennsylvania Dutch) **b :** BOCCARO **c :** red-firing European 18th century stoneware imitative of boccaro

red-wat \ˈre,dwät\ *adj* [¹*red* + *wat*, Sc var. of *wet*] *Scot* **:** wet with blood **:** BLOODSTAINED, BLOODY

red water *n* **1 :** any of certain diseases of cattle characterized by hematuria: as **a :** a babesiasis (as Texas fever) in which hemoglobin liberated by destruction of red blood cells appears in the urine **b :** a chronic disease affecting cattle esp. at the end of winter attributed to oxalic acid in the forage and marked by escape of blood into the urine from lesions in the bladder **c :** EAST COAST FEVER **d :** an acute febrile septicemia that is caused by a bacterium (*Clostridium hemolyticum*), is marked by hemoglobinuria and sometimes by intestinal hemorrhages, and less commonly affects horses, sheep, and swine **e :** bovine leptospirosis **2 :** any of various diseases of other animals of which hematuria is a prominent symptom **3 a :** water that is colored red (as by iron compounds) **b :** RED TIDE

red-wat-shod \ˈ=,=,=\ *adj* [*red-wat* + *shod*] *Scot* **:** having bloodstained shoes **:** wading in blood

redweed \ˈ=,=\ *n* **1** *dial Eng* **:** CORN POPPY **2 :** POKEWEED

red whelk *n* **:** an edible European whelk (*Neptunea antiqua*) with a slightly ridged yellowish or reddish shell — called also *buckie*

red whortleberry *n* **:** any of various cranberries; *esp* **:** MOUNTAIN CRANBERRY

red willow *n* **1 :** any of several willows (as a sandbar willow) with reddish or purplish twigs; *esp* **:** PURPLE WILLOW **2 a :** SILKY CORNEL **b :** RED OSIER 2

red wine *n* **:** a wine with a predominantly red color derived during fermentation from the natural pigment in the skins of red or otherwise dark-colored grapes — compare ROSÉ, WHITE WINE

redwing \ˈ=,=\ *n* **1** *or* **red-winged thrush** \ˈ=,=-\ **:** a European thrush (*Turdus musicus* syn. *T. iliacus*) having the underwing coverts red **2 :** REDWING BLACKBIRD **3 :** a southern African francolin (*Francolinus levaillanti*) **4 :** GADWALL

redwing blackbird *or* **red-winged blackbird** *n* **:** a bird (*Agelaius phoeniceus*) of the family Icteridae which is widely distributed in No. America, breeds in swampy places, and collects in the fall in large flocks for migration and whose adult male is black with a patch of bright scarlet bordered behind with white or buff on the wing coverts while the female and the young of both sexes are brown with dusky streaks —called also *maizebird, maizer*

red wolf *n* **1 :** MANED WOLF **2 :** a member of any of several races of a small wolf (*Canis niger*) of the southeastern U.S. that survives chiefly in Texas and has reddish hairs interspersed with black and the short hairs shading from yellow to red

¹redwood \ˈ=,=\ *adj* [¹*red* + *wood* (mad)] *Scot* **:** stark mad

²redwood \ˈ=,=\ *n* [¹*red* + *wood* (growth of trees)] **1 a :** a wood yielding a red dye: as **a :** BRAZILWOOD **b :** CAMWOOD **c :** SAPPANWOOD **d :** LIMA WOOD **e :** BARWOOD **2 :** a tree that yields a red dyewood or that produces wood of a red or reddish color: as **a :** RED SANDALWOOD **b :** AMBOYNA 1 **c :** ROHUN **d :** any of various So. American trees of the genera *Caesalpinia* and *Erythroxylon* **e :** MAHOGANY **f :** SCOTCH PINE **g :** CORNELIAN CHERRY **h :** an Asiatic buckthorn (*Rhamnus erythroxylon*) **i :** a tree (*Melhania erythroxylon*) of the family Sterculiaceae of St. Helena **j :** an African tree (*Ochna arborea*) with reddish wood **k :** FALSE LOGWOOD **1 :** a snakebark (*Colubrina ferruginosa*) of the West Indies **3 a :** a commercially important coniferous timber tree (*Sequoia sempervirens*) of California found only on the Coast Range sometimes reaching a height of 360 feet **b :** the brownish red light wood of the California redwood tree that resists decay and is much used commercially **4 :** a variable color averaging a moderate reddish brown that is lighter and stronger than mahogany, yellower, lighter, and stronger than roan, and lighter, stronger, and very slightly redder than oxblood

red worm *n* **1 :** BLOODWORM; *esp* **:** a small reddish aquatic oligochaete worm (genus *Tubifex*) that is often fed to aquarium fish **2 a :** GAPEWORM **b :** PALISADE WORM

redworm disease \ˈ=,=-\ *n* **:** strongylosis of horses

red zinc ore *n* **:** ZINCITE

¹ree \ˈrē, ˈrā\ *vt* [ME *reien*] *dial Eng* **:** SIFT

²ree \ˈrē, ˈrā\ *adj* [origin unknown] *chiefly Scot* **:** IRRATIONAL, BEFUDDLED

³ree \ˈrē\ *n* -s *usu cap* **:** ARIKARA

reebok *var of* RHEBOK

reech \ˈrēch\ *dial var of* REEK

re·echo \(ˈ)rē+\ *vi* **:** to repeat or return an echo **:** echo again or repeatedly ⟨the words . . . ~ through the book —Eila Campbell⟩ **:** REVERBERATE, RESOUND ⟨thunder ~*ed* through the valley⟩ ⟨the house ~*ed* with laughter⟩ ~ *vt* **:** to send (an echo) back **:** cause an echo of to return

reechy \ˈrēchē\ *adj* -ER/-EST [ME *rechy*, fr. *rech, rek* reek + *-y* — more at REEK] **1** *archaic* **:** having a strong odor **:** RANCID **2** *archaic* **:** blackened by smoke

¹reed \ˈrēd\ *n* -s *often attrib* [ME *rede, reod*, fr. OE *hrēod*; akin to MD *ried, riet* reed, OS *hriod*, OHG *hriot, riot* reed, Lith *krutėti* to stir, move, Toch A *kru* reed] **1 a :** any of various tall grasses with slender stems: as **(1) :** DITCH REED **(2) :** GIANT REED 1 **b :** a stem of such a grass **c :** a person or thing too weak to rely on **:** one easily swayed or overcome **2 a :** a growth or mass of reeds **:** reeds for thatching or for plastering on **b :** reeds as a material **c** *dial Eng* **:** straw prepared for thatching **d :** the strong fibrous core of rattan used in basket weaving **3 :** ARROW **4 :** a musical instrument made of the hollow joint of a plant (as of reed or cane) with a mouthpiece and finger holes **:** PIPE ⟨heard the shepherd's ~ —Sir Walter Scott⟩ **5 :** an ancient Hebrew unit of length equal to 6 cubits or about 10.25 feet ⟨the foundations . . . measured a full ~ of six long cubits —Ezek 41:8 (RSV)⟩ **6 a :** a thin elastic tongue (as of cane, wood, metal, or plastic) fastened at one end to the mouthpiece of a musical instrument (as the clarinet or the organ reed pipe) or to a reed block or other fixture over an air opening (as in the reed organ or accordion) and set in vibration by the breath or other air current **b :** the immediate mechanism (as the beak of a clarinet) surrounding and comprising the reed proper **c :** a reed instrument ⟨the ~s of an orchestra⟩ **d :** REED STOP **7 a (1) :** a device on a loom that resembles a comb and is attached to the lay, set with a series of flat parallel wires called dents, and used to space the warp yarns evenly and to beat up the filling **(2) :** the fineness of cloth as determined by the number of dents and therefore of threads per inch of the reed **b :** a comb of boxwood or other hard material for pressing down the weft of tapestry **8 a :** REEDING 1 a **b :** one of a series of corrugations on the edge of a coin

²reed \"\ *vt* -ED/-ING/-S [ME *reden*, fr. *rede* reed] **1 a :** to cover with reed or thatch **b :** to prepare (as straw) for use in thatching **2 :** to decorate with reeds or reeding ⟨the foot posts are deeply ~*ed* —*Antiques*⟩ **3 :** to draw (yarns) through the reed of a loom ⟨~ the warp⟩ **4 :** to make corrugations on (the edge of a coin)

³reed \"\ *var of* REDE

⁴reed \"\ *var of* READ

reed-back \ˈ=,=\ *adj, of a chair* **:** having a back of vertical and flat or curved and narrow balusters often with a connecting member at the center

reedbed \ˈ=,=\ *n* **:** a bed of reeds

reed bent *or* **reed bent grass** **1 :** a grass of the genus *Calamagrostis* **2 :** a perennial grass (*Arctagrostis arundinacea*) of northern No. America and Asia

reedbird \ˈ=,=\ *n* **1 :** BOBOLINK — used esp. of this bird when flocking in reedy marshes in fall and winter **2 :** any of several small Asiatic timaliine birds of the genera *Schoenicola* and *Laticilla* **3 :** SEDGE WARBLER

reed·buck \ˈrēd,bək\ *n, pl* **reedbuck** *also* **reedbucks** [trans. of Afrik *rietbok*] **:** any of several African antelopes (as the bohor, nagor, reitbok) that are related to the waterbuck and kobs but smaller, constitute the genus *Redunca*, and are of a brownish fawn color with horned males and hornless females

reed bunting *n* **1 :** a European bunting (*Emberiza schoeniclus*) frequenting marshy places and having the face and head chiefly black, the wings and back chestnut, and the underparts white — called also *reed sparrow* **2 :** BEARDED TIT

reed canary grass *n* **:** a perennial grass (*Phalaris arundinaceae*) occurring commonly in marshy meadows and ditches of Europe and No. America, used in some areas for forage, and having broad leaves and narrow dense panicles — called also *lady's-laces*

reede *obs var of* REED

reed·en \ˈrēdᵊn\ *adj* [ME, fr. ¹*reed* + *-en*] **:** made or consisting of reed

reed·er \-də(r)\ *n* -s [ME *redare*, fr. *reden* to reed + *-are* -er] **1 :** one that reeds: as **a :** one that thatches with reeds **b :** a textile worker who replaces the broken reeds of a loom or draws the warp threads through the reeds **c :** a worker who tapes a reed or wire on sweatband leathers **2 :** a reed-covered frame to protect drying china clay

reed fescue *n* **:** a tall robust fescue that is usu. considered a variety (*Festuca elatior arundinacea*) of meadow fescue

reedfish \ˈ=,=\ *n* **:** a long slender West African freshwater fish (*Erpetoichthys calabaricus* or *Calamoichthys calabaricus*) that lacks pelvic fins, in many respects resembles an eel, and is closely related to the bichir — see CLADISTIA

reed grass *n* **1 :** any of various reeds or reedy grasses: as **a :** a tall perennial grass of the genus *Calamagrostis* sometimes used for hay; *esp* **:** an Australian grass (*C. quadriseta* or *Deyeuxia quadriseta*) **b :** a grass of the genus *Arundo*; *esp* **:** GIANT REED 1 **c :** WOOD GRASS 1 **d :** a grass of the genus *Phragmites*; *esp* **:** DITCH REED **2 :** BUR REED

reed green *n* **:** a light yellow green that is yellower and duller than glass green and yellower and less strong than sky green

reed horn *n* **:** a lighthouse and lightship sound signal obtained by vibrating a steel reed with compressed air

reedier *comparative of* REEDY

reediest *superlative of* REEDY

re·edification \(ˌ)rē+\ *n* [ME *reedification*, fr. MF or LL; MF *reedification*, fr. LL *reaedification-, reaedificatio*, fr. *reaedificatus* (past part. of *reaedificare* to rebuild) + L *-ion-, -io* -ion] **:** the act or process of rebuilding

re·edify \(ˈ)rē+\ *vt* [ME *reedifien*, fr. MF *reedifier*, fr. LL *reaedificare*, fr. L *re-* + *aedificare* to build — more at EDIFY] **:** REBUILD

reed·i·ly \ˈrēdᵊlē, -də̇lē, -li\ *adv* **:** with a reedy quality

reed·i·ness \-dēnə̇s, -din-\ *n* -ES **:** the quality or state of being reedy

reed·ing \ˈrēdiŋ\ *n* -s [fr. gerund of ²*reed*] **1 a :** a small convex molding — called also *reed*; compare FLUTING; see MOLDING illustration **b :** decoration by series of parallel reeds (as on chair or table legs) **2 :** corrugations on the edge of a coin

re·edit \(ˈ)rē+\ *vt* **:** to edit again **:** make a new edition of

re·edition \ˌrē+\ *n* **:** the act, process, or result of reediting **:** a new edition

reed·less \ˈrēdlə̇s\ *adj* **1 :** having no reed **2** *of a pipe-organ stop* **:** lacking a reed but producing a reedlike tone

reedlike \ˈ=,=\ *adj* **:** resembling a reed (as in slender form or upright growth) or that of a reed ⟨a ~ grass⟩ ⟨a ~ tone⟩

reed·ling \ˈrēdliŋ\ *n* -s [¹*reed* + *-ling*] **:** BEARDED TIT

reed mace *n* **:** CATTAIL

reed mark *n* **:** a warp mark in cloth caused by defective reeds or a faulty setting of the loom or yarns

reed meadow grass *n* **:** a pasture grass (*Glyceria grandis*) found in moist places throughout No. America

reed organ *n* **:** a keyboard wind instrument (as the harmonium, American organ) in which the wind acts on a set of free metal reeds

reed pheasant *n* **:** BEARDED TIT

reed pipe *n* **1 :** a musical instrument made of a reed **:** PIPE **2 :** a pipe of a pipe organ producing its musical tone by vibration of a beating reed in a current of air — compare FLUE PIPE

reeds *pl of* REED, *pres 3d sing of* REED

reed-shade \ˈ=,=\ *n* **:** a shade constructed of reeds for the protection of plants in hot locations

reed sparrow *n* [ME *rede sparowe*, fr. *rede* reed + *sparowe* sparrow — more at REED, SPARROW] **:** REED BUNTING

reed stop *n* **:** a set of reed pipes in a pipe organ controlled by a single stop knob and constructed to be generally imitative of some orchestral instrument

reed thrush *n* **:** GREAT REED WARBLER

re·educate \(ˈ)rē+\ *vt* [*re-* + *educate*] **1 :** to train the physically disabled in the use of muscles in new functions or of prosthetic appliances in old functions in an effort to replace or restore lost competence ⟨~ the amputee⟩ **2 :** to cause to develop new attitudes or habits replacing others held to be undesirable or unsatisfactory usu. as the result of faulty training ⟨~ a delinquent⟩

re·education \(ˌ)rē+\ *n* [*reeducate* + *-ion*] **:** the act or process of reeducating **:** rehabilitative training ⟨~ for youthful offenders aimed at their restoration to society⟩

re·educative \(ˈ)rē+\ *adj* [*reeducate* + *-ive*] **:** having the purpose or power to reeducate

reed vole *n* **:** a large long-tailed Chinese vole (*Microtus fortis*) in color resembling the Norway rat

reed warbler *n* **:** a small chiefly European warbler (*Acrocephalus scirpaceus*) that is brown above and buffy white below, is often mistaken for the marsh warbler, and is usu. seen about reedbeds and other marshy areas; *broadly* **:** any of various birds of the genus *Acrocephalus* (as a great reed warbler or a marsh warbler)

reed wolf *n* **:** a jackal that inhabits reed beds of the Danube valley

reedwork \ˈ=,=\ *n* [¹*reed* + *work*] **:** the reed stops of a pipe organ — compare FLUEWORK

reed wren *n* **1 :** a reed warbler (*Acrocephalus scirpaceus*) **2 :** LONG-BILLED MARSH WREN

reedy \ˈrēdē, -di\ *adj* -ER/-EST [ME, fr. ¹*reed* + *-y*] **1 :** abounding in or covered with reeds ⟨~ marshes⟩ **2 :** made of or resembling reeds **:** long and slender like a reed ⟨thin ~ arms⟩ **:** FRAIL, WEAK **3 :** having the tone quality of a reed instrument ⟨~ music⟩ ⟨~ singing⟩ **4 :** showing reed marks ⟨~ cloth⟩

reed yellow *n* **:** CHALCEDONY YELLOW

¹reef \ˈrēf\ *n* -s [ME *riff*, fr. ON *rif*; prob. akin to OE *rāw* row — more at ROW] **1 :** a part of a sail that is taken in or let out by means of the reef points in order to regulate the size of the sail **:** a strip of sail set off by a reef band **2 :** the reduction in area of a sail by reefing

²reef \"\ *vb* -ED/-ING/-S *vt* **1 a :** to reduce the area of (a sail) by rolling or folding a portion at the head (as of a square sail) or at the foot (as of a fore-and-aft sail) and securing to the yard or spar with reef points **b :** to lower or bring inboard (a spar) wholly or partially ⟨~ the topmast⟩ **2 :** to move the floats of (a paddle wheel) toward the center so that they will not dip so deeply **3 :** to roll or fold up in the manner of a sail ⟨~ a parachute⟩ ~ *vi* **1 :** to reduce a sail by taking in a reef **2** *slang* **:** to pick a pocket esp. by drawing up the lining — **reef one's sails :** to reduce the scope of one's activities **:** curtail one's efforts **:** withdraw in part

³reef \"\ *n* -s [earlier *riff*, fr. D *rif*, prob. of Scand origin; akin to ON *rif* reef of a sail] **1 a (1) :** a chain or range of rocks or ridge of sand lying at or near the surface of the water; *esp* **:** one where there is not more than six fathoms at low water — see BARRIER REEF, CORAL REEF, FRINGING REEF, SAND REEF; compare BANK, SHOAL **(2) :** a hazardous obstruction to the achievement of an objective ⟨helped themselves over early financial ~s by working in the . . . store —W.F.Longgood⟩ **b :** a sedimentary rock or part thereof composed almost or exclusively of the remains of reef-building organisms **:** BIOHERM **2 a :** a deposit of ore **:** VEIN, LODE **b :** the barren rock and shale surrounding the diamondiferous rock in the diamond mines of southern Africa **3 :** REEF SPONGE

⁴reef \"\ *n* -s [ME *ref, reof* rough, scabby, fr. OE *hrēof* rough, scabby, leprous — more at DANDRUFF] *dial Brit* **:** an eruption on the skin **:** ITCH

reef·able \ˈrēfəbəl\ *adj* **:** that can be reefed

reef band *n* **:** a piece of canvas sewed across a sail to strengthen it at the eyelet holes for reef points

reef bass *n* **:** CHANNEL BASS

reef crab *n* **:** a small Australian crab (*Ozius truncatus*) that is a great nuisance in reef netting because of its entering the nets in great numbers and cutting them to escape

reef cringle *n* **:** one of the cringles on the leech of a sail at the end of a reef band through which a rope passes binding the edge of a reefed sail to the yard or spar

¹reef·er \ˈrēfə(r)\ *n* -s **1 a :** one that reefs **b :** MIDSHIPMAN **2 a :** a close-fitting usu. double-breasted jacket or short coat of thick cloth **b :** a woman's usu. princess style single-breasted or double-breasted coat with a collar

²reefer \"\ *n* -s [*reef* to roll up (i.e., a cigarette) + *-er*, n. suffix] **:** a cigarette containing the dried leaves and flowers of marijuana

³ree·fer \"\ *n* -s [by shortening & alter.] **1 :** REFRIGERATOR **2 :** a refrigerator car, truck, trailer, or ship

reef goose *n* **:** CANADA GOOSE

reef heron *n* **:** a white or slaty-blue heron (*Demigretta sacra*) of the coasts of southern Asia, Australia, and Oceania

reef jig *or* **reef jigger** *n* **:** a light tackle on a yard for stretching the reef band before reefing

reef knoll *n* **:** a mass of coralline limestone within a sedimentary series **:** a fossil coral or algal reef

reef knot *n* **:** a square knot used in tying reef points

reef–knot \ˈ=,=\ *vt* **:** to make a reef knot in

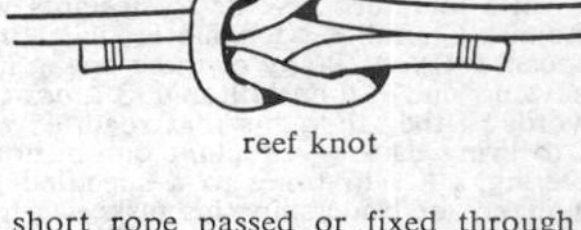

reef knot

reef line *n* **:** REEF POINT

reef netting *n* **:** fishing with a net suspended between two boats anchored off a reef

reef pendant *n* **:** a short rope passed or fixed through a reef cringle and used to fasten the clew to the boom or the leach to the reef tackle in reefing a sail

reef point *also* **reefing point** *n* **:** one of the pieces of small rope passing through the eyelet holes of a reef band and used in reefing the sail — called also *point*; see SAIL illustration

reefs *pl of* REEF, *pres 3d sing of* REEF

reef sponge *n* **:** a soft close-grained fine-textured West Indian commercial sponge (*Spongia obliqua*)

reef tackle *n* **:** a tackle by which the reef cringles of a square sail are hauled up and out to the yardarm to give slack for reefing — see SAIL illustration

reefy \ˈrēfē\ *adj* -ER/-EST [³*reef* + *-y*] **1 :** full of reefs or rocks **2 :** containing sedimentary material resembling that of a sedimentary reef

reeing *pres part of* REE

¹reek \ˈrēk\ *n* -s [ME *rek, reke*, fr. OE *rēc*; akin to OFris *rēk* smoke, OS *rōk*, OHG *rouh*, ON *reykr*, OE *rēocan* to reek] **1** *chiefly dial* **:** SMOKE **2 :** VAPOR, MIST, FOG ⟨the wettest imaginable blanket of sea ~ enveloped us —Osbert Sitwell⟩ **3 :** a strong or disagreeable fume or odor ⟨exuded the sharp, spiced ~ of tobacco —A.W.Turnbull⟩ ⟨the overpowering ~ of sewage⟩

²reek \"\ *vb* -ED/-ING/-S [ME *reken*, fr. OE *rēocan*; akin to OFris *rēka* to smoke, OHG *rouhhan* to smoke, smoke up, ON *rjūka* to smoke, steam] *vi* **1 :** to emit smoke or vapor ⟨a marsh ~*ing* in the sun⟩ **2 a :** to give off or become permeated with a strong often offensive odor ⟨horses that ~ with sweat⟩ ⟨a restaurant that ~s of garlic⟩ **b :** to give a strong impression of some constituent quality or feature **:** show permeation with a dominant quality or feature ⟨a mean building which ~*ed* of poverty —D.G.Gerahty⟩ ⟨historical best sellers ~ with sentiment —A.L.Guérard⟩ **3 :** EMANATE, ISSUE, RISE, FUME ⟨smoke which still away did ~ . . . from that eternal pyre —John Keats⟩ ⟨an atmosphere . . . which ~*ed* up from decayed trees —E.A.Poe⟩ ~ *vt* **1 :** to subject to the action of smoke or vapor **2 :** to give off as or as if a reek **:** EXHALE, EXUDE, VENT ⟨his manner ~s prosperity⟩ **syn** see EMIT

³reek \"\ *vt* -ED/-ING/-S [origin unknown] *Scot* **:** EQUIP, OUTFIT

⁴reek \"\ *n* -s [prob. alter. of ¹*rick*] *dial Brit* **:** HEAP, PILE

⁵reek \"\ *vt* -ED/-ING/-S *dial Brit* **:** to pile up **:** HEAP

⁶reek \"\ *Scot var of* REACH

reek·er \ˈrēkə(r)\ *n* -s **:** one that reeks

reek·ing·ly *adv* **:** in a reeking manner **:** with a reek

reeky \ˈrēkē\ *adj* -ER/-EST [ME *reky*, fr. *rek* reek + *-y*] **:** emitting or permeated with a reek **:** REEKING ⟨~ fen —Sir Walter Scott⟩

¹reel \ˈrēl, *esp before pause or consonant* ˈrēəl\ *n* -s *often attrib* [ME, fr. OE *hrēol*; akin to ON *hræll* weaver's sley, Latvian *krekls* shirt, Gk *krekein* to weave] **1 a** : a revolving device used in winding yarn or thread into hanks or skeins and in winding raw silk from cocoons and consisting usu. of a light frame with radial arms on a central axle **b** : any of various revolving devices (as a flanged cylinder) for winding up or paying out something flexible (as rope, wire, strip metal or plastic, hose) ⟨lamps that pull down from overhead tension ~*s*⟩ ⟨a surveyor's ~ containing a tape measure⟩ ⟨a garden hose ~ on wheels⟩ ⟨an industrial ~ for feeding coiled steel stock to a punch press⟩ **c** (1) : a flanged metal cylinder and crank attached to the butt of a fishing rod for winding up or letting out line (2) *chiefly Brit* : a spool or bobbin of wood to hold sewing thread ⟨a cotton ~⟩ (3) : a shaft or drum on which the full-width sheet coming from a papermaking machine is wound (4) : a flanged spool on which image-bearing motion-picture film or signal-bearing tape or wire is wound ⟨a standard ~ of 35 mm. film containing 1000 or 2000 feet⟩ **d** : a reel with its contents : the amount on a reel ⟨steel rope in ~*s* of 1800 feet⟩: as (1) WEB; *specif* : the part of a web in process of manufacture that has passed the driers of a paper machine (2) : a strip of image-bearing motion picture film (3) : a roll of postage stamps for use in a dispenser **2 a** : a rotating conveyer used in dyeing **b** : a frame carrying the bolting cloth or mesh wire screen used to sift ground grain (as wheat, corn) or to grade and size hulled rice **c** : the upright revolving wheel in a reel oven consisting of connected pairs of radial arms from which the trays holding the baking pans are suspended **d** : a revolving set of bars that feed grain stalks through a harvester **e** : the spiral blading of a lawn mower **f** : a clothes dryer consisting of lines on a frame of usu. radial arms revolving on a vertical pole **3** : a humming noise like that made by a moving reel ⟨a kingfisher . . . with his loud clicking ~ —John Burroughs⟩ — **off the reel** *adv* **1** : in straight succession : without interruption ⟨can sell 20 percent more cars right *off the reel* —*Time*⟩ **2** : without hesitation : as if reeled off : DIRECTLY ⟨write his impressions *off the reel*⟩

²**reel** \"\ *vb* -ED/-ING/-S [ME *reelen, relen*, fr. ¹*reel*] *vt* **1 a** : to wind (as yarn, thread, fishline) upon a reel **b** : to unwind (silk) from a cocoon onto a reel **c** : to roll up (as postage stamps) into a pack **2** : to draw by reeling a line ⟨~ a fish in⟩ **3** : to straighten (as pipe, rail, rod) by passing above two rolls and under a third ~ *vi* : to wind on a reel

³**reel** \"\ *vb* -ED/-ING/-S [ME *relen*, prob. fr. ¹*reel*] *vi* **1** : to turn or move round and round : WHIRL: **a** *of the eyes* : to roll with dizziness or excitement **b** : to be giddy : be in a whirl ⟨her head ~*ed* under the blow —Kathleen Freeman⟩ ⟨feats of heroism . . . so stupendous and so numerous that the mind ~*s* absorbing them —Douglas Stewart⟩ **2** : to behave in a violent disorderly manner : run riot ⟨the ~*ing* days of faction fights —Sean O'Faolain⟩ **3** : to waver or fall back from a blow ⟨~*s* under the impact⟩ ⟨a fierce attack that sent the enemy ~*ing*⟩ : RECOIL ⟨~*ed* back in horror⟩ **4 a** : to sway unsteadily on one's feet (as from dizziness or intoxication) ⟨~ down the street⟩ ⟨having no strap to hold to, she ~*ed* and staggered and pitched with every sudden start or jerking stop of the car —Clara Morris⟩ **b** : to move with great irregularity and unsteadiness (as of a ship in a storm, a building in an earthquake) **5** *dial* : to twist one's foot in walking ~ *vt* **1** : to cause to reel ⟨~ his partner in a dance⟩ **2** *obs* : to cause (as a stone) to roll **3** *obs* : to stagger through (a street)

⁴**reel** \"\ *n* -S **1** : a reeling motion **2** : TUMULT **3 reels** *pl, obs* : REVELS

⁵**reel** \"\ *n* -S **1 a** : a lively dance of the Scottish Highlanders marked by circular figures and performed with gliding movements **b** : music for or having the rhythm of this dance in moderately quick duple time **2** : VIRGINIA REEL **3** *dial* : a dance song

⁶**reel** \"\ *vi* -ED/-ING/-S : to dance a reel

⁷**reel** \"\ *n* -S [prob. fr. ³*reel*] : a paver's hammer of from 5 to 7 pounds in weight having rectangular ends and used for finishing small paving blocks

reel·able \'rēləbəl\ *adj* : capable of being wound on a reel

re·elect \¦rē+\ *vt* [*re-* + *elect*] : to elect for another term in office — **re·election** \"+\ *n*

reeled \'rē(ə)ld\ *adj* **1** : wound on a reel ⟨partly ~ cocoons⟩ **2** : disposed in a zigzag line : STAGGERED ⟨~ rivet holes⟩

reeled silk *n* : high quality raw silk reeled in one continuous filament from the cocoon directly into a skein — compare SPUN SILK

reel·er \'rēlə(r)\ *n* -S **1** : one that reels or works with a reel: as **a** : a worker who reels (as thread or yarn) by hand or by machine **b** : an instrument or machine for reeling **c** : a leather worker who uses a beam machine to transfer hides from one vat of solution to another **2** : a motion picture having a given number of reels ⟨a two-*reeler*⟩

reel foot *n, Scot* : CLUBFOOT

re·eligibility \(¦)rē+\ *n* : the quality or state of being re-eligible

re·eligible \(')rē+\ *adj* : capable of being reelected or reappointed to office

reeling *pres part of* REEL

reeling hammer *n* : ⁷REEL

reel·ing·ly *adv* : in a reeling manner : with a reeling motion

reel off *vt* [²*reel*] : to tell or recite fluently ⟨*reeled* off the story of his life⟩ ⟨*reeled* the figures *off* without hesitation⟩

reel oven *n* : an oven with a revolving wheel equipped with suspended trays holding food (as meat or bread) in the process of baking that is adjusted to bake the contents in one revolution of the wheel and is automatically controlled to stop when a tray is level with the loading door

¹**reel·rall** \'rēl,ral, -,räl\ *n* -S [prob. redupl. of ⁴*reel*] *Scot* : DISTURBANCE, FUSS

²**reelrall** \"\ *adv, dial Brit* : TOPSY-TURVY

reels *pl of* REEL, *pres 3d sing of* REEL

reel seat *n* : the part of a fishing rod butt upon which the reel is mounted

re·embodiment \¦rē+\ *n* **1** : the act or process of reembodying **2** : a person or thing that reembodies another

re·embody \"+\ *vt* : to embody again or anew : put in or into a new form : RESHAPE, REINCORPORATE, REORGANIZE

re·emerge \"+\ *vi* : to emerge again after concealment, retirement, suppression, quiescence — **re·emergence** \"+\ *n* — **re·emergent** \"+\ *adj*

reem·ing beetle \'rēmiŋ-\ *n* [*reeming* fr. (assumed) ME (dial.) *reming*, pres. part. of *remen* to open up, clear — more at REAM] : the largest mallet used by a calker

reeming iron *n* : a chisel for reaming the seams of planks in calking ships

re·emission \¦rē+\ *n* [*re-* + *emission*] : an act or process of emitting anew

re·emphasis \(')rē+\ *n* : an act or instance of reemphasizing

re·emphasize \"+\ *vt* : to emphasize again or anew; *specif* : to declare one's continued faith in (as a questioned doctrine)

re·employ \¦rē+\ *vt* : to hire back ⟨workers were ~*ed* after the layoff⟩ — **re·employment** \"+\ *n*

reen \'rēn, 'rān\ *var of* RHINE

re·enact \¦rē+\ *vt* [*re-* + *enact*] **1** : to enact (as a law) again **2** : to act or perform again ⟨the actor will ~ the role he made famous⟩ ⟨taken to the scene shortly after he confessed to ~ the crime —*Springfield (Mass.) Daily News*⟩ ⟨a land rush that ~*ed* on a minor scale scenes associated with the opening of the Cherokee Strip —*Amer. Guide Series: Ark.*⟩ — **re·enactment** \"+\ *n*

re·enforce \"+\ *var of* REINFORCE

re·engrave \"+\ *vt* [*re-* + *engrave*] : to cut decorative lines or patterns into (an etched halftone plate)

reengraving *n* [*re-* + *engraving*] : a reengraved plate

re·enlist \¦rē+\ *vb* : to enlist again ⟨found civilian life too hard and ~*ed* in the army⟩ ⟨~ the same volunteer help⟩

re·enlistment \"+\ *n* **1** : the act of reenlisting **2** : the term served in consequence of reenlisting **3** : a person who has reenlisted

re·enter \(')rē+\ *vb* [ME *reentren* fr. *re-* + *entren* to enter — more at ENTER] *vt* **1** : to enter again **2** : to cut (as engraved lines on a plate of metal) deeper ~ *vi* : to enter again

reentering angle *or* **reentrant angle** *n* : an angle pointing inward; *specif* : an angle in a line of troops or of fortifications with its apex turned away from the enemy — opposed to *salient angle*

reentering order of battle : a formation of attacking or rarely defending forces in lines converging away from the enemy that is feasible only when both flanks are protected against being turned or when they overlap the enemy's lines

re·entrance \(')rē+\ *n* **1** : REENTRY **2** *also* **re·en·tran·cy** \(')=¦en·trənsē\ -ES : the quality or state of being reentrant **3** : REENTERING ANGLE

¹**re·entrant** \(')rē+\ *adj* **1** : directed inward **2** : having its ends closed on itself ⟨~ armature winding⟩

²**reentrant** \"\ *n* **1** : one that reenters or is reentrant **2 a** : REENTERING ANGLE ⟨a ~ in a fortification⟩ **b** : an indentation between two salients in a horizontal plane ⟨a ~ in a coastline⟩

re·entry \(')rē+\ *n* [ME *reentre*, fr. *re-* + *entre* entry — more at ENTRY] **1** : a retaking possession; *esp* : entry by a lessor or grantor on premises leased or granted in exercise of a right reserved on the tenant's failure to perform the covenants or conditions of the lease, grant, or other conveyance **2** : a second or new entry ⟨a ~ into public life⟩ ⟨granted a ~ permit by the consulate⟩ **3 a** : a regaining of the right to lead by winning a trick in bridge **b** : a playing card that will win a trick in the hand of a player who has previously had the right to lead **4** : a double impression on a line-engraved stamp produced in the transfer of the design to the printing plate; *also* : DOUBLE TRANSFER **5** : the action of reentering the earth's atmosphere after traveling into space — used of a missile or vehicle ⟨a nose cone, or ~ body, that would not burn up like a meteor when it plunged back into the atmosphere —Clay Blair⟩

ree·per \'rēpə(r)\ *n* -S [Marathi *rip*] : a strip of wood used in India as a batten or a lath

re·equip \¦rē+\ *vt* [*re-* + *equip*] : to equip again

rees *pres 3d sing of* REE, *pl of* REE

ree·shle \'rēshəl\ *or* **ree·sle** \'rēsəl\ *chiefly Scot var of* RUSTLE

¹**reest** \'rēst, 'rāst\ *adj* [ME *reest, rest*, alter. of *resty* — more at REASTY] *dial* : REASTY

²**reest** \'rēst\ *vt* -ED/-ING/-S [origin unknown] *Scot* : to cure (as meat) by smoking

³**reest** \"\ *vi* -ED/-ING/-S [prob. short for E dial. (Sc) *arreest* to arrest, fr. ME (Sc) *arreisten*, fr. MF *arester* — more at ARREST] *chiefly Scot, of a horse* : BALK

⁴**reest** \"\ *dial var of* REST

re·establish \¦rē+\ *vt* [*re-* + *establish*] **1** : to establish again in or to a former place, position, or state : set up, fix, or confirm again : RESTORE ⟨~ the air base closed after the war⟩ ⟨a campaign to ~ orthodoxy in the school⟩ **2** : to establish anew in a different place, position, or state : REFOUND, RESETTLE ⟨~ the flooded town on a higher site⟩ ⟨~ the refugees uprooted by war in new homes⟩ — **re·establishment** \"+\ *n*

re·esterification \¦rē+\ *n* [*re-* + *esterification*] : TRANSESTERIFICATION

rees·ty \'rēsti, 'rās-\ *var of* REASTY

reet \'rēt\ *chiefly dial var of* RIGHT

re·etch \(')rē+\ *vt* : to etch again (as a lithographic stone in continuation of a partial etching) : touch up (a plate) with a brush dipped in acid — **re·etcher** \"+\ *n*

re·evaluate \¦rē+\ *vt* [*re-* + *evaluate*] : to evaluate again ⟨forcing one to reexamine and ~ its merits —R.H.Popkin⟩

re·evaluation \"+\ *n* [*re-* + *evaluation*] : the act or result of evaluating again ⟨remarks . . . meant to stimulate a ~ of present-day procedure —*Long Island Med. Jour.*⟩

re·evaporation \"+\ *n* : evaporation a second time; *specif* : evaporation in a steam engine of the moisture from condensation due to the steam temperature falling below that of the cylinder walls in expansion

¹**reeve** \'rēv\ *n* -S [ME *reve, ireve*, fr. OE *gerēfa*, fr. *ge-* (perfective, associative, and collective prefix) + *-rēfa* (fr. OE *-rōf* number, array); akin to OHG *ruova* number, array — more at CO-] **1** : a local administrative agent of the king in Anglo-Saxon times having a position and function similar to that of the bailiff under the Norman kings ⟨away from court, the king's estates were managed by resident ~*s*, who also collected the dues which the king's subjects owed —R.F.Treharne⟩ — see PORTREEVE; compare SHERIFF **2** : an officer on a medieval English manor orig. chosen by the villeins to represent their interests but later becoming the lord's agent associated with the bailiff and responsible for maintaining order and overseeing the discharge of feudal obligations (as rents) **3 a** : the chief magistrate of a town; *specif* : the president of the council in rural municipalities and in some villages in central and western Canada **b** : an official charged with the enforcement of local regulations in various English and American communities ⟨field ~⟩ ⟨deer ~⟩ — see HOGREEVE; compare WARDEN

²**reeve** \"\ *vb* **rove** \'rōv\ *or* **reeved; rove** *or* **reeved; reeving; reeves** [origin unknown] *vt* **1 a** : to pass (as the end of a rope) through a hole or opening in a block, thimble, cleat, ringbolt, cringle, or similar device **b** : to fasten by passing through a hole or around something — usu. used with *on, about, to, around, over* ⟨they *rove* a rope over the yard⟩ **c** : to pass a rope through ⟨~ a block⟩ **2** : to pass cautiously through : THREAD ⟨the ship *reeved* the shoals⟩ ~ *vi, of a rope* : to pass through a block or similar device ⟨two strong lines *reeving* through ringbolts on the deck head —Peter Heaton⟩

³**reeve** \"\ *n* -S [prob. alter. of *ruff*] : the female of the ruff

reeve·land *also* **reve·land** \'rēv,land\ *n* [OE *gerēfland*, fr. *gerēfa* reeve + *land* — more at LAND] : land having reverted to the king and not being granted to tenants but placed in charge of a reeve

reeves's pheasant \'rēvz(əz)-\ *n, usu cap R* [prob. after the name *Reeves*] : a pheasant (*Syrmaticus reevesii*) native to China having in the male plumage that is largely buffy with dark edgings on the feathers, black collar, white nape and throat, and black belly and having a white head with a dark facial band and a very long tail

reeving line bend *n* : a bend for joining two lines without making a bulky knot so that they will reeve through an opening

re·evoke \¦rē+\ *vt* : to evoke again; *specif* : to recall to life or to the imagination

ree wheatgrass \'rē-\ *n* [*ree* prob. fr. ³*ree*] : INTERMEDIATE WHEATGRASS

re·examination \"+\ *n* : a second or new examination; *esp* : an examination made by a party calling a witness after and upon matters arising out of the cross-examination : REDIRECT EXAMINATION

re·examine \"+\ *vt* : to subject to reexamination — **re·examiner** \"+\ *n*

re·exchange \"+\ *n* **1** : a renewed or second exchange **2 a** : the process by which is recovered the expense chargeable on a bill of exchange or draft which has been dishonored in a foreign country and returned to the country in which it was made or endorsed to be there taken up **b** : the draft so drawn or the expense or percentage included in it

¹**re·export** \(¦)rē+\ *vt* : to export again (something imported) — **re·exportation** \"+\ *n* — **re·exporter** \"+\ *n*

²**re·export** \(')rē+\ *n* **1** : the act of reexporting **2** : a reexported commodity

re·extent \¦rē+\ *n* : a second extent or execution made in old English law on complaint that a former one was wrong

¹**ref** \'ref\ *n* -S [short for *referee*] : the referee of a game or sport

²**ref** \"\ *vb* **reffed; reffed; reffing; refs** : REFEREE

ref *abbr* **1** referee **2** reference **3** referred **4** refinery; refining **5** reformation; reformed; reformer **6** refrain **7** refrigeration; refrigerator **8** refunding

re·face \(')rē+\ *vt* [*re-* + *face*] **1** : to supply with a new front : renew the front or appearance of ⟨~ a church⟩ **2** : to renew a faced surface on (as the end of a cylindrical piece) by re-cutting or regrinding

refacimento *var of* RIFACIMENTO

refaction *n* -S [F *réfaction* rebate, repairs, fr. *refaire* to remake, do over again, repair, after such pairs as F *satisfaire* to satisfy (fr. L *satisfacere*) : *satisfaction* (fr. L *satisfaction-, satisfactio*)] *obs* : RECOMPENSE

re·fait \rə'fā\ *n* -S [F, fr. *refait*, past part. of *refaire* to remake, do over again, repair, deal (cards) over again, fr. OF, to remake, do over again, repair, fr. *re-* + *faire* to make, do, fr. L *facere* — more at DO] : a drawn or inconclusive game or coup in the game of trente-et-quarante requiring a new deal or turn to effect a decision

re·fall \(')rē+\ *vi* [*re-* + *fall*] *archaic* : to fall again : fall repeatedly

re·fashion \(')rē+\ *vt* [*re-* + *fashion*] : to make again : make over : ALTER ⟨spiritual enthusiasm which ~*ed* the forms of religious devotion in the twelfth century —R.W.Southern⟩ — **re·fashioner** \"+\ *n*

re·fasten \"+\ *vt* [*re-* + *fasten*] : to fasten again ⟨nervously unfastening and ~*ing* her glove⟩

refd *abbr* **1** referred **2** reformed

re·fect \rə'fekt, rē'-\ *vt* -ED/-ING/-S [L *refectus*, past part. of *reficere* to remake, renew, restore] *archaic* : to restore after hunger or fatigue : refresh with food or drink

re·fect·ed \-təd\ *adj* [fr. *refection*, after such pairs as E *correction: corrected*] : in a state of refection ⟨~ rats⟩

re·fec·tion \rə'fekshən, rē'-\ *n* -S [ME *refeccioun*, fr. MF *refection*, fr. L *refection-, refectio* refreshment, repairing, fr. *refectus* (past part. of *reficere* to remake, renew, restore, fr. *re-* + *facere* to make, do) + *-ion-, -io* -ion] **1** : refreshment of mind, spirit, or body esp. after hunger or fatigue : NOURISHMENT, RELIEF **2 a** : the taking of refreshment : satisfaction of hunger and thirst **b** : food and drink : REPAST **3 a** : the eating of feces esp. by the animal producing them **b** : spontaneous recovery of vitamin-depleted animals on a high starch diet presumably resulting from consumption of feces enriched with vitamins synthesized by intestinal bacteria

re·fec·tion·er \-sh(ə)nə(r)\ *n* -S : REFECTORIAN

refection sunday *n, usu cap R&S* [prob. so called because the gospel for the day relates the miracle of feeding the five thousand (Jn 6: 1-14)] : MID-LENT SUNDAY

re·fec·tive \-tiv\ *adj* [*refect* + *-ive*] **1** : REFRESHING, RESTORING **2** : designed to induce refection ⟨a ~ diet⟩

re·fec·to·rar·i·an \rə,fektə'ra(a)rēən\ *n* -S [ML *refectorarius* refectorian (fr. LL *refectorium* refectory + L *-arius* -ary) + E *-an*] : REFECTORIAN

re·fec·to·rer \rə'fektərə(r)\ *n* -S [*refectory* + *-er*] : REFECTORIAN

re·fec·to·ri·al \¦rē,fek¦tōrēəl\ *adj* [*refectory* + *-al*] : of, relating to, or used for refection

re·fec·to·ri·an \,rē,fek'tōrēən\ *n* -S [*refectory* + *-an*] : one in charge of a refectory or of refections — called also *refectioner*

re·fec·to·ry \rə'fekt(ə)rē, rē'f-\ *n* -ES [LL *refectorium*, fr. L *refectus* (past part. of *reficere* to remake, renew, restore) + *-orium* -ory] : a dining hall; *esp* : a dining hall in a monastery, convent, or religious college

refectory table *n* : a long narrow table with heavy legs and long heavy stretcher

refectory table

refel *vt* **refelled; refelled; refelling; refels** [L *refellere* to refute, disprove, fr. *re-* + *fallere* to deceive — more at FAIL] **1** *obs* : REFUTE, DISPROVE, DISCREDIT **2** *obs* : REJECT, REPULSE

re·fer *R* rə'fər, rē'f-, + *vowel* -fər·; *-R* -fə, + *suffixal vowel* -fər· *also* -fər, + *vowel in a following word* -fər· *or* -fə *also* -fər\ *vb* **referred; referred; referring; refers** [ME *referren, referen*, fr. L *referre*, lit., to carry back, fr. *re-* + *ferre* to carry — more at BEAR] *vt* **1 a** : to think of, regard, or classify under a subsuming principle or with a general group : explain in terms of a general cause ⟨the Anthocerotes cannot certainly be *referred* to this common stock —D.H.Campbell⟩ ⟨*referred* the dearth to the Civil War —Katharine F. Gerould⟩ **b** : to allot to a particular place, stage, or period ⟨legend *refers* the tying of knots in strings to about 2800 B.C. —Edward Clodd⟩ **c** : to regard as coming from or localized in a certain portion of the body or of space ⟨visual sensations are *referred* to external space⟩ ⟨the pain of appendicitis may be *referred* to any region of the abdomen —*Encyc. Americana*⟩ **2 a** : to send or direct for treatment, aid, information, decision ⟨~ a student to a dictionary⟩ ⟨~ a bill to a committee⟩ ⟨~ a patient to a specialist⟩ **b** : to direct for testimony or guaranty as to one's character or ability ⟨~ an office to a former employer⟩ **3** *obs* : to reserve for subsequent discussion : DEFER **4** *obs* : to submit or entrust (oneself) for aid or advice ~ *vi* **1** *obs* : RECUR, RETURN **2 a** : to have relation or logical or factual connection : POINT, RELATE ⟨the superscript numerals ~ to notes at the foot of the page⟩ ⟨red pepper may ~ to cayenne —J.W. Parry⟩ **b** : to direct attention : ALLUDE ⟨his remarks *referred* only indirectly to the opposing party⟩ ⟨for *referring* to these familiar facts the excuse is made —Herbert Spencer⟩ **3** : to have recourse : APPLY, APPEAL ⟨pausing frequently in his speech to ~ to his notes⟩ ⟨*referred* to his watch and hurried away⟩ **syn** see ASCRIBE

refer·able \'ref(ə)rəbəl, rə'fər·əb- rē'f- *also* -'fərəb-\ *adj* [*refer* + *-able*] : capable of being considered in relation to something else : ASSIGNABLE, ASCRIBABLE ⟨decide to which of these motives such extraordinary scenes were ~ —Charles Dickens⟩ ⟨in head injuries . . . persistent symptoms ~ to trauma should be carefully considered —H.G.Armstrong⟩ ⟨such differences are ~ to the particular environments within which the members of various societies are reared —Ralph Linton⟩

¹**ref·er·ee** \,refə¦rē, (')re¦frē\ *n* -S [*refer* + *-ee*] **1** : one to whom a thing is referred: as **a** : a person to whom a matter (as a private bill) is referred by parliament to examine and report upon **b** (1) : a person orig. in equity practice a master to whom a matter in dispute has been referred that he may settle it (2) : an attorney at law appointed to act as an officer of the court in determining or reporting on an issue referred to him in a pending proceeding or suit with or without the consent of the parties — distinguished from *arbitrator* (3) : a qualified person appointed by a judge in a juvenile or domestic relations case to investigate and report the facts and often to make recommendations **2** : an official in a sports contest usu. having final authority for administering the game — compare UMPIRE **3** *Brit* : REFERENCE 5a

²**referee** \"\ *vb* **refereed; refereed; refereeing; referees** *vt* **1** : to administer (as a match, a game) as referee **2** : to arbitrate (a dispute) as a judge or third party ~ *vi* : to act as referee ⟨the teacher . . . ~*ing* in the rain on Saturday morning —*Scots Mag.*⟩

¹**ref·er·ence** \'refərn(t)s, -f(ə)rən-\ *n* -S [*refer* + *-ence*] **1** : the act of referring ⟨~ to a map will make the position clear⟩ or consulting ⟨~ to an almanac⟩ ⟨items arranged alphabetically for ease of ~⟩ ⟨a manual designed for ready ~⟩ ⟨the report was filed for future ~⟩ **2** : the act of referring a matter in dispute to a referee **3** : the capability or character of alluding to or bearing on or directing attention to something : RELATION, RESPECT ⟨with ~ to his suggestion⟩ ⟨in ~ to your letter of the 14th⟩ **4** : something that refers to something else: as **a** : ALLUSION, MENTION ⟨omitted all ~ to his prison record⟩ ⟨the play is full of ~*s* to contemporary events⟩ **b** : a specific direction of the attention : a sign or indication referring a reader to another passage or book ⟨a list of ~*s* is appended⟩ **c** : consultation of sources of information ⟨books more suitable for ~ than for reading⟩ ⟨volumes for ready ~⟩ **d** : TAB 1a(4) **5** : one that is referred to or consulted: as **a** : a person of whom inquiries can be made as to the character or capacity of another **b** : a written statement of the qualifications of a person seeking employment or appointment given by his previous employer or by someone familiar with his character, ability, experience, or training : RECOMMENDATION ⟨three ~*s* must accompany each application⟩ **c** : a book or a passage in a work to which a reader is referred **d** : DENOTATION, MEANING **6** : the direction of others' attention or behavior to one's self ⟨delusions of ~⟩ — see IDEAS OF REFERENCE

²**reference** \"\ *vt* -ED/-ING/-S **1** : to supply with references ⟨the work is fully *referenced*⟩ **2** : to put in a form (as a table, list) adapted to easy reference

³**reference** \"\ *adj* : used or usable for reference : taken or laid down as standard for measuring, reckoning, or constructing ⟨~ point⟩ ⟨~ plane⟩; *specif* : of known potency and used as a standard in the biological assay of a sample of the same drug of unknown strength

reference book *n* **1** : a book (as a dictionary, encyclopedia, atlas) intended primarily for consultation rather than for consecutive reading **2** : a library book that may be used on the premises but may not be taken out

reference frame *n* : FRAME OF REFERENCE

reference gage *n* : MASTER GAGE

reference group *n, sociol* **:** a group toward whose interests, attitudes, and values the individual is oriented
reference library *n* **1 :** a collection of books often about a particular subject useful for consultation ⟨a *reference library* of science⟩ **2 :** a library the books of which may be used on the premises but may not be taken out
reference line *n* **:** an arbitrary fixed line (as an x-axis or a polar axis) from which coordinates of a point are computed
reference mark *n* **:** a conventional mark (as *, †, ‡, §, ‖, ¶, ☞) or a superior figure or letter placed in a text for directing attention to a footnote or a key on the same or another page — see respectively ASTERISK, DAGGER, DOUBLE DAGGER, SECTION, PARALLEL, PARAGRAPH, INDEX
ref·er·en·dal \ˌrefəˈrendᵊl\ *adj* [*referendum* + *-al*] **:** REFERENDARY
[1]**ref·er·en·da·ry** \ˌrefəˈrendərē\ *n* -ES [LL *referendarius*, fr. L *referendus* to be referred (gerundive of *referre* to refer) + *-arius* -ary] **1 :** an official at various imperial, papal, and royal courts charged with investigative or advisory duties — used as a title **2 :** REFEREE, ARBITRATOR **3** *obs* **:** one who furnishes news **:** REPORTER
[2]**referendary** \ˌ≈≈ˈ≈≈≈\ *adj* [*referendum* + *-ary*] **:** of or relating to a referendum
ref·er·en·dum \ˌrefəˈrendəm\ *n, pl* **referen·da** \-də\ *or* **referendums** \-dəmz\ [L, neut. of *referendus* to be referred, gerundive of *referre* to refer — more at REFER] **1 a :** the principle or practice of submitting to popular vote a measure passed upon or proposed by a legislative body or by popular initiative **b :** a vote on a measure so submitted **c :** a similar practice or method for ascertaining the will of members of an organized group (as a union, club, faculty) **:** POLL **2 :** a diplomatic agent's note asking his government for instructions
[1]**refer·ent** \rəˈfərənt, rēˈf-, ˈref(ə)rənt\ *n* -S [L *referent-, referens*, pres. part. of *referre*] **1 :** someone that is referred to or consulted **2 a :** a word or a term that refers to another **b** *logic* **:** the term (as *a* in the proposition *a* has the relation R to *b*) from which a relation proceeds **:** the first term of a relation (as *a* in R*a, b, c*) — compare RELATUM **3 :** that which is denoted or named by an expression or a statement **:** a spatiotemporal object or event to which a term, sign, or symbol refers **:** the object of a reference
[2]**referent** \"\ *adj* [L *referent-, referens*, pres. part. of *referre*] **:** that refers **:** having reference ⟨judgments ∼ to the entirety of life —L.T.Hobhouse⟩ — **refer·ent·ly** *adv*
ref·er·en·tial \ˌrefəˈrenchəl\ *adj* [fr. [1]*reference*, after such pairs as E *difference*: *differential*] **1 :** containing or constituting a reference **:** pointing to something out of itself ⟨symbols are inherently ∼⟩ ⟨∼ rather than emotive use of words⟩ **2 :** of, relating to, or intended for reference ⟨notes for ∼ use⟩ — **ref·er·en·tial·ly** \-chəlē\ *adv*
re·fer·ral \rəˈfərəl, rēˈf- *also* -ˈfərəl\ *n* -S [*refer* + *-al*] **1 :** the act of referring: as **a :** the passing along or forwarding of an applicant for employment after an initial interview to a selected employer, placement officer, or bureau **b :** the process of directing or redirecting (as a medical case, a patient) to an appropriate specialist or agency for definitive treatment **2 a :** one that is referred ⟨50 percent of its ∼*s* are turned down at the plant —*Survey Graphic*⟩ **b :** an instance or case of referring ⟨need to make ∼*s* to family agencies more frequently —Bernard Kogon⟩
referred *past of* REFER
referred pain *n* **:** a pain subjectively localized in one region though due to irritation in another region
re·fer·rer \rəˈfərə(r), rēˈf-, *-R also* -ˈfərə(r\ *n* -S [*refer* + *-er*] **:** one that refers
re·fer·ri·ble \rəˈfərəbəl, rēˈf- *also* -ˈfərəb-\ *adj* [*refer* + *-able*] **:** REFERABLE
referring *pres part of* REFER
refers *pres 3d sing of* REFER
reff *abbr* references
reffed *past of* REF
reffing *pres part of* REF
ref·fo \ˈre(ˌ)fō\ *n* -S [*ref-* (fr. *refugee*) +*-o*] *Austral* **:** a refugee from Europe
refg *abbr* refrigerating; refrigerator
re·fight \(ˈ)rē+\ *vt* [*re-* + *fight*] **:** to fight over again (as in imagination) ⟨spent every Saturday ∼*ing* the Revolution — visiting homes, battlefields, museums, forts —Dorothy Barclay⟩
re·figure \"+\ *vt* [*re-* + *figure*] **:** to figure again
[1]**re·fill** \"+\ *vb* [*re-* + *fill*] *vt* **:** to fill again **:** REPLENISH ∼ *vi* **:** to become filled again
[2]**re·fill** \ˈrē+ˌ-\ *n* **1 :** a commercial product designed to fill again a container with its appropriate contents ⟨∼ for a vanity case⟩ ⟨a loose-leaf notebook ∼⟩ **2** *med* **:** a replacement in a cavity of removed liquid or other material or a substitution (as of gas) for such material ⟨pneumothorax ∼⟩ **3 :** a prescription compounded and dispensed for the second time without an order from the physician **4 :** a second serving of food or drink
re·fill·able \(ˈ)rēˈfiləbəl\ *adj* **:** capable of being refilled ⟨∼ prescription⟩ ⟨∼ notebook⟩
re·film \(ˈ)rē+\ *vt* [*re-* + *film*] **:** to film again
re·filter \(ˈ)rē+\ *vt* [*re-* + *filter*] **:** to filter again
re·finance \(ˈ)rē+\ *vt* [*re-* + *finance*] **:** to renew or reorganize the financing of **:** provide capital for afresh **:** provide for (an outstanding indebtedness) by making another loan or a larger loan on fresh terms
re·find \(ˈ)rē+\ *vt* [*re-* + *find*] **:** to find again **:** REDISCOVER, RECOVER
[1]**re·fine** \rəˈfīn, rēˈf-\ *vb* -ED/-ING/-S [*re-* + *fine* (to refine)] *vt* **1 :** to reduce to a fine, unmixed, or pure state **:** separate from extraneous matter **:** free from dross or alloy ⟨∼ silver⟩ **:** free or cleanse from impurities ⟨∼ sugar⟩ **2 a** (1) **:** to give a final mechanical treatment to (paper stock) so as to put in the best possible condition for the grade of paper being made (2) **:** to prepare (pulp screenings) for manufacture into coarse paper **b :** to treat (pig iron) in the refinery furnace so as to remove the silicon and other unwanted elements **c :** to manufacture (petroleum products) by distilling crude petroleum and purifying the resulting successive distillates **d :** to subject (raw sugar) to a series of processes (as defecation or carbonation, filtration through bone black or activated carbon, and crystallization) to produce white sugar **3 :** to free (as the mind or soul) from moral imperfection, grossness, dullness, earthiness **:** SPIRITUALIZE, ELEVATE ⟨tried in sharp tribulation and *refined* by faith and faithful works —John Milton⟩ **4 :** to improve or perfect by pruning, polishing, or rarefying ⟨∼ a poetic style⟩ ⟨the imagination cannot escape from the literal but at best can only ∼ it —Bernard DeVoto⟩ **5 :** to attenuate or reduce in vigor, intensity, vitality by pruning, polishing, or purifying ⟨much of the really nutritive material actually was *refined* out of the foods —W.H.Camp⟩ **6 :** to increase or heighten the discriminatory power of **:** SUBTILIZE ⟨∼ a method of analysis⟩ ⟨spent . . . years patiently *refining* the crude statistics of economic change —*Times Lit. Supp.*⟩ **7 :** to free from what is coarse, vulgar, uncouth **:** cause to become fastidious, elegant, cultivated ⟨sent to a finishing school to ∼ her taste and manners⟩ ∼ *vi* **1 :** to become pure or perfected **:** become free or freer from what is extraneous or crude or debasing **2 :** to make improvement by adding or introducing subtleties or distinctions — used with *on* or *upon* ⟨the earlier science had only *refined* upon the ordinary notions of ordinary people —A.N.Whitehead⟩
[2]**refine** *adj, obs* **:** REFINED
re·fined \-nd\ *adj* **1 :** free from impurities ⟨to gild ∼ gold, to paint the lily —Shak.⟩ **2 :** FASTIDIOUS, CULTIVATED, HIGHBRED ⟨she spoke in a painfully ∼ accent⟩ ⟨sensitive, ∼ face⟩ ⟨belief that the function of music is to cause a ∼ sort of sensuous pleasure —Susanne K. Langer⟩ **3 :** marked by subtlety of discrimination or precision of method or technique **:** carried to a fine point **:** PRECISE, EXACT ⟨drawn out with that ∼ analysis of terms which I always find a waste of time —H.J.Laski⟩ ⟨men learned the necessity of exact measurement and ∼ calculations —J.H.Randall⟩ — **re·fined·ly** \-n(ə)dlē\ *adv* — **re·fined·ness** \-nədnəs, -n(d)nəs\ *n* -ES
refined madder *n* **:** FLOWERS OF MADDER
refined wool fat *n* **:** LANOLIN b
re·fine·ment \rəˈfīnmənt, rēˈf-\ *n* -S **1 :** the action or process of refining ⟨∼ of metals⟩ ⟨∼ of torture⟩ ⟨∼ of measuring techniques⟩ **2 :** the quality or state of being refined **:** CULTIVATION, ELEGANCE, POLISH ⟨always comparing immigrant vitality with native ∼ —M.D.Geismar⟩ ⟨sniffed with exquisite ∼ —Elinor Wylie⟩ **3 a :** something that is the product or outcome of a refining process or that conduces to refining **:** a refined feature or method ⟨pursued the delicate art of suggestion to its furthest ∼*s* —Maurice Bowra⟩ **b :** subtlety in reasoning ⟨∼*s* of logic⟩ ⟨∼ is what characterizes our intellectualist philosophies —William James⟩ **c :** a contrivance, device, or feature intended to improve or perfect ⟨introduce ∼*s* into a machine⟩ ⟨this ∼ will increase the cost of the automobile⟩ **d :** a slight departure from mechanical exactness or uniformity of line intended to enhance the beauty of a building or overcome undesirable optical effects
re·fin·er \-īnə(r)\ *n* -S **:** one that refines: as **a :** one whose work is refining a specified thing ⟨lard ∼⟩ ⟨oil ∼⟩ **b :** a machine that gives the final mechanical treatment to paper stock
re·fin·er·man \-mən, -ˌman\ *n, pl* **refinermen :** a millman who refines reclaimed rubber
refiners' sirup *n* **:** the residual liquid product obtained in the process of refining raw sugars
re·fin·ery \rəˈfīn(ə)rē, rēˈf-, -ri\ *n* -ES **:** a building and equipment for refining or purifying metals, oil, or sugar; *specif* **:** a furnace with a shallow hearth for refining pig iron to wrought iron or to iron suitable for puddling
re·finger \(ˈ)rē+\ *vt* [*re-* + *finger*] **:** to alter or replace the fingering of (a musical passage)
refining *n* -S **:** the action or process of removing impurities from a crude or impure material: as **a** *of metals* **:** subjection to high heat or other purification methods (as electrolysis or treatment with chemicals) ⟨fire ∼ of copper⟩ — compare PARTING **b** *of glass* **:** FINING 1b **c** *of sugar* **:** processing in a series of steps ending with crystallization **d** *of petroleum* **:** fractional distillation usu. followed by other processing (as cracking)
refining engine *n* **:** REFINER b
re·finish \(ˈ)rē+\ *vt* [*re-* + *finish*] **:** to give (as furniture) a new surface
re·finisher \"+\ *n* **:** one that refinishes furniture
[1]**re·fit** \(ˈ)rē+\ *vb* [*re-* + *fit*] *vt* **:** to prepare for use again **:** fit out or supply again **:** restore after damage or decay ⟨∼ a ship⟩ ∼ *vi* **:** to get refitted **:** obtain repairs or fresh supplies or equipment ⟨the fleet returned to ∼⟩
[2]**re·fit** \ˈrē+ˌ-, ≈ˈ≈\ *n* **:** a refitting or fitting out again **:** a repairing of damages or replacing of what is worn or useless; *esp* **:** a refitting and renovating of a ship ⟨assisting with ∼*s* of other submarines as they came and went —E.L.Beach⟩
re·fit·ment \(ˈ)rēˈfitmənt\ *n* **:** REFIT
re·fix \(ˈ)rē+\ *vt* [*re-* + *fix*] **:** to fix again **:** set up again **:** attach again or in a new place
re·fixture \"+\ *vt* [*re-* + *fixture*] **:** to renew or replace the fixtures of (as a store, an office)
refl *abbr* **1** reflection; reflective; reflectively; reflector **2** reflex; reflexive
re·flash \(ˈ)rē+\ *n* [*re-* + *flash*] **:** a rekindling and bursting into flame ⟨prevent possible ∼ by cooling the hot surface and any glowing material —*Training Manual for Auxiliary Firemen*⟩
re·flate \rəˈflāt, rēˈf-\ *vb* -ED/-ING/-S [back-formation fr. *reflation*] *vi* **:** to expand again the quantity of currency and credit after a period of deflation ∼ *vt* **:** to expand again the amount of (currency and credit)
re·fla·tion \-āshən\ *n* -S [*re-* + *-flation* (as in *inflation*)] **:** restoration of deflated prices to a desirable level by the use of monetary powers
[1]**re·flect** \rəˈflekt, rēˈf-\ *vb* -ED/-ING/-S [ME *reflecten*, fr. L *reflectere*, fr. *re-* + *flectere* to bend, turn] *vt* **1** *archaic* **:** to turn into or away from a certain course **:** turn aside **:** DEFLECT, DIVERT **2 a :** to turn, throw, or bend off or backward at an angle ⟨light ∼*ed* from the moon⟩ ⟨heat ∼*ed* by the light surface⟩ **b :** to cast back **:** cause to rebound or reverberate **:** to project out ⟨his internal stresses ∼*ed* a dry bitterness upon the world —H.G.Wells⟩ ⟨new music . . . ∼*s* just as much emotion as any other kind of music —Aaron Copland⟩ **3 a :** to bend or fold back **:** impart a backward curve, bend, or fold to **:** make retrorse in form ⟨petals ∼*ed* at the tops⟩ **b :** to push or lay aside (as tissue, an organ) during surgery in order to gain access to the part to be operated on **4 :** to give back or exhibit as an image, likeness, or outline **:** reproduce or show as a mirror does ⟨the trees on the shore line were ∼*ed* in the clear water⟩ ⟨dignity was ∼*ed* in her vivid blue eyes —Ellen Glasgow⟩ ⟨this body, with full power to enact laws, more truly ∼*ed* the popular will —*Amer. Guide Series: Pa.*⟩ **5 :** to bring or cast as a result **:** bring about as an attribute, characterization, designation ⟨his attitude would ∼ little credit on his political judgment —W.H.Chamberlin⟩ **6 :** to make manifest or apparent as a likely cause, plausible conditioning factor, fitting background element, or concomitant **:** SHOW ⟨the influence of the lumbering period is ∼*ed* in Bay City's many large frame dwellings —*Amer. Guide Series: Mich.*⟩ ⟨the pulse generally ∼*s* the condition of the heart —Morris Fishbein⟩ ⟨the structure of the compound sentence often ∼*s* a simple artlessness —R.M.Weaver⟩ **7 :** to remember with thoughtful consideration **:** come to recollect, realize, or consider in a course of thought — used with a following clause ⟨Blake's poetry . . . told me that he must be an Irishman before ever I ∼*ed* that his name was Irish —A.T.Quiller-Couch⟩ ∼ *vi* **1** *obs* **a :** to become turned or thrown back **:** REBOUND ⟨the sun darts forth his rays at right angles which ∼ back upon themselves —Nathanael Carpenter⟩ **b :** to cast light **:** SHINE ⟨whose virtues will, I hope, ∼ on Rome, as Titan's rays on earth —Shak.⟩ **2 :** to throw back light or sound **:** return rays, beams, or waves **3 :** to think and consider esp. after the immediate event **:** think quietly and calmly **:** RECONSIDER ⟨∼ on the role of philosophy in a liberal civilization —M.R.Cohen⟩ **4** *obs* **:** to bounce back **:** spring back after impact **:** RECOIL **5 a :** to tend to bring reproach **:** cast or bring censure, discredit, reproach, doubt, or suspicion ⟨the investigation ∼*s* on the integrity of the officials involved⟩ ⟨did not ∼ on the general's character in his speech⟩ **b :** to have a bearing or influence ⟨the steel strike naturally ∼*ed* in the sale of plastics⟩ **6 :** to become mirrored **:** produce a mirrored image ⟨clouds ∼*ing* on the lake⟩ **syn** see THINK — **reflect in a plane :** to construct a figure each of whose points P' is related with a corresponding point P of a given figure in such a way that the line joining P and P' is bisected perpendicularly by the plane
[2]**reflect** *n* -S *obs* **:** REFLECTION
re·flec·tance \-tən(t)s\ *n* -S **:** the fraction of the total luminous flux incident upon a surface that is reflected and that varies according to the wave-length distribution of the incident light — called also *reflection coefficient, reflection factor;* compare ALBEDO
reflected *adj* [ME, fr. past part. of *reflecten* to reflect] **1 :** bent or sent back **:** MIRRORED; *specif* **:** derived through the reflection of waves or rays ⟨∼ heat⟩ ⟨∼ color⟩ **2 :** coming indirectly or from a source other than oneself or itself **:** received from another ⟨enjoying the ∼ glory of his famous brother⟩ **3 :** turned back upon itself ⟨a sea shell with a ∼ lip⟩ — **re·flect·ed·ly** *adv* — **re·flect·ed·ness** *n* -ES
reflected impedance *n* **:** a part of the impedance of an electric circuit that is due to the influence of another coupled circuit
reflecterize *var of* REFLECTORIZE
reflecting *adj* **:** that reflects or causes reflection: as **a :** having some contrivance or apparatus to reflect light or heat ⟨∼ microscope⟩ ⟨∼ projector⟩ ⟨∼ oven⟩ **b :** THOUGHTFUL ⟨in our less ∼ moments we are apt to claim a very intimate acquaintance with matter —James Jeans⟩ — **re·flect·ing·ly** *adv*
reflecting galvanometer *n* **:** a galvanometer in which the deflections of the needle or coil are read by means of a mirror attached to it that reflects a ray of light or the image of a scale
reflecting telescope *n* **:** REFLECTOR 4
re·flec·tion \rəˈflekshən, rēˈf-\ *n* -S [ME, alter. (influenced by *reflecten* to reflect) of *reflexion*, fr. MF, fr. LL *reflexion-, reflexio* action of bending back, fr. L *reflexus* (past part. of *reflectere* to reflect, bend back) + *-ion-, -io* -ion] **1 :** the partial or complete return of a wave motion (as of light or sound) from a surface that it encounters into the medium that it originally traversed and in a manner that is usu. diffuse or irregular — compare SPECULAR REFLECTION **2 :** the production of an image by or as if by a mirror ⟨the eye sees not itself but by ∼ —Shak.⟩ ⟨the officers were a ∼ of their men, more restrained —John Steinbeck⟩ **3 a :** the action of bending or folding back **b :** a reflected part ⟨the mesentery is a ∼ of the peritoneum⟩ **:** FOLD **4 :** something produced by reflecting: **a :** reflected light or heat **b :** reflected brilliance (as of wit) or warmth (as of emotion) ⟨joy is only the ∼ of what is sought, a will-o'-the wisp —Gouverneur Paulding⟩ **c :** an image given back by a reflecting surface **:** a reflected counterpart **d :** an effect produced by an influence ⟨∼*s* of ancient Celtic legend in Italian literature⟩ **5 :** reproach cast or brought to bear **:** CENSURE, BLAME, IMPUTATION ⟨the ∼*s* on certain named persons' chastity and honesty —*Geog. Jour.*⟩ **6 :** a thought, idea, or opinion formed or a remark made as a result of meditation ⟨random ∼*s* and essays by one of our finest stylists —Orville Prescott⟩ **7 a :** consideration of some subject matter, idea, or purpose often with a view to understanding or accepting it or seeing it in its right relations ⟨as . . . walking gave him a better chance for ∼, the prospect slowly brightened —John Buchan⟩ **b :** introspective contemplation of the contents or qualities of one's own thoughts or remembered experiences ⟨∼ can be practiced on every experience —Edmund Husserl⟩ **8** *obs* **:** turning back **:** RETURN **9** *obs* **:** RELATION, CONNECTION **10** *obs***:** RECOLLECTION
re·flec·tion·al \-shənᵊl, -shnəl\ *adj* **:** relating to or caused by reflection
reflection coefficient *n* **:** REFLECTANCE
reflection factor *n* **:** REFLECTANCE
reflection grating *n* **:** a diffraction grating whose lines are ruled on a mirror surface
reflection plane *n* **:** a mirror plane of symmetry of a crystal
reflection twin *n* **:** a twin crystal in which the individuals are so related that one is a mirror image of the other — compare ROTATION TWIN
re·flec·tive \rəˈflektiv, rēˈf-, -tēv *also* -təv\ *adj* **1 :** capable of throwing back light, images, sound waves **:** REFLECTING ⟨∼ surfaces⟩ ⟨∼ insulation⟩ **2 :** marked by reflection **:** concerned with ideas or with introspective pondering **:** THOUGHTFUL, DELIBERATIVE ⟨∼ reading of history⟩ ⟨∼ temperament⟩ **3 :** of, relating to, or caused by reflection ⟨∼ glare of the beach⟩ ⟨poise and swoop of a gull's flight casts in addition a ∼ beauty on its animal structure —Lewis Mumford⟩ **4 :** REFLEXIVE ⟨∼ verb⟩ — **re·flec·tive·ly** \-təvlē, -li\ *adv* — **re·flec·tive·ness** \-tivnəs, -tēv- *also* -təv-\ *n* -ES
reflective judgment *n, Kantianism* **:** a judgment that proceeds from given particulars to the discovery of a general concept or universal principle under which the particulars may be subsumed — contrasted with *determinative judgment*
re·flec·tiv·i·ty \(ˌ)rēˌflekˈtivədˌē, rəˌf-\ *n* -ES **1 :** ability to reflect beams or rays **:** reflective power ⟨the high ∼ of snow fields⟩ **2 :** REFLECTANCE
re·flec·tom·e·ter \-ˈtäməd·ə(r)\ *n* [[1]*reflect* + *-o-* + *-meter*] **:** a photometric or electronic device for measuring the reflectances of light or other radiant energy
re·flec·tor \rəˈflektə(r), rēˈf-\ *n* -S [[1]*reflect* + *-or*] **1** *obs* **a :** one that meditates or considers **b :** one that casts reflections **:** CRITIC **2 :** a polished body or surface for reflecting light or other radiation: as **a :** a device used to modify the distribution of light from an illuminant, to shade the source, to direct the beams, and to produce artistic effect **b :** a highly polished curved usu. parabolic metal piece for reflecting the light forward in a head lamp **c :** a bowl-shaped device commonly of polished metal placed behind lamps to increase the amount of light reaching a scene to be photographed **d :** a panel (as of wallboard covered with metallic foil) used to reflect light onto the subject (as in portraiture or motion pictures) **e :** a utensil designed to reflect heat from an open fire and used in baking **f :** a device for reflecting sound toward an audience **3 :** a portion of an antenna array that serves to reverse the direction of part of the radio waves sent out from the radiating portion and is often used to improve the directional quality of the antenna **4 :** a telescope in which the principal focusing element is a mirror usu. of spherical or paraboloidal shape **5 :** a part of a nuclear reactor that reflects neutrons back toward the reactor core
re·flec·tor·ize *or* **re·flect·er·ize** \-təˌrīz\ *vt* -ED/-ING/-S [*reflectorize* fr. *reflector* + *-ize; reflecterize* alter. (influenced by *-er*) of *reflectorize*] **1 :** to prepare (a surface) so as to make reflecting **2 :** to provide with reflectors ⟨∼ a road sign⟩ ⟨∼ a curved margin of a highway⟩
reflects *pres 3d sing of* REFLECT, *pl of* REFLECT
re·flesher \(ˈ)rē+\ *n* [*re-* + *flesher*] **:** a leather worker who removes from hides any flesh left by the fleshing machine operator
re·flet \rəˈflā, rēˈf-\ *n* -S [F, modif. (influenced by L *reflectere*) of It *riflesso*, fr. *riflesso*, adj., reflected, fr. L *reflexus*, past part. of *reflectere* to reflect] **:** special brilliance of surface **:** metallic luster esp. on ceramic ware ⟨gold ∼ of majolica ware⟩
[1]**re·flex** \ˈreˌfleks *sometimes* rəˈf- *or* rēˈf-\ *n* -ES [L *reflexus*, past part. of *reflectere* to reflect] **1 :** reflected heat, light, or color; *specif* **:** light represented as reflected from an illuminated surface to one in shade (as in a painting) **2 a :** a mirrored image ⟨like the ∼ of the moon seen in a wave —P.B.Shelley⟩ **b :** a copy that reflects an original in essential features or peculiar characteristics ⟨to make legislation a ∼ of the popular will —W.E.H.Lecky⟩ **3 a** *obs* **:** a considered thought or statement **b** *obs* **:** a glancing reference **:** ALLUSION **4 a** *or* **reflex act :** an act (as a movement) performed automatically and without conscious volition in consequence of a nervous impulse transmitted inward by afferent fibers from a receptor to a nerve center and commonly through adjustor neurones outward by efferent fibers to an effector (as a muscle or gland) **b** *or* **reflex action :** the whole process comprising reception, transmission, and reaction that culminates in such an act **c reflexes** *pl* **:** the power of acting or responding with adequate speed ⟨his strength and the agility in his legs were gone and his ∼*es* no longer as they had been —Ernest Hemingway⟩ ⟨his ∼*es* are gone . . . I will never okay him to fight again —*Time*⟩ **d :** an automatic or strongly habitual and predictable way of thinking or behaving ⟨to obscure emotion was becoming for him a natural ∼ —Truman Capote⟩ ⟨the dangers of this wholesale conditioning of human mental ∼*es* —*New Republic*⟩ **5 a :** a phonemic, grammatical, or vocabulary element as found in a language in a form determined by development from an earlier stage of the language **b :** a cognate element
[2]**reflex** \"\ *adj* [L *reflexus*, past part. of *reflectere*] **1 :** bent, turned, or directed back **:** reversed in direction or course **:** REFLECTED ⟨∼ current in a river⟩ ⟨stem with ∼ leaves⟩ **2 :** directed back upon the mind or its operations **:** INTROSPECTIVE **3 :** produced in reaction, in resistance, or in return ⟨monetary deflation is the ∼ consequence of undue inflation⟩ **4** *of an angle* **:** greater than two and less than four right angles **:** being between 180° and 360° — see ANGLE illustration **5 a :** of, relating to, or produced by stimulus without necessarily the intervention of consciousness ⟨∼ contraction of the iris⟩ **b :** relating to, marked by, connected with, or constituting a reflex ⟨∼ center⟩ **6 :** having an amplifier tube functioning simultaneously as both a radio-frequency and an audio-frequency amplifier by leading the current through a tube both before and after detection ⟨∼ receiving set⟩ **7 :** relating to the reproduction of print or other graphic matter by means of a contact printing method in which light transmitted through light-sensitive material is reflected back onto the material from the matter to be reproduced ⟨∼ paper⟩ ⟨∼ copying⟩
reflex arc *n* **:** the complete nervous path that is involved in a reflex
reflex camera *n* **:** a camera in which the image formed by the lens is reflected by a mirror onto a ground-glass screen for focusing and composition
re·flexed \-kst\ *adj* [ME *reflexid*, fr. L *reflexus* (past part. of *reflectere*) + *-id*, *-ed* -ed] **1** *obs* **:** thrown back **:** caused or

produced by reflection **2 :** bent or curved backward or downward ⟨~ petals⟩ ⟨~ leaves⟩

reflexed bow *n* **:** a bow whose limbs curve away from the string side when unbraced

re·flex·i·bil·i·ty \rə̇ˌfleksəˈbiləd·ē, (ˌ)rēˌf-\ *n* -ES **:** the quality or state of being reflexible

re·flex·i·ble \rə̇ˈfleksəbəl, rēˈf-\ *adj* [L *reflexus* (past part. of *reflectere*) + E *-able*] **:** capable of being reflected

re·flex·ion *Brit var of* REFLECTION 1

re·flex·ism \ˈrēˌflekˌsizəm *sometimes* rə̇ˈf- *or* rēˈf-\ *n* -S **:** the limitation of psychological research to the study of reflexes

¹**re·flex·ive** \rə̇ˈfleksiv, rēˈf-, -sēv *also* -səv\ *adj* [ML *reflexivus* reflected, turned back, fr. L *reflexus* (past part. of *reflectere* to reflect) + *-ivus* -ive] **1 :** capable of bending back **2 a :** directed or turned back upon itself **:** INTROSPECTIVE — used of a mental act **b :** marked by or capable of reflection **:** REFLECTIVE **3 :** relating to, characterized by, or being a relation that exists between an entity and itself ⟨the relation *is equal to* is ~ but the relation *is the father of* is not⟩ **4 :** of, relating to, or constituting an action (as in "the witness perjured himself" or "I bethought myself") that is directed back upon the agent or the grammatical subject **5 :** relating to or consisting of a reflex or reflexes ⟨the nervous process which forms the basis of all ~ actions —A.L.Schniermann⟩ — **re·flex·ive·ly** \-səvlē, -li\ *adv* — **re·flex·ive·ness** \-sivnəs, -sēv- *also* -səv-\ *n* -ES

²**reflexive** \"\ *n* -S **:** a reflexive pronoun or verb

reflexive pronoun *n* **:** a pronoun referring to the subject of the sentence, clause, or verbal phrase in which it stands; *specif* **:** a personal pronoun compounded with *-self*

re·flex·iv·i·ty \(ˌ)rēˌflekˈsivəd·ē, rə̇ˌf-\ *n* -ES **:** the quality or state of being reflexive

re·flex·ly *adv* **:** in a reflex manner ⟨~ induced contractions⟩ **:** by means of reflexes ⟨~ contracting the iris⟩

re·flex·ness *n* -ES **:** the quality or state of being reflex

re·flexo·gen·ic \rə̇ˌfleksəˈjenik\ *or* **re·flex·og·e·nous** \ˌrēˌflekˈsäjənəs\ *adj* [¹*reflex* + *-o-* + *-genic* or *-genous*] **1 :** causing reflexes; *esp* **:** being the point of origin of reflexes ⟨a ~ zone⟩ **2 :** originating reflexly ⟨~ components of respiration⟩

re·flexo·log·ic \rə̇ˌfleksəˈläjik\ *adj* **:** relating to reflexology — **re·flexo·log·i·cal·ly** \-jə̇k(ə)lē\ *adv*

re·flex·ol·o·gist \ˌrēˌflekˈsäləjə̇st\ *n* -S **:** one who interprets behavior as consisting of reflexes

re·flex·ol·o·gy \-jē\ *n* -ES [ISV ¹*reflex* + *-o-* + *-logy*; orig. formed as Russ *refleksologiya*] **1 :** the study and interpretation of behavior in terms of simple and complex reflexes **2 :** the reflex component of the function of a body part or system or of a particular kind of activity ⟨the ~ of locomotion⟩

re·float \(ˈ)rē+\ *vt* [*re-* + *float*] **:** to set afloat again ⟨~ a grounded ship⟩

re·florescence \ˌrē+\ *n* [L *reflorescere* to blossom again (fr. *re-* + *florescere* to begin to bloom) + E *-ence* — more at FLORESCENCE] **:** a renewed blossoming

re·florescent \"+\ *adj* [L *reflorescent-, reflorescens*, pres. part. of *reflorescere* to blossom again] **:** flowering again

re·flourish \(ˈ)rē+\ *vi* [ME *reflorissen*, fr. *re-* + *florissen, florisshen* to flourish] **:** to flourish again

¹**re·flow** \(ˈ)rē+\ *vi* [ME *reflowen*, fr. *re-* + *flowen* to flow] **1 :** to flow back **:** EBB **2 :** to flow in again **:** FLOOD ⟨universal deluge . . . that ebbs but to ~ —Lord Byron⟩

²**re·flow** \ˈrē+ˌ-\ *n* **1 :** REFLUX, EBB **2 :** renewed flowing or flooding

re·flower \(ˈ)rē+\ *vi* [*re-* + *flower*] **:** to blossom or flourish anew

ref·lu·ence \ˈreˌflüən(t)s, -fləwən-\ *n* -S [L *refluere* to flow back (fr. *re-* + *fluere* to flow) + E *-ence* — more at FLUID] **:** refluent action **:** REFLUX

ref·lu·ent \-nt\ *adj* [L *refluent-, refluens*, pres. part. of *refluere* to flow back] **:** flowing back ⟨~ blood in the veins⟩ **:** EBBING, SUBSIDING ⟨~ tides⟩

¹**re·flux** \ˈrēˌfləks\ *n* [ME, fr. ML *refluxus*, fr. L *re-* + *fluxus* flow — more at FLUX] **1 a :** a flowing back **:** REFLUENCE ⟨the flux and ~ of the tides⟩ ⟨the fluxes and ~*es* of the mind when agitated by the great and simple affection —William Wordsworth⟩ **b :** a process of refluxing or the condition of being refluxed **2 :** a reflux apparatus; *esp* **:** REFLUX CONDENSER **3 :** the liquid condensed from the vapors in a refluxing operation

²**reflux** \"\ *adj* **1 :** of or relating to reflux **:** RETURNING, EBBING **2 :** admitting or controlling reflux ⟨~ tower in an oil field⟩

³**reflux** \"\ *vt* -ED/-ING/-ES **:** to cause to flow back or return; *esp* **:** to heat (as under a reflux condenser) so that the vapors formed condense to a liquid that flows back to be heated again

reflux condenser *n* **:** a condenser usu. placed upright so that the condensed vapors flow back into the distilling flask and continued boiling of easily volatile substances is possible with little loss from evaporation

reflux valve *n* **:** a back-pressure valve

re·fly \(ˈ)rē+\ *vb* [*re-* + *fly*] *vi* **:** to fly again **:** fly back ~ *vt* **1 :** to travel or cover (a course) again in flight **2 :** to transport again or back in flight

re·focil·late \rēˈfäsəˌlāt, -fōs-\ *vt* -ED/-ING/-S [LL *refocillatus, refocilatus*, past part. of *refocillare, refocilare* to warm into life again, fr. L *re-* + *focilare, foculare* to revive or refresh by warmth, fr. *foculum* chafing dish, brazier, fr. *fovēre* to warm, keep warm — more at DAY] **:** REFRESH, REVIVE ⟨*refocillating* their spirits with whiskey and soda⟩ — **re·focil·la·tion** \(ˌ)ˌ=ˌ=ˈlāshən\ *n* -S

re·focus \(ˈ)rē+\ *vb* [*re-* + *focus*] **:** to focus again

re·fold \"+\ *vt* [*re-* + *fold*] **:** to fold again **:** return to a folded state

re·fold·er \"ə(r)\ *n* **:** one that inspects and refolds garments

re·foot \(ˈ)rē+\ *vt* [*re-* + *foot*] **:** to provide (as a stocking, a pillar) with a new foot

re·ford \"+\ *vt* [*re-* + *ford*] **:** to ford again

re·forest \"+\ *vt* [*re-* + *forest*] **:** to renew forest cover on (denuded land) by natural seeding or artificial planting — **re·forestation** \(ˌ)rē+\ *n*

re·forge \(ˈ)rē+\ *vt* [ME *reforgen*, fr. MF *reforgier*, fr. *re-* + *forgier* to forge] **:** to forge again or anew **:** fashion or fabricate anew **:** make over ⟨*reforging* of the raw materials into a new and valid film form —Arthur Knight⟩

¹**re·form** \rə̇ˈfȯ(ə)rm, rēˈf-, -ȯ(ə)m\ *vb* [ME *reformen*, fr. MF *reformer*, fr. OF, fr. L *reformare*, fr. *re-* + *formare* to form, fr. *forma* form — more at FORM] *vt* **1** *obs* **:** RESTORE, RENEW **2 a :** to restore to a former good state **:** bring from bad to good ⟨hopes that Congress may, somehow, ~ itself —T.H. Eliot⟩ **b :** to amend or improve by change of form or by removal of faults or abuses ⟨the fact is that the world does not care to be ~*ed* —S.M.Crothers⟩ ⟨need for ~*ing* news writing in order to make it more readable —F.L.Mott⟩ **c :** to put or change into a new and improved form or condition ⟨his ambition to ~ the map of the world —Benjamin Farrington⟩ **3 :** to put an end to (an evil) by enforcing or introducing a better method or course of action or behavior ⟨~ the abuses of political patronage⟩ **4 :** to induce or cause to abandon an evil manner of living and follow a good one **:** change from worse to better ⟨attempts to ~ the criminal⟩ ⟨~ a drunkard⟩ **5** *obs* **:** CENSURE, REPROVE **6** *obs* **:** to improve by cutting **:** PRUNE ⟨labor to ~ yon flowery arbors —John Milton⟩ **7 a :** to correct the errors in **:** EMEND ⟨~ the calendar⟩ **b :** to rectify (as an error in a legal instrument) in accordance with the real intention of the parties to a transaction **8 a** *obs* **:** to form (a military unit) into a new organization (as by reduction in number) **b** *obs* **:** DISBAND **c :** RE-FORM **9 a :** to subject (hydrocarbon oils or gases) to reforming **b :** to produce by reforming ⟨~*ed* gasoline⟩ ⟨~*ed* refinery oil gas⟩ ~ *vi* **:** to change for the better **:** amend or correct one's character or habits ⟨if given more time, I think the Church would have ~*ed* from within —A.N.Whitehead⟩ **syn** see CORRECT

²**reform** \"\ *n* -S [prob. fr. F *réforme*, fr. *réformer* to reform, fr. OF *reformer*] **1 a :** amendment of what is defective, vicious, corrupt, or depraved ⟨~ of the law courts⟩ ⟨a school for ~ of young criminals⟩ **b :** a removal or correction of an abuse, a wrong, or errors ⟨calendar ~⟩ ⟨~ of election procedures⟩ **2** *usu cap* **:** REFORMATION 2 **3** *usu cap* **:** REFORM JUDAISM

³**reform** \"\ *adj* **:** relating to or favoring reform ⟨~ movement⟩ ⟨~ bill⟩ ⟨~ candidate⟩

re-form \(ˈ)rē¦f-\ *vb* [*re-* + *form*] *vt* **:** to form again ⟨the Mexicans *re-formed* their lines and came on again and again —*Amer. Guide Series: Texas*⟩ ⟨the cartel has recently been *re-formed*⟩ ~ *vi* **:** to take form again ⟨clouds were dissolving and *re-forming*⟩ **:** come together again in a formation ⟨escaped . . . by an epic retreat . . . later to *re-form* and become the spearhead of the Allied offensive —*Atlantic*⟩

re·form·abil·i·ty \rə̇ˌfȯ(r)məˈbiləd·ē, (ˌ)rēˌf-\ *n* **:** the capability of being reformed ⟨question of the ~ of alcoholics⟩

re·form·able \=ˈ=məbəl\ *adj* [ME *reformabyll*, fr. *reformen* to reform + *-abyll, -able* -able] **:** capable of being reformed ⟨a ~ type of criminal offender⟩

reformade *n* -S [by alter.] *obs* **:** REFORMADO

ref·or·ma·do \ˌrefə(r)ˈmä(ˌ)dō, -mā(-\ *n, pl* **reformados** *or* **reformadoes** [Sp, fr. *reformado*, past part. of *reformar* to reform, reorganize, fr. L *reformare* to reform] **1 a :** an officer deprived of command by the reorganization or disbandment of his troops but retaining rank and receiving full or half pay **b :** a volunteer serving without a commission but with an officer's rank **2** *obs* **:** a reformed person **3** *obs* **:** a supporter of reform

ref·or·ma·tion \ˌrefə(r)ˈmāshən\ *n* -S [ME *reformacion*, fr. MF *reformation*, fr. L *reformation-, reformatio*, fr. *reformatus* (past part. of *reformare* to reform) + *-ion-, -io* -ion] **1 :** the act of reforming or state of being reformed: as **a** *obs* **:** RESTORATION, REESTABLISHMENT **b :** improvement in form or condition ⟨urging a radical ~ of society⟩ **c :** amendment of moral behavior ⟨satire lashes vice into ~ —John Dryden⟩ **d :** correction or improvement of what is faulty, defective, inefficient, or objectionable ⟨~ of the postal service⟩ **e :** the correction by a court of equity of errors and mistakes in or arising out of the execution of a written instrument to make the instrument conform to the real intention of the parties thereto **2** *usu cap* **:** a 16th century religious movement aimed at correcting real or assumed abuses in the Roman Catholic Church and marked ultimately by rejection of the supremacy of the pope, rejection or modification of much of Roman Catholic doctrine, and establishment of the Protestant churches

re-formation \¦rē(ˌ)fȯ(r)¦māshən\ *n* [*re-* + *formation*] **:** a shaping or forming again or anew ⟨*re-formation* of a granitic magma⟩ ⟨*re-formation* of a regiment⟩

ref·or·ma·tion·al \¦refə(r)¦māshən°l, -shnəl\ *adj* **:** of or relating to reformation ⟨~ zeal⟩

re·for·ma·tive \rə̇ˈfȯ(r)məd·iv, rēˈf-, -mətiv\ *adj* [¹*reform* + *-ative*] **:** tending or disposed to reform ⟨~ and rehabilitative agencies⟩ ⟨the puritan conscience of the middle class was rousing itself for a final ~ fling —Roy Lewis & Angus Maude⟩ — **re·for·ma·tive·ly** \-əvlē, -li\ *adv* — **re·for·ma·tive·ness** \-ivnə̇s\ *n* -ES

¹**re·for·ma·to·ry** \-məˌtōrē, -tȯr-, -ri\ *adj* [¹*reform* + *-atory*] **:** intended for reformation **:** REFORMATIVE ⟨~ measures⟩

²**reformatory** \"\ *n* -ES **:** a penal institution to which young or first offenders or women are committed and in which repressive and punitive measures are held to be subordinated to training in industry and exercise of the physical, mental, and moral faculties — compare TRAINING SCHOOL 2

¹**reformed** *adj* **1 :** restored to purity or excellence **:** AMENDED, IMPROVED, CORRECTED ⟨~ calendar⟩ **2** *usu cap* **a :** of or relating to the whole body of Protestant Christianity stemming from the Reformation **:** PROTESTANT ⟨*Reformed* theological doctrines⟩ **b :** of or relating to a Protestant church other than Lutheran formed in various European continental countries — used in official titles of several churches ⟨Dutch *Reformed*⟩ ⟨Christian *Reformed* Church⟩ **3 :** observing a religious discipline more strictly conformable to the original rule or set of directives — used of a branch or congregation of a religious order ⟨the ~ Benedictines of that era⟩ **4** *obs, of an officer* **:** left without a command and retired on half or full pay **5** *usu cap* **:** of or relating to Reform Judaism

²**reformed** *n, pl* **reformed** *usu cap* **:** a member of a Protestant church; *esp* **:** a member of a Reformed church

reformed spelling *n* **:** any of several methods of spelling English words that use letters with more phonetic consistency than conventional English spelling and usu. discard some of the silent letters (as in *thoro* for *thorough, markt* for *marked, laps* for *lapse*)

re·form·er \rə̇ˈfȯrmər, rēˈf-, -ȯ(ə)mə(r\ *n* -S **1 :** one that effects or tries to effect a reformation or amendment **:** one that works for or urges reform ⟨once the moralist, the religionist, or the puritan ~ becomes the censor of art —Hunter Mead⟩ **2** *usu cap* **:** a leader of the Reformation in the 16th century ⟨this is not what the *Reformers* meant by faith —B.E.Meland⟩ **3 :** an advocate or promoter of political reform: **a :** an advocate or promoter of parliamentary reform; *esp* **:** a participator in the reform movement in Great Britain in 1831–32 **b** *usu cap* **:** a member of a reform party (as in Canada or New Zealand) **4 :** an apparatus for reforming hydrocarbon materials (as naphtha or natural gas) ⟨catalytic ~⟩

reforming *n* -S [fr. gerund of ¹*reform*] **:** cracking of various hydrocarbon oils or gases to form specialized products: as **a :** cracking of petroleum naphtha or straight-run gasoline of low octane number usu. to form gasoline containing lighter constituents and having a higher octane number — compare HYDROFORMING **b :** cracking of natural gas or other hydrocarbon gases often in the presence of steam to reduce the heating value or to produce hydrogen

re·form·ing·ly *adv* [*reforming* (pres. part. of ¹*reform*) + *-ly*] **:** in a reforming manner **:** so as to reform

re·form·ism \-ˌmizəm\ *n* -S [ISV ¹*reform* + *-ism*] **:** a doctrine or policy or movement of reform ⟨moral ~⟩ ⟨economic ~⟩

¹**re·form·ist** \-ˌmə̇st\ *n* -S [¹*reform* + *-ist*] **1 a :** REFORMER **b :** one that advocates gradual rather than revolutionary change **2 :** a member of a reformed branch or congregation of a religious group

²**reformist** \"\ *or* **re·form·is·tic** \=¦=¦mistik\ *adj* **:** relating or belonging to a policy or movement of reform ⟨~ elements in the labor movement⟩ ⟨~ views⟩

reform jew *n, usu cap R&J* **:** an adherent of Reform Judaism

reform judaism *n, cap R&J* **:** a development of Judaism that began in Germany in the early part of the 19th century and is marked by an effort to promote faith in God through a rationalization of belief according to the truths of modern sciences, by an acceptance of the doctrine of ethical monotheism and a rejection of the legal authority of the Talmud, by a simplification of many ritual and ceremonial observances, and by the affirmation of the essentially religious rather than national character of Judaism — called also *Liberal Judaism;* compare CONSERVATIVE JUDAISM, ORTHODOX JUDAISM

reforms *pres 3d sing of* REFORM, *pl of* REFORM

reform school *n* **:** a reformatory for boys or girls

re·formulate \(ˈ)rē+\ *vt* [*re-* + *formulate*] **:** to formulate again; *esp* **:** to formulate in a different way — **re·formulation** \(ˌ)rē+\ *n*

re·fortify \(ˈ)rē+\ *vt* [*re-* + *fortify*] **:** to fortify again or afresh

¹**re·found** \"+\ *vt* [*re-* + *found* (to establish)] **:** to establish again

²**refound** \"\ *past of* REFIND

³**refound** \"\ *vt* [*re-* + *found* (to cast)] **:** to cast again ⟨~ type⟩

re·founder \(ˈ)rē+\ *n* [¹*refound* + *-er*] **:** one that founds again ⟨~ of a monastery⟩

refr *abbr* **1** refraction **2** refrigerate; refrigerating; refrigeration

¹**re·fract** \rə̇ˈfrakt, rēˈf-\ *vt* -ED/-ING/-S [L *refractus*, past part. of *refringere* to refract, break off, fr. *re-* + *frangere* to break — more at BREAK] **1** *obs* **:** REFLECT **2** *obs* **:** to break up **:** DIVIDE **3 :** to subject (rays of light) to refraction **4 :** to determine the refracting power or abnormality of refraction in (as an eye or a lens)

²**refract** *adj* [L *refractus*, past part. of *refringere*] *obs* **:** REFRACTED

re·frac·ta·ry \rə̇ˈfraktərē, rēˈf-, -təri\ *adj* [L *refractarius*, fr. *refractus* (past part. of *refringere* to refract, break off) + *-arius* -ary] **:** REFRACTORY

re·fract·ed \-təd\ *adj* [fr. past part. of ¹*refract*] **:** bent backward angularly as if half-broken ⟨~ stem⟩ ⟨~ spines⟩

re·frac·tile \-t°l\ *adj* **:** capable of refracting **:** REFRACTIVE ⟨~ cells⟩ — **re·frac·til·i·ty** \=ˌ=ˈtiləd·ē\ *n* -ES

refracting angle *n* **:** the dihedral angle (as of a prism) included between the planes of the two sides through which the refracted beam passes — compare REFRACTION ANGLE

refracting system *n* **:** REFRACTIVE SYSTEM

refracting telescope *n* **:** REFRACTOR

re·frac·tion \rə̇ˈfrakshən, rēˈf-\ *n* -S [LL *refraction-, refractio*, fr. L *refractus* (past part. of *refringere*) + *-ion-, -io* -ion] **1 :** the action of refracting or the state of being refracted: as **a :** the deflection from a straight path undergone by a light ray or a wave of energy in passing obliquely from one medium (as air) into another (as water, glass) in which its velocity is different **b** *obs* **:** REFLECTION, REBOUND **c** *obs* **:** a breaking up **d :** the change in the apparent position of a celestial body that is due to the bending of the light rays emanating from it as they pass through the earth's atmosphere; *also* **:** the correction to be applied to the apparent position of a body because of this bending **2** *obs* **:** reduction of a bill **:** REBATE **3 a :** the refractive power of the eye **b :** the act or technique of determining ocular refraction and identifying abnormalities as a basis for the prescription of corrective lenses **4 :** the action of distorting an image by viewing through a medium ⟨looking at the world . . . observing it without the ~ of moral judgment —Janet Flanner⟩

refraction angle *n* **1 :** the difference between the geometrical and observed altitude of a celestial body that is produced by atmospheric refraction **2 :** ANGLE OF REFRACTION

re·fractionate \(ˈ)rē+\ *vt* [*re-* + *fractionate*] **:** to fractionate again (as by distillation) — **re·fractionation** \(ˌ)rē+\ *n*

refraction circle *n* **:** an instrument with a graduated circle for measuring deviations due to refraction

re·frac·tion·ist \rə̇ˈfraksh(ə)nə̇st, rēˈf-\ *n* -S **:** one skilled in the practical application of the laws of refraction esp. to the determination of errors of refraction in the eye

re·frac·tive \-ktiv, -ktēv *also* -ktəv\ *adj* **1 :** having power to refract ⟨~ lens⟩ **2 :** relating to or due to refraction ⟨~ phenomena⟩ ⟨~ dispersion of light⟩ — **re·frac·tive·ly** \-tə̇vlē, -li\ *adv* — **re·frac·tive·ness** \-tivnəs, -tēv- *also* -təv-\ *n* -ES

refractive index *n* **:** INDEX OF REFRACTION

refractive power *n* **:** the ability of a substance to refract light expressed quantitatively by either its index of refraction or its refractivity

refractive system *n* **:** an optical system in which lenses instead of mirrors are used for focusing light, forming an image, or changing the path of a beam of light by refraction; *specif* **:** a mode of lighting in lighthouses by a central lamp surrounded by a combination of lenses — called also *refracting system*

re·frac·tiv·i·ty \rə̇ˌfrakˈtivəd·ē, (ˌ)rēˌf-, -vətē, -i\ *n* -ES **:** REFRACTIVE POWER; *specif* **:** the index of refraction minus one — compare SPECIFIC REFRACTIVITY

re·frac·tom·e·ter \-ˈtämədˑə(r)\ *n* [ISV *refraction* + *-o-* + *-meter*] **:** an instrument for measuring indices of refraction

re·frac·to·met·ric \rə̇¦fraktə¦me·trik, rēˈf-\ *adj* **:** of or relating to refractometry

re·frac·tom·e·try \rəˌfrakˈtäməˑtrē, (ˌ)rēˌf-\ *n* -ES [ISV *refraction* + *-o-* + *-metry*] **:** the art or process of measuring indices of refraction **:** the use of the refractometer

re·frac·tor \rə̇ˈfraktə(r), rēˈf-\ *n* -S **:** something that refracts light rays; *specif* **:** a telescope in which the principal focusing element is a lens that is usu. an achromat with crown glass and flint glass components

re·frac·to·ri·ly \-kt(ə)rəlē, -ˌfrakˈtōrəlē, -ȯr-, -li\ *adv* **:** in a refractory manner

re·frac·to·ri·ness \-rēnə̇s, -rin-\ *n* -ES **:** the quality or state of being refractory: as **a :** the ability of a material to resist a high temperature **b :** the insensitivity to further immediate stimulation that develops in nervous or other irritable tissue as a result of intense or prolonged stimulation

¹**re·frac·to·ry** \rə̇ˈfrakt(ə)rē, rēˈf-, -)ri\ *adj* [alter. (influenced by *-ory*) of *refractary*] **1 :** resisting control or authority **:** STUBBORN, UNMANAGEABLE, PERVERSE ⟨to persuade her ~ daughter to agree to the propriety of what she was going to do —Anthony Trollope⟩ ⟨bold attempts to reduce ~ material to poetic treatment —F.B.Millett⟩ ⟨the boy was solitary and ~ to all education save that of wide and desultory reading —F.J.Mather⟩ **2 a :** resistant to treatment or cure ⟨a ~ fulminating lesion⟩ **b :** unresponsive to stimulus ⟨the ~ period of a muscle fiber⟩ **c :** resistant or not responding to an infectious agent **:** IMMUNE, INSUSCEPTIBLE ⟨after recovery the animals were completely ~ to reinfection⟩ **3 :** resisting treatment under ordinary or various extraordinary conditions **:** difficult to fuse, corrode, reduce, or draw out ⟨~ ore⟩ ⟨~ metals⟩; *esp* **:** capable of enduring or resisting high temperature ⟨~ clays⟩ ⟨~ brick⟩ ⟨~ mortar⟩ **syn** see UNRULY

²**refractory** \"\ *n* -ES **1** *obs* **:** a refractory person **2 :** a refractory material: as **a :** any of various nonmetallic ceramic substances that are characterized esp. by their suitability for use as structural materials at high temperatures usu. in contact with metals, slags, glass, or other corrosive materials (as in furnaces, crucibles, or saggers), that are classified chemically as acid (as silica and fireclay), basic (as magnesite and dolomite), or neutral (as high-alumina refractories, carbon, and silicon carbide), and that are produced in the form of brick and other shapes, finely ground cementing materials, castable concretes, plastics, and granular materials in bulk **b :** a substance resistant to corrosion by chemical agents and used esp. in chemical plants and laboratories

refractory clay *n* **:** FIRECLAY

refractory period *or* **refractory phase** *n* **:** the brief period immediately following the response of a muscle, nerve, or other irritable element before it recovers its capacity to make a second response

refractory rock *n* **:** a naturally occurring rock material that has refractory qualities and is used in the form of blocks for lining certain types of furnaces

refractory ware *n* **:** clayware so composed as to resist a high temperature and suitable for saggers, crucibles, blocks and pots for glass furnaces, blast-furnace linings, and heating elements

refracts *pres 3d sing of* REFRACT

¹**re·frain** \rə̇ˈfrān, rēˈf-\ *vb* -ED/-ING/-S [ME *refreynen*, fr. MF *refraindre* to restrain, moderate, echo, fr. OF, alter. (influenced by *fraindre* to break, fr. L *frangere*) of *refreindre*, fr. L *refringere* to refract, break off — more at REFRACT] *vt* **1** *archaic* **:** to hold back **:** put a restraint upon **:** CURB, GOVERN, RESTRAIN **2** *obs* **:** to abstain from **:** give up **:** AVOID, SHUN ~ *vi* **:** to keep oneself from doing, feeling, or indulging in something **:** hold aloof **:** FORBEAR, ABSTAIN ⟨had an impulse to speak, but on second thought ~*ed*⟩ ⟨promised to obey our laws, support our government and ~ from treachery —Kenneth Roberts⟩ ⟨carefully ~*s* from setting too great a store by miracle and prophecy —*Times Lit. Supp.*⟩

syn ABSTAIN, FORBEAR: REFRAIN is more suitable than ABSTAIN or FORBEAR to indicate checking or inhibiting an inclination or impulse, especially a momentary or passing one ⟨no tolerable parent could *refrain* from praising a child when it first walks and when it first says an intelligible word —Bertrand Russell⟩ ⟨I have since tried, not very successfully, to *refrain* from muttering proudly when the brighter young minds among contemporaries are mentioned: "Former student of mine!" —Irwin Edman⟩ ABSTAIN is applicable to deliberate self-denial, renunciation, or nonparticipation on principle ⟨the early Christians avoided contact with the State, *abstained* from the responsibilities of office, and were even reluctant to serve in the army —J.E.E.Dalberg-Acton⟩ ⟨in time of war it was incumbent upon all wives who were left behind to live chaste lives, to make offerings to the gods, and to *abstain* from cutting their hair —J.G.Frazer⟩ FORBEAR may apply to instances of restraining, checking, or withholding motivated by self-restraint, patience, stoicism, compassion, or clemency ⟨her prudent mother, occupied by the same ideas, *forbore* to invite him to sit by herself —Jane Austen⟩ ⟨he was not a seaman but a merchant who could not *forbear* the fun of setting sail with his merchandise —*Times Lit. Supp.*⟩

²**refrain** \"\ *n* -S [ME *refreyn*, fr. MF *refrain*, fr. *refraindre* to restrain, moderate, echo] **:** a phrase or verse which recurs regularly esp. at the end of each stanza or division of a poem or song **:** BURDEN, CHORUS; *also* **:** the musical setting of such a phrase or verse

refraination *n* -S [by alter. (influenced by ¹*refrain*)] *obs* **:** REFRENATION

re·frain·ment \rə̇ˈfrānmənt, rēˈf-\ *n* -S **:** the act of refraining

re·frame \(ˈ)rē+\ *vt* [*re-* + *frame*] **:** to frame or construct again or afresh **:** put in or provide with a new frame ⟨~ a statement⟩ ⟨~ a picture⟩

refranation *n* -s [by alter.] *obs* : REFRENATION

re·fran·gent \rə'franjənt, rē'f-\ *adj* [*refrang-* (as in *refrangible*) + *-ent*] : REFRACTING

re·fran·gi·bil·i·ty \ˌ=ˌ=jə'bilədē\ *n* -ES : the quality or state of being refrangible

re·fran·gi·ble \=ˈ==bəl\ *adj* [fr. ¹*refract*, after L *fractus* (past part. of *frangere* to break): ML *frangibilis* frangible, breakable — more at BREAK, FRANGIBLE] : capable of being refracted ⟨a prism divides the differently ~ rays of sunlight⟩ — **re·fran·gi·ble·ness** *n*

re·freeze \(ˈ)rē+\ *vb* [*re-* + *freeze*] *vt* : to freeze again after thawing ~ *vi* : to become frozen again

ref·re·na·tion \ˌrefrə'nāshən\ *n* -s [ME *refrenacion*, fr. L *refrenation-, refrenatio*, fr. *refrenatus* (past part. of *refrenare* to restrain, fr. *re-* + *frenare* to bridle, restrain, fr. *frenum* bridle) + *-ion-, -io* -ion — more at FRENUM] **1** *obs* : the act of restraining or refraining **2** : the failure of an expected planetary aspect to occur because one of the planets becomes retrograde

re·fresh \rə'fresh, rē'f-\ *vb* [ME *refresshen*, fr. MF *refreschir*, *refreschier*, fr. OF, fr. *re-* + *freis* fresh (fem. *fresche*) — more at FRESH] *vt* **1** : to restore strength and animation to (as through food or rest) : relieve from fatigue or depression : REVIVE, REINVIGORATE ⟨rode many hours, but a brief rest and change of position ~*ed* him —Oliver La Farge⟩ ⟨~*ed* himself with a cold shower and rubdown⟩ : CHEER ⟨~*ing* himself with a little tobacco —Winston Churchill⟩ ⟨it ~*es* me to find a woman so charmingly direct, so completely feminine —Louis Bromfield⟩ **2** : to freshen up (as by cleaning, trimming) : RENOVATE **3 a** : to restore or maintain by renewing supply : REPLENISH ⟨English middle classes . . . continually renewed and ~*ed* themselves from the countryside —Roy Lewis & Angus Maude⟩ ⟨the steward ~*ed* our glasses —A.J.Liebling⟩ ⟨supply ship ~*ed* the attacking submarines⟩ **b** : QUICKEN ⟨let me ~ your memory of the events with this letter⟩ **4** : to make fresh by wetting or cooling; *specif* : to restore water to (dehydrated food) ~ *vi* **1** : to become fresh again : REVIVE **2** : to refresh oneself : take refreshment **3** : to lay in fresh provisions ⟨harbors where ships can ~⟩

re·fresh·ant \-shənt\ *n* -s : something that invigorates or reanimates : REFRESHER ⟨caffeine is a real stimulant and ~ —*Arthur Little's Industrial Bull.*⟩

re·fresh·en \(ˈ)rē¦freshən\ *vt* [*re-* + *freshen*] : make fresh again : REFRESH, RENOVATE ⟨~*ing* of old disciplines —W.H. Whyte⟩

re·fresh·er \rə'freshə(r), rē'f-\ *n* -s [ME *refressher*, fr. *refresshen* to refresh + *-er*] **1 a** : something (as a drink) that refreshes or revives ⟨stopped in the bar for a quick ~⟩ **b** : something that makes fresh or vivid again : REMINDER **c** : something that provides review or additional instruction after a period of inactivity or gives instruction designed to keep one abreast of developments in scholarly investigation or new professional techniques and developments ⟨for those who need a simple ~ on the basic science involved in atomic energy —Alfred Friendly⟩ ⟨the serviceman is called to London for a ~ course whenever a new machine is marketed —Bryan Morgan⟩ **2 a** *Brit* : an extra fee paid to counsel in a case adjourned from one term to another or unusually protracted ⟨my retainer is reasonable, my ~*s* modest —Hervey Allen⟩ **b** *Austral* : an extra fee paid counsel for each day of trial beyond the first five hours

re·fresh·ful \-shfəl\ *adj* : full of power to refresh : REFRESHING — **re·fresh·ful·ly** \-fəlē\ *adv*

refreshing *adj* **1** : giving new life or vigor : STIMULATING ⟨the complicated challenge of the world he was facing had been ~ —Victor Canning⟩ : HEARTENING ⟨a letter from you this morning was ~ beyond words —H.J.Laski⟩ **2** : giving an unexpected pleasant or agreeable sensation : providing relief from boredom : contrasting with what is commonplace or hackneyed ⟨a new and ~ informality⟩ ⟨has the ~ good sense to say favorable things about his own work —M.W. Fishwick⟩ — **re·fresh·ing·ly** *adv* — **re·fresh·ing·ness** *n* -ES

re·fresh·ment \rə'freshmənt, rē'f-\ *n* -s [ME *refresshement*, fr. MF *refreschement*, fr. *refreschier* to refresh + *-ment*] **1** : the act of refreshing or state of being refreshed: **a** : spiritual restoration : reanimation of the soul ⟨often turned for guidance, inspiration, and ~ to the masters of his boyhood —B.R.Redman⟩ **b** : restoration of strength, spirit, vigor, or liveliness esp. after fatigue or depression ⟨walking . . . for the ~ of the frosty air —Charles Dickens⟩ **2 a** : something (as food, drink) that refreshes : means of restoration or reanimation **b refreshments** *pl* : a light meal : LUNCH ⟨serve ~*s* at a card party⟩ ⟨a booth for ~*s* was set up on the fairgrounds⟩

refreshment sunday *n*, *usu cap R&S* [prob. so called because the gospel for the day relates the miracle of feeding the five thousand (Jn 6:1–14)] : MID-LENT SUNDAY

¹**re·frig·er·ant** \rə'frij(ə)rənt, rē'f-\ *adj* [MF or L; MF, fr. L *refrigerant-, refrigerans*, pres. part. of *refrigerare*] : COOLING ⟨~ latitudes⟩ : allaying heat or fever ⟨~ medicines⟩ : REFRESHING

²**refrigerant** \"\ *n* -s : a refrigerant agent or agency: as **a** : a medicine or an application for allaying fever or its symptoms **b** : a substance (as ice, ammonia, carbon dioxide) used in refrigeration

¹**refrigerate** *adj* [ME, fr. L *refrigeratus*, past part. of *refrigerare*] **1** *obs* : REFRIGERATED **2** *obs* : REFRIGERANT

²**re·frig·er·ate** \-jəˌrāt, *usu* -ād.+V\ *vb* -ED/-ING/-S [L *refrigeratus*, past part. of *refrigerare*, fr. *re-* + *frigerare* to make cool, fr. *frigor-, frigus* coolness, frost, cold — more at FRIGID] *vt* **1** : to cause to become cool : make or keep cold or cool; *specif* : to freeze or chill (food) for preservation **2** : to extract heat from (as a body, a substance) by lowering the temperature of the body and by keeping its temperature below that of its surroundings ~ *vi* : to become cool or cold

refrigerating engine *or* **refrigerating machine** *n* : an apparatus working in a reversed heat-engine cycle for utilizing mechanical energy (as by compressing and expanding ammonia gas) to extract heat from a substance (as circulating brine) — compare BRAYTON CYCLE

re·frig·er·a·tion \rəˌfrijə'rāshən, rēˌf-\ *n* -s [ME *refrygeracion*, fr. L *refrigeration-, refrigeratio* coolness, cooling, fr. *refrigeratus* (past part. of *refrigerare*) + *-ion-, -io* -ion] : the action or process of refrigerating: as **a** : the cooling or freezing of food or perishables for storage — see ELECTRIC REFRIGERATION, MECHANICAL REFRIGERATION **b** : a deliberate lowering of the temperature of the body or of a part (as a leg) for therapeutic purposes or to facilitate surgery — compare HYPOTHERMIA

re·frig·er·a·tive \=ˈ==ˌrād·iv\ *adj* [MF *refrigeratif*, fr. LL *refrigerativus*, fr. L *refrigeratus* (past part. of *refrigerare* to refrigerate) + *-ivus* -ive] : tending to cool : allaying heat : COOLING

re·frig·er·a·tor \-ˌrād·ə(r), -ātə-\ *n* -s : something that refrigerates or keeps cool: **a** : a cabinet or room for keeping food or other articles cool **b** : an apparatus for rapidly cooling heated liquids or vapors in a distilling process : CONDENSER 2 f

refrigerator car *n* : a freight car constructed and used primarily as a refrigerator in transporting fresh meats, fruits, vegetables and usu. also adaptable by the installation of heating units for transporting commodities that must be protected from cold

refrigerator van *n*, *Brit* : REFRIGERATOR CAR

refrigerator a

¹**re·frig·er·a·to·ry** \rə'frij(ə)rəˌtōrē, rē'f-, -tȯr-, -ri\ *n* -ES [²*refrigerate* + *-ory*] : something that cools or refrigerates: **a** : an apparatus (as in a still) for condensing vapors **b** : the chamber or tank in which ice is formed in an ice machine **c** : a place of cooling or getting cooled

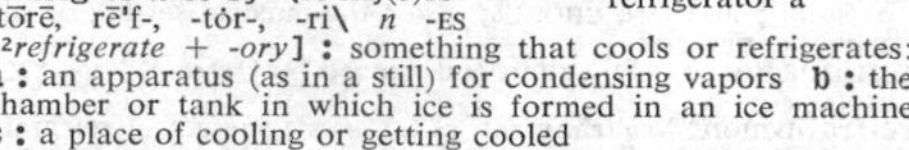

²**refrigeratory** \"\ *adj* [L *refrigeratorius*, fr. *refrigeratus* (past part. of *refrigerare*) + *-orius* -ory] : REFRIGERATIVE

re·frin·gen·cy \rə'frinjənsē\ *also* **re·frin·gence** \-jən(t)s\ *n*, *pl* **refringencies** *also* **refringences** [*refringency* fr. *refringent* + *-cy*; *refringence* ISV, fr. *refringent*, after such pairs as E *evident: evidence*] : REFRACTIVITY

re·frin·gent \-jənt\ *adj* [L *refringent-, refringens*, pres. part. of *refringere* to refract, break off — more at REFRACT] : REFRACTIVE, REFRACTING — compare BIREFRINGENT

re·front \(ˈ)rē+\ *vt* [*re-* + *front*] : to change or renew the front of ⟨~ a house⟩

refs *pl of* REF, *pres 3d sing of* REF

¹**reft** *past of* REAVE

²**reft** \'reft\ *n* -s [alter. (prob. influenced by *cleft*) of *rift*] : CLEFT, FISSURE

re·fuel \(ˈ)rē+\ *vb* [*re-* + *fuel*] *vt* : to provide with fresh fuel : replenish the fuel supply of ~ *vi* : to take on a fresh fuel supply

¹**ref·uge** \'re(ˌ)fyüj, *esp before a syllable-increasing suffix* -ˌfyəj\ *n* -s [ME, fr. MF, fr. L *refugium*, fr. *refugere* to run away, avoid, escape, fr. *re-* + *fugere* to run away, flee — more at FUGITIVE] **1** : shelter or protection from danger or distress ⟨seek ~ in flight⟩ ⟨take ~ in the home of a friend⟩ ⟨a house of ~⟩ **2 a** : a home for those who are destitute, homeless, or in disgrace **b** : a sanctuary for birds or wild animals **c** : a mountain hut or cabin erected to serve as sleeping quarters for mountaineers **d** : a safety zone for pedestrians crossing a street in heavy traffic : SAFETY ISLAND **3** : a means of resort for help in difficulty : RESOURCE ⟨patriotism is the last ~ of a scoundrel —Samuel Johnson⟩ ⟨the ivory tower . . . as a place of ~ from unpleasant reality —H.N.Russell⟩

²**refuge** \"\ *vb* -ED/-ING/-S *vt* : to give refuge to ~ *vi* : to seek or take refuge

³**ref·uge** \", 'refij\ *n* [by alter.] *chiefly dial* : ³REFUSE

¹**ref·u·gee** \ˌrefyə¦jē, -efyü,j-, ˌ==ˈ=\ *n* -s [F *réfugié*, past part. of *réfugier* to put in a place of safety (*se réfugier* to take refuge), fr. L *refugium* refuge] **1** : one that flees to a place of safety; *esp* : one who flees to a foreign country or power to escape danger or persecution in his own country or habitual residence because of his race, religion, or political beliefs **2** : one who flees from justice : FUGITIVE **3** : COWBOY 2a

²**refugee** \"\ *vi* **refugeed; refugeed; refugeeing; refugees** : to flee as a refugee

³**refugee** \"\ *adj* **1** : that is a refugee ⟨~ slaves⟩ **2** : that has taken flight from unfavorable investment conditions or from invading armies to carry on in another country ⟨~ capital⟩ ⟨~ government⟩

ref·u·gee·ism \-ē,izəm\ *n* -s : the state of being a refugee

re·fu·gi·um \rə'fyüjēəm, rē'f-\ *n*, *pl* **refu·gia** \-ēə\ [L, refuge — more at REFUGE] : an area of relatively unaltered climate that is inhabited by plants and animals during a period of continental climatic change (as a glaciation) and remains as a center of relic forms from which a new dispersion and speciation may take place after climatic readjustment

re·ful·gence \rə'fəljən(t)s, rē'f-\ *also* **re·ful·gen·cy** \-nsē, -nsi\ *n*, *pl* **refulgences** *also* **refulgencies** [L *refulgentia*, fr. *refulgent-, refulgens* (pres. part. of *refulgēre*) + *-ia* -y] : the quality or state of being refulgent : BRILLIANCE, SPLENDOR, RADIANCE ⟨came into the ~ of the headlights —Kay Boyle⟩

re·ful·gent \-nt\ *adj* [L *refulgent-, refulgens*, pres. part. of *refulgēre* to shine brightly, glitter, fr. *re-* + *fulgēre* to shine, flash — more at FULGENT] : giving out a bright light : richly radiant ⟨~ sunset⟩ : SHINING, BRILLIANT ⟨in arms . . . of golden panoply, ~ host —John Milton⟩ **syn** see BRIGHT

¹**re·fund** \rə'fənd, (ˈ)rē¦f-\ *vt* -ED/-ING/-S [ME *refunden*, fr. MF & L; MF *refonder, refunder* to reimburse, fr. L *refundere* to pour back, give or put back, fr. *re-* + *fundere* to pour — more at FOUND] **1 a** *obs* : to pour back **b** : to give or put back **2** : to return (money) in restitution, repayment, or balancing of accounts ⟨~ the price of a defective article⟩ ⟨~ the excess on a tax⟩ **3** : REPAY, REIMBURSE

²**re·fund** \'rē,fənd *sometimes* rə'f- *or* rē'f-\ *n* -s **1** : the act of refunding **2** : a sum that is paid back : REPAYMENT

³**re·fund** \(ˈ)rē¦fənd\ *vt* [*re-* + *fund*] : to fund again or anew; *specif* : to borrow usu. by the sale of bonds in order to pay off an existing loan with the proceeds ⟨~ a debt⟩ ⟨~ a mortgage⟩

re·fund·able \rə'fəndəbəl, rē'f-\ *adj* [¹*refund* + *-able*] : capable of being refunded ⟨overpayment of a tax is ~ at the end of the year⟩ ⟨~ deposit⟩

refund annuity *n* : an annuity payable until annuitant's death when if total payments have not equalled all or a stated part of the purchase price the difference is paid to the annuitant's estate or to a designated beneficiary

refunding bond *n* [*refunding* fr. gerund of ³*refund*] : a bond issued to pay off an outstanding issue

re·furbish \(ˈ)rē+\ *vt* [*re-* + *furbish*] : to brighten or freshen up : to make as if new : RENOVATE ⟨~ an old house⟩ ⟨~ an antique table⟩ ⟨~ an old legend⟩

re·fur·bish·ment \"mənt\ *n* -s : the act or result of refurbishing : RENEWAL ⟨various kinds of adjustments and ~*s* of beliefs —W.W.Howells⟩ ⟨spring ~ of houses⟩

re·furl \(ˈ)rē+\ *vt* [*re-* + *furl*] : to furl again

re·furnish \"+\ *vt* [*re-* + *furnish*] : to furnish anew; *specif* : TOPWORK

re·fus·able \rə'fyüzəbəl, rē'f-\ *adj* [¹*refuse* + *-able*] **1** : capable of being refused : admitting of refusal **2** *obs* : meriting refusal or rejection

re·fus·al \-zəl\ *n* -s [ME *refusell*, fr. *refusen* to refuse + *-ell*, *-aille* -al] **1** : the act of refusing or denying : rejection of something demanded, solicited, or offered for acceptance ⟨~ to answer questions⟩ ⟨her ~ of all marriage proposals⟩ ⟨the horse was disqualified by his ~ at the first fence⟩ **2** : the opportunity or right of refusing or taking before others : the choice of refusing or taking (as a purchase) ⟨promised to give him the first ~ of my house⟩ **3** *obs* : one that has been refused or rejected **4 a** : stoppage of a driven bolt or pile because of resistance greater than the driving force **b** : the point of such stoppage **c** : the distance a pile sinks under a single blow **d** : the total distance a pile sinks under a volley of blows

¹**re·fuse** \rə'fyüz, rē'f-\ *vb* -ED/-ING/-S [ME *refusen*, fr. MF *refuser*, fr. OF, fr. (assumed) VL *refusare*, fr. L *refusus*, past part. of *refundere* to pour back, give or put back — more at REFUND] *vt* **1** *obs* : AVOID, SHUN **2** : to decline to accept : REJECT ⟨~ an office⟩ ⟨~ a gift⟩ ⟨~ advice⟩; *specif* : to decline to have as husband **3 a** : to show or express a positive unwillingness to do or comply with (as something asked, demanded, expected) — used with a following infinitive ⟨*refused* to answer the question⟩ ⟨motor *refused* to start⟩ **b** : DENY ⟨*refused* to give his permission⟩ ⟨has never *refused* his help before⟩ ⟨was *refused* entrance at the club door⟩ **4** *obs* : to give up : RENOUNCE ⟨still ~ this world, to do their Father's will —John Bunyan⟩ ⟨deny thy father and ~ thy name —Shak.⟩ **5** *of a horse* : to decline to jump or leap over (as a fence or ditch) **6** : to fail to follow with a card from (the suit led) because of not having one **7** : to bend back or keep back (as the flank of one's defensive position) ~ *vi* **1** : to withhold acceptance, compliance, or permission ⟨that the King had offered him the Garter, but that he had asked permission to ~ —Valentine Heywood⟩ **2** *of a horse* : to decline to jump **3** : to fail to follow suit in a card game **syn** see DECLINE — **refuse stays** *of a ship* : to fail to go about : miss stays

²**refuse** \"\ *n* -s *dial chiefly Eng* : REFUSAL

³**ref·use** \'re,fyüs, -üz\ *n* -s [ME, fr. MF *refus* refusal, rejection, fr. OF, fr. *refuser* to refuse] **1** : the worthless or useless part of something : LEAVINGS, DREGS, DROSS ⟨~ from silver mining⟩ ⟨sugar cane ~⟩ ⟨propertyless gentlemen . . . have to be content nowadays with the ~ of middle class employment —G.B.Shaw⟩ **2** : RUBBISH, TRASH, GARBAGE

syn WASTE, RUBBISH, TRASH, DEBRIS, GARBAGE, OFFAL: REFUSE applies to any matter or materials rejected as useless and fit only to be thrown out or away ⟨there was a huge stinking heap of week-old *refuse* . . . old clothes, sad boots with calloused heels, and hats that were just misshapen basins of felt; old books and magazines, stained with tea leaves and the sodden heterogeneous mass of household garbage —Ruth Park⟩ WASTE is also comprehensive; it may indicate that unused or rejected in one operation but possible for use in another capacity or under different circumstances ⟨mechanics using cotton *waste* to clean their hands⟩ ⟨*waste* in lumbering, the parts of trees that could be used but are not⟩ ⟨barnyard *wastes*⟩ ⟨tea *waste* — slack bushes, waste leaf, and crushed sugarcane leaf and pulp —Eve Langley⟩ RUBBISH now is likely to indicate a heterogeneous accumulation of worn-out, used-up, broken, rejected, or worthless materials or things ⟨*rubbish*. This material includes the household and business wastes that are not classified as garbage or ashes. It includes paper, rags, excelsior and other packing, wood, glass, crockery, and metals —V.M.Ehlers & E.W.Steel⟩ TRASH in general use has about the same suggestion as RUBBISH; it may refer to a somewhat lighter welter of discarded material and may be less likely to suggest separate objects and more likely to suggest a crumpled mass ⟨cleaning the old newspapers, rags, tin cans and other *trash* out of the cellar⟩ DEBRIS is likely to indicate broken fragments of bricks, rocks, walls, or buildings ⟨cleaning up the *debris* after the fire⟩ ⟨the *debris* left after mining operations⟩ GARBAGE now usu. indicates animal or vegetable refuse from the processes of shipping, preparing, and serving food ⟨egg shells, orange peels, coffee grounds and the rest of the *garbage* after breakfast⟩ OFFAL may refer to anything cut off or allowed to fall off in processing (as animal entrails or feet or fish heads or chicken heads); it may suggest the offensive but does not always do so, since such meat offal as hearts and livers may be sought for eating ⟨"*Offal!*" she gasped. "Take that carrion out" —Kenneth Roberts⟩

⁴**refuse** \"\ *adj* [ME, fr. *refuse*, n.] : thrown aside or left as worthless or of no value : REFUSED, REJECTED, WORTHLESS, USELESS ⟨~ land⟩ ⟨~ wood⟩

¹**re-fuse** \(ˈ)rē¦fyüz\ *vt* [*re-* + *fuse* (to melt)] : to melt again

²**re-fuse** \"\ *vt* [*re-* + *fuse* (to equip with a fuse)] : to replace a fuse in

re·fus·er \rə'fyüzə(r), rē'f-\ *n* -s [ME, fr. *refusen* to refuse + *-er*] **1** : one that refuses ⟨that horse has become a chronic ~⟩ **2** : RECUSANT

re·fus·ible \(ˈ)rē¦fyüzəbəl\ *adj* [²*re-fuse* + *-able*] : capable of renewal with a new fuse ⟨~ plug in a safety valve⟩

re·fu·sion \rə'fyüzhən, rē'f-\ *n* -s [F *réfusion* act of giving or putting back, fr. LL *refusion-, refusio* restitution, overflowing, fr. L *refusus* (past part. of *refundere* to pour back, give or put back) + *-ion-, -io* -ion] : the act of pouring back : REINFUSION

re-fusion \(ˈ)rē¦fyüzhən\ *n* [*re-* + *fusion*] : a second or fresh melting ⟨~ of rocks⟩

re·fut·abil·i·ty \rəˌfyüd·ə'bilədē, rēˌfyü|, ˌrefyə|, |tə'-, -lətē, -i\ *n* : capability of being refuted

re·fut·able \rə'fyüd·əbəl, rē'fyü|, 'refyə|, |təb-\ *adj* [LL *refutabilis*, fr. L *refutare* to refute + *-abilis* -able] : capable of being refuted — **re·fut·ably** \-blē, -bli\ *adv*

re·fut·al \rə'fyüd·ᵊl, rē'f-, -ütᵊl\ *n* -s : REFUTATION

ref·u·ta·tion \ˌrefyə'tāshən\ *n* -s [L *refutation-, refutatio*, fr. *refutatus* (past part. of *refutare* to refute) + *-ion-, -io* -ion] : the act or process of refuting : proof of falsehood or error : overthrowing by argument or proof : DISPROOF, CONFUTATION ⟨some of his blunders seem rather to deserve a flogging than a ~ —T.B.Macaulay⟩

re·fut·ative \rə'fyüd·əd·iv, rē'f-, -ütətiv\ *adj* [fr. *refutation*, after such pairs as E *negation: negative*] : tending to refute : relating to refutation ⟨~ force of his argument⟩

re·fut·ato·ry \-üd·əˌtōrē, -ütə-, -tȯr-, -ri\ *adj* [LL *refutatorius*, fr. L *refutatus* (past part. of *refutare*) + *-orius* -ory] : REFUTATIVE

re·fute \rə'fyüt, rē'f-, *usu* -üd.+V\ *vt* -ED/-ING/-S [L *refutare* to check, drive back, refute, fr. *re-* + *-futare* to beat — more at BEAT] : to overthrow by argument, evidence, or proof : prove to be false or erroneous : CONFUTE ⟨~ arguments⟩ ⟨~ testimony⟩ ⟨*refuted* the charge of laziness by working hard⟩ **syn** see DISPROVE

re·fut·er \-üd·ə(r), -ütə-\ *n* -s : one that refutes something

reg \'reg\ *n* -s [of Hamitic origin; akin to Amharic *'arăgă* rise, ascend] : ²ERG

reg *abbr* **1** regent **2** regiment **3** [L *regina*] queen **4** region **5** register; registered **6** registrar; registry **7** regius **8** regular; regularly **9** regulate; regulation; regulator

¹**re·gain** \(ˈ)rē+\ *vt* [*re-* + *gain*] **1** : to gain anew : get again : RECOVER ⟨~ health⟩ ⟨~*ed* his position in society⟩ **2** : to get back to : reach again ⟨~ the shore⟩ **syn** see RECOVER

²**regain** \"\ *n* **1** : an act or instance of regaining **2** : an amount regained; *specif* : the percentage based on the bone-dry weight of materials of moisture that a textile material absorbs in a standard atmosphere

re·gain·er \-nə(r)\ *n* : one that regains something

re·gain·ment \-mənt\ *n* -s : an act or instance of regaining ⟨waiting for her ~ of composure⟩

¹**regal** *n* -s [ME, kingdom, royal jewel, fr. MF *regale* kingdom, royal garment, fr. OF, fr. fem. of (assumed) OF *regal* royal, regal (whence MF *regal*), fr. L *regalis*] *obs* : something relating or belonging to royalty: as **a** : a royal jewel ⟨the ~ of France⟩ **b** : a regal privilege **c** : a chalice used in the Communion at English coronations

²**re·gal** \'rēgəl\ *adj* [ME, fr. MF or L; MF, fr. L *regalis* royal, regal — more at ROYAL] **1** : of, relating to, suitable to, or like a king **2** : of notable excellence or magnificence : STATELY, SPLENDID

³**regal** \"\ *n* -s [MF *regale*, perh. fr. fem. of *regal* royal, regal] : a small portable organ of the 16th and 17th centuries having orig. reed pipes only but later incorporating flue pipes and having keys played with one hand while the bellows are worked with the other

¹**re·gale** \rə'gālē, rē'-\ *n*, *pl* **re·ga·lia** \-lyə, -lēə\ [ML, royal prerogative, royal ornament, fr. L, neut. of *regalis* royal, regal] **1 a** : the right, power, or privilege of a king : royal prerogative — usu. used in pl. **b** [F & ML; F *régale*, fr. ML *regale*, fr. L, neut. of *regalis*] : a right or prerogative of enjoying the revenues of vacant sees and abbacies and of presenting to benefices dependent on them claimed by rulers in the middle ages **2** *regalia pl* **a** : the emblems, symbols, or paraphernalia (as crown, scepter, or standard) indicative of royal state **b** : decorations, insignia, or special costume indicative of an office or of membership in a group (as a social or fraternal order) ⟨the lord mayor in full *regalia*⟩ **3** *regalia pl* : costume devoted to a particular situation or use : special costume : FINERY ⟨unrecognizable in his Sunday *regalia*⟩

²**re·gale** \rə'gāl, rē-, *esp before pause or consonant* -āəl\ *vb* -ED/-ING/-S [F *régaler*, fr. MF *regaler*, fr. *regale*, *rigalle*, n.] *vt* **1 a** : to entertain (as a person) sumptuously or agreeably : feast with delicacies ⟨*regaled* her guests with the best of everything⟩ **b** : to indulge, refresh, or renew (oneself) with food or drink and esp. with delicacies ⟨*regaling* himself with a vast platter of chitterlings⟩ **c** : to serve as a delicacy for : REFRESH ⟨good ale to ~ our throats⟩ **2** : to offer pleasant entertainment to (as the senses) : give pleasure or amusement to : affect pleasurably ⟨a sight that ~*s* the eye⟩ ⟨*regaled* the meeting with the tale of the committee's troubles⟩ ~ *vi* : to feast oneself : FEED ⟨*regaling* on dewberries —George Meredith⟩ **syn** see PLEASE

³**regale** \"\ *n* -s [F *régal*, fr. MF *regale*, *rigalle*, fr. *re-* + *gale* pleasure, merrymaking — more at GALLANT] **1 a** : a choice or sumptuous repast : FEAST **b** : a ration or treat of food or drink **2** : REGALEMENT

reg·a·lec·i·dae \ˌregə'lesəˌdē\ *n pl*, *cap* [NL, fr. *Regalecus*, type genus + *-idae*] : a family of large marine fishes (order Allotriognathi) constituted by the oarfishes

re·gal·e·cus \rə'galəkəs\ *n*, *cap* [NL (intended as trans. of Norw *sildekonge* oarfish, fr. *sild* herring + *konge* king), fr. L *reg-, rex* king + *allec* fish pickle — more at ROYAL] : the type and sole genus of the family Regalecidae

re·gale·ment \rə'gā(ə)lmənt, rē'-\ *n* -s **1** : an act of regaling **2** : something that regales : ENTERTAINMENT, REFRESHMENT

re·gal·er \-ālə(r)\ *n* -s : one that regales

regal fern *n* : ROYAL FERN

regal fritillary *n* : a common fritillary butterfly (*Speyeria idalia*) of the eastern U. S.

¹**regalia** *pl of* REGALE

²**regalia** *or* **regalio** *obs var of* REGALO

³**re·ga·lia** \rə'gālyə, -lēə, ˌrāgə'lēə\ *n* -s [AmerSp *regalía*, fr. Sp, royal prerogative, fr. ML *regalia*, pl. of *regale* royal prerogative] : a cigar of large size and superior quality; *also* : the size in which such cigars are classed

re·ga·lian \rə'gālyən, rē'-, -lēən\ *adj* [F *régalien*, fr. L *regalis* royal, regal + F *-en* -an (fr. L *-anus*)] : of or belonging to a royal ruler : REGAL, SOVEREIGN ⟨~ rights⟩

re·gal·ism \'rēgəˌlizəm\ *n* -s : the doctrine of royal supremacy esp. in church affairs

re·gal·ist \-ˌləst\ *n* -s **:** an advocate of regalism

re·gal·i·ty \rə'galəd·ē, rē'-, -lətē, -i\ *n* -ES [ME *regalite*, fr. MF & ML; MF *regalité*, fr. ML *regalitat-, regalitas*, fr. L *regalis* royal, regal + *-tat-, -tas* -ty] **1 a :** sovereign right or privilege **:** sovereign jurisdiction or prerogative **b regalities** *pl* **:** REGALIA **2 :** a country or territory subject to royal jurisdiction or to such jurisdiction in the hands of a subject **3 :** a royal grant under former English or Scots law permitting a lord of a particular territory to exercise jurisdiction similar in civil matters to that of a sheriff and with more extensive jurisdiction to hear criminal cases — see LORD OF REGALITY

re·gal lily \'rēgəl-\ *also* **re·ga·le lily** \rə'gālē-\ *n* [*regal lily* fr. ²*regal* + *lily; regale lily* fr. NL *regale* (specific epithet of *Lilium regale*) (fr. L, neut. of *regalis* royal, regal) + E *lily*] **:** a widely cultivated garden lily (*Lilium regale*) of western China grown for its showy flowers that are white and yellow inside but streaked or flushed with pink or light lilac purple on the outer surface of the petals

re·gal·ly \'rēgəlē, -li\ *adv* [ME *regaliche*, fr. ²*regal* + *-liche* -ly] **:** in a regal manner **:** so as to be or appear regal

regal moth *n* **:** a large showy American moth (*Citheronia regalis*) having the forewings olive spotted with yellow and heavily veined with red and the hind wings orange-red spotted with yellow — see HICKORY HORNED DEVIL

re·gal·ness *n* -ES **:** the quality or state of being regal

re·ga·lo \rə'gä(ˌ)lō, -gä(ˌ)-, -ga(ˌ)-\ *n* -s [Sp, fr. MF *regale* feast — more at REGALE] *archaic* **:** GIFT, BONUS, TREAT; *esp* **:** an offering of superior food or drink

regal purple *n* **:** ROYAL PURPLE 2

regals *pl of* REGAL

regalty *n* -ES [ME *regalte*, prob. modif. of MF *regalité*] *obs* **:** REGALITY

re·galvanize \(ˈ)rē+\ *vt* [*re-* + *galvanize*] **:** to restore vitality or activity to as if by galvanizing

regal water *n* [trans. of NL *aqua regia*] *archaic* **:** AQUA REGIA

¹**re·gard** \rə'gärd, rē'-, -gȧd\ *n* -s [ME, fr. MF *regard, regart*, fr. OF, fr. *regarder*, v.] **1** *archaic* **:** ASPECT, APPEARANCE, MIEN **2 a :** attention of the mind with a feeling of interest **:** attention or respect as shown in action or conduct **:** CONSIDERATION, HEED, CONCERN **b :** LOOK, GLANCE, GAZE ⟨fixed on him his magisterial ~⟩ **c :** inspection of a forest by officials under old English law to learn if any trespasses have been committed **:** the right or office of such inspection; *also* **:** a district under the jurisdiction of such an official **3 a :** the worth or estimation in which something is held ⟨a man of small ~⟩ **b** (1) **:** a feeling of blended approval, appreciation, respect, liking, and affection usu. based on attractive characteristics of the object ⟨their ardor and their faithful endurance of all the hardships have won them the ~ of their British comrades —Sir Winston Churchill⟩ (2) **:** friendly greetings implying such a feeling — usu. used in pl. ⟨give them our ~*s*⟩ **c :** an evidence of affection or kindly feeling **:** a protective interest based on esteem **:** CARE ⟨a man with any ~ for his health⟩ **4 :** something that is considered as a ground of action or opinion **:** CONSIDERATION, MOTIVE **5 :** an aspect to be taken into consideration or significant to the matter in question **:** RELATION, RESPECT ⟨knowing nothing of the divine will in our ~⟩ ⟨considered with some ~ for its effect on my health⟩ ⟨in ~ to internal policy —M.R.Cohen⟩ ⟨in doubt in ~ to its aims —J.H.Robinson †1936⟩ ⟨no melodramatics with ~ to art —J.C.Powys⟩ ⟨this agreement, with ~ to which there was an express understanding —Ellen Wilkinson⟩ **6** *obs* **:** INTENTION

syn RESPECT, ESTEEM, ADMIRATION: REGARD is the least connotative in this group and is often accompanied by a modifier like *high* to indicate a favorable feeling ⟨a pilot held in high *regard*⟩ REGARD may be used to suggest friendly feelings without impulse to emulation or closer relationship ⟨gave her their affection in full measure . . . with a manly *regard*, in which there was nothing akin to what is distinctively called love —Nathaniel Hawthorne⟩ RESPECT may add to REGARD implications of deference to or veneration of on the part of an inferior or junior. It may suggest that the feeling implied is justly due ⟨an important form of rewards and punishments for young children, and also for older boys and girls if conferred by a person who inspires *respect* —Bertrand Russell⟩ It may suggest deference to rank with or without implications of accompanying liking ⟨the *respect* which he felt for her high rank, and his veneration for her as his patroness —Jane Austen⟩ ⟨but nobody really liked her: malignity commands *respect*, not liking —Robert Graves⟩ ESTEEM may suggest more genuine feeling than RESPECT; it may connote warmth of feeling or conviction of a worthiness to be emulated ⟨if Stephen did disclose himself to him, it would be a signal mark of *esteem* —Archibald Marshall⟩ ⟨expressing my *esteem* for his character —Edmund Burke⟩ ADMIRATION is a strong term suggesting pleasure, delight, and wonder, often with impulse to emulate or possess; it stresses feeling, sometimes, although certainly not always, implying a subordination of thoughtful judgment ⟨his own romantic *admiration* of Mary, Queen of Scots —S.M.Crothers⟩ ⟨should not hold up military conquerors to *admiration* —Bertrand Russell⟩ ⟨in proportion to his *admiration* for his father —George Meredith⟩ REGARD stresses the fact of feeling, RESPECT due feeling suitably expressed, ESTEEM genuine warm and lasting feeling, and ADMIRATION strong feeling with less suggestion of judicious analysis.

— **in regard of** *prep* **1** *archaic* **:** in comparison with **2 :** in respect to **:** as to **3** *obs* **:** on account of **:** because of **4** *obs* **:** out of consideration or respect for

²**regard** \"\ *vb* -ED/-ING/-S [ME *regarden*, fr. MF *regarder, reguarder* to regard, look at, fr. OF, fr. *re-* + *garder, guarder* to guard — more at GUARD] *vt* **1 a :** to pay attention to **:** notice or remark particularly ⟨don't ~ this very seriously⟩ **b** *obs* **:** to look after **:** take care of or for **2 a** *obs* **:** to treat (a thing) as something of peculiar value, sanctity, or worth **b :** to have care for **:** heed in conduct or practice **:** have respect for (as a person) **:** show respect or consideration for ⟨each must ~ the rights of all⟩ **c :** to hold (one) in high esteem **:** care for **3 a :** to keep in view **:** look at **:** gaze upon ⟨your niece ~*s* me with an eye of favor —Shak.⟩ **b** *obs* **:** to face toward **4 :** to take into consideration or account **:** take account of ⟨neither ~*ing* that she is my child nor fearing me as if I were her father —Shak.⟩ **5 :** to have relation to or bearing upon **:** relate to **:** touch on ⟨your argument does not ~ the question⟩ **6 :** to look at from a particular point of view **:** think of **:** CONSIDER, EVALUATE, JUDGE — usu. used with *as* ⟨~*ed* their chief as a brave soldier and a resourceful leader⟩ ⟨he ~*ed* no task as to humble for him to undertake —Aldous Huxley⟩ ~ *vi* **1 :** to look attentively **:** GAZE **2** *obs* **:** to take heed or pains **3 :** to pay attention **:** HEED **syn** see CONSIDER

re·gard·able \-dəbəl\ *adj* **:** fit for or deserving of notice

re·gar·dant \rə'gärd³nt, -gȧd-\ *adj* [ME, fr. MF *regardant, reguardant*, pres. part. of *regarder, reguarder* to look at] **1 :** annexed to a particular manor whoever owned it — used of a medieval English villein; compare *in gross* at ²GROSS **2** *also* **re·guar·dant** \"\ **a :** GUARDANT **b :** looking backward over the shoulder — used of a heraldic representation of an animal

regarded *past of* REGARD

re·gard·er \rə'gärdər, rē'-, -gȧdə(r\ *n* -s [²*regard* + *-er*; trans. of AF *regardour*] **1 :** an officer having the right and duty under Old English law to inspect the royal forests and ascertain the presence or absence of trespasses or violations of the law **2 :** one that regards

re·gard·ful \=ˈ=fəl\ *adj* **1 :** HEEDFUL, OBSERVANT **2 :** full or expressive of regard or respect **:** RESPECTFUL — **re·gard·ful·ly** \-fəlē, -li\ *adv* — **re·gard·ful·ness** *n* -ES

regarding *prep* **:** with respect to **:** CONCERNING

¹**re·gard·less** \=ˈ=ləs\ *adj* **1 :** having no regard **:** HEEDLESS, CARELESS ⟨crushing the bloom with ~ tread⟩ **2** *archaic* **:** not meriting regard — **re·gard·less·ly** *adv* — **re·gard·less·ness** *n* -ES

²**regardless** \"\ *adv* **:** without regard to impeding elements (as of prudence, expense, or effort) ⟨everything's been done ~ —James Montgomery⟩ ⟨insisted we have dinner ~⟩

regardless of *prep* **:** without taking into account **:** in spite of ⟨*regardless of* our mistakes⟩

regards *pl of* REGARD, *pres 3d sing of* REGARD

re·gather \(ˈ)rē+\ *vb* [*re-* + *gather*] *vt* **:** to gather anew **:** bring together once more **:** REUNITE **:** RECRUIT ⟨~*ing* our forces⟩ ~ *vi* **:** to come together anew **:** become whole again ⟨storm clouds ~*ing* over the hills⟩ ⟨the crowd ~*ed* after the storm⟩

re·gat·ta \rə'gad·ə, rē'-, -gatə, -gäd·ə, -gätə\ *n* -s [It *regatta, regata*, fr. It (Venetian dial.)] **1 a :** a gondola race in Venice **b :** a rowing, speedboat, or sailing race; *esp* **:** an organized series of such races **2 :** a strong twilled English cotton fabric for clothing usu. with colored stripes or checks **3 :** LIBERTY 6

regd *abbr* registered

re·gear \(ˈ)rē+\ *vt* [*re-* + *gear*] **:** to alter so as to be suitable for a new purpose or condition ⟨~*ing* the national economy for war⟩

re·ge·late \'rējəˌlāt, ˌ==ˈ=\ *vi* [back-formation fr. *regelation*] **:** to freeze together again **:** undergo regelation

re·gelation \ˌrē+\ *n* [*re-* + *gelation* (freezing)] **:** the refreezing of water derived from the melting of ice under pressure when the pressure is relieved

re·gel's privet \'rāgəlz-\ *or* **regel privet** *n* [prob. after Edward August von *Regel* †1892 Ger. botanist in Russia] **:** a deciduous Asiatic shrub (*Ligustrum obtusifolium regehanum*) with horizontally spreading branches and pubescent branchlets and leaves that is used as a hedge plant and is notably tolerant of shade and soil

re·gence \'rējən(t)s\ *adj* [F *Régence* belonging to or characteristic of the regency of Philippe II, Duc d'Orléans †1723 regent of France 1715–23 during the minority of Louis XV, fr. *régence*, n., regency, fr. MF *regence* rule, fr. ML *regentia* regency, rule] **:** of, relating to, or being furniture or a furniture style characteristic of the regency of the Duke of Orleans, prevalent between about 1680 and 1725, and marked by a gradual transition from the earlier severely angular and massive to the delicate curvatures of Louis XV style

¹**re·gen·cy** \-nsē, -si\ *n* -ES [ME *regencie*, fr. ML *regentia*, fr. *regent-, regens* ruler, regent + L *-ia* -y — more at REGENT] **1 a :** the office, jurisdiction, or dominion of a regent or vicarious ruler or of a body of regents **b** *archaic* **:** the office or position of ruler **:** royal office or state **:** RULE **2 :** a territory governed by a regent or regency **3 a** *obs* **:** a governing body of various cities or states **b :** a body of men entrusted with vicarious government ⟨a ~ constituted during a king's minority⟩ **4 :** a period during which a regent or body of regents governs

²**regency** \"\ *adj, often cap* [¹*regency;* fr. the regency of George, Prince of Wales (afterwards George IV †1830 King of Great Britain and Ireland) during the period (1811–20) when his father George III was still alive but permanently deranged] **:** of, relating to, typical of, or adapted from early 19th century England, its customs, or its styles ⟨a ~ poem⟩ ⟨~ furniture⟩ ⟨~ dress⟩

re·gen·er·a·ble \(ˈ)rē¦jen(ə)rəbəl, rə'-\ *adj* [³*regenerate* + *-able*] **:** capable of being regenerated

re·gen·er·a·cy \-n(ə)rəsē\ *n* -ES [¹*regenerate* + *-cy*] **:** the quality or state of being regenerated

re·gen·er·ant \-n(ə)rənt\ *n* -s [³*regenerate* + *-ant*] **:** a regenerating agent

¹**re·gen·er·ate** \-n(ə)rət, *usu* -əd·+V\ *adj* [ME *regenerat*, fr. L *regeneratus*, past part. of *regenerare* to regenerate, fr. *re-* + *generare* to beget — more at GENERATE] **1 :** formed or created again **2 :** spiritually reborn or converted **:** having undergone regeneration; *specif* **:** having become a Christian **3 :** restored to a better, higher, or more worthy state ⟨~ by redemption from error or decay⟩

²**regenerate** \"\ *n* -s **:** a regenerated thing or person: as **a :** an individual who is spiritually reborn **b** (1) **:** an organism that has undergone regeneration (2) **:** a regenerated body part or structure

³**regenerate** \-nəˌrāt, *usu* -ād·+V\ *vb* [L *regeneratus*, past part. of *regenerare*] *vi* **1 :** to become formed again **:** become shaped anew **2 :** to become regenerate **:** REFORM **3 :** to undergo regeneration ~ *vt* **1 a :** to cause to be spiritually born again **:** subject to spiritual regeneration **b :** to make a radical change for the better in **:** reform completely ⟨forces that will ~ society⟩ **2 a :** to generate or produce anew **:** REPRODUCE, RE-CREATE, REVIVE ⟨~ hatred⟩; *esp* **:** to replace (a body part) by a new growth of tissue ⟨lizards that ~ lost tails⟩ **b** (1) **:** to form (a compound) again chemically from a derivative (2) **:** to produce again from a modified form by chemical treatment in a form changed physically but usu. not to a great extent chemically from the original raw material ⟨*regenerated* fibers⟩ **3 :** to reestablish on a new and usu. better basis **4 :** to restore (a material) to original strength (as by adding salt to a brine that has been weakened by the absorption of atmospheric moisture) or to restore original properties to (a material) **5 :** to increase the amplification of (an electron current) by causing a part of the power in the output circuit to act upon the input circuit by means of electron tubes

regenerated cellulose *n* **:** cellulose obtained in a changed form by sulfuric acid or other chemical treatment of an extruded coagulated solution (as of viscose or cuprammonium solution) or a stretched acetate fiber ⟨*regenerated cellulose* and acetate fibers⟩ — see CELLOPHANE, ²RAYON 1b

re·gen·er·ate·ly *adv* **:** in a regenerate manner **:** as if regenerated

re·gen·er·ate·ness *n* -ES **:** the quality or state of being regenerate

re·gen·er·a·tion \(ˌ)rēˌjenə'rāshən, rəˌ-\ *n* [ME *regeneracioun*, fr. MF & LL; MF *regeneration*, fr. LL *regeneration-, regeneratio*, fr. L *regeneratus* (past part. of *regenerare*) + *-ion-, -io* -ion] **1 :** an act of regenerating or the condition of being regenerated **2 :** spiritual rebirth **:** spiritual renewal, re-creation, or revival **:** a radical spiritual transformation in which the center of one's life is shifted under the action of a divine agency (as the Holy Spirit) from a self-centered ultimate concern to a God-centered ultimate concern **3 :** the renewal, regrowth, or restoration of a body or a bodily part, tissue, or substance after injury or as a normal bodily process ⟨~ of a plant from a cutting⟩ ⟨~ of a lost claw by a lobster⟩ ⟨continual ~ of epithelial cells⟩ ⟨~ of the contractile substance of muscle after exercise⟩ — compare REGULATION **4 a :** the process by which part of the power in the output circuit of an amplifying device is caused to act upon the input circuit so as to increase the amplification **:** FEEDBACK **b :** the utilization by special devices of heat or other products that would ordinarily be lost — see REGENERATOR 4

re·gen·er·a·tive \rē'jenəˌrād·|iv, rə'-, -n(ə)rə|, |t|, |ēv\ *adj* [ME, fr. ML *regenerativus*, fr. L *regeneratus* (past part. of *regenerare*) + *-ivus* -ive] **1 :** of, relating to, marked by, or using regeneration **:** tending to regenerate ⟨~ influences⟩ ⟨a ~ furnace⟩ ⟨the ~ phase of the cycle⟩ **2 :** constituting or relating to the returning of energy to a supply system (as when a descending motor-driven hoist returns energy to the line by acting as a generator); *specif* **:** relating to a method of amplification with electron tubes in which a part of the power in the output circuit acts upon the input circuit to increase the amplification — **re·gen·er·a·tive·ly** \|əvlē, -li\ *adv*

regenerative braking *n* **:** electric braking in which electrical energy that is produced by the motor is transferred to the supply line

regenerative cooling *n* **:** a cryogenic method in which the rapid expansion of a portion of a gas to be liquefied is utilized to lower the temperature of the remainder

regenerative cycle *n* **:** a cycle in a steam engine using heat that would ordinarily be lost: as **a :** a multiple-expansion steam-engine cycle in which the receivers are used as successive feed-water heaters **b :** a steam-turbine cycle in which the condensate or feed water is heated to a temperature that is much higher than that corresponding to saturation at the exhaust pressure by means of steam that has been bled from the turbine at points intermediate between the throttle and exhaust

regenerative furnace *n* **:** a gas-burning furnace equipped with a regenerator

regenerative motor *n* **:** a jet or rocket motor in which the incoming combustion air is heated by passage through the motor cooling jacket

re·gen·er·a·tor \rē'jenəˌrād·ə(r), -ātə-\ *n* [LL, fr. L *regeneratus* (past part. of *regenerare* to regenerate) + *-or*] **1 :** one that regenerates **2 :** a heavy swinging counterpoise or other balancing device for a mine pump rod to permit a higher engine speed **3 :** a hypothetical body (as used with a reversible engine operating on a Stirling cycle) that stores heat from the working substance of an engine so that each part of the body and the contiguous gas or vapor have the same temperature, each increment of heat is maintained at the temperature at which it was received, and the stored heat is returned to the working substance by the reversal of the process **4 :** a device used esp. with hot-air engines or gas-burning furnaces in which the incoming air or gas is heated by contact with masses (as of iron, brick) previously heated by the outgoing hot air or gas or by being passed through a pipe or pipes heated by a flow of the hot air or gas escaping in the opposite direction — compare HEAT EXCHANGER

re·gen·er·a·trix \=ˌ==ˈrā(ˌ)triks\ *n* [NL, fem. of LL *regenerator* — more at -TRIX] **:** a female regenerator ⟨regarded herself as fit to be the ~ of the world —Mortimer Collins⟩

re·genesis \(ˈ)rē+\ *n* [*re-* + *genesis*] **:** new birth **:** RENEWAL

re·gens·burg \'rāgənzˌbərg, -bəg, -bəig, -gənsˌbu̇r|g, -üə|, |k\ *adj, usu cap* [fr. *Regensburg*, city in southern Germany] **:** of or from the city of Regensburg, Germany **:** of the kind or style prevalent in Regensburg

¹**re·gent** \'rējənt\ *adj* [ME, fr. ML *regent-, regens*, fr. L, pres. part. of *regere* to rule — more at RIGHT] **1** *archaic* **:** functioning as a presiding officer over academic debates and disputations — used postpositively of a master of arts of less than five years standing at Oxford or Cambridge universities **2** [²*regent*] **:** exercising vicarious authority **:** acting as a regent (as of a country) **3** [L *regent-, regens*, pres. part. of *regere*] *archaic* **:** RULING, GOVERNING, REGNANT

²**regent** \"\ *n* -s [ME, fr. MF or ML; MF, ruler, regent, fr. ML *regent-, regens*, fr. L, pres. part. of *regere* to rule] **1 a** *archaic* **:** something that rules or governs **:** a ruling authority or principle **b :** one who rules or reigns **:** GOVERNOR, RULER **2 :** one invested with vicarious authority **:** one who governs a kingdom in the minority, absence, or disability of the sovereign: as **a :** a member of a former governing body of some European cities **b :** a native official in the former Dutch administration of Java through whom a resident and his assistants carry out the details of the government of a residency **3 a** (1) **:** a regent master of arts (2) **:** an instructor in a Scottish college in charge of students through the entire course **:** PROFESSOR **b** *obs* **:** the headmaster of a school **c :** a member of an academic or cultural governing board (as of a state university) **4** *or* **regent pump :** a woman's pump having a circular vamp and a quarter unbroken at the heel

regent bird *n* [so called in honor of George, Prince of Wales (afterward George IV †1830 King of Great Britain and Ireland), regent during the period (1811-20) when his father George III was still alive but permanently deranged] **:** a showy Australian bowerbird (*Sericulus chrysocephalus*) that in the male has the head, neck, and large patches on the wings bright golden yellow and the rest of the plumage deep velvety black

regent honey eater *n* [*regent* (as in *regent bird*) + *honey eater*] **:** FLYING COACHMAN

regent parrot *n* [*regent* (as in *regent bird*) + *parrot*] **:** a predominantly yellowish green Australian parrot (*Polytelis anthopeplus*) with dark bluish green outer and black under tail feathers and dark red markings on the wings

re·gent·ship \'==ˌship\ *n* **:** the office or state of a regent

re·germinate \(ˈ)rē+\ *vi* [*re-* + *germinate*] **:** to grow or develop anew **:** REGENERATE — **re·germination** \(ˌ)rē+\ *n*

reges *pl of* REX

reg·ga \'regə\ *n, pl* **regga** *or* **reggas** *usu cap* **:** a member of a Bantu-speaking people northwest of Lake Tanganyika

reg·gia·no \re'jä(ˌ)nō\ *also* **reggiano cheese** *n* -s *usu cap R* [It *reggiano*, fr. *reggiano*, adj., of or from the city of Reggio nell'Emilia, Italy] **:** a high quality Parmesan cheese that is usu. aged for several years before use

reg·gio \'re(ˌ)jō\ *also* **reg·gian** \-jən\ *adj, usu cap* [*reggio* fr. *Reggio* di Calabria, city in southern Italy; *reggian* fr. It *reggiano*, fr. *Reggio* di Calabria + It *-ano* -an (fr. L *-anus*)] **1 :** of or from the city of Reggio di Calabria, Italy **:** of the kind or style prevalent in Reggio di Calabria **2** [*reggio* fr. *Reggio* nell'Emilia, city in northern Italy; *reggian* fr. It *reggiano*, fr. *Reggio* nell'Emilia + It *-ano* -an (fr. L *-anus*)] **:** of or from the city of Reggio nell'Emilia, Italy **:** of the kind or style prevalent in Reggio nell'Emilia

regia dona *pl of* REGIUM DONUM

reg·i·ci·dal \ˌrejə'sīd³l\ *adj* **:** relating to regicide or a regicide **:** constituting or disposed to regicide

reg·i·cide \'rejəˌsīd\ *n* -s [prob. fr. (assumed) NL *regicida*, fr. L *regi-* (fr. *reg-, rex* king) + *-cida* -cide — more at ROYAL] **1 :** one who kills, murders, or shares overt responsibility (as by acting as judge or executioner) for the death of a king esp. to whom he is naturally subject **2** [prob. fr. (assumed) NL *regicidium*, fr. L *regi-* (fr. *reg-, rex* king) + *-cidium* -cide] **:** the killing or murder of a king

reg·i·cid·ism \-ˌdizəm\ *n* -s **:** the practice of regicide

re·gi·dor \ˌrāhē'thō(ə)r\ *n, pl* **regido·res** \-ō(ˌ)rās\ [Sp, fr. *regir* to rule, fr. L *regere*] **:** one of a body of officers charged with the government of a Spanish or Latin American municipality and corresponding to the English alderman

re·gie \rā'zhē, 'ˌ=\ *n* -s [F *régie*, fr. MF *regie* government, jurisdiction, fr. *regir* to rule, fr. L *regere*] **1 a :** a government monopoly (as on tobacco or salt) used chiefly as a means of taxation **b :** tobacco or tobacco products bought or supplied by agents of such a monopoly ⟨a ~ cigarette⟩ **2 :** direct management of public finance or public works by agents of the government for government account as distinguished from a system under which such public business is done under contract **3 :** the system of collecting taxes by officials who have either no interest or a very small interest in the proceeds as distinguished from the system of farming them out

re·gild \(ˈ)rē+\ *vt* [*re-* + *gild*] **:** to gild anew **:** BRIGHTEN, FRESHEN ⟨~*ing* his renown with new triumphs⟩

re·gime *also* **ré·gime** \rā'zhēm, rə'-, rē'- *sometimes* -'jēm\ *n* -s [F *régime*, fr. L *regimin-, regimen*] **1 a :** REGIMEN 1 **b :** a regular pattern of occurrence or action (as of seasonal rainfall) **2 a :** a method of ruling or management **:** a manner of administration **b :** a form of government or administration ⟨totalitarian ~⟩; *specif* **:** a governmental or social system ⟨Nazi ~⟩ **c :** the period during which a regime prevails **3 :** the condition of a river with respect to the rate of its flow as measured by the volume of water passing different cross sections in a given time **4 :** a fruiting cluster of the African oil palm

regime dotal *n* [F *régime dotal*, lit., dotal system of management] **:** the right and power of a husband under civil law to administer during his life his wife's dotal property under the rules of law safeguarding its return upon the dissolution of the marriage by death or other cause

reg·i·men \'rejəmən, -ˌmen\ *n* -s [ME, fr. L *regimin-, regimen* rule, government, fr. *regere* to rule — more at RIGHT] **1 a :** a systematic plan (as of diet, therapeutic and sanitary measures, and medication) designed to improve and maintain the health of a patient or to control a particular ailment **b :** a regulation or treatment intended to benefit by gradual operation **2 :** GOVERNING, GOVERNMENT, RULE, ADMINISTRATION **3 :** GOVERNMENT 5a **4 :** the characteristic behavior or orderly procedure of a natural phenomenon or process (as of a river or a glacier)

¹**reg·i·ment** \'rejəmənt *sometimes* -jm-\ *n* -s [ME, fr. MF, fr. LL *regimentum*, fr. L *regere* to rule + *-mentum* -ment] **1 a :** governmental rule **b** *obs* **:** REGIMEN 2, REGIME 2a **2** *obs* **a :** RULERSHIP, GOVERNORSHIP; *also* **:** the period of a particular reign **b :** GOVERNANCE, MANAGEMENT, GUIDANCE **c :** a region or district governed **3 :** a body of soldiers commanded by a colonel and consisting of a variable number of companies, troops, or batteries: as **a :** a parent military organization that may include many battalions or other units which rarely serve together but share a common history, traditions, uniforms, and other matters **b :** a military unit composed basically of a headquarters and two or more battalions — compare GROUP **4 a** *obs* **:** a group (as of dogs, birds, devils) forming a particular class or kind **b** *chiefly dial* **:** a large quantity ⟨a ~ of company for Sunday dinner⟩ ⟨put up a ~ of peaches last summer⟩

²**regiment** \-jəˌment, -j(ə)mənt — *see* ²-MENT\ *vt* -ED/-ING/-S **1 a :** to form (military personnel) into a regiment **b :** to place in or assign to a regiment **2 a :** to organize into groups, classes, or other units esp. for the sake of central regulation or control ⟨~ the industries of a country⟩ **b :** to subject to systematization or rigid discipline **:** reduce to strict order or uniformity ⟨an education that ~*s* children⟩

¹reg·i·men·tal \ˌrejəˈmentᵊl\ *adj* **1 :** belonging to, used by, or concerning a regiment ⟨~ officers⟩ ⟨~ supplies⟩ **2 :** serving to regiment **:** tending to regimentation

²regimental \"\ *n* -s **1 a :** the uniform worn by the officers and soldiers of a regiment **:** military dress — usu. used in pl. **b regimentals** *pl* **:** special clothing required for a particular activity **2 :** a grayish purplish blue that is redder and duller than Wedgwood blue (sense 2) or average delft and redder and lighter than average navy blue — called also *Persian blue*

regimental color *also* **regimental flag** *or* **regimental standard** *n* **:** a flag, ensign, or pennant usu. bearing symbols associated with the regiment by which it is carried as a mark of identification ⟨for many years . . . state flags continued to be carried as *regimental colors* —Leslie Thomas⟩

regimental combat team *n* **:** a tactical organization usu. formed by attaching artillery, engineers, or other special details to an infantry regiment for a particular mission

reg·i·men·tal·ly \-ᵊlē, -ᵊli\ *adv* **:** in a regimental manner **:** by regiment

reg·i·men·ta·ry \-tərē\ *adj* **:** involving or tending toward regimentation

reg·i·men·ta·tion \ˌrejəmən·ˈtāshən, -ˌmen·ˈ-\ *n* -s **:** the act or process of regimenting; *esp* **:** reduction to strict order or uniformity

re·gim·i·nal \rəˈjimənᵊl\ *adj* [L *regimin-, regimen* rule, government + E *-al* — more at REGIMEN] **:** of, relating to, or constituting regimen ⟨~ rules⟩

¹re·gi·na \rəˈjīnə, rēˈ-, -jēnə\ *n, pl* **regi·nae** \-jī(ˌ)nē, -jēˌnī\ [L, fem. of *reg-, rex* king — more at ROYAL] **:** QUEEN

²re·gi·na \rəˈjīnə, rēˈ-\ *adj, usu cap* [fr. *Regina*, capital of Saskatchewan, province in western Canada] **:** of or from Regina, the capital of Saskatchewan **:** of the kind or style prevalent in Regina

re·gi·nal \ˌ=ˈjīnᵊl, -jēn-\ *adj* [MF or ML; MF, fr. ML *reginalis*, fr. L *regina* + *-alis* -al] **:** of or relating to a queen **:** QUEENLY

re·gion \ˈrējən\ *n* -s [ME *regioun*, fr. MF *region* territory, region, fr. L *region-, regio* direction, territory, region, fr. *regere* to guide, rule + *-ion-, -io* -ion — more at RIGHT] **1 a** *obs* **:** REALM, KINGDOM **b :** an administrative area, division, or district (as in Rome under Augustus or in Soviet Russia) **2 a :** a major indefinite division of inanimate creation ⟨in the dark ~*s* of the night sky⟩ ⟨the aquatic ~*s* of the earth⟩ **b :** a sphere (as of activity or interest) subject to expressed or implied forces ⟨the abstract ~ of higher mathematics⟩ **:** FIELD 2a **3 :** a particular part of the world or universe (as natural waters, the sky, a particular galaxy): as **a :** a large tract of land **:** one of the large districts or quarters into which a space or surface is conceived of as divided; *broadly* **:** an indefinite area of land (as a country, province, district, or tract) ⟨there are few unknown ~*s* left on earth⟩ **b :** a broad geographical area containing a population whose members possess sufficient historical, cultural, economic, and social homogeneity to distinguish them from others ⟨the ~ of the Southwest in the U. S.⟩ **c** (1) **:** a major area of the world that is to some degree isolated by climatic or physical barriers and that supports a characteristic fauna differing both qualitatively and quantitatively from that of other regions ⟨faunal overlap of the Ethiopian and Oriental ~*s*⟩ (2) **:** an area often with distinct natural boundaries that is characterized by the prevalence of one or more vegetational climax types or by a mosaic of such types ⟨the oak-chestnut ~ of the deciduous forest formation of eastern No. America⟩ **4 a :** one of the major subdivisions into which the body or one of its parts may logically be divided ⟨the nine ~*s* of the abdomen⟩ **b :** an indefinite area surrounding a specified body part ⟨a pain in the heart ~⟩ **c :** space occupied by something **:** part in question, engaged, occupied, or under discussion ⟨the ~ of highest concentration⟩ **5 :** one of the portions or zones into which the atmosphere is divided according to height or the sea according to depth ⟨the dark abyssal ~ of the sea⟩ **6 :** a mathematical aggregate consisting of the totality of all values of an aggregate of continuous variables each varying over an interval

re·gion·al \-jənᵊl, -jnəl\ *adj* [L *regionalis*, fr. *region-, regio* + *-alis* -al] **1 a :** of or relating esp. to a geographical region ⟨allowing local needs to take precedence over ~⟩ **b :** of, relating to, or located in the peripheral parts of a district as distinguished from its central or major part **:** PROVINCIAL ⟨what items should properly be ~ and what central —*Brit. Book News*⟩ ⟨transactions on all ~ exchanges (those exchanges located outside New York City) —*Los Angeles (Calif.) Times*⟩ ⟨a ~ turn of speech⟩ **2 a :** of or relating to a region of a country **:** SECTIONAL, LOCAL ⟨~ governments⟩ **b :** of, relating to, or affecting a particular bodily region **:** LOCALIZED ⟨~ enteritis⟩ **3 :** marked by or having an effect of regionalism ⟨~ art⟩ — **re·gion·al·ly** \-ᵊlē, -əlē, -i\ *adv*

regional anatomy *n* **:** a branch of anatomy dealing with regions and levels of the body esp. with reference to diagnosis and treatment of disease or injury

regional anesthesia *n* **:** anesthesia of a region of the body accomplished by a series of encircling injections of an anesthetic — compare BLOCK ANESTHESIA

regional climax *n* **:** CLIMAX 4

regional ileitis *n* **:** ileitis that involves the distal portion of the ileum, sometimes spreads to the colon, and is characterized by diarrhea, cramping, loss of appetite and weight with local abscesses and scarring which produce a thickened, indurated, inelastic, and stenosed intestine

re·gion·al·ism \ˈrējənᵊlˌizəm, -jnəˌli-\ *n* -s [ISV *regional* + *-ism*] **1 a :** consciousness of and loyalty to a distinct subnational or supranational area usu. characterized by a common culture, background, or interests **b :** development of a political or social system based on one or more such areas **2 :** the theory or practice of selecting a particular locale or region for subject matter and stressing its characteristic aspects in art or literature **3 :** a peculiarity (as of speech) that predominates or persists in a particular geographic area **4 :** the study of regional societies as distinct geographical and sociocultural complexes esp. in their relationship to other regions and to the composite national societies of which they form a part

re·gion·al·ist \-ləst\ *n* -s [ISV *regional* + *-ist*] **:** an advocate or practitioner of regionalism

re·gion·al·is·tic \ˌrējənᵊlˈistik, -jnəˈli-\ *also* **regionalist** *adj* **:** of or relating to regionalism

re·gion·al·i·ty \ˌrējəˈnalədē\ *n* -ES **:** arrangement or ordering in regions ⟨~ in embryonic differentiation⟩

re·gion·al·iza·tion \ˌrējənᵊləˈzāshən, -jnələˈz-, -ᵊlˌīz-, -əˌlīˈz-\ *n* -s **:** an act or instance of regionalizing

re·gion·al·ize \ˈrējənᵊlˌīz, -jnəˌlīz\ *vt* -ED/-ING/-S **:** to divide into regions or administrative districts **:** arrange regionally

regional library *n* **:** a public library system serving and supported by several contiguous counties usu. in the same state

regional metamorphism *n* **:** geological metamorphism involving a wide area

regional servant *n* **:** one of six major leaders of the Jehovah's Witnesses who is responsible for one of six geographical areas of the U.S.

re·gion·ary \ˈrējəˌnerē\ *adj* [LL *regionarius*, fr. L *region-, regio* + *-arius* -ary] **:** REGIONAL

re·gioned \ˈrējənd\ *adj* **:** divided into regions **:** occupying a particular region

regions *pl of* REGION

ré·gis·seur \R ˌrāzhēˈsər, + V -ˈsər·; –R -ˈsə̄, + *vowel in a word following without pause* -ˈsər· *or* -ˈsə̄ *also* -ˈsər\ *n* -s [F *régisseur*, fr. *régiss-* (stem of *régir* to direct, rule, fr. L *regere* to guide, rule) + *-eur* -or — more at RIGHT] **:** DIRECTOR 1c; *sometimes* **:** STAGE MANAGER

¹reg·is·ter \ˈrejəstə(r)\ *n* -s [ME *registre*, fr. MF, fr. OF, fr. ML *registrum*, alter. of LL *regesta* (pl.) list, register, fr. L, neut. pl. of *regestus*, past part. of *regerere* to bring back, transcribe, fr. *re-* + *gerere* to bear, wage, cherish — more at CAST] **1 :** a written record containing regular entries of items or details **:** an official or formal enumeration, description, or record of particulars **:** a memorial record ⟨a municipal ~ of births, marriages, and deaths⟩ **2 a :** a book or system of public records ⟨a ~ of births⟩ ⟨a ~ of patents⟩ **b :** the records of landed property under Scots law — called also *register of sasines* **c :** a record containing the names of seamen of a district or country or a list and description of the merchant vessels belonging to a port, district, or country **d :** the formal record maintained by a corporation of names and addresses of holders of its registered securities **e :** a roster of individuals qualified or available for some particular end or service ⟨a civil service ~⟩ ⟨the medical ~⟩ ⟨an employment ~⟩ **3 :** a list of signatures printed in some early books for the guidance of the binder **4 :** an entry in a register ⟨could find no ~ of her death⟩ **5 a :** a set of pipes of the same quality in a pipe organ **:** STOP **b** (1) **:** the compass or range of a human voice (2) **:** the series of musical tones of like quality within the compass of a voice that are produced by a particular adjustment of the vocal cords **c :** the compass of a musical instrument; *also* **:** a special portion of the compass (as a series of tones similarly produced and of the same quality) ⟨the ~ of the clarinet⟩ **6 :** a lid, stopper, or sliding plate in a furnace, stove, or other heating device for regulating the admission of air to the fuel; *also* **:** an arrangement containing dampers or shutters (as in the floor or wall of a room or passage or in a chimney) for admitting or excluding heated air or for regulating ventilation **7 :** REGISTRATION, REGISTRY ⟨a port of ~⟩ **8 a :** something that registers or records: as (1) **:** a device for registering automatically a cumulative number (as of persons admitted, fares taken) (2) **:** the part of a gas, water, or electric meter that consists of the mechanism and dials for indicating the total quantity consumed (3) **:** a contrivance for automatically noting the performance of a machine or the rapidity of a process **b :** a number or amount registered by such a device **9 a :** exact correspondence in position of a page with its counterpart on the other side of a leaf or sheet ⟨the printed matter on both sides of the sheet was in perfect ~ —W.T.Berry⟩ **b :** exact placement (as of the successive impressions that make a multicolor illustration or of folds or creases) ⟨knife folders sometimes have creasings and foldings out of ~ on 32-page signatures —*Book Production*⟩ **c :** complete or virtual agreement with respect to position (as in the component images in a three-color photograph) **10 :** a certificate signed by the commissioner of navigation and issued by the customs collector of a port to the owner of a ship engaged in foreign trade that sets forth the description, name, ownership, and other identifying data of the ship and serves as evidence of nationality and as a muniment of title **11 :** a telegraphic recorder **12 :** a piece of registered mail **13 :** a range or row esp. when one of a series ⟨the upper ~ of a design in fresco⟩ **14 :** a condition of being in correct alignment or in proper relative position

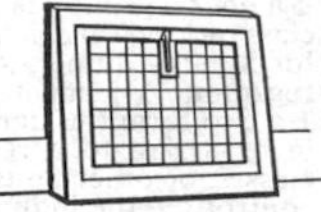

register 6

²register \"\ *vb* **registered; registered; registering** \-t(ə)riŋ\ **registers** [ME *registeren, registren*, fr. MF *registrer*, fr. OF, fr. ML *registrare*, fr. *registrum*, n.] *vt* **1 a :** to record formally and exactly **:** make an accurate entry of in a formal record **b :** to make or secure an official entry of in a register ⟨~*ed* the birth of his child⟩ ⟨~ a car⟩ **c :** to enroll formally as a voter ⟨a time set for ~*ing* new voters⟩ **d :** to record automatically **:** INDICATE **e :** to enter (a security) in the name of the owner in a formal record ⟨a ~*ed* security, bearing the name of its owner on its face, is transferable only on written assignment of the owner of record and actual surrender of the certificate⟩ **f :** to engage or assist in the formal enrollment of in a school or course ⟨spent the morning ~*ing* graduate students⟩ **2 a :** to make correspond exactly **:** adjust so as to secure correspondence **b :** to superimpose (two or more images) exactly (as in photographic printing or projection) **c :** to place or adjust (as a form, paper, or a cut) to print in register **3 a :** to record (a piece of mail) in the post office of mailing and at each successive point of transmission guaranteeing special care in delivery or for a fee above the minimum guaranteeing indemnity in case of loss, rifling, or damage **b :** to have (a piece of mail) registered **4 :** to convey an impression of ⟨his whole bearing ~*ed* intense fear⟩; *esp* **:** to convey (as a piece of information, a mood, or awareness of a situation) by expression and bodily movements without the use of words — used esp. of actors in motion pictures ~ *vi* **1 :** to enroll one's name in a register ⟨~*ed* at the hotel⟩: as **a :** to enroll one's name in a list of voters — compare REGISTRATION 5 **b :** to enroll formally as a student in a school or course ⟨planned to ~ for the second semester⟩ **2 a :** to correspond exactly **:** fit correctly in relative position **:** be in correct alignment one with another ⟨the holes for the bolts ~ perfectly⟩ **b** *of printed matter* **:** to be in register **c :** to adjust gunfire (as by artillery) on a visible point which preferably can be located on a map in order to permit prompt shifts to other visible targets or to secure data for corrections in firing on targets located on the map but not visible **3 a :** to manipulate organ registers **b** *of an actor* **:** to convey (as by bodily movement or facial expression) an emotion, information, or other matter without the use of words **4 :** to make an impression ⟨the name simply didn't ~ with me⟩

³register \"\ *n* -s [prob. alter. of *registrer*] **:** one who registers or records **:** REGISTRAR, RECORDER; *esp* **:** a public officer charged with recording specific documents, transactions, or events or with keeping them in a public office ⟨a ~ of deeds⟩ ⟨~ of probate⟩

registerable *var of* REGISTRABLE

registered *adj* **1 a :** having the owner's name entered in a register ⟨a ~ security⟩ **b :** recorded as the owner of a security ⟨~ holders of a stock⟩ **2 :** recorded on the basis of pedigree, possession of breed characteristics, or both in the studbook of a recognized breed association ⟨a ~ Holstein⟩ ⟨a ~ Percheron⟩ **3 a :** qualified formally or officially (as by passage of an examination or licensing) to perform a specified function or practice a specified skill or function ⟨a ~ lobbyist⟩ ⟨a ~ architect⟩ ⟨a ~ hospital⟩ **b :** qualified officially to vote ⟨as a ~ Democrat he maintains his legal residence in New Mexico —*Current Biog.*⟩

registered bond *n* **:** a bond registered in the name of the holder on the books of the company and issued with the name of the holder written on the bond certificate

registered envelope *or* **registration envelope** *n, Brit* **:** a government-stamped envelope for use in sending a registered letter

registered mail *n* **:** mail recorded in the post office of mailing and at each successive point of transmission so as to guarantee special care in delivery or for a fee above the minimum to guarantee indemnity in case of loss, rifling, or damage — compare CERTIFIED MAIL

registered mail insurance *n* **:** insurance against loss due to the theft or destruction of property that is sent by registered mail

registered nurse *n* **:** a graduate trained nurse who has been licensed by a state authority (as a board of nursing examiners) after successfully passing examinations for registration

registered representative *n* **:** an employee of a brokerage house authorized (as by the New York Stock Exchange) to obtain orders from customers for a commission

registered seed *n* **:** seed or seed stock (as of potatoes) that is produced from foundation stock and is used for the production of additional registered seed or of commercial certified seed

registered tonnage *n* **:** REGISTER TONNAGE

reg·is·ter·er \ˈrejəst(ə)rə(r)\ *n* -s [²*register* + *-er*] **:** one that registers **:** REGISTRAR

registering *pres part of* REGISTER

registering thermometer *n* **:** a thermometer that indicates the maximum or the minimum temperature or both between settings and is commonly of the liquid-in-glass type

register office *n* **:** an office (as an employment office) where a register or record is kept

register of sasines **:** REGISTER 2b

registers *pl of* REGISTER, *pres 3d sing of* REGISTER

reg·is·ter·ship \ˈ===ˌship\ *n* [³*register* + *-ship*] **:** REGISTRARSHIP

register tonnage *n* **:** the gross tonnage of a ship less deductions (as of space occupied by engines and crew) and consisting of the part actually available for commercial use (as in the transport of freight or passengers)

reg·is·tra·bil·i·ty \ˌrejəstrəˈbilədē\ *n* **:** the quality or state of being registrable

reg·is·tra·ble \ˈrejəstrəbəl\ *also* **reg·is·ter·able** \-st(ə)rəbəl\ *adj* [¹*register* + *-able*] **:** capable of being registered **:** subject to registration

reg·is·trant \ˈrejəstrənt\ *n* -s [¹*register* + *-ant*] **:** one who registers; *esp* **:** one who by virtue of securing an official registration obtains a specific right or title of possession and use (as to a trademark)

reg·is·trar \ˈrejəˌsträr, -strä(r, ˌ==ˈ=\ *n* -s [alter. (prob. influenced by ML *registrarius*) of *registrer*] **1 :** one who registers **:** an official recorder or keeper of records ⟨a ~ of voters⟩ ⟨a ~ of a diocese⟩: as **a :** an officer of an educational institution charged with registering students, keeping academic records, issuing official information (as catalogs and bulletins), corresponding with candidates for admission, and evaluating their credentials **b :** an agent of a corporation (as a bank or trust company) appointed to keep account of and to authenticate issues of stocks and bonds **c :** an admitting officer at a hospital **d :** a guard at the entrance to a national forest who tells people of the forest laws and who keeps records of hunters and the game they bring out **2 :** a registering contrivance **:** REGISTER 8 **3** *Brit* **:** RESIDENT 4a

registrar-general *n, pl* **registrars-general :** the head of a general register office

reg·is·trar·ship \-ˌship\ *n* **:** the office or dignity of a registrar

reg·is·trary \ˈrejəstrəri\ *n* -ES [ML *registrarius*, fr. *registrum* register + L *-arius* -ary — more at REGISTER] **:** REGISTRAR

¹registrate *adj* [ME (Sc) *registrat*, fr. ML *registratus*, past part. of *registrare* to register] *obs* **:** REGISTERED

²reg·is·trate \ˈrejəˌstrāt, *usu* -ād.+V\ *vb* -ED/-ING/-S [ML *registratus*, past part. of *registrare*] *vt* **:** REGISTER ~ *vi* **:** to select and adjust pipe organ stops

reg·is·tra·tion \ˌ==ˈstrāshən\ *n* -s [MF or ML; MF, fr. ML *registration-, registratio*, fr. *registratus* (past part. of *registrare* to register) + L *-ion-, -io* -ion — more at REGISTER] **1 :** an act or the fact of registering ⟨completed ~ for a course of study⟩ ⟨the office will be open for the ~ of the unemployed⟩ **2 :** something registered (as a name or fact) **:** an entry in a register ⟨search for a particular ~⟩ **3 :** the number of individuals registered **:** ENROLLMENT ⟨a course with a large ~⟩ **4 a :** the art or act of registrating **b :** the combination of stops selected for the performing of a particular musical composition on an organ **5 :** an act whereby a person by appearing publicly before the proper officials gives oath about matters (as citizenship, age, residence) required of a qualified voter and signs a register to afford proof of his right to vote at a caucus, primary, or election **6 :** the act of bringing together (as two or more images in color photography or in animation motion picture photography) in complete agreement with respect to position **7 :** REGISTER 9 **8 :** a document certifying an act of registering ⟨carried his automobile ~ in his wallet⟩

reg·is·tra·tion·al \ˌ==ˈstrāshənᵊl, -shnəl\ *adj* **:** of or relating to registration

registration area *n* **:** the part of the U.S. having a public registration of births or deaths that meets the standards set by the Census Bureau and including more than 95 percent of the population of the U.S.

registration statement *n* **:** a comprehensive statement required to be filed (as with the Securities and Exchange Commission) by all issuers of securities in the U.S. except those specifically exempted

reg·is·trer \ˈrejəstrə(r)\ *n* -s [ME *registrer, registrere*, modif. (influenced by ME *-er, -ere* -er) of MF *registreur*, fr. *registrer* to register + *-eur* -or — more at REGISTER] **1** *obs* **:** REGISTRAR **2** [²*register* + *-er*] **:** a registering device

reg·is·try \-strē, -ri\ *n* -ES [²*register* + *-ry*] **1 :** an act of registering **:** ENROLLMENT, REGISTRATION **2 a :** the condition or fact of being entered in a register ⟨a certificate of ~⟩; *specif* **:** the particular nationality of a ship as evidenced by such an entry **:** FLAG **b :** a certificate of registry of a ship ⟨ships of Greek ~⟩ **3 :** the place where a register is kept **:** a place of registration **:** REGISTER OFFICE **4 :** an official record book; *also* **:** an entry in one

re·gi·um do·num \ˌrējēəmˈdōnəm\ *n, pl* **re·gia do·na** \-jēəˈdōnə\ [NL, royal gift] **:** a former annual grant of public money in England for the Presbyterian clergy in Ireland

re·gius professor \ˈrēj(ē)əs-\ *n* [NL, royal professor] **:** a holder of a professorship founded by royal bounty or dependent on royal patronage at the older British universities

re·give \(ˈ)rē+\ *vt* [*re-* + *give*] **:** to give again **:** RESTORE

regl *abbr* regimental

re·glaze \(ˈ)rē+\ *vt* [*re-* + *glaze*] **:** to provide (as windows) with new glass **:** replace damaged or lost glass of

regle *vt* [MF *regler*, fr. LL *regulare* to regulate — more at REGULATE] *obs* **:** RULE, GOVERN

reglement *n* -s [MF, fr. *regler* + *-ment*] *obs* **:** REGULATION

reg·le·men·ta·ry \ˌregləˈmentərē, -n·trē\ *adj* [F *réglementaire*, fr. *réglement* regulation (fr. MF *reglement*) + *-aire* -ary] **:** of, relating to, or involving regulations

reg·let *also* **rig·let** \ˈreglət, *chiefly Brit* ˈrig-\ *n* -s [F *réglet* reglet, straightedge, fr. MF *reglet* straightedge, fr. *regle* straightedge, rule (fr. L *regula*) + *-et* — more at RULE] **1 :** a flat narrow molding used in architecture chiefly to separate parts or members of compartments or panels or doubled, turned, and interlaced to form knots, frets, or other ornaments or to cover joints between boards **:** FILLET, BATTEN **2 a :** a strip of wood less than type high and ranging in thickness from 3 point to 24 point or more used as spacing material in the makeup and lockup of type — compare FURNITURE, ⁴LEAD 2e **b :** reglets or material for them

re·glow \(ˈ)rē+\ *vi* [*re-* + *glow*] **:** to glow again or anew

re·glue \"+\ *vt* [*re-* + *glue*] **:** to make fast, whole, or secure again with glue ⟨~ a loose cover⟩

reg·nal \ˈregnᵊl\ *adj* [ML *regnalis*, fr. L *regnum* kingly government, rule, reign, kingdom + *-alis* -al — more at REIGN] **:** of or relating to a reign, kingdom, or king — **reg·nal·ly** \-nəlē, -li\ *adv*

regnal year *n* **:** a year of a sovereign's reign dating from the moment or anniversary of the moment of accession ⟨the first *regnal year* of George V was from May 6, 1910 to May 5, 1911⟩ — used esp. in the citation of laws

reg·nan·cy \ˈregnənsē, -si\ *n* -ES [*regnant* + *-cy*] **:** the quality or state of being regnant **:** SOVEREIGNTY, RULE

reg·nant \-nənt\ *adj* [L *regnant-, regnans*, pres. part. of *regnare* to reign — more at REIGN] **1 :** exercising rule or authority **:** REIGNING ⟨a queen ~⟩ **2 a :** having the chief power **:** exercising sway **:** DOMINANT ⟨filled with a ~ determination to defend herself —Gilbert Parker⟩ **b :** of common or widespread occurrence **:** PREVALENT ⟨the vices ~ —Jonathan Swift⟩

re·gnault's formula \rənˈyōz-\ *n, usu cap R* [after Henri V. *Regnault* †1878 Fr. chemist and physicist] **:** an empirical formula giving the specific enthalpy of steam at any centigrade temperature in calories per gram **:** $H = 606.5 + 0.305\ t$

regnault's law *n, usu cap R* **:** a statement in physics: the specific heat of a gas at constant pressure is the same whatever the pressure

reg·num \ˈregnəm\ *n, pl* **reg·na** \-nə\ [L] **1 a :** DOMINION, RULE **b :** tenure of power **2 :** any of the major divisions of animal, plant, and nonliving things into which natural objects fall **:** KINGDOM 6

reg·o·lith \ˈregəˌlith\ *n* -s [Gk *rhēgos* blanket + E *-lith*; akin to Gk *rhezein* to dye — more at RAGA] **:** MANTLEROCK

re·gorge \(ˈ)rē+\ *vb* [F *regorger*, fr. MF, fr. *re-* + *gorger* to gorge — more at GORGE] *vt* **1 :** to vomit up or out **:** throw back **:** DISGORGE **2** [*re-* + *gorge*] **:** to swallow again **:** swallow or suck back ⟨tides at highest mark *regorge* the flood —John Dryden⟩ ~ *vi* **:** to gush again **:** be thrown back

reg·o·sol \ˈregəˌsäl, -sȯl\ *n* -s [*rego-* (as in *regolith*) + L *solum* ground, soil — more at SOLE] **:** an azonal soil consisting chiefly of soft and imperfectly consolidated material (as sand or recent volcanic ash), exhibiting little or no pedological development, and having no clear-cut and specific morphology

regr *abbr* registrar

re·grade \(ˈ)rē+\ *vt* [*re-* + *grade*] **1 :** to provide (as a road or slope) with a new grade **2 :** to assign to a new category or grade ⟨*regrading* stored apples⟩; *often* **:** to regroup (students) for purposes of more effective instruction

¹re·grant \"+\ *vt* [*re-* + *grant*] **:** to grant back or again ⟨the charter was not ~*ed*⟩

²regrant \"\ *n* **:** a granting again (as back to a former proprietor or by way of renewal of a grant)

re·grasp \"+\ *vt* [*re-* + *grasp*] **:** to take again into one's grasp **:** seize hold of anew ⟨seeking to ~ lost liberties⟩
re·grass \"+\ *vt* [*re-* + *grass*] **:** to plant again with grass **:** cause grass to grow on (as barren or cutover land)
¹re·grate \rə'grāt, rē'-\ *archaic Scot var of* REGRET
²regrate \"\ *vt* -ED/-ING/-S [ME *regraten*, fr. MF *regrater*, fr. *regratier* regrater] **1 :** to buy up (necessities of life) at a market or fair with the intention of reselling in or near the same place at a profit — compare ENGROSS **2 :** to sell or dispose of (commodities bought in regrating) usu. at retail
³regrate \"\ *vt* -ED/-ING/-S [F *regratter*, fr. *re-* + *gratter* to scratch, scrape, fr. MF *grater* — more at GRATE] **:** to remove the outer surface of (masonry) so as to freshen in appearance
re·grat·er *also* **re·gra·tor** \-ād·ə(r)\ *n* -S [*regrater* fr. ME *regrater, regratere*, fr. MF *regratier*, fr. OF; *regrator* fr. ME *regratour*, fr. AF, alter. (influenced by AF *-our* -or, fr. OF *-eor, -eur*) of MF *regratier;* akin to OSp *regatero* regrater, OIt *rigattiere*] **1 a** *chiefly Brit* **:** one that regrates supplies or necessities **b** *dial* **:** a middleman who travels about the country buying up farm produce for market **2** *chiefly Brit* **:** one that gets profits or credits due another esp. by irregular means
re·grede \rə'grēd\ *vi* -ED/-ING/-S [L *regredi* to go back] *astron* **:** to go back **:** RETROGRADE
¹re·greet \(')rē+\ *vt* [*re-* + *greet*] **1** *obs* **:** to greet again **2** *archaic* **:** to return the salutation of **:** offer a greeting to
²regreet *n* **1** *obs* **:** a greeting in return **:** a return salutation **2 regreets** *pl, obs* **:** a message or words of greeting **:** GREETINGS
¹re·gress \'rē,gres\ *n* -ES [ME *regresse*, fr. L *regressus*, fr. *regressus*, past part. of *regredi* to go back, fr. *re-* + *gradi* to step, go — more at GRADE] **1 :** an act or the privilege of going or coming back **:** WITHDRAWAL, EGRESS ⟨free ingress and ~ for ships⟩; as **a :** the right or power of falling back on another as primarily liable **:** RECOURSE **b :** reentry or right of reentry (as upon lands redeemed from forfeiture or default or upon a vacated benefice) **2 :** RETROGRESSION, RETROGRADATION **3 :** the act of reasoning backward (as from effect to cause)
²re·gress \rə'gres, rē'-\ *vb* -ED/-ING/-ES [L *regressus*, past part. of *regredi* to go back] *vi* **:** to make or undergo regress **:** be subject to or exhibit regression **:** RETROGRADE; *often* **:** to tend to approach or revert to a mean ~ *vt* **:** to induce a state of psychological regression in (as by hypnosis or suggestion)
re·gres·sion \-'greshən\ *n* -S [L *regression-, regressio*, fr. *regressus* (past part. of *regredi* to go back) + *-ion-, -io* -ion] **1 a :** an act or the fact of regressing **:** REGRESS, RETROGRESSION, REVERSION **b :** a hypothetical reversal of direction in a biological evolutionary process that is sometimes invoked to explain the extinction of the graptolites and similar paleontologic phenomena **2 :** a trend or shift toward a mean or toward a lower or less perfect state (as of function or differentiation): as **a :** apparent trend of offspring in respect to heritable characters away from specializations exhibited by their parents and toward the mean development characteristic of their biotype **b :** a functional relationship between two or more correlated variables that is often empirically determined from data and is used esp. to predict values of one variable when given values of the others ⟨the ~ value of *y* on *x* is linear⟩; *specif* **:** a function that yields the mean value of a random variable under the condition that one or more independent variables have specified values **c :** a gradual spontaneous diminution or fading of a latent or developed photographic image **d** (1) **:** progressive decline (as in size, severity, or intensity) of a manifestation of disease ⟨marked ~ of a tumor often follows radiation⟩ ⟨~ of symptoms followed the climax⟩ (2) **:** gradual loss of specific differentiation and function by a body part esp. as a physiological change accompanying aging ⟨menopausal ~ of the ovaries⟩ **e** (1) **:** reversion in behavior, thinking, attitudes, or identifications to an earlier mental or behavioral level or to an earlier stage of psychosexual development in response to organismic stress or to suggestion — compare FIXATION (2) **:** gradual loss of memories and acquired skills (as in old age) in which the order of development is reversed so that the most recent memories are lost first and the earliest acquisitions are the last to go **3 :** retrograde motion esp. of an astronomical orbital characteristic
regression coefficient *n* **:** a coefficient in a regression equation **:** the slope of the regression line
regression curve *n* **:** a curve that best fits particular data according to some principle (as the principle of least squares)
regression equation *n* **:** the equation of a regression curve
regression line *n* **:** a regression curve that is a straight line
re·gres·sive \rə'gresiv, rē'-, -sēv *also* -səv\ *adj* **1 :** that regresses or tends to regress **:** RETROGRESSIVE **2 :** characterized by or derived from reasoning backward (as from effect to cause or from observed facts to a principle) **3 :** constituting or relating to a technique of micrological staining in which the stain is applied to excess and the excess later removed in order to enhance the specificity of the staining **4 a :** of, relating to, typical of, or tending to produce regression ⟨~ tissue changes⟩ **b :** being, characterized by, or developing in the course of an evolutionary process involving increasing simplification of bodily structure **5 :** having the nature of the first of two sounds dependent on the nature of the second ⟨~ assimilation⟩ **6 :** decreasing in rate as the base increases — used of taxation and methods of apportioning taxes **7 :** DEGRESSIVE **b** — **re·gres·sive·ly** \-sə̇vlē, -li\ *adv* — **re·gres·sive·ness** \-sivnə̇s, -sēv- *also* -səv-\ *n* -ES
regressive sorites *n* **:** a sorites in which the order of the premises is reversed
re·gres·siv·i·ty \,rē,gre'sivəd·ē\ *n* -ES **:** the quality or state of being regressive **:** tendency toward regression
re·gres·sor \rə'gresə(r), rē'-\ *n* -S **:** one that regresses or is regressing
re·gres·sus \-səs\ *n* -ES [L — more at REGRESS] **:** REGRESS
¹re·gret \rə'gret, rē'-, *usu* -ed·+V\ *vb* **regretted; regretted; regretting; regrets** [ME *regretten*, fr. MF *regreter, regrater*, fr. OF, fr. *re-* + *-greter, -grater* (of Scand origin; akin to ON *grāta* to weep) — more at GREET] *vt* **1 :** to remember with sorrow or grief **:** mourn the loss or death of **:** miss poignantly ⟨that fair lady whom thou dost ~ —P.B.Shelley⟩ **2 :** to have dissatisfaction, misgivings, or distress of mind concerning **:** be keenly sorry for ⟨~ one's mistakes⟩ ⟨~ my inability to be present⟩ ~ *vi* **:** to experience regret
²regret \"\ *n* -S [MF, fr. OF, lamentation, fr. *regreter, regrater*, v.] **1 :** sorrow aroused by circumstances beyond one's control or power to repair **:** grief or pain tinged with disappointment, dissatisfaction, longing, remorse, or comparable emotion ⟨a scene that awakens ~⟩ ⟨keen ~ for past deeds⟩ **2 a :** an expression of sorrow, disappointment, or other distressing emotion ⟨weary him with vain ~*s*⟩ **b regrets** *pl* **:** a reply politely declining an invitation ⟨send ~*s*⟩ **syn** see SORROW
re·gret·ful \-'=fəl\ *adj* **:** full of regret **:** REPINING — **re·gret·ful·ly** \-fəlē, -li\ *adv* — **re·gret·ful·ness** \-lnə̇s\ *n* -ES
re·gret·less \-'=lə̇s\ *adj* **:** feeling no regret **:** free from regrets
re·gret·ta·ble *also* **re·gret·able** \rə'gred·əbəl, rē'-, -etəb-\ *adj* **:** admitting of or deserving regret — **re·gret·ta·ble·ness** \-bəlnə̇s\ *n* -ES — **re·gret·ta·bly** \-blē, -li\ *adv*
re·gret·ter \-'gred·ə(r), -etə-\ *n* -S **:** one that regrets
re·gret·ting·ly *adv* **:** in a regretting manner **:** with regret
re·grind \(')rē+\ *vt* [*re-* + *grind*] **:** to grind anew **:** to reshape or refit by grinding ⟨had his valves *reground*⟩
re·group \"+\ *vb* [*re-* + *group*] *vt* **:** to form into a new grouping ⟨in order to subtract 129 from 531 ~ 531 into 5 hundreds, 2 tens, and 11 ones⟩ ⟨~*ed* the products to make a better display⟩; *esp* **:** to alter the tactical formation of (a military force) usu. preparatory to beginning a new phase of an operation ~ *vi* **:** to form a new group (as in altering the tactical formation of a military force) — **re·group·ment** \"+\ *n*
re·grow \"+\ *vb* [*re-* + *grow*] *vt* **:** to grow (as a missing part) anew ⟨many lower vertebrates can ~ lost limbs or tails⟩ ~ *vi* **:** to grow again **:** continue to grow after interruption or injury ⟨forests ~ but slowly after a severe fire⟩
re·growth \"+\ *n* [*re-* + *growth*] **:** a product of regrowing; *esp* **:** the vegetation that appears after denudation of land (as by clearing, burning, or excessive grazing)
regs *pl of* REG
regt *abbr* **1** regent **2** regiment
regtl *abbr* regimental
reguardant *var of* REGARDANT
¹re·guer·don \rə'gərdᵊn\ *vt* [ME *reguerdonen*, fr. MF *reguerdoner*, fr. OF *reguerdoner, reguerredoner*, fr. *re-* + *guerdoner, guerredoner* to reward — more at GUERDON] *archaic* **:** REWARD
²reguerdon \"\ *n* [ME *reguerdoun*, fr. MF *reguerdon*, fr. OF, fr. *reguerdoner, reguerredoner*, v.] *archaic* **:** REWARD
reg·u·la \'regyələ\ *n, pl* **regu·lae** \-,lē\ [L *regula* straightedge, rule] **1 :** an architectural band or fillet esp. when one of a series beneath the taenia in a Doric architrave of which each corresponds to a triglyph above and has a row of six guttae on its lower side **2 :** RULE ⟨the authoritative ~ for community life⟩
reg·u·la·ble \'regyələbəl\ *adj* [*regulate* + *-able*] **:** capable of being regulated
reg·u·lant \-lənt\ *n* -S [*regulate* + *-ant*] **:** a substance or agent that regulates something (as plant growth)
¹reg·u·lar \'regyələ(r), ÷ -g(ə)l-\ *adj* [ME *reguler*, fr. MF, fr. LL *regularis* canonical, regular, containing a set of rules, fr. L, of or belonging to a bar, fr. *regula* straightedge, rule + *-aris* -ar — more at RULE] **1 :** belonging to a Christian monastic order or community **:** living under or relating to a monastic rule ⟨the ~ clergy⟩ — opposed to *secular* **2 a :** formed, built, arranged, or ordered according to some established rule, law, principle, or type **:** harmonious in form, structure, or arrangement **:** SYMMETRICAL ⟨~ verse⟩ ⟨a man with ~ features⟩ ⟨a disciplined ~ landscape⟩ **b** (1) **:** both equilateral and equiangular ⟨a ~ polygon⟩ (2) **:** having faces that are congruent regular polygons and all the polyhedral angles congruent ⟨a ~ polyhedron⟩ **c** *of a flower* **:** having the members of each whorl symmetrical with respect to form **:** ACTINOMORPHIC — compare IRREGULAR **d :** having or constituting an isometric system ⟨~ crystals⟩ **3 a :** steady or uniform in course, practice, or occurrence **:** not subject to unexplained or irrational variation **:** steadily pursued **:** ORDERLY, METHODICAL ⟨~ habits⟩ **b** (1) **:** returning, recurring, or received at stated, fixed, or uniform intervals ⟨a ~ income⟩ ⟨in the ~ course of events⟩ (2) **:** functioning at proper intervals — used esp. of the bowels **4 a :** constituted, selected, conducted, made, or otherwise handled in conformity with established or prescribed usages, rules, or discipline ⟨a ~ meeting⟩ ⟨a ~ election⟩ **b :** NORMAL, STANDARD, CORRECT: as (1) **:** undeviating in conformance to a standard set (as by convention, established authority, or a particular group) (2) **:** being such without any doubt **:** THOROUGH, COMPLETE, UNMITIGATED ⟨a ~ scoundrel⟩ (3) *slang* **:** like other good fellows in views and ways **c** (1) **:** conforming to the normal or usual manner of inflection ⟨~ English nouns take *-s* or *-es* plurals⟩ (2) **:** WEAK 8a **d** *of a postage stamp* **:** issued without restriction for the payment of all types of postage ⟨the list included stamps of the ~ issue as well as airmails, special deliveries, and commemoratives⟩ **5 a :** of, relating to, or constituting the regular army of a state ⟨a ~ soldier⟩ **b :** constituting or made up of individuals properly recognized as legitimate combatants in war **6** *usu cap* **:** of, relating to, or belonging to the Regular Baptists **7 :** of, relating to, or being a transaction on a stock exchange requiring delivery of the securities involved on the third full business day after purchase
syn NORMAL, TYPICAL, NATURAL: REGULAR may imply conformity to a prescribed rule, standard, or established pattern ⟨a *regular* meeting of the society⟩ ⟨following the *regular* procedure of the legislature⟩ ⟨their action was made *regular* and legal —J.R.Green⟩ NORMAL suggests falling within the limits of a norm ⟨if a boy has abnormal mental powers in some direction, combined with poor physique and great nervousness, he may be quite incapable of fitting into a crowd of *normal* boys —Bertrand Russell⟩ ⟨her intensity, which would leave no emotion on a *normal* plane, irritated the youth into a frenzy —D.H.Lawrence⟩ TYPICAL applies to whatever shows to a marked degree characters or characteristics of a type, class, or group, sometimes to the exclusion of distinctive individual characteristics ⟨peculiar to himself, not *typical* of Greek ideas —G.L.Dickinson⟩ ⟨until twenty years ago a *typical* English country town with wide High Street, narrow Market Street, picturesque Market Square, two ancient hostelries, fine old church, gabled almshouses —Compton Mackenzie⟩ ⟨what he had to do was to give plot and accurate delineation of character to the winds, make his personages *typical* rather than individual —Richard Garnett †1906⟩ NATURAL describes whatever conforms with its nature, kind, or essence ⟨the *natural* love of a mother for her child⟩ ⟨water as the *natural* environment of a fish⟩ These words are often interchangeable and are often used together ⟨a mode of thinking, a distinctive type of reaction, gets itself established, in the course of a complex historical development, as typical, as *normal* —Edward Sapir⟩
²regular \"\ *n* -S **1 :** a member of a Christian monastic order or community following a rule **:** one of the regular clergy ⟨controversy between the seculars and the ~*s*⟩ **2 :** a soldier in a regular army — usu. used in pl. **3 a :** one (as a customer or contributor) that is regular esp. in pursuing a fixed or recurrent routine **b :** one that can be trusted or depended upon with assurance **c :** a player on an athletic team who usu. starts every game **4 :** a clothing size designed to fit the person of average height
³regular \"\ *adv, chiefly dial* **:** REGULARLY
⁴regular \"\ *adj* [NL *Regularia* & NL *Regulares*] **:** of or relating to the Regularia or Regulares
regular army *n* **:** a permanently organized body constituting the army of a state and being often identical with the standing army that is maintained by a federal government
regular baptist *n, usu cap R&B* **1 :** a member of a moderately Calvinistic Baptist sect that is found chiefly in the southern U.S., represents the original English Baptists before the division into Particular and General Baptists, and observes close communion and foot washing **2 :** a Baptist who belongs to the General Association of Regular Baptist Churches formed in 1932 by churches which had withdrawn from the Northern Baptist Convention
regular canon *n, sometimes cap R&C* **:** CANON REGULAR
regular canoness *n* **:** a canoness bound by a vow of poverty and following a strict religious rule
regular clerk *n* **:** CLERK REGULAR
regular clerk of st. paul *usu cap R&C&S&P* [after *St. Paul* *ab* A.D. 67 Christian apostle to the Gentiles] **:** a member of a Roman Catholic congregation founded in 1530 in Milan — called also *Barnabite*
regular deposit *n* **:** SPECIAL DEPOSIT
reg·u·lar·es \,regyə'la(a)(,)rēz\ *n pl, cap* [NL, fr. LL, pl. of *regularis* regular] *in former classifications* **:** an order or other group comprising all symmetrical Blastoidea
¹reg·u·lar·ia \,==' la(a)rēə\ *n pl, cap* [NL, fr. LL, neut. pl. of *regularis* regular] *in some classifications* **:** a division of Echinoidea including the ordinary sea urchins that have a more or less globular symmetrical shell with 20 meridional rows of plates and the mouth and anus at opposite poles
²regularia \"\ [NL, fr. LL, neut. pl. of *regularis* regular] *syn of* REGULARES
reg·u·lar·i·ty \,regyə'larəd·ē, -rətē, -i *also* -ler-\ *n* -ES [F *régularité*, fr. MF *regularité*, fr. LL *regularis* regular + MF *-té* -ty] **1 :** the quality or state of being regular ⟨~ of outline⟩ ⟨~ of habits⟩ **2 :** something that is regular
regularity theory *n* **:** a view held by Humeans: an event may be the cause of another event without there being a necessary connection between the two
reg·u·lar·iza·tion \,regyələrə̇'zāshən, -,rī'z-\ *n* -S **:** the act or an instance of regularizing ⟨his ~ of their informal marriage⟩
reg·u·lar·ize \'===,rīz\ *vt* -ED/-ING/-S *see -ize in Explan Notes* **:** to make regular (as by conformance to law, rules, or custom) **:** make steady or uniform
reg·u·lar·iz·er \-,rīzə(r)\ *n* -S **:** one that regularizes
regular lay *n* **:** MEDIUM LAY
regular–lay rope *n* **:** a wire rope having the wires in the strands twisted in directions opposite to the strands in the rope
regular lot *n* **:** a number or amount regularly intended when the number or amount is not specified; *esp* **:** a standard unit of trade (as on an exchange) of a commodity or stock
reg·u·lar·ly \'regyələ(r)lē ÷ -gyə(r)l|, ÷ -g(ə)lə(r)l|, |i\ *adv* **:** in a regular, orderly, lawful, or methodical way **:** SYMMETRICALLY, CORRECTLY, PROPERLY
regular ode *n* **:** an ode that is divided into sections each having a strophe and an antistrophe of identical and an epode of contrasting form
regular peloria *n* **:** peloria in which symmetry is attained by decrease in number of normally irregular parts — compare IRREGULAR PELORIA
regular pyramid *n* **:** a pyramid whose base is a regular polygon and whose vertex is on the perpendicular to the base through its center
regular reflection *n* **:** reflection such that the angle of reflection of the light is equal to the angle of incidence and on the opposite side of the normal to the point of incidence
regulars *pl of* REGULAR
regular sequence *n* **:** a sequence possessing a limit **:** a convergent sequence
regular solid *n* **:** any of five regular polyhedrons **:** a regular tetrahedron, hexahedron, octahedron, dodecahedron, or icosahedron
regular year *n* **:** a common year of 354 days or a leap year of 384 days in the Jewish calendar — see YEAR table
reg·u·lat·able \'regyə,lād·əbəl, -lātə-, ,=='===\ *adj* **:** capable of being regulated
reg·u·late \'==,lāt, *usu* -ād·+V\ *vb* -ED/-ING/-S [LL *regulatus*, past part. of *regulare*, fr. L *regula* straightedge, rule — more at RULE] *vt* **1 :** to govern or direct according to rule ⟨laws which ~ the succession of seasons⟩; *usu* **:** to bring under the control of law or constituted authority **:** make regulations for or concerning ⟨~ the industries of a country⟩ **2 a :** to reduce to order, method, or uniformity **:** REGULARIZE ⟨~ one's habits⟩ **b** *obs* **:** DISCIPLINE **3 :** to fix the time, amount, degree, or rate of (as by adjusting, rectifying) ⟨~ the pressure of a tire⟩; *also* **:** to adjust so as to work accurately or regularly ⟨~ a clock⟩ ~ *vi* **:** to make regulations
regulated company *n* **:** a mercantile association holding by government charter exclusive trading rights with specified lands and combining freedom for the individual to trade on his own capital with regulations limiting trade in order to keep up prices
regulating box *n* **:** a rheostat for regulating the electric current passing through the field-magnet coils (as of a dynamo)
regulating station *n* **:** a military command agency that controls all movements of personnel and supplies into and out of a given area
¹reg·u·la·tion \,=='lāshən\ *n* -S [*regulate* + *-ion*] **1 :** an act of regulating or the condition of being regulated ⟨the ~ of her mind⟩ ⟨business suffering from undue ~⟩ **2 a :** an authoritative rule or principle dealing with details of procedure; *esp* **:** one intended to promote safety and efficiency (as in a school or factory) **b :** a rule or order having the force of law issued by an executive authority of a government usu. under power granted by a constitution or delegated by legislation: as (1) **:** a piece of subordinate legislation issued by a British administrative unit under the authority and subject to the veto of parliament — compare PROVISIONAL ORDER, STATUTORY ORDER (2) **:** one issued by the president of the U. S. or by an authorized subordinate — called also *executive order* (3) **:** an administrative order issued by an executive department or a regulatory commission of the U. S. government to apply and supplement broad congressional legislative enactments **3 :** the percentage variation in some characteristic quantity (as voltage) as a machine or apparatus becomes loaded; *also* **:** the ratio of deviation of such a quantity at rated load to its normal value at no load **4 a :** redistribution of material (as in an embryo) to restore a damaged or lost part independent of new tissue growth — compare REGENERATION **b :** the mechanism by which an early embryo maintains essentially normal development in the face of abnormal conditions **c :** DETERMINATION **syn** see LAW
²regulation \;==;==\ *adj* **:** prescribed by or being in accord with regulations ⟨the ~ cap of a nurse⟩; *broadly* **:** USUAL, CUSTOMARY ⟨the ~ accompaniments of a Thanksgiving dinner⟩
¹reg·u·la·tive \'==,lā|d·|iv, -lə|, |t|, |ēv *also* |əv\ *adj* **1 :** tending to regulate **:** having regulation as an aim ⟨a ~ statute⟩ **2 a :** directing or regulating in the manner of a rule to be followed or an end to be attained — compare REGULATIVE PRINCIPLE **b :** constituting in Kantianism the ideas of reason (as First Cause) that arise in the mind because ideal knowledge requires the conception of the totality of conditions for anything given as conditioned — contrasted with *constitutive* **3 :** capable of regulation **:** involving progressive determination and restriction of initially totipotent material — used of a developing zygote or its state; compare MOSAIC
²regulative \"\ *n* -S **:** something (as a principle or enactment) that has regulative force
reg·u·la·tive·ly \|əvlē, -li\ *adv* **:** in a regulative manner **:** so as to be regulative
regulative principle *n* **:** a rule or principle of procedure: as **a** *archaic* **:** the principle underlying syllogistic inference or in accordance with which any particular inference is drawn **b :** a rule of procedure to which there is no alternative if the desired end is to be secured although it cannot itself assure attainment
reg·u·la·tor \'==,lād·ə(r), -lātə-\ *n* -S **:** one that regulates: as **a** (1) **:** one of a board of seven appointed by King James II in 1687 with powers to appoint and remove officers and freemen at their discretion for the purpose of influencing the election of members of Parliament (2) *usu cap* **:** a member of any of various associations of the poorer people in No. Carolina existing from 1767 to 1771, formed to resist official extortion, refusing to pay taxes, and committing many deeds of violence (3) **:** a member of any of various bands or volunteer committees in the U.S. formed in newly occupied or settled regions before the establishment of local government to preserve order, prevent crime, and administer justice **b** (1) **:** a person who regulates mechanisms (as clocks) or conditions (as of traffic) (2) **:** a worker who hangs or bolts up ship plates on the frame of a ship **c** (1) **:** an automatic device for maintaining the current, voltage, speed, or other characteristic of a machine, transformer, or comparable device at a specified value or for adjusting these quantities at will (2) **:** a lever or index in a watch for altering the effective length of the hairspring to make the watch go faster or slower (3) **:** an accurate master clock used for timing watches and clocks — compare ASTRONOMICAL CLOCK (4) **:** GOVERNOR 4b (5) **:** a sliding door for controlling ventilation in a mine (6) **:** a balance valve for controlling the admission of steam to the steam chest in a locomotive (7) **:** a reducing valve or steam= pressure regulating device (8) *Brit* **:** a throttle on a locomotive **d** (1) **:** a substance added in a reaction to regulate the amount of another substance formed (2) **:** GROWTH REGULATOR (3) **:** PLANT REGULATOR
regulator pin *n* **:** either of two short upright thin cylindrical pins that are fitted in a watch regulator bearing or banking the hairspring in such a manner that moving the regulator into a position in which the pins touch the hairspring closer to its center shortens the spring and causes the watch to run faster
reg·u·la·to·ry \'==lə,tōrē, -tȯr-, -ri\ *adj* **1 :** of or relating to regulation **:** making or concerned with the making of regulations **:** REGULATIVE ⟨~ measures⟩ ⟨a local ~ body⟩ **2 :** subject to regulation ⟨~ products that are considered dangerous and may be shipped only under stipulated conditions of packaging, labeling, and handling⟩
¹reg·u·line \'regyə,līn, -,lən\ *adj* [prob. fr. (assumed) NL *regulinus*, fr. ML *regulus* + L *-inus* -ine] **:** of, relating to, or being a regulus ⟨~ silver⟩ ⟨a ~ deposit⟩
²reguline \-lən, -līn\ *n* -S **:** a smooth coherent electrodeposit of metal
reg·u·lus \'regyələs\ *n* [ML, metallic antimony, fr. L, petty king, fr. *reg-, rex* king + *-ulus* — more at ROYAL] **1** *pl* **reguluses** \-ləsə̇z\ *or* **reg·u·li** \-,lī\ **a :** the more or less impure button, globule, or mass of metal or metallic substance formed beneath the slag in smelting and reducing ores ⟨~ of antimony⟩ **b :** the material of such a mass **:** coarse metal **:** MATTE **2** *pl* **reguluses** *or* **reguli** [L] **:** a petty king **:** a ruler of little power or consequence **3 a** *pl* **reguluses** *or* **reguli** [LL, fr. L] **:** KINGLET **b** *cap* [NL, fr. LL] **:** a genus (the type of the family Regulidae) of passerine birds consisting of the kinglets **4** *pl* **reguluses** *or* **reguli** [LL, fr. L] **:** a mythical Nubian snake believed to kill its victim by its hiss — compare BASILISK, COCKATRICE

re·gur \ˈrēgər, ˈräg-\ *n* -s *sometimes cap* [Hindi *regar*] **:** a rich black loam of India similar to the Russian chernozem

re·gurge \rəˈgərj, rēˈ-, -gə̄j, -gəij\ *vb* [by shortening & alter.] **:** REGURGITATE

re·gur·gi·tant \-jəd·ənt, -ətənt *also* -tᵊnt\ *adj* [ML *regurgitant-, regurgitans*, pres. part. of *regurgitare*] **:** throwing or flowing back **:** REGURGITATING

re·gur·gi·tate \-jə,tāt, *usu* -ād·+V\ *vb* -ED/-ING/-S [ML *regurgitatus*, past part. of *regurgitare*, fr. L *re-* + LL *gurgitare* to engulf — more at GURGITATION] *vi* **:** to become thrown or poured back **:** gush, rush, or surge back **~** *vt* **:** to throw, cast, or pour back or out again (as from a cavity)

re·gur·gi·ta·tion \(ˌ)rē,gərjəˈtāshən, -gə̄j-,-gəij-, rə,=ˈ=\ *n* [ML *regurgitation-, regurgitatio*, fr. *regurgitatus* (past part. of *regurgitare*) + L *-ion-, -io* -ion] **:** an act of flowing, pouring, or gushing back or out again; *specif* **:** reversal of the natural direction in which the current or contents flow through a tube or cavity of the body (as the casting up of incompletely digested food by some birds feeding their young or the backward flow of blood through a defective heart valve) ⟨mitral ~⟩ — **re·gur·gi·ta·tion·al** \-shənᵊl, -shnəl\ *adj*

reh \ˈrā\ *n* -s [Hindi *rēh*] **:** a mixture of soluble sodium salts appearing as an efflorescence on the ground in arid or semiarid regions in India

re·ha·bil·i·tant \,rē(h)əˈbilətənt *sometimes* ,rēhaˈb-\ *n* -s [*rehabilitation* + *-ant*] **:** a disabled person undergoing rehabilitation

re·ha·bil·i·tate \-lə,tāt, *usu* -ād·+V\ *vt* -ED/-ING/-S [ML *rehabilitatus*, past part. of *rehabilitare*, fr. L *re-* + LL *habilitare* to habilitate — more at HABILITATE] **1 a :** to restore (as a delinquent) by a formal act or declaration to a former right, rank, or privilege lost or forfeited **:** invest or clothe again with some right, authority, or dignity **:** restore to a former capacity **:** qualify again **:** REINSTATE ⟨the judges . . . were *rehabilitated* by the payment of a fine —William Stubbs⟩ **b :** to restore to good repute by vindicating **:** clear of unjust or unfounded charges **:** reestablish the good name of ⟨a campaign to ~ the memory of . . . England's wickedest king —*N.Y. Times*⟩ ⟨wish to ~ this country in the eyes of those nations whose good opinion we value —Edith Summerskill⟩ **2 a :** to put on a proper basis or into a previous good state **:** restore (as something damaged or decayed) to a state of efficiency and good management ⟨~ . . . forests that once supplied a large share of the country's timber —*Amer. Guide Series: Minn.*⟩ ⟨~ wastelands⟩ ⟨~ slum areas⟩ **b :** to restore to a condition of health or normal activity by a process of medical rehabilitation ⟨~ a person after he has lost his sight —*Current Biog.*⟩ **c :** to restore to a useful and constructive place in society through social rehabilitation ⟨nuns who attempt to ~ a prostitute —Curtis Harrington⟩ **d :** to restore to a state of solvency or efficiency ⟨~ a company financially⟩ ⟨~ equipment⟩

re·ha·bil·i·ta·tion \,==,==ˈtāshən\ *n* -s *often attrib* [ML *rehabilitation-, rehabilitatio*, fr. *rehabilitatus* (past part. of *rehabilitare* to rehabilitate) + L *-ion-, -io* -ion] **1 :** the action or process of rehabilitating or of being rehabilitated: as **a :** the reestablishment of the reputation or standing of a person **:** the vindication of one's character **b :** the physical restoration of a sick or disabled person by therapeutic measures and reeducation to participation in the activities of a normal life within the limitations of his physical disability ⟨the ~ of patients with a lower extremity amputation —*Jour. Amer. Med. Assoc.*⟩ ⟨~ after coronary occlusion⟩ **c :** the process of restoring an individual (as a convict, mental patient, or disaster victim) to a useful and constructive place in society through some form of vocational, correctional, or therapeutic retraining or through relief, financial aid, or other reconstructive measure **d :** the restoration of something damaged or deteriorated to a prior good condition **:** improvement to a higher level or greater value ⟨the ~ of devastated libraries —*Amer. Library Assoc. Bull.*⟩ ⟨the ~ of the power of Britain —R.H.Gabriel⟩ ⟨~ of buildings in a slum area⟩ **2 :** the result of rehabilitating **:** the state of being rehabilitated ⟨the ultimate aim of any antituberculosis program is the ~ of the patient —*Jour. Amer. Med. Assoc.*⟩ ⟨this inmate's . . . struggle toward ~ —*Saturday Rev.*⟩

re·ha·bil·i·ta·tive \,==ˈ==,tād·|iv, -āt|, |ēv *also* |əv\ *adj* [*rehabilitate* + *-ive*] **:** of, relating to, or designed to accomplish rehabilitation ⟨from a penal to a ~ philosophy —J.B.Costello⟩ ⟨~ treatment⟩

re·ha·bil·i·tee \,==,==ˈtē\ *n* -s [*rehabilitate* + *-ee*] **:** one who is in the process of being rehabilitated ⟨this form of therapy fitted . . . our ~*s*' needs —M.C.Bettis⟩

re·hair \(ˈ)rē+\ *vt* [*re-* + *hair*] **:** to attach new hair to (a bow of a musical instrument)

re·hallow \"+\ *vt* [*re-* + *hallow*] **:** to hallow again ⟨though it is sullied . . . your august coldness shall ~ it —Gordon Bottomley⟩

re·hammer \"+\ *vt* [*re-* + *hammer*] **:** to hammer again

re·handle \"+\ *vt* [*re-* + *handle*] **:** to handle again ⟨~ tobacco before using⟩; *esp* **:** to give a new and different treatment to (as a subject or theme) ⟨*rehandled* the legend⟩

re·hang \"+\ *vt* [*re-* + *hang*] **:** to hang again esp. in a new and different way ⟨~ the portraits in the gallery⟩ ⟨take off the dust covers and ~ the curtains⟩

re·harmonize \"+\ *vt* [*re-* + *harmonize*] **:** to harmonize again or anew; *specif* **:** to provide (as a melody or musical passage) with a different harmony

¹re·hash \"+\ *vt* [*re-* + *hash*] **:** to hash over again **:** present or use again in another form without real change or improvement in substance **:** restate (as old arguments) in new language ⟨~*ed* the previous night's ball —Lillian Ross⟩ ⟨does more than ~ an old tale —T.H.Williams⟩ ⟨~*ed* all their old propaganda charges —*N.Y. Times*⟩

²re·hash \ˈrē+,-, =ˈ=\ *n* **1 :** a product of rehashing **:** something presented in a new form without change of substance ⟨the text . . . is simply a dull ~ of the operatic plots —John Haverstick⟩ ⟨popular ~*es* of history and legend are many —T.F.Reddaway⟩ ⟨a ~ of stale ideas hurriedly dashed off —J.F.McComas⟩ **2 :** the action or process of rehashing ⟨in the course of the long ~ of old arguments —A.H. Vandenberg †1951⟩

rehave *vt* [ME *rehaven*, fr. *re-* + *haven* to have] *obs* **:** to have or get again **:** REGAIN

re·hear \(ˈ)rē+\ *vt* [back-formation fr. *rehearing*] **:** to hear judicially again or anew ⟨the Interstate Commerce Commission . . . proceeded to ~ the matters appertaining to that application —*McLean v. Keith*⟩

re·hearing \(ˈ)rē+\ *n* [*re-* + *hearing*] **:** a second or new hearing (as of a trial or an argument on appeal) by the same tribunal and upon the pleadings and depositions already in the case

re·hears·al \rəˈhərsəl, rēˈh-, -hə̄s-,-həis-\ *n* -s [ME *rehersaille*, fr. *rehersen* to rehearse + *-aille* -al] **1 :** the action of rehearsing ⟨a series of blackout ~*s* —Winifred Bambrick⟩ ⟨require a ~ of the whole of American history —H.S.Commager⟩ ⟨seemed like a ~ of her own life, terrible in its vividness —Sherwood Anderson⟩ **2 :** a private recital, performance, or practice session held in preparation for a public appearance ⟨much confusion at the ~⟩

re·hearse \-s\ *vb* -ED/-ING/-S [ME *rehersen, rehercen*, fr. MF *rehercier* to repeat, to harrow over again, fr. *re-* + *hercier* to harrow, fr. *herce* harrow — more at HEARSE] *vt* **1 a :** to repeat or say again (as something already said or heard) ⟨the term is duly *rehearsed* in most of the history books —S.L.Faison⟩ ⟨no need to ~ here in detail the familiar story —F.L.Allen⟩ **b :** to recite or repeat aloud in a formal manner **:** say or tell over usu. from beginning to end ⟨as if she had been in the dock she *rehearsed* her poor tale —Maurice Hewlett⟩ **2** *archaic* **:** to present an account of **:** describe at length **:** NARRATE, RECOUNT, RELATE, TELL ⟨~*s* to a youth . . . the checkered story of her life —J.L.Lowes⟩ **3 :** to recount in order **:** mention one by one or one after another **:** ENUMERATE ⟨an address which *rehearsed* the wrongs suffered by the army —H.E.Scudder⟩ ⟨the multitude of things produced by . . . savages and peasants —John Dewey⟩ **4 a :** to practice or go through (as a play, scene, or part) in private in preparation for a more formal and public presentation **:** recite or repeat (as lines) in such a practice ⟨*rehearsed* the shooting of a rural story —Andrew Buchanan⟩ ⟨while his grandfather *rehearsed* campaign speeches —*Current Biog.*⟩ ⟨familiar symphonies . . . rarely get *rehearsed* —Virgil Thomson⟩ **b :** to train, instruct, or make proficient by rehearsal ⟨staff members have been *rehearsed* for the gala opening —*Springfield (Mass.) Union*⟩ ⟨~*s* the orchestra three times for each of his programs —Virgil Thomson⟩ **5 :** to perform or practice as if in a rehearsal ⟨the kitten ~*s* the kind of actions the cat employs in catching its prey —John Dewey⟩ ⟨the Pacific Fleet will ~ . . . a mission they might be called to perform —*N.Y. Times*⟩ **~** *vi* **:** to recite something esp. for practice **:** engage in a rehearsal ⟨dominant actors who *rehearsed* in submissive roles —Helen H. Nowlis⟩ **syn** see RELATE

re·hears·er \-sə(r)\ *n* -s **:** one that rehearses; *specif* **:** a person who conducts rehearsals of an orchestra

¹re·heat \(ˈ)rē+\ *vt* [*re-* + *heat*] **:** to heat again

²re·heat \ˈrē+,-, =ˈ=\ *n* **1 :** a device (as an afterburner) used to recover heat for improved efficiency of a jet engine **2 :** AFTERBURNING 2

re·heater \(ˈ)rē+\ *n* [*re-* + *heater*] **:** one that reheats: as **a :** a furnaceman who reheats metal **b :** a receiver furnished with means for heating the steam in a compound engine or turbine **c :** an apparatus for reheating compressed air before use to prevent excessively low temperatures due to expansion

reheating furnace *n* **:** a furnace used in steel making in which bars are reheated before being rolled

reh·fuss tube \ˈrāfəs-\ *n, usu cap R* [after Martin E. *Rehfuss* b1887 Am. physician] **:** a flexible tube fitted with a slotted endpiece at the end that passes into the stomach and a syringe at the upper end and used esp. for withdrawing gastric juice for gastric analyses

re·ho·bo·am \,rēəˈbōəm *sometimes* ,rēhə-\ *n* -s *usu cap* [after *Rehoboam fl ab* 925 B.C. son of King Solomon and first king of the southern kingdom of Judah, fr. Heb *Rĕḥabh'ām*, lit., the nation is enlarged] **:** an oversize wine bottle holding about five quarts ⟨a *Rehoboam* of champagne⟩

re·ho·both \ˈrēə,bōth, rəˈhōbəth\ *also* **re·he·both** \ˈrēə,bōth\ *n* -s *usu cap* [prob. after *Rehoboth*, site where Isaac dug a well for which the herdsmen of Abimelech did not fight and that he named (Gen 26:22), fr. Heb *Rĕḥōbhōth*, lit., wide spaces] **:** a member of a community or company of peoples in southwestern Africa of mixed European and native and esp. Hottentot and Herero origin

re·house \(ˈ)rēˈhau̇z\ *vt* [*re-* + *house*] **:** to establish in a new or different housing unit of a better quality ⟨get rid of slums and ~ slum dwellers —Catherine Bauer⟩ ⟨county boroughs . . . must ~ a large surplus population outside their own areas —*Economist*⟩

rehs *pl of* REH

re·hy·drat·able \ˌrē,hīˈdrād·əbəl, rēˈhī,dr-\ *adj* **:** capable of being rehydrated ⟨~ rice⟩

re·hydrate \(ˈ)rē+\ *vt* [*re-* + *hydrate*] **:** to hydrate again: as **a :** to restore moisture to (dehydrated foods) **b :** to restore body fluid lost in dehydration to ⟨~ the patient⟩

re·hydration \ˌrē+\ *n* [*re-* + *hydration*] **:** the action or process of rehydrating

re·hypothecation \ˌrē+\ *n* [*re-* + *hypothecation*] **:** the action of a broker who pledges with a bank or other lender securities already left on deposit with him by a customer as a pledge for their purchase on margin

rei *pl of* REUS

reichert-meissl number *or* **reichert-meissl value** \ˈrīkə(r)t, ˈmīsəl-\ *n, usu cap R&M* [after Karl *Reichert* and E. *Meissl*, 19th cent. Ger. chemists] **:** a Reichert value expressed as the milliliters of tenth-normal alkali required to neutralize the acids obtained from five grams of fat by a specified method of saponification and distillation

reichert value *or* **reichert number** *n, usu cap R* [after Karl *Reichert*, 19th cent. Ger. chemist] **:** a value that indicates the content in butter or other fat of the water-soluble volatile fatty acids (as butyric acid, caproic acid, caprylic acid); *esp* **:** REICHERT-MEISSL NUMBER

reichs·mark \ˈrīks+,-\ *n, pl* **reichsmarks** *also* **reichsmark** *sometimes cap* [G, fr. *reichs* (gen. of *reich* empire, realm, fr. OHG *rīhhi*) + *mark* — more at RICH, MARK] **:** the German mark from 1925 to 1948

reichs·pfennig \"+,-\ *n, pl* **reichspfennigs** *also* **reichspfennige** *sometimes cap* [G, fr. *reichs* (gen. of *reich* realm) + *pfennig* — more at PFENNIG] **1 :** the German pfennig from 1925 to 1948 equal to ¹⁄₁₀₀ reichsmark **2 :** a coin representing one reichspfennig

reichs·taler \"+,-\ *n* -s *often cap* [G, fr. *reichs* (gen. of *reich* realm) + *taler* — more at TALER] **:** the old German taler of legal weight and fineness as distinguished from one of the many local varieties — called also *speciestaler*

reid \ˈrēd\ *Scot var of* RED

reif \ˈrēf\ *n* -s [ME (Sc) *ref, reif*, fr. OE *rēaf*; akin to OHG *roubōn* to rob — more at REAVE] *chiefly Scot* **:** ROBBERY, PLUNDER ⟨keep the house frae ~ and wear —Sir Walter Scott⟩

re·ifi·ca·tion \,rēəfəˈkāshən\ *n* -s [L *res* thing + E *-i-* + *-fication* — more at REAL] **:** the process or result of reifying **:** HYPOSTATIZATION ⟨~*s* of idealized abstractions —Joseph Katz⟩

re·ify \ˈrēə,fī\ *vt* -ED/-ING/-ES [L *res* + E *-ify*] **:** to regard (as an abstraction, a mental construction) as a thing **:** convert mentally into something concrete or objective **:** give definite content and form to **:** MATERIALIZE ⟨~*ing* both space and time⟩ ⟨a culture can be *reified* into a body of traditions —M.J. Herskovits⟩

¹reign \ˈrān\ *n* -s [ME *rein, regne*, fr. OF *reigne, regne*, fr. L *regnum* reign, fr. *reg-, rex* king — more at ROYAL] **1 a :** royal authority **:** the power or rule of a monarch **:** SOVEREIGNTY ⟨crown prince . . . assumed active ~ from his father —*Current Biog.*⟩ ⟨under the ~ of the Stuart kings⟩ **b :** the dominion, sway, or influence of one resembling or held to resemble a monarch ⟨the ~ of the . . . Puritan ministers was stern and intolerant —W.L.Sperry⟩ ⟨the full ~ of egotism as the ideal behind action —S.L.A.Marshall⟩ ⟨assuring the ~ of justice for all —*Loyola Univ. Bull.*⟩ **2** *archaic* **:** the territory or sphere that is reigned over **:** EMPIRE, KINGDOM, REALM ⟨the pole, Nature's remotest ~ —P.B.Shelley⟩ **3 :** the period of time during which someone (as a monarch) or something reigns ⟨the 20th year of the queen's ~⟩ ⟨at the beginning of his ~ as president of the college⟩ ⟨the ~ of Sanskrit . . . was longer than that of Greek and Latin —*Times Lit. Supp.*⟩

²reign \"\ *vi* -ED/-ING/-S [ME *reignen, regnen*, fr. OF *regner*, fr. L *regnare*, fr. *regnum* reign] **1 a :** to possess or exercise sovereign power **:** hold supreme authority in a state **:** govern as king, emperor, or other royal ruler **:** hold supreme power and dignity in a kingdom or empire **:** GOVERN, RULE ⟨Holy City . . . where Christ, the Lamb, doth ~ —W.R.Bowie⟩ **b :** to hold office as chief of state (as in a kingdom) without exercising more than minimal powers of making and executing governmental policy **:** have limited or nominal sovereignty ⟨the queen . . . ~*s* but does not rule —*Brit. Parliament*⟩ ⟨an Arab sultan ~*s* but British administrators . . . rule —Orville Prescott⟩ ⟨the royal governor both ~*ed* and ruled —D.W. Brogan⟩ ⟨will be the constitutional head of his country and will be above party and politics, an arbitrator and conciliator. He will not govern but will ~ —*N.Y. Times*⟩ **2 :** to exercise authority or hold sway in the manner of a monarch ⟨the archbishop . . . ~*s* as supreme moral authority on this island —George Weller⟩ ⟨in the countryside . . . the priest ~*s* more completely —Paul Blanshard⟩ ⟨the campus queen ~*ed* over the weekend festivities⟩ **3 :** to be predominant or prevalent **:** PREDOMINATE, PREVAIL ⟨these forests have ~*ed* supreme for countless millennia —W.H.Hodge⟩ ⟨commotion . . . ~*ed* through the house —E.J.Simmons⟩ ⟨a complete silence still ~*ed* inside —T.B.Costain⟩

reign of terror [fr. *Reign of Terror*, a period of the French Revolution between the executions of Louis XVI and Robespierre that was conspicuous for the mass executions of political suspects] **1 :** a state characterized by conditions (as violence, threats of violence, or actions as injurious as physical violence) that produce terror among the people involved ⟨created a *reign of terror* throughout . . . the state —*Amer. Guide Series: Oreg.*⟩ ⟨no overt *reign of terror* among our intellectuals —W.G.Carleton⟩ **2 :** a period of time during which such conditions prevail ⟨gave ordinary prisoners some measure of confidence that the *reign of terror* . . . was finished —*N.Y. Herald Tribune*⟩

¹rei·hen·grä·ber \ˈrīən,grābə(r)\ *n pl, usu cap* [G, lit., graves in rows, fr. *reihen* (pl. of *reihe* row, fr. MHG *rihe* line) + *gräber*, pl. of *grab* grave, fr. OHG; fr. their being arranged in rows — more at GRAVE] **:** long barrows that are found in southern Germany

²reihengräber \"\ *n pl, usu cap* **:** the prehistoric prob. Teutonic people that are buried in the Reihengräber

re·illumine \ˌrē+\ *vt* [*re-* + *illumine*] **:** to illumine again

re·im·burs·able \ˌrēəmˈbərsəbəl, -bə̄s-,-bəis-\ *adj* [*reimburse* + *-able*] **:** REPAYABLE ⟨~ indebtedness⟩ ⟨replacement of . . . equipment on a ~ basis —*U.S.Code*⟩

re·im·burse \-s\ *vt* -ED/-ING/-S [*re-* + obs. E *imburse* to pocket money, make rich, pay, fr. MF *embourser* to pocket money, fr. OF *em-* en- + *borser* to get money — more at DISBURSE] **1 :** to pay back (an equivalent for something taken, lost, or expended) to someone **:** REPAY ⟨costs shall be . . . *reimbursed* from such funds —*U.S. Code*⟩ **2 :** to make restoration or payment of an equivalent to (as a person) **:** INDEMNIFY ⟨~ government employees for travel expenses⟩ **syn** see PAY

re·im·burse·ment \,==ˈ=mənt\ *n* -s [prob. fr. F *remboursement*, fr. MF, fr. *rembourser* to reimburse (fr. *re-* + *embourser* to pocket money) + *-ment*] **:** the action of reimbursing **:** REPAYMENT ⟨make direct ~*s* to private corporations for federal income taxes —*New Republic*⟩ ⟨~ for out-of-pocket expenditures⟩

reimer-tiemann reaction \ˈrīmə(r)ˈtēmən-, -ē,män-\ *n, usu cap R & T* [after Karl *Reimer* 19th cent. Ger. chemist and Ferdinand *Tiemann* †1899 Ger. chemist] **:** either of two similar chemical reactions: **a :** a reaction for producing phenolic aldehydes by the action of chloroform and caustic alkali on phenols **b :** a reaction for producing phenolic acids from carbon tetrachloride, alkali, and phenols

re·impose \ˌrē+\ *vt* [*re-* + *impose*] **:** to impose again ⟨~ recently relaxed . . . restrictions —*Current Biog.*⟩ ⟨duties are to be *reimposed* for a further ten years —*Contemporary Rev.*⟩ ⟨*reimposing* the ban on parking⟩

re·imposition \(ˌ)rē+\ *n* [*re-* + *imposition*] **:** the action of reimposing ⟨~ of installment credit controls —*Wall Street Jour.*⟩ ⟨~ of taxes⟩

re·impression \ˌrē+\ *n* [*re-* + *impression*] **:** a second or repeated impression (as of a book) without change **:** a reprint as distinguished from a new edition

reims *also* **rheims** \ˈrēmz, *F* raaⁿs\ *adj, usu cap* [fr. *Reims* (*Rheims*), France] **:** of or from the city of Reims, France **:** of the kind or style prevalent in Reims **:** RHEMISH

¹rein \ˈrān\ *n* -s [ME *reine, rene*, fr. MF *reine, resne*, fr. (assumed) VL *retina*, fr. L *retinere* to hold back — more at RETAIN] **1 :** a line (as a leather strap) which is fastened to a bit on each side and through which a rider or driver exerts pressure on the bit for governing or guiding an animal (as a horse) ⟨use of the ~ . . . to lead the horse's head and neck to the right —Harry Disston⟩ — usu. used in pl. ⟨seize the ~*s* from the grasp of the slumbering coachman —Thomas De Quincey⟩ — see BRIDLE illustration **2 :** something held to resemble the rein of a horse: as **a :** a restraining influence **:** CURB, CHECK ⟨let their eyes move without ~ —John Milton⟩ ⟨regulation . . . imposes ~*s* on consumer credit —John Elliott⟩ ⟨hold him under a tight ~ in his youth —R.A.Hall b. 1911⟩ **b :** the controlling or guiding power **:** position of command ⟨the ~*s* of government . . . have been handed to men of one party —A.N.Holcombe⟩ ⟨without the ~*s* of patronage . . . the forces of party organization lack guidance —Gladwin Hill⟩ **3 :** the part of a horse on which the reins exert leverage ⟨a horse with a good ~ has a well-sloped shoulder, rather long neck, and well-set head⟩ — **give rein to :** to give freedom, unlimited scope, or full course to ⟨*gave* full *rein to* his mingled exasperation and boredom —S.H.Adams⟩ ⟨the military forces *given free rein to* quell the rebellion —Virginia Valentine⟩ ⟨*giving free rein to* his commanding general⟩

²rein \"\ *vb* -ED/-ING/-S [ME *reinen*, fr. *reine* rein] *vt* **1** *obs* **:** to fasten or tie up (as a horse) to something by means of reins ⟨alight thy steed and ~ his proud head to the saddlebow —Shak.⟩ **2** *archaic* **:** to provide with a rein ⟨~*ed* with gold his foaming steeds —Alexander Pope⟩ **3 a :** to check or stop and hold by a pull at the reins **:** pull up by means of reins ⟨cowboys ~*ed* their sweating ponies to a halt —J.C.MacDonald⟩ — often used with *back, in,* or *up* ⟨the squire . . . ~*ed* in his horse —T.B.Costain⟩ **b :** to put a check or restraint upon as if by the use of reins — often used with *in* or *up* ⟨unable to ~ in his impatience any longer —Vicki Baum⟩ ⟨~ the tongue⟩ ⟨tries hard to ~ in his imagination —Kendall Smith⟩ **4 a :** to control, direct, or turn with the reins ⟨~ a horse to the left⟩ ⟨they ~*ed* their horses through the chaparral —*Underworld Detective*⟩ **b :** to guide, manage, or govern as if by the use of reins ⟨~*ed* our conversation round to . . . future prospects —Joseph Furphy⟩ **~** *vi* **1** *archaic* **:** to submit or yield to the use of reins ⟨will bear you easily and ~*s* well —Shak.⟩ **2 :** to move or pull in or as if in response to tightened reins — usu. used with *back, in,* or *up* **3 :** to stop or slow up one's horse or oneself by or as if by pulling the reins — often used with *back, in,* or *up* ⟨cavalrymen ~*ed* up⟩ ⟨~*ed* in to a jog⟩ ⟨~ back and take your places —J.H.Wheelwright⟩

³rein \"\ *n* -s [Norw, fr. ON *hreinn* — more at REINDEER] **:** REINDEER

rei·na \ˈrānə\ *n* -s [Sp, queen, fr. L *regina*, fem. of *reg-, rex* king — more at ROYAL] **:** a California rockfish (*Sebastodes elongatus*)

¹re·incarnate \(ˌ)rē+\ *vt* [*re-* + *incarnate*] **:** to incarnate again or anew — compare TRANSMIGRATE

²re·incarnate \"+\ *adj* [*re-* + *incarnate*, adj.] **:** incarnate again

re·incarnation \"+\ *n* [*re-* + *incarnation*] **1 a :** the action of reincarnating or the state of being reincarnated **b :** rebirth in new bodies or forms of life; *esp* **:** a rebirth of a soul in a new human body **2 :** a belief (as in metempsychosis and transmigration) that the souls of the dead successively return to earth in new forms or bodies **3 :** one that has been reincarnated **:** a fresh embodiment of someone or something ⟨a lively ~ of the busy . . . colonial capital —*Amer. Guide Series: Va.*⟩

re·in·car·na·tion·ist \"əst\ *n* -s [*reincarnation* + *-ist*] **:** a believer in reincarnation

re·incorporate \ˌrē+\ *vt* [trans. of F *reincorporer*] **:** to incorporate again

¹rein·deer \ˈrān+,-\ *n, pl* **reindeer** *also* **reindeers** [ME *reindere*, fr. ON *hreinn* reindeer (prob. akin to ON *horn* horn) + ME *dere* deer — more at HORN, DEER] **:** any of several deers of the genus *Rangifer* that inhabit the northern parts of Europe, Asia, and America, have large crescentic hooves with very large dewclaws, antlers present in both sexes with those of the male long, sweeping, often somewhat palmate at the ends, and with broad greatly developed brow antlers and with those of the female much smaller and simpler, and are often domesticated and used esp. in Lapland for drawing sleds and as a source of food — compare CARIBOU, ELK, MOOSE

European reindeer

²reindeer \"\ *adj, usu cap* **:** of, belonging to, or constituting a Paleolithic period in central Europe when reindeer were esp. numerous **:** MAGDALENIAN

reindeer moss *or* **reindeer lichen** *n* **:** any fruticose lichen of the genus *Cladonia*; *esp* **:** a gray erect tufted and much-branched lichen (*C. rangiferina*) that is found in extensive patches on the ground in arctic and even in north temperate regions and forms a large part of the food of reindeer and caribou in the far north (as in Lapland) and is sometimes eaten by man — called also *arctic moss*

reindeer pest *or* **reindeer plague** *n* **:** an enzootic highly fatal malignant edema of reindeer characterized by excitement, lack of appetite, staggering gait, difficult respiration, and edematous swellings

rei·nec·kate \\'rīnə,kāt\\ *n* -s *sometimes cap* [*reinecke* + *-ate*] **:** a salt of reinecke acid

rei·nec·ke acid \\'rīnəkə-, -kē-\\ *n, usu cap R* [after A. *Reinecke*, 19th cent. Ger. chemist] **:** the monobasic acid $HCr(NH_3)_2(SCN)_4$ of which Reinecke salt is the ammonium salt

reinecke salt *n, usu cap R* [after A. *Reinecke*, 19th cent. Ger. chemist] **:** a red crystalline coordination complex $NH_4[Cr(NH_3)_2(SCN)_4].H_2O$ that is formed by adding ammonium dichromate to hot ammonium thiocyanate and that with heavy-metal ions and with organic bases, alkaloids, and basic antibiotics gives precipitates useful in separations and characterizations

re·infection \\¦rē+\\ *n* [*re-* + *infection*] **:** an additional infection following recovery from or superimposed on a previous infection of the same type ⟨reactivation of a lesion which has become temporarily arrested is not in the pathologic sense a "~" but rather . . . delayed progression —F.D.Gunn⟩

[1]**re·inforce** *also* **re·enforce** \\¦rē+\\ *vb* -ED/-ING/-S [*reinforce* fr. *re-* + *inforce*, alter. of *enforce; reenforce* fr. *re-* + *enforce*] *vt* **1 a :** to strengthen with additional force, assistance, material, or support **:** make stronger or more pronounced ⟨walls . . . *reinforced* with mud —*Amer. Guide Series: Minn.*⟩ ⟨details piled upon details ~ the picture —Emory Ross⟩ ⟨~ the elbows of a jacket⟩ ⟨the atmosphere *reinforced* by candle fumes was stifling —Ronald Storrs⟩ **b :** to strengthen (a military or naval force) with additional units ⟨~ the regular troops —Manfred Nathan⟩ ⟨the Englishman . . . was *reinforced* by three other ships of the line —*U.S. Naval Inst. Proceedings*⟩ **c :** to strengthen or increase (a group or number) by fresh additions ⟨the faculty . . . was *reinforced* from the ranks of its students —R.M.Lovett⟩ ⟨the reformers were *reinforced* in the assembly —B.K.Sandwell⟩ ⟨trout eggs can be treated by the same solution provided it is *reinforced* after each lot —*Transactions of the Amer. Fisheries Society*⟩ **d :** to make more forcible, cogent, or convincing ⟨movements we make with face, head, hands, feet to ~ our words —Stuart Chase⟩ ⟨~ an argument⟩ **e :** to make greater (as by the provision of fresh force or additional units) ⟨~ the collections on government . . . science, and technology —L.H.Evans⟩ ⟨~ their own productivity by the creation of . . . marvelous machinery —R.W.Emerson⟩ **2** *obs* **:** to renew or repeat with fresh force **3** *obs* **:** to enforce again ⟨~ . . . the laws against the conventicles —Andrew Marvell⟩ **4 :** to increase the likelihood of (a response) by a reward **~** *vi* **:** to seek or get reinforcements **syn** see STRENGTHEN

[2]**re·inforce** \\"\\ *n* -s **:** something that reinforces or strengthens; *specif* **:** the metal band placed over the chamber and rear part of the bore of a gun — see CANNON illustration

reinforced bow *n* **:** a bow backed with sinew — called also *sinew-backed bow*

reinforced concrete *n* **:** concrete in which metal (as steel) in the form of rods, bars, or meshwork is embedded in such a manner that the two materials act together in resisting forces — called also *ferroconcrete*

re·inforcement \\¦rē+\\ *n* -s [*reinforce* + *-ment*] **1** *obs* **:** a fresh or renewed assault ⟨with a sudden ~ struck . . . like a planet —Shak.⟩ **2 a :** the action of reinforcing or the state of being reinforced **:** augmentation of strength or force ⟨willow mattresses used for ~ of caving banks —*Amer. Guide Series: La.*⟩ ⟨his task is the factual ~ of Christian theology by ethnology —Rodney Needham⟩ ⟨heavy ~ of credit supplies . . . had taken place —*Financial Times* (*London*)⟩ **b :** the strengthening of the response to one stimulus by the concurrent action of another stimulus (as a reward) — compare RECRUITMENT **3** *archaic* **:** the action of enforcing again or anew **4 :** something that reinforces: as **a :** an additional unit (as of troops or ships) to augment the strength of an army, fleet, or other military force ⟨received . . . a ~ of 30,000 men —Thomas Lediard⟩ — often used in pl. ⟨without ~*s* he would not be able to maintain his position —*U.S. Naval Inst. Proceedings*⟩ **b :** an additional supply or contribution ⟨great ~*s* of sympathy —Walter Pater⟩ **c :** something designed to provide additional strength (as in a weak area) ⟨leather ~*s* on the jacket and trouser pockets —*N.Y. Times*⟩ ⟨gummed ~*s* . . . prevent paper from tearing —J.R.Gregg⟩

re·inforcer \\"+\\ *n* -s [*reinforce* + *-er*] **:** one that reinforces

reinforcing *n* -s [fr. gerund of [1]*reinforce*] **:** REINFORCEMENT 4c

reinforcing agent *n* **:** a substance (as carbon black or other pigment) used esp. in compounding rubber to improve the physical properties (as resilience, toughness, and tensile strength)

re·inform \\¦rē+\\ *vt* [*re-* + *inform*] **:** to form anew **:** invest again with form ⟨~ features and attributes that have long been laid . . . in the quiet of the grave —R.L.Stevenson⟩

reining *pres part of* REIN

rein·less \\'rānləs\\ *adj* [[1]*rein* + *-less*] **1 :** having no reins **:** ungoverned by reins ⟨~ steeds⟩ **2 :** lacking control or guidance **:** UNCHECKED, UNRESTRAINED ⟨the ~ play of the imagination —John Ruskin⟩

rein orchis \\'rān-\\ *n* [*rein* prob. back-formation fr. *reins;* fr. the kidney-shaped lip in some species] **:** any of several orchids of *Habenaria* or a related genus usu. with a kidney-shaped lip to the flower

[1]**reins** \\'rānz\\ *n pl* [ME *reins*, fr. MF & L; MF *reins*, fr. L *renes*] **1 :** KIDNEYS ⟨cleaveth my ~ asunder —Job 16:13 (AV)⟩ **2 :** the region of the kidneys **:** LOINS ⟨girdled about the ~ with a curse —A.C.Swinburne⟩ **3 :** the seat of the feelings, affections, or passions ⟨my ~ also instruct me —Ps 16:7 (AV)⟩ ⟨searcheth the ~ and hearts —Rev 2:23 (AV)⟩ **4 :** the parts of a vault between the crown and the spring or abutment including the filling behind the vault shell

[2]**reins** *pl of* REIN, *pres 3d sing of* REIN

re·insert \\¦rē+\\ *vt* [*re-* + *insert*] **:** to insert again ⟨~ a letter in an envelope⟩

reins·man \\'rānzmən\\ *n, pl* **reinsmen** [*reins* (gen. of [1]*rein*) + *man*] **:** a person skilled in handling reins; *specif* **:** a skillful jockey or harness driver ⟨30-year-old ~ . . . won the two major driving titles —*N.Y. Times*⟩

re·instate \\¦rē+\\ *vt* [*re-* + *instate*] **1 :** to instate again **:** place again (as in possession or in a former position) ⟨*reinstated* in British favor —*Amer. Guide Series: Fla.*⟩ ⟨*reinstated* in his former government and university posts —*Current Biog.*⟩ ⟨able to ~ law and order —Michael Blundell⟩ ⟨~ an insurance policy⟩ **2 :** to restore to a proper condition **:** replace in an original or equivalent state ⟨the broken glass hacked out and *reinstated* —Samuel Butler †1902⟩

re·instatement \\"+\\ *n* [*reinstate* + *-ment*] **1 a :** the action of reinstating (as in a post or position formerly held but relinquished) ⟨~ of the postmaster⟩ ⟨~ to amateur status of a tennis star turned professional⟩ **b :** the action of replacing or restoring the effectiveness of (as something damaged, worn out, or lapsed) ⟨the cost of ~ may exceed the market value of the whole farm —*Country Life*⟩; *esp* **:** the action of restoring an insurance policy to its previous status or amount after it has been reduced by the payment of a claim or allowed to lapse **2 :** the state or condition of being reinstated ⟨his ~ in popular favor quickly followed⟩

re·in·sta·tion \\,rēənz'tāshən, -ən'st-\\ *n* -s [*reinstate* + *-ion*] **:** REINSTATEMENT ⟨his ~ in the service —George Meredith⟩

re·insurance \\¦rē+\\ *n* [*re-* + *insurance*] **1 :** an insurance by another insurer of all or a part of a risk previously assumed by the direct-writing company **2 :** the amount assumed in reinsurance **3 :** the action of reinsuring — see EXCESS-LOSS REINSURANCE, EXCESS REINSURANCE, FACULTATIVE REINSURANCE, FLAT REINSURANCE, TREATY REINSURANCE

reinsurance reserve *n* **:** RESERVE 6b(2)

re·insure \\"+\\ *vb* [*re-* + *insure*] *vt* **1 :** to insure again by transferring to another insurance company the liability in whole or in part assumed by the direct-writing company **:** transfer (the whole or part of a risk) to another company **2 :** to insure again by assuming the liability in whole or in part of an insurance company which is already covering the risk **:** assume (the whole or part of a risk) in reinsurance **~** *vi* **:** to provide increased insurance ⟨tried to ~ against invasion by making concessions to the enemy⟩ ⟨~ by hanging on to regions important . . . for supply or defense —*Economist*⟩

re·insurer \\"+\\ *n* [*reinsure* + *-er*] **:** one that reinsures

re·integrate \\(')rē+\\ *vt* [ML *reintegratus*, past part. of *reintegrare* to renew, reinstate, fr. L *re-* + *integrare* to integrate — more at INTEGRATE] **1** *archaic* **:** REINSTATE 1 ⟨all . . . should be *reintegrated* in their former possessions —Edward Herbert⟩ **2 :** to cause or bring about the reintegration of: as **a :** to integrate again into an entity ⟨if . . . her economy is not *reintegrated* into the European and world economy —Heinz Eulau⟩ **b :** to restore to unity after disintegration ⟨magical practices . . . ~ the individual and organize society —A.L.Kroeber⟩

re·integration \\(¦)rē+\\ *n* [ML *reintegration-, reintegratio*, fr. *reintegratus* (past part. of *reintegrare* to reinstate) + L *-ion-, -io* -ion] **:** repeated or renewed integration ⟨the ~ of veterans into an expanding civilian economy —H.S.Truman⟩

re·integrative \\(')rē+\\ *adj* [*reintegrate* + *-ive*] **1 :** tending to reintegrate ⟨~ phenomena⟩ **2 :** favoring or implementing reintegration ⟨~ trends⟩

re·interpret \\¦rē+\\ *vt* [*re-* + *interpret*] **:** to interpret again; *specif* **:** to give a new or different interpretation to ⟨patterns which the lapse of time has ~*ed* beyond recognition —Edward Sapir⟩ ⟨the New Testament . . . needs constantly to be ~*ed* for each succeeding generation —Walter Murdoch⟩

re·interpretation \\"+\\ *n* [*re-* + *interpretation*] **:** the action of reinterpreting or the state of being reinterpreted ⟨~ of borrowed behavior patterns —Ralph Linton⟩ ⟨the scholarly revaluation and ~ of form —*Yale Rev.*⟩

re·inthrone \\¦rē+\\ *vt* [*re-* + *inthrone*, alter. of *enthrone*] *archaic* **:** to enthrone again

re·introduce \\(¦)rē+\\ *vt* [*re-* + *introduce*] **:** to introduce again

re·invasion \\¦rē+\\ *n* [*re* + *invasion*] **:** a second or another invasion

re·invest \\"+\\ *vb* [*re-* + *invest*] *vt* **1 :** to invest again or anew ⟨great poetry . . . searches how to ~ words with meaning —C.S.Kilby⟩ **2 a :** to invest (as the income or repaid capital from old investments) in the purchase of additional securities **b :** to invest (as a part of earnings) in a business rather than making a distribution of dividends or profits **~** *vi* **:** to make a reinvestment ⟨before you ~, weigh the alternatives carefully⟩

re·investiture \\"+\\ *n* [*re-* + *investiture*] **:** the action of reinvesting or the state of being reinvested **:** REINSTATEMENT ⟨~ in their prerogatives —J.P.Peters⟩

re·investment \\"+\\ *n* [*re-* + *investment*] **:** the action of reinvesting or the state of being reinvested **:** a second or repeated investment

re·invigorate \\"+\\ *vt* [*re-* + *invigorate*] **:** to give renewed or fresh vigor to ⟨studies designed to ~ the humanities —W.H.Whyte⟩

re·invigoration \\"+\\ *n* [*re-* + *invigoration*] **:** the action of reinvigorating or the state of being reinvigorated ⟨his strong ~ of the forces of democracy —F.R.Dulles⟩

rein·wardt·ia \\rīn'wärd·ēə, rān-\\ *n, cap* [NL, fr. Caspar G. C. *Reinwardt* †1854 Du. botanist + NL *-ia*] **:** a small genus of East Indian undershrubs (family Linaceae) having alternate and rather large leaves and yellow flowers with fugacious petals

[1]**reis** *pl of* REAL

[2]**reis** *var of* RAIS

reis·ner work \\'rīz|nə(r)-, -īs|\\ *n* [after *Reisner*, 17th cent. Ger. cabinetmaker] **:** wooden inlaid work of different colors

reiss·ner's fiber \\'rīsnə(r)z-\\ *n, usu cap R* [after Ernst *Reissner* †1878 Ger. anatomist] **:** a band of fibers arising from the roof of the midbrain in many vertebrates, passing along the aqueduct and fourth ventricle to enter the central canal of the spinal cord, ending in the regions of the spinal nerves, being esp. large in fishes, and probably taking part in visual reflexes or regulating flexion of the body

reissner's membrane *n, usu cap R* [after Ernst *Reissner* †1878 Ger. anatomist] **:** a thin cellular membrane separating the vestibular and cochlear canals of the inner ear

[1]**re·issue** \\(')rē+\\ *vb* [*re-* + *issue*] *vi* **:** to come forth again ⟨it ~*s* into the ocean at the northerly end of the gulf —Thomas Jefferson⟩ **~** *vt* **:** to issue again; *esp* **:** to cause to appear or become available after a period of absence or unavailability ⟨~ a film⟩ ⟨~ a book⟩ ⟨~ a stamp⟩

[2]**reissue** \\"\\ *n* [*re-* + *issue*, n.] **1 :** a second or repeated issue (as of a publication) with change only in price or form ⟨a ~ in one volume of the two-volume . . . edition —Harvey Breit⟩ ⟨~ of a recording long unavailable⟩ ⟨~ of a postage stamp⟩ **2 :** a postage stamp (as of an earlier time no longer available) that has been reissued for postal use — compare REPRINT

reist \\'rēst\\ *var of* REEST

reister *n* -s [MF *reistre*, fr. G *reiter* rider] *obs* **:** REITER

reit·bok *also* **reit·boc** \\'rēt,bäk\\ *or* **reit·buck** \\-,bək\\ *or* **riet·bok** *or* **riet·boc** *n, pl* **reitbok** *or* **reitboks** [Afrik *rietbok*, fr. D *riet* reed (fr. MD) + *bok* buck, fr. MD *bok, boc;* akin to OE *buc* buck — more at REED, BUCK] **:** any of several reedbucks (esp. *Redunca arundinum*) of southern Africa having a bushy tail and in the male small ringed horns that curve forward

rei·ter \\'rīd·ə(r)\\ *n* -s [G, lit., rider, fr. MHG *rīter*, fr. OHG *rītāri*, fr. *rītan* to ride + *-āri* -er — more at RIDE] **:** a German cavalry soldier esp. of the 16th and 17th centuries

re·it·er·ant \\rē'id·ərənt, -itər-\\ *adj* [L *reiterant-, reiterans*, pres. part. of *reiterare* to repeat] **:** iterant to an increased degree ⟨a meaningless ~ jangle of noise —Julian Maclaren-Ross⟩ ⟨~ cry⟩

[1]**re·it·er·ate** \\-rət\\ *adj* [ME *reiteraten*, fr. L *reiteratus*, past part. of *reiterare* to repeat, fr. *re-* + *iterare* to iterate — more at ITERATE] **:** REITERATED, REPEATED ⟨in ~ refrain —Frances Bushnell⟩

[2]**re·it·er·ate** \\rē'id·ə,rāt, -itə-, *usu* -ād·+V\\ *vt* -ED/-ING/-S [ME reitterate, fr. L *reiteratus*, past part. of *reiterare* to repeat] **1 :** to say or do over again or repeatedly **:** repeat often or continually sometimes with a wearying effect ⟨information . . . *reiterated* day after day by every organ of publicity —John Dewey⟩ ⟨the sharp *reiterated* strokes of a woodpecker —J.C.Powys⟩ ⟨on a fence built around the mill he *reiterated* his warning against anyone attempting entrance —*Amer. Guide Series: Minn.*⟩ **2** *obs* **:** to repeat the application or use of (as a medicine) **syn** see REPEAT

re·it·er·at·ed·ly \\=='==,===, =,=='===\\ *adv* **:** in a reiterated or repeated manner **:** REPEATEDLY

re·it·er·a·tion \\(,)rē,idə'rāshən, -itə-\\ *n* -s [ML *reiteration-, reiteratio*, fr. L *reiteratus* (past part.) + *-ion-, -io* -ion] **1 :** the action of reiterating **:** REPETITION ⟨development by ~ of short simple motifs —Henry Cowell⟩ ⟨the poem is concluded with a ~ of the initial idea —C.S.Kilby⟩ **2** *archaic* **a :** a form printed on the reverse side of a sheet already printed on one side **b :** the action of printing a reiteration **:** PERFECTING **c :** matter printed by reiteration

re·it·er·a·tive \\='==,rād·iv, -,rəd·-\\ *adj* [[1]*reiterate* + *-ive*] **:** exhibiting or marked by reiteration ⟨~ imagery⟩

re·it·er·a·tive·ly \\-əvlē\\ *adv* **:** in a reiterative manner

rei·ter's disease \\'rīd·ə(r)z-\\ *also* **reiter's syndrome** *n, usu cap R* [after Hans *Reiter* *b*1881 Ger. physician] **:** a disease of unknown cause characterized by arthritis, conjunctivitis, and urethritis

rei·thro·don·to·mys \\,rīthrə'däntə,mis\\ *n, cap* [NL, fr. *reithr-* (fr. Gk *rheithron* that which flows, stream, fr. *rhein* to flow) + *odont-* + *-mys* — more at STREAM] **:** a genus of cricetid rodents comprising the harvest mice

reive \\'rēv\\ *vb* -ED/-ING/-S [ME (Sc) *reifen*, fr. OE *rēafian* to rob, despoil — more at REAVE] *Scot* **:** RAID

reiv·er \\'rēvər\\ *n* -s [ME (Sc) *reiffar*, fr. OE *rēafere*, fr. *rēafian* to rob + *-ere* -er] *Scot* **:** RAIDER ⟨a hiding place of stolen cattle in the days of the Border ~*s* —Janet MacPherson⟩ ⟨defense against sea ~*s* —D.G.Duff⟩

reiz·ianum \\,rītsē'anəm, -'än-,-'ān-\\ *n* -s [NL, fr. F. W. *Reiz* †1790 Ger. metrist + NL *-anum* (fr. L *-ianus* -ian)] **1 :** an acephalous pherecratic (as ⏒–⏑⏑–⏓) **2 :** a combination of an anapest or sometimes an iambus or a trochee with a bacchius

re·ja \\'rā(,)hä\\ *n* -s [Sp] **:** a grille or screen made usu. of wrought or cast metal and used in Spanish architecture to protect a window in a house or to enclose a chapel or a tomb in a church

re·jane green \\rā'zhän-\\ *n, often cap R* [prob. after Gabrielle Charlotte *Réjane* †1920 Fr. actress] **:** a moderate yellowish green that is greener and paler than tarragon and yellower and paler than malachite green

rejang *usu cap, var of* REDJANG

rejd *abbr* rejoined

[1]**re·ject** \\rə'jekt, rē'j-\\ *vt* -ED/-ING/-S [ME *rejecten*, fr. L *rejectus*, past part. of L *reicere, rejicere*, fr. *re-* + *-icere, -jicere* (fr. *jacere* to throw) — more at JET] **1 :** to refuse to acknowledge, adopt, believe, acquiesce in, receive, or submit to **:** decline to accept **:** REFUSE ⟨considered a proposition fairly and ~*ed* it —Willa Cather⟩ ⟨~ a diplomatic note⟩ ⟨~ a claim⟩ **2** *obs* **:** to cast off (as a person) **:** FORSAKE **3 :** to refuse to have, use, or take for some purpose **:** cast or throw away as useless, unsatisfactory, or worthless **:** DISCARD ⟨several publishers ~*ed* the manuscript —*Amer. Guide Series: N.Y.*⟩ ⟨memory . . . ~*s* what has not interested and impressed it —Laurence Binyon⟩ ⟨~*ed* by the recruiting station —O.S.J. Gogarty⟩ **4 a :** to refuse to hear, receive, or admit **:** REBUFF, REPEL ⟨parents who ~ the child —A.L.Porterfield⟩ ⟨underprivileged people who feel basically ~*ed* by society —Frank Fremont-Smith⟩ **b :** to refuse (a person) as lover or spouse ⟨~*ed* by her lover —J.T.Farrell⟩ **5 :** to refuse to grant, consider, or accede to ⟨the demand was at once ~*ed* by the baronage —J.R.Green⟩ **6 a :** to throw or cast back **:** REPULSE **b** *obs* **:** to cut off (as a person) from something ⟨the young men were . . . ~*ed* from any hopes of the kingdom —William Whiston⟩ **7 :** to spew out (as from the mouth or stomach) **:** EJECT **syn** see DECLINE

[2]**re·ject** \\'rē,jekt *sometimes* rə'j- *or* rē'j-\\ *n* -s **:** one that is or has been rejected: as **a :** one rejected as not wanted, unsatisfactory, or not fulfilling standard requirements ⟨good eggs found in the ~*s* by recandling —*Experiment Station Record*⟩ ⟨how often the deepest convictions of one generation are the ~*s* of the next —Learned Hand⟩ **b :** a partly chipped stone once started as an implement and then rejected **c :** a person rejected as unfit for military service ⟨army culls, physical or mental ~*s* from overseas duty —Taliaferro Boatwright⟩

re·ject·able \\rə'jektəbəl, rē'j-\\ *adj* **:** capable of being rejected **:** suitable for rejection

re·ject·age \\-tij\\ *n* -s [[1]*reject* + *-age*] **:** rejected material or objects ⟨from examination of large quantities of ~ —*Popular Science Monthly*⟩

re·jec·ta·men·ta \\rə,jektə'mentə, (,)rē,j-\\ *n pl* [NL, pl. of *rejectamentum*, fr. L *rejectare* (freq. of *rejicere* to reject) + *-mentum* -ment] **:** things rejected **:** a quantity of rejects **:** RUBBISH, REFUSE, WRACK

rejectaneous *adj* [L *rejectaneus*, fr. *rejectus* (past part. of *rejicere* to reject) + *-aneus* (as in *subterraneus* subterranean)] *obs* **:** deserving rejection **:** REJECTABLE ⟨profane, ~, and reprobate people —Isaac Barrow⟩

reject back *n* **:** a back veneer (as of a table top) concealed from view and having specified allowable imperfections or open joints

re·ject·ee \\rə¦jek¦tē, rē¦j-, ¦rē,j-\\ *n* -s [[1]*reject* + *-ee*] **:** one that is or has been rejected; *specif* **:** REJECT c ⟨selective service ~*s*⟩

re·ject·er \\rə'jektə(r), rē'j-\\ *n* -s **:** one that rejects

re·jec·tion \\-kshən\\ *n* -s [MF or L; MF *rejection*, fr. L *rejection-, rejectio*, fr. *rejectus* (past part. of *rejicere* to reject) + *-ion-, -io* -ion] **1 :** the action of rejecting or the state of being rejected ⟨an intellectual ~ of liberalism —Raymond Walters b. 1912⟩ ⟨~ of the atypical child by the . . . group —G.S.Speer⟩ ⟨criminal behavior is sometimes ~ of existing institutions —H.A.Murray & C.K.Kluckhohn⟩ **2 :** something rejected

rejection slip *n* **:** a printed slip enclosed with a rejected manuscript returned by an editor (as of a magazine) to an author or his agent

rejectitious *adj* [[1]*reject* + *-itious*] *obs* **:** deserving or requiring rejection **:** REJECTABLE ⟨persons spurious and ~ —Edward Waterhouse⟩

re·jec·tive \\rə'jektiv, rē'j-\\ *adj* **:** rejecting or tending to reject ⟨~ or overcritical attitudes of disappointed parents —Rudolf Hirschberg⟩

re·jec·tor \\-tə(r)\\ *n* -s **1 :** REJECTER **2 :** a circuit that combines inductance and capacitance in parallel so as to offer high impedance to a given impressed frequency and to resonate to all other frequencies — compare ACCEPTOR, FILTER, WAVE TRAP

re·jigger \\(')rē+\\ *vt* [*re-* + *jigger*] **:** to alter or rearrange again **:** manipulate in a new or different way ⟨executives ~ their organization charts —*Management Rev.*⟩ ⟨the government ~*ed* price ceilings on various pork cuts —*Chicago Daily Drovers Jour.*⟩

re·joice \\rə'jȯis, rē'j-\\ *vb* -ED/-ING/-S [ME *rejoicen, rejoisen*, fr. MF *rejoiss-*, extended stem of *rejoir* to rejoice, fr. *re-* + *joir* to rejoice, fr. L *gaudēre* — more at JOY] *vt* **:** to give joy to **:** make joyful **:** GLADDEN ⟨this book will ~ his many admirers —*advt*⟩ ⟨my enforced silence *rejoiced* me all the more —Kay Boyle⟩ ⟨a letter from you *rejoiced* my heart —H.J.Laski⟩ ⟨dispelled the clouds and *rejoiced* the optimists —S.B.Fay⟩ **~** *vi* **:** to feel joy or great delight **:** experience gladness or pleasurable satisfaction ⟨*rejoiced* that the Fates had agreed —George Meredith⟩ ⟨a layman can only ~ at the legal subtlety —Robert Lekachman⟩ ⟨truly *rejoiced* to be preserved —Jane Austen⟩ **syn** see PLEASE — **rejoice in :** HAVE, OWN, POSSESS ⟨it *rejoices in* the name of pigweed —Rachel Henning⟩ ⟨the mountains *rejoice in* an average annual rainfall of thirty inches —Oliver La Farge⟩

re·joice·ful \\-sfəl\\ *adv* **:** JOYFUL ⟨makes the season . . . ~ —*N. Y. Herald Tribune*⟩

re·joice·ment \\-smənt\\ *n* -s **:** REJOICING ⟨a golden festival of ~ was taking place —Jack Kerouac⟩

re·joic·er \\-sə(r)\\ *n* -s **:** one that rejoices

rejoicing *n* -s [ME *rejoising*, fr. gerund of *rejoisen* to rejoice] **1 a :** the action of one that rejoices **:** the feeling and expression of joy ⟨sounds of ~ from the distant camp —T.B.Macaulay⟩ **b :** an instance, occasion, or expression of joy **:** FESTIVITY **2** *obs* **:** something that causes one to rejoice **:** an occasion of joy or gladness ⟨thy testimonies . . . are the ~ of my heart —Ps 119:111 (AV)⟩

rejoicing in the law *or* **rejoicing of the law** *or* **rejoicing over the law** [trans. of Heb *simhāth tōrah*] *usu cap R&L* **:** SIMHATH TORAH

re·joic·ing·ly *adv* **:** in a rejoicing manner **:** with joy or exultation ⟨a fact to be thankfully and ~ accepted —A.C.Swinburne⟩

re·join \\rə'jȯin, rē'j-, *in vt senses 1 & 2* (')rē¦j-\\ *vb* [ME *rejoinen* to answer to a legal charge, join one's own plea to that of the plaintiff, fr. MF *rejoin-*, stem of *rejoindre* to rejoin, fr. *re-* + *joindre* to join, fr. OF — more at JOIN] *vi* **:** to make a reply to a legal charge or pleading; *esp* **:** to answer the replication of the plaintiff **~** *vt* **1 :** to join (as two things together or one with another) again **:** reunite after a separation ⟨~ the broken pieces⟩ ⟨the road ~*s* the highway two miles east⟩ **2 :** to join (as a person or group) again ⟨~*ed* his regiment⟩ ⟨~*ed* the Republican party⟩ **3 :** to say in answer or as a rejoinder **:** state in reply **syn** see ANSWER

re·join·der \\rə'jȯində(r), rē'j-\\ *n* -s [ME *rejoiner*, fr. MF *rejoindre* to rejoin (taken as a n.)] **1 :** the defendant's answer to the plaintiff's replication **2 :** REPLY; *specif* **:** an answer to a reply ⟨her remarks . . . met with no ~ —Owen Wister⟩ ⟨drew the sharpest ~*s* in the panel discussion which ensued —H.W. Sams⟩ ⟨a statement in ~⟩

re·join·dure \\-d(y)ə(r)\\ *n* -s [F *rejoindre* to rejoin + E *-ure*] *obs* **:** a joining again **:** REUNION ⟨rudely beguiles our lips of all ~ —Shak.⟩

re·joint \\(')rē+\\ *vt* -ED/-ING/-S [*re-* + *joint*] **1 :** to reunite the joints of **:** join or unite anew **2 :** to fill up the joints of (as stones in buildings when the mortar has been dislodged)

re·jon \\rā'hōn\\ *n* -s [Sp *rejón*, fr. *rejo* iron nail, sharp point, fr. *reja* plowshare, fr. L *regula* iron bar, straight piece of wood, ruler — more at RULE] **:** a short barbed spear used by the rejoneador in bullfighting

re·jo·ne·a·dor \\rā¦hōnēə¦dȯ(ə)r, -ēə¦thȯ-\\ *n* -s [Sp, fr. *rejón*] **:** the mounted man who thrusts a rejon into the shoulder muscles of the bull in bullfighting

re·jo·neo \\,rāhō'nā(,)ō\\ *n* -s [Sp, fr. *rejón*] **:** the art of bullfighting from on horseback with a short barbed spear

re·judge \\(')rē+\\ *vt* [*re-* + *judge*] **:** to judge again **:** deliver a new judgment upon **:** REEXAMINE, REVIEW

re·junction \"+\ *n* [*re-* + *junction*] **:** REUNION ⟨where burnt bodies went . . . to await ~ to their souls —Bruce Marshall⟩
re·ju·ve·nate \rə̇'jüvə,nāt, rē'j-, *-usu* -ād·+V\ *vb* -ED/-ING/-S [*re-* + L *juvenis* young person + E *-ate*] *vt* **1 a :** to make young or youthful again **:** restore to youth **:** impart renewed vitality to **:** REINVIGORATE ⟨the fruit . . . ~*s* even the most decrepit old men —Robert Graves⟩ ⟨~ and reorganize . . . economic and social life —A.R.Williams⟩ **b :** to restore to a condition resembling an original or new state ⟨fenders . . . that can be *rejuvenated* and kept —*Buick Mag.*⟩ ⟨~ four tired chairs —*McCall's Needlework*⟩ **2 :** to restore to a more youthful condition; *specif* **:** to restore sexual vigor in (as by hormones or an operation) **3 a :** to stimulate (as by uplift) to renewed erosive activity — used of streams **b :** to develop youthful features of topography in (an area previously worn down nearly to base level) ⟨recently *rejuvenated* glaciated mountains —R.L.Ives⟩ **~** *vi* **1 :** to cause or bring about rejuvenation ⟨creams that ~ as you sleep —Lois Long⟩ ⟨nothing ~*s* like being on the offensive —Mollie Panter-Downes⟩ **2 :** to undergo rejuvenation ⟨her novices continued to ~ till their mental outlook was almost that of eight-year-olds —*Times Lit. Supp.*⟩
re·ju·ve·na·tion \rə̇,jüvə'nāshən, (,)rē,j-\ *n* -S **1 :** the action of rejuvenating or the state of being rejuvenated **:** restoration of youthful vigor ⟨~ of streams⟩ ⟨schemes for the ~ of the drama —Arnold Bennett⟩ ⟨poured half a billion dollars into Italy's post-war ~ —A.H.Vandenberg †1951⟩ **2 :** the restoration of vigor to a tree by pruning, spraying, soil treatment, or other means
re·ju·ve·na·tor \=ˈ==,nād·ə(r), -ātə-\ *n* -S **:** one that rejuvenates
re·ju·ve·nes·cence \rə̇,jüvə'nesᵊn(t)s, (,)rē,j-\ *n* -S [ML *rejuvenesc*ere to become young again (fr. L *re-* + *juvenescere* to become young, fr. *juvenis* young person) + E *-ence*] **1 :** a renewal of youth **:** a restoration of physical, mental, or spiritual youthfulness **:** REJUVENATION 1 ⟨secure a new lease of life and ~ of his divine energies —E.O.James⟩ **2 :** reinvigoration of an individual or strain esp. when following and dependent on some change in its vital behavior (as associated with zoospore formation in various lower algae or held to follow conjugation in some protozoans)
re·ju·ve·nes·cen·cy \-ᵊnsē\ *n* -ES [ML *rejuvenesc*ere + E *-ency*] *archaic* **:** REJUVENESCENCE
re·ju·ve·nes·cent \rə̇'jüvə'nesᵊnt, (')rē¦j-\ *adj* [*rejuvenescence* + *-ent*] **:** becoming or causing to become rejuvenated **:** becoming youthful again **:** growing young **:** REJUVENATING
re·ju·ve·nize \=ˈ==,nīz\ *vt* -ED/-ING/-S [*re-* + L *juvenis* young person + E *-ize*] **:** REJUVENATE
rekh·ta \'rektə\ *or* **rekh·ti** \-tē\ *n* -S [Hindi *rekhta*, fr. Per] **:** a very highly persianized form of Urdu used in Urdu poetry
re·ki \'rākē\ *n, pl* **reki** *or* **rekis** *usu cap* **1 :** a group of nomadic peoples in the deserts of Baluchistan **2 :** a member of the Reki peoples
¹**re·kindle** \(')rē+\ *vt* **:** to kindle again **:** arouse again ⟨*rekindled* the ancient flame of Indian religion —*Amer. Guide Series: Ind.*⟩ ⟨the timely arrival . . . *rekindled* hope —R.A. Billington⟩ **~** *vi* **:** to ignite anew ⟨in the event that the fire ~*s* —*Fire Manual (Mass.)*⟩
²**rekindle** \"\ *n* [fr. gerund of ¹*rekindle*] **:** an instance of rekindling (as of a fire) **:** a fire believed to be extinguished that starts up again
re·knit \(')rē+\ *vt* [*re-* + *knit*] **:** to knit up or together again **:** REFASTEN ⟨~ the severed integrations of peace —Edmond Taylor⟩
rel \'rel\ *n* -S [*rel*uctance] **:** a unit of reluctance equal to one ampere turn per maxwell
rel *abbr* **1** related; relating; relative; relatively **2** relay **3** release; released **4** relief; relieve; relieved; relieving **5** religion **6** [L *reliquae*] relics
relaid *past of* RELAY
re·lamp \(')rē+\ *vt* [*re-* + *lamp* (n.)] **:** to replace the incandescent units of (as a light fixture)
¹**re·lapse** \rə̇'laps, rē'-, 'rē,l-\ *n* [L *relapsus*, past part. of *relabi* to slide back, sink back, relapse, fr. *re-* + *labi* to slide, glide, fall — more at SLEEP] **1 :** the act or fact of backsliding, becoming worse, or subsiding ⟨~ into barbarism⟩ ⟨~ of the stock market⟩ **2 :** a recurrence of illness; *esp* **:** recurrence of symptoms of a disease after a prolonged abatement — compare RECRUDESCENCE
²**re·lapse** \rə̇'laps, rē'-\ *vi* [L *relapsus*, past part. of *relabi*] **1 :** to slip or fall back into a former state (as of illness, vice) after a change for the better ⟨he *relapsed* when allowed out of bed⟩ ⟨reformed drunkards often ~⟩ **2 :** SINK, SUBSIDE, LAPSE ⟨*relapsed* into obscurity⟩ **3** *obs* **:** to fall away **:** WITHDRAW ⟨~ into silence⟩ **4 :** to fall back into paganism, evil, error, heresy, or unbelief **:** BACKSLIDE
³**re·lapse** \"\ *n* [L *relapsus*, past part. of *relabi*] **:** one who has relapsed **:** BACKSLIDER
re·laps·er \-sə(r)\ *n* **:** one that relapses
relapsing fever *n* **:** any of several forms of an acute epidemic infectious disease marked by sudden recurring paroxysms of high fever lasting from five to seven days, articular and muscular pains, and sudden crisis and caused by a spirochete (genus *Borrelia*) transmitted by the bites of lice and ticks and found in the circulating blood
re·last·er \(')rē'lastə(r)\ *n* [*re-* + *last* + *-er*] **:** a worker who puts shoes on a finishing last after the sole has been sewed to the upper
relata *pl of* RELATUM
re·lat·abil·i·ty \rə̇,lād·ə'biləd·ē\ *n* **:** the quality or state of being relatable
re·lat·able \rə̇'lād·əbəl\ *adj* [¹*relate* + *-able*] **:** that may be related
¹**re·late** \rə̇'lāt, rē'-, *usu* -ād·+V\ *vb* -ED/-ING/-S [L *relatus* (suppletive past part. of *referre* to carry back, refer, relate), fr. *re-* + *latus*, suppletive past part. of *ferre* to carry — more at REFER, TOLERATE] *vt* **1 a :** to give an account of **:** TELL ⟨tradition ~*s* that he once rode horseback all the way to Washington —*Amer. Guide Series: N. C.*⟩ **b** *archaic* **:** SAY, ASSERT, REPUTE **2 :** to show or establish a logical or causal connection between ⟨seeks to ~ poverty and crime⟩ ⟨~ the flow of individual consciousness to large political and social contours —Warren Beck⟩ ⟨utterly unable to ~ these two events⟩ **~** *vi* **1 :** to apply or take effect retroactively ⟨a will upon approval ~*s* back to the date of testator's death⟩ **2** *obs* **:** to give an account or report ⟨I might ~ of thousands —John Milton⟩ **3 :** to be in relationship **:** have reference ⟨public acts that ~ to crime prevention⟩ ⟨most of the lecture *related* to the causes of common ailments⟩ **4** *of a person* **:** to have meaningful social relationships **:** interact realistically ⟨a boy with a long history of emotional maladjustment and inability to ~ well to people —Edwin Powers & Helen Witmer⟩
syn RELATE, REHEARSE, RECITE, RECOUNT, NARRATE, DESCRIBE, STATE, and REPORT can all mean to tell orally or in writing the details or circumstances of a situation or combination of events. RELATE implies the giving of an account, usu. detailed or orderly, of something one has experienced ⟨*related* how it screamed, how it followed him in the brush, how he took to his boat, how its eyes gleamed from the shore —John Burroughs⟩ REHEARSE usu. suggests a repetition, a summary, a retold account, or a going over as in one's mind ⟨these defects arise out of the difficulties which have been *rehearsed* in these opening pages —*Orient Bk. World*⟩ ⟨in the interval . . . I *rehearsed* a great many ways of meeting him —Mary Austin⟩ RECITE and the more common RECOUNT imply a particularity, often enumeration, of detail, RECOUNT often implying a retelling ⟨would be asked to fill out a questionnaire *reciting* what the condition of the lot was, the view of the lot, the orientation of the lot, the size of their family, their needs, what they wanted to achieve —J.W.Rouse⟩ ⟨a review that merely *recited* the contents of a book —Raymond Walters b.1912⟩ ⟨often *recounts* the conversations with which they filled the long, hot days of driving —L.P.Smith⟩ ⟨*recounted* the story he had heard from the soldier —Hanama Tasaki⟩ NARRATE suggests a chronological account often with the use of devices of literary narration as plot or movement toward a climax ⟨this is not the place to *narrate* the achievements of the Canadian forces in that tremendous struggle —B.K.Sandwell⟩ ⟨it *narrates* the story of the shepherd Aminta and his love for the shepherdess Silvia —R.A.Hall b.1911⟩ DESCRIBE emphasizes details which provide a picture or a representation to other than visual senses ⟨bitter sea and glowing light, bright clear air, dry as dry, — that *describes* the place —Richard Jefferies⟩ ⟨a woman to be *described* as stout or thin, as jolly or crabbed, but always mature —Joseph Conrad⟩ ⟨the water, rich in iron and sulphur, is *described* as similar to that of the Vichy springs in France —*Amer. Guide Series: Minn.*⟩ STATE suggests definiteness of detail and economy of presentation ⟨*state* the case rather than render an opinion⟩ ⟨*state* facts, then explain them⟩ REPORT implies a recounting, esp. factual, for the information of others, as the readers of a newspaper ⟨the human tedium which the skilled novelist suggests without *reporting* in grim detail —*Time*⟩ ⟨newspapers are already *reporting* the ravages of dysentery —Justina Hill⟩ ⟨similar practices . . . are *reported* from other parts of the world —J.G.Frazer⟩ **syn** see in addition JOIN
²**relate** \"\ *n* -S [L *relatus*, suppletive past part. of *referre*] **:** something related to something else; *esp* **:** the first term in a relationship — compare CORRELATE
related *adj* [fr. past part. of ¹*relate*] **1 :** having relationship **:** connected by reason of an established or discoverable relation ⟨painting and the ~ arts⟩ ⟨including the ~ species of quartz⟩ ⟨chemistry and ~ sciences⟩ ⟨church-*related* colleges⟩ **2 :** allied by kindred; *esp* **:** connected by consanguinity ⟨persons ~ in the first degree⟩ **3 :** having similar properties **:** belonging to the same family of chemical elements ⟨cobalt, iron, and nickel are ~ elements⟩ **4 :** having a close harmonic connection — used of tones, chords, or tonalities — **re·lat·ed·ly** *adv*
related key *n* **:** a key having important tones in common with another key and hence admitting of ready modulation; *esp* **:** a key whose tonic chord is a triad of tones in the original key (as, for C major, the keys F major, G major, A minor, D minor, and E minor)
re·lat·ed·ness *n* -ES **1 :** the state or character of being related **2 :** a particular manner of being related or of being constituted by relations; *esp* **:** the manner of being related which characterizes a type of reality or level of existence ⟨the specific ~ of the organic⟩ ⟨relativity means ~ and not mere chaos or anarchy —N.E.Nelson⟩
re·lat·er \rə̇'lād·ə(r)\ *n* -S **:** one that relates; *esp* **:** NARRATOR
relates *pres 3d sing of* RELATE, *pl of* RELATE
relating *pres part of* RELATE
re·la·tion \rə̇'lāshən, rē'-\ *n* -S [ME *relacioun*, fr. MF *relation*, fr. L *relation-*, *relatio*, fr. *relatus* (suppletive past part. of *referre* to carry back, refer, relate) + *-ion-*, *-io* -ion — more at RELATE] **1 :** the act of telling or recounting **:** RECITAL, ACCOUNT, NARRATION ⟨was the hero of the affair according to his own ~⟩ ⟨tedious ~ of circumstantial details⟩ **2 :** an extended account or report ⟨the Jesuit ~*s* of missionary work in the New World⟩ **3 :** an aspect or quality (as resemblance, direction, difference) that can be predicated only of two or more things taken together **:** something perceived or discovered by observing or thinking about two or more things at the same time **:** CONNECTION ⟨discovered a ~ between dreams and waking actions⟩ ⟨the ~*s* between the objects in the picture are all wrong⟩ **4 :** the referring of an act to a prior date as the time of its taking effect **:** the giving force or operation to an act or proceeding as of some previous date or time by the fiction that it had happened or begun at that time **5 a** (1) **:** a person connected by consanguinity or affinity **:** KINSMAN, KINSWOMAN, RELATIVE (2) **:** a person who in case of intestacy would be legally entitled to a share of the property of the intestate under the statute of distributions in force in the jurisdiction in question — compare CONSANGUINITY **b** *dial* **:** RELATIVES **c :** relationship by consanguinity or affinity **:** KINSHIP **6 :** REFERENCE, RESPECT — used esp. in the phrase *in relation to* ⟨had a lot to say in ~ to that affair⟩ ⟨stingy only in ~ to his family⟩ **7 a :** the mode in which one thing or entity stands to another, itself, or others ⟨the ~ of father to son, parent to children⟩ or in which two or more entities stand to one another ⟨the ~ of members of the same community⟩ **b :** a logical bond; *specif* **:** a dyadic or polyadic predicate or propositional function — compare ASYMMETRIC, INTRANSITIVE, IRREFLEXIVE, ONE-ONE, REFLEXIVE, SYMMETRICAL, TRANSITIVE **8 a :** the state of being mutually or reciprocally interested (as in social or commercial matters) **b relations** *pl* **:** DEALINGS, AFFAIRS ⟨the foreign ~*s* of a country⟩ **:** INTERCOURSE ⟨broke off all ~*s* with him and his family⟩ **:** sexual union ⟨charged with having ~*s* with a woman not his wife⟩
re·la·tion·al \-shənᵊl, -shnəl\ *adj* **1 :** of or relating to kinship ⟨~ duties⟩ **2 :** characterized by or constituted by relations ⟨~ nature of space⟩ ⟨the form of propositions we classify as ~ is expressed as a function of two or more arguments —Alice Ambrose & Morris Lazerowitz⟩ ⟨~ anatomy⟩ ⟨~ plant morphology⟩ **3 :** having the function chiefly of indicating a relation of syntax ⟨~ words⟩ — distinguished from *notional*
re·la·tion·ary \-shə,nerē\ *adj* **:** RELATIONAL
re·la·tion·ism \-,nizəm\ *n* -S **1 :** RELATIVITY 2c **2 :** a doctrine holding that relations exist as real entities **3 :** a theory holding that any ideological perspective or system is conditioned by its sociocultural context
re·la·tion·ist \-sh(ə)nə̇st\ *n* -S **:** one who supports or follows a doctrine of relationism
re·la·tion·less \-shənlə̇s\ *adj* **:** not related **:** not having relations
re·la·tion·ship \-n,ship\ *n* **1 :** the state or character of being related or interrelated **:** a connection by way of relation ⟨show the ~ between two things⟩ ⟨this text's ~ to that is obvious but difficult to account for⟩ ⟨study language ~*s*⟩ **2 :** KINSHIP, CONSANGUINITY, AFFINITY ⟨claimed a ~ with the deceased⟩; *also* **:** a specific instance or type of this ⟨a list of family ~*s*⟩ **3 :** a state of affairs existing between those having relations or dealings; ⟨improve church ~*s*⟩ ⟨a psychologist's study of the mother-child ~⟩ ⟨a good doctor-patient ~⟩
rel·a·ti·val \,relə'tīvəl\ *adj* [¹*relative* + *-al*] **:** relating to or resembling a relative pronoun or other relative word ⟨~ construction⟩ ⟨~ use of *that*⟩
¹**rel·a·tive** \'reləd·iv, -ətiv\ *n* -S [ME, fr. MF *relatif* (adj.) or LL *relativus* (adj.)] **1 :** a word (as a relative pronoun) referring grammatically to an antecedent **2 :** a thing having a relation to or connection with or necessary dependence upon another thing **:** a being or object posited by virtue of its relations — opposed to *absolute* **3 a :** a person connected with another by blood or affinity; *esp* **:** one allied by blood **:** RELATION, KINSMAN ⟨gifts to friends and ~*s*⟩ **b :** an animal or plant related to another by common descent ⟨teosinte, corn's closest ~ —P.C. Mangelsdorf⟩ **4 :** a relative term ⟨using the ~*s father* and *son* instead of the absolutes *man* and *boy*⟩ **5 :** one of two or more related chemical substances: as **a :** one of a group of chemical compounds derived from a common parent **b :** one of a series of isomeric compounds **6 :** a statistical figure obtained by taking the value of a variable (as a price, a production total) for one time or place, dividing it by the value of the same variable for another time and place, and multiplying by 100
²**relative** \"\ *adj* [MF or LL; MF *relatif*, fr. LL *relativus*, fr. L *relatus* (suppletive past part. of *referre* to carry back, refer, relate) + *-ivus* -ive — more at RELATE] **1 :** referring to an antecedent **:** introducing a subordinate clause qualifying an expressed or implied antecedent ⟨a ~ connective⟩; *also* **:** introduced by a connective referring to an expressed or implied antecedent — see RELATIVE ADJECTIVE, RELATIVE ADVERB, RELATIVE CLAUSE, RELATIVE PRONOUN **2 a** *archaic* **:** having mutual relation with each other **:** RELATED, CORRESPONDING ⟨several different yet ~ designs —Nathaniel Hawthorne⟩ **b :** correlating with a right or duty of another **:** CORRESPONDING ⟨~ rights of husband and wife⟩ **3 :** having relation, reference, or application **:** PERTAINING, RELEVANT, PERTINENT ⟨matters ~ to maintenance of international peace —Vera M. Dean⟩ **4 :** arising from relation **:** resulting from or existing in connection with or reference to something else **:** not absolute or independent **:** COMPARATIVE — distinguished from *positive* ⟨~ velocity⟩ ⟨~ value of dollars and pounds⟩ ⟨~ isolation of life in the country⟩ **5 :** having the same key signature — used of major and minor keys and scales ⟨G major and E minor are ~ keys⟩ **6 :** expressed as the ratio of the specified quantity to the total magnitude or to the mean of all the quantities involved ⟨~ constant error in measuring⟩ ⟨~ probable error⟩
relative adjective *n* **:** a pronominal adjective that introduces a clause qualifying an antecedent (as *which* in "our next meeting will be on Monday, at which time a new chairman will be elected") or a clause functioning as a substantive (as *which* in "I do not know which course I should follow")
relative advantage *n* **:** COMPARATIVE ADVANTAGE
relative adverb *n* **:** an adverb that introduces a clause qualifying an antecedent (as *when* in *the season when roses bloom; where* in *entered the room where they were sitting;* and *why* in *the reason why he did it*)
relative aperture *n* **:** a measure of the angle of the cone of light rays from an object that traverse an optical system; *specif* **:** the effective aperture of a camera lens expressed as a fraction of its focal length with the symbol *f* being used instead of 1 as the numerator or expressed as the ratio of the effective aperture to the focal length ⟨a lens having an effective aperture that is 1/4.5 of its focal length has a *relative aperture* of f/4.5 or 1:4.5⟩
relative bearing *n* **:** a bearing relative to the heading of a ship or airplane
relative clause *n* **1 :** an adjective clause introduced by a relative pronoun expressed or suppressed, relative adjective, or relative adverb and having either a purely descriptive force (as in *John, who often tells fibs*) or a limiting one (as in *boys who tell fibs*) **2 :** a substantive clause introduced by an indefinite relative (as in *he belittles whatever his sister tries to do*)
relative error *n* **:** the ratio of an error in a measured or calculated quantity to the magnitude of that quantity
relative frequency *n* **:** the ratio of the frequency of a particular event in a statistical experiment to the total frequency
relative fugacity *n* **:** ACTIVITY 6b
relative humidity *n* **:** the ratio of absolute humidity to the maximum possible density of water vapor in the air at the same temperature
relative impediment *n* **:** an impediment that forbids marriage only with certain persons (as close relations)
relative inclinometer *n* **:** an inclinometer that shows the attitude of an airplane with reference to apparent gravity — compare TURN INDICATOR
relative index of refraction : the ratio of the velocity of light in two different media
relative-in-law \'====,=\ *n, pl* **relatives-in-law :** a connection by marriage **:** a relative of one's spouse
relative location *n* **:** the marking and arrangement of library books with relation to each other and not to particular shelves
rel·a·tive·ly \'reləd·əvlē, -ətə-, -li\ *adv* **:** in a relative manner **:** in relation or respect to something else **:** not absolutely ⟨foreign policy . . . determined by ~ small but strongly organized groups —Vera M. Dean⟩
relative motion *n* **1 :** motion as observed from or referred to some material system constituting a frame of reference (as two adjacent walls and floor of a room) — see RELATIVITY 3 **2 :** the motion of one body with respect to another regarded as fixed — compare RELATIVE VELOCITY
rel·a·tive·ness \-d·ivnə̇s, -tiv-\ *n* -ES **:** the quality or state of being relative **:** RELATIVITY
relative nullity *n* **:** nullity existing only in favor of particular persons
relative personal equation *n* **:** the deviation between values obtained by different observers — compare ABSOLUTE PERSONAL EQUATION
relative pitch *n* **1 :** the pitch of a musical tone as determined by its position in a scale — distinguished from *absolute pitch* **2 :** the ability to recognize or produce a musical tone at its correct pitch according to its relative position in a scale ⟨she has good *relative pitch*⟩
relative pronoun *n* **1 :** a pronoun (as *who, which, that*) that introduces a clause modifying an antecedent (as in *the man who would be king*) **2 :** an indefinite relative (as *who, whoever, what, whatever*) that introduces a clause functioning as a substantive (as in *order what you like* or *invite whomever you please*)
relative rank *n* **1 :** the rank in a service or branch of the armed services other than an officer's own which corresponds with the rank held by him — distinguished from *lineal rank* **2 :** comparative rank according to date of commission among officers holding the same grade
relative refractive index *n* **:** RELATIVE INDEX OF REFRACTION
relatives *pl of* RELATIVE
relative term *n* **:** a term (as *father, predecessor, employee*) which names either a relationship or an object as standing in a certain relation — compare ABSOLUTE 9a
relative velocity *n* **:** the vector difference between the velocities of two bodies **:** the velocity of a body with respect to another regarded as being at rest — compare RELATIVE MOTION
relative wind *n* **:** the motion of the air relative to a body in it usu. determined so as to exclude disturbance at the surfaces of the body
rel·a·tiv·ism \'reləd·ə,vizəm, -ətə,-\ *n* -S [ISV ²*relative* + *-ism*] **1 :** a doctrine of relationism or of relativity: as **a :** a theory that knowledge is relative to the limited nature of the mind and the conditions of knowing and hence not true to the nature of independent reality and that holds that absolutely true knowledge is impossible because of the limitations and variability of sense perceptions or that reality as it is in itself cannot be known by mind whose modes of thinking and perception are essentially subjective or that thinking and perception seize relations of one thing to another only and not the intrinsic nature of an object and hence are merely symbolic — called also *epistemological relativism* **b :** a view that theories of what is right and good are relative in that ethical truths depend upon the individuals and groups holding them so that what is considered right and good by one person or group may be considered wrong and bad by another — called also *ethical relativism* **2 :** RELATIVITY
rel·a·tiv·ist \-.vəst\ *n* -S [ISV ²*relative* + *-ist*] **:** a believer in, or advocate of relativity, relativism, or the theory of relativity
rel·a·tiv·is·tic \¦====¦vistik\ *adj* **1 :** of, relating to, or characterized by relativity or relativism; *specif* **:** tending to regard human nature and values as subject to changing sociocultural conditions rather than as absolute or universal **2 :** of or relating to the physical theory of relativity — **rel·a·tiv·is·ti·cal·ly** \-stə̇k(ə)lē\ *adv*
rel·a·tiv·i·ty \,relə'tivəd·ē, -ətē, -i\ *n* -ES [prob. fr. F *relativité*, fr. *relatif* relative + *-ité* -ity — more at RELATIVE] **1 :** the quality or state of being relative **:** relativeness ⟨~ of means to ends⟩ **2 :** the fact or condition of being relative as opposed to absolute or independent **:** the state of being dependent for existence or determined in nature, value, or some other quality by relation to something else: as **a :** the quality of variability arising from necessary connection with or reference to something contingent ⟨the ~ of beauty to taste or of rights to law⟩ **b :** the mutual dependence or concomitant variability of two or more related things **c :** dependence on the subjective nature of man or upon limitations and peculiar character of individuals ⟨the ~ of knowledge⟩ **3 a :** the study of the relative motion of bodies and of the associated phenomena **b :** a theory formulated by Albert Einstein and leading to the assertion of the equivalence of mass and energy and of the increase of the mass of a body with increased velocity and based on the two postulates that if two systems are in relative motion with uniform linear velocity it is impossible for observers in either system by observation and measurement of phenomena in the other to learn more about the motion than the fact that it is relative motion and that measurements of the velocity of light in either system regardless of the position of the source of light always give the same numerical value — called also *special theory of relativity* **c :** an extension of the theory to include a discussion of gravitation and related phenomena — called also *general theory of relativity* **4 :** a theory of culture which holds that societal systems of value, ethical standards, and social norms must be understood as inevitably related to their specific cultural context of historical development and which questions the extension of moral judgments arising out of a single tradition to another culture
rel·a·tiv·iza·tion \,reləd·ivə'zāshən\ *n* -S **:** the act or result of making relative or regarding as relative rather than absolute ⟨assert again the dignity of human action against modern historical contemplation and ~ —Hannah Arendt⟩ ⟨~ of space and time determinations⟩

rel·a·tiv·ize \'reləd·i,vīz\ *vt* -ED/-ING/-S [²*relative* + *-ize*] **1 :** to make relative **:** reduce from absoluteness to relativity **:** treat as contingent or limited to particular conditions **2 a :** to describe (a physical process) in relativistic terms **b :** to modify (an equation or formula) to accord with relativity theory

re·la·tor \rə'lād·ə(r)\ *n* -S [L, fr. *relatus* (suppletive past part. of *referre* to carry back, refer, relate) + *-or* — more at RELATE] **1 :** one that relates **:** RELATER, NARRATOR ⟨~ of folk tales⟩ **2 :** a private person at whose relation or in whose behalf an information in the nature of a quo warranto or mandamus is filed

re·la·trix \-ā·triks\ *n* -ES [LL, fem. of L *relator*] **:** a female relator

re·la·tum \rə'lād·əm\ *n, pl* **rela·ta** \-d·ə\ [NL, fr. L, neut. of *relatus*] **:** a thing or term related **:** one of a group of related things **:** CORRELATIVE; *specif* **:** one of the terms to which a logical relation proceeds **:** the second or one of the succeeding terms of a relation — compare REFERENT 2b

¹**re·lax** \rə'laks, rē'-\ *vb* -ED/-ING/-ES [ME *relaxen*, fr. L *relaxare*, fr. *re-* + *laxare* to loosen, slacken, fr. *laxus* loose — more at SLACK] *vt* **1** *obs* **:** to make less close in structure, texture, or formation **:** lessen the density or compactness of **2 :** to make less tense or rigid **:** lessen the tension or pressure of **:** SLACKEN ⟨alternately contracting and ~*ing* his muscles⟩ ⟨pain forced him to ~ his grip⟩ ⟨after a mile of hard driving he ~*ed* the pace⟩ ⟨unsafe to ~ our vigilance for an instant⟩ **3 :** to make less severe or strict **:** lessen the stringency, austerity, or harshness of ⟨~*es* its rigid immigration laws for all members of learned professions —*Report: (Canadian) Royal Commission on Nat'l Development*⟩ ⟨wartime is well known to ~ conventions —C.W.Cunnington⟩ **4 :** to make soft or enervated **:** deprive of energy, zeal, strength of purpose ⟨this ~*ing* of his critical faculties —Steven Marcus⟩ **5 :** to relieve from nervous tension **:** cause to unbend in manner or behavior ⟨a shampoo soothed and ~*ed* him⟩ **6 :** to relieve from constipation ⟨~ a horse's bowels by putting him on wet bran⟩ ~ *vi* **1 :** to become lax, weak, or loose **:** REST ⟨lay back and let his eyes and mind ~⟩ **2 :** to abate in intensity **:** let up ⟨set up a standard of perfection which seldom permitted him to ~ —Edward Ryerson⟩ **3 a** *of a muscle or muscle fiber* **:** to become inactive and lengthen **b** *of yarn* **:** to shrink to original length after release of stress **4 :** to cast off social restraint, nervous tension, or attitude of anxiety or suspicion ⟨found it hard to ~ in the presence of his social inferiors⟩ ⟨the country ~*es* into its habitual tolerance of free expression —H.L.Smith b.1906⟩ **5 :** to seek rest or recreation **:** escape from pressure of duty or responsibility ⟨~ at the seashore⟩ ⟨is ushered into a private anteroom to ~ before addressing the convention⟩

²**relax** *n* -ES **1** *obs* **:** RELAXATION **2** *obs* **:** DIARRHEA

¹**re·lax·ant** \-sənt\ *adj* [L *relaxant-, relaxans*, pres. part. of *relaxare*] **:** of, relating to, or producing relaxation ⟨~ effect of a drug⟩

²**relaxant** \"\ *n* -S **1 :** a drug that relaxes; *specif* **:** one that relieves tension of smooth or striated muscle — compare PARALYTIC 2 **2 :** LAXATIVE

relaxate *vb* -ED/-ING/-S [L *relaxatus*, past part. of *relaxare*] *obs* **:** RELAX, RELEASE

re·lax·a·tion \(,)rē,lak'sāshən, rə,-\ *n* -S [MF or L; MF, fr. L *relaxation-, relaxatio*, fr. *relaxatus* (past part. of *relaxare* to relax) + *-ion-, -io* -ion — more at RELAX] **1 :** the act or fact of relaxing or of being relaxed ⟨~ of the muscles⟩ ⟨the ~ of discipline⟩ ⟨~ of a law⟩ **2 :** an abatement or remission of a penalty or payment ⟨ask for ~ in war reparations⟩ ⟨a ~ of a fine⟩ **3 :** a relaxing or recreative state, activity, or pastime; DIVERSION, RECREATION ⟨play golf as a ~⟩ ⟨seek ~ in the country⟩ **4** *Scots law* **:** release from or cancellation of legal restriction or penalty; *esp* **:** release from a penalty (as outlawry) judicially imposed **5 :** the lengthening that characterizes inactive muscle fibers or muscles **6 :** the adjustment of a system to a state of equilibrium following the abrupt removal of some influence (as a magnetic force, a high temperature) **syn** see REST

relaxation oscillation *n* **:** a mechanical, electric, or acoustic oscillation (as of a road scraper, wires singing in wind) that consists of a build-up of displacement followed by sudden release of the displaced system

relaxation oscillator *n* **:** an electric oscillator by which are produced rapid surges due to the alternate charging and discharging of a condenser, the discharges being initiated by a thyratron when the condenser voltage reaches a certain value

relaxation time *n* **1 :** the time required for an exponentially decreasing variable (as the amplitude of a damped oscillation) to drop from an initial value to 1/*e* or 0.368 of that value (where *e* is the base of natural logarithms) **2 :** the period required for the attainment of statistical equipartition of energy (as of motion) within the Milky Way galaxy, any other galaxy, groups of galaxies, clusters, stars or any selected group of similar celestial bodies **3 :** the time required for a viscous substance to recover from shearing stress after flow has ceased

re·lax·a·tive \rə'laksəd·iv\ *adj* [*relaxation* + *-ive*] **:** that relaxes or tends to relax ⟨light, ~ reading⟩

re·lax·a·to·ry \-sə,tōrē\ *adj* [*relaxation* + *-ory*] **:** RELAXATIVE

re·laxed \rə'lakst, rē'-\ *adj* **1 :** not strict, not exact, nor severe **:** lacking in precision or stringency ⟨~ rules of procedure⟩ ⟨~ restrictions on imports⟩ ⟨person of somewhat ~ morals⟩ **2 :** set at rest or at ease ⟨found him in one of his rare ~ moments smoking a pipe⟩ **3 :** easy of manner **:** free from stiffness **:** INFORMAL, EASYGOING ⟨~ style of comedy⟩ ⟨a characteristic poem of his . . . the record of a moment of free and undirected consciousness —F.R.Leavis⟩ — **re·laxed·ly** \-sədlē, -stlē, -li\ *adv* — **re·laxed·ness** \-sədnəs, -s(t)nəs\ *n* -ES

re·lax·er \-sə(r)\ *n* -S **:** one that relaxes ⟨music is often an excellent ~⟩

re·lax·in \-sən\ *n* -S [¹*relax* + *-in*] **:** a sex hormone that is apparently a neutral polypeptide, that is produced by the corpus luteum, and that facilitates childbirth by causing relaxation of the pubic symphysis

re·lax·om·e·ter \(,)rē,lak'sämәd·ə(r)\ *n* [¹*relax* + *-o-* + *-meter*] **:** an instrument for measuring relaxation times in the study of anelastic stress relaxation in plastic or viscous substances

¹**re·lay** \'rē,lā\ *n* -S [ME, fr. MF *relais*, fr. *relaier*] **1 :** a supply arranged beforehand for successive relief: as **a :** a supply of hunting horses or dogs kept in readiness at certain places to continue the pursuit of game if it comes that way **b :** a supply of horses placed at stations to be ready to relieve others so that a traveler may proceed without delay; *also* **:** the post or station at which the fresh supply is obtained **c :** a number of men who relieve others in carrying on some work **:** a relief gang ⟨working in ~*s* around the clock⟩ **2 a :** RELAY RACE **b :** one of the legs or divisions of a relay race **c relays** *pl* **:** a track meet featuring relay races **3 :** an electromagnetic device for remote or automatic control that is actuated by a variation in conditions of an electric circuit and that operates in turn other devices (as switches, circuit breakers) in the same or a different circuit **4 :** SERVOMOTOR **5 :** the act of passing along (a message, a signal, a ball) by stages; *also* **:** one of such stages ⟨the shortstop's ~ from center field was too late to catch the runner at the plate⟩ **6 :** an arrangement by which water is pumped through two or more pumping engines in order to increase the pressure in a fire hose **7 :** a bundle of relayed mail **8 :** RADIO RELAY

²**relay** \", rə'lā, rē'-\ *vb* -ED/-ING/-S [ME *relayen*, fr. MF *relaier*, fr. OF, fr. *re-* + *laier* to leave — more at DELAY] *vt* **1 a :** to place or dispose in relays **b :** to provide with relays **c :** to divide up (mail) into bundles each of which is to be placed in a storage box along a carrier's route to be picked up by him **2 :** to pass along by relays ⟨news was ~*ed* to distant points⟩ ⟨promised to ~ my message⟩ **3 :** to control or operate (as a circuit, a switch) by a relay **4 :** to pump (water) through two or more pumping engines in order to increase the pressure in a fire hose ~ *vi* **1 :** to obtain a fresh relay ⟨gained time by ~*ing* at each town⟩ **2 :** to operate the contacts of a relay

³**re·lay** \(')rē+\ *vt* [*re-* + ¹*lay*] **:** to lay again ⟨the flagstones will have to be taken up and *relaid*⟩ ⟨~*ing* several miles of track⟩

relay broadcast *n* **:** REBROADCAST

relay governor *n* **:** a speed regulator (as a waterwheel governor) embodying the relay principle

relay nucleus *n* **:** a nucleus of the brain that serves primarily to relay stimuli from lower receptor centers to coordinating cortical centers

relay race *n* **:** a race between teams of two or more contestants with each team member covering a specified portion of the entire course — see MEDLEY RELAY

relay rail *n* **:** worn rail that is suitable for relaying in sidings and guardrails

relay station *n* **:** RADIO RELAY

reld *abbr* relieved

re·learn \(')rē+\ *vt* [*re-* + *learn*] **:** to learn again what has been partly or completely forgotten or lost

re·leas·abil·i·ty *also* **re·leas·ibil·i·ty** \rə,lēsə'biləd·ē\ *n* -ES **:** the quality or state of being releasable

re·leas·able *also* **re·leas·ible** \rə'lēsəbəl\ *adj* [¹*release* + *-able* or *-ible*] **:** capable of being released; *esp* **:** PUBLISHABLE — **re·leas·ably** \-blē\ *adv*

¹**re·lease** \rə'lēs, rē'-\ *vt* -ED/-ING/-S [ME *relesen, relessen*, fr. OF *relessier, relaissier*, fr. L *relaxare* to loosen, relax — more at RELAX] **1** *obs* **:** to loosen or remove the force or effect of **:** ALLEVIATE **2 :** to set free from restraint, confinement, or servitude **:** set at liberty **:** let go ⟨~ a bent bow⟩ ⟨ordered all prisoners *released*⟩ ⟨~ a caged bird⟩ ⟨treated as an inferior himself and he has to ~ his frustrations somewhere —Darrell Berrigan⟩ **3 :** to relieve from something that confines, burdens, or oppresses ⟨waiting for death to ~ him from his agony⟩ ⟨asked her to ~ him from his promise⟩ **4 :** to give up (a claim, title, right) in favor of another **:** SURRENDER, RELINQUISH, RESIGN, QUIT ⟨~ a claim to property⟩ ⟨~ all claims or demands regarding personal injury⟩ ⟨~ a reserved seat in a plane flight⟩ **5 :** to give permission for the publication, performance, exhibition, or sale of (as a film, news article, phonograph record) on but not before a specified date **6 a** *obs* **:** to grant remission of (a debt, tax) **b :** MITIGATE **syn** see FREE

²**release** \"\ *n* -S [ME *reles*, fr. MF *reles, relais*, fr. OF, fr. *relessier, relaissier*] **1 a :** relief or deliverance from sorrow, suffering, or trouble ⟨unconsciousness brought a merciful ~ from his pain⟩ **b :** salvation or spiritual liberation from all earthly bondage and temporal contingencies **:** MOKSHA **2 a :** discharge from obligation or responsibility (as a debt, penalty, or claim) **:** a giving up (as of a right or claim) **:** RELINQUISHMENT **b :** an act or instrument by which a legal right is discharged **:** QUITCLAIM; *specif* **:** a conveyance of a man's right in lands or tenements to another having an estate in possession — compare ACQUITTANCE **3 a :** the act of liberating or freeing **:** discharge from restraint ⟨awaiting ~ from jail⟩ ⟨sudden ~ of free oxygen caused the explosion⟩ ⟨~ of homing pigeons⟩ ⟨~ of gas from a balloon⟩ **b :** the mode of holding and loosing an arrow in shooting with a bow — compare MEDITERRANEAN RELEASE, MONGOLIAN RELEASE, PRIMARY RELEASE **c :** the act or manner of concluding a musical tone or phrase — compare ATTACK **d :** the act or manner of ending a sound **:** the movement of one or more vocal organs in quitting the position for a speech sound **e :** a relaxation of the muscles after contraction in dancing **4 :** an instrument formally discharging from restraint or custody **5 a :** the act of permitting a working fluid (as steam) to escape from the cylinder at the end of the working stroke **b :** the point in the cycle of operations or on the corresponding indicator diagram at which this act occurs **c :** the period during exhaust from the point of escape to where the pressure of the exhausting fluid is sensibly that of the condenser or of the outside air **6 a :** the state of being liberated or freed ⟨the long summer ~ from school⟩ **b :** a freeing (as of a young forest tree) from the competing effects of taller overshadowing vegetation ⟨a statistical analysis of the value of ~ cuttings⟩ ⟨the time of ~ is apparent in cross section because of the sudden increase in growth increment —E. Lucy Braun⟩ **7 :** a device adapted to hold and later release a mechanism as required: as **a :** a catch on a motor-starting rheostat that automatically releases the rheostat arm and so stops the motor in case of a break in the field circuit **b :** the catch on an electromagnetic circuit breaker for a motor which acts in case of an overload **c :** a device for releasing the cocked shutter of a camera during picture taking **8 a :** the act of permitting performance or publication **b :** the matter released; *esp* **:** a statement prepared for the press by a public figure, a government agency, an organization **c :** a printed card conveying information and instructions to be used with a block-signaling system at intermediate sidings or at offices lacking telegraphic stations **9 :** the usu. contrasting middle portion of a popular song

re–lease \(')rē+\ *vt* [*re-* + *lease*] **:** to lease again **:** grant a new lease of

released rate *n* **:** a transportation rate reduced as a result of partial release of a carrier (as a railroad) from liability

released time *n* **:** a time set aside for dismissing children from public school once a week to receive religious instruction in the faith of their parents

released valuation *n* **:** a value lower than the usual commercial value of a commodity agreed upon by carriers and shippers to obtain a released rate and reduced carrier liability — compare AGREED VALUATION

re·leas·ee \rə¦lē¦sē\ *n* -S [¹*release* + *-ee*] **:** one to whom a release is given

re·lease·ment \rə'lēsmənt\ *n* -S **1** *archaic* **:** the act of releasing or fact of being released **2** *obs* **:** RELAXATION

release print *n* **:** a positive print of a motion picture used for exhibition

re·leas·er \-sə(r)\ *n* -S **:** one that releases; *specif* **:** a stimulus that esp. in lower organisms serves as the initiator of complex reflex behavior ⟨exposure to changing day length may be a ~ for nidification in many migratory birds⟩

release therapy *n* **:** psychiatric therapy in which the patient acts out his inner conflicts

releasible *var of* RELEASABLE

re·lea·sor \-sə(r)\ *n* -S [¹*release* + *-or*] **:** one that gives a release

re·lec·tion \rə'lekshən\ *n* -S [LL *relection-, relectio*, fr. L *relectus* (past part. of *relegere* to read again, fr. *re-* + *legere* to gather, select, read) + *-ion-, -io* -ion — more at LEGEND] **1** *obs* **:** REREADING **2** *obs* **:** a revised reading **:** EMENDATION

rel·e·ga·ble \'reləgəbəl\ *adj* [*relegate* + *-able*] **:** that may be relegated

rel·e·gate \'relə,gāt, *usu* -ād.+V\ *vt* -ED/-ING/-S [L *relegatus*, past part. of *relegare*, fr. *re-* + *legare* to send with a commission or charge — more at LEGATE] **1 a :** to send into exile **:** BANISH **b :** to put out of sight or mind **:** consign to insignificance or oblivion ⟨~ this sofa to the trash heap⟩ ⟨details *relegated* to the footnotes⟩ **c :** DEGRADE, DEMOTE ⟨in the oldest Neolithic settlements . . . hunting has been *relegated* to a secondary role —V.G.Childe⟩ ⟨the living tongues are *relegated* to a lower plane than Greek and Latin —C.H.Grandgent⟩ **2 :** to consign by classifying or appraising ⟨muscular atrophies . . . are not properly *relegated* to the group of neuromuscular disorders —W.A.D.Anderson⟩ ⟨no wrong is done to a great and influential work by *relegating* it to rhetoric, to philosophy —René Wellek & Austin Warren⟩ **3 :** to submit or refer for decision, judgment, or execution ⟨smaller companies can ~ the job of planning to a semiclerical level —E.J.Mann⟩ ⟨much of the work was *relegated* to special committees⟩ **syn** see COMMIT

rel·e·ga·tion \,==ˈgāshən\ *n* -S [L *relegation-, relegatio*, fr. *relegatus* + *-ion-, -io* -ion] **1** *Roman law* **:** a mild banishment not entailing loss of property or civil rights — compare DEPORTATION **2 :** the act of relegating or state of being relegated **:** REMOVAL, BANISHMENT **3 :** ASSIGNMENT, DELEGATION ⟨~ of minor decisions to his subordinates⟩

¹**re·lent** \rə'lent, rē'-\ *vb* -ED/-ING/-S [ME *relenten*, perh. fr. *re-* + L *lentus* flexible, slow — more at LITHE] *vi* **1** *obs* **:** MELT, LIQUEFY **2 :** to become less severe, harsh, or strict **:** become mollified, compassionate, or forgiving ⟨when a second appeal, couched in more urgent terms, was dispatched to him, he ~*ed* —Bennett Cerf⟩ **3 :** to let up **:** SLACKEN ⟨the wind blast would have to ~ . . . nothing like that could keep on and on —G.W. Brace⟩ ~ *vt* **1** *obs* **:** cause to be less harsh or severe **:** SOFTEN, MOLLIFY **2** *obs* **:** SLACKEN, ABATE ⟨oftentimes he would ~ his pace —Edmund Spenser⟩ **3** *obs* **:** to give up ⟨no discouragement shall make him once ~ his . . . intent to be a pilgrim —John Bunyan⟩ **4** *obs* **:** REPENT, REGRET **syn** see YIELD

²**relent** \"\ *n* -S *archaic* **:** an act of relenting, yielding, or slackening

re·lent·ing·ly *adv* **:** with relentment **:** MERCIFULLY

re·lent·less \-tləs\ *adj* **:** that cannot or does not relent or give way to appeals or to pity **:** mercilessly hard or harsh **:** immovably stern or persistent ⟨~ avenger⟩ ⟨~ pursuer⟩ ⟨~ judge⟩ ⟨~ and unsparing criticism⟩ — **re·lent·less·ly** *adv* — **re·lent·less·ness** *n* -ES

re·lent·ment \-tmənt\ *n* -S **:** an act of relenting

re·les·see \rə¦le¦sē\ *n* [by alter. (influence of *lessee*)] **:** RELEASEE

re·les·sor \-sȯ(ə)r\ *n* [by alter. (influence of *lessor*)] **:** RELEASOR

re·let \(')rē+\ *vt* [*re-* + *let*] **:** to let again **:** renew the lease of

re·letter \"+\ *vt* [*re-* + *letter*] **1 :** to renew the lettering of **2 :** to change the lettering of

rel·e·vance \'reləvən(t)s\ *also* **rel·e·van·cy** \-nsē, -si, *substand* 'revələn-\ *n, pl* **relevances** *also* **relevancies :** relation to the matter at hand **:** PERTINENCE ⟨a scholar's activities should have ~ to the immediate future of our civilization —J.B.Conant⟩

rel·e·vant \-nt\ *adj* [ML *relevant-, relevans*, fr. L, pres. part. of L *relevare* to raise up, lift up — more at RELIEVE] **1 :** bearing upon or properly applying to the matter at hand **:** affording evidence tending to prove or disprove the matters at issue or under discussion **:** PERTINENT ⟨began work on the problem by reading all the ~ literature⟩ ⟨~ testimony⟩ **2 :** CORRESPONDENT, PROPORTIONAL, COMMENSURATE ⟨the human concepts of one inch in length, and one second in time . . . are purely ~ to human life —A.N.Whitehead⟩ **3** *Scots law* **:** VALID, SUFFICIENT ⟨~ defense⟩

syn RELEVANT, GERMANE, MATERIAL, PERTINENT, APPOSITE, APPLICABLE, APROPOS can signify, in common, having a relation to or a bearing upon a matter in hand or upon present circumstances. A thing is RELEVANT when it has a connection, esp. a logical connection, with a matter under consideration ⟨nor shall any amendment not germane or *relevant* to the subject matter contained in the bill be received —*U.S.Code*⟩ ⟨what the cartman is saying is *relevant* to his case —John Hersey⟩ ⟨had thoroughly familiarized himself with all the knowledge *relevant* to his new duties —Benjamin Farrington⟩ GERMANE is interchangeable with RELEVANT but usu. adds to it the idea of unquestionable closeness and fitness or appropriateness of relationship as in spirit, tone, or quality ⟨almost every fact — religious, social, political, economic — was, somehow or other, *germane* to the war or the peace —Katharine F. Gerould⟩ ⟨the fierce aversions and the passionate cravings which are *germane* to the hermit life —H.O.Taylor⟩ A thing is MATERIAL when it has so close a relationship with a case in hand that it cannot be dispensed with without serious alteration of the case ⟨the motion is supported by an affidavit showing that the evidence is *material* —B.F.Tucker⟩ ⟨information *material* to the solution of a problem⟩ PERTINENT is interchangeable with RELEVANT, although it often stresses a more decisive or significant relationship, characterizing what not only bears upon but also contributes materially to the understanding or solution as of a problem or matter in hand ⟨had something *pertinent* to say about every horse that was brought out —Gerald Beaumont⟩ ⟨relatively few studies *pertinent* to the transplantation of lung tissue have been made —C.A.Hardin & C.F.Kittle⟩ ⟨deal in a specific kind of emotional conflict for *pertinent* dramatic ends —Irving Kolodin⟩ APPOSITE usu. applies to what is relevant and germane to the point of felicitousness ⟨*apposite* quotations from the classics came easily to his pen to grace the pellucid flow of his English —V.L.Parrington⟩ ⟨his sermons . . . are replete with *apposite* arguments and quotations from the Latin classics in support of the teachings of Christianity —G.C.Sellery⟩ A thing is APPLICABLE when it can be brought to bear upon or be used fittingly in reference to a matter in hand ⟨beauty in this broad sense is *applicable* to widely differing artistic achievements —C.W.H.Johnson⟩ ⟨this assumption is not *applicable* to many economic problems —Robert Dorfman⟩ A thing is APROPOS when it is opportunely appropriate ⟨once asked him, *apropos* of his liberal politics . . . what ideal of society he would approve —George Santayana⟩ ⟨she stays glued to her easel, creating futuristic pictures *apropos* of which the author observes, "She had a moderate talent for painting" —S.J. Perelman⟩

rel·e·vant·ly *adv* **:** with relevance

relevate *vt* -ED/-ING/-S [L *relevatus*, past part. of *relevare* — more at RELIEVE] *obs* **:** RAISE, RELIEVE; *esp* **:** to restore to good spirits

re·le·vé \,relə'vā\ *n* -S [F, lit., raised, fr. past part. of *relever* to raise — more at RELIEVE] **:** a rise to the toes from the flat foot in ballet dancing

re·li·abil·i·ty \rə,līə'biləd·ē, rē,-, -ətē, -i\ *n* **:** the quality or state of being reliable; *specif* **:** the extent to which an experiment, test, or measuring procedure yields the same result on repeated trials

reliability coefficient *n* **:** a measure of the accuracy of a test or measuring instrument obtained by measuring the same individuals twice and computing the correlation of the two sets of measures

re·li·able \rə'līəbəl, rē'-\ *adj* [*rely* + *-able*] **:** suitable or fit to be relied on ⟨~ witness⟩ ⟨~ history⟩ **:** worthy of dependence or reliance **:** of proven consistency in producing satisfactory results ⟨~ recipe⟩ ⟨~ remedy⟩; *specif* **:** giving the same results on successive trials ⟨~ intelligence test⟩ ⟨~ measuring device⟩

syn DEPENDABLE, TRUSTWORTHY, TRUSTY, TRIED: RELIABLE describes what can be counted on or trusted in to do as expected or to be truthful ⟨a *reliable* employee⟩ ⟨*reliable* guards at the gates⟩ ⟨*reliable* on duty, but a wild, desperate fellow off the deck of his ship —A. Conan Doyle⟩ ⟨a *reliable* machine⟩ ⟨*reliable* testimony⟩ DEPENDABLE is a close synonym for RELIABLE and may indicate a steady predictability or trustworthiness or reliability worthy of fullest confidence ⟨a *dependable* workman⟩ ⟨*dependable* amounts of rainfall⟩ ⟨a *dependable* hard-working physician⟩ ⟨the most *dependable* of our allies⟩ TRUSTWORTHY indicates meriting confidence for proved soundness, integrity, veracity, judgment, or ability ⟨after considerable deliberation on the part of the captain and mate, four of the seamen were pitched upon as the most *trustworthy* —Herman Melville⟩ ⟨his careful use of sources makes him the first *trustworthy* American historian —*Amer. Guide Series: Mass.*⟩ TRUSTY implies that the person or thing described has been tested and found dependable ⟨*trusty* servants who have been with us for some time —A.Conan Doyle⟩ TRIED likewise stresses proved dependability ⟨the men who fought there were the *tried* fighters, the hammered, the weather-beaten, the very hard-dying men —S.V.Benét⟩

re·li·able·ness *n* -ES **:** RELIABILITY

re·li·ably \-blē, -li\ *adv* **:** in a reliable manner **:** with certainty

re·li·ance \rə'līən(t)s, rē'-\ *n* -S [*rely* + *-ance*] **1 :** the act of relying ⟨~ on income tax revenues to carry government costs⟩ **2 :** the condition or attitude of one who relies **:** DEPENDENCE, CONFIDENCE ⟨~ on promises⟩ **3 :** something or someone relied upon **:** MAINSTAY ⟨long a main ~ of the administration in foreign affairs⟩ **syn** see TRUST

re·li·ant \-nt\ *adj* [back-formation fr. *reliance*] **1 :** having reliance on something or someone ⟨~ on sleeping pills⟩ ⟨~ on her brother for news of the family⟩ **2 :** DEPENDENT, TRUSTING — **re·li·ant·ly** *adv*

rel·ic \'relik, -lēk\ *n* -S [ME *relik*, fr. OF *relique*, fr. ML *reliquia*, back-formation fr. LL *reliquiae*, pl., remains of a martyr, fr. L, remains, leavings, remains of a deceased person, fr. *relinquere* to leave behind — more at RELINQUISH] **1 a :** an object (as a bone, an article of clothing or of personal use) kept in esteem and veneration because of its association with a saint or martyr **b :** something that serves as a remembrance of a person, place, or event **:** SOUVENIR, MEMENTO ⟨snapshots and other ~*s* of her youth⟩ **2 relics** *pl* **:** REMAINS, CORPSE ⟨sacred earth where his dear ~*s* lie —William Wordsworth⟩ **3 :** something that is left behind after decay, disintegration, or disappearance (as of a structure, a race, a nation) **:** a surviving ruin or specimen or remnant ⟨~*s* of ancient cities⟩ ⟨the chimney . . . may be a ~ of the earlier building —*Amer. Guide Series: Conn.*⟩ ⟨residual landforms many of which are capped by isolated ~s of once continuous dolerite sills —Arthur Holmes⟩ **4 :** a trace of some past or outmoded practice, custom, or belief **:** SURVIVAL, VESTIGE ⟨the prison . . . is an anachronistic ~ of medieval concepts of crime and punishment —R.S.Banay⟩ **5 :** RELICT 4 **6 :** RELICT 5 **7 :** a term, form, or pronunciation once common over a wide area but now occurring only in a usu. isolated place

relic area *n* **:** a region that retains characteristic speech features from an earlier stage of a language which have been lost or have undergone greater change in other regions — compare FOCAL AREA, GRADED AREA

rel·i·cary \ˈreləˌkerē\ *n* -ES [Sp *relicario*, fr. ML *reliquiarium* — more at RELIQUARY] **:** RELIQUARY

¹rel·ict \ˈrelikt, -lēkt\ *n* -s [in sense 1, fr. L *relictum*, neut. of *relictus*, past part. of *relinquere* to leave behind; in sense 2, fr. L *relicta*, neut. pl. of *relictus;* in sense 3, fr. LL *relicta*, fr. L, fem. of *relictus;* in senses 4 & 5, fr. ²*relict* — more at RELINQUISH] **1** *obs* **:** RELIC 1a **2 relicts** *pl, archaic* **:** RELIC 2 **3 :** WIDOW ⟨the ~ of a famous general⟩ ⟨a banker's wife who behaved as if she had been his ~ —George Meredith⟩ **4 :** a persistent remnant of an otherwise extinct flora or fauna or kind of organism ⟨various Australian cycads are probably Carboniferous ~s⟩ ⟨the metasequoia is a ~ of a once abundant genus⟩ **5 :** a relict relief feature or rock ⟨older view that the Scandinavian mountain range is simply a ~ of the higher ancient Caledonian range —*Jour. of Geol.*⟩

²re·lict \rəˈlikt, rēˈ-\ *adj* [L *relictus*, past part. of *relinquere*] **1** *obs* **:** left behind by death; *specif* **:** WIDOWED **2** *also* **relic a :** remaining after other parts have been removed or have disappeared **:** RESIDUAL ⟨~ lake⟩ ⟨~ mountain⟩ ⟨~ quartz⟩ **b :** left behind in a process of change ⟨~ sulfides in a partly oxidized ore body⟩ **3** *also* **relic :** surviving as a remnant of a vanishing race, type, or species **:** belonging to an otherwise extinct class or kind ⟨such ~ animals as the opossum —Weston La Barre⟩

re·lict·ed \-təd\ *adj* **:** RELICT 2

re·lic·tion \-kshən\ *n* -s [L *reliction-, relictio* act of leaving behind, fr. *relictus* (past part. of *relinquere*) + *-ion-, -io* -ion] **:** the gradual withdrawal of the water in the sea, a lake, or a stream leaving permanently exposed and uncovered land whose title then vests in the abutting owner of adjacent land; *also* **:** the land so left uncovered — compare ACCRETION

relied *past of* RELY

¹re·lief \rəˈlēf, rēˈ-\ *n* -s [ME *relefe, releve, relief*, fr. MF *relief*, fr. OF, fr. *relever* to raise again, relieve — more at RELIEVE] **1 a :** a fine or money composition (as a year's rent or a fixed sum) formerly paid by the heir of a deceased tenant to his lord for the privilege of taking up the landed estate which on strict feudal principles had escheated — distinguished from *heriot* **b :** an acknowledgment made by the heir of his vassal tenure of a lord as a condition of being received or had as a vassal **2 :** removal or lightening of something oppressive, burdensome, painful, dangerous, or distressing ⟨expressing his secret fears gave him great ~⟩ ⟨it was a ~ to take off his tight shoes⟩ **: a :** aid in the form of money or necessities for the indigent, aged, or handicapped ⟨public ~⟩ ⟨work ~⟩ ⟨disaster ~⟩ **b** *obs* **:** FEEDING, SUSTENANCE **c :** military assistance in or rescue from a position of extreme difficulty or encirclement ⟨sent to the ~ of a besieged city⟩ **d :** diversion or amusement serving to ease or relax the mind ⟨have no ~ but in passing their afternoons in visits . . . and their evenings at cards —Jonathan Swift⟩ **e :** means of breaking or avoiding monotony, tedium, or prolonged straining of attention ⟨the appearance on the horizon of even the swagman's silhouette may be a welcome ~ —William Power⟩ **3 :** release from a post or from the performance of duty by the intervention of others, by discharge, or by relay ⟨~ of a sentry⟩ ⟨the ~ of the commanding general was to be expected⟩ **4 a :** one that relieves from performance of duty by taking the place of another ⟨explained their duties and equipment to their ~s —G.J.Dufek⟩ **:** RELAY, REPLACEMENT ⟨send up a ~ to consolidate the position —Bill Mauldin⟩ **b :** SCRUB 3b(2) **5 a :** legal remedy or redress **b** *Scots law* **:** release from an obligation or contribution from a joint obligor for his proportionate share of liability **6** [F; trans. of It *rilievo*, fr. *rilevare* to raise, fr. L *relevare* — more at RELIEVE] **a :** a mode of sculpture in which forms and figures are distinguished (as by modeling of soft material, hammering of thin malleable material, or cutting away the surface in a hard material) from a surrounding plane surface — compare INTAGLIO, *in the round* at ROUND; see BAS-RELIEF, FLAT RELIEF, MEZZO-RELIEVO, SUNK RELIEF **b :** sculpture or a sculptural form executed in this mode ⟨a stone ~ above the arch⟩ **c :** projecting detail, ornament, or figures in sculpture ⟨the sharp edges of the ~ cannot stand the test of time⟩ **7 a :** the suggestion in pictorial art of spatial dimensions and relations communicated by the arrangement of lines, colors, or shadings **b :** vividness or sharpness of outline due to contrast (as of color or shading) ⟨a roof in bold ~ against the sky⟩ **8 :** the difference of level between the highest part of a fortification works and the bottom of the ditch or trench **9 :** the elevations or inequalities of a land surface **:** the difference in elevation between the hilltops or summits and the lowlands of a region **10 :** the character of the surface of a mineral section as observed under the microscope **11 a :** a passage in a tailstock center for the facing or parting tool made by cutting away one side of the center so that the tool may be advanced to or almost to the center of the work **b :** a slight modification in the dimension of a part of a machine to secure clearance **c :** the lessening of excessive pressure (as of a tool, a moving part, a confined gas) **d :** CLEARANCE 2e

²relief \"\ *adj* **1 :** providing relief from distress, pressure, strain, congestion ⟨~ measures during a famine⟩ ⟨~ highway⟩ **2 :** characterized by surface inequalities **3 :** of or used in letterpress ⟨~ form⟩ ⟨~ plate⟩ ⟨~ engraving⟩

³relief \"\ *adj, usu cap* [fr. the *Relief* Church, founded in 1761 in Scotland by Thomas Gillespie †1774 Scottish clergyman and his followers] **:** of or relating to the Relief Church that was founded to provide relief from the evils of patronage and that joined in 1847 with the United Secession to form the United Presbyterian Church (of Scotland)

re·lief·er \-fə(r)\ *n* -s [¹*relief* + *-er*] **1 :** RELIEF PITCHER **2 :** one who receives public relief

relief frame *n* **:** a frame or ring interposed between the back of a slide valve and the inside of the steam-chest cover in some large engines to prevent access of the steam to the greater part of the valve thereby relieving the pressure on the valve and materially reducing friction

relief map *n* **:** a map representing topographic relief by contour lines, hachures, coloring, shading, or similar graphic means

relief model *n* **:** a three-dimensional scale model of a part of the earth's surface

relief pitcher *n* **:** a baseball pitcher who takes over for another during a game; *esp* **:** one who is regularly held in readiness for relief

relief printing *n* **:** LETTERPRESS 1a

relief process *n* **:** a process for making subtractive color prints that employs photographic images of varying thickness in a material (as gelatin) that may contain a pigment or may be dyed to show variations in optical density in proportion to thickness

relief valve *n* **:** a valve for the escape of steam or fluid under excessive pressure

relief well *n* **:** a vertical drain used for the drainage of a deep pervious stratum to relieve waterlogging of the surface soil

re·li·er \rəˈlī(ə)r\ *n* -s [*rely* + *-er*] **:** one that relies

relies *pres 3d sing of* RELY

re·liev·able \rəˈlēvəbəl\ *adj* **:** capable of being relieved ⟨~ wrongs⟩

re·lieve \rəˈlēv, rēˈ-\ *vb* -ED/-ING/-s [ME *releven*, fr. MF *relever* to lift up, raise, relieve, fr. L *relevare*, fr. *re-* + *levare* to raise — more at LEVER] *vt* **1 :** to free from a burden, evil, pain, or distress **:** give ease, comfort, or consolation to ⟨knowing the truth will ~ anxious parents⟩ **:** give aid, help, or succor to **:** RESCUE, DELIVER ⟨~ a besieged city⟩ ⟨a society for *relieving* the poor⟩ **2 a :** to bring about the removal or alleviation of **:** make less burdensome or afflicting **:** MITIGATE, LESSEN, ALLEVIATE ⟨strenuous efforts to ~ the food shortage⟩ ⟨frequently smokes to ~ nervous tension⟩ ⟨no words can ~ her sorrow⟩ **b :** to remove something from the possession of **:** ROB, DEPRIVE ⟨crooks . . . eager to ~ the Texas cowboys of their pay —E.V.Buckholder⟩ **3 a :** to release from a post, station, or duty ⟨asked to be *relieved* of command of the army⟩ ⟨he was *relieved* of further responsibility for the program⟩ **b :** to take the place of **:** take over from ⟨sent to ~ the gate sentry⟩ **:** SUCCEED ⟨tulips bloom . . . to be *relieved* by roses when their time is up —E.O.Hauser⟩ ⟨*relieved* the operator for lunch and a smoke⟩ **4 :** to set free from an obligation, condition, or restriction **5 :** to acquire or take (a feudal estate) by paying or rendering a relief **6 :** to ease of an imposition, burden, wrong, or oppression by judicial or legislative interposition **:** RIGHT ⟨a zoning law cannot constitutionally ~ land . . . from lawful restrictions affecting its use, imposed by convenants —*Amer. Jurisprudence*⟩ **7 :** to remove or lessen the monotony of by contrast or variety ⟨brown hills *relieved* by patches of green⟩ **8 a :** to give prominence or conspicuousness to **:** set off by contrast **:** give sharp outline to ⟨her tall figure *relieved* against the blue sky —Sir Walter Scott⟩ **b :** to raise (as figures, letters) in relief **9 :** to supply with food, munitions, stores ⟨~ a lighthouse by ship⟩ ⟨~ an arctic weather station⟩ **10 a :** to furnish (as a cutting tool) with a relief angle **b :** to free from tightness in relative movement **c :** to cut away a small amount of material from a part of (a machine) to obtain clearance **11 :** to empty the bladder or bowels of (oneself) ⟨children are likely to ~ themselves on any street —*Time*⟩ ~ *vi* **1 :** to bring or give relief **2 :** to stand out in relief **3 :** to clear one from a legal obligation, condition, or restriction ⟨a *relieving* clause⟩

syn ALLEVIATE, LIGHTEN, ASSUAGE, MITIGATE, ALLAY: RELIEVE indicates a lifting, perhaps temporary, of a burden, pain, or anxiety, so that it is no longer quite oppressive ⟨particularly zealous in taking steps to control the fire and *relieve* the suffering it entailed —Donald Milner⟩ ⟨a sex offender, deeply guilty over his past acts and *relieved* by analysis of the neurotic demands that had prompted them —Walter Goodman⟩ ALLEVIATE indicates a temporary lightening of pain, distress, or difficulty, and may contrast with *cure* or *eliminate* ⟨no dentists to care for them; not even any oil of cloves to *alleviate* the ache —C.C.Furnas⟩ ⟨activation of the Parking Authority in order to help *alleviate* New York's chronic traffic problem —*Current Biog.*⟩ LIGHTEN may suggest a cheering, buoying up, or refreshing abatement of depression or oppression ⟨forever grumblingly attempting to *lighten* their sufferings —Kenneth Roberts⟩ ⟨his experience in copyreading and criticizing other people's efforts at expression ought to *lighten* the task of the editor to whom he eventually submits something —R.L.Greene⟩ ASSUAGE suggests a moderating of pain, vexation, or sorrow by soothing, softening, or mollifying ⟨the fugitive breezes, the life-giving zephyrs that *assuage* the torment of the summer heat —Stuart Cloete⟩ ⟨grief that Professor Abbott did not live to enjoy the fame he had earned is *assuaged* by the knowledge that he survived to complete his great work —Godfrey Davies⟩ MITIGATE also suggests moderating, by any means, or countering the force or intensity of something painful ⟨*mitigate* the barbarity of criminal law —W.R.Inge⟩ ⟨group friction and conflict are generally *mitigated* when people realize their common interests —M.R.Cohen⟩ ⟨the torment of his thirst *mitigated* a trifle by a drenching in the brine —C.G.D.Roberts⟩ ALLAY applies to any effective calming, soothing, quieting, or pacifying ⟨the approach of winter *allayed* the fear of Indian raids —G.R.Stewart⟩ ⟨the president, in a TV chat intended to *allay* the country's fears —W.L.Miller⟩ ⟨something must be done to *allay* growing public discontent and to still the disagreements —*New Statesman & Nation*⟩

re·lieved \-vd\ *adj* **:** experiencing or showing relief esp. from anxiety or pent-up emotion ⟨answered presently in a ~ tone⟩ ⟨greatly ~ or disappointed . . . to find that there is little or no sensation of speed —H.G.Armstrong⟩ — **re·lieved·ly** \-vədlē, -vd-, -li\ *adv*

re·liev·er \-və(r)\ *n* -s **:** one that relieves: **a :** any of various mechanical devices for relieving strain **b :** something that relieves pain or distress **c :** RELIEF PITCHER

relieving arch *n* **:** an arch built over a lintel to relieve or distribute the weight of the wall above — called also *discharging arch*

relieving arch

relieving officer *n, Brit* **:** an official administering public relief

relieving tackle *n* **1 :** a temporary tackle rigged to a ship's tiller during gales or in battle to assist or replace the steering gear **2 :** a tackle to a careened ship to prevent her from going over entirely and to assist in righting her

¹re·lie·vo \rēˈlē(ˌ)vō; rēlˈyä(-, -ye(-\ *n* -s [It *rilievo* — more at RELIEF] **:** RELIEF 6

²re·lie·vo \rəˈlē(ˌ)vō\ *n* -s [prob. fr. *relieve* + *-o*] **:** a game in which members of one team are given time to hide, then are sought by those of the other team who try to capture them, take them to a place of confinement, and keep them from being released by their teammates — called also *ring-a-lievo*

rel·i·gate \ˈreləˌgāt\ *vb* -ED/-ING/-s [L *religatus*, past part. of *religare* to tie back, tie up, tie fast — more at RELY] **:** to bind together **:** CONSTRAIN — **rel·i·ga·tion** \ˌ==ˈgāshən\ *n* -s

re·light \(ˈ)rē+\ *vt* [*re-* + *light*] **:** to light again

re·lig·i·fy \rəˈlijəˌfī\ *vt* -ED/-ING/-s [*religious* + *-fy*] **:** to make religious in form, content, appearance, or function

religio- *comb form* [*religion*] **:** religion ⟨*religio*centric⟩ **:** religious and ⟨*religio*philosophical⟩

re·li·gio·ethical \-ˈlijē(ˌ)ō+\ *adj* [*religio-* + *ethical*] **:** religious and ethical

re·li·gion \rəˈlijən, rēˈ-\ *n* -s [ME *religioun*, fr. L *religion-, religio* reverence, piety, religion, prob. fr. *religare* to tie back, tie up, tie fast + *-ion-, -io* -ion — more at RELY] **1 :** the personal commitment to and serving of God or a god with worshipful devotion, conduct in accord with divine commands esp. as found in accepted sacred writings or declared by authoritative teachers, a way of life recognized as incumbent on true believers, and typically the relating of oneself to an organized body of believers ⟨ministers of ~⟩ **2 :** the state of a religious ⟨retire into ~⟩ ⟨the nun died in her thirtieth year of ~⟩ **3 a :** one of the systems of faith and worship **:** a religious faith ⟨monotheistic ~s⟩ ⟨tolerant of all ~s⟩ ⟨forbidding discrimination because of race, color, or ~⟩ **b :** the body of institutionalized expressions of sacred beliefs, observances, and social practices found within a given cultural context ⟨the ~ of this primitive people⟩ **4 :** the profession or practice of religious beliefs **:** religious observances ⟨the kernel of his practical ~ was that it was respectable, and beneficial to one's business, to be seen going to services —Sinclair Lewis⟩ **5** *archaic* **:** scrupulous conformity **:** CONSCIENTIOUSNESS, FIDELITY **6 a :** a personal awareness or conviction of the existence of a supreme being or of supernatural powers or influences controlling one's own, humanity's, or all nature's destiny ⟨only man appears to be capable of ~⟩ **b :** the access of such an awareness or conviction accompanied by or arousing reverence, gratitude, humility, the will to obey and serve **:** religious experience or insight ⟨in middle life he suddenly got ~⟩ **7 a :** a cause, principle, system of tenets held with ardor, devotion, conscientiousness, and faith **:** a value held to be of supreme importance ⟨by making democracy our ~ and by practicing as well as preaching its doctrines —W.O.Douglas⟩ ⟨Marxism was his ~⟩ ⟨he has made a ~ of pleasure, and it is a brave thing to do these days —Gerald Sykes⟩ **b :** a quality, condition, custom, or thing inspiring zealous devotion, conscientious maintenance, and cherishing ⟨a ~ with him to preserve in good condition all that had lapsed from his mother's hands —Thomas Hardy⟩

syn FAITH, CHURCH, CREED, COMMUNION, DENOMINATION, SECT, CULT, PERSUASION: RELIGION is a general term esp. applicable to the great revelations and the larger subdivisions among their believers ⟨the Christian *religion*⟩ ⟨the Roman Catholic or Methodist *religion*⟩ FAITH is applicable to any formulated and established major religious group; it may or may not suggest ardent, complete acceptance ⟨the Muhammadan *faith*⟩ ⟨the Mormon *faith*⟩ ⟨men of all *faiths*⟩ CHURCH is likely to stress the existence of an established formal organization and procedure; it may suggest a Christian rather than non-Christian context ⟨the Orthodox *Church*⟩ ⟨the Presbyterian *Church*⟩ CREED differs from FAITH in more strongly suggesting formal doctrinal expression of what is believed — accord on the basis of doctrinal assent — but is applicable to most religious groups ⟨men of the Lutheran *creed*⟩ ⟨the *creed* of Hebraism⟩ COMMUNION may suggest accord on liturgical or sacramental practice and earnest, close fellowship in worship; it is applicable to both larger and smaller groups. DENOMINATION is likely to suggest a smaller section called by a distinctive name of a larger group ⟨various Protestant *denominations*⟩ SECT now indicates a smaller group which has split off from a larger through discontent with some matter of doctrine or observance ⟨the Uniat *sect*⟩ ⟨a *sect* composed of the followers of John Huss⟩ CULT suggests a small group holding to unusual, grotesque, or secret spurious notions and rituals ⟨forbade the practice of certain eastern *cults*, and expelled from Rome Greek and Asiatic magicians —John Buchan⟩ PERSUASION may suggest conviction arising from evangelism or exhortation; often it is more or less interchangeable with FAITH ⟨chapel goers, people of Wesleyan *persuasion*⟩

¹religionary *n* -ES [*religion* + *-ary* (n. suffix)] *obs* **:** one whose vocation is religion

²re·li·gion·ary \-jəˌnerē\ *adj* [*religion* + *-ary* (adj. suffix)] **:** RELIGIOUS

re·li·gion·er \-jənə(r)\ *n* -s **:** RELIGIONIST

re·li·gion·ism \-jəˌnizəm\ *n* -s **:** strict practice of or devotion to religion; *also* **:** exaggerated religious zealotry

re·li·gion·ist \-ˌnəst\ *n* -s **:** one earnestly devoted or attached to a religion **:** a religious zealot — **re·li·gion·is·tic** \=ˌ==ˈnistik\ *adj*

re·li·gion·ize \=ˈ==ˌnīz\ *vt* -ED/-ING/-s **:** to make religious **:** imbue with religious principles **:** bring into conformity with religious standards **:** interpret or understand (a thing) from a religious framework ⟨~ our politics⟩ ⟨~ death⟩

re·li·gion·less \rəˈlijənləs\ *adj* **:** lacking religion

religions *pl of* RELIGION

re·li·gio·political \-ˈlijē(ˌ)ō+\ *adj* [*religio-* + *political*] **:** religious and political

re·li·gi·ose \rəˈlijēˌōs\ *adj* [*religion* + *-ose*] **:** excessively or obtrusively or sentimentally religious ⟨a leader of a ~ nationalism —Percy Winner⟩ ⟨modern advertising methods will not long need to lack leaders who can use the ~, fanatical technique —*English Jour.*⟩

re·li·gi·os·i·ty \rəˌlijēˈäsəd·ē, rē,-, -ətē, -i\ *n* -ES [ME *religiosite*, fr. L *religiositas* religiousness, fr. *religiosus* religious + *-itas* -ity] **:** intense, excessive, or affected religiousness ⟨~ of the converted worldling and intellectual —Douglas Bush⟩ ⟨it was precisely sadness and ~ and grandiloquence that first attracted me in poetry —George Santayana⟩

re·li·gi·o·so \rəˌlijēˈō(ˌ)sō\ *adj (or adv)* [It, religious, fr. L *religiosus*] **:** religious in style and feeling — used as a direction in music

¹re·li·gious \rəˈlijəs, rēˈ-\ *adj* [ME, fr. OF *religieus*, fr. L *religiosus*, fr. *religio* religion + *-osus* -ous — more at RELIGION] **1 :** relating to that which is acknowledged as ultimate reality **:** manifesting devotion to and reflecting the nature of the divine or that which one holds to be of ultimate importance **:** exemplifying the influence of religion **:** PIOUS, GODLY ⟨a ~ purpose⟩ ⟨a ~ man⟩ ⟨~ attitude⟩ **2 :** committed, dedicated, or consecrated to the service of the divine **:** set apart to religion ⟨a Buddhist monk of a ~ order⟩ ⟨the ~ life of a nun⟩ ⟨~ offerings⟩ **3 :** of or relating to religion **:** concerned with religion **:** teaching or setting forth religion ⟨~ liberty⟩ ⟨a ~ duty⟩ ⟨a ~ poet⟩; *also* **:** SACRED, HOLY ⟨a ~ book⟩ ⟨~ rites⟩ **4 a :** scrupulously and conscientiously faithful ⟨~ in his observance of rules of health⟩ **b :** FERVENT, ZEALOUS **syn** see DEVOUT

²religious \"\ *n, pl* **religious** [ME, fr. OF *religieus*, fr. *religieus*, adj.] **:** one (as a monk or nun) who is bound by vows, sequestered from secular concerns, and devoted to a life of piety

religious education *n* **1 :** instruction in religion as a subject of general education **2 :** instruction in the principles of a particular religious faith

religious house *n* **:** CONVENT, MONASTERY

religious humanism *n* **:** a modern American movement composed chiefly of nontheistic humanists and humanist churches and dedicated to achieving the ethical goals of religion without beliefs and rites resting upon supernaturalism

re·li·gious·ly *adv* [ME, fr. *religious* + *-ly*] **:** in a religious manner **:** FAITHFULLY, CONSCIENTIOUSLY ⟨clock which my father ~ wound each Sunday morning —Della Lutes⟩ ⟨kept his diary ~⟩ **:** in favor of religion ⟨she was ~ inclined⟩

religious naturalism *n* **:** PROCESS PHILOSOPHY

re·li·gious·ness *n* -ES [ME *religiousnesse*, fr. *religious* + *-nesse* -ness] **:** the quality or state of being religious **:** RELIGIOSITY

religious of the cenacle *usu cap R&C* **:** a member of the Roman Catholic Society of Our Lady of the Cenacle, a congregation of nuns established in France in 1826 and devoted esp. to directing retreats for women

religious of the sacred heart *usu cap R&S&H* **:** a member of the Roman Catholic Society of the Sacred Heart, a religious community of women founded in France in 1800 and devoted to the education of girls

re·line \(ˈ)rē+\ *vt* [*re-* + *line*] **1 :** to put new or fresh lines on **2 :** to put a new lining in ⟨~ brakes⟩

re·lin·quent \rəˈliŋkwənt\ *adj* [L *relinquent-, relinquens*, pres. part. of *relinquere*] **:** RELINQUISHING

re·lin·quish \rəˈliŋkwish, rēˈ-, -ink-, -wēsh, *esp in pres part* -wəsh\ *vb* -ED/-ING/-ES [ME *relinquissen, relinquisshen*, fr. MF *relinquiss-*, lengthened stem of *relinquir*, fr. L *relinquere*, lit., to leave behind, fr. *re-* + *linquere* to leave — more at LOAN] *vt* **1 a** *obs* **:** FORSAKE **b :** to withdraw or retreat from **:** ABANDON ⟨the shores they have ~ed shrink to . . . remoteness —George Meredith⟩ **2 a :** to desist from **:** leave off **:** cease from considering, practising, exercising, or cherishing ⟨~ing the law, Webster resumed teaching —H.E.Scudder⟩ ⟨the . . . scheme had been deferred, not ~ed —Jane Austen⟩ **b :** to assent to withdrawal, dropping, or cessation of **:** give up **:** RENOUNCE ⟨his concealment from herself of the name he had ~ed —Charles Dickens⟩ ⟨refused to ~ his claim to the inheritance⟩ ⟨~ed all hope of finding survivors⟩ **3 a :** to let go of physically **:** stop holding **:** RELEASE ⟨~ed his grip on his armchair⟩ **b :** to give over possession or control of **:** YIELD, SURRENDER ⟨the ambition which incites a man to seize power seldom allows him to ~ it —*Times Lit. Supp.*⟩ ~ *vi, obs* **:** to go away **:** DISAPPEAR, VANISH

syn LEAVE, ABANDON, WAIVE, RESIGN, CEDE, YIELD, SURRENDER: RELINQUISH, a word wide in meaning, as the preceding definitions indicate, usu. does not suggest forceful action or strong feeling in dropping, desisting, renouncing; it sometimes suggests regret at giving up or delay in the process ⟨and your system . . . have courage to cast the dream of it out of you; *relinquish* an impossible project —George Meredith⟩ ⟨did not lightly *relinquish* his hope of victory —*Amer. Guide Series: Ind.*⟩ ⟨it cost him a few struggles to *relinquish* her —Jane Austen⟩ LEAVE may connote more peremptory and definite action than RELINQUISH (“he has *left* me,” Sophia interrupted him in her weak and fatigued voice —Arnold Bennett⟩ ⟨always carries his mouth open, a practice which, it is prophesied, he will soon *leave* off in this land of flies —Rachel Henning⟩ ABANDON may stress finality and completeness in giving up, esp. before dangers, hostile advances, encroachments that cannot be checked, or against the claims of duty or loyalty ⟨the stations were withdrawn . . . and northern Texas *abandoned* to the savages —R.A.Billington⟩ ⟨*abandoning* wife and children, home and business, and renouncing normal morality and humanity —G.B.Shaw⟩ WAIVE may suggest either temporary or permanent forgoing; it often connotes a voluntary, complaisant giving up of something in the interests of conciliation or convenience ⟨from that time onward the office rule was *waived* —E.H.Collis⟩ RESIGN may suggest either a formal and definite giving up or relinquishing or a wistful, stoic, or confiding yielding or acceptance without struggle ⟨Britain rightly refused to budge from the position that it would not *resign* its trusteeship —*Nation*⟩ ⟨these saintly self-deniers, these *resigned* sufferers, who would not strive nor cry —Matthew Arnold⟩ CEDE suggests giving up or granting formally by or as if by treaty, negotiation, or arbitration holdings, either willingly or under duress and compulsion, but always peacefully ⟨strongly urging the states to *cede* these lands to the United States —R.B.Taney⟩ ⟨the Dutch were forced to *cede* New Amsterdam —Stringfellow Barr⟩ YIELD may suggest a giving up through diplomatic concession but is more likely to connote submitting and giving over to superior force ⟨he already saw that his friend and employer was a man who knew no moderation in his requests and impulses and he *yielded* gracefully —Thomas Hardy⟩ ⟨after a spirited contest lasting three quarters of a century, theocratic Puritanism *yielded* to ecclesiastical democracy —V.L.Parrington⟩ SURRENDER is likely to indicate giving up under compulsion to superior forces, esp. after resistance or preparation for or show of resistance ⟨Fort Orange *surrendered* to the English —A.C.Flick⟩

re·lin·quish·ment \-shmənt\ *n* -s **1 :** the act of relinquishing **:** a giving up **:** SURRENDER, RENUNCIATION **2 :** a piece of relinquished or abandoned land

1rel·i·quary \ˈreləˌkwerē, -ri\ *n* -ES [F *reliquaire*, fr. ML *reliquiarium*, fr. *reliquia* relic + L *-arium* -ary — more at RELIC] **:** a casket, shrine, or container for keeping or exhibiting relics

2reliquary \"\ *adj* [ML *reliquia* relic + E *-ary*] **:** of, relating to, or serving as relics ⟨~ case⟩ ⟨the general tendency . . . was towards a circular form for devotional and ~ pendants —Joan Evans⟩

rel·ique \ˈrelik, rəˈlēk\ *archaic var of* RELIC

re·liq·ui·ae \rəˈlikwəˌē\ *n pl* [L — more at RELIC] **:** remains of the dead **:** organic remains **:** RELICS

re·liq·ui·al \-wēəl\ *adj* [L *reliquiae* remains + E *-al*] **:** RELICT 3

re·liq·ui·an \-ən\ *adj* [L *reliquiae* + E *-an*] **:** being or resembling a relic **:** RELIQUARY

rel·i·quism \ˈreləˌkwizəm\ *n* -s [*relic* + *-ism*] **:** practice of keeping or venerating relics

1rel·ish \ˈrelish, -lēsh\ *n* -ES [alter. of ME *reles* taste, aftertaste, odor, scent, fr. OF *reles*, *relais* something left behind, release — more at RELEASE] **1 :** characteristic flavor; *esp* **:** pleasing or zestful flavor **:** TANG, SAVOR ⟨now I have better things to write of — things that have some ~ of good in them —Irving Bacheller⟩ **2 :** a quantity just sufficient to flavor or characterize **:** TRACE, DASH ⟨your lordship . . . hath yet some smack of age in you . . . some ~ of the saltness of time —Shak.⟩ **3** *obs* **:** power to discern and appreciate; *often* **:** personal taste **:** LIKING **4 a :** enjoyment of or delight in something that satisfies one's tastes, inclinations, desires **:** GRATIFICATION ⟨men have a keener ~ for privileges and honors than for equality —Réne Sédillot⟩ ⟨with the ~ of a child digging into a dish of ice cream⟩ **b :** APPETITE, STOMACH, INCLINATION ⟨a studious boy with little ~ for sports⟩ **5 a :** something served to add a zestful flavor to a plain dish **:** CONDIMENT ⟨horseradish sauce is a favorite ~ with boiled beef⟩; *esp* **:** a savory pickled or preserved food prepared from mixed chopped vegetables or fruits and usu. served with meat ⟨corn ~⟩ ⟨beet ~⟩ ⟨pickle ~⟩ **b :** APPETIZER, HORS D'OEUVRE **syn** see TASTE

2relish \", *esp in pres part* -ləsh\ *vb* -ED/-ING/-ES *vt* **1 :** to add a relish, flavor, or zest to **:** serve as a condiment to ⟨a savory bit that served to ~ wine —John Dryden⟩ **2 :** to be pleased or gratified by **:** approve of **:** ENJOY ⟨~*ed* the relaxed attentiveness and technical aplomb of the instrumentalists —Herbert Weinstock⟩ ⟨could not expect them to ~ the prospect of a cut in salary⟩ **3 a :** to eat or drink with pleasure **:** like the taste of ⟨so hungry that he will ~ plain food⟩ **b :** to delight in **:** take keen pleasure in ⟨bargains . . . with a fruit vendor, both of them laughing and ~*ing* the process and each other —Roger Angell⟩ **4 :** to appreciate with taste and discernment ⟨a people trained by oratory to ~ virtuosity of speech —H.M.Reynolds⟩ ⟨~*es* literature with his palate as well as with his brain —Henri Peyre⟩ **5** *obs* **:** to have a savor or suggestion of **:** smack of **~** *vi* **:** to have a characteristic or pleasing taste ⟨find ways in which the soldiers' food could be made more ~*ing* —*Current Biog.*⟩ ⟨his style ~*es* perhaps too much of the schoolroom⟩ **syn** see LIKE

3relish \"\ *n* -ES [perh. fr. ¹*relish*] **:** a grace or embellishment in early English music

4relish \"\ *vt*, *obs* **:** to sing with embellishments **:** WARBLE ⟨~ a love song, like a robin redbreast —Shak.⟩

5relish \"\ *n* -ES [F *relais*] **:** the projection or shoulder at the side of or around a tenon — compare MORTISE

6relish \"\ *vt* **:** to cut or shape the shoulder on (a tenon)

rel·ish·able \-shəbəl\ *adj* **:** capable of being relished **:** TASTY ⟨~ to readers hungry for spiritual fare —H.M.Robinson⟩

relishing *adj* [fr. pres. part. of ²*relish*] **:** that relishes or gives a relish **syn** see PALATABLE

re·live \(ˈ)rē+\ *vb* [*re-* + *live*] *vt* **1** *obs* **:** to recall to life **:** REVIVE **2 :** to live over again **:** experience again imaginatively ⟨*reliving* his battle experiences⟩ **~** *vi* **:** to return to life **:** live again

re·lle·no \rālˈyā(ˌ)nō\ *n* -s [Sp, fr. *rellenar* to refill, stuff, fr. *re-* (fr. L) + *llenar* to fill, fr. *lleno* full, fr. L *plenus* — more at FULL] **:** stuffed pepper

rel·ly·an \ˈrelēən\ *adj*, *usu cap* [James Relly †1778 British theologian who organized a Universalist congregation in London soon after 1750 + E *-an*] **:** of or relating to the theologian Relly or to a short-lived minority group of Universalists named after him — **rel·ly·an·ism** \-əˌnizəm\ *n* -s *usu cap* — **rel·ly·an·ite** \-ˌnīt\ *n* -s *usu cap*

1re·load \(ˈ)rēˈlōd\ *vt* [*re-* + *load*] **:** to load again: as **a :** to put fresh ammunition into after firing ⟨~ a shotgun⟩ **b :** to load (a cartridge) by hand ⟨a ~*ing* tool⟩

2reload \ˈ=,=\ *n* **:** the act or result of reloading: as **a :** a gun cartridge loaded by hand **b :** worthless securities or real estate sold to a person who has already bought

re·load·er \-də(r)\ *n* **:** one that reloads; *esp* **:** a salesman skilled in selling reloads of securities or property

re·lo·cat·able \ˌrēlōˈkādəbəl\ *adj* **:** capable of being relocated ⟨~ partitions⟩

re·lo·cate \(ˈ)rē,lōˌkāt, ˌrēlōˈkāt, *usu* -ād·+V\ *vt* [*re-* + *locate*] **:** to locate or allocate again **:** establish or lay out in a new place ⟨~ families forced out by floods⟩ ⟨~ the roadbed of a washed-out railroad line⟩

re·lo·ca·tion \ˌrēlōˈkāshən\ *n* [*re* + *location*] **1** *Roman, civil, & Scots law* **:** renewal of a lease — see TACIT RELOCATION **2** [*relocate* + *-ion*] **:** removal and establishment in a new place ⟨~ of war refugees⟩

re·lo·ca·tor \(ˈ)rēˌlōˌkād·ə(r), ˈrēlōk-\ *n* **:** one that relocates: as **a :** an instrument used in seacoast fortifications for obtaining the range and position of a target from the range and position as determined with respect to the end of the base line **b :** one that relocates an abandoned or forfeited mining claim

re·lu·cence \rəˈlüsᵊn(t)s, rē- *also* rəlˈyü *or* rel-\ *n* -s **:** the quality of being relucent **:** BRIGHTNESS

re·lu·cent \-nt\ *adj* [L *relucent-, relucens*, pres. part. of *relucēre* to shine back, fr. *re-* + *lucēre* to shine — more at LIGHT] **:** reflecting light **:** RADIANT, REFULGENT, SHINING ⟨large, dark, ~ eyes set widely apart —Compton Mackenzie⟩

re·luct \rəˈləkt, rē-\ *vi* -ED/-ING/-S [L *reluctari*] **1 :** to make a determined resistance **:** STRUGGLE **2 :** to feel or show repugnance or reluctance **:** REVOLT ⟨many readers . . . ~ at works containing dialect —L.P.Smith⟩

re·luc·tance \-tən(t)s\ *n* -s [L *reluctari* + E *-ance*] **1** *obs* **:** the act of struggling against or opposing **:** OPPOSITION **2 :** the quality or state of being reluctant **:** UNWILLINGNESS, AVERSION, REPUGNANCE ⟨obeyed with ~⟩ ⟨showed a ~ to accept charity⟩ **3 :** a quantity in a magnetic circuit analogous to the resistance of an electric circuit or conductor; *specif* **:** the ratio of the magnetic potential difference to the corresponding flux — compare PERMEANCE

reluctance cartridge *n* **:** a device for converting phonograph-record groove undulations into an electrical voltage by electromagnetic means

re·luc·tan·cy \-nsē, -si\ *n* -ES [L *reluctari* + E *-ancy*] **1 a :** a mental conflict **b :** OPPOSITION, RESISTANCE **c :** REGRET ⟨memories bring regrets and *reluctancies* of the spirit —Victor Canning⟩ **2 :** DISINCLINATION, RELUCTANCE, REPUGNANCE ⟨~ to testify in court⟩

re·luc·tant \-nt\ *adj* [L *reluctant-, reluctans*, pres. part. of *reluctari* to struggle against, oppose, resist, be reluctant, fr. *re-* + *luctari* to struggle, wrestle — more at LOCK] **1 :** offering opposition **:** RESISTING **2 :** hesitant from or as if from dislike, doubt, fear, or scruple **:** AVERSE, UNWILLING ⟨~ to charge a dead man with an offense from which he could not clear himself —Edith Wharton⟩ ⟨persuaded him into ~ consent⟩ ⟨trying to scratch a living from ~ soil⟩ **syn** see DISINCLINED

re·luc·tant·ly *adv* **:** with reluctance **:** UNWILLINGLY, GRUDGINGLY

re·luc·tate \rəˈləkˌtāt\ *vb* -ED/-ING/-S [L *reluctatus*, past part. of *reluctari*] *vi* **:** to show reluctance **:** RELUCT **~** *vt* **:** to struggle against **:** REPUDIATE, REPEL

rel·uc·ta·tion \ˌreləkˈtāshən, ˌrē,ləkˈ-\ *n* -s [LL *reluctation-, reluctatio*, fr. L *reluctatus* + *-ion-, -io* -ion] **:** RELUCTANCE, RELUCTANCY

re·luc·tiv·i·ty \-ˈtivədˌē\ *n* -ES [*reluctance* + *-ivity* (as in *conductivity*)] **:** the reciprocal of magnetic permeability

re·lume \rəˈlüm, rē- *also* rəlˈyüm *or* rel-\ *vt* -ED/-ING/-S [irreg. fr. LL *reluminare*] **:** to light or light up again **:** RELLUMINE, REKINDLE ⟨jets of affection which ~ a young world for me —R.W.Emerson⟩ ⟨then shall be no lamp *relumed* in heaven —Rupert Brooke⟩

re·lu·mine \-mən\ *vt* -ED/-ING/-S [LL *reluminare*, fr. L *re-* + *luminare* to light up — more at ILLUMINATE] **:** RELUME

re·ly \rəˈlī, rē-\ *vb* **relied; relied; relying; relies** [ME *relien*, fr. MF *relier* to connect, fasten together, repair, rally, fr. L *religare* to tie back, tie up, tie fast, fr. *re-* + *ligare* to tie — more at LIGATURE] *vt* **1** *obs* **:** to gather together (as soldiers) **:** RALLY **2** *obs* **:** BASE, REST, REPOSE **~** *vi* **1** *obs* **:** HOLD, CLEAVE, BELONG — used with *to* **2** *obs* **:** CONSIST, SUBSIST — used with *in* **3** *obs* **:** LEAN, REST — used with *on* or *upon* **4 :** to have confidence **:** have a feeling of security **:** place faith without reservation **:** TRUST — used with *on*, *upon*, or sometimes *in* ⟨~ on his own wits⟩ ⟨can this rope be *relied* upon⟩ ⟨*relied* on the letter reaching you in time⟩ **:** expect with confidence or certainty ⟨dangerous to ~ on higher market prices⟩ **5 :** to find support **:** DEPEND ⟨~ on a well for all their water needs⟩ ⟨~ on foreign sources of rubber⟩

syn COUNT (*on*), RECKON (*on*), BANK (*on*), TRUST, DEPEND (*on*): RELY, COUNT, RECKON, and BANK are about equal in force and are often interchangeable. RELY may connote an objectivity of judgment based on previous experience with whatever is in question ⟨that unskilled copyists cannot be *relied* on in matters of punctuation, line structure —Van Wyck Brooks⟩ COUNT (*on*) may suggest a situation involving calculation or computation ⟨a special sum set apart . . . in addition to her pin money; *on* that she may absolutely *count* —Edith Wharton⟩ RECKON (*on*) likewise connotes calculating or planning. In affirmative situations it is common in reference to the known or determined as of one nature or another ⟨the king scarcely knew *on* what members of his cabinet he could *reckon* —T.B.Macaulay⟩ BANK (*on*), which is the least formal in this series, may carry connotations from the noun *bank* (meaning "financial institution") and suggest the certainty of money in a bank. BANK (*on*) is wide in its use in applying to persons, things, facts, and ideas, and to either their general existence as such or their utility and benefit to the speaker ⟨today, as hitherto, we *bank on* war —J.H. Holmes⟩ ⟨you can *bank on* Jeeves —P.G.Wodehouse⟩ TRUST may or may not suggest more complete belief or confidence in on the basis of faith rather than empirical fact ⟨let us to Providence *trust* —A.H.Clough⟩ ⟨better not *trust* her instinct —George Meredith⟩ ⟨*trusting* to common sense as well as Allah —Aldous Huxley⟩ DEPEND (*on*) may suggest weakness or lack of forethought, invention, or self-sufficiency. It may apply to situations in which no alternate recourse or measure has been planned ⟨he was always getting himself into crusades, or feuds, or love, or debt, and *depended on* the woman to get him out —Henry Adams⟩

rem \ˈrem\ *n*, *pl* **rem** *or* **rems** [roentgen equivalent man] **:** the dosage of any ionizing radiation that will cause the same amount of biological injury to human tissue as one roentgen of X-ray or gamma-ray dosage — compare REP

rem *abbr* **1** remain; remainder **2** remark **3** remit; remitted; remittance **4** remove

remade *past of* REMAKE

remade milk *n* **:** RECONSTITUTED MILK

1re·main \rəˈmān, rē-\ *vb* -ED/-ING/-S [ME *remainen*, fr. MF *remanoir*, *remaindre*, fr. L *remanēre* to stay behind, be left, fr. *re-* + *manēre* to stay, remain — more at MANSION] *vi* **1 a :** to be a part not destroyed, taken away, or used up **:** be still extant, present, or available **:** be left when the rest is gone ⟨ruins . . . of the officers' quarters ~ —*Amer. Guide Series: Texas*⟩ ⟨the pulpy . . . substance ~*ing* after the juice is ground from sugarcane —*Amer. Guide Series: La.*⟩ ⟨in the two weeks that ~*ed* to us —Kenneth Roberts⟩ **b :** to be something yet to be shown, done, or treated ⟨how it will work ~*s* to be seen⟩ ⟨looked around to see what work ~*ed*⟩ ⟨it ~*s* to add that the author has read very widely in the subject —C.E.Bazell⟩ **2 a :** to stay in the same place or with the same person or group ⟨will ~ in town for two days⟩ ⟨the matter ~*ed* with Congress —A.G.Larke⟩; *specif* **:** to stay behind while others withdraw ⟨asked the student to ~ after school⟩ **b** *obs* **:** RESIDE, DWELL **3 :** to continue unchanged in form, condition, status, or quantity **:** continue to be ⟨the pact was to ~ in force for 50 years —*Americana Annual*⟩ **:** STAND ⟨population ~*s* at around eight hundred —Fred Zimmer⟩ ⟨stir well and let the mixture ~ until morning⟩ ⟨a lubricant that ~*s* liquid at low temperatures⟩ ⟨~ silent rather than sounding off —Stuart Chase⟩ ⟨~*s* primarily a livestock state —*Amer. Guide Series: Nev.*⟩ **4** *of land* **:** to stay or continue for the benefit of another than the grantor ⟨after life estate the land still ~*ed* for the grantor's children⟩ — see REMAINDER 1a **~** *vt*, *obs* **:** AWAIT **syn** see STAY

2remain \"\ *n* -s [ME, fr. MF, fr. *remaindre* to remain — more at ¹REMAIN] **1** *obs* **:** the state of remaining **:** STAY ⟨my here ~ in England —Shak.⟩ **2 :** a remaining part or trace — usu. used in pl. ⟨the crumpled ~*s* of stone chimneys —Frederick Nebel⟩ ⟨repacked the ~*s* of the supper —C.S. Forester⟩ ⟨fossil ~*s* of prehistoric animals —*Amer. Guide Series: Minn.*⟩ ⟨a female of advanced years with the ~*s* of irresistible beauty —G.B.Shaw⟩ **3 remains** *pl* **:** the works of a writer who has died; *esp* **:** writings left unpublished by a writer at his death ⟨edited his dead friend's literary ~*s*⟩ **4 remains** *pl* **:** a dead body ⟨the custom of filing past the open casket to view the ~*s*⟩ ⟨secondary burials sometimes comprise masses of bone with the ~*s* of several individuals —G.R. Willey⟩

1re·main·der \-də(r)\ *n* -s [ME, fr. AF, fr. MF *remaindre* to remain] **1 a :** an estate (as land) in expectancy that becomes an estate in possession upon the determination of a particular prior estate created at the same time and by the same instrument ⟨if land be conveyed to A for life, and on his death to B, A's life interest is a particular estate and B's interest is a ~⟩ — distinguished from *reversion* **b :** the right to succeed to a title or dignity upon the death of the holder ⟨the earl marshalship was granted anew . . . with many specific ~*s* —J.H.Round⟩; *specif* **:** the right of succession to a peerage assigned to a specified person or line of descent in default of male issue in the direct line ⟨living members in ~ to the title —*Burke's Peerage*⟩ **2 a :** a remaining group, part, or trace **:** REST ⟨half of whom are transported by regular bus service . . . and the ~ by private conveyances —H.W.H.King⟩ ⟨for the second year's work, and throughout the ~ of his course —*Bull. of Meharry Med. Coll.*⟩ **b :** the number left after subtraction or deduction; *specif* **:** the undivided part less or lower in degree than the divisor left after division **c** *obs* **:** a person remaining out of a number **3 a :** a book belonging to or forming a supply sold at a reduced price by the publisher after sales have become unprofitable ⟨guess that a half of all fiction books . . . and a quarter of the nonfiction end up as ~*s* —*N.Y. Times Bk. Rev.*⟩ **b :** a stamp of an unsold post office supply of a demonetized issue — usu. used in pl.

2remainder \"\ *adj* **1 :** not taken, used, or gone **:** LEFTOVER, REMAINING ⟨as dry as the ~ biscuit after a voyage —Shak.⟩ **2 :** of, forming, or selling publishers' remainders ⟨a ~ counter⟩ ⟨~ prices⟩

3remainder \"\ *vb* **remaindered; remaindered; remaindering** \-d(ə)riŋ\ **remainders** *vt* **1 :** to sell the unsold copies of (a publication) at a lowered price **2 :** to sell usu. at a discount the remaining supply of (a demonetized postage stamp) to collectors or dealers **~** *vi* **:** to sell remainders

remainder binding *n* **:** an inferior binding put (as by a jobber) on remainders sold unbound by the publisher

remainder cancellation *n* **:** a cancellation on a remainder stamp making it invalid for postal use and available as a philatelic item

re·main·der·man \=ˈ==mən\ *n*, *pl* **remaindermen** [*remainder* + *man*] **:** one who holds or is entitled to a legal remainder

remainder theorem *n* **:** a theorem in algebra: if $f(x)$ is a polynomial in x then the remainder on dividing $f(x)$ by $x-a$ is $f(a)$

1re·make \(ˈ)rē+\ *vt* [*re-* + *make*] **:** to give a different form to **:** TRANSFORM ⟨eastern Germany . . . is being *remade* according to the Soviet image —*Americana Annual*⟩ **:** REVISE ⟨~ their plans for the weekend —Josephine Y. Case⟩ — **re·maker** \"+\ *n*

2remake \ˈ=,=\ *n* **:** a refilmed version of a previously made motion picture

re·mak's fiber \ˈrāˌmäks-\ *n*, *usu cap R* [after Robert *Remak* †1865 Ger. physician, its discoverer] **:** an unmyelinated peripheral nerve fiber serving to conduct impulses that arise in pain receptors

re·man \(ˈ)rē+\ *vt* [*re-* + *man*] **1 :** to man (as a ship or gun) again or anew **2 :** to imbue with courage or manliness again

re·man·ci·pate \rəˈman(t)səˌpāt\ *vt* [L *remancipatus*, past part. of *remancipare* to remancipate, fr. *re-* + *mancipare* to deliver as property, transfer — more at MANCIPATE] *Roman law* **:** to reconvey (a person or thing) by mancipation to the mancipant or to a third person — **re·man·ci·pa·tion** \=,==ˈpāshən\ *n*

1re·mand \rəˈmand, rē-, -maa(ə)nd, -månd\ *vt* -ED/-ING/-S [ME *remaunden*, fr. MF *remander*, fr. LL *remandare* to send back word, fr. L *re-* + *mandare* to hand over, order, send word — more at MANDATE] **1 :** to cause to go back to a place (as by an authoritative command) **:** order back **:** consign again **2 :** to return (a case) from one court to another esp. lower court or from a court to an administrative agency **3 :** to send (a person charged with a crime) back into custody by court order (as pending trial) ⟨the judge discharges him or ~*s* him⟩ **:** to turn (a prisoner) over for continued detention ⟨she temporarily ~*ed* him to . . . New York's detention home for boys —Marjorie Rittwagen⟩ ⟨those . . . in need of further treatment are usually ~*ed* to state or private institutions —S.R.Cutolo⟩

2remand \"\ *n* -s **:** the act of remanding or state of being remanded **:** an order to remand an accused person ⟨a prisoner appearing on ~⟩ **:** detention under an order to remand ⟨use ~ for studying the child's background and attitude⟩

remand center *n* **:** a British institution to which the court may commit for temporary detention juvenile offenders too unruly or depraved for a remand home

remand home *n* **:** a British institution to which juvenile offenders may be committed by the court for temporary detention **:** DETENTION HOME ⟨children from 8 to 16 sent to *remand homes* for periods up to one month⟩ — compare BORSTAL

rem·a·nence \ˈremənən(t)s\ *n* -s [²*remanent*, after such pairs as E *excellent: excellence*] **1 :** the property of being residual or enduring **2 :** the magnetic induction remaining in a magnetized substance when the external magnetizing force has become zero — compare COERCIVE FORCE

1remanent *n* -s [L *remanent-, remanens*, pres. part. of *remanēre* to be left, remain — more at REMAIN] *obs* **:** REMAINDER, REMNANT, RESIDUE

2rem·a·nent \-nənt\ *adj* [ME, fr. L *remanent-, remanens*] **1** *obs* **:** PERMANENT, LASTING, ENDURING **2 :** left after the rest has been used, removed, done **:** REMAINING, RESIDUAL ⟨~ sugar in new wine⟩ **3** *chiefly Scot* **:** SUPPLEMENTARY, FURTHER **4 :** of, relating to, or characterized by magnetic remanence

remanent magnetism *n* **:** RESIDUAL MAGNETISM

rem·a·net \ˈreməˌnet, *usu* -ed·+V\ *n* -s [L, it is left, remains, 3rd sing. pres. indic. of *remanēre* to be left, remain] **:** something remaining; *specif* **:** a case or proceeding the hearing of which is postponed

re·ma·nié \rəˌmänˈyā\ *n* -s [F, past part. of *remanier* to rework, rehandle, fr. *re-* + *manier* to handle, fr. OF, fr. *main* hand, fr. L *manus* — more at MANUAL] **:** a part or fragment (as a pebble or fossil) of an older formation incorporated in a younger deposit **:** RELICT, RESIDUAL

1re·manufacture \(ˈ)rē+\ *n* [*re-* + *manufacture*, n.] **:** the process of remanufacturing ⟨paper . . . for ~ into shell wrappings —*Literary Digest*⟩

2remanufacture \"\ *vt* [*re-* + *manufacture*, v.] **:** to manufacture (used or scrap material) into a new product ⟨~ calculating machines⟩ ⟨~ the refuse of cotton and woolen yarn⟩

re·margin \(ˈ)rē+\ *vb* [*re-* + *margin*] *vt* **1 :** to put a fresh margin on (the leaves of a book) **2 :** to make good the margin on ⟨~ a loan⟩ **~** *vi* **:** to replenish or add to an existing margin (as one decreased by a change in prices)

1re·mark \rəˈmärk, rē-, -mȧk\ *vb* [F *remarquer*, fr. MF, fr. *re-* + *marquer* to mark — more at MARQUE] *vt* **1** *obs* **a :** to mark in a notable manner **:** distinguish clearly ⟨his manacles ~ him; there he sits —John Milton⟩ **b :** to direct attention to **:** point out **2 :** to take notice of **:** OBSERVE, PERCEIVE, NOTE ⟨a passer-by would have ~*ed* an elderly shopkeeper bent apparently on a day in the country —John Buchan⟩ ⟨~*ed* no stiffness in her speech, but thought she spoke in music —William Black⟩ **3 :** to express as an observation or comment in speech or writing **:** STATE, SAY — usu. used with a direct or indirect quotation ⟨"Nice day!" he ~*ed*⟩ ⟨a metropolitan newspaper ~*ed* that no one today hopes for progress —Robert Bierstedt⟩ **~** *vi* **:** to make an observation or comment — used with *on* or *upon* ⟨~*ed* on the prosperous look of the countryside⟩ **syn** see SEE

2remark \"\ *n* [F *remarque*, fr. MF, fr. *remarquer* to remark] **1** *obs* **:** the quality or state of deserving special consideration **:** IMPORTANCE **2 :** the act of remarking **:** NOTICE, OBSERVATION **3 a :** the expression in speech or writing of something remarked or noticed **:** the mention of that which deserves attention or notice ⟨worthy of special ~ in a social history —G.M. Trevelyan⟩ **b :** a casual expression of an opinion or judgment ⟨began to pass ~*s* at the new guy —Harvey Granite⟩ **4** *obs* **a :** a notable sign or characteristic **:** an indicative mark **b :** TOKEN, INDICATION **c :** something noteworthy

re·mark·abil·i·ty \=,=kəˈbiləd·ē, -ləte, -i\ *n* **:** the quality or state of being remarkable

1re·mark·able \=ˈ=kəbəl\ *adj* [F *remarquable*, fr. *remarquer* to remark + *-able*] **1 a :** worthy of being or likely to be noticed **b :** UNCOMMON, EXTRAORDINARY ⟨~ for his generosity⟩ ⟨the ~ features of a place⟩ ⟨~ beauty⟩ **2** *obs* **:** that can be seen or observed **:** DISCERNIBLE **syn** see NOTICEABLE

2remarkable \"\ *n* -ES *archaic* **:** a remarkable thing or occurrence

re·mark·able·ness *n* -ES **:** the quality or state of being remarkable

re·mark·ably \-kəblē, -li\ *adv* **:** in a remarkable manner or to a remarkable degree **:** UNUSUALLY, EXTRAORDINARILY ⟨~ tall trees⟩ ⟨~ few fences⟩

re·mark·ed·ly \-kədlē, -li\ *adv* [*remarked* (past part. of ¹*remark*) + *-ly*] **:** MARKEDLY, NOTABLY ⟨the megalithic relics . . . have ~ constant features —Lancelot Hogben⟩

re·mark·er \rəˈmärkər, rē-, -mȧkə(r\ *n* -s **:** one that remarks

re·marque *also* **re·mark** \rəˈmärk, rē-, -mȧk\ *n* -s [F *remarque* remark — more at REMARK] **1 :** a drawn, etched, or incised scribble or sketch done on the margin of a plate or stone and removed before the regular printing **2 :** REMARQUE PROOF

remarque proof *n* **:** a proof taken before remarques have been removed

re·marriage \(ˈ)rē+\ *n* [*re-* + *marriage*] **:** an act or instance of remarrying **:** the state of being remarried ⟨lost the inheritance by ~⟩

re·marry \"+\ *vb* [*re-* + *marry*] **:** to marry again ⟨were *remarried* in a religious ceremony after the civil marriage⟩ ⟨the mothers . . . had *remarried* soulless loafers who treated the children's pensions as a life income —*Sydney (Australia) Bull.*⟩ ⟨~ his divorced wife after a reconciliation⟩ ⟨waited a year after his wife's death before he *remarried*⟩

re·match \'rē,mach\ *n* [*re-* + *match*] **:** a second match between the same two sports contestants or teams **:** a return match

re·ma·te \rā'mätā\ *n* -s [Sp, lit., end (fr. its usually being the last of a series of pases), fr. *rematar* to finish off, end, fr. *re-* (fr. L) + *matar* to kill, perh. fr. L *mattus* stupid, drunk — more at MAT] **:** a whirling pase used by a matador to fix the position of the bull

rem·a·zol dye \'remə,zōl-, -zōl-\ *n, usu cap R* [origin unknown] **:** any of several fiber-reactive dyes — see DYE table I

rem·ba·ran·ga \,rembə'raŋgə\ *n, pl* **rembaranga** *or* **rembarangas** *usu cap* **1 :** an aboriginal people of central Arnhem-land, Australia **2 :** a member of the Rembaranga people

rem·brandt \'rem,brant\ *n* -s *often cap* [after *Rembrandt* van Rijn †1669 Dutch painter] **:** a dark grayish brown that is very slightly yellower and paler than Liberia and slightly less strong than average chocolate brown

rem·brandt·esque \¦rem,brant·¦esk, -n·¦te-\ *adj, usu cap* [*Rembrandt* van Rijn + E *-esque*] **:** resembling the style or manner of the Dutch painter Rembrandt (as in his use of strongly contrasted light and shade) ⟨*Rembrandtesque* setting for the moving throng of figures —Mrs Humphry Ward⟩

rem·brandt·ish \'rem,brantish\ *adj, usu cap* [*Rembrandt* van Rijn + E *-ish*] **:** REMBRANDTESQUE

rem·brandt·ism \-nt·,izəm, -n·,ti-\ *n* -s *usu cap* [*Rembrandt* van Rijn + E *-ism*] **:** Rembrandtesque style

rembrandt's madder *n, often cap R* [after *Rembrandt* van Rijn] **:** ANTIQUE RED

rembrandt tulip *n, usu cap R* **:** any of various Darwin tulips with blotched or mottled coloring that result from color breaks

re·mede *or* **re·mead** \rə'mēd\ *n* [ME, fr. MF, fr. L *remedium* remedy] *chiefly Scot* **:** REMEDY, REDRESS

re·me·di·able \rə'mēdēəbəl, rē'-\ *adj* [ME, fr. MF, fr. L *remediabilis*, fr. *remediare* to remedy + *-abilis* -able] **:** capable of being remedied ⟨not a crime but only a ∼ blunder —T.E. Ennis⟩ ⟨children with ∼ defects in vision⟩ — **re·me·di·a·ble·ness** *n* -ES — **re·me·di·a·bly** \-blē, -li\ *adv*

re·me·di·al \-dēəl\ *adj* [LL *remedialis*, fr. L *remedium* remedy + *-alis* -al] **1 :** affording a remedy **:** intended for a remedy or for the removal or abatement of a disease or of an evil ⟨∼ surgery⟩ ⟨∼ legislation⟩ — compare DECLARATORY **2 :** concerned with the correction of faulty study habits, the improvement of skills imperfectly learned, and the raising of a pupil's general competence ⟨∼ reading⟩ ⟨∼ instruction⟩ — **re·me·di·al·ly** \-əlē, -li\ *adv*

remedial loan society *n* **:** a bank or other financial institution that lends small sums to needy borrowers at a relatively moderate rate of interest

remedial right *n* **:** a right (as of self-defense) arising on a violation of and for the protection of a substantive right

remediate *adj* [L *remedium* remedy + E *-ate*] *obs* **:** REMEDIAL

re·me·di·a·tion \rə,mēdē'āshən\ *n* -s [L *remediation-*, *remediatio*, fr. *remediatus* (past part. of *remediare* to remedy) + *-ion-*, *-io* -ion] **:** the act or process of remedying ⟨∼ of reading difficulties⟩

rem·e·di·less \'remədēləs, -dəl-\ *adj* [ME *remedilesse*, fr. ¹*remedy* + *-lesse* -less] **1 a** *obs* **:** lacking hope of assistance or relief **:** being beyond help **b :** having no legal remedy **2 :** not admitting of remedy **:** IRREMEDIABLE, IRREPARABLE — **rem·e·di·less·ly** *adv* — **rem·e·di·less·ness** *n* -ES

¹**rem·e·dy** \-dē, -di\ *n* -ES [ME *remedie*, fr. AF, fr. L *remedium*, fr. *remederi* to heal again, cure, fr. *re-* + *mederi* to heal — more at MEDICAL] **1 :** something that relieves or cures a disease **:** a medicine or application that serves or helps to terminate disease and restore health **2 :** something that corrects or counteracts an evil **:** CORRECTIVE, COUNTERACTIVE, REPARATION ⟨whose simple ∼ for discontent was the wall and the firing-squad —H.J.Laski⟩ **3 :** TOLERANCE 3a **4 :** the legal means to recover a right or to prevent or obtain redress for a wrong **:** the relief (as damages, restitution, specific performance, an injunction) that may be given by a court for a wrong **5 :** a half-holiday in an English school

syn CURE, MEDICINE, MEDICAMENT, MEDICATION, SPECIFIC, PHYSIC: REMEDY applies to a substance or treatment that is known or regarded as effective in bringing about recovery or restoration of health or the normal functioning of the body ⟨patent medicines and cold *remedies*⟩ ⟨a toothache *remedy*⟩ ⟨much has been written on the subject of fear and many inspirational and emotional *remedies* have been suggested —W.J. Reilly⟩ ⟨a homely *remedy* is to rub a moist cake of carbolic soap over the skin —F.D.Smith & Barbara Wilcox⟩ ⟨psychoanalysis as a *remedy* for mental ills⟩ CURE, more positive than REMEDY in implying complete recovery or restoration of health, is a common term to designate anything advocated as being or thought to be conducive to complete recovery ⟨no known specific *cure* for tuberculosis —*Therapeutic Notes*⟩ ⟨the climate was advertised during the eighties as a *cure* for tuberculosis —*Amer. Guide Series: Minn.*⟩ ⟨reaching into the medicine cabinet for a *cure* for the baby —W.J.Reilly⟩ ⟨all current surgical intervention in mental disease is not proposed as a *cure* —*Collier's Yr. Bk.*⟩ MEDICINE is the ordinary term for any substance or preparation taken internally in treating a disturbance of the normal functions of the body ⟨most *medicines* are alleviative in their action and not definitely curative —A.C. Morrison⟩ ⟨the witch doctor is there to give them some magic *medicine* to drink —J.G.Frazer⟩ MEDICAMENT OR MEDICATION are general terms esp. used by doctors and pharmacists for all medicinal substances and preparations whether taken internally or applied externally ⟨doctors admit that they can do more for their patients now that they do not have to worry about the size of their bills and the cost of *medicaments* —*New Statesman & Nation*⟩ ⟨made the rounds of her five patients with a *medicament* of her own — a quart of Chesterfield's best bonded bourbon —J.A.Maxwell⟩ ⟨prescribe several kinds of *medication* hoping to hit on a cure⟩ SPECIFIC is applied to something, usu. a drug, known to be effective in curing a specific disease ⟨various rheumatism *specifics* containing cinchophen, found to have notably injurious effects on the liver —*Encyc. Americana*⟩ PHYSIC is the archaic equivalent of MEDICINE ⟨this first revolt against authority took the form of refusing *physic* when he was ill —Agnes Repplier⟩; in modern use it has specialized to become synonymous with *purgative* or *cathartic*.

²**remedy** \"\ *vt* -ED/-ING/-ES [ME *remedien* to provide remedy for, fr. MF *remedier*, fr. L *remediare*, fr. L *remedium*] **1** *obs* **:** to give legal redress to **:** render justice to **2 :** to provide or serve as a remedy for **:** RELIEVE, REPAIR ⟨certain mental blocks can be *remedied* —Stuart Chase⟩ ⟨some defect in total mobilization to be *remedied* in time —H.W.Neuberg⟩ **syn** see CORRECT, CURE

re·meid \rə'mēd\ *var of* REMEDE

¹**re·melt** \(')rē¦melt\ *vt* [*re-* + *melt*] **:** to melt (as a metal) again

²**remelt** \'=,=\ *n* **:** something remelted (as a metal) or to be remelted (as sugar)

re·mem·ber \rə'membə(r), rē'-\ *vb* **remembered; remembered; remembering** \-b(ə)riŋ\ **remembers** [ME *remembren*, fr. MF *remembrer*, fr. LL *rememorari*, fr. *re-* + *memorari* to be mindful of, fr. L *memor* mindful — more at MEMORY] *vt* **1 :** to have (a notion or idea) come into the mind again as previously perceived, known, or felt **:** have a renewed apprehension of **:** bring to mind again **:** think of again ⟨∼ events of one's childhood⟩ ⟨racked his brain to ∼ the name⟩ **2** *archaic* **a :** to take thought of ⟨now, I ∼ me, I'm married —William Congreve⟩ **b :** to put in mind **:** bring to recollect ⟨∼*ing* them the truth of what they themselves know —John Milton⟩ **3 :** to hold in memory with some feeling or intention **:** keep the recollection of: as **a :** to keep in mind so as to bestow attention or consideration upon **:** be continually thoughtful or regardful of ⟨∼ one's friends at Christmas⟩ ⟨∼ the Sabbath day to keep it holy —Exod 20:8 (RSV)⟩ **b** (1) **:** to keep in mind as deserving a reward (2) **:** REWARD ⟨was ∼*ed* in the will⟩ **4 :** to hold or bear in mind **:** retain in the memory ⟨∼ the dates until after the examination⟩ **5 a :** to recall to the mind of another **b :** to convey greetings from ⟨∼ me to your father when you get home⟩ **6 :** MENTION, RECORD, COMMEMORATE ⟨tradition and history have not ∼*ed* their names —V.L.Parrington⟩ ∼ *vi* **1 :** to exercise or have the power of memory ⟨some ∼ better than others⟩ ⟨give him time to ∼⟩ **2 :** to have a recollection or remembrance ⟨ask your grandmother about it — she'll ∼⟩ — sometimes used with *of* ⟨you'll find conditions very different to what you ∼ of —Henry Green⟩

syn RECOLLECT, RECALL, REMIND, REMINISCE, BETHINK, MIND: REMEMBER may indicate an effortless or unwilled permitting of something held in one's memory to occupy one's attention, vividly or not ⟨when people talked about things they could *remember* Matey always wondered which kind of *remembering* they meant — the kind that was just a sort of knowing how something in the past had happened or the other kind when suddenly everything seemed to be happening all over again —Dorothy C. Fisher⟩ RECOLLECT may differ from REMEMBER in involving a bringing back, sometimes with conscious effort, of something of which one has not thought for a time ⟨I can *recollect* my reply to the postscript, but not the whole letter —W.F.DeMorgan⟩ ⟨I had begun by making simple notes after our various conversations on the ship, so that I shouldn't forget details; later, as certain aspects of the thing began to grip me, I had the urge to do more, to fashion the written and *recollected* fragments into a single narrative —James Hilton⟩ Used of persons, RECALL may suggest a process whereby the mind is summoned to bring back in toto rather than slowly reassembling; used of things, it indicates evoking or calling forth a memory ⟨"had you any conversation with the prisoner on that passage across the Channel?" "Yes, sir." "*Recall* it." In the midst of a profound stillness, she faintly began —Charles Dickens⟩ ⟨that tree always awakened pleasant memories, *recalling* a garden in the South of France where he used to visit young cousins —Willa Cather⟩ REMIND suggests the evoking of something forgotten or hard to think of again, sometimes by way of admonition; when used reflexively of persons it indicates a conscious jogging of memory ⟨the young soldier was *reminded* by his sister of their childhood hideout —*Amer. Guide Series: La.*⟩ ⟨the drone of the remorse-mongers as they *remind* him that he is partially to blame —E.M.Forster⟩ ⟨might *remind* ourselves that criticism is as inevitable as breathing —T.S.Eliot⟩ REMINISCE may imply a casual, unguided, and perhaps nostalgic consideration of the past ⟨cut me short to *reminisce* of his schoolmates —Hervey Allen⟩ ⟨listening to papa *reminisce* how he had gone around Thanksgiving Day as a boy —Betty Smith⟩ BETHINK applies to thinking back and recollecting with reflection ⟨he *bethought* him of certain meals his mother had cooked at home —Stephen Crane⟩ MIND, close in meaning and suggestion to RECOLLECT, often seems dialectal or quaint in suggestion ⟨I can *mind* her well as a nursing mother — a comely woman in her day —A.T.Quiller-Couch⟩

re·mem·ber·able \-b(ə)rəbəl\ *adj* [*remember* + *-able*] **:** capable of being remembered **:** MEMORABLE ⟨describe our feelings in ∼ words —Aldous Huxley⟩

re·mem·ber·er \-b(ə)rə(r)\ *n* -s [*remember* + *-er*] **:** one that remembers ⟨the forgetter . . . has fewer facts but many more ideas than the ∼ —Odell Shepard⟩

re·mem·ber·ing·ly *adv* [*remembering* (pres. part. of *remember*) + *-ly*] **:** in a remembering manner

re·mem·brance \rə'membrən(t)s, rē'- *also* -bər-\ *n* -s [ME, fr. MF, fr. *remembrer* to remember + *-ance*] **1 :** the state of bearing in mind ⟨Roman soldiers . . . keep the Jews in ∼ of their provincial status —L.C.Douglas⟩ **2 a :** the ability to remember **:** the function of memory **:** present consciousness of past experience ⟨paints largely from ∼, from a wealth of rich experiences —Henry Miller⟩ **b :** the period over which one's memory extends **:** the reach of personal knowledge **3 :** an act of recalling to mind ⟨put in a fresh rage by the ∼ of their past offenses⟩ **4 :** a memory of a person, thing, or event ⟨how the rest of the night was passed . . . I have only the dimmest ∼ —John Burroughs⟩ **5 a :** something that serves to keep in or bring to mind **:** REMINDER, SOUVENIR ⟨the wreck of the armor-plated vessel . . . is a ∼ of the war —*Saturday Rev.*⟩ **b :** an act or thing evoking or honoring the memory of a person or event **:** COMMEMORATION, MEMORIAL ⟨the sabbath is to be kept in ∼ of the deliverance from Egypt —G.E.Wright⟩ ⟨in lieu of flowers ∼*s* may be made —*N. Y. Herald Tribune*⟩ **c :** a greeting or gift recalling or expressing friendship or affection ⟨give my ∼*s* to them⟩ ⟨shopping for some little ∼ to send her friend at Christmas⟩ **syn** see MEMORY

remembrance day *n, usu cap R&D, Brit* **:** ARMISTICE DAY

re·mem·branc·er \-nsə(r)\ *n* -s [ME, fr. AF, fr. MF *remembrance* + AF *-er*] **1** *usu cap* **:** any of several officials of the Court of Exchequer in England having orig. the duty of bringing various matters to the attention of the proper persons — see KING'S REMEMBRANCER, QUEEN'S REMEMBRANCER **2** *usu cap* **:** an official of the City of London who represents that corporation before parliamentary committees and at council and treasury boards — called also *City Remembrancer* **3 :** a person who brings things to the mind of another **:** one that reminds **4 :** a thing that serves to bring to or keep in mind **:** REMINDER, MEMENTO, MEMORIAL

re·mem·o·rate \rə'memə,rāt\ *vi* -ED/-ING/-S [LL *rememoratus*, past part. of *rememorari* to remember — more at REMEMBER] *obs* **:** REMIND, REMEMBER — **re·mem·o·ra·tion** \=,==='rāshən\ *n* -s *archaic*

remercy *vt* [ME *remercien*, fr. MF *remercier*, fr. *re-* + *mercier* to thank, fr. *merci* favor, mercy, thanks — more at MERCY] *obs* **:** THANK

re·mex \'rē,meks\ *n, pl* **rem·i·ges** \'remə,jēz\ [NL *remig-*, *remex*, fr. L, oarsman, fr. *remus* oar + *-ig-* (fr. *agere* to drive) — more at ROW, AGENT] **:** a primary or secondary quill feather of the wing of a bird

re·mi \'rē,mī\ *n pl, usu cap* [L] **:** an ancient people in Gaul forming a division of the Belgae and allied to Caesar in the campaign of 57 B.C.

remi- *comb form* [L, fr. *remus* oar — more at ROW] **:** oar ⟨*remiform*⟩ ⟨*remiped*⟩

rem·i·cle \'reməkəl\ *n* -s [NL *remiculum*, irreg. dim. of *remex*] **:** a small remex

re·mig·i·al \rə'mijēəl\ *adj* [NL *remig-*, *remex* + E *-ial*] **1 :** of or relating to the remiges **2** [NL *remigium* + E *-al*] **:** of or relating to a remigium

re·mig·i·um \-ēəm\ *n* -s [NL, fr. L, oarage, fr. *remig-*, *remex* oarsman — more at REMEX] **:** the anterior rigid part of the wing of an insect that is acted on by the muscles and is the chief effector of flight

rem·i·grant \'reməgrənt\ *n* [L *remigrant-*, *remigrans*, pres. part. of *remigrare*] **:** a migrant who returns; *specif* **:** an aphid of the winged generation that returns to its former host

re·migrate \(')rē+\ *vi* [L *remigratus*, past part. of *remigrare* to remigrate, fr. *re-* + *migrare* to migrate — more at MIGRATE] **:** to migrate again or back — **re·migration** \(¦)rē+\ *n*

re·mij·ia \rə'mijēə\ *n, cap* [NL, fr. *Remijo*, 19th cent. surgeon + NL *-ia*] **:** a genus of tropical So. American shrubs and trees (family Rubiaceae) having leaves with large stipules and racemes of small white woolly flowers — see CUPREA BARK

re·militarization \(¦)rē+\ *n* [*re-* + *militarization*] **1 :** the act or process of remilitarizing **2 :** the state of being remilitarized

re·militarize \(')rē+\ *vt* [*re-* + *militarize*] **:** to equip again with military forces and defenses

re·mind \rə'mīnd, rē'-\ *vt* [*re-* + *mind*] **1** *obs* **:** to recall to mind **2 :** to put (one) in mind of something **:** cause to remember ⟨∼ him to stop for groceries⟩ ⟨a man whose appearance ∼*ed* her of her father⟩ **syn** see REMEMBER

re·mind·er \-də(r)\ *n* -s [*remind* + *-er*] **:** one that reminds: as **a :** something that reminds by association ⟨areas of rubble that stand as grim ∼*s* of the war⟩ ⟨occasional sawmills, ∼*s* of the once-active lumber industry —*Amer. Guide Series: Maine*⟩ **b :** a device designed to prompt or aid the memory ⟨tied a string around his finger as a ∼⟩

re·mind·ful \-dfəl\ *adj* [*remind* + *-ful*] **1 :** MINDFUL, REGARDFUL **2 :** tending to remind **:** SUGGESTIVE, EVOCATIVE ⟨the river's scarred sides . . . are ever ∼ of the destruction its floodwaters have wrought —*Amer. Guide Series: Texas*⟩

re·mind·ing·ly *adv* [*reminding* (pres. part. of *remind*) + *-ly*] **:** in a reminding way

rem·i·nisce \,remə'nis\ *vb* -ED/-ING/-S [back-formation fr. *reminiscence*] *vi* **:** to indulge in reminiscence ⟨got to *reminiscing* about the old days —F.D.Roosevelt⟩ ∼ *vt* **:** to write or say in reminiscence **syn** see REMEMBER

rem·i·nis·cence \-sᵊn(t)s\ *n* -s [MF or LL; MF *reminiscence*, fr. LL *reminiscentia* (trans. of Gk *anamnēsis*, lit., recollection, remembrance), fr. L *reminiscent-*, *reminiscens* + *-ia* — more at REMINISCENT] **1 :** the apprehension of a form (as an idea) as if it had been known in a previous existence **2 a :** the recall to mind of a long-forgotten experience or fact **b :** the process or practice of thinking or telling about past experiences ⟨after another quarter of an hour of ∼ they had got around to the things that had happened to each of them since they had last met —Mary Austin⟩ **3 a :** a remembered experience **b :** an oral or written account of a memorable experience ⟨the ∼ of his trip into the family vault . . . borders on the macabre —F.E.Coenen⟩ — often used in pl. ⟨published the ∼*s* of the old settler⟩ **4 :** something (as a phrase, custom, feature) so suggestive of something else as to be regarded as an unconscious repetition, imitation, or survival **5 :** improvement of the memory for an experience despite the lapse of time since that experience **syn** see MEMORY

¹**rem·i·nis·cent** \¦==¦nisᵊnt\ *adj* [L *reminiscent-*, *reminiscens*, pres. part. of *reminisci* to recall to mind, remember, fr. *re-* + *-minisci* (fr. the root of *ment-*, *mens* mind) — more at MIND] **1 :** of the character of or relating to reminiscence; *also* **:** having or marked by reminiscence of something previously known or experienced ⟨some other state of existence of which we have been previously conscious and are now ∼ —William Hamilton †1856⟩ **2 :** given to or indulging in reminiscences **:** characterized by reminiscing **:** abounding in reminiscences ⟨∼ old men⟩ ⟨a ∼ mood⟩ ⟨a ∼ essay⟩ **3 :** that reminds one of something previously seen or known **:** SUGGESTIVE ⟨dignity and elegance ∼ of powdered ladies and gentlemen of the eighteenth century —*Amer. Guide Series: N.H.*⟩

²**reminiscent** \"\ *n* -s **:** a relater of reminiscences

rem·i·nis·cen·tial \¦remənə¦senchəl\ *adj* [LL *reminiscentia* reminiscence + E *-al*] **:** REMINISCENT ⟨the chatty, anecdotal, ∼ record of persons and places —Leon Edel⟩ — **rem·i·nis·cen·tial·ly** \-chəlē\ *adv*

rem·i·nis·cent·ly *adv* **:** in a reminiscent manner ⟨talked ∼ of his early struggles⟩

rem·i·nis·cer \,remə'nisə(r)\ *n* -s **:** one that reminisces

rem·i·nis·ce·re sunday \¦remə¦nisərē-\ *n, usu cap R&S* [L *reminiscere* remember, imper. of *reminisci*; fr. the first word of the Introit for the day — more at REMINISCENT] **:** the second Sunday in Lent

rem·i·nis·cing·ly *adv* [*reminiscing* (pres. part. of *reminisce*) + *-ly*] **:** REMINISCENTLY

re·mint \(')rē+\ *vt* [*re-* + *mint*] **:** to mint (an old coin) again **:** RECOIN; *also* **:** to resume the minting of (an obsolete coin)

¹**rem·i·ped** \'remə,ped\ *n* -s [F *rémipède*, fr. L *remiped-*, *remipes* oar-footed, fr. *remi-* + *ped-*, *pes* foot — more at FOOT] **:** a crustacean or insect with feet or legs used as oars

²**remiped** \"\ *adj, of a crustacean or insect* **:** having feet or legs that are used as oars

¹**re·mise** \rə'mīz, rē'-\ *n* -s [ME, fr. MF, fr. *remis* (past part. of *remettre* to put back, fr. L *remittere* to send back), fr. L *remissus*, past part. of *remittere* — more at REMIT] **1** *archaic* **:** a legal surrender or release (as of a claim) **2** *obs* **:** a remittance of money **3 a :** a carriage house **b :** a livery carriage superior to a hackney **4 :** the second of two fencing thrusts delivered on the same lunge (as on failure of the opponent to riposte)

²**remise** \"\ *vb* -ED/-ING/-S [ME *remisen*, partly fr. MF *remis*, past part. of *remettre* to put back, partly fr. ¹*remise*] *vt* **1** *obs* **:** to send or put back **:** REPLACE, RETURN **2 :** to give, grant, or release a claim to **:** make over or surrender by deed ∼ *vi* **:** to make a remise in fencing

re·miss \rə'mis, rē'-\ *adj* [ME, fr. L *remissus* slack, loose, fr. past part. of *remittere* to let go back, relax — more at REMIT] **1** *obs* **a :** LIQUEFIED, DISSOLVED **b :** DILUTED, FAINT, PALE **2 :** negligent in the performance of one's work, duty, or duties **:** CARELESS, INATTENTIVE, SLACK ⟨a ∼ correspondent⟩ ⟨∼ in paying one's bills⟩ **3 a :** manifesting lack of energy or care or due strictness **:** unduly lenient **:** LAZY, LANGUID ⟨in one's ∼ hours⟩ ⟨∼ discipline⟩ **b :** showing neglect or inattention **:** negligently performed **:** LAX ⟨the service in this hotel is very ∼⟩ **4** *obs* **:** GENTLE, MILD, MODERATE, RELAXED **syn** see NEGLIGENT

re·miss·ibil·i·ty \rə,misə'bilədē\ *or* **re·miss·ible·ness** *n* -ES [*remissible* + *-ity*, *-ness*] **:** the quality or state of being remissible

re·miss·ible \rə'misəbəl\ *adj* [MF or LL; MF *remissible*, fr. LL *remissibilis*, fr. L *remissus* (past part. of *remittere* to remit) + *-ibilis* -ible] **:** that may be forgiven ⟨∼ sins⟩ — **re·miss·ibly** \-blē\ *adv*

re·mis·sion \rə'mishən, rē'-\ *n* -s [ME, fr. OF, fr. L *remission-*, *remissio*, fr. *remissus* (past part. of *remittere* to remit) + *-ion-*, *-io* -ion] **:** the act of remitting: as **a :** the act of pardoning sin or offense **:** FORGIVENESS ⟨∼ of his sins through the sacrament of penance⟩ **b** (1) **:** cancellation or relinquishment of the whole or a part of a financial obligation ⟨tax ∼*s*⟩ (2) **:** the voluntary release of a debt or claim to a debtor or person liable by a creditor or claimant having legal capacity to alienate **c :** pardon granted (as by the British parliament) for a legal offense **d** (1) **:** relief from a forfeiture or penalty (as by the surrender by the government to a former owner of property forfeited for violation of revenue laws) (2) **:** the act or procedure of so restoring property or of so remitting a penalty **e :** a temporary abatement of the symptoms of a disease — distinguished from *intermission*

remission thursday *n, usu cap R&T* **:** MAUNDY THURSDAY

re·mis·sive \rə'misiv\ *adj* [ML *remissivus*, fr. L *remissus* + *-ivus* -ive] **1** *obs* **:** REMISS **2 :** granting or bringing about remission or pardon **3 :** causing or permitting abatement **4 :** marked by diminution or abatement — **re·mis·sive·ly** \-sᵊvlē\ *adv* — **re·mis·sive·ness** \-sivnəs\ *n* -ES

re·miss·ly *adv* **:** in a remiss manner

re·miss·ness *n* -ES **:** the quality or state of being remiss

¹**re·mit** \rə'mit, rē'-, *usu* -id·+V\ *vb* **remitted; remitted; remitting; remits** [ME *remitten*, fr. L *remittere* to let go back, send back, relax, give up, forgive, fr. *re-* + *mittere* to let go, send — more at SMITE] *vt* **1 a** (1) **:** to release one from the guilt or penalty of **:** PARDON, FORGIVE ⟨held that God had granted to . . . the apostles and through them to the priests the power to ∼ sins —K.S.Latourette⟩ (2) *obs* **:** to set free (as a prisoner) **:** RELEASE **b :** to refrain from exacting (as a payment) ⟨the rents of the husbandman and other taxes were *remitted* —James Mill⟩ **c :** to cancel or refrain from inflicting (a penalty) ⟨in sentences involving loss of pay and confinement, the loss of pay is frequently *remitted* —*Naval Orientation*⟩ **d :** to give relief from (suffering) ⟨grace that turned staleness sweet, peace that *remitted* pain —Edmund Wilson⟩ **2 a :** to lay aside (a mood or disposition) partly or wholly **b** *obs* **:** to give up (a right or possession) **:** SURRENDER, RESIGN **c :** to desist from (an activity) **d :** to let (as attention, diligence) slacken **:** MITIGATE, RELAX **3 a :** to submit or refer (something) for consideration, judgment, decision or action esp. to one in authority ⟨∼ the question to a special committee⟩; *specif* **:** REMAND 2 **b :** REMAND 3 **c :** to refer (a person) for information or help (as to a book or person) **d :** to refer, assign, or allot to **4 :** to restore or consign to a former status or condition; *specif* **:** to restore to a former and more valid title **5 :** to put off **:** POSTPONE, DEFER ⟨∼ consideration of the matter until the next session⟩ **6 :** to send (money) to a person or place (as in payment of a demand, account, draft) ∼ *vi* **1 a :** to abate in force or intensity **:** MODERATE **b** *of a disease or abnormality* **:** to abate symptoms for a period **:** be remittent or go into a remission **2 :** to send money (as in payment) ⟨please ∼ promptly by check or money order⟩ **syn** see SEND

²**remit** \"\ *n* -s **:** an act of remitting or a matter, cause, or proceeding remitted to another person or authority for consideration or judgment

re·mit·ment \-itmənt\ *n* -s [*remit* + *-ment*] **1 :** an act of remitting **2 :** a sum of money remitted

re·mit·ta·ble \-id·əbəl\ *adj* [*remit* + *-able*] **:** that may be remitted

re·mit·tal \-d·ᵊl\ *n* -s [*remit* + *-al*] **:** REMISSION

re·mit·tance \rə'mitᵊn(t)s, rē'-\ *n* -s [*remit* + *-ance*] **1 a :** a sum of money sent to another person or place **b :** an instrument by which money is remitted **2 :** transmittal of money (as to a distant place)

remittance man *n* **:** a person living on a remittance; *esp* **:** one living away from the British Isles but subsisting chiefly on remittances from home

re·mit·tee \rə,mi'tē\ *n* -s [*remit* + *-ee*] **:** one to whom a remittance is sent

¹**re·mit·tent** \rə'mitᵊnt, rē'-\ *adj* [L *remittent-*, *remittens*, pres. part. of *remittere* to remit] *of a disease* **:** characterized by

alternating periods of abatement and of increase of symptoms ⟨a ~ fever⟩ — **re·mit·tent·ly** *adv*
²**remittent** \"\ *n* -s : a remittent fever
¹**re·mit·ter** \-id·ə(r), -itə-\ *n* -s [*remit* + -*er* (as in *cesser*)] **1** : the principle or operation of law by which a person who obtains possession of property under a defective title is placed in the same legal position as if he had entered under some prior and more valid title which he also holds **2** : an act remitting a person to a former status or a cause to another court
²**remitter** \"\ *n* -s [*remit* + -*er*, agent suffix] : one that remits; *specif* : one that sends a remittance
re·mit·ti·tur \rəˈmid·əd·ə(r)\ *n* -s [L, it is sent back, remitted, 3d sing. pres. indic. pass. of *remittere* to send back, remit] **1 a** : a remission to a defendant by a plaintiff of the portion of a verdict for damages considered excessive by trial or appellate court **b** : the formal agreement or stipulation of the plaintiff waiving or releasing his right to receive such portion representing the excessive damages **c** : the direction or order of the court approving such stipulation and judgment for the reasonable portion of damages or ordering a new trial unless such remission is made by the plaintiff **2** : a sending back from an appellate or superior to a trial or inferior court of a case and its record for further proceedings (as additional findings of fact) or for entry of a final judgment in accordance with instructions or the decision of the appellate or superior court
re·mix \(ˈ)rē+\ *vb* [*re-* + *mix*] : to mix again
¹**rem·nant** \ˈremnənt\ *n* -s [ME, contr. of *remenant*, fr. MF, fr. pres. part. of *remenoir, remanoir* to be left, remain — more at REMAIN] **1** : a usu. small part, member, or trace remaining ⟨her rather sweet expression . . . was the only ~ of a former prettiness —Osbert Sitwell⟩ ⟨occasional erosion ~s stand above the general land surface —P.G.Worcester⟩ : REMAINDER, REST ⟨more at ease during the ~ of the London season —G.B.Shaw⟩ ⟨the ship came up and the ~ on the boat were saved —B.N.Cardozo⟩ : SURVIVOR — often used in pl. ⟨the ~s of a camp group that had suffered misfortune —C.D. Forde⟩ ⟨the crumbled ~s of a business section —*Amer. Guide Series: Oregon*⟩ **2** : an unsold or unused end of piece goods **3** *often cap* : a minority of Israel preserved by God from the calamities visited upon the wicked to become the nucleus of a new and holy community
²**remnant** \"\ *adj* [modif. (influenced by ¹*remnant*) of MF *remenant*, pres. part. of *remenoir* to be left] : yet left : REMAINING ⟨always thereafter . . . would carry in his heart some ~ feeling of disgrace —Bernard DeVoto⟩
rem·nant·al \(ˈ)remˈnantᵊl\ *adj* : of the nature of a remnant
re·mod·el \(ˈ)rēˈmädᵊl\ *vt* [*re-* + *model*] : to model anew : RECONSTRUCT **syn** see MEND
re·mod·el·er *or* **re·mod·el·ler** \-d(ᵊ)lə(r)\ *n* : one that remodels
remolade *var of* REMOULADE
re·mold \(ˈ)rē+\ *vt* [*re-* + *mold*] : to mold again ⟨~*ing* the world to the heart's desire —H.J.Muller⟩
re·monetization \(ˌ)rē+\ *n* [*remonetize* + -*ation*] : the act of remonetizing
re·monetize \(ˈ)rē+\ *vt* [*re-* + *monetize*] : to restore to use as legal tender ⟨~ silver⟩
re·mon·strance \rəˈmän(t)strən(t)s, rēˈ-\ *n* -s [MF, fr. *remonstrer* to remonstrate (fr. ML *remonstrare*) + -*ance* — more at REMONSTRATE] **1 a** *archaic* : a written or spoken representation or demonstration of a matter **b** : an earnest presentation of reasons in opposition to something; *specif* : a document formally stating points of opposition or grievance **2** *archaic* : a demonstration or manifestation of a fact or quality : PROOF, EVIDENCE **3** : an act or instance of remonstrating : EXPOSTULATION ⟨a plan that provoked violent ~⟩ ⟨the vociferous ~s of a football team's supporters when a doubtful offside has been awarded —E.A.Armstrong⟩ **4** : MONSTRANCE
remonstrancer *n* -s *often cap* [*remonstrance* + -*er*] *obs* : REMONSTRANT 1
¹**re·mon·strant** \-ənt\ *n* -s [ML *remonstrant-, remonstrans*, fr. pres. part. of *remonstrare* to remonstrate] **1** : one who remonstrates; *specif, usu cap* : one of 46 ministers of Arminian views who in 1610 addressed a remonstrance to the States General of Holland and West Friesland containing five articles which set forth their differences from the strict Calvinists and which were condemned by the Synod of Dort in 1619 when the remonstrating ministers were removed from their ministry — compare ARMINIANISM **2** *usu cap* : a member of a small Arminian sect in Holland deriving from the Remonstrants of 1610
²**remonstrant** \"\ *adj* [in sense 1, fr. ¹*remonstrant*; in sense 2, fr. ML *remonstrant-, remonstrans*, pres. part. of *remonstrare*] **1** *usu cap* : of or relating to the Remonstrants **2** : vigorously objecting or opposing : making a protest : REMONSTRATING ⟨a quality urgent, piercingly ~ in those quacks —Owen Wister⟩
re·mon·strant·ly *adv* : in a remonstrant manner
re·mon·strate \rəˈmän(t)ˌstrāt, rēˈ- *sometimes* ˈremənzˌt- *or* ˈremənˌst-, *usu* -ād·+V\ *vb* -ED/-ING/-S [ML *remonstratus*, past part. of *remonstrare* to point out, demonstrate, fr. L *re-* + *monstrare* to show — more at MUSTER] *vt* **1** *obs* : to point out : DEMONSTRATE **2** *obs* : to call attention to (as a fault, wrong, or aggrieving condition) by way of censure, complaint, or protest **3** : to say or plead in protest, reproof, or opposition ~ *vi* : to present and urge reasons in opposition (as to an act, measure, or proceedings) : EXPOSTULATE ⟨~ with a person regarding his habits⟩ **syn** see OBJECT
re·mon·strat·ing·ly *adv* [*remonstrating* (pres. part. of *remonstrate*) + -*ly*] : in a remonstrating way
re·mon·stra·tion \ˌrēˌmänˈstrāshən, ˌremənzˈt-, ˌremənˈst-\ *n* -s [ME, fr. MF or ML; MF *remonstration*, fr. ML *remonstration-, remonstratio*, fr. *remonstratus* + L -*ion-, -io* -ion] : the act or an instance of remonstrating : PROTEST
re·mon·stra·tive \rəˈmän(t)strəd·iv\ *adj* [*remonstrate* + -*ive*] : having the character of a remonstrance : expressing a remonstrance — **re·mon·stra·tive·ly** \-d·əvlē\ *adv*
re·mon·stra·tor \-(t)ˌstrād·ə(r)\ *n* -s [*remonstrate* + -*or*] : one that remonstrates
re·mon·stra·to·ry \-(t)strəˌtōrē\ *adj* [*remonstrate* + -*ory*] : REMONSTRANT
¹**re·mon·tant** \rəˈmäntᵊnt, rēˈ- -tənt\ *adj* [F, lit., rising again, fr. pres. part. of *remonter* to remount] : flowering again ⟨~ roses⟩ ⟨a ~ plant⟩
²**remontant** \"\ *n* -s : a hybrid perpetual rose
rem·on·toir *or* **rem·on·toire** \ˌremənˌtwär\ *n* -s [F *remontoir* device for winding clocks, fr. *remonter* to remount, rewind — more at REMOUNT] : a device to give a uniform impulse to a pendulum or balance
rem·o·ra \ˈremərə\ *n* [L, delay, echeneid (fr. its supposed ability to delay ships), fr. *remorari* to delay, fr. *re-* + *morari* to delay — more at MORATORY] **1 a** -s : any of several highly specialized fishes constituting *Echeneis* and various related genera (order Discocephali), having the anterior dorsal fin converted into an oval transversely lamellate suctorial disc on the top of the head, by means of which they adhere firmly to sharks and other large fishes and to ships but are able to let go at will, and being distributed throughout tropical and warm temperate seas — called also *shark sucker, sucking fish* **b** *cap* : an important genus of such fishes **2** -s : something that holds back or delays : CLOG, DRAG — **rem·o·rid** \-rəd\ *adj*
re·mord \rəˈmȯ(ə)rd\ *vt* [ME *remorden* to afflict with remorse, fr. MF *remordre*, fr. L *remordēre* to bite again, vex — more at REMORSE] *archaic* : AFFLICT
re·morse \rəˈmȯ(ə)rs, rēˈ-, -ȯ(ə)s\ *n* -s [ME *remors, remorse*, fr. MF *remors*, fr. ML *remorsus*, fr. L, act of biting again, fr. *remorsus*, past part. of *remordēre* to bite again, vex, fr. *re-* + *mordēre* to bite — more at SMART] **1 a** : a gnawing distress arising from a sense of guilt for past wrongs (as injuries done to others) : SELF-REPROACH ⟨knew ~ for sermon times spent in daydreams —Rose Macaulay⟩ ⟨felt a twinge of ~ for having been so brusque⟩ **b** : an attack of remorse **2** *obs* : sympathetic sorrow : COMPASSION **3** *obs* : a lessening or break in a process or action **4** *obs* : a solemn obligation **syn** see PENITENCE
re·morse·ful \-sfəl\ *adj* [*remorse* + -*ful*] **1** : springing from or characterized by remorse ⟨a ~ confession⟩ **2** *obs* : COMPASSIONATE — **re·morse·ful·ly** \-fəlē, -li\ *adv* — **re·morse·ful·ness** *n* -ES
re·morse·less \-sləs\ *adj* [*remorse* + -*less*] **1** : being without remorse : PITILESS, MERCILESS ⟨a monster of . . . ~ cruelty —Leslie Stephen⟩ **2** : continuing without lessening or break : RELENTLESS ⟨the drive of technology was so ~ that younger economists . . . turned from philosophy to research —C.A. & Mary Beard⟩ — **re·morse·less·ly** *adv* — **re·morse·less·ness** *n* -ES
¹**re·mote** \rəˈmōt, rēˈ-, *usu* -ōd·+V\ *adj*, *often* -ER/-EST [L *remotus*, fr. past part. of *removēre* to move back, move away — more at REMOVE] **1 a** : separated by intervals greater than usual : far apart **b** : not extending the full distance from the margin of the pileus to the stipe ⟨a mushroom with a ~ veil⟩ **2** : far removed in space, time, relation, or likeness : not near or immediate : FAR, DISTANT ⟨the church was too ~ for a walking bridal party —Thomas Hardy⟩ ⟨from ~ antiquity up to modern times —S.F.Mason⟩ ⟨work to which ~ generations may look back with pride —Benjamin Farrington⟩ ⟨fourth cousins and *remoter* relatives⟩ : DIVERGENT ⟨nations as ~ in culture and civilization as Poland and China, . . . Czechoslovakia and Morocco —H.A.Rusk⟩ ⟨fantastically unreal and utterly ~ from the slightest vestige of truth —John Russell b.1872⟩ : SEPARATED, ABSTRACTED ⟨the ideas of an ether, of waves in it . . . are ~ from ordinary experience —A. N.Whitehead⟩ **3** : located out of the way : SECLUDED ⟨the Coast Guard Service renders invaluable aid to natives living along the ~ seacoast —G.A.Parks⟩ ⟨the ~ atmosphere of these retired wold villages —*Brit. Book News*⟩ **4 a** : not proximate or acting directly : not primary **b** : not arising from the effect of that which is primary or proximate in its action ⟨~ damages⟩ — compare CONSEQUENTIAL **5** : small in degree : SLIGHT ⟨if one solves the economic difficulties, the danger of war becomes ~ —F.D.Smith & Barbara Wilcox⟩ ⟨hasn't the *remotest* notion what time it is⟩ **6** : distant in manner : ALOOF, INACCESSIBLE ⟨they can be cold or warm, ~ or friendly —John Mason Brown⟩ **7 a** : arising elsewhere than from the part of the body that makes a movement — opposed to *resident* **b** : not present to the senses at the moment
²**remote** \"\ *n* -s **1** : one that is remote **2** : a radio or television program or portion of a program (as sports and news events) originating outside the studio
³**remote** \"\ *adv*, *often* -ER/-EST : at a distance
remote control *n* : control (as by a switch or switchboard or by a radio signal) of operation from a point at some distance removed
remoted *adj* [L *remotus* + E -*ed*] *obs* : REMOTE
remote indication *n* : transfer and repetition (as by telemetering) of information from one point to another more or less remote
re·mote·ly *adv*, *sometimes* -ER/-EST : in a remote manner or to a remote extent ⟨a sphinx who smiles ~⟩ ⟨every man she had ever known closely or ~ —Ellen Glasgow⟩ : at or from a distance ⟨processes controlled ~ by the tiny brain —W.E. Swinton⟩ : DISTANTLY
remote matter *n* : MATTER OF A SYLLOGISM 2
re·mote·ness *n* -ES : the quality or state of being remote
re·mo·tion \rəˈmōshən\ *n* -s [ME *remocion, remosion*, fr. L *remotion-, remotio* removal, fr. *remotus* (past part. of *removēre* to remove) + -*ion-, -io* -ion — more at REMOVE] **1** : the quality or state of being remote : REMOTENESS **2 a** : the act of removing : REMOVAL **b** *obs* : DEPARTURE **3** [MF, fr. L *remotion-, remotio* removal] : the process of reaching or defining a conception by the successive elimination of what is extraneous
re·mo·tive \-ōd·iv\ *adj* [L *remotus* (past part. of *removēre* to remove) + E -*ive*] **1** : REMOVING **2** : REMOVABLE
remotive proposition *n* : PRIVATIVE PROPOSITION; *esp* : one that asserts the absence of something to be of the essence of the subject
re·mou·lade *also* **re·mo·lade** \ˌrāməˈläd\ *n* -s [F *rémolade, rémoulade*, fr. F dial. *rémola, rémolat* horseradish (modif. of L *armoracea, armoracium*) + F -*ade*] : a pungent sauce or dressing resembling mayonnaise but usu. made with cooked egg yolks and often with savory herbs or condiments
¹**re·mount** \(ˈ)rē+\ *vb* [ME *remounten*, partly fr. *re-* + *mounten* to mount, partly fr. MF *remonter* to remount, fr. *re-* + *monter* to mount — more at MOUNT] *vt* **1** : to mount (something) again ⟨~ this map on the other wall⟩ ⟨reaching the mouth of the stream, they ~*ed* it to its source⟩ **2** : to furnish remounts to ⟨the regiment must be ~*ed*⟩ ~ *vi* **1** : to mount again ⟨~ at once and ride back⟩ **2** : to go back (as during a study) to a point or period
²**re·mount** \ˈrē+ˌ-, ≈ˈ≈\ *n* **1** : a fresh horse to replace one no longer available (as by reason of fatigue, disablement, loss, or age); *specif* : a green or incompletely trained cavalry horse **2** : a group, stud, or supply of remounts
³**remount** \"\ *adj* [²*remount*] : of or relating to a remount
re·mov·abil·i·ty \rəˌmüvəˈbiləd·ē, rēˌ-, -lətē, -i\ *n* : the quality or state of being removable
re·mov·able \rəˈmüvəbəl, rēˈ-\ *adj* [¹*remove* + -*able*] : capable of being removed, displaced, transferred, dismissed, or eradicated ⟨~ partition⟩ ⟨a ~ bed⟩ ⟨a headman appointed and ~ by the mayor —G.M.Harris⟩ — **re·mov·able·ness** *n* -ES — **re·mov·ably** \-blē\ *adv*
removable truck-type switchboard *n* : a switchboard in which the instruments and main control equipment are mounted upon a removable structure that runs on guide rails
re·mov·al \rəˈmüvəl, rēˈ-\ *n* -s [*remove* + -*al*] : the act of removing or fact of being removed ⟨surgical ~ of the growth⟩ : dismissal from office : shift of location : change of residence
removal of causes **1** : the taking of pending cases from a state to a federal court because of diversity of citizenship or because of federal question **2 a** : the transfer of a case from one federal court to another **b** : the transfer of a case from one to another court within the same state for original hearing or trial — compare APPEAL, REVIEW
¹**re·move** \rəˈmüv, rēˈ-\ *vb* [ME *removen, remeven*, fr. OF *remouvoir, removoir*, fr. L *removēre*, fr. *re-* + *movēre* to move — more at MOVE] *vt* **1** : to change or shift the location, position, station, or residence of (as in order to reestablish) : SHIFT, TRANSFER — usu. used with *to* and specified place ⟨~ the troops to the front⟩ ⟨~ the family to the seashore⟩; *specif* : to transfer (a pending case) for original hearing or trial from one court to another in the same or another jurisdiction — compare REMOVAL OF CAUSES **2** : to move by lifting, pushing aside, or taking away or off : put aside, apart, or elsewhere ⟨~*s* his hat in the house⟩ ⟨~ a book from a shelf to examine it⟩ **3** : to force (one) to leave a place or to go away: as **a** : to dismiss from office **b** : ASSASSINATE **c** : to take away by death **4** : to get rid of as though by moving : ERADICATE, ELIMINATE ⟨~ the causes of poverty⟩ ~ *vi* **1** : to change location, station, or residence ⟨~ from their town house to the country⟩ **2** : to go away : DISAPPEAR, DEPART **3** : to be capable of being removed ⟨a bottle cap that ~*s* easily⟩ **syn** see MOVE
²**remove** \"\ *n* -s **1 a** : REMOVAL; *specif* : the transfer of one's business or of one's domestic belongings from one location or dwelling house to another : MOVE **b** *archaic* : the act of removing a horse's shoe to dress the hoof **c** *Brit* : a change of dishes during a meal **d** *Brit* : promotion of a pupil to the next form **2 a** : a distance (as a space, time, or divergence of state) separating one person or thing from another : distance apart or away ⟨at a short ~ upon the same platform was an officer —Ambrose Bierce⟩ ⟨her poems . . . work best at a slight ~ from the personal —Richard Wilbur⟩ **b** (1) : a degree distant (as in derivation or relationship) : a grade or stage of separation from the immediate or direct : a step apart or away ⟨such a popular song . . . simply repeats, at many ~*s*, a motif of the conventional behavior of the courtly lover —R.A.Hall b.1911⟩ ⟨a primary and intense experience . . . which men at best know only at second ~ —M.F.A. Montagu⟩ — compare FIRSTHAND (2) : a degree of lineal consanguinity : a generation removed ⟨only at one ~ from the villager —G.M.Trevelyan⟩ ⟨the sixteen sire lines . . . of these famous racehorses at the fourth ~ —Dennis Craig⟩ **3** *obs* : ABSENCE **4** : an intermediate form between two others in an English school
removed *adj* [fr. past part. of ¹*remove*] **1 a** : distant in degree of relationship **b** *of a cousin* : belonging to a generation separated from the propositus by a given degree of lineal consanguinity : of a younger or older generation — used in law only of cousins of a younger generation ⟨a second cousin's child is a second cousin once ~⟩ ⟨a first cousin's grandchild is a first cousin twice ~⟩ **2** : separate or remote (as in space, time, or character) from something : DISTANT, AWAY, OFF ⟨with peace as far ~ as it had been at the time of his election —F.L.Paxson⟩ ⟨considerations entirely ~ from politics⟩ — **re·moved·ly** \-vədlē, -vd-\ *adv* — **re·moved·ness** \-vədnəs, -v(d)n-\ *n* -ES
re·move·ment \-vmənt\ *n* -s [¹*remove* + -*ment*] : REMOVAL
¹**re·mov·er** \-və(r)\ *n* -s [*remove* + -*er*, agent suffix] **1** : one that removes something: as **a** *Brit* : MOVER a(4) **b** : a solvent or chemical used in removing a substance (as from a surface) ⟨paint and varnish ~⟩ ⟨rust ~⟩ ⟨dye ~⟩ ⟨hair ~⟩ **2** *obs* : a changeable or unsettled person
²**remover** \"\ *n* -s [¹*remove* + -*er* (as in *cesser*)] : transfer of a proceeding from one tribunal to another
rem·scheid \ˈremˌshīt\ *adj*, *usu cap* [fr. *Remscheid*, city of northwestern Germany] : of or from the city of Remscheid, Germany : of the kind or style prevalent in Remscheid
rem·sen cooler \ˈremzən-\ *n*, *usu cap R* [prob. fr. the proper name *Remsen*] : a cooler the base of which is gin
re·mu·da \rəˈmüdə\ *n* -s [AmSp, relay, shift of horses or oxen, fr. Sp, exchange, fr. *remudar* to exchange, fr. *re-* + *mudar* to change, fr. L *mutare* — more at MISS] : the herd of saddle horses from which are chosen those to be used for the day by the ranch hands : a relay of remounts
re·mu·ner·a·ble \rəˈmyün(ə)rəbəl\ *adj* [ML *remunerabilis*, fr. L *remunerare* to reward + -*abilis*] : admitting or worthy of remuneration — **re·mu·ner·a·bly** \-blē\ *adv*
re·mu·ner·ate \rəˈmyünəˌrāt, rēˈ-, *usu* -ād·+V\ *vt* -ED/-ING/-S [L *remuneratus*, past part. of *remunerare* to recompense, reward, fr. *re-* + *munerare* to give, present, fr. *muner-, munus* gift — more at MEAN] **1** : to pay an equivalent for (as a service, loss, expense) **2** : to pay an equivalent to (a person) for a service, loss, or expense : RECOMPENSE, COMPENSATE **syn** see PAY
re·mu·ner·a·tion \≈ˌ≈≈ˈrāshən\ *n* -s [ME *remuneracion*, fr. MF or L; MF *remuneration*, fr. L *remuneration-, remuneratio*, fr. *remuneratus* + -*ion-, -io* -ion] **1** : an act or fact of remunerating **2** : something that remunerates : RECOMPENSE, PAY
re·mu·ner·a·tive \rəˈmyünəˌrād·iv, rēˈ-, -n(ə)rəl, |t|, |ēv *also* |əv\ *adj* [*remunerate* + -*ive*] **1** : serving to remunerate : REWARDING ⟨~ justice⟩ **2** : affording remuneration : PROFITABLE, GAINFUL ⟨a ~ business⟩ ⟨a ~ salary⟩ — **re·mu·ner·a·tive·ly** \|əvlē\ *adv* — **re·mu·ner·a·tive·ness** \|ivnəs\ *n* -ES
re·mu·ner·a·tor \-nəˌrād·ə(r)\ *n* -s [LL, fr. L *remuneratus* (past part. of *remunerare* to remunerate) + -*or*] : one that remunerates
re·mu·ner·a·to·ry \-nərəˌtōrē\ *adj* [*remunerate* + -*ory*] : REMUNERATIVE
remuneratory sanction *n* : a sanction in the form of a reward withheld for failure to comply with the law
re·murmur \(ˈ)rē+\ *vb* [L *remurmurare*, fr. *re-* + *murmurare* to murmur] *vi* : to murmur repeatedly ~ *vt* : to repeat, echo, utter again, or reply in murmurs
¹**ren·ais·sance** \ˌrenəˈsän(t)s *also* -ˈzä- *sometimes* -äⁿs *or* -äⁿ(t)s, *chiefly Brit* rəˈnāsᵊn-\ *n* -s [F, fr. MF, rebirth, fr. *renais-* (stem of *renaistre* to be born again, fr. L *renasci*, fr. *re-* + *nasci* to be born) + -*ance* — more at NATION] **1** *often cap* **a** : enthusiastic and vigorous activity along literary, artistic, and cultural lines distinguished by a revival of interest in the past, by an increasing pursuit of learning, and by an imaginative response to broader horizons generally ⟨conceptions of the nature of the *Renaissance* —W.K.Ferguson⟩ ⟨the transcendental movement that marked the full flowering of the New England ~ —V.L.Parrington⟩ **b** : the period of such a revival ⟨the *Renaissance* of the eighth and ninth centuries —Kemp Malone⟩ ⟨that second *Renaissance*, the Victorian Age —Edwin Benson⟩ ⟨the period conventionally known as the *Renaissance* —David Daiches⟩ **2** *usu cap* : the neoclassic style of art prevailing during the Renaissance period **3** : a return of youthful vigor, freshness, zest, or productivity : a renewal of life or interest in some aspect of it : REBIRTH ⟨a postwar ~ —Granville Hicks⟩ ⟨grand opera . . . is currently enjoying a ~ —Joseph Wechsberg⟩ ⟨the biggest tennis ~ ever known in this country —*Holiday*⟩
²**renaissance** \"\ *adj* **1** : of or relating to a renaissance **2** *usu cap* : of, relating to, or typical or suggestive of the transitional movement in Europe between medieval and modern times beginning in the 14th century in Italy, lasting into the 17th century, and marked by a humanistic revival of classical influence expressed in a flowering of the arts and literature and by the beginnings of modern science ⟨*Renaissance* painting⟩ ⟨the *Renaissance* ideal of the universal man —*Horizon*⟩
renaissance architecture *n*, *usu cap R* : the style of building and decoration that arose in the early 15th century in Italy based on the study and adaptation of the Roman classic orders and design and that spread later through western Europe succeeding the Gothic style
renaissance furniture *n*, *usu cap R* : a style of furniture developed early in the Renaissance distinguished in its national types but in general of oak or walnut richly carved, massive and palatial in structure, and classical in decorative motifs
renaissance lace *n*, *usu cap R* : a lace of braid or tape used for curtains and dresses : GUIPURE — called also *Battenberg lace*
ren·ais·sant \-nt\ *adj*, *usu cap* [back-formation fr. ¹*renaissance*] : of or relating to the Renaissance
re·nal \ˈrēnᵊl\ *adj* [F or LL; F *rénal*, fr. LL *renalis*, fr. L *renes* (pl.) kidneys + -*alis* -al] : of, relating to, or involving the kidneys : located in the region of the kidneys : NEPHRIC
renal artery *n* : any of the branches of the abdominal aorta that supply the kidneys being in man one to each kidney, arising immediately below the origin of the superior mesenteric artery, dividing into four or five branches which enter the hilum of the kidney, and giving off smaller branches to the ureter, adrenal gland, and adjoining structures
renal calculus *n* : a calculus in the kidney — called also *kidney stone*
renal cast *n* : a cast of a renal tubule consisting of granular, hyaline, albuminoid, or other material formed in and discharged from the kidney in renal disease
renal clearance *n* : CLEARANCE 2g
renal colic *n* : the severe pain produced by the passage of a calculus from the kidney through the ureter
renal corpuscle *n* : MALPIGHIAN CORPUSCLE
renal glycosuria *or* **renal diabetes** *n* : excretion of glucose associated with increased permeability of the kidneys without increased sugar concentration in the blood
renal papilla *n* : one of the eminences projecting into the pelvis of a vertebrate kidney through which the collecting tubules discharge
renal plexus *n* : the sympathetic plexus supplying the kidney
renal portal vein *n* **1** : one of the portal veins carrying blood from some of the posterior parts of the body to the kidneys in most lower vertebrates and including typically two trunks formed one for each kidney by the bifurcation of the caudal vein but enlarged or largely replaced by branches from the hind limbs in many of the higher forms **2** : either of a pair of veins in birds that originate like the renal portal veins of lower forms but pass through the corresponding kidney and enter the femoral vein without breaking into capillaries in the kidney
renal splanchnic nerve *n* : either of a pair of sympathetic nerves that arise from the lower ganglia of the sympathetic chain and end in the renal plexus and the lower part of the solar plexus
renal threshold *n* : the concentration level up to which a substance (as glucose) in the blood is prevented from passing through the kidneys into the urine
renal vein *n* : any of the veins that return the blood from the kidneys to the vena cava being in man one from each kidney and lying in front of the renal arteries
re·name \(ˈ)rē+\ *vt* [*re-* + *name*] : to name again or anew
re·nan·i·an \rəˈnanēən\ *adj*, *usu cap* [Joseph Ernest *Renan* †1892 Fr. philologist and historian + E -*ian*] : of or relating to the French philologist and historian Ernest Renan or resembling his thought or style
re·nard·ite \rəˈnärˌdīt\ *n* -s [F, Alphonse Francois *Renard* †1903 Belg. geologist + F -*ite*] : a mineral $Pb(UO_2)_4(PO_4)_2$-

$(OH)_4.7H_2O$ consisting of a hydrous basic lead and uranyl phosphate

re·nas·cence \rə'nas°n(t)s, rē'-, -naas-, -nais-\ *n* -s *often cap* [alter. (influenced by *renascent*) of *renaissance*] : RENAISSANCE ⟨blossomed into new freedom, an artistic ~, of eager and elaborate experimentation —Marjory S. Douglas⟩

re·nas·cent \-°nt\ *adj* [fr. L *renascent-*, *renascens*, pres. part. of *renasci* to be born again — more at RENAISSANCE] : springing or rising again into being or vigor : being born again or reproduced ⟨~ paganism⟩

re·na·tur·a·tion \(¦)rē,nāchə¦rāshən\ *n* -s [*renature* + *-ation*] : the process of renaturing ⟨denaturation and ~ of proteins⟩

re·nature \(')rē+\ *vt* [*re-* + *nature*] : to restore (as denatured material) to its original nature ⟨silk fibroin is the first protein to be completely *renatured* after denaturation —J.W.McBain⟩

ren·con·tre \ren'käntə(r)\ *or* **ren·coun·ter** \-kaůn-\ *n* -s [*rencounter* fr. MF *rencontre* chance or hostile meeting, fr. *rencontrer* to rencounter; *rencontre* fr. F, fr. MF] **1** : a hostile meeting between forces or individuals : COMBAT, ACTION, DUEL **2** : a personal contest (as in debate or repartee) ⟨a lively ~ of two famous wits⟩ **3** : a casual meeting with a person or thing ⟨a lucky ~ with a friend⟩ **4** *archaic* : a sudden meeting or collision of two bodies

ren·coun·ter \-kaůn-\ *vb* [MF *rencontrer*, fr. *re-* + *encontrer* to encounter, fr. OF — more at ENCOUNTER] *vt* **1** *obs* **a** : to meet in hostility : encounter in combat or fight **b** : to meet forcibly : collide with **2** : to meet (as a friend) casually ~ *vi* : to come together in rencontre

rend \'rend\ *vb* **rent** \-nt\ *also* **rended**; **rent** *also* **rended**; **rending**; **rends** [ME *renden*, fr. OE *rendan*; akin to OFris *renda* to tear, rend, Skt *randhra* split, opening, hole] *vt* **1** : to pull violently from a person or thing : remove from place by violence : tear out or away : WRENCH, WREST ⟨glaciers may . . . ~ boulders from their beds —G.W.Tyrrell⟩ ⟨~ manhood out of him in fear —G.D.Brown⟩ **2 a** : to split or tear apart or in pieces by violence : CLEAVE ⟨saw lightning ~ a tree⟩ : DISMEMBER ⟨many a carcass they left . . . for the horny-nibbed raven to ~ —Alfred Tennyson⟩ **b** : to convert straight-grained wood into (laths) by splitting **3** : to tear (the hair or clothing) as a sign of anger, grief, or despair ⟨foam, fling myself flat, ~ my clothes to shreds —Robert Browning⟩ **4** : to affect as if tearing or splitting: as **a** : to lacerate (as the heart) with painful feelings ⟨look in his face . . . and ~ him with her scorn —Ellen Glasgow⟩ **b** : to pierce with sound ⟨suddenly this dead stillness was *rent* by a shot —Zane Grey⟩ **c** : to divide (as a nation) into parties : DISINTEGRATE ⟨a long dispute over where it should be built *rent* the community —*Amer. Guide Series: Va.*⟩ ~ *vi* **1** : to perform an act of tearing or splitting ⟨a time to ~ and a time to sew —Eccles 3:7 (RSV)⟩ **2** : to become torn or split ⟨made of rotten black cloth . . . or else it would not have *rent* —Edmund Hickeringill⟩ **syn** see TEAR

1**ren·der** \'rendə(r)\ *vb* **rendered**; **rendered**; **rendering** \-d(ə)riŋ\ **renders** [ME *rendren*, fr. MF *rendre* to give back, deliver, yield, cause to become, fr. (assumed) VL *rendere*, alter. (influenced by L *prendere* to take, contr. of *praehendere*) of L *reddere*, partly fr. *red-* re- + *dare* to give, partly fr. *red-* + *-dere* to put — more at PREHENSILE, DATE, DO] *vt* **1** *obs* : to say over : RECITE, REPEAT **2 a** : to melt down : extract or clarify by melting : TRY ⟨~ lard, oil, or wax⟩ **b** : to treat so as to extract the fat ⟨~ garbage⟩ **3 a** : to hand over to another (as the intended recipient) : DELIVER, TRANSMIT ⟨his father left him gold . . . which was not ~*ed* to him —Alfred Tennyson⟩ **b** : to give up : SURRENDER, YIELD ⟨~ one's life for a cause⟩ ⟨a term . . . so sacrosanct that the material goods of this life must be mysteriously ~*ed* up for it —R.M.Weaver⟩ **c** : to furnish for consideration, approval, or information ⟨~*ed* a report to . . . Congress concerning plant disposal —D.D.Eisenhower⟩ ⟨~ an annual account to the court of his trusteeship⟩ as (1) : to send (a bill) to a customer ⟨~ accounts at the first of the month⟩ (2) : to hand down (a legal judgment) : give as a verdict ⟨in the Federal District Court . . . a verdict of $1,295 and costs was ~*ed* against them —*Amer. Guide Series: Mich.*⟩ **d** *archaic* : to present (oneself) at a place ⟨the most distant members . . . may probably ~ themselves at Philadelphia in fifteen to twenty days —Benjamin Franklin⟩ **4 a** (1) : to give in reward or retribution ⟨~ them their due reward —Ps 28:4 (RSV)⟩ ⟨see that none ~ evil for evil —1 Thess 5:15 (AV)⟩ (2) : to give (thanks) for something received ⟨thanksgiving . . . we ~ to God for you —1 Thess 3:9 (RSV)⟩ (3) *archaic* : to give reward or retribution for : REQUITE ⟨~ to every man his righteousness —1 Sam 26:23 (AV)⟩ **b** (1) : to give back : REPAY, RESTORE ⟨~ to the earth the bodies of the dead⟩ (2) : to cause (an image or sound) to return : REFLECT, ECHO ⟨the heart's echoes ~ no song when the spirit is mute —P.B.Shelley⟩ **c** : to give (as rent, honor) in acknowledgment of dependence or obligation : give (something due) to another : PAY ⟨the serf . . . might enjoy his land so long as he ~*ed* three days' work in the week to his lord —G.G.Coulton⟩ ⟨the failure of those living to . . . ~ due respect to its memory —*Amer. Guide Series: Del.*⟩ **d** : to do (a service) for another ⟨thanked them for the service they had ~*ed* him⟩ : give (as help) to another ⟨having ~*ed* at least five years of service as such an officer —*U.S. Code*⟩ ⟨stand by and ~ help if help be needed —Rafael Sabatini⟩ ⟨the protection they ~ in winter against the cold winds from the interior —Samuel Van Valkenburg & Ellsworth Huntington⟩ **5** *obs* : to give out : EMIT ⟨cedar, which ~*s* a fine fragrancy —Samuel Gale⟩ **6 a** : to put into a state ⟨a novelist of more meager talents . . . would ~ this sugary situation into pure hokum —Martin Levin⟩ **b** (1) : to cause to be or become : MAKE ⟨enough rainfall in the average year to ~ irrigation unnecessary —P.E.James⟩ ⟨the building of the railroad . . . ~*ed* a road of even less importance —G.R.Stewart⟩ ⟨this literalness . . . ~*s* it a fine introduction to twelve-tone music —Arthur Berger⟩ (2) : to cause something to have : IMPART ⟨the college is one of the great social institutions which ~*s* form and continuity to American culture —*Encyc. Americana*⟩ **c** (1) : to put into artistic or verbal form : reproduce or represent by artistic or verbal means (as music, painting, writing) : execute in an artistic or verbal medium : DEPICT, EXPRESS ⟨music has set itself to ~*ing* the modern mood —Irving Babbitt⟩ ⟨a society painter must ~ a likeness of his subject —Arnold Isenberg⟩ ⟨the problem of ~*ing* every unique sensation, never merely pointing, naming, summarizing —H.J.Muller⟩ ⟨aimed at ~*ing* its meaning in an English that would not become dated —*Current Biog.*⟩ (2) *obs* : to describe or represent as having a given character or being in a given condition : give out to be ⟨I have heard him speak of that same brother, and he did ~ him the most unnatural that lived amongst men —Shak.⟩ (3) : to give an interpretation or performance of (an artistic work or element or dramatic role) ⟨called upon to ~ duets at every stop —*Current Biog.*⟩ (4) : to produce a copy or version of ⟨the documents are ~*ed* in their original French —Robert Lawrence⟩ (5) : to execute the motions of (as a salute) ⟨a . . . major appeared before us to ~ a meticulous salute —*Infantry Jour.*⟩ **d** : to put into another language or into other words : TRANSLATE ⟨every document . . . must be ~*ed* into several languages —R.H.Jackson⟩ : REWORD ⟨a famous sea song now ~*ed* down for landsmen's hearing —Gavin Douglas⟩ **7** : to direct the execution of (as justice) : ADMINISTER ⟨in ancient Ireland it was either the local king or the high king . . . who ~*ed* justice —E.D.Chapple & C.S.Coon⟩ **8** : to apply a coat of plaster or cement directly to ⟨buildings should be made as ratproof as possible by ~*ing* the walls with cement —F.D.Smith & Barbara Wilcox⟩ **9 a** : to cause (a rope) to pass or run through a block or loop (as by slackening it off) **b** : to coil (a rope) so as to ensure kink-free redelivery when wanted **10** *chiefly Brit* : to apply a medium (as ink, crayon, ink wash) to (a drawing) so as to bring out form and modeling ~ *vi* **1** : to give recompense ⟨for he will ~ to every man according to his works —Rom 2:6 (RSV)⟩ **2** : to pass or run smoothly (as through a block or off a coil) **3** : to extract fat, oil, or wax by melting (as in boiling water, steam, benzine) **4** *chiefly Brit* : to finish a perspective drawing so as to bring out form and modeling

2**render** \"\ *n* -s **1** *obs* : SURRENDER **2** : a return in kind, services, or money due from a tenant to his superior in feudal England ⟨the normal ~ due to a lord from a ten-hide estate —F.M.Stenton⟩ **3** *archaic* : the act of rendering an account or statement **4** : a coat of plaster or cement applied directly on a wall

3**rend·er** \"\ *n* -s [*rend* + *-er*] : one that rends

ren·der·able \-d(ə)rəbəl\ *adj* [1*render* + *-able*] : capable of being rendered

ren·der·er \-rə(r)\ *n* -s [1*render* + *-er*] : one that renders; *specif* : one that operates a rendering plant

rendering *n* -s [fr. gerund of 1*render*] **1** : a work forming a presentation, expression, or interpretation (as of an idea, theme, or part) : RENDITION, VERSION: as **a** : TRANSLATION **b** : a finished perspective drawing of a proposed building or product : VISUALIZATION ⟨nicely colored ~*s* of buildings on the drawing boards . . . from a huge cement plant to a modest church —A.W.Baum⟩ **c** : a rendered illustration of an object of art ⟨made ~*s* of Spanish colonial arts in New Mexico for the *Index of American Design* —*Southwest Review*⟩ **2 a** : a coat of plaster laid directly on brickwork or stonework **b** *Brit* : the finish coat of mortar on a concrete floor or roof on which tiles are laid **c** : the finish application of a material on a wall usu. for decorative purposes

rendering plant *n* : a plant that converts packing house waste, kitchen grease, and livestock carcasses into industrial fats and oils (as tallow for soap) and various other products (as fertilizer)

rendering works *n pl but sing or pl in constr* : RENDERING PLANT

renderset \'⸗,⸗\ *or* **render-and-set** \¦⸗⸗⸗¦⸗\ *adj* [1*render* + *set*] : consisting of two coats of plaster

1**ren·dez·vous** \'rändə,vü, -dē,-, -dā,-\ *n*, *pl* **rendezvous** \-üz\ [MF, fr. the phrase *rendez vous* present yourselves, fr. *rendez* (2d pl. imper. of *rendre* to render, deliver) + *vous* you, fr. L *vos*; akin to Gk *hymeis* you, Skt *vas*, OSlav *vy*] **1 a** : a place appointed for assembling or meeting ⟨met him at the ~ agreed on the night before⟩; *specif* : a place appointed for the assembly of troops, ships, or airplanes before or after an operation ⟨the belated arrival of this division at the ~ —*Amer. Guide Series: Fla.*⟩ ⟨there were three ports of . . . ~, any one of which the whaling fleet might make at the end of a season to transship the catch to the schooner tenders —H.A. Chippendale⟩ **b** : a place to which people customarily come in numbers : a place of popular resort : HAUNT ⟨Lower City Park, a favorite ~ for anglers seeking small panfish —*Amer. Guide Series: Mich.*⟩ **c** : a place used (as by a band of outlaws or pirates) as a headquarters to work out of **2 a** : a meeting at an appointed place and time ⟨blue-jacketed sailors hurry to some long-anticipated ~ —*Amer. Guide Series: Va.*⟩ ⟨~ was made with a tanker and escort and . . . the ships of the task group refueled —Martin Dibner⟩ **b** : an agreement to meet each other or with another person or thing ⟨kept their ~⟩ ⟨I have a long-delayed ~ with the city beneath the sea —H.E.Rieseberg⟩ **c** : an annual gathering of fur trappers for trade and fun **3** *obs* : RETREAT, REFUGE **4** *obs* : a gathering or assemblage of persons or things **syn** see ENGAGEMENT

2**rendezvous** \"\ *vb* **rendezvoused**; **rendezvoused** \-üd\ **rendezvousing** \-üiŋ\ **rendezvouses** \-üz\ *vi* **1** : to come together at a place; *esp* : to meet or assemble by appointment ⟨all the cars ~ each night at prearranged destinations —*Ford Times*⟩ **2** *obs* : to mobilize one's forces ~ *vt* : to bring together at a rendezvous ⟨decided to ~ two fleets . . . and to decoy U.S. ships away with a third fleet —*Newsweek*⟩

rend·ible \'rendəbəl\ *adj* [*rend* + *-ible*] : capable of being rent

rending *pres part of* REND

ren·di·tion \ren'dishən\ *n* -s [obs. F, fr. MF, alter. (influenced by *rendre* to render) of *reddition* — more at REDDITION] **1** : the act or result of rendering ⟨timely and adequate ~ of medical care —*Jour. Amer. Med. Assoc.*⟩ : INTERPRETATION ⟨his sensitive ~ gave the lyrics a haunting and dramatic quality⟩ : TRANSLATION ⟨the first ~ of the work into English⟩ : PERFORMANCE ⟨the whole ~ lasted only a minute⟩ : EXPRESSION ⟨read it . . . for its pleasing ~ of a state of mind —David Daiches⟩ **2** : EXTRADITION 1

ren·dle·wood \'ren(d)°l,wůd\ *n* [perh. fr. *rend*] *dial Eng* : wood (as oak) with the bark off

rendrock \'⸗,⸗\ *n* [*rend* + *rock*] : a dynamite used in blasting and consisting of nitroglycerin, potassium nitrate, wood pulp, and paraffin or pitch

rends *pres 3d sing of* REND

ren·du \'rän(,)dü\ *n* -s [F, rendering, fr. past part. of *rendre* to render, fr. MF — more at RENDER] : an artistically finished architectural drawing representing a design problem

ren·dzi·na \ren'jēnə\ *n* -s [Pol, rich limy soil] : an intrazonal group of dark grayish-brown soils developed in humid to subhumid grassy regions from soft calcareous marl or chalk and having brown friable upper layer and grayish or yellowish underlayers

re·neague \rə'nēg\ *dial Brit var of* RENEGE

ren·e·al·mia \,renē'almēə\ *n*, *cap* [NL, fr. Paul de *Reneaulme* †1624 Fr. botanist + NL *-ia*] *in some classifications* : a genus of tropical American and African herbs (family Zingiberaceae) having leafy or naked stems and racemose showy flowers

1**ren·e·gade** \'renə,gād, -nē,-\ *n* -s [Sp *renegado*, fr. ML *renegatus*, fr. past part. of *renegare* to deny, fr. L *re-* + *negare* to deny — more at NEGATION] **1** : a person who leaves one religious faith for another : a religious apostate **2** : a deserter from one cause, principle, party, or allegiance to another often hostile one : TURNCOAT, TRAITOR ⟨venom the ~ can summon up against his former beliefs and associates —*New Yorker*⟩ **3** : an individual who rejects the restraints of law or convention

2**renegade** \"\ *vi* -ED/-ING/-S : to become a renegade

3**renegade** \"\ *adj* : that is a renegade; *specif* : having deserted a cause, principle, or allegiance for a hostile one : TRAITOROUS, APOSTATE ⟨better to be . . . an honest animal than a ~ human being —Eleanor Dark⟩

ren·e·ga·do \,renə'gä(,)dō, -gā(-\ *n* -ES [Sp — more at RENEGADE] : RENEGADE

renegate *n* -s [ML *renegatus* — more at RENEGADE] *obs* : RENEGADE

1**re·nege** \rə'nig, rē'- *also* -neg *sometimes* -nēg *or* -nāg\ *vb* -ED/-ING/-S [ML *renegare* — more at RENEGADE] *vt* **1** : DENY, RENOUNCE, DESERT, RETRACT **2** : REFUSE, DECLINE ~ *vi* **1** *obs* : to make a denial **2** : REVOKE 2 **3** : to break one's word : go back on a promise ⟨I'll wed him, and I'll not ~ —J.M.Synge⟩ ⟨both had *reneged* on paying off the loan —*Time*⟩ **4** : to reverse a stand or plan : back out : back down ⟨can do this without *reneging* on our traditions of due legal procedure —*New Republic*⟩

2**renege** \"\ *n* -s : REVOKE 2

re·neg·er \-gə(r)\ *n* -s : one that reneges

re·negotiable \¦rē+\ *adj* [*renegotiate* + *-able*] : that can be renegotiated : subject to renegotiation ⟨a sale becomes ~ if the purchaser, or some subsequent purchaser, uses the material or article in the performance of a ~ contract —*Jour. of Accountancy*⟩

re·negotiate \"+\ *vb* [*re-* + *negotiate*] *vt* : to negotiate anew; *specif* : to determine under statutory procedure the existence and amount of excessive profits on (a government defense contract or subcontract or the price stipulated) in order to eliminate or to obtain a refund of such profits ~ *vi* : to adjust a defense contract price in order to eliminate or recover excessive profits — **re·negotiation** \"+\ *n* — **re·negotiator** \"+\ *n*

re·nerve \(')rē+\ *vt* [*re-* + *nerve*] : to nerve again : REINVIGORATE

re·nest \"+\ *vi* [*re-* + *nest*] : to nest again after the failure, disturbance, or destruction of the first nesting

ren·ette \(')re¦net\ *n* -s [L *renes* kidneys + E *-ette*] : a specialized excretory cell in some nematode worms

re·new \rə'n(y)ü, rē'-\ *vb* -ED/-ING/-S [ME *renewen*, fr. *re-* + *new*] *vt* **1** : to make new again : restore to freshness, perfection, or vigor ⟨steams . . . to ~ felt, suede, velvet —*Sears, Roebuck Cat.*⟩; *also* : to gain again as new : REASSUME ⟨~ his strength⟩ **2** : to make new spiritually : REGENERATE ⟨be ye transformed by the ~*ing* of your mind —Rom 12:2 (AV)⟩ **3** : to restore to existence : REESTABLISH, RECREATE, REBUILD ⟨~ the old splendor of a palace⟩ : REVIVE, RESUSCITATE ⟨~ the sentiments of youth⟩ **4** : to go over again : make or do again : REPEAT ⟨~ a motion⟩ **5** : to begin again : RECOMMENCE, RESUME ⟨felt reluctant to rise and ~ my ramble —W.H.Hudson †1922⟩ **6** : to restore to fullness or sufficiency : REPLACE ⟨twisting the knob that ~*ed* the film —Arthur Gordon⟩ ⟨~ water in a tank⟩ ⟨~ one's equipment⟩ **7 a** : to grant or obtain an extension of : continue in force for a fresh period ⟨~ a lease⟩ **b** : to grant or obtain an extension of the loan of ⟨~*ed* the library book for another two weeks⟩ ~ *vi* **1** : to become new or as new : grow again : REVIVE **2** : to begin again : RESUME ⟨their friendship ~*ed*⟩ **3** : to make a renewal (as of a lease) **4** *obs* : to come back (as to a fresh attack) — **re·new·abil·i·ty** \rə,n(y)üə'bilǝd·ē\ *n* -ES — **re·new·able** \rə'n(y)üəbəl\ *adj* — **re·new·ably** \-blē\ *adv*

renewable fuse *n* [*renew* + *-able*] : a cartridge fuse permitting the replacement of a burned-out link

re·new·al \rə'n(y)üəl, rē'-, -(y)ůəl *also* -ül\ *n* -s [*renew* + *-al*] **1** : the act or process of renewing ⟨a ~ of the copyright by the publisher⟩ : REPETITION ⟨the 15th ~ of the . . . winter carnival —*Springfield (Mass.) Union*⟩ **2** : the quality or state of being renewed **3** : something renewed; *specif* : an expiring agreement (as a library loan or a subscription to a periodical) renewed for an additional period **4** : something used for renewing; *specif* : an expenditure that betters (as by prolonging useful lives, increasing output) existing fixed assets and is usu. capitalized in the accounts — usu. used in pl; compare REPAIR, REPLACEMENT **5** : a forbearance from enforcing an obligation (as on commercial paper) in virtue of an agreement by which the obligee relinquishes his right of action for a definite period or until a specified date

renewed bark *n* [fr. past part. of *renew*] : the new growth appearing on a cinchona under mossed bark — compare NATURAL BARK

re·newed·ly \-üədlē, -üd-\ *adv* [*renewed* + *-ly*] : in a renewed manner : ANEW

re·newed·ness \-dnəs\ *n* -ES : the quality or state of being renewed

re·new·er \-üə(r)\ *n* -s [ME, fr. *renewen* to renew + *-er*] : one that renews

ren·frew·shire \'ren,frü,shi(ə)r, -shiə, -,shə(r)\ *or* **ren·frew** \-ü\ *adj*, *usu cap* [fr. *Renfrewshire*, county of southwestern Scotland] : of or from the county of Renfrew, Scotland : of the kind or style prevalent in Renfrew

ren·gas \'reŋ,gäs\ *n* -ES [Malay *rĕngas*] : BLACK-VARNISH TREE

reng·ma \'reŋmə\ *n*, *pl* **rengma** *or* **rengmas** *usu cap* **1** : a Naga people inhabiting the Mikir hills of Assam **2** : a member of the Rengma people

ren·gue \'reŋgā\ *n* -s [AmerSp] : a coarse piña cloth made in the Philippines

ren·gue·ra \ren'gerə\ *n* -s [AmerSp, lameness, fr. *rengo* lame, fr. Sp *renco*, prob. of Gmc origin; akin to OE *wrencan* to twist — more at WRENCH] *Peru* : swayback of sheep

reni- *comb form* [L *renes* kidneys] **1** : kidney ⟨*reni*form⟩ ⟨*reni*puncture⟩ **2** : nephridial and ⟨*reni*cardiac⟩ ⟨*reni*pericardial⟩

re·ni·fleur \,renə'flər\ *n* -s [F, sniffer, fr. *renifler* to sniff (fr. MF, fr. OF *re-* + *nifler* to sniff, prob. of imit. origin) + *-eur* -er] : one who receives sexual gratification from smells (as of urine)

ren·i·form \'renə,fȯrm, 'rēn-, -ȯ(ə)m\ *adj* [NL, fr. *reni-* + *-formis* -form] : resembling a mammalian kidney in shape : NEPHROID; *specif* : bean-shaped in outline ⟨a ~ leaf⟩ ⟨a ~ table⟩ — see LEAF illustration

re·nig \rə'nig, rē'-\ *vi* **renigged**; **renigged**; **renigging**; **renigs** [alter. of *renege*] : RENEGE

re·nil·la \rə'nilə\ *n* [NL, fr. L *renes* kidneys + NL *-illa*] **1** *cap* : a genus (the type of the family Renillidae) comprising the sea pansies **2** -s : SEA PANSY

1**re·nil·lid** \-ləd\ *adj* [NL *Renillidae*] : of or relating to the Renillidae

2**renillid** \"\ *n* -s : a coelenterate of the family Renillidae

re·nil·li·dae \-lə,dē\ *n pl*, *cap* [NL, fr. *Renilla*, type genus, + *-idae*] : a family of colonial alcyonarians (order Pennatulacea) having a circular or reniform rachis with the polyps dorsal

re·nin \'rēnən\ *n* -s [L *renes* kidneys + ISV *-in*] : a proteolytic enzyme that is found in kidney and that hydrolyzes hypertensinogen to hypertensin

reni·portal \¦renə, ¦rēnə+\ *adj* [*reni-* + *portal*] : renal portal

ren·i·ten·cy \'renəd·ənsē, rə'nīt°nsē\ *also* **ren·i·tence** \'renəd·ən(t)s, rə'nīt°n(t)s\ *n*, *pl* **renitencies** *also* **renitences** [*renitency* fr. LL *renitentia*, fr. L *renitant-*, *renitens* + *-ia* -y; *renitence* fr. F *rénitence*, fr. MF, fr. LL *renitentia*] : the quality or state of being renitent : RESISTANCE, OPPOSITION, RELUCTANCE

ren·i·tent \'renəd·ənt, rə'nīt°nt\ *adj* [F or L; F *rénitent* fr. L *renitent-*, *renitens*, pres. part. of *reniti* to struggle against, fr. *re-* + *niti* to lean, push, strive — more at NISUS] **1** : resisting pressure or the effect of it : acting against impulse by elastic force **2** : resisting constraint or compulsion : persistently opposed : RECALCITRANT ⟨the Italians . . . have a traditional way of being subtly and stubbornly ~ to any government —Eric Mettler⟩

rennes \'ren\ *adj*, *usu cap* [fr. *Rennes*, city of northwest France] : of or from the city of Rennes, France : of the kind or style prevalent in Rennes

1**ren·net** \'renət, *usu* -əd·+V\ *n* -s [ME, fr. (assumed) *rennen* to cause to coagulate (fr. OE *gerennan*, fr. *ge-* together + — assumed — *rennan* to cause to run — akin to OHG *rennen* to cause to run, ON *renna*, Goth ur*rannjan*; all fr. a prehistoric causative of the verb represented by OE *rinnan* to run) + *-et* — more at CO-, RUN] **1 a** : the contents of the stomach of an unweaned calf or other animal **b** : the lining membrane of the stomach (as the fourth stomach of ruminants) used for curdling milk; *also* : a preparation of the stomach of animals that is used for this purpose **c** : RENNIN **d** *or* **rennet bag** *or* **rennet stomach** : ABOMASUM **2** : something used to curdle milk ⟨vegetable ~⟩

2**rennet** \"\ *vt* -ED/-ING/-S : to add rennet to (milk) in cheese making to promote formation of curd

rennet casein *n* : CASEIN C

ren·nin \-nən\ *n* -s [*rennet* + *-in*] : a crystallizable enzyme that coagulates milk, that occurs esp. with pepsin in the gastric juice of young animals and is obtained as a yellowish powder, grains, or scales usu. by extraction of the mucous membrane of the fourth stomach of calves, and that is used chiefly in making cheese, junkets, and casein for plastics — called also *chymosin*

reno- *comb form* [L *renes* kidneys] **1** : kidney ⟨*reno*graphy⟩ **2** : renal and ⟨*reno*cutaneous⟩ ⟨*reno*gastric⟩ ⟨*reno*intestinal⟩ ⟨*reno*pulmonary⟩

re·nominate \(')rē+\ *vt* [*re-* + *nominate*] : to nominate again or anew esp. for a term of office in immediate succession — **re·nomination** \(¦)rē+\ *n*

ren·o·trophic \¦renə·¦träfik, ¦rēn-\ *adj* [*reno-* + *-trophic*] : tending to induce enlargement of the kidney ⟨~ hormonal agents⟩

ren·o·trop·ic \-äpik\ *adj* [*reno-* + *-tropic*] **1** : RENOTROPHIC **2** : specifically attracted to kidney tissue ⟨~ infective agents⟩

1**re·nounce** \rə'naůn(t)s, rē'-\ *vb* -ED/-ING/-S [ME *renouncen*, fr. MF *renoncer*, fr. L *renuntiare* to report back, retract, renounce, fr. *re-* + *nuntiare* to report, fr. *nuntius* message, messenger — more at NUNCIO] *vt* **1** *obs* : ANNOUNCE, DECLARE, PROCLAIM **2** : to announce one's abandonment of the ownership of : give up, abandon, or resign usu. formally (something possessed) ⟨~ a title⟩ ⟨~ a claim⟩ **3** : to give up or abandon (something practiced, professed, intended) ⟨~ his errors⟩ ⟨~ faith⟩ ⟨~ a purpose⟩ ⟨~ the use of nuclear weapons⟩ **4** : to refuse further to follow, obey, or recognize : cast off : DISCLAIM, REPUDIATE ⟨~ one's son⟩ ⟨~ the authority of the church⟩ **5 a** : REVOKE *vt* 2 **b** : REFUSE *vt* 6 ~ *vi* **1** : to make a renunciation **2 a** : REVOKE *vi* 2 **b** : REFUSE *vi* 3 **3** : to abandon, decline, or resign formally some legal right or trust (as citizenship) **syn** see ABJURE

2**renounce** \"\ *n* -s [F *renonce*, fr. *renoncer* to renounce] **1** : failure to follow suit when able to do so **2** : a failure to follow suit

re·nounce·able \-səbəl\ *adj* : that can be renounced

re·nounce·ment \-smənt\ *n* -s [MF *renoncement*, fr. *renoncer* to renounce + *-ment*] : RENUNCIATION

re·nounc·er \-sə(r)\ *n* -s : one that renounces

ren·o·vate \'renə,vāt, *usu* -ād·+V\ *vb* -ED/-ING/-S [L *renovatus*, past part. of *renovare* to renovate, fr. *re-* + *novare* to make new, fr. *novus* new — more at NEW] *vt* **1** : to restore to life, vigor, or activity : REVIVE, REGENERATE **2 :** to restore to a former state (as of freshness, soundness, purity, or newness of appearance) : make over : RENEW ⟨~ a house⟩ **3 a :** to prune (old shrubs or trees) so that the old wood is subsequently replaced by new growth **b :** to invigorate (old lawns, fields, or pastures) by fertilization or cultivation ~ *vi* **:** to become renewed : REVIVE

renovated butter *n* [fr. past part. of *renovate*] : PROCESS BUTTER

ren·o·vat·ing·ly *adv* [*renovating* (pres. part. of *renovate*) + *-ly*] : in a renovating manner

ren·o·va·tion \ˌ==ˈvāshən\ *n* [ME *renovacion*, fr. MF or L; MF *renovation*, fr. L *renovation-*, *renovatio*, fr. *renovatus* (past part. of *renovare* to renew) + *-ion-*, *-io* -ion — more at RENOVATE] **1 :** the act or process of renovating : making over : REVIVAL **2 :** the state of being renovated

ren·o·va·tion·ist \-sh(ə)nəst\ *n* -s [*renovation* + *-ist*] : an advocate of renovation (as of a government)

ren·o·va·tor \ˈ==ˌvād·ə(r), -ātə-\ *n* [LL, fr. L *renovatus* + *-or*] **1 :** one that renovates (as worn or damaged articles) **2 :** a nozzle attachment for the suction pipe of a vacuum cleaner

[1]**re·nown** \rəˈnau̇n, rēˈ-\ *n* -s [ME *renoun*, fr. MF *renon*, fr. OF, fr. *renomer* to celebrate, fr. *re-* + *nomer* to name, fr. L *nominare*, fr. *nomin-*, *nomen* name — more at NAME] **1 :** the state of being widely acclaimed and highly honored (as for signal achievement) ⟨poet of great ~⟩ ⟨the increasing ~ of the university⟩ ⟨win ~ by a deed of heroism⟩ **2** *obs* **a :** REPORT, RUMOR; *also* **:** good report **b :** REPUTATION; *also* : NOTORIETY **3 :** something renowned (as a deed) **syn** see FAME

[2]**renown** \"\ *vt* -ED/-ING/-S [MF *renommer*, fr. OF *renomer*] : to give renown to : make renowned

re·nowned \-nd\ *adj* [ME *renouned*, fr. past part. of *renoun* to renown] : having renown : CELEBRATED ⟨one of the most ~ shrines on the continent⟩ — **re·nowned·ly** \-nədlē, -nd-\ *adv* — **re·nowned·ness** \-nədnəs, -n(d)n-\ *n* -ES

re·nown·er \-nə(r)\ *n* -s [*renown* + *-er*] : one that gives renown

rens·se·laer·ite \ˈren(t)sələˌrīt, ¦ren(t)sə¦liˌrīt\ *n* -s [Stephen Van *Rensselaer* †1839 Am. army officer and politician + E *-ite*] : a soft compact talc that is an altered pyroxene and is often worked in a lathe into articles (as inkstands)

[1]**rent** \ˈrent\ *n* -s *often attrib* [ME *rente*, fr. OF, income from a property, fr. (assumed) VL *rendita*, fr. fem. of past part. of (assumed) *rendere* to yield — more at RENDER] **1** *also* **rents** *pl, chiefly dial* **:** a piece of property that the owner allows another to use in exchange for a payment in services, kind, or money : a rented property; *esp* **:** an apartment or house that rents **2** *obs* **a :** REVENUE, INCOME **b :** TRIBUTE, TAX, TOLL **3 a :** a return made by a tenant or occupant of land or corporeal hereditaments to the owner for the possession and use thereof : a fixed periodical profit in money, provisions, chattels, or services issuing out of lands and tenements in payment for use; *esp* **:** a pecuniary sum agreed upon between a tenant and his landlord and paid at fixed intervals by the tenant to the landlord for the use of land or its appendages ⟨~ for a house⟩ **b :** the amount paid by a hirer or lessee of personal property (as farming stock, machinery) to the owner for the use thereof whether combined with rent for land or not **c :** a royalty under a mineral lease **d :** compensation for use and occupation of real estate not arising out of a lease in writing **4 a :** the portion of the income of an economy (as of a nation) attributable to land as a factor of production in addition to capital and labor : the income of landowners as a class — compare PROFIT, WAGE **b :** the income earned by a unit of production (as a market garden, a repairman) beyond the minimum required to make employment in such production worth while by meeting costs and at least equaling other possible employments in returns : the difference between the actual return from a commodity or service and the supply price : ECONOMIC RENT **c :** income or gain that is a differential return (as the excess of personal earnings of a producer of rare ability over those of an average producer) or as a surplus above costs ⟨entrepreneur's ~ denotes the profits of an ably managed . . . enterprise, conceived of as a differential above the return secured by a marginal undertaking which is barely able to meet its costs —A.A.Young⟩ — see CONSUMER'S SURPLUS, PRODUCER'S SURPLUS — **for rent :** available for use or service in return for payment : to let ⟨a house *for rent*⟩ : for hire ⟨costumes *for rent*⟩

[2]**rent** \"\ *vb* -ED/-ING/-S [ME *renten*, fr. *rente* rent] *vt* **1** *obs* **:** to give revenues or an endowment to : ENDOW **2 :** to take and hold under an agreement to pay rent : pay rent for ⟨the tenant ~*s* the house by the month under a one-year lease⟩ **3 :** to grant the possession and enjoyment of for rent : hire out : LET ⟨the owner ~*s* the house at a reasonable figure⟩ ~ *vi* **1 :** to be for rent ⟨the largest apartment ~*s* for $800 a year⟩ **2 a :** to obtain the possession and use of a place or article for rent ⟨~*s* from the family in the other apartment⟩ **b :** to allow the possession and use of property for rent ⟨~*s* to families with children⟩

[3]**rent** *past of* REND

[4]**rent** \ˈrent\ *vb* [ME *renten*, alter. (influenced by [3]*rent*) of *renden* to rend] *dial chiefly Eng* : REND, TEAR

[5]**rent** \"\ *n* -s **1 :** an opening (as a tear in cloth, a cleft in the earth, a gorge, a crack in wood) made by or as if by rending **2 :** a split in a party or organized group : SCHISM **3 :** an act or an instance of rending **syn** see BREACH

rent·abil·i·ty \ˌrentəˈbiləd·ē\ *n* **:** the quality or state of being rentable

rent·able \-təbəl\ *adj* [[2]*rent* + *-able*] : that can be rented

rent·age \ˈrentij\ *n* -s [[1]*rent* + *-age*] : RENT, RENTAL

[1]**rent·al** \-tᵊl\ *n* -s [ME, fr. ML *rentale*, fr. ME *rente* rent + L *-ale*, neut. of *-alis* -al] **1 :** RENT-ROLL **2 :** an amount paid or collected as rent : income from rent ⟨collected the most ~ of the city's apartment house owners⟩ : return (as a sum of money) given or received as rent : the amount of rent ⟨the average ~ (including gas, electricity, heat, and janitor service) is $8.08 per month for each room —*Amer. Guide Series: N.J.*⟩ **3** *Scots law, obs* **:** a tack usu. for life for a low customary rent granted to kindly tenants **4 :** a property (as an apartment, automobile, dinner jacket) that is given for use in return for payment : something rented ⟨moved to a cheaper ~⟩ **5 :** an act of renting ⟨~*s* are made only to . . . established film societies —*Saturday Rev.*⟩ **6 :** a business that rents something

[2]**rental** \"\ *adj* **1 :** of or relating to rent ⟨~ charges⟩ **2 :** that can be or has been rented ⟨~ housing⟩ ⟨a ~ car⟩ ⟨~ books⟩ **3 :** dealing in rental property ⟨a ~ agency⟩

rental collection *n* **:** a collection of books in an otherwise free library (as in a college) that may be borrowed at a daily fee

rentaler *or* **rentaller** *n* -s [[1]*rental* + *-er*] *obs* : KINDLY TENANT

rental library *n* **:** a commercially operated library (as in a store) that lends books at a usu. fixed charge per book per day ⟨a drug store with a *rental library* serviced by a concession company⟩ — called also *lending library*

rental value insurance *n* **:** insurance against loss to the occupant of the rental value of described premises because of specified damage to such premises

rent charge *n, pl* **rents charge** [[1]*rent*] **1 :** a periodical payment made a charge on land by reservation in a conveyance of land for life or in fee simple or granted by deed and expressly giving to the holder who has no reversionary interest in the land the right of distress for arrears — compare RENT SECK **2** *Brit* **:** an annual sum charged on land or payable out of the income of land to which attaches a statutory power of distress for arrears

rent charger *n* **:** the owner of a rent charge

rent control *n* **:** government regulation of the amount charged as rent for housing and often also of eviction

rente \ˈränt\ *n* -s [F, income, rent, fr. OF — more at RENT] **1 :** annual income under French law on property forever alienated of the same type as the English rents charge, rents seck, and annuities **2 a :** interest payable by the government of France and some other European countries on the consolidated debt **b :** a government security yielding rente

ren·ten·mark \ˈrentᵊnˌmärk\ *n, sometimes cap* [G, fr. *rente* income (fr. OF) + *mark* — more at RENT, MARK] : a temporary German monetary unit used for bank notes issued in 1923 to stabilize currency, made equivalent to one billion inflated imperial marks, and superseded by the reichsmark

[1]**rent·er** \ˈrentə(r)\ *n* -s [ME, fr. *renten* to enjoy the possession of for rent + *-er*] : one that rents: as **a :** the lessee or tenant of lands, tenements, or other property **b** *chiefly Brit* **:** a motion-picture distributor

[2]**ren·ter** \"\ *vt* -ED/-ING/-S [F *rentrer*, alter. (influenced by *rentrer* to enter again, fr. OF, fr. *re-* + *entrer* to enter) of MF *rentraire*, fr. *re-* + *entraire* to draw in, fr. OF, fr. *en-* in- (fr. L *in-*) + *traire* to draw, fr. L *trahere* — more at ENTER, DRAW] : to fine-draw rents in cloth

[3]**rent·er** \"\ *n* -s [[4]*rent* + *-er*] : CHIPPER d

ren·tier \ˈrän·(ˌ)tyā\ *n* -s [F, fr. OF, fr. *rente* + *-ier* -er] **1 :** one who owns rentes **2 :** a person who receives a fixed income (as from land, stocks, bonds) : one who lives on income from investments

renting *pres part of* RENT

rent insurance *n* [[1]*rent*] : insurance against loss to a landlord because of suspension of rents resulting from specified damage to rented premises

[1]**rent·less** \ˈrentləs\ *adj* [[1]*rent* + *-less*] **1** *obs* **:** not yielding rent **2 :** rent free **3 :** UNRENTABLE

[2]**rentless** \"\ *adj* [[5]*rent* + *-less*] : not torn

rent of assize [[1]*rent*] : a fixed rent paid by freeholders or ancient copyholders of an English manor

rent party *n* **:** a party to which admission is charged with the profits going to pay the host's rent

rent resolute *n, Old Eng law* **:** crown rents from lands formerly in possession of now dissolved religious bodies

rent–roll \ˈ=ˌ=\ *n* [[1]*rent* + *roll*] : a register of rents including the names of tenants and the amounts due; *also* **:** the total income indicated by such a register

rents *pl of rent, pres 3d sing of* RENT

rent seck *n, pl* **rents seck** [ME *rent sek*, fr. AF *rente seque*, lit., dry rent] : a rent reserved or granted like a rent charge orig. not having the right of distress but in England having a power of distress annexed in 1730

rent service *n* [[1]*rent*] : rent reserved out of land held by fealty or other corporeal service and under the common law having attached the right of distress

rents, issues, and profits *n pl* **:** the total wealth or profit either gross or net after the satisfaction of reasonable expenses arising from the ownership or possession of property

rent table *n* **:** a round or polygonal table made during the second half of the 18th century in England with small drawers often labeled with the days of the week and possibly used for a simple filing system for rent collecting

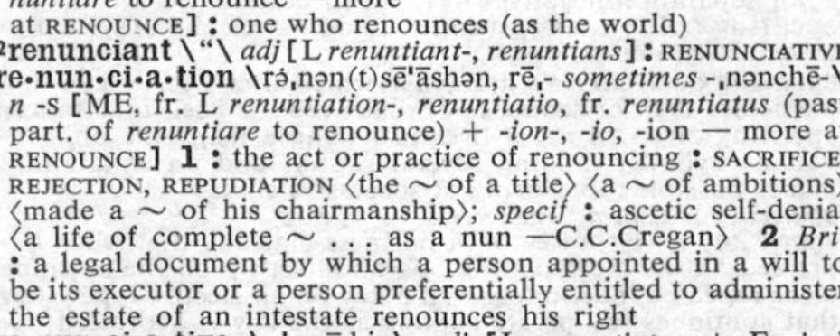

rent table

re·number \(ˈ)rē+\ *vt* [ME *renombren*, fr. *re-* + *nombren* to number] : to number again (as with different numbers) ⟨~ the street⟩ ⟨~ pages 15 to 34⟩

[1]**re·nun·ci·ant** \rəˈnən(t)sēənt\ *n* -s [L *renuntiant-*, *renuntians*, pres. part. of *renuntiare* to renounce — more at RENOUNCE] : one who renounces (as the world)

[2]**renunciant** \"\ *adj* [L *renuntiant-*, *renuntians*] : RENUNCIATIVE

re·nun·ci·a·tion \rəˌnən(t)sēˈāshən, rēˌ- *sometimes* -ˌnənchē-\ *n* -s [ME, fr. L *renuntiation-*, *renuntiatio*, fr. *renuntiatus* (past part. of *renuntiare* to renounce) + *-ion-*, *-io*, -ion — more at RENOUNCE] **1 :** the act or practice of renouncing : SACRIFICE, REJECTION, REPUDIATION ⟨the ~ of a title⟩ ⟨a ~ of ambitions⟩ ⟨made a ~ of his chairmanship⟩; *specif* **:** ascetic self-denial ⟨a life of complete ~ . . . as a nun —C.C.Cregan⟩ **2** *Brit* **:** a legal document by which a person appointed in a will to be its executor or a person preferentially entitled to administer the estate of an intestate renounces his right

re·nun·ci·a·tive \=ˈ==ˌād·iv\ *adj* [L *renuntiatus* + E *-ive*] : marked by or expressive of renunciation

re·nun·ci·a·to·ry \=ˈ==əˌtōrē\ *adj* [L *renuntiatus* + E *-ory*] : of or relating to renunciation : RENUNCIATIVE

[1]**ren·verse** \renˈvərs\ *vt* -ED/-ING/-S [MF *renverser*, fr. *re-* + *enverser* to invert, fr. OF, fr. *envers* upside down, fr. L *inversus* — more at INVERSE] *archaic* **:** to turn back : REVERSE, OVERTURN, OVERTHROW

[2]**ren·ver·sé** \¦ränˌver¦sā\ *adj* [F, lit., turned back, fr. past part. of *renverser* to turn back, fr. MF] : consisting of or accompanied by a bending of the head and body from the waist while turning in ballet : REVERSED ⟨a ~ movement⟩

ren·verse·ment \renˈvərsmənt\ *n* -s [F, reversal, inversion, fr. MF, fr. *renverser* to turn back, turn over + *-ment* — more at RENVERSE] : an airplane maneuver consisting of a half-roll followed by a half-loop

ren·voi \renˈvȯi\ *n* -s [F, act of sending back, reference, fr. MF, fr. *renvoyer* to send back, fr. OF, fr. *re-* + *envoyer*, *envoier* to send — more at ENVOY] **1 :** the return by a government of an alien to his own country **2 :** the reference of a matter involving a conflict of jurisdiction in private international law to the law or courts of a jurisdiction other than the local jurisdiction involved

re·occupy \(ˈ)rē+\ *vt* [*re-* + *occupy*] : to occupy again

re·occur \¦rē+\ *vi* [*re-* + *occur*] : to occur again

re·occurrence \"+\ *n* [*re-* + *occurrence*] : a second or another occurrence

re·odorization \(¦)rē+\ *n* **:** the act or process of reodorizing or the state of being reodorized

re·odorize \(ˈ)rē+\ *vt* [*re-* + *odorize*] : to change the odor of — compare DEODORIZE

re·open \(ˈ)rē+\ *vb* [*re-* + *open*] *vt* **1 :** to open again ⟨~*ed* his eyes⟩ ⟨~*ed* the school⟩ **2 a :** to take up again : RESUME ⟨the right to ~ discussion of matters affecting international peace —Vera M. Dean⟩ **b :** to resume the discussion or consideration of (a closed matter) ⟨~ the contract to discuss wages —*Wall Street Jour.*⟩ **c :** to try or hear (a legal suit or action) anew esp. for the purpose of hearing new evidence **3 :** to begin again ⟨~ fire⟩ ⟨~ hostilities⟩ ~ *vi* **:** to open again; *specif* **:** to resume operations after an interruption or suspension ⟨the store ~*ed* after a one-week shutdown⟩

re·opener \"+\ *n* : REOPENING CLAUSE

reopening clause *n* **:** a clause in a collective bargaining contract providing for a reconsideration of an issue (as wages) during the life of the contract

[1]**re·order** \(ˈ)rē+\ *vb* [*re-* + *order*] *vt* **1 :** to order again or anew : arrange in a different way : REORGANIZE ⟨our greatest opportunity to ~ our city patterns —Charles Abrams⟩ **2 :** to give a reorder for ⟨~*ed* two dozen blouses of the same style⟩ ~ *vi* **:** to place a reorder ⟨when I sell these, I'll ~⟩

[2]**reorder** \"\ *n* **:** an order for the same goods previously ordered from a particular firm or supplier

re·ordination \(¦)rē+\ *n* [LL *reordination-*, *reordinatio*, fr. *reordinatus* (past part. of *reordinare* to ordain again, fr. L *re-* + LL *ordinare* to ordain) + L *-ion-*, *-io* -ion — more at ORDAIN] : a second or repeated ordination

re·organization \"+\ *n* **1 :** the act of reorganizing or the state of being reorganized ⟨a thorough-going ~ of our entire body of subject-matter along new lines —*School & Society*⟩ **2 a :** the rehabilitation of the finances of a business concern under procedures prescribed by federal bankruptcy legislation **b :** any of various procedures (as recapitalizations or mergers) that affect the tax structure of a corporation under federal income tax legislation **3 :** the alteration of the existing structure of governmental units (as bureaus or legislative committees) and the lines of control and authority between them usu. to promote greater efficiency and responsibility

re·organize \(ˈ)rē+\ *vb* [*re-* + *organize*] *vt* **:** to organize again or anew : change the organization of ⟨~ the department to increase efficiency⟩ ~ *vi* **:** to effect a reorganization ⟨with the option then to continue, suspend, or ~ —W.Z.Ripley⟩ — **re·organizer** \"+\ *n*

re·orient \"+\ *vt* [*re-* + *orient*] : to orient again or anew : change the orientation of ⟨suggests that American institutions of higher learning ~ their programs to include professional or vocational training for all —H.J.Carman⟩

re·orientate \"+\ *vt* [*re-* + *orientate*] : REORIENT

re·orientation \(¦)rē+\ *n* [*re-* + *orientation*] : a changed orientation ⟨a ~ of attitudes toward this part of the world —Robert Trumbull⟩

[1]**rep** \ˈrep\ *n* -s [short for *reputation*] *slang* **:** REPUTATION; *esp* **:** status in a group (as a street gang)

[2]**rep** \"\ *n* -s [prob. short for [3]*reprobate*] : a person given to immoral behavior

[3]**rep** *or* **repp** \ˈrep\ *n* -s [modif. of F *reps*, modif. of E *ribs*, pl. of [1]*rib*] : a clothing and upholstery fabric in plain weave with prominent rounded crosswise ribs that is usu. made by alternating fine and coarse yarns or by the slacking and tensioning of yarns and that is woven from various fibers singly or in combination

[4]**rep** \"\ *n* -s [short for [2]*representative*] : REPRESENTATIVE; *specif* **:** a cowboy who rides in a roundup as the representative of a particular ranch ⟨a ~ from each ranch in the area would see that everything was done fair and square —S.E.Fletcher⟩

[5]**rep** \"\ *vi* **repped**; **repped**; **repping**; **reps :** to act as a rep in a roundup ⟨inquired what brand we were *repping* for —Emma Yates⟩

[6]**rep** \"\ *n* -s [by shortening] : REPERTORY

[7]**rep** \"\ *or* **rep unit** *n, pl* **rep** *or* **reps** [*rep* fr. *r*oentgen *e*quivalent *p*hysical] : the dosage of any ionizing radiation that will develop the same amount of energy upon absorption in human tissues as one roentgen of X-ray or gamma-ray dosage — compare REM

rep *abbr* **1** repair **2** repeat **3** report; reported; reporter **4** republic; republican

re·pack \(ˈ)rē+\ *vt* [ME *repakken*, fr. *re-* + *pakken* to pack] : to pack again or anew; *specif* **:** to put into a different container ⟨~*ed* tomatoes⟩

re·package \"+\ *vt* [*re-* + *package*] : to package again or anew; *specif* **:** to put into a more efficient or attractive form

[1]**re·paint** \"+\ *vt* [*re-* + *paint*] : to paint again or anew ⟨figures of the past whom I should like to ~ for this generation —H.J.Laski⟩ ⟨~ the house⟩; *specif* **:** to paint over (part of a picture) ⟨the painting turned up again heavily ~*ed* —*Time*⟩

[2]**re·paint** \ˈrē+ˌ-, =ˈ=\ *n* **1 :** the fact of having been repainted ⟨is marred by a clumsy ~⟩ **2 :** something repainted

[1]**re·pair** \rəˈpa(a)|(ə)r, rēˈp-, -pe|, |ə\ *vi* -ED/-ING/-S [ME *repairen*, fr. MF *repairer*, *repairier* to return, go back to one's own country, dwell, fr. OF *repairier*, fr. LL *repatriare* to go back to one's own country, fr. L *re-* + LL *-patriare* (fr. L *patria* native country) — more at EXPATRIATE] **1 a :** to betake oneself : GO ⟨summoned me to ~ immediately to the lobby —Horace Sutton⟩ **b :** to go habitually : RESORT ⟨sacred trees to which they ~ at various times, but especially before harvest —J.G.Frazer⟩ **c :** to go to a specified place for a specified purpose ⟨~ to the second-floor cafe to drink tea and coffee —C.S.Coon⟩ ⟨~*ing* to their villages in the rainy season to plant their plots —R.H.Lowie⟩ **d :** to go for the purpose of assembling : RALLY ⟨raise a standard to which the wise and honest can ~ —George Washington⟩ ⟨a standard of ethical professional conduct to which all architects of good will might ~ —G.B.Cummings⟩ **2** *obs* **:** RETURN ⟨all to Athens back again ~ —Shak.⟩

[2]**repair** \"\ *n* -s [ME *repair*, *repaire*, fr. MF *repaire* return, dwelling, fr. OF, fr. *repairier*, v.] **1 :** the act or fact of repairing to a place : RESORT ⟨as the day gets warm, ~ is had to the shade of a tree —James Stevenson-Hamilton⟩ **2** *chiefly Scot* **:** a concourse esp. of people : FLOCKING **3 :** a place of resort : HAUNT ⟨his house became a ~ for rising politicians⟩

[3]**repair** \"\ *vb* -ED/-ING/-S [ME *repairen*, *reparen*, fr. MF *reparer*, fr. L *reparare*, fr. *re-* + *parare* to prepare — more at PARE] *vt* **1 a :** to restore by replacing a part or putting together what is torn or broken : FIX, MEND ⟨so neatly ~*ed* that he could see no trace of the once familiar rents —T.B.Costain⟩ ⟨~ a house⟩ ⟨~ a shoe⟩ **b :** to restore to a sound or healthy state : RENEW, REVIVIFY ⟨~ his strength⟩ ⟨resume his law practice in order to ~ his private fortune —E.M.Coulter⟩ ⟨~ the tissues of the body⟩ **2 :** to make good : REMEDY ⟨the material and moral damage took long to ~ —Jacquetta & Christopher Hawkes⟩ ⟨~ the lack of early education —E.H. Collis⟩ ⟨will ~ his ignominious failure —Bernard DeVoto⟩ **3 :** to make up for : compensate for ⟨~ an insult⟩ ⟨~ an injustice⟩ ~ *vi* **:** to make repairs **syn** see MEND

[4]**repair** \"\ *n* -s **1 a :** the act or process of repairing : restoration to a state of soundness, efficiency, or health ⟨the boat was beyond ~⟩ ⟨a thorough ~ of the crazy fabric of human nature —T.L.Peacock⟩ **b :** an instance or result of repairing ⟨the coat needed only a simple ~⟩ ⟨made a few ~*s* to the stairs where some boards had come loose⟩ ⟨the ~ to the rug was evident to the eye⟩ **c :** the replacement of destroyed cells or tissues by new formations **2 a :** relative condition with respect to soundness or need of repairing ⟨the car is in reasonably good ~⟩ ⟨the building is in poor ~⟩ **b :** the state of being in good or sound condition ⟨the house is in ~⟩ ⟨the house is out of ~⟩ ⟨his judgment was in constant ~ —F.A.Swinnerton⟩ **3 repairs** *pl* **:** the portion of maintenance charges expended to keep fixed assets in adequate and efficient operating condition and recorded on the books as expense — contrasted with *renewal* and *replacement*

re·pair·able \-pa(a)rəbəl, -per-\ *adj* **:** capable of being repaired

re·pair·er \-pa(a)rə(r), -perə-\ *n* -s **:** one that repairs; *specif* **:** one whose work is repairing ⟨shoe ~⟩ ⟨watch ~⟩

re·pair·man \-pa(a)rmən, -per-\ *n, pl* **repairmen :** one who repairs; *specif* **:** one whose occupation is to make repairs or readjustments in a mechanism ⟨a typewriter ~⟩ ⟨a radio ~⟩

repair ship *n* **:** a naval auxiliary vessel fitted with shops for the handling of repairs to naval vessels

repair shop *n* **:** an establishment where repairs are made ⟨a small *repair shop* that mends all sorts of items⟩

re·pand \rəˈpand, rēˈp-\ *adj* [L *repandus* bent backward, turned up, fr. *re-* + *pandus* bent, crooked; akin to ON *fattr* bent backward and perh. to L *pandere* to spread — more at FATHOM] *of a leaf* **:** having a slightly undulating margin

rep·a·ra·ble \ˈrep(ə)rəbəl *also* ÷ *like* REPAIRABLE\ *adj* [L *reparabilis*, fr. *reparare* to repair + *-bilis* -able] **1 :** capable of being mended or put into sound condition : REPAIRABLE ⟨when inspected parts are found defective but ~ —G.J.Stegemerten⟩ **2 :** capable of being remedied or made good ⟨~ damage⟩

rep·a·ra·tion \ˌrepəˈrāshən\ *n* -s [ME *reparacioun*, fr. MF *reparation*, fr. LL *reparation-*, *reparatio*, fr. L *reparatus* (past part. of *reparare* to repair) + *-ion-*, *-io* -ion — more at REPAIR] **1 a :** the act or process of mending or restoring : a repairing or keeping in repair ⟨the ~ of wasted tissue⟩ ⟨a church in need of constant ~⟩ **b reparations** *pl* **:** REPAIRS **2 a :** the act of making amends, offering expiation, or giving satisfaction for a wrong or injury ⟨the treatment may consist of ~ to and propitiation of the offended spirit —*Notes & Queries on Anthropology*⟩ **b :** something done or given as amends or satisfaction ⟨was educated in France at royal expense as ~ for the death of his father —H.C.Nixon⟩ **3 :** the payment of damages : INDEMNIFICATION; *specif* **:** compensation in money or in materials (as commodities or capital equipment) payable by a defeated nation as war indemnity for direct damages to or expenditures sustained by another nation as a result of hostilities with the defeated nation — usu. used in pl. ⟨extract maximum ~*s* by dismantling and transferring plants —Karl Loewenstein⟩

re·par·a·tive \rəˈparəd·iv, rēˈp-\ *adj* [LL *reparativus*, fr. L *reparatus* (past part. of *reparare*) + *-ivus* -ive] **1 :** of, relating to, or effecting repair **2 :** serving to make amends ⟨does a fine ~ job for several neglected poets —George Dillon⟩

re·par·a·to·ry \-arəˌtōrē\ *adj* [fr. *reparative*, after such pairs as E *preparative: preparatory*] : REPARATIVE

[1]**rep·ar·tee** \¦repə(r)¦tē, -ˌpär¦t-, -ˌpȧ¦t-, -tā\ *n* -s [F *repartie*, fr. *repartir* to retort, fr. MF, fr. *re-* + *partir* to divide, go away — more at PART] **1 a :** a quick and witty reply : a clever retort ⟨won the applause of the audience with his ~ to a heckler⟩ **b :** a succession of clever retorts ⟨beneath the surface of ~ and mock seriousness —R.M.Weaver⟩ ⟨the constant ~ is artificial and wearying⟩ **2 :** adroitness and cleverness in reply : quickness and sharpness in retort ⟨was noted for his ~ and impromptu wit⟩ **3 :** the uttering of clever retorts ⟨her skill at ~ has made her many enemies⟩ **syn** see WIT

[2]**repartee** \"\ *vi* **reparteed**; **reparteed**; **reparteeing**; **repartees :** to make or be able to make clever retorts

re·par·ti·mi·en·to \rəˌpärd·əmēˈen·(ˌ)tō, ˌrāˌpärd·əmˈyen·-\ *n* -s [AmerSp, fr. Sp, distribution, fr. *repartir* to distribute (fr. *re-* — fr. L — + *partir* to divide, fr. L *partire*, *partiri*) + *-miento* -ment (fr. L *-mentum*) — more at PART] : a grant or distribution formerly made to Spanish colonists or establishments in America; *esp* **:** a grant of Indian forced labor (as for use in agriculture, in mining, or in construction) — compare ENCOMIENDA

re·partition \ˌrē+, *in sense 1* ˈrē *or* ˌre+\ *n* [prob. fr. Sp *repartición*, fr. *repartir* to distribute, after Sp *partir* to divide: *partición* division (fr. L *partition-, partitio* division, partition)] **1 :** DISTRIBUTION ⟨the relative ~ of land and water is very different from what prevails on the earth —*Popular Science Monthly*⟩ **2 :** a second or additional partition ⟨the ~ of the country⟩

re·pass \(ˈ)rē+\ *vb* [ME *repassen*, fr. MF *repasser*, fr. OF, fr. *re-* + *passer* to pass] *vi* **:** to pass again esp. in the opposite direction **:** RETURN ⟨they pass and they ~ with pallid eyes —Robert Browning⟩ ~ *vt* **1 a :** to cross again in returning ⟨~ the desert⟩ ⟨~ the ocean⟩ **b :** to pass through, over, or by again ⟨~ the gate⟩ ⟨~ the road⟩ ⟨~ the house⟩ **2 :** to cause to pass again ⟨~ the needle through the cloth⟩ **3** [*re-* + *pass*] **:** to adopt again ⟨~*ed* the bill over the presidential veto⟩ ⟨~*ed* the resolution⟩

re·passage \"+\ *n* [ME, fr. MF, fr. *repasser* + *-age*] **:** the act or privilege of repassing **:** passage back or freedom to repass ⟨granted them passage and ~ through his territory⟩

¹re·past \rəˈpast, rēˈp-, -paa(ə)st,-paist,-pȧst *also* ˈrē,p-\ *n* -S [ME, fr. MF, food, fr. OF, fr. *repaistre* to give a meal to, feed (fr. *re-* + *paistre* to feed, fr. L *pascere*), after OF *paistre* to feed: *past* food, meal (fr. L *pastus*, past part. of *pascere* to feed — more at FOOD] **1 :** something that is taken as food ⟨crow is hardly a palatable ~ for the average citizen —*Phoenix Flame*⟩; *specif* **:** a supply of food and drink served as a meal ⟨a delicious ~ of simple but perfectly cooked food⟩ **2 a :** the act of taking food ⟨if, before ~, it shall please you to gratify the table with a grace —Shak.⟩ **b :** the time or occasion of eating a meal ⟨preferred to be alone during his evening ~⟩

²repast \"\ *vb* -ED/-ING/-S [ME *repasten*, fr. *repast*, n.] *vt*, *obs* **:** to supply food to **:** FEED ⟨~ them with my blood —Shak.⟩ ~ *vi* **:** to take food **:** FEAST — usu. used with *on* or *upon*

repastination *n* -S [L *repastination-, repastinatio*, fr. *repastinatus* (past part. of *repastinare* to dig again, fr. *re-* + *pastinare* to dig and trench in preparation for the planting of vines, fr. *pastinum* 2-pronged dibble) + *-ion-, -io* -ion] *obs* **:** the act of digging over again ⟨this continual motion, ~, and turning of the mold with the spade —John Evelyn⟩

re·patri·a·ble \rēˈpā·trēəbəl *also* -pa··\ *adj* [ˈ*repatriate* + *-able*] **:** capable of being repatriated

¹re·patri·ate \(ˈ)ˌ≈ˈ≈≈,āt, *usu* -ˌād.+V\ *vt* -ED/-ING/-S [LL *repatriatus*, past part. of *repatriare* to go back to one's own country — more at REPAIR] **1 :** to restore or return to one's country of origin, allegiance, or citizenship ⟨*repatriated* prisoners of war as quickly as they could be processed⟩ **2 :** to restore to the country of origin ⟨has at the moment no dollars to remit any profits or ~ any capital —*Time*⟩

²re·patri·ate \-ˌət, -ˌāt, *usu* |d.+V\ *n* -S **:** one who is repatriated

re·patri·a·tion \(ˌ)≈,≈≈ˈāshən\ *n* -S [ML *repatriation-, repatriatio*, fr. LL *repatriatus* (past part. of *repatriare*) + L *-ion-, -io* -ion] **:** the act of repatriating or the state of being repatriated

¹re·pay \(ˈ)rēˈpā, rəˈpā\ *vb* [*re-* + *pay*] *vt* **1 a :** to pay back **:** REFUND ⟨~ the investment in the first year of operation —R.E.Cross⟩ **b :** to give or inflict in return or requital ⟨evil pursueth sinners; but to the righteous good shall be *repaid* —Prov 13:21 (AV)⟩ ⟨~ her scorn for scorn —John Keats⟩ **2 :** to make a return payment to **:** COMPENSATE, REQUITE ⟨if the traveller would only leave the boat and wander inland, he would be *repaid* by the revelation of marvellous beauties of Nature —Anthony Trollope⟩ **3 :** to make requital for **:** RECOMPENSE ⟨a friendly act that was later *repaid* with treachery —*Amer. Guide Series: Maine*⟩ ⟨a society which will well ~ intensive study —W.H.Goodenough⟩ ~ *vi* **:** to make return payment or requital ⟨loans are judged on . . . the ability of the borrower to ~ —*Collier's Yr. Bk.*⟩ **syn** see PAY

²repay \"\ *n* **:** REPAYMENT

re·pay·able \≈ˈ≈əbəl\ *adj* **:** subject to repayment

repaying *adj* **:** PROFITABLE, REWARDING ⟨the necessary, ~ effort to acquire command of the realities masked by musical terminology —*N.Y.Herald Tribune Bk. Rev.*⟩

re·pay·ment \rəˈpāmənt, rēˈp-\ *n* [ME, fr. *re-* + *payment*] **1 :** the act or an instance of paying back **:** REIMBURSEMENT ⟨was unable to make ~ of the loan at the time specified⟩ **2 :** REQUITAL ⟨this ingratitude was a poor ~ for his sacrifices⟩

¹re·peal \rəˈpēl, rēˈp-, *esp before pause or consonant* -ēəl\ *vt* -ED/-ING/-S [ME *repelen*, fr. MF *repeler, rapeler*, fr. OF, fr. *re-* + *apeler* to appeal, call — more at APPEAL] **1 :** to rescind or revoke (as a sentence or law) from operation or effect **:** ABROGATE, ANNUL ⟨pledged that laws forbidding strikes for the duration of the rebellion would be ~*ed* —*Current Biog.*⟩ **2 :** to give up **:** ABANDON, RENOUNCE ⟨all past forgiveness it ~*ed* —William Wordsworth⟩ **3 a** *obs* **:** to summon to return **:** recall from exile ⟨I here forget all former griefs, cancel all grudge, ~ thee home again —Shak.⟩ **b** *obs* **:** to bring back or attempt to bring back **:** restore or seek to restore ⟨she ~*s* him for her body's lust —Shak.⟩ **syn** see REVOKE

²repeal \"\ *n* -S [MF *rapel*, fr. OF, fr. *repeler, rapeler*, v.] **1** *obs* **:** RECALL; *esp* **:** a summoning back from exile ⟨rash in the ~ —Shak.⟩ **2 :** the act or an instance of repealing **:** ABROGATION, REVOCATION ⟨the ~ of a law⟩ ⟨the ~ of the 18th amendment to the U.S. Constitution⟩ ⟨the ~ of a too hasty resolution⟩

re·peal·able \-ēləbəl\ *adj* **:** capable of being repealed

re·peal·er \-ēlə(r)\ *n* -S **1 :** one that repeals; *specif* **:** a legislative act that abrogates an earlier act **2 a :** one who seeks a repeal **b** *usu cap* **:** a supporter of a political campaign initiated about 1830 to repeal the Articles of Union between Great Britain and Ireland

re·peal·ist \-ēləst\ *n* -S **:** one who advocates repeal (as of some specific legislative measure)

¹re·peat \rəˈpēt, rēˈp-, *usu* -ēd· +V\ *vb* -ED/-ING/-S [ME *repeten*, fr. MF *repeter*, fr. L *repetere* to repeat, go back to, fr. *re-* + *petere* to go to or toward — more at FEATHER] *vt* **1 a :** to say or state again **:** REITERATE ⟨~*ed* his command⟩ ⟨~*ed* his question⟩ **b :** to say over from memory **:** RECITE ⟨remember the rest of her lesson, and ~ correctly all those verses —Robert Browning⟩ **c :** to say after another ⟨~ the following words after me⟩ **d :** to make public **:** relate to others **:** DIVULGE ⟨I will not ~ your words . . . outside this cloister; because the consequences to you would certainly be fatal —Henry Adams⟩ ⟨the child ~*s* everything he hears⟩ **2 a :** to make, do, or perform again ⟨~*ed* his earlier protests⟩ ⟨was sent on a similar errand and ~*ed* the theft —Edward Clodd⟩ ⟨for several years this annual fete was ~*ed* —*Amer. Guide Series: Minn.*⟩ **b :** to make appear again **:** cause to recur **:** PRESENT, SHOW, REPRODUCE ⟨two end pavilions ~ the dominant motif of the central pavilion —*Amer. Guide Series: Minn.*⟩ ⟨a game that ~*ed* the pattern of many previous ones between the same teams⟩ ⟨a program ~*ed* on tape⟩ **c :** to go through or experience again ⟨expected to ~ the years of practical banishment endured by his father —W.C.Ford⟩; *specif* **:** to take (a grade or course in school or college) again esp. to make up a failure ⟨had to ~ the fourth grade⟩ ⟨~*ed* English composition⟩ **3 :** to express or present (oneself) again in the same words, terms, or form as before ⟨history sometimes seems to ~ itself⟩ ⟨a writer who ~*s* himself shamelessly⟩ ⟨wrote innumerable songs without ever ~*ing* himself⟩ ~ *vi* **1 :** to say, do, or accomplish something again ⟨there were, to ~ and to conclude, three saving accidents —R.P.Blackmur⟩ ⟨is favored to ~ as batting champion⟩; as **a :** to vote illegally more than once in a particular election ⟨registration of voters is designed to eliminate ~*ing*⟩ **b** *of a timepiece* **:** to strike again the last hour and sometimes the last half hour, quarter hour, or minute if so adjusted **2** *of food* **:** to seem to rise in the gullet **:** give one its taste again ⟨boiled onions always ~ on me⟩

syn ITERATE, REITERATE, INGEMINATE: REPEAT is a general term centering attention on the fact of uttering, saying, or presenting again one or a number of times. ITERATE and REITERATE may stress the fact of frequent repetitive utterance ⟨the bird in the dusk *iterating* . . . his one phrase —C.P.Aiken⟩ ⟨*reiterated* the words until her voice died away in a mumble —Gertrude Atherton⟩ INGEMINATE may indicate a single repetition, a saying twice ⟨comes . . . with his olive branch *ingeminating* peace —*Pall Mall Gazette*⟩ **syn** see in addition QUOTE

²re·peat \", ˈrē,p-\ *n* -S *often attrib* **1 :** the act of repeating ⟨blooom usu. from the later part of June to the end of July, with an occasional ~ late in August —*New Yorker*⟩ **2 :** something that is repeated **:** REPETITION: as **a** (1) **:** a musical passage to be repeated in performance (2) **:** a sign consisting typically of a vertical series of two or four dots that are placed before and after or often only at the end of a passage to be repeated **b :** a repeated pattern in a textile design **c :** a reorder of merchandise **d :** a repeated telegraph message **e :** a rebroadcast of a radio or television program **3 :** the number of threads necessary to make the basic unit of a weave

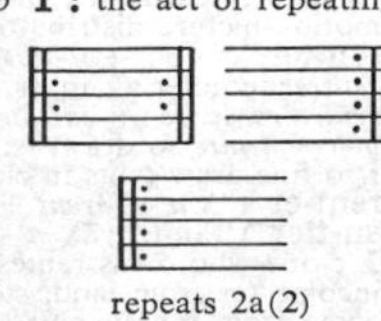

repeats 2a(2)

re·peat·abil·i·ty \rə,pēd·əˈbiləd·ē, rē,p-, -pētə-, -lətē, -i\ *n* **:** the quality or state of being repeatable

re·peat·able \≈ˈ≈≈bəl\ *adj* **:** capable of being repeated or fit to be repeated

repeated *adj* **1 :** renewed or recurring again and again **:** CONSTANT, FREQUENT ⟨~ absences⟩ ⟨~ mistakes⟩ ⟨~ changes of plan⟩ **2 :** said, done, or presented again ⟨an often ~ excuse⟩ ⟨an eloquently ~ speech⟩ ⟨an easily ~ pattern⟩ — **re·peat·ed·ly** *adv*

repeated twinning *n* **:** twinning in which more than two simple crystals are involved

re·peat·er \rəˈpēd·ə(r), rēˈp-, -pētə-\ *n* -S **:** one that repeats: as **a :** one who relates or recites ⟨a ~ of old stories and ballads⟩ **b :** a watch or clock with a striking mechanism that upon pressure of a spring will indicate the time in hours and quarters or sometimes minutes **c :** a rifle or shotgun having a magazine that holds a number of cartridges that are loaded shot by shot into the firing chamber by the operation of the action of the piece **d** (1) **:** an arrangement for receiving signals from one telegraph line and retransmitting corresponding signals into another line (2) **:** a vacuum-tube or electronic amplifier inserted at proper intervals in long-distance telephone or television transmission lines and capable of delivering to the line an amplified copy of the received message **e :** RECIDIVIST **f :** one who votes again in an election **:** FLOATER 3a **g :** a pennant used to repeat a flag above it in signal hoist so that no two flags in one hoist are the same **h :** a gyrocompass device having a compass card and lubber's line and receiving electrically the indications from the master compass — called also *gyro repeater* **i :** a performer (as an animal or athlete) who duplicates or repeats a feat **j :** a member of a theatrical audience who has attended a previous performance of the same production **k :** a student enrolled in a grade, class, or course for the second or a subsequent time **l :** a trough-shaped semicircular horizontal guide in a rolling mill to deflect the rod from one pass into the next

repeating *pres part of* REPEAT

repeating back *n* **:** an arrangement of parts for a camera permitting the exposure through suitable color filters of three-color separation negatives in rapid succession

repeating coil *n* **:** a transformer used in a telephone system to associate two circuits

repeating decimal *n* **:** a decimal in which after a certain point a particular digit or sequence of digits repeats itself indefinitely

repeating firearm *n* **:** a firearm having a magazine or a revolving cylinder holding several rounds and an action that makes possible rapid firing of successive shots

repeating watch *n* **:** REPEATER b

repeat key *n* **1 :** a key on a business machine that when depressed allows a calculating operation set up on the machine to be repeated indefinitely **2 :** a key on an electric typewriter that continues to operate as long as the key is depressed

repeat order *n* **:** REORDER

repeats *pres 3d sing of* REPEAT, *pl of* REPEAT

re·pe·chage \,repəˈshäzh, rəˈpesh,äzh\ *n* -S [F *repêchage* second chance, supplementary examination for a candidate that has previously failed, fr. *repêcher* to rescue, fish out (fr. *re-* + *pêcher* to fish, fr. L *piscari*, fr. *piscis* fish) + *-age* — more at FISH] **:** a second-chance trial heat (as in olympic rowing) in which losers in the first round of competition are given another chance to qualify for the semifinals

re·pel \rəˈpel, rēˈp-\ *vb* **repelled; repelled; repelling; repels** [ME *repellen*, fr. L *repellere*, fr. *re-* + *pellere* to drive — more at FELT] *vt* **1 a :** to drive back **:** beat off **:** REPULSE ⟨~ the enemy⟩ ⟨execute the laws of the Union, suppress insurrections, and ~ invasions —*U.S.Constitution*⟩ ⟨~ onslaughts by starveling barbarians —V.G.Childe⟩ **b :** to fight against **:** RESIST ⟨cannot claim the assistance of the law in *repelling* the trade competition of rivals —C.A.Cooke⟩ **c :** to keep in check **:** REPRESS ⟨~ the temptation to take the easy way out⟩ **d :** to reverse the advance or movement of ⟨the rocks ~ the waves⟩ **2 :** to turn away **:** refuse to receive or credit **:** REJECT ⟨*repelled* the suggestion when it was made to him and opposed it wherever he decently could —J.C.Fitzpatrick⟩ ⟨*repelled* the insinuation⟩ **3 a :** to drive away **:** DISCOURAGE ⟨foul words and frowns must not ~ a lover —Shak.⟩ ⟨concerned about the effect his actions will have in attracting or *repelling* votes —E.N.Griswold⟩ **b :** to be incapable of adhering to, mixing with, taking up, or holding ⟨a fabric that ~*s* moisture⟩ ⟨oil ~*s* water⟩ **c :** to force away or apart or tend to do so by mutual action at a distance ⟨two like electric charges ~ one another⟩ **4 :** to cause aversion in **:** DISGUST ⟨a tendency toward suspicion and sarcasm that *repelled* people —W.A.Swanberg⟩ ⟨their cold intelligence, their stereotyped, unremitting industry ~ me —L.P.Smith⟩ ~ *vi* **:** to cause aversion **:** exercise repulsion ⟨so malodorous as to be more calculated to ~ than to invite —*Irish Digest*⟩ ⟨when a picture of little merit attracts or a recognized masterpiece ~*s* —C.W.H.Johnson⟩

re·pel·lence *also* **re·pel·lance** \-lən(t)s\ *n* -S [fr. ¹*repellent, repellant*, after such pairs as E *evident: evidence* and such pairs as E *abundant: abundance*] **:** REPELLENCY

re·pel·len·cy *also* **re·pel·lan·cy** \-nsē,-nsi\ *n* -ES [¹*repellent, repellant* + *-cy*] **:** the quality or capacity of repelling **:** REPULSION ⟨has none of the ~ of textbooks —*New Yorker*⟩ ⟨the attraction or ~ of the odor —*Jour. of Economic Entomology*⟩

¹re·pel·lent *also* **re·pel·lant** \-nt\ *adj* [*repellent* fr. L *repellent-, repellens*, pres. part. of *repellere* to repel; *repellant* alter. (influenced by *-ant*, adj. suffix) of *repellent*] **1 :** serving or tending to drive away or ward off ⟨put forth her hands with an involuntary ~ gesture —Nathaniel Hawthorne⟩ — often used in combination ⟨a mosquito-*repellent* spray⟩ ⟨a water-*repellent* coat⟩ **2 :** arousing aversion or disgust **:** REPUGNANT ⟨his peculiar and ~ characteristic was the fantastic manner in which he was deformed —P.I.Wellman⟩ ⟨finds the paintings mostly meaningless and ~ —Havelock Ellis⟩ **syn** see HATEFUL

²repellent *also* **repellant** \"\ *n* -S [*repellent* fr. ¹*repellent*; *repellant* alter. (influenced by *-ant*, n. suffix) of *repellent*] **:** something that repels: as **a :** a substance obnoxious to insects and employed to prevent their attacks **:** INSECTIFUGE **b :** a solution used (as on fabrics) to resist absorption of a liquid (as water or ink)

re·pel·lent·ly *adv* **:** in a repellent manner

re·pel·ler \-lə(r)\ *n* -S **:** one that repels

re·pel·ling·ly *adv* **:** in a repelling manner ⟨made no sign of greeting but looked at him ~⟩

¹re·pent \rəˈpent, rēˈp-\ *vb* -ED/-ING/-S [ME *repenten*, fr. OF *repentir*, fr. *re-* + *pentir* to be sorry, fr. L *paenitēre* to be sorry, cause to be sorry — more at PENITENCE] *vi* **1 :** to turn from sin out of penitence for past wrongdoings, abandon sinful or unworthy purposes and values, and dedicate oneself to the amendment of one's life ⟨unless you ~ you will all likewise perish —Lk 13:3 (RSV)⟩ **2 a :** to feel regret or contrition for what one has done or omitted to do ⟨marry in haste and ~ at leisure⟩ — often used with *of* ⟨~*ed* of his decision to give up the study of medicine⟩ **b :** to change one's mind about something one has done or said ⟨begins with a sweeping condemnation of his opponent's views, but later ~*s* somewhat and finds some good in them⟩ ⟨take him up on his promise before he ~*s*⟩ ~ *vt* **1 :** to cause (one or oneself) to feel regret or contrition for a past action, course of conduct, or decision ⟨it ~*ed* the Lord that he had made man on the earth —Gen 6:6 (AV)⟩ ⟨it ~*ed* me of my boldness —Grant Allen⟩ **2 a :** to feel sorrow or regret for **:** be dissatisfied or regretful about ⟨he ~*ed* his marriage and suffered from it —George Eliot⟩ ⟨~*ed* her rashness⟩ ⟨~*ed* his bargain⟩ **b :** to feel repentance for **:** do penance for ⟨~ his sins⟩ ⟨~ the evil of his ways⟩

²re·pent \ˈrēpənt\ *adj* [L *repent-, repens*, pres. part. of *repere* to creep — more at REPTILE] **:** CREEPING, PROSTRATE

re·pent·ance \rəˈpentᵊn(t)s, rēˈp-, -entən-\ *n* -S [ME *repentaunce*, fr. MF *repentance*, fr. OF, fr. *repentant*, after such pairs as OF *abundant: abundance*] **:** the act or process of repenting; *specif* **:** contrition for one's sins together with the dedication of oneself to the abandonment of unworthy purposes and values and to the amendment of one's life ⟨there's no ~ in the grave —Isaac Watts⟩ **syn** see PENITENCE

¹re·pent·ant \-ᵊnt,-ənt\ *adj* [ME *repentaunt*, fr. OF *repentant*, pres. part. of *repentir* to repent] **1 :** experiencing repentance **:** PENITENT ⟨the ~ little prodigal —W.M.Thackeray⟩ **2 :** expressing or showing repentance ⟨~ tears⟩ — **re·pent·ant·ly** *adv*

²repentant \"\ *n* -S *archaic* **:** PENITENT

re·pent·er \-entə(r)\ *n* -S **:** one that repents

re·pent·ing·ly *adv* **:** in a repenting manner **:** REPENTANTLY

re·people \(ˈ)rē+\ *vt* [MF *repeupler*, fr. OF *repuepler*, fr. *re-* + *puepler* to people] **1 :** to people anew **2 :** RESTOCK

re·percolation \(ˌ)rē+\ *n* [*re-* + *percolation*] **:** percolation again or anew; *specif* **:** the process of repeatedly percolating the same menstruum through fresh material

reper·cuss \ˌrēpə(r)ˈkəs *also* ˌrep-\ *vt* -ED/-ING/-ES [L *repercussus*, past part. of *repercutere*, fr. *re-* + *percutere* to beat, strike — more at PERCUSSION] **:** to drive or beat back **syn** see REBOUND

reper·cus·sion \ˌ≈≈ˈkəshən\ *n* [L *repercussion-, repercussio*, fr. *repercussus* (past part. of *repercutere*) + *-ion-, -io* -ion] **1 a** *archaic* **:** a driving or forcing back of one thing by another or the state of being driven back **:** RECOIL, REPULSE **b :** REFLECTION, REVERBERATION ⟨if the sun's glory were not endlessly caught, splintered and thrown back by atmospheric ~*s* —Thomas De Quincey⟩ **2 a :** an impact, action, or effect given or exerted in return **:** a reciprocal action or effect ⟨caught up in the ~*s* of the movement —Stuart Cloete⟩ **b :** a widespread, indirect, or unforeseen effect of an act, action, or event ⟨this drastic depletion must have ~*s* elsewhere and play a part in lowering the country's water table —*Farmer's Weekly (So. Africa)*⟩ ⟨the accelerated rate of mobility produced complex social ~*s* —Oscar Handlin⟩ **3 a :** the dominant in a Gregorian chant **b :** the reentrance of a fugue subject and answer after the development or after an episode **4 :** BALLOTTEMENT

reper·cus·sive \ˌ≈≈ˈkəsiv\ *adj* [ME *repercussif* serving to drive away, prob. fr. (assumed) ML *repercussivus*, fr. L *repercussus* (past part. of *repercutere*) + *-ivus* -ive] **1 a :** REVERBERATING ⟨the ~ banjos and sobbing saxophones —Carl Sandburg⟩ **b :** thrown back **:** REFLECTED, REVERBERATED ⟨rages loud the ~ roar —James Thomson †1748⟩ **2 :** serving to throw back a sound ⟨a ~ cave⟩

re·perforator \rē+\ *n* [*re-* + *perforator*] **:** a device that receives a message and perforates a tape that can then be used to retransmit the message

rep·er·toire *R* ˈrepə(r)·,twär *sometimes* -wȯ(ə)r; *–R* -pə-·,twä(r *sometimes* -wȯə(r *or* -wȯ(r\ *n* -S [F *répertoire* repertory, repertoire, fr. LL *repertorium* repertory] **1 a :** a list or supply of dramas, operas, pieces, or parts that a company or a person has thoroughly rehearsed and is prepared to perform ⟨a fine pianist but with a very limited ~⟩ **b :** a supply of skills, devices, or expedients possessed by a person or necessary to him in his occupation **:** BAG OF TRICKS, STOCK-IN-TRADE ⟨essential to the ~ of the right halfback —Josephine Lees⟩ ⟨has a small but dependable ~ of jokes designed to amuse the young —Frank Sullivan⟩ ⟨blackmail, seduction and plain old-fashioned lying . . . are all part of her ~ —*Theatre Arts*⟩ **c :** the dishes available at a particular restaurant or in a particular place ⟨both serve good inexpensive food, though their ~ is small —Frederic Morton⟩ **2 a :** the complete list or supply of dramas, operas, or musical works available for performance ⟨our modern orchestral ~⟩ **b :** the complete list or supply of skills, devices, methods, or ingredients used in a particular field, occupation, or practice ⟨has done almost everything in the ~ of modern criticism —S.E.Hyman⟩ ⟨tracer methodology already is well established in the biochemical ~ —M.D. Kamen⟩

rep·er·to·ri·al \ˌrepə(r)ˈtōrēəl, -tȯr-\ *adj* **:** of or relating to a repertory

rep·er·to·ri·um \ˌ≈≈ˈ≈ēəm\ *n*, *pl* **reperto·ria** \-ēə\ [LL, repertory] **:** REPOSITORY ⟨constitute *repertoria* of source material —Joshua Whatmough⟩

rep·er·to·ry *R* ˈrepə(r),tōrē, -tȯr-, -ri, *–R* -pə,t-\ *n* -ES [LL *repertorium*, fr. L *repertus* (past part. of *reperire* to find, find out, acquire, fr. *re-* + *parere, parire* to bring forth, produce) + *-orium* -ory — more at PARE] **1 :** an ordered list, index, or catalog **2 a :** a place where something may be found **:** REPOSITORY ⟨suggests the shop of a country job printer — until a closer look takes in the type ~ —*Printing & Graphic Arts*⟩ **3 :** REPERTOIRE ⟨whose ~ of dialects and characters is large —*Current Biog.*⟩ ⟨the violin ~⟩ ⟨has introduced the whole ~ of the supposed feats of mesmerism —Edmund Wilson⟩ **4 :** the practice of presenting with a resident company a number of different productions (as plays or dances) during a season either successively or alternately

repet *abbr* [L *repetatur*] let it be repeated — used as a direction in medical prescriptions

rep·e·tend \ˈrepə,tend, ˌ≈≈ˈ≈\ *n* -S [L *repetendum* something to be repeated, neut. of *repetendus*, gerundive of *repetere* to repeat] **:** a repeated or recurrent sound, cadence, word, or phrase or one that is to be repeated for conformity to a pattern; *specif* **:** REFRAIN ⟨in the deepening music of the vowels, in subtle and haunting ~*s* —*Atlantic*⟩

re·pe·ti·teur \ˌrā,pād·əˈtər(·), -ped-·\ *n* -S [F *répétiteur* singing coach, tutor, fr. L *repetitus* (past part. of *repetere* to repeat) + F *-eur* -or] **:** a singing coach; *esp* **:** one who coaches singers in operatic roles

rep·e·ti·tion \ˌrepəˈtishən\ *n* -S [L *repetition-, repetitio*, fr. *repetitus* (past part. of *repetere* to repeat) + *-ion-, -io* -ion — more at REPEAT] **1 a :** the act or an instance of repeating something that one has already said or done ⟨she heard again that he was a widower and a grandfather but there seemed to be design in his ~ —Lenard Kaufman⟩ ⟨no more than two ~*s* of the same course will be allowed to any student —*Loyola Univ. Bull.*⟩ **b :** the act of repeating or saying something over in order to learn it **:** REHEARSAL **c :** the act of reciting something learned ⟨listened with delight to her ~*s* of her favorite passages —T.L.Peacock⟩ **d :** MENTION, RECITAL ⟨yawning at the ~ of delights which she saw no likelihood of sharing —Jane Austen⟩ **2** *Scots law* **:** a demand for restitution or repayment; *broadly* **:** RESTITUTION, RECOVERY, RESTORATION **3 a :** the fact of occurring, appearing, or being repeated again ⟨wait a long time for a ~ of this feat⟩ ⟨the design consists of a ~ of the same geometrical figure⟩ **b :** COPY, REPRODUCTION ⟨when Greek art, even in Roman copies, was the only indisputable art, except for some Renaissance ~*s* —Roger Fry⟩ **c :** spore germination in various fungi in which a spore is produced at the end of a stalk arising from another spore and in turn often germinates in the same way **4 :** the ability of a musical instrument to respond to the repeated striking of the same key in rapid succession ⟨an organ defective in ~⟩ ⟨a piano with excellent ~⟩

rep·e·ti·tion·al \ˌ≈≈ˈtishənᵊl, -shnəl\ *adj* **:** REPETITIOUS ⟨something deadening and ~ has been happening to even the best modernist art —Janet Flanner⟩

repetition compulsion *n* **:** an irresistible tendency to repeat an emotional experience or to return to a previous psychological state

rep·e·ti·tious \ˌrepəˈtishəs\ *adj* [fr. *repetition*, after such pairs as E *ambition: ambitious*] **1 :** marked by repetition **:** containing frequent repetitions **:** tediously repeating ⟨the tiresome ~ analyses . . . which sometimes make him so exasperating to read —Edmund Wilson⟩ **2 :** repeating the same process or action again and again ⟨the industrial revolution has freed man's hands from much dull and ~ work —Bryan Morgan⟩ — **repetitiously** *adv* — **repetitiousness** *n* -ES

re·pet·i·tive \rəˈped·əd·iv, rēˈp-, -etətiv\ *adj* [fr. *repetition*, after such pairs as E *action: active*] **1 :** containing repetition

: REPEATING ⟨~ combinations of the symbols for one and ten —Lancelot Hogben⟩ **2** : REPETITIOUS ⟨the vast deluge of ~ verbiage found in legal documents —W.H.Wright⟩ ⟨a ~ job that might drive you or me crazy —Stuart Chase⟩ — **re·pet·i·tive·ly** \-əvlē, -li\ *adv* — **re·pet·i·tive·ness** \-ivnəs\ *n* -ES

repha·im \'refēəm, rə'fāəm\ *n pl, usu cap* [Heb *rĕphā'īm*] : ancient giants reported in the Old Testament to have flourished in Canaan and its vicinity prior to the Hebrews

re·phonemicize \¦rē+\ *vt* [*re-* + *phonemicize*] : to transcribe (a phoneme) or all amenable phonemes of (a language) with multiple symbols that are more accurately descriptive than single symbols of the phonetic makeup involved — **re·phonemicization** \"+\ *n*

¹re·photograph \(')rē+\ *vt* [*re-* + *photograph*] : to photograph (a scene or object) again : RETAKE ⟨no unusual experience to find myself ~*ing* a group of trees⟩

²rephotograph \"\ *n* **1** : a photographing again of a scene or object : RETAKE **2** : a picture resulting from rephotographing

re·phrase \(')rē+\ *vt* [*re-* + *phrase*] : to phrase anew or in a new form

¹re·pine \rə'pīn, rē'p-\ *vb* -ED/-ING/-S [*re-* + *pine* (to languish)] *vi* **1** : to feel or express dejection or discontent : COMPLAIN, FRET ⟨we may regret but not ~ at the disappearance of much of interest and value as the result of progress —Edwin Benson⟩ ⟨courage, when misfortune comes, to bear without *repining* the ruin of our hopes —Bertrand Russell⟩ **2** : to wish discontentedly ⟨~ for an unwritten masterpiece —T.S.Eliot⟩ ~ *vt, archaic* : to complain or fret about **syn** see COMPLAIN

²repine \"\ *n* -S : DISCONTENT

re·pin·er \-nə(r)\ *n* -S : one that repines

re·pin·ing·ly *adv* : COMPLAININGLY

re·pique *or* **re·pic** \rə'pēk\ *n* -S [F *repic*, fr. *repiquer* to prick again, fr. MF, fr. *re-* + *piquer* to prick — more at PIKE] : the making of 30 or more points in combinations alone before an opponent in the game of piquet scores; *also* : a bonus of 60 points given for this

repl *abbr* replace; replacement

repla *pl of* REPLUM

re·place \rə'plās, rē'p-\ *vt* [*re-* + *place*] **1** : to place again : restore to a former place, position, or condition ⟨*replaced* the card in the file⟩ ⟨*replaced* the king on the throne⟩ **2** : to take the place of : serve as a substitute for or successor of : SUCCEED, SUPPLANT ⟨the saw and sawmill rapidly *replaced* the ax —*Amer. Guide Series: Mich.*⟩ ⟨the dried wood . . . has long been *replaced* by steel and concrete —T.H.Matthews⟩ **3** : to put in place of : provide a substitute or successor for ⟨necessary to ~ all the machinery in the plant⟩ **4** : to fill the place of : supply an equivalent for ⟨a broken toy should not be immediately *replaced* —Bertrand Russell⟩ ⟨promised to ~ the money he had stolen⟩

syn DISPLACE, SUPPLANT, SUPERSEDE: REPLACE implies supplying a substitute or equivalent for someone or something, often something lost, worn out, broken, dismissed, destroyed, or otherwise no longer usable ⟨Doe *replacing* Roe in the line-up⟩ ⟨nor would I admit that the human actor can be *replaced* by a marionette —T.S.Eliot⟩ ⟨an old bridge *replaced* by a new one⟩ DISPLACE implies an ousting, dislodging, putting out, discharging, or crowding out, preceding a replacing ⟨prehistoric Siouan tribes have been *displaced* almost entirely by Indians of Algonquian stock —*Amer. Guide Series: Minn.*⟩ ⟨when large-scale commercial farms *displaced* the old peasant holdings —Oscar Handlin⟩ ⟨since machinery has *displaced* manual labor —Karl Meyer⟩ ⟨in this realm of science symbols first *displace* words —T.H.Savory⟩ SUPPLANT is now likely to indicate an uprooting and eradication followed by a replacing or displacing by something newer, better, more modern or effective ⟨horse cars *supplanted* by trolleys⟩ ⟨rock fireplaces *supplanted* those of sapling and mud construction —*Amer. Guide Series: Tenn.*⟩ ⟨a valuable means of *supplanting* editorial guesswork with facts —F.L.Mott⟩ ⟨a secure national government *supplanting* the provisional one⟩ SUPERSEDE is rarely without suggestions of replacement by something better or newer ⟨the old-fashioned fishing luggers with their varicolored sails have been *superseded* by motorboats —*Amer. Guide Series: La.*⟩ ⟨frame houses soon *superseded* the original log ones —*Amer. Guide Series: N.C.*⟩ ⟨that is the worst of erudition — that the next scholar sucks the few drops of honey that you have accumulated, sets right your blunders, and you are *superseded* —A.C.Benson⟩

re·place·abil·i·ty \¦=¦=bilǝd·ē\ *n* : the quality or state of being replaceable

re·place·able \=¦=əbəl\ *adj* : capable of being replaced ⟨a cheap, standardized, and ~ product —Lewis Mumford⟩

replaced crystal *n* : PSEUDOMORPH

re·place·ment \=¦=mənt\ *n* -S **1** : the act of replacing or the state of being replaced : SUBSTITUTION ⟨the problem of blood loss and its ~ is ever present in this type of surgery —*Jour. Amer. Med. Assoc.*⟩: as **a** : the removal of an edge or an angle of a crystal by one or more faces **b** : substitution of one substance in a rock fabric for another by solution and redeposition **2** : something that replaces : SUBSTITUTE: as **a** : an individual available for assignment to a military unit to replace a loss or complete a quota **b** : a new fixed asset or portion of an asset that takes the place of a discarded one **c** : an artificial substitute for a lost or amputated body part : PROSTHESIS

replacement cost *n* : the current cost of replacing a fixed asset with a new one of equal effectiveness

replacement depot *n* : a military installation usu. in a theater of operations where replacements are assembled and then assigned to fill vacancies in military units

replacement set *n* : a set of elements any one of which may be used to replace a given variable or placeholder in a mathematical phrase or sentence — compare DOMAIN

replacement therapy *n* : therapy involving the supplying of something (as nutrients or blood) lacking from or lost to the system

replacement vein *also* **replacement deposit** *n* : SUBSTITUTION VEIN

re·plac·er \-sə(r)\ *n* : one that replaces; *specif* : RERAILER

replaces *pres 3d sing of* REPLACE

replacing *pres part of* REPLACE

re·pla·cive \-siv\ *n* -S [*replace* + *-ive*] : a difference of phonemes in the word stem of two or more grammatically distinct forms ⟨the vowel of *feet* as compared with that of *foot* displays a ~ plural form instead of the usual suffix *-s*⟩

¹re·plant \(')rē+\ *vt* [*re-* + *plant*] **1 a** : to plant again or anew ⟨~ a tree⟩ ⟨~ a bulb⟩ **b** : RESETTLE ⟨move people out of submarginal and blighted areas and ~ them in communities which have a resource base —Stuart Chase⟩ **2** : to provide with new plants ⟨~ the flower bed⟩

²re·plant \'rē+,-, =¦=\ *n* : something planted again or anew; *specif* : a plant used to fill a vacancy in a row or planting esp. after a first or initial planting

re·plantation \¦rē+\ *n* **1** : a new or second planting **2** : the implantation of a drawn tooth in its socket

re·plate \'rē+,-\ *n* [*re-* + *plate*, v.] : a printing of an edition of a newspaper or periodical in which new material is inserted by an alteration or resetting of a plate

¹re·play \(')rē+\ *vt* [*re-* + *play*] : to play again or over ⟨acted the part more effectively each time he ~*ed* it⟩ ⟨ruled that the entire game would have to be ~*ed*⟩

²re·play \'rē+,-, =¦=\ *n* : something that is replayed

replay duplicate *n* : a game of duplicate whist or bridge in which two pairs compete and in which the boards are played twice with each pair holding the same hands on the second play that its opponents held before

re·plead \(')rē+\ *vt* [*re-* + *plead*] : to plead again; *specif* : to file a new legal pleading appropriate under the circumstances (as after a demurrer has been overruled)

re·plead·er \"ə(r)\ *n* [*replead* + *-er* (as in *cesser*)] **1** : a second legal pleading or course of pleadings **2** : the right of pleading again even after trial or verdict

re·pledge \(')rē+\ *vt* [MF *replegier* to become surety for, fr. OF, fr. *re-* + *plegier* to guarantee, become surety for — more at PLEDGE] *Scots law* : to remove from the jurisdiction of another court to one's own

re·ple·gi·ate \rə'plējē,āt\ *vt* [ML *replegiatus*, past part. of *replegiare*, fr. OF *replegier*] : REPLEDGE

re·plen·ish \rə'plenish, rē'p-, *esp in pres part* -nəsh\ *vb* [ME *replenisshen, replenissen*, fr. MF *repleniss-*, stem of *replenir* to fill, supply abundantly, fr. OF, fr. *re-* + *-plenir* (fr. *plein* full, fr. L *plenus*) — more at FULL] *vt* **1 a** : to fill with persons or animals : people or stock ⟨be fruitful and multiply and ~ the earth —Gen 1:28 (AV)⟩ **b** *archaic* : to supply fully : equip completely : PERFECT ⟨his hive had so long been ~*ed* with honey —William Wordsworth⟩ ⟨the most ~*ed* villain in the world —Shak.⟩ **c** : to fill with some quality or source of inspiration or power : provide with intellectual or spiritual sustenance : NOURISH ⟨the American mind should cease to ~ itself with the mighty wonders of Europe —Van Wyck Brooks⟩ **d** : to fill completely : occupy or pervade all parts of ⟨their vacant heart ~*ed* with a child —Robert Browning⟩ ⟨she saw the blood his cheeks ~ —Shak.⟩ **2 a** : to fill up again ⟨she kept his glass ~*ed* —Charles Dickens⟩ ⟨the heavy demands for his legal services that promised to ~ his exchequer —A.C. Cole⟩ ⟨remains below the surface until he needs to ~ his lungs with another gulp —John Tassos⟩ **b** : to build up again : RENEW, RESTORE ⟨he ~*ed* the fire and drew up close to it —T.B. Costain⟩ ⟨the plants are still growing, and ~*ing* their food reserves —*Farm Jour.*⟩ ⟨the supply of oil will have ~*ed* itself —*Amer. Guide Series: Pa.*⟩ **c** : to supply again : REFIT ⟨finds it cheaper and faster to ~ its ships while under way —George Weller⟩ **d** : to make good : REPLACE ⟨how fast have the shipyards . . . been able to ~ these losses —*Fortune*⟩ **3** : to add replenisher to (as a photographic developer or fixing bath) ~ *vi* : to become full : fill up again

re·plen·ish·er \-shə(r)\ *n* -S : one that replenishes ⟨enormous deposits of marl or bog lime, a valuable soil ~ —*Amer. Guide Series: Minn.*⟩; *specif* : a chemical solution added to a photographic working solution (as a developer or fixing bath) for restoring or maintaining chemical activity

re·plen·ish·ment \-shmənt\ *n* -S **1** : something that replenishes : a new supply ⟨organizations accustomed to recruit new members from among the new immigrants were now cut off from ~*s* —Oscar Handlin⟩ **2** : the act or process of replenishing or the state of being replenished ⟨propagates cutthroat trout, chiefly for the ~ of mountain streams —*Amer. Guide Series: Oregon*⟩ ⟨promised him rest and ~ —Winifred Bambrick⟩

¹re·plete \rə'plēt, rē'p-, *usu* -lēd·+V\ *adj* [ME *repleet*, fr. MF & L; MF *replet*, fr. L *repletus*, past part. of *replēre* to fill up, fr. *re-* + *plēre* to fill — more at FULL] **1 a** : fully or abundantly provided : well supplied ⟨the race itself is ~ with thrills, sometimes with spills —*Amer. Guide Series: Ind.*⟩ ⟨~ with hard and book-learned words, impressively sonorous —R.W.Southern⟩ **b** : fully or richly charged, imbued, or impregnated ⟨a warmly affectionate book, ~ with both human and religious value —Frances Witherspoon⟩ ⟨a life ~ with charm —P.E.More⟩ **2** : FILLED ⟨a thin limestone bed ~ with characteristic echinoids —*Science*⟩ **b** : abundantly fed : GORGED, SURFEITED ⟨could not face the thought of being ~ in a starving world —A.L.Guérard⟩ **c** : filled out : FAT, STOUT ⟨richly and healthily ~, though with less of his substance in stature; a frankly fat gentleman —Henry James †1916⟩ **3** : COMPLETE, FULL ⟨the text is too ~ to be used in abbreviated survey or cultural courses —*Rev. of Scientific Instruments*⟩

²replete \"\ *vt* -ED/-ING/-S [ME *repleten*, fr. L *repletus*, past part. of *replēre* to fill up] **1** : to fill to satiety : STUFF ⟨fat with *repleted* appetite —Charles Dickens⟩ **2** : REPLENISH ⟨mostly stolen . . . later *repleted* —Eleanor Clark⟩

³replete \"\ *n* -S [¹*replete*] : a worker ant capable of greatly distending its abdomen and serving as a reservoir of liquid food for the rest of the colony — called also *plerergate*; compare HONEY ANT

re·plete·ness *n* -ES : the quality or state of being replete

re·ple·tion \-ēshən\ *n* -S [ME *replecioun* surfeit, condition of being filled up, fr. MF & LL; MF *repletion* surfeit, fr. LL *repletion-, repletio* completion, fr. L *repletus* (past part. of *replēre* to fill up) + *-ion-, -io* -ion] **1 a** : the act of overeating or the state of being overfed : SURFEIT ⟨made sick by ~⟩ ⟨eat to ~⟩ **b** : fullness of blood : PLETHORA **2** : the condition of being filled up or overcrowded ⟨a hall filled to ~⟩ **3** : fulfillment of a need or desire : SATISFACTION ⟨the peace and spiritual ~ of the evening's rest —R.L.Stevenson⟩

re·ple·tive \-ēd·iv\ *adj* [LL *repletivus* complementary, fr. L *repletus* (past part. of *replēre*) + *-ivus* -ive] : serving or tending to make replete : FILLING

re·plevi·able \rə'plevēəbəl, rē'p-\ *adj* : capable of being replevied

¹re·plev·in \-vən\ *n* -S [ME, fr. AF *replevine*, fr. *replevir* to give security, fr. OF, to give security for, fr. *re-* + *plevir* to pledge, fr. (assumed) LL *plebere* — more at PLEDGE] **1 a** : the return to or recovery by a person of goods or chattels claimed to be wrongfully taken or detained upon the person's giving security to try the matter in court and return the goods if defeated in the action **b** : the writ by or the common-law action in which goods and chattels are replevied **2** : the act of bailing a person or the bail given

²replevin \"\ *vt* -ED/-ING/-S : REPLEVY

replevin bond *n* : a bond required of a plaintiff in a replevin action to indemnify the defendant or the court officer seizing the property in the defendant's possession and transferring it to the plaintiff in the event the plaintiff loses his case

re·plev·i·sa·ble \-vəsəbəl\ *adj* [AF *replevisable, replevissable*, fr. OF *repleviss-* (stem of *replevir*) + *-able*] : REPLEVIABLE

re·plev·i·sor \-sə(r), -,sȯ(ə)r\ *n* -S [*replevis-* (as in *replevisable*) + *-or*] : the plaintiff in a replevin action

¹re·plevy \-vē\ *n* -ES [ME, fr. AF *replevir*, v.] : REPLEVIN

²replevy \"\ *vb* -ED/-ING/-ES [AF *replevir*] *vt* **1** *archaic* : to bail or admit to bail **2** : to take or get back by a writ for replevin ~ *vi* : to recover goods by replevin

re·pli·ant \rə'plīənt, rē'p-\ *n* -S [¹*reply* + *-ant*] : one who makes replication

rep·li·ca \'repləkə, -lēkə\ *n* -S [It, repetition, fr. *replicare* to repeat, fr. LL, fr. L, to fold back — more at REPLY] **1** : a reproduction, facsimile, or copy (as of a picture or statue) done by the maker of the original or under his direction **2** : a facsimile of an original work of art **3** : COPY, DUPLICATE ⟨a legislative body which would not be merely a ~ of the lower house —R.M.Dawson⟩ ⟨bored by their conversation, which was the ~ of a conversation he had heard a thousand times before —Victoria Sackville-West⟩

replica grating *n* : a diffraction grating formed by molding a film (as of collodion) on a ruled grating

¹rep·li·cate \'replə,kāt\ *vt* -ED/-ING/-S [LL *replicatus*, past part. of *replicare* to reply, repeat, fr. L, to fold back] **1** : to give as an answer : REPLY **2** : DUPLICATE, REPEAT ⟨the sequence of elementary responses necessary in the act of *replicating* the outline of the triangle —D.M.MacKay⟩ ⟨~ a statistical experiment⟩ ⟨*replicated* row plantings⟩ **3** [L *replicatus*, past part. of *replicare*] : to fold or bend back ⟨a *replicated* leaf⟩

²rep·li·cate \-ləkət\ *n* -S [LL *replicatus*, past part. of *replicare* to repeat] **1** : a repeated musical tone one or more octaves above or below a given tone **2** : an experiment or procedure that repeats another done at the same time

³replicate \"\ *adj* [L *replicatus*, past part. of *replicare* to fold back] **1** : folded over or backward : folded back upon itself **2** [LL *replicatus*, past part. of *replicare* to repeat, fr. L, to fold back] : MANIFOLD, REPEATED ⟨~ samples of 10 gm. were used for determining total nitrogen —*Jour. of Agric. Research*⟩

re·plic·a·tile \rə'plikə,tīl, rē'p-, -kəd·ᵊl, -kə(,)tīl\ *adj* [¹*replicate* + *-ile*] : capable of being folded back on itself ⟨~ wings of an insect⟩

rep·li·ca·tion \,replə'kāshən\ *n* -S [ME *replicacioun*, fr. MF *replication*, fr. LL *replication-, replicatio*, fr. L, action of folding back, fr. *replicatus* (past part. of *replicare* to fold back) + *-ion-, -io* -ion] **1 a** : ANSWER, REPLY ⟨what ~ should be made by the son of a king —Shak.⟩ **b** (1) : an answer to a reply : REJOINDER ⟨by way of ~ to your answer —O.W.Holmes †1935⟩ (2) : a plaintiff's or complainant's reply in matters of fact to a defendant's plea, answer, or counterclaim (3) *Roman law* : a plaintiff's reply to a defendant's exceptio **2** : ECHO, REVERBERATION ⟨trembled underneath her banks to hear the ~ of your sounds made in her concave shores —Shak.⟩ **3 a** : COPY, REPRODUCTION ⟨a home conceived as a ~ of a medieval castle⟩ **b** : the act or action of reproducing ⟨halftone plate and addressing machine methods of ~ —*Library Science Abstracts*⟩ **4** : repetition of an experiment or procedure at the same time and place; *esp* : a systematic or random repetition of agricultural test rows or plats to reduce error (as due to variation in soil)

re·pli·er \rə'plī(ə)r, rē'p-, -īə\ *n* -S : one that replies

rep·lum \'repləm\ *n, pl* **rep·la** \-lə\ [L, part of a door (prob. bolt for covering the gap in a folding door), fr. *replēre* to fill up — more at REPLETE] : a thin false dissepiment separating the two valves of some fruits (as siliques and some legumes) from which the valves fall away at maturity

re·plume \(')rē+\ *vt* [*re-* + *plume*] : to plume anew : PREEN

¹re·ply \rə'plī, rē'p-\ *vb* -ED/-ING/-ES [ME *replien* (influenced in meaning by LL *replicare* to reply, fr. L, to fold back), fr. MF *replier* to fold again, fr. L *replicare* to fold back, fr. *re-* + *plicare* to fold — more at PLY] *vi* **1 a** : to respond in words or writing : ANSWER ⟨*replied* to the speech with a few words of thanks⟩ ⟨received your letter a week ago but have waited to ~⟩ **b** : ECHO, RESOUND **c** : to answer a defendant's original plea or response **2** : to do something in response ⟨the ship *replied* to the flagship's signal⟩; *specif* : to return an attack or gunfire ⟨poured broadside after broadside into the forts, which *replied* continuously —*Amer. Guide Series: La.*⟩ ⟨~*ing* with rifles and bayonets —*Newsweek*⟩ ~ *vt* : to give as an answer ⟨*replied* not a word⟩ ⟨did not know what to ~⟩ **syn** see ANSWER

²reply \"\ *n* -ES **1** : something that is said, written, or done in answer or response ⟨made a long-winded ~ to the teacher's question⟩ ⟨a letter in ~ to a request for a loan⟩ ⟨only three or four of the train guard had been able to fire a ~ —F.V.W. Mason⟩ **2** : REPLICATION 1b(2)

reply brief *n* : a brief required by some courts of a party to a legal action in answer to points of law raised in an opponent's brief but not in his own

reply card *n* **1** *or* **reply postal card** : DOUBLE POSTAL CARD **2** : any card for use in mailing a reply that is provided by the one who requests the reply and who sometimes offers to pay the postage for the reply

reply coupon *n* : a coupon sold by a post office in one country and exchangeable in another country for a stamp to be used on a letter of reply

reply envelope *n* : BUSINESS REPLY ENVELOPE

reply-paid postcard *n* : DOUBLE POSTAL CARD

reply-paid telegram *n* : a telegram to which a reply is prepaid by the sender

re·pone \rə'pōn, rē'p-\ *vt* -ED/-ING/-S [L *reponere* to put back — more at REPOSIT] **1** *Scots law* : to restore (as a minister) to former standing or office **2** *Scots law* : to restore (as a defaulting party in an action) to former legal status in order to try the action again : REHABILITATE

¹re·port \rə'pō(ə)r\t, rē'p-, -pȯ(ə)r\, -pōə\, -pȯ(ə)\ *sometimes* 'rē,p-; *usu* \d·+V\ *n* -S [ME, fr. MF, statement, account, fr. OF, fr. *reporter*, v.] **1 a** : common talk or an account spread by common talk : a story or statement casually repeated and generally believed : RUMOR ⟨denies the common ~ that he ghosted the whole document —Bruce Bliven b.1889⟩ **b** : FAME, REPUTATION ⟨evil ~ beset him early and pursued him throughout his active life —S.H.Adams⟩ ⟨member, 27, well experienced all branches, and of good ~ —*Veterinary Record*⟩ **2 a** : something that gives information : a usu. detailed account or statement ⟨a weather ~⟩ ⟨an intelligence ~⟩ ⟨a news ~⟩ ⟨a stock market ~⟩ **b** : NOTIFICATION ⟨the health authorities had received no new ~*s* of typhoid cases for 24 hours⟩ **c** (1) : an account or statement of the facts of a legal case heard and of the decision and opinion of the court or quasi-judicial administrative agency determining the case (2) : a written submission of a question of law (as by a lower court) to an appellate court for review before final decision is entered **d** : a record of the speeches and remarks delivered and the actions taken during a meeting or session (as of a convention) esp. as formally published ⟨a ~ of the proceedings of the nominating convention⟩ **3** : an explosive noise ⟨the roar of airplane engines and the sharp ~*s* of opening parachutes filled the skies —O.N.Bradley⟩ ⟨the ~ of a gun served to scare some hundreds more —C.L.Barrett⟩ **4 a** : a usu. formal and sometimes official statement giving the conclusions and recommendations of a person or group authorized or delegated to consider a proposal ⟨the committee made an unfavorable ~ on the bill⟩ **b** : a usu. formal account of the results of an investigation given by a person or group authorized or delegated to make the investigation ⟨an audit ~⟩ ⟨after exhaustive study the committee made its ~ on the causes of the accident⟩ ⟨the committee presented its ~ on the teaching of science in the high schools⟩ **c** : an analysis of operations and progress and a statement of future plans made at stated intervals by an administrator or executive to his superiors or those to whom he is responsible ⟨gave his departmental ~ to the president of the company⟩ ⟨the board of directors issued its annual ~ to the stockholders⟩ **d** : a statement of a student's academic record for a particular period often including also an evaluation of his rate of progress — **on report** : required to appear before one's commanding officer to answer for an infraction of regulations : subject to disciplinary action ⟨perhaps he could put somebody *on report*, get him some extra duty —K.M.Dodson⟩

²report \=¦=\ *vb* -ED/-ING/-S [ME *reporten*, fr. MF *reporter* to report, carry back, fr. OF, fr. L *reportare*, fr. *re-* + *portare* to carry — more at FARE] *vt* **1 a** : to give an account of : NARRATE, RELATE, TELL ⟨fiction should confine itself solely to ~*ing* emotion and behavior —Bernard De Voto⟩ ⟨it was ~*ed* that she exercised great political influence over her husband —Martha T. Stephenson⟩ **b** : to describe as being in a specified state or condition ⟨a servant came to the door and ~*ed* her asleep —Sherwood Anderson⟩ ⟨~*ed* him much improved⟩ **2 a** : to serve as carrier of (a message) ⟨the ambassador ~*ed* the president's answer to his government⟩ **b** : to relate the words or sense of (something said) ⟨what she confessed I must ~ —Shak.⟩ ⟨~ what he actually did say —Benjamin Farrington⟩ **c** (1) : to make a written record or summary of ⟨~ a speech⟩ ⟨~ a trial⟩ (2) : to make a shorthand record of ⟨most radio speakers talk too fast, and trying to ~ them is often discouraging —C.I.Blanchard & C.E.Zoubek⟩ **d** (1) : to watch for and write about the newsworthy aspects or developments of : COVER ⟨a newsman assigned to ~ the trial⟩ ⟨a foreign correspondent ~*ing* events in the Far East⟩ (2) : to prepare or present an account of for radio or television broadcast ⟨~*s* the news every evening at seven⟩ ⟨the excited enthusiastic voice of a commentator ~*ing* a baseball game —Maritta Wolff⟩ **3 a** (1) : to give a formal or official account or statement of : state formally ⟨the treasurer ~*ed* a balance of ten dollars⟩ ⟨the company ~*ed* a sales total of over a million dollars for the month⟩ (2) : to return or present (a matter officially referred for consideration) with conclusions or recommendations; *specif* : report out **b** : to announce or relate as the result of a special search, examination, or investigation ⟨~*ed* the discovery of new diamond mines⟩ ⟨~*ed* no sign of disease⟩ ⟨~*ed* new evidence bearing on the authorship of the play⟩ **c** : to announce the presence, arrival, or sighting of ⟨~*ed* himself present⟩ ⟨while waiting for the tower to ~ the general's plane —J.G.Cozzens⟩ ⟨~*ed* land straight ahead⟩ **d** : to make known to the proper authorities : give notification of ⟨~ a fire⟩ ⟨~ an accident⟩ ⟨~ a case of diphtheria⟩ **e** : to make a charge of misconduct against ⟨the stationmaster all but threatened to ~ me —Walter de la Mare⟩ ⟨~*ed* the abusive student to the principal⟩ ~ *vi* **1 a** : to give an account of someone or something : TELL ⟨he did not simply ~: he criticized and reflected —Ilse Lind⟩ **b** : to give an account of oneself : make one's whereabouts or activities known to someone ⟨promised to ~ by letter⟩ ⟨hasn't ~*ed* for days⟩ **c** : to present oneself ⟨~ for duty⟩ ⟨~ to the commanding officer⟩ ⟨the children will ~ for class each day whether the school is open or not —*New Republic*⟩ — often used with *in* or *back* ⟨~*ed* in every morning⟩ ⟨time to ~ back for work⟩ **2** : to make, issue, or submit a report : present a formal statement or account ⟨the committee will ~ at twelve o'clock⟩ ⟨the inspector has not yet ~*ed* on the condition of the mine⟩ **3** : to act in the capacity of a reporter : furnish news reports ⟨~*ing* for a living⟩ **syn** see RELATE

re·port·able \=¦=əbəl\ *adj* **1** : admitting of or meriting a report ⟨ten years of research that produced no ~ results⟩ **2** : required by law to be reported ⟨~ income⟩

re·port·age \=¦=ij, -ēj, *esp for 2* ,repər'täzh *or* -,pȯr- *or* -täzh\ *n* -S [F, fr. *reporter*, n., news reporter (fr. E) + *-age*] **1 a** : the act or process of reporting news ⟨in which he described some of the new skills in ~ required to carry out such an assignment —*Time*› **b :** a news story ‹their front pages are usu. divided between local scandals and romantic ~s —*Atlantic*› **c :** DOCUMENTATION ‹the superiority of pictures over the written word as a means of ~ —*Coming Events in Britain*› **2 :** writing intended to give a factual and detailed account of directly observed or carefully documented events and scenes ‹seem to be saying that straightforward ~ is the only branch of literature that matters —George Orwell›

report card *n* **:** a report on a student that is periodically submitted by a school to the student's parents or guardian

re·port·ed·ly \\=ˈ=ədlē, -li\\ *adv* **:** according to report **:** REPUTEDLY ‹has ~ made many anonymous benefactions to hospitals —*Current Biog.*›

re·port·er \\=ˈ=ə(r)\\ *n* -s [alter. (influenced by *-er*) of ME *reportour*, fr. MF *reporteur*, fr. *reporter* to report + *-eur* -or] **:** one that reports ‹a ~ of spiritual and physical reality —H.S. Canby› ‹ask him to continue being a ~ and judge of what is new in the arts —Malcolm Cowley›: as **a :** an officer or person who makes authorized statements of law proceedings and decisions or of legislative debates **b :** one who makes a shorthand record of a speech or proceeding; *specif* **:** COURT REPORTER **c** (1) **:** one who is employed by a newspaper or magazine to gather and write news for publication ‹a sports ~› ‹a financial ~› ‹a society ~› (2) **:** one who reports news events on a radio or television program **:** COMMENTATOR **d** *archaic* **:** PISTOL

reporting pay *n* **:** a payment made to a worker who reports for work without having previously been told that no work is available — called also *call-in pay*

repor·to·ri·al \\ˌrepə(r)ˈtōrēəl, -tȯr- *also* ˈrēp- *or* -ˌpōr- *or* -ˌpȯr-\\ *adj* [irreg. (influenced by *-or*) fr. *reporter* + *-ial*] **1 :** of, relating to, or characteristic of a reporter ‹a long ~ career› ‹~ curiosity› ‹~ skills› **2 :** of, resembling, or characteristic of a report ‹a ~ book› ‹~ prose› ‹it is too topical, too transitory, too ~ —C.P.Aiken› — **repor·to·ri·al·ly** \\-ēəlē, -li\\ *adv*

report out *vt, of a legislative committee* **:** to return (a bill) after consideration and often with revisions to a legislative body for debate and vote ‹on the fifteen-man body there are eight sure votes for *reporting* the measure *out* —*Newsweek*›

reports *pl of* REPORT, *pres 3d sing of* REPORT

report stage *n* **:** the stage in the British legislative process that occurs prior to the third reading and that involves the receipt by the legislative body of the report of the committee to which the bill has been assigned, consideration of amendments made in committee, and usu. discussion esp. of details and amendment — compare LEGISLATION 1

reposal *n* -s *obs* **:** the act of reposing ‹the ~ of any trust, virtue, or worth in thee —Shak.›

¹re·pose \\rə̇ˈpōz, rēˈp-\\ *vt* -ED/-ING/-S [ME *reposen* to replace, put back, irreg. (influenced by such verbs as ME *deposen* to depose) fr. L *reponere* (perfect stem *repos-*) — more at REPOSIT] **1** *archaic* **:** to put away or set down **:** DEPOSIT **2 :** to place (as confidence or trust) **:** SET — usu. used with *in* ‹~ full confidence in their leader —T.B.Macaulay› ‹the complete trust *reposed* in him and his policies —*Newsweek*› **3 :** to place for control, management, or use ‹~s the judicial power in a supreme court —*Amer. Guide Series: La.*›

²repose \\"\\ *vb* -ED/-ING/-S [ME *reposen*, fr. MF *reposer*, fr. OF, fr. LL *repausare*, fr. L *re-* + LL *pausare* to stop, rest — more at PAUSE] *vt* **1 a :** to lay at rest **:** place in a restful or resting position **:** REST ‹upon that cottage bench *reposed* his limbs —William Wordsworth› **b :** to give rest to **:** refresh by rest ‹enter in the castle and there ~ you for the night —Shak.› **2 :** to cause to be calm or quiet **:** COMPOSE ‹extraordinarily difficult to ~ a man whose leg troubled him, whose war troubled him, whose bank troubled him and whose wife troubled him —Francis Hackett› **~** *vi* **1 a :** to lie at rest ‹during the hot afternoon, the entire town ~s› **b :** to lie dead ‹*reposing* in state› **c :** to remain still or concealed **:** lie quiet or hidden ‹under the soil . . . there ~ vastly greater quantities of raw materials —F.C.James› ‹the existence of similar sunken lands now *reposing* on the bottom of the Pacific —J.F. McComas› **2 :** to take rest **:** cease from activity, exertion, or movement ‹she did not ~; she could not . . . she sat thinking —Arnold Bennett› **3** *archaic* **:** to rest in confidence **:** RELY ‹upon whose faith and honor I ~ —Shak.› **4 :** to rest for support **:** LIE — usu. used with *on* or *upon* ‹cutting generous portions with a huge knife from the loaf *reposing* on a round wooden base —Sidney Lovett› ‹medieval justice *reposed* so greatly on the system of fines —G.G.Coulton›

³repose \\"\\ *n* -s [MF *repos*, fr. OF, fr. *reposer*, v.] **1 a :** a state of resting after exertion or strain **:** temporary mental or physical inactivity used to restore vigor; *esp* **:** rest in sleep ‹a little feast that would make other men heavy and desirous of ~ —Willa Cather› ‹earned one's night's ~ —H.A.Overstreet› **b :** relief from excitement, danger, or difficulty **:** restful change **:** RELAXATION ‹where at last he could find warmth and the brief, treacherous ~ of dissipation —J.T.Soby› **2 a :** a place or state of rest; *esp* **:** eternal or heavenly rest ‹to pray for the ~ of a soul› **b :** freedom from something that disturbs or excites **:** CALM, PEACE, TRANQUILLITY ‹the unfailing ~ of the bayou —*Christian Science Monitor*› ‹induce a sense of ~ and contentment —S.P.B.Mais› **c :** a harmony in the disposition of parts and colors that is restful to the eye ‹his painting was criticized as lacking ~› **3 a :** QUIESCENCE ‹the volcano was in ~› **b :** cessation or absence of activity, movement, or animation ‹his face in ~ is grave and thoughtful —R.C.Doty› ‹~ again freezes the burning features of his face —C.L.Sulzberger› **4 :** composure of manner **:** quiet dignity **:** EASINESS, POISE **syn** see REST

re·pose·ful \\-fəl\\ *adj* **:** full of repose **:** QUIET, RESTFUL ‹a graveled alley vaulted with fine straight green oaks, which seemed marvellously cool and ~ —Edmund Wilson› **syn** see COMFORTABLE

re·pose·ful·ly \\-fəlē, -li\\ *adv* **:** in a reposeful manner **:** RESTFULLY

re·pose·ful·ness \\-fəlnə̇s\\ *n* -ES **:** the quality or state of being reposeful **:** RESTFULNESS

reposing room *n* **:** a room (as in a funeral home) used for the viewing of the deceased by mourners

re·pos·it \\rə̇ˈpäzə̇t, rēˈp-\\ *vt* [L *repositus*, past part. of *reponere* to replace, put back, fr. *re-* + *ponere* to put, place — more at POSITION] **1 :** to lay away **:** DEPOSIT, STORE ‹buried sedimentary rocks which have entrapped the water in which the rocks were originally ~*ed* —*Westralian Farmers Co-op Gazette*› **2 :** to put back in place **:** REPLACE ‹he ~*ed* the stomach in the abdomen —John Kobler›

¹repo·si·tion \\ˌrēpəˈzishən, ˌrep-\\ *n* [LL *reposition-*, *repositio*, fr. L *repositus* (past part. of *reponere*) + *-ion-*, *-io* -ion] **1 :** the act of repositing or the state of being reposited **2** *Scot* **:** restoration to a position, possession, or office **:** REINSTATEMENT

²re·po·si·tion \\ˌrēpəˈzishən\\ *vt* [*re-* + *position*] **:** to change the position of ‹a malposition of the lower jaw . . . may be assumed and the jaw temporarily ~*ed* —H.G.Armstrong› ‹advise the receiver pilot to ~ his craft —*Ethyl News*›

¹re·pos·i·to·ry \\rə̇ˈpäzəˌtōrē, rēˈp-, -tȯr-, -ri\\ *n* -ES [L *repositorium*, fr. *repositus* (past part. of *reponere*) + *-orium* -ory] **1 :** a place, room, or container where something is deposited or stored **:** DEPOSITORY ‹the child's desk . . . as a ~ for his music papers and other oddments —Marcia Davenport›: as **a :** a building or room for the exhibition of a collection (as of works of art) **:** MUSEUM ‹a single museum serves not only as local ~ for cultural monuments but also as a community center —Lincoln Kirstein› **b :** a burial vault **c :** a place where something is kept or shown for sale **:** a warehouse, store, or showroom ‹now had an office and a clerk and they had a ~ . . . for their finished work —Ben Riker› **d :** a side altar or niche in a Roman Catholic church where the consecrated Host is deposited from Maundy Thursday until Good Friday — called also *altar of repose* **2 :** one that contains or stores something nonmaterial **:** STOREHOUSE ‹although well written and attractively printed, is little more than a ~ of linguistic superstitions —R.A.Hall b.1911› ‹theoretically the mob is the ~ of all political wisdom and virtue —H.L.Mencken› **3 :** a place or region richly supplied with some natural resource ‹the ~ of fabulous oil resources —A.E.Stevenson b.1900› **4 :** a person to whom something is confided or entrusted ‹he had been an entranced ~ of many secrets —John Buchan›

²repository \\"\\ *adj, of a drug* **:** designed to act over a prolonged period **:** slowly absorbed **:** DEPOT ‹~ penicillin›

re·possess \\ˌrē+\\ *vt* [*re-* + *possess*] **1 a :** to possess again **:** regain possession of ‹~*ed* her vanity bag —Christopher Morley› ‹a young playwright, seeking a way to ~ the great classical tradition of comedy —William Becker› **b :** to resume possession of (an item purchased on installment) in default of the payment of installments due ‹~*ed* the car› ‹~*ed* the sofa› **2** *Scot* **:** REINSTATE ‹for the purpose of ~*ing* his uncle again in the lodge —Sir Walter Scott› **3 :** to restore to possession **:** put in possession again ‹theology has ~*ed* itself of a good conscience and a sense of authority —A.N.Wilder› — **repossessor** \\"+\\ *n*

re·possession \\"+\\ *n* **:** the act or state of possessing again **:** RECOVERY; *specif* **:** the act of resuming possession of property when the purchaser fails to keep up payments on it

repost *var of* RIPOSTE

re·pot \\(ˈ)rē+\\ *vt* [*re-* + *pot*] **:** to transfer a plant from one pot to another usu. with the addition of fresh soil

re·pous·sage \\rə̇ˈpüˈsäzh\\ *n* -s [F, fr. *repousser* + *-age*] **1 :** the art or process of hammering out or pressing thin metal from the reverse side **2 :** the hammering out of an etching and photoengraving plate from behind to level up any part that has been worked into a depression

¹re·pous·sé \\-ˈsā\\ *adj* [F, past part. of *repousser* to press back, thrust back, fr. MF, fr. *re-* + *pousser* to push, thrust, fr. OF *poulser* — more at PUSH] **1** *of metal work* **a :** shaped or ornamented with patterns in relief made by hammering or pressing on the reverse side ‹~ work› ‹a silver dish with a ~ rim› **b :** formed in relief ‹a ~ pattern› **2 :** resembling or giving the effect of repoussé work ‹an elongated box bag of crushed silver or gold kid stitched in a ~ design —Marion Miller›

²repoussé \\"\\ *n* -s **:** repoussé work

repp *var of* REP

rep·pe chemistry \\ˈrepə-\\ *n, usu cap R* [after Walter *Reppe* b1892 Ger. chemist] **:** a branch esp. of industrial chemistry that is based on reactions of acetylene under pressure and also of the products so obtained and that includes vinylation, ethynylation, polymerization to cyclic compounds, and carbonylation

repped \\ˈrept\\ *adj* [³*rep* + *-ed*] **:** resembling rep **:** having a ribbed surface ‹~ paper›

repping *pres part of* REP

rep·ple dep·ple \\ˌrepəlˈdepəl\\ *n* [by shortening & alter.] *slang* **:** REPLACEMENT DEPOT

repr *abbr* **1** repair **2** represent; representative; represented; representing **3** reprint; reprinted

rep·re·hend \\ˌreprə̇ˈhend, -prēˈ-\\ *vt* -ED/-ING/-S [ME *reprehenden*, fr. L *reprehendere* to hold back, seize, reprehend, fr. *re-* + *prehendere* to grasp, seize — more at PREHENSILE] **:** to voice disapproval of esp. after judgment **:** find fault with usu. with sternness and as a rebuke **:** BLAME, CENSURE, CHIDE, REPRIMAND, REPROVE ‹~ not the imperfection of others —George Washington› ‹I severely ~*ed* him on this occasion —Samuel Richardson› **syn** see CRITICIZE

reprehender *n* -s *obs* **:** one that voices disapproval

rep·re·hen·si·bil·i·ty \\ˌreprə̇ˌhen(t)səˈbilədē\\ *n* -ES **:** the quality or state of being reprehensible

rep·re·hen·si·ble \\-en(t)səbəl\\ *adj* [ME, fr. LL *reprehensibilis*, fr. L *reprehensus* (past part. of *reprehendere*) + *-ibilis* -able] **:** worthy of or deserving reprehension **:** BLAMABLE, CENSURABLE, CULPABLE, REPROVABLE ‹to capitalize on his ignorance is morally ~ —Nicholas Samstag› ‹it is my ~ nature to welcome excitement —Carl Van Doren› ‹when a work of art excites . . . ~ passions —Samuel Alexander›

rep·re·hen·si·bly \\-blē, -bli\\ *adv* **:** in a reprehensible manner or degree ‹those laws . . . were in his judgment ~ lenient —T.B.Macaulay›

rep·re·hen·sion \\ˌ==ˈhenchən\\ *n* -s [ME *reprehensioun*, fr. MF or L; MF *reprehension*, fr. L *reprehension-*, *reprehensio*, fr. *reprehensus* (past part. of *reprehendere*) + *-ion-*, *-io* -ion] **1 :** the act of reprehending **:** REPROOF ‹if they are corrupt, they merit . . . blame and ~ —Edmund Burke› ‹lifted no voice in ~ of his corrupt deals —S.H.Adams› **2** *archaic* **:** an instance of reprehending ‹his writings contained . . . severe ~s —Thomas Brown›

rep·re·hen·sive \\ˌ==ˈhen(t)siv, -sēv *also* -səv\\ *adj* [fr. *reprehension*, after such pairs as E *apprehension: apprehensive*] **:** serving to reprehend **:** conveying reprehension or reproof ‹~ aspects and unfortunate results of unwarranted charges —*New Republic*› — **rep·re·hen·sive·ly** \\-sə̇vlē, -li\\ *adv*

rep·re·hen·so·ry \\-n(t)s(ə)rē\\ *adj* [fr. *reprehension*, after such pairs as E *commendation: commendatory*] *archaic* **:** REPREHENSIVE ‹no reason for making any ~ complaint —Samuel Johnson›

rep·re·sent \\ˌreprə̇ˈzent, -prēˈz-, *in rapid speech often* ÷ -pəˈz, *chiefly in substand speech* -pərˈz-\\ *vb* -ED/-ING/-S [ME *representen*, fr. MF *representer*, fr. L *repraesentare*, fr. *re-* + *praesentare* to present — more at PRESENT] *vt* **1 :** to bring clearly before the mind **:** cause to be known, felt, or apprehended **:** present esp. by description **2 :** to serve as a sign or symbol of **3 :** to portray by pictorial, plastic, or musical art **:** DELINEATE, DEPICT **4** *archaic* **:** to make manifest **:** DISPLAY, EXHIBIT, SHOW **5 :** to exhibit by delineation, depiction, or portrayal — used esp. of a work of art **6 :** to present by means of something standing in the place of **:** serve as the counterpart or image of **:** TYPIFY **7 :** to exhibit dramatically: **a :** to produce on the stage **b :** to act the part or role of **:** personate in acting or on the stage **8 a :** to supply the place, perform the duties, exercise the rights, or receive the share of **:** take the place of in some respect **:** fill the place of for some purpose **:** substitute in some capacity for **:** act the part of, in the place of, or for (as another person) usu. by legal right **b :** to serve (as in a legislative body) by delegated or deputed authority usu. resulting from election ‹the state was ~*ed* in Congress by two Republicans› **9 :** to describe as having a specified character or quality **10 :** to set forth or place before someone (as by statement, account, or discourse) **:** exhibit (a fact) to another mind in language **:** give one's own impressions and judgment of **:** state with advocacy or with the design of affecting action or judgment **:** point out by way of protest or remonstrance **11 :** to serve as a specimen, example, or instance of **12 a :** to form an image or representation of in the mind **b** (1) **:** to apprehend (an object) by means of an idea (2) **:** to recall in memory (an object of previous experience) **13 :** to correspond to in kind **~** *vi* **:** to make representations against something **:** present objections **:** PROTEST

syn REPRESENT, DEPICT, PORTRAY, DELINEATE, PICTURE, and LIMN can mean to present an image or lifelike imitation of, as in art. REPRESENT implies a placing before the mind as if real or as if living, as by a picture, description, or piece of sculpture ‹the statue *represented* the great man as even more heroic than he was in fact› ‹the stage setting *represents* a hotel lobby› ‹seemed to think that music could *represent* physical objects and literary or historical events —*New Republic*› DEPICT suggests specifically a graphic representation ‹*depicted* hill-country scenes in woodcuts and etchings —*Amer. Guide Series: Ark.*› ‹miniature tapestries that *depict* quaint eighteenth-century scenes —Horace Sutton› ‹action can tell a story, display all the most vivid relations between men, and *depict* every kind of human emotion, without the aid of a word —O.W. Holmes †1935› PORTRAY suggests specifically a detailed representation as of a character by means of a portrait ‹a picture vividly *portraying* the passion of Joan of Arc› ‹in literature are portrayed all human passions, desires, and aspirations —C.W.Eliot› DELINEATE, suggesting a line drawing, stresses a care for accuracy of detail and fullness of outline ‹his brush did its work with a steady and sure stroke that indicated command of his materials. He could *delineate* whatever he elected with technical skill —Richard Jefferies› ‹various clinical studies which fairly well *delineated* the usefulness of this drug —R.R.Tompsett & Walsh McDermott› ‹those who perform on the screen have to *delineate* character and to display the emotions —P.W.Tell› PICTURE suggests perhaps more pictorial quality or definiteness of representation ‹on the walls were *pictured* buffalo and reindeer› ‹the writer is a master of vivid illustrations from nature and history, of rhythmical period or terse antithesis, of emotional appeal and concrete *picturing* of facts —*Encyc. Americana*› ‹*picture* things as they were in the golden thirteenth century —G.G.Coulton› LIMN is chiefly a literary equivalent of DEPICT or DELINEATE ‹prosecution *limned* a somewhat different picture —*Newsweek*› ‹his talent for dialogue as a means for *limning* character —Margaret Hexter› ‹the life of the community is drawn in detail and the sorrows and sacrifices *limned* with deep compassion —Mary L. Dunn›

re-present \\ˌrē + *pronunc at verb* PRESENT\\ *vt* [*re-* + *present*] **:** to present again, anew, or through the medium of art

rep·re·sent·able *pronunc at* REPRESENT + əbəl\\ *adj* **:** capable of being represented

rep·re·sen·ta·men \\ˌreprə̇ˌzenˈtāmən, -prē-, -ˌzən-\\ *n, pl* **represen·tam·i·na** \\-tamənə\\ [fr. *representation*, after such pairs as L *putation-*, *putatio* act of pruning (fr. *putatus* — past part. of *putare* to cut, prune — + *-ion-*, *-io* -ion): *putamen* that which falls off in pruning — more at PUTAMEN] **:** the product as distinguished from the act of philosophical representation — compare REPRESENTATION 1e

rep·re·sent·ant \\ˌreprə̇ˈzentᵊnt, -prēˈ-, -zentənt\\ *n* -s [F *représentant*, fr. MF *representant*, fr. *representant*, pres. part. of *representer* to represent] **:** one that represents another **:** REPRESENTATIVE ‹the greatest literary ~ of the revolution —*Nineteenth Century & After*›

rep·re·sen·ta·tion \\ˌreprə̇ˌzenˈtāshən, -prēˌz-, -zən-, *in rapid speech often* ÷ -pə(ˌ)z-, *chiefly in substand speech* -pər(ˌ)z-\\ *n* -s [ME *representacion*, fr. MF *representation*, fr. L *repraesentation-*, *repraesentatio*, fr. *repraesentatus* (past part. of *repraesentare* to represent) + *-ion-*, *-io* -ion] **1 :** one that represents or is represented: as **a :** a likeness, picture, model, or other reproduction ‹~s in pottery of frogs and turtles —*Times Lit. Supp.*› ‹an allegorical ~ . . . decorates the main pediment —*Amer. Guide Series: Mich.*› **b** (1) **:** a statement or account esp. made to convey a particular view or impression of something with the intention of influencing opinion or action ‹his ~s . . . influenced the president to investigate —*Amer. Guide Series: Minn.*› ‹make no false ~s to me —Thomas Hardy› ‹defendant's ~s that said automobile was new —*Southeastern Reporter*› (2) **:** a statement of fact incidental or collateral to a contract made orally or in writing and on the faith of which the contract is entered into — compare ¹AFFIRMATIVE 3b, PROMISSORY, WARRANTY ‹written ~s obtained from officials of the client —R.S.Johns› ‹the contract of sale contains a ~ by the purchaser —*U.S.Code*› **c :** a dramatic production or performance ‹a theatrical ~› **d** (1) **:** a usu. formal and serious statement (as of facts, reasons, or arguments) made against something or to effect a change ‹the colonial secretary made ~s on behalf of the Uitlanders —Ethel Drus› (2) **:** a usu. formal protest **:** EXPOSTULATION, REMONSTRANCE ‹the tenants had decided not to pay the increase until they had made ~s to the Native Affairs Department —H.S.Warner› **e** (1) **:** an image or idea formed by the mind (2) **:** an idea that is the direct object of thought and the mental counterpart or transcript of the object known by means of it **2 :** the act or action of representing or the state of being represented: as **a :** the action of representing (as by portrayal or delineation) in a visible image or form ‹a strict ~ of nature would require that it curve —Hunter Mead› ‹entrance of light rays into the eye and their final ~ in the brain —F.A.Geldard› ‹an exponent of ~ rather than abstraction in art› **b :** the action of setting forth or placing before another (as by a statement, account, or discourse) esp. with a view to affecting action ‹the ~ of student opinion to the administration —*Seton Hall Univ. Bull.*› ‹yielding to the artful ~ of ambitious hypocrites —Sir Walter Scott› **c** (1) **:** the action or fact of one person standing for another so as to have to a greater or less extent the rights and obligations of the person represented; *specif* **:** the relation of an heir to his predecessor when both the rights and obligations of the predecessor devolve upon the heir (as in Roman and Scots law) (2) **:** the substitution of an individual or class of individuals in place of a person (as when a child or children take the share of an estate that would have fallen to a deceased parent) **d** (1) **:** the action of representing or the fact of being represented in a legislative body ‹~ of territory . . . rather than of population —G.A.Graham› ‹raise the issue of Chinese ~ —*New Statesman & Nation*› ‹the ancient world knew nothing of the device of ~ —Woodrow Wilson› (2) **:** the action or fact of being represented in some other grouping, body, or aggregation ‹in . . . such universities and colleges there is no ~ of any non-West European culture —*Amer. Council of Learned Soc. Newsletter*› ‹~ of classic issues in the collection› **e** (1) **:** the action or process by which the mind forms an image or idea of an object (2) **:** recurrent as opposed to simple presentation **3 :** the whole body of persons representing a constituency ‹when vacancies happen in the ~ of any state in the Senate —*U. S. Constitution*› ‹chosen head of the U. S. ~ —*Current Biog.*› ‹small ~s from the Baltic states —Henry Giniger›

re-presentation \\(ˌ)rē + *pronunc at* PRESENTATION\\ *n* [*re-present* + *-ation*] **:** a presentation again or anew ‹the revision and *re-presentation* of established favorite titles —Louise S. Bechtel› ‹a *re-presentation* of facts previously stated›

rep·re·sen·ta·tion·al \\ˈ==(ˌ)= *as in* REPRESENTATION + ˈtāshənᵊl *or* -shnəl\\ *adj* **1 :** of, based upon, or of the nature of representation ‹~ art› ‹~ powers› ‹~ office› **2 :** of, relating to, or supporting representationalism ‹~ school› ‹~ theory›

rep·re·sen·ta·tion·al·ism \\ˌ==(ˌ)=ˈtāshənᵊlˌizəm, -shnəˌli-\\ *n* -s **1** *also* **rep·re·sen·ta·tion·ism** \\-shəˌnizəm\\ **:** the philosophical doctrine asserting that the immediate or direct object of knowledge is an idea in the mind distinct from the external or independent object which is the occasion of perception and holding sometimes that the idea is a mental counterpart or true copy of the external object and sometimes that the idea is a modification of the consciousness determined in part by the nature of the independent object and in part by the nature or limitations of the mind **2 :** REPRESENTATIVE ART ‹unorthodox ~ in his work —J.J.Sweeney› ‹~ is better left to the action film —Delmore Schwartz›

rep·re·sen·ta·tion·al·ist \\-shənᵊlə̇st, -shnəl-\\ *n* -s **:** one that practices or advocates representative art — compare ABSTRACTIONIST 2

rep·re·sen·ta·tion·ist \\-sh(ə)nə̇st\\ *n* -s **:** an adherent of philosophical representationism

¹rep·re·sent·a·tive \\ˌreprə̇ˈzentədˌiv, -prēˈz-, -təiv, *in rapid speech often* ÷ -pəˈz-, *chiefly in substand speech* -pərˈz-\\ *adj* [ME, fr. MF or ML; MF *representatif*, fr. ML *repraesentativus*, fr. L *repraesentatus* (past part. of *repraesentare* to represent) + *-ivus* -ive] **1 :** serving to represent, portray, or typify **:** characterized by representation ‹a painting ~ of a battle› **2 :** standing for or in the place of another **:** acting for another or others **:** constituting the agent for another esp. through delegated authority **3 :** of, based upon, or constituting a form of government in which the many are represented by persons chosen from among them usu. by election ‹~ government› ‹~ democracy› ‹development of the ~ system› **4 :** serving as a characteristic example **:** illustrative of a class **:** conveying an idea of others of the kind **:** TYPICAL ‹a ~ modern play› ‹a ~ romantic poem› **5 a :** having the character of a mental representation — compare REPRESENTATION 1e **b :** of or relating to the doctrine of representationalism ‹the ~ theory of knowledge›

²representative \\"\\ *n* -s **1 a :** one that stands for a number or class (as of persons or things) **:** one that in some way corresponds to, replaces, or is equivalent to someone or something else **:** SAMPLE, SPECIMEN ‹many ~s of the Protozoa —R.E.Coker› ‹the student body includes ~s of 36 states —*Amer. Guide Series: N.C.*› ‹where distinctly different biological ~s are found —*Amer. Guide Series: Minn.*› **b :** a typical embodiment of some quality or abstract concept **:** TYPE ‹the most authoritative ~ . . . of the ideal of priestly stewardship —V.L.Parrington› ‹of the Semitic family Arabic is the chief living ~ —A.L.Kroeber› ‹the sole ~ . . . of the feelings and the knowledge of the middle ages —H.T.Buckle› **2** *obs* **:** a representative body or assembly ‹debate in the grand ~ of the kingdom —Nathaniel Bacon› **3 :** one that represents another or others in a special capacity: as **a** (1) **:** one that represents a constituency as a member of a legislative or other governing body ‹the people exercises this sovereignty . . . through the votes of its ~s —D.W.S.Lidderdale› ‹committee . . . to which no ~ of an Arab state had been named —*U. N. Bull.*› ‹summoned ~s of the shires and the boroughs to parliament› (2) **:** a member of the House of Representatives of the U.S. Congress (3) **:** a member of a house of representatives in a state legislature **b** (1) **:** one that represents another as agent, deputy, substitute, or delegate usu. being invested with the authority of the principal (2) : one appointed to represent a sovereign or government abroad ⟨the permanent ~ of Canada to the North Atlantic Council —*Current Biog.*⟩ ⟨served as ~ of the president of the U.S. in conferences with the allies⟩ **c** : one who legally represents or stands in the place of a deceased person : LEGAL REPRESENTATIVE a, PERSONAL REPRESENTATIVE **d** : one that in some respect stands for or in the place of another ⟨money is only a commodious ~ of the commodities which may be purchased with it —Joseph Priestley⟩ **e** : one that represents a business organization : SALESMAN ⟨local ~ of an insurance company⟩ **f** : one that represents another as successor or heir : one representing a line or tradition ⟨the last ~ of one of the founding families⟩ ⟨do not know if his large family has left any ~s today —*Notes & Queries*⟩

representative art *n* : art that is concerned with the representation of reality and esp. the characteristic or verisimilar representation of nature or life ⟨the earliest works of art from the caves of Europe are not only realistic, but meritoriously *representative art* —Clark Wissler⟩

representative–at–large *n, pl* **representatives–at–large** \ˌ==-ˌ====ˌ=\ : CONGRESSMAN-AT-LARGE

representative democracy *n* : DEMOCRACY 1b(2)

representative firm *n* : a model firm not necessarily in existence which as an abstract construction is used to illustrate the operations of a market as a whole

representative fraction *n* : a map scale in which figures representing units (as centimeters, inches, or feet) are expressed in the form of the fraction 1/*x* (as 1/250,000) or of the ratio 1:*x* to indicate that one unit on the map represents *x* units (as 250,000 centimeters) on the earth's surface

representative legislature *n* : a British colonial legislature in which at least one half of the members are elected by the people of the colony — compare LEGISLATIVE COUNCIL 2

rep·re·sent·a·tive·ly \-əvlē, -li\ *adv* [ME *representatyfliche*, fr. *representatyf, representative* representative + *-liche* -ly] : in a representative manner

representative money *n* : paper money backed by an equal amount of gold or silver coin or bullion held by a government

rep·re·sent·a·tive·ness \-ivnəs\ *n* -ES **1** : the quality or state of being representative ⟨his ~ as an American⟩ **2** : the characteristic of a specific scientific experiment that makes it an adequate sample of the general case

representative peer *n* : a peer chosen to represent other peers in the House of Lords: **a** : one of 16 Scottish peers elected as their representatives for the duration of a single parliament by persons holding Scottish peerages only **b** : one of 28 Irish peers elected as their representatives for life by persons holding Irish peerages only

representative sampling *n* : sampling in which the relative sizes of sub-population samples are chosen equal to the relative sizes of the sub-populations

representative theory *n* : REPRESENTATIONALISM 1

representative town meeting *n* : a town meeting in which a usu. small number of representatives previously elected by the townspeople vote and transact business although other residents may attend and often are allowed to speak

representator *n* -S [LL *repraesentator*, fr. L *repraesentatus* (past part. of *repraesentare* to represent) + *-or*] *obs* : REPRESENTER

represented *past of* REPRESENT

representee *n, obs* : a parliamentary representative

rep·re·sent·er \ˌ==ˈzentə(r)\ *n* -S : one that represents (as by exhibition, acting, or presentation)

representing *pres part of* REPRESENT

rep·re·sent·ment \ˌ==ˈzentmənt\ *n, archaic* : REPRESENTATION ⟨the presentments of sense or the ~s of memory —E.R. Conder⟩ ⟨expect to prevail . . . by a bare ~ of the unreasonableness of their actions —Henry Dodwell⟩

representor *n* -S *obs* : REPRESENTATIVE

represents *pres 3d sing of* REPRESENT

¹re·press \rəˈpres, rēˈp-\ *vb* -ED/-ING/-ES [ME *repressen*, fr. L *repressus*, past part. of *reprimere* to check, repress — more at REPRIMAND] *vt* **1** : to check by or as if by pressure : keep or hold in check : restrain from spreading, increasing, or doing harm : CONTROL, CURB ⟨obstruction of justice . . . is sternly ~*ed* —Edward Jenks⟩ ⟨developed psychic interests . . . but then these were ~*ed* by her parents —A.G.N.Flew⟩ ⟨law tended to foster rather than ~ grammar —H.O.Taylor⟩ ⟨~ bleeding⟩ **2** : to keep down or under by self-control : restrain oneself from expression (as by showing, feeling, or uttering) of : keep under control ⟨could not ~ a smile at the comical figure —Ellen Glasgow⟩ ⟨~*ed* the temptation to talk about it —Kathleen Freeman⟩ ⟨a remarkable ability to ~ his home worries while on the job —W.H.Whyte⟩ **3 a** : to reduce to subjection or quietness : put down by force : SUBDUE ⟨a hopeless undertaking . . . to try to ~ such powerful subjects —H.T.Buckle⟩ **b** : to suppress by exercising force : put down : QUELL ⟨the royal commissioners sent to ~ the tumult —J.R.Green⟩ **4** : to prevent the natural or normal expression, activity, or development of : cause repression of or in ⟨chill penury ~*ed* their noble rage —Thomas Gray⟩ ⟨natural instinct ~*ed* by a perpetual stern control —Havelock Ellis⟩ **5** : to exclude from consciousness : subject to repression ⟨new experiential material . . . ~*ed* in the personality to the level of the unconscious —H.W.Dunham⟩ ⟨~ conflicts⟩ ~ *vi* : to cause or bring about repression : take repressive action ⟨the dominant minority's will to ~ —A.J.Toynbee⟩ ⟨taboos against the gentler emotion force him to ~ —Howard Griffin⟩

²re·press \ˈrē,pres\ *n* : a machine for re-pressing brick

re–press \(ˈ)rē¦pres\ *vt* [*re-* + *press*] : to press again ⟨~ bricks in a mold after coming from the brick machine and before burning in kiln⟩ ⟨was ~*ed* into government service —Whitney Balliett⟩ ⟨~ a record⟩

repressed *adj* **1 a** : subjected to repression ⟨a ~ child⟩ ⟨~ ambition⟩ **b** : characterized by restraint ⟨the ~ delicacy of its general design —*Amer. Guide Series: Conn.*⟩ **2** : affected by repression ⟨infantile anxiety based on ~ phantasies —Christine Olden⟩ ⟨~ hostilities and guilt reactions —Louise Heathers⟩

repressed inflation *n* : a condition in which direct economic controls (as price and wage controls and rationing) are utilized to prevent inflation without removing the underlying inflationary pressures

re·press·er \rəˈpresə(r), rēˈp-\ *n* -S [ME, fr. *repressen* to repress + *-er*] : one that represses

repressing *n* -S [*re-press* + *-ing*] : a phonograph record by one other than the original manufacturer or under a different label than that originally used when first released ⟨concertos . . . now available in domestic ~*s* —C.M.Smith⟩

re·pres·sion \rəˈpreshən, rēˈp-\ *n* -S [ME *repressioun* ability to repress, fr. ML *repression-, repressio*, fr. LL, suppression, fr. L *repressus* (past part. of *reprimere* to check, repress) + *-ion-, -io* -ion] **1 a** : the action of repressing or the state of being repressed ⟨relentless ~ of all Christian sects —R.H. Jackson⟩ ⟨auxiliary units dealing with vice ~ —F.A.Ogg & P.O.Ray⟩ ⟨~ of unpopular opinions⟩ **b** : an instance of repressing ⟨religious wars and the ~s which followed —G.C. Sellery⟩ ⟨racial ~s are more harmful to well-being —Charles Abrams⟩ **2 a** : a process or mechanism of ego defense whereby wishes or impulses that are incapable of fulfillment are kept from or made inaccessible to consciousness except in disguised form (as conversion in neurosis or sublimation or symbolization in normality) **b** : an idea, memory, or experience that has been extruded from consciousness into the unconscious — contrasted with *suppression;* compare MECHANISM OF DEFENSE

re·pres·sive \-esiv,-esəv *also* -esav\ *adj* [ML *repressivus*, fr. L *repressus* (past part. of *reprimere* to check, repress) + *-ivus* -ive] : having power or tending to repress : causing or intended to cause repression ⟨~ measures⟩ ⟨~ taxation⟩ ⟨~ policy⟩

re·pres·sive·ness *n* -ES : the quality or state of being repressive ⟨a ~ in the man —G.D.Brown⟩

re·pres·sor \-sə(r)\ *n* -S [L, fr. *repressus* (past part. of *reprimere*) + *-or*] : one that represses

re·pressure \(ˈ)rē+\ *vt* [*re-* + *pressure*] : to raise the pressure of (an oil-bearing formation) by pumping in air or gas with the object of forcing out additional oil

re·price \(ˈ)rē+\ *vt* [*re-* + *price*] : to give a new price to : fix a new price schedule for ⟨stock that does not move may be *repriced* —*Dry Goods Economist*⟩ ⟨give the government authority to ~ any orders —Helen Fuller⟩

re·priev·al \rəˈprēvəl, rēˈp-\ *n* -S *archaic* : REPRIEVE ⟨~s and prolongings of this present life —Robert Leighton⟩ ⟨brought no ~ from anguish —Robert Southey⟩

¹re·prieve \rəˈprēv, rēˈp-\ *vt* -ED/-ING/-S [alter. (perh. influenced by obs. E *repreve* to reprove, fr. ME *repreven*) of earlier *repry*, perh. fr. MF *repris*, past part. of *reprendre* to take back — more at REPRISE, REPROVE] **1** *obs* : to put off (as something evil) : DELAY, POSTPONE ⟨since we cannot death ~ —Katherine Philips⟩ **2** : to delay the punishment of (as a condemned prisoner) : suspend the execution of sentence on : RESPITE **3** : to give relief or deliverance to for a time : preserve temporarily ⟨whose hard hand *reprieved* the empire from its fate —Robert Browning⟩

²reprieve \"\ *n* -S **1 a** : the act of reprieving or the state of being reprieved **b** : a formal temporary suspension of the execution of a sentence ⟨the president . . . shall have power to grant ~s and pardons for offenses against the United States —*U.S. Constitution*⟩; *esp* : a remission or commutation of a capital sentence **c** : something resembling such a formal suspension : a respite from a decision or penalty ⟨unless there is an eleventh-hour ~ the . . . elevated will cease operating at midnight —*N.Y. Times*⟩ **2** : an order or warrant for a formal suspension (as of a capital sentence) ⟨a messenger was dispatched with a ~ —*Amer. Guide Series: Conn.*⟩ **3** : a respite or temporary escape (as from death, pain, or trouble) ⟨the first relief over the ~ from a railway strike —*Blackwood's*⟩

¹rep·ri·mand \ˈreprə,mand, -maa(ə)nd, -mänd\ *n* -S [F *réprimande*, alter. of MF *reprimende*, fr. L *reprimenda*, fem. of *reprimendus* that is to be checked or repressed, gerundive of *reprimere* to check, repress, fr. *re-* + *-primere* (fr. *premere* to press) — more at PRESS] : a severe or formal reproof : a sharp rebuke : CENSURE; *esp* : one given with authority

²reprimand \", ˌ==ˈ=\ *vt* -ED/-ING/-S [F *réprimander*, fr. *réprimande*, n.] : to reprove severely : chide for a fault : censure formally and esp. with authority : REPREHEND ⟨had done something naughty and knew that she was going to be ~*ed* —I.V.Morris⟩ ⟨this member was found guilty . . . and voted by the House to be ~*ed* —D.G.Hitchner⟩ ⟨the court can ~ them . . . in the event of negligence —F.W.Crofts⟩ **syn** see REPROVE

¹re·print \(ˈ)rē+\ *vt* [*re-* + *print*] : to print again : make a reprint of

²re·print \ˈrē+,- *also* =ˈ=\ *n* **1 a** (1) : a subsequent printing of a book already published having the identical text of the previous printing (2) : such a printing with cheaper paper and binding and put out by a different publisher **b** : a second or new impression of printed matter **c** : an article or extract issued separately after being first published as part of a collection or in a periodical : OFFPRINT **d** : printed text used as copy for something to be typeset **e** (1) : matter (as in a periodical) that has appeared in print before (2) : a later printing of material published in more than one edition of the same newspaper; *esp* : matter in one day's early edition printed in a late edition of the previous day **2 a** : a government or private reprinting of a postage stamp no longer current usu. on different paper or in a different color or perforation from the first printing and esp. for other than postal use — compare REISSUE **b** : a stamp so reprinted **3** : REPRESSING

re·printer \(ˈ)rē+\ *n* : one that publishes a reprint

re·pri·sal \rəˈprīzəl, rēˈp-\ *n* -S [ME *reprisail*, fr. MF *reprisaille*, modif. (influenced by MF *repris*, past part. of *reprendre* to take back) of OIt *ripresaglia*, fr. *ripreso* (past part. of *riprendere* to take back, recapture, fr. L *reprehendere* to hold back, seize, reprehend, recover) + *-aglia* -al (fr. L *-alia*, neut. pl. of *-alis* -al)] **1 a** : the act or practice in international law of resorting to force short of war (as by embargo, sequestration, forcible seizure, retortion, or retaliatory acts of the nature of those complained of) to procure redress of grievances **b** : an instance of such action **2** *obs* : PRIZE ⟨this rich ~ is so nigh and yet not ours —Shak.⟩ **3** : the regaining of something (as by recapture) **4** : something (as an amount or sum of money) given or paid in restitution : COMPENSATION — usu. used in pl. **5** : an action of retaliation (as for injury or attack)

¹re·prise \rəˈprīz, rēˈp-, *in senses 5 & 6* rəˈprēz\ *n* -S [ME, fr. MF, reprise, action of taking back, fr. OF, action of taking back, fr. fem. of *repris*, past part. of *reprendre* to take back, fr. L *reprehendere* to hold back, seize, reprehend, recover — more at REPREHEND] **1** : a deduction or charge (as rent charge, rent seck, pensions, or annuities) to be made yearly out of a manor or estate — usu. used in pl. ⟨the clear yearly value above all ~s of the rectory —*Stat. 1 & 2 William IV*⟩ **2** *archit* : a return in an internal angle **3** *archaic* : REPRISAL 4 ⟨by exchanging an apartment . . . he might well have got a ~ of several million francs —Carleton Lake⟩ **4** *obs* : a retaliatory act : REPRISAL **5 a** : a recurrence, renewal, or resumption of an action : a separate or repeated occurrence ⟨were plunged . . . not once or twice but in frequent ~s —George MacKenzie⟩ **b** : a renewal of attack following a return to guard in fencing **6 a** : the second section of pieces in binary form in 17th century French music **b** : a musical repetition: (1) : the repetition of the exposition preceding the development (2) : RECAPITULATION **c** : something resembling or held to resemble a reprise in a musical score : a subsequent and identical performance : REPETITION

²re·prise \-īz, *in sense 3* -ēz\ *vt* -ED/-ING/-S [ME *reprisen* to begin again, fr. MF *repris*, past part. of *reprendre* to take back] **1** *archaic* : to take back; *esp* : to recover by force ⟨might ~ the arms . . . forfeited —George Chapman⟩ **2** *archaic* : COMPENSATE **3** : to repeat the performance of ⟨~ a song⟩

re·pris·ti·nate \(ˈ)rē¦pristə,nāt\ *vt* -ED/-ING/-S [*re-* + *pristine* + *-ate*] : to restore to an original state or condition : REVIVE ⟨~ the cosmic order as of before the Fall —H.M.Rosenthal⟩

re·pris·ti·na·tion \(ˌ)rē,pristəˈnāshən\ *n* -S : the act or action of restoring to a pristine state or condition : renewal of purity : RESTORATION ⟨~ of the American Idea as a fighting faith in freedom —H.M.Kallen⟩

re·privatization \(ˌ)rē+\ *n* -S [*re-* + *private* + *-ization*] : the act or action of privatizing again : restoration to private ownership or control (as after nationalization) ⟨the ~ of the subways is . . . to be desired —Henry Hazlitt⟩

¹re·proach \rəˈprōch, rēˈp-\ *n* -ES [ME *reproche*, fr. MF, fr. OF, fr. *reprochier*, v.] **1 a** : a source of disgrace or shame : a cause of blame or censure : an occasion of discredit : something (as a fact, matter, feature, or quality) producing disgrace or blame ⟨make us see in our whole prison system a ~ —B.N. Cardozo⟩ ⟨made their calling a ~ and a hissing —A.M. Young⟩ **b** : the quality or state (as disgrace, shame, blame, discredit, or opprobrium) so incurred ⟨these rare exceptions did not take away the ~ which lay on the whole body —T.B. Macaulay⟩ **2** : the act or action of reproaching sometimes sternly or abusively and sometimes mildly and gently as an upbraiding ⟨a term of ~⟩ ⟨was above ~⟩ ⟨turned a look of keen ~ on him —George Eliot⟩ ⟨the abstainers are not regarded with ~ —Freeman Lincoln⟩ **3** : an expression of censure, disapproval, or rebuke ⟨raged at . . . him with contradictory ~*es* —Joseph Conrad⟩ ⟨answer . . . letters sadly and patiently and with no ~*es* —Margaret Deland⟩ ⟨her greeting was a playful ~ —Willa Cather⟩ **4** *obs* : one subjected to censure or scorn : an object of contempt ⟨we are become a ~ to our neighbors —Ps 79:4 (AV)⟩ **5 reproaches** *pl, usu cap* : a series of antiphons that are made up of sentences represented as addressed by Christ to his people to remind them of his services to mankind and their ingratitude and are individually followed by the Trisagion sung as a respond and that constitute a service or part of a service on Good Friday in the Roman Catholic and some Anglican churches

²reproach \"\ *vt* -ED/-ING/-ES [MF *reprocher*, fr. OF *reprochier*, fr. (assumed) VL *repropiare*, fr. L *re-* + LL *-propiare* (as in *appropiare* to approach) — more at APPROACH] **1** : to cast up to someone as deserving reproach : bring up as a fault or demerit : allude to as blameworthy : make a matter of reproach — usu. used with *to* or *against* ⟨his conscience ~*ed* him nothing —Andre Ambron⟩ ⟨the mere fact . . . should not be ~*ed* against them —*London Daily News*⟩ **2** : to utter a reproach to: **a** : to upbraid, censure, or tax with something blameworthy or reprehensible esp. through hurt disappointment or chagrin : rebuke strongly or sternly : SCOLD ⟨I should like to . . . ~ her for being false —George Meredith⟩ **b** : to chide gently or in a friendly spirit often in an appeal for amendment : reprove constructively and helpfully : express disappointment and disapproval to ⟨she was very glad to see me and ~*ed* me for giving her no notice of my coming —Jane Austen⟩ **3** : to bring into discredit : constitute a cause of reproach to ⟨you might ~ your life —Shak.⟩ **4** : to cast reproach, blame, or discredit on ⟨the triviality with which we often ~ the remarks of the chorus —Matthew Arnold⟩ **syn** see REPROVE

re·proach·able \-chəbəl\ *adj* [ME *reprochable*, fr. OF, fr. *reprochier* + *-able*] *archaic* : deserving reproach : CENSURABLE ⟨conduct . . . in the highest degree ~ —George Keate⟩

re·proach·er \-chə(r)\ *n* -S : one that reproaches

re·proach·ful \-chfəl\ *adj* **1** : full of reproach or reproaches : expressing censure or rebuke ⟨~ words⟩ ⟨a ~ glance⟩ **2** *archaic* : involving or incurring reproach, shame, or censure : BLAMEWORTHY, DISGRACEFUL, SHAMEFUL ⟨a most ~ death —Samuel Parker †1688⟩

re·proach·ful·ly \-fəlē, -li\ *adv* **1** : in a reproachful manner ⟨my hostess was annoyed . . . and looked at me ~ —Maude Hutchins⟩ **2** *obs* : in a shameful or disgraceful manner ⟨publicly and ~ executed —Edward Hyde⟩

re·proach·ful·ness \-fəlnəs\ *n* -ES : the quality or state of being reproachful

re·proach·ing·ly *adv* : REPROACHFULLY ⟨seemed to look at him ~ —Charlotte Smith⟩

rep·ro·ba·cy \ˈreprəbəsē\ *n* -ES [²*reprobate* + *-cy*] : the quality or state of being reprobate ⟨committed defiantly, in open ~ —J.A.Symonds⟩

rep·ro·bance \-bən(t)s\ *n* -S [²*reprobate* + *-ance*] *archaic* : REPROBATION ⟨fallen to ~ —A.C.Swinburne⟩

¹rep·ro·bate \-,bāt, *usu* -ād·+V\ *vt* -ED/-ING/-S [ME *reprobaten*, fr. LL *reprobatus*, past part. of *reprobare* to disapprove, condemn — more at REPROVE] **1** : to disapprove of : reject as unworthy or evil : censure strongly and forcefully : CONDEMN, DISCOUNTENANCE ⟨*reprobated* the decoration of churches with images —G.G.Coulton⟩ ⟨such sentiments . . . are now severely *reprobated* —Walter Moberly⟩ ⟨she genuinely *reprobated* . . . disorderliness —Margery Sharp⟩ **2** : to reject from Himself : foreordain to damnation : EXCLUDE — used of God **3** : to refuse to accept : REJECT ⟨every scheme . . . recommended by one of them was *reprobated* by the other —T.B.Macaulay⟩ **4** : to reject (as an instrument or deed) as not binding on account of forgery, perjury, or reliance upon incompetent evidence : take exception to : put away : DISALLOW — compare APPROBATE 1b **syn** see CRITICIZE

²rep·ro·bate \" *sometimes* -,bət *or* +V -bəd·\ *adj* [LL *reprobatus*, past part. of *reprobare*] **1** *archaic* : rejected as not enduring proof or trial : inferior in purity or fineness when compared to a standard : CONDEMNED, WORTHLESS **2 a** : condemned or rejected by God's decree : lost in sin **b** : morally abandoned : lost to all sense of religious or moral obligation : DEPRAVED, UNPRINCIPLED **3** : expressing or involving reprobation ⟨the ~ sense of a word⟩ **4** : of, relating to, or having the characteristics of a reprobate : CORRUPT ⟨~ conduct⟩

³reprobate \"\ *n* -S **1** : one rejected or foreordained to condemnation by God : one not of the elect : one fallen from grace : a lost soul **2 a** : a depraved, vicious, or unprincipled person : one whose character is utterly bad : SCOUNDREL **b** : one held to resemble such a scoundrel : SCAMP

rep·ro·ba·tion \ˌreprəˈbāshən\ *n* -S [ME *reprobacion* action of raising objections, fr. LL *reprobation-, reprobatio* rejection by God's decree, fr. *reprobatus* (past part. of *reprobare*) + L *-ion-, -io* -ion] : the act of reprobating or the state of being reprobated: as **a** : the act of raising legal exceptions or objections — compare REPROBATOR **b** : rejection by God's decree : predestination or foreordination to eternal damnation ⟨the election, ~, and fatality of Calvinism are rejected —F.S.Mead⟩ — compare ELECTION 1d, PRETERITION 3 **c** *archaic* : rejection as inferior or spurious : condemnation as worthless ⟨a brand of ~ on clipped poetry and false coin —John Dryden⟩ **d** : severe disapproval : CENSURE, REPROOF ⟨the result of this almost universal ~ . . . was his ruin —G.C.Sellery⟩ ⟨first to fix a mark of ~ upon the African slave trade —R.B.Taney⟩ ⟨the shaken head of moral ~ —S.H.Adams⟩

rep·ro·ba·tive \ˈreprə,bād·iv\ *adj* [¹*reprobate* + *-ive*] : expressing or conveying reprobation ⟨employed language more stern and ~ —Isaac Taylor⟩ ⟨the curious ~ force . . . acquired by the term —R.M.Weaver⟩

rep·ro·ba·tor \-ād·ə(r)\ *n* [¹*reprobate* + *-or*] : a onetime proceeding in Scots law to disqualify or reject a witness

rep·ro·ba·to·ry \ˈreprəbə,tōrē\ *adj* [¹*reprobate* + *-ory*] : REPROBATIVE ⟨wagged a ~ head —Marguerite Steen⟩

re·processed \(ˈ)rē+\ *adj* [*re-* + *processed* (past part. of *process*)] *of wool fibers* : obtained from finished but unused wool products (as mill ends and clippings from wholesale clothing manufacture) and remade into merchandise — compare REUSED

re·pro·duce \ˌrēprə¦d(y)üs *sometimes* ˌrep-\ *vb* [*re-* + *produce*] *vt* : to produce again: as **a** : to produce (new individuals of the same kind) by a sexual or an asexual process : cause the existence of (something of the same class, kind, or nature as another thing) ⟨~ a rose⟩ ⟨an animal which can ~ a lost part⟩ **b** : to cause to exist again or anew ⟨~ water from steam⟩ **c** : to cause to be or seem to be repeated : bring about again : REPEAT ⟨actors *reproduced* the sound of running horses by pounding . . . pillows —*Amer. Guide Series: N.Y.*⟩ **d** : to bring forward, present, or exhibit again ⟨letter from which I ~ a few characteristic passages —Havelock Ellis⟩ ⟨~ a play⟩ **e** (1) : to make an image, copy, or other representation of : PORTRAY ⟨~ a face on canvas⟩ (2) : to copy by a different process or method than that orig. employed ⟨~ an oil painting by color lithography⟩ **f** : to cause to exist in the mind or imagination : create again mentally : represent clearly to the mind **g** : to revive mentally : have a mental image of : REMEMBER **h** : to translate (a recording) into sound or into an electrical voltage ~ *vi* **1** : to turn out in a specified way in reproduction ⟨the original will ~ clearly in a . . . photocopy —*Dun's Rev.*⟩ **2** : to produce offspring ⟨the young couples did not ~ freely —Willa Cather⟩

re·pro·duc·er \-sə(r)\ *n* : one that reproduces: as **a** : a device (as a record player, magnetic-recorder playback, or a photoelectric amplifier for cinema sound tracks) for utilizing recordings to produce an electrical voltage that may be amplified and usu. reproduced as sound ⟨disc ~⟩ ⟨film ~⟩ ⟨tape ~⟩ **b** : a device in a manograph for reproducing the engine stroke on a reduced scale

re·pro·duc·ibil·i·ty \ˌ==,d(y)üsəˈbiləd·ē, -lətē, -i\ *n* -ES : capability of being reproduced ⟨a product giving excellent ~ on the spectrograph —*Economic Geology*⟩ ⟨~ of results in successive tests —F.A.Geldard⟩

re·pro·duc·ible \ˌ==¦d(y)üsəbəl\ *adj* : capable of being reproduced : permitting reproduction ⟨astonishingly ~ results can be obtained —S.E.Luria⟩

reproducing characteristic *n* : a relation between system amplification change and frequency in tape, disc, or film record reproduction necessary to compensate for record and recording characteristics

reproducing head *n* : a device for utilizing a tape or disc recording to produce an electrical voltage that is usu. amplified and used to produce sound

reproducing tube *or* **reproduction tube** *n* : the cathode ray tube in which the image is reproduced in television

re·pro·duc·tion \ˌ==¦dəkshən\ *n* -S [fr. *reproduce*, after E *produce: production*] **1** : the act or process of reproducing: as **a** : the act of forming, creating, or bringing into existence again ⟨the squire interposed his authority towards the ~ of peace —T.L.Peacock⟩ ⟨~ of capital⟩ ⟨sound ~⟩ **b** : REGENERATION **c** : the process by which plants and animals give rise to offspring that fundamentally consists of the segregation of a portion of the parental body and its subsequent growth and differentiation into a new individual, that in its simpler forms is asexual or vegetative and involves the multiplication of a single parent by building, fission, or the formation of specialized bodies (as tubers, corms, or gemmules) any of which normally grows and differentiates into a new living unit genetically identical with the parent, that may also be sexual involving union of gametes of two parents in fertilization to form a new individual combining genetic characters from each parent although in various modifications offspring may be produced by a single parent in an essentially sexual manner, and that among the higher plants and in many invertebrate animals is characterized by sexual generations alternating with asexual in a characteristic pattern so that long-continued vegetative reproduction without genetic recombination is the exception rather than the rule — compare CLONE, HERMAPHRODITE, PARTHENOGENESIS **d** : a revival of what has been previously learned or experienced : RECALL **e** : the process of producing a representation in another form or medium (as a copy or likeness) **2** : something reproduced: as **a** : a representation in another form or medium ⟨printed ~s of the great masters⟩ : COPY, LIKENESS, COUNTERPART, RECONSTRUCTION ⟨to make a ~ of the Elizabethan theater⟩ **b** : an exact copy : REPLICA **c** : an imprint, impression, engraving, etching, woodcut, cast, or statuette of a work of art subject to copyright after being published if embracing artistic elements apart from the original **d** : young seedling trees in a forest ⟨fires . . . killed all small ~ and larger trees —*Ecology*⟩ **3** : the capacity of plants and animals to give rise to offspring

reproduction cost *n* : PHYSICAL VALUE

reproduction factor *or* **reproduction constant** *n* : MULTIPLICATION FACTOR

re·pro·duc·tion·ist \\,=='dəksh(ə)nəst\\ *n* : one who makes reproductions or copies

¹re·pro·duc·tive \\;==;dəktiv, -tēv *also* -təv\\ *adj* [fr. *reproduce*, after E *produce: productive*] : of, relating to, or capable of reproduction : tending to reproduce : resembling, employed in, or effecting reproduction ⟨~ organs⟩ ⟨~ industries⟩ ⟨records and other ~ devices⟩ — compare VEGETATIVE — **re·pro·duc·tive·ness** *n* -ES

²reproductive \\"\\ *n* **1** : an individual engaging in reproduction : an actual or potential parent **2** : a member of the termite caste that subserves the reproductive function of the colony — compare SOLDIER, WORKER

reproductive imagination *n* : IMAGINATION 1

re·pro·duc·tive·ly \\-tәvlē, -li\\ *adv* : in respect to reproduction : in reproductive terms ⟨amphibians . . . were still ~ bound to the water —Weston La Barre⟩

reproductive potential *n* : the relative capacity of a species to reproduce itself under optimum conditions

re·pro·duc·tiv·i·ty \\,==,dək'tivəd·ē, -vətē, -i\\ *n* [ISV ¹*reproductive* + *-ity*] : the state of or capacity for being reproductive

repromission *n* -S [ME *repromissioun*, fr. L *repromission-, repromissio*, fr. *repromissus* (past part. of *repromittere* to promise in return, fr. *re-* + *promittere* to promise) + *-ion-, -io* -ion — more at PROMISE] *obs* : a promise made in return

re·proof \\rə'prüf, rē'p-\\ *n* [ME *reprof, repref, reprove, repreve*, fr. MF *reprove, repreuve*, fr. OF, fr. *reprover* to reprove] **1** : censure for a fault : an expression of censure or blame : REBUKE, REPRIMAND ⟨the latter action is almost like a ~ to the players —Warwick Braithwaite⟩ ⟨pained by the severity of his father's ~ —Jane Austen⟩ ⟨highly sensitive . . . and cannot bear ~ —Robert Littell⟩ **2** *archaic* : DISPROOF, REFUTATION ⟨in . . . ~ and conviction of Roman errors —Jeremy Taylor⟩

re pro proof \\'rē(,)prō\\ *or* **repro** *or* **reproduction proof** *n* -S [*repro* short for *reproduction*] : a clean sharp proof made esp. from a letterpress printing surface to serve as photographic copy for a printing plate (as for letterpress, offset, or gravure)

reprovable *adj* [ME, fr. MF *reprouvable*, fr. *reprouver, reprover* to reprove + *-able*] *obs* : deserving reproof or censure : BLAMEWORTHY, REPREHENSIBLE

re·prove \\rə'prüv, rē'p-\\ *vb* [ME *reproven, repreven*, fr. MF *reprouver, reprover* (3d pers. sing. pres. indic. *repreuve*), fr. OF, fr. LL *reprobare* to disapprove, condemn, fr. L *re-* + *probare* to test, prove — more at PROVE] *vt* **1** : to chide as blameworthy : administer a rebuke to : call attention to remissness in often in a kindly or gentle way : seek to correct esp. by mild rebuke, suasion, or implication ⟨embarrassed to hear the children *reproved* in this way —Victoria Sackville-West⟩ **2** : to express disapproval of (as conduct, actions, or beliefs) : indicate disapprobation of esp. by contrast or implication : CENSURE, CONDEMN ⟨it is not for me to ~ popular taste —D.W.Brogan⟩ **3** *obs* : to prove (as an idea or statement) to be false or erroneous : DISPROVE, REFUTE ⟨~ my allegation, if you can —Shak.⟩ **4** *obs* : CONVINCE, CONVICT ⟨will ~ the world of sin and of righteousness —Jn 16:8 (AV)⟩ ~ *vi* : to express rebuke or reproof ⟨came . . . to ~ and exhort —Mary E. Braddon⟩

syn REBUKE, REPRIMAND, REPROACH, CHIDE, ADMONISH: REPROVE indicates an expression of disapproval made without harshness and with mild and kindly urging of betterment ⟨a light to guide, a rod to check the erring, and *reprove* —William Wordsworth⟩ REBUKE indicates a sharper and more severe expression of disapproval, designed to rebuff and check shortly or sharply ⟨must *rebuke* this drunkenness of triumph —P.B.Shelley⟩ REPRIMAND may indicate a severe, formal or official rebuke ⟨in *reprimanding* an officer —T.B.Macaulay⟩ REPROACH indicates upbraiding faultfinding often arising from vexed disappointment of hopes or expectations ⟨bitterly *reproach* him in your own heart and seriously think that he has behaved very badly to you —Oscar Wilde⟩ CHIDE is likely to indicate mild pointing out of errors, esp. venial ones, and lightly scolding for them ⟨there stood he *chiding* dilatory grooms —Robert Browning⟩ ADMONISH indicates earnest sympathetic or friendly warning, counsel, or exhortation; the notion of reproving for a fault is not stressed ⟨wife who "told a lie, not a pernicious lie, but unadvisedly" was simply *admonished* —Agnes Repplier⟩ ⟨softly *admonished* the child⟩

re·prov·er \\-və(r)\\ *n* -S [ME *reprovere*, fr. *reproven* to reprove + *-ere* -er] : one that reproves

re·prov·ing·ly *adv* : in a reproving manner ⟨looks at me ~ —Willa Cather⟩

reps *pl of* REP

rept *abbr* **1** receipt **2** report

¹rep·tant \\'reptənt\\ *adj* [L *reptant-, reptans*, pres. part. of *reptare* to creep, fr. *reptus*, past part. of *repere* to creep] : REPENT

²reptant \\"\\ *n* -S [NL *Reptantia*] : a member of the Reptantia

rep·tan·tia \\rep'tanch(ē)ə, -ntēə\\ *n pl, cap* [NL, fr. L, neut. pl. of *reptant-, reptans*, pres. part. of *reptare* to creep] : a suborder of decapod crustaceans comprising lobsters, crabs, hermit crabs, and related forms and having no stylocerite, the abdomen well developed to greatly reduced and frequently depressed but never laterally compressed, the rostrum reduced or absent and usu. depressed if present, and the second antennal scale reduced or absent

rep·ta·to·ri·al \\;reptə;tōrēəl\\ *or* **rep·ta·to·ry** \\'==,tōrē\\ *adj* [*reptatorial* fr. *reptatory* + *-al*; *reptatory* prob. fr. (assumed NL *reptatorius*, fr. L *reptatus* (past part. of *reptare* to creep) + *-orius* -ory] : REPTANT

reptd *abbr* **1** reported **2** reprinted

¹rep·tile \\'rept³l, -,tīl\\ *n* -S [ME *reptil*, fr. MF or LL; MF *reptile* (fem.), irreg. fr. LL *reptile* (neut.), fr. neut. of *reptilis*, adj., reptant, fr. L *reptus* (past part. of *repere* to creep) + *-ilis* -ile; akin to OHG *reba* tendril, Lith *rėplioti* to creep] **1** : an animal that crawls or moves (as a snake) on its belly or (as a lizard) on small short legs **2 a** : a vertebrate of the class Reptilia **b** : AMPHIBIAN 1b — not used technically **3** : one held to resemble a reptile : a person having a low, groveling, mean, repulsive, or despicable character

²reptile \\"\\ *adj* [LL *reptilis*] **1** : moving on the belly or on small and short legs : CREEPING, REPTANT **2** : having characteristics associated with a reptile : GROVELING, DESPICABLE, LOW, MALIGNANT, MEAN ⟨a false ~ prudence, the result not of caution but of fear —Edmund Burke⟩ ⟨~ press⟩ **3** : of, of the nature of, or relating to a reptile, reptiles, or the Reptilia

rep·tile·like \\-t³l,(l)īk\\ *adj* : resembling a reptile

rep·til·ia \\rep'tilēə, -lyə\\ *n pl, cap* [NL, fr. LL, pl. of *reptile*] : a class of Vertebrata comprising air-breathing animals that have lungs but never gills, usu. a three-chambered heart, two aortic arches from which the systemic arteries arise, a bony skeleton in which the skull articulates with the vertebral column by a single occipital condyle, the vertebrae gastrocentral, and the compound mandible articulate with the skull through a quadrate bone, that lack hair or feathers and have the skin more or less covered with horny epidermal plates or scales and relatively free from glands, that are known since the Carboniferous and as the dominant form of life in the Mesozoic, and that are represented in the recent fauna by the snakes and lizards, the turtles, the loricates, and the aberrant tuatara — see COTYLOSAURIA, LORICATA, MESOSAURIA, PELYCOSAURIA, PTEROSAURIA, RHYNCHOCEPHALIA, SQUAMATA, TESTUDINATA, THERAPSIDA

¹rep·til·ian \\(')rep;tilēən, -lyən\\ *adj* [NL *Reptilia* + E *-an*, adj. suffix] **1 a** : resembling or having the characteristics of the Reptilia or a reptile ⟨his light green ~ eye —Jean Stafford⟩ **b** : held to resemble a reptile in nature or character : MEAN ⟨a ~ villain —Theodore Dreiser⟩ **2** : of or relating to the Reptilia or a reptile ⟨a ~ skull⟩

²reptilian \\"\\ *n* -S [NL *Reptilia* + E *-an*, n. suffix] : one of the Reptilia : REPTILE 2

reptilian age *n* : the Mesozoic era during which reptiles were the dominant form of life

rep·ti·loid \\'reptə,lȯid\\ *adj* [¹*reptile* + *-oid*] : resembling a reptile

¹re·pub·lic \\rə'pəblik, rē'p-, -lēk\\ *n* -S [F *république*, fr. MF *republique*, fr. L *respublica, res publica*, fr. *res* thing, fact, matter + *publica*, fem. of *publicus* public — more at REAL, PUBLIC] **1** *obs* : COMMONWEAL, STATE **2 a** (1) : a government characterized by having a chief of state who is not a monarch and who in modern times is usu. a president (2) : a political unit (as a nation or state) having such a form of government ⟨the ~ of England, Scotland, and Ireland under Oliver Cromwell —E.E.Reynolds⟩ ⟨the ~s of South America have been the happy hunting ground of dictators —L.A.Mills⟩ ⟨the ancient Roman ~⟩ **b** (1) : a government in which supreme power resides in a body of citizens entitled to vote and is exercised by elected officers and representatives responsible to them and governing according to law : REPRESENTATIVE DEMOCRACY (2) : a political unit (as a nation or state) having such a form of government ⟨pledge allegiance to the flag of the United States of America and to the ~ for which it stands —Francis Bellamy⟩ ⟨the German people . . . by creating a federal ~ resting upon a democratic constitution —*U.S.Code*⟩ **c** : a usu. specified republican government of a political unit ⟨France's ~s are numbered . . . consecutively —*Times Lit. Supp.*⟩ ⟨the Fourth *Republic*⟩ **3 a** : a community of beings that resembles in organization a political republic and is usu. characterized by a general equality among members ⟨a curious ~ of industrious hornets —M.G.J.deCrèvecoeur⟩ **b** : a body of persons freely engaged in a specified activity ⟨the ~ of art⟩ ⟨the ~ of letters⟩ **4** : an organization modeled after a junior republic ⟨establish a boys' ~ in this state —*Springfield (Mass.) Daily News*⟩ **5** : a constituent political and territorial unit of the U.S.S.R. and Yugoslavia ⟨our visits to four of the ~s of Yugoslavia —G.E.Shipler⟩ ⟨the Ukraine and the other ~s within the U.S.S.R. —Bogdan Raditsa⟩

²republic *also* **republical** *adj* [*republic* fr. ¹*republic; republical* fr. ¹*republic* + *-al*] *obs* : REPUBLICAN 1 ⟨the ~ cities . . . of Greece —Roger Boyle⟩ ⟨devoted to the . . . *republical* party —Edward Hyde⟩

¹re·pub·li·can \\rə'pəbləkən, rē'p-, -lēk-\\ *adj* [modif. (influenced by E *-an*, adj. suffix) of F *républicain*, fr. MF *republicain*, fr. *republique*] **1 a** : of, relating to, or having the characteristics of a republic : having the form or based on the principles of a republic ⟨the United States shall guarantee to every state in this union a ~ form of government —*U.S.Constitution*⟩ ⟨the success of ~ institutions in So. American countries —John Dewey⟩ **b** : favoring, supporting, or advocating a republic ⟨so little ~ and so much aristocratic sentiment —Philip Marsh⟩ ⟨a ~ party⟩ **c** : held to belong to or be appropriate for one living in or supporting a republic ⟨our ~ and artistic simplicity —Nathaniel Hawthorne⟩ ⟨a ~ indifference to the majesty of office —H.S.G.Saunders⟩ **2** *usu cap* **a** : of, relating to, or constituting the Democratic-Republican party **b** : of, relating to, or constituting one of the two major political parties in the U.S. evolving in the mid-19th century from the Whigs, Free-Soilers, and Democrats primarily for the purpose of opposing the extension of slavery and becoming usu. associated with business, financial, and some agricultural interests and with favoring a restricted governmental role in social and economic life — compare DEMOCRATIC 2, LIBERAL REPUBLICAN, NATIONAL REPUBLICAN **3** : living, nesting, or breeding in large flocks or communities

²republican \\"\\ *n* -S **1** : one that favors or supports a republican form of government **2** *usu cap* **a** : a member of a political party advocating republicanism **b** : a member of the Democratic-Republican party **c** : a member of the Republican party of the U.S.

re·pub·li·can·ism \\-kə,nizəm\\ *n* -S [¹*republican* + *-ism*] **1** : adherence to or sympathy for a republican form of government : republican practices or spirit : attachment to republican principles or institutions ⟨~, driven underground by the era of reaction, was kept alive —*Times Lit. Supp.*⟩ ⟨popular democratic sentiment came forth as ~ —Alfredo Mendizábal Villalbo⟩ **2** : a republican form of government : the principles or theory of republican government ⟨maintenance of ~ in Latin America —Alexander Marchant⟩ ⟨~ in the seventeenth century was . . . an aristocratic doctrine —G.H.Sabine⟩ **3** *usu cap* **a** : the principles, policy, or practices of the Republican party of the U.S. ⟨the leading theorist of modern *Republicanism* —Stewart Alsop⟩ **b** : the Republican party or its members ⟨a rousing battle between midwest *Republicanism* and Democratic liberalism —*N.Y.Times*⟩

re·pub·li·can·ize \\-,nīz\\ *vt* -ED/-ING/-S [F *républicaniser*, fr. *républicain* republican + *-iser* -ize] **1** : to make republican in character, form, or principle : change (as a state) into a republic ⟨the first public measure which tended . . . to ~ France —William Taylor †1836⟩ **2** : to alter or reorganize on republican principles ⟨took France at least thirty years . . . to ~ its civil service —Arnold Brecht⟩

republican marriage *n, usu cap R* [trans. of F *mariage républicain*] : a method of execution practiced during the French Revolution consisting of binding a man and woman together and throwing them into the water — compare NOYADE

republican pawnee *n, usu cap R&P* : KITKEHAHKI

republican swallow *n* : CLIFF SWALLOW

re·publication \\(;)rē+\\ *n* [*re-* + *publication*] **1** : the act or action of republishing or the state of being republished : a new or second publication (as of a will, code, religion, literary work, or law) ⟨two novels . . . that highly deserve ~ —*N.Y. Herald Tribune Bk. Rev.*⟩ ⟨~ of a former will revokes one of a later date —William Blackstone⟩ **2** : something (as a book) that has been republished : a fresh publication (as of a literary work)

republic day *n, usu cap R&D* : a day established as a holiday in various countries to commemorate the foundation of a republic

re·publish \\(')rē+\\ *vt* [*re-* + *publish*] : to publish again or anew: as **a** : to publish a reprint of (as a book or statement) **b** : to execute (a will) anew ⟨subsequent to the purchase . . . the devisor ~*ed* his will —William Blackstone⟩

re·publisher \\"+\\ *n* : one that republishes

re·pub·lo·crat *also* **re·pub·li·crat** \\rə'pəblə,krat, -rē'p-\\ *n* -S *usu cap* [*republocrat* fr. ²*republican* + *democrat; republicrat* blend of ²*republican* and *democrat*] : a member of the Democratic party esp. in the southern states who supports to a large extent the policy and measures of the Republican party ⟨if the Democratic convention appeases the Southern *Republocrats* —Bruce Bliven b.1889⟩ — compare DIXIECRAT

¹re·pu·di·ate \\rə'pyüdē,āt, rē'p-, *usu* -ād·+V\\ *vt* -ED/-ING/-S [L *repudiatus*, past part. of *repudiare* to cast off, reject, divorce, fr. *repudium* casting off, divorce, fr. *re-* + *-pudium* (perh. akin to L *pudēre* to be ashamed) — more at PUDIC] **1** : to divorce, put away, or discard (a wife) : separate formally from (a woman to whom one is betrothed or married) **2** : to cast off : refuse to have anything to do with : DISOWN, RENOUNCE **3 a** : to refuse to accept as having rightful authority or obligation : reject as unauthorized or as having no binding force ⟨~ a contract⟩ ⟨~ a will⟩ **b** : to refuse approval or belief to : reject as untrue or unjust ⟨~ a charge⟩ **4** : to refuse to acknowledge or to pay ⟨~ a debt⟩ **syn** see DECLINE, DISCLAIM

²repudiate *adj* [L *repudiatus*, past part. of *repudiare*] *obs* : REPUDIATED : DIVORCED

re·pu·di·a·tion \\=,=='āshən\\ *n* -S [L *repudiation-, repudiatio*, fr. *repudiatus* (past part. of *repudiare*) + *-ion-, -io* -ion] : the action of repudiating or the state of being repudiated: as **a** : divorce or legal separation from a woman **b** : the action of refusing to be bound by the terms of a contract (as in refusing to acknowledge or pay a debt); *specif* : such an action on the part of public authorities against whom no claim can be enforced ⟨~ of the state debt⟩ ⟨~ is bad for credit —Stringfellow Barr⟩ **c** : the action in canon law of refusing a benefice **d** : the act or action of rejecting or refusing to accept something ⟨resulted in the magistrate's ~ by both parties —*Current Biog.*⟩ ⟨the ~ of a great tradition —J.L.Lowes⟩ ⟨expressed his ~ of this counsel —G.B.Shaw⟩

re·pu·di·a·tion·ist \\-sh(ə)nəst\\ *n* -S : one that favors repudiation esp. of a public debt

re·pu·di·a·tor \\='==,ād·ə(r), -,ātə-\\ *n* -S [LL, fr. L *repudiatus* (past part. of *repudiare*) + *-or*] : one that repudiates or advocates repudiation (as of a public debt)

re·pugn \\rə'pyün, rē'p-\\ *vb* -ED/-ING/-S [ME *repugnen*, fr. MF & L; MF *repugner*, fr. L *repugnare*] *vi, archaic* : to make resistance : offer opposition, objection, or resistance : fight against someone : strive against something : OBJECT, OPPOSE, RESIST ~ *vt* **1** *obs* : to be contrary to, inconsistent with, or opposed to **2** : to contend against : OPPOSE, REFUTE, REJECT, REPEL ⟨stubbornly he did ~ the truth —Shak.⟩

re·pug·nance \\rə'pəgnən(t)s, rē'p-\\ *n* -S [ME *repugnaunce*, fr. MF *repugnance*, fr. L *repugnantia*] **1 a** : the quality or fact of being opposed and esp. reciprocally opposed : contradictory opposition or disagreement (as of ideas, opinions, or statements) : INCOMPATIBILITY, INCONGRUITY, INCONSISTENCY ⟨no inconsistency or natural ~ between this poetical and religious faith in the same mind —William Hazlitt⟩ **b** : an instance of such contradiction or inconsistency ⟨preparing the draft . . . seeing that it is free from errors or ~s —James Bryce⟩ **2** : deep-rooted antagonism : settled aversion : strong dislike, distaste, or antipathy ⟨the ~ which vulgarity inspires —Albert Dasnoy⟩ ⟨her instinctive dignity and ~ to any show of emotion —George Eliot⟩ ⟨his ~ toward the political philosophy of the Fascist states —Maurice Halperin⟩

re·pug·nan·cy \\-gnənsē, -si\\ *n* -ES [L *repugnantia*, fr. *repugnant-, repugnans* (pres. part. of *repugnare*) + *-ia* -y] **1** : REPUGNANCE 1 ⟨local legislation is void for ~ to the terms of the mandate —Martin Wight⟩; *specif* : a contradiction or inconsistency between sections of a legal instrument ⟨risks of ~ being discovered between the text . . . and the explanatory matter —T.E.May⟩ **2 a** : opposition or resistance (as of feeling) usu. based upon aversion or antipathy **b** : REPUGNANCE 2

re·pug·nant \\-gnənt\\ *adj* [ME *repugnaunt*, fr. MF *repugnant*, fr. L *repugnant-, repugnans*, pres. part. of *repugnare* to resist, fr. *re-* + *pugnare* to fight — more at PUGNACIOUS] **1** : characterized by opposition and esp. contradictory opposition : INCOMPATIBLE, INCONSISTENT, OPPOSED ⟨where there are ~ provisions in a statute the one last in order shall . . . govern —Roscoe Pound⟩ ⟨the statute . . . is ~ to the Constitution —C.P.Curtis⟩ ⟨such procedure was ~ to fair employment practices —Dwight Macdonald⟩ **2** *archaic* : disposed to fight against something : making or offering resistance : HOSTILE ⟨tempering the ~ mass —P.B.Shelley⟩ **3** : distasteful to a high degree : exciting distaste or aversion : LOATHSOME, OBJECTIONABLE, REPULSIVE ⟨unclean and ~ food —Willa Cather⟩ ⟨one custom ~ to nature —G.G.Coulton⟩ ⟨found the idea thoroughly ~ to him⟩ **syn** see HATEFUL, OFFENSIVE

repugnant condition *n* : a condition given no effect because inconsistent with and contrary to the quality and nature of an estate previously granted or an obligation already imposed in a deed : an insensible condition

re·pug·nant·ly *adv* : in a repugnant manner

re·pug·na·to·ri·al \\rə;pəgnə;tōrēəl, rē;p-\\ *adj* [L *repugnatorius* repugnatorial (fr. *repugnatus* — past part. of *repugnare* — + *-orius* -ory) + E *-al*] : serving to repel enemies ⟨the ~ pores of millipedes⟩

repugnatorial gland *n* : a gland of some insects that by emitting an offensive secretion or vapor serves to repel enemies — called also DEFENSIVE GLAND

re·pullulate \\(')rē+\\ *vi* -ED/-ING/-S [L *repullulatus*, past part. of *repullulare*, fr. *re-* + *pullulare* to sprout — more at PULLULATE] *archaic* : to bud or sprout again ⟨whose branches . . . are withered, never to ~ again —Eliza Nathan⟩

re·pullulation \\(;)rē+\\ *n, archaic* : the action of budding or sprouting again : the state of having budded or sprouted again ⟨the ~ of the pure love —Henry More⟩

re·pulp \\(')rē +\\ *vt* [*re-* + *pulp*] : to pulp again

¹re·pulse \\rə'pəls, rē'p- *also* -lts\\ *vt* -ED/-ING/-S [L *repulsus*, past part. of *repellere* to repel — more at REPEL] **1** : to drive or beat back (as an assault or an enemy) : repel usu. by force of arms ⟨police charging the plant gates were *repulsed* at every attempt —*Amer. Guide Series: Mich.*⟩ ⟨*repulsed* an Indian attack here —*Amer. Guide Series: Tenn.*⟩ **2** : to repel by discourtesy, coldness, or denial : REBUFF, REFUSE, REJECT ⟨*repulsed* every attempt . . . at conversation —Jane Austen⟩ ⟨she had learned to . . . ~ advances that were disagreeable —Ellen Glasgow⟩ ⟨repudiate and ~ any suggestion that we are making a questionable compromise —Sir Winston Churchill⟩ **3** : to cause a feeling of repulsion in : DISGUST ⟨*repulsed* by the sight of . . . green flies feeding upon the putrefying flesh of a crocodile —Bernice Matlowsky⟩ ⟨*repulsed* by his own weakness —Carson McCullers⟩

²repulse \\"\\ *n* -S [in sense 1, fr. L *repulsa*, fr. fem. of *repulsus*, past part. of *repellere;* in other senses, fr. L *repulsus* action of driving back, fr. *repulsus*, past part. of *repellere*] **1** : refusal of a request or suit : DENIAL, REBUFF, REJECTION ⟨court ~ from her husband —Thomas Hardy⟩ ⟨reap nothing but ~ and hate —John Milton⟩ **2** : the action of repelling (as an assailant or a hostile force) or the fact of being repelled in hostile encounter **3** *archaic* : the action of forcing or driving back : the state of being forced or driven back — opposed to *impulse* ⟨what a most powerful suction that ~ will create —George Semple⟩

re·pul·sion \\rə'pəlshən, rē'p-\\ *n* -S [MF, fr. ML *repulsion-, repulsio*, fr. LL, refutation, fr. L *repulsus* (past part. of *repellere*) + *-ion-, -io* -ion] **1** : the action of repulsing or the state of being repulsed : the action of driving off, back, or away : the state of being driven off, back, or away ⟨the ~ of the Spanish army —Alexander Ranken⟩ ⟨magnetic attraction and ~⟩ **2** : a force (as between like electric charges, like magnetic poles, or antiparallel electric currents) tending to produce separation **3** : feeling of aversion : strong dislike : REPUGNANCE ⟨towards whom . . . she felt strong physical ~ —T.S.Eliot⟩ ⟨voice tinged with fastidious ~ —Agatha Christie⟩ **4** : the tendency of particular genetic characters to be inherited separately presumably because of linkage of dominant genes that control expression of one character and recessive genes of another — compare COUPLING

repulsion-induction motor *n* : an alternating current motor with both a commutated and squirrel-cage rotor winding

repulsion motor *n* : an alternating current motor with a stator winding and a rotor winding with the latter short-circuited by a commutator and jumper

re·pul·sive \\rə'pəlsiv, rē'p-, -sēv *also* -səv\\ *adj* **1** : tending to repel or reject (as by denial or coldness of manner) : having or motivated by an intention to reject (as advances) : COLD, FORBIDDING ⟨his reserve may be a little ~ —Jane Austen⟩ ⟨her manner became daily colder and more ~ —Emily Eden⟩ **2** : serving to repulse : able to repel : characterized by repulsion ⟨~ of his might the weapon stood —Alexander Pope⟩ ⟨two bodies endowed with a ~ power —Tobias Smollett⟩ ⟨~ force⟩ **3** : repellent to the mind : arousing aversion or disgust : DISGUSTING ⟨contracted a ~ disease —V.G.Heiser⟩ ⟨the most ~ character in recent novels —John Farrelly⟩ ⟨the idea . . . was utterly ~ to her —J.C.Powys⟩ **syn** see OFFENSIVE

re·pul·sive·ly *adv* : in a repulsive or repelling manner

re·pul·sive·ness *n* -ES : the quality or state of being repulsive ⟨the moral ~ of the race theory —A.J.Toynbee⟩

rep unit *var of* REP

¹re·purchase \\(')rē+\\ *vt* [*re-* + *purchase*] : to buy back or again : regain by purchase : REDEEM ⟨~ the family estate —*Quarterly Rev.*⟩

²repurchase \\"+\\ *n* : the action of repurchasing ⟨an option of ~⟩

repurchase agreement *n* **1** : a contract giving the seller the right to repurchase property sold on specified terms; *specif* : one giving a dealer the right to repurchase government securities sold to Federal Reserve banks **2 :** a contract that requires a dealer to buy back a durable good (as an automobile) on which payments have been defaulted to the finance company

repure *vt* [*re-* + *pure*] *obs* : to make pure again ⟨nor state nor honor can ~ dishonored sheets —William Barksted⟩

rep·u·ta·bil·i·ty \ˌrepyəd·əˈbiləd·ē, -pyətə-, -lətē, -i, *chiefly in substand speech* -pə-\ *n* : the quality or state of being reputable ⟨conspicuous consumption . . . is a means of ~ to the gentleman of leisure —Thorstein Veblen⟩

rep·u·ta·ble \ˈ===ˌbəl\ *adj* [ˡ*repute* + *-able*] **1 :** enjoying good repute : of excellent reputation : held in esteem : ESTIMABLE, RESPECTABLE ⟨quite a ~ scientist in his day —Benjamin Farrington⟩ ⟨the most ~ newspaper of a hundred years ago —H.L.Smith b.1906⟩ ⟨~ conduct⟩ **2 :** employed widely or sanctioned by good writers ⟨~ use is the use of no single writer —Barrett Wendell⟩ ⟨not . . . ~ speech at all but jargon —A.T.Quiller-Couch⟩

rep·u·ta·bly \-blē,-bli\ *adv* : in a reputable manner

rep·u·ta·tion \ˌrepyəˈtāshən, *chiefly in substand speech* -pə-\ *n* -s [ME *reputacioun*, fr. L *reputation-, reputatio* consideration, fr. *reputatus* (past part. of *reputare*) + *-ion-, -io* -ion] **1 :** the fact of being highly esteemed : the condition of being regarded as worthy or meritorious : public esteem either attained or in the process of attainment : good name : high regard : CELEBRITY, DISTINCTION, NOTE ⟨native artists . . . made their ~*s* abroad —*Amer. Guide Series: Mich.*⟩ ⟨a younger illustrator who is gaining a ~ —*Amer. Guide Series: Ark.*⟩ ⟨a man of ~⟩ **2 :** the estimation in which one is generally held : the character commonly imputed to one as distinct from real or inherent character ⟨a task of some difficulty to disentangle him from his ~ —T.S.Eliot⟩ ⟨cases which hold that evidence about the ~ of the accused is inadmissable —F.W.Lacey⟩ ⟨a good ~⟩ **3 a :** the honor or credit belonging to one : one's good name : one's place in public esteem or regard ⟨save the ~*s* of several ladies —Mary W. Montagu⟩ **b :** a particular good name ⟨laughs at the ~*s* she has torn —William Cowper⟩ **4 :** a particular character in popular estimation or ascription — used with *of* ⟨had the ~ of being a hard worker⟩ **syn** see FAME

re·pu·ta·tive \rəˈpyüd·əd·iv, rēˈp-\ *adj* [ˡ*repute* + *-ative*] *archaic* : PUTATIVE

re·pu·ta·tive·ly \-əvlē\ *adv, archaic* : by repute : PUTATIVELY ⟨have this . . . ~ by divine appointment —Cotton Mather⟩

ˡ**re·pute** \rəˈpyüt, rēˈp-, *usu* -üd·+V\ *vb* -ED/-ING/-S [ME *reputen*, fr. MF *reputer*, fr. L *reputare* to compute, think over, fr. *re-* + *putare* to consider, think — more at PAVE] *vt* **1 :** to hold in thought : ACCOUNT, ESTEEM, THINK ⟨Negroes were *reputed* the good workers —Oscar Handlin⟩ ⟨men and women who are *reputed* moral —Samuel Butler †1902⟩ ⟨she is *reputed* to make nocturnal visits to the guest room —*Amer. Guide Series: La.*⟩ ~ *vi, obs* : to hold an appraising opinion; *esp* : to hold a high opinion ⟨you should ~ highly . . . of your own endowments —Ben Jonson⟩

²**repute** \"\ *n* -s **1** *obs* : OPINION, ESTIMATION, JUDGMENT ⟨their judgment and ~ of these is true —William Tomlinson⟩ **2 :** the character or status commonly ascribed to one : the popular opinion of one : reputation of a specified kind ⟨a large farmer of good ~ —Thomas Hardy⟩ ⟨the popular ~ of . . . later empresses —John Buchan⟩ ⟨a work held in high ~⟩ **3** *obs* : POSITION, RANK, STATUS ⟨these cardinals have the ~ of princes —James Howell⟩ **4 :** the state of being widely and favorably known, spoken of, or esteemed : DISTINCTION, HONOR ⟨the gentleman was of ~ in Paris —Charles Dickens⟩ ⟨only a general of ~ could get recruits —John Buchan⟩ ⟨won him a deserved ~ —Irving Kolodin⟩ **5** *obs* : the reputation of having or being something ⟨who had then the ~ of an honest man —Donald Mackay⟩ **6 :** the reputation of a particular person or thing ⟨jeopardizing the company's ~⟩ ⟨threats to the ~ of an honest man⟩ **syn** see FAME

reputed *adj* **1 :** held in repute and esp. high repute : having a good repute : held in estimation : REPUTABLE 1 ⟨a member of a ~ legal firm —Edith Wharton⟩ ⟨selected from ~ vineyards —*Farmer's Weekly* (*So. Africa*)⟩ **2 :** according to reputation or popular belief : supposed, thought, or reckoned to be the thing specified : generally accepted : PUTATIVE ⟨the ~ father of the child⟩ — compare REPUTED MANOR

re·put·ed·ly *adv* : by repute : in common estimation : according to reputation or general belief ⟨fishes with ~ poisonous flesh —R.E.Coker⟩ ⟨small, conservative, and ~ aristocratic town —Helen Martin⟩

reputed manor *n* : a manor that has lost its manorial status by the lack of some necessary adjunct (as the absence of a court baron)

reputed quart *n, Brit* : an amount about equal to a quart : ⅙ gallon

re·pute·less \-ütləs\ *adj, obs* : devoid of good repute : INGLORIOUS ⟨left me in ~ banishment —Shak.⟩

req *abbr* **1** request **2** require; required **3** requisition

reqmt *abbr* requirement

re·queen \(ˈ)rē+\ *vt* [*re-* + *queen*] : to replace an old queen of (a hive of bees) with a young one of the same season's raising

ˡ**re·quest** \rəˈkwest, rēˈk-\ *n* -s [ME *requeste*, fr. MF, fr. OF, fr. (assumed) VL *requaesita*, fr. fem. of (assumed) VL *requaesitus*, past part. of (assumed) VL *requaerere* to need, seek for, inquire after — more at REQUIRE] **1 :** the act of asking for something (as an object, a favor, or some action desired) : an expression of a desire or wish : ENTREATY, PETITION ⟨I will marry her, sir, at your ~ —Shak.⟩ ⟨let me renew my ~ that you would repeat the tale —Benjamin Jowett⟩ **2 a :** an instance of asking for something : an expressed desire ⟨~*s* for murals . . . are more numerous —*Amer. Guide Series: Minn.*⟩ ⟨staff personnel answer individual ~*s* for specific information —*U.S. Atomic Energy Commission*⟩ **b :** a document or other writing embodying such an expressed desire : PETITION ⟨first-class mail bearing the sender's return ~ —*U.S. Post Office Manual*⟩ **3 :** the thing that is asked for : the matter or subject of the asking ⟨his own bank has refused him . . . because his ~ exceeds its legal limit —*Nation's Business*⟩ ⟨turned down the growers' ~ for a . . . council —*Farmer's Weekly* (*So. Africa*)⟩ ⟨granted a ~⟩ **4 :** the condition or fact of being requested ⟨the pamphlet . . . is available on ~ —*Official Register of Harvard Univ.*⟩ ⟨tickets will be available only upon ~⟩ **5 :** the state of being asked for or held in such estimation as to be sought after : DEMAND ⟨his scientific knowledge . . . brought him otherwise into moderate ~ —Charles Dickens⟩ ⟨much in ~ as an after-dinner speaker⟩ ⟨a book in great ~⟩ — **by request** *or* **at request** *adv* : in compliance with or in response to a request ⟨the bills were introduced *by request*⟩

²**request** \"\ *vt* -ED/-ING/-S [MF *requester*, fr. OF, fr. *requeste*, n.] **1 a :** to ask (as a person or an organization) to do something ⟨they ~*ed* her to write —Ellen Glasgow⟩ ⟨I ~ you to give my poor host freedom —Shak.⟩ ⟨~*ed* the Parliament to act —*Current Biog.*⟩ **b :** to ask (as a person or an organization) for something ⟨~ the board for an opinion⟩ **2 :** to ask for permission or opportunity (to do something) : express a wish or desire (to do something) ⟨he . . . ~*s* to be excused from the ungrateful task —G.S.Faber⟩ ⟨we had ~*ed* to sleep in the straw-loft —G.J.Cayley⟩ **3** *obs* : to ask (a person) to come or go to something or someplace ⟨I was ~*ed* to supper last night —Ben Jonson⟩ **4 :** to ask for ⟨~*ed* a brief delay —Vera M. Dean⟩ ⟨officials ~*ed* the area for Indian families —*Amer. Guide Series: Minn.*⟩ ⟨~*ed* that seven physicians withdraw from the . . . organization —*Current Biog.*⟩ **syn** see ASK

re·quest·er \-tə(r)\ *n* -s : one that requests something

request note *n* : a legal request directed to an English revenue officer for permission to remove goods subject to excise

ˡ**requi·em** \ˈrekwēəm *also* ˈrāk- *or* ˈrēk- *sometimes* -ēˌem\ *n* -s [ME, fr. L *requiem* (first word of the introit of the requiem mass), accus. of *requies* rest, fr. *re-* + *quies* rest, quiet — more at WHILE] **1** *or* **requiem mass** *sometimes cap R* : a mass for the repose of one or more departed souls commonly sung at funerals and on All Souls' Day **2** *obs* : an invitation to rest or repose **3 a :** a dirge or other solemn chant for the repose of the dead **b :** something resembling or held to resemble such a dirge or chant ⟨the book, then, is a ~ . . . for the old life of laissez-faire —Albert Hubbell⟩ **4** *archaic* : a state or time of repose : PEACE, QUIET, REST ⟨in his presence alone is to be found the ~ of their troubled souls —George Walker⟩ **5** *usu cap* **a** (1) : a musical setting of the mass for the dead including the Requiem, Kyrie, several stanzas of the hymn Dies Irae, the Domine Jesu Christe, Sanctus, Benedictus, Agnus Dei, and the Lux Aeterna (2) : a piece of like character on other words from Scripture or elsewhere **b :** a grand musical service or hymn in honor of the dead

²**requiem** \"\ *or* **requiem shark** *n* -s [obs. F *requiem*, alter. (influenced by F *requiem* requiem mass, fr. L) of F *requin*] : REQUIN

re·qui·es·cat \ˌrekwēˈeˌskät, -kat\ *n* -s [L, may he (or she) rest, 3d pers. sing. pres. subj. of *requiescere* to rest, fr. *re-* + *quiescere* to be quiet, fr. *quies* rest, quiet] : a prayer for the repose of a dead person

req·ui·es·cence \ˌrekwēˈesᵊn(t)s\ *n* -s [L *requiescere* + E *-ence*] : REPOSE ⟨retire to silence and ~ —N.W.Wraxall⟩

re·quin \rəˈkan\ *also* **requin shark** *n* -s [F *requin*] : a voracious shark of the family Carcharhinidae (as a cub shark or sometimes the man-eater)

re·quir·able \rəˈkwīrəbəl, rēˈk-\ *adj* : capable of being required : REQUISITE

ˡ**re·quire** \-ī(ə)r, -īə\ *vb* -ED/-ING/-S [ME *requeren, requiren*, fr. MF *requerre* (3d pers. sing. pres. indic. *requiert*), fr. (assumed) VL *requaerere* to need, seek for, inquire after, alter. (influenced by L *quaerere* to seek, ask) of L *requirere*, fr. *re-* + *-quirere* (fr. *quaerere*)] *vt* **1** *obs* : to ask, request, or desire (a person) to do something ⟨in humblest manner I ~ your Highness that it shall please you to declare —Shak.⟩ ⟨when he was *required*, he . . . put forth his tongue —2 Mach 7:10 (NCE)⟩ **2 a :** to ask for authoritatively or imperatively : claim by right and authority : insist upon usu. with certainty or urgency : DEMAND, EXACT ⟨this night your soul is *required* of you —Lk 12:20 (RSV)⟩ ⟨informed . . . that his lord *required* to speak with him —Sir Walter Scott⟩ **b** *archaic* : to ask for as a favor : REQUEST ⟨they go commission'd to ~ a peace —John Dryden⟩ **3 a :** to call for as suitable or appropriate in a particular case : need for some end or purpose ⟨contributions to American art ~ more detailed treatment —*Amer. Guide Series: Minn.*⟩ **b :** to demand as necessary or essential (as on general principles or in order to comply with or satisfy some regulation) : make indispensable ⟨the inference . . . is not absolutely *required* by the facts —Edward Sapir⟩ ⟨no religious test shall ever be *required* as a qualification —*U.S. Constitution*⟩ **c :** to demand as a necessary help or aid : need as an essential : stand in urgent need of : NEED, WANT ⟨growing children ~ more food⟩ **4** *archaic* : to search for as needed or wanted : seek after ⟨the brave chiefs . . . wandering o'er the camp, *required* their lord —Alexander Pope⟩ **5 :** to impose a compulsion or command upon (as a person) to do something : demand of (one) that something be done or some action taken : enjoin, command, or authoritatively insist (that someone do something) ⟨a farmer will be *required* to comply with all acreage allotments —*Nation's Business*⟩ **6 :** to feel or be under the necessity of (doing or being something specified) — used with a following infinitive ⟨one does not ~ to be a specialist —Elizabeth Bowen⟩ ⟨a candidate ~*s* to hold a . . . certificate —*Achievement in the Gold Coast*⟩ ~ *vi* **1** *archaic* : to make request or demand : ASK ⟨they must . . . ~ of Heaven with upward eyes for all that they desire —John Keats⟩ **2** *archaic* : to be necessary or requisite **syn** see DEMAND, LACK

²**require** \"\ *n* -s *archaic* : REQUIREMENT

re·quire·ment \-ī(ə)rmənt, -īəm-\ *n* -s : something required: **a :** something that is wanted or needed : NECESSITY ⟨production was not sufficient to satisfy both civilian and governmental ~*s* for automobiles⟩ ⟨permit agriculturalists to buy their ~*s* upon favorable conditions —*Nineteenth Century*⟩ **b :** something called for or demanded : a requisite or essential condition : a required quality, course, or kind of training ⟨two ~*s* are necessary . . . for a material to rate as an insulation —P.D.Close⟩ ⟨compel the school board to revoke the oath ~ —David Clinton⟩ ⟨the doctoral student must satisfy the language ~ —H.R.Bowen⟩ ⟨fulfill the ~*s* for college entrance⟩

re·quir·er \-īrə(r)\ *n* -s *archaic* : one that requires ⟨Christ . . . a ~ of mercy —E.B.Pusey⟩

ˡ**req·ui·site** \ˈrekwəzət, *usu* -əd·+V\ *adj* [ME, fr. L *requisitus*, past part. of *requirere* to need, seek for, inquire after] : required by the nature of things or by circumstances or by the end in view : ESSENTIAL, INDISPENSABLE, NECESSARY ⟨the ~ quorum of forty members was not present —R.L.Schuyler⟩ ⟨food ~ for the journey —P.A.Rollins⟩ ⟨lacked the skill ~ for delicate execution —H.O.Taylor⟩ **syn** see NEEDFUL

²**requisite** \"\ *n* -s : something that is required or necessary : an indispensable or essential thing or quality ⟨neither of these ~*s* for an heuristic work . . . is fulfilled —L.C.Feldstein⟩ ⟨intellectual freedom . . . is the prime ~ for a free people —*Science*⟩ ⟨the first ~ in the storyteller's art is to tell a story —W.S.Maugham⟩

req·ui·site·ness *n* -ES : the quality or state of being requisite : NECESSITY ⟨proof of the ~ of attending to the customs of the East —Thomas Harmer⟩

ˡ**req·ui·si·tion** \ˌrekwəˈzishən\ *n* -s [MF or ML; MF, fr. ML *requisition-, requisitio*, fr. L, examination, fr. *requisitus* (past part. of *requirere*) + *-ion-, -io* -ion] **1 a** *archaic* : the act of requesting or requiring **b** *archaic* : a request or demand made by a person **c :** a necessary condition : REQUIREMENT ⟨~*s* of a position⟩ ⟨~ of a science⟩ **2 a :** the act of formally requiring or calling upon someone to perform some action **b :** a formal demand in civil and Scots law for the performance of an obligation; *esp* : one made through a notary **c :** a formal demand made by one international jurisdiction (as a nation) upon another for the surrender or extradition of a fugitive from justice ⟨the prisoner . . . had been arrested in England on the ~ of the Swiss Government —*In Re Castioni*⟩ — compare EXTRADITION **3 a :** the act of requiring something to be furnished **b :** a demand or application made usu. with authority: as (1) : a demand made by military authorities upon civilians (as the people of an invaded country) for supplies, labor, shelter, or other military needs — compare CONTRIBUTION 1 (2) : a written request for something (as materials, supplies, or personnel) authorized but not made available automatically ⟨sent a ~ to the purchasing department⟩ ⟨a ~ for clothing⟩ **4 :** the state of being demanded or called for : the condition of being put into service or use — used with *in* or *into* ⟨every sort of vehicle is put in ~ —Tyrone Power †1841⟩ ⟨the hangman . . . was in constant ~ —Charles Dickens⟩

²**requisition** \"\ *vt* **requisitioned; requisitioned; requisitioning** \-sh(ə)niŋ\ **requisitions** : to make a requisition for : demand or call for with authority : require to be furnished ⟨officers have been authorized . . . to ~ billeting facilities —H.S.Truman⟩ ⟨during the war most of the hotels were ~*ed* —S.P.B.Mais⟩ ⟨~ equipment from the supply officer⟩

req·ui·si·tion·ist \-sh(ə)nəst\ *also* **req·ui·si·tion·er** \-nə(r)\ *n* -s [*requisitionist* fr. ˡ*requisition* + *-ist*; *requisitioner* fr. ²*requisition* + *-er*] : one that makes or signs a requisition

re·quis·i·to·ri·al \rəˌkwizəˈtōrēəl, rēˌk-\ *adj* [ˡ*requisitory* + *-al*] : making requisition : expressing a request : REQUISITORY ⟨letters ~ came into use —Manfred Nathan⟩

ˡ**re·quis·i·to·ry** \=ˈ==ˌtōrē\ *adj* [ME *requisitorie*, fr. ML *requisitorius*, fr. L *requisitus* (past part. of *requirere* to need, seek for, inquire after) + *-orius* -ory — more at REQUIRE] : containing or constituting a requisition : making a requisition ⟨a ~ letter⟩

²**requisitory** \"\ *n* -ES [modif. (influenced by ˡ*requisitory*) of F *réquisitoire*, fr. MF *requisitorie*, fr. *requisitoire*, adj., requisitory, fr. ML *requisitorius*] : the formal demand made in French law by the public prosecutor for the punishment of an accused person on the charges stated

re·quit·al \rəˈkwīd·ᵊl, rēˈk-, -ītᵊl\ *n* -s **1 :** the act or action of requiting or the state of being requited : return or repayment for something (as a service, an injury) ⟨to receive benefits as long as there is hope of ~ —Thomas Hobbes⟩ ⟨in ~ of those well-intended offices —Samuel Johnson⟩ ⟨the distribution of good rather than . . . the ~ of evil —Lucius Garvin⟩ **2 :** something that requites : something given in return, compensation, or retaliation ⟨an ungrateful ~ of the unquestioned services of the company —H.H.Wilson⟩

re·quite \-īt, *usu* -īd·+V\ *vt* -ED/-ING/-S [*re-* + obs. E *quite* to set free, discharge, repay, fr. ME *quiten* — more at QUIT] **1 a :** to make return for (as a kindness, service, benefit) : REPAY, REWARD ⟨cards left without a visit are *requited* by cards similarly left —Agnes M. Miall⟩ ⟨whose patronage is happily *requited* with . . . ritual slaughter —John Marks⟩ **b :** to make retaliation for (as a wrong or an injury) : AVENGE ⟨thought . . . incumbent on a man to ~ injuries —Henry Sidgwick⟩ **2** *archaic* : to give, pay, or do in return : make return of ⟨~ like for like —J.C.Geikie⟩ **3 :** to make return to (as a person, a community) for a benefit or service ⟨you will ~ me . . . by the sight of your ardor for what is noble —A.T. Quiller-Couch⟩ or for an injury ⟨~ a traitor with death⟩ **4** *obs* : to take the place of : compensate or make up for ⟨deserves that short delight, the nauseous qualms of . . . travel to ~ —John Dryden⟩ **syn** see RECIPROCATE

re·quit·er \rəˈkwīd·ə(r), -ītə-\ *n* -s : one that requites something ⟨ungrateful ~ of the kindness of such friends —*American*⟩

re·radiate \(ˈ)rē+\ *vt* [*re-* + *radiate*] : to radiate again or anew

re·radiation \(ˌ)rē+\ *n* [*re-* + *radiation*] : radiation again or anew; *specif* : radiation emitted by a body or system as a result of its absorbing radiation incident on it ⟨the intensity of the sun's radiation . . . not dissipated by ~ —*Experiment Station Record*⟩

re·rail \(ˈ)rē+\ *vt* [*re-* + *-rail* (as in *derail*)] : to replace (as a railway engine) on the rails

re·rail·er \(ˈ)rēˈrālə(r)\ *n* -s : a device for putting derailed cars or locomotives back on the rails

ˡ**rerd** *or* **rerde** \ˈre(ə)rd\ *n* -s [ME, fr. OE *reord* voice, speech; akin to OHG *rarta* modulation, ON *rödd* voice, Goth *razda* tongue, speech, Skt *rasati* he roars, yells] *dial* : a noisy cry : DIN, CLAMOR, ROAR

²**rerd** \"\ *vi* -ED/-ING/-S [ME *rerden* to roar, speak, fr. OE *reordian* to speak, fr. *reord*, n.] *dial* : to make a noise : cry out : ROAR

rere- *comb form* [ME, fr. MF *rere, riere* backward, behind, fr. L *retro* — more at RETRO-] : subsequent : rear ⟨*rere*-banquet⟩

rere-account \ˈri(ə)r+=ˌ=\ *n* [ME *rereaccompt*, fr. *rere-* + *acount, accompt* account] *archaic* : a subsequent or later accounting

re·read \(ˈ)rē+\ *vt* [*re-* + *read*] : to read again or anew

rere-arch *var of* REAR ARCH

rere-banquet *n, obs* : a repast taken after the noon or evening meal

rere·brace \ˈri(ə)rˌbrās\ *n* [ME, fr. *rere-* + *brace* armor esp. for the arm — more at BRACE] : plate armor for the upper part of the arm

re·record \ˌrē+\ *vt* [*re-* + *record*] : to record again or anew; *specif* : to transfer (sound records) electrically from one or more films, magnetic recordings, or discs to other films, tapes, or discs

rere-dorter \ˈri(ə)r+ˌ-\ *n* [ME *rere-dortour*, fr. *rere-* + *dorter, dortour* dorter] : a latrine situated at the rear of a medieval convent or monastery

rere·dos \ˈrerəˌdäs *also* ˈrirə- *sometimes* ˈri(ə)rˌd- *or* ˈriəˌd-\ *n* -ES [ME, modif. of AF *areredos*, fr. MF *arere, arrere* behind, backward + *dos* back, fr. L *dorsum* — more at ARREAR] **1 a :** a screen or partition wall usu. ornamental and of wood or stone located behind an altar ⟨a high altar with a vast late Gothic ~ —Nikolaus Pevsner⟩ **b :** CHOIR SCREEN **2** *obs* : a wall drapery back of an altar **3 :** the back of a fireplace or in some ancient halls of an open hearth immediately under the louver in the center of the hall **4 :** BRAZIER ⟨no suggestion of fire in the ~ —T.B.Costain⟩

rerefief \ˈri(ə)r+ˌ-\ *n* [MF *rerefief, rierefief, rierefié*, fr. OF, fr. *rere, riere* backward, behind + *fief, fié* fief, fee — more at FEE] : ARRIERE FEE

rere·mouse \ˈri(ə)r+ˌ-\ *n, pl* **rere·mice** [ME *reremous*, fr. OE *hrēremūs*, prob. fr. *hrēran* to move, stir + *mūs* mouse — more at CRATER, MOUSE] *archaic* : BAT

rere·supper \ˈri(ə)r+ˌ-\ *n* [ME *reresoper*, fr. AF *rere super*, fr. OF *rere, riere* + *soper, super* supper] : a late or second supper ⟨trestles still stood from last night's ~ —T.B.Costain⟩

rere·ward \ˈri(ə)rˌwȯrd, ˈriəˌwȯ(ə)d\ *n* [ME *rerewarde*, fr. AF, fr. OF *rere* backward, behind + ONF *warde* guard; akin to OF *garde, guarde* guard — more at RETRO-, GUARD] *obs* : REAR GUARD ⟨the Lord will go before you; and the God of Israel will be your ~ —Isa 52:12 (AV)⟩

re·roll \(ˈ)rē+\ *vt* [*re-* + *roll*] : to roll again or anew

re·roller \"+\ *n* : one that rolls again or anew: as **a :** a textile worker who winds cloth from large rolls onto separate tubes **b :** a worker who repairs defective cigars

ˡ**re·run** \(ˈ)rē+\ *vt* [*re-* + *run*] : to run again or anew

²**re·run** \ˈrē+ˌ-, =ˈ=\ *n* **1 :** the act or action of running something again or anew; *esp* : the presentation of a motion picture or television film after its first run — compare REISSUE **2 :** an instance of running something again or anew : a subsequent identical presentation **3 :** a film presented in a rerun

ˡ**res** *pl of* RE

²**res** \ˈrās, ˈrēz\ *n, pl* **res** \"\ [L — more at REAL] : THING; *usu* : a particular thing : MATTER, POINT, SUBJECT — used esp. in various chiefly legal phrases

res *abbr* **1** resawed **2** research **3** reserve **4** residence; residency; resident; residential **5** residue **6** resigned **7** resistance **8** resistor **9** resolution **10** resort

RES *abbr* reticuloendothelial system

re·saca \rəˈsäkə\ *n* -s [AmSp, fr. Sp *resacar* to draw back, fr. *re-* re- (fr. L) + *sacar* to draw, take out, perh. fr. L *saccus* sack — more at SACK] *Southwest* : the dry channel or the former often marshy course of a stream

res·acetophenone \(ˌ)rez+\ *n* [ISV *resorcinol* + *acetophenone*] : a crystalline phenolic ketone $(HO)_2C_6H_3COCH_3$ made from resorcinol, acetic acid, and zinc chloride; 2,4-dihydroxy-acetophenone

res ad·ju·di·ca·ta \ˈrāˌsädˌyüdəˈkäd·ə, ˌrēzəˌjüdəˈkād·ə\ *n* [LL] : RES JUDICATA

resai *var of* REZAI

re·sail \(ˈ)rē+\ *vb* [*re-* + *sail*] *vt* : to sail (as a race or course) again ~ *vi* : to sail back or again ⟨planned to ~ about sundown⟩

re·sak \rəˈsak\ *n* -s [fr. native name in Malaysia] : durable hard heavy Malaysian wood from trees of the family Dipterocarpaceae and esp. of the genus *Shorea*

re·salable \(ˈ)rē+\ *adj* [*re-* + *salable*] : fit for resale : that may be sold again usu. to the next link in a chain of distribution

re·sale \ˈrē+ˌ-, =ˈ=\ *n* [*re-* + *sale*] **1 :** the act of selling again usu. to the next link in a chain of distribution ⟨the wholesaler lives by ~ to the retailer⟩ **2 a :** a sale at second hand **b :** an additional sale to the same buyer

resale price *n* **1 :** a price at which an article is resold by a business concern that buys it for resale **2 a :** a price suggested (as by a producer) as proper to be charged on resale of an article usu. to the ultimate consumer **b :** a stipulated price under the various state price maintenance laws at which a branded article must be resold as agreed with the brand owner or a minimum price below which such article cannot be lawfully resold

re·salutation \(ˌ)rē+\ *n* [L *resalutation-, resalutatio*, fr. *resalutatus* (past part. of *resalutare* to greet in return) + *-ion-, -io* -ion] : the giving of a salutation in response to one given

re·salute \ˌrē+\ *vt* [ME *resaluten* to salute in return, fr. L *resalutare*, fr. *re-* + *salutare* to salute] : to salute in return or anew

ˡ**re·saw** \(ˈ)rē+\ *vt* [*re-* + *saw*] : to saw over again; *specif* : to saw into boards or dimension lumber

²**re·saw** \ˈrē+ˌ-, =ˈ=\ *n* : a machine for resawing lumber — compare HEADSAW

re·sawer \(ˈ)rē+\ *n* [ˡ*resaw* + *-er*] : RESAWYER

re·sawyer \"+\ *n* [fr. ˡ*resaw*, after E *saw: sawyer*] : one that resaws something; *esp* : an operator of a resaw

re·say \"+\ *vt* [*re-* + *say*] **1 :** to say in answer : REPLY **2 :** to say again : REPEAT

res·azurin \(ˈ)rezˈazhərən\ *n* -s [ISV *resorcinol* + *azure* + *-in*] : a blue crystalline dye $C_{12}H_7NO_4$ of the phenoxazine class made by the action of nitrous acid on resorcinol and used chiefly as an oxidation-reduction indicator in the resazurin test for bacteria

resazurin test *n* : a test of the keeping quality of milk based on the speed with which a standard quantity of the dye resazurin is reduced by a sample of milk

re·scale \(ˈ)rē+\ *vt* [*re-* + *scale*] : to plan, establish, or formulate on a new and usu. smaller scale ⟨*rescaling* our living to conform to our budget⟩

re·scind \rə'sind, rē's-\ *vt* -ED/-ING/-S [L *rescindere* to cut loose, annul, fr. *re-* + *scindere* to cut, split — more at SCHISM] **1 :** to do away with **:** take away **:** REMOVE ⟨~ this needless outlay⟩ **2 a :** to take back **:** ANNUL, CANCEL ⟨refused to ~ his harsh order⟩ **b :** to abrogate (a contract) by tendering back or restoring to the opposite party what one has received from him (as in cases of fraud, duress, mistake, or minority) **3 :** to vacate or make void (as an act) by the enacting or a superior authority **:** REPEAL ⟨~ a law⟩ ⟨~ a judgment⟩ **syn** see REVOKE

re·scind·able \-dəbəl\ *adj* **:** capable of being rescinded

re·scind·er \-də(r)\ *n* -S **:** one that rescinds something

re·scind·ment \-in(d)mənt\ *n* -S [*rescind* + *-ment*] **:** an act of withdrawing **:** ABROGATION, ANNULMENT, CANCELLATION

re·scis·si·ble \-isəbəl, -izə-\ *adj* [L *resciss*us + E *-ible*] **:** capable of being rescinded

re·scis·sion \-izhən, -ish-\ *n* -S [LL *rescission-*, *rescissio* annulment, fr. L *rescissus* (past part. of *rescindere* to rescind) + *-ion-*, *-io* -ion] **1** *obs* **:** an act of cutting off **2 :** an act of rescinding, annulling, or vacating or of cancelling or abrogating (as by restoring to another party to a contract or transaction what one has received from him)

re·scis·so·ry \-isərē, -izə-\ *adj* [LL *rescissorius*, fr. L *rescissus* + *-orius* -ory] **:** relating to, tending to, or having the effect of rescission **:** REVOKING ⟨a ~ action⟩

res co·gi·tans \(')rās'kōgə,tän(t)s, (')rēz'käjə,tanz\ *n* [NL] **:** a thinking thing (as the mind or soul)

res com·mu·nes \,rāskə'mü,nās, ,rēzkə'myü(,)nēz\ *n pl* [LL, lit., common things] *Roman & civil law* **:** things owned by no one and subject to use by all **:** things (as light, air, the sea, running water) incapable of entire exclusive appropriation

re·score \(')rē+\ *vt* [*re-* + *score*] **:** to score again or anew; *specif* **:** to arrange (a musical ensemble instrumental composition) for a different combination of instruments

res cor·po·ra·les \'rā,skȯ(r)pə'rä,lās, 'rēz,kȯ(r)pə'rā(,)lēz\ *n pl* [L] *Roman & civil law* **:** corporeal or tangible things or those perceptible to the senses

rescounter *n* [It *riscontro*, fr. *riscontrare* to check an account, fr. *ri-* re- (fr. L *re-*) + *scontrare* to meet, fr. L *ex-* out of + *contra* opposite, against — more at EX-, COUNTER] *obs* **:** settlement of accounts

res·cous \'reskəs\ *n* -ES [ME *rescous*, *rescus*, fr. MF *rescousse*, fr. OF, fr. *rescourre* to rescue — more at RESCUE] **:** RESCUE 2

re·scramble \(')rē+\ *vt* [*re-* + *scramble*] **:** to rearrange in a scrambled or disorderly fashion

re·screen \"+\ *vt* [*re-* + *screen*] **:** to screen anew; *esp* **:** to assort once more often according to more liberal specifications

re·scribe \"+\ *vt* -ED/-ING/-S [L *rescribere*, fr. *re-* + *scribere* to write — more at SCRIBE] **1** *obs* **:** to write in reply **2 :** to write over again **:** REWRITE

re·script \'rē,skript\ *n* [L *rescriptum*, fr. neut. of *rescriptus*, past part. of *rescribere* to write in reply] **1 a :** a written answer of a Roman emperor or of a sovereign or a pope to an inquiry upon some matter of law or state **b** *Roman Catholicism* **:** an official written reply from the Holy See or an ordinary answering a private petition or a question covering a particular case **c :** a written message of the Japanese emperor carrying both temporal and religious authority and defining the position of the state **2 :** an official or authoritative order, decree, or formal announcement **3 a :** an act of rewriting **b :** something that is rewritten **:** REWRITING

re·scrip·tion \rə'skripshən, rē's-\ *n* -S [MF or LL; MF fr. LL *rescription-*, *rescriptio*, fr. L *rescriptus* + *-ion-*, *-io* -ion] **1** *obs* **a :** RESCRIPT, REWRITING **b :** a reply in writing **2 :** a promissory note or warrant formerly issued by a government

re·scrip·tive \-ptiv\ *adj* [*rescript* + *-ive*] **:** relating to or serving for a rescript; *also* **:** DECIDING, SETTLING — **re·scrip·tive·ly** \-ptəvlē\ *adv*

res·cu·able \'reskyəwəbəl, -(,)skyüəb-\ *adj* [*rescue* + *-able*] **:** that may be rescued

1res·cue \'re(,)skyü\ *vb* **rescued**; **rescued**; **rescuing** \-,skyəwiŋ, -(,)skyüiŋ\ **rescues** [ME *rescuen*, *rescowen*, fr. MF *rescourre*, fr. OF, fr. *re-* + *escourre* to shake out, wrest away, fr. L *excutere*, fr. *ex-* + *-cutere* (fr. *quatere* to shake) — more at QUASH] *vt* **1 a :** to free from confinement, violence, danger, or evil **:** liberate from actual restraint **:** SAVE, DELIVER ⟨~ a prisoner of war from the enemy⟩ ⟨*rescued* a drowning child⟩ **b :** to take forcibly from the custody of the law **2 :** to recover by force: as **a :** to deliver (as a place besieged) by force of arms **b :** to effect a rescue of (a prize) **3 :** to bid over a bid by (one's partner or oneself) in a card game on the assumption that the previous bid would entail a serious penalty ~ *vi* **:** to bring about deliverance

syn DELIVER, REDEEM, RANSOM, RECLAIM, SAVE **:** RESCUE indicates freeing from capture, assault, evil, death, or destruction by ready prompt action ⟨*rescuing* a soldier from the enemy⟩ ⟨*rescuing* the guards held as hostages⟩ ⟨the seamen *rescued* from the lost ship⟩ ⟨*rescue* his nation from defeat⟩ DELIVER signifies setting free from confinement, suffering, tribulation, embarrassment, or vexation ⟨*delivered* the prisoners from the Bastille⟩ ⟨*deliver* us from evil —Mt 6:13 (RSV)⟩ ⟨the population of Russia had only just been *delivered*, nominally at least, from serfdom —Havelock Ellis⟩ REDEEM applies to releasing from captivity, retribution, sequestration, or deterioration by some necessary expenditure ⟨let me *redeem* my brothers both from death —Shak.⟩ ⟨he labored for eighty years, *redeeming* them to Christianity from their magical and bloodthirsty practices —Norman Douglas⟩ ⟨a plot of land *redeemed* from the heath, and after long and laborious years brought into cultivation —Thomas Hardy⟩ RANSOM usu. applies specifically to buying a captive out of his captivity ⟨*ransom* a child held by kidnappers⟩ ⟨back in Quebec with a number of Iroquois captives whom he had *ransomed* —J.J. Wynne⟩ RECLAIM indicates a bringing back or returning to a former sound, good, or valuable condition of something that has undergone error, degenerating, waste, neglect, or abandonment ⟨the priest labored zealously to *reclaim* those of the redmen that had listened to Baptist teachings —Louise P. Kellogg⟩ ⟨I fear he is not to be *reclaimed;* there is scarcely a hope that anything in his character or fortunes is reparable now —Charles Dickens⟩ ⟨a large-scale program of *reclaiming* land and of bringing new land into cultivation —H.S.Truman⟩ SAVE is a general term that can be used in place of any of the preceding; it may imply a freeing from danger, evil, or trial and a maintaining or preserving for continued existence, security, use, or service ⟨*saved* a tired swimmer from drowning⟩ ⟨firemen *saving* the rear wing of the house⟩

2rescue \"\ *n* -S [ME *rescue*, *rescowe*, fr. *rescuen*, *rescowen* to rescue] **1 :** an act of rescuing **:** deliverance or aid in delivering from restraint, violence, or danger ⟨three ~*s* to his credit⟩ ⟨come to their ~⟩ **2 a :** the forcible taking of a person or goods from the custody of the law (as in retaking or taking away against law of things lawfully distrained or in the forcible liberation of a person from an arrest or imprisonment) **b** (1) **:** the retaking of a prize by those captured with it resulting in the restoration of the property to the owner by the effect of the right of postliminium — compare RECAPTURE (2) **:** succor rendered by the arrival of outside help before the succored party is entirely overcome

rescue breathing *n* [*2rescue*] **:** MOUTH-TO-MOUTH METHOD

rescue buoy *n* **:** BREECHES BUOY

rescued *past of* RESCUE

res·cue grass \'re(,)skyü-\ *or* **rescue brome** *n* [prob. alter. of *fescue grass*] **:** a tall American bromegrass (*Bromus catharticus*) that somewhat resembles chess and is cultivated for hay and forage in the southern U.S. and other mild regions

res·cue·less \'re(,)skyüləs, -,skyəl-\ *adj* **:** lacking rescue

rescue mission *n* **:** a city mission established to help persons esp. of low income who are unable to help themselves and are in desperate need of moral and spiritual rehabilitation

res·cu·er \-,skyəwə(r), -(,)skyüə(-\ *n* -S **:** one that rescues

rescues *pres 3d sing of* RESCUE, *pl of* RESCUE

rescuing *pres part of* RESCUE

res do·mi·nans \(')rās'dōmə,nän(t)s, (')rēz'dämə,nanz\ *n* [NL] **:** the dominant property or tenement entitled to enjoy a servitude

1re·seal \(')rē+\ *vt* [*re-* + *seal*] **:** to seal again or anew

2re·seal \'=,=\ *adj* **:** designed to be resealed ⟨~ jars⟩

1re·search \rə'sərch, rē's-, 'rē,s-, -sēch,-səich\ *n* [MF *recerche*, fr. *recercher* to research] **1 :** careful or diligent search **:** a close searching ⟨~*es* after hidden treasure⟩ **2 a :** studious inquiry or examination; *esp* **:** critical and exhaustive investigation or experimentation having for its aim the discovery of new facts and their correct interpretation, the revision of accepted conclusions, theories, or laws in the light of newly discovered facts, or the practical applications of such new or revised conclusions, theories, or laws ⟨gave his time to ~⟩ **b** (1) **:** a particular investigation of such a character **:** a piece of research (2) **:** a presentation (as an article or book) incorporating the findings of a particular research **3 :** capacity for or inclination to research ⟨a scholar of great ~⟩ **syn** see INQUIRY

2research \"\ *vb* [MF *recercher* to research, seek out, fr. OF, fr. *re-* + *cercher* to search — more at SEARCH] *vt* **:** to search or investigate exhaustively **:** make researches into ~ *vi* **:** to make researches or investigations

re-search \(')rē¦sərch, -sēch,-səich\ *vt* [*re-* + *search*] **:** to search again or anew ⟨decided to *re-search* the chest for the lost letters⟩

researched *adj* [fr. past part. of *2research*] **:** based on thorough investigation of pertinent data ⟨a carefully ~ study⟩ ⟨a show with accurate obviously ~ costumes⟩

re·search·er *pronunc at* 1RESEARCH +ə(r)\ *n* [*2research* + *-er*] **:** one that researches **:** a person who devotes himself to research

re-search·er *pronunc at* RE-SEARCH +ə(r)\ *n* [*re-search* + *-er*] **:** a worker who cleans tobacco a second time to remove dirt and stems

re·search·ful *pronunc at* 1RESEARCH + fəl\ *adj* [*1research* + *-ful*] **:** making researches or evincing research **:** SCHOLARLY

re·search·ist \"+əst\ *n* -S [*1research* + *-ist*] **:** one engaged in research **:** RESEARCHER

research professor *n* [*1research*] **:** a professor in a college or university who is free to devote his whole time to research

re·seat \(')rē+\ *vt* [*re-* + *seat*] **1 :** to seat or set again ⟨had his valves ~*ed*⟩ **2 :** to fit with a new seat ⟨the chair needs to be ~*ed*⟩ or equip with new seats ⟨~ a theater⟩

re·seau \rā'zō, rə'-\ *n, pl* **reseaus** \-ōz\ *or* **re·seaux** \-ō(z)\ [F *réseau*, fr. OF *resel*, dim. of *rais*, *rois* net, fr. L *retis*, *rete* — more at RETINA] **:** NETWORK: as **a :** a system of lines forming small squares of standard size that is photographed by a separate exposure on the same plate with star images (as to facilitate measurements or detect changes of the film) **b :** a net ground or foundation in lace **c :** a screen with minute elements of three colors in a regular geometric pattern used for taking and viewing additive color photographs **d :** a group of meteorological stations under common direction or cooperating in some common purpose

re·secrete \¦rē+\ *vt* [*re-* + *secrete*] **:** to secrete again or anew

re·sect \rə'sekt, rē's-\ *vt* -ED/-ING/-S [L *resectus*, past part. of *resecare* to cut off, fr. *re-* + *secare* to cut — more at SAW] **1** *obs* **:** to cut or pare off, away, or out **:** EXCISE **2 :** to perform the surgical operation of resection on

re·sect·abil·i·ty \=,sektə'bilәd·ē\ *n* [*resectable* + *-ity*] **:** the condition of being resectable — compare OPERABILITY

re·sect·able \='sektəbəl\ *adj* **:** capable of being resected **:** suitable for resection ⟨~ cancer⟩ — compare OPERABLE

re·sec·tion \='sekshən\ *n* [L *resection-*, *resectio*, fr. *resectus* (past part. of *resecare* to cut off) + *-ion-*, *-io* -ion — more at RESECT] **1** *obs* **:** an act of cutting or paring off **2 :** the surgical removal of part of an organ or structure ⟨gastric ~⟩ ⟨~ of the lower bowel⟩ — sometimes distinguished from *excision* **3 :** a method in surveying by which one determines a position on a map after it has been properly oriented by drawing lines from two or more distant objects through their plotted positions on the map

re·sec·tion·al \-shənᵊl,-shnəl\ *adj* [*resection* + *-al*] **:** of or relating to resection

re·sec·to·scope \='sektə,skōp\ *n* [*resection* + *-o-* + *-scope*] **:** an instrument consisting of a tubular fenestrated sheath with a sliding knife within it that is used for surgery within cavities (as of the prostate through the urethra)

re·se·da \rə'sēdə, rē's-\ *n* [NL, fr. L, a plant used to reduce tumors] **1 a** *cap* **:** a genus of Old World herbs (family Resedaceae) having racemose flowers with cleft petals, numerous stamens, and an urn-shaped horned capsule opening at the summit — see DYER'S ROCKET, MIGNONETTE 1 **b** -S **:** any plant of the genus *Reseda* **2** *or* **reseda green** -S **a :** a variable color averaging a grayish green that is yellower and darker than average bayberry, yellower, lighter, and stronger than slate green, and yellower and slightly lighter than average blue spruce (sense 2a) — called also *mignonette* **b :** a light olive that is greener and less strong than citrine and darker than grape green **c** *of textiles* **:** a grayish to dark grayish green

res·e·da·ce·ae \,resə'dāsē,ē\ *n pl, cap* [NL, fr. *Reseda*, type genus + *-aceae*] **:** a family of mainly Mediterranean herbs (order Parietales) having alternate or fascicled leaves, glandular stipules, and racemose irregular flowers and including several that are cultivated as ornamentals — compare MIGNONETTE — **res·e·da·ceous** \¦resə¦dāshəs\ *adj*

re·see \(')rē+\ *vt* [*re-* + *see*] **:** to see again or anew

re·seed \"+\ *vb* [*re-* + *seed*] *vt* **1 :** to sow seed on again or anew ⟨had to ~ the lower land⟩ **2 :** to maintain (itself) by self-sown seed ⟨some plants will ~ themselves indefinitely⟩ ~ *vi* **:** to maintain itself by self-sown seed

re·seize \"+\ *vt* [MF *resaisir*, fr. OF, fr. *re-* + *saisir* to seize — more at SEIZE] **1** *or* **re·seise** \"+\ **:** to put into possession or seizin again **:** reinvest with seisin — used with *of*, *in*, and sometimes *with* **2 :** to seize again or anew

1re·seiz·er *or* **re·seis·er** \(')rē¦sēzə(r)\ *n* -S [*reseize* + *-er* (as in *cesser*)] **:** resumption of possession by a feudal lord after a tenant's default

2reseizer \"\ *n* [*reseize* + *-er*, agent suffix] **:** one that seizes again

re·seizure \(')rē+\ *n* [*re-* + *seizure*] **:** the action or an act of reseizing

re·select \¦rē+\ *vt* [*re-* + *select*] **:** to select again or anew; *esp* **:** to select among (the progeny of a selected breeding population) for individuals exhibiting to best advantage a desired quality

re·sell \(')rē+\ *vb* [*re-* + *sell*] **:** to sell again

re·sem·blance \rə'zemblən(t)s, rē'z-\ *n* -S [ME, fr. AF, fr. OF *resembler* to resemble + *-ance*] **1** *obs* **a :** a thing or person resembling or suggesting another **b :** SYMBOL **c :** SIMILE, COMPARISON **2 :** the quality or state of resembling **:** LIKENESS, SIMILITUDE, SIMILARITY; *also* **:** a point of likeness ⟨there is no ~ between the two⟩ ⟨family ~⟩ **3 :** REPRESENTATION, IMAGE **4** *archaic* **:** characteristic appearance of nature **:** outward aspect or manifestation **:** SEMBLANCE **5** *obs* **a :** DEMONSTRATION **b :** PROBABILITY

re·sem·blant \-nt\ *adj* [ME, fr. MF, pres. part. of *resembler* to resemble] **1 :** manifesting or characterized by resemblance **2 :** dealing with resemblances or representations of things

re·sem·ble \rə'zembəl, rē'z-\ *vb* **resembled**; **resembled**; **resembling** \-b(ə)liŋ\ **resembles** [ME *resemblen*, fr. MF *resembler*, fr. OF, fr. *re-* + *sembler* to be like, seem, fr. L *similare*, *simulare* to copy, imitate, fr. *similis* like, resembling — more at SIMILAR] *vt* **1 :** to be like or similar to **:** bear the similitude of in appearance or qualities ⟨these brothers ~ each other⟩ **2** *archaic* **:** to represent as like **:** LIKEN, COMPARE **3** *obs* **:** to make a likeness or image of **:** REPRESENT, PORTRAY, DEPICT; *also* **:** SYMBOLIZE **4 :** to cause to be like **:** make like ~ *vi* **1** *obs* **:** to seem in outward show **:** APPEAR **2 :** to have a resemblance **:** bear a likeness **3 :** to be alike **:** resemble each other

re·sem·bler \-b(ə)lə(r)\ *n* -S **:** one that resembles

resemblingly *adv* [*resembling* (fr. pres. part. of *resemble*) + *-ly*] *obs* **:** in a resembling manner **:** so as to resemble

re·seminate \(')rē+\ *vt* [L *reseminatus*, past part. of *reseminare* to sow again, fr. *re-* + *seminare* to sow, fr. *semin-*, *semen* seed — more at SEMEN] **:** to produce again by or as if by means of seed

re·send \(')rē+\ *vt* [*re-* + *send*] **1 a :** to send again or anew **b :** to send back **2 :** to send on (a telegraphic message) by means of a repeater

res·ene \'re,zēn\ *n* -S [ISV *resin* + *-ene*] **:** any of various mixtures of neutral alkali-resistant compounds that are found in rosin and other natural resins and that contain carbon, hydrogen, and oxygen — not used systematically

re·sensitize \(')rē+\ *vt* [*re-* + *sensitize*] **:** to render sensitive (as to light, an allergen) again or anew

re·sent \rə'zent, rē'z-\ *vt* -ED/-ING/-S [F *ressentir*, fr. OF *resentir*, *ressentir*, fr. *re-* + *sentir* to feel, fr. L *sentire* — more at SENSE] **1** *obs* **:** to be sensible of: as **a :** to receive with satisfaction, appreciation, pleasure, or similar response; *also* **:** to remember gratefully **b :** to feel (oneself) affected by sorrow, pain, or distress **c :** to take (something) well or ill **2 :** to feel, express, or exhibit indignant displeasure at ⟨~ undue familiarity⟩ **3** *archaic* **:** to have the quality of **:** SUGGEST

re·sent·ful \-ntfəl\ *adj* **1 :** full of resentment or inclined to resent **2 :** caused or marked by resentment — **re·sent·ful·ly** \-fəlē, -li\ *adv* — **re·sent·ful·ness** *n* -ES

resentiment *n* -S [MF — more at RESENTMENT] *obs* **:** RESENTMENT

re·sent·ing·ly *adv* [*resenting* (fr. pres. part. of *resent*) + *-ly*] **:** in a resenting manner **:** with resentment

resentive *adj* [*resent* + *-ive*] *obs* **:** that resents or tends to resent

re·sent·ment \rə'zentmənt, rē'z-\ *n* -S [F *resentiment*, *ressentiment*, fr. MF, fr. *resentir*, *ressentir* to resent (fr. OF) + *-ment*] **1 :** a feeling of indignant displeasure because of something regarded as a wrong, insult, or other injury **:** UMBRAGE **2 a** *obs* **:** a state of feeling an emotion or sentiment or a sensation (as of smell); *sometimes* **:** a keenly felt emotion **:** a sharp sense, perception, or realization **b** *archaic* **:** a specific emotion or expression of an emotion (as appreciation, interest, good will) **syn** see OFFENSE

re·se·quent \(')rē¦sēkwənt, 'rēsək-\ *adj* [*re-* + *-sequent* (as in *consequent*, *subsequent*)] **1 :** of, relating to, or being a stream that flows down the dip of underlying formations in the same direction as an original consequent stream but developed later and generally tributary to a subsequent stream **2 :** of, relating to, or being a fault-line scarp that faces in the same direction as an initial fault scarp but is due to differential erosion rather than to crustal movement

reserate *vt* -ED/-ING/-S [L *reseratus*, past part. of *reserare* to unlock, unbar, fr. *re-* + *sera* bar, bolt] *obs* **:** UNLOCK, OPEN

re·ser·pic acid \rə's¦ərpik-, rē'-, -'z¦\ *n* [ISV *reserp*ine + *-ic*] **:** a pentacyclic acid $C_{21}H_{27}N_2O_3COOH$ obtained by hydrolysis of reserpine and derived from both harmine and isoquinoline

reser·pine \rə'sərpən, rē'-, -'zər-, -,pēn; 'resər,pēn, 'rezə-\ *n* -S [G *reserpin*, fr. *reserp-* (prob. irreg. fr. NL *Rauwolfia serpentina*, fr. *Rauwolfia* + *serpentina*, fr. LL, fem. of *serpentinus* serpentine) + G *-in* -ine] **:** a crystalline pentacyclic sedative hypotensive alkaloid $C_{33}H_{40}N_2O_9$ that is extracted esp. from the root of shrubs of the genus *Rauwolfia* (as *R. serpentina*) and is used in the treatment of hypertension and various mental diseases and tension states

re·serv·able \rə'zərvəbəl, rē'z-, -zēv-,-zəiv-\ *adj* **:** that may be reserved

res·er·va·tion *R* ,rezər'vāshən *or sometimes* -zə'v- *by r-dissimilation*, *–R* -zə'v-\ *n* -S [ME *reservacioun*, fr. MF *reservation*, fr. *reserver* to reserve + *-ation*] **1 :** an act of reserving something (as for a particular use or the use of a particular person or group) ⟨~ of rights by the states⟩: as **a** *Christian relig* (1) **:** retention of tithes (2) **:** retention of the right of nomination to a vacant benefice (3) **:** retention of the power of absolution in particular cases (4) **:** retention of a portion of the eucharistic elements for adoration by those worshiping at the church or for the administration of communion to the sick **b** (1) **:** the act or fact of a grantor's reserving some new thing out of the thing granted and not in esse as such before; *also* **:** the right or interest so reserved or the clause by which it is reserved — distinguished from *exception* (2) **:** EXCEPTION 4b, PROVISO **c** (1) *obs* **:** a keeping concealed of something pertinent **:** a holding back (2) **:** the setting of limiting conditions or withholding from complete exposition ⟨answered without ~⟩ **d :** an engaging in advance of some accommodation or service ⟨the ~ of a hotel room⟩; *also* **:** a promise, guarantee, or record of such engagement ⟨it is advisable to telegraph for ~*s*⟩ **2 :** something that is reserved: as **a** (1) **:** a limiting condition **:** LIMITATION ⟨agreed with several ~*s* to their plan⟩ (2) *obs* **:** something kept hidden **:** a deceptively expressed statement (as an answer) **b** (1) **:** a tract of public land set aside for a particular purpose (as schools, forest, or the use of Indians) (2) **:** an area in which hunting is not permitted; *esp* **:** one set aside as a secure breeding place for game birds or mammals **syn** see CONDITION — **off the reservation :** free from the usual restraints and controls

res·er·va·tion·ist \-sh(ə)nəst\ *n* -S [*reservation* + *-ist*] **:** one who has or makes reservations

re·serv·ato·ry \rə'zərvə,tōrē\ *n* -ES [ML *reservatorium*, fr. L *reservatus* (past part. of *reservare* to reserve) + *-orium* -ory] *archaic* **:** a place (as a cupboard or reservoir) in which things are kept

1re·serve \rə'sərv, rē'z-, -zēv,-zəiv\ *vb* [ME *reserven*, fr. MF *reserver*, fr. L *reservare* to keep back, save up, fr. *re-* + *servare* to save, protect, keep — more at CONSERVE] *vt* **1 a :** to keep in store for future or special use **:** hold or keep in reserve **b** (1) **:** to retain power of absolution of to oneself — used of a religious superior (as the pope, a bishop) (2) **:** to set apart (a case) for such action on the part of a superior (3) **:** to retain or set aside (a portion of the consecrated elements) at the time of a celebration of the Eucharist for future use (as for communion of the sick) **c :** to keep back **:** retain or hold over to a future time or place **:** fail to deliver, make over, or disclose at once **:** defer the discussion or determination of **d :** to make legal reservation of **:** withhold from the operation of a grant, agreement, or release **2 a :** to keep or leave safe, sound, or intact **:** SPARE, SAVE **b** *obs* **:** to keep unaltered or free from decay **c :** to continue to have or show **d :** to retain particular areas (as in porcelain) in the same color as the original surface **3 a :** to set aside or apart — usu. used with *for* or *to* ⟨*reserved*, and destined to eternal woe —John Milton⟩ **b :** to have set aside (as for one's use) ⟨~ seats at the opera⟩ **4** *archaic* **:** to make an exception of or in favor of **:** EXCEPT **5** *obs* **:** to keep from being known to others ~ *vi*, *obs* **:** to continue to be (as in existence or a specified condition) **:** REMAIN **syn** see KEEP

2reserve \"\ *n* -S [F *réserve*, fr. MF, fr. *reserver* to reserve] **1 :** something that is reserved **:** something kept back or held available (as for future use) **:** STORE, STOCK **2 :** something reserved or set aside for a particular purpose, use, or reason (as a tree in a part of a wood that is to be felled or a part of a lode): as **a** (1) **:** a military force intended to be withheld temporarily from action for use by a commander when he desires to commit it to influence decisively the course of an engagement — usu. used in pl.; compare SUPPORT (2) **:** forces not in the field for any reason but available (3) **:** the military forces of a country not part of the regular services or in the U.S. of the National Guard; *also* **:** a member of these forces **:** RESERVIST **b :** a tract (as of public land) set apart for a particular purpose **:** RESERVATION ⟨forest ~*s*⟩ **c :** a distinction in an exhibition that indicates that the recipient will get a prize if another should be disqualified **d :** an area left the natural color of the background or original surface color **3 :** an act of reserving **:** EXCEPTION, RESTRICTION, QUALIFICATION — usu. used with reference to adherence to a principle, belief, or standard ⟨a mental ~⟩ **4 a :** self-restraint, closeness, or caution in one's words and bearing toward others **:** self-control in expression (as of one's thoughts, feelings, plans) **:** lack of effusiveness or sometimes of cordiality **b :** forbearance from making a full explanation, complete disclosure, or free expression of one's mind (as in casuistry or religious instruction) **:** intentional withholding or suppression of truth when it is regarded as inconvenient to disclose it (as from people who are regarded as unable to understand it or receive it with benefit) **5** *archaic* **:** a case of withholding information or knowledge; *also* **:** a piece of information not fully disclosed **:** SECRET **6 :** money or its equivalent kept in hand or set apart usu. to meet a specified liability or anticipated liabilities: as **a** (1) **:** uninvested cash kept on hand by a bank (2) **:** such cash together with deposits in a central depository (as a Federal Reserve bank or the Bank of England) — see LEGAL RESERVE **b** (1) **:** the portion of an insurance company's assets set aside for some special purpose as evidenced by showing the reserve as a liability on the books (2) **:** the amount of funds or assets calculated on net premiums to be necessary for a life insurance company to have at any given time to enable it with interest and premiums paid as they shall accrue to meet all claims on the insurance then in force as they would mature according to the particular mortality table accepted **:** the theoretical difference between the present value of the total insurance and the present value of the future premiums on the insurance constituting the amount for which another insurance company could afford to take over the insurance and often regarded as a reinsurance fund — called also *reinsurance reserve;* see CATASTROPHE RESERVE, INITIAL RESERVE, INSURANCE RESERVE, INVESTMENT RESERVE, LEGAL RESERVE, LOSS RESERVE, MEAN RESERVE, TERMINAL RESERVE, UNEARNED PREMIUM RESERVE **c :** RESERVE ACCOUNT **d** (1) **:** the portion of the earnings of a corporation set aside for a specific purpose such as to meet future losses or contingent liabilities — compare SURPLUS (2) **:** a deduction from the book value of an asset to bring its valuation into line with current market conditions or possible future losses ⟨a ~ against losses on bank loans⟩ ⟨a ~ for depreciation of securities of an investment company⟩ — called also *valuation reserve* **e :** the liquid resources (as gold and foreign exchanges) of a nation for meeting international payments **7 a :** RESIST 2a **b :** the capacity of a solution to neutralize alkali or acid when its reaction is shifted from one hydrogen-ion concentration to another; *esp* **:** the capacity of blood or bacteriological media to react with acid or alkali within predetermined and usu. physiological limits of hydrogen-ion concentration — compare BUFFER 4a, BUFFER SOLUTION **c :** a preparation used on an object in electroplating to fix the limits of the deposit **8 :** SUBSTITUTE — **in reserve** *adv* **:** held back for other or future use **:** still available ⟨had other arguments *in reserve*⟩ ⟨kept *in reserve*⟩ — **without reserve** *adv* **1 :** freely and openly **:** so as to give complete information ⟨answered *without reserve*⟩ **2 :** without qualification, condition, or restriction; *usu* **:** without a fixed minimum price or other restriction to sale

³reserve \"\ *adj* **:** constituting or having the form or function of a reserve ⟨a ~ supply⟩ ⟨~ strength⟩

re-serve \(ˈ)rē+\ *vt* [*re-* + *serve*] **:** to serve again or anew ⟨*re-served* the warrant⟩

reserve account *n* [³*reserve*] **1 :** a valuation account that shows the estimated or actual decline in value of an asset and is always subtracted on a balance sheet from the related asset account to show net value ⟨a *reserve account* for depreciation⟩ ⟨*reserve accounts* for bad debts⟩ ⟨*reserve account* to reduce investments to market value⟩ — called also *allowance account, provision account, valuation account* **2 :** an account that shows an accrued usu. estimated liability ⟨*reserve account* for income taxes⟩ **3 :** an account that shows profits or surplus segregated or appropriated for a particular purpose ⟨*reserve account* for contingencies⟩ ⟨*reserve account* for replacement of fixed assets⟩

reserve air *n* **:** SUPPLEMENTAL AIR

reserve bank *n* [²*reserve*] **1 :** any of 12 Federal Reserve banks in the U.S. **2 :** a central bank holding reserves of other banks ⟨the South African *Reserve Bank*⟩

reserve buoyancy *n* [³*reserve*] **:** the volume of a ship above the water plane that can be made watertight and thus increase the ship's buoyancy — called also *reserve of buoyancy*

reserve capacity *n* **:** installed equipment (as in an electric power plant) that is in excess of that required to carry peak load

reserve card *n* [¹*reserve*] **:** a postal card notifying a library patron that a book he was previously unable to consult or borrow is now available

reserve city *n* [²*reserve*] **:** a city of the U.S. designated by the Board of Governors of the Federal Reserve system in which member banks of the system are required to maintain higher legal reserves than in other areas — compare CENTRAL RESERVE CITY, COUNTRY BANK

re·served \-vd\ *adj* [fr. past part. of ¹*reserve*] **1 :** marked by a disposition to be restrained in words and actions: as **a :** checking free expression of knowledge or ideas through caution **:** not open, communicative, or candid ⟨habitually was ~ in speech, withholding her opinion —Victoria Sackville-West⟩ **b :** checking easy free conversation or activity through formality, stiffness, or other inhibition **:** not spontaneous, natural, or hearty ⟨a certain vulgar gusto in his movement that divided him from the ~, watchful rest of the family —D.H.Lawrence⟩ **2 :** kept or set apart or aside for future or special use or for an exigency **3 :** left of the same color as the background or as the original color of the surface of the material **syn** see SILENT

reserved book *n* **:** a book (as in a college library) used for students' required or collateral reading in courses and segregated from the general collections

reserved list *n* **:** a list of officers in the British navy retired from active service on half pay but available to be called upon to serve in time of war or emergency

re·serv·ed·ly \-vədlē, -li\ *adv* **:** in a reserved manner **:** with reserve

re·serv·ed·ness \-dnəs\ *n* -ES **:** the quality or state of being reserved

reserved power *n* **:** a political power reserved by a constitution or similar constituent instrument to the exclusive jurisdiction of a specified political authority (as a state or executive) usu. held to constitute the original source of powers undergoing allocation and distinguished from those delegated to other authority ⟨some *reserved powers* in the U.S. federal system belong to the states⟩ ⟨the *reserved powers* at the disposal of a British colonial governor⟩ — compare IMPLIED POWER, RESIDUAL POWER

re·serve·less \-vləs\ *adj* **:** lacking reserve or a reserve

reserve of buoyancy [²*reserve*] **:** RESERVE BUOYANCY

reserve officer *n* [²*reserve*] **:** an officer in a military reserve

reserve price *n* [³*reserve*] **:** a price announced at an auction as the least that will be entertained — compare BY-BIDDER

reserver *n* -S *obs* **:** one that reserves; *esp* **:** RESERVOIR

reserve ratio *n* [²*reserve*] **:** the ratio of the cash reserves of a bank to liabilities; *esp* **:** the ratio of gold certificates to combined deposit liabilities and outstanding Federal Reserve notes of the Federal Reserve banks

reserve ration *n* [³*reserve*] **:** a ration consisting of concentrated foods packed in a sealed container for use only in emergency

reserves *pres 3d sing of* RESERVE, *pl of* RESERVE

reserving *pres part of* RESERVE

re·serv·ist \-vəst\ *n* -S [²*reserve* + *-ist*] **:** a member of the reserves of the armed forces

¹res·er·voir *R* ˈrezəv,wär (-zəv- *by* r-*dissimilation*), -zə,vȯ(ə)r *also* -zərv,w- *or* -zər,v- *or* -v,wȯ(ə)r *or* ÷ -,vȯi *sometimes* -,vär *or by* r-*dissimilation* -v,wä *or* -,vȯ *or* -,vä; *-R* -zəv,wä(r, -,vȯ(ə) *also* -v,wȯ(ə) *or* ÷ -,vȯi *sometimes* -,vä(r\ *n* -S [F *réservoir*, fr. MF, fr. *reserver* to reserve + *-oir* -ory] **1 :** a place where something is kept in store: as **a :** a place where water is collected and kept in quantity for use when wanted; *esp* **:** an artificial lake in which water is impounded for domestic and industrial use, irrigation, hydroelectric power, flood control, or other purposes **b :** a part of an apparatus in which a liquid is held ⟨the ~ of an oil lamp⟩ **c :** a tank on the back of an old-fashioned kitchen range in which water is kept hot by escaped heat from the oven **2 a :** a space (as an enlargement of a vessel or the cavity of a glandular acinus) in which a body fluid or other product is stored ⟨oil ~*s* on a leaf⟩ **b :** the enlarged posterior portion of the gullet of some flagellates **3 :** an extra supply **:** RESERVE, STORE **4 a :** a body of rock sufficiently porous to permit the accumulation of water, petroleum, or natural gas **b :** the gathering ground where snow collects to form a glacier **:** the area covered by the névé **c :** a space within the earth occupied by molten rock or magma **5 :** STORAGE BELLOWS **6 a** *also* **reservoir host :** an organism in which a parasite that is pathogenic for some other species lives and multiplies without damaging its host; *broadly* **:** a noneconomic organism within which a pathogen of economic or medical importance flourishes without regard to its pathogenicity for the reservoir ⟨rats are ~*s* of plague⟩ ⟨*reservoir hosts* are important in the epidemiology of virus diseases⟩ **b :** a colony or group of organisms (as noxious animals) that persists when the general population of the species declines and serves as a breeding nucleus ⟨small ~ populations persist with control operations⟩

²reservoir \"\ *vt* -ED/-ING/-S **1 :** to provide with a reservoir **2 :** to collect, store, or keep in or as if in a reservoir

reservoir rock *n* **:** a permeable rock that contains oil or gas in appreciable quantity

¹re·set \rəˈset\ *n* -S [ME *recet, resset*, fr. OF *recet*, fr. L *receptus* retreat, retirement, place of refuge, fr. *receptus*, past part. of *recipere* to take back, receive — more at RECEIVE] **1** *obs* **:** an opportunity or right of refuge or shelter **:** SUCCOR, HELP; *also* **:** a place of refuge or shelter **:** ABODE, RESORT **2** *obs* **:** one who shelters another **3** *Scots law* **a :** the receiving of goods obtained by theft, robbery, swindling, or embezzlement with intent to deprive the owner of them by one knowing the goods to have been so obtained **b** *obs* **:** the harboring of an outlaw

²reset \"\ *vt* [ME *recetten, resetten*, fr. OF *recetter*, fr. L *receptare*, freq. of *recipere* to receive] **1** *chiefly Scot* **:** to give shelter to **:** WELCOME **2** *Scots law* **:** to receive and secrete (stolen goods)

³re·set \(ˈ)rē+\ *vt* [*re-* + *set*] **:** to set again or afresh ⟨~ type⟩ ⟨~ a diamond⟩ ⟨~ a field with tomato plants⟩

⁴re·set \ˈrē+,-,≈ˈ≈\ *n* **1 :** something that is reset: as **a :** matter set up in print again **b :** REPLANT **2 :** an act of resetting **3 :** something used in resetting: as **a :** a device for releasing the brakes of a train after they have been applied by automatic train control **b :** a device for restoring a contact or pointer to its normal or prior position

re·settable \(ˈ)rē+\ *adj* [³*reset* + *-able*] **:** capable of being reset

¹re·set·ter \rəˈsetər\ *n* [ME *recettor, ressettour*, fr. MF *recetteur*, fr. OF *recetter* to give shelter to + *-eur* -or] **1** *obs* **:** one that harbors or assists criminals **2** *chiefly Scot* **:** a receiver of stolen goods

²re·setter \(ˈ)rē+\ *n* [³*reset* + *-er*] **1 :** one that resets something (as type) **2 :** a leather worker who smooths and stretches hides by applying tallow and rubbing with a dull blade

resetter-out \(ˈ)≈ˈ≈≈,≈\ *n* **:** a leather worker who improves the grain of and removes the moisture from leather by stretching with a dull blade

re·settle \(ˈ)rē+\ *vb* [*re-* + *settle*] *vt* **:** to settle again or anew; *esp* **:** to settle (people) in a new place or a new way of life ~ *vi* **:** to become settled again or anew (as after disturbance or upheaval) — **re·settlement** \"+\ *n*

re·sew \"+\ *vb* [*re-* + *sew*] **:** to sew again

res ex·ten·sa \ˌrā,sekˈsten(t)sə, ˌrēzik-\ *n, pl* **res exten·sae** \-n,sī, -n,sē\ [NL] **:** an extended thing or substance **:** material substance — compare CARTESIANISM

res ges·tae \(ˈ)rāsˈge,stī, (ˈ)rēzˈje,stē\ *n pl* [L] **:** things done **:** TRANSACTIONS, DEEDS, EXPLOITS; *esp* **:** the facts that form the environment of a litigated issue **:** the things or matters and spontaneous oral statements accompanying and incident to a transaction or event and admissible in evidence as illustrating or explaining it

¹resh \ˈrāsh\ *n* -ES [Heb *rēsh*, lit., head] **1 :** the 20th letter of the Hebrew alphabet — symbol ר; see ALPHABET table **2 :** the letter of the Phoenician alphabet or of any of various other Semitic alphabets corresponding to Hebrew resh

²resh \ˈresh\ *dial var of* RUSH

re·shape \(ˈ)rē+\ *vb* [*re-* + *shape*] *vt* **:** to give a new form or orientation to ⟨*reshaping* the nation's foreign policy⟩ ~ *vi* **:** to take on a new form

re·shaper \"+\ *n* **:** one that reshapes something; *esp* **:** a worker who does the final blocking of hats

re·shearer \"+\ *n* [*re-* + *shearer*] **:** a worker who shears steel sheets to specified sizes

re·shelve \"+\ *vt* [*re-* + *shelve*] **:** to restore (as books) to a shelf

re·ship \"+\ *vb* [*re-* + *ship*] *vt* **:** to ship again: as **a :** to put on board of a ship a second time **:** transfer to another ship ⟨~ bonded merchandise⟩ **b :** to put in place or set up again ~ *vi* **:** to embark on a ship again or anew; *esp* **:** to sign again or anew for service on a ship

re·shipment \"+\ *n* [*reship* + *-ment*] **1 :** an act of reshipping **2 :** something that is reshipped

re·shipper \"+\ *n* [*reship* + *-er*] **1 :** one that reships **2 :** a container used for reshipping; *usu* **:** a case or box used to ship empty unit containers (as glass jars) and reused for the subsequent shipping of the filled containers

re·show \"+\ *vt* [*re-* + *show*] **:** to show again or anew; *specif* **:** to show (a motion picture) on a second or later run

resht \ˈresht\ *adj, usu cap* [fr. *Resht*, city of northwest Iran] **:** of or from the city of Resht, Iran **:** of the kind or style prevalent in Resht

¹re·shuffle \(ˈ)rē+\ *vt* [*re-* + *shuffle*] **1 :** to shuffle (cards) again **2 :** to reorganize (as a cabinet or a political alignment) usu. by reordering of forces without other major changes (as of personnel)

²reshuffle \"\ *n* **:** an act or a result of reshuffling

res·i·ance \ˈrezēən(t)s\ *also* **res·i·an·cy** \-nsē\ *n, pl* **resiances** *also* **resiancies** [*resiance* fr. MF *reseance*, fr. *reseoir* to reside (fr. L *residēre*) + *-ance*; *resiancy* fr. *resiant* + *-cy*] *archaic* **:** ABODE, RESIDENCE

¹res·i·ant \-nt\ *n* -S [ME *resceant*, fr. MF *reseant*, fr. *reseant*, adj.] *archaic* **:** RESIDENT

²resiant \"\ *adj* [ME *reseant*, fr. MF, fr. OF, fr. pres. part. of *reseoir* to reside, fr. L *residēre*] *archaic* **:** abiding in a place **:** RESIDENT

¹re·side \rəˈzīd, rēˈz-\ *vi* -ED/-ING/-S [ME *residen*, fr. MF or L; MF *resider*, fr. L *residēre* to sit back, remain, abide, fr. *re-* + *sedēre* to sit — more at SIT] **1** *obs* **:** to settle oneself or a thing in a place **:** be stationed **:** REMAIN, STAY **2 a :** to be in residence as the incumbent of a benefice or an office **b :** to dwell permanently or continuously **:** have a settled abode for a time **:** have one's residence or domicile **3 :** to have an abiding place **:** be present as an element or inhere as a quality **:** be vested as a right — usu. used with *in* ⟨the power of decision ~*s* in the electorate⟩

syn LIVE, DWELL, SOJOURN, LODGE, STAY, PUT (*up*), STOP: RESIDE, despite the fact that it is somewhat formal, may be the preferred term for expressing the idea that a person keeps or returns to a particular dwelling place as his fixed, settled, or legal abode ⟨all persons born or naturalized in the United States, and subject to the jurisdiction thereof, are citizens of the United States and of the State wherein they *reside* —*U.S. Constitution*⟩ LIVE is the more general word for indicating that one has one's home in a place, often with special reference especially to hours away from work ⟨those who *lived* apart in temples —Agnes Repplier⟩ ⟨he works in New York but *lives* in New Jersey⟩ ⟨officially *residing* in Pennsylvania but *living* most of the time in Washington⟩ ⟨*living* in an old farmhouse⟩ DWELL is a somewhat elevated or bookish synonym for LIVE in this sense ⟨a young Indian girl whose people *dwelt* on the west side of the gorge —Ted Sumner⟩ ⟨in far-flung crown colonies and other dependencies *dwell* millions of people for whom political authority requires to be expressed in terms of tangible, visible personality —F.A.Ogg & Harold Zink⟩ SOJOURN is used in connection with a temporary habitation held for a limited or uncertain time ⟨artists who *sojourned* for a time amidst the western scene —*Amer. Guide Series: Oregon*⟩ LODGE applies to having sleeping and general living accommodations at a place, sometimes implying that meals are taken elsewhere ⟨*lodging* at the inn nearby⟩ ⟨a house in the Outer Bailey where you may *lodge* until morning —J.H. Wheelwright⟩ STAY is now perhaps the most usual common equivalent for SOJOURN; it may be used in reference to paid quarters, as in a hotel, or to visits with friends or relatives ⟨*stay* and eat at middle-class British hotels —Richard Joseph⟩ ⟨*staying* in the country in a house where . . . was also a guest —W.S.Maugham⟩ PUT (*up*) is a colloquial equivalent for STAY ⟨*put up* at a motel⟩ STOP is commonly used to indicate breaking a trip or journey and staying for a period ⟨*stop* at a hotel⟩ ⟨*stop* in Chicago for the night⟩

²reside *vi* [L *residere* to sink back, fr. *re-* + *sidere* to sit down, settle, sink; akin to L *sedēre* to sit] *obs* **:** SINK, SUBSIDE, SETTLE

¹res·i·dence \ˈrez(ə)dən(t)s, -zədᵊn-, *sometimes* -zə,den- *or chiefly substand South* ˌ≈≈ˈden(t)s\ *n* -S [ME, fr. MF, fr. ML *residentia*, fr. L *resident-, residens* (pres. part. of *residēre* to reside, abide) + *-ia* -y] **1 a :** the act or fact of abiding or dwelling in a place for some time **:** an act of making one's home in a place ⟨a center of fashionable ~⟩ ⟨where scepter'd angels held their ~ —John Milton⟩ **b :** the act or fact of living or regularly staying at or in some place either in or as a qualification for the discharge of a duty or the enjoyment of a benefit ⟨the governor was in ~⟩ **c :** the presence of an incumbent in his benefice **2 a** (1) **:** the place where one actually lives or has his home as distinguished from his technical domicile (2) **:** a temporary or permanent dwelling place, abode, or habitation to which one intends to return as distinguished from a place of temporary sojourn or transient visit (3) **:** a domiciliary place of abode **b** (1) **:** the place of the principal office of a corporation or business concern designated in its articles of incorporation or originally registered in accordance with law (2) **:** a place of doing business or maintaining an office of a corporation or business concern that is registered in accordance with law — used in some statutes (3) **:** a place in which in fact business is being done, an office is being maintained, or lawful powers or rights are being exercised by a corporation or business concern — used in broad statutory interpretations **c :** the place where something is permanently established **:** a seat or center of something (as power or prerogative) **3** *obs* **:** continuance or insistence in action **4 a :** a building used as a home **:** DWELLING; *esp* **:** a house of superior or pretentious character **b :** housing or a unit of housing provided for students and administered by a department of an educational institution; *also* **:** the department administering such residence **5 a :** the period or duration of one's abode in a place ⟨after a ~ of some 30 years⟩ **b :** the period during which one is actively engaged in academic duties or study or research at a college or university

²residence *n* -S [²*reside* + *-ence*] **1** *obs* **:** matter that falls or settles to the bottom of liquors **:** SEDIMENT; *also* **:** RESIDUUM **2** *obs* **:** depositing of sediment **:** SETTLING

res·i·denc·er \ˈrez(ə)dənsə(r), -zədᵊns- *sometimes* -zə,den(t)s-\ *n* -S [ME, residentiary (adj.), fr. AF, fr. ML *residentiarius* — more at RESIDENTIARY] **1** *obs* **:** a clergyman in residence **2 :** a resident representative or minister

res·i·den·cia \ˌrezəˈden(t)sēə, -)thēə\ *n* -S [Sp, lit., residence, fr. ML *residentia*] **:** a court or inquiry held in Spanish countries for a period of 70 days by a specially commissioned judge to examine into the conduct of a retiring high official (as a viceroy, captain general, governor)

res·i·den·cy \ˈrez(ə)dənsē, -zədᵊns-, -si *sometimes* -zə,den(t)s-\ *n* -ES [*resident* + *-cy*] **1 :** place of residence **:** DWELLING **2 a :** the official residence of a resident diplomatic agent or governor **b :** a territory in a protected state in which the powers of the protecting state are executed by a resident agent; *specif* **:** such an administrative division in parts of the East Indies (as formerly in India or Java) **3 :** a period of advanced medical training and education that normally follows graduation from medical school and completion of an internship and that consists of supervised practice of a specialty in a hospital and in its outpatient department and instruction from specialists on the hospital staff

¹res·i·dent \-nt, *chiefly substand South* ˌrezəˈdent\ *adj* [ME, fr. L *resident-, residens*, pres. part. of *residēre* to reside] **1 :** dwelling or having an abode for a continued length of time **:** being in residence **:** RESIDING ⟨while ~ at college⟩ ⟨a ~ landowner⟩ **2 :** PRESENT, INHERENT ⟨energy ~ in matter⟩ **3 a** *obs* **:** not moving **:** FIXED, STABLE, RESTING **b :** not migratory **4 :** appertaining directly to a moving part of the body ⟨~ sensations⟩ — opposed to *remote* **5 :** involving, requiring, or taken during residence at an educational institution ⟨degree requirements include a year of ~ study⟩

²resident \"\ *n* -S **1 :** one who resides in a place **:** one who dwells in a place for a period of some duration — often distinguished from *inhabitant* **2 a :** a diplomatic agent residing at a foreign court or seat of government; *esp* **:** MINISTER RESIDENT 1 **b :** the governor of a residency **3 :** an ecclesiastical incumbent who is in residence **4 a :** a physician serving a residency usu. in preparation for independent practice in a specialty — compare HOUSE PHYSICIAN, INTERN **b :** a graduate student or postgraduate who resides in an educational institution to assist in its administration, pursue his own further studies, or gain practical experience

resident buyer *n* [¹*resident*] **:** a market representative located in a central market area and acting as buyer and consultant to one or more retailers in a line (as women's clothing) subject to much variation and rapid change

resident commissioner *n* **1 :** a representative of a dependency in the U.S. House of Representatives having the right to speak but not to vote **2 :** an administrator in a colony or possession who is the resident representative of the British government

res·i·dent·er \ˈreza,dentə(r), ˌ≈≈ˈ≈≈\ *n* -S [²*resident* + *-er*] *chiefly dial* **:** RESIDENT, INHABITANT

resident-general \ˌ≈(≈)(,)≈ˈ≈(≈)≈\ *n, pl* **residents-general** *or* **resident-generals** [F *résident général*, fr. *résident* resident (fr. L *resident-, residens*) + *général* general, fr. L *generalis*] **:** a political resident of high rank; *specif* **:** one serving as the principal administrative officer in a French North African territory

res·i·den·tial \ˌrezəˈdenchəl *sometimes* (ˈ)rezˈd-\ *adj* [fr. ¹*residence*, after such pairs as E *essence: essential*] **1 a :** used, serving, or designed as a residence or for occupation by residents ⟨a ~ hotel⟩ **b** (1) **:** providing and administering living accommodations for students ⟨a ~ college⟩ (2) **:** requiring or involving attendance of classes on a campus ⟨~ study⟩ ⟨a ~ course⟩ **2 :** adapted or restricted to or occupied by residences ⟨a ~ quarter⟩ **3 :** of, relating to, or connected with residence or residences ⟨~ trade⟩ ⟨a ~ zone⟩ ⟨~ construction⟩ — **res·i·den·ti·al·i·ty** \ˌrezə,dencheˈaləd·ē, -lətē, -i\ *n* -ES — **res·i·den·tial·ly** \ˌrezəˈdench(ə)lē, -li *sometimes* (ˈ)rezˈd-\ *adv*

¹res·i·den·ti·ary \ˌrezəˈdenchē,erē, -chərē\ *n* -ES [ML *residentiarius*, fr. *residentia* residence + *-arius* -ary] **1 :** an ecclesiastic who is or who is obliged to be in residence for a certain time **2 :** one who is resident **:** RESIDENT

²residentiary \"\ *adj* [ML *residentiarius*, fr. *residentia* residence + *-arius* -ary] **1 :** having residence **:** RESIDING, RESIDENT ⟨a ~ guardian⟩; *specif* **:** under ecclesiastical obligation to be in residence for a certain time (as at a cathedral) ⟨a canon ~⟩ **2 :** RESIDENTIAL

res·i·den·ti·ary·ship \-,ship\ *n* [¹*residentiary* + *-ship*] **:** the position or state of an ecclesiastical residentiary

res·i·dent·ship *pronunc at* ¹RESIDENT +,ship\ *n* [²*resident* + *-ship*] **:** the position or state of a resident

re·sid·er \rəˈzīdə(r), rēˈz-\ *n* -S [¹*reside* + *-er*] **:** one that resides **:** RESIDENT

resides *pres 3d sing of* RESIDE

residing *pres part of* RESIDE

residua *pl of* RESIDUUM

¹re·sid·u·al \rəˈzij(ə)wəl, rēˈz-, -jəl\ *adj* [L *residuum* residue + E *-al*] **1 :** of, relating to, or constituting a residue **:** remaining after a part is taken **:** left as a residuum **2 :** relating to or like a residue or remainder ⟨~ analysis⟩ ⟨a ~ quantity⟩ **3 :** remaining in a body cavity after maximum normal expulsion has occurred ⟨~ urine⟩ — compare RESIDUAL AIR **4 a :** leaving a residue that remains effective for some time after application ⟨~ insecticides⟩ **b :** of or relating to a residual insecticide ⟨a ~ spray⟩

²residual \"\ *n* -S **:** REMAINDER, RESIDUUM: as **a** (1) **:** a binomial expression with one negative term (2) **:** the difference of the results obtained by observation and by computation from a formula (3) **:** the difference between the mean of several observations and any one of them **b :** a product or substance remaining over (as at the end of a chemical process, distillation, extraction) ⟨the various ~*s* of metabolic activity⟩ **c** (1) **:** an internal aftereffect of experience or activity that influences later behavior **:** a memory trace ⟨the ~*s* of past training⟩ (2) **:** the disability (as a scar or a limp) remaining after satisfactory recovery from a disease or operation

residual affinity *n* [¹*residual*] **:** RESIDUAL VALENCE

residual air *n* **:** the volume of air still remaining in the lungs after the most forcible expiration possible and amounting usu. to 60 to 100 cubic inches — compare SUPPLEMENTAL AIR

residual charge *n* **:** a comparatively feeble charge that appears on a condenser whose dielectric is not homogeneous a short time after being discharged — compare ABSORPTION 3

residual claimant theory *n* **:** a theory in economics: wages are a residual after the distributive shares of other factors of production are determined

residual dextrin *n* **:** LIMIT DEXTRIN
residual error *n* **:** the difference between a group of values observed and their arithmetical mean
residual estate *n* **:** RESIDUARY ESTATE
re·sid·u·al·ly \-əlē, -əli\ *adv* [¹*residual* + *-ly*] **:** as a residue **:** in a residual manner
residual magnetism *or* **residual induction** *n* **:** magnetization remaining in a magnetized body no longer under external magnetic influence **:** the magnetism of a permanent magnet
residual phenomena *n pl* **:** the phenomena that remain to be explained after the effects of known causes are subtracted — compare METHOD OF RESIDUES
residual placer *n* **:** a placer deposit consisting of decomposed rock or residual portions of such rock and lying at the locality of origin
residual power *n* **:** power held to remain at the disposal of a governmental authority (as an executive or the central government of a federation) after an enumeration or delegation of specified powers to other authorities ⟨the *residual power* of the Dominion could not be employed . . . except in the case of extraordinary national emergency —Alexander Brady⟩ — compare RESERVED POWER
residual product *n* **:** BY-PRODUCT ⟨coke and coal tar from gasworks are *residual products*⟩
residual ray *n* **:** any of the infrared rays that remain in a beam of thermal radiation after a series of reflections from a crystal
residual soil *n* **:** soil formed in situ by rock decay and left as a residue after the leaching out of the more soluble products
residual sound *n* **:** echoing sound audible in a place after the source has become silent **:** REVERBERATION
residual stress *n* **:** a stress that exists within a solid body though no external stress-producing forces are acting and that is due to some inequality of previous treatment of adjacent parts ⟨poorly annealed glass may be highly unstable because of *residual stresses* and shatter from a slight shock⟩ — compare RUPERT'S DROP
residual valence *n* **:** unemployed valence; *esp* **:** combining power that is not utilized when the elements combine to form simple molecules and so leads to such phenomena as association and hydration — compare HYDROGEN BOND
¹**re·sid·u·ary** \rə'zijə,werē, rē'z-, -jər|, |i\ *adj* [L *residuum* residue + E *-ary*] **:** of, relating to, consisting of, or constituting a residue, residuum, or remainder ⟨the ~ part of an estate⟩
²**residuary** \"\ *n* -ES **:** a residuary legatee
residuary clause *n* [¹*residuary*] **:** the part of a testator's will in which the residue of his estate is disposed of to one or more persons — compare BEQUEATH 1a
residuary estate *n* **:** the residue of a testator's estate
residuary legacy *n* **:** a legacy that includes all of a testator's estate not specifically distributed in other legacies or in charges against the estate
residuary legatee *n* **:** a legatee inheriting a testator's residuary estate
res·i·due \'rezə,d(y)ü\ *n* -S [ME, fr. MF *residu*, fr. L *residuum*, fr. neut. of *residuus* left over, remaining, fr. *residēre* to sit back, remain — more at RESIDE] **:** something that remains after a part is taken, separated, removed, or designated **:** REMNANT, REMAINDER, REST: as **a :** the part of a testator's estate or of any part thereof remaining after the satisfaction of all debts, charges of administration, statutory allowances for support of a widow and children, and previous devises and bequests **b** *obs* **:** REMAINDER 2b **c :** the part of a molecule that remains after the removal of a portion of its constituents **:** an atom or group regarded as a portion of a molecule **:** UNIT ⟨fatty acid ~*s* in fats⟩ ⟨like starch they [glycogens] are based upon maltose ~*s*, and like amylopectin . . . the branches contain less than half as many maltose units —J.W.McBain⟩ — compare RADICAL **d :** GRUFFS
re·sid·u·ous \rə'zij(ə)wəs, rē'z-\ *adj* [L *residuus* — more at RESIDUE] *archaic* **:** REMAINING, RESIDUAL
re·sid·u·um \-j(ə)wəm\ *n, pl* **resid·ua** \-wə\ *also* **residuums** [L — more at RESIDUE] **:** something that remains behind (as after charges are met or a process completed): as **a :** RESIDUE a **b :** a residual product (as from the distillation of crude petroleum) **:** DEPOSIT, SEDIMENT **c :** RESIDUAL c
re·sign \rə'zīn, rē'z-\ *vb* -ED/-ING/-S [ME *resignen*, fr. MF *resigner*, fr. L *resignare* to unseal, cancel, resign, fr. *re-* + *signare* to mark, sign, seal — more at SIGN] *vt* **1** *obs* **:** to refrain from **:** give over or desist from **2 :** to give up deliberately **:** renounce by a considered or formal act **:** RELINQUISH ⟨the publisher did not hesitate to ~ all claims to the copyright on these terms —Jane Austen⟩ ⟨~*ing* all his rights in the property⟩ ⟨tempted to ~ the search —*Times Lit. Supp.*⟩ **3 a :** to give over or consign (as to the care or possession of another) **:** let go into another's possession or control, often submissively or confidingly **:** RELEGATE, COMMIT ⟨she loves me all that she can, and her ways to my ways ~ —Edna S.V. Millay⟩ ⟨~*ed* the child to the care of an aunt⟩ **b :** to give (oneself) over unresistingly, typically to effects of an indicated dominance, control, or influence, with stoic acceptance, calm resignation, or confidence ⟨we must ~ ourselves to such epidemics of human pugnacity and egotism —G.B.Shaw⟩ ⟨had ~*ed* himself to playing a minor role⟩ ~ *vi* **1 a :** to give up, relinquish, or forswear one's office, rank, membership, post, or charge esp. formally and definitely — often used with *from* ⟨~*ed* from the club⟩ or with *as* ⟨~ as chairman⟩ **b** *obs* **:** ABDICATE **2 :** to accept something as inevitable **:** SUBMIT — usu. used with *to* ⟨we must ~ to our fate⟩ **syn** see RELINQUISH
re–sign \(')rē¦sīn\ *vt* [*re-* + *sign*] **:** to sign again **:** affix one's signature to a second time
re·sig·na·tary \rə'zignə,terē\ *n* -ES [F *résignataire*, fr. L *resignatus* + F *-aire* -ary] **:** one in whose favor a resignation is made
res·ig·na·tion \,rezəg'nāshən, |ēg- *sometimes* -es|\ *n* -S [ME, fr. MF, fr. ML *resignation-, resignatio*, fr. L *resignatus* (past part. of *resignare* to resign) + *-ion-, -io* -ion] **1 a :** the act or fact of resigning something (as a claim, possession, office) **:** SURRENDER **b :** a formal notification of relinquishment (as of an office or position) ⟨wrote out his ~ the same day⟩ **2 :** the quality or state of being resigned **:** SUBMISSION, ACQUIESCENCE; *esp* **:** quiet and patient submissiveness (as to the rule or will of another) **3 :** the formal return by a vassal of a fee to the superior from whom it was held under former Scots law **syn** see PATIENCE
resignation bond *n* **:** a bond given by a beneficed clergyman of the Church of England to secure resignation of his benefice on some contingency
res·ig·na·tion·ism \-shə,nizəm\ *n* -S [*resignation* + *-ism*] **:** resignation as a mood, pose, or form of emotional indulgence
res·ig·na·tion·ist \-sh(ə)nəst\ *n* -S [*resignation* + *-ist*] **:** a person (as a writer) devoted to or exhibiting resignationism
re·signed \rə'zīnd, rē'z-\ *adj* [fr. past part. of *resign*] **1 a :** given up **:** SURRENDERED ⟨a ~ post⟩ **b :** having resigned from office ⟨the ~ vice president⟩ **2 :** being resigned to something **:** characterized by resignation **:** SUBMISSIVE, ACQUIESCENT — **re·sign·ed·ly** \-nədlē, -li\ *adv* — **re·sign·ed·ness** \-nədnəs\ *n* -ES
re·sign·ee \rə'zī¦nē, rē¦z-\ *n* -S [*resign* + *-ee*] **1 :** one to whom or in whose favor something is resigned **2 :** a person who resigns from something (as a job)
re·sign·er \-'zīnə(r)\ *n* -S [*resign* + *-er*] **:** one that resigns; *specif* **:** one that resigns a fee under Scots law — compare RESIGNATION 3
re·sign·ful \-nfəl\ *adj* [*resign* + *-ful*] **:** full of or expressive of resignation
re·sign·ment \-nmənt\ *n* -S [ME *resignement*, fr. *resignen* to resign + *-ment*] **:** the act of resigning **:** RESIGNATION
resigns *pres 3d sing of* RESIGN
re·sile \rə'zīl, rē'z-, *esp before pause or consonant* -īəl\ *vi* -ED/-ING/-S [MF & LL; MF *resilir* to withdraw from an agreement, fr. LL *resilire* to rebound, withdraw, fr. L to jump back, rebound — more at RESILIENT] **:** to draw back **:** RECOIL, RETRACT, RETREAT, RECEDE; *esp* **:** to return to a prior or original position ⟨~ from an agreement⟩ ⟨give a tube time to ~ after being stretched⟩ **syn** see REBOUND
resilia *pl of* RESILIUM
re·sil·i·ate \-zilē,āt\ *vt* -ED/-ING/-S [F *résilier* (alter. of MF *resilir* to withdraw from an agreement) + E *-ate* — more at RESILE] **:** CANCEL
re·sil·ience \rə'zilyən(t)s, -lēən-\ *n* -S [L *resilire* to rebound + E *-ence*] **1 a :** an act of springing back **:** REBOUND, RECOIL, ELASTICITY **b :** capability of a strained body to recover its size and shape after deformation, esp. when the strain is caused by compressive stresses — called also *elastic resilience* **2 :** the recoverable potential energy of an elastic solid body or structure due to its having been subjected to stress not exceeding the elastic limit
re·sil·ien·cy \-nsē,-nsi\ *n* -ES [*resilient* + *-cy*] **:** the property of being resilient **:** RESILIENCE 1
re·sil·ient \-nt\ *adj* [L *resilient-, resiliens*, pres. part. of *resilire* to jump back, rebound, fr. *re-* + *salire* to jump, leap — more at SALLY] **:** returning freely to a previous position, shape, or condition: as **a :** moving swiftly back **:** RECOILING **b :** capable of withstanding shock without permanent deformation or rupture ⟨~ bodies⟩ **c :** SPRINGY ⟨a ~ turf⟩ **d :** looking backward **e :** tending to regain strength or high spirits after weakness or depression **:** BUOYANT **syn** see ELASTIC, FLEXIBLE
resilient escapement *n* **:** a lever escapement in a timepiece having yielding banking pins designed to resist sudden shock
re·sil·ient·ly *adv* **:** in a resilient manner **:** with resilience
re·sil·i·fer \-ləfə(r)\ *n* -S [NL *resilium* + E *-fer*] **:** a spoon-shaped process on the hinge plate of some bivalve mollusks (as members of the genus *Mactra*) supporting the resilium
re·sil·i·om·e·ter \-,zilē'ämәd·ə(r)\ *n* [*resilience* + *-o-* + *-meter*] **:** an instrument for testing resilience
resilition *n* -S [fr. *resilient*, after such pairs as E *ebullient: ebullition*] *obs* **:** RESILIENCE
re·sil·i·um \rə'zilēəm, rē'z-\ *n, pl* **resil·ia** \-lēə\ [NL, fr. L *resilire* to rebound — more at RESILIENT] **:** the internal part of the hinge ligament of a bivalve shell resembling in consistency and often described as cartilage but being in fact chitinous
re·silver \(')rē+\ *vt* [*re-* + *silver*] **:** to silver again or anew ⟨~ an old mirror⟩
¹**res·in** \'rez°n\ *n* -S [ME, fr. MF *resine*, fr. L *resina*, fr. Gk *rhētinē* resin of the pine] **1 a :** any of various hard brittle solid to soft semisolid amorphous fusible flammable substances (as amber, copals, dammars, mastic, guaiacum) that are usu. transparent or translucent and yellowish to brown in color with a characteristic luster, that are formed esp. in plant secretions and are obtained as exudates of recent or fossil origin (as from tropical trees or pine or fir trees) or as extracts of plants, that contain usu. resin acids and their esters and are soluble in ether and other organic solvents but not in water, that are electrical nonconductors, and that are used chiefly in varnishes, printing inks, plastics, and sizes, in medicine, and as incense ⟨the spirit soluble ~*s* are in general of the soft variety, while the oil soluble are usually hard —*Natural Resins Handbook*⟩ — called also *natural resin;* compare BALSAM, FOSSIL RESIN, GUM, GUM RESIN, LAC, MINERAL RESIN, OLEORESIN, PITCH **b :** ROSIN **c :** a solid pharmaceutical preparation consisting chiefly of the resinous principles of a drug or drugs usu. extracted by solvents (as by alcohol followed by precipitation with water) or by driving off the essential oil from an oleoresin ⟨~ of jalap⟩ ⟨~ of podophyllum⟩ **2 a :** any of a large class of synthetic products (as alkyd resins or phenolic resins) usu. of high molecular weight that have some of the physical properties of natural resins but typically are very different chemically, that may be thermoplastic or thermosetting, that are made by polymerization or condensation, and that are used chiefly as plastics or the essential ingredients of plastics, in varnishes and other coatings, in adhesives, and in ion exchange ⟨when the ~ itself is capable of being shaped into a finished article without a plasticizer, as polystyrene, the terms resin and plastic are interchangeable for that material —G.M.Kline⟩ ⟨in industrial terminology the unfabricated material is sometimes called a ~ and the fabricated article a plastic —L.F. & Mary Fieser⟩ — called also *synthetic resin;* compare ION-EXCHANGE RESIN, SYNTHETIC RUBBER **b :** any of various resinlike products made from a natural resin (as rosin) or a natural high polymer (as cellulose or rubber) by chemical modification
²**resin** \"\ *vt* -ED/-ING/-S **:** to treat (as by rubbing or coating) with resin **:** apply resin to
re·si·na \rə'zīnə\ *n* -S [L — more at RESIN] **:** RESIN 1a
res·in·a·ceous \¦rez°n¦āshəs\ *adj* [L *resinaceus*, fr. *resina* resin + *-aceus* -aceous] **:** RESINIFEROUS, RESINOUS
resin acid *n* **:** any of the acids (as abietic acid or pimaric acid) found free or in the form of esters in rosin, other natural resins, and tall oil and used chiefly in the form of salts (as sodium resinate or metallic soaps)
resin alcohol *n* **:** any of the alcohols found in the form of esters in natural resins
¹**res·in·ate** \'rez(ə)nət, -z°n,āt\ *n* -S [*resin* + *-ate*, n. suffix] **:** a salt or ester of a resin acid, of a mixture of such acids, or of rosin
²**res·in·ate** \-z°n,āt\ *vt* -ED/-ING/-S [*resin* + *-ate*, v. suffix] **:** to impregnate or flavor with resin
resinback \'=,=\ *n* **:** a circus horse used in bareback riding, vaulting, and tumbling acts
resin bee *n* **:** a solitary bee (genus *Anthidium*) that uses resin as cement in constructing its nest
resinbush \'=,=\ *n* **1 :** a low southern African shrub (*Euryops athanasiae*) of the family Compositae having smooth pinnately parted leaves and abounding in resin **2 :** a much-branched tropical African shrub (*Heeria insignis*) of the family Anacardiaceae having narrowly oblong leaves usu. in groups of three and with a silvery lower surface, small whitish flowers, black oval fruit, and very resinous sap
resin canal *or* **resin duct** *n* **:** a tubular intercellular space in gymnosperms and some angiosperms that occurs either normally or in response to injury, is formed either by dissolution of cells or by splitting of the walls of adjacent layers of cells, and is lined with epithelial cells which secrete resin
resin cell *n* **:** a plant cell that secretes or stores resin
resin cerate *n* **:** BASILICON OINTMENT 2
res in cor·po·ra·les \'rā,sin,kȯ(r)pə'rä,lās, 'rē,zin,kȯ(r)pə'rā(,)lēz\ *n pl* [L] **:** incorporeal things — used esp. in Roman and civil law
resin emulsion paint *n* **:** a paint either ready-mixed or in paste form having as its binder or nonvolatile vehicle an emulsion of synthetic and generally alkyd resin
res·in·er \'rez°nə(r)\ *n* -S [²*resin* + *-er*] **1 :** one that resins something **2** [¹*resin* + *-er*] **:** one that collects resin from trees
re·sing \(')rē+\ *vt* [*re-* + *sing*] **:** to sing again or anew
resin gnat *or* **resin midge** *n* [¹*resin*] **:** any of various small two-winged flies (genus *Retinodiplosis*) with larvae that injure pine trees by causing an exudation of resin in which they live
res·in·ic \(')re¦zinik\ *adj* [¹*resin* + *-ic*] **:** of, relating to, or obtained from resin ⟨~ acids⟩
res·in·if·er·ous \¦rez°n¦if(ə)rəs\ *adj* [¹*resin* + *-iferous*] **:** secreting or bearing resin ⟨~ vessels⟩
re·sin·i·fi·ca·tion \re,zinəfə'kāshən\ *n* -S [F *résinification*, fr. *résinifier* to resinify, after such pairs as F *gratifier* to gratify: *gratification*] **:** the action or process of resinifying ⟨~ takes place in the stumps of the fallen trees —E.L.Kropa⟩
res·in·i·fy \re'zinə,fī\ *vb* -ED/-ING/-ES [F *résinifier*, fr. *résine* resin + *-ifier* -ify] *vt* **:** to convert into or treat with resin ~ *vi* **1 :** to change into or become resin **2 :** to form a gummy material — used of an oil evaporating to such a residue
resining *pres part of* RESIN
res·in·ize \'rez°n,īz\ *vt* -ED/-ING/-S [¹*resin* + *-ize*] **:** to treat with resin **:** apply resin to
resinlike \'=,=\ *adj* [¹*resin* + *like*] **:** resembling resin esp. in properties or texture
resino- *comb form* [L *resina* resin] **1 :** resin ⟨*resinography*⟩ ⟨*resinogenous*⟩ **2 :** resinous and ⟨*resinoextractive*⟩ ⟨*resinovitreous*⟩
res·in·og·e·nous \¦rez°n¦äjənəs\ *adj* [*resino-* + *-genous*] **:** RESINIFEROUS
res·in·og·ra·phy \,rez°n'ägrəfē\ *n* -ES [*resino-* + *-graphy*] **:** the micrography of polished or etched surfaces of resins or plastics
¹**res·in·oid** \'rez°n,ȯid\ *adj* [¹*resin* + *-oid*] **:** somewhat like resin **:** more or less resinous
²**resinoid** \"\ *n* -S **1 :** a resinoid substance; *esp* **:** a thermosetting synthetic resin either before or after curing ⟨~ bonds for abrasives⟩ **2** *pharmacy* **a :** any of a class of resinlike preparations introduced by the eclectics and made by pouring a concentrated alcoholic extract of a drug into cold water and separating and drying the precipitate formed **b :** GUM RESIN **c :** any of various flower essences used in the perfume industry
resin oil *n* **:** an oil distilled from resin; *esp* **:** ROSIN OIL
res·in·ol \'rez°n,ȯl, -,ōl\ *n* -S [ISV ¹*resin* + *-ol*] **:** any of various alcohols found as esters in resins
resin opal *n* **:** opal with a resinous appearance
res·in·osis \,rez°n'ōsəs\ *n, pl* **resino·ses** \-ō,sēz\ [NL, fr. L *resina* resin + NL *-osis*] **:** an excessive outflow of resin from coniferous plants usu. resulting from injury or disease
res·in·ous \'rez(°)nəs\ *adj* [L *resinosus*, fr. *resina* resin + *-osus* -ous] **1 :** of, relating to, containing, like, or obtained from resin ⟨~ exudates⟩ ⟨~ products⟩ **2 :** of or relating to a luster of certain minerals and rocks (as sphalerite, pitchstone) that on fractured surfaces have the appearance of resin
res·in·ous·ly *adv* **:** in a resinous manner **:** so as to be resinous
res·in·ous·ness *n* -ES **:** the quality or state of being resinous
resin plant *n* **:** INCIENSO
resins *pl of* RESIN, *pres 3d sing of* RESIN
resin soap *n* **1 :** soap made from resin as well as fat and containing sodium or potassium resinates; *esp* **:** ROSIN SOAP **2 :** a soapy substance formed from a resin (as rosin) and alkali, composed essentially of sodium or potassium resinates, and used esp. in sizing paper or as an insecticide
resin spirit *n* **:** ROSIN SPIRIT
res in·tegra \'rā'sintəgrə, ,rās°n'tegrə, rē'zi-, ,rēz°n-\ *n* [L, lit., thing untouched] **:** a case or a question that has not been examined or passed upon — used chiefly in law and diplomacy
res in·ter ali·os ac·ta \'rā,sintə,rälē,ō'saktə\ *n* [LL, lit., thing done among others] **:** the act of a person who is a stranger to the matter under adjudication
resinweed \'=,=\ *n* [¹*resin* + *weed*] **:** ROSINWEED
res·iny \'rez(°)nē, -ni\ *adj* [*resin* + *-y*] **:** RESINOUS 1
res·i·pis·cence \,resə'pis°n(t)s\ *n* -S [LL *resipiscentia*, fr. L *resipiscent-, resipiscens* (pres. part. of *resipiscere* to recover one's senses, fr. *re-* + *-spiscere*, fr. *sapere* to taste, have sense, be wise) + *-ia* -y — more at SAGE] **:** change of mind or heart **:** REFORMATION; *often* **:** return to a sane, sound, or correct view or position
res ip·sa lo·qui·tur \'rā,sipsə'lōkwə,tù(ə)r\ *n* [L, the thing speaks for itself] **:** a case in which mere proof that an accident took place is sufficient under the circumstances to warrant an inference that it was caused by defendant's negligence unless otherwise explained
¹**re·sist** \rə'zist, rē'z-\ *vb* -ED/-ING/-S [ME *resisten*, fr. MF or L; MF *resister*, fr. L *resistere*, fr. *re-* + *sistere* to take a stand, cause to stand; akin to L *stare* to stand — more at STAND] *vt* **1 :** to withstand the force or the effect of **:** be able to repel or ward off ⟨armor that ~*s* all weapons⟩ ⟨a constitution that ~*s* disease⟩ ⟨metal that ~*s* acid⟩ **2 :** to exert oneself to counteract or defeat **:** strive against **:** OPPOSE ⟨~ the enemy valiantly⟩ ⟨~*ing* arrest⟩ ⟨~*ed* temptation⟩ ⟨~ the lowering of moral standards⟩ **3** *obs* **:** to be distasteful to ~ *vi* **:** to exert force in opposition ⟨it can overrule him, yes, but he must somehow ~ —H.D.Thoreau⟩ **syn** see CONTEST
²**resist** \"\ *n* -S **1** *obs* **:** RESISTANCE **2 :** something (as a coating) that resists or prevents a particular action: as **a :** a substance (as a paste) used in textile printing to prevent either by mechanical or chemical means or both the fixing of a color or mordant on parts of the fabric ⟨additions of inert substances to chemical ~*s* . . . are often useful —Ellis Clayton⟩ **b :** a substance applied to a surface to render it nonconducting during electroplating and thus prevent deposition **c :** a protective acid-proof coating on the printing area of a photo-engraving undergoing etching — called also *acid resist*
³**resist** \"\ *adj* [²*resist*] **:** decorated by or involving decoration by a process in which blank areas of design are made by coating ceramic materials with washable resist before applying glaze, luster, or other finish ⟨a pink and bronze ~ jug⟩ ⟨a ~ technique⟩
re·sist·ance \rə'zistən(t)s, rē'z-\ *n* -S [ME, fr. MF *resistence* resistance, fr. LL *resistentia*, fr. L *resistent-, resistens*, (pres. part. of *resistere* to resist) + *-ia* -y] **1 :** the act or an instance of resisting **:** passive or active opposition; *also* **:** a means or method of resisting ⟨unfold to us some warlike ~ —Shak.⟩ **2 :** power or capacity to resist; *esp* **:** the inherent ability of an animal or plant body to resist untoward circumstances (as disease, toxic agents, or infection) — compare IMMUNITY, SUSCEPTIBILITY **3 :** an opposing force **:** a force tending to prevent motion or other action **:** a retarding force ⟨the ~ of the air to a body passing through it⟩ ⟨good ~ to wear⟩ ⟨grade ~ of a railroad⟩ **4 a :** the property of a body whereby it opposes and limits the passage through it of a steady electric current — see OHM'S LAW; compare ACOUSTIC RESISTANCE **b :** a source of resistance; *specif* **:** RESISTOR **5 :** the retardation of a boat passing through the water due to (1) the friction between its wetted surface and the water, (2) the making of eddies or dead water, or (3) the formation of waves — called also respectively (1) *frictional resistance, skin resistance*, (2) *eddy resistance*, (3) *wave resistance* **6 :** a mechanism of ego defense wherein a psychoanalysis patient rejects, denies, or otherwise opposes therapeutic efforts by the analyst — compare MECHANISM OF DEFENSE **7** *often cap* **:** an organized underground movement of a conquered country made up of groups of fighters engaged in sabotage and secret operations to thwart, waylay, and otherwise wear down occupation forces and often also in punishing collaborators among fellow countrymen — often used with *the* ⟨a former member of the French ~⟩
resistance box *n* **:** an instrument for measuring and comparing electrical resistances
resistance coil *n* **:** a coil of wire introduced into an electrical circuit to provide resistance
resistance derivatives *n pl* **:** quantities expressing the variation of the forces and moments on aircraft due to disturbance of steady motion
resistance drop *n* **:** the voltage drop in an electrical circuit due to the current traversing a nonreactive resistor — see IMPEDANCE DROP, REACTANCE DROP
resistance furnace *n* **:** an electric furnace in which heat is obtained from the energy loss of a resistor
resistance heating *n* **:** heating by means of energy produced by the passing of electric current through resistance units
resistance point *n* **:** a point at which a trend meets with opposing or nullifying forces; *esp* **:** the price at which a security on a declining market tends to stabilize or reverse its downward trend
resistance thermometer *n* **:** a thermometer utilizing a wire as the thermoelectric element and indicating variations in temperature by corresponding changes of the electrical resistance of the wire
resistance welding *n* **:** a form of electric pressure welding in which the necessary heat is produced by a flow of current through the parts to be welded and sufficient pressure to make the weld is applied simultaneously with the flow of current — compare BUTT WELDING, PERCUSSIVE WELDING, SEAM WELDING, SPOT WELDING
¹**re·sist·ant** *also* **re·sist·ent** \-stənt\ *adj* [*resistant* fr. MF *resistent, resistant*, fr. L *resistent-, resistens*, pres. part. of *resistere* to resist; *resistent* fr. L *resistent-, resistens*] **:** making or having powers of resistance **:** RESISTING ⟨a constitution ~ to disease⟩ — often used in combination ⟨corrosion-*resistant* materials⟩
²**resistant** \"\ *n* -S **:** one that resists **:** RESISTER
re·sist·ant·ly *adv* **:** in a resistant manner **:** so as to resist
resist–dye *vt* [²*resist*] **1 :** to print (a fabric) by repeatedly putting a resist on different parts of the pattern and placing the fabric in successive dye baths — compare BATIK **2 :** to cross-dye (fabric) by weaving with an undyed yarn and a dyed yarn that will resist further dyeing of the completed fabric
resisted *past of* RESIST
re·sist·er \-stə(r)\ *n* -S [ME, fr. *resisten* to resist + *-er*] **:** one that resists
re·sist·ful \-stfəl\ *adj* [*resist* + *-ful*] **:** inclined to resistance **:** making much resistance
re·sist·ibil·i·ty \-,zistə'biləd·ē\ *n* -ES **1 :** the quality or state of being resistible ⟨the ~ of divine grace⟩ **2 :** ability to resist **:** power of resistance ⟨the ~ of granite to erosion⟩
re·sist·ible \-'zistəbəl\ *adj* [¹*resist* + *-ible*] **:** capable of being resisted, withstood, opposed, or frustrated ⟨a ~ attack⟩ ⟨such ~ temptations⟩ — **re·sist·ible·ness** \-bəlnəs\ *n* -ES — **re·sist·ibly** \-blē,-bli\ *adv*
resisting *pres part of* RESIST
re·sist·ing·ly *adv* **:** in a resisting manner **:** so as to resist
re·sist·ive \-stiv\ *adj* [*resist* + *-ive*] **:** tending to resist **:** dis-

posed to resistance : RESISTANT ⟨fire-*resistive* materials⟩; *esp* : exhibiting or relating to electrical resistance — **re·sist·ive·ly** \-təvlē\ *adv* — **re·sist·ive·ness** \-tivnəs\ *n* -ES

re·sis·tiv·i·ty \rə,zi'stivəd·ē, (,)rē,z-\ *n* -ES [*resistive* + *-ity*] **1** : capacity for resisting : RESISTANCE ⟨high chemical ~⟩ **2 a** : a characteristic of a given substance upon which depends the electrical resistance of a body of that substance **b** : the longitudinal electrical resistance of a uniform rod of unit length and unit cross-sectional area — called also *specific resistance*

re·sist·less \-'zistləs\ *adj* [ˡ*resist* + *-less*] **1** : incapable of being resisted **2** : having no power to resist : making no opposition — **re·sist·less·ly** *adv* — **re·sist·less·ness** *n* -ES

re·sis·tor \-istə(r)\ *n* -S [*resist* + *-or*] : a device possessing electrical resistance used in an electric circuit for protection, operation, or current control

resist printing *n* [²*resist*] : a method of printing textiles by roller printing a pattern in resist paste on a white fabric, placing the fabric in a dye bath, and subsequently removing the resist to leave a white pattern on a colored ground

resists *pres 3d sing of* RESIST, *pl of* RESIST

res·ite \'re,zīt\ *n* -S [ISV ˡ*resin* + *-ite*; prob. orig. formed as G *resit*] : an infusible insoluble resin formed as the final cured stage in the alkaline condensation of a phenol and an aldehyde to a phenolic resin — called also *C-stage resin;* compare RESITOL, RESOL

re-site \(')rē+\ *vt* [*re-* + *site*] : to place on another site

res·i·tol \'rezə,tȯl, -tōl\ *n* -S [prob. fr. ˡ*resite* + *resol*] : a thermoplastic resin that is insoluble in alkali, that is formed as the second resin stage in the alkaline condensation of a phenol and an aldehyde to a phenolic resin, and that is used chiefly in molding powders and as an adhesive for wood — called also *B-stage resin;* compare RESITE, RESOL

re·sitting \(')rē+\ *n* [*re-* + *sitting*] : a sitting (as of a legislature) for a second time : another sitting

re·size \(')rē+\ *vt* [*re-* + *size*] : to shape again to size : bring again to a correct size after deformation ⟨~ a cartridge shell by driving it with a mallet into a hardened steel die⟩

re·sizer \"+\ *n* -S [*resize* + *-er*] : one that resizes: as **a** : a die for resizing shells **b** : a die through which a bullet purposely made a trifle larger than standard size is forced to bring it to a correct final shape and size

res ju·di·ca·ta \'rās,yüdə'kād·ə, 'rēz,jüdə'kād·ə\ *n* [L] : a thing or matter that has been finally decided on its merits (as between the parties) by a court having jurisdiction of the subject of the litigation and of the defendant if the judgment is a personal one against him and that cannot be litigated again between the same parties — called also *former adjudication*

re·slant \(')rē+\ *vt* [*re-* + *slant*] : to slant again or anew; *specif* : to orient in accord with a new outlook ⟨the writers who sat down to ~ Czechoslovakia's schoolbooks —*Time*⟩

res man·ci·pi \(')rā'smäŋkə,pē, (')rēz'man(t)sə,pī\ *n pl* [L, lit., things of mancipium] : property subject under Roman law to transfer by the formal ceremony of mancipation

res mo·bi·les \-'smōbə,lās, -z'mōbə,lēz\ *n pl* [L] *civil law* : movable things

re·smooth \(')rē¦smüth\ *vt* [*re-* + *smooth*] : to make smooth anew

res·na·tron \'reznə-,trän\ *n* -S [*resonator* + *-tron*] : a high-power wide-frequency electron tube used esp. in World War II to jam enemy radar

res nec man·ci·pi \'rā,snek'mäŋkə,pē, 'rēz,nek'man(t)sə,pī\ *n pl* [L, lit., things not of mancipium] : things other than res mancipi

res nul·li·us \,rāsnə'lēəs, rā'snůlē-; ,rēznə'līəs, rēz'nəlēəs\ *n* [LL, lit., thing of no one] **1** : a thing belonging to no one whether because never appropriated (as a wild animal) or because abandoned by its owner but acquirable by appropriation **2** : property not subject to private ownership under Roman law

re·socialization \(¦)rē+\ *n* [*re-* + *socialization*] : readjustment of an individual (as a psychotic, a physically handicapped person) to life in society : REHABILITATION

re·sod \(')rē+\ *vt* [*re-* + *sod*] : to cause to become covered anew with sod (as by seeding with grass)

re·soil \"+\ *vt* [*re-* + *soil*] **1** : to make dirty again **2** : to cover anew with soil ⟨~*ing* a terrace⟩

reso·jet engine \'rezō,jet-\ *n* [*resonance* + *jet* + *engine*] : a jet engine consisting essentially of a continuously open air inlet, a diffuser, a combustion chamber, and an exhaust nozzle, having fuel admitted continuously, and having resonance established within the engine so that there is a pulsating thrust produced by the intermittent flow of hot gases

res·ol *or* **res·ole** \'re,zōl, -zōl\ *n* -S [ISV ˡ*resin* + *-ol*; prob. orig. formed as G *resol* (pl. *resole*)] : a fusible resin soluble in alkali and alcohol that is formed as the first resin stage in the alkaline condensation of a phenol and an aldehyde to a phenolic resin, that consists essentially of a mixture of phenol alcohols, and that is used chiefly in laminating and impregnating paper and fabrics — called also *A-stage resin;* compare RESITE, RESITOL

re·sole \(')rē+\ *vt* [*re-* + *sole*] : to put a new sole on (as a shoe)

ˡ**re·sol·u·ble** \rə'zälyəbəl, rē'zäl-, 'rezəl-\ *adj* [LL *resolubilis*, fr. L *resolvere* to resolve + *-bilis* capable of (being acted upon)] : admitting of being resolved

²**re·sol·u·ble** \(')rē¦sälyəbəl\ *adj* [*re-* + *soluble*] : capable of being redissolved

ˡ**res·o·lute** \'rezə,lüt *also* -əl,yü| *sometimes* -zələ|; *usu* |d·+V\ *adj, sometimes* -ER/-EST [L *resolutus*, past part. of *resolvere* to resolve] **1** *obs* : PAID **2** *obs* : DECIDED, POSITIVE **3** : having or characterized by a decided purpose : DETERMINED, RESOLVED ⟨stood ~ against the enemy⟩ ⟨~ for peace⟩; *also* : BOLD, FIRM, STEADY ⟨a ~ man⟩ ⟨this ~ purpose⟩ **syn** see FAITHFUL

²**resolute** \"\ *n* -S [in sense 1 fr. L *resolutum*, neut. of *resolutus*, past part. of *resolvere* to resolve, pay; in sense 2 fr. ˡ*resolute*] **1** *obs* : PAYMENT **2** : one who is resolute or daring

³**res·o·lute** \'rezə,lü| *also* -əl,yü|\ *vi* -ED/-ING/-S [back-formation fr. *resolution*] : to draw up, pass, or express a resolution

res·o·lute·ly \'rezə,lütlē, -tli *also* -əl,yüt- *or* ,==¦== *sometimes* 'rezələt-\ *adv* : in a resolute manner : with resolution

res·o·lute·ness \'==(,)=nəs, ,==¦==\ *n* -ES : the quality or state of being resolute

res·o·lu·tion \,rezə'lüshən *also* -zəl'yü-\ *n* -S [ME, fr. MF or L; MF *resolution*, fr. L *resolution-, resolutio*, fr. *resolutus* (past part. of *resolvere* to resolve) + *-ion-, -io* -ion] **1** : the act or process of reducing to simpler form: as **a** : the act of analyzing or converting a complex notion into simpler ones or into its elements **b** : the act of solving **c** : the act of determining **d** : the passing of a musical voice part from a dissonant to a consonant tone or the progression of a chord from dissonance to consonance — see SUSPENSION illustration **e** : the act of separating a chemical compound into its elements or a mixture into its component parts; *specif* : separation of a racemic compound or mixture into its two components **f** (1) : the division of a prosodic element into its component parts (as the components of a long syllable in ancient Greek and Latin verse into two short syllables) (2) : the substitution in Greek or Latin prosody of two short syllables for a long syllable **g** : the analysis of a vector into two or more vectors of which it is the sum; *esp* : the finding of the components of a vector (as a force) in specified directions **h** : the act, process, or capability of rendering distinguishable the individual parts of an object, closely adjacent optical images (as with a microscope) or sources of light (as with a telescope), nearly identical wavelengths of light (as with a spectrograph), particles of nearly the same energy, particles of nearly the same mass (as with a mass spectrograph), or events occurring at nearly the same time (as with a nuclear radiation detector) **2 a** *archaic* : the dissipation of unhealthy matter (as of humors or a contagium) from the body **b** *archaic* : weakening or relaxation of control of a bodily part **c** : the subsidence of inflammation; *specif* : the solution and enzymic digestion of lung exudates in pneumonia and their absorption by the blood resulting in restoration of a normal aerated condition to the lung — compare CONSOLIDATION, ORGANIZATION **3** : a result of resolution : something that is resolved: as **a** : something separated into its component parts or reduced to a simpler form (as by dissolution or melting); *also* : conversion into liquid **b** : something that is determined upon : settled determination; *also* : firmness or constancy of resolve **c** (1) *archaic* : a decisive or clarifying statement or verdict (2) : a formal expression of opinion, will, or intent by an official body or assembled group ⟨the committee sent a ~ of sympathy⟩; *also* : a declaration submitted to an assembly for adoption — see CONCURRENT RESOLUTION, JOINT RESOLUTION **d** : the consonant tone or consonance in which a musical dissonance is resolved **e** : a product of prosodic resolution ⟨two short syllables forming the ~ of a long⟩ **f** (1) : the precision with which a television picture is or can be reproduced usu. measured in terms of the number of lines that can be distinguished in a picture (2) : the minimum separation at which two targets can be distinguished by radar **4 a** : the quality of mind or spirit admitting or productive of resolution (as of problems) : decision of character : RESOLUTENESS **b** *obs* : firmness in opinion : assured knowledge : CERTAINTY **5** : the point in a play or other work of literature at which the chief dramatic complication is worked out **syn** see COURAGE

re-solution \¦rēsə¦lüshən *also* -səl¦yü-\ *n* [*re-* + *solution*] : the act of solving or dissolving again

res·o·lu·tion·ary \,rezə'lüshə,nerē *also* -zəl'yü-\ *adj* [*resolution* + *-ary*] : involving resolution

res·o·lu·tion·er \-sh(ə)nə(r)\ *n* -S [*resolution* + *-er*] **1** : one that makes a resolution or joins with others in a declaration **2** *usu cap* : one of a party among the Covenanters favoring the resolution of 1650 that all persons not professed enemies to the Covenant or excommunicated should be allowed to serve in the army — compare PROTESTER

res·o·lu·tion·ist \-nəst\ *n* -S [*resolution* + *-ist*] : RESOLUTIONER

ˡ**re·sol·u·tive** \rə'zälyəd·iv, 'rezə,lüd-·\ *adj* [ME, fr. MF *resolutif*, fr. ML *resolutivus*, fr. L *resolutus* (past part. of *resolvere* to resolve) + *-ivus* -ive] **1** : serving to dissolve or relax : designed to dissolve ⟨a ~ medical application⟩ **2** : operating to resolve or annul ⟨a ~ condition in an agreement⟩ **3** : ANALYTICAL, EXPLICATIVE — used chiefly in formal logic

²**resolutive** \"\ *n* -S [ME, fr. MF *resolutif*, fr. *resolutif*, adj.] *archaic* : RESOLVENT

re·sol·u·to·ry \rə'zälyə,tōrē, 'rezələ,tōrē, ¦rezə¦lüd·ərē\ *adj* [LL *resolutorius*, fr. L *resolutus* + *-orius* -ory] **1** *obs* : serving to explain **2** : RESOLUTIVE

resolutory condition *n* : a condition that under civil and Scots law upon fulfillment terminates a contract and entitles the parties to be restored to the status quo

re·solv·abil·i·ty \rə,zälvə'biləd·ē, rē,z-, -zȯlv-, -lətē, -i *also* -zä(ů)v- *or* -zōv-\ *n* : the quality or state of being resolvable

re·solv·able *also* **re·solv·ible** *adj* \-vəbəl\ : capable of being resolved ⟨a ~ quarrel⟩; *esp* : capable of optical resolution ⟨a ~ image⟩ ⟨~ stars⟩ — **re·solv·able·ness** *n* -ES

re·solv·an·cy \vənsē\ *n* -ES [ˡ*resolve* + *-ancy*] : the state of being resolved

ˡ**re·solve** \rə'zälv, rē'z-, -zȯlv *also* -zä(ů)v *or* -zōv\ *vb* [L *resolvere* to unloose, dissolve, break up, pay back, fr. *re-* + *solvere* to loosen, release, pay — more at SOLVE] *vt* **1** *obs* : DISSOLVE, MELT ⟨O, that this too too solid flesh would melt, thaw, and ~ itself into a dew —Shak.⟩ **2** : to separate or break up : change or convert by disintegration : reduce by or as if by analysis — used with *into* or formerly with *in* ⟨the prism *resolved* the light into a play of color⟩ ⟨winter will ~ the sods into mellow loam⟩ ⟨*resolving* the nation into warring factions⟩ ⟨~ the problem into simple elements⟩ **3** : to cause to disintegrate : break into bits or separate into constituent elements ⟨fall plowing allows winter to ~ the clods⟩: as **a** : to perform the operations required and solve (a mathematical equation) **b** : to distinguish between or render independently visible adjacent parts of ⟨~ the lines of a spectrum⟩ ⟨~ a galaxy into its stars and nebulas⟩ **c** : to split up (as a force or velocity) into two or more components esp. in assigned directions : find a component of in a given direction usu. with the assumption of one other component in a direction at right angles ⟨*resolved* force *AB* along *AC*⟩ **d** : to separate (a racemic compound or mixture) into two components — opposed to *racemize* **4 a** : to cause (as inflammation, pain) to dissipate : cause resolution of **b** *obs* (1) : to make weak or slack : RELAX (2) : to cause to become lax (as in conduct) **5 a** *archaic* : to free (as a person) from doubt or uncertainty : make certain or assured : INFORM, CONVINCE **b** : to take away (as a doubt or impediment) : clear up : DISPEL ⟨gradually *resolved* his doubts⟩ **c** : to find an answer to : make clear or certain : SOLVE, UNRIDDLE ⟨~ a problem⟩ **6 a** : to bring oneself or another to (as a course of action) : DECIDE ⟨having *resolved* his fate⟩ — usu. used with a following clause ⟨we *resolved* that we must part⟩ or infinitive ⟨if you ~ to go⟩ **b** : to reach a decision about : SETTLE ⟨determined to ~ all disputed points⟩ **7 a** : to express (as an opinion or determination) by resolution and vote : declare or decide by a formal vote — used with a following clause ⟨the house *resolved* that no money should be appropriated⟩ or infinitive ⟨*resolved* to censure the speaker⟩ **b** : to change or convert (itself) by resolution or formal vote ⟨the house *resolved* itself into a committee⟩ **8** : to make (as one or more voice parts or the total musical harmony) progress from a dissonance into a consonance **9** : to work out the resolution of (as a play) ~ *vi* **1** *archaic* : to become fluid : MELT, DISSOLVE **2** : to become separated into its component parts or elements : DISINTEGRATE; *also* : to become reduced by or as if by dissolving or analysis ⟨physiological processes ultimately ~ into the integration of matter and the dissipation of motion —James Ward⟩ **3** : to undergo resolution — used esp. of a disease or inflammation **4** : to form a purpose or resolution; *esp* : to determine after reflection ⟨~ on a better course of life⟩ **5** *obs* **a** : to become of opinion : become convinced **b** : CONSULT, DELIBERATE **6** *archaic* : to determine to start or leave — used with *for* **7** : to progress from a dissonance to a consonance — used of a voice part or of the total musical harmony **8** : to become void : LAPSE **syn** see ANALYZE, DECIDE, SOLVE

²**resolve** \"\ *n* -S **1** : something that has been resolved : RESOLUTION **2** : resolute quality : fixity of purpose **3** : a legal or official determination; *esp* : a legislative declaration : a formal resolution **4** *obs* : an act of resolving or expounding

re·solv·ed·ly \-vədlē\ *adv* : in a resolved manner : RESOLUTELY

re·solv·ed·ness \-dnəs\ *n* -ES : the quality or state of being resolved

resolved rhyme *n* : rhyme exhibiting resolution

ˡ**re·solv·ent** \-vənt\ *adj* [L *resolvent-, resolvens*, pres. part. of *resolvere* to resolve] : having power to resolve : causing solution : SOLVENT ⟨a ~ drug⟩

²**resolvent** \"\ *n* **1** : an agent that has power to disperse inflammatory or other lesions : something that aids the absorption of effused products **2** : something that can cause solution : SOLVENT **3** : a means of solving something (as a problem)

re·solv·er \-və(r)\ *n* -S [ˡ*resolve* + *-er*] : one that resolves

re·solv·ible \-vəbəl\ *var of* RESOLVABLE

resolving power *n* [fr. gerund of ˡ*resolve*] **1** : the ability of an optical system to form distinguishable images of objects separated by small angular distances **2** : the ability of a photographic film or plate to reproduce the fine detail of an optical image commonly evaluated in lines per millimeter **3** : the ability of observing equipment to give evidence of the existence and nature of celestial objects of very small angular dimensions depending esp. on the wavelength of the received radiation and being least for longest wavelengths

resolving time *n* : the shortest time interval between pulses in a nuclear counter that will permit them to be separately detected — compare DEAD TIME

res·o·nance \'rez(ᵊ)nən(t)s\ *n* -S *often attrib* [ME, fr. L *resonantia* echo, fr. *resonant-, resonans*, pres. part. of *resonare* to echo, resound — more at RESOUND] **1 a** : the quality or state of being resonant **b** (1) : a vibration of large amplitude in a mechanical or electrical system caused by a relatively small periodic stimulus of the same or nearly the same period as the natural vibration period of the system (as when a child in a swing is given pushes with the natural frequency of the swing, when an organ pipe responds to a tuned reed, or when a radio receiving circuit is tuned to a broadcast frequency) (2) : the state of adjustment that produces resonance in a mechanical or electrical system ⟨a violin string in ~ with a vibrating tuning fork⟩ ⟨two circuits in ~ with each other⟩ **2 a** : the intensification and enriching of a musical tone by supplementary vibration that is either sympathetically or mechanically induced **b** : a quality imparted to voiced sounds by the resonance-chamber action of mouth and pharynx configurations and in some cases of the nostrils in addition **3** : the sound elicited on percussion of the chest **4** : the complex of internal bodily processes that occur in emotional states : RAPPORT, EMPATHY **5** : a phenomenon that is shown by a molecule, ion, or radical to which two or more structures differing only in the distribution of electrons can be assigned, that is detected by shortened atomic distances and by lessened heats of hydrogenation or combustion over those expected from comparable structures not exhibiting this phenomenon, and that gives rise to a general stabilization of the structure because of the several orbital paths that the electrons may take among the atoms concerned ⟨~ is usually responsible for the deep color of certain organic compounds —J.A.Leermakers & Arnold Weissberger⟩ — called also *mesomerism;* compare HYPERCONJUGATION, TAUTOMERISM

resonance absorption *n* **1** : the absorption of electromagnetic energy at a frequency such that the photon energy is equal to a quantum excitation energy of the absorbing system **2** : the abnormally strong absorption by atomic nuclei of neutrons having certain definite energies

resonance acceleration *n* : an imparting of high speeds to electric particles by periodically varying the accelerating electric field so as to give a fresh impulse at the beginning of each successive segment of the path — compare CYCLOTRON

resonance band *n* : a frequency region in a sound spectrum that has relatively great intensity

resonance curve *n* : a curve whose abscissas are frequencies lying near to and on both sides of the natural frequency of a vibrating system and whose ordinates are the corresponding amplitudes of the near-resonant vibrations

resonance hybrid *n* : a compound, molecule, ion, or radical exhibiting resonance and having a structure represented in the written form as the average of two or more structural formulas separated each from the next by a double-headed arrow ⟨the *resonance hybrid* of carbon dioxide is represented by $^{-}O{-}C{\equiv}O^{+}\longleftrightarrow O{=}C{=}O\longleftrightarrow {}^{+}O{\equiv}C{-}O^{-}$⟩

$$CH_3C(=O)O^{-} \longleftrightarrow CH_3C(O^{-})=O$$

resonance hybrid of the acetate ion

resonance pipe *n* : a pipe in a musical instrument (as an organ) for increasing its sonority

resonance potential *n* : the energy in volts required to remove an electron from a normal orbit to the next nearest orbit

resonance radiation *n* : radiation emitted by atoms or molecules excited by radiation of the same wavelength and constituting one type of fluorescence

resonance spectrum *n* : a spectrum of resonance radiation

resonance theory *n* **1** : a theory of hearing: different sections of the basilar membrane of the organ of Corti are tuned to different vibration rates and set up sympathetic vibrations that stimulate sensory nerve endings when the cochlear endolymph is vibrating at a corresponding frequency **2** : a theory in physiology: different forms of excitation arise in the central nervous system, are transmitted diffusely to the endorgans, but are individually capable of effectively stimulating only those muscles or other motor organs that are responsive to their particular frequency

ˡ**res·o·nant** \-z(ᵊ)nənt\ *adj* [L *resonant-, resonans*, pres. part. of *resonare* to resound — more at RESOUND] **1** : continuing or capable of continuing to sound : able to resound : echoing back ⟨a harsh ~ boom⟩ **2 a** : capable of inducing resonance in sound : tending to reinforce or cause prolongation of sound ⟨violins of fine ~ wood⟩ **b** : relating to or exhibiting resonance : adjusted so as to respond to vibrations of a given frequency **3 a** : intensified and enriched by or as if by resonance : having a resounding quality ⟨a ~ voice⟩ ⟨the ~ beauty of his prose⟩ **b** : marked by or suggestive of the loud, oratorical, or grandiloquent ⟨a new and more ~ sort of headline, the streamer —H.G.Wells⟩ **c** *of colors* : producing mutual enhancement by contrast ⟨richer impasto and more ~ color —*Nat'l Gallery of Art*⟩ **4** : characterized by phonetic resonance : being a phonetic resonant

syn RESOUNDING, RINGING, VIBRANT, SONOROUS, OROTUND: RESONANT may indicate the full effect of the possibilities of vibration or the ready reactive effect of similar stimuli ⟨the beating small drums — a hollow *resonant* sound —C.B. Nordhoff & J.N.Hall⟩ ⟨the connotative words . . . have a quality and tone which is *resonant* in combination as though a tuning fork had been struck —R.L.Cook⟩ It may suggest clear and lasting carrying power and consequent force, intensity, or effect ⟨it was *resonant* with feeling and through long centuries gave voice to emotions —H.O.Taylor⟩ RESOUNDING adds the notion of echoing, reechoing, or reverberating as vibrations are thrown back ⟨the sound of a great underground river, flowing through a *resounding* cavern —Willa Cather⟩ Through the suggestion of repetition to make clear and unequivocal, it may connote the certain, positive, unreserved, and convincing ⟨the queen of Egypt was not ill-pleased by the Parthian failure, since a *resounding* success would have made Antony independent of her —John Buchan⟩ RINGING may be associated with bell-like sounds, ample and full, made without external or contrived vibrating devices ⟨a perfect ecstasy of song — clear, *ringing*, copious —John Burroughs⟩ Used of speech or composition, it connotes the clear, vigorous, and fervent ⟨his *ringing* appeal for independence . . . was followed in December by another shrill cry to the people, rallying them to the patriot side —C.A. & Mary Beard⟩ VIBRANT calls attention to attendant vibrations and overtones in actualizing sound, but, unlike the preceding words, does not imply their reflection, continuation, or amplification ⟨the speaker paused a moment, his low *vibrant* tones faltering into silence —Israel Zangwill⟩ ⟨a deep strong voice, more musical than any merely human voice, richer, warmer, more *vibrant* with love and yearning and compassion —Aldous Huxley⟩ In other uses it connotes keen sensitivity, pleasing or invigorating awareness or aliveness ⟨Latin verses that were freed from the dead rules of quantity, and were already *vibrant* with a vital feeling for accent and rhyme —H.O.Taylor⟩ ⟨there was something *vibrant* and clean about the sense of conviction and affirmation that was rising within us as the challenge crystallized —Norman Cousins⟩ SONOROUS is likely to suggest fullness or loudness of sound without much suggestion of vibration or timbre ⟨the deep, *sonorous* voice of the red-bearded Duke, which boomed out like a dinner gong —A. Conan Doyle⟩ Applied to speeches and writing it suggests the imposing or high-flown ⟨here all day long rolled forth, in *sonorous* Latin, the interminable periods of episcopal oratory —Lytton Strachey⟩ ⟨a *sonorous* declaimer . . . he went out of his way to invite majestic effects —V.L.Parrington⟩ OROTUND, etymologically suggesting maximum opening of the mouth, likewise connotes full sound ⟨to be sung to the tune of Yankee Doodle, yet in a slower, more *orotund* fashion —Vachel Lindsay⟩ Applied to style of composition or delivery it may indicate the pompous or bombastic ⟨the phrase needs be fitly *orotund* —J.B.Cabell & A.J.Hanna⟩

²**resonant** \"\ *n* -S **1 a** : a sound characterized by resonance : a resonant sound **b** *phonetics* : a speech sound (as a vowel, semivowel, nasal, lateral, or any of certain varieties of \r\) that is articulated without occlusion or friction — compare OBSTRUENT **2** : a resonant body

resonant cavity *n* [ˡ*resonant*] : CAVITY RESONATOR

resonant frequency *or* **resonance frequency** *n* : a frequency capable of exciting a resonance maximum in a given body or system

res·o·nant·ly *adv* : in a resonant manner : with resonance

res·o·nate \'rez°n,āt, *usu* -ād·+V\ *vb* -ED/-ING/-S [L *resonatus*, past part. of *resonare* to resound — more at RESOUND] *vi* **1** : to produce or exhibit resonance : vibrate sympathetically (as with some source of sound or electric oscillations) ⟨the geometry of the *resonating* ions —K.J.Brunings & A.H.Corwin⟩ **2** : to respond as if by resonance : REECHO ⟨a boy reared in a minister's home may all his life ~ . . . to moral dogmas —C.W. Shumaker⟩ ~ *vt* : to subject to resonating : make resonant

res·o·na·tor \-ād·ə(r), -ātə-\ *n* -S [*resonate* + *-or*] **1** : something that resounds or resonates: as **a** : a hollow acoustic vessel with two openings one of which is to be held to the ear and the other directed toward a source of sound which may be intensified in certain frequencies by the resonance of the enclosed air **b :** an electric circuit in which are incorporated inductance and capacitance so connected that a periodic electromotive force of suitable frequency causes the circuit to resonate with electric oscillations of maximum amplitude **c :** CAVITY RESONATOR **d :** a device (as the piano soundboard, the body of a stringed instrument) for increasing the power or beauty of tone of a musical instrument by sympathetic vibration **e :** any of the pharynx, mouth, or nose cavities that serve to reinforce tones in the formation of speech sounds **f :** an open box for containing a telegraph sounder and designed to concentrate and amplify the sound **2 :** a small auxiliary muffler behind the regular muffler in the exhaust system of an automobile

re·sorb \rə'sȯ(ə)rb, (')rē'-, -'zȯ-\ *vb* -ED/-ING/-S [L *resorbēre*, fr. *re-* + *sorbēre* to suck up, swallow — more at ABSORB] *vt* **1 :** to swallow or suck in again **:** take up again **2** *of a living organism* **:** to lyse and assimilate (the substance of a differentiated structure previously produced by the body) ⟨~*ed* the fetuses⟩ ~ *vi* **:** to undergo resorption ⟨the injected protein ~*s* after some days⟩

re·sorb·ent \-bənt\ *adj* [L *resorbent-, resorbens*, pres. part. of *resorbēre*] **:** swallowing or sucking in again **:** REABSORBING

res·orcin \rə'zȯrs°n, (')rez+\ *n* -S [ISV *res-* (fr. L *resina* resin) + *orcin*] **:** RESORCINOL — not used systematically

resorcin brown *n, often cap R&B* **:** an acid dye — see DYE table I (under *Acid Orange 24*)

resorcin dark brown *n, often cap R&D&B* **:** an acid dye — see DYE table I (under *Acid Brown 14*)

res·orcinol \"+\ *n* -S [ISV *resorcin* + *-ol*] **:** a sweetish crystalline phenol $C_6H_4(OH)_2$ that turns pink in air, that is obtained from various resins (as galbanum or asafetida) or tannins by degradation but is usu. made by fusion of *meta*-benzene-disulfonic acid with sodium hydroxide, and that is used chiefly in making dyes, pharmaceuticals, phenolic resins esp. for adhesives, and rubber products and in medicine in the treatment of skin diseases; *meta*-dihydroxy-benzene

res·or·cyl·ic acid \¦re,zȯr¦silik-\ *n* [ISV *resorcin* + *-yl* + *-ic*] **:** any of three isomeric crystalline acids $C_6H_3(OH)_2COOH$ that are both carboxyl derivatives of resorcinol and dihydroxy derivatives of benzoic acid; *esp* **:** the crystalline beta or 2,4-dihydroxy derivative used chiefly in making dyes, pharmaceuticals, and fine chemicals

re·sorp·tion \rə'sȯrpshən, -'zȯ-, (')rē¦-\ *n* -S [L *resorptus* (past part. of *resorbēre* to resorb) + E *-ion*] **:** the act or process of resorbing **:** REABSORPTION ⟨the ~ of a tooth root⟩

resorption border *or* **resorption rim** *n* **:** one of a series of borders of one or more minerals around a central larger crystal representing recrystallizations of material dissolved by a molten magma from previously crystallized minerals — called also *corrosion border;* compare REACTION RIM

re·sorp·tive \-ptiv\ *adj* [L *resorptus* + E *-ive*] **:** relating to or caused by resorption **:** tending to cause resorption **:** capable of being resorbed

¹re·sort \rə'zȯ(ə)r|t, rē'z-, -ȯ(ə)|\ *sometimes* -'sȯ-; *usu* |d.+V\ *n* -S [ME, fr. MF, resource, jurisdiction to which one has recourse, fr. *resortir* to resort] **1 a :** something to which or someone to whom one looks for help **:** a source of aid or refuge **:** RESOURCE, EXPEDIENT ⟨an appeal to his uncle seemed his last ~⟩ **b :** an act of going to or making application (as in seeking aid) **:** RECOURSE ⟨have ~ to force⟩ **2 a :** frequent, habitual, or general going or repairing to or visiting ⟨a place of popular ~⟩ **b :** persons who frequent a place **:** ASSEMBLAGE, COMPANY, THRONG **c** (1) **:** a place to which one betakes himself or persons go habitually **:** a place of frequent assembly **:** HAUNT (2) **:** a popular place of entertainment or recreation **3** *obs* **a :** frequenting in numbers **:** CONCOURSE **b :** a going of one person with others or to a place **4** *obs* **a :** a mechanical spring **b :** motive power **:** CAUSE, SOURCE **syn** see RESOURCE

²resort \"\ *vb* -ED/-ING/-S [ME *resorten*, fr. MF *resortir* to come out again, rebound, recoil, resort, fr. OF, fr. *re-* + *sortir* to escape] *vi* **1 :** to have recourse (as to a source of aid or for a purpose) **:** to seek aid, relief, or advantage ⟨~*ed* to a trick⟩ ⟨knew no one to whom he could ~ for help⟩ **2 :** to betake oneself **:** REPAIR; *esp* **:** to go frequently, customarily, or usually **3** *obs* **:** to fall back **:** REVERT, RETURN **4** *obs* **:** to direct one's attention **:** TURN ~ *vt, obs* **:** VISIT

re-sort \(')rē¦sȯ(ə)r|, -ȯ(ə)|\ *vt* [*re-* + *sort*] **:** to separate again **:** classify anew

re·sort·er *pronunc at* ¹RESORT +ə(r)\ *n* -S [¹*resort* + *-er*] **:** a frequenter of a resort or resorts

re-sort·er *pronunc at* RE-SORT +ə(r)\ *n* [*re-sort* + *-er*] **:** one that re-sorts

res·o·ru·fin \,rezə'rüfən\ *n* -S [ISV *resorcin* + L *rufus* red + ISV *-in* — more at RED] **:** a red-brown crystalline dye $C_{12}H_7NO_3$ of the phenoxazine class that gives fluorescent red or pink solutions, that is formed by the action of nitrosylsulfuric acid on resorcinol or by reduction of resazurin, and that on reduction yields a colorless dihydro derivative

¹re·sound \rə'zaund, rē'z- *sometimes* -'saü-\ *vb* [ME *resounen*, fr. MF *resoner*, fr. L *resonare* to sound again, echo, resound, fr. *re-* + *sonare* to sound — more at SOUND] *vi* **1 :** to become filled with sound **:** RING, ECHO, REVERBERATE ⟨the earth ~*ed* with his praise⟩ **2 :** to produce an echoing sound ⟨through the dell his horn ~*s* —Sir Walter Scott⟩ **3 :** to become proclaimed or renowned ⟨a name to ~ for ages —Alfred Tennyson⟩ ~ *vt* **1 :** to proclaim (as someone's praises or virtues) **:** celebrate in music, song, or story **:** extol loudly or widely **2 :** to cause (a sound) to be repeated **:** REECHO **3 :** to sound or utter in full resonant tones

²resound \"\ *n* **:** something that resounds (as an echo)

re-sound \(')rē¦saund\ *vb* [*re-* + *sound*] *vt* **:** to sound (as a horn) again or anew ~ *vi* **:** to sound again or anew

resounding *adj* [ME *resouning*, fr. pres. part. of *resounen* to resound] **1 a :** producing or characterized by resonant sound **:** echoing or awakening echoes **:** RESONATING ⟨a ~ harp⟩ ⟨a ~ hall⟩ **b :** giving an effect of resonance through repetition or multiplication ⟨~ cries⟩ **2 a :** sounding inflated or orotund **:** excessively sonorous or unduly impressive ⟨"Princess Patricia Pattipam of Patagonia", a ~ name for a slipper-chewing puppy⟩ **b :** admitting or designed to admit of no equivocation or doubt **:** FORCEFUL, EMPHATIC, UNEQUIVOCAL ⟨a ~ denial⟩ ⟨a ~ success⟩ **syn** see RESONANT

re·sound·ing·ly *adv* **:** in a resounding manner **:** so as to resound ⟨a voice rang out ~⟩

re·source \'rē,s|ō(ə)rs, rə's|, rē's|, |ȯ(ə)rs, |ōəs, |ȯ(ə)s *also* -,z| *or* -'z|\ *n* -S [F *ressource*, fr. OF *ressourse* relief, resource, fr. *resourdre* to rise again, relieve, fr. L *resurgere* to rise again — more at RESURRECTION] **1 a :** a new or a reserve source of supply or support **:** a fresh or additional stock or store available at need **:** something in reserve or ready if needed ⟨exhausted every ~⟩ ⟨open up new ~*s* to an impoverished culture⟩ **b resources** *pl* **:** available means (as of a country or business) **:** computable wealth (as in money, property, products) **:** immediate and possible sources of revenue ⟨rich natural ~*s*⟩ ⟨the book value of a company's ~*s*⟩ **2 :** something to which one has recourse in difficulty **:** means of resort in exigency **:** EXPEDIENT, STRATAGEM ⟨her usual ~ was confession⟩ **3 :** possibility of relief or recovery — usu. used in negative construction ⟨lost without ~⟩ **4 :** a means of spending or utilizing one's leisure time ⟨Boston at that time offered few healthy ~*s* for boys or men —Henry Adams⟩ **5 :** capability of or skill in meeting a situation **:** ability to rise to an occasion **:** RESOURCEFULNESS **6 :** an accounting asset — usu. used in pl.

syn RESORT, EXPEDIENT, SHIFT, MAKESHIFT, STOPGAP, SUBSTITUTE, SURROGATE: RESOURCE may refer to any asset or means benefiting or assisting one, often to an additional, new, previously unused, or reserve asset ⟨the nursing mother feeds the newborn from the resources of her own vitality —H.M.Parshley⟩ ⟨almost the only *resource* upon which people can depend for a living appears to be fish and other animals —Samuel Van Valkenburg & Ellsworth Huntington⟩ ⟨in their relative inexperience of the variety of humans and of human beliefs, they all tend to turn inward upon their own limited *resources:* the primitive to his sacred tribalism, the child to his narcissistic self and body, and the psychotic to the inward resources of his autistic thinking —Weston La Barre⟩ RESORT in this sense is now uncommon except in the phrases *last resort* and *to have resort to*, in which it is close synonym to RESOURCE ⟨brotherhood was invoked more wholeheartedly, as the last *resort* against nihilist desperation —Ignazio Silone⟩ ⟨except in revolutionary unions, the strike is used only as a last *resort* —G.S.Watkins⟩ EXPEDIENT may apply to any continuance, means, or plan for solution of a particular immediate problem, especially to one not commonly or customarily used ⟨if all fears arise from suggestion, they can be prevented by the simple *expedient* of not showing fear or aversion before a child —Bertrand Russell⟩ ⟨but is not this a desperate *expedient*, a last refuge likely to appeal only to the leaders of a lost cause —J.W.Krutch⟩ ⟨as the war endures, this spirit replaces the aims with which the war was begun by *expedients* forced on the rulers by the character of the gigantic conflict itself —D.W.Brogan⟩ SHIFT may refer to a temporary or tentative expedient, admittedly imperfect; in reference to plans and stratagems it may suggest dubiousness or trickery ⟨most people who were brought into intimate contact with the two-roomed cottage, not always perhaps including the inhabitants, who had grown up amidst the *shifts* they enforced, heartily condemned them —G.E.Fussell⟩ MAKESHIFT usu. designates that which is frankly temporary and inferior and either adopted through urgent need or countenanced through indifference and carelessness ⟨the premises . . . being only a *makeshift* until the works . . . should be finished —F.W.Crofts⟩ ⟨like all attempts to pigeonhole human emotions, these classifications are, of course, *makeshifts*. They have no scientific value whatsoever —H.W.Van Loon⟩ STOPGAP refers to something used or employed momentarily or temporarily as an emergency measure ⟨both vigilantes and mass meeting were looked upon as temporary *stopgaps*, to be disbanded as soon as governmental machinery was provided by the United States —R.A.Billington⟩ SUBSTITUTE indicates anything which replaces a thing or article originally or customarily used; it does not necessarily connote anything about merit or cause ⟨peat as a coal *substitute*⟩ ⟨a *substitute* for milk itself could be manufactured from the soya bean —V.G.Heiser⟩ ⟨this mock king who held office for eight days every year was a *substitute* for the king himself —J.G.Frazer⟩ SURROGATE is a more learned word for SUBSTITUTE, often used of synthetic products or of replacement figures in psychological and sociological analyses ⟨that is why slang is so insidious and so pervasive; it too is a facile *surrogate* for thought —J.L.Lowes⟩ ⟨his accounts are full, informed, trustworthy, but he does not pretend to the depersonalized objectivity that too often serves as a *surrogate* for authority in such writing —Howard M. Jones⟩ ⟨usually each child thus receives his turn to act as parent-*surrogate* to a younger child —Allison Davis⟩

re·source·ful \-'=fəl *also* '=,=fəl\ *adj* [*resource* + *-ful*] **1 :** characterized by resource in the meeting of situations **:** fertile in devising ways and means **2 :** having great resources richly endowed (as with natural products) — **re·source·ful·ly** \-fəlē, -li\ *adv* — **re·source·ful·ness** *n* -ES

re·source·less \'=,=ləs, =¦=ləs\ *adj* **:** lacking or deficient in resources — **re·source·less·ness** *n* -ES

resources *pl of* RESOURCE

re·sow \(')rē+\ *vt* [*re-* + *sow*] **:** to sow (as land or seed) again or anew

resp *abbr* **1** respective; respectively **2** respiration; respiratory **3** respondent

re·spar \(')rē+\ *vt* [*re-* + *spar*] **:** to install new spars (as in a ship's rigging)

re·speak \"+\ *vb* [*re-* + *speak*] *vt* **:** ECHO, RESOUND ~ *vi* **:** to speak further **:** make additional utterance

¹re·spect \rə'spekt, rē's-\ *n* -S [ME, fr. L *respectus* act of looking back, regard, consideration, fr. *respectus*, past part. of *respicere* to look back — more at ²RESPECT] **1 a :** a relation to or concern with something usu. specified ⟨the final questions had ~ to her financial situation⟩ **b :** a relation or reference to a particular thing or situation **:** RELEVANCE ⟨remarks having ~ to an earlier plan⟩ **c** *obs* **:** ASPECT **2 a :** an act of noticing with attention **:** the giving of particular attention to **:** CONSIDERATION ⟨having ~ to the views of another⟩ **b** *obs* **:** HEED, CARE, CIRCUMSPECTION **c respects** *pl, obs* **:** attention to diverse matters **3 a :** high or special regard **:** deferential regard (as from a servant to his master) **:** ESTEEM ⟨a great ~ for his judgment⟩ — often used in negative construction ⟨having no ~ for class distinctions⟩ **b :** the quality or state of being esteemed **:** HONOR ⟨a man generally held in high ~⟩ **c** *obs* **:** STANDING, REPUTATION **d respects** *pl* (1) *obs* **:** COURTESIES (2) **:** expressions of respect or deference ⟨paid his ~*s*⟩ **4** *obs* **:** CONSIDERATION, MOTIVE, INTEREST **5 a** *obs* **:** COMPARISON — used chiefly in the phrase *in respect* **b :** a point regarded **:** PARTICULAR, DETAIL ⟨in all ~*s* perfect⟩ **syn** see REGARD — **in respect** *or* **in respect that** *archaic* **:** seeing that **:** SINCE — **in respect of** *prep* **1 :** as to **:** as regards **:** insofar as concerns **:** with respect to **2** *archaic* **:** in consideration of **:** on account of — **in respect to** *prep* **:** in relation to **:** with regard to **:** as respects — **with respect to** *prep* **:** as regards **:** insofar as concerns **:** with reference to ⟨*with respect to* your last letter⟩

²respect \"\ *vb* -ED/-ING/-S [L *respectus*, past part. of *respicere* to look back, look back at, regard, have respect for, fr. *re-* + *specere* to look — more at SPY] *vt* **1** *obs* **:** RESPITE, POSTPONE, NEGLECT **2 a** *obs* (1) **:** CONSIDER, DEEM, HEED (2) **:** to look for **:** ANTICIPATE (3) **:** to look toward or at **:** front upon or toward (4) **:** to look upon **b :** to be depicted facing (as one another) — used of heraldic figures **3 a :** to consider worthy of esteem **:** regard or treat with respect ⟨loved and ~*ed* his parents⟩ **:** ESTEEM, VALUE **b :** to refrain from obtruding upon or interfering with ⟨~ a person's privacy⟩ **4 :** to have regard or reference to **:** relate to **:** be concerned with ⟨the treaty ~*s* our commerce⟩ ~ *vi* **:** LOOK, FRONT, FACE — usu. used in heraldry — **as respects :** as regards **:** with regard to **:** as to ⟨perfectly tolerant except *as respects* his personal honor⟩ — **respect the person 1 :** to consider a case or question with reference to the person involved and one's bias for or against him **2** *archaic* **:** to have regard for the quality (as of rank, station, outward aspect) of a person

re·spect·abil·i·ty \-,spektə'bilədē, -lətē, -i\ *n* **1 a :** the quality or state of being respectable **b :** the status of being respectable **:** CONSEQUENCE **2 a :** a respectable person **:** respectable persons ⟨the ~ of the town⟩ **b :** a respectable convention **:** DECENCY ⟨those little *respectabilities* that make group life bearable⟩

re·spect·abi·lize \=¦==bə,līz\ *vt* -ED/-ING/-S [*respectable* + *-ize*] **:** to make respectable **:** give an apparent respectability to

¹re·spect·able \rə'spektəbəl, rē's-\ *adj* [²*respect* + *-able*] **1 :** worthy of note **:** having claims to consideration **:** of consequence ⟨everything relating to bulls is popular and ~ in Thebes —P.B.Shelley⟩ **2 :** worthy of esteem or deference **:** ESTIMABLE, RESPECTED ⟨a highly ~ authority⟩ **3 a :** decent in behavior or character **:** morally estimable ⟨a ~ innkeeper⟩ **b :** exhibiting respect for the decencies or proprieties **:** conventionally correct in conduct ⟨many persons find it easier to be good than ~⟩ **4 :** being such to a significant degree **:** TOLERABLE: as **a :** fair in size or quantity ⟨a ~ amount⟩ ⟨a ~ volume of work⟩ **b :** moderately good **:** pleasing but not exceptional ⟨a house with a ~ view⟩ ⟨a ~ performance⟩ **5 :** decent in appearance or standing **:** PRESENTABLE ⟨a ~ coat⟩ ⟨a ~ address⟩ — **re·spect·able·ness** \-nəs\ *n* -ES — **re·spect·ably** \-blē, -bli\ *adv*

²respectable \"\ *n* -S **:** a respectable person

re·spect·ant \-ktənt\ *adj* [L *respectant-, respectans*, pres. part. of *respectare* to look back, look back at — more at RESPITE] **1 :** depicted upright and facing one another — used of heraldic representations of fishes and mammals; compare AFFRONTÉ, COMBATANT **2 :** looking back

re·spect·er \-ktə(r)\ *n* -S [²*respect* + *-er*] **:** one that respects esp. unduly or to the point of partiality — usu. used in negative constructions ⟨death is no ~ of preachers⟩ ⟨wombats are no ~*s* of fences or crops —Bill Beatty⟩

re·spect·ful \-ktfəl, *in rapid speech* -kfəl\ *adj* [¹*respect* + *-ful*] **1 :** full of respect: as **a** *obs* **:** HEEDFUL, CAREFUL — usu. used with *of* **b** *obs* **:** deserving or receiving respect **c :** marked or characterized by respect **:** showing deference ⟨~ deportment⟩ ⟨a ~ glance⟩ — **re·spect·ful·ly** \-fəlē, -li\ *adv* — **re·spect·ful·ness** *n* -ES

respecting *prep* [fr. pres. part. of ²*respect*] **1 :** in view of **:** CONSIDERING ⟨~ what a rancorous mind he bears —Shak.⟩ **2 :** with regard or relation to **:** REGARDING, CONCERNING ⟨~ his conduct there is but one opinion⟩

re·spec·tive \rə'spektiv, rē's-, -tēv *also* -təv\ *adj* [partly fr. ML *respectivus* having respect to, fr. L *respectus* (past part. of *respicere* to look back at) + *-ivus* -ive; partly fr. ²*respect* + *-ive* — more at RESPECT] **1 a** *obs* **:** noticing with attention **:** REGARDFUL, ATTENTIVE **b** *archaic* **:** CAREFUL, HEEDFUL **2** *obs* **:** rendering respect **:** COURTEOUS **3** *obs* **a :** having reference **:** RELATED, CORRESPONDENT **b :** RELATIVE **4** *obs* **:** fitted to awaken respect **:** RESPECTABLE **5** *obs* **a :** regardful of particular persons or things **b :** PARTIAL, DISCRIMINATIVE **6 :** proper or relating to particular persons or things each to each **:** PARTICULAR, SEVERAL ⟨their ~ homes⟩ ⟨assembling the ~ parts according to the diagram⟩

re·spec·tive·ly \-təvlē, -li\ *adv* **:** in a respective manner **:** so as to be respective; *usu* **:** as relating to each **:** in particular **:** each to each **:** each in the order given ⟨two philosophers who stressed ~ deductive and empirical aspects of science⟩ ⟨when the daughters were 12, 10, and 7 years old ~⟩

re·spec·tive·ness \-tivnəs, -tēv- *also* -təv-\ *n* -ES **:** the quality or state of being respective

re·spect·less \-ktləs\ *adj* **:** not having or not showing respect **:** CARELESS, DISRESPECTFUL

respectlessly *adv* [*respectless* + *-ly*] *obs* **:** without respect

respects *pl of* RESPECT, *pres 3d sing of* RESPECT

respectuous *adj* [MF *respectueux*, fr. L *respectus* respect + F *-eux* -ous] *obs* **:** deserving or showing respect

respectworthy \=¦=,==\ *adj* **:** worthy of respect

re·spell \(')rē+\ *vt* [*re-* + *spell*] **:** to spell again, anew, or in another way; *esp* **:** to spell out according to a phonetic system ⟨words ~*ed* to show the pronunciation⟩

re·spin \"+\ *vt* [*re-* + *spin*] **:** to spin again or anew

res·pi·ra·bil·i·ty \,resp(ə)rə'bilədē, rə,spīr-, rē,spīr-\ *n* **:** the quality or state of being respirable

res·pi·ra·ble \'resp(ə)rəbəl, rə'spīr-,rē'spīr-\ *adj* [F or LL; F *respirable*, fr. LL *respirabilis*, fr. L *respirare* to respire + *-abilis* -able] **1 :** suitable for being breathed **:** adapted for respiration ⟨a ~ atmosphere⟩ **2 :** capable of respiration ⟨~ beings⟩ — **res·pi·ra·ble·ness** *n* -ES

res·pi·rat·ing \'respə,rād·iŋ\ *adj* [fr. *respiration*, after such pairs as E *inspiration: inspirating*, pres. part. of *inspirate*] **:** functioning in respiration ⟨~ muscles⟩

res·pi·ra·tion \,respə'rāshən\ *n* -S [ME *respiracioun*, fr. L *respiration-, respiratio*, fr. *respiratus* (past part. of *respirare* to breathe) + *-ion-, -io* -ion — more at RESPIRE] **1 a :** the placing of air or dissolved gases in intimate contact with the circulating medium (as blood) of a multicellular organism whether by breathing, diffusion through gills or body surface, or other means ⟨most fishes use gills in ~⟩ **b :** a single complete act of breathing ⟨30 ~*s* per minute⟩ **2 :** the physical and chemical processes by which an organism supplies its cells and tissues with the oxygen needed for metabolism and relieves them of the carbon dioxide formed in energy-producing reactions and which typically involve osmotic exchange between regions of greater and lesser concentration, mechanical transport in a fluid medium (as blood), and chemical storage by mean of carriers (as hemoglobin) or buffers **3 :** any of various energy-yielding oxidative reactions in living matter that typically involve transfer of oxygen and production of carbon dioxide and water as end products — called also *cellular respiration;* compare FERMENTATION

res·pi·ra·tion·al \¦==¦rāshən°l, -shnəl\ *adj* **:** of or relating to respiration **:** RESPIRATORY ⟨~ disorders⟩

respiration calorimeter *n* **:** an apparatus for measuring the gaseous exchange between a man or lower animal and the surrounding atmosphere with particular reference to the oxygen consumed and carbon dioxide eliminated and simultaneously the quantity of energy given out in the form of heat and work in order to determine the relation of these factors to the food and drink consumed and to body activity

res·pi·ra·tor \'respə,rād·ə(r), -ātə- *sometimes* -,sprā-\ *n* -S [L *respiratus* (past part. of *respirare* to breathe) + E *-or* — more at RESPIRE] **1 :** a device (as a gas mask) for protecting the respiratory tract (as against irritating and poisonous gases, fumes, smoke, dusts) with or without equipment supplying oxygen or air ⟨filter ~*s* provide protection against any particulate matter, either solid, mist, or spray in an atmosphere containing a sufficient amount of oxygen —F.A. Van Atta⟩ ⟨air line ~*s*⟩ **2 :** a device for maintaining artificial respiration ⟨chest and tank ~*s*⟩ — compare CUIRASS 4b, IRON LUNG

res·pi·ra·to·ri·um \,resprə'tōrēəm, rə,spīr-\ *n, pl* **respi·rato·ria** \-ēə\ [NL, fr. LL, neut. of *respiratorius*] **:** a tracheal gill (as of a dipterous larva)

res·pi·ra·to·ry \'resp(ə)rə,tōrē, ÷'respə,t- (*by r-dissimilation*), -tȯr-, -ri *also* rə'spīrə,- *or* rē'spīrə,- *sometimes* (')re¦spīrə,-\ *adj* [LL *respiratorius*, fr. L *respiratus* (past part. of *respirare* to breathe) + *-orius* -ory — more at RESPIRE] **:** of or relating to respiration ⟨~ function⟩ **:** serving for or functioning in respiration ⟨~ organs⟩ ⟨~ nerves⟩

respiratory center *n* **:** a region in the medulla oblongata that regulates respiratory movements

respiratory enzyme *n* **:** an enzyme (as an oxidase, dehydrogenase, or catalase) associated with the processes of cellular respiration; *esp* **:** CYTOCHROME OXIDASE

respiratory leaf *or* **respiratory leaflet** *n* **:** one of the laminae of a book lung

respiratory nerve *n* **:** any of four nerves supplying the muscles of respiration and comprising two internally located phrenic nerves and two externally located posterior thoracic nerves

respiratory pigment *n* **:** any of various conjugated proteins that function in the transfer of oxygen in cellular respiration and that are permanently colored (as hemoglobin), alternate between a colored and a colorless phase (as hemocyanin) depending on their degree of oxygenation, or are permanently colorless (as the pigment of a few marine mollusks)

respiratory plate *n* **:** a flattened expansion of the body wall of an insect larva or other aquatic invertebrate that serves as a gill

respiratory quotient *also* **respiratory ratio** *n* **:** a ratio indicating the relation of the volume of carbon dioxide given off in respiration to that of the oxygen consumed and having a value near 1 when the organism is burning chiefly carbohydrates, near 0.7 when chiefly fats, and near 0.8 when chiefly proteins but sometimes exceeding 1 when carbohydrates are being changed to fats for storage — abbr. *RQ*

respiratory system *n* **:** a system of organs subserving the function of respiration and in air-breathing vertebrates consisting typically of the lungs and their nervous and circulatory supply, the channels by which these are continuous with the outer air, various supportive and protective structures, and usu. the muscles and skeletal structures concerned with emptying and filling the lungs

respiratory tree *n* **1 :** an internal arborescent usu. paired tubular appendage of the cloaca of some holothurians that is considered to be an organ of respiration **2 :** the trachea, bronchi, and bronchioles

respiratory trumpet *n* **:** either of the two trumpet-shaped projections that bear the thoracic spiracles in the pupae of mosquitoes and midges

re·spire \rə'spī(ə)r, rē's-, -īə\ *vb* -ED/-ING/-S [ME *respiren*, fr. MF & L; MF *respirer* to revive, fr. L *respirare* to blow back, breathe, breathe again, recover breath, fr. *re-* + *spirare* to blow, breathe — more at SPIRIT] *vi* **1 :** to have or enjoy a breathing space or respite **:** REVIVE; *also* **:** to recover hope or courage **2** *obs, of the wind* **:** BLOW **3 a :** BREATHE; *specif* **:** to inhale air into the lungs and exhale it from them successively in carrying on the gaseous exchange of the blood **b :** to engage in or perform respiration **4** *of a cell or tissue* **:** to take up oxygen and produce carbon dioxide through oxidation ~ *vt* **1 :** to breathe (as air) in and out **:** inspire and expire **2 :** to give off as or as if an exhalation **:** EXHALE

re·spirit \(')rē+\ *vt* [*re-* + *spirit*] **:** to put new spirit or courage in

res·pi·rom·e·ter \,respə'rämәd·ə(r)\ *n* [L *respirare* to breathe + E *-o-* + *-meter*] **1 :** an instrument for studying the character and extent of respiration **2 :** a diver's headdress having a receptacle for compressed oxygen for replenishing the oxygen in the expired air after its harmful ingredients have been chemically removed

res·pi·rom·e·try \-mə·trē\ *n* -ES [L *respirare* + E *-o-* + *-metry*] : the study of respiration (as cellular respiration) by means of a respirometer

¹res·pite \'respə̇t *sometimes* 're,spī| *or* rə̇'spī| *or* rē'spī|; *usu* |d·+V\ *n* -S [ME *respit*, fr. OF, fr. ML *respectus*, fr. L, act of looking back — more at RESPECT] **1** : a putting off of that which was appointed : extension of time : POSTPONEMENT, DELAY: as **a** : temporary suspension of the execution of a capital offender : REPRIEVE **b** : a delay of appearance at court granted to a jury **2** : temporary intermission of labor or of any process or operation : interval of rest **3** *obs* : delay in acting **4** *obs* : LEISURE, OPPORTUNITY **5** : one that is reprieved

²respite \"\ *vb* -ED/-ING/-S [ME *respiten*, fr. MF *respiter*, fr. ML *respectare* to respect, delay, respite, fr. L, to look back repeatedly, wait for, respect, freq. of *respicere* to look back — more at RESPECT] *vt* **1** : to give or grant a respite to: as **a** : to delay or postpone : put off **b** : to keep back from execution : REPRIEVE **2** *archaic* : to desist from : FORBEAR, SUSPEND **3 a** : to suspend temporarily the necessity for meeting (as an obligation) or paying (a penalty) **b** *obs* : to relieve by a pause or interval of rest **4** *obs* : PROLONG ~ *vi*, *archaic* : to take a respite : REST

res·pite·less \-tlə̇s\ *adj* : having no respite

re·splend \rə̇'splend, rē's-\ *vi* -ED/-ING/-S [ME *resplenden*, fr. L *resplendēre* — more at RESPLENDENT] : to shine resplendently : be resplendent ⟨natural moral values ~ among all other values —Dietrich von Hildebrand⟩

re·splen·dence \-dən(t)s\ *n* -S [ME, fr. LL *resplendentia*, fr. L *resplendent-, resplendens* + *-ia* -y] : the quality or state of being resplendent : brilliant luster : SPLENDOR

re·splen·den·cy \-dənsē, -si\ *n* -ES [LL *resplendentia*] **1** : RESPLENDENCE **2** : a resplendent thing (as a garment) ⟨her folds and *resplendencies* —H.L.Davis⟩

re·splen·dent \-dənt\ *adj* [L *resplendent-, resplendens*, pres. part. of *resplendēre* to shine back, fr. *re-* + *splendēre* to shine — more at SPLENDID] : shining brilliantly : LUSTROUS **syn** see SPLENDID

re·splen·dent·ly *adv* : in a resplendent manner : with resplendence

¹re·spond \rə̇'spänd, rē's-\ *n* -S [ME, fr. MF *respondre* to respond] **1** : something sung or said after or in reply to the officiant in a liturgy : a response to or as if to a versicle : RESPONSORY **2** : an engaged pillar supporting an arch or closing a colonnade of arcade ⟨the nave arcade will be of nine pillars and two ~*s*⟩; *also* : a corbel so used or a pilaster that backs up a free column **3** : ANSWER, REPLY

²respond \"\ *vb* -ED/-ING/-S [MF *respondre* to answer, correspond, fr. L *respondēre* to promise in return, answer, correspond, fr. *re-* + *spondēre* to promise — more at SPOUSE] *vi* **1** *archaic* : to correspond or accord with something **2** : to say something in return : make an answer ⟨~*ed* negatively to the question⟩: as **a** : to make a respond or response in a liturgy **b** (1) : to make a bid in bridge based wholly or partly on strength promised by a previous bid by one's partner (2) : to bid as directed by a forcing bid made by one's partner **3** : to show some reaction to a force or stimulus ⟨the pupil of the eye ~*s* to change of light intensity⟩ : react in response ⟨a horse ~*ing* to kindly treatment⟩ ⟨~*ed* with rage to the insult⟩ ⟨the abscess ~*ed* well to heat treatment⟩; *often* : to react favorably in response ⟨is at last ~*ing* to medication⟩ **4** : to render satisfaction : be answerable ~ *vt*, *archaic* : to answer to : correspond to **syn** see ANSWER

re·spon·de \-n,dē\ *n* -S [L, 2nd sing. imper. of *respondēre* to respond] *Scots law* : an entry formerly made in a book of record in chancery of a nonentry or relief duty payable by an heir taking a precept from chancery; *also* : the amount of the duties in such an entry

re·spon·de·at ouster \-.dēət-\ *n* [L *respondeat* let him make answer (3d sing. pres. subj. of *respondēre* to respond) + AF *ouster, oustre* further, beyond, alter. of OF *outre*, fr. L *ultra* — more at ULTERIOR] : a judgment or order used upon denial of a dilatory plea to direct the party who made it to plead to the merits

respondeat superior *n* [ML, let the superior give answer] : the responsibility of a principal for his agent's acts ⟨the power of control is the test of liability under the doctrine of *respondeat superior* —J.D.Johnson⟩

re·spon·dence \rə̇'spändən(t)s, rē's-\ *also* **re·spon·den·cy** \-dənsē\ *n, pl* **respondences** *also* **respondencies** [L *respondēre* to answer, correspond + E *-ence, -ency*] : the act of responding : the quality or state of being respondent : ANSWERING, RESPONSE; *also* : CORRESPONDENCE, AGREEMENT

¹re·spon·dent \-dənt\ *n* -S [L *respondent-, respondens*, pres. part. of *respondēre* to answer, correspond — more at RESPOND] : one that responds (as with a reply): as **a** : one that maintains a thesis in reply — distinguished from *opponent* **b** (1) : one that answers in various legal proceedings that are usu. not according to the course of the common law (as in equity, admiralty, ecclesiastical, or statutory cases) (2) : the prevailing party in the lower court — distinguished from *appellant*

²respondent \"\ *adj* [L *respondent-, respondens*] **1** *obs* : serving to correspond **2** : making response : ANSWERING, RESPONSIVE; *esp* : being a defendant or respondent at law

re·spon·den·tia \,rē,spän'dench(ē)ə\ *n* -S [NL, fr. L *respondent-, respondens* + *-ia* -y; fr. the fact that it is only a personal obligation on the borrower who is bound to answer the contract] : a loan upon goods laden on a ship conditioned to be repaid with maritime interest only in the event of the safe arrival of some part of the goods — compare BOTTOMRY

re·spond·er \rə̇'spändə(r), rē's-\ *n* -S : one that responds: **a** : a person that responds (as to a question, a bid, a kindness) **b** : something that reacts responsively: as (1) : the main charge of an explosive that requires an initiator to set it off (2) : the part of a transponder that transmits a radio signal

responsa *pl of* RESPONSUM

¹responsal *adj* [ME *responsaill*, fr. ML *responsalis* of a reply, answerable, fr. L *responsum* reply + *-alis* -al — more at RESPONSE] **1** *obs* : ANSWERABLE, RESPONSIBLE **2** *obs* : RESPONSIVE

²re·spon·sal \rə̇'spän(t)səl, rē's-\ *n* -S **1** [ME, fr. ML *responsalis* of a reply] **a** *obs* : REPLY, ANSWER **b** *archaic* : a respond in a liturgy **2** [ML *responsalis*, fr. *responsalis* of a reply] *obs* : the respondent in a disputation **3** : RESPONSALIS

re·spon·sa·lis \-,spän'sāləs\ *n, pl* **responsa·les** \-'sā(,)lēs\ [LL *responsalis* (trans. of LGk *apokrisiarios*), fr. L *responsum* reply + *-alis* -al — more at RESPONSE] : one who gives answers as the representative of an ecclesiastic : APOCRISIARIUS

re·spon·sa pru·den·ti·um \-sə(,)prü'dentēəm, -dench(ē)əm\ *n pl* [LL] : the responses or opinions of eminent lawyers or professional jurists on legal questions addressed to them — compare OBITER DICTUM

re·spon·sa·ry \-n(t)sərē\ *n* -ES [*response* + *-ary*] : RESPONSORY, RESPONSE

re·sponse \rə̇'spän(t)s, rē's-\ *n* -S [ME & L; ME *respounse*, fr. MF *respons*, fr. L *responsum* reply, fr. neut. of *responsus*, past part. of *respondēre* to answer — more at RESPOND] **1** : an act or action of responding (as by an answer) : a responsive or corresponding act or feeling : a responding to a motive force or situation : REACTION ⟨the sensitive and wistful ~ of a poet to the gentler phase of beauty —*Amer. Guide Series: Minn.*⟩ ⟨the ~ of a wire to the flow of electric current⟩: as **a** : a liturgical answer in the form of a verse, sentence, phrase, or word sung or said by the people or choir after or in reply to the officiant at a religious service and often indicated in liturgical books by R or ℟ : RESPOND, RESPONSORY; *also* : an anthem sung after or during a lection **b** : a supernatural answer (as by an oracle) **c** (1) : ANSWER 5 (2) : the chorus or refrain of a folk song or rhyme **d** : reply to an objection in formal disputation **e** (1) : activity or inhibition of previous activity of an organism or of any of its parts resulting from stimulation ⟨a motor ~⟩ ⟨a native ~⟩ (2) : such activity or inhibition existing in a covariant relationship with drive, cue, and reinforcement **f** : the output of a transducer or detecting device resulting from a given input; *specif* : the voltage output of a microphone per unit amplitude of sound pressure at the diaphragm — compare RESPONSE CURVE **g** : a bridge bid made by a player who responds **2** : a half pier or pillar that supports an arch

response curve *n* : a curve graphically exhibiting the magnitude of the response of a sensitive device to a varying stimulus (as of a microphone to sounds of varying intensity)

re·sponse·less \-sləs\ *adj* [*response* + *-less*] : making no response : UNRESPONSIVE

re·spons·er \-sə(r)\ *n* -S [*response* + *-er*] : RESPONDER

re·spon·si·bil·i·ty \rə̇,spän(t)sə'biləd·ē, rē,s-, -lətē, -i\ *n* -ES **1** : the quality or state of being responsible: as **a** : moral, legal, or mental accountability ⟨assume the ~ for another's debt⟩ ⟨prove the ~ of the accused⟩ ⟨a person completely lacking in ~⟩ **b** : RELIABILITY, TRUSTWORTHINESS; *sometimes* : ability to pay ⟨the ~ of one seeking a loan⟩ **2** : something for which anyone is responsible or accountable ⟨leadership carries great *responsibilities*⟩ ⟨sought relief from his ~⟩ ⟨a ~ he had never asked for⟩

¹re·spon·si·ble \-'spän(t)səbəl\ *adj*, *sometimes* -ER/-EST [L *responsus* (past part. of *respondēre* to answer, correspond) + E *-ible* — more at RESPOND] **1** *obs* : CORRESPONDENT, ACCORDANT **2 a** : likely to be called upon to answer ⟨a man is ~ for his acts⟩ **b** : answerable as the primary cause, motive, or agent whether of evil or good : creditable or chargeable with the result — used with *for* ⟨~ for her injury⟩ ⟨a committee ~ for assembling supplies⟩ **c** : liable or subject to legal review or in case of fault to penalties ⟨a guardian is ~ to the court for his conduct in office⟩ **3 a** : able to respond or answer for one's conduct and obligations : trustworthy in respect to financial or other matters ⟨a ~ citizen⟩ **b** : of decent appearance : PRESENTABLE **c** (1) : having the character of a free moral agent : capable of determining one's own acts (2) : capable of being deterred by consideration of sanctions or consequences **4** : involving responsibility : involving a degree of accountability ⟨a ~ office⟩ **5** : politically answerable (as to a legislature or an electorate); *esp* : required to submit to the electorate if defeated by the legislature — used esp. of the British cabinet

syn ANSWERABLE, ACCOUNTABLE, AMENABLE, LIABLE: RESPONSIBLE may differ from ANSWERABLE and ACCOUNTABLE in centering attention on a formal organizational role, function, duty, or trust ⟨while held *responsible* for the bank's operations, the president has powers considered largely nominal —*Current Biog.*⟩ ⟨chief of personnel for the *New York Herald Tribune*, where she is also *responsible* for special editorial work in the field of industrial relations —*Current Biog.*⟩ ANSWERABLE is likely to be used in situations involving moral or legal obligation or duty under judgment ⟨we must take heed, however, that we do not load their memory with infamy which of right belongs to their master. For the treaty of Dover the King himself is chiefly *answerable* —T.B.Macaulay⟩ ⟨there was something ineradicably corrupt inside her for which her father was not *answerable* —E.K.Brown⟩ ACCOUNTABLE may be used in situations involving imminence of retribution for unfulfilled trust or violated obligation ⟨the president is invested with certain important political powers, in the exercise of which he is to use his own discretion, and is *accountable* only to his country in his political character and to his own conscience —John Marshall⟩ AMENABLE may indicate the fact of subjection to review, judgment, or control by a higher agency ⟨certain boats are sometimes not *amenable* to the rules of the right-of-way. A naval boat, for instance, on official business, may demand and take the right-of-way —H.A. Calahan⟩ ⟨scholar and teacher alike ranked as clerks, free from lay responsibilities or the control of civil tribunals, and *amenable* only to the rule of the bishop and the sentence of his spiritual courts —J.R.Green⟩ LIABLE may indicate the fact of being legally answerable without making further indication or implication ⟨judgment in cases of impeachment shall not extend further than to removal from office, and disqualification to hold and enjoy any office of honor, trust, or profit under the United States; but the party convicted shall, nevertheless, be *liable* and subject to indictment, trial, judgment, and punishment, according to law —*U. S. Constitution*⟩

²responsible \"\ *n* -S : one that accepts responsibility; *esp* : an actor prepared to fill various important roles as occasion demands

re·spon·si·ble·ness *n* -ES : the quality or state of being responsible

re·spon·si·bly \-blē,-bli\ *adv* : in a responsible manner : so as to exhibit responsibility

re·spon·sion \-nchən\ *n* -S [ME, fr. MF or ML; MF *responsion* answer, sum to be paid, fr. ML *responsion-, responsio*, fr. L, answer, fr. *responsus* (past part. of *respondēre* to answer) + *-ion-, -io* -ion — more at RESPOND] **1** *obs* : a sum required to be paid; *esp* : an annual payment required of a member of a military order of knighthood **2 a** : an act of answering : ANSWER, RESPONSE **b responsions** *pl* : the first examination taken by a candidate for the B.A. degree at Oxford University and required for matriculation — called also *smalls*; compare PREVIOUS EXAMINATION

re·spon·sive \-n(t)siv, -sēv *also* -səv\ *adj* [MF or LL; MF *responsif*, fr. LL *responsivus*, fr. L *responsus* + *-ivus* -ive] **1** : giving or serving as an answer : constituting a response or made in response to something ⟨a ~ glance⟩ ⟨prairie fires sprang up ~ to the draught⟩ **2** *obs* : CORRESPONDENT, CORRESPONDING **3** : readily inclined to respond or react appropriately or sympathetically to influences, suggestions, impressions : SENSITIVE : not dull, apathetic, unreceptive, impassive, or unaffected ⟨sensitive to atmospheric conditions, ~ to every varying shift of wind and weather —J.C.Powys⟩ ⟨efforts . . . to keep government in America ~ to the will of the people —V.L.Parrington⟩ **4** : involving the use of responses ⟨~ worship⟩ **syn** see TENDER

re·spon·sive·ly \-səvlē, -li\ *adv* : in a responsive manner

re·spon·sive·ness \-sivnə̇s, -sēv- *also* -səv-\ *n* -ES [*responsive* + *-ness*] : the quality or state of responding or being responsive; *esp* : the rapidity with which a member (as an instrument pointer) comes to rest after a change of any kind

responsive reading *n* : textual matter read aloud as part of a religious service or exercise in which a verse or sentence by the leader is followed by a verse or sentence by the congregation; *also* : a liturgical form or process in which leader and congregation read passages aloud alternatively

re·spon·siv·i·ty \rə̇,spän'sivəd·ē, (,)rē,s-\ *n* -ES [*responsive* + *-ity*] : RESPONSIVENESS

re·spon·sor \rə̇'spän(t)sə(r), rē's-\ *n* -S [L, one that answers, fr. *responsus* + *-or*] : the receiver component of an interrogator

¹re·spon·so·ri·al \rə̇¦spän¦sōrēəl, (')rē¦s-\ *adj* [¹*responsory* + *-al*] : relating to or consisting of responses : ANTIPHONAL

²responsorial \"\ *n* -S [ML *responsoriale*, fr. LL *responsorium* responsory + L *-ale* (neut. of *-alis* -al)] : a book of religious responsories

¹re·spon·so·ry \rə̇'spän(t)sərē, rē's-, -ri\ *n* -ES [ME, fr. LL *responsorium*, fr. L *responsus* (past part. of *respondēre* to answer) + *-orium* -ory — more at RESPOND] : a liturgical response; *esp* : an anthem that is sung or said after or during a lection

²responsory *adj* [ML *responsorius*, fr. L *responsus* + *-orius* -ory] *obs* : relating to or constituting an answer : ANSWERING, RESPONSIVE

re·spon·sum \rə̇'spän(t)səm, rē's-\ *n, pl* **respon·sa** \-)sə\ [NL, fr. L, reply, formal opinion of a jurisconsult — more at RESPONSE] : a written decision from a rabbinical authority in response to a submitted question or problem

re·spooler \(')rē+\ *n* [*re-* + *spooler*] : a worker who winds yarn from one spool to another

re·spot \"+\ *vt* [*re-* + *spot*] : to replace (as a tenpin) precisely in position

re·spray \"+\ *vt* [*re-* + *spray*] : to spray (as fruit trees) an additional time ⟨had to ~ the orchard because of rain⟩

re·spring \"+\ *vb* [*re-* + *spring*] *vi* : to spring up again ~ *vt* : to equip with new springs ⟨had the chair *resprung*⟩

res pu·bli·ca \rā'spüblə̇,kä\ *n, pl* **res publi·cae** \-,kī\ [L — more at REPUBLIC] : COMMONWEAL, COMMONWEALTH, STATE, REPUBLIC

res publicae *n pl* [LL, public things] : things (as the sea, navigable waters, and highways) that are construed under Roman and civil law as owned by no one but subject to use by the public

re·spue \rə̇'spyü\ *vt* [L *respuere* to spit back, fr. *re-* + *spuere* to spit — more at SPEW] : to reject vigorously

ressala *var of* RISALA

ressaldar *var of* RISALDAR

res·sault·ed \rə̇'sȯltə̇d, (')rē¦s-\ *adj* [F *ressault, ressaut* projection (fr. It *risalto*, fr. *risaltare* to spring back, project, fr. *ri-* re- — fr. L *re-* — + *saltare* to leap, fr. L) + E *-ed* — more at SALTANT] : having projections from the plane of a wall or surface

res ser·vi·ens \'rās'servē,en(t)s, 'rēz'sərvē,enz\ *n* [NL] : a servient property or tenement subject to a servitude

¹rest \'rest\ *n* -S [ME, fr. OE *ræst, rest* rest, bed; akin to OHG

rests 5a(2)

rasta rest, a measure of distance between two resting places, ON *rǫst* a measure of distance, mile, Goth *rasta* mile, OE *rōw* rest, calm, OHG *ruowa*, ON *rō*, Gk *erōē* rest, respite, and perh. to OE *ærn, ren* house, OFris *-ern*, ON *rann*, Goth *razn*] **1** : refreshment or repose of body or mind due to more or less complete cessation of activity esp. to sleep ⟨eight hours of ~ a night⟩ ⟨for this I had deprived myself of ~ and health —Mary W. Shelley⟩ **2 a** (1) : cessation or temporary interruption of motion, exertion, or labor : freedom from activity or labor ⟨~ from hard physical effort⟩ ⟨a ten-minute ~ period⟩ ⟨for the purpose of drawing a line between such bodily motions and ~*s* —O.W.Holmes †1935⟩ (2) : a bodily state (as that attained by a fasting individual lying supine) characterized by minimal functional and metabolic activities ⟨the patient must have complete ~⟩ (3) : a position on any gymnastic apparatus in which the body is supported wholly or mainly by the hands or arms, the elbows are above the point of support, and the center of gravity is below the shoulders **b** : absence or cessation of motion as a physical phenomenon : continuance in the same place ⟨a body will continue in a state of ~ unless acted upon⟩ **c** : the repose of death ⟨went to his final ~⟩ **3** : a place where one may rest or abide: as **a** : a permanent or transitory lodging place ⟨found their ~ in the shelter of a wayside tree⟩ ⟨whether that luxurious roadside ~ is a hotel or motel —Frances W. Browin⟩ **b** : a halting place or breathing spot (as a landing between flights of a stair) ⟨a steep trail with little ~*s* chipped out of the rock⟩ **c** : an establishment for the accommodation of a particular group or class (as when out of work or off duty) ⟨a sailors' ~⟩ **4** : freedom from anything that fatigues, disturbs, or troubles : peace of mind or spirit ⟨there was ~ now, not disquietude, in the knowledge —Ellen Glasgow⟩ **5 a** (1) : a rhythmic silence in music or in one of its parts (2) : a character that stands for such silence ⟨half ~⟩ ⟨quarter ~⟩ **b** : a brief pause in reading : CAESURA **6** : something on which anything rests or leans or may rest or lean for support ⟨chin ~ for a violin or viola⟩ ⟨a rail serving as a ~ for the feet⟩: as **a** : a support for a gun when firing **b** : a part in a lathe or similar machine that supports the cutting tool or steadies the work **c** *Brit* : BRIDGE 3e **d** : the part of a partial denture that rests on an abutment tooth, distributes stresses, and holds the clasp in position **e** : a sand-filled pillow or similar firm but moldable cushion used to raise or support a portion of the body during surgery ⟨kidney ~⟩ **7** : renewed vigor

syn REST, RELAXATION, LEISURE, REPOSE, EASE, COMFORT: of these closely related terms the first three — REST, RELAXATION, and LEISURE — stress the condition of being free from labor or from the tension or necessity of effort; the second three — REPOSE, EASE, and COMFORT — stress more the frame of mind or condition of body incident to such a condition. REST, the most general of the terms, emphasizes primarily the fact of cessation or intermission of activity, esp. fatiguing activity or effortful movement, although it also usu. indicates the consequent relief, refreshment, or reinvigoration ⟨night came and with it but little *rest* —Thomas Hardy⟩ ⟨to enjoy a *rest* from struggling —Leslie Rees⟩ RELAXATION emphasizes the release of the muscular or spiritual tension necessary to work or worry; it may be identical with REST or achieved in it so that in some uses it has come to be synonymous with *recreation* ⟨throughout the hours of busiest work and closest application, as well as in the preceding and following moments of leisure and occasional intervals of *relaxation* —W.C.Brownell⟩ ⟨the active amusements and *relaxations* of life can only rest certain of our faculties —John Galsworthy⟩ LEISURE is rather the time exempt from labor as well as the freedom from the necessity of effort; it usu., but not necessarily, implies rest or relaxation, and frequently indicates the unhurriedness of life incident to such a sense of freedom ⟨he who knows how to employ rationally any amount of *leisure* that may fall to his lot —Norman Douglas⟩ ⟨the absence of worry and anxiety about oneself . . . has always been assumed to be a prerequisite condition of *leisure* —R.A.Beals & Leon Brody⟩ ⟨the capacity for civilized enjoyment, for *leisure* and laughter —Bertrand Russell⟩ REPOSE usu. indicates a rest distinguished by physical or mental tranquillity, a freedom from any agitation or disturbance as in peaceful sleep, and has therefore developed to indicate such tranquillity or freedom itself or the appearance of it ⟨a certain woodenness when her face was in *repose* —Scott Fitzgerald⟩ ⟨the pleasant *repose* of the upper valley villages —*Amer. Guide Series: Vt.*⟩ ⟨a langorous *repose* in keeping with the season —Elinor Wylie⟩ EASE indicates a physical or mental condition from which tension, anxiety, effort, or pain have been removed; it may carry a range of meanings from a pleasant release from pain to a rather luxurious absence of all physical or mental effort; by extension from this it has come to signify a relaxed effortlessness in movement, conduct, or accomplishment ⟨a mild sedative brought a certain *ease*⟩ ⟨to live in *ease* and comfort⟩ ⟨the *ease* which he displayed in the conduct of practical affairs —Arnold Bennett⟩ ⟨*ease* and strength, effort and weakness, go together —G.B.Shaw⟩ COMFORT indicates essentially the physical or mental state induced by relief from what disturbs or troubles, but more widely indicates a state not only in which all things that disturb or pain are absent but in which usu. there is a positive physical if passive pleasure. COMFORT stresses more than EASE does the physical pleasurableness of the state and in usu. implying an outside agency which induces the state it has come to signify the thing or things that bring such relief or pleasure ⟨every word brought *comfort* rather than grief —Virginia D. Dawson & Betty D. Wilson⟩ ⟨it was a great *comfort* to me to get back home alive⟩ ⟨if it went on long there would be no *comfort* in the home for anybody —Stuart Cloete⟩ ⟨he is a layman which will be a *comfort* to those of his readers who have not had a scientific training —*London Calling*⟩

at rest 1 : resting or reposing esp. in sleep or death ⟨after so long a sickness it was merciful that she was finally *at rest* and in her grave⟩ **2** : QUIESCENT, MOTIONLESS ⟨the center of buoyancy of a floating body which is *at rest* —*Water & Sewage Control Engineering*⟩ ⟨no small child is ever really *at rest*⟩ **3** : free of anxieties : CALM ⟨set your mind *at rest*⟩

²rest \"\ *vb* -ED/-ING/-S [ME *resten*, fr. OE *ræstan, restan*; akin to OE *ræst* rest] *vi* **1 a** : to take or get repose by lying down; *esp* : to get refreshment of body by sleep **b** : to be in the repose of death : be dead or in the grave **c** : SLEEP, SLUMBER **2** : to cease from action or motion : desist from labor or exertion ⟨planned to ~ during her vacation⟩ **3** : to be free from whatever wearies or disturbs : be quiet or still **4** : to have place : sit or lie fixed or supported : SETTLE ⟨a column ~*s* on its pedestal⟩ ⟨one wing of the army ~*ed* on the hills⟩ **5 a** : to remain confident : put trust **b** : to lean in confidence : repose without anxiety : TRUST, RELY ⟨~ secure on his word⟩ **c** : to become based or founded : have a use as a foundation — usu. used with *on* or *upon* ⟨the verdict ~*ed* on several sound precedents⟩ ⟨a charge ~*ing* upon one man's unsupported statement⟩ **6 a** : to become vested **b** *obs* : CONSIST **c** : to remain or lie for action or accomplishment ⟨the maintenance of peace ~*s* with him alone⟩ **7** *of farmland* : to remain idle or uncropped **8** : to bring to an end voluntarily the introduction of evidence in a law case and thereby lose the right to introduce fresh evidence except in rebuttal ~ *vt* **1 a :** to give rest or repose to : refresh by repose : lay or place at rest : allow to remain inactive, quiet, or undisturbed ⟨~*ed* his horse before starting up the grade⟩ ⟨you should ~ your eyes from so much reading⟩ **b :** to permit (as soldiers in ranks) to move, talk, and smoke while keeping one foot in place ⟨~*ed* his men between the drill exercises⟩ **2 :** to set (as oneself) at rest ⟨~ yourself before the fire⟩ — often used formerly in greetings ⟨God ~ you merry, Sir —Shak.⟩ **3 :** to place or lay on a support : support on or with something ⟨~ the book against the lamp⟩ ⟨~*ed* his gouty foot on a cushion⟩ **4 a :** to cause to be firmly fixed : GROUND ⟨was ~*ing* all his hopes on his son⟩ ⟨~*ed* her case on this argument⟩ **b :** to desist voluntarily from presenting evidence pertinent to (a case at law) **5 :** to allow (land) to remain idle **syn** see BASE — **rest with :** to be the prerogative or province of ⟨any further investigation *rests with* the supervisor⟩

³rest \"\ *n* -s [ME, short for *arest* — more at ARREST] **1** *obs* **:** a checking or halting by or as if by arrest; *specif* **:** legal arrest **2 :** a projection from or attachment on the side of the breastplate of medieval armor intended to support the butt of the lance **3 :** CLARION 5

⁴rest \"\ *vt* [ME *resten*, short for *aresten* — more at ARREST] *chiefly dial* **:** ARREST

⁵rest \"\ *n* -s [ME, fr. MF *reste*, fr. *rester* to remain, rest] **1 :** something that remains over: as **a rests** *pl* **:** REMAINS, RELICS **b** (1) *obs* **:** an amount still unpaid : a balance due (2) *Brit* **:** a reserve (as of a bank) consisting of profits remaining undivided after payment of dividends : SURPLUS **c :** the part remaining after removal of a part in fact or contemplation : all that is left : REMAINDER, RESIDUE — used with *the* ⟨if you will take the baby we can care for the ~⟩ ⟨used the ~ of the butter at breakfast⟩ **d :** a mass of surviving embryonic cells or of cells misplaced in development ⟨some neoplasms probably always arise from embryonic ~*s*⟩ ⟨adrenal *rests* in the kidney⟩ **2 :** a series of repeated returns (as in a game of tennis) : a spell of uninterrupted returning — compare RALLY

⁶rest \"\ *vi* -ED/-ING/-S [ME *resten*, fr. MF *rester* to remain, be left over, fr. L *restare* to stand back, stop behind, be left over, fr. *re-* + *stare* to stand — more at STAND] **1** *obs* **:** to remain unpaid **2 :** to be left over : remain after something is taken away : continue to exist

rest *abbr* restored

re·staff \(ˈ)rē+\ *vt* [*re-* + *staff*] **:** to provide with a new staff ⟨had to ~ the entire hotel⟩

re·stage \"+\ *vt* [*re-* + *stage*] **:** to present again or anew on the stage; *esp* **:** to present (as a play) with a new setting

re·stain \"+\ *vt* [*re-* + *stain*] **:** to stain again or anew; *esp* **:** to re-treat with a stain ⟨destaining and ~*ing* histological slides⟩

rest and residue *or* **rest, residue, and remainder** *n* [⁵*rest*] **:** the residuary estate of a testator

re·start \(ˈ)rē+\ *vb* [*re-* + *start*] *vt* **1 :** to start again or anew ⟨~*ed* his car⟩ **2 :** to resume (as an activity) after interruption ~ *vi* **:** to commence once more : resume operation

re·starter \"+\ *n* [*restart* + *-er*] **:** one that restarts; *esp* **:** a device for automatically restarting an apparatus or mechanism (as a phonograph)

re·state \"+\ *vt* [*re-* + *state*] **:** to state again or in a new form — **re·statement** \"+\ *n*

re·staur *or* **re·stor** \rəˈstȯ(ə)r\ *n* -s [*restaur* fr. F, alter. (influenced by *restaurer* to restore) of OF *restor* restoration, reparation; *restor*, alter. (influenced by *restore*) of *restaur* — more at RESTAURANT, RESTORE, n.] **1 :** the legal recourse that insurers have against each other according to the date of their insurance **2 :** the recourse of an insurer against the master of a ship if loss occurs through his negligence; *also* **:** the recourse of one against a guarantor or against one under obligation to indemnify

res·tau·rant \ˈrest(ə)rənt, -stə,ränt *also* -,stränt *or* -,stərnt\ *n* -s [F, food that restores, restaurant, fr. pres. part. of *restaurer* to restore, fr. L *restaurare* — more at RESTORE] **:** an establishment where refreshments or meals may be procured by the public : a public eating house

restaurant car *n*, *Brit* **:** DINING CAR

res·tau·rant·er \-ntə(r)\ *n* -s [*restaurant* + *-er*] **:** RESTAURATEUR

res·tau·ra·teur \ˌrestə|rəˈtər(·), |,räˈ-, -ˈtü(ə)r\ *also* **res·tau·ran·teur** \|,rän·ˈt- *also* |,ran-\ *n* -s [*restaurateur* fr. F, fr. LL *restaurator* restorer, fr. L *restauratus* (past part. of *restaurare* to restore) + *-or; restauranteur*, modif. (influenced by *restaurant*) of F *restaurateur* — more at RESTORE] **:** the operator or proprietor of a restaurant

¹res·tau·ra·tion \ˌrestəˈrāshən, -e,stȯˈr-\ *archaic var of* RESTORATION

²res·tau·ra·tion \restȯräsyō͞\ *n* -s [F, lit., restoral, restoration, fr. MF — more at RESTORATION] **:** RESTAURANT; *also* **:** the purveying of food (as by a restaurant)

res·tau·ra·tor \ˈrestə,rād·ə(r)\ *n* -s [LL] *archaic* **:** RESTORER

res·tau·ra·trice \ˌrestərəˈtrēs\ *n* -s [F, fr. LL *restauratric-, restauratrix*, fem. of *restaurator* restorer — more at RESTAURATEUR] **:** a woman who operates or owns a restaurant

¹restbalk \ˈ=,=\ *n* [¹*rest* + *balk*] **:** a ridge of land between furrows

²restbalk \"\ *vt* **:** to leave restbalks in (land) in ploughing

rest cure *n* [¹*rest*] **:** treatment of disease (as neurasthenia or tuberculosis) by rest and isolation in a good hygienic environment

rest day *n* **:** a day which is set aside for rest or on which one departs from a normal or usual routine: as **a** (1) **:** SABBATH (2) **:** a day of equivalent religious import in religions other than Judaism and Christianity **b :** a day that is not a workday **c :** any of the days sometimes introduced into an open season on which hunting is not permitted

rested *past of* REST

re·steel \(ˈ)rē+\ *vt* [*re-* + *steel*] **:** to equip with or as if with new steel ⟨~*ed* himself to meet the challenge⟩

re·stem \"+\ *vt* [*re-* + *stem*] **:** to stem again ⟨a ship *restemming* its way⟩

rest·er \ˈrestə(r)\ *n* -s **:** one that rests

rest·ful \ˈrestfəl\ *adj, sometimes* **restfuller** \-fələ(r)\ *sometimes* **restfullest** \-fələst\ [ME, fr. ¹*rest* + *-ful*] **1 :** marked by, affording, or suggesting rest and repose : offering freedom from toil, agitation, or effort ⟨something so beautiful and ~ about his method . . . so free from that fretful haste, that vehement striving —J.K.Jerome⟩ **2 :** enjoying rest : being at ease : RELAXED, TRANQUIL, PLACID ⟨as if no . . . circumstances could put her for long together out of temper . . . her lips were full and ~ —Samuel Butler †1902⟩ **syn** see COMFORTABLE

rest·ful·ly \-fəlē, -li\ *adv* [ME, fr. *restful* + *-ly*] **:** in a restful manner or style : so as to be restful

rest·ful·ness *n* -ES [ME *restfulnes*, fr. *restful* + *-nes* -ness] **:** the quality or state of being restful

restharrow \ˈ=,=(,)=\ *n* [⁴*rest* + *harrow*] **:** a plant of the genus *Ononis*; *esp* **:** a European woody herb (*O. repens*) with pink flowers, unifoliolate leaves, and long tough roots

rest home *n* [¹*rest*] **:** an establishment for the care and housing of persons (as the aged, convalescents) that need special attention or services

rest house *n* **1 :** a house or building for the rest and shelter of travelers; *specif* **:** a dak bungalow **2 :** a resort facility (as a boarding house) featuring a quiet relaxing life and simple wholesome food and appealing esp. to a clientele seeking rest and relaxation

restie *obs var of* RESTY

restier *comparative of* RESTY

restiest *superlative of* RESTY

res·tiff *or* **res·tif** \ˈrestəf\ *adj* [ME *restife, restiffe* — more at RESTIVE] **:** RESTIVE 1c

res·ti·form body \ˈrestə,fȯrm-\ *n* [L *restis* rope, cord + E *-form* — more at RUSH] **:** either of a pair of prominent bands of nerve fibers on the dorsal surface of the medulla oblongata that form part of the lateral boundaries of the fourth ventricle and are continued upward as the inferior peduncles of the cerebellum

re·stimulate \(ˈ)rē+\ *vt* [*re-* + *stimulate*] **:** to reactivate by stimulation

resting *adj* [ME, fr. pres. part. of *resten* to rest, repose] **1 :** not in growing condition : not physiologically active : DORMANT, QUIESCENT ⟨a ~ lily bulb⟩ ⟨~ nerve cells⟩; *also* **:** of, relating to, or marked by dormancy ⟨a ~ period⟩ ⟨~ stages⟩ **2 :** not undergoing or marked by mitosis or other form of division though otherwise physiologically active ⟨a ~ stage⟩

resting cell *n* **1 :** RESTING SPORE **2 :** a living cell with a resting nucleus

resting egg *n* **:** WINTER EGG

resting nucleus *n* **:** a cell nucleus when not undergoing reproduction (as by mitosis)

resting-place \ˈ==,=\ *n* [ME, fr. *resting* (gerund of *resten* to rest, repose) + *place*] **1 :** a place where rest may be taken **2 :** the place where a dead person is laid **3 :** a landing in a staircase : HALFPACE, QUARTERPACE

resting spore *n* [*resting*] **:** a spore (as many zygospores) that remains dormant for a period before germination and is usu. invested with a thickened cell wall to withstand adverse conditions (as of desiccation, heat, or cold) — see CHLAMYDOSPORE

resting wandering cell *n* **:** a fixed histiocyte of the loose connective tissue of the body

res·tio \ˈrestē,ō\ *n, cap* [NL, fr. L, maker of rope, fr. *restis* rope, cord — more at RUSH] **:** a large genus of leafless southern African and Australian herbs (family Restionaceae) having one-celled anthers and many-flowered spikelets with imbricated glumes — see CORDLEAF, ROPE GRASS

res·ti·o·na·ce·ae \ˌrestēəˈnāsē,ē\ *n pl, cap* [NL, fr. *Restion-, Restio*, type genus + *-aceae*] **:** a family of monocotyledonous herbs (order Xyridales) that resemble rushes and have either no leaves or tiny sheathing ones and glumaceous panicled flowers — **res·ti·o·na·ceous** \¦===¦nāshəs\ *adj*

re·stipulation \(ˌ)rē+\ *n* [*re-* + *stipulation*] **:** an act of stipulating anew : RESTATEMENT

res·ti·tute \ˈrestə,tüt, -stə-,tyüt\ *vb* -ED/-ING/-S [L *restitutus*, past part. of *restituere* to restore — more at RESTITUTION] *vt* **1 :** to restore to a former state or position : REHABILITATE **2 :** to give back : REFUND ~ *vi* **:** to become restored, rehabilitated, or refunded : undergo restitution

res·ti·tu·tio in in·te·grum \ˌrestəˈtüd·ē,ōiˈnintəgrəm, -,ō-(,)inin·ˈteg-\ *n* [LL] *Roman & civil law* **:** restoration to a whole or uninjured condition : restoration to the status quo ante

res·ti·tu·tion \ˌrestəˈtüshən, -stəˈtyü-\ *n* -s [ME, fr. OF, fr. L *restitution-, restitutio*, fr. *restitutus* (past part. of *restituere* to set up again, restore, fr. *re-* + *-stituere* — fr. *statuere*, to set up) + *-ion-, -io* -ion — more at STATUTE] **1 :** an act of restoring or a condition of being restored: as **a :** restoration of something to its rightful owner : the making good of or giving an equivalent for some injury (as a loss of or damage to property) **b :** the final restoration of all things and persons to harmony with God's will **c :** restoration of a person to a former position or status; *also* **:** the condition of one so restored : REINSTATEMENT **d :** restoration of a thing or institution to its original state or form **e** *Brit* **:** restoration of conjugal rights **f :** a return to or recovery of a former physical state ⟨the ~ of an elastic body⟩ — compare COEFFICIENT OF RESTITUTION **2 :** something intended to cause or serving to cause restoration of a previous state: as **a** (1) *Brit* **:** a legal action to compel resumption of cohabitation between a husband and wife who have separated that is now used only as preliminary to divorce (2) **:** an action based upon equitable principles to recover money or property that in good conscience belongs to the plaintiff or to prevent a defendant from being unjustly enriched at the expense of the plaintiff (3) **:** an action to restore the parties to a transaction that is being rescinded or avoided to the respective positions they occupied prior to entering into the transaction **b :** a movement of rotation that usu. occurs in childbirth after the head has been delivered and that causes it to point toward the side to which it was directed at the beginning of labor

res·ti·tu·tion·ism \-shə,nizəm\ *n* -s [*restitution* + *-ism*] **:** RESTORATIONISM

res·ti·tu·tion·ist \-sh(ə)nəst\ *n* -s *often cap* [*restitution* + *-ist*] **:** one who holds some form of religious doctrine based on the belief that everything is ultimately to be restored to its pristine form and purity : RESTORATIONIST

restitution nucleus *n* **:** a cell nucleus that contains a diploid or double number of chromosomes and that results typically from failure of completion of a division in mitosis

res·ti·tu·tive \ˈrestə,tüd·iv, -stə-,tyü-\ *adj* [ML *restitutivus*, fr. L *restitutus* (past part. of *restituere* to restore) + *-ivus* -ive — more at RESTITUTION] **:** constituting or tending toward restitution

res·ti·tu·to·ry \ˌrestəˈtüd·ərē, -stəˈtyü-; rəˈsticha,tōrē\ *adj* [LL *restitutorius*, fr. L *restitutus* + *-orius* -ory] **:** of, relating to, or aiming at restitution

res·tive \ˈrestiv, -tēv *also* -təv\ *adj* [ME *restife, restiffe* stationary (of animals), refusing to go forward, resisting control, fr. MF *restif*, (fr. *rester* to remain, stop behind) + *-if* -ive — more at REST] **1** *archaic* **a :** disposed to rest : INACTIVE, SLUGGISH **b :** standing firm : unwilling to yield or adjust : PERSISTENT, STUBBORN, INFLEXIBLE **c :** stubbornly resisting control or guidance : obstinate in refusal : BALKY **2 a** *of a horse* **:** high-spirited and unwilling to submit to discipline or to stand at ease : FRACTIOUS **b :** marked by uneasiness and lack of quietness or attentive interest : FIDGETY ⟨a ~ crowd⟩ **syn** see CONTRARY

res·tive·ly \-təvlē, -li\ *adv* **:** in a restive manner

res·tive·ness \-tivnəs, -tēv- *also* -təv-\ *n* -ES **:** the quality or state of being restive

rest·less \ˈrestləs, *in rapid speech* -sl-\ *adj* [ME *restles*, fr. ¹*rest* + *-les* -less] **1 a :** deprived of rest or sleep : finding no rest : UNEASY ⟨the patient was ~ from pain⟩ **b :** not affording rest : UNRESTFUL ⟨a ~ night⟩ **2 a :** continuing without end : UNCEASING ⟨~ change⟩ **b :** moving or operating continuously : UNQUIET ⟨the ~ sea⟩ **3 :** characterized by or manifesting unrest esp. of mind : lacking in repose : averse to inaction; *also* **:** CHANGEFUL, UNSETTLED, DISCONTENTED

restless cavy *n* **:** APEREA

restless flycatcher *n* **:** a small flycatcher (*Seisura inquieta*) of Australia that is steely blue above and white below and has the habit of hovering with the body arched and wings quivering

rest·less·ly *adv* **:** in a restless manner

rest·less·ness *n* -ES **:** the quality or state of being restless

rest mass *n* [¹*rest*] **:** the mass of a body exclusive of additional mass acquired by the body when in motion according to the theory of relativity

re·stock \(ˈ)rē+\ *vt* [*re-* + *stock*] **:** to stock again : provide new stock for ⟨~*ing* a forest with seedlings⟩ ⟨~*ed* the stream with trout⟩

restor *var of* RESTAUR

re·stor·able \rəˈstōrəbəl, -rēˈs-, -tȯr-\ *adj* [¹*restore* + *-able*] **:** fit for restoring or reclaiming; *esp* **:** capable of being rehabilitated ⟨~ prisoners⟩

re·stor·al \-ōrəl, -ȯrəl\ *n* -s [¹*restore* + *-al*] **:** RESTORATION

¹res·to·ra·tion \ˌrestəˈrāshən\ *n* -s [alter. (influenced by ¹*restore*) of ME *restauracion*, fr. MF or LL; MF *restauration*, fr. LL *restauration-, restauratio*, fr. L *restauratus* (past part. of *restaurare* to restore) + *-ion-, -io* -ion — more at RESTORE] **1 :** an act of restoring or the condition or fact of being restored: as **a :** a bringing back to or putting back into a former position or condition : REINSTATEMENT, RENEWAL, REESTABLISHMENT ⟨the ~ of peace⟩ ⟨the ~ of the monarchy⟩ ⟨behold the different climes agree rejoicing in thy ~ —John Dryden⟩ **b :** a putting back into consciousness or health : recovery of health or strength ⟨~ from sickness⟩ **c :** the ultimate bringing of the whole universe including all men into harmony with the will of God — called also *final restoration* **d :** the act of giving back something to one deprived of it : RESTITUTION **e :** a putting back into an unimpaired or much improved condition ⟨the ~ of a painting⟩ **f :** the act or fact of replacing missing teeth or crowns or associated structures; *also* **:** the replacement (as a denture) used **g :** the reinstatement of the amount or penalty of a fidelity bond (as by a special payment) **2 :** something that is restored; *specif* **:** a representation of the original form (as of a fossil animal or of a building) **3 :** the process of putting a building back into nearly or quite the original form; *also* **:** the making of drawings or models or both designed to show the conceived original form of a building (as a ruin)

²restoration \¦==¦=\ *adj, usu cap* **:** of, relating to, or constituting a period in English history often held to coincide with the reign of Charles II but sometimes considered to extend from his accession to that of Queen Anne ⟨*Restoration* drama⟩

res·to·ra·tion·er \ˌrestəˈrāsh(ə)nə(r)\ *n* -s [*restoration* + *-er*] **:** RESTORATIONIST

res·to·ra·tion·ism \-shə,nizəm\ *n* -s [*restauration* + *-ism*] **:** the belief or doctrines of the restorationists

res·to·ra·tion·ist \-sh(ə)nəst\ *n* -s [*restoration* + *-ist*] **1 :** one who believes in a temporary future punishment and a final restoration of all to the favor and presence of God **2 :** one who makes restorations of buildings

restoration style *n, usu cap R* **:** an English style esp. of furniture and architecture characteristic of the period of the restoration of Charles II

¹re·stor·ative \rəˈstōrəd·iv, -tȯr-\ *adj* [ME *restoratif*, alter. (influenced by ¹*restore*) of *restauratif*, fr. MF, fr. L *restauratus* (past part. of *restaurare* to restore) + MF *-if* -ive — more at RESTORE] **:** of or relating to restoration : having power to restore — **re·stor·ative·ly** *adv* — **re·stor·ative·ness** *n* -ES

²restorative \"\ *n* -s [ME *restoratif*, fr. *restoratif*, adj.] **:** something (as a food or medicine) that serves to restore esp. a person to consciousness or rapidly to normal vigor

res·to·ra·tor \ˈrestə,rād·ə(r)\ *n* -s [modif. (influenced by E ¹*restore*) of F *restaurateur* — more at RESTAURATEUR] *archaic* **:** RESTAURATEUR; *also* **:** RESTAURANT

¹re·store \rəˈstō(ə)r, rēˈs-, -tō(ə)r, -tōə, -tȯ(ə)\ *vb* -ED/-ING/-S [ME *restoren*, fr. OF *restorer*, fr. L *restaurare* to put back into an original state, renew, fr. *re-* + *-staurare* (fr. *instaurare* to renew, restore, perform) — more at STORE] *vt* **1 :** to give back (as something lost or taken away) : make restitution of : RETURN ⟨*restored* the lost child to its parents⟩ **2 :** to put or bring back (as into existence or use) ⟨~ harmony among foes⟩ ⟨*restored* a city-manager plan of government⟩ **3 :** to bring back to or put back into a former or original state : RENEW: as **a :** REBUILD, RECONSTRUCT **b** (1) **:** to put back into or replace in a former state of favor or grace : deliver from the consequences of sin (2) **:** to reinstate in a former position or office **c :** to bring back to a healthy state : cause to recover ⟨and his hand was *restored* whole as the other —Mk 3:5 (AV)⟩ **d :** to make calm or tranquil in mind **e** (1) **:** to bring back from a state of injury or decay or from a changed condition (as by repairing or retouching) : RENOVATE ⟨~ a painting⟩ (2) **:** to repair and alter (a building) with the aim of putting back into the original form ⟨~ a cathedral⟩ **f :** to form a picture or model of the original form of (as something lost or mutilated) : represent or reproduce in the original form ⟨~ ancient ruins⟩ **g :** to place in a text as conjecturally the original reading **4 :** to bring (as a person) back to some former state ⟨*restored* the child to health⟩ : put again in possession of something ⟨~ the king to his throne⟩ **5 a** *obs* **:** to make amends or compensation for **b** *Scots law* **:** to give or make restitution to **c** *archaic* **:** to make good the loss or damage due to **d :** to put back into (a processed food) the original nutritive value by adding elements lost in processing or equivalents of such elements **6 a :** to put (itself) back into the original position or form ⟨an elastic body automatically ~*s* itself after deformation⟩ **b :** to bring (as steel damaged by overheating) back to normal condition **c :** to put back into a former or proper position ⟨*restored* the book to the shelf⟩ ~ *vi* **1** *obs* **:** RECOVER, REVIVE **2 :** to restore a person or thing — **restore in blood :** to readmit to rights (as of a title or inheritance) forfeited under English law by attainder either of the person himself or of his ancestors — compare CORRUPTION OF BLOOD

²restore *n* -s [ME, fr. MF *restor*, fr. OF, fr. *restorer* to restore] *obs* **:** RESTORATION

restorement *n* -s [ME, fr. MF, fr. OF, fr. *restorer* to restore + *-ment*] *obs* **:** RESTORATION

re·stor·er \rəˈstōrə(r), rēˈs-, -tȯr-\ *n* -s [¹*restore* + *-er*] **:** one that restores or makes restorations

restoring force *or* **restoring torque** *n* [fr. pres. part. of ¹*restore*] **:** any one of the forces or torques that tend to restore a system or parts thereof to equilibrium after displacement

restoring moment *n* **:** RIGHTING MOMENT

restoritie *or* **restority** *n, pl* **restorities** [by alter.] *obs* **:** RESTORATIVE

re·stow \(ˈ)rē¦stō\ *vt* [*re-* + *stow*] **:** to stow (as freight) again or anew — **re·stow·al** \-ōəl\ *n* -s

rest period *n* [¹*rest*] **1 :** a period when the internal condition of a wood plant is unfavorable for the growth of buds even though external conditions are favorable **2 :** a period (as during winter or in a dry season) when bulbous plants lose their foliage and mature their bulbs

restr *abbr* restaurant

re·straighten \(ˈ)rē+\ *vt* [*re-* + *straighten*] **:** to straighten again or anew ⟨bent to ~ the seams of her hose⟩

re·strain \rəˈstrān, rēˈs-\ *vb* -ED/-ING/-S [ME *restreynen, restraynen*, fr. MF *restreindre, restraindre*, fr. L *restringere* to draw back tight, restrain, restrict, fr. *re-* + *stringere* to draw tight — more at STRAIN] *vt* **1 a :** to hold (as a person) back from some action, procedure, or course : prevent from doing something (as by physical or moral force or social pressure) ⟨~*ing* her charges . . . from overt acts of violence —C.H. Grandgent⟩ **b :** to limit or restrict to or in respect to a particular action or course : keep within bounds or under control ⟨~*ing* state banks which were inclined to do unsound business —*Dict. of Amer. Biog.*⟩ **2 a :** to moderate or limit the force, effect, development, or full exercise of : prevent or rule out excesses or extremes of ⟨~*ing* lax management⟩ **b :** to keep from being manifested or performed : REPRESS ⟨could hardly ~ her astonishment from being visible —Jane Austen⟩ **3** *obs* **:** to draw back (as a rein) tightly **4 a :** to deprive of liberty : place under arrest or restraint **b :** to deprive (as of liberty) by restraint : abridge the freedom of — used with *of* **5** *obs* **:** FORBEAR, FORBID ~ *vi* **1** *archaic* **:** REFRAIN **2 :** to restrain a person or thing

syn CHECK, CURB, BRIDLE, SNAFFLE, INHIBIT: RESTRAIN is a general term suggesting use of force, pressure, or strenuous persuasion to hold back a person or thing from a course or action or to prevent the action itself ⟨Delaware, in commissioning its delegates, *restrained* them from assenting to any change in the "rule of suffrage" —E.K.Alden⟩ ⟨one wants to produce in the child the same respect for the garden that *restrains* the grown-ups from picking wantonly —Bertrand Russell⟩ RESTRAIN may also be used with any moderating action, any action that prevents extremes ⟨a law of 17 B.C. gave a legal position to slaves informally manumitted . . . but drastically *restrained* their power to acquire and bequeath property —John Buchan⟩ CHECK indicates a restraining of a course, activity, impetus, or effect; its suggestions may rest on uses of the word in horsemanship, chess, or military affairs ⟨if you, my dear father, will not take the trouble of *checking* her exuberant spirits . . . she will soon be beyond the reach of amendment —Jane Austen⟩ ⟨the ambition of churchmen to shine in worldly contests is disciplined and *checked* by the broader interests of the church —Henry Adams⟩ CURB, BRIDLE, and SNAFFLE likewise carry suggestions from horsemanship, CURB indicating drastic and quick checking, BRIDLE indicating a steady, continued guiding, controlling, holding from excess, and SNAFFLE indicating a light curbing ⟨control of money, bills, and the right of electing the councillors *curbed* somewhat the Governor's immense power —*Amer. Guide Series: Mass.*⟩ ⟨endowed . . . with zest, with abundance, with romping blood. She had never been *bridled* in mind or body —Francis Hackett⟩ ⟨whose potential violence of feeling is *bridled* by good form —*N. Y. Herald Tribune Bk. Rev.*⟩ INHIBIT, largely psychological or scientific in its suggestions, is likely to bring into consideration repressive or curbing effects of custom, morality, precept, or conscience ⟨the inherent immorality of the acts has become as strong an *inhibiting* factor as the fear of punishment —T.L.Karsten & J.H.Mathias⟩ ⟨a more and more courageous, a less and less *inhibited* medium of expression —F.B.Millett⟩

re·strain·able \-nəbəl\ *adj* **:** capable of being or subject to being restrained

re·strain·ably \-blē\ *adv* **:** in a restrainable manner

re·strained \-nd\ *adj* [fr. past part. of *restrain*] **:** marked by or manifesting restraint (as in art) : devoid of excess or extravagance : DISCIPLINED — **re·strain·ed·ly** \-n(ə)dlē, -li\ *adv* — **re·strain·ed·ness** \-nədnəs, -n(d)nəs\ *n* -ES

restrained beam *n* **:** a beam built in at the supports : an encastre beam

re·strain·er \-nə(r)\ *n* -s **:** one that restrains; *esp* **:** a chemical (as potassium bromide) used to retard the action of a photographic developer esp. on unexposed silver salts

restraining *adj* [fr. pres. part. of *restrain*] **:** used for restraining : designed to restrain (as from a course of action) — see RESTRAINING ORDER — **re·strain·ing·ly** *adv*

restraining order *n* : a preliminary legal order sometimes issued to keep a situation unchanged pending decision upon an application for an injunction

re·straint \rə'strānt, rē's-\ *n* -s [ME, fr. MF *restrainte*, fr. fem. of *restraint*, past part. of *restraindre* to restrain — more at RESTRAIN] **1 a** : an act of restraining, hindering, checking, or holding back from some activity or expression ⟨to act upon his own choice and judgment free from ~s . . . imposed by the arbitrary will of other human beings —John Dewey⟩ **b** : a means, force, or agency that restrains, checks free activity, or otherwise controls ⟨if a woman has no inclination to do what is wrong, being secured from it is no ~ to her —James Boswell⟩ ⟨the ~s of an academic habit —Irwin Edman⟩ **c** : the condition of being restrained, checked, or controlled : deprivation of liberty : CONFINEMENT ⟨absolute liberty is absence of ~ —Henry Adams⟩ ⟨facilities for the accommodation and ~ of so large a number of frenzied patients —V.G. Heiser⟩ **2** : a check on free commercial or business activity : EMBARGO ⟨production being hindered by governmental ~s⟩ **3** : a check or control over free, easy, or unruly expression : CONSTRAINT : reserved expression avoiding extravagance or excess : stiffness and lack of easy naturalness and liveliness ⟨a ~ which kept them mutually silent on the subject —Jane Austen⟩ ⟨so much ~ of feeling, so much impersonality, so much coldness —Manny Farber⟩ ⟨designed with . . . ~ without overemphasis of decoration —*Amer. Guide Series: Del.*⟩ **syn** see FORCE

restraint of marriage : a condition attached to a gift or bequest or in a contract that nullifies the grant if the donee or grantee marries and is usu. void if general and unlimited in scope

restraint of princes *archaic* : EMBARGO

restraint of trade : an attempt or intent to eliminate or stifle competition, to effect a monopoly, to maintain prices artificially, or otherwise to hamper or obstruct the course of trade and commerce as it would be if left to the control of natural and economic forces

re·strengthen \(')rē+\ *vt* [*re-* + *strengthen*] : to make strong again (as by recruiting or reinforcing) : impart new strength to

re·stress \"+\ *vt* [*re-* + *stress*] : to subject to phonetic stress (as a form or vowel that originated by loss of stress) and in so doing produce a stressed form different from the original stressed form ⟨\ˌfrəm\ *from* yielded \ˌfrəm\, which by ~*ing* yields \ˈfrəm\⟩

re·strict \rə'strikt, rē's-\ *vt* -ED/-ING/-S [L *restrictus*, past part. of *restringere* to restrain, restrict — more at RESTRAIN] **1** : to set bounds or limits to : hold within bounds: as **a** : to check free activity, motion, progress, or departure of : RESTRAIN ⟨intellectual snobbery which has tended to ~ men and women from an understanding of religion —A.H. Compton⟩; *also* : HAMPER, DIMINISH **b** : to check, bound, or decrease the range, scope, or incidence of : set what is to be included or embraced by : bar or carefully govern addition or increment to ⟨countries where literacy was largely ~*ed* to the upper classes —Helen Sullivan⟩ **2** : to place (land) under restrictions as to use (as by zoning ordinances) **syn** see LIMIT

restricted *adj* [fr. past part. of *restrict*] : subject or subjected to restriction: as **a** : limited to the use of particular classes of people or specifically excluding others (as members of a class or ethnic group felt to be inferior) ⟨a ~ residential area⟩ ⟨~ hotels⟩ **b** : not given a security classification but not for general circulation or release ⟨a ~ publication⟩ — used officially by the U.S. prior to Nov. 1953; see RESTRICTED DATA — **re·strict·ed·ly** *adv* — **re·strict·ed·ness** *n* -ES

restricted area *n* : an area from which military personnel are excluded for reasons of security or safety unless specially authorized : an off limits area

restricted data *n pl* : all data concerning the design, manufacture, and utilization of atomic weapons, the production of special nuclear material, or the use of special nuclear material in the production of energy but not including data declassified by the proper lawful authority

re·stric·tion \-kshən\ *n* -s [ME *restriccioun*, fr. LL *restriction-, restrictio* limitation, fr. L *restrictus* (past part. of *restringere* to restrict) + *-ion-, -io* -ion — more at RESTRAIN] **1** : something that restricts : QUALIFICATION: as **a** : a regulation that restricts or restrains ⟨new ~s for hunters⟩ **b** : a limitation placed on the use or enjoyment of real or other property; *esp* : an encumbrance on land restricting the uses to which it may be put **c** : a limitation that is imposed upon a class or ethnic group and that excludes its members from a fairly competitive use and enjoyment of the facilities of a community (as housing, employment, or education) **d** : limitation of the opening two or three moves in a game of checkers to one series chosen by lot from an accepted list **2** : an act of restricting or the condition of being restricted : confinement within bounds ⟨undue ~ of children⟩ **3** : a tacit or expressed qualification : RESERVATION ⟨a mental ~⟩ **4** : TIGHTENING, CONSTRICTION

re·stric·tion·ary \-shəˌnerē\ *adj* [*restriction* + *-ary*] : RESTRICTIVE

re·stric·tion·ism \-ˌnizəm\ *n* -s [*restriction* + *-ism*] : a policy or philosophy advocating restriction or restrictions: as **a** : a policy or practice of trade restraints (as by internal restrictive practices or by import restrictions) : a monopolistic policy **b** (1) : a policy of labor resistance to mechanization and automation based on a desire to increase the number of available jobs (2) : a policy of curtailing the individual worker's output to make the job last longer

¹re·stric·tion·ist \-sh(ə)nəst\ *n* -s [*restriction* + *-ist*] : an advocate of restriction or restrictionism

²restrictionist \"\ *adj* : of, relating to, or concerned with restrictionism or restrictionists ⟨~ opinions⟩ ⟨a ~ policy⟩

¹re·stric·tive \rə'striktiv, rē's-, -ktēv *also* -ktəv\ *adj* [ME, fr. MF *restrictif*, serving to restrict, astringent, fr. L *restrictus* (past part. of *restringere* to restrict) + MF *-if* -ive — more at RESTRAIN] **1** *obs* : ASTRINGENT, BINDING, STYPTIC **2** : serving or tending to restrict : conveying restrictions ⟨a ~ tariff⟩ ⟨~ regulations⟩ ⟨a ~ railroad signal⟩ **3** : expressing a limitation of the reference of the term qualified ⟨a ~ adjective⟩ ⟨~ phrases⟩ — see RESTRICTIVE CLAUSE **4** : prohibiting further negotiation or giving authority to deal with an instrument as directed but not to transfer ownership ⟨a ~ endorsement of a negotiable instrument⟩ — **re·stric·tive·ly** \-tə̇vlē, -li\ *adv* — **re·stric·tive·ness** \-tivnəs, -tēv- *also* -təv-\ *n* -ES

²restrictive \"\ *n* -s : a restrictive term or expression

restrictive clause *n* : an adjective clause so closely attached to its noun as to be essential to the definiteness of the noun's meaning (as *who succeeded* in "the boy who succeeded had worked hard") — called also *determinative clause*

restrictive covenant *n* : an agreement generally running with the land and restricting the free use of land (as to particular purposes or to occupancy by members of a particular ethnic group)

restrictive endorsement *n* : an endorsement transferring commercial paper for a particular purpose (as for deposit or collection or payment to a named person only) thereby indicating negotiability is to cease — compare SPECIAL ENDORSEMENT

restricts *pres 3d sing of* RESTRICT

¹re·strike \(')rē+\ *vb* [¹*re-* + *strike*] *vt* : to strike again or anew ~ *vi* : to strike again or anew

²re·strike \'rē+,-, ⸗'⸗\ *n* **1** : a coin or medal struck from an original die at some time after the original issue and usu. esp. for collectors **2** : an impression made from a surface that has already been printed from; *typically* : a new print made from an old woodcut, lithographic stone, or metal engraving **3** : a coin struck on another coin

re·string \(')rē+\ *vt* [*re-* + *string*] : to fit (as a violin, a tennis racket) with new strings

re·stringe \rə'strinj\ *vt* -ED/-ING/-S [L *restringere* to draw back tight, restrict — more at RESTRAIN] **1** *obs* : to make costive : BIND **2** *archaic* : CONFINE, RESTRICT

re·strin·gen·cy \-njənsē\ *n* -ES [¹*restringent* + *-cy*] : the quality or state of being restringent

¹re·strin·gent \-jənt\ *adj* [L *restringent-, restringens*, pres. part. of *restringere* to draw back tight, restrict — more at RESTRAIN] *archaic* : BINDING, ASTRINGENT, STYPTIC

²restringent \"\ *n* -s *archaic* : something (as a word or a medication) with restringent properties

rest room *n* [¹*rest*] : a room or suite of rooms in a public or semipublic building or a business establishment provided with lavatory, toilet, and other facilities for clients', visitors', or employees' rest or comfort

re·structure \(')rē+\ *vt* [*re-* + *structure*] : to give a new structure or organization to

rests *pl of* REST, *pres 3d sing of* REST

re·study \(')rē+\ *vt* [*re-* + *study*] : to study again or anew : make a new appraisal or evaluation of ⟨had to ~ the whole program in terms of recent developments in technique⟩

re·stuff \"+\ *vt* [*re-* + *stuff*] : to provide with a new stuffing ⟨~*ed* the old cushions⟩

rest up *vi* [²*rest*] : to get a complete rest : rest oneself thoroughly

rest·ward \'restwə(r)d\ *also* **rest·wards** \-dz\ *adv* [¹*rest* + *-ward*] : toward rest or a resting place

res·ty \'restē\ *adj* -ER/-EST [alter. of *restive*] **1** : SLUGGISH, INDOLENT **2** *chiefly dial* : RESTIVE

re·style \(')rē+\ *vt* [*re-* + *style*] : REFASHION: **a** : to make in a new style **b** : to design or set a new style for

re·subject \ˌrē+\ *vt* [*re-* + *subject*] : to bring again into subjection — **re·subjection** \"+\ *n*

re·sublime \"+\ *vt* [*re-* + *sublime*] : to sublime again ⟨*resublimed* iodine⟩

re·submission \"+\ *n* [*re-* + *submission*] : an act of resubmitting

re·submit \"+\ *vt* [*re-* + *submit*] : to offer (as a question for popular vote) again or anew

re·sue \rə'sü\ *vt* -ED/-ING/-S [origin unknown] : to mine (a very narrow vein) by first stoping the rock wall on one side and then removing the ore

¹re·sult \rə'zəlt, rē'z-\ *vi* -ED/-ING/-S [ME *resulten*, fr. ML *resultare*, fr. L, to leap back, spring back, fr. *re-* + *-sultare* (fr. *saltare* to leap) — more at SALTANT] **1** : to proceed, spring, or arise as a consequence, effect, or conclusion : come out or have an issue : TERMINATE, END — used with *from* or *in* ⟨this measure will ~ in good⟩ ⟨an injury ~*ing* from a fall⟩ **2** *archaic* : to leap or spring back : REBOUND, RECOIL **3** *law* **a** : REVERT ⟨the estate will ~ to him⟩ **b** *archaic* : DEVOLVE — used with *to*

²result \"\ *n* -s **1** : a decision or resolution of a deliberative or legislative body **2** : something that results as a consequence, effect, issue, or conclusion ⟨suffer from the ~s of war⟩ ⟨the causes and ~s of sleeping sickness⟩; *sometimes* : beneficial or tangible effect : FRUIT ⟨an inquiry without ~⟩ ⟨get ~s from a new treatment⟩ **3** : something obtained, achieved, or brought about by calculation, investigation, or similar activity (as an answer to a problem or knowledge gained by scientific inquiry) ⟨he added the long column of figures and offered the ~⟩ ⟨his thesis was the ~ of his study⟩ **4 results** *pl* : a synoptic publication of the outcome of related competitive events ⟨the race ~s are on the back page⟩ ⟨have you seen the football ~s⟩ **syn** see EFFECT — **in result** *adv* : as a result ⟨the dam broke and *in result* the land was flooded⟩

re·sult·ance \-t'n(t)s, -tən-\ *also* **re·sult·an·cy** \-nsē\ *n*, *pl* **resultances** *also* **resultancies** [¹*result* + *-ance*, *-ancy*] **1** *obs* : a combined result : AGGREGATE, GIST **2** *obs* : EMANATION, REFLECTION **3** *obs* : the fact or character of being resultant **4** : RESULT, OUTCOME

¹re·sult·ant \-nt\ *adj* [ML *resultant-, resultans*, pres. part. of *resultare* to result] : being derived from or consequent upon something else : having the character of a result or consequence : RESULTING ⟨a ~ force⟩ ⟨~ measures⟩

²resultant \"\ *n* -s [partly fr. ¹*resultant*, partly fr. F *résultante*, fr. fem. of *résultant* resultant (adj.), fr. ML *resultant-, resultans*] : something that results or constitutes a result : a resulting quality, character, condition, or product : OUTCOME: as **a** (1) : a mathematical vector sum (2) : the single vector that is equivalent to a given set of vectors (as of forces or velocities) and is usu. the sum of these vectors (3) : ELIMINANT **b** (1) : COMBINATION TONE (2) *also* **resultant bass** : ACOUSTIC BASS **c** : an effective force that results from the cooperation and antagonism of varied individual forces : a product or mean of conflicting and cooperating elements ⟨life in a democracy is . . . the ~ of millions of individual decisions —A.A.Berle⟩ ⟨social adjustment of an individual is the ~ of two complementary forces —L.E. Rosenzweig⟩ **d** : a substance formed in a chemical reaction : PRODUCT — opposed to *reactant*

re·sult·ant·ly *adv* [¹*resultant* + *-ly*] : so as to be resultant : in the manner of a resultant

re·sult·ative \-ltəd·iv\ *adj* [¹*result* + *-ative*] : RESULTANT; *esp* : expressive of result ⟨German *ergreifen* is a ~ verb⟩

re·sult·ful \-ltfəl\ *adj* [²*result* + *-ful*] : bearing or full of results : FRUITFUL ⟨a ~ investigation⟩ ⟨passed ~ hours in the library⟩ — **re·sult·ful·ly** \-fəlē\ *adv*

re·sult·ing·ly *adv* [*resulting* + *-ly*] : as a result

resulting trust *n* : a trust based upon the presumed intentions of the parties as inferred from all the circumstances that the one holding legal title to trust property holds it for the benefit of the other — compare CONSTRUCTIVE TRUST, EXPRESS TRUST

resulting use *n* : a use raised in a court of equity in favor of a grantor or donor transferring property to uses when failing to declare the use for a particular person or when a use declared has come to an end or cannot possibly vest and no other person is designated to enjoy it

re·sult·less \-ltləs\ *adj* [²*result* + *-less*] : productive of no result : INEFFECTIVE — **re·sult·less·ly** *adv* — **re·sult·less·ness** *n* -ES

results *pres 3d sing of* RESULT, *pl of* RESULT

re·sum·able \rə'züməbəl, rē'z-\ *adj* : capable of being resumed : fit to be resumed

¹re·sume \-m\ *vb* -ED/-ING/-S [ME *resumen*, fr. MF or L; MF *resumer* fr. L *resumere* to take up again, take back, resume, fr. *re-* + *sumere* to take up, take, fr. *sub-* under, up + *emere* to take — more at SUB-, REDEEM] *vt* **1** : to assume or take again : put on anew : REOCCUPY ⟨don't ~ the habit⟩ ⟨~ her place in society⟩ ⟨*resumed* our coats and hats⟩ **2** : to enter upon or begin again : take up after interruption ⟨sat down and *resumed* her work⟩ ⟨~ reading where you left off⟩ **3** : to take back to oneself ⟨on default the grantor does not automatically ~ title⟩ **4** : to take or pick up again : go back to using **5** : to make repetition of (as a sentence); *also* : REITERATE, SUMMARIZE, EPITOMIZE ~ *vi* **1** : to take possession again **2** : to recommence something (as a discourse, work, business) interrupted : go on again after an interruption

²ré·su·mé *or* **re·su·me** *or* **re·su·mé** \ˌrezəˌmā *also* ˌrā| *or* |(ˌ)ü|mā *sometimes* |zh|\ *n* -s [F, fr. past part. of *résumer* to recapitulate, sum up, fr. MF, to resume] : a summing up : a condensed statement : ABRIDGMENT, SUMMARY; *specif* : a brief account of one's education and professional experience

³résumé \"\ *vt* -ED/-ING/-S : SUMMARIZE

re·sum·er \rə'züma(r), rē'z-\ *n* -s : one that resumes

re·summon \(')rē+\ *vt* [*re-* + *summon*] : to summon again or anew

re·summons \"+\ *n* [ME *resommons*, fr. AF *resomons*, fr. past part. of *resomondre*, *resemondre* to resummon, fr. OF *re-* + *semondre* to summon — more at SUMMON] : a summons to a party or witness already once summonsed : another summons issued in a case after the original

re·sump·tion \rə'zəm(p)shən, rē'- *sometimes* -'sə-\ *n* -s [ME fr. MF or LL; MF *resomption* act of resuming, fr. LL *resumption-, resumptio*, fr. L *resumptus* (past part. of *resumere* to resume) + *-ion-, -io* -ion] **1 a** : the taking again by the crown or other authority of lands or tenements previously granted (as on the ground of false suggestions or other error) **b** : the taking back or recovery of something previously given up or lost ⟨a ~ of power by the opposition⟩ **2 a** : the act or fact of taking up again : RECOMMENCEMENT ⟨the ~ of her duties after the holiday⟩ **b** : a return to payment in specie ⟨~ seems unlikely in the U. S. under present conditions⟩

re·sump·tive \-m(p)tiv\ *adj* [L *resumptus* + E *-ive*] **1** : constituting a résumé : SUMMARIZING **2** : tending toward or indicative of resumption — **re·sump·tive·ly** \-tə̇vlē\ *adv*

res uni·ver·si·ta·tis \'rāˌsünəˌversə'täd·əs, 'rēˌzünəˌvərsə'täd-\ *n pl* [L] : things belonging under Roman or civil law to a society, corporation, university, or other community or public or private group for the use of the group and not the constituent members thereof

re·supinate *also* **re·supinated** \(')rē+\ *adj* [L *resupinatus*, past part. of *resupinare* to bend back to a supine position, fr. *re-* + *supinus* supine] **1** : inverted in position : appearing by a twist of the axis to be upside down or reversed ⟨many orchids have ~ flowers⟩ **2** : having or being a fruiting body that forms a hyphal mat on the substrate with the hymenium at the periphery or over the whole surface ⟨a ~ fungus⟩

re·supination \(ˌ)rē+\ *n* [L *resupinatus* + E *-ion*] **1** : the act of lying on the back or the position of one so lying **2** : a turning or twisting (as of a flower) to an inverted or apparently upside-down position; *also* : a resupinate condition

re·supine \"+\ *adj* [L *resupinus*, fr. *resupinare*] : SUPINE

¹re·supply \ˌrē+\ *vt* [*re-* + *supply*] : to supply again : provide anew with supplies; *esp* : to provide (a military force in action) with replacement or supplementary matériel

²resupply \"\ *n* : an act or system of resupplying

re·surface \(')rē+\ *vb* [*re-* + *surface*] *vt* : to provide with a new or fresh surface: as **a** : to dress the surface of anew ⟨~ a tool⟩ **b** : to renew the surface pavement of ⟨~ a street⟩ ~ *vi*, *of a submarine* : to come again to the surface of the water

¹re·surge \rə'sərj, rē's-\ *vi* [L *resurgere* — more at RESURRECTION] : to rise again : become resurrected ⟨the *resurging* of nationalism⟩

²re·surge \(')rē+\ *vi* [*re-* + *surge*] : to surge back or to and fro ⟨as the battle ~s⟩

re·sur·gence \rə'sərjən(t)s, rē's-, -sōj-, -soij-\ *n* -s [fr. ²*resurgent*, after such pairs as E *excellent*: *excellence*] : a rising again into life, activity, or prominence ⟨a ~ of religious feeling⟩

re·sur·gen·cy \-nsē, -nsi\ *n* -ES [²*resurgent* + *-cy*] : the quality or state of being resurgent : RESURGENCE

¹re·sur·gent \-nt\ *n* -s [L *resurgent-, resurgens*, pres. part. of *resurgere*] : one that experiences resurgence

²resurgent \"\ *adj* [L *resurgent-, resurgens*, pres. part. of *resurgere* to rise again — more at RESURRECTION] **1** : rising again from an inferior state (as death, torpor, decadence) to a superior state ⟨~ life of spring —W.P.Smith⟩ **2** : tending to produce resurgence ⟨nationalism is a powerful, even a ~ force —*New Republic*⟩

resurgent water *n* : water that having once been at the surface of the earth has supposedly been incorporated in molten magma and again reached the surface by expulsion

res·ur·rect \ˌrezə'rekt\ *vb* -ED/-ING/-S [back-formation fr. *resurrection*] *vt* **1 a** : to raise from the dead : restore to life **b** : to bring to view again (something forgotten or lost) **2** : to disinter or exhume (a body) in the character of a resurrectionist **3** : to bring again (a feature buried beneath sedimentary deposits) to the surface by erosion ⟨~*ed* peneplain⟩ ~ *vi* : to become risen again from the dead

¹res·ur·rec·tion \ˌrezə'rekshən\ *n* -s [ME, fr. LL *resurrection-, resurrectio* act of rising from the dead, Easter festival, fr. *resurrectus* (past part. of *resurgere* to rise from the dead, fr. L, to rise again, fr. *re-* + *surgere* to rise) + L *-ion-, -io* -ion — more at SURGE] **1 a** *usu cap* : a service or festival (as Easter) commemorating the rising of Jesus Christ from the dead ⟨*Resurrection* services at the cathedral⟩ **b** *often cap* : the rising again to life of all the human dead before the final judgment that is predicted in Christian religions ⟨there will be a ~ of both the just and the unjust —Acts 24:15 (RSV)⟩ **c** : the state of one risen from the dead ⟨for in the ~ they neither marry nor are given in marriage —Mt 22:30 (RSV)⟩ **d** *usu cap* : a representation of Christ's resurrection (as in art or drama) **2** : the act or fact of rising again from an inferior state (as death, decay, disuse) into a superior : RESURGENCE, REVIVAL **3** : an agent, cause, or exemplar of a rising of the dead ⟨I am the ~ and the life —Jn 11:25 (RSV)⟩ **4** *Christian Science* : spiritualization of thought : material belief yielding to spiritual understanding

²resurrection \ˌ⸗⸗'⸗⸗\ *vt* -ED/-ING/-S [¹*resurrection*] : RESURRECT

res·ur·rec·tion·al \ˌrezə'rekshən°l, -shnəl\ *adj* : of or relating to resurrection

res·ur·rec·tion·ary \ˌrezə'rekshəˌnerē\ *adj* [¹*resurrection* + *-ary*] : constituting resurrection; *also* : of or relating to resurrectionism

resurrection body *n* : man's body as restored by resurrection

res·ur·rec·tion·er \ˌrezə'reksh(ə)nə(r)\ *n* -s [²*resurrection* + *-er*] : RESURRECTIONIST 1

resurrection fern *n* [¹*resurrection*] : GRAY POLYPODY

res·ur·rec·tion·ism \ˌrezə'rekshəˌnizəm\ *n* -s [¹*resurrection* + *-ism*] : the practice of body snatchers

res·ur·rec·tion·ist \-sh(ə)nəst\ *n* -s [¹*resurrection* + *-ist*] **1** : a stealer of dead bodies : BODY SNATCHER **2** : one who resurrects (as by restoring, reviving, or reemploying) **3** : one who believes in the resurrection of the body

res·ur·rec·tion·ize \-shəˌnīz\ *vt* -ED/-ING/-S [¹*resurrection* + *-ize*] : RESURRECT

resurrection man *n* [¹*resurrection*] : BODY SNATCHER

resurrection plant *n* **1** : any of several club mosses of the genus *Selaginella* (as *S. convoluta* and *S. lepidophylla*) that close up when dry but expand again when moistened **2** : ROSE OF JERICHO **3** : a fig marigold (*Mesembryanthemum tripolium*)

resurrection woman *n* : a body snatcher who is a woman

res·ur·rec·tive \ˌrezə'rektiv\ *adj* [LL *resurrectus* (past part. of *resurgere* to rise from the dead) + E *-ive* — more at RESURRECTION] : of, relating to, or causing resurrection

res·ur·rec·tor \-tə(r)\ *n* -s [*resurrect* + *-or*] : one that resurrects ⟨a ~ of things past⟩

resurrects *pres 3d sing of* RESURRECT

re·surrender \ˌrē+\ *vt* [*re-* + *surrender*] : to yield anew

¹re·survey \(ˌ)rē+\ *vt* [*re-* + *survey*] : to survey again or anew; *esp* : to recheck the boundaries of by surveying

²resurvey \"+\ *n* [*re-* + *survey*] : a second or fresh survey ⟨made a ~ of 15th century Irish writings⟩

re·sus·ci·ta·ble \rə'səsəd·əbəl, rē's-\ *adj* [L *resuscitare* to revive + E *-able*] : capable of resuscitation — **re·sus·ci·ta·bly** \-blē, -bli\ *adv*

re·sus·ci·tate \-'səsəˌtāt, *usu* -ād·+V\ *vb* -ED/-ING/-S [L *resuscitatus*, past part. of *resuscitare* to stir up again, revive, fr. *re-* + *suscitare* to stir up, rouse, fr. *sus-* up (var. of *sub-*) + *citare* to put in motion, stir — more at SUB-, CITE] *vt* **1** : to revive from apparent death or from unconsciousness ⟨try to ~ a nearly drowned person by artificial respiration⟩ **2** : to restore from a state of desuetude or decay ⟨withered plants *resuscitated* by rain⟩ ⟨plans to ~ the liberal party⟩ ~ *vi* : to come to : regain vigor or vitality : REVIVE

re·sus·ci·ta·tion \rəˌsəsə'tāshən, (ˌ)rēˌs-\ *n* -s [LL *resuscitation-, resuscitatio*, fr. L *resuscitatus* + *-ion-, -io* -ion] : an act of resuscitating or the state of being resuscitated : RESTORATION, REVIVAL, RENEWAL ⟨~ by means of artificial respiration or cardiac massage⟩

re·sus·ci·ta·tive \⸗'⸗⸗ˌtād·iv\ *adj* [*resuscitate* + *-ive*] : tending to resuscitate : REVIVING, REVIVIFYING ⟨lifeguards were taught the basic ~ methods⟩

re·sus·ci·ta·tor \-ād·ə(r)\ *n* -s [*resuscitate* + *-or*] : one that resuscitates; *specif* : an apparatus that delivers oxygen or a mixture of oxygen and carbon dioxide to and induces a renewal of respiration in the asphyxiated

re·swear \(')rē+\ *vt* [*re-* + *swear*] : to swear to or cause to swear anew or again

re·symbolization \(ˌ)rē+\ *n* [*re-* + *symbolization*] : symbolization again or anew; *specif* : a mental transformation either for better or for worse consisting in the finding of new meanings and new forms of expression for one's thoughts and desires

re·symbolize \(')rē+\ *vt* [*re-* + *symbolize*] : to provide with new symbols : symbolize anew

re·synthesis \"+\ *n* [*re-* + *synthesis*] : a reuniting usu. in a new combination of parts or elements that have been separated (as by prior analysis)

re·synthesize \"+\ *vt* [*re-* + *synthesize*] : to synthesize again : subject to resynthesis : practice resynthesis upon

¹ret \'ret, *usu* -ed·+V\ *vb* **retted; retted; retting; rets** [ME *reten*, fr. MD *reten, reeten*] *vt* **1** : to soak or expose (as flax or hemp) to moisture in order to promote the loosening of the fiber from the woody tissue by bacterial action; *also* : to treat chemically for loosening of the fiber from the woody tissue **2** : to rot or injure by exposure to moisture ~ *vi* : to become retted : undergo loosening of the fiber from the woody tissue after soaking ⟨it finally ~s, and the black inner fiber . . . can be gathered up and baled —Thomas Barbour⟩

²ret \"\ *n* -s : RETTING ⟨dew-*ret*⟩ ⟨water-*ret*⟩

ret *abbr* **1** retain; retainer; retaining **2** retard **3** retired **4** return; returned

re·ta·ble \rə'tābəl, rē'-\ *n* -s [F, fr. Sp *retablo*, modif. of Catal *reataula*, fr. *rea-* backward, behind (fr. L *retro-*) + *taula* table, fr. L *tabula* tablet, board] **:** a raised shelf or ledge behind an altar on which are placed the altar cross, the altar lights, and vases of flowers; *also* **:** an elaborate framework rising behind the altar and enclosing a panel decorated with painting, sculpture, or mosaic — compare PREDELLA

re·ta·blo \rä'tä(,)blō\ *n* -s [Sp, retable] **1 :** a votive offering made in the form of a religious picture typically portraying Christian saints, painted on a panel, and hung in a church or chapel esp. in Spain and Mexico **2 :** REREDOS 1

¹re·tail \'rē,tāl; *in sense 2* rə't- *or* rē't-, *esp before pause or consonant* -āəl\ *vb* -ED/-ING/-S [ME *retailen*, fr. MF *retaillier* to cut off, diminish, divide into pieces, fr. OF, fr. *re-* + *taillier* to cut — more at TAILOR] *vt* **1 :** to sell in small quantities (as the single yard, pound, gallon) **:** to sell directly to the ultimate consumer ⟨~ cloth⟩ ⟨~ groceries⟩ **2 :** to relate in detail or to one person after another **:** tell again or again and again ⟨~ a conversation⟩ ⟨~ gossip⟩ ⟨~ a story⟩ **~** *vi* **:** to sell at retail ⟨a book that ~s for $10⟩

²re·tail \'rē,tāl\ *n* -s [ME, fr. MF, cut, piece, fr. OF, fr. *retaillier* to cut off; influenced in meaning by ME *retailen* to retail] **:** the sale of commodities or goods in small quantities to ultimate consumers — opposed to WHOLESALE — **at retail** *adv* **:** at a price customarily asked by a retailer **:** RETAIL ⟨sold *at retail*⟩

³retail \"\ *adj* **:** of, relating to, or engaged in the sale of commodities at retail ⟨~ trade⟩ ⟨~ merchant⟩ ⟨~ business⟩ ⟨~ selling⟩ ⟨~ price⟩

⁴retail \"\ *adv* **:** in small quantities **:** from a retailer ⟨a blend costing five cents more a pound ~ —W.H.Ukers⟩ ⟨cartridge sells ~ for less —E.T.Canby⟩

retail credit *n* **:** CONSUMER CREDIT

re·tail·er \-lə(r)\ *n* -s [ME, fr. *retailen* to retail + *-er*] **:** one that retails something ⟨a ~ of gossip⟩; *specif* **:** a merchant middleman who sells goods mainly to ultimate consumers

re·tail·ing \-liŋ\ *n* -s [ME, fr. gerund of *retailen* to retail] **:** the activities involved in the selling of goods to ultimate consumers for personal or household consumption **:** selling at retail

re·tail·ment \-lmənt\ *n* -s [¹*retail* + *-ment*] **:** act of retailing ⟨~ of the news⟩

retail store *n* **:** a place of business usu. owned and operated by a retailer but sometimes owned and operated by a manufacturer or by someone other than a retailer in which merchandise is sold primarily to ultimate consumers

re·tain \rə'tān, rē'-\ *vb* -ED/-ING/-S [ME *reteinen, retainen*, fr. MF *retenir*, fr. OF, fr. L *retinēre*, fr. *re-* + *-tinēre* (fr. *tenēre* to hold) — more at THIN] *vt* **1** *obs* **:** RESTRAIN, PREVENT **2 a :** to hold or continue to hold in possession or use **:** continue to have, use, recognize, or accept **:** maintain in one's keeping ⟨a person does not always ~ his human form or qualities —Frederica de Laguna⟩ ⟨some of the terms are ~*ed* today because of constant use —R.L.Whistler⟩ ⟨~*ed* his seat on the bench of the Supreme Court —T.P.Abernethy⟩ **b :** to keep in pay or in one's service ⟨was ~*ed* to make a survey of operations of the agency —*Current Biog.*⟩ ⟨~*s* the clinic to examine all its employees —Stuart Chase⟩; *specif* **:** to employ (a lawyer) by paying a preliminary fee that secures a prior claim upon services in case of need **c :** to keep in mind or memory **:** REMEMBER ⟨each of the principals in his way has ~*ed* the imprint of a hideous scene —Sylvia Berkman⟩ **3 :** to hold secure or intact (as in a fixed place or condition) **:** prevent escape, loss, leakage, or detachment of ⟨the habit of chewing betel leaf and ~*ing* the cud against the mucous lining of the cheek —*N.Y. Times Mag.*⟩ ⟨available water which could be . . . ~*ed* by small dams —F.J.R.Rodd⟩ ⟨modern mammals . . . ~*ed* the egg within the body after fertilization —Weston La Barre⟩ **~** *vi, obs* **:** to serve as a retainer **:** BELONG, PERTAIN **syn** see KEEP

retained income *n* **:** EARNED SURPLUS

retained object *n* **:** an object in a passive construction that is identical with the direct or indirect object in the corresponding active construction ⟨*me* in *a book was given me* and *book* in *I was given a book* are *retained objects*⟩

¹re·tain·er \-nə(r)\ *n* -s [ME *reteiner*, prob. fr. MF *retenir* to retain (vb. taken as n.)] **1 a :** the act of withholding what one has in his hands by virtue of some right (as where a creditor pays his own claim out of the debtor's property that has come into his hands as representative of the debtor) **b** (1) **:** the act of a client by which he engages the services of a lawyer, counselor, or adviser (2) **:** the document expressing such engagement or the authority so conferred **c :** a fee paid to a lawyer to maintain a cause or to a professional adviser for advice or for a claim upon his services in case of need — called also *retaining fee*; see GENERAL RETAINER **2 :** engagement for a position or job **:** EMPLOYMENT

²retainer \"\ *n* -s [*retain* + *-er*] **1 :** one that retains **:** MAINTAINER **2 :** one that is retained **:** a person attached or owing service to a household **:** one that serves a person of high position or rank **:** DEPENDENT, SERVANT ⟨an old family ~⟩ ⟨civil affairs were belatedly put into the hands of native ~*s* of the French —R.H.Rovere⟩ ⟨recruited from the landowning class and their ~*s* —*Amer. Scholar*⟩; *broadly* **:** EMPLOYEE ⟨old civil service ~*s*⟩ **3 :** a civilian employee of a military camp or unit ⟨~*s* and persons accompanying or serving with the armies of the United States in the field —*U.S. Manual for Courts-Martial*⟩ **4 :** any of various devices used for holding something: as **a :** a cage or frame for keeping the balls or rollers in a ball or roller bearing properly spaced **b :** a rebound clip in a leaf spring **c :** a pressure valve on a railroad car for retaining part of the brake cylinder pressure to aid in slowing the train on a long grade while increasing the brake pipe pressure to recharge the auxiliary reservoirs **d :** the part of a bridge or other dental replacement by which it is made fast to adjacent natural teeth

retaining fee *n* **:** RETAINER 1c

retaining wall *n* **:** a wall built to resist lateral pressure other than wind pressure; *esp* **:** one to prevent an earth slide — compare BREAST WALL

¹re·take \(')rē+\ *vt* **retook; retaken; retaking; retakes** [ME *retaken*, fr. *re-* + *taken* to take — more at TAKE] **1 :** to take or receive again **:** take back **2 :** to take from a captor **:** RECAPTURE **3 :** REPHOTOGRAPH ⟨~ a motion-picture scene⟩

²retake \'rē+,-\ *n* -s **1 :** a rephotographing of a scene or object ⟨~ of a scene in a motion picture⟩ **2 :** a picture made by rephotographing

re·taker \(')rē+\ *n* -s **:** one that retakes

re·tal·i·ate \rə'talē,āt, rē'-, *usu* -ād.+V\ *vb* [LL *retaliatus*, past part. of *retaliare* to retaliate, fr. L *re-* + *-taliare* (akin to *talio* talion) — more at TALION] *vt* **1 :** to return the like for **:** repay or requite in kind (as an injury) **2 :** to put or inflict in return ⟨~ a wrong⟩ ⟨~ a charge upon the accuser⟩ **~** *vi* **:** to return like for like **:** make requital; *esp* **:** to return evil for evil ⟨terrorist violence erupts in Algeria and Morocco — troops ~ quickly —Henry Giniger⟩ ⟨schoolmates quick to recognize a victim who would never ~ —Geoffrey Gorer⟩ ⟨the judicial process . . . permits society to ~ against the transgressor —Walter Goodman⟩ ⟨one person stands as the butt of the other's wit, and though he can ~ he must not take offense —*Notes & Queries on Anthropology*⟩ ⟨easy for anyone of moderate genius, and some erudition, who was desirous of ~*ing* upon those authors, to compose a work with this title —H.W.Church⟩ **syn** see RECIPROCATE

re·tal·i·a·tion \=,==ʹāshən\ *n* -s [L *retaliatus* (past part. of *retaliare* to retaliate) + E *-ion*] **:** an act of retaliating **:** REQUITAL; *esp* **:** return of evil for evil ⟨sanguinary ~ on the part of a rejected office seeker —W.A.Swanberg⟩ ⟨~ by revenge or blood feud on a collective scale —*Notes & Queries on Anthropology*⟩ ⟨~ against aggression at places of our own choosing —Arthur Krock⟩

re·tal·i·a·tive \=ʹ==,ād·iv\ *adj* **:** RETALIATORY

re·tal·i·a·tor \-d·ə(r)\ *n* -s **:** one that retaliates

re·tal·ia·to·ry \rə'talyə,tōrē, rē'-, -lēə,-, -tōr-, -ri, ÷-lə,-\ *adj* **:** tending to, involving, or having the nature of retaliation ⟨from ~ political revenge the transition was easy to pillage and wholesale murder —J.A.Froude⟩ ⟨deterrent force of our ~ air power —Dean Acheson⟩ ⟨the ~ sanction of blood revenge on the part of animal ghosts —W.H.Gilbert⟩

retaliatory tariff *n* **:** a tariff imposed as a means of coercing a foreign government and intended to compel the grant of reciprocity privileges

¹re·ta·ma \rə'tämə, rē'-, -tāmə\ [NL, fr. Sp, shrub of the genus *Genista*, fr. Ar *ratam* retem] *syn of* GENISTA

²retama \"\ *also* **ra·ta·ma** \"\ *n* -s **1 a :** JERUSALEM THORN 2 **b :** PALOVERDE **2** [AmerSp, *retama*, fr. Sp, canary broom] **:** any of several yellow-flowered tropical American shrubs of the genus *Cassia*

¹re·tan \'rē+,-\ *adj* [*re-* + *tan*] **:** produced by a combination of two different tanning methods ⟨~ leather uppers⟩

²retan \"\ *n* -s **:** retan leather — compare CHROME RETAN

¹re·tard \rə'tärd, rē'-, -täd\ *vb* -ED/-ING/-S [L *retardare*, fr. *re-* + *tardare* to make slow, to delay, fr. *tardus* slow — more at TARDY] *vt* **1 :** to make slow or slower **:** delay or impede the progress, course, or event of **:** slow up by preventing or hindering advance or accomplishment **:** keep back ⟨the rate of downcutting in the section of the channel upstream from the gap was ~*ed* —*Jour. of Geol.*⟩ ⟨frequent wars, lack of roads and railroads, and bad government long combined to ~ this area —Samuel Van Valkenburg & Ellsworth Huntington⟩ ⟨language is at one and the same time helping and ~*ing* us in our exploration of experience —Edward Sapir⟩ ⟨mental evolution has perhaps ~*ed* the progress of physical changes —W.R.Inge⟩ **2 :** to delay academic progress by failure to promote (a pupil) **3 :** to restrain (a plant) from growing **4 :** to readjust the timing of (an ignition spark) so that ignition occurs later with reference to top dead center in the piston stroke ⟨with a ~*ed* spark and a late explosion, the combustion or burning of the charge of gas is not complete —A.L.Dyke⟩ **~** *vi* **:** to become delayed **:** undergo retardation **syn** see DELAY

²retard \"\ *n* -s [F, fr. MF *retarder* to retard, fr. L *retardare*] **1 :** delay through being retarded **:** RETARDATION ⟨a ~ was needed in one passage of the *Te Deum* —*Time*⟩ **2 :** a device for retarding an automotive ignition spark — **in retard** *archaic* **:** in the rear **:** BEHIND — usu. used with *of*

re·tard·ance \-dᵊn(t)s\ *n* -s [MF, fr. *retarder* to retard + *-ance*] **:** RETARDATION

re·tard·an·cy \-nsē\ *n* -ES [¹*retard* + *-ancy*] **:** the quality or capacity of retarding ⟨a paint having fire ~⟩

¹re·tard·ant *also* **re·tard·ent** \-nt\ *adj* [¹*retard* + *-ant* or *-ent*] **:** serving or tending to retard ⟨a flame-*retardant* paint⟩ ⟨rust-*retardant* coatings⟩

²retardant \"\ *n* -s **:** something that is retardant **:** RETARDER ⟨a fire ~⟩ ⟨a rust ~⟩

¹retardate *vt* -ED/-ING/-S [L *retardatus*, past part. of *retardare* to retard] *obs* **:** RETARD

²re·tard·ate \rə'tär,dāt\ *n* -s [L *retardatus*, past part.] **:** one who is mentally retarded; *esp* **:** a pupil who is retarded in school

re·tar·da·tion \,rē,tär'dāshən, -tä'-\ *n* -s [ME *retardacioun*, fr. MF *retardation*, fr. L *retardation-, retardatio*, fr. *retardatus* (past part.) + *-ion-, -io* -ion] **1 :** the action or an instance of retarding ⟨the amount of ~ obtained by the braking system of a vehicle —*Principles of Automotive Vehicles*⟩ — opposed to *acceleration* **2 :** the extent to which anything is retarded **:** the amount of retarding or delay ⟨the percent ~ in speed of reading —M.A.Tinker⟩ **3 a :** a musical suspension; *esp* **:** one that resolves upward **b :** a slackening of the tempo **4 a :** an abnormal slowness of thought or action **b :** slowness or limitation in development or progress **c :** the act or process of falling behind the norm for one's age **d :** the amount of such falling behind ⟨a ~ of two years in intelligence⟩ **5 :** backwardness in progress through school as a result of nonpromotion

retardation of the tide 1 : LUNITIDAL INTERVAL **2 :** RETARD OF THE TIDE **3 :** LAG OF THE TIDE

re·tard·a·tive \rə'tärdəd·iv\ *adj* [¹*retardate* + *-ive*] **:** relating to, expressing, or tending to cause retardation

re·tard·a·to·ry \-də,tōrē, -tōr-, -ri\ *adj* [¹*retardate* + *-ory*] **:** RETARDING, RETARDATIVE

retarded *adj* [fr. past part. of ¹*retard*] **:** slow or limited in intellectual development, in emotional development, or in academic progress ⟨physically precocious, mentally ~, overripe and immature at the same time —Arthur Koestler⟩ ⟨~ children are frequently subjected to tasks which they cannot possibly understand or perform —Elise Martens⟩

retarded depression *n* **:** a depression marked by slowness of thought and action; *specif* **:** the depressed phase of manic-depressive psychosis — contrasted with AGITATED DEPRESSION

re·tard·er \rə'tärdər, rē'-, -tädə(r\ *n* -s [¹*retard* + *-er*] **:** one that retards: as **a :** a substance that when added to a cement or to gypsum plaster prolongs the setting time **b :** RESTRAINER **c :** a power-operated braking device placed in the classification tracks of hump yards to control the speed of moving railroad cars **d :** a substance added in small proportion to a rubber compound for retarding vulcanization

retarding *pres part of* RETARD

re·tard·ing·ly *adv* **:** in a retarding manner

re·tard·ment \-dmənt\ *n* -s [F *retardement*, fr. MF, fr. *retarder* to retard + *-ment* — more at RETARD] **:** an act of retarding **:** RETARDATION

retard of the tide : the interval between the moon's transit at which a tide originates and advent of the tide itself which is not principally due to the transit immediately preceding but to a transit which has occurred some time before — compare LUNITIDAL INTERVAL

re·taste \(')rē+\ *vt* [*re-* + *taste*] **:** to taste again

¹retch \'rech, *chiefly Brit* 'rēch\ *vb* -ED/-ING/-ES [alter. of ³*reach*] *vi* **:** to make an effort to vomit **:** strain to vomit **~** *vt* **:** to throw up **:** VOMIT

²retch \"\ *n* -ES **:** an act or instance of retching

³retch *dial var of* REACH

⁴retch \"\ *dial past of* REACH

retd *abbr* **1** retained **2** retired **3** returned

re·te \'rēd·ē, 'rētē\ *n, pl* **re·tia** \'rēshēə, 'rēd·ēə, 'rētēə\ [ME *riet*, fr. L *rete* net — more at RETINA] **1 :** a circular plate with many holes used on the astrolabe to indicate the positions of the principal fixed stars **2** [NL, fr. L, net] **a :** NET, NETWORK; *esp* **:** a plexus of blood vessels or nerves **b :** an anatomical part resembling or including a network; *specif* **:** MALPIGHIAN LAYER

rete cord *n* **:** one of the strands of cells that grow from the region of the mesonephros into the developing gonad of the vertebrate embryo

retel *abbr* referring to telegram

re·tell \(')rē+\ *vt* **retold; retold; retelling; retells** [*re-* + *tell*] **1 :** to count again **2 :** to tell in another form ⟨simple as these myths are, they are *retold* with dignity and understanding —Irene Smith⟩

retelling *n* -s [fr. gerund of *retell*] **:** a new version of an old story ⟨a charming ~ of the great Greek, Roman and Norse myths —Bennett Cerf⟩

re·tem \'rē,tem\ *also* **rae·tam** \-tam\ *n* -s [Ar *ratam*] **:** a desert shrub (*Retama raetam*) that constitutes the juniper of the Old Testament, that has tiny white flowers, and that is found in Syria and Arabia

rete mi·rab·i·le \-mə'rabə,lē\ *n, pl* **retia mir·a·bil·ia** \-,mirə'bilēə\ [NL, fr. L, wonderful net] **:** a small but dense network of blood vessels formed by the breaking up of a larger vessel into branches that usu. reunite into one trunk and believed esp. important as an oxygen-storing mechanism in aquatic mammals

re·temper \(')rē+\ *vt* [*re-* + *temper*] **:** to mix (concrete or mortar) again with or without additional water after initial set has taken place

retene \'rē,tēn, 're,-\ *n* -s [Gk *rhētinē* resin] **:** a crystalline hydrocarbon $C_{18}H_{18}$ isolated esp. from pine tar, rosin oil, and various fossil resins but usu. prepared from abietic acid and related compounds by dehydrogenation; 1-methyl-7-isopropyl-phenanthrene

re·tent \rə'tent\ *n* -s [L *retentum*, neut. of *retentus*] **:** something that is retained esp. in the mind

re·ten·tion \rə'tenchən, rē'-\ *n* -s [ME *retencioun*, fr. L *retention-, retentio*, fr. *retentus* (past part. of *retinēre* to retain) + *-ion-, -io* -ion — more at RETAIN] **1 a :** the act of retaining or state of being retained **b :** continuance in use (as of a name or custom) ⟨specific African cultures came to predominate, and recognizable ~*s* of these customs are present —M.J.Herskovits⟩ **c :** abnormal retaining in a canal, reservoir, or tissue of the body of a fluid or secretion which is to be voided ⟨~ of urine⟩ ⟨~ of bile⟩ **d** (1) **:** a retaining or an ability to retain things in mind **:** MEMORY ⟨recall, recognition, and relearning are the three experimental tests of ~ —R.S.Woodworth⟩ (2) **:** the preservation of aftereffects of experience and learning so that recall or recognition is possible or that relearning is easier than the learning of new material **e :** a keeping in one's own possession or control ⟨the ~ by the railways of about 3,500 trucks —Alzada Comstock⟩ ⟨her ~ of the world figure skating title —*Current Biog.*⟩ ⟨the ~ of part of the medical personnel taken prisoner —J.S.Pictet⟩ **f** (1) **:** a retaining or holding fixed in some place, position, or condition ⟨~ is the fixation of a removable partial denture in the mouth in such a manner that . . . it may be inserted and retained with sufficient firmness —*Rev. of Dentistry*⟩ (2) **:** state of being kept in place **2 :** power or capacity of retaining **:** RETENTIVENESS ⟨shape, crease, and pleat-*retention* are not obtainable with any of the natural fibers —J.B.Goldberg⟩ ⟨good initial color and color ~, are properties that can be attained by alkyds —H.E.Hillman⟩ **3 :** something that is retained ⟨the amount of precipitation that falls on an area but does not run off is the ~⟩ **4 :** a possessory lien **5 :** the portion of the insurance on a particular risk not reinsured or ceded by the originating insurer

re·ten·tion·ist \-chənəst\ *n* -s **:** one who advocates the retention of something (as territory or a policy)

¹re·ten·tive \rə'tentiv, rē'-, -tēv *also* -təv\ *adj* [ME *retentif, retentive*, fr. MF & ML; MF *retentif*, fr. ML *retentivus*, fr. L *retentus* (past part.) + *-ivus* -ive] **:** tending to retain **:** having the power, property, or capacity of retaining ⟨soils ~ of moisture⟩: as **a :** retaining knowledge **:** having a good memory **:** TENACIOUS ⟨a ~ memory⟩ ⟨a ~ mind⟩ ⟨a ~ person⟩ **b :** PARSIMONIOUS **c :** holding in place or custody **:** preventive of escape **:** RESTRAINING **d :** RESTRAINED, RETICENT — **re·ten·tive·ly** \-tәvlē, -li\ *adv* — **re·ten·tive·ness** \-tivnəs, -tēv- *also* -təv-\ *n* -ES

²retentive \"\ *n* -s **:** something that retains or confines **:** RESTRAINT

re·ten·tiv·i·ty \,rē,ten'tivəd·ē, -ətē, -i\ *n* -ES **:** the power of retaining **:** retentive force ⟨moisture ~⟩; *specif* **:** the capacity for retaining magnetism after the action of the magnetizing force has ceased measured by the ratio of the residual magnetism to the maximum previously attained

re·ten·tor \rə'tentə(r)\ *n* -s [L, one that holds back, fr. *retentus* (past part. of *retinēre* to hold back, retain) + *-or*] **:** a muscle that serves to retain a part in place esp. when retracted

rete peg *n* **:** any of the inwardly directed prolongations of the Malpighian layer of the epidermis that intermesh with the dermal papillae of the skin

re·test \'rē+,-\ *n* [*re-* + *test*] **:** a repeated test

rete testis *n, pl* **retia testium** [NL, lit., network of the testis] **:** the network of tubules in the mediastinum of the testis

ret·ger·site \'retgə(r),sīt\ *n* -s [Jan Willem *Retgers* †1896 Du. chemical crystallographer + E *-ite*] **:** a mineral $NiSO_4.6H_2O$ consisting of hydrous nickel sulfate

re·think \(')rē+\ *vb* [*re-* + *think*] **:** to think again **:** RECONSIDER

re·throne \"+\ *vt* -ED/-ING/-S [*re-* + *throne*] **:** to enthrone again

retia *pl of* RETE

re·ti·al \'rēshēəl\ *adj* [NL *rete* + E *-al*] **:** of or relating to a rete

re·ti·ar·i·us \,rēshē'a(a)rēəs\ *n, pl* **retiar·ii** \-rē,ī\ [L, fr. *rete* net + *-arius* -ary — more at RETINA] **:** a Roman gladiator armed with a net and a trident

re·ti·ary \'rēshē,erē\ *adj* [L *retiarius* one armed with a net, retiarius] **1 :** armed with a net **2 :** skillful to entangle

ret·i·cel·la \,red·ə'chelə\ *also* **reticel·lo** \-che(,)lō\ *n* -s [*reticella* fr. It, little net, dim. of *rete* net, fr. L; *reticello* alter. (prob. influenced by *cello*) of *reticella*] **:** an early needlepoint lace derived from cutwork and drawnwork and made by buttonholing geometric patterns on or over a fabric foundation and cutting away the foundation

ret·i·cence \'red·əsən(t)s, -etəs-\ *n* -s [F *réticence*, fr. L *reticentia*, fr. *reticent-, reticens* (pres. part. of *reticēre* to keep silent) + *-ia* -y] **1 :** the quality or state or an instance of being reticent **:** restraint in speaking or communicating **:** RESERVE ⟨people who speak their minds and their souls without ~ —Gerald Bullett⟩ ⟨difference between stony ~ and a torrent of impulsive unbosoming —W.S.Gilbert⟩ ⟨after the death of a writer certain ~*s* need no longer be observed —Leon Edel⟩ ⟨a man of few ~*s*, the disc jockey must rank among the most thoroughly overt —C.W.Morton⟩ **2 :** restraint in behavior, expression, or performance ⟨the value of ~ in art —Thomas Wood †1950⟩ ⟨accompaniment in duo-piano playing requires even more ~ than is necessary in accompanying a voice or another instrument —A.E.Wier⟩ ⟨family was Quaker-like in its emotional ~ —H.S.Canby⟩

ret·i·cen·cy \-nsē, -si\ *n* -ES [L *reticentia*] **:** RETICENCE

ret·i·cent \-nt\ *adj* [L *reticent-, reticens*, pres. part. of *reticēre* to keep silent, fr. *re-* + *-ticēre* (fr. *tacēre* to be silent) — more at TACIT] **1 :** inclined to keep silent or uncommunicative **:** given to reserve in speech ⟨particularly ~ about their knowledge — Irving Kristol⟩ ⟨though ~ about his personal history, on other matters he was garrulous —W.J.Ghent⟩ ⟨~ of his opinions —D.C.Peattie⟩ ⟨~ persons who are afraid to express themselves in a company —F.H.Allport⟩ **2 :** restrained in expression, presentation, or appearance ⟨magnificently ~ study of a housewife —Roger Manvell⟩ ⟨the room has an aspect of ~ dignity —A.N.Whitehead⟩ ⟨art is thoughtful, ~, and stern, being composed of black and gray striations —*Saturday Rev.*⟩ **syn** see SILENT

ret·i·cent·ly *adv* **:** in a reticent manner

ret·i·cle \'red·|əkəl, -et|, |ēk-\ *n* -s [L *reticulum* little net, reticulum] **:** a system of lines, dots, cross hairs, or wires in the focus of the eyepiece of an optical instrument (as a gunsight, microscope, telescope, or transit) used typically for estimating speed or distance, for measuring or counting, or as a centering or aiming device

reticul- *or* **reticulo-** *also* **reticuli-** *comb form* [L, fr. *reticulum*] **1 :** a reticulum ⟨*reticulo*cyte⟩ **2 :** the reticulum ⟨*reticul*itis⟩ **3 :** reticulose and ⟨*reticulo*ramose⟩ ⟨*reticulo*venose⟩

reticula *pl of* RETICULUM

re·tic·u·lar \rə'tikyələ(r), rē'-\ *adj* [NL *reticularis*, fr. L *reticulum* little net, reticulum + *-aris* -ar — more at RETICULE] **1 :** resembling a net in appearance or structure **:** RETICULATED, RETICULATE; *specif* **:** of or relating to a reticulum **:** taking on the form of or being a reticulum **2 :** resembling a net in operation or effect **:** INTRICATE

reticular cartilage *n* **:** ELASTIC CARTILAGE

reticular cell *n* **:** RETICULUM CELL; *esp* **:** one that gives rise to blood cells

reticular formation *n* **:** nervous tissue within the brain made up of intermingled neuropil and medullated fibers

reticular layer *n* **:** the deeper layer of the dermis formed of interlacing fasciculi of white fibrous tissue

re·tic·u·lar·ly *adv* **:** in a reticular manner

reticular theory *n* **:** a theory in cytology: protoplasm consists essentially of a reticulum of more solid consistency containing a more fluid substance with spaces or granules in its interstices

¹re·tic·u·late \rə'tikyələt, rē'-, -yə,lāt, *usu* -d.+V\ *adj* [L *reticulatus*, fr. *reticulum* little net + *-atus* -ate] **1 :** resembling network **:** having the form or appearance of a net **:** NETTED; *specif* **:** having veins, fibers, or lines crossing like the threads or fibers of a network ⟨a ~ leaf⟩ ⟨a ~ wing⟩ **2 :** covered with small polygonal scales — used of the tarsus of a bird **3 :** involving repeated intercrossing between a number of lines; *specif* **:** of or relating to evolutionary change dependent on complex recombination of genes from varied strains of a diversified interbreeding population ⟨~ evolution⟩ — compare POLYPLOID COMPLEX

²re·tic·u·late \-yə,lāt, *usu* -ād.+V\ *vb* -ED/-ING/-S [back-formation fr. *reticulated*] *vt* **1 a :** to divide, mark, or construct so as to resemble or form network **b :** to distribute (as electricity, water, or goods) by means of a network **c :** to form a reticulation in (a photographic material) ⟨~ gelatin⟩

⟨~ a print⟩ **2 :** to provide or construct with a reticle **~** *vi* **:** to become reticulated

re·tic·u·lat·ed \-ˌād·əd, -ātəd\ *adj* [L *reticulatus* reticulated + E *-ed*] **1 :** RETICULATE **2 a :** having lines or roads intercrossed **:** forming or formed like a network or a web ⟨~ canals⟩ ⟨a ~ system of transportation⟩ **:** pierced or open in a pattern resembling a net ⟨a ~ pottery jar⟩ **b :** constructed or faced with diamond-shaped stones or square stones placed diagonally ⟨~ masonry⟩

reticulated glass *n* **:** ornamental ware made from glass in which one set of white or colored lines seems to meet and interlace with another set

reticulated python *n* **:** a very large python (*Python reticulatus*) of southeastern Asia that is usu. considered the largest of recent snakes

reticulated tracery *n* **:** NET TRACERY

re·tic·u·late·ly *adv* **:** in a reticulate manner

re·tic·u·la·tion \ˌ=ˌ==ˈlāshən\ *n* -s [¹*reticulate* + *-ion*] **1 :** reticulated formation or appearance **:** NETWORK; *also* **:** something reticulated (as a system of transportation) **2 :** a network of corrugations produced accidentally or intentionally by a treatment producing rapid expansion and shrinkage of the swollen photographic gelatin and displacement of the image particles in processing

reticulato- *comb form* [L *reticulatus* reticulated (fr. *reticulum* + *-atus* -ate) + E *-o-*] **:** reticulately ⟨*reticulato*coalescent⟩ ⟨*reticulato*granulate⟩ ⟨*reticulato*ramose⟩ ⟨*reticulato*venose⟩

ret·i·cule \ˈred·əˌkyül, -etə-\ *n* -s [F *réticule*, fr. L *reticulum* little net, network, dim. of *rete* net — more at RETINA] **1 :** RETICLE **2 :** a woman's small drawstring bag used as a pocketbook, workbag, or carryall

re·tic·u·lin \rəˈtikyələn\ *n* -s [ISV *reticul-* + *-in*] **:** a protein substance similar to collagen and held to be a constituent of reticular tissue

re·tic·u·li·termes \rəˌtikyələ+\ *n, cap* [NL, fr. *reticul-* + *Termes*] **:** a widely distributed genus of termites that includes several forms common in the U.S.

re·tic·u·li·tis \rəˌtikyəˌlīd·əs\ *n* -ES [NL, fr. *reticul-* + *-itis*] **:** inflammation of the reticulum of a ruminant

reticulo- — see RETICUL-

re·tic·u·lo·cyte \rəˈtikyəlōˌsīt\ *n* -s [ISV *reticul-* + *-cyte*] **:** a young red blood cell that contains a fine basophilic reticulum representing the remains of the nucleus and is present in small numbers in normal blood and greatly increased following hemorrhage or other conditions in which many red cells are lost or destroyed — **re·tic·u·lo·cyt·ic** \=ˌ=ˌ===ˈsid·ik\ *adj*

re·tic·u·lo·cy·to·sis \=ˌ==ˌsīˈtōsəs\ *n, pl* **reticulocyto·ses** \-ˌōˌsēz\ [NL, fr. ISV *reticulocyte* + NL *-osis*] **:** an increase in the number of reticulocytes in the blood typically following hemorrhage or accompanying hemolytic anemia and representing an attempt of the system to restore the blood balance by hastening the maturation of red blood cells

re·tic·u·lo·endothelial \rəˌtikyəlō+\ *adj* [*reticul-* + *endothelial*] **:** of, relating to, or being the reticuloendothelial system

reticuloendothelial system *n* **:** a diffuse system of cells arising from mesenchyme, including reticulum cells and endothelial cells of capillaries and various other ducts and cavities, comprising all the phagocytic cells of the body except the circulating leukocytes, functioning to rid the body of debris, and according to some authorities being the ultimate source of all blood cells and playing a major role in hemoglobin conservation and synthesis

re·tic·u·lo·en·do·the·li·o·sis \rəˌtikyəlōˌendōˌthēlēˈōsəs\ *or* **re·tic·u·lo·sis** \rəˌtikyəˈlōsəs\ *n, pl* **reticuloendothelio·ses** \-ˈōˌsēz\ *or* **reticulo·ses** \-ˈlōˌsēz\ [*reticuloendotheliosis* fr. NL, fr. *reticuloendothelium* + *-osis*; *reticulosis* fr. NL, fr. *reticul-* + *-osis*] **:** an abnormal state characterized by proliferation of reticuloendothelial cells or their derivatives and their collection in bone and soft tissue (as Gaucher's disease, Hand-Schüller-Christian disease, or Niemann-Pick disease) **:** EOSINOPHILIC GRANULOMA

re·tic·u·lo·endothelium \rəˌtikyəlō+\ *n* [NL, fr. *reticul-* + *endothelium*] **:** the cells of the reticuloendothelial system regarded as a tissue

re·tic·u·lo·sarcoma \"+\ *n* [NL, fr. *reticul-* + *sarcoma*] **:** a sarcoma derived from reticulum cells

re·tic·u·lose \rəˈtikyəˌlōs, rēˈ-\ *adj* [*reticul-* + *-ose*] **:** RETICULATE 1

re·tic·u·lum \-yələm\ *n, pl* **reticu·la** \-lə\ [NL, fr. L, little net, network — more at RETICULE] **1 :** the second stomach of a ruminant in which folds of the mucous membrane form hexagonal cells — called also *honeycomb stomach*; see TRIPE **2 :** a netlike structure **:** NETWORK: as **a :** interstitial tissue composed of reticulum cells **b :** the network often visible in fixed protoplasm both of the cell body and nucleus of many cells and according to the reticular theory regarded as an essential structural part of the protoplasm

reticulum cell *n* **:** one of the branched anastomosing cells of the reticuloendothelial system that form an intricate interstitial network ramifying through other tissues and organs and being esp. abundant in perivascular connective tissue

ret·i·form \ˈreˌd·əˌfȯrm, ˈrē|, |tə-, -ō(ə)m\ *adj* [NL *retiformis*, fr. L *rete* net + *-iformis* -iform] **:** composed of crossing lines and interstices **:** RETICULAR, NETLIKE; *specif* **:** being the connective tissue cells of the framework of the lymphatic glands

re·timber \(ˈ)rē+\ *vt* [*re-* + *timber*] **:** to furnish with new timber **:** to plant with timber again

¹retin- *or* **retini-** *also* **retina-** *comb form* [NL, fr. Gk *rhētinē* resin] **:** resin ⟨*Retinispora*⟩ ⟨*retinoid*⟩ ⟨*retinalite*⟩

²retin- *or* **retino-** *comb form* [fr. *retina*] **:** retina ⟨*retinitis*⟩ ⟨*retinoscope*⟩

ret·i·na \ˈretᵊnə *sometimes* -tnə\ *n, pl* **retinas** \-əz\ *or* **reti·nae** \-ᵊnˌē\ [ME *rethina*, fr. ML *retina*, prob. fr. L *rete* net; akin to Gk *erēmos* desolate, lonely, Lith *rėtis* sieve, OSlav *oriti* to loosen, Skt *ṛte* without, except; basic meaning: loose] **:** the sensory membrane that lines most of the large posterior chamber of the vertebrate eye, receives the image formed by the lens, is the immediate instrument of vision, is connected to the brain by the optic nerve, and consists essentially of supporting and protective structures, nervous elements, and sensory end organs arranged in several layers of which the sensory layer composed of small rodlike bodies interspersed with shorter conical bodies both of which are the specialized terminal parts of neuroepithelial cells is one of the outermost — see CONE, FOVEA, MACULA LUTEA, ROD

ret·i·nac·u·lar \ˌretᵊnˈakyəl(ə)r\ *adj* [NL *retinaculum* + E *-ar*] **:** relating to or resembling a retinaculum

ret·i·nac·u·late \-yələt, -yəˌlāt\ *adj* [NL *retinaculum* + E *-ate*] **:** having a retinaculum

ret·i·nac·u·lum \ˌ==ˈnakyələm\ *n, pl* **retinacu·la** \-lə\ [NL, fr. L, that which holds or binds, band, fr. *retinēre* to hold back, retain — more at RETAIN] **1 a :** a small structure on the forewings of many moths and butterflies that catches and holds the frenulum **b :** a small organ on the underside of the abdomen of a springtail that articulates with the apex of the springtail **c :** a connecting or retaining band **:** FRENUM **2 a :** any of the small glands or bodies resembling glands at the base of the stalk of a pollinium **b :** the hooklike funicle of a seed of a plant of the family Acanthaceae

ret·i·nal \ˈretᵊnəl *sometimes* -tnəl\ *adj* [²*retin-* + *-al*] **:** of, relating to, involving, or being a retina

re·tin·a·lite \rəˈtinᵊlˌīt\ *n* -s [¹*retin-* + *-lite*] **:** a massive variety of serpentine of a honey-yellow or greenish color and a waxy or resinous luster

retinal purple *n* **:** VISUAL PURPLE

retinal rivalry *n* **:** the oscillating perception of first one then the other of two visual stimuli which differ radically in color or form when they are presented simultaneously to congruent areas of both eyes

ret·in·as·phalt \ˌretᵊnˈaˌsfȯlt\ *or* **ret·in·as·phal·tum** \ˌ==ˌaˈsfaltəm\ *n* [*retinasphalt* fr. NL *retinasphaltum*; *retinasphaltum* fr. NL, fr. Gk *rhētinē* resin + NL *asphaltum* asphalt — more at ASPHALT] **:** a fossil resin usu. found with lignite

ret·i·nene \ˈretᵊnˌēn\ *n* -s [²*retin-* + *-ene*] **:** either of two carotenoid pigments that are aldehydes corresponding to the two vitamin A alcohols from which they are formed reversibly by oxidation: **a :** a light yellow crystalline compound $C_{19}H_{27}CHO$ related to vitamin A_1 and formed from rhodopsin or iodopsin by the action of light — called also *retinene₁* **b :** an orange-red crystalline compound $C_{19}H_{25}CHO$ related to vitamin A_2 and formed from porphyropsin by the action of light — called also *retinene₂*

¹ret·i·nis·po·ra \ˌretᵊnˈispərə\ [NL, fr. ¹*retin-* + *-spora*] *syn of* CHAMAECYPARIS

²retinispora \"\ *or* **ret·i·nos·po·ra** \-ˈäs-\ *n* -s [NL] **1 :** any of various Japanese ornamental dwarf shrubs of the genus *Chamaecyparis* that resemble cypresses; *esp* **:** any of several shrubs that are horticultural varieties derived from the sawara cypress or the sun tree **2 :** any of several shrubs of the genus *Thuja* that retain the needlelike juvenile foliage permanently and are propagated by cuttings or grafting

ret·i·nite \ˈretᵊnˌīt\ *n* -s [F *rétinite*, fr. *rétin-* ¹*retin-* + *-ite*] **:** a fossil resin of variable composition

ret·i·ni·tis \ˌretᵊnˈīd·əs\ *n, pl* **reti·nit·i·des** \-ˈid·əˌdēz\ [NL, fr. ²*retin-* + *-itis*] **:** inflammation of the retina

retino- — see RETIN-

ret·i·no·blas·to·ma \ˌretᵊnōˌblaˈstōmə\ *n* [NL, fr. ²*retin-* + *blast-* + *-oma*] **:** a malignant tumor of the retina derived from retinal germ cells and believed to be hereditary

ret·i·no·cho·roid·i·tis \ˌretᵊnōˌkōrˌȯiˈdīd·əs\ *n* [NL, fr. ²*retin-* + *choroid* + *-itis*] **:** inflammation of the retina and the choroid

ret·i·noid \ˈretᵊnˌȯid\ *adj* [¹*retin-* + *-oid*] **:** resembling a resin

ret·i·no·pap·il·li·tis \ˌretᵊnōˌpapəˈlīd·əs\ *n* [NL, fr. ²*retin-* + *papilla* + *-itis*] **:** inflammation of both the retina and the optic papilla

ret·i·nop·a·thy \ˌretᵊnˈäpəthē\ *n* -ES [²*retin-* + *-pathy*] **:** a noninflammatory disease of the retina ⟨hypertensive ~⟩ ⟨diabetic ~⟩

ret·i·noph·o·ral \ˌ==ˈäfərəl\ *adj* [*retinophore* + *-al*] **:** of or relating to a retinophore

ret·i·no·phore \ˈretᵊnəˌfō(ə)r\ *n* -s [²*retin-* + *-phore*] **:** one of a group of cells enclosing a crystalline cone in the distal portion of an ommatidium

ret·i·no·scope \-ˌskōp\ *n* [²*retin-* + *-scope*] **:** an apparatus for viewing the retina; *specif* **:** an apparatus for retinoscopy

ret·i·no·scop·ic \ˌ===ˈskäpik\ *adj* [*retinoscopy* + *-ic*] **:** relating to or made by means of retinoscopy ⟨a ~ study⟩ — **ret·i·no·scop·i·cal·ly** \-pək(ə)lē\ *adv*

ret·i·nos·co·py \ˌretᵊnˈäskəpē\ *n* -ES [²*retin-* + *-scopy*] **:** observation of the retina of the eye; *specif* **:** a method of determining the state of refraction of the eye by illuminating the retina with a mirror and observing the direction of movement of the retinal illumination and adjacent shadow when the mirror is turned — called also *skiascopy*

ret·i·nos·po·ra \ˌretᵊnˈäspərə\ [NL, alter. of *Retinispora*] *syn of* CHAMAECYPARIS

ret·i·nue \ˈretᵊnˌ(y)ü\ *n* -s [ME *retenue*, fr. MF, fr. fem. of *retenu*, past part. of *retenir* to retain — more at RETAIN] **:** the body of retainers who follow a prince or other distinguished person **:** a train of attendants **:** SUITE ⟨the largest ~ ever to accompany a candidate for the vice-presidency —R.H.Rovere⟩ ⟨a ~ of slave-servants —J.R.Perkins⟩ ⟨a school for a devoted ~ of students —Stuart MacClintock⟩ ⟨there were two assisting priests, and a ~ of altar boys —Mary Deasy⟩

re·tin·u·la \rəˈtinyələ\ *n, pl* **retinu·lae** \-yəˌlē\ [NL, dim. of *retina*, fr. ML — more at RETINA] **:** the neural receptor of a single facet of an arthropodan compound eye — **re·tin·u·lar** \-yələ(r)\ *adj*

ret·i·nule \ˈretᵊnˌyül\ *n* -s [NL *retinula*] **:** RETINULA

re·tir·a·cy \rəˈtīrəsē\ *n* -ES [fr. ¹*retire*, after such pairs as E *conspire: conspiracy*] **1 :** RETIREMENT, SECLUSION **2 :** sufficient means or property to make possible retirement from business

ret·i·rade \ˌred·əˈräd\ *n* -s [F, fr. It *ritirata* retreat, fr. fem. of *ritirato*, past part. of *ritirare* to retreat, withdraw, fr. *ri-* re- (fr. L *re-*) + *tirare* to draw, pull, shoot — more at TIRADE] **:** a fortification retrenchment usu. of two faces making a reentering angle

re·tir·al \rəˈtīrəl\ *n* -s [¹*retire* + *-al*] **:** an act of retiring: as **a :** RETREAT, WITHDRAWAL **b** *Brit* **:** RETIREMENT ⟨headmaster must be approaching the ~ age —*Scots Mag.*⟩ ⟨rumor about my ~ —Harry Lauder⟩ ⟨~ from a directorship⟩

re·tir·ant \-rənt\ *n* -s [¹*retire* + *-ant*] **:** RETIREE

¹re·tire \rəˈtī(ə)r, rēˈ-, -īə\ *vb* -ED/-ING/-S [MF *retirer*, fr. *re-* + *tirer* to draw, pull, fr. OF — more at TIRADE] *vi* **1 a :** to withdraw from action or danger **:** RETREAT ⟨the raiders *retired* by this route —H.L.Merillat⟩ ⟨ordered his command to ~ —*Amer. Guide Series: La.*⟩ **b :** to give ground in fencing **:** take a step back **c :** to cease batting in cricket and leave the field (as when dismissed or injured) **2 :** to withdraw, go away, or betake onself esp. for the sake of privacy, seclusion, or protection **:** go into retreat ⟨the men usually remain at table or ~ to the library —June Platt⟩ ⟨the alligator is generally considered as disposed to ~ from man —*Encyc. Americana*⟩ ⟨~ to the nearest wineshop —Norman Douglas⟩ ⟨*retired* to comb his hair —John Pudney⟩ ⟨*retired* to a cloister —H.O. Taylor⟩ **3 :** to move, fall, or bend back **:** recede or appear to recede ⟨*retired* a few yards —William Black⟩ ⟨plants and animals . . . closely followed the *retiring* ice —John Muir †1914⟩ **4 :** to withdraw from office, public station, business, occupation, or active duty ⟨~ from the diplomatic service⟩ ⟨~ from the editorship⟩ ⟨~ as a soldier⟩ ⟨~ from the sea⟩ **5 :** to go to bed ⟨perhaps she was tired and would like to ~ —P.B.Kyne⟩ **~** *vt* **1 a :** WITHDRAW **b :** to march (a military force) away from the enemy esp. in order to avoid decisive combat **2 :** to draw or pull back ⟨~ a reddy⟩ **3** *obs* **:** to remove or bring by or as if by leading **4 a :** to withdraw from circulation or from the market **:** take up or pay **:** RECALL, REDEEM ⟨the bonds would be *retired* inside the Treasury's walls —G.B.Robinson⟩ ⟨unwanted currency is returned to the Federal Reserve banks where it is either *retired* or held for future demand —J.A.Leavitt & C.O.Hanson⟩ ⟨~ a loan⟩ ⟨~ a bond⟩ ⟨~ stock⟩ ⟨~ indebtedness⟩ ⟨~ a note⟩ **b :** to withdraw from usual use or service ⟨~ this poor land from agriculture and plant extensive forests —*Amer. Guide Series: Ind.*⟩ ⟨worn-out equipment was *retired* from service —*Yrbk. of Railroad Information*⟩ **5 a :** to cause to retire ⟨any employee who has served at least 15 years is automatically *retired* at the end of the month in which he reaches age 70 —*Your Retirement System*⟩ ⟨once a man is put on a committee, he stays on it . . . until the voters ~ him —Bruce Catton⟩ **b :** to release from active duty and place on the retired list ⟨~ a military officer⟩ **6 :** to put out (a batter or side) in baseball or cricket **syn** see GO

²retire \"\ *n* -s **:** RETIREMENT, WITHDRAWAL; *also* **:** a place to which one retires

³re·ti·ré \rəˌtiˈrā\ *n* -s [F, past part. of *retirer* to retire, fr. MF] **:** a ballet movement in which the foot of one leg is brought to the knee of the other

retired *adj* [fr. past part. of ¹*retire*] **1 :** SECLUDED, SEQUESTERED ⟨a ~ life⟩ ⟨a ~ village⟩ ⟨a ~ path⟩ **2 :** withdrawn into oneself **:** RESERVED **3** *obs* **a :** PRIVATE, SECRET ⟨~ thoughts⟩ **b :** ABSTRUSE, RECONDITE **4 :** withdrawn from active duty or business ⟨a ~ officer⟩ ⟨a ~ physician⟩ **5 :** received by or due to a person on a retired status ⟨~ pay⟩ ⟨~ pension⟩ — **re·tired·ly** *adv* — **re·tired·ness** *n* -ES

retired list *n* **:** a list of officers or enlisted men who by reason of age, length of service, failure of promotion, or physical disability are relieved from active military service and retired with reduced pay

re·tir·ee \rəˌtīˈrē\ *n* -s [¹*retire* + *-ee*] **:** one who retires from his vocation

re·tire·ment \rəˈtī(ə)rmənt, rēˈ-, -ˈtīəm-\ *n* -s [MF, fr. *retirer* to retire + *-ment*] **1 :** an act of retiring or state of being retired: as **a :** a falling back ⟨~ of an army⟩ **b :** a withdrawing into seclusion or retreat **c :** withdrawal from office, active service, or business **d :** secluded condition or state **:** withdrawal from society or publicity **:** PRIVACY; *also* **:** a time or occasion of this **2 :** a place of seclusion or privacy **:** a place to which one withdraws or retreats **:** a private abode **:** RETREAT

retirement annuity *n* **:** accumulation of net premiums and interest used to purchase a life annuity at the time annuitant reaches specified retirement date

retirement income insurance *n* **:** a policy providing a death benefit should the insured die before reaching a stated age or a life income should he survive to that age

retirement plan *n* **:** a systematic arrangement established by an employer for guaranteeing an income to employees upon retirement according to definitely established rules with or without employee contributions but usu. funded — compare PENSION PLAN

re·tir·er \-īrə(r)\ *n* -s [¹*retire* + *-er*] **:** one that retires

retiring *adj* **:** RESERVED, SHY **:** not forward or obtrusive ⟨a ~ man⟩ ⟨~ manners⟩ ⟨~ disposition⟩ ⟨~ habits⟩ — **re·tir·ing·ly** *adv* — **re·tir·ing·ness** *n* -ES

retnr *abbr* retainer

retold *past of* RETELL

ret·o·na·tion wave \ˌretᵊnˈāshən-\ *n* [*retonation* fr. *re-* + *-tonation* (as in *detonation*)] **:** a compressional wave propagated backward from the starting point of an explosion wave in a gaseous mixture

retook *past of* RETAKE

re·tool \(ˈ)rē+\ *vt* [*re-* + *tool*] **1 :** to reequip (as a factory or an industry) with tools (as dies and punches) for manufacturing ⟨~ an aircraft plant to build prefabricated houses⟩ ⟨~ an industry for armaments work⟩ ⟨~ a nation to war production —*Nat'l Geographic*⟩ **2 :** REORGANIZE ⟨~*ing* of our academic structure —Mortimer Graves⟩ ⟨period of economic and social ~*ing* —Vera M. Dean⟩

re·tor·sio fac·ti \rəˈtȯ(r)shēˌōˈfakˌtī\ *n, pl* **retorsiones facti** [NL] **:** the infliction of retaliatory injuries by one nation on another equal to those it has suffered

ré·tor·sion de droit \rātȯrsyōⁿdədrwä\ *n, pl* **rétorsions de droit** [F] **:** lawful retaliation or reprisal in international law

¹re·tort \rəˈtȯ(ə)r|t, rēˈ-, -ō(ə)|, *usu* |d·+V\ *vb* -ED/-ING/-S [L *retortus*, past part. of *retorquēre* to turn back, bend back, retort, fr. *re-* + *torquēre* to bend, twist — more at TORTURE] *vt* **1 :** to pay, cast, or hurl back **:** RETURN, REPAY ⟨~ an accusation⟩ ⟨~ a wrong⟩ ⟨~ a censure⟩ ⟨~ an incivility⟩ **2 :** to make a like reply to **:** answer in kind **:** say in reply ⟨will ~ the question . . . by another question —Sir Winston Churchill⟩ ⟨triumph on being able to ~ . . . the comfort of having a daughter well married —Jane Austen⟩ ⟨"it is false," he ~*ed*⟩ **3 :** to answer or meet (as an argument) by a counter argument of a like kind **4 a** *obs* **:** to throw back (as a spear) **:** REVERBERATE ⟨~ sound⟩ **:** REFLECT ⟨~ heat⟩ **b :** to turn, twist, or curve back ⟨our driver's head was ~*ed* to harangue the back seat —Christopher Morley⟩ **~** *vi* **1** *obs* **:** to turn or spring back **:** RECOIL **2 :** to make retort **:** return an argument or charge ⟨I ~ upon the ethnologists —A.T.Quiller-Couch⟩ ⟨~*ed* upon the teasers, without stammering —Arnold Bennett⟩ **3 :** RETALIATE ⟨~*ed* with worse revenge of his own sort —Arthur Morrison⟩ ⟨there exists in the animals the impulse to ~ upon offenders —Samuel Alexander⟩ **syn** see ANSWER

²retort \"\ *n* -s **1 :** a quick sharp witty cutting or severe reply; *esp* **:** one that turns the first speaker's statement or argument against him or counters it ⟨make some quick ~ that silenced her tormenters —T.S.Eliot⟩ ⟨wrote an article in the *Standard* (as a ~ to my criticism of her) —Arnold Bennett⟩ **2 :** the act or practice of making retorts ⟨the ~ courteous —Shak.⟩

³retort \"\ *n* -s [MF *retorte*, fr. ML *retorta*, fr. fem. of L *retortus*, past part. of *retorquēre* to bend back; fr. its bent shape] **1 :** a vessel in which substances are subjected to distillation or decomposition by heat and which may be made in various forms and of various materials for different uses: as **a :** a bulb of glass or metal with a curved or slanting beak to enter a receiver for general chemical operations **b :** a long semicylinder now usu. of fireclay or silica for the manufacture of coal gas **2 :** MAGAZINE 5b

two forms of retort 1a

⁴retort \"\ *vt* -ED/-ING/-S **1 :** to treat (as oil shale) by heating in a retort **2 :** AUTOCLAVE ⟨~ canned food⟩

re·tort·er \|d·ə(r)\ *n* -s **:** one that retorts

re·tor·tion \rəˈtȯrshən, rēˈ-, -tȯ(ə)sh-\ *n* -s [ML *retortion-*, *retortio*, fr. L *retortus* (past part.) + *-ion-*, *-io* -ion] **1 :** an act of retorting **:** a turning, twisting, bending, or throwing back **:** REFLECTION **2** *obs* **:** ²RETORT **3** *or* **re·tor·sion** \"\ **:** RETALIATION — used chiefly of acts by which an aggrieved state treats the subjects of another state giving provocation in a manner similar to that in which the subjects of the state using retortion are treated by the state giving provocation

retort stand *n* **:** a stand for holding a retort — compare RING STAND

re·toss \(ˈ)rē+\ *vt* [*re-* + *toss*] **:** to toss back or again

¹re·touch \(ˈ)rē|təch\ *vb* [F *retoucher*, fr. MF, fr. *re-* + *toucher* to touch — more at TOUCH] *vt* **1 :** to touch again or rework in order to improve **:** amend by retouches **:** touch up ⟨~ a picture⟩ ⟨~ a written record⟩ ⟨~ makeup⟩ **2 :** to alter (a photographic negative or print or an engraving plate) so as to produce a more desirable appearance (as by disguising physical defects of the subject or of the photographic material) **3 :** to color (new growth of hair) to match previously dyed, tinted, or bleached hair **~** *vi* **:** to make or give retouches

²retouch \ˈ=ˌ=, =ˈ=\ *n* **1 :** the act, process, or an instance of retouching; *specif* **:** the retouching of a new growth of hair **2 :** a retouched detail or part

re·touch·er \-chə(r)\ *n* -s **:** one that retouches

¹re·tour \rəˈtu̇(ə)r\ *n* [ME, fr. MF, fr. *retourner* to return — more at RETURN] **1** *chiefly Scot* **:** RETURN **2** *Scots law* **a :** the return made to the court of chancery on a brieve of inquest with the jury's verdict thereon **b :** a copy or extract of such return

²retour \"\ *vt, Scots law* **:** to make a retour of

re·tour·able \-rəbəl\ *adj* [²*retour* + *-able*] *Scots law* **:** RETURNABLE

¹re·trace \(ˈ)rē-|trās\ *vt* [F *retracer*, fr. MF *retracier*, fr. *re-* + *tracier* to trace — more at TRACE] **:** to trace again or back: as **a :** to trace the origin or early history of by going back over previous steps ⟨~ one's family line⟩ **b :** to go over again with the eyes **:** reinspect closely **c :** to go over again in memory **:** RECALL **d :** to go back upon (as one's steps) **:** go over again usu. in a reverse direction ⟨decided to ~ his course⟩ **e :** to trace over again or renew the outline of ⟨~ a drawing⟩ ⟨~ letters⟩

²retrace \ˈ=ˌ=, =ˈ=\ *n* **:** the return of the electron beam to the starting point in a cathode ray tube after completion of all or a part of the scanning process **:** FLYBACK

re·trace·ment \-smənt\ *n* -s **:** an act or result of retracing ⟨~ of the outline made it sharper⟩

re·track \(ˈ)rē+\ *vt* [*re-* + *track*] **:** to track or trace again

re·tract \rəˈtrakt, rēˈ-\ *vb* -ED/-ING/-S [ME *retracten*, fr. L *retractus*, past part. of *retrahere* to draw back, withdraw — more at RETREAT] *vt* **1 a :** to draw or pull back or in ⟨a cat can ~ its claws⟩ ⟨flipped out its wings and ~*ed* them again —E.A.Armstrong⟩ ⟨throwing out and ~*ing* their left fists —G.B.Shaw⟩ **b** (1) **:** to move (the tongue) further back (2) **:** BACK 3b **2** *obs* **a :** to draw or bring (a person) back **b :** to hold back **:** PREVENT, RESTRAIN **c :** to take away **:** REMOVE **3** [MF *retracter*, fr. L *retractare* to pull back, withdraw, retract, freq. of *retrahere* to draw back] **:** to take back (as an accusation or promise) **:** RECALL, RECANT, DISAVOW ⟨~ the wish as brutal —Thomas Hardy⟩ ⟨~ everything we had previously said —L.L.Snyder⟩ ⟨a confession she later ~*ed* —Robert Parris⟩ ⟨refused to ~ his previous naturalism —*Americana Annual*⟩ **~** *vi* **1 :** to draw back **:** undergo retraction ⟨beds automatically ~ into the walls —*Current Biog.*⟩ ⟨watched the boat ~ from the beach —K.M.Dodson⟩ ⟨she did not ~ in horror; but laughed —Elizabeth Taylor⟩ **2 :** to withdraw, recant, or disavow something (as an accusation, statement, opinion) ⟨was tarred, feathered, and carried several miles in a cart, but refused to ~ —E.K.Alden⟩ **syn** see ABJURE, RECEDE

re·tract·able \-ktəbəl\ *adj* **:** capable of being retracted ⟨~ wheels⟩ ⟨a ~ landing gear⟩

re·trac·ta·tion \ˌrēˌtrakˈtāshən\ *n* -S [L *retractation-, retractatio*, fr. *retractatus* (past part. of *retractare* to retract) + *-ion-, -io* -ion] **:** RETRACTION, RECANTATION

retracted *adj* [fr. past part. of *retract*] **:** drawn, pulled, or moved back **:** WITHDRAWN, RECANTED

re·trac·tile \rəˈtrakt°l\ *adj* [*retract* + *-ile*] **:** capable of, or exhibiting retraction **:** capable of being drawn back or in ⟨the claws of a cat are ~⟩ ⟨a ~ spring⟩ — compare PROTRACTILE — **re·trac·til·i·ty** \ˌrēˌtrakˈtiləd·ē\ *n* -ES

re·trac·tion \rəˈtrakshən, rēˈ-\ *n* -S [ME *retraccioun*, fr. MF *retraction*, fr. L *retraction-, retractio* hesitation, refusal, fr. *retractus* (past part. of *retrahere* to draw back) + *-ion-, -io* -ion] **1 :** an act of withdrawing a declaration, accusation, promise **:** RECANTATION, REVOCATION, RECALL; *also* **:** a statement made by one retracting ⟨a ~ of a charge or decree⟩ ⟨insist upon a ~⟩ **2 :** an act of retracting or drawing back or in **:** a state of being retracted **:** ability to retract ⟨the ~ of claws⟩ ⟨the ~ of rubber . . . the property which causes rubber to return to its original shape —*Science*⟩ ⟨~ of the oceans from the polar areas —*Jour. of Geol.*⟩ ⟨fear of life and ~ from its exigencies and challenges —John Dewey⟩ ⟨print a ~ of errors —Lister Hill⟩

re·trac·tor \-ktə(r)\ *n* -S **:** one that retracts: as **a :** a surgical

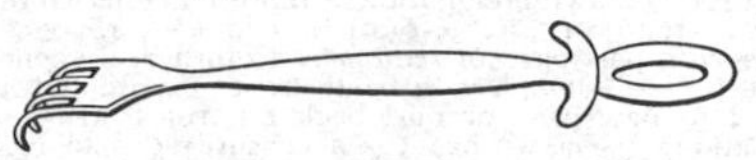

retractor a

instrument for holding tissues away from the field of operation **b :** a muscle that draws in an organ or part — opposed to *protractor*

re·trad \ˈrēˌtrad, ˈreˌ-\ *adv* [L *retro* backward + E *-ad* — more at RETRO-] **:** BACKWARD, POSTERIORLY

re·tra·hent \ˈrētrəhənt\ *adj* [L *retrahent-, retrahens*, pres. part. of *retrahere* to withdraw — more at RETREAT] **:** that retracts ⟨~ muscles⟩

retraict *n* -S [MF, alter. of *retrait* retreat] *obs* **:** RETREAT

re·train \(ˈ)rēˈtrān\ *vb* [*re-* + *train*] *vt* **:** to train again ⟨~ a muscle⟩ ⟨~ men⟩ **~** *vi* **:** to become trained again ⟨vocational ~*ing*⟩ ⟨a reemployment, ~*ing*, and rehabilitation program for returning veterans —*Current Biog.*⟩

re·tral \ˈrētrəl\ *adj* [L *retro* backward + E *-al* — more at RETRO-] **1 :** situated at or toward the back **:** POSTERIOR **2 :** BACKWARD, RETROGRADE — **re·tral·ly** \-lē\ *adv*

re·transmission \¦rē+\ *n* [*re-* + *transmission*] **:** transmission back or again

re·transmit \(¦)rē+\ *vt* [*re-* + *transmit*] **:** to transmit back or again

re·traverse \¦rē+\ *vt* [*re-* + *traverse*] **:** to traverse again ⟨caves whose cunning twists and turns no one could possibly ~ —Florette Henri⟩

re·trax·it \rəˈtraksət\ *n* -S [L, he has withdrawn] **:** the withdrawing of a suit in court by the plaintiff personally by which he loses his right of action

¹retread \(ˈ)rē¦tred\ *vt* -ED/-ING/-S [*re-* + *tread*, n.] **:** to furnish with a new tread; *specif* **:** to cement, mold, and vulcanize an entire new tread of camelback upon the bare cord fabric of (a worn pneumatic tire) after the buffing off of the remains of the old tread — distinguished from *recap*

²retread \ˈ=ˌ=\ *n* -S **1 :** a new tread on a tire **2 :** a retreaded tire **3** *slang* **:** a person returned to military service after a period as a civilian ⟨~*s* — officers or veterans of the last World War who came forward to serve their country again —J.J.McCloy⟩

re-tread \(ˈ)=¦=\ *vt* **:** to tread again

¹re·treat \rəˈtrēt, rēˈ-, *usu* -rēd·+V\ *n* -S [ME *retret*, fr. MF *retret, retrait*, fr. *retrait*, past part. of *retraire* to withdraw, fr. L *retrahere* to draw back, withdraw, fr. *re-* + *trahere* to draw, pull — more at DRAW] **1 a :** an act of retiring or withdrawing (as from what is difficult, dangerous, or disagreeable or as into privacy from business, public life, or society) **:** the process of receding ⟨this ~ from reality characterizes much of our thinking about social and criminal problems —D.W. Maurer & V.H.Vogel⟩ ⟨the squalor of the medieval village had long been in ~ before the homely dignity and comfort of the rural middle class —G.M.Trevelyan⟩ ⟨an escape from the world of men, a refusal to accept the responsibility of social and adult life, a ~ into the egocentric —*Times Lit. Supp.*⟩ ⟨the ~ of the forest —*Amer. Guide Series: Minn.*⟩ ⟨the final ice ~ during the Ice Age —W.J.Miller⟩ **b** (1) **:** the withdrawal esp. when forced of troops from the presence of an enemy or from ground occupied to ground farther from the enemy or from an advanced position (2) **:** a signal for retreating or retiring (3) **:** a signal given by bugle with or without drums at the beginning of the flag-lowering ceremony at a military installation (4) **:** the flag-lowering ceremony at a military installation that may constitute part of the ceremony of evening parade **2 a :** a place to which someone retires**:** a place of seclusion, privacy, safety, or resort **:** a retired abode **:** hiding place **:** REFUGE ⟨quiet city that is becoming a ~ for writers and artists —R.F.Warner⟩ ⟨three acres for a country ~ —Green Peyton⟩ ⟨regard the hut as a ~ and a camp rather than a home —H.S.Canby⟩ **b :** ASYLUM ⟨a charitable ~ for down-and-outs —Van Wyck Brooks⟩ ⟨the provincial house and novitiate . . . is a ~ for aged or invalid members —*Amer. Guide Series: Md.*⟩ **3 :** recessed work **:** a retired part **:** RETIREMENT, RECESS ⟨a facade in ~⟩ **4 :** a special period of group withdrawal to a place of seclusion for the purpose of deepening the spiritual life of participants through such means as prayer, meditation, study, and instruction under a director ⟨priests and religious usually make a retreat every year for a week or eight days —Cyprian Emanuel⟩ **5 :** the extent to which an aeronautical structure (as an airplane wing tip) or similar structure recedes

²retreat \ˈ"\ *vb* -ED/-ING/-S [ME *retreten*, fr. *retret* retreat] *vi* **1 :** to make a retreat **:** retire from a position or place **:** WITHDRAW ⟨the army ~*ed*⟩ ⟨stared after the ~*ing* cab —G.B.Shaw⟩ ⟨labor determined not to ~ from the position it had attained —Oscar Handlin⟩ ⟨became despondent, and ~*ed* within herself —*Jour. of Child Psychiatry*⟩ ⟨as though a glacier had just ~*ed* —Walter Bernstein⟩ ⟨a ~*ing* chin⟩ **2 :** to slope backward — used of an airplane wing tip **~** *vt* **:** to draw or lead back **:** WITHDRAW, REMOVE ⟨~*ing* his chair with intense disgust —George Meredith⟩ ⟨no hurt ~*s* us from this calm —Genevieve Taggard⟩; *specif* **:** to move (a piece) back in chess **syn** see RECEDE

re-treat \(ˈ)rē+\ *vt* **:** to treat again **:** RECONSIDER

re·treat·al \rəˈtrēd·°l\ *adj* **:** of or relating to retreat

re·treat·ant \-ēt°nt\ *n* -S **:** one who is on a religious retreat

re·treat·ism \-ēdˌizəm\ *n* -S **:** the attitude of being resigned to abandonment of an original goal or the means of attaining it (as in political or cultural matters)

re-treatment \(ˈ)rē+\ *n* **:** further treatment

re·tree \rəˈtrē\ *or* **retree paper** *n* -S [*retree* prob. fr. F *retrait* withdrawal, retreat, fr. MF] **:** paper that is imperfect or slightly damaged (as by dirty stains, specks, or pinholes occurring in the process of manufacture) ⟨packages of ~ are often marked *R* in the U.S. and *XX* in Great Britain⟩ — compare CASSIE PAPER

re·trench \rəˈtrench, rēˈ-\ *vb* [obs. F *retrencher* (now *retrancher*), fr. MF *retrenchier*, fr. *re-* + *trenchier* to trench — more at TRENCH] *vt* **1** *obs* **a :** to cut short **:** REPRESS **b :** to cut off **:** INTERCEPT **2 :** to cut down **:** LESSEN, REDUCE, CURTAIL ⟨must expect to have her pay ~*ed* —Mary W. Montagu⟩ ⟨a long speech . . . but I could be glad you would ~ it —Thomas Gray⟩ ⟨the gentry, compelled to ~ their expenses —T.B. Macaulay⟩ **3 :** to cut out **:** EXCISE, OMIT ⟨~ a paragraph⟩ **4 :** to cut off **:** pare away **:** do away with **:** REMOVE **5 :** to furnish with a retrenchment in fortifying **~** *vi* **:** to make retrenchments or reductions; *specif* **:** to cut down living expenses **:** ECONOMIZE ⟨the lords are ~*ing* visibly —Nancy Mitford⟩ **syn** see SHORTEN

re·trench·ment \-chmənt\ *n* -S [MF *retrenchement*, fr. *retrenchier* + *-ment*] **1 :** an act or process of retrenching **:** REDUCTION, CURTAILMENT, EXCISION **:** cutting down of expenses ⟨~ of their way of living —Willa Cather⟩ ⟨~ both in public expenditures and international commitments —Max Ascoli⟩ **2 :** a defense work (as a simple traverse or parapet and ditch) constructed within another to prolong the defense when the enemy has gained the outer work

retrg *abbr* retracting

re·trial \(ˈ)rē+\ *n* [*re-* + *trial*] **:** a second trial, experiment, or test **:** a second judicial trial (as of an accused person)

re·trib·ute \rəˈtriˌbyüt, ˈretrəˌ-\ *vb* -ED/-ING/-S [L *retributus*, past part. of *retribuere* to retribute] *vt* **:** to pay back **:** give in return **:** REQUITE **~** *vi*, *obs* **:** to make requital

ret·ri·bu·tion \ˌre.trəˈbyüshən\ *n* -S [ME *retribucioun*, fr. MF *retribution*, fr. LL *retribution-, retributio*, fr. L *retributus* (past part. of *retribuere* to retribute, fr. *re-* + *tribuere* to bestow) + *-ion-, -io* -ion — more at TRIBUTE] **1 :** RECOMPENSE, RETURN, REWARD ⟨denied just ~ for their services⟩ **2 :** the dispensing or receiving of reward or punishment according to the deserts of the individual esp. in the hereafter ⟨interpret justice in terms of ~ —Lucius Garvin⟩ ⟨by a whimsical ~, his own novels have passed for pantomimes —Richard Garnett †1906⟩; *specif* **:** LAST JUDGMENT ⟨the day of ~⟩ **3 a :** something given or exacted in recompense **b :** PUNISHMENT ⟨a visitation of divine ~ in the form of elemental phenomena —*Amer. Guide Series: Texas*⟩ ⟨knew the ~ in store for them if they misbehaved —*Time*⟩; *esp* **:** condign punishment in the hereafter

re·trib·u·tive \rəˈtribyəd·iv, rēˈ-, -ətiv\ *adj* [*retribute* + *-ive*] **:** of, relating to, or having the nature of retribution **:** involving condign punishment ⟨his ultimate fate of ~ assassination —*Times Lit. Supp.*⟩ ⟨~ murderer —Warren Ramsey⟩ ⟨the righteousness of God is both ~ and forgiving —*Lutheran Quarterly*⟩ ⟨~ punishment is the essential of medieval justice —M.R.Cohen⟩ — **re·trib·u·tive·ly** \-əd·əvlē, -ətəv-, -li\ *adv*

retributive justice *n* **:** justice concerned with punishing or rewarding an individual

re·trib·u·tor \-əd·ə(r)\ *n* -S [LL, fr. L *retributus* (past part.) + *-or*] **:** one that exacts or pays retribution

re·trib·u·to·ry \-yəˌtōrē, -tór-, -ri\ *adj* [L *retributus* (past part.) + E *-ory*] **:** involving, causing, or characterized by retribution **:** RETRIBUTIVE ⟨in that era of ~ religion —*Times Lit. Supp.*⟩

re-tried *past of* RE-TRY

re-tries *pres 3d sing of* RE-TRY

re·triev·able \rəˈtrēvəbəl, rēˈ-\ *adj* **:** capable of being retrieved **:** admitting of retrieval

re·triev·al \-vəl\ *n* -S **1 :** an act or process of retrieving ⟨the application of punched-card machines for the organization and ~ of information —*Amer. Documentation*⟩ ⟨any ~ of his error became more and more difficult —George Eliot⟩ **2 :** possibility of being retrieved or of recovering ⟨beyond ~⟩

¹re·trieve \rəˈtrēv, rēˈ-\ *vb* -ED/-ING/-S [ME *retreven, retriven*, modif. of MF *retrover, retrouver* to find again, fr. *re-* + *trouver* to find, prob. fr. (assumed) VL *tropare* to compose — more at TROUBADOUR] *vt* **1 a** *obs* **:** to discover again (game once sprung); *esp* **:** to flush (partridges) a second time **b :** to discover and bring in (killed or wounded game) **2 :** to call to mind again (as by study or an effort of memory) **:** find again ⟨memory withdrew further, *retrieved* the visit of two summers ago —George Green⟩ ⟨a gesture *retrieved* from long ago —*New Yorker*⟩ **3 :** REGAIN, REPOSSESS ⟨*retrieved* his fortune —H.E.Scudder⟩ ⟨go back to the box and ~ the letter —Elizabeth M. Roberts⟩ ⟨*retrieved* his position of preeminence —*Current Biog.*⟩ **4 a** *obs* **:** to bring back **:** make return **:** RECALL **b :** to reel in **:** draw back ⟨allowing the fly to sink beneath the surface of the water before *retrieving* it —Alexander MacDonald⟩ **c :** to get possession of **:** RESCUE, SALVAGE ⟨Greek sculpture *retrieved* from the ruins of Roman Carthage —A.J. Liebling⟩ ⟨built his shanty from lumber *retrieved* from steamboat disasters —*Amer. Guide Series: Ark.*⟩ **d :** to successfully return (a ball or shuttlecock that is difficult to reach) **5 :** RESTORE, REVIVE ⟨wrote . . . to ~ the heroic past —Van Wyck Brooks⟩ ⟨*retrieved* himself by deciding to become a lawyer —C.R.Williams⟩ **6 :** to remedy the evil consequences of **:** make good **:** REPAIR, CORRECT ⟨third edition . . . ~*s* many of the faults of the second —F.L.Pick & G.N.Knight⟩ ⟨the defeat was *retrieved* —Jacquetta & Christopher Hawkes⟩ ⟨*retrieving* the fundamental error of underestimating the skill of the enemy general —*New Republic*⟩ ⟨~ the situation⟩ **~** *vi* **1 :** to bring in game; *also* **:** to bring back an object thrown by a person ⟨teach a dog to ~⟩ **2** *obs* **:** RECUPERATE **3 :** to reel or draw in a fishing line ⟨allow the lure to sink close to the bottom, then give a sharp jerk and ~ for a few feet —*Fishing Tackle Cat.*⟩ **syn** see RECOVER

²retrieve \ˈ"\ *n* -S **1** *obs* **:** the rediscovery or second flushing of game (as birds once sprung) **2 :** RETRIEVAL ⟨surface . . . baits always float upon the surface of the water and remain there during the ~ —*Fishing Tackle Cat.*⟩ **3 :** the successful return of a ball that is difficult to reach or control (as in tennis or volleyball)

re·trieve·less \-vləs\ *adj* **:** IRRETRIEVABLE

re·trieve·ment \-vmənt\ *n* -S **:** RETRIEVAL

re·triev·er \-və(r)\ *n* -S [ME *retriver*, fr. *retriven* to retrieve + *-er*] **1 :** a dog used or trained primarily for retrieving game; *usu* **:** a dog of any of several strains or breeds of vigorous active medium-sized dogs with heavy water-resistant coats developed by crossbreeding and noted for ability to retrieve — see CHESAPEAKE BAY RETRIEVER, CURLY-COATED RETRIEVER, GOLDEN RETRIEVER, LABRADOR RETRIEVER **2 :** one that retrieves ⟨the most dogged ~ tennis has seen —*Time*⟩ ⟨~ of foreign orders and pledges —H.G.Wells⟩ **3 :** TROLLEY RETRIEVER

retrim \(ˈ)rē+\ *vt* [*re-* + *trim*] **:** to trim again or anew

retro- *prefix* [ME, fr. L, fr. *retro*, adv., backward, back, behind, fr. *re-* back, again + *-tro* (as in *intro* inwardly) — more at RE-, INTRO-] **1 a :** backward **:** back **:** retroverse ⟨*retro*mingent⟩ ⟨*retro*-rocket⟩ ⟨*retro*serrate⟩ **b :** back in time **:** past ⟨*retro*dict⟩ ⟨*retro*cognition⟩ **2 a :** situated behind ⟨*retro*choir⟩ **b :** situated behind a (specified) part ⟨*retro*auricular⟩ ⟨*retro*pubic⟩ **3 :** contrary to the usual or natural course **:** retrograde ⟨*retro*infection⟩

ret·ro·act \¦re.trō +, *sometimes* ¦rē·trō+\ *vi* [*retro-* + *act*] **:** REACT

ret·ro·action \ˈ"+\ *n* [*retroactive* + *-ion*] **1 :** retroactive or retrospective operation (as of a law or tax) **2** [*retro-* + *action*] **:** a reciprocal action **:** REACTION

ret·ro·active \ˈ"+\ *adj* [F *rétroactif*, fr. L *retroactus* (past part. of *retroagere* to turn back, drive back, fr. *retro-* + *agere* to drive, act) + F *-if* -ive — more at AGENT] **:** having relation or reference to or efficacy in a prior time: as **a :** operative, binding, and taking effect prior to enactment, promulgation or imposition ⟨the ~ effect of the Redemption⟩ ⟨~ decree⟩ ⟨~ tax⟩ **b :** consisting of an increase in wages effective as of an earlier date ⟨~ pay⟩ — **ret·ro·actively** \ˈ"+\ *adv*

retroactive inhibition *n* **:** obliteration of the results of learning by immediately subsequent activity

retroactive law *or* **retroactive statute** *n* **:** a law that operates to make criminal or punishable or in any way expressly affects an act done prior to the passing of the law — compare EX POST FACTO LAW

ret·ro·activity \ˈ"+\ *n* **1 :** the quality or state of being retroactive **2 :** the capacity of a bacterial agent in biological warfare to react upon the user

ret·ro·bulbar \ˈ"+\ *adj* [ISV *retro-* + *bulbar*] **:** situated behind a bulbar structure; *specif* **:** being behind the eyeball

ret·ro·caval \ˈ"+\ *adj* [*retro-* + *caval*] **:** situated behind the vena cava

ret·ro·cecal *or* **ret·ro·caecal** \ˈ"+\ *adj* [*retro-* + *cecal, caecal*] **:** situated behind the cecum ⟨the vermiform appendix is considered ~ when directed upward behind the cecum⟩

ret·ro·cede \ˌre.trəˈsēd *sometimes* ˌrē·t-\ *vb* [L *retrocedere*, fr. *retro-* + *cedere* to go — more at CEDE] *vi* **:** to go back **:** RECEDE **~** *vt* [F *rétrocéder*, fr. ML *retrocedere*, fr. L, to go back] **1 :** to cede back (a territory or jurisdiction) ⟨there is hereby *retroceded* to the state of New Mexico the exclusive jurisdiction heretofore acquired from the state of New Mexico by the United States —*U.S.Code*⟩ **2 :** to reassign (all or a part of a risk) to another reinsurer

ret·ro·ced·ence \-d°n(t)s\ *n* -S **:** RETROCESSION

¹ret·ro·ces·sion \-ˈseshən\ *n* -S [LL *retrocession-, retrocessio*, fr. L *retrocessus* (past part. of *retrocedere* to go back, go backward) + *-ion-, -io* -ion] **1 :** the act or process of retroceding **:** RECESSION **2 :** an instance of retrocession

²retrocession \ˈ"\ *n* [*retro-* + *cession*] **1 a** *Scots law* **:** the assignment by an assignee of a right to the cedent **b :** the return of a title to property to its former or its true owner **:** the confirmation of the original title in its true owner **2** [F *rétrocession*, fr. ML *retrocession-, retrocessio* retreat, fr. LL, act of going back] **:** the act of ceding back ⟨a ~ of jurisdiction over a territory⟩ **3 a :** a process of reassigning or ceding by a reinsurer to another insurance company all or a part of the risks assumed **b :** the amount reassigned or ceded

ret·ro·ces·sion·al \-shən°l\ *n* -S [¹*retrocession* + *-al*] **:** RECESSIONAL

ret·ro·ces·sive \¦==¦sesiv\ *adj* [L *retrocessus* (past part. of *retrocedere* to go backward) + E *-ive*] **:** RETROGRADE

ret·ro·choir \ˈre.trō+,-, *sometimes* ˈrē·trō+,-\ *n* [*retro-* + *choir*] **1 :** the space left in a church behind the high altar or choir enclosure sometimes used as a chapel and occas. containing a second choir enclosure **2 :** the space beyond the line of the eastern face of the altar in an apsidal church

ret·ro·cognition \¦re.trō+, *sometimes* ¦rē·trō+\ *n* [*retro-* + *cognition*] **:** direct or extrasensory perception of past events

ret·ro·cognitive \ˈ"+\ *adj* [*retro-* + *cognitive*] **:** of, relating to, or having the characteristics of retrocognition

ret·ro·dict \ˌre.trəˈdikt *sometimes* ˌrē·t-\ *vt* -ED/-ING/-S [*retro-* + *-dict* (as in *predict*)] **:** to infer (a past state of affairs) from present observational data ⟨future and past eclipses . . . can be predicted and ~*ed* equally successfully —Maurice Cranston & J.W.N.Watkins⟩ — **ret·ro·dic·tion** \-kshən\ *n* — **ret·ro·dic·tive** \¦==¦diktiv\ *adj*

ret·ro·displacement \¦re.trō+, *sometimes* ¦rē·trō+\ *n* [*retro-* + *displacement*] **:** backward displacement of a bodily organ

ret·ro·duc·tion \ˌre.trəˈdəkshən *sometimes* ˌrē·t-\ *n* -S [*retro-* + *-duction* (as in *abduction, induction*)] **:** an inference in induction leading to a hypothesis

ret·ro·duc·tive \¦==¦dəktiv\ *adj* [*retroduction* + *-ive*] **:** of or relating to retroduction

ret·ro·fec·tion \ˌ==ˈfekshən\ *n* -S [*retro-* + *infection*] **:** infection with pinworms in which the eggs hatch on the anal skin and mucosa and the larvae migrate up the bowel to the cecum where they mature

ret·ro·fit \ˈre.trō+,-, *sometimes* ˈrē·trō+,-\ *n* [*retro-* + *fit*] **:** a modification or addition of equipment (as on an aircraft or automobile) to include changes made for later production models

ret·ro·flex \ˈre.trəˌfleks *sometimes* ˈrē·t-\ *or* **ret·ro·flexed** \-st\ *adj* [*retroflex* ISV, fr. NL *retroflexus* bent backward, fr. *retro-* + L *flexus*, past part. of *flectere* to bend; *retroflexed* fr. NL *retroflexus* bent backward + E *-ed*] **1 :** turned or bent abruptly backward **:** REFLEXED **2 a :** articulated with or involving the participation of the tongue tip curled up and back until its under surface touches the hard palate — used esp. of various consonants in Asiatic-Indian languages **b** *of a vowel* **:** articulated with or involving the participation of the tongue tip raised and retracted toward the hard palate

ret·ro·flex·ion *or* **ret·ro·flec·tion** \ˌ==ˈflekshən\ *n* [prob. fr. (assumed) NL *retroflexion-, retroflexio*, fr. NL *retroflexus* bent backward + L *-ion-, -io* -ion] **1 :** the act or process of bending back **2 :** the state of being bent back; *specif* **:** the bending back of the body of the uterus upon the cervix which is little if at all out of its normal axis — compare RETROVERSION **3** [*retroflex* + *-ion*] **:** retroflex articulation

retrog *abbr* retrogression; retrogressive

ret·ro·gra·da·tion \ˌre.trōgrāˈdāshən *sometimes* ˌrē·t-\ *n* [LL *retrogradation-, retrogradatio*, fr. L *retrogradare* to retrograde (fr. *retrogradus* retrograde) + *-ation-, -atio* -ation] **1 :** the act or process of retrograding: as **a :** REGRESSION 3 **b :** a step-by-step reexamination of an investigation or argument backward from the conclusion to the first fact or premise **c :** a backward movement **:** RETREAT ⟨the ~ of a coastline⟩ **d :** RETROGRESSION 2 **e :** reversal of a fluid colloidal solution to an insoluble or gelled state on standing or on cooking — used esp. of starch solutions

ret·ro·gra·da·to·ry \¦==¦grādəˌtōrē\ *adj* [*retrogradation* + *-ory*] **:** causing retrogradation

¹ret·ro·grade \ˈre.trəˌgrād *sometimes* ˈrē·t-\ *adj* [ME, fr. L *retrogradus*, fr. *retro-* + *gradus* step — more at GRADE] **1 a** *of a celestial body* **:** having a direction contrary to that of the general motion of similar bodies **:** exhibiting regression **b :** moving, directed, or tending in a backward direction **:** contrary to the previous direction **:** RETREATING ⟨fight a ~ action —A.E.Younger⟩ ⟨a ~ step⟩ ⟨~ telescope⟩ **c** (1) **:** contrary to the normal order **:** INVERSE, INVERTED ⟨a ~ order of enumeration⟩ (2) **:** repeated backward ⟨a ~ melody in a contrapuntal composition⟩ ⟨~ imitation⟩ **2 :** tending towards or resulting in a worse state ⟨a ~ people⟩ ⟨~ ideas⟩ ⟨a ~ measure⟩ **3** *archaic* **:** OPPOSED, CONTRADICTORY ⟨it is most ~ to our desires —Shak.⟩ **4 :** characterized by retrogression **5 :** affecting memories of a period immediately prior to a shock or seizure ⟨~ amnesia⟩

²retrograde \ˈ"\ *n* **1 :** one that degenerates **2 :** RETROGRESSION

³retrograde \ˈ"\ *adv* **:** BACKWARD, REVERSELY

⁴retrograde \ˈ"\ *vb* [L *retrogradi*, fr. *retro-* + *gradi* to step, go — more at GRADE] *vt*, *archaic* **:** to turn back **:** REVERSE ⟨events . . . which seem to retard or ~ the civility of ages —R.W.Emerson⟩ **~** *vi* **1** *of a celestial body* **:** to move in a direction contrary to the normal: as **a :** to move opposite to the general eastward movement in the solar system **:** move westward on the sky **b :** to move backward in an orbit **:** turn and move actually or apparently for a while in the direction opposite to its own usual direction **2 a :** to recede over the path of a previous advance **:** RETREAT ⟨a glacier ~*s*⟩ ⟨the army ~*s* from the front⟩ **b :** to go back over something (as a narrative or argument) **:** RECAPITULATE **3 :** to decline from a better to a worse condition **:** fall back from a higher to a lower state of development ⟨~ in intelligence⟩ ⟨manufacturing *retrograding* to a cottage industry⟩ **syn** see RECEDE

ret·ro·grade·ly *adv* **:** in a retrograde manner

retrograde pyelogram *n* **:** a roentgenogram of the kidney made after injection of opaque material through the ureter — compare PYELOGRAPHY

¹ret·ro·gress \ˈre.trəˌgres *sometimes* ˈrē·t-\ *n* -ES [LL *retrogressus*, fr. L, past part. of *retrogradi* to retrogress] **:** retrogression

²retrogress \¦==¦=\ *vb* -ED/-ING/-ES [L *retrogressus*, past part. of *retrogradi* to retrogress] *vi* **:** to move backward **:** revert to an earlier state or condition **~** *vt* **:** REGRESS

ret·ro·gres·sion \¦==¦greshən\ *n* -S [L *retrogressus* (past part.) + E *-ion*] **1 :** REGRESSION 3 **2 :** a reversal in development or condition: as **a :** a passing from a higher to a lower or from a more to a less specialized state or type of organization or structure in the course of the development of an organism **b :** subsidence or decline of symptoms or manifestations of a disease **c :** retrograde imitation in contrapuntal music

ret·ro·gres·sive \¦==¦gresiv, -sēv *also* -səv\ *adj* [L *retrogressus* (past part.) + E *-ive*] **:** characterized by or tending to retrogression **:** RETROGRADE: as **a :** going or directed backward ⟨the senses represent to us the course of the planets as now progressive, now retrogressive —L.W.Beck⟩ **b :** declining from a better to a worse state **c :** passing from a higher to a lower organization ⟨~ metamorphosis⟩ — **ret·ro·gres·sive·ly** \-səvlē, -li\ *adv*

ret·ro·hypophyseal \¦re.trō+, *sometimes* ¦rē·trō+\ *adj* [*retro-* + *hypophyseal*] **:** POSTPITUITARY

ret·ro·infection \ˈ"+\ *n* [*retro-* + *infection*] **:** infection contrary to the usual course; *specif* **:** infection communicated to a mother by her fetus

ret·ro·ject \ˈre.trəˌjekt *sometimes* ˈrē·t-\ *vt* -ED/-ING/-S [*retro-* + *-ject* (as in *project*)] **:** to project into the past ⟨~ an hallucination into one's childhood⟩ — **ret·ro·jec·tion** \ˌ==ˈjekshən\ *n* -S

ret·ro·len·tal \¦==¦lent°l\ *adj* [*retro-* + NL *lent-, lens* lens + E *-al* — more at LENS] **1 :** situated or occurring behind a lens **2 :** of or involving the parts of the eye behind the lens

retrolental fibroplasia *n* **:** a disease of the retina in premature infants of low birth weight characterized by the presence of an opaque fibrous membrane behind the lens of the eye

ret·ro·lenticular \¦re·trō+, *sometimes* ¦rē·trō+\ *adj* [*retro-* + *lenticular*] : situated behind the lens of the eye

ret·ro·lingual \"+\ *adj* [*retro-* + *lingual*] : situated behind or near the base of the tongue ⟨~ salivary glands⟩

1ret·ro·min·gent \ˌre·trəˈminjənt *sometimes* ˌrē·t-\ *n* -s [*retro-* + L *mingent-, mingens*, pres. part. of *mingere* to urinate — more at MIXEN] : an animal that urinates backward

2ret·ro·min·gent \¦==¦==\ *adj* : urinating backward ⟨the male cat is a ~ animal⟩ — **ret·ro·min·gent·ly** *adv*

ret·ro·molar \¦re·trō+, *sometimes* ¦rē·trō+\ *adj* [*retro-* + *molar*] : distal to the last molar

ret·ro·ne·cine \ˌre·trōˈnēˌsēn, -ˌsən *sometimes* ˌrē·t-\ *n* -s [*retror*sine + se*necionine*] : a crystalline amino dihydroxy bicyclic alcohol $C_8H_{13}NO_2$ derived from pyrrole and formed by hydrolysis of various alkaloids (as senecionine or monocrotaline)

ret·ro–ocular \¦re·trō+, *sometimes* ¦rē·trō+\ *adj* : situated behind the eye : RETROBULBAR

retro–operative \"+\ *adj* : RETROACTIVE

ret·ro·peritoneal \"+\ *adj* [*retro-* + *peritoneal*] : situated behind the peritoneum — **ret·ro·per·i·to·ne·al·ly** *adv*

ret·ro·pubic \"+\ *adj* [*retro-* + *pubic*] **1** : situated behind the pubis **2** : constituting a pad of fat behind the pubic symphysis

ret·ro·pul·sion \ˌre·trəˈpəlshən *sometimes* ˌrē·t-\ *n* [ISV *retro-* + *pulsion*] : a disorder of locomotion attending paralysis agitans that is marked by a tendency to walk backwards

ret·ro·reflective \¦re·trō+, *sometimes* ¦rē·trō+\ *adj* [*retro-* + *reflective*] : REFLECTIVE

ret·ro–rocket \"+\ *n* : an auxiliary rocket or jet engine on a rocket or artificial satellite that thrusts in a direction opposite to or at an oblique angle to the motion of the vehicle in order to decelerate it for a landing upon a celestial body

re·trorse \rə̇ˈtrȯ(ə)rs\ *adj* [L *retrorsus*, contr. of *retroversus* retroverse — more at RETROVERSION] : bent backward or downward — compare ANTRORSE, EXTRORSE, INTRORSE — **re·trorse·ly** *adv*

re·tror·sine \rə̇ˈtrȯrˌsēn, -ˌsən\ *n* -s [NL *retrorsus* (specific epithet of *Senecio retrorsus*) (fr. L, bent backwards) + E *-ine*] : a poisonous crystalline alkaloid $C_{18}H_{25}NO_6$ found in various plants of the genus *Senecio* (as *S. retrorsus*)

ret·ro·serrate \¦re·trō+, *sometimes* ¦rē·trō+\ *adj* [*retro-* + *serrate*] : having retrorse teeth or barbs ⟨a ~ leaf⟩

ret·ro·serrulate \"+\ *adj* [*retro-* + *serrulate*] : having minute retrorse teeth or barbs ⟨~ spicules⟩

1ret·ro·spect \ˈre·trəˌspekt *sometimes* ˈrē·t-\ *n* -s [L *retrospectus*, past part. of *retrospicere* to look back at, fr. *retro-* + *specere* to look at, see — more at SPY] **1** *archaic* : reference to or regard of a precedent or authority ⟨we may introduce a song without ~ to the old comedy —W.S.Landor⟩ **2** : a review of or meditation upon past events ⟨the essence of memory, the vital, tangible ~ —William Beebe⟩ ⟨feel that wise historical ~ as well as the decent opinion of mankind will confirm it —S.F.Bemis⟩ ⟨the new chapter starts with a ~⟩ ⟨accomplished results that in ~ pleased him —W.C.Ford⟩ ⟨shivered in ~ when I thought of that afternoon meeting in that freezing hall —Anna L. Strong⟩

2retrospect \"\ *adj* : retrospective

3retrospect \"\ *vb* -ED/-ING/-S [L *retrospectus*, past part. of *retrospicere* to look back at] *vi* **1** : to practice retrospection ⟨able to ~ at fairly long distances backward —*Vancouver (Canada) Morning Star*⟩ **2** : to refer back : REFLECT ⟨it may be useful to ~ to an early period —Alexander Hamilton⟩ ~ *vt* : to go back over in thought : consider or think of with reference to the past ⟨~*ed* the faces and minds of grown people —Samuel Richardson⟩

ret·ro·spec·tion \ˌ==ˈspekshən\ *n* -S [L *retrospect*us (past part. of *retrospicere*) + E *-ion*] **1** *archaic* : reference or allusion to a past event **2 a** : the act or process of surveying the past ⟨he lives in anticipation, not in ~⟩ **b** : an instance of retrospection **3** : observation of mental processes through primal memory immediately after their occurrence

1ret·ro·spec·tive \¦==¦spektiv, -tēv *also* -təv\ *adj* [L *retrospect*us (past part. of *retrospicere*) + E *-ive*] **1** : contemplative of or relative to past events : characterized by, given to, or indulging in retrospection ⟨a ~ exhibit of an artist's work⟩ ⟨after the decline of interest in nature ancient culture became introspective and ~ —John Dewey⟩ ⟨~ self-justification⟩ ⟨~ octogenarian⟩ **2** : affecting things past : RETROACTIVE — compare EX POST FACTO **3** *of a view* : that is in the direction of the rear (as of a house) — **ret·ro·spec·tive·ly** \-tə̇vlē, -li\ *adv*

2retrospective \"\ *n* -S : a generally comprehensive exhibition showing the work of an artist over a span of years ⟨the big ~ of his works at the Museum of Modern Art —R.M.Coates⟩

retrospective rate *n* : an insurance premium rate computed for a particular risk at the close of the period of coverage by adding the expense constant and the actual losses incurred with the final rate being subject to an agreed maximum

ret·ro·stal·sis \ˌre·trəˈstȧlsə̇s, -stal- *sometimes* ˌrē·t-\ *n, pl* **retrostal·ses** \-lˌsēz\ [NL, fr. *retro-* + peri*stalsis*] : backward motion of the intestines : reversed peristalsis

ret·ro·stal·tic \¦==¦stȯltik, -stal-\ *adj* [*retro-* + *-staltic* (as in *peristaltic*)] : of or relating to retrostalsis

1ret·rous·sage \ˌre·trəˈsäzh\ *n* -S [F, act of tucking up, turning up, fr. *retrousser* to tuck up, turn up + *-age*] : the wiping of an inked engraved plate with a cloth so as to draw up a slight amount of ink to the edges of the filled lines and soften the definition of the lines when printed

2retroussage \"\ *vt* -ED/-ING/-S : to treat (an engraved plate) by retroussage

ret·rous·sé *also* **ret·rous·sée** \¦re·trə¦sā\ *adj* [*retroussé* fr. F, fr. past part. of *retrousser* to turn up, tuck up, fr. MF, fr. *re-* + *trousser* to tuck up, truss up; *retroussée* fr. F, fem. of *retroussé* — more at TRUSS] : turned up ⟨a ~ nose⟩

ret·ro·vaccination \¦re·trō+, *sometimes* ¦rē·trō+\ *n* [*retro-* + *vaccination*] : vaccination in which smallpox virus from human vesicles is used as seed virus in producing smallpox vaccine in cattle

ret·ro·verse \¦re·trə¦vərs *sometimes* ¦rē·t-\ *adj* [L *retroversus*] : turned backward : REVERSED

ret·ro·ver·sion \ˌ==ˈvərzhən, -vəzh-, -vəizh-\ *n* [L *retrovers*us turned backward (fr. *retro-* + *versus* toward, in the direction of — fr. *versus*, past part. of *vertere* to turn) + E *-ion* — more at WORTH] **1 a** : the act or process of turning back **b** : regression to a lower stage of development ⟨these political and moral ~*s*, the totalitarian states —Max Eastman⟩ **c** : translation into the original language **2** : the bending backward of the uterus and cervix out of the normal axis so that the fundus points toward the sacrum and the cervix toward the pubic symphysis — compare RETROFLEXION

ret·ro·vert·ed \¦==¦vərd·ə̇d\ *adj* [fr. past part. of obs. E *retrovert* to turn back, fr. E *retro-* + L *vertere* to turn] : turned back : REVERTED ⟨~ uterus⟩

re·trude \rə̇ˈtrüd\ *vt* -ED/-ING/-S [L *retrudere* to thrust backward] : to produce retrusion of

re·tru·sion \-üzhən\ *n* -S [L *retrus*us (past part. of *retrudere* to thrust backward, fr. *re-* + *trudere* to thrust) + E *-ion* — more at THREAT] **1** : a condition in which a tooth or the jaw is posterior to its proper occlusal position **2** : the act of moving a tooth posteriorly

re·tru·sive \-üsiv\ *adj* [*retrus*ion + *-ive*] : marked by retrusion

re–try \(ˈ)rē+\ *vt* : to try again ⟨*re-try* on the same charges persons who had already faced trial —Tom Fitzsimmons⟩

rets *pres 3d sing of* RET

ret·si·na *also* **ret·zi·na** \ˈretsənə\ *n* -S [NGk *retsina*, perh. fr. It *resina* resin, fr. L] : resin-flavored wine of Greek origin

retted *past of* RET

ret·ter \ˈred·ə(r)\ *n* -S [1*ret* + *-er*] : one that rets

ret·tery *also* **ret·tory** \-ərē\ *n* -ES [1*ret* + *-ery* or *-ory*] : a place or establishment where flax is retted

retting *pres part of* RET

re·tube \(ˈ)rē+\ *vt* [*re-* + *tube*] : to equip (as a gun or a boiler) with a new tube ⟨~ a larger gun to 4.7 in. caliber —*Mech. Engineering*⟩

re·tund \rə̇ˈtənd\ *vt* -ED/-ING/-S [L *retundere*, fr. *re-* + *tundere* to beat — more at STUTTER] *archaic* : to beat or drive back : make impotent or ineffective : BLUNT, REFUTE ⟨~ the edge of a sword⟩

1re·turn \rə̇ˈtərn, rēˈ-, -tən, -təin\ *vb* -ED/-ING/-S [ME *retournen, retornen*, fr. MF *retourner, retorner*, fr. *re-* + *torner* to turn — more at TURN] *vi* **1 a** : to go back or come back again (as to a place, person, or condition) ⟨~*s* to his home⟩ ⟨~ to the mainland —R.W.Hatch⟩ ⟨~*ing* to his former associates⟩ ⟨consciousness ~*s* quickly —H.G.Armstrong⟩ ⟨the same themes ~*ing* later in the movement⟩ **b** : to go back in thought or practice : REVERT 1 ⟨now, to ~ to my story⟩ ⟨her mind ~*ed* to her early youth —Ellen Glasgow⟩ ⟨~*s* to a . . . representational mode of painting —Herbert Read⟩ **2** : to pass back to an earlier possessor : REVERT 2 ⟨now shall the kingdom ~ to the house of David —1 Kings 12:26 (AV)⟩ **3** : to speak or write in answer : REPLY, RETORT ⟨"very well," ~*ed* the reviewer . . . "that's the way I see the book" —Edward Bok⟩ ~ *vt* **1 a** : to give (an official account or report) to a superior (as by a list or statement) ⟨~ the names of all residents of the ward⟩ ⟨~ a list of jurors⟩ **b** : to elect (a candidate) as attested by official report or returns ⟨~*ing* a Labor candidate, the first ever elected in that constituency⟩ **c** : to bring back (as a writ or verdict) to an office or tribunal ⟨~ a verdict of not guilty⟩ ⟨grand jury ~*ed* 214 indictments —P.M.Angle⟩ **2 a** : to bring, send, or put (a person or thing) back to or in a former position ⟨~ the lever to the first position⟩ ⟨~*ed* his handkerchief to his pocket⟩ ⟨~ your swords to their scabbards⟩ ⟨the pilot ~*ed* his attention to the controls —Joseph Wechsberg⟩ **b** : to restore to a former or to a normal state ⟨~*ing* the mansion to the way it looked when erected —Betty Pepis⟩ ⟨these lands will be ~*ed* to forest —*Amer. Guide Series: Conn.*⟩ **3 a** : to send back upon : VISIT — usu. used with *on* or *upon* ⟨the Lord shall ~ thy wickedness upon thine own head —1 Kings 2:44 (AV)⟩ **b** *obs* : to retort (as an accusation) upon ⟨recollecting what he had said . . . I ~*ed* it back upon him —Daniel Defoe⟩ **4** : to bring in or produce (as earnings or profit) : YIELD ⟨subscription concerts barely ~*ed* the musicians a living wage —*Amer. Guide Series: Mich.*⟩ **5 a** : to give or perform (something) in return : REPAY ⟨~ good for evil⟩ ⟨~ a courtesy call⟩ ⟨the devotion it was not in her nature to ~ —Naomi Lewis⟩ ⟨~ thanks for the repast —T.B.Macaulay⟩ **b** : to give back (as a greeting) ⟨~ an answer⟩ ⟨~*ed* his greeting with a friendly smile⟩ **c** : to give (something) back to the owner ⟨a man who would even ~ a borrowed umbrella —R.W.Emerson⟩ **d** : REFLECT ⟨~ an echo⟩ **6** : to cause (as a wall or molding) to continue in a different direction esp. at a right angle **7** : to lead (a specified suit or specified card of a suit) in response to one's partner's earlier lead ⟨~*ing* a seven of spades to partner's spade lead⟩ **8 a** : to play back (as a ball) to an opponent (as in tennis) ⟨found his service difficult to ~⟩ **b** : to throw back (as a fielded ball in baseball or cricket) ⟨~*ed* the ball from deep centerfield to the first baseman⟩ **c** : to hit (a bowled ball in cricket) back to the bowler **syn** see RECIPROCATE

2return \"\ *n* -S [ME *retourn, retorn*, fr. *retournen, retornen* to return] **1 a** : the act of coming back to or from a place or condition ⟨his ~ to civilian life⟩ ⟨on their ~ from a long trip⟩ ⟨the ~ of health⟩ ⟨a ~ to nationalism⟩ ⟨the ~ of the blood pressure to normal —H.G.Armstrong⟩ **b** : a regular or frequent returning to the same place or condition : RECURRENCE ⟨the ~ of the seasons⟩ ⟨the ~ of the tide⟩ ⟨wished him on his birthday many happy ~*s* of the day⟩ ⟨sorry to hear you had a ~ of your rheumatism —Walt Whitman⟩ **c** : REVERSION ⟨~*s* to a childhood form of functioning —H.A.Overstreet⟩ **d** : RESTORATION ⟨the ~ of the monarchy after a generation⟩ **2 a** (1) : the delivery of a legal order (as a writ, precept, or execution) to the proper officer or court (2) : the endorsed certificate of an official stating what he has done in or about the execution of such a legal order ⟨required to make a ~ of his proceedings in the matter⟩ (3) : the sending back of a commission with the certificate of the commissioners (4) : RETURN DAY **b** : an account or formal report (as of an action performed or a duty discharged or of facts or statistics) ⟨a ~ of government revenue and expenditure⟩ ⟨census ~*s*⟩; *esp* : a set of tabulated statistics prepared for general information — usu. used in pl. **c** (1) : a report of the results of balloting — usu. used in pl. ⟨election ~*s*⟩ (2) : an official declaration of the election of a candidate ⟨each house shall be the judge of the elections, ~*s*, and qualifications of its own members —*U.S. Constitution*⟩ (3) *chiefly Brit* : ELECTION ⟨his ~ to parliament on his first try for public office⟩ **d** : an official report or statement submitted by a military officer to his superior; *esp* : one accounting for personnel, property, or supplies **e** (1) : a formal document executed in accordance with law on a required form showing taxable income, allowable deductions and exemptions, and the computation of the tax due ⟨income tax ~*s*⟩ — called also *tax return* (2) : a list of taxable property **3 a** : the continuation in a different direction and usu. at a right angle of the face or of any member of a building (as a colonnade or molding) or of a molding or group of moldings (as in the mitering of a picture frame at the corners) : the short wall at an angle to a longer wall ⟨a facade of 60 feet east has a ~ of 20 feet north⟩ **b** : one of the two flats on the sides of a stage that are fastened at right angles to the downstage ends of the set and run parallel to the footlights and that both mask the backstage and complete the set **c** : a turn, bend, or winding (as in a line, rod, stream, mining gallery, or military trench) back to or toward itself **d** : a short branch track (as in a mining gallery) to hold returning trucks as others pass on the main track **e** : a means (as a channel, pipe, or duct) for conveying something (as steam, water, or gas) back to its source or starting point; *specif* : the conductor that conveys an electric current to the source after its energy is utilized **f** : AIRWAY 1 **g** : the track on which a bowling ball is returned from the pit to the bowler **4 a** : a quantity of goods, consignment, or cargo coming back in exchange for goods sent out as a mercantile venture **b** : the value of or profit from such venture ⟨enterprises which . . . yield their promoters a handsome ~ —R.E.Cameron⟩ **c** (1) : the profit from labor, investment, or business : income or profit in relation to its source : YIELD ⟨had a good cash ~ from his writings⟩ — often used in pl. ⟨box-office ~*s*⟩ (2) **returns** *pl* : RESULTS ⟨showing ~*s* from his long hours of study⟩ **d** : the rate of profit in a process of production per unit of cost — compare LAW OF CONSTANT RETURN, LAW OF DIMINISHING RETURNS **5 a** : the act of returning something to a former place, condition, or ownership : RESTITUTION ⟨arranged for the ~ of the toppled statue to its pedestal⟩ ⟨demands the ~ of the property to its rightful owner⟩ **b** : something returned: as (1) : a paper calling for payment (as a check or draft) returned by a bank to the clearinghouse (as the London Bankers' Clearing House) because of lack of funds, insufficient endorsement or other defect (2) **returns** *pl* : unsold books, periodicals, or newspapers returned to publishers for cash or credit (3) **returns** *pl* : mail received as the result of an advertising appeal (as by mail, radio, or television) ⟨the ~*s* on the mailing were running about 3%⟩ **c returns** *pl* (1) : refuse tobacco made up of fragments and siftings (2) : tobacco prepared by returning shag for recutting **6 a** : something given to repay or reciprocate : REQUITAL ⟨gives all and expects no ~ —Eden Phillpotts⟩ ⟨making some ~ to society for the educational opportunities one has enjoyed —*Bull. of Bates Coll.*⟩ **b** : ANSWER, RETORT ⟨when he criticizes, can . . . be sure of a responsive ~ —Fred Rodell⟩ **c** : a lead in a suit previously led by one's partner (as in bridge) **d** : an answering or retaliatory play: as (1) : the act of returning a ball to an opponent (as in tennis, badminton, handball, or cricket) ⟨his ~ of service was a strong backhand drive⟩ (2) : a counterthrust in fencing : RIPOSTE (3) : the runback of the ball after a kick by the other team in football **7** *chiefly Brit* : a round-trip ticket

3return \"\ *adj* **1 a** : having or formed by a return or change of direction ⟨a ~ facade⟩ **b** : turned back : doubled upon itself ⟨a ~ flue⟩ **2** : played, delivered, or given in return ⟨a ~ game⟩ ⟨a ~ blow⟩ ⟨a ~ courtesy⟩ **3** : used or taken on returning or on a trip back ⟨a ~ cargo⟩ ⟨the ~ road has been blocked —Gail Kennedy⟩ **4** : returning or permitting return ⟨a ~ current⟩ ⟨a ~ valve⟩ **5** : of, relating to, causing, or permitting a return to a place or condition : RECURRING ⟨~ orders⟩ ⟨a ~ bout with tuberculosis —E.P.Snow⟩

re·turn·abil·i·ty \rə̇ˌtərnəˈbiləd·ē\ *n* [*returnable* + *-ity*] : the quality or state of being returnable

re·turn·able \rə̇ˈtərnəbəl, -tən-, -təin-\ *adj* [ME *retournable, retornable*, fr. *retournen, retornen* to return + *-able* — more at RETURN] **1** : legally required to be returned, delivered, or argued at a specified time or place ⟨a writ ~ at the next court session⟩ ⟨a verdict ~ to the court⟩ ⟨an interlocutory matter ~ on the date indicated⟩ **2 a** : capable of being returned (as for reuse) ⟨~ bottles⟩ **b** : permitted to be returned ⟨~ fees⟩ ⟨a ~ deposit⟩ ⟨the merchandise is not ~⟩ **3** : able to return ⟨a source of . . . short-term power could make the military glider a ~ weapon —G.E.Pendray⟩

returnable container *n* : a heavy-duty drum or shipping case or box that can be used for several trips : a glass container (as a milk bottle) that can be returned for cleaning and refilling

return address *n* : an address at which shipped or mailed articles may be returned to the sender

return ball *n* : a child's ball held by an elastic string so that it returns to the hand or cup from which it is thrown

return bead *n* : a bead molding that is nearly a complete circle in section

return bend *n* : a bend (as in a pipe fitting) that alters the direction of its center line 180 degrees

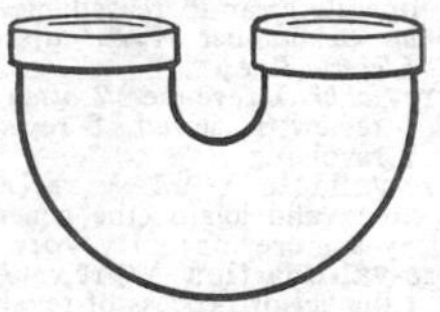

return bend

return block *n* : SNATCH BLOCK

return card *n* **1** : a card sent out by an advertiser with other printed matter to be filled in (as with an order) and returned to the sender **2** : sender's name and address in the upper left-hand corner of the face of a piece of mail for assuring its return if undeliverable — called also *corner card*

return–cocked bead \=ˈ=ˌ=-\ *n* : a bead that projects from an angle and is not flanked by quirks — compare COCK BEAD, QUIRK BEAD

return connecting rod *n* : a connecting rod having its crankpin end on the same side of the crosshead as the engine cylinder

return crease *n* : a line at each end of and at right angles to the bowling crease in cricket

return day *n* : a day when a return is to be made: as **a** : a day on which the defendant in an action or proceeding is to appear in court and answer the writ or other mandate which is to be then returned **b** : a day fixed for the return of all writs issued subsequent to the next prior return day **c** : a day fixed by law for canvassing election returns

returned *past of* RETURN

returned shipment rate *n* : a reduced railroad rate on containers returned empty

re·turn·ee \rə̇¦tər¦nē\ *n* -S [1*return* + *-ee*] : one that has returned (as from a sojourn abroad or from exile or imprisonment); *esp* : a person who has served overseas and been returned (as for leave, reassignment, or discharge) to the continental U.S.

return envelope *n* : a usu. stamped and self-addressed envelope enclosed with a mailed communication for the requested reply

re·turner \(ˈ)rē+\ *n* [*re-* + *turner*] : one that helps fasten metal bands around bales of cotton by turning ends of bands under the bales as they come through the press

return game *or* **return match** *n* **1** : a second game or match (as of tennis or bridge) played by the same contestants to give the loser of the first a chance to recoup the loss **2** : the second of a pair of games (as of basketball) scheduled between two teams for the same season often in a home-and-home series

returning *pres part of* RETURN

returning board *n* : an official body (as a state commission or a court) designated by law to canvass election returns

returning officer *n* : an English government official (as a mayor or sheriff) designated to receive nominations and to conduct and report on elections

re·turn·less \rə̇ˈtərnlə̇s\ *adj* : allowing no return from or way out of : INESCAPABLE ⟨an almost ~ depth of misery and crime —*Blackwood's*⟩

return piece *n* : one of the two wings connected to an interior setting that turn off the stage back of each side of the proscenium opening

return postage *n* : postage enclosed in a letter for the expected reply

return receipt *n* : a postal receipt sent back to the sender of a piece of insured or registered mail on payment of a special fee that shows to whom and at what time the mail was delivered

returns *pres 3d sing of* RETURN, *pl of* RETURN

return shock *n* : an electric shock that follows electric discharge from a cloud and is due to the sudden release of electricity induced on bodies on the earth by the charge of the cloud

return ticket *n, chiefly Brit* : a round-trip ticket

return trace *n* : RETRACE

return trap *n* : a trap in a return pipe

return trip *n, chiefly Brit* : ROUND TRIP

return wall *n* : a wall that makes a decided angle with and is approximately the same height as an outer wall of a building and that is distinguished from a partition or a low wall carrying a partition

re·tuse \rə̇ˈtüs, rəˈtyüs\ *adj* [L *retusus*, past part. of *retundere* to beat back, to dull — more at RETUND] : having the apex rounded or obtuse with a slight notch ⟨a ~ leaf⟩ — compare EMARGINATE, OBCORDATE

ret·zian \ˈretsēən\ *n* -S [Sw, fr. Anders Jahan *Retzius* †1821 Swed. botanist] : a mineral consisting of a basic arsenate of manganese, calcium, and the yttrium earths occurring in brown orthorhombic crystals

retzina *var of* RETSINA

ret·zi·us's vein \ˈretsēəs(ə̇z)-\ *n, usu cap R* [after Anders Adolf *Retzius* †1860 Swed. anatomist and anthropologist] : any of various veins in the dorsal part of the abdomen forming anastomoses between the inferior vena cava and the superior and inferior mesenteric veins

reu·ben·ite \ˈrübəˌnīt\ *n* -S *usu cap* [*Reuben*, oldest son of Jacob and ancestor of the tribe (fr. LL *Ruben*, fr. Heb *R'ūbhēn*) + E *-ite*] : a member of the Hebrew tribe of Reuben

re·une \rēˈyün\ *vi* -ED/-ING/-S [back-formation fr. *reunion*] : to hold a reunion (as of college alumni) ⟨two dinners will be held for each class . . . *reuning* this summer —*Dartmouth Alumni Mag.*⟩

re·unification \(¦)rē+\ *n* [*re-* + *unification*] : the act or process of reunifying ⟨advocating ~ of the divided country⟩

re·unify \(ˈ)rē+\ *vt* [*re-* + *unify*] : to restore the unity or integrity of (as a divided country)

re·union \(ˈ)rē¦yünyən\ *n* [*re-* + *union*] **1** : a union formed again after separation or discord ⟨a ~ of the dissident sect with its parent body⟩ **2 a** : a meeting of persons long separated ⟨the lovers' ~ after the war⟩ ⟨a family ~⟩ **b** : an assembly of persons associated by former membership in a group (as a college class) ⟨alumni ~*s* on the campus during commencement week⟩ ⟨a regimental ~⟩ **c** : a social gathering held at a more or less customary time and place : GET-TOGETHER ⟨the moments of their weekly ~ —Joseph Conrad⟩

re·un·ion·ist \-ənə̇st\ *n* : an advocate of reunion (as of sects or parties) — **re·un·ion·is·tic** \(¦)rē¦yünyə¦nistik\ *adj*

re·u·nit·able \¦rēyü¦nīd·əbəl\ *adj* [*reunite* + *-able*] : capable of being reunited ⟨separated but ~ parts⟩

re·unite \¦rē+\ *vb* [ML *reunitus*, past part. of *reunire* to reunite, fr. L *re-* + LL *unire* to unite — more at UNITE] *vt* : to bring together again or unite (persons or things) after a separation ⟨the beach patrols *reunited* parents and their lost children⟩ ⟨both *reunited* in the splendid tomb —Henry Riddell⟩ ~ *vi* : to come together or unite again : REJOIN ⟨will manage . . . sooner or later to ~ under one color —A.J. Toynbee⟩

re·u·ni·tion \ˌrēyüˈnishən\ *n* [ML *reunit*us (past part.) + E *-ion*] : the act or process of reuniting; *esp* : the reassembling of an organism from its separated constituent parts or cells ⟨~ may be observed to occur experimentally with various sponges⟩

re–up \(ˈ)rē+\ *vi, slang* : REENLIST ⟨refusing in droves to *re-up* —*Time*⟩

re·us \ˈrēəs\ *also* **rea** \-ēə\ *n, pl* **rei** \-ēˌī\ *also* **re·ae** \-ēˌē\ [*reus* fr. L; *rea* fr. L, fem. of *reus*; perh. akin to L *res* thing, fact — more at REAL] *Roman, civil, & canon law* : DEFENDANT 2 — opposed to *actor*

re·us·able \(ˈ)rē¦yüzəbəl\ *adj* [¹*reuse* + *-able*] **:** capable of being used again or repeatedly ⟨a new 55-gallon ~ drum . . . suitable for shipping oils —*Scientific Monthly*⟩
¹re·use \(ˈ)rē+\ *vt* [*re-* + *use* (v.)] **:** to use again **:** to use (as a container) again or repeatedly ⟨the oil-saturated water is *reused* —R.N.Shreve⟩
²re·use \"+\ *n* [*re-* + *use* (n.)] **:** repeated use ⟨waste paper is pulped for ~ —*Chem. Abstracts*⟩
reused *adj, of wool fibers* **:** obtained from finished wool products used by the ultimate consumer, sanitized, and re-made into merchandise — compare REPROCESSED
¹rev \ˈrev\ *n* -s [short for *revolution*] **:** a revolution of a motor ⟨300 ~*s* per minute⟩
²rev \"\ *vb* **revved; revved; revving; revs** *or* **revvs** *vt* **:** to step up the number of revolutions per minute of (a motor) ⟨*revving* the engine and slamming the clutch in —Richard McCloskey⟩ — often used with *up* ⟨three people *revving* up motor-bikes —*London Calling*⟩ **~** *vi, of a motor* **:** to operate at an increased speed of revolution — usu. used with *up* ⟨a bomber *revved* up on the hangar apron —*General Electric Rev.*⟩
rev *abbr* **1** revenue **2** *often cap* reverend **3** reverse; reversed **4** review; reviewed **5** revise; revised; revision **6** revolution **7** revolving
re·validate \(ˈ)rē+\ *vt* [*re-* + *validate*] **:** to make (as a law) valid again ⟨the general assembly . . . may ~ the law by a mere majority vote —*Amer. Guide Series: Conn.*⟩
re·val·i·da·tion \(¦)rē,valəˈdāshən\ *n* [*revalidate* + *-ion*] **:** the act or process of revalidating
re·valorization \(¦)rē+\ *n* [*re-* + *valorization*] **:** the act or process of revalorizing
re·valorize \(ˈ)rē¦valə,rīz\ *vt* [back-formation fr. *revalorization*] **:** to change the valuation of (as assets or currency) following an inflation ⟨~ assets on a balance sheet⟩ ⟨~ the treasury's gold stock⟩
re·val·u·ate \(ˈ)rē¦valyə,wāt, *usu* -ād.+V\ *vt* [back-formation fr. *revaluation*] **:** to valuate (as currency) again **:** make a new or different evaluation of ⟨*revaluated* on a par with the U.S. dollar⟩ ⟨*revaluating* great . . . works of fiction —J.T.Farrell⟩
re·valuation \(¦)rē+\ *n* [*re-* + *valuation*] **1 :** a revised or new valuation or estimate **:** REAPPRAISAL ⟨this ~ of primitive art —Herbert Read⟩ **2 :** the act or process of revaluating ⟨the ~ of property⟩
re·value \(ˈ)rē+\ *vt* [*re-* + *value*] **:** to value (as currency) again or afresh **:** make a second or new valuation or appraisal of **:** REAPPRAISE ⟨prepared, if necessary, to ~ the dollar —Leon Halden⟩ ⟨*revalued* everything in his house according to the measure of response it drew from her —Scott Fitzgerald⟩
re·vamp \"+\ *vt* [*re-* + *vamp*] **:** to vamp again or anew: as **a :** to put in repair (as an old house) **:** RENOVATE, RECONSTRUCT ⟨~*ed* cherry wood showcases —*Jewelers' Circular-Keystone*⟩ ⟨~*ing* old cars⟩ **b :** to revise (as a play) by bringing up to date or by fitting to a new need ⟨a story a hundred years old, ~*ed* every few years —Edward Bok⟩ ⟨~ much of what was heretofore believed true —*Science News Letter*⟩
re·vanche \rəˈväⁿch\ *n* -s [F, fr. MF, alter. of *revenche*, *revenge* revenge — more at REVENGE] **:** REVENGE; *esp* **:** the policy of a government intent on the recovery of lost territory
¹re·vanch·ist \-chəst\ *adj* **:** of, relating to, or marked by a policy of revanche
²revanchist \"\ *n* -s **:** one who advocates a policy of revanche
revd *abbr, often cap* reverend
¹re·veal \rəˈvēl, rēˈ-\ *vt* -ED/-ING/-S [ME *revelen*, fr. MF *reveler*, fr. L *revelare* to reveal, unveil, fr. *re-* + *velare* to veil, fr. *velum* veil] **1 :** to communicate or make known by superhuman means or agency **:** disclose or make manifest through divine inspiration (as in a vision) **2 :** to make (something secret or hidden) publicly known **:** DIVULGE ⟨~ a confidence⟩ ⟨~*ed* his plans for the nation⟩ **3 :** to open up to view **:** show plainly or clearly **:** DISPLAY ⟨the rising curtain ~*ed* a street scene⟩ ⟨the painting ~*s* the painter⟩ ⟨the dress ~*ed* nearly everything⟩
syn DISCOVER, DISCLOSE, DIVULGE, TELL, BETRAY, BEWRAY: REVEAL indicates a making known or setting forth sometimes comparable to unveiling; it may apply to supernatural or inspired revelation, to simple disclosure, or to indication by signs, symptoms, or similar evidence ⟨laws divine deduced by reason or to faith *revealed* —William Wordsworth⟩ ⟨the artist, the man of genius, raises this veil and *reveals* nature to us —Havelock Ellis⟩ ⟨he *revealed* his gift for patient diplomacy —John Buchan⟩ ⟨conversation *revealed* a persistent, if muted, snobbery —Francis King⟩ DISCOVER indicates a making known or showing by or as if by uncovering; it is commonly used in connection with matters kept secret and not previously known ⟨a test which we may apply to all figure painters—a test which will often *discover* the secret of unsatisfactory design —Laurence Binyon⟩ DISCLOSE is more common than DISCOVER to indicate these notions ⟨the stress of passion often *discloses* an aspect of the personality completely ignored till then by its closest intimates —Joseph Conrad⟩ ⟨did not *disclose* his objective —Willa Cather⟩ DIVULGE indicates disclosing, often with a degree of publicity or with a suggestion of impropriety or breach of confidence, real or implied ⟨knew of the conspiracy and did not *divulge* it —Hilaire Belloc⟩ ⟨the prefaces written for it . . . *divulged* the closest workshop secrets that any novelist has yet confided to nonnovelists —C.E.Montague⟩ TELL may simply indicate giving necessary or helpful information ⟨kiss and *tell*⟩ ⟨*tell* him the news⟩ BETRAY is stronger than DIVULGE in centering attention on breaches of confidence and than REVEAL when outward signs or indications are involuntary ⟨letters that would *betray* the conspiracy he had entered into —Sherwood Anderson⟩ ⟨the deep fondness of her heart *betrayed* itself by a faint smile —Anne D. Sedgwick⟩ BEWRAY is an archaic synonym for REVEAL or BETRAY ⟨silence in love *bewrays* more woe than words —Walter Raleigh⟩
²reveal \"\ *n* -s **:** REVELATION, DISCLOSURE
³reveal \"\ *n* -s [alter. (influenced by ²*reveal*) of earlier *revale*, fr. ME *revalen*, v., to lower, bring down, fr. MF *revaler*, fr. *re-* + *-valer* (fr. *val* valley) — more at VALE] **1 :** the side of an opening (as for a window or doorway) between a doorframe or window frame and the outer surface of a wall; *also* **:** the whole thickness of the wall where the opening is not filled (as with a door) **:** JAMB **2 :** the border surrounding a window of an automobile
re·veal·able \-ləbəl\ *adj* **:** capable of being revealed **:** fit for revealing
re·veal·ed·ly \-ēlədlē, -ld-\ *adv* **:** in a revealed manner **:** with or as if with revelation
revealed religion *n* **:** religion based on revelation — compare NATURAL RELIGION
revealed theology *n* **:** theology based on and attainable from revelation only
re·veal·er \-ˈvēlə(r)\ *n* -s **:** one that reveals
re·veal·ing·ly *adv* **:** in a revealing manner **:** so as to reveal
re·veal·ing·ness *n* -ES **:** the quality or state of being revealing
re·veal·ment \-lmənt\ *n* -s **:** an act or instance of revealing **:** REVELATION
re·vegetate \(ˈ)rē+\ *vt* [*re-* + *vegetate*] **:** to provide anew with vegetation; *esp* **:** to provide a new vegetative cover for (land previously stripped of vegetation) — **re·vegetation** \(¦)rē+\ *n*
rev·e·hent \ˈrevəhənt, rəˈvē(h)ə-\ *adj* [L *revehent-*, *revehens*, pres. part. of *revehere* to carry back, fr. *re-* + *vehere* to carry — more at WAY] **:** carrying back ⟨~ veins⟩
¹reveil *vt* [alter. (influenced by *veil*) of ¹*reveal*] *obs* **:** to make known **:** DISCLOSE
²reveil \(ˈ)rē+\ *vt* [*re-* + *veil*] **:** to cover again or conceal with or as if with a veil
rev·eil·le \ˈrevəlē, -li, *Brit* rəˈvali *or* -veli\ *n* -s [modif. of F *réveillez*, imper. pl. of *réveiller* to awaken, arouse, fr. MF *reveiller*, fr. *re-* + *eveiller* to rouse, watch, fr. OF *esveillier*, fr. (assumed) VL *exvigilare*, fr. L *evigilare*, fr. *e-* + *vigilare* to wake, watch, fr. *vigil* awake, watchful — more at VIGIL] **1 a** (1) **:** a signal usu. sounded by bugle at about sunrise summoning soldiers or sailors to the day's duties (2) **:** a military formation held after the sounding of such a signal **b :** a signal to arise or commence **2 :** a time of arising or commencing
reveille gun *n* **:** a firing of a gun immediately preceding the first note of reveille or sometimes the first note of a march that immediately precedes reveille
ré·veil·lon \,rāvāˈyōⁿ\ *n* -s [F, fr. MF *reveillon*, fr. *reveiller* to awaken, arouse] **:** a festive supper commonly eaten in France following Christmas midnight mass
¹rev·el \ˈrevəl\ *vi* **reveled** *or* **revelled; reveled** *or* **revelled; reveling** *or* **revelling** \-v(ə)liŋ\ **revels** [ME *revelen*, fr. MF *reveler* to rebel, make noise, be merry, fr. L *rebellare* to rebel, make war again — more at REBEL] **1 :** to be festive in a riotous or noisy manner **:** indulge or take part in a revel ⟨they ~*ed* the night away⟩ **2 :** to take great or intense delight or satisfaction — used with *in* ⟨~*ing* in pride⟩ ⟨~*ed* in her unhappiness —Agnes Repplier⟩
²revel \"\ *n* -s [ME, fr. MF, rebellion, disorder, feast, fr. *reveler* to rebel, be merry] **1 :** MERRYMAKING, REVELRY, CAROUSING, CONVIVIALITY ⟨he fishes, drinks, and wastes the lamps of night in ~ —Shak.⟩ **2 a :** a merry or noisy celebration (as of a feast or wedding) **b revels** *pl* **:** the entertainment (as dances, games, pageants, and masques) provided at a revel **3** *dial Eng* **:** a parish festival **4 revels** *pl* **:** REVELS OFFICE — used with *the*
³revel *vt* [L *revellere* — more at REVULSION] *obs* **:** to draw back **:** WITHDRAW
rev·el·a·bil·i·ty \,revələˈbiləd.ē\ *n* [L *revelare* to reveal + E *-ability*] **:** the quality or state of being revealable
reveland *var of* REEVELAND
rev·e·la·tion \,revəˈlāshən\ *n* -s [ME *revelacioun*, fr. MF *revelation*, fr. LL *revelation-*, *revelatio*, fr. L *revelatus* (past part. of *revelare* to reveal, unveil) + *-ion-*, *-io* -ion — more at REVEAL] **1 a :** an act of revealing or communicating divine truth; *esp* **:** God's disclosure or manifestation of himself or of his will to man ⟨the ~ to the Jews assembled around Mount Sinai⟩ **b :** something that is revealed by God to man **c :** something that contains or serves to communicate revelation or that purports to do so ⟨the *Revelations* of Bartholomew⟩ **2 a :** an act of revealing or opening to view **:** the disclosing or discovering to others of what was before unknown to them **b :** something that is revealed **:** DISCLOSURE **3 :** something that tends (as by its unexpectedness, excellence, charm, or worth) to create surprise ⟨her alert keenness was a ~⟩ ⟨the ease of handling of the new machine was a ~ to me⟩
rev·e·la·tion·al \¦==ˈlāshənᵊl\ *adj* **:** of or relating to revelation ⟨prophets who claim divine inspiration for their message . . . as a ~ religion —E.A.Nida⟩
rev·e·la·tion·ist \,==ˈlāshənəst\ *n* -s **1 :** one who makes a revelation **2 :** one who accepts revelation as a religious principle; *esp* **:** one who holds that knowledge of God or ultimate reality has its basis in and can be attained only from revelation
re·vel·a·tive \rəˈveləd.iv, rēˈ-; ˈrevə,lād.-\ *adj* [L *revelatus* (past part. of *revelare* to reveal) + E *-ive*] **:** REVEALING
rev·e·la·tor \ˈrevə,lād.ə(r)\ *n* -s [LL, fr. L *revelatus* (past part.) + *-or*] **:** REVEALER; *esp* **:** one that reveals the will of God
re·vel·a·to·ry \rəˈvelə,tōrē, rēˈ-; ˈrevəl-\ *adj* [L *revelatus* (past part.) + E *-ory*] **:** relating to or having the nature of revelation; *usu* **:** serving to disclose something (as character or conditions) ⟨~ glimpses of their home life⟩ ⟨a ~ account⟩
rev·el·er *or* **rev·el·ler** \ˈrev(ə)lə(r)\ *n* -s [alter. (influenced by *-er*) of ME *revelour*, fr. *revelen* to revel + *-our* -or — more at REVEL] **:** one that revels
¹re·vel·lent \rəˈvelənt\ *n* -s [L *revellent-*, *revellens*, pres. part. of *revellere* to draw back, pull away — more at REVULSION] **:** a revulsive agent (as a medicine)
²revellent \"\ *adj* [L *revellent-*, *revellens*] **:** causing revulsion **:** REVULSIVE
revelling *pres part of* REVEL
rev·el·ly \rəˈvelē\ *n* -ES [F *réveillez* — more at REVEILLE] *chiefly dial* **:** REVEILLE
rev·el·ment \ˈrevəlmənt\ *n* -s [¹*revel* + *-ment*] **:** an act of reveling **:** REVELRY
rev·el·rous \-lrəs\ *adj* [*revelry* + *-ous*] **:** marked by or full of revelry ⟨a ~ night⟩
revelrout \ˈ==,=\ *n* [²*revel* + *rout*] **1** *obs* **:** REVELRY, CAROUSAL; *also* **:** REVEL **2** *archaic* **:** a troop of revelers
rev·el·ry \ˈrevəlrē, -ri\ *n* -ES [ME *revelrie*, fr. *revelen* to revel + *-rie* -ry — more at REVEL] **:** an act of reveling **:** boisterous merrymaking
revels *pres 3d sing of* REVEL, *pl of* REVEL
revels office *n, usu cap R&O* **:** a former office in the English royal household of which the master of the revels was head and which had charge of court entertainment
¹rev·e·nant \ˈrevənənt, ¦revə¦näⁿ\ *n* -s [F, fr. pres. part. of *revenir* to come back, fr. MF — more at REVENUE] **:** one that returns: as **a :** the ghost of a dead person **:** SPECTER, WRAITH ⟨a lovely woman's wistful ~, surviving in disembodied beauty —John Bennett⟩ **b :** one who returns to a former place after prolonged absence ⟨our ~ from a hundred years ago —K.K. Darrow⟩ **c :** a person having qualities characteristic of another age or time as if returned therefrom ⟨a ~ from Regency times⟩
²revenant \"\ *adj* [F, pres. part. of *revenir* to come back] **1 :** coming back **:** RECURRING ⟨a ~ spirit⟩ **2 :** of, relating to, or typical of a revenant ⟨~ shrieks⟩
re·ven·di·cate \rəˈvendə,kāt\ *vt* -ED/-ING/-S [back-formation fr. *revendication*] **1 :** to recover by a formal demand for restoration **2 a :** to bring action under civil law to enforce rights in specific property whether corporeal or incorporeal or movable or immovable **b :** to proceed to recover goods sold for which the price has not been paid when vendee becomes insolvent and goods are in the same condition — compare STOPPAGE IN TRANSITU
re·ven·di·ca·tion \=,==ˈkāshən\ *n* -s [F, fr. MF, prob. fr. *revendiquer* to revendicate (fr. *re-* + *vendiquer* to lay claim to something, fr. L *vindicare*) + *-ation* — more at VENGEANCE] **:** an act or instance of revendicating
¹re·venge \rəˈvenj, rēˈ-\ *vb* -ED/-ING/-S [ME *revengen*, fr. MF *revengier*, *revenchier*, fr. OF, fr. *re-* + *vengier*, *venchier* to avenge — more at VENGEANCE] *vt* **1 :** to inflict harm or injury in return for (as an injury or insult) **:** exact satisfaction for under a sense of injury ⟨~ his father's murder⟩ ⟨the gods are just, and will ~ our cause —John Dryden⟩ **2 :** to avenge or seek vengeance for a wrong done (oneself or another) ⟨~ oneself on one's enemies⟩ **3** *obs* **:** PUNISH **~** *vi* **:** to take vengeance — used with *upon* **syn** see AVENGE
²revenge \"\ *n* -s [MF *revenge*, *revenche*, fr. *revengier*, *revenchier* to revenge] **1 :** the disposition or desire to seek vengeance ⟨a prey to ~⟩; *also* **:** the gratification of such a desire ⟨determined to have his ~⟩ **2 :** an act or instance of revenging or returning evil for evil **:** vindictive retaliation ⟨a terrible ~⟩ **3** *obs* **a :** AVENGING ⟨none would strike a stroke in his ~ —Shak.⟩ **b :** PUNISHMENT **4 :** an opportunity of getting satisfaction or retrieving oneself (as by a return match) ⟨give one his ~⟩
re·venge·ful \-jfəl\ *adj* **:** full of or prone to revenge **:** desirous of vengeance ⟨a harsh ~ spirit⟩ **syn** see VINDICTIVE
re·venge·ful·ly \-fəlē\ *adv* **:** in a revengeful manner
re·venge·ful·ness *n* -ES **:** the quality or state of being revengeful **:** VINDICTIVENESS
re·venge·less \-jləs\ *adj* **1 :** free from revengefulness **:** lacking in vindictiveness **2** *obs* **:** UNREVENGED
re·venge·ment \-jmənt\ *n* -s **:** REVENGE
re·veng·er \-jə(r)\ *n* -s **:** one that revenges **:** AVENGER
re·veng·ing·ly *adv* **:** in a revenging manner
re·vent \(ˈ)rē+\ *vt* [*re-* + *vent*] **:** to fit with a new vent ⟨~*ed* the plumbing⟩
rev·e·nue \ˈrevə,n(y)ü\ *n* -s *often attrib* [ME, fr. MF, fr. fem. of *revenu*, past part. of *revenir* to come back, fr. L *revenire*, fr. *re-* + *venire* to come — more at COME] **1 a** *obs* **:** the return from landed property or other source of income — used with *of* **b :** the income that comes back from an investment (as in real or personal property) **:** the annual or periodical rents, profits, interest, or issues of any species of real or personal property; *often* **:** investment income as distinguished from salary, wages, or donations **c :** the annual or periodical yield of taxes, excises, customs, duties, and other sources of income that a nation, state, or municipality collects and receives into the treasury for public use **:** public income of whatever kind **2 :** an item of income **:** the total income produced by a given source ⟨a property expected to yield an annual ~ of 10,000 dollars⟩ **3 a :** a government department concerned with the collection of the national revenue **b :** REVENUE STAMP
revenue account *n* **:** INCOME ACCOUNT 1
revenue act *or* **revenue law** *n* **:** a statute imposing a tax to defray the expenses of government; *esp* **:** a federal revenue act making a major change in existing tax law
revenue bond *n* **:** a bond issued by a public agency authorized to build, acquire, or improve a revenue-producing property and payable solely out of revenue derived from such property
revenue cutter *n* **:** an armed government vessel employed esp. to enforce revenue laws and prevent smuggling
rev·e·nued \-üd\ *adj* **:** provided with a revenue
revenue expenditure *n* **:** an expenditure allocable to and chargeable against revenue — contrasted with *capital expenditure*
rev·e·nu·er \-(y)üə(r), -(y)ů(ə)r, -(y)ůə\ *n* -s **:** a revenue officer or cutter ⟨a fast ~⟩
revenue stamp *n* **:** a stamp for use as evidence of payment of a tax (as on a package of cigarettes, a proprietary article, a lease, or a mortgage) — called also *fiscal stamp*
revenue tariff *n* **:** a tariff intended wholly or primarily to produce public revenue — compare PROTECTIVE TARIFF
re·ver \rəˈver\ *n* -s [F *revers* — more at REVERS] **:** REVERS
re·ver·able \rəˈvirəbəl\ *adj* [¹*revere* + *-able*] **:** meriting reverence
¹re·verb \rəˈvərb\ *vb* [L *reverberare*] **:** REVERBERATE
²reverb \"\ *n* -s [by shortening] **:** REVERBERATION
re·ver·ba·to·ry \rəˈvərbə,tōrē, rēˈ-, -vəb-, -vəib-\ *adj* [by contr.] **:** REVERBERATORY
re·ver·ber·ance \-b(ə)rən(t)s\ *n* -s **:** the quality or state of being reverberant
re·ver·ber·ant \-nt\ *adj* [L *reverberant-*, *reverberans*, pres. part. of *reverberare* to reverberate] **:** tending to reverberate **:** marked by reverberation **:** RESONANT ⟨~ rooms⟩ ⟨~ voices⟩ ⟨sound of the waves, made weirdly hollow and ~ by the fog —Jack London⟩ — **re·ver·ber·ant·ly** *adv*
¹re·ver·ber·ate \rəˈvərbə,rāt, rēˈ-, -vəb-, -vəib-, *usu* -ād.+V\ *vb* -ED/-ING/-S [L *reverberatus*, past part. of *reverberare* to strike back, cause to rebound, fr. *re-* + *verberare* to lash, whip, beat, fr. *verber* rod — more at VERVAIN] *vt* **1 :** to return or send back **:** force or drive back: as **a :** REPEL **b :** ECHO **c :** REFLECT ⟨a mirror *reverberating* the glaring light⟩; *esp* **:** to drive from one side to another (as flame in a furnace) **2 :** to subject to the action of a reverberatory furnace **:** fuse by reverberated heat **~** *vi* **1 :** to become driven or sent back **:** become reflected (as from a surface) ⟨warmth *reverberating* from the sunny court⟩ **2 :** to continue or become repeated in or as if in a series of echoes ⟨his call *reverberated* from the hills⟩ **3 :** to be forced to strike or go — used with *upon* or *over* ⟨so arranged that the flames ~ upon the charge of ore⟩ ⟨*reverberating* over the surface to be heated⟩ **syn** see REBOUND
²re·ver·ber·ate \-bərət, -bə,rāt\ *adj* [L *reverberatus*, past part. of *reverberare*] **:** REVERBERATED, REVERBERATING, REVERBERANT, REFLECTED ⟨~ sound⟩
re·ver·ber·a·tion \=,==ˈrāshən\ *n* -s [ME *reverberacioun*, fr. MF *reverberation*, fr. ML *reverberation-*, *reverberatio*, fr. L *reverberatus* (past part.) + *-ion-*, *-io* -ion] **1 a** *obs* **:** the fact of being sent forcibly back (as by or after impact) **b :** a reflecting of something (as light or heat); *also* **:** the repetitive effect or impact resulting from such reflecting **2** *obs* **:** the reflecting action of some medium or body **3 :** an act of reverberating ⟨the ~ of voices in the narrow corridor⟩: as **a :** an act of reflecting radiation (as sound, heat, or light); *also* **:** the reflected condition of such radiation **b :** subjection to the action of a reverberatory furnace **4 :** something that is reverberated: as **a :** a sound persisting because of repeated reflections after the source has been cut off — distinguished from *echo*; compare RESIDUAL SOUND **b :** a reflected light or color
reverberation time *n* **:** the time that it takes a sound made in a room to diminish to one millionth of its original intensity
re·ver·ber·a·tive \=ˈ==,rād.|iv, -b(ə)rə|, |t|, |ēv *also* |əv\ *adj* [¹*reverberate* + *-ive*] **:** constituting reverberation **:** tending to reverberate **:** REFLECTIVE ⟨the ~ light of the beach outside —R.M.Coates⟩
re·ver·ber·a·tor \-bə,rād.ə(r)\ *n* -s [¹*reverberate* + *-or*] **:** something (as a reflector) that produces reverberation
¹re·ver·ber·a·to·ry \rəˈvərb(ə)rə,tōrē, rēˈ-, -vəb-, -vəib-, -bə,-, -tòr-, -ri\ *adj* [¹*reverberate* + *-ory*] **:** acting by reverberation **:** forced back or diverted onto material under treatment ⟨a ~ fire⟩ ⟨~ heat⟩
²reverberatory \"\ *n* -ES **:** a furnace or kiln in which heat is radiated from the roof onto the material (as cast iron or copper ore) treated
re·ver·brate \rəˈvər,brāt\ *adj* [contr. of ²*reverberate*] **:** REVERBERATING, RESOUNDING, ECHOING ⟨~ hills⟩
re·ver·di *or* **re·ver·die** \rəˈverdē\ *n* -s [OF *reverdie*, lit., foliage, verdure, fr. *reverdier*, *reverdoier* to grow green again, fr. *re-* + *verdier*, *verdoier* to grow green — more at VERDANT] **:** an old French song signalizing the return of spring
¹re·vere \rəˈvi(ə)r, rēˈ-, -iə\ *vt* -ED/-ING/-S [L *reverērī*, fr. *re-* + *verērī* to respect, revere, fear — more at WARY] **:** to regard with reverence or profound respect and affection **:** practice an affectionate deference toward **:** show love and honor to ⟨whom he rather *revered* as his father than treated as his partner —Joseph Addison⟩
syn REVERENCE, VENERATE, WORSHIP, ADORE: one REVERES, usu. with tenderness and deference, persons or often institutions, or their accomplishments or attributes, entitled to respect and honor, or objects closely associated with or symbolic of such people or institutions ⟨academic idols which they, in their turn, had been taught to *revere* —Joanne Wheeler⟩ ⟨*revere* past national glories, almost to the point of worship —T.H. Fielding⟩ ⟨*revered* for the wisdom of his counsels and the nobility of his character —Theodore Collier⟩ REVERENCE, applying more often to things than persons, suggests more the fact of holding in high respect and with a certain self-abnegation, esp. a respecting of things commonly respected or regarded as inviolable ⟨brought up to love and *reverence* her mother —Margaret Deland⟩ ⟨pledged to *reverence* the name of God —F.B.Steck⟩ VENERATE applies commonly to persons or things regarded as holy, sacred, or sacrosanct because of character, associations, or age ⟨those who *venerate* . . . Dante and Shakespeare and Milton —Havelock Ellis⟩ ⟨*venerate* and obey natural law —W.R.Inge⟩ ⟨revered him as much as he *venerated* her —Osbert Sitwell⟩ One commonly WORSHIPS a divine being when one pays homage by word or ceremonial, but more broadly one WORSHIPS anyone or anything to whom he attributes an esp. exalted character or before whom he abases himself in great respect or adoration ⟨*worship* God each Sunday⟩ ⟨*worship* the flag of one's country⟩ ⟨the grave of a famous hunter, where they *worship* his spirit —J.G.Frazer⟩ ⟨the unwavering *worship* of a good dog for his master —Elizabeth Goudge⟩ ADORE is often used in the sense of WORSHIP in its application to a divine being although suggesting a more personal emotion; but commonly and much more generally it applies to any extremely great and usu. unquestioning love, however manifest ⟨his staff *adored* him, his men worshiped him —W.A.White⟩ ⟨music that he *adored* —Marcia Davenport⟩ ⟨still *adores* baseball and never expects to tire of it⟩
²revere \"\ *n* -s [alter. of *revers*] **:** REVERS
rev·er·ee \,revəˈrā\ *n* -s [prob. fr. F *révérée*, fem. past part. of *révérer* to revere, fr. L *reverērī*] **:** MINIATURE PINK
¹rev·er·ence \ˈrevərn(t)s *also* -v(ə)rən-\ *n* -s [ME, fr. OF, fr. L *reverentia*, fr. *reverent-*, *reverens* (pres. part. of *reverērī* to revere) + *-ia* -y — more at REVERE] **1 a :** honor or respect felt or manifested **:** deference duly paid or expressed ⟨a seemly ~ may be paid to power —William Wordsworth⟩ **b :** profound respect mingled with love and awe (as for a holy or exalted being or place or thing) ⟨pray with ~⟩ — often used with *in* ⟨a child reared in ~ of his parents⟩ **2 a :** a gesture of respect (as an obeisance, bow, or curtsy) ⟨made a slight ~ in passing⟩ **b :** a deep bow performed in a court dance or ballet **3 a :** the character or state of being revered or honored **:** exalted position ⟨remembering the ~ of the place in which he stood⟩ ⟨attained great ~ among the citizens⟩ **b :** something held in reverence **:** an object of honor and respect ⟨one's private ~*s*⟩ **4 :** CLERGYMAN — used as a respectful form of

address (as in the phrases *his Reverence, saving your reverence*) **syn** see HONOR

²**reverence** \"\ *vt* -ED/-ING/-S [ME, fr. *reverence*, n.] **:** to regard or treat with reverence, respect, honor, or veneration **:** show reverence to or respect for **:** esteem highly ⟨~ the gods⟩ ⟨those who ~ the laws of their country⟩ ⟨truly *reverenced* honest effort⟩ **syn** see REVERE

rev·er·enc·er \-nsə(r)\ *n* -S **:** one that reverences

¹**rev·er·end** \ˈrevərnd *also* -v(ə)rən-\ *adj, sometimes* -ER/-EST [ME, fr. MF, fr. L *reverendus*, gerundive of *reverērī* to revere] **1 :** worthy of reverence **:** entitled to respect or honor (as on account of age or position) **:** inspiring reverence **:** REVERED ⟨these ~ halls⟩ ⟨my ~ father⟩ — often used in respectful address ⟨you may trust my aim, ~ sir⟩ **2** *obs* **:** SACRED, HOLY **3 :** REVERENT ⟨experienced a ~ awe at the sight⟩ **4 a :** of, relating to, or characteristic of the clergy **b** *usu cap* **:** belonging to the clergy **:** being a clergyman — used in a form of address usu. preceded by *the*, followed by a title or a full name, and sometimes qualified by an honorific ⟨the *Reverend* Dr. Doe⟩; abbr. *Rev.* ⟨*Rev.* John Doe⟩; compare MOST REVEREND, RIGHT REVEREND, VERY REVEREND **5** *chiefly Midland* **:** STRONG, POTENT, UNDILUTED ⟨a ~ whiskey⟩

²**reverend** \"\ *n* -S **:** a member of the clergy **:** MINISTER, PRIEST, PASTOR ⟨churches don't hire ~*s*, they hire families —Monte Linkletter⟩ ⟨saw the ~ walking down the road⟩ ⟨good morning, *Reverend*⟩

reverendly *adv* [ME, fr. ¹*reverend* + *-ly*] **1** *obs* **:** REVERENTLY **2** *obs* **:** in a manner to inspire reverence

rev·er·end·ship \-n(d),ship\ *n* **:** the condition of being a clergyman

rev·er·ent \ˈrevərnt *also* -v(ə)rən-\ *adj* [in sense 1, fr. ME, alter. (influenced by L *reverent-, reverens*) of MF *reverend*; in sense 2, fr. ME, fr. L *reverent-, reverens*, pres. part. of *reverērī* to revere — more at REVERE] **1** *obs* **:** REVEREND 1, 4 **2 :** disposed to revere **:** expressing or characterized by reverence or veneration **:** very or profoundly respectful ⟨~ disciples⟩ ⟨~ conduct⟩ **3 :** REVEREND 5 — **rev·er·ent·ly** *adv* — **rev·er·ent·ness** *n* -ES

rev·er·en·tial \ˌrevəˈrenchəl\ *adj* **1 :** proceeding from or expressing reverence **:** having a reverent quality ⟨~ awe⟩ **2 :** inspiring reverence **:** VENERABLE ⟨a ~ judge with a long white beard⟩ — **rev·er·en·ti·al·i·ty** \ˌ==ˌrenchēˈaləd·ē\ *n* -ES — **rev·er·en·tial·ly** \ˌ==ˈrenchəlē, -li\ *adv* — **rev·er·en·tial·ness** *n* -ES

re·ver·er \rə̇ˈvirə(r)\ *n* -S **:** one that reveres

reveres *pres 3d sing of* REVERE, *pl of* REVERE

rev·er·ie *or* **rev·ery** \ˈrev(ə)rē, -ri\ *n, pl* **reveries** [F *rêverie*, fr. MF *resverie, raverie, reverie* delirium, rage, revelry, fr. *resver, raver, rever* to wander, be delirious + *-erie* -ery] **1 :** an extravagant or fanciful product of the mind **:** a theory or notion marked by strangeness or impracticality **:** a purely visionary or theoretical concept ⟨the scheme was pure ~⟩ **2 a :** the condition of being lost in thought or abstracted musing ⟨passed the day in ~ before the fire⟩ **b :** a sequence of thoughts or images not purposively directed ⟨had a ~ about the children's future⟩

re·verification \(ˌ)rē+\ *n* [*re-* + *verification*] **:** a new or second act of verifying

re·verify \(ˈ)rē+\ *vt* [*re-* + *verify*] **:** to verify again or anew **:** RECHECK

revering *pres part of* REVERE

rev·er·ist \ˈrevərə̇st\ *n* -S **:** one who indulges in reveries

re·vers *n, pl* **revers** \rə̇ˈvi(ə)r, rēˈ-, |ə *also* -ve| *or* -va(ə)|\ [F, lit., reverse, fr. MF] **1 :** a wide turned-back or applied facing that is usu. one of a pair along the front edges of a garment (as a coat or dress), sometimes includes a continuous section for a collar, and often extends to the hemline **2 :** a lapel on women's garments

re·ver·sal \-səl\ *n* -S [ME, fr. *reversen* to reverse + *-al*] **1 :** an act or the process of reversing: as **a :** a change or overthrowing of some legal proceeding or judgment ⟨the ~ of an attainder⟩ **b :** the causing to move or face in an opposite direction or to appear in an inverted position ⟨the ~ of a rotation⟩ ⟨the ~ of objects by a lens⟩ **c :** a method of testing or determining the collimation (as of a transit) by inverting the telescope in its supports **d :** INVERSION 2c **e :** an act or instance of going from the defensive position to the position of advantage in amateur wrestling — compare TAKEDOWN **2 a :** a conversion in whole or part of a photographic positive into a negative or vice versa **b :** SOLARIZATION

reversal process *n* **:** a photographic process in which the reverse of the image formed by direct development is obtained (as by destroying the primary developed negative image with a bleach and developing the residual silver halide to form the reversed image)

¹**re·verse** \rə̇ˈvərs, rēˈ-, -vȯs, -vəis\ *adj* [ME *revers*, fr. MF, fr. L *reversus*, past part. of *revertere* to turn back — more at REVERT] **1 a :** turned back **:** opposite or contrary to one another or to a thing specified ⟨came back in the ~ order⟩ **b :** having the back presented to the observer or opponent — opposed to *obverse* **2** *obs* **:** BACKHANDED ⟨a ~ blow⟩ ⟨~ thrust⟩ **3 :** relating to, facing, or commanding the rear of a military force **4 :** acting or operating in opposite or contrary fashion esp. to what is usual **5 :** effecting reverse movement or operation ⟨a ~ gear⟩ **6 a** (1) **:** so made that the part of a print normally black is white and vice versa ⟨a ~ photoengraving⟩ (2) **:** FLOPPED **b :** constituting a mirror image ⟨the ~ symbols ☞ and ☜⟩ ⟨a ~ positive image⟩

²**reverse** \"\ *vb* -ED/-ING/-S [ME *reversen*, fr. MF *reverser*, fr. LL *reversare* to turn round, freq. of L *revertere* to turn back] *vt* **1** *obs* **:** to cause to return **2** *obs* **:** OVERTHROW, SUBVERT **3 :** to turn completely about in position or direction **:** change to the opposite as regards position **:** TRANSPOSE ⟨a picture *reversed* in reproduction⟩ **4 :** to turn upside down **:** INVERT ⟨*reversing* his glass as a signal that he would drink no more⟩ **5 :** ANNUL: as **a :** to overthrow (a legal decision) by a contrary decision **:** make void (as for error) ⟨the higher court may ~ the judgment⟩ **b :** to take an opposite stand from that formerly held by (oneself) — usu. used with *about* or *over* ⟨*reversed* himself about the superiority of mother's cooking⟩ **c :** to change to the contrary in character or trend ⟨~ a policy⟩ **6 :** to cause to go or move in the opposite direction ⟨~ the flow of a stream⟩; *esp* **:** to cause (as an engine or machine) to perform its revolutions or action in the opposite direction **7 a :** to use (as a tool) or do (as an experiment) in the opposite way **b :** to produce by or use in reverse printing ⟨*reversed* plates⟩ ⟨*reversing* lettering into a color panel⟩ ~ *vi* **1** *obs* **a :** to draw or move back **:** turn away **:** RECOIL **b :** to fall down **:** turn over **c :** RETURN **2 :** to alter or revoke a decision (as on a point of law) **3 :** to turn or move in the opposite direction (as in waltzing) **:** become reversed **4 :** to put a mechanism (as an engine or a machine) in reverse **5 :** to make a reverse bid in bridge **syn** see REVOKE

³**reverse** \"\ *n* -S [ME *revers*, fr. MF, fr. *revers*, adj.] **1 :** something that is directly opposite or contrary to something else **:** CONTRARY, OPPOSITE ⟨hoped for a sunny day but the fact was just the ~⟩ — often followed by *of* or *to* ⟨the ~ of good luck⟩ **2** *obs* **:** a backhanded thrust, cut, or stroke (as with a sword) **3 :** an act or instance of reversing: as **a :** a turning completely about (as in dancing) **:** a complete change or reversal ⟨an unexpected ~ of plans⟩ **b :** a change from better to worse **:** MISFORTUNE, CHECK, DEFEAT — often used in pl. ⟨meet with heavy ~*s*⟩ **4 a :** matter that appears or is presented when something is reverted or is turned or viewed oppositely to the position or direction in which it is ordinarily seen ⟨the ~ of a leaf⟩ **b :** the side of a coin, token, medal, seal, or currency note that is considered the back **c :** the back of a book leaf **:** VERSO **d :** an inverted utterance (as a phrase or sentence) **e :** something (as a negative or lettering) produced by or used in reverse printing **5 :** the rear of a military force **6 a** (1) **:** a gear that reverses something; *also* **:** the mechanical train brought into play when such a gear is used ⟨something out of order in the ~⟩ ⟨put the transmission in ~⟩ (2) **:** movement or course in reverse **b :** a turn or fold made in bandaging by which the direction of the bandage is changed **c :** an offensive play in football in which a back moving in one direction passes or hands the ball to a player moving in the opposite direction **7 :** REVERSE BID **syn** see CONVERSE — **in reverse** *adv* **:** in an opposite manner or direction **:** BACK, BACKWARD

⁴**reverse** \"\ *adv* [ME *revers*, fr. *revers*, adj.] **:** so as to oppose **:** REVERSELY ⟨acted ~ to his own best interests⟩

reverse arms *n* **:** a position of a soldier in which a rifle is held between the right elbow and the body at an angle of 45 degrees with the barrel downward and the muzzle down and to the rear

reverse bar *n* **:** a portion or section of a reverse frame in a ship; *also* **:** REVERSE FRAME

reverse bearing *n* **:** a bearing in surveying resulting from a backsight

reverse bid *n* **:** a bridge rebid in a suit higher in rank than a suit previously bid by the same player made at a level of two or higher and usu. requiring a strong hand

reverse casehardening *n* **:** a condition in wood resulting from excessive steaming (as in an attempt to correct casehardening) and characterized by the surface layers being under tension and the inner layers under compression

reverse circulation *n* **:** flow in a direction opposite to the normal

reverse current *n* **:** flow of direct electric current in a reverse direction or of alternating current in phase opposition to normal

reverse-current circuit breaker *n* **:** a circuit breaker that opens the circuit controlled upon the reversal of the direction of the flow of power

reverse curve *n* **:** an S-shaped curve (as in a railway line or a highway) made by joining two simple curves turning in opposite directions; *broadly* **:** a stretch formed of two oppositely turning simple curves joined by a tangent

reversed *adj* [fr. past part. of ²*reverse*] **1 :** turned backward or the contrary way **:** turned side for side or end for end: as **a :** RESUPINATE **b :** SINISTRAL — used esp. of a univalve shell **c :** INVERTED 1c **d :** exhibiting sexual behavior characteristic of the opposite sex **2 :** having the edges turned back to give the appearance of greater thickness — used of sheet-metal work **3 :** set aside **:** ANNULLED, VACATED ⟨a ~ decision⟩ — **re·versed·ly** \-sə̇dlē, -stlē, -li\ *adv*

reversed calf *n* **:** calf leather finished on flesh side by light buffing and used flesh side out (as for shoes)

reversed collar *n* **:** CLERICAL COLLAR

reversed foot *n* **:** a foot in which the prevailing cadence of a metrical series or of an adjacent foot is reversed or inverted by exchanging the positions of stressed and unstressed or long and short elements ⟨a trochee in an iambic series is a *reversed foot*⟩ — compare INVERSION

reverse discard *n* **:** a discard or play in bridge or whist of two or more losing cards in some order other than that conventionally expected by one's partner as a signal — compare ECHO, HIGH-LOW

reverse dive *n* **:** one of several competitive dives in which the body rotates backward around a transverse axis from a front takeoff — compare BACK DIVE, FRONT DIVE, INWARD DIVE, TWIST DIVE

reversed line *also* **reversed spectrum line** *n* **:** a strong line in an emission spectrum that has a dark line down its middle due to absorption by the colder vapor which surrounds the central luminous vapor

reverse english *n, usu cap E* **1** *or* **reverse side :** English imparted to a cue ball causing it to rebound at a more obtuse angle and at a slower speed — compare RUNNING ENGLISH **2 :** something that is an apparent contradiction or inverted application ⟨putting *reverse English* on one's words —Richard Wilbur⟩

reverse fault *n* **:** a geological fault in which the hanging wall appears to have been pushed up along the footwall

reverse flush *vt* **:** to circulate water or a cleansing fluid through (the cooling system of an automobile) in reverse of the normal circulation to dislodge an accumulation of sludge

reverse frame *n* **:** a part of the frame of a steel ship formed by an angle iron placed opposite the frame proper but with its flanges reversed in direction from those forming the frame — see SHIP illustration

reverse graft *n* **:** a plant graft in which the scion is inserted in an inverted position usu. in order to develop a dwarf plant

reverse half nelson *n* **:** a half nelson applied (as from a cross-body ride) with the arm under the opponent's opposite rather than corresponding arm — see GUILLOTINE 7

reverse hydrant *n* **:** a hydrant through which water is pumped into a main from another source

reverse indention *n* **:** HANGING INDENTION

reverse index *n* **:** a list (as an index or glossary) in which items are arranged alphabetically under their final element

reverse keys *n pl* **:** an arrangement of keys or wedges resembling a stonemason's plug and feather used for forcing apart two pieces previously fastened by a key or cotter

reverse·ly *adv* **:** in an opposite way **:** so as to be reversed

re·verse·ment \rə̇ˈvərsmənt\ *n* -S **:** REVERSAL; *esp* **:** a flight maneuver consisting of a half-roll and a half-loop performed in that order

reverse of the medal : an opposite and usu. less favorable aspect of an affair or question

reverse painting *n* **:** the art or method of painting on the back of a glass panel in which the details are done first so that the finished work may be seen correctly from the opposite side; *also* **:** an example of such painting

reverse perspective *n* **:** visual perspective (as in Byzantine painting and medieval illumination) characterized by divergence of parallel lines and diminution of objects toward the observer — compare LINEAR PERSPECTIVE

reverse-phase relay *n* **:** a phase-rotation relay applied to protect electric motors against damage by reversal of phase sequence

reverse pitch *n* **:** propeller blade pitch in which the thrust produced is opposite to that normally obtained

re·vers·er \-sər\ *n* -S **1 :** one that reverses ⟨a signal ~⟩: as **a :** a device for reversing an electric current or polarity **b :** a switching device for interchanging electrical circuits to reverse the direction of motor rotation **2** *Scots law* **a :** REVERSIONER **b :** MORTGAGOR; *also* **:** one granting a wadset of his land

reverses *pres 3d sing of* REVERSE, *pl of* REVERSE

reverse slope *n* **:** a slope that descends away (as from an enemy force) esp. when marked by a hill or ridge

reverse spelling *n* **:** an unphonetic and unetymological spelling imitating the same spelling in words where it is etymological but no longer phonetic (as *limb* from *lim*, compare *lamb*, where *b* is etymological; *delight* from *delit*, compare *light*; *Swanage* from *Swanwich* \ˈswänij\ compare *savage*)

reverse taper *n* **:** a planform configuration in which the chord of the wing of an airplane increases with distance outboard from the root

reverse turn *n* **1 :** IMMELMANN TURN **2 a :** counterclockwise rotation **b :** a counterclockwise turn in dancing

re·ver·si \rə̇ˈvərsē\ *n* -S [F, fr. obs. F *reversin*, modif. (influenced by F *revers* reverse, fr. MF) of It *rovescina*, fr. *rovescio*, adj., reverse, inside out, fr. *rovesciare* to reverse, turn inside out, fr. (assumed) VL *reversiare*, fr. LL *reversare* to turn round; fr. the fact that the game is won by losing — more at REVERSE] **1 :** a card game in which the player who makes the fewest points and takes the fewest tricks wins **2 :** a game for two which is played on a checkerboard with 64 pieces having one color on one side and another on the other and in which if a player can so place his men as to enclose one of the opponent's he may reverse it and use it as one of his own

re·vers·ibil·i·ty \rə̇ˌvərsəˈbiləd·ē, rē,-, -vəs-, -vəis-, -lətē, -i\ *n* -S **:** the quality or state of being reversible

reversibility principle *n* **:** a principle in optics: if light travels from a point *A* to a point *B* over a particular path, it can travel over the same path from *B* to *A*

¹**re·vers·ible** \=ˈ=səbəl\ *adj* [²*reverse* + *-ible*] **:** capable of being reversed or of reversing ⟨a chair with a ~ back⟩ ⟨a ~ judgment⟩: as **a :** capable of going through a series of actions (as movements or changes) in either direction backward or forward ⟨a ~ chemical reaction⟩ — see REVERSIBLE PROCESS **b** (1) **:** having two finished usable sides often with different patterns or colors ⟨~ fabric⟩ ⟨~ panels⟩ — compare DAMASK 1 (2) **:** made to be worn with either side out and often with a different fabric on each side ⟨~ overcoat⟩ ⟨~ jacket⟩ **c :** capable of being corrected **:** not permanent or irrevocable ⟨~ hypertension⟩ — **re·vers·ible·ness** *n* -ES — **re·versibly** \-blē, -li\ *adv*

²**reversible** \"\ *n* -S **:** a reversible cloth

reversible cell *or* **reversible element** *n* **:** an electrical cell the chemical action in which can be reversed by passing through it a current opposite in direction to that generated by the cell ⟨a storage cell is a *reversible cell*⟩

reversible colloid *n* **:** a colloid that can be precipitated as a gel and then again dispersed as a sol

reversible disc plow *n* **:** a disc plow having the disc reversible so that the soil can be thrown in the same direction regardless of the direction of travel

reversible electrode *n* **:** a metallic electrode that will dissolve when a current is passed from it into a solution and that will have plated on it metal from the solution when the current is passed in the reverse direction

reversible error *n* **:** error justifying the vacating of a judgment or decree, sustaining an exception or appeal, or remanding a case for new trial or hearing

reversible lock *n* **:** a lock that may be applied to a door opening in either direction or hinged to either jamb

reversible-pitch propeller *n* **:** a propeller whose blade pitch may be adjusted to produce thrust in a direction opposite to that normally obtained

reversible process *n* **:** an ideal process or series of changes of a system which is in complete equilibrium at each stage such that when the process is reversed each of the changes both internal and external is reversed but with the amount of transferred energy unaltered

reversible reaction *n* **:** a reaction that takes place in either direction according to conditions (as the formation of hydriodic acid by union of hydrogen and iodine or its decomposition into these elements) — compare EQUILIBRIUM 1b

re·versify \(ˈ)rē+\ *vt* [*re-* + *versify*] **:** to formulate anew in verse

reversing *pres part of* REVERSE

reversing eyepiece *n* **:** an eyepiece (as of a telescope) equipped with a prism or mirror to interchange opposite sides of the field and give a mirror image — compare REVERSING PRISM

reversing layer *n* **:** the lowest layers of the sun's chromosphere which are perhaps a few hundred miles in depth and in which occurs the absorption that produces most of the dark lines in the solar spectrum; *also* **:** a corresponding region in the atmosphere of a star

reversing link *n* **:** the slotted link of a link motion

re·vers·ing·ly *adv* **:** so as to reverse **:** in a reversing manner

reversing prism *n* **:** a right-angled prism that reverses in one coordinate the images of objects viewed through it by total reflection — compare PORRO PRISM

reversing switch *n* **:** an electric switch that has four terminals capable of being connected in pairs in two different ways so as to reverse the direction of current flow

reversing thermometer *n* **:** a thermometer for registering temperature in deep water by means of the breaking of a column of mercury when the thermometer inverts at a specified depth

re·ver·sion \rə̇ˈvər|zhən, rēˈ-, -vȯ|, -vəi| *also* |shən\ *n* -S [ME, fr. MF, fr. L *reversion-, reversio* act of turning back, fr. *reversus* (past part. of *revertere* to turn back) + *-ion-, -io* -ion — more at REVERT] **1 a** (1) **:** the returning of an estate upon its termination to its former owner or his successor in interest (2) **:** the part of a simple estate remaining in its owner after he has granted therefrom a lesser particular estate (as the future reversionary interest when a term for years, a life estate, a fee tail, or a contingent remainder) that will upon the termination of the lesser estate automatically return to the possession of the owner **b :** the right of redemption under Scots law from wadset existing during the time allowed for the payment of the debt secured thereby **c :** a future interest in property left in a grantor or his successor in interest that is not subject to a condition precedent **2 a** *archaic* **:** the residue of food or drink left over (as from a meal) **:** SCRAPS, LEFTOVERS **b** *obs* **:** a small amount or number **:** REMAINDER, REMNANT **3 :** the right of succession or of future possession or enjoyment (as of an office or of material or immaterial goods) **4 :** an act or instance of returning (as to a former condition or faith) **:** RECONVERSION: as **a :** the act of reverting an algebraic series **b :** a return toward some ancestral type or condition **:** the reappearance of an ancestral character **:** ATAVISM **5 :** an act or instance of turning the opposite way or the state of being so turned ⟨the breeze underwent an abrupt ~⟩ **6 :** a product of reversion: as **a :** an organism with an atavistic character **:** THROWBACK **b :** a reversionary annuity **c :** a virus disease of black currants transmitted by a gall mite and characterized by narrow rugose leaves, abnormally elongated and partially or completely sterile flowers, and degeneration of the plant as a whole

re·ver·sion·able \-nəbəl\ *adj* **:** capable of reversion

re·ver·sion·al \|zhənᵊl, |zhnəl, |sh-\ *adj* **:** of, relating to, or constituting a reversion **:** REVERSIONARY — **re·ver·sion·al·ly** \-ᵊlē, -əlē, -i\ *adv*

re·ver·sion·ary \|zhəˌnerē, |sh-, -ri\ *adj* **:** of, relating to, constituting, or involving a reversion and esp. a legal reversion to be enjoyed in succession or after the termination of a particular estate ⟨a ~ interest⟩

reversionary annuity *n* **:** an annuity payable to some person upon another becoming for any reason unable to receive it and usu. equivalent to a survivorship annuity

reversion duty *n, chiefly Brit* **:** a duty levied on a lessor at the termination of a long lease based on increase of property valuation during the period of the lease

re·ver·sion·er \|zh(ə)nə(r), |sh-\ *n* -S **:** one that has or is entitled to a reversion; *broadly* **:** someone having a vested right to a future estate

re·ver·sion·ist \-nə̇st\ *n* -S **1 :** REVERSIONER **2 :** an advocate of reversion to some previous state (as of political affiliation)

reversion to type : REVERSION 4b

reversis *pl of* REVERSI

re·ver·sive \rə̇ˈvərsiv\ *adj* [²*reverse* + *-ive*] **:** relating to or marked by reversion **:** tending to reverse or revert

re·verso \rə̇+\ *n* [*re-* + *verso*] **:** VERSO

¹**re·vert** \rə̇ˈvər|t, rēˈ-, -vȯ|, -vəi|, *usu* |d·+V\ *vb* -ED/-ING/-S [ME *reverten*, fr. MF *revertir*, fr. OF, fr. L *revertere* to turn back, fr. *re-* + *vertere* to turn — more at WORTH] *vi* **1 :** to come or go back (as to a place, person, condition, or topic) ⟨a people that ~*ed* to savagery⟩ **2 :** to return to the proprietor or his heirs or assigns after the termination of a particular estate or reversion granted by him **3 :** to undergo reversion **:** return toward some ancestral type **4 :** to return to a former chemical state — used esp. of solubilized phosphoric acid or phosphate in fertilizer that becomes insoluble again **5 :** to develop an off-flavor — used esp. of a fat or a fatty oil ~ *vt* **1** *obs* **a :** to cause to return to; *esp* **:** RESTORE **b :** to turn, force, or throw back **c :** REVOKE, REVERSE, ANNUL **2 :** to turn to the contrary **:** REVERSE, INVERT **3 :** to turn (as the eyes) or direct back or to the rear **4 :** to cause (as phosphates) to revert — **revert a series :** to so treat an infinite algebraic series (as $y=a+bx+cx^2+$etc.) as to find x in a series in powers of y

²**revert** \"\ *n* -S **:** one that reverts or is reverted; *esp* **:** one that returns to a former faith

³**revert** \"\ *adj* **:** REVERTED

reverted *adj* **:** turned or curled back or the wrong way ⟨a ~ leaf⟩ **:** directed back ⟨with eyes ~⟩ **:** REVERSED; *also* **:** affected with reversion ⟨a ~ culture of bacteria⟩ ⟨~ black currants⟩

reverted train *n* **:** an epicyclic train in which the first and last wheels revolve on the same axis so that when these two wheels are nearly equal a very slow relative rotation is secured

¹**re·vert·er** \|d·ə(r)\ *n* -S [ME, fr. AF *reverter* to return (taken as a n.), fr. OF *revertir* to return, revert] **1 :** REVERSION **2 a :** a possibility of reversion of an estate in land ⟨land subject to a ~⟩

²**reverter** \"\ *n* -S [¹*revert* + *-er*] **:** one that reverts

re·vert·ible \|d·əbəl\ *adj* [ME, fr. *reverten* to revert + *-ible*] **:** that may revert or be reverted

re·ver·tive \|d·iv\ *adj* **:** reverting or tending to revert **:** RE-

revery *var of* REVERIE

re·vest \rəˈvest, rēˈ-\ *vb* -ED/-ING/-S [ME *revesten*, fr. OF *revestir*, fr. LL *revestire* to clothe again, fr. L *re-* + *vestire* to clothe, fr. *vestis* garment — more at WEAR] *vt* **1 a** *obs* **:** to clothe in clerical vestments **:** ROBE **b** *obs* **:** to clothe (as oneself) anew **:** dress with fresh or different garments **c :** to put on (as a costume) again **:** RESUME **2 :** to vest again **:** REIN-

STATE, REINVEST ⟨~ a king in his kingdom⟩ ⟨lands ~*ed* in a former owner⟩ ~ *vi* : to take effect or vest again (as of a title) : revert to a former owner ⟨the title ~*ed* in A⟩
re·ves·ti·ary \-tē,erē\ *n* -ES [ME *revestiarie*, fr. MF] : REVESTRY
re·ves·try \-trē\ *n* [ME, modif. (influenced by *vestrie* vestry) of MF *revestiarie*, fr. ML *revestiarium*, fr. *re-* + *vestiarium* vestry — more at VESTRY] : a place for the vesting of priests : VESTRY
re·vet \rə'vet, rē'-, *usu* -ed·+V\ *vt* **revetted**; **revetted**; **revetting**; **revets** [F *revêtir*, lit., to clothe again, dress up, dress, fr. OF *revestir*] : to face (as an embankment) with a revetment
re·vête \rə'vet\ *vt* -ED/-ING/-S [F *revêtir*] : REVET
re·vête·ment \rə'vetmäⁿ\ *n* -S [F, fr. MF *revestement*, fr. OF *revestir* to clothe again + *-ment*] : REVETMENT
re·vet·ment \rə'vetmənt, rē'-\ *n* -S [F *revêtement*] **1** : a facing of stone, concrete, fascines, or other material to sustain an embankment **2** : EMBANKMENT; *esp* : a bank or barricade (as of earth or sandbags) built up to provide shelter (as for planes, magazines, or personnel) against bomb splinters, strafing, or overrun of landing space
re·victual \(')rē+\ *vb* [*re-* + *victual*] *vt* : to supply (as an army) with a fresh stock of provisions ~ *vi* : to obtain fresh stocks of provisions — **re·victual·ment** \"+mənt\ *n* -S
¹re·vie \(')rē¦vī\ *vb* -ED/-ING/-S [MF *renvier*, fr. *re-* + *envier* to challenge, vie — more at VIE] *vt* : to meet a wager on (as the taking of a trick in a card game) with a higher wager ~ *vi* **1** *obs* : to exceed an adversary's wager **2** *obs* : to make a retort : bandy words
²revie *n* -S [MF *renvi*, fr. *re-* + *envi* challenge, vie, fr. *envier*] *obs* : a higher wager (as in a card game) than an adversary's
¹re·view \rə'vyü, rē'-\ *n* [MF *revue*, fr. fem. of *revu*, past part. of *revoir* to look over, fr. *re-* + *voir* to look, see — more at VIEW] **1** : a looking over or examination with a view to amendment or improvement : REVISION ⟨an author's ~ of his works⟩ **2** : an inspection (as of troops under arms or of a naval force) by a high officer (as for the purpose of ascertaining the state of discipline and equipment); *specif* : a march past a reviewing officer usu. following an inspection **3** : a general survey or view (as of the events of a period) ⟨take a ~ of the war⟩ ⟨pass one's life in ~⟩ **4** : an act of inspecting or examining : REVIEWING **5** : judicial reexamination (as of the proceedings of a lower tribunal by a higher) **6 a** : an explanatory and critical account of an artistic production or performance (as a book, play, exhibition, or concert) usu. in a periodical : CRITICISM, CRITIQUE **b** : a periodical containing primarily critical articles **7 a** : a second or repeated view : REEXAMINATION **b** : a retrospective view or survey (as of one's life) **c** (1) : renewed study (as at the end of a course or before an examination) of material previously studied (2) : an exercise designed to facilitate such study **8** : REVUE
²review \", *in senses 1&2* (')rē¦vyü\ *vb* [*re-* + *view*] *vt* **1** *archaic* : to view or see again **2** : to examine again : make a second or additional inspection of : study anew ⟨the officers viewed and ~*ed* the fortifications⟩ **3** [¹*review*] **a** : to take a view of : examine with consideration or attention : SURVEY ⟨on ~*ing* all the circumstances⟩ **b** : to look back on : take a retrospective view of **4** : to reexamine judicially ⟨a higher court may ~ the proceedings and judgments of a lower one⟩ **5** : to go over or examine critically or deliberately: as **a** *obs* : to subject to revision (as a manuscript before printing or a book for a new edition) **b** : to go over with critical examination in order to discover excellences or defects; *also* : to give a critical examination of ⟨~ a new novel⟩ **6** : to make a formal or official examination of the state of (as troops) : hold a review of ⟨~ a regiment⟩ **7** : to recapitulate (previous calls in the auction of the current deal) in a bridge game ~ *vi* : to make a review ⟨~*ing* for a test⟩; *usu* : to write reviews : be a reviewer
re·view·abil·i·ty \rə,vyüə'bilәd·ē\ *n* : the quality or state of being reviewable
re·view·able \rə'vyüəbəl\ *adj* : subject to review : capable of being reviewed
re·view·al \-üəl\ *n* -S **1** : an act of reviewing : REVISION **2** : a literary review : CRITICISM
re·view·er \rə'vyüə(r), rē'-, -yü(ə)r, -yüə\ *n* : one that reviews or reexamines: as **a** : one that examines publications critically and writes his opinion of them for publication : a professional critic of books : a review writer **b** *obs* : REVISER **c** *obs* : one that looks back **d** : a clerk that examines insurance applications to see whether they are properly filled out and whether they introduce suitable risks
reviewing authority *n* : one having authority to review some decision; *esp* : a military commander to whom the record of a court-martial trial is submitted for review and approval
re·view·less \-yüləs\ *adj* : receiving or meriting no review ⟨~ paperbacks⟩
re·vig·or·ate \rə'vigə,rāt\ *vt* -ED/-ING/-S [ML *revigoratus*, past part. of *revigorare* to make strong again, fr. L *re-* + LL *vigorare* to make strong, fr. L *vigor* strength — more at VIGOR] : REINVIGORATE
¹re·vile \rə'vīl, rē'-, *esp before pause or consonant* -īəl\ *vb* -ED/-ING/-S [ME *revilen*, fr. MF *reviler* to despise, regard as vile, fr. *re-* + *-viler* (fr. *vil* vile) — more at VILE] *vt* : to subject to verbal abuse : address or assail with opprobrious language : rail at ~ *vi* : to use contemptuous or opprobrious language : RAIL **syn** see SCOLD
²revile *n* -S *obs* : a reviling remark or speech; *also* : REVILING
re·vile·ment \-lmənt\ *n* -S : an act or instance or the practice of reviling
re·vil·er \-lə(r)\ *n* -S : one that reviles
re·vil·ing·ly *adv* : in a reviling manner
re·vindicate \(')rē+\ *vt* [*re-* + *vindicate*] : to vindicate again; *esp* : to demand and take back — **re·vindication** \(¦)rē+\ *n*
re·vi·res·cence \,revə'resᵊn(t)s\ *n* -S : the condition or fact of being revirescent
rev·i·res·cent \¦==¦resᵊnt\ *adj* [L *revirescent-, revirescens*, pres. part. of *revirescere* to grow green again, fr. *re-* + *virescere* to grow green — more at VIRESCENT] : growing fresh or young again : REVIVING
re·vis·abil·i·ty \rə,vīzə'bilәd·ē\ *n* : the quality or state of being revisable
re·vis·able \rə'vīzəbəl\ *adj* : capable of being revised : subject to or meriting revision ⟨~ estimate⟩
re·vis·al \-zəl\ *n* -S : an act of revising : REVISION ⟨the ~ of a manuscript⟩
¹re·vise \rə'vīz, rē'-\ *vb* -ED/-ING/-S [MF *reviser*, fr. L *revisere* to look back, look again, freq. of *revidēre* to see again, fr. *re-* + *vidēre* to see — more at WIT] *vi* **1** *obs* : to look again, often, or back : look in retrospect : REFLECT **2** : to make a revision : be engaged in revision (as of a manuscript) ~ *vt* **1** : to look at or over again for the purpose of correcting or improving : go or read over to correct errors or make improvements ⟨~ a manuscript⟩ **2 a** : to make a new, amended, improved, or up-to-date version of : subject to revision ⟨~ a dictionary⟩ ⟨*revised* the game laws⟩ **b** : to provide with a new taxonomic arrangement ⟨*revising* the alpine ferns⟩ **syn** see CORRECT
²revise \"\ *n* -S **1** : an act of revising : REVIEW, REVISION, REEXAMINATION **2** : a printing proof taken from matter that incorporates changes marked in a previous proof **3** : a revised form
revised edition *n* : an edition (as of a book) incorporating major revisions by the author or an editor and often supplementary matter designed to bring it up to date — compare REISSUE, REPRINT
re·vis·er \-zə(r)\ *n* -S : one that revises something (as printer's proofs)
re·vis·ible \-zəbəl\ *adj* [¹*revise* + *-ible*] : REVISABLE
re·vi·sion \rə'vizhən, rē'-\ *n* -S [F, fr. LL *revision-, revisio* fact of seeing again, fr. L *revisus* (past part. of *revidēre* to see again) + *-ion-, -io* -ion] **1 a** : an act of revising : reexamination or careful reading over for correction or improvement ⟨the ~ of a book⟩ **b** : something made by revising : a revised form or version **2** : a seeing again
re·vi·sion·ary \-zhə,nerē, -ri *also* **re·vi·sion·al** \-zhənᵊl, -zhnəl\ *adj* : of, relating to, or made up of revision
re·vi·sion·ism \-zhə,nizəm\ *n* -S **1** : advocacy of revision (as of an original doctrine or treaty) : the theory or practice of a revisionist **2** : a movement among socialists to modify Marxian socialism esp. so as to be evolutionary rather than revolutionary in spirit
¹re·vi·sion·ist \-zh(ə)nəst\ *n* -S [*revision* + *-ist*] **1** : an advocate of revision (as of a court decision or an accepted attitude or point of view) **2** : REVISER **3** : an advocate of revisionism
²revisionist \"\ *adj* : advocating revision or revisionism; *esp* : seeking to reanalyze and re-present historical data in light of subsequent knowledge
¹re·visit \(')rē+\ *vt* [*re-* + *visit* (v.)] **1** *obs* : to inspect or check anew : REEXAMINE **2** : to visit again : return to
²revisit \"\ *n* [*re-* + *visit* (n.)] : a second or subsequent visit
re·vis·i·tant \(')rē¦vizətᵊnt\ *adj or n* [¹*revisit* + *-ant*] : REVISITING
re·vis·i·ta·tion \(¦)rē,vizə¦tāshən\ *n* [¹*revisit* + *-ation*] : an act of revisiting
re·vi·sor \rə'vīzə(r), rē'-\ *n* -S [¹*revise* + *-or*] : REVISER
re·vi·so·ry \-z(ə)rē, -ri\ *adj* [¹*revise* + *-ory*] : having the power or purpose to revise : making or intended to make revision ⟨~ body⟩ ⟨a ~ function⟩
re·visualize \(')rē+\ *vt* [*re-* + *visualize*] : to bring again into view esp. as a mental image
re·vi·tal·iza·tion \(¦)rē,vīd·ᵊlə¦zāshən\ *n* [*revitalize* + *-ation*] **1** : an act or instance of revitalizing **2** : something that is revitalized
re·vitalize \(')rē+\ *vt* [*re-* + *vitalize*] : to impart new life or vigor to : restore to a vigorous active state — **re·vitalizer** \"+\ *n*
re·viv·abil·i·ty \rə,vīvə'bilәd·ē\ *n* : the quality or state of being revivable
re·viv·able \rə'vīvəbəl\ *adj* [*revive* + *-able*] : capable of being revived; *usu* : not wholly or permanently lifeless — **re·viv·ably** \-blē\ *adv*
re·viv·al \rə'vīvəl, rē'-\ *n* -S [*revive* + *-al*] **1** : an act or instance of reviving or the state of being revived : RESTORATION: as **a** : renewed attention to something (as to letters, a technique, or a custom) ⟨a ~ of the old independent spirit⟩ ⟨enjoyed the ~ of costume parties that season⟩ **b** : renewed performance of or interest in the drama and literature : a new presentation or publication (as of a play or book) **c** : a period of religious awakening : renewed interest in religion ⟨plans of the American Baptists to promote a nationwide ~ this year⟩; *also* : an evangelistic meeting or a series of evangelistic meetings often characterized by emotional excitement **d** (1) : reanimation from a state of languor or depression — used esp. of the health, spirits, or similar qualities (2) : restoration to consciousness or life **e** : renewed pursuit or cultivation or flourishing state of something (as commerce, arts, agriculture) ⟨a ~ of weaving⟩ **f** : renewed prevalence of something (as a practice or a fashion); *esp* : the reappearance of Gothic forms in 19th century architecture **2** : restoration of force, validity, or effect (as to a legal judgment) ⟨the ~ of a debt barred by limitation⟩ ⟨the ~ of a revoked will⟩ **3** : RECALL 2
re·viv·al·ism \-ə,lizəm\ *n* -S **1** : the spirit or kind of religion or the methods characteristic of religious revivals **2** : a tendency or desire to revive or restore
re·viv·al·ist \-ləst\ *n* -S **1** : a clergyman or layman who promotes religious revivals : an advocate of or participator in religious revivals; *specif* : a clergyman (as an evangelist) without a particular charge who goes about to promote revivals **2** : a reviver or restorer of something disused (as an earlier architectural or literary style) — **re·viv·al·is·tic** \¦=¦==¦listik\ *adj*
re·vive \rə'vīv, rē'-\ *vb* -ED/-ING/-S [ME *reviven*, fr. MF *revivre*, fr. L *revivere* to live again, fr. *re-* + *vivere* to live — more at QUICK] *vi* **1** : to return to consciousness or life : recover life, vigor, or strength : become reanimated or reinvigorated : become active, operative, valid, or flourishing again ⟨hope *revived* in him⟩ ⟨the drooping plants *revived* in the rain⟩ **2** : to recover the metallic state — used esp. of a metal ~ *vt* **1** : to restore to consciousness or life : REANIMATE, REVITALIZE **2** : to raise from languor, depression, or discouragement : bring into action after a suspension : make active, operative, valid, or flourishing again : REINVIGORATE **3** : to raise from a state of neglect or disuse : bring back (as into currency, use, performance) ⟨~ a play⟩ **4** : to renew in the mind or memory : bring to recollection : recall attention to ⟨*reviving* the scene in his mind⟩ **5 a** : to reduce or restore (as a metal after calcination) to the metallic state **b** : REVIVIFY **6** : REJUVENATE 3
re·vive·ment \-īvmənt\ *n* -S **1** *archaic* : REVIVAL **2** *obs* : a reviving influence : a cause of revival
¹re·viv·er \-īvə(r)\ *n* -S : one that revives: as **a** : STIMULANT **b** : a preparation for restoring finish **c** : one that restores to use, reestablishes, or reintroduces something **d** : a renovator of old or outworn things (as buildings or clothes)
²reviver *n* -S *obs* : REVIVAL, REESTABLISHMENT
re·viv·i·ca·tion \(,)rē,vivə'kāshən\ *substand var of* REVIVIFICATION
re·vivification \(¦)rē+\ *n* [LL *revivification-, revivificatio*, fr. *revivificatus* (past part. of *revivificare* to restore to life) + *-ion-, -io* -ion] **1** : renewal or restoration of life : an act of recalling or restoring or the state of being recalled from death or apparent death or torpidity to life **2** : the process of chemically reviving (as a metal) or revivifying (as char) **3** : REVIVAL, RENEWAL, REINVIGORATION
re·viv·i·fi·er \(')rē¦vivə,fī(ə)r, rə'v-\ *n* [*revivify* + *-er*] : one that revivifies : REVIVER
re·viv·i·fy \-,fī\ *vb* [F *révivifier*, fr. LL *revivificare* to restore to life, fr. L *re-* + LL *vivificare* to make alive, vivify — more at VIVIFY] *vt* : to impart new life to : cause to revive: as **a** : REANIMATE, REINVIGORATE **b** : to restore to life : RESUSCITATE **c** (1) : REVIVE 5a (2) : to restore to a chemically active state : REACTIVATE ~ *vi* : REVIVE
reviving *adj* **1** : regaining an active state **2** : RESUSCITATIVE **3** : RENEWING — **re·viv·ing·ly** *adv*
rev·i·vis·cence \,revə'visᵊn(t)s\ *also* **rev·i·vis·cen·cy** \-ᵊnsē\ *or* **rev·i·ves·cence** \-'vesᵊn(t)s\ *or* **rev·i·ves·cen·cy** \-ᵊnsē\ *n, pl* **reviviscences** *also* **reviviscencies** [*reviviscence, reviviscency* fr. L *reviviscere* to revive + E *-ence* or *-ency*; *revivescence, revivescency* alter. (influence of *-escence*) of *reviviscence, reviviscency*] : an act of reviving or the condition of being revived : renewal of life : restoration to life, vigor, or activity
rev·i·vis·cent \-'visᵊnt\ *adj* [L *reviviscent-, reviviscens, revivescent-, revivescens*, pres. part. of *reviviscere, revivescere* to come to life again, fr. *re-* + *viviscere, vivescere* to come to life, incho. of *vivere* to live — more at QUICK] : able or disposed to revive : causing revival
re·vi·vor \rə'vīvə(r)\ *n* -S [alter. (influenced by *-or*) of ²*reviver*] : revival under English law of a suit that is abated
rev·o·ca·bil·i·ty \,revəkə'bilәd·ē, -lətē, -i *also* ÷rə,vōk- *or* ÷rē,-\ *n* : the quality or state of being revocable
rev·o·ca·ble \'revəkəbəl *also* ÷rə'vōk- *or* ÷rē'-\ *adj* [ME, fr. MF, fr. L *revocabilis*, fr. *revocare* to call back, revoke + *-abilis* -able] : capable of being revoked — **rev·o·ca·ble·ness** *n* -ES — **rev·o·ca·bly** \-blē, -li\ *adv*
rev·o·ca·tion \,revə'kāshən, ,rē(,)vō'-\ *n* [ME *revocacioun*, fr. MF *revocation*, fr. L *revocation-, revocatio*, fr. *revocatus* (past part. of *revocare* to revoke) + *-ion-, -io* -ion] **1** *archaic* : an act of recalling or calling back or the condition of being recalled **2** : an act of revoking : the act by which one having the right annuls something previously done, a power or authority given, or a license, gift, or benefit conferred : REPEAL, REVERSAL, WITHDRAWAL ⟨the ~ of an edict⟩ ⟨subject to ~ of a license⟩ **3** *obs* : RECANTATION, RETRACTION
rev·o·ca·tive \'revə,kād·iv, rə'väkəd-\ *adj* [L *revocatus* (past part.) + E *-ive*] : able or serving to revoke : REVOKING
rev·o·ca·to·ry \'revəkə,tōrē, rə'väk-\ *adj* [ME, fr. LL *revocatorius*, fr. L *revocatus* (past part. of *revocare* to revoke) + *-orius* -ory] : of or relating to revocation : tending to or involving a revocation : REVOKING, RECALLING
revoice \(')rē+\ *vt* [*re-* + *voice*] **1** : to voice again : ECHO **2 a** : to refurnish with a voice **b** : to adjust (as an organ pipe) in tone
re·vok·able \rə'vōkəbəl\ *adj* [*revoke* + *-able*] : REVOCABLE
¹re·voke \rə'vōk, rē'-\ *vb* -ED/-ING/-S [ME *revoken*, fr. MF *revoquer*, fr. L *revocare*, fr. *re-* + *vocare* to call — more at VOICE] *vt* **1** : to bring or call back: as **a** *obs* : RESTRAIN, CHECK, PREVENT **b** : to call or summon back **c** : to call back to mind or memory **d** *obs* : to restore to use or operation : REVIVE **2** : to annul by recalling or taking back (as something granted by a special act) : RESCIND, CANCEL, REPEAL ⟨~ a will⟩ ⟨~ a privilege⟩ **3** *obs* : WITHDRAW: as **a** : RECANT, RETRACT **b** : to take back : REASSUME, RECOVER **c** : to draw back ~ *vi* **1** : to make revocation **2** : to fail to follow suit when able in a card game in violation of the rule of the game : RENEGE
syn REVERSE, REPEAL, RESCIND, RECALL: REVOKE indicates an annulling or abrogating, esp. of something given or assigned, with formality or not ⟨*revoke* a license⟩ ⟨*revoke* a grant⟩ ⟨his power of attorney . . . has never been *revoked* —Hamilton Basso⟩ REVERSE may be a close synonym for REVOKE, esp. in indicating decision directly opposed to that previously made; it is often used of a higher agency or instrumentality acting on a lower ⟨the plate umpire *reversing* his decision after conferring with the others⟩ ⟨the superior court *reversing* the decision of the lower court⟩ REPEAL is likely to be used in reference to formal abrogation by constituted authority ⟨the legislature *repealed* the unpopular law the next year⟩ ⟨the eighteenth article of amendment to the Constitution of the United States is hereby *repealed* —*U.S. Constitution*⟩ RESCIND applies to abolishing, abrogating, or making void, sometimes with suggestions of summary or definitive procedure ⟨one body of customs after another was swept away; ordinances were overhauled or *rescinded* —F.A. Ogg & Harold Zink⟩ ⟨the legislature refused to function until martial law was *rescinded* —*Current Biog.*⟩ RECALL in this sense indicates a calling back, suspending, or abrogating, either finally as erroneous or ill-advised or tentatively for deliberation ⟨would have done anything to *recall* the word, as soon as it was out of his mouth —Margaret Kennedy⟩ ⟨*recall* a bridge bid⟩ ⟨*recall* a stringent edict⟩
²revoke \"\ *n* -S **1** : ANNULLING, CANCELLATION; *also* : RECALL **2** : an act or instance of revoking in a card game
revokement *n* -S *obs* : REVOCATION
re·vok·er \-kə(r)\ *n* -S : one that revokes
re·vok·ing·ly *adv* : in a revoking manner : so as to revoke
revol *abbr* revolution
re·volatilize \(')rē+\ *vt* [*re-* + *volatilize*] : to volatilize again or anew
¹re·volt \rə'vōlt, rē'- *sometimes* -vòlt\ *vb* -ED/-ING/-S [MF *revolter*, fr. OIt *rivoltare* to turn over, overthrow, fr. (assumed) VL *revolvitare*, freq. of L *revolvere* to roll back, revolve — more at REVOLVE] *vi* **1** : to renounce allegiance or subjection : desert (as a party, leader, or formerly a religion) for another : go over to another : turn away from a party, leader, or duty **2 a** : to be disgusted, shocked, or grossly offended : feel disgust or nausea : turn or rise in disgust or repugnance — used with *at* or *against* ⟨the stomach ~*s* at such food⟩ ⟨his nature ~*s* against such treatment⟩ **b** : to turn away or shrink with disgust or loathing — usu. used with *from* ⟨~*ing* from such a scene of carnage⟩ ~ *vt* **1** *obs* : to cause to turn back **2** : to cause to turn away or shrink with disgust or abhorrence : affect with disgust or loathing : NAUSEATE ⟨such acts ~ the conscience⟩ ⟨is ~*ed* by the indecency of hanging —R.G.G.Price⟩
²revolt \"\ *n* -S [MF *revolte*, fr. *revolter* to revolt] **1** : a casting off of allegiance : an uprising against legitimate authority : a renunciation of allegiance and subjection (as to a government) : INSURRECTION ⟨the ~ of a province⟩; *also* : the act of revolting **2** : a movement or expression of vigorous dissent or refusal to accept ⟨iconoclasm is a ~ against image worship⟩ **3** : a change of party or opinion ⟨transitory parties rising in ~ against rigid old guard conservatism⟩ **syn** see REBELLION
³revolt \"\ *n* : REVOLTER
re·volt·er \-tə(r)\ *n* -S : one that revolts : REBEL
re·volt·ing *adj* : giving rise to disgust or shock : strongly offensive : NAUSEATING ⟨~ cant about the duty of obedience —Henry Adams⟩ **syn** see OFFENSIVE
re·volt·ing·ly *adv* : in a revolting manner : so as to be revolting ⟨~ sordid details⟩
re·volt·ress \-l·trəs\ *n* -ES [*revolter* + *-ess*] : a female revolter
rev·o·lu·ble \'revəlyəbəl, rə'väl-\ *adj* [L *revolubilis*, fr. *revolvere* to revolve + *-ibilis* -ible] : capable of revolving : REVOLVABLE, ROTATING — **rev·o·lu·bly** \-blē\ *adv*
¹rev·o·lute \'revə,lüt, -əl,yüt, *usu* -üd·+V\ *adj* [L *revolutus*, past part. of *revolvere* to revolve] : rolled backward or downward ⟨a leaf with ~ margins⟩ — compare CONVOLUTE, INVOLUTE
²revolute \"\ *vi* -ED/-ING/-S [back-formation fr. ¹*revolution*] : to make or undergo revolution
rev·o·lut·ed \-üd·əd\ *adj* [L *revolutus* (past part. of *revolvere* to revolve) + E *-ed*] : REVOLUTE
¹rev·o·lu·tion \,revə'lüshən *also* -əl'yü-\ *n* -S [ME *revolucioun*, fr. MF *revolution*, fr. LL *revolution-, revolutio*, fr. L *revolutus* (past part. of *revolvere* to roll back, revolve) + *-ion-, -io* -ion — more at REVOLVE] **1 a** (1) : the act of a celestial body of going around in an orbit or elliptic course; *also* : apparent movement of such a body around the earth — usu. distinguished from *rotation* (2) : the time taken by a celestial body to make a complete round in its orbit (3) : the rotation of a celestial body on its axis — not used technically **b** : completion of a course (as of years); *also* : the period made by the regular succession of a measure of time or by a succession of similar events **c** *obs* : CYCLE, EPOCH **d** *archaic* : RECURRENCE, REPETITION **e** (1) : a progressive motion of a body around a center or axis such that any line of the body remains throughout parallel to its initial position to which it returns on completing the circuit (2) : motion of any figure about a center or axis in which each point of the figure traces a circular arc of the same angular size about its projection on the axis as center ⟨the ~ of a right-angled triangle about one of its legs generates a cone⟩ (3) : ROTATION 1b ⟨a bell rings for each ~ of the hectograph⟩ **2** : alteration or change in some matter or respect: as **a** : a sudden, radical, or complete change ⟨a ~ in thought⟩ : a basic reorientation and reorganization ⟨a ~ in technology⟩ **b** : a fundamental change in political organization or in a government or constitution : the overthrow or renunciation of one government or ruler and the substitution of another by the governed **c** : profound crustal movement involving mountain-making and other physical changes on a continent-wide or world-wide scale; *also* : the interval of time during which such a movement occurs **3 a** *archaic* : a turning over in the mind or in discussion : PONDERING, CONSIDERATION **b** *obs* : a winding or curving form or course : TWIST, BEND **syn** see REBELLION
²revolution \"\ *vt* -ED/-ING/-S : REVOLUTIONIZE
rev·o·lu·tion·al \¦revə¦lüshənᵊl, -shnəl *also* -əl¦yü-\ *adj* : REVOLUTIONARY — **rev·o·lu·tion·al·ly** \-ᵊlē, -əlē, -i\ *adv*
rev·o·lu·tion·ar·i·ly \¦==¦=shə¦nerəlē\ *adv* : in a revolutionary manner : so as to be revolutionary
rev·o·lu·tion·ar·i·ness \,==¦==,nerēnəs\ *n* -ES : the quality or state of being revolutionary
¹rev·o·lu·tion·ary \¦revə¦lüshə,nerē, -ri *also* -əl¦yü-\ *adj* [¹*revolution* + *-ary*] **1** : of, relating to, or having the nature of a revolution ⟨a ~ war⟩ ⟨a ~ party⟩ **2** : tending to, promoting, or involving revolution ⟨~ motion⟩ ⟨a ~ speech⟩ ⟨~ improvements in technique⟩; *often* : RADICAL, EXTREMIST ⟨a ~ outlook⟩ **3** *usu cap* : of or relating to the American Revolution or to the period in which it occurred ⟨*Revolutionary* history⟩ ⟨*Revolutionary* costume⟩
²revolutionary \"\ *n* -ES : REVOLUTIONIST
revolution counter *n* : a mechanism tallying the elapsed revolutions of a piece of apparatus and often indicating as well the instantaneous rotational speed
rev·o·lu·tion·eer·ing \,==,=='niriŋ\ *n* -S [¹*revolution* + *-eering* (as in *engineering*)] : the promoting or conducting of revolutions
rev·o·lu·tion·er \,=='=sh(ə)nə(r)\ *n* -S : one that supports or is engaged in a revolution : REVOLUTIONIST
rev·o·lu·tion·ism \-shə,nizəm\ *n* -S : revolutionary acts or practices : revolutionary doctrines or principles : advocacy of such doctrines or principles
¹rev·o·lu·tion·ist \-sh(ə)nəst\ *n* -S [¹*revolution* + *-ist*] : one engaged in a revolution : a favorer of revolution : one who advocates revolutionary doctrines or principles

²**revolutionist** \ˌ=ˈ=(ˌ)=\ *adj* **:** of or relating to revolution or revolutionists ⟨~ doctrines⟩
rev·o·lu·tion·ize \ˌ==ˈ=shə,nīz\ *vb* -ED/-ING/-S *see -ize in Explan Notes* [¹*revolution* + *-ize*] *vt* **1 :** to change fundamentally or overthrow completely the established government of **2 :** to make revolutionary **:** imbue with revolutionary doctrines or principles **3 :** to change completely or fundamentally ~ *vi* **:** to undergo revolution
rev·o·lu·tion·iz·er \-zə(r)\ *n* -S **:** one that revolutionizes ⟨~ of heavy industry⟩
re·volv·able \rəˈvälvəbəl\ *adj* **:** capable of being revolved — **re·volv·ably** \-blē\ *adv*
¹**re·volve** \rəˈvälv, rē'-, -ˈvȯlv *also* -ˈvä(ù)v *or* -ˈvȯv\ *vb* -ED/-ING/-S [ME *revolven*, fr. L *revolvere* to roll back, fr. *re-* + *volvere* to roll — more at VOLUBLE] *vt* **1** *obs* **:** to turn (the eyes or sight) back or around **2 :** to consider or meditate upon at length or repeatedly considering various aspects and phases (as in seeking a solution or reaching a decision) ⟨*revolving* a scheme to get a pension for his brother⟩ ⟨*revolved* the story in his mind as he waited⟩ **3** *obs* **:** to turn or bring back **:** RESTORE **4** *archaic* **:** to skim or search through (as a book) **:** turn the pages of; *also* **:** to read through **:** STUDY **5** *obs* **:** to wrap up **:** BIND **6 a :** to cause to go around in an orbit **b :** to cause to turn around on or as if on an axis **:** ROTATE ~ *vi* **1 a** *obs* **:** RETURN **b :** to come around again **:** RECUR **2 a :** to meditate on something **:** consider deliberately **:** PONDER ⟨with thoughts *revolving* upon his holiday plans⟩ **b :** to be a source or cause of meditation ⟨the idea continued to ~ in his mind⟩ **3 a :** to move in a curved path around a center or axis ⟨the planets ~ around the sun⟩ — compare REVOLUTION 1e(1) **b :** to turn or roll around on or as if on an axis like a wheel **:** ROTATE — compare REVOLUTION 1e(2) **4 :** to come to a center or focal point **:** PIVOT ⟨the whole household ~*s* about the baby⟩ **syn** see CONSIDER, TURN
²**revolve** \"\ *n* -S **:** an act or instance of revolving **:** REVOLUTION
re·volve·ment \-vmənt\ *n* -S **:** an act of revolving or the condition of being revolved ⟨the periodic ~ of funds⟩
re·vol·ven·cy \-vənsē\ *n* -ES **:** a capacity or tendency to revolve
re·volv·er \-və(r)\ *n* -S [¹*revolve* + *-er*] **1 :** a handgun having a cylinder of several chambers that are brought successively into line with the barrel and discharged with the same hammer — compare PISTOL **2 :** the particular indeterminate form assumed by the three-point problem in surveying or navigating when the point of observation falls on a circle through the three fixed points **3 :** one that revolves; *esp* **:** a revolving device
re·volv·ered \-(r)d\ *adj* **:** bearing a revolver
revolving *adj* **1 :** that revolves or rotates or recurs ⟨grief returns with the ~ year —P.B.Shelley⟩; *esp* **:** recurrently available ⟨scrap metal is our one great ~ industrial resource —*Canadian Purchasor*⟩ — see REVOLVING CREDIT, REVOLVING FUND **2** *of a firearm* **:** having a cylinder or a series of barrels that turn about a common longitudinal axis — **re·volv·ing·ly** *adv*
revolving credit *n* **:** a credit which may be used repeatedly up to the limit specified after partial or total repayments have been made
revolving die holder *n* **:** a releasing die head
revolving door *n* **:** an outer door (as of a public building) consisting of two or more flaps revolving together on a common vertical axis within a cylindrical vestibule and having the flaps so constructed or arranged as to prevent the direct passage of air through the vestibule
revolving field alternator *n* **:** an alternator operating by stationary conductors and rotating field magnets
revolving fund *n* **:** a fund set up for specified purposes with the proviso that repayments to the fund may be used again for these purposes ⟨a *revolving fund* to make loans to disabled veterans going into business ventures⟩

revolving door

revolving letter of credit : a letter of credit authorizing drafts up to a specified amount and permitting additional drafts to be drawn up to the amount of accepted drafts previously paid off
revolving light *n* **:** FLASHLIGHT a(2)
revolving plug *n* **:** the rotating part of a cylinder lock **:** the part into which the key is inserted
revolving storm *n* **:** CYCLONE
re·vomit \(ˈ)rē+\ *vt* [*re-* + *vomit*] **:** to vomit up **:** vomit forth again
re·vote \"+\ *vt* [*re-* + *vote*] **:** to regrant by voting
revs *pl of* REV, *pres 3d sing of* REV
re·vue \rəˈvyü, rē'-\ *n* -S [F, fr. MF, review — more at REVIEW] **:** a light theatrical entertainment consisting of brief items (as sketches, songs, monologues) in which recent events and esp. plays of the past year are satirically reviewed **:** a medley of songs, tableaux vivants, and chorus dances with light skits
re·vu·ist \-üəst\ *n* -S [F *revuiste*, fr. *revue* + *-iste* -ist] **:** a writer of revues
re·vulsed \rəˈvəlst\ *adj* [L *revulsus* (past part. of *revellere* to draw back) + E *-ed*] **:** affected with or having undergone revulsion
re·vul·sion \rəˈvəlshən, rē'- *sometimes* -lzh-\ *n* -S [L *revulsion-, revulsio* act of pulling away, fr. *revulsus* (past part. of *revellere* to pull away, fr. *re-* + *vellere* to pull, pluck) + *-ion-, -io* -ion — more at VULNERABLE] **1 :** an act or technique of turning or diverting a disease or blood from a diseased region in one part of the body to another (as by counterirritation) **2 :** a strong pulling or drawing back or away **:** WITHDRAWAL ⟨public ~ from such political cynicism⟩ **3 a :** a sudden or strong reaction, reversion, or change ⟨a ~ of mood⟩ **b :** a sense or mood of utter distaste or repugnance **:** REPULSION ⟨met his advances with ~⟩ ⟨a scene of utmost ~⟩
re·vul·sion·ary \-ə,nerē\ *adj* **:** of, relating to, or constituting a revulsion
¹**re·vul·sive** \rəˈvəlsiv, rē'-, -sēv *also* -səv\ *adj* [L *revulsus* (past part.) + E *-ive*] **:** causing or tending to revulsion — **re·vul·sive·ly** \-səvlē, -li\ *adv*
²**revulsive** \"\ *n* -S **:** something that causes revulsion
revved *past of* REV
revving *pres part of* REV
revvs *pres 3d sing of* REV
rew \ˈrü\ *chiefly dial var of* RUE
re·wake \(ˈ)rē+\ *or* **re·waken** \"+\ *vb* [*re-* + *wake* or *waken*] *vt* **:** to waken again or anew ~ *vi* **:** to become once more awake ⟨~ to her opportunity⟩
¹**re·ward** \rəˈwȯ(ə)rd, rē'-, -ȯ(ə)d\ *vb* -ED/-ING/-S [ME *rewarden*, fr. ONF *rewarder* to reward, regard, look at, fr. *re-* + *warder* to watch over, guard, of Gmc origin; akin to OHG *wartēn* to watch, take care — more at WARD] *vt* **1** *obs* **a :** to give or assign to as due **:** recompense or requite with **b :** to give (as a hawk or hound) a share or particular part of prey usu. when taken **2 :** to make a return or give a reward to (as a person) or for (as a service or accomplishment) ⟨~*ing* his friends and repaying his enemies⟩ ⟨~ small personal services generously⟩ ~ *vi* **:** to give rewards **:** make requital
²**reward** \"\ *n* -S [ME, fr. ONF, fr. *rewarder* to reward] **1 :** something that is given in return for good or evil done or received ⟨one of our fine old members . . . who passed to his ~ —R.T.Smith⟩ and esp. that is offered or given for some service or attainment (as a prize for excellence in studies, a sum of money for the return of something lost or for the capture of a criminal) **:** RECOMPENSE, REQUITAL ⟨thy great misdeeds have met a due ~ —John Dryden⟩ **2** *obs* **a :** ¹QUARRY 1a **b :** REMUNERATION; *esp* **:** extra pay **c :** an extra supply of food **:** an extra dish **3 :** compensation for services **:** a sum of money paid or taken for doing or forbearing to do some act (as for furnishing information leading to the arrest and conviction of criminals or for restoring lost property) **4 :** PROFIT
re·ward·able \-dəbəl\ *adj* **:** subject to or meriting reward — **re·ward·able·ness** *n* -ES
re·ward·ed·ly \-dədlē\ *adv* **:** in a rewarded manner
re·ward·er \-də(r)\ *n* -S [ME, fr. *rewarden* to reward + *-er*] **:** one that rewards
re·ward·ful \-dfəl\ *adj* **:** offering or productive of reward ⟨~ pursuits⟩ — **re·ward·ful·ness** *n* -ES
rewarding *adj* **1 :** valuable and pleasing **:** yielding or likely to yield a reward ⟨reading is a ~ pastime⟩ ⟨a most ~ meeting⟩ **2 :** offered by way of reward **:** serving as or suitable for a reward ⟨a warmly ~ smile of thanks⟩ — **re·ward·ing·ly** *adv*
re·ward·less \-dləs\ *adj* **:** receiving no reward
re·warehouse \(ˈ)rē+\ *vt* [*re-* + *warehouse*] **:** to return to a warehouse **:** store anew under warehouse conditions
re·wa-re·wa \ˈrewəˈrewə\ *n* -S [Maori] **1 :** a slender New Zealand tree (*Knightia excelsa*) resembling the Lombardy poplar in habit but yielding a valuable timber **2 :** the strong heavy mottled red wood of the rewa-rewa — called also *New Zealand honeysuckle*
re·warm \(ˈ)rē+\ *vt* [*re-* + *warm*] **:** to make warm again
re·warper \"+\ *n* [*re-* + *warper*] **:** a textile worker who rewinds yarn from the warp beam for dyeing
rewash \"+\ *vt* [*re-* + *wash*] **:** to wash anew or again and again ⟨waves ~ and undermine the cliffs⟩ ⟨~*ing* mine tailings for color⟩
re·water \"+\ *vt* [*re-* + *water*] **:** to provide anew with water ⟨rains ~*ing* the hills⟩
re·waybill \"+\ *vt* [*re-* + *waybill*] **:** to provide (as freight at a junction point) with a new waybill
re·weaken \"+\ *vb* [*re-* + *weaken*] *vt* **:** to cause to become weak again ⟨wind had ~*ed* the timbers⟩ ~ *vi* **:** to become weak again **:** yield anew to weakness ⟨afraid she would ~ and agree to go⟩
re·weave \"+\ *vt* [*re-* + *weave*] **:** to make whole by or as if by weaving
re·wed \"+\ *vb* [*re-* + *wed*] **:** REMARRY
re·weigh \"+\ *vt* [*re-* + *weigh*] **:** to weigh again or anew — **re·weigher** \"+\ *n*
re·weld \"+\ *vt* [*re-* + *weld*] **:** to reunite or make secure by or as if by welding
re·wet \"+\ *vt* [*re-* + *wet*] **:** to make wet again
re·win \"+\ *vt* [*re-* + *win*] **:** REGAIN
¹**re·wind** \"+\ *vt* [*re-* + *wind*] **:** to wind again ⟨~ yarn⟩; *esp* **:** to reverse the winding of (a motion-picture film, magnetic tape, or wire) on a reel usu. so as to place the beginning on the outside of the roll
²**re·wind** \ˈrē+,- =ˈ=\ *n* **1 :** something that has been rewound **2 :** an act of rewinding **3 :** a device for rewinding something; *esp* **:** a mechanism for rewinding motion-picture film consisting of a mounted reel or roll hub rotated manually or by an electric motor
re·winder \(ˈ)rē+\ *n* **:** one that rewinds something: as **a :** an operator of a machine for rewinding yarn, cloth, paper **b** [*re-* + *winder*] (1) **:** REWIND 3 (2) **:** a machine that takes paper from a reel and winds it onto a core and usu. slits and trims the edges at the same time
re·wir·able \(ˈ)rē¦wīrəbəl\ *adj* **:** capable of being rewired ⟨a ~ electric fixture⟩
re·wire \(ˈ)rē+\ *vt* [*re-* + *wire*] **1 :** to wire (as a house, a cable, an electric machine) anew **2 :** to telegraph (as a message) or telegraph to (as a person) in return
re·wood \"+\ *vt* [*re-* + *wood*] **:** REFOREST
re·word \"+\ *vt* [*re-* + *word*] **1 :** to put into words again **:** repeat in the same words **2 :** to alter the wording of **:** restate in other words ⟨~ a message⟩
re·work \"+\ *vt* [*re-* + *work*] **:** to work again or anew ⟨decided to ~ the old mine⟩: as **a :** to reorganize and revise ⟨~*ing* an old legend in a contemporary scene⟩ **b :** to reprocess (used, imperfect, or discarded material) for further use ⟨~ condemned butter⟩ **c :** to subject again after a lapse of time to the action of a geologic agent ⟨sediment . . . has been ~*ed* and redeposited —G.L.Knight⟩
re·workable \"+\ *adj* **:** fit to be reworked ⟨~ scrap⟩
reworked wool *n* **:** wool that has been used and is subsequently reprocessed for further use — compare SHODDY
re·wound \"+\ *vt* [*re-* + *wound*] **:** to wound again or afresh
¹**re·write** \"+\ *vb* [*re-* + *write*] *vt* **1 :** to write in reply **:** answer in writing **2 :** to make a revision or recast of (as a paragraph, story, or article): as **a :** to put (material supplied to a newspaper or periodical by a collector or contributor) into form for publication **b :** to alter (previously published material) for use in another publication ~ *vi* **:** to revise or recast something previously written ⟨an author usu. spends a good deal of time *rewriting*⟩: as **a :** to rewrite material supplied to a newspaper or periodical by a collector or contributor **b :** to alter previously published material for use in another publication
²**re·write** \ˈrē+,-\ *n* -S **:** a piece of writing (as an article or news story) constructed by rewriting ⟨a complete ~ of the first draft of a novel⟩
rewrite man *n* **:** a newspaperman who specializes in rewriting
re·writer \(ˈ)rē¦rīd·ə(r), -ītə-\ *n* [¹*rewrite* + *-er*] **:** one that rewrites; *specif* **:** REWRITE MAN
¹**rex** *n pl* [origin unknown] *obs* **:** PRANKS — used in the phrase *to play rex*
²**rex** \ˈreks\ *n, pl* **re·ges** \ˈrē,jēz\ [L, king — more at ROYAL] **1 :** KING **2** *usu cap* **:** the presiding masquer in a Mardi Gras festival or parade (as at New Orleans)
³**rex** \"\ *n, pl* **rexes** *or* **rex** [NL, fr. L, king] **1 :** a genetic variation esp. of the domestic rabbit and various rodents which behaves as a simple recessive and in which the guard hairs are shorter than the undercoat or entirely lacking **2 :** an animal or pelt exhibiting the rex characteristic
⁴**rex** \"\ *vt* -ED/-ING/-ES **:** to breed (as rabbits) selectively for the establishment of the rex variation
rex begonia *n* **:** any of various rhizomatous begonias derived from an East Indian species (*Begonia rex*) and having variegated heavily-veined rough-textured leaves, thick hairy stems, and usu. insignificant flowers
rex·ine \ˈrek,sīn\ *n* -S [²*rex* + *-ine*] *Brit* **:** a strong coated cloth usu. imitating leather and used esp. for bookbinding
rex·ist \ˈreksəst\ *n* -S *usu cap* [F *rexiste*, fr. *rex-* (fr. *Christus Rex*, title of a publication issued by founders of the party) + *-iste* -ist] **:** a member of a Belgian fascist political party established in 1935
rey \ˈrā\ *n, pl* **re·yes** \ˈrā,(y)ās\ [Sp, fr. L *reg-, rex*] **:** KING
rey·kja·vik \ˈrākyə,vēk, -vik\ *adj, usu cap* [fr. *Reykjavik*, Iceland] **:** of or from Reykjavik, the capital of Iceland **:** of the kind or style prevalent in Reykjavik
reyn \ˈrān\ *chiefly Scots var of* REIN
rey·nard \(ˈ)rā¦närd, ˈre,n-, -nȧd, ˈrānə(r)d, ˈrenə(r)d\ *n* -S *often cap* [ME *Renard*, fox who is the hero of the French medieval beast epic *Roman de Renart*, fr. MF *Renart, Renard, Regnard*] **:** FOX
reyn·olds number \ˈrenᵊldz-\ *n, usu cap R* [after Osborne *Reynolds* †1912 Eng. physicist] **:** an abstract number characteristic of the flow of a fluid in a pipe or past an obstruction used esp. in the testing of scale models of airplanes in a wind tunnel **:** the ratio of the product of the density of the fluid, the flow velocity, and a characteristic linear dimension of the body under observation to the coefficient of absolute viscosity
re·youth \(ˈ)rē+\ *vt* -ED/-ING/-S [*re-* + *youth*] **:** to make (as oneself) young again
re·zai *or* **re·sai** \rəˈzīē\ *n* -S [Hindi *razāī*, fr. Per] **:** a cotton-filled coverlet or mattress of India
rez·ban·yite \ˈrez'ban,yīt\ *n* -S [G *rezbanyit*, fr. *Rézbánya*, Hungary (now *Băiţa*, Romania) + G *-it* -ite] **:** a mineral $Pb_3Cu_2Bi_{10}S_{19}$ consisting of lead, copper, and bismuth sulfide and occurring in metallic-gray granular masses (sp. gr. 6.1–6.4)
rez-de-chaus·sée \,rāchōˈsā\ *n* -S [F, lit., level of the street] **:** the ground story of a building whether on a level with the street or slightly above it — used esp. of a building on the continent of Europe
re·zone \(ˈ)rē+\ *vt* [*re-* + *zone*] **:** to zone anew **:** alter the zoning of ⟨~ a street⟩
rf *abbr* **1** refunding **2** rinforzando **3** roof
RF *abbr* **1** *often not cap* radio frequency **2** range finder **3** rapid fire **4** reducing flame **5** representative fraction **6** reserve force **7** rheumatic fever **8** right field **9** right foot **10** right forward **11** right front **12** rough finish
RFB *abbr* right fullback
RFC *abbr* radio-frequency choke
RFD *abbr* rural free delivery
rfg *abbr* **1** refunding **2** roofing
RFG *abbr* rapid-fire gun
rfl *abbr* refuel
rfn *abbr* rifleman
rfr *abbr* roofer
rf station *n, usu cap R&F* [Radio Frequency] **:** a radio beacon that transmits radio signals equally in all directions
rfz *abbr* rinforzando
RG *abbr* **1** red-green **2** *often not cap* reduction gear **3** right guard **4** rolled gold
rgr *abbr* ringer
rgt *abbr* regiment
rh *usu cap R, var of* RH FACTOR
rH *symbol* the negative logarithm of the pressure in atmospheres of hydrogen gas that would exist at an electrode in equilibrium with an oxidation-reduction system and that serves as a measure of the state of oxidation-reduction of the system ⟨where linear relationships hold ~ is of importance and care should be taken to restrict its use only to such systems —H.T.S.Britton⟩ — compare PH
RH *abbr* **1** *often not cap* relative humidity **2** right halfback **3** right hand **4** Rockwell hardness **5** roundhouse **6** Royal Highness
Rh *symbol* rhodium
rhabd \ˈrabd\ *n* -S [NL *rhabdus*] **:** RHABDUS
rhabd- *or* **rhabdo-** *comb form* [LGk, fr. Gk, fr. *rhabdos* rod — more at VERVAIN] **1 :** rod **:** stick ⟨*rhabdo*nema⟩ **2 :** rodlike structure ⟨*rhabdo*lith⟩ ⟨*rhabdo*some⟩
rhab·di·on \ˈrabdē,än\ *n* -S [NL, fr. Gk, little rod, dim. of *rhabdos* rod] **:** any of the sclerotized segments making up the lining of the buccal cavity of a nematode worm
rhab·dite \ˈrab,dīt\ *n* -S [*rhabd-* + *-ite*] **1 :** one of the minute, smooth, rodlike or fusiform structures produced in the cells of the epidermis or in cells sunk within the underlying parenchyma of many turbellarians and a few trematodes and discharged in great numbers in the mucous secretions of these animals **2 :** one of the paired appendages that unite to form the ovipositor in some insects
¹**rhab·ditid** \(ˈ)rab¦dīd·əd, -ˌdid·əd\ *adj* [NL *Rhabditidae*] **:** of or relating to the Rhabditidae or Rhabditida
²**rhabditid** \"\ *n* -S **:** a rhabditid worm
rhab·dit·i·da \rab'did·ədə\ *n pl, cap* [NL, fr. *Rhabditis* + *-ida*] **:** a large order of Aphasmidia comprising free-living and parasitic nematode worms having the esophagus more or less clearly divided into three regions, usu. three or six lips, and the musculature meromyarian or polymyarian
rhab·dit·i·dae \-id·ə,dē\ *n pl, cap* [NL, fr. *Rhabditis*, type genus + *-idae*] **:** a large family of nematode worms that with related forms comprises a superfamily of the order Rhabditida
rhab·dit·i·form \-id·ə,fȯrm\ *adj* [NL *Rhabditis* + E *-iform*] **:** RHABDITOID
rhab·di·tis \rab'dēd·əs\ *n, cap* [NL, fr. Gk *rhabdos* rod] **:** a genus (the type of the family Rhabditidae) of minute nematode worms having the esophagus clearly divided into three regions, dwelling in soil and organic debris, and occas. behaving as facultative parasites
rhab·di·toid \ˈrabdə,tȯid\ *adj* [NL *Rhabditis* + E *-oid*] **1 :** resembling or related to the genus *Rhabditis* **2** *of a larval nematode* **:** having the esophagus functional and with an enlarged pharyngeal bulb like that of a rhabditid
rhab·di·um \ˈrabdēəm\ *n, pl* **rhab·dia** \-ēə\ [NL, fr. Gk *rhabdion*, dim. of *rhabdos* rod] **:** a striated muscle fiber
rhab·do·car·pon \,rabdōˈkär,pän\ *or* **rhab·do·car·pum** \-,pəm\ [NL, fr. *rhabd-* + *-carpon, -carpum* (fr. Gk *karpos* fruit) — more at HARVEST] *syn of* RHABDOCARPUS
rhab·do·car·pus \-,pəs\ *n, cap* [NL, fr. *rhabd-* + *-carpus*] **:** a form genus of Paleozoic fossil plants based on seeds and now known to belong for the most part to the genus *Cordaites*
rhab·do·coel *or* **rhab·do·coele** \ˈrabdə,sēl\ *adj* [NL *Rhabdocoela*] **:** of or relating to the order Rhabdocoela
rhab·do·coe·la \,rabdəˈsēlə\ *n pl, cap* [NL, fr. *rhabd-* + *-coela -coele*] **:** an order of Turbellaria comprising small marine, freshwater, or rarely terrestrial flatworms with simple unbranched intestine — **rhab·do·coe·lan** \¦==¦=lən\ *adj or n* — **rhab·do·coe·lid** \-ləd\ *or* **rhab·do·coe·lous** \-ləs\ *adj*
rhab·do·coele \ˈrabdə,sēl\ *n* -S [NL *Rhabdocoela*] **:** a flatworm of the order Rhabdocoela
¹**rhab·do·coe·li·da** \,rabdəˈsēlədə\ *n pl, cap* [NL, fr. *Rhabdocoela* + *-ida*] *in former classifications* **:** an order or other division of Turbellaria including the Alloiocoela, the Rhabdocoela, and sometimes the Acoela — **rhab·do·coe·li·dan** \¦==¦=lədᵊn\ *adj or n*
²**rhabdocoelida** \"\ [NL, fr. *rhabd-* + *coel-* + *-ida*] *syn of* RHABDOCOELA
¹**rhab·doid** \ˈrab,dȯid\ *adj* [NL *rhabdoides*, fr. Gk *rhabdoeidēs* like a rod, striped, fr. *rhabd-* + *-oeidēs* -oid — more at RHABD-] **1 :** shaped like a rod **2 :** RHABDOIDAL
²**rhabdoid** \"\ *n* -S **:** a rhabdite or similar body in the integument of a flatworm
³**rhabdoid** \"\ *n* -S **:** a rod-shaped protoplasmic body in the sensitive cells of leaves of various plants of the family Droseraceae — **rhab·doi·dal** \(ˈ)rab¦dȯidᵊl\ *adj*
rhab·do·lith \ˈrabdə,lith\ *n* -S [ISV *rhabd-* + *-lith*] **:** a minute calcareous rodlike structure found both at the surface and on the bottom of the ocean
rhab·dom \ˈrab,däm, -,dəm\ *or* **rhab·dome** \-,dōm\ *n* -S [LGk *rhabdōma* bundle of rods, fr. Gk *rhabdos* rod] **:** one of the minute rodlike structures in the retinulae in the compound eyes of arthropods — **rhab·do·mal** \(ˈ)=¦dōməl, ¦=,dəm-\ *adj*
rhab·do·man·cer \ˈrabdə,man(t)sə(r)\ *n* -S [*rhabdomancy* + *-er*] **:** one who practices rhabdomancy
rhab·do·man·cy \-sē\ *n* -ES [LGk *rhabdomanteia*, fr. Gk *rhabd-* (fr. *rhabdos* rod) + *manteia* divination — more at VERVAIN, -MANCY] **:** divination by rods or wands
rhab·do·mere \ˈrabdə,mi(ə)r\ *n* -S [*rhabdom* + *-mere*] **:** a division of a rhabdom
rhab·dom·o·nas \rab'dämənəs, -,nas\ *n, cap* [NL, fr. *rhabd-* + *-monas*] **:** a genus of motile, elongated, often spindle-shaped sulfur bacteria (family Thiorhodaceae) usu. rose-red in color
rhab·do·myoma \¦rab(,)dō+\ *n* [NL, fr. *rhabd-* + *myoma*] **:** a benign tumor composed of striated muscle fibers
rhab·do·myosarcoma \"+\ *n* [NL, fr. *rhabd-* + *my-* + *sarcoma*] **:** a malignant rhabdomyoma
rhab·doph·a·ga \rab'däfəgə\ *n, cap* [NL, fr. *rhabd-* + *-phaga*] **:** a widely distributed genus of gall midges
rhab·do·phane \ˈrabdə,fān\ *n* -S [G *rhabdophan*, fr. *rhabd-* + *-phan* -phane] **:** a brown, pinkish, or yellowish white hydrous phosphate (Ce, Y, La, etc.)$(PO_4).H_2O$ of cerium, yttrium, and rare-earth elements occurring massive
rhab·doph·a·nite \rab'däfə,nīt\ *n* -S [G *rhabdophan* + E *-ite*] **:** RHABDOPHANE
rhab·doph·o·ra \rab'däfərə\ [NL, fr. *rhabd-* + *-phora*] *syn of* GRAPTOLITOIDEA
rhab·doph·o·ran \-fərən\ *n* -S **:** GRAPTOLITE
rhab·do·pleu·ra \,rabdōˈplùrə\ *n, cap* [NL, fr. *rhabd-* + Gk *pleura* side, rib — more at PLEURISY] **:** a widely distributed genus of marine compound animals having two tentacle-bearing arms and usu. classed as hemichordates in the order Pterobranchia
rhab·do·pod \ˈrabdə,päd\ *n* -S [*rhabd-* + *-pod*] **:** one of the rodlike styles of the males of many insects
rhab·do·some \ˈrabdə,sōm\ *n* -S [*rhabd-* + *-some*] **:** a colonial graptolite derived from a single individual
rhabds *pl of* RHABD
rhab·dus \ˈrabdəs\ *n* -ES [NL, fr. Gk *rhabdos* rod — more at VERVAIN] **:** a simple uniaxial sponge spicule
rhachi- *or* **rhachio-** — see RACHI-
rha·chi·a·nec·tes \,rākēəˈnek(,)tēz\ *n, cap* [NL, fr. Gk *rhachia* surf, beach + NL *-nectes*] **:** a genus of whalebone whales comprising solely the gray whale
rhach·i·tome \ˈrakə,tōm\ *n* -S [NL *Rhachitomi*] **:** an amphibian of the order Rhachitomi

rha·chit·o·mi \rə'kid·ə,mī, ra'k-\ *n pl, cap* [NL, fr. *rachi-* + *-tomi* (fr. Gk *tomos* cut, slice) — more at TOME] : an order of Labyrinthodontia including most of the larger Permian amphibians and comprising forms having rhachitomous vertebrae, relatively stocky salamandriform bodies, and in some cases external gills

rha·chit·o·mous *also* **ra·chit·o·mous** \rə'kid·əməs, (')ra¦k-\ *adj* [*rachi-* + *-tomous*] : being, having, or relating to vertebrae with centra of which the parts remain separate, an intercentrum wedge-shaped and ventral, and separate pleurocentra above and behind the intercentra

rhaco·mit·ri·um \,rakō'mi·trēəm, ,rāk-\ *n, cap* [NL, fr. Gk *rhakos* ragged garment + *mitrion*, dim. of *mitra* headband — more at MITER] : a genus of acrocarpous mosses (family Grimmiaceae) growing chiefly on sandstone rocks and having often hair-pointed leaves and sinuous leaf cells

rha·coph·o·rus \rə'käfərəs, ra'k-\ [NL, fr. Gk *rhakos* ragged garment + NL *-phorus*] *syn of* POLYPEDATES

rhad·a·man·thine \,radə¦man(t)thən, -an,thīn\ *adj, often cap* [*Rhadamanthus*, one of the judges in the lower world + E *-ine*] : of, relating to, or characteristic of Rhadamanthus; *esp* : rigorously just ⟨a ~ judgment —A.C.Benson⟩ ⟨morals to become less ~ —*Times Lit. Supp.*⟩

rhad·a·man·thus \-an(t)thəs\ *n* -ES *usu cap* [after *Rhadamanthus*, son of Zeus and Europa in Greek mythology who for his exemplary justice was made one of the judges of souls in the lower world, fr. L, fr. Gk *Rhadamanthos, Rhadamanthys*] : an extremely strict judge

¹**rhae·tian** *also* **rhe·tian** \'rēsh(ē)ən\ *n* -S *cap* [L *rhaetus* rhaetian + E *-an*] **1** : a native or inhabitant of ancient Rhaetia **2** : RHAETO-ROMANIC

²**rhaetian** *also* **rhetian** \"\ *adj, usu cap* [L *Rhaetia*, ancient Roman province south of the Danube river corresponding with Tirol and the Grisons (fr. *Rhaeti* Rhaetians + *-ia* -y) + E *-an*] **1** : of or relating to ancient Rhaetia **2** : of or relating to the people of ancient Rhaetia

rhae·tic \'rēd·ik\ *n, cap* [L *rhaeticus* of Rhaetia, fr. *Rhaetia* + *-icus* -ic] **1** : an ancient language of Rhaetia of unknown relationship **2** : RHAETO-ROMANIC

rhaeto-romanic *or* **rhaeto-romance** *or* **rhaeto-romansh** *or* **rheto-romanic** *or* **rheto-romance** *or* **rheto-romansh** \¦rēd·(,)ō+\ *n, cap both Rs* [*rhaeto-, rheto-* (fr. L *rhaetus* Rhaetian) + *romanic* or *romance* or *romansh*; trans. of G *rätoromanisch*] : a Romance language of eastern Switzerland, northeastern Italy, and adjacent parts of Austria — see FRIULIAN, ROMANSH

rhag·a·des \'ragə,dēz\ *n pl* [L, fr. Gk, pl. of *rhagas* rent, chink, fissure on the skin; akin to Gk *rhēgnynai* to break, OSlav *rězati* to cut, slaughter] : linear cracks or fissures in the skin, occurring esp. at the angles of the mouth or about the anus

rha·gad·i·form \rə'gadə,fȯrm\ *adj* [Gk *rhagad-, rhagas* fissure + E *-iform*] : having or characterized by cracks or fissures ⟨~ eczema⟩

rha·gio·crine cell \'rājēə,krin-, -rīn-, -rēn-\ *n* [*rhagiocrine* ISV *rhagio-* (fr. Gk *rhagion*, dim. of *rhag-, rhax* berry, grape) + *-crine* (fr. Gk *krinein* to separate) — more at RAISIN, CERTAIN] : HISTIOCYTE

¹**rhag·i·o·nid** \'rajēə,nid\ *adj* [NL *Rhagionidae*] : of or relating to the Rhagionidae

²**rhagionid** \"\ *n* -S : an insect of the family Rhagionidae

rhag·i·on·i·dae \,rajē'änə,dē\ *n pl, cap* [NL, fr. *Rhagion-, Rhagio*, type genus (fr. Gk *rhagion*, a spider, dim. of *rhag-, rhax* malmignatte, grape, berry) + *-idae*] : a widely distributed family of predaceous two-winged flies having usu. a tapering body, long slender legs, and sometimes a conspicuous downward-projecting proboscis

rha·go·dia \rə'gōdēə\ *n, cap* [NL, fr. Gk *rhagōdēs* like grapes (fr. *rhag-, rhax* grape + *-ōdēs* -ode) + NL *-ia*] : a genus of Australian shrubs or herbs (family Chenopodiaceae) with small greenish spicate or panicled flowers succeeded by fleshy berries

rhag·o·le·tis \,ragə'lēd·əs\ *n, cap* [NL, irreg. fr. Gk *rhag-, rhax* malmignatte] : a genus of trypetid flies containing many whose larvae feed on fruits and berries — see APPLE MAGGOT, CHERRY FRUIT FLY

rhagon \'rā,gän, 'ra,-\ *n* -S [NL, fr. Gk *rhag-, rhax* grape, berry] **1** : LEUCON **2** : a sponge or sponge larva of leuconoid structure in which the flagellated chambers are few in number and often adjoin the paragaster — **rhagonoid** *adj or n*

rhamn- *comb form* [ISV, fr. NL *Rhamnus*] : buckthorn : rhamnose ⟨*rhamn*itol⟩

rham·na·ce·ae \ram'nāsē,ē\ *n pl, cap* [NL, fr. *Rhamnus*, type genus + *-aceae*] : a widely distributed family (order Rhamnales) of thorny shrubs and trees having undivided stipulate leaves and cymose flowers with the stamens opposite the petals and a superior ovary that becomes a 3-celled capsule or a drupe — **rham·na·ceous** \(')ram¦nāshəs\ *adj*

rham·na·les \ram'nā(,)lēz\ *n pl, cap* [NL, fr. *Rhamnus* + *-ales*] : an order of dicotyledonous woody plants in which the stamens are equal in number with the sepals and alternate with them and the ovary is surrounded by a disk

rham·na·zin \'ramnəzən, ram'naz°n\ *n* -S [*rhamn-* + *-azin* (fr. *azine*)] : a pale yellow crystalline dye $C_{17}H_{14}O_7$ occurring as a glycoside esp. in Persian berries; a dimethyl ether of quercetin

rham·ne·tin \'ramnətən\ *n* -S [ISV *rhamn-* + *-etin* (as in *quercetin*)] : a yellow crystalline dye $C_{16}H_{12}O_7$ that is obtained by hydrolysis of xanthorhamnin from Persian berries and is a methyl ether of quercetin

rham·ni·nose \-nōs *also* -nōz\ *n* -S [ISV *rhamn-* + *-in* + *-ose*] : a crystalline reducing trisaccharide sugar $C_{18}H_{32}O_{14}$ obtained by hydrolysis of xanthorhamnin and on further hydrolysis yielding rhamnose and galactose

rham·ni·tol \'ramnə,tōl, -tōl\ *n* -S [*rhamn-* + *-itol*] : a crystalline pentahydroxy alcohol $C_6H_9(OH)_5$ obtained by reducing rhamnose

rham·nonic acid \(')ram¦nänik-, -¦nōnik\ *n* [ISV *rhamn-* + *-onic*] : an acid $CH_3(CHOH)_4COOH$ obtained by oxidation of rhamnose

rham·nose \'ram,nōs *also* -ōz\ *n* -S [ISV *rhamn-* + *-ose*] : a crystalline aldose sugar $CH_3(CHOH)_4CHO$ obtained in the common dextrorotatory L form usu. by hydrolysis of xanthorhamnin, quercitrin, and other rhamnosides; 6-deoxy-mannose — compare GLUCOSE

rham·no·side \'ramnə,sīd\ *n* -S [*rhamnose* + *-ide*] : a glycoside (as xanthorhamnin, quercitrin, frangulin, hesperidin) that yields rhamnose on hydrolysis

rham·nus \'ramnəs\ *n, cap* [NL, fr. Gk *rhamnos* buckthorn — more at VERVAIN] : a genus (the type of the family Rhamnaceae) of trees and shrubs having strongly pinnately veined leaves, small perfect or polygamous flowers with the ovary free from the disk, and a fruit that is an oblong or globular drupe with two to four stones — compare RHAMNALES; see BUCKTHORN, LOKAO

rhamph- *or* **rhampho-** *comb form* [Gk, fr. *rhamphos*; akin to Gk *rhabdos* rod — more at VERVAIN] : beak : crooked beak ⟨*Rhampho*charus⟩ ⟨*rhamph*oid⟩

rham·phas·ti·dae \ram'fastə,dē\ [NL, fr. *Rhamphastos* + *-idae*] *syn of* RAMPHASTIDAE

rhamphastos [NL — more at RAMPHASTOS] *syn of* RAMPHASTOS

rham·phoid *also* **ram·phoid** \'ram,fȯid\ *adj* [*rhamph-* + *-oid*] : shaped like a beak ⟨~ cusp⟩

¹**rham·pho·rhyn·chid** \¦ram(p)fə¦riŋkəd\ *adj* [NL *Rhamphorynchidae*] : of or relating to the genus *Rhamphorhynchus* or the family Rhamphorhynchidae

²**rhamphorhynchid** \"\ *n* -S : a rhamphorhynchid pterosaur

rham·pho·rhyn·choid \¦==¦=,kȯid\ *adj* [NL *Rhamphorynchus* + E *-oid*] : resembling or related to the genus *Rhamphorhynchus*

rham·pho·rhyn·chus \,==ˈ=,kəs\ *n, cap* [NL, fr. *rhamph-* + *-rhynchus*] : a genus (the type of the family Rhamphorhynchidae) of pterosaurs having an elongated tail supporting a leathery expansion at the tip and slender forwardly directed teeth

rham·pho·the·ca \,ram(p)fə'thēkə\ *n* -S [NL, fr. *rhamph-* + *theca*] : the horny sheath composed of modified scales of a bird's bill

rh antigen *n, usu cap R* : RH FACTOR

rhap *abbr* rhapsody

rhaphe *var of* RAPHE

rha·pon·tic \rə'päntik\ *n* [NL *rhaponticum*, fr. *rha ponticum* pontic rhubarb, fr. LL *rha* rhubarb + L *ponticum*, neut. of *ponticus* pontic — more at RHUBARB, PONTIC] **1** *archaic* : either of two European knapweeds (*Centaurea centaurium* and *C. rhaponticum*) **2** *archaic* **a** : a rhubarb (*Rheum rhaponticum*) **b** : the root of this plant used in pharmacy

rha·pon·ti·gen·in \rə,päntə'jenən\ *n* -S [ISV *rhapontin* + *-genin*] : a crystalline phenol $C_{15}H_{14}O_4$ derived from stilbene and obtained by hydrolysis of rhapontin

rha·pon·tin \rə'pänt°n\ *or* **rha·pon·ti·cin** \-təsən\ *n* -S [ISV *rhapontic* + *-in*] : a crystalline glucoside $C_{21}H_{24}O_9$ found in rhubarb

rhap·sode \'rap,sōd\ *n* -S [F, fr. Gk *rhapsōidos* — more at RHAPSODY] : RHAPSODIST

rhapsoder *n* -S [*rhapsody* + *-er*] *obs* : a collector of literary pieces

rhap·sod·ic \(')rap¦sädik, -dēk\ *adj* [Gk *rhapsōidikos*, fr. *rhapsōidos* rhapsodist + *-ikos* -ic] **1** **a** : characteristic or suggestive of a rhapsody : having the form or manner of a rhapsody ⟨the first movement . . . is loose and ~ in form —Douglas Watt⟩ ⟨a ~ gypsy air —Sara R. Watson⟩ **b** : given to expression or composition in the form or manner of the rhapsody ⟨a ~ composer whose music is fed on the most outspoken type of romantic fervor —Nicolas Slonimsky⟩ **2** : extravagantly emotional : RAPTUROUS ⟨the ~ quality of the program notes —Robert Lawrence⟩ ⟨the most laudatory, if not downright ~, adjectives —Bernard Kalb⟩ ⟨a terrible bliss of self-love, a ~ egotism —Peggy Bennett⟩ ⟨sent ~ greetings —Sidney Wallach⟩ **3** : of or relating to the recitation of rhapsodies ⟨the ~ exhibitions of ancient Greek festivals⟩

rhap·sod·i·cal \-dəkəl, -dēk-\ *adj* [Gk *rhapsōidikos* rhapsodic + E *-al*] **1** *archaic* : of a disconnected or fragmentary style ⟨the reader of this ~ work —Laurence Sterne⟩ **2** : RHAPSODIC

rhap·sod·i·cal·ly \-dək(ə)lē, -dēk-, -li\ *adv* : in a rhapsodic manner : RAPTUROUSLY

rhap·so·dist \'rapsədəst\ *n* -S [¹*rhapsody* + *-ist*] **1** *obs* : ANTHOLOGIST **2** : one who recites a rhapsody; *esp* : a professional reciter of epic poems (as of Homer) **3** : one who recites or sings poems for a livelihood **4** : one who writes or speaks rhapsodically ⟨any ~ of motorcars —Edmund Wilson⟩ — **rhap·so·dis·tic** \¦==¦distik, -tēk\ *adj*

rhap·so·dize \'rapsə,dīz\ *vb* -ED/-ING/-S [¹*rhapsody* + *-ize*] *vt* **1** *archaic* : to patch together (as stories) : make a medley of ⟨*rhapsodizing* all these affairs —Laurence Sterne⟩ **2** : to utter or recite as or in the manner of a rhapsody ~ *vi* : to indulge in rhapsody : utter rhapsodies ⟨~ about a new book⟩ ⟨heard friends ~ about a dinner —*Harper's Bazaar*⟩

¹**rhap·so·dy** \'rapsədē, -di\ *n* -ES [L *rhapsodia*, fr. Gk *rhapsōidia*, fr. *rhapsōidos* rhapsodist (fr. *rhaptein* to sew, stitch together + *ōidē* ode, song) + *-ia* -y; akin to Gk *rhepein* to bend, incline, *rhapis* rod, ON *orf*, *orb* handle of a scythe, OHG *worf* handle of a scythe, Lith *verpti* to spin, and prob. to L *repens* sudden — more at ODE] **1** : a recitation or song of a rhapsodist : a portion of an epic poem (as a book of the *Iliad* or *Odyssey*) adapted for recitation **2** *archaic* : a literary work consisting of disconnected pieces; *also* : a miscellaneous collection or disconnected series : MEDLEY, JUMBLE ⟨a ~ of words —Shak.⟩ **3** **a** : an ecstatic or highly emotional utterance or literary work : effusively incoherent and extravagant discourse ⟨a speech that bordered upon ~⟩ ⟨recite a long ~ to the joys of viewing America from a caboose —R.P.Cooke⟩ ⟨the novel ends in a kind of meditative ~ —Mark Schorer⟩ **b** : RAPTURE, ECSTASY ⟨reading poetry often seems a state of ~ in which rhyme and meter and sound stir the mind as wine and dance stir the body —Virginia Woolf⟩ **4** : an instrumental composition that is irregular in form like an improvisation or free fantasia **syn** see BOMBAST

²**rhapsody** \"\ *vb* -ED/-ING/-ES : RHAPSODIZE

rha·son *or* **ra·son** \'rā,sən\ *n* -S [MGk *rhason*, a napless woolen cloth, rhason, perh. fr. L *rasus*, past part. of *radere* to scrape, scratch, shave — more at RAT] *Eastern Church* **1** : an ecclesiastical garment resembling the cassock **2** : a long loose cloak worn over the rhason — called also *exorhason*

rhas·o·phore *or* **ras·o·phore** \'razə,fō(ə)r\ *n* -S [MGk *rhasophoros* fr. *rhason* + Gk *-phoros* -phore] *Eastern Church* : a member of a monastic order who has not yet passed through the novitiate : NOVICE

rhat·a·ny \'rat°nē\ *n* -ES [Sp *ratania* & Pg *ratânhia*, fr. Quechua *ratánya*] **1** : the dried root of either of two American shrubs (*Krameria triandra* and *K. argentea*) that is used as an astringent — see PARÁ RHATANY, PERUVIAN RHATANY **2** : a plant that yields rhatany

rha·thy·mia \rə'thīmēə\ *n* -S [Gk, fr. *rhathymos* lighthearted, easy-tempered, carefree (fr. *rha* easy, ready + *thymos* spirit, mind, courage) + *-ia* -y — more at FUME] : the state of being carefree : LIGHT-HEARTEDNESS

RHB *abbr* right halfback

rhd *abbr* railhead

rhe \'rē\ *n* -S [Gk *rhein* to flow — more at STREAM] : the cgs unit of fluidity : the reciprocal of poise

¹**rhea** \'rēə\ *n* [NL, prob. fr. *Rhea*, mother of Zeus and other gods in Greek mythology, fr. L, fr. Gk] **1** *cap* : a genus of large tall flightless So. American birds (order Rheiformes) that resemble but are smaller than the African ostrich, have three toes, a fully feathered head and neck, an undeveloped tail, and pale gray to brownish feathers that droop over the rump and back **2** -S : any bird of the genus *Rhea* or broadly of the order Rheiformes comprising as surviving forms only a larger bird (*R. americana*) ranging from Brazil to Patagonia and a smaller (*Pterocnemia pennata*) from the highlands of Peru to the Straits of Magellan — called also *nandu*

²**rhea** \", rē'ä\ *n* -S [Assamese *rihā*] : CHINA GRASS

rhe·a·dine *or* **rhoe·a·dine** \'rēə,dēn, -,d°n\ *n* -S [ISV *rhead-, rhoead-* (fr. NL *rhoeas*, *rhoeas* — specific epithet of the corn poppy *Papaver rhoeas* — fr. Gk *rhoiad-, rhoias* corn poppy) + *-ine*] : a nonpoisonous crystalline alkaloid $C_{21}H_{21}NO_6$ found in various poppies (as the corn poppy)

rhe·bok *or* **ree·bok** \'rē,bäk\ *n, pl* **rhebok** *or* **rheboks** [Afrik *reebok*, fr. MD *reeboc* male of the roe deer, fr. *ree* roe deer + *boc* buck; akin to OE *rā* roe deer and to OE *buc* buck — more at ROE, BUCK] : a southern African antelope (*Pelea capreolus*) nearly as large as the fallow deer but having the form and habits of the chamois and being light gray with short upright horns

rhe·buck \'rē,bək\ *n, pl* **rhebuck** *or* **rhebucks** [part trans. of Afrik *reebok*] : RHEBOK

rheg·nop·teri \reg'näptə,rī\ [NL, fr. Gk *rhēgnynai* to break, break loose, burst forth + *pteron* wing, feather — more at RHAGADES, FEATHER] *syn of* POLYNEMOIDEA

rhe·ic acid \'rēik-\ *n* [*rheic* fr. *rhe-* (fr. NL *Rheum*) + *-ic*] : CHRYSOPHANIC ACID

rhe·idae \'rēə,dē\ *n pl, cap* [NL, fr. *Rhea*, type genus + *-idae*] : a family of birds coextensive with the order Rheiformes

rhe·ifor·mes \,rēə'fȯr(,)mēz\ *n pl, cap* [NL, fr. *Rhea* + *-iformes*] : an order of birds that are intermediate in some respects between the ostriches and the emus and cassowaries and that comprise the recent and extinct rheas

rheims *usu cap, var of* REIMS

rhe·in \'rēən\ *n* -S [ISV *rhe-* (fr. NL *Rheum*) + *-in*] : a yellow crystalline acid $C_{15}H_8O_6$ occurring esp. in rhubarb and senna leaves; 4,5-dihydroxy-2-anthraquinone-carboxylic acid

rhe·mish \'rēmish\ *adj, usu cap* [*Rheims* (*Reims*), city in northeastern France + E *-ish*] : REIMS

rhenish \'renish, 'rēn-, -nēsh\ *adj, usu cap* [L *Rhenus* Rhine, river in western Europe flowing from Switzerland through Germany and the Netherlands into the North Sea + E *-ish*] : of or relating to the river Rhine or the region on or near it esp. in Germany ⟨*Rhenish* wine⟩ ⟨*Rhenish* Confederation⟩

rhenish architecture *n, usu cap R* : the German Romanesque architecture of the Rhine valley combining native elements with others derived from Byzantine and esp. Lombard architecture

rhe·ni·um \'rēnēəm\ *n* -S [NL, fr. L *Rhenus* Rhine river + NL *-ium*] : a rare heavy polyvalent metallic element that resembles manganese chemically, that occurs esp. in molybdenite, gadolinite, columbite, or platinum ores, that is obtained either as a black or grayish powder by ignition in hydrogen usu. of a perrhenate or as a silver-white hard metal (as by sintering the powder), and that is usu. used in catalysts for dehydrogenation and in thermocouples — symbol *Re*; see ELEMENT table

rheo- *comb form* [Gk *rheos* anything flowing, stream, fr. *rhein* to flow — more at STREAM] : flow : current ⟨*rheo*taxis⟩ ⟨*rheo*stat⟩

rheo *abbr* rheostat

rheo·base \'rēō+,-\ *n* [ISV *rheo-* + *base*] : the minimal electrical current required to excite a tissue (as nerve or muscle) given indefinitely long time during which the current is applied — compare CHRONAXIE — **rheo·basic** \¦rēō+\ *adj*

rhe·o·log·i·cal \¦rēə¦läjəkəl\ *also* **rhe·o·log·ic** \-jik\ *adj* [*rheology* + *-ical* or *-ic*] : of or relating to rheology or to the phenomena of flowing matter ⟨the fundamental ~ properties of metals —*Technical News Bull.*⟩ ⟨~ properties of cheddar cheese —*Biol. Abstracts*⟩ — **rhe·o·log·i·cal·ly** \-jək(ə)lē\ *adv*

rhe·ol·o·gist \rē'äləjəst\ *n* -S [*rheology* + *-ist*] : a specialist in rheology

rhe·ol·o·gy \-jē\ *n* -ES [ISV *rheo-* + *-logy*] : a science dealing with the deformation and flow of matter

rhe·om·e·ter \rē'ämədə(r)\ *n* [ISV *rheo-* + *-meter*] : an instrument for measuring the flow of viscous substances — **rheo·met·ric** \¦rēə¦me·trik\ *adj* — **rhe·om·e·try** \rē'ämə·trē\ *n* -ES

rheo·mor·phic \¦rēə¦mȯrfik\ *adj* [*rheomorphism* + *-ic*] : of or relating to rheomorphism

rheo·mor·phism \¦rēə¦mȯr,fizəm\ *n* -S [*rheo-* + *-morphism*] : metamorphism in which flow of the solid rock fabric is conspicuous

rheo·pexy \'rēə,peksē\ *n* -ES [*rheo-* + *-pexy*] : the accelerated gelation of a thixotropic sol brought about by jarring the containing vessel, by slow stirring, or by pouring

rheo·phil·ic \,rēə'filik\ *or* **rheo·phile** \'rēə,fīl\ *also* **rheo·phil** \'==,fil\ *or* **rhe·oph·i·lous** \(')rē¦äfələs\ *adj* [ISV *rheo-* + *-philic, -phile, -phil, -philous*] : preferring or living in flowing water ⟨~ fauna⟩

rheo·plankton \¦rēō+\ *n* [*rheo-* + *plankton*] : plankton of running waters (as of rivers)

rhe·o·stat \'rēə,stat, *usu* -ad·+V\ *n* -S [*rheo-* + *-stat*] : a resistor for regulating a current by means of variable resistances — compare RESISTANCE BOX — **rhe·o·stat·ic** \¦==¦stad·|ik, -at|, |ēk\ *adj*

rheo·tac·tic \¦rēə¦taktik\ *adj* [*rheo-* + *-tactic*] : relating to or exhibiting rheotaxis ⟨~ response⟩

rheo·taxis \¦rēə¦taksəs\ *n, pl* **rheotaxes** [NL, fr. *rheo-* + *-taxis*] : a taxis in which mechanical stimulation by a stream of fluid (as water) is the directive factor

rheo·trope \'rēə,trōp\ *n* -S [ISV *rheo-* + *-trope*] : a commutator for reversing a current

rheo·trop·ic \¦rēə¦träpik\ *adj* [*rheotropism* + *-ic*] : relating to or exhibiting rheotropism

rhe·ot·ro·pism \rē'ä·trə,pizəm\ *n* [ISV *rheo-* + *tropism*] : a tropism in which mechanical stimulation by a stream of fluid (as water) is the orienting factor ⟨many motile animals . . . exhibit either positive or negative ~ —P.S.Welch⟩

rhes *pl of* RHE

rhe·sus factor *or* **rhesus antigen** \'rēsəs-\ *n* : RH FACTOR

rhesus monkey *or* **rhesus** *also* **rhesus macaque** *n* -ES [*rhesus* fr. NL] : a pale brown Indian monkey (*Macaca mulatta*) of active and playful disposition often kept in zoological gardens and much used in medical research

rhetian *usu cap, var of* RHAETIAN

rhetor \'rēd·ə(r), 'red·-\ *n* -S [ME *rethor*, modif. of L *rhetor*, fr. Gk *rhētōr*] : RHETORICIAN 1

rhet·o·ric \'red·ərik, -etə-\ *n* -S [ME *rethorik*, fr. MF *rethorique*, modif. of L *rhetorica*, fr. Gk *rhētorikē*, fr. fem. of *rhētorikos* rhetorical, oratorical, fr. *rhētor-, rhētōr* orator + *-ikos* -ic — more at WORD] **1** : the art of expressive speech or discourse; *specif* : **a** : the study of principles and rules of composition formulated by ancient critics (as Aristotle and Quintilian) and interpreted by classical scholars for application to discourse in the vernacular **b** : the art or practice of writing or speaking as means of communication or persuasion often with special concern for literary effect ⟨freshman composition is a course in ~ —H.C.Bowersox⟩ ⟨the cultivation of grammar and ~ —John Dewey⟩ **2** **a** : skill in the effective use of speech : ELOQUENCE **b** (1) : artificial elegance of language : discourse without conviction or earnest feeling (2) : inflated language : VERBOSITY, BOMBAST ⟨that passage, sir, is not empty ~ —Virginia Woolf⟩ ⟨the enemy of ~ and every kind of artifice and virtuosity —Philip Rahv⟩ ⟨the mocking ~ upon a tombstone —J.C.Powys⟩ **c** : style of language ⟨his ~ would not have been commended at Cambridge⟩ ⟨large, and sometimes loose, exalted simplicities of his ~ —*Times Lit. Supp.*⟩ **3** **a** : verbal communication : DISCOURSE, SPEECH ⟨the temptation to establish peace by ~ —W. Van Kirk⟩ ⟨a ~ of fantastic slang —Edmund Wilson⟩ **b** : the verbal content of a composition (as a poem) or a body of literature ⟨the deep hold that the symbols of free speech and other civil liberties have in the American ~ —Max Lerner⟩ **c** : the verbal elements employed in or characteristic of discourse relating to a particular subject or area ⟨made effective use of the ~ of liberalism —Sidney Hook⟩ **4** : persuasive or moving power ⟨mastery of expressive musical ~ —Carl Parrish & J.F.Ohl⟩ ⟨sweet, silent ~ of persuading eyes —Samuel Daniel⟩ **5** : a treatise on rhetoric; *esp* : a textbook on literary composition ⟨the authors of freshman ~*s* —C.W.Shumaker⟩

rhe·tor·i·cal \rə'tȯrəkəl, -tär-, -rēk-\ *also* **rhe·tor·ic** \rə'tȯrik, -tär-, -rēk\ *adj* [*rhetorical* fr. ME, fr. L *rhetoricus* rhetorical (fr. Gk *rhētorikos*) + E *-al*; *rhetoric* fr. ME *rethorick*, fr. MF *rethorique*, modif. of L *rhetoricus*] **1** **a** : of, relating to, or concerned with rhetoric ⟨accepted two or three verbal and ~ changes that I suggested —W.A.White⟩ ⟨make science, in part, at least, a subject for ~ discourse —*Quarterly Journ. of Speech*⟩ ⟨the ~ sin of the meaningless variation —Lewis Mumford⟩ **b** : employed for rhetorical effect ⟨don't remember a single decorative or ~ word in his first ten cantos —Ezra Pound⟩ — often used without regard to some actual condition or circumstance qualifying or negating the literal significance of the statement ⟨must have known that he was acting too late to stay the legislators' stampede to vote and adjourn, so his message was partly ~ —*New Republic*⟩ ⟨the offer was ~, with no certainty . . . that the money would be paid at all —T.E. Lawrence⟩ ⟨an essentially ~ charge —Rupert Emerson⟩ **2** **a** : given to rhetoric : emphasizing style often at the expense of thought : GRANDILOQUENT, BOMBASTIC ⟨wrote long ~ speeches like operatic solos, regarding my plays as musical performances —E.R.Bentley⟩ ⟨an essay on friendship, high-flown, ~ —H.S.Canby⟩ ⟨flamboyant and ~ tastes, which produced the most beautiful architecture of the past —Stephen Spender⟩ **b** : employing or relating to speech or oratory esp. in contradistinction to other modes of communication or contest ⟨the actual thought of a real war, not a ~ one —Vincent Sheean⟩ ⟨has finally repudiated color caste — at the ~ level —Carey McWilliams⟩

rhetorical accent *n* : ACCENT 6c

rhe·tor·i·cal·ly \-rək(ə)lē, -rēk-, -li\ *adv* : with respect to rhetoric : for rhetorical effect : in a rhetorical manner ⟨aim has been to punctuate as lightly as possible, and ~ rather than grammatically —J.R.Sutherland⟩ ⟨threw up her hands and asked ~ what was going to happen to them now —Louis Auchincloss⟩

rhe·tor·i·cal·ness \-rəkəlnəs, -rēk-\ *n* -ES : the condition of being rhetorical

rhetorical question *n* : a question not intended to elicit an answer but asked for rhetorical effect often with an assumption that only one answer is possible (as in "Who does not love his country?")

rhetorical syllogism *n* : a truncated syllogism that is persuasive but not necessarily valid

rhe·tor·i·cate \-rə,kāt\ *vi* -ED/-ING/-S *archaic* [*rhetoric* + *-ate*] : to use rhetorical language

rhet·o·ri·cian \,red·ə'rishən, -etə-\ *n* -S [ME *rethoricien*, fr. MF, fr. *rethorique* rhetoric + *-ien* -ian] **1** **a** : a master or teacher of rhetoric (as in ancient Greece and Rome) : one concerned with rhetoric ⟨he was a ~ and cared little for give-and-take —Jean Stafford⟩ **b** : ORATOR ⟨the only university whose ~*s* have twice won the . . . tournament, outtalking all opponents in that oratorical round robin —T.D.Durrance⟩ **2** **a** : an eloquent writer or speaker ⟨a great ~, a master of telling phrases and emphatic effects —Maurice Bowra⟩ **b** : one who writes or speaks in an inflated or bombastic style ⟨so often, too often, to have been but a pompous ~ —W.S.Maugham⟩

rhet·o·rize \'red·ə,rīz\ *vi* -ED/-ING/-S [ML *rhetorizare* to play the orator, fr. Gk *rhētorizein* to be an orator, fr. *rhētor-*, *rhētōr* orator + *-izein* -ize] *archaic* : to use rhetorical language

rheto-romance *or* **rheto-romansh** *usu cap both Rs, var of* RHAETO-ROMANIC

¹**rheum** \'rüm, 'rům\ *n* -S [ME *reume*, fr. MF, fr. L *rheuma*, fr. Gk — more at RHEUMATISM] **1 a** : a watery discharge from the mucous membranes esp. of the eyes or nose **b** : a condition marked by such discharge (as a cold or catarrh) **2** *archaic* : TEARS ⟨indisposed by a very great ~ —John Evelyn⟩

²**rhe·um** \'rēəm\ *n, cap* [NL, fr. Gk *rhēon* rhubarb — more at RHUBARB] : a genus of Asiatic herbs (family Polygonaceae) with large leaves, loose stipular sheaths, and small flowers in ample paniculate racemes, the perianth 6-parted, the fruit 3-winged — see RHUBARB

¹**rheu·mat·ic** \(')rü¦mad·ik, -at|, |ēk *also* (')rů¦m- *or* rə'm-\ *adj* [ME *rewmatik*, fr. L *rheumaticus* troubled with rheum, fr. Gk *rheumatikos* subject to rheum or flux, fr. *rheumat-*, *rheuma* rheum, flux + *-ikos* -ic] **1** *obs* : derived from or being rheum : full of rheum : suffering from rheum : tending to cause rheum **2 a** : of, relating to, or characteristic of rheumatism : attending or caused by rheumatism ⟨~ pain⟩ **b** : affected with rheumatism ⟨a ~ joint⟩ — **rheu·mat·i·cal·ly** \|ək(ə)lē, |ēk-, -li\ *adv*

²**rheumatic** \", *in sense 2* -iks,-ēks, 'rüma,tiks *also* 'rům-\ *n* -S **1** : one affected with rheumatism **2 rheu·matics** *pl, dial* : RHEUMATISM — often used with *the*

rheu·mat·i·cal \(')rü¦mad·|əkəl, -at|, |ēk- *also* (')rů¦m- *or* rə'm-\ *archaic var of* RHEUMATIC

rheumatic disease *n* : any of several diseases (as rheumatoid arthritis, rheumatic fever, fibrositis) characterized by inflammation and pain in muscles or joints from various causes

rheumatic fever *n* : an acute often recurrent disease occurring chiefly in children and young adults and characterized by fever, inflammation, pain, and swelling in and around the joints, inflammatory involvement of the pericardium and valves of the heart, and often the formation of small nodules chiefly in the subcutaneous tissues and the heart

rheumatic heart disease *n* : active or inactive disease of the heart resulting from rheumatic fever and characterized by inflammatory changes in the myocardium or scarring of the valves that reduce the functional capacity of the heart

rheu·mat·icky \(')rü¦mad·əkē, -atə-, -ki *also* rə'm-; 'rüma,tik- *also* 'rům-\ *adj* [²*rheumatic* + *-y*] : RHEUMATIC

rheu·ma·tism \'rüma,tizəm *also* 'rům-\ *n* -S [L *rheumatismus* rheum, fr. Gk *rheumatismos*, fr. *rheumatizesthai* to suffer from a flux, fr. *rheumat-*, *rheuma* flux, rheum; akin to Gk *rhein* to flow — more at STREAM] **1** : any of numerous conditions characterized by inflammation or pain in muscles, joints, or fibrous tissue ⟨muscular ~⟩ **2** : RHEUMATOID ARTHRITIS

rheumatism root *n* **1** : TWINLEAF **2** : SPOTTED WINTERGREEN

rheumatism weed *n* : any of several No. American plants used esp. formerly in folk medicine for pain or inflammation in the joints: as **a** : PIPSISSEWA **b** : either of two common dogbanes (*Apocynum cannibinum* and *A. androsaemifolium*)

rheu·ma·tiz \'==,tiz\ *n* -ES [by shortening & alter.] *chiefly dial* : RHEUMATISM

¹**rheu·ma·toid** \-,tȯid\ *adj* [ISV *rheumatism* + *-oid*; orig. formed as F *rhumatoïde*] : characteristic of or affected with rheumatoid arthritis

²**rheumatoid** \"\ *n* -S : one affected with rheumatoid arthritis

rheumatoid arthritis *n* : a constitutional disease of unknown cause characterized by inflammation and swelling of joint structures and marked by a chronic progressive course ending in complete stiffening of one or more joints, permanent disability, and invalidism — compare DEGENERATIVE ARTHRITIS

rheumatoid spondylitis *n* : rheumatoid arthritis of the spine

rheu·ma·tol·o·gist \,rümə'täləjəst *also* ,rům-\ *n* -S [*rheumatology* + *-ist*] : a specialist in rheumatic diseases

rheu·ma·tol·o·gy \-jē\ *n* -ES [ISV *rheumatism* + *-o-* + *-logy*] : a branch of medicine dealing with rheumatic diseases

rheumed \'rümd, 'růmd\ *adj* [¹*rheum* + *-ed*] : RHEUMY

rheum·i·ly \'rüməlē, 'rům-\ *adv* : in a rheumy manner

rheums *pl of* RHEUM

rheumy \-mē\ *adj* [¹*rheum* + *-y*] **1** : consisting of or full of rheum ⟨his blinking and ~ eyes—Margery Sharp⟩ **2** : affected with or subject to catarrh or rheumatism : RHEUMATIC ⟨falsetto voice, ~ with age and grief —Ellen Glasgow⟩ **3** : causing or tending to cause catarrh or rheumatism ⟨~ mists of winter —*Architect & Building News*⟩

rhex·ia \'reksēə\ *n* [NL, fr. L, a plant] **1** *cap* : a small genus of herbs (family Melastomaceae) having 3-nerved leaves and red or yellow flowers with 4 petals and 8 equal anthers — see DEER GRASS **2** -S : any plant of the genus *Rhexia*

rhex·is \'reksəs\ *n, pl* **rhex·es** \-k,sēz\ [NL, fr. Gk *rhēxis* act of breaking, fr. *rhēgnynai* to break — more at RHAGADES] : RUPTURE ⟨~ of a blood vessel⟩ ⟨~ of an organ⟩

rh factor *also* **rh** \'ä'rāch-, ä'(r)äch-\ *n, usu cap R* [*rhesus* monkey (in which it was first detected)] : a substance or one of a group of substances that is present in the red blood cells of a large majority of persons and in those of other higher animals, is prob. an agglutinogen, is inherited according to Mendelian principles, and is capable of inducing intense antigenic reaction under suitable circumstances (as in repeated transfusion of Rh-positive blood to an Rh-negative person) — called also *Rh antigen, rhesus factor*; compare HR FACTOR

RHI *abbr* range-height indicator

rhig·o·lene \'rigə,lēn, -lən\ *n* -S [Gk *rhigos* cold + E *-ol* + *-ene* — more at FRIGID] : a petroleum product intermediate between cymogene and gasoline containing chiefly pentanes and used formerly in medicine as a local anesthetic

rhin- *or* **rhino-** *comb form* [NL, fr. Gk, fr. *rhin-*, *rhis* nose; perh. akin to Skt *sarā* flowing, Gk *oros* whey — more at SERUM] **1 a** : nose ⟨*rhin*itis⟩ ⟨*rhino*logy⟩ **b** : nose and ⟨*rhino*laryngology⟩ ⟨*rhino*pharyngitis⟩ **2 a** : nasal ⟨*rhino*lith⟩ ⟨*rhino*caul⟩ **b** : nasal and ⟨*rhino*pharyngeal⟩

rhi·na \'rīnə\ *n* [NL, fr. L, a shark, fr. Gk *rhinē*, a shark, file, rasp — more at WRITE] *syn of* SQUATINA

-rhi·na \"\ *n comb form* [NL, fr. Gk *rhin-*, *rhis* nose] : one or ones having (such) a nose — in taxonomic names in zoology ⟨Amphi*rhina*⟩ ⟨Phyllo*rhina*⟩

rhi·nal \'rīn°l\ *adj* [*rhin-* + *-al*] : of or relating to the nose : NASAL, NARIAL

¹**rhi·nan·tha·ce·ae** \,rī,nan'thāsē,ē\ *n pl, cap* [NL, fr. *Rhinanthus*, type genus + *-aceae*] *in some esp former classifications* : a family of dicotyledonous plants that includes those figworts having the lower lip or lateral lobes of the corolla external in the bud

²**rhinanthaceae** \"\ *syn of* SCROPHULARIACEAE

rhi·nan·thus \rī'nan(t)thəs\ *n, cap* [NL, fr. *rhin-* + *-anthus*] : a small genus of partially parasitic herbs (family Scrophulariaceae) that have an inflated 4-toothed calyx, bilabiate corolla, four unequal stamens, and winged seeds — see RATTLE

rhi·nar·i·um \rī'na(a)rēəm\ *n, pl* **rhinar·ia** \-ēə\ [NL, fr. Gk *rhin-*, *rhis* nose + NL *-arium*] **1** : the lower part of the clypeus in some insects (as dragonflies) **2** : the hairless area of roughened skin at the tip of the snout of a mammal

rhinc·odon \'riŋkə,dän\ *n, cap* [NL, fr. *rhinc-* (irreg. fr. L *rhina*, a shark) + *-odon*] : a genus of elasmobranch fishes that contains only the whale shark and is now usu. isolated in a separate family though formerly often included in Orectolobidae

rhine \'rēn\ *n* -S [earlier *royne*, prob. alter. of ME *rune* watercourse, fr. OE *ryne* course, flow, watercourse; akin to OFris *rene* flow; derivative fr. the root of E ¹*run*] *dial chiefly Eng* : a drainage ditch : RUNNEL

-rhine — see -RRHINE

rhine·grave \'rīn,grāv\ *n* [MD *rijngrave*, fr. *Rijn* Rhine river + *grave* count — more at BURGRAVE] : a count who has possessions bordering the Rhine

rhine·land·er \'rīn,landə(r), -lən-\ *n* -S *cap* [G *rheinländer*, fr. *Rheinland* Rhineland, part of Germany west of the Rhine river] **1 a** : a native or inhabitant of the part of Germany west of the Rhine river **b** : a native or inhabitant of the Rhine province of Prussia **2** : a native speaker of one of the Rhenish dialects of the German language — compare BAVARIAN, SWABIAN, WESTPHALIAN

rhin·encephalic \(¦)rīn+\ *also* **rhin·encephalous** \¦rīn+\ *adj* [*rhinencephalic* fr. F *rhinencéphalique*, fr. NL *rhinencephalon* + F *-ique* -ic; *rhinencephalous* fr. NL *rhinencephalon* + E *-ous*] : of or relating to the rhinencephalon

rhin·encephalon \¦rīn+\ *n, pl* **rhinencephala** [NL, fr. *rhin-* + *encephalon*] : the anterior inferior part of the forebrain that is chiefly concerned with olfaction

rhi·ne·odon \'rīnēə,dän, rī'n-\ *n* [NL, fr. L *rhina*, a shark + *-odon* — more at RHINA] *syn of* RHINCODON

rhine·stone \'rīnz,tōn, -īn,st-\ *n* [*Rhine*, river in western Europe + E *stone*; trans. of F *caillou du Rhin*] : a colorless imitation stone of high luster made of glass, paste, or gem quartz

rhine·stoned \-ōnd\ *adj* : set with or as if with rhinestones

rhin·eura \rī'n(y)urə\ *n, cap* [NL, fr. *rhin-* + Gk *eurys* broad — more at EURY-] : a genus of limbless burrowing lizards (family Amphisbaenidae) that includes solely the thunderworm

rhine wine \'rīn-\ *n, usu cap R* [*rhine* fr. *Rhine*, river in western Europe flowing from Switzerland through Germany and the Netherlands into the North sea] **1** : a wine that is produced in the valley of the Rhine; *esp* : one that is light-bodied, dry, and white and that averages 7 to 10 percent ethyl alcohol by volume **2** : a wine that is similar to the white wine of the Rhine but is produced elsewhere (as in California or New York state)

rhin·i·on \'rinē,än\ *n* -S [NL, fr. Gk, dim. of *rhin-*, *rhis* nose — more at RHIN-] : a point at the lower end of the median suture joining the nasal bones — see CRANIOMETRY illustration

rhi·ni·tis \rī'nīd·əs\ *n, pl* **rhinit·i·des** \-'nid·ə,dēz\ [NL, fr. *rhin-* + *-itis*] **1** : inflammation of the mucous membrane of the nose from infectious, allergic, or other causes: as **a** : COMMON COLD **b** : CORYZA b **2** : bullnose of swine

¹**rhi·no** \'rī(,)nō\ *n, pl* **rhino** [origin unknown] : MONEY, CASH

²**rhino** \"\ *n, pl* **rhino** *or* **rhinos** [by shortening] : RHINOCEROS

³**rhino** \"\ *or* **rhino ferry** *n* -S : a pontoon or group of pontoons propelled by outboard motor and used esp. by a naval force during landing operations for transportation of vehicles, docking facilities, and other functions

rhino- — see RHIN-

rhi·no·bat·i·dae \,rīnō'bad·ə,dē\ *n pl, cap* [NL, fr. *Rhinobatos*, type genus + *-idae*] : a family of viviparous elasmobranch fishes of warm seas comprising the guitarfishes, fiddlers, and related forms that are included among the rays but somewhat approach the sharks in the long narrow body and the possession of a tail fin

rhi·nob·a·tos \rī'näbəd·əs\ *n, cap* [NL, fr. Gk, a fish, perh. of the genus *Rhinobatos*, fr. *rhinē*, a shark, file, rasp + *batos* skate (fish) — more at WRITE] : a genus (the type of the family Rhinobatidae) of viviparous elasmobranch fishes

rhi·nob·a·tus \"\ [NL, fr. Gk *rhinobatos*] *syn of* RHINOBATOS

rhi·no·cer·i·cal \¦rīnə¦serəkəl\ *adj* [prob. fr. ¹*rhino* + *-cer* (as in *rhinoceros*) + *-ical*] *archaic* : full of money : RICH

rhi·noc·er·ine \rī'näsə,rīn, -sərən\ *or* **rhi·noc·er·oid** \-sə,rȯid\ *adj* [*rhinoceros* + *-ine* or *-oid*] : RHINOCEROTIC

rhinoceroid \"\ *n* -S [NL *Rhinoceros* + E *-oid*] : RHINOCEROTID

rhi·noc·er·os \rī'näs(ə)rəs\ *n* [ME *rinoceros*, fr. L *rhinocerot-*,

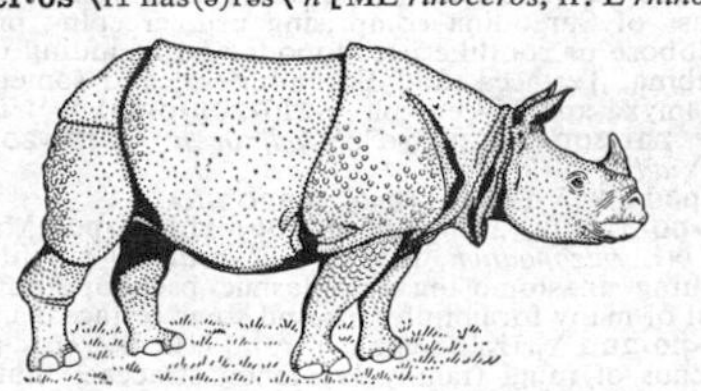

Indian rhinoceros

rhinoceros, fr. Gk *rhinokerōt-*, *rhinokerōs*, fr. *rhin-*, *rhis* nose + *-kerōt-*, *-kerōs* (fr. *keras* horn) — more at RHIN-, HORN] **1** *pl* **rhi·noceroses** \-rəsəz\ *or* **rhinoceros** \-rəs\ *or* **rhi·noc·eri** \-ä,sə,rī\ *also* **rhinoc·er·o·tes** \(,)rī,näsə'rōd·(,)ēz\ : any of various large powerful herbivorous thick-skinned perissodactyl mammals of the family Rhinocerotidae that have one or two heavy upright horns on the snout or that in some extinct genera are hornless — see BLACK RHINOCEROS, WHITE RHINOCEROS, WOOLLY RHINOCEROS **2** *cap* [NL, fr. L] : a genus (the type of the family Rhinocerotidae) that contains the Indian and Malayan rhinoceroses

rhinoceros auklet *n* : an auklet (*Cerorhinca monocerata*) of the northern Pacific that has a deciduous horn on the bill

rhinoceros beetle *n* : any of various chiefly tropical very large beetles of *Dynastes* and closely related genera having projecting horns on thorax and head and large larvae that bore in living or decaying plant tissue and are sometimes eaten by man; *esp* : a lustrous greenish gray dark spotted beetle (*Dynastes tityus*) of tropical America and southeastern U.S.

rhinoceros bird *n* **1** : OXPECKER **2** : RHINOCEROS HORNBILL

rhinoceros hornbill *n* : any of various hornbills; *esp* : a hornbill (*Buceros rhinoceros*) of the Malay peninsula and islands of Indonesia having a casque on the bill that is very large and turned up in front

rhinoceros viper *n* : a heavy-bodied brightly-colored West African viper (*Bitis nasicornis*) with a pair of hornlike outgrowths on the snout — called also *river jack*

rhi·noc·er·ot \rī'näsə,rät\ *n* -S [L *rhinocerot-*, *rhinoceros*] *archaic* : RHINOCEROS

rhi·noc·er·ot·ic \(¦)rī¦näsə¦räd·ik\ *adj* [LL *rhinoceroticus*, fr. L *rhinocerot-*, *rhinoceros* + *-icus* -ic] : of, relating to, or resembling a rhinoceros

¹**rhi·noc·er·o·tid** \-sə¦rōd·id\ *adj* [NL *Rhinocerotidae*] : of or relating to the Rhinocerotidae

²**rhinocerotid** \"\ *n* -S : a mammal of the family Rhinocerotidae : RHINOCEROS

rhi·noc·er·oti·dae \(,)rī,näsə'räd·ə,dē, -'rōd-\ *n pl, cap* [NL, fr. *Rhinocerot-*, *Rhinoceros*, type genus + *-idae*] : a family of mammals that contains all the true rhinoceroses and that is often considered to constitute together with extinct related forms a distinct superfamily of Perissodactyla

rhi·noc·er·oti·form \(¦)==¦==,fȯrm\ *adj* [L *rhinocerot-*, *rhinoceros* + E *-iform*] : resembling a rhinoceros

rhi·noc·er·o·tine \rī'näsərə,tīn\ *adj* [L *rhinocerot-*, *rhinoceros* + E *-ine*] : RHINOCEROTIC

rhi·noc·er·o·toid \-,tȯid\ *adj* [L *rhinocerot-*, *rhinoceros* + E *-oid*] : RHINOCEROTIC

rhi·no·cryp·ti·dae \,rīnə'kriptə,dē\ *n pl, cap* [NL, fr. Rhinocrypta, type genus (fr. *rhin-* + *-crypta*, fr. Gk *kryptos* hidden) + *-idae* — more at CRYPT] : a family of So. American birds closely related to Furnariidae — see TAPACOLO

rhino ferry *var of* RHINO

rhi·no·gen·ic \¦rīnə¦jenik\ *or* **rhi·nog·e·nous** \(')rī¦näjənəs\ *adj* [*rhin-* + *-genic* or *-genous*] : originating in or transmitted by way of the nose ⟨~ meningitis⟩

rhi·no·la·lia \,rīnə'lālēə, -ālyə\ *n* -S [NL, fr. *rhin-* + *-lalia*] : nasal tone in speech esp. when caused by excessive closure or openness of the posterior nares

rhi·no·laryngology \¦rī(,)nō+\ *n* [*rhin-* + *laryng-* + *-logy*] : a branch of medical science that deals with the nose and larynx and their diseases

rhi·no·laryngoscope \"+\ *n* [*rhin-* + *laryng-* + *-scope*] : a scope fitted with mirrors and a lighting system used for examination of the nose and larynx — **rhi·no·laryngoscopic** \"+\ *adj*

rhi·no·lith \'rīnə,lith\ *n* -S [ISV *rhin-* + *-lith*] : a concretion formed within the cavities of the nose — **rhi·no·lith·ic** \¦==¦lithik\ *adj*

rhi·no·log·ic \¦==¦läjik\ *or* **rhi·no·log·i·cal** \-jəkəl\ *adj* [*rhinology* + *-ic* or *-ical*] : of or relating to the nose

rhi·nol·o·gist \rī'näləjəst\ *n* -S [*rhinology* + *-ist*] : a physician who specializes in rhinology

rhi·nol·o·gy \-jē\ *n* -S [*rhin-* + *-logy*] : a branch of medical science that deals with the nose and its diseases

rhi·nol·o·phid \rī'näləfəd\ *n* -S [NL *Rhinolophidae*] : a leaf-nosed bat of the family Rhinolophidae

rhi·no·loph·i·dae \,rīnə'läfə,dē\ *n pl, cap* [NL, fr. *Rhinolophus*, type genus (fr. *rhin-* + Gk *lophos* crest) + *-idae*] : a family of Old World leaf-nosed bats that includes many common horseshoe bats

¹**rhi·nol·o·phine** \rī'nälə,fīn, -,fən\ *adj* [NL *Rhinolophina* (syn. of *Rhinolophidae*), fr. *Rhinolophus* + *-ina*] : of or relating to the family Rhinolophidae

²**rhinolophine** \"\ *n* -S : a bat of the family Rhinolophidae

rhi·no·nic·ter·is \,rīnō'niktərəs\ *n, cap* [NL, fr. *rhin-* + Gk *nykteris* bat — more at NYCTERIS] : a genus of Australian bats related to *Hipposideros* and including solely the orange horseshoe bat

rhi·no·nys·si·dae \-'nisə,dē\ *n pl, cap* [NL, fr. *Rhinonyssus*, type genus (fr. *rhin-* + Gk *nyssein* to prick, sting) + *-idae* — more at NUMEN] : a widely distributed family of mites that are parasitic in the nasal passages of birds

rhi·no·pharyngitis \¦rī(,)nō+\ *n* [NL, fr. *rhin-* + *pharyngitis*] : inflammation of the mucous membrane of the nose and pharynx

rhi·no·pharynx \"+\ *n* [NL, fr. *rhin-* + *pharynx*] : NASOPHARYNX

rhi·noph·i·dae \rī'näfə,dē\ [NL, fr. *Rhinophid-*, *Rhinophis* + *-idae*] *syn of* UROPELTIDAE

rhi·no·phis \'rīnəfəs\ *n, cap* [NL, fr. *rhin-* + *-ophis*] : a genus of shieldtail snakes of the family Uropeltidae

rhi·no·pho·nia \,rīnə'fōnēə\ *n* -S [NL, fr. *rhin-* + *-phonia*] : marked nasal resonance

rhi·no·phore \'rīnə,fō(ə)r\ *n* -S [*rhin-* + *-phore*] : one of the two tentacles that are considered to be olfactory organs on the back of the head or neck of a mollusk of the order Opisthobranchia

rhi·no·phyma \¦rīnə+\ *n* [NL, fr. *rhin-* + *phyma*] : a nodular swelling and congestion of the nose in an advanced stage of acne rosacea

rhi·no·plas·tic \¦rīnə¦plastik\ *adj* [*rhin-* + *-plastic*] : of or relating to rhinoplasty

rhi·no·plas·ty \'==,plastē\ *n* -ES [ISV *rhin-* + *-plasty*] : plastic surgery of the nose

rhi·no·po·ma \,rīnə'pōmə\ *n, cap* [NL, fr. *rhin-* + Gk *pōma* lid, cover; akin to OE *fōdder* case, sheath — more at FUR] : a genus (coextensive with the family Rhinopomatidae) of insectivorous bats comprising the mouse-tailed bats

rhi·nop·tera \rī'näpt(ə)rə\ *n, cap* [NL, fr. *rhin-* + *-ptera*] : a genus of rays comprising the cow-nosed rays and being sometimes placed in a separate family but usu. included among the Myliobatidae

rhi·nor·rha·gia \,rīnə'rāj(ē)ə\ *n* -S [NL, fr. *rhin-* + *-rrhagia*] : NOSEBLEED

rhi·nor·rhea *or* **rhi·nor·rhoea** \-'rēə\ *n* -S [NL, fr. *rhin-* + *-rrhea*, *-rrhoea*] : excessive mucous secretion from the nose

rhinos *pl of* RHINO

rhi·no·scleroma \¦rī(,)nō+\ *n, pl* **rhinoscleromata** [NL, fr. *rhin-* + *scleroma*] : a chronic inflammatory disease of the nasopharyngeal mucosa that is characterized by the formation of granulomas and by dense induration of the tissues and nodular deformity

rhi·no·scope \'rīnə,skōp\ *n* [ISV *rhin-* + *-scope*] : an instrument for examining the cavities and passages of the nose

rhi·no·scop·ic \¦==¦skäpik\ *adj* [ISV *rhinoscopy* + *-ic*] : of or relating to rhinoscopy

rhi·nos·co·py \rī'näskəpē\ *n* -ES [ISV *rhin-* + *-scopy*] : examination of the nasal cavity and passages (as by means of a speculum or laryngoscopic mirror introduced into the pharynx)

rhi·no·spo·rid·i·o·sis \¦rī(,)nōspə,ridē'ōsəs\ *n, pl* **rhinosporidio·ses** \-dē'ō,sēz\ [NL, fr. *Rhinosporidium* + *-osis*] : a fungous disease of the external mucous membranes (as of the nose) that is characterized by the formation of pinkish red, friable, sessile, or pedunculate polyps and is believed to be caused by a microparasite (*Rhinosporidium seeberi*)

rhi·no·sporidium \¦rī(,)nō+\ *n* [NL, fr. *rhin-* + *sporidium*] **1** *cap* : a genus of microparasites that are associated with some types of nasal polyps in man and in horses and that are sometimes regarded as chytrids related to the Olpidiaceae but are now often held to be protozoans possibly related to the Sarcosporidia **2** *pl* **rhinosporidia** : a microparasite of the genus *Rhinosporidium*

rhi·no·ter·mit·i·dae \¦rī(,)nō(,)tər'mid·ə,dē\ *n pl, cap* [NL, fr. *Rhinotermit-*, *Rhinotermes*, type genus (fr. *rhin-* + *Termit-*, *Termes*) + *-idae*] : a large and widely distributed family of termites that occur in temperate, subtropical, and tropical regions

rhi·no·theca \¦rīnə+\ *n, pl* **rhinothecae** [NL, fr. *rhin-* + *theca*] : the sheath of the upper mandible of a bird — **rhi·no·thecal** \"+\ *adj*

-rhi·nus \'rīnəs\ *n comb form* [NL, fr. Gk *rhin-*, *rhis* nose — more at RHIN-] : one having (such) a nose — in generic names in zoology ⟨Mega*rhinus*⟩

rhipi- *comb form* [NL, fr. Gk *rhipid-*, *rhipis* fan] : RHIPID-

rhipi·ceph·a·lus \,ripə'sefələs\ *n, cap* [NL, fr. *rhipi-* + *-cephalus*] : a large and widely distributed genus of ixodid ticks that are parasitic on many mammals and some birds and include vectors of serious diseases (as Rocky Mountain spotted fever and east coast fever)

rhipid- *or* **rhipido-** *comb form* [NL, fr. Gk, fr. *rhipid-*, *rhipis* fan; akin to Gk *rhip-*, *rhips* wickerwork, *rhiptein* to throw, OHG *rīban* to grate, rub, turn, twist, MD *wriven* to rub, twist; basic meaning: turning] : fan — chiefly in taxonomic names ⟨*Rhipid*istia⟩ ⟨*Rhipido*glossa⟩

rhip·i·date \'ripə,dāt\ *adj* [*rhipid-* + *-ate*] : FAN-SHAPED

rhi·pid·i·a·ce·ae \rə,pidē'āsē,ē\ *n pl, cap* [NL, fr. *Rhipidium*, type genus + *-aceae*] : a family of phycomycetous fungi (order Leptomitales) that have the thallus differentiated into holdfast, basal cell, and hyphal branches

rhip·i·dist \'ripədəst\ *n* -S [NL *Rhipidistia*] : a fish or fossil of the order Rhipidistia

rhip·i·dis·tia \,ripə'distēə\ *n pl, cap* [NL, fr. *rhipid-* + Gk *histia*, pl. of *histion* sail; akin to Gk *histanai* to cause to stand — more at STAND] : an order of extinct crossopterygian fishes that have the basal bones of the median fins united into one mass — see HOLOPTYCHIIDAE, OSTEOLEPIDAE — **rhip·i·dis·ti·an** \¦==¦distēən\ *adj or n* — **rhip·i·dis·tid** \-təd\ *adj or n*

rhi·pid·i·um \-'pidēəm\ *n* -S [NL, fr. Gk *rhipidion* small bellows, dim. of *rhipid-*, *rhipis* fan] : a fan-shaped cymose inflorescence (as in some sedges) in which the branches lie in the same plane and are suppressed alternately on each side

rhip·i·do·glos·sa \,ripədō'gläsə, -lȯsə\ *n pl, cap* [NL, fr. *rhipid-* + *-glossa*] : a suborder of Aspidobranchia that comprises gastropod mollusks (as the abalones, the top shells, and the keyhole limpets) having a long radula with teeth that are long and hooklike in each transverse row and with indefinitely numerous marginal teeth becoming smaller toward the edges — see HELICINA — **rhip·i·do·glos·sal** \-səl\ *adj* — **rhip·i·do·glos·sate** \-sət, -,sāt\ *adj*

rhip·i·dop·tera \,ripə'däpt(ə)rə\ [NL, fr. *rhipid-* + *-ptera*] *syn of* STREPSIPTERA

rhip·i·dop·ter·ous \¦==¦däpt(ə)rəs\ *adj* [NL *Rhipidoptera* + E *-ous*] : STREPSIPTERAL

¹**rhi·piph·o·rid** \rə'pifərəd\ *adj* [NL *Rhipiphoridae*] : of or relating to the Rhipiphoridae

²**rhipiphorid** \"\ *n* -S : a beetle of the family Rhipiphoridae

rhip·i·phor·i·dae \,ripə'fȯrə,dē\ *n pl, cap* [NL, fr. *Rhipiphorus*, type genus (fr. *rhipi-* + *-phorus*) + *-idae*] : a family of small beetles that are parasitic on wasps and other insects, having a pointed abdomen, and undergo hypermetamorphosis

rhi·pip·tera \rə'pipt(ə)rə\ [NL, fr. *rhipi-* + *-ptera*] *syn of* STREPSIPTERA

rhi·pip·ter·ous \-)rəs\ *adj* [NL *Rhipiptera* + E *-ous*] : STREPSIPTERAL

rhip·sa·lis \rip'sāləs\ *n, cap* [NL, fr. Gk *rhip-*, *rhips* wickerwork + L *-alis* -al — more at RHIPID-] : a genus consisting of chiefly tropical American unarmed cacti that have fleshy mostly cylindrical stems of very diverse habit and small flowers with 6 to 10 petals followed by a berrylike fruit and are often epiphytes with pendent branches — see MISTLETOE CACTUS

rhip·to·glos·sa \,riptə'gläsə, -lȯsə\ *n pl, cap* [NL, fr. Gk *rhiptos* thrown (fr. *rhiptein* to throw) + NL *-glossa* — more at RHIPID-] : a division of reptiles often considered a superfamily of Lacertilia that comprises the Old World chameleons

rhiz- *or* **rhizo-** *comb form* [NL, fr. Gk, fr. *rhiza* — more at ROOT] : root ⟨*rhiz*anthous⟩ ⟨*Rhizo*mys⟩ ⟨*rhizo*philous⟩

-rhi·za or **-r·rhi·za** \'rīzə\ *n comb form, pl* **-rhi·zae** \-(,)zē\ or **-rhizas** or **-r·rhi·zae** or **-rrhizas** [NL, fr. Gk *rhiza* root] **1 :** root : part resembling or connected with a root ⟨coleo*rhiza*⟩ ⟨myco*rrhiza*⟩ **2 :** plant having (such) a root — in genus names in botany ⟨Balsamo*rrhiza*⟩

rhi·zan·thous \(')rī¦zan(t)thəs\ *adj* [ISV *rhiz-* + *-anthous*] **:** producing flowers apparently directly from the root

rhiz·autoicous \¦rīz+,ȯ¦tȯikəs\ *adj* [*rhiz-* + *autoicous*] **:** having the antheridia on a branch connected by rhizoids to the archegonial branch — used of mosses; compare CLADAUTOICOUS

rhi·zid·i·a·ce·ae \rə,zidē'āsē,ē\ *n pl, cap* [NL, fr. *Rhizidium*, type genus (fr. *rhiz-* + *-idium*) + *-aceae*] **:** a family of fungi (order Chytridiales) that are mostly ectoparasites on various algae and that have a plant body with a globose fertile portion and a vegetative portion of tapering rhizoidal branches

¹rhi·zi·na \rə'zīnə, -zēnə\ *n, cap* [NL, fr. *rhiz-* + *-ina*] **:** a genus of ascomycetous fungi (family Pezizaceae) that form flat ascocarps with rootlike outgrowths

²rhizina \"\ also **rhi·zine** \'rī,zīn, -zᵊn\ *n* -s [NL *rhizina*, fr. *rhiz-* + *-ina* -ine] **:** RHIZOID — **rhi·zi·nous** \rə'zīnəs, -'zēn-; 'rīzᵊn-\ *adj*

rhi·zo·bi·a·ce·ae \(,)rī,zōbē'āsē,ē\ *n pl, cap* [NL, fr. *Rhizobium*, type genus + *-aceae*] **:** a small family of rod-shaped or irregular usu. flagellated and gram-negative aerobic bacteria (order Eubacteriales) that includes saprophytes, important nitrogen-fixing symbionts of plants, and some plant pathogens — see AGROBACTERIUM, RHIZOBIUM

rhi·zo·bi·um \rī'zōbēəm\ *n* [NL, fr. *rhiz-* + *-bium*] **1** *cap* **:** the type genus of Rhizobiaceae comprising small heterotrophic soil bacteria capable of forming symbiotic nodules on the roots of leguminous plants and of there becoming bacteroids that fix atmospheric nitrogen **2** *pl* **rhizo·bia** \-ēə\ *often cap* **:** any bacterium of the genus *Rhizobium*

rhi·zo·caline \¦rī(,)zō+\ *n* [*rhiz-* + *caline*] **:** a hormone or hormonelike factor distinct from auxin that is held to play a role in the formation of plant roots — compare CAULOCALINE

rhi·zo·car·pous \¦rīzō¦kärpəs\ or **rhi·zo·car·pic** \-pik\ *adj* [*rhizocarpous* fr. *rhiz-* + *-carpous*; *rhizocarpic* ISV *rhiz-* + *-carpic*] **1 :** having perennial underground parts but annual stems and foliage — used of perennial herbs **2 :** producing hypogeal cleistogamous flowers

rhi·zo·caul \'rīzə,kȯl\ or **rhi·zo·cau·lus** \,==¦kȯləs\ *n, pl* **rhizocauls** \'==,kȯlz\ or **rhizocau·li** \,==¦kȯ,lī\ [NL *rhizocaulus*, fr. *rhiz-* + Gk *kaulos* stalk — more at COLE] **:** HYDRORHIZA

rhi·zo·ceph·a·la \,rīzō'sefələ\ *n pl, cap* [NL, fr. *rhiz-* + *-cephala*] **:** an order of Cirripedia comprising extremely degenerate forms that live as parasites on crabs and hermit crabs, are hermaphroditic though complementary males occur, when young pass through stages similar to those of a developing barnacle, and afterward attach themselves to suitable hosts where after a complex series of changes they become limbless unsegmented tumid sacs attached by a short peduncle from which rootlike processes penetrate to all parts of the host and absorb its juices — see PELTOGASTER, SACCULINA

rhi·zo·ceph·a·lan \-lən\ or **rhi·zo·ceph·a·lid** \-ləd\ *n* -s [NL *Rhizocephala* + E *-an* or *-id*] **:** a crustacean of the order Rhizocephala

rhi·zo·ceph·a·lous \¦==¦==ləs\ *adj* [NL *Rhizocephala* + E *-ous*] **:** of or relating to the Rhizocephala

rhi·zo·chlor·i·da·les \,rīzō,klōrə'dā(,)lēz\ *n pl, cap* [NL, fr. *Rhizochlorid-*, *Rhizochloris*, genus of yellow-green algae (fr. *rhiz-* + L *Chlorid-*, *Chloris*, goddess of flowers) + *-ales* — more at CHLORIS] **:** an order of yellow-green algae (class Xanthophyceae) that have the vegetative cells permanently amoeboid, are naked or partially surrounded by an envelope, and are often joined in groups by cytoplasmic bridges — see RHIZOCHRYSIDALES

rhi·zo·chrys·i·da·les \-,krisə'dā(,)lēz\ *n pl, cap* [NL, fr. *Rhizochrysid-*, *Rhizochrysis*, genus of yellow-green algae (fr. *rhiz-* + Gk *chrysid-*, *chrysis* vessel of gold) + *-ales* — more at CHRYSIS] **:** an order of yellow-green algae (class Xanthophyceae) that have the vegetable cells either amoeboid or with temporary flagellated stages but in other respects resemble the Rhizochloridales

rhi·zoc·to·nia \,rī,zäk'tōnēə\ *n* [NL, fr. *rhiz-* + Gk *ktonos* murder + NL *-ia* — more at -CTONUS] **1** *cap* **:** a form genus of imperfect fungi (order Mycelia Sterilia) that formerly included numerous fungi which since the discovery of their perfect stages have been placed in other genera (as *Corticium* and *Pellicularia*) **2** -s **:** any fungus now or formerly belonging to the form genus *Rhizoctonia*

rhizoctonia disease also **rhizoctonia** *n* -s [NL *Rhizoctonia*] **1 :** a disease caused by fungi of *Rhizoctonia* or closely related genera **2 :** a disease of potatoes caused by a fungus (*Pellicularia filamentosa* syn. *Rhizoctonia solani*) and characterized esp. by black scurfy spots on the tubers — called also *little potato, rosette, russet scab, stem canker;* compare DAMPING-OFF

rhi·zoc·to·ni·ose \-ē,ōs also -ōz\ *n* -s [NL *Rhizoctonia* + E *-ose*] **:** RHIZOCTONIA DISEASE 1

rhi·zo·dermis \¦rīzō+\ *n* -ES [ISV *rhiz-* + *-dermis*] **:** EPIBLEM

rhi·zo·din·i·a·les \,rīzō,dinē'ā(,)lēz\ *n pl, cap* [NL, prob. fr. *rhiz-* + *dini-* (fr. Gk *deinos* terrible) + *-ales* — more at DIRE] **:** an order of colorless marine algae (class Dinophyceae) having the vegetative cells naked and amoeboid

rhi·zo·gen \'rīzəjən, -,jen\ *adj* [ISV *rhiz-* + *-gen*] **:** RHIZOGENIC

rhi·zo·genesis \,rīzə+\ *n* [NL, fr. *rhiz-* + *genesis*] **:** root development

rhi·zo·gen·ic \¦rīzə¦jenik\ or **rhi·zo·ge·net·ic** \-jə¦ned·ik\ or **rhi·zog·e·nous** \(')rī¦zäjənəs\ *adj* [*rhiz-* + *-genic* or *-genetic* or *-genous*] **:** producing roots — used of the tissue of the pericycle in the roots of seed plants that gives rise to rootlets endogenously

rhi·zog·ly·phus \rī'zägləfəs\ *n, cap* [NL, fr. *rhiz-* + Gk *glyphē* carved work — more at GLYPH] **:** a widely distributed genus of mites including some that are injurious to winter wheat and rye and to lily and other bulbs — see BULB MITE

rhi·zo·graph \'rīzə,graf, -räf\ *n* [*rhiz-* + *-graph*] **:** a device to trace the movement of roots in the soil

¹rhi·zoid \'rī,zȯid\ *adj* [ISV *rhiz-* + *-oid*] **:** resembling a root

²rhizoid \"\ *n* -s [*rhiz-* + *-oid*] **:** a rootlike structure: as **a :** one of the slender unicellular or multicellular filaments that attach the gametophyte of a fern, moss, or liverwort to the substrate and that function as absorptive organs **b :** a similar process in a thallophyte that often forms a specially differentiated basal holdfast — called also *rhizina* **c :** any of various processes of animals (as those by which a rhizocephalan attaches to its host) — **rhi·zoi·dal** \(')rī¦zȯidᵊl\ *adj*

rhi·zo·ma \rī'zōmə\ *n, pl* **rhizoma·ta** \-məd·ə\ [NL] **:** RHIZOME

rhi·zo·mas·ti·gi·na \¦rī(,)zō,mastə'jīnə\ *n pl, cap* [NL, fr. *Rhizomastig-*, *Rhizomastix*, genus of protozoa (fr. *rhiz-* + Gk *mastig-*, *mastix* whip, scourge) + *-ina* — more at MASTIG-] **:** an order of Zoomastigina that comprises protozoans which have both flagella and pseudopods and which chiefly are obscure soil or water organisms though a few are commensals and one (*Histomonas meleagris*) causes the serious blackhead of turkeys and other fowl

rhi·zo·mat·ic \¦rīzə¦mad·ik\ *adj* [ISV *rhizomat-* (fr. NL *rhizomat-*, *rhizoma*) + *-ic*] **:** of, relating to, or resembling a rhizome

rhi·zom·a·tous \(')rī¦zäməd·əs, -zōm-\ *adj* [ISV *rhizomat-* (fr. NL *rhizomat-*, *rhizoma*) + *-ous*] **:** having the characteristics of or resembling a rhizome

rhizomatous begonia *n* **:** any of a group of begonias that have prominent horizontal or creeping shaggy stems or rhizomes — compare FIBROUS-ROOTED BEGONIA, TUBEROUS BEGONIA

rhi·zome \'rī,zōm\ *n* -s [NL *rhizoma*, fr. Gk *rhizōma* mass of roots (of a tree), stem, race, fr. *rhizoun* to cause to strike root, fr. *rhiza* root — more at ROOT] **1 :** a more or less elongate stem or branch of a plant that is often thickened or tuber-shaped as a result of deposits of reserve food material, is usu. horizontal and underground, produces shoots above and roots below, and is distinguished from a true root in possessing buds, nodes, and usu. scalelike leaves — called also *rootstalk;* compare BULB 1, CORM **2 :** STOLON 2

rhi·zomic \-zōmik, -zäm-\ *adj* [*rhizome* + *-ic*] **:** of, relating to, or made up of rhizomes

rhi·zo·morph \'rīzə,mȯrf\ *n* [NL *rhizomorpha*, fr. *rhiz-* + *-morpha*, fem. sing. of *-morphus* -morphous] **1 :** an aggregation of fungous threads intertwining like the strands of a rope that frequently resembles a root and is characteristic of many basidiomycetes (as *Armillaria mellea*) **2** [*rhiz-* + *-morph*] **:** the lower part of the short cormoid axis from which the true roots develop in members of the genus *Isoetes* and various other lower vascular plants — **rhi·zo·mor·phic** \¦==¦mȯrfik\ *adj*

rhi·zo·mor·phoid \¦==¦mȯr,fȯid\ *adj* [*rhiz-* + *morph-* + *-oid*] **:** RHIZOMORPHOUS

rhi·zo·mor·phous \-,fəs\ *adj* [ISV *rhiz-* + *-morphous*] **:** having the form of a root

rhi·zo·mycelial \¦rī(,)zō+\ *adj* [NL *rhizomycelium* + E *-al*] **:** of, relating to, or resembling a rhizomycelium

rhi·zo·mycelium \"+\ *n, pl* **rhizomycelia** [NL, fr. *rhiz-* + *mycelium*] **:** an aggregate of gradually attenuated hyphal branches (as in the fungi of the family Cladochytriaceae) having fertile regions developed at various points

¹rhi·zo·my·id \¦rīzō¦mīəd\ *adj* [NL *Rhizomyidae*] **:** of or relating to the Rhizomyidae

²rhizomyid \"\ *n* -s **:** a rodent of the family Rhizomyidae

rhi·zo·my·i·dae \,rīzō'mīə,dē\ *n pl, cap* [NL, fr. *Rhizomys*, type genus + *-idae*] **:** a family of Asiatic and African fossorial rodents that are related to but somewhat more specialized than the common murid rodents — see RHIZOMYS

rhi·zo·mys \'==,mis\ *n, cap* [NL, fr. *rhiz-* + *-mys*] **:** the type genus of Rhizomyidae comprising the oriental bamboo rats

rhi·zo·per·tha \,rīzō'pərthə\ *n, cap* [NL, fr. *rhiz-* + Gk *perthein* to plunder, sack; perh. akin to Gk *pherein* to carry — more at BEAR] **:** a genus of minute beetles (family Bostrychidae) that feed on grain and other seeds

rhi·zoph·o·ra \rī'zäfərə\ *n, cap* [NL, fr. *rhiz-* + *-phora*] **:** a small genus (the type of the family Rhizophoraceae) of tropical trees and shrubs that have tetramerous flowers and a partly inferior ovary forming a fleshy berry — see MANGROVE

rhi·zopho·ra·ce·ae \rī,zäfə'rāsē,ē, ,rīzəf-\ *n pl, cap* [NL, fr. *Rhizophora*, type genus + *-aceae*] **:** a family of trees and shrubs (order Myrtales) that usu. form dense jungles along tropical seacoasts and that have opposite coriaceous leaves, flowers with valvate calyx and 2- to 6-celled ovary, and seeds that germinate while the fruit is still attached — compare MANGROVE — **rhi·zopho·ra·ceous** \=¦==¦rāshəs, ¦===-\ *adj*

rhi·zo·phore \'rīzə,fō(ə)r\ *n* -s [ISV *rhiz-* + *-phore*] **:** one of the downward-growing leafless dichotomous shoots in club mosses of the genus *Selaginella* that bear tufts of adventitious roots at the apex

rhi·zo·plane \-,plān\ *n* [*rhiz-* + *plane*] **:** the external surface of roots together with closely adhering soil particles and debris ⟨the ~ forms a particular subdivision of a rhizosphere⟩

rhi·zo·plast \-,plast\ *n* -s [ISV *rhiz-* + *-plast*] **:** a fibril that connects the blepharoplast with the nucleus in flagellated cells or organisms

¹rhi·zo·pod \-,päd\ *adj* [NL *Rhizopoda*] **:** of or relating to the Rhizopoda

²rhizopod \"\ *n* -s **:** a protozoan of the subclass Rhizopoda

¹rhi·zop·o·da \rī'zäpədə\ *n pl, cap* [NL, fr. *rhiz-* + *-poda*] **:** a subclass of Sarcodina comprising usu. creeping protozoans with lobose or rootlike pseudopods and including the orders Amoebina, Testacea, and Foraminifera, and sometimes also Proteomyxa and Mycetozoa — **rhi·zop·o·dal** \(')rī¦zäpədᵊl\ *adj* — **rhi·zop·o·dan** \-dᵊn\ *adj or n* — **rhi·zop·o·dous** \-dəs\ *adj*

²rhizopoda \"\ [NL] *syn of* SARCODINA

rhi·zo·po·di·um \,rīzə'pōdēəm\ also **rhi·zo·pod** \'rīzə,päd\ *n* -s [NL *rhizopodium*, fr. *rhiz-* + *-podium*] **:** a filamentous branching anastomosing ectoplasmic pseudopodium that is typical of many foraminiferans and some testaceans

rhi·zo·po·gon \,rīzə'pō,gän\ *n, cap* [NL, fr. *rhiz-* + *-pogon*] **:** a genus of fungi (family Hymenogastraceae) that produce subterranean sporophores resembling tubers with 2-spored to 8-spored basidia in a compact gleba of irregular chambers

rhi·zop·ter·in \rī'zäptərən\ *n* -s [*rhiz-* + *pterin*] **:** a pale yellow crystalline aldehydo amino acid $C_{15}H_{12}N_6O_4$ obtained in the fumaric acid fermentation by a black mold (*Rhizopus nigricans*) that promotes the growth of several streptococci **:** a formyl derivative of pteroic acid

rhi·zo·pus \'rīzəpəs\ *n, cap* [NL, fr. *rhiz-* + *-pus*] **:** a genus of fungi (family Mucoraceae) that have columellate hemispherical aerial sporangia formed in fascicles anchored to the substrate and tufts of rhizoids or root hyphae connected by stolons — see BREAD MOLD, ²LEAK 3, RHIZ ROT; compare MUCOR, SOFT ROT

rhi·zo·sphere \'rīzə+,-\ *n* [ISV *rhiz-* + *sphere*] **:** soil that surrounds and is influenced by the roots of a plant — see RHIZOSPHERE EFFECT

rhizosphere effect *n* **:** the enhancement of the growth of a soil microorganism resulting from physical and chemical alteration of the soil and the contribution of excretions and organic debris of roots within a rhizosphere

rhi·zos·to·mae \rī'zästə,mē\ *n pl, cap* [NL, fr. *Rhizostoma*, genus of jellyfishes, fr. *rhiz-* + *-stoma*] **:** an order of Scyphozoa comprising jellyfishes that are related to the Semaeostomeae but are distinguished from them by fused oral lobes, by numerous small mouths replacing the primary mouth, and by the absence of tentacles and including various large jellyfishes that are dried and used as food in China and Japan — **rhi·zo·stoma·tous** \¦rīzə¦stōməd·əs, -täm-\ *adj* — **rhi·zo·stome** \'rīzə,stōm\ *n* -s — **rhi·zos·to·mous** \(')rī¦zästəməs\ *adj*

rhi·zo·sto·ma·ta \,rīzə'stōməd·ə\ [NL, fr. *rhiz-* + *-stomata*] *syn of* RHIZOSTOMAE

rhi·zo·ta \rī'zōd·ə\ *n pl, cap* [NL, irreg. fr. Gk *rhizoun* to cause to strike root — more at RHIZOME] *in some classifications* **:** an order of rotifers that when adult are attached by the truncated end of the tail — **rhi·zote** \'rī,zōt\ *adj* — **rhi·zotic** \(')rī¦zōd·ik, -zäd-\ *adj*

rhi·zot·o·my \rī'zäd·əmē\ *n* -ES [ISV *rhiz-* + *-tomy*] **:** the operation of cutting the anterior or posterior spinal nerve roots for therapeutic purposes

rhm \'rəm\ *n* -s [roentgen per hour at one meter] **:** a unit of gamma-ray source intensity equal to the intensity of a source that delivers one roentgen of gamma-ray dosage per hour at a distance of one meter

rh–negative *adj, usu cap R* **:** lacking Rh factor in the red blood cells

rho \'rō\ *n* -s [Gk *rhō*, of Sem origin; akin to Heb *rēsh*] **:** the 17th letter of the Greek alphabet — symbol P or ρ; see ALPHABET table

rhod- or **rhodo-** *comb form* [NL, fr. L, fr. Gk, fr. *rhodon* rose — more at ROSE] **:** rose : red ⟨*rhod*ium⟩ ⟨*rhodo*plast⟩

rho·damine \'rōdə,mēn, -,mən; rō'damən\ *n, often cap* [ISV *rhod-* + *amine*] **:** any of a group of yellowish red to blue fluorescent xanthene dyes: as **a** or **rhodamine B :** a brilliant bluish red basic dye made usu. by fusing *meta*-diethyl-aminophenol with phthalic anhydride and used chiefly in coloring paper, lacquers, and stains, in making organic pigments esp. for printing inks, and as a biological stain — see DYE table I (under *Basic Violet 10, Pigment Violet 1*, and *Solvent Red 49*) **b** or **rhodamine 6G :** a brilliant yellowish red basic dye made similarly from *meta*-ethyl-aminophenol and phthalic anhydride and used similarly — see DYE table I (under *Basic Red 1* and *Pigment Red 81*)

rho·danate \'rōdᵊn,āt, rō'danət\ *n* -s [*rhodan-* (in *rhodanic acid*) + *-ate*] **:** THIOCYANATE — not used systematically

rho·da·nese \'rōdᵊn,ēz, -ēs\ *n* -s [prob. irreg. fr. *rhodanic* (in *rhodanic acid*)] **:** a crystallizable enzyme that catalyzes the conversion of cyanide and thiosulfate or thiosulfonate to thiocyanate and sulfite and that occurs in animal tissues and bacteria

rho·dan·ic acid \(')rō¦danik-\ *n* [*rhodanic* ISV *rhodan-* (modif. of Gk *rhodon* rose) + *-ic*] **1 :** THIOCYANIC ACID — not used systematically **2 :** RHODANINE

rho·da·nide \'rōdᵊn,īd, rō'danəd\ *n* -s [ISV *rhodan-* (in *rhodanic acid*) + *-ide*] **:** THIOCYANATE — not used systematically

rho·danine \'rōdᵊn,ēn, rō'danən\ *n* -s [ISV *rhodan-* (in *rhodanic acid*) + *-ine*] **:** a pale yellow crystalline acidic derivative $C_3H_3NOS_2$ of thiazole that is formed by reaction of sodium chloroacetate, ammonia, and carbon disulfide or from ammonium thiocyanate and that condenses with aldehydes and many ketones to give colored products

¹rho·dan·the \rō'dan(t)thē\ [NL, fr. *rhod-* + Gk *anthos* flower — more at ANTHOLOGY] *syn of* HELIPTERUM

²rhodanthe \"\ *n* -s **:** an Australian annual everlasting (*Helipterum manglesii*) having nodding flower heads with scarious involucral bracts

rhode is·land \(')rō¦dīlənd, *before a consonant often* -n\ *adj, usu cap R&I* [fr. *Rhode Island*, northeastern state of the U. S., prob. modif. (influenced by D *Rood Eiland* Rhode Island, lit., red island, fr. *rood* red — fr. MD *root* — + *eiland* island — fr. MD *eilant*) of *Rhodes*, island of the eastern Mediterranean + E *island;* akin to OHG *rōt* red and to OFris *eiland* island; prob. fr. the belief that it was the size of the isle of Rhodes and that its Atlantic coast had a red appearance — more at RED, ISLAND] **:** of or from the state of Rhode Island **:** of the kind or style prevalent in Rhode Island

rhode island bent *n, usu cap R&I* **:** a lawn grass (*Agrostis tenuis*) of eastern No. America with very slender culms

rhode is·land·er \rō'dīləndə(r)\ *n, cap R&I* [*Rhode Island*, state of the U. S. + E *-er*] **:** a native or resident of the state of Rhode Island

rhode island red *n* [so called fr. its being bred first in Rhode Island] **1** *usu cap both Rs & I* **:** a leading American breed of general-purpose domestic fowls having a long heavy body, smooth yellow or reddish legs, rich brownish red plumage, and single or rose comb **2** *usu cap 1st R&I & often cap 2d R* **:** a bird of the Rhode Island Red breed

rhode island white *n* **1** *usu cap R&I&W* **:** an American breed of domestic fowls resembling Rhode Island reds but having pure white plumage **2** *usu cap R&I & often cap W* **:** a bird of the Rhode Island White breed

rho·de·ose \'rōdē,ōs *also* -,ōz\ *n* -s [Gk *rhodeos* of roses, rosy, fr. *rhodon* rose] **:** FUCOSE

rhodes grass \'rōdz-\ *n, usu cap R* [after Cecil J. *Rhodes* †1902 Eng. statesman and financier in So. Africa] **:** a perennial grass (*Chloris gayana*) native to southern Africa and introduced into the U. S. that is cultivated as a forage grass esp. in dry regions

rhodes–grass scale *n, usu cap R* **:** a mealybug (*Antonina graminis*) that is a serious pest on grass in the southern U. S.

rho·de·sia \rō'dēzh(ē)ə\ *adj, usu cap* [fr. *Rhodesia*, region in southern Africa] **:** of or from the region of Rhodesia **:** of the kind or style prevalent in Rhodesia

¹rho·de·sian \(')rō¦dēzh(ē)ən\ *adj, usu cap* [*Rhodesia* + E *-an*] **1 :** of, relating to, or characteristic of Rhodesia **2 :** of, relating to, or characteristic of the people of Rhodesia

²rhodesian \"\ *n* -s *cap* **:** a native or inhabitant of Rhodesia

rhodesian mahogany *n, usu cap R* **:** either of two African trees: **a :** POD MAHOGANY **b :** a southern African leguminous timber tree (*Copaifera coleosperma*) with very hard reddish wood used esp. for high-grade flooring

rhodesian man *n, usu cap R* [so called fr. the fact that remains of the type were found in Northern Rhodesia] **:** an extinct primitive African man (*Homo rhodesiensis* or *Africanthropus rhodesiensis*) of doubtful age and obscure affinities having long bones of modern type and prob. upright posture and a skull with very prominent brow ridges and large face but thoroughly human palate and dentition and a simple but relatively large brain — compare BOSKOP MAN

rhodesian ridgeback *n* **1** *usu cap both Rs* **:** an African breed of powerful long-bodied hunting dogs of uncertain ancestry having a dense harsh short coat in some shade of tan with a characteristic ridge or crest of reversed hair along the spine **2** *usu cap 1st R & often cap 2d R* **:** a dog of the Rhodesian Ridgeback breed used in its native area esp. for hunting the larger cats (as leopards or lions)

rhodesian teak *n, usu cap R* **:** a southern African leguminous timber tree (*Baikiaea plurijuga*) with very hard moderately heavy reddish brown wood that is highly resistant to insect attack and is used esp. for railroad ties and block flooring

rho·de·soid \rō'dē,zȯid\ *adj, usu cap* [*rhodesian* (in *rhodesian man*) + *-oid*] **:** resembling or having the characteristics of Rhodesian man

rhodes scholar \'rōdz'(s)kälə(r), -d'sk-\ *n, usu cap R* [after Cecil J. *Rhodes* †1902] **:** a holder of a Rhodes scholarship

rhodes scholarship *n, usu cap R* [after Cecil J. *Rhodes* †1902 Eng. statesman and financier in South Africa] **:** one of numerous scholarships founded under the will of Cecil J. Rhodes that are tenable at Oxford University for a term of two or three years and are distributed among candidates from the British Commonwealth, the U. S., and Germany

rhodes·wood \'rōdz,wu̇d\ *n* [prob. trans. of F *bois de Rhodes*] **:** a torchwood (*Amyris balsamifera*)

¹rho·di·an \'rōdēən\ *adj, usu cap* [L *rhodius* Rhodian (fr. *Rhodos*, *Rhodus* Rhodes, fr. Gk *Rhodos*) + E *-an*, adj. suffix] **1 :** of, relating to, or characteristic of Rhodes, an island of the eastern Mediterranean **2 :** of, relating to, or characteristic of the people of Rhodes

²rhodian \"\ *n* -s *cap* [L *rhodius*, adj., Rhodian + E *-an*, n. suffix] **:** a native or inhabitant of Rhodes

rho·din \'rōdᵊn\ also **rho·dine** \", -,dēn\ *n* -s [ISV *rhod-* + *-in*, *-ine*] **:** any of several derivatives of chlorophyll b that are formyl derivatives of the chlorins

rho·di·nal \'rōdᵊn,al\ *n* -s [ISV *rhodin-* (as in *rhodinol*) + *-al*] **:** levorotatory citronellol

rho·di·nol \'rōdᵊn,ōl, -,ȯl\ *n* -s [ISV *rhodin-* (fr. L *rhodinus* made from roses, fr. Gk *rhodinos*, fr. *rhodon* rose) + *-ol* — more at ROSE] **1 :** a liquid obtained usu. from geranium oil or rose oil, consisting essentially of citronellol and geraniol, and used in perfumes esp. of the rose type **2 :** levorotatory citronellol

rho·dite \'rō,dīt\ *n* -s [NL *rhodium* + E *-ite*] **:** a mineral consisting of a native alloy of rhodium and gold

rho·di·um \'rōdēəm\ *n* -s [NL, fr. *rhod-* + *-ium*] **:** a bright white hard ductile metallic element that is one of the platinum metals, that is chiefly trivalent and is resistant to attack by acids and other corrosive agents at ordinary temperatures, that occurs esp. in platinum ores, and that is used chiefly in alloys with platinum (as for catalysts, thermocouples, or spinnerets for rayon) and in plating for reflectors, electrical contacts, or jewelry — symbol *Rh;* see ELEMENT table

rhodium oil *n* [*rhodium* (*wood*) + *oil*] **1 :** a thick yellowish essential oil with roselike odor obtained from rhodium wood — called also *rosewood oil* **2 :** a commercial mixture containing rose oil

rhodium wood *n* [part trans. of NL *lignum rhodium*, fr. L *lignum* wood + NL *rhodium*, neut. of *rhodius* of the rose, fr. Gk *rhodon* rose] **:** the fragrant wood of the root and stem of either of two shrubs (*Convolvulus scoparius* and *C. virgatus*) native to the island of Teneriffe

rhodi·zite \'rōdə,zīt, 'räd-\ *n* -s [G *rhodizit*, fr. Gk *rhodizein* to be rose-red (fr. *rhodon* rose + *-izein* -ize) + G *-it* -ite; fr. its reddening effect on the blowpipe flame] **:** a mineral $NaKLiAl_4Be_3B_{10}O_{27}$ consisting of a borate of aluminum, beryllium, lithium, potassium, and sodium occurring in white isometric crystals (hardness 8, sp. gr. 3.4)

rho·di·zon·ic acid \¦rōdə¦zänik-\ *n* [G *rhodizon-* (in *rhodizonsäure* rhodizonic acid, fr. Gk *rhodizein* to be rose-red + G *säure* acid) + E *-ic*] **:** a cyclic acid $C_6H_2O_6$ known in an unstable colored enediol form and a colorless more stable tautomeric form but obtained usu. in the form of a colored salt (as the red disodium salt by passing carbon monoxide into a solution of sodium in liquid ammonia)

rhod·ni·us \'rädnēəs\ *n, cap* [NL, prob. irreg. fr. Gk *rhodon* rose; fr. the pink body fluid] **:** a genus of reduviid bugs including some that are intermediate hosts of the trypanosome causing Chagas' disease

rhodo- — see RHOD-

rho·do·bac·te·ri·a·ce·ae \¦rō(,)dō(,)bak,tirē'āsē,ē\ *n pl, cap* [NL, fr. *Rhodobacterium*, type genus (fr. *rhod-* + *Bacterium*) + *-aceae*] *in some classifications* **:** a family of Thiobacteriales coextensive with Rhodobacteriinae

rho·do·bac·te·ri·a·les \-ā(,)lēz\ *n pl, cap* [NL, fr. *Rhodobacterium* + *-ales*] *in some classifications* **:** an order of bacteria coextensive with Rhodobacteriinae

rho·do·bac·te·ri·inae *n pl, cap* \-rē'ī(,)nē\ [NL, fr. *Rhodobacterium* + *-inae*] **:** a suborder of Pseudomonadales comprising bacteria that contain bacteriochlorophyll or a related green pigment and carry on a form of photosynthesis not resulting in release of free oxygen but requiring extraneous oxidizable material (as hydrogen, reduced sulfur compounds, or alcohols) which is dehydrogenated with concurrent reduction of carbon dioxide to form water as a metabolic end product

rho·do·chro·site \ˌrōdəˈkrōˌsīt, rōˈdäkrəˌs-\ *n* -s [G *rhodochrosit*, fr. *rhod-* + Gk *chrōsis* coloring (fr. *chrōs*, *chroos* color, skin) + G *-it* -ite — more at CHROMATIC] **:** a characteristically rose red mineral $MnCO_3$ consisting essentially of manganese carbonate that is isomorphous with calcite and siderite and commonly occurs massive with rhombohedral cleavage like calcite (hardness 3.5–4.5, sp. gr. 3.45–3.60)

rho·do·den·dron \ˌrōdəˈdendrən\ *n* [NL, fr. L, fr. Gk, fr. *rhodon* rose + *dendron* tree — more at ROSE, DENDR-] **1** *cap* **:** a genus of shrubs or trees (family Ericaceae) that are native to the cooler regions of the northern hemisphere and are cultivated widely and that have alternate short-petioled often leathery leaves scattered or in clusters at the branch ends and flowers in terminal umbellate racemes **2** -s **:** any of various plants of the genus *Rhododendron* with persistent leathery leaves and campanulate flowers — compare AZALEA

rho·do·lite \ˈrōdᵊlˌīt\ *n* -s [*rhod-* + *-lite*] **:** a pink or purple garnet intermediate between pyrope and almandite that is used as a gem

rho·dom·e·la·ce·ae \rōˌdämōˈlāsēˌē\ *n pl, cap* [NL, fr. *Rhodomela*, type genus (fr. *rhod-* + Gk *melas* black) + *-aceae* — more at MULLET] **:** a large family of filamentous red algae (order Rhodymeniales) characterized by a much-branched thallus in which the main axis and branches consist of a polysiphonic arrangement of filaments — **rho·dom·e·la·ceous** \ˌ=ˌ==ˈlāshəs\ *adj*

rho·do·microbium \ˌrō(ˌ)dō+\ *n, cap* [NL, fr. *rhod-* + *microbium*] **:** a genus of reddish nitrogen-fixing soil bacteria (family Hyphomicrobiaceae)

rhodomontade *var of* RODOMONTADE

rho·do·nite \ˈrōdᵊnˌīt\ *n* -s [G *rhodonit*, fr. Gk *rhodon* rose + G *-it* -ite] **:** a pale red triclinic mineral $MnSiO_3$ consisting essentially of manganese silicate that commonly occurs massive and is used as an ornamental stone esp. in Russia (hardness 5.5–6.5, sp. gr. 3.40–3.68) — called also *manganese spar*

rhodonite pink *n* **:** a dark purplish pink that is redder and less strong than clover pink or Persian lilac

rhod·o·pe \ˈrädə(ˌ)pē\ *n, cap* [NL, prob. fr. Gk *Rhodopē*, nymph of a Thracian well] **:** a genus of minute marine animals that resemble planarians but are commonly regarded as degenerate nudibranch mollusks because of the structure of their nervous system

rho·do·phy·ce·ae \ˌrōdōˈfīsēˌē\ *n pl, cap* [NL, fr. *rhod-* + *-phyceae*] **:** a class of chiefly marine multicellular algae (division Rhodophyta) comprising algae in which red phycoerythrin and sometimes blue phycocyanin mask the chlorophyll, in which no motile form or stage exists, and in which there is a well-marked and often complex alternation of generations — compare RED ALGA — **rho·do·phyce·ous** \ˌ=ˌ=ˈfisēəs, -ˈfis-\ *adj*

rho·doph·y·ta \rōˈdäfədə\ *n pl, cap* [NL, fr. *rhod-* + *-phyta*] **:** a division or other category of lower plants coextensive with the class Rhodophyceae

rho·do·plast \ˈrōdəˌplast\ *n* -s [ISV *rhod-* + *-plast*] **:** one of the reddish chromatophores occurring in the red algae — compare PHAEOPLAST

rho·dop·sin \rōˈdäpsən\ *n* -s [ISV *rhod-* + *ops-* (fr. Gk *opsis* sight) + *-in* — more at -OPSIS] **:** a brilliant red photosensitive pigment in the retinal rods of marine fishes and most higher vertebrates that is important in vision in dim light and that is quickly bleached by light to a mixture of opsin and the retinene related to vitamin A_1 and is regenerated in the dark — called also *visual purple;* compare OPTOGRAM, PORPHYROPSIN

rho·do·ra \rəˈdōrə\ *n* [NL, fr. L, a plant] **1** *cap* **:** a genus closely related to *Rhododendron* and comprising shrubs that are found in Canada and New England and have delicate pink flowers produced before or with the leaves in the spring **2** -s **:** any plant of the genus *Rhodora*

rho·do·sper·me·ae \ˌrōdəˈspərmēˌē\ *n pl, cap* [NL, fr. *rhod-* + *-spermeae*] *syn of* RHODOPHYCEAE

rho·do·sper·min \-mən\ *n* [ISV *rhod-* + *sperm-* + *-in*] **:** PHYCOERYTHRIN

rho·do·sper·mous \ˌ=ˌ=ˈspərməs\ *adj* [*rhod-* + *-spermous*] **:** RHODOPHYCEOUS

rho·do·spirillum \ˌrō(ˌ)dō+\ *n, cap* [NL, fr. *rhod-* + *Spirillum*] **:** a genus of spiral actively motile bacteria (family Athiorhodaceae) that live in mud and stagnant water and are held to fix atmospheric nitrogen

rho·do·ty·pos \ˌrōdəˈtīpəs\ *n, cap* [NL, fr. *rhod-* + Gk *typos* model — more at TYPE] **:** a genus of Japanese shrubs (family Rosaceae) having solitary white tetramerous flowers and shining black persistent drupelets — see JETBEAD

rho·dy·me·nia \ˌrōdəˈmēnēə\ *n, cap* [NL, fr. *rhod-* + Gk *hymēn* membrane + NL *-ia* — more at HYMEN] **:** a genus of red algae (the type of the family Rhodymeniaceae) having a thallus that consists of numerous leaflike divisions — see DULSE

rho·dy·me·ni·a·ce·ae \ˌrōdəˌmēnēˈāsēˌē\ *n pl, cap* [NL, fr. *Rhodymenia*, type genus + *-aceae*] **:** a family of red algae (order Rhodymeniales) — **rho·dy·me·ni·a·ceous** \ˌrōdəˌmēnēˈāshəs\ *adj*

rho·dy·me·ni·a·les \ˌrōdəˌmēnēˈā(ˌ)lēz\ *n pl, cap* [NL, fr. *Rhodymenia* + *-ales*] **:** an order of red algae (subclass Florideae) that resemble those of the order Ceramiales but are distinguished by having the auxiliary cell formed prior to fertilization

rhoe·ada·les \ˌrēəˈdā(ˌ)lēz\ *n pl, cap* [NL, fr. Gk *rhoiad-*, *rhoias* corn poppy + NL *-ales*] **:** an order of dicotyledonous plants including the families Papaveraceae, Fumariaceae, and Cruciferae and having regular or irregular cyclic flowers with hypogynous stamens and a superior compound ovary

rhoeadine *var of* RHEADINE

rhoeo \ˈrē(ˌ)ō\ *n, cap* [NL] **:** a monotypic genus of herbs (family Commelinaceae) — see OYSTER PLANT 3

rhomb \ˈräm(b)\ *n* -s [MF *rhombe*, fr. L *rhombus*, fr. Gk *rhombos* rhombus, spinning top, magic wheel; akin to Gk *rhembein* to whirl — more at VERVAIN] **1 :** RHOMBUS **2** *obs* **:** CIRCLE, WHEEL **3 :** RHOMBOHEDRON

rhomb- *or* **rhombo-** *comb form* [MF, fr. L, fr. Gk, fr. *rhombos* rhomb] **1 :** rhomb ⟨*rhomb*encephalon⟩ ⟨*rhombo*hedron⟩ **2 :** rhombic and ⟨*rhombo*quadratic⟩ ⟨*rhombo*vate⟩

rhomb·encephalon \ˌräm,b+\ *n, pl* **rhombencephala** [NL, fr. *rhomb-* + *encephalon*] **:** the parts of the definitive vertebrate brain that develop from the embryonic hindbrain; *sometimes* **:** HINDBRAIN 1a

rhombi *pl of* RHOMBUS

¹rhom·bic \ˈrämbik\ *adj* [*rhomb-* + *-ic*] **1 :** having the form of a rhombus **2 :** ORTHORHOMBIC

²rhombic \"\ *or* **rhombic antenna** *also* **rhombic aerial** *n* -s **:** an aerial antenna with pronounced directional characteristics

rhombic sulfur *n* **:** the familiar yellow orthorhombic crystalline form of sulfur of density 2.07 that changes to the monoclinic form at 95.5° C

rhom·bi·form \ˈrämbəˌfȯrm\ *adj* [*rhomb-* + *-iform*] **1 :** RHOMBIC **2 :** RHOMBOID

rhom·bo·clase \ˈrämbəˌklās, -āz\ *n* -s [Hung *rhomboklas*, fr. *rhomb-* + *-klas* -clase] **:** a mineral $HFe(SO_4)_2.4H_2O$ consisting of a hydrous acid ferric sulfate and occurring in colorless rhombic plates with basal cleavage

rhom·bo·gan·oid \ˌrämbōˈgaˌnȯid\ *n* [NL *Rhomboganoidei*] **:** HOLOSTEAN

rhom·bo·ga·noi·dei \ˌräm(ˌ)bōgəˈnȯidēˌī\ *n pl, cap* [NL, fr. *rhomb-* + *Ganoidei*] *in some classifications* **:** an order or other group coextensive with Holostei in its narrowest scope

rhom·bo·gen \ˈrämbəjən, -ˌjen\ *or* **rhom·bo·gene** \-ˌjēn\ *n* -s [*rhomb-* + *-gen*, *-gene*] **:** the form of a mesozoan of the order Dicyemida that occurs in the sexually mature host, arises from a final generation of nematogens, and gives rise to free-swimming ciliated larvae — compare INFUSORIGEN — **rhom·bo·gen·ic** \ˌrämbəˈjenik\ *adj* — **rhom·bog·e·nous** \(ˈ)rämˈbäjənəs\ *adj*

rhom·bo·he·dral \ˌrämbōˈhēdrəl *sometimes chiefly Brit* -ˈhed-\ *adj* [NL *rhombohedron* + E *-al*] **1 :** relating to or having the form of a rhombohedron or a form derivable from a rhombohedron **2 :** of or relating to the rhombohedral system — **rhom·bo·he·dral·ly** \-drəlē\ *adv*

rhombohedral iron ore *n* **1 :** HEMATITE **2 :** ²SIDERITE

rhombohedral system *n* **:** a crystal system characterized by three equal and interchangeable axes at equal angles to each other and usu. classed as a division of the hexagonal system — compare TETRAGONAL SYSTEM

rhom·bo·he·dric \-drik\ *adj* [ISV *rhombohedr-* (fr. NL *rhombohedron*) + *-ic;* orig. formed as F *rhombohédrique*] **:** RHOMBOHEDRAL

rhom·bo·he·dron \-drən *sometimes* -ˌdrän\ *n, pl* **rhombohedrons** \-drənz\ *or* **rhombohe·dra** \-drə\ [NL, fr. *rhomb-* + *-hedron*] **:** a parallelepiped whose faces are rhombuses

¹rhom·boid \ˈrämˌbȯid\ *n* -s [MF *rhomboïde*, fr. L *rhomboides*, fr. Gk *rhomboeidēs* rhombus-shaped, rhomboidal, fr. *rhombos* rhomb + *-oeidēs* -oid — more at RHOMB] **:** a parallelogram in which the angles are oblique and adjacent sides are unequal

rhomboid

²rhomboid \"\ *adj* [*rhomb-* + *-oid*] **1 :** shaped somewhat like a rhombus **2 :** RHOMBOIDAL

rhom·boi·dal \(ˈ)rämˈbȯidᵊl\ *adj* [¹*rhomboid* + *-al*] **:** shaped somewhat like a rhomboid

rhom·boi·des \rämˈbȯi(ˌ)dēz\ *n* [L] **1** *archaic* **:** RHOMBOID **2** *archaic* **:** RHOMBOIDEUS

rhom·boi·de·us \rämˈbȯidēəs\ *n, pl* **rhomboi·dei** \-ēˌī\ [NL, lit., rhomb-like, fr. L *rhomboides* + *-eus* -eous] **:** either of two muscles that lie beneath the trapezius muscle and connect the spinous processes of various vertebrae with the medial border of the scapula: **a** *or* **rhomboideus minor :** a muscle arising from part of the ligamentum nuchae and the last cervical and first thoracic vertebrae **b** *or* **rhomboideus major :** a muscle arising from the four or five upper thoracic vertebrae and the supraspinous ligament

rhomboid fossa *n* **:** the floor of the fourth ventricle of the brain

rhom·boid·ly *adv* [²*rhomboid* + *-ly*] **:** in a rhomboid form

rhom·bo·zoa \ˌrämbəˈzōə\ [NL, fr. *rhomb-* + *-zoa*] *syn of* MESOZOA

rhombs *pl of* RHOMB

rhomb spar *n* **:** dolomite esp. in rhombohedral crystals

rhom·bus \ˈrämbəs\ *n, pl* **rhombuses** \-bəsəz\ *or* **rhom·bi** \-ˌbī\ [L — more at RHOMB] **:** an equilateral parallelogram

rhombus

rhon·chi·al \ˈräŋkēəl\ *adj* [LL *rhonchus* + E *-ial*] **1 :** of or relating to a rhonchus **2 :** due to rhonchi

rhon·chus \-ŋkəs\ *n, pl* **rhon·chi** \-nˌkī, -ŋ,-, -ˌkē\ [LL, act of snoring, fr. Gk *rhonchos*, *rhonkos* snoring, wheezing — more at RHYNCH-] **:** a whistling or snoring sound heard on auscultation of the chest when the air channels are partly obstructed — compare RALE

rhon·dda \ˈrändə, -nthə\ *adj, usu cap* [fr. *Rhondda*, Wales] **:** of or from the urban district of Rhondda **:** of the kind prevalent in Rhondda

rhopal- *or* **rhopalo-** *comb form* [LL, fr. Gk, fr. *rhopalon*] **:** club ⟨*Rhopalo*cera⟩ ⟨*Rhopal*ura⟩ — in taxonomic names in zoology

¹rho·pal·ic *or* **ro·pal·ic** \(ˈ)rōˈpalik\ *adj* [LL *rhopalicus*, fr. Gk, *rhopalikos* rhopalic, like a club (i.e., thicker toward the end), fr. *rhopalon* club + *-ikos* -ic; perh. akin to Gk *rhabdos* rod — more at VERVAIN] **:** having each succeeding unit in a prosodic series larger or longer than the preceding one: **a :** having each successive word in a line or verse longer by one syllable than its predecessor **b :** having successive lines of a stanza increasing in length by the addition of one element (as a syllable or metrical foot)

²rhopalic \"\ *n* -s **:** a rhopalic line, verse, or stanza

rho·pa·li·oid \rōˈpalēˌȯid\ *n* -s [NL *rhopalium* + E *-oid*] **:** an organ of some scyphozoans that resembles a rhopalium

rho·pa·lism \ˈrōpəˌlizəm\ *n* -s [¹*rhopalic* + *-ism*] **1 :** the quality or state of being rhopalic **2 :** the use or production of rhopalic forms **3 :** an instance of rhopalic form in verse

rho·pa·li·um \rōˈpalēəm\ *n, pl* **rhopa·lia** \-ēə\ [NL, fr. Gk *rhopalion*, dim. of *rhopalon* club] **:** one of the marginal sensory bodies of a discomedusan

rho·pa·loc·era \ˌrōpəˈläsərə\ *n pl, cap* [NL, fr. *rhopal-* + *-cera*] **:** a division of Lepidoptera consisting of the butterflies — compare HETEROCERA — **rho·pa·loc·er·al** \ˌrōpəˈläsərəl\ *adj* — **rho·pa·loc·er·ous** \-sərəs\ *adj*

rho·pa·lo·cer·cous \ˌrōpəlōˈsərkəs\ *adj* [*rhopal-* + *-cercous* (fr. Gk *kerkos* tail)] *of a cercaria* **:** having a tail as wide as or wider than the body

rho·pa·lo·si·phum \-ˈsīfəm\ *n, cap* [NL, prob. fr. *rhopal-* + Gk *siphōn* tube, pipe — more at SIPHON] **:** a widely distributed genus of aphids including several that attack numerous crop plants and some that are vectors of plant viruses — see APPLE GRAIN APHID, CORN LEAF APHID

rho·pa·lu·ra \ˌrōpəˈlurə\ *n, cap* [NL, fr. *rhopal-* + *-ura*] **:** the chief genus of Orthonectida

rhos *pl of* RHO

rho·ta·cism \ˈrōdəˌsizəm\ *also* **rho·ta·cis·mus** \ˌ==ˈsizməs\ *or* **ro·ta·cism** \ˈ==ˌsizəm\ *n* -s [NL *rhotacismus*, fr. MGk *rhōtakizein* to make too much or wrong use of the letter rho or r (fr. *rhō* rho) + L *-ismus* -ism — more at RHO] **1 :** a defective pronunciation of *r; esp* **:** substitution of some other sound for that of *r* **2 :** the change of the sound \z\ to \r\ esp. common between vowels (as in forlo*r*n [lose] or Latin gene*r*is [Sanskrit janasas])

rho·ta·cize \-ˌsīz\ *vi* -ED/-ING/-S [MGk *rhōtakizein*] **:** to undergo or produce rhotacism

rh–positive *adj, usu cap R* **:** containing Rh factor in the red blood cells

RHQ *abbr* regimental headquarters

RHS *abbr, often not cap* right-hand side

rhu·barb \ˈrüˌbärb, -ˌbȧb\ *n* -s [ME *rubarbe*, fr. MF *rubarbe*, *reubarbe*, prob. fr. ML *reubarbum*, alter. of *reubarbarum*, prob. alter. of *rha barbarum* barbarian rhubarb, fr. LL *rha* rhubarb (fr. Gk *rha*, *rhēon*, perh. fr. *Rha* Volga river) + L *barbarum*, neut. of *barbarus* barbarous, barbarian — more at BARBAROUS] **1 :** a plant of the genus *Rheum* (as *R. rhaponticum*, *R. officinale*, or *R. palmatum*) having large leaves with thick succulent petioles that are often eaten as a sauce, in pies, or in preserves **2 :** the dried rhizome and roots of any of several herbs of the genus *Rheum* (as *R. officinale* and *R. palmatum*) grown in China and Tibet and used as a purgative and stomachic bitter **3 :** CITRINE 1 **4 :** a heated dispute or controversy **:** ROW ⟨election was no hotter than the ∼ which followed it —*News of Orange County (Hillsboro, N.C.)*⟩; *specif* **:** a dispute on the field during a baseball game ⟨beanball throwing, deliberately manufactured ∼s and umpire baiting —John Durant⟩ **5** *chiefly dial* **:** an aerial strafing mission against targets of opportunity ⟨when a fighter pilot flies low over France, strafing whatever he finds — trains, troops, airdromes — he is on a ∼ —*Time*⟩ **6** *slang* **:** an out-of-the-way sparsely populated countrified area ⟨the slick chick from the deep ∼ —W.M.Swann⟩

rhum \ˈrəm, ˈrȯm\ *n* -s [F, fr. E *rum* — more at RUM] **:** RUM

rhumb \ˈrəm(b)\ *n* -s [earlier *rumb*, fr. OSp *rumbo* or MF *rumb*, prob. modif. (influenced by L *rhombus* rhomb) of MD *ruum*, *rume* space, room, hold (of a ship); akin to OHG *rūm* space, room — more at RHOMB, ROOM] **1 :** RHUMB LINE **2 :** one of the points of the mariner's compass — compare COMPASS CARD

rhum·ba \ˈrəmbə, ˈrüm-, ˈrüm-\ *var of* RUMBA

rhum·ba·tron \-bəˌträn\ *n* -s [*rhumba* + *-tron;* fr. the rhythmic oscillation of the waves inside it] **:** the buncher and catcher singly or in combination in a klystron

rhumb line \ˈrəmˌlīn\ *n* **:** a line on the surface of the earth that makes equal oblique angles with all meridians, that is a spiral coiling round the poles but never reaching them, and that is the path of a ship sailing always oblique to the meridian in the direction of one and the same point of the compass ⟨the only projection on which the *rhumb line* on the earth is reduced to a straight line on the map is the Mercator projection —C.H. Deetz⟩ — called also *loxodrome*, *loxodromic curve*

rhu·punt \ˈrēˌpint\ *n* -s [W] **:** a Welsh verse composed of three, four, or five four-syllable sections linked by cynghanedd and rhyme, the first three sections made to rhyme with each other and the fourth section to rhyme with the fourth of the next verse, and the whole written as a single line or divided into as many lines as it has rhyming sections

rhus \ˈrəs, ˈrüs\ *n* [NL, fr. L, sumac, fr. Gk *rhous*] **1** *cap* **:** a genus of shrubs and trees (family Anacardiaceae) native to temperate and warm regions having simple or pinnate leaves and small polygamous flowers in panicles with persistent calyx and one-ovuled ovary that produces a small one-seeded drupe — see POISON IVY, POISON OAK, STAGHORN SUMAC **2** *pl* **rhuses** *or* **rhus :** any plant of the genus *Rhus*

rhus dermatitis *n* **:** dermatitis caused by contact with various plants of the genus *Rhus* and esp. with the common poison ivy (*R. toxicodendron*)

rhus gla·bra \-ˈglābrə, -läb-\ *n* [NL, lit., bald rhus] **:** the dried ripe fruit of the smooth sumac used as an astringent, in gargles, and as a refrigerant

rhu·sio·path·ia \ˌrüzēōˈpathēə\ *n* -s [NL, prob. fr. Gk *rhysos* shriveled, wrinkled + NL *-pathia* — more at RHYSSA] **:** SWINE ERYSIPELAS

rhy·ac·o·lite \rīˈakəˌlīt\ *n* -s [G *ryakolith*, fr. *ryako-* (fr. Gk *rhyak-*, *rhyax* stream, stream of lava) + *-lith* -lite; akin to Gk *rhein* to flow — more at STREAM] **:** SANIDINE

rhy·aco·phil·i·dae \(ˌ)rīˌakōˈfiləˌdē, ˌrīakōˈf-\ *n pl, cap* [NL, fr. *Rhyacophila*, type genus (fr. Gk *rhyak-*, *rhyax* stream + NL *-phila*) + *-idae*] **:** a large and widely distributed family of caddis flies

¹rhyme *or* **rime** \ˈrīm\ *n* -s [*rhyme* alter. (influenced by L *rhythmus* rhythm) of *rime; rime* fr. ME *rime*, *ryme*, fr. OF *rime*, prob. modif. (influenced by OHG *rīm* number, series) of L *rhythmus* rhythm — more at RITE, RHYTHM] **1 a :** correspondence in terminal sounds of two or more words, lines of verse, or other units of composition or utterance: as (1) *also* **rhyme proper :** correspondence of the last accented vowels and all succeeding sounds in two lines or units esp. (as in English verse) when the sounds preceding the last accented vowel are different in the two rhyming units (2) **:** ASSONANCE 2 b (3) **:** CONSONANCE 2 d **b :** one of two or more words thus corresponding in sound ⟨*fall*, *appall*, *haul*, and *awl* are approved ∼*s*⟩ ⟨there were no more ∼*s* for *sky* —Lord Dunsany⟩ **c :** correspondence of other than terminal word sounds: as (1) **:** BEGINNING RHYME (2) **:** ALLITERATION (3) **:** INTERNAL RHYME **d :** RHYME SCHEME **2 a** (1) **:** rhyming verse ⟨some love of yours has writ to you in ∼ —Shak.⟩ (2) **:** POETRY ⟨there is no such thing as a dialect for ∼, or a language for verse —John Ruskin⟩ ⟨in the style of folk ∼ —H.W.Wells⟩ ⟨writers of pleasant ∼*s* —*Australasian*⟩ **b :** a composition in verse that rhymes ⟨my passionate ∼ —W.B. Yeats⟩ ⟨gave us an extraordinary English doggerel ∼ —J.M. Synge⟩ **3 :** RHYTHM, MEASURE ⟨gay broad leaves shone and swung in ∼ —John Galsworthy⟩

²rhyme *or* **rime** \"\ *vb* **rhymed** *or* **rimed; rhymed** *or* **rimed; rhyming** *or* **riming; rhymes** *or* **rimes** [*rhyme* alter. (influenced by ¹*rhyme*) of *rime; rime* fr. ME *rimen*, *rymen*, fr. OF *rimer*, fr. *rime* rhyme] *vi* **1 :** to make rhymes **:** compose rhyming verse ⟨talked nothing but blank verse for the rest of the afternoon, except once or twice when she *rhymed* —J.B.S. Haldane⟩ ⟨how vilely doth this cynic ∼ —Shak.⟩ **2 a** *of a word or verse* **:** to end in syllables that rhyme **:** form a rhyme ⟨the middle line of each terzina, or triplet, ∼*s* with the first and third lines of the next —J.A.Macy⟩ **b** *of a word or syllable* **:** to be a rhyme ⟨since stressed can ∼ with unstressed syllables the number of possible full rhymes in English is greatly extended —G.S.Fraser⟩ ⟨*cover* ∼*s* with *lover*⟩ **3 :** to be in accord **:** HARMONIZE ⟨the sun, the banners, the rose leaves, the young children . . . ∼ with the new joy and innocence to be achieved —George Santayana⟩ ∼ *vt* **1 a :** to relate or praise in rhyming verse ⟨∼*s* the struggles of the first settlers —Katharine L. Bates⟩ **b :** to put into rhyme ⟨if I could have the wish I ∼ —H.A.Blood⟩ **c :** to compose (verse) in rhyme ⟨I *rhymed* out poetry in my youth —Donagh MacDonagh⟩ **d :** to cause to rhyme **:** use as rhyme ⟨*sleight* is *rhymed* with *counterfeit* as well as *height* —*Notes & Queries*⟩ **2 :** to drive or bring to a particular state or condition by rhyming or a rhyme ⟨pretty friendship 'tis to ∼ your friends to death before their time —A.E.Housman⟩

rhyme·less \ˈrīmləs\ *adj* **:** lacking rhyme **:** UNRHYMED

rhyme or reason *n* [trans. of F (*sans*) *rime ni raison* (without) rhyme or reason] **:** GOOD SENSE, REASON, REASONABLENESS ⟨the order of entries is utterly without *rhyme or reason* —*Saturday Rev.*⟩

rhym·er *or* **rim·er** \ˈrīmə(r)\ *n* -s [*rhymer* alter. (influenced by ¹*rhyme*) of *rimer; rimer* alter. (influenced by *-er*) of ME *rymor*, fr. MF *rimeur*, fr. OF, fr. *rime* rhyme + *-eur* -or] **:** one that makes rhymes **:** VERSIFIER; *specif* **:** a mediocre poet

rhyme royal *n, pl* **rhyme royals :** a stanza of seven lines in iambic pentameter in which the first and third, the second, fourth, and fifth, and the sixth and seventh lines rhyme — compare BALLADE ROYAL, CHANT ROYAL, SEPTET

rhyme scheme *n* **:** the arrangement of rhymes in a stanza or a poem

rhyme·ster *or* **rime·ster** \ˈrīmztə(r), -m(p)st-\ *n* -s [*rhymester* alter. (influenced by ¹*rhyme*) of *rimester; rimester* fr. *rime*, n. + *-ster*] **:** an inferior poet **:** a maker of poor verse ⟨contended with the easy vernacular solution of the ∼ —W.F. DeMorgan⟩

rhyme–tag \ˈ=ˌ=\ *n* **:** a word or phrase used primarily to produce a rhyme

rhyming dictionary *n* **:** a dictionary that groups rhyme words under the rhymes they form

rhyming slang *n* **:** slang in which a word whose meaning is intended is replaced by a word or phrase that rhymes with it (as *jimmygrant* for *immigrant*) or by part of a rhyming phrase (as *turtles* for *turtle doves* for *gloves*)

rhym·ist \ˈrīməst\ *n* -s [²*rhyme* + *-ist*] **:** POET; *esp* **:** one that uses rhymes

rhynch- *or* **rhyncho-** *comb form* [NL, fr. Gk, fr. *rhynchos* snout, bill, beak; prob. akin to Gk *rhonchos*, *rhonkos* snoring, wheezing, *rhenchein*, *rhenkein* to snore, snort, OIr *srennim* I snore] **:** snout — chiefly in taxonomic names in zoology

rhyn·chob·del·lae \ˌriŋˌkäbˈde(ˌ)lē\ [NL, fr. *rhynch-* + *-bdellae*] *syn of* RHYNCHOBDELLIDA

¹rhyn·chob·del·lid \ˌ=ˌ=ˈ=ləd\ *adj* [NL *Rhynchobdellida*] **:** of or relating to the Rhynchobdellida

²rhynchobdellid \"\ *n* -s **:** a leech of the order Rhynchobdellida

rhyn·chob·del·li·da \ˌ=ˌ=ˈ=lədə\ *n pl, cap* [NL, fr. *rhynch-* + Gk *bdella* leech + NL *-ida*] **:** an order of leeches with an exsertile proboscis, without jaws, and with colorless blood

rhyn·cho·ceph \ˈriŋkəˌsef\ *n* -s [NL *Rhynchocephalia*] **:** a reptile of the order Rhynchocephalia

rhyn·cho·ceph·a·la \ˌriŋkōˈsefələ\ *or* **rhyn·cho·ceph·a·li** \-ˌlī\ [NL, fr. *rhynch-* + *-cephala* or *-cephali*] *syn of* RHYNCHOCEPHALIA

rhyn·cho·ce·pha·lia \ˌriŋ(ˌ)kōsəˈfālyə, -ālēə\ *n pl, cap* [NL, fr. *rhynch-* + *cephal-* + *-ia*] **:** an order of Reptilia that comprises forms resembling lizards but having biconcave vertebrae, immovable quadrate bones, and other peculiar osteological characters and that includes *Sphenodon* and numerous fossil genera — compare TUATARA — **rhyn·cho·ce·pha·lian** \ˌ=(ˌ)=ˌ=ˈfālyən, -lēən\ *adj or n* — **rhyn·cho·ce·phal·ic** \-ˈfalik\ *adj* — **rhyn·cho·ceph·a·lous** \ˌ=(ˌ)=ˈsefələs\ *adj*

rhyn·cho·coel *also* **rhyn·cho·coele** \ˈriŋkōˌsēl\ *or* **rhyncho·coelom** *or* **rhyn·cho·coelome** \ˈriŋkō+\ *n* -s [*rhynch-* + *-coel*, *-coele* or *coelom*, *coelome*] **:** a tubular cavity that holds the introverted proboscis of a nemertean worm and is sometimes considered homologous with the coelom

rhyn·cho·coe·la \-ˈsēlə\ [NL, fr. *rhynch-* + *-coela* -coele] *syn of* NEMERTEA

rhyn·cho·coe·lic \ˌ=ˌ=ˈsēlik\ *or* **rhyn·cho·coe·lous** \-ləs\ *adj* [NL *Rhynchocoela* + E *-ic* or *-ous*] **:** NEMERTEAN

rhyn·cho·lite \ˈriŋkəˌlīt\ *n* -s [*rhynch-* + *-lite*] **:** the calcified tip of a jaw of a Triassic nautiloid cephalopod

rhyn·cho·nel·la \ˌriŋkəˈnelə\ *n, cap* [NL, fr. *rhynchon-* (irreg. fr. Gk *rhynchos* snout) + *-ella*] **:** a genus (the type of the family Rhynchonellidae) of articulate brachiopods having a sharply beaked ridged shell with the dorsal valve convex and the ventral more or less flattened — **rhyn·cho·nel·lid** \-ləd\ *n* -s — **rhyn·cho·nel·loid** \ˌ=ˌ=ˈ=ˌlȯid\ *adj or n*

rhyn·cho·nel·li·dae \ˌ=ˌ=ˈneləˌdē\ *n pl, cap* [NL, fr. *Rhynchonella*, type genus + *-idae*] **:** a family of articulate brachiopods that is known from the Ordovician to the Recent and is usu. placed in a distinct suborder or superfamily of Telotremata but is sometimes considered to form a separate order

rhyn·choph·o·ra \riŋˈkäfərə\ *n pl, cap* [NL, fr. *rhynch-* + *-phora*] **:** a large and economically important group of beetles consisting of the weevils that usu. have the head more or less prolonged in front to form a snout — **rhyn·choph·o·ran** \(ˈ)=ˌ==rən\ *adj or n* — **rhyn·cho·phore** \ˈriŋkəˌfō(ə)r\ *n* -s

rhyn·choph·o·rous \(ˈ)riŋˈkäfərəs\ *adj* [*rhynch-* + *-phorous*] **1 :** having a beak **2** [NL *Rhynchophora* + E *-ous*] **:** of or relating to the Rhynchophora

rhyn·cho·sia \riŋˈkōzh(ē)ə\ *n, cap* [NL, fr. Gk *rhynchos* snout + NL *-ia;* fr. the shape of the pod] **:** a large genus of chiefly tropical often twining plants (family Leguminosae) with trifoliolate stipulate leaves and racemose yellow flowers

rhyn·chos·po·ra \riŋˈkäspərə\ *n, cap* [NL, fr. *rhynch-* + *-spora*] **:** a genus of widely distributed sedges (family Cyperaceae) having leafy culms, clustered spikelets, a perianth usu. of barbed bristles, and an achene crowned by the persistent style base

rhyn·cho·ta \riŋˈkōd·ə\ [NL, fr. Gk *rhynchos* snout] *syn of* HEMIPTERA

¹rhyn·chote \ˈriŋˌkōt\ *or* **rhyn·cho·tal** \(ˈ)riŋˈkōd·ᵊl\ *or* **rhyn·cho·tous** \-d·əs\ *adj* [*rhynchote* fr. NL *Rhynchota; rhynchotal, rhynchotous* fr. NL *Rhynchota* + E *-al* or *-ous*] **:** of or relating to the Hemiptera

²rhynchote \"\ *n* -s [NL *Rhynchota*] **:** HEMIPTERON, BUG

-rhyn·chus \ˈriŋkəs\ *n comb form* [NL, fr. Gk *rhynchos* — more at RHYNCH-] **:** one having a snout, bill, or beak of a (specified) kind — in generic names in zoology ⟨Calyptorhynchus⟩

rhyn·cos·to·mi \riŋˈkästəˌmī\ [NL, fr. *rhync-* (fr. Gk *rhynchos* snout) + *-stomi*] *syn of* ACARINA

rhy·nia \ˈrīnēə\ *n* [NL, fr. *Rhynie*, Scotland, where the fossil plant was discovered + *-ia*] **1** *cap* **:** a genus (the type of the family Rhyniaceae) of small leafless dichotomously branching fossil plants with terminal sporangia, a primitive stele, and smooth branching rhizomes — compare HORNEOPHYTON **2** -s **:** any plant or fossil of *Rhynia* or a closely related genus

rhy·ni·a·ce·ae \ˌrīnēˈāsēˌē\ *n pl, cap* [NL, fr. *Rhynia*, type genus + *-aceae*] **:** a family of Paleozoic plants (order Psilophytales) known chiefly from the genera *Rhynia* and *Horneophyton*

rhy·noch·e·ti \rīˈnäkəˌtē\ *n pl, cap* [NL, fr. *Rhynochetos, Rhinochetus*, genus of kagus, fr. *rhyn-, rhin-* (fr. Gk *rhin-, rhis* nose) + *-ochetos, -ochetus* (fr. Gk *ochetos* channel, duct, means of carriage); akin to Gk *ochos* carriage — more at RHIN-, WAY] **:** a suborder of Gruiformes comprising the kagus

rhyns·bur·ger \ˈrīnzˌbərgə(r)\ *n* -s *usu cap* [D *rijnsburger*, fr. *Rijnsburg* Rhynsburg, village near Leiden in the southwestern Netherlands where the Collegiants first held independent services] **:** COLLEGIANT

rhyo·dacite \ˌrīō+\ *n* [*rhyolite* + *dacite*] **:** a rock intermediate between rhyolite and dacite that is the extrusive equivalent of granodiorite

rhy·o·lite \ˈrīəˌlīt\ *n* -s [G *rhyolith*, fr. *rhyo-* (irreg. fr. Gk *rhyak-, rhyax* stream of lava) + *-lith* -lite — more at RHYACOLITE] **:** a very acid volcanic rock that consists typically of phenocrysts of quartz, sanidine, and sometimes oligoclase embedded in a groundmass of minute crystals usu. mixed with glass and is the lava form of granite — **rhy·o·lit·ic** \ˌrīəˈlid·ik\ *adj*

rhyo·tax·it·ic texture \ˌrī(ˌ)ōˌtakˈsid·ik-\ *n* [*rhyotaxitic* modif. (influenced by *-ic*) of G *rhyotaxitisch*, fr. *rhyo-* (in *rhyolith* rhyolite) + *taxitisch* taxitic, fr. *taxit* taxite + *-isch* -ish — more at TAXITE] **:** FLUIDAL TEXTURE

rhypa·rog·ra·pher \ˌripəˈrägrəfə(r), ˌrip-\ *n* -s [Gk *rhyparographos* painting sordid subjects + E *-er*] **:** a painter who practices rhyparography

rhypa·ro·graph·ic \ˌ;==ˌrōˈgrafik\ *adj* [F *rhyparographique*, fr. Gk *rhyparographos* + F *-ique* -ic] **:** of or relating to rhyparography

rhypa·rog·ra·phy \ˌ==ˈrägrəfē\ *n* -ES [Gk *rhyparographos* painting sordid subjects (fr. *rhyparos* filthy, dirty + *-graphos* writing, painting — fr. *graphein* to write —) + E *-y* — more at CARVE] **1 :** the painting or literary depiction of mean, unworthy, or sordid subjects **2 :** the painting of genre or still-life pictures

rhys·sa \ˈrisə\ *n, cap* [NL, fr. Gk *rhyssos, rhysos* shriveled, wrinkled; akin to Gk *rhytid-, rhytis* wrinkle — more at RHYTIDOME] **:** a genus of ichneumon flies parasitic on the larvae of wood-boring insects

¹rhythm \ˈrithəm\ *n* -s [MF & L; MF *rhythme*, fr. L *rhythmus*, fr. Gk *rhythmos* measure, rhythm, measured motion; akin to Gk *rhein* to flow — more at STREAM] **1** *obs* **:** RHYME **2 a :** an ordered recurrent alternation of strong and weak elements in the flow of sound and silence in speech including the grouping of weaker elements around stronger, the distribution and relative disposition of strong and weak elements, and the general quantitative relations of these elements and their combinations **b :** a particular example or form of rhythm ⟨the ~ of Homeric verse⟩ ⟨Sapphic ~⟩ ⟨iambic ~⟩ **3 a :** the forward movement of music **:** the temporal pattern produced by the grouping and balancing of varying stresses and tone lengths in relation to an underlying steady and persisting succession of beats **:** the aspect of music comprising all the elements (as accent, meter, time, tempo) that relate to forward movement as contrasted with pitch sequence or tone combination **b :** a symmetrical and regularly recurrent grouping of tones according to accent and time value ⟨rumba ~⟩ **c :** a particular typical accent pattern that groups the beats of a composition or movement into measures ⟨six-eight ~⟩ **d** *or* **rhythm section :** the group of instruments (as in a dance or jazz band) that supplies the rhythm ⟨the sound of the cornet . . . is a very stirring sound indeed, especially when accompanied by clarinet, trombone, and ~ —Wilder Hobson⟩ — see RHYTHM BAND **4 a :** the regular recurrence of similar features in a literary, musical, or artistic composition ⟨the effect of a pitched or a flat roof or a dome, the ~ of projections and recessions —Nikolaus Pevsner⟩ — compare PROPORTION, SYMMETRY **b :** an ordered sequence of harmonious or related compositional elements **5 a :** harmonious or orderly movement, fluctuation, or variation with recurrences of action or situation at fairly regular intervals ⟨investigators, concentrating on recurrent processes, have been able to demonstrate the existence of many ~s with a definite temporal sequence of phases repeated again and again —P.A. Sorokin⟩ ⟨the discipline of the factory hooter . . . had to be accepted by a people used to the entirely different ~s of country life —Roy Lewis & Angus Maude⟩ **b :** a segment of a rhythm ⟨the rising ~ of border incidents —*Atlantic*⟩ **6 :** a regularly recurrent quantitative change in a variable biological process: as **a :** the pattern of recurrence of the cardiac cycle ⟨an irregular ~ marked by dropped systoles⟩ **b :** the recurring pattern of physical and functional changes associated with the mammalian and esp. human sexual cycle — see RHYTHM METHOD **7 a :** a patterned succession of various combinations in long and short time divisions of impulse and release in dancing that is usu. regularly recurrent in folk and simple art dances and often irregular and complex in modern dance when representative of erratic moods and their correlated movements **b :** easy muscular coordination (as in running, swimming, skating) **8 :** the repetition in a literary work at varying intervals and in an altered form or under changed circumstances of phrase, incident, character type, or symbol **9 :** the effect created by the elements in a play, motion picture, or novel that relate to the temporal development of the action (as the length and diversity of scenes, language, lighting, and the timing of the actors); *specif* **:** a sense of emotional intensity or of logical development in the plot of a motion picture produced by the use of montage ⟨a series of alternate long and short scenes securing a quicker ~ —Herbert Read⟩ ⟨even as the emotional ~ catches hold, the mood is continually jolted by meaningless digressions —*Time*⟩

syn CADENCE, METER: RHYTHM is wider in its use than CADENCE or METER. It is applicable to sound in poetry and music and also to any recurrent sound, movement, arrangement, or condition in virtually any sphere. Sometimes the word connotes little more than regular alternation ⟨the alternating *rhythm* of conquest and rebellion, repression and reprisal —Lewis Mumford⟩ ⟨a mysterious *rhythm* of elation and depression —Cyril Connolly⟩ Often it suggests subtlety and variation in recurrence ⟨prose *rhythm* should not have a conspicuous movement of sound —Allen Tate⟩ ⟨the shaking of the house was periodic but without rhythm —Christopher La Farge⟩ Often it suggests a recurrence pattern too varied to be easily grasped ⟨the wavering, lovely *rhythms* of the sea —Rose Macaulay⟩ ⟨a *rhythm*, even though not reducible to law, is manifest in the history of supreme court adjudication —Felix Frankfurter⟩ CADENCE is used mostly in relation to sound or to coordinated motion and is mainly applicable to shorter phrases or series. While RHYTHM stresses orderly recurrence with possible variety, CADENCE stresses variety in ordered sequence, often with falling or rising effects ⟨the song of the ruby-crowned wren, or kinglet — the same liquid bubble and *cadence* which characterize the wren songs generally . . . beginning in a fine, round, needlelike note, and rising into a full sustained warble —John Burroughs⟩ It may suggest the quite subtle or affective ⟨leaves in the mind of the sensitive reader an intangible residuum of pleasure; a *cadence*, a quality of voice that is exclusively the writer's own —Willa Cather⟩ METER applies almost entirely to more mechanical and more obvious poetic measures ⟨iambic pentameter is the most common *meter* in English poetry⟩

²rhythm *vb, obs* **:** RHYME

rhyth·mal \ˈrithməl\ *adj* **:** RHYTHMIC

rhythm band *n* **:** a band usu. composed of schoolchildren in the lowest grades who play simple percussion instruments (as rhythm sticks, sleigh bells, cymbals, or tambourines) to learn fundamentals of coordination and music

rhythmed \ˈrithəmd\ *adj* [fr. past part. of ²*rhythm*] **:** RHYTHMIC ⟨~ dialogue which gradually rises into song —W.P.Eaton⟩

rhyth·mic \ˈrithmik, -mēk *sometimes* -th-\ *adj* [LL *rhythmicus*, fr. Gk *rhythmikos*, fr. *rhythmos* rhythm + *-ikos* -ic — more at RHYTHM] **:** marked by or moving in pronounced rhythm **:** regularly recurrent **:** CADENCED ⟨the ~ chiming of church bells —John Galsworthy⟩

rhyth·mi·cal \-mәkəl, -mēk-\ *adj* [LL *rhythmicus* + E *-al*] **1** *obs* **:** RHYMING, RHYMED **2 :** RHYTHMIC ⟨~ prose⟩ **3 :** of, relating to, or involving rhythm ⟨~ skill⟩ ⟨~ systems⟩

rhythmical accent *n* **:** ACCENT 6d

rhyth·mi·cal·ly \-k(ə)lē, -li\ *adv* **1 :** in a rhythmic manner **2 :** with regard to rhythm

rhyth·mic·i·ty \rithˈmisəd·ē, -sətē, -i\ *n* -ES [*rhythmic* + *-ity*] **:** the state of being rhythmic or of responding rhythmically

rhythmic precipitation *n* **:** the process of forming Liesegang rings

rhyth·mics \ˈrithmiks, -mēks *sometimes* -th-\ *n pl but usu sing in constr, also* **rhyth·mic** \-k\ [*rhythmics* fr. ¹*rhythm* + *-ics; rhythmic* fr. LL *rhythmicus* rhythmical] **1 :** the science or theory of rhythms **2 :** rhythmical system

rhyth·mist \ˈrith(ə)məst\ *n* -s **:** one who studies, produces, or has a feeling for rhythm

rhyth·miz·able \ˈrith(ə)ˌmīzəbəl\ *adj* [*rhythmize* + *-able*] **:** capable of being rhythmized

rhyth·mi·za·tion \ˌrith(ə)məˈzāshən, -thəˌmīˈz-\ *n* -s [*rhythmize* + *-ation*] **:** the organization of a series of events or processes into a rhythmic whole ⟨~ transforms walking into marching, prancing into dancing —Susanne K. Langer⟩

rhyth·mize \ˈrith(ə)ˌmīz\ *vt* -ED/-ING/-S [¹*rhythm* + *-ize*] **:** to make rhythmic

rhythm·less \ˈrithəmləs\ *adj* **:** devoid of rhythm

rhythm method *n* **:** a method of birth control involving continence during the period of the sexual cycle in which ovulation is most likely to occur — compare SAFE PERIOD

rhyth·mol·o·gist \rithˈmäləjəst\ *n* -s [Gk *rhythmos* rhythm + E *-log* + *-ist*] **:** a specialist in rhythm

rhyth·mo·poe·ia *or* **rhyth·mo·pe·ia** \ˌrithməˈpē(y)ə\ *n* -s [LL *rhythmopoeia* making of rhythm, fr. Gk *rhythmopoiia*, fr. *rhythmos* rhythm + *-poiia* making (fr. *poiein* to make) — more at RHYTHM, POET] **:** rhythmic composition or art

rhythms *pl of* RHYTHM

rhythm section *n* **:** RHYTHM 3d

rhythm stick *n* **:** one of a pair of plain or notched wood sticks that are struck or rubbed together to produce percussive sounds and are used esp. by children in rhythm bands

rhyth·mus \ˈrithməs\ *n, pl* **rhyth·mi** \-ˌmī\ [L — more at RHYTHM] **:** RHYTHM

rhy·tid·odon \rəˈtidəˌdän\ [NL, fr. Gk *rhytid-, rhytis* wrinkle + NL *-odon*] *syn of* RUTIODON

rhyt·i·dome \ˈrid·əˌdōm\ *n* -s [prob. fr. (assumed) NL *rhytidoma*, fr. Gk *rhytidōma* wrinkle, fr. *rhytidoun* to wrinkle, fr. *rhytid-, rhytis* wrinkle; perh. akin to Gk *eryein* to drag, draw, L *rudent-, rudens* ship's rope] **:** the part of the bark external to the last formed periderm — called also *scale bark, shell bark*

¹rhy·ti·na \rəˈtīnə, -tēnə\ [NL, fr. *rhyt-* (fr. Gk *rhytis* wrinkle) + *-ina*] *syn of* HYDRODAMALIS

²rhytina \"\ *n* -s **:** STELLER'S SEA COW

rhy·tis·ma \rəˈtizmə, rīˈt-\ *n, cap* [NL, fr. Gk *rhytisma* patch] **:** a genus of fungi (family Phacidiaceae) forming black stromata — see TAR SPOT

rhy·ton \ˈrīˌtän\ *n, pl* **rhytons** *also* **rhy·ta** \-tə\ [Gk *rhyton*, neut. of *rhytos* flowing; akin to Gk *rhein* to flow — more at STREAM] **:** an ancient drinking horn usu. with a base formed as the head of an animal, woman, or mythological creature

¹ri *var of* RIG

²ri \ˈrē\ *n, pl* **ri** [Jap, fr. Chin *li*³] **:** a Japanese unit of distance equal to about 2.44 miles

RI *abbr* **1** refractive index **2** reinsurance **3** repulsion induction

ria \ˈrēə\ *n* -s [Sp *ría*, fr. *río* river — more at RIO] **:** a long narrow inlet that gradually gets shallower inward and that is caused by submergence of the lower part of a narrow river valley **:** CREEK

¹ri·al \ˈrīəl\ *adj* [ME, fr. MF *rial, real, royal* — more at ROYAL] *archaic Scot* **:** ROYAL, MAGNIFICENT

²rial *var of* RYAL

³rial *var of* REAL

⁴rial *var of* RYAL

⁵ri·al \rēˈ(y)ȯl,-)äl\ *n* -s [Per, fr. Ar *riyāl* riyal] **1 a** (1) **:** the basic monetary unit of Iran or Oman — see MONEY table (2) *or* **riyal :** the basic monetary unit of Yemen Arab Republic — see MONEY table **b :** a coin or note representing the rial **2 a :** a Sudanese monetary unit equal to 1/10 pound **b :** a coin representing one rial

ri·al·to \rēˈal(ˌ)tō\ *n* -s [fr. *Rialto*, island and district on the Grand Canal, Venice, Italy in which the exchange was situated] **1 :** an exchange or market place **2 :** the theater district of a town

ri·ant \ˈrīənt\ *adj* [MF, pres. part. of *rire* to laugh, fr. L *ridēre* — more at RIDICULOUS] **:** pleasingly mirthful or gay ⟨a ~ landscape⟩ — **ri·ant·ly** *adv*

ri·ata \rēˈad·ə, -ˈä-\ *n* -s [modif. of AmerSp *reata* — more at LARIAT] **:** LARIAT

¹rib \ˈrib\ *n* -s [ME *rib, ribbe*, fr. OE *rib, ribb;* akin to OHG *rippi* rib, ON *rif*, OSlav *rebro*, Gk *erephein* to roof over] **1 a :** one of the paired curved bony or partly cartilaginous rods that stiffen the lateral walls of the body of most vertebrates and protect the viscera, that are usu. movably articulated with the spinal column at the dorsal end and sometimes connected also at the ventral end with the sternum by costal cartilages morphologically considered unossified segments, that occur in mammals exclusively or almost exclusively in the thoracic region, and that form in man normally 12 pairs — see FALSE RIB, TRUE RIB; COW illustration **b :** one of the swimming bands of a ctenophore **c :** a cut of meat including a rib ⟨~ roast⟩ — see BEEF illustration, LAMB illustration **d** [so called fr. the biblical account of Eve's creation from Adam's rib, Gen 2:21–22] **:** WIFE **2 :** an elongated elevation running the length of an object: as **a** (1) **:** the quill of a feather (2) **:** a vein of an insect's wing (3) **:** one of the primary veins of a leaf **b** (1) **:** a strip of land lying between furrows (2) **:** STRATUM, DIKE *specif* **:** a small ridge on a steep mountainside **c** *chiefly Scot* **:** a bar of a gate **d** (1) **:** one of the vertical ridges formed in knitting by ribbing and containing one or more wales (2) **:** one of the horizontal or vertical ridges in a woven fabric that are in a close regular pattern and made by the use of coarser yarns in the warp or weft **e** (1) **:** a ridge, fin, or wing (as on a plate, cylinder, or beam) used to strengthen, stiffen, or dissipate heat (2) **:** a metal strip running the length or most of the length of a shoulder weapon (as a shotgun) or of a handgun (as a target pistol) and designed to facilitate alignment of the sights or to bring the sighting plane into prominence **f :** RAISED BAND **3 :** an object designed to provide lateral, longitudinal, or horizontal support: as **a :** a framing timber in a house or other similar building **b** (1) **:** a transverse member of the frame of a ship that runs from keel to deck and carries the bending or plating (2) **:** a light fore-and-aft member in the wing of an airplane that supports the fabric covering or metal skin and that determines the form of the wing section **c :** a stiff strip (as of metal) supporting the fabric in an umbrella **d :** one of a number of parallel members supporting a bridge **e** (1) **:** one of the quadrantal or otherwise curved members of the framing for a dome (2) **:** an arched longitudinal frame of timber or one of a set of such frames parallel and equidistant supporting the transverse laggings and with them forming the centering of an arch (3) **:** one of the arches in Romanesque and Gothic vaulting meeting and crossing one another and dividing the whole vaulted space into triangles (4) **:** a projecting band in a vault or arched ceiling **f** (1) **:** solid coal on the side of a gallery or solid ore in a vein (2) **:** an elongated pillar of ore or coal left as a support in a mine **4 :** an object so curved as to resemble a human rib: as **a :** a curved side connecting the top and back of a musical instrument of the violin class **b :** a piece of thin wood or slate used in ceramic work that is cut to the shape of the section or profile of a cup and that is employed in smoothing the inner surface of the clay

²rib \"\ *vt* **ribbed; ribbed; ribbing; ribs 1 :** to furnish, strengthen, or enclose with or as if with ribs ⟨~ a vessel⟩ ⟨~ a structure⟩ **2 :** to form vertical ridges in in knitting by alternating knit and purl stitches in a regular pattern

³rib \"\ *n* -s [IrGael *ribe, ruibe*] *Irish* **:** a single hair **:** BRISTLE

⁴rib \"\ *vt* **ribbed; ribbed; ribbing; ribs** [prob. fr. ¹*rib;* fr. the tickling of one's ribs to cause laughter] **:** to poke fun at **:** KID ⟨players *ribbing* an umpire⟩

⁵rib \"\ *n* -s **1 :** JOKE ⟨always enjoying a ~ on someone else⟩ **2 :** PARODY ⟨an uproarious ~ of a Western⟩

rib- *or* **ribo-** *comb form* [*ribose*] **1 :** related to ribose ⟨*ribitol*⟩ ⟨*riboflavin*⟩ **2** *ribo-, usu ital* **:** having the stereochemical arrangement of atoms or groups found in ribose ⟨*D-ribo-3-hexulose*⟩

¹ri·bald \ˈribəld *also* ˈriˌbȯld *or* ÷ˈrīˌbȯld *or* ÷ˈrībəld\ *n* -s [ME *ribald, ribaud*, fr. OF *ribauld, ribaut* wanton, rascal, fr. *riber* to be wanton, of Gmc origin; akin to OHG *rīban* to be wanton, lit., to turn, twist, rub — more at RHIPID-] **1 a :** a retainer employed in a feudal household in the meanest positions and in the field as an irregular soldier **b :** ROGUE, RASCAL **2 :** a person coarse or lewd in appearance, speech, writing, or thought

²ribald \"\ *adj* **1 :** marked by coarseness and indecency **:** OFFENSIVE **2 :** characterized by broad indecent humor ⟨a ~ tale⟩ **:** capable of, displaying, or suggesting rough convivial wit ⟨a ~ mind⟩ ⟨a ~ company⟩ **syn** see COARSE

rib·ald·ly *adv* [²*ribald* + *-ly*] **:** in a ribald manner ⟨stayed only to hoot ~ at the delegates —W.A.White⟩

rib·al·drous \-drəs\ *adj* [*ribaldry* + *-ous*] *archaic* **:** RIBALD

rib·al·dry \-drē,-dri\ *n* -ES [ME *ribaldrie, ribaudrie*, fr. MF *ribaulderie, ribauderie*, fr. OF, fr. *ribauld* ribald + *-erie* -ery] **1** *obs* **:** lewd or licentious acts **:** DEBAUCHERY **2 a :** ribald quality, nature, or element ⟨the ~ in an author's works⟩ ⟨the lusty ~ of peasant humor —*Times Lit. Supp.*⟩ **b :** ribald language, jesting, or wit ⟨the ~ of a stag party⟩

rib·and *also* **rib·band** \ˈribən(d)\ *n* -s [ME *riband, ribband*, alter. (prob. influenced by ¹*band*) of *riban* ribbon — more at RIBBON] **1 :** a ribbon used esp. as a decoration **2 :** RIBBON 2a

ri·bat \rəˈbät\ *n* -s [Ar *ribāṭ* station, inn, religious house] **:** an Islamic monastery

¹rib·band \ˈri(b)ˌban(d), -ibən(d)\ *n* [¹*rib* + *band*] **1 a :** a long narrow strip or bar used in shipbuilding that is bent and bolted longitudinally to the frames to hold them in position **b :** a timber secured along the ground ways in shipbuilding to keep the sliding ways from spreading to the side **2 :** a scantling, spar, or plank used in construction work (as in making a corduroy road or a pontoon bridge)

²ribband \"\ *vt* -ED/-ING/-S **:** to provide, secure, or fasten with a ribband

ribbed \ˈribd\ *adj* [¹*rib* + *-ed*] **:** furnished, marked, or strengthened with a rib ⟨a ~ structure⟩ ⟨~ land⟩ ⟨a ~ sweater⟩

ribbed-knit *var of* RIB-KNIT

ribbed vault *n* **:** a vault in which solid ribs carry the vaulted surface

¹rib·ber \ˈribə(r)\ *n* -s [²*rib* + *-er*] **:** one that ribs: as **a :** one that builds or installs ribs in construction work **b :** a knitting machine that produces ribbed fabrics or that makes ribbing for cuffs, waistbands, or similar pieces of clothing

²ribber \"\ *n* -s [⁴*rib* + *-er*] **:** one that mocks or teases

ribbier *comparative of* RIBBY

ribbiest *superlative of* RIBBY

¹rib·bing \ˈribiŋ, -bēŋ\ *n* -s [¹*rib* + *-ing*] **:** a pattern, system, or structure composed of ribs: as **a** (1) **:** a framework (as of a building or ship) made up chiefly of ribs (2) **:** the ribwork in vaulting **b :** the veins of a leaf **c :** a strip of ribbed fabric (as a semielastic band of ribs used as a close-fitting edge finish on sweaters, socks, and mittens) **d :** a part of an artificial fly wound over the body material and often added to simulate the stripes on a natural insect — see FLY illustration

²ribbing \"\ *n* -s [fr. gerund of ⁴*rib*] **:** an act of teasing or mocking

rib·bok \ˈriˌbäk\ *n, pl* **ribbok** *or* **ribboks** [by alter.] **:** RHEBOK

¹rib·bon \ˈribən *also* -bᵊm\ *n* -s *often attrib* [ME *riban*, fr. MF *riban, ruban*, prob. fr. a Gmc compound whose first element is akin to OE *hring* ring and whose second element is akin to ME *band*] **1 a :** a flat or tubular narrow fabric (as of silk, rayon, nylon, or cotton) closely woven in various constructions (as in velvet, satin, taffeta, or grosgrain) and used for trimmings, decorations, or knitting **b :** a narrow fabric (as of paper or textile fibers pasted on tape) used chiefly for tying packages **c :** a piece of usu. multicolored ribbon that serves as a decoration (as for military service) or that is worn in place of a medal represented by its colors ⟨campaign ~⟩ ⟨service ~⟩ **d :** a strip of imprinted red, blue, white, or yellow satin often attached to a button or badge and given in recognition of winning one of the first three or four places in competition (as at a horse show, livestock show) **2 :** a long narrow strip resembling or suggestive of a ribbon: as **a :** a single bendlet that surmounts the other heraldic bearings and is borne as a difference mark **b :** a board framed into the studs to support the ceiling or floor joists **c :** a straight or crumpled varicolored stripe across slate that shows the location of the original bedding **d** (1) **:** RADULA (2) **:** an egg case (as of a mollusk) when produced in a long string **e** (1) **:** a strip of inked fabric (as in a typewriter) on which the type faces strike and which prints the type characters on a sheet below (2) **:** a continuous roll of paper that regulates casting in the monotype **f** (1) **:** the form in which molten glass is taken from the furnace in the manufacture of some types of glass (2) **:** a pressed and flattened sliver ready for spinning **g :** a bookmark consisting of a length of material often attached by one end to the top headband of the book **3 ribbons** *pl* **:** REINS **4 :** FRAGMENT, PIECE, SHRED — usu. pl. ⟨torn to ~s⟩ **5 :** RIBBAND

²ribbon \"\ *vt* **ribboned** \-bənd,-bᵊmd\ **ribboned** \"\ **ribboning** \-bəniŋ\ **ribbons** \-bənz,-bᵊmz\ **1 a :** to adorn or mark out with or as if with a ribbon ⟨gaily *~ed* schoolgirls⟩ **b :** to divide into ribbons ⟨~ material for bandages⟩ **2 :** to rip to shreds ⟨a flag *~ed* by the wind⟩

ribbonback \ˈ==ˌ=\ *adj* **:** having a back with open slats carved to represent intertwined ribbons ⟨a ~ chair⟩

ribbon bed *n* **:** a flower bed in which the plants are set in parallel lines or rows with one kind to a row

ribbon brake *n* **:** BAND BRAKE

ribbon bush *n* **:** CENTIPEDE PLANT

ribbon candy *n* **:** a thin brittle usu. colored sugar candy made in the form of a ribbon folded back and forth upon itself and bought esp. at Christmastime

ribbon conveyor *n* **:** a spiral continuous conveyor having an open space between the shaft and the ribbon flight so that damp or sticky material cannot build up around the shaft

ribbon copy *n* **:** a copy (as of a document) made by the typewriter ribbon **:** ORIGINAL — compare CARBON COPY

ribbon development *or* **ribbon building** *n* **:** a system of buildings built side by side or adjoining that follow in succession along a road ⟨the drear *ribbon developments* of British industrial areas⟩ — called also *string development*

rib·bon·er \ˈribənə(r)\ *n* -s [¹*ribbon* + *-er*] **:** one that produces, processes, or handles ribbon; *specif* **:** one that inserts ribbon or tape into a tubing or beading on garments

ribbon fern *n* **1 :** a fern of the genus *Vittaria* having grasslike fronds **2 :** a commonly cultivated Asiatic fern (*Pteris serrulata*) naturalized in tropical America **3 :** an Australian adder's-tongue (*Ophioglossum pendulum*)

ribbon figure *or* **ribbon grain** *or* **ribbon stripe** *n* **1 :** ²ROE 2 **2 :** a banded figure fundamentally similar to roe but having the dark marks elongated to extend the length of the piece

ribbonfish \ˈ=,=\ *n* **1 :** any of various elongate greatly compressed marine fishes: as **a :** DEALFISH **b :** any of numerous elongated fishes constituting the family Cepolidae — called also *bandfish* **c :** OARFISH **d :** CUTLASS FISH **2 :** any of several fishes of the genus *Equetus* (family Sciaenidae) having striping usu. in gray and black

ribbon grass *n* **:** a reed canary grass (*Phalaris arundinacea picta*) grown for its white-striped leaves — called also *gardener's-garters, lady's-laces, painted grass*

ribbon gum *n* **:** an Australian eucalypt (*Eucalyptus viminalis*) with long slender leaves; *also* **:** any of several closely related trees (as the peppermint gum)

rib·bon·ism \ˈribə,nizəm\ *n* -s *usu cap* **:** the principles or practices of Ribbonmen

ribbon jasper *n* **:** jasper having stripes (as of red and green)

ribbon lightning *n* **:** a more or less continuous lightning discharge over an appreciable time producing a picture in the shape of a ribbon in a rotating camera

ribbonlike \ˈ==,=\ *adj* **:** resembling a ribbon

ribbon loom *n* **:** a narrow fabric loom usu. wide enough to weave forty or more pieces at one time

rib·bon·man \-,man\ *n, pl* **ribbonmen** *usu cap* [¹*ribbon* + *man;* fr. the green ribbon worn as a badge by members of the society] **:** a member of a Roman Catholic secret society founded in Ireland in 1808 in opposition to the landlord class

ribbon microphone *n* **:** a dynamic microphone in which the pick-up device is a thin metallic ribbon

ribbon movement *n* **:** the mechanism for moving the ribbon of a typewriter

ribbon park *n* **:** an extended area a few hundred feet wide landscaped like a park through which a highway winds

ribbon reverse *n* **:** a mechanism on a typewriter that works both automatically and manually to reverse the direction of travel of the ribbon

ribbon rock *n* **:** vein rock usu. quartz banded with stripes of darker mineral

ribbons *pl of* RIBBON, *pres 3d sing of* RIBBON

ribbon saw *n* **:** BAND SAW

ribbon seal *n* **:** a No. Pacific seal (*Histriophoca fasciata* or *Phoca fasciata*) of which the adult male is broadly banded with brown and yellowish white

ribbon snake *n* **:** a common No. American garter snake (*Thamnophis saurita*) found chiefly in wet places that is slender and striped with bright yellow and dark brown

ribbon structure *n* **:** a structure common in quartz veins consisting of narrow layers of quartz separated by thin dark seams of altered wall rock

ribbon tree *n* **:** a New Zealand tree (*Plagianthus betulinus*) from whose inner bark a strong fiber resembling flax is obtained — see NEW ZEALAND COTTON

ribbon vibrator *n* **:** a device behind the printing point indicator of a typewriter that carries the ribbon and raises it into printing position each time a character key is struck

ribbon windows *n pl* **:** a series of windows set side by side to form a continuous band horizontally across a facade

ribbonwood \ˈ==,=\ *n* **1 :** a New Zealand shrub or small tree (*Hoheria populnea*) of the family Malvaceae having bark that is used for cordage and a profusion of small snow-white flowers in close axillary clusters — called also *houhere* **2 :** RIBBON TREE **3** *West* **:** a small tree or shrub (*Adenostoma sparsifolium*) related to the chamiso

ribbon worm *n* **:** NEMERTINE

ribbony \ˈribənē\ *adj* [¹*ribbon* + *-y*] **:** of, adorned with, or like ribbon

ribbon windows

rib·by \ˈribē\ *adj* -ER/-EST [¹*rib* + *-y*] **:** showing or characterized by ribs ⟨~ fabric⟩

rib cage *n* **:** the bony enclosing wall of the chest consisting chiefly of the ribs and their connectives — called also *thoracic cage*

ribe \ˈrīb\ *n* -s [origin unknown] *dial* **:** a scrawny or thin person or animal

ri·bes \ˈrī(,)bēz\ *n, cap* [NL, fr. ML, currant, fr. Ar *rībās* rhubarb] **:** a genus of shrubs (family Saxifragaceae) having small racemose variously colored flowers with four or five scalelike petals, four or five stamens, two styles, a wholly inferior ovary, and a pulpy few-seeded to many-seeded berry that disarticulates from its pedicel — see CURRANT 2

rib eye *n* **:** the large piece of meat that lies along the outer side of the rib (as of a steer) and is a continuation of the longissimus dorsi muscle

rib-faced deer \ˈ=,=-\ *n* [¹*rib* + *faced*] **:** a muntjac (*Muntiacus muntjak*)

ribgrass \ˈ=,=\ *n* **:** ¹PLANTAIN; *usu* **:** an Old World plantain (*Plantago lanceolata*) with long narrow ribbed leaves that is now generally established in temperate regions — called also *buckhorn, English plantain, ribwort*

ri·bi·tol \ˈrībə,tōl, -tȯl\ *n* -s [*rib-* + *-itol*] **:** ADONITOL

ri·bi·tyl \-,til\ *n* -s [*ribitol* + *-yl*] **:** the univalent radical $HOCH_2(CHOH)_3CH_2-$ formed by removal of one of the terminal hydroxyl groups of adonitol

rib-knit *also* **ribbed-knit** \ˈrib(d),nit\ *n* **1 :** a knitting with a ribbed pattern **2 :** a fabric or a piece of fabric knitted with a ribbed pattern ⟨a dress with collars and cuffs of *rib-knit*⟩

rib lath *n* **:** metal lath with ribs at intervals to increase its rigidity

rib·less \ˈribləs\ *adj* **:** having no ribs or no visible ribs

rib·let \-lət\ *n* -s [¹*rib* + *-let*] **:** one of the rib ends in the strip of breast of lamb or veal cut from the rack — see LAMB illustration

riblike \ˈ=,=\ *adj* **:** resembling a rib

rib meristem *n* **:** a meristem in which cell divisions occur chiefly in one plane at right angles to the longitudinal axis and give rise to vertical rows or columns of cells — called also *file meristem;* compare MASS MERISTEM, PLATE MERISTEM

ribo- — see RIB-

ri·bo·fla·vin \,rībəˈflāvən, ˈ==,==\ *also* **ri·bo·fla·vine** \ˈ", -,vēn\ *n* [ISV *rib-* + *flavin*] **:** a yellow fluorescent crystalline flavin pigment $C_{17}H_{20}N_4O_6$ derived from ribose that is a growth-promoting member of the vitamin B complex occurring both free (as in milk) and combined as nucleotides and flavoprotein enzymes (as in liver, green leafy vegetables, yeast, anaerobic fermentation bacteria), that is made synthetically or by fermentation, and that is used in nutrition (as in vitamin preparations, enriching flour and bread, and poultry feed) and in medicine (as in treating lesions of the tongue, lips, and face) — called also *lactoflavin, vitamin B_2, vitamin G;* see ARIBOFLAVINOSIS 1

riboflavin phosphate *n* **:** a yellow crystalline mono-phosphoric ester $C_{17}H_{21}N_4O_9P$ of riboflavin that is a coenzyme of several flavoprotein enzymes — called also *flavin mononucleotide, riboflavin 5′-phosphate;* compare FLAVIN ADENINE DINUCLEOTIDE

ri·bon·ic acid \(ˈ)rīˈbänik-\ *n* [part trans. of G *ribonsäure,* fr. *ribon* (alter. by transposition of letters of *arabinose*) + *säure* acid] **:** an acid $HOCH_2(CHOH)_3COOH$ obtained by oxidation of ribose

ri·bo·nu·cle·ase \,rībōˈn(y)üklē,ās, -āz\ *n* -s [*ribonucleic* + *-ase*] **:** a crystalline enzyme found esp. in the pancreas that acts on ribonucleic acid by catalyzing its hydrolysis only to nucleotides and also by catalyzing the transfer but not liberation of phosphate groups from the nucleotides

ri·bo·nu·cle·ate \-ēət, -ē,āt\ *n* [*ribonucleic* + *-ate*] **:** a salt of a ribonucleic acid

ri·bo·nu·cle·ic acid \,rībō;n(y)ü;klēik-\ *n* [*rib-* + *nucleic*] **:** any of various nucleic acids that yield ribose as one product of hydrolysis, that are found in cytoplasm and some nuclei, and that are associated with the control of cellular chemical activities — abbr. *RNA;* called also *yeast nucleic acid;* compare DEOXYRIBONUCLEIC ACID

ri·bo·nu·cleo·protein \,rībō;n(y)üklēō+\ *n* [*ribonucleic* + *-o-* + *protein*] **:** a nucleoprotein that yields a ribonucleic acid on hydrolysis

ri·bose \ˈrī,bōs *also* -ōz\ *n* -s [ISV *ribonic* + *-ose*] **:** a crystalline aldose sugar of the pentose class $C_5H_{10}O_5$ found esp. as the D-form as a constituent of many nucleosides (as adenosine, cytidine, guanosine) and obtained usu. from ribonucleic acid by hydrolysis or from altrose by degradation

ri·bo·side \ˈrībə,sīd, -,səd\ *n* -s **:** a glycoside that yields ribose on hydrolysis

riboso *var of* REBOZO

ri·bo·syl \ˈrībə,sil\ *n* -s [*rib-* + glyco*syl*] **:** a glycosyl radical $C_5H_9O_4$ derived from ribose

ribroast \ˈ=,=\ *vt* [¹*rib* + *roast,* v.] *archaic* **:** THRASH

rib roast *n* [¹*rib* + *roast,* n.] **:** a cut of meat containing the rib eye with rib or with rib removed — see BEEF illustration

ribs *pl of* RIB, *pres 3d sing of* RIB

rib stitch *n* **:** a ribbed knitting pattern — see ²RIB 2

ri·buck \ˈrī,bək\ *adj* [origin unknown] *slang Austral* **:** FIRST-RATE, GENUINE — often used interjectionally

ri·bu·lose \ˈribyə,lōs *also* -ōz\ *n* -s [*rib-* + *-ulose*] **:** a ketose $C_5H_{10}O_5$ that is formed from ribose or arabinose during epimerization and that plays a role in carbohydrate metabolism

rib-vault \ˈ=,=\ *n* **:** RIBBED VAULT

ribwork \ˈ=,=\ *n* **:** a ribbed structure, arrangement, or pattern

ribwort \ˈ=,=\ *or* **ribwort plantain** *n* **:** a ribgrass (*Plantago lanceolata*)

ri·car·di·an \rəˈkärdēən\ *adj, usu cap* [David *Ricardo* †1823 Eng. economist + E *-ian*] **:** of or relating to the English political economist Ricardo or to his theory of rent as an economic surplus

ric·cia \ˈrichēə\ *n, cap* [NL, fr. P.F.*Ricci* 18th cent. Ital. nobleman + NL *-ia*] **:** a genus (the type of the family Ricciaceae) of floating liverwort resembling duckweed and characterized by a dichotomously branched thallus which may be floating, submerged, or rooted on damp soil

ric·ci·a·ce·ae \,richēˈāsē,ē\ *n pl, cap* [NL, fr. *Riccia,* type genus + *-aceae*] **:** a family comprising fleshy and typically rosette-forming liverworts that are nearly cosmopolitan in distribution and being usu. included in Marchantiales but sometimes isolated in a separate order — see RICCIA

ric·cio·car·pus \,richēōˈkärpəs\ *n, cap* [NL, fr. *Riccia* + *-o-* + *-carpus*] **:** a genus of liverworts closely resembling and often included in *Riccia* but distinguished by the arrangement of archegonia and antheridia along the median groove of the gametophyte

ric·co's law \ˈri(,)kōz-\ *n, usu cap R* [after *Ricco,* its formulator] **:** a statement in physiology: when a light source of a given size and intensity is just capable of producing visual sensation reduction of either size or intensity will make it invisible

¹**rice** \ˈrīs\ *n* -s [ME *ris, rise,* fr. OE *hrīs;* akin to OHG & ON *hrīs* twig — more at CREST] **1** *chiefly dial* **:** TWIG, BRANCH **2** *chiefly dial* **:** BRUSHWOOD

²**rice** \ˈ"\ *n, pl* **rice** [ME *rys, ryce,* fr. OF *ris,* fr. It *riso,* fr. Gk *oryzon, oryza,* of non-IE origin; akin to the source of Skt *vrīhi* rice] **:** an annual cereal grass (*Oryza sativa*) widely cultivated in warm climates for its seed that is used for human food, for its hulls and other by-products that are used to feed livestock, and for its straw that is used in making paper

³**rice** \ˈ"\ *vt* -ED/-ING/-S [²*rice*] **:** to put through a ricer

⁴**rice** \ˈ"\ *adj* **1 :** consisting of, containing, or concerned with rice **2 :** made from nubby seedlike yarns ⟨~ fabrics⟩ **3 :** finished to resemble rice paper

rice bean *n* [²*rice*] **:** an annual half-twining bean (*Phaseolus calcaratus*) adapted to about the same area as the cowpea and cultivated for its seed to a limited extent in Asia and the East Indies

ricebird \ˈ=,=\ *n* **1 :** any of several small birds common in rice fields: as **a :** JAVA SPARROW **b :** BOBOLINK **c :** YELLOW-BREASTED BUNTING **d :** FLORIDA GALLINULE **2** *usu cap* **:** SOUTH CAROLINIAN — used as a nickname

rice body *n* **:** a smooth glistening ovoid particle like a grain of rice in joints and the sheaths of tendons and bursae occurring as a result of chronic inflammation — usu. used in pl.

rice borer *n* **:** any of several small caterpillars that are the larvae of pyralidid moths and that feed on rice plants

rice bowl *n* **:** an area (as southeast Asia) that produces large quantities of rice

rice bran *n* **:** a product obtained by milling rice consisting of the seed coat, a fraction of the grain removed in milling, the germ, and broken grains, and used as a stock feed and medicinally as a source of thiamine

rice bug *n* **:** an unpleasant smelling coreid bug (*Leptocorixa varicornis*) that is injurious to rice in India and the Far East — called also *rice sapper*

rice bunting *n* **:** BOBOLINK

rice christian *n, usu cap C* **:** a convert to Christianity who accepts baptism not on the basis of personal conviction but out of a desire for food, medical services, or other benefits

rice coal *n* **:** anthracite coal of a small size **:** number 2 buckwheat coal — see ANTHRACITE table

rice cut-grass *n* **:** a rough-leaved marsh grass (*Leersia oryzoides*) of eastern No. America having grains that somewhat resemble those of rice

rice drier *n* **:** an installation employing a series of tempering bins and blasts of heated air to dry and cure newly threshed rice

rice-field eel *n* **:** any of several small dark-colored eel-shaped Asiatic and East Indian fishes (family Synbranchidae) common in ditches and flooded rice fields from China to India

rice-field mouse *or* **rice-field rat** *n* **:** RICE RAT

rice-field rail *n* **:** SORA

rice-field tire *n* **:** a large rubber tire with deep lugs on the tread used on self-propelled machines working in wet rice fields

rice flower *n* **:** any of several commonly cultivated shrubs of the genus *Pimelea* whose small unopened flower buds suggest grains of rice

rice glue *n* **:** a cement made by boiling ground rice in soft water and used somewhat like papier-maché to make various molded articles (as statuary)

rice grain *n* **:** the granular structure of the sun's surface or photosphere when observed in white light

rice-grain decoration *n* **:** ceramic decoration consisting of translucent spots produced by piercing the greenware before firing and allowing glaze to fill the openings

ricegrass \ˈ=,=\ *n* **1 :** a stoloniferous marsh grass (*Leersia hexandra*) of tropical America cultivated (as in the Philippines and southern Africa) for green forage **2 :** a European spartina (*Spartina townsendi*) used as a fodder and soil-binding plant **3 :** any of several grasses of the genus *Oryzopsis* (esp. *O. oryzoides*)

rice grub *n* **:** the larva of any of several beetles injurious to the rice plant in the southern U.S.

rice hen *n* **:** FLORIDA GALLINULE

rice meal *n* **:** the ground by-product of rice milling consisting of rice bran, polishings, and some rice flour and used chiefly as a feedstuff for livestock

rice paddy *n* **:** PADDY 2

rice paper *n* [so called fr. its resemblance to paper made from rice straw] **:** a thin delicate material resembling paper made by cutting the pith of the rice-paper tree into one roll or sheet and flattening under pressure

rice-paper tree *or* **rice-paper plant** *n* **:** a small Asiatic tree or shrub (*Tetrapanax papyriferum*) of the family Araliaceae widely cultivated in China and Japan and having large leaves with five to seven lobes, small white flowers, and stems with pith from which rice paper is made

rice polish *also* **rice dust** *n* **:** a finely powdered material obtained in milling white rice consisting of the inner bran layer with a little of the starchy interior that is rubbed off the kernels and used as a source of thiamin, riboflavin, and niacin and as stock feed

rice polishings *n pl* **:** the inner bran layer of rice that is rubbed off in milling

rice powder *n* **:** a face powder derived from rice

ric·er \ˈrīsə(r)\ *n* -s [³*rice* + *-er*] **:** a kitchen utensil designed for pressing cooked soft vegetables or uncooked soft foods through a perforated container so that the resulting product emerges as strings about the diameter of a grain of rice

rice rail *n* [²*rice*] **:** SORA

rice rat *or* **rice mouse** *n* **:** any of various cricetid rats (genus *Oryzomys*) abundant in moist or swampy areas from New Jersey to Venezuela; *esp* **:** a rodent (*O. palustris*) of the southeastern U. S. that greatly resembles the Norway rat

ricer

ri·cer·car \,rēˌcherˈkär\ *or* **ri·cer·ca·re** \-ä(,)rā\ *n, pl* **ricercars** \-ärz\ *or* **ricerca·ri** \-ä(,)rē\ [It, fr. *ricercare* to seek again, seek out, fr. *ri-* re- (fr. L *re-*) + *cercare* to seek (fr. LL *circare* to go about, traverse); fr. the disguising of the subjects by various alterations — more at SEARCH] **1 :** a contrapuntal instrumental composition analogous to the motet in vocal music usu. consisting in the 16th century of a series of fugal expositions on different subjects and in the 17th century developing into the true fugue on a single subject **2 :** a learned and elaborate fugue esp. in the 18th century

ri·cer·ca·ta \-ädə\ *n* -s [It, fr. fem. of *ricercato,* past part. of *ricercare*] **:** RICERCAR

rice root *n* [²*rice*] **1** *also* **rice-root grass :** BROOMROOT **2** *also* **rice-root lily :** CHECKERED LILY

rices *pl of* RICE, *pres 3d sing of* RICE

rice sapper *n* **:** RICE BUG

rice shell *n* **:** any of numerous small white olive shells of *Olivella* or related genera

rice stalk borer *n* **:** a rice borer that is the larva of a moth (*Chilo plejadellus*)

rice stinkbug : a pentatomid bug (*Oebalus pugnax*) that feeds on developing rice grains in the southern U.S.

rice tenrec *n* **:** a tenrec of the genus *Oryzorictes*

rice water *n* **:** a drink chiefly for invalids made by boiling a small quantity of rice in water

rice-water stool *n* **:** a watery stool containing white flecks of mucus, epithelial cells, and bacteria and discharged from the bowels in Asiatic cholera and other severe forms of diarrhea

rice water weevil *n* **:** a weevil (*Lissorhoptrus oryzophilus*) that feeds as a larva on the roots of the rice plant when under water and as an adult on the rice leaves

rice weevil *n* **1 :** a small weevil (*Sitophilus oryzae*) destructive esp. of stored rice, wheat, flour, and biscuit — called also *black weevil* **2 :** RICE WATER WEEVIL

ric·ey \ˈrīsē\ *adj;* **riceyer; riceyest** [²*rice* + *-y*] **:** of or resembling rice ⟨~ texture⟩ ⟨~ color⟩

¹**rich** \ˈrich\ *adj* -ER/-EST [ME *riche,* fr. OE *rīce;* akin to OHG *rīhhi* rich, ON *rīkr,* Goth *reiks* mighty, ruler, OE *rīce* kingdom, realm, rule, OHG *rīhhi,* ON *rīki,* Goth *reiki;* all fr. prehistoric Gmc borrowings fr. Celt words whose root is represented by OIr *rī* (gen. *rīg*) king — more at ROYAL] **1** *obs* **:** possessed of great temporal power **:** MIGHTY **2 :** possessing or controlling great wealth **:** WEALTHY ⟨~ bankers⟩ **3 a :** possessed of high intrinsic or estimated value ⟨~ jewels⟩ ⟨the best uranium, that is to say the ~*est* rock in the world —J.D.Hillaby⟩ **b :** abounding in natural wealth (as ore, water, productive soil) — often used with *in* ⟨a kingdom ~ in forests and mines and lush pastureland⟩ **4 a** (1) **:** burdened with every luxury **:** SUMPTUOUS ⟨a ~ banquet⟩ (2) **:** gorgeously and pleasingly showy ⟨~ garments⟩ **:** splendidly costly ⟨~ tapestries⟩ (3) **:** magnificently impressive **:** gorgeously replete with pomp and ceremony ⟨a ~ military funeral⟩ **b** (1) **:** elaborately adorned **:** sumptuously ornamented ⟨a ~ altar⟩ (2) **:** fabricated from the best material and with the best skill and care ⟨~ furnishing⟩ ⟨~ interior decorations⟩ **5 a** (1) *of color* **:** vivid but pleasing; *specif* **:** of high or very high saturation and commonly of low lightness ⟨a ~ red⟩ (2) **:** warmly and pleasingly colorful ⟨a ~ landscape⟩ ⟨a ~ sunset⟩ **b :** full and mellow in tone and quality ⟨a ~ voice⟩ ⟨~ music⟩ **c** (1) **:** possessed of strong pleasant fragrance ⟨~ perfume⟩ (2) **:** pleasantly pungent ⟨a ~ barnyard odor⟩ **6 a :** ABUNDANT, PLENTIFUL — often used with *in* ⟨a mixture ~ in lime⟩ or postposed and hyphenated ⟨an iron-*rich* soil⟩ ⟨manganese-*rich* ore⟩ **b :** producing abundantly or yielding large returns **:** PRODUCTIVE ⟨a ~ mine⟩ ⟨~ farmland⟩ **7 a :** abundantly supplied with plant nutrients ⟨~ soil⟩ **b :** abounding in resinous heartwood ⟨~ stumps⟩ **c :** containing a large proportion of cementing material ⟨~ mortar⟩ ⟨~ concrete⟩ ⟨~ plaster⟩ **d :** containing a pronounced complement of fat or fatty substances ⟨turkey, pork, and other ~ meats⟩ ⟨~ eggnogs⟩ **e :** high in the combustible component — used esp. of a fuel mixture for an internal-combustion engine ⟨the ~ mixtures are generally used at high power output —*Aircraft Power Plants*⟩ — opposed to *lean* **8 a :** high in entertainment ⟨a ~ first act⟩ **:** strongly amusing ⟨a ~ humor⟩ **b :** pregnant with meaning, import, or significance ⟨~ words⟩ ⟨~ allusions⟩ **c :** LUSH ⟨~ foliage⟩ ⟨~ meadows⟩ **9 :** containing coarse, shocking, or scurrilous expressions ⟨~ abuse⟩ **10 :** pure or very nearly pure ⟨~ lime⟩ **11 :** PLASTIC — used in ceramics of clay

syn WEALTHY, AFFLUENT, OPULENT: applied to persons and to groups, RICH and WEALTHY are often interchangeable in indicating possession of considerable wealth ⟨was indeed *rich,* according to the standards of the Square; nay, *wealthy* —Arnold Bennett⟩ RICH may occasionally apply to greater possession than WEALTHY ⟨a *wealthy* but not a *rich* man —*Times Lit. Supp.*⟩ but it is more likely to be used in extended senses than WEALTHY ⟨lived alone, poor in worldly goods to the verge of distress, but *rich* beyond avarice in his vast and unique collection of snow-crystal pictures —W.J.Humphreys⟩ WEALTHY may suggest along with the fact of ownership its established, accustomed, or lasting enjoyment ⟨many of the *wealthy* supporters of the drama in Providence bought boxes by the season and were served wines and sherbets between the acts —*Amer. Guide Series: R.I.*⟩ AFFLUENT often is interchangeable with WEALTHY but may suggest a comfortably increasing wealth ⟨ride in larger and larger cars so that we may seem more *affluent* than we actually are —J.D.Adams⟩ OPULENT, applied less often to persons than to things, may suggest extreme wealth attended with lavish, luxuriant, or splendid expenditure ⟨an *opulent* frock of gold brocade —Jean Stafford⟩ ⟨an *opulent* blue mink coat —*Time*⟩ ⟨an *opulent* and glittering eastern throne —John Buchan⟩

²**rich** \ˈ"\ *n, pl* **rich** *or* **riches** \ˈrichəz\ **1** *pl rich* **:** a rich person ⟨the ~ has many friends —Prov 14:20 (RSV)⟩ — usu. used collectively ⟨respected by both ~ and poor⟩ ⟨the ~ all belong to the same clubs here⟩ **2** *riches pl* [ME (sing. or pl.), fr. *richesse* richness, wealth, fr. OF, fr. *riche* rich, of Gmc origin; akin to OE *rīce* rich — more at RICH] **:** something that makes one rich **:** rich possessions **:** abundant means **:** WEALTH ⟨spiritual ~*es*⟩ ⟨what care I in ~*es* to wallow —Robert Burns⟩

¹**ri·char·dia** \rəˈchärdēə\ *n, cap* [NL, fr. *Richard* Richardson †1741 Eng. physician and botanist + NL *-ia*] **:** a small genus of tropical American hairy herbs (family Rubiaceae) with inconspicuous flowers in dense heads and an ovary of two to four cells — see MEXICAN CLOVER

²**ri·char·dia** \rəˈshärdēə\ [NL, fr. L.C.M.*Richard* †1821, Fr. botanist + NL *-ia*] *syn of* ZANTEDESCHIA

rich·ard miles \,richə(r)dˈmī(ə)lz\ *n, usu cap R&M* [fr. the name *Richard Miles*] **:** a party to legal proceedings whose true name is unknown; *esp* **:** the fourth such party when four are unknown — compare JOHN DOE, JOHN STILES, RICHARD ROE

richard roe \-ˈrō\ *n, usu cap both Rs* [fr. the name *Richard Roe*] **:** a party to legal proceedings whose true name is unknown; *esp* **:** the second such party when two are unknown — compare JOHN DOE, JOHN STILES, RICHARD MILES

rich·ard·so·nia \ˌrichə(r)dˈsōnēə\ *n* [NL, fr. Richard *Richardson* †1741 Eng. botanist + NL *-ia*] *syn of* RICHARDIA
rich·ard·so·ni·an \ˌ¦==¦=nēən\ *adj, usu cap* [Samuel *Richardson* †1761 Eng. novelist + E *-ian*] : of or relating to the English novelist Richardson or to the sentimental or psychological fiction he produced
rich·ard·son's grouse \ˈrichə(r)dsənz-\ *n, usu cap R* [after Sir John *Richardson* †1865 Scot. naturalist] : a northern dusky grouse (*Dendragapus obscurus richardsonii*)
richardson's jaeger *n, usu cap R* [after Sir John *Richardson*] : PARASITIC JAEGER
richardson's owl *n, usu cap R* [after Sir John *Richardson*] : a small gray white-speckled owl (*Aegolius funereus richardsoni*) of the boreal forests of No. America
rich·ards's indicator \ˈrichə(r)dz(əz)-\ *n, usu cap R* [after Charles B. *Richards* †1919 Am. engineer, its inventor] : a steam-engine indicator using a straight-line reducing motion between the working piston and the recording stylus or pencil which makes it suitable for use on high-speed engines
richard's weed *n* [after *Richard* Richardson †1741 Eng. physician and botanist] : MEXICAN CLOVER
rich·ea \ˈrishēə\ *n, cap* [NL, fr. Col. A. *Riche* †1791 Fr. naturalist] : a genus of chiefly Tasmanian and usu. evergreen shrubs or trees (family Epacridaceae) with elongated sheathing leaves often in terminal tufts that resemble those of the ti
ri·chell·ite \rəˈsheˌlīt\ *n* -s [F *richellite*, fr. *Richelle*, near Visé, Liége prov., Belgium + F *-ite*] : a mineral $Ca_3Fe_{10}(PO_4)_8(OH,F)_{12}.nH_2O(?)$ consisting of a basic hydrous fluophosphate of iron and calcium in yellow masses
rich·en \ˈrichən\ *vt* -ED/-ING/-S [¹*rich* + *-en*] : to make rich or richer ⟨~ a mixture⟩ ⟨he used a privately furnished slush fund to ~ himself —R.C.Ruark⟩
richer *comparative of* RICH
rich·esse \ˈriˌches, rəˈch-\ *n* -s [ME — more at RICH] : RICHNESS
richest *superlative of* RICH
rich·ling \ˈrichliŋ\ *n* -s [¹*rich* + *-ling*] : a rich youth
rich·ly *adv* [ME *richely*, fr. OE *rīclīce*, fr. *rīce* rich + *-līce* -ly] **1** : in a rich manner **2** : in full measure : FULLY, AMPLY ⟨~ deserving of praise⟩
rich·mond \ˈrichmənd\ *adj, usu cap* **1** [fr. *Richmond*, capital of Virginia] : of or from Richmond, the capital of Virginia ⟨a *Richmond* historical site⟩ : of the kind or style prevalent in Richmond **2** [fr. *Richmond*, borough of New York City, N.Y.] : of or from the borough of Richmond, New York, N.Y. ⟨*Richmond* officials⟩ : of the kind or style prevalent in Richmond
rich·mon·de·na \ˌrichmənˈdēnə\ *n, cap* [NL, irreg. fr. Charles W. *Richmond* †1932 Am. ornithologist] : a genus of birds (family Fringillidae) consisting of the cardinals
rich·mond·er \ˈrichməndə(r)\ *n* -s *cap* [*Richmond*, capital of Virginia + E *-er*] : a native or resident of Richmond, Virginia
rich·ness *n* -ES [ME *richenesse*, fr. *riche* rich + *-nesse* -ness] : the quality or state of being rich ⟨the ~ of a country⟩ ⟨~ of allusion⟩
rich oil *n* : an absorbent oil rich in gasoline (as used in the manufacture of natural gasoline)
rich-pine \ˈ=ˌ=\ *n* [¹*rich*] *chiefly Midland* : KINDLING WOOD
rich rhyme *n* [trans. of F *rime riche*] : RIME RICHE
richt \ˈrikt\ *Scot var of* RIGHT
rich·ter·ite \ˈriktəˌrīt\ *n* -s [G *richterit*, fr. Theodor *Richter* †1898 Ger. metallurgical chemist + G *-it* -ite] : a mineral $(Na,K)_2(Mg,Mn,Ca)_6Si_8O_{22}(OH)_2$ that is a variety of amphibole containing as bases sodium, magnesium, manganese, potassium, and calcium
richweed \ˈ=ˌ=\ *n* [¹*rich* + *weed*] **1** : a plant of the genus *Pilea* — called also *clearweed* **2** : RAGWEED 2 a **3** : WHITE SNAKEROOT **4** : HORSE BALM 1
ricin \ˈrīsᵊn, ˈris-\ *n* -s [L *ricinus* castor-oil plant] : an amorphous and violently poisonous protein in the castor bean
ricin·elaidic acid \ˌ¦risᵊn, ¦risᵊn+. . .-\ *n* [*ricinoleic* + *elaidic*] : a crystalline unsaturated hydroxy fatty acid $HOC_{17}H_{32}COOH$ obtained from ricinoleic acid; the trans isomer of ricinoleic acid
ricing *pres part of* RICE
ri·cin·i·dae \rəˈsinəˌdē, rīˈs-\ *n pl, cap* [NL, fr. *Ricinus*, type genus (fr. L *ricinus* tick, louse) + *-idae*] : a large family of biting lice that includes numerous parasites of land and water birds
ri·ci·nine \ˈrisᵊnˌēn, -ᵊnən\ *n* -s [L *ricinus* castor-oil plant + E *-ine*] : a crystalline compound $C_8H_8N_2O_2$ derived from pyridone and obtained from castor beans
ricin·ole·ate \ˌ==ˈōlēˌāt, -ēˌāt\ *n* [*ricinoleic* + *-ate*] : a salt or ester of ricinoleic acid
ricin·oleic acid \ˌ¦==+. . .-\ *n* [L *ricinus* castor-oil plant + E *oleic*] : an oily unsaturated hydroxy fatty acid $HOC_{17}H_{32}COOH$ that is found in castor oil in the form of a glyceride and that readily polymerizes on heating; 12-hydroxy-oleic acid
ricin·ole·in \ˌ==ˈōlēən\ *n* [*ricinoleic* + *-in*] : an ester of glycerol and ricinoleic acid; *esp* : the tri-ricinoleate $C_3H_5(C_{18}H_{33}O_3)_3$ constituting the chief component of castor oil
ri·ci·nu·lei \ˌrisᵊnˈ(y)üleˌī\ *n pl, cap* [NL, pl. dim. of L *ricinus* tick] : a small order of Arachnida comprising living and fossil forms with an oval hard body bearing a large movable hood that folds down in front over the mouthparts — **ri·ci·nu·le·id** \-ēəd\ *n or adj*
ri·ci·nus \ˈrisᵊnəs\ *n* [NL, fr. L, tick, castor-oil plant (perh. fr. the resemblance of its seed to a tick)] **1** *cap* : a genus of plants (family Euphorbiaceae) having large palmate leaves and monoecious flowers with very numerous stamens — see CASTOR-OIL PLANT **2** -ES : any plant of the genus *Ricinus*
ricinus oil *n* [NL *Ricinus*] : CASTOR OIL
¹**rick** \ˈrik\ *n* -s [ME *reke*, *reek*, fr. OE *hrēac*; akin to ON *hraukr* rick, and perh. to OE *hrycg* ridge — more at RIDGE] **1** : an elongated stack or pile (as of grain, straw, or hay) in the open air and often protected from wet with thatching **2** : a pile of cordwood, stave bolts, or other material split from short logs; *specif* : a cord eight feet long by four feet high and of a width equal to the length of one stick **3** : a framework of wood or metal used in a warehouse to hold barrels of whiskey during the aging period
²**rick** \"\ *vt* -ED/-ING/-S : to heap up (as hay) in ricks : pile up
³**rick** \"\ *vt* -ED/-ING/-S [perh. fr. ME *wrikken* to move unsteadily] *chiefly Brit* : WRENCH, SPRAIN
⁴**rick** \"\ *n* -s *chiefly Brit* : SPRAIN
rick·ard·ite \ˈrikə(r)ˌdīt\ *n* -s [Thomas A. *Rickard* †1953 Am. mining engineer + E *-ite*] : a mineral Cu_4Te_3 consisting of a copper telluride and occurring in deep metallic purple masses
¹**rick·er** \ˈrikə(r)\ *n* -s [origin unknown] : POLE, SPAR
²**ricker** \"\ *n* -s [²*rick* + *-er*] : one that ricks; *specif* : one that places barrels of whiskey in ricks
rick·et·i·ly \ˈrikəd·ᵊlē\ *adv* [*rickety* + *-ly*] : in a rickety manner
rick·et·i·ness \-əd·ēnəs, -ətin-\ *n* -ES : the quality or state of being rickety
rick·ets \ˈrikəts\ *n pl but sing in constr* [origin unknown] **1** : a nutritional disturbance affecting the young of animals and man characterized by defective nutrition of the entire body and esp. faulty ossification of bone due to defective deposition and utilization of minerals (as calcium and phosphorus) owing to inadequate exposure to sunlight or deficient intake of vitamin D **2** : OSTEOMALACIA
rick·etts·emia \ˌrikətˈsēmēə\ *n* -s [NL, fr. *Rickettsia* + *-emia*] : the abnormal presence of rickettsiae in the blood
rick·ett·sia \rəˈketsēə\ *n* [NL, fr. Howard T. *Ricketts* †1910 Am. pathologist + NL *-ia*] **1** *cap* : the type genus of Rickettsiaceae comprising pleomorphic rod-shaped nonfilterable microorganisms that live intracellularly in biting arthropods and when transmitted to man by the bite of an arthropod host cause a number of serious diseases (as Rocky Mountain spotted fever and typhus) **2** *pl* **rickettsi·ae** \-sēˌē\ *or* **rickettsias** *also* **rickettsia** *sometimes cap* : any member of the genus *Rickettsia* or the family Rickettsiaceae
rickettsia body *n, sometimes cap R* : RICKETTSIA 2
rick·ett·si·a·ce·ae \rəˌketsēˈāsēˌē, (ˌ)riˌk-\ *n pl, cap* [NL, fr. *Rickettsia*, type genus + *-aceae*] : a family of microorganisms (order Rickettsiales) resembling bacteria and being typically inhabitants of arthropod tissues but capable in some cases of causing serious disease in man and other vertebrates — compare COWDRIA, RICKETTSIA

rick·ett·si·al \rəˈketsēəl, (ˈ)ri¦k-\ *adj* [NL *Rickettsia* + E *-al*] : of, relating to, or caused by rickettsiae ⟨a ~ disease⟩ ⟨~ vaccines⟩
rick·ett·si·a·les \rəˌketsēˈā(ˌ)lēz, (ˌ)riˌk-\ *n pl, cap* [NL, fr. *Rickettsia* + *-ales*] : an order of small pleomorphic gram-negative microorganisms of uncertain biological position that are obligate parasites living in vertebrates or in arthropods which often serve as vectors of those parasitic in vertebrates — see BARTONELLACEAE, RICKETTSIACEAE; compare CHLAMYDIACEAE
rickettsialpox \(ˌ)=¦===ˌ=\ *n* [*rickettsial* + *pox*] : a disease characterized by fever, chills, headache, backache, and a spotty rash and caused by a rickettsia (*Rickettsia akari*) thought to be transmitted to man by the bite of a mite living on mice
rick·ett·si·o·sis \rəˌketsēˈōsəs, (ˌ)riˌk-\ *n, pl* **rickettsio·ses** \-ōˌsēz\ [NL *Rickettsia* + *-osis*] : infection with or disease caused by a rickettsia ⟨a mild ~⟩
rick·ett·sio·stat·ic \rə¦ketsēō¦stad·ik\ *adj* [NL *Rickettsia* + *-o-* + Gk *statikos* causing to stand — more at STATIC] : growth-inhibiting for rickettsiae
rick·ety \ˈrikəd·ē, -ətˌ ¦i\ *adj* [*rickets* + *-y*] **1** : affected with rickets : RACHITIC **2 a** : feeble in the joints : TOTTERING ⟨a ~ old man⟩ **b** : SHAKY, UNSOUND ⟨a ~ building⟩
rick·ey \ˈrikē, -ki\ *n* -s [prob. fr. the name *Rickey*] **1** : a tall drink consisting of a spirituous liquor, lime juice, sugar, and soda water and served with ice cubes and the peel of the used lime in the glass ⟨gin ~⟩ **2** : a nonalcoholic carbonated drink usu. containing lime juice or orange juice
¹**rick·le** \ˈrikəl\ *n* -s [perh. of Scand origin; akin to Norw dial *rikl*, *rukl* small heap of stones] **1** *dial Brit* : a small stack : loose heap : PILE ⟨a ~ of stones⟩ **2** *dial Brit* : something loosely put together; *specif* : a lanky loose-jointed person
²**rickle** \"\ *vt* -ED/-ING/-S *dial Brit* : to make into a pile
rick·ma·tic \ˈrikməˌtik\ *n* -s [origin unknown] *chiefly Scot* : CONCERN, BUSINESS ⟨the whole ~ was a wreck⟩
rick·rack *or* **ric·rac** \ˈriˌkrak\ *n* -s [redupl. of ⁴*rack*] : a flat braid usu. of cotton or rayon woven under tension to form small even zigzags and used as a decorative trimming or an openwork insertion on clothing

rickrack

ricks *pl of* RICK, *pres 3d sing of* RICK
rick·sha *or* **rick·shaw** \ˈrikˌshȯ\ *n* -s [by shortening & contr.] : JINRIKISHA
rickstand \ˈ=ˌ=\ *n* [¹*rick* + *stand*] : a flooring or frame for a rick
rickyard \ˈ=ˌ=\ *n* [¹*rick* + *yard*] : the part of a farm in which hay or fodder is ricked or stacked : STACKYARD
¹**ric·o·chet** \ˈrikəˌshā, ˌ==ˈ=, *chiefly Brit* -shet\ *n* -s [F] **1** : a glancing rebound or skipping (as of a projectile along the ground when a gun is fired at a low angle of elevation or of a flat stone thrown along the surface of water); *also* : an object that ricochets **2** : a bounding or thrown staccato played or to be played in one bow stroke (as on the down bow) — used as a musical direction for bowed stringed instruments
²**ricochet** \"\ *vi* **ricocheted** \-ād\ *or* **ricochetted** \-etəd\ **ricocheted** *or* **ricochetted; ricocheting** \-āiŋ\ *or* **ricochetting** \-etiŋ\ **ricochets** **1** : to skip with a glancing rebound or series of rebounds ⟨a *~ing* bullet⟩ **2** : to move, fly, or strike in the manner of a ricochet
ricochet fire *n* : fire in which the projectile glances from a surface after impact
ric·o·let·ta·ite \ˌrikəˈled·əˌīt\ *n* -s [*Ricoletta*, locality in Tirol + E *-ite*] : an igneous rock that is a basic granogabbro composed of anorthite, some orthoclase, and pyroxene with accessory biotite, olivine, and magnetite
ri·cot·ta \riˈkȯd·ə, -ˈōt(ˌ)tä\ *n* -s [It, fr. L *recocta*, fem. of *recoctus*, past part. of *recoquere* to cook again, boil again, fr. *re-* + *coquere* to cook — more at COOK] : a white unripened whey cheese of Italian origin that resembles cottage cheese
ric·tal \ˈriktᵊl\ *adj* [NL *rictus* + E *-al*] : of or relating to the rictus
ric·tus \-təs\ *n, pl* **rictus** *or* **rictuses** [NL, fr. L, open mouth, fr. *rictus*, past part. of *ringi* to open the mouth, show the teeth; akin to OSlav *ręgnąti* to gape, and perh. to OE *wrencan* to twist — more at WRENCH] **1** : the gape of the mouth of a bird **2 a** : the mouth orifice **b** : a gaping grin or grimace ⟨a face frozen in a ~ of terror⟩
¹**rid** \ˈrid, *dial* ˈred\ *vb* **rid** *also* **ridded; rid** *also* **ridded; ridding; rids** [ME *ruden, rudden, ridden*, fr. ON *rythja*; akin to OE *āryddan* to plunder, OHG *riutan* to clear land, Av *raoiδya-* to prepare for cultivation, L *ruere* to dig up — more at RUIN] *vt* **1** *archaic* **a** : to clear or free (as land) of obstructions, waste, or encumbrances **b** : to clear away : clean up **2 a** *archaic* : to set free : DELIVER — often used with *of* or *from* **b** : to make (someone or something) free : RELIEVE — often used in the phrase *be rid of* or *get rid of* ⟨succeeded in getting ~ of a huge billboard —Edward Bok⟩ ⟨was glad to ~ herself of the burden —C.S.Forester⟩ **3** : to take away : clear off : REMOVE **4** *chiefly dial* : to get through (work) : DISPATCH **5** *dial* : ²REDD ~ *vi, chiefly dial* : to become dispatched
syn CLEAR, UNBURDEN, DISABUSE, PURGE: RID is a rather general term but is likely to refer to concrete or specific matters which are burdensome or pestiferous ⟨England had in the meantime *ridded* herself of the Stuarts, worried along under the Hanoverians —Agnes Repplier⟩ ⟨a lazy man's expedient for *ridding* himself of the trouble of thinking and deciding —B.N.Cardozo⟩ CLEAR is likely to be used to refer to tangible matters which obstruct progress, clutter an area, or block vision ⟨wars which . . . enabled the United States first to *clear* its own territory of foreign troops —S.F.Bemis⟩ ⟨rose from the food she had barely tasted and began to *clear* the table —Ellen Glasgow⟩ and may be used also in relation to ideas that hinder progress ⟨of service to his fellow Methodists in *clearing* away obstructions to modern thinking —H.K. Rowe⟩ UNBURDEN is likely to indicate freeing oneself from something taxing or something distressing the mind or spirit, in the latter situation often by confessing, revealing, frankly discussing ⟨insisted that he *unburden* himself of most of the weighty chores that go with the job of majority leader —*Time*⟩ ⟨conquers his own submissiveness and *unburdens* himself, before his domineering wife, of all the accumulated resentment and dislike —S.M.Fitzgerald⟩ DISABUSE is likely to refer to freeing the mind from an erroneous notion or an attitude or feeling making clear straightforward thought difficult ⟨if men are now sufficiently enlightened to *disabuse* themselves of artifice, hypocrisy, and superstition —John Adams⟩ ⟨neither familiarity with the history and institutions of Old World nations nor contact with them during two wars *disabused* the average American of his feeling of superiority —H.S.Commager⟩ PURGE may refer to cleansing out of or purification from that which is impure or alien or extrinsic ⟨*purged* of all its unorthodox views —G.B.Shaw⟩ ⟨the room had never quite been *purged* of the bad taste of preceding generations —Edmund Wilson⟩ In political matters it may suggest ruthless elimination ⟨the dictator has *purged* academic faculties of every savant suspected of being opposed to his regime —Howard M. Jones⟩
²**rid** [ME *riden* (past pl. & past part.), fr. OE *ridon* (past pl.), *geriden* (past part.)] *chiefly dial past of* RIDE
³**rid** \ˈrid\ *dial var of* ⁵REDD
⁴**rid** \"\ *dial var of* RED
rid·abil·i·ty \ˌrīdəˈbiləd·ē, -lətē, -i\ *n* : the quality or state of being ridable
rid·able *or* **ride·able** \ˈrīdəbəl\ *adj* [¹*ride* + *-able*] **1** : capable of being ridden (as a horse) : fit for riding **2** : fit to be ridden over (as a road or ford) — **ridably** *adv*
rid·dance \ˈridᵊn(t)s\ *n* -s [¹*rid* + *-ance*] **1** : an act of ridding, freeing, or cleaning : CLEARANCE ⟨the experiments showed high rates of kill with some of them showing 100 percent ~ —J.B.Robson⟩ **2** *obs* : progress with a task : dispatch of work **3** : DELIVERANCE, RELIEF — often used in the phrase *good riddance* ⟨it's gone — and good ~ too —Weston LaBarre⟩

rid·del *also* **rid·dle** \ˈridᵊl\ *n* -s [ME *ridel, riddel*, perh. fr. *riddil* riddle (sieve)] : a church curtain : one of the side curtains of an altar
¹**ridden** [ME *riden*, fr. OE *geriden*] *past part of* RIDE
²**rid·den** \ˈridᵊn\ *adj* **1** : extremely concerned with or bothered by — usu. used in combination ⟨conscience-*ridden*⟩ **2** : excessively full of or supplied with — usu. used in combination ⟨slum-*ridden*⟩
¹**rid·der** \ˈridə(r)\ *n* -s [ME, fr. OE *hrider, hridder* — more at *riddle* (sieve)] *chiefly Eng* : a sieve esp. for sifting grain
²**ridder** \"\ *n* -s [¹*rid* + *-er*] : one that rids
rid·ding \ˈridiŋ\ *n* -s [fr. gerund of ¹*rid*] *dial Eng* : a clearing in the woods — used esp. in place names
¹**rid·dle** \ˈridᵊl\ *n* -s [ME *redels, redel, ridel*, fr. OE *rǣdels, rǣdelse* opinion, conjecture, riddle; akin to MHG *rātsel* riddle, OE *rǣdan* to advise, interpret — more at READ] **1** : a mystifying, misleading, or puzzling question posed as a problem to be solved or guessed often as a game : CONUNDRUM, ENIGMA **2** : something or someone difficult to understand : a problematical event, situation, or person : MYSTERY ⟨the eternal ~ of nominalism and realism —B.N.Cardozo⟩ ⟨will help the scientist to solve one of the many *~s* of cancer —Waldemar Kaempffert⟩ **syn** see MYSTERY
²**riddle** \"\ *vb* **riddled; riddled; riddling** \-d(ᵊ)liŋ\ **riddles** *vt* **1** : to find the solution of : EXPLAIN, INTERPRET **2** : to create or set a riddle for : MYSTIFY, PERPLEX, PUZZLE ~ *vi* : to speak in or propound riddles
³**riddle** \"\ *n* -s [ME *riddil*, fr. OE *hriddel*, alter. of *hrider*, *hridder* — more at CERTAIN] **1** : a coarse sieve: as **a** : a sieve for grading potatoes **b** : a device for sifting coal **c** : a sieve for panning gold **d** : a sieve for sand used in a foundry **e** : a strainer kept in motion to sift middlings in flour milling **2** *archaic* : a compartmented case or container or its contents; *esp* : a 13-bottle case of wine **3** *archaic* : a board set with zigzag pins between which wire is drawn to straighten it

riddle 1d

⁴**riddle** \"\ *vb* -ED/-ING/-S [ME *ridlen, riddlen*, fr. *riddil* sieve] *vt* **1** : to separate (as grain from the chaff) with a riddle : pass through or as if through a riddle : SCREEN, SIFT ⟨*riddled* the coal to grade it by size⟩ **2 a** : to fill (something or someone) as full of holes as a sieve : puncture often and thoroughly ⟨he stood up, *riddled* them with fire and flopped down again —Dave Richardson⟩ ⟨*riddled* the ship with a broadside⟩ ⟨it had become badly *riddled* by termites —*Amer. Guide Series: La.*⟩ **b** : to spread throughout : PERMEATE ⟨the graft that *~s* virtually every metropolitan police force —August Heckscher⟩ ⟨its lawn *riddled* with weeds —Bernard Kalb⟩ ~ *vi* : to use a riddle : sift through : PENETRATE, PIERCE ⟨cold winds ~ through the thin walls⟩
riddle and shears *n pl but sing in constr* [³*riddle*] *dial Brit* : SIEVE AND SHEARS
riddle canon *n* [¹*riddle*] : a musical canon esp. popular in the 15th and 16th centuries in which the entrances of the successive parts were indicated by monograms, symbols, or other cabalistic devices — called also *enigma canon*
rid·dle·me·ree \¦ridᵊlmə¦rē\ *n* -s [by shortening and alter. fr. the phrase *riddle my riddle*] *archaic* : RIGMAROLE
¹**rid·dler** \ˈrid(ᵊ)lə(r)\ *n* -s [²*riddle* + *-er*] : one that propounds, speaks in, or tries to solve riddles
²**riddler** \"\ *n* -s [⁴*riddle* + *-er*] : a worker who sifts with a riddle: as **a** : one who screens cut tobacco to remove coarse pieces **b** : one who cleans metal parts by shaking them in a riddle to remove loose chips
¹**riddling** *n* -s [fr. gerund of ²*riddle*] : a posing of or play with riddles
²**riddling** *adj* [fr. pres. part. of ²*riddle*] **1** : speaking in riddles : containing or presenting riddles : EQUIVOCAL, ENIGMATIC ⟨the hero's own language is often ~ —Maynard Mack⟩ **2** : riddle-solving : DIVINING — **rid·dling·ly** *adv*
³**riddling** *n* -s [fr. gerund of ⁴*riddle*] **1** : the act of sifting : SCREENING **2 riddlings** *pl* : coarse material left in a riddle after shaking : SIFTINGS
¹**ride** \ˈrīd\ *vb* **rode** \ˈrōd\ *or chiefly dial* **rid** \ˈrid\ *or* **rade** \ˈrād\ **rid·den** \ˈridᵊn\ *or chiefly dial* **rid** *or* **rode; riding** \ˈrīdiŋ\ **rides** [ME *riden*, fr. OE *rīdan* to ride, travel, swing; akin to OHG *rītan* to ride, ON *rītha* to ride, travel, swing, OIr *rīadaim* I ride, travel, Gaulish *rēda* wagon] *vi* **1 a** : to sit and be carried on the back of an animal (as a horse) that one directs and controls **b** : to participate in a raid or military or vigilante action of mounted men **c** : to travel or become conveyed by a vehicle (as a carriage, an automobile, or a railroad train) : become carried (as in a litter or on men's shoulders) **2** : to seem to move or become borne along by an intangible agency : become sustained, supported, or forwarded ⟨*rode* on the wave of popularity⟩ **3** : to seem to float : FLOAT: as **a** : LIE, REST ⟨the squadron *rode* safely at anchor⟩ **b** : to sail, skim, or become driven over the water ⟨the little boat *rode* lightly before a breeze⟩ **c** : to move like a floating object ⟨a full moon *rode* in the night sky⟩ **4** : to become supported at rest or in motion on an axle, pivot, or other bearing point or surface ⟨the lever carries two studs, both of which ~ in the cam —William Landon & George Hafferkamp⟩ **5** *of a male animal* : to mount in copulation **6** : to travel over a surface ⟨a big powerful car that *~s* smoothly and quietly⟩ **7** *archaic* : PROJECT **8** : to take its course : continue without interference ⟨let it ~⟩ **9** : to be contingent : DEPEND ⟨his party's hopes seemed to ~ on his renomination⟩ **10** : to climb up on the body : bunch up in folds or ridges ⟨my skirt had *ridden* up above my knees, the way a tight skirt will —S.A.Offit⟩ **11 a** : to become bet ⟨his money is *riding* on the favorite⟩ **b** : to remain as a bet — used of an original bet or stake plus accumulated winnings ⟨he let his winnings ~⟩ **12** : to improvise variations freely on a jazz theme ~ *vt* **1 a** : to sit and be carried on while directing and controlling ⟨a jockey who had *ridden* many a winner⟩ ⟨*rode* a bicycle daily to a ripe age⟩ **b** : to move with or be carried by like a rider ⟨*rode* the waves with an experienced swimmer's ease⟩ ⟨bad news *~s* the lightning —Irving Stone⟩ **2 a** : to traverse (as a route or distance) on horseback or by vehicle ⟨*rode* a mail route daily for years⟩ ⟨abolishing the requirement that supreme court judges ~ circuit —C.B.Swisher⟩ ⟨*rode* hundreds of miles⟩ **b** : to ride a horse in ⟨~ a winning race⟩ **3 a** : to endure without great damage : SURVIVE, LAST ⟨a large sailing vessel . . . *riding* the storm —*Western Mail*⟩ — usu. used with *out* ⟨*rode* out the gale in safety —R.H.Dana⟩ ⟨can ~ out the current adjustment without having to make drastic price revisions —*Newsweek*⟩ **b** : to move with (something fluctuating or dangerous) so as to emerge unharmed : SURMOUNT, SURVIVE ⟨~ an adverse situation⟩ ⟨were now trying to ~ the devastating postwar slump in agriculture —Roy Lewis & Angus Maude⟩ **4** : to traverse on horseback in order to inspect or maintain ⟨~ fence⟩ **5** : to mount in or as if in copulation — used of a male animal **6 a** : to burden or oppress as if by the weight of a rider : weigh down ⟨only a man, *ridden* by anxiety and impotence, by desire and guilt —L.A.Fiedler⟩ ⟨was *ridden* by a veritable devil —E.P.Hanson⟩ **b** (1) : to harass persistently (as by carping criticism, ridicule, or abuse) : subject to pertinacious or concerted annoyance, irritation, or distress ⟨the officers in that tropic outpost *rode* the artist mercilessly⟩ (2) : TEASE, RIB, BANTER **7 a** : to convey like a rider : give a ride to ⟨*rode* the youngster on his back⟩ ⟨exposed him and *rode* him out of town on a rail⟩ **b** : to convey in a vehicle ⟨*rode* a shipment of castings back to the plant in the truck on his return trip⟩ **c** *archaic* : to keep (a ship) anchored or moored **8** : to project over : OVERLAP, OVERRIDE **9** : to urge (a racehorse) to the limit **10** : to aim too long at (a moving target) thereby losing coordination and proper lead and making a miss more likely **11** : to manipulate (a log drive) while standing on floating logs **12** : to recoil from or give with (a landing punch or blow) in order to soften the impact **13** : to legally charge (an opponent who has possession of the ball) in lacrosse **14** : to improvise variations on (a jazz theme) at will **syn** see BAIT — **ride a hobby** : to pursue a favorite topic

or activity — **ride and tie** *archaic* **:** to share a single horse with someone by taking turns in riding and walking, each rider leaving the horse tied at the end of his ride for the use of the man following on foot — **ride circuit :** to hold court in the various towns where court may be lawfully held in a judicial circuit under laws requiring the judge to travel for that purpose — **ride for a fall :** to court danger **:** behave recklessly — **ride herd on :** to look out for **:** keep in check **:** OVERSEE, POLICE ⟨here comes an officer to *ride herd on* us —Erle Stanley Gardner⟩ — **ride roughshod over :** to treat with disdain or abuse ⟨warn him not to *ride roughshod over* the younger children⟩ — **ride rusty** *archaic* **:** to grow obstinate or refractory — **ride the brake** *or* **ride the clutch :** to keep in partial engagement by resting a foot continuously on the pedal with resultant unnecessary mechanical wear — **ride the gain :** to control the output of sound reproducing equipment manually to prevent blasting at high volume — **ride the line :** to ride around the edges of a herd of cattle to round up strays — **ride the marches** *archaic* **:** to ride along boundaries to inspect or reaffirm them — **ride the rods :** to ride the truss rods beneath a railroad car as a hobo — **ride the vents :** to prepare a submarine to submerge — **ride to hounds :** to chase a fox on horseback with hounds

²**ride** \"\ *n* -s **1 :** an act of riding; *esp* **:** a journey or trip on horseback or by vehicle **2 :** MOUNT **3 :** a way (as a road or path) suitable for riding; *specif* **:** a lane in a forest **4 :** any of various mechanical devices at an amusement park or carnival for riding on **5 a :** a trip on which gangsters take a victim in order to murder him ⟨this case has the earmarks of a ~ —Jack Heise⟩ — usu. used in the phrase *take for a ride* **b :** GOING-OVER ⟨has some confused ideas that the reviewer takes for a ~⟩ **c :** HOODWINKING, SWINDLING ⟨do not want to be taken for a ~ by foreign financiers who would take our money and let us whistle for repayment —Alvin Johnson⟩ **6 :** any of various positions in which a wrestler is astride or above a prone opponent **7 a :** a means of transportation ⟨advertised for a daily ~ to the city⟩ **b :** a person providing transportation ⟨my ~ said he would be late⟩ **8 :** public interest or attention **:** NOTICE ⟨disk jockeys were giving the one-week-old recording a big ~ —*Newsweek*⟩ **9 :** the qualities of travel comfort provided by a vehicle — **for the ride :** for the satisfaction of an activity **:** for fun ⟨I just go along *for the ride* —W.J.Reilly⟩

³**ride** \"\ *n* -s [perh. fr. ¹*ride*] *chiefly dial* **:** the strap of a hinge

rideable *var of* RIDABLE

rideal-walker test \rə'dē(ə)l'wȯkə(r)-\ *n, usu cap R&W* [after Samuel *Rideal* †1929 & J.T.A.*Walker* Eng. chemists] **:** a test for determining the phenol coefficient esp. of a disinfectant

ri·deau \rə'dō\ *n* -s [F, fr. MF, lit., curtain; perh. fr. ME *ridel, riddel* curtain — more at RIDDEL] **:** a small ridge or mound of earth **:** ground slightly elevated

ride down *vt* **1 :** to tread under one's horse's feet **:** OVERTHROW, TRAMPLE **2 :** to bear down on (as a halyard when hoisting a sail)

ri·dent \'rīdᵊnt\ *adj* [L *rident-, ridens*, pres. part. of *ridēre* to laugh — more at RIDICULOUS] *archaic* **:** broadly smiling

ride off *vt* **1 :** to ride so as to deflect (an opposing polo player) **2 :** RIDE OUT 1

rideoff \'=,=\ *n* -s [*ride off*] **:** an act or instance of riding alongside a polo opponent and pushing him away from the line of the ball to prevent his hitting it

ride out *vt* **1 :** to cut out or separate by riding ⟨*rode* the bull *out* of the herd⟩ **2 :** to urge (a racehorse) to the limit

rid·er \'rīdə(r)\ *n* -s [ME, fr. OE *rīdere*, fr. *rīdan* to ride + *-ere* -er] **1 :** one that rides horseback: as **a** *archaic* **:** a mounted highwayman, freebooter, or moss-trooper **b :** COWBOY 3a **c :** a circus performer who rides horses **d :** a mounted agent employed on a plantation — compare DITCH RIDER **e :** JOCKEY **2 :** one that rides a vehicle ⟨train ~⟩ ⟨motorcycle ~⟩ **3 a** [trans. of D *rijder*] **:** a Dutch ryder **b :** a Scotch gold coin issued by James III and his successor **4 a :** an addition or amendment to a manuscript, printer's proof, or other document often attached on a separate piece of paper **:** ALLONGE, ANNEX, CODICIL **b :** something added as an extra to a seemingly completed statement or act **c** *Brit* **:** a recommendation by a jury appended to its verdict **d :** a clause appended to a legislative bill to secure an object usu. entirely distinct from that of the bill itself ⟨wantonly violates the Constitution in attaching legislative ~*s* to appropriation bills —*New Republic*⟩ **5 :** something used to overlie or cover another (as an upper tier of casks, a turn of a rope, or a tree placed on a wall) **6 a :** a rail laid slanting in the forks of the cross stakes at the corner of a worm fence as a reinforcement **b :** a small movable adjusting weight on the beam of a balance resembling the weight on a steelyard **c :** a pipe above and parallel to a main pipe into which part of the flow is diverted over a considerable distance and from which the flow is redirected into the main **7** *archaic* **:** TRAVELING SALESMAN **8 a :** the top raker of a set of raking shores **b :** the strap of a hinge **9 :** ENDORSEMENT 2 b **10 a :** a thin parallel coal seam or mineral vein overlying a larger seam or vein **b :** the country rock between them **c :** a body of barren or country rock occurring as a horse within a vein **11 :** a vibrating steel roller that rests on and rotates in contact with a form roller to augment the distribution of printing ink **12 :** a man who rides a freight car being switched over the hump of a railroad classification yard in order to set the brakes and stop the car at the proper point **13 :** an extra rib timber set in between the frames of a wooden ship **14 :** a logger who drives a horse or mule to haul rigging equipment back to the woods after each log has been skidded to the yard or landing

rid·ered \'rīdə(r)d\ *adj* [*rider* + *-ed*] **:** having riders across the stakes — used of a fence

rider embolus *n* **:** SADDLE EMBOLUS

rid·er·ess \'rīdərəs\ *n* -ES [*rider* + *-ess*] **:** a female rider

rider keelson *n* **:** a line of timber or plates fastened to the top of a ship's keelson

rid·er·less \'rīdə(r)ləs\ *adj* **:** having no rider

rider plate *n* **:** a continuous horizontal flat plate connected to the top of a ship's vertical keel

rider's bone *n* **:** a bony deposit in the muscles of the upper and inner part of the thigh due to pressure and chronic irritation that are caused by the saddle in riding — called also *cavalry bone*

ride up *vi* **:** to work up on the person **:** climb up — used of clothing ⟨a girdle that won't *ride up*⟩

¹**ridge** \'rij\ *n* -s [ME *rigge*, fr. OE *hrycg*; akin to OHG *hrukki* back, spine, mountain ridge, ON *hryggr* back, spine, mountain ridge, L *cruc-, crux* stake used for punishment, cross, Skt *kruñcati* it curves, L *curvus* curved — more at CROWN] **1 a** *obs* **:** the back or backbone of a man or an animal **b :** the projecting or elevated part of the back along the line of the backbone **c :** an elevated body part projecting from a surface ⟨the urogenital ~⟩ **2 a :** a range of hills or mountains or the upper part of such a range **:** an extended elevation between valleys **b :** an elongate elevation on an ocean bottom **3 :** a top or upper part esp. when long and narrow **:** CREST **4 a :** a raised line or strip (as of ground thrown up by a plow between furrows) **b :** BEACH RIDGE **c :** a small raised line on the surface of metal, cloth, or bone **5 a :** the line of intersection at the top between the opposite slopes or sides of a roof **b :** a shingle, tile, or slate adjacent to the ridge of a roof **c :** the horizontal beam to which the upper ends of the rafters of a roof are fixed **:** RIDGEPOLE **d :** the internal angle of a vault **6 :** either of the two projections of a bound book parallel to the joint and formed by the bend put in the sections in the backing operation — called also *shoulder* **7 :** a wedge-shaped extension of a high-pressure area — opposed to *trough* **8 :** the upper part of the narrow posterior end of the body of a whale **9 :** the raised knitting pattern formed by garter stitch made by two rows of knit stitch

²**ridge** \"\ *vb* -ED/-ING/-S *vt* **1 :** to form into a ridge **:** furnish or mark with ridges **2 a :** to plow alternate strips in by turning the furrow onto an unplowed strip **b :** to throw soil toward (a crop row) from both sides ⟨*ridged* his corn⟩ **c :** to spade or plow (ground) into alternate ridges and troughs ⟨if low lands must be used for the bean crop, they should be *ridged* —E.V.Wilcox⟩ ~ *vi* **:** to form into or become marked with ridges **:** extend in ridges ⟨the land ~*s* northward⟩

ridgeband \'=,=\ *n* [¹*ridge* + *band*] *dial Brit* **:** the part of a harness that passes over the saddle and supports the shafts of a cart

ridge beech *n* **:** a common beech (*Fagus grandifolia*) of No. America

ridgeboard \'=,=\ *n* **:** RIDGEPOLE 1

ridgebone \'=,=\ *n* [ME *riggebone*, fr. OE *hrycgbān*, fr. *hrycg* ridge + *bān* bone] *archaic* **:** BACKBONE

ridge buster *n* **:** a cultivator equipped with disks for tearing down ridges and filling the furrows

ridgecap \'=,=\ *n* **:** a wood or metal covering placed over the ridge of a roof

ridged \'rijd\ *adj* [¹*ridge* + *-ed*] **:** having a ridge **:** RIDGY

ridge fillet *n* **1 :** a ridge between flutes of a column or other depressions **2 :** a main runner for molten metal

ridge harrow *n* **:** a harrow hinged longitudinally so as to run partly on the side of a ridge

ridg·el \'rijəl\ *n* -s [perh. fr. ¹*ridge*] **:** RIDGELING

ridge·let \'rijlət\ *n* -s [¹*ridge* + *-let*] **:** a small ridge

ridgelike \'=,=\ *adj* **:** resembling a ridge

ridgeline \'=,=\ *n* **:** a line marking or following a ridge top

ridge·ling *or* **ridg·ling** \'rijliŋ\ *n* -s [perh. fr. ¹*ridge* + *-ling*; fr. the supposed remaining of the undescended testes near the animal's back] **1 :** a male animal having one or both testes undescended; *esp* **:** a horse exhibiting such abnormality and being typically male in conformation and behavior but sterile when the condition is bilateral **2 :** an imperfectly castrated male animal — compare HALF-CASTRATE

ridge plow *n* **:** ²LISTER 1

ridgepole \'=,=\ *n* **1 :** the highest horizontal timber in a roof and the receiver of the upper ends of the rafters — see ROOF illustration **2 :** the horizontal pole at the top of a tent

¹**ridg·er** \'rijə(r)\ *n* -s [¹*ridge* + *-er*] *dial Brit* **:** RIDGEBAND

²**ridger** *n* -s [²*ridge* + *-er*] **:** one that ridges: as **a :** ²LISTER 1 **b :** LISTER CULTIVATOR **c :** an implement for making levees in the check system of irrigation

ridge rib *n* **:** a rib marking the ridge of a vault

ridge roll *n* **:** a metal, tile, or wood strip rounded at the top and used as finishing for the ridge of a roof

ridge roof *n* **:** GABLE ROOF

ridgerope \'=,=\ *n* [¹*ridge* + *rope*] **1 :** a lifeline alongside the bowsprit of a ship **2 :** a rope just above and parallel to a ship's rail **3 a :** the backbone of a ship's awning **b :** a rope along a ship's side to which the side of an awning is made fast **c :** a rope forming the backbone or ridgepole of a tent

ridge runner *n, chiefly Midland* **:** a mountain farmer **:** HILLBILLY, HICK

ridges *pl of* RIDGE, *pres 3d sing of* RIDGE

ridge stone *n* **1 :** a stone for the margin of a well or shaft **2 :** APEX STONE

ridge tile *n* **:** an often decorative tile of bent or curved section used in covering the ridge of a roof — compare HIP TILE

ridgetop \'=,=\ *n* **:** the crest of a ridge ⟨climbed away from the river . . . toward the ~ —A.W.Peterson⟩

ridgetree \'=,=\ *n, archaic* **:** RIDGEPOLE

ridgeway \'=,=\ *n* **:** a road following the ridge of a hill or of a range of hills ⟨on road and on ~, on sea and on land —J.M.Synge⟩

ridging *n* -s [fr. gerund of ²*ridge*] **1 a :** the making of a ridge **b :** the throwing of soil toward a crop row from both sides ⟨the ~ of potatoes⟩ ⟨the ~ of sugarcane⟩ **2 :** the material of which the ridge of a roof is made or with which it is covered

ridging plow *n* **:** ²LISTER 1

ridgy \'rijē\ *adj* -ER/-EST [¹*ridge* + *-y*] **:** having ridges **:** rising in a ridge

¹**rid·i·cule** \'ridə,kyül, -dē,k-\ *n* -s [F or L; F *ridicule* fr. L *ridiculum* laughing matter, jest — more at RIDICULOUS] **1** *archaic* **:** something or someone absurd or laughable **2 :** the arousing of laughter, mockery, or scorn at someone or something **:** the casting of an absurd or derisive light on a person or thing ⟨my early work was written in secret to escape ~ —Ellen Glasgow⟩ **3** *archaic* **:** the quality or state of being laughable **:** RIDICULOUSNESS ⟨gave an air of ~ to his greatest actions —Oliver Goldsmith⟩

²**ridicule** \"\ *vt* -ED/-ING/-S **:** to subject to ridicule or mockery **:** make fun of **:** DERIDE ⟨death and disease ~ man's petty arrogance —Harriet Zinnes⟩ ⟨pointed a moral or *ridiculed* his opponents —*Amer. Guide Series: La.*⟩

syn RIDICULE, DERIDE, MOCK, TAUNT, TWIT, and RALLY agree in meaning to make someone or something the object of laughter. RIDICULE implies the belittling, often malicious, of the person or thing ridiculed ⟨gouge, expose, and *ridicule* the stupidity of human beings —Edwin Edwards⟩ ⟨the man who wants to preserve his personal identity is *ridiculed* as an eccentric or resented as a snob —S.J.Harris⟩ DERIDE implies bitterness against or contempt for the person or thing derided ⟨took his revenge on the fate that had made him sad by fiercely *deriding* everything —Aldous Huxley⟩ ⟨books were likely to be *derided* or ignored by the critics —E.A.Davidson⟩ MOCK stresses the scorn, often ironic, of the person mocking ⟨anger seized her at the suspicion that he was *mocking* them —Ellen Glasgow⟩ ⟨now taking on one expression and then another, in imitation of various people he was *mocking* —D.H.Lawrence⟩ TAUNT implies mockery and suggests jeeringly provoking insults ⟨*taunt* a boy into a fight⟩ ⟨the mill foreman so *taunted* the workers, so badgered them and told them that they dared not quit —Sinclair Lewis⟩ TWIT formerly implied taunts or throwing something up to someone, but now, like RALLY, implies a bantering, good-humored teasing or mockery, though sometimes coming close to taunting ⟨the absence of ideas with which Matthew Arnold *twits* them —W.R.Inge⟩ ⟨*twit* Victorian manners and morals —*Time*⟩ ⟨all the charming witticisms of English lecturers who *twitted* us about our standardization and materialism —Eric Sevareid⟩ ⟨he loved his mistress . . . no one dared . . . *rally* him on his weakness —G.B.Shaw⟩ ⟨it would be amusing to *rally* her friend . . . for neglecting his wife —Edith Sitwell⟩

³**ridicule** \', -kəl\ *n* -s [F, alter. of *réticule* — more at RETICULE] *chiefly dial* **:** RETICULE 2

rid·i·cul·er \-,kyülə(r)\ *n* -s [²*ridicule* + *-er*] **:** one that engages in ridicule

ri·dic·u·los·i·ty \rə,dikyə'läsəd·ē\ *n* -ES [L *ridiculosus* + E *-ity*] **1 :** the quality or state of being ridiculous **:** RIDICULOUSNESS **2 :** something ridiculous

ri·dic·u·lous \rə'dikyələs, *chiefly in substand speech* -k(ə)ləs\ *adj* [L *ridiculosus* or *ridiculus*; *ridiculosus* fr. *ridiculum* laughing matter, jest (fr. neut. of *ridiculus* laughable, ridiculous) + *-osus* -ous; *ridiculus* fr. *ridēre* to laugh; akin to Skt *vrīḍate* he is ashamed] **1 :** fit or likely to excite ridicule **:** unworthy of serious consideration **:** ABSURD, COMICAL, FUNNY, LAUGHABLE, PREPOSTEROUS ⟨here surely is the world's record in the domain of the ~ and the contemptible —Sir Winston Churchill⟩ ⟨to be made ~ before her increased his humiliation —W.S. Maugham⟩ **2** *dial* **:** violating decency or moral sense **:** INDECENT, OUTRAGEOUS, SCANDALOUS **syn** see LAUGHABLE

ri·dic·u·lous·ly *adv* **:** in a ridiculous manner **:** ABSURDLY, LAUGHABLY ⟨was ~ absent-minded, and many stories circulated regarding her peculiarities —H.E.Starr⟩

ri·dic·u·lous·ness *n* -ES **:** the quality or state of being ridiculous **:** LAUGHABLENESS

¹**ri·ding** \'rīdiŋ, -dēŋ\ *n* -s [ME *riding, rithing*, by simplification of *-th th-, -t th-* in (assumed) *north thriding, east thriding, west thriding*, fr. (assumed) OE *thriding, thrithing* (whence ML *treding, trehinga*), fr. ON *thrithjungr* third part, fr. *thrithi* third + *-ungr* -ing — more at THIRD, -ING (one of a kind)] **1 :** one of the three administrative jurisdictions into which Yorkshire, England, was formerly divided ⟨East *Riding*⟩ ⟨West *Riding*⟩ ⟨North *Riding*⟩ **2 :** an administrative jurisdiction or electoral district in an English county other than Yorkshire or in one of the British dominions (as New Zealand or Canada)

²**rid·ing** \"\ *n* -s [ME, fr. gerund of *riden* to ride] **1 :** the action of one that rides **:** a trip or journey made by a rider on horseback or in a vehicle **2** *chiefly Brit* **a :** a festival or pageant marked by a procession **b :** SHIVAREE, SKIMMINGTON **3 :** an avenue or lane cut in a wood esp. as a place for riding **4 :** ANCHORAGE **5 :** OVERLAP 1 a **6 :** the harassment of someone who has made himself unpopular, conspicuous, or offensive ⟨the Old Man's favorite often takes a hard ~ for this good reason —J.G.Cozzens⟩

³**rid·ing** \"\ *adj* **1 :** used for riding on ⟨a ~ horse⟩ **2 a :** used for riding or when riding **:** devoted to riding ⟨a ~ whip⟩ ⟨a ~ academy⟩ **b :** worn when riding **3 :** operated or driven by a rider ⟨a ~ plow⟩ ⟨a ~ cultivator⟩

⁴**rid·ing** \'ridᵊn\ *var of* RIDDING

riding bitts *n pl* [³*riding*] **:** massive bitts formerly used to secure the anchor cables of a ship riding at anchor

riding boot *n* **:** a leather boot esp. for horseback riding; *specif* **:** TOP BOOT — compare COWBOY BOOT, JODHPUR 2

riding breeches *n pl* **:** breeches made wide through the lower thighs and with tight-fitting calf-length legs and worn for horseback riding

riding breeches

riding buckler *n, naut* **:** a buckler with a hole for the passage of a cable

riding chair *n, archaic* **:** ¹CHAIR 3 b

riding chock *n* **:** a chock often fitted with a pawl and used to relieve the strain of an anchor cable on a windlass **:** CABLE STOPPER

riding habit *n* **:** an outfit for horseback riding; *esp* **:** a woman's outfit including jacket with breeches for riding astride or with a skirt for riding sidesaddle

riding hood *n* **:** an enveloping hood or hooded cloak worn for riding and as an outdoor wrap by women and children

riding interest *n* **:** a creditor's interest resting upon the share of a claimant in multiplepoinding or other action under Scots law

riding light *n* [³*riding*] **:** ANCHOR LIGHT

ridingman *n, pl* **ridingmen** [*riding*, pres. part. of ¹*ride*] **:** a man bound by feudal law to do service on horseback as an escort or messenger but not to do military service

riding master *n* [³*riding*] **:** an instructor in horsemanship

riding rhyme *n* **:** a rhymed couplet in iambic pentameter (as used by Chaucer and Lydgate) **:** an early form of heroic couplet

riding roller *n* [*riding*, pres. part. of ¹*ride*] **:** RIDER 11

riding sail *n* [³*riding*] **:** a triangular sail sometimes set usu. on the aftermast to keep a vessel head to wind when riding at anchor

riding whip *or* **riding crop** *n* **:** a short whip used by horsemen

rid·ley \'ridlē\ *n* -s [prob. fr. the name *Ridley*] **:** a marine turtle (*Caretta kempii* or *Lepidochelys kempii*) of the family Cheloniidae found off the Atlantic coast of the U.S. — called also *bastard turtle*

ri·dot·to \rə'däd·(,)ō, -'dȯd·-\ *n* -s [It, retreat, place of entertainment, redoubt — more at REDOUBT] **1 :** a public entertainment consisting of music and dancing often in masquerade introduced from Italy and very popular in England in the 18th century **2 :** an arrangement or abridgment of a musical composition from the full score

rids *pres 3d sing of* RID

ridy-horse \'rīdē,=\ *n* [alter. of *riding horse*] *Midland* **:** SEESAW, TEETER

RIE *abbr, often not cap* retirement income endowment

rie·beck·ite \'rē,be,kīt\ *n* -s [G *riebeckit*, fr. Emil *Riebeck* †1885 Ger. explorer + G *-it* -ite] **:** a black monoclinic amphibole $Na_2Fe_5Si_8O_{22}(OH)_2$ containing much iron and sodium

rief \'rēf\ *var of* REIF

rief·ler clock \'rēflə(r)-\ *n, cap R* [after Siegmund *Riefler* †1912 Ger. engineer] **:** a high-precision standard clock having a pin escapement and a partially free mercurial pendulum

rie·gel \'rēgəl\ *n* -s [G, lit., crossbar] **:** a low transverse rock ridge on the floor of a glaciated valley commonly situated at the down-valley end of a flat

riel \'rē(ə)l\ *n* -s [origin unknown] **:** the basic monetary unit of Cambodia from 1954 divided into 100 sen — see MONEY table

riem \'rēm\ *n* -s [Afrik, strap, belt, fr. MD *rieme* — more at RIM] *Africa* **:** a pliable strip usu. of rawhide **:** THONG

rie·man·ni·an \(')rē¦mänēən, -man-\ *adj, usu cap* [G.F.B. *Riemann* †1866 Ger. mathematician + E *-ian*] **:** relating to or discovered by the German mathematician Riemann

riemannian geometry *n, usu cap R* **:** a non-Euclidian geometry in which straight lines are geodesics and in which the parallel postulate is replaced by the postulate that every pair of straight lines intersects

riem·pie \'rēmpē\ *n* -s [Afrik *riempje* thong, dim. of *riem* strap, belt — more at RIEM] *southern Africa* **:** a rawhide strip used esp. as webbing in making furniture seats ⟨dozing in her wide *riempie*-bottomed chair —Stuart Cloete⟩

ries·ling \'rēzliŋ, -ēsl-, -lēŋ\ *n* -s *usu cap* [G] **:** a dry white table wine resembling Rhine wine

rietbok *or* **rietboc** *var of* REITBOK

riever *var of* REAVER

RIF \'rif\ *n* -s [*r*eduction *i*n *f*orce] **1 :** a process of reduction of personnel (as of a government organization) esp. for reasons of economy — compare ⁹RIFF **2 :** the act of dismissing a person esp. from government employment for reasons of economy; *also* **:** a notice of such dismissal

ri·fa·ci·men·to \(,)rē,fächē'men·(,)tō\ *or* **re·fa·ci·men·to** \rā,f-\ *n, pl* **rifacimen·ti** \-(,)tē\ *or* **rifacimentos** *or* **refacimen·ti** *or* **refacimentos** [It *rifacimento*, fr. *rifaci-* (stem of *rifare* to make over, fr. *ri-* re- — fr. L *re-* — + *facere, fare* to make, do, fr. L *facere*) + *-mento* -ment (fr. L *-mentum*) — more at DO] **:** a recasting or adaptation of a literary work or musical composition

¹**rife** \'rīf\ *adj* -ER/-EST [ME *rif, rive, ryfe*, fr. OE *rȳfe*; akin to MLG *rīve* abundant, ON *rīfr* munificent, abundant] **1 a :** existing generally **:** PREVALENT ⟨similar magical practices were ~ in antiquity —J.G.Frazer⟩ ⟨speculation was ~ as to a possible alliance —*Americana Annual*⟩ ⟨manipulation in the stock was ~ —Harold Wincott⟩ ⟨disease and starvation were ~ —*Collier's Yr. Bk.*⟩ **b :** commonly reported **:** CURRENT ⟨rumors of overwhelming evidence to convict him were ~ —George Meredith⟩ ⟨legends were ~ of its extraordinary wealth —John Buchan⟩ **c :** frequently heard or used ⟨what's the adage ~ in man's mouth —Robert Browning⟩ **2 a :** ABUNDANT, PLENTIFUL, NUMEROUS ⟨a considerable poet himself in days when poets were ~ —O.S.J.Gogarty⟩ ⟨genius . . . is nearly extinct, and talent is unprecedentedly ~ —G.D.Painter⟩ ⟨berets are ~ here —Lois Long⟩ **b :** RANK, STRONG ⟨in the deep jungle . . . everything was damp and ~ and hot —Norman Mailer⟩ ⟨when issues are hotly contested and prejudices are ~ —F.L. Mott⟩ **3 :** ABOUNDING, REPLETE — usu. used with *with* ⟨the district is ~ with legends —Richard Joseph⟩ ⟨the science of animal behavior is ~ with controversy —*Scientific American Reader*⟩ **4** *dial* **:** QUICK, READY, INCLINED ⟨could see that Katty's eyes were ~ for mischief —Daniel Corkery⟩ **syn** see PREVAILING

²**rife** \"\ *adv* -ER/-EST [ME *rif, rife*, fr. *rif, rife* rife, adj.] **:** RIFELY ⟨weeds grew ~ in the vacant lots⟩

rife·ly *adv* [ME *rively*, fr. *rive* rife + *-ly*] *obs* **:** in a rife manner

rife·ness *n* -ES [ME *ryfenes*, fr. *ryfe* rife + *-nes* -ness] **:** the quality or state of being rife ⟨appalling ~ of the terrain —Norman Mailer⟩

¹**riff** \'rif\ *n* -s [D *rif* — more at REEF] *dial* **:** REEF ⟨giant rays frequent the tidal ~*s* —Hodding Carter & Anthony Ragusin⟩ ⟨Long *Riff*, Virgin Islands⟩

²**riff** *n* -s [back-formation fr. *midriff*] *obs* **:** DIAPHRAGM

³**riff** *also* **rif** \'rif\ *n, pl* **riffs** \-fs\ *or* **riffi** \-fē\ *or* **riff** *cap* [fr. Er *Rif*, coastal area of northern Morocco] **:** a Berber of Er Rif, a hilly coastal region of northern Morocco — called also *Riffian*

⁴**riff** \'rif\ *n* -s [short for ¹*riffle*] *dial* **:** RIFFLE, RIPPLE ⟨beyond the breakers or in the ~*s* at the inlet —E.A.Weeks⟩

⁵**riff** \"\ *vb* -ED/-ING/-S [short for ²*riffle*] **:** RIFFLE, SKIM ⟨~ through the pages of a book⟩ ⟨~ through items on a bargain counter⟩

⁶**riff** \"\ *n* -s [prob. by shortening and alter. fr. *refrain*] **:** a short rhythmic jazz figure repeated without melodic development and often serving as background of a solo improvisation; *also* **:** a piece constructed on such a repeated figure

⁷**riff** \"\ *vi* -ED/-ING/-S **:** to perform or make use of riffs esp. in jazz

⁸**riff** \"\ *n* -s [origin unknown] **:** a tap dance step of foot swing and ball-heel or heel-ball impact in any direction

⁹**riff** *also* **rif** \"\ *vt* **riffed; riffed; riffing; riffs** *also* **rifs**

[*RIF*] **:** to discharge esp. from government service for reasons of economy

riff·ian \'rifēən\ *n* -s *cap* [Er *Rif*, coastal area of northern Morocco + E *-ian*] **:** RIFF

¹rif·fle \'rifəl\ *n* -s [perh. alter. (influenced by *ripple*) of *ruffle*] **1 a :** a shallow extending across the bed of a stream over which the water flows swiftly so that the surface of the water is broken in waves ⟨passed a very bad ~ of rocks in the evening —G.R.Clark⟩; *also* **:** any expanse of shallow bottom causing broken water ⟨channel into the port was hard to navigate due to reef patches and ~ —Michael Rosene⟩ **b :** a stretch of water flowing over a riffle ⟨fish the ~*s*; cast in swift white water —Richard Salmon⟩ **c :** a wave of a riffle ⟨white-topped ~*s* racing past their heads out in midstream —H.L. Davis⟩ **2 a :** a small wave or succession of small waves **:** RIPPLE ⟨a ~ of laughter passed among them —Virginia A. Oakes⟩ ⟨flats and slow swells, breaking here and there into ~*s* of rounded foothills —Russell Lord⟩ **b :** a patch of ripples or small waves (as caused by a light breeze) on an otherwise calm or unbroken surface of water ⟨the march of ~*s* across the water marked the approach of the breeze —R.J.Smith⟩ ⟨could see a little ~ of dark coming along where the morning northerly was making up —G.W.Brace⟩ ⟨a ~ caused by a school of fish⟩ **3** [*²riffle*] **a :** the act or process of shuffling (as cards) ⟨the dealer merely manipulated the ~ so that a disproportionate number of splits appeared —C.B.Davis⟩; *specif* **:** RIFFLE-SHUFFLE **b :** the sound made while doing this ⟨heard the stiff ~ of cards —Wallace Stegner⟩

²riffle \"\ *vb* **riffled; riffled; riffling** \-f(ə)liŋ\ **riffles** *vi* **1 :** to form a riffle **:** flow over a riffle **:** move in riffles ⟨a fish nosed the surface . . . and the water *riffled* and lay quiet again —A.B.Guthrie⟩ ⟨*riffling* brooks⟩ ⟨our flags *riffling* in the breeze —Shelby Foote⟩ **2 :** to engage in turning or mixing lightly or hastily (as in cursory search of something) **:** RUN, SKIM — usu. used with *through* ⟨*riffled* through hundreds of letters and cards —M.L.Bach⟩ ⟨~ through one's files⟩ ⟨~ through a manuscript⟩ ⟨watched a child ~ through the gifts under a tree —*New Yorker*⟩ ~ *vt* **1 a :** to ruffle slightly **:** form undulations in **:** RIPPLE ⟨flag *riffled* by the breeze⟩ ⟨fish-*riffled* sloughs —*Ford Times*⟩ **b :** to produce as riffles ⟨choppy waves, *riffled* by the wind —Wyman Richardson⟩ **2 a :** to stir or shift lightly or hastily (as in cursory search of something) **:** leaf through (as a book) rapidly or hastily ⟨*riffled* my field guidebook —D.C.Peattie⟩ ⟨~ the papers on the desk top⟩ **b :** to leaf or thumb (a stack of pieces of paper) by holding in one hand and sliding the thumb of the other hand along the edge so as to release sheets successively from the pressure of the thumb or by holding against a flat surface and thumbing similarly by lifting one side or corner with the thumb of the same hand ⟨would ~ the cards . . . then deal —C.B.Davis⟩ ⟨*riffling* the cards with his white hands —Grace Metalious⟩ ⟨~ the bills⟩ **c :** to shuffle (playing cards) by separating the deck into two parts that are laid flat on the table, elevating a corner or side of each part of the pack slightly, and thumbing in such a manner that the two parts are intermixed and then sliding the entire pack together **d :** to manipulate (a stack of objects) idly between the fingers of one hand or of both hands ⟨fingers of his right hand, rapidly *riffling* a little pile of chips —Richard Donovan & H.M.Greenspun⟩ ⟨the sheriff *riffled* his coins —H.L.Davis⟩

³riffle \"\ *n* -s [prob. fr. *¹riffle*] **1 a** (1) **:** any of various contrivances (as blocks, rails, poles, or iron bars often combined with sacking, matting, or hides with the hair up) laid on the bottom of a sluice or launder to make a series of grooves or interstices to catch and retain a mineral (as gold) (2) **:** a groove or interstice so formed **b** *or* **riffle bar :** a bar or cleat in a riffle, table, cradle, or similar gold-washing apparatus **2** *also* **riffle block a** (1) **:** a cleat or bar fastened to an inclined surface (as of a Wilfley table) to catch and hold mineral grains (2) **:** the groove formed by two such parallel cleats or bars **b :** one of a series of cleats or bars used (as in a trough) to separate foreign matter from any material (as paper pulp) suspended in flowing water **3 :** a device for dividing ground ore or other material (as in sampling) consisting usu. of an even number of narrow sloping troughs of equal width with adjacent troughs discharging in opposite directions or of a series of parallel troughs separated by gaps of the same width as the troughs **4 :** a transverse board in a fishway to check the flow of the current and afford a resting pool for ascending fish

⁴riffle \"\ *vt* -ED/-ING/-S **1 :** to run (a material) through a riffle or over a series of riffles ⟨~ ground ore in sampling⟩ ⟨~ pulp in paper manufacture⟩ **2 :** to run the point of the trowel along the center of a spread of (mortar) in bricklaying

riffle file *n* [back-formation fr. *¹riffler*] **:** RIFFLER

rif·fle·man \-mən\ *n, pl* **rifflemen** [*³riffle* + *man*] **:** a worker who scoops gold particles from behind the riffles of gold-washing apparatus

¹rif·fler \'rif(ə)lə(r)\ *n* -s [modif. of F *rifloir*, fr. MF, fr. *rifler*

riffler

to file + *-oir* -ory — more at RIFLE] **:** a small file with ends curved to various shapes used for working in depressions (as in die sinking)

²riffler \"\ *n* -s [*⁴riffle* + *-er*] **:** a trough used in papermaking containing upright partitions that slow the flow of pulp and permit heavy irregular particles to drop out

riffler man *n* [*²riffler*] **:** a worker who uses a riffler to remove impurities from pulp stock

riffle-shuffle \'==,==\ *n* [*¹riffle* + *shuffle*] **:** the act or process of shuffling playing cards by first separating the pack into two parts

¹riff-raff \'ri,fraf, -raa(ə)f, -raif\ *n* [ME *riffe raffe*, fr. *rif and raf* every single one, fr. MF *rif et raf* completely, fr. *rifler* to plunder + *raffe* act of sweeping — more at RIFLE, RAFFLE] **1 a :** persons of the lowest or most disreputable class ⟨beachcombers, adventurers, rough traders, and general ~ —Ellen La Motte⟩; *broadly* **:** any group of persons looked upon as common, disreputable, or very unconventional ⟨all the ~ for miles around have been using my garden as if it were their own —P.G.Wodehouse⟩ ⟨painters, authors, and other vagrant ~ who frequented the premises —Norman Douglas⟩ **b :** the lowest or most disreputable element of the populace **:** RABBLE, MOB, CANAILLE ⟨the ~ might sack the town —*Harper's*⟩ **c :** one of the riffraff **:** a disreputable person ⟨will not have some ~ . . . trailing about with us —Elizabeth Janeway⟩ **2 :** REFUSE, RUBBISH, TRASH ⟨waistcoats of dirty damask, legs of velvet breeches—in a word, all the cast-off ~ of centuries —W.W.Story⟩ ⟨had once actually said that pigeons were mere ~ —Sean O'Faolain⟩

²riffraff \"\ *adj* **:** composed of, belonging to, or characteristic of the rabble **:** DISREPUTABLE, TRASHY, WORTHLESS ⟨a score of ~ gunslingers, barroom brawlers —*New Yorker*⟩ ⟨~ opinions⟩ ⟨a ~ army⟩ ⟨row of ~ dwellings —Booth Tarkington⟩

riffs *pl of* RIFF, *pres 3d sing of* RIFF

¹ri·fle \'rīfəl\ *vb* **rifled; rifled; rifling** \-f(ə)liŋ\ **rifles** [ME *riflen*, fr. MF *rifler* to scratch, file, plunder, fr. OF, of Gmc origin; akin to obs. D *riffelen* to scrape, groove, MD *riven* to rake — more at RIVEL] *vt* **1 :** to ransack and rob or plunder **:** pillage thoroughly **:** despoil completely ⟨his mail was repeatedly *rifled* —William MacDonald⟩ ⟨not only dug deep into local archives but *rifled* the memories of farmers —*Newsweek*⟩ **2 :** to steal and carry away **:** snatch away **:** carry off ⟨till time shall ~ every youthful grace —Alexander Pope⟩ ~ *vi* **:** to engage in ransacking and pillaging ⟨*rifling* through her desk in a desperate search for writing materials —Brand Blanshard⟩ **syn** see ROB

²rifle \"\ *n* -s [ME, fr. ONF, perh. fr. OF *rifler* to scratch, file] **1 :** a strip of wood covered with emery or similar material and used for sharpening scythes **2** *Brit* **:** a bent stick fastened at the butt of a scythe and serving to lay the mowed grain in rows

³rifle \"\ *vt* **rifled; rifled; rifling** \-f(ə)liŋ\ **rifles :** to whet with a rifle ⟨*rifling* scythes and filing hoes —William Humphrey⟩

⁴rifle \"\ *vt* **rifled; rifled; rifling** \-f(ə)liŋ\ **rifles** [F *rifler* to scratch, file, fr. MF] **:** to cut spiral grooves into the bore of (as a firearm or piece of ordnance) ⟨*rifled* arms⟩ ⟨*rifled* pipe⟩

⁵rifle \"\ *n* -s **1** *archaic* **:** one of the spiral grooves in the bore

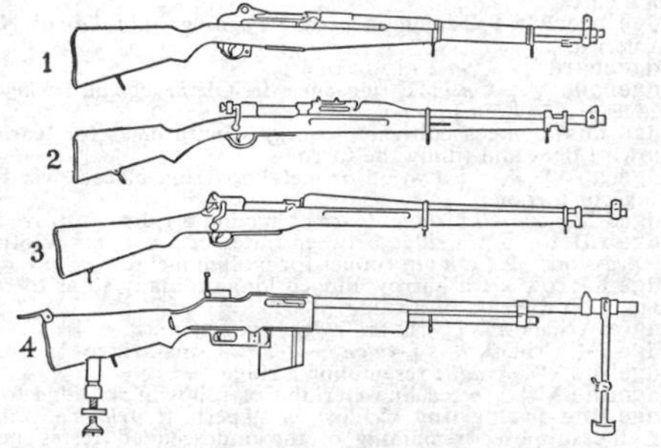

rifles 2: *1* Garand semiautomatic, *2* Springfield, *3* Enfield, *4* Browning automatic

of a rifled firearm **2 a :** a firearm having a rifled bore and intended to be fired from the shoulder — see CARBINE; compare MUSKET, PISTOL, SHOTGUN **b :** a rifled artillery piece ⟨startling crack of a single great fourteen-inch ~, carefully aimed —K.M. Dodson⟩ **3 a :** RIFLEMAN ⟨appointed captain of a Maryland company of ~*s* —*Amer. Guide Series: Md.*⟩ **b rifles** *pl* **:** a body of soldiers armed with rifles ⟨the 6th Gurkha *Rifles*⟩ **4** *or* **rifle green :** a dark grayish olive green to black **5 :** a mobile lighting unit with a spirally ribbed parabolic reflector throwing a narrow beam that is used esp. in television and motion-picture making

⁶rifle \"\ *vt* **rifled; rifled; rifling** \-f(ə)liŋ\ **rifles** [*⁵rifle*] **:** to hit or throw (a ball) with great force ⟨*rifled* a single to center field⟩

rifle bar *n* [*⁵rifle*] **:** a rifled steel bar used for rotating drill steel in a machine drill

riflebird \'==,=\ *n* [*⁵rifle*; fr. the sound of its cry] **:** any of several birds of paradise of *Ptiloris* or a related genus; *esp* **:** a bird of paradise (*P. paradisea*) of New So. Wales and Queensland the male of which is chiefly velvety black with greenish and purplish iridescence on the head, underparts, and middle tail feathers

rifle drill *n* **:** a drill designed to create long straight holes of small diameter (as for a rifle)

rifled slug *n* [fr. past part. of *⁴rifle*] **:** a shotgun projectile having a round nose, a hollow base, and sides cut with a series of oblique grooves that increase the accuracy of the projectile by causing it to rotate as it passes through the smooth bore of the shotgun

rifle frock *n* [*⁵rifle*] *archaic* **:** a rifleman's tunic

rifle grenade *n* **:** a grenade projected from a launching device attached to the muzzle of a rifle or carbine and requiring a special cartridge

rifle gun *n* **:** RIFLE; *esp* **:** a muzzle-loading rifle

ri·fle·man \'rīfəlmən\ *n, pl* **riflemen 1 :** a soldier armed with a rifle **2 :** one skilled in shooting with a rifle — **ri·fle·man·ship** \-,ship\ *n*

rifleman bird *n* [so called fr. the resemblance of its plumage to the uniform of the early British volunteer rifle corps] **1 :** RIFLEBIRD **2 :** a small passerine bird (*Acanthisitta chloris*) of New Zealand with green-and-bronze plumage

rifle pit *n* **:** a short trench or excavation with a parapet of earth in front to shelter one or more riflemen

¹ri·fler \'rīf(ə)lə(r)\ *n* -s [ME *riffler, rifeler*, fr. *riflen* to rifle, plunder + *-er*] **:** one that rifles **:** ROBBER

²rifler \"\ *n* -s [*⁴rifle* + *-er*] **:** one that grooves rifling by machine

ri·fle·ry \'rīfəlrē\ *n* -ES [*⁵rifle* + *-ry*] **1 :** rifle shots ⟨storm of ~ cracked and rattled among the northern foothills —Richard Dehan⟩ **2 :** rifle shooting; *esp* **:** the practice of shooting with a rifle at a target

rifles *pres 3d sing of* RIFLE, *pl of* RIFLE

rifle salute *n* [*⁵rifle*] **:** a position in the manual of arms in which the disengaged hand extended is brought across the body touching the rear of the receiver of the rifle when held at shoulder arms or near its muzzle when held at order or trail arms

ri·fle·scope \'rīfəl,skōp, -l,sk-\ *n* [*⁵rifle* + *-scope*] **:** a telescopic sight for a rifle

rifleshot \'==,=\ *n* **:** one who shoots a rifle skillfully

rifle tie *n* **:** a tie with the pith of the tree at or near the center of the ends

rifle whiskey *n* **:** inferior or cheap whiskey

rifling *n* -s [fr. gerund of *⁴rifle*] **1 :** the act or process of making spiral grooves (as in a gun barrel) **2 a :** a system of spiral grooves cut in the surface of the bore of a gun leaving intervening lands that cut into the projectile when fired or into a metal band secured to it and rotate it about its longer axis **b :** a system of spiral grooves (as in a pipe or drill core)

rifle salute

¹rift \'rift\ *n* -s [ME, of Scand origin; akin to ON *ript* breach of contract, *rifa* to rive, Dan & Norw *rift* rent, fissure — more at RIVE] **1 a :** an opening made by cracking or splitting **:** FISSURE, CREVASSE ⟨a ~ in the ice⟩ ⟨spring that gushes from a ~ in a red sandstone bluff —*Amer. Guide Series: Texas*⟩ ⟨widened lattice intervals are evidently ~*s* in the crystal lattice, produced initially by plastic deformation —*Science*⟩; *broadly* **:** any crack or flaw caused by stress or conflict — often used of minute or immaterial things ⟨little ~ within the lute —Alfred Tennyson⟩ ⟨first split Western man's acts from his ideals, for only by such a ~ in his mind could he hold on to these mutually destroying beliefs —Lillian Smith⟩ **b** (1) **:** a normal fault; *esp* **:** one along which movement has occurred in comparatively recent geologic time (2) **:** a depression or valley along the trace of a fault or fault zone — compare RIFT VALLEY **2 a :** an open space **:** a clear interval ⟨glimpsed occasionally through ~*s* in the dense foliage —*Amer. Guide Series: Pa.*⟩ ⟨high ~*s* of blue, white-cloud-dappled sky —Flora Thompson⟩ ⟨had one of those ~*s* of lucidity in which I saw him whole and limited —Mary Austin⟩ **3 :** wood split or cut radially from the log ⟨~ flooring⟩ **4 :** the direction of easiest splitting esp. of a granite — used esp. by quarrymen **5 :** a divergence (as of interests or beliefs) resulting in disagreement or dispute ⟨this little ~ it was that had widened to a now considerable breach —H.G.Wells⟩ ⟨a growing ~ and an atmosphere of suspicion between the two parties —*Farmer's Weekly (So. Africa)*⟩ ⟨developments in the industrial crisis which reveal significant ~*s* among his own supporters —*New Statesman & Nation*⟩ **syn** see BREACH

²rift \"\ *vb* -ED/-ING/-S [ME *riften*, of Scand origin; akin to ON *ripta* to break a contract, *ript* breach of contract] *vt* **1 a :** CLEAVE, RIVE, SPLIT, DIVIDE ⟨mica ~*ed* into sheets⟩ ⟨the mist is ~*ed* and we can look straight at the words —R.P.Warren⟩ **b :** to saw (wood) radially from the log so as to have the annual rings perpendicular or nearly so to the face **2 :** to penetrate by or as if by cleaving ⟨the intellect is a cleaver; it discerns and ~*s* its way into the secret of things —H.D.Thoreau⟩ ~ *vi* **1 :** to burst open **:** SPLIT ⟨the clouds ~*ed*⟩ **2 :** to form a rift in the earth's crust ⟨sedimentary deposits surviving the denudation following the ~*ing* —*E. African Agric. Jour.*⟩

³rift \"\ *vi* -ED/-ING/-S [ME *riften*, fr. ON *rypta*; prob. akin to Skt *rauti* he roars — more at RUMOR] *chiefly dial* **:** to belch or break wind

⁴rift \"\ *n* -s [prob. alter. of *¹riff*] **:** a shallow or rocky place in a stream forming either a ford or a rapid ⟨trout waters, where the ~*s* and pools harbor flashing rainbows —G.P.Manning⟩

⁵rift \"\ *adj* [by shortening] **:** RIFT-SAWED ⟨~ fir⟩ ⟨~ laths⟩

rift crack *n* [*¹rift*] **:** HEART SHAKE

rift·er \'riftə(r)\ *n* -s [*¹rift* + *-er*] **:** a crack in sea ice **:** an open space in a floe

rift grain *n* [*¹rift*] **:** edge grain of quarter-sawed or rift-sawed boards with the annual rings nearly perpendicular to the surface

rift·less \'riftləs\ *adj* **:** having no rift

rift saw *n* [*²rift* + *saw*] **:** a saw for rifting timber (as into boards and laths); *esp* **:** a circular saw having four or more toothed projecting arms for sawing cants into flooring strips

rift saw

rift-sawed *or* **rift-sawn** \'=,=\ *adj* [*¹rift* + *sawed* or *sawn*] **1 :** sawed radially from the log so as to have the annual rings perpendicular or nearly so to the face **2 :** QUARTERSAWED

rift valley *n* [*¹rift*] **:** an elongated valley formed by the depression of a block of the earth's crust between two faults or fault zones of approximately parallel strike **:** a graben having surface expression

rift valley fever \'=,==-\ *n, usu cap R&V* [fr. *Rift Valley*, western Kenya, Africa] **:** a virus disease of east African sheep and sometimes cattle characterized by fever and destructive hepatitis and occasionally transmitted to man in a much-attenuated form

¹rig \'rig\ *n* -s [ME *ryg*, of Scand origin; akin to ON *hregg* storm, Faroese *reiggj* powerful movement, Icel *hragla* to rain slowly, Dan *ræg* frost] *dial Eng* **:** a high wind **:** STORM

²rig \"\ *n* -s [ME (northern dial.), back, ridge, fr. OE *hrycg* — more at RIDGE] **1** *chiefly Scot* **:** RIDGE **2** *chiefly Brit* **:** RIDGELING **3 :** a measure of land in Scotland ⟨will buy me ~*s* o'land —Robert Burns⟩

³rig \"\ *vb* **rigged; rigged; rigging; rigs** [ME *riggen*, prob. of Scand origin; akin to Norw *rigga* to bind, wrap up, Sw *rigga* (*på*) to harness (up)] *vt* **1 a :** to fit out (as a ship) with the necessary tackle **:** fit the shrouds, stays, and braces of (as a ship) to their respective masts and spars **:** make (as a ship) ready for sea **b :** to fit shrouds, stays, or similar devices to (as a mast or spar) ⟨~ the mainmast⟩ **2 :** to fit out or provide with clothes **:** CLOTHE, DRESS ⟨*rigged* him in moccasins —H.L. Davis⟩ — usu. used with *out* ⟨~ him out in garments like the British noblemen wore —F.B.Gipson⟩ ⟨she was *rigged* out in Victorian style —Ellery Queen⟩ **3 a :** to furnish with apparatus or gear **:** provide with equipment **:** fit up **:** EQUIP ⟨some of the craft are *rigged* for dredging —H.M.Parshley⟩ ⟨crushing stone *rigged* with an ox yoke and pole —*Amer. Guide Series: Conn.*⟩ **b :** to fit out in some way ⟨why the book should have been *rigged* out as a liturgy —*Times Lit. Supp.*⟩ **4 a :** to put into proper position or condition for use **:** set up in working order **:** ADJUST, FIX ⟨*rigged* the tarpaulins over stakes —Rex Ingamells⟩ ⟨alarm clocks are *rigged* to turn on radios —Gladwin Hill⟩ ⟨*rigged* up a Christmas tree in the town hall —W.A. White⟩ **b :** to move (as a boom on a sailing vessel) in a desired direction or to the proper position ⟨~ in a boom⟩ ⟨~ out a boom⟩ **5 :** to fit up as a makeshift **:** set up as an expedient ⟨~ jury masts⟩ — often used with *out* or *up* ⟨*rigged* up an affair . . . to take the place of a bed —D.B.Putnam⟩ ⟨*rigged* up a temporary shelter⟩ **6 :** to assemble, adjust, and align the component parts including the control surfaces of (an airplane) to assure satisfactory flight-handling characteristics ~ *vi, obs* **:** to become or get rigged — used of a ship

⁴rig \"\ *n* -s **1 :** the distinctive shape, number, and arrangement of sails and masts differentiating types of vessels without reference to the hull ⟨schooner ~⟩ ⟨ship ~⟩ — compare ⁵BARK 2, ¹BRIG, CATBOAT, HERMAPHRODITE BRIG, KETCH, KNOCKABOUT 3, LUGGER, SCHOONER, SLOOP, YAWL; see FORE-AND-AFT RIG, SQUARE RIG **2 :** TURNOUT, EQUIPAGE; *esp* **:** a carriage with its horse **3 :** DRESS 2; *esp* **:** clothing designed for a special purpose or worn as a distinctive costume ⟨dressed in festive ~ —Mollie Panter-Downes⟩ ⟨an English judge in full ~ —F.J.Warburg⟩ ⟨boats' crews should be correctly . . . dressed in the ~ ordered —*Manual of Seamanship*⟩ **4 :** tackle, apparatus, or machinery fitted up for a specified purpose: as **a** (1) **:** a derrick complete with enginehouse and other equipment necessary for operation that is used for boring and afterwards pumping an oil well (2) **:** an oil derrick (3) **:** a similar apparatus used for other types of drilling (as pile-driving or drilling for water) **b** (1) **:** a cultivator gang composed of a combination of beam, shank, and shovels (2) **:** such a combination in a cultivator **c :** a thresher with a tractor and other equipment **:** a threshing outfit **d :** a fisherman's terminal tackle or gear **e :** FIRE ENGINE **f :** a trailer truck **:** a tractor-trailer **:** a tractor hitched to a trailer **g** (1) **:** the complete station of an amateur radio operator (2) **:** a high fidelity sound system **5** *West* **:** SADDLE

⁵rig \"\ *vi* **rigged; rigged; rigging; rigs** [perh. by shortening & alter. fr. *wriggle*] **1** *chiefly dial* **:** to romp and wriggle about **2** *chiefly dial* **:** to behave lewdly

⁶rig \"\ *n* -s *dial Eng* **:** a wanton immoral woman

⁷rig \"\ *n* -s [origin unknown] **1** *chiefly Brit* **:** the action of ridiculing **:** BANTER, RIDICULE, SPORT **2 a** *chiefly Brit* **:** a fraudulent or cheating trick **:** SWINDLE **b :** manipulation of prices to a desired level in a securities or commodity market by artificial means (as a corner) **3** *chiefly Brit* **:** a wanton or mischievous act **:** PRANK

⁸rig \"\ *vt* **rigged; rigged; rigging; rigs 1** *dial Eng* **:** to play tricks on **:** FOOL, HOAX **2 a :** to arrange or manage esp. by deceptive means **:** manipulate in an underhanded manner **:** achieve or carry out by fraudulent means **:** control by dishonest means ⟨attempt to ~ the scales —*Adelaide S. A. Sunday Mail*⟩ ⟨~ an election⟩ ⟨~ the stock market⟩ **b :** to fix in advance to secure or show a desired result ⟨dealers had combined to ~ the auction price very low —James Higgins & Gordon Donald⟩ ⟨~ a quiz by furnishing the contestants with answers⟩ ⟨~ prices⟩

⁹rig *or* **ri** \'rē\ *n* -s [IrGael *rī* (gen. *rīogh, rīgh*, dat. *rīgh*), fr. OIr, (gen., dat., & acc. *rīg*) — more at ROYAL] **:** an ancient Irish king

ri·ga \'rēgə\ *adj, usu cap* [fr. *Riga*, Latvia] **:** of or from Riga, the capital of Latvia **:** of the kind or style prevalent in Riga

rig·a·doon \ˌrigəˈdün\ *or* **ri·gau·don** \rēgōdōⁿ\ *n, pl* **rigadoons** \-ünz\ *or* **rigaudons** \-ōⁿ\ [F *rigaudon, rigodon*, perh. fr. the name *Rigaud*] **1 :** a lively dance performed with a jumping step and popular in the 17th and 18th centuries **2 :** the music for the rigadoon usu. in spirited duple or quadruple time

riga fir *or* **riga pine** *n, usu cap R* **:** SCOTCH PINE

rig·a·ma·jig \'rig(ə)mə,jig\ *n* -s [alter. (influenced by *⁴rig*) of *thingumajig*] **:** something the name of which is unknown or not remembered **:** THINGUMBOB ⟨the ~ they keep track of the rooms on —Sinclair Lewis⟩

rigamarole *var of* RIGMAROLE

rig-and-fur \ˌrigənˈfər\ *adj* [*²rig*] *chiefly Scot* **:** ridged and furrowed **:** RIBBED ⟨*rig-and-fur* stockings⟩

rig·a·ree \'rigə,rē, ,==ˈ=\ *n* -s [origin unknown] **:** ornamentation on glass (as of early wine decanters) consisting of narrow applied bands forming parallel ribs

rigation *n* -s [L *rigation-, rigatio*, fr. *rigatus* (past part. of *rigare* to water) + *-ion-, -io -ion* — more at RAIN] *obs* **:** IRRIGATION

rig·a·to·ni \ˌrigəˈtōnē\ *n, pl* **rigatoni** [It, pl., fr. *rigato*, past part. of *rigare* to draw a line, make a furrow, make fluting, fr. *riga* line, of Gmc origin; akin to OHG *riga* line — more at ROW] **:** hollow alimentary paste made in short curved fluted pieces

rigged *past of* RIG

rig·ger \'rigə(r)\ *n* -s [*³rig* + *-er*] **1 :** one that rigs: as **a :** one whose occupation is fitting the rigging of ships **b :** one that manipulates something (as the stock market or an auction) usu. by dishonest means **c :** one who installs or operates the rigging involved in skidding logs from a forest with a power-drawn cable **d :** one of a crew of men who build oil and gas well rigs — called also *climber* **e :** one who assists in the installation and repair of underground electric cables **f :** one who assembles the parts of awnings that are to be hung **g :** a netmaker who sews the outer edges of netting to ropes **h :** one employed in assembling and aligning aircraft or parachutes **i :** one that works with rigging or similar equipment or tends a rigging machine ⟨crane ~*s*⟩ ⟨scaffold ~*s*⟩ **j :** one that rigs a racing shell **2 :** a band pulley or drum

3 : a long slender and pointed sable brush used in painting pictures **4** : a ship of a specified rig ⟨square-*rigger*⟩ **5** : OUTRIGGER 1 **6** : a scaffold erected in building operations to protect passersby from falling objects

rigger's screw *n* : RIGGING SCREW 1

¹rig·ging \'rigən, -giŋ\ *n* -S [ME (northern dial.), fr. *rig* back, ridge + *-ing* — more at RIG (ridge)] **1** *chiefly Scot* : the ridge or roof of a building **2** *chiefly Scot* : the back of an animal or human being

²rig·ging \-giŋ\ *n* -S [fr. gerund of ³*rig*] **1 a** : the ropes, chains, and other lines used aboard a vessel esp. in working sail and supporting masts and spars — see RUNNING RIGGING, STANDING RIGGING; SHIP illustration **b** : a similar network of ropes or wires used for support and manipulation (as in scaffolding or in theater scenery) **2** : CLOTHING 1 a ⟨the tall old woman in the dark ~ —Sir Walter Scott⟩ **3** : the exterior leather trappings of a saddle — see STOCK SADDLE illustration **4** : the cables, blocks, and other equipment used in power skidding and hauling logs **5** : the system of cords and wires that distribute the load of an aerostat over the envelope **6** : the network of thongs used to attach a snowshoe to the foot **7** : pattern and related equipment for making a mold in founding

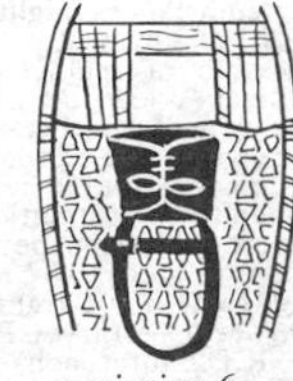
rigging 6

rigging loft *n* **1** : a loft in which rigging is prepared for use on ships **2** : an open floor of beams over the stage and under the roof of a theater from which the scenery is raised and lowered

rigging screw *n* **1** : a screw clamp or vise for bending rope around a thimble for splicing or seizing **2** *Brit* : TURNBUCKLE

rig·gish \'rigish\ *adj* [⁶*rig* + *-ish*] *chiefly dial* : WANTON ⟨~ embraces —C.E.Montague⟩

rig·got \'rigət\ *n* -S [fr. obs. F *rigot*, fr. MF, prob. alter. of *rigole* drain, irrigation ditch, canal — more at RIGOLET] *dial Eng* : a surface drain, esp. for rain water : GUTTER

riggs' disease \'rigz-\ *n, usu cap R* [after John M. *Riggs* †1885 Am. dentist] : PERIODONTITIS

righi-leduc effect \¦rēgēlə¦dük-, ¦ri|\ *n, usu cap R&L* [after Augusto *Righi* †1920 Ital. physicist and Sylvestre Anatole *Leduc*, 20th cent. Fr. physicist] : a transverse temperature gradient observed in a metal when the metal is in a magnetic field whose lines of force are perpendicular to the heat flux — called also *Leduc effect*

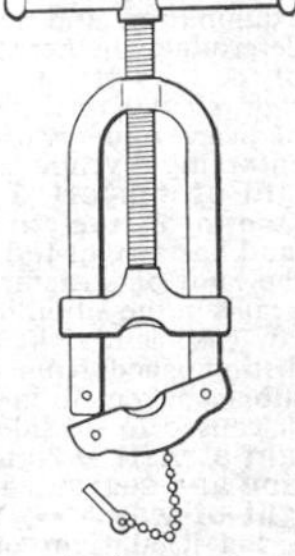
rigging screw

¹right \'rīt, *usu* -īd·+V\ *adj, sometimes* -ER/-EST [ME *riht, right*, fr. OE *riht*; akin to OHG *reht* right, ON *rēttr*, Goth *raihts* right, L *rectus* straight, right, *regere* to lead straight, guide, rule, *rogare* to ask, Gk *oregein* to stretch out, *orektos* stretched out, upright, Skt *ṛjyati, ṛñjati* he stretches, hastens, *raji* straightening up, straight; basic meaning: straight] **1** : disposed to do what is just or good : RIGHTEOUS, UPRIGHT ⟨a God of faithfulness . . . just and ~ is he —Deut 32:4 (RSV)⟩ ⟨the ~ soul, high and true and pure —W.L.Sullivan⟩ ⟨a ~ conscience⟩ ⟨a ~ man⟩ **2 a** : being in accordance with what is just, good, or proper ⟨conflicting notions of ~ conduct —B.N.Cardozo⟩ ⟨teach young girls ~ behavior when faced with . . . temptations —*London Calling*⟩ ⟨it is ~ that we should do this⟩ ⟨religious teachings as to what is ~ and what is wrong⟩ ⟨doing something he thought not quite ~⟩ **b** : held to be in accordance with justice, morality, and goodness usu. because approved by a person or group ⟨asserted that he was on the ~ side of the controversy⟩ ⟨of course the ~ cause and the ~ men won —*Times Lit. Supp.*⟩ **3 a** : agreeable to a standard or principle : FIT, SUITABLE ⟨educating by a ~ use of pleasure —Benjamin Jowett⟩ ⟨the perfectioning of our countrymen in . . . the ~ use of their native language —Samuel Foote⟩ **b** : agreeing with or conforming to facts : characterized by strict accordance with fact or truth : devoid of error or fault : CORRECT, EXACT ⟨a ~ description of our sport —Shak.⟩ ⟨the answer to a sum is either ~ or wrong —Bertrand Russell⟩ **c** : leading in the proper direction or toward a desired objective ⟨took the ~ road⟩ ⟨set out in the ~ direction⟩ ⟨the ~ way to salvation⟩ **4** : satisfying the requirements of necessity, propriety, or suitability : APPROPRIATE, FITTING ⟨the ~ man for the job —B.R. Redman⟩ ⟨knew that he said the ~ thing —Elizabeth Goudge⟩ ⟨marry when she has found the ~ chap —Robert Reid⟩ ⟨an audience that . . . applauded at the ~ moments —Joseph Wechsberg⟩ **5** *obs* : having proper title or right : LAWFUL, RIGHTFUL ⟨they slew their ~ king —Thomas Becon⟩ ⟨he has a great estate, only the ~ owner keeps him out —Jonathan Swift⟩ **6** : devoid of bends or curves : STRAIGHT ⟨a ~ line⟩ ⟨streets made very broad and ~ —Richard Tomson⟩ **7 a** : justly entitled to the name : having the true character of : ACTUAL, GENUINE, REAL ⟨manifested themselves to be ~ barbarians —John Milton⟩ ⟨a ~ woman⟩ ⟨a spillway rather than a ~ river —H.S.Canby⟩ ⟨~ deer⟩ — compare RIGHT WHALE **b** : having a genuine rather than a counterfeit or spurious character ⟨an ounce of ~ Virginia tobacco —Richard Steele⟩ ⟨wainscoted with ~ wainscot —John Entick⟩ **8** : properly relating or attached to one ⟨give it its ~ name⟩ **9** : characterized by normality : SANE, SOUND ⟨offers no man in his ~ mind could resist —Bennett Cerf⟩ ⟨no rancher in his ~ senses goes into business on borrowed capital —Green Peyton⟩ **10 a** (1) : of, relating to, or constituting the hand that in most persons is stronger, the side of the body on which it is located, or the parts of that side of the body ⟨her ~ foot⟩ ⟨the ~ side of a human body⟩ ⟨delivered a ~ hook to the jaw⟩ (2) : of, relating to, or constituting a similarly located part of another object **b** : located on, designed for, or used on that side of the body ⟨the ~ pocket of a shirt⟩ ⟨a ~ glove⟩ **c** : located on an observer's right or directed as his right hand would point ⟨the ~ side of a house⟩ ⟨took the ~ fork in the road⟩ **d** : located on the right of an observer facing in the same direction as the object involved ⟨stage ~⟩ ⟨the ~ wing of an army⟩ ⟨the ~ bank of a river⟩ **11** : erect from a base : having its axis perpendicular to the base : upright rather than oblique — compare RIGHT ANGLE, RIGHT SPHERE **12** : of, relating to, or constituting the side of something that is usu. held to be the principal one or the one naturally or by design turned up, outward, or toward one or the one that is most finished or polished ⟨turn your socks ~ side out⟩ ⟨the ~ side of a piece of velvet⟩ ⟨in the ditch beside the road, ~ side up . . . rested a new coupe —Scott Fitzgerald⟩ **13** : held to presage good luck or good spirits during the day ⟨got up on the ~ side of the bed⟩ ⟨get the project started off on the ~ foot⟩ **14** : acting, thinking, or judging in accordance with truth or the facts (as of a case) : correct in opinion, judgment, or procedure : stating truth ⟨he was ~ in refusing the offer⟩ ⟨time proved him ~⟩ ⟨~ you are, sir⟩ **15 a** : mentally normal or sound : SANE ⟨not ~ in his head⟩ ⟨not ~ in her mind⟩ **b** : well in physical health : being in good health and spirits : being in good physical condition : SOUND, WELL ⟨the patient doesn't look quite ~ yet⟩ ⟨a few days' rest would put him ~ —Max Peacock⟩ **16** : being in a proper or satisfactory state : being in good order ⟨everything will come out ~ in the end⟩ ⟨get something ~⟩ ⟨that will make it ~⟩ ⟨hunches which turned out ~ —A.G.N.Flew⟩ **17** : being in a correct or properly directed state ⟨we'll set the world ~ —Eden Phillpotts⟩ ⟨the readiness . . . to put things ~ —*London Calling*⟩ ⟨proceeded to set him ~⟩ **18** : most favorable, convenient, or desired : ADVANTAGEOUS, PREFERABLE ⟨I'm still on the ~ side of 50 —Alan Villiers⟩ ⟨get on the ~ side of the law —Hugo Wall⟩ ⟨the ~ side of the tracks⟩ **19** *often cap* : of, adhering to, or constituted by the Right esp. in politics — compare RIGHT WING **20 a** : producing or likely to produce a winning roll or series of rolls in craps and other dice games ⟨the dice are ~ tonight⟩ ⟨bet he's ~⟩ **b** : hopeful that a roll or series of rolls on which a bet is placed in craps and other dice games will result in a natural or a point made ⟨a ~ bet⟩ ⟨a ~ bettor⟩ **21** : socially acceptable, prominent, or correct ⟨did not know the ~ people except in a business way —J.P.Marquand⟩ ⟨a ~ school⟩ ⟨belongs to the ~ clubs —H.N.Maclean⟩ **22 a** : ALL RIGHT 3 ⟨a ~ guy⟩ **b** : held by criminals to be trustworthy and sympathetic or made safe through bribery ⟨a ~ official⟩ ⟨in ~ territory⟩ **syn** see CORRECT

²right \"\ *n* -S [ME *riht, right*, fr. OE *riht* (akin to OS & OHG *reht*, OFris *riucht*), fr. *riht*, adj.] **1** : an ethical or moral quality that constitutes the ideal of moral propriety and involves various attributes (as adherence to duty, obedience to lawful authority, whether divine or human, and freedom from guilt) : something morally just or consonant with the light of nature : the straight course **2** : something to which one has a just claim: as **a** : the power or privilege to which one is justly entitled (as upon principles of morality, religion, law, or custom) ⟨held their lands by ~ of the sword —Kemp Malone⟩ ⟨might, not ~ . . . put her in the position she occupied —J.H.Blunt⟩ ⟨accorded of grace and not of ~⟩ ⟨primacy by ~ of merit⟩ **b** : a power, privilege, or condition of existence to which one has a natural claim of enjoyment or possession ⟨the ~*s* of the people⟩ ⟨~ of liberty⟩ — see NATURAL RIGHT **c** : a power, privilege, or immunity vested in one (as by authority or social custom) **d** (1) : a power or privilege vested in a person by the law to demand action or forbearance at the hands of another : a legally enforceable claim against another that the other will do or will not do a given act : a capacity or privilege the enjoyment of which is secured to a person by law — see ABSOLUTE RIGHT, REMEDIAL RIGHT, SUBSTANTIVE RIGHT; compare PERSON OF INCIDENCE, PERSON OF INHERENCE (2) : a claim recognized and delimited by law for the purpose of securing it (3) : the aggregate of the capacities, powers, liberties, and privileges by which a claim is secured (4) : the capacity to assert a legally recognized claim (5) : the interest or share that one has in a piece of property (6) : a claim or title to property or a possession — often used in pl. ⟨bought land and water ~*s* here —*Amer. Guide Series: Md.*⟩ ⟨leased some mineral ~*s* —*Lamp*⟩ ⟨his ~*s* to the throne⟩ (7) **rights** *pl* : the property interest possessed under common law, copyright law, or custom and agreement in an intangible thing esp. of a literary and artistic nature ⟨sold the film ~*s* of the novel for $50,000 —Arnold Bennett⟩ ⟨promised me the Australian ~*s* of his play —Mrs. Patrick Campbell⟩ ⟨publishing ~*s* under a contract⟩ **e** : a power, privilege, or immunity vested in an animal or group of animals (as by custom) ⟨grazing ~*s* of a herd of antelope⟩ **3 a** : something that justly accrues or falls to one : something that one may properly claim : one's due ⟨claim your ~*s*⟩ ⟨honor and admiration are her ~*s* —John Fletcher⟩ **b** *archaic* : an estate, dominion, or other territory belonging to one; *esp* : the piece of land allocated by a colonial New England town to an individual settler **4** : just or equitable treatment : righteous action : fairness in decision : JUSTICE ⟨in ~ to his majesty and the service —Thomas Hale⟩ ⟨had fortune done him ~ —John Dryden⟩ **5 a** : the cause of truth or justice; *esp* : a cause alleged to be true or just by the party supporting it **b** : the person, party, or cause that maintains what is right **6 a** : the right hand ⟨sneaked his ~ home to the jaw —Donn Byrne⟩ **b** (1) : the location or direction lying on the right side of one's body ⟨on our ~ was a large house⟩ (2) : a similar location or direction with respect to another object ⟨as you look at the . . . flag, its ~ is on your own left —*Boy Scout Handbook*⟩ **c** : the part of something (as the wing of an army, the stage of a theater, or the portion of a line of men) that is on the right side of an observer facing in the direction it faces **d** : the road (as of a pair diverging from a point) lying to one's right ⟨take the ~ at the fork⟩ **e** : RIGHT FIELD ⟨sent a nice single to ~ —*Springfield (Mass.) Republican*⟩ **7** : one of the principal tines of a stag's antler (as a brow antler, bay antler, or royal antler) — usu. used in pl. **8** : the true account or correct interpretation of something (as a story, matter, or dispute) ⟨could not . . . learn the very ~ of it —Henry Fielding⟩ — usu. used in pl. ⟨have never heard the ~*s* of that story —Frederick Marryat⟩ **9** : the quality or state of being factually correct : consonance with fact : truthfulness of statement : freedom from error or falsehood : adherence to truth or fact : CORRECTNESS ⟨some mixture of ~ and wrong in their reasoning —Edmund Burke⟩ **10** : the member of a pair situated or used on the right side: as **a** : a shoe or other article of footwear for the right foot **b** : a glove or other article of apparel for the right hand **11** *often cap* **a** : the part of a legislative chamber located to the right of the presiding officer and usu. occupied in continental European and other countries having a similar political pattern by members professing a more conservative or rightist position on political issues than other members ⟨loud applause from benches of the ~⟩ ⟨the ~ is occupied by a neo-Fascist group⟩ — compare CENTER 3 c, LEFT 3 a **b** : the members of a legislative body occupying such seats as a result of their political views **12 a** (1) *usu cap* : individuals or groups sometimes professing views characterized by opposition to change in the established political, social, and economic order and favoring the preservation of traditional attitudes and practices and sometimes advocating the establishment of an authoritarian political order by revolution or other forceful means ⟨a sweeping victory for the conservative *Right* —F.A.Magruder⟩ ⟨brickbats from the extreme *Right*—Al Hine⟩ — compare AUTHORITARIAN, CONSERVATIVE, FASCIST, LEFT 4 a, NAZI, REACTIONARY, TRADITIONALIST (2) : a group or party in another organization that favors conservative, traditional, or sometimes authoritarian attitudes and policies ⟨the ~ in a labor union⟩ ⟨left and ~ in the literary world⟩ **b** *often cap* : the symbolic position occupied by persons professing such views : a conservative or rightist as distinguished from a radical position ⟨drove the Government to the ~⟩ ⟨people ranging from center to extreme ~ —*Harper's*⟩ **13** : a blow (as given by a boxer) with the right fist ⟨a hard ~ to the jaw —*Amer. Guide Series: N.Y.*⟩ **14 a** : a privilege given stockholders of a corporation to subscribe pro rata to a new issue of securities generally at a price below that prevailing in the market ⟨the prospective offering of ~*s* to . . . railroad stockholders —*N.Y. Times*⟩ **b** : the negotiable certificate evidencing such privilege — usu. used in pl. **15** *dial* **a** : DUTY, OBLIGATION ⟨you have a ~ to behave better⟩ **b** : likely reason or excuse ⟨a ~ to fall in if you skate on thin ice⟩

syn RIGHT, PREROGATIVE, PRIVILEGE, PERQUISITE, APPANAGE, BIRTHRIGHT can signify, in common, something to which one has a just or legal claim. RIGHT, the most inclusive, can designate anything, as a power, condition of existence, or possession to which one is entitled by nature, legal or moral law, a grant, or purchase ⟨the *right* to life, liberty, and the pursuit of happiness⟩ ⟨the *right* to freedom of speech⟩ ⟨the *right* to property⟩ ⟨the *right* to command⟩ ⟨the *right* to respect⟩ PREROGATIVE is a right by reason of one's sex, rank, office, character giving precedence, superiority, or advantage over others ⟨entitled to the full *prerogative* of his office —F.M. Stenton⟩ ⟨it may at times exercise the *prerogative* of art by a deliberate use of vague language or imagery —C.S.Kilby⟩ ⟨endurance and stamina in the last analysis are the *prerogatives* of the male —Gerald Beaumont⟩ PRIVILEGE is a special right granted as a favor or concession or belonging to one as a prerogative ⟨the installment buyer must usually pay extra for the *privilege* of deferring payment for what he has bought —J.A.Leavitt & C.O.Hanson⟩ ⟨a propertied class struggling for its *privileges* which it honestly deems to be its rights —W.A.White⟩ ⟨took over all the chartered rights and *privileges* of the existing power companies —*Amer. Guide Series: Maine*⟩ PERQUISITE signifies something, usu. money or something of value, to which one is entitled, esp. by custom, in addition to one's regular salary or wages ⟨the petty graft and favoritism which are normal *perquisites* of machine rule —Green Peyton⟩ ⟨salary is generally supplemented by a rent-and-rate-free house, fuel, and sometimes other *perquisites* —*Auctioneering, Estate Agency & Land Agency*⟩ ⟨shipwrecks and their jetsam are treated as an age-old *perquisite* of the native —*Times Lit. Supp.*⟩ APPANAGE denotes anything to which one has a claim through custom, tradition, or natural necessity but sometimes extends to signify merely an appurtenance ⟨armaments at one's own discretion must be regarded as no longer an *appanage* of nationhood —W.H.B.Beveridge⟩ ⟨fashion at Court and their acquired prestige as a token of power and dignity made gloves an *appanage* of the ruling classes —Anny Varron⟩ ⟨whose literary work had become a mere *appanage* of his domestic life —Van Wyck Brooks⟩ BIRTHRIGHT is a right to which one is entitled by reason of one's birth or the appurtenances of it, as the fact that one is a man, or a citizen of a particular country, descendant of a given family line ⟨the poetic imagination that was his Elizabethan *birthright* —V.L.Parrington⟩ ⟨free public education was the *birthright* of every child —*Proposals for Public Education*⟩ ⟨a group which regarded creative painting as its special *birthright* —Rosamund Frost⟩ ⟨if the college holds to its *birthright* and remains committed as a matter of purpose to serious concern with the issues of conscience —J.S.Dickey⟩

— **by rights** *adv* : with reason or justice : PROPERLY, RIGHTLY ⟨I should not *by rights* have told you —H.R.Haggard⟩ ⟨which is *by rights* the job of a trained psychologist —J.P.Warburg⟩ — **in one's own right** : by title vested in oneself rather than through the ownership or title of another : by virtue of qualifications or properties belonging to someone or something ⟨a life peeress *in her own right* —*N.Y. Times*⟩ ⟨a man of letters *in his own right* —*Amer. Guide Series: N.H.*⟩ ⟨an excellent novel *in its own right* —B.R.Redman⟩ — **in right of** : through right or title derived from or belonging to ⟨claiming the dukedom *in right of* his wife —J.M.Jephson & L.A.Reeve⟩ — **in the right** : with justice, reason, or fact on one's side : RIGHT, CORRECT ⟨in the disagreement he was *in the right*⟩ — **in the right of** : by title vested in the person specified rather than through the ownership or title of another — **of right 1** : as an absolute right not depending on discretion or favor ⟨asserting that all land belongs *of right* to the Crown —*Times Lit. Supp.*⟩ ⟨the provision, as *of right*, of an income —J.F.Golay⟩ **2** : legally or morally demandable : properly exactable ⟨bail in misdemeanors is *of right*⟩ — **right now** *adv* : at once : IMMEDIATELY, INSTANTANEOUSLY ⟨came alive *right now* —Ross Santee⟩ — **to rights** *adv* **1** : in order : into a proper condition ⟨put things *to rights*⟩ ⟨set matters *to rights*⟩ ⟨set the rooms *to rights* —Agnes S. Turnbull⟩ **2 a** *chiefly dial* : at once : without delay : DIRECTLY, STRAIGHTWAY ⟨ordered him to be carried *to rights* to the tower —Thomas Tryon⟩ **b** *obs* : COMPLETELY, ALTOGETHER ⟨the hulk . . . sunk *to rights* —Jonathan Swift⟩

³right \"\ *adv* [ME *riht, right*, fr. OE *rihte*, fr. *riht*, adj.] **1** : in conformity with the standard of justice and duty : in accordance with righteousness : according to right : in harmony with the moral standard of actions : RIGHTEOUSLY, UPRIGHTLY ⟨live ~⟩ ⟨act ~⟩ **2** : EXACTLY, PRECISELY, JUST, ALTOGETHER ⟨~ where you are⟩ ⟨~ at his fingertips⟩ ⟨~ here and now⟩ ⟨~ outside the door⟩ **3 a** : in a suitable, proper, fitting, or desired manner : in the required or necessary way : DULY, WELL ⟨my boys . . . dress ~ —Jack Kramer⟩ ⟨with strict discipline instructed ~ —Wentworth Dillon⟩ ⟨you counsel ~ —Oliver Goldsmith⟩ ⟨hold your pen ~⟩ **b** : in a fortunate, desirable, or satisfactory way ⟨everything will come out ~⟩ **4 a** : in a straight line or direct course : DIRECTLY, STRAIGHT ⟨I'm going ~ home⟩ ⟨his tea came ~ from China⟩ ⟨I'll come ~ back⟩ **b** *archaic* : in the proper course ⟨directed them that went ~ —Ecclus 49:9(AV)⟩ **5** : according to fact or truth : ACCURATELY, CORRECTLY, TRULY ⟨tell a story ~⟩ ⟨estimate a distance ~⟩ ⟨guess ~⟩ ⟨she couldn't believe she had heard ~ —Virgie Roger⟩ **6 a** : all the way ⟨first . . . to take his ship ~ round the world —A.L.Rowse⟩ ⟨windows coming ~ down to the floor —Sacheverell Sitwell⟩ ⟨cut it back . . . ~ back —Audrev Barker⟩ ⟨~ through the hot summer⟩ **b** : COMPLETELY ⟨get ~ away from any such historical basis —Christopher Hawkes⟩ ⟨streamlined square-root ~ out of the curriculum —Bice Clemow⟩ ⟨running ~ out of soap —Elizabeth Bowen⟩ ⟨blurted the words ~ out⟩ **7 a** : IMMEDIATELY ⟨~ after his marriage —Janet Flanner⟩ ⟨~ after an early breakfast —W.A. White⟩ **b** : without delay : very soon : almost at once ⟨I'll be ~ with you —Scott Fitzgerald⟩ ⟨go ~ out of the business course here and get jobs —Hannah Lees⟩ **8** : in a great degree : EXTREMELY, VERY ⟨knew ~ well what was happening —W.A.White⟩ ⟨~ graciously he smiled on us —E.C.Stedman⟩ ⟨it's ~ pleasant sitting here —Ellen Glasgow⟩ — see RIGHT HONORABLE, RIGHT REVEREND, RIGHT WORSHIPFUL **9** : on or to the right ⟨he looked neither ~ nor left —Sir Walter Scott⟩ ⟨the local elections showed that the country was moving ~⟩ **10** : on the shooter or the dice to win ⟨consistently bets ~⟩

⁴right \"\ *vb* -ED/-ING/-S [ME *rihten, righten*, fr. OE *rihtan*; akin to OHG *rihten* to straighten, make right, rule, regulate, ON *rētta* to straighten, make right, adjust, Goth *garaihtjan* to guide; causative-denominative fr. the root of E ¹*right*] *vt* **1 a** : to do justice to : make reparation to : relieve from wrong : restore rights to : assert or regain the rights of : redress the injuries of ⟨so just is God to ~ the innocent —Shak.⟩ ⟨the injured person would be . . . coming back to ~ himself —Leslie Stephen⟩ **b** : to set right : JUSTIFY, VINDICATE ⟨felt the need to ~ himself at court⟩ **2 a** : to make right (something that has been wrong) : bring into accordance with truth : make correct or exact ⟨~ the stupidities in our immigration laws —*New Republic*⟩ ⟨false habits which must be consciously ~*ed* —J.M. Barzun⟩ **b** : to correctly inform or otherwise set right (as a person) ⟨endeavor to ~ the public mind⟩ **3** : AVENGE ⟨~ all wrongs⟩ **4 a** : to restore to the proper state or condition : put right : ADJUST ⟨~ all matters to our satisfaction⟩ **b** *chiefly dial* : to set in order : clear from a disorderly condition : REPAIR — often used with *up* ⟨air the beds and ~ the room —St. John Honeywood⟩ ⟨the old fence . . . was ~*ed* up to keep creatures out —George Washington⟩ **5 a** : to bring (as a ship or conveyance) back into the proper, normal, or natural position : restore to an upright or vertical position ⟨the room ~*ed* itself —Agnes S. Turnbull⟩ ⟨~ a capsized boat⟩ ⟨in the hope that things will ~ themselves —Bernard De Voto⟩ **b** : to bring (oneself) back to one's balance or footing : recover the balance, equilibrium, or footing of (oneself) ⟨tripped but ~*ed* himself⟩ ~ *vi* : to reassume the proper position : recover the natural position : become upright ⟨the ship slowly ~*ed* again⟩ — **right the helm** : to put the helm in line with the keel

⁵right \"\ *n* -S [by alter.] *archaic* : RITE

right-about \'==,=\ *n* -S [fr. *(to the) right about!*] **1** : the position arrived at by turning directly about by the right or sometimes by the left so as to face in the opposite direction : the quarter directly opposite — usu. used with *to* ⟨the officer is . . . not to face his guard to the *right-about* —*Army Regulations & Ordinances*⟩ ⟨the fox took the opportunity to swing to the *right-about* —E.P.Elmhirst⟩ **2** : RIGHT-ABOUT-FACE

¹right-about-face \¦==,=¦=\ *vi* [fr. the imper. phrase *right about face*] **1** : to execute a right-about-face **2** : to turn to the right-about esp. as a military maneuver

²right-about-face \"\ *n* : a complete reversal of attitude, point of view, or policy ⟨another change in the party line, pretty nearly a *right-about-face* —Upton Sinclair⟩

right along *adv* : without cessation ⟨worked *right along*⟩ ⟨busy *right along* with court work —O.W.Holmes †1935⟩

¹right and left *adv* **1** : on or toward the right and the left : toward the right and then the left ⟨dodged *right and left*⟩ **2** : on both or all sides : in both or all directions ⟨troops looting *right and left* —A.N.Dragnich⟩ ⟨social events . . . have been rained out *right and left* —*Springfield (Mass.) Daily News*⟩

²right and left *n* : a dance figure in which the men and the women winding in and out in opposite directions clasp right and left hands alternately as they pass one another

right-and-left \¦=¦=\ *adj* **1 a** : of or relating to the right and the left **b** : designed for right and left feet or for right and left hands **2** : of, relating to, or constituting a screw, pipe coupling, coupling, turnbuckle, or sleeve nut formed with right-handed threads at one end and left-handed threads at the other

right angle *n* [ME *riht angle*] : the angle bounded by two radii that intercept a quarter of a circle : an angle formed by two lines perpendicular to each other — see ANGLE illustration — **at right angles** *adv* : in a perpendicular direction : in a direction perpendicular to something ⟨the teeth are filed straight across the saw *at right angles* to the blade —*U. S. War Dept. Technical Manual*⟩ ⟨set in a plane *at right angles* to the table —*Machinery & Tools*⟩

right-angle \(')ꞏ¦ꞏꞏ\ *vb* [*right angle*] *vt* **:** to bend, direct, or locate at a right angle ⟨white benches were *right-angled* to every doorstep —Anna Cunningham⟩ ~ *vi* **:** to proceed at a right angle ⟨the car . . . *right-angled* sharply north —J.D. Salinger⟩

right-angle clamp *n* **:** a clamp whose clamping face and supporting arm make a right angle

right-angled *also* **right-angle** \(')ꞏ¦ꞏꞏ\ *adj* **1 :** containing or forming a right angle ⟨*right-angled* triangle⟩ ⟨*right-angle* streets⟩ ⟨*right-angled* change of course —P.H.Taylor⟩ — see TRIANGLE illustration **2 :** characterized by right angles ⟨this most *right-angled* of cities —J.L.Motley⟩

right-angle gauge *n* **:** TRY SQUARE

right-angular \(')ꞏ¦ꞏꞏꞏ\ *adj* **:** forming a right angle or right angles ⟨*right-angular* bends⟩ ⟨*right-angular* fences⟩

right ascension *n* **:** one of the equator coordinates of a heavenly body; *specif* **:** the arc of the celestial equator between the vernal equinox and the point where the hour circle through the given body intersects the equator reckoned eastward commonly in terms of the corresponding interval of sidereal time in hours, minutes, and seconds

right at *adv* [ME] *dial* **:** APPROXIMATELY ⟨fetch *right at* three hundred dollars apiece —H.L.Davis⟩

right away *adv* **:** without delay or hesitation **:** at once **:** IMMEDIATELY, STRAIGHTWAY ⟨said he couldn't do the job *right away* —H.B.Hough⟩ ⟨sign you on *right away* —H.A.Chippendale⟩

right azygous vein *n* **:** the azygous vein on the right side of the vertebral column

right-bank \ꞏ¦ꞏ\ *vb* **:** to bank to the right — used esp. of an airplane or a bird in flight

right bower *n* **:** the jack of trumps (as in euchre and five hundred)

right boy *n, usu cap R* **:** a member of a secret association formed in Ireland in the late 18th century principally to obtain redress of agrarian grievances

right-center \ꞏ¦ꞏꞏ\ *n, often cap R&C* **:** a political group or an organized party belonging to the Center but closely associated with the Right in policies and practice — compare LEFT-CENTER

right circular cone *or* **right cone** *n* **:** CONE 2a

right cylinder *or* **right-circular cylinder** *n* **:** a cylinder whose side is perpendicular to its base

¹**right-down** \ꞏ¦ꞏ\ *adj* [²*right* + *down*] **:** characterized by genuineness or thoroughness **:** COMPLETE, THOROUGH ⟨a real *right-down* New York trotter —T.C.Haliburton⟩ ⟨many *right-down* vices —Richard Free⟩

²**right-down** \"\ *adv* **:** without reserve or limitation **:** POSITIVELY, THOROUGHLY, VERY ⟨a regular *right-down* bad 'un —Charles Dickens⟩

righted *past of* RIGHT

right·en \ˈrītᵊn\ *vt* -ED/-ING/-S [¹*right* + *-en*] **:** to restore to original or proper condition **:** set right **:** STRAIGHTEN ⟨the agility to ~ himself at once —Robert Rankin⟩ ⟨old confusions which his reason must ~ —H.B.Alexander⟩

righ·teous \ˈrīchəs\ *adj* [alter. (influenced by *-eous*) of earlier *rightwise, rightuous,* fr. ME *rightwise, rightwos,* fr. OE *rihtwīs,* fr. *riht,* n., right + *wīs* wise — more at RIGHT, WISE] **1 :** doing that which is right **:** acting rightly or justly **:** conforming to the standard of the divine or the moral law **:** free from guilt or sin **:** JUST, UPRIGHT, VIRTUOUS ⟨the gift of God Almighty makes a man essentially ~ —Walter Lowrie⟩ ⟨he who is ~ in the treatment of his slaves —Benjamin Jowett⟩ **2 a :** according with that which is right **:** characterized by uprightness or justice **:** morally right or justifiable **:** free from wrong **:** EQUITABLE ⟨the ~ authority of God's chosen rulers —V.L.Parrington⟩ ⟨fearless in his ~ cause —John Milton⟩ **b :** arising from an outraged sense of justice, morality, or fair play ⟨~ indignation⟩ ⟨~ wrath⟩ **c :** characterized by or expressing satisfaction based on a belief in the correctness or moral uprightness of something (as an action) ⟨meets the resultant gossip . . . with a ~ indifference to either its unfairness or his share in it —*Harper's Bazaar*⟩ **syn** see MORAL

righ·teous·ly *adv* [alter. of earlier *rightwisely,* fr. ME, fr. OE *rihtwīslīce,* fr. *rihtwīs* + *-līce* -ly] **:** in a righteous manner ⟨~ indignant with anything so vague —Havelock Ellis⟩ ⟨acting ~ in separating husband and wife —George Meredith⟩

righ·teous·ness *n* -ES [alter. of earlier *rightwiseness,* fr. ME *rightwisenes,* fr. OE *rihtwīsnes,* fr. *rihtwīs* + *-nes* -ness] **1 :** the quality or state of being righteous **:** conformity to the divine or the moral law **:** RECTITUDE, UPRIGHTNESS ⟨walking before thee in holiness and ~ all our days —*Bk. of Com. Prayer*⟩ ⟨belief that ~ lies on the side of . . . property —H.L.Matthews⟩ **2** *obs* **:** a righteous act, deed, or quality **:** righteous conduct ⟨all our ~*es* are as filthy rags —Isa 64 : 6 (AV)⟩ **3 :** the quality or state of being rightful or just ⟨the ~ of one's claim⟩ **4 :** the state of acceptance with God **:** a right relationship to God **:** JUSTIFICATION

¹**righter** *comparative of* RIGHT

²**right·er** \ˈrīd·ə(r), -ītə-\ *n* -S **:** one that sets right **:** one that does justice or redresses wrong ⟨a ~ of wrongs⟩

rightest *superlative of* RIGHT

right-eyed \ꞏ¦ꞏ\ *adj* **1 :** having the right eye dominant **2 :** using the right eye rather than the left esp. in sighting

right face *n* [fr. the imper. phrase *right, face*] **:** an act of turning 90 degrees to the right from the halted position of attention as a military maneuver — often used as a command; compare ABOUT-FACE, LEFT FACE

right field *n* **1 :** the part of the baseball outfield to the right facing from the plate **2 :** the station of the right fielder

right fielder *n* [*right field* + *-er*] **:** the player defending right field in baseball or softball — see BASEBALL illustration

right·ful \ˈrītfəl\ *adj* [ME *rihtful, rightful,* fr. *riht, right,* n., right + *-ful* — more at RIGHT] **1** *archaic* **:** disposed to do right **:** RIGHTEOUS, UPRIGHT ⟨most ~ judge —Shak.⟩ **2 :** conforming to what is right, just, or moral **:** thoroughly fair **:** EQUITABLE ⟨a ~ cause⟩ **3 :** having a right or just claim according to established laws **:** being or holding by right **:** LEGITIMATE ⟨~ owner⟩ ⟨~ king⟩ ⟨~ heir⟩ **4 :** having an appropriate character or status **:** FITTING, PROPER ⟨proceeded in the ~ order —F.W.Robertson⟩ ⟨grimy colliery villages having no ~ place in a rural landscape —L.D.Stamp⟩ ⟨~ objectives⟩ **5 :** held by right **:** possessed by just claim **:** LEGAL ⟨~ share⟩ ⟨~ inheritance⟩ ⟨~ authority⟩ **syn** see DUE

right·ful·ly \-f(ə)lē, -li\ *adv* [ME *rihtfully, rightfully,* fr. *rihtful, rightful* + *-ly*] **1 :** in accordance with right or justice **:** FAIRLY, JUSTLY ⟨no man can ~ be condemned without reference to some definite law —S.T.Coleridge⟩ **2 :** in a correct or proper manner **:** RIGHTLY ⟨those things which we dread . . . so ~ —*Key Reporter*⟩

right·ful·ness \-fəlnəs\ *n* -ES [ME *rihtfulnes, rightfulnes,* fr. *rihtful, rightful* + *-nes* -ness] **:** the quality or state of being right **:** the justness or equity of something **:** accordance with right and justice ⟨feeling the ~ of the world —Willard Luce⟩

right hand *n* [ME, fr. OE *riht hond, riht hand*] **1 a :** the hand on a person's right side **b :** the hand of greeting, welcome, or friendship **c :** a reliable or indispensable person **:** a useful or efficient helper ⟨indispensable as the *right hand* and instrument of the gods —George Grote⟩ **2 a :** the right side **:** the direction toward the right **b :** a place of honor or precedence ⟨sitteth on the *right hand* of God —*Bk. of Com. Prayer*⟩

right-hand \ꞏ¦ꞏ\ *adj* [*right hand*] **1 :** situated on the right **:** nearer the right hand than the left ⟨*right-hand* room⟩ ⟨*right-hand* side of the road⟩ ⟨the *right-hand* upper vest pocket —Sinclair Lewis⟩ **2 a :** of, using, or performed with the right hand ⟨*right-hand* blow⟩ ⟨*right-hand* dexterity⟩ **b :** designed for or used on the right hand ⟨a *right-hand* glove⟩ **3 :** chiefly relied on **:** almost indispensable — compare RIGHT-HAND MAN 2 **4 :** having, operating in, or delivering power in a right-handed direction ⟨a *right-hand* motor⟩ ⟨*right-hand* engine revolution⟩ **5 a** *of a door* **:** opening to the right away from one **b** *of a hinge* **:** fitting or designed to fit a right-hand or right-hand reverse bevel door **c** *of a lock* (1) **:** fitting or designed to fit on a right-hand or right-hand reverse bevel door or on a left-hand reverse bevel door if both sides of the lock operate (2) **:** throwing or designed to throw right **6 a** *of a turning tool* **:** designed to cut to the right **b** *of a thread chaser* **:** designed to cut a right-hand screw thread **c** *of a milling cutter* **:** designed to rotate counterclockwise **7** *of a rope* **:** RIGHT-LAID **8 a :** of or relating to a division of non-Brahmanical castes in southern India engaging in social and ceremonial rivalry with the left-hand castes **b :** of or relating to a division of Shaktism marked by public Vedic and puranic rites

right-hand convention *n* **:** RIGHT-HANDED SCREW CONVENTION

¹**right-handed** \ꞏ¦ꞏꞏ\ *adj* [ME *right handed,* fr. *right hand* + *-ed*] **1 :** having the right hand more apt or usable than the left **:** preferring the right hand ⟨a *right-handed* pitcher⟩ **2 a :** of, belonging to, or designed for the right hand ⟨a *right-handed* glove⟩ ⟨a *right-handed* implement⟩ **b :** done or made with or as if with the right hand ⟨a *right-handed* stroke⟩ ⟨a *right-handed* blow⟩ **3 :** having the same direction or course as the movement of the hands of a watch viewed from in front **:** CLOCKWISE — used of a twist, rotary motion, or spiral curve as viewed from a given direction with respect to the axis of rotation ⟨a *right-handed* propeller⟩ **4 :** dextrally spiral ⟨most univalve shells are *right-handed*⟩ **5** *of a rope* **:** RIGHT-LAID **6 :** RIGHT-HAND ⟨*right-handed* door⟩ **7 a :** having a crystal structure that has a mirror-image relationship to another enantiomorphous structure regarded as left-handed in which the same compound can crystallize ⟨*right-handed* quartz⟩ **b :** having crystal faces that result from and may be used to characterize such a structure **c :** DEXTROROTATORY — **right-handed·ly** *adv* — **right-handed·ness** *n*

²**right-handed** \"\ *adv* **:** with the right hand **:** in a right-handed manner ⟨throws and bats *right-handed*⟩

right-handed rope *or* **right-hand rope** *n* **1 :** a right-laid rope in which the strands are formed of yarns with left-handed twist **:** a plain-laid rope — compare LEFT-HANDED ROPE **2 :** any right-laid rope

right-handed screw *n* **:** a screw the threads of which (as of a common wood screw) wind spirally in such a direction that the screw advances away from the observer when turned with a right-handed rotation in a fixed nut

right-handed screw convention *n* **:** a convention in mathematics: if linear motion is produced perpendicular to a plane by a rotation in the plane in a given direction, the direction of the linear motion will be that of the motion along its axis of a right-handed screw with axis perpendicular to the plane and with the given direction of rotation in a resisting medium

right-hand·er \ꞏ¦ꞏə(r)\ *n* [*right hand* + *-er*] **1 :** a blow struck with the right hand **2 :** a right-handed person

right-hand lady *n* **:** the woman of the couple to a man's right in a square dance set — compare CORNER LADY, OPPOSITE LADY, PARTNER

right-hand man *n* **1** *obs* **:** a soldier holding a position of responsibility or command on the right of a troop of horse **2 :** a valuable assistant upon whom one is accustomed to rely

right hand of fellowship : a handclasp with the right hand given in some Christian communions in token of the fellowship of the church at occasional ceremonies (as a formal public welcome of new members by the pastor of a congregation or as the installation or ordination of a minister)

right-hand regular lock *n* **:** a right-hand lock for a door that opens inward

right-hand reverse bevel *adj, of a cupboard or closet door* **:** opening to the right toward one

right-hand reverse lock *n* **:** a right-hand lock for a door that opens outward

right-hand rule *n* **:** a rule in electricity: if the thumb, the forefinger, and the middle finger of the right hand are bent at right angles to one another with the thumb pointed in the direction of motion of a conductor relative to a magnetic field and the forefinger in the direction of the field, then the middle finger will point in the direction of the induced electromotive force — compare THUMB-AND-FINGER RULE

right-hand screw thread *n* **:** a screw thread whose helix moves downward when the screw is inserted vertically from above in a fixed mating thread and turned clockwise

right-hand·wise \ꞏ¦ꞏꞏ\ *adv* **:** CLOCKWISE

right heart *n* **:** the right auricle and ventricle **:** the half of the heart by which blood is passed through the pulmonary circulation

right heir *n* **1 :** an heir at law by blood **2 :** the particular heir granted or devised an estate tail as distinguished from the heirs in general

right helicoid *n* **:** a helicoid with generating line perpendicular to its axis

right honorable — used as a courtesy title or an official title for earls, viscounts, and barons, for peers' sons and daughters having courtesy titles, and for various high governmental officials (as members of the Privy Council)

righting *pres part of* RIGHT

righting moment *n* **:** a moment that tends to restore an airplane or a naval vessel to its previous attitude after any small rotational displacement — called also *restoring moment*

right·ism \ˈrīd·ˌizəm, -ī,ti-\ *n* -S *sometimes cap* [²*right* + *-ism*] **1 :** the principles and views of the Right; *also* **:** the movement embodying these principles **2 :** advocacy of or adherence to the doctrines of the Right

¹**right·ist** \ˈrīd·əst, -ītə-\ *n* -S *often cap* [²*right* + *-ist*] **1 :** a member of a group (as a political party) belonging to the Right **2 :** one that believes in or advocates principles associated with the Right

²**rightist** \"\ *adj, often cap* **1 :** of, relating to, or favoring the Right or a group belonging to the Right **2 :** favoring, characterized by, or based upon the principles of the Right

right-laid \ꞏ¦ꞏ\ *adj, of rope* **:** formed of strands twisted together counterclockwise

righ·tle \ˈrītᵊl\ *vt* -ED/-ING/-S [¹*right* + *-le*] *dial Eng* **:** to put right **:** set in order **:** MEND

right·less \ˈrītləs\ *adj* **:** deprived of rights **:** without rights

right·less·ness *n* -ES **:** the quality or state of being rightless ⟨the serf's ~ as regards his lord —Frederick Pollock & F.W. Maitland⟩

right·ly *adv* [ME *rihtly, rightly,* fr. OE *rihtlīce,* fr. *rihtlīc* right, proper, fr. *riht* right + *-līc* -ly — more at RIGHT] **1 :** according to justice or equity **:** in conformity with the divine will or moral rectitude **:** in accordance with right conduct **:** FAIRLY, JUSTLY ⟨wondering if he did quite ~ in supporting the Fascists —*Hibbert Jour.*⟩ **2 :** in the right or proper manner **:** APPROPRIATELY, FITLY ⟨~ proud of its ancient buildings —John Durant⟩ ⟨being ~ cast for the role —Warwick Braithwaite⟩ ⟨the courts are ~ reluctant to thrust themselves into the administrative process —H.S.Commager⟩ **3 :** according to truth or fact **:** ACCURATELY, CORRECTLY, EXACTLY ⟨could ~ identify her if we . . . meet —Hartley Howard⟩ ⟨advised ~ or wrongly by his colleagues —Ed Nellor⟩

right lymphatic duct *n* **:** a short vessel discharging into the right subclavian vein, the lymph from the right side of the head, neck, and thorax, the right arm, right lung, right side of the heart, and convex surface of the liver

right-minded \ꞏ¦ꞏꞏ\ *adj* **:** having a right or honest mind **:** possessing a mind disposed or inclined toward what is right **:** purposing well ⟨that respect for law which every *right-minded* citizen ought to have —Bertrand Russell⟩

right-mind·ed·ness *n* **:** the quality or state of being right-minded ⟨confidence in the *right-mindedness* of his fellow men —J.R.Lowell⟩

right·most \ˈrīt,mōst\ *adj* **:** farthest on the right

right·ness *n* -ES [ME *rihtnes, rightnes,* fr. OE *rihtnes,* fr. *riht* right + *-nes* -ness] **1 :** the quality or state of being right (as in character or conduct) **:** moral rectitude **:** INTEGRITY **2 :** factual correctness **:** ACCURACY, TRUTH **3 :** the quality or state of being appropriate **:** FITNESS, SUITABILITY

righto \ˈrī(,)tō, (')ꞏ¦ꞏ\ *interj* [¹*right* + *-o*] *chiefly Brit* — used to express cheerful concurrence, assent, or understanding

right of action 1 : a right to begin and enforce an action in the courts (as for the purpose of enforcing a right or redressing a wrong) **2 :** CHOSE IN ACTION 1

right of approach : the right of a man-of-war to approach and in time of war to board and inspect a merchant ship at sea in order to ascertain her nationality without interfering with her voyage

right of assembly : the principle of popular government often constitutionally guaranteed that it is the right of the people peaceably to assemble for any purpose not expressly prohibited by law — compare UNLAWFUL ASSEMBLY

right of asylum : the right of receiving protection at a place (as the residence of a sovereign or an ambassador or a foreign state) recognized by custom or treaty

right of common : ²COMMON 4

right of confrontation : the right of one accused of a crime to hear the witnesses testify against him and to cross-examine them

right of drip : an easement or servitude existing only as acquired by grant or prescription that gives one the right to have the water running or dripping from his house fall on the land of his neighbor

right of emption *or* **right of sole emption :** the right formerly exercised by the English Crown of buying commodities at its need or for its use at such price or on such terms of payment as circumstances might warrant

right of entry 1 a : the legal right of taking or resuming possession of real estate in a peaceable manner **b :** POWER OF TERMINATION **c :** a legal right to enter upon land in the possession of another for a special purpose (as of an owner to show land to a prospective purchaser or of a landlord to make repairs) without being guilty of a trespass **2 :** the right of an alien to enter a nation, state, or other political jurisdiction for some special purpose (as of a journalist to report or of a student to study)

right off *adv* **:** right away ⟨the catalog copy caught our eye *right off* —Harvey Breit⟩ ⟨three things should be said *right off* —R.E.Lauterbach⟩

right of privacy : the qualified legal right of a person to have reasonable privacy in not having his private affairs made known or his likeness exhibited to the public having regard to his habits, mode of living, and occupation

right of redemption : the legal right to regain ownership of property that one has formerly enjoyed by freeing it from a debt, charge, or lien, (as by paying to the creditor what is due to release the secured property) — compare EQUITY OF REDEMPTION

right of search 1 : the right of a belligerent to stop a merchant vessel of a neutral state on the high seas and make such examination and search as may be reasonably necessary to determine whether it has become liable to capture by violation of the laws of war (as by carrying contraband goods) **2 :** a right similar to the wartime right of search that arises in time of peace under various circumstances (as for the purpose of enforcing revenue law or preventing piracy)

right of support 1 : the easement or servitude acquired by grant or by prescription by which an owner of a structure on land has a right to rest or support it in whole or in part upon the land or structure of an adjoining owner (as by inserting beams in the adjoining wall on the boundary) **2 :** the common law easement right of an owner of land to have his soil (as distinguished from the structures thereon) both lateral and subjacent remain in its natural condition without being moved or caused to subside without his consent

right of visit *or* **right of visit and search** *or* **right of visitation and search :** RIGHT OF SEARCH

right-of-way \ꞏꞏ¦ꞏ\ *n, pl* **rights-of-way** *or* **right-of-ways** **1 :** a legal right of passage over another person's ground — compare EASEMENT, SERVITUDE **2 :** the area or way over which a right-of-way exists: as **a :** a path or thoroughfare which one may lawfully use (as in crossing the property of another) **:** one established by persons exercising the right to pass over the property of another **b :** the strip of land devoted to or over which is built a public road ⟨miles of *right-of-way* at the sides of improved highways —A.W.Wells⟩ **c :** the land occupied by a railroad for its tracks, yards, and buildings but esp. for its main line **d :** the land used by a public utility (as for an electric power transmission line or a natural gas pipeline) **3 :** a precedence in passing accorded to one vehicle (as an automobile, an airplane, a railroad train, or a boat) over another either by custom, by decision of an appropriate officer (as a train dispatcher), by municipal ordinance, or by statute **4 :** the customary or legal right of traffic to take precedence over any other traffic (as from a certain direction) ⟨usu. street or road traffic in the U.S. has the *right-of-way* over all intercepting traffic except that approaching on the right-hand side and over all following traffic⟩ ⟨a sailing vessel ordinarily has the *right-of-way* over a steam or motor ship⟩ **5 :** the right to take precedence over others (as in speaking, acting, or being brought to the attention of a person or group) **:** permission or opportunity to proceed usu. in precedence over others ⟨if the rules committee refuses to give a bill *right-of-way* —Harold Zink⟩ ⟨the generals were given the *right-of-way* where they should have been checked —J.T.Shotwell⟩

right out *adv, obs* **:** OUTRIGHT ⟨swears he will . . . be a boy *right out* —Shak.⟩

right reverend — used as a courtesy title for various high ecclesiastical officials (as Anglican bishops, some Roman Catholic abbots and abbesses, vicars general, prothonotaries apostolic and domestic prelates, the moderator of the Church of Scotland)

right rudder *n* **:** a position of a ship's rudder that will turn the ship to the right — often used as a command

rights *pl of* RIGHT, *pres 3d sing of* RIGHT

right sailing *n* **:** the movement of a vessel when it sails on one of the four cardinal points so as to alter either its latitude or longitude but not both

right section *n* **:** a cross section (as of a cylinder)

right shoulder arms *n* [fr. the imper. phrase *right shoulder, arms*] **:** a position in the manual of arms in which the rifle is held in the right hand with the barrel resting against the right shoulder and the muzzle inclined to the rear — often used as a command; compare LEFT SHOULDER ARMS

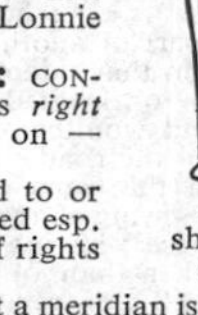
right shoulder arms

right side *n* **1 :** WIRE SIDE **2 :** FELT SIDE

¹**right smart** *adj* [²*right* + *smart*] *chiefly Midland* **:** CONSIDERABLE, LARGE ⟨a *right smart* distance⟩

²**right smart** *n, South & Midland* **:** a large amount, number, or quantity **:** a good deal ⟨suffered a *right smart* with a misery in his side —Elizabeth M. Roberts⟩ ⟨she'll leave him a *right smart* when she passes on —Lonnie Coleman⟩

³**right smart** *adv, South & Midland* **:** CONSIDERABLY, VERY ⟨the hill there . . . is *right smart* steeper than the side we were on —Alder Jernigan⟩

rights on *adv* **:** with the rights attached to or accruing to the security mentioned — used esp. of stock sold or bought with the value of rights included in the price

right sphere *n* **1 :** a sphere so placed that a meridian is parallel to the horizon or plane of projection **2 :** the celestial sphere as seen from all stations on the equator where all bodies rise and set at right angles to the horizon

¹**right stage** *n* **:** the half of a theatrical stage to the right of an actor facing the audience

²**right stage** *adv (or adj)* [¹*right stage*] **:** toward or on the half of a theatrical stage to the right of an actor facing the audience ⟨exit *right stage*⟩ — compare DOWNSTAGE, LEFT STAGE, UPSTAGE

right triangle *n* **:** a triangle having a right angle

right·ward \ˈrītwə(r)d\ *also* **right·wards** \-dz\ *adv (or adj)* [¹*right* + *-ward, -wards*] **:** toward or on the right ⟨looked ~ across the cliffs —*Listener*⟩ ⟨signs of . . . a ~ turn in politics —*Newsweek*⟩

right whale *n* **:** a large whalebone whale of the family Balaenidae having no dorsal fin, the baleen very long, the head enormous and about one third the total length, the throat unfurrowed, and the small eye situated near the angle of the mouth: as **a :** GREENLAND WHALE **b:** SOUTHERN RIGHT WHALE

right whale porpoise *n* **:** a porpoise of the genus *Lissodelphis*

right wing *n* **1 :** the division of a group (as a political party) that believes in or advocates rightist principles and practices ⟨the *right wing* of the Republican party⟩ ⟨member of the fascist *right wing*⟩ — compare LEFT WING **2 :** RIGHT 12 ⟨the *right wing* in British politics⟩

right-wing \ꞏ¦ꞏ\ *adj* [*right wing*] **:** of, adhering to, or favoring the Right ⟨in most European countries the Liberals today are a *right-wing* party —A.M.Schlesinger b.1917⟩ ⟨a *right-wing* majority in the legislative elections —Lionel Durand & Calvin Tomkins⟩ ⟨*right-wing* views⟩

right-wing·er \'ˌ=ˌwiŋə(r)\ *n* -s **1** : a member of a right wing **2** : RIGHTIST

right worshipful — used as a title of honor for various British municipal officials (as mayors, sheriffs, aldermen)

rig·id \'rijəd\ *adj* [MF or L; MF *rigide*, fr. L *rigidus*, fr. *rigēre* to be stiff; perh. akin to L *regere* to lead straight, guide, rule — more at RIGHT] **1 a** : very firm rather than pliant in composition or structure : lacking or devoid of flexibility : inflexible in nature : HARD ⟨metals are not perfectly ~ but elastic —Charles Babbage⟩ ⟨a ~ totalitarian system —Harrison Smith⟩ ⟨~ governmental controls⟩ **b** : stiff and unyielding in appearance ⟨his face was ~ with pain⟩ **2 a** : inflexibly fixed or set in opinion : scrupulously exact with respect to opinions or observances ⟨~ on points of theology —G.R.Crone⟩ ⟨a ~ Catholic⟩ **b** : strictly observed : characterized by scrupulous exactness in observance ⟨~ principles of honesty⟩ ⟨~ adherence to rules⟩ ⟨condemns the ~ observance of artistic conventions —Laurence Binyon⟩ **3** : rigorous or harsh in character : inflexible rather than lax or indulgent : SEVERE ⟨~ inquiry⟩ ⟨a ~ schoolmaster⟩ ⟨~ treatment⟩ **4** : precise and accurate in procedure : exact in method : characterized by an undeviating adherence to strict accuracy ⟨~ control of chemical composition and processing methods —*Steel*⟩ **5 a** : having the gas containers enclosed within compartments of a fixed fabric-covered framework or hull that carries cabins, gondolas, and motors ⟨a ~ airship⟩ **b** : having the outer shape maintained by a fixed framework **6** : of, relating to, or constituting a branch of dynamics in which the bodies whose motions are considered are treated as being absolutely invariable in shape and size under the application of force

syn RIGOROUS, STRICT, STRINGENT: RIGID may suggest stiff, uncompromising or unbending inflexibility ⟨a *rigid* system, faithfully administered, would be better than a slatternly compromise —A.C.Benson⟩ ⟨the Mosaic conception of morality as a code of *rigid* and inflexible rules, arbitrarily ordained, and to be blindly obeyed —Havelock Ellis⟩ RIGOROUS suggests a harsh, severe, inflexible exaction or imposition unabated or unmitigated and entailing hardship and difficulty ⟨the king, therefore, although far from clement, was not extremely *rigorous*. He refused the object of the appeal, but he did not put the envoys to death —J.L.Motley⟩ ⟨to stay in the harsh, cruel, cold climate and endure the cramped and *rigorous* life of the struggling back-country settlement —B.K.Sandwell⟩ ⟨a time-table almost as *rigorous* as that of the locomotive engineer —Lewis Mumford⟩ STRICT implies tight conformity ruling out deviation, looseness, laxity, latitude, or mitigation ⟨*strict* enforcement of the speed laws⟩ ⟨ritual is not easy compliance with usage; it is *strict* compliance with detailed and punctilious rule —W.G.Sumner⟩ STRINGENT suggests severe, tight restriction, constriction, or limitation that checks, curbs, circumscribes, or coerces ⟨he bound me in the most *stringent* terms to say no further word to himself, his methods, or his successes —A. Conan Doyle⟩ ⟨the law was so *stringent* that magazines containing patent medicine advertising could not be shipped into the Philippines unless the formulae were published —V.G.Heiser⟩ ⟨the legal terms of his bondage became more *stringent*, the possibility of emancipation narrower, and the regulation of the emancipated more restrictive —Oscar Handlin⟩ **syn** see in addition STIFF

rigid conduit *n* : firm thick-wall metallic conduit for electric wiring — compare THIN-WALL CONDUIT

rigid constitution *n* : a constitution that is difficult or slow to change usu. because of a prescribed process of amendment that is detailed and lengthy in execution

ri·gid·i·fi·ca·tion \rəˌjidəfə'kāshən\ *n* -s : the action of rigidifying or the state of being rigidified ⟨an increasing ~ of policy —G.D.H.Cole⟩

ri·gid·i·fy \-'=ˌ=ˌfī\ *vb* -ED/-ING/-ES [*rigid* + *-ify*] *vt* : to make rigid ⟨this historical conception has been *rigidified* by the Stalinists —J.T.Farrell⟩ ~ *vi* : to become rigid ⟨relations that ~ into fixed patterns⟩

ri·gid·i·ty \rə'jidəd·ē, -idətē, -i\ *n* -ES [L *rigiditas*, fr. *rigidus* rigid + *-itas* -ity — more at RIGID] **1** : the quality or state of being rigid: as **a** : the quality or state of resisting change of form : want of pliability : HARDNESS ⟨the ~ of armor —V.H.S. Mercier⟩ ⟨that perfect state of flux between ~ and liquefaction —C.J.Phillips⟩ ⟨the distinctions . . . had lost much of their ~ —Douglas Bush⟩ ⟨wage ~⟩ ⟨emotional ~⟩ **b** : stiffness of appearance, manner, opinion, or conduct ⟨there had come into his face a ~ —John Galsworthy⟩ **c** : abnormal stiffness of muscle (as over a site of inflammation or from systemic disease) ⟨~ of abdominal wall in peritonitis⟩ ⟨nuchal ~⟩ **d** : the quality or state of being strict or severe : HARSHNESS, INFLEXIBILITY **e** : the quality or state of being fixed in position — used esp. of a movable object **2** : an instance of being rigid : someone or something that is rigid (as in form or conduct) ⟨the *rigidities* of small-town life —*Times Lit. Supp.*⟩ ⟨create *rigidities* in the economic system —H.G.Johnson⟩ ⟨new *rigidities* of thought —C.J.Rolo⟩ **3** : the amount of resistance of a body to change of form **4** or **rigidity modulus** : SHEAR MODULUS

rig·id·ly *adv* : in a rigid manner : with rigidity : STIFFLY, SEVERELY, STRICTLY ⟨a ~ suspended, electrically operated car —*Amer. Guide Series: Minn.*⟩ ⟨a ~ stratified society —Ralph Linton⟩ ⟨restricting ~ the exchange of information —Raymond Daniell⟩

rig·id·ness *n* -ES : the quality or state of being rigid : RIGIDITY

rig irons *n pl* [⁴*rig*] : the hardware with nails excluded necessary to complete an oil-well drilling rig

riglet *var of* REGLET

rig·ling \'riglən, -liŋ\ *n* -s [²*rig* + *-ling*] *chiefly Scot* : RIDGELING

rig·ma·ree \'rigməˌrē\ *n* -s [NL *Reg. Maria*, abbr. for *Regina Maria* Queen Mary that appeared on coins struck during the reign of Mary Stuart †1587 Queen of Scots] **1** *chiefly Scot* : a small coin **2** *chiefly Scot* : TRIFLE

¹**rig·ma·role** *or* **rig·a·ma·role** \'rig(ə)məˌrōl *sometimes* -ˌrō\ *n* -s [alter. of *ragman roll*] **1** : a succession of confused, meaningless, or foolish statements : prolix and rambling or incoherent talk ⟨a snarling violent ~ . . . kept on coming from him —Claud Cockburn⟩ ⟨never heard such a ~ —George Meredith⟩ **2** : a complex and ritualistic procedure that is characterized more by form than genuine meaning ⟨the odd procedures and mysterious ~*s* of industrial laboratories —John McCarten⟩ ⟨the whole academic ~ of scales and exercises was unnecessary —Winthrop Sargeant⟩

²**rigmarole** \"\ *also* **rig·ma·rol·ish** \-ōlish\ *adj* : consisting of or marked by rigmarole ⟨babbling its indistinct ~ story —Edmund Wilson⟩ ⟨read some long *rigmarolish* old records —Samuel Lover⟩

rig·o·let \ˌrigə'let\ *n* -s [AmerF (Mississippi Valley), dim. of F *rigole* drain, irrigation ditch, canal, fr. OF *regol*] *South* : a small stream : CREEK, RIVULET

rig·or \'rigə(r), *in sense 2* " *or chiefly Brit* 'rīˌgȯ(ə)(r *or* -īgə(r\ *n* -s *see -or in Explan Notes* [ME *rigour*, fr. MF *rigueur*, fr. L *rigor* stiffness, hardness, inflexibility, fr. *rigēre* to be stiff + *-or* — more at RIGID] **1 a** (1) : often harsh inflexibility in opinion, temper, or judgment : SEVERITY, STERNNESS ⟨the moral ~ . . . which prohibits . . . such innocent pleasures as . . . dancing at the crossroads —H.M.Reynolds⟩ (2) : the quality of being unyielding or inflexible : exactingness without allowance, deviation, or indulgence : STRICTNESS ⟨juries are the device by which the ~ of the law is modified —C.E.Wyzanski⟩ (3) : strictness or severity of life : AUSTERITY **b** : an act or instance of strictness, severity, harshness, oppression, or cruelty ⟨the humanist must recognize the normality, the practical necessity of the very ~*s* he is trying to soften —H.J.Muller⟩ **2 a** : a chill or chilliness, with contraction of muscle and convulsive shuddering or tremor (as in the chill preceding a fever) **3** : a condition that makes life difficult, challenging, or uncomfortable; *esp* : extremity of cold ⟨the ~*s* of a northern winter⟩ ⟨did not intend to let the ~*s* of a strange land frighten her away —Green Peyton⟩ **4** : strict precision : EXACTNESS ⟨built upon systems of postulates by means of theorems developed with logical ~ —Joshua Whatmough⟩ **5 a** *obs* : the quality or state of being rigid : RIGIDITY, STIFFNESS **b** : a state of rigidity in organs, tissues, or cells during which they are incapable of responding to stimuli and which is induced by factors arising in the organism (as accumulation of toxic substances) or impinging on the organism from without (as excessive but not immediately lethal temperature) — see RIGOR MORTIS **syn** see DIFFICULTY

rig·or·ism \'rigəˌrizəm\ *n* -s [F *rigorisme*, fr. L *rigor* + F *-isme* -ism] **1** : rigidity in principle or practice: as **a** : austerity of life **b** : strictness in ethical principles — usu. used of ascetic ethics **2** : a system of moral theology holding that when doubt exists as to whether a law of Roman Catholicism is binding in a particular case the law must always be obeyed

¹**rig·or·ist** \-gərəst\ *n* -s [F *rigoriste*, fr. L *rigor* + F *-iste* -ist] **1** : one who is strict in adherence to or enforcement of rules, standards, laws, or principles **2** : one who professes rigorism

²**rigorist** \"\ *or* **rig·or·is·tic** \ˌrigə'ristik\ *adj* **1** : rigid in principles or actions : STRICT **2** : of or relating to the doctrine of rigorism

rig·or mor·tis \ˌrigər'mȯrd·əs, \təs, -gə'mȯ(ə)\, *chiefly Brit* \ˌrīˌgȯ(ə)'m- *or* ˌrigə'm-\ *n* [L, stiffness of death] : rigidity of muscles after death depending in time of onset and duration upon variable factors in the body and in the environment

rig·or·ous \'rig(ə)rəs\ *adj* [ME, fr. ML *rigorosus*, fr. L *rigor* + *-osus* -ous] **1 a** : manifesting, exercising, or favoring rigor : allowing no abatement or mitigation : inflexibly strict : INEXORABLE ⟨liquor smuggling . . . has been another problem . . . to vex governments seeking to maintain a ~ policy of liquor control —D.W.McConnell⟩ **b** : extremely or excessively strict : HARSH, STERN ⟨a ~ academy where the girls wore uniforms, were forbidden to correspond with male contemporaries . . . and were not given diplomas until they passed college entrance examinations —Robert Rice⟩ ⟨juries are now ~, now indulgent —F.A.Ogg & Harold Zink⟩ **2** : marked by extremes of temperature or climate, barrenness of comforts or necessities, or other strenuous challenging obstacles ⟨the life was ~, conditions primitive —*Amer. Guide Series: Texas*⟩ ⟨a combination of high altitudes, ~ climate, poor drainage and thin soils giving rise to poor land —G.P.Wibberley⟩ **3** : scrupulously accurate : EXACT, PRECISE ⟨the reader, missing . . . poets whom he expected to find, may complain that my criterion of significance is too ~ —F.R.Leavis⟩ **syn** see RIGID

rig·or·ous·ly *adv* [ME, fr. *rigorous* + *-ly*] : in a rigorous manner : with rigor

rig·or·ous·ness *n* -ES : the quality or state of being rigorous

rig-out \'=ˌ=\ *n* -s [fr. *rig out*, v.] *Brit* : a suit of clothes : OUTFIT

rigs *pl of* RIG, *pres 3d sing of* RIG

rigs·by \'rigzbi\ *n* -ES [⁶*rig* + *-sby* (as in the name *Crosby*)] *dial Eng* : a rough or loose woman

rigs·da·ler \'rigzˌdälə(r)\ *n* -s [Dan, fr. *rig* kingdom, realm (fr. ON *rīki*) + *daler* — more at RICH] : an old Danish dollar coin similar to the German reichstaler

rig up *vt* : to assemble or improvise (as equipment)

rijder *var of* RYDER

rijks·daal·der \'rīksˌdäl(d)ə(r)\ *n* -s [D, alter. of *rijksdaler*, fr. *rijk* kingdom, realm (fr. MD *rike*, *rijc*) + *daler* taler; akin to OHG *rīhhi* kingdom, realm — more at RICH, DOLLAR] **1** : an old Dutch dollar similar to the German reichstaler **2** : the modern Dutch 2½ guilder piece

rijst·ta·fel \'rīˌstäfəl\ *n* -s [D, fr. *rijst* rice (fr. MD *rijs*, fr. MF *ris*) + *tafel* table, fr. MD *tavele*, *tafele*, fr. (assumed) VL *tavola*, fr. L *tabula* tablet — more at RICE, TABLE] : an Indonesian midday meal consisting chiefly of rice to which are added small portions of a wide variety of meats and vegetables, fish, chicken, fruit, eggs, curries, pickles, and condiments

ri·ker mount \ˌrīkə(r)-\ *n*, *usu cap R* [after Albert Joyce *Riker* *b*1894 Am. botanist] : a flat pasteboard container having a glass cover, containing cotton wool, and used for mounting a specimen (as a plant or insect)

rik·i·sha *or* **rik·sha** *or* **rik·shaw** \'rikˌ(ˌ)shȯ\ *n* -s [short for *jinrikisha*, *jinriksha*, *jinrikshaw*] : JINRIKISHA

riks·da·ler \'riksˌdälə(r)\ *n* -s [Sw, fr. *rike* kingdom, realm (fr. ON *rīki*) + *daler* — more at RICH] : an old Swedish dollar serving as the basic monetary unit of Sweden from the 16th century to 1878

riks·mål *or* **riks·maal** \'rikˌsmȯl\ *n* -s *often cap* [Norw *riksmål* (formerly spelled *riksmaal*), fr. *rik* kingdom, realm + *mål* speech, fr. ON *māl* — more at MAIL] : a literary form of Norwegian developed by the gradual reform of written Danish in conformity to Norwegian usage — compare LANDSMÅL

ril·a·wa \'riləˌwä\ *n* -s [Sinhalese *rilavā*] : TOQUE MACAQUE

rile \'rīl, *esp before pause or consonant* -īəl\ *vt* -ED/-ING/-S [alter. of ¹*roil*] **1** : ¹ROIL 1 ⟨a shower would quickly ~ many streams with the runoff from dirt roads —Christopher Rand⟩ **2** : to make angry : arouse resentment in ⟨in our complex world of overorganization, we cannot get at the people who ~ us —T.V.Smith⟩ **syn** see IRRITATE

ril·ey *also* **rily** \'rīlē\ *adj* **1** : TURBID, ROILED **2** : ANGRY, IRRITATED

¹**rill** \'ril\ *n* -s [D *ril* or LG *rille* furrow, channel made by a small stream, rill; akin to Fris *ril* narrow passage, narrow path, OE *rīth*, *rithe* brook, stream, OS *rīth* gushing brook, MLG *rīde* brook, and prob. to OE *rīsan* to rise — more at RISE] **1 a** : a very small brook : RIVULET, STREAMLET **b** : a small depression or channel eroded by a rill **2** : a transient runnel in which the water of a wave returns to the sea or a lake after breaking on a beach

²**rill** \"\ *vi* -ED/-ING/-S : to run in a small stream : flow like a rill

³**rill** \"\ *adj* : GROOVE

⁴**rill** \'ril\ *or* **rille** \", 'rilə\ *n* -s [G *rille*, lit., furrow, channel made by a small stream, fr. LG] : one of several long, narrow telescopic valleys on the surface of the moon

rill·et \'rilət\ *n* -s [¹*rill* + *-et*] : a little rill

ril·lett *or* **ril·lette** \rə'let\ *n* -s [F *rillette*, dim. of *rille* piece of pork, fr. MF, dial. var. of *reille* board, plank, lath, fr. L *regula* rule, straightedge — more at RULE] : highly seasoned potted pork

rillstone \'=ˌ=\ *n* [¹*rill* + *stone*; intended as trans. of G *rillenstein*, fr. *rille* furrow + *stein* stone] : VENTIFACT

rill stope *n* : an overhand stope in which the back is carried up like a series of inverted steps

¹**rim** \'rim\ *n* -s [ME *rime*, *rim*, fr. OE *rima*; akin to OFris *rim* edge, ON *rimi* strip of land, *rim* fence rail, Goth *rimis* quietness, OIr *forim-* to set, put, Gk *ērema* gently, softly, slowly, Lith *remti* to support, Skt *ramate* he stands still, rests; basic meaning: to rest, support] **1 a** : the outer often curved or circular edge or border of something : BRIM, LIP, MARGIN ⟨~ of a coin⟩ ⟨~ of a tabletop⟩ ⟨~ of a bowl⟩ ⟨~ of a cup⟩ ⟨~ of an ocean⟩ ⟨hayricks on the ~ of a field —Gladys B. Stern⟩ ⟨each sheet written to the ~ in Swift's crabbed little hand —Virginia Woolf⟩ ⟨a glow along the ~ of the hills —Lord Dunsany⟩ **b** : BRINK ⟨close to the ~ of world war —M.W.Straight⟩; *specif* : RIMROCK 2 ⟨~ of a plateau⟩ ⟨north ~ of the canyon⟩ **2 a** : the outer circular part of a wheel joined to the hub usu. by spokes **b** : a removable outer metal band on an automobile wheel to which the tire is attached **3 a** : a raised or projecting outer edge or border ⟨~ of a plate⟩ ⟨inside ~ of a turntable⟩ **b** : something applied as a border ⟨licking the ~ of milk from her upper lip —Nicholas Monsarrat⟩ **4** : FRAME 3m(1) — compare HORN-RIMMED **5** : the outer edge of a usu. horseshoe-shaped copydesk where the copyreaders as distinguished from the copy editor sit ⟨from the ~ to the slot to the city editor to the reporter —Bruce Westley⟩ ⟨because he couldn't write a headline to fit the allotted space, he persuaded a fellow ~ man to do the job for him —*Newsweek*⟩ —compare SLOT **syn** see BORDER

rim 2b

²**rim** \"\ *vb* **rimmed**; **rimmed**; **rimming**; **rims** *vt* **1** : to furnish with a rim : serve as a rim for : BORDER, ENCLOSE ⟨*rimmed* the outline of another letter in gold —Gordon Webber⟩ ⟨a balcony *rimming* the second floor —Morris Gilbert⟩ ⟨high mountains which *rimmed* the region —R.A. Billington⟩ ⟨nails *rimmed* black with grease —Kay Boyle⟩ **2** *of a ball* : to run around the rim of ⟨a putt that *rimmed* the cup⟩ ~ *vi* : to form or show a rim, edge, or border ⟨opened the door. The yellow light from inside *rimmed* about her —R.J.Hogan⟩ ⟨till *rimmed* into the east the risen sun —Walter de la Mare⟩ ⟨the biotite . . . does not ~ or interfinger with hornblende —*Economic Geology*⟩

³**rim** \"\ *n* -s [ME *reme*, *rime*, *rim* membrane, fr. OE *rēama*, *rēoma* membrane, ligament; akin to OS & OHG *riomo* strap, MD *rieme*, MLG *rēme*] *archaic* : PERITONEUM

ri·ma \'rīmə\ *n*, *pl* **ri·mae** \-ī,mē\ [NL, fr. L, slit, fissure, crack — more at ROW] **1** : a long narrow aperture : CLEFT, FISSURE **2** *also* **rima glot·ti·dis** \-'gläd·ədəs\ [*rima glottidis*, NL, lit., rima of the glottis] : the passage in the glottis between the true vocal cords — **ri·mal** \-məl\ *adj*

ri·mas \'rēməs\ *n* -ES [Tag] *Philippines* : BREADFRUIT

ri·mate \'rīˌmāt\ *adj* [L *rima* + E *-ate*] : having fissures : FISSURED

ri·ma·tion \rī'māshən\ *n* -s [NL *rima* + E *-ation*] : RIMA

rim·base \'rimˌbās\ *n* **1** : the mass of metal connecting a trunnion with the trunnion band or the body of a cannon — see CANNON illustration **2** : the shoulder of the stock of a firearm on which the breech of the barrel rests

rim blight *n* : a disease of tea caused by a fungus of the genus *Cladosporium* and characterized by yellowing of the leaf margins followed by browning

rim-bound \'=ˌ=\ *adj* : having the tips and margins of the leaves curved downward (as in tobacco suffering from potash hunger)

rim clutch *n* : a friction clutch having for one of the friction contacting members a cylindrical rim that is gripped (as by lever action, fitted ring segments, or shoes) on both cylindrical surfaces

rim-drive \'=ˌ=\ *n* : a method of driving a disc recorder or phonograph turntable by frictional contact between a motor shaft and the rim of the turntable and often by interposing a rubber-covered wheel between shaft and turntable

¹**rime** \'rīm\ *n* -s [ME *rim*, fr. OE *hrīm*; akin to OS *hrīpo* frost, OHG *hrīffo*, *rīffo*, MHG *rīm*, ON *hrīm*, *hrīmi* frost, Latvian *kreims* cream, Lith *krėna*] **1** *or* **rime frost** : FROST 1c(1) **2** : an accumulation of granular ice tufts on the windward sides of exposed objects slightly resembling hoarfrost but formed only from undercooled fog or cloud and always built out directly against the wind **3** : CRUST, INCRUSTATION ⟨~ of snow —D.C.Peattie⟩ ⟨dust settled down . . . making a gray ~ on eyebrows, nose —Thomas Wood †1950⟩ ⟨a ~ of alkali on flatland⟩

²**rime** \"\ *vt* -ED/-ING/-S : to cover with or as if with rime ⟨hedgerows were *rimed* and stiff with frost —William Faulkner⟩ ⟨age had *rimed* his beard —Kay Rogers⟩ ⟨wagons *rimed* with clay —Hamilton Basso⟩

³**rime** *var of* RHYME

⁴**rime** \'rīm\ *n* -s [L *rima* — more at ROW] : CHINK, CRACK, FISSURE

⁵**rime** \"\ *dial chiefly Eng var of* REAM

rime couée \ˌrēmkü'ā\ *n*, *pl* **rimes couées** \"\ [F] : TAIL RHYME

rime·less \'rīmləs\ *adj* : being without rime : FROSTLESS

rime riche \rēm'rēsh\ *n*, *pl* **rimes riches** \"\ [F, lit., rich rhyme] : a rhyme produced by agreement in sound not only of the last accented vowel and any succeeding sounds but also of the consonant preceding this rhyming vowel ⟨in English, *church spire* and *aspire* would be *rimes riches*⟩ — called also *identical rhyme*; distinguished from *rime suffisante*

rime suf·fi·sante \ˌrēmˌsüfē'zäⁿt\ *n*, *pl* **rimes suffisantes** \"\ [F, lit., sufficient rhyme] : end rhyme produced by agreement in sound of an accented final vowel and following final consonant or consonants if any ⟨in English, *dip* and *ship*, *flee* and *see* are *rimes suffisantes*⟩ — distinguished from *rime riche*

¹**rimfire** \'=ˌ=\ *adj* [¹*rim* + *fire* (v.)] **1** *of a cartridge* : having the percussion compound in a rim surrounding the base — distinguished from *center-fire* **2** : designed for or adapted to the use of rimfire cartridges ⟨~ rifle⟩

²**rimfire** \"\ *n* [¹*rim* + *fire* (n.)] : the burning of the leaf margins (as in tobacco) caused by potash hunger

rim·land \'rimˌland, -ˌlaa(ə)nd, -ˌlənd\ *n* : a region on the periphery of the heartland

rim·less \'rimləs\ *adj* **1** : lacking a rim or frame ⟨wearing ~ glasses⟩ **2** *of a cartridge case* : having a rim diameter equal to or less than that of the body of the case

rim lighting *n* : BACKLIGHTING

rim lock *or* **rim latch** *n* : a lock or latch made to be fastened to the face of a door — compare MORTISE LOCK

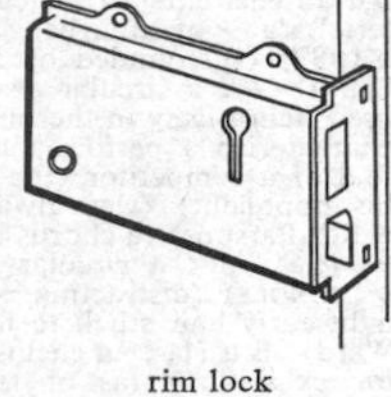

rim lock

rimmed \ˌrimd\ *adj* [¹*rim* + *-ed*] **1** : having a rim — usu. used in combination ⟨gold-*rimmed*⟩ ⟨narrow-*rimmed*⟩ ⟨red-*rimmed*⟩ **2** *of a cartridge case* : having a diameter at the rim greater than that of the body of the case and no extractor groove around the base of the case at the rim **3** *of a letter* : bordered all round by white space enclosed by a continuous fine line ⟨a ~ type face⟩ **4** *of steel* : incompletely deoxidized so that after solidification the outside portion is distinctly different in constitution from the interior of the ingot — compare KILL *vt* 6b

rim·mer \'rimə(r)\ *n* -s [²*rim* + *-er*] : one that rims: as **a** : an implement for cutting, trimming, or ornamenting the rim of something **b** : a worker who forms edge wires that are used as top frames of bedspring assemblies or one who attaches rims to the top coils of bedsprings

²**rimmer** \"\ *n* -s [⁵*rim* + *-er*] : REAMER

rimming *pres part of* RIM

rim of sa·nio \-'sänēˌō\ *usu cap S* [after Carl *Sanio*, 19th cent. botanist] : CRASSULA

ri·mose \(')rī'mōs\ *or* **ri·mous** \'rīməs\ *adj* [L *rimosus*, fr. *rima* slit, crack, fissure + *-osus*, -ose, -ous — more at ROW] : having numerous clefts, cracks, or fissures ⟨the ~ bark of a tree⟩ — **ri·mose·ly** *adv* — **ri·mos·i·ty** \rī'mäsəd·ē\ *n* -ES

¹**rim·ple** \'rimpəl\ *n* -s [ME, fr. OE *hrympel* — more at RUMPLE] : FOLD, WRINKLE, RUMPLE, RIPPLE

²**rimple** \"\ *vb* -ED/-ING/-S : RUMPLE, WRINKLE, RIPPLE

rimp·tion \'rim(p)shən\ *n* -s [origin unknown] *South & Midland* : ABUNDANCE, LOT — usu. used in pl. ⟨~*s* of food⟩

¹**rimrock** \'=ˌ=\ *n* [¹*rim* + *rock*] **1** : a top stratum or overlying strata of resistant rock of a plateau outcropping to form a more or less vertical face (as in the wall of a canyon) ⟨mesas topped with ~ —Agnes M. Cleaveland⟩ — compare ¹CAP 2a(3) **2** : the edge or face of an outcropping of rimrock ⟨stopping the car on the high ~, we looked down —Frank Waters⟩ ⟨a high flat mesa, with ~*s* all around —Will James⟩

²**rimrock** \"\ *vt*, *West* : to destroy (as a flock of sheep) by driving over a cliff

rims *pl of* RIM, *pres 3d sing of* RIM

rim saw *n* : a disk saw having the teeth on a separate ring

rim·stone \'rimzˌtōn, -m,st-\ *n* : a calcareous deposit formed as a ring around an overflowing basin (as of a mineral hot spring)

ri·mu \'rē(ˌ)mü\ *n* -s [Maori] **1** : a tall New Zealand timber tree (*Dacrydium cupressinum*) with a small head, drooping terminal branches covered with tiny keeled linear leaves, and an ovoid terminal nut with a fleshy red receptacle **2** : the wood of the rimu tree used for furniture and general construction — called also *imou pine*, *red pine*

rim·u·la \'rimyələ\ *n*, *pl* **rimu·lae** \-yəˌlē\ [NL, dim. of *rima*] : a small fissure (as in the brain or spinal cord)

rim·u·lose \-yəˌlōs\ *adj* [NL *rimula* + E *-ose*] : having small chinks or fissures

ri·mur \'rēmə(r)\ *n pl* [ON *rīmur*, pl. of *rīma*, fr. *rīm* rhyme, fr. MLG, fr. OF *rime* — more at RHYME] : a complex form of versified saga or treatment of episodes from the sagas popular in Iceland from the 15th century

rimy \'rīmē\ *adj* -ER/-EST [fr. (assumed) ME, fr. OE *hrīmig*, fr. *hrīm* frost + *-ig* -y — more at RIME] : covered with rime : FROSTY

¹**rin** \'rin\ *chiefly Scot var of* RUN

²**rin** \"\ *n*, *pl* **rin** [Jap] **1** : a Japanese monetary unit equal to ⅒ sen **2** : a coin representing one rin

rin·ceau \raⁿ'sō\ *n*, *pl* **rin·ceaux** \-ō(z)\ [F, fr. MF *rainsel* branch, fr. (assumed) VL *ramuscellus*, alter. of LL *ramusculus* small branch, dim. of *ramus* branch — more at RAMIFY] : an ornamental motif consisting essentially of a sinuous and branching scroll elaborated with leaves and other natural forms (as derived from the acanthus)

rin·con \riŋˈkōn\ *n, pl* **rincons** \-ōnz\ *or* **rinco·nes** \-ō,nās\ [Sp *rincón,* lit., corner, nook, alter. of *recón, rencón,* fr. Ar dial. (Spain) *rukun* (Ar *rukn*)] **1** *Southwest* **:** a small secluded valley **2** *Southwest* **:** an alcove or angular recess in a cliff **3** *Southwest* **:** a bend in a river

¹rind \ˈrīnd, *dial or before consonant or pause* ˈrīn\ *n* -s [ME *rind, rinde,* fr. OE; akin to MD *rinde, rende & runde* bark, OS *rinda,* OHG *rinda, rinta* bark, G dial (Hesse) *runde* scab, Norw *rind* strip, OE *rendan* to rend — more at REND] **1 :** BARK, CORTEX ⟨~ of a tree⟩ **2 a :** PEEL ⟨watermelon ~⟩ ⟨grated lemon ~⟩ **b :** a piece of peel **:** PEELING ⟨grapefruit ~s⟩ **3 a :** an outer layer or covering **:** CRUST, SKIN ⟨~ of cheese⟩ ⟨~ of ham⟩ ⟨atmosphere, the earth's invisible ~ —Waldemar Kaempffert⟩ ⟨dreams that lie hidden beneath the ~ of the commonplace —H.A.Overstreet⟩ **b :** a piece of skin or other outer layer ⟨bacon ~s⟩ **4 :** a strip of cloth under the leather grip of a golf club

²rind \"\ *vt* -ED/-ING/-S **:** to remove the rind of **:** BARK

³rind *or* **rynd** \ˈrīnd, ˈrind\ *n* -s [ME *rynd;* akin to MD *rijn* millrind, MLG *rin, ryn*] **:** MILLRIND 1

⁴rind \"\ *vt* -ED/-ING/-S [alter. of earlier *rend,* fr. ME *renden,* fr. MF *rendre* to render — more at RENDER] *dial Brit* **:** RENDER ⟨~ tallow⟩ ⟨~ butter⟩

⁵rind \ˈrīn(d)\ *n* -s [alter. of ¹*rime*] *dial chiefly Brit* **:** FROST 1c(1)

rind disease *n* **:** a disease of sugarcane formerly thought to be caused by a fungus (*Melanconium sacchari*) that is now known to be an accompaniment of other diseases (as red rot) and characterized by dark bluish shrunken wrinkled lesions on the stems

rind·ed \ˈrīndəd\ *adj* [¹*rind* + *-ed*] **:** having a rind — usu. used in combination ⟨smooth-*rinded*⟩ ⟨green-*rinded*⟩

rin·der·pest \ˈrində(r),pest\ *n* [G, fr. *rinder* (pl. of *rind* head of cattle, fr. OHG *hrind, rind*) + *pest,* fr. L *pestis* — more at RUNT] **:** an acute highly infectious febrile disease of cattle and less often of sheep, goats, and wild game animals caused by a filterable virus and producing diphtheritic inflammation of the mucous membranes and esp. of the intestines — called also *cattle plague*

rind gall *n* **:** a defect in timber caused by the growth of annual layers of wood over a bruise in the bark

rind graft *n* **:** BARK GRAFT

rin·dle \ˈrindᵊl, -nᵊl\ *n* -s [alter. of earlier *rinel* — more at RUNNEL] *dial chiefly Eng* **:** RUNNEL

rind·less \ˈrīn(d)ləs\ *adj* **:** lacking a rind ⟨~ cheese⟩

rindy \-ndē\ *adj* [¹*rind* + *-y*] **:** having a rind or skin

rin·for·zan·do \ˌrēnfȯrˈtsän(,)dō\ *adj* (*or adv*) [It, reinforcing, strengthening, verbal of *rinforzare* to reinforce, strengthen, fr. *ri-* re- (fr. L *re-*) + *inforzare* to enforce, strengthen, fr. OIt, fr. MF *enforcier* — more at ENFORCE] **:** played with a sudden increase of force — used as a direction in music usu. for special emphasis of a note, chord, or short phrase; abbr. *rf* or *rfz;* compare SFORZANDO

rin·for·za·to \-ˈädˌ(,)ō\ *adj* (*or adv*) [It, past part. of *rinforzare*] **:** RINFORZANDO

¹ring \ˈriŋ\ *n* -s *often attrib* [ME, fr. OE *hring;* akin to OFris, OS, & OHG *hring* ring, ON *hringr,* Crimean Goth *rinck, ringo* ring, Umbrian *krenkatrum* belt, OSlav *krǫgŭ* circle, L *curvus* curved — more at CROWN] **1 a :** a circular or curved band (as of metal, wood, fabric, or plastic) used for holding, connecting, hanging, or pulling ⟨curtain ~⟩ ⟨key ~⟩ ⟨towel ~⟩ ⟨the ~ of a drawer pull⟩ ⟨the ~ of an anchor⟩ **b :** one of the small iron circles used in making chain mail **c :** a usu. circular band of metal or other material used for packing or sealing ⟨rubber ~s for sealing fruit jars⟩; *specif* **:** PISTON RING **2 a :** a circlet of metal or other material often set with a gem that is worn on the finger as an ornament, token, or amulet or for use as a seal ⟨diamond ~⟩ ⟨fraternal ~⟩ — see ENGAGEMENT RING, SIGNET RING, WEDDING RING; compare ³BAND 6e **b :** a circlet of metal or other material worn as an ornament on any part of the body (as the arm, ankle, toe) — compare EARRING **3 :** the rim or border of a circular object ⟨the ~ of the horizon⟩ **4 a :** any circular or continuous round line, figure, or object ⟨coffee cup ~s on a table⟩ ⟨dog with a ~ of white around his neck —F.B.Gipson⟩ ⟨smoke ~s⟩ ⟨~ of scum in a washbasin⟩ **b :** an encircling arrangement (as of persons, things, or material) ⟨a ~ of suburbs⟩ ⟨a ~ of encircling hills —G.H.Reed b.1887⟩ ⟨surrounded by a wide ~ of suspicion —Bradford Smith⟩ **c :** a circular or spiral course ⟨run in ~s⟩ — often used figuratively in the pl. with *around* and often with *run* to characterize a performance that easily or greatly surpasses that of a competitor ⟨the mayoral candidate ran ~s around his opponent⟩ ⟨was always working ~s around the boys —R.P.Parsons⟩ ⟨a chorus that can dance ~s around any other —*Time*⟩ **d :** a circular ripple on the surface of a liquid **e :** RINGLET ⟨distracting ~s of her hair —Mary Austin⟩ ⟨her light curly hair stuck to her forehead in baby ~s —Mary J. Ward⟩ **5 a** (1) **:** an enclosed often circular or oval space esp. for exhibitions (as of riding) or competitions (as races) ⟨stock sales ~⟩ ⟨exercise ~⟩ (2) **:** a structure containing such a ring; *specif* **:** BULLRING **b :** a usu. circular space in the arena of a circus covered with tanbark or sawdust and used for performances (as of animal trainers and their charges) — see THREE-RING CIRCUS **c :** the occupation of a circus performer — used with *the* ⟨abandoning the stage for the ~ —T.W. Duncan⟩ **6 a :** an enclosure usu. about 20 feet square marked by ropes attached to posts at the corners and raised on a platform in which boxers or wrestlers contest; *also* **:** this enclosure together with its supporting platform — see PRIZE RING **b :** PRIZEFIGHTING ⟨fought a few professional bouts only to decide against continuing in the ~ —*Current Biog.*⟩ ⟨end of his ~ career⟩ **7 :** a cut made into or through the bark and around the trunk or a limb of a tree **8 :** one of the ridges increasing in number with age that encircle the horns of cattle **9 :** one of three concentric bands usu. believed to be composed of meteoric fragments revolving around the planet Saturn **10 rings** *pl* **:** the cage at masthead for lookout (as on a whaling vessel) — compare CROW'S NEST **11 a :** ANNULUS 5 **b :** GROWTH RING **12 a :** an enclosure or space devoted to betting at a horse race **b :** those who bet in a ring; *esp* **:** the bookmakers of a ring **13 a :** an archivolt made up of a half ring of voussoirs **b :** a parallel course of half bricks or other small voussoirs forming a rowlock arch **c :** an encircling architectural element (as a corridor or a series of rooms) **14 a :** an exclusive combination of persons for a selfish and often corrupt purpose (as to control the market, distribute offices, or obtain contracts) ⟨not a member of the inner party ~ —*Times Lit. Supp.*⟩ ⟨had the courage to tackle price ~s —Seamus Brady⟩ ⟨organized ~s stealing cars —*Springfield (Mass.) Union*⟩ ⟨innocent women were frequently framed by a ~ consisting of police officers, stool pigeons, bondsmen and lawyers —Morris Ploscowe⟩ **b :** a temporary group of persons working cooperatively **:** POOL ⟨organization of spray ~s where a group of growers uses one spraying outfit —*Experiment Station Record*⟩ **15 a :** a series of buyers and sellers in a produce exchange in which each buyer is the seller in the same amount of the same goods to another buyer so that the entire series of transactions can be settled by ringing out **b :** ¹PIT 1b(9) **16 :** the field of a political contest **:** RACE ⟨threw his hat into the presidential ~⟩ **17 :** a circle drawn around a marginal marking on a proof to indicate that the change ordered is not in correction of a printer's error, that the circled writing is a query to the author, or that a circled arabic numeral or abbreviation is to be spelled out **18 a :** SPINNING RING **b :** RING SPINNER **19 :** food in the shape of a circle: as **a :** cooked food folded in a circle ⟨noodle ~⟩ ⟨~ cake⟩ **b :** a long sausage tied together at the ends ⟨Polish ~⟩ **20 :** WATER RING **21 :** a circle of worked stitches used to form patterns in tatting **22 :** an arrangement of atoms represented in formulas or models in a cyclic manner or as a closed chain and commonly consisting of five or six atoms although smaller and also much larger rings are known ⟨carbocyclic and heterocyclic ~s⟩ — called also *cycle;* compare BENZENE RING, NUCLEUS 2j, OPEN CHAIN, STRUCTURAL FORMULA **23** *chiefly Brit* **:** a band attached (as to the leg of a bird) to identify **24 :** a pair of meiotic chromosomes associated end-to-end due to the formation of terminal chiasmata at both ends of the pair **25 :** one of a pair of heavy usu. leather covered metal circles suspended from the ceiling or a crossbar and used for gymnastic exercise **26 :** a round disk of rattan or metal with intertwined thongs used to prevent a ski pole from sinking into the snow **27** *Austral* **:** ²RINGER 4 **28 :** an aggregate in which addition is commutative, the product of two elements is unique, and multiplication is distributive with respect to addition and associative

²ring \"\ *vb* -ED/-ING/-S [ME *ringen,* fr. *ring,* n.] *vt* **1 :** to place or form a ring entirely or nearly around **:** station or take position around in a ring or cordon **:** mark by drawing a ring around **:** ENCIRCLE ⟨~*ed* on three sides by mountains —*Amer. Guide Series: N.H.*⟩ ⟨a guard was set that he might not flee — a score of bayonets ~*ed* the tree —Rudyard Kipling⟩ ⟨a name that has ~*ed* the world —*advt*⟩ **2 :** to place a ring on **:** provide with a ring: as **a :** to put a ring in the nose or around the neck in order to subdue, check, or shackle ⟨hogs ~*ed* to prevent rooting⟩ **b** *chiefly Brit* **:** to place a ring around the leg of (a bird or animal) to classify or identify **:** BAND **3 :** to wheel around **:** run or ride around encircling (as to prevent straying or escape) **:** move in a circle ⟨eagles sailing round and round them like sheep dogs ~*ing* a flock —Francis Ratcliffe⟩ ⟨herders ~*ing* cattle⟩ **4 :** GIRDLE 3 **5 :** to throw a ring over (the mark) in a game where rings or other curved objects (as horseshoes) are tossed at a standing or projecting mark **6 :** to exhibit or exercise in a ring **:** introduce into a ring (as at a dog or horse show or a circus) **7 :** to settle (a contract) by ringing out **8 :** to enter (as a horse or dog) in a contest as a ringer ~ *vi* **1 a :** to move in a ring **b :** to rise in the air spirally **2 :** to form or take the shape of a ring **syn** see SURROUND — **ring an anchor :** to haul the anchor up until its ring is at the hawsehole or cathead — usu. used with *up*

³ring \"\ *vb* **rang** \ˈraŋ, -aiŋ\ *also* **rung** \ˈrəŋ\ **rung; ringing; rings** [ME *ringen,* fr. OE *hringan;* akin to MD *ringen* to ring, ON *hringja* to ring, *hrang* noise, din, Toch B *krañko* cock, Lith *krañkti* to croak, Skt *kruñ* curlew, and perh. to OE *hrǣfn* raven — more at RAVEN] *vi* **1 :** to sound clearly and resonantly ⟨the ~*ing* of many bells⟩ ⟨the doorbell *rang*⟩ ⟨dense porcelaneous ware usually high fired enough to ~ —W.E. Cox⟩ ⟨weird ~*ing* voices of veeries —W.P.Smith⟩ **2 :** to sound loudly and sonorously ⟨cheers *rang out*⟩ ⟨his voice *rang* with indignation⟩ ⟨the trumpet *rang*⟩ ⟨oaths *rang* across the stable yard —Margaret Kennedy⟩ **3 a :** to be filled with a ringing or reverberating sound **:** RESOUND, ECHO ⟨woods *rang* with the sound of the ax⟩ **b :** to have the sensation of being filled with a humming sound ⟨his ears *rang*⟩ **4 :** to cause something to ring (as in giving a summons) ⟨~ for breakfast⟩ **5 :** to engage in bell ringing or making music with bells **6 a :** to become filled with talk or report ⟨newspapers *rang* with the unknown author's story —W.E.Smith⟩ ⟨the world *rang* with his fame⟩ ⟨their letters ~ with sincere praise —*advt*⟩ **b :** to cause much talk **:** have great renown ⟨his deeds *rang* through the country⟩ **c :** to sound repetitiously **:** DIN ⟨their praises *rang* in our ears⟩ ⟨a tune that ~s in one's memory⟩ **7 :** to have a particular sound or character expressive of some quality ⟨a spirited story that ~s true in all its incidental details —Frances Gaither⟩ ⟨piece of empty heroics, which must ~ false from the screen —Lee Rogow⟩ ⟨a well-meant effort *rang* hollow —S.L.A.Marshall⟩ ⟨his heroine . . . is a little too sensitive to ~ true —James Yaffe⟩ **8** *chiefly Brit* **:** to place a telephone call **:** TELEPHONE — usu. used with *up* or *through* ~ *vt* **1 :** to cause (a metallic body) to sound esp. by striking ⟨the soldier *rang* each dollar against his bayonet to test the purity of the coin —Nora Waln⟩; *specif* **:** to sound (a church bell) with a full swing from a mouth-up position — compare CHIME, CLOCK **2 :** to make (a sound) by or as if by ringing a bell ⟨the shard-borne beetle, with his drowsy hums, hath *rung* night's yawning peal —Shak.⟩ **3 :** to announce or proclaim by or as if by ringing **:** usher in or out by ringing a bell ⟨~ an alarm⟩ ⟨~ in the new year, ~ out the old⟩ **4 :** to repeat often, loudly, or earnestly ⟨~ denunciations⟩ ⟨~ the praises of a compatriot⟩ **5 a :** to summon esp. by bell **b** *chiefly Brit* **:** TELEPHONE — usu. used with *up* **6 :** to cause (a machine or device) to register **:** ring up ⟨~ a cash register⟩ ⟨~ a time clock⟩ ⟨~ a sale⟩ — **ring a bell :** to arouse a response **:** strike a sympathetic chord **:** call out recognition **:** stir a memory ⟨his remarks on federal aid and increased taxes *rang a bell* —J.A.Morris b.1904⟩ ⟨have a sense of the ridiculous which *rings a bell* with us —Henry Baerlein⟩ ⟨if the name *rings no bell* in your mind —Howard Nemerov⟩ — **ring down the curtain 1 a :** to give the signal for lowering the curtain in a theater or auditorium **b :** to lower the curtain in a theater or auditorium **2 :** to conclude a performance or action ⟨this sorry episode *rang down the curtain* on what was planned to be a spectacular adventure⟩ — **ring the bell :** to be convincing or successful ⟨this last advantage *rang the bell* with bankers —*Newsweek*⟩ ⟨good title, a good blurb, army lingo; it *rang the bell* —R.A.Robinson⟩ — **ring the changes** *or* **ring changes :** to run through the whole range of possible variations **:** reiterate in exhaustive variety of expression ⟨*rings the changes* on possible meanings of words —David Daiches⟩ ⟨clever at *ringing the changes* with a black frock and a white one —Frances Towers⟩ — **ring up the curtain 1 a :** to give the signal for raising the curtain in a theater or auditorium **b :** to raise the curtain in a theater or auditorium **2 :** to begin a performance or action

⁴ring \"\ *n* -s **1 :** a set of church bells; *esp* **:** one tuned in scale for change ringing **2 :** a clear resonant sound made by or resembling that made by vibrating metals ⟨the ~ of a bell⟩ ⟨the ~ of hammer upon anvil —Elizabeth Goudge⟩ ⟨each ~ of the telephone filled me with dread —Ralph Ellison⟩ ⟨the ~ of laughter⟩ **3 :** resonant tone (as in response to plucking or striking) **:** SONORITY ⟨the ~ of a glass goblet⟩ ⟨the ~ of a porcelain dish⟩ ⟨the ~ of a coin⟩ ⟨a voice of ~ and warmth —Irving Kolodin⟩ **4 :** a loud sound **:** a sound continued, repeated, or reverberated ⟨hear the ~ in your ears of wind from the solitude of mountain heights —Alicita & Warren Hamilton⟩ **5 :** a sound or character (as of speech or writing) expressive of some particular quality ⟨a ~ of ardent sincerity in his voice —G.G.Carter⟩ ⟨strange circumlocutions that . . . still have the ~ of natural speech —Arthur Knight⟩ ⟨such generalizations have the ~ of plausibility —Alexander Gerschenkron⟩ ⟨scheme has a fantastic ~ about it —O.S. Nock⟩ **6 a :** the act or an instance of sounding a bell or similar device **b :** the act or an instance of summoning (as by a bell or buzzer) **c :** a telephone call — often used with *give*

⁵ring \"\ *Scot var of* REIGN

ring–a–lievo \ˌriŋəˈlē(,)vō\ *or* **ring–a–levio** \-ēvē,ō\ *n* -s [alter. of *ring relievo*] **:** ²RELIEVO

ring–a–rosy \ˈriŋəˈrōzē\ *n* -ES **:** RING-AROUND-A-ROSY

ring–around–a–rosy *or* **ring–around–the–rosy** \ˈ⸗,⸗⸗ˈ⸗⸗\ *n* -ES **:** a children's singing game in which the players dance around in a circle and at a given signal squat

rin·gas \ˈriŋgəs\ *n* -ES [Malay *rĕngas*] **:** BLACK-VARNISH TREE

rin·ga·tu \ˌriŋgəˈtü\ *n* -s *cap* [Maori, fr. *ringa* hand + *tu* to stand] **:** a semi-Christian Maori sect in New Zealand that was a milder development from an antichristian cult evolved by the Maoris when fighting against the English

ring auger *n* **:** an auger turned by a bar inserted in a ring or eye at the upper end of the shank

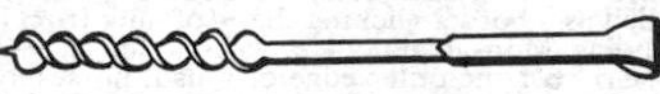

ring auger

ringbark \ˈ⸗,⸗\ *vt* **:** ²GIRDLE 3

ring–barked \ˈ⸗ˈ⸗\ *adj* **:** having the periderm in more or less complete concentric layers often with the bark shedding in sheets (as in birch trees) ⟨a herd . . . grazing among the *ring-barked* trees on the slope above —Francis Ratcliffe⟩

ringbarker \ˈ⸗,⸗⸗\ *n* **:** a large gregarious Australian phasmid (*Podocanthus wilkinsoni*) that defoliates eucalyptus and some other trees

ringbill \ˈ⸗,⸗\ *n* **:** RING-NECKED DUCK

ring–billed duck *or* **ring–billed blackhead** *or* **ring–billed bluebill** \ˈ⸗,⸗-\ *n* **:** RING-NECKED DUCK

ring–billed gull *n* **:** a rather small American gull (*Larus delawarensis*) having when adult a black band on the bill

ring binder *n* **:** a loose-leaf binder in which split metal rings attached to a metal back hold the perforated leaves

ringbird \ˈ⸗,⸗\ *n* **:** REED BUNTING

ring blackbird *n* **:** RING OUZEL

ringbolt \ˈ⸗,⸗\ *n* **:** an eyebolt with a ring through its eye

ringbolt

ringbone \ˈ⸗,⸗\ *n* **:** an exostosis on the pastern bones of the horse usu. producing lameness — compare SIDEBONE — **ring-boned** \ˈ⸗,⸗\ *adj*

ring boot *n* **:** a rubber ring placed around the fetlock of a horse to prevent injury from brushing, cutting, or interfering

ring budding *n* **:** ANNULAR BUDDING

ring bunting *n* **:** REED BUNTING

ring buoy *n* **:** a life buoy in the shape of a ring

ring canal *n* **1 :** the circular water tube that surrounds the esophagus of echinoderms **2 :** the circular canal in the edge of the umbrella of a jellyfish that links the radial canals

ring carrier *n, obs* **:** GO-BETWEEN

ring cell *n* **:** one of the cells in the annulus of a fern

ring–chain isomerism *n* **:** isomerism between a cyclic and an open-chain form esp. when the two forms are tautomeric

ring closure *n* **:** a chemical reaction in which an open chain of atoms is closed to form a ring **:** CYCLIZATION

ring clutch *n* **:** RIM CLUTCH

ring complex *n* **:** an occurrence of diverse igneous rocks characterized by approximately circular outcropping of a dike rock

ring compound *n* **:** a cyclic compound containing one or more rings in the molecule

ring cowrie *n* **:** a cowrie (*Cypraea annulus*)

ringcraft \ˈ⸗,⸗\ *n* **:** the tactics, strategy, and skill of a boxer

ring dance *n* **:** ROUND DANCE 1

ring dial *n* **:** a small portable dial in the shape of a cylindrical ring for determining time

ring dike *n* **:** a dike of igneous rock having an arcuate outcrop that if fully developed is elliptical or circular in plan

ring disease *n* **1 :** RING ROT 2b **2 :** BROWN ROT 1c

ring dollar *n* **:** HOLEY DOLLAR

ring dotterel *also* **ringed dotterel** *n* **:** a European ring plover

ringdove \ˈ⸗,⸗\ *n* **1 :** a common European pigeon (*Columba palumbus*) larger than the stock dove or rock pigeon and having on each side of the neck a whitish patch and the wing edged with white **2 :** a small dove (*Streptopelia risoria*) of southeastern Europe and much of Asia that is related to the common turtledove, is often kept as a cage bird, and is buffy with a black collar

ring dropper *n* **:** a sharper who pretends to have found a ring dropped by himself and fraudulently tries to induce one to buy it

ring dropping *n* **:** a method of swindling practiced by ring droppers

ringed *adj* **1 :** encircled or marked with or as if with a ring **:** forming or shaped like a ring **:** composed or formed of rings **:** ANNULAR **2 :** wearing a wedding ring **:** lawfully wedded ⟨a ~ wife —Alfred Tennyson⟩

ringed perch *var of* RING PERCH

ringed plover *var of* RING PLOVER

ringed seal *n* **:** a seal (*Phoca hispida*) of northern waters having ringlike white spots on the body

ringed snake *or* **ring snake** *n* **1 :** a harmless European colubrid snake (*Natrix natrix*) common in England **2 :** RING-NECKED SNAKE

ringed worm *n* **:** ANNELID

ring·elnat·ter \ˈriŋəl,nädə(r)\ *n* -s [G, fr. *ringel* small ring (dim. of *ring,* fr. OHG *hring*) + *natter* adder, fr. OHG *nātara* — more at RING, ADDER] **:** RINGED SNAKE 1

rin·gent \ˈrinjənt\ *adj* [L *ringent-, ringens,* pres. part. of *ringi* to open the mouth, show the teeth — more at RICTUS] **1 :** having the lips widely separated and gaping like an open mouth ⟨~ corolla⟩ **2 :** gaping irregularly ⟨the ~ valves of various bivalves⟩

¹ring·er \ˈriŋə(r)\ *n* -s [ME, fr. *ringen* to ring (a bell) + *-er* — more at RING] **1 :** one that sounds esp. by ringing; *specif* **:** BELL RINGER **2 :** a device providing electric current for operating telephone bells **3 a :** one that enters a competition under false representations esp. as to identity or past performances; *esp* **:** a horse entered fraudulently in a race under a false name to obtain better odds in the betting **b :** one that strongly resembles another — often used with *dead* ⟨a man who is a dead ~ for the senator⟩

²ringer \"\ *n* -s [²*ring* + *-er*] **1 :** one that encircles or puts a ring around (something): as **a :** one who puts rings or bands on articles (as on bottles or cigars) **b :** one that rings trees; *specif* **:** a fitter who prepares logs for peeling by cutting through the bark **c :** a quoit or horseshoe that lodges so as to surround the peg; *also* **:** the throw by which it is so lodged **2 :** a billiard ball encircled with a distinguishing band of color (as usu. any of those numbered from nine to fifteen) **3 :** a game of marbles in which marbles are placed in a cross in the center of a ring marked on the ground and players try to knock them out of the ring **4** *Austral* **a :** SHEEPSHEARER; *esp* **:** a very fast and competent one **b :** STOCKMAN, COWBOY

ring·er's solution \ˈriŋə(r)z-\ *or* **ringer solution** *also* **ring·er's fluid** *n, usu cap R* [after Sydney *Ringer* †1910 Eng. physician] **:** a balanced aqueous solution of the chlorides of sodium, potassium, and calcium, sodium bicarbonate, and sodium dihydrogen phosphate used in physiological experiments to provide a medium essentially isotonic to many animal tissues esp. of poikilothermic vertebrates — compare PHYSIOLOGICAL SALINE

ring fence *n* **:** a fence that encircles a large area or a whole estate within one enclosure

ring–fence \ˈ⸗,⸗\ *vt* [*ring fence*] **:** to enclose in or as if in a ring fence

ring finger *n* **:** the third finger of the left hand on which engagement and wedding rings are placed; *also* **:** the corresponding finger of the right hand

ring formula *n* **:** a structural formula containing one or more rings

ring frame *n* **:** RING SPINNER

ring gage *n* **1 :** an external gage in the form of a cylindrical ring or washer often provided with a bushing of hardened steel **2 a :** a tapered stick with graduated markings for measuring finger rings **b :** a set of ring blanks for determining the size of ring worn by an individual

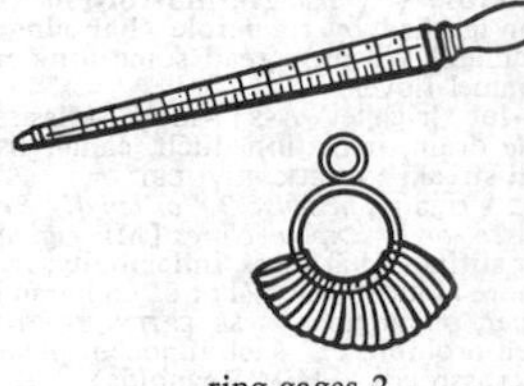

ring gages 2

ring gear *n* **:** a gear cut on a ring-shaped rim; *specif* **:** the large gear in the differential of an automobile that is driven by the propeller shaft pinion and transmits the power through the differential to the live axle

ring gland *n* **:** an endocrine organ of various two-winged flies that lies about the aorta and is apparently concerned with the initiation of metamorphosis

ring grass *also* **ring muhly** *n* **:** a No. American perennial muhly (*Muhlenbergia torreyana*) having scaly rhizomes and a slender cylindrical panicle of purplish spikelets

ring growth *n* **:** the tendency of various plants (as grasses) to grow in rings — compare FAIRY RING

ring·hals \ˈriŋ,hals\ *also* **rin·kals** \ˈriŋ,kals\ *n* -ES [Afrik *rinkals* (formerly spelled *ringhals*), fr. *ring* (fr. MD *rinc*) + *hals* neck, fr. MD; akin to OHG *hring* ring and to OHG *hals* neck — more at RING, COLLAR] **:** a venomous African elapid snake (*Haemachates haemachatus*) that is closely related to the true cobras but has keeled scales and that seldom strikes but spits or sprays its venom aiming at the eyes of its victim where

the poison causes intense pain and possible blindness — called also *spitting snake*
ring head *n* **:** a magnetic head in which the magnetic core is ring-shaped and contains one or more very short air gaps and in which the magnetic tape or wire is in contact with or close proximity to the outer surface of the ring and bridges one of these gaps
ringier *comparative of* RINGY
ringiest *superlative of* RINGY
ring in *vt* **1 :** to cause (a bell) to take part in the changes in change ringing **2 :** to introduce unwelcomely, surreptitiously, or fraudulently **:** FOIST ⟨*ring in* a horse in a race under a false name⟩ ⟨*ring in* marked cards on one's opponents⟩ **~** *vi* **:** to register one's arrival by ringing a time clock **:** begin work
ring·i·ness \ˈriŋēnəs\ *n* -ES **:** the state of being ringy; *specif* **:** the state of having the annual rings of wood easily separable — compare RING SHAKE
¹ring·ing \ˈriŋiŋ, ˈriŋēŋ\ *n* -s [ME, fr. gerund of *ringen* to ring — more at RING (make sounds)] **1 :** the sounding of a bell or other sonorous body **2 :** a sound of ringing or a sensation like that caused by the sound of ringing ⟨a ~ in the ears⟩
²ringing \"\ *adj* [ME, fr. pres. part. of *ringen* to ring] **1 :** sounding like a bell **:** clear and full in tone **:** SONOROUS, OROTUND, RESOUNDING ⟨her beautiful, ~, honest voice —Havelock Ellis⟩ ⟨gave me a ~ crack on the head —Vincent McHugh⟩ **2 :** vigorously unequivocal **:** DECISIVE, FERVID ⟨find some opportunity of sealing this document by a ~ declaration —*Economist*⟩ ⟨a ~ appeal⟩ **syn** see RESONANT
³ringing \"\ *n* -s [ME, fr. gerund of *ringen* to ring — more at RING (make a ring)] **1 :** the act or result of putting a ring on or about something **2 :** the state of being encircled or marked by a ring
ringing engine *n* **:** a simple form of pile driver in which the pile hammer is lifted by men pulling on ropes
ringing loft *n* **:** a floor for bell ringers in the tower of a church
ring·ing·ly *adv* [²*ringing* + *-ly*] **:** in a ringing manner ⟨~ denounced the proposal⟩
ring·ing·ness *n* -ES **:** the quality of being ringing
ring joint *n* **:** the joint between the proximal and middle phalanges of a finger
ring·le \ˈriŋəl\ *n* -s [¹*ring* + *-le*] **1** *dial Eng* **:** a metal ring; *esp* **:** one placed in an animal's nose **2** *obs* **:** CIRCLE
ring·lead \ˈriŋ,lēd\ *vb* [back-formation fr. *ringleader*] *vt* **:** to act as ringleader to **~** *vi* **:** to act as ringleader
ringleader \ˈ=,==\ *n* [¹*ring* (group) + *leader*] **:** a leader of a group of individuals engaged esp. in violation of law or an improper enterprise ⟨one of the ~*s* of the abortive revolution —Ethel Drus⟩ ⟨vengeful murder of the mutiny's bloodthirsty ~ —F.R.Dulles⟩
ringle-eyed \ˈ=,=ˈēd\ *adj, Scot* **:** WALLEYED
ring·less \ˈriŋləs\ *adj* **:** lacking a ring **:** being without rings ⟨~ knitting⟩
¹ring·let \-lət, *usu* -əd·+V\ *n* -s [¹*ring* + *-let*] **1** *archaic* **a :** a small ring **:** a small circle **b :** FAIRY RING **2 :** CURL; *esp* **:** a long curl of hair **3 :** any of various butterflies belonging to *Coenonympha, Erebia,* and closely related genera of the family Satyridae
²ringlet \"\ *vt* **ringleted** *also* **ringletted; ringleted** *also* **ringletted; ringleting** *also* **ringletting; ringlets :** to form in ringlets ⟨each head tenderly is ~*ed* —James Stephens⟩ ⟨the bay was ~*ed* with rain —James Daugherty⟩
ringleted *also* **ringletted** *adj* [¹*ringlet* + *-ed*] **:** having ringlets **:** worn in ringlets ⟨bearded and ~ men —*Time*⟩ ⟨~ locks⟩
ringlike \ˈ=,=\ *adj* **:** resembling a ring in form ⟨~ spots⟩
ring lock *n* **:** a combination lock in which a series of grooved rings surrounding the bolt must be arranged so as to bring their grooves in line before the bolt can be shot
ringlock nail \ˈ=,=-\ *n* **:** a nail with annular grooving for better holding power
ring lubrication *n* **:** lubrication of a shaft bearing by means of a ring riding on the shaft in rotation and bringing up oil from a well into which it dips
ring·man \ˈriŋmən\ *n, pl* **ringmen :** ¹BOXER
ringmaster \ˈ=,==\ *n* **1 :** one in charge of the performance of trained horses in a ring (as of a circus) **2 :** EQUESTRIAN DIRECTOR
ring money *n* **:** annular pieces of metal used as money among primitive peoples
ring muscle *n* **:** ORBICULARIS
ringneck \ˈ=,=\ *n* **:** a ring-necked bird or animal (as a ring plover, a ring-necked duck, or a ring-necked pheasant)
ring-necked \ˈ=ˈ=\ *or* **ring-neck** \ˈ=,=\ *adj* **:** having a ring of color about the neck
ring-necked duck *n* **:** an American scaup duck (*Aythya collaris*) the male of which has the head, neck, and breast black, a narrow chestnut ring encircling the neck, the sides vermiculated with black, and the belly mostly white

ring-lock nail

ring-necked lizard *n* **:** COLLARED LIZARD
ring-necked parrakeet *n* **:** a medium-sized parrakeet (*Psittacula krameri*) found from western Africa to the Red sea and in India that is green with a rose-colored collar and reddish bill and is often kept as a pet
ring-necked pheasant *n* **:** a pheasant that is a Chinese variety (*Phasianus colchicus torquatus*) of the common Old World pheasant distinguished by a white neck ring; *broadly* **:** any of various pheasants widely introduced in temperate regions as game birds that are varieties of or hybrids between varieties of the common pheasant
ring-necked plover *n* **:** RING PLOVER
ring-necked snake *also* **ringneck snake** *n* **:** any of numerous small smooth colubrid snakes having a yellowish ring about the neck and constituting a genus (*Diadophis*) with representatives in all parts of the U. S.
ring necrosis *n* **:** a browning of the vascular ring in stems or tubers (as that characteristic of fusarium wilt and a form of necrosis of the potato caused by frost)
ring nematode *n* **:** a nematode worm of a genus (*Criconemoides*) of the family Criconematidae having cuticle divided into annuli that give an effect of pseudosegmentation, being soil-dwelling, and feeding on roots and possibly causing winter injury of the peach
ring net *n* **:** a fishing net somewhat resembling a purse seine used esp. in the European herring fishery — **ring-netter** \ˈ=,==\ *n*
ring off *vi* **1** *chiefly Brit* **:** to terminate a telephone call **:** HANG UP **2** *chiefly Brit* **:** to stop talking
ring of saturn *usu cap R&S* [after *Saturn,* Roman god connected with the sowing of seed, fr. L *Saturnus*] **:** a small line forming a semicircle around the base of the finger of Saturn and usu. held by palmists to indicate a lack of stability or purpose and often failure in life
ring of sol·o·mon \-ˈsäləmən\ *usu cap R&S* [after *Solomon,* †*ab*933 B.C. king of Israel noted for his wisdom] **:** a small line forming a semicircle around the base of the finger of Jupiter and usu. held by palmists to indicate a love of and possible proficiency in occult studies
ring-oil \ˈriŋ,ȯil\ *vt* [back-formation fr. *ring oiler*] **:** to oil (a bearing) by conveying the oil to the point to be lubricated by means of a ring that rests upon and turns with the journal and dips into a reservoir containing the lubricant
ring oiler *n* **:** a ring-oiling device
¹ring out *vi* [²*ring*] **:** to settle or close a transaction (as in futures) in a produce exchange by forming into a series a number of buyers and sellers in which the first and the last deal with each other to complete the ring and all settle by paying differences
²ring out *vi* [³*ring*] **:** to register one's departure from work by ringing a time clock
ring ouzel *n* **:** a thrush (*Turdus torquatus*) that is related to the European blackbird and the American robin, is black with a white bar across the breast, and breeds in mountainous regions of northern Europe and migrates to Africa — called also *ring blackbird, ring thrush*
ring parrakeet *or* **ring parrot** *n* **:** any of several Old World chiefly green parrakeets having a red ring around the neck (as *Psittacula krameri* found in India and Africa and *P. alexandri* of Java)
ring perch *or* **ringed perch** *n* **:** YELLOW PERCH
ring pin *n* **:** a pin whose head is in the form of a ring for receiving a label
ring plain *n* **:** a lunar crater of exceptional diameter with relatively smooth interior
ring plover *or* **ringed plover** *n* **:** any of various small plovers of the widely distributed genus *Charadrius* (as the common European species *C. hiaticula* and the American semipalmated, piping, and killdeer plovers) having the upper part chiefly brownish or buffy and the underparts white and a black breast band or collar
ring-porous \ˈ=ˈ==\ *adj* **:** having vessels more numerous and usu. larger in cross section in the springwood with a resulting more or less distinct line between the springwood and the wood of the previous season — used of woody stems and roots (as of oaks); compare DIFFUSE-POROUS
ring relievo *n* **:** ²RELIEVO
ring road *n, chiefly Brit* **:** BELT HIGHWAY
ring-roll mill *n* **:** a crusher or pulverizer in which the material is squeezed by rolling between rings
ring rope *n* **1 :** a rope rove through sheaves in the cathead and the ring of an anchor to haul the latter close up under the former **2 :** a rope for bending a cable to an anchor
ring rot *n* **1 :** decay in a log following closely the annual rings **2 a :** a disease of sweet potatoes caused by a fungus (*Rhizopus stolonifer*) in which the roots are girdled by bands of dry rot **b :** a disease of potatoes caused by a bacterium (*Corynebacterium sepedonicum*) and characterized by browning of the ring of vascular bundles — called also *ring disease* **c :** BROWN ROT 1c
rings *pl of* RING, *pres 3d sing of* RING
ring screw *n* **:** a screw having a ring formed on its end (as for attaching chain or rope)
ring seal *n* **:** an engraved gem or precious stone set in a ring and used as a seal
ring settlement *n* **:** a settlement made in a produce exchange by ringing out
ring shake *n* **:** a defect in timber consisting of shrinkage and separation of the annual rings — called also *cup shake;* compare HEART SHAKE
ring shout *n* **:** a dance of African origin done by Negro slaves and revivalists in which all form a circle and shuffle counterclockwise usu. with much shouting
¹ringside \ˈ=,=\ *n* [¹*ring* + *side*] **:** the area just outside a ring esp. in which a contest (as boxing or racing) occurs; *broadly* **:** a place from which one may have a close view (as of a show)
²ringside \"\ *adj* **:** at or from the ringside ⟨a ~ table in a nightclub⟩ ⟨shiny-topped ~ clientele —T.H.Fielding⟩
³ringside \"\ *adv* **:** at the ringside ⟨sit ~ at a hockey game⟩
ring·sid·er \ˈriŋ,sīdə(r)\ *n* -s [¹*ringside* + *-er*] **:** one that watches a performance (as a boxing or wrestling match) at or near ringside
ring sight *n* **:** a gunsight having a ring or series of concentric rings through which one sights
ring-silicate \ˈ=,==(,)=\ *n* **:** CYCLOSILICATE
ring snake *var of* RINGED SNAKE
ring spinner *n* **:** a machine for spinning in which the twist given to the yarn by a revolving bobbin is regulated by a small metal loop sliding on a ring around the bobbin — called also *ring frame*
ring spinning *n* **:** a method of spinning employing a ring spinner
ring spot *n* **1 :** a lesion of plant tissue consisting of yellowish, purplish, or necrotic, often concentric rings **2 :** any plant disease of which ring spots are the characteristic lesion: as **a :** a virus disease of tobacco and related plants producing chlorotic rings on the leaves **b :** a disease of sugarcane caused by a fungus (*Leptosphaeria sacchari*) and characterized by purplish bordered spots **c :** a disease of the lower leaves of cauliflower and related crucifers caused by a fungus (*Mycosphaerella brassicicola*) **d :** an anthracnose of lettuce caused by a fungus (*Marssonina panathoniana*) **e :** FROGEYE a(1) **f :** FAIRY RING SPOT
ring stand *n* **:** a stand (as of iron) consisting of a long upright rod attached to a heavy rectangular base and used with rings and clamps fastened to the rod to support laboratory apparatus (as distilling flasks, retorts, condensers)
ring·ster \ˈriŋztə(r), -ŋ(k)st-\ *n* -s [¹*ring* + *-ster*] **:** a member of an esp. political or price-fixing ring
ring stick *n* **:** RING GAGE 2
ring stone *n* **:** a voussoir showing on the face of the wall
ring stopper *n* **1** *archaic* **:** a cathead stopper **2 :** a chain passing under and around the shank of an anchor near the ring and made fast to the releasing tumbler in securing an anchor on the billboard
ringstraked \ˈ=,=\ *adj, archaic* **:** marked with circular stripes ⟨removed that day the he-goats that were ~ and spotted —Gen 30:35 (AV)⟩
ring system *n* **:** the structure typical of a cyclic chemical compound and consisting of one or more rings (as fused rings) ⟨five- and six-membered *ring systems*⟩ — compare SKELETON
ringtail \ˈ=,=\ *n* **1 a** *dial Eng* **:** the female or immature hen harrier **b :** an immature golden eagle **c :** HUDSONIAN GODWIT **2 a :** CACOMISTLE **b :** RING-TAILED OPOSSUM **c :** RACCOON **3 :** a studding sail set on the gaff of a fore-and-aft sail abaft the leech **4** *or* **ringtail monkey** *also* **ring-tailed monkey :** CAPUCHIN
ring-tailed \ˈ=ˈ=\ *adj* **1 :** having a tail marked with rings of differing colors **2 :** having a tail carried in the form of a circle ⟨a *ring-tailed* dog⟩
ring-tailed cat *n* **:** CACOMISTLE
ring-tailed eagle *n* **:** an immature golden eagle
ring-tailed lemur *n* **:** MADAGASCAR CAT
ring-tailed marlin *or* **ringtail marlin** *n* **:** HUDSONIAN GODWIT
ring-tailed opossum *n* **:** any of several relatively small herbivorous arboreal marsupials (genus *Pseudocheirus*) common in much of Australia and in New Guinea and having strongly prehensile tails
ring-tailed roarer *n* **:** an imaginary animal
ring-tail perch *n* **:** YELLOW PERCH
ringtaw \ˈ=,=\ *n* **:** a game of marbles in which marbles are placed in a circle on the ground and shot at from a line about two yards distant with the object of knocking them out of the circle
ring tennis *n* **:** DECK TENNIS
ring test *n* **:** a test for antigens or antibodies in which a layer of diluted material suspected of containing antigen is placed over a column of known antiserum in a small test tube or a layer of diluted known antigen is placed over serum suspected of containing antibodies and is then examined for a positive reaction signaled by formation of a thin plane or ring of precipitate
ring thrush *n* **:** RING OUZEL
ringtoss \ˈ=,=\ *n* **:** a game the object of which is to toss a ring so that it will fall over an upright stick
ring traveler *n* **:** TRAVELER 5
ring up *vt* [³*ring*] **1 :** to total and record esp. by means of a cash register ⟨the groceries were *rung up*⟩ ⟨*ring up* a sale⟩ **2 :** RECORD ⟨below the margin *rung up* in the last election⟩ ⟨highest figure so far *rung up* elsewhere is $50 million —J.N. Wallace⟩ ⟨*rang up* social triumphs —*Sat. Eve. Post*⟩
ringwalk \ˈ=,=\ *n, archaic* **:** a walk made by hunters around a wood or other covert
ringwall \ˈ=,=\ *n* **:** a wall that encircles an area
ring watch *n* **:** a very small timepiece set in a case mounted on a finger ring
ring willow *n* **:** a weeping willow (*Salix babylonica crispa*) with folded and spirally curved leaves
ring winding *n* **:** armature winding in which the wire is wound round the outer and inner surfaces alternately of an annular or cylindrical core — distinguished from *drum winding*
ringworm \ˈ=,=\ *n* [ME, fr. *ring* + *worm*] **1 :** any of several contagious diseases of the skin, hair, or nails of man and domestic animals caused by fungi esp. of the genera *Trichophyton* and *Microsporum* and characterized on the skin by ring-shaped discolored patches covered with vesicles and scales **2 :** MILLIPEDE
ringworm bush *or* **ringworm cassia** *n* **:** a tropical American shrub (*Cassia alata*) whose leaves yield a juice used as a cure for ringworm and poisonous bites
ringy \ˈriŋē\ *adj* -ER/-EST **:** resembling or suggesting a ring
¹rink \ˈriŋk\ *n* -s [ME (Sc dial.) *renk, rinc* area in which a combat or contest takes place, fr. MF *renc, ranc, reng, rang* line, place, row, rank — more at RANK] **1 a :** a smooth level extent of ice marked off for curling or ice hockey — see CURLING illustration, ICE HOCKEY illustration **b :** an enclosed sheet of ice usu. artificial and under cover for ice-skating; *also* **:** a building containing such a rink **c :** a covered enclosure for roller-skating **2 :** a division of a bowling green 19 to 21 feet in width and running the length of the green and large enough for a match **3 a :** a team of four players in a game of bowls or curling **b :** a game of bowls or curling played by four players on each side
²rink \"\ *vi* -ED/-ING/-S **:** to skate at a rink
rin·ka·fad·da \ˈriŋkəˈfäᵺə\ *also* **rin·ka** \ˈriŋkə\ *n* -s [IrGael *rinnce fada,* fr. *rinnce* dance + *fada* long] **:** an Irish dance resembling the Virginia reel
rinkals *var of* RINGHALS
rink·ite \ˈriŋ,kīt\ *n* -s [G *rinkit,* fr. Hinrich J. *Rink* †1893 Dan. explorer + G *-it* -ite] **:** a mineral $Na(Ca,Ce)_2(Ti,Ce)(SiO_4)_2F$ consisting chiefly of a yellowish crystalline silicate of cerium
rink·man \ˈriŋkmən\ *n, pl* **rinkmen :** one who takes care of a skating rink and assists and instructs skaters
rin·ko·lite \ˈriŋkə,līt\ *n* -s [Russ *rinkolit,* alter. of *rinkit* rinkite, fr. G] **:** a strontian variety of rinkite
rink·tum dit·ty \ˈriŋktəmˈdidˌē\ *n* [origin unknown] **:** a mixture of tomato sauce, onion, cheese, egg, and seasonings served on toast
rin·man's green *or* **rin·mann's green** \ˈrinmənz-\ *n, usu cap R* [after Sven Rinman †1792 Swedish mineralogist] **:** COBALT GREEN 1
rin·ne·ite \ˈrinē,īt\ *n* -s [G *rinneit,* fr. W. B. *Rinne* †1933 Ger. mineralogist + G *-it* -ite] **:** a mineral NaK_3FeCl_6 consisting of a chloride of iron, potassium, and sodium and occurring in colorless, pink, violet, or yellow granular masses (hardness 3, sp. gr. 2.3)
rin·ne·mann's green \ˈrin(ə)mənz-\ *n, usu cap R* [after Sven *Rinman* †1792 Swedish mineralogist] **:** COBALT GREEN 2
rin·ner \ˈrinə(r)\ *dial Brit var of* RUNNER
rins·abil·i·ty *or* **rins·ibil·i·ty** \,rin(t)səˈbilədē\ *n* -ES **:** capability of being rinsed
rins·able *or* **rins·ible** \ˈrin(t)səbəl\ *adj* **:** capable of being rinsed
¹rinse \ˈrin(t)s, *dial* ˈrench *or* ˈren(t)s *or* ˈrinch\ *vb* -ED/-ING/-S [ME *rincen,* fr. MF *rincer,* fr. OF *recincier,* fr. (assumed) VL *recentiare,* fr. L *recent-, recens* fresh, young, recent — more at RECENT] *vt* **1 :** to cleanse by the introduction of water or other liquid ⟨~ a bottle⟩ — often used with *out* ⟨~ out the mouth⟩ **2 a :** to cleanse by dipping into water **:** cleanse (as from the soap used in washing) by agitating in clear water or by pouring clear water over ⟨~ clothes⟩ ⟨~ the hands⟩ **b :** to treat (the hair) with a rinse **3 :** to remove (dirt or impurities) by washing lightly or in water only **4 :** to cleanse (a surface) by the application of any suitable substance ⟨*rinsed* his hands in snow —W.V.T.Clark⟩ ⟨counters were *rinsed* with a very dilute solution of lacquer in amyl acetate —*Physical Rev.*⟩ **~** *vi* **:** to be removable by the use of water ⟨a soap that ~*s* easily⟩
²rinse \"\ *n* -s **1 a :** the act or process of rinsing **b :** DOUCHE **2 a :** water or other liquid used for rinsing **b** (1) **:** any of various cosmetic solutions that remove soap, bring out highlights of the hair's color, or temporarily tint the hair another color (2) **:** an application of such a solution
rins·er \"+ə(r)\ *n* -s **1 :** one that rinses **2 :** a utensil used to hold water for rinsing
rinsing *n* -s [fr. gerund of ¹*rinse*] **1 :** water that has been used for rinsing — usu. used in pl. **2 :** the last dregs **:** RESIDUE — usu. used in pl. ⟨the ~*s* of an unwashed wineglass —O.W. Holmes †1894⟩
¹rio \ˈrē(,)ō\ *adj, usu cap* [fr. *Rio,* nickname for *Rio de Janeiro,* Brazil] **:** RIO DE JANEIRO
²rio \"\ *n* -s *usu cap* [fr. *Rio,* nickname for *Rio de Janeiro*] **:** a Brazilian coffee
rio de ja·nei·ro \ˈrē(,)ō,dāzhəˈne(,)rō, -dē|, |jə'-, -ˈni(,)-\ *adj, usu cap R&J* [fr. *Rio de Janeiro,* Brazil] **:** of or from the city of Rio de Janeiro, Brazil **:** of the kind or style prevalent in Rio de Janeiro
ri·o·din·i·dae \,rīəˈdinə,dē\ *n pl, cap* [NL, fr. *Riodina,* type genus + *-idae*] **:** a family of small or medium-sized often brightly colored butterflies having metallic spots on the wings and the first pair of legs reduced in the males and occurring mostly in the New World tropics
rio grande disease \ˈrē(,)ōˈgrand-, -aand-, -dē-, -di- *sometimes* ˈrī| *or* |ə'-\ *n, usu cap R&G* [fr. the *Rio Grande,* river in the southwestern U.S.] **:** a disease of lettuce of unknown cause first reported from the Rio Grande valley and causing the older leaves to become reddish esp. on the tips while the younger central ones blanch and do not grow to normal size
rio ipecac *n, usu cap R* **:** IPECAC 2a
rio pie·dras *or* **rio pie·dras** \ˈrē(,)ōˈpyādrəs\ *adj, usu cap R&P* [fr. *Rio Piedras,* Puerto Rico] **:** of or from the city of Rio Piedras, Puerto Rico **:** of the kind or style prevalent in Rio Piedras
¹ri·ot \ˈrīət, *usu* -əd·+V\ *n* -s *often attrib* [ME *riot, riote,* fr. OF *riot, rihot, riote, rihote* quarrel, dispute, fr. *ruihoter, rihoter, rioter* to quarrel, dispute, perh. fr. *ruire* to roar, fr. L *rugire* — more at BRUIT] **1** *archaic* **a :** profligate or wanton behavior **:** DEBAUCHERY, EXCESS, EXTRAVAGANCE **b :** unrestrained revelry or merrymaking **c :** noise, uproar, or disturbance made by revelers **2 :** an assemblage of three or more persons in a public place for the purpose of accomplishing by concerted action and in a turbulent and disorderly manner a common purpose irrespective of the lawfulness of the purpose **3 :** a hunting dog's following of the scent of an animal the hunter does not want **4 :** a random or disorderly profusion esp. of color ⟨a rhythmic ~ of color —*Amer. Guide Series: Oregon*⟩ **5 :** something or someone wildly amusing **:** a cause or occasion of mirth or hilarity ⟨her latest hat is a ~⟩ **syn** see BRAWL
²riot \"\ *vb* -ED/-ING/-S [ME *rioten,* fr. *riote, riot,* n.] *vi* **1 :** to indulge in revelry or wantonness **:** practice license or excess **2** *archaic* **:** to take great pleasure — used with *in* or *upon* **3 :** to create or engage in a disturbance or tumult; *specif* **:** to disturb the peace by a riot **4** *of a hound* **:** to follow the scent of an animal which it is not intended to hunt **~** *vt* **1 :** to waste or spend recklessly ⟨would hardly care to see him ~*ing* away her whole property —Leslie Ford⟩ **2 :** ATTACK, DESPOIL
riot act *n* [fr. the *Riot Act,* an English law of 1715 that provided for the dispersal of gatherings disturbing the peace] **:** a vigorous reproof, reprimand, or warning **:** DRESSING DOWN — used in the phrase *read the riot act* ⟨read me the *riot act* for what I'd done —J.B.Benefield⟩
ri·ot·er \ˈrīəd·ə(r), -ətə-\ *n* -s [ME *rioter,* alter. of *riotour,* fr. *rioten* + *-our* -or] **:** one that riots: as **a** *archaic* **:** a profligate liver **:** REVELER, ROISTERER **b :** one that creates or takes part in a disturbance, tumult, or riot
riot gun *n* **:** a small arm used to disperse rioters rather than to inflict serious injury or death; *esp* **:** a short-barreled shotgun
ri·ot·ing·ly *adj* **:** RIOTOUSLY
riotise *n* -s [¹*riot* + obs. *-ise* -ice (fr. ME *-ice, -ise*)] *obs* **:** LICENTIOUSNESS, EXCESS, REVELRY
ri·ot·ous \ˈrīəd·əs, -ətəs\ *adj* [ME, fr. *riote, riot* debauchery, riot + *-ous* — more at RIOT] **1 a :** practicing or marked by license or excess **:** PROFLIGATE, WANTON **b :** ABUNDANT, EXUBERANT, PROFUSE ⟨a ~ display of color⟩ ⟨~ slapstick⟩ **2 :** of the nature of a riot **:** marked by public uproar and disturbance **:** participating in riot **:** TURBULENT, SEDITIOUS
ri·ot·ous·ly *adv* **:** in a riotous manner
ri·ot·ous·ness *n* -ES **:** the quality, state, or habit of being riotous
ri·ot·ry \ˈrīətrē\ *n* -ES [²*riot* + *-ry*] **1** *archaic* **:** RIOTING **2** *archaic* **:** rioting persons
¹rip \ˈrip\ *n* -s [ME *rippe, ripp,* fr. ON *hrip;* akin to OHG *href* carrying basket, Latvian *kribas,* pl., wicker bottom of a sled, and perh. to L *curvus* curved — more at CROWN] **1** *dial* **:** a wicker basket (as for fish) **2** *dial* **:** a coop for fowl
²rip \"\ *vb* **ripped; ripped; ripping; rips** [prob. fr. Flem *rippen* to rip, strip off roughly; prob. akin to MD *reppen, rippen* to set in motion, pull, touch, MLG *reppen* to touch, move, OE *hreppan, hrepian* to touch — more at RAFFLE] *vt* **1 a :** to cut or tear apart **:** split open **:** slash off ⟨machinery commenced *ripping* up the earth —G.S.Perry⟩ ⟨something the dogface hopefully *ripped* open with anxious hands only to dis-

cover a can —J.P.O'Neill⟩ ⟨its passage *ripped* away the crown of the arch, and immediately the whole bridge collapsed —O.S. Nock⟩ **b :** to saw or split (wood) with the grain **c** *dial Brit* **:** to remove and replace (tiles) on a roof **d :** to cut, break, ravel, take out, or undo (stitches) in sewing **:** separate (as a garment) into its parts **2 a :** to slash or slit with or as if with a sharp blade ⟨*ripped* up his waistcoat to feel if he was not wounded —Daniel Defoe⟩ **b** *archaic* **:** to tear open (an old sore or grievance) **3** *archaic* **:** to recall to notice or reopen (as a closed issue or an unpleasant business) **4 :** to utter violently (as an oath) **:** burst out with **:** spit out ⟨*ripped* out vituperation, cursing, and blasphemy⟩ ~ *vi* **1 :** to pull or tear apart **:** REND ⟨the strain was too great; the sleeve *ripped* away from the coat⟩ **2 :** to move unchecked **:** proceed without restraint **:** rush headlong ⟨a smart convertible coupe came *ripping* up the short steep drive —Christopher Morley⟩ **3 :** to burst out with violent or profane utterance — usu. used with *out* ⟨*ripped* out with an oath⟩ **syn** see TEAR — **rip into :** to tear into like a buzz saw **:** ATTACK ⟨*ripped into* his antagonist with fury⟩ — **rip up the back :** to assail with hostile comment esp. behind the victim's back **:** BACK-BITE

³rip \"\ *n* -s **1 :** a rent made by ripping **:** a torn place **:** a gap left by a seam giving way **:** TEAR **2 :** a cut of wood along the grain (as by a ripsaw) **3** *dial Brit* **:** RUSH, SPEED

⁴rip \'rip\ *Scot var of* ²REAP

⁵rip \"\ *n* -s [perh. fr. ³*rip*] **1 :** a body of water made rough by the meeting of opposing tides or currents **:** TIDE RIP **2 :** a current roughened by passing over an irregular bottom — used esp. of tidal currents and sometimes of currents in rivers; compare UNDERTOW

⁶rip \"\ *n* -s [perh. alter. of ²*rep*] **1 :** a worn-out worthless horse ⟨left the spavin-legged old ~ standing there —Bruce Siberts⟩ **2 :** a reckless or dissolute person **:** LIBERTINE, RAKE ⟨his elder brother was a bit of a ~ —Ngaio Marsh⟩

rip *abbr* **1** ripieno **2** ripped

RIP *abbr* **1** [L *requiescat in pace*] may he (she) rest in peace **2** [L *requiescant in pace*] may they rest in peace

¹ri·par·i·an \rə'perēən, (')rī¦p-, -pa(a)r-,-pār-\ *also* **ri·par·i·al** \-ēəl\ *adj* [L *riparius* riparian + E *-an* or *-al* — more at RIVER] **1 :** of or relating to or living or located on the bank of a watercourse (as a river or stream) or sometimes a lake ⟨~ vegetation⟩ ⟨~ states⟩ ⟨~ scenery⟩ **2 :** LITTORAL

²riparian \"\ *n* -s **:** one that lives or has property on the bank of a river

riparian right *n* **:** the right of one owning riparian land to have access to and use of the shore and water — compare LITTORAL RIGHT, WATER RIGHT

ri·par·i·ous \-ēəs\ *adj* [L *riparius*] **:** RIPARIAN

rip cord *n* **1 :** a cord by which the gasbag of a balloon may be ripped open for a limited distance to release the gas quickly and so cause immediate descent **2 :** a cord or wire pulled manually or automatically in making a descent to release the pilot parachute which lifts the main parachute out of its container ready to open **3 a :** a cord inserted longitudinally in a sheathed electric cable for use in ripping the sheath at the ends for easier removal (as in making connections) **b :** an electric cord consisting of two individually insulated wires readily separable by ripping usu. for a short distance to make a connection

rip current *n* [⁵*rip*] **:** a strong surface current flowing outward from a shore — called also *riptide*

¹ripe \'rīp\ *adj* -ER/-EST [ME, fr. OE *rīpe;* akin to OS *rīpi* ripe, MD *ripe*, OHG *rīfi;* derivative fr. the root of E *reap*] **1 :** fully grown and developed **:** MATURE: as **a :** ready for reaping or harvesting ⟨~ grain⟩ ⟨a ~ field⟩ **b** *of fruit* (1) **:** having mature seed (2) **:** fully developed and so usable as food **c :** mature enough for use as cuttings — used of stems or other plant parts **d** *of timber or a forest* **:** ready to be cut **e :** free from budding cells — used of a yeast **2 :** having the full development and powers of maturity: as **a :** having full mental and physical maturity **b :** having mature knowledge, understanding, or judgment **:** CONSUMMATE, PERFECTED ⟨a ~ scholar⟩ ⟨~ wisdom⟩ **c :** stemming from thorough consideration or reflection **:** based on full deliberation ⟨they deal with many subjects and are characterized by ~ reflection and consummate mastery of style —*Encyc. Americana*⟩ **3 :** marked by maturity or fullness of time: as **a :** exhibiting full mental or physical powers ⟨a ~ time of life⟩ ⟨a ~ age⟩ **b :** of advanced years **:** LATE ⟨lived to the ~ age of 90⟩ **c :** fully arrived **:** SUITABLE ⟨the time seemed ~ to proceed to . . . evangelization —Kemp Malone⟩ **4 :** ready for some action or purpose **:** fully prepared for some use or object **:** fit for consummation ⟨a state of affairs ~ for axis exploitation —H.M.Sachar⟩ ⟨the classical type of monopoly capitalism ~ for public ownership —*New Statesman & Nation*⟩ ⟨here is a mixed-up character, ~ for the analyst —Lucy Crockett⟩ **5 :** brought by aging to full flavor or to the height of desirability as food or drink **:** MELLOW ⟨~ cheese⟩ ⟨a ~ port⟩ ⟨~ venison⟩ **6 :** ready to discharge **:** MATURED — used of an abscess or boil **7** *archaic* **:** DRUNK — used in the phrase *reeling ripe* **8 :** ruddy, plump, or full like ripened fruit ⟨the invitation of ~ young lips⟩ **9 :** due or ready for action, trial, or payment (as a lawsuit or a claim) **10 :** sufficiently developed to be removed by surgery — used of a cataract in the eye **11 a :** ready to be discharged — used of eggs **b :** containing ripe eggs or spermatozoa — used of a fish; compare GREEN

²ripe \"\ *vb* -ED/-ING/-S [ME *ripen*, fr. OE *rīpian*, fr. *rīpe* ripe] *chiefly dial* **:** RIPEN, MATURE

³ripe \"\ *vb* -ED/-ING/-S [ME *ripen*, fr. OE *rȳpan;* akin to OHG *roufen* to pluck, ON *ruppa, rupla*, Goth *raupjan* to pluck, ON *rögg* tuft of hair — more at RUG] *vt* **1** *chiefly Scot* **a :** to make a thorough search of **b :** to subject to thorough examination or investigation **2** *chiefly Scot* **:** to steal from **:** ROB **3** *chiefly Scot* **:** to clear of something that obstructs **:** clean out **4** *chiefly Scot* **:** to break up or remove stones from (rough ground) ~ *vi, chiefly Scot* **:** to make a search

⁴ripe \"\ *chiefly dial var of reap*

⁵ripe \"\ *n* -s [ME, fr. L *ripa* — more at RIVER] *archaic* **:** RIVERBANK, SEASHORE

ripe·ly *adv* [ME, fr. *ripe* + *-ly*] **1** *obs* **:** with mature deliberation **2 :** in a ripe manner **:** with mature or developed appearance **:** AMPLY

rip·en \'rīpən, -pᵊm\ *vb* **ripened** \-pənd,-pᵊmd\ **ripened** \"\ **ripening** \-p(ə)niŋ\ **ripens** \-pənz,-pᵊmz\ [¹*ripe* + *-en*] *vi* **1 :** to grow ripe **:** become mature (as of grain, fruit, or a microorganism) **2 :** to approach or come to full development **:** arrive at completeness or perfection **:** become fit for use, for action, or for an appropriate purpose **3 :** to become ready to discharge — used of an abscess or boil **4** *of a photographic emulsion* **:** to increase in average grain size as a result of physical treatment (as prolonged heating) or in sensitivity as a result of chemical treatment ~ *vt* **1 :** to make ripe ⟨the grower may . . . ~ the fruit in transit or on arrival by means of ethylene —G.L.Jenkins & W.H.Hartung⟩ ⟨time had ~*ed* his life and mellowed its fruits —Van Wyck Brooks⟩ **2 :** to bring to maturity, completeness, or perfection **:** cause full development of **:** fit or prepare for some use or purpose: as **a :** to sour (cream) by bacterial action as a prelude to churning for butter to reduce fat loss and improve the flavor of the finished product **b :** to age or cure (cheese) to develop characteristic flavor, odor, body, texture, and color **c :** to improve flavor and tenderness of (beef or game) through the action of enzymes in the meat during a period of refrigeration **3 :** to cause to become ready to discharge — used of an abscess or boil **syn** see MATURE

rip·en·er \'rīp(ə)nə(r)\ *n* -s **:** one that ripens

ripe·ness \'rīpnəs\ *n* -ES [ME *ripenes*, fr. OE *rīpnes*, fr. *rīpe* ripe + *-nes* -ness — more at RIPE] **:** the quality or state of being ripe **:** MATURITY, COMPLETENESS, PERFECTION

riper *comparative of* RIPE

ripe rot *n* **:** decay of ripe fruit caused by a fungus; *esp* **:** BITTER ROT 1

ripest *superlative of* RIPE

ripgut \'=,=\ *or* **ripgut grass** *n* [²*rip* + *gut*] **:** a troublesome weedy European grass (*Bromus rigidus*) adventive in California

ri·pic·o·lous \rə'pikələs, (')rī¦p-\ *adj* [fr. L *ripa* bank + E *-i-* + *-colous*] **:** RIPARIAN

ri·pid·o·lite \rə'pidᵊl,īt, rī'p-\ *n* -s [G *ripidolith*, irreg. fr. *rhipid-* + *-lith* -lite] **:** a mineral $(Mg,Fe)_9Al_6Si_5O_{20}(OH)_{16}$ consisting of a basic magnesium iron aluminum silicate of the chlorite group

ri·pie·nist \rə'p'yānəst\ *n* -s [²*ripieno* + *-ist*] **:** one that plays a ripieno

¹ri·pie·no \-ā(,)nō\ *adj* [It, filled up, stuffed, supplementary, fr. *ri-* re- (fr. L *re-*) + *pieno* full, fr. L *plenus* — more at FULL] **1 :** of or relating to a musical instrument or performer serving solely to swell the mass of an orchestra **:** SUPPLEMENTARY **2 :** TUTTI

²ripieno \"\ *n, pl* **ripie·ni** \-ā(,)nē\ *or* **ripienos** [It, fr. *ripieno*, adj.] **:** a supplementary musical instrument or performer or the group playing the ripieno part — compare CONCERTINO

¹ri·poste *also* **re·post** \rə'pōst, rē'p-\ *n* -s [F *riposte*, alter. of *risposte*, fr. It *risposta*, lit., answer — more at RISPOSTA] **1 :** a fencer's quick return thrust following a successful parry **2 :** a retaliatory verbal sally **:** RETORT ⟨the critic's ~ might be that most of these stories are machine-made too —Harrison Smith⟩ **3 :** a retaliatory maneuver or measure **:** COUNTERATTACK ⟨the raid upriver was a successful ~ to the enemy's earlier attack⟩

²riposte *also* **repost** \"\ *vb* -ED/-ING/-S [F *riposter*, fr. *riposte*] *vi* **1 :** to make a riposte in fencing **2 :** to deliver a verbal counterthrust **:** make a telling retort ⟨the two men argued and *riposted* —Janet Flanner⟩ **3 :** to deliver a counterblow or counterattack ⟨the general evaded pursuit and *riposted*⟩ ~ *vt* **:** to deliver (a verbal counterthrust) in reply **:** RETORT

rip panel *n* **:** a strip in the upper part of the fabric of a balloon or semirigid or nonrigid airship which is torn off when immediate deflation is desired

ripped *past of* RIP

¹rip·per \'ripə(r)\ *n* -s [²*rip* + *-er*] **1 :** a worker who rips: as **a :** one who opens seams to prepare them for resewing **b :** an operator of a ripsaw or variety saw **c :** a member of a fish-dressing gang who opens the belly of fish and removes the viscera **2 :** a tool, device, or machine that rips: as **a :** a long bar or thin steel blade used to remove damaged roofing slates and notched for drawing nails **b :** a device for opening stitched seams in cloth **c :** RIPSAW **d :** a machine with revolvable knives for cutting millboard **e :** a road machine to break up worn or disintegrated pavement **f :** a subsoiler or chisel implement that loosens surface soil and subsoil **3 :** any of the larger blocks on which the first few drawings are effected in wiredrawing **4 a :** an excellent example or instance of a kind **:** HUMDINGER ⟨a ~ — American musical comedy in the highest gear —*Newsweek*⟩ **b :** a wild or reckless person **5** *chiefly NewEng* **:** ¹BOBSLED 2 **6 :** a madman or criminal who slashes his victims with a knife

²ripper \"\ *adj* **:** designed to make drastic changes in a governmental agency for purely partisan purposes ⟨~ legislation⟩ ⟨~ bill⟩ ⟨~ amendment⟩

rip·pet *or* **rip·pit** \'ripət\ *n* -s [origin unknown] *dial* **:** a noisy quarrel **:** FUSS, UPROAR

rip·pi·er *or* **rip·i·er** \'ripēə(r)\ *n* -s [¹*rip* + *-ier*] *archaic* **:** a fish peddler

rip·ping \'ripiŋ, -pēŋ\ *adj* [prob. fr. pres. part. of ²*rip*] **:** GRAND, SWELL ⟨also some ~ letters from you —O.W.Holmes †1935⟩

ripping bar *n* **:** a steel bar having one end formed into a ripping

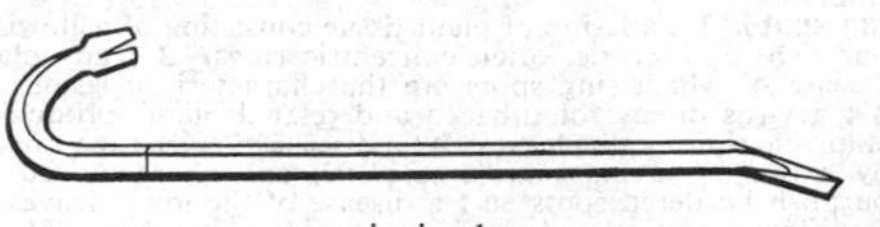

ripping bar

chisel and the other end shaped like a gooseneck with a claw for pulling nails

ripping chisel *n* **:** a long slender chisel sometimes with a slightly bent and cleft cutting end used for cleaning mortises or for heavy prying

ripping cord *n* **:** RIP CORD 1

ripping iron *n* **:** RAVEHOOK

rip·ping·ly *adv* **:** SPLENDIDLY

ripping panel *or* **ripping strip** *n* **:** RIP PANEL

ripping punch *n* **:** a tool with a rectangular point used in a punching machine for crosscutting metal plates

ripping saw *n* **:** RIPSAW

ripping size *n* **:** the size of rough wood stock required for the production of a finished product

¹rip·ple \'ripəl\ *vt* -ED/-ING/-S [ME *riplen;* akin to MD *repelen* & *repen* to ripple, MLG *rēpelen*, MHG *reffen* to ripple, OHG *riffilōn* to saw] **1 :** to remove (seeds) from flax or hemp with a ripple **2 :** to draw (flax) through a ripple

²ripple \"\ *n* -s [ME *repylle, ryppyll;* akin to MLG *rēpel* ripple, OHG *riffila* saw, *riffilōn* to saw — more at ¹RIPPLE] **:** a large instrument like a comb for removing seeds and other matter from flax or hemp

³ripple \"\ *vi* -ED/-ING/-S [ME *replen*, of Scand origin; akin to Norw *ripla* & *ripa* to scratch, Sw *repa* — more at REAP] *dial Brit* **:** to scratch slightly

⁴ripple \"\ *n* -s *dial Brit* **:** a slight cut **:** SCRATCH

⁵ripple \"\ *vb* **rippled; rippling** \-p(ə)liŋ\ **ripples** [perh. fr. ²*rip* + *-le*] *vi* **1 a :** to become fretted or lightly ruffled on the surface (as water) **:** become covered with or form in small waves or undulations ⟨a blue river *rippled* into the bay —Israel Zangwill⟩ ⟨the ripened cornfields *rippled* up to the doorsteps of the cottages —Flora Thompson⟩ ⟨his lean, sun-bronzed upper body *rippled* all over with long, graceful muscle —Frank Yerby⟩ **b :** to flow in small waves ⟨the brook *rippled* onward below her⟩ **c :** to fall in soft undulating folds or wavy lines ⟨the cloth *rippled* to the floor⟩ **2 :** to flow with a light rise and fall of sound or inflection ⟨laughter *rippled* over the audience⟩ **3 :** to move with an undulating motion or so as to cause ripples ⟨the canoe *rippled* through the water⟩ **4 :** to run irregularly through a crowd, group, or population ⟨had watched discontent ~ through the seaports and back country —Oscar Handlin⟩ ~ *vt* **1 :** to stir up small waves on (water) **:** move or disturb lightly ⟨a moderate breeze was *rippling* the lagoon —Ernest Beaglehole⟩ **2 :** to impart a wavy motion or appearance to ⟨began to stretch and ~ his muscles —*Time*⟩ **3 :** to utter or play with a slight rise and fall of sound **:** make a light rapid cadence or melody of ⟨*rippling* a boogiewoogie beat on the piano —Noel Houston⟩

⁶ripple \"\ *n* -s **1 a :** a shallow stretch of running water in a stream roughened or broken by rocky or uneven bottom **b** (1) **:** the fretting or ruffling of the surface of water (as by wind) (2) **:** a small wave **c :** a small wave propagated by both surface tension and gravity — distinguished from *gravity wave* **2 :** something resembling or suggesting a ripple of water: as **a :** RIPPLE MARK 2 **b :** a soft fold (as in a full skirt) or a wavy outline (as in a hat brim) **c :** CHATTER MARK 1 **d :** a sound like that of rippling water ⟨a ~ of laughter⟩ ⟨a ~ of conversation⟩ **3 :** ¹RIFFLE 1 **4 :** a slight fluctuation in the intensity of an otherwise steady electrical current

ripple fire *n* **:** the discharge of rockets in quick succession

ripple grass *n* **:** a ribgrass (*Plantago lanceolata*)

ripple index *n* **:** the horizontal distance from crest to crest divided by the vertical distance from crest to trough of the ripples on a ripple-marked surface

rip·ple·less \'ripəl(l)əs\ *adj* **:** having no ripples **:** GLASSY, SMOOTH

ripple mark *n* **1 a :** the undulating surface of a ridge or trough produced in incoherent granular material (as loose sand) by wind, currents of water, or the agitation of waves **b :** one of the ridges on such a surface **2 :** a striation across the grain of wood esp. on the tangential surface caused by storied cambial and other cells — **ripple-marked** \'==,=\ *adj*

rip·pler \'rip(ə)lə(r)\ *n* -s **:** one that ripples; *esp* **:** ²RIPPLE

rip·plet \'rip(ə)lət\ *n* -s **:** a small ripple

ripple voltage *n* **:** the alternating component of unidirectional voltage from a rectifier or generator

ripple weld *n* **:** a weld having a rippled surface

ripple-weld \'==,=\ *vt* [*ripple weld*] **:** to unite by means of a ripple weld

rip·pling·ly *adv* **:** in a rippling manner **:** WAVILY

rip·ply \'rip(ə)lē, -li\ *adj* [⁵*ripple* + *-y*] **1 :** having ripples ⟨~ water⟩ **2 :** resembling the sound of rippling water

rip·pon \'ripən\ *n* -s [fr. *Rippon* (Ripon), Yorkshire, England] *archaic* **:** a horseman's spur

¹rip·rap \'ri,prap\ *n* [fr. obs. *riprap* sound of rapping, redupl. of ¹*rap*] **1 :** a foundation or sustaining wall of stones thrown together without order (as in deep water, on a soft bottom, or on an embankment slope to prevent erosion) **2 :** stone used for riprap

²riprap \"\ *vt* **:** to form a riprap in or upon **:** strengthen or support with a riprap ⟨*riprapped* the breakwater with stone⟩

riprapping *n* -s **:** a riprap foundation or wall

rip-roaring \'ri,prōriŋ, -prȯr-\ *adj* [alter. of *rip-roarious*] **:** noisily excited or exciting **:** HILARIOUS

rip-roarious \(')ri¦prōrēəs, -prȯr-\ *adj* [²*rip* + *-roarious* (as in *uproarious*)] **:** HILARIOUS

rips *pl of* RIP, *pres 3d sing of* RIP

ripsack \'=,=\ *n* [²*rip* + *sack*] **:** GRAY WHALE

¹ripsaw \'=,=\ *n* [²*rip* + *saw*] **:** a coarse-toothed saw for cutting wood in the direction of the grain — compare CROSSCUT SAW

²ripsaw \"\ *vt* **:** to saw (wood) in the direction of the grain

rip·sawyer \'rip+,-\ *n* [²*ripsaw* + *-yer* (as in *sawyer*)] **:** a worker who uses a ripsaw

ripsnorter \'=¦==\ *n* [²*rip* + *snorter*] **1 :** a violently energetic or noisily outspoken person **:** someone using slambang methods ⟨that venerable old ~ defended the right of the clergy to drive fast horses —Phil Stong⟩ **2 :** something extreme **:** HUMDINGER ⟨yesterday's performance was a ~ for gaiety, vigor, and general run-around —Virgil Thomson⟩ — compare SNORTER — **ripsnorting** \'=¦==\ *adj*

riptide \'=,=\ *n* [⁵*rip* + *tide*] **1 :** RIP CURRENT **2 :** a situation in which confused overwhelming forces play on someone **:** a destructive vortex ⟨creators and culture heroes who crack up in a ~ of alcohol —Richard Chase⟩

rip track *n* **:** a siding on which railroad cars are given minor repairs

¹rip·u·ar·i·an \¦ripyə¦werēən, -wa(a)r-,-wār-\ *adj, usu cap* [ML *Ripuarius* Ripuarian + E *-an*] **:** of or relating to a group of Franks settling in the 4th century on both banks of the Rhine near the present city of Cologne

²ripuarian \"\ *n* -s *cap* **:** a Ripuarian Frank

rip van win·kle \,rip,van'wiŋkəl\ *n* -s *usu cap R&V&W* [after *Rip Van Winkle*, fictional ne'er-do-well in the Catskill mountains of N.Y. state in colonial days who slept for 20 years, as portrayed in a story of *The Sketch Book* (1820) by Washington Irving †1859 Am. writer] **:** someone not alert to current conditions ⟨some *Rip Van Winkle* in an obscure corner . . . who has read nothing for four years —*Manchester Guardian Weekly*⟩

rir·o·ri·ro \,rirə'rē(,)rō\ *n* -s [Maori] **:** GRAY WARBLER

ri·sa·la *or* **res·sa·la** \rə'sälə\ *n* -s [Hindi *risāla* troop, fr. Per, fr. Ar *risālah* mission] **:** a troop of irregular cavalry in the Anglo-Indian army

ri·sal·dar *or* **ris·sal·dar** \rə'säl,där, 'risəl,-\ *or* **res·sal·dar** \rə'säl,där, 'resəl,-\ *n* -s [Hindi *risāldār*, fr. Per *risāladār*, fr. *risāla* + *-dār* holder — more at BHUMIDAR] **:** a native commander of a risala in the Anglo-Indian army

risco *n* -s [It *risco, risico, rischio*] *obs* **:** RISK, VENTURE

¹rise \'rīz\ *vb* **rose** \'rōz\ *or archaic* **rise** *or dial* **riz** \'riz\ **ris·en** \'rizᵊn\ *or dial* **riz; ris·ing** \'rīziŋ\ **ris·es** \'rīzəz\ [ME *risen*, fr. OE *rīsan;* akin to OHG *rīsan* to rise, climb, fall, ON *rīsa* to rise, Goth *urreisan* to get up, L *oriri* to rise, *rivus* brook, stream, Gk *ornynai* to urge on, cause to rise, *oros* mountain, Skt *arṇa* wave, *ṛṣva* high, *raya* stream, Hitt *arāi* he rises] *vi* **1 a :** to assume an upright or standing position **:** get up from lying, kneeling, or sitting **b :** to get up from sleep or from one's bed **c :** to get back on one's feet after a fall **d :** to regain standing after a lapse, disgrace, or failure **e** (1) **:** to stand erect (as of a terrified person's hair) (2) **:** to resume an upright position (as of flattened grass or grain) **2 :** to come back to life **:** return from death or the grave ⟨witnesses who ate and drank with him after he *rose* from the dead —Acts 10:41 (RSV)⟩ **3 a :** to go to war **:** take up arms **:** launch an attack **:** make insurrection ⟨the people of Boston *rose* and seized all of the Dominion officers who could be found —Viola F. Barnes⟩ — usu. used with *against* ⟨the Lord will cause your enemies who ~ against you to be defeated before you —Deut. 28:7 (RSV)⟩ **b** *obs* (1) **:** to break camp (2) **:** to withdraw a besieging force **4 a** *obs* **:** to show respect **:** DEFER — used with *up* **b :** to respond warmly **:** show enthusiasm **:** APPLAUD, CHEER — usu. used with *to* ⟨the audience *rose* to his verve and wit⟩ **5 :** to end a session **:** ADJOURN ⟨when the committee *rose* on Friday the clerk had read through section 203 —*Congressional Record*⟩ **6 a :** to move up from the horizon **:** climb the skies **:** come up ⟨a pale sun *rose* in lowering skies⟩ — opposed to *set* **b :** to come in view (as of a ship at sea) above the horizon or to appear larger on nearer approach **7 a :** to ascend into the air **:** move upward ⟨smoke *rose* quietly from cottage chimneys all through the valley below⟩ **b :** to grow taller **:** increase in height ⟨~ to heights unusual for other trees⟩ **8 :** to swell in size or volume **:** reach a higher level ⟨the river *rose* rapidly with the heavy rains⟩ ⟨becomes an island each time the tide *rises*⟩ ⟨a blister *rose* at the burn⟩ ⟨bread dough *rises*⟩ **9 :** to extend upward **:** grow in process of construction **:** incline or reach above other objects ⟨at a little distance above him *rose* a small butte —Oliver La Farge⟩ ⟨octagonal towers ~ a story higher than the main body of the structure —*Amer. Guide Series: Texas*⟩ ⟨a meeting place or assembly hall will ~ —Sidonie M. Gruenberg⟩ ⟨between the valleys of the gorge ~ miniature mountain peaks —*Amer. Guide Series: La.*⟩ **10 a :** to become lifted up or raised **:** swell with joy **:** increase in cheer, hope, or courage **:** become elated ⟨spirits *rose* as the danger passed⟩ **b :** to increase in fervor **:** grow heated or ardent **:** INTENSIFY ⟨members of his staff watched indignation ~ in him —Stewart Cockburn⟩ **11 :** to move aloft **:** become lifted higher **:** go up **:** SOAR ⟨the curtain *rose* on a lovely set⟩ ⟨birds *rose* all around in alarm⟩ **12 a :** to come up to the surface (as of the water or the ground) ⟨a diver *rose* near him in the water⟩ ⟨the spring ~*s* cool and fresh from great depths⟩ **b :** to move up through the water to take food or bait ⟨trout were *rising* hungrily⟩ **13** *of locked-up printing type* **a :** LIFT **b :** to work up **14 a :** to attain a higher level **:** gain in vigor, clarity, grace, or effectiveness ⟨his painting *rose* to a fresh expressiveness and revealed a shrewder, gentler insight⟩ ⟨*rose* to heights of passionate eloquence⟩ **b :** to increase in quantity or number ⟨funds available for investment *rose* sharply —R.P.Edmunds⟩ ⟨cotton acreage *rose* over 50 percent —*Americana Annual*⟩ **c :** to advance in rank, position, or esteem ⟨*rose* to the rank of brigadier general of cavalry when still in his twenties —J.H.Easterby⟩ **d :** to increase in price **:** grow dearer ⟨the cost of paper *rose*⟩ **e :** to become higher in pitch or louder ⟨her voice *rose* then in a shrill crescendo⟩ **15 a :** to grow stronger or more resolute ⟨his courage *rose* as difficulties multiplied about him⟩ **b :** to increase in force or rate of speed ⟨the wind *rose* rapidly⟩ ⟨storms *rose* often to wild fury⟩ **16 :** to take place **:** HAPPEN, OCCUR ⟨then *rose* a little circumstance that was to have far-reaching results⟩ **17 a :** to attain existence **:** come on the scene **:** become born **:** APPEAR ⟨search and you will see that no prophet is to ~ from Galilee —Jn 7:52 (RSV)⟩ ⟨great regimes *rose*, based upon the irrational and negative in man's nature —M.W.Straight⟩ **b** *archaic* **:** to spring up **:** GROW — used of a plant **18 :** to follow as a consequence **:** become derived **:** ORIGINATE, RESULT ⟨wars had *risen* out of incidents more trivial —L.C.Douglas⟩ **19 :** to gain currency **:** CIRCULATE ⟨a rumor *rose* in city hall circles that the mayor would resign⟩ **20 a :** to have source or origin **:** SPRING ⟨the river ~*s* in the foothills⟩ **b :** to have a beginning ⟨great nations ~ and fall⟩ **21 :** to exert oneself to meet a challenge or provocation **:** show oneself equal to a demand or test **:** prove adequate — usu. used with *to* ⟨their ministerial leaders *rose* ably to the occasion with consummate theological arguments —*Amer. Guide Series: Conn.*⟩ **22 :** to become raised (as of a vowel) ~ *vt* **1 :** to cause to rise; *esp* **:** to lure (a fish) to rise **2** *chiefly dial* **:** to make higher **:** INCREASE — used of price **3** *archaic* **:** to reach the top of **:** SURMOUNT

syn RISE, ARISE, ASCEND, MOUNT, SOAR, TOWER, ROCKET, LEVITATE, SURGE can mean, in common, to move or come up from a lower to a higher level. RISE is the most general, interchangeable with all the others ⟨the fountain *rose* to a 6-foot spout⟩ ⟨she felt the color *rising* in her face —Anne D. Sedgwick⟩ ⟨the building *rose* a story at a time⟩ ⟨the balloon *rose* into the heavens⟩ ⟨the table *rose* from the floor and seemed to poise in midair⟩ ⟨the wave *rose* and crashed against the cliff⟩ It is usu. used in some idioms that refer to getting up from a lying, sitting, or kneeling position ⟨awake and *rise* at dawn⟩ ⟨*rise* from a chair⟩ or to objects as the sun, moon, or a mountain that seem to get up or lift themselves in this way ⟨the moon rose at 10:35 in the evening⟩ ⟨stairways *rising* diagonally across the porch —*Amer. Guide Series: La.*⟩ ⟨cliffs around the bay *rise* steep from the waters —Leonard Lyons⟩ or to a fluid under the influence of a natural force ⟨the mercury *rose* steadily until the temperature was over 100 degrees⟩ ⟨in the flood the river *rose* five feet⟩ ARISE is narrower in application and is used to indicate literal movement upward usu. to getting up after a sleep; in figurative applications it is more synonymous with *appear* or *come into existence* ⟨an apparition *arose* before us⟩ ⟨city after city *arose* —R.W. Murray⟩ ⟨an eager babbling *arose* from the shore —Kenneth Roberts⟩ ⟨a haze of dust *arose* —Melvin Van den Bark⟩ ASCEND and MOUNT carry a strong idea of continuous, progressive upward movement ⟨*ascend* a mountain⟩ ⟨*mount* a long flight of stairs⟩ ⟨the smoke rose and *ascended* to the treetops⟩ ⟨after the initial rise the temperature *mounted* steadily⟩ ⟨*ascend* a stream in a canoe⟩ ⟨as the road *mounted*, the air became sharper —Joseph Wechsberg⟩ SOAR, always suggesting the straight upward flight of a bird, therefore indicates continuous, usu. swift ascent to high altitudes, literal or figurative ⟨the flight of hawks is impressive . . . *soaring* in intricate spirals —*Amer. Guide Series: Pa.*⟩ ⟨snowy mountains *soaring* into the sky twelve and thirteen thousand feet —John Muir †1914⟩ ⟨food items, the prices of which may *soar* or plummet —Carey Longmire⟩ TOWER usu. applies to things that attain conspicuous height through growth or building up, connoting extension to a height considerably above neighboring objects ⟨peaks that *tower* in the distance —Laurence Binyon⟩ ⟨surrounded by mountains which *tower* thousands of feet higher —Tom Marvel⟩ ⟨great chimneys *tower* above its roof —*Amer. Guide Series: Md.*⟩ ⟨the great men *tower* over the young making their authority manifest in the land —H.J.Laski⟩ ROCKET suggests the startlingly swift speed, usu. upward, of a projectile ⟨teal *rocketed* over the treetops —*New Yorker*⟩ ⟨prices have *rocketed* sky-high —Patrick Kent⟩ LEVITATE implies a force that causes something to rise through actual or induced buoyancy, usu., however, being associated with spiritualistic practices and illusory risings of a person or thing ⟨had once *levitated* himself three feet from the ground by a simple act of the will —Katherine A. Porter⟩ ⟨in other experiments . . . with *levitated* tables —H.H.U.Cross⟩ SURGE, often with *up*, suggests the heaving upward or forward of a large wave ⟨water forced in by the ocean waves would *surge* up through it and trickle down the mountains —*Amer. Guide Series: Oregon*⟩ ⟨strong emotions *surged* through him as he strode on —O.E. Rölvaag⟩ **syn** see in addition SPRING

²**rise** \" *sometimes* -īs\ *n* -s **1** : an act of rising or a state of being risen: as **a** : a movement upward : an ascent to a higher plane **b** : the emergence of the sun or some other celestial body above the horizon **c** *obs* (1) : a leap upward esp. from a running start (2) : a place providing a takeoff point for such a leap **d** : the upward movement of a fish to seize food or bait **e** (1) : an increase in the pitch of sound or an upward change of key ⟨a ~ of a tone or semitone⟩ (2) : a rising-pitch intonation in speech — compare ²FALL 3d **f** (1) : the reaching of a higher level by an increase of quantity or bulk (2) : the amount or height of such an increase ⟨the ~ of the river was six feet⟩ **g** : the distance from the firing line to the traps in trapshooting **2** : BEGINNING, DERIVATION, ORIGIN, SOURCE, START ⟨with the ~ of tin mining in more recent years, the community has once again regained its position of importance —P.E.James⟩ **3** : the distance or elevation of one point above another: as **a** : the height of an arch from base to apex **b** : the height of a step in a staircase measured from one tread to the next **4** : an increase in amount, number, or volume: as **a** : an increase in the loudness of the voice ⟨the ordinary ~*s* and falls of the voice —Francis Bacon⟩ **b** *chiefly Brit* : an increase in wages or salary ⟨five shillings a week ~ from the first of January —Victoria Sackville-West⟩ **c** : an increase in price, value, rate, or sum ⟨the corn shortage that followed land expropriation caused a ~ in corn prices —Virginia Prewett⟩ ⟨it had no concomitant provision for a tax ~ —J.C.Ingraham⟩ ⟨a general ~ in the cost of living —C.L.Guthrie⟩ ⟨a walkout, a fare ~ — or both — appeared inevitable —*N.Y. World-Telegram*⟩ **d** : the difference in diameter between two points on a log : TAPER **5 a** : an upward slope : INCLINE ⟨hopes for a ~ in the road —*Amer. Guide Series: Fla.*⟩ ⟨a ~ in the ocean bottom⟩ **b** : a spot higher than the surrounding ground : HILLTOP ⟨the road breaks suddenly over a ~ —*Amer. Guide Series: Wash.*⟩ **6** : ²RAISE 4 **7** : an irritated or retaliatory response to provocation : an angry reaction : RETORT ⟨got a ~ out of him⟩ **8** : the vertical displacement of the center of gravity of a seaplane float or hull from an arbitrary reference level **9 a** : the distance from the crotch to the waistline on pants **b** : the distance above the waistline on skirts

³**rise** \"\ *chiefly dial var of* ¹RICE

rise and fall *n* : the vertical up and down movement of the tide resulting from but not necessarily coincident with its flow and ebb

rise and shine *vi* : to get out of bed — often used as a command

risen [ME, fr. OE] *past part of* RISE

rise of floor : DEAD RISE

ris·er \ˈrīzə(r)\ *n* -s [ME, fr. *risen* to rise + *-er* — more at RISE] **1** : one that rises: as **a** : one that gets up from sleep ⟨birds are early ~*s*⟩ **b** : INSURGENT **c** : a part in a machine that operates by rising **2 a** : the upright member between two stair treads — compare OPEN RISER **b** : an upright face (as of a platform or veranda) suggesting a stair riser **c** : a topographic feature resembling a stair riser (as a steep slope between terraces of different altitude or between flat parts of a stepped glaciated valley floor) **3** : ²RAISE 4 **4 a** : FEEDHEAD **b** : a channel or head in a foundry mold (as to permit escape of air) **5** : a block on which a printing plate (as a stereotype or electrotype) is mounted **6** : a device or structure used to increase elevation: as **a** : one of two members placed below a seat to raise it **b** : any of various movable platforms for stage use on which performers are placed for better visibility ⟨portable ~*s* adequate for a full orchestra⟩ **7 a** : a vertical supply or return pipe for steam, water, or gas **b** : a vertical wire connecting two floors in the electric wiring system of a building **8** : a raised or marked spot where the warp passes over the weft or over the filling in a weaving pattern — compare SINKER 8 **9** : one of four straps attaching a parachutist's harness to the parachute — see PARACHUTE illustration

riser plate *n* : a plate used with a railroad gage or tie plate to raise and support a point rail above the base of the rail and maintain minimum gage

rises *pres 3d sing of* RISE, *pl of* RISE

rishi *also* **rsi** \ˈrishē\ *n* -s [Skt *ṛṣi*; akin to Skt *rasa* juice, fluid — more at ROSEMARY] : a holy Hindu sage, saint, or inspired poet

ris·i·bil·i·ty \ˌrizəˈbiləd·ē, -lətē, -i\ *n* -ES [LL *risibilitas*, fr. *risibilis* + L *-itas* -ity] **1** : the ability or inclination to laugh : alertness or sensitiveness to the ridiculous, incongruous, or absurd — often used in pl. ⟨our *risibilities* support us as we skim over the surface of a deep issue —J.A.Pike⟩ **2** : LAUGHTER, MERRIMENT ⟨excites much ~ by being tossed in a blanket —Wilmot Harrison⟩

ris·i·ble \ˈrizəbəl\ *adj* [LL *risibilis*, fr. L *risus* (past part. of *ridēre* to laugh) + *-ibilis* -ible — more at RIDICULOUS] **1** : capable of laughing : disposed to laugh ⟨heaven is not for pallid saints but raging and ~ men —Christopher Morley⟩ **2** : arousing, exciting, or provoking laughter : FUNNY, RIDICULOUS ⟨~ courtroom antics —Robert Hatch⟩ ⟨my salary is ~ —W.J. Locke⟩ **3** : associated with, relating to, or used in laughter ⟨~ muscles⟩ ⟨something would be said to touch his ~ faculties —W.H.Hudson †1922⟩ **syn** see LAUGHABLE

ris·i·bles \-lz\ *n pl* : sense of the ridiculous : SENSE OF HUMOR ⟨an article which tickled my ~ immensely —Vinnie Hicks⟩

¹**rising** *n* -s [ME, action of rising, fr. gerund of *risen* to rise — more at RISE] **1** *chiefly dial* : a pathological excrescence : a puffing up : BOIL, PUSTULE **2** *chiefly dial* : a leavening agent (as yeast) used to make dough rise **3** : ²RAISE 4 **4 a** : a narrow strake to support the thwarts of a boat **b** : fore-and-aft bearers to support a deck

²**rising** *adj* [fr. pres. part. of ¹*rise*] **1** *heraldry* : having the wings opening as if for flight **2** *chiefly Midland* : more than : EXCEEDING — often used with *of* **3** : passing from a less vigorous to a more vigorous physical condition : IMPROVING — used esp. of domestic livestock; compare FALLING

³**rising** *adv* : on the verge of being a stated age : NEARLY, ALMOST ⟨a mare ~ nine⟩

rising diphthong *n* : a diphthong in which the final vowel element is more prominent than the beginning element (as the \yä\ in \ˈyät\ *yacht*) — compare FALLING DIPHTHONG, ²GLIDE 3b

rising hinge *n* : a door hinge designed so that the door is lifted a little when opened

rising line *n* : a line drawn in the plan of a ship to show the heights of the floors

rising rhythm *n* : a rhythm in which the stresses regularly fall on the last syllable of each foot (as in iambic or anapestic lines) — opposed to *falling rhythm*; compare CADENCE 5, UNDULATING CADENCE

rising seat *n* : one of the tiered seats facing the congregation in a Friends' meetinghouse that are occupied by the elders

rising timbers *n pl* : the floor timbers in the forward or afterparts of a wooden ship inclined up from the rest of the deck

rising hinge

rising vote *n* : a vote in which the voters on each side rise in turn to be counted — compare DIVISION, VOICE VOTE

rising wood *n* **1** : timber used to fill in at the junctions of a wooden ship's keelson with the stem and stern posts **2** : the upper timber of a wooden ship's keel when composed of two timbers

¹**risk** \ˈrisk, *dial* ˈresk\ *n* -s [F *risque*, fr. It *risco, risico, rischio*] **1** : the possibility of loss, injury, disadvantage, or destruction : CONTINGENCY, DANGER, PERIL, THREAT ⟨the infinite care and ~ which are involved in the dangerous mission of bomb disposal —E.A.Weeks⟩ ⟨foreign ships and planes refused to run the ~ of attack —*Collier's Yr. Bk.*⟩ **2** : someone or something that creates or suggests a hazard or adverse chance : a dangerous element or factor — often used with qualifiers to indicate the degree or kind of hazard ⟨the wife who didn't fix her husband a good breakfast . . . wasn't a good ~ —W.H.Whyte⟩ ⟨must be kept clean and free from fire ~*s* —Peter Heaton⟩ ⟨a poor ~ for surgery⟩ **3 a** (1) : the chance of loss or the perils to the subject matter of insurance covered by a contract (2) : the degree of probability of such loss **b** : AMOUNT AT RISK **c** : a person or thing judged as a (specified) hazard to an insurer ⟨a poor ~ for insurance⟩ **d** : an insurance hazard from a (specified) cause or source ⟨war ~⟩ ⟨disaster ~⟩ **4** : the product of the amount that may be lost and the probability of losing it — compare EXPECTATION 6b **syn** see DANGER

²**risk** \"\ *vb* -ED/-ING/-S [F *risquer*, fr. It *riscare, risicare, rischiare*, fr. *risco, risico, rischio*] *vt* **1** : to expose to hazard or danger ⟨wasn't going to ~ his neck —Barnaby Conrad⟩ ⟨father and son were ready to ~ their futures on the book business alone —A.E.Peterson⟩ **2** : to incur the risk or danger of : venture upon ⟨these privateers ~*ed* being hung as pirates —*Amer. Guide Series: N. H.*⟩ ~ *vi* : to take risks **syn** see VENTURE

³**risk** \ˈrisk\ *vi* -ED/-ING/-S [prob. of imit. origin] *Scot* : to make a crackling or grating sound

risk capital *n* : VENTURE CAPITAL

risk·er \ˈriskə(r), *dial* ˈres-\ *n* -s : one that risks

risk·ful \-kfəl\ *adj* : RISKY — **risk·ful·ness** *n* -ES

risk·i·ly \ˈriskəlē, -li\ *adv* : in a risky manner : HAZARDOUSLY ⟨lost the game by playing too ~⟩

risk·i·ness \-kēnəs, -kin-\ *n* -ES : the quality or state of being risky : CHANCINESS

risk·less \-kləs\ *adj* : having no danger : free of adverse chance : CERTAIN, SAFE ⟨relatively ~ financial arrangements —Albert Lepawsky⟩ ⟨the return on ~ investments is not sufficiently attractive —John Ryan⟩

risk premium *n* : NET PREMIUM

risky \-kē, -ki\ *adj, usu* -ER/-EST [¹*risk* + *-y*] **1** : attended with risk or danger : HAZARDOUS ⟨pretty ~ going out there in the tide and in the fog —D.B.Putnam⟩ **2** [modif. of F *risqué* — more at RISQUÉ] : RISQUÉ ⟨~ anecdotes were discouraged —Gamaliel Bradford⟩ ⟨she had on the *riskiest* dress she'd bought —Ring Lardner⟩ **syn** see DANGEROUS

ris·ley act \ˈrizlē-\ *n, usu cap R* [after the *Risley* family, 19th cent. circus trio consisting of Richard Risley Carlisle †1874 Am. gymnast and circus performer and his two sons] : a circus act in which an acrobat lying on his back juggles barrels or fellow acrobats with his feet

ri·so·lu·to \ˌrēsəˈlü(ˌ)tō, -ēzə-\ *adv (or adj)* [It, resolute, fr. L *resolutus* — more at RESOLUTE] : resolutely and with marked accent — used as a direction in music

ri·sor·gi·men·to \(ˌ)rē,sȯ(r)jəˈmen·(ˌ)tō\ *n* -s [It, fr. *risorgere* to rise again (fr. L *resurgere*) + *-i-* + *-mento* -ment (fr. L *-mentum*) — more at RESURRECTION] : a time of renewal or renaissance : REVIVAL ⟨a ~ of culture —R.P.Casey⟩ ⟨an industrial and agricultural ~ —B.A.Javits⟩ ⟨a betrayal of the men of the *Risorgimento* who made Italy a free nation —*Times Lit. Supp.*⟩

ri·so·ri·us \rəˈsōrēəs, rī'-, -ˈzō-\ *n, pl* **riso·rii** \-ē,ī\ [NL, fr. L *risus* (past part. of *ridēre* to laugh) + *-orius* -ory — more at RIDICULOUS] : a narrow band of muscle fibers arising from the fascia over the masseter muscle and inserted into the tissues at the corner of the mouth

ri·sot·to \rəˈsȯd·(ˌ)ō, -ˈz|, |äd-\ *or* **ri·zot·to** \-ˈz\ *n* -s [It *risotto*] : rice cooked in meat stock and seasoned in any of various ways (as with butter and cheese or with wine and saffron)

¹**risp** \ˈrisp\ *vb* [ME *rispen*, fr. ON *rispa* to scratch; akin to G *rispeln* to scrape together, LG *rispe* hackle, and perh. to Norw *ripa* to scratch — more at REAP] *Scot* : RASP, SCRATCH

²**risp** \"\ *n* -s [origin unknown] *dial chiefly Eng* : a stem or stalk of a plant

ri·spet·to \rəˈsped·(ˌ)ō\ *n* -s [It, lit., respect, fr. L *respectus* — more at RESPECT] : an Italian verse stanza of from 6 to 10 lines with rhymes

ri·spos·ta \rəˈspōstə\ *n* -s [It, lit., answer, fr. fem. of *risposto*, past part. of *rispondere* to answer, fr. L *respondēre* to answer, respond — more at RESPOND] : the answer in a musical fugue or the consequent in a canon

ris·qué \rəˈskā, (ˈ)ri¦s-\ *adj* [F, fr. past part. of *risquer* to risk — more at RISK] : verging on impropriety or indecency : DARING, OFF-COLOR ⟨a ~ story⟩

¹**riss** \ˈris\ *n* -ES *usu cap* [fr. the *Riss* river, tributary of the Danube in southwestern Germany] : the third stage of Pleistocene glaciation in Europe

²**riss** \"\ *or* **riss·ian** \-sēən\ *adj, usu cap* : of or relating to the Riss glaciation

rissaldar *var of* RISALDAR

ris·soa \ˈrisəwə, rəˈsōə\ *n, cap* [NL, after Giovanni A. *Risso* †1845 Fr. naturalist] : a genus (the type of the family Rissoidae) of small snails that live in brackish water and have an acuminate often finely sculptured shell with a corneous operculum

¹**ris·soid** \ˈrisəwəd, -ˌsȯid\ *or* **ris·soid·e·an** \¦risə¦widēən, rəˈsȯid-\ *adj* [*rissoid* fr. NL *Rissoidae*; *rissoidean* fr. NL *Rissoidae* + E *-an*] : of or relating to the Rissoidae

²**rissoid** \"\ *n* -s : a snail of the family Rissoidae

ris·soi·dae \rəˈsōə,dē, -ˈsȯi(ˌ)dē\ *n pl, cap* [NL, fr. *Rissoa*, type genus + *-idae*] : a large family of marine and freshwater snails (suborder Taenioglossa) with a long snout, ciliated tentacles, and eyes on small prominences at the base of the tentacles — see RISSOA

¹**ris·sole** \rəˈsōl, ˈri,s-\ *n* -s [F, fr. MF *roissole*, fr. (assumed) VL *russeola*, fr. L *russeus* reddish, fr. *russus* red — more at RUSSET] : minced meat or fish covered with pastry and fried in deep fat

²**ris·so·lé** \ˈrisəlē, ¦==¦lā\ *adj* [F, fr. past part. of *rissoler* to brown by frying in deep fat, fr. *rissole*] : browned by frying in deep fat ⟨~ potatoes⟩

ris·som \ˈrisəm, ˈrizəm\ *n* -s [ME *risom*, of Scand origin; akin to Sw dial. *resma, resme* ear of oats, Norw *risla* bush, treetop, ear of grain; akin to OHG *hrīs* twig — more at CREST] **1** *chiefly dial* : an ear or stalk of grain : STRAW 2 **2** *chiefly dial* : a tiny bit : PARTICLE

riss-würm \ˈriˈs|wərm, |wü(ə)rm, |vi(ə)rm, *G* |vu̇rm\ *n* -s *usu cap R&W* [fr. the *Riss* river, a tributary of the Danube in southwestern Germany, and the *Würm*, a small stream of southern Bavaria, Germany] : the third interglacial interval during the Pleistocene glaciation of Europe

ri·sus sar·do·ni·cus \ˌrēsə(s)ˌsärˈdänəkəs, ¦rīs-\ *n* [NL, lit., sardonic laugh] : a facial expression characterized by raised eyebrows and grinning distortion of the face resulting from spasm of facial muscles esp. in tetanus

rit \ˈrit\ *vt* **rit·ted**; **rit·ted**; **rit·ting**; **rits** [ME *ritten*; akin to OHG *rizzōn, rizzen* to scratch, tear; derivative fr. the stem of OE *wrītan* to scratch (on something), write — more at WRITE] *dial Brit* : to scratch or cut esp. with a sharp instrument

rit *abbr* ritardando

RIT *abbr* refining in transit

rita *also* **rta** \ˈrid·ə\ *n* -s [Skt *ṛta*, fr. *ṛta* fit, right, true — more at ARTICLE] : the cosmic-moral principle of order that in Vedic tradition establishes regularity and righteousness in the world

ri·tard \rəˈtärd, ˈrē,t-\ *n* -s [by shortening] : RITARDANDO

¹**ri·tar·dan·do** \ˌrē,tärˈdän(ˌ)dō, -dan-\ *adv (or adj)* [It, fr. L *retardandum*, gerund of *retardare* to retard — more at RETARD] : with a gradual slackening in tempo : RALLENTANDO — used as a direction in music

²**ritardando** \"\ *n* -s **1** : a movement or passage in gradually slackening tempo **2** : a gradually slackening tempo

¹**rite** \ˈrīt, *usu* -īd·+V\ *n* -s [ME, fr. L *ritus*; akin to OE *rīm* number, OHG, series, number, ON, calculation, OIr, number, Gk *arithmos* number, *arariskein* to fit — more at ARM] **1 a** : a prescribed form or manner governing the words or actions of a ceremony esp. of considerable religious, courtly, social, or tribal significance ⟨the introduction into a particular ~ of features not sanctioned by the texts —L.P.Smith⟩ **b** *often cap* : LITURGY; *esp* : one of the historical forms of the eucharistic service ⟨Charlemagne introduced the Roman ~ throughout his territories⟩ **2** : a ceremonial act or action or series of such acts esp. in established religious usage, in tribal custom, or occas. in bizarre practices or unduly formalized conduct in ordinary life ⟨~ of baptism⟩ ⟨~*s* of a fraternal organization⟩ ⟨at puberty, initiation ~*s* are held —*African Abstracts*⟩ ⟨woman engaged in the ~*s* of good grooming —Agnes Rogers⟩ ⟨making an apologetic ~ of pulling up his trousers and stuffing in his shirt —Richard Llewellyn⟩ — see RITE OF INTENSIFICATION, RITE OF PASSAGE **3** *sometimes cap* : a division of the Christian church as determined by liturgy ⟨Eastern Orthodox of the Byzantine ~⟩ ⟨Protestants of the Anglican ~⟩ — see LATIN RITE **syn** see FORM

²**ri·te** \ˈrīd·ē, -ī,tē\ *adv (or adj)* [NL, fr. L, in accordance with religious usage, fitly, aptly; akin to L *ritus* rite] : with a pass — used as a mark of undistinguished achievement in the academic requirements for graduation

rite de pas·sage \ˌrētdəpaˈsäzh\ [F] : RITE OF PASSAGE

rite·less \ˈrītləs\ *adj* : lacking a rite : devoid of ceremony

rite·less·ness *n* -ES : the state of being riteless

ritely *adv, obs* : according to rite or ritual : DULY

riten *abbr* ritenuto

ri·te·nen·te \ˌrēd·əˈnentē, -en·(ˌ)tā\ *adv (or adj)* [It, fr. L *retinent-, retinens*, pres. part. of *retinēre* to hold back, detain, restrain, retain — more at RETAIN] : RITARDANDO — used as a direction in music

ri·te·nu·to \ˌrēd·əˈnü(ˌ)tō\ *adj* [It, past part. of *ritenere* to hold back, detain, restrain, retain, fr. L *retinēre*] : held back in tempo — used as a direction in music usu. indicating an abrupt slowing down

rite of intensification : a ritualistic procedure associated with periodic events or seasonal crises affecting a societal group as a whole

rite of passage : a ritualistic procedure associated with a nonperiodic crisis or a transitional change of status for an individual (as initiation, marriage, illness, or death)

rithe \ˈrīth\ *n* -s [ME, fr. OE *rīth, rīthe* — more at RILL] *dial Eng* : a small stream : RUNNEL, RIVULET ⟨in the channels and ~*s* of Colchester Harbor —Alan Moore⟩

rit·ling \ˈritlən\ *var of* RECKLING

ri·tor·nel·lo \ˌrid·ərˈne(ˌ)lō, ˌri,tȯrˈn-\ *or* **ri·tor·nelle** *or* **ri·tor·nel** \¦=(,)=¦nel\ *n, pl* **ritornelli** *or* **ritornellos** *or* **ritornelles** *or* **ritornels** [It *ritornello*, dim. of *ritorno* return, fr. *ritornare* to return, fr. *ri-* re- (fr. L *re-*) + *tornare* to turn, return, fr. L, to turn in a lathe — more at TURN] **1 a** : a short instrumental passage in a vocal musical composition often consisting of a burden or refrain **b** : an instrumental interlude between the parts of an opera **2** : a tutti passage in a concerto **3** : the last two lines of a 14th century madrigal serving as a concluding passage or section

¹**ritsch·li·an** \ˈrichlēən\ *adj, usu cap* [Albrecht *Ritschl* †1889 Ger. theologian + E *-ian*] : of, relating to, or in accordance with the theological principles of Ritschl who rejected the metaphysical development of theology emphasizing its ethical-social content and held that religious judgments are judgments of value and that Christian theology should rest mainly on an appreciation of the inner life of Christ

²**ritschlian** \"\ *n* -s *usu cap* : an advocate of Ritschlian views

ritsch·li·an·ism \-ēə,nizəm\ *n* -s *usu cap* : Ritschlian theological views and principles

ri·tsu \ˈrit(ˌ)sü, ˈrēt-\ *n* -s [Jap, lit., law, moral law] : a Hinayana Buddhist school founded in Japan in A.D. 754

rit·ter \ˈrid·ə(r)\ *n, pl* **ritter** *or* **ritters** [G, fr. MHG *riter*, fr. MD *riddere, ridder* horseman, knight, prob. alter. (influenced by an assumed n. akin to OE *ridda* horseman, fr. the stem of *rīdan* to ride) of *ridere, rider*, fr. *riden* to ride + *-ere, -er* -er; akin to OE *rīdan* to ride — more at RIDE] : KNIGHT; *specif* : a member of one of the lowest orders of German or Austrian nobility

ritt·master *or* **rit·master** \ˈrit+,-\ *n* [part trans. of G *rittmeister*, fr. *ritt* troop of horsemen (fr. *reiten* to ride, fr. OHG *rītan*) + *meister* master — more at RIDE] *archaic* : a captain of cavalry

¹**rit·u·al** \ˈrich(ə)wəl, -chəl\ *adj* [L *ritualis*, fr. *ritus* rite + *-alis* -al — more at RITE] : of, relating to, or employed in rites or a ritual : forming a ritual : CEREMONIAL ⟨a ~ dance of Haiti —Nicolas Slonimsky⟩ ⟨the kind of material and the kind of knot have great ~ importance —N.F.Busch⟩ ⟨relatives and most ardent disciples, paying their ~ calls —*Time*⟩ ⟨our favorite ~ phrases —James Blish⟩ ⟨sedate little colonial tribe, with its ~ tea parties and tennis parties —Nadine Gordimer⟩

²**ritual** \"\ *n* -s **1** : the forms of conducting a devotional service esp. as established by tradition or by sacerdotal prescription : the prescribed order and words of a religious ceremony ⟨the rain ~ is simple —M.A.Jaspan⟩ ⟨thus the religion becomes more and more of an empty ~ —C.W.Thayer⟩ **2 a** : a code or system of rites (as of a fraternal society) ⟨the opposition party is compelled by parliamentary ~ to vote no —V.O.Key⟩ **b** : any practice done or regularly repeated in a set precise manner so as to satisfy one's sense of fitness and often felt to have a symbolic or quasi-symbolic significance ⟨busy among her pots and pans, making a ~ of her household duties —W.S.Maugham⟩ ⟨essential to reach a cave round the next headland where she would sit down facing the sea before she thought about anything — thus making a little ~ against despair —Audrey Barker⟩ **3 a** : a book containing the rites or ceremonial forms to be observed by an organization (as a church or fraternal society) **b** : the verbal formulas of ritual **4** : an act of ritual ⟨to take your girl to the flicks on Saturday night is a ~ —John Berger⟩ ⟨the neurotic is isolated by his very ~*s* —David Riesman⟩ ⟨the elaborate ~*s* of present-day medicine —*Jour. Amer. Med. Assoc.*⟩ **syn** see FORM

rit·u·al·ism \-ə,lizəm\ *n* -s **1** : a conducting of religious worship according to a ritual : the use of ritual **2** : adherence to or observance of a ritual or ritualistic forms; *often* : excessive devotion to prescribed ritual forms in worship **3** : the study of ritual and its use

rit·u·al·ist \-ələst\ *n* -s **1** : one skilled in or attached to a ritual : one who studies ritual **2 a** : one who advocates or practices the increased use of religious ritual esp. to an extent often

deemed excessive by others **b** *usu cap* **:** a member of the High Church party in the Anglican communion **3 :** one rigidly conforming to established procedures or institutional norms ⟨the syndrome of the social ~ —R.K.Merton⟩ ⟨like a trout fisherman he is a fanatical ~ —Bernard DeVoto⟩
rit·u·al·is·tic \ˌrich(ə)wə¦listik, -chə¦l-, -tēk\ *adj* **1 :** of, in accordance with, or characterized by the use of ritual ⟨~ work of a lodge⟩ **2 :** stressing the use of ritual forms **:** adhering to or devoted to ritualism ⟨a feudal or ~ society —Michael Polanyi⟩ — **rit·u·al·is·ti·cal·ly** \-tək(ə)lē, -tēk-, -li\ *adv*
rit·u·al·i·ty \ˌ(ˌ)rich(ə)ˈwalədē\ *n* -ES **:** ritual quality **:** RITUALISM ⟨openings, seasons, closings, all accomplished with majestic ~ —Arnold Gifford⟩
rit·u·al·iza·tion \ˌrich(ə)wələˈzāshən, -chəl-, -ˌlīˈz-\ *n* -S **:** the act of ritualizing **:** the condition of being ritualized
rit·u·al·ize \ˈ=(=)=ˌlīz\ *vb* -ED/-ING/-S *see -ize in Explan Notes*, *vi* **:** to practice ritualism ~ *vt* **1 :** to make a ritual of ⟨the *ritualized* spectacle of a bullfight —Wallace Stegner⟩ **2 :** to impose a ritual upon ⟨a highly *ritualized* society —Ernest Beaglehole⟩
rit·u·al·less \ˈrich(ə)wəl(l)əs, -chəl-\ *adj* **:** devoid of ritual **:** lacking a ritual
rit·u·al·ly \-chəlē, -ch(ə)wəlē, -li\ *adv* **:** by rites or by a particular rite **:** by or according to a ritual **:** as a ritual
ritual murder *n* **:** the sacrificial slaying of a human as a propitiatory offering to a deity
rit·wan \ˈritwən\ *n, pl* **ritwan** *or* **ritwans** *usu cap* **1 :** a language stock of northern California comprising Wiyot and Yurok and possibly related to Algonquian — see WEITSPEKAN, WISHOSKAN **2 a :** the peoples speaking Ritwan languages **b :** a member of any such peoples
¹ritz \ˈrits\ *vt* -ED/-ING/-ES [fr. the Ritz hotels] *slang* **:** to behave superciliously toward **:** SNUB
²ritz \"\ *n* -ES [fr. the Ritz hotels] *slang* **:** ostentatious display — used in the phrase *put on the ritz*
ritz·i·ly \-tsəlē, -li\ *adv* **:** in a ritzy manner
ritz·i·ness \-tsēnəs, -tsin-\ *n* -ES **:** the condition of being ritzy **:** OSTENTATION
ritzy \-sē, -si\ *adj* -ER/-EST [*Ritz* hotels (esp. the *Ritz-Carlton* in New York City) founded by or named for César *Ritz* †1918 Swiss entrepreneur + E -*y*] **1 :** ostentatiously smart in appearance or manner **:** ULTRAFASHIONABLE ⟨stayed at ~ hotels⟩ **2 :** HAUGHTY, SNOBBISH
ri·vage \ˈrīvij, ˈriv-\ *n* -S [ME, fr. MF, fr. *rive* bank, shore (fr. L *ripa*) + *-age* — more at RIVE] **1** *archaic* **:** SHORE, COAST, BANK **2** *old Eng law* **:** a duty paid to the crown for the passage of ships on various rivers
ri·vage green \rəˈväzh-\ *n* **:** a moderate yellow green to light yellowish green
¹ri·val \ˈrīvəl\ *n* -S [MF or L; MF, fr. L *rivalis* one having water rights to the same stream as another, rival in love, fr. *rivalis*, adj., of a brook or stream, fr. *rivus* brook, stream + *-alis* -al — more at RISE] **1 a :** one of two or more striving for what only one can possess ⟨~*s* for the throne⟩ **b :** one striving for competitive advantage ⟨~*s* in business⟩ **2** *obs* **:** ASSOCIATE, COMPANION ⟨the ~*s* of my watch —Shak.⟩ **3 :** one that equals another in the possession of desired qualities or aptitudes **:** PEER ⟨was easily Carson's ~ as a pistol shot —Willa Cather⟩ ⟨a cathedral that is the ~ of any in Christendom⟩
²rival \"\ *adj* **:** having the same pretensions or claims **:** COMPETING, CONTESTING ⟨problem of the ~ claims of sense and reason —Benjamin Farrington⟩ ⟨a world where ~ propagandists are perpetually blazing falsehoods at us —Bertrand Russell⟩ ⟨tried to make myself persona grata to ~ factions —V.G.Heiser⟩ ⟨~ labor unions⟩
³rival \"\ *vb* **rivaled** *or* **rivalled**; **rivaled** *or* **rivalled**; **rivaling** *or* **rivalling** \-v(ə)liŋ\ **rivals** *vi* **:** to act as a rival **:** COMPETE ⟨friends ~*ing* in good deeds⟩ ~ *vt* **1 :** to be in competition with **:** strive to gain some object in opposition to **2 :** to strive to equal or excel **:** EMULATE **3 :** to possess qualities or aptitudes that equal (those of another) ⟨such ancient glass as we have in our parish churches ~*s* any in the world —Ivor Bulmer-Thomas⟩ ⟨growing rich in a boom that ~*ed* the Yukon gold rush —*Amer. Guide Series: Mich.*⟩ **syn** see MATCH
ri·val·i·ty \rīˈvalədē\ *n* -ES [L *rivalitas*, fr. *rivalis* rival + *-itas* -ity — more at RIVAL] **:** RIVALRY
ri·val·ize \ˈrīvəˌlīz\ *vi* -ED/-ING/-S **:** to act as a rival ⟨her urge to ~ with menfolk in the things of the mind —Frank Budgen⟩
ri·val·less \-vəl(l)əs\ *adj* **:** being without a rival
ri·val·rous \-vəlrəs\ *adj* [*rivalry* + *-ous*] **:** given to rivalry **:** COMPETITIVE ⟨ascendant, expansive, and ~ students —F.H. Allport⟩ ⟨one of the leading families has shown a ~ attitude toward the others —M.C.Yang⟩ — **ri·val·rous·ness** *n* -ES
ri·val·ry \ˈrīvəlrē, -ri\ *n* -ES [¹*rival* + *-ry*] **1 :** the act of rivaling **:** the state of being a rival **:** COMPETITION ⟨sibling ~ in our society —Weston LaBarre⟩ ⟨~ and even antagonism between the two nations —Edward Shils⟩ ⟨excitable subjects are prone to overstimulation through ~ —F.H.Allport⟩ **2 :** an instance of rivalry ⟨public reaction to the *rivalries* of the court factions —Evelyn G. Cruickshanks⟩ **3 :** RETINAL RIVALRY
ri·val·ship \-lˌship\ *n* **:** RIVALRY
¹rive \ˈrīv\ *vb* **rived** \ˈrīvd\ *also* **rove** \ˈrōv\ **riv·en** \ˈrivən\ *also* **rived** \ˈrīvd\ **riv·ing** \ˈrīviŋ\ **rives** \ˈrīvz\ [ME *riven*, fr. ON *rífa*; akin to OFris *rīva* to tear, rend, L *ripa* bank, shore, Gk *ereipein* to dash down, tear down, OE *rāw* row — more at ROW] *vt* **1 a :** to wrench open or tear apart or to pieces ⟨great gray masses of cloud, *riven* by the hurricane —William Black⟩ **b :** to split or break up by or as if by a sharp instrument **:** CLEAVE, SEVER ⟨new highways *riving* the green —Donald Davidson⟩ **c :** to break or crack by or as if by a shock or impact **:** BURST ⟨*riven* pinnacles of stone gnawed by the waves into bizarre shapes —Norman Douglas⟩ **d :** PIERCE ⟨not dug by the hand of man, these tunnels, but *riven* by nature —I.L.Idriess⟩ **e** (1) **:** to divide into many pieces or factions **:** SHATTER ⟨were *riven* with fears and alarms about subversion at home —Reinhold Niebuhr⟩ ⟨the union is *riven* with discord —Earl Brown⟩ ⟨bellows of triumph ~ the night —H.H.Martin⟩ (2) **:** FRACTURE ⟨a country so often *riven* by earthquakes —G.B.Sansom⟩ ⟨detrital beds . . . *riven* by a series of faults —*Amer. Guide Series: Md.*⟩; *specif* **:** to crack or break up by the alternate freezing and thawing of water contained in fissures ⟨where massive rock . . . is exposed in polar regions and on high mountain summits, frost *riving* is the dominant weathering process —O. D. Von Engeln⟩ ⟨brecciated bedrock, perhaps largely frost-*riven* —*Jour. of Geol.*⟩ **2 a :** to wrench or tear away ⟨cloak *riven* from his back⟩ — often used with *off* or *away* ⟨bark of the trunk was *riven off*⟩ ⟨a few stout heaves *rived* off the upper part of the lid —Harvey Graham⟩ **b :** to pull or tear down or out ⟨storms . . . that ~ the trunks of tallest cedars down —Thomas Otway⟩ **c :** to split off ⟨huge rocks, *riven* by frost action from the side of the mountain —*Amer. Guide Series: N. H.*⟩ **3 :** to affect (as the heart or soul) with painful thoughts **:** stir by strong emotion ⟨all thoughts to ~ the heart are here —A.E.Housman⟩ ⟨his soul does not appear to have been *riven* by a consciousness of sin —H.O.Taylor⟩ ⟨a sudden craving *rived* him to be working again —Richard Llewellyn⟩ ⟨was plainly *riven* by anger —T.R.Fyvel⟩ **4 :** to make or form (as laths or boards) by splitting ⟨hand-*riven* shingles⟩ ⟨*rived* staves⟩ — often used with *out* ⟨went to work on those old cypress logs, sawing, chopping, hewing, and *riving* out boards to cover the house —Marjory S. Douglas⟩ **5** *Scot* **:** PLOW 1 ~ *vi* **1 :** to become split **:** CRACK ⟨the oak . . . *riving* and splitting round about the passage of the bullet —Thomas Fuller⟩ **2 :** to break esp. with sorrow **:** BURST ⟨he prays you as his heart would ~ . . . to save his dear son's soul alive —D.G.Rossetti⟩ **syn** see TEAR
²rive \ˈrīv\ *n* -S **1** *dial Eng* **:** PULL, TUG **2** *dial Eng* **:** CLEFT, RENT
¹riv·el \ˈrivəl\ *vb* **riveled** *or* **rivelled**; **riveled** *or* **rivelled**; **riveling** *or* **rivelling** \-v(ə)liŋ\ **rivels** [ME *rivelen*, fr. OE *gehriflian*; akin to LG *riffel* furrow, MD *riven* to rake, *rive* rake, OFris *rīve* rake, ON *hrīfa* to rake, and prob. to OE *sceran* to cut, shear — more at SHEAR] **:** WRINKLE, SHRIVEL
²rivel \"\ *n* -S **:** WRINKLE
¹riv·er \ˈrivə(r)\ *n* -S *often attrib* [ME *rivere*, *river*, fr. OF *rivere*, *riviere* riverbank, land along a river, river, fr. (assumed) VL *riparia*, fr. L, fem. of *riparius* riparian, fr. *ripa* bank, shore + *-arius* -ary — more at RIVE] **1 a :** a natural surface stream of water of considerable volume and permanent or seasonal flow ⟨~ channel⟩ ⟨~ gravel⟩ ⟨~ engineer⟩ — compare BROOK, CREEK **b :** WATERCOURSE ⟨dry ~⟩ ⟨underground ~⟩ **c :** ESTUARY, TIDAL RIVER ⟨York *River*, Va.⟩ ⟨Neponset *River*, Mass.⟩; *also* **:** INLET, STRAIT ⟨East *River*, N.Y.⟩ ⟨Sakonnet *River*, R.I.⟩ ⟨Indian *River*, Fla.⟩ **2 a :** something resembling a river ⟨~ of ice⟩ ⟨~ of air⟩ ⟨~*s* of lava glow an angry red —*Read Mag.*⟩ ⟨the enormous oceanic ~ of the Gulf Stream —Marjory S. Douglas⟩ ⟨costumes . . . made a rippling, many-colored ~ of the street —H.A.Sinclair⟩ ⟨the never-failing ~ of student life —J.B.Conant⟩ **b rivers** *pl* **:** copious flow **:** large or overwhelming quantities **:** OUTPOURING ⟨~*s* of birds pouring against the sunset back to the rookeries —Marjory S. Douglas⟩ ⟨rain, pouring down through the blackness in solid ~*s* —C.S.Forester⟩ ⟨~*s* of print that gushed forth about her —Mollie Panter-Downes⟩ ⟨drank ~*s* of coffee⟩ **3 :** a pure white diamond of very high grade occas. with a prismatic blue radiance **4 :** a white typically irregular streak or area running through several lines of close-set printed matter and caused by a series of wide spaces that appear to form a continuous line — called also *channel*, *gutter*, *staircase* — **down the river** *adv* (*or adj*) **:** into a less desirable situation than formerly **:** in an abandoned and inconsiderate manner **:** with damage to prestige, reputation, or status — used with *sell* — **up the river** *adv* (*or adj*) **:** to or in prison ⟨takes the rap and goes *up the river* —Nigel Balchin⟩
²riv·er \ˈrīvə(r)\ *n* -S [ME, one that rives, fr. *riven* to rive + *-er* — more at RIVE] **:** one that rives; *specif* **:** a worker who splits blocks of wood with a froe to make pickets, posts, or rails
¹riv·er·ain \ˈrivəˌrān, ˌ==ˈ=\ *adj* [F, fr. MF *riveran*, fr. *rivere*, *riviere* river — more at RIVER] **:** relating to a riverbank **:** situated or dwelling near or on a river **:** RIPARIAN ⟨wooded ~ districts —Cuthbert Christy⟩ ⟨~ tribes⟩ ⟨an immemorial ~ right —Eliot Gregory⟩
²riverain \"\ *n* -S [F, fr. *riverain*, adj.] **:** a district situated beside a river
river ash *n* **:** RED ASH 1a
riverbank \ˈ==ˌ=\ *n* **:** the bank of a river
riverbank grape *n* **:** a wild grape (*Vitis riparia*) abundant along riverbanks in the eastern U.S. and characterized by high climbing stems and acid blackish fruit
riverbank willow *n* **:** SANDBAR WILLOW a
river basin *n* **:** BASIN 3d
riverbed \ˈ==ˌ=\ *n* **:** the channel occupied or formerly occupied by a river
river birch *n* **1 :** an American birch (*Betula nigra*) having reddish brown bark and growing in swamps and river bottoms throughout the eastern U.S. **2 :** the hard close-grained brownish wood of the river birch tree **3 :** SWEET BIRCH
river blackfish *n* **:** a medium-sized food fish (*Gadopsis marmoratus*) of the Murray river system of Australia noted for its rich oily flesh
river black oak *n* **:** an Australian beefwood (*Casuarina suberosa*)
river blue *n* **:** a grayish blue to moderate greenish blue
riverboat \ˈ==ˌ=\ *n* **:** a boat (as a towboat, a barge, a shallow-draft passenger boat, or a rowboat) used on or plying a river
riv·er·boat·man \-mən\ *n, pl* **riverboatmen 1 :** the navigator of a riverboat **2 :** one employed on a riverboat
river bottom *n* **:** low-lying land along a river
river bottom disease *n* **:** INFECTIOUS ANEMIA
river brethren *n pl, usu cap R&B* [fr. the Susquehanna *river*, near which the denomination was formed] **:** members of a body of Christians formed about 1770 in Pennsylvania among Swiss and German immigrants, resembling the Mennonites in doctrines and practices, and now divided into the Brethren in Christ, the Yorker Brethren, and the United Zion Church
river bulrush *or* **river club rush** *n* **:** a stout perennial herb (*Scirpus fluviatilis*) with numerous spikelets in a large terminal umbel
riverbush \ˈ==ˌ=\ *n* **:** BUTTONBUSH
river carpsucker *n* **:** a carpsucker (*Carpiodes carpio*)
river chub *n* **:** HORNYHEAD CHUB
river coal *n* **:** coal dredged from riverbeds downstream from mining areas whence it has been washed
river cottonwood *n* **:** SWAMP COTTONWOOD
river crab *n* **1 :** a freshwater crab of the family Potamonidae; *esp* **:** a common crab (*Potamon fluviatile*) of flowing waters of southern Europe **2 :** a Central American grapsid crab (*Platychirograpsus typicus*) living in burrows along riverbanks
rivercraft \ˈ==ˌ=\ *n* **:** RIVERBOAT
river crawfish *n* **:** a crayfish living chiefly in rivers; *esp* **:** a small white crayfish (*Cambarus blandingi*) of the southeastern U.S.
river cress *n* **:** LAKE CRESS
river deer *n* **:** a small deer (*Hydropotes inermis*) of the river marshes in southern China the males of which have no antlers but are provided with tusklike canine teeth
river dog *n* **:** HELLBENDER 1a
river dolphin *n* **:** any of several So. American and Asiatic long-snouted dolphins (family Platanistidae) of medium size that are chiefly confined to freshwater
river driver *n* **:** one who drives logs on a river
river duck *n* **:** any of various rather small ducks chiefly of the genus *Anas* that typically nest and live about freshwater and usu. feed by dabbling
riv·ered \ˈrivə(r)d\ *adj* [¹*river* + *-ed*] **:** supplied with rivers ⟨such dew as only ~ lands beget —Eileen Duggan⟩
riveret *n* -S [MF *riverete*, dim. of *rivere*, *riviere* river — more at RIVER] *obs* **:** RIVULET
riverfront \ˈ==ˌ=\ *n* **:** the land or area along a river; *esp* **:** an area (as in a city) devoted to business done on the river
river-god \ˈ==ˌ=\ *n* **:** a deity supposed to preside over a river as its tutelary divinity
river grape *n* **:** CHICKEN GRAPE
river grass *n* **:** TEXAS MILLET
river gum *n* **:** an often somewhat crooked and irregular Australian red gum (*Eucalyptus rostrata* or *E. camaldulensis*) that grows chiefly along rivers, has lanceolate leaves, and yields a durable reddish lumber used in heavy construction
riverhead \ˈ==ˌ=\ *n* **:** the source of a river
river hog *n* **:** any of several stream-frequenting African wild hogs constituting the genus *Koiropotamus* — compare BUSHPIG, PAINTED PIG
river horse *n* **:** HIPPOPOTAMUS
riv·er·ine \ˈrivəˌrīn\ *adj* [¹*river* + *-ine*] **1 :** of, relating to, formed by, or resembling a river ⟨~ traffic⟩ ⟨~ gold-bearing deposits⟩ **2 :** living or situated on the banks of a river ⟨~ villages⟩ ⟨elephant feeding in the ~ thickets —*African Wild Life*⟩
river jack *n* **:** RHINOCEROS VIPER
river lamprey *n* **:** a river-dwelling lamprey; *esp* **:** LAMPERN
riv·er·less \ˈrivə(r)ləs\ *adj* **:** lacking a river
riv·er·let \ˈrivə(r)lət\ *n* -S [¹*river* + *-let*] **:** a little river
riverlike \ˈ==ˌ=\ *adj* **:** resembling a river
river limpet *n* **:** FRESHWATER LIMPET
river locust *n* **:** a false indigo (*Amorpha fruticosa*)
riv·er·ly \ˈrivə(r)lē\ *adj* **:** RIVERINE ⟨rivers . . . go about their ~ business of flowing into the seas —*Lamp*⟩
riv·er·man \-)mən\ *n, pl* **rivermen 1 :** one who lives and works on or along a river **2 :** RIVER DRIVER **3 :** a deckhand on a riverboat
river mangrove *n* **:** an Old World tropical tree (*Aegiceras majus*) of the family Myrsinaceae having the habit of a mangrove
river maple *n* **:** SILVER MAPLE
river mussel *n* **:** MUSSEL 2
river novel *n* [trans. of F *roman-fleuve*] **:** ROMAN-FLEUVE
river oak *n, Austral* **:** SHE-OAK
river pear *n* **:** ANCHOVY PEAR
river peppermint *n* **:** a medium-sized fast-growing peppermint gum (*Eucalyptus lindleyana*) that grows chiefly along watercourses
river perch *n* **:** YELLOW PERCH
river pine *n* **:** JERSEY PINE
river pink *n* **:** PINXTER FLOWER
river poplar *n* **:** BALSAM POPLAR
river prawn *n* **:** a large edible freshwater prawn (*Palaemon australis*) common in Australian rivers where it may reach a length of a foot or more — called also *long-clawed prawn*
river rat *n* **1 :** RIVERMAN 1 **2 :** one who spends his leisure time on or along a river
river red gum *n* **:** RIVER GUM
river rock *n* **:** a dark variety of phosphate rock obtained from stream beds
rivers *pl of* RIVER
river shad *n* **:** a shad that spawns in one of the streams of the Mississippi drainage and is prob. identical with the common American shad (*Alosa sapidissima*) but is sometimes considered a distinct species (*A. chrysochloris*)
river shark *n* **:** a small but ferocious shark (*Carcharinus lamia*) of tropical coastal waters and rivers
rivershed \ˈ==ˌ=\ *n* **:** the watershed of a river
river shrew *n* **:** OTTER SHREW
river shrimp *n* **:** a common commercial freshwater shrimp (*Macrobrachium ohionis*) of the southeastern U.S.
riverside \ˈ==ˌ=\ *n* [ME, fr. *river* + *side*] **:** the side or bank of a river **:** RIVERFRONT ⟨the ~*s* had been only partly drained —D.R.Macgregor⟩
riverside grape *n* **1 :** CHICKEN GRAPE **2 :** RIVERBANK GRAPE
riverside tobacco *n* **:** WILD TOBACCO 3
river tern *n* **:** a tern (*Sterna aurantia*) of India that frequents rivers
river terrace *n* **:** STREAM TERRACE
river trout *n* **1 :** a small brownish green trout that is a variety of the European brown trout **2 :** WALLEYE 4
riv·er·ward \ˈrivə(r)wə(r)d\ *or* **riv·er·wards** \-dz\ *adv* (*or adj*) [¹*river* + *-ward*, *-wards*] **:** toward a river ⟨door on the ~ side —D.C.Peattie⟩
riverwash \ˈ==ˌ=\ *n* **:** soil material transported and deposited by streams
riverway \ˈ==ˌ=\ *n* **:** a river used to convey traffic ⟨battled up the ~*s* of the unhappy land —John Craig⟩
riverweed \ˈ==ˌ=\ *n* **:** a plant of the genus *Podostemon*
riverweed family *n* **:** PODOSTEMONACEAE
riv·ery \ˈriv(ə)rē, -)ri\ *adj* **1 :** having many streams of water ⟨amid the thresh of weirs in the ~ lands —Louis Golding⟩ **2 :** of, relating to, or resembling a river ⟨a ~ field spread out below —W.B.Yeats⟩ ⟨~ pleasures —*Times Lit. Supp.*⟩
rives *pres 3d sing of* RIVE, *pl of* RIVE
¹riv·et \ˈrivət, *usu* -əd·+V\ *n* -S [ME *ryvette*, *revette*, fr. MF *river* to be attached] **:** a headed pin or bolt of some malleable material (as wrought iron, mild steel, or copper) used for uniting two or more pieces by passing the shank through a hole in each piece and then beating or pressing down the plain end so as to make a second head

rivets: *1* steeple-head, *2* button-head, *3* countersunk, *4* conehead

²rivet \"\ *vt* **riveted** *also* **rivetted**; **riveted** *also* **rivetted**; **riveting** *also* **rivetting**; **rivets** [ME *rivetten*, *reveten*, fr. *ryvette*, *revette*, n.] **1 :** to fasten with or as if with rivets ⟨~ two pieces of iron⟩ ⟨copper ~*ing* for pants —*Fortnight*⟩ ⟨could not drink tea from ~*ed* china —Elizabeth Taylor⟩ **2 :** to upset the end or point of (as a metallic pin, rod, or bolt) by beating or pressing so as to form a head **:** PEEN **3 :** to fasten firmly **:** make firm, strong, or immovable **:** fix closely (as the eye, gaze, or mind) ⟨made abundant gifts to ~ this fealty —Bernard DeVoto⟩ ⟨stood ~*ed* to the earth . . . in the fascination of that dreaded gaze —Sheridan Le Fanu⟩ ⟨reporters' attention was temporarily ~*ed* on some pelicans —Percy Sillitoe⟩ **4 :** to attract and hold engrossingly (as the attention) ⟨another part of the room soon ~*ed* her gaze —Thomas Hardy⟩
rivet buster *n* **:** a tool that resembles a chisel and is used for knocking off rivet heads
riv·et·er *also* **riv·et·ter** \-əd·ə(r), -ətə-\ *n* -S **1 :** a worker who inserts and upsets rivets by hand or by machine **2 :** a riveting machine
rivet forge *or* **riveting forge** *also* **rivet hearth** *n* **:** a forge for heating rivets
rivet heater *n* **1 :** RIVET FORGE **2 :** a worker who heats rivets in a rivet forge
rivet hole *n* **:** the drilled or punched hole in which a rivet is to be inserted
riveting *n* -S [¹*rivet* + *-ing*] **1 :** the act of one who rivets **2 :** the work of a riveter **3 :** a set of rivets
riveting die *n* **:** SETTING PUNCH
riveting hammer *n* **:** a hammer usu. with a flat face and cross peen used for driving rivets and beating metal
riveting stake *n* **:** a block of steel used in watchmaking that is pierced with holes for the reception of arbors so that the pinion or collet to be riveted finds a resting place round the edge of a suitable hole
rivet knob *or* **riveting knob** *n* **:** SETTING PUNCH
riv·et·less \-ətləs\ *adj* **:** made without rivets
rivet line *n* **:** a line through the centers of a row of rivets
rivet pitch *n* **:** the distance between the centers of adjacent rivets that hold together the parts of a built member
rivet set *or* **riveting set** *n* **:** SETTING PUNCH
rivet snap *n* **:** SNAP 11a
rivet weld *n* **:** a weld having the form of a countersunk-head rivet and serving as a rivet
rivet wheat *n* **:** POULARD WHEAT
riv·i·era \ˌrivēˈerə, rəvˈye-ˌrevˈye-\ *n* -S *often cap* [fr. the *Riviera*, region much frequented as a resort area on the Mediterranean in southeastern France and northwestern Italy] **:** a coastline much frequented as a resort area and usu. having a mild climate ⟨the Cornish *Riviera*⟩ ⟨other men were living riotously on ~*s* —Clare & Harris Wofford⟩
riv·i·ère \ˌrivē¦e(ə)r, rəvˈye-, revˈye-\ *n* -S [F, lit., river, fr. OF *rivere*, *riviere* riverbank, land along a river, river — more at RIVER] **:** a necklace of diamonds or other precious stones
ri·vi·na \rəˈvīnə, -vēnə\ *n, cap* [NL, after August Q. *Rivinus* (Bachmann) †1723 Ger. botanist and physiologist] **:** a small genus of tropical American herbs (family Phytolaccaceae) having small racemose pink flowers succeeded by flattened red berries — see BLOODBERRY
riving *pres part of* RIVE
riving knife *n* **:** FROE
riving machine *n* **:** a machine for splitting wood (as for making staves or shingles)
rivo *interj* [prob. modif. of Sp *arriba* up, up with (often used in interjectional phrases), fr. *a* to (fr. L *ad*) + *riba* slope, embankment, fr. L *ripa* bank, shore — more at AT, RIVE] *obs* — used as an encouragement to drink and be merry
ri·vol·ta·sia \ˌrivəlˈtāzh(ē)ə\ *n, cap* [NL] **:** a genus of mites that occur on the skin and feathers of birds
riv·u·lar·ia \ˌrivyəˈla(a)rēə\ *n, cap* [NL, fr. L *rivulus* rivulet + NL *-aria* — more at RIVULET] **:** a genus (the type of the family Rivulariaceae) of blue-green algae with radially arranged filaments exhibiting false branching and forming spherical to irregular somewhat gelatinous colonies
riv·u·lar·i·a·ce·ae \ˌ==ˌ==ˈāsēˌē\ *n pl, cap* [NL, fr. *Rivularia*, type genus + *-aceae*] **:** a family of freshwater blue-green algae (order Hormogonales) consisting of slender gradually attenuated or hair-tipped filaments usu. growing in tufts attached to the substrate and frequently mucilaginous — see CALOTHRIX, RIVULARIA — **riv·u·lar·i·a·ceous** \ˌ==ˌ==¦āshəs\ *adj*
riv·u·let \ˈrivyələt, *usu* -əd·+V\ *n* -S [modif. (influenced by L *rivulus* rivulet) of It *rivoletto*, dim. of *rivolo*, fr. L *rivulus*, dim. of *rivus* brook, stream — more at RISE] **:** a small stream **:** BROOK, RUNNEL, STREAMLET ⟨rills running down the steepest slopes develop into ~*s* —C.A.Cotton⟩ ⟨~*s* of melted snow coursing along the ruts —F.V.W.Mason⟩ ⟨~*s* of perspiration ran down their flushed cheeks —Kenneth Roberts⟩
riv·u·lose \ˈrivyəˌlōs\ *adj* [L *rivulus* rivulet + E *-ose*] **:** marked with irregular, narrow, sinuous, or crooked lines ⟨a ~ thallus⟩
riv·u·lus \-ləs\ *n, cap* [NL, fr. L, rivulet — more at RIVULET] **:** a large genus of brightly colored but often sluggish So. and Central American killifishes several species of which are sometimes kept in a tropical aquarium
rix \ˈriks\ *dial var of* ¹RUSH 1a
rix·da·ler \ˈriksˌdälə(r)\ *n* [fr. obs. D *rijksdaler* — more at RIJKSDAALDER] **:** RIJKSDAALDER

rix-dollar \"\ *n* [part trans. of obs. D *rijksdaler*] **1 :** any of various old dollar coins of Germany, the Netherlands, or Scandinavia **:** REICHSTALER, RIGSDALER, RIKSDALER, RIJKSDAALDER **2 :** any of several silver coins formerly issued by England for colonies (as Ceylon, Cape Colony) **3 :** RIJKSDAALDER 2

rixy \ˈriksi\ *n, pl* **rix·ies** [origin unknown] *dial Eng* **:** TERN

ri·yadh \rēˈ(y)äd\ *adj, usu cap* [fr. *Riyadh*, Saudi Arabia] **:** of or from Riyadh, a capital of Saudi Arabia **:** of the kind or style prevalent in Riyadh

ri·yal *or* **ri·al** \rēˈ(y)ȯl, -)äl\ *n, pl* **riyal** *or* **riyals** *or* **rial** *or* **rials** [Ar *riyāl*, fr. Sp *real* — more at REAL (coin)] **1 :** a silver coin of Saudi Arabia equivalent to 1/10 pound sterling when first issued in 1928 **2 :** MARIA THERESA DOLLAR **3 :** a coin of Iraq equivalent to 1/5 dinar **4 a :** the basic monetary unit of Qatar and Saudi Arabia — see MONEY table **b :** a coin or note representing one riyal

riz *dial past of* RISE

ri·zal day \rəˈzäl-, rēˈsäl-\ *n, usu cap R&D* [after José *Rizal* †1896 Philippine patriot] **:** December 30, observed as a legal holiday in the Philippines in commemoration of the death of the Filipino patriot José Rizal in 1896

rizotto *var of* RISOTTO

¹riz·zar \ˈrizər\ *n* -s [prob. fr. obs. F *ressoré* dried in the sun] *Scot* **:** RED CURRANT

²rizzar \"\ *n* -s [prob. fr. obs. F *ressoré* dried in the sun] **1** *Scot* **:** the act or process of drying or curing in the sun **2** *Scot* **:** a dry haddock cured in the sun

³rizzar \"\ *vt* -ED/-ING/-s *Scot* **:** to dry or cure (fish) in the sun

riz·zom *var of* RISSOM

RJ *abbr* road junction

rk *abbr* rock

RK *abbr* run of kiln

rkt *abbr* rocket

RKVA *abbr, often not cap* reactive kilovolt-ampere

rky *abbr* rocky

RL *abbr* **1** radiolocation **2** *often not cap* random lengths **3** reduced level **4** rhumb line **5** right line **6** rocket launcher

RL and R *abbr* rail, lake, and rail

r-less \ˈärləs, ˈäl-\ *adj, of a dialect of English* **:** having with varying regularity as the speech counterpart of a prepausal or preconsonantal orthographic *r* the sound \ə\ or greater duration or nothing at all instead of the retroflex sound of some dialects

RLF *abbr* retrolental fibroplasia

RLO *abbr* returned letter office

rls *abbr* release

rly *abbr* railway

rm *abbr* **1** ream **2** room

RM *abbr* **1** radioman **2** reichsmark **3** resident magistrate **4** royal mail

r-meter \ˈär,mēd·ər\ *n* **:** an instrument or device for measuring the intensity of X rays or gamma radiation

RMI *abbr* radio magnetic indicator

r month *n, usu cap R* [so called fr. the fact that the letter *r* appears in the name of each month] **:** one of the months from September to April during which oysters are traditionally in season in the northern hemisphere

RMS *abbr* **1** railway mail service **2** *often not cap* root-mean-square **3** royal mail ship; royal mail steamer

rmt *abbr* remount

RN *abbr* **1** registered nurse **2** Reynolds number

Rn *symbol* radon

RNA *abbr or n* -s ribonucleic acid

rnd *abbr* round

rng *abbr* range

rnwy *abbr* runway

ro \ˈrō\ *n* -s *usu cap* [coined 1906 by Edward P. Foster †1937 Am. clergyman] **:** an artificial language intended to be international that rejects all existing words and roots and is based on analysis and classification of ideas — **ro·ist** \ˈrōəst\ *n* -s *usu cap*

ro *abbr* **1** recto **2** road **3** roan **4** rood **5** [F *rouble*] ruble

RO *abbr* **1** radar operator **2** receiving office **3** reconnaissance officer **4** recruiting officer **5** regimental order **6** royal observatory **7** royal octavo

¹roach \ˈrōch\ *n* -ES [ME *roche*, fr. OF, rock, fr. (assumed) VL *rocca* — more at ROCK] **1** *dial Eng* **:** a stony hill **:** ROCK **2 :** gravelly or stony soil **:** refuse stone

²roach \"\ *n, pl* **roach** *also* **roaches** [ME *roche*, fr. MF, fr. OF, of unknown origin] **1 a :** a silver-white European freshwater cyprinid fish (*Rutilus rutilus*) with a greenish back **b :** any of various other cyprinid fishes (as the No. American golden shiner) **2 :** any of several American freshwater sunfishes (family Centrarchidae) **3 :** SPOT 7

³roach \"\ *vt* -ED/-ING/-ES [origin unknown] **1 :** to cause to arch; *specif* **:** to brush (the hair) in a roach — often used with *up* **2 :** to cut off (as a horse's mane) so the part left stands upright **3 :** to cut (a sail) with a roach

⁴roach \"\ *n* -ES **1 :** a curved cut in the edge of a sail and esp. in the leech or foot to prevent chafing or to secure a better fit **2 :** a roll of hair brushed straight back from the forehead or occas. the side of the head **3 :** a sheet of water thrown upwards behind the float of a seaplane

⁵roach \"\ *n* -ES [short for *cockroach*] **1 :** COCKROACH **2 :** the butt of a marijuana cigarette

roachback \ˈ=,=\ *n* [³*roach* + *back*, n.] *West* **:** GRIZZLY BEAR

roach back \ˈ=ˈ=\ *n* [³*roach* + *back*, n.] **:** an arched back

¹road \ˈrōd\ *n* -s [ME *road*, *rode*, fr. OE *rād* ride, riding, journey; akin to MD *rede* ride, manner of riding, ON *reith* vehicle, riding; derivative fr. the root of OE *rīdan* to ride — more at RIDE] **1** *obs* **a** (1) **:** the act of riding on a horse (2) **:** a journey on horseback **b :** an armed hostile incursion on horseback against a person or place **:** FORAY, RAID **2 :** ROADSTEAD — often used in pl. ⟨shipping lying in the ~s —Mary Johnston⟩ ⟨Hampton *Roads*, Virginia⟩ **3 a :** an open way or public passage for vehicles, persons, and animals **:** a track for travel or transportation to and fro serving as a means of communication between two places usu. having distinguishing names **b :** a public way outside of an urban district **:** HIGHWAY — contrasted with *street* **c :** the part of a thoroughfare over which vehicular traffic moves **:** the space between curbs **:** ROADWAY **d :** a vehicular way for local traffic: as (1) **:** a private way (2) **:** one that is unpaved (3) **:** one located in a rural area **e :** STREET, AVENUE — used esp. in arterial street names **4 a :** a route followed on a journey **:** WAY, PATH ⟨get out of my ~⟩ ⟨knew that the Arkansas river, with its tributaries . . . was the ~ to the southwest —*Amer. Guide Series: Ark.*⟩ **b :** the course or route to an end, conclusion, or circumstance ⟨the path of promotion lay through the schools rather than along the ~ of military service —R.W.Southern⟩ **5 :** public highways ⟨take to the ~⟩ **6 :** RAILROAD, RAILWAY **7 :** GANGWAY 4 **8 :** the places and routes frequented on a tour (as of a theatrical troupe or a sports team) ⟨community theater attempted to fill the need which the professional ~ either failed to meet or failed to find —W.C.Glackin⟩ — **for the road** *adv* **:** as a friendly gesture of farewell ⟨gave me a final glass *for the road* —T.H.White b.1906⟩ ⟨gave the passenger ship one more blast *for the road* —R.F.Mirvish⟩ — **on the road** *adv* (*or adj*) **1 :** away from home usu. in regular travel on business esp. as a traveling salesman **2 :** in transit through a circuit of scheduled performances or games in several centers ⟨a brief stage career *on the road*, in summer stock, and on Broadway —*Current Biog.*⟩ ⟨the team is *on the road*⟩ — **over the road** *adv* **:** to prison

²road *vt* -ED/-ING/-s **1** *of a dog* **:** to track (a game bird) by the foot scent **2 :** to put or drive onto or carry on a road

road·abil·i·ty \,rōdəˈbiləd·ē, -lətē, -i\ *n* [¹*road* + *-ability*] **:** the qualities (as steadiness, flexibility in speed, and balance) that are desirable in an automobile on the road

road·able \ˈrōdəbəl\ *adj* [¹*road* + *-able*] **1 :** capable of being driven along roads like an automobile usu. under power delivered to one or more wheels **2** *of an airplane* **:** capable of being transformed into an automobile by removal or folding of wings and tail

road actor *n* **:** a performer in a company playing only on the road

road agent *n* **:** a highwayman esp. on stage routes

road band *n* **:** a steel rim attached to steel tractor wheels to prevent damage to the road by the lugs on the tractor wheels

roadbed \ˈ=,=\ *n* **1 a :** the bed or foundation of a railroad on which the ties, rails, and ballast rest **b :** the ballast or the upper surface of the ballast on which the ties rest **2 a :** the earth foundation of a highway or street, graded and prepared for paving or surfacing **b :** the part of the surface of a highway or street traveled by vehicles

¹roadblock \ˈ=,=\ *n* **1 a :** a barricade (as of concrete, logs, boards, sandbags, barbed wire) often with traps or mines for holding up an enemy's advance at a point on the road covered by heavy fire from shelter **b :** a road barricade set up esp. by law enforcement officers **c :** an obstruction in a road caused by wrecked vehicles, fallen trees, landslides, or debris **2 :** a fact, condition, or countermeasure that blocks progress along a course or that prevents accomplishment of an objective ⟨the hope that something could be done to remove the ~ of the filibuster —P.H.Douglas⟩

²roadblock \"\ *vt* -ED/-ING/-s **:** to put a roadblock in the way of

roadbook \"\ *n* **:** a guidebook esp. devoted to routes and distances

road brand *n* **:** a lightly burned brand marked upon all the cattle of a herd driven beyond a county line when the herd is composed of cattle from various owners

road breaker *n* **:** a powered tool to break up road pavements

road builder *n* **:** one that builds roads

road cart *n* **:** a light 2-wheeled vehicle often with a back

road coach *n* **:** the stagecoach as revived in England during the last half of the 19th century

road commissioner *n* **:** a local or county official who supervises the construction of roads

road donkey *n* **:** a stationary donkey engine mounted on a sled for dragging logs along a skid road by a cable wound on a drum

road drag *n* **:** a drag for smoothing dirt roads with an unpacked surface

road·ed \ˈrōdəd\ *adj* **:** provided with roads

road engine *n* **:** a locomotive used in line-haul service — compare SWITCH ENGINE

road·eo \ˈrōdē,ō\ *n* -s [blend of ¹*road* and *rodeo*, n.] **:** a contest featuring events that test driving skill esp. of professional truck drivers

road·er \ˈrōdə(r)\ *n* -s **1 :** a craft anchored in a roadstead **2 :** ROADSTER 1 **3 :** ROAD DONKEY

road freight conductor *n* **:** a railroad employee who takes charge of the makeup for freight trains and the removal of freight at destinations

road game *n* **:** a sports contest (as a baseball or basketball game) played while a team is on the road; *broadly* **:** a game played at an opponent's field, court, or stadium

road gang *n* **:** a crew of men building or working on a road

road goose *n, Brit* **:** a brant (*Branta bernicla*)

road grade *n* **:** the level and gradient of a roadway determined along the center line

road grader *or* **road machine** *also* **road scraper** *n* **:** a wheeled device having a long inclined vertically adjustable steel blade used to throw earth and other surface material from the side to the center of a road

road hack *n* **:** a fast trotting horse for saddle or harness use

road harrow *n* **:** a harrow designed to reshape a disturbed surface of a gravel-covered or stone-covered road

roadhead \ˈ=,=\ *n* **:** the end of a road: as **a :** one where men and goods must continue on foot or on animals ⟨heroic bands of soldiers labor . . . to keep the trucks moving through to the ~, where mules or porters will take over the traffic —G.H. Johnston⟩ **b :** the farthest point reached by a road under construction

road hog *n* **:** a driver esp. of an automotive vehicle who selfishly obstructs others using the road esp. by occupying part of another's traffic lane

road horse *n* **:** a driving or carriage horse for use on a road

roadhouse \ˈ=,=\ *n* **1 a :** an inn furnishing meals and lodging to travelers **b :** an often rudely constructed hotel or lodge in Alaska and northern Canada **2 :** an inn or tavern usu. located outside city limits and set up for serving liquor and usu. meals, for dancing, and often for gambling

road·ing \ˈrōdiŋ\ *n* -s **:** highway construction and maintenance

road·less \-dləs\ *adj* **1 :** having no roads **2 :** legally barred to the construction of permanent roads but open to temporary roads (as for logging or driving cattle) — **road·less·ness** *n* -ES

roadmaker \ˈ=,==\ *n* **:** one that makes roads

road making *n* **:** the process or technique of constructing roads

road·man \ˈrōd,man, -,mən\ *n, pl* **roadmen** **1 a :** one who works at the building and repairing of roads and esp. of logging roads **b :** one who makes, repairs, or keeps clean the roads of a mine **2 a :** PEDDLER, CANVASSER, TRAVELING SALESMAN **b :** one who manages the sales and distribution of a newspaper within a specific county district

road map *n* **:** a map showing roads esp. for automobile travel

roadmaster \ˈ=,==\ *n* **1 :** a railroad maintenance official in charge of a division of from 50 to 150 miles of roadway **2 :** a public overseer of repairs of roads

road mender *n* **:** one that repairs roads

road metal *n* **:** broken stone or cinders used in making and repairing roads or ballasting railroads

road mix *n* **:** a mixture of aggregate and bituminous binder rolled down to provide a road surface

road monkey *n* **:** a man who inspects and repairs a logging road

roadnet \ˈ=,=\ *n* **:** the system of roads within an area

road oil *n* **:** oil (as from asphalt-base petroleum) put on roads to lay the dust and act as a waterproof binder

road pen *n* **:** a special pen with two points used by map makers

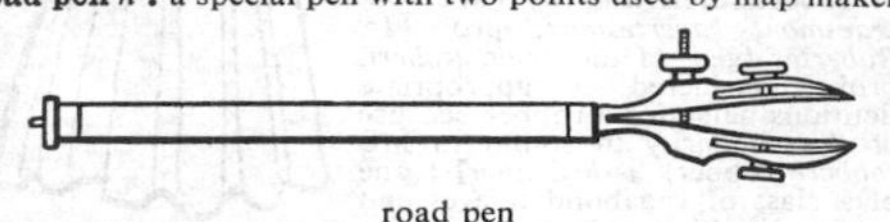

road pen

in representing roads

road ripper *n* **:** SCARIFIER

road roller *n* **:** one that rolls roadways; *specif* **:** a machine equipped with heavy wide smooth rollers for compacting roads and pavements

roadrunner \ˈ=,==\ *n* **1 :** a bird (*Geococcyx californianus*) of largely terrestrial habits that resembles a cuckoo and is noted for running with great speed and that ranges from California to Mexico and eastward to Texas — called also *chaparral bird* **2 :** a Mexican bird (*Geococcyx velox*) similar and closely related to the roadrunner

roads *pl of* ROAD, *pres 3d sing of* ROAD

road shock *n* **:** the sensation experienced at the steering wheel of a vehicle traveling over a rough pavement

road show *n* **1 :** a theatrical performance given by a troupe on tour **2 :** a special engagement of a new motion picture usu. at advanced prices

road-show \ˈ=,=\ *vt* [*road show*] **:** to present (a motion picture) as a road show

¹roadside \ˈ=,=\ *n* **:** the strip of land adjoining a road **:** the side of a road

²roadside \"\ *adj* **:** situated at the side of a road; *specif* **:** located along a highway and accessible to motorists ⟨~ café⟩

roadside thistle *n* **1 :** BULL THISTLE **2 :** TALL THISTLE

road sign *n* **:** a sign bearing information about a road

roads·man \ˈrōdzmən\ *n, pl* **roadsmen** [*road's* (gen. of ¹*road*) + *man*] **:** ROADMAN 1

road·stead \ˈrōdz,ted, -dst-, -ōd,st-\ *n* **:** a place less sheltered or enclosed than a harbor where ships may ride at anchor

road·ster \ˈrōdztə(r), -dst-\ *n* -s **1 a :** ROAD HORSE **b :** a utility saddle horse of the hackney type — distinguished from *hunter* and *charger* **2 a :** HIGHWAYMAN **b :** TRAMP **3 a** *Brit* **:** a sturdy bicycle adapted for ordinary use on common roads **b :** a light carriage **:** BUGGY **c :** an automobile with an open body having one cross seat and a luggage compartment in the rear or sometimes a rumble seat

roadstone \ˈ=,=\ *n* **:** stone for making roads

¹road test *n* **:** a test of a vehicle or driver under practical operating conditions on the road

²road test *vt* **:** to administer a road test on or to

road wagon *n* **:** a wagon for use on common roads; *esp* **:** BUGGY

roadway \ˈ=,=\ *n* **1 a :** the strip of land through which a road is constructed and which is physically altered **b :** ROAD; *specif* **:** the part of a road over which the vehicular traffic travels **2 :** the right of way of a railroad with tracks, structures, and appurtenances necessary for the operation of trains **3 :** the part of a bridge used by vehicles

road wheel *n* **:** a vehicular wheel that holds to the track or road but on which no driving power is exerted

roadwork \ˈ=,=\ *n* **:** work done on a road; *specif* **:** conditioning exercise in preparation for an athletic contest (as a boxing match or track event) consisting mainly of long runs in the open country

roadworthiness \ˈ=,===\ *n* **:** the quality or state of being roadworthy

roadworthy \ˈ=,==\ *adj* **:** fit for or for use on the road

¹roam \ˈrōm\ *vb* -ED/-ING/-s [ME *romen*; perh. akin to OE *ārǣman* to raise, ON *reimt* haunted, OE *rīsan* to rise — more at RISE] *vi* **1 a :** to go from place to place without a specific purpose or direction **:** ROVE, WANDER ⟨while various bands had moved to their reservations . . . they showed an increasing tendency to ~ —*Amer. Guide Series: Minn.*⟩ **b :** to travel purposefully throughout a wide area unhindered ⟨a mobile and elusive floating air base that can ~ at will over three-quarters of the globe —R.A.Ofstie⟩ **2** *obs* **:** to direct one's course **:** GO, PROCEED **3 :** to contemplate a wide range of thoughts or memories ⟨scientists have more to do . . . than to allow their imaginations to ~ at large —Joan Younger⟩ ~ *vt* **:** to range over **:** wander about ⟨cattle and sheep ~ hillside meadows — *Amer. Guide Series: N.C.*⟩ ⟨~*ing* the streets⟩ ⟨his imagination ~*ed* a continent —H.S.Commager⟩

²roam \"\ *n* -s **:** an act of roaming **:** WANDERING, RAMBLE

ro·a·mai·na \,rōəˈmīnə\ *n, pl* **roamaina** *or* **roamainas** *usu cap* **1 a :** a people of Ecuador and northern Peru of uncertain linguistic affiliation **b :** a member of the Roamaina people **2 :** the language of the Roamaina people

roam·er \ˈrōmə(r)\ *n* -s [ME *romere*, fr. *romen* to roam + *-ere* -er] **:** one that roams

roaming *adj* **:** that roams

¹roan \ˈrōn *sometimes* -ōən\ *adj* [MF, fr. OSp *roano*, prob. irreg. fr. Goth *rauths* red — more at RED] **1** *of an animal's coat* **:** having the base color (as black, red, gray, or brown) muted and lightened by a liberal admixture of white hairs — compare BLUE-ROAN, RED-ROAN, STRAWBERRY ROAN **2 :** of the color roan **3** [²*roan*] **:** made of roan ⟨~ binding⟩

²roan \"\ *n* -s **1 a :** an animal (as a horse) with a roan coat — usu. used of a red roan when unqualified; see BLUE-ROAN **b :** ROAN ANTELOPE **2 a :** the color of a roan horse — used esp. when the base color is red **b :** a moderate reddish brown that is redder and slightly lighter and stronger than mahogany, redder, less strong, and slightly lighter than oxblood, and redder and paler than Tuscan red **3 :** a sheepskin used esp. for bookbinding generally made from skins that are tanned with sumac and colored and finished to imitate morocco — distinguished from *basil*

roan antelope *n* **:** a southern African antelope (*Hippotragus equinus*) slightly larger and lighter-colored than the sable antelope

ro·a·noke \ˈrō(ə),nōk\ *n* -s [fr. *rawranoke* shell money (in some Algonquian language of Virginia), prob. fr. *rarenawok* smoothed shells, fr. *rar* to smooth, rub] **:** WAMPUM

roanoke bell *n, usu cap R* [fr. *Roanoke*, city in west central Virginia] **:** VIRGINIA COWSLIP

¹roar \ˈrō(ə)r, ˈrȯ(ə)r, -ōə, -ō(ə)\ *vb* -ED/-ING/-s [ME *roren*, fr. OE *rārian*; akin to MD *reren* to roar, OHG *rērēn* to bleat, Skt *rāyati* he barks] *vi* **1 a :** to utter or emit a full loud heavy prolonged sound ⟨the lions ~*ed*⟩ ⟨the little brass cannon ~*ed* again and again —*Amer. Guide Series: Tex.*⟩ **b :** to sing or shout with full force ⟨the lumbermen had their own songs, ~*ed* in the forests and in mill-town saloons —*Amer. Guide Series: Mich.*⟩ **2 a :** to make or emit a loud mixed confused sound (as background reverberation or rumbling) ⟨a city that normally grumbles and screeches and ~*s* —I.J.C.Brown⟩ **b :** to laugh out loudly and continuously with fullest enjoyment ⟨the audience ~*ing* at the pantomime⟩ **3 a :** to be boisterous **:** act or proceed in a riotous turbulent disorderly way ⟨desperadoes from the hills regularly ~*ed* in to take over the town —R.A.Billington⟩ **b :** to show surprising or extravagant activity or noise ⟨around which all this controversy ~*s* —A.H.Vandenberg †1951⟩ **c :** to proceed or rush with great speed, activity, or impetus and with great noise or commotion ⟨rivers ~*ed* in the abandoned channels of the glaciers —John Muir †1914⟩ ⟨get a good view of the express as she ~*ed* through —O.S.Nock⟩ **4 :** to make a loud noise in breathing (as horses afflicted with roaring) ~ *vt* **1 :** to utter or proclaim with a roar ⟨~*ing* names . . . like a railway porter shouting out a list of stations —Robert Lynd⟩ ⟨delegates to the union's . . . convention ~*ed* approval of a resolution —Mary K. Hammond⟩ ⟨~ defiance⟩ **2 :** to bring into a specified state by roaring ⟨the river ~*ed* him to sleep⟩ **3 :** to cause to roar ⟨pressed on the accelerator, savagely ~*ing* the engine —Russell Thacher⟩

syn HOWL, ULULATE, BELLOW, BAWL, BLUSTER, CLAMOR, VOCIFERATE: ROAR suggests the full loud reverberating sound made by lions or the booming sea or by persons in rage or boisterous merriment ⟨far away guns *roar* —Virginia Woolf⟩ ⟨the harsh north wind . . . *roared* in the piazzas —Osbert Sitwell⟩ ⟨*roared* the blacksmith, his face black with rage —T.B.Costain⟩ HOWL indicates a higher, less reverberant sound often suggesting the doleful or agonized or the sounds of unrestrained laughter ⟨frequent *howling* of jackals and hyenas —James Stevenson-Hamilton⟩ ⟨how the wind does *howl* —J.C.Powys⟩ ⟨*roared* at his subject . . . *howled* at . . . inconsistencies —Martin Gardner⟩ ULULATE is a literary synonym for HOWL but may suggest mournful protraction and rhythmical delivery ⟨an *ululating* baritone mushy with pumped-up pity —E.B.White⟩ BELLOW suggests the loud, abrupt, hollow sound made typically by bulls or any similar loud, reverberating sound ⟨most of them were drunk. They went *bellowing* through the town —Kenneth Roberts⟩ BAWL suggests a somewhat lighter, less reverberant, unmodulated sound made typically by calves ⟨a woman *bawling* abuse from the door of an inn —C.E.Montague⟩ ⟨the old judge was in the hall *bawling* hasty orders —Sheridan Le Fanu⟩ BLUSTER suggests the turbulent noisiness of gusts of wind; it often suggests swaggering and noisy threats or protests ⟨expressed her opinion gently but firmly, while he *blustered* for a time and then gave in —Sherwood Anderson⟩ ⟨swagger and *bluster* and take the limelight —Margaret Mead⟩ CLAMOR suggests sustained, mixed and confused noisy outcry as from a number of agitated persons ⟨half-starved men and women *clamoring* for food —Kenneth Roberts⟩ ⟨easy . . . for critics . . . to *clamor* for action —Sir Winston Churchill⟩ VOCIFERATE suggests loud vehement insistence in speaking ⟨was not willing to break off his talk; so he continued to *vociferate* his remarks —James Boswell⟩

²roar \"\ *n* -s [ME *rore*, fr. *roren*, v.] **:** the sound of roaring: **a :** the deep loud cry of some wild beasts ⟨the ~ of a lion⟩ **b :** a loud deep cry of emotion (as pain or anger) **c :** a loud continuous confused sound ⟨the ominous, steady ~ of airplane engines —Erle Stanley Gardner⟩ ⟨a ~ of conversation coming from the bar —Claud Cockburn⟩ ⟨able to make his thin whistling rise above the ~ of the stream —T.B.Costain⟩ **d :** a boisterous outcry or shouting ⟨a ~ of laughter⟩

roar·er \ˈrōrə(r), ˈrȯr-\ *n* -s **:** one that roars: as **a** *obs* **:** a riotous swaggering disorderly person **:** BULLY **b :** a horse subject to roaring **c :** a person having esp. in his own opinion remarkable abilities (as of fighting or rafting) **d :** GUSHER; *esp* **:** a noisy gassy oil well

¹roaring *n* -s [ME *roringe*, *roring*, fr. OE *rārung*, fr. *rārian* to roar + *-ung* -ing] **1 a :** a loud deep prolonged sound (as an utterance or cry of an animal or of a person in distress, anger or mirth) **b :** a loud indistinct steady sound (as of wind, waves, or a crowd) **2 :** noisy respiration in a horse caused by paralysis of the left recurrent laryngeal nerve and atrophy of the muscles of the arytenoid cartilage on that side, occurring only during exercise, and constituting an unsoundness in the horse — compare GRUNTING, THICK WIND

²roaring *adj* [ME *roring*, alter. (influenced by *roringe*, *roring*, n.) of *rorende*, pres. part. of *roren* to roar] **1 :** making or characterized by a noise like a roar **:** LOUD ⟨~ applause⟩

2 : RIOTOUS, DISORDERLY 3 : marked by prosperity or bustle esp. of a temporary nature : THRIVING, BOOMING ⟨overnight the sleepy post became a ~ construction camp —Tom Marvel⟩ ⟨doing a ~ trade⟩ — **roar·ing·ly** *adv*

³roaring *adv* : EXTREMELY — used in the phrase *roaring drunk*

roaring boy *or* **roaring lad** *n* : a noisy bullying street roisterer of Elizabethan and Jacobean England intimidating passersby (as if to commit robbery) — called also *circling boy*

roaring forties *n pl* : either of two stormy tracts of ocean between 40 degrees and 50 degrees latitude north or south

roaring meg \-ˈmeg\ *n, usu cap M* [fr. *Meg*, nickname fr. the name *Margaret*] *obs* : CANNON

¹roast \ˈrōst\ *vb* -ED/-ING/-S [ME *rosten*, fr. OF *rostir*, of Gmc origin; akin to MD *roosten* to roast, OHG *rōsten* (both derivatives fr. a noun represented by MD *roost* gridiron, grill, OHG *rōst*)] *vt* **1 a :** to cook by exposure to radiant heat before a fire or in an oven open toward the fire and having reflecting surfaces within — distinguished from *bake* ⟨~ meat on a spit⟩ **b :** to cook in an oven by dry heat **c :** to cook by surrounding with hot embers, ashes, sand, or stones ⟨~ a potato in ashes⟩ **d :** to dry and parch by exposure to heat ⟨~ coffee⟩ ⟨~ chestnuts⟩ **2 :** to heat (inorganic material) with access of air and without fusing in order to effect useful physical changes: as **a :** to expel volatile matter **b :** to effect oxidation **c :** to remove sulfur from sulfide ores — compare CALCINE **3 a :** to heat to excess ⟨after supper, when the sun no longer ~*ed* the valley —Oliver La Farge⟩ **b** *obs* **:** to cause to be hot with fury **4 :** to ridicule or criticize severely ⟨the critics ~*ed* the elaborately staged work —*Newsweek*⟩ ~ *vi* **1 :** to cook meat, fish, or vegetables by heat (as before a fire or in an oven) **2 :** to undergo the process of being roasted or of getting heated as if being roasted

²roast \ˈ"\ *n* -S [in sense 1, fr. ME *rost*, fr. MF, fr. OF, fr. *rostir*, v.; in other senses, fr. ¹*roast*] **1 :** a piece of meat which has been roasted or is suitable for being roasted; *esp* **:** a roast of beef ⟨pork ~⟩ — see BEEF illustration **2 :** a party or social gathering at which the main food is prepared by roasting before an open fire or in hot ashes or sand ⟨corn ~⟩ ⟨wienie ~⟩ **3 :** an act or process of roasting; *specif* **:** severe banter, ridicule, or criticism **4 :** a class or variety of roasted coffee as determined by length of roasting or extent of change during that process

³roast \ˈ"\ *adj* [ME *rost*, past part. of *rosten*, v.] **:** ROASTED ⟨~ beef⟩

roast·er \-tə(r)\ *n* -S [ME *roostare*, fr. *roosten*, *rosten* to roast + *-er*, *-ere*, *-are* -er] **1 :** one that roasts something (as meat, coffee, cacao beans, or nuts) **2 :** a machine or contrivance for roasting: as **a :** a device for roasting coffee or peanuts **b :** a pan for roasting meat **c :** a furnace for roasting ore **3 :** something adapted to roasting esp. whole: as **a :** a sucking pig **b :** a young domestic fowl for table use weighing more than four pounds **c :** any animal (as a rabbit) suitable for roasting **4 :** BURNER 1a(2) **5 :** SCORCHER 1b

roasting *adv* **:** to a roasting degree ⟨~ hot meat⟩

roasting ear *n* **1 :** an ear of sweet corn roasted or suitable for roasting usu. in the husk in hot ashes, before an open fire, or in an oven **2** *often* ˈrōsᵊn,i(ə)r, -ō,sni(ə)r, -iə\ *chiefly South & Midland* **:** an ear of sweet corn boiled or steamed after removal of the husk or suitable for boiling or steaming ⟨picked an armful of *roasting ears* in the garden⟩ **:** an ear of corn on the cob

roasting jack *n* **:** a device for turning a spit on which meat is roasted or barbecued

roast·ing·ly *adv* **:** in a roasting manner

roast set *n* **:** CARVING SET

roast sintering *n* **:** BLAST ROASTING

roat *or* **roate** *obs var of* ROTE

¹rob \ˈräb\ *vb* **robbed; robbed; robbing; robs** [ME *robben*, fr. OF *rober*, of Gmc origin; akin to OHG *roubōn* to rob — more at REAVE] *vt* **1 a** (1) **:** to take something away from (a person) by force **:** steal from ⟨~*s* me of that which not enriches him —Shak.⟩ ⟨*robbed* the messenger as he left the bank⟩ (2) **:** to take personal property from (the person or presence of another) feloniously and by violence or threat of violence **b** (1) **:** to remove valuables without right from (a place) ⟨~ a safe⟩ ⟨where the coyotes gathered most often they had *robbed* the henhouse —Jean Stafford⟩ (2) **:** to take the contents of (a receptacle) ⟨~ a hive of honey⟩ ⟨raising, *robbing*, baiting, and lowering the traps —Ronald Sercombe⟩ **c :** to take away as loot **:** STEAL ⟨contrive to ~ the honey and subvert the hive —John Dryden⟩ **2 a :** to deprive of something due, expected, or desired ⟨speechless death, which ~*s* my tongue from breathing native breath —Shak.⟩ ⟨racketeering rings that were *robbing* guileless citizens —J.A.Morris b. 1904⟩ ⟨not ready to agree that air power had changed the principles of warfare or *robbed* sea power of its sovereign values —S.L.A.Marshall⟩ **b :** to withhold unjustly or injuriously from a person or thing ⟨concave surfaces are troublesome in that they tend to focus sound in some spots and ~ sound energy from others —J.F.Nickerson⟩ **c :** to deprive (an opponent) of a hit or run in baseball by a spectacular play **3 :** to exchange a less valuable card in one's hand for (another card) **4 a :** to mine coal or ore without provision for the preservation of (a mine): as (1) **:** to take out pillars of coal or ore from (a mine) as a final operation before the abandonment of the mine (2) **:** to take out the richer and more accessible ores from (a mine) leaving valuable material behind while destroying the mine **b :** to mine (coal or ore) without provision for the preservation of the mine ~ *vi* **:** to take without right or permission and usu. by violence something belonging to another **:** commit robbery

syn PLUNDER, RIFLE, LOOT, THIEVE, BURGLARIZE: ROB indicates the taking of another's property either by such felonious methods as violence, intimidation, or fraud, or, by extension, by any unjust procedure ⟨to *rob* a bank⟩ ⟨to *rob* one's partners by embezzlement⟩ ⟨*robbed* of his good name by slander⟩ PLUNDER suggests despoiling and robbing in force, as by gangs, bandits, or soldiery, or on a massive scale ⟨a band of Tories who were escaping after *plundering* the home of a patriotic resident —*Amer. Guide Series: Conn.*⟩ ⟨went to prison for his activities as head of a ring which *plundered* at least $75,000,000 from the city —Paul Blanshard⟩ RIFLE suggests a ransacking or more or less complete despoliation, sometimes done systematically ⟨a boat presently came alongside with a gang of desperadoes, who boarded her, and *rifled* her of everything valuable —Francis Parkman⟩ ⟨tomb was *rifled* by the sexton after her burial for the sake of her jewelry which had been buried with her —S.P.B.Mais⟩ LOOT may add suggestions of extreme reprehensibility, as in situations involving barbarism, desperation, or colossal venality; sometimes it applies to pillaging by undisciplined soldiery or by mobs ⟨*looting* the bodies of those killed in the wreck⟩ ⟨a group of officials *looting* the state treasury⟩ THIEVE may imply stealthy taking of another's possessions, often habitual or accustomed ⟨thousands of these people have, since the liberation, become almost nomads, wandering about, *thieving* for their food —Ernest Bevin⟩ BURGLARIZE technically implies a breaking and entering of premises, often with notable force ⟨the house had been *burglarized*⟩ ⟨*burglarizing* fur storage lofts⟩

— rob the cradle : to select as a companion or spouse a person much younger than oneself

²rob \ˈ"\ *n* -S [MF, fr. Ar *rubb*] **:** the thickened juice of ripe fruit obtained by evaporation of the juice over a fire till it has the consistency of a syrup and afterward sometimes mixed with honey or sugar

ROB *abbr, often not cap* remain on board; remaining on board

ro·ba·lo \rōˈbä(,)lō\ *n, pl* **robalos** *or* **ro·balo** [Sp *róbalo*, *robalo*, prob. modif. of (assumed) Sp *lobaro*, irreg. fr. Sp *lobo* wolf, fr. L *lupus* — more at WOLF] **:** SNOOK 1a

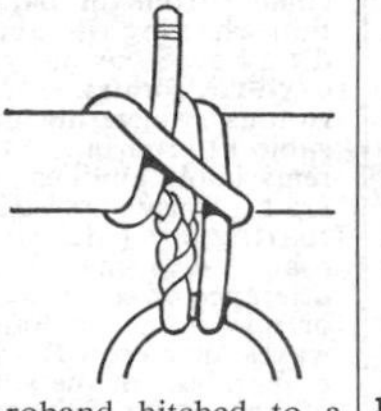

roband hitched to a ring and tied around a spar

roband \ˈrōbən, ˈräb-, -band\ *also* **rob·bin** \ˈräbən\ *or* **rope·band** \ˈrōp,ban(d)\ *n* -S [*roband* prob. fr. (assumed) ME *roband*, prob. fr. MD *rabant*, fr. *ra* sail yard + *bant* band, hoop (akin to OHG *bant* fetter); *robbin* fr. ME *robyn*, prob. alter. (influenced by *Robin*, nickname fr. the name *Robert*) of (assumed) ME *roband*; *ropeband* by folk etymology fr. *roband*; MD *ra* sail yard akin to MHG *rahe* pole, sail yard, ON *rā* sail yard, Lith *rėklės* wooden frame for drying or smoking foods — more at BAND] **:** a small piece of spun yarn or marline used to fasten the head of a sail to a spar

rob·ber \ˈräbə(r)\ *n* -S *often attrib* [ME *robbere*, *robbour*, fr. OF *robere*, *robeor*, fr. *roben* to rob + *-ere*, *-eor* -er] **:** one that robs: as **a :** one that commits the crime of robbery **b** *or* **robber bee :** a honeybee worker that steals honey from a colony not its own **c :** a miner who rips out the supporting pillars of coal after the regular mining has been done

robber ant *n* **:** any of various slave-making ants (as *Formica sanguinea* and *Polyergus rufescens*)

robber baron *n* **1 :** a medieval lord subsisting by robbing, holding for ransom, or exorbitantly taxing travelers through his domain **2 :** an American capitalist of the latter part of the 19th century grown wealthy through exploitation of natural resources, governmental influence, or low wage scales

robber crab *n* **1 :** PURSE CRAB **2 :** HERMIT CRAB

robber fly *n* **:** any of numerous often large predaceous flies of the family Asilidae that usu. are covered with coarse bristly hair and have a slender body and long legs but sometimes closely resemble the bumblebees and that as larvae prey upon other insect larvae and as adults prey upon other insects

robber frog *n* **:** any of several frogs of the genus *Eleutherodactylus* with a call like the bark of a dog that are chiefly native to Central America though one species extends into extreme southern Texas

robber gull *n* **:** JAEGER 3

robbers' roost *n* **:** an outlaw hideout esp. in the western U. S.

rob·bery \ˈräb(ə)rē, -)ri\ *n* -ES [ME *robberie*, fr. OF *roberie*, fr. *rober* to rob + *-erie* -ery] **:** the act or practice of robbing; *specif* **:** a larceny from the person or immediate presence of another by violence or threat of violence — compare MIXED LARCENY, THEFT

robbery insurance *n* **:** insurance against loss by theft of property from the person or immediate presence of the possessor

robbia work *n, usu cap R* **:** DELLA ROBBIA WARE

rob·bin *Brit var of* ROBIN

robbing *pres part of* ROB

¹robe \ˈrōb\ *n* -S [ME, fr. OF, robe, booty, of Gmc origin; akin to OE *rēaf* garment, armor, booty, OHG *roub* booty, *roubōn* to rob — more at REAVE] **1 a :** a long loose outer garment cut in flowing lines and used for ordinary wear by men and women during the middle ages and in modern times esp. in Asian and African countries ⟨supply purple ~*s* for the courtiers —Connop Thirlwall⟩ ⟨the Indians wove their own heavy cotton ~*s* —C.B.Hitchcock⟩ **b :** a similar garment often of special or elegant style and material used for state, ceremonial, and official occasions or as a symbol of office or profession ⟨the Sovereign has . . . been invested with the Royal *Robe* of cloth of gold in which he is crowned —L.E. Fanner⟩ ⟨the judge was already rising and arranging his ~*s* —Frances P. Keyes⟩ **c :** a usu. loose wraparound garment of varying length for informal wear esp. at home (as a bathrobe or dressing gown) ⟨found him . . . wearing a natty red lounging ~ and white pajamas —*New Yorker*⟩ ⟨the girls . . . have beach ~*s* and hats —Bernard De Voto⟩ **2 :** something resembling or suggesting a long loose enveloping garment ⟨a vast and fruitful land . . . clad with a ~ of plants —Russell Lord⟩ ⟨the glorious congregation of peaks . . . in their ~*s* of snow and light—John Muir †1914⟩ ⟨shed your ~ of sanctity —Rafael Sabatini⟩ **3 :** the legal profession — usu. used with preceding *the* ⟨the cadets of many of our good families follow the ~ as a profession —W.M.Thackeray⟩ **4 a :** a covering for the lower body made from pelts finished with the fur on the top side and often a lining of fabric on the underside that resembles a blanket and is used while driving or at outdoor events — see BUFFALO ROBE, LAP ROBE **b :** a similar covering of fabric ⟨warm woolen auto ~*s*⟩ **5 :** WARDROBE ⟨double-door cedar ~*s* —*advt*⟩

²robe \ˈ"\ *vb* -ED/-ING/-S [ME *roben*, fr. *robe*, n.] *vt* **1 :** to clothe or invest with a robe ⟨helped to ~ him in . . . a quilted robe of scarlet silk —Nora Waln⟩ ⟨bathers must immediately ~ themselves upon leaving the water —*Time*⟩ **2 :** to dress or cover as if with a robe ⟨~*s* himself in moonlight —John Foster⟩ ⟨love *robed* her in a blush —T.T.Lynch⟩ ~ *vi* **:** to put on a robe ⟨in the early morning, he *robed* . . . and drove abroad —Mary Lindsay⟩

robe de cham·bre \rōbdəshäⁿbr(ᵊ), -b(rə)\ *n, pl* **robes de chambre** \ˈ"\ [F] **:** DRESSING GOWN

robe de nuit \-dənwyē\ *n, pl* **robes de nuit** \ˈ"\ [F] **:** NIGHTGOWN

robe de style \-dəstēl\ *n, pl* **robes de style** \ˈ"\ [F] **:** a usu. long formal gown with a tight bodice and a bouffant skirt

robe de style

robe·less \ˈrōbləs\ *adj* **:** lacking a robe

ro·ben·hau·si·an \ˌrōbənˈhaùzēən\ *adj, usu cap* [*Robenhausen*, locality in northeast central Switzerland where evidences of such a culture have been found + E *-an*] **:** of or relating to a stage of Neolithic culture characterized by lake dwellings, polished stone tools, agriculture, weaving, and domestic animals

rob·er \ˈrōbə(r)\ *n* -S **:** one that robes

rob·erds·man \ˈräbə(r)dzmən\ *n, pl* **roberdsmen** *usu cap* [ME *roberdesman*, *robertesman*, prob. fr. *Robertes* (gen. of the name *Robert*, prob. considered an appropriate fictitious name for a robber because of the similarity in sound to ME *robbere* robber) + ME *man*] **:** one of a class of vagabond thieves and robbers in 14th century England

rob·ert of lin·coln \ˌräbərd·ə(v)ˈliŋkən\ *usu cap R&L* [alter. (influenced by the name *Robert* and by E *of*) of obs. E *Bob-o-Lincoln* — more at BOBOLINK] **:** BOBOLINK

ro·ber·val's balance \ˈrōbə(r),vōlz-\ *n, usu cap R* [after Gilles Personne de *Roberval* †1675 Fr. mathematician] **:** a balance in which the pans are fixed to the prolonged vertical sides of a jointed parallelogram whose two other sides are pivoted in their midpoints to a vertical post

robes·pierr·ist \ˈrōb,spirəst, -bz,pyer-\ *n* -S *usu cap* [F *robespierriste*, fr. Maximilien F. M. I. de *Robespierre* †1794 Fr. revolutionist + F *-iste* -ist] **:** a follower or supporter of Robespierre

ro·bi·ga·lia \ˌrōbəˈgālēə\ *n* -S *usu cap* [L, fr. *Robigus*, Roman god associated with wheat blight] **:** an ancient Roman festival celebrated April 25 including a procession and the sacrifice of a dog to the god Robigus to avert blight from the fields

rob·in \ˈräbən *sometimes* -bᵊm\ *n* -S [in sense 1, short for *robin redbreast*; in other senses, fr. *Robin*, nickname fr. the name *Robert*] **1 a :** a small European thrush (*Erithacus rubecola*) resembling a warbler and having a brownish olive back and yellowish red throat and breast — called also *redbreast* **b :** any of various Old World songbirds (as members of the genera *Petroica*, *Melanodryas*, *Saxicola*, and *Saxicoloides*) that are related to or resemble in size, color, or habits the European robin — compare WOOD ROBIN **c :** a large No. American thrush (*Turdus migratorius*) with olivaceous gray upper parts, blackish head and tail, black and whitish streaked throat, and chiefly dull reddish breast and underparts that often nests in orchard or shade trees close to human habitations and lays pale greenish blue eggs **d :** any of various other American birds — usu. used in combination ⟨golden ~⟩; compare TOWHEE, VARIED THRUSH **e** *Jamaica* **:** GREEN TODY **2** *dial Eng* **:** any of various plants: as **a :** RAGGED ROBIN **b :** RED CAMPION **c :** HERB ROBERT **3 :** SEA ROBIN

robin accentor *n* **:** a small Asiatic songbird (*Prunella rubeculoides*) somewhat resembling the European robin in color

robin chat *n* **:** any of various African thrushes of *Cossypha* and closely related genera that are slaty blue with orange breasts

robin dipper *n* **:** BUFFLEHEAD

rob·in·et \ˈräbənət\ *n* -S [ME, short for *robinet redbrest*, fr. *Robinet* (dim. of *Robin*, nickname fr. the name *Robert*) + ME *redbrest* redbreast] **1 a** *dial Eng* **:** ROBIN **b :** CHAFFINCH **2** [fr. *Robinet*, dim. of *Robin*, nickname fr. the name *Robert*] **:** a light cannon of the 16th century throwing a projectile weighing about half a pound

robi·ne·tin \ˌrōbəˈnētᵊn, ˌräb-\ *n* -S [*robin-* (fr. NL *Robinia*) + *-et-* + *-in*] **:** a yellow crystalline flavone pigment $C_{15}H_{10}O_7$ obtained esp. from the stem wood of a locust (*Robinia pseudoacacia*)

rob·ing \ˈrōbiŋ\ *n* -S [ME, fr. gerund of *roben* to robe] **1 :** ROBE 1 **2** *also* **rob·in** \-bən\ **:** a band or flounce for trimming a robe or gown

robing room *n* **:** a small room in a church where robes or ecclesiastical vestments are put on before a service

rob·in hood \ˈräbənˌhùd, *sometimes* -bᵊmˈ-\ *n, usu cap R&H* [*Robin Hood*, legendary Eng. outlaw, hero of a cycle of ballads, first mentioned *ab*1377] **1 :** a person or group whose acts lie partly or wholly outside accepted standards of legality, morality, or propriety; *esp* **:** one that robs the wealthy to aid the needy ⟨a kind of primitive and rather unscrupulous *Robin Hood* — taking from the rich to give to the poor and keeping undisclosed amounts for itself —J. Halero Ferguson⟩ **2 :** a spectacular hero ⟨interstellar *Robin Hoods* . . . on rocket-motor bikes and space-sphere junkets —T.H.Robsjohn-Gibbings⟩

robin hood's barn *n, usu cap R&H* **:** a long circuitous route ⟨tortuous meanderings around *Robin Hood's barn* —H.P. Fairchild⟩

ro·bin·ia \rōˈbinēə\ *n* [NL, fr. Jean *Robin* †1629 Fr. botanist + NL *-ia*] **1** *cap* **:** a genus of No. American trees and shrubs (family Leguminosae) having showy racemose pink or white flowers — see BRISTLY LOCUST, CLAMMY LOCUST, LOCUST **2** -S **:** any plant of the genus *Robinia*

robi·nin \ˈrōbənən, ˈräb-\ *n* -S [*robin-* (fr. NL *Robinia*) + *-in*] **:** a yellow crystalline glycoside $C_{33}H_{40}O_{19}$ derived from kaempferol and found in the flowers of a locust (*Robinia pseudoacacia*)

robi·nose \-ˌnōs *also* -ōz\ *n* -S [*robin-* (fr. NL *Robinia*) + *-ose*] **:** a trisaccharide sugar $C_{18}H_{32}O_{14}$ obtained from robinin by hydrolysis and yielding one part of galactose and two of rhamnose on hydrolysis

robin redbreast *n* [ME *robin redbrest*, fr. *Robin* (nickname fr. the name *Robert*) + ME *redbrest* redbreast] **1 :** ROBIN 1a **2 :** ROBIN 1c

robin runaway *n* **1 :** DEWDROP **2 :** GROUND IVY 1

robins *pl of* ROBIN

robin sandpiper *or* **robin snipe** *n* **1 :** *also* **robin breast :** ³KNOT **2 :** DOWITCHER

robin's egg *n* **:** a grayish blue that is greener and paler than electric or copenhagen, lighter, stronger, and slightly greener than Gobelin, and greener and lighter than old china — compare ROBIN'S-EGG BLUE

robin's-egg blue *n* **1 :** a variable color averaging a light greenish blue that is bluer and paler than average turquoise (sense 2a) or average turquoise blue and bluer and deeper than average aqua blue — compare ROBIN'S EGG **2 :** a light bluish green that is greener and duller than average aqua green (sense 1) and greener and paler than average turquoise green — called also *bird's-egg green*, *eggshell blue*

robin snow *n, chiefly New Eng* **:** a light snowfall after the return of the first robin

rob·in·son·ade \ˌräbənsəˈnād, ˌrōbənzōˈnädə\ *n, pl* **robinson·ades** \-ādz\ *also* **robinson·aden** \-ädᵊn\ *often cap* [G *robinsonade*, fr. *Robinson Crusoe*, sailor who survives by great resourcefulness when marooned on a desert island in the fictional prose narrative *Robinson Crusoe* (1719) by Daniel Defoe †1731 Eng. journalist and novelist] **:** a fictitious narrative of often fantastic adventures in real or imaginary distant places; *esp* **:** a story of the adventures of a person marooned on a desert island ⟨the *Robinsonade* in world literature —E.G. Gudde⟩

robinson crusoe *n, usu cap R&C* **:** CRUSOE

rob·in·son·ite \ˈräbənsəˌnīt *also probably by* n-*dissimilation* -ˌbəs-\ *n* -S [Stephen C. *Robinson b*1911 Canadian geologist + E *-ite*] **:** a mineral $Pb_7Sb_{12}S_{25}$ consisting of a sulfide of lead and antimony that is found in Pershing county, Nev.

robin's plantain *n* **:** a common perennial herb (*Erigeron pulchellus*) of eastern No. America having flower heads with violet purple rays

ro·bi·son ester \ˈrōbəsən-\ *n, usu cap R* [after Robert *Robison* †1941 Eng. biochemist] **:** GLUCOSE PHOSPHATE b

ro·ble \ˈrō(,)blā, -ōbəl\ *n* -S [AmerSp, fr. Sp, oak, fr. L *robur* — more at ROBUST] **1 :** any of several oaks of California and Mexico: as **a :** CALIFORNIA WHITE OAK **b :** CANYON LIVE OAK **2 :** any of several hard-timbered tropical American trees: as **a :** a quira (*Platymiscium polystachyum*) **b :** any of various trees of the genera *Catalpa*, *Tabebuia*, and *Tecoma* **c :** UMBU-RANA **3 :** a So. American tree of the genus *Nothofagus* (as *N. obliqua* or *N. dombeyi*)

ro·bomb \ˈrō+ˌ-\ *n* [blend fr. *robot bomb*] **:** ROBOT BOMB

¹robo·rant \ˈräbərənt, ˈrōb-\ *n* -S [L *roborant-*, *roborans*, pres. part. of *roborare* to strengthen] **:** an invigorating drug **:** TONIC

²roborant \ˈ"\ *adj* [L *roborant-*, *roborans*, pres. part. of *roborare*] **:** STRENGTHENING

roborate *vt* [ME *roboraten*, fr. L *roboratus*, past part. of *roborare* to strengthen, confirm, fr. *robor-*, *robur* strength — more at ROBUST] **1** *obs* **:** RATIFY, CORROBORATE **2** *obs* **:** STRENGTHEN — **roboration** *n* -S

ro·bot \ˈrō,bät, -ˌbət, *usu* -äd· *or* -əd· +V; *sometimes* -(,)bō *or* -,bət *or* (+V) -,bəd·\ *n* -S *often attrib* [Czech, fr. *robota* work, compulsory service; akin to OSlav *rabota* servitude, OE *earfothe* hardship, labor, OHG *arabeit* trouble, distress, ON *erfithi* toil, distress, Goth *arbaiths* labor, L *orbus* orphaned, bereft — more at ORPHAN] **1 a :** a machine in the form of a human being that performs the mechanical functions of a human being but lacks emotions and sensitivity ⟨electronically controlled ~*s* with hands, eyebrows, and bodies that move —*Time*⟩ ⟨a world of men and women — not of cast iron ~*s* —*Spectator*⟩ — compare AUTOMATON, GOLEM **b :** an automatic apparatus or device that performs functions ordinarily ascribed to human beings or operates with what appears to be almost human intelligence; *esp* **:** such an apparatus that is started by means of radiant energy or sound waves ⟨a ~ mechanism that steers a cultivator precisely along a row of crops —*Newsweek*⟩ ⟨a ~ taking pictures at intervals⟩ **c** (1) **:** a mechanism that operates without human assistance; *esp* **:** one that is guided by automatic controls ⟨automatic percolator ~⟩ ⟨~ airplane⟩ ⟨~ factory⟩ (2) *southern Africa* **:** TRAFFIC SIGNAL (3) **:** ROBOT BOMB **2 :** an efficient, insensitive, and often brutalized person ⟨social ~*s*, taking whatever is brought to us, always grateful —Gilbert Seldes⟩ ⟨the average worker who has functioned from adolescence as a ~ —Henry Miller⟩

robot bomb *n* **:** a small pilotless jet-propelled airplane that is steered by a gyroscopic device, that is heavily loaded with explosives, and that descends as an aerial bomb — called also *buzz bomb*, *flying bomb*, *robomb*, *V-1*

ro·bot·ism \ˈ=(,)=ˌizəm\ *n* -S **:** machinelike behavior in a human being

ro·bot·iza·tion \ˌ=(,)=əˈzāshən, -ˌīˈz-\ *n* -S **1 :** the act or process of turning a human being into a robot **2 :** AUTOMATION

ro·bot·ize \ˈ=(,)=ˌīz\ *vt* -ED/-ING/-S **1 :** to make automatic ⟨chemical process plants so highly *robotized* that their complex operations are controlled by one or two operators at a push-button panel —Gerard Piel⟩ **2 :** to turn (a human being) into a robot

rob roy \ˈräˈbrȯi\ *n, usu cap both Rs* [prob. fr. *Rob Roy*, nickname of Robert Macgregor †1734 Scot. freebooter] **:** a cocktail consisting of Scotch whisky, sweet vermouth, and bitters stirred with ice, strained, and served garnished with a maraschino cherry

robs *pres 3d sing of* ROB, *pl of* ROB

ro·bur \ˈrōbə(r)\ *n* -S [L, oak] **:** ENGLISH OAK

ro·bust \rōˈbəst, ˈrō,bəst *also* ˈrō,b-\ *adj, often* -ER/-EST [L *robustus* oaken, hard, strong, fr. *robor-*, *robur* oak, strength; perh. akin to L *ruber* red — more at RED] **1 a :** having or exhibiting strength or vigorous health **:** POWERFUL, MUSCULAR, VIGOROUS ⟨a new land, full of ~ people —Green Peyton⟩ ⟨a hearty, ~ man in his middle sixties —Jule Mannix⟩ **b :** firm and assured in purpose, opinion, or outlook ⟨this embodied moral healthiness, this ~ sayer of Yea and Nay . . . this genuine man —W.L.Sullivan⟩ ⟨the ~ skepticism of science —M.R.Cohen⟩ ⟨a faith so ~ as to outlive shock upon shock of disillusion —Irving Babbitt⟩ **c :** exceptionally sound : FLOURISHING ⟨men and women of ~ health and keen intelligence —W.R.Inge⟩ ⟨protected by history, by geography and . . . by its ~ liberal tradition —A.M.Schlesinger b. 1917⟩ **d :** strongly formed or constructed : STURDY ⟨~ flowering plants such as veratrum, larkspur, lupine —John Muir †1914⟩ ⟨the furniture is structurally as ~ as the society it served —John Gloag⟩ ⟨sex in any race is shown by the general proportion of the bones . . . the male frame being more ~ and the bones . . . more rugged —R.W.Murray⟩ **2 :** ROUGH, RUDE ⟨appease their hunger with pemmican and their spirits with roistering songs and ~ stories —*Amer. Guide Series: Minn.*⟩ **3 :** requiring strength or vigor ⟨the physical weakling . . . of little material value to the group in the ~ economy of the hunters —R.W. Murray⟩ **4 :** FULL-BODIED, STRONG ⟨splendidly ~ soups and stews —*New Yorker*⟩ ⟨~ coffee⟩ **syn** see HEALTHY

ro·bus·ta coffee \rō'bəstə-\ *n* [NL *robusta* (specific epithet of *Coffea robusta*, syn. of *Coffea canephora*), fr. L, fem. of *robustus*] **1 :** a coffee (*Coffea canephora*) that is indigenous to Central Africa but grown in Java and elsewhere and has high resistance to coffee rust **2 a :** the seed of robusta coffee **b :** coffee brewed from the seed of robusta coffee

ro·bus·tic·i·ty \(,)rō,bə'stisəd·ē, ,rō_b-\ *n* -ES [obs. E *robustic* robust (fr. E *robust* + *-ic*) + E *-ity*] : ROBUSTNESS

ro·bus·tious \(')rō¦bəschəs, rə'b-\ *adj* **1 :** ROBUST, STOUT, HEALTHY **2 :** rudely vigorous : BOISTEROUS, ROUGH ⟨a likeable fellow, direct and ~ —S.H.Adams⟩ ⟨~ times when broadcloth in politics had gone out of fashion and homespun had come in —V.L.Parrington⟩ — **ro·bus·tious·ly** *adv* — **ro·bus·tious·ness** *n* -ES

ro·bust·ly *adv* : in a robust manner

ro·bust·ness \rō'bəs(t)nəs, 'rō,b- *also* 'rō_b-\ *n* -ES : the quality or state of being robust

ro·bus·tu·ous \(')rō¦bəsch(əw)əs\ *adj* [*robust* + *-uous* (as in *contemptuous*)] : ROBUSTIOUS

roc \'räk\ *n* -S [Ar *rukhkh*] **1 :** a legendary bird of great size and strength believed to inhabit the Indian ocean area — compare SIMURGH **2 :** an aerial bomb with a television apparatus for transmitting information used to guide the bomb by remote radio control to the target

ROC *abbr* reserve officer candidate

ro·caille \rō'kī, rə'-\ *n* -S [F, fr. *roc* rock, fr. MF, irreg. fr. *roche* rock, fr. (assumed) VL *rocca* — more at ROCK] **1 :** a style of ornamentation developed in the 18th century and characterized by forms derived from the artificial rockwork and pierced shellwork of the period **2 :** ROCOCO

roc·am·bole *or* **roc·om·bole** \'räkəm,bōl\ *n* -S [F *rocambole*] : a European leek (*Allium scorodoprasum*) often cultivated like the shallot and similarly used

roc·cel·la \rō'chelə\ *n, cap* [NL, fr. It, archil (plant), alter. of *oricello*] : a genus (the type of the family Roccellaceae) of chiefly maritime rock-inhabiting lichens that have a fruticulose or pendulous thallus and include some (esp. *Roccella tinctoria*) which are the chief sources of the dye archil and some which furnish litmus — compare LECANORA, PERTUSARIA — **roc·cel·line** \-elən, -e,līn\ *adj*

roc·cel·lic acid \rō'chelik-\ *n* [*roccellic* ISV *roccell-* (fr. NL *Roccella*) + *-ic*] : a crystalline dicarboxylic acid $C_{17}H_{32}O_4$ derived from succinic acid and found in various lichens (as *Roccella tinctoria*)

roc·cus \'räkəs\ *n, cap* [NL, perh. irreg. fr. E *rockfish*] : a genus of fishes (family Serranidae) including the common marine striped bass

roch \'räk\ *Scot var of* ROUGH

roch·dale principles \'räch,dāl-\ *n pl, usu cap R* [fr. *Rochdale*, city in northwest England where such cooperative marketing was begun in 1844] : a system of cooperative marketing in which no credit is given and all profits are distributed among the customers

roche \'rōch\ *n* -S [obs. E *roche* stony hill, rock, fr. ME — more at ROACH] *dial Eng* : any of various rocks, stones, or geological strata

ro·chea \'rōshēə\ *n, cap* [NL, fr. François Dela-*Roche* †1813 Swiss botanist] : a small genus of southern African fleshy undershrubs (family Crassulaceae) with showy cymose salver-shaped flowers of various colors

roche limit \'rȯsh-, 'rōsh-\ *or* **roche's limit** \-shəz-\ *n, usu cap R* [after E. A. *Roche* †1883 Fr. mathematician] : the distance between a planet's center and its satellite within which the satellite cannot approach without suffering disruption; *specif* : the distance 2.44 times the planet's radius from its center when the planet and the satellite are of the same density

ro·chelle powders \(')rō¦shel-\ *n pl, usu cap R* [fr. La *Rochelle*, city in western France] : SEIDLITZ POWDERS

rochelle salt *n, usu cap R* : a crystalline salt $KNaC_4H_4O_6 \cdot 4H_2O$ that has a cooling saline taste, that is a mild purgative, and that is used also esp. in the silvering of mirrors and in piezoelectric devices — often used in pl.; called also *potassium sodium tartrate, Seignette salt*

roche mou·ton·née \¦rȯsh,müt°n'ā, ¦rōsh-\ *n, pl* **roches moutonnées** \-ā(z)\ [F, lit., fleecy rock] : an elongate rounded ice-sculptured knob or hillock of bedrock

roch·es·ter \'rächəstə(r), -,ches-\ *adj, usu cap* [fr. *Rochester*, city in western New York] : of or from the city of Rochester, N.Y. ⟨the *Rochester* business district⟩ : of the kind or style prevalent in Rochester

roch·es·te·ri·an \,rächə'stirēən, -,che's-\ *n* -S *cap* [*Rochester* (any of several cities including one in southeast England and one in western New York) + E *-an*] : a native or resident of Rochester, esp. Rochester, New York

1**roch·et** \'rächət\ *n* -S [ME *rochet*, *roget*, *ruget*, fr. MF *rouget*, fr. OF, fr. *rouge* red + *-et* — more at ROUGE] : RED GURNARD

2**rochet** \"\ *n* -S [ME, fr. MF, fr. OF, fr. (assumed) OF *roc* coat (of Gmc origin; akin to OHG *roc* coat) + OF *-et* — more at FROCK] **1 :** a close-fitting white ecclesiastical vestment resembling a surplice usu. with long close sleeves but sometimes winged or sleeveless that is worn esp. by bishops and privileged prelates in some ceremonies **2** *archaic* : a loose smock or cloak worn as an outer garment

ro·chet·ta \rō'ked·ə\ *n* -S [It *rocchetta*, dim. of *rocca* rock, fr. (assumed) VL *rocca* — more at ROCK] *archaic* : POLVERINE

ro·chon prism \(')rō¦shōⁿ-\ *n, usu cap R* [after Alexis M. *Rochon* †1817 Fr. astronomer and optician] : a polarizing prism consisting of two equal prisms of calcite or other doubly refracting material cut so that the optic axis of one of the prisms is parallel to its refracting edge, the axis of the other is perpendicular to its refracting edge, and the directions of the optic axes make angles of 90 degrees with each other

1**rock** \'räk\ *vb* -ED/-ING/-S [ME *rokken*, fr. OE *roccian*; akin to OHG *rucken* to cause to move, shift, ON *rykkja* to jerk] *vt* **1 a :** to move (as a child) back and forth in or as if in a cradle **b :** to bring into or maintain in a state of rest, sleep, or serenity by gentle motion to and fro ⟨~*ing* the child on her breast⟩ **c :** to wash (placer gravel) in a cradle **d :** to prepare the surface of (a mezzotint plate) by the use of a cradle **2 a :** to cause (as a cradle) to sway gently backward and forward ⟨a warning sea bell ~*ed* by rising waves —J.C.Powys⟩ ⟨the languid spring breeze ~*ed* the little green bombshells of maple sprays —*New Republic*⟩ **b** (1) **:** to cause to shake violently ⟨when artillery maneuvers are held . . . the quiet countryside is shattered and ~*ed* by the roaring thunder of the big guns —*Amer. Guide Series: Vt.*⟩ ⟨she began to cry, great sobs that ~*ed* her —Robert Lowry⟩ (2) **:** to daze with a vigorous blow ⟨three smashing right crosses that ~*ed* him —Nat Fleischer⟩ (3) **:** to astonish or disturb esp. by upsetting cherished opinions or customary ways of life ⟨~*ing* the solid beliefs they had never dreamed of questioning —Virginia D. Dawson & Betty D. Wilson⟩ ⟨the news of the coming degree had ~*ed* the household with surprise —Agnes S. Turnbull⟩ **c** (1) **:** to dislodge (something stuck or wedged) by rhythmic back and forth movement ⟨set up on your towline and we'll ~ her out of here —K.M. Dodson⟩ (2) **:** to move clumsily first from one side and then from the other ⟨~*ed* his shoulders up the stairs —Scott Fitzgerald⟩ ⟨~*ed* the box across the platform⟩ (3) **:** to move (airplane wings) up and down usu. as a signal ⟨~*ed* my wings to let the landing signal officer know that I needed to land at once —D.A.Bryla⟩ **d :** to move (a vehicle or animal) at a steady fairly rapid pace ⟨~*ing* my mule right along but riding him as easy as I could —Jackson Burgess⟩ ~ *vi* **1 a :** to move violently backward and forward under impact : REEL, TOTTER ⟨the tower ~*ed* under the impact of the hurricane⟩ **b** (1) **:** to move gently and rhythmically back and forth ⟨~*ing* on the balls of his feet —Richard Llewellyn⟩ ⟨the speedometer was ~*ing* between sixty and sixty-five —Charley Robertson⟩ ⟨a low, steady breeze drove the little waves ~*ing* to the shore —John Burroughs⟩ (2) **:** to sit and move back and forth in a rocking chair ⟨~*ed* all day on her veranda —Laura Krey⟩ **c :** to sway gently under outside impact ⟨boats ~*ing* on the yellow river —W.G.Hardy⟩ **2 a :** to react with intense emotion ⟨the continent ~*ed* with surprise —*Woman*⟩ ⟨the audience was ~*ing* with laughter —H.J.Laski⟩ **b :** to seem to sway as if in response to human illness or emotion ⟨felt a blow against the back of his head, saw the walls of the house ~*ing* in sick blackness, and slid out on the hot steps —Josephine Johnson⟩ ⟨the room with its portions of shells ~*ed* more frequently with laughter than with explosives —*N.Y. Times Bk. Rev.*⟩ **3 a :** to move forward at a steady rhythmic pace ⟨the chuffing doubleheaders of the narrow-gage ~*ed* cautiously along the tracks —Helen Rich⟩ **b :** to move forward at high speeds ⟨~*ed* around town at furious speeds —R.L.Taylor⟩ **4 :** to sing, play music, or dance in a quick lively tempo — **rock the boat :** to do something that disturbs the equilibrium of a project ⟨trips should not be timed to *rock the boat* in countries where elections are being held —*Reporter*⟩ **syn** see SHAKE

2**rock** \"\ *n* -S : a rocking movement; *specif* : a change of balance in a step dance from one foot to the other with feet crossed

3**rock** \"\ *n* -S [ME *roc*, *rokke*, fr. MD *rocke*; akin to OHG *rocko* distaff, ON *rokkr* distaff, OHG *roc* coat — more at FROCK] **1 :** DISTAFF; *esp* : one with wool or flax on it **2 :** the wool or flax on a distaff

4**rock** \"\ *n* -S *often attrib* [ME *rokke*, fr. ONF *roque*, fr. (assumed) VL *rocca*, prob. of non-IE origin] **1 a :** a usu. bare cliff, promontory, peak, or hill that is one mass ⟨the ~ of Gibraltar⟩ **b :** a mass of stone lying at or near the surface of the water ⟨scattered ~*s* with 3¾–6 fathoms . . . of water over them —*U. S. Coast Pilot: West Indies*⟩ ⟨a reef, with four ~*s* showing above water —*U. S. Coast Pilot: West Indies*⟩ **c :** a barren islet **d :** a jagged rocky coastline esp. when a source of danger to shipping — often used in pl. ⟨the schooner was driven onto the ~*s*⟩ **2 a :** extremely hard dense stone ⟨hewn out of adamant ~ —Edmund Spenser⟩ **b** (1) **:** a large concreted mass of stony material : a large fixed stone (2) **:** stony material broken from such a mass **c** (1) **:** consolidated or unconsolidated solid mineral matter composed of one or usu. two or more minerals or partly of organic origin (as coal) that occurs naturally in large quantities or forms a considerable part of the earth's crust ⟨granite, sand, gravel, clay, and glacial ice are ~*s*⟩ (2) **:** a particular mass or kind of such material within the earth's surface (3) **:** an often jagged fragment of rock ranging in size from a boulder to a pebble ⟨chunkin' ~*s* at my granddaddy —Stetson Kennedy⟩ (4) **:** ore as mined; *esp* : Lake Superior copper ore **3 a** (1) **:** something that resembles a rock in firmness : FOUNDATION, SUPPORT ⟨the concept of a law that is independent of any sovereign, which cannot be repealed . . . is the ~ on which our society rests —Herbert Agar⟩ (2) **:** something that serves as a defense or refuge ⟨the Lord is my ~, and my fortress —2 Sam 22:2 (RSV)⟩ (3) **:** something that threatens or causes a disaster or wreck — often used in pl. ⟨the university, so near the ~*s* in preceding years, had become one of the best-rounded educational institutions in the country —*Current Biog.*⟩ ⟨our political parties must never flounder on the ~*s* of moral equivocation —A.E.Stevenson †1965⟩ **b :** a small island that is a place of confinement or of dangerous or monotonous duty ⟨three divisions of Marines . . . on the hottest ~ of them all —L.M.Uris⟩ **4 :** STRIPED BASS a **5 a** (1) **:** a hard stick candy with color running through and variously flavored (as with peppermint, clove, or anise) (2) **:** ROCK CANDY 1 **b** *or* **rock cake :** a cookie that is made of firm dough dropped from a spoon to a cookie sheet and that when baked retains an uneven form and contour **6 a :** a piece of money; *esp* : a dollar bill **b rocks** *pl* : MONEY ⟨a pocket full of ~*s*⟩ **7 :** PLYMOUTH ROCK **8** *slang* **a :** GEM **b :** DIAMOND **9 :** a mass consisting of lime soap obtained in a process for saponifying fats by heating them with lime and water under pressure **10 :** a stupid mistake : BONER ⟨pulled a ~ . . . in right field —Casey Stengel⟩ **11 :** ROCK 'N' ROLL — **of the old rock :** of proved and seasoned excellence — used esp. of a gem — **on the rocks** *adv (or adj)* **1 a :** in or into a state of destruction or wreckage ⟨lived together six years and had one daughter before the marriage went *on the rocks* —F.B.Gipson⟩ **b :** in or into a state of bankruptcy or destitution ⟨in a brief space of time the company went *on the rocks* —*Amer. Guide Series: La.*⟩ **2 :** on ice cubes ⟨bourbon *on the rocks*⟩

5**rock** \"\ *vt* -ED/-ING/-S : to throw stones at

rock·a·by *or* **rock·a·bye** \'räkə,bī\ *v imper* [1*rock* + *-aby*, *-abye* (as in *hushaby*, *hush-a-bye*)] : HUSHABY

rock·a·hom·i·ny \,räkə'hämənē\ *n* [perh. fr. *rokahaměn* (in some Algonquian language of Virginia)] *obs* : parched corn finely ground

rock along *vi* : to continue steadily and easily along the same path ⟨an industry that . . . would *rock along* quietly from one decade to the next —*New Yorker*⟩

rock and roll *var of* ROCK 'N' ROLL

rock and rye *n* : an American rye whiskey flavored with orange, lemon, and occas. pineapple and cherry

rock arm *n* : ROCKER ARM

rock asphalt *n* : ASPHALT ROCK

rock·a·way \'räkə,wā\ *n* -S [perh. fr. *Rockaway*, town in northern New Jersey where carriages were made] **1 :** a light low American four-wheel carriage with a fixed top and open sides that may be covered by waterproof curtains **2 :** a heavy carriage enclosed at sides and rear with a door on each side

rock badger *n* : 2HYRAX

rock barnacle *n* : ACORN BARNACLE

rock basin *n* : a depression in solid rock often resulting from ice erosion in mountain regions and usu. containing small lakes

rock bass *n* **1 :** a sunfish (*Ambloplites rupestris*) that is widely distributed in eastern No. America west of the Alleghenies and esp. the upper Mississippi valley and Great Lakes region that is a good food fish though little esteemed as food — called also *rock sunfish* **2 a :** STRIPED BASS a **b :** any of several sea basses (genus *Paralabrax*) that are widely distributed along the California and adjoining Mexican coast — called also *cabrilla*

rock beauty *n* : a European alpine perennial herb (*Draba pyrenaica*) having fragrant lilac purple flowers

rock·bell \'räk,bel\ *n* : COLUMBINE 1a

rock·ber·ry \'räk- — *see* BERRY\ *n* **1 :** BEARBERRY 1 **2 a :** CROWBERRY 1a **b :** RED CROWBERRY 1

rockbird \'=,=\ *n* **1 :** a seabird (as a murre) that breeds in rocky cliffs **2 :** COCK OF THE ROCK **3 :** PURPLE SANDPIPER

rock bit *n* : a hardened drill for making holes in hard rock

rock borer *n* : any of several marine bivalve mollusks (as various members of the genera *Petricola*, *Pholas*, and *Lithophaga*) that bore holes in rock

rock-boring isopod \'=,==-\ *n* : a marine isopod (*Sphaeroma pentodon*) of the Pacific Coast of No. America that burrows into stone or wood by biting off pieces with its powerful mandibles

rock bottom *n* : the absolute bottom, foundation, or core ⟨all human beings . . . are, at *rock bottom*, psychologically primitive —Edward Sapir⟩

rock-bottom \'=¦==\ *adj* [*rock bottom*] : the very lowest ⟨a ~ price⟩

rockbound \'=,=\ *adj* **1 :** fringed, surrounded, or covered with rocks : ROCKY ⟨a stern and ~ coast —Felicia D. Hemans⟩ ⟨as desolate a stretch of ~ desert as may be found —*Geog. Jour.*⟩ **2 :** stern, rigid, and unyielding in character, doctrine, or moral views ⟨breaks through the barrier of ~ custom —F.C.Laubach⟩ ⟨a square, hulking man who . . . believed with all his ~ soul —P.B.Martin⟩

rock brake *n* : any of several ferns that grow chiefly on or among rocks: as **a :** CLIFF BRAKE **b :** a fern of the genus *Cryptogamma* **c :** POLYPODY

rock breaker *n* : STONE CRUSHER

rock·bridge·ite \'räk,bri,jīt\ *n* -S [*Rockbridge* County, west central Virginia, its locality + E *-ite*] : a mineral ($Fe^{II}Fe_4^{III}(PO_4)_3(OH)_5$) consisting of a basic phosphate of iron isomorphous with frondelite

rock-built \'=,=\ *adj* : made of or built on rock

rock burst *n* : a violent expulsion of rock from the walls of a mine opening caused by heavy pressure on brittle rocks in deep mines where mining has deprived the rock of support on one side — compare BUMP

rock cake *n* : ROCK 5b

rock candy *n* **1 :** boiled sugar crystallized in large masses on lightweight string and used esp. in rock and rye **2 :** ROCK 5a(1)

rock catchfly *n* : a wild pink (*Silene caroliniana*)

rock cavy *n* : MOCO

rock cedar *n* : a juniper (*Juniperus mexicana*) of the southwestern U.S. and Mexico that closely resembles the red cedar and has valuable wood used for ties and telegraph poles — called also *mountain cedar*

rock chestnut oak *n* : a common chestnut oak (*Quercus prinus*)

rock chute *n* : ROCK HOLE

rock-climber \'=,==\ *n* : one that engages in rock-climbing

rock-climbing \'=,==\ *n* : mountain climbing up difficult rocky faces

rock club moss *n* : FESTOON PINE

rock cock *n* : COCK OF THE ROCK

rock cockle *n* : any of several comparatively small edible clams (family Veneridae) of the Pacific coast of No. America that have thick rounded ridged shells resembling those of the cockles

rock cod *n* **1 :** ROCKFISH **2 :** any of several groupers of the genus *Epinephelus*; *esp* : BLACK ROCK COD **3 :** a cod that is a variety of the true cod

rock cork *n* : MOUNTAIN CORK

rock cornish *n, usu cap R&C* : a crossbred domestic fowl produced by breeding Cornish and White Rock fowls and used esp. for the production of small well-fleshed roasters

rock crab *n* : any of several crabs inhabiting rocky shores: as **a :** a crab (*Cancer irroratus*) of the east coast of No. America **b :** a crab (*Cancer antennarius*) of the Pacific coast **c :** SALLY LIGHTFOOT **d :** an Australian crab (*Nectocarcinus integrifrons*)

rockcraft \'=,=\ *n* **1 a :** the art of building with rock **b :** skill in rockcraft **2 :** skill in climbing over rocks and ledges

rock cranberry *n* : MOUNTAIN CRANBERRY

rock cress *n* : any of several rock-loving cresses (as members of the genus *Arabis*)

rockcrusher \'=,==\ *n* **1 :** STONE CRUSHER **2 :** a very strong hand of cards held by one player

rock crystal *n* : transparent quartz : CRYSTAL 2

rock dash *n* : a stucco finish in which crushed rock or pebbles are embedded in the stucco base

rock dassie *n* : KLIPDASSIE

rock day *n, usu cap R&D* [3*rock*; fr. the resumption of domestic duties after the Christmas holidays] : the day after Epiphany

rock dove *n* : ROCK PIGEON 1

rock drill *n* : a machine (as a hammer drill or piston drill) for making holes in rock

rock dust *n* : pulverulent rock (as shale or limestone) used in rock-dusting — called also *stone dust*

rock-dust \'=,=\ *vt* [*rock dust*] : to spread or distribute rock dust in (coal mine workings) to reduce the explosion hazard

rocked *past of* ROCK

rock eel *n* **1 :** GUNNEL **2 :** a blackish green blenny (*Xiphister mucosus*) common in the intertidal zone from Alaska to southern California

rock elm *n* **1 a :** a tall widely distributed elm (*Ulmus thomasii*) of eastern No. America that has broadly obovate leaves narrowing abruptly to a point, grayish deeply fissured bark, and light brown wood **b :** the strong tough durable springy wood of the rock elm **2 :** SLIPPERY ELM **3 :** AMERICAN ELM

1**rock·er** \'räkə(r)\ *n* -S [ME *rokkere*, fr. *rokken* to rock + *-ere* -er] **1** *archaic* : one that rocks a cradle **2 a :** either of two curving pieces of wood or metal on which an object (as a cradle or chair) rocks **b :** any of various objects that rock upon rockers: as (1) **:** CRADLE 1a (2) **:** ROCKING CHAIR (3) **:** an infant's toy having a seat placed between side pieces that are usu. constructed to resemble an animal **c :** any of various objects having the form of a rocker or with parts resembling a rocker: as (1) **:** ROCKER PANEL (2) **:** a skate with a curved blade (3) **:** a curved dentate blade used in mezzotint to roughen the surface of the plate (4) **:** a boat with a rockered keel (5) **:** one of the curved stripes under the three chevrons that indicate the grade of a sergeant (as in the U.S. Army and Marine Corps) **3 :** any of various devices that work with a rocking motion: as **a :** CRADLE 3a **b** *or* **rocker pit** *or* **rocker vat :** a vat equipped with frames on which hides are hung and which rock continuously in order to keep the hides in motion **c** (1) **:** a lever (as in some link motions and gas-engine gears) that is pivoted at or near its center and operates with an up-and-down motion (2) **:** ROCKSHAFT **d :** an adjustable brush holder for a dynamo or motor **e :** a steel or cast-iron pedestal supporting the end of a truss or girder and permitting rotation and horizontal movement caused by expansion and contraction **f :** ROCKING BAR **4 :** a miner or engraver that uses a rocker **5 :** a three-lobed school skating figure performed on either edge and either forward or backward in which the skater executes a turn at each junction of the three lobes in the direction of the natural rotation of the curve being skated and remains on the same edge throughout — compare 5COUNTER 11 — **off one's rocker :** in a state of insanity or confusion ⟨went *off her rocker*, and had to be put away in a mental home —Mervyn Wall⟩

rocker 2b(3)

2**rocker** \"\ *vt* -ED/-ING/-S : to build (as a boat keel) with a camber like a rocker

3**rocker** \"\ *n* -S [4*rock* + *-er*] : ROCK PIGEON

rocker arm *n* : a center-pivoted lever to push an automotive engine valve down when the camshaft pushes the lift rod against the other end of the lever

rocker bent *n* : a bent supporting a bridge span hinged at one or both ends to provide for expansion and contraction of the span

rocker cam *n* : a cam (as on a rockshaft) with a rocking or reciprocating movement

rocker keel *n* : a rockered keel

rocker panel *n* : the portion of the body paneling of a vehicle that is situated below the doorsills of the passenger compartment

rocker shaft *n* : ROCKSHAFT

rocker-stamp \'==,=\ *vt* : to impress a continuous design on (pottery) with an implement rocked at successive points

rock·ery \'räkərē, -əri\ *n* -ES [4*rock* + *-ery*] : ROCK GARDEN

1**rock·et** \'räkət, *usu* -əd·+V\ *n* -S [ME *roket*, fr. ONF *roquet*, fr. (assumed) OF *roc* coat + OF *-et* — more at ROCHET] *chiefly dial* : ROCHET

2**rocket** \"\ *n* -S [MF *roquette*, fr. OIt *rochetta*, *ruchetta*, dim. of *ruca* garden rocket, fr. L *eruca* — more at ERUCA] **1 :** GARDEN ROCKET 1 **2 a :** a plant of the genus *Hesperis*; *esp* : DAME'S VIOLET **b :** any of several plants resembling dame's violet

3**rocket** *n* -S *often attrib* [It *rocchetta* rocket, small distaff, dim. of *rocca* distaff, of Gmc origin; akin to OHG *rocko* distaff — more at ROCK] **1 :** a firework consisting of a cylindrical case partly filled with a combustible composition (as potassium nitrate, charcoal, and sulfur), fastened to a guiding stick, projected through the air by gases liberated when the charge is ignited by a fuse, and used for pyrotechnic display (as stars, gold or silver rain, floral designs) and for signaling **2 :** an incendiary weapon consisting of a tailpiece, fuse and powder charge, and a round-nosed hollow warhead filled with pitch, powder, tallow, and potassium nitrate and fired upward at about 45 degrees through a metal pipe in a wooden chute leading to a square hole in the side of a ship ⟨the ~*s*' red glare —F.S.Key⟩ **3 :** a device consisting of a case containing a combustible composition projected through the air by reaction from the rearward discharge of gases liberated by combustion and used as an incendiary or explosive missile or as a propelling unit (as for a lifesaving line or a whaling harpoon) **4** *also* **rocket engine** *or* **rocket motor : a** jet engine that operates on the same principle as the firework rocket, that consists essentially of a combustion chamber and an exhaust nozzle, that carries either liquid or solid propellants which provide the fuel and oxygen needed for combustion and thus make the engine independent of the oxygen of the air, and that is used esp. for the propulsion of a missile (as a bomb or shell) or a vehicle (as an airplane or automobile) **5 :** a rocket-propelled bomb, missile, or other projectile **6** *chiefly Brit* **:** REBUKE

⁴rocket \"\ *vb* -ED/-ING/-S *vt* **1 :** to attack with rockets ⟨bombing, strafing and *~ing* enemy frontline troops and rear-area supply lines —*N.Y.Times*⟩ **2 :** to convey by means of a rocket ⟨~ a satellite into orbit⟩ **3 :** to bring into prominence ⟨coal . . . suddenly *~ed* this railroad flag stop . . . into industrial importance —*Amer. Guide Series: Va.*⟩ ~ *vi* **1 :** to rise straight up and swiftly when flushed — used esp. of pheasants **2 a :** to rise up swiftly, spectacularly, and with force ⟨*~ed* to stardom almost overnight —*Time*⟩ **b :** to travel rapidly ⟨the salesmen . . . piled back into their cars and *~ed* off to the next live account —Richard Bissell⟩ **syn** see RISE

rocket bomb *n* **1 :** an aerial bomb designed for release at low altitude and equipped with a rocket apparatus for giving it added momentum **2 :** a rocket-propelled bomb launched from the ground

rocket candytuft *n* **:** a European candytuft (*Iberis amara*) having large and full flower clusters

rocket cress *n* **:** a winter cress (*Barbarea vulgaris*)

rock·e·teer \ˌräkəˈti(ə)r, -iə\ *n* -s **1 :** one who fires, pilots, or rides in a rocket **2 :** a scientist who specializes in rocketry; *specif* **:** a designer of rockets

rock·et·er \ˈräkəd·ə(r), -ətə-\ *n* -s **1 :** a game bird that rockets **2 :** ROCKETEER

rocket larkspur *n* **:** a commonly cultivated annual larkspur (*Delphinium ajacis*) of southern Europe with showy blue or sometimes violet or pinkish flowers

rocket launcher *n* **:** a launcher consisting of a tube or cluster of tubes (as a three-tube unit placed on the underside of an airplane wing) for firing rocket shells — see BAZOOKA

rocket plane *n* **:** an airplane propelled by rockets or armed with rocket launchers

rocket-propelled \ˈ==ˌ=ˈ=\ *adj* **:** propelled by a rocket engine

rocket propulsion *n* **:** propulsion by means of a rocket engine

rock·et·ry \ˈräkətrē, -tri\ *n* -ES **:** the study of, experimentation with, or use of rockets

rocket salad *n* **:** GARDEN ROCKET 1

rocket ship *n* **1 :** a rocket-propelled ship **2 :** a small warship equipped with rocket launchers **3 :** a rocket-propelled craft capable of navigation beyond the earth's atmosphere

rocket sled *n* **:** a rocket-propelled sled on a rail

rock face *n* **1 :** a weather-worn quarry face **2 :** FACE 7c

rock-faced \ˈ=ˌ=\ *adj* **:** having a face of or resembling rock

rock falcon *n* **1** *or* **rock hawk :** MERLIN **2 :** PEREGRINE FALCON

rockfall \ˈ=ˌ=\ *n* **:** a mass of falling or fallen rocks — compare ROCKSLIDE

rock fastener *n* **:** an interlocking seal formed by looped ends of wire binding a wood box

rock fence *n, chiefly South* **:** STONE WALL 1

rock fern *n* **:** any of various ferns that grow chiefly on or among rocks: as **a :** EVERGREEN WOOD FERN 1 **b :** a finely divided tropical Asiatic and Australasian fern (*Cheilanthes tenuifolia*) that has been implicated in Australia in an acute intoxication of cattle **c :** any of several chiefly tropical ferns of the genus *Asplenium*

rock-fill \ˈ=ˌ=\ *adj* [⁴*rock* + *fill*, n.] **:** composed of large rock or stone loosely placed ⟨*rock-fill* dam⟩

rockfish \ˈ=ˌ=\ *n* **:** any of various fishes that live among rocks or on rocky bottoms: as **a :** any of several fishes of the family Scorpaenidae including the black rockfish, the cabezone, the priestfish, and the red rockfish that are all valuable market fishes — see GOPHER 4 **b :** STRIPED BASS **a c :** any of several groupers **d :** GREENLING 1a

rock flour *n* **:** finely powdered rock material produced by grinding action (as of a glacier on its bed) — called also *glacial meal*

rockfoil \ˈ=ˌ=\ *n* [⁴*rock* + *foil* (leaf)] **:** SAXIFRAGE

rock garden *n* **:** a garden laid out among rocks or decorated with rocks and adapted for the growth of particular kinds of plants (as alpines) — compare ALPINE GARDEN

rock gas *n* **:** NATURAL GAS

rock geranium *n* **:** ALUMROOT 1

rock glacier *n* **:** a rock stream having the general appearance of a valley glacier

rock goat *n* **:** IBEX

rock goldenrod *n* **:** a perennial goldenrod (*Solidago pumila*) of western No. America having tufted basal leaves, a very short stem, and yellow flower heads

rock goose *n* **:** KELP GOOSE

rock grouper *n* **:** RED ROCKFISH 2

rock grouse *n* **1 :** ROCK PTARMIGAN **2 :** SANDGROUSE

rock guenon *n* **:** PATAS

rock gypsum *n* **:** massive coarsely crystalline to fine-grained gypsum

rockhair \ˈ=ˌ=\ *n* **:** a slender rock-inhabiting tufted lichen (*Alectoria jubata*) used in dyeing

rock hare *n* **:** any of several very fleet short-eared usu. reddish hares (genus *Pronolagus*) of southern Africa — called also *red hare*

rock hind *n* **:** any of various spotted groupers commonly found about rocky coasts or reefs; *esp* **:** a common small form (*Epinephelus adscensionis*) of the tropical Atlantic and Mediterranean typically grayish green with red or red-brown spots and white blotches — compare HIND

rock hole *n* **:** a raise in a coal mine driven from a gangway or breast to an overlying coal seam — called also *rock chute*

rock hopper *n* **:** any of several small penguins (genus *Eudyptes*) of the Falkland Islands, New Zealand, and antarctic waters that have a short thick bill and a yellow crest — called also *crested penguin*

rock hound *n* **1 :** GEOLOGIST; *esp* **:** one who searches for oil **2 :** one who hunts and collects gemstones or minerals as a hobby

rock hyrax *n* **:** a hyrax that frequents barren rocky areas: **a :** KLIPDASSIE **b :** SYRIAN HYRAX

rockier *comparative of* ROCKY

rockies *pl of* ROCKY

rockiest *superlative of* ROCKY

rock·i·ness \ˈräkēnəs, -kin-\ *n* -ES **:** the quality or state of being rocky

¹rock·ing \ˈräkiŋ, -kēŋ\ *adj* [ME *rokkinge*, pres. part. of *rokken* to rock] **1 a :** having a swaying, rolling, or back-and-forth movement **b :** used for rocking **2 :** held up by a horizontal quarter circle — see BRAND illustration

²rock·ing \ˈräkən, -kiŋ\ *n* -s [³*rock* + *-ing*] *Scot* **:** an evening gathering; *esp* **:** a spinning party

rocking bar *n* **1 :** a bascule-shaped plate in a watch that contains the winding wheels and rocks them alternately to engage first the winding and then the hand setting mechanism **2 :** a device in an alarm clock or watch that engages the time and alarm mainsprings

rocking bed *n* **:** a powered bed that uses gravity as an artificial respirator by raising a person's head above the feet so that the weight of the abdominal organs stretches the diaphragm and raising the feet above the head so that the weight of the organs compresses the diaphragm

rocking cam *n* **:** ROCKER CAM

rocking chair *n* **:** a chair mounted on rockers

rocking furnace *n* **:** an often electrically heated horizontal cylindrical melting furnace rolling back and forth in a usu. geared cradle

rock·ing·ham \ˈräkiŋˌham, -ŋəm\ *or* **rockingham ware** *n, usu cap R* [after Charles Watson-Wentworth, Marquis of *Rockingham* †1782 Eng. statesman on whose estate at Swinton, England, it was originally made] **:** a usu. buff or white earthenware with an often spattered brown glaze; *also* **:** an ornately decorated and gilded 19th century bone chinaware from the same source

rocking horse *n* **:** a toy consisting of a figure of a horse mounted on rockers or on a mechanism permitting rocking on which a child may sit and rock — called also *hobbyhorse*

rocking horse

rock·ing·ly *adv* **:** in a rocking manner

rocking pier *n* **:** a bridge pier hinged so as to allow a slight longitudinal motion of the bridge when the latter expands or contracts

rocking rhythm *n* **:** UNDULATING CADENCE

rocking shaft *n* **:** ROCKSHAFT

rocking stone *n* **:** an often large stone so balanced upon its foundation that it can be rocked or slightly moved with little force

rocking tool *n* **:** ROCKER 2c(3)

rocking valve *or* **rocking slide valve** *n* **:** a steam engine valve consisting of a disk or cylindrical piece with the necessary openings that oscillates or revolves on its seat

rock jasmine *n* **:** a plant of the genus *Androsace*

rock kangaroo *n* **:** ROCK WALLABY

rock kelp *n* **:** ROCKWEED

rock lark *n* **:** ROCK PIPIT

rock larkspur *n* **:** DWARF LARKSPUR

rock·lay \ˈräˌklā\ *chiefly Scot var of* ROQUELAURE

rock leather *n* **:** MOUNTAIN LEATHER

rock·less \ˈräkləs\ *adj* **:** lacking rocks

rock·let \-lət\ *n* -s **:** a small rock

rock lever *or* **rocking lever** *n* **:** a hinged lever that works with a rocking movement **:** an equalizing bar for draft animals hinged by a knuckle joint

rocklike \ˈ=ˌ=\ *adj* **:** resembling a rock esp. in hardness

rock lily *n* **1 :** a tropical American club moss (*Selaginella convoluta*) that grows in dense tufts **2 :** an Australian orchid (*Dendrobium speciosum*) having large green pseudobulbs and dense racemes of creamy white flowers that is usu. found growing on rocks **3 :** any of several rock-loving herbs: as **a :** COLUMBINE **b :** PASQUEFLOWER

rock·ling \ˈräkliŋ\ *n, pl* **rocklings** *also* **rockling** [⁴*rock* + *ling*] **1 :** any of several small rather elongate marine cods (family Gadidae); *esp* **:** a fish (*Gadus mustela* or *Motella mustela*) that is common in tide pools along European coasts and has four barbels on the snout and one beneath the chin — called also *five-bearded rockling* **2 :** an Australian and New Zealand fish (genus *Genypterus*) of the family Ophidiidae

rock lobster *n* **1 :** SPINY LOBSTER **2 :** the flesh of the Cape crawfish esp. when canned or frozen for use as food

rock louse *n* **:** a small innocuous Australian isopod (*Deto marina*) living under rocks along the seashore

rock madwort *n* **:** BASKET-OF-GOLD

rock·man \ˈräkmən, -ˌman\ *n, pl* **rockmen 1 :** a worker who removes rocks or ledges by blasting **2 :** a worker in a mine: **a** *Brit* **:** a miner who gets out slate rock in a slate mine **b :** SLATEMAN **3 :** a jackhammer operator **4 :** TOWERMAN d

rock manakin *n* **:** COCK OF THE ROCK

rock maple *n* **:** a sugar maple (*Acer saccharum*)

rock martin *n* **:** ROCK SWALLOW

rock mat *n* **:** any of several evergreen prostrate subshrubs constituting a genus (*Petrophytum*) of the family Rosaceae

rock melon *n* **:** CANTALOUPE

rock milk *n* **:** AGARIC MINERAL

rock moss *n* **1 :** a rock-loving lichen **2 :** WIDOW'S-CROSS

rock mouse *n* **:** a small southern African murid rodent (*Petromyscus collinus*) living in rocky areas

rock 'n' roll *or* **rock and roll** \ˌräkənˈrōl\ *n* **1 :** popular music characterized by a strong beat and much repetition of simple phrases often with elements of blues, folk song, and country music **2 :** an improvisatory style of popular dancing associated with rock 'n' roll music

rock 'n' roller *or* **rock and roller** \ˌ==ˈrōlə(r)\ *n* **:** one who composes or plays rock 'n' roll or who is an enthusiastic dancer or listener to rock 'n' roll

rock oak *n* **:** any of several American oaks: as **a :** BASKET OAK **b :** CHESTNUT OAK **c :** BLUE OAK

rock oil *n* [trans. of ML *petroleum*] **:** PETROLEUM

rock·oon \(ˈ)räˈkün\ *n* -s [³*rocket* + *balloon*] **:** a small rocket carried to a high altitude by a balloon and then fired

rock opossum *n* **:** a rock wallaby (*Petrogale xanthopus*)

rock ouzel *n* **:** RING OUZEL

rock oyster *n* **:** any of various oysters or other bivalves occurring attached to rocks: **a :** a mollusk of the genus *Hinnites* represented on the west coast of No. America by a large flattened bivalve (*H. giganteus*) **b :** a mollusk of *Chama* or related genera **c :** JINGLE SHELL

rock painting *n* **:** a painting on rock (as a cave wall, cliff, or boulder) made by primitive peoples

rock parrakeet *or* **rock parrot** *n* **:** a small chiefly greenish Australian parrakeet (*Neophema petrophila*) that nests in holes in cliffs

rock partridge *n* **:** a partridge (*Alectoris graeca*) having many varieties widely distributed in southern and eastern Asia and about the Mediterranean esp. in dry uplands — compare CHUKAR, GREEK PARTRIDGE, RED-LEGGED PARTRIDGE

rock phosphate *n* **:** phosphate rock used as a fertilizer

rock pigeon *n* **1 :** a bluish gray wild pigeon (*Columba livia*) with a purplish breast, white rump, and dark wing bars that is found chiefly along rocky coasts of Europe and Asia — called also *rock dove* **2 :** SANDGROUSE

rock pile *n* [so called fr. the custom of requiring prisoners to work at breaking rock] **:** JAIL

rock pine *n* **1 :** a cypress pine (*Callitris verrucosa*) **2 :** a ponderosa pine (*Pinus ponderosa scopulorum*)

rock pink *n* **:** a pink-flowered perennial herb (*Talinum calycinum*) of the western U. S.

rock pipit *n* **:** a European pipit (*Anthus spinoletta petrosus*) that frequents rocky shores — called also *rock lark*

rock plant *n* **:** a plant that grows on or among rocks or is suited to a rock garden

rock plover *n* **1 :** PURPLE SANDPIPER **2 :** TURNSTONE

rock pool *n* **:** a tide pool in a rocky shoreline or reef

rock pressure *n* **1 :** the pressure on fluids in subsurface formation **2 :** the pressure indicated in a closed well

rock ptarmigan *n* **:** any of various ptarmigans (esp. *Lagopus mutus*)

rock purslane *n* **:** a plant of the genus *Calandrinia*

rock python *n* **:** a very large python (*Python sebae*) of tropical and southern Africa — called also *rock snake*

rock rabbit *n* **1 :** ²HYRAX **2 :** PIKA

rock rat *n* **:** any of several African rodents of rocky uplands; *esp* **:** a small southern African hystricomorph rodent (*Petromys typicus*) having four grinding teeth on each side in each jaw

rock-ribbed \ˈ=ˌ=\ *adj* **1 :** ROCKY **2 :** firm and inflexible in doctrine or integrity

rock river *n* **:** an exceptionally long and narrow rock stream

rockrose \ˈ=ˌ=\ *n* **1 :** a plant of the Cistaceae (esp. of the genera *Cistus, Helianthemum,* and *Crocanthemum*) **2 :** any of several Australian shrubs (as of the genus *Hibbertia*)

rockrose family *n* **:** CISTACEAE

rocks *pres 3d sing of* ROCK, *pl of* ROCK

rock salmon *n* **1 :** AMBERJACK **a 2 :** a common silvery pink to bright red snapper (*Lutjanus argentimaculatus*) of the tropical Indo-Pacific highly esteemed for food and sport **3 :** any of several fishes (as the pollack, the wolffish, or the dogfish) used as food in England but not esteemed as food fishes under their usual names

rock salt *n* **:** common salt occurring in solid form as a mineral esp. in rocklike masses and usu. more or less colored by iron **:** HALITE; *sometimes* **:** salt artificially prepared in large crystals or masses

rock samphire *n* **:** SAMPHIRE 1, 2

rock sand *n* **:** the detritus of eroded or abraded rock commonly used for cores in casting

rock sandwort *n* **:** a low perennial tufted herb (*Arenaria stricta*) of northeastern No. America with subulate rigid leaves and small white flowers in dichotomous cymes

rock saw *n* **:** a small coarse-toothed saw that cuts into a log ahead of the main saw and protects the latter by removing small stones or pebbles embedded in the log

rock saxifrage *n* **:** EARLY SAXIFRAGE

rock seal *n* **:** HARBOR SEAL

¹rockshaft \ˈ=ˌ=\ *n* [¹*rock* + *shaft*] **:** a shaft that oscillates on its journals instead of revolving and that usu. carries levers or projecting pieces (as arms, wipers, or tumblers) to receive and communicate reciprocating motion

²rockshaft \"\ *n* [⁴*rock* + *shaft*] **:** a shaft through which rock filling is introduced into a mine

rock shell *n* **:** a gastropod mollusk of the family Muricidae

rock-shelter \ˈ=ˌ==\ *n* **:** a natural shelter between or under standing rocks in which the debris and campfires of prehistoric peoples are found

rock·skip·per \ˈ=ˌ==\ *n* **:** any of several blennies; *esp* **:** a small Indo-Pacific fish (*Alticops periophthalmus*) that is extremely agile in and about rocky tide pools and reefs

rockslide \ˈ=ˌ=\ *n* **1 :** a usu. rapid downward movement of rock fragments that slide over an inclined surface **2 :** a rock mass moved by a rockslide — compare ROCKFALL

rock snake *n* **1 :** any of several large pythons: as **a :** ROCK PYTHON **b :** INDIAN PYTHON **c :** CARPET SNAKE **2 :** a snake of the genus *Bungarus* (as the krait)

rock snipe *n* **:** PURPLE SANDPIPER

rock soap *n* **:** MOUNTAIN SOAP

rock sparrow *n* **1 :** any of several Old World sparrows of the genus *Petronia* (as *P. petronia* and *P. superciliaris*) **2 :** a sparrow (*Aimophila ruficeps eremoeca*) of Mexico and Texas

rock spiraea *n* **:** a plant of the genus *Holodiscus* — compare OCEAN SPRAY

rock spray *n* **:** any of several plants of the genus *Cotoneaster; esp* **:** a prostrate evergreen Himalayan shrub (*C. horizontalis*) cultivated for its solitary white flowers and bright red fruits

rock squirrel *n* **1 :** a large ground squirrel (*Citellus variegatus grammurus*) of western No. America having better developed tail and ears than the more strictly burrowing species **2 :** any of several relatively large terrestrial squirrels (genus *Sciurotamias* or *Rupestes*) of the rocky uplands of east central Asia

rockstaff \ˈ=ˌ=\ *n* [¹*rock* + *staff*] **:** an oscillating bar (as the lever of a forge bellows)

rock starling *n* [⁴*rock* + *starling*] **:** RING OUZEL

rock stream *n* **:** a mass of rock fragments that moves or has moved slowly down a slope under its own weight usu. aided by frost action and sometimes by interstitial ice — compare ROCK GLACIER, ROCK RIVER

rock sturgeon *n* **:** LAKE STURGEON

rock sucker *n* **:** LAMPREY

rock sunfish *n* **:** ROCK BASS 1

rock swallow *n* **:** any of several swallows that nest on rocky crags; *esp* **:** a common Eurasiatic bird (*Ptyonoprogne rupestris*) — called also *crag martin, rock martin*

rock tar *n* **:** PETROLEUM

rock terrace *n* **:** a terrace of more durable bedrock left on the side of a valley cut by erosion in flat-lying sedimentary or volcanic strata of varying resistance

rock thrush *or* **rock shrike** *n* **:** any of various Old World thrushes of the genus *Monticola*

rock tripe *n* **:** a lichen of the genus *Umbilicaria* or of the related genus *Gyrophora* that has a flat coriaceous blackish thallus, is common on rocks in arctic, subarctic, and north temperate regions, and is used as food in cases of extremity

rock trout *n* **:** GREENLING 1a

rock turn *n* **:** a turn in ballroom dancing in which the couple use a rocking step

rock turquoise *n* **:** turquoise matrix

rock violet *n* **:** a green alga (*Trentepohlia iolithus*) occurring on rocks at high elevations and exhaling an odor of violets

rock vole *n* **:** a light-colored vole (*Microtus chrotorrhinus*) of rocky highlands of northeastern No. America

rock wallaby *n* **:** any of various medium-sized kangaroos of the genus *Petrogale* having a completely naked muzzle and a slender tufted tail and inhabiting rocky regions — called also *rock kangaroo*

rock warbler *n* **:** a small Australian singing bird (*Origma rubricata*) that frequents rocky ravines

rock waste *n* **:** the material resulting from the disintegration and decomposition of rock by weathering

rockweed \ˈ=ˌ=\ *n* **:** a coarse seaweed of the family Fucaceae growing attached to rocks; *esp* **:** a member of the genera *Fucus* or *Ascophyllum*

rockweed bird *n* **:** PURPLE SANDPIPER

rock·well hardness \ˈräˌkwel-, -ˌkwəl-\ *n, usu cap R* [after Stanley P. *Rockwell*, 20th cent. Am. metallurgist] **:** the hardness of a metal or alloy measured by an apparatus in which a diamond-pointed cone is pressed into the metal to a standard depth to determine the relative resistance to penetration as indicated automatically by a number on a dial

rock whiting *n* **:** KELPFISH b

rock wool *n* **:** mineral wool made by blowing a jet of steam through molten rock (as limestone or siliceous rock) or through slag and used chiefly for heat and sound insulation

rockwork \ˈ=ˌ=\ *n* **1 :** a mass of rocks **2 a :** ROCK GARDEN **b :** artificial rock ledges and waterfalls in gardens **3 a :** stonework with a surface left broken and rough **b :** rock-faced masonry **4 :** ROCKCRAFT 2

rock wren *n* **1 :** a wren (*Salpinctes obsoletus*) of arid parts of the western U. S. and Mexico **2 :** a small short-tailed passerine bird (*Xenicus gilviventris*) of New Zealand

¹rocky \ˈräkē, -ki\ *adj* -ER/-EST [ME *rokky*, fr. *rokke* rock, cliff + *-y*, adj. suffix] **1 :** abounding in or consisting of rocks ⟨a ~ shore⟩ **2 :** difficult to impress or affect **:** HARD, INSENSITIVE, OBDURATE ⟨may he also move my mind, and ~ heart so strike and rend —James Howell⟩ **3 :** firmly held **:** STEADFAST ⟨eccentrics . . . have their ~ rightness even when the world judges them to have been wildly wrong —*Times Lit. Supp.*⟩

²rocky \"\ *adj* [¹*rock* + *-y*] **1 :** prone to rock or totter **:** UNSTABLE ⟨wore high ~ heels —Wright Morris⟩ **2 :** ill at ease, physically upset, or mentally confused (as from a blow, drinking excessively, or sickness) ⟨feeling pretty ~ on account of the siege I went through last night —E.A.Robinson⟩ ⟨wound up with a two-inch cut under the left eye and was ~ at the final bell —*N.Y. Times*⟩ **3 a :** appearing likely to fail **:** UNPROMISING ⟨the wedding got off to a ~ start —R.L.Taylor⟩ **b :** marked by obstacles **:** DIFFICULT ⟨eight ~ months in business — *Time*⟩ **4 :** tending towards craziness **:** DAFT **5 :** UNCOUTH, OBSCENE ⟨a ~ story⟩

³rocky \"\ *n* -ES [⁴*rock* + *-y*, n. suffix] *Austral* **:** ROCK CRAB

rocky ford \ˈ==ˌ=\ *n, usu cap R&F* [fr. *Rocky Ford*, city in southeast Colorado that is the trade center for a region producing such muskmelons] **:** any of various netted muskmelons that are typically of superior shipping quality

rocky mountain \ˌ==ˈ==\ *adj, usu cap R&M* [fr. *Rocky mountains*, mountain system in western No. America] **:** of or relating to the Rocky mountains

rocky mountain bee plant *n, usu cap R&M* **:** a spiderflower (*Cleome serrulata*) of north central and western No. America sometimes used as an ornamental — called also *stinking clover*

rocky mountain canary *n, usu cap R&M, chiefly West* **:** BURRO

rocky mountain elk *n, usu cap R&M* **:** a wapiti (*Cervus canadensis nelsoni*)

rocky mountain fir *n, usu cap R&M* **:** ALPINE FIR

rocky mountain garrot *n, usu cap R&M* **:** BARROW'S GOLDENEYE

rocky mountain goat *n, usu cap R&M* **:** MOUNTAIN GOAT 1

rocky mountain grape *n, usu cap R&M* **:** OREGON GRAPE

rocky mountain grasshopper *or* **rocky mountain locust** *n, usu cap R&M* **:** a No. American grasshopper (*Melanoplus spretus*)

rocky mountain jay *n, usu cap R&M* **:** a Canada jay (*Perisoreus canadensis capitalis*) having a white head and being widely distributed in the Rocky mountain area from Montana to Arizona and New Mexico

rocky mountain juniper *or* **rocky mountain red cedar** *n, usu cap 1st R&M* **:** a small to medium-sized conical evergreen tree (*Juniperus scopulorum*) that is native to the Rocky mountain region, has reddish brown shreddy bark, often drooping branchlets, and gray-green foliage, and is used for hedges and other ornamental purposes

rocky mountain maple *n, usu cap R&1stM* **:** DWARF MAPLE

rocky mountain oyster *n, usu cap R&M* **:** MOUNTAIN OYSTER

rocky mountain sheep *n, usu cap R&M* : BIGHORN

rocky mountain spotted fever *n, usu cap R&M* : an acute febrile disease that is characterized by chills, fever, prostration, pains in muscles and joints, and a red to purple eruption and is caused by a microorganism (*Rickettsia rickettsii*) transmitted by the bite of the Rocky Mountain wood tick

rocky mountain whitefish *n, usu cap R&M* : a whitefish (*Prosopium williamsonii*) of the western U. S. and Canada

rocky mountain white oak *n, usu cap R&M* : any of several Rocky Mountain trees of the genus *Quercus*

rocky mountain white pine *n, usu cap R&M* : LIMBER PINE

rocky mountain willow *n, usu cap R&M* : a low much-branched shrubby willow (*Salix saximontana*) of the boreal regions of northwestern No. America, having oblong-oval to orbicular leaves

rocky mountain wood tick *n, usu cap R&M* : a widely distributed wood tick (*Dermacentor andersoni*) of western No. America that is a vector of Rocky Mountain spotted fever and sometimes causes tick paralysis

[1]**ro·co·co** \rə'kō(,)kō, rō'k- *also* 'rōkə,kō\ *adj* [F, irreg. fr. *rocaille;* fr. the prevalence of rocaille ornamentation in 18th century France] **1** : OUTMODED, QUAINT, OLD-FASHIONED **2 a** : of, relating to, or having the characteristics of a style of artistic expression prevalent esp. during the 18th century chiefly in interior decoration, furniture, porcelain, and tapestry and characterized by an often fanciful and frivolous use of curved spatial forms, light and fantastic often flowing, reversed, or unsymmetrical curved lines, and ornament of pierced shellwork ⟨the explosive energy of the baroque . . . lessens as the ~ spirit of the new century lightens the motives it has inherited, and replaces gusto with a slighter vivacity —*History of World Art*⟩ — compare BAROQUE, LOUIS QUINZE **b** : of, relating to, or having the characteristics of a style of painting esp. prevalent during the 18th century exemplified by Watteau and often depicting scenes from classical mythology inspired by the fêtes champêtres **c** : of, relating to, or having the characteristics of a style of literature prevalent esp. in Germany in the first half of the 18th century and typified esp. by lighthearted playful lyric pieces often with suggestive erotic hints **d** : of, relating to, or having the characteristics of a style of music esp. of the 18th century marked by light gay ornamentation and the departure from thorough bass and polyphony **e** : excessively ornate or intricate ⟨his bed was covered with a lavishly embroidered velvet slip, far too ~ for any interior decorator's parlor but more like evidence of an adolescent and painfully mistaken idea of what a prince might choose —Kay Boyle⟩ ⟨the lush and heartbreakingly ~ writings of . . . a society reporter of long ago whose prose gyrations must be read to be believed —Stanley Walker⟩ ⟨caught out with a ~ phrase or an overstuffed image —*Los Angeles* (*Calif.*) *Times*⟩ **syn** see ORNATE

[2]**rococo** \"\ *n* -s [F, fr. *rococo*, adj.] : rococo work or style

rocombole *var of* ROCAMBOLE

rocou *var of* ROUCOU

rocs *pl of* ROC

[1]**rod** \'räd\ *n* -s [ME, fr. OE *rodd;* akin to ON *rudda* club and perh. to OHG *riutan* to clear land — more at RID] **1 a** (1) : a straight slender stick growing upon or cut from a tree or bush : SHOOT, WAND (2) : OSIER (3) : WALKING STICK (4) : a stick or bundle of twigs used for punishing ⟨he who spares the ~ hates his son —Prov 13:24 (RSV)⟩ (5) : a short club or stick with a bulging end used by shepherds as a cudgel to protect their flocks from wolves (6) *obs* : a stick or switch used while riding (7) : FISHING POLE (8) : a bar or staff for measuring (9) : a narrow board, lath, batten, or strip usu. cut to a fixed length and marked with feet and inches or usu. the heights and other dimensions of work to be done — called also *staff* (10) : a long wooden straightedge used with the edge against fresh plaster to bring the plaster to a true surface **b** : a slender bar resembling a wand of wood: as (1) : FISHING ROD (2) *dial Brit* : a wagon shaft (3) : RAMROD (4) : a member used in tension (as for sustaining a suspended weight) or in tension and compression (as for transmitting reciprocating motion) : CONNECTING ROD (5) : any of various parts of the metal framework below the body of a railroad car — usu. used in the phrase *ride the rods* ⟨then I rode the ~s east —Earle Birney⟩ (6) *slang* : REVOLVER, PISTOL (7) : a wood or metal often expandable bar used for hanging household items (as window or shower curtains, clothes, and towels) (8) : LIGHTNING ROD **c** (1) : SCEPTER (2) : a wand or staff carried as a badge of office by a marshal, usher, or similar official **2 a** (1) : a means of punishment (2) : punishment inflicted **b** : POWER, AUTHORITY, TYRANNY ⟨shall rule them with a ~ of iron —Rev 2:27 (RSV)⟩ **3 a** : a unit of length equal to 5½ yards or 16½ feet — see MEASURE table **b** : a square rod **4** : any of the long rod-shaped sensory bodies in the retina responsive to faint light — compare CONE 3c; see SCOTOPIA **5** : a bacterium shaped like a rod **6** : WHIP 3a **7** : FISHERMAN **8** : HOT ROD

[2]**rod** \"\ *vt* **rodded**; **rodded**; **rodding**; **rods** **1** : to provide with lightning rods **2** : to pack tight, smooth, or pulverize (as concrete) by pounding with a rod **3** : to remove obstacles from or clean (a receptacle) by running a rod through

rod adaptation *n* : DARK ADAPTATION

rod breaker *n* : a breaker whose moldboard is replaced by bent rods to reduce friction

rod cell *n* : MACROSCLEREID

rod–cone theory *n* : DUPLICITY THEORY

rod·der \'rädə(r)\ *n* -s [[1]*rod* + *-er*] : a textile worker who folds double-width goods

[1]**rode** [ME *rood, rode* (past), fr. OE *rād*] *past and chiefly dial past part of* RIDE

[2]**rode** \'rōd\ *dial Brit var of* RUD

[3]**rode** \"\ *n* -s [origin unknown] : a light rope for a boat's anchor

rode goose \"-\ *n* [alter. of *road goose*] *Brit* : a brant (*Branta bernicla*)

[1]**ro·dent** \'rōdᵊnt\ *adj* [L *rodent-, rodens*, pres. part. of *rodere* to gnaw — more at RAT] **1** : GNAWING, BITING, CORRODING **2** [NL *Rodentia*] : of or relating to the Rodentia or a rodent

[2]**rodent** *n* -s [NL *Rodentia*] **1** : a mammal of the order Rodentia **2** : a small mammal suggesting a member of the Rodentia (as a shrew or a pika)

ro·den·tia \rō'dench(ē)ə, -ntēə\ *n pl, cap* [NL, fr. L, neut. pl. of *rodent-, rodens*, pres. part. of *rodere* to gnaw] **1** : an order of Eutheria comprising relatively small gnawing mammals with a single pair of upper incisors that grow from persistent pulps and bear enamel chiefly in front to produce a chisel-shaped edge — compare HYSTRICOMORPHA, MYOMORPHA, SCIUROMORPHA **2** *in some classifications* : an order coextensive with Glires — **ro·den·tian** \-ən\ *adj or n*

ro·den·tial \-əl\ *adj* [NL *Rodentia* + E *-al*] : of or relating to the Rodentia — **ro·den·tial·ly** \-əlē\ *adv*

ro·den·ti·ci·dal \rō¦dentə¦sīdᵊl\ *adj* [[2]*rodent* + *-i-* + *-cidal*] **1** : destroying or controlling rodents **2** [*rodenticide* + *-al*] : of or relating to a rodenticide

ro·den·ti·cide \=ˈ==,sīd\ *n* -s [[2]*rodent* + *-i-* + *-cide*] : an agent that kills rodents; *broadly* : an agent that repels or controls rodents

rodent ulcer *n* : a chronic persisting ulcer of the exposed skin and esp. of the face destructive locally and spreading slowly that is usu. a basal-cell carcinoma

[1]**ro·deo** \÷'rōdē,ō, rō'dā(,)ō *sometimes* 'rōdā,ō *or* rə'dā(,)ō; *the stress in Spanish is* =ˈ==\ *n* -s [Sp, roundup, action of surrounding, fr. *rodear* to surround, fr. *rueda* wheel, fr. L *rota* — more at ROLL] **1 a** : ROUNDUP **b** : a place where cattle are brought together **2 a** : a public performance that features esp. contests in bareback bronco riding, calf roping, saddle bronco riding, steer wrestling, and Brahma bull riding **b** : an assembly or contest likened to a rodeo ⟨combine forces with one or more other troops and hold a bicycle ~ —*Girl Scout Handbook*⟩ ⟨parachute ~⟩ ⟨annual sailfish ~ held each spring⟩

[2]**rodeo** \"\ *vi* -ED/-ING/-S : to compete in a rodeo

rod epithelium *n* : epithelium having the cells striated so as to appear as if divided at one end into a bundle of rods and lining parts of various glands

rod fiber *n* : the terminal fiber of a retinal rod

rod granule *n* : the cell body of a retinal rod

rod·ham \'räd,ham\ *n* -s [[1]*rod* + *ham*] : a patch of land bearing willow trees

rod·ing \'rōdiŋ\ *n* -s [[4]*rode* + *-ing*] : the anchor line of a dory or similar small fishing boat

rod in pickle : a reproof, punishment, or penalty ready for future application

rod·knight \'räd,=\ *n* [ME, fr. OE *rādcniht* — more at RADKNIGHT] : RADKNIGHT

rod·less \'rädləs\ *adj* : lacking a rod

rod·let \-dlət\ *n* -s : a small rod

rodlike \'=,=\ *adj* : resembling a rod

rod·man \'rädmən, -,man\ *n, pl* **rodmen** **1** : CHAINMAN 4 **2** : a worker who puts reinforcing steel into concrete forms **3** : a textile worker who steams cloth in a chamber

rod mill *n* **1** : a mill that produces rods of steel or other metal **2** : a pulverizing machine that uses loose iron rods as the grinding media — compare BALL MILL

rod·ney \'rädni\ *n* -s [prob. fr. the name *Rodney*] *dial Eng* : IDLER, BUM

rod of cor·ti \-'kȯrd·ē, -r,tē\ *usu cap C* [after Alfonso *Corti* †1876 Ital. anatomist] : any of the minute modified epithelial elements that rise from the basilar membrane of the organ of Corti in two spirally arranged rows so that the free ends of the members incline toward and interlock with corresponding members of the opposite row and enclose the tunnel of Corti

ro·do·lia \rō'dōlyə\ *n, cap* [NL] : a genus of predaceous ladybugs including the vedalia

rodo·mont \'rädə,mänt, 'rōd-\ *n* -s [It *rodomonte*, fr. *Rodomonte, Rodamonte*, fierce and boastful Moorish king of Algiers in the epic *Orlando Innamorato* (1487) by Matteo M. Boiardo †1494 Ital. poet and in the epic *Orlando Furioso* (1516) by Lodovico Ariosto †1533 Ital. poet] : a vain or blustering boaster : BRAGGART, BRAGGADOCIO

[1]**rodo·mon·tade** \¦==_mən·¦tād, -,män·-, -täd\ *or* **rodo·mon·ta·do** \,==(,)='tä(,)dō\ *also* **rhodo·mon·tade** \¦rädə-, ¦rōd-\ *n* -s [MF *rodomontade*, fr. *Rodomonte, Rodamonte* + MF *-ade*] **1 a** : a vain exaggerated boast : a bragging speech **b** : vain boasting : empty bluster : RANT **2** : BRAGGART **syn** see BOMBAST

[2]**rodomontade** *also* **rhodomontade** \"\ *vi* : BOAST, BRAG, RANT

[3]**rodomontade** \"\ *or* **rodomontado** \"\ *also* **rhodomontade** \"\ *adj* : BOASTFUL, RANTING

rods *pl of* ROD, *pres 3d sing of* ROD

rods·man \'rädzmən\ *n, pl* **rodsmen** [*rod's* (gen. of [1]*rod*) + *man*] **1** : CHAINMAN 4 **2** : one who eases jammed oil-shale retorts by pushing with long iron rods

rod·ster \'rädztə(r), -dst-\ *n* -s : ANGLER

rod weeder *n* : an implement that destroys weeds in plowed land by means of a square rod that revolves backward as it is drawn forward across a field a few inches below the surface of the soil and lifts weeds and clods to the surface

[1]**roe** \'rō\ *n, pl* **roe** *or* **roes** [ME *ro, roo*, fr. OE *rā;* akin to OHG *rēh* roe deer, ON *rā* roe deer, OIr *rīabach* dappled, Lith *raĩbas*] **1** : ROE DEER **2 a** : HIND **b** : DOE

[2]**roe** \"\ *n* -s [ME *roof, roughe, row;* akin to OHG *rogo* roe, ON *hrogn* roe, Lith *kurkulaĩ* frog's eggs] **1 a** : the eggs of a fish esp. when still enclosed in the ovarian membrane ⟨shad ~⟩ — compare SOFT ROE **b** : the eggs or ovaries of an invertebrate (as the coral of a lobster) **2** : a dark mottled or flecked figure appearing esp. in quartersawed lumber of wood with an interlocked grain (as a figured mahogany)

roe·bling·ite \'rōbliŋ,īt\ *n* -s [Washington A. *Roebling* †1926 Am. civil engineer + E *-ite*] : a mineral supposedly $Ca_7Pb_2H_{10}(SO_4)_2(SiO_4)_6$ consisting of an acid lead calcium silicate and sulfate occurring in white crystalline masses (hardness 3, sp. gr. 3.4)

roe·buck \'rō,bək\ *n, pl* **roebuck** *or* **roebucks** [ME *robucke, roobucke*, fr. *ro, roo* roe deer + *buck, bucke* buck] : ROE DEER; *esp* : the male roe deer

roed \'rōd\ *adj* : filled with roe ⟨a ~ salmon⟩

roe deer *n* : a small European and Asiatic deer (*Capreolus capreolus*) that has erect cylindrical antlers forked at the summit and approximate at the base, is reddish brown in summer and grayish in winter, has a white rump patch, and is noted for its nimbleness and gracefulness

roeier *comparative of* ROEY

roeiest *superlative of* ROEY

roe·mer·ite \'rāmə,rīt, 'rərm-\ *n* -s [G *römerit*, fr. Friedrich A. *Roemer* †1869 Ger. geologist + G *-it* -ite] : a mineral $FeFe_2(SO_4)_4.14H_2O$ consisting of a hydrous sulfate of ferrous and ferric iron

[1]**roent·gen** *also* **rönt·gen** \'ren|tgən, 'rən| *also* |chən *or* |tjən\ *adj* [ISV, fr. Wilhelm Conrad *Röntgen* †1923 Ger. physicist] : of or relating to the physicist Röntgen or to X rays ⟨~ examinations⟩ ⟨~ therapy⟩

[2]**roentgen** *also* **röntgen** \"\ *n* -s [ISV, fr. Wilhelm Conrad *Röntgen*] : the international unit of X radiation or gamma radiation that is the amount of radiation producing under ideal conditions in one cubic centimeter of air at 0° C and 760 millimeters mercury pressure ionization of either sign equal to one electrostatic unit of charge

roent·gen·iza·tion *also* **rönt·gen·iza·tion** \,==ə'zāshən, -,ī'z-\ *n* -s [ISV *roentgen-, röntgen-* (fr. Wilhelm Conrad *Röntgen*) + *-ization*] **1** : the act or process of using X rays **2** : discoloration (as of glass) by prolonged action of X rays

roent·gen·ize *also* **rönt·gen·ize** \'==,īz\ *vt* -ED/-ING/-S [ISV *roentgen-, röntgen-* (fr. Wilhelm Conrad *Röntgen*) + *-ize*] **1** : to make (air or other gas) conductive of electricity by the passage of X rays **2** : to subject to the action of X rays (as for the treatment of a tumor)

roent·gen·kymogram \¦==+\ *n* [ISV [1]*roentgen* + *kymogram*] : a kymogram made on an X-ray film

roent·gen·kymographic \"+\ *adj* [ISV *roentgenkymography* + *-ic*] : of or relating to roentgenkymography

roent·gen·kymography \"+\ *n* [ISV [1]*roentgen* + *kymography*] : kymography on a moving X-ray film

roentgen meter *n* [[1]*roentgen* + *meter*] : R-METER

roent·gen·o·gram \'==ə,gram\ *n* [ISV [1]*roentgen* + *-o-* + *-gram*] : a photograph made with X rays : RADIOGRAPH

[1]**roent·gen·o·graph** \-graf,-grȧf\ *n* [[1]*roentgen* + *-o-* + *-graph*] : ROENTGENOGRAM

[2]**roentgenograph** \"\ *vt* : to photograph with X rays

roent·gen·o·graph·ic \¦===¦grafik\ *adj* [ISV *roentgenography* + *-ic*] : of or relating to roentgenography — **roent·gen·o·graph·i·cal·ly** \-fək(ə)lē\ *adv*

roent·gen·og·ra·phy \,=='ägrəfē\ *n* -ES [ISV [1]*roentgen* + *-o-* + *-graphy*] : photography by means of X rays

roent·gen·o·log·ic \¦==_ə¦läjik\ *or* **roent·gen·o·log·i·cal** \-jəkəl\ *adj* [*roentgenologic* ISV *roentgenology* + *-ic; roentgenological* fr. *roentgenology* + *-ical*] : of or relating to roentgenology — **roent·gen·o·log·i·cal·ly** \-jək(ə)lē\ *adv*

roent·gen·ol·o·gist \,=='äləjəst\ *n* -s [*roentgenology* + *-ist*] : a specialist in roentgenology

roent·gen·ol·o·gy \-ləjē\ *n* -ES [ISV [1]*roentgen* + *-o-* + *-logy*] : a branch of radiology that deals with the use of X rays for diagnosis or treatment of disease

roent·gen·om·e·ter \,=='äməd·ə(r)\ *n* [[1]*roentgen* + *-o-* + *-meter*] : R-METER

roent·gen·om·e·try \-mə·trē\ *n* -ES [[1]*roentgen* + *-o-* + *-metry*] : measurement of X rays esp. of their dosage for therapeutic purposes

roent·gen·o·scope \'==_ə,skōp\ *n* [[1]*roentgen* + *-o-* + *-scope*] : FLUOROSCOPE

roent·gen·o·scop·ic \¦==ə¦skäpik\ *adj* [*roentgenoscope* + *-ic*] : FLUOROSCOPIC — **roent·gen·o·scop·i·cal·ly** \-pək(ə)lē\ *adv*

roent·gen·os·co·py \,=='äskəpē\ *n* -ES [ISV [1]*roentgen* + *-o-* + *-scopy*] : examination by means of fluoroscopy

roent·gen·o·ther·a·py \¦==_ō¦therəpē\ *n* [ISV [1]*roentgen* + *-o-* + *therapy*] : radiotherapy by means of X rays

roentgen ray *n, often cap 1st R* [[1]*roentgen* + *ray*] : X RAY

roentgen–ray tube *n* : X-RAY TUBE

roentgen sickness *n* [[1]*roentgen* + *sickness*] : radiation sickness from overexposure to X rays

roent·gen·ther·a·py \¦==¦therəpē\ *n* [ISV [1]*roentgen* + *therapy*] : ROENTGENOTHERAPY

roer \'rü(ə)r\ *n* -s [Afrik, fr. D, firelock (gun), pipe, fr. MD, firelock (gun), pipe, reed; akin to OHG *rōr* reed, ON *reyrr*, Goth *raus*] : a heavy long-barreled gun formerly used for hunting big game in southern Africa

roes *pl of* ROE

roess·ler·ite \'reslə,rīt, 'rə(r)s-\ *n* -s [G *rösslerit*, fr. Karl *Rössler*, 19th cent. resident of Hanau, Germany + G *-it* -ite] : a mineral $MgH(AsO_4).7H_2O$ consisting of a hydrous acid arsenate of magnesium

roes·te·lia \re'stēlyə, ,rə(r)'s-\ *n, cap* [NL, fr. *Roestel fl ab* 1800 Ger. pharmacist + NL *-ia*] : a form genus of rust fungi comprising forms now known to be aecial stages of fungi of the genus *Gymnosporangium*

roestone \'=,=\ *n* [[2]*roe* + *stone*] : OOLITE

ro·ey \'rōē\ *adj* **roeier**; **roeiest** [[2]*roe* + *-y*] : having a mottled or streaked grain ⟨~ mahogany⟩

ROG *abbr, often not cap* receipt of goods

ro·ga·te sunday \rō,gäd·ē-\ *n, usu cap R&S* [*rogate* prob. fr. L, 2d pers. pl. imper. of *rogare*] : ROGATION SUNDAY

ro·ga·tion \rō'gāshən\ *n* -s [ME *rogacioun*, fr. L *rogation-, rogatio*, fr. *rogatus* (past part. of *rogare* to ask, beg) + *-ion-, -io* -ion — more at RIGHT] **1 a** : LITANY, SUPPLICATION **b** **rogations** *pl* : the ceremonies of the Rogation Days **2 a** : the inquiry made by the consuls or tribunes of ancient Rome as to the will of the people on a proposed decree or law **b** : the consuls' or tribunes' proposal of a law or decree for passage by the people **c** : the law or decree proposed by the consuls or tribunes **3** *obs* : a formal petition : REQUEST

rogation days *n pl, usu cap R&D* [ME *rogacioun dayes*] : the three days before Ascension Day observed by some Christians as days of special supplication

rogation flower *n* [so called fr. a former practice of making it into garlands that were carried in processions on Rogation Days] **1** : a branched perennial herbaceous Old World milkwort (*Polygala vulgaris*) with pink, white, or blue flowers **2** : a pink-flowered milkwort (*Polygala incarnata*) of eastern No. America

rogation sunday *n, usu cap R&S* : the Sunday immediately before the three Rogation Days : the fifth Sunday after Easter

rogationtide \='==,=\ *n, usu cap* : the period of the Rogation Days

rogation week *n, usu cap R* : the week in which the Rogation Days occur

rog·a·to·ry \'rägə,tōrē\ *adj* [F *rogatoire*, fr. ML *rogatorius* supplicatory, fr. L *rogatus* (past part. of *rogare*) + *-orius* -ory] : seeking information; *specif* : authorized to examine witnesses or ascertain facts ⟨a ~ commission⟩

[1]**rog·er** \'räjə(r)\ *vb* -ED/-ING/-S [obs. E *roger*, n., penis, fr. the name *Roger*] *vt* : to copulate with — usu. considered vulgar ⟨occasionally . . . ~*ed* the lady —Ezra Pound⟩ ~ *vi* : COPULATE — usu. considered vulgar ⟨should not a half-pay officer ~ for sixpence —James Boswell⟩

[2]**roger** \"\ *n* -s *usu cap* [fr. the name *Roger*] : JOLLY ROGER

[3]**roger** \"\ *usu cap* [fr. the name *Roger*] — a communications code word for the letter *r*

[4]**roger** \"\ *interj* [fr. [3]*roger* (standing for the initial letter *r* of *received*)] — used esp. in radio and signaling to indicate that a message has been received and understood or that the speaker agrees with what has been said

roger de coverley *or* **roger of coverley** [*roger de coverley* alter. (influenced by *Sir Roger de Coverley*, fictitious country gentleman appearing in many numbers of the daily periodical *The Spectator* conducted 1711–12 in England, fr. *roger of coverley*) of *roger of coverley*, prob. fr. *Roger* (the name) + *of* + *Coverley* (a fictitious place name)] : SIR ROGER DE COVERLEY

rog·er·ene \¦räjə¦rēn\ *or* **rog·er·ine** \", -ə¦rīn\ *n* -s *usu cap* [*rogerene* fr. John *Rogers* †1721 Am. religious leader + E *-ene* (as in *nazarene*); *rogerine* alter. (influenced by E *-ine*, adj. suffix) of *rogerene*] : a follower of the religious leader John Rogers holding such principles as nonparticipation in war, religious liberty, and freedom in ecclesiastical matters

ro·get's spiral \(')rō¦|zhāz-, 'rä'|\ *n, usu cap R* [after Peter M. *Roget* †1869 Eng. physician] : an open helix of elastic wire that contracts in length when an electric current passes through it and thereby demonstrates the attraction of parallel currents

ro·gnon \(')rōn¦yōⁿ, (')rȯn-\ *n* -s [F, lit., kidney, fr. (assumed) VL *renion-, renio*, fr. L *renes* (pl.) kidneys] : a small rounded mass of rock usu. embedded in rock of a different type

[1]**rogue** \'rōg\ *n* -s [origin unknown] **1 a** : VAGRANT, TRAMP, BEGGAR **b** : a wandering, disorderly, or dissolute person formerly accountable under various vagrancy acts — usu. used in the phrase *rogues and vagabonds* **2 a** : a dishonest unprincipled person; *specif* : SWINDLER **b** : a worthless fellow : SCOUNDREL **3** : a pleasantly mischievous person ⟨tell me about . . . the dear little ~*s* —Walt Whitman⟩ **4 a** (1) : ROGUE ELEPHANT (2) : a large animal with habits like those of a rogue elephant **b** : a horse inclined to shirk or misbehave **5 a** : an individual exhibiting a chance biological variation or deviating from the type of a variety or breed — usu. used of an inferior, diseased, or abnormal plant **b** : a normal plant (as of a named variety) that is accidentally mixed in with plants of another kind (as a red tulip in a field of white tulips) **syn** see VILLAIN

[2]**rogue** \"\ *vb* **rogued**; **rogued**; **rogu·ing** *or* **rogue·ing**; **rogues** *vi* **1** : to wander or act like a rogue **2** : to weed out inferior, diseased, or abnormal individuals from a crop ⟨by careful selection and *roguing* the . . . strain was evolved —*Gardeners' Chronicle*⟩ ~ *vt* **1** : to weed out (as an inferior plant or a field) **2** : to act like a rogue toward : SWINDLE

[3]**rogue** \"\ *adj* **1** *of an animal* : vicious and destructive ⟨~ otter⟩ **2** : resembling a rogue elephant in being separated or vicious ⟨the ~ male self-exiled from society —E.O.Hauser⟩ ⟨wrecked by a ~ mine —Alfred Bester⟩

rogue elephant *n* : a vicious elephant that separates from the herd and roams alone

rogu·er \'rōgə(r)\ *n* -s : one that rogues

rogu·ery \'rōgərē, -əri\ *n* -ES **1** : the practices or conduct of a rogue ⟨more often the victim than the practitioner of ~ —S.T. Williamson⟩ **2** : an act characteristic of a rogue ⟨dismissed . . . for unspecified *rogueries* —Wolcott Gibbs⟩ **3** : mischievous play ⟨little wretches . . . stealing back through the shrubbery so as not to be seen all bedraggled from some ~ —Virginia Woolf⟩ **4** : the world of rogues ⟨a thing at which all ~ rejoiced —Walter Besant⟩

rogue's badge *n* **1** : a red ribbon on the tail of a hunting horse that kicks **2 a** : a hood worn by a racehorse **b** : blinkers worn by a racehorse

rogue's badge 2

rogues' gallery *n* **1** : a collection of portraits of criminals ⟨the *rogues' gallery* in the post office⟩ **2** : a collection resembling a collection of portraits of criminals ⟨this interesting *rogues' gallery* of the insect world includes detailed snapshots of a feeding bedbug —John Pfeiffer⟩

rogue·ship \'rōg,ship\ *n* : the quality or state of being a rogue

rogue's march *n* : a tune of English origin formerly played to accompany the expulsion of a soldier from the army

rogue's yarn *n* : a yarn of a different twist, material, or color inserted into navy cordage esp. to identify it if stolen or to trace the maker in case of defect

rogu·ish \'rōgish, -gēsh\ *adj* **1** : of, relating to, or having the characteristics of a rogue : DISHONEST, UNPRINCIPLED ⟨had some ~ intentions of his own about the money —W.M. Thackeray⟩ ⟨~ stories emphasizing ingenuity⟩ **2** : pleasantly mischievous ⟨a ~ wink⟩ — **rogu·ish·ly** *adv* — **rogu·ish·ness** *n* -ES

roguy \-gē,-gi\ *adj, obs* : ROGUISH

ro·hil·la \rō'hilə\ *n, pl* **rohilla** *or* **rohillas** *usu cap* : a member of an Afghan people settling in the district of Rohilkhand in northern India early in the 18th century

rohr bor·dun \¦rōr(,)bȯr¦dün\ *n* [G *rohrbordun*, fr. G *rohr* reed, pipe (fr. OHG *rōr* reed) + *bordun* bourdon, fr. F *bourdon*, fr. MF, bass horn, of imit. origin — more at ROER] : a rohrflöte of 16-foot pitch

rohr·flö·te \'rōr,flœtə\ *n* -s [G, fr. *rohr* reed, pipe + *flöte* flute, fr. MHG *floite, flöute*, fr. MD *flute, floyte*, fr. OF *flaute, flahute, fleute* — more at FLUTE] : a pipe-organ flute stop having closed metal pipes with chimneys

rohr na·sat \'rōr,nä,zät\ *or* **rohr quin·te** \'rōr,kvintə\ *n* [*rohr nasat* fr. G *rohrnasat*, fr. *rohr* reed, pipe + *nasat* nazard; *rohr quinte* fr. G *rohrquinte*, fr. *rohr* reed, pipe + *quinte* fifth in music, fr. F, fr. MF, fem. of *quint*, adj., fifth, fr. L *quintus* — more at NASAT, QUINT] **:** a rohrflöte speaking at 2⅔-foot pitch

ro·hu \(ˈ)rō¦hü\ *n, pl* **rohu** *or* **rohus** [Hindi *rohū*] **:** a large small-mouthed Indian cyprinid fish (*Labeo rohita*) valued for food and sport

ro·hun \ˈrōən\ *or* **ro·hu·na** \-ənə\ *also* **ro·han** \-ən\ *n* -s [Hindi *rohan*, fr. Skt *rohaṇa*] **:** an East Indian tree (*Soymida febrifuga*) of the family Meliaceae having hard durable wood and tonic bark

roi fai·né·ant \rə¦wä,fā(,)nāˈäⁿ, ¦rw-\ *n, pl* **rois fainéants** \"\ [F, faineant king] **:** a do-nothing king; *esp* **:** one who has delegated or lost his royal power while still reigning

¹roil \ˈrȯil, *esp before pause or consonant* -ȯiəl\ *vb* -ED/-ING/-S [origin unknown] *vt* **1 a :** to make turbid by stirring up the sediment or dregs ⟨something of the rubbery aspect of fish seen under ~*ed* water —John McCarten⟩ ⟨looked down into the ~*ed* wine —Lionel Trilling⟩ **b :** to stir up **:** DISTURB, DISORDER ⟨fine white marl which becomes . . . ~*ed* by the waves —S.E.Morison⟩ ⟨activities . . . certain to keep American politics ~*ed* —Douglass Adair⟩ **2 :** RILE 2 ⟨she's trying to be clever . . . don't let her ~ you —Frances G. Patton⟩ ~ *vi* **1 :** to move turbulently from one place to another ⟨the clouds ~*ed* up about the dome again and hid it —W.A.Dorrance⟩ ⟨the chatter of that busy little beck as it ~*ed* over its shallows —T.B.Costain⟩ **2 :** to be in a state of turbulence ⟨the air ~*ed* and eddied in the heat —Richard Thruelsen & Elliott Arnold⟩ ⟨floods from . . . ~*ing* gullies —*Time*⟩ **syn** see IRRITATE

²roil \"\ *n* -s **1 :** AGITATION ⟨feeling the ~ of waters on the flanks, the dangerous turbulence —Richard Eberhart⟩ **2 :** a small section of rapidly moving turbulent water ⟨the river showed steely ~*s* of slick water —H.L.Davis⟩

³roil \"\ *vi* -ED/-ING/-S [origin unknown] *dial Eng* **:** to romp or play esp. in a rough manner

roily \ˈrȯilē\ *adj* -ER/-EST [¹*roil* + -*y*] **1 :** full of sediment or dregs **:** MUDDY **2 :** TURBULENT ⟨always building higher the dams of their emotions until they broke and the ~ waters rushed out in a wasting flood —V.L.Parrington⟩ **syn** see TURBID

roint \ˈrȯint\ *vt* [by shortening] *dial chiefly Eng* **:** AROINT

¹rois·ter *also* **roys·ter** \ˈrȯistə(r)\ *n* -s [prob. fr. MF *rustre* boor, lout, alter. of *ruste*, fr. *ruste*, adj., rude, rough, fr. L *rusticus* rustic, rural — more at RUSTIC] *archaic* **:** ROISTERER

²roister *or* **royster** \"\ *vi* **roistered** *or* **roystered; roistered** *or* **roystered; roistering** *or* **roystering** \-t(ə)riŋ\ **roisters** *or* **roysters :** to have a noisy disorderly good time esp. under the influence of alcohol **:** CAROUSE, REVEL ⟨had gambled and ~*ed* and drunk until he dropped in his tracks —Donn Byrne⟩

rois·ter·er *or* **roys·ter·er** \-tərə(r)\ *n* -s **:** one that roisters

roistering *or* **roystering** *adj* **:** characterized by or associated with noisy revelry ⟨usual for hilarious youths to pull off the bride's garters . . . but this was no ~ wedding —Francis Hackett⟩ ⟨good rich ~ ribald words —D.W.Maurer⟩

rois·ter·ous *or* **roys·ter·ous** \-t(ə)rəs\ *adj* [¹*roister* + -*ous*] **:** ROISTERING ⟨take the play . . . and rush it through to a ~ conclusion —Brooks Atkinson⟩ — **rois·ter·ous·ly** *or* **roys·ter·ous·ly** *adv*

roist·ing *or* **royst·ing** \-tiŋ\ *adj* [fr. pres. part. of obs. E *roist*, *royst* to roister, back-formation fr. E ¹*roister*] *archaic* **:** ROISTERING

roi·te·let \¦rȯid·ᵊl¦et, rwä·tlā\ *n, pl* **roitelets** \-ets,-ā\ [F, fr. MF, fr. *roitel*, *roietel* petty king (fr. OF, dim. of *roi* king, fr. L *reg-*, *rex*) + -*et* — more at ROYAL] *archaic* **:** a petty king

rok \ˈräk\ *n* -s *usu cap* [Republic of Korea, republic constituting the southern part of Korea] **:** a member of the armed forces of the Republic of Korea

ro·ka \ˈrōkə\ *n* -s [Ar *ruqʿ*] **:** MAFURA

¹roke \ˈrōk\ *n* -s [ME, prob. fr. MD *roke*, *rooc* smoke; akin to OHG *rauh* smoke — more at REEK] **1** *dial chiefly Brit* **:** VAPOR: as **a :** FOG, MIST **b :** STEAM **2** *dial chiefly Brit* **:** SMOKE, REEK

²roke \"\ *vt* [origin unknown] *dial Eng* **:** to poke around **:** STIR

rok·e·lay \ˈräkə,lā, -ä,klā\ *chiefly Scot var of* ROQUELAURE

ro·ker \ˈrōkə(r)\ *n* -s [prob. fr. Dan *rokke*, fr. MLG *roche*, *ruche*; akin to OE *reohhe* ray and prob. to OE *rūh* rough — more at ROUGH] **1 :** any of various rays; *esp* **:** THORNBACK RAY **2** *dial Eng* **:** ROCKLING

roky \ˈrōki\ *adj* -ER/-EST [¹*roke* + -*y*] *dial chiefly Brit* **:** FOGGY, MISTY

ro·lan·dic \rō¦landik\ *adj, usu cap R* [Luigi *Rolando* †1831 Ital. anatomist + E -*ic*] **:** of, relating to, or discovered by Luigi Rolando

rolandic area *n, usu cap R* **:** the motor area of the cerebral cortex comprising the anterior wall of the central sulcus, the anterior central gyrus, and the paracentral lobule

rolandic fissure *n, usu cap R* **:** CENTRAL SULCUS

role *also* **rôle** \ˈrōl\ *n* -s [F *rôle*, lit., roll, fr. OF *role* — more at ROLL] **1 a** (1) **:** a character assigned to or assumed by someone ⟨to prove his point he went to sea in the ~ of a castaway, on an inflated rubber raft —Walter Hayward⟩ ⟨given the ~ of peacemaker⟩ ⟨cast in the ~ of scapegoat⟩ (2) **:** a socially prescribed pattern of behavior corresponding to an individual's status in a particular society **b** (1) **:** a part played by an actor (as in a play or movie) ⟨in succeeding months played a long list of comedy and farcical ~*s* —W.P.Eaton⟩ (2) **:** a part assumed by a singer (as in an opera or oratorio) ⟨one of the most taxing tenor ~*s* in the repertoire⟩ **2 :** a function performed by someone or something in a particular situation, process, or operation ⟨the ~ of the teacher in the educational process⟩ ⟨plays an important ~ in city politics⟩ ⟨the ~ of automobiles in leisure has been significant —A.P.James⟩ ⟨the ~ of peroxidation in vitamin E deficiency —*Current Biog.*⟩

ro·leo \ˈrōlē,ō\ *n* -s [²*roll* + -*eo* (as in *rodeo*)] **:** a logrolling tournament

roley-poley *var of* ROLY-POLY

rolfs' oak \ˈrälfs-\ *n, cap R* [after Frederick M. *Rolfs* †1956 Am. botanist] **:** a Florida coastal scrub oak (*Quercus rolfsii*) with hard rigid branches, small leathery leaves, and acorns usu. in pairs and half-covered by the funnel-shaped cups

¹roll \ˈrōl\ *n* -s [ME *rolle*, fr. OF *rolle*, *role*, fr. L *rotulus*, *rotula* little wheel, dim. of *rota* wheel; akin to OFris *reth* wheel, OHG *rad* wheel, ON *röthull* halo, sun, W *rhod* wheel, Latvian *rats* wheel, Skt *ratha* wagon] **1 a** (1) **:** a written document (as on parchment or paper) that is rolled up for carrying or storing **:** SCROLL ⟨reading a certain passage from the ~ —Robert Browning⟩; *specif* **:** a written document containing an official or formal record (as of the proceedings of a court or political body) ⟨chancery ~*s*⟩ ⟨~*s* of parliament⟩ ⟨keeper of the ~*s*⟩ — compare MASTER OF THE ROLLS (2) **:** a manuscript book ⟨medieval ~*s* of arms⟩ **b :** a list of names or related items **:** CATALOG, REGISTER ⟨place at the head of the ~ of science has not been challenged —*Times Lit. Supp.*⟩ ⟨a slipshod work that hardly belongs in the ~ of his novels⟩ ⟨belongs in the ~ of great actors⟩ **c :** an official list ⟨the ~ of registered voters⟩ ⟨the public relief ~*s*⟩: as (1) **:** MUSTER ROLL (2) **:** a list of members of a school or class ⟨when students other than day students are permitted to withdraw, or are dropped from the ~ —*College of William & Mary Cat.*⟩ ⟨the teacher called the ~⟩ (3) **:** a list of members of a legislative body ⟨the clerk called the ~ and recorded the votes⟩ (4) *Brit* **:** a list of those qualified to practice as solicitors — usu. used in pl. (5) **:** a list of practitioners in a court or in the courts of a state — usu. used in pl. (6) **:** TAX LIST **2 :** something that is rolled up into or as if into a cylinder or ball ⟨great ~*s* of fat around his middle —T. B.Costain⟩ ⟨his head, which is bald on top, is outlined by a thick ~ of curly black hair —*Current Biog.*⟩ ⟨a ~ of twine⟩: as **a** (1) **:** a quantity (as of fabric or paper) rolled up to form a single package; *also* **:** a number of separate sheets or papers rolled together ⟨a ~ of wrapping paper⟩ ⟨a ~ of paper towels⟩ (2) **:** a bolt of wallpaper (3) **:** WEB **b :** a hairdo in which some or all of the hair is rolled or curled up or under ⟨pageboy *roll*⟩ **c :** a continuous strand of textile fiber (as wool) that is formed by slightly twisting, rolling, or rubbing the fibers **d :** any of

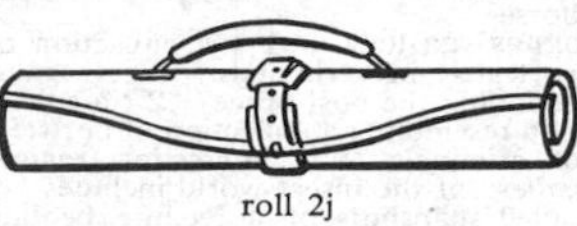

roll 2j

various food preparations rolled up for cooking or serving: as (1) **:** a small piece of yeast dough baked in any of numerous forms (2) **:** meat rolled and cooked (3) **:** JELLY ROLL (4) **:** sweet dough that is spread with a filling and then rolled up and baked ⟨a blackberry ~⟩ **e :** a rounded molding or similar architectural element (as a volute of the Ionic order) **f :** a cylindrical twist of tobacco **g :** any of a series of rounded strips of wood over which the ends of the roofing plates of a lead or other metal roof are turned and lapped **h :** BLANKET ROLL 1 **i :** MUSIC ROLL **j :** a flat flexible case (as of leather) in which articles may be rolled and fastened by straps or metal clasps; *also* **:** a cylindrical case **k** (1) **:** a number of pieces of paper money folded or rolled into a wad to be carried in the pocket ⟨a man of the world who has a ~ of bills in his pocket —Donald Windham⟩ (2) *slang* **:** BANKROLL ⟨producers themselves anxiously cast about for angels willing to shoot their ~*s* on shows —Seymour Peck⟩ **3 :** something that performs a rolling action or movement **:** a cylindrical body set in bearings and used singly or in pairs or sets to crush, flatten, shape, move, or operate something **:** ROLLER: as **a :** a roller used to break clods or level soil **b :** a metal wheel for making decorative lines on book covers; *also* **:** a design impressed by such a tool **c rolls** *pl* **:** a set of two or more similar parallel cylinders placed a small distance apart in bearings and made to rotate in opposite directions so as to draw material between them in order to crush it (as rock or ore) or compress and shape it (as malleable metal) **d :** a typewriter platen **e :** BREAK ROLL

²roll \"\ *vb* -ED/-ING/-S [ME *rollen*, *rolen*, fr. MF *roller*, *roler*, fr. (assumed) VL *rotulare*, fr. L *rotulus*, *rotula* small wheel] *vt* **1 a :** to impel forward by causing to turn over and over on a surface ⟨~*ed* the barrel down the hill⟩ ⟨~*ed* the hoop along the street⟩ **b :** to cause to revolve by turning over and over **:** move by turning on or as if on an axis ⟨were placed on the sheets and ~*ed* in the flour —*Amer. Guide Series: La.*⟩ **c** (1) **:** to move or cause to move in a circular manner **:** turn from one side to another ⟨already the girl was ~*ing* her eyes and giggling —Ellen Glasgow⟩ ⟨~*ed* his head round in the direction of the curtained window —Elizabeth Bowen⟩ ⟨~*ing* his shoulders —F.M.Ford⟩ (2) **:** to swing or sway from side to side ⟨~*ed* the great bomber like a jet fighter —*Time*⟩ **d :** to cause to take shape as a mass by turning over and over **:** heap up in a mass ⟨the wind blowing over the empty prairies can ~ tumbleweed as big as a bushel basket —Frances Gaither⟩ **e :** to impel forward with an easy, continuous motion ⟨the river ~*s* its waters to the ocean⟩ **f** (1) **:** to make a cast of (dice or a specified number on the dice) (2) **:** to cast dice in competition with ⟨I'll ~ you to see who pays⟩ **2 :** to reflect on **:** CONSIDER, PONDER ⟨my thoughts the matter ~, and solve and oft resolve the whole —R.W.Emerson⟩ **3 a :** to put a wrapping around **:** ENFOLD, ENVELOP ⟨very pleasant to lie snugly ~*ed* in blankets —John Seago⟩ **b :** to wrap round on itself or on something else **:** cause to take a relatively spherical or cylindrical form **:** shape into a ball or roll ⟨~*ed* his hamlike hands into fists —Irene Kuhn⟩ ⟨~*ed* his own cigarettes⟩ ⟨~*ed* up the cloth⟩ ⟨~*ed* the bandage around his leg⟩ **4 a** (1) **:** to press, spread, or level with a roller **:** make smooth, even, or compact ⟨~ steel rails⟩ ⟨~ sheet-brass⟩ ⟨~ a field⟩ ⟨~ the dough⟩ ⟨~ cracker crumbs⟩ ⟨had seen too many minds ~*ed* flat by academicism —T.M.Longstreth⟩ (2) **:** to form a screw thread on (a rod) by cold-rolling between dies or rollers having suitably shaped ridges that displace the metal from the thread space and force it up above the original surface of the work on each side **b :** to make smooth and rounded by attrition ⟨implements should be examined to see whether they are ~*ed* . . . or wind-worn, or relatively fresh —*Notes & Queries on Anthropology*⟩ **c** (1) **:** to ink with a roller or rollers ⟨~ a form⟩ (2) **:** to make (a stereotype matrix) or mold (a form) in a mangle **d :** to spread out **:** EXTEND ⟨if the weather was good we ~*ed* our beds on the ground and slept in the open —Ross Santee⟩ ⟨in the grave throw me and ~ the sod o'er me —*Western Folklore*⟩ ⟨~ out the red carpet⟩ **5 a :** to cause to move on wheels ⟨~*ed* the baby carriage to the store⟩ **b :** to transport in a wheeled vehicle ⟨loved to be ~*ed* through the park in an old-fashioned hansom cab⟩ **c :** to traverse in or by a wheeled vehicle ⟨tried to believe the hardest miles were ~*ed* —A.B. Guthrie⟩ **d :** to move or cause to be moved by means of rollers ⟨had the log house ~*ed* to its present site —*Amer. Guide Series: La.*⟩ **e :** to cause to begin operating or moving ⟨~ the cameras⟩ **6 a :** to sound with a full, reverberating tone ⟨~*ed* the psalm to wintry skies —Alfred Tennyson⟩ — often used with *out* ⟨~*ed* out the words so that everyone could hear⟩ **b :** to make a continuous beating sound upon **:** sound a roll upon ⟨local constables in remote hamlets ~*ed* their drums to bring out the villagers —*Time*⟩ **c :** to utter with a trill ⟨they might ~ their r's and use their noses as trombones of conversation —Corra Harris⟩ **d :** to play (a chord) in arpeggio style (as on a harp or piano) **7 :** to rob (a person) usu. by going through his pockets while he is drunk, asleep, or unconscious **:** JACKROLL ⟨~*ing* lushes in the subway —Wolcott Gibbs⟩ ⟨had been doped, beaten up, and ~*ed* —R.G.Martin⟩ ~ *vi* **1 a :** to move forward along a surface by rotation ⟨the ball ~*ed* along the floor⟩ **b** (1) **:** to turn over and over ⟨the children ~*ed* in the grass, or waded in the brook —Henry Adams⟩ ⟨the dog ~*ed* in the mud⟩ (2) **:** to luxuriate in an abundant supply **:** WALLOW — used with *in* ⟨tragic to think that a man may be short of money whilst his children are ~*ing* in it —J.D.Sheridan⟩ **c :** to move onward or around as if by completing a revolution ⟨the months ~ on⟩ ⟨five summers have ~*ed* round since then —Douglass Cater⟩ **:** ELAPSE, PASS ⟨the years ~ by —*Fortnight*⟩ **d :** to move in an orbit ⟨the planets ~ around the sun⟩ **2 a :** to look in one direction after another in quick succession **:** to shift the gaze continually ⟨a pair of eyes which ~*ed* with malevolent curiosity —T.B.Costain⟩ **b** *archaic* **:** to revolve in the mind **c :** to revolve on or as if on an axis ⟨long has the globe been ~*ing* round —Walt Whitman⟩ **3 :** to move about **:** ROAM, WANDER **4 a :** to flow with a rising and falling motion ⟨the waves ~ on⟩ ⟨the clouds ~ past⟩ **:** go forward in an easy, gentle, or undulating manner ⟨mists ~*ing* down the mountain —*Irish Digest*⟩ ⟨the fog, which from the foot of the lawn ~*ed* away . . . like a sea —R.M.Lovett⟩ **b :** to flow in a continuous stream **:** to arrive, become produced, or become received in abundant quantities or amount **:** POUR ⟨cars ~*ing* off the assembly line⟩ ⟨delegates ~*ed* in from all parts of the country⟩ ⟨the money was ~*ing* in⟩ **c :** to flow as part of a stream of words ⟨catchy phrases, and sharp retorts that ~ so freely from the tongues of the people he characterizes —H.H. Reichard⟩ **d :** to have an undulating contour **:** display a gently rising and falling surface ⟨most of it is prairie, but the prairie ~*s* and dips and curves —Sinclair Lewis⟩ **e :** to lie extended **:** STRETCH ⟨the flowers ~*ed* away in dizzy unbroken patterns to the horizon —Alan Moorehead⟩ ⟨to the west and south ~ the grainfields —O.A.Fitzgerald⟩ **5 a :** to become carried in a vehicle ⟨got in the car and were soon ~*ing* at high speed⟩ **b :** to become carried on a stream ⟨the scattered debris ~*ed* down the flooded river⟩ **c :** to move on wheels ⟨with a smooth hard-packed surface of snow, trucks can ~ right along —Harold Griffin⟩ **6 a :** to make a deep reverberating sound ⟨the thunder ~*s*⟩ ⟨the drums ~⟩ ⟨a roar from the crowd ~*ed* all around enveloping us —A.P.Gaskell⟩ **b :** to make a deep and sonorous sound ⟨listen to a rich voice which ~*ed* out into the dusk —Margaret Kennedy⟩ **c :** TRILL — used of a bird **7 a :** to incline first to one side and then to the other **:** swing from side to side ⟨the ship still heaved and ~*ed* on the heavy sea —C.S.Forester⟩ ⟨as he swam he ~*ed* like a sick fish —Kenneth Roberts⟩ **b :** to walk with a swinging gait **:** SWAY ⟨a heavy elderly peasant ~*ed* in his gait —F.M.Ford⟩ **c :** to move so as to cushion the impact of a blow — used with *with* ⟨~*ed* with the punch, but it caught his nose nevertheless —Edwin Corle⟩ **8 a :** to take the form of a cylinder or ball ⟨this cloth ~*s* unevenly⟩ ⟨laid my tarp on the ground and *rolled* up in every blanket I had —Ysabel Rennie⟩ **b :** to respond to rolling in a specified way **:** be in a specified condition after being rolled ⟨the tennis courts ~*ed* easily after the shower⟩ ⟨the metal ~*ed* out in flat bars⟩ **9 a :** to get under way **:** begin to move ⟨the fire engines ~*ed* while the alarm bell was still ringing⟩ ⟨the company commander gave the signal to ~ and the tanks moved out⟩ **b :** to move forward **:** develop and maintain impetus ⟨not enough real sting in demand to get business ~*ing* at the speed many steelmakers had hoped for —*Wall Street Jour.*⟩ ⟨~*ed* to a fourth term —*Time*⟩ ⟨the team was held scoreless during the third period, but in the fourth period they started to ~ again⟩ **c :** to go into action or operation ⟨the cameras were ready to ~⟩ ⟨the presses started to ~⟩ **d :** to go to press ⟨they went home after the late edition had ~*ed*⟩ **10 a :** BOWL **b :** to execute a forward or backward roll in tumbling — **roll one's hoop** *slang* **:** to attend to one's own business — often used after the verb *go* — **roll the bones :** to roll dice; *esp* **:** to shoot craps — **roll up one's sleeves :** to get to work vigorously **:** make a determined effort

³roll \"\ *n* -s **1 a :** a prolonged sound produced by rapid and regular strokes on a drum **b :** a sonorous and often rhythmical flow of speech ⟨no amount of circumlocution in English can do justice to the heavy ~ of the Latin periods —R.W.Southern⟩ **c :** a heavy reverberatory sound ⟨the ~ of cannon⟩ ⟨the ~ of thunder⟩ ⟨heard the slow, steady ~ of the surf —Hamilton Basso⟩ **d :** a chord in arpeggio style produced on a keyboard instrument or a harp **e :** a trill of some birds; *esp* **:** any of various trills in the song of the canary ⟨bass ~⟩ ⟨bell ~⟩ ⟨water ~⟩ **2 :** a rolling movement or an action or process involving such movement ⟨the ~ of the waves⟩ ⟨the ~ of the ball⟩ ⟨a ~ of the dice⟩ ⟨eyes with the hint of a ~ in them —Clemence Dane⟩: as **a :** a swaying movement of the body ⟨she walks slowly, easily, but with a slight ~ —Constance Walsh⟩ **b :** a side to side movement (as of a ship or train) **c** (1) **:** an angular displacement about the longitudinal axis of an airplane (2) **:** a flight maneuver in which a complete revolution about the longitudinal axis is made with the horizontal direction of flight being approximately maintained **d** (1) **:** any of several acrobatic and modern dance exercises in which the body is rotated on the floor ⟨back ~⟩ ⟨chest ~⟩ ⟨shoulder ~⟩ (2) **:** a pivot of ballroom dance partners away from or toward each other or toward a new partner **e :** a tumbling stunt in which the body is rotated in a circle on the mat either forward or backward about its lateral axis while in a tuck position **f :** the movement of a curling stone after impact with another stone **3 a :** an undulation in the roof or floor of a coal seam or in one or both walls of a mineral vein **b :** an undulation on a land surface **:** a low rounded ridge ⟨the trees around the more distant spring are hidden behind a ~ of the ground —G. R. Stewart⟩

roll·able \ˈrōləbəl\ *adj* **:** capable of being rolled

roll-and-fillet molding \ˌ≈≈¦≈-\ *n* **:** a nearly cylindrical molding that is larger than a bead and has a projecting fillet on one side

¹rollaway \ˈ≈≈,≈\ *dial var of* ROLLWAY 2

²rollaway \"\ *or* **rollaway bed** *n* -s [fr. *roll away*, v.] **:** a bed that can be folded and rolled away (as into a closet)

roll back *vt* **1 :** to reduce (a commodity price) to or toward a previous level on a national scale by government control devices ⟨taking measures to *roll* commodity prices *back*⟩ **2 :** to cause to retreat or withdraw **:** push back ⟨confident that he could *roll back* the ragtag, disorganized force that barred his way —F.V.W.Mason⟩

rollback \ˈ≈,≈\ *n* -s [*roll back*] **1 :** the cam on the knob spindle for moving the bolt of a lock **2 :** the act or an instance of rolling back **:** a driving or forcing back to a previous level or position ⟨a ~ of prices⟩ ⟨a ~ of the invading army⟩

rollaway

roll book *n* **:** a book in which a teacher keeps a record of the attendance or classwork of his pupils

roll call *n* [¹*roll* + *call*, after the phrase *call the roll*] **1 a :** the act or an instance of calling off a list of names (as for checking attendance or recording a vote) ⟨the first sergeant began the *roll call*⟩ ⟨the teacher never skips *roll call*⟩ ⟨demanded a *roll call* on the measure⟩ **b :** a regularly scheduled time for calling the roll ⟨was unable to get back before *roll call*⟩ **c :** a signal for a roll call ⟨the bugler blew *roll call*⟩ **2 :** REGISTER, ROLL ⟨in his own *roll call* of heroes —M.Y.Hughes⟩

roll-call \ˈ≈,≈\ *vt* [*roll call*] **:** to call the roll of ⟨efforts . . . to have the delegations *roll-called* —*Springfied (Mass.) Union*⟩

roll ceiling *n* **:** a removable stage ceiling that can be rolled up for storage

roll-cumulus \ˈ≈,≈≈≈\ *n* **:** a stratocumulus in which the clouds near the horizon resemble long bars

rolled \ˈrōld\ *adj* [ME, fr. past part. of *rollen*, *rolen* to roll — more at ROLL] **:** subjected to or produced by rolling

rolled barley *n* **:** steamed and flattened barley grains used for feeding livestock and poultry

rolled glass *n* **1 :** a flat glass of considerable thickness that is made by passing a roller over molten glass between thickness strips placed on the edges of the casting table **2 :** CYLINDER GLASS

rolled gold *or* **rolled gold plate** *n* **1 :** a base metal (as brass) with a thin plate of gold rolled over it **2 :** a gold electroplate rolled or drawn out so that the gold becomes very thin

rolled oats *n* **:** hulled oats steamed and then flattened by being passed between rollers

rolled roast *n* **:** a boned and rolled rib roast of beef — compare STANDING ROAST

¹roll·er \ˈrōlə(r)\ *n* -s *often attrib* [ME, fr. *rollen*, *rolen* to roll + -*er* — more at ROLL] **1 :** a revolving cylinder over or on which something is moved: as **a** (1) **:** a usu. wooden cylinder over which an endless towel passes (2) **:** any of the cylinders in a papermaking machine for carrying forward the web of paper or over and around which the machine clothing travels **b :** a hard steel cylinder used (as in a roller bearing) to reduce friction — see ROLLER BEARING illustration **c :** a cylinder on which heavy objects (as logs or steel rails) are rolled for ease in moving **d :** a wheel of a caster or roller skate **e :** ROLL 3d **f :** a disk mounted on the balance staff of a timepiece and containing the roller jewel **2 :** a revolving cylinder used alone or in pairs or sets to press, shape, or smooth something: as **a :** a device with one or more heavy broad-rimmed wheels that is pulled or driven over ground (as soil, lawn, or a macadam surface) to smooth or compact it — see BAR ROLLER, ROAD ROLLER **b :** one of a pair or set of rolls used to flatten and shape material (as metal) drawn between them **c** (1) **:** a revolving cylinder for inking or dampening a printing surface or forming one unit of the inking or dampening mechanism of a press (2) **:** PAINT ROLLER **d :** either of the hard revolving cylinders in a mangle or wringer between which material to be ironed or squeezed dry is passed **e** (1) **:** ROLLER DIE (2) **:** THREAD ROLLER **f :** MANGLE 4 **g :** BREAK ROLL **h :** a forging die fuller of such shape that the stock may be rolled on it **3 a** *or* **roller bandage :** a long rolled bandage **b :** a wide band of webbing buckled around a horse to keep his blanket in place **4 :** a cylindrical stick or rod on which something (as a map or shade) is rolled up **5 :** one that performs or supervises a rolling operation: as **a** (1) **:** one that operates a rolling mill (2) **:** one that operates a bar mill for reducing the thickness of bars of metal (as gold or silver) **b** (1) **:** one that rolls up textiles usu. by machine (2) **:** one that operates a machine for winding rolls of wallpaper **c :** one that rolls wrapper leaves around the bunches of cigars **d :** one that rolls candy centers to shape or that rolls candy in nuts **6 a :** one of a series of long heavy waves that roll in upon a coast (as after a storm) ⟨the canoe, carried helpless on the top of a big ~, grounded on the beach —A.A.Grace⟩ **b :** a tumbler pigeon; *esp* **:** one of any of several varieties in which the characteristic action is markedly developed — see ORIENTAL ROLLER **c :** a small burrowing snake of the family Aniliidae **d :** a ship that rolls ⟨a bad ~ in heavy seas⟩ **e :** a batted ball that rolls along the ground **:** a soft grounder **7 :** a woman's hat with a small crown and a narrow brim that is curved upward all around

²roller \"\ *n* -s [G, fr. *rollen* to roll, reverberate (fr. MHG, to roll, fr. MF *roller*, *roler*) + -*er* (fr. OHG -*āri*, fr. L -*arius*) — more at ROLL] **1 :** any of numerous mostly brightly colored nonpasserine Old World birds of the family Coraciidae that are related to the motmots and todies and include a common European bird (*Coracias garrulus*) that is chiefly blue and greenish in various shades with the back reddish brown — see

GROUND ROLLER **2 :** a canary having a song with a long rich recurrent trill in which the notes are soft and run together — distinguished from *chopper*
roller-backer \ˈ==,==\ *n* **:** a machine that backs a book by a roller action and forms shoulders but does not round the book except as the rollers perfect the round already imparted — compare ROUNDER AND BACKER
roller bearing *n* **:** a bearing in which the journal rotates in peripheral contact with a number of rollers usu. contained in a cage — compare BALL BEARING
roller-blind shutter *n* **:** FOCAL-PLANE SHUTTER
roller chain *n* **:** a block chain in which hollow transverse blocks or cylinders turning on steel pins act as rollers to lessen friction

roller bearing: *1* outer race, *2* cage, *3* roller, *4* inner race

roll·er coaster \ˈrōlə(r),- *also* -lē,- *or* -li,-\ *n* **1 :** an elevated railway (as in an amusement park) constructed with curves and inclines at different levels and having cars rolling upon it **2 :** a car that runs on a roller coaster
roller-coat \ˈ==,=\ *vt* **:** to apply (as paint or enamel) to a surface by means of a roller
roller conveyor *n* **:** a conveyor consisting of fixed-location rollers over which materials are moved by gravity or propulsion
roller derby *n* **:** a contest between two roller skating teams on a circular track in which each attempts to maneuver a skater into position to score points by circling the track and orientating one or more opponents within a given time limit
roller die *n* **:** one of a set of flat block or cylindrical dies used in a thread roller for rolling screw threads
roller freight car *n* **:** a freight car equipped with roller bearings
roller gate *n* **:** a hollow drum placed horizontally at the crest of a dam and rolled up or down an inclined track by pinion and rack to regulate water elevation
roller gin *n* **:** a cotton gin in which the lint is pulled from the seed by a roller covered with walrus hide and assisted by a fixed knife and a moving knife
roller jewel *n* **:** a usu. ruby or sapphire pin set upright in the roller disk and pushed by the pallet fork — called also *impulse pin*
roller leather *n* **:** vegetable-tanned leather from sheep, lamb, or calf skins used for covering the rollers of textile machinery
roll·er·man \ˈrōlə(r)mən\ *n, pl* **rollermen :** one who tends a rolling machine or performs a rolling action: as **a :** BRAKER **b :** JACKMAN **c :** a calender man who makes imitation leather **d :** a mine worker who keeps in repair the pulleys over which haulageway cables pass **e :** an auto worker who runs the motors of finished cars to check their performance, to detect unusual noises, to test parts subject to vibration, and to check the operation of gages **f :** LEVERMAN
roller mill *n* **:** a mill for crushing or grinding material (as grain) by passing it between rolls
roller nest *n* **:** a group of steel rollers assembled together in a frame and placed under the end of a bridge truss or girder and on a bearing plate to permit expansion and contraction to occur without restraint
roller print *n* **:** a fabric with a design made by roller printing
roller printing *n* **:** a method of printing textiles that uses a series of engraved metal rollers each of which contains the parts of the pattern to be printed in one color
roller shade *n* **:** a window shade mounted on a roller
roller skate *n* **:** a skate with small wheels instead of a runner for skating on a surface other than ice
roller-skate \ˈ==,=\ *vi* [*roller skate*] **:** to move on roller skates — **roller skater** *n*
roller stock *n* **:** a metal bar forming the core of a composition printing roller
roller table *n* **:** a double roller disk sometimes used in timepieces instead of a single roller
roller-top \ˈ==,=\ *n* **:** ROLL TOP
roller towel *n* **:** an endless towel hung from a roller
roller tube *n* **:** a culture tube (as for normal or malignant tissue cells) in which the material to be cultivated is immobilized on the side of the tube by a film of serum or other medium and which is rotated (as in a water bath) to insure adequate and uniform aeration

roller skate

roller-up \ˈ==ˈ=\ *n, pl* **rollers-up** [*roll up* + *-er*] **:** one that rolls up; *specif* **:** a textile worker who rolls skeins of yarn
roll film *n* **:** a strip of sensitized film for still-camera use that is wound on a spool with backing paper for light protection and daylight loading
roll-forming machine \ˈ=,==-\ *n* **:** a machine that shapes sheet metal to a desired curve by means of rollers
¹**rol·lick** \ˈrälik, -lēk\ *vi* -ED/-ING/-S [origin unknown] **1 :** to move or behave in a carefree joyous manner **:** FROLIC, ROMP ⟨she loved to ~; persiflage was her natural expression —W.A. White⟩ ⟨the puppies ~ about —Emily Hahn⟩ ⟨begins like an 18th century minuet and ~s suddenly into a jig —Waldo Frank⟩ **2 :** to revel in something ⟨would certainly roll and ~ in women unless there was work for him to do —H.G.Wells⟩
syn see PLAY
²**rollick** \"\ *n* -S **1 :** enthusiastic gaiety **:** EXUBERANCE, JOYOUSNESS ⟨filled the English theater with such ~ as it had scarcely known before —*Time*⟩ **2 :** ESCAPADE, LARK
rol·lick·er \-kə(r)\ *n* -S **:** one that rollicks **:** a boisterous person
rollicking *adj* **1 :** unrestrained in speech or behavior **:** BOISTEROUS, SWAGGERING ⟨a reckless, ~ set —Herman Melville⟩ ⟨with all his ~ rudeness, curiosity, and crudeness of dress —E.M.Coulter⟩ **2 :** light-heartedly gay **:** having or expressing a carefree joyousness ⟨the comic novels . . . are jolly, ~ affairs —John Barkham⟩ ⟨weep at the songs of sorrow, stamp their feet in joy at the ~ songs —Louise L. Davis⟩ — **rol·lick·ing·ly** *adv* — **rol·lick·ing·ness** *n* -ES
rol·lick·some \-ksəm\ *adj* **:** ROLLICKING — **rol·lick·some·ness** *n* -ES
roll in *vi* **:** to go to bed **:** turn in
roll-in \ˈ=,=\ *n, pl* **roll-ins** *or* **rolls-in** [fr. *roll in,* v.] **:** a play in field hockey by which a ball that has been hit out of bounds over either side line is rolled onto the field from beyond the side line by a member of the opposing team
rol·lin film \ˈrälən-\ *n, usu cap R* [prob. fr. the name *Rollin*] **:** a very thin film produced by capillary creeping of liquid helium II over a solid surface
¹**roll·ing** \ˈrōliŋ, -lēŋ\ *n* -S [ME, fr. gerund of *rollen, rolen* to roll — more at ROLL] **:** an act, action, or effect of one that rolls
²**rolling** \"\ *adj* [fr. pres. part. of ²*roll*] **1 a :** rotating on or as if on an axis or moving along a surface by rotation ⟨~ wheels⟩ **b :** moving on wheels or rollers ⟨this leaves only forty feet, or three lanes for ~ traffic —J.M.Lawrence⟩ **2 a :** moving from side to side or up and down ⟨~ eyes⟩ **b :** swinging from side to side **:** LURCHING, SWAYING ⟨a ~ gait⟩ **3 :** turned over upon or toward itself **:** COILING ⟨a ~ hat brim⟩ ⟨bought him a ~ Byronic collar —W.A.White⟩ **4 a :** RESOUNDING, REVERBERATING ⟨see the splintering lightning, and hear the ~ thunder —*Phoenix Flame*⟩ ⟨the traditional ~ phrases of the American declamatory style —*Time*⟩ **b :** TRILLED ⟨~ notes⟩ **5 a** (1) **:** surging or rising upward in billows or rolls ⟨the ~ sea⟩ ⟨the ~ fog⟩ (2) **:** moving in waves **:** progressing or acting in stages **:** STAGGERED ⟨the economy was going through a ~ adjustment in which first one industry and then another was affected⟩ **b :** having gradual rounded undulations of surface ⟨ahead of us was a ~ green plain, with dark mountains beyond it —Ernest Hemingway⟩ ⟨~ hills⟩ **6 :** coming in regular rotation **:** RECURRING ⟨the ~ seasons⟩ ⟨the ~ years⟩ — **roll·ing·ly** *adv*
rolling barrage *n* **:** a barrage that moves forward by bounds at a fixed rate in advance of attacking infantry — called also *creeping barrage*
rolling bridge *n* **:** a revolving drawbridge
rolling chair *n* **:** a wheeled chair; *esp* **:** one adapted for recreational use and propelled by an attendant outdoors (as on a boardwalk)
rolling chock *n* **:** BILGE KEEL
rolling circle *n* **1 :** the generating circle of cycloidal and similar curves **2 :** PITCH CIRCLE
rolling colter *n* **:** a colter consisting of a sharp-edged steel disk
rolling eight *n* **:** a flight maneuver in which an airplane flies two horizontal eights side by side in immediate succession
rolling friction *n* **:** resistance to motion by bodies that are in rolling contact
rolling grass *n* **:** SPINY ROLLING GRASS
rolling hitch *n* **:** a hitch for fastening a line to a spar or to the standing part of another line that will not slip when the pull is parallel to the spar or line — see MAGNUS HITCH
rolling inspection *n* **:** a check of moving trains (as for signs of a hotbox or dragging equipment) made by track workers and the crews of passing trains
rolling jack *n* **:** a machine for rolling leather
rolling key clutch *n* **:** a friction clutch in which a set of rollers surrounding a shaft is wedged (as by a locking pawl) between this shaft and a hub on a second shaft to be connected with it
rolling kitchen *n* **:** a kitchen set up in a truck or trailer for cooking food and conveying it to troops in the field
rolling landside *n* **:** a landside consisting of a metal disk wheel that revolves on an axle
rolling mill *n* **1 :** an establishment where metal is rolled into plates and bars of various sections **2 :** a machine for shaping material (as heated metal, molten glass, or leather) by passing and repassing it between rolls
rolling moment *n* **:** a moment that tends to rotate an airplane about its longitudinal axis
rolling pin *n* **:** a long cylinder (as of wood or plastic) fitted with a handle or knob at each end and used for rolling out paste or dough
rolling press *n* **1 :** a calender that operates by means of rollers **2 :** a printing press with a D-shaped roller used in copperplate printing
rolling reef *n* **:** a reef made by rolling up the sail around a spar at the foot

rolling pin

rolling road *n* **:** a road formerly used for rolling hogsheads of tobacco to market
rolling spar *n* **:** BOAT BOOM
rolling stock *n* **1 :** the wheeled vehicles (as locomotives, passenger cars, or freight cars) owned and used by a railroad **2 :** the wheeled vehicles (as trucks or tractor-trailers) owned and used by a motor carrier
rolling stone *n* **:** a person who changes his habitation, business, or pursuits with great frequency **:** one who leads a wandering or unsettled life ⟨a rover perhaps, but not a thriftless *rolling stone* —*Dial*⟩
rolling tackle *n* **:** a tackle used to steady a yard when the ship rolls in bad weather
rolling weed *n* **:** TUMBLEWEED
rol·lin·ia \rəˈlinēə\ *n, cap* [NL, fr. Charles *Rollin* †1741 Fr. educator + NL *-ia*] **:** a small genus of tropical American trees and shrubs (family Annonaceae) distinguished by the wing-appendaged petals of the flower — see BIRIBA
roll-ins *pl of* ROLL-IN
roll joint *n* **:** a joint in sheet metal made by rolling up overlapped edges and pressing flat
roll-leaf \ˈ=,=\ *n* **:** gold or foil laid on thin glazed paper and put up in rolls for feeding out mechanically in a stamping press
roll·man \ˈrōlmən\ *n, pl* **rollmen :** one who operates a rolling machine: as **a :** an operator of a power roll for smoothing sheets of metal **b :** an operator of a rolling machine for crushing already broken ore in preparation for mineral extraction **c :** an operator of a machine for cooling melted lard by contact with a refrigerated roll
roll·mops \ˈrōl,mäps\ *n, pl* **rollmops** \"\ *also* **rollmop·se** \-səs\ [G, fr. *rollen* to roll + *mops* simpleton, pugnosed dog, fr. LG — more at ROLLER, MOPPET] **:** a fillet of freshened salt herring rolled up with pickle or onion and skewered and then pickled in a marinade of vinegar, sliced onion, peppercorns, celery seed, bay leaves, or other spices
rollock *var of* ROWLOCK
roll-off \ˈ=,=\ *n* -S [fr. *roll off,* v.] **1 :** a tendency of an airplane esp. at high speed to lower one wing **2 :** a gradual decrease in efficiency of transmission in a sound recording system with a rise or lowering of the frequency range past a particular frequency **3 :** a play-off match in bowling
roll-on \ˈ=,=\ *n* -S [fr. *roll on,* v.] **:** a woman's girdle of rubber or elasticized fabric
roll out *vi* **:** to get out of bed ⟨*rolled out* about three o'clock in the morning to ride guard till daylight —F.B.Gipson⟩
roll-out \ˈ=,=\ *n* -S [fr. *roll out,* v.] **:** the rolling out to public view of a new airplane prototype
roll over *vt* **:** to refinance a maturing obligation (as a short-term government security) by offering a new obligation of the same type in exchange
roll-over arm \ˈ=,==-\ *n* **:** a fully upholstered chair or sofa arm curving outward from the seat
roll-over plow *n* **:** SWIVEL PLOW
roll pass *n* **:** ²PASS 3
roll roofing *n* **:** PREPARED ROOFING
rolls *pl of* ROLL, *pres 3d sing of* ROLL
roll scale *n* **:** MILL SCALE
rolls-in *pl of* ROLL-IN
rolls·man \ˈrōlzmən\ *n pl* **rollsmen :** one who passes cold steel boiler plate through a roll machine to shape it to desired curvature
roll sulfur *n* **:** sulfur in the form of rods or sticks made by casting molten sulfur
roll top *n* **1 :** the flexible cover of a rolltop desk **2 :** ROLLTOP DESK
rolltop desk \ˈ=,=-\ *n* **:** a writing desk having a sliding cover made of parallel slats fastened to a flexible backing
roll train *n* **:** a set of plain or grooved rolls (as in a rolling mill) for rolling metal into various forms
roll up *vt* **1 :** to increase by successive accumulations **:** build up **:** ACCUMULATE ⟨*rolled up* a huge fortune⟩ ⟨*rolled up* a large majority⟩ ⟨*rolled up* a big sale⟩ **2 :** to apply developing ink to (a lithographic plate) ~ *vi* **1 :** to become larger by successive accumulations

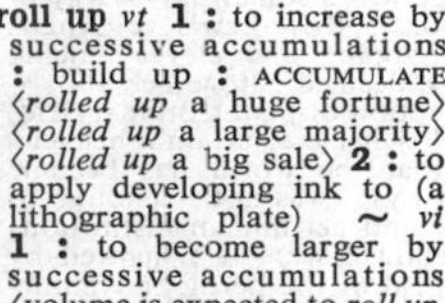

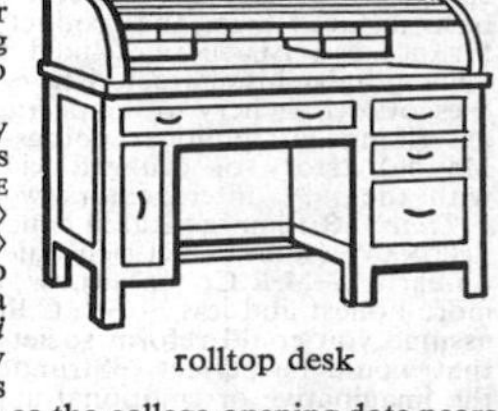

rolltop desk

⟨volume is expected to *roll up* as the college opening date nears —*Women's Wear Daily*⟩ **2 a :** to arrive in a vehicle ⟨turning in at the bridge, *rolled up* to the front porch —Ellen Glasgow⟩ **b** *Austral* **:** to congregate in large numbers; *esp* **:** to attend a meeting
¹**roll-up** \ˈ=,=\ *n* -S [fr. *roll up,* v.] **1 :** long hose worn by men esp. in the 18th century **2 :** a food preparation that is rolled up with or without a filling ⟨a ham *roll-up*⟩ **3** *Austral* **:** a gathering of people **4 :** a developing ink used in rolling up a lithographic plate
²**roll-up** \"\ *adj* [fr. *roll up,* v.] **:** capable of being rolled up ⟨*roll-up* blinds⟩ ⟨a *roll-up* tobacco pouch⟩
rollway \ˈ=,=\ *n* **1 a :** a natural or prepared slope for rolling logs into a stream **b** (1) **:** a pile of logs stored at a landing (2) **:** LANDING 2b **2 :** an outside entrance to a cellar
roll welding *n* **:** forge welding by pressure rolls
rolock wall *or* **rolok wall** *var of* ROWLOCK WALL
rol·o·way \ˈrälə,wā\ *n* -S [origin unknown] **:** DIANA MONKEY
¹**ro·ly-po·ly** *also* **ro·ley-po·ley** \ˈrōlēˈpōlē\ *n, pl* **roly-polys** *or* **roly-polies** [redupl. of *roly, roley,* fr. ²*roll* + *-y*] **1 :** any of various games in which a ball is rolled or thrown into holes, hats, or circles or at pins **2 :** a dessert made of rolled-out dough spread with a filling, rolled up into a cylinder shape, and baked or steamed **3 :** an Australian tumbleweed (*Bassia muricata*) that resembles the rose of Jericho **4 a :** a roly-poly person or thing **b :** a toy usu. made to resemble a person and so formed and weighted as to rock when touched and return to an erect position — called also *tumbler*
²**roly-poly** \ˈ==ˈ==\ *adj* **:** short and pudgy in stature **:** ROTUND ⟨she was so round and *roly-poly* I used to wonder how she ever moved fast enough to catch hold of a bird —Astrid Peters⟩
rom \ˈrōm\ *n* -S *usu cap* [Romany, married man, husband, gypsy man, fr. Skt *ḍomba, ḍoma* man of a low caste of musicians] **:** a male gypsy
rom *abbr* **1** roman **2** romance
ROM *abbr, often not cap* run of mine
ro·ma·dur \ˌrōməˈdu̇(ə)r\ *n* -S *usu cap* [G] **:** a cheese similar to Limburger in flavor and aroma
rom·age \ˈrämij\ *chiefly Scot var of* RUMMAGE
¹**ro·ma·gnese** \ˌrōmäˌnyēz, -ēs\ *adj, usu cap* [It, adj. & n., fr. *Romagna,* area in northern Italy + It *-ese*] **1 :** of, relating to, or characteristic of the Romagna **2 :** of, relating to, or characteristic of the people of the Romagna
²**romagnese** \"\ *n, pl* **romagnese** *cap* **:** a native or inhabitant of the Romagna
ro·ma·gnole *also* **ro·ma·gnol** \ˌ==ˈnyōl\ *n* -S *cap* [It *romagnolo, romagnuolo,* fr. *Romagna*] **1 :** ROMAGNESE **2 :** one who speaks an Italian dialect of the Romagna
¹**ro·maic** \rōˈmāik, -āēk\ *adj, usu cap* [NGk *Rhōmaïkos,* fr. Gk, Roman, fr. *Rhōmē, Rhōma* Rome + *-ikos* -ic] **:** of or relating to modern Greece or modern Greek
²**romaic** \"\ *n* -S *cap* **:** the modern Greek vernacular
ro·ma·i·ka \rōˈmäēkə\ *n* -S [NGk *rhōmaikē,* fr. fem. of *Rhōmaïkos*] **:** a modern Greek folk dance
ro·maine \(ˈ)rōˈmān\ *also* **romaine lettuce** *n* -S [F *romaine,* fr. fem. of *romain* Roman, fr. L *Romanus* — more at ROMAN] **:** COS LETTUCE
ro·ma·ji \ˈrōməjē\ *n* -S *usu cap* [Jap *rōmaji*] **:** a method of writing Japanese in Roman characters
¹**ro·mal** \rəˈmal\ *n* -S [modif. of MexSp *ramal,* fr. Sp. strand of rope, fr. *rama* branch — more at RAMADA] **:** a thong usu. braided and divided into two lashes and attached to the saddle or reins for use as a quirt
²**romal** *var of* RUMAL
¹**ro·man** \ˈrōmən\ *n* [partly fr. ME, fr. OE, fr. L *Romanus,* adj. & n., fr. *Roma* Rome + *-anus* -an; partly fr. ME *Romain,* fr. OF, fr. L *Romanus*] **1** -S *cap* **a :** a native or resident of Rome **b :** a Christian inhabitant of ancient Rome — usu. used in pl. ⟨the Epistle to the *Romans*⟩ **2** -S *usu cap* **:** ROMAN CATHOLIC — often taken to be offensive **3** -S **:** roman letters or type ⟨set this word in ~⟩ **4** -S *cap* **a** *archaic* **:** LATIN **b** *archaic* **:** ¹ROMANCE 5 **c :** the Italian dialect of Rome **5 a** *usu cap* **:** an Italian breed of small stocky short-necked white geese **b** -S *often cap* **:** any bird of this breed **6** -S **:** a bright red sparid sea fish (*Chrysoblephus laticeps*) of southern Africa valued for sport and food — called also *red roman*
²**roman** \"\ *adj* [partly fr. ME, fr. L *Romanus;* partly fr. ME *Romain,* fr. OF, fr. L *Romanus*] **1** *usu cap* **a :** of, relating to, or characteristic of Rome, Italy, esp. ancient Rome **b :** of, relating to, or characteristic of the people of Rome; *specif* **:** having characteristics (as fortitude, courage, justice, or manliness) attributed to the ancient Romans ⟨by his *Roman* bearing in adversity, has earned a great deal of public sympathy —*Economist*⟩ **2** *usu cap* **:** of, relating to, or characteristic of the language of the ancient Romans **3 a :** UPRIGHT — used of numbers and the letters of English and other languages whose capital forms are modeled on ancient Roman inscriptions esp. as distinguished from italic, black letter, and the letters of non-Latin alphabets **b** *usu cap* **:** being round, bold, and clear — used of handwriting **4** *usu cap* **a :** of or relating to the Roman Catholic Church ⟨*Roman* practices⟩ **b :** of or relating to the Latin rite ⟨the *Roman* liturgy⟩ **5 :** having a semicircular intrados **:** ROUND ⟨a ~ arch⟩ **6** *usu cap* **:** having a prominent bridge of a slightly aquiline cast ⟨a *Roman* nose⟩ **7** *usu cap* **:** of, relating to, or constituting a mosaic formed by the ends of short slender sticks of colored glass fixed in cement **8** *usu cap* **:** of, relating to, or characteristic of the Roman ride
ro·man à clef \rōmäⁿnäklā\ *n, pl* **romans à clef** \"\ [F, lit., novel with a key] **:** a novel in which real persons or actual events figure under disguise ⟨a *roman à clef* of show business —Burton Rascoe⟩
roman alphabet *n, usu cap R* **:** LATIN ALPHABET
roman alum *n, usu cap R* **:** alum crystallized in cubes; *esp* **:** alum formerly made from alunite at Tolfa near Rome that was reddish because of a very small amount of iron oxide though otherwise very pure
roman architecture *n, usu cap R* **:** the classic architectural style of the Roman empire marked by the use of the orders, pediment, arch, dome, and vault
roman brick *n, often cap R* **:** a building brick having the dimensions of 1½ in. x 4 in. x 12 in.
roman candle *n, usu cap R* **1 :** a firework in the form of a straight cylindrical case characterized by the continued emission of sparks and the ejection at intervals of balls or stars of fire in high arching trajectories **2 :** SPANISH DAGGER
roman canvas *n, usu cap R* **:** a fine linen canvas primed on one side for oil painting
roman capital *n, sometimes cap R* **1 :** a letter belonging to a

ROMAN CAPITALS

style of alphabet modeled upon the simple erect characters of Roman inscriptions **2 roman capitals** *pl* **:** a mode of writing consisting of roman capital letters
¹**roman catholic** *n, usu cap R&C* **:** a member of the Roman Catholic Church
²**roman catholic** *adj, usu cap R&C* **:** of, relating to, or being a Christian church with a hierarchy headed by the pope, a usu. Latin rite centering in the Mass, seven sacraments, veneration of the Virgin Mary and the saints, clerical celibacy, many religious orders, and dogma including transubstantiation and papal infallibility
roman catholicism *n, cap R&C* **:** the faith, doctrine, or polity of the Roman Catholic Church
¹**ro·mance** \rōˈman(t)s, -maa(ə)n-, ˈ=,=\ *n* -S [ME *romauns, romance,* fr. OF *romans, romanz* French, something composed in French, tale in verse, fr. L *Romanice* in the Roman manner, fr. *Romanicus* Roman, fr. *Romanus* Roman + *-icus* -ic — more at ROMAN] **1** *often cap* **a :** a tale in verse written in medieval times based chiefly on legend, chivalric love and adventure, or the supernatural — called also *metrical romance;* compare EPIC **b :** a prose tale written in medieval times and resembling a metrical romance **c :** a prose narrative having romantic qualities or characteristics: as (1) **:** one treating imaginary characters involved in events unrelated to everyday life — compare FANTASY FICTION (2) **:** one dealing with the remote in time or place, the heroic, the adventurous, and often the mysterious — compare HISTORICAL NOVEL **d :** a class or division of literature comprising romance or romantic fiction **2 :** something (as an extravagant invention or wild exaggeration) that lacks basis or foundation in fact ⟨new institutions were growing up to fight the speculation and ~ that passed for science —Mari Sandoz⟩ ⟨the critic . . . has given us what is really merely a ~ exploiting the supposed working of the mechanism, in place of an actual study that sticks close to the facts —C.I.Glicksberg⟩ **3 :** the quality or state of being romantic ⟨there is real ~ in the way words have come to have their present meanings —A.T.Weaver⟩ ⟨there is such ~ attaching to all who explore uncharted seas in cockleshell boats —*Times Lit. Supp.*⟩ ⟨~ of the pioneer⟩ ⟨~ of steel and steam⟩ ⟨~ of history⟩ ⟨~ of whaling⟩ **4 a** (1) **:** a love, love affair, or marriage of a romantic nature ⟨high school ~⟩ ⟨the ~ reportedly developed on ski jaunts —*Current Biog.*⟩ ⟨a fairy tale of love and ~ with a beautiful . . . girl —L.O.Coxe⟩ ⟨he and his wife are reported to have lived a ~ lasting almost sixty years —W.S.Rusk⟩ (2) **:** LOVEMAKING **b :** an attraction or aspiration of an emotional or romantic character ⟨the dream of travel . . . was his ~ —George Meredith⟩ ⟨the League of Nations was his first real ~ —James Cameron⟩ ⟨religion was their ~ —Van Wyck Brooks⟩ **5** *cap* **a :** the languages developed from Latin (as Portuguese, Spanish, French, Italian, Romanian) that constitute a division of the Italic branch of the Indo-European language family — see INDO-EUROPEAN LANGUAGES table **b :** any of such languages
²**romance** \(ˈ)=ˈ=\ *adj* **1** *usu cap* **:** of, relating to, or constituting the Romance languages **2 :** of or relating to the countries

succeeding the Roman Empire in the medieval period **3 :** of, relating to, or characterized by romance or the romantic ⟨~ accounts of the last Gaulish invasions —Thomas Arnold⟩

³romance \ˈ=,=, ˈ=,=\ *vb* -ED/-ING/-S *vi* **1 :** to exaggerate or invent detail or incident in a romantic manner ⟨would ~ about the notables he met or the books he read —R.B.Morris⟩ ⟨the great scandal . . . was his habit of unscrupulous *romancing* —Edmund Wilson⟩ **2 :** to entertain romantic thoughts or ideas ⟨looking in at the windows . . . and *romancing* over the pictures —L.P.Smith⟩ ~ *vt* **1 :** to exaggerate or invent (as detail or incident) in a romantic manner ⟨the book exceeds and ~*s* the factual material —Donald Sutherland⟩ ⟨this *romanced* account of his wanderings, his turpitudes, and his squabbles —A.L.Guérard⟩ **2 :** to seek the favor or influence of by personal attention, flattery, or gifts ⟨was nice to the press and *romanced* the disc jockeys —*Time*⟩ **3 :** to make love to **:** carry on a love affair with ⟨a favorite spot . . . to ~ their girl friends —Budd Schulberg⟩

⁴romance \"\ *n* -S [F, fr. Sp, fr. OSp, Spanish, something written in Spanish, tale, ballad, fr. L *Romanice* in the Roman manner — more at ¹ROMANCE] **1 :** a short lyric tale set to music **2 :** a song or short instrumental piece in ballad style

roman cement *n, usu cap R* **:** a natural cement prepared by calcining septaria and grinding it dry to a fine powder

ro·manc·er \-sə(r)\ *n* -S [¹*romance* + -*er*] **1 :** a writer of romance or romantic fiction **2 :** one that romances

romance stanza *n* **:** a six-line verse stanza common in metrical romances in which lines 1, 2, 4, and 5 of 4 accents each are rhymed and lines 3 and 6 of 3 accents each are rhymed

roman chamomile *n, usu cap R* **:** ENGLISH CHAMOMILE

roman chamomile oil *n, usu cap R* **:** CHAMOMILE OIL a

romanche *usu cap, var of* ROMANSH

ro·man·ci·cal \rōˈman(t)səkəl\ *adj* [¹*romance* + -*ical*] **1 :** of, relating to, or consisting of romance or romantic fiction ⟨~ books⟩ **2 :** writing or inventing romance or romantic fiction ⟨~ writers⟩

ro·manc·ist \rōˈman(t)səst\ *n* -S [¹*romance* + -*ist*] **:** ROMANCER 1

roman club *n, usu cap R* **:** a system of bidding at contract bridge employing an artificial opening bid of one club for hands that are barely strong enough to bid or for some hands that are quite strong

roman collar *n, usu cap R* **:** CLERICAL COLLAR

roman-dutch law *n, usu cap R&D* **:** the civil-law system developed by Dutch jurists and used in So. Africa and other parts of the world colonized by the Dutch

ro·ma·nes·ca \,rōməˈneskə\ *n* -S [It, fr. fem. of *romanesco* Roman, fr. *romano* Roman (fr. L *Romanus*) + -*esco* -esque — more at ROMAN] **:** GALLIARD 2

¹ro·man·esque \ˌrōməˈnesk\ *adj, usu cap* [²*Roman* + -*esque*] **1 :** ROMANCE 1 **2 a :** of, relating to, or constructed in the Romanesque style or architecture **b :** of or relating to art contemporary with the Romanesque style and marked by religious solemnity, decorativeness, and symbolism **3 :** ROMANTIC 4 ⟨this *Romanesque* fantasy, nostalgic with adolescence and written with imagination and flourish —Janet Flanner⟩

²romanesque \"\ *n* -S **1** *cap* **:** ¹ROMANCE 5 **2** *usu cap* **:** the Romanesque style of art or architecture

romanesque architecture *or* **romanesque style** *n, usu cap R* **:** the architecture or style that developed in Italy and various parts of western Europe between the periods of the Roman and the Gothic styles: **a :** a continuation before A.D. 1000 of the Early Christian style in unvaulted basilican churches marked by the development of the cruciform plan with choirs and transepts without sculptural treatment **b :** any of several advanced and differentiated styles (as Lombard, Norman, Rhenish architecture) having as common features the use of the round arch and vault with narrowing and heightening of the nave, the substitution for columns of piers often with engaged shafts, the decorative use of arcades and colonnettes, and profuse carved ornament esp. on capitals, stringcourses, and the moldings of doorways — see ARCHITECTURE table

romanesque revival *n, usu cap 1st R* **:** a nostalgic stylistic return in the late 19th century to pre-Gothic architectural forms

ro·ma·nes·ta red MT-2544 \ˌrōməˈnestə-\ *n, usu cap both Rs* [*romanesta* of unknown origin] **:** an organic pigment — see DYE table I (under *Pigment Red 15*)

roman fern *n, usu cap R* **:** DEER FERN

ro·man-fleuve \rōmä^nflœv\ *n, pl* **romans-fleuves** \"\ [F, lit., river novel] **:** a distinctively French novel having the form of a long, multivolume, and usu. easygoing chronicle of persons comprising a family, community, or other social group

roman foot *n, usu cap R* **:** an ancient Roman unit of length equal to 11.64 English inches

roman gold *n, usu cap R* **:** gold having a yellow mat finish

roman green *n, often cap R* **:** a moderate olive color that is redder than average olive green and redder, lighter, and stronger than average olive color

roman holiday *n, usu cap R* [so called fr. the bloody combats staged as entertainment in ancient Rome] **1 a :** an event or occasion resembling the games or gladiatorial combats of the ancient Roman circus (as for spectacle or savagery provided or demanded as a source of sadistic pleasure for onlookers) **b :** a time of enjoyment derived from the sufferings or losses of others or the source of such enjoyment ⟨our own fliers seemed to be letting the Jerries have a *Roman holiday* at our expense —E.V.Westrate⟩ ⟨diplomats who felt themselves merely victims to be sacrificed every four years to make a *Roman holiday* for a new President —Emily Bax⟩ **2 :** a public dispute, investigation, or turmoil in which the participants inflict embarrassment, degradation, or ignominy on each other or themselves often at the direction or to the satisfaction of nonparticipants ⟨persons charging police brutality have had a *Roman holiday* in making these charges but not following them up —*Springfield* (*Mass.*) *Union*⟩ ⟨the investigation was accompanied by reams of publicity and millionaires were summoned by the score to make a *Roman holiday* —*Amer. Mercury*⟩

roman hyacinth *n, usu cap R* **:** a hyacinth (*Hyacinthus orientalis albulus*) with loosely flowered spikes several of which grow from one bulb

romani *cap, var of* ROMANY 2

ro·ma·nia \rōˈmānēə, -nyə\ *or* **ru·ma·nia** *or* **rou·ma·nia** \rü'-\ *adj, usu cap* [fr. *Romania*, country in eastern Europe] **:** of or from Romania **:** of the kind or style prevalent in Romania **:** ROMANIAN

¹ro·ma·nian *or* **ru·ma·nian** *or* **rou·ma·nian** \-ən\ *adj, usu cap* [*Romania, Roumania, Rumania*, country in eastern Europe + E -*an*] **1 a :** of, relating to, or characteristic of Romania **b :** of, relating to, or characteristic of the Romanians **2 :** of, relating to, or characteristic of the Romanian language

²romanian *or* **rumanian** *or* **roumanian** \"\ *n* -S *cap* **1 :** a native or inhabitant of Romania; *esp* **:** one of the dominant ethnic group prob. descended from Roman provincial colonists of Dacia and Moesia **2 :** the Romance language of the Romanian people

¹ro·man·ic \rōˈmanik, -nēk\ *adj* [L *Romanicus* Roman — more at ROMANCE] **1** *usu cap* **:** ROMANCE 1 **2** *usu cap* **:** descended from the Roman people ⟨the *Romanic* races⟩ — compare LATIN, ROMANCE 2

²romanic \"\ *n* -S *cap* **:** ROMANCE 5

ro·man·i·cist \-nəsəst\ *n* -S *usu cap* **:** ROMANIST 3

romanies *pl of* ROMANY

roman indiction *n, usu cap R* **:** the indiction of the system that began on Dec. 25, A.D. 312 or as still used in modern chronology Jan. 1, 313 — called also *pontifical indiction*

ro·man·ish \ˈrōmənish, -nēsh\ *adj, usu cap* [²*Roman* + -*ish*] **:** of or relating to the Roman Catholic Church — usu. used disparagingly; compare ROMISH

ro·man·ism \-mə,nizəm\ *n* -S [²*Roman* + -*ism*] **1** *cap* **:** ROMAN CATHOLICISM **2** *usu cap* **:** the polity, institutions, or prevailing spirit of ancient Rome

¹ro·man·ist \-,nəst\ *n* -S *usu cap* [NL *Romanista*, fr. L *Romanus* Roman + -*ista* -ist — more at ROMAN] **1 :** one who adheres to Roman Catholicism — usu. used disparagingly **2 :** a specialist in the language, culture, or law of ancient Rome **3 :** a person skilled or informed in Romance languages or philology — called also *Romanicist* **4 :** an historian who magnifies the influence of Roman institutions in the development of European civilization — compare GERMANIST

²romanist \"\ *or* **ro·man·is·tic** \ˌ==ˈnistik\ *adj, usu cap* **1 :** adhering to or inclining toward Roman Catholicism **2 :** of or relating to the law of ancient Rome

ro·man·i·ty \rōˈmanəd·ē\ *n* -ES *usu cap* **:** ROMANISM

ro·ma·ni·um \rōˈmānēəm\ *n* -S [NL, fr. R. I. *Roman*, 19th cent. metallurgist, its inventor + NL -*ium*] **:** an alloy consisting of aluminum having an admixture of less than one percent of tungsten together with a little copper, nickel, antimony, and tin

ro·man·iza·tion \,rōmənəˈzāshən, -mə,nīˈ-\ *n* -S *usu cap* **:** the act or process of Romanizing

ro·man·ize \ˈrōmə,nīz\ *vb* -ED/-ING/-S [²*Roman* + -*ize*] *vt* **1** *often cap* **a :** to cause to acquire traits or characteristics distinctly Roman or become adapted to Roman customs or outlook **b :** to bring (as an area or people) under the political, cultural, or commercial influence of Rome **2** *sometimes cap* **a :** to write or print (as a language) in roman characters — compare ROMAJI **b :** to represent (as pagination) in roman numerals **3** *usu cap* **a :** to convert to Roman Catholicism **b** (1) **:** to give a Roman Catholic character to (2) **:** to subject to the principles and usages of the Roman Catholic Church ~ *vi, usu cap* **:** to become Roman Catholic; *also* **:** to adhere to or incline toward Roman Catholicism

roman lake *n, often cap R* **:** CARMINE 2

roman law *n, usu cap R* **:** the legal system of the ancient Romans that includes the customary or unwritten law and the written law, is based on the traditional law and the legislation of the city of Rome, and in form comprises legislation of the law-making assemblies, resolves of the senate, enactments of the emperors, the edicts or praetorian law, the writings of the jurisconsults, and the codes of the later emperors — see CIVIL LAW; compare JUS GENTIUM, NATURAL LAW

ro·man·ly *adv, usu cap* **:** in a manner characteristic of the ancient Romans

roman nettle *n, usu cap R* **:** an annual herb (*Urtica pilulifera*) with stinging foliage and small clusters of green flowers

roman numeral *n, often cap R* **:** one of the symbols in a system of numerical notation based upon the ancient Roman system — see NUMBER table

ro·ma·no \rōˈmä(,)nō\ *also* **romano cheese** *n* -S *usu cap R* [It *romano* Roman, fr. L *Romanus* — more at ROMAN] **:** a sharp hard cheese of pale color and granular texture with a blackish green rind made of ewe's milk and now also of milk from cows and goats

romano- *comb form, usu cap* [²*Roman*] **:** Roman **:** Roman and ⟨*Romano*-Etruscan⟩ ⟨*Romano*-German⟩

roman ocher *n, usu cap R* **1 :** an orange-yellow ocher **2 :** OCHER BROWN

roman order *n, usu cap R* **1 :** the composite order in architecture **2 :** ARCH ORDER

ro·ma·nov \ˈrōmə,nȯf\ *n* [after the *Romanov* dynasty that ruled Russia 1613–1917] **1** *usu cap* **:** a Russian breed of prolific strong-wooled sheep **2** -S *often cap* **:** any sheep of the Romanov breed

ro·ma·now·sky stain \ˌrōməˈnȯfskē-\ *n, usu cap R* [after Dimitri L. *Romanowsky* †1921 Russ. physician] **:** a stain made from water-soluble eosin, methylene blue, and absolute methanol and used in parasitology

roman pace *n, usu cap R* **:** an ancient Roman unit of length that is equal to five Roman feet or 4.85 English feet and is measured in pacing from the heel of one foot to the heel of the same foot when it next touches the ground

roman peace *n, usu cap R* [trans. of L *pax Romana*] **:** a peace imposed and maintained by force of arms **:** PAX

roman pearl *n, usu cap R* **:** an imitation pearl made of a glass bulb coated with pearl essence and filled with wax

roman plant *n, usu cap R* **:** GOOD-KING-HENRY

roman purple *n, often cap R* **:** a moderate violet that is redder and deeper than Parma violet (sense 2a) and redder and stronger than damson

roman revival *n, usu cap 1st R* **:** a late Renaissance return to the simpler forms of classic Roman architecture

roman ride *n, usu cap 1st R* **:** a style of riding in which the rider stands with one foot on the back of each of two horses driven as a pair ⟨first came the *Roman ride*, a wild gallop about the ring . . . on two horses —Eduard Bass⟩

roman rings *n pl, usu cap 1st R* **:** large pendent rings used by an acrobat or gymnast in performing gymnastic feats in midair

romans *pl of* ROMAN

roman sandal *n, usu cap R* **:** a shoe on which the vamp is composed of a series of buckled straps equally spaced

Roman sandal

roman sepia *n, often cap R* **:** VANDYKE BROWN 2

romans-fleuves *pl of* ROMAN-FLEUVE

ro·mansh *or* **ro·mansch** *or* **ro·manche** \rōˈmanch, -mänch\ *or* **ru·mansch** \rüˈ-\ *n, pl* **romanshes** *or* **romansches** *or* **romanches** *or* **rumansches** *usu cap* [Romansh *rumansch, rumonsch, romonsch*] **:** the Rhaeto-Romanic dialects spoken in the Grisons, Switzerland; *esp* **:** those west of the Engadine

roman snail *n, usu cap R* **:** a European edible snail (*Helix pomatia*)

roman striking *n, usu cap R* **:** a system of striking the time in some older clocks that employs two bells of different pitch with the lower-toned bell representing the Roman figure V and the higher-toned bell the Roman figure I

roman stripe *n, usu cap R* **1 roman stripes** *pl* **:** bright varicolored stripes of equal or unequal widths used as a continuous textile pattern **2 :** a fabric with a pattern of Roman stripes

¹ro·man·tic \rōˈmantik, -maan- -tēk *sometimes* rəˈ-\ *adj* [F *romantique*, fr. obs. *romant* romance (fr. MF, fr. OF *romans, romanz* French, something composed in French, tale in verse) + -*ique* -ic — more at ROMANCE] **1 :** consisting of or similar in form or content to a romance ⟨my advance toward ~ composition —Sir Walter Scott⟩ ⟨~ fiction⟩ **2 :** having no basis in fact **:** being the product of invention or exaggeration **:** FABULOUS, IMAGINARY ⟨liked to make observations all his own and give his characteristic ~ report afterward —Glenway Wescott⟩ ⟨treachery to the peerage was a somewhat ~ way of describing his political goings-on —Roy Lewis & Angus Maude⟩ ⟨story of drugged kidnapping and clever fencing with the . . . interrogators was deemed altogether too ~ —*Time*⟩ **3 :** impractical in conception or plan **:** UNREALISTIC, VISIONARY ⟨some ~ get-rich-quick scheme to attain a heaven-on-earth —M.R.Cohen⟩ ⟨now that the world has become more honest and less ~ —L.C.Powys⟩ ⟨was not ~ enough to assume you could reform society and get human institutions that would be perfect —Stringfellow Barr⟩ **4 :** marked by the imaginative or emotional appeal of the heroic, adventurous, remote, mysterious, or idealized characteristics of things, places, people ⟨collecting ~ articles of commerce — the pearl oyster, arrowroot, ambergris, sandalwood, coconut oil —Herman Melville⟩ ⟨a noble chase of great extent, beautifully wild and ~, well stored with game of all sorts, and abounding with excellent timber —Tobias Smollett⟩ ⟨had become so ~ a figure that his appearance on the street of any border town started lurid tales of bloodshed and sudden death —Mari Sandoz⟩ ⟨reminiscing about his childhood, he almost invariably is drawn into a nostalgic mood where events and characters assume ~ proportions —Rose Feld⟩ ⟨makes a deep impression on the mind; far deeper than the less ~, everyday thing which shows the real state of an island in the statistical sense —R.A.W.Hughes⟩ **5 :** having an inclination or desire for romance **:** responsive to the appeal of the imaginative or emotional qualities of human experience ⟨most people are ~ at 20, owing to lack of experience —E.M. Forster⟩ ⟨was once young and passionate, ~ about the schemes which he realistically carried out —Carl Van Doren⟩ ⟨children are, and ought to be, ~ —C.H.Grandgent⟩ **6 a** *often cap* **:** of, relating to, or having the characteristics of romanticism or the romantic movement ⟨the modern ~ tradition, however, can be traced to one important literary source —Mabel Elliott & Francis Merrill⟩ ⟨the generating and generic element in the *Romantic* doctrine —A.O.Lovejoy⟩ ⟨characteristic of the *Romantic* period —W.H.Auden⟩ ⟨the ~ poets⟩ — compare CLASSICAL **b** *of art, literature, or music* **:** marked by freedom, spontaneity, or freedom of conception and expression **7 a :** characterized by a strong personal sentiment, highly individualized feelings of affection, or the idealization of the beloved or the love relationship **:** ARDENT, FERVENT 2 ⟨give the impression of having married for ~ love —James Jones⟩ ⟨her first ~ admiration of his lofty bearing —George Meredith⟩ ⟨the period of ~ love among the newly married —Lewis Mumford⟩ **b :** marked chiefly by sexual passion or its gratification ⟨in popular speech, today, a ~ novel or film is one concerned . . . with sexual passion —*Times Lit. Supp.*⟩ **8 :** of, relating to, or constituting the part of the hero in a light or romantic comedy ⟨played the ~ lead⟩ **syn** see SENTIMENTAL

²romantic \"\ *n* -S **1 :** a characteristic or component of or suggestive of romance or romantic writing — usu. used in pl. ⟨there you are with your ~*s* again —William Black⟩ ⟨love for the banker's daughter takes care of the ~*s* —*Newsweek*⟩ **2 a :** a person of romantic temperament or disposition **:** one given to romance ⟨is still essentially a ~ — capable of seeing the world as he wishes to see it —T.R.Fyvel⟩ ⟨by temperament and training the ~ who feels first and thinks afterwards —Edward Cushing⟩ **b** *usu cap* **:** ROMANTICIST 1 ⟨the *Romantics* convert nature into a solace for the trials of civilization —Philip Rahv⟩ ⟨was characteristic of the *Romantics* to seek experience for its own sake —Edmund Wilson⟩

ro·man·ti·cal \-təkəl\ *adj* [F *romantique* + E -*al*] **:** ROMANTIC

ro·man·ti·cal·ly \-tək(ə)lē, -tēk-, -li\ *adv* **:** in a romantic manner ⟨~ the village fireman hangs on with one hand —S.R. Gain⟩ ⟨~ in love —W.F. De Morgan⟩ ⟨the house ~ decorated with battlemented towers and high mullioned windows —*Amer. Guide Series: Md.*⟩

ro·man·ti·cal·ness *n* -ES **:** the quality or state of being romantic

romantic green *n* **:** WARBLER GREEN

ro·man·ti·cism \-tə,sizəm\ *n* -S [¹*romantic* + -*ism*] **1 :** the quality or state of being romantic ⟨passed through a period of ~ when a broken love affair somehow seemed noble —G.R. Carlsen⟩ ⟨pure ~ to expect any solution of isolated issues —J.A. del Vayo⟩ ⟨no time for vague ~ in foreign policy —*New Republic*⟩ **2** *often cap* **a** (1) **:** a literary, artistic, and philosophical movement originating in Europe in the 18th century, characterized chiefly by a reaction against neoclassicism with its stress on reason and intellect and an emphasis on the imagination and emotions and their freely individualized expression or realization in all spheres of activity, and marked esp. in English literature by sensibility and the use of autobiographical material of an introspective cast, an exaltation of the primitive and the common man, an appreciation and often a worship of external nature, an interest in the remote in time and space, a predilection for melancholy, and the use in poetry of older verse forms (as the ballad stanza and the sonnet) — compare CLASSICISM 3 (2) **:** an aspect of romanticism (as sentimentalism, primitivism, or medievalism) **b :** adherence to or practice of romantic doctrine or assumptions ⟨the ~ of Byron⟩ ⟨the ~ of early 19th century music⟩ ⟨the ~ of Turner's landscapes⟩ ⟨the ~ of Rodin⟩

¹ro·man·ti·cist \-,səst\ *n* -S [¹*romantic* + -*ist*] **1** *often cap* **:** an advocate of or participant in romanticism or the romantic movement esp. in art, literature, or music **2 :** ROMANTIC 2a

²romanticist \"\ *also* **ro·man·ti·cis·tic** \ˌ=,==ˈsistik\ *adj, often cap* **:** of, relating to, or having the characteristics of romanticism or the romantic movement ⟨is clearly of the ~ type —W.M.Wheeler⟩ ⟨built around the two most ~ nations —A.F.Buchan⟩

ro·man·tic·i·ty \,rō,manˈtisəd·ē\ *n* -ES *archaic* **:** ROMANTICISM

ro·man·ti·ci·za·tion \rō,mantəsəˈzāshən\ *n* -S **:** the act or process of romanticizing

ro·man·ti·cize \rōˈmantə,sīz *sometimes* rəˈ-\ *vb* -ED/-ING/-S [¹*romantic* + -*ize*] *vt* **:** to make romantic **:** add romance to ⟨old forms of drudgery are *romanticized*, old forms of slavery forgotten —H.J.Muller⟩ ⟨rebuke the press for alleged *romanticizing* of gangsterism —F.L.Mott⟩ ~ *vi* **1 :** to hold romantic ideas **:** indulge in romantic fancies ⟨had *romanticized* a great deal about Indians —*Southern Observer*⟩ **2 :** to present or portray details, incidents, or people in a romantic light or manner ⟨has been . . . successful in resisting the impulse to dramatize, though she has yielded occasionally to the impulse to ~ —Howard Lindsay⟩ ⟨refuses to ~, glamorize, or otherwise adopt the strange combination of true confession and movie magazine technique —Abraham Veinus⟩

ro·man·tic·ly *archaic var of* ROMANTICALLY

romantico- *comb form* [¹*romantic*] **:** romantic and ⟨*romantico*-heroic⟩ ⟨*romantico*-literary⟩

romantics *pl of* ROMANTIC

ro·man·tism \rōˈman,tizəm\ *n* -S [F *romantisme*, fr. *romantique* + -*isme* -ism] **:** ROMANTICISM ⟨moonshine ~ idealizing slave-holding aristocrats —J.F.Dobie⟩

roman umber *n, often cap R* **:** RAW UMBER 2

roman violet *n, often cap R* **:** PANSY VIOLET 3

roman wormwood *n, usu cap R* **1 a :** a European wormwood (*Artemisia pontica*) that is a minor source of absinthe **b :** RAGWEED 2a **2 :** a glaucous No. American corydalis (*Corydalis sempervirens*) with loose racemes of yellow-tipped pink flowers

¹rom·a·ny \ˈrämənē, ˈrōm-, -ni\ *also* **rom·ma·ny** \ˈräm-\ *n* -ES [Romany *romano, romani*, adj., gypsy, fr. *rom* married man, husband, gypsy man — more at ROM] **1** *cap* **:** GYPSY 1 **2** *also* **rom·a·ni** \"\ *cap* **:** the Indic language of the gypsies — see INDO-EUROPEAN LANGUAGES table **3** *often cap* **:** a blackish blue that is redder and less strong than average midnight

²romany \"\ *also* **rommany** \"\ *adj, usu cap* [Romany *romano, romani*] **1 :** of, relating to, or characteristic of the Romanies **2 :** of, relating to, or characteristic of the Romany language

ro·man·za \rōˈmanzə\ *n* -S [It, fr. Sp *romance* — more at ROMANCE] **:** ⁴ROMANCE

ro·maunt \rōˈmänt, -mȯnt\ *n* -S [ME, fr. MF *romant* — more at ROMANTIC] *archaic* **:** ROMANCE 1

ro·mayne work \(ˈ)rō¦mān-\ *n, often cap R* [prob. fr. F *romaine*, fem. of *romain* Roman — more at ROMAINE] **:** the ornamentation of furniture with carved medallions, knobs, or finials in the form of human or grotesque heads found esp. in 17th century England

rom·berg sign \ˈräm,bərg-\ *n, usu cap R* [after Moritz H. *Romberg* †1873 Ger. neurologist] **:** a diagnostic sign of locomotor ataxia and other diseases of the nervous system consisting of a swaying of the body when the feet are placed close together and the eyes are closed

rom·bow·line \ˈrämˈbōlən\ *or* **rum·bow·line** \,rəm-\ *n* [origin unknown] **1 :** old condemned canvas or rope unfit for use except as chafing gear aboard ship **2 :** an inferior rope used as lashing

¹rome \ˈrōm\ *n* -S *cap* [ME, fr. *Rome*, Italy] **:** ROMAN CATHOLICISM ⟨was loyal to *Rome* less because it was Catholic than because it was Roman —D.C.Williams⟩

²rome \"\ *adj, usu cap* [fr. *Rome*, Italy] **:** of or from Rome, capital of Italy ⟨the *Rome* correspondent⟩ **:** of the kind or style prevalent in Rome **:** ROMAN

ro·me·ite \ˈrōmē,īt\ *n* -S [modif. (influenced by -*ite*) of F *roméine*, fr. Jean B. L. *Romé* de Lisle + F -*ine*] **:** a mineral $(Ca,Fe,Mn,Na)_2(Sb,Ti)_2O_6(O,OH,F)$ consisting of a hyacinth or honey yellow oxide of calcium, iron, manganese, sodium, antimony, and titanium related to bindheimite and occurring in minute octahedrons

rom·el·dale \ˈräməl,dāl\ *n* [blend of *Romney, Rambouillet*, and *Corriedale*] **1** *usu cap* **:** an American breed of utility sheep developed by crossbreeding Romneys and Rambouillets with the intention of retaining a heavy fleece of fine wool while producing a quickly maturing high-grade market lamb **2** -S *often cap* **:** a sheep of the Romeldale breed

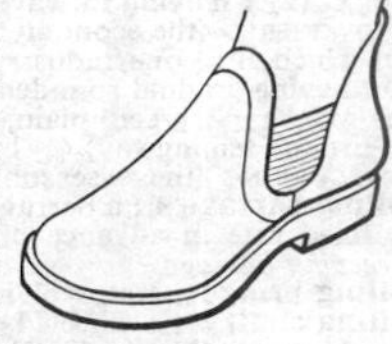

romeo 2

¹ro·meo \ˈrōmē,ō\ *n* -S [after *Romeo*, ill-fated lover in Shakespeare's *Romeo and Juliet*] **1** *usu cap* **:** one given over to a love affair or lovemaking ⟨his hair slicked down like any dance hall

Romeo's —*Time*) ⟨deserting art and science for beauty, he became a celebrated international *Romeo* —Alva Johnston⟩ **2 :** a man's slipper or shoe with a high backing quarter, high front, and usu. U-shaped elastic gores at the sides — compare CONGRESS GAITER, GAITER, JULIET

²romeo \"\ *usu cap* [after *Romeo*] — a communications code word for the letter *r*

rome penny *n, usu cap R* **:** PETER'S PENCE

ro·mer·il·lo \ˌrōməˈri(ˌ)lō\ *n* -S [AmerSp, dim. of *romero* rosemary, fr. L *ros maris*, lit., dew of the sea, fr. *ros* dew + *maris*, gen. of *mare* sea — more at RORIC, MARINE] **1 :** any of several tropical American plants with an aromatic odor most of which yield native remedies or dyes: as **a :** a So. American herb (*Heterothalamus brunioides*) of the family Compositae whose flower heads yield a yellow dye **b :** a Mexican shrubby milkweed (*Asclepias linaria*) that yields a violent purge **c :** any of several Mexican plants of the family Compositae (esp. *Porophyllum scoparium* and *Chrysactinia mexicana*) **2 :** the dye yielded by the So. American herb romerillo

ro·me·ro \rōˈme(ˌ)rō\ *n* -S [Sp, lit., pilgrim, alter. of *romeo*, fr. ML *romaeus* Byzantine Greek, pilgrim headed for Rome, fr. MGk *rhōmaios*, fr. Gk, Roman, fr. *Rhōmē* Rome] **:** PILOT FISH 1

rome·scot \ˈrōmz,kät, -m,sk-\ *n, usu cap* [ME, fr. OE *Rōmescot*, fr. *Rōm* Rome + *scot*] **:** PETER'S PENCE

rome·ward \ˈrōmwə(r)d\ *adv (or adj), usu cap* [ME, fr. *Rome* + *-ward*] **:** toward Rome or Roman Catholicism ⟨the church service is oriented *Romeward*⟩ ⟨*Romeward* tendency⟩ ⟨*Romeward* doctrine⟩

rom·ish \ˈrōmish, -mēsh\ *adj, usu cap* [*Rome* + E *-ish*] **:** of or relating to the Roman Catholic Church — **rom·ish·ly** *adv* — **rom·ish·ness** *n* -ES

rom·ist \-məst\ *n* -S *usu cap* [*Rome* + E *-ist*] *archaic* **:** ROMAN CATHOLIC

rom·mack \ˈräməkl\ *vi* [origin unknown] *dial Eng* **:** to romp or play boisterously

rommany *usu cap, var of* ROMANY

rom·ney \ˈrämnē-\ *or* **romney marsh** *n* [fr. *Romney Marsh*, coastal pasture tract in southwestern England] **1** *usu cap R & sometimes cap M* **:** a British breed of hardy long-wooled mutton-type sheep esp. adapted to damp or marshy regions **2** -S *often cap R & sometimes cap M* **:** an animal of the Romney breed

rom·neya \ˈrämnēə, ˌ=ˈ==\ *n, cap* [NL, after Thomas *Romney* Robinson †1882 Brit. astronomer] **:** a genus of shrubs (family Papaveraceae) having the stigmata united in a ring at the base

romney hut *n, usu cap R* [fr. the name *Romney*] **:** a large strong building similar to the smaller Nissen hut

¹romp \ˈrämp *sometimes* ˈrȯmp\ *n* -S [partly alter. of ⁴*ramp*; partly alter. of ²*ramp*] **1 :** one that romps; *esp* **:** a romping girl or woman **2 a :** lively, frisky, or boisterous play or sport **:** FROLIC, GAMBOL ⟨both dogs loose, it is quite possible that a joyful ~ rather than a dogfight would result —J.W.Cross⟩ ⟨students' day features a parade through town with all manner of ~ and hilarity —Ernest Stock⟩ ⟨a high-spirited ~ which is the American version of country dancing —Angelica Gibbs⟩ **b :** a romp marked by lovemaking ⟨had made a tryst for a twilight ~ —Lucy M. Montgomery⟩ ⟨the lovers . . . going out onto the porch in a ~ every little while —Elizabeth M. Roberts⟩ **3 :** a pace or rate of progress in a race or contest by which one wins easily or outdistances competitors by a large margin **:** RUNAWAY ⟨a gray colt who beat 18 other well fancied youngsters in a ~ —G.F.T.Ryall⟩ ⟨is expected to win the political race in a ~⟩ ⟨a 65-yard touchdown ~⟩ **4 :** a literary or dramatic production consisting chiefly of a series of lively fast-moving loosely organized incidents or episodes ⟨it was a semiautobiographical ~ through the sophisticated continental and domestic settings —Edward Lueders⟩ ⟨a play that begins like another ~ about a junior miss up to junior mischief —*Time*⟩ ⟨the plot is no more than an artfully regulated ~ —*Newsweek*⟩ **syn** see PLAY

²romp \"\ *vb* -ED/-ING/-S [alter. of ¹*ramp*] *vi* **1 a :** to play in a lively, frisky, or boisterous manner **:** FROLIC, GAMBOL ⟨found the general ~*ing* in the living room with his five children —*Newsweek*⟩ ⟨the hugest playmate that ever ~*ed* with fairies and the aery sprites of merry mischief —G.K. Chesterton⟩ **b :** to engage in lovemaking ⟨~ with one's . . . pretty serving girl when wifie's busy bathing —Robert Browning⟩ ⟨during the trial of a paternity suit it was brought out that . . . the footmen ~*ed* with the servant girls —R.D.Altick⟩ **2 a :** to proceed, move, or go in a gay, animated, or vigorous manner ⟨the wind was ~*ing* through the streets like a boisterous country visitor —Rebecca West⟩ ⟨girls . . . ~ down the stone steps with such a deafening clatter —Sam Heppner⟩ ⟨boats that ~*ed* over the bay —Jean Stafford⟩ **b :** to run or advance in a race or contest with such progress as to win easily or outdistance the competitors by a large margin ⟨~*ed* home a winner . . . in his first start —G.F.T.Ryall⟩ ⟨~*ed* for four touchdowns and three conversion points —*Newsweek*⟩ ⟨~*ing* home with 51 of the 52 seats up for election —Alex Josey⟩ **3 a :** to act a part in a play in a lively, fast, or informal manner ⟨aiming at speed, achieves it by letting his smooth cast ~ gayly and ripple off the script's cute lines at a fast rate —P.T.Hartung⟩ ⟨~ throughout the half hour flubbing and gagging, sticking to script and bouncing off into ad lib —*Newsweek*⟩ **b :** to play music in a buoyant spontaneous manner usu. with flourishes or improvisations ⟨the two ~ through chase choruses, sometimes trading every four bars, which is . . . quite exciting as they play it —Bill Simon⟩ ⟨watching the piano player take his chorus, with a fine ~*ing* offbeat in the treble —Vincent McHugh⟩ ⟨~*ed* through a few popular songs, backed up by a drummer and a bass player —Douglas Watt⟩ ~ *vt* **:** to convey or urge in a sportive or boisterous manner ⟨~ the children to bed⟩ **syn** see PLAY

romp·er \-pə(r)\ *n* -S **1 :** one that romps ⟨a cry like every kind of bell rang from these ~*s* as they raced —John Masefield⟩ **2 a :** a child's one-piece garment consisting of waist and short bloomers — usu. used in pl. **b :** any of various garments of somewhat similar design worn by adults — usu. used in pl.

romping *adj* **1 :** engaging in a romp **:** given to romps ⟨a lively ~ boy⟩ **2 :** having the characteristics of a romp ⟨had a big ~ party and ended by gathering around the piano and singing —W.A.White⟩ — **romp·ing·ly** *adv*

romp·ish \-pish, -pēsh\ *adj* **:** ROMPING ⟨a ~ girl⟩ ⟨a series of ~ square dances —K.M.Dodson⟩ — **romp·ish·ness** *n* -ES

rom·pu \ˈräm(ˌ)pü\ *adj* [F, past part. of *rompre* to break, fr. L *rumpere* — more at REAVE] *of a heraldic ordinary* **:** depicted as broken usu. with the broken piece pushed up — compare FRACTED 2

rompy \ˈrämpē\ *adj* -ER/-EST [²*romp* + *-y*] **:** ROMPING

roms *pl of* ROM

ron·ca·dor \ˌräŋkəˈdō(ə)r\ *n, pl* **roncadors** \-rz\ *or* **roncado·res** \-ōˌrās\ [Sp, lit., one that snores, fr. *roncado* (past part. of *roncar* to snore, fr. LL *rhonchare*, fr. *rhonchus* snore) + *-or* — more at RHONCHUS] **1 :** any of several croakers (family Sciaenidae) of the American Pacific coast (as the yellowfin croaker or the black croaker) **2 :** any of various grunts (esp. *Haemulon steindachneri*) of both the Atlantic and Pacific coasts

ron·cet \ränˈsā\ *n* -S [F, dim. of *ronce* bramble, blackberry bush, fr. L *rumic-, rumex* sorrel — more at RUMEX] **:** COURT-NOUÉ

ron·co \ˈräŋ(ˌ)kō\ *n* -S [AmerSp, fr. Sp, hoarse, modif. (influenced by *roncar* to snore) of L *raucus*] **1 :** any of several grunts (genus *Haemulon*); *esp* **:** a small gray brown-streaked food fish (*H. parra*) of the tropical western Atlantic from the Florida Keys and Cuba to Brazil — called also *sailor's-choice* **2 :** ATLANTIC CROAKER

ron·dache \(ˈ)ränˈdash\ *n* -S [F, fr. MF *rudache, rondache*] **:** a small round shield carried by a foot soldier

ron·da·vel \ˈrändəˌvel\ *n* -S [Afrik *rondawel*] **1 :** a round native hut of southern Africa usu. made of mud and having a thatched roof of grass **2 :** a round house resembling a native hut often used as a guesthouse or tourist dwelling in southern Africa

rond de jambe \ˌrändəˈzhäm\ *n, pl* **ronds de jambe** \-n(z)d-\ [F, lit., circle of the leg] **:** a circular movement of the leg in ballet either par terre or en l'air

ronde \ˈränd\ *n* -S [F, fr. fem. of *rond* round, fr. OF *roont, rount, ront* — more at ROUND] **:** script with heavy strokes nearly upright **:** ROUND HAND

ron·deau \ˈrän(ˌ)dō, =ˈ=\ *n, pl* **ron·deaux** \-ō(z)\ [MF, lit., small circle, alter. of *rondel*] **1 a :** a fixed form of verse running on two rhymes and consisting usu. of 15 lines of eight or ten syllables divided into three stanzas with the beginning of the first line of the first stanza serving as the refrain of the second and third stanzas — called also *rondel* **b :** a poem in this form **2 a :** a medieval monophonic French song characterized by the many repetitions of its two themes or sections **b :** ¹RONDO 3 **3** [LaF, fr. F] **:** ²RONDO

rondeau re·dou·blé \-rəˌdüˈblā\ *n, pl* **rondeaux redoublés** [F, lit., double rondeau] **1 :** a fixed form of verse running on two rhymes that usu. consists of five quatrains in which the lines of the first quatrain are used consecutively to end each of the remaining four quatrains and which are sometimes followed by an envoi of four lines that terminates with the opening words of the poem **2 :** a poem in the rondeau redoublé form

ron·del \ˈrändᵊl, -nˌdel\ *or* **ron·delle** \ränˈdel\ *n* -S [ME, fr. OF, lit., small circle — more at ROUNDEL] **1** *usu rondelle* **:** something that forms a circle **:** a circular object: as **a :** a tiny jeweled circle or ring-shaped bead usu. strung between larger stones or sections of a necklace **b :** a flat circular disk usu. of sapphire or ruby from which a jewel bearing is made **c :** a flat circular diamond with approximately 128 facets around the edge **2 a** *usu rondel* **:** a form of verse running on two rhymes and consisting usu. of 14 lines of eight or ten syllables divided into three stanzas with the first two lines of the first stanza serving as the refrain of the second and third stanzas **b :** a poem in this form **c :** RONDEAU 1

ron·de·let \ˌrändəˈlet\ *n* -S [MF, dim. of *rondel*] **:** a modified rondeau running on two rhymes and consisting usu. of seven lines in which the first line of four syllables is repeated as the third line and as the final line or refrain with the remaining lines made up of eight syllables each

ron·de·le·tia \ˌrändəˈlēshēə\ *n* [NL, fr. Guillaume *Rondelet* †1566 French naturalist + NL *-ia*] **1** *cap* **:** a genus of tropical American trees and shrubs (family Rubiaceae) having salver-shaped fragrant flowers with a long tube **2** -S **:** any plant of the genus *Rondeletia*

ron·delle \ränˈdel\ *or* **ron·dle** \ˈrändᵊl\ *n* -S [F *rondelle* — more at RONDEL] **:** the crust or scale on molten metal in the crucible

ron·di·no \ränˈdē(ˌ)nō\ *or* **ron·do·let·to** \ˌrändəˈled·(ˌ)ō\ *n* -S [It, dim. of *rondò*] **:** a short rondo

¹ron·do \ˈrän(ˌ)dō\ *n* -S [It *rondò*, fr. F *rondeau* — more at RONDEAU] **1 :** ⁵ROUND 3 **2 :** the musical setting of a rondeau or similar verse form **3 :** an instrumental composition or movement in which the principal theme or first subject occurs at least three times in the same key with contrasting themes or sections in between and which is often the last movement of a sonata — called also *rondeau* **4 :** a dance composition that has a recurrent movement theme alternating with new themes and is derived from a medieval round dance with singing of verse and refrain

²rondo \"\ *n* -S [LaF *rondeau* — more at RONDEAU] **:** a gambling game in which balls are pushed from one corner of a pocket billiard table to the opposite and bets are decided by the number of odd or even balls that remain on the table —called also *rondeau*

ron·dure \ˈränjə(r)\ *n* -S [modif. (influenced by *-ure*) of F *rondeur* roundness, fr. MF, fr. *rond* round + *-eur* -or — more at RONDE] **1 :** ROUND 1a ⟨the whole ~ of the turning globe —J.C.Powys⟩ **2 :** gracefully rounded curvature ⟨the bare swelling ~*s* of the mountains —Meridel Le Sueur⟩ ⟨a pretty girl of agreeable ~ —Wolcott Gibbs⟩

¹rone \ˈrōn\ *n* -S [ME, prob. of Scand origin; akin to ON *runnr* bush, grove, Norw dial. *runn*, *runne* bush, *runne* twig; akin to OHG *rono* trunk of a tree, block of wood, OE *rīsan* to rise — more at RISE] *chiefly Scot* **:** BRUSHWOOD, THICKET

²rone \"\ *n* -S [origin unknown] *Scot* **:** a rain spout or pipe

ro·neo \ˈrōnēˌō\ *vt* -ED/-ING/-S [fr. *roneo*, a kind of duplicating machine, fr. *rotary* + *Neo*style, a trademark for a kind of duplicating machine] **:** to produce (printed copies) on a duplicating machine that is similar in principle to the mimeograph

ro·neo·graph \ˈrōnēəˌgraf, -räf\ *vt* -ED/-ING/-S [*roneo*, a kind of duplicating machine + *-graph* (as in *mimeograph*)] **:** RONEO

rong \ˈräŋ\ *also* **rong-pa** \-ˈpä\ *n, pl* **rong** *or* **rongs** *also* **rongpa** *or* **rongpas** *usu cap* **:** LEPCHA

ron·ga \ˈräŋgə\ *n, pl* **ronga** *or* **rongas** *usu cap* **1 a :** a group of Bantu peoples chiefly of southern Mozambique **b :** a member of a Ronga people **2 :** a Bantu language of the Ronga peoples

¹ron·geur \rō(ⁿ)ˈzhər\ *n* -S [F, lit., one that gnaws, fr. MF, fr. *ronger* to gnaw (fr. — assumed — VL *rodicare*, fr. *rodere* to gnaw) + *-eur* -or — more at RAT] **:** a heavy-duty forceps for removing small pieces of bone or tough tissue

²rongeur \"\ *vt* -ED/-ING/-S **:** to remove (bone) with a rongeur

rô·nier \rōˈnyā\ *n* -S [F *rondier, rônier*] **:** PALMYRA

ron·quil \ˈräŋkəl\ *n* -S [AmerSp *ronquillo*, dim. of *ronco* — more at RONCO] **:** any of several marine percoid fishes (family Bathymasteridae) of the northwest coast of No. America that resemble the jawfishes

rons·dorf·er \ˈränzˌdȯrfə(r)\ *also* **rons·dorf·i·an** \(ˈ)=ˈdȯrfēən\ *n* -S *usu cap* [*Ronsdorfer* fr. G, fr. *Ronsdorfer*, adj., of Ronsdorf, fr. *Ronsdorf*, city (now part of Wuppertal) in northern Germany where the sect was founded; *Ronsdorfian* fr. *Ronsdorf* + E *-ian*] **:** one of a small sect of 18th century German millenarians — called also *Zionite*

röntgen *var of* ROENTGEN

ronyon *n* -S [perh. modif. of F *rogue* scab, mange] *obs* **:** a mangy or scabby creature

roo \ˈrü\ *n* -S [by shortening] *Austral* **:** KANGAROO

roocooyen *usu cap, var of* RUCUYEN

rood \ˈrüd\ *n* -S [ME *rod, rood*, fr. OE *rōd* rod, cross, rood; akin to OFris *rōd, rōde* gallows, OHG *ruota* rod, pole, OS *rōda* gallows, ON *rathi* oar, OSlav *ratište, ratovište* shaft of a lance, and perh. to L *retae* trees on a river bank or in a stream] **1 :** a cross or crucifix symbolizing the cross on which Jesus Christ died ⟨by the holy ~ —Shak.⟩; *specif* **:** a large crucifix at the entrance of the chancel of a medieval church **2 a :** any of various units of land area: as (1) **:** a unit used in England and Scotland equal to 40 square rods or ¼ acre (2) **:** a Dutch unit used in South Africa equal to 148.752 square feet **b :** any of various units of length: as (1) **:** a unit used in England and Scotland equal to 7 or 8 yards or sometimes a rod (2) **:** a Dutch unit used in South Africa equal to 12.396 feet

rood altar *n* **:** an altar placed against the outer side of a rood screen

rood arch *n* **1 :** a central arch in a rood screen above which appears the rood **2 :** an arch between the nave and the chancel immediately above the rood

rood beam *n* **:** the beam at the entrance of a church chancel that supports a large cross or crucifix esp. in a medieval church

rood cloth *n* **:** a violet or black veil used to cover the rood during Lent

rood day *n, usu cap R&D* **:** HOLY-ROOD DAY

roo·de·bok \ˈrüdəˌbäk\ *n, pl* **roodebok** *or* **roodeboks** [Afrik *rooibok* (previously spelled *roodebok*), fr. *rooi* red (fr. MD *root, rood*) + *bok* male goat, male antelope, fr. MD *boc* male goat; akin to OE *rēad* red and to OE *buc, bucca* male goat — more at RED, BUCK] **1 :** IMPALA **2 :** a reddish duikerbok (*Cephalophus patalensis*)

rood goose *n* **:** BRANT

roo·dle \ˈrüdᵊl\ *n* -S [G *rudel* pack, flock, troop] **:** one hand of a round of hands in poker usu. played after an esp. high hand (as four of a kind or a full house) with the special provision that the round will consist of jackpots or sometimes of stud poker or dealer's choice with the pot limit usu. doubled

rood loft *n* [ME *rodeloft*, fr. *rod, rood, rode* rood + *loft*] **:** a loft or gallery over the rood screen in a medieval church used for display of the rood and its appendages and for the reading of the Gospel and the Epistle

rood screen *n* **:** a screen separating the chancel of a church from the nave and often surmounted by a cross or crucifix — called also *jube*

rood spire *or* **rood steeple** *n* **:** a rood tower with a spire

rood stair *n* **:** a stairway leading to the rood loft

roodstone \ˈ=ˌ=\ *n* **:** a stone cross or crucifix

rood tower *n* **:** a tower at the intersection of the nave and transept of a church

¹roof \ˈrüf, ˈru̇f, *dial* ˈrəf\ *n, pl* **roofs** \-fs\ *also* **rooves** \ˈrüvz\ *often attrib* [ME *rof, roof, rouf, ruf*, fr. OE *hrōf*; akin to OFris *hrōf* roof, MLG *rōf, rūf* cover, sheltering roof, MD *roef, roof* cover, roof, ON *hrōf* roof of a boathouse, boathouse, OSlav *stropŭ* roof] **1 a :** the outside cover of a building or structure including the roofing and all the materials and construction necessary to maintain the cover upon its walls or other support: (1) **:** such a cover or its inner shell on the interior of a structure; *esp* **:** a high vaulted or spacious ceiling ⟨the long interior . . . has a handsome open timber ~ decorated in polychrome —*Amer. Guide Series: Conn.*⟩ ⟨its principal room is the Livery Hall, high ceilinged, with decorated ~, chandeliers, and tall marble pillars —Gerard Foy⟩ (2) **:** such a cover of a house or home ⟨finds herself without a ~ over her head —H.M. Parshley⟩ ⟨placing . . . the most distressed families under ~ —*U. S. Code*⟩ **b :** a shelter, house, or other domicile used as a home ⟨had his ~ and taught physics in a boy's school —D. C.Peattie⟩ ⟨why not . . . share the same ~ —Virginia Woolf⟩ **c :** ROOFING ⟨the house has a slate ~⟩ ⟨slag or gravel ~⟩ ⟨coal tar, pitch, and felt ~⟩ **2 a** (1) **:** the highest point or reach of something **:** SUMMIT, CULMINATION ⟨in the desolate mountains at the ~ of the . . . world —*Newsweek*⟩ (2) **:** CEILING 7 ⟨what the nation needed . . . was a floor under some prices and a ~ over others —*Time*⟩ ⟨both wool and rubber . . . have gone through the ~ —*America*⟩ **b :** something that covers in, includes, or completes ⟨agency to put a permanent ~ over the temporary consolidation of the independent housing agencies —*Time*⟩ **c :** the vault of the heavens ⟨this majestic ~ fretted with golden fire —Shak.⟩ ⟨beneath this small blue ~ of vernal sky —S.T.Coleridge⟩ **d :** something resembling a roof in form or function: as (1) **:** the canopy of leaves and branches formed by trees or other vegetative growth ⟨from under shady arborous ~ —John Milton⟩ ⟨some do rise above the jungle ~ —C.H.Curran⟩ (2) **:** the cover of a vehicle (as a car or airplane) **:** TOP **3 a :** the vaulted upper boundary of the mouth supported largely by the palatine bones and limited anteriorly by the dental ridge and posteriorly by the uvula and upper part of the fauces **b :** TEGMENTUM **c :** a covering structure of any of various other parts of the body ⟨~ of the skull⟩ ⟨~ of a cavity⟩ **4 a** (1) **:** the rock immediately above a tabular deposit (as a coal seam or vein) (2) **:** the overhead of an excavation or tunnel in a mine (3) **:** the invaded rock above a batholith **b :** a passage excavated in quarrying slate from below upward **:** RAISE

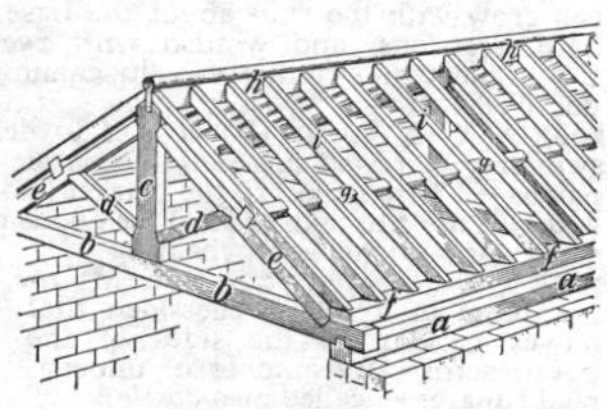

roof 1a: timbers in a gable roof: *a* wall plate; *b* tie beam; *c* king post; *d, d,* struts; *e, e,* principal rafters; *f* pole plate; *g, g,* purlins; *h* ridgepole; *i, i,* common rafters

²roof \"\ *vt* -ED/-ING/-S [ME *rofen*, fr. *rof, roof*, n.] **1 a :** to cover or provide (a structure) with a roof ⟨had the passage at the entrance of the house repaired and ~*ed* —Thomas Carlyle⟩ ⟨the thatcher mounts his ladder . . . with his burden of straw, ~*ing* the corn built to be its own storehouse —Adrian Bell⟩ **b :** to provide (a roof) with a protective or weatherproof exterior ⟨originally ~*ed* with handmade shingles —*Amer. Guide Series: La.*⟩ **2 a :** to constitute or form a roof over (something) ⟨maple trees ~*ed* every street with gold —Janet Whitney⟩ ⟨the mountains which ~ their mines —*Christian Science Monitor*⟩ **b :** to provide shelter for **:** HOUSE

roof·age \-fij\ *n* -S [¹*roof* + *-age*] **:** ROOFING

roof comb *or* **roof crest** *n* **:** a wall rising from the center line of a roof to give an appearance of greater height

roof–deck \ˈ=ˌ=\ *n* **:** a flat portion of a roof used as a walk or terrace

roofed ingle *n* **:** CHIMNEY CORNER 1

roof·er \-fə(r)\ *n* -S **1 :** one who builds or repairs roofs **2 :** a plank or timber used in roofing; *also* **:** a low-grade board

roof garden *n* **:** a restaurant at the top of a building or hotel where food and beverages are sold and facilities usu. provided for music and dancing

roof houseleek *n* **:** HOUSELEEK

roof·ing \-fiŋ, -fēŋ\ *n* -S [ME *rovyng*, fr. *rof, roof* roof + *-ing* — more at ROOF] **1 :** a material used or suitable for the construction of a roof; *specif* **:** a material designed for application to a roof as protection from the weather ⟨slate ~⟩ ⟨aluminum ~⟩ ⟨mineral-surfaced ~⟩ **2 :** ROOF ⟨constructing the ~ for the chicken house⟩ **3 :** the wedging (as of a horse or car) against the top of an underground passage in a mine

roofing nail *n* **:** a short nail usu. with a large flat head and a barbed shank used for securing roofing paper or asphalt shingles to roof boards

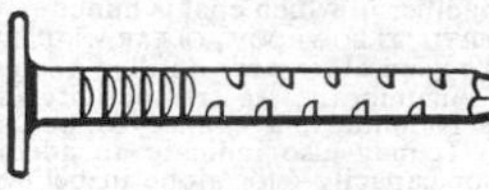

roofing nail

roof·less \-fləs\ *adj* **1 :** having no roof **2 :** having no house **:** HOMELESS

roof·let \-lət\ *n* -S **:** a small roof

roof·man \-fmən\ *n, pl* **roofmen :** a mine or quarry worker who inspects roofs and walls after blasting and dislodges loose blocks with a bar

roof nucleus *n* **:** a nucleus lying in the roof of the cerebellum

roof pendant *n* **:** a downward projection or sag of the roof of a batholith

roof plate *n* **:** PLATE 5a(1)

roof prism *n* **:** a glass prism used in an optical range finder and other instruments that performs the double function of changing the direction of the light rays by 90 degrees and reversing the image right to left — compare PORRO PRISM

roof rat *n* **:** a grayish brown rat that is a variety (*Rattus rattus alexandrinus*) of the black rat, is common in warm regions, and often nests in trees or the upper parts of buildings

roofs *pl of* ROOF, *pres 3d sing of* ROOF

roof–spotter \ˈ=ˌ==\ *n, Brit* **:** SPOTTER 2b(3)

roof stay *n* **:** a stay rod or tie rod connecting the crown sheet of a boiler with the shell

rooftop \ˈ=ˌ=\ *n* **:** ROOF; *esp* **:** the roof of a house ⟨every balcony and ~ on the steep hills lining the streets was crowded with spectators —*N.Y. Times*⟩

rooftree \ˈ=ˌ=\ *n* [ME, fr. *rof, roof* roof + *tre, tree* tree — more at TREE] **1 :** RIDGEPOLE **2 :** ROOF 1a(2) ⟨a dozen players are housed under his ~ —Nike Anderson⟩ ⟨assured of a welcome under any ~, great or humble —I.S.Cobb⟩

roo·i·bok *also* **roo·ye·bok** \ˈrüēˌbäk\ *n, pl* **rooibok** *or* **rooiboks** [Afrik *rooibok* — more at ROODEBOK] **:** IMPALA

roo·i·bos tea \ˈrüēˌbäs-\ *or* **roo·i·bosch tea** \-sh-\ *n* [part trans. of Afrik *rooibostee* (formerly spelled *rooiboschtee*), fr. *rooibos*, the shrub from which it is made (fr. *rooi* red + *bos* bush, fr. MD *busch, bosch* bush forest) + *tee* tea — more at ROODEBOK, BUSH] **:** a beverage that is made from a southern African shrub (*Aspalathus cedarbergensis*) of the family Leguminosae

roo·i·gras \ˈrüēˌgras\ *also* **rooi grass** \ˈrüē-\ *n* -ES [Afrik *rooigras*, fr. *rooi* red + *gras* grass, fr. MD; akin to OHG *gras* grass — more at GRASS] **:** an African veldt grass (*Themeda triandra*) that is valued for grazing and is represented by similar or identical grasses in parts of southern Asia and Australia — see KANGAROO GRASS

roo·i·nek \ˈrüēˌnek\ *n* -S [Afrik, fr. *rooi* red + *nek* neck, nape of the neck, fr. MD *neche* nape of the neck; akin to OHG *hnac* nape of the neck — more at NECK] *southern Africa* **:** BRITISHER — usu. used disparagingly

rooi rhebok *or* **rooi ribbok** \ˈrüē-\ *n* [Afrik *rooireebok, rooiribbok*, fr. *rooi* red + *reebok, ribbok* rhebok — more at RHEBOK] **:** an African upland reedbuck (*Redunca fulvorufula*)

¹rook \'ru̇k\ *n* -s [ME *rok, rook,* fr. OE *hrōc;* akin to OHG *hruoh, ruoho* rook, ON *hrōkr* rook, Goth *hrukjan* to crow, Gk *krōzein, krazein* to croak, Skt *khargalā* owl, OE *hræfn* raven — more at RAVEN] **1 a :** a common Old World gregarious bird (*Corvus frugilegus*) about the size and color of the American crow with the skin about the base of the bill becoming bare, scabrous, and whitish with age **b :** RUDDY DUCK **2 :** a cheat or swindler esp. in gaming **3** *obs* **:** one easily deceived **:** DUPE

²rook \"\ *vb* -ED/-ING/-S *vt* **1 :** to defraud by cheating or swindling ⟨arrested for ~*ing* the public in door-to-door campaigns —*Time*⟩ ⟨takes to the market and gets ~*ed* —*Commonweal*⟩ **2** *obs* **:** to take or steal (as goods or money) by cheating ~ *vi, obs* **:** to engage in cheating

³rook \"\ *n* -s [ME *rok, roke,* fr. MF *roc,* fr. Ar *rukhkh,* fr. Per] **:** a piece in a set of chessmen that moves parallel to the sides of the board across any number of unoccupied squares — called also *castle*

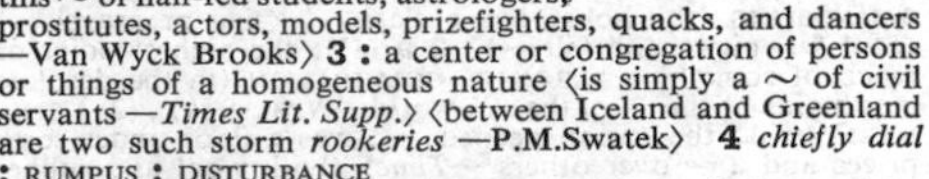
rook

rook·er \'ru̇kə(r)\ *n* -s [origin unknown] **:** a raker for a baker's oven

rook·ery \'ru̇kərē, -ri\ *n* -ES [¹*rook* + *-ery*] **1 a :** the group of nests or the breeding place of a colony of rooks; *also* **:** a colony of rooks **b :** a breeding ground or common haunt of other gregarious birds or animals (as herons, penguins, or seals); *also* **:** a colony of such birds or animals **:** ROOST 1d **2 a :** a dilapidated tenement or rundown group of dwellings ⟨typhoid ran rampant in the *rookeries* which masqueraded as homes —*Sat. Eve. Post*⟩ **b :** a building with many rooms or occupants often of a diverse sort ⟨in this ~ of half-fed students, astrologers, prostitutes, actors, models, prizefighters, quacks, and dancers —Van Wyck Brooks⟩ **3 :** a center or congregation of persons or things of a homogeneous nature ⟨is simply a ~ of civil servants —*Times Lit. Supp.*⟩ ⟨between Iceland and Greenland are two such storm *rookeries* —P.M.Swatek⟩ **4** *chiefly dial* **:** RUMPUS **:** DISTURBANCE

rook·ie \'ru̇kē, -ki\ *n* -s *often attrib* [alter. (influenced by ¹*rook*) of *recruit*] **1 :** a raw recruit **:** NOVICE, BEGINNER ⟨a ~ in the army⟩ ⟨a ~ on the police force⟩ **2 :** a new member of or candidate for an athletic team; *esp* **:** a baseball player in his first season with a major league team ⟨was chosen ~ of the year⟩

rook's tour *n* **:** a chess problem in which a rook makes a circuit of the board touching each square once

rookus *var of* RUCKUS

rooky \'ru̇kē\ *adj* -ER/-EST [¹*rook* + *-y*] **:** full of or containing rooks ⟨the crow makes wing to the ~ wood —Shak.⟩

¹room \'rüm, 'ru̇m\ *n* -s *often attrib* [ME *roum,* fr. OE *rūm;* akin to OHG, ON, & Goth *rūm* room, space; all fr. a prehistoric Gmc n. derived fr. an adj. represented by OE *rūm* roomy, spacious, OHG *rūmi,* ON *rūmr,* Goth *rūms;* akin to L *rur-, rus* country, open land, MIr *rōe, rōi* level field, Av *ravah-* space, distance] **1 a :** unoccupied area **:** SPACE ⟨increasing population requires more ~⟩ ⟨infinity of ~ in the reaches of the universe⟩ **b :** unoccupied area or space sufficient for additional accommodation ⟨~ at the inn⟩ ⟨~ for pasture⟩ ⟨~ to swing a cat in⟩ ⟨tearing down tenements to make ~ for new building⟩ **2 a :** a particular area or limited portion of space **:** COMPASS ⟨plenty of ~ between the houses⟩ ⟨a small car requires little ~⟩ ⟨the sonnet's narrow ~ of 14 lines —O.S.J.Gogarty⟩ **b** *Scot* **:** a piece of land **:** HOLDING, FARM **3 a** *obs* **:** a place or station assigned to a person or thing **b** *obs* **:** an office or position attributed to a particular person **:** RANK, POST ⟨and therein placed a race of upstart creatures, to supply perhaps our vacant ~ —John Milton⟩ **c** (1) **:** a place or station formerly occupied by another ⟨in whose ~ I am now assuming the pen —Sir Walter Scott⟩ ⟨be thou in Adam's ~ the head of all mankind —John Milton⟩ (2) *archaic* **:** PLACE, STEAD ⟨substitute judgment in the ~ of sensation —Joseph Butler⟩ **4 a :** a part of the inside of a building, shelter, or dwelling usu. set off by a partition ⟨15 ~ colonial mansion . . . for rest or convalescent home —*advt*⟩ **:** CHAMBER; *esp* **:** such a part used as a lodging ⟨goes back to his furnished ~ —Norman Mailer⟩ ⟨the individual who actually assigns guests to their ~*s* —Don Short⟩ **b rooms** *pl* **:** a suite or set of rooms used for lodging **:** APARTMENT, FLAT ⟨sells his house and takes ~*s* in the city⟩ **c :** lodging consisting of a room usu. specifically earned or furnished ⟨~, board, and the return trip home . . . were paid for —*Newsweek*⟩ — compare ROOM AND BOARD **d :** the people or an assemblage gathered in a room ⟨attract the attention of the whole ~⟩ **5 :** the opportunity, occasion, or capacity for something (as an action, development, or mental process) ⟨~ to hope⟩ ⟨~ to improve⟩ ⟨~ for argument⟩ ⟨~ in morality for the high aspiration, the courageous decision —Havelock Ellis⟩ ⟨~ in art and in civilization for many kinds of art —Thomas Munro⟩ ⟨no ~ in his mind for that malaise —Van Wyck Brooks⟩ **6 :** a chamber in which coal is mined — called also *breast, stall*

syn BERTH, ELBOWROOM, CLEARANCE, LEEWAY, MARGIN, PLAY: ROOM is a general term for unfilled open space without obstruction or encumbrance to free activity ⟨space is *room* . . . and *room* is roominess, a chance to be, live and move —John Dewey⟩ It may also indicate an adequate occasion, opportunity, or capacity ⟨not alone in believing Mexico's behavior left no *room* for peaceful settlement —R.A.Billington⟩ ⟨which never arrived at so high a point of definition but that it left great *room* for disputes —G.G.Coulton⟩ BERTH, orig. maneuvering space for a ship, still indicates a separation by wide clear space in various idioms ⟨classified as the only venomous snake and is deservedly given a wide *berth* —*Amer. Guide Series: Del.*⟩ ELBOWROOM indicates adequate free space for physical activity or, by extension, freedom from cramping constraint ⟨the Swiss, who have always liked plenty of *elbowroom* in their business dealings, are considerably irked by the restrictions of postwar trading —Mollie Panter-Downes⟩ CLEARANCE as a synonym in this series stresses lack of obstruction; it is used in connection with the physical fact of a clear space around a moving object or with the indication that there is no objection, reservation, or check against free procedure ⟨the new tunnels provide *clearance* for the largest trucks⟩ ⟨the steel industry refused to make any wage proposals until it obtained federal *clearance* for higher steel prices —*Current History*⟩ LEEWAY may indicate a reserve resource or advantageous characteristic not earmarked or calculated on, an allowed tolerance, or a measure of personal discretion or freedom from restriction in activity ⟨*leeway* of a few minutes to change planes⟩ ⟨in many more or less routine matters the Union government allows them a considerable amount of *leeway* —F.A.Ogg & Harold Zink⟩ MARGIN in this sense is like LEEWAY in suggesting a reserve for contingencies and emergencies or a reserve of any sort facilitating free and easy procedure ⟨the most dogged, strong-minded ones, who find themselves with a *margin* of intellectual freshness and inquisitiveness at the end of the day —W.N.Francis⟩ PLAY applies to the fact of free movement or action without severe checks or cramping surroundings, esp. to reactions to force or stress without more than incidental suggestions about ample space or roominess ⟨the *play* of a gusty wind —Amy Lowell⟩ ⟨planning versus the *play* of the free market —*Times Lit. Supp.*⟩ ⟨a world in which affection has free *play,* in which love is purged of the instinct for domination —Bertrand Russell⟩

²room *adv, usu* -ER/-EST [obs. *room,* adj., roomy, spacious, fr. ME *roum, rom, room,* fr. OE *rūm* — more at ¹ROOM] *obs* **:** LARGE 2

³room \'rüm, 'ru̇m\ *vt* -ED/-ING/-S [ME *roumen,* fr. *roum,* adj.] *archaic* **:** to clear (a space) from encumbrance **:** make roomy or void

⁴room \"\ *vb* -ED/-ING/-S [¹*room*] *vi* **:** to occupy a room **:** LODGE ⟨the students ~ together in the dormitory⟩ ~ *vt* **:** to accommodate (a guest or roomer) with lodgings; *also* **:** to convey to or install in a room ⟨a bellman ~*s* the guests at the hotel⟩

room·age \-mij\ *n* -s [¹*room* + *-age*] **:** SPACE, ACCOMMODATION

room and board *n* **:** lodging and food usu. specifically earned or furnished ⟨receives wages plus *board and room*⟩ — compare ROOM 4c, BOARD 4c, FOUND

room-and-pillar \ˌ⸗⸗ˈ⸗⸗\ *adj* **:** BORD-AND-PILLAR

room and space *n* **:** the distance from one side of a frame of a boat to the corresponding side of the next frame

room boss *n* **:** one who inspects the rooms in mines to ensure that mining is done properly and safety regulations are observed

room clerk *n* **:** a hotel clerk who is in charge of the assignment of rooms to guests

room divider *n* **:** an article of furniture (as a rack, chair, or table) used to divide a room into separate areas ⟨drafts are avoided by high-backed seats that are also *room dividers* —Edgar Kaufmann⟩

roomed \ˈrümd, ˈru̇md\ *adj* [¹*room* + *-ed*] **:** containing or furnished with rooms — usu. used in combination ⟨a nine-*roomed* house⟩

room·er \'rümə(r), 'ru̇m-\ *n* -s [⁴*room* + *-er*] **:** LODGER

room·ette \(ˈ)rüˈmet, (ˈ)ru̇ˈ-\ *n* -s [¹*room* + *-ette*] **:** a small private single room on a railroad sleeping car with a folding bed and toilet facilities

room·ful \'rüm,fu̇l, 'ru̇m-\ *n* -s **:** as much or as many as a room will hold ⟨a ~ of men⟩; *also* **:** the persons or objects in a room ⟨the whole ~⟩ ⟨the group is one of the handsomest and most impressive ~*s* —R.M.Coates⟩

room·ie *also* roomy \'rümē, 'ru̇mē\ *n, pl* roomies [¹*room* + *-ie, -y*] **:** ROOM-MATE

room·i·ly \'rüməlē, 'ru̇m-, -li\ *adv* **:** with ample room **:** SPACIOUSLY

room·i·ness \-mēnəs, -min-\ *n* -ES **:** the quality or state of being roomy

rooming house *n* **:** a house where rooms are provided and let **:** LODGING HOUSE

rooming-in \ˈ⸗⸗ˌ⸗\ *n* -s [fr. gerund of *room in,* v.] **:** the arrangement in a hospital whereby a newborn infant is kept in a crib at or near the mother's bedside instead of in a nursery

roommate \ˈ⸗ˌ⸗\ *n* **:** one of two or more persons occupying or sharing the same room

rooms *pl of* ROOM, *pres 3d sing of* ROOM

room service *n* **:** the service provided by a hotel or lodging house for guests in their rooms and usu. carried out by bellboys or waiters ⟨ring for *room service* and have breakfast in bed —J.R.Ullman⟩; *also* **:** the department of a hotel or lodging house responsible for room service ⟨calling *room service*⟩

roomsome *adj* [¹*room* + *-some*] *obs* **:** ROOMY

room·stead \'rümz,ted, 'ru̇m-, -m,st-\ *n, archaic* **:** a division of space **:** COMPARTMENT

roomth \'rüm(p)th\ *n* -s [alter. (influenced by obs. *room, adj.,* roomy, spacious) of ME *rimth,* fr. OE *rȳmth,* fr. *rūm* roomy, spacious — more at ²ROOM] *dial chiefly Eng* **:** ROOM, PLACE

room trader *n* **:** FLOOR TRADER

roomy \'rümē, 'ru̇mē, -mi\ *adj, often* -ER/-EST [¹*room* + *-y*] **1 :** having ample room **:** SPACIOUS, CAPACIOUS ⟨a ~ mansion⟩ ⟨a ~ ship⟩ ⟨~ pockets⟩ ⟨a ~ novel⟩ ⟨his voice . . . with its ~, rich qualities —Whitney Balliett⟩ **2** *of a female animal* **:** having a large or well-proportioned body suited for breeding ⟨a strong, healthy, ~ mare —*Horse*⟩ ⟨a ~ bitch⟩

roon \'rün, 'rün\ *chiefly Scot var of* ROUND

roond \-nd\ *Scot var of* ROUND

roop \'rüp\ *var of* ROUP

roor·back *also* roor·bach \'ru̇r,bak, 'ru̇(ə),-\ *n* -s [after Baron von Roorback, fictional author of *Roorback's Tour through the Western and Southern States,* an imaginary book from which an alleged passage was quoted in the Ithaca (N.Y.) *Chronicle* of 1844 that made scurrilous charges against James K. Polk, then Democratic candidate for president] **:** a defamatory falsehood published for political effect usu. before an election ⟨strategists on both sides on the alert for ~*s* —*Newsweek*⟩

roos *pl of* ROO

¹roose \'rüz\ *n* -s [ME *ros, roos,* of Scand origin; akin to Icel *hrōs* praise, ON *hrōsa* to praise, boast; prob. akin to ON *hrōthr* praise — more at CADUCEUS] **1** *chiefly dial* **:** BOASTING, BRAGGING **2** *chiefly dial* **:** PRAISE

²roose \"\ *vt* -ED/-ING/-S [ME *rosen, rusen,* fr. ON *hrōsa* to praise, boast] *chiefly dial* **:** to commend highly **:** EXTOL, FLATTER

roo·se·velt elk \'rōz(ə),velt- *also* -ˌvəlt- *sometimes* 'rüz-\ *n, usu cap R* [after Theodore *Roosevelt*] **:** the largest of the American wapitis (*Cervus canadensis occidentalis*) now restricted to the Olympic peninsula of the state of Washington

roo·se·velt·ian \ˌrōz(ə)ˈveltēən *sometimes* ˌrüz-\ *adj, usu cap* [Theodore *Roosevelt* †1919, 26th U. S. president and Franklin Delano *Roosevelt* †1945, 32d U. S. president + E *-ian*] **1 :** of, relating to, or supporting Theodore Roosevelt or his views or policies ⟨*Rooseveltian* doctrine of speaking softly . . . and of carrying the big stick —*Nation*⟩ **2 :** of, relating to, or supporting F. D. Roosevelt or his views or policies ⟨*Rooseveltian* tendencies toward currency expansion —Jeannette P. Nichols⟩

roo·se·velt·iana \ˌ⸗(⸗)ˌveltēˈanə, -ˈänə, -ˈänə\ *n pl, usu cap* [Theodore & Franklin D. *Roosevelt* + E *-i-* + *-ana*] **:** matter (as papers, books, letters, relics) relating to Theodore Roosevelt or Franklin D. Roosevelt

roo·se·velt·ism \'rōz(ə),vel,tizəm *also* -ˌvəl- *sometimes* 'rüz-\ *n* -s *usu cap* [Theodore & Franklin D. *Roosevelt* + E *-ism*] **:** a system or views formulated by or attributed to either Theodore Roosevelt or Franklin D. Roosevelt

roo·se·velt·ite \-l,tīt\ *n* -s [F. D. *Roosevelt* + E *-ite*] **:** a bismuth arsenate found in Santiaguilo, Potosí, and Bolivia

roosevelt trout *n, usu cap R* [after Theodore *Roosevelt*] **:** a trout of western No. America prob. identical to the golden trout but often considered a separate species (*Salmo roosevelti*)

¹roost \'rüst\ *n* -s [ME *roost,* fr. OE *hrōst;* akin to MD *roest* roost, palate, OS *hrōst* framing of a roof, attic, MHG *rāz, rāze* bonfire, honeycomb, ON *hrōt* roof, Goth *hrot* roof, OSlav *krada* pile of wood, bonfire] **1 a :** a pole or other support on which birds or fowls rest esp. at night **:** PERCH **b :** a place where any birds customarily roost ⟨the starlings in these vast ~*s* —*Brit. Birds in Colour*⟩ **c :** a hen house or section of a building used for roosting ⟨barns and chicken ~*s* that have been converted into living quarters —Dwight MacDonald⟩ **d :** a group of fowls or birds roosting together ⟨alarms the whole ~ into flight⟩ **2 :** a resting place **:** LODGING ⟨the only ~ was in the garret, which . . . contained 11 double beds —J.R.Lowell⟩ **3 :** ROOKERY 3 ⟨rededicated that ~ of B-36 intercontinental bombers —*N. Y. Times*⟩ ⟨a ~ of party members and supporters —Anthony West⟩ ⟨the informal ~ for most designers —D.M.Oenslager⟩

²roost \"\ *vb* -ED/-ING/-S *vi* **1 a :** to settle down for rest or sleep **:** PERCH ⟨coveys ~ like quail on the ground during the night in stubble, under grass, and under low bushes —L.W. Wing⟩ ⟨grasshoppers have a habit of ~*ing* on sagebrush on warm nights —*Ecology*⟩ ⟨killed 90 percent of the flies that ~*ed* on the walls and ceilings overnight —*Science News Letter*⟩ ⟨chickens ~ at night⟩ **b :** to place or seat oneself as on a roost ⟨the old men ~*ed* on benches in front of the courthouse —Grace Metalious⟩ ⟨men ~*ing* on the car roofs of freight trains —A.F.Harlow⟩ ⟨flyers ~*ing* on the float of their overturned plane —E.L.Beach⟩ **2 :** to lodge or stay for a night or a period of time usu. in an informal or temporary manner ⟨vagrants wandered up and down the country, ~*ing* in hedgerows —J.A.Symonds⟩ ⟨the hotels had been abandoned, and we ~*ed* in them —A.J.Liebling⟩ ⟨planes . . . ~*ed* in the supposedly safe Inland sea —*Newsweek*⟩ ~ *vt* **:** to supply a roost for **:** put to roost ⟨so named because Indians ~*ed* their turkeys here —Cecile Johnson⟩

roost cock *n, archaic* **:** ROOSTER 1

roost·er \'rüstə(r) *sometimes* 'ru̇s-\ *n* -s **1 a :** an adult male domestic fowl **:** COCK **b :** an adult male of various other birds or fowl ⟨a ringneck pheasant ~⟩ ⟨ptarmigan ~*s*⟩ **2 :** a person having characteristics (as cockiness, pride) usu. attributed to a rooster ⟨professor who considered himself quite a ~ in his history —Jo Mora⟩ ⟨was just a young ~ then . . . breaking horses for four bits a day —F.B.Gipson⟩ **3 :** GOOSENECK b **4 :** PAPAGALLO

roosterfish \ˈ⸗⸗ˌ⸗\ *n* **:** PAPAGALLO

rooster heads *n pl but sing in constr* **:** SHOOTING STAR 2

roost·ers \-(r)z\ *n pl but sing in constr* **1 :** a common No. American blue violet (*Viola palmata*) **2 :** WHITE ADDER'S-TONGUE

rooster tail *n* **:** the arching white water and spray cast up astern by a motorboat or other object moving through the water at a fast rate

¹root \'rüt, 'ru̇t, *usu* |d·+V\ *n* -s *often attrib* [ME *rot, root,* fr.

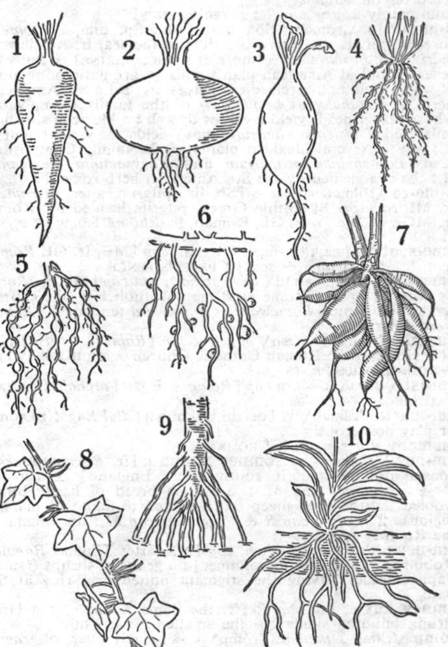

roots 1a: *1* conical, *2* napiform, *3* fusiform, *4* fibrous, *5* moniliform, *6* nodulose, *7* tuberous, *8* adventitious root, *9* prop root, *10* aerial root

OE *rōt,* fr. ON; akin to OE *wyrt* herb, plant, root, OHG *wurz* herb, plant, ON *urt* herb, Goth *waurts* root, L *radix* root, Gk *rhadix* branch, *rhiza* root, Toch B *witsako,* Alb *rrãnzë*] **1 a :** the portion of the plant body of a seed plant that originates usu. from the radicle at the extremity of the hypocotyl, functions as an organ of absorption, aeration, and food storage or as a means of anchorage and support, and differs from a stem in lacking nodes, buds, and leaves, in possessing an endodermis and a protective cap over the apical meristem, and in producing its branches normally in acropetal succession **b** (1) **:** a subterranean part of a plant (as a true root, bulb, tuber, rootstock, or other modified stem); *specif* **:** a large fleshy edible root or similar organ (as a carrot, turnip, radish, potato) (2) **:** the substance, material, or tissue of a root — often used in combination ⟨beet*root*⟩ (3) **roots** *pl, Brit* **:** ROOT CROPS **2 :** something that resembles a root in position or function esp. as a source of nourishment or as a support: as **a :** the part of a tooth lying within the socket; *also* **:** any of the processes into which this part is often divided — see TOOTH illustration **b :** the enlarged basal part of a hair consisting of the hair follicle, papilla, and developing hair shaft that lie within the skin **c :** the proximal end of a nerve; *esp* **:** one or more bundles of nerve fibers joining the cranial and spinal nerves with their respective nuclei and gray columns — see DORSAL ROOT, VENTRAL ROOT **d :** the part of an organ or physical structure by which it is attached to the body ⟨~ of a nail⟩ **3 a** (1) **:** the origin or cause of a condition, tendency, or quality ⟨tackling not only the psychological and emotional causes of race conflicts but also their economic ~*s* —M.F.A. Montagu⟩ ⟨the ~ of civil violence lay in the unequal distribution of the land —*Current Biog.*⟩; *specif* **:** an attribute that brings about an action or condition ⟨the love of money is the ~ of all evil —1 Tim 6:10 (AV)⟩ ⟨from the ~ of hate grows war⟩ (2) **:** the line of evolutionary development of a condition, trend, or branch of human activity — usu. used in pl. ⟨although its ~*s* go back . . . before the 19th century, fascism emerged after World War I —*Collier's Yr. Bk.*⟩ **b** (1) **:** a race, family, or progenitor that is the source or beginning of a group or line of descendants ⟨should be the ~ and father of many kings —Shak.⟩ ⟨the ~ out of which sprang two distinct people —John Locke⟩ ⟨the ~*s* of science, however, ran deep, stretching back to the period before the appearance of civilization —S.F.Mason⟩ ⟨beginnings of these types of literature had ~*s* reaching well back —R.A.Hall b. 1911⟩ (2) *obs* **:** a descendant or offshoot of a line or family **:** SCION **c** (1) **:** the underlying support or foundation of something **:** BASIS ⟨respect for the rights and intelligence of others which is the ~ of the democratic society —*Official Register of Harvard Univ.*⟩ ⟨has loosened the ~*s* of the slave system —C.L.Carmer⟩ ⟨have created a real opposition, which is the main ~ of continued social peace —H.J.Laski⟩ ⟨nourishing a strong ~ of loyalty⟩ ⟨tear out the evil by the ~*s*⟩ (2) **:** a culture or cultural tradition underlying subsequent related cultures in a limited area **d :** the inner core or essential nature or part of something **:** HEART ⟨~ of the matter⟩ ⟨delving into the ~*s* of the inner life —R.W.Southern⟩ ⟨the two dogmas are identical at ~ —Albert Hofstadter⟩ **e :** an indigenous relationship or close and sympathetic bond usu. with or in the social environment **:** TIE — usu. used in pl. ⟨the feeling that modern life has no ~*s* —E.R.Bentley⟩ ⟨depriving youngsters of that extra stability which comes when ~*s* can grow in one place —Martha M. Eliot⟩ ⟨industrial workers who would never put their ~*s* down in the countryside —Sam Pollock⟩ **4 a :** the time (as a birth date, the position of a planet, or a point in time) from which to reckon in making astronomical or astrological calculations **b** (1) **:** a quantity that when taken as a factor the number of times indicated by the index produces another quantity ⟨either +3 or −3 is a second ~ of 9 because either taken twice as a factor produces 9⟩ (2) **:** a value that when substituted for the unknown quantity in an equation satisfies the equation **5 a** (1) **:** the base or lower part of a material thing **:** BOTTOM ⟨~ of a hill⟩ ⟨~*s* of the sea⟩ (2) **:** the basal extension of a geological formation ⟨lateral compression . . . forces the granitic part of the crust downward to form a solid ~ —W.H.Bucher⟩ **b :** the part of a material thing by which it is attached to something else: as (1) **:** the part of a weir or dam adjoining or penetrating the bank or sides of a stream or river (2) **:** the portion of an airplane wing nearest the fuselage (3) **:** the portion of the blade of a propeller or rotor nearest the hub **6 a** (1) **:** the simple element inferred as the basis from which a word is derived by phonetic change or by extension (as composition and addition of a prefix, suffix, inflectional ending, or replacive) (2) **:** the simple element (as Latin *sta*) inferred as common to all the words of a group in a language (as in Latin *stamus* "we stand" with a personal ending, *sistimus* "we place" with reduplication and personal ending, *statio* "standing place" with a suffix, and *constituere* "to establish" with a prefix) or in related languages **b :** the sequence of consonants recurring with various vowel sequences and affixes in a set of related words in Semitic **c :** a meaningful morpheme (as *hold*) esp. as recurring with various affixes or replacives in grammatically different forms (as *holds, held, beholders, withholding*) **7 a :** the musical tone from whose harmonics or overtones a chord is composed **b :** the lowest tone of a chord in its normal position **8 a :** the part of an open gear tooth between the pitch circle and the minor diameter **b** (1) **:** the surface between the threads at the minor diameter of a screw or at the major diameter of a nut — compare CREST 6 (2) **:** a similar surface on the blading of a turbine **9 :** the bottom zone of the space provided for a fusion weld **10** *slang* **:** a kick usu. delivered to the posterior ⟨caught him a great ~ with his boot on the backside —Bruce Marshall⟩ **syn** see ORIGIN

²root \"\ *vb* -ED/-ING/-S [ME *roten*, fr. *rot, root*, n.] *vt* **1 a :** to furnish with or enable to develop roots ⟨~ the seedlings in the hotbed⟩ ⟨two deeply ~*ed* and far-flung cultures —A.W. Hummel⟩ **b :** to fix or firmly attach by or as if by roots ⟨the lichen is ~*ed* to the rock⟩ ⟨he stands ~*ed* to the spot⟩ ⟨as firmly ~*ed* to their homesteads as the stone walls and fences —*Amer. Guide Series: N. J.*⟩ ⟨pension and seniority rights ~ workers to their jobs —Jules Abels⟩ **c :** to set firmly or establish usu. by implanting in something ⟨a peace ~*ed* in justice and law —H.S.Truman⟩ ⟨lack of a well-*rooted* tradition —R.W.Southern⟩ ⟨the ~*ed* beliefs of a lifetime are not easily shaken —T.B.Costain⟩ ⟨~*ed* in love, he grows and lives in peace⟩ ⟨wants to ~ his work in the reality of his own time —M.D.Geismar⟩ **d :** to furnish or give an origin or cause to (an action or development) ⟨a neurosis . . . is often ~*ed* in some childhood difficulty —*Irish Digest*⟩ ⟨many dental ailments are ~*ed* in psychosomatic disturbances —*Collier's Yr. Bk.*⟩ ⟨her problems are ~*ed* in temperament rather than economic handicaps —E.B.George⟩ **2 :** to pull, tear out, or remove often by force **:** root out ⟨~ these evils from the land⟩ ⟨launched his jet at the gun and tried to ~ it from its cave —J.A.Michener⟩ **~** *vi* **1 :** to grow roots in or as if in the earth **:** to strike or take root ⟨seedlings ~ quickly with plenty of water and sunlight⟩ ⟨prevent a few viruses from ~*ing* in nerve endings —*Monsanto Mag.*⟩ ⟨theories . . . ~*ing* in the savage mind, growing up strongly —Emma Hawkridge⟩ **2 :** to become fixed or firmly established **:** to establish oneself ⟨now I'll redeem my error and ~ forever here —Samuel Foote⟩ ⟨the patriots in whom the stock of freedom ~*s* —R.W.Emerson⟩ ⟨the new science of human behavior ~*s* in the study of concrete cases —H.A.Overstreet⟩ **3 :** to have or find an origin, basis, or cause in something ⟨the sin of self-righteousness which not infrequently ~*s* in sectional pride —B.G.Gallagher⟩ ⟨like everything else in human conduct, gesture ~*s* in the reactive necessities of the organism —Edward Sapir⟩

³root \"\ *vb* -ED/-ING/-S [alter. (influenced by ¹*root*) of earlier *wroot*, fr. ME *wroten*, fr. OE *wrōtan;* akin to MLG *wrōten* to root, MD *wroeten*, OHG *ruozzen*, ON *rōta* to root, and prob. to OE *wrītan* to incise, write — more at WRITE] *vi* **1 :** to turn up or dig in the earth with the snout **:** GRUB ⟨~, hog, or die⟩ ⟨pigs ~*ing* for truffles⟩ ⟨fish ~*ing* in the mud for food⟩ **2 :** to poke or dig down or into usu. in search of something ⟨chickens ~*ing* about in the rubbish —Alan Moorehead⟩ ⟨~*ed* in the bog and began to eat the cherries —Katherine Mansfield⟩ ⟨~*ing* about in the kitchen —Valentine Williams⟩ **~** *vt* **:** root out ⟨the razor-back type was able to ~ its living and to do battle with . . . most foes —E.D.Ross⟩

⁴root \"\ *vi* -ED/-ING/-S [perh. alter. of ⁵*rout*] **1 :** to shout for or otherwise noisily applaud or encourage a contestant or team **:** CHEER ⟨a band of students ~*ing* for the school football team —Lucius Garvin⟩ ⟨going to the races to ~ for her brown colt —*Time*⟩ **2 :** to wish for the success of or lend support to someone or something ⟨can't be successful unless everyone loves him and ~*s* for him —Delmore Schwartz⟩ ⟨the communities which it served were ~*ing* for it —S.H.Adams⟩

root·age \"+ij\ *n* -S [¹*root* + *-age*] **1 :** a developed system of roots **:** a firm rooting ⟨the heavy ~ of bunchgrass necessitated ploughing the land a year in advance —*Amer. Guide Series: Wash.*⟩ ⟨it is among the ignorant that all sorts of superstitions and panaceas take ~ and flourish —*Automobilist*⟩ **2 :** the origin or beginnings of something **:** ROOT 3a(1) ⟨a man of lowly ~ —Raymond Moley⟩ ⟨all these philosophies had a Greek ~ and were developed further in the Hellenistic world —K.S.Latourette⟩ ⟨the disquiet to conscience . . . has ~ in the religious and ethical soil —B.G.Gallagher⟩ ⟨repentance has a deep ~ in the spirit of man —O.J.Raab⟩

root beer *n* **:** a sweetened effervescent beverage prepared by carbonating or fermenting a watery mixture of extractions from roots and herbs, natural flavoring oils (as nutmeg, cloves, anise, and wintergreen), and sugar

root blindness *n* **:** a lack of roots caused by disease or nematodes

root borer *n* **:** an insect or insect larva that bores into the roots of plants: as **a :** the large larva of a beetle (*Prionus laticollis*) of the family Cerambycidae that infests the roots of the grapevine and of various trees **b :** the larva of any of various moths (as *Paranthrene polistiformis*) that bores in grapevine roots

root-bound \ˈ≠,≠\ *adj* **1 :** POT-BOUND **2 :** having the roots matted ⟨deep in shaggy untended lawns of old trees and ~ scented and flowering shrubs —William Faulkner⟩

root canal *n* **:** PULP CANAL

root cap *n* **:** a protective cap or thimble-shaped mass of parenchyma cells usu. irregularly arranged that covers the terminal meristem in most root tips and is constantly renewed from the meristem as the cells are sloughed off by penetration of the root apex through the soil — compare HISTOGEN

root celery *n* **:** CELERIAC

root cellar *n* **:** an underground or partly underground pit that is used for the storage of root crops, potatoes, or other vegetables and is usu. covered over with earth and entered from a stairway at one end

root circle *n* **:** DEDENDUM CIRCLE

root climber *n* **:** a plant that climbs by its adventitious roots (as the common ivy and many tropical aroids)

root collar *n* **:** CROWN 12a

root crop *n* **:** a crop grown for its enlarged roots (as turnips, mangels, sugar beets, sweet potatoes)

root cutting *n* **1 :** a piece of root used in propagating a plant (as blackberry, horseradish, or oriental poppy) — compare CUTTING 1a **2 :** the basal sections of jute fibers unsuitable for use in the spinning process — usu. used in pl. ⟨*root-cuttings* are separated from the other fibers⟩

root determinative *n* **:** DETERMINATIVE 3

root disease *n* **:** a disease affecting a root system or attacking a plant primarily through the roots; *esp* **:** a stunting and deterioration of sugarcane caused by unfavorable soil conditions and attacks of fungi of the genus *Pythium* (esp. *P. arrhenomanes*) — called also *Lahaina disease*

root division *n* **:** the propagation of plants by dividing the root stocks or the crowns

rooted *adj, of a tooth* **:** having a contracted root nearly closing the pulp cavity and preventing further growth

root·ed·ly *adv* **:** in a firm or well established manner

root·ed·ness *n* -ES **:** the quality or state of being rooted ⟨a ~ in his environment which made him almost immovable —Stephen Spender⟩

¹root·er \ˈrüd·ə(r), ˈru̇|, |tə(r)\ *n* -S [³*root* + *-er*] **:** a heavy plowing device for tearing up the ground surface esp. for a roadbed

²rooter \"\ *n* -S [⁴*root* + *-er*] **:** one that roots; *esp* **:** an enthusiastic supporter

root·ery \-ərē\ *n* -ES [¹*root* + *-ery*] **:** a pile of roots and soil set with plants

root fly *n* **:** CABBAGE FLY

root fungus *n* **:** a fungus (as a saprophyte, parasite, or symbiont) typically growing upon or associated with the roots of a plant — compare MYCORRHIZA

root gall *n* **1 :** an abnormal enlargement or swelling of or on the root of a plant commonly due to a parasitic organism **2 :** ROOT KNOT

root graft *n* **1 :** a plant graft in which the stock is a root or piece of a root ⟨whip grafts of apple are usu. *root grafts*⟩ **2 :** a natural anastomosis between roots of compatible plants growing near one another ⟨oak wilt is said to be transmitted through *root grafts*⟩

root hair *n* **:** one of the many hairlike tubular outgrowths of epidermal or sometimes cortical cells commonly found just behind the root apex that function in absorption and are continually replaced as the root elongates

root-hardy \ˈ≠¦≠≠\ *adj* **:** having a hardy root or rootstock

roothold \ˈ≠,≠\ *n* **1 :** anchorage of a plant to soil through the growth and spreading of roots ⟨the transplants should be watered carefully until they get a new ~⟩ **2 :** a place where plants may obtain a roothold ⟨the sheer face of the mountain offered scarcely a ~⟩

root house *n* **:** a shed or a wing of a building usu. used for the storage of foodstuffs

rootier *comparative of* ROOTY

rootiest *superlative of* ROOTY

root in *vi* **:** to hog in

root knot *n* **:** a disease of many kinds of wild or cultivated plants caused by eelworms that produce characteristic enlargements on the roots and stunt the growth of the plant — called also *root gall;* compare ROOT-KNOT NEMATODE

root-knot nematode *also* **root-knot eelworm** *n* **:** any of several small plant-parasitic nematodes formerly regarded as varieties of a single species (*Heterodera marioni*) but now usu. referred as separate species to the related genus *Meloidogyne*, invading roots of most cultivated and many wild plants, and inducing the formation of galls in which they live and on which they feed — compare MEADOW NEMATODE

roo·tle \ˈrüd·ᵊl\ *vi* -ED/-ING/-S [freq. of ³*root*] **:** ³ROOT ⟨lean black pigs ~ for filth —*Manchester Guardian Weekly*⟩ ⟨*rootled* at the bottom of a deep drawer —John Buchan⟩

root·less \ˈrütləs, ˈru̇t-\ *adj* **:** having no roots: as **a :** lacking firmness or a solid basis **:** UNSTABLE ⟨this explanation we find unconvincing and biologically ~ —Weston La Barre⟩ ⟨family and environmental factors which determine the ~ behavior of adolescents —Frances Keene⟩ **b :** lacking a tie or sympathetic relationship with or in the social environment ⟨have become ~ individuals who do not find a home either with their communal environment or with a Christian atmosphere —J.M.Van der Kroef⟩ ⟨all are strangers, ~ in place or time, in the nervous new civilization —T.H.White b.1915⟩ **c** *of a tooth* **:** retaining a pulp cavity widely open at the bottom that permits an abundant supply of nutriment

root·less·ness *n* -ES **:** the quality or state of being rootless

root·let \-lət\ *or* **root·ling** \-liŋ\ *n* -S **:** a small root; *also* **:** one of the ultimate divisions of a growing root

rootlike \ˈ≠,≠\ *adj* **:** having the appearance or acting in the manner of a root

root line *n* **:** DEDENDUM CIRCLE

root maggot *n* **:** a legless grub that is the larva of any of numerous insects (as the cabbage fly) and that feeds in roots

root-mean-square \ˈ≠,≠ˈ≠\ *n* **:** the square root of the arithmetical mean of the squares of a set of numbers — abbr. *RMS, rms*

root-mean-square deviation *n* **:** STANDARD DEVIATION

root metaphor *n* **:** a fundamental perspective or viewpoint based on a supposition of similarity of form between mental concepts and external objects which though not factually supportable determines the manner in which an individual structures his knowledge — compare CATEGORY

root nodule *or* **root tubercle** *n* **:** NODULE 2b(3)

root of unity : a real or complex solution of the equation $x^n - 1 = 0$ where n is an integer

¹root out *vt* [²*root*] **:** to remove altogether **:** ERADICATE, DESTROY ⟨attempting to *root out* his mistakes —A.T.Weaver⟩ ⟨powers to *root out* organized crime and political corruption —*N.Y.Times*⟩ ⟨movement to *root* the radicals *out* of American life —Oscar Handlin⟩

²root out *vt* [³*root*] **:** to turn over, dig up, or discover and bring to light ⟨hogs *rooting out* truffles⟩ ⟨spent the whole of March 8 *rooting out* those treasured possessions from holes and corners —Kenneth Roberts⟩ ⟨a game which could *root out* our grandfathers *out* of their beds at three o'clock in the morning —Stanislaus Lynch⟩

root pressure *n* **:** the chiefly osmotic pressure or force by which water rises into the stems of plants from the roots

root-prune \ˈ≠,≠\ *vt* **:** to prune the roots of (woody plants) in order to check top growth, develop a mass of small fibrous roots, or induce flowering and fruiting

root pulper *n* **:** a machine used for reducing root crops to a pulp for stock feed

root rake *n* **:** a tree dozer or rooter with heavy teeth (attached to the front of a tractor) that is used for uprooting small trees, stumps, or brush and pushing them into piles

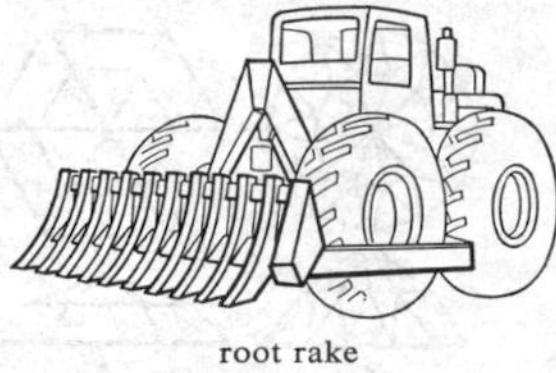

root rake

root rot *n* **:** a plant disease characterized by a decay of the roots (as those caused by fungi of the genera *Armillaria, Oozonium, Thielavia, Rhizoctonia*, or *Sphaerostilbe*) — compare ROSELLINIA

root-run \ˈ≠,≠\ *n* **:** a space or area for root development

roots *pl of* ROOT, *pres 3d sing of* ROOT

root sheath *n* **1 a :** a many-layered epidermal sheath surrounding an aerial root (as the velamen in an epiphytic orchid) **b :** COLEORHIZA **2 :** the epidermal lining of a hair follicle comprising two principal layers of cells that make up an inner and an outer root sheath

rootstalk \ˈ≠,≠\ *n* **:** RHIZOME

rootstock \ˈ≠,≠\ *n* **1 a :** a rhizomatous underground part of a plant **b :** a stock for grafting consisting of a root or a piece of root; *broadly* **:** STOCK **2 :** HYDRORHIZA **3 :** a source of offshoots **:** ORIGIN ⟨going back to one of the ~*s* of economic thought —*Times Lit. Supp.*⟩

root sucker *n* **:** a shoot springing from the roots of a plant (as wild plum or raspberry)

root symbiosis *n* **:** the mycorrhizal association of bacteria and fungi with the roots of certain plants — compare MYCORRHIZA

root tip *n* **:** the terminal portion of a root or root branch usu. including the root cap and the meristematic region behind it and often the regions of differentiation, elongation, and root hair formation

root vole *n* **:** any of various voles of the genus *Microtus; esp* **:** a Siberian vole (*M. oeconomus*) that stores up roots and tubers for future use

root weevil *n* **1 :** any of several Australian weevils of the genus *Baryopadus; esp* **:** a larva (*B. squalidus*) that bores in the roots of the apple and pear **2 :** WATER WEEVIL

rootworm \ˈ≠,≠\ *n* **1 :** an insect larva (as the corn rootworm) that feeds on the roots of plants **2 :** a nematode worm that infests roots

rooty \ˈrü|d·ē, ˈru̇|, |t|, |i\ *adj* -ER/-EST [ME *ruty*, fr. *rot, root, rut* root + *-y* — more at ROOT] **1 :** full or consisting of roots ⟨~ soil⟩ **2 :** similar to or of the quality of roots ⟨a ~ fragrance of pine and moss and bracken —John Buchan⟩

roove *var of* ROVE

rooves *pl of* ROOF

rooyebok *var of* ROOIBOK

ROP *abbr* **1** record of performance; record of production **2** *often not cap* run-of-paper

rop·able *or* **rope·able** \ˈrōpəbəl\ *adj* **1 :** capable of being roped **2** *Austral* **:** in a bad temper **:** ANGRY

ropalic *adj var of* RHOPALIC

¹rope \ˈrōp\ *n* -S *often attrib* [ME, fr. OE *rāp;* akin to OHG *reif* hoop, ON *reip* rope, Goth *skaudaraip* sandal strap] **1 a** (1) **:** a large stout cord made of strands of natural or artificial fibers (as hemp, Manila hemp, sisal, jute, flax, cotton, or nylon) twisted or braided together esp. in a thickness an inch or more in circumference or ¼ inch to 5 inches in diameter (2) **:** a large stout cord made of strands of wire twisted or braided together (3) **:** a cord having a wire core with fiber strands braided around it (4) **:** a large stout cord made of nonfibrous artificial material (as glass or a plastic) **b :** a braided or unbraided long slender strip of material used as rope ⟨rawhide ~⟩ **c :** a piece of rope cut to a suitable length for a particular function: as (1) **:** a cord for hanging a person **:** a hangman's noose (2) **:** any of various lines aboard or connected to a ship ⟨wheel ~⟩ — see SHIP illustration (3) *obs* **:** TIGHTROPE (4) **:** LASSO (5) **:** one of the usu. three cords stretched one above the other at intervals of about 18 inches that mark off a boxing or wrestling ring **2 :** a unit of length **:** ROOD **3 :** a line aboard a ship before it is used ⟨a ~ stored in a coil⟩ **4 a :** a row or string consisting of a number of things united (as by braiding, twining, or threading) ⟨a ~ of pearls⟩ ⟨a ~ of onions⟩ **b :** two or more mountain climbers fastened at intervals to a single rope for security **5 :** slimy strands in food substances (as milk, flour, or bread) caused by contamination with bacteria or fungi — compare ROPINESS, ROPY BREAD **6 :** a device usu. consisting of long streamers of aluminum foil dropped from an airplane to confuse enemy radar equipment **7 a** (1) **:** something that binds, confines, or holds in check (2) **:** a condition, event, or action that helps a person in a disadvantageous state ⟨redeemed me . . . from the ~*s* of sin —Maurice Samuel⟩ **b :** something twisted and braided like a rope ⟨the soft ~ of her hair tossed from side to side —James Joyce⟩ **c :** something long, elongated, and strung out ⟨far ahead in the dark I saw the monumental bridge, ~*s* of light across the dark river —Ralph Ellison⟩ **d :** SEQUENCE — used in panguingue and other card games of the rummy family **8 :** freedom of action esp. when likely to cause harm ⟨enough ~ to hang himself⟩ ⟨allowing himself sufficient ~ to wander beyond the city —Isolde Farrell⟩ **9 ropes** *pl* **:** the special techniques or procedures involved **:** INS AND OUTS ⟨postponed everything . . . with the excuse that he was learning the ~*s* —T.R.Ybarra⟩ — **on the ropes** *adv (or adj)* **1 :** in a groggy defenseless state upon the ropes of a boxing ring **2 :** in a helpless condition ⟨emotionally, physically and financially I was *on the ropes* —Polly Adler⟩

²rope \"\ *vb* -ED/-ING/-S *vt* **1 a :** to bind, fasten, or tie with a rope or cord ⟨I'll ~ myself here so that I won't be swept overboard —Richard Sale⟩ **b :** to partition, separate, or divide by means of a rope so as to include or exclude ⟨*roped* away from the entrance among a herd of other waiting people —J.B. Benefield⟩ ⟨to ~ off the street near the fire⟩ **c :** to capture by means of a rope **:** LASSO ⟨~ cattle⟩ ⟨~ a steer⟩ ⟨~ out a mustang⟩ **d :** to connect or fasten together (a party of mountain climbers) with a rope — usu. used with *up* **2** *of a sail* **:** to sew a boltrope on the edge of **3 :** to draw as if with a rope: **a :** to inveigle into joining an undertaking or organization ⟨the conspirators *roped* into their scheme a whole network of the magnates —Hilaire Belloc⟩ **b** *slang* **:** to take in **:** SWINDLE ⟨an old confidence man wrote with nostalgia of fat marks he had *roped* and taken for their bankrolls —R.B.Gehman⟩ — often used with *in* **c** *slang* **:** to attract by the use of sexual charms esp. into an engagement — often used with *in* **~** *vi* **1 :** to take the form of or twist in the manner of rope **:** to extend in a filament or thread (as by means of a glutinous or adhesive quality) ⟨the saliva *roping* from his jowls —Ralph Ellison⟩ **2 :** to connect or fasten together a party of mountain climbers with a rope ⟨today soft snow lay on ice . . . so we *roped* up —W.H.Murray⟩

³rope \"\ *n* -S [ME *rop*, fr. OE *ropp, hrop;* akin to MD *rop* animal entrails] *dial Brit* **:** ENTRAIL, INTESTINE

ropeband *var of* ROBAND

ropebark \ˈ≠,≠\ *n* **:** LEATHERWOOD 1a

rope brake *n* **:** a band brake or absorption dynamometer in which the band is replaced by a rope — compare PRONY BRAKE

rope brown *n* **:** a brown paper esp. of excellent quality made from old Manila ropes

rope clip *n* **:** a clamp (as a U-bolt) for clamping together two ropes (as wire ropes) or two parts of a rope

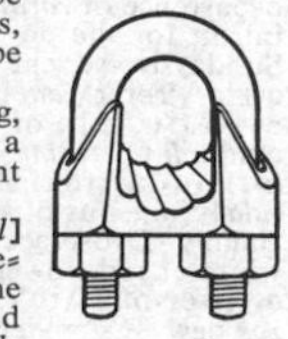

ropedancer \ˈ≠,≠≠\ *n* **:** one that dances, walks, or performs acrobatic feats on a rope extended through the air at some height

ropedancing \ˈ≠,≠≠\ *n* **:** the art of dancing, walking, or performing acrobatic feats on a rope extended through the air at some height

rope down *vb* **:** to make a rappel

rope drilling *n* [*drilling* fr. gerund of *drill*] **:** a method of sinking wells or making boreholes in which the tools are attached to the lower end of a rope or cable and lifted and dropped alternately — called also *cable drilling, cable system, percussion drilling*

rope clip

rope drive *n* **:** one or more ropes transmitting torque from one parallel grooved pulley to another

rope grass *n* **:** a plant of the genus *Restio*

rope-grass family *n* **:** RESTIONACEAE

rope hose tool *n* **:** a rope having a hook and often a ring attached used by firemen esp. to hold hose in place while in use

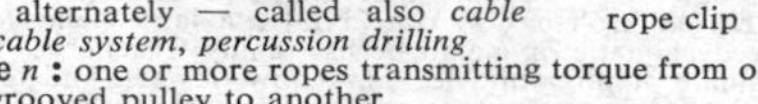

rope hose tools

rope house *n* **1 :** a storehouse for rope **2 :** an open-sided shed in which salt is crystallized out from brine on ropes down which the brine trickles

rope key *n* **:** TENT SLIDE

rope ladder *n* **:** a ladder with sidepieces of rope and rungs of rope, wood, or metal

rope-lay cable *n* **:** a cable in which the separate wires are spirally stranded before being spiraled together

rope molding *n* **:** a molding in a pattern twisted like the strands of a rope

rope of sand : something of no cohesion or stability **:** a feeble union or tie

rop·er \ˈrōpə(r)\ *n* -S [ME *ropere* maker of ropes, fr. ¹*rope* + *-ere* -er] **1 :** a maker of ropes; *specif* **:** an operator of a machine for twisting yarn into rope **2 :** one that ropes cattle or horses **:** COWBOY **3 a :** one that entices customers to a gambling establishment esp. with a fixed game **b :** a detective who hides his identity and tries to make a suspect give himself away **c :** a strikebreaker who circulates among strikers in search of men tempted to return to work **4 :** a jockey who checks his horse to prevent it from winning **5 :** a hat blocker who forms brims

rope race *n* **:** a race in a pulley through which a rope runs

rope railway *n* **:** ROPEWAY

¹roperipe \ˈ≠,≠\ *adj* **1** *archaic* **a** *of a deed* **:** punishable by hanging **b** *of a person* **:** deserving to be hung **2** *obs* **:** BOMBASTIC

²roperipe \"\ *n* -S **:** one that deserves to be hung **:** RASCAL

rop·ery \ˈrōp(ə)rē\ *n* -ES [ME *roperie*, fr. ¹*rope* + *-erie* -ery] **1 :** a place where ropes are made **2** *archaic* **:** roguish tricks or banter

ropes *pl of* ROPE, *pres 3d sing of* ROPE

rope's end *n* [ME *roppys end*, fr. *roppys, ropes* (gen. of ¹*rope*) + *end, ende* end] **1 :** a piece of rope esp. for use as a lash for punishing **2 :** a hangman's noose

rope's-end \ˈ≠,≠\ *vt* [*rope's end*] **:** to punish with a rope's end

rope spear *n* **:** a spear used to recover rope lost in an oil well

rope stitch *n* **:** an embroidery stitch made by overlapping small slanted stitches

rope system *n* **:** a method of training dewberries in which the canes are tied to one or two horizontal wires strung above the plants between posts

rope tow *n* **:** SKI TOW 1

ropetrick *n, obs* **:** ROGUERY

rope walk *n* **1** *or* **rope yard :** a long path devoted to the manufacture of rope down which the worker carries and lays the strands **2 :** a long narrow building containing a rope walk

ropewalker \ˈ≠,≠≠\ *n* **:** an acrobat that walks on a rope extended through the air at some height

ropeway \ˈ≠,≠\ *n* **1 :** a fixed cable or a pair of fixed cables suspended between supporting towers serving as a track for passenger or freight carriers that are self-propelled or move by gravity **2 :** an endless aerial cable suspended between supports that revolve, upon drums turned by a stationary engine and used to transport logs, ore, and other freight suspended free or in carriers **:** CABLEWAY

ropework \ˈ≠,≠\ *n* **1 :** an establishment where ropes are made **2 a :** the art of tying knots **b :** work (as knots) made of entwined ropes

rope yarn *n* **1 a :** the yarn or thread composing the strands of a rope **b :** a yarn of fibers loosely twisted up right-handedly **2 :** something of small account **:** TRIFLE

rope-yarn knot *n* **:** a knot made by splitting rope yarns and joining the ends with half knots and used to tie rope yarns together

rope-yarn knot

ropeyarn sunday \'⸗,⸗-\ *n, often cap R & usu cap S* [prob. so called fr. a former practice on sailing ships of setting aside one afternoon a week for the mending of clothes] *slang* **:** an afternoon during the week in which no work is required

rop·i·ly \'rōpəlē, -li\ *adv* **:** in a ropy manner

rop·i·ness \-pēnəs, -pin-\ *n* -ES **1 :** the quality or state of being ropy **2 a :** a stringy condition of milk caused by contamination with some strains of bacteria **b :** a slimy condition of flour or bread caused by bacterial or fungal contamination

¹rop·ing \'rōpiŋ\ *adj* [ME *ropinge*, fr. pres. part. of (assumed) ME *ropen* to be ropy, fr. ME *¹rope*] *archaic* **:** ROPY

²roping \"\ *n* -S [*¹rope* + *-ing*] **1 :** ROPES, CORDAGE **2 :** BOLT-ROPE **3 :** ROVING; *specif* **:** a wool sliver delivered from the finisher card ready for spinning

roping needle *n* **:** a sailmaker's large needle

ropy *also* **rop·ey** \'rōpē, -pi\ *adj* **ropier; ropiest** [ME *ropy*, fr. *¹rope* + *-y*] **1 a :** capable of being drawn into a thread **:** VISCOUS, GLUTINOUS ⟨a ~ froth had dried on his lips —John Bennett⟩ **b :** having a gelatinous quality (as milk) or slimy quality (as bread or flour) from bacterial or fungal contamination **c** *of a paint* **:** having a quality or characteristic that causes it to act stringy under the brush and not level out properly **2 :** resembling rope: as **a :** long, gnarled, and often roughly fibrous ⟨their ~ vines twisted around strands of wire strung between five-foot stakes —*Amer. Guide Series: Pa.*⟩ **b :** MUSCULAR, SINEWY ⟨a scrawny Yankee with a cloth cap and a ~ neck —Nancy Hale⟩ **3** *usu* **ropey**, *slang* **:** extremely unsatisfactory or inauspicious

ropy lava *n* **:** lava marked with wrinkles resembling rope **:** PAHOEHOE

roque \'rōk\ *n* -S [alter. of *¹croquet*] **:** croquet played on a hard-surfaced court having a raised border used as a cushion in bank shots

Roque·fort \'rōkfərt\ *trademark* — used for a cheese made of ewes' milk and ripened in caves

roque·laure \¦räkə¦lō(ə)r, ¦rōk-\ *n* -S [F, fr. Antoine Gaston Jean Baptiste, Duc de *Roquelaure* †1738 Fr. marshal] **:** a knee-length cloak buttoned in front worn esp. in the 18th and early 19th centuries

¹ro·quet \(')rō¦kā\ *vt* -ED/-ING/-S [prob. alter. of *²croquet*] **:** to hit (another's ball) in croquet — used of a croquet ball or of the player who strikes it

²roquet \"\ *n* -S **:** the act of roqueting

ro·quette \rō'ket\ *n* -S [F — more at ROCKET] **:** GARDEN ROCKET 1

ro·ral \'rōrəl\ *adj* [L *ror-, ros* dew + E *-al*] *archaic* **:** DEWY

ro·ram hat \'rōrəm-\ *n* [*roram* (of unknown origin) + *hat*] **:** a hat made of a woolen cloth with a fur face worn esp. in the 19th century

ro·ra·te sunday \rō'räd-ē-\ *n, cap R&S* [*rorate* fr. L, 2d pers. pl. imper. of *rorare* to drip moisture, fr. *ror-, ros* dew; fr. the occurrence of *rorate* as the first word in the Latin form of the introit for the day in some Christian churches] **:** the fourth Sunday in Advent

ro·ric \'rōrik\ *adj* [ISV *ror-* (fr. L *ror-, ros* dew) + *-ic* — more at ROSEMARY] **:** of or relating to dew **:** DEWY

rorid *adj* [L *roridus*, fr. *ror-, ros* dew] *obs* **:** DEWY

ro·rid·u·la \rō'rijələ\ *n, cap* [NL, prob. fr. L *roridus* dewy + *-ula*] **:** a genus of southern African insectivorous undershrubs (family Droseraceae) having entire or pinnatifid leaves and white or red flowers with a 3-celled ovary

ro·rif·er·ous \rō'rif(ə)rəs\ *adj* [L *rorifer* roriferous (fr. *ror-, ros* dew + *-fer* -ferous) + E *-ous*] **:** generating dew

ro·rip·pa \rō'ripə\ *n, cap* [NL] **:** a large genus of chiefly weedy aquatic or marsh herbs (family Cruciferae) that have pinnate or pinnatifid leaves, yellow flowers, and terete pods with seeds in two rows in each cell and that include some forms used for salad greens or pot herbs — see MARSH CRESS

ror·qual \'rȯrkwəl\ *n* -S [F, fr. Norw *røyrhval*, fr. ON *reytharhvalr*, fr. *reythr* rorqual (fr. *rauthr* red) + *hvalr* whale — more at RED, WHALE] **:** a whalebone whale (as a blue whale, finback, or sei) of the genus *Balaenoptera* or *Sibbaldus* having a rather small head, the skin of the throat marked with deep longitudinal furrows, and relatively short slender forelimbs one-seventh or less of the length of head and body

¹ror·schach \'rō(ə)r,shäk\ *n* -S *usu cap* [after Hermann *Rorschach* †1922 Swiss psychiatrist] **1** *or* **rorschach test :** a psychological test of personality and intelligence consisting of 10 standard black or colored inkblot designs that the subject describes in terms of what they look like to him and reveals through his selectivity the manner in which intellectual and emotional factors are integrated in his perception of environmental stimuli **2** *or* **rorschach protocol :** the data obtained by a Rorschach

²rorschach \"\ *vt* -ED/-ING/-S *often cap* **:** to test by means of the Rorschach

ror·schach·er \-kə(r)\ *or* **ror·schach·ist** \-kəst\ *n* -S *usu cap* [Hermann *Rorschach* + E *-er* or *-ist*] **:** one who is skilled in the administration, scoring, and interpretation of the Rorschach test

rort \'rȯ(ə)rt\ *n* -S [perh. back-formation fr. *rorty*] *Austral* **:** a fraudulent scheme **:** TRICK

ror·ty \'rȯ(ə)rti\ *adj* -ER/-EST [origin unknown] *slang Brit* **:** FINE, GAY, SPORTY

rory-tory \¦rōri¦tōri\ *adj* [prob. alter. of *tory-rory*] *dial Eng* **:** DASHING, FLAMBOYANT, GAY

ros *pl of* RO

¹ro·sa \'rōzə\ *n, cap* [NL, fr. L, rose — more at ROSE] **:** a large genus of erect or sometimes climbing or creeping mostly prickly shrubs (family Rosaceae) that are widely distributed esp. in temperate regions and have compound leaves and regular 5-petaled red, white, pink, or yellow flowers with many stamens

²rosa \"\ *adj, usu cap* [*Rosa*, locality in north central New Mexico] **:** of or belonging to a culture in north central New Mexico A.D. 700–900 characterized by stockades and pit houses having a large and variable floor plan

rosa americana *n, usu cap R&A* [NL, American rose] **:** one of a series of brass coins in twopence, penny, and halfpenny denominations issued in 1722–23 for use in America that bear on the reverse a rose and an inscription containing the words *Rosa Americana*

ro·sace \(')rō¦zās, rō'zäs\ *n* -S [F, fr. MF, irreg. fr. *rose*, fr. L *rosa*] **:** a circular ornamental architectural member that is usu. a panel enclosing a richly sculptured rosette

ro·sa·cea \rō'zāshēə\ *n* -S [NL, fem. of *rosaceus* rose-colored, fr. L, made of roses, fr. *rosa* rose + *-aceus* -aceous] **:** ACNE ROSACEA

ro·sa·ce·ae \-āsē,ē\ *n pl, cap* [NL, fr. *Rosa*, type genus + *-aceae*] **:** a large family of nearly cosmopolitan trees, shrubs, and herbs (order Rosales) having alternate usu. stipulate leaves, 5-petaled regular flowers with numerous stamens, and dry fruits sometimes on pulpy receptacles — see AMYGDALACEAE

ro·sa·ceous \(')rō¦zāshəs\ *adj* [NL *Rosaceae* + E *-ous*] **1 a :** of or relating to the Rosaceae **b :** of, relating to, or resembling a rose esp. in having a 5-petaled regular corolla **2** [NL *rosaceus* rose-colored] **:** of the color rose **:** ROSY

rosa-de-montana \,rōzədəmən·'tän(y)ə\ *n, pl* **rosa-de-montanas** [AmerSp *rosa de montaña*] **:** PINK VINE

rosaker *n* -S [alter. of earlier *rosealgar*, fr. ME *rosalgere*, fr. OPg *rosalgar*, fr. Ar *rahj al-ghār* powder of the mine] *obs* **:** REALGAR

ro·sa·les \rō'zā(,)lēz\ *n pl, cap* [NL, fr. *Rosa* + *-ales*] **:** an order of dicotyledonous plants having flowers with the petals separate or in some members of the family Leguminosae more or less united, a partly united calyx, epigynous or perigynous stamens, and one or more carpels

ro·sa·lia \rō'zālyə\ *n* -S [It, fr. *Rosalia* (feminine name); fr. the occurrence of *Rosalia* as the first word in an old song employing such repetition] **:** a melody in which a phrase or passage is successively repeated each time a step or half step higher

ro·sa·line \'rōzə,lēn\ *n* -S [prob. irreg. fr. *²rose*] **:** a lace with rose designs made by needlepoint or bobbin method

ro·sa·may \'rōzə,mā\ *n* -S [prob. irreg. fr. *²rose*] **:** AUSTRALIAN ROSEWOOD 2

ros·aniline \(')rōz+\ *n* [ISV *ros-* (fr. L *rosa* rose) + *aniline* — more at ROSE] **1 a** *or* **rosaniline base :** a white crystalline base $H_2N(CH_3)C_6H_3C(OH)(C_6H_4NH_2)_2$ that is the methyl derivative of pararosaniline and likewise is the parent compound of many triphenylmethane dyes — see DYE table I (under *Solvent Red 41*) **b :** FUCHSINE **2 :** any of a series of bases or dyes related to rosaniline and fuchsine

ro·sar·i·an \rō'za(a)rēən\ *n* -S [*²rose* + *-arian*] **:** a cultivator of roses **:** a rose fancier

¹ro·sa·rio \rō'zärē,ō, -'sä-\ *n* -S [perh. fr. *Rosario*, municipality in southern Luzon, Republic of the Philippines] **:** ARMY BROWN

²rosario \"\ *adj, usu cap* [fr. *Rosario*, city in east central Argentina] **:** of or from the city of Rosario, Argentina **:** of the kind or style prevalent in Rosario

ro·sar·i·um \rō'za(a)rēəm\ *n* -S [L] **:** a rose garden

ro·sa·ry \'rōz(ə)rē, -)ri\ *n* -ES [in sense 1, fr. ME *rosarie*, fr. L *rosarium* rose garden, fr. neut. of *rosarius* of roses, fr. *rosa* rose + *-arius* -ary; in other senses, fr. ML *rosarium* string of beads used in counting prayers, series of prayers, fr. L, rose garden — more at ROSE] **1 a :** a bed or bush of roses **b :** a place where roses grow **2 :** a string of beads used in counting prayers; *specif* **:** a string of beads by which the prayers of the Roman Catholic rosary are counted — compare CHAPLET **3 a** *often cap* **:** a form of devotion to the Virgin Mary in the Roman Catholic Church that consists of the recitation of usu. five decades of Ave Marias preceded each by a paternoster and ended with a gloria **b :** a devotional exercise among other religious groups marked by the use of beads ⟨a Buddhist ~⟩ **4** *med* **:** BEADING f

rosary 2

rosary pea *n* **1 :** INDIAN LICORICE **2 :** JEQUIRITY

rosary vine *n* **:** a prostrate or trailing vine (*Ceropegia woodii*) of the family Asclepiadaceae having dark green fleshy white-veined leaves and purplish flowers usu. in pairs on a long pedicel

ro·sa·site \'rōzə,sīt, -zə,zīt\ *n* -S [It, fr. *Rosas* mine, Sulcis, Sardinia, its locality + It *-ite*] **:** a mineral $(Cu,Zn)_2(OH)_2(CO_3)$ consisting of a basic carbonate of copper and zinc that is prob. a zincky malachite

ro·sa so·lis \,rōzə'sōləs\ *n, pl* **rosa solises** [NL, alter. (influenced by L *rosa* rose) of ML *ros solis* — more at ROSOLIO] **:** a cordial flavored with juice from the sundew or other herbs and spices

roscher·ite \'räshə,rīt, 'rōsh-\ *n* -S [G *roscherit*, fr. Walter *Roscher*, 20th cent. Ger. mineral collector) + G *-it* -ite] **:** a mineral $(Ca,Mn,Fe)_2Al(PO_4)_2(OH).2H_2O$ consisting of a hydrous basic phosphate of aluminum, manganese, calcium, and iron and occurring in dark brown monoclinic crystals

ros·ci·an \'räsh(ē)ən\ *adj, usu cap* [L *roscianus* of Roscius, fr. *Roscius* (Roman gentile name borne by several prominent persons including Quintus Roscius) + L *-anus* -an] **:** of, relating to, or skilled in acting

ros·cid \'räsəd\ *adj* [L *roscidus*, fr. *ror-, ros* dew — more at ROSEMARY] *archaic* **:** DEWY

ros·coe \'rä(,)skō\ *n* -S [prob. fr. the name *Roscoe*] *slang* **:** PISTOL

ros·coe·lite \'rä(,)skō,līt\ *n* -S [Sir Henry E. *Roscoe* †1915 Eng. chemist + E *-lite*] **:** a mineral approximately $K_2(Mg,Fe,V,Al)_4(Si,Al)_8O_{20}(OH)_4$ consisting of a brownish mica in minute scales that contains vanadium

ros·com·mon \(')rä¦skämən\ *adj, usu cap* [fr. *Roscommon*, county in north central Ireland] **:** of or from County Roscommon, Ireland **:** of the kind or style prevalent in County Roscommon

¹rose [ME *roos, rose*, fr. OE *rās*] *past of* RISE

²rose \'rōz\ *n* -S [ME, fr. OE, fr. L *rosa*, prob. fr. Gk *rhodon*, prob. of Iranian origin; akin to the source of Per *gul* rose; akin to OE *word*, a bush] **1 :** a plant or flower of the genus *Rosa* **2 :** something resembling a rose in form: as **a :** any of various heraldic representations of a rose that usu. have five petals opened wide with barbs between and stamens or seeds in a circular center and when blazoned proper the barbs vert and the seeds or and that are often used as a cadency mark representing the seventh son **b** (1) **:** the card of the mariner's compass (2) **:** COMPASS ROSE (3) **:** a chart showing true and magnetic courses (4) **:** a circular card with radiating lines used in other instruments **c :** a rosette esp. on a shoe **d** *or* **rose cut** (1) **:** a form in which diamonds and other gems are cut that usu. has a flat circular base and facets in two ranges rising to a point and is used esp. when the loss to the stone in cutting it as a brilliant would be too great — compare BRABANT ROSE, DOUBLE ROSE, DUTCH ROSE (2) **:** a gem (as a diamond) with a rose cut (3) **:** a diamond so small that it can be cut little if at all **e** (1) **:** a perforated nozzle for delivering water in fine jets (2) **:** ROSE BOX **f :** ROSE WINDOW **g** (1) **:** an often ornamental fixture supporting or encircling a gas pipe, electric-light wire, or other conduit (as where it passes through a ceiling or wall) — called also *rosette* (2) **:** a round plate designed for attaching to a door surface and for receiving the shank of a doorknob **3 a :** a perfume having an odor like that of roses **b :** a constituent of such a perfume consisting of rose oil or a formulated preparation with a similar odor **4 a :** a person and esp. a woman of great charm, excellence, or virtue **b :** a comfortable situation or an easily accomplished task ⟨it began to look as if things might be ~s, ~s all the way —J.P.O'Donnell⟩ **5 a :** a variable color averaging a moderate purplish red that is redder and paler than violine pink, magenta rose, average fuchsia rose, or average raspberry rose, redder and stronger than mallow, and bluer and paler than solferino **b :** the hue of health **:** a pink or ruddy flush — usu. used in pl. ⟨the ~s in her cheeks⟩ **c :** ERYSIPELAS **6 :** the decoration of the circular sound hole in the top of a lute or similar musical instrument sometimes serving as a trademark — **under the rose** *adv* (*or adj*) **:** in secret **:** in private

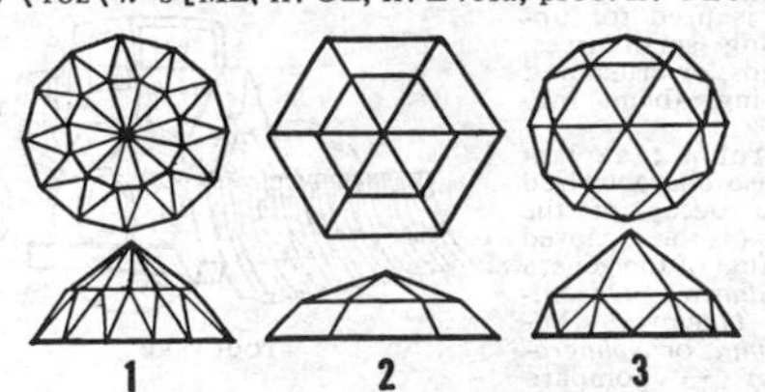

rose 2d(1): *1* rose recoupé, *2* brabant, *3* Dutch

³rose \"\ *vt* -ED/-ING/-S **:** to make of the color rose **:** FLUSH

⁴rose \"\ *adj* **1 a :** of or relating to a rose ⟨~ petal⟩ ⟨~ wreath⟩ **b :** bordered or overgrown with roses **:** used for roses ⟨a ~ arbor⟩ ⟨~ bower⟩ ⟨~ jar⟩ **c :** flavored, scented, or colored with or like roses ⟨~ bowl⟩ ⟨~ water⟩ **2 :** of the color rose — used esp. of gems ⟨~ opal⟩ ⟨~ topaz⟩ ⟨~ tourmaline⟩

⁵ro·sé \(')rō¦zā\ *n* -S [F, fr. *rosé*, adj., pink, fr. OF, fr. *rose*, n., rose, fr. L *rosa* — more at ²ROSE] **:** a table wine made from red grapes by removing the skins after fermentation has begun and thereby imparting a light pink rather than a red color to the wine — compare RED WINE, WHITE WINE

rose acacia *n* **:** BRISTLY LOCUST

ro·se·al \'rōzēəl\ *adj* [L *roseus* rosy (fr. *rosa* rose + *-eus* -eous) + E *-al*] *archaic* **:** resembling or suggesting a rose

rose alder *n* **:** an Australian shrub (*Duboisia myoporoides*) resembling the related pituri

rose aphid *n* **:** any of several plant lice that feed on the foliage of the rose; *esp* **:** a green and pinkish aphid (*Macrosiphum rosae*) that feeds chiefly on new shoots and buds

rose apple *n* **1 :** any of several tropical plants of the genus *Eugenia* or their fruits: as **a :** a tropical tree (*E. jambos*) with large thick leaves and pink flowers; *also* **:** its large edible fleshy fruit with a woolly surface and a roselike fragrance **b :** MALAY APPLE **c :** BRUSH CHERRY **d :** JAVA PLUM **2** *Austral* **:** BURDEKIN PLUM

rose ash *n* **:** a grayish red that is duller and slightly bluer than bois de rose and yellower and duller than appleblossom

ro·se·ate \'rōzēət, -ē,āt, *usu* \d·+V\ *adj* [L *roseus* rosy + E *-ate*] **1 a :** resembling a rose esp. in color **b :** overly optimistic or pleasing **:** viewed in or inclined to view in a favorable light ⟨the most fashionable variety of prewar liberalism was a hopeful and ~ internationalism —F.B.Millett⟩ **2** *archaic* **:** full of, consisting of, or made from roses — **ro·se·ate·ly** *adv*

roseate cockatoo *n* **:** GALAH 1

roseate spoonbill *n* **:** a spoonbill (*Ajaia ajaja*) found from the southern U. S. to Patagonia that has the head and throat bare and chiefly pink plumage

roseate tern *n* **:** a cosmopolitan tern (*Sterna dougalli*) having the breast roseate in the breeding season and when adult the tail deeply forked and the cap black, mantle pearl, and feet red

rose·bay \'rōz,bā\ *n* **1 :** OLEANDER **2 :** a plant of the genus *Rhododendron; esp* **:** BIG LAUREL **3** *or* **rosebay willow** *or* **rosebay willow herb :** FIREWEED b

rose beetle *n* **1 :** ROSE CHAFER **2 :** ROSE WEEVIL

rose beige *n* **:** a variable color averaging a light brown that is yellower and slightly duller than alesan, paler than cork, and yellower, less strong, and slightly darker than blush

rose bengal \(,)rōz+ *pronunc at* BENGAL\ *also* **rose ben·gale** \-gäl,-gəl\ *n, pl* **rose bengals** *often cap R&B* [prob. fr. F *rose bengale*, fr. *rose* (fr. L *rosa*) + *Bengale* Bengal, region of the Indian subcontinent — more at ROSE] **:** either of two bluish red acid dyes that are iodinated and chlorinated derivatives of fluorescein — see DYE table I (under *Acid Red 94*)

rose bisque *n* **:** ROSE HORTENSIA

rose bit *n* **:** a rose countersink or reamer

rose bloom *n* **:** FALSE BLOSSOM

rose blotch *n* **:** BLACK SPOT 1c

rose blush *n* **1 :** BLUSH 4a **2 :** a light reddish brown that is redder, lighter, and slightly stronger than copper tan and slightly darker than monkey skin

rose box *n* **:** a strainer for the end of the suction pipe of a pump

rose-breasted \'⸗¦⸗⸗\ *adj* **:** having the breast marked with rose

rose-breasted grosbeak *n* **:** a grosbeak (*Pheucticus ludovicianus*) found in eastern No. America that in the male is chiefly black and white with the breast and linings of the wings rose red and in the female is grayish brown streaked with paler tints with the lining of the wings orange

rose breath *n* **:** a pale to light pink

rose brown *n* **:** a variable color averaging a dark grayish red that is lighter and slightly bluer than average cordovan (sense 3b)

rosebud \'⸗,⸗\ *n* **1 :** the flower of a rose before it opens or when but partly open **2 :** a moderate to strong purplish pink

rosebud cherry *n* **:** a large shrub or small shrubby tree (*Prunus subhirtella*) that is native to Japan and is often cultivated as an ornamental for the sake of its rose-pink flowers borne on long slender often drooping branches

rosebush \'⸗,⸗\ *n* **1 :** a shrubby rose **2** *Austral* **:** a small timber tree (*Eupomatia laurina*) with soft coarse-grained yellowish brown wood

rose cake *n, obs* **:** rose petals pressed into a cake and used for perfume

rose campion *n* **1 :** MULLEIN PINK **2 :** CORN COCKLE

rose car·o·line \-'karə,līn, -,lən\ *n, often cap C* [perh. fr. the name *Caroline*] **:** a moderate yellowish pink that is yellower and less strong than coral pink and redder and duller than peach pink

rose car·thame \-,kär'täm\ *n, often cap C* [*carthame* fr. F, fr. NL *Carthamus*] **:** CARTHAMUS RED

rose cen·dre \-'sändr(ᵊ), -d(rə)\ *n* [*cendre* fr. F, ash, ashes, fr. L *ciner-, cinis* — more at INCINERATE] **:** a moderate yellowish pink that is paler and much yellower than coral pink and yellower and less strong than peach pink

rose chafer *n* **1** *also* **rose bug :** a common No. American melolonthid beetle (*Macrodactylus subspinosus*) whose larva feeds on plant roots and the adults on leaves and flowers of various plants (as rosebushes, fruit trees, or grapevines) **2 :** a common metallic green European scarabaeid beetle (*Cetonia aurata*) that feeds on plant roots as a larva and on leaves and flowers (as of roses) as an adult

rose-cheeked \'⸗¦⸗\ *adj* [*²rose* + *-cheeked*] having (such) cheeks (fr. *cheek* + *-ed*)] **:** having rose-colored cheeks

rose chestnut *n* **:** an East Indian timber tree (*Mesua ferrea*) that has very heavy hard wood used for railroad ties and flowers yielding a perfume

rose clover *n* **:** an Asiatic winter annual clover (*Trifolium hirtum*) introduced into the U.S. as a forage crop esp. on poor rangeland

rose cold *n* **:** ROSE FEVER

rose-colored \'⸗,⸗⸗\ *adj* **1 :** having a rose color **2 :** seeing or seen in a promising light **:** OPTIMISTIC ⟨delivers a final . . . talk, capping the *rose-colored* impression of life in this particular branch of the service —*Christian Science Monitor*⟩

rose-colored spectacles *or* **rose-colored glasses** *n pl* **:** optimistic eyes **:** favorably disposed opinions ⟨view the world through *rose-colored spectacles*⟩

rose-colored starling *or* **rose-colored pastor** *n* **:** a glossy black chiefly Asian bird (*Pastor sturnus* or *P. roseus*) of the family Sturnidae with a pink back and abdomen that is chiefly Asian though often appearing in flocks in Europe and sometimes in England

rose comb *n* [*²rose* + *comb*] **1 :** a flat rather broad comb of a domestic fowl that has the upper surface studded with small tubercles and terminates posteriorly in a fleshy spike — see COMB illustration **2 :** a disorder of mushrooms in which the caps are much distorted and which is prob. caused by chemical irritants (as oily sprays or heater fumes)

rose-comb \'⸗,⸗\ *also* **rose-combed** \'⸗¦kōmd\ *adj* [*rose-comb* fr. *rose comb; rose-combed* fr. *²rose* + *combed*] **:** having a rose comb

rose coral *n* **:** any of several corals (genus *Isophyllia*) similar to the brain corals but with deeply incised clefts which make them resemble full-blown roses

rose countersink *n* **:** a countersink with radial teeth on its conical end — see COUNTERSINK illustration

rose curculio *n* **:** a small bright red weevil (*Rhynchites bicolor*) with black snout and underside that is common on roses and produces larvae that feed on the seed pods

rose cut *n* **:** ROSE 2d(1)

rose-cut \'⸗,⸗\ *adj* [*rose cut*] *of a gem* **:** cut as a rose

rose cutter *n* **:** a milling cutter having a hemispherical end milling surface

rosed *adj* [fr. past part. of *³rose*] **:** tinged with rose

rose d'al·thaea \,rōz,dal'thēə\ *n, often cap A* [prob. fr. F] **:** a strong pink that is yellower and less strong than carnation rose, yellower and duller than coral (sense 3b), and yellower, lighter, and stronger than sea pink

rose daphne *n* **:** a low evergreen shrub (*Daphne cneorum*) with trailing pubescent branches and fragrant rose-pink flowers in sessile many-flowered heads

rose de nymphe \,rōzdə'nim(p)f, -nam-\ *n* [prob. fr. F] **:** a pale yellow that is slightly greener and darker than average ivory and duller than cream

rose du bar·ry \,rōzd(y)ü'barē\ *or* **rose pompadour** \'rōz + *pronunc at* POMPADOUR\ *n, usu cap B & P* [*rose du barry* prob. fr. F, fr. Marie Jeanne Bécu, Comtesse *du Barry* †1793 mistress of King Louis XV of France; *rose pompadour* prob. fr. F, fr. Jeanne Antoinette Poisson, Marquise de *Pompadour* †1764 mistress of King Louis XV of France] **:** an opaque pink ceramic overglaze color developed in France during the 18th century

rose diamond *n* **:** a diamond cut as a rose

rose do·rée \,rōzdə'rā\ *n* [*dorée* fr. F, fr. fem. of *doré* gilded, past part. of *dorer* to gild — more at DORÉ] **:** a deep pink to moderate red that is yellower and stronger than laurel pink and very slightly bluer and less strong than watermelon

rosedust \'⸗,⸗\ *n* **:** a grayish red to reddish brown

rose ear *n* **:** an ear (as of some dogs) that folds backward so as to display part of the inside

rose end *n* **:** the end of a potato or other tuber opposite the point of attachment

rose engine *n* **:** a machine or a lathe attachment for producing an eccentric relative movement between the rotating mandrel and a cutting point so as to form on the work (as paper currency) a variety of curved lines resembling a rosette — see ENGINE TURNING

rose family *n* **:** ROSACEAE

rose fever *n* **:** hay fever occurring in the spring or early summer — called also *rose cold*

rosefish \ˈ=,=\ *n* **:** a large marine food fish (*Sebastes marinus*) of the family Scorpaenidae found on the northern coasts of Europe and America that when mature is usu. bright rose red or orange red and when young, usu. mottled with red and dusky brown — called also *ocean perch*

rose–flowering locust \ˈ=,=(=)=-\ *n* **:** CLAMMY LOCUST

rose france \=ˈ=\ *n, often cap F* [*France*, country of west central Europe] **:** PEACH BLOOM

rose geranium *n* **:** any of several southern African herbs of the genus *Pelargonium* (esp. *P. graveolens*) grown for their fragrant 3- to 5-lobed leaves and small pink flowers

rose–geranium oil *n* **:** geranium oil esp. when obtained by distillation of leaves to which rose petals have been added

rose gold *n* **:** gold with a ruddy mat surface finish

rose gray *n* **1 :** ASHES OF ROSE 1 **2 :** a brownish gray that is slightly less strong than mouse gray and lighter than castor

rose gum *n* **:** a flooded gum (*Eucalyptus grandis*)

rosehead \ˈ=,=\ *n* **:** ROSE 2e(1)

rosehead nail *or* **roseheaded nail** *n* **:** a nail with a many-sided pyramidal head, used esp. as decoration in upholstery

rose her·mo·sa \,rōz(,)hərˈmōsə, -z,her-\ *n* [*hermosa* fr. Sp, fem. of *hermoso* beautiful, fr. L *formosus* — more at FORMOSITY] **:** a moderate pink that is yellower and darker than arbutus pink and deeper than chalk pink or hydrangea pink — called also *pink pearl*

rose·hill \ˈrōz,hil\ *or* **rose·hill·er** \-lə(r)\ *or* **rosehill parakeet** *n* [*rosehill* fr. *Rosehill*, district near Sydney, southeast Australia; *rosehiller* fr. *Rosehill* + E *-er; rosehill parakeet* fr. *Rosehill* + E *parakeet*] **:** ROSELLA

rose hip *or* **rose haw** *n* **:** HIP

rose hor·ten·sia \ˈ=,hȯ(r)ˈten(t)sēə, -nch(ē)ə\ *n, often cap H* [²*rose* + NL *Hortensia* (syn. of *Hydrangea*), fr. *Hortense* van Nassau, sister of Prince Charles Henri Nicolas Othon de Nassau-Siegen †1808 military adventurer who in French service accompanied Bougainville in his voyage around the world (1766–69) + NL *-ia*] **:** a light reddish brown that is redder, lighter, and slightly stronger than copper tan and lighter than monkey skin — called also *rose bisque*

ros·el \ˈräzəl\ *n* -s [ME *rosell, rosyle*, alter. of *rosin, rosine* rosin] *dial Eng* **:** RESIN

rose lake *n* **:** a dark reddish orange that is yellower and duller than average lacquer red and redder and darker than burnt sienna or ocher red

rose lashing *n* **:** a lashing made by passing the parts alternately over and under and finished by securing the hauling parts over the crossing — called also *rose seizing*

rose lathe *n* **:** a lathe provided with a rose engine

rose laurel *n* **1 :** OLEANDER **2 :** BIG LAUREL

roseleaf \ˈ=,=\ *n* **:** a moderate pink that is yellower and darker than arbutus pink and deeper than hydrangea pink

rose leafhopper *n* **:** a cicadellid bug (*Edwardsiana rosae*) native to Europe but now widespread in No. America that is a general plant feeder and is esp. injurious to roses and apples

rose lashing

rose·less \ˈrōzləs\ *adj* **:** lacking a rose

roselike \ˈ=,=\ *adj* **:** resembling a rose

ro·se·lite \ˈrōzə,līt\ *n* -s [Gustav *Rose* †1873 Ger. mineralogist + E *-lite*] **:** a mineral $(CaCoMg)_3(AsO_4)_2.2H_2O$ consisting of a rose-red arsenate of calcium, cobalt, and manganese in small triclinic crystals

ro·sel·la \rōˈzelə\ *n* -s [irreg. fr. *Rosehill*, district near Sydney, southeast Australia] **:** an Australian parrakeet (*Platycercus eximius*) often kept as a cage bird having the head and back of the neck scarlet and the cheeks white, the back dark green varied with lighter green, and the breast red and yellow; *broadly* **:** any parrakeet of the genus *Platycercus* **2** *Austral* **:** a sheep that has shed a portion of its wool

ro·selle \rōˈzel\ *also* **ro·sel·la** \-lə\ *or* **ro·zelle** \-l\ *n, pl* **roselles** *also* **rosellas** *or* **rozelles** [origin unknown] **1 :** an East Indian annual herb (*Hibiscus sabdariffa*) cultivated for its fleshy calyxes that are used for making tarts and jelly and an acid drink and for its bast fiber that is used as a substitute for hemp **2 :** the fiber from the roselle

ro·sel·lin·ia \,räsəˈlinēə, -äzə-\ *n, cap* [NL, fr. Ferdinando P. *Rosellini*, 19th cent. Ital. botanist + NL *-ia*] **:** a genus of fungi (family Xylariaceae) having smooth perithecia with dark one-celled ascospores

rose madder *n* **1 :** MADDER ROSE **2 :** a pale rose pigment made now usu. from alizarin and hydrated alumina — compare MADDER LAKE 2b

rose mahogany *n* **:** AUSTRALIAN ROSEWOOD 2

ro·se·ma·ling \ˈrōzə¦māliŋ\ *n* -s [Norw, fr. *rose* (fr. ON *rōs, rōsa*, fr. L *rosa*) + *maling* painting, fr. *male* to paint, fr. MLG *mālen*; akin to OHG *mālēn, mālōn* to paint, ON *mæla* to paint, Goth *meljan* to write, Gk *melas* black — more at ROSE, MULLET] **:** painted or carved decoration (as on furniture, walls, or wooden dinnerware) in Scandinavian peasant style that consists of colorful floral and other designs and inscriptions

rose mallow *n* **1 :** any of several plants of the genus *Hibiscus* with large rose-colored flowers; *esp* **:** a showy plant (*H. moscheutos*) of salt marshes of the eastern U.S. **2 :** HOLLYHOCK

rose malmaison *n* **:** MALMAISON ROSE

rose mandarin *n* **:** a twisted-stalk (*Streptopus roseus*) of eastern No. America with rosy purple flowers

rose ma·rie \,rōzməˈrē\ *n, often cap M* [prob. fr. the name *Marie*] **:** a deep pink that is bluer and lighter than average coral (sense 3b) and deeper than fiesta or begonia

rose·mary \ˈrōz,merē, -,mər-\ *n* -ES [ME, by folk etymology (influence of ME ²*rose* and of the name *Mary*) fr. *rosmarine*, fr. L *rosmarinus*, fr. *ror-, ros* dew + *marinus* of the sea; akin to Gk *exeran* to pour out, Skt *rasa* juice, ON *rās* race, course — more at RACE, MARINE] **1 :** a fragrant shrubby mint (*Rosmarinus officinalis*) of southern Europe and Asia Minor that has a warm pungent bitterish taste and is used as a culinary herb and in perfumery **2 :** COSTMARY

rosemary oil *n* **:** a pungent essential oil obtained from the flowering tops of rosemary and used chiefly in soaps, colognes, hair lotions, and pharmaceutical preparations

rosemary pine *n* **1 :** any of three common pines of the southeastern U.S. with fine-grained wood: **a :** LOBLOLLY PINE 1 **b :** LONGLEAF PINE **c :** SHORTLEAF PINE **2 :** lumber from a rosemary pine

rose mauve *n* **:** a variable color averaging a grayish purple that is redder and deeper than telegraph blue, mauve gray, or average orchid gray

rose midge *n* **:** a minute brownish gall midge (*Dasyneura rhodophaga*) whose larvae develop in the flower buds of roses

rose mildew *n* **:** a powdery mildew (*Sphaerotheca pannosa*) common on the foliage of cultivated roses

rose mill *n* **:** a milling cutter with a rounded cutting edge

rose mist *n* **:** a grayish to moderate pink

rose mon·tée \,rōzmänˈtā\ *n* [*montée* fr. F, fem. of *monté* mounted, set, past part. of *monter* to mount — more at MOUNT] **:** a doublet of paste

rose morn *n* **:** PEACH BLOOM

rose moss *n* **:** a portulaca (*Portulaca grandiflora*)

rose nail *n* **:** ROSEHEAD NAIL

ro·sen·ber·gia \,rōzᵊnˈbərgēə, -rjēə\ [NL, perh. fr. Caroline *Rosenberg* †1902 Dan. amateur botanist + NL *-ia*] *syn of* COBAEA

ro·sen·busch·ite \ˈrōzᵊn,bu̇,shīt\ *n* -s [Norw *rosenbuschit*, fr. Harry *Rosenbusch* †1914 Ger. geologist + Norw *-it* -ite] **:** a mineral $(Ca,Na)_3(Zr,Ti)Si_2O_8F$ consisting of a silicate and fluoride of zirconium, titanium, sodium, and calcium

rose ney·ron \,rōz,nāˈrōⁿ\ *n, often cap N* [*neyron* perh. fr. F, variety of grape] **:** a strong red to purplish red that is lighter and stronger than spinel red

rose nils·son \rōzˈnilsən *also* -lts-\ *n, often cap N* [perh. after Christine *Nilsson* †1921 Swed. soprano] **:** a deep pink that is bluer, lighter, and stronger than average coral (sense 3b) and bluer and deeper than fiesta or begonia

rose noble *n* [ME, fr. ²*rose* + *noble*, n.] **:** RYAL 1

rose nude *n* **:** a grayish yellowish pink to brownish pink

roseo- *comb form* [ISV, fr. L *roseus* rosy — more at ROSEAL] **:** specif. in names of rose-red coordination complexes (as of cobalt or chromium) containing five molecules of ammonia and one of water and also of analogous usu. yellow complexes of chromium ⟨*roseo*cobaltic chloride $[Co(H_2O)(NH_3)_5]Cl_3$⟩

rose of china *usu cap C* **:** CHINA ROSE 2

rose of heaven *n* **:** an annual herb (*Lychnis coeli-rosa*) of the Mediterranean region that is cultivated for its rose-purple flowers

rose of jer·i·cho \-ˈjerə,kō\ *usu cap J* [ME, fr. *Jericho*, ancient city in Palestine north of the Dead sea] **1 :** an Asiatic plant (*Anastatica hierochuntica*) that rolls up when dry and expands when moistened — called also *resurrection plant* **2 :** a xerophytic plant (*Odontospermum pygmaeum*) of the family Compositae with an involucre that closes firmly over the flower head when dry

rose of shar·on \-ˈsha(a)rən, -ˈsher-,-ˈshār-\ *n, usu cap S* [Plain of *Sharon*, coastal plain in western Palestine] **1 :** a showy flowering plant mentioned in the Bible and commonly considered to have been a tulip, narcissus, or meadow saffron **2 :** a Eurasian St.-John's-wort (*Hypericum calycinum*) often cultivated for its large yellow flowers **3 :** a commonly cultivated Asiatic shrub or small shrubby tree (*Hibiscus syriacus*) having mostly 3-lobed leaves and showy bell-shaped rose, purple, or white flowers

rose oil *n* **:** a fragrant essential oil obtained from roses and used chiefly in perfumery and in flavoring; *esp* **:** ATTAR OF ROSES

ro·se·o·la \rōˈzēələ\ *n* -s [NL, fr. L *roseus* rosy — more at ROSEAL] **1 :** a rose-colored eruption in spots; *specif* **:** RUBELLA **2** *or* **roseola in·fan·tum** \-ləinˈfantəm\ [NL *roseola infantum*, lit., roseola of infants] **:** a mild disease of infants and children characterized by fever lasting three days followed by an eruption of rose-colored spots — **ro·se·o·lar** \-lə(r)\ *adj*

rose parrakeet *n* **:** ROSELLA 1

rose pastor *or* **rose starling** *also* **rose ouzel** *n* **:** ROSE-COLORED STARLING

rose–petty \ˈ=,==\ *n* **:** ROBIN'S PLANTAIN

rose pink *n* [²*rose* + *pink*, n.] **1 :** an American centaury (*Sabbatia angularis*) **2 :** a variable color averaging a moderate pink that is bluer and deeper than hydrangea pink or arbutus pink and bluer, stronger, and slightly darker than chalk pink

rose–pink \ˈ=¦=\ *adj* [²*rose* + *pink*, adj.] **:** of the color rose pink

rose plum *n* **:** a variable color averaging a grayish purplish red that is bluer and paler than Aztec maroon and bluer and duller than tourmaline pink or daphne pink

rose pogonia *n* **:** SNAKEMOUTH

rose point *n* **:** needlepoint lace of Venetian origin made with rose designs in low relief connected by brides

rose purple *n* **:** a light reddish purple that is bluer and duller than crocus (sense 3b)

rose quartz *n* **:** a rose-red variety of quartz

rose reamer *n* **:** a straight reamer that cuts on its end only and is used esp. when considerable stock is to be removed

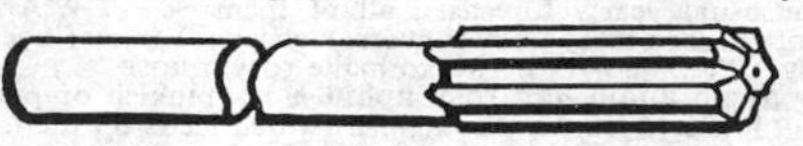

rose reamer

rose re·cou·pé \-rə¦kü¦pā\ *n* [*recoupé* fr. F, past part. of *recouper* to cut again, cut back — more at RECOUP] **:** a rose (as of a diamond or other gem) having 36 triangular facets — see ROSE illustration

rose–red \ˈ=¦=\ *adj* [ME *rose red*, fr. ²*rose* + *red*] **:** of the color rose red

rose red *n* [ME fr. *rose red* adj.] **:** a variable color averaging a deep red that is bluer, lighter, and stronger than cherry wine

rose–ringed \ˈ=¦=\ *adj* **:** having a red collar — used of the ring parrakeets

roseroot \ˈ=,=\ *n* **:** a perennial fleshy herb (*Sedum rosea*) whose roots have the odor of roses

rose rust *n* **1 :** any of several rusts that attack roses: as **a :** a rust of the genus *Phragmidium* **b :** a rust of the genus *Earlea* **2 :** disease caused by a rose rust

ros·ery \ˈrōz(ə)rē, -)ri\ *n* -ES [²*rose* + *-ery*] **:** ROSARY 1

rose ryal *n* **:** a 30-shilling gold piece bearing the ryal design issued by James I of England

roses *pl of* ROSE, *pres 3d sing of* ROSE

rosés *pl of* ROSÉ

rose sawfly *n* **:** a sawfly injurious to roses: as **a :** an adult rose slug **b :** a similar European sawfly (*Hylotoma rosarum*)

rose scale *n* **:** a scale (*Aulacaspis rosae*) that is injurious to roses

rose seizing *n* **:** ROSE LASHING

rose slug *n* **:** either of two slimy green larval sawflies that feed on the parenchyma of and skeletonize the leaves of rose-bushes: **a :** the bristly whitish green larva of a sawfly (*Cladius isomerus*) — called also *bristly rose slug* **b :** the velvety yellowish green larva of a sawfly (*Endelomyia aethiops*) that is native to Europe but now common in the eastern and central U. S.

rose soirée *n* **:** a deep pink that is bluer, lighter, and stronger than average coral (sense 3b), bluer and deeper than fiesta, and yellower and deeper than begonia

rose star *n* **:** a common usu. grayish shallow-water starfish (*Crossaster papposus*) of northern seas that is marked with two concentric rose-red bands

¹**ro·set** \(ˈ)rōˈzet\ *n* -s [ME, fr. MF *rosete, rosette*, lit., small rose, fr. OF — more at ROSETTE] **1** *obs* **:** a red color used by painters **2 :** BRAZIL 2

²**ros·et** \ˈräzət\ *n* -s [alter. of ME *rosin, rosine* rosin] *chiefly Scot* **:** RESIN

³**roset** \"\ *vt, Scot* **:** to rub with resin

rose·tan \ˈrōz,tan, -taa(ə)n\ *n* **:** PEARL BLUSH

rosetangle \ˈ=,==\ *n* **:** a red alga belonging to the Ceramiaceae or a related family — see CERAMIUM

rose taupe *n* **:** a variable color averaging a dark reddish gray that is stronger and slightly yellower and lighter than blue fox and yellower, lighter, and slightly stronger than average mauve taupe

rose tree *n* **:** TREE ROSE

ro·set·ta stone \rōˈze|d·ə-, |tə-\ *n, usu cap R* [*Rosetta stone*, stone found in 1799 that is celebrated for having furnished the first clue to the decipherment of Egyptian hieroglyphics since it bears an inscription in hieroglyphics, demotic characters, and Greek, fr. *Rosetta*, city in northern Egypt near which it was found] **:** something that furnishes the first clue to the decipherment of a previously incomprehensible system of ideas or state of affairs ⟨the book can be its own *Rosetta stone* and it is an interesting game to try to ferret out meanings by comparing passages till the puzzle is solved —Ellsworth Faris⟩

¹**ro·sette** \(ˈ)rōˈzet, *usu* -ed·+V\ *n* -s [F, lit., small rose, fr. OF *rosete, rosette*, fr. *rose* (fr. L *rosa*) + *-ete, -ette* -ette — more at ROSE] **1 :** a thin disk (as of copper) formed by chilling the surface of molten metal with water **2 :** an ornament resembling a rose usu. made of gathered or pleated material and worn as a badge of office, as evidence of having one of several decorations (as the Medal of Honor), or as trimming (as on a hat, shoe, or dress) **3 :** an ornamental disk consisting of leafage or a floral design usu. in relief used as a decorative motif — compare ROUNDEL **4 :** a structure or color marking on an animal suggestive of a rosette: as **a :** the group of five petal-shaped ambulacra on a spatangid or clypeastroid sea urchin **b :** one of the clusters of dark spots on the pelt of a leopard **5 :** a cluster of leaves developed in crowded circles or spirals from a crown either basally (as in a dandelion) or at the apex (as in many tropical palms) **6** *also* **rosette disease a** (1) **:** any of several plant diseases that are characterized by the grouping of the leaves in dense clusters and result from various causes (as the attack of fungi, virus infections, or nutritional disturbances) (2) **:** a symptom of rosette **b :** RHIZOCTONIA DISEASE **c :** a virus disease of the peanut characterized by yellowing of the leaves and extreme stunting **7 :** any of various fixtures: as **a :** ROSE 2g(1) **b :** an ornamental ring surrounding a cylinder lock **c :** an ornamental head for a screw used for fastening mirrors **d :** a ceiling device having terminals for connecting to an electric line and other terminals to which a drop cord may be attached **8 :** a small piece of boneless veal encircled by a bacon strip and skewered to be held flat for braising or frying **9 a :** an iron used with the handle of a timbale iron **b :** a pastry shell fried with a rosette

rosette 3

²**rosette** \"\ *vt* -ED/-ING/-S **1 :** to obtain in the form of rosettes by superficial chilling **2 :** to cause (the leaves of a plant) to form in dense clusters **3 :** to affect (a plant) with rosette

rosette plate *n* **:** one of the small perforated plates by which the zooecia of many marine bryozoans communicate

ro·sett·er \rōˈzed·ə(r)\ *n* -s **:** one that ties ribbon bows on candy boxes

rose water *n* [ME, fr. ²*rose* + *water*] **:** a watery solution of the odoriferous constituents of the rose made by distilling the fresh flowers with water or steam and used as a perfume

rosewater *also* **rosewatered** \ˈ=,==\ *adj* [*rosewater* fr. *rose water; rosewatered* fr. *rose water* + *-ed*] **1 :** scented with or having the odor of rose water **2 :** affectedly nice or delicate **:** SENTIMENTAL ⟨it will take more than a ~ biography to cover up his throttling of the press, rough treatment of critics, army domination —Hubert Herring⟩

rose water ointment *n* **:** COLD CREAM

rose weevil *n* **:** a weevil (*Pantomorus godmani*) that destroys the leaves and flowers of the rose and other plants and whose larva feeds on the roots — called also *rose beetle*

rose willow *n* **1 :** any of several willows with purple or reddish twigs; *esp.* **:** PURPLE WILLOW **2 :** SILKY CORNEL

rose window *n* **:** a circular window filled with tracery — called also *rose;* compare WHEEL WINDOW

rose wine *n* **:** a variable color averaging a grayish red that is bluer and deeper than appleblossom, bois de rose, or Pompeian red

rose window

rosewood \ˈ=,=\ *n* -s **1 a :** any of various tropical trees yielding valuable cabinet woods of a dark red or purplish color streaked and variegated with black: as (1) **:** BRAZILIAN ROSEWOOD (2) **:** HONDURAS ROSEWOOD — see AFRICAN ROSEWOOD, BLACKWOOD (3) **:** AMBOYNA **b :** the wood of a rosewood **2 a :** AUSTRALIAN ROSEWOOD **b :** a small Australian tree (*Heterodendron oleaefolium*) of the family Sapindaceae with very hard wood **c :** BASTARD ROSEWOOD **3 a :** a moderate reddish brown that is lighter and stronger than mahogany and yellower, lighter, and stronger than roan **b :** a light grayish reddish brown

rosewood brown *n* **:** a moderate reddish brown that is yellower and less strong than roan and yellower and paler than mahogany

rosewood oil *n* **1 :** RHODIUM OIL **2 :** BOIS DE ROSE OIL

rosewood tan *n* **:** a variable color averaging a light reddish brown to moderate reddish brown

rose worm *n* **:** the larva of a small brown tortricid moth (*Archips rosana*) that lives on the rose and various other plants, rolling up the leaves for a nest and devouring both the leaves and buds

rosewort \ˈ=,=\ *n* **:** ROSEROOT

ro·sha grass \ˈrōshə-\ *n* [*rosha* fr. Hindi *rūsā*] **:** any of several Asiatic grasses of the genus *Cymbopogon* that yield pleasantly scented oils (esp. *C. martinii*)

rosh ha·sha·nah *or* **rosh ha·sha·na** *also* **rosh ha·sho·noh** \,rōsh(h)əˈshōnə, ,rōsh-, ,räsh-, -ˈshōnə, -ˈshänə *also* ¦r . . . sh-, häshəˈnä\ *n, cap R&H* [Mishnaic Heb *rōsh hashshānāh*, lit., beginning of the year] **:** Jewish New Year **:** NEW YEAR 2

rosh ho·desh \=ˈkō,desh\ *or* **rosh chodesh** *n, usu cap R&H&C* [Heb *rōsh ḥōdhesh*, lit., beginning of the new moon] **:** the beginning of each month in the Jewish calendar marked by a special liturgy

ro·sic·ky·ite \rōˈzitskē,īt\ *n* -s [G *rosickýit*, fr. V. *Rosický*, 20th cent. Czechoslovak mineralogist + G *-it* -ite] **:** a mineral γ-S consisting of native sulfur in the gamma crystal form

rosi·cru·cian \,rōzəˈkrüshən, ,räz-\ *n* -s *usu cap, often attrib* [irreg. fr. NL Frater *Rosae Crucis* (latinization of the name of Christian *Rosenkreutz*, reputed 15th cent. founder of the secret Rosicrucian Society) + E *-an*] **1 :** one who claimed to belong to a secret society of philosophers in the 17th century and the early part of the 18th deeply versed in the secrets of nature **2 :** a member of one of several organizations held to be descended from the Rosicrucians and devoted to esoteric wisdom

rosi·cru·cian·ism \-shə,nizəm\ *n* -s *usu cap* **:** the principles, institutions, or practices of Rosicrucians

rosied *past of* ROSY

¹**rosier** *comparative of* ROSY

²**ro·sier** \ˈrōzhər, ˈrōzē(ə)r\ *n* -s [MF, rosebush, rose garden, fr. L *rosarium* rose garden — more at ROSARY] *archaic* **:** ROSEBUSH

ro·si·er·e·site \,rōzēˈerə,sīt\ *n* -s [F *rosiérésite*, fr. *Rosières*, copper mine near Carmaux, southern France + F *-ite*] **:** a mineral consisting of a hydrous aluminum phosphate containing lead and copper and occurring in yellow to brown stalactitic masses (sp. gr. 2.2)

rosies *pres part of* ROSY

rosiest *superlative of* ROSY

ro·silla \rōˈzilə, -ˈsilə, -ˈsē(y)ə\ *n* -s [AmerSp] **1 :** a sneezeweed (*Helenium puberulum*) of southern California **2 :** a shrub or small tree (*Eysenhardtia polystachya*) of the family Leguminosae of Arizona and adjacent Mexico with small white flowers in long racemes — see NEPHRITIC WOOD

ros·i·ly \ˈrōzəlē, -li\ *adv* **1 :** with a rosy color or tinge **2 :** CHEERFULLY, PLEASANTLY

¹**ros·in** \ˈräzᵊn *also* ˈrȯz-, *dial* ˈrōzəm\ *n* -s [ME *rosin, rosine*, modif. of MF *resine* resin] **:** a translucent pale yellow or amber to dark red or darker brittle friable resin that is obtained from the oleoresin or dead wood of pine trees by removal of the volatile turpentine or from tall oil by removal of the fatty acid components, that contains abietic acid and other resin acids as principal components, and that is used in the unmodified form, in modified form (as hydrogenated rosin or polymerized rosin), or in the form of a derivative (as a salt or ester) chiefly in making varnishes, lacquers, printing inks, driers, sizes for paper, and soaps, in adhesives, binding materials, soldering fluxes, and polishes, and for rosining bows for violins and other string instruments — called also *colophony;* see GUM ROSIN, WOOD ROSIN

²**rosin** \"\ *vt* **rosined; rosined; rosining** \-z(ᵊ)niŋ, *dial* -zəmiŋ\ **rosins** [ME *rosinen*, fr. *rosin, rosine*, n.] **1 :** to rub with rosin (as the bow of a violin) **2 :** to add rosin in some form to (as soap)

ros·i·nan·te \,räzᵊnˈantē, ,rȯz-\ *n* -s [after *Rocinante*, Don Quixote's bony horse in the novel *Don Quixote* by Miguel de Cervantes Saavedra †1616 Span. novelist] **:** a broken-down horse **:** NAG

ros·in·ate \ˈräzᵊnət, -ᵊn,āt *also* ˈrōz-\ *n* -s [¹*rosin* + *-ate*] **:** a salt or ester or mixture of salts and esters prepared from rosin **:** RESINATE ⟨copper ~⟩

rosinback \ˈ==,=\ *n* **:** a circus horse with a broad level back ridden by bareback riders and acrobats

rosin brush *n* **:** GREASEWOOD

rosin cerate *n* **:** BASILICON OINTMENT

ros·i·ness \ˈrōzēnə̇s, -zin-\ *n* -ES **:** the quality or state of being rosy: **a :** a rosy color or complexion **b :** a cheerful appearance or outlook ⟨there is a kind of musical-comedy bounce and ~ about the good-natured score —Douglas Watt⟩

rosin ester *n* **:** an ester or mixture of esters of the acid components of rosin; *esp* **:** ESTER GUM

rosing *pres part of* ROSE

rosin oil *n* **:** an oily liquid obtained by destructive distillation of rosin and composed principally of hydrocarbons with some resin acids; *esp* **:** the viscous fraction that boils higher than rosin spirit, that when crude is dark-colored and fluorescent and has a sharp odor, and that is used chiefly in making lubricating greases and printing inks, in impregnating paper coverings for electric cables, and in compounding with other oils

ros·in·ous \ˈräzᵊnəs *also* ˈrōz-\ *adj* **:** containing or resembling rosin

rosin plant *n* **:** ROSINWEED

rosin rose *n* **:** KLAMATH WEED

rosin soap *n* **1** *or* **rosined soap :** soap (as yellow soap) made from rosin as well as fat **2 a :** a resin soap made from rosin **b :** DISPROPORTIONATED ROSIN

rosin spirit *n, pl* **rosin spirits** *but sing or pl in constr* **:** a volatile liquid that is obtained as the first fraction in the destructive distillation of rosin, that has a sharp odor before refining, and that is used chiefly as a thinner for varnish and wood stains and as an adulterant of turpentine

rosinweed \ˈ==,=\ *n* **:** any of various American plants having resinous foliage or a resinous odor: as **a :** COMPASS PLANT a **b :** GUMWEED **c :** a golden aster (*Chrysopsis villosa*) of western No. America **d :** PRAIRIE DOCK 1

rosinwood \ˈ==,=\ *n* **:** ROSINWEED c

ros·iny \ˈräzᵊnē *also* ˈrōz-\ *adj* **:** abounding in, resembling, or having the odor of rosin

ros·kopf \ˈrä,skäpf\ *n* -s *usu cap* [after G. F. *Roskopf* †1889 Swiss watchmaker] **:** a watch with a barrel whose diameter is greater than the radius of the watch

ros·lyn blue \ˈräzlən-\ *n, often cap R* [perh. fr. the name *Roslyn*] **:** MAZARINE BLUE

rosmarine *n* -s [ME — more at ROSEMARY] *obs* **:** ROSEMARY

¹**ros·mini·an** \(ˈ)räzˈminēən, -mēn-\ *adj, usu cap* [ISV *rosmini-* (fr. Antonio *Rosmini*-Serbati †1855 Ital. philosopher and founder of the Institute of Charity) + *-an*, adj. suffix] **:** of or relating to Antonio Rosmini-Serbati or his doctrines

²**rosminian** \"\ *n* -s *usu cap* [ISV *rosmini-* (fr. Antonio *Rosmini*-Serbati) + *-an*, n. suffix] **1 :** an adherent of Rosminianism **2 :** a member of the congregation of the Institute of Charity of the Roman Catholic Church

ros·mini·an·ism \-ēə,nizəm\ *n* -s *usu cap* **:** the philosophy of the Rosminian teaching that the idea of being is innate and that through it true knowledge is made possible

ro·solic acid \(ˈ)rōˈzälik-, -zōlik-\ *n* [*rosolic* fr. G *rosol-* (in *rosolsäure* rosolic acid) (fr. *ros-* — fr. L *rosa* rose — + *-ol-* — fr. L *oleum* oil) + E *-ic* — more at ROSE, OIL] **:** either of two phenolic quinonoid derivatives of triphenylmethane: **a :** a crystalline compound that is red by transmitted light, that is made usu. from a mixture of phenol and *ortho*-cresol or from rosaniline, and that differs from aurin in containing one or possibly two methyl groups — called also *coralline* **b :** AURIN

ro·so·lio *also* **ro·so·glio** \rōˈzōlē,ō, -ōl(,)yō\ *n* -s [It *rosolio*, prob. fr. ML *ros solis* sundew, fr. L *ros* dew + *solis*, gen. of *sol* sun — more at ROSEMARY, SOLAR] **:** a cordial made from spirits and sugar flavored variously (as with petals of roses, orange blossom water, cinnamon, or cloves)

ro·so·lite \ˈrōzə,līt\ *n* -s [²*rose* + *-o-* + *-lite*] **:** a pink variety of garnet

ro·so·ri·al \rōˈzōrēəl, -ˈsō-\ *adj* [NL *Rosores* (syn. of *Rodentia*) (fr. LL, pl. of *rosor* gnawer, fr. L *rosus* — past part. of *rodere* to gnaw — + *-or*) + E *-ial* — more at RAT] **:** of or relating to the rodents **:** GNAWING

¹**ross** \ˈrȯs *also* ˈräs\ *n* -ES [origin unknown] **:** the rough often scaly exterior of bark

²**ross** \"\ *vt* -ED/-ING/-ES **:** to remove the ross from

ross·er \-sə(r)\ *n* -s **:** one that rosses: **a :** a logger who peels the bark and smooths the wood on one side of logs so they can be dragged more easily — called also *barker, scalper, slipper* **b :** one who peels bark from pulpwood to save wood that would be wasted if peeling were done by machine **c :** PEELER 1b **d** (1) **:** an attachment for a circular saw to remove scaly and gritty bark ahead of the kerf (2) **:** a machine for removing bark from pulpwood

rossi–forel scale *n, usu cap R&F* \ˌrō|sēfəˈrel-, ˌrä|\ [after Michele Stefano De *Rossi* †1898 Ital. geologist and François Alphonse *Forel* †1912 Swiss naturalist] **:** an arbitrary numerical scale of intensity of seismic disturbances ranging from one for a barely perceptible tremor to 10 for an earthquake of the highest intensity

ross·ite \ˈrȯ,sīt\ *n* -s [Clarence S. *Ross* b1880 Am. geologist + E *-ite*] **:** a rare mineral $CaV_2O_6·4H_2O$ consisting of a hydrous calcium vanadate

ros·so an·ti·co \ˌrō(,)sō,anˈtē(,)kō, ˌrȯ(-, ˌrä(-, -sō,än-\ *n* [It] **1 a :** a deep red Grecian marble used esp. by the ancient Romans **b :** a porphyritic diorite used esp. by the ancient Egyptians and Romans **2 :** a hard red unglazed Wedgwood stoneware resembling boccaro

ross's goose \ˌrȯ|sə̇z- *also* ˌrä|\ *n, usu cap R* [after Bernard R. *Ross* †1874 Irish fur trader] **:** a very small white goose (*Chen rossii*) that breeds in arctic America and migrates through western No. America

ross's gull *n, usu cap R* [after Sir James Clark *Ross* †1862 Scot. polar explorer] **:** a small rare gull (*Rhodostethia rosea*) of the far north having the tail wedge-shaped and the lower parts rosy when in full plumage

ross's seal *n, usu cap R* [after Sir James Clark *Ross*] **:** an antarctic seal (*Ommatophoca rossi*) having but two upper incisors, very small teeth, small claws on the forefeet, and none on the hind feet

rost *obs var of* ROAST

ros·tel·lar \(ˈ)räˈstelə(r)\ *adj* [*rostell*um + *-ar*] **:** of, relating to, or having the form of a rostellum

ros·tel·late \ˈrästə,lāt, (ˈ)räˈstelə̇t\ *adj* [prob. fr. (assumed) NL *rostellatus*, fr. NL *rostellum* + L *-atus* -ate] **:** having a rostellum

ros·tel·li·form \räˈstelə,fȯrm\ *adj* [*rostell*um + *-iform*] **:** shaped like a rostellum

ros·tel·lum \räˈsteləm\ *n* -s [NL, fr. L, small beak, small snout, dim. of *rostrum* beak — more at ROSTRUM] **1 a :** a small process resembling a beak **:** a diminutive rostrum **b :** the apex of the gynaecium of an orchid flower that resembles a beak **2 a** (1) **:** the sucking beak of a louse (2) **:** the beak of a hemipteran **b :** an anterior prolongation of the head of a tapeworm bearing hooks — see ECHINOCOCCUS illustration

¹**ros·ter** \ˈrästə(r) *sometimes* ˈrȯs- *or* ˈrōs-\ *n* -s [D *rooster* list, gridiron, fr. MD, gridiron, fr. *roosten* to roast + *-er*; fr. the parallel lines — more at ROAST] **1 :** a roll or list of officers or enlisted men; *esp* **:** a list which gives the order in which units or individuals are due to perform a prescribed duty ⟨guard ~⟩ **2 :** an itemized listing of a group or collection ⟨membership ~⟩ ⟨the season's ~ of new music by world-famous foreign masters —Virgil Thomson⟩

²**roster** \"\ *vt* -ED/-ING/-S **:** to list in a roster

ros·tock \ˈrä,stäk, ˈrȯ,stȯk\ *adj, usu cap* [fr. *Rostock*, city in northern Germany] **:** of or from the city of Rostock, Germany **:** of the kind or style prevalent in Rostock

ros·tov \rəˈstȯ|f, (ˈ)rä|s-, -tȯl, |v\ *adj, usu cap* [fr. *Rostov-on-Don*, city in the southeastern part of European Russia, U.S.S.R.] **:** of or from Rostov-on-Don, U.S.S.R. **:** of the kind or style prevalent in Rostov-on-Don

rostr- *or* **rostri-** *or* **rostro-** *comb form* [L *rostr-*, fr. *rostrum*] **1 :** beak **:** rostrum ⟨*rostr*ad⟩ ⟨*rostri*form⟩ **2 :** rostral and ⟨*rostro*lateral⟩

ros·trad \ˈrä,strad\ *adv* [*rostr-* + *-ad*] **:** toward a rostrum

¹**ros·tral** \-strəl\ *adj* [NL *rostralis*, fr. L *rostrum* beak, ship's beak + *-alis* -al] **1 :** of or relating to a rostrum; *specif* **:** of, relating to, or being a scale or plate bordering the median part of the upper lip in some reptiles **2 :** adorned with rostra ⟨~ pillar⟩ **3 a** *of a part of the spinal cord* **:** SUPERIOR **b** *of a part of the brain* **:** anterior or ventral — **ros·tral·ly** \-əlē\ *adv*

²**rostral** \"\ *n* -s **:** a rostral plate or shield

rostral column *n* **:** a memorial column commemorating esp. a naval victory

rostral crown *n* **:** NAVAL CROWN 1

ros·tralis \räˈstraləs, -strāl-,-strāl-\ *n* -ES [NL, fr. *rostralis*, adj., rostral] **:** the suctorial organ of a bug or related insect (order Hemiptera) consisting of the elongated and closely associated mandibles and maxillae

ros·trate \ˈrä,strāt, -ˌstrə̇t\ *adj* [L *rostratus*, fr. *rostrum* + *-atus* -ate] **:** having a rostrum

ros·trat·ed \-,strād·ə̇d\ *adj* [*rostrate* + *-ed*] **1 :** ROSTRATE **2 :** ROSTRAL 2

¹**ros·tro·carinate** \ˌrä(,)strō+\ *adj* [*rostr-* + *carinate*] **:** of, relating to, or constituting a chipped flint artifact shaped somewhat like an eagle's beak and found in eastern England

²**rostrocarinate** \"\ *n* -s **:** a rostrocarinate artifact

ros·tru·lar \ˈrästrələ(r)\ *adj* [*rostrul*um + *-ar*] **:** of or relating to a rostrulum

ros·tru·lum \-ləm\ *n, pl* **rostru·la** \-lə\ [NL, fr. L *rostrum* beak + *-ulum*] **:** a small rostrum; *specif* **:** the proboscis of a flea

ros·trum \ˈrästrəm *sometimes* ˈrȯs-\ *n, pl* **rostrums** \-trəmz\ *or* **ros·tra** \-trə\ [L *rostrum* muzzle, beak, ship's beak, & L *Rostra* (fr. pl. of *rostrum*) platform for speakers in the Forum of ancient Rome decorated with the beaks of ships captured in war, fr. *rodere* to gnaw — more at RAT] **1 a** *usu rostra pl but sing in constr* **:** any of various ancient Roman platforms for public orators **b :** a stage for public speaking **:** a pulpit or platform occupied by an orator or public speaker **c :** a raised platform; *specif* **:** one upon the stage of a theater usu. with a removable top and hinged sides for flat storage and often reached by stairs or a ramp **2 :** the curved often ornamental end of a ship's prow; *esp* **:** the beak or ram of a war galley — compare ACROTERION **3 :** a part suggesting a bird's bill: as **a :** the beak, snout, or proboscis of any of various insects and arachnids **b :** the often spinelike anterior median prolongation of the carapace of a crustacean (as a lobster) **c :** the snout of a gastropod mollusk when nonretractile **d :** the grooved extension of any of many gastropod shells protecting the siphon **e :** GUARD 7c **f :** the interior median spine of the body of the basisphenoid bone articulating with the vomer **g :** the reflected anterior portion of the corpus callosum below the genu **h :** a differentiated scale forming the snout of snakes **i :** the anterior projecting element in the chondrocranium of elasmobranch fishes **4 a :** process or prolongation resembling a beak; *specif* **:** one of the inner segments of the corolla of a milkweed

rosu·late \ˈrōzələt, ˈräz-\ *adj* [LL *rosula* small rose (fr. L *rosa* rose + *-ula*) + E -ate — more at ROSE] **:** arranged in the form of a rosette or in rosettes

¹**rosy** \ˈrōzē, -zi\ *adj* -ER/-EST [ME, fr. ²*rose* + *-y*] **1 a** (1) **:** of the color rose (2) **:** having a rose-colored complexion **:** HEALTHY, BLOOMING (3) **:** suffused with blushes **:** BLUSHING **b :** perfumed with or as if with roses **c** *obs* **:** abounding in or adorned with roses **2 :** characterized by or tending to promote optimism ⟨the individual episodes are uneven in quality, but all are enveloped in a ~ romanticism —John Barkham⟩ ⟨the ~ era when men thought physical science would soon make Earth so pleasant that Heaven would no longer be desired —Webb Garrison⟩ ⟨big businessmen made their usual yearly forecasts, all of them ~ —T.W.Arnold⟩ — often used in combination ⟨*rosy*-cheeked⟩ ⟨*rosy*-fingered⟩

²**rosy** \"\ *vt* -ED/-ING/-ES **:** to make rosy **:** ROSE

rosy apple aphid *also* **rosy aphid** *n* **:** a pinkish or purplish plant louse (*Dysaphis plantaginea*) which feeds on the foliage and fruit of the apple and whose summer generations occur on plantain

rosy barb *n* **:** a small silvery green Indian cyprinid fish (*Barbus conchonius*) the male of which becomes flushed with rose during the breeding season and which is a favorite in tropical aquariums

rosy bush *n* **:** HARDHACK 1

rosy finch *n* **:** any of several finches of western No. America and eastern Asia constituting the genus *Leucosticte* and having chiefly brownish plumage suffused in the adult with rose or white on the upper tail coverts

rosy gull *n* **:** ROSS'S GULL

¹**rot** \ˈrät, *usu* -äd.+V\ *vb* **rotted; rotted; rotting; rots** [ME *roten, rotien*, fr. OE *rotian*; akin to OHG *rōzzēn* to rot, ON *rotna* to rot, L *rudus* rubble, broken stone — more at RUDE] *vi* **1 a :** to undergo natural decomposition **:** decay as a result of the action of bacteria or fungi ⟨causes the bones to ~⟩ ⟨*rotting* wood⟩ **b :** to become unsound or weak (as from extended use or chemical action) ⟨the rich silk damasks . . . were the first to ~ away —Sheila O'Callaghan⟩ ⟨ships *rotting* in the harbor⟩ ⟨*rotting* ice⟩ **2 a :** to go to ruin **:** DETERIORATE ⟨sent to die on some jungle island . . . or to ~ there month after month —Irwin Shaw⟩ ⟨~ in jail⟩ **b :** to become morally corrupt **:** DEGENERATE ⟨a civilization that *rotted* and disappeared⟩ **3 :** to suffer from rot — used esp. of a plant **4** *chiefly Brit* **:** to talk nonsense **:** JOKE ⟨I know I did, silly, but I was only *rotting* —*Strand Mag.*⟩ ~ *vt* **1 :** to cause to decompose ⟨the heavy rains *rotted* the wheat⟩ ⟨dampness had *rotted* spots of the plaster —Marcia Davenport⟩ **2 :** to affect (as sheep) with rot **3 :** to cause to deteriorate **:** CORRUPT ⟨infected with the same decay as had *rotted* other great civilizations of the past —F.H.Cramer⟩ **4 :** to expose (as flax) to a process of maceration for the purpose of separating the fiber **:** RET **5** *chiefly Brit* **:** to make fun of **:** TEASE ⟨all felt that the family was being *rotted* —John Galsworthy⟩ **syn** see DECAY

²**rot** \"\ *n* -s [ME, of Scand origin; akin to Icel *rot*; akin to ON *rotna* to rot] **1 a :** the process of rotting or state of being rotten **:** DECAY, PUTREFACTION ⟨the ~ begins as soon as the fish are killed⟩ **b :** something that is rotten or rotting ⟨the moist ferny odors, the ~ and ordure . . . filled their senses —Norman Mailer⟩ **2 a** *archaic* **:** a wasting putrescent disease in people ⟨then the ~ returns to thine own lips again —Shak.⟩ **b :** any of several parasitic diseases that chiefly attack sheep and are characterized by tissue necrosis and progressive emaciation; *specif* **:** LIVER ROT **3 a :** social or spiritual deterioration or corruption ⟨the creeping ~ of the society to which he belonged —*Times Lit. Supp.*⟩ **b :** confusion or disorder esp. in a government organization ⟨organize the affairs of . . . the little state and stop the financial ~ —Stephen Spender⟩ **4 :** breakdown or decay of plant tissues caused esp. by fungi or bacteria — see BITTER ROT, BLACK ROT, DRY ROT **5 :** NONSENSE ⟨talked ~ about getting on in the world —A.H. Hawkins⟩ — often used interjectionally to express disbelief or disgust **6 :** the falling of several cricket wickets in quick succession

rot *abbr* **1** rotary **2** rotating; rotation **3** rotten

¹**ro·ta** \ˈrōd·ə\ *n* -s [L, wheel — more at ROLL] **1** *chiefly Brit* **a :** a fixed order of rotation (as of persons or duties) **b :** a roll or list of persons **:** ROSTER **2** *usu cap* [ML, fr. L] **:** a tribunal of the Roman Catholic curia consisting of ten auditors exercising jurisdiction usu. of an appellate nature esp. in matrimonial cases appealed from diocesan courts **3 :** a round or other musical composition with frequent repeats or refrains

²**rota** \"\ *n* -s [ML — more at ROTE] **:** HURDY-GURDY

³**rota** *var of* ROTE

rotacism *var of* RHOTACISM

ro·tal \ˈrōd·ᵊl\ *adj* [LL *rotalis* wheeled, fr. L *rota* + *-alis* -al] **1 a :** of or relating to wheels **b :** of or relating to rotary motion **:** ROTARY **2** [NL *rotalis*, fr. LL] **:** of or relating to the Rota

ro·ta·la \rōˈtālə, -tälə\ *n, cap* [NL, irreg. fr. LL *rotalis*] **:** a genus of annual weedy herbs (family Lythraceae) with 4-angled stems, opposite or whorled leaves, and small, axillary, and mostly solitary flowers — see TOOTHCUP

ro·ta·lia \rōˈtālēə\ *n, cap* [NL, fr. LL *rotalis* + NL *-ia*] **:** a genus of foraminiferans having a finely perforated test with the segments in a turbinoid spiral and with septa composed of two lamellae between which are anastomosing canals — **ro·ta·li·an** \-lēən\ *adj or n* — **ro·ta·li·form** \-lə,fȯrm\ *or* **ro·ta·li·iform** \-lēə,fȯrm\ *adj*

ro·tame·ter \ˈrōd·ə,mēd·ə(r), rōˈtamə̇d·ə-\ *n* [L *rota* wheel + E *-meter*] **1 :** an instrument for measuring curved lines by running over them a small wheel connected with a recording dial — compare ODOMETER, OPISOMETER **2 :** a gage that consists of a graduated glass tube containing a free float for measuring the flow of a liquid or a gas

rotan *var of* RATTAN

ro·tar·i·an \rōˈterēən, -ta(a)r-, -tār-\ *n* -s *usu cap* [*Rotary* (*club*) + E *-an*] **:** a member of one of the major service clubs

ro·tar·i·an·ism \-ēə,nizəm\ *n* -s *usu cap* **:** the principles or practices of Rotarians

¹**ro·ta·ry** \ˈrōd·ərē, ˈrōtə-, -əri *sometimes* -ō,ter-\ *adj* [ML *rotarius*, fr. L *rota* wheel + *-arius* -ary — more at ROLL] **1 a :** of, relating to, or resembling a wheel turning on its axis ⟨~ blades⟩ **b :** resembling the motion of a rotating body ⟨~ motion⟩ ⟨~ movement⟩ — compare ROTATIONAL, ROTATORY **2 :** having an important part that turns on an axis ⟨~ cutter⟩ **3 :** characterized by rotation of persons ⟨employment . . . under a ~ hiring system —Stanley Levey⟩ **4 :** produced by or used in a rotary press ⟨~ gravure⟩ ⟨~ printing⟩ ⟨~ plates⟩

²**rotary** \"\ *n* -ES **1 :** a rotary machine: as **a :** ROTARY PRESS **b :** a rig for drilling a well by the rotary method **c :** a drill-pipe turntable and the mechanical assembly for supporting and rotating it **d** *or* **rotary converter :** SYNCHRONOUS CONVERTER **2** *also* **rotary intersection :** a road junction formed around a central more or less circular plot about which traffic moves in one direction only — called also *circle, traffic circle*

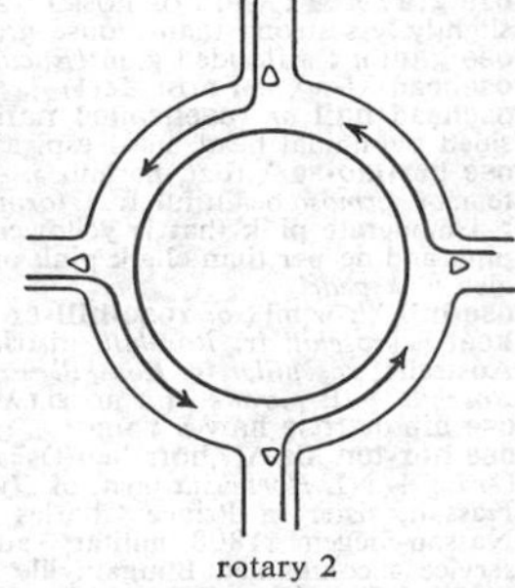

rotary 2

rotary beater *n* **:** a beater having single or double metal blades that rotate when a geared wheel with which they are meshed is operated by hand; *specif* **:** EGGBEATER

rotary blower *n* **:** a machine for producing artificial draft by centrifugal force of rotating vanes

rotary bridge crane *n* **:** a bridge crane that has one end of the beam or bridge pivoted and the other running on a circular track

rotary condenser *n* **:** SYNCHRONOUS CONDENSER

rotary cultivator *n* **:** a cultivator having blades or claws that revolve rapidly

rotary–cut \ˌ===ˈ=\ *adj* **:** spirally sliced from a log with a rotary lathe ⟨*rotary-cut* veneers⟩

rotary discard *n* **:** a discard from a suit in bridge or whist to denote strength in the suit next in rank (as the discard of a heart to show strength in spades)

rotary drill *n* **:** a rock drill that bores by a rotary action

rotary engine *n* **1 :** any of various engines (as a turbine) in which power is applied to vanes, disks having buckets, or similar parts constrained to move in a circular path **2 :** a radial engine in which the cylinders revolve about a stationary crankshaft

rotary fault *n* **:** a fracture in the earth's crust in which the displacement of rock is downward at one point and upward at another point along the strike — called also *pivotal fault*

rotary file *n* **:** a file of cylindrical or modified cylindrical form that is given a rotating rather than a reciprocating motion

rotary gap *or* **rotary spark gap** *n* **:** a spark gap in which one of the electrodes rotates thereby causing a regular change in gap length and timing the condenser discharge

rotary hoe *n* **:** an implement consisting essentially of a series of rotating hoe wheels each having many sharp curved steel prongs

rotary kiln *n* **:** a rotated cylinder lined with refractory and slightly inclined axially for manufacture of cement, gypsum plaster, and lime

rotary microtome *n* **:** a microtome in which the object to be cut moves vertically downward against the knife — compare SLIDING MICROTOME

rotary milling machine *n* **:** a milling machine having a rotary table and one or more cutters

rotary planer *n* **:** a machine for milling plane surfaces on large work by moving the work secured to the table of the machine past a revolving cutter

rotary plow *n* **1 :** a plow having a rotating propeller-shaped element for throwing snow aside **2 :** a rotary tiller **:** a plow with rapidly revolving blades or hooked fingers

rotary press *n* **:** a press in which paper carried by an impression cylinder is printed by rotation in contact with a curved printing surface attached to a plate cylinder or (as in photo-offset) a blanket cylinder — compare CYLINDER PRESS, PLATEN PRESS

rotary pump *n* **:** a valveless pump in which the fluid is positively pushed by meshing vanes on parallel revolving shafts and meshing screws into the discharge pipe

rotary reflection axis *n* **:** ROTOFLECTION AXIS

rotary shear *n* **1 :** a rotating bedplate of a lathe **2 rotary shears** *pl* **:** a machine having a pair of rotary overlapped cutter wheels for shearing sheet metal along a curved line

rotary table oven *n* **:** an oven comprising one or more horizontal circular tables on a vertical axis that turns so that work can be introduced at one radial position and removed at another after heat and rotation have completed the process

rotary transformer *n* **:** SYNCHRONOUS CONVERTER

rotary valve *n* **:** a valve acting by continuous or partial rotation

rotary–wing aircraft *n* **:** an aircraft supported in flight partially or wholly by rotating airfoils

ro·tat·able \ˈrō,tād·əbəl, -ātə-, =ˈ===\ *adj* **:** capable of being rotated — **ro·tat·ably** \-blē, -bli\ *adv*

¹**ro·tate** \ˈrō,tāt, *usu* -ād.+V\ *adj* [L *rota* wheel + E *-ate*] **:** having the parts flat and spreading or radiating like the spokes of a wheel ⟨~ blue flowers⟩

²**ro·tate** \ˈrō,tāt, *usu* -ād.+V; *chiefly Brit* =ˈ=\ *vb* -ED/-ING/-S [L *rotatus*, past part. of *rotare*, fr. *rota* wheel — more at ROLL] *vi* **1 :** to turn about an axis or a center **:** REVOLVE ⟨the magnetic drums ~ —Magnus Pyke⟩ ⟨a pivoted seat which can ~ in an arc of 180 degrees —*Scientific American*⟩ ⟨the earth ~*s* around the sun —Hugh Odishaw⟩; *specif* **:** to move in such a way that all particles follow circles with a common angular velocity about a common axis **2 :** to perform an act, function, or operation in turn **:** pass or alternate in a series ⟨the 17 judges who ~ through the court —Marjorie Rittwagen⟩ ⟨these typewriters ~ through all the classrooms —Naomi L. Engelsman⟩ ⟨*rotating* internships⟩ **3 a :** to move a joint with a circular motion in dancing **b :** to progress in a circular path around a central axis in dancing ~ *vt* **1 :** to cause to turn about an axis or a center **:** REVOLVE ⟨the crankshaft is *rotated* —Joseph Heitner⟩ ⟨asked the patient to ~ his eyes⟩ **2 :** to cause to grow in rotation **:** vary by rotational planting ⟨~ crops⟩ **3 :** to cause to pass or act in a series **:** ALTERNATE ⟨every food used was *rotated* . . . so that each food was repeated at a specified interval —H.J.Rinkel⟩ ⟨*rotated* the honor between them so that neither should feel hurt —Ernest Beaglehole⟩ **4 :** to exchange (individuals or units) with personnel more comfortably situated ⟨a buddy of his . . . was to be *rotated* home —E.J.Kahn⟩ **5 :** to move (a joint) with a circular motion in dancing

syn ROTATE and ALTERNATE mean to succeed or cause to succeed each other in turn. ROTATE may apply to two or more things and implies an indefinite repetition of an order of succession, usu. a predetermined order ⟨to *rotate* crops is to grow different crops on the same land in successive seasons in an order designed to maintain soil fertility⟩ ⟨workers may *rotate* in jobs when they periodically interchange jobs according to a predetermined scheme⟩ ⟨a repertory company of veteran actors who could rotate in the playing of starring, featured, and minor roles —*Current Biography*⟩ ALTERNATE may be used interchangeably with ROTATE ⟨workers may *alternate* in their jobs⟩ but in such use it usu. puts strong stress on the succession of one upon another rather than the interchange of all even though in a given order ⟨the three plots *alternate* in the representation —L.P.Goggin⟩ ⟨a large number of vertical fountains, which *alternate* in a series of sprays —*Amer. Guide Series: Mich.*⟩ More usu. ALTERNATE applies to only two things and generally does not put strong stress on repetition or continuity ⟨a region of rich and varied productivity, in which oil fields and cultivated lands *alternate* —*Encyc. Americana*⟩ **syn** see in addition TURN

ro·tat·ed \ˈrō,tād·əd, -ātəd\ *adj* [L *rota* wheel + E *-ate* + *-ed*] **:** ROTATE

ro·tat·ee \ˌrō,tād·ˈē, ==ˈ=; ˌrōd·əˈtē\ *n* -s [²*rotate* + *-ee*] **:** a member of the armed forces returned from combat or other arduous service because of length of stay or type of duty

rotating band *or* **rotating ring** *n* **:** a soft metal band around the lower part of a projectile to prevent the escape of gas and by fitting into the rifling to give the projectile its spin

rotating die head *n* **:** a device that revolves and chases threads on work held stationary in a machine

rotating internship *n* **:** a medical internship in which the intern works under supervision in several departments or services in succession ⟨had his *rotating internship* in medicine, surgery, obstetrics, and pediatrics⟩ — compare STRAIGHT INTERNSHIP

rotating-wing aircraft *n* **:** ROTARY-WING AIRCRAFT

ro·ta·tion \rōˈtāshən\ *n* -s [L *rotation-, rotatio*, fr. *rotatus* (past part. of *rotare* to rotate) + *-ion-, -io* -ion] **1 a :** the act of turning about an axis or a center ⟨the ~ of a shaft⟩ ⟨the ~ of the earth about the sun⟩ ⟨body ~ in slalom skiing⟩ — see DEXTROROTATION, LEVOROTATION, SPECIFIC ROTATION; compare OPTICAL ROTATION, POLARIZATION, REVOLUTION **b :** one complete turn **:** the angular displacement required to return a rotating body or figure to its original orientation — called also *revolution* **2 a :** return or succession in a series ⟨the ~ of the seasons⟩ ⟨retired by ~⟩ **b :** the action of placing in succession in a series ⟨the resolution provided for ~ of the chairmanship —Vera M. Dean⟩ **3 :** the growing of different crops in succession on one field usu. in regular sequence **4 :** the turning of a limb or other body part about its long axis as if on a pivot ⟨~ of the head to look over the shoulder⟩ **5 :** the time required or estimated to be required to bring timber crops to a specified state of maturity **6 :** the direction in which the turn to deal, bid, and play passes from player to player in a card game **7 :** the exchange of individuals or units with personnel more comfortably situated ⟨was due for ~ back home soon —Marcus Duffield⟩ **8** *also* **rotation pool :** fifteen-ball pool in which the object balls are played upon in numerical order

ro·ta·tion·al \(ˈ)=ˈtāshənᵊl, -shnəl\ *adj* **:** of, relating to, or characterized by rotation — **ro·ta·tion·al·ly** \-ᵊlē, -əl, \|ī\ *adv*

rotational fault *n* **:** ROTARY FAULT

rotational inertia *n* **:** MOMENT OF INERTIA 1

rotational loss *n* **:** the power or energy loss incurred by friction and windage as an object is revolved

rotational motion *n* **1 :** motion of rotation **2 :** VORTICAL MOTION

rotational quantum number *n* **:** a vector quantum number that determines the angular momentum of a molecule rotating about an axis through its center of mass

rotational specific heat *n* **:** the contribution made to the specific heat of a substance by change in mean energy of molecular rotation with change in temperature — compare VIBRATIONAL SPECIFIC HEAT

rotational spectrum *n* **:** the part of a molecular spectrum in which the bands arise from quantized changes in the energy of molecular rotation — compare VIBRATIONAL SPECTRUM

rotational vector *n* **:** a vector field whose curl is not zero

rotation axis *n* **:** a simple axis of symmetry in a crystal about which the whole crystal configuration is brought into coincidence with its original aspect by a rotation of one half, one third, one fourth, or one sixth of a turn about the axis

rotation crossing *n* **:** a system of breeding domestic animals in which the female offspring resulting from a cross between two breeds are bred to a sire of a third breed and the female offspring resulting from the second cross are then bred to a sire of one of the two breeds used in the original cross — compare CRISSCROSSING

rotation grazing *n* **:** the shifting of livestock to different units of a pasture or range in regular sequence to permit the recovery and growth of the pasture plants after grazing

rotation spectrum *n* **:** ROTATIONAL SPECTRUM

rotation twin *n* **:** a twin crystal in which the individuals are so related that one can be made to coincide with the other by a rotation of 180 degrees or occas. 60, 90, or 120 degrees — compare REFLECTION TWIN

ro·ta·tive \ˈrō,tād·iv, rōˈt-\ *adj* [L *rotatus* (past part. of *rotare* to rotate) + E *-ive*] **1 :** turning like a wheel **:** ROTARY, ROTATIONAL ⟨~ velocity⟩ **2 :** occurring in a regular series **:** characterized by rotation ⟨the ~ plan of the rectorship —A. L.Vogel⟩ **3 :** causing rotation — **ro·ta·tive·ly** \-d·əvlē\ *adv*

ro·ta·tor \ˈrō,tād·ə(r) -ātə-, *chiefly Brit* =ˈ==\ *n, pl* **rotators** \-ə(r)z\ *or* **ro·ta·to·res** \ˌrōd·əˈtōr(,)ēz, ,rōtə-, -ˈtòr-\ *see numbered senses* [NL, fr. L, one who rotates something, fr. *rotatus* (past part. of *rotare* to rotate) + *-or*] **1 :** a muscle that partially rotates a part on its axis; *specif* **:** any of several small muscles in the dorsal region of the spine arising from the upper and back part of a transverse process and inserted into the lamina of the vertebra above **2** *pl rotators* **:** a machine or a mechanical part that causes rotation: as **a :** the screw-shaped part of a ship's log that causes the log to rotate in the water **b :** a small fast electric motor specially adapted for rotating disks and Geissler tubes **c :** a device for rotating a television antenna

ro·ta·to·ria \ˌrōd·əˈtōrēə\ [NL, fr. neut. pl. of *rotatorius* rotatory] *syn of* ROTIFERA

¹**ro·ta·to·ri·an** \ˌ==ˈ==ən\ *adj* [NL *Rotatoria* + E *-an*, adj. suffix] **:** ROTIFERAL

²**rotatorian** \"\ *n* -s [NL *Rotatoria* + E *-an*, n. suffix] **:** ROTIFER

ro·ta·to·ry \ˈrōd·ə,tōrē, ˈrōtə-, -,tòr-, -ri\ *adj* [prob. fr. NL *rotatorius*, fr. L *rotatus* (past part. of *rotare* to rotate) + *-orius* -ory] **1 a :** of or relating to rotation **:** ROTARY ⟨~ motion⟩ **b :** producing rotation ⟨~ substances⟩ — compare DEXTROROTATORY, LEVOROTATORY **2 :** occurring in rotation ⟨become . . . wearied with the repetition of ~ acts —William Godwin⟩

rotatory dispersion *n* **:** the production of colors that results from passing white light through an optically active substance (as quartz) that causes the amount of optical rotation to vary with the wavelength

rotatory reflection axis *n* **:** ROTOFLECTION AXIS

rotch *or* **rotche** \ˈräch\ *n, pl* **rotch·es** [origin unknown] **:** DOVEKIE 2

¹**rote** \ˈrōt\ *also* **ro·ta** \ˈrōd·ə\ *or* **rot·ta** \ˈräd·ə\ *or* **rotte** \ˈrät\ *n* -s [*rote* fr. ME, fr. OF, of Gmc origin; akin to OHG *hruozza* crowd, prob. of Celt origin; akin to MIr *crott* harp; *rota, rotta, rotte* fr. ML *rota, rotta*, fr. OF *rote* — more at CROWD] **:** CRWTH

²**rote** \ˈrōt, *usu* -ōd·+V\ *n* -s [ME, rote, custom, perh. fr. L *rota* wheel — more at ROLL] **1 a :** the use of the memory usu. with little intelligence — usu. used in the phrase *by rote* ⟨an arrogant adolescent repeating by ~ —Harold Garfinkel⟩ **b :** something learned by memorizing ⟨the tongue in his mouth would have waggled strange ~ if they had encouraged him —Peggy Bennett⟩ **2 :** routine carried out without understanding of its meaning or purpose **:** mechanical repetition of a pattern ⟨bewildered by the entrance of science and technology into his realm where ~ had ruled so long —F.L.Paxson⟩ ⟨the champions of the liberal arts . . . have seemed content to live on ~ and reputation —A.W.Griswold⟩ ⟨unreasoning ~ learning⟩ ⟨only in the later Inca period do evidences of mass and ~ production begin to present themselves —John Collier b.1884⟩ ⟨copying their teachers by ~ —C.W.Shumaker⟩ ⟨we cannot guarantee loyalty . . . or patriotism by ~ or by oath —J.B. Oakes⟩

³**rote** \"\ *vt* -ED/-ING/-S *archaic* **:** to repeat by rote — **rot·er** \-ōd·ə(r), -ōtə-\ *n* -s

⁴**rote** \"\ *or* **rut** \ˈrət, *usu* -əd·+V\ *n* -s [perh. of Scand origin; akin to ON *rauta* to roar — more at ROUT] **:** the noise of the surf crashing on the shore

⁵**rote** \"\ *vi* -ED/-ING/-S [L *rotare* to rotate] *archaic* **:** to go out or change by rotation

ro·te·noid \ˈrōtᵊn,òid\ *n* -s [*rotenone* + *-oid*] **:** any of various compounds (as deguelin or toxicarol) related chemically to rotenone and usu. occurring with it

ro·te·none \ˈrōtᵊn,ōn\ *n* -s [ISV *roten-* (fr. Jap *roten* derris plant) + *-one*] **:** a crystalline pentacyclic compound $C_{23}H_{22}O_6$ that is related to isoflavone, found esp. in derris and cube roots, used in insecticides and in primitive fish and arrow poisons, and of low toxicity to warm-blooded animals

rot grass *n, dial Brit* **:** any of several marsh or bog plants believed to cause rot in sheep: as **a :** VELVET GRASS **b :** BUTTERWORT

rotgut \ˈ=,=\ *n, slang* **:** bad liquor

roth·er·ham \ˈrät͟hərəm\ *adj, usu cap* [fr. *Rotherham*, county borough in northern England] **:** of or from the county borough of Rotherham, England **:** of the kind or style prevalent in Rotherham

roth·lie·gen·de *or* **rot·lie·gen·de** \ˈrōt,lēgəndə\ *adj, usu cap* [obs. G *rothliegende* (now *rotliegende*), fr. obs. G *roth* red (now *rot*) (fr. OHG *rōt*) + G *liegende*, weak nom. sing. neut. of *liegend*, pres. part. of *liegen* to lie, fr. OHG *ligen*; fr. the red beds of sandstone near Eisenach, central Germany — more at RED, LIE] **:** of, relating to, or constituting a subdivision of the European Permian — see GEOLOGIC TIME table

roth·rock grama \ˈrä,thräk-, -,thrək-\ *n* [prob. after Joseph T. *Rothrock* †1922 Am. physician and botanist] **:** an erect perennial grass (*Bouteloua rothrockii*) with pectinately arranged spikelets

ro·ti·fer \ˈrōd·əfə(r), -ōtəf-\ *n* -s [NL *Rotifera*] **:** one of the Rotifera

ro·tif·era \rōˈtif(ə)rə\ *n pl, cap* [NL, fr. L *rota* wheel + *-i-* + *-fera* (neut. pl. of *-fer*) — more at ROLL] **:** a class of Aschelminthes comprising minute usu. microscopic but many-celled aquatic animals having the anterior end modified into a retractile disk bearing one or two circles of strong cilia that often give the appearance of rapidly revolving wheels — **ro·tif·er·al** \-)rəl\ *adj* — **ro·tif·er·an** \-)rən\ *n or adj* — **ro·tif·er·ous** \-)rəs\ *adj*

ro·ti·form \ˈrōd·ə,fòrm\ *adj* [NL *rotiformis*, fr. L *rota* wheel + *-iformis* -iform] **:** ROTATE

ro·tis·ser·ie \rōˈtisərē, -əri\ *n* -s [F *rôtisserie*, fr. MF *rostisserie*, fr. *rostiss-* (stem of *rostir* to roast) + *-erie* -ery — more at ROAST] **1 a :** a shop where meats are roasted and sold **b :** a restaurant that specializes in broiled and barbecued meats **2 :** a cooking appliance fitted with a spit on which food is rotated before or over a source of heat

rotl \ˈräd·ᵊl\ *n, pl* **rotls** \-ᵊlz\ *also* **ar·tal** \(ˈ)ärˈtal\ *or* **ar·tel** \-tel\ [Ar *raṭl, riṭl*] **:** any of various units of weight of Mediterranean and Near Eastern countries ranging from slightly less than one pound to more than six pounds

rotn *abbr* rotation

ro·to \ˈrōd·(,)ō, ˈrō(,)tō\ *n* -s [by shortening] **:** ROTOGRAVURE

roto- *comb form* [L *rota* wheel + E *-o-* — more at ROLL] **:** rotary ⟨*roto*spray⟩ ⟨*roto*-planer⟩

ro·to·beater \ˈrōd·(,)ō+,-\ *n* [*roto-* + *beater*] **:** a rotating beater with flails used to macerate potato vines and weeds before digging

ro·to·flec·tion axis \ˌrōd·ōˈflekshən-\ *n* [*rotoflection* fr. *roto-* + *flection*] **:** a compound symmetry element that requires identity of the structure and form of a crystal with its former configuration after a combination of rotation of 60, 90, 120, or 180 degrees with reflection across the plane normal to the axis

¹**ro·to·graph** \ˈrōd·ə,graf, -räf\ *n* [*roto-* + *-graph*] **:** a photographic white-on-black print (as of a manuscript or book) made directly on bromide paper by the use of a reversing prism without a negative

²**rotograph** \"\ *vt* -ED/-ING/-S **:** to make a rotograph of

ro·to·gra·vure \ˌrōd·əgrəˈvyů(ə)r, -ōtə-, -üə\ *n* [*roto-* + *gravure*] **1 a :** a photogravure process in which the impression is produced by a rotary press **b :** a print made by rotogravure **2 :** a section of a newspaper devoted to rotogravure pictures

ro·tome·ter \ˈrōd·ə,mēd·ə(r), rōˈtämәd-\ *n* [*roto-* + *-meter*] **:** ROTAMETER

ro·ton \ˈrō,tän\ *n* -s [L *rotare* to rotate + E *-on*] **:** one of the hypothetical energy quanta that are concerned along with phonons in the behavior of liquid helium II — compare SECOND SOUND

rotonda *var of* ROTUNDA

ro·tor \ˈrōd·ə(r), -ōtə-\ *n* -s [short for *rotator*] **1 :** a part that revolves in a stationary part: as **a :** the rotating member of an electrical machine **b :** the rotating wheel or group of wheels in a steam turbine — compare STATOR **2 :** a revolving vertical cylinder of a rotor ship **3 :** a complete system of rotating airfoils that supplies all or a major part of the lift supporting an aircraft ⟨the ~ of a helicopter⟩

rotor blade *n* **:** a blade in a rotor assembly

rotorcraft \ˈ==,=\ *n* **:** ROTARY-WING AIRCRAFT

rotor disk *n* **:** the plane circular area swept through by the blades of a helicopter rotor

rotor plane *n* **:** ROTARY-WING AIRCRAFT

rotor ship *n* **:** a ship propelled by the pressure and suction of the wind acting on one or more revolving vertical cylinders

ro·to·till \ˈrōd·ō,til\ *vt* [back-formation fr. *Rototiller*] **:** to stir with a rotary plow or a rotary tiller

Ro·to·till·er \-lə(r)\ *trademark* — used for a power-driven implement with a series of revolving blades or prongs that break up or pulverize the soil

rotproof \ˈ=,=\ *adj* **:** proof against damage by rot

rots *pres 3d sing of* ROT, *pl of* ROT

rot·se \ˈrätsə\ *n, pl* **rotse** *or* **rotses** *usu cap* **:** LOZI

rotta *or* **rotte** *var of* ROTE

rot·tan *also* **rot·ten** \ˈrätᵊn\ *n* -s [ME *rotten*, alter. of *ratoun* — more at RATTON] *chiefly dial* **:** RAT

rotted *past of* ROT

¹**rot·ten** \ˈrätᵊn\ *adj* -ER/-EST [ME *roten*, fr. ON *rotinn*; akin to OE *rotian* to rot — more at ROT] **1 a :** having rotted **:** DECAYED, PUTRID ⟨people who are dead and ~ in their graves —Mary Deasy⟩ ⟨a ~ tomato⟩ ⟨a little paint on a ~ house —Eric Linklater⟩ ⟨some granites are exceedingly ~ —K.A. Henderson⟩ ⟨~ ice⟩ **b** *obs* **:** characterized by rot ⟨the ~ diseases of the South —Shak.⟩ **2 a :** morally corrupt ⟨people . . . have become aware of something ~ in our democracy —Garrett Mattingly⟩ ⟨his heart . . . went ~ with vanity —Maurice Cranston⟩ **b :** very badly behaved **:** SPOILED ⟨a ~ child⟩ **3 a** *of a sheep* **:** affected with rot **b :** causing or characteristic of rot in sheep **4 :** extremely unpleasant **:** DISAGREEABLE ⟨a ~ day⟩ ⟨a ~ humor⟩ ⟨soldiering is a ~ job —J.O. Hannay⟩ ⟨it's ~ waiting for things —John Galsworthy⟩ **5 :** marked by weakness or unsoundness ⟨a commando group whose special operations are canceled one after another until the group goes ~ —Curtis Bradford⟩ **6 :** very uncomfortable (as from sickness or low spirits) ⟨caught a cold and felt ~⟩ ⟨was looking ~⟩ **7 :** marked by extremely poor quality **:** ABOMINABLE ⟨a ~ book⟩ ⟨paid $50 for ~ seats —Barnaby Conrad⟩ ⟨~ luck⟩ ⟨a ~ failure⟩ — **rot·ten·ly** \-ᵊnlē, -li\ *adv* — **rot·ten·ness** \-ᵊn(n)əs\ *n* -ES

²**rotten** \"\ *vb* -ED/-ING/-S *chiefly dial* **:** ROT

rotten borough *n* **:** an election district that has many fewer inhabitants than other election districts with the same voting power — compare POCKET BOROUGH

rotten–egg \ˌ==ˈ=\ *vt* [fr. the phrase *rotten egg*] **:** to throw rotten eggs at

rotten neck *n* **:** rice blast

rottenstone \ˈ==,=\ *n* **:** a friable siliceous stone that is the residue of siliceous limestone from which the calcareous matter has been removed by the action of natural waters

rotten stop *n* **:** a light temporary lashing put around a sail to hold it in a bundle while it is being hoisted

rot·ter \ˈräd·ə(r), -ätə-\ *n* -s **1 :** one that rots **2 :** an unprincipled, lazy, or weak person ⟨~s who will trip, gouge, beat, sneak, lie, cheat, and steal to win —*Emporia (Kans.) Gazette*⟩ ⟨a drunken ~⟩ ⟨the brave man's courage, the ~'s cowardice —Dixon Wecter⟩

rot·ter·dam \ˈräd·ə(r),dam, -ätə-, -,daa(ə)m\ *adj, usu cap* [fr. *Rotterdam*, city in the western Netherlands] **:** of or from the city of Rotterdam, Netherlands **:** of the kind or style prevalent in Rotterdam

rotting *pres part of* ROT

rott·lera \ˈrätlərə\ *n* -s [NL *Rottlera* (syn. of *Mallotus*), fr. Johann Peter *Rottler* †1836 Dan. missionary] **:** KAMALA 2

rott·ler·in \-lərən\ *n* -s [ISV *rottler-* (fr. NL *Rottlera*) + *-in*] **:** a salmon-colored crystalline phenolic ketone $C_{30}H_{28}O_8$ that is the active principle of kamala

rott·wei·ler \ˈrät,wī,lə(r)\ *n* [G, fr. *Rottweil*, city in southwest Germany + G *-er*] **1** *usu cap* **:** a German breed of tall vigorous black cattle dogs having short hair, tan or brown marking, a short tail, small drooping ears, and a pronounced stop **2** -s *often cap* **:** a dog of the Rottweiler breed

rot·u·la \ˈrächələ\ *n, pl* **rotulas** \-ləz\ *or* **rotu·lae** \-,lē\ [in sense 1, fr. ME, fr. ML, fr. L, little wheel; in other senses, fr. NL, fr. L — more at ROLL] **1 :** PATELLA 2a **2 :** one of the five radial pieces intervening between the alveoli and extending inward toward the esophagus in the Aristotle's lantern of a sea urchin **3 :** TROCHE — **rot·u·lar** \-ˌlə(r)\ *adj* — **ro·tu·li·an** \räˈtülēən, räˈtyü-, räˈchü-\ *adj*

rot·u·lad \ˈrächə,lad\ *adv* [*rotula* + *-ad*] **:** toward the patella

rot·u·let \ˈrächələt\ *n* -s [ML *rotulus* roll, register (fr. L, little wheel) + E *-et* — more at ROLL] **:** a small scroll or register

rot·u·li·form \ˈrächələ,fòrm, räˈtü-, räˈtyü-, räˈchü-\ *adj* [*rotula* + *-iform*] **1 :** ROTATE **2 :** PATELLIFORM

¹**ro·tund** \(ˈ)rōˈtənd\ *n* -s *archaic* [by shortening] **:** ROTUNDA

²**rotund** \"\ *adj* [L *rotundus* round — more at ROUND] **1 :** marked by roundness **:** ROUNDED ⟨no less smooth and ~ than the gorgeous melons and watermelons —George Santayana⟩ **2 :** marked by fullness **:** SONOROUS ⟨the ~ and reverberating phrase —Aldous Huxley⟩ ⟨a deep ~ voice⟩ **3 :** marked by plumpness **:** CHUBBY ⟨a ~ little man⟩ **syn** see FAT

ro·tun·da \rōˈtəndə\ *or* **ro·ton·da** \-tän-\ *n* -s [*rotunda* alter. (influenced by L *rotundus*) of *rotonda*, fr. It, fr. L *rotunda*, fem. of *rotundus* round] **1 :** a round building; *esp* **:** one that is round both outside and inside and is covered by a dome **2 a :** a large round room **b :** a large central area in a hotel or other public building **3 :** a round script black letter type design

Rotunda

rotunda 3

ro·tun·date \-ˈtəndət, -,dāt\ *adj* [L *rotundatus*, past part. of *rotundare* to make round, fr. *rotundus* round] **:** rounded at the end or corners

ro·tun·di·ty \-ndəd·ē, -ətē, -i\ *n* -ES [L *rotunditat-, rotunditas*, fr. *rotundus* round + *-itat-, -itas* -ity] **1 a :** the quality or state of being rotund **:** ROUNDNESS ⟨the thick ~ o' the world —Shak.⟩ **b :** a round mass or object ⟨laid his hand caressingly upon the consoling ~ of a five-gallon keg —Elinor Wylie⟩ **2 a :** rounded fullness of language ⟨scholars disputing . . . with leisured ~ of phrase —R.W.Southern⟩ **b :** a rotund phrase ⟨its adorable simplicities compensate even for its Johnsonian *rotundities* —H.J.Laski⟩ **3 a :** roundness of the body **:** PLUMPNESS ⟨a sparer diet had checked the movement towards ~ —John Buchan⟩ **b :** a rounded part of the body ⟨a cozy creased ~ between waistcoat and table —Clemence Dane⟩

ro·tund·ly *adv* **:** in a rotund manner

ro·tun·do \rōˈtən(,)dō\ *n* -s [by alter.] **:** ROTUNDA

ro·tu·ri·er \rōˈtůrē,ā, rō·ˈtyů-, F rōtüryā\ *n* -s [MF, fr. *roture* land tenure of a person not of noble birth, newly cleared land, action of breaking (fr. OF *routure* action of breaking, fr. L *ruptura* fracture, break) + *-ier* — more at RUPTURE] **1 :** a person not of noble birth; *specif* **:** a freeman holding land by payment of rent in money or kind without feudal duties and charges **2 :** a rich person of plebeian origin **:** NOUVEAU RICHE

ro·ty·len·chus \ˌrōd·ᵊlˈeŋkəs, ,räd-·\ *n, cap* [NL, prob. irreg. fr. *Tylenchus*] **:** a genus of plant-parasitic nematodes (family Tylenchidae) that attack plant roots and underground stems

rou·baix \(ˈ)rüˈbe, -bā\ *adj, usu cap* [fr. *Roubaix*, city of northern France] **:** of or from the city of Roubaix, France **:** of the kind or style prevalent in Roubaix

rouble *var of* RUBLE

rou·cou \(ˈ)rüˈkü\ *also* **ro·cou** \(ˈ)rōˈ-\ *n* -s [F, fr. Tupi *urucú*] **1 :** ANNATTO TREE **2 :** ANNATTO

roucouyenne *usu cap, var of* RUCUYEN

roué \(ˈ)rüˈā\ *n* -s [F, lit. broken on the wheel, fr. past part. of *rouer* to break on the wheel, fr. ML *rotare*, fr. L, to rotate; fr. the feeling that such a person deserved this punishment — more at ROTATE] **:** a man devoted to a life of sensual pleasure esp. in his relations with women **:** DEBAUCHEE, RAKE ⟨an elderly ~ . . . had invited her to call him Daddy —Jean Stafford⟩

¹**rou·en** \(ˈ)rüˈän, -äⁿ\ *adj, usu cap* [fr. *Rouen*, city of northern France] **:** of or from the city of Rouen, France **:** of the kind or style prevalent in Rouen

²**rouen** \"\ *n* [¹*rouen*] **1** *usu cap* **:** a breed of domestic ducks resembling Pekins in form and size and wild mallards in plumage coloring **2** -s *often cap* **:** a duck of the Rouen breed

³**rouen** \"\ *or* **rouen ware** *n* -s [¹*rouen*] **:** often ornate faience and soft paste porcelain produced at Rouen, France mostly in the 17th and 18th centuries

⁴**rou·en** \ˈrüən\ *dial Eng var of* ROWEN

¹**rouge** \ˈrüzh, *esp South sometimes* ˈrüj\ *n* -s [F, fr. MF, fr. *rouge* red, fr. L *rubeus* reddish; akin to L *ruber* red — more at RED] **1 :** any of various cosmetics that give a red coloring to the cheeks or lips ⟨didn't need any powder or lip ~ to make her pretty —Nora Caplan⟩ **2 a :** a red powder consisting essentially of ferric oxide and usu. prepared by calcining ferrous sulfate; *esp* **:** a comparatively light-colored form (as jewelers' rouge) used chiefly in polishing glass, metal, or gems and as a pigment — compare CROCUS 2a, IRON RED 1 **b :** any of various oxide or other materials (as black rouge or green rouge) used similarly ⟨white ~ . . . is made from pure alumina —*Materials & Methods*⟩ ⟨lampblack, known as satin ~, finds some use for polishing celluloid and bone —*Industrial Minerals & Rocks*⟩ **3 :** the red compartments in roulette when a bet is made on them ⟨played the ~ six times in a row⟩

²**rouge** \"\ *vb* -ED/-ING/-S *vt* **1 :** to apply rouge to (as the face or the cheeks) **2 :** to cause to blush **:** REDDEN ⟨lovely features, *rouged* by a hectic glow —Augusta Evans⟩ ~ *vi* **1 :** to use rouge **2 :** BLUSH ⟨you would have seen me ~ —Herbert Gold⟩

³**rouge** \"\ *adj* [F, fr. MF] **:** RED

⁴**rouge** \ˈrüj\ *n* -s [origin unknown] **1 a :** a scrimmage in the Eton and similar football games **b :** a one-point score in such football games made by the opponents when a defender touches the ball down behind his own goal line **2 :** CANADIAN FOOTBALL

rouge·berry \ˈ=- — *see* BERRY\ *also* **rouge plant** *n* [³*rouge*] **:** BLOODBERRY

rouge de cuiv·re \ˌrüzhdəˈkwēv(rə), -vr(ᵊ)\ *n* [F] **:** COPPER 5a

rouge de feu \-ˈfə\ *n* [F, fire red] **:** FLAME RED

rouge et noir \ˈrüzhāˈnwär\ *n* [F, lit., red and black] **:** a gambling game in which two rows of cards are dealt and designated as rouge and noir and the players may bet on which row will have a count nearer 31, on whether the first card of the winning row will be of the color for that row, or on whether it will not — called also *trente-et-quarante*

rouge flam·bé \ˌrüzh,flämˈbā\ *n* [F, fr. *rouge* red + *flambé* — more at FLAMBÉ] **:** mottled purplish red

rou·geot \rüˈzhō\ *n* -s [F, fr. *rouge* red] **:** a nonparasitic disease of the grape characterized by an arrested growth of the tips of shoots and a red discoloration of the leaves along the margin and between the main veins

rou·get cell \(ˈ)rüˈzhā-\ *n, usu cap R* [after Charles *Rouget* †1904 Fr. physiologist] **:** one of numerous branching cells adhering to the endothelium of capillaries and regarded as a contractile element in the capillary wall

rouge ve·ge·tal \ˈrüzh,vāzhāˈtal\ *n* [F *rouge végétal*, lit., vegetable red] **:** CARTHAMUS RED

¹**rough** \ˈrəf\ *adj* -ER/-EST [ME, fr. OE *rūh*; akin to OHG *rūh* rough, hairy, L *runcare* to weed, *ruga* wrinkle, Gk *orychein*, *oryssein* to dig, *orygē* act of digging, Skt *rūkṣa* rough, ON *rögg* tuft, shagginess — more at RUG] **1 a :** marked by inequalities (as rises and falls, ridges, protuberances, projections, breaks, or seams) on the surface **:** not smooth or plain **:** COARSE ⟨a ~ board⟩ ⟨~ stone⟩ ⟨a tunic of ~ serge —G.B. Shaw⟩ ⟨a ~ roadway made of cinders and slag —Louis Bromfield⟩ **b :** covered with hair, fleece, or bristles **:** SHAGGY, UNSHORN ⟨~ satyrs danced —John Milton⟩ ⟨a ~ hog⟩ ⟨~ sheep⟩ ⟨a face ~ with two days' beard⟩ **c** (1) **:** having a broken, uneven, or bumpy surface ⟨~ hilly country⟩ (2) **:** difficult to

travel over or penetrate : WILD ⟨~ country . . . covered with dense jungle⟩ **2 a :** marked by turbulence or storminess : TEMPESTUOUS ⟨the ~ waters of the channel⟩ ⟨~ winds⟩ ⟨~ weather⟩ ⟨a ~ voyage⟩ ⟨airsickness brought about by flight through ~ air —H.G.Armstrong⟩ **b** (1) **:** characterized by harshness or violence : unduly or offensively forceful ⟨a ~ breed of men⟩ ⟨~ usage⟩ ⟨used ~, abusive language to the umpire⟩ ⟨a very ~ society where men . . . violated the rights of others with impunity —W.P.Webb⟩ (2) **:** marked by struggle or difficulty : TRYING ⟨a ~ day⟩ ⟨a ~ assignment⟩ ⟨things are ~ all over —Hamilton Basso⟩ ⟨she had a bit of ~ going —*Fashion Digest*⟩ **3 a :** coarse, rugged, or unpolished in character or appearance : UNREFINED: as (1) **:** lacking smoothness of outline or form ⟨a ~ landscape⟩ (2) **:** harsh or rasping to the ear ⟨a radio emitting only ~ sounds⟩ (3) **:** harsh or sharp to the taste ⟨~ whiskey⟩ ⟨a ~ red wine⟩ (4) **:** poor in quality ⟨~ food⟩ ⟨~ clothes⟩ (5) **:** crude in style or expression ⟨~ rhymes⟩ (6) **:** INDELICATE ⟨a ~ anecdote for such an audience⟩ **b** (1) **:** marked by a lack of civility, refinement, or grace : UNCOUTH, PRIMITIVE ⟨~ farm workers⟩ ⟨~ hospitality⟩ (2) **:** crudely amiable : BLUFF ⟨the ~ kindness of . . . people —Harold Griffin⟩ **4 a :** marked by crudeness or lack of finish : UNPOLISHED ⟨~ leather⟩ ⟨~ rice⟩ ⟨a ~ performance⟩ ⟨sheets of ~ . . . plate glass —Ellis Humphreys⟩ **b :** prepared or executed hastily, tentatively, or imperfectly : MAKESHIFT, APPROXIMATE ⟨a ~ draft⟩ ⟨a ~ estimate⟩ ⟨~ data⟩ ⟨~ justice⟩ ⟨a ~ idea of how a machine operates⟩ ⟨a ~ wigwam fashioned of fir boughs —F.V.W.Mason⟩ **c :** qualified for only the cruder or simpler operations of a trade ⟨a ~ carpenter⟩ **d :** demanding mainly physical force rather than intellect ⟨~ work⟩ **5 a :** pronounced with aspiration ⟨a ~ vowel⟩ **b** *of a stop consonant in ancient Greek* **:** voiceless, aspirated, and fortis — compare MEDIAL 2b **6 :** relatively poor — used esp. of a poker hand (as in lowball) — compare SMOOTH **7 :** forming rough colonies usu. made up of organisms that form chains or filaments and tend to marked decrease in capsule formation and virulence — used of dissociated strains of bacteria; compare MUCOID

syn UNEVEN, RUGGED, HARSH, SCABROUS: ROUGH is a general term wide in its use. In its first meaning ROUGH simply indicates noticeable inequality of surface perceptible to touch ⟨a *rough* edge⟩ ⟨a *rough* stone⟩ From this the word has spread to indicate lack of regularity, modulation, and polish, with most but not all of its suggestions unpleasant ⟨the *rough* blow of sheer force —J.R.Green⟩ ⟨the people of Teutonic speech had their *rough* verse —H.O.Taylor⟩ ⟨*rough* and graceless would be such a greeting —R.W.Emerson⟩ UNEVEN in its first uses simply indicated lack of evenness ⟨an *uneven* road⟩ ⟨an *uneven* floor⟩ In later senses it often indicates lack of uniformity or consistency of treatment ⟨the book as a whole is an *uneven* achievement; for its writing ranges from the human and impassioned to the dully academic —David Hall⟩ In its first use in reference to land surfaces RUGGED applies to land made very irregular and difficult by a series of irregularities, of hills and gullies, mountains and gorges ⟨with much labor and puffing we drew ourselves up the *rugged* declivity —John Burroughs⟩ Used in relation to style of composition, it stresses lack of smoothness and easy fluency ⟨the most *rugged*-seeming of prose dialogue, the kind of dialogue that people sometimes praise as "simply a page torn from life" —C.E.Montague⟩ In other uses it may suggest robust strength and endurance ⟨I am not of a *rugged* constitution, and it irked me to be so feeble —C.B.Nordhoff & J.N.Hall⟩ ⟨the *rugged* countenance of the stoic Julia Shane —Louis Bromfield⟩ ⟨Litchfield was as *rugged* in its faith as the hills it nestled among —V.L.Parrington⟩ Orig. meaning unpleasant to the touch because of irregularity, HARSH has come to indicate that which is strongly unpleasant to any sense ⟨the cognac was *harsh* —Winifred Bambrick⟩ ⟨that cold unfeeling prison, with the *harsh* noise of the large key and the fetters —Anthony Trollope⟩ It is never complimentary. In other senses it applies to either that which may make one physically uncomfortable or that which may offend feelings of kindliness or justice ⟨the genial influence of summer commonly prevails over the *harsh* austerity of winter —J.G. Frazer⟩ ⟨could not recall a *harsh* word that had been uttered by Amelia. She had been all sweetness and kindness —W.M. Thackeray⟩ SCABROUS orig. simply indicated presence of raised protuberances, points, or dots and had no value judgments or implications ⟨the *scabrous* leaf of the slippery elm⟩ Possibly through an imagined relation with *scabby*, the word now has often the connotation of *encrusted* and may suggest the squalid or vile ⟨tiny, *scabrous* stone cottages with squealing pigs on the first floor —*Time*⟩ ⟨collects the scandals of the day; on these he is . . . a connoisseur who is consulted upon *scabrous* discoveries —Osbert Sitwell⟩ **syn** see in addition RUDE

[2]**rough** \"\ *n* -s [ME *ruhe, rouch,* fr. *ruhe, rough,* adj.] **1 a :** ground that is uneven and covered with high grass, brush, and stones ⟨an acre of ~ covered with . . . sumac —*Gardeners' Chronicle*⟩; *specif* **:** such ground bordering the fairway of a golf course and providing a poor lie for a golf ball ⟨the stretch of ~ for the next 15 . . . feet from the fairway is allowed to grow four or five inches high —R.T.Jones⟩ — compare FAIRWAY 3 **b** (1) **:** vegetative cover which has been undisturbed by fire or clearing (2) **:** the accumulation of underbrush, herbaceous growth, and litter characteristic of such cover **2 :** the harsh or disagreeable side or aspect of something : severe treatment ⟨learn to take the ~ with the smooth⟩ **3 a :** refuse material from mineral workings **b roughs** *pl* **:** coarse poor sands from tin dressing **4 :** something in a crude, unfinished, or preliminary state: as **a :** an uncut gem stone ⟨the huge piece of ~ was cut to a superb gem of 128 carats —*Jewelers' Circular-Keystone*⟩ **b :** broad outline : general terms — often used with *in* ⟨the question . . . has been discussed in ~ —*Manchester Guardian Weekly*⟩ **c :** a hasty preliminary drawing or layout made by an artist or designer ⟨has both ~*s* and finished work to show as samples —*Illustrator*⟩ **d :** ROUGH PROOF **e :** the state of tanned leather before it has been finished — compare CRUST 6 **5 :** a coarse uncivil person; *esp* **:** one who is disorderly or violent : ROWDY, TOUGH ⟨a gang of these ~*s* broke in —Alan Paton⟩ **6 :** a spike or calk inserted in a horseshoe to prevent the horse from slipping **7 :** the side of a tennis racket on which the binding strings form loops around the regular lengthwise strings at the top and at the throat end of the racket — **in the rough 1 :** in a crude, unfinished or uncultivated state : UNPOLISHED ⟨a diamond *in the rough*⟩ ⟨the boy will go far, but he's *in the rough* now —Agnes S. Turnbull⟩ **2 :** in the ordinary everyday state : under informal conditions ⟨you must take us *in the rough*⟩ ⟨eating fried chicken *in the rough*⟩

[3]**rough** \"\ *adv, often* -ER/-EST [[1]*rough*] **:** ROUGHLY ⟨ride ~⟩ ⟨the wood is ~ shaped —C.L.Walker⟩

[4]**rough** \"\ *vb* -ED/-ING/-S *vt* **1 a :** to make rough : ROUGHEN ⟨~ the edges of glass⟩ ⟨satin garments are very easily ~*ed* —C.B.Randall b.1901⟩ — often used with *up* ⟨a stiff breeze ~*ing* up the sea⟩ **b :** RUFFLE ⟨a bird ~*ing* his feathers⟩ **2 a :** to use physical force upon : MANHANDLE, BEAT ⟨not accustomed to being ~*ed* about —Angus Mowat⟩ — usu. used with *up* ⟨was ~*ed* up and pushed into the street —*Springfield (Mass.) Daily News*⟩ **b :** to subject (an opponent) to unnecessary and intentional violence in a sport (as football, soccer, or ice hockey) ⟨deliberately ~*ed* the . . . goalkeeper —*Newsweek*⟩ **3 a :** to calk or otherwise roughen (a horse's shoes) to prevent slipping — compare CALK **b** *chiefly Austral* **:** to break or train (a horse); *esp* **:** to partially break (a horse) that is later to be trained for some special use (as military service) — now usu. used with *off* **4 a :** to shape, make, or dress (something) in a rough or preliminary way ⟨~ the pieces of wood to approximately the size desired⟩ — often used with *down, off, out* ⟨~ down coarse iron⟩ ⟨~ off timber⟩ ⟨~ out lenses⟩ ⟨~ out disks and housings in the quantities . . . needed —*Aero Digest*⟩ **b :** to mark or indicate the outline or chief lines of — usu. used with *out,* sometimes with *in* ⟨~*ed* out the general structure —M.F.A.Montagu⟩ ⟨~*ing* out my preliminary ideas for this novel —Rex Ingamells⟩ ⟨~*ing* in the voice parts —Deems Taylor⟩ ~ *vi* **:** to subject a player to unnecessary violence in a sport ⟨sent off the field by the referee for ~*ing*⟩ — **rough it :** to endure hard or primitive living conditions : live without ordinary comforts ⟨*rough it* on a camping trip⟩

rough·age \-fij, -fēj\ *n* -s [[1]*rough* + *-age*] **1 :** coarse bulky food for domestic animals that is relatively high in fiber and low in digestible nutrients (as bran, hay, silage) : COARSE FODDER — opposed to *concentrate;* compare FODDER 2 **2 a :** food for humans with a considerable proportion of indigestible material that by its bulk stimulates the intestines to peristalsis **b :** the indigestible material taken in by humans as bulk; *esp* **:** CELLULOSE

rough alpine fern *n* **:** HOLLY FERN a

rough amaranth *n* **:** PIGWEED a

rough-and-ready \ˌ⸗⸗ˈ⸗⸗\ *adj* [[1]*rough*] **1** *of a thing* **:** lacking finish or polish but good enough for a temporary or limited purpose : MAKESHIFT, APPROXIMATE ⟨a *rough-and-ready* method⟩ ⟨a *rough-and-ready* estimate⟩ ⟨a *rough-and-ready* description of the development of feudalism —G.G.Coulton⟩ **2** *of a person* **:** lacking delicacy or refinement but forthright, vigorous, and roughly competent ⟨a *rough-and-ready,* loud-spoken man —Zane Grey⟩

[1]**rough-and-tumble** \ˌ⸗⸗ˈ⸗⸗\ *n* [prob. fr. [4]*rough*] **:** rough, disorderly, and hazardous fighting or struggling with much random knocking about and no holds barred : SCUFFLE, FREE-FOR-ALL ⟨could have handled him in a *rough-and-tumble* —Elmer Davis⟩ ⟨a *rough-and-tumble* among the boys in the playground⟩ ⟨the *rough-and-tumble* of frontier life⟩ ⟨the *rough-and-tumble* of politics⟩

[2]**rough-and-tumble** \"\ *adj* **1 :** marked by or suited for rough-and-tumble : roughly vigorous ⟨a good *rough-and-tumble* fight⟩ ⟨grew up in a *rough-and-tumble* atmosphere —E.J.Kahn⟩ ⟨stands up to *rough-and-tumble* wear —*N. Y. Times Mag.*⟩ **2 :** put together haphazardly : MAKESHIFT ⟨a *rough-and-tumble* fence⟩

rough-bark \ˈ⸗ˌ⸗\ *or* **rough-bark disease** *n* **1 :** any of several virus diseases of woody plants (as cherry, apple, citrus) characterized by generalized roughening and often longitudinal splitting of the bark **2 :** a disease of apples that is caused by a fungus (*Phomopsis mali*) and produces rough cankers on the twigs and branches **3 :** a nonparasitic disease of fruit trees (as apples and pears) characterized by a general roughening of the bark and not by local cankers

rough bedstraw *n* **:** a perennial bedstraw (*Galium asprellum*) of central and eastern No. America having stems branched below and rough with hooked bristles along the four angles

rough bent *or* **rough bent grass** *n* **:** a slender grass (*Agrostis scabra* or *A. hiemalis*) with widely spreading capillary panicles that is sometimes used for dried bouquets

rough bindweed *n* **:** a European smilax (*Smilax aspera*) the root of which yields a kind of sarsaparilla

rough bluegrass *or* **rough-stalked bluegrass** *n* **:** a European forage grass (*Poa trivialis*) naturalized in eastern No. America and having stems that are sometimes harsh below the panicle

rough breathing *n* [trans. of LL *spiritus asper*] **1 :** a mark ʽ used in Greek over some initial vowels or over ρ to show that they are aspirated (as in ὡς pronounced \ˈhōs\ or ῥήτωρ pronounced \ˈhrātōr\) **2 :** the sound indicated by a mark ʽ over a Greek vowel or ρ — called also *spiritus asper;* compare BREATHING 2, SMOOTH BREATHING

rough buttonweed *n* **:** BUTTONWEED 1

[1]**roughcast** \ˈ⸗ˌ⸗\ *n* [[3]*rough* + *cast,* past part. of *cast*] **1 :** the rudimentary unfinished form of something : rough model **2 :** a plastering made of lime mixed with shells or pebbles and used for covering buildings usu. by being thrown from a trowel forcibly against the wall **3 :** a rough surface finish (as of a wall made of plaster or concrete) : SPATTER DASH

[2]**roughcast** \"\ *vt* **1 :** to plaster (as a wall) with roughcast **2 :** to shape or form (something) roughly without polish, revision, or correction ⟨~ a clay model⟩ ⟨~ a poem⟩

rough cinquefoil *n* **:** a rough-hairy annual or biennial weed (*Potentilla norvegica*) with long-petioled usu. 3-foliolate leaves

rough coat *n* **:** the first coat (as of paint or plaster)

rough-coat \ˈ⸗ˌ⸗\ *vt* [*rough coat*] **:** to apply a rough coat of plaster to (a wall or lath)

rough comfrey *n* **:** PRICKLY COMFREY

rough diamond *n* **1 :** an uncut diamond **2 :** a person of exceptional qualities or abilities but lacking in social graces and refinement of manner : DIAMOND IN THE ROUGH

roughdraw \ˈ⸗ˌ⸗\ *vt* [[3]*rough* + *draw*] **:** to draw (a metal rod) into wire crudely or roughly

[1]**roughdry** \ˈ⸗ˌ⸗\ *vt* [[3]*rough* + *dry*] **:** to dry (laundry) without smoothing or ironing ⟨clothes *roughdried*⟩

[2]**roughdry** \ˈ⸗ˌ⸗\ *adj* **1 :** washed and dried but not ironed ⟨a basket of ~ laundry⟩ ⟨a pile of ~ clothes was on the bed —P.E.Green⟩ **2 :** of or relating to a laundry service in which washed articles are returned dry but not ironed ⟨has her laundry done ~⟩

roughed *past of* ROUGH

rough·en \ˈrəfən\ *vb* -ED/-ING/-S [[1]*rough* + *-en*] *vt* **:** to make (something) rough ⟨her hands were ~*ed* by work —Ellen Glasgow⟩ ~ *vi* **:** to become rough ⟨the terrain ~*s* somewhat as the watershed . . . is approached —*Amer. Guide Series: Texas*⟩

[1]**rougher** *comparative of* ROUGH

[2]**rough·er** \ˈrəfə(r)\ *n* -s [[4]*rough* + *-er*] **:** one that roughs or roughs out work: as **a :** a glass cutter that makes the first heavy incisions or grinds the edges to a rough finish **b :** one that guides heated steel bars, rods, or sheets through the roughing rolls repeatedly until steel is reduced to the desired gauge — called also *bulldogger* **c :** a poultry dresser that pulls out tail and wing feathers only

roughest *superlative of* ROUGH

rough fig *n* [[1]*rough*] *Austral* **:** PURPLE FIG

rough file *n* **:** a file of the grade having the coarsest cutting ridges

rough fish *n* **:** a fish that is neither a sport fish nor an important food for sport fishes — compare FORAGE FISH, TRASH FISH

rough-footed \ˈ⸗ˈ⸗⸗\ *adj* [ME *rouh foted,* fr. *rouh, rough* rough + *foted* footed] **:** having feathered feet ⟨the *rough-footed* eagles⟩

rough fox *n* **:** CRAB-EATING FOX

rough gentian *n* **:** SOAPWORT GENTIAN

rough-gilt \ˈ⸗ˈ⸗\ *adj* [[3]*rough* + *gilt,* past part. of *gild*] *of a book edge* **:** gilded before sewing ⟨a ~ book⟩

rough goldenrod *n* **:** a very common No. American rough-stemmed herb (*Solidago rugosa*) with scabrous foliage and yellow flowers in large secund panicles

rough grazing *n, Brit* **:** unimproved pasture or range

rough green snake *n* **:** a green snake (*Ophiodrys aestivus*) of the southern and eastern U.S. having strongly keeled light to dark green scales above and smooth pale yellow to yellowish white ventral plates — see SMOOTH GREEN SNAKE

rough hawkbit *n* **:** a rough-hairy European weed (*Leontodon nudicaulis*) with a rosette of basal leaves and a solitary long-stalked head of yellow flowers that is adventive in No. America

roughhearted \ˈ⸗ˈ⸗⸗\ *adj* [[1]*rough* + *hearted*] **:** lacking sympathy or benevolence : UNFEELING, CALLOUS, HARDHEARTED

roughhew \ˈ⸗ˈ⸗\ *vt* [[3]*rough* + *hew*] **1 :** to hew (as timber) coarsely without smoothing or finishing ⟨~ a statue out of a large block of marble⟩ **2 :** to give the first form or shape to : form crudely or roughly : ROUGHCAST ⟨~*s* his novels rapidly but then polishes them slowly over a long period⟩ ⟨a divinity that shapes our ends ~ them how we will —Shak.⟩

roughhewn \ˈ⸗ˈ⸗\ *adj* [[3]*rough* + *hewn*] **1 :** crudely shaped : left in a rough, unsmoothed, or unfinished state ⟨~ beams⟩ **2 :** lacking polish : UNCULTIVATED, PLAIN ⟨a ~ seaman —Francis Bacon⟩ ⟨he was rather attractive, in a ~ kind of way —Jan Speas⟩

rough horsetail *n* **:** a scouring rush (*Equisetum hyemale*)

[1]**rough·house** \ˈrəfˌhau̇s\ *n* [[1]*rough* + *house*] **:** an outbreak of violence or rough boisterous play esp. among occupants of a house or room ⟨the horseplay turned to a ~: snatching of trousers and smacks with the flat of hard hands, followed by clumsy steeplechases over the obstacles of beds —T.E. Lawrence⟩

[2]**rough·house** \"\ *also* -au̇z\ *vb* **roughhoused; roughhoused; roughhousing** \-au̇ziŋ *also* -au̇siŋ\ **roughhouses** \-au̇zəz *also* -au̇səz\ *vt* **1 :** to handle or deal with roughly often in a spirit of fun : MANHANDLE **2** ⟨intimidated and *roughhoused* their opponents⟩ ⟨young men engage in gymnastics and ~ each other —*Amer. Guide Series: N.Y.City*⟩ **2 :** to fondle (as a child) with playful roughness ⟨babies . . . tickled or *roughhoused* —Benjamin Spock⟩ ~ *vi* **:** to engage in roughhouse ⟨got to *roughhousing* in the rooms and nobody got any sleep —Henry La Cossitt⟩

[3]**rough·house** \-au̇s\ *adj* **:** of, relating to, or characterized by roughhouse ⟨~ tactics⟩

roughies *pl of* ROUGHY

rough in *vt* **:** to install in a building (the concealed part of the plumbing equipment)

roughing *n* -s [fr. gerund of [4]*rough*] **:** the act or process of removing (as by stippling or pebbling) a high finish on paper stock

roughing-in \ˈ⸗⸗ˈ⸗\ *n* -s [fr. gerund of [4]*rough*] **1 a :** the first coat of plaster (as on brick) **b :** the act or process of applying such a coat **2 :** the installation in a building of the part of the plumbing equipment that is concealed (as in walls or under floors)

roughing mill *n* **1 :** a set of roughing rolls **2 :** a revolving metal disk charged with an abrasive that is used in various processes (as the grinding of gems)

roughing rolls *n pl* **:** a series of rolls in which wrought metal is first given the form of a bar preparatory to being reheated and finished or through which an ingot of steel or other metal first passes in the rolling process

rough·ish \ˈrəfish\ *adj* [[1]*rough* + *-ish*] **:** somewhat rough ⟨two ~ . . . chaps —Arnold Bennett⟩ ⟨~ spots in a summer that glided by —Booth Tarkington⟩

rough leaf *n* **:** ARBUTUS 3

rough-leaf tree *n* **:** CHAPARRO 3

rough-leaved fig \ˈ⸗ˌ⸗-\ *n, Austral* **:** PURPLE FIG

rough-legged hawk \ˈ⸗ˌ⸗(⸗)-\ *or* **roughleg** \ˈ⸗ˌ⸗\ *n* **:** any of several large heavily built hawks of the genus *Buteo* (as the European *B. lagopus*) that are closely related to the true buzzards but have the tarsus feathered to the base of the toes, feed chiefly on rodents (as mice), and are beneficial to the farmer — see FERRUGINOUS ROUGHLEG

rough lemon *n* **1 :** a hybrid lemon with a large spreading thorny tree and rough-skinned nearly globular acid fruits that prob. originated in India but has become naturalized in tropical America and southern Africa and is important chiefly as rootstock for sweet and mandarin oranges and the grapefruit **2 :** the fruit of a rough lemon

rough lock *n* **1 :** a chain or rope fastened around the runner of a sled to retard its movement downhill **2 :** a chain tied around the rim of a rear wheel of a wagon and fastened to the wagon reach so that the skidding wheel will retard the movement of the wagon downhill

rough-lock \ˈ⸗ˌ⸗\ *vt* [*rough lock*] **:** to fasten a rough lock on ⟨*rough-locking* the wagon wheels, to keep the wagon from pushing the mules when we went down —J.H.Stuart⟩

rough lumber *n* **:** lumber that has not been dressed since it was sawed

rough·ly *adv* [ME *rohly,* fr. *roh, rough* rough + *-ly*] **:** in a rough manner: as **a :** with harshness or violence : SEVERELY ⟨women were treated ~ —Theodor Reik⟩ ⟨closed the door ~ —Marcia Davenport⟩ **b :** without finish : COARSELY ⟨local gray stone, ~ dressed —*Amer. Guide Series: Minn.*⟩ **c :** without completeness or exactness : APPROXIMATELY ⟨~ speaking⟩ ⟨in ~ chronological order⟩ ⟨must know ~ what each act will contain —John Van Druten⟩

rough-machine \ˈ⸗⸗ˌ⸗\ *vt* [[3]*rough* + *machine*] **:** to machine (work) approximately to size usu. by taking heavy cuts with the object chiefly of removing excess metal rather than of obtaining a correct size and finish

rough music *n* [[1]*rough*] *dial Brit* **:** SHIVAREE

[1]**rough·neck** \ˈrəfˌnek\ *n* [[1]*rough* + *neck*] **1 :** a rough or uncouth person; *esp* **:** one markedly inclined to violent, quarrelsome, or mischievous behavior : ROWDY, TOUGH ⟨a gang of ~*s*⟩ ⟨stopped her boy from playing with the neighborhood ~*s*⟩ **2 :** a member of a crew that builds and repairs oil wells

[2]**roughneck** \"\ *also* **rough·necked** \-kt\ *adj* **:** having the characteristics of or suitable for a roughneck : UNCOUTH, BARBAROUS ⟨~ language⟩ ⟨the world's gone ~ —Ellen Glasgow⟩ ⟨went out to a ~ dance —Sinclair Lewis⟩

rough·ness *n* -ES [ME *roughnesse,* fr. [1]*rough* + *-nesse* -ness] **1 :** the quality or state of being rough: as **a :** inequality or unevenness of surface ⟨the ~ of the path⟩ ⟨place his fingers on the paper . . . to perceive ~ —R.S.Woodworth⟩ **b :** a sensation of harshness or sharpness (as to the taste or hearing) ⟨the tea . . . strong with that ~ which sets one's teeth on edge —G.E.Fussell⟩ ⟨the ~ of their voices grating on his nerves⟩ **c :** harsh, rude, or violent speech or behavior ⟨a riverside town well known for ~ —Harvey Day⟩ **d :** violent agitation : STORMINESS ⟨the ~ of the sea⟩ ⟨the ~ of the weather⟩ **e :** lack of refinement or polish : CRUDENESS ⟨the life of the people had lost . . . its broad pioneer ~ —*Amer. Guide Series: Tenn.*⟩ **2 :** a rough place or part ⟨the ~*es* remaining after the first revision of an essay⟩ **3** *Midland* **:** roughage used as fodder

rough·om·e·ter \ˌrəˈfäməd·ə(r)\ *n* [[1]*rough* + *-o-* + *-meter*] **:** an instrument for measuring the roughness of a road surface

rough out *vt* **:** to maintain (a horse) solely on pasture or roughage ⟨an experienced steeplechaser *roughed out* at grass —*Veterinary Record*⟩

rough pea *n* **:** SINGLETARY PEA

rough pigweed *n* **:** a pigweed (*Amaranthus retroflexus*)

rough-point \ˈ⸗ˈ⸗\ *vt* [[3]*rough* + *point*] **:** to point (stone) with a pick or with heavy points so as to leave projections from about half an inch to an inch in height

rough proof *n* **:** a printer's proof made quickly by hand without the use of special proof paper, positioning, or makeready

rough rice *n* **:** PADDY

rough·ride \ˈrəfˌrīd\ *vi* [back-formation fr. *roughrider*] **:** to ride as or in the manner of a roughrider

rough·rid·er \-də(r)\ *n* [[1]*rough* + *rider*] **1 :** one that breaks horses to the saddle or who is noted for or accustomed to riding little-trained horses; *specif* **:** a trooper in the British cavalry who is assigned as a horse trainer **2 a :** an irregular cavalryman **b** *usu cap* **:** an officer or enlisted man in the 1st U.S. Volunteer Cavalry regiment in the Spanish-American War composed mostly of western cowboys and hunters and eastern college athletes and sportsmen commanded by Theodore Roosevelt

roughs *pl of* ROUGH, *pres 3d sing of* ROUGH

roughscuff *also* **rough-scruff** \ˈ⸗ˌ⸗\ *n* [[1]*rough* + *scuff, scruff*] **:** RIFFRAFF ⟨the political ~ of Europe —*Atlantic*⟩

roughseed bulrush \ˈ⸗ˌ⸗-\ *n* [[1]*rough* + *seed*] **:** a perennial Old World rush (*Scirpus mucronatus*) that occurs as a weed in California rice fields and has seeds with barbed bristles

roughshod \ˈ⸗ˈ⸗\ *adj* [[3]*rough* + *shod*] **1 :** shod with shoes armed with points or calks ⟨a ~ horse⟩ **2 :** marked by inhumanity or tyranny ⟨~ condemnation proceedings⟩ ⟨~ reign⟩

rough·some \ˈrəfsəm\ *adj* [[1]*rough* + *-some*] *chiefly Scot* **:** ROUGH, UNCOUTH, BOORISH

rough-spoken \ˈ⸗ˈ⸗⸗\ *adj* [[3]*rough* + *spoken*] **:** rough or crude in speech ⟨a ~ old sailor⟩

rough-stalked meadow grass \ˈ⸗ˌ⸗-\ *n* [[1]*rough*] **:** ROUGH BLUEGRASS

rough stop *n* **1 :** any one of the three Greek consonants ϕ, θ, χ that were orig. the voiceless stops \p\, \t\, \k̟\ followed by an \h\ sound or aspiration — called also *aspirata* **2 :** a voiceless aspirated stop in any language

roughstring \ˈ⸗ˌ⸗\ *n* **:** a board notched out to fit the steps and fixed to the inside of an open string to strengthen it — compare FACE STRING

[1]**roughstuff** \ˈ⸗ˌ⸗\ *n* [[1]*rough* + *stuff*] **1 :** an undercoat of paint used to level inequalities of a surface **2** *usu* **rough stuff :** boisterous behavior : violent treatment ⟨allowed no *rough stuff* in his dance hall⟩ ⟨if the fellow didn't pay off, they went in for *rough stuff* —A.J.Liebling⟩

[2]**roughstuff** \"\ *vt* **:** to paint (a surface) with roughstuff

rought [alter. of *raught*] *dial chiefly Brit past of* REACH

roughtail \ˈ⸗ˌ⸗\ *n* [[1]*rough* + *tail*] **:** a burrowing snake of the family Uropeltidae having large scales or shields on the tail

roughtailed \ˈ⸗ˈ⸗\ *adj* [[1]*rough* + *tailed*] **1 :** having a rough tail ⟨~ mice⟩ **2 :** having a tail that is characteristic of a roughtail

rough-tree rail *n* [*rough-tree* small timber used as a rail (perh. alter. of *rooftree*) + *rail*] **:** the rail at the top of a ship's main bulwarks and below the topgallant bulwarks

rough-weed \ˈ⸗ˌ⸗\ *n* [[1]*rough*] **:** HEDGE NETTLE

rough whelk *n* **:** DRILL 4

rough-winged swallow \ˈ⸗ˌ⸗-\ *n* **:** a swallow of the American genus *Stelgidopteryx* or of the African genus *Psalidoprocne* having the outer web of the first primary developed into a series of minute hooks

roughy \ˈrəfē\ *n* -ES [prob. fr. [1]*rough* + *-y*] **1 :** a small but highly esteemed Australian marine percoid food fish (*Arripis georgianus*) — called also *Tommy rough* **2 :** a small reddish brown Australian slime head (*Trachichthys australis*)

rougy \ˈrüzhē\ *adj* [[1]*rouge* + *-y*] **:** covered with or like rouge

rouk \ˈrōk\ *var of* ROKE

rouky \-ki\ *adj* -ER/-EST [*rouk* + *-y*] *chiefly Scot* **:** FOGGY, MISTY

roul *abbr* roulette

[1]**rou·lade** \rüˈläd\ *n* -S [F, lit., act of rolling, roll, fr. *rouler* to roll (fr. MF *roller*) + *-ade* — more at ROLL] **:** a series of rapid musical notes or tones inserted in a musical composition as ornamentation; *specif* **:** a vocal ornament or coloratura (as an arpeggio or quick run) sung to one syllable

[2]**roulade** \"\ *vi* -ED/-ING/-S **:** to sing with roulades

[3]**roulade** \"\ *n* -S [F, lit., act of rolling, fr. MF] **:** a slice of meat rolled with or without a stuffing and braised or sauteed ⟨~ of beef⟩

roule *obs var of* ROLL

rou·leau \rüˈlō\ *n, pl* **rou·leaux** \-ō(z)\ *or* **rouleaus** [F, fr. MF *rolel*, dim. of *role* roll — more at ROLE] **:** a little roll: as **a :** a roll of coins put up in paper ⟨held out *rouleaux* of pennies —Richard Llewellyn⟩ **b :** a group of red blood corpuscles resembling a stack of coins **c :** a decorative piping or rolled trimming for women's clothing **d :** a bundle of fascines used in groups in siege operations

[1]**rou·lette** \rüˈlet, *usu* -ed·+V\ *n* -S [F, lit., small wheel, fr. OF *roelete*, dim. of *roele* small wheel, circular object, fr. LL *rotella*, dim. of L *rota* wheel — more at ROLL] **1 :** a gambling game in which players bet on which numbered red or black compartment of a revolving wheel a small ball spun in the opposite direction will come to rest in and in which the bets are placed on a table marked to correspond with the compartments of the wheel **2 :** any of various toothed wheels or disks (as for producing rows of dots on engraved plates, for roughening a plate in altering a mezzotint or for making short consecutive incisions in paper to facilitate subsequent division) **3 :** FILLET 5a **4 a :** a series of tiny slits made between rows of stamps as an aid to separation of the stamps — compare PERFORATION 2b(1) **b :** a row of teeth, scallops, or dashes along the edge of a detached stamp from a rouletted sheet **c :** one of the slits or teeth of a roulette

[2]**roulette** \"\ *vt* -ED/-ING/-S **1 :** to make roulettes in (as a sheet of stamps) or on the edge of (a stamp) **2 :** to make (a design) by rocker-stamping

rouletting *n* -S [fr. gerund of [2]*roulette*] **:** ROULETTE 4

rou·man \ˈrümən\ *adj or n, usu cap* [F *Roumain*, fr. Romanian *Român* — more at RUMAN] **:** ROMANIAN

roumania *usu cap, var of* ROMANIA

roumanian *usu cap, var of* ROMANIAN

roumelian *usu cap, var of* RUMELIAN

rou·mi \ˈrümē\ *n* -S [Ar *rūmīy* Roman, fr. L *Roma* + Ar *-īy* (gentilic suffix)] **:** a non-Muslim — usu. used disparagingly

roun \ˈrün\ *Scot var of* ROUND

[1]**rounce** \ˈrau̇n(t)s\ *n* -S [D *rondse*, *rons*, prob. fr. *rond* round, fr. MF, fr. OF *roont* (fem. *roonde*) — more at ROUND] **:** a handle by which the bed of a hand printing press is run in under the platen and out again; *also* **:** the whole apparatus for moving the bed under the platen

[2]**rounce** \"\ *vi* -ED/-ING/-S [origin unknown] **:** to be agitated **:** flounce around **:** FUSS ⟨mother is kind of *rouncing* round, all right —Sinclair Lewis⟩

[1]**rounceval** *adj* [fr. *Roncesvalles*, *Roncevaux*, mountain pass in northern Spain; fr. the gigantic bones shown there as those of the paladins of Charlemagne slain in battle in 778] *obs* **:** HUGE, LARGE

[2]**roun·ce·val** \ˈrau̇n(t)səvəl\ *n* -S **1** *obs* **a :** something very large **:** GIANT, MONSTER **b :** a big loud woman **:** VIRAGO **2 :** MARROWFAT 1

roun·cy \ˈrau̇n(t)sē\ *n* -ES [ME, fr. MF *ronci* charger] *archaic* **:** a riding horse

[1]**round** \ˈrau̇nd\ *vb* -ED/-ING/-S [ME *rounen*, fr. OE *rūnian*; akin to OHG *rūnēn* to whisper, ON *rȳna* to converse confidentially; all fr. a prehistoric NGmc-WGmc denominative verb fr. the source of OE *rūn* mystery, secret — more at RUNE] *vi, archaic* **:** WHISPER ~ *vt* **1 :** to whisper (something) **2 :** to speak to (someone) in a whisper

[2]**round** \"\ *adj, usu* -ER/-EST [ME *round*, *rounde*, fr. OF *roont*, *rount* (fem. *roonde*, *rounde*) fr. L *rotundus*; akin to L *rota* wheel — more at ROLL] **1 a :** having every part of the surface or of the circumference equally distant from a center within **:** SPHERICAL, CIRCULAR, ANNULAR, SPIRAL **b :** circular in cross section **:** CYLINDRICAL **c :** having a curved outline or form esp. like the arc of a circle or an ellipse or a part of the surface of a sphere **d** *of an arch* **:** having a semicircular intrados — see ARCH illustration **e** *archaic* **:** having a full or circular form — used of a garment **f** *of shoulders* **:** bent forward from the line or plane of a person's back **2 :** well fleshed **:** well filled out **:** PLUMP, SHAPELY **3 a :** COMPLETE, FULL — used of a number or quantity ⟨a ~ dozen⟩ ⟨a ~ million men⟩ ⟨a ~ ton of irreclaimable scrap⟩ **b :** approximately correct; *esp* **:** exact only to the nearest ten, hundred, or multiple of these ⟨his year's profit was about $5000 as a ~ figure⟩ **c :** substantial in amount **:** AMPLE, LARGE ⟨will be taken off our hands quickly and at a good ~ price —T.B.Costain⟩ **4 a :** showing severity or violence **:** HARSH ⟨gave him a ~ hiding —Ellery Queen⟩ **b :** marked by bluntness, directness, or forthrightness **:** BOLD, PLAIN, OUTSPOKEN ⟨asserted with a ~ oath . . . that all sergeants were liars —Haldane Macfall⟩ **c :** BRISK, FAST, VIGOROUS ⟨set a ~ pace —John Buchan⟩ **5 a :** traversing a course that ends at its starting point after retracing itself or making a circuit — used esp. in the phrase *round trip* **b :** moving in or forming a circle — compare ROUND DANCE **6 a :** brought to completion or perfection **:** thoroughly wrought **:** FINISHED **b :** imaginatively presented or drawn with lifelike fullness or vividness **:** seen from all sides or in many aspects ⟨the characters and their motives are as ~ and deep as those we might hope to find in a serious novel —*Times Lit. Supp.*⟩ **7 :** delivered with a more or less full swing of the arm ⟨a ~ blow⟩ **8 :** having full or unimpeded resonance or tone **:** MELLOW, RICH, SONOROUS **9 :** pronounced with rounded lips **:** LABIALIZED **10 :** of or relating to handwriting that is predominantly curved rather than angular ⟨a ~ schoolboy hand⟩ **11 :** of or relating to a transaction in securities that includes both buying and selling (as the sale of issues previously bought or a purchase made to cover a short sale) **12** *of a fish* **:** not gutted or dressed **:** ENTIRE

[3]**round** \"\ *adv* [ME *round*, *rounde*, fr. [2]*round*] **1 a :** in a circular or curved path or progression **:** in a course that follows a circle, ellipse, orbit, or spiral **:** AROUND ⟨our plane circled ~ at dusk —Noel Barber⟩ **b :** in close from all sides so as to surround, confine, or ring about ⟨walls and towers girdled ~ with radiance and splendor —Brooks Atkinson⟩ **c :** by a circuitous or curving route **:** in an indirect or roundabout way ⟨brought the milk ~ to the back door⟩ ⟨did not shine at golf but went ~ in the middle 80s⟩ **d :** to each of a group or number in succession **:** in turn **:** in rotation ⟨handed ~ water in an enamel mug —Margaret Kennedy⟩ ⟨cigars enough to go ~⟩ **2 :** on every side **:** in all or various directions from a fixed point ⟨the peasants ~ about his father's parish —O.S.J.Gogarty⟩ ⟨made frequent excursions in the country ~⟩ **3 :** with revolving or rotating motion ⟨the wheel turns ~⟩ **4** *obs* **:** DIRECTLY, OUTSPOKENLY **5 :** to a place or person either specified or understood ⟨sent ~ for the doctor⟩ ⟨invited them ~ to meet his guest⟩ ⟨called his car ~⟩ **6 :** APPROXIMATELY, NEARLY ⟨happened at the corner or ~ there⟩ **7 :** from beginning to end **:** THROUGH ⟨about 700 workers are employed at the plant the year ~ —*Amer. Guide Series: Md.*⟩ **8 a :** in the reverse or opposite direction **:** to the rear ⟨turned ~ in his chair to look⟩ **b :** from one opinion or attitude to another **:** to a different or altered position ⟨see if you can talk me ~ —Dorothy Sayers⟩ **9 a :** here and there **:** from one place to another **:** all about ⟨word got ~ quickly⟩ **b :** over a property to inspect it ⟨showed the visitors ~⟩ **10 :** back to normal health or equilibrium ⟨brought a woman ~ after a faint⟩ **11 :** in a series or progression **:** in order ⟨seemed to be going about things the wrong way ~⟩

[4]**round** \"\ *prep* **1 a :** so as to progress around or make the circuit of ⟨had the great thrill of flying ~ Africa —C.B. Randall b.1891⟩ **b :** so as to revolve or rotate about (an axis or center) ⟨pointed out that the planets move ~ the sun in the same direction and nearly in the same plane —H.S. Jones⟩ **c :** so as to make a partial circuit of **:** so as to reach the other side of by a curving course ⟨whether he sailed directly across the bay . . . or coasted ~ it is uncertain —Stanley Casson⟩ **d :** so as to follow the curving line of **:** along the bend of ⟨it was a mile by water, four miles ~ the shore —David Walker⟩ **e :** beyond the projection of ⟨it stood just ~ the corner from his father's house —Van Wyck Brooks⟩ **2 a :** so as to encircle or enclose **:** on all sides of ⟨the fat thus formed is to be found in large masses . . . ~ the kidneys —S.J.Watson⟩ ⟨they swarmed close ~ her to hear —C.S.Forester⟩ ⟨pulled her shawl closer ~ her —T.H.Barnardo⟩ **b :** in the vicinity of **:** adjacent to **:** NEAR ⟨the lands ~ the city —Herbert Agar⟩ **c :** so as to form a group or mass about ⟨will tend to gather ~ him the best minds in America —*New Republic*⟩ ⟨a great puddle formed ~ the hole⟩ **d** (1) **:** from point to point or from person to person in **:** here and there in ⟨took his way ~ the city, passing a discreet word here and a mere look there as he went⟩ ⟨refreshes the students' memories by asking a few simple questions ~ the class —D.H.Spencer⟩ (2) **:** throughout the extent of **:** all over **:** all through ⟨the blood circulates ~ the body⟩ **3 a :** in all directions from ⟨we cannot measure it by what we see ~ us —Lewis Galantiere⟩ **b :** so as to have a center or basis in ⟨the flame . . . was yellow on the outside, bluish in the middle, but there was no color ~ the wick —Stuart Cloete⟩ ⟨the biography is centered ~ the individual —Richard Pares⟩ **4 a :** all during a specified period of time **:** THROUGHOUT ⟨the perfect satisfaction which is one equation of love — ~ the days, the weeks —Ethel Wilson⟩ **b :** at about a specified time or season ⟨~ 1900 his repute was still untarnished⟩ ⟨he had to find gunpowder and guns to keep the army from dissolving ~ Christmas —*Times Lit. Supp.*⟩

[5]**round** \"\ *n* -S [ME *rounde*, fr. [2]*round*; in some senses prob. fr. MF or F *rond*, *ronde*, fr. *rond* (adj.), fr. OF *roont*, *rount*] **1 :** something round: as **a :** a spherical object or surface **:** BALL, GLOBE **b** (1) **:** a circular area or surface or its circumference **:** CIRCLE, RING (2) *obs* **:** CROWN ⟨and wears upon his baby brow the ~ and top of sovereignty —Shak.⟩ **c :** a cylindrical object ⟨maintained a stock of bar steel that included ~*s* up to 2½ inches in diameter⟩ **d :** a circular building, wall, or other structure or a rounded or circular part of one (as a turret) **e :** a knot of people or a circle of things **f :** a topographical circle, bend, or curve **2 :** ROUND DANCE 1 ⟨a light fantastic ~ —John Milton⟩ **3 :** a polyphonic vocal composition in which three or four voices follow each other around in a canon at the unison or octave **:** CIRCULAR CANON **4 a :** a rung of a ladder or of a chair **b :** a round rod constituting a machine part (as a cylindrical bar of a lantern pinion) **c :** a rounded molding **5 a :** a circling or circuitous path or course **b :** motion in a circle or about a curving track ⟨won his race only with a final fast ~ of the track⟩ **6 :** a route or circuit habitually covered: as **a :** the circuit covered by a military watch at a camp or other installation; *also* **:** a military patrol that makes rounds to keep order in a community or to keep sentinels alert **b :** the beat or route regularly covered by a watchman or policeman — usu. used in pl. **c** *Brit* **:** the route of a newspaper delivery boy, milkman, or other vendor **d :** a series of professional calls on patients in a hospital made by a doctor or nurse — usu. used in pl. **e :** a series of social calls or visits **:** a routine of social activity ⟨a busy ~ of dances and parties⟩ **f :** a circuit or progression of similar calls or stops ⟨undertook a ~ of nightclubs after the play⟩ ⟨hurriedly made the ~*s* of his ice cream customers⟩ **g :** a line or course by which rumor, news, or other communication spreads among people — often used in pl. ⟨rumors calling his solvency in question were going the ~*s* of the brokerage offices⟩ ⟨knew he could expect any gossip that might be going the ~*s*⟩ **h rounds** *pl, Brit* **:** a circuit from farm to farm formerly followed by agricultural laborers **7** *obs* **:** a piece of sculpture modeled in full form unattached to a background **8 :** a drink of liquor apiece served at one time to each person in a group ⟨this ~ is on me⟩ **9 :** a series or sequence of actions, events, or affairs that recur in routine or repetitive manner ⟨politics exist that men may live the daily ~ in security —J.M. Cameron⟩ ⟨life for them is one ~ of committees and council meetings —Margaret Stewart⟩ **10 :** a cycle of time **:** a period that recurs in a fixed pattern ⟨the ~ of the hours⟩ ⟨the annual ~⟩ **11 a :** one shot fired by a weapon or by each man in a military unit **:** SALVO, VOLLEY **b :** a unit of ammunition consisting of all the parts (as a projectile, a propellant, an igniting charge, and a primer) necessary in the firing and functioning of one shot **12 :** a unit of card play constituted by each player's having had his turn (as in playing a card, receiving a card in the deal, dealing, or betting) **13 :** a unit or division of play in a sports contest or game which occupies a stated period of time, covers a prescribed distance, includes a specified number of moves or plays, or gives each player one turn: as **a :** any of various archery events in which a specified number of arrows are shot at prescribed distances **b :** one of the three-minute periods into which a boxing match is divided **c :** the playing of 18 holes of golf or one circuit of the course **d :** a series of 25 shots in trapshooting or skeet **e :** a match in an elimination tournament **14** *Brit* **:** a brewer's vessel in which fermentation is carried out **15 :** an outburst of applause ⟨took half a dozen curtain calls in response to repeated ~*s* of applause⟩ **16 a :** a hind leg of beef esp. between the rump and the lower leg ⟨a roast ~ of beef⟩ — see BEEF illustration **b** a small beef casing **c :** a slice of food ⟨a ~ of bread⟩ ⟨a ~ of rolled dough⟩ ⟨a ~ of celeriac root⟩ **17 rounds** *pl* **:** the original striking order of a set of bells in change ringing ⟨the return to ~*s* concludes a set of changes⟩ **18 :** a rounded or curved part: as **a :** the shaft of a paddle **b :** the convex backbone or concave fore edge of a book **19 :** a group or series of drill holes blasted in sequence in advancing mine working places **20 :** an artist's brush having a round tapered point — compare BRIGHT, FLAT **21 :** a row in circular needlework (as kn. ting or crocheting) — **in round** *adv, of a book* **:** in the process or state of having the backbone rounded from side to side — **in the round** *adv (or adj)* **1 :** in full sculptured form unattached to a background **:** FREESTANDING ⟨an athlete superbly represented *in the round*⟩ ⟨a head shown *in the round*⟩ — distinguished from *relief* **2 :** with an inclusive or comprehensive view or representation ⟨a wise physician who saw his patients *in the round*⟩ ⟨the flat people of a novelist too little perceptive or skilled to show us humanity *in the round*⟩ **3 :** with a centered stage that is surrounded by an audience on all sides **4** *of a fish* **:** not eviscerated **:** WHOLE — **out of round :** in a distorted or imperfectly generated state of roundness ⟨great care and skill are required in machining long thin cylindrical work if it is not to be *out of round*⟩ ⟨a roll of newsprint should be stored on its end or it will get *out of round* and feed badly in the press⟩

[6]**round** \"\ *vb* -ED/-ING/-S [ME *rounden*, fr. [2]*round*] *vt* **1 a :** to make circular, spherical, or cylindrical **:** give a round or convex shape to (as the backbone of a book) **b :** to curve or curl into a ring or ball ⟨had ~*ed* her body into a little circular heap while she slept⟩ **c** (1) **:** to make (the lips) more or less round and protruded by lessening the distance between the corners of the mouth (as in the pronunciation of \ü\) (2) **:** to pronounce (a vowel or consonant) with rounding of the lips **:** LABIALIZE **2** *archaic* **a :** to trim (hair) short around the head **b :** to crop the hair of (a person) **c :** to trim the lobe of (a dog's ear) **3 a :** to go around **:** make the circuit of **b :** to pass part way around **:** reach the other side of by a curving course **:** go about (a point or corner) **:** DOUBLE ⟨whenever you ~ a turn, there's a view —E.W.Smith⟩ ⟨the railroad had ~*ed* the hill —*Amer. Guide Series: Ark.*⟩ ⟨slipped in loose dirt ~*ing* first base —Bob Broeg⟩ **4 :** to ring about **:** ENCIRCLE, ENCOMPASS, SURROUND ⟨the inclusive verge of golden metal that must ~ my brow —Shak.⟩ **5 a :** to bring to fullness or completion **:** perfect the form of **:** finish off ⟨has ~*ed* the characters by giving each a claim for sympathy —Henry Hewes⟩ **b :** to bring to perfection of style **:** POLISH ⟨music rose from paragraph after ~*ed* paragraph⟩ ⟨an epigram ~*ed* the sentence with a flourish⟩ **6 :** to cause to face about **:** turn or swing around ⟨with a dexterous swerve he ~*ed* the yawl about —Frederick Way⟩ **7 :** to express (a number) in briefer or less exact form **:** state as a round number: as **a :** to drop decimal figures to the right of a specified number of places after increasing the final remaining figure by 1 if the first digit dropped is 5 or greater ⟨11.3572 ~*ed* to three decimals becomes 11.357⟩ ⟨9.419 ~*ed* to two decimals is 9.42⟩ **b :** to express as an approximate round number rather than as the exact figure ⟨we are ~*ing* all figures to the nearest hundred million —G.V.Cox⟩ **8 a :** to cut (fleshed hides) in sections for treatment **:** TRIM **b** (1) **:** to cut (sole leather) to required shape with a knife rather than a die (2) **:** to cut (the sole of a shoe) to conform to the shape of a last after a sole has been attached ~ *vi* **1** *obs* **:** to go rounds as a guard or watchman **2 a :** to become circular or spherical **:** grow round or plump **:** attain a shapely form ⟨her body now ~*s* into womanhood⟩ **b :** to reach fullness, adequacy, or completion **:** DEVELOP, GROW ⟨the sales campaign he had outlined was now ~*ing* into final shape⟩ ⟨the century ~*ed* into its third decade —R.B. Fosdick⟩ **3 :** to take a curving line or direction **:** follow a winding course **:** BEND ⟨leaning wide on the turns like jockeys ~*ing* into the home stretch —H.L.Davis⟩ — **round on 1 :** to inform against **:** BETRAY **2 :** to turn against (a friend or ally) in anger or hostility **:** ASSAIL ⟨she *rounded on* him fiercely —Kathleen Freeman⟩ ⟨was always *rounding on* his own side on the eve of victory —L.B.Nicolson⟩

[1]**round about** *adv* [ME, fr. [3]*round* + *about*] **1 :** around in a circle or circular course **:** on all sides or in all directions **:** in the vicinity **:** NEARBY ⟨rows of orange trees . . . contrast pleasantly with the white walls *round about* —Samuel Van Valkenburg & Ellsworth Huntington⟩ **2 :** in an opposite direction ⟨turned *round about* and stalked off⟩ **3 :** in an indirect way ⟨came *round about* and slowly to these conclusions⟩

[2]**round about** *prep* **1 :** in an encircling course about **:** so as to move around ⟨danced lightly *round about* the maypole⟩ **2 :** in a circle about **:** so as to surround **:** here and there around **:** in the vicinity of ⟨took up positions in the desert *round about* a walled city⟩ **3 :** at approximately a specified time ⟨*round about* the turn of the century another science was lying in wait for the artist —Herbert Read⟩

[1]**roundabout** \ˈ⸗⸗,⸗\ *n* -S [[1]*round about*] **1 :** something circular: as **a** *archaic* **:** a circular course or path **b** *archaic* **:** a circular encampment **c** *chiefly dial* **:** a surrounding hedge **2 a :** a circuitous way to a destination or object **:** an indirect route **:** DETOUR ⟨the painting had reached the U. S. in the typical ~ of forgotten masterpieces, after a journey that began in 1909 —*Time*⟩ **b :** an oblique or indirect expression **:** CIRCUMLOCUTION **3** *Brit* **:** MERRY-GO-ROUND ⟨it looks like some new and terrifying ~ at a fairground —Ivor Jones⟩ ⟨what the public lose materially on the swings as consumers they will more than gain on the ~*s* as producers —*Economist*⟩ **4** *archaic* **:** ROUND DANCE 1 **5** *also* **roundabout jacket :** a short close-fitting jacket worn by men and boys esp. in the 19th century **6** *Brit* **:** ROTARY 2 **7 a :** ROUND TRIP **b :** a rambling excursion

[2]**roundabout** \"\ *adj* [[1]*round about*] **1 :** marked by circuitousness or indirection: as **a :** deviating from a straight line or course **:** CURVING, MEANDERING, WINDING ⟨the train has to come a ~ way —Cortland Fitzsimmons⟩ **b :** oblique or devious in speech or conduct ⟨write ~ paragraphs —C.E.Kellogg⟩ ⟨his approach to her was ~ —Jean Stafford⟩ **2 :** rounded in figure **:** PLUMP ⟨a little ~ woman with rosy cheeks —Elizabeth Goudge⟩ — **round·about·ness** *n* -ES

roundabout chair *n* [[2]*roundabout*] **:** CORNER CHAIR

round angle *n* [[2]*round*] **:** the plane angle swept through by a half line in turning positively in a plane about its extremity as a center until it returns to its original position ⟨a *round angle* is 360 degrees⟩ — compare RIGHT ANGLE, STRAIGHT ANGLE

round–arm \ˈ⸗,⸗\ *adj* [[2]*round* + *arm*] **:** marked by an outward or horizontal swing of the arm ⟨a *round-arm* blow⟩

round back *n* [[2]*round*] **:** the backbone of a book when distinctly convex — compare SQUARE BACK

round bale *n* **:** a cotton bale containing a rolled-up sheet of cotton fiber wrapped in burlap and averaging 250 pounds in weight

round–bale press *n* **:** a hay press that binds a cylindrical bale with twine and leaves an air space running lengthwise through its center

round barrow *n* **:** a Neolithic British burial mound of rounded shape built by a brachycephalic people — compare LONG BARROW

round bass *n* **:** FLIER 3

round bracket *n* **:** BRACKET 4c

round buffalo *n* **:** BLACK BUFFALO 1

round cell *n* **:** a small lymphocyte or a closely related cell esp. occurring in an area of chronic infection or as the typical cell of some sarcomas

round church *n* **1 :** a church of circular plan usu. having a ring of columns dividing a tower nave from a surrounding aisle **2 :** a church of polygonal plan with central or radial rather than longitudinal disposition

round clam *n* **:** QUAHOG 1

round dance *n* **1 :** a folk or ritual group or couple dance in which participants form a ring and move in a prescribed direction **2 :** a ballroom dance in which couples progress around the room

round–dealing *adj, obs* **:** CANDID, OPEN, PLAIN DEALING

rounded *adj* [fr. past part. of [6]*round*] **1 a :** convex, curving, or round in shape **:** flowing rather than jagged or angular ⟨every ~ knoll was torn open in the hope of finding clues —*Amer. Guide Series: Minn.*⟩ ⟨scoop neckline; smooth, ~ shoulders —*Americana Annual*⟩ **b :** showing a norm or ideal of bodily perfection **:** SHAPELY ⟨~ like a swimmer or a wrestler —Carl Van Doren⟩ **c :** built with round rather than pointed arches **2 :** fully developed **:** COMPLETE, PERFECTED: as **a :** marked by generous attainment or developed character ⟨a ~ human being, compellingly vivid and alive —*Saturday Rev.*⟩ ⟨a mind well ~ and austere, clear with himself as with others —Robert Lawrence⟩ **b :** marked by full or many-sided perfection or excellence ⟨the ~ analysis and estimate of a great novel by a critic both firm and sensitive —E.K.Brown⟩ ⟨~ culture⟩ **c :** conceived, drawn, or presented in full form or in all aspects **:** shown perceptively or penetratingly **:** comprehensively realized ⟨a sympathetic, ~ and complete picture of a young girl growing up —*advt*⟩ **d :** polished in phrasing or style **:** deftly turned **:** FINISHED ⟨significance and effect closely mated in the telling word and the ~ period⟩ **3 a :** having full unmuted resonance **:** MELLOW, SONOROUS ⟨fine ~ sound, especially of the piano —Irving Kolodin⟩ **b :** produced with rounded lips **:** ROUND, LABIALIZED **4 :** numerically exact only to a convenient degree **:** APPROXIMATE ⟨the figures given are slightly ~ statements of the average —W.C.Allee⟩ — **round·ed·ness** *n* -ES

roun·del *or* **roun·dle** \ˈrau̇ndᵊl\ *n* -S [ME *roundel*, *roundell*, *rundel*, fr. OF *rondel*, *rondelle*, fr. *roont* (fem. *ronde*) round + *-el*, *-elle*, dim. suffix — more at ROUND] **1 :** something circular **:** a round figure: as **a** *chiefly dial* **:** a circle marked out or otherwise formed **b :** a circular group or ring of things or persons **c :** a plain or colored glass disk (as for a railway signal lamp or a theatrical lighting device) **d :** a circular tray, trencher, or small table **2 :** a circular panel, window, or niche; *esp* **:** a recessed circular niche for a bust — compare ROSETTE **3 :** any of various small circular subordinaries representing balls or plates of metal or color — compare BEZANT, GOLPE, GUZE, [4]HURT, PELLET, TORTEAU **4 :** RONDEL 1b(1) **5 a :** ROUND 3 **b :** ROUND DANCE 1 **6 a :** RONDEL 2a **b :** an English modified rondeau whose refrain comes after the first and last of three tercets and fits into the rhyme scheme *aba B, bab, aba B*

roun·de·lay \ˈrau̇ndə,lā *also* ˈrän-\ *n* -S [modif. (influenced by [4]*lay*) of MF *rondelet*, dim. of *rondel* small circle, rondeau, fr. OF — more at ROUNDEL] **1 a :** RONDEAU 2a **b :** a simple lively-spirited song or air ⟨water nymphs that were singing their ~*s* under me —H.W.Longfellow⟩ **2 :** ROUND DANCE **3 :** a poem with a refrain that recurs frequently or at fixed intervals as in a rondel

[1]**rounder** *comparative of* ROUND

[2]**round·er** \ˈrau̇ndə(r)\ *n* -S [partly fr. [5]*round* + *-er*; partly fr. [6]*round* + *-er*] **1 a** *archaic* **:** a guard or watchman who makes rounds **b :** a Methodist local preacher who rides a circuit **2 :** a dissolute or rakish person **:** WASTREL ⟨nightclub ~*s* and pool players —*Newsweek*⟩ **3 a rounders** *pl but sing in constr*

: an English game that is played with ball and bat and somewhat resembles baseball **b** : a circuit of the bases made on a single hit in the game of rounders **4** : one that rounds by hand or by machine: as **a** : a dividing machine operator who rolls cut pieces of dough into balls **b** : a shoe worker who trims insoles or outsoles according to a pattern **c** : one that rounds the backs of books **d** : an operator of a turning machine that rounds and trims barrel heads or basket bottoms **e** : one that cuts hat brims to prescribed width **5** : any of various boring or shaping tools **6** : a boxing match lasting a specified number of rounds ⟨went on to win a dull 10-*rounder* —*Sports Illustrated*⟩ **7 rounders** *pl but sing in constr* : ROUNDSTERS

rounder and backer *n* : a machine that accepts a book with a flat backbone, rolls it out to accept concave front and convex back edges, and completes the shaping by backing — compare ROLLER-BACKER

roundest *superlative of* ROUND

round-eyed \ˈ=ˈ=\ *adj* [²*round* + *eyed*] : having the eyes wide open (as with astonishment)

round file *n* : a file of circular cross section used for filing round holes — compare RATTAIL FILE

roundfish \ˈ=,=\ *n* **1** : an ordinary fish as distinguished from a flatfish **2** : an entire fish as distinguished from a dressed fish

round game *n* : a game usu. for four or more players in which every participant plays for himself and has no partner

round hand *n* : a bold plain handwriting ⟨write a fair *round hand* —C.S.Forester⟩

round haul net *or* **round haul seine** *n* : a fishnet (as a purse seine or a lampara) designed for surrounding a school of fishes so that they can be hauled in en masse

roundhead \ˈ=,=\ *n* [²*round* + *head*] **1** *usu cap* : a Puritan or member of the Parliamentary party in England at the time of Charles I and Oliver Cromwell — compare CAVALIER **2** : a brachycephalic person

roundheaded \ˈ=ˈ==\ *adj* [²*round* + *headed*] : having a round head: as **a** : BRACHYCEPHALIC **b** *usu cap* (1) : having the hair closely cropped like the Roundheads (2) : PURITANICAL ⟨*Roundheaded* criticism —Heywood Broun⟩ **c** : rounded on the top or end ⟨a ~ screw⟩ **d** : having the head or upper part semicircular ⟨a ~ window⟩ ⟨~ door⟩ — **round·head·ed·ness** *n* -ES

roundheaded apple tree borer *n* : APPLE TREE BORER b

roundheaded borer *n* : a larval beetle (family Cerambycidae) with a small head with large strong mandibles, a large prothorax, and the legs vestigial or absent that develops and feeds in woody plant tissues — compare BARDEE, HUHU

round-heart \ˈ=,=\ *n* [²*round* + *heart*] : PURPLE MEADOW PARSNIP

round heart disease *n* : an obscure disease of poultry in which affected birds often die suddenly without previous signs of illness of a dilated hypertrophied heart with fatty infiltration of its muscles and usu. passive hyperemia of the lungs and viscera

roundheel \ˈ=,=\ *n* [²*round* + *heel*] : PUSHOVER ⟨a luscious ~ with a heart of gold —J.T.Latouche⟩

round herring *n* : any of numerous small mostly tropical marine fishes (family Dussumieriidae) resembling the herrings but having the belly smooth and rounded

roundhouse \ˈ=,=\ *n* [in sense 1, fr. ⁵*round* patrol; in other senses fr. ²*round*] **1** *archaic* : a constable's jail : GUARDHOUSE, LOCKUP **2** : a circular building for housing and repairing locomotives **3 a** : a cabin or apartment on the afterpart of a quarterdeck having the poop for its roof (as on 18th century sailing ships) **b** : a privy on deck near the bow **4** : a meld of one king and queen of each suit scoring 240 in every form of pinochle except two-handed pinochle in which it scores at most 220 — called also *round trip* **5** : a hook in boxing delivered with a wide or exaggerated swing **6** : a wide slow outcurve in baseball with little or no drop

round·house·man \ˈ=,=mən\ *n, pl* **roundhousemen** : one who is employed in a railroad roundhouse

round in *vt* [⁶*round*] : to haul in on (a rope, esp. a weather brace)

¹**rounding** *n* -S [fr. gerund of ⁶*round*] **1 a** : the act or process of making or becoming round **b** : the trimming and cutting of hides **c** : the act or result of pronouncing with rounded lips — called also *lip-rounding* **2** : something that has been made round : a rounded object, surface, or corner **3** : rope rejected for other use and wound round a ship's cable as chafing gear **4** : the expressing of a number with only a convenient degree of exactness (as by dropping decimals beyond a stated number of places or by substituting zeros for final integers)

²**rounding** *adj* [fr. pres. part. of ⁶*round*] **1** : ENCIRCLING, ENCOMPASSING **2** : tending towards roundness : becoming round **3** : circling round **4** : of, relating to, or used for trimming or shaping to roundness ⟨a ~ tool⟩

round iron *n* [²*round*] : a bulbous-headed iron tool used when hot to smooth off soldered joints

round·ish \ˈraůndish, -dēsh\ *adj* [²*round* + *-ish*] : somewhat round

roundle *var of* ROUNDEL

round-leaved dogwood \ˈ=,=-\ *or* **round-leaf dogwood** *n* [²*round* + *leaved* or *leaf*] : GREEN OSIER b

round-leaved wintergreen *n* : a wintergreen (*Pyrola americana*) with small broadly elliptic or round leaves

round·let \ˈraůndlət, rapid -nl-; *usu* -əd·+V\ *n* -S [ME *roundelet*, fr. MF *rondelet* — more at ROUNDELAY] **1** : a little circle or round object : DISK **2** : a 15th century hat for men with a round padded edge and loose drapery forming the crown and hanging over the edge **3** : RUNDLET **4** *heraldry* : ROUNDEL 3

round ligament *n* [²*round*] **1** : a fibrous cord resulting from the obliteration of the umbilical vein of the fetus and passing from the umbilicus to the notch in the anterior border of the liver and along the under surface of that organ **2** : either of a pair of rounded cords arising from each side of the uterus and traceable through the inguinal canal to the tissue of the labia majora into which they merge **3** : a triangular ligament of the hip joint implanted by its apex into a depression near the middle of the head of the femur and by its broad base into the margins of the cotyloid notch of the innominate bone

roundline \ˈ=,=\ *n* : a 3-strand right-handed line used for seizings — compare HAMBROLINE

round lot *n* **1** : a lot of 100 or a multiple of 100 shares of active stock traded on an exchange **2** : a lot of 10 or a multiple of 10 shares of a few designated inactive stocks traded on an exchange — compare ODD LOT

round·ly \ˈraůndlē, -li, *rapid* -nl-\ *adv* [ME, fr. ²*round* + *-ly*] **1 a** : COMPLETELY, FULLY, WHOLLY ⟨returned to France feeling he had been ~ snubbed —C.G.Bowers⟩ **b** : in a bold, open or plainspoken manner : BLUNTLY, CANDIDLY ⟨~ criticized his uncongenial master —R.A.Hall b.1911⟩ **2 a** : in a brisk or vigorous manner : PROMPTLY, SMARTLY **b** : BITTERLY, SCATHINGLY, SHARPLY ⟨~ denounced him for quitting —F.J. Haskin⟩ **3** *obs* : with ready or unimpeded speech : FLUENTLY **4** : CIRCULARLY, PLUMPLY, ROTUNDLY **5** : in a general way : in round numbers : COMPREHENSIVELY ⟨although he has some specialized knowledge, he is ~ and exhaustively general —Elizabeth Hardwick⟩

round·man \ˈraůn(d)mən\ *n, pl* **roundmen** [⁵*round* + *man*] : a slaughterhouse worker who cleans rounds for use as casings

round·ness \ˈraůnnəs *also* -ndnəs\ *n* -ES [ME *roundnesse*, fr. ²*round* + *-nesse* -ness] : the quality or state of being round

roundnose \ˈ=,=\ *or* **roundnosed** \ˈ=ˈ=\ *adj* [²*round* + *nose* or *nosed*] : having a round or rounded nose : rounded on corners or edges; *specif* : having a cutting edge rounded to increase tool life ⟨a ~ turning tool⟩ or to make a curving or gouging cut ⟨a ~ chisel⟩ : having the working end rounded ⟨~ pliers⟩

round of beam [⁵*round*] : the camber of a ship's deck beams

round off *vt* [⁶*round*] **1** : to trim or finish into curved or rounded form **2** : to bring to symmetry or completion ⟨*rounded off* his property by purchase of the additional land⟩ ⟨a term in Congress *rounded off* his career⟩ **3** : ⁶ROUND 7a ⟨*round* all decimals *off* to the nearest thousandth⟩

roundoff \ˈ=,=\ *n* -S [*round off*] : a tumbling stunt in which the body makes one revolution from feet to hands to feet incorporating a half twist — compare CARTWHEEL

round out *vb* [⁶*round*] *vt* : to bring to completion or fullness : finish out ⟨*round out* my quartet of Americana with an autobiography —E.A.Weeks⟩ ⟨the republic had *rounded out* a century of independence —Sidney Warren⟩ ~ *vi* : to grow round or plump

round pompano *n* [²*round*] : a small pompano (*Trachinotus falcatus*) found from Brazil northward sometimes to Cape Cod

round robin *n* **1 a** : a written petition, memorial, or protest to which the signatures are affixed in a circle so as not to indicate who signed first **b** : a statement signed by several persons ⟨a *round robin* signed by 15 senators, who declared that . . . they would not vote to convict the governor —Hodding Carter⟩ **c** : a letter sent in turn to the members of a group (as a college class) each of whom signs and forwards it sometimes after adding information or comment ⟨a *round robin* letter to religious leaders in the community requesting that they pass the bibliography on to the next person on a list —*Amer. Library Assoc. Bull.*⟩ **2** : a talk or meeting in which several participants share : ROUND TABLE ⟨got together on a *round robin* telephone hookup —*Newsweek*⟩ **3** : a tournament in which every contestant meets every other contestant in turn **4** : SERIES, SEQUENCE, ROUND ⟨another *round robin* of price boosts —*Newsweek*⟩ ⟨*round robin* of colorcasts for all the regular shows on the network —*Advertising Age*⟩ **5** : ROUND SCAD

round rush *n* : SOFT RUSH

rounds *pl of* ROUND, *pres 3d sing of* ROUND

round scad *n* : a small fusiform carangid fish (*Decapterus punctatus*) of the western Atlantic related to and often included among the mackerel scads — called also *cigarfish, quiaquia*

round scale *n* : any of various armored scales (as the San Jose scale) that constitute the genus *Aspidiotus* and have a nearly circular covering

rounds chef *n* [⁵*round*] : ROUNDSMAN 3

roundseam \ˈ=,=\ *n* [²*round*] : a seam used to join the edges of canvas without lapping (as when sewing the bottom into a sea bag)

round-seeded spinach \ˈ=,==-\ *n* : a spinach (*Spinacia oleracea inermis*) having the fruit without spines

round seizing *n* : a seizing in which the lines seized are parallel to each other and a double binding layer is used — compare FLAT SEIZING

round shot *n* : an obsolete spherical projectile for ordnance

round-shouldered \ˈ=ˈ==\ *adj* : having the shoulders stooping or rounded

rounds·man \ˈraůn(d)zmən\ *n, pl* **roundsmen** [⁵*round*] **1** : an English laborer receiving parish relief and working for various farmers in turn under a system now obsolete **2** : one that makes rounds: as **a** : a supervisory police officer of the grade of sergeant or just below **b** *Brit* : ROUTE MAN ⟨a butcher's ~ in London —Flora Thompson⟩ **c** : WATCHMAN **3** : a cook capable of substituting for or assisting any of the specialty cooks — called also *rounds chef, swingman, tournant* **4** : one who patrols a petroleum refinery to supervise the watchmen and porters

round splice *n* [²*round*] : a long splice keeping the shape of the rope

round stave basket *n* : a basket used chiefly for fruits and vegetables that is usu. circular and of greater diameter than depth and is made in standard capacities ranging from ⅛ bushel to 2 bushels

round steak *n* [⁵*round*] : a steak cut from the whole round of beef including the bone — compare BOTTOM ROUND, TOP ROUND; see BEEF illustration

round·sters \ˈraůn(d)ztə(r)z, -n(t)st-\ *n pl but sing in constr* [irreg. fr. ⁵*round*] : the privilege in marbles of shooting from any point on the ring line ⟨if your shooter goes outside the ring, you may take ~⟩

round stingray *n* [²*round*] : a small round-bodied stingray (*Urobatis halleri*) common in shallow water along the southern California coast — called also *stingaree*

roundstone \ˈ=,=\ *n* **1** : any naturally rounded stone — compare BOULDER, COBBLE, PEBBLE **2** : a paving cobblestone

round table *n* [ME; fr. the Round Table of Arthurian legend] **1** *often cap* **a** : any of various knightly assemblies or tournaments modeled on King Arthur's Round Table **b** : any of various English sites, structures, or natural formations associated in legend with King Arthur's Round Table **2 a** : a conference for discussion or deliberation by several participants often seated at a round table so that no precedence in rank can be indicated **b** : the participants in such a conference **c** : the discussion carried on at a round table conference

roundtail \ˈ=,=\ *n* [²*round* + *tail*] : BONYTAIL

round-tailed muskrat \ˈ=,=-\ *n* : a large swamp-living vole (*Neofiber alleni*) of Florida resembling a small muskrat but having the tail cylindrical and tapering instead of keeled

round-the-clock *adj* : AROUND-THE-CLOCK

round-the-corner \ˈ==ˈ==\ *adj* : of or relating to a card sequence in which the king and deuce both connect with the ace

round-the-head \ˈ==ˈ=\ *adj* : played forehanded on the backhand side of the body (as the left side of a right-handed player) — used of a circular stroke in badminton

round timber *n* [²*round*] **1** : timber used (as for poles) without being squared by sawing or hewing **2** *South & Midland* : untapped turpentine-yielding pine trees

round to *vi* [⁶*round*] : to come about with head to the wind in either direction usu. preparatory to heaving to or coming to anchor

roundtop \ˈ=,=\ *n* [²*round*] : a round platform at a masthead

round tower *n* : a circular stone tower ranging in height from 60 to 150 feet, having a conical cap, and built in considerable numbers in Ireland from the 9th to the 13th centuries as refuges from Viking invaders

roundtree \ˈ=,=\ *n* [alter. of *rowan tree*] : AMERICAN MOUNTAIN ASH

round trip *n* [²*round*] **1** : a trip to a place and back usu. over the same route **2** : ROUNDHOUSE 4

round turn *n* **1** : one turn of a rope round a timber or belaying pin or around a bollard on a pier to stop a ship suddenly **2** : a foul hawse resulting from a 720-degree turn made by a ship riding at two anchors — compare ELBOW IN HAWSE

round up *vb* [⁶*round*] *vt* **1** : to haul up (as slack rope through its leading block or a tackle by its fall) **2 a** : to collect (cattle) by riding around them and driving them in **b** : to gather in or bring together (scattered persons or things) ⟨police *rounded up* members of a gambling ring⟩ ⟨*rounds up* the news in a nightly 11 o'clock broadcast⟩ ~ *vi* : to collect in a group

roundup \ˈ=,=\ *n* -S [in sense 1, fr. ⁶*round* + *up*; in other senses fr. *round up*] **1** : an upward curvature (as in a ship's deck) : CAMBER **2 a** : the gathering together of cattle by riders (as for branding or for shipment to market) **b** : the men and horses engaged in a roundup **3** : a gathering in of scattered persons or things ⟨a ~ of criminals⟩ **4 a** : a summary (as in a printed or broadcast news report) of related information of various kinds or from various sources ⟨a ~ of the year's financial news⟩ **b** : a brief résumé of late news ⟨said he heard it on the 11 o'clock news ~⟩

roun·dure \ˈraůnjə(r)\ *n* -S [²*round* + *-ure*] *archaic* : ROUNDNESS

round window *n* : the cochlear fenestra of the ear

roundwise *adv (or adj)* [²*round* + *-wise*] *obs* : in a circular form or manner

roundwood \ˈ=,=\ *n* [*round* (alter. of *rowan*) + *wood*] **1** : AMERICAN MOUNTAIN ASH **2** : ROUND TIMBER 1

roundworm \ˈ=,=\ *n* [²*round*] : a nematode worm and sometimes also a gordian or acanthocephalan worm as distinguished from a flatworm or tapeworm

round yam *n* : BURDEKIN VINE

roun·tree \ˈrōn·,trē\ *Scot var of* ROWAN TREE

¹**roup** \ˈrōp, ˈrüp\ *vb* -ED/-ING/-S [ME *roupen*, fr. MD *roepen* to cry out, call; akin to OE *hrōpan* to cry out, call, OHG *hruoffan*, ON *hrōpa* to slander, Goth *hropjan* to cry out, call, and perh. to OE *hrēth* glory — more at CADUCEUS] *vi, dial chiefly Brit* : to call or shout hoarsely : CROAK ~ *vt, Scot* : to sell at auction

²**roup** \"\ *n* -S **1** *Scot* : CLAMOR, SHOUTING **2** *chiefly Scot* : a public auction

³**roup** \ˈrüp\ *n* -S [origin unknown] : any of various respiratory disorders of poultry: as **a** : coryza of chickens esp. when in an advanced stage and marked by the presence of thick cheesy mucus — compare PIP **b** : INFECTIOUS SINUSITIS **c** : FOWL POX **b d** : avitaminosis A of poultry

roup·et \ˈrōpət, ˈrüp-\ *adj* [Sc *roup* hoarseness + *-et* -ed] *Scot* : afflicted with a sore throat : HOARSE

roupy \-pi\ *adj* -ER/-EST [Sc *roup* hoarseness (prob. of imit. origin) + *-y*] *chiefly Scot* : HOARSE

rous·ant \ˈraůzᵊnt\ *adj* [¹*rouse* + *-ant*] : RISING — used of a heraldic bird, esp. a swan

¹**rouse** \ˈraůz\ *vb* -ED/-ING/-S [ME *rousen, rowsen*] *vi* **1** *obs* **a** : to erect and shake the feathers — used esp. of a hawk **b** : to stand on end ⟨my fell of hair would . . . ~, and stir as life were in't —Shak.⟩ **2 a** : to become aroused from or as if from sleep : AWAKEN, STIR ⟨laughed and dozed, then *roused* and read again —Vachel Lindsay⟩ ⟨before she could ~ from this insult —Grace Kinnicut⟩ — often used with *up* ⟨from under . . . ragged blankets figures *roused* up from the dirt floor —F.V.W. Mason⟩ **b** : to gather strength : MOUNT, INTENSIFY ⟨our indignation ~s —Adam Smith⟩ **3** *slang Austral* : to speak angrily : RANT, RAVE ~ *vt* **1** *archaic* : to cause to break from cover ⟨*roused* a hart —Charles Kingsley⟩ **2** *obs* **a** : to cause to erect and shake (the feathers) : RUFFLE **b** : to lift up : RAISE ⟨being mounted, and both *roused* in their seats —Shak.⟩ **3 a** : to call forth : set in motion : RAISE, STIMULATE ⟨names in the railway time-table . . . first ~ romantic images in the mind of the boy —Edmund Wilson⟩ ⟨these questions . . . sometimes *roused* charges and countercharges —Alan Valentine⟩ **b** : to kindle to intensity : EXCITE, INFLAME ⟨such wars ~ limited passions —Herbert Agar⟩ ⟨the nobility that is in us is *roused* to respond —H.A.Overstreet⟩ **c** : to arouse from sleep or torpor : AWAKEN, STIR ⟨use . . . histrionics to ~ her audience —Andrea Parke⟩ ⟨the government was *roused* to unparalleled activity —B.E.Supple⟩ ⟨the boat ~s wild ducks to flight —*Amer. Guide Series: Mich.*⟩ ⟨made an effort . . . to ~ herself from sorrow —Margaret A. Barnes⟩ — often used with *up* ⟨*roused* up his brothers, who were in bed —William Black⟩ **d** (1) : to alert for action — used with *out* ⟨*roused* out his anchor watch —K.M.Dodson⟩ (2) : to haul strongly (as on a rope or hawser) **syn** see STIR

²**rouse** \"\ *n* -S : an act or instance of rousing; *esp* : an excited stir ⟨a ~ of voices —Carl Sandburg⟩

³**rouse** \"\ *n* -S [alter. (resulting fr. incorrect division of *drink carouse*) of ¹*carouse*] **1** *obs* : DRINK, TOAST **2** *archaic* : CAROUSAL

⁴**rouse** \"\ *vt* -ED/-ING/-S [by shortening fr. earlier *arrouse* to sprinkle, bedew, fr. ME *arousen*, fr. MF *aroser*, fr. (assumed) VL *adrosare*, fr. L *ad-* + *ros* dew — more at ROSEMARY] : to cure (as herring) by salting

⁵**rouse** \ˈrüz\ *var of* ROOSE

rouseabout \ˈ==,=\ *n* -S [¹*rouse* + *about*] *Austral* : a man of all work; *specif* : a handyman on a sheep farm : KNOCKABOUT

rouse·ment \ˈraůzmənt\ *n* -S [¹*rouse* + *-ment*] : an act or instance of stirring up : AROUSAL

rous·er \ˈraůzə(r)\ *n* -S : one that rouses: as **a** : one that awakens or excites **b** : an implement for stirring a fermenting brew **c** : something superlative of its kind : HUMDINGER ⟨a real ~ of a storm —R.L.Taylor⟩

¹**rousing** *n* -S [fr. gerund of ¹*rouse*] **1** : an act or instance of stirring up : AGITATION, DISTURBANCE **2** *slang Austral* : SCOLDING ⟨the women and the youngsters gave me a ~ —*Melbourne (Australia) Argus*⟩

²**rousing** *adj* [fr. pres. part. of ¹*rouse*] **1 a** : having the power to rouse : EXCITING, STIRRING ⟨a ~ speech⟩ ⟨brought the meeting to a close with a ~ hymn —Agnes S. Turnbull⟩ **b** : BRISK, LIVELY ⟨a ~ ballet about three sailors on shore leave —Walter Terry⟩ ⟨milliners doing a ~ trade at Easter⟩ **2** : exceptional of its kind : SUPERLATIVE ⟨wrote three ~ best sellers in a row —Bennett Cerf⟩ — **rous·ing·ly** *adv*

rous sarcoma *also* **rous' sarcoma** *or* **rous's sarcoma** \ˈraůs(əz)-\ *n, usu cap R* [after F. Peyton *Rous* b1879 Am. physician] : a readily transplantable malignant spindle-cell sarcoma of chickens that is transmissible by cell-free filtrate and so is regarded as due to a specific carcinogenic virus

rous·seau·ean *or* **rous·seau·ian** \rüˈsōēən\ *adj, usu cap* [Jean Jacques *Rousseau* †1778 Fr. philosopher & author + E *-ean* or *-ian*] : ROUSSEAUISTIC

rous·seau·esque \ˌrüsōˌesk\ *adj, usu cap* [Jean Jacques *Rousseau* + E *-esque*] : ROUSSEAUISTIC

rous·seau·ism \rüˈsōˌizəm\ *n* -S *usu cap* [Jean Jacques *Rousseau* + E *-ism*] : the philosophy of Jean Jacques Rousseau or his followers and esp. the doctrines of the inherent equality of men, the general will as the basis of government, and the corruption and degradation of human nature by civilization — compare SOCIAL CONTRACT

rous·seau·ist \-ōəst\ *or* **rous·seau·ite** \-ōˌīt\ *n* -S *usu cap* [Jean Jacques *Rousseau* + E *-ist* or *-ite*] : a follower of Rousseau or adherent to Rousseauism

rous·seau·is·tic \ˌrüsōˈistik\ *adj, usu cap* [Jean Jacques *Rousseau* + E *-istic*] : of, relating to, or characteristic of Rousseau or Rousseauism

rous·sette \rüˈset\ *n* -S [F, fr. MF, fr. fem. of *rousset* reddish, fr. OF — more at RUSSET] : a small shark or dogfish of the genus *Scyliorhinus*

rous·sin's salt \ˈrüsənz-\ *n, usu cap R* [after François-Zacharie *Roussin* †1894 Fr. chemist] : any of two series of alkali metal salts that are nitrosyl and sulfur complexes of iron: **a** : a red unstable salt having the general formula $M[Fe(NO)_2S]$ and obtainable by reaction of nitric oxide with ferrous sulfide **b** : a black more stable salt having the general formula $M[Fe_4(NO)_7S_3]$ and obtainable (as by treatment with alkali) from a red salt

¹**roust** \ˈraůst\ *vb* -ED/-ING/-S [alter. of ¹*rouse*] *vt, dial* : to rout esp. out of bed : cause to appear : ROUSE — usu. used with *out* or *up* ⟨would roll back into his blankets . . . till the sound of another boat ~*ed* him out again —H.L.Davis⟩ ⟨the bartender ~*ed* up an odd bottle of . . . port —Jack Kerouac⟩ ~ *vi* [Sc, to shout, roar, fr. *roust* voice, shout, fr. ME *rowst*, fr. ON *raust* voice] *slang Austral* : ¹ROUSE 3

²**roust** \ˈrüst\ *n* -S [of Scand origin; akin to ON *röst* current] *dial Eng* : a strong tide or current esp. in a narrow channel

roustabout \ˈ==,=\ *n* -S [¹*roust* + *about*] **1 a** : a dock worker or deckhand ⟨~ and chore boy on a dirty trawler —L.C. Douglas⟩ **b** : an unskilled or semiskilled laborer; *esp* : one working in an oil field or refinery : FLOORMAN ⟨~s . . . maintain the oil wells once they are brought in —*Newsweek*⟩ **c** : a member of the working crew of a circus responsible for erection and dismantling of tents, care of the grounds, and handling of animals and equipment **2** *Austral* : ROUSEABOUT

roust·er \ˈraůstə(r)\ *n* -S [¹*roust* + *-er*] : ROUSTABOUT 1

¹**rout** \ˈraůt, *usu* -d·+V\ *vi* -ED/-ING/-S [ME *routen*, fr. OE *hrūtan*; akin to OHG *hrūzan* to snore, ON *hrjōta*, and prob. to OE *hrot* thick fluid — more at CORYZA] *archaic* : SNORE

²**rout** \"\ *n* -S [ME *rute, route*, fr. MF *route*, troop, band, defeat, fr. (assumed) VL *rupta*, fr. L, fem. of *ruptus*, past part. of *rumpere* to break — more at REAVE] **1 a** : a crowd of people : MOB, THRONG ⟨succeeded by a ~ of rabbis, reverends, and monsignors —Dwight MacDonald⟩; *specif* : RABBLE ⟨the butler, the parlormaid, and the ~ from belowstairs —J.C. Trewin⟩ **b** *or* **route** \"\ *archaic* : a company of animals : FLOCK ⟨restless ~s of sheep —John Clare⟩ **c** : a large number : MULTITUDE ⟨the ~ of series of books and pamphlets on the war —*Times Lit. Supp.*⟩ **d** : NUMBER, HERD ⟨you will not swell the ~ of lads that wore their honors out —A.E.Housman⟩ ⟨a vulgar comment . . . by the common ~ —Shak.⟩ **2** : a disturbance of the peace by persons assembled with intent to do something and actually making a motion toward its execution which if executed would make them rioters **3** *archaic* **a** : DISTURBANCE, UPROAR **b** : FUSS ⟨make such a ~ about it —Harriet Granville⟩ **4** : a fashionable gathering : RECEPTION, SOIREE ⟨foreign potentates at diplomatic ~s —Robert Rice⟩ **syn** see CROWD

³**rout** \"\ *vb* -ED/-ING/-S [ME *rowten*, fr. ON *rauta*; akin to OE *rēotan* to cry, weep, OHG *riozan*, L *rudere* to roar, Skt *roditi* he weeps, cries, and prob. to OE *rēon* to lament — more at RUMOR] *vi* **1** *dial chiefly Brit* : to low loudly : BAWL, BELLOW — used of cattle **2** : to make a loud noise : ROAR ~ *vt, dial chiefly Brit* : to shout out : ROAR ⟨have no . . . inclination to ~ out my name to the countryside —R.L.Stevenson⟩

⁴**rout** \"\ *n* -S *dial chiefly Brit* : a loud noise : CLAMOR, UPROAR

⁵**rout** \"\ *vb* -ED/-ING/-S [alter. of ³*root*] *vi* **1** : to poke around with the snout : ROOT ⟨pigs ~*ing* in the earth⟩ **2** : to make a haphazard search : RUMMAGE ⟨~*ed* in a corner and came back with . . . thread and needle —G.W.Brace⟩ **3** : to

perform a gouging operation ⟨carve, ~, shape and grind on this versatile machine —*advt*⟩ ~ *vt* **1 a** *archaic* **:** to dig up with the snout ⟨~*ing* up the moss . . . in search of acorns —Peter Beckford⟩ **b :** to gouge out or make a furrow in: as (1) **:** to scoop out or cut away (as blank parts) from a printing surface (as an engraving or electrotype) with a router (2) **:** to remove (as metal or wood) with a gouge or other hand-operated cutting tool **2 a :** to expel by force **:** EJECT — usu. used with *out* ⟨whole families are . . . ~*ed* out of house and home —Arthur Murphy⟩ **b :** to cause to emerge esp. from bed **:** drag out **:** ROUST ⟨~*ed* . . . from his garret by loud rings at the bell —Floyd Dell⟩ ⟨~*ed* me out of bed to help place the target —A.C.Fisher⟩ ⟨~ the enemies of Calvinism from the inmost keep of their stronghold —V.L.Parrington⟩ **3 :** to dig out **:** come up with **:** UNCOVER ⟨went . . . to his cellar and ~*ed* out a bottle of port —John Masefield⟩

6rout \"\ *n* -s **:** an act, process, or result of routing ⟨this house, with its strange clutter . . . gives the effect of ~ —Howard Griffin⟩

7rout \"\ *n* -s [prob. of Scand origin; akin to ON *hrota* barnacle goose] *chiefly dial* **:** BRANT

8rout \"\ *n* -s [MF *route* troop, band, defeat — more at 2ROUT] **1 :** a state of wild confusion or disorderly retreat ⟨charging tanks put the infantry to ~⟩ ⟨reason had been clearly put to ~ by nineteenth-century Romanticism —Edmund Wilson⟩ **2 a :** a disastrous defeat **:** DEBACLE ⟨the battle became a ~, a shambles —*Amer. Guide Series: Texas*⟩ **b :** a precipitate flight ⟨everybody was for saving his own skin in this frantic ~ —L.C.Douglas⟩ **c :** an act or instance of routing ⟨the ~ of the Democrats . . . resulted in the candidacy of Republican incumbents —V.O.Key⟩ ⟨most crushing defeat since its 61–0 ~ last year⟩ **3** *archaic* **:** a fleeing force ⟨disordered the rank . . . whereupon their men were in ~*s* —Mary Wroth⟩

9rout \"\ *vt* -ED/-ING/-S **1 a :** to disorganize completely **:** put to precipitate flight **:** DEMORALIZE, STAMPEDE ⟨the large and well-mechanized army . . . had been ~*ed* and was in part surrounded —Upton Sinclair⟩ ⟨charged the main body of Russian cavalry . . . and ~*ed* it —Al Newman⟩ **b :** to defeat decisively **:** OVERWHELM ⟨suffered the discomfiture of seeing their party ~*ed* at the polls —A.N.Holcombe⟩ ⟨the team ~*ed* their traditional Thanksgiving Day rivals 41–0⟩ **2 :** to drive out **:** cause to disappear **:** DISPEL ⟨virtues are discredited and decency is ~*ed* —Frank Mac Shane⟩ **syn** see CONQUER

1route \'rüt, 'raůt, *usu* |d·+V\ *also* **rout** \'raůt\ *n* -s [ME *rute, route,* fr. OF *route* troop, band, route, fr. (assumed) VL *rupta (via),* lit., broken way, beaten way, fr. L *rupta,* fem. of *ruptus,* past part. of *rumpere* to break — more at REAVE] **1 a :** a traveled way **:** ROAD, HIGHWAY ⟨expressways, toll roads, turnpikes, and similar large-scale ~*s* —P.F.Griffin⟩ ⟨because of its position on a water ~, the village soon became a river-traffic center —*Amer. Guide Series: Mich.*⟩ **b :** a means of access **:** CHANNEL, PATH ⟨preparedness was offered as a ~ to peace —F.L.Paxson⟩ ⟨liberal arts courses . . . as a ~ to the graduate schools —*Univ. of Chicago Round Table*⟩ **2 a :** a regular routine **:** customary progression **b :** a method of transmitting a disease or of administering a remedy ⟨the airborne ~ of . . . infection —M.L.Furcolow⟩ ⟨may be injected into . . . patients who cannot for any reason take the material by the oral ~ —*Collier's Yr. Bk.*⟩ **3 :** a line or direction of travel **:** COURSE, TRACK ⟨bayous change their ~*s* with each flood —*Lamp*⟩ ⟨U.S. 19 follows the general ~ of the old Catawba Trail —*Amer. Guide Series: N.C.*⟩ **4 a :** an established itinerary **:** a selected or regularly traversed passage esp. between two distant points ⟨soon I'll be over the panhandle . . . if I've not drifted north of ~ —C.A.Lindbergh b.1902⟩ ⟨permission . . . for 53 new domestic air ~*s* —*Americana Annual*⟩ ⟨the preponderance of shipping traffic along the north Atlantic ~ —R.S.Thoman⟩; *specif* **:** a telephone line ⟨a new procedure . . . enables operators to use the circuits on busy ~*s* more efficiently —C.F.Craig⟩ **b :** an assigned territory to be systematically covered ⟨postal ~⟩ ⟨paper ~⟩ **c :** a prescribed manner of shipment that may include selected carriers, junctions, and delivery point ⟨inform me by what ~ they had sent an order —Georgina Grahame⟩ **5** *archaic* **:** marching orders ⟨our ~ came for a march —Robert Bage⟩ **6 :** a horse race of a mile or more ⟨a horse trained for ~*s* does not do well in sprints⟩ **syn** see WAY

2route \"\ *also* **rout** \"\ *vt* -ED/-ING/-S **1 a :** to plan an itinerary for **:** send by a selected route **:** DIRECT ⟨~ lines through the richest inland spots —*Amer. Guide Series: Minn.*⟩ ⟨*routed* volunteers to the guerilla frontiers —E.P.Snow⟩ **b :** to divert in a specified direction ⟨~ the high voltage to the various engine cylinders in the correct sequence —*Aircraft Power Plants*⟩ ⟨took to *routing* their business through his . . . colleague —S.H.Adams⟩ **c :** to select the course to be followed by a shipment by designating carrier, intermediate points, junctions, and final delivery **2 :** to put (the mail for a postal route) in order for delivery **3 :** to prearrange and direct the order and execution of (a series of processes or transactions) in a factory or business **:** dispatch documents or materials to appropriate destinations ⟨~ an invoice to the accounting department⟩ **syn** see SEND

route agent *n* [1*route*] **:** a postal employee accompanying mail being transported by train and receiving, canceling, and delivering mail along the route

route chart *n* **:** FLOW CHART

route locking *n* **:** electric locking that prevents the movement of any switch, movable point frog, or derail in advance of a train after it has passed a signal to proceed

route·man \'=mən\ *n, pl* **routemen** [1*route* + *man*] **1 a :** a salesman or deliveryman on an assigned route **b :** the supervisor of a group of news carriers responsible for helping to establish routes, taking care of complaints, making out bills, and paying carriers **2 :** a shipyard worker who plans the most efficient routing of work through a department

route march *n* **:** a practice march in peacetime or one at a distance from the enemy in wartime in which troops maintain the prescribed interval and distance but are not required to keep step, maintain silence, or hold their arms in any one position

1rout·er \'raůd·ə(r), -aůtə-\ *n* -s [5*rout* + *-er*] **:** one that routs: as **a :** ROUTER PLANE **b :** a machine with a rapidly revolving vertical spindle and cutter for milling out the surface of wood or metal (as in woodworking or photoengraving) **c** *or* **router-bit** \'==,=\ **:** the lip on a bit (as a center bit) that cuts the radius of the nicker **d :** an aircraft worker who shapes sheet metal blanks with a routing machine **e :** an operator of a machine for cutting designs in wooden stock

2rout·er \'rüd·ə(r), 'raů|, |tə(r)\ *n* -s [2*route* + *-er*] **:** one that routes: as **a :** a clerk who sorts articles according to delivery routes **b :** a floor boy who keeps shoe workers supplied with material

3router \"\ *n* -s [1*route* + *-er*] **:** a horse trained for distance races — compare SPRINTER

router plane *n* [1*router*] **:** a plane consisting of a horizontal bar with a handle at each end supporting a vertically inserted narrow cutter operated by pulling and pushing and used for cutting recesses and smoothing the bottom of grooves — see PLANE illustration

route step *n* [1*route*] **:** the out-of-step manner of executing a route march — used as a military command ⟨we were never given *route step* until after we'd cleared the last of the company streets —Richard Yates⟩

route transposition *n* **:** encipherment in which the plaintext letters are placed along a more or less complex path (as a set of lines, a zigzag, a spiral) and then copied out in order as they are found to lie along a differently defined path — compare COLUMNAR TRANSPOSITION

routeway \'=,=\ *n* **:** ROUTE 3 ⟨the one natural ~ across the desert waste would appear to be the River Nile —L.D.Stamp⟩

1routh \'rüth, 'raůth\ *n* -s [origin unknown] *chiefly Scot* **:** PLENTY, ABUNDANCE

2routh \"\ *also* **routhy** \-thi\ *adj* **1** *chiefly Scot* **:** PLENTIFUL, ABUNDANT **2** *chiefly Scot* **:** ABOUNDING

1rou·tine \(')rü'tēn\ *n* -s [F, fr. MF, fr. *route* traveled way] **1 a :** a standard practice **:** regular course of procedure ⟨the old speakeasy ~ of having a guard inspect you with one eye through a peephole —Robert Shaplen⟩ ⟨the usual ~ of appointment: tutor, 1871–74; assistant professor, 1875–80; professor, 1880–1916 —J.M.Berdan⟩ **b :** the habitual method of performance of established procedures ⟨the matter-of-fact laconic ~ of the hospital —Leslie Rees⟩ ⟨housewives, their ~ quickened by the pace of wartime living —*Monsanto Mag.*⟩ **c :** a repetitive speech or formula ⟨that old ~ about his welfare, and what was best for it —Gregor Felsen⟩ ⟨the "visit your dentist twice a year" ~ —*Spokane (Wash.) Spokesman Rev.*⟩ **2 a :** adherence to a pattern of behavior characterized by mechanical repetition ⟨most of us are blind — made so by custom and ~ —C.S.Kilby⟩ **b :** the quality or state of being humdrum ⟨sell out quickly . . . to avoid the dull ~ of development —*Amer. Guide Series: Nev.*⟩ **3 a :** an established sequence of operations (as in a factory or business establishment) **b :** a sequence of computer instructions for performing a particular task **4 a :** a standardized piece of entertainment or showmanship **:** ACT, BIT ⟨went through the hat ~ for distinguished guests —*Time*⟩; *specif* **:** a theatrical number ⟨a breathtaking ~ on a tightrope —*New Yorker*⟩ ⟨sitting out front at rehearsals, he jots down . . . a description of each ~ —H.W.Wind⟩ **b :** a fixed series of dance steps or rhythmic movements ⟨can pick up a difficult tap ~ at a single rehearsal —Agnes de Mille⟩

2routine \(')=¦=\ *adj* **1 :** of a commonplace or repetitious character **:** ORDINARY, USUAL ⟨the level of artistry . . . was altogether ~ and uninspired —Winthrop Sargeant⟩ ⟨read about the spectacular flights, but . . . seldom read anything about the hundreds of ~ flights made over the same country —Harold Griffin⟩ ⟨a few phrases of ~ patriotism —James Joll⟩ ⟨the car performs well with only ~ maintenance⟩ **2 :** of, relating to, or in accordance with established procedure ⟨the ~ settlement of boundary disputes —S.F.Bemis⟩ ⟨the ~ use of the blood-pressure test —F.A.Faught⟩ ⟨the purser's ~ book . . . lists everything that has to be done —*Saturday Rev.*⟩ — **rou·tine·ly** *adv* — **rou·tine·ness** *n* -ES

3routine \=¦=\ *vt* -ED/-ING/-S **:** ROUTINIZE ⟨a horse should not be *routined* in any one test —*Notes on Dressage*⟩ ⟨~*s* the sequence of dialogue —Maurice Zolotow⟩

rou·ti·neer \,rütə'ni(ə)r\ *n* -s [1*routine* + *-eer*] **:** one that adheres to or insists on routine ⟨hacks and ~*s* were making the fascinating game of business and finance appear endlessly dull —M.S.Rukeyser⟩

routine orders *n pl* **:** orders relating to military matters other than operations in the field — compare COMBAT ORDERS

1routing *n* -s [fr. gerund of 5*rout*] **1 :** the removal of excess material (as from a printing plate) by cutting, milling, or gouging **2 :** a groove or indentation produced by routing

2routing *n* -s [fr. gerund of 2*route*] **1 a :** a course of travel **:** ITINERARY **b :** transmission over a selected course **:** CIRCULATION ⟨selective ~ of messages —Eunice Cooper & Helen Dinerman⟩ **2 :** the sorting of mail into proper sequence for delivery **3 :** the scheduling or standardization of a flow of work **4 a :** the determination of a course and method of shipment (as of freight) **b :** ROUTE 4c

rou·tin·ist \rü'tēnəst\ *n* -s [1*routine* + *-ist*] **:** ROUTINEER

rou·tin·iza·tion \rü,tēnə'zāshən\ *n* -s **:** an act or instance of routinizing ⟨specialization and ~ have reduced the creative aspects of their work —R.K.Burns⟩

rou·tin·ize \rü'tē,nīz\ *vt* -ED/-ING/-S [1*routine* + *-ize*] **:** to discipline in or reduce to a routine ⟨*routinized* assembly-line workers —J.B.Martin⟩ ⟨we can ~ this process —F.J.Gruenberger⟩

rout·ous \'raůd·əs\ *adj* [2*rout* + *-ous*] *archaic* **:** NOISY, UPROARIOUS

rout·ous·ly *adv* [*routous* + *-ly*] **1** *archaic* **:** UPROARIOUSLY, NOISILY **2 :** in violation of a law against routs

routs *pl of* ROUT, *pres 3d sing of* ROUT

rout-seat \'=,=\ *n* [2*rout*] *Brit* **:** a light bench supplied for parties ⟨knocked . . . off the end of a *rout-seat* at a ball —W.F. DeMorgan⟩

roux \'rü\ *n, pl* **roux** \'rü(z)\ [F, fr. (*beurre*) *roux* browned butter, fr. *roux* reddish brown, russet, fr. OF *rous* — more at RUSSET] **:** a mixture of flour and fat cooked sometimes until the flour browns and used to thicken soups and sauces

1rove [ME *roof*] *past of* RIVE

2rove \'rōv\ *n* -s [ME *rewe, rufe, rove,* fr. ON *rō*] **1** *or* **roove** \'rüv\ **:** BURR 3 b **2 :** the bight of a rope sling that receives the hook

3rove \"\ *vb* -ED/-ING/-S [ME *roven*] *vi* **1 :** to shoot at rovers in archery **2 a :** to move aimlessly **:** ROAM, STRAY ⟨criminals . . . *roving* about freely without either arrest or custodial restraint —H.E.Barnes⟩ ⟨members . . . *roved* restlessly from one committee meeting to another —Allan Nevins⟩ **b :** to follow a random course **:** RAMBLE, WANDER ⟨at first he did not follow her, his thoughts had *roved* so far —Ellen Glasgow⟩ ⟨feebly his glance *roved* over the figures by the bed —Mary Austin⟩ **3** *obs* **a :** to deviate from the point ⟨from that mark how far they ~ —John Milton⟩ **b :** to take random aim **c :** GUESS **4** *archaic* **:** to troll with live bait ⟨~ for a perch with a minnow —Izaak Walton⟩ **5** *dial Brit* **:** to be light-headed or delirious **:** RAVE ~ *vt* **:** to traverse aimlessly **:** wander through or over **:** ROAM ⟨permit their progeny . . . to ~ the forest —S.H.Adams⟩ ⟨letting her eyes ~ the room as if she were planning . . . its decoration —Jean Stafford⟩ ⟨saw the searchlights *roving* the sky —Howard Hunt⟩

4rove \"\ *n* -s **:** an act or instance of wandering ⟨a sidelong ~ of the eye —A.L.Kroeber⟩

5rove *n* -s [modif. of Sp & Pg *arroba*] *obs* **:** ARROBA

6rove *past of* REEVE

7rove \'rōv\ *vt* -ED/-ING/-S [origin unknown] **:** to join (textile fibers) with a slight twist and draw out into roving

8rove \"\ *n* -s [origin unknown] **:** 3ROVING 1

rove beetle \'rōv-\ *n* [perh. fr. 3*rove*] **:** any of numerous beetles constituting the family Staphylinidae, having a long body and very short wing covers beneath which the wings are folded transversely, often occurring on decaying animal and vegetable matter, and many of them being predatory and the larvae of some parasitic

rove-over \'=,==\ *adj* [prob. fr. 6*rove* + *over*] **:** having an extrametrical syllable at the end of one line that forms a foot with the first syllable of the next line — used of a type of verse in sprung rhythm

1ro·ver \'rōvə(r)\ *n* -s [ME, fr. MD *rover* robber, plunderer, fr. *roven* to rob + *-er*; akin to OE *rēafian* to reave — more at REAVE] **:** PIRATE ⟨the accumulated loot of all the sea ~*s* —H.E.Rieseberg⟩

2rov·er \"\ *n* -s [ME, fr. *roven* to shoot at random, wander + *-er* — more at ROVE] **1 a :** a random mark at an uncertain distance used as a target in archery — usu. used in pl. ⟨in shooting at ~*s* the archer whose arrow comes nearest the mark selects the next target⟩ **b :** one of a series of fixed marks at long range **c :** a strong arrow used in shooting at rovers **d :** an archer shooting at rovers **2 :** one that wanders: as **a :** a habitual roamer **:** TRAVELER, STRAY ⟨as much night life . . . as any vacation ~ can safely stand —C.L.Biemiller⟩ ⟨cattle, some ~*s* always excepted . . . remain on a given range —J.F.Dobie⟩ **b :** FLIRT, MASHER ⟨my true love's a ~ —Edna S. V. Millay⟩ **c** *chiefly Brit* **:** a boy scout over 17 years old who takes part in advanced scouting activities **d :** an architectural molding that follows a curve **e** *usu cap* **:** COLORADAN — used as a nickname **3 a** *or* **rover ball :** a croquet ball that has been through all the wickets and would be out if it hit the stake but is continued in play **b :** the player of a rover ball — **at rovers** *adv, obs* **:** at random **:** HAPHAZARDLY ⟨speaketh not *at rovers* —Arthur Golding⟩

3rov·er *n* -s [7*rove* + *-er*] **:** one that makes roving

rover bellflower *n* [2*rover*] **:** a coarse European perennial herb (*Campanula rapunculoides*) widely naturalized esp. in eastern No. America and having racemes of nodding flowers with campanulate corollas

rov·er boy *n, usu cap R&B* [fr. the *Rover boys,* heroes of a series of juvenile books (1899–1925) by Edward Stratemeyer †1930 Am. writer] **:** a physically brave and morally excellent person of somewhat limited outlook and experience ⟨trying to be the *Rover Boy* of the beachhead —R.M.Ingersoll⟩

rovescio *adv* [by shortening] **:** a rovescio

1roving *n* -s [ME, fr. gerund of *roven* to shoot at random, wander — more at ROVE] **1 :** an act or instance of shooting at random archery targets and esp. at natural targets in fields or woodlands **2 :** an act or instance of roaming ⟨every year this animal's ~*s* are restricted —Washington Irving⟩ ⟨found dial ~ common in the early parts of a program —George Fisk⟩

2roving *adj* [fr. pres. part. of 3*rove*] **1** *obs* **:** based on guesswork **:** CONJECTURAL **2 a :** traversing a random course **:** NOMADIC, WANDERING ⟨a ~ band of gypsies⟩ ⟨a ~ vixen wanting cubs —John Masefield⟩ **b :** traversing an assigned route or capable of being shifted from place to place **:** MOBILE ⟨~ judge⟩ ⟨~ reporter⟩ ⟨serving as a ~ police force for . . . the Territory of Arizona —Ross Santee⟩ **c :** of a general nature **:** unrestricted as to location or area of concern ⟨~ envoy⟩ ⟨~ assignment⟩ **d :** DISCURSIVE, RAMBLING ⟨a ~ wit⟩ ⟨unrelated subjects that happen to strike a ~ fancy —Dorothy Sayers⟩ **3 :** inclined to travel or stray **:** PERIPATETIC, ROAMING ⟨a large and ~ cast subsidiary to the main characters —Sylvia Berkman⟩ ⟨alas for poor Madame, he had a ~ eye —HenryS.Jones⟩

3roving *n* -s [fr. gerund of 7*rove*] **1 a :** a slightly twisted roll or strand of textile fibers **b :** material in an intermediate stage between sliver and yarn **2 :** the final process of reducing and drawing out sliver preliminary to spinning — compare SLUBBING

roving reel *n* [3*roving*] **:** a device for measuring the length of textile rovings

1row \'rō\ *vb* -ED/-ING/-S [ME *rowen,* fr. OE *rōwan;* akin to MHG *rüejen* to row, ON *rōa,* L *remus* oar, Gk *eressein* to row, *eretmon* oar, Skt *aritra*] *vi* **1 a :** to propel a boat by means of oars ⟨got into the dinghy and ~*ed* out to the sloop⟩ **b :** to be a member of a racing crew ⟨~*ed* on the varsity eight⟩ **c :** to take part in a rowing competition ⟨~*s* against the champions in the annual regatta⟩ **2** *archaic* **:** to struggle to advance ⟨no one shall find me ~*ing* against the stream . . . I write for general amusement —Sir Walter Scott⟩ **3 :** to move by or as if by the propulsion of oars ⟨as the boats ~*ed* in . . . we could hear groans and lamentations —Kenneth Roberts⟩ ⟨pelicans ~ by on slow, powerful wings —Juana Vogt⟩ ~ *vt* **1 a :** to propel with or as if with oars ⟨~ a boat⟩ **b :** to be equipped with (a specified number of oars) ⟨the ceremonial barge ~*ed* 14 oars⟩ **c** (1) **:** to participate in (a rowing match) ⟨~ a race⟩ (2) **:** to compete against in a rowing match ⟨~*s* the champion in the regatta⟩ (3) **:** to pull (an oar) in a crew ⟨~*ed* stroke for the class crew⟩ **2 :** to transport in or as if in a boat propelled by oars ⟨charged a small fee to ~ us across the river⟩ ⟨sailors on shore leave ~ their girls around the lake in the park⟩

2row \"\ *n* -s **:** an act or instance of rowing ⟨go for a ~ on the lake⟩

3row \'raů\ *chiefly Scot var of* RAW

4row \'rō\ *n* -s [ME *rawe, rowe,* fr. OE *rāw, rǣw;* akin to OHG *rīga* line, L *rima* slit, fissure, crack, Skt *rikhati* he scratches, *rekhā* scratch, line] **1 a :** a number of objects in an orderly series **:** STRING ⟨a double ~ of sodium vapor highway lamps —*Amer. Guide Series: Va.*⟩ **b :** an uninterrupted sequence **:** SUCCESSION ⟨utter . . . ~*s* of platitudes —Joyce Cary⟩ ⟨won the state tourney for four years in a ~ —*Bull. of Bates Coll.*⟩ **c :** an arbitrary series or arrangement of the twelve-tone chromatic scale used as a basis or organizational device for modern musical compositions **2** *archaic* **:** a homogeneous group **:** CATEGORY, SET ⟨an only daughter . . . who is, at least, approaching the old maid's ~ —Manasseh Cutler⟩ **3** *obs* **:** a written line esp. metrical ⟨the first ~ of the pious chanson —Shak.⟩ **4 a :** 1BLOCK 5c(2) ⟨street after street exactly alike, lined with ~*s* —T.F.Hamlin⟩ **b :** a way for passage **:** ALLEY, STREET ⟨on Catfish ~ and down Ramcat Alley —Shelby Foote⟩ ⟨two of the island's main arteries, Royal Poinciana Way and Coconut ~ —Walter Cartwright⟩ **c :** a street or area dominated by a specific kind of enterprise or occupancy ⟨in most cities a separate automobile ~ has arisen on the edge of the central business district —C.D.Harris & E.L. Ullman⟩ ⟨rumors fly along diplomatic ~⟩ ⟨zigzag from movie house to movie house like a barfly on whiskey ~ —Nathaniel Bart⟩ **5 :** a continuous strip usu. running horizontally or parallel to a base line: as **a :** a line of seats in a theater ⟨a pair of seats in the fifth ~ center⟩ **b :** a line of cultivated plants ⟨hoe between the ~*s*⟩ **c :** a horizontal line (as of figures) — distinguished from *column* ⟨~ totals are added to get the column total⟩ **d :** a line of stitches across a piece of needlework ⟨a ~ of knitting⟩ **e** (1) **:** a line of tufts in a carpet ⟨there is usu. one ~ of pile tufts for each cycle of back weaving⟩ (2) **:** the average number of tufts per inch in a carpet counted in the direction of the warp — **a row to hoe :** a task to accomplish — usu. used with a modifying adjective ⟨have had a hard *row to hoe* —*Coast Artillery Jour.*⟩ ⟨I'd like to be a surgeon, but it's a long *row to hoe* —*Sat. Eve. Post*⟩

5row \"\ *vt* -ED/-ING/-S **:** to form into or furnish with rows ⟨above the . . . heads of the students ~*ed* before me —Ralph Ellison⟩ ⟨a bare room ~*ed* with dusty windows —R.M. Coates⟩

6row \'raů\ *n* -s [origin unknown] **1 a :** a noisy disturbance **:** BRAWL, RUCKUS ⟨a first-class ~ between a brutal ranger . . . and an inoffensive citizen —S.E.White⟩ **b :** a heated argument **:** QUARREL, SQUABBLE ⟨a terrific ~ . . . between husband and wife because the former put a 15¢ stamp too much on a letter —H.J.Laski⟩ ⟨during the recent ~ over atomic-energy legislation their feuding was epic —Alfred Friendly⟩ **2** *slang chiefly Brit* **a :** a loud sound **:** NOISE, RACKET ⟨would make a beastly ~ with that instrument —F.M. Ford⟩ **b :** MOUTH ⟨she give him a big apple to shut his ~ —Richard Llewellyn⟩ **syn** see BRAWL

7row \"\ *vb* -ED/-ING/-S *vt* **1** *archaic* **:** to subject to assault **:** rough up **2** *chiefly Brit* **:** to speak angrily to **:** BERATE, SCOLD ⟨~*ed* the driver about the fare —*McClure's*⟩ ~ *vi* **:** to have a quarrel **:** FIGHT, SQUABBLE ⟨wrangled and ~*ed* with . . . other editors —W.A.White⟩

ROW *abbr* right of way

row·able \'rōəbəl\ *adj* [1*row* + *-able*] **:** capable of being rowed or rowed upon

row·an \'raůən, 'rōən\ *n* -s [of Scand origin; akin to ON *reynir* rowan; akin to OE *rēad* red — more at RED] **1 :** ROWAN TREE **2 :** ROWANBERRY

row·an·berry \'==- — *see* BERRY\ *n* [*rowan* + *berry*] **:** the fruit of the rowan tree

rowan tree *n* **1 :** a Eurasian tree (*Sorbus aucuparia*) with pinnate leaves and flat corymbs of small white flowers followed by red pomes resembling berries — called also *European mountain ash* **2 :** AMERICAN MOUNTAIN ASH

row-barge \'rō,=\ *n* [1*row* + *barge*] **:** a ship's barge or a passenger boat propelled by oars

row binder \'rō,=\ *n* [4*row*] **:** CORN BINDER

rowboat \'rō,=\ *n* [1*row* + *boat*] **:** a small boat of shallow draft usu. having a flat or rounded bottom, a squared-off or V-shaped stern, cross thwarts for rowers and passengers, and rowlocks for the oars with which it is propelled

row crop \'rō-\ *n* [4*row*] **:** a crop (as corn or cotton) that is usu. planted in rows

row culture \'rō-\ *n* **:** cultivation of crops in rows

row·di·ly \'raůdᵊl|ē, -dəl|, |i\ *adv* **:** in a rowdy manner

row·di·ness \-dēnəs, -din-\ *n* -ES **:** the quality or state of being rowdy

row down \(')rō-\ *vt* [1*row*] **:** to overtake (as another racing shell) in a rowing match

1row·dy \'raůdē, -di\ *adj* -ER/-EST [perh. irreg. fr. 6*row*] **1 a :** lacking in refinement **:** noisily turbulent **:** BOISTEROUS, ROUGH ⟨a shouting ~ game —Marjory S. Douglas⟩ ⟨a ~ little girl, who gave way upon the slightest provocation to uncontrollable laughter —Scott Fitzgerald⟩ ⟨~ mountain brooks —*Amer. Guide Series: Conn.*⟩ **b :** of a disreputable character **:** RAFFISH, VULGAR ⟨lackeys, housemaids and yokels of all sorts formed the most ~, but also the most enraptured, group in the . . . theater —W.S.Clark⟩ ⟨the comedy is often broad, even ~ —Hollis Alpert⟩ **2** *Austral* **:** lacking in docility **:** STUBBORN, UNRULY — used of livestock

2rowdy \"\ *n* -ES **:** one that is boisterous or pugnacious ⟨a favorite pastime of these . . . *rowdies* was to ride through the town at great speed while shooting with both hands —S.H. Holbrook⟩ ⟨the tough eggs, the *rowdies* in the crew —E.L. Burdick⟩

3rowdy \"\ *vi* -ED/-ING/-ES **:** to behave in a rowdy manner ⟨there was a lot of gambling and *rowdying* —Bruce Siberts⟩

row·dy·dow *or* **row-de-dow** \'raůdē,daů\ *n* -s [irreg. fr. 6*row*] **1 :** noisy excitement **:** HUBBUB, TO-DO ⟨piqued by all the ruffle and ~ —M.G.Bishop⟩ **2 a :** a noisy disturbance or spirited contest **:** BRAWL, FIGHT **b :** a boisterous party **:** SPREE

row·dy·dow·dy \¦raůdē¦daůdē\ *adj* [irreg. fr. *rowdydow*] **:** BOISTEROUS, VULGAR

row·dy·ish \ˈrau̇dēish, -di·ish\ *adj* [²*rowdy* + *-ish*] **:** tending to be crude or noisy
row·dy·ism \-dē,izəm, -di·iz-\ *n* -s [²*rowdy* + *-ism*] **:** rowdy character or behavior
rowed \ˌrōd\ *adj* [⁴*row* + *-ed*] **:** formed into or furnished with rows — often used in combination ⟨a six-*rowed* ear of corn⟩
rowe·ite \ˈrō,īt\ *n* -s [George *Rowe* 20th cent. Am. mineralogist] **:** a mineral (Mn,Mg,Zn)$Ca(BO_2)_2(OH)_2$, consisting of a basic borate of calcium, manganese, magnesium, and zinc
¹**row·el** \ˈrau̇(ə)l\ *n* -s [ME *rowelle, ruel*, fr. MF *rouelle* small wheel, fr. OF *roele* — more at ROULETTE] **1 a :** a revolving disk at the end of a spur with a varying number of sharp points for goading a horse ⟨the size of the ~ and the number of spokes determine the extent of spur cruelty —N.W.McKelvey⟩ **b** *obs* **:** a small knob on a horse's bit ⟨the iron ~s into frothy foam he bit —Edmund Spenser⟩ **2 :** something that resembles the rowel of a spur; *specif* **:** a spiked wheel on a soil pulverizer **3 :** a roll (as of hair or silk) passed through the flesh of an animal to induce localized drainage of widespread infection — compare SETON
²**rowel** \"\ *vt* **roweled** *or* **rowelled; roweled** *or* **rowelled; roweling** *or* **rowelling; rowels 1 a :** to goad with a rowel **:** SPUR ⟨~s his horse to a fresh burst of speed⟩ **b** (1) **:** to rake as if with a rowel **:** dig into **:** REND ⟨bathers *rowelling* the sand with horny heels —Louis Kent⟩ (2) **:** to disturb or incite to action **:** TROUBLE, PRICK ⟨blurted out the question that was *roweling* each one's mind —Joseph Bryan & P.G. Reed⟩ **c :** to furnish with a rowel ⟨a *roweled* spur⟩ **2 :** to insert a rowel of hair or silk into an animal
¹**row·en** \ˈrau̇ən\ *n* -s [ME *rewayn, roweyn*, fr. (assumed) ONF *rewain* (whence Picard *rouain*); akin to OF *regain* aftermath, fr. *re-* + *gaaigner* to till — more at GAIN] **1 :** a stubble field left unplowed till late in the autumn to be grazed by cattle **2 :** AFTERMATH 1 — often used in pl.
²**row·en** \ˈrōən\ *chiefly Scot var of* ROWAN
row·er \ˈrō(ə)r, -ōə\ *n* -s [ME, fr. *rowen* to row + *-er*] **:** one that rows a boat **:** OARSMAN
row·et \ˈrau̇ət\ *n* -s [prob. fr. E dial. *row* rough, fr. ME, fr. OE *rūw-, rūh* rough — more at ROUGH] *dial* **:** AFTERMATH 1
row galley \ˈrō-\ *n* [¹*row*] *archaic* **:** a galley propelled by oars
row house *n* [⁴*row*] **:** one of a series of houses connected by common sidewalls and forming a continuous group
row·ing \ˈrōiŋ, -ōēŋ\ *n* -s *often attrib* [ME, fr. OE, fr. *rōwan* to row + *-ing*] **1 :** the propulsion of a boat by means of oars **2 :** the art or practice of racing in shells as a sport **:** CREW
rowing boat *n, chiefly Brit* **:** ROWBOAT
rowing machine *n* **:** a machine used in a gymnasium for exercising the muscles used in rowing
row·land·ite \ˈrōlən,dīt\ *n* -s [Henry A. *Rowland* †1901 Am. physicist + E *-ite*] **:** a massive grayish green yttrium silicate containing iron and fluorine

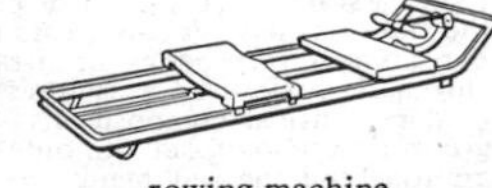
rowing machine

row·lock \ˈräl·ək, ˈrəl·ək (*usual nautical pronunciations*), ˈrō,läk\ *or* **rol·lock** *or* **rul·lock** *n* [prob. alter. (influenced by ¹*row*) of *oarlock*] **1 :** OARLOCK **2 a :** a course of brick laid on edge with the ends exposed **b :** the end of a brick exposed in a rowlock
rowlock arch *n* **:** an arch in which voussoirs are arranged in separate concentric rings each forming an arch
rowlock-back wall *n* **:** a wall with a face of brick laid flat and a back of brick laid on edge
rowlock wall *also* **rolock wall** *or* **rolok wall** *n* **:** a hollow wall made of brick on edge placed as headers and stretchers in Flemish bond
rown \ˈrau̇n\ *dial Brit var of* ROWAN
row out \(ˈ)rō-\ *vt* [¹*row*] **:** to exhaust by rowing ⟨number three had *rowed* himself *out* and was slumped over his oar at the finish line⟩

rowlock arch

rowport \ˈrō,=\ *n* [¹*row* + *port*] **:** an opening in the side of a small sailing ship to allow for the use of sweeps in calm weather
rows *pres 3d sing of* ROW, *pl of* ROW
rowse *obs var of* ROUSE
rowt *dial chiefly Brit var of* ³ROUT, ⁴ROUT
rowth *var of* ROUTH
rowy \ˈrōē\ *adj* [⁴*row* + *-y*] **:** of uneven texture or appearance **:** STREAKED
rox·burgh·shire \ˈräks,bərə,shi(ə)r, -,b(ə)rə-, -,shər\ *or* **rox·burgh** *adj, usu cap* [fr. *Roxburgh, Roxburghshire*, county of southeast Scotland] **:** of or from the county of Roxburgh, Scotland **:** of the kind or style prevalent in Roxburgh
rox·bury waxwork \ˈräksb(ə)rē-, -,ber|, |i-\ *n, usu cap R* [fr. *Roxbury*, residential district of Boston, Mass.] **:** BITTERSWEET 2 b
rox·o·la·ni \,räksəˈlā(,)nē, -lä,nī\ *n pl, usu cap* [L] **:** an ancient Sarmatian people living northeast of the Black sea, sometimes preying upon the Roman provinces, and sometimes serving as Roman auxiliaries
¹**roy·al** \ˈrói(ə)l, ˈrō(i)yəl\ *adj* [ME, fr. MF, fr. L *regalis* of a king, royal, regal, fr. *reg-, rex* king + *-alis* -al; akin to Skt *rājan* king, OIr *rī* (gen. *rig*), L *regere* to guide, rule — more at RIGHT] **1 a :** of kingly ancestry **:** belonging to royalty ⟨English princes of the blood ~ —Virginia Cowles⟩ **b :** of, relating to, owned by, or subject to the jurisdiction of the crown ⟨the limitation of ~ power under a constitutional monarchy⟩ ⟨a special train for the queen and members of the ~ party⟩ ⟨the prince and his bride honeymooned on the ~ yacht⟩ ⟨courts had been effectively centralized under ~ control —C.H.McIlwain⟩ **c :** indicative of royalty ⟨~ title⟩ ⟨~ crown⟩ ⟨~ crest⟩ **d :** reserved for the sovereign **:** not to be hunted or captured without a license from the crown ⟨giraffes rank as ~ game —L.G.Green⟩ **e :** being in the crown's service ⟨~ prosecutor⟩ ⟨*Royal* Air Force⟩ **2 a :** of a nobility or splendor worthy of royalty **:** MAGNIFICENT, REGAL ⟨there is something . . . ~ in the stately carriage of a stag's head —R.F.Kilvert⟩ ⟨was treated with the ~ acclaim of a visiting statesman —W.A.White⟩ ⟨coffee ~ . . . with brandy or whiskey mixed up in it —J.W.Ellison b.1929⟩ **b** *archaic* **:** limited to a chosen few **:** ELITE ⟨the ~ dynasty of the apostles —J.H.Newman⟩ **c :** requiring no exertion **:** marked by special privilege **:** EASY ⟨there is no ~ road to logic and really valuable ideas can only be had at the price of close attention —Justus Buchler⟩ **3 a :** having attributes of royalty **:** MAJESTIC ⟨the lion is a ~ beast⟩ **b :** of great size or magnitude **:** BIG, IMPOSING ⟨wielded a patronage of ~ dimensions —J.H.Plumb⟩ ⟨a battle ~ that covers miles and lasts for hours —Arthur Knight⟩ ⟨stop being such a ~ pain in the neck —F.C.Thorne⟩ **c** (1) **:** of superior quality **:** EXCELLENT, SUPERB ⟨a ~ view⟩ ⟨cow of ~ breeding —*Amer. Guide Series: Minn.*⟩ (2) **:** of a highly pleasurable kind **:** GLORIOUS ⟨would have a ~ time . . . sailing the wherry —Archibald Marshall⟩ **d :** playing the part of royalty ⟨place the crowns on the ~ pair . . . elected by popular campus vote —*Springfield (Mass.) Daily News*⟩ **4 a :** established or chartered by the crown **:** enjoying the king's patronage ⟨*Royal* Academy⟩ ⟨the *Royal* Burghs of Scotland⟩ ⟨Massachusetts was once a ~ colony⟩ ⟨*Royal* Swedish Yacht Club⟩ **b :** granted or performed by the king ⟨whatsoever she asked . . . Solomon gave her of his ~ bounty —1 Kings 10:13 (AV)⟩ ⟨honored by several ~ visits —T.B. Macaulay⟩ **5 :** of, relating to, or being a part (as a mast, sail, or yard) next above the topgallant — see SHIP illustration **6 :** resisting chemical action **:** NOBLE ⟨~ gases⟩ ⟨~ metals⟩
²**royal** \"\ *n* -s **1 a :** ROYAL ANTLER **b :** a stag of eight years or more having antlers with at least twelve points **2 a :** RYAL 1 **b :** ⁴REAL **3 :** a small sail on the royal mast that is the highest usu. carried on a square-rigged ship and is located immediately above the topgallant sail — see SAIL illustration **4 :** a royal personage ⟨there are . . . titles for all spouses of ~s —V.W.Turner⟩ **5 :** a standard British size of paper usu. 20 x 25 or 19 x 24 inches **6 :** change ringing on ten bells **7 a :** a blue or green crown used as the symbol for the fifth suit in some five-suit packs of playing cards **b :** ROYAL FLUSH **c :** ROYAL SPADE **8** *or* **royal blue a :** a variable color averaging a vivid purplish blue **b** *of textiles* **:** a deep blue that is duller than Yale blue and redder and duller than imperial blue **c :** SMALT 2 **d :** PRUSSIAN BLUE 2 **9 :** ROYAL PALM ⟨mast-straight ~s lining the avenue —C.S.Lloyd⟩ **10** [trans. of F *royale*] **:** ROYALE 2
royal agaric *n* **:** a widely distributed edible mushroom (*Amanita caesarea*) resembling the poisonous fly agaric and having a smooth deep orange pileus, yellow gills, a large membranaceous annulus, and a white volva
royal antelope *n* **:** a tiny western African antelope (*Neotragus pygmaeus*) that is one of the smallest of ruminants standing only 12 inches high at the shoulder and has in the male short spikelike horns and bright russet above and white below — called also *kleeneboc*
royal antler *n* **:** the third tine above the base of a stag's antler — called also *tres-tine;* see ANTLER illustration
royal arch mason *n, usu cap R&A&M* **:** a member of a Royal Arch lodge
royal assent *n* **:** the official but purely formal approval of the sovereign required for the passage of all legislation under English parliamentary law
royal auction bridge *n* **:** auction bridge in which the spade suit is bid either as the lowest-ranking suit counting 2 points per odd trick or as the highest-ranking suit counting 9 points per odd trick — compare ROYAL SPADE
royal bay *n* **:** LAUREL 1 a
royal casino *n* **:** a casino in which each jack is worth 11, queen 12, and king 13 and may be so used in builds
royal cell *n* **:** a special chamber in most termite nests for the king and queen of the colony
royal coachman *n* **:** COACHMAN 2
royal colony *n* **:** a colony governed directly by the crown through a governor and council appointed by it — compare CHARTER COLONY, PROPRIETARY COLONY
royal copenhagen *n, usu cap R&C* **:** hard paste porcelain produced at Copenhagen, Denmark, since the late 18th century and orig. under royal auspices
royal demesne *n* **:** the lands belonging to the British crown including both the ancient demesne and property acquired later (as by forfeiture or gift) **:** CROWN LAND 1 ⟨the bulk of the cities were situated in the *royal demesne* —J.R.Green⟩
royal doors *n pl, often cap R&D* **1 :** HOLY DOORS **2 :** the central doors in some Eastern churches leading from the narthex into the nave
royal dresden *n, usu cap R&D* **:** a superior grade of Dresden china
roy·ale \(ˈ)rói¦al, (ˈ)rō(i)¦yal\ *n* -s [F, fr. fem. of *royal*, adj. — more at ROYAL] **1 :** an egg custard cooked and set in a mold, cut into various shapes when cold, and added as a garnish to clear soups **2 :** a changement de pied with a beating together of the legs while in the air
royal eagle *n* **:** GOLDEN EAGLE
royal fern *also* **royal osmund** *n* **:** a common and widely distributed fern (*Osmunda regalis*) with large bipinnate fronds bearing the panicled globose sporangia at their summit — called also *ditch fern, French bracken, king fern*
royal fish *n* **1** *Eng law* **:** marine animals (as whale, sturgeon or porpoises) of superior excellence that belong to the crown when cast ashore or caught in territorial waters **2** *Scots law* **a :** whales of such large size as to entitle the sovereign to claim them **b :** salmon in the sea and mussels and oysters that can be lawfully taken in public or private rivers only by license of the crown although the latter do not belong officially to the crown
royal fizz *n* **:** a fizz made from lemon juice, gin, a whole egg, and sugar
royal flush *n* **:** a straight flush in poker with the ace the highest card — see POKER illustration
royal flycatcher *n, usu cap R&F* **:** a small tyrant flycatcher (*Onychorhynchus coronatus*) of tropical America having a head with a large fan-shaped crest that is bright red edged with black — called also *king tody*
royal green *n* **1 :** LIGHT BRUNSWICK GREEN **2 :** PARIS GREEN 1
royal hart *n* **:** a red deer with fully developed antlers
royal highness *n* **1 a :** a child, brother, sister, uncle, aunt, or grandchild in the male line of the British sovereign — used as a title before 1917 **b :** a child or grandchild of the British sovereign — used as a title since 1917 **c :** someone on whom the British sovereign chooses to bestow the designation **d :** any of various members of imperial and royal families of other countries **2 :** a person properly addressed as Royal Highness ⟨eight *royal highnesses* attended the coronation⟩
roy·al·ism \-ə,lizəm\ *n* -s [¹*royal* + *-ism*] **:** MONARCHISM
¹**roy·al·ist** \-ələst\ *n* -s [¹*royal* + *-ist*] **1** *often cap* **:** an adherent of a king or of monarchical government: as **a :** a supporter of Charles I in his struggles with the Puritans and parliament **:** CAVALIER — compare ROUNDHEAD **b :** an adherent of George III or the British government in the American Revolution **:** TORY **c :** an adherent of the Bourbon dynasty in France during and since the French Revolution **2 :** a reactionary business tycoon or powerful trust ⟨take unwarranted power out of the hands of economic or social ~s —Louis Filler⟩
²**royalist** \"\ *or* **roy·al·is·tic** \ˌróiəˈlistik, ˌrō(i)yəˈ-, -tēk\ *adj* **:** of, relating to, or characteristic of royalism or royalists
roy·al·ize \ˈ==,līz\ *vb* -ED/-ING/-S *vt, archaic* **:** to make royal ⟨to ~ his blood I spilled my own —Shak.⟩ ~ *vi, obs* **:** to assume royal power
royal jelly *n* **:** a highly nutritious secretion of the pharyngeal glands of the honeybee that is fed to the very young larvae in a colony and to all queen larvae
roy·al·ly \ˈróiəlē, ˈrō(i)yə-, -li\ *adv* [ME, fr. ¹*royal* + *-ly*] **1 a :** by the crown ⟨an edict published ~⟩ **b :** with the pomp and ceremony due a sovereign ⟨treated the ambassador ~⟩ **c :** with the utmost care and consideration **:** INDULGENTLY ⟨a small breeding stock was put inside fences and treated ~ —R.M.Yoder⟩ **2 :** in a splendid manner **:** MAGNIFICENTLY ⟨~ mounted upon one of the emperor's horses —Richard Knolles⟩ **3 :** on a large scale **:** GRANDLY, GLORIOUSLY ⟨~ duped by them and their accomplices —R.A.Hall b.1911⟩
royal marriage *n* **:** the king and queen of trumps in a card game (as pinochle or bezique)
royal moth *n* **:** any of various large handsome moths (as the regal moth and imperial moth) of *Citheronia* and related genera
royal palm *n* **1 :** any of several palms of the genus *Roystonea; esp* **:** a tall graceful pinnate-leaved palm (*R. regia*) of southern Florida and Cuba having a whitish trunk often enlarged or swelled out at the base and being widely planted for ornament throughout the tropical world **2 :** CABBAGE PALM 1b
royal peculiar *n* **:** a church or parish within the jurisdiction of the British sovereign and exempt from that of the ordinary in whose territory it is situated
royal pendulum *n* **:** a clock pendulum long enough to beat seconds
royal pink *n* **:** a deep pink that is bluer, stronger, and slightly darker than average coral (sense 3b) and bluer and deeper than fiesta or begonia
royal poinciana *n* **:** a showy tropical tree (*Delonix regia* syn. *Poinciana regia*) native to Madagascar but now widely planted for its immense racemes of scarlet and orange flowers, producing flat woody pods often two feet long, and having graceful twice-pinnate leaves — called also *flamboyant, flame tree, peacock flower*
royal purple *n* **1 :** a dark reddish purple that is redder, lighter, and stronger than average plum (sense 6a), redder and paler than imperial, and stronger than grape wine **2 :** a strong violet that is less strong and slightly lighter than pansy and bluer, less strong, and slightly darker than clematis — called also *king's purple, regal purple*
royal python *n* **1 :** BALL PYTHON **2 :** RETICULATED PYTHON
royal red *n* **1 :** VERMILIONETTE **2 :** vermilion or a color resembling it
royal rock snake *n* **:** BALL PYTHON 2
royals *pl of* ROYAL
royal scarlet *n* **:** red mercury iodide HgI_2
royal scyth *n, usu cap R&S* **:** a member of the noble class in Scythian society acting as an integrative force for the whole nomadic group of Scythians
royal spade *n* **:** a spade trump in royal auction bridge when every trick over six taken by the successful bidder scores 9
royal standard *n* **:** an emblem of royal authority that is usu. a flag or square banner smaller than the national flag; *specif* **:** a flag bearing the arms of England quartered with those of Scotland and Ireland used as a naval flag of command or as evidence of the actual presence of the sovereign in a palace or castle or on board a ship
royal tennis *n* **:** COURT TENNIS
royal tern *n* **:** a large tern (*Thalasseus maximus*) of the southern U.S. and farther southward that is white with a black crown and crest and pearl-gray mantle
roy·al·ty \ˈrói(ə)ltē, ˈrō(i)yəl-, -ti\ *n* -ES [ME *roialte*, fr. MF *roialté*, fr. OF, *roial* royal (fr. L *regalis*) + *-té* -ty — more at ROYAL] **1 a :** royal status or power **:** SOVEREIGNTY ⟨gain ~ by conquest⟩ **b royalties** *pl, archaic* (1) **:** the prerogatives of sovereignty ⟨assume these *royalties*, and not refuse to reign —John Milton⟩ (2) **:** emblems of sovereignty ⟨*royalties* which he was wont to adorn himself with when he sat in state —Benjamin Church⟩ **c** *archaic* **:** KINGDOM, REALM ⟨republics were formed upon the ruin of . . . *royalties* —Thomas Carte⟩ **2 a** *obs* **:** splendid appearance **:** GLORY, MAGNIFICENCE **b :** regal character or bearing **:** MAJESTY, NOBILITY ⟨happiness depends upon the inward ~ of the spirit —W.F.Hambly⟩ **3 a** (1) **:** persons of royal lineage ⟨marriage customs among the ~ of the Peruvian Inca —Weston La Barre⟩ (2) **:** an embodiment of sovereignty ⟨she was ~ and a symbol of the British Empire —*United Press*⟩ **b :** a person of royal rank ⟨the crowd hangs about . . . in the hope of seeing a ~ or a raja's jewels —*Manchester Guardian Weekly*⟩ ⟨how to address *royalties* and persons possessing complicated titles —George Santayana⟩ **c :** a privileged class ⟨the twenty-five hundred a year that marked the economic ~ of Gopher Prairie —Sinclair Lewis⟩ **4 a :** a right delegated (as to an individual or corporation) by a sovereign ⟨the ~ is vested in the lord of the manor —M.C. Greenwell⟩ **b :** a landed estate or right of exploitation granted by a sovereign — usu. used in pl. ⟨landed proprietors . . . became anxious to lease their *royalties* —F.S.Williams⟩ **c** *Scots law* **:** a township or territory subject to royal jurisdiction **d** *Brit* **:** a tract of coal-mining land or a portion thereof **5 a :** a seigniorage on gold and silver coined at the mint **b :** a percentage paid to the British crown of gold or silver taken from mines or a tax exacted in lieu thereof **c :** a share of the product or profit of property reserved by the owner when the property is sold, leased, or used or a payment (as a percentage of the amount of property used) to the owner for permitting another to exploit, use, or market such property (as natural resources, patents, or copyrights) which is often subject to depletion with use **6 :** BONUS 4b
royal walnut *n* **1 :** ENGLISH WALNUT **2 :** a hybrid between two black walnuts (*Juglans nigra* and *J. californica*)
royal water lily *n* **1 :** a So. American water lily (*Victoria amazonia*) with large circular leaves — called also *Amazon water lily, giant water lily* **2 :** a lily (*Victoria cruziana*) of Paraguay that is closely related to the royal water lily for which it is often substituted in the horticultural trade and has flowers which turn pinkish red
royal worcester *n, usu cap R&W* **:** Worcester china made after 1788
royal yellow *n* **:** ORPIMENT 2
royc·ean \ˈróisēən\ *adj, cap* [Josiah *Royce* †1916 Am. philosopher + E *-an*] **:** of or relating to the American philosopher Josiah Royce or his objective idealism
roy·e·na \róiˈēnə, rō(i)ˈyē-\ *n, cap* [NL, fr. Adrian van *Royen* †1779 Du. botanist] **:** a genus of southern African shrubs or trees (family Ebenaceae) having monoclinous flowers with bell-shaped accrescent calyx and reflexed corolla lobes — see AFRICAN BLADDERNUT
roy·et \ˈróiət\ *adj* [prob. alter. of earlier *riot*, fr. ME, fr. ¹*riot*] **1** *Scot* **:** UNRULY, WILD **2** *Scot* **:** MISCHIEVOUS, ROMPING
roy·nish \ˈróinish\ *adj* [ME, fr. *royne* scurf, scab (fr. MF *rogne*, fr. — assumed — VL *ronea*, prob. alter. — influenced by L *rodere* to gnaw — of L *aranea* spider, spider web) + *-ish* — more at ARACHN-, RAT] **1** *archaic* **:** MANGY, SCABBY **2** *archaic* **:** BASE, COARSE
royster *var of* ROISTER
roys·ton crow \ˈróistən-\ *n, usu cap R* [fr. *Royston*, urban district of northern Hertfordshire, England] **:** HOODED CROW 1
roy·sto·nea \rói'stōnēə\ *n* [NL, fr. General *Roy Stone* †1905 Am. engineer] **1** *cap* **:** a genus of chiefly West Indian pinnate-leaved palms with smooth often spindle-shaped stems and large graceful leaves — see CABBAGE PALM, ROYAL PALM **2** -s **:** any palm of the genus *Roystonea*
rozelle *var of* ROSELLE
ro·zi \ˈrōzē\ *or* **ro·zwi** \ˈräzwē\ *n, pl* **rozi** *or* **rozis** *or* **rozwi** *or* **rozwis** *usu cap* **:** LOZI
roz·zer \ˈräzə(r)\ *n* -s [origin unknown] *slang Brit* **:** POLICEMAN
rp *abbr* **1** rappen **2** recipe **3** *often cap R&P* reprint; reprinted; reprinting **4** rupiah
RP *abbr* **1** Received Pronunciation **2** refilling point **3** regius professor **4** reply paid **5** [L *res publica*] republic **6** return of post **7** return premium **8** [L *reverendus pater*] reverend father **9** rust preventive
RPC *abbr* reply post card
rpf *abbr* reichspfennig
RPM *abbr, often not cap* revolutions per minute
RPO *abbr* railway post office
RPP *abbr* reply paid postcard
RPS *abbr, often not cap* revolutions per second
rpt *abbr* **1** repeat **2** report; reported; reporting
rptd *abbr* **1** repeated **2** reported **3** reprinted **4** ruptured
RQ *abbr* respiratory quotient
rqn *abbr* requisition
rr *abbr* **1** [L *rarissime*] very rarely **2** rear
RR *abbr* **1** railroad **2** right rear **3** right reverend **4** rights reserved **5** rural route
RRC *abbr* regular route carrier
-r·rha·chis \ˌrəkəs\ *n comb form* -ES [NL, fr. Gk *rhachis* — more at RACHI-] **:** spine ⟨hematorrhachis⟩
-r·rha·gia \ˈrāj(ē)ə\ *n comb form* -s [NL, fr. Gk, fr. *rhēgnynai* to break, burst, rend — more at RHAGADES] **:** abnormal or excessive discharge or flow ⟨enterorrhagia⟩ ⟨metrorrhagia⟩
-r·rha·phy \ˌrəfē, -fi\ *n comb form* -ES [F *-raphie, -rrhaphie*, fr. Gk *-rrhaphia*, fr. *rhaptein* to sew together — more at RHAPSODY] **:** suture **:** sewing ⟨cardiorrhaphy⟩ ⟨nephrorrhaphy⟩
-r·rhea *also* **-r·rhoea** \ˈrēə\ *n comb form* -s [ME *-ria*, fr. LL *-rrhoea*, fr. Gk *-rrhoia*, fr. *rhoia*, fr. *rhein* to flow — more at STREAM] **:** flow **:** discharge ⟨logorrhea⟩ ⟨Melanorrhoea⟩ ⟨mucorrhea⟩
-r·rhex·is \ˈreksəs\ *n comb form, pl* **-r·rhex·es** \-k,sēz\ [NL, fr. Gk *rhēxis* action or process of breaking, fr. *rhēgnynai* to break, burst, rend] **:** rupture ⟨hysterorrhexis⟩ **:** splitting ⟨onychorrhexis⟩
-r·rhine *or* **-rhine** \,rīn\ *adj comb form* [ISV, fr. Gk *-rrhin-, -rrhis*, fr. *rhin-, rhis* nose — more at RHIN-] **:** having (such) a nose ⟨mesorrhine⟩ ⟨monorhine⟩ ⟨platyrrhine⟩
-r·rhi·za — see -RHIZA
RRL *abbr* regimental reserve line
rs *abbr, often cap* **1** reis **2** rupees
RS *abbr* **1** rabbinical supervision **2** radio station **3** recording secretary **4** recruiting service; recruiting station **5** reformed spelling **6** report of survey **7** revised statutes **8** right side
r's *or* **rs** *pl of* R
r salt *n, usu cap R* **:** the disodium salt $HOC_{10}H_5(SO_3Na)_2$ of R acid
rsi *var of* RISHI
RSM *abbr* regimental sergeant major
RSO *abbr* **1** railway sorting office **2** railway suboffice **3** regimental supply officer
r star *n, usu cap R* **:** a star of spectral type R — see SPECTRAL TYPE table
RSVP \,ä,res,vēˈpē, ,á,es-\ *abbr* [F *répondez s'il vous plaît*] please reply
RSWC *abbr* right side up with care
rt *abbr* right
ˈ**rt** \(ə)rt\ *vb* [by contr.] *archaic* **:** ART
RT *abbr* **1** radio technician **2** radio telegraphy **3** radio telephone **4** reading test **5** register ton **6** released time **7** re-

turn ticket **8** right tackle **9** room temperature **10** round trip **11** running title
rta *var of* RITA
RTA *abbr* reciprocal trade agreement
RTC *abbr* **1** replacement training center **2** reserve training corps
rtd *abbr* **1** retired **2** returned
rte *abbr* route
RTN *abbr* registered trade name
RTO *abbr* railroad transportation officer; railway transportation officer
rty *abbr* rarity
RU *abbr* rat unit
Ru *symbol* ruthenium
ru·ade \rü'äd\ *n* -s [F, lit., action of bucking (of a horse), fr. MF, fr. *ruer* to buck, fling, throw (fr. ML *rutare* to throw down, fr. L *rutus*, past part. of *ruere* to rush, fall) + *-ade* — more at RUG] **:** a preparatory movement for a parallel turn in skiing that consists of a bucking motion lifting the tails of the skis
ruala *usu cap, var of* RWALA
ru·a·na \rü'änə\ *n* -s [AmerSp, fr. Sp, woolen fabric] **:** a woolen covering resembling a poncho worn esp. in Colombia
ru·an·da \rü'ändə\ *n, pl* **ruanda** *or* **ruandas** *usu cap* **1 a :** a Bantu people in the region around the Virunga mountains in East Africa **b :** a member of such people **2 :** the Bantu language of the Ruanda people used as one of the two trade languages of Ruanda-Urundi — compare RUNDI
ru·a·shid \rü'äshəd\ *n, pl* **ruashid** *or* **ruashids** *usu cap* **1 :** an Arab people of inner Oman **2 :** a member of the Ruashid people
¹rub \'rəb\ *vb* **rubbed; rubbed; rubbing; rubs** [ME *rubben;* akin to Fris *rubben* to rub, scratch, Icel *rubba* to scrape, and prob. to OE *rēafian* to take away by stealth or force — more at REAVE] *vi* **1 a :** to move along the surface of a body with pressure **:** GRATE ⟨if the journal ~*s* against the bearing surface . . . too hard . . . the bearing surface will be scratched —H.F. Blanchard & Ralph Ritchen⟩ **b** (1) **:** to fret or chafe with friction ⟨~ upon a sore⟩ (2) **:** to cause discontent, irritation, or anger ⟨it ~*s* to be presided over by a vast . . . aggressively paternal indifference —R.W.Flint⟩ **2 :** to continue in a course, situation, or way of life usu. with slight difficulty or hindrance ⟨the great mass of modern men could ~ along happily enough without works of art —Roger Fry⟩ **3** *of a bowl* **:** to come in contact with an impediment on the green **4 :** to respond to rubbing (as for erasure or obliteration) **:** become rubbed ⟨dull inks . . . sometimes ~ off, even though the engraving is completely dry —R.N.Steffens⟩ **~** *vt* **1 a** (1) **:** to subject (as a body or a surface) to the action of something moving esp. back and forth with pressure and friction ⟨bent over and *rubbed* his sore ankle⟩ (2) **:** to scour, smooth, burnish, polish, or brighten by rubbing ⟨could see his reflection in the well *rubbed* wood⟩ — often used with *up* ⟨~ up the brass⟩ (3) **:** to spread a substance thinly over **:** SMEAR ⟨~ dressed fish generously with cut lemons —Jane Nickerson⟩ (4) **:** to roughen, wear, or make worn by the friction of rubbing **b** (1) **:** to cause (a body) to move with pressure and friction along a surface ⟨*rubbing* grubby knuckles in his eyes as he wept —T.B.Costain⟩ (2) **:** to remove, reduce to powder, spread, erase, or otherwise treat by rubbing ⟨*rubbed* the rust from old muskets —Dana Burnet⟩ ⟨the paste had hardened, and it was then vigorously *rubbed* in —H.E.Scudder⟩ (3) **:** to start (as a flame) by the friction of rubbing (4) **:** to straighten (as a wire or needle) by rubbing while hot **c :** to bring into reciprocal back and forth or rotary contact ⟨~ two sticks to make fire⟩ ⟨*rubbing* his hands in glee⟩ **d :** to take a rubbing of **2 a** *archaic* **:** to arouse a remembrance or a memory in ⟨~ him on this point, for his recollection becomes rusty —Sir Walter Scott⟩ **b :** to arouse pain, distress, or anger in **:** ANNOY, IRRITATE — **rub elbows** *or* **rub shoulders :** associate closely **:** MINGLE ⟨men and women of assorted ages and degrees of prosperity *rub elbows* and exchange opinions —Lowell Brentano⟩ ⟨reports on social products *rub shoulders* with book reviews and notes —*Friends' Intelligencer*⟩ — **rub the wrong way :** to arouse the antagonism, antipathy, or displeasure of **:** IRRITATE ⟨a knack of understanding my fellow creatures . . . and not being *rubbed the wrong way* by their faults —Max Beerbohm⟩
²rub \"\ *n* -s **1 a** (1) **:** an unevenness or inequality of surface of the ground in lawn bowling (2) *archaic* **:** an unevenness or inequality of surface that impedes movement ⟨there will be ~*s* in the smoothest road —Sir Walter Scott⟩ **b :** an obstruction or difficulty that hinders, stops, or alters the course of an argument, chain of thought, or action ⟨the ~ is that so few of the scholars have any sense of this truth themselves —Benjamin Farrington⟩ **c** (1) **:** something that mars the smoothness of a surface **:** ROUGHNESS ⟨leave no ~*s* nor botches in the work —Shak.⟩ (2) **:** something grating to the feelings (as a gibe, sarcasm, or harsh criticism) ⟨I got many severe ~*s*, often unconsciously given —T.B.Aldrich⟩ (3) **:** something that mars or upsets a usu. serene state of affairs or way of life ⟨even the mildest occupation produces its ~*s* and frictions —W.H. Chamberlin⟩ **2 :** the application of friction with pressure **:** RUBBING **3** *dial Eng* **:** RUBSTONE
rub *abbr* **1** rubbed **2** [L *ruber*] red **3** rubber
rub-a-dub \'rəbə,dəb\ *n* -s [imit.] **:** the sound of drumbeats
ru·ba'i \rü'bä,ē\ *n, pl* **ru·bai·yat** \'rübē,(y)ät, -bə,yät, -,bī-,(y)ät, *usu* -äd·+V\ *also* **rubais** [Ar *rubā'iyah*, fr. *rubā'īy* composed of four elements] **:** QUATRAIN
rubaiyat stanza *n, usu cap R* [*Rubáiyát*, collection of quatrains by Omar Khayyám †*ab*1123 Pers. poet and astronomer] **:** an iambic pentameter quatrain in which the first, second, and fourth lines rhyme — called also *Omar stanza*
ru·ban \'rübən\ *n* -s [ME (Sc), fr. MF — more at RIBBON] *archaic* **:** RIBBON
ru·barth's disease \'rü,bärt(h)s-\ *n, usu cap R* [after C. Sven *Rubarth b*1905 Swed. veterinarian] **:** a highly fatal febrile virus hepatitis of dogs marked by shivering, incoordination, spasms, and collapse accompanied by engorgement of visceral blood vessels and edema and cloudy swelling of liver, spleen, and lymph nodes
ru·basse \(')rü¦bas\ *n* -s [F *rubace*, irreg. fr. *rubis* ruby, fr. MF *rubi, rubis* — more at RUBY] **:** a quartz stained a ruby red — called also *Mont Blanc ruby*
ru·ba·to \rü'bäd·(,)ō, -bä|,|(,)tō\ *n, pl* **ruba·ti** \|d·(,)ē, |(,)tē\ *or* **rubatos** [It, past part. of *rubare* to rob, of Gmc origin; akin to OHG *roubōn* to rob — more at REAVE] **:** fluctuation of speed within a musical phrase or measure typically against a rhythmically steady accompaniment
rub·bage \'rəbij\ *chiefly dial var of* RUBBISH
rubbed brick *n* **:** brick rubbed with sandstone to produce a smoother surface of a lighter color and used esp. in colonial Virginia
¹rub·ber \'rəbə(r)\ *n* -s **1 a :** one that rubs: as (1) **:** one who polishes a finish (as of wood or metal furniture) (2) **:** one that massages esp. in a public bath (3) **:** a textile worker who removes processing marks from cloth **b :** an instrument or object used in rubbing, polishing, scraping, or cleaning: as (1) **:** a towel or brush used for cleaning (2) **:** WHETSTONE, RUBSTONE (3) **:** ERASER; *esp* **:** one made of rubber (4) **:** a piece of firm cloth used in grooming a horse esp. for rubbing down the coat when wet or for giving a final gloss after brushing and currying **c :** something that operates by or is used to prevent rubbing, chafing, or friction: as (1) **:** a wooden strip protecting the outside of the gunwales of an open boat (2) **:** a rough or prepared surface to ignite a match by friction **d** (1) **:** a rough uneven place in a bowling green (2) **:** IMPEDIMENT, DIFFICULTY (3) **:** MISFORTUNE, TROUBLE **e :** a soft brick **:** CUTTER **2** [so called fr. its use in erasers] **a :** a substance that is obtained from the latex of many tropical plants esp. of the genera *Hevea* and *Ficus*, is usu. characterized by its elasticity though its properties vary widely depending upon its source and preparation, is usu. prepared by coagulating the latex (as with formic acid), collecting the sticky coagulum, and either milling into rough sheets of crepe rubber or rolling into smooth or ribbed sheets and drying often by smoking, and is used chiefly in crepe soles and rubber cements — called also *caoutchouc, india rubber, natural rubber;* see PARA RUBBER 1, PLANTATION RUBBER, WILD RUBBER **b :** any of various rubberlike substances that like natural rubber can be vulcanized **:** a vulcanizable elastomer **:** SYNTHETIC RUBBER **c :** natural or synthetic rubber that has been modified to increase its useful properties (as elasticity, toughness, resistance to abrasive wear) usu. by masticating, compounding with sulfur or other vulcanizing agents and with various chemicals (as accelerators, zinc oxide, carbon black or other reinforcing pigments, fillers, softeners, extenders, and antioxidants), forming, and vulcanizing and that is used chiefly in tires, hose, belting, friction materials, containers, electric insulation, and waterproof materials, often in combination with textile fabrics, metals, or other materials **3 :** something made of rubber or felt to resemble rubber (as in composition or elasticity): as **a :** an overshoe of rubber; *esp* **:** one having no buckles and not extending as high as the ankle — compare GALOSH, STORM RUBBER, TOE RUBBER **b :** RUBBER BAND **c** (1) **:** a rubber tire (2) **:** the set of tires on a vehicle ⟨I'll road test her for you after we get new ~ on —Gregor Felsen⟩ **d :** the puck used in ice hockey **e** (1) **:** the pitcher's plate in baseball or softball (2) **:** HOME PLATE **f :** CONDOM **4** [by shortening] **:** RUBBERNECK **5 :** a security issued by a tire and rubber company
²rubber \"\ *adj* **1 :** made of rubber **2 :** producing rubber
³rubber \"\ *vt* **rubbered; rubbered; rubbering** \-b(ə)riŋ\ **rubbers 1 :** to make of rubber **2 :** to coat with rubber **:** RUBBERIZE
⁴rubber \"\ *n* -s [origin unknown] **1 :** a contest consisting of a specified odd number of games so that to win one side must take a majority (as two out of three, three out of five, or four out of seven) **2 :** a victory determined by the winning of a majority of a series of games **3** *or* **rubber game :** an odd game played to determine the winner when two sides have reached a tie
⁵rubber \"\ *vi* -ED/-ING/-S [by shortening] **:** RUBBERNECK
rubber band *n* **:** an endless cord, string, or band of rubber used variously (as for holding together a sheaf of papers)
rubber-base paint *n* **1 :** a paint having chlorinated rubber as its binder or nonvolatile vehicle **2 :** an emulsion paint having a latex of styrene-butadiene copolymer or other synthetic resin latex as its nonvolatile vehicle
rubber belt *n* **:** a belt made of rubber belting
rubber belting *n* **:** belting made of cotton duck held together by a rubber mixture
rubber boa *or* **rubber snake** *n* **:** a harmless blunt-tailed snake (*Charina bottae*) of the family Boidae that is rubbery in smoothness and suppleness of appearance, usu. less than 18 inches long, and found in the moister regions of western No. America — called also *ball snake, two-headed snake*
rubber boot *n* **:** a boot made of fabric heavily coated with rubber
rubber bridge *n* **:** a form of bridge in which the cards are dealt at random and not replayed as in duplicate bridge and in which settlement is made at the end of each rubber
rubber cement *n* **:** an adhesive consisting typically of a dispersion of unvulcanized rubber in an organic solvent (as petroleum naphtha or benzene)
rubber check *n* [so called because it comes back like a bouncing rubber ball] **:** a check returned by the bank as not good because of insufficient funds in the account on which the check is drawn
rubber dam *n* **:** a thin sheet of rubber that is stretched around a tooth to keep it dry during dental work or is used in strips to provide drainage in surgical wounds
rubber dog *n* **:** PUPPY 4
rubber-down \'==,=\ *n, pl* **rubbers-down** [*rub down* + *-er*] **:** one that rubs down (as in smoothing leather or wood or in reducing pulp)
rubber hydrocarbon *n* **:** a white highly polymerized hydrocarbon $(C_5H_8)_n$ or $(C_{10}H_{16})_n$ that is amorphous at ordinary temperatures and that is stereoisomeric with gutta hydrocarbon and constitutes the principal component of natural rubber **:** a cis form of polyisoprene
rubber hydrochloride *n* **:** a thermoplastic substance made by treating a dispersion of natural rubber with hydrogen chloride and used chiefly in the form of thin strong stretchable moistureproof film for making raincoats, as packaging material, and as fruit wrapping — compare CHLORINATED RUBBER
rubber ice *n* **:** soft flexible ice on a body of water
rub·ber·ize \'rəbə,rīz\ *vt* -ED/-ING/-S **:** to coat or impregnate with rubber or a rubber solution ⟨~ cloth⟩
rubber jaw *n* **:** osteomalacia of the dog marked by softening and degenerative changes of the jaw and facial skeleton and commonly occurring in company with renal insufficiency and uremia
rubber latex *n* **:** a milky juice that is extracted from any of various plants and is the source of natural rubber
rubberlike \'==,=\ *adj* **:** resembling rubber esp. in physical properties (as elasticity and toughness)
rubberlip perch *or* **rubberlip sea-perch** \'==,=-\ *n* [*rubberlip* fr. ²*rubber* + *lip*] **:** a medium-sized silvery or bluish purple surf fish (*Rhacochilus toxotes*) of the California coast that is a leading market fish of the area
rub·ber·man \'rəbə(r)mən, -,man\ *n, pl* **rubbermen :** a worker who renews rubber tubing in electrolytic cells and purifies water for use in them
¹rubberneck \'==,=\ *also* **rub·ber·neck·er** \'==,=ə(r)\ *n* [*rubberneck* fr. ²*rubber* + *neck; rubbernecker* fr. ²*rubberneck* + *-er*] **1 :** an extremely inquisitive person ⟨two cars had smashed together . . . and a cluster of ~*s* had gathered around —John Brooks⟩ **2 :** TOURIST; *esp* **:** one on a guided tour
²rubberneck \"\ *vi* -ED/-ING/-S [¹*rubberneck*] **1 :** to look about, stare, or listen with exaggerated curiosity ⟨limping out of bed to join the ~*ing* patients at the windows —Earle Birney⟩ **2 :** to go on a tour **:** SIGHT-SEE
rubber neck \'==,=\ *n* [²*rubber* + *neck*] **:** CANDLEPINS
rubbernose \'==,=\ *or* **rubbernose sturgeon** *n* **:** LAKE STURGEON
rubber plant *n* **:** a plant (as the Colorado rubber plant) that yields rubber; *esp* **:** a tropical Asian tree (*Ficus elastica*) with strongly buttressed trunk that may exceed 100 feet in height, is the source of Assam rubber, and is frequently dwarfed in pots for use as an ornamental
rubber plating *n* **:** the deposition of rubber from rubber latex or other rubber dispersion containing negatively charged rubber particles usu. on a metal by electrophoresis or by coagulation with positively charged ions
rubber point *n* **:** a point credited to the side that wins a game in whist, the number of points so credited depending on the difference between the winners' and losers' scores in the game
rubbers *pl of* RUBBER, *pres 3d sing of* RUBBER
rubber-seed oil *n* **:** a fatty oil obtained esp. from the seeds of the Para rubber tree and used chiefly in soap
rubber sheet *n* **:** a sheet of rubber or a cloth coated with rubber for use esp. on a hospital bed or a child's crib
rubber stamp *n* **1 :** a stamp of rubber for making imprints **2 a :** a person who echoes the words, opinions, or mannerisms of others **:** one without originality **b :** a group (as a legislative body) or a person that approves or endorses a program or policy with little or no dissent or discussion ⟨it is probably not fair to consider the council merely a *rubber stamp* —F.A.Ogg & Harold Zink⟩ ⟨others have been more amenable *rubber stamps* for administration policy —*Economist*⟩ **3 a :** something (as an expression) that duplicates without originality a common mode or pattern **:** STEREOTYPE, CLICHÉ ⟨the usual *rubber stamps* of criticism —H.L.Mencken⟩ ⟨your windows can be . . . rich without being *rubber stamp* —*Amer. Home*⟩ **b :** an endorsement or approval esp. when given with slight study or discussion

rubber stamp 1

rubber-stamp \¦==¦=\ *vt* [*rubber stamp*] **1 :** to cancel, endorse, approve, or otherwise mark with a rubber stamp **2 :** to approve, endorse, or dispose of (as a document or policy) as a matter of routine usu. without the exercise of judgment or at the expressed or implied command of another person or body ⟨wanted to *rubber-stamp* the appropriations and leave —*Newsweek*⟩ ⟨citizen committees which expect the board to *rubber-stamp* their findings —*Education Digest*⟩
rubber thread *n* **:** a fine square or round filament of rubber used esp. for elastic and elasticized thread and fabrics
rubber tree *n* **:** a tree that yields rubber; *esp* **:** PARA RUBBER 2 — compare RUBBER PLANT
rubber vine *n* **1 :** INDIA-RUBBER VINE **2 :** MADAGASCAR RUBBER VINE **3 :** Jamaican woody vine (*Forsteronia floribunda*) of the family Apocynaceae that yields rubber
rubberweed \'==,=\ *n* **:** PINGUE
rub·bery \'rəb(ə)rē, -)ri\ *adj* **:** resembling natural rubber (as in elasticity, consistency, or texture) **:** RUBBERLIKE ⟨mud so tough and ~ that . . . it would pull the hooves off a horse —H.L.Davis⟩ ⟨had a ~ face that lent itself beautifully to mugging —E.J.Kahn⟩
rub·bidge \'rəbij\ *dial var of* RUBBISH
rubbing *n* -s [ME *rubbinge*, fr. gerund of *rubben* to rub] **1 :** the action or process of chafing, polishing, or otherwise treating or affecting a surface or body by the motion of applied pressure upon it **2 :** an image of a raised, indented, or textured surface obtained by placing paper over it and rubbing the paper (as with heelball, charcoal, graphite)
rubbing alcohol *n* **:** a liquid for external use containing usu. denatured alcohol or isopropyl alcohol and water
rubbing block *n* **1 :** an abrasive block that is commonly of sandstone and is used for cleaning, smoothing, or polishing (as marble, building stone, bricks) **2 :** the part of an electric railway plow that makes contact with a conductor rail in a conduit
rubbing varnish *n* **:** varnish used to form a hard surface for rubbing
rub·bish \'rəbish, -bēsh\ *n* -ES [ME *robous, robys, robishe;* perh. akin to ME *rubben* to rub — more at RUB] **1 a :** useless fragments of stone or other material left over in building or broken from ruined buildings **:** RUBBLE **b :** miscellaneous useless valueless waste or rejected matter **:** TRASH, DEBRIS ⟨three buildings surrounded by logs and stumps, carpenters' and masons' debris, and other ~ —*Amer. Guide Series: Mich.*⟩ ⟨letters, journals, estate accounts, locks of hair, shreds of silk, sentimental ~ of all sorts —Mollie Panter-Downes⟩ **2 :** vapid, worthless, or nonsensical writing, talk, or art ⟨of our dramatic literature few real masterpieces are forgotten and not much ~ survives —W.B.Adams⟩ ⟨it is often said that editors and publishers do not order or commission stories — which, of course, is ~ —Robert Moses⟩ **syn** see REFUSE
rub·bish·ing \-bəshiŋ\ *adj* **:** RUBBISHY — **rubbishingly** *adv*
rub·bish·ly \-bishlē\ *adj* **:** RUBBISHY
rubbish pulley *or* **rubbish wheel** *n* **:** GIN BLOCK
rub·bishy \-bəshē, -shi\ *adj* **1 :** consisting of or covered with rubbish ⟨a ~ heap of corrugated paper boxes —Berton Roueché⟩ **2 :** of the quality of rubbish **:** TRASHY, WORTHLESS ⟨the ~ newspapers which form almost the sole reading of the majority —W.R.Inge⟩
¹rub·ble \'rəbəl\ *n* -s [ME *robyl, rubel;* perh. akin to ME *rubben* to rub] **1 a :** broken fragments of stone and other matter resulting from the decay or destruction of a building ⟨fortifications knocked into ~ —C.S.Forester⟩ **b :** a miscellaneous confused mass, pile, or group of usu. broken or worthless things ⟨lay in a pile of ~, only this time there was more of it, additional gear having hit the deck —K.M.Dodson⟩ ⟨lonely in his box the dead man lay, with his ~ of mourners behind him —Bruce Marshall⟩ **2 a :** waterworn or rough broken stones or bricks used in coarse masonry or to fill up between the facing courses of walls **b :** masonry composed of rubble **:** RUBBLEWORK **3 a :** rough stone as it comes from the quarry **b :** the upper fragmentary and decomposed portion of a mass of stone esp. in a quarry **:** BRASH **c :** a mass or layer of fragments of rock lying under alluvium **d :** ¹TALUS 2 **4 :** floating or grounded sea ice in hard roughly rounded blocks from two to five feet in diameter
²rubble \"\ *vt* -ED/-ING/-S **:** to reduce to rubble **:** DESTROY ⟨the city has twice been *rubbled* in battle —H.G.Nickels⟩
rubble ashlar *n* **:** ashlar with rubble backing
rubble concrete *n* **:** concrete in which large stones are added to the freshly placed concrete while it is still soft and plastic
rubble drain *n* **:** FRENCH DRAIN
rub·ble·man \'rəbəlmən, -,man\ *n, pl* **rubblemen :** a foreman in charge of the drilling and splitting of stone
rubble masonry *n* **:** masonry composed of unsquared stone
rubblestone \'==,=\ *n* **:** RUBBLE
rubblework \'==,=\ *n* **:** masonry of unsquared or rudely squared stones that are irregular in size and shape
rub·bly \'rəb(ə)lē\ *adj* **:** relating to, abounding in, composed of, or resembling rubble ⟨~ formation⟩ ⟨~ coal⟩
rub down *vt* **:** to rub from top to bottom or head to foot; *specif* **:** to dry (a horse) of sweat or rain (as with a straw wisp or a rubber)
rubdown \'=,=\ *n* -s [*rub down*] **:** a rubbing of the body (as after a bath) ⟨a brisk ~ with a rough towel⟩; *esp* **:** a massage given after or during the course of an athletic contest to promote the removal of fatigue products through improved circulation

rubblework

rube \'rüb\ *n* -s [fr. *Rube*, nickname fr. the name *Reuben*] **:** an awkward unpolished unsophisticated usu. gullible rustic ignorant of urban ways ⟨the era of the backwoods ~ is gone —Jeff McDermid⟩ ⟨jumpin around from one ~ town to another —Richard Bissell⟩ **syn** see BOOR
ru·be·an·ic acid \¦rübē¦anik-\ *n* [*rubeanic* ISV *rube-* (fr. L *rubeus* red, reddish) + *-ane* + *-ic*] **:** an intensely colored thioamide $(CSNH_2)_2$ that is a weak acid, that is made by addition of hydrogen sulfide to cyanogen, and that forms deeply colored heat-stable nickel salts; dithio-oxamide
¹ru·be·fa·cient \¦rübə¦fāshənt\ *adj* [L *rubefacient-, rubefaciens*, pres. part. of *rubefacere* to make red, fr. *rubeus* red, reddish + *facere* to make — more at RUBY, DO] **:** causing redness (as of the skin)
²rubefacient \"\ *n* -s **:** a substance for external application that produces redness of the skin
ru·be·faction \-'fakshən\ *n* -s [prob. fr. (assumed) NL *rubefaction-, rubefactio*, fr. L *rubefactus* (past part. of *rubefacere*) + *-ion-, -io* -ion] **1 :** the act or process of causing redness **2 :** redness due to a rubefacient
rube gold·berg \'rüb'gōl(d),bərg, -bəg,-bəig\ *also* **rube gold·berg·ian** \-gēən\ *adj, usu cap R&G* [*Rube Goldberg* (Reuben L. Goldberg) *b*1883 Am. cartoonist known for comic drawings of ridiculously complicated mechanical contrivances] **:** accomplishing by extremely complex roundabout means what actually or seemingly could be done simply ⟨crowded with a *Rube Goldberg* phantasmagoria of furnaces, grinders, tanks, mixers and countless unrecognizable contraptions —Webb Waldron⟩
ru·bel·la \rü'belə\ *n* -s [NL, fr. L, fem. of *rubellus* reddish] **:** an acute contagious disease usu. affecting children and young adults characterized by a red skin eruption, mild symptoms, and short course, but causing organic damage to the fetus in early pregnancy — called also *German measles;* see MATERNAL RUBELLA
ru·bel·lite \rü'be,līt, 'rübə,l-\ *n* -s [L *rubellus* reddish (fr. *ruber* red) + E *-ite* — more at RED] **1 :** a mineral consisting of a tourmaline varying from a pale rose red to a deep ruby red and found esp. in California, Brazil, and the Ural mountains **2 :** a vivid purplish red that is bluer and duller than Indiana and bluer and darker than malmaison rose
ru·ben·esque \¦rübə¦nesk\ *adj, usu cap* [Peter Paul *Rubens* †1640 Flem. painter + E *-esque*] **:** of, relating to, or having the characteristics of the painter Rubens or his work ⟨the high ceiling was painted blue with a sky in which floated fat *Rubenesque* cherubs discreetly veiled in wisps of cloud —Vivian Ellis⟩ ⟨the walls . . . were a blaze of magnificent form and color: a *Rubenesque* room —Hewlett Johnson⟩
ru·ben·si·an \(')rü¦benzēən\ *adj, usu cap* [Peter Paul *Rubens* + E *-an*] **:** RUBENESQUE
ru·bens' madder \'rübənz(əz)-\ *n, often cap R* **:** a dark reddish orange that is less strong and very slightly redder and lighter than average lacquer red and redder, stronger, and slightly lighter than burnt sienna

ru·be·o·la \rü'bēələ\ *n* -s [NL, fr. neut. pl. of (assumed) NL *rubeolus* reddish, fr. L *rubeus* red, reddish] : MEASLES — **ru·be·o·lar** \-lə(r)\ *adj*

rub·eryth·ric acid \ˌrübəˌrithrik-\ *n* [ruberythric ISV *rub-* (fr. NL *Rubia*) + *erythr-* + *-ic*] : a yellow crystalline acidic glycoside $C_{25}H_{26}O_{13}$ occurring in madder root and yielding alizarin and primeverose on hydrolysis

rub·eryth·rin·ic acid \ˌrübəˌri¦th¦rinik-, ˌrüˌberə¦th¦\ *n* [*ruberythrinic* fr. G *ruberythrin-* (in *ruberythrinsäure* ruberythric acid) (fr. *rub-* — fr. NL *Rubia* — + *erythr-* + *-in* -ine) + E *-ic*] : RUBERYTHRIC ACID

ru·bes·cence \rü'besᵊn(t)s\ *n* -s [fr. *rubescent*, after such pairs as E *adolescent*: *adolescence*] : the quality or state of being rubescent

ru·bes·cent \-ᵊnt\ *adj* [L *rubescent-, rubescens*, pres. part. of *rubescere* to grow red, incho. of *rubēre* to be red; akin to L *ruber* red — more at RED] : growing or becoming red : ERUBESCENT, REDDENING, FLUSHING

ru·bia \'rübēə\ *n, cap* [NL, fr. L, madder; akin to L *ruber* red] : a genus (the type of the family Rubiaceae) of Old World herbs having pentamerous flowers and fleshy fruit — see MADDER

ru·bi·a·ce·ae \ˌrübē'āsēˌē\ *n pl, cap* [NL, fr. *Rubia*, type genus + *-aceae*] : a family of mostly tropical herbs, shrubs, and trees (order Rubiales) of very diverse habits having opposite stipulate leaves and regular flowers with the stamens borne on the corolla tube and a 1- to 10-celled ovary usu. with numerous ovules that becomes in fruit a capsule, a berry, or one or more distinct nutlets — **ru·bi·a·ceous** \ˌrübē¦āshəs\ *adj*

ru·bi·a·les \ˌrübē'ā(ˌ)lēz\ *n pl, cap* [NL, fr. *Rubia* + *-ales*] : an order of dicotyledonous plants having opposite leaves, an inferior compound ovary, and epigynous stamens equal in number to the lobes of the corolla

ru·bi·celle \ˌrübə¦sel\ *n* -s [alter. of earlier *rubacelle*, prob. fr. F, dim. of *rubace* rubasse — more at RUBASSE] : a ruby spinel of a yellow or orange-red color

¹ru·bi·con \'rübəˌkän *sometimes* -bəkən *or* -bēkən\ *n* -s [L *Rubicon-, Rubico*, small river in north central Italy which in the time of the ancient Roman republic formed part of the boundary between Cisalpine Gaul and Italy, and over which Julius Caesar crossed into Italy with his army in 49 B.C. against the orders of the government to begin the civil war in which he overthrew Pompey] **1** *usu cap* : a bounding or limiting line; *esp* : one that when crossed commits a person to an irrevocable change or decision ⟨the little lads think they have crossed the *Rubicon* when they first get trousers —Cahir Healy⟩ **2** : the winning of a card game before the loser has reached a certain prescribed score or with a score so low that it is at least twice as great as the loser's score and usu. with the effect that the winner's score is doubled ⟨~ bezique⟩ — compare LURCH

²rubicon \"\ *vt* -ED/-ING/-S : to defeat (as in piquet or bezique) with a score so low that it is added to the winner's

ru·bi·cund \'rübəkənd, -bēkə-, -bəˌkə-\ *adj* [L *rubicundus*; akin to L *ruber* red — more at RED] : inclining to redness : RUDDY, RED ⟨as a result of a judicious mixture of wind, rain and beer the . . . farmer's face is ~ and jovial —S.P.B.Mais⟩

ru·bi·cun·di·ty \ˌrübə'kəndədē, -ndətē, -i\ *n* -ES [ML *rubicunditat-, rubicunditas*, fr. L *rubicundus* + *-itat-, -itas* -ity] : the quality or state of being rubicund : RUDDINESS

ru·bid·ic \(')rü¦bidik\ *adj* [ISV *rubid-* (fr. NL *rubidium*) + *-ic*] : of or relating to rubidium

ru·bid·i·um \rü'bidēəm\ *n* -s [NL, fr. L *rubidus* red + NL *-ium*; fr. two red lines in its spectrum; akin to L *ruber* red] : a soft silvery metallic element of the alkali metal group that is found combined in small amounts in many minerals and mineral waters and the ashes of many plants usu. accompanied by still smaller amounts of cesium, that is produced in metallic form by electrolysis or chemical reduction of its compounds, and that decomposes water with violence and inflames spontaneously in air — symbol *Rb*; see ELEMENT table

ru·bied \'rübēd, -bid\ *adj* [¹*ruby* + *-ed*] : made like a ruby in color

rubier *comparative of* RUBY

rubies *pl of* RUBY, *pres 3d sing of* RUBY

rubiest *superlative of* RUBY

ru·bi·fy \'rübəˌfī\ *vt* -ED/-ING/-ES [ME *rubifyen*, fr. MF *rubifier, rubefier*, modif. (influenced by MF *-fier* -fy) of L *rubefacere* — more at RUBEFACIENT] : to make red : REDDEN

ru·big·i·nous \(')rü¦bijənəs\ *also* **ru·big·i·nose** \-ˌnōs\ *adj* [L *robiginosus, rubiginosus* rusty, fr. *robigin-, rubigin-, robigo, rubigo* + *-osus* -ose; akin to L *ruber* red] : of or marked with a rusty red color : FERRUGINOUS

ru·bi·jervine \ˌrübə+\ *n* [¹*ruby* + *jervine*] : a nonpoisonous crystalline alkaloid $C_{27}H_{43}NO_2$ found with jervine in green and white hellebore

rub in *vt* : to insist on, harp on, continue to recall, or emphasize (as something unpleasant) ⟨if they failed he never *rubbed in* their failure —F.W.Crofts⟩ ⟨trying to *rub* it *in* that they had won their freedom —J.H.Huizinga⟩

rubine *or* **rubin** *n* -s [ML *rubinus*, fr. L *rubeus* red, reddish — more at RUBY] *obs* : RUBY

ru·bin test \'rübən-\ *n, usu cap R* [after I.C.*Rubin* b1883 Am. gynecologist] : a test to determine the patency or occlusion of the fallopian tubes by insufflating them with carbon dioxide by transuterine injection

ru·bi·ous \'rübēəs\ *adj* [¹*ruby* + *-ous*] : RED, RUBY

ru·ble *also* **rou·ble** \'rübəl\ *n* -s [Russ *rubl'*, fr. Old Russian *rublĭ*, lit., block of wood, fr. *rubiti* to build; akin to Lith *rumbas* scar on a tree and perh. to MHG *rumph* trunk, torso — more at RUMP] **1** : the basic monetary unit of the U.S.S.R. — see MONEY table **2** : a coin representing one ruble

rub of the green : something happening to a golf ball in play that affects its course or status not caused by a player or caddie involved in the match

ru·bor \'rüˌbó(ə)r, -ˌbər\ *n* -s [L, redness; akin to L *ruber* red — more at RED] : redness of the skin (as in inflammation or from dilated capillaries)

rub out *vt* **1** : to obliterate or extinguish by rubbing ⟨*rubbed out* the shovel marks and all their tracks —W.F.Davis⟩ ⟨*rubbed out* the end of his cigarette —Kay Boyle⟩ **2** : to destroy completely ⟨much of the older section of town was *rubbed out* in the air raids —Richard Joseph⟩; *specif* : MURDER, KILL ⟨somebody *rubbed* him *out* this afternoon with a twenty-two —Raymond Chandler⟩

rub rail *n* : a metal rail to protect against rubbing: as **a** : a projecting steel or aluminum strip that protects a truck or bus body against damage by gliding contact **b** : a brass rail on a boat to take wear of the lines

ru·brene \'rüˌbrēn\ *n* -s [ISV *rubr-* (fr. L *rubr-, ruber* red) + *-ene*] : an orange-red fluorescent crystalline polycyclic hydrocarbon $C_{42}H_{28}$ that is decolorized by oxygen with the reversible formation of a peroxide; tetraphenyl-naphthacene

¹ru·bric \'rü(ˌ)brik, -ˌbrēk\ *n* -s [ME *rubrike* red ocher, heading in red letters of a part of a book, fr. MF *rubrique*, fr. L *rubrica*, fr. *rubr-, ruber* red — more at RED] **1** *archaic* **a** : BOLE **b** : RED OCHER **2** : a heading of a chapter, a section, or other part of a book or manuscript distinguished by being done or underlined in a color (as red) different from the rest of the text or by some other device **3 a** (1) : a section heading of a discourse or writing (2) : NAME, TITLE ⟨as botany, zoology and geography have become increasingly technical . . . they too have dropped the ~ of natural history —*Amer. Naturalist*⟩ (3) : something under which a thing is classed : CONCEPT, CLASS, CATEGORY ⟨a variety of names has been applied to the sensations falling under the general ~, "pressure" —F.A. Geldard⟩ **b** (1) : the title of a statute or law (2) : a statute, law, commandment, or dictum regarded as authoritative (3) : a collection or group of statutes, laws, or dicta : CANON; *specif* : a collection of ecclesiastical rules (4) : a rule for the conduct of a liturgical service ⟨the ~s of the Order of Confirmation⟩ (5) : PURITY RUBRIC **c** : a formula, commentary, or gloss that elucidates or sets within a context ⟨like accepting a fairy tale as history, through ignoring the prefatory ~ "once upon a time, in a world that never was" —A.G.N. Flew⟩; *specif* : an editorial interpolation ⟨clarity is promoted by the use of numbered paragraphs with marginal ~s —J.C. Stewart⟩ **4** : a technique, custom, form, or thing established or settled (as by authority) ⟨hand engraving is an art in its own right, with its own ~s —O.L.Harvey⟩ ⟨no longer wore high laced boots, because the ~s had changed in these matters —Bruce Marshall⟩ **5** *obs* : a calendar of saints **6** *or* **ru·bri·ca** \-brəkə, -brēkə\ [Sp *rúbrica* paraph, heading, fr. L *rubrica*] : PARAPH

²rubric \"\ *or* **ru·bri·cal** \-brəkəl, -brēk-\ *adj* [*rubric* fr. ME *rubrike*, fr. *rubrike*, n.; *rubrical* fr. ¹*rubric* + *-al*] **1 a** : colored, written, printed in, or marked with red **b** : RED-LETTER ⟨~ day⟩ **2** : of, relating to, or in accordance with a rubric — **ru·bri·cal·ly** \-brək(ə)lē, -brēk-, -li\ *adv*

³rubric \"\ *vt* -ED/-ING/-S [¹*rubric*] : to adorn with red : REDDEN

ru·bri·cate \'rübrəˌkāt\ *vt* -ED/-ING/-S [LL *rubricatus*, past part. of *rubricare* to color red, fr. L *rubrica* red ocher] **1 a** : to write or print as a rubric ⟨*rubricated* capital letter⟩ ⟨*rubricated* title in a manuscript⟩ **b** : to add a rubric to or provide with a rubric ⟨*rubricated* manuscript⟩ ⟨*rubricated* calendar⟩ **2** : to arrange as in a rubric : fix in form

ru·bri·ca·tion \ˌ==¦kāshən\ *n* -s **1** : the act or process of rubricating **2** : something (as a letter or word) that is rubricated

ru·bri·ca·tor \'==ˌkād·ə(r)\ *n* -s : one that rubricates; *esp* : a member of a medieval brotherhood with the duty of rubricating books and manuscripts produced in a monastery

ru·bri·cian \rü'brishən\ *n* -s : one skilled in the knowledge of or tenaciously adhering to a rubric

ru·bric·i·ty \rü'brisədē\ *n* -ES [²*rubric* + *-ity*] : REDNESS

ru·bro·cortical \¦rü(ˌ)brō+\ *adj* [*rubro-* (fr. L *rubr-, ruber* red + E *-o-*) + *cortical*] : connecting or relating to the red nucleus and the cortex of the brain

ru·brofu·gal \¦rübrō¦fyügəl, (')rü¦bräfyəg-\ *adj* [*rubro-* (fr. L *rubr-, ruber* red + E *-o-*) + *-fugal*] : passing or leading away from the red nucleus

ru·bro·petal \¦rübrō¦pedᵊl, -¦ped-, (')rü¦bräpəd-\ *adj* [*rubro-* (fr. L *rubr-, ruber* red + E *-o-*) + *-petal*] : passing or leading into the red nucleus

ru·bro·spinal \¦rü(ˌ)brō+\ *adj* [*rubro-* (fr. L *rubr-, ruber* red + E *-o-*) + *spinal* — more at RED] **1** : of, relating to, or connecting the red nucleus and the spinal cord **2** : of, relating to, or constituting a tract of crossed nerve fibers passing from the red nucleus to the spinal cord and relaying impulses from the cerebellum and corpora striata to the motor neurons of the cord

rubs *pres 3d sing of* RUB, *pl of* RUB

rubstone \'=ˌ=\ *n* [ME *rubston*, fr. *rubben* to rub + *ston, stoon* stone] : a sandstone or grit for scouring, polishing, or sharpening; *esp* : WHETSTONE

rub up *vt* **1** : to revive or refresh knowledge of : RECALL ⟨*rubbed up* his Latin in an epitaph for the tomb of some pet dog —Virginia Woolf⟩ **2** : to improve the keenness of (a mental faculty) ⟨have begun a course of history . . . to *rub up* my memory before I touch on classic ground —Sydney Morgan⟩ **3** : to daub (a lithographic stone or plate) with ink preparatory to proofing or running

ru·bus \'rübəs\ *n, cap* [NL, fr. L, blackberry] : a genus of often prickly shrubs (family Rosaceae) having 3- to 7-foliolate or simple lobed leaves, white or pink flowers with a flat persistent calyx bearing the numerous stamens, and a mass of carpels ripening into an aggregate fruit composed of many drupelets — see BLACKBERRY, DEWBERRY, RASPBERRY

¹ru·by \'rübē, -bi\ *n* -ES [ME, fr. MF *rubi*, fr. OF, irreg. fr. L *rubeus* red, reddish; akin to L *ruber* red — more at RED] **1 a** (1) : a precious stone that is a red corundum and is found esp. in Burma, Ceylon, and Thailand — see RUBY SPINEL (2) *obs* : any of various precious stones of red color **b** : something made of ruby; *esp* : a watch bearing, pin, roller, or other part made of ruby or of a substitute material **2 a** (1) *or* **ruby red** : the color of the ruby : a dark red that is bluer, lighter, and stronger than average garnet or average wine and less strong and very slightly yellower than cranberry (2) *of textiles* : a deep purplish red that is redder and paler than magenta (sense 2a) and bluer and slightly lighter than American beauty **b** (1) : something resembling a ruby in color (2) : RUBY GLASS **3** *Brit* : AGATE 4 **4** : a Brazilian hummingbird of the genus *Clytolaema* whose male has a ruby-colored throat or breast

²ruby \"\ *adj* -ER/-EST : of the color ruby

³ruby \"\ *vt* -ED/-ING/-ES [²*ruby*] : to make of the color ruby : REDDEN

ruby-and-topaz hummingbird *n* : a showy hummingbird (*Chrysolampis mosquitus*) of northern So. America

ruby blende *n* : a red or reddish brown transparent sphalerite

ruby copper *or* **ruby copper ore** *n* : CUPRITE

ruby-crowned kinglet *or* **ruby-crowned wren** \'==ˌ=-\ *n* : an American kinglet (*Regulus calendula*) having a notable song and in the male a bright red crown patch

ruby glass *n* : glass of a deep red color produced by the use of selenium or esp. formerly by the addition of an oxide of copper or the use of gold chloride

ruby grass *n* : NATAL GRASS

ruby port *n* : a port wine of a deep red color

ruby silver *or* **ruby silver ore** *n* **1** : PYRARGYRITE **2** : PROUSTITE

ruby spaniel *n* : an English toy spaniel of a solid red color

ruby spinel *n* : a spinel used as a gem — see BALAS, RUBICELLE, SPINEL RUBY

rubytail \'==ˌ=\ *or* **ruby-tailed fly** \'==ˌ=-\ *n* : any of various cuckoo wasps; *esp* : a common European insect (*Chrysis viridula*) having part of the abdomen metallic red

rubythroat \'==ˌ=\ *n* **1** : RUBY-THROATED HUMMINGBIRD **2** : any of several red-throated Asiatic thrushes of the genus *Calliope*

ruby-throated hummingbird \¦==¦==-\ *n* : a hummingbird (*Archilochus colubris*) of eastern No. America having a bright bronzy green back, whitish underparts, and in the adult male a red throat with metallic reflections

ruby wasp *or* **ruby-tail wasp** *or* **ruby fly** *n* : CUCKOO WASP

ruby wine *n* : a dark red that is yellower and duller than cranberry and bluer, stronger, and slightly lighter than average garnet or average wine

ruby wood *n* **1** : RED SANDALWOOD 1 b **2** : SHEA TREE

ruby zinc *n* **1** : RUBY BLENDE **2** : ZINCITE

ru·cer·vine \rü'sərvən, -ˌvīn\ *adj* [NL *Rucervus* (fr. *Rusa* + *Cervus*) + E *-ine*] : of, relating to, or like a deer of a genus (*Rucervus*) that is now usu. made a subgenus of *Cervus*

rucervine antler *n* : an antler with long and simple brow tine and doubly dichotomous beam

¹ruche \'rüsh\ *n* -s [F, fr. ML *rusca* bark, rind, of Celt origin; akin to W *rhisgl* bark, ScGael *rūsg* rind, IrGael *rusc* bark] : RUCHING

²ruche \"\ *vt* -ED/-ING/-S : to trim with ruching

ruch·ing \'rüshiŋ\ *n* -s [¹*ruche* + *-ing*] : a pleated, fluted, or gathered strip of fabric (as lace, net, ribbon) used for trimming usu. in rows and esp. on women's garments

¹ruck \'rək\ *n* -s [ME *ruke, roke*, of Scand origin; akin to Norw dial. *rūka* heap, ON *hraukr* rick — more at RICK] **1** *chiefly dial* : HEAP, STACK, PILE, RICK ⟨coral ~s sticking out of the water —*Blackwood's*⟩ **2 a** : a large number or quantity taken esp. as indistinguishable in the aggregate : ASSEMBLAGE ⟨successes emerge from a ~ of smaller undertakings —Carl Van Doren⟩ **b** : the usual run of persons or things : GENERALITY, CROWD, MULTITUDE ⟨wrote the common ~ of the songs I was listening to —Max Beerbohm⟩ ⟨qualities that are bound to raise a man out of the ~ —G.W.Johnson⟩ ⟨from the ~ of routine, there arose a diversion —A.R.Griffin⟩ **c** : MASS, JUMBLE ⟨what I feel about the ~ of recent verse —J.L.Lowes⟩ ⟨a great ~ of textbooks —*Springfield (Mass.) Union*⟩ ⟨picked our way through the ~, lighting matches . . . when we found ourselves trapped in blind alleys between bales —W.D.Steele⟩ ⟨marked the land with the ~ of buffalo bones —Meridel Le Sueur⟩ **3 a** : the racehorses running in a group behind those that set the pace ⟨come up from the ~⟩ **b** : any aggregation of persons or things following the winners or vanguard ⟨finish a yacht race in the ~⟩ ⟨the ~ of wagons came after them —Irving Bacheller⟩ ⟨war and chaos in its ~ —S.L.A. Marshall⟩ **4** : a group of players of each team in rugby that are close together but not in a set formation

²ruck \"\ *vt* -ED/-ING/-S *chiefly dial* : to rake into a heap

³ruck \"\ *n* -s [of Scand origin; akin to ON *hrukka* wrinkle; akin to MHG *runke* wrinkle, OE *scrincan* to shrink — more at SHRINK] : CREASE, PUCKER, WRINKLE

⁴ruck \"\ *vb* -ED/-ING/-S *vi* : to draw or work into wrinkles or creases : PUCKER ⟨more micaceous rocks may show a ~*ing* or even small folds —*Economic Geology*⟩ — often used with *up* ⟨keeping the shirt from ~*ing up* —*advt*⟩ ~ *vt* : CREASE, PUCKER, WRINKLE ⟨those whose natures have been ~*ed* and wrinkled with suffering —R.S.Ellery⟩ — often used with *up* ⟨page was so wet, so ~*ed* up —Elizabeth Taylor⟩ ⟨top of the world, here ~*ed* up into gleaming ridges —Phil Stong⟩

⁵ruck \'rək, 'rük\ *n* -s [prob. fr. ³*ruck*] *dial Brit* : RUT, FURROW

¹ruck·le \'rəkəl, 'rük-\ *vi* **ruckled; ruckled; ruckling** \-k(ə)liŋ\ **ruckles** [of Scand origin; akin to ON *hrygla* to rattle in the throat; akin to MHG *rückeln, rüheln* to rattle in the throat, roar, OE *hrog* mucus, phlegm, Lith *kraũkti* to croak, groan, OSlav *krukŭ* raven, L *corvus* raven, *crepare* to crack, creak — more at RAVEN] *dial Brit* : to make a hoarse rattling sound (as from suffocation) ⟨asses braying and camels *ruckling* —I.M.Lask⟩

²ruck·le \'rəkəl\ **ruckled; ruckled; ruckling** \-k(ə)liŋ\ **ruckles** *vb* [³*ruck* + *-le*] *Brit* : to form or work into folds : CRUMPLE, WRINKLE

ruck·sack \'rəkˌsak, 'rük-\ *n* [G, fr. *ruck-* (prob. alter. of *rücken* back, spine, fr. OHG *hrukki*) + *sack* sack, fr. OHG *sac* — more at RIDGE, SACK] : KNAPSACK

rück·umlaut \'rœk+ˌ-\ *n* [G lit., back umlaut, fr. *rück-* (fr. *zurück* back, backward, fr. MHG *ze rücke*, fr. *ze* to — fr. OHG *zi* — + *rücke* back, fr. OHG *hrukki*) + *umlaut* — more at TO, RIDGE, UMLAUT] : the absence of umlaut of the stem vowel in the past tense and past participle of some Germanic weak verbs as a result of the loss of *i* in the following syllable before the umlaut period

ruck·us \'rəkəs, 'rük-\ *also* **roo·kus** \'rük-\ *n* -ES [*ruckus* prob. blend of *ruction* and *rumpus*; *rookus* alter. of *ruckus*] **1** : a noisy fight; *esp* : one involving a number of people : FRACAS **2** : CONTROVERSY, ROW, DISTURBANCE ⟨old ~*es* he stirred up among the critics —*New Yorker*⟩ ⟨political ~⟩ ⟨raise a ~⟩

ruc·ta·tion \ˌrək'tāshən\ *n* -s [LL *ructation-, ructatio*, fr. L *ructatus* (past part. of *ructare* to belch) + *-ion-, -io* -ion — more at ERUCT] *archaic* : BELCH

ruc·tion \'rəkshən\ *n* -s [perh. by shortening & alter. fr. *insurrection*] **1** : a noisy rough-and-tumble fight : FREE-FOR-ALL **2** : a heated quarrel esp. among a number of people ⟨raise a ~⟩ **3** : a state of disturbance or uproar : vociferous or belligerent disagreement : CONTENTION, DISSENSION, FRICTION ⟨herds were pushed with constant ~ by following waves of farmers —Russell Lord⟩

ruc·tious \'rəkshəs\ *adj* [*ruction* + *-ious*] *dial* : causing a ruction : QUARRELSOME, CONTENTIOUS, UNRULY, VEXED ⟨~ ghosts called poltergeists —*Time*⟩

ru·cu·yen *also* **roo·coo·yen** *or* **rou·cou·yenne** \ˌrüˌkü¦yen\ *n, pl* **rucuyen** *or* **rucuyens** *usu cap* **1 a** : a Cariban people of the Tumuc-Humac mountains between Brazil and the Guianas **b** : a member of such people **2** : a language of the Rucuyen people

¹rud *also* **rudd** \'rəd\ *n* -s [ME *rude, rudde, rode*, fr. OE *rudu*; akin to OE *rēad* red — more at RED] **1** *dial* **a** : a ruddy color : REDNESS **b** : HUE, COMPLEXION **2** *archaic* : RED OCHER

²rud *also* **rudd** \"\ *vt* **rudded; rudded; rudding; ruds** *also* **rudds** [ME *ruden, rudden, roden*, fr. *rude, rudde, rode* rud] : REDDEN

rud *abbr* rudder

ru·das \'rüdəs\ *n* -ES [origin unknown] *Scot* : an ugly foul-mouthed old hag : BELDAM

rud·beck·ia \ˌrəd'bekēə, rüd-\ *n* [NL, fr. Olof *Rudbeck* †1702 Swed. scientist + NL *-ia*] **1** *cap* : a genus of No. American perennial herbs (family Compositae) having showy pedunculate flower heads with a hemispherical involucre, mostly yellow ray flowers, and a conical chaffy receptacle — see BLACK-EYED SUSAN, GOLDEN GLOW **2** -s : any plant of the genus *Rudbeckia*

rudd \'rəd\ *n* -s [prob. fr. ¹*rud*] : a freshwater European cyprinid fish (*Scardinius erythrophthalmus*) resembling the roach but having the dorsal fin farther back, a stouter body, and red irises and fins — called also *redeye*

¹rud·der \'rədə(r)\ *n* -s *often attrib* [ME *rother*, fr. OE *rōther* paddle; akin to OHG *ruodar* rudder, ON *rōthr* act of steering; derivative fr. the root of E ¹*row*] **1 a** : a flat piece or structure of wood or metal attached upright to the sternpost or in single-screw ships to the rudderpost by hinges or by pintles and gudgeons so that it can be turned (as by a tiller) causing the ship's head to turn in the same direction because of the resistance offered to the water by the rudder **b** : a hinged or movable auxiliary airfoil usu. attached at the rear end that serves to control direction of flight in the horizontal plane by impressing yawing moments on an airplane **2** : RUDDER ANGLE ⟨what ~, if any, the ship is carrying —*Manual of Seamanship*⟩ **3** : one that resembles a rudder in being a guide or governor ⟨for rhyme the ~ is of verses —Samuel Butler †1680⟩ **4** : a plate or wheel at the rear end of a lister to guide and steady the moldboards and assist in bearing the weight **5** : a tail esp. of an otter **6** : a swinging support for the leaf of a drop-leaf table

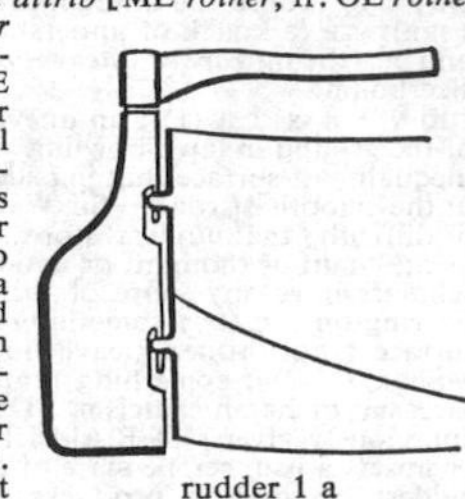

rudder 1 a

²rudder \"\ *vt* -ED/-ING/-S **1** : STEER **2** : to provide with a rudder

rudder angle *n* : the acute angle between the rudder and the fore-and-aft line of a ship or airplane

rudder bar *n* : a foot bar for operating the central cables leading to the rudder of an airplane

rudder bird *or* **rudder duck** *n* : RUDDY DUCK

rudder brake *n* : an eccentric friction band for controlling the motion of a rudder (as in a seaway)

rudder breeching *n* : a rope for lifting a rudder so as to ease the strain on the pintles

rudder chain *n* : one of a pair of loose chains or ropes that lead from a rudder to the quarters for operating it in case the tiller or rudderhead is broken

rudder crosshead *n* : an athwartship metal bar or casting which is secured to a rudderhead in lieu of a tiller and to which the connecting rods of the steering gear are secured

rudderfish \'==ˌ=\ *n* [¹*rudder* + *fish*] : any of various fishes reputed to follow or accompany ships: as **a** : PILOT FISH 1 **b** : BANDED RUDDERFISH **c** : any of several butterfishes (family Stromateidae) **d** : any of various fishes of the family Kyphosidae; *esp* : BERMUDA CHUB **e** : the opaleye or other fish of the family Girellidae

rudderhead \'==ˌ=\ *n* [¹*rudder* + *head*] : the upper end of a rudderstock to which the tiller is attached

rudderhole \'==ˌ=\ *n* [¹*rudder* + *hole*] : a hole in a deck through which a rudderstock passes

rudder iron *n* : a pintle or gudgeon for a ship's rudder

rud·der·less \'rədə(r)ləs\ *adj* : lacking a rudder

rudder lug *n* : a projection on a rudder frame at the forward edge for taking a pintle

rudderpost \'==ˌ=\ *n* [¹*rudder* + *post*] **1** : RUDDERSTOCK **2** : an additional sternpost in a single-screw ship to which the rudder is attached

rudderstock \'==ˌ=\ *n* [¹*rudder* + *stock*] : the shaft of a rudder

rudder stop *n* : a fitting on the stern frame or structure of a ship to limit the swing of the rudder

rudder tackle *n* : emergency tackle for use when mechanical steering gear fails to function

rudder torque *n* : a twisting effect exerted by the rudder of an airplane on the fuselage due to the lateral displacement of the center of pressure of the rudder

rudder trunk *n* : a watertight enclosure around a rudderstock

rud·der·va·tor *also* **rud·de·va·tor** \'rədə(r)ˌvād·ə(r)\ *n* -s [blend of *rudder* and *elevator*] : a movable airfoil at the trailing edge of a vee tail designed to perform the functions of both a rudder and an elevator

rud·di·ly \'rədᵊlē, -dəl|, |i\ *adv* : with a ruddy hue or tinge

rud·di·ness \'rədēnəs, -din-\ *n* -ES : the quality or state of being ruddy

1rud·dle \ˈrədᵊl\ *n* -s [dim. of 1*rud*] **1** *also* **red·dle** \ˈred-\ : RED OCHER **2** : 2BOLE 3

2ruddle \"\ *vt* **ruddled; ruddled; ruddling** \-d(ᵊ)liŋ\ **ruddles** **1** : to mark, paint, or color with red ocher ⟨~ sheep⟩ **2** : ROUGE **3** : REDDEN, FLUSH ⟨faces *ruddled* by the light of bobbing lanterns —Sinclair Lewis⟩

rud·dle·man \-dᵊlmən\ *also* **red·dle·man** \ˈred-\ *n, pl* **rud·dlemen** [1*ruddle* or *reddle* + *man*] : a dealer in red ocher

rud·dock \ˈrədək\ *n* -s [ME *ruddok*, fr. OE *ruddoc*; akin to OE *rudu* rud] **1** : ROBIN 1 a **2** *obs* : a piece of gold money

rudds *pl of* RUD, *pres 3d sing of* RUD

1rud·dy \ˈrədē, -di\ *adj* -ER/-EST [ME *rudi, rudie*, fr. OE *rudig*, fr. *rudu* rud + *-ig* -y — more at RUD] **1** : having or marked by a reddish color associated with the glow of good health or a suffusion of blood (as from exercise, excitement, exposure) ⟨a ~ complexion⟩ ⟨~ face⟩ ⟨stout ~ countryman⟩ **2 a** : of the color red **b** : RED, REDDISH ⟨~ glares from the blast furnaces —D.E.Keir⟩ **3** : GLOWING, LIVELY, VIVID ⟨~ memories⟩ **4** *Brit* — used as a generalized expression of intensification ⟨a ~ lie⟩ ⟨a ~ shame⟩ often losing all force ⟨what's the ~ matter⟩; often considered vulgar

2ruddy \"\ *vt* -ED/-ING/-ES : to make ruddy : REDDEN ⟨sunlight *ruddied* the windows⟩

3ruddy \"\ *adv, Brit* — an intensive ⟨could ~ well do as he liked⟩; often considered vulgar

ruddy diver *n* : RUDDY DUCK

ruddy duck *n* : an American duck (*Oxyura jamaicensis rubida*) having a broad bill and a wedge-shaped tail of stiff sharp feathers, the adult male having the upper parts largely rich brownish red and the female and young male being dull brown mixed with blackish on the back and grayish below

ruddy plover *n* : SANDERLING

ruddy sheldrake *n* : a sheldrake (*Tadorna ferruginea*) of southern Europe, Asia, and northern Africa that is chiefly orange-brown with the quills of the wings and tail blackish and the speculum bronzy green and with the male in summer having a black collar

ruddy turnstone *n* : an American turnstone (*Arenaria interpres morinella*) similar to the common turnstone

rude \ˈrüd\ *adj* -ER/-EST [ME, fr. MF, fr. L *rudis*; akin to L *rudus* rubble, broken stone, *rullus* coarse, rustic, MIr *rūad* ruin, MD *ruten* to tear, plunder, ON *reyta* to tear up, pluck out, L *ruere* to rush, fall, dig up — more at RUG] **1** : being in or marked by a rough, plain, or unfinished condition: **a** : lacking in craftsmanship or artistic finish : UNPOLISHED ⟨a ~ sketch⟩ ⟨a few ~ benches on which the players usually sat —Edna Ferber⟩ ⟨ornate window facings had broken off, leaving ~ gaps in the design —Marcia Davenport⟩ **b** : *of sound* : DISCORDANT, JARRING ⟨a ~ serenade⟩ ⟨the frowning-down of ~ intonations and laughing-out of oddities —D.L.Bolinger⟩ **c** : NATURAL, RAW, UNMANUFACTURED ⟨~ cotton⟩ ⟨examines, bit by bit, the ~ material of knowledge —T.L.Peacock⟩ **d** *of land* : RUGGED, WILD ⟨a ~ and rocky gorge commences —Tom Marvel⟩ ⟨shelter in a ~ country of forests —*Amer. Guide Series: Va.*⟩ **e** : STORMY, TURBULENT, BITTER ⟨winter's ~ winds⟩ ⟨~ seas⟩ **f** : hastily executed and admittedly imperfect or imprecise ⟨~ estimates⟩ **g** : being in or characteristic of a primitive or undeveloped state ⟨succeeded in constructing a ~ steam engine —T.B. Macaulay⟩ ⟨peasants use ~ wooden plows —Jack Raymond⟩ ⟨idea that man has progressed from ~ beginnings to civilized society —S.F.Mason⟩ **h** : IMMODERATE, UNMITIGATED ⟨the bright ~ sun —Gordon Merrick⟩ **i** : being in the rough state : UNDRESSED, UNFINISHED ⟨~ monoliths⟩ **j** : SIMPLE, ELEMENTARY, ELEMENTAL, UNSUBTLE ⟨community on the outskirts of civilization which continues to maintain itself in ~ plenty and comfort —W.H.Mallock⟩ ⟨landscape done in ~ whites, blacks, deep browns —Richard Harris⟩ **2** : lacking refinement or delicacy: **a** : lacking education : IGNORANT, UNLEARNED, UNTUTORED ⟨~ mountaineers⟩ **b** : lacking polish : INELEGANT, UNCOUTH ⟨even the ~ dialects of the illiterate began to acquire dignity —Josiah Royce⟩ ⟨gave to his historical compositions a ~ dramatic vigor —Roger Fry⟩ **c** : offensive in manner or action : DISCOURTEOUS, UNMANNERLY, IMPUDENT ⟨made a ~ reply⟩ ⟨his brusqueness did not make him ~ —O.S.J. Gogarty⟩ **d** : marked by a lack of gentleness or by the use of force ⟨place a ~ hand upon our little mare's bridle —Kenneth Roberts⟩ ⟨dragged him with ~ cuffs before the magistrate —A.C.Whitehead⟩ ⟨self-discipline and single-mindedness must have been needed to make this ~ initiation to the stage endurable —*Times Lit. Supp.*⟩ **e** : UNCIVILIZED, BARBAROUS, SAVAGE ⟨in the ~ ages of society —Adam Smith⟩ ⟨during ~ times no man can be useful or faithful to his tribe without courage —C.R.Darwin⟩ **f** : UNAFFECTED, GUILELESS, OPEN ⟨arguments for ~ virtue are almost inevitably less stimulating than those for sophisticated corruption —Wolcott Gibbs⟩ ⟨ought to . . . speak the ~ truth in all ways —R.W.Emerson⟩ **g** : COARSE, RIBALD, VULGAR ⟨exchanged banter in ~ phrases, which at first shocked her —Theodore Dreiser⟩ ⟨paint on which someone had scratched a ~ picture —F.D.Ommanney⟩ ⟨unimportant work with a few small, ~ words in it —Anthony West⟩ **3** : marked by lack of training or skill : INEXPERIENCED, INEXPERT ⟨~ workmanship⟩ ⟨was but a ~ scholar⟩ **4** : ROBUST, STURDY, VIGOROUS ⟨spoke of the ~ health of their children —Joseph Conrad⟩ ⟨the ~ strength of the idiom —Gilbert Millstein⟩ **5 a** : sudden and disconcerting or unpleasant : ABRUPT ⟨freedom that is due for a ~ awakening sooner or later —W.J.Reilly⟩ ⟨the change may not be so ~ or so sweeping —Douglas Cater⟩ **b** : GRAVE, IMPERATIVE, UNAVOIDABLE ⟨inner strength to endure in the face of ~ realities —*Americas*⟩

syn ILL-MANNERED, DISCOURTEOUS, IMPOLITE, UNCIVIL, UNGRACIOUS: in this set RUDE is the strongest word. It implies either a general and habitual deficiency in manners, grace, or polish or a coarse insensitivity to another's feelings or even a desire to wound them ⟨she thought he was *rude*, and so did he — and tried to philosophize himself out of his sense of social maladjustment —H.S.Canby⟩ ⟨I don't see why we should go to a house where the host apparently enjoys flatly contradicting you . . . probably he doesn't even know when he's being *rude* —Sinclair Lewis⟩ ILL-MANNERED stresses great want of knowledge of proprieties, usages, and graces of good society ⟨our Royal Family are getting a little tired of the well-meant, but at the same time *ill-mannered* homage of well-dressed crowds —*London Daily News*⟩ ⟨the pompous *ill-mannered* police —*Harper's*⟩ DISCOURTEOUS is likely to imply a consciousness of offending or wounding another if not the intent ⟨*discourteous* enough to slam the door in another's face⟩ ⟨*discourteous* in pointedly refusing to acknowledge his greeting⟩ IMPOLITE suggests less obvious and egregious departures from better conduct ⟨had been somewhat *impolite* in failing to answer her invitation as quickly as good manners demanded⟩ UNCIVIL indicates lack of decent consideration usually expected among men but not prescribed by any code of etiquette ⟨"comfortable seat, and be damned to you!" was the patient's *uncivil* reply —Anthony Trollope⟩ UNGRACIOUS may indicate lack of grace and consideration ensuing through gaucheness, callowness, surliness, irritation ⟨an interesting person, this stern Australian nurse — taciturn, suspicious, *ungracious* —A. Conan Doyle⟩

syn CRUDE, ROUGH, CALLOW, RAW, GREEN: except for CALLOW and GREEN, words in this series follow much the same pattern of semantic expansion. They are here compared only as indicating lack of social refinement in persons and in their actions and thoughts. RUDE may indicate complete lack of social polish or civility ⟨to be ill-bred and *rude* is intolerable, and the way to be kicked out of company —Earl of Chesterfield⟩ It may suggest intentional discourtesy or ill treatment of others ⟨I do not know whether it came from his own innate depravity or from the promptings of his master, but he was *rude* enough to set a dog at me —A. Conan Doyle⟩ CRUDE may emphasize a predisposition to the gross, simple, obvious, or primitive and an ignorance of the amenities ⟨they seem pleasant and good-humored, but a little *crude*, and lacking in the subtler forms of wit and understanding —Rose Macaulay⟩ More than others in this series, CRUDE may suggest an enduring characteristic rather than one from a passing phase ⟨the marks of the thoroughbred were simply not there. The man was blatant, *crude*, overly confidential . . . One often observed in him a certain pathetic wistfulness, a reaching out for a grand manner that was utterly beyond him —H.L.Mencken⟩ ROUGH suggests harsh, uncivil, unfeeling action or conduct, but may be concerned more with manifest conduct than inner character ⟨men of a *rough* and unsparing address should take great care that they be always in the right, the justice and propriety of their sentiments being the only tolerable apology . . . for such conduct —William Cowper⟩ It may thus suggest outer bluffness rather than inner incivility ⟨a *rough* old charitable mercifulness, better than sentimental ointment —George Meredith⟩ CALLOW, GREEN, and RAW all suggest novices' experiences and situations as causes for lack of savoir faire without indicating stupidity, truculence, or obduracy and without suggesting future inadequacy or gaucherie. CALLOW almost always denotes the immaturity of adolescence or early manhood ⟨not the aggregation of *callow* schoolboys fresh from the playing fields which in prewar times filled the academic halls, but an assemblage of men whose maturity has been forged in the holocaust of battle —Amy Loveman⟩ GREEN suggests unfamiliarity with a new environment or pursuit ⟨young men who were *green* recruits last autumn have matured into self-assured and hardened fighting men —F.D.Roosevelt⟩ It may also suggest rustic gullibility ⟨he has taken me for a *green* country girl, impressed with him because he is from the city and dressed in fine clothes —Sherwood Anderson⟩ RAW suggests outward uncertainty or awkward blundering due to lack of experience and training ⟨they think him *raw*, brusque, and uncultivated. He does not know the ritual . . . knowledge of which, acquired by long experience, is the mark of fit membership in the society —W.G. Sumner⟩

rude·ly *adv* [ME, fr. *rude* + *-ly* — more at RUDE] **1** : in a rude manner ⟨spoke ~ to him⟩ ⟨laughed ~⟩ ⟨~ made⟩ ⟨~ awakened⟩ **2** : APPROXIMATELY, IMPRECISELY ⟨estimated ~⟩ ⟨~, 75 by 125⟩

rude·ness *n* -ES [ME, fr. *rude* + *-ness*] **1** : the quality or state of being rude ⟨shocked by the ~ of frontier life —*Amer. Guide Series: Tenn.*⟩ **2** : a rude action ⟨an unpardonable ~⟩

ru·den·ture \(ˈ)rü¦denchə(r)\ *n* -s [F, fr. L *rudent-, rudens* ship's rope + F *-ure* — more at RHYTIDOME] *archit* : CABLING

ru·dera \ˈrüdərə\ *n pl* [L, pl. of *rudus* rubble, broken stone — more at RUDE] *archaic* : RUINS, DEBRIS

1ru·der·al \ˈrüdərəl\ *adj* [NL *ruderalis*, fr. L *rudera* + *-alis* -al] *of a plant* : growing in rubbish or in a waste or disturbed place

2ruderal \"\ *n* -s : a weedy and commonly introduced plant growing where the native vegetational cover has been interrupted; *esp* : a weed other than a grass growing where the vegetation has been disturbed by man (as in old fields or along roadsides)

ru·der·ate \ˈrüdə,rāt\ *vt* [L *ruderatus*, past part. of *ruderare* to pave with broken stone, fr. *rudus* rubble] *archaic* : to pave with broken stone

ru·der·a·tion \,rüdəˈrāshən\ *n* -s [L *ruderation-, ruderatio*, fr. *ruderatus* (past part.) + *-ion-, -io* -ion] *archaic* : the process of paving with broken stone

rudes·by \ˈrüdzbē\ *n* -ES [*rude* + *-sby* (as in the name *Crosby*)] *archaic* : an uncivil turbulent person ⟨a madbrain ~ full of spleen —Shak.⟩

rudge \ˈrəj\ *chiefly dial var of* RIDGE

ru·di·ment \ˈrüdəmənt\ *n* -s [L *rudimentum* first attempt, beginning, fr. *rudis* raw, rough, rude + *-mentum* -ment — more at RUDE] **1 a** : a first principle : a basic element ⟨my tactics missed a ~ —Emily Dickinson⟩ ⟨the single leaf is the ~ of beauty in the landscape —Isaac Taylor⟩ — usu. used in pl. ⟨assume that the judges know the ~s of law —B.N.Cardozo⟩ **b rudiments** *pl* : fundamental skills taught or learned (as in an elementary school) ⟨carefully grounded in the ~s —W.B. Parker⟩ ⟨acquired the mere ~s of a common-school education —Edna Yost⟩ **2 a** : something that is unformed or undeveloped : BEGINNING ⟨must admit he had the ~ of decency —Christopher Morley⟩ — usu used in pl. ⟨experiments . . . which seem to show the ~s of a human type of intelligence in the chimpanzee —R.W.Murray⟩ ⟨the ~s of a plan⟩ ⟨gave himself the ~s of a wash —Maurice Walsh⟩ ⟨~s of a headache⟩ **b** : a body part or organ so deficient in size or in both size and structure as to entirely prevent its performing its normal function: (1) : an organ or part just beginning to develop : ANLAGE (2) : one whose development has been arrested at an early stage (3) : the remains of a part functional only in an earlier stage of the same individual or in his ancestors : VESTIGE

ru·di·men·tal \¦rüdə¦mentᵊl\ *adj* : RUDIMENTARY

ru·di·men·tar·i·ly \¦rüdə(,)men·¦terəlē, -,mən-·, -li\ *adv* : in a rudimentary manner ⟨~ and geometrically Cubist —Janet Flanner⟩

ru·di·men·ta·ri·ness \,rüdəˈmentərēnəs, -rin-\ *n* -ES : the quality or state of being rudimentary

1ru·di·men·ta·ry \¦rüdə¦mentərē, -n·trē, -ri *sometimes* -dəmən·,ter-\ *adj* [*rudiment* + *-ary*] **1** : of or relating to rudiments: as **a** : consisting in first principles : BASIC, FUNDAMENTAL ⟨these ~ truths —M.R.Cohen⟩ **b** : of a primitive kind : UNDEVELOPED, ELEMENTARY ⟨a ~ sort of building —Henry Wynmalen⟩ ⟨man with a ~ conscience —Greer Williams⟩ ⟨conditions which do not meet ~ standards of decency —F.D. Roosevelt⟩ **c** : of or relating to the basic skills taught esp. in elementary school ⟨received four years of ~ education —*Current Biog.*⟩ **2** : having the character of a rudiment : very imperfectly developed or represented only by a vestige

2rudimentary \"\ *n* -ES : RUDIMENT 2b

ru·di·men·ta·tion \,rüdə(,)men·ˈtāshən, -,mən-\ *n* -s [*rudiment* + *-ation*] : the formation of a vestigial organ by continuous lagging in development — compare APHANISIA

rud·ish \ˈrüdish\ *adj* [*rude* + *-ish*] : somewhat rude

ru·dis·ta \rüˈdistə\ *n pl, cap* [NL, fr. L *rudis* rude, raw + *-ista* -ist] *in some classifications* : a division of Eulamellibranchia comprising extinct chiefly Cretaceous bivalve mollusks with one valve elongate, conical, and thick-shelled and the other small and fitting like a lid on the first — **ru·dis·tan** \(ˈ)=¦=stən\ *adj or n* — **ru·dis·tid** \(ˈ)=¦=stəd\ *adj or n*

ru·dis·tae \=ˈ=(,)stē\ [NL] *syn of* RUDISTA

rud·mas·day \ˈrədməs,dā, ˈrüd-\ *n, usu cap* [alter. of earlier *roodmas day*, fr. *roodmas* (fr. *rood* + *mas* — fr. ME *masse* mass —) + *day* — more at MASS] : HOLY-ROOD DAY

ru·dol·phine tables \(ˈ)rü¦dälfən-\ *n, usu cap R* [*rudolphine* fr. *Rudolph* (Rudolf) II †1612 Holy Roman emperor + E *-ine*] : a set of astronomical tables computed by Kepler (1571–1630) and founded on observations by Tycho Brahe (1546–1601)

ruds *pl of* RUD, *pres 3d sing of* RUD

1rue \ˈrü\ *vb* -ED/-ING/-S [ME *ruen, rewen*, fr. OE *hrēowan*; akin to OHG *hriuwan* to grieve, regret, ON *hryggr* sorrowful and perh. to Gk *krouein* to strike, push & Lith *krušti* to stamp, smash] *vt* **1 a** : to repent of (wrongdoing) : feel penitence or remorse for **b** : to feel regret for (as an act or a choice) : wish undone or done differently ⟨several used us unconsciously and *rued* the results —A.B.Guthrie⟩ ⟨I ~ that day —Emmett Gowen⟩ **2** *obs* **a** : to affect with pity or compassion **b** : to regard with pity or compassion ~ *vi* **1** *archaic* : to be repentant : feel contrition **2 a** : to regret an act or choice **b** *Scot* : to be dissatisfied with a bargain : try to go back on an agreement — often used with *of* **3** *obs* : to feel sorrow, regret, or reluctance **4** *archaic* : to have compassion : feel pity : show mercy — often used with *on* or *upon* — **rue back** *South & Midland* : to repent and try to withdraw from an agreement or bargain

2rue \"\ *n* -s [ME *rewe*, fr. OE *hrēow*; akin to MD *rouwe* sorrow, OHG *hriuwa* sorrow, *hriuwan* to grieve] **1 a** : REGRET, SORROW ⟨although she mocked his ~, he knew she shared it —Kathryn Grondahl⟩ **b** : REPENTANCE **2** : COMPASSION, PITY

3rue \"\ *n* -s [ME *rue, ruwe, rewe*, fr. MF *rue*, fr. L *ruta*, fr. Gk *rhytē*] : a European strong-scented perennial woody herb (*Ruta graveolens*) having yellow flowers and decompound leaves with a bitter taste — called also *herb of grace*

rue anemone *n* [3*rue*] : a delicate vernal herb (*Anemonella thalictroides*) of the family Ranunculaceae having decompound leaves and white flowers resembling those of the wood anemone

rue bargain *n* **1** *dial Brit* : a bargain that one regrets **2** *dial Brit* : a forfeit (as of money) given for withdrawing from an agreement

rue family *n* [3*rue*] : RUTACEAE

rue·ful \ˈrüfəl\ *adj* [ME *rewful*, fr. *rewe* rue + *-ful*] **1** : exciting pity or sympathy : PITIABLE, WOEFUL ⟨~ squalid poverty that crawled by every wayside —John Morley⟩ **2** : feeling or expressing sorrow or pity : MOURNFUL, REGRETFUL, SAD ⟨troubled her with a ~ disquiet —W.M.Thackeray⟩; *often* : quizzically mournful ⟨looked up . . . with a ~ grin —Elmer Davis⟩

rue·ful·ly \-f(ə)lē, -li\ *adv* [ME *rewfully*, fr. *rewful* rueful + *-ly*] : in a rueful manner

rue·ful·ness \-fəlnəs\ *n* -ES [ME *rewfulnes*, fr. *rewful* rueful + *-nes* -ness] : the quality or state of being rueful

ru·elle \(ˈ)rü¦el\ *n* -s [ME *ruel*, fr. MF *ruele*, lit., alley, dim. of *rue* street, fr. L *ruga* wrinkle, fold — more at ROUGH] **1** *archaic* : the space between a bed and the wall **2** : a morning reception held in their bedrooms by fashionable French ladies of the 17th and 18th centuries **3** : a narrow street or alley ⟨the smaller ~s were in pitch-darkness —Donald Stokes⟩

ru·el·lia \rüˈelēə\ *n* [NL, fr. Jean *Ruel* (latinized *Ruellius*) †1539 Fr. physician and botanist + NL *-ia*] **1** *cap* : a very large genus of chiefly tropical American herbs and shrubs (family Acanthaceae) that have showy solitary or paniculate flowers with the simple or 2-lobed style recurved at the apex and the ovary 2-celled **2** -s : any plant or flower of the genus *Ruellia*

rue oil *n* [3*rue*] : a colorless to yellow usu. fluorescent essential oil with an intense odor obtained from rue and other plants of the genus *Ruta* and used chiefly in perfumery and in medicine as a local irritant

rue·ping process \ˈrü¦piŋ-, ˈrē¦-\ *n, usu cap R* [after Max *Rüping* 20th cent. Ger. timber engineer, its originator] : a treatment for preserving wood with the use of a minimum amount of coal-tar creosote by alternating pressure and vacuum so that only the walls of the wood cells are coated and the cells themselves are not filled

ru·fes·cence \rüˈfesᵊn(t)s\ *n* -s : the quality or state of being rufescent : a reddish or bronze color

ru·fes·cent \(ˈ)rü¦fesᵊnt\ *adj* [L *rufescent-, rufescens*, pres. part. of *rufescere* to become reddish, fr. *rufus* red — more at RED] : REDDISH

1ruff \ˈrəf\ *n* -s [ME *ruf, roffe*, prob. fr. *ruffe, rowe* sea bream, perh. fr. *row, ruh, rough*, adj., rough — more at ROUGH] **1** *also* **ruffe** : a small freshwater European perch (*Acerina cernua*) **2** : a pumpkinseed (*Lepomis gibbosus*)

2ruff \"\ *n* -s [prob. back-formation fr. 1*ruffle*] **1** : a wheel-shaped collar made of several layers of lace or lace-edged muslin or linen starched and goffered usu. in S-shaped folds and worn tied on at the front by men and women of the late 16th and early 17th centuries **2** : RUFFLE 4a **3** : something suggestive of a ruff: as **a** : a fringe or frill of long hairs or a set of lengthened or otherwise modified feathers around or on the neck of a mammal or bird ⟨the ~ of a Persian cat⟩ **b** : a collar to prevent endwise motion (as at either end of a shaft journal) **c** : a loose ornamented boot top common in the 17th century **4 a** : a common sandpiper (*Philomachus pugnax*) of Europe and Asia whose male during the breeding season has a large ruff of erectile feathers on the neck and yellowish naked tubercles on the face, is polygamous, and is noted for pugnacity — compare REEVE **b** : a domestic pigeon having a ruff on its neck **5** [influenced in meaning by 1*ruffle*] *obs* **a** : the highest degree (as of pride or prosperity) : the top extreme or limit : APEX, CREST, ZENITH **b** : ELATION, PRIDE **c** : fury or violence of passion

ruff 1

3ruff \"\ *vt* -ED/-ING/-S **1 a** : to make into a ruff **b** : 1RUFFLE 7a **2** *of a stooping falcon* : to strike but fail to secure (a bird) **3** : to comb (hair) by taking hold of a strand and pushing the short hairs toward the scalp with the comb

4ruff \"\ *n* -s [MF *roffle, ronfle*] **1** : a 16th century game from which whist was developed **2** : the playing of a trump when another suit is led

5ruff \"\ *vb* -ED/-ING/-S : TRUMP

6ruff \"\ *n* -s [imit.] *archaic* : a low drumbeat : RUFFLE

7ruff \"\ *vb* -ED/-ING/-S **1** *Scot* : to beat a ruffle on a drum **2** *Scot* : to stamp with the feet in applause

ruff and honours *n* : 4RUFF 1

ruffed *adj* [fr. past part. of 3*ruff*] : having, wearing, or furnished with a ruff

ruffed bustard *n* : HOUBARA

ruffed grouse *n* : a No. American grouse (*Bonasa umbellus*) valued as a game bird in wooded parts of the U.S. and Canada whose male is about 17 inches long, is varied with rufous, black, and gray and has a dark band on the tail and tufts of large glossy black feathers on the sides of the neck, and is noted for drumming with its wings in the breeding season — compare PARTRIDGE, PHEASANT

ruffed lemur *n* : a large black-and-white lemur (*Lemur varius*) having the face framed by thick fringes of long hair on the sides of the head

1ruf·fi·an \ˈrəfēən\ *n* -s [MF *rufian*] **1** : a coarse, brutal, or cruel fellow : a man of crime or violence : BULLY, ROWDY, TOUGH **2** *obs* : a keeper and companion of whores : PANDER, PIMP

2ruffian \"\ *adj* : of, relating to, or behaving like a ruffian : BRUTAL, COARSE, ROWDY

3ruffian \"\ *vi* -ED/-ING/-S *archaic* : to play the ruffian : act rough

ruf·fi·an·ish \-ēənish\ *adj* : RUFFIANLY

ruf·fi·an·ism \-ēə,nizəm\ *n* -s : the action, conduct, or qualities of a ruffian

ruf·fi·an·ize \-,nīz\ *vb* -ED/-ING/-S *vi* : to act in a ruffianly manner ~ *vt* : to make ruffianly

ruffianlike \ˈ=,=,=\ *adj* : appropriate to or resembling a ruffian

ruf·fi·an·ly \ˈrəfēənlē, -li\ *adj* : of or relating to a ruffian : behaving as a ruffian : COARSE, ROUGH, ROWDY ⟨always appeals to the more ~ elements —A.M.Young⟩

ruf·fi·a·no \,rüfēˈä(,)nō\ *n, pl* **ruffia·ni** \-nē\ [It] *archaic* : RUFFIAN

1ruf·fle \ˈrəfəl\ *vb* **ruffled; ruffled; ruffling** \-f(ə)liŋ\ **ruffles** [ME *ruffelen*; akin to LG *ruffelen* to crumple] *vt* **1 a** : to roughen or disturb the smoothness of : agitate the surface of **b** : to rub (a surface) rough : ABRADE, GRAZE **c** : to disturb the composure of : DISTRACT, TROUBLE, VEX ⟨said this to try to ~ her husband —Rex Ingamells⟩ **2** *obs* : to throw into confusion or perplexity **3** *chiefly dial* : to annoy with insults : ATTACK, BULLY **4** : to erect (as feathers) in or like a ruff : cause to rise or bristle : STIFFEN **5** : to act the braggart : roister about : SWAGGER — used with *it* ⟨*ruffled* it with the other gunmen who infested the town —W.M.Raine⟩ **6 a** : to flip through (as the pages of a book) ⟨ran with it to the piano, *ruffling* the pages to find the place —Marcia Davenport⟩ : shuffle (playing cards) rapidly **b** *obs* : to rumple or tousle (a woman) familiarly or rudely **c** *obs* : to seize rudely **7 a** : to make into a ruffle : GATHER, PLEAT **b** : to finish or trim with ruffles ~ *vi* **1 a** *archaic* : to strive or contest against another or on behalf of another : engage in combat — used with *with* or *for* **b** *archaic* : to grow rough, boisterous, or turbulent (as the wind) **2** : to become discomposed, irritated, or angered ⟨their dispositions ~ perceptibly —*Life*⟩ **3** : to flutter or stir into an uneven surface : rise or form into folds or irregularities ⟨a flag on a tall pole *ruffled* in the breeze⟩ **4** : to swagger arrogantly : act the bully or braggart : show bravado : BLUSTER ⟨gets drunk, ~s, and roisters —Charles Kingsley⟩ ⟨one that *ruffled* in a manly pose —W.B.Yeats⟩

2ruffle \"\ *n* -s **1 a** : a disturbance of calm or equanimity : a state of irritation, vexation, or discomposure ⟨recuperate after the ~ of breakfast —Elizabeth Taylor⟩ **b** : something that causes annoyance or vexation **2 a** : a rough brawl, fight, or dispute : COMMOTION, SKIRMISH ⟨all the ~ and rowdydow —M.G.Bishop⟩ **b** *obs* : busy ostentation : vainglorious pomp or display **3** : a roughness, unevenness, or disturbance of surface : RIPPLE ⟨give the water a glistening ~ —Vincent McHugh⟩ **4 a** : a strip of fabric that is gathered or pleated on one edge and attached along that edge as a trimming or finish ⟨curtains with a ~ at the bottom⟩ ⟨a blouse trimmed with lace ~s⟩ — compare 4FLOUNCE **b** : 2RUFF 3a **c** : 2RUFF 3c **5** : the mesentery of a slaughtered meat animal **6** : the group of wings on a metal gudgeon for a wooden shaft

3ruffle \"\ *vi* -ED/-ING/-S [6*ruff* + *-le*] **1** *of a drum* : to beat with a ruffle **2** : to beat a ruffle on a drum

4ruffle \"\ *n* -s : a low vibrating drumbeat less loud than a roll — compare RUFFLE AND FLOURISH

ruffle and flourish *n* **:** a ruffling drumbeat and fanfare played in honor of a high official at a ceremonial reception

ruf·fled \-fəld\ *adj* [fr. past part. of [1]*ruffle*] **1 :** having ruffles **:** trimmed with ruffles **2** *hort* **:** having a distinctly waved margin

ruffle fat *n* **:** the fat of the mesentery attached to the intestines of slaughtered animals

ruf·fler \-f(ə)lə(r)\ *n* -s [[1]*ruffle* + *-er*] **1** *archaic* **:** a vagabond rogue or beggar of the 16th century often professing to be an injured soldier **2 :** a swaggering roistering fellow ⟨strut like the bold ~s they fancied themselves to be —T.B.Costain⟩ **3 :** DISTURBER ⟨a great ~ of pat orthodoxies⟩ **4 :** a sewing-machine attachment for making ruffles

ruffling *n* -s [fr. gerund of [1]*ruffle*] **:** fabric gathered or pleated into ruffles; *also* **:** RUFFLE

ruf·fly \-f(ə)lē, -li\ *adj* [[2]*ruff* + *-ly*] **:** having plaits, folds, or puckers **:** RUFFLED

ruff out *vt* **:** to establish (a bridge suit) by trumping leads on which the opponents' high cards must fall

ruffs *pl of* RUFF, *pres 3d sing of* RUFF

ru·fin·ic \(ˈ)rü¦finik\ *adj* [L *rufus* red + *-inic* (as in *albinic*)] *biol* **:** REDDISH — **ru·fi·nism** \ˈrüfə,nizəm\ *n* -s

ru·fos·i·ty \rüˈfäsəd·ē\ *n* -ES [*rufous* + *-ity*] **:** the quality or state of being rufous

ru·fous \ˈrüfəs\ *adj* [L *rufus* red — more at RED] **1 :** of any of several colors averaging a strong yellowish pink to moderate orange **2 :** REDDISH; *esp* **:** having reddish hair and a freckling skin ⟨the ~, foxy little dentist —Nancy Hale⟩

rufous hornbill *n* **:** CALAO

rufous hummingbird *n* **:** a hummingbird (*Selasphorus rufus*) of the western U.S. with a chiefly reddish brown male

ruf·ter hood \ˈrəftə(r)-\ *also* **rufter** *n* -s [*rufter* prob. fr. [3]*ruff*] *falconry* **:** a hood for a newly taken hawk

ru·fus \ˈrüfəs\ *adj* [L] **:** RUFOUS

[1]**rug** \ˈrəg, ˈrüg\ *vb* **rugged; rugged; rugging; rugs** [ME *rugen, ruggen*, of Scand origin; akin to ON *rugga* to rock; akin to ON *rykkja* to jerk — more at ROCK] *dial Brit* **:** PULL, TEAR, WRENCH

[2]**rug** \"\ *n* -s [ME, fr. *rugen* to rug] **1** *dial Brit* **:** PULL, TUG, HAUL **2** *dial Brit* **:** a good bargain **:** FIND

[3]**rug** \ˈrəg\ *n* -s [of Scand origin; akin to Norw dial. *rugga* coarse rug, Sw *rugg* entangled hair, ON *rögg* tuft, shagginess; akin to Goth *riurs* fleeting, perishable, MIr *rūam* spade, shovel, L *ruere* to rush, fall, dig up, Gk *erysichthōn* tearing up earth, OSlav *ryti* to dig, Skt *ravate* he breaks up, smashes, *ruta* shattered, divided; basic meaning: breaking up, tearing] **1 a :** a coarse rough woolen clothing fabric of the 16th and 17th centuries **b :** a garment of this fabric **2 a :** a piece of thick heavy fabric usu. with a nap or pile and commonly of wool that is used as a floor covering, is usu. woven either in one piece of a definite shape and design or in widths so made as to form a definite design when they are united, and is not intended to cover an entire floor — compare CARPET, ORIENTAL RUG **b :** a floor mat made of an animal pelt ⟨bearskin ~⟩ **c :** a warm covering for the lap and feet (as of one riding in a sleigh or sitting on a ship's deck) **:** LAP ROBE — compare BEARSKIN, BUFFALO ROBE **3 :** a covering or blanket for an animal (as a horse or cow) **4** *slang* **:** TOUPEE 2

[4]**rug** \"\ *vt* **rugged; rugged; rugging; rugs :** to cover with a rug or blanket — often used with *up* ⟨~ up a sick goat⟩

[5]**rug** \"\ *adj* [origin unknown] *archaic* **:** COMFORTABLE, COZY, SNUG

ru·ga \ˈrügə\ *n, pl* **ru·gae** \-ü,gī, -ü(,)jē\ [NL, fr. L, wrinkle, fold] **:** a visceral fold or wrinkle — used chiefly in pl. — **ru·gal** \-ügəl\ *adj*

ru·gate \ˈrü,gāt, -gət\ *adj* [L *rugatus*, past part. of *rugare* to crease, wrinkle, fr. *ruga* wrinkle, fold — more at ROUGH] **:** WRINKLED, RUGOSE

ru·gat·ed \ˈrü,gād·əd\ *adj* [L *rugatus* (past part. of *rugare* to wrinkle) + E *-ed*] **:** RUGOSE

rug·be·ian \ˈrəgbēən, ,=ˈ==\ *n* -s *usu cap* [irreg. fr. *Rugby* School + E *-an*] **:** a pupil or alumnus of Rugby School

rug brick *n* [[3]*rug*] **:** a face brick with a surface rough like the pile of a rug

rug·by \ˈrəgbē, -bi\ *or* **rugby football** *n* -ES *often cap R* [fr.

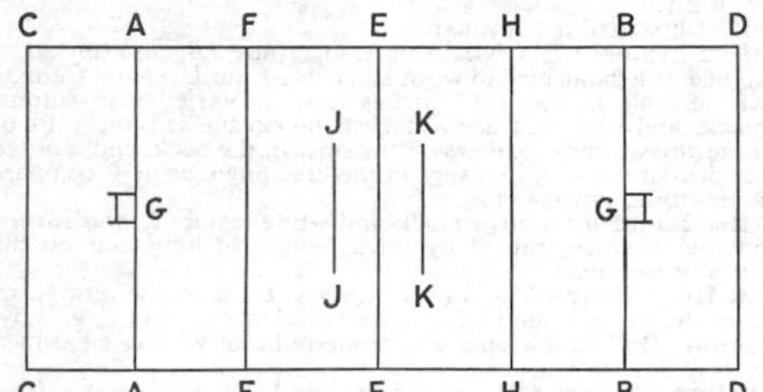

diagram of rugby field: field of play, ABBA; goal lines, AA and BB; touchlines, AB and AB; touch-in-goal lines, AC, AC, BD, and BD; in-goals, ACCA and BDDB; dead-ball lines, CC and DD; halfway line, EE; 10 yard lines, JJ and KK; 25 yard lines, FF and HH; goals, G and G

Rugby School, Rugby, Warwickshire, England, where it was first played] **:** an amateur football game which is played with an oval ball by teams of 15 players each and in which play is continuous, kicking, dribbling, lateral passing, tackling, and the scrum are featured, and interference and substitution are not permitted — compare RUGBY LEAGUE FOOTBALL

rugby game *or* **rugby fives** *n, usu cap R* **:** the game of fives played on a court having rear as well as front and side walls — compare ETON GAME

rugby league football *n, usu cap R&L* [*Rugby League*, unofficial name of *The Rugby Football League*, football league formed in England in 1895] **:** a modified form of rugby which is played under professional rules with 13 players to a team and in which a try counts 3 points and any goal 2 points — called also *Northern Union football*

rugby tan *n* **:** ARAB 4

rugby union football *n, usu cap R&U* [*Rugby Union*, unofficial name of *The Rugby Football League* (originally called *The Northern Rugby Football Union*), football league formed in England in 1895] **:** RUGBY

rug-cutter \ˈ=,==\ *n* **:** a jitterbug dancer ⟨an editorial page which will appeal primarily to *rug-cutters* and jive hounds —*Saturday Rev.*⟩

rug-cutting \ˈ=,==\ *n* **:** JITTERBUG

ru·gel's plantain \ˈrügəlz-\ *n* [after Ferdinand *Rugel* †1879 Ger. botanist, its discoverer] **:** a broad-leaved No. American plantain (*Plantago rugelii*) having reddish petioles and slender spikes of flowers — called also *broad-leaved plantain*

rugg *var of* RUG

rug·ged \ˈrəgəd\ *adj, often* -ER/-EST [ME, fr. (assumed) *rug* rag, tuft (of Scand origin) + *-ed*; akin to ON *rögg* tuft, shagginess — more at RUG] **1** *obs* **a :** rough with bristles or hair **:** SHAGGY **b :** having a coarse or hairy texture — used of clothing and textiles **2 :** having a rough, uneven, or irregular surface or broken jagged outline or contour ⟨a ~ mountain range⟩ ⟨a steep and ~ ascent —John Burroughs⟩ ⟨cascades, canyons, deep gorges, and ~ profiles —*Amer. Guide Series: Maine*⟩ **3 :** marked by storm or tempest **:** WILD ⟨the ~*est* weather in all No. America — dull, damp, chilly, and beset unendingly by storms —A.H.Farnsworth⟩ **4 :** rough to the ear **:** harsh-sounding ⟨a book so ~ in its style, that an attempt to polish it seemed an Herculean labor —William Cowper⟩ **5 a :** seamed with wrinkles and furrows **:** VIGOROUS, WEATHERED — used of a human face **b :** showing facial signs of physical or moral strength **:** STURDY ⟨a certain determination that was inseparable from the ~ countenance —Louis Bromfield⟩ **6 a :** austere or stern in aspect, conduct, or character **:** HARSH, UNGENTLE **b :** wanting in civility or cultivation **:** COARSE, RUDE **c :** unpolished but sturdy **7 a :** strongly built or constituted **:** HARDY, ROBUST, VIGOROUS ⟨those that survive are stalwart, ~ men —L.D.Stamp⟩ ⟨the ~ steel sections are given a heavy coating of pure zinc —*advt*⟩ **b :** presenting a severe test of ability, stamina, or resolution ⟨a ~ competitive exam⟩ ⟨the ~ conditions of frontier life⟩ **syn** see ROUGH

rugged individualism *n* **:** the practice or advocacy of individualism in social and economic relations emphasizing personal liberty and independence, self-reliance, resourcefulness, self-direction of the individual, and free competition in enterprise

rug·ged·iza·tion \,rəgədəˈzāshən, -,dīˈz-\ *n* -s **:** the act of ruggedizing or the state of being ruggedized

rug·ged·ize \ˈrəgə,dīz\ *vt* -ED/-ING/-S [*rugged* + *-ize*] **:** to strengthen and reinforce (as a machine, structure, instrument) for better resistance to wear, stress, and abuse ⟨the new *ruggedized* camera solves the particular problems presented by airborne applications —*Industrial Equipment News*⟩

rug·ged·ly *adv* **:** in a rugged manner

rug·ged·ness *n* -ES **:** the quality or state of being rugged

rug·ger \ˈrəgə(r)\ *n* -s [by alter.] *Brit* **:** RUGBY

rug·ging \ˈrəgiŋ\ *n* -s [[3]*rug* + *-ing*] **:** a coarse plainwoven woolen cloth with a thick nap used as floor covering

rug gown *n* **1** *obs* **:** a gown made of rug **2** *obs* **:** someone (as a watchman) wearing a rug gown

rug·gy \ˈrəgē\ *adj* [ME, prob. alter. (influenced by *-y*) of *rugged*] *dial* **:** RUGGED, ROUGH

rugheaded *adj* [[3]*rug* + *headed*] *obs* **:** having shaggy hair

ru·go·sa \rüˈgōsə\ [NL, fr. L, fem. neut. pl. of *rugosus* wrinkled, rugose] *syn of* TETRACORALLA

rugosa rose *n* **:** any of various garden roses descended from a Japanese rose (*Rosa rugosa*)

ru·gose \ˈrü,gōs, -ōz\ *adj* [L *rugosus* wrinkled, fr. *ruga* wrinkle + *-osus* -ose — more at ROUGH] **1 :** full of wrinkles ⟨~ cheeks⟩ **2** *bot* **:** having the veinlets sunken and the spaces between elevated ⟨the ~ leaves of the sage and the horehound⟩ — compare BULLATE — **ru·gose·ly** *adv*

rugose mosaic *n* **:** a highly destructive virus disease of potatoes due to the combined action of the viruses responsible for vein-banding and latent virus disease and causing dwarfed, wrinkled, and mottled leaves, stunting, and premature death — compare POTATO MOSAIC

ru·gos·i·ty \rüˈgäsəd·ē, rəˈg-\ *n* -ES [LL *rugositat-, rugositas*, fr. L *rugosus* wrinkled + *-itat-, -itas* -ity] **:** the quality or state of being rugose **:** a wrinkled place **:** WRINKLE

ru·gous \ˈrügəs\ *adj* [L *rugosus*] **:** WRINKLED, RUGOSE

rugs *pres 3d sing of* RUG, *pl of* RUG

ru·gu·la \ˈrügyələ\ *n, pl* **rugu·lae** \-,lē\ [NL, fr. L *ruga* wrinkle, fold + *-ula* -ule] **:** a small fold

ru·gu·lose \-,lōs\ *adj* [prob. fr. (assumed) NL *rugulosus*, fr. NL *rugula* + L *-osus* -ose] **:** having small rugae **:** finely wrinkled **:** having rugulae

ruhm·korff coil \ˈrüm,kȯrf-\ *n, usu cap R* [after Heinrich *Ruhmkorff* †1877 Ger. physicist, its inventor] **:** INDUCTION COIL

[1]**ru·in** \ˈrüən, ˈrü| *also* |,in, *dial* ˈrərn\ *n* -s [ME *ruine*, fr. MF, fr. L *ruina*; akin to L *ruere* to rush, fall — more at RUG] **1 a** *archaic* **:** a falling down esp. of a building **:** COLLAPSE **b :** the decay or fall of an individual or a group **:** physical, moral, economic, or social collapse ⟨bankruptcy, dishonor, and ~ were now his lot⟩ **2 a** *archaic* **:** the condition of something that has collapsed **:** a state of destruction or abjectness **b :** the remains of something that has been destroyed **:** decayed or broken fragments — usu. used in pl. ⟨went back to the ~*s* of their city —Weston La Barre⟩ **3 :** a cause or agent of destruction **:** DESTROYER, WRECKER ⟨this carelessness . . . was to be his ~ —Mary A. Hamilton⟩ ⟨drink was his ~⟩ **4 a :** the destruction, laying waste, or wrecking of something **:** DEVASTATION, OVERTHROW ⟨~ can make a hideous modern building seem beautiful —Stephen Spender⟩ ⟨the ~ of modern drama —T.S.Eliot⟩ ⟨risked . . . his own political ~ —C.H.Sykes⟩ **b :** DAMAGE, INJURY, IMPAIRMENT ⟨the ~ of misspent years cannot be quickly undone⟩ **5 :** the moral or social downfall of a woman (as by vice or seduction) ⟨a daughter's ~ unhinged the old man's mind⟩ **6 :** a building, person, or other object that has tumbled down or fallen into decay ⟨a ~ that was now a home of bats and lizards⟩ ⟨should write the biography of this shambling ~ —Lee Rogow⟩

[2]**ruin** \"\ *vb* **ruined** \-nd, *dial* -nt\ **ruined; ruining; ruins** [MF or ML; MF *ruiner* to ruin, fr. ML *ruinare*, fr. L *ruina* ruin] *vt* **1 a :** to lay waste **:** reduce to wreckage **:** DEVASTATE, OVERTHROW ⟨~*ed* temple⟩ ⟨~*ed* city⟩ ⟨the ~*ed* land⟩ **b** *obs* **:** to root out or lay low **2 a :** to damage or destroy irredeemably **:** inflict irreparable injury on ⟨rain had ~*ed* her hat⟩ ⟨crops ~*ed* by hail⟩ ⟨a car ~*ed* in a smashup⟩ ⟨in danger of being ~*ed* by prosperity⟩ **b :** to overthrow the fortunes of **:** bring to financial ruin **:** BANKRUPT, IMPOVERISH ⟨was ~*ed* during the great crash⟩ ⟨had been ~*ed* by speculation⟩ **c :** to bring (a woman) to degradation or dishonor **3 :** to subject to entire frustration, failure, or disaster ⟨~*ed* hopes⟩ ⟨an illness that ~*ed* his chances of promotion⟩ ~ *vi* **1 a :** to crash down **:** fall headlong to destruction **b :** to become decayed or dilapidated **2 :** to come to moral, financial, or social ruin **:** be impoverished, degraded, or dishonored **syn** see DESTROY

ruin agate *n* **:** a usu. brown agate showing on a polished surface markings suggestive of ruined buildings

[1]**ru·in·ate** \ˈrüə,nāt, ˈrüə-, *usu* -ād·+V\ *adj* [ML *ruinatus*, past part. of *ruinare* to ruin] **:** RUINED

[2]**ruinate** \"\ *vb* -ED/-ING/-S [ML *ruinatus*, past part. of *ruinare* to ruin] *vt* **1** *chiefly dial* **a :** to bring down **:** DEMOLISH, DESTROY, OVERTHROW **b :** to reduce to poverty or wretchedness **:** DEGRADE, DISHONOR **2** *obs* **:** to bring to nothing **:** SUBVERT ~ *vi* **1** *chiefly dial* **:** to fall into ruin **2** *obs* **:** CRASH

ru·in·a·tion \,==ˈnāshən\ *n* -s [[2]*ruinate* + *-ion*] **1 :** the act of ruining or the state of being ruined **:** DESTRUCTION **2 a :** cause of ruin **:** a destructive agent or factor ⟨the olive is the ~ of the martini —*Saturday Rev.*⟩

ru·in·a·tor \ˈ==,nād·ə(r), -ātə-\ *n* -s [[2]*ruinate* + *-or*] **:** DESTROYER, RUINER

ru·in·er \-,nə(r)\ *n* -s [[2]*ruin* + *-er*] **:** one that ruins

ruing *pres part of* RUE

ru·in·i·form \ˈrüənə,fȯrm, ˈrüə-, rüˈin-\ *adj* [[1]*ruin* + *-iform*] **:** having the appearance of ruins — used of minerals

ruin marble *n* **:** a brecciated limestone giving a mosaic effect when cut and polished that suggests a picture of ruins

ru·in·ous \ˈrüənəs, ˈrüə-\ *adj* [ME *ruinose*, fr. LL *ruinosus*, fr. L *ruina* ruin + *-osus* -ose — more at RUIN] **1 :** fallen into decay or dilapidation **:** RUINED ⟨the high paling was broken by the mossy and ~ posts of an old gateway —John Buchan⟩ **2 :** causing or tending to cause ruin **:** DESTRUCTIVE, DISASTROUS, PERNICIOUS ⟨the excessive wages paid for unskilled labor were ~ to the farmer —Ellen Glasgow⟩

ru·in·ous·ly *adv* **:** in a ruinous manner

ru·in·ous·ness *n* -ES **:** the quality or state of being ruinous

rul·able \ˈrüləbəl\ *adj* [ME *reuleable*, fr. *reule* rule + *-able*] **1** *obs* **:** capable of being ruled **2 :** permissible according to the rules

[1]**rule** \ˈrül\ *n* -s [ME *riwle, reule, riule*, fr. OF *reule, riule*, fr. L *regula* straightedge, rule, fr. *regere* to lead straight, guide — more at RIGHT] **1 a :** a prescribed, suggested, or self-imposed guide for conduct or action **:** a regulation or principle ⟨his parents laid down the ~ that he must do his homework before going out to play⟩ ⟨a very sound ~ for any hiker is to mind his own business —F.D.Smith & Barbara Wilcox⟩ ⟨made it a ~ never to lose his temper⟩ **b :** the laws or regulations prescribed by the founder of a religious order for observance by its members ⟨the ~ of St. Dominic⟩ **c :** an accepted procedure, custom, or habit having the force of a regulation ⟨we are bound by the ~s of our culture to conceal such matters —Marjorie Fischer⟩ ⟨the ~ of the house was an early bedtime⟩ **d** (1) **:** a usu. written order or direction made by a court regulating court practice or the action of parties but not making a final judgment on the merits of a controversy (2) **:** a legal precept applied to a given set of facts as stating the law applicable to a case (3) **:** a statement or doctrine accepted as part of the common law — see RULE AGAINST PERPETUITIES **e :** a regulation or bylaw governing procedure in a public or private body (as a legislature or club) or controlling the conduct of its members ⟨a ~ for limiting debate⟩ ⟨a ~ against insulting language⟩ ⟨a ~ for the admission of new members⟩ **f :** one of a set of usu. official regulations by which an activity (as a sport) is governed ⟨the infield fly ~⟩ ⟨the ~s of professional basketball⟩ **2 a** (1) **:** a statement of a fact or relationship generally found to hold good **:** a usu. valid generalization ⟨the exception proves the ~⟩ (2) **:** a generally prevailing condition, quality, state, or mode of activity or behavior ⟨fair weather was the ~ yesterday afternoon over most of the nation —*N.Y. Times*⟩ ⟨persons in whose families high blood pressure was the ~ rather than the exception —Morris Fishbein⟩ **b :** a standard by which something is judged or valued **:** CRITERION ⟨"good enough" becomes the ~ and enters into the character of our theater life —Leslie Rees⟩ **c** (1) **:** a principle regulating or held to regulate the practice of an art or science ⟨the ~s of perspective⟩ ⟨the ~s of harmony⟩ ⟨the ~*s* of versification⟩ (2) **:** a principle regulating or held to regulate the form and use of words ⟨a knowledge of the irrefragable ~*s* of the comma was mistaken for a knowledge of language —Charlton Laird⟩ **d** (1) **:** a determinate method prescribed for performing a mathematical operation and attaining a certain result (2) *dial* **:** RECIPE **3 a** (1) **:** the exercise of authority or control **:** DOMINION, GOVERNMENT, SWAY ⟨under his firm ~, however, conditions quickly improved —C.M.Fuess⟩ ⟨establishing a single ~ throughout the kingdom far and wide —B.N.Cardozo⟩ (2) **:** a period during which a specified ruler or government exercises control ⟨during the ~ of the Caesars⟩ ⟨in the first year of the ~ of the republic⟩ **b :** the state of being governed **:** CONTROL ⟨to a child, winter . . . was confinement, school, ~, discipline —Henry Adams⟩ **4 a** (1) **:** an instrument for measuring or ruling off lengths that consists of a strip or strips of material (as wood, metal, or tape) marked off in units of length (as inches or centimeters) (2) **:** RULER 2a **b** (1) **:** a metal strip with a type-high face that prints a linear design (2) *Brit* **:** DASH 3e (3) **:** LINE GAUGE (4) **:** COMPOSING RULE (5) **:** MAKEUP RULE **5** *obs* **:** BEHAVIOR, CONDUCT ⟨this uncivil ~ —Shak.⟩ **6 a rules** *pl* **:** a limited area formerly established near a prison for the residence of prisoners of certain categories (as debtors) **b :** the freedom to live in such an area ⟨was a prisoner on ~⟩ **syn** see LAW — **as a rule** *adv* **:** as a general thing **:** ORDINARILY, USUALLY ⟨*as a rule* sick people recover without treatment —L.J.Henderson⟩ — **under the rule** *adv* **:** in accordance with a stock-exchange rule providing for sales or purchases to be made by an officer of the exchange for the account of members not fulfilling their contracts made on the floor

[2]**rule** \"\ *vb* -ED/-ING/-S [ME *riwlen, reulen, rulen*, fr. OF *reuler, riuler*, fr. L *regulare*, fr. *regula* rule] *vt* **1 a :** to control, direct, or influence the mind, character, or actions of ⟨so long as she could ~ her own mind she was not afraid of the forces without —Ellen Glasgow⟩ ⟨what ~*s* an Admission Dean's judgment in the midwinter heat of competition —V.S. Carruthers⟩ ⟨be *ruled* by me and have a care o' the crowd —Robert Browning⟩ **b :** to curb or moderate by the use of self-control ⟨went on a diet but found it difficult to ~ her appetite⟩ **c :** to exercise control over **:** GUIDE, MANAGE ⟨~ a horse⟩ **2 a :** to exercise authority or power over **:** GOVERN ⟨became Speaker and for nearly two years *ruled* the Assembly with a rod of iron —E.H.Collis⟩ ⟨the territory is *ruled* by a high commissioner —*Americana Annual*⟩ **b :** to hold preeminence in (as by ability, strength, or position) **:** DOMINATE ⟨an actor who ~*s* the Shakespearean stage⟩ ⟨*ruled* the featherweight division —*Providence (R.I.) Evening Bull.*⟩ **c :** to play a dominant role in or exert a controlling influence over ⟨profit taking *ruled* the stock market yesterday —*Wall Street Jour.*⟩ ⟨the monsoon seasons, which ~ the climate in a great part of Asia —Owen & Eleanor Lattimore⟩ **3 a :** to declare authoritatively **:** DECIDE, DECREE, DETERMINE; *specif* **:** to require or command by judicial rule **:** give as a direction, order, or determination of a court **b :** to consider as **:** JUDGE ⟨at the risk of really being *ruled* a maverick —Irving Kolodin⟩ **4 a** (1) **:** to mark with lines drawn along the straight edge of a ruler ⟨~ a sheet of paper⟩ **:** print or mark with lines by means of a rule ⟨a pad of *ruled* yellow paper⟩ (2) **:** to mark (a line) on a paper with a ruler ⟨*ruled* vertical lines on the sheet⟩ **b :** to arrange in a straight line or mark off in lines as if with a ruler ⟨nor were the eyebrows bushy like most old men's, but smoothly *ruled* —Clemence Dane⟩ ⟨flowering shrubs which *ruled* the mountain walls like a sheet of paper —John Muir †1914⟩ ~ *vi* **1 a :** to have power or command **:** exercise supreme authority ⟨*ruled* wisely over his subjects —*Time*⟩ ⟨a king who reigns but does not ~⟩ **b :** to exercise control **:** PREDOMINATE ⟨the physical did not ~ in her nature —Sherwood Anderson⟩ **2 a :** to prevail at a specified rate or level ⟨prices had *ruled* high —Robert Hunter⟩ ⟨in the offshore islands . . . temperature and humidity ~ higher than on the mainland —*Internat'l Reference Service*⟩ **b :** to exist in a specified state or condition **3 a :** to lay down a legal rule or order of court **b :** to decide an incidental legal point **c :** to enter a rule — **rule the roast** *or* **rule the roost :** to be at the head of things **:** have full authority or control ⟨wouldn't you like to *rule the roast*, and guide this university —W.S.Gilbert⟩ ⟨a little-boy school in which I and my gang had *ruled the roost* —Donald Moffat⟩ **syn** see DECIDE

rule against perpetuities : a rule at common law that makes void any estate so limited that it will not necessarily take effect or vest within a life or lives in being at the time of the creation of the estate and 21 years thereafter with the addition of the period of gestation in the case of a person entitled to the estate being conceived but unborn

ruled surface *n, math* **:** a surface generated by a moving straight line

rule joint *n* **:** a knuckle joint having shoulders that abut when the connected pieces are opened out fully and thus permit folding in one direction only

rule·less \ˈrülləs\ *adj* [ME *rewleless*, fr. *rewle, riwle* rule + *-less* — more at RULE] **:** not curbed or ruled by law **:** LAWLESS

rule nisi *n* **:** a rule or order upon condition that is to become absolute unless cause is shown to the contrary

rule of adjunction : a rule in logic: if each of two statements (as *p* and *q*) has been asserted then their conjunct (as *p·q*) may be asserted

rule of deduction : TRANSFORMATION RULE

rule of eleven : a rule in bridge and whist: when a player leads his fourth-best card of a suit the number of its spots subtracted from eleven gives the number of higher cards of the same suit not in the leader's hand — called also *eleven rule*

rule off *vt* **:** to debar (as a horse, jockey, player) from a race or contest **:** DISQUALIFY ⟨*ruled* him *off* for rough riding⟩

rule of faith 1 : a standard for testing truth in religion; *esp* **:** an ultimate theological criterion **2 :** an authoritative statement of religious belief **:** a creedal formulation designed to sum up major orthodox beliefs and to exclude heresy

rule of law 1 : a legal rule **:** a determination of the applicable rule as distinguished from a finding of fact **2 :** adherence to due process of law **:** government by law

rule of the air : a provision of the code of regulations governing matters of air traffic (as the meeting and overtaking of other aircraft, the use of defined air lanes of travel, or the height of flying over cities)

rule of the road 1 : any of the various regulations imposed upon travelers by land or water for their mutual convenience or safety **2 :** any of the rules making up a code governing ships as to the lights to be carried, the signals to be made, and the action of one ship with respect to another when risk of collision exists

rule of three : a rule in mathematics: the product of the means in a proportion equals the product of the extremes — used for finding the fourth term of a proportion where three are given

rule of thumb 1 : a method of procedure or analysis based upon experience and common sense and intended to give generally or approximately correct or effective results ⟨seems to have run the ship by *rule of thumb* and word of mouth —William McFee⟩ **2 :** a general principle regarded as roughly correct and helpful but not intended to be scientifically accurate ⟨a good *rule of thumb* is that smart youngsters prepared to enter college at the age of 16 have not been accelerated too much —L.M.Spencer⟩

rule of two and three : a bidding principle in contract bridge: a player who makes a preemptive bid should not overbid by more than two tricks when vulnerable or three tricks when not vulnerable

rule out *vt* **1 a :** to exclude or eliminate ⟨was *ruled out* on a technicality that required members to be experienced lawyers —*Current Biog.*〉 〈*rule* such subjective and moral judgments *out* of our biology —A.L.Kroeber〉 **b :** to eliminate as a possibility 〈a positive diagnosis can be made only after *ruling out* gastric and duodenal ulcer —H.G.Armstrong〉 **2 :** to make impossible **:** PREVENT 〈heavy rain *ruled* the picnic *out* for that day〉 **syn** see EXCLUDE

rul·er \'rülə(r)\ *n* -s [ME *reuler*, fr. *reulen* to rule + *-er* — more at RULE] **1 a :** one that exercises authority, command, or dominating influence 〈the old male was even in captivity the undisputed guardian and ~ of all the other members —Weston La Barre〉 〈the ~*s* of modern art〉 〈an ambition that became the ~ of his life〉; *specif* **:** one who rules over a nation or people 〈an able and vigorous ~ who reunited his country〉 〈their position in our democratic system as the informants of our ~*s*, the people —F.L.Mott〉 **b :** one who exercises control in some limited field 〈was the ~ of Admiralty Room 40 —*Brit. Book News*〉 **2 :** one that rules lines: as **a :** a straight or curved strip (as of wood or metal) with a smooth edge usu. marked off in units (as inches or centimeters) and used for guiding a pen or pencil in drawing lines or for measuring **b :** an operator of a machine for drawing ink lines on paper

rul·er·ship \-,ship\ *n* **:** the office, function, or status of a ruler **:** RULE, SOVEREIGNTY

rules committee *n* **:** a committee of a legislative house that determines the rules and procedure for expediting the business of the house and has the power to control the date and nature of debate of a proposed bill

rules of court : the regulations covering practice and procedure before a particular court

rules of practice : the published regulations relating to the presentation of evidence and appearance of witnesses before a particular administrative agency or regulatory body

¹rul·ing \'rüliŋ, -lēŋ\ *n* -s [ME *riwling*, fr. gerund of *riwlen* to rule] **1 :** an official or authoritative decision, decree, or statement 〈his own experience and judgment carried more weight with him than the ~*s* of any of the surgical authorities —Harvey Graham〉: as **a :** a decision or rule of a judge or a court **b :** an interpretation by an administrative agency of the law under which it operates applicable to a given statement of facts **2** *math* **:** a generatrix of a ruled surface

²ruling \"\ *adj* **1 a :** exerting power or authority 〈~ family〉 〈~ party〉 **b :** CHIEF, PREDOMINATING 〈a ~ passion〉 〈a ~ ambition〉 〈a ~ idea〉 **2 :** generally prevailing **:** CURRENT 〈~ prices in the world market —F.D.Smith & Barbara Wilcox〉

ruling elder *n* **:** ³ELDER 4b

ruling engine *n* **:** an exceedingly accurate and delicately adjusted machine for ruling lines (as of a diffraction grating)

ruling grade *n* **:** the grade on any particular road regarded as limiting the weight of a train that can be drawn by one engine — compare PUSHER GRADE

ruling pen *n* **:** a draftsman's pen for ruling lines that has a pair

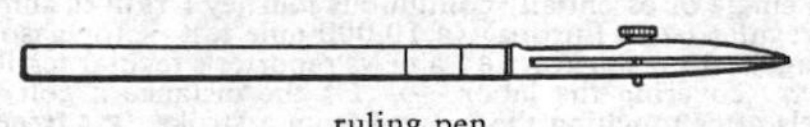

ruling pen

of adjustable metal blades or points between which the ink is contained with the thickness of the line being regulated by a screw that closes the blades or allows them to open

rul·lion \'rəlyən\ *n* -s [prob. fr. obs. E (Sc) *rullion* shoe made of untanned leather, prob. alter. of ME (Sc) *rewelin, rewling* shoe of rawhide, fr. OE *rifeling*; perh. akin to OE *gehriflian* to wrinkle, shrivel — more at RIVEL] *chiefly Scot* **:** a large rough-looking person or creature

rullock *var of* ROWLOCK

ruly \'rülē\ *adj* [back-formation fr. *unruly*] *archaic* **:** OBEDIENT, ORDERLY

¹rum \'rəm\ *adj* **rummer; rummest** [earlier *rome*, perh. fr. Romany *rom* married man, husband, gypsy man — more at ROM] **1** *chiefly Brit* **:** unusually fine **:** EXCELLENT **2** *chiefly Brit* **a :** characterized by queerness, peculiarity, or unusualness 〈writing is a ~ trade . . . and what is all right one day is all wrong the next —Angela Thirkell〉 **b :** marked by difficulty, danger, or a threatening appearance — often used as a generalized expression of disapproval 〈had a ~ time from the weather —*Newsweek*〉 〈she's ~ about the eyes —Arthur Morrison〉

²rum \"\ *n* -s [prob. short for *rumbullion*] **1 :** an alcoholic liquor prepared by fermenting molasses, macerated sugarcane, or other saccharine cane product, distilling, coloring with caramel, and aging — compare RUM ESSENCE **2 :** alcoholic liquor 〈the crimes due to ~〉

³rum \"\ *var of* RUMMY

ru·mal \(')rü¦mäl\ *or* **ro·mal** \rō'm-\ *n* -s [Hindi *rūmāl*, fr. Per, fr. *rū* face + *māl* wiper] **1 :** a usu. silk plainwoven Indian fabric used for dresses and handkerchiefs **2 :** an often checked cotton or silk kerchief used as a scarf and in India as a headdress by men

¹ru·man \'rümən\ *n* -s *cap* [Romanian *Rumân, Român*, fr. L *Romanus* Roman — more at ROMAN] **:** ROMANIAN

²ruman \"\ *n* -s *cap* [Romanian *rumân*] **:** WALLACHIAN

rumania *usu cap, var of* ROMANIA

rumanian *usu cap, var of* ROMANIAN

rumansch *usu cap, var of* ROMANSH

rum·ba *also* **rhum·ba** \'rəmbə, 'rùm-,'rüm-\ *n* -s [AmerSp *rumba*, fr. *rumbo* carousal, spree, fr. Sp, pomp, ostentation, looseness, perh. fr. *rumbo* bearing, course, direction, rhumb line, fr. OSp — more at RHUMB] **1 a :** a Cuban Negro dance marked by violent movements **b :** an American ballroom dance imitative of the Cuban rumba **2 :** the music for a rumba characterized by strong rhythmic syncopations

¹rum·ble \'rəmbəl\ *vb* **rumbled; rumbled; rumbling** \-b(ə)liŋ\ **rumbles** [ME *rumblen, romblen*; akin to MHG *rummeln* to rumble, OSw *rumbla* and prob. to ON *rymja* to roar, grumble — more at RUMOR] *vi* **1 a :** to make a low heavy rolling sound 〈thunder which ~*s* ominously, yet, because of distance, is all but inaudible —Erle Stanley Gardner〉 〈the camels' bellies *rumbling* to the water they held —I.L.Idriess〉 〈the dark spaces between the walls ~ with strange and appalling noises —Sherwood Anderson〉 **b** (1) **:** to travel as a low reverberating sound 〈*rumbling* through the racy air — the unmistakable sound of a horn —Blanche E. Baughan〉 (2) **:** to travel or go with an accompanying low heavy sound 〈mule-drawn freight wagons *rumbled* through the town —*Amer. Guide Series: Texas*〉 **c :** to speak in a low rolling tone 〈heard him *rumbling* to himself as they went out —Grace Campbell〉 **2 :** to constitute or create a disturbing factor **:** represent a state of unrest 〈there had been *rumbling* in the Head Camp a controversy of no mean proportions —C.W. Ferguson〉 **3** *slang* **:** to engage in a rumble 〈the Cherubs are *rumbling* —Walter Bernstein〉 ~ *vt* **1 a :** to utter or emit in a low rolling voice 〈*rumbled* that one of his children liked frogs —*Yankee*〉 **b** *chiefly Brit* **:** to stir up or knock about with a rumbling sound **2 a** *slang* **:** to detect or see through (as a trick, a trickster) 〈dice are almost never gaffed so that the same numbers always come up because even the greenest mark would ~ that in short order —John Scarne & Clayton Rawson〉 **b** *slang* **:** to give oneself away to or become detected by (as the intended victim) while in the act of committing a crime **:** excite the suspicion of 〈I read the financial pages and the investment journals so I won't slip up and ~ the mark —D.W.Maurer〉 **3 :** to polish or otherwise treat (metal parts) in a tumbling barrel

²rumble \"\ *n* -s [ME *rumbel*, fr. *rumblen, romblen* to rumble] **1 a :** a low heavy continuous reverberating often muffled sound (as of heavy vehicles, distant thunder) 〈as the train lost speed the smooth ~ of wheels over rails broke into a series of rattling thumps —John Dos Passos〉 〈could hear the ~ of a man's voice . . . but I couldn't hear the words —Erle Stanley Gardner〉 **b :** low-frequency noise in disc recording or reproduction caused by low-frequency vibration mechanically transmitted to the turntable or pickup **2 a** [short for *rumble-tumble*] **:** a seat for servants behind the body of a carriage **b** [by shortening] **:** RUMBLE SEAT **3 :** TUMBLING BARREL **4 :** something that breaks in upon or upsets a peaceful state of affairs: as **a :** a generalized or widespread expression of dissatisfaction or unrest 〈~*s* of opposition arose in the counties —J.N.Popham〉 **b :** RUMOR, COMPLAINT 〈picked up the ~ . . . and thought he'd pass it on just in case —P.A.Brodeur〉 **c :** QUARREL, DISTURBANCE **d** *slang* (1) **:** detection in a criminal act (2) **:** a search by law enforcement officials of premises or a neighborhood for narcotics or narcotics peddlers **e** *slang* **:** a street fight esp. among teenage gangs 〈down in the basement of a candy store, getting their switchblade knives, zip guns, and Molotov cocktails ready for a ~ —Marjorie Rittwagen〉

rumble-bumble \¦rəmbəl¦bəmbəl\ *n* **:** a miscellaneous mass or mixture **:** JUMBLE, HODGEPODGE

rum·ble·ga·rie \¦rəm(b)əl¦gärì\ *adj* [prob. fr. ²*rumble* + connective *-g-* + *-arie* -ary] *Scot* **:** careless and disorderly in action or manner **:** HARUM-SCARUM

rum·ble·gump·tion *also* **rum·el·gump·tion** \'rəm(b)əl-,gəm(p)shən\ *n* [alter. (influenced by ²*rumble*) of obs. E (northern dial.) *rumgumption*, prob. fr. E ¹*rum* + *gumption*] *Scot* **:** good judgment **:** SENSE, INTELLIGENCE

rum·bler \'rəmb(ə)lə(r)\ *n* -s [¹*rumble* + *-er*] **:** one that rumbles as: **a :** TUMBLING BARREL **b :** an operator of a machine (as a tumbling barrel) that cleans small articles by tumbling them with abrasives or cleaning fluid

rumble seat *n* **:** a folding seat in the back of an automobile (as a coupe or roadster) not covered by the top

rumble-tumble \¦rəmbəl¦təmbəl\ *n* **1 :** RUMBLE 2a **2 :** a heavy coach or cart that moves with a deep rumbling sound

rum·bling·ly *adv* **:** in a rumbling manner

rum·bly \'rəmb(ə)lē, -li\ *adj* [²*rumble* + *-y*] **:** tending or causing to rumble or rattle

rum·bo \'rəm(,)bō\ *n* -s [*rumb-* (fr. *rumbullion*) + *-o*] *archaic* **:** GROG

rumbowline *var of* ROMBOWLINE

rum·bow·ling \,rəm'bōlən, -liŋ\ *n* -s [alter. of *rumbullion*] **:** GROG

rumbullion *n* -s [origin unknown] *obs* **:** RUM

rum·bus·ti·cal \¦rəm¦bəstəkəl\ *adj* [*rumbustic* (prob. alter. of obs. E *robustic* robust, robustious, fr. E *robust* + *-ic*) + *-al*] **:** RAMBUNCTIOUS

rum·bus·tious \-schəs\ *adj* [alter. (prob. influenced by ²*rumble*) of *robustious*] **:** RAMBUNCTIOUS

rum cherry *n* **:** BLACK CHERRY 2a

rum–dum *also* **rum–dumm** \'rəm,dəm\ *adj* [prob. fr. ²*rum* + G *dumm* dumb (fr. OHG *tumb* mute, stupid) — more at DUMB] **:** reeling from drunkenness **:** INTOXICATED

rumdum \"\ *n* -s [*rum-dum*] **:** DRUNKARD

¹ru·me·lian *or* **rou·me·lian** \(')rü¦mēlēən, -lyən\ *adj, usu cap* [*Rumelia*, former division of the Turkish empire that included Albania, Macedonia, and Thrace + E *-an*] **1 :** of, relating to, or characteristic of Rumelia, former European division of the Turkish Empire **2 :** of, relating to, or characteristic of the people of Rumelia

²rumelian *or* **roumelian** \"\ *n* -s *cap* [*Rumelia* + *-an* (n. suffix)] **:** a native or inhabitant of Rumelia

ru·men \'rümən\ *n, pl* **rumi·na** \-mənə\ *or* **rumens** [NL, fr. L, gullet — more at RUMINATE] **:** the large first compartment of the stomach of a ruminant from which food is regurgitated for rumination and in which cellulose is broken down by the action of bacterial and protozoan symbionts **:** PAUNCH; *broadly* **:** the first three compartments of the ruminant stomach — distinguished from *abomasum*; compare OMASUM, RETICULUM

ru·men·itis \,rümə'nīd·əs\ *n*, -ES [NL, fr. *rumen* + *-itis*] **:** inflammation of the rumen

rumeno- *comb form* [NL, fr. *rumen*] **:** rumen 〈*rumenotomy*〉

ru·meno·centesis \¦rümənō+\ *n* [NL. fr. *rumeno-* + *centesis*] **:** puncture of the rumen with a trocar and cannula to permit the escape of gas

ru·men·ot·o·my \,rümə'näd·əmē\ *n* -ES [*rumeno-* + *-tomy*] **:** incision into the rumen

rum essence *n* **:** ethyl butyrate or a prepared mixture of esters and oils used in the manufacture of imitation rum

ru·mex \'rü,meks\ *n, cap* [NL, fr. L, sorrel] **:** a genus of herbs and shrubs (family Polygonaceae) that are mainly native to north temperate regions and have small flowers in axillary clusters often aggregated in a large panicle and 3-angled wingless fruit enclosed in a persistent perianth whose inner segments often bear conspicuous tubercles — see CANAIGRE, ¹DOCK 1

rum·fus·tian \¦rəm¦fəschən\ *n* [prob. fr. ²*rum* + *fustian*] **:** a hot drink composed of strong beer, wine, gin, egg yolks, sugar, and spices

rum–hole \'=,=\ *n, slang* **:** BAR, SALOON

ru·mi·nal *also* **ru·men·al** \'rümənᵊl\ *adj* [NL *rumin-, rumen* + E *-al*] **:** of or relating to the rumen

¹ru·mi·nant \'rümənənt\ *n* -s [L *ruminant-, ruminans*, pres. part. of *ruminare, ruminari* to chew the cud] **:** a ruminant mammal

²ruminant \"\ *adj* [L *ruminant-, ruminans*, pres. part. of *ruminare, ruminari*] **1 a :** chewing the cud **:** characterized by chewing again what has been swallowed **b :** of or relating to the Ruminantia **2 :** given to or engaged in contemplation **:** MEDITATIVE — **ru·mi·nant·ly** *adv*

ru·mi·nan·tia \,rümə'nanch(ē)ə\ *n pl, cap* [NL, fr. L *ruminant-, ruminans* (pres. part. of *ruminare, ruminari*) + NL *-ia*] **:** a suborder of Artiodactyla comprising even-toed hoofed mammals (as sheep, giraffes, deer, and camels) that chew the cud and have a complex 3- or 4-chambered stomach — compare ABOMASUM, OMASUM, RETICULUM, RUMEN; see PECORA, TRAGULINA, TYLOPODA

¹ru·mi·nate \'rümə,nāt, *usu* -ād·+V\ *vb* -ED/-ING/-S [L *ruminatus*, past part. of *ruminare, ruminari* to chew the cud, think over, ruminate fr. *rumin-, rumen* gullet; akin to Skt *romantha* chewing the cud] *vt* **1 :** to muse upon **:** contemplate over and over **:** ponder over 〈*ruminating* the contents of that last batch of letters she had received —Aldous Huxley〉 〈*ruminating* a judgment in his solemn dull brain —Edmond Taylor〉 **2 :** to chew repeatedly for an extended period 〈looked over my head in a trance, occasionally *ruminating* her gum —Nathaniel Burt〉 ~ *vi* **1 :** to chew again what has been chewed slightly and swallowed **:** chew a cud 〈the cows . . . stood in the yards all day, *ruminating* and steaming —Adrian Bell〉 **2 :** to consider something for a period or at intervals **:** engage in contemplation **:** REFLECT 〈the old woman sat *ruminating* for a moment —Guy McCrone〉 〈it is fascinating to ~ on what a really intelligent program might accomplish —Aaron Copland〉 **syn** see PONDER

²ru·mi·nate \-,nə̇t, -,nāt, *usu* |d·+V\ *adj* [L *ruminatus*, past part. of *ruminare, ruminari* to chew the cud] **:** mottled as if chewed — used of the endosperm of a seed (as of the nutmeg) in which the dark inner layer of the testa is infolded into the lighter endosperm

ru·mi·nat·ing·ly *adv* **:** in a ruminant manner

ru·mi·na·tion \,rümə'nāshən\ *n* -s [L *rumination-, ruminatio* act of chewing the cud, act of thinking over, fr. *ruminatus* (past part.) + *-ion-, -io* -ion] **:** the act or process of ruminating: **a :** the act or process of regurgitating and rechewing previously swallowed food **b** (1) **:** the act or process of considering at more or less length **:** deliberate meditation or reflection 〈these changes call not for argument but for ~ —Thornton Wilder〉 (2) **:** obsessive or abnormal reflection upon an idea or deliberation over a choice

ru·mi·na·tive \'rümə,nād·|iv, -nəl, |t|, |ēv *also* |əv\ *adj* [¹*ruminate* + *-ive*] **1 :** inclined to or engaged in rumination **2 :** marked by careful consideration **:** fully meditated — **ru·mi·na·tive·ly** \|əvlē, -li\ *adv*

ru·mi·na·tor \-,nād·ə(r), -ātə-\ *n* -s [L, fr. *ruminatus* (past part.) + *-or*] **:** one that ruminates 〈a writer who combines the beauty and precision of an artist with the wit and illumination of a ~ —E.A.Weeks〉

rum·kin \'rəm(p)kən\ *n* -s [prob. fr. obs. D *roomerken*, prob. fr. D *roemer, romer* rummer + *-ken* -kin] *archaic* **:** a drinking vessel

rum·less \'rəmləs\ *adj* [²*rum* + *-less*] **:** lacking rum

¹rum·mage \'rəmij, -mēj\ *n* -s [obs. E *rummage* act of packing or arranging cargo, modif. of MF *arrimage*, fr. *arrimer, arimer, aruner* to pack or arrange cargo (fr. *a-* — fr. L *ad-* — + *-rimer, -rumer*, prob. of Gmc origin) + *-age*; akin to OHG *rūm* room, space — more at ROOM] **1 :** *chiefly Scot* **:** a noisy bustling turmoil **:** UPROAR **2 :** a thorough search esp. among a variety or confusion of objects or into every section of an area 〈went off on a back-of-the-store ~ —*New Yorker*〉 **3 a :** a confused miscellaneous collection **:** a nondescript mass or group 〈a fabulous brown ~ of encyclopedias, world globes, maps, photographs, holy pictures, mirrors . . . and too much furniture —J.F.Powers〉 **b** *or* **rummage goods :** the items for sale at a rummage sale **4 :** RUMMAGE SALE

²rum·mage \", *esp in pres part* -məj\ *vb* -ED/-ING/-S *vt* **1 a** *obs* **:** to pack or rearrange (as cargo or ballast) in the hold of a ship **b** *obs* **:** to set in order (as a ship or hold) by rearranging the cargo **2 a :** to put into confusion **:** mix up **:** DISORDER **b** *obs* **:** to mix together by stirring **:** STIR **3 a** (1) **:** to make a thorough search in **:** look through every section of **:** RANSACK 〈one of you boys go ~ the storeroom for the corn popper —S.E.White〉 (2) **:** to search thoroughly for contraband 〈when the import cargo is discharged the examining officer finally ~*s* the ship —G.D.Ham〉 **b :** to discover by or as if by a thorough search **:** produce by searching **:** hunt out 〈*rummaged* a sword and red sash from somewhere —Mary B. Chesnut〉 〈*rummaged* up his sexton and his verger as witnesses —J.C.Powys〉 〈*rummaged* a conclusion from some odd corner of his soul —Samuel Butler †1902〉 **c :** to examine minutely and completely **:** scrutinize carefully 〈another . . . prowl through the most thoroughly *rummaged* era in our history —*New Yorker*〉 ~ *vi* **1 :** to stow or rearrange cargo in or clean the hold of a ship **2 a :** to make a thorough search or investigation 〈by dint of *rummaging* through various special lists and imported series, . . . it may be possible to assemble the entire series —Edward Sackville-West & Desmond Shawe-Taylor〉 **b :** to engage in an undirected fumbling haphazard search 〈the men ransacked the thatched huts, *rummaged* among the pots, the fishing gear, the shell ornaments —Marjory S. Douglas〉 〈all my books are packed and gone and . . . I can't browse or ~ —H.J.Laski〉 **syn** see SEEK

rum·mag·er \-jə(r)\ *n* -s [*rummage* + *-er*] **:** one that searches (as for contraband)

rummage sale *n* **1 :** a clearance sale of unclaimed or shopworn goods at a store or warehouse or of seized contraband **2 :** a sale of donated articles to raise money (as for a church)

¹rum·mer \'rəmə(r)\ *n* -s [G or D; G *römer*, fr. D *roemer, romer*, perh. fr. *roem* boast, praise, fr. MD; akin to OHG *hruom* honor, praise — more at BREME] **:** a large tall glass or drinking cup used esp. for wine

²rummer *comparative of* RUM

rum·mery \'rəmərē\ *n* -ES [²*rum* + *-ery*] **:** a commercial establishment where alcoholic beverages are sold **:** BAR, SALOON

rummest *superlative of* RUM

rum–mill \'=,=\ *n, slang* **:** BAR, SALOON

¹rum·my \'rəmē, -mi\ *adj* -ER/-EST [¹*rum* + *-y*] **:** marked by oddness or idiosyncrasies **:** QUEER

²rummy \"\ *adj* -ER/-EST [²*rum* + *-y*] **:** of, relating to, or affected by rum 〈~ taste〉 〈his face was blotched . . . his eyes were ~, his jaw was uncertain —W.A.White〉

³rummy \"\ *n* -ES [²*rum* + *-y* (n. suffix)] **1 :** one who drinks rum **:** DRUNKARD 〈I sat at the bar along with the usual collection of winos and *rummies* —Ed Barcolo〉 **2 :** a dealer in or distiller of intoxicating liquor

⁴rummy \"\ *also* **rum** \'rəm\ *n, pl* **rummies** *also* **rums** [*rummy* perh. fr. ¹*rummy*; *rum* back-formation fr. ⁴*rummy*] **1 :** one of numerous card games whose common essential features are that each player in turn draws one card from the stock of undealt cards or the discard of the previous player, tries to assemble in his hand groups of three or more cards of the same rank or suit usu. in order to meld them, and further tries to go out by being the first to meld all his cards **2 :** the condition of a player in rummy who has melded all his cards

⁵rummy \"\ *interj* — used by a player in some games of rummy to announce discovery that an opponent has neglected to take a discard he could add to a meld and to invest himself in the delinquent player's rights

rum·ness *n* -ES [¹*rum* + *-ness*] *chiefly Brit* **:** the quality or state of being rum **:** ODDITY, IDIOSYNCRACY

¹ru·mor \'rümə(r)\ *n* -s *see -or in Explan Notes* [ME *rumour*, fr. MF, fr. L *rumor*; akin to OE *rēon* to lament, MHG *rienen* to moan, complain, ON *rymja* to roar, grumble, *rymr* coarse voice, L *ravus* hoarse, *ravis* hoarseness, Gk *ōryesthai* to howl, roar, Skt *rauti* he roars, cries] **1 a :** common talk or opinion **:** widely disseminated belief having no discernible foundation or source **:** HEARSAY 〈~ puts the amount at about 5000 kegs —W.Z.Ripley〉 〈we make our blunders . . . as ~ has it that you make your own —B.N.Cardozo〉 **b :** an instance of rumor **:** a statement or report current without any known authority for its truth 〈almost every newspaper issue brought ~*s* of reduction in their salaries —V.G.Heiser〉; *esp* **:** an unconfirmed piece of information or explanation disseminated among the public by other than formal news agencies or sources 〈one of the community's most creative gossips begins to circulate the ~ that she is either a spy or a saboteur —Charles Lee〉 〈tips and ~*s* . . . would send shares . . . up to thousands, and down again to the gutter —*Amer. Guide Series: Nev.*〉 **c** *archaic* **:** talk or report of a notable person or event **:** FAME 〈great is the ~ of this dreadful knight and his achievements of no less account —Shak.〉 **2 a** *archaic* **:** a prolonged indistinct noise **:** CLAMOR, UPROAR **b :** a soft low indistinct sound **:** MURMUR 〈a ~ of vespers in the chapel〉

²rumor \"\ *vt* **rumored; rumored; rumoring** \-m(ə)riŋ\ **rumors** *see -or in Explan Notes* **:** to tell by rumor **:** give out tidings of **:** noise abroad

ru·mor·er \-mərə(r)\ *n* -s **:** RUMORMONGER

rumormonger \'==,==\ *n* [¹*rumor* + *monger*] **:** one that spreads rumors

ru·mor·ous \'rümərəs\ *adj* **1 :** MURMURING **2 a :** of the nature of rumor **b :** filled with rumor

¹rump \'rəmp\ *n* -s, *often attrib* [ME *rumpe*, of Scand origin; akin to Icel *rumpr* rump, buttocks, Dan *rumpe* buttocks; akin to MHG *rumph* trunk, torso, MD *romp* trunk] **1 a :** the upper more or less rounded part of the hindquarters of a quadruped mammal — see COW illustration **b :** BUTTOCKS 1a **c :** the sacral or dorsal part of the posterior end of a bird — see BIRD illustration **d :** the hind end of the body of any of various animals in which well-defined landmarks are lacking **2 :** a cut of beef between the loin end and the round — see BEEF illustration **3 :** a small fragment or remainder: as **a :** a parliament, committee, or other group carrying on in the name of the original body after the departure or expulsion of a large number of its members 〈the ~ of the National Assembly sits from time to time to endorse the . . . policy of the Government —*Statesman's Yr. Bk.*〉 〈reduced his congregation to a determined and inveterate ~ of faithful souls —Robertson Davies〉 〈~ peasant and bourgeois groups are kept in the Government as window dressing —*Economist*〉 **b :** a small group usu. claiming to be representative of a larger whole that arises independently or breaks off from a parent body 〈set up a ~ Government . . . with no effective authority —Sir Winston Churchill〉 **c :** a fragment of a country left after partition or after secession, occupation, or annexation of a part 〈this small truncated ~ of a country . . . is a viable economic unity —Edward Crankshaw〉 〈partitioned into two ~ states —M.S.Handler〉 **4 :** a geographical feature (as a ridge or a cape) resembling a rump

²rump \"\ *vt* -ED/-ING/-S **1 :** to turn one's back upon esp. as a sign of contempt **2 :** to remove (hide) from the hind leg of a slaughtered beef animal

rump bone *n* **:** SACRUM

rumped \'rəmpt\ *adj* [¹*rump* + *-ed*] **:** having a specified kind of rump — usu. used in combination 〈*white-rumped*〉

rump·er \'rəmpə(r)\ *n* -s [*Rump* Parliament, remnant of the Long Parliament in England after the expulsion of most of its members by the army of Cromwell in 1648 (fr. ¹*rump*) + *-er*] **1** *usu cap* **:** a member or supporter of the Rump Parliament **2** [¹*rump* + *-er*] **:** a slaughterhouse worker who removes the hide from the tail bone, rump, and hind legs

rumpf \'rüm(p)f\ *n* -s [G, trunk, torso, fr. MHG *rumph*] **:** CORE 1t

¹rum·ple \'rəmpəl\ *n* -s [dim. of ¹*rump*] *Scot* **:** RUMP, TAIL

²rumple \"\ *n* -s [MLG *rumpel*; akin to MD *rumpelen, rompelen* to rumple] **:** FOLD, WRINKLE

³rumple \"\ *vb* **rumpled; rumpled; rumpling** \-p(ə)liŋ\ **rumples** [D *rompelen*, fr. MD *rumpelen, rompelen*; akin to OE *hrympel* wrinkle, OHG *rimpfan* to crease, wrinkle, LGk *krambos* dry, withered, L *curvus* curved — more at CROWN]

vt **1 :** to cause to form into irregular folds **:** WRINKLE, CRUMPLE **2 :** to make unkempt **:** TOUSLE, MUSS ⟨*rumpled* hair⟩ **~** *vi* **:** to become mussed or wrinkled

rump·less \'rəmpləs\ *adj* [[1]*rump* + *-less*] **:** lacking the coccygeal vertebrae ⟨~ domestic fowls⟩ **:** TAILLESS

rum·ply \'rəmp(ə)lē\ *adj* -ER/-EST [[2]*rumple* + *-y*] **:** RUMPLED

rumpot \'=,=\ *n* [[2]*rum* + *pot*] *slang* **:** DRUNKARD

rump steak *n* **:** a steak cut from the rump

[1]**rum·pus** \'rəmpəs\ *n* -ES [origin unknown] **1 :** COMMOTION 4, DISTURBANCE, FRACAS **2 :** a hotly debated division of opinion **syn** see BRAWL

[2]**rumpus** \"\ *vi* **rumpussed** *or* **rumpused; rumpussed** *or* **rumpused; rumpussing** *or* **rumpusing; rumpusses** *or* **rumpuses :** to cause a disturbance **:** make a rumpus

rumpus room *n* **:** a room usu. in the basement of a home that is set apart and furnished for games, parties, and recreation

[1]**rumpy** \'rəmpē\ *n* -ES [[1]*rump* + *-y* (n. suffix); fr. its rudimentary tail] **:** MANX CAT

[2]**rumpy** \"\ *adj* -ER/-EST [[1]*rump* + *-y* (adj. suffix)] **:** having a prominent rump **:** STEATOPYGOUS

rumrunner \'=,==\ *n* [[2]*rum* + *runner*] **:** a person or ship engaged in bringing prohibited alcoholic liquor ashore or across a border

rum-running \'=,==\ *n* **:** the act or process of bringing prohibited alcoholic liquor ashore or across a border

rums *pl of* RUM

rumshop \'=,=\ *n* **:** a commercial establishment where alcoholic liquors are sold **:** BAR, SALOON

rum sucker *n* **:** a moss (*Polytrichum commune*)

rum tum ditty *also* **rum tum tiddy** *n* [origin unknown] **:** RINKTUM DITTY

[1]**run** \'rən\ *vb* **ran** \'ran, 'raa(ə)n\ *or nonstand* **run; run; running; runs** [ME *runnen, ronnen;* in intransitive senses, alter. of *rinnen, irnen,* partly fr. OE *rinnan, iernan,* partly fr. ON *rinna;* akin to OS, OHG, & Goth *rinnan* to run; in transitive senses, alter. of *rennen, ernen,* partly fr. OE *ærnan,* partly fr. ON *renna;* akin to OS *rennian* to cause to run, OHG *rennen* to cause to run, Goth ur*rannjan* to cause to rise; causatives fr. the root of OE *rinnan, iernan;* akin to OE *rīsan* to rise — more at RISE] *vi* **1 a :** to go by moving the legs quickly **:** go faster than a walk; *specif* **:** to go steadily by springing steps so that both feet leave the ground for an instant in each step **b** *of a horse* **:** to move at a fast gallop as distinguished from a canter **:** move with each leg acting in turn as a propeller and supporter and all four legs being for an instant in the air under the body **c :** FLEE, RETREAT, ESCAPE ⟨afraid to fight but ashamed to ~⟩ ⟨dropped his gun and *ran*⟩ ⟨obliged to cut and ~⟩ **d :** to make a bid in a card game in an effort to escape the consequences of a previous bid ⟨refrained from doubling four spades for fear he would ~ to five clubs⟩ — sometimes used with *out* **2 a :** to go without restraint **:** move freely about at will ⟨let his chickens ~ loose⟩ ⟨liked to ~ barefoot in the summer⟩ **b :** to keep company **:** CONSORT — used with *with* chiefly of male animals ⟨a ram *running* with his ewes⟩ **c :** to sail before the wind in distinction from reaching or sailing close-hauled **d :** ROAM, ROVE, GAD — usu. used with *about* or *around* ⟨spends his time *running* around nights and sleeping all day⟩ ⟨caught cold *running* about with no overcoat⟩ **e :** to deviate from a correct path — used of a saw cut **3 a :** to go rapidly or hurriedly **:** HASTEN ⟨~ and fetch the doctor⟩ **b :** to go in urgency or distress **:** RESORT ⟨~*s* to his mother at every little difficulty⟩ ⟨don't come *running* to me when you get in trouble⟩ **c :** to make a quick, easy, or casual trip or visit ⟨*running* up to town every week or so⟩ ⟨just *ran* over to borrow some sugar⟩ **4 a :** to contend in a race ⟨will be able to ~ tomorrow⟩; *also* **:** to finish a race in a specified place ⟨*ran* a poor third⟩ **b :** to enter into an election contest **:** become a candidate ⟨I do not choose to ~ —Calvin Coolidge⟩ **5 a :** to move on or as if on wheels **:** GLIDE ⟨the hoist ~*s* on an overhead track⟩ ⟨file drawers *running* on ball bearings⟩ ⟨the tractor ~*s* on an endless chain tread⟩ **b** (1) **:** to roll forward rapidly or freely ⟨the cue ball *ran* straight into the side pocket⟩ (2) *of a golf ball* **:** to bound or roll along after touching the ground subsequent to the carry ⟨*ran* some 10 yards onto the green⟩ **c :** to pass or slide freely along ⟨rope ~*s* through the pulley⟩ **d :** to ravel lengthwise owing to a dropped or broken stitch ⟨stockings guaranteed not to ~⟩ **6 :** to sing or play a musical passage quickly ⟨~ up the scale⟩ **7 a :** to go back and forth **:** PLY ⟨a ferry ~*s* to the island each hour⟩ **b** *of fish* **:** to migrate or move in schools; *esp* **:** to ascend a river to spawn **8 a :** TURN, ROTATE ⟨a swiftly *running* grindstone⟩ ⟨let the motor ~ until it warms up⟩ **b :** FUNCTION, OPERATE, WORK ⟨an engine that ~*s* on kerosine or gasoline⟩ ⟨things are *running* smoothly at the office now⟩ ⟨expense of keeping the old car *running*⟩ **9 a :** to continue in force or operation **:** remain effective ⟨the contract has two more years to ~⟩ ⟨six months on each charge, the sentences to ~ concurrently⟩ **b :** to accompany as a valid obligation or right ⟨covenants the rights and liabilities of which pass to assignees ~ with the land⟩ **c :** to continue to accrue or become payable in an amount increasing with the passing of time ⟨interest on the loan ~*s* from last July 1st⟩ **10 :** to pass from one state to another ⟨~ into trouble⟩ ⟨~ into debt⟩ **11 a :** to flow rapidly ⟨a brook *running* high with meltwater⟩ or under pressure ⟨someone left the hot water *running*⟩ ⟨feelings were *running* high on both sides of the dispute⟩ ⟨tide *running* out⟩ **b :** to change to a liquid state **:** MELT, FUSE ⟨heat a pipe joint until the solder ~*s*⟩ ⟨the icing had begun to ~⟩ **c :** to spread out, diffuse, or dissolve ⟨colors guaranteed not to fade or ~⟩ ⟨the writing was blurred where the ink had ~ on the wet pages⟩ **d :** to discharge pus or serum ⟨a *running* sore⟩ **e** *dial* **:** CURDLE **f** *of soil* **:** to become fluid or pasty when wet **12 a :** to develop rapidly in some specific direction; *esp* **:** to throw out an elongated and often vining shoot of growth ⟨the early squashes are beginning to ~ and flower⟩ **b :** to tend to produce or develop a specified quality or feature — usu. used with *to* ⟨they ~ to big noses in that family⟩ ⟨this tree ~*s* to quite tart fruit⟩ **13 a :** to lie in or take a certain direction ⟨the boundary line ~*s* east from the stone⟩ ⟨his action ~*s* counter to prevailing practice⟩ ⟨the printed matter on this page ~*s* the short way of the page⟩ ⟨a red thread ~*s* through the cloth⟩ **b :** to lie or extend in relation to something ⟨where the road ~*s* close to the shore⟩ ⟨a path ~*s* along the ridge⟩ ⟨the fence ~*s* along two sides of the field⟩ ⟨heating pipes *ran* overhead⟩ **c :** to go back **:** REACH ⟨a custom since the time that no man's mind ~*s* to the contrary⟩ ⟨born of a line *running* back to King Alfred⟩ **d :** to be in a certain form or expression ⟨his letter ~*s* as follows⟩ or order of succession ⟨the house numbers in this block ~ in odd numbers from 3 to 57⟩ **14 a :** to occur intermittently and persistently **:** RECUR — usu. used with *through* or *in* ⟨a note of despair ~*s* through the whole narrative⟩ ⟨musical talent seems to ~ in his family⟩ ⟨tune kept *running* in his head⟩ ⟨thoughts and memories of home kept *running* through his mind⟩ **b :** to continue to be of a specified size or character or quality ⟨peaches are *running* unusually large this year⟩ ⟨profits were *running* high⟩ **c :** to continue at a certain rate or value ⟨this ore ~*s* as high as $200 to the ton⟩ **d :** to exist or occur in a continuous range of variation ⟨guesses at his real age ~ from 39 to 45 or higher⟩ **e :** to play on a stage a number of successive days or nights ⟨the piece *ran* for six months⟩ **15 a :** to spread or pass quickly from point to point ⟨chills *ran* up his spine⟩ ⟨a whisper *ran* through the crowd⟩ ⟨a shout *ran* down the line of soldiers⟩ ⟨fire *ran* swiftly over the oily sea⟩ **b :** to be current **:** spread abroad **:** pass from mouth to mouth ⟨the story ~*s* that they have been secretly married for months⟩ ⟨speculation *ran* rife on who the candidate would be⟩ **~** *vt* **1 a :** to cause (an animal) to go at speed **:** ride or drive fast **b :** to bring to a specified condition by or as if by running ⟨he almost *ran* himself to death⟩ ⟨fie, now you ~ this humor out of breath—Shak.⟩ **c :** to go in pursuit of **:** HUNT, CHASE ⟨~ a deer⟩ ⟨the dog was caught *running* sheep and had to be shot⟩ **d :** to follow the trail of backwards **:** TRACE ⟨*ran* the rumor to its source⟩ **e :** to enter, register, or enroll as a contestant in a race ⟨*ran* the filly in the half mile⟩ **f :** to put forward as a candidate for office ⟨*ran* him for governor⟩ **2 a :** to drive (livestock) esp. to a grazing place ⟨~ cattle to pasture⟩ **b :** to provide pasturage for (livestock) ⟨land that will ~ three sheep to the acre⟩ **c :** to keep or maintain (livestock) on or as if on pasturage ⟨~ a few head of stock⟩ ⟨~ 2,000,000 chickens a year⟩ **d :** to put (a male animal) with females for breeding ⟨flush the ram before *running* him with the ewes⟩ **3 a :** to pass over, traverse, or cover by or as if by running ⟨quick at fielding and *running* bases⟩ ⟨the disease has *run* its course⟩ ⟨her acting *ran* the whole range of emotions⟩ **b :** to accomplish or perform by or as if by running ⟨*ran* a great race⟩ ⟨*running* errands for a bank⟩ **c :** to flee from ⟨*ran* the country after the robbery⟩ **d :** to slip through or past ⟨~ a blockade⟩ ⟨~ a guard⟩ ⟨~ a traffic signal⟩ **4 a :** to cause to slip into or through **:** THRUST ⟨*ran* the spear through his body⟩ ⟨*ran* a splinter into his toe⟩ ⟨*ran* his hand into his pocket⟩ **b :** STITCH; *esp* **:** to sew with running stitches ⟨~ a basting to mark the waistline⟩ ⟨~ a line of stitching⟩ **c :** to cause to pass **:** LEAD ⟨~ a rope through a pulley⟩ ⟨~ a wire in from the antenna⟩ **d :** to cause to collide ⟨*ran* his head into a post⟩ **e :** SMUGGLE **5 :** to cause to pass lightly or quickly over, along, or into something ⟨*ran* his eye down the list⟩ ⟨*ran* his fingers along the shelf⟩ ⟨~ your hand over the tabletop to see if the varnish is dry⟩ ⟨*ran* his tongue over his parched lips⟩ **6 a :** to cause or allow (as a vehicle, a vessel) to go in a specified manner or direction ⟨*ran* the ship aground on a sandbar⟩ ⟨*ran* his car off the road⟩ **b :** OPERATE ⟨~ a lawn mower⟩ ⟨~ a taxi⟩ **c :** to carry on **:** MANAGE, CONDUCT ⟨~ a factory⟩ ⟨~ a travel bureau⟩ ⟨the men who ~ things in this city⟩ **7 a :** to be full of or drenched with **:** flow with ⟨the streets *ran* blood⟩ ⟨all the brooks *ran* gold —A.E.Housman⟩ **b :** CONTAIN, ASSAY ⟨tailing ~*s* 2 percent zinc⟩ **8 a :** to cause to move or flow in a specified way or into a specified position ⟨~ sheets through a wringer⟩ ⟨~ cards into a file⟩ **b :** FAN 7b **9 a :** to melt and cast in a mold ⟨~ bullets⟩ **b :** to make (a resin) soluble in oil by subjecting to thermal processing **c :** TREAT, PROCESS, REFINE ⟨~ oil in a still⟩ **d :** to pour into the cracks and joints of a pavement ⟨~ tar⟩ or into a form ⟨~ concrete⟩ **e :** to apply (as paint) by flowing ⟨~ a wash⟩; *also* **:** to cover (a surface) by flowing on ⟨~ a wall⟩ **f :** to form (a molding) with plaster **g :** to pass (starch slurry) down a run **10 :** to make oneself liable to **:** expose oneself to **:** INCUR ⟨*ran* the risk of discovery by lighting a fire⟩ **11 :** to mark out **:** cause to be drawn ⟨~ a contour line in surveying land⟩ ⟨~ a line through the word to be deleted⟩ **12 :** to permit (as charges, accounts, bills) to accumulate before settling ⟨~ an account at the grocery⟩ **13 a :** to run off ⟨a book to be ~ on lightweight paper⟩ ⟨a job to be ~ 4-up⟩ **b :** to carry in a printed medium **:** PRINT ⟨every newspaper *ran* the story⟩ ⟨~ this advertisement for 3 days⟩ **c :** to use as a direct printing surface ⟨you may stereotype these woodcuts but do not ~ them⟩ **14 a :** to make (a series of counts) without a miss ⟨~ 19 in an inning in billiards⟩ **b** *card games* **:** to lead winning cards of (a suit) successively and usu. until no more remain **15 :** to make (a golf ball) roll forward after alighting ⟨*ran* his ball past the cup⟩ **16** *croquet* **:** to play one's ball through (a wicket) or against (a stake)

syn RACE, COURSE, CAREER: RUN is the general term in this set, indicating either a rapid or more-or-less normal movement or motion ⟨a halfback *running* laterally⟩ ⟨busses *running* on Elm Street⟩ ⟨the watch had stopped *running*⟩ RACE almost always indicates great speed or rapidity, often in or as though in urgent situations with freedom from normal inhibitions ⟨he *raced* for a small dune and flung himself down behind it —Irwin Shaw⟩ ⟨thoughts were under control no longer: they *raced* desperately — as she had once seen a dog *race* . . . running desperately and hopelessly from inescapable terror —Margery Sharp⟩ COURSE in this sense may indicate rapid or pulsating motion or activity, often following a definite or expected course or channel ⟨reconnaissance aircraft *coursed* North Korea —*N.Y.Times*⟩ ⟨her hand became a closer prisoner. All at once an alarming delicious shudder went through her frame. From him to her it *coursed* —George Meredith⟩ ⟨new life *coursing* through Europe's stagnant economic system —R.A.Billington⟩ CAREER is likely to indicate high speed with headlong impetus or, occas., with veering or rocking motion ⟨*careering* through the salons on a bicycle —*Time*⟩ ⟨blind historians *careering* on their juggernauts of theory —*Times Lit. Supp.*⟩ ⟨intoxicated cats *careering* through our houses —F.A.Swinnerton⟩

— **run across :** to meet with or discover by chance ⟨years later I *ran across* him in a bar in Paris⟩ — **run after 1 :** PURSUE, CHASE ⟨*running after* a pickpocket⟩; *esp* **:** to seek the company of ⟨old enough now to start *running after* the girls⟩ **2 :** to take up with **:** FOLLOW ⟨*runs after* every new fashion⟩ ⟨*run after* new theories⟩ — **run against 1 :** to meet suddenly or unexpectedly **2 :** to work or take effect unfavorably to **:** DISFAVOR, OPPOSE ⟨time is now *running against* us in this affair⟩ ⟨do nothing that would *run against* his moral principles⟩ — **run at check** *of a hunting dog* **:** to follow base game — **run a temperature :** to have a fever — **run cunning :** to run false — **run division** *obs* **:** to play variations **:** elaborate upon a theme or topic — **run down the latitude :** to sail north or south on a meridian until the latitude of the destination is reached — **run false :** to save distance by running directly for the hare or game instead of following the scent or track — **run foul of :** to collide with ⟨*ran foul* of a hidden reef⟩ **:** run into conflict with or hostility to ⟨*run foul of* the law⟩ — **run free :** to sail with the wind coming from abaft the beam **:** RUN *vi* 2 c — **run heelway :** to run the wrong way on the trail of the quarry — **run in the blood :** to be a family, national, or racial trait — **run into 1 a :** to change or transform into **:** BECOME ⟨reverence for law and prescription . . . which *runs* sometimes *into* pedantry —T.B. Macaulay⟩ **b :** to merge with ⟨little lakes that all *run into* one another⟩ ⟨a dreamy state in which one day seemed to *run into* another⟩ **c :** to mount up to ⟨keeping a boat like that one *runs into* money⟩ ⟨his yearly income often *runs into* six figures⟩ **2 a :** to collide with ⟨veered off the road and *ran into* a telephone pole⟩ **b :** ENCOUNTER, MEET ⟨*ran into* an old classmate⟩ ⟨*run into* difficulties⟩ — **run in with :** to make toward **:** NEAR ⟨*run in with* the land⟩ — **run mad :** to run wildly about under the influence of hydrophobia **:** become affected with hydrophobia — **run ragged :** to wear out **:** EXHAUST ⟨children and housework were *running* her *ragged*⟩ ⟨the word "character," meaning a person . . . of eccentricity has been *run ragged* —John McNulty⟩ — **run rings around :** to show marked superiority over **:** defeat decisively or overwhelmingly — **run riot 1 a :** to act wildly or without restraint ⟨*ran riot* with Chinese red in the living room⟩ **b :** to occur in profusion ⟨puns *ran riot* in his style⟩ **2 :** to pursue the wrong scent or base game — **run scared :** to bend every effort (as in a political campaign) through or as if through fear of defeat — **run short :** to become insufficient ⟨drinking water was *running short* before the voyage was over⟩ — **run short of :** to use up **:** become lacking in sufficient quantity of ⟨we are *running short of* time to finish the job⟩ ⟨army *ran short of* provisions⟩ — **run the cards :** to deal the requisite cards in seven-up when the eldest hand begs — **run to cover :** to flee from danger or financial risk ⟨short sellers of stock *run to cover* by buying back the stock when the market rises⟩ — **run to earth :** to hunt to its hiding place, home, starting place, or origin ⟨after much searching I *ran* him *to earth* in a dingy hotel⟩ — **run to seed 1 :** to expend or exhaust vitality in producing seed **2 :** to cease growing **:** lose vital force ⟨let his mind *run to seed*⟩ — **run track :** to compete in running events as distinguished from field events — **run upon :** to run across **:** meet with — **run wild 1 :** to go unrestrained or out of control **:** run riot ⟨prices were *running wild* all over Miami —Alva Johnston⟩ **2 :** to live or grow without cultivation or training ⟨gardens and lawns neglected and *running wild*⟩

[2]**run** \"\ *n* -S [ME *rune,* fr. *runnen, ronnen* to run — more at [1]RUN] **1 a :** an act or the action of running **:** continued and usu. rapid movement ⟨walked faster and faster finally breaking into a ~⟩ ⟨let the dogs out for a ~⟩ ⟨police arrived on the ~⟩ **b :** a quickened gallop **c** (1) **:** the act of migrating or ascending a river to spawn — used of fish (2) **:** an assemblage or school of fishes that migrate or ascend a river to spawn **d :** a running race ⟨a mile ~⟩ — distinguished from *dash* **e** (1) **:** a score made in cricket each time the batsmen safely change ends after a hit or when the ball is in play — compare BOUNDARY, EXTRA (2) **:** a score made in baseball by a runner reaching home plate safely after touching the three bases in order — compare HOME RUN **f :** strength or ability to run ⟨the first two laps took most of the ~ out of him⟩ **2 a** *chiefly Midland* **:** CREEK 2 **b :** a swift tidal current **c :** a pronounced swell or markedly choppy condition of the surface of the water ⟨there was a ~ of sea in the harbor —John Masefield⟩ **d :** something that flows in the course of a certain operation or during a certain time ⟨a ~ of must in wine making⟩ ⟨the first ~ of sap in sugar maple⟩ — compare FORERUN **3 a :** the afterpart of the underwater body of a ship from where it begins to curve or slope upward and inward to the stern — compare ENTRANCE 7; see SHIP illustration **b :** the direction in which a vein of ore lies **c :** a direction of secondary or minor cleavage **:** GRAIN ⟨~ of a mass of granite⟩ — compare RIFT 4 **d :** an irregular body of ore having an approximately horizontal direction **e :** the horizontal distance to which a mine drift is or may be carried **f** (1) **:** the length of the base of a right triangle (2) **:** the horizontal distance measured from the face of one riser to that of the next (3) **:** the horizontal distance covered by a flight of steps (4) **:** the horizontal distance from the wall plate to the center line of a building ⟨the rise of a rafter per foot of ~⟩ (5) **:** extent measured linearly ⟨the bridge carries a load of 500 pounds per foot ~⟩ **g :** the distance irrigation water must flow from the supply ditch to the end of the field or to the lower level **h :** general tendency or direction ⟨kept in touch with the general ~ of the stock market⟩ **4 :** a continuous series esp. of things of identical or similar sort ⟨a ~ of poor poker hands⟩: as **a :** a rapid scale passage in vocal or instrumental music **b** *dancing* **:** a number of rapid, small, elastic steps executed in even tempo **c :** the act of making successively a number of successful shots or strokes; *also* **:** the score thus made ⟨~ of 15 balls in pool⟩ ⟨a ~ of 20 in billiards⟩ **d :** an unbroken course of being repeated (as of a play on the stage) **e** (1) **:** a set of consecutive measurements, readings, or observations (2) *math* **:** a maximal subsequence of elements of like kind in any ordered sequence of elements of two kinds **f :** a train of cars in a mine **g :** persistent and heavy demands from depositors, creditors, or customers ⟨a ~ on a bank⟩ ⟨a ~ on limited stocks of goods in a store⟩ **h :** a heavy demand for a printing sort not ordinarily needed in quantity **i :** SEQUENCE 2b **j :** a stereotyped passage of narrative or description introduced into Gaelic popular tales **5 :** the quantity of work turned out in a continuous operation: as **a :** the paper made in a continuous operation (as to fill a given order or part of an order) **b :** a single distillation of a given amount of material **c :** PIPELINE RUN **d :** the quantity of lumber cut from a log **e :** a numbering unit for woolen yarns based on the number of 1,600-yard hanks to a pound ⟨a two-*run* yarn has 3,200 yards to a pound⟩ **6 :** the usual or normal kind, character, type, or group ⟨the general ~ of modern fiction⟩ ⟨average ~ of college graduates⟩ ⟨his whole appearance was . . . out of the common ~ —Washington Irving⟩ **7 a :** a caving in of a mine working **b :** a fall of a cage in a mine shaft **c :** deviation of a tool from a correct path **8 a :** the distance covered in a period of continuous traveling or sailing ⟨betting on the day's ~ of the ship⟩ **b :** a course or route mapped out and traveled with regularity ⟨the ~ of the "Twentieth Century Limited" between New York and Chicago⟩ **c :** a single or essentially continuous journey **:** TRIP ⟨a ship on her regular ~ to Europe⟩ ⟨a 10,000 mile test ~ for gasoline mileage⟩ **d :** BOMB RUN **e :** a news reporter's regular territory **:** BEAT ⟨covering the labor ~⟩ **f :** the distance a golf ball travels after touching the ground from a stroke **g :** freedom of movement in or access to a place or area ⟨has the ~ of the whole neighborhood⟩ ⟨has the ~ of his friend's house including the kitchen⟩ **9 a :** the period during which a machine or plant is in continuous operation; *specif* **:** the period in the manufacture of water gas during which steam is admitted at the end of the blow and the gas is produced — compare BACK RUN **b :** a test or proof of a process, a material (as ore), or a machine ⟨a laboratory ~⟩ **10 a :** a way, track, or path frequented by animals ⟨a rabbit ~⟩ ⟨a beaver ~⟩ ⟨poisoning rat ~*s*⟩ **b :** an enclosure for livestock where they may feed and exercise — often used in combination ⟨fowl ~⟩ ⟨hog ~⟩ **c** *Austral* **:** a large area of land used for grazing ⟨sheep ~⟩ **:** RANCH, STATION ⟨*run*-holder⟩ **d :** the bower of a bowerbird **e :** an inclined passage between levels in a mine **f :** an inclined plane for a passageway (as in a theater) **:** RAMP **g :** the clear space not less than 15 feet in length and immediately back of the foul line from which a bowler delivers his ball **11 a :** an inclined course for coasting, skiing, or bobsledding **b :** a support (as a track, pipe, trough) on which something runs ⟨sash ~ in a window frame⟩ ⟨overhead ~ for a traveling hoist⟩ **c :** a settling trough for slimes used in working ore **d :** a long slightly inclined table used in washing starch free from gluten, fiber, and other impurities **12 a :** a ravel in a knitted fabric (as in hosiery) caused by the breaking or dropping of one or more stitches **b :** a paint defect occurring at the time of application caused by excessive flow **13 :** a pair of millstones **14 :** the distance between two degrees or assigned points on an arc or curved scale (as of a surveying instrument); *also* **:** the value of a division of the scale in seconds of arc **15 runs** *pl but sing or pl in constr* **:** DIARRHEA — not often in polite use — **by the run** *adv* **1 :** so as to run freely — used of letting go in contrast to slacking away gradually ⟨lower sail *by the run*⟩ **2 :** according to a measure of work equivalent to a linear yard of breast excavated — sometimes used in estimating the pay of miners — **in the long run :** in the course of sufficiently prolonged time, trial, or experience ⟨integrity succeeds best *in the long run*⟩

[3]**run** \"\ *adj* [fr. past part. of [1]*run*] **1 a :** MELTED ⟨~ butter⟩ ⟨~ honey⟩ **b :** made from molten material **:** cast in a mold ⟨~ metal⟩ ⟨~ joint⟩ **2 :** SMUGGLED ⟨~ diamonds⟩ **3** *Scot* **a :** THOROUGH, OUTRIGHT **b :** CONTINUOUS, RUNNING **4** *of fish* **:** having made a migration or spawning run ⟨a fresh ~ salmon⟩ **5 :** exhausted or winded from running

runabout \'==,=\ *n* -S [fr. *run about,* v.] **1 :** a young child ⟨special problems of toddlers and ~*s* —*New Republic*⟩ **2 :** one who wanders or gads about **:** VAGABOND, STRAY, STRAGGLER **3 a :** a light uncovered wagon **b :** a light roadster **c :** a light motorboat **:** SPEEDBOAT

run·a·gate \'rənə,gāt\ *n* -S [alter. (influenced by [1]*run*) of *renegate*] **1 :** RENEGADE **2 a :** FUGITIVE, RUNAWAY **b :** VAGABOND, WANDERER

run along *vi* **:** to go away **:** be on one's way **:** DEPART ⟨it's late, I must *run along*⟩

run around *vi* **:** to seek amusement or companionship restlessly or incessantly ⟨that crowd he used to *run around* with⟩ ⟨never home, evenings, always *running around*⟩; *specif* **:** to engage in extramarital relations ⟨suspected her husband of *running around*⟩ **~** *vt* **:** to set or arrange (type matter) as a runaround

runaround \'==,=\ *n* -S [fr. *run around,* v.] **1 :** a whitlow encircling the fingernail **2 :** a track, way, or channel provided for bypassing an obstacle or tie-up **3 :** the distance that a scraper traverses in completing one cycle of operations (as loading, transporting, dumping, and returning to the starting point) **4 :** a passage driven in a shaft pillar to connect mine workings on opposite sides of a shaft **5 :** matter typeset in shortened measure to run down one or both sides of something (as a cut or box) inserted in running text matter **6 :** deliberately deceptive or delaying action esp. in response to a request **:** substitution of evasive or misleading replies for definite and candid refusal ⟨tried to get contracts and have been given the familiar official ~ —*New Republic*⟩

run away *vi* **1 :** FLEE, DESERT, ABSCOND **2 :** to leave home ⟨had *run away* twice before he was ten⟩; *esp* **:** ELOPE ⟨*ran away* with a man twice her age⟩ **3 :** to run out of control **:** STAMPEDE, BOLT ⟨realized that his horse was *running away*⟩ — **run away with 1 :** to take away in haste or secretly; *often* **:** STEAL **2 :** to take in a hauling part (as of a fall, tackle, or brace) by holding fast to it and running along the deck **3 :** to become conspicuous in or outshine the others in (a theatrical performance) ⟨in the minor role of the hero's uncle he succeeded in *running away with* the show⟩ **4 :** to carry or drive beyond prudent or reasonable limits ⟨let his imagination *run away with* him⟩

[1]**runaway** \'==,=\ *n* -S [*run away*] **1 :** one that flees from danger, duty, or legal or parental restraint **:** FUGITIVE **2 :** the act of running away out of control; *also* **:** a horse that is running out of control **3 :** excessive or uncontrolled speed (as of a turbine or locomotive) or flow (as of an oil well) **4 :** a one-sided or overwhelming victory

[2]**runaway** \"\ *adj* [*run away*] **1 :** running away **:** fleeing or escaping from danger, duty, or restraint ⟨~ slave⟩ ⟨~ team⟩ ⟨~ railroad car⟩ **2 :** accomplished by elopement or during

flight ⟨a ~ marriage⟩ **3 :** won by a long lead ⟨a ~ race⟩ **:** DECISIVE **4** *of prices* **:** subject to rapid changes usu. toward higher levels ⟨~ inflation⟩
run-away-robin \ˈ==,=ˈ==\ *n* **:** GROUND IVY 1
runaway shop *n* **:** an industrial plant moved by its owners from one location to another to escape union labor regulations or state laws
runback \ˈ=,=\ *n* -s [fr. *run back*, v.] **1 :** a run made in football after catching an opponent's kick **2 :** the area of a tennis court behind the base line **3 :** a return pipe or duct (as in a still, a heating system)
runboard \ˈ=,=\ *n* **:** RUNNING BOARD
runboat \ˈ=,=\ *n* **:** a boat that collects the catches of individual fishermen at prearranged points
runby \=,ˈrən,bī\ *n, pl* **runbys** \-īz\ [fr. *run by*, v.] **1 :** the clearance space between the top of the car frame and the lowest portion of the overhead work in a hoistway or elevator shaft **2 :** an extra piece of track to permit a train to back past a crossover without using it
runcation *n* -s [L *runcation-, runcatio*, fr. *runcatus* (past part. of *runcare* to weed) + *-ion-, -io* -ion — more at ROUGH] *obs* **:** removal of weeds
¹runch \ˈrənch\ *n* -ES [origin unknown] **1 :** CHARLOCK **2 :** JOINTED CHARLOCK
²runch \"\ *vb* -ED/-ING/-ES [prob. by alter.] *Scot* **:** CRUNCH
runchweed \ˈ=,=\ *n* **:** CHARLOCK
run·ci·ble spoon \ˈrən(t)səbəl-\ *n* [coined with an obscure meaning in 1871 by Edward Lear †1888 Eng. landscape painter and writer of nonsense verse] **:** a fork with three broad curved prongs and a sharpened edge used with pickles or hors d'oeuvres
run·ci·nate \ˈrən(t)sənət, -sə,nāt, *usu* -d.+V\ *adj* [L *runcinatus*, past part. of *runcinare* to plane off, fr. *runcina* plane, prob. modif. (influenced by *runcare* to weed) of Gk *rhykanē*; akin to Gk *orychein, oryssein* to dig — more at ROUGH] **:** pinnately cut with the lobes pointing downward ⟨the ~ leaf of the dandelion⟩ — see LEAF illustration
rund \ˈrən(d)\ *chiefly Scot var of* RAND
rundale \ˈ=,=\ *n* [¹*run* + *dale* (portion of land)] **:** a distribution of lands among tenants or owners in Scotland and Ireland by which the land is apportioned so that a single tenant's or owner's holding consists of strips lying between those of others
run·di \ˈründē\ *n, pl* **rundi** *or* **rundis** *usu cap* **1 a :** a Bantu-speaking people of Urundi, East Africa **b :** a member of such people **2 :** a Bantu language of the Rundi people used as one of the two trade languages of Ruanda-Urundi — compare RUANDA
¹run·dle \ˈrəndᵊl\ *n* -s [ME *rundel* — more at ROUNDEL] **1** *obs* **:** CIRCLE, SPHERE **2 a :** a step of a ladder **:** RUNG **b :** one of the pins of a lantern pinion **3 :** the drum of a windlass or capstan
²run·dle \ˈrünᵊl, ˈrənᵊl\ *dial var of* RUNNEL
rund·let \ˈrəndlət\ *also* **run·let** \-nl-\ *n* -s [ME *roundelet* — more at ROUNDLET] **1 :** a small barrel **:** KEG **2 :** an old unit of liquid capacity equal to 15 imperial gallons or 18 U. S. gallons
run down *vt* **1 a :** to collide with and knock down (as with an automobile) ⟨*ran down* an old man in the rain⟩ **b :** to run against and sink ⟨*ran* a fishing boat *down* in the harbor⟩ **2 a :** to chase until exhausted **:** pursue until overtaken or captured ⟨finally *ran* the fugitive *down* in a blind alley⟩ **b :** to find by search **:** trace the source of ⟨had quite a time *running down* the technical words —Tom Marvel⟩ **c :** to tag out (a base runner) between bases **3 :** DISPARAGE ⟨nags her husband and *runs* him *down* in company⟩ **4 :** to cause to diminish in value or quantity ⟨*run* a stock *down*⟩ ~ *vi* **1 :** to cease to operate because of the exhaustion of motive power ⟨that clock *ran down* hours ago⟩ **2 :** to decline in physical condition ⟨his health *ran down* to a dangerous level⟩ ⟨the railroads have been permitted to *run down* alarmingly⟩ **3** *Brit, of a stream* **:** to fall to normal level after a flood
run-down \ˈ=ˈ=\ *adj* [fr. *run down*, past part. of *run down*] **1 :** in poor repair **:** DILAPIDATED ⟨rehabilitation of *run-down* houses and neighborhoods⟩ **2 :** in poor health or physical condition **:** worn out **:** EXHAUSTED **3 :** completely unwound **:** stopped for want of winding
rundown \ˈ=,=\ *n* [*run down*] **1 :** a baseball action in which a runner is caught off base on a base path with two or more opponents throwing the ball back and forth in an attempt to tag him out **2 :** an item-by-item check, investigation, report, analysis, or summary ⟨~ of a suspect's police record⟩ ⟨gave a ~ on current foreign affairs, country by country⟩ ⟨his ~ of the kinds of people who read a newspaper —Edmund Fuller⟩
rune \ˈrün\ *n* -s [ON & OE *rūn* secret, mystery, character of the runic alphabet, writing; akin to OE *rūnian* to whisper, OHG *rūna* secret discussion, *rūnēn* to whisper, ON *reyna* to whisper, Goth *rūna* secret, mystery, and prob. to L *rumor* — more at RUMOR] **1 a :** one of the characters of the runic alphabet **b :** OGHAM **c :** one of the characters of the alphabet of the Orkhon inscriptions **d :** one of the characters of the Szekler alphabet **2 :** a magic incantation **:** CHARM, SPELL **3** [Finn *runo*, of Gmc origin; akin to ON *rūn* secret, mystery, character of the runic alphabet, writing] **a :** a Finnish poem (as the Kalevala or one of its divisions) **b** (1) **:** an old Norse poem (2) **:** POEM, SONG ⟨the ~s that I rehearse —R.W.Emerson⟩
runed \-nd\ *adj* **:** inscribed with runes ⟨~ helmet⟩
runelike \ˈ=,=\ *adj* **:** resembling a rune ⟨~ symbol⟩
rune-master \ˈ=,==\ *n* **:** maker of runes **:** MAGICIAN ⟨Odin was also the greatest *rune-master* of the ancient Germanic world —Anna C. Paues⟩
runesmith \ˈ=,=\ *n* **:** one that writes in or deciphers runes
rune-staff \ˈrün,staf\ *n* [trans. of Sw *runstav*, fr. *runa* rune + *stav* staff] **:** CLOG ALMANAC
run fish *n* [*run* fr. past part. of ¹*run*] **:** a spent salmon
¹rung [ME rungen (past pl. & past part.), alter. prob. influenced by *sungen* sung) of *ringden* (past pl.), *ringed* (past part.), fr. OE *hringdon* (past pl.), *gehringed* (past part.)] *past of* RING
²rung \ˈrəŋ\ *n* -s [ME *rung, rong*, fr. OE *hrung*; akin to MLG & MHG *runge* spoke of a wagon, Goth *hrunga* staff, and perh. to OE *hring* ring — more at RING] **1** *archaic Scot* **:** a heavy stick of wood **:** a stout staff or cudgel **2 a :** a spoke of a wheel **b :** one of the radial handles projecting from the rim of a steering wheel **c :** one of the pins or trundles of a lantern pinion **d :** one of the stakes of a cart **3 a :** a crosspiece between the legs of a chair **b :** one of the crosspieces of a ladder **c :** STAIR, TREAD **4 :** a stage in an ascent **:** STEP, GRADE, DEGREE ⟨reached the top ~ of Hollywood fame —*Irish Digest*⟩ ⟨the son must rise a few ~s on the social scale by studying law —H.W. Van Loon⟩
³rung \"\ *adj* [fr. *rung*, obs. past part. of ²*ring*, alter. (influenced by ¹*rung*) of *ringed*] **:** RINGED ⟨fallen trunks of ~ giants have rotted —I.M.Mudie⟩ ⟨sows are ~ to prevent rooting⟩ **:** HOOPED ⟨piles with ~ heads to prevent splitting⟩
rung·less \-ŋləs\ *adj* **:** lacking rungs ⟨~ chair⟩
runholder \ˈ=,==\ *n, Austral* **:** one that owns or leases a run
ru·nic \ˈrünik, -nēk\ *adj* [*rune* + *-ic*] **1 a :** of, relating to, or consisting of runes ⟨~ inscription⟩ ⟨~ verses⟩ **b :** having secret or magical meaning ⟨~ markings⟩ ⟨~ rhymes⟩ **2 :** of or relating to the ancient Scandinavians ⟨~ poetry⟩ ⟨~ mythology⟩ — **ru·ni·cal·ly** \-nək(ə)lē\ *adv*
runic alphabet *n* **1 :** an alphabet orig. of 24 and later of some 16 angular characters prob. derived from both Latin and Greek and used for inscriptions and magic signs by the Germanic peoples from about the 3d to the 13th centuries and esp. by the Scandinavians and Anglo-Saxons — called also *futhark;* compare THORN 3, WEN, YOGH **2 :** the runiform alphabet of the Orkhon inscriptions
runic cross *n* **:** CELTIC CROSS
runic knot *n* **:** an interlaced ornament found on monuments, jewelry, and metalwork of the early northern European peoples
runic staff *n* **:** CLOG ALMANAC
run·i·form \ˈrünə,fȯrm\ *adj* [*rune* + *-iform*] **:** resembling the ancient runes in form or appearance
run in *vt* **1 a :** to make (typeset matter) continuous without a paragraph or other break **b :** to insert as additional matter **c :** to give paragraph indention to (a subhead) and make part of the running text **d :** to load (matrices) into a typesetting machine in which matrix distribution is automatic **2 :** to arrest for a minor offense ⟨got drunk the other night and the coppers *run* me *in* —Carl Sandburg⟩ ⟨*run in* for speeding⟩ **3 :** to operate (a newly built machine) long enough and at the proper speeds to cause the bearing surfaces to so wear that the machine may be satisfactorily operated under service conditions ~ *vi* **1** *of typeset matter* **:** to come short of filling the estimated space **2 :** to pay a casual visit ⟨lived close by and was used to *running in* whenever he liked⟩
run-in \ˈ=,=\ *n* -s [*run in*] **1 :** something inserted as a substantial addition in copy or typeset matter **2** *Brit* **:** the finish of a race or hunt **3 :** TIFF, ALTERCATION, QUARREL ⟨*run-ins* of tourists with taximen —A.D.Sheffield⟩ **4 :** the operation of running in a new engine or machine
run-in groove \ˈ=,=-\ *n* **:** LEAD-IN GROOVE
r unit *n* **:** ROENTGEN
ru·nite \ˈrü,nīt\ *n* -s [*rune* + *-ite*] **:** GRAPHIC GRANITE
run lace *n* **:** needlerun lace
run·less \ˈrənləs\ *adj* **:** scoring no runs ⟨held the visiting team ~ for eight innings⟩
¹runlet *var of* RUNDLET
²run·let \ˈrənlət\ *n* -s [²*run* + *-let*] **:** RUNNEL
run·na·ble \ˈrənəbəl\ *adj* [¹*run* + *-able*] **:** capable of being run; *esp* **:** suitable to be hunted ⟨~ stag⟩
run·nel \ˈrənᵊl\ *n* -s [alter. (influenced by ¹*run*), of earlier *rinel*, fr. ME, fr. OE *rynel*, fr. the stem of *rinnan* to run, flow — more at RUN] **1 :** RIVULET, BROOK, STREAMLET **2 a :** the channel eroded by a small stream **b :** a small trough formed by wave or current action on a sea or lake bottom just offshore
run·ner \ˈrənə(r)\ *n* -s [ME *rinner, renner*, fr. *rinnen, rennen* to run + *-er*] **1 :** one capable of running ⟨the cheetah is the fastest ~ of all animals⟩ **:** RACER **2 a :** a horse entered in a race ⟨eight ~s in the final race of the day⟩ **b** (1) **:** a cricket batsman attempting to score a run; *specif* **:** a substitute allowed to run for an injured batsman (2) **:** BASE RUNNER (3) **:** a football player in possession of a live ball **c :** a man in backgammon that starts from the opponent's home table **d :** a bird that characteristically runs or scuttles along the ground; *specif* **:** WATER RAIL **e :** a wounded bird that moves fast but cannot fly **f :** a popular fast-selling item of merchandise **3 :** one whose occupation requires physical movement from place to place: as **a :** one that delivers messages, reports, materials, or products for a business organization either within the establishment or to outside locations **b :** a police officer or police detective in 18th century London — see BOW STREET RUNNER **c :** one that makes a business of running for things in return for the gratuities received ⟨a ~ called a cab for him⟩ **d :** COMMISSIONAIRE **e :** a messenger between headquarters of military units esp. during action **f :** an agent who accepts, transmits, and pays bets for a numbers game or a bookmaker **g :** one that smuggles or distributes illegal drugs ⟨dope ~⟩ **4 :** one that operates or manages something: **a :** a workman that operates a carrying vehicle (as in a mine) **:** DROPPER **b :** one that operates a machine **c :** a seaman engaged for a short single voyage **d :** the driver of a locomotive **5 a :** any of various large active carangid fishes: as (1) **:** RAINBOW RUNNER (2) **:** BLUE RUNNER (3) **:** LEATHERJACKET 1b **b** *Africa* **:** COBIA **c :** INDIAN RUNNER **d :** BLACKSNAKE 1a **6 a :** a ship of exceptional speed used for dispatches without convoy **b :** a ship that runs a blockade or carries smuggled goods **c :** RUNBOAT **7 a :** either of the longitudinal pieces on which a sled or sleigh slides **b :** the part of a skate that slides on the ice **:** BLADE **c :** ²SKATE 1a **d :** a horizontal longitudinal timber on the top of a scaffold or staging carrying a line of rails (as for a hoisting apparatus) **:** STRINGER, STRINGPIECE **e :** the support of a drawer or a sliding door **8 a :** a growth produced by a plant in running; *usu* **:** STOLON 1 **b :** a plant that forms or spreads by means of runners **c :** a twining vine — not used technically; see SCARLET RUNNER **9 a :** a rope rove through a single movable block and usu. attached to a luff tackle **b :** a backstay running from mast to rail of a sailing ship and adjustable by means of a tackle or lever **10 runners** *pl, chiefly dial* **:** the small intestine of a domestic animal **11 a :** a carpet adapted by its long and narrow shape for extending along a hall or passageway or staircase **b :** a narrow decorative cloth cover for the top of a piece of furniture (as a table, dresser) **12 a :** the rotating stone of a set of millstones **b :** a movable slab used in grinding or polishing stone or glass **13 a :** a movable pulley block running on a fall that is fixed at one end **b :** IDLER WHEEL **c :** the impeller of a pump **d :** either of the sliding centers of a watchmaker's lathe **e :** a train of wheels for regulating the speed of striking in a repeating watch **f :** the revolving part of a turbine **g :** the driven member of an automotive hydraulic coupling or transmission **h :** a rotary tool for running a nut on a bolt or screw **14 a :** the sliding piece of an umbrella to which the ribs are attached **b :** a piece bearing a hairline that slides along the outer scale of a slide rule **15 :** a channel or trough for conducting molten metal into a mold **16 :** RUN 12a **17** *Brit* **:** any of the numbers placed consecutively at the ends of lines of a printed text
runner bean *also* **runner** *n* -s *chiefly Brit* **:** SCARLET RUNNER
runner peanut *n* **:** a peanut having a low prostrate plant with pods at the base and along procumbent rooting stems — compare BUNCH PEANUT
runner stick *n* **:** GATE PIN
runner-up \ˈ=,=ˈ=\ *n, pl* **runners-up 1 :** one that raises or runs up bids at an auction **2 :** a competitor receiving a prize or special recognition but not winning first place in a contest ⟨a thousand-dollar prize for the best window display . . . "crinkly fifty-dollar bills" to the ten *runners-up* —Bennett Cerf⟩; *esp* **:** one winning second place ⟨won the conference . . . in addition to one third place, three *runners-up*, and three state championships —*Athletic Jour.*⟩
run·net \ˈrənət, ˈrün-\ *dial var of* RENNET
runnier *comparative of* RUNNY
runniest *superlative of* RUNNY
run·ni·ness \ˈrənēnəs\ *n* -ES **:** the quality or state of being runny **:** FLUIDITY
¹run·ning \ˈrəniŋ, -nēŋ\ *n* -s [ME *running, ronning, rinning, renning*, fr. gerund of *runnen, ronnen, rinnen, rennen* to run — more at RUN] **1 :** the act of racing **:** RACE **2 :** strength or ability to run ⟨still had a lot of ~ left in him at the finish **3 :** the condition of a surface to be run on ⟨kept to the outside of the track where the ~ was better⟩ **4 :** the quantity of a liquid that flows (as in a certain time or during a particular operation) ⟨the first ~ of a still⟩ ⟨early ~ of sap⟩ **5 :** control of operation **:** MANAGEMENT, CARE ⟨has the ~ of two machines at the same time⟩ — **in the running 1 :** entered as a competitor in a contest **2 :** having a chance of winning a contest
²running \"\ *adj* [ME *running, ronning, rinning, renning*, fr. pres. part. of *runnen, ronnen, rinnen, rennen*] **1 :** FLUID, RUNNY ⟨~ bog⟩ **2 :** continuing step by step or from place to place without pause **:** CONTINUOUS ⟨~ fire of machine guns and rifles⟩ ⟨retreating troops fought a ~ battle⟩ ⟨the text forms a ~ comment on the pictures⟩ ⟨~ record of cash expenditures⟩ **3 :** measured linearly **:** LINEAR ⟨cost of lumber per ~ foot⟩ **4 :** FLOWING, EASY, CURSIVE ⟨~ hand in writing⟩ ⟨a ~ rhythm in music⟩; *specif* **:** having the flow natural to ordinary expression or statement ⟨pronunciation of a word in ~ speech⟩ **5 :** not fixed or definite in its effect or application but left open for future determination ⟨~ lease⟩ ⟨~ insurance policy⟩ ⟨~ writ⟩ **6 :** initiated or performed with impetus from running **:** executed with a running start or with emphasis on running ⟨the team's ~ plays worked better than its pass plays⟩ **7 :** fitted or trained for running rather than walking, trotting, jumping ⟨~ horse⟩
³running \"\ *adv* [fr. pres. part. of ¹*run*] **:** in unbroken succession **:** CONSECUTIVELY ⟨won the championship 3 years ~⟩
running account *n* **:** CURRENT ACCOUNT 1
running backstay *n* **:** RUNNER 9 b
running bale *n* **:** a bale of cotton as it comes from the gin weighing 500 to 508 lbs
running birch *n* **:** CREEPING SNOWBERRY
running blackberry *n* **:** DEWBERRY
running block *n* **:** a movable pulley block that rises or sinks with the weight that is raised or lowered — distinguished from *standing block*
running board *n* **:** a footboard on the side of an automobile or locomotive or on the roof of a freight car
running bond *n* **:** a masonry bond in which each brick is laid as a stretcher overlapping the bricks in the adjoining courses
running bowline *n* **:** a slip noose made by tying a bowline knot with the end of a line around its own standing part
running bowsprit *n* **:** a bowsprit that can be run in or rigged in when headsails are taken off
running brand *n* **:** a cattle brand made by drawing a figure with a simple iron instead of stamping with a set shape
running days *n pl* **:** the consecutive calendar days occupied on a voyage (as under a charter party)
running-down clause \ˌ==ˈ=-\ *n* **:** COLLISION CLAUSE
running english *n, usu cap E* **:** side spin imparted to a cue ball so as to increase the angle of rebound — compare REVERSE ENGLISH
running expenses *n pl* **:** daily, current, or ordinary and necessary expenses **:** operating costs

running bowline

running fit *n* **:** contact of mechanical parts that permits free rotation or movement
running fits *n pl but sing or pl in constr* **:** CANINE HYSTERIA
running fix *n* **:** a navigational position determined by the intersection of two or more lines of position taken at different times and then advanced to a common time
running gate *n* **:** a gate through which molten metal runs into a mold
running gear *n* **1 :** RUNNING RIGGING **2 a :** the wheels and axles of a wagon or carriage in distinction from the body **b :** the parts of an automobile chassis (as the frame, springs, axles, and wheels) not used in developing, transmitting, and controlling power **c :** the working and carrying parts of a locomotive or a machine in distinction from the framework
running hand *n* **:** handwriting in which the letters are usu. slanted and the words formed without lifting the pen
running head *or* **running headline** *n* **:** RUNNING TITLE; *also* **:** a line at the head of a page (as of a book or magazine) carrying the title or publication name and sometimes other matter (as folio, dateline, chapter number, part number)
running inventory *n* **:** PERPETUAL INVENTORY
running iron *n* **:** a branding iron with which a brand is drawn freehand on the hide of an animal
running key *n* **:** an unpredictable keying sequence (as a text used as a key by prearrangement)
running knot *n* **:** a knot that slips along the rope or line round which it is tied **:** a knot used to form a running noose; *esp* **:** an overhand slip knot
running light *n* **:** one of the lights carried by a ship under way at night and comprising a green light on the starboard side, a red light on the port side, and on a steamer a white light at the foremast head; *also* **:** one of a similar set of lights carried on the wingtips and fuselage of an airplane
running line *n* **1 :** a line carried from a ship by boat to a wharf, buoy, or other ship **:** GUESS-WARP 1 **2 :** a light line used in hauling a heavy line (as a mooring or towing cable)
run·ning·ly *adv* **:** in a running, rapid, or flowing manner
running mallow *n* **:** DWARF MALLOW
running mate *n* **1 :** a horse entered in a race to set the pace for a horse of the same owner or stable that is being ridden to win **2 :** a candidate running for a subordinate place on a ticket; *esp* **:** the candidate for vice-president considered in relation to the candidate for president **3 :** a staff officer's opposite on the line officers' promotion list with whose promotion the staff officer is advanced in grade on the same date **4 :** a person frequently seen in close association with another **:** COMPANION
running milkweed *n* **:** NEGRO VINE
running myrtle *n* **:** PERIWINKLE 1 a
running oak *n* **:** MOUNTAIN MISERY
running ornament *n* **:** an ornamental decoration (as on a band) formed with a continuous design **:** FRET, WAVE
running part *n* **:** the part of a tackle that is hauled upon — distinguished from *standing part*
running pine *n* **:** CORAL EVERGREEN
running rail *n* **:** a rail that acts as a running surface for the flanged wheels of a car or locomotive — compare GUARDRAIL, THIRD RAIL
running rigging *n* **:** rigging that is used primarily in setting, furling, and otherwise handling sails and movable spars or in handling cargo and that usu. runs through blocks or pulleys — compare STANDING RIGGING
running rope *n* **:** rope used in running rigging **:** hoisting or hauling rope — distinguished from *standing rope*
runnings *pl of* RUNNING
running set *n* **:** a folk dance of Kentucky and the Great Smoky mountains that combines couple figures of square dancing with the circular progression of a round
running shoe *n* **:** a soft leather shoe with spiked soles esp. designed for foot racing
running shooting *n* **:** shooting at a running target
running side *n, Brit* **:** RUNNING ENGLISH
running spider *n* **:** a spider that builds no web but hunts its prey by running
running start *n* **1 :** a start effected by setting off the competitors in a race from a point behind the starting line so that they are in rapid motion when crossing that line **2 :** a great initial impetus or advantage in carrying out a project
running stitch *n* **:** a small even stitch usu. run on a needle in groups (as for seaming, gathering, quilting)
running story *n* **1 :** a story that is continued in two or more issues of a newspaper or magazine **2 :** a newspaper story received or sent to the composing room in takes
running strawberry-bush *n* **:** a deciduous prostrate shrub (*Euonymus obodatus*) of eastern No. America that has rooting branches and obovate finely serrate leaves
running text *n* **:** straight matter
running title *n* **:** the title or short title of a volume printed at the top of left-hand text pages or sometimes of all text pages — called also *running head*
running toad *n* **:** NATTERJACK
running track *n* **1 :** a track reserved for movement through a railroad yard **:** a thoroughfare track **2 :** a track for running foot races
running trap *n* **:** a trap (as a U trap) in a pipe permitting liquid flow but forming a barrier against sewer gases

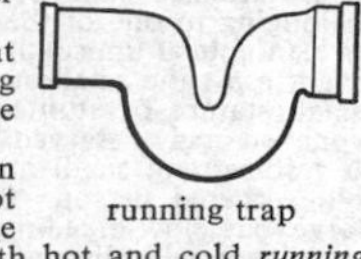
running trap

running walk *n* **:** a slow easy 4-beat gait of a horse in which one hindleg touches the ground just before the opposite foreleg
running water *n* **1 :** water flowing in a stream or river **:** water that is not stagnant or brackish **2 :** water made available through a pipe ⟨cabins with hot and cold *running water*⟩
running wheel *n* **:** TREADWHEEL
run·ny \ˈrənē, -ni\ *adj, sometimes* -ER/-EST [¹*run* + *-y*] **:** having a tendency to run: as **a :** excessively soft and liquid ⟨a ~ dough⟩ ⟨meringue that will not hold its shape but turns ~⟩ **b :** secreting mucus ⟨watery eyes and a ~ nose⟩
run off *vt* **1 a :** to recite or compose rapidly or glibly **:** dash off ⟨*run off* a letter⟩ **b :** to produce by a printing press or an analogous process ⟨*ran off* 10,000 copies of the first edition⟩ ⟨*run* a batch of mimeographed sheets *off*⟩ **c :** to cause (a race) to be run **:** cause (as a match, a tournament) to be played to a finish **d :** to decide (as a race) by a runoff **e :** to carry out (a test) **2 :** to cause (as molten metals) to flow away **:** draw off **:** drain off **3 a :** to drive off (as trespassers) or dispossess ⟨soldiers . . . raided the town's laundry, *ran off* the Chinese proprietor, and took all the clothing —*Amer. Guide Series: Wash.*⟩ **b :** to steal (as cattle) by driving away ⟨most of his stock was *run off* by Indians⟩ ~ *vi* **1 :** to run away ⟨snatched up the purse and *ran off*⟩ **2** *of bills payable* **:** to cease to exist by being paid at maturity — **run off with :** to carry off **:** STEAL
runoff \ˈ=,=\ *n* -s [*run off*] **1 a :** the portion of the precipitation on the land that ultimately reaches streams and thence the sea; *esp* **:** the water from rain or melted snow that flows over

the surface **b :** syrup that has been drawn off the sugar crystals **2 :** a final race, contest, or election to decide an earlier one that has not resulted in a decision in favor of any one competitor **3 :** a gradually increasing superelevation applied to a tangent on a railroad track or highway just adjacent to the easement to a curve **4** *NewZeal* **:** an area of pastureland not adjacent to the farm

runoff primary *n* **:** a second primary election held in some states to decide which of the two highest candidates for an office in the first primary will be awarded the party nomination

run of mine : ore or coal as it comes from the mine without grading or sorting for size or quality

run-of-mine \ˌ==ˈ=\ *or* **run-of-the-mine** \ˌ===ˈ=\ *adj* [*run of mine*] **1 :** UNGRADED, UNSORTED, CRUDE, UNREFINED **:** not ground or treated **2 :** ORDINARY, MEDIOCRE, RUN-OF-THE-MILL ⟨*run-of-mine* college graduate⟩

run-of-paper \ˌ==ˈ==\ *adj* **:** to be placed anywhere in a newspaper at the option or discretion of the editor ⟨*run-of-paper* advertisement⟩ — abbr. *R.O.P.*

run-of-river \ˌ==ˈ==\ *adj* **:** operating on the flow of the river without modification by upstream storage ⟨*run-of-river* power plant⟩

¹run-of-the-mill \ˌ===ˈ=\ *n* **:** manufactured goods not graded or sorted for quality

²run-of-the-mill *adj* **:** not outstanding in quality or rarity **:** AVERAGE, MEDIOCRE ⟨*run-of-the-mill* politician⟩ ⟨*run-of-the-mill* boxing⟩

ru·no·log·i·cal \ˌrünəˈläjəkəl\ *adj* **:** of or relating to runology

ru·nol·o·gist \rüˈnäləjəst\ *n* -s **:** a specialist in the study of runes and runic writings

ru·nol·o·gy \-jē\ *n* -ES [*rune* + *-o-* + *-logy*] **:** the study of runes and runic writings

run on *vi* **1 :** to keep going **:** CONTINUE ⟨if the disease is allowed to *run on* unchecked⟩ ⟨let an account *run on*⟩ **2 :** to talk or narrate at length ⟨*ran on* endlessly about his family⟩ ⟨apt to *run on* at the slightest provocation⟩ ~ *vt* **1 :** to carry on (matter in type) without a break or a new paragraph **:** run in **2 :** to place or add (as an entry in a dictionary) at the end of a paragraphed item

¹run-on \ˈ=ˌ=\ *adj* [fr. *run on*, past part. of *run on*] **:** continuing without rhetorical pause from one line of verse into another **:** characterized by enjambment — contrasted with *end-stopped*

²run-on \ˈ=ˌ=\ *n* -s **:** something (as a dictionary entry) that is run on

run-on couplet *n* **:** OPEN COUPLET

run-on sentence *n* **1 :** a sentence formed with a comma fault **2 :** a sentence that rambles on by the slipshod adding on of clauses

run out *vi* **1 a :** to come to an end **:** EXPIRE ⟨the lease *runs out* next month⟩ **b :** to become exhausted or used up **:** FAIL ⟨food supplies had *run out* toward the end of the trip⟩ ⟨his patience had *run out*⟩ **c :** to come to the end of a supply ⟨have we enough milk so that we won't *run out* before the next delivery⟩ **d :** to lose distinguishing breed or varietal characters esp. as a result of inbreeding or indiscriminate breeding **2 :** ⟨a herd of Herefords had been allowed to *run out*⟩ **2 :** to jut out ⟨where the land *runs out* to form a cape⟩ ~ *vt* **1 :** to finish out (as a course, a series, a contest) **:** COMPLETE; *specif* **:** *of a baseball batter* **:** to run hard to first base after (a hit) esp. when a put-out is likely ⟨the runner must *run* everything *out* if he wants the breaks —W.L.Myers⟩ **2 a :** to fill out (a line) with quads, leaders, or ornaments **b :** to set (as the first line of a paragraph) with a hanging indention **3 :** to exhaust (oneself) in running ⟨*ran* himself *out* in the first mile⟩ **4 :** FAN 7b **5 :** to put out (a cricket batsman) during an attempted run by breaking the wicket with a fielded ball **6 :** to cause to leave by force or coercion **:** EXPEL ⟨if the gamblers don't leave town they will be *run out*⟩ — **run out of :** to use up or come to the end of the available supply of ⟨*ran out of* gas a mile from home⟩ ⟨always *running out of* money before payday⟩ — **run out on :** to fail to support **:** leave in the lurch **:** DESERT ⟨his former allies *ran out on* him⟩ **:** FORSAKE ⟨if the boy senses that his girl is *running out on* him he too is hurt —Evelyn M. Duvall⟩

runout \ˈ=ˌ=\ *n* -s [*run out*] **1 :** the amount that one surface (as the outside surface of a cylindrical sleeve) lacks of being true with another surface of the same part (as the inside surface of the sleeve) **2 :** the greatest distance that a moving part of a machine can travel away from a fixed reference point ⟨~ of the plunger of a hydraulic press⟩ **3 :** an instance of running out a cricket batsman ⟨on no account throw hard to the bowler unless there is a good chance of a *runout* —*Calling All Cricketers*⟩ **4 :** an act of escape or desertion ⟨a divorce caused by an agrarian ~ on the partnership is labor's nightmare —*N.Y. Times*⟩

run-out groove \ˈ=ˌ=-\ *n* **:** a lead-out groove on a phonograph record

runout powder *n*, *slang* **:** RUNOUT, DESERTION, ESCAPE — used chiefly in the phrase *take a runout powder*

run over *vi* **1 :** OVERFLOW ⟨my cup *runneth over* —Ps 23:5 (AV)⟩ **2 :** to exceed a limit ⟨delay caused by the radio program *running over*⟩ **3** *of a steam engine* **:** to throw over ~ *vt* **1 :** to go over, examine, repeat, or rehearse ⟨considered all possible ways of escape, *running* them *over* swiftly in his mind⟩ ⟨let's *run* this song *over* a couple of times⟩ **2 :** to collide with, knock down, and often drive over

run-over \ˈ=ˌ==\ *adj* [fr. *run over*, past part. of *run over*] **1 :** extending beyond the allotted space ⟨*run-over* matter in printing⟩ **2 :** worn at one side ⟨*run-over* heels⟩

runover \ˈ=ˌ==\ *n* -s [in sense 1, fr. *run-over;* in sense 2, fr. *run over*] **1 :** typeset matter that exceeds the space estimated or allotted **2 :** BREAKOVER ⟨a two-column front-page lead story with a three-column ~ —A.J.Liebling⟩

runproof \ˈ=ˌ=\ *adj* **:** resistant to runs ⟨~ stockings⟩ ⟨~ dye⟩

run·rig \ˈrən,rig\ *n* [ME *rynrig*, fr. *ryn*, *rin* run + *rig* — more at RUN] **:** RUNDALE

runround \ˈ=ˌ=\ *n* -s [fr. *run round*, v.] **:** RUNAROUND 1

runs *pres 3d sing of* RUN, *pl of* RUN

run sheep run *n* **:** a game in which one group of players hide and their leader tries to guide them safely home by calling "run, sheep, run" when he thinks they can escape being caught by those searching

runt \ˈrənt\ *n* -s *except sense 5 a* [origin unknown] **1 a** *chiefly dial* **:** the dead stump or trunk of a tree **b** *chiefly Scot* **:** a usu. hardened stalk or stem of a plant **2 :** an ox or cow belonging to one of the breeds of small British upland cattle **3 :** an animal unusually small as compared with others of its kind; *esp* **:** the smallest of a litter of pigs **4 a :** a person of small stature or stunted growth — usu. used disparagingly ⟨one scraggly, starved little ~ of a man —Ira Wolfert⟩ **b :** something small and contemptible **c** *chiefly Scot* **:** an old withered person **5 a** *usu cap* **:** an old breed of very large but slow-breeding domestic pigeons usu. white, blue, or silvery with barred wings and iridescent neck **b** *sometimes cap* **:** a bird of this breed **6 :** a poor hand in poker and some other card games; *specif* **:** a poker hand of less value than a pair

runt·ed \-təd\ *adj* **:** RUNTY, STUNTED ⟨discarding the ~ ears of corn⟩

run through *vt* **1 :** to pierce with or as if with a sword **2 :** to spend or consume wastefully ⟨inherited a fortune but *ran* it *through* in no time⟩ **3 :** to read or rehearse without pausing ⟨the cast *ran through* the whole play once without lights or scenery⟩

run-through \ˈ=ˌ=\ *n* -s [*run through*] **1 a :** a cursory reading **b :** a rapid or cursory summary ⟨a *run-through* of the week's events⟩ **c :** a single rehearsal of an entire piece or program **2** *Brit* **:** FOLLOW SHOT

runt·i·ness \ˈrəntēnəs, -tin-\ *n* -ES **:** the quality of being small or poorly developed

runt·ish \-tish\ *adj* **:** RUNTY, STUNTED — **runt·ish·ly** *adv* — **runt·ish·ness** *n* -ES

runty \-tē, -ti\ *adj* -ER/-EST **1 :** like a runt **:** UNDERSIZED **2** *dial* **:** MEAN, SURLY

run up *vi* **:** to grow rapidly **:** shoot up ⟨his debts *ran up* alarmingly by the week⟩ ~ *vt* **1 :** to increase by bidding **:** bid up ⟨professional traders had *run* the price *up*⟩ **2 :** to stitch quickly ⟨to *run up* a seam⟩ ⟨to *run up* a dress in a morning⟩ **3 :** to erect hastily ⟨*run up* an apartment house⟩ ⟨*run up* a circus tent⟩ **4 :** to add (a column of figures) rapidly **5 :** to shuffle (the pack) so that certain combinations of cards shall come out in desired order **6 :** to operate (an aircraft engine) at a high rate of speed either in a stationary aircraft or on a test stand in order to test, check, or warm the engine

run-up \ˈ=ˌ=\ *n* -s [*run up*] **:** the act of running up something ⟨a *run-up* of a golf ball to the putting green⟩ ⟨a *run-up* of a polo ball to the goal⟩ ⟨a *run-up* of prices in the stock market⟩; *specif* **:** acceleration of an aircraft engine on the ground for testing and checking

runway \ˈ=ˌ=\ *n* [¹*run* + *way*] **1 :** the channel of a stream **2 :** the beaten path made by animals in passing to and from their feeding grounds **:** TRAIL, RUN **3 a :** a passageway for animals **b :** a space provided for exercise ⟨~ for chickens⟩ **4 :** a road on which logs are skidded **5 a :** a way or gauged track for wheeled vehicles, conveyors, overhead hoist **b :** an artificially surfaced or paved strip of ground on a landing field for the landing and takeoff of airplanes **6 :** a narrow platform or bridge leading from a stage into the auditorium to enable the players to perform in the midst of the audience **7 a :** a path along which a jumper or pole vaulter runs in approaching the takeoff **b :** the area behind the foul line on which a bowler makes his approach and delivers the ball

ru·pee \rüˈpē, ˈ=(ˌ)=\ *n* -s [Hindi *rūpaiyā*, *rupīyā*, fr. Skt *rūpya* silver, coined silver, fr. *rūpa* form, beauty] **1 :** the basic monetary unit of India, Mauritius, Nepal, Pakistan, Seychelles, and Sri Lanka — see MONEY table **2 :** a coin or note representing one rupee

ru·pert's drop \ˈrüpərts-\ *n*, *usu cap R* [after Prince *Rupert* of Germany †1682 who first brought it to England to his uncle Charles I of England] **:** a congealed blob of glass formed by dropping melted glass into water and setting up such residual stresses that the globule explodes violently when the surface is scratched or a piece broken off

ru·pes·tri·an \rüˈpestrēən\ *or* **ru·pes·tral** \-rəl\ *adj* [NL *rupestris* rupestrian (fr. L *rupes* rock + *-estris*, as in *terrestris* terrestrial) + E *-an* or *-al;* akin to L *rumpere* to break — more at REAVE] **:** composed of rock **:** inscribed on rocks

ru·pes·trine \rüˈpestrən\ *adj* [L *rupes* rock + E *-trine* (as in *palustrine*)] **:** RUPICOLOUS

¹ru·pia \ˈrüpēə\ *n* -s [NL, irreg. fr. Gk *rhypos* dirt, filth + NL *-ia;* perh. akin to OSlav *strupŭ* wound] **:** an eruption occurring esp. in tertiary syphilis consisting of vesicles having an inflamed base and filled with serous purulent or bloody fluid which dries up and forms large blackish conical crusts — **ru·pi·al** \-əl\ *adj*

²ru·pia \rüˈpēə\ *n* -s [Pg, fr. Hindi *rūpaiyā*, *rupīyā* rupee — more at RUPEE] **:** the rupee of Portuguese India

ru·pi·ah \rüˈpēə\ *n*, *pl* **rupiah** *or* **rupiahs** [Hindi *rūpaiyā*, *rupīyā* rupee] **1 :** the basic monetary unit of Indonesia — see MONEY table **2 :** a note representing one rupiah

ru·pi·cap·ra \ˌrüpəˈkaprə\ *n*, *cap* [NL, fr. L, chamois, fr. *rupes* rock + *-i-* + *capra* she-goat — more at RUPESTRIAN, CAPRA] **:** a genus of mammals (family Bovidae) consisting of the chamois

ru·pi·cap·rine \ˌ==ˈkaˌprīn, -ˌprən\ *adj* [NL *Rupicapra* + E *-ine*] **:** of or relating to the genus *Rupicapra*

ru·pic·o·la \rüˈpikələ\ *n*, *cap* [NL, fr. L *rupi-* (fr. *rupes* rock) + NL *-cola*] **:** a genus of birds (family Cotingidae) containing the cock of the rock

ru·pic·o·lous \-ləs\ *or* **ru·pic·o·line** \-kəˌlīn, -kələn\ *adj* [L *rupi-* + E *-colous*, *-coline*] **:** living among, inhabiting, or growing on rocks

rup·pia \ˈrəpēə\ *n*, *cap* [NL, fr. Heinrich B. *Ruppius* (Rupp) †1719 Ger. botanist + NL *-ia*] **:** a small genus of widely distributed submerged marine herbs (family Hydrocharitaceae) having capillary stems, slender alternate leaves, and monoecious flowers destitute of perianth — see DITCH GRASS

¹rup·ture \ˈrəpchə(r), -psh-\ *n* -s [ME *ruptur*, fr. MF or L; MF *rupture*, fr. L *ruptura* fracture, break, fr. *ruptus* (past part. of *rumpere* to break) + *-ura* -ure — more at REAVE] **1 a :** breach of peace or concord; *specif* **:** open hostility or war between nations ⟨could not assume the responsibility of a ~ and would support the principle of arbitration —C.L. Jones⟩ **b :** a breach of the harmonious relationship between two parties ⟨mother and son avoided an open ~ —George Santayana⟩ **2 a :** the tearing apart by force, disease, or other cause of an organ or structure ⟨the ~ of the heart muscle⟩ ⟨the ~ of an intervertebral disk⟩ **b** [ML *ruptura*, fr. L, fracture, break] **:** HERNIA **3 :** a break in the earth's surface (as a gorge or ravine) **4 :** a breaking apart **:** SEPARATING **:** the state of being broken apart ⟨the last telegram sent . . . before the ~ of the wire —W.H.G.Kingston⟩ ⟨the ~ of the moral code can break down the power of principle —E.T.Thurston⟩ **syn** see BREACH

²rupture \ˈ"\ *vb* **ruptured; ruptured; rupturing** \-pchəriŋ, psh(ə)riŋ\ **ruptures** *vt* **1 a :** to part by violence **:** BREAK, BURST ⟨her nurse became alarmed and said she would ~ her stitches —Marcia Davenport⟩ **b :** to create or induce a breach of ⟨even at the expense of *rupturing* Arab unity —Denis Healey⟩ **2 :** to produce a hernia in ~ *vi* **:** to have a break or rupture

ruptured *adj* **1 :** torn apart **:** burst asunder **:** BROKEN ⟨~ water mains increased the misery of the flood victims⟩ ⟨beyond the ~ wire fence lay . . . cramped frame houses —W.B.Marsh⟩ **2 :** having a rupture or a hernia ⟨a ~ appendix⟩

ruptured duck *n*, *slang* **:** the symbol of an eagle with outspread wings depicted in the honorable service emblem for men and women of the U.S. armed forces

rupturewort \ˈ==ˌ=\ *n* **:** a plant of the genus *Herniaria; esp* **:** a common prostrate Old World herb (*H. glabra*) formerly reputed to cure ruptures and sometimes used as a ground cover

¹ru·ral \ˈru̇rəl, ˈrür-\ *adj* [ME, fr. MF, fr. L *ruralis*, fr. *rur-*, *rus* country, open land + *-alis* -al — more at ROOM] **1 :** living in country areas **:** engaged in agricultural pursuits ⟨a ~ people⟩ ⟨elected by constituencies which are basically ~ —*New Republic*⟩ **2 :** characterized by simplicity **:** lacking sophistication **:** UNCOMPLICATED ⟨in search of ~ life —Christopher Rand⟩ ⟨poetry is very, very ~ —Robert Frost⟩ ⟨programs of ballads and ~ dances —Marinobel Smith⟩ **3 :** of, relating to, or characteristic of people who live in the country ⟨his long knotty ~ fingers —Edmund Wilson⟩ ⟨modern warfare no longer calls for ~ stamina —Alfred Vagts⟩ ⟨a gardener who looked excessively ~ —Rebecca West⟩ **4 :** of, relating to, associated with, or typical of the country ⟨~ architecture was reflected in houses with low, plain walls —*Amer. Guide Series: Mich.*⟩ ⟨crowds welcomed us at each ~ town —A.C.Fisher⟩ ⟨under this legislation, a ~ area includes most places with fewer than 1,500 people —J.H. Ferguson & D.E.McHenry⟩ **5 :** of, relating to, or constituting a tenement in land adapted and used for agricultural or pastoral purposes — opposed to *urban*

²rural \ˈ"\ *n* -s **:** one who lives in the country

rural dean *n* **:** an ecclesiastic ranking immediately under an archdeacon and appointed as a diocesan official to supervise the affairs of a group of parishes constituting a division of an archdeaconry

rural district *n* **:** a subdivision of an administrative county that usu. embraces several country parishes and is governed by a council — see DISTRICT COUNCIL; compare URBAN DISTRICT

ru·ra·les \rüˈräˌlās\ *n pl* [MexSp, fr. Sp, adj., pl. of *rural*, fr. L *ruralis* — more at RURAL] **:** the Mexican rural mounted constabulary

rural free delivery *also* **rural delivery** *n* **:** the free delivery of mail by the U.S. postal service usu. from the nearest post office having carrier service to a rural area not served directly by a post office or having only a small post office without carriers — abbr. *RFD, RD*

ru·ral·ism \ˈru̇rəˌlizəm, ˈrür-\ *n* -s **1 :** the quality or state of being rural **2 :** a rural idiom or expression

ru·ral·ist \-ləst\ *or* **ru·ral·ite** \-ˌlīt\ *n* -s [¹*rural* + *-ist* or *-ite*] **1 :** an inhabitant of the country **:** FARMER **2 :** one who advocates life in the country as contrasted with life in a city

ru·ral·i·ty \ru̇ˈralədē\ *n* -ES [¹*rural* + *-ity*] **:** RURALISM **:** a rural place

ru·ral·iza·tion \ˌru̇rələˈzāshən\ *n* -s **:** the act of becoming ruralized

ru·ral·ize \ˈru̇rəˌlīz, ˈrür-\ *vb* -ED/-ING/-S [¹*rural* + *-ize*] *vt* **:** to make rural **:** give a rural appearance to ~ *vi* **:** to go into the country **:** RUSTICATE ⟨*ruralizing* with my ancient cousin —*Lippincott's Mag.*⟩

ru·ral·ly \-əlē\ *adv* **:** in a rural manner

rural route *or* **rural delivery route** *n* **:** a mail-delivery route in a rural free delivery area served by a regular postal carrier and beginning and ending at the same post office — compare STAR ROUTE

rural servitude *n*, *Roman, civil, & Scots law* **:** a servitude affecting chiefly or solely the soil or land and imposed upon a rural tenement or estate — compare URBAN SERVITUDE

rural sociology *n* **:** a branch of sociology dealing with the study of rural communities and the rural way of life — compare URBAN SOCIOLOGY

rur·ban \ˈrərbən, ˈru̇r-\ *adj* [blend of ¹*rural* and *urban*] **1 :** relating to or living in a community, zone, or town which is primarily residential but where some farming is engaged in **2 :** situated or living outside the city limits but not on a farm

ru·ri·decanal \ˌru̇rə+\ *adj* [L *ruri-* (fr. *rur-*, *rus* country) + E *decanal* — more at ROOM] **:** of or relating to a rural dean

ru·rig·e·nous \ru̇ˈrijənəs\ *adj* [L *ruri-* + E *-genous*] **:** born or living in the country

ru·ri·ta·ni·an \ˌru̇rəˈtānēən\ *adj*, *usu cap* [*Ruritania*, fictional kingdom in the romantic novel *The Prisoner of Zenda* (1894) by Anthony Hope (Sir Anthony Hope Hawkins) †1933 Eng. writer + E *-an*] **:** of, relating to, or having the characteristics of an imaginary place of high romance ⟨indulged in a sort of *Ruritanian* flirtation with the Queen —H.G.Wells⟩ ⟨a *Ruritanian* existence — sumptuously gay, flitting, free of earnest obligations, infused with a fierce devotion to royalty —*Times Lit. Supp.*⟩

ru·ru \ˈrü(ˌ)rü\ *n* -s [Maori] **:** the New Zealand boobook owl

ru·sa \ˈrüsə\ *n* [Hindi *rūsā*] **1** -s **:** SAMBAR **2** *cap* [NL, fr. Hindi *rūsā*] **:** a genus of deers now usu. regarded as a subgenus of *Cervus* and comprising the sambars and related forms — **ru·sine** \ˈrüˌsīn, -üsən\ *adj*

rus·cus \ˈrəskəs\ *n* [NL, fr. L, butcher's-broom] **1** *cap* **:** a small genus of European evergreen shrubs (family Liliaceae) with leaflike phylloclades, small greenish flowers, and red berries — see BUTCHER'S-BROOM **2** -ES **:** any plant of the genus *Ruscus*

ruse \ˈrüs, ˈrüz\ *n* -s [F, fr. MF, dodging of game to evade hunters, trick, ruse, fr. MF *reuser*, *ruser* to put to flight, retreat, to dodge to evade hunters, trick, deceive — more at RUSH] **:** a stratagem or trick usu. intended to deceive **:** a wily subterfuge ⟨succeeded through a ~ in turning back an English expedition —*Amer. Guide Series: La.*⟩ ⟨has a strong bias toward ~ and cunning —G.C.Sellery⟩ **syn** see TRICK

ru·sell \ˈrüsᵊl, ˈrōsᵊl\ *n* -s [Yiddish *rosel* pickle, broth, stew, rusell, fr. Russ *rosol*, *rossol* salt water, beef tea, broth, fr. *roz-* out of, separate from + *sol* salt; akin to L *sal* salt — more at SALT] **:** vinegar made of fermented beet juice and used during Passover

¹rush \ˈrəsh\ *n* -ES *often attrib* [ME *rish*, *resh*, *rush*, fr. OE *risc*, *resc*, *rysc;* akin to MLG *risch*, *rüsch* rush, MD & MHG *rusch*, Norw *rusk*, *ryskje* hair grass, L *restis* rope, cord, Skt *rajju* rope, cord, Lith *reksti* to plait, bind, tie] **1 a :** any of various plants esp. of the genera *Juncus* and *Scirpus* the cylindrical and often hollow stems of which are used in bottoming chairs and plaiting mats and the pith of which is used in some places for wicks and rushlights **b :** any of various other plants resembling rush **c :** CATTAIL **2 :** the merest trifle **:** STRAW ⟨not even worth a ~⟩

²rush \ˈ"\ *vb* -ED/-ING/-ES [ME *russhen*, fr. *rish*, *resh*, *rush*, n.] *vt* **:** to strew with, work with, or make with rushes ~ *vi* **:** to gather rushes

³rush \ˈ"\ *vb* -ED/-ING/-ES [ME *russhen*, fr. MF *reuser*, *ruser*, to put to flight, repel, retreat, fr. L *recusare* to object to, reject, refuse — more at RECUSANT] *vi* **1 a :** to move forward or progress with speed often impetuously and sometimes with violence or tumult ⟨servants ~*ed* in and out piling up a variety of food —Heinrich Harrer⟩ ⟨the gate was open and the Indians ~*ed* in —*Amer. Guide Series: Pa.*⟩ **b :** to act with haste, precipitation, or eagerness, typically with impatience at delay or without due consideration or preparation ⟨the complaining parties . . . ~ blindly on the superficial causes of their immediate distress —J.A.Froude⟩ ⟨~*ing* in with brand-new solutions without consulting the party —Leslie Roberts⟩ ⟨men who should have known better ~*ed* into print —W.E.Swinton⟩ **2 a :** to flow or fall very rapidly and often noisily **:** dart or move quickly ⟨flames . . . ~*ing* up in long lances —John Muir †1914⟩ ⟨skim along . . . at fifty miles an hour with the air ~*ing* in —Tom Marvel⟩ ⟨the brook . . . ~*es* over a precipice in two cascades —*Amer. Guide Series: Conn.*⟩ **b :** to surge up rapidly and forcefully to a dominating degree ⟨all the horror ~*ed* over her afresh —Ellen Glasgow⟩ ⟨tenderness ~*ed* upon him —Christine Weston⟩ ⟨old times ~*ed* back upon me — the remembrance of old services —W.M.Thackeray⟩ **3 :** to act as carrier of a football in a running play ~ *vt* **1** *obs* **:** to thrust or force often ruthlessly or violently ⟨thy fault our law calls death; but the kind Prince . . . hath ~*ed* aside the law —Shak.⟩ **2 :** to cause to go forward at a high rate of speed ⟨able to guess when new gales . . . would ~ the line of snowstorms out to sea —J.A.Michener⟩ **3 a :** to move quickly and often heedlessly without thought ⟨seemed to be ~*ing* himself and others into trouble —Walter Lippmann⟩ **b :** to impel or hurry on or forward with marked speed, impetuosity, or violence ⟨was able to ~ into the field three regiments of militia —*Amer. Guide Series: N.H.*⟩ ⟨~*ed* her to the hospital —Morris Fishbein⟩ ⟨didn't want to be ~*ed* into marriage —Floyd Dell⟩ **c :** to perform, execute, or deliver in a notably short time or at high speed ⟨decided that the work . . . was to be ~*ed* —Mary Austin⟩ ⟨the same class of ambitious leaders ~*ed* it into statehood —D.Y.Thomas⟩ **4 :** to urge to an unnaturally rapid progress or pace ⟨better not to ~ young children too much, even if they are unusual —Charles Angoff⟩ ⟨the department stores always seem to ~ the season⟩ ⟨had been really ~*ed* yesterday⟩ **5 :** to run towards or against in attack **:** VANQUISH, OVERPOWER **:** break in by charge or onset ⟨~*ed* the enemy group, bayoneted their leader —H.L.Merillat⟩ ⟨if you hear three shots, ~ the door —Laura Krey⟩ **6 :** to roquet (a ball) so that it travels a considerable distance **7 a :** to carry (a ball) forward in a running play **b :** to move in quickly on (a kicker or passer) so as to hinder, prevent, or block a kick or pass **8 a :** to lavish attention on **:** court assiduously **:** have frequent dates with ⟨has been ~*ing* that girl for nearly three months⟩ **b :** to entertain esp. at parties and dances in order to secure a pledge of membership ⟨the sorority decided to ~ fewer girls this year⟩

syn DASH, TEAR, SHOOT, CHARGE: RUSH suggests either impetuosity or intense hurry on account of some exigency, with carelessness about the concomitant effects of the precipitate action ⟨a flying rout of suns and galaxies, *rushing* away from the solar system —E.M.Forster⟩ ⟨business *rushed* forward into the glittering years —*Amer. Guide Series: Ind.*⟩ DASH is now likely to suggest running or moving at a wild unrestrained top speed ⟨gyroscopically controlled trains that can make 150 miles an hour . . . and *dash* across an abyss on a steel cable —Waldemar Kaempffert⟩ ⟨*dash'd* on like a spurred blood-horse in a race —Lord Byron⟩ TEAR, in this sense, may suggest extreme swiftness with impetus, violence, and abandon ⟨then he *tore* out of the study —Agnes S. Turnbull⟩ ⟨disheveled atoms *tear* along at 100 miles a second —Waldemar Kaempffert⟩ SHOOT may imply the precipitate headlong rushing or darting of something impelled, as though discharged from a gun ⟨leaped to one side and out of reach of those wicked horns. The bull *shot* past —F.B.Gipson⟩ ⟨the Bridal Veil *shoots* free from the upper edge of the cliff by the velocity the stream has acquired —John Muir †1914⟩ ⟨*shooting* out in their motorcars on errands of mystery —Virginia Woolf⟩ CHARGE is likely to suggest a rapid, violent onslaught gathering forceful momentum calculated to overpower ⟨down we swept and *charged* and overthrew —Alfred Tennyson⟩ ⟨one morning he *charged* — he was a very burly man — into Rossetti's studio —Osbert Sitwell⟩ — **rush the growler :** to fetch beer from a saloon esp. in a pail or pitcher

⁴rush \ˈ"\ *n* -ES [ME, fr. *russhen*, v.] **1 a :** a moving forward with rapidity and force or eagerness **:** a swift sometimes violent motion or course **:** ONSET ⟨a ~ was made at the first three food-laden wagons —F.V.W.Mason⟩ ⟨a whole load of earth fell with a ~ —Liam O'Flaherty⟩ **b :** a sound of or as if of swift movement ⟨the idea may come with a ~ of wings —Harriet Monroe⟩ ⟨heard the ~ of the distant waterfall⟩ **c :** a surging usu. of some deeply felt emotion ⟨a ~ of moral indignation —V.S.Pritchett⟩ ⟨sat back with a curious little ~ of excitement —Ann Bridge⟩ ⟨a quick ~ of sympathy —Gordon Cuyler⟩ **2 a :** an unusual burst of activity, productivity, or speed usu. because of pressure or accumulation ⟨the ~ . . . to locate and tap new and improved sources of raw materials —V.G. Iden⟩ ⟨buy in a wild Saturday morning ~ or go without what you need —Nathaniel Peffer⟩ ⟨the patient had peristaltic ~es⟩ **b :** a sudden insistent and usu. eager demand ⟨caused a ~ among American banking houses to retain him as their legal counsel —*Current Biog.*⟩ ⟨was assured of a box-office ~ —*Newsweek*⟩ ⟨the height of the Christmas ~ —Wynford Vaughan-Thomas⟩ **3 :** a thronging of many people usu. to some new place; *esp* **:** GOLD RUSH ⟨the second season of the great California ~ —Cliff Farrell⟩ ⟨most men who have known the excitement of a ~ always remain prospectors at heart —*Amer. Guide Series: Nev.*⟩ **4 :** the act of carrying a football during a game **:** running play ⟨sped 56 yards with the kickoff and got three more on a ~ —Allison Danzig⟩ **5 :** a contest or trial of strength between two classes or delegations of two classes usu. in a school or university ⟨the day of the big freshman ~, in which the sophomores would . . . try to prevent the freshmen from charging —Edmund Wilson⟩ **6 :** a round of assiduous attention usu. involving extensive social activity ⟨seem to be giving her quite a ~ —Hamilton Basso⟩ **7 :** an advance positive print of a motion-picture scene processed directly after the shooting for review by the director or producer — often used in pl. — **at a rush** *adv* **:** in a great hurry ⟨victory had to be won *at a rush* or not at all —*Times Lit. Supp.*⟩

⁵rush \"\ *adj* **1 :** involving haste **:** requiring special speed usu. in preparation, process, or action ⟨~ orders for coffee and doughnuts —Robertson Davies⟩ **2 :** characterized by a press of activity for students being considered for fraternity or sorority membership ⟨~ week⟩ **3 :** characterized by maximum activity ⟨transatlantic liner business will swing into the annual ~ season —George Horne b.1902⟩ ⟨the worst delays . . . took place not in cities but in suburban towns at the ~ commuting hours —Hal Burton⟩

rush-bearing \'ˌ=\ *n* **:** a festival formerly held in rural England on the anniversary of the dedication of a church and marked by the bringing of rushes by the parishioners to strew the church

rush-bottomed \'=ˌ==\ *adj* **:** having a seat made of rushes ⟨admired the antique *rush-bottomed* chair⟩

rush candle *n* **:** RUSHLIGHT

rushed \'rəsht\ *adj* [¹*rush* + *-ed*] **:** overgrown or overlaid with rushes

rush·ee \(ˌ)rə'shē\ *n* -s [³*rush* + *-ee*] **:** a college or university student (as a freshman) who is being rushed by a fraternity or sorority

rush·en \'rəshən, 'rüsh-\ *adj* [ME *russchen*, fr. OE *riscen*, fr. *risc, resc, rysc* rush + *-en* — more at RUSH] *chiefly dial* **:** made of rushes

¹rush·er \'rəshə(r)\ *n* -s [³*rush* + *-er*] **:** one that rushes: as **a :** one that does things rapidly **:** a quick energetic person **b :** one that acts hastily without thought **c :** one who joins in the rush to a freshly discovered ore field **d :** a football player who carries the ball in a running play

²rusher \"\ *n* -s [¹*rush* + *-er*] **:** one who weaves rushes into frames of chairs

rushes *pl of* RUSH, *pres 3d sing of* RUSH

rush family *n* **:** JUNCACEAE

rush grass *n* **:** a grass of the genus *Sporobolus* having wiry stems and sheathed panicles

rush hour *n* **:** the period of the day when the demands esp. of traffic or business are at the peak ⟨the rapidity of subway transit . . . outside of *rush hours* is one of the wonders of the world —Irwin Edman⟩

¹rushing *adj* [fr. pres. part. of ³*rush*] **1 :** moving with extreme rapidity **:** IMPETUOUS, PRECIPITATE ⟨give the impression that the typical mountain stream is a ~ torrent —Alexander MacDonald⟩ **2 :** briskly active ⟨women in shawls and boots did a ~ business in evergreen wreaths —Horace Sutton⟩ — **rush·ing·ly** *adv*

²rushing *n* -s [fr. gerund of ³*rush*] **:** the extensive social activity characteristic of the rushes of a fraternity or sorority ⟨about to ban the house from interfraternity activities, including ~ —J.D.May⟩

rush-leaved daffodil \'=ˌ=-\ *n* **:** JONQUIL

rushlight \'=ˌ=\ *n* **1 :** a candle made of the pith of various rushes, peeled except on one side, and dipped in grease ⟨draw the curtain, and kindle the ~ —Mary Webb⟩ **2 :** one that is singularly insignificant ⟨told him that good scholars were looked upon here as mere ~s —*Yale Literary Mag.*⟩

rushlike \'=ˌ=\ *adj* **:** resembling a rush

rush lily *n* **:** a large-flowered plant of the genus *Sisyrinchium*; *esp* **:** a blue-eyed grass (*S. angustifolium*)

rush nut *n* **:** CHUFA

rush pink *n* **:** a plant of the genus *Lygodesmia* (family Compositae); *esp* **:** a No. American perennial rushlike herb (*L. juncea*) with finely grooved leaves and pink or white flowers

rush ring *n* **:** a ring made of plaited rushes and used as a wedding ring

rush seat *n* **:** a theatre or concert seat usu. in a separate section of the balcony that may be occupied by the first ticket holder securing it

rush toad *n* **:** NATTERJACK

rushwork \'=ˌ=\ *n* [¹*rush* + *work*] **:** the art or craft of weaving rushes

rushy \'rəshē\ *adj* -ER/-EST [ME *resshy, russhy*, fr. *rish, resh, rush* rush + *-y* — more at RUSH] **1 :** made of or resembling rushes **2 :** abounding with rushes

rusine antler *n* [*rusine* fr. NL *Rusa* + E *-ine*] **:** an antler with the brow tine simple and the beam simply forked at the tip

¹rusk \'rəsk\ *n* -s [modif. of Sp & Pg *rosca* coil, screw, twisted roll] **1 :** hard crisp bread orig. used as ship's stores **2 :** a sweet or plain twice-baked bread that is first prepared and baked and then sliced and baked a second time until it is dry and crisp

²rusk \"\ *vt* -ED/-ING/-S **:** to toast or crisp (bread or cake) into rusk

ruski *var of* RUSSKI

rus·kin \'rəskən\ *n* -s [IrGael *ruscān*, dim. of *rusc* bark — more at RUCHE] *dial Eng* **:** a receptacle for butter often made of bark

rus·kin·ian \ˌrə'skinēən\ *adj, usu cap* [John *Ruskin* †1900 Eng. art critic and sociological writer + E *-ian*] **:** of, relating to, or resembling the writings of the critic Ruskin

rus·kin·ize \'rəskəˌnīz\ *vb* -ED/-ING/-S *usu cap* [John *Ruskin* + E *-ize*] *vt* **:** to convert to ideas resembling those of John Ruskin ⟨it is too late to *Ruskinize* our civilization —Katharine F. Gerould⟩ ~ *vi* **:** to adopt or plead for the principles of Ruskin ⟨don't *Ruskinize* to me —*Scribner's*⟩

rus·ot \'rəsət\ *or* **rus·wut** \-swət\ *n* -s [Hindi *rasaut, raswat*] **:** an extract from the wood or roots of various shrubs of the genus *Berberis* that is used in India mixed with opium as an application to infected eyelids

¹russ \'rəs\ *n, pl* **russ** *or* **russes** *cap* [Russ *Rus'*, old name for Russia and the Russian people (first applied to the Scandinavian Varangians that settled and came to power in the Novgorod and Kiev area in the 9th cent.), of Scand origin like Finn *Ruotsi* Sweden, MGk *rhōsisti* Scandinavian, ML *Rusios* Norsemen; akin to ON *rōthr* art of rowing, *rōa* to row — more at ROW] **1 :** a native or inhabitant of Russia **2 :** the Russian language

²russ \"\ *adj, usu cap* **:** of or relating to the Russians

rus·sel \'rəsəl\ *n* -s [ME *ryssill*, prob. fr. *Rijssel* (Lille), city in northern France] **:** a strong twilled woolen cloth for clothing and shoes

rus·se·lia \ˌrə'sēlēə, -lyə\ *n, cap* [NL, fr. Alexander *Russell* †1768 Brit. physician at Aleppo + NL *-ia*] **:** a genus of often nearly leafless Mexican shrubs (family Scrophulariaceae) having red flowers with a tubular corolla, four stamens, and a nearly globose 2-celled capsule — see CORAL PLANT 2 c

rus·sell·ian \ˌrə'selēən\ *adj, usu cap* [Bertrand *Russell* b1872 Eng. mathematician and philosopher + E *-ian*] **:** of or relating to the philosopher Bertrand Russell or his theories

rus·sell·ite \'rəsəˌlīt\ *n* -s *usu cap* [Charles Taze *Russell* †1916 Am. religious leader + E *-ite*] **:** one of the Jehovah's Witnesses — often taken to be offensive

rus·sell's paradox \'rəsəlz-\ *n, usu cap R* [after Bertrand *Russell*] **:** a paradox that discloses itself in forming a class of all classes that are not members of themselves and in observing that the question of whether it is true or false if this class is a member of itself can be answered both ways — compare LIAR PARADOX, VICIOUS CIRCLE PRINCIPLE

russell's viper *n, usu cap R* [after Patrick *Russell* †1805 Brit. physician at Aleppo] **:** a strikingly marked highly venomous snake (*Vipera russellii* syn. *Daboia russelli*) of southeastern Asia that is light brown above with three longitudinal rows of black light-margined rings which sometimes encircle reddish dots — called also *daboia*

rus·sene *or* **ru·sin** \'rüˌsēn, rü'-, '=ˌ=\ *n* -s *usu cap* [Russ *rusin*, fr. *Rus'*, old name for Russia — more at RUSS] **:** RUTHENIAN

¹rus·set \'rəsət, *usu* -əd·+V\ *n* -s [ME, fr. OF *rosset, rousset*, fr. *rosset, rousset*, adj., russet, fr. *ros, rous* russet, fr. L *russus* red; akin to L *ruber* red — more at RED] **1 :** coarse homespun cloth in reddish brown or natural colors formerly used by country people **2 :** a variable color averaging a strong brown that is duller and slightly redder than rust, paler and slightly redder than average copper brown, and redder and deeper than gold brown — compare RUSSET BROWN **3 :** any of various winter apples having rough skins of a russet color ⟨the Roxbury ~⟩ **4 :** russet leather **5 :** RUSSETING 3

²russet \"\ *adj* [ME, fr. MF *rousset*] **1 :** reddish brown or reddish gray or yellowish brown ⟨the morn in ~ mantle clad —Shak.⟩ **2 :** of the color russet **3 a :** made of russet **b** *obs* **:** wearing clothing made of russet **4 :** of, relating to, or constituting leather that is finished except for the coloring and polishing

³russet \"\ *vb* **russeted** *also* **russetted; russeted** *also* **russetted; russeting** *also* **russetting; russets** *vt* **1 :** to cast a russet glow over **2 :** to cause russeting ~ *vi* **1 :** to become russet in color ⟨leaves ~ in autumn⟩ **2 :** to become russet **:** undergo russeting

russet-backed thrush \'==ˌ=-\ *n* **:** a common thrush (*Hylocichla ustulata*) of the Pacific coast somewhat darker than the related olive-backed thrush of eastern No. America

russet brown *n* **:** a variable color averaging a moderate to strong brown that is redder and darker than oak and yellower and darker than Vassar tan or Arabian brown

russet coat *n* **:** a coat of russet color or russet cloth; *also* **:** a wearer of such a coat

russet dwarf *n* **:** a virus disease of the potato characterized by dwarfing, browning, or rusting of the leaves and leaf fall

russet green *n* **:** a grayish to moderate greenish yellow that is redder and darker than citron green

rus·set·ing *also* **rus·set·ting** \'rəsəd·iŋ, -ət|, |ēŋ\ *n* -s [¹*russet* + *-ing*] **1** *obs* **:** one wearing russet **:** RUSTIC **2 :** RUSSET 3 **3 :** a brownish roughened area on the skin of fruit (as apples, pears, and citrus fruit) that resembles the normal skin of a russet apple and is caused by frost, insect or fungous injury, or spraying — compare SCURF

rus·set·ish \|ish\ *adj* **:** somewhat russet in color

russet mite *n* **:** RUST MITE

russet orange *n* **1 :** a variable color averaging a strong orange that is yellower and darker than pumpkin, yellower than mandarin orange, and redder and deeper than cadmium yellow **2 :** CHROME SCARLET

russet scab *n* [¹*russet*; fr. the roughened area on the tubers] **:** RHIZOCTONIA DISEASE 2

russet tan *n* **:** a moderate reddish brown that is yellower and paler than roan, mahogany, oxblood, or rustic brown

rus·sety \|ē\ *adj* **:** somewhat russet in color

¹rus·sia \'rəshə, *dial* 'rüshə\ *adj, usu cap* [fr. *Russia*, country in eastern Europe] **:** of or from Russia **:** of the kind or style prevalent in Russia

²russia \"\ *n* -s **:** RUSSIA LEATHER

russia duck *or* **russian duck** *n, usu cap R* **:** a strong linen duck formerly used for summer clothing

russia iron *n, usu cap R* **:** a sheet iron having a lustrous blue black coating of oxide for protection against corrosion

russia leather *or* **russia calf** *n, usu cap R* **1 :** leather made from various skins by tanning with barks of the willow, birch, or oak and then rubbing the flesh side with birch-tar oil which imparts a peculiar odor and protects from insects **2 :** a chrome-tanned or vegetable-tanned fancy leather that resembles the original Russia leather and is generally made from calf or small cattle hides

¹rus·sian \-shən\ *adj, usu cap* [*Russia*, country in eastern Europe + E *-an*] **:** of or relating to Russia, its inhabitants, or their language

²russian \"\ *n* -s *usu cap* **1 a :** one of the people of Russia; *esp* **:** a member of the dominant Slavic-speaking Great Russian ethnic group of Russia **b :** one that is of Russian descent **2 a :** a Slavic language of the Russian people **:** the official language of the Soviet Union **b :** the three Slavic languages of the Russian people collectively including Belorussian and Ukrainian

russian almond *n, usu cap R* **:** an Asiatic dwarf almond (*Prunus tenella*) cultivated for its rosy red flowers

russian backgammon *n, usu cap R* **:** a variation of backgammon in which all the pieces are entered on the same table as determined by throws of the dice and proceed in the same direction around the board

russian bagatelle *n, usu cap R* **:** a childish variation of bagatelle employing holes, pins, arches, and bells — called also *cockamaroo*

russian ballet *n, usu cap R* **1 :** ballet developed early in the 20th century by teachers and students of the Russian Imperial Ballet Academy with characteristic emphasis upon the execution of dramatic, symbolic, or interpretative pantomime through rhythmic plastic movements and postures with the aid of appropriate costumes and setting **2 :** a group of dancers trained in the Russian ballet

russian bank *n, usu cap R* **:** a card game in its procedure similar to most forms of solitaire but always played by two persons in which each player has his own pack of cards and attempts to play all of them while impeding the opponent's plays — called also *crapette*

russian bassoon *n, usu cap R* **:** an obsolete brass musical instrument similar to the bass horn

russian bath *n, usu cap R* **:** a vapor bath variously modified consisting essentially in a prolonged exposure of the body to steam followed by washings, friction, and a cold plunge

¹russian blue *n, often cap R* **:** a bluish gray to pale blue

²russian blue *n, usu cap R & often cap B* **:** a slender long-bodied large-eared domestic cat with short silky bluish gray fur

russian boot *n, usu cap R* **:** a leather boot extending to the calf and having a wide cuff and sometimes a tassel

russian cactus *n, usu cap R* **:** RUSSIAN THISTLE

russian calf *n, usu cap R* **:** a moderate brown that is deeper and slightly redder than chestnut brown, deeper and yellower than auburn or bay, and redder, stronger, and slightly lighter than coffee — called also *Cappagh brown, carob brown, judge, India tan, Kis Kilim*

russian dandelion *n, usu cap R* **:** KOK-SAGHYZ

russian dressing *n, usu cap R* **:** mayonnaise dressing with pungent additions that may include chili sauce, chopped pickles, or pimientos

russian flax *n, usu cap R* **:** FLAX 1

russian fly *n, usu cap R* **:** SPANISH FLY

russian gray *n, usu cap R* **:** SLATE GRAY

russian green *n, usu cap R* **:** a dark yellowish green to grayish green — called also *vert russe*

rus·sian·ism \-shəˌnizəm\ *n* -s *usu cap* **1 :** a special interest in or attachment to Russia or the Russian people **2 :** a quality or group of qualities characteristic of Russia, its people, or its language

rus·sian·iza·tion \ˌrəshənə'zāshən\ *n* -s *usu cap* **:** the act or process of russianizing

rus·sian·ize \'rəshəˌnīz\ *vt* -ED/-ING/-S *often cap* [¹*Russian* + *-ize*] **1 a :** to cause to acquire Russian characteristics, qualities, culture, beliefs, or political practices **b** (1) **:** to bring (a region or esp. a national group) under the national control of Russia (2) **:** to force to conform to a Russian cultural pattern or political organization **2 :** to treat (leather) by a process similar to or intended to produce results similar to that used on Russia leather

russian knapweed *n, usu cap R* **:** a Eurasian herb (*Centaurea picris*) introduced into the central U.S. where it has become a troublesome weed

russian mulberry *n, usu cap R* **:** a small bushy mulberry that is a variety (*Morus alba tatarica*) of the white mulberry

russian muskrat *n, usu cap R* **:** DESMAN 1 a, 2

russian olive *n, usu cap R* **:** a large shrub or small tree (*Elaeagnus angustifolia*) that has silvery twigs, lanceolate to oblong-lanceolate leaves which are light green above and silvery below, fragrant axillary flowers which are yellow within and silvery without, and small yellow fruits covered with silvery scales and that is native to western Asia and southern Europe and is widely cultivated in arid windy regions as an ornamental, as a coarse hedge or shelterbelt plant, or for wildlife food — called also *oleaster*

russian orthodox *adj, usu cap R&O* **:** of, relating to, or being the autocephalous Eastern Orthodox Church of Russia headed by the Patriarch of Moscow and using an Old Church Slavonic liturgy or one of its autonomous 20th century branches chiefly outside Russia

russian pigweed *n, usu cap R* **:** an annual Asiatic herb (*Axyris amaranthoides*) of the family Chenopodiaceae naturalized in No. America having unisexual flowers of which the pistillate ones have a 3- or 4-parted perianth

russian red clover *n, usu cap 1st R* **:** a drought-resistant red clover that is usu. considered a variety (*Trifolium pratense pallidum*) of the common red clover

russian roulette *n, usu cap 1st R* **:** an act of bravado consisting of spinning the cylinder of a revolver loaded with one cartridge, pointing the muzzle at one's own head, and pulling the trigger

russian sable *n, usu cap R* **:** SIBERIAN SABLE

russian sheet iron *n, usu cap R* **:** RUSSIA IRON

russian spring-summer encephalitis *n, usu cap R* **:** a tick-borne encephalitis

russian sunflower *n, usu cap R* **:** a large-seeded sunflower that is a variety of the common sunflower (*Helianthus annuus*) and is used as food in Russia

russian thistle *or* **russian tumbleweed** *n, usu cap R* **:** a prickly European herb (*Salsola kali tenuifolia*) that is a serious pest in No. America — called also *Russian cactus*

russian turnip *n, usu cap R* **:** RUTABAGA

russian turpentine *n, usu cap R* **:** turpentine obtained chiefly from the Scotch pine

russian walnut *n, usu cap R* **:** ENGLISH WALNUT

russian whist *n, usu cap R* **:** VINT

russian wild rye *n, usu cap 1st R* **:** an Asiatic ryegrass (*Elymus junceus*) introduced into No. America and used as a forage grass

russian wolfhound *n, usu cap R* **:** BORZOI 2

russian wormwood *n, usu cap R* **:** an Asiatic gray-pubescent subshrub (*Artemisia sacrorum*) used as an ornamental and having nodding flower heads in slender racemes

russia sheet iron *n, usu cap R* **:** RUSSIA IRON

rus·si·fi·ca·tion \ˌrəsəfə'kāshən\ *n* -s *sometimes cap* **:** the act or process of being russified

rus·si·fy \'rəsəˌfī\ *vt* -ED/-ING/-ES *often cap* [²*Russ* + *-ify*] **1 :** RUSSIANIZE **2 :** to modify (language or a word or expression) to conform to characteristics distinctive of the Russian language ⟨*Russified* more than any other of the Balto-Finnic languages —F.J.Oinas⟩

rus·sism \'rəˌsizəm\ *n* -s *usu cap* [²*Russ* + *-ism*] **:** a word, expression, or language characteristic or distinctive of Russian

russ·ki *also* **russ·ky** *or* **rus·ki** \'rəskē\ *n, pl* **russkies** *or* **russkis** *also* **ruskies** *or* **ruskis** *usu cap* [Russ *russkii*, adj. & n., Russian, fr. *Rus'*, old name for Russia — more at RUSS] **:** a native of Russia **:** RUSSIAN — often taken to be offensive

russ·ni·ak \'rəsnēˌak\ *n* -s *cap* [Ukr *rusnyak, rusnak*] **:** RUTHENIAN

russo- *comb form, usu cap* [*Russia* & ¹*Russian*] **1 :** Russia **:** Russians ⟨*Russo*phobia⟩ **2 :** Russian and ⟨*Russo*-Japanese⟩

rus·so-byzantine \ˌrə(ˌ)sō, -shō+\ *adj, usu cap R&B* [*Russo-* + *Byzantine*] **:** having Byzantine characteristics modified by Russian influence; *esp* **:** of or relating to the typical Russian architecture previous to 1700

rus·so·phil \'rəsəˌfil\ *or* **rus·so·phile** \-fīl\ *n* -s *usu cap* [*Russo-* + *-phil, -phile*] **:** one who admires or supports Russia or Russian policy

rus·so·pho·bia \ˌ=='fōbēə\ *n, usu cap* [NL, fr. *Russo-* + *-phobia*] **:** fear or dislike of Russia or Russian policy

rus·sud \'rəˌsəd\ *n* -s [Hindi *rasad*, lit., income, revenue, contribution, fr. Per] **:** grain or forage provided by local Indian officers at a military camping ground

rus·su·la \'rəsyələ\ *n, cap* [NL, fr. LL, fem. of *russulus* reddish, fr. L *russus* red — more at RUSSET] **:** a large genus that comprises stout-stemmed white-spored fungi (family Agaricaceae) with neither annulus nor volva, includes some edible species, and may be distinguished from the related *Lactarius* by the absence of milky juice and by the brittle pileus of red, purple, yellow, green, or blue

¹rust \'rəst\ *n* -s [ME, fr. OE *rūst*; akin to OS, OHG, & OSw *rost* rust; derivative fr. the stem of E ¹*red*] **1 a :** the reddish porous brittle coating that is formed on iron esp. when chemically attacked by moist air and that consists essentially of hydrated ferric oxide but usu. contains some ferrous oxide and sometimes iron carbonates and iron sulfates — compare CORROSION 1a, ⁵SCALE 4a **b :** the somewhat similar coating produced on any of various other metals by corrosion — compare PATINA 2 **c :** something resembling rust **:** ACCRETION ⟨this poem . . . under its accumulated ~ and dirt of five centuries is fresh and living even today —G.G.Coulton⟩ **2 a** *obs* **:** corrosive or injurious accretion or influence ⟨how he glisters thorough my ~ —Shak.⟩ **b :** an ill effect usu. caused by idleness, inaction, or neglect ⟨read to keep your mind from ~⟩ ⟨lest through the ~ of time . . . they should be lost to the world forever —Laurence Sterne⟩ **3 a** (1) *or* **rust disease :** any of numerous destructive diseases of plants produced by fungi of the order Uredinales and characterized by reddish brown pustular lesions on stems, leaves, or other plant parts — see APPLE RUST, LEAF RUST, STEM RUST, STRIPE RUST, WHEAT RUST; compare MILDEW, SMUT (2) *or* **rust fungus :** a fungus of the order Uredinales — compare PUCCINIA, UROMYCES **b :** any of several other fungus diseases of plants — usu. used with a descriptive term; see WHITE RUST **c :** an abnormal reddish or brownish discoloration of vegetation or fruit **4 :** a strong brown that is stronger and slightly yellower and lighter than average russet, lighter, stronger, and very slightly redder than average copper brown, and redder and deeper than gold brown **5 :** a composition used in making a rust joint

²rust \"\ *vb* -ED/-ING/-S [ME *rusten*, fr. *rust*, n.] *vi* **1 :** to form rust **:** become oxidized — compare CORRODE *vi* 2, TARNISH **2 :** to degenerate in idleness **:** become dull, slow, or impaired esp. by inaction, lack of use, or the passage of time ⟨once-functioning objects now ~ed and moldered in this cellar —Marcia Davenport⟩ ⟨no man to let his power ~ —*Time*⟩ **3 :** to turn or become the color of rust **:** become reddish brown as if with rust ⟨the leaves slowly ~⟩ **4 a :** to be affected with a rust fungus **b :** to acquire a rusty appearance ~ *vt* **1 :** to cause (a metal) to form rust ⟨keep up your bright swords, for the dew will ~ them —Shak.⟩ — compare CORRODE *vt* 1 **2 :** to impair or corrode by or as if by time, inactivity, or deleterious use ⟨a six-year layoff . . . had not ~ed his technique —*Newsweek*⟩ **3 :** to blast or wither by or as if by the rust fungus **4 :** to turn to the color of rust **:** cause to become reddish brown ⟨the wind brought salt . . . ~ing the crops —*N.Y.Times*⟩

rust brown *n* **:** RUSSET 2

rust cement *n* **:** IRON CEMENT

¹rus·tic \'rəstik, -tēk\ *adj* [ME *rustyk*, fr. MF *rustique*, fr. L *rusticus*, fr. *rus* country, open land — more at ROOM] **1 :** of or relating to the country **:** RURAL ⟨rude carts, bespattered with ~ mire —Charles Dickens⟩ **2 :** of or relating to rustic work **3 a :** having an appearance or manner held to resemble country folk ⟨a splendid primeval ~ figure —Osbert Lancaster⟩

b : living in a rural area : engaged in country occupations (as farming) ⟨one of the few victories in all history of ~ untrained volunteers over professional soldiers —Budd Schulberg⟩ **4** : having or exhibiting qualities held to be characteristic of rural people: as **a** : marked by awkwardness : lacking polish : COARSE, RUDE ⟨~ readiness to jeer at the unusual —H.O. Taylor⟩ **b** : marked by simplicity : ARTLESS ⟨if education had not meddled with her ~ nature —Jean Stafford⟩ ⟨participating in these ~ occasions —P.L.Fermor⟩ **5** : adapted or appropriate to the country or country living : ROUGH, STURDY : lacking in ornamentation ⟨had a ~ shanty and arbor —Herman Melville⟩ ⟨dotted with tourist cabins and hotels — from the luxurious to the ~ —*Amer. Guide Series: Ariz.*⟩

²rustic \"\ *n* -s **1 a** : an inhabitant of a rural area ⟨new emphasis on the preciousness of the . . . soil affected both ~ and townsman —John Buchan⟩ **b** : one who is rude, coarse, or dull **c** : a rural person thought to be naturally simple in character or manners : one without sophistication ⟨where had my simple ~ procured it —Jacob Hay⟩ **2** : brick with a rough textured surface often multicolored : a style of masonry resembling rockwork **3** : RUSTIC MOTH **4** : a ceramic surface artificially roughened

¹rus·ti·cal \-tə̇kəl\ *adj* [ME *rusticall*, fr. MF *rustical*, fr. *rustique* rustic + *-al*] : RUSTIC

²rustical \"\ *n* -s : RUSTIC

rus·ti·cal·ly \-k(ə)lē\ *adv* : in a rustic manner

rus·ti·cate \ˈrəstə̇ˌkāt, *usu* -ād·+V\ *vb* -ED/-ING/-S [L *rusticatus*, past part. of *rusticari* to live in the country, fr. *rusticus* rustic] *vi* : to go into or reside in the country : pursue a rustic life ⟨*rusticating* in . . . villages off the beaten track —T.H. Fielding⟩ ~ *vt* **1** : to punish by requiring temporary absence : suspend from school or college ⟨did not stand high in the esteem of the faculty and was once *rusticated* —G.H.Genzmer⟩ **2** : to bevel or rebate (as the edges of stone blocks) to make the joints conspicuous ⟨a *rusticated* stone pavilion —H.S. Morrison⟩ **3** : to compel to reside in the country ⟨*rusticated* himself so long that he is become an absolute wild Irishman —Henry Fielding⟩ **4** : to cause to become rustic : implant rustic mannerisms in

rus·ti·ca·tion \ˌ==ˈkāshən\ *n* -s [L *rustication-, rusticatio*, fr. *rusticatus* + *-ion-, -io* -ion] **1** : the act of rusticating : the state of being rusticated : retirement to or residence in the country ⟨a period of ~ before taking up his new duties⟩ **2 a** : suspension from a college, university, or professional society ⟨anything from a small fine to ~ . . . —*Time*⟩ **b** : the act of suspending or the state of being suspended **3 a** : the practice of rusticating masonry **b** : masonry having the surface textured, reticulated, or otherwise accented or the joints emphasized

rus·ti·ca·tor \ˈ==ˌkād·ə(r)\ *n* -s : one that rusticates

rustic brown *n* : a moderate reddish brown that is yellower and less strong than roan, yellower and slightly paler than mahogany, and yellower, less strong, and slightly lighter than oxblood — called also *casserole, Eskimo, gingerspice*

rustic capital *n* : a Latin book hand much used from the 1st to the 7th centuries and occas. until the 10th with the letters formed in a manner natural to the pen

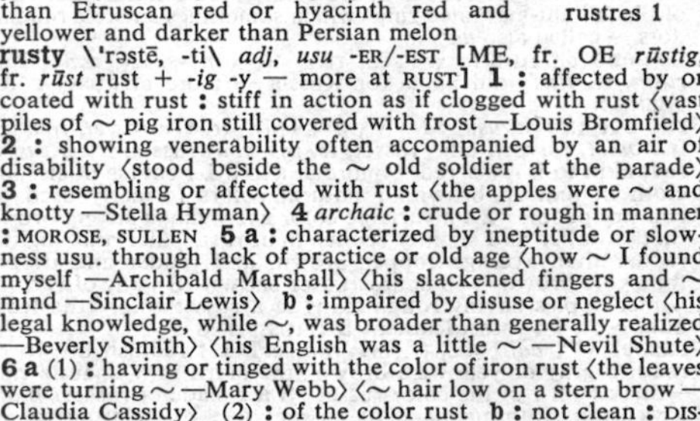

rustic capitals

rustic drab *n* : DRAB 2a

rus·ti·cism \ˈrəstə̇ˌsizəm\ *n* -s : a rustic phrase, manner of speaking, habit, or custom ⟨now and then a home ~ is fresh and startling —Charles Lamb⟩

rus·tic·i·ty \ˌrəˈstisəd·ē, -ətē, -i\ *n* -ES [MF *rusticité*, fr. L *rusticus* + MF *-ité* -ity] **1** : a lack of ease or refinement : awkwardness of manner : GAUCHERIE ⟨any little ~ of gait or pronunciation . . . was so quickly and completely lost —Samuel Butler †1902⟩ **2** : gracelessness of language : failure to reveal polish or elegance ⟨had the ~ of the average freshman theme⟩ **3** : a lack of perception or knowledge : IGNORANCE, STUPIDITY ⟨was ashamed of my own ~ in that distinguished company⟩ **4** : the quality or state of being rustic ⟨the ~ of . . . country towns —*Amer. Guide Series: Ind.*⟩

rus·ti·cize \ˈrəstə̇ˌsīz\ *vt* -ED/-ING/-S [¹*rustic* + *-ize*] : to give a rustic aspect to ⟨moved out . . . where accent and manner were *rusticized* —A.J.Liebling⟩

rustic joint *n* : a sunken joint between building stones

rus·tic·ly *adv* : RUSTICALLY

rustic moth *n* : any of various moths (family Noctuidae) belonging to *Agrotis* and related genera and having larvae that are cutworms

rusti·coat \ˈrəstēˌkōt\ *adj* [¹*rusty* + *coat*] : rusty coated ⟨dine . . . upon ~ potatoes —John Quincy Adams⟩

rustic servitude *n* : RURAL SERVITUDE

rustic ware *n* : terra cotta that is light brown in color with a brown glaze and is often used in architectural work

rustic work *n* **1** : cut stone facing that has the joints rusticated : stone with the face cut to a rough or jagged surface in imitation of nature **2** : summerhouses or furniture for summerhouses or for outdoor use made of rough limbs of trees

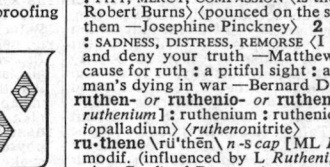

chair in rustic work 2

rustier *comparative of* RUSTY

rustiest *superlative of* RUSTY

rust·i·ly \ˈrəstə̇lē\ *adv* : in a rusty manner ⟨his cart is rickety, the wheels creak ~ —R.P. Casey⟩

rust·i·ness \-tēnə̇s\ *n* -ES [ME *rustynes*, fr. *rusty* + *-nes* -ness] : the quality or state of being rusty

rust joint *n* : a joint made with iron cement that causes the formation of rust between iron or steel surfaces

¹rus·tle \ˈrəsəl\ *vb* **rustled; rustled; rustling** \-s(ə)liŋ\ **rustles** [ME *rustelen, rustlen, rouschelen*, prob. of imit. origin; in some senses, influenced in meaning by *hustle*] *vi* **1 a** : to make a quick succession of small clear sounds usu. by moving ⟨the piny needles *rustled* down —Zane Grey⟩ ⟨their footsteps *rustled* in the fallen golden leaves —Anne D. Sedgwick⟩ ⟨the audience ~*s* in anticipation —Alfred Bester⟩ **b** : to wear clothing that produces soft sounds as one moves ⟨heard his wife ~⟩ **2 a** : to act or move with great energy and forthrightness ⟨the only thing to do is to ~ around —C.G. Poore⟩ ⟨as the jobs began to get scarce, he began to ~ harder —F.B.Gipson⟩ **b** : to forage food ⟨he wanted longhorns . . . they could ~ for themselves, fatten, and make a man money —F.B.Gipson⟩ **3** : to steal cattle ~ *vt* **1** : to cause to move with quick successive small clear sounds : stir with a rustling noise ⟨*rustled* the papers nervously⟩ **2 a** : to get by hustling : obtain by one's own exertions : handle actively and energetically ⟨took over all household chores, cleaning and cooking, *rustling* firewood —Bill Wolf⟩ ⟨~ some dinner together —J.B.Benefield⟩ **b** : FORAGE ⟨cows . . . died of starvation because they didn't know how to ~ a living in among the cactus —Paul Schubert⟩ **3** : to take (as cattle) feloniously : STEAL ⟨they caught him *rustling* cattle and hung him⟩

²rustle \"\ *n* -s **1** : a quick succession or confusion of small clear sounds ⟨a ~ of a window shade —R.P.Warren⟩ ⟨the sharp hiss and ~ of the wind —John Muir †1914⟩ ⟨heard the ~ of a newspaper —Lyle Saxon⟩ ⟨listened to the ~ of her skirts —Gilbert Parker⟩ **2** : an act of engaging actively and energetically in some pursuit : HUSTLE

rus·tler \ˈrəs(ə)lə(r)\ *n* -s : one that rustles: as **a** : a plant whose leaves make a rustling sound in the wind **b** : an alert energetic driving person : HUSTLER **c** : a cattle thief **d** : a domestic animal that can care for itself ⟨herefords make good ~*s*⟩ **e** : a mine worker who helps to operate the haulage system

¹rus·tling \ˈrəs(ə)liŋ, -lēŋ\ *n* -s [ME *rouschelynge*, fr. gerund of *rustelen, rustlen, rouschelen* to rustle — more at RUSTLE] **1** : the continuous small clear sounds made by movement ⟨the ~*s* of the birds⟩ **2** : the stealing of cattle ⟨this story of ranch life, ~ . . . and mystery —*Saturday Rev.*⟩

²rustling \"\ *adj* [fr. pres. part. of ¹*rustle*] : making continuous small clear sounds ⟨~ silk⟩ ⟨~ leaves⟩ — **rus·tling·ly** *adv*

rust mite *n* : any of various small gall mites that burrow in the surface of leaves or fruits usu. producing brown or reddish patches — see CITRUS RUST MITE

rustproof \ˈ=ˌ=\ *adj* : incapable of rusting ⟨the manufacture of some specialties such as ~ steel —*N.Y.Times*⟩

rust-proof \"\ *vt* [*rustproof*] : to make rustproof

rust·proof·er \"+ə(r)\ *n* : a worker who applies rust-proofing material to metal

rus·tre \ˈrəstə(r)\ *n* -s [F *ruste, rustre*] **1** *heraldry* : a lozenge pierced with a round opening to show the tincture of the field behind **2** : a metal scale of oval or lozenge shape used on medieval armor

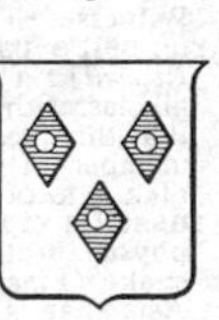
rustres 1

rus·tred \-(r)d\ *adj* : having or composed of rustres — used of medieval armor

rusts *pl of* RUST, *pres 3d sing of* RUST

rust tan *n* : a grayish reddish orange that is yellower, darker, and slightly less strong than Etruscan red or hyacinth red and yellower and darker than Persian melon

¹rusty \ˈrəstē, -ti\ *adj*, *usu* -ER/-EST [ME, fr. OE *rūstig*, fr. *rūst* rust + *-ig* -y — more at RUST] **1** : affected by or coated with rust : stiff in action as if clogged with rust ⟨vast piles of ~ pig iron still covered with frost —Louis Bromfield⟩ **2** : showing venerability often accompanied by an air of disability ⟨stood beside the ~ old soldier at the parade⟩ **3** : resembling or affected with rust ⟨the apples were ~ and knotty —Stella Hyman⟩ **4** *archaic* : crude or rough in manner : MOROSE, SULLEN **5 a** : characterized by ineptitude or slowness usu. through lack of practice or old age ⟨how ~ I found myself —Archibald Marshall⟩ ⟨his slackened fingers and ~ mind —Sinclair Lewis⟩ **b** : impaired by disuse or neglect ⟨his legal knowledge, while ~, was broader than generally realized —Beverly Smith⟩ ⟨his English was a little ~ —Nevil Shute⟩ **6 a** (1) : having or tinged with the color of iron rust ⟨the leaves were turning ~ —Mary Webb⟩ ⟨~ hair low on a stern brow —Claudia Cassidy⟩ (2) : of the color rust **b** : not clean : DISCOLORED ⟨bales of cotton, ~ from exposure to the elements⟩ **c** : dulled in color or appearance by age and long use : revealing hard wear ⟨a slender woman in a ~ black robe —Ralph Ellison⟩ ⟨wore . . . baggy trousers so short as to show his ~ boots —G.F.Milton⟩ **7** : characterized by staleness : HOARY, OUTMODED ⟨followed by a magic-lantern show and some ~ jokes —R.L.Taylor⟩ **8** : harsh and grating in tone as if from disuse : HOARSE ⟨gave a ~ chuckle as if unaccustomed to laughing —J.H.Wheelwright⟩ ⟨a ~, willfully ancient voice —Edith Sitwell⟩

²rusty \ˈrůsti, ˈrəsti\ VAR OF REASTY

³rus·ty \ˈrəstē\ *adj* -ER/-EST [alter. (influenced by ¹*rusty*) of *resty*] **1** : RESTIVE ⟨~ horses⟩ **2** *chiefly dial* : having a surly manner : ILL-TEMPERED ⟨~ ever since that business over the oil shares —John Galsworthy⟩

rusty blackbird *or* **rusty grackle** *n* : a blackbird (*Euphagus carolinus*) of the eastern U.S. whose adult male has a white iris and a uniformly blue-black color in spring but in the fall has the edges of the feathers become rusty

rusty blotch *n* : a disease of barley caused by an imperfect fungus (*Helminthosporium californicum*) characterized by irregular brown blotches on the leaves

rusty dab *n* : a rusty-brown yellow-tailed flatfish (*Limanda ferruginea*) of the east coast of No. America that is a small but good food fish

rusty fig *n* : a fig (*Ficus rubiginosa*) having rusty hairs on twigs, buds, petioles, and lower leaf surfaces

rusty gold *n* : native gold having on it some coating which prevents it from amalgamating readily

rusty grain beetle *n* : a reddish brown cucujid beetle (*Cryptolestes ferrugineus*) that is destructive to stored grain products

rusty mottle *n* : a virus disease of cherry characterized by retarded blossom and leaf development in spring, followed by necrotic spotting and shot-holing and frequently by yellowish rusty chlorotic spotting of leaves and considerable defoliation

rusty plum aphid *n* : a common plant louse (*Hysteroneura setariae*) that attacks plum, sorghum, and some other plants esp. in southwestern U.S.

rusty tiger cat *n* : FLATHEADED CAT

rusty woodsia *n* : a common rock-inhabiting fern (*Woodsia ilvensis*) of the north temperate zone with rusty-brown stipes and lanceolate pinnate fronds and with the pinnae crowded and sessile

ruswut *var of* RUSOT

¹rut \ˈrət, *usu* -d·+V\ *n* -s [ME *rutte*, fr. MF *rut, ruit* noise, roar, rut, fr. LL *rugitus* roar, fr. L, past part. of *rugire* to roar — more at BRUIT] **1** : an annually recurrent state of sexual excitement in the male deer; *broadly* : sexual excitement in a mammal esp. when recurring periodically : ESTRUS, HEAT **2** : the period during which rut occurs in most sexually mature members of a natural population — often used with *the*

²rut \"\ *vi* **rutted; rutted; rutting; ruts** : to be in or enter into a state of rut

³rut \"\ *n* -s [perh. modif. of MF *route* way, route, track of an animal — more at ROUTE] **1** : a track worn by a wheel or by habitual passage of anything : a groove in which anything runs ⟨~*s* of the wagon trains are still to be seen —Veda Conner⟩; *broadly* : CHANNEL, FURROW ⟨~*s* of old stream beds⟩ ⟨~*s* in wrinkled skin⟩ **2** : a usual or fixed practice : a regular course; *esp* : an esp. monotonous routine method of action or procedure from which one is not easily stirred ⟨shock of death had pushed men's minds out of habitual ~*s* —Dixon Wecter⟩ ⟨fall into a conversational ~⟩

⁴rut \"\ *vt* **rutted; rutted; rutting; ruts** : to make a rut in : FURROW ⟨wagon trains were *rutting* the prairies —*Amer. Guide Series: Texas*⟩ ⟨the *rutted* snow underfoot —I.S.Cobb⟩ ⟨*rutted* his brow⟩

⁵rut \"\ *var of* ROTE

⁶rut *or* **ruth** \"\ *n* -s [Hindi *rath*, fr. Skt *ratha* wagon, chariot — more at ROLL] **1** : a carriage drawn by a pony or by oxen **2** : a cart for carrying images in a procession

ru·ta \ˈrüd·ə\ *n*, *cap* [NL, fr. L, rue — more at RUE (herb)] : a large genus (the type of the family Rutaceae) of Eurasian strong-scented herbs and undershrubs having yellow or greenish flowers and 4- to 5-toothed petals that are borne on the receptacle — see RUE

ru·tab \rüˈtäb\ *adj* [Ar] : of, relating to, or constituting the third of four recognized stages in the ripening of the date in which the tip becomes soft and loses the bright color of the previous stage — compare KHALAL, KIMRI, TAMAR

ru·ta·ba·ga \ˌrüd·əˌbāgə, -üt·-\ *n* -s [Sw dial. *rotabagge*, fr. *rot* root (fr. ON *rōt*) + *bagge* bag, ram — more at ROOT] : a turnip (*Brassica napobrassica*) commonly with a very large yellowish root that is used as food both for stock and for human beings — called also *swede, Swedish turnip, Russian turnip*

ru·ta·ce·ae \rüˈtāsēˌē\ *n pl*, *cap* [NL, fr. *Ruta*, type genus + *-aceae*] : a family of herbs, shrubs, and trees (order Geraniales) often glandular and strong scented and having flowers that are tetramerous or pentamerous with a compound ovary of four or five distinct or somewhat united carpels — **ru·ta·ceous** \-āshəs\ *adj*

ru·tae·car·pine *or* **ru·te·car·pine** \ˌrüd·ēˈkärˌpēn, -ˌpə̇n\ *n* -s [NL *rutaecarpa* (specific epithet of *Evodia rutaecarpa*, prob. fr. L *rutae* — gen. of *ruta* rue — + *-carpa*, fr. Gk *karpos* fruit) + E *-ine* — more at RUE (herb), HARVEST] : a light yellow crystalline alkaloid $C_{18}H_{13}N_3O$ found in the fruit of an Asiatic shrub or small tree (*Evodia rutaecarpa*)

rutch \ˈrůch\ *vi* -ED/-ING/-ES [G *rutschen* to slide, slither, fr. MHG *rützen, rütschen*] : to move with a crunching or shuffling noise ⟨no sound except the ~*ing* of heavily loaded bare feet on the paving stones —Talbot Mundy⟩

ru·te·li·an \rüˈtēlēən\ *n* -s [NL *Rutela* + E *-ian*] : a beetle of the family Rutelidae

ru·tel·id \rüˈteləd\ *adj* [NL *Rutelidae*] : of or relating to the Rutelidae

ru·tel·i·dae \rüˈteləˌdē\ *n pl*, *cap* [NL, fr. *Rutela*, type genus (irreg. fr. L *rutilus* red) + *-idae*; prob. akin to L *ruber* red — more at RED] : a family of vegetable-feeding often brilliantly colored scarabaeoid beetles — compare GOLDSMITH BEETLE

ru·te·mark \ˈrüd·əˌmärk\ *n* [Norw *rutemark*, fr. *rute* route + *mark*] **1** : a surface marking found in arctic regions, consisting of a row of loose stones enclosing a polygonal area, and usu. occurring in groups **2** : a mud or soil crack similar to a rute-mark in form

ruth \ˈrüth\ *n* -s [ME *rewthe, routhe, ruthe*, fr. *ruen, rewen* to rue — more at RUE] **1** : sorrow for the misery of another : PITY, MERCY, COMPASSION ⟨is there no pity, no relenting ~ —Robert Burns⟩ ⟨pounced on the snails without ~ and trampled them —Josephine Pinckney⟩ **2** : sorrow for one's own faults : SADNESS, DISTRESS, REMORSE ⟨I seek . . . not in ~, to curse and deny your truth —Matthew Arnold⟩ **3** : a reason or cause for ruth : a pitiful sight : a sad thing ⟨the ~ of a young man's dying in war —Bernard DeVoto⟩ **syn** see SYMPATHY

ruthen- *or* **ruthenio-** *or* **rutheno-** *comb form* [ISV, fr. NL *ruthenium*] : ruthenium : ruthenious ⟨*ruthenammines*⟩ ⟨*ruthenio*palladium⟩ ⟨*ruthenonitrite*⟩

ru·thene \rüˈthēn\ *n* -s *cap* [ML *Rutheni, Ruteni*, pl., Russians, modif. (influenced by L *Rutheni, Ruteni*, a people of Aquitanian Gaul) of Russ *rusin* — more at RUSSENE] : RUTHENIAN

ru·the·ni·an \-nēən\ *n* -s *cap* [*Ruthenia*, a part of the Ukraine + E *-an*] **1 a** : one of a branch of the Little Russians formerly chiefly of Galicia in Austria and the eastern part of Czechoslovakia and recently annexed to the Ukrainian S.S.R. along with the Ruthenian-speaking parts of former southeastern Poland **b** : the Ukrainian language as used in Galicia **2** : a member of a former Eastern Orthodox body entering into communion with Rome at the end of the 16th century and becoming the Uniate Church of the Little Russians

ru·then·ic \-thenik, -thēn-\ *adj* [*ruthen-* + *-ic*] : of, relating to, or derived from ruthenium — used esp. of compounds in which this element has a relatively high valence

ru·the·ni·ous \rüˈthēnēəs\ *also* **ru·the·nous** \ˈrüthənəs\ *adj* [*ruthenious* fr. NL *ruthenium* + E *-ous*; *ruthenous* fr. *ruthen-* + *-ous*] : of, relating to, or derived from ruthenium — used esp. of compounds in which this element has a relatively low valence

ru·the·ni·um \rüˈthēnēəm\ *n* -s [NL, fr. ML *Ruthenia* Russia, where it was first found + NL *-ium*] : a hard brittle grayish white polyvalent rare metallic element that is one of the platinum metals and resembles osmium but is more resistant to corrosion (as by oxidizing acids), that occurs in platinum ores esp. in iridosmine, and that is used chiefly in hardening platinum and palladium alloys — symbol *Ru*; see ELEMENT table

ruthenium oxide *n* : an oxide of ruthenium: as **a** : the dark blue crystalline dioxide RuO_2 formed by heating ruthenium in air **b** : the explosive volatile poisonous yellow crystalline tetroxide RuO_4 having a disagreeable odor

ruthenium red *n* : an ammoniated ruthenium chloride obtained as a brownish red powder and used as a microscopic stain and as a test esp. for pectin and gums

ruth·er·ford \ˈrəthə(r)fə(r)d\ *n* -s [after Baron Ernest *Rutherford* †1937 Brit. physicist] : a unit strength of a radioactive source corresponding to one million disintegrations per second

rutherford atom *n*, *usu cap R* [after Baron Ernest *Rutherford*] : the atom consisting of a small dense positively charged nucleus surrounded by planetary electrons

ruth·er·ford·ine \-fə(r)ˌdēn, -ˌdə̇n\ *n* -s [G *rutherfordin*, fr. Baron Ernest *Rutherford* + G *-in* -ine] : a mineral $(UO_2)(CO_3)$ consisting of uranyl carbonate in dense yellow masses of minute fibers

rutherford scattering *n*, *usu cap R* [after Baron Ernest *Rutherford*] : a scattering of alpha particles on passage through thin metal foils in an angular distribution that indicates a concentration of positive charge at the atomic nucleus

ruth·er·glen bug \ˈrəthə(r)ˌglen-\ *n*, *usu cap R* [fr. *Rutherglen*, Scotland] : a common Australian lygaeid bug (*Nysius vinitor*) that attacks many plants (as citrus, peach, plum, potato, and grapes)

ruth·ful \ˈrüthfəl\ *adj* [ME *rewtheful, routheful, rutheful*, fr. *rewthe, routhe, ruthe* pity + *-ful* — more at RUTH] **1** : full of ruth : PITIFUL, TENDER ⟨had never known a woman so ~ —Budd Schulberg⟩ **2** : full of sorrow : WOEFUL, RUEFUL ⟨a ~ smile —*Times Lit. Supp.*⟩ **3** : causing sorrow — **ruth·ful·ness** *n* -ES

ruth·ful·ly \-fəlē\ *adv* [ME *rewthfully, routhfully, ruthfully*, fr. *rewthful, routhful, ruthful*, adj.] : in a ruthful manner

ruth·less \ˈrüthlə̇s *sometimes* ˈrůth-\ *adj* [ME *rewtheles, routheles, rutheles*, fr. *rewthe, routhe, ruthe* pity, ruth + *-les* -less] : having no ruth : MERCILESS, PITILESS, RELENTLESS, UNSPARING ⟨act of savage, ~ ferocity —J.A.Froude⟩ ⟨savage and ~ energy in the shedding of innocent blood —Agnes Repplier⟩ ⟨~ enforcement of the game laws —G.B.Shaw⟩ ⟨~ disregard for the exhaustibility of the resources they exploited —J.K.Howard⟩ ⟨fearless and ~ honesty in expressing his opinions —F.W.Scott⟩

ruth·less·ly *adv* : in a ruthless manner : MERCILESSLY

ruth·less·ness *n* -ES : the quality or state of being ruthless

ruths *pl of* RUTH

ru·ti·do·sis \ˌrüd·əˈdōsə̇s\ *n*, *pl* **rutido·ses** \-ōˌsēz\ [NL, irreg. fr. Gk *rhytidōsis* wrinkling, fr. *rhytidoun* to wrinkle + *-sis* — more at RHYTIDOME] : a wrinkling esp. of the cornea

ru·ti·lant \ˈrüd·ᵊlənt\ *adj* [ME *rutilaunt*, fr. L *rutilant-, rutilans*, pres. part. of *rutilare* to make red, fr. *rutilus* red; akin to L *ruber* red — more at RED] : having a reddish glow : SHINING ⟨sun, which put a ~ sheen on their skin —Louis Adamic⟩

rutilate *vi* [L *rutilatus*, past part. of *rutilare*] *obs* : SHINE

ru·ti·lat·ed quartz \ˈrüd·ᵊlˌād·əd-\ *n* [*rutile* + *-ate* + *-ed*] : quartz characterized by the presence of enclosed rutile needles — compare SAGENITE

ru·tile \ˈrüˌtēl, -ˌtīl\ *n* -s [G *rutil*, fr. L *rutilus* red — more at RUTILANT] **1** : a mineral TiO_2 that consists of titanium dioxide, is trimorphous with anatase and brookite, is usu. of a reddish brown color but when deep red or black is sometimes cut into a gem, has a brilliant metallic or adamantine luster, occurs in tetragonal crystals which are commonly prismatic with striations and often geniculate as a result of twinning or occas. occurs massive, and usu. contains a little iron **2** : a synthetic gem in any of several colors and of the same composition as rutile that because of its dispersion and refractive power rivals the diamond in beauty

ru·tin \ˈrütᵊn\ *n* -s [ISV *rut-* (fr. NL *Ruta*) + *-in*] : a yellow crystalline flavonol glycoside $C_{27}H_{30}O_{16}$ that is found in rue leaves, tobacco leaves, buckwheat, flower buds of the Japanese pagoda tree, and other plants, that yields quercetin and rutinose on hydrolysis, and that is used chiefly for strengthening capillary blood vessels (as in cases of hypertension and radiation injury)

ru·tin·ose \-ᵊnˌōs\ *n* -s [ISV *rutin* + *-ose*] : a hygroscopic reducing disaccharide sugar $C_{12}H_{22}O_{10}$ that is obtained from rutin and yields D-glucose and L-rhamnose on hydrolysis

rut·i·o·don \ˈrəd·ēəˌdän\ *n*, *cap* [NL, irreg. fr. Gk *rhytis* wrinkle + NL *-odon* — more at RHYTIDOME] : a genus of subaquatic Triassic reptiles (order Thecodontia) with very elongate narrow skull and four or more rows of dermal scutes

rut·land beauty \ˈrətlənd-\ *n*, *usu cap R* [prob. fr. *Rutland* county, England] : HEDGE BINDWEED

rutland leather *n*, *usu cap R* [fr. *Rutland* county, England] : a high-grade flexible roan used esp. in bookbinding

rut·land·shire \-n(d)ˌshi(ə)r, -ˌshiə, -ˌshə(r)\ *or* **rutland** *adj*, *usu cap* [fr. *Rutlandshire* or *Rutland* county, Eng.] : of or from the county of Rutland, England : of the kind or style prevalent in Rutland

ruts *pl of* RUT, *pres 3d sing of* RUT

rutted *adj* [fr. past part. of ⁴*rut*] : having or marked by ruts ⟨~, odorous alleys and byways —Foster Fitz-Simons⟩

rut·tee *also* **rat·ti** \ˈrəd·ē\ *n* -s [Hindi *ratti*, fr. Skt *raktikā*, fr. *rakta* red, fr. *rajyati* it is dyed or colored — more at RAGA] : any of various Indian units of weight equal to around one or two grains troy

¹rut·ter \ˈrəd·ə(r)\ *n* -s [D *ruiter*, fr. MD *ruter, rutter, ruiter*, fr. OF *routier*, fr. *route* band, troop, route + *-ier* — more at ROUTE] *archaic* : a horseman or trooper orig. of German forces common in the 15th and 16th centuries

²rutter \"\ *n* -s [⁴*rut* + *-er*] **1** : one that ruts **2** : a plow for cutting ruts in a logging road for the runners of the sleds to run in

rut·ti·ness \ˈrəd·ēnə̇s, -ət|, |in-\ *n* -ES : the quality or state of being rutty

rutting *pres part of* RUT

rut·tish \|ish, |ēsh\ *adj* [²*rut* + *-ish*] : inclined to rut : LUSTFUL, SALACIOUS — **rut·tish·ly** *adv* — **rut·tish·ness** *n* -ES

1rut·tle \'rət°l, 'ru̇t°l\ *vi* -ED/-ING/-S [ME *rutelen;* akin to ME *ratelen* to rattle — more at RATTLE] *dial Brit* **:** RATTLE

2ruttle \"\ *n* -S *dial Brit* **:** RATTLE; *specif* **:** DEATH RATTLE

1rut·ty \'rəd·\|ē, -ət\|, \|i\ *adj* -ER/-EST [3*rut* + *-y*] **:** full of ruts ⟨lane had shriveled to a ~ track —Berton Roueché⟩

2rutty \"\ *adj* -ER/-EST [1*rut* + *-y*] **:** RUTTISH, LUSTFUL

ru·tu·bu·ri \ˌrüd·ə'bu̇rē\ *n* -S [MexSp, fr. Tarahumara] **:** a ritual round dance of the Mexican Tarahumara Indians

rut·u·li \'rəchəˌlī\ *n pl, cap* [L] **:** an ancient Italian people having their capital in 442 B.C. at Ardea and probably representing an early Indo-European people

rutway \'=ˌ=\ *n* [3*rut* + *way*] **:** a way for the passage and guidance of wheeled vehicles formed by stone blocks laid end to end in parallel lines

ru·vet·tus \rə'ved·əs\ *n, cap* [NL, fr. It *rovetto* escolar, dim. of *rovo* briar, bramble, fr. L *rubus* blackberry bush, bramble] **:** a genus of marine fishes (family Gempylidae) containing the escolars

RV *abbr* rendezvous

RVA *abbr, often not cap* reactive volt-ampere

RVSVP *abbr* [F *répondez vite s'il vous plaît*] please reply at once

rw *abbr* railway

RW *abbr* **1** radiological warfare **2** *often not cap* random widths **3** reverse work **4** right of way **5** right wing **6** right worshipful or worthy

rwa·la *or* **ru·wa·la** *or* **ru·wal·la** \rə'wälə\ *also* **ru·a·la** \rü'älə\ *n, pl* **rwala** *or* **rwalas** *or* **ruwala** *or* **ruwalas** *or* **ruwalla** *or* **ruwallas** *usu cap* **:** a member of a powerful Arabian people supposed to be descended from Abraham, regarded as the true pure Bedouins, and related to the Anezeh group of peoples

rwan·da \rə'wändə\ *adj, usu cap* [fr. *Rwanda*, central Africa] **:** of or from the country of Rwanda **:** of the kind or style prevalent in Rwanda

rwan·dan \-dən\ *n* -S *cap* [*Rwanda*, Africa + E *-an*] **:** a native or inhabitant of Rwanda — **rwandan** *adj, usu cap*

rwy *abbr* railway

Rx *n* -S [fr. *Rx*, symbol] **:** a medical prescription

Rx *symbol* **1** recipe **2** tens of rupees

-ry \rē, ri\ *n suffix* -ES [ME *-rie*, fr. OF, short for *-erie* -ery] **:** -ERY ⟨pilot*ry*⟩ ⟨wizard*ry*⟩ ⟨pheasant*ry*⟩ ⟨citizen*ry*⟩ ⟨musket*ry*⟩ ⟨ribald*ry*⟩ ⟨sloven*ry*⟩ ⟨prelat*ry*⟩ ⟨sergeant*ry*⟩ ⟨bandit*ry*⟩ ⟨peasant*ry*⟩

ry *abbr* **1** *often cap* railway **2** Rydberg

ry·al *also* **ri·al** \'rī(ə)l\ *n* -S [ME, fr. *ryal, rial* royal — more at RIAL] **1 :** an old English gold coin weighing 120 grains orig. equivalent to 10 shillings but later under Elizabeth to 15 shillings, first issued by Edward IV in place of the debased noble of Henry IV, and bearing the design of the noble with a rose added — called also *rose noble* **2 :** one of two Scottish coins: **a :** a gold coin equivalent to 60 shillings or 3 pounds issued by Mary Queen of Scots **b :** a silver coin worth 30 shillings issued by Mary and James VI

ry·a·nia \rī'ānēə\ *n* -S [NL *Ryania* (genus name of *Ryania speciosa*, the shrub from which it is made), fr. John *Ryan*, 18th cent. Brit. physician + NL *-ia*] **1 :** an insecticide made of a mixture of alkaloids from the ground stems of a tropical So. American shrub (*Patrisia pyrifera* syn. *Ryania speciosa*) and used esp. against the European corn borer **2 :** the plant that yields ryania

ry·an·o·dine \rī'anəˌdēn, -ˌdən\ *n* -S [irreg. fr. NL *Ryania* (genus name of *Ryania speciosa*) + E *-ine*] **:** a crystalline insecticidal alkaloid $C_{25}H_{35}NO_9$ that is toxic to mammals and is obtained from the root and stem of the ryania

ryd·berg \'ridˌbərg\ *n* -S *usu cap* [after Johannes R. *Rydberg* †1919 Swedish physicist] **:** the Rydberg constant esp. when expressed in energy terms with maximum possible value of about 2.179×10^{-11} ergs

rydberg constant *or* **rydberg unit** *n, usu cap R* [after Johannes R. *Rydberg*] **:** a wave number characteristic of the atomic spectrum of each element equal to the constant factor in the wave-number formula for all the spectral series of the elements and having a value from 109,678 cm^{-1} for hydrogen to 109,737 cm^{-1} for the heaviest elements

ry·der *or* **rij·der** \'rīdə(r)\ *n* -S [*ryder* fr. ME *rydar*, fr. MD *rider*, fr. *riden* to ride + *-er; rijder* fr. D, fr. MD *rider;* akin to OHG *rītan* to ride — more at RIDE] **:** an old gold coin of the Netherlands bearing a horseman on the obverse

1rye \'rī\ *n* -S [ME, fr. OE *ryge;* akin to OFris *rogga* rye, OS *roggo*, OHG *rocko*, ON *rugr*, Russ *rozh'*, Lith *rugỹs*] **1 :** a hardy annual cereal grass (*Secale cereale*) that has loose spikes with an articulate rachis and long-awned lemmas and is widely cultivated esp. in northern continental Europe where its grain is the chief ingredient of black bread and in No. America where it is used esp. as a cover crop and for soil improvement and frequently for forage **2 :** the seeds of rye used for bread flour, whiskey manufacture, feed for poultry and other farm animals, and esp. formerly in the roasted state a coffee substitute **3 :** RYE WHISKEY **4 :** RYE BREAD ⟨ham on ~⟩

2rye \"\ *n* -S [Romany *rai*, fr. Skt *rājan* king — more at ROYAL] **:** GENTLEMAN; *specif* **:** a gypsy gentleman

rye and indian *n, usu cap I* **:** bread made of rye flour and corn meal and in colonial days often baked in a pot or a brick oven

rye bread *n* **:** any bread made wholly or in part from rye flour (as black bread, pumpernickel, knäckebröd, and a light loaf usu. containing caraway seed)

ryecorn \'=ˌ=\ *n, Austral* **:** 1RYE 1

ryegrass \'=ˌ=\ *n* **1 :** any of several grasses of the genus *Lolium; esp* **:** PERENNIAL RYEGRASS — see ITALIAN RYEGRASS **2 :** LYME GRASS — see GIANT RYEGRASS

rye·land \'rīlənd\ *n* [fr. *Ryelands*, district and hamlet in Herefordshire, Eng.] **1** *usu cap* **:** an old English breed of hardy hornless white-faced sheep producing high quality wool and quick-maturing lambs of good size **2** -S *often cap* **:** an animal of the Ryeland breed

rye rust *n* **:** any of the several rusts of the genus *Puccinia* attacking rye

rye smut *n* **:** a smut (as the stem smut) attacking rye

rye waltz *n* **:** a ballroom dance with a waltz step alternately in duple and in triple time

rye whiskey *n* **:** a whiskey distilled from rye or from a mixture of rye and malt

ryke \'rēk\ *Scot var of* REACH

ryme \'rīm\ *n* -S [obs. E *ryme, rime* rim, fr. ME *rime* — more at RIM] *archaic* **:** the surface of water ⟨the gate was backed against the ~ —John Masefield⟩

ryn·chops \'riŋˌkäps\ *n, cap* [NL, irreg. fr. *rhynch-* + *-ops*] **:** a genus of birds consisting of the skimmers and constituting a family of the order Charadriiformes

ryn·chos·po·ra \riŋ'käspərə\ [NL, irreg. fr. *rhynch-* + *-spora*] *syn of* RHYNCHOSPORA

ryn·chos·po·rous \-rəs\ *adj* [irreg. fr. *rhynch-* + *-sporous*] **:** having a beaked fruit or seed

rynd *var of* RIND

ry·o·bu \rē'ō(ˌ)bü\ *or* **ryobu shinto** *n, cap R&S* [Jap *ryō bu*, lit., two parts] **:** a Shinto sect fostering a mixture of Shinto and Buddhism and being greatly popular in Japan between the 9th and 18th centuries

ry·ot *or* **rai·yat** \'rīət\ *n* -S [Hindi *raiyat, ra'īyat*, fr. Per, fr. Ar *ra'īyah* flock, herd] **:** a peasant, tenant farmer, or cultivator of the soil in India

1ry·ot·war \¦rīə·¦twär, -ət·¦w-\ *or* **ry·ot·wa·ri** *or* **ry·ot·wa·ry** *or* **rai·yat·wa·ri** \-rē\ *n, pl* **ryotwars** *or* **ryotwaris** *or* **ryotwaries** *or* **raiyatwaris** [Hindi *raiyatwār, raiyatwārī* by or with individual cultivators, fr. *raiyat, ra'īyat*] **:** a system of collecting land rent or taxes in which the government settlement is made directly with the ryots

2ryotwar \"\ *or* **ryotwari** *or* **ryotwary** *or* **raiyatwari** \"\ *adj* [Hindi *raiyatwār, raiyatwārī*] **:** of or relating to the ryotwar system

ry·pe \'rüepə, 'rīp\ *n, pl* **rype** *or* **rypes** [Dan & Norw; akin to ON *rjūpa* ptarmigan, Latvian *rubenis* moorhen] **:** PTARMIGAN

1ryt·i·na \'rit°nə\ [NL, irreg. fr. *rhyt-* + *-ina*] *syn of* HYDRODAMALIS

2rytina \"\ *n* -S [NL 1*Rytina*] **:** STELLER'S SEA COW

ryu·kyu \rē'(y)ü(ˌ)kyü, rə'-\ *n, usu cap* [fr. the *Ryukyu* islands, southwest of Japan] **:** the language of the Ryukyuan people that is related to Japanese

ryu·kyu·an \-kyüən\ *n* -S *usu cap* [*Ryukyu* islands + E *-an*] **1 :** the people of the Ryukyu islands **2 :** a member of the Ryukyuan people

¹s \'es\ *n, pl* **s's** *or* **ss** \'esəz\ *often cap, often attrib* **1 a :** the 19th letter of the English alphabet **b :** an instance of this letter printed, written, or otherwise represented — see LONG S **c :** a speech counterpart of orthographic *s* (as *s* in *sister, basin,* or French *sang*) **2 :** a printer's type, a stamp, or some other instrument for reproducing the letter *s* **3 :** someone or something arbitrarily or conveniently designated *s* esp. as the 18th or when j is used for the 10th the 19th in order or class **4 a** [*satisfactory*] **:** a grade assigned by a teacher or examiner rating a student's work as satisfactory **b :** one graded or rated with an s **5 :** something having the shape of the letter S ⟨an *S* curve in the road⟩

²s *abbr, often cap* **1** sabbath **2** sacral **3** sacred **4** saeculum **5** saint **6** sand **7** satang **8** scalar **9** schilling **10** school **11** science **12** scribe **13** seaman **14** search **15** seat **16** second; secondary **17** secretary **18** section **19** see **20** semi **21** senate **22** September **23** [L *sepultus*] buried **24** series **25** set **26** sharp **27** shilling **28** ship **29** side **30** sign; signed **31** [L *signa*] write **32** signature **33** signor **34** silicate **35** silver **36** silversmith **37** simplex **38** [L *sine*] without **39** sine **40** single **41** singular **42** [L *sinister*] left **43** sink **44** sire **45** slip **46** slow **47** small **48** smooth **49** snow **50** socialist **51** society **52** [L *socius* or *sodalis*] fellow **53** soft **54** sol **55** solid **56** solidus **57** solo **58** solubility **59** son **60** soprano **61** sou **62** south; southerly; southern **63** special **64** species **65** speed **66** sphere; spherical **67** staff **68** standard **69** station **70** statute **71** steamer **72** steel **73** stem **74** stere **75** stock **76** straight **77** subito **78** subject **79** submarine **80** substantive **81** succeeded **82** sucre **83** sun **84** superb **85** superior **86** surfaced **87** surplus **88** survey **89** switch **90** symmetrical

³s *symbol, cap* **1** sulfur **2** entropy **3** the subject of a proposition in logic

¹s- — see SYM-

²s- \'sekən,derē; ¦es\ *abbr, usu ital* secondary — esp. in names of organic radicals ⟨*s*-butyl⟩

¹-s \s *after a voiceless consonant sound,* z *after a voiced consonant sound or a vowel sound*\ *n pl suffix* [ME *-es, -s,* fr. OE *-as,* nom. & acc. pl. ending of some masc. nouns; akin to OS *-os,* nom. & acc. pl. ending of some masc. nouns, and prob. to Skt (Vedic) *-āsas,* nom. pl. ending of some masc. nouns] **1 a** — used to form the plural of most nouns that do not end in *s, z, sh, ch,* or postconsonantal *y* ⟨head*s*⟩ ⟨book*s*⟩ ⟨boy*s*⟩ ⟨belief*s*⟩ ⟨parade*s*⟩ ⟨state*s*⟩ — compare ¹-ES 1 **b** — used to form the plural of proper nouns that end in postconsonantal *y* ⟨Italy*s*⟩ ⟨Mary*s*⟩ **c** — used to form the plural of abbreviations, numbers, letters, and symbols used as nouns ⟨MC*s*⟩ ⟨4*s*⟩ ⟨#*s*⟩ and often preceded by an apostrophe ⟨B'*s*⟩ ⟨p'*s*⟩ ⟨&'*s*⟩ **2** [ME *-es, -s,* pl. ending of nouns, fr. *-es, -s,* gen. sing. ending of nouns (functioning adverbially, as in *nedes* needs, *alweys* always), fr. OE *-es*] — used to form plural nouns with adverbial function denoting usual or repeated action or state ⟨always at home Sunday*s*⟩ ⟨can reach him there mealtime*s*⟩ ⟨morning*s* he stops by the newsstand⟩ — compare ¹-ES 2

²-s \"\ *n suffix* — used to form nicknames expressing affection or familiarity ⟨Mom*s*⟩ ⟨Dad*s*⟩ or designating a characteristic feature or activity of the person named ⟨Fat*s*⟩ ⟨Freckle*s*⟩ ⟨Cuddle*s*⟩ ⟨Smile*s*⟩ or an object characteristically associated with the person named ⟨Boot*s*⟩ ⟨Spark*s*⟩

³-s \"\ *vb suffix* [ME (Northern & North Midland dial.) *-es,* fr. OE (Northumbrian dial.) *-es, -as,* prob. fr. *-es, -as,* 2d pers. sing. pres. indic. ending — more at -EST] **1** — used to form the third person singular present of most verbs that do not end in *s, z, sh, ch,* or postconsonantal *y* ⟨fall*s*⟩ ⟨take*s*⟩ ⟨play*s*⟩ — compare ²-ES 1 **2** *substand* — used to form the historical present first person singular ⟨then I say*s* to him⟩ — compare ²-ES 2

-'s \s *after voiceless consonant sounds other than* s, sh, ch; *z after vowel sounds or voiced consonant sounds other than* z, zh, j; əz *after* s, sh, ch, z, zh, j\ *n suffix or pron suffix* [ME *-s, -es,* gen. sing. ending of nouns, fr. OE *-es,* gen. sing. ending of some masc. & neut. nouns; akin to OHG *-es,* gen. sing. ending of some masc. & neut. nouns, ON *-s,* Goth *-is,* Gk *-ou,* Gk (Homeric) *-oo, -oio,* Skt *-asya*] — used to form the possessive of singular nouns ⟨boy'*s*⟩, of plural nouns not ending in *s* ⟨children'*s*⟩, of some pronouns ⟨anyone'*s*⟩, and of word groups functioning as nouns ⟨the man in the corner'*s* hat⟩ or pronouns ⟨someone else'*s*⟩

-s' *like* ¹-s\ *n pl suffix* [ME *-s,* alter. of *-es* — more at -ES'] — used to form the plural possessive of most nouns that do not end in *s, z, sh,* or postconsonantal *y* ⟨girl*s'*⟩ ⟨worker*s'*⟩ ⟨voter*s'*⟩

¹'s *like* -'s\ *vb* [contr. of *is, has, does*] **1 :** IS ⟨she'*s* here⟩ **2 :** HAS ⟨he'*s* seen them⟩ **3 :** DOES ⟨what'*s* he want?⟩ ⟨what'*s* it mean?⟩

²'s \s\ *pron* [by contr.] **:** US — used with *let* ⟨let'*s*⟩

³'s *like* -'s\ *adj* [by contr.] *archaic* **:** HIS ⟨I cut off'*s* head —Shak.⟩

⁴'s *before a vowel sound:* z; *before a consonant sound that can follow word-initial s in English:* s; *before a voiced consonant that does not follow word-initial s:* z *or (with alteration of the voiced to the corresponding voiceless consonant)* s\ *n* [contr. of *God's,* gen. of *God*] **:** God's — often used in mild oaths ⟨'*s*blood⟩ ⟨'*s*death⟩

⁵'s \z\ *conj* [by contr.] *dial* **:** AS ⟨so'*s* you can come⟩

⁶'s *or* **'se** *also* **s'** \s\ *vb* [contr. of *sall*] *dial Brit* **:** SHALL ⟨I'*se* repeat each poor man's prayer —Robert Burns⟩

sa \(ˈ)sä, ˌsə\ *dial var of* SO

sa *abbr* sable

SA *abbr* **1** salt added **2** seaman apprentice **3** *often not cap* [L *secundum artem*] according to art **4** semiannual **5** semiautomatic **6** sex appeal **7** *often not cap* [L *sine anno*] without year **8** small arms **9** [F] société anonyme **10** *often not cap* [L *sub anno*] under the year **11** subject to approval

SAA *abbr* small arms ammunition

saa·di·an \'sädēən\ *n* -s *usu cap* [*Saadi,* 16th and 17th cent. dynasty of sherifs in Morocco + E *-an*] **:** a member of a dynasty of sherifs of Arab descent ruling Morocco between 1550 and 1688 and noted for their splendid tombs in Marrakech

¹saa·nen \'sänən, 'zä-\ *n* [fr. *Saanen,* locality in southwest Switzerland] **1** *usu cap* **:** a Swiss breed of white or light-colored usu. hornless short-haired dairy goats **2** -s *often cap* **:** an animal of the Saanen breed

²saanen \"\ *also* **saanen cheese** *n* -s *often cap* **:** a cheese similar to Emmenthal cheese that is cooked longer, requires three to nine years to cure, and keeps longer

saar·land·er \'s|är,landər, 'z|, |ä,landə(r, -laan-\ *n* -s *cap* [G *saarländer,* fr. *Saarland,* coal-producing and industrial region in southwest Germany + G *-er*] **:** a native or inhabitant of Saarland

sab *abbr, often cap* sabbath

SAB *abbr* **1** science advisory board **2** soprano, alto, baritone

sa·ba \sə'bä\ *n* -s [Tag *sabá*] **1 :** a common cooking banana (*Musa sapientum* var. *compressa*) in the Philippines **2 :** a fine textile from the fiber of the saba plant

sab·a·dil·la \ˌsabə'dilə, -'dē(y)ə\ *also* **ceb·a·dil·la** \ˌseb-\ *n* -s [Sp *cebadilla,* dim. of *cebada* barley, fr. *cebo* feed, fr. L *cibus* food — more at CIBARIAL] **1 :** a Mexican plant (*Schoenocaulon officinale*) of the family Liliaceae — called also *cevadilla* **2 :** the seeds of the sabadilla plant used as a source of veratrine and in the preparation of an insecticide used esp. for stock and for garden crops

sab·a·dine \'sabə,dēn, -ˌdən\ *n* -s [ISV *sabad-* (fr. NL *Sabadilla* — syn. of *Schoenocaulon* — fr. E *sabadilla*) + *-ine*] **:** a crystalline alkaloid $C_{29}H_{51}NO_8$ that is found in sabadilla seeds

sa·bad·i·nine \sə'badᵊn,ēn, -ᵊnən\ *n* -s [ISV *sabadine* + *-ine*] **:** CEVINE

¹sa·bae·an *or* **sa·be·an** \sə'bēən\ *adj, usu cap* [L *sabaeus* Sabaean (fr. Gk *sabaios,* fr. *Saba* Sheba, ancient kingdom in southwestern Arabia, fr. Ar *Saba'*) + E *-an*] **1 :** of or relating to the ancient people and kingdom of Saba flourishing in southwestern Arabia from about 950 to 115 B.C., attaining their prime about the middle of the first millennium B.C., and anciently renowned for wealth and trade (as in spices) — compare HIMYARITE, MINAEAN **2 :** of or relating to the language and alphabet of the Sabaeans

²sabaean *or* **sabean** \"\ *n* -s **1** *cap* **a :** a native or inhabitant of Saba in southern Arabia **b :** the Semitic language of the Sabaean people that is a form of South Arabic **2** *usu cap* **:** MANDAEAN

sa·bai grass \sə'bī-\ *n* [Hindi *sabai*] **:** BHABAR 1

sabakha *var of* SEBKHA

sa·bal \'sā,bal\ *n* [NL] **1** *cap* **:** a small genus of American dwarf fan palms having creeping horizontal or subterranean stems and long petioled leaves with obscure or rudimentary midribs — see CABBAGE PALMETTO **2** -s **:** the partly dried ripe fruit of the saw palmetto used as a diuretic

sa·ba·lo \'sabə,lō\ *n* -s [AmerSp *sábalo,* fr. Sp, shad, perh. of Celt origin; akin to OIr *sam* summer — more at SUMMER] **1 :** TARPON **2** *also* **sa·ba·lo·te** \ˌsabə'lōd·ē\ [*sabalo* fr. AmerSp *sábalo,* fr. Sp, shad; *sabalote* fr. AmerSp, fr. *sábalo*] **:** MILKFISH 1

sabal palmetto *n* **:** CABBAGE PALMETTO

sa·ba·na \sə'b|änə, -'v|, |a-\ *n* -s [Sp — more at SAVANNA] **:** SAVANNA 2

sa·ba·thé's cycle \ˌsabə¦tāz-\ *n, usu cap S* [prob. fr. the name *Sabathé*] **:** a cycle of operations in internal-combustion engines in which the combustion takes place partly explosively and partly at constant pressure and which resembles partly the Otto cycle and partly the Diesel cycle

sabaton *var of* SABBATON

sa·ba·yon \sȧbȧyōⁿ\ *n, pl* **sabayons** \"\ [F, modif. of It *zabaione* zabaglione, perh. of Illyrian origin; akin to the source of LL *sabaia,* an Illyrian drink made from grain; akin to OE *sæp* sap — more at SAP] **:** ZABAGLIONE

sab·bat \'sabət\ *n* -s *often cap* [F, lit., sabbath, fr. L *sabbatum* — more at SABBATH] **:** a midnight assembly of witches and sorcerers held in medieval and Renaissance times at intervals (as on Walpurgis Night, Halloween) to renew allegiance to the devil sometimes present in a form like a goat and to celebrate rites (as the Black Mass) and orgies — called also *sabbath, witches' sabbath*

¹sab·ba·tar·i·an \ˌsabə'terēən, -ta(a)r-,-tär-\ *n* -s *often cap* [L *sabbatarius,* n., sabbatarian (fr. *sabbatum* sabbath + *-arius* -ary) + E *-an,* n. suffix] **1 :** one who regards and keeps the seventh day of the week as holy in conformity with the letter of the decalogue **2 :** one who favors strict observance of the sabbath ⟨were strict *Sabbatarians,* would not even read Sunday papers —*Time*⟩ **3 :** a member of a non-Jewish religious sect originating in Russia distinguished by observance of Jewish rites and festivals including Saturday as the day of rest

²sabbatarian \¦==¦===\ *adj, often cap* [LL *sabbatarius,* adj., sabbatarian (fr. L *sabbatum* sabbath + *-arius* -ary) + E *-an,* adj. suffix] **1 :** of or relating to the sabbath or to sabbatarians ⟨~ regulations⟩ **2 :** rigidly strict in the manner advocated by sabbatarians ⟨a soberer crowd . . . almost ~ in its decorousness —Robert Lynd⟩

sab·ba·tar·i·an·ism \ˌ==¦==ə,nizəm\ *n* -s *often cap* **:** the principles and practices of sabbatarians; *esp* **:** the puritanical suppression on Sunday of all avoidable work and enjoyment as an enforcement of pious devotion and sobriety

sab·bath \'sabəth\ *n* -s *often attrib* [ME *sabath, sabat,* fr. OF *sabat, sabbat* & OE *sabat,* fr. L *sabbatum,* fr. Gk *sabbaton,* fr. Heb *shabbāth,* fr. *shābath* to rest] **1** *often cap* **a** (1) *also* **sabbath day** [ME *sabat day,* fr. *sabat* sabbath + *day*] **:** the day of rest and solemn assembly observed as sacred to God by Jews and some Christian churches on the seventh day of the week from sunset Friday until sunset Saturday ⟨six days thou shalt labor and do all thy work: but the seventh day is the ~ of the Lord thy God; in it thou shalt not do any work —Deut 5:13–14 (AV)⟩ (2) **:** some other Scriptural period (as the sabbatical year) of solemn rest or cessation from usual activity ⟨the tenth day of this seventh month is the day of atonement; it shall be for you . . . a ~ of solemn rest —Lev 23:27–32 (RSV)⟩ ⟨six years shall you sow in your field . . . but in the seventh year there shall be a ~ of solemn rest for the land —Lev 25:3–4 (RSV)⟩ **b** *also* **sabbath day :** the day of rest and public worship observed on Sunday by most Christian churches in commemoration of the resurrection of Christ on the first day of the week; *specif* **:** the Lord's Day observed strictly as a day of solemn rest and devotion continuing the Old Testament Sabbath **c :** the day of the week regularly set aside by some other religion for public observances ⟨although it was Friday, the Moslem *Sabbath,* people were at work —Francis Ofner⟩ **2** *often cap* **:** a time of rest or repose **:** a cessation of effort, pain, or care **3** *sometimes cap* **:** SABBAT

sab·bath·ar·i·an \ˌsabə'therēən\ *n* -s *often cap* [by alter. (influence of *sabbath*)] **:** SABBATARIAN

sabbath-day house *n, often cap S* **:** a house formerly built (as in colonial Connecticut) near a church and heated on winter Sundays as a place for worshipers living at a distance to warm themselves and eat between morning and afternoon services in an unheated church

sabbath-day's journey *n, often cap S* **:** a distance of 2000 cubits that under rabbinic law a Jew might travel on the sabbath from the walled limits of a town or city

sab·bath·less \'sabəthləs\ *adj, often cap* **:** having no sabbath ⟨*Sabbathless* Satan —Charles Lamb⟩

¹sab·bath·ly \-thlē\ *adv, often cap* [*sabbath* + *-ly,* adv. suffix] **:** every sabbath

²sabbathly \"\ *adj, often cap* [*sabbath* + *-ly,* adj. suffix] **:** occurring every sabbath

sabbath school *n, often cap 1st S* **:** a school held on the sabbath for purposes of religious education; *also* **:** the pupils or teachers and pupils of such a school

sab·ba·tia \sə'bash(ē)ə, -bad·ēə\ *n* [NL, fr. Liberatus *Sabbati,* 18th cent. Ital. botanist + NL *-ia*] **1** *cap* **:** a genus of smooth slender No. American herbs (family Gentianaceae) with opposite leaves and showy white or rose-pink cymose flowers — see MARSH PINK **2** -s **:** any plant of the genus *Sabbatia* — see AMERICAN CENTAURY

¹sab·ba·tian \sə'bash(ē)ən\ *n* -s *usu cap* [*Sabbatius,* 4th cent. A.D. Novatian presbyter + E *-an*] **:** one of the followers of the Novatian presbyter Sabbatius who held that Easter and the feast of the Passover should be kept at the same time by Christians and Jews

²sab·ba·ti·an \ˌsabə'tīən\ *or* **shab·ba·thai·an** *or* **shab·be·thai·an** \ˌshabə'tīən\ *n* -s *usu cap* [*sabbatian* fr. *Sabbatius* (latinized form of the name of Sabbatai Zebi †1676 Hebrew mystic) + E *-an; shabbathaian, shabbethaian* fr. *Shabbethai* (Sabbatai Zebi) + E *-an*] **:** a follower of the cabalist Sabbatai Zebi who proclaimed himself the Messiah and was accepted as such by many Jews — compare DÖNMEH

¹sab·bat·i·cal \sə'bad·ə̇kəl, -atǀ, ǀēk-\ *or* **sab·bat·ic** \ǀik, ǀēk\ *adj* [*sabbatical* fr. LL *sabbaticus* sabbatical (fr. Gk *sabbatikos,* fr. *sabbaton* sabbath + *-ikos* -ic) + E *-al; sabbatic* fr. LL *sabbaticus*] **1** *sometimes cap* **:** of, relating to, or suited to the sabbath ⟨~ laws⟩ ⟨~ peace⟩ **2 :** having the character of a recurring period of rest or renewal

²sabbatical \"\ *n* -s **:** SABBATICAL YEAR 2 **:** LEAVE ⟨studied in Europe on his ~⟩

sabbatical year *n* **1** *often cap S* **:** a year of rest for the land observed every seventh year in ancient Judea by allowing the fields and vineyards to lie without tilling, sowing, pruning, or reaping from autumn to autumn in accordance with a Levitical commandment — compare JUBILEE **2** *or* **sabbatical leave :** a leave with full or half pay granted (as every seventh year) to one holding an administrative or professional position (as college professor) for rest, travel, or research

sab·ba·tine \'sabə,tīn, -tēn\ *adj, usu cap* [ML *sabbatinus* of the sabbath, fr. L *sabbatum* sabbath + *-inus* -ine] **:** of, relating to, or constituting an indulgence granted the Carmelite order and its confraternities based orig. on a spurious bull of 1322 promising liberation from Purgatory the Saturday after death, ratified in modified form by later popes, and promising the intercession of the Virgin Mary to those observing given conditions ⟨the *Sabbatine* privilege⟩

sab·ba·tism \-,tizəm\ *n* -s [LL *sabbatismus* celebration of the sabbath, fr. Gk *sabbatismos,* fr. *sabbatizein* to keep the sabbath] **:** the strict observance of the sabbath

sab·ba·ti·za·tion \ˌsabəd·ə̇'zāshən, -bə,tī'z-\ *n* -s *often cap* [ML *sabbatization-, sabbatizatio,* fr. LL *sabbatizatus* (past part. of *sabbatizare*) + L *-ion-, -io* -ion] **:** the act or process of sabbatizing

sab·ba·tize \'sabə,tīz\ *vb* -ED/-ING/-S *sometimes cap* [ME *sabatisen,* fr. LL *sabbatizare,* fr. Gk *sabbatizein,* fr. *sabbaton* sabbath + *-izein* -ize — more at SABBATH] *vi* **:** to keep the sabbath ~ *vt* **:** to keep as the sabbath

sab·ba·ton *or* **sab·a·ton** \'sabə,tän\ *n* -s [ME *sabaton, sabatoun,* fr. OProv *sabato, sabaton,* fr. *sabata* shoe — more at SABOT] **:** a piece of armor covering the foot; *specif* **:** a solleret broad and blunted at the toes

sabbats *pl of* SABBAT

sab·be·ka \'sabəkə\ *n* -s [Aram *śabbĕkhā*] **:** TRIGON

sab-cat \'sab,=\ *n* [*sabotage* + *cat*] **:** SABOTEUR

¹sa·be \'savē, -vi\ *vb* **sabed; sabed; sabeing; sabes** [Sp, 2nd pers. (formal) & 3d pers. sing. pres. indic. of *saber* to know — more at SAVVY] **:** SAVVY

²sabe \"\ *n* -s **:** SAVVY

sabean *usu cap, var of* SABAEAN

sa·bel·la \sə'belə\ *n* [NL, fr. L *sabulum* sand + NL *-ella* — more at SAND] **1** *cap* **:** a genus (the type of the family Sabellidae) of tube-dwelling marine polychaete worms with the prostomial palps modified into semicircular plumose gills **2** -s **:** any worm of the genus *Sabella* — **sa·bel·li·form** \-lə,fȯrm\ *adj* — **sabel·loid** \sə'be,lȯid, 'sabə,l-\ *adj or n*

sab·el·lar·ia \ˌsabə'la(a)rēə\ *n, cap* [NL, prob. fr. *Sabella* + *-aria*] **:** a genus (the type of the family Sabellariidae) of tube-dwelling marine worms with greatly developed peristome and the posterior end of the body tapering like a tail

¹sab·el·lar·i·id \¦==¦=rēəd\ *adj* [NL *Sabellariidae*] **:** of or relating to the Sabellariidae

²sabellariid \"\ *n* -s [NL *Sabellariidae*] **:** a worm of the family Sabellariidae

sab·el·la·ri·idae \ˌsabələ'rīə,dē, sə,bel-\ *n pl, cap* [NL, fr. *Sabellaria,* type genus + *-idae*] **:** a family of typically colonial and sometimes reef-building polychaete worms — see SABELLARIA

¹sa·bel·li·an \sə'belēən\ *n* -s *usu cap* [ME, fr. LL *sabellianus,* fr. *Sabellius,* 3d cent. A.D. Roman Christian prelate and theologian + L *-anus* -an] **:** a follower of Sabellius, a leader of the Modalistic Monarchians in the 3d century who held in general that there is one divine essence and that the Father, the Logos, and the Holy Spirit are three different manifestations of the one God; *also* **:** a Modalistic Monarchian

²sabellian \"\ *adj, usu cap* **1 :** of or relating to the Sabellians **2 :** of or adhering to Modalistic Monarchianism

³sabellian \"\ *n* -s *cap* [L *Sabellus,* n., Sabine + E *-an,* n. suffix] **1 :** a member of one of a group of early Italian peoples comprising Sabines, Samnites, and others **2 :** one or all of a number of poorly known languages or dialects of ancient central Italy that are presumably closely related to Oscan and Umbrian

⁴sabellian \"\ *adj, usu cap* [L *Sabellus,* n., Sabine + E *-an,* adj. suffix] **:** of, relating to, or forming the Sabellians or their languages or dialects

sa·bel·li·an·ism \sə'belēə,nizəm\ *n* -s *usu cap* **:** the theological doctrines of the Sabellians **:** MODALISTIC MONARCHIANISM — compare PATRIPASSIANISM

sa·bel·lic \-lik\ *n* -s *cap* [L *sabellicus* of the Sabines, fr. *Sabellus,* n., Sabine + *-icus* -ic] **:** ³SABELLIAN

¹sa·bel·lid \sə'beləd\ *adj* [NL *Sabellidae,* family of worms, fr. *Sabella,* type genus + *-idae*] **:** of or relating to the genus *Sabella* or the family Sabellidae

²sabellid \"\ *n* -s [NL *Sabellidae*] **:** a worm of the genus *Sabella* or the family Sabellidae

¹sa·ber *or* **sa·bre** \'sābə(r)\ *n* -s [F *sabre,* modif. of G dial.

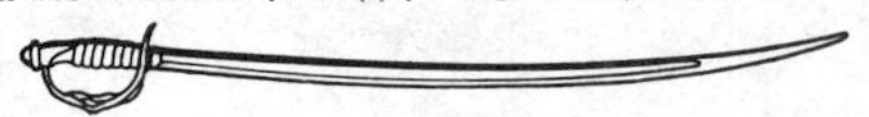

saber 1

sabel, fr. MHG *sabel, sebel,* of Slav origin; akin to Russ *sablya* saber, Pol *szabla*] **1 :** a heavy military sword with a usu. curved blade having a cutting edge, a thick back, and a guard for the hand and used esp. by cavalry men **2 a :** a light fencing or dueling sword with an arc-shaped guard and tapering flexible blade of fluted H section that is not more than 41⅜ inches long and has one full cutting edge and an 8-inch cutting edge on the back at the tip — compare ÉPÉE, FOIL **b :** the art or practice of fencing with the saber that limits the target to the trunk and counts hits by cut as well as thrust

²saber *or* **sabre** \"\ *vt* **sabered** *or* **sabred; sabered** *or* **sabred; sabering** *or* **sabring** \-b(ə)riŋ\ **sabers** *or* **sabres :** to strike, cut, or kill with a saber

saberbill \'==,=\ *n* **1 :** CURLEW **2 :** a So. American dendrocolaptine bird of the genus *Campylorhamphus* having a long decurved bill

saber fish *n* **:** CUTLASS FISH

saber leg *n* **:** an incurved chair leg square in cross section — see LEG illustration

saber-legged \¦==¦=(=)\ *adj* **:** being sickle-hocked

saber rattling *n* **:** an ostentatious, offensive, or threatening display of military power or prowess

saber saw *n* **:** a portable electric jigsaw

saber shin *n* **:** a tibia with a pronounced anterior convexity that occurs in congenital syphilis

sabertooth \'==,=\ *n* -s **:** SABER-TOOTHED TIGER

saber-toothed \¦==¦=\ *adj* **:** having long trenchant canine teeth **:** MACHAIRODONT

saber-toothed tiger *n* **1 :** any of numerous extinct cats widely distributed in the Oligocene through the Pleistocene of both the Old and New World, differing from the typical cats chiefly in the extreme development of the upper canines into curved swordlike piercing or slashing weapons and in enlargement of the gape with corresponding muscular and skeletal changes, and constituting a distinct feline subfamily that reaches its climax in the New World Pleistocene genus *Smilodon* **2 :** any of various chiefly No. American and Miocene or Pliocene cats of *Nimravus* and related genera that resemble but are less specialized than the typical saber-toothed tigers — called also *false saber-toothed tiger*

saberwing \'==,=\ *n* **:** any of various So. American hummingbirds of the genera *Campylopterus* and *Eupetomena* in which the outer primaries are strongly falcate

sabes *pres 3d sing of* SABE, *pl of* SABE

sa·bha \sə'bä\ *n* -s [Hindi *sabhā,* fr. Skt — more at SIB] **1 :** a public meeting in India **:** ASSEMBLY **2 :** an organized group in India **:** SOCIETY, COUNCIL

¹sa·bia \'sābēə\ *n, cap* [NL, prob. fr. native name in India] **:** a genus (the type of the family Sabiaceae) of tropical Asiatic erect or climbing shrubs having alternate petioled leaves and small axillary regular flowers and having the stamens, petals, and sepals opposite throughout

²sa·bia \səb'yä\ *n* -s [Pg *sabiá,* fr. Tupi] **:** any of several thrushes of the genus *Mimus* popular as songbirds in Brazil

sa·bi·a·ce·ae \ˌsābē'āsē,ē\ *n pl, cap* [NL, fr. *Sabia,* type genus + *-aceae*] **:** a family of tropical shrubs and trees (order Sapindales) having small paniculate flowers with a compressed or lobed ovary of two or three cells and fruit consisting of one-seeded nutlets — **sa·bi·a·ceous** \¦==¦āshəs\ *adj*

¹sa·bi·an \'sābēən, 'säb-\ *n* -s *usu cap* [Ar *Ṣābi'* Sabian + E *-an*] **1 :** one of a group mentioned in the Koran as entitled to Muslim religious toleration along with Jews and Christians and usu. identified with the Mandaeans or the Elkesaites **2 :** a Syrian pagan of a Hauranitic group orig. of star worshipers claiming toleration from the Muslim conquerors under the pretense of belonging to the Sabian group tolerated by the Koran and including scholars and astronomers noted under the caliphate

²sabian \"\ *adj, usu cap* **:** of or relating to the Sabians

sa·bi·an·ism \-ēə,nizəm\ *n* -s *usu cap* **:** the religion of the Sabians

sa·bi·cu *or* **sabicu wood** \'sabə,kü\ *n* -s [AmerSp *sabicú*] **1 :** the hard dark brown wood of a West Indian tree (*Lysiloma sabicu*) resembling mahogany in texture and valued for furniture making **2 :** the tree that yields sabicu wood

sabin \'sābən, 'sab-\ *n* -s [after Wallace C. W. *Sabine* †1919 Am. physicist] **:** a unit of acoustic absorption equivalent to the absorption by one square foot of a perfect absorber (as an open window)

sa·bi·na \sə'bīnə, -bēnə\ *or* **sab·ine** \'sabən\ *n* -s [L *sabina*] : SAVIN 1

sab·i·nane \'sabə,nān\ *n* -s [ISV *sabin-* (fr. NL *sabina* — specific epithet of the savin *Juniperus sabina* — fr. L *sabina* savin) + *-ane*] : THUJANE

¹sabine \'sā,bīn, 'sa,b-\ *n* -s *usu cap* [ME *Sabyn*, fr. L *Sabinus*, n. & adj.] **1** : a member of an ancient people inhabiting chiefly the Apennines northeast of Latium and conquered and incorporated by Rome in 290 B.C. — compare SAMNITE **2** : the Italic language of the Sabine people

²sabine \"\ *adj, usu cap* [L *Sabinus*] : of or relating to the Sabines

sab·i·nene \'sabə,nēn\ *n* -s [ISV *sabin-* (fr. NL *sabina*) + *-ene*] : a liquid bicyclic unsaturated terpene hydrocarbon $C_{10}H_{16}$ found esp. in savin oil that is the isomer of thujene containing a double bond outside of the rings; 4(10)-thujene

sabine pine \'sā\|bən-, 'sa\|, \|,bīn-\ *n* [after Joseph *Sabine* †1837 Brit. horticulturist] *n, usu cap S* **1** : DIGGER PINE **2** : TORREY PINE

sabine's gull \-nz-\ *n, usu cap S* [after Sir Edward *Sabine* †1883 Brit. physicist and explorer] : a small gull (*Xema sabini*) breeding in arctic regions that has a dark gray head, black collar, white wing tips, and a slightly forked tail

sa·bi·no \sə'bē(,)nō\ *n* -s [AmerSp *sabino, sabina*, fr. Sp *sabina* savin, fr. L] **1 a** (1) : a bald cypress (*Taxodium distichum*) (2) : AHUEHUETE **b** : ROCK CEDAR **2** : a Puerto Rican forest tree (*Magnolia splendens*) with hard heavy durable wood that is used for furniture and general construction

sa·bir \sə'bi(ə)r\ *n* -s [F, fr. the word for "know" in a concocted lingua franca used by Molière †1673 Fr. playwright in his comedy *Le Bourgeois Gentilhomme* (1670) as the vehicle of a song (of which the first two lines are *Se ti sabir, Ti respondir* meaning "if you know, answer"), prob. fr. Sp *saber* to know — more at SAVVY] : a French-based pidgin language of No. Africa

sabkha *var of* SEBKHA

¹sa·ble \'sābəl\ *n* -s *see sense 2a* [ME, sable (heraldic color, color, animal, and fur), fr. MF, fr. OF (animal and fur), fr. MLG *sabel*, fr. MHG *zabel, zobel*, fr. OHG *zobel*, of Slav origin; akin to Russ *sobol'* sable (animal and fur), Pol *sobol*; perh. akin to Skt *śabara, śabala* spotted — more at CERBERUS] **1 a** : the heraldic color black **b** : the color black **c** : black clothing worn as a sign of mourning — usu. used in pl. **2 a** *or pl* **sable** (1) : a carnivorous mammal (*Martes zibellina*) of northern Europe and parts of northern Asia that attains a length of about 18 inches exclusive of the tail, varies from yellowish to dark brown above with grayish markings on the face and tawny on the throat and underparts, and is one of the most valued of fur-bearing animals esp. for its very dark skin (2) : any of various related animals; *esp* : PINE MARTEN **b** (1) : the fur or pelt of a sable (2) : a trimming or article of this fur ⟨she wore her ~s with a tailored suit⟩ — usu. used in pl. **3** *or* **sable's hair pencil** : an artist's brush of sable hair **4** : SABLE ANTELOPE **5 a** : the color of the fur of the sable **b** : WOODBARK

²sable \"\ *adj* [ME, fr. *sable*, n.] **1 a** : of the heraldic color black — abbr. *sa* **b** : black in color : dressed in black : darkened as by night ⟨down the ~ flood we glided —Charlotte Brontë⟩ **c** *of a dog* : having a black-shaded outer coat over an undercoat of lighter color **2 a** : SAD, GLOOMY, DISMAL **b** : darkly mysterious or threatening **3** : SATANIC ⟨his ~ majesty⟩

sable antelope *n* : a large handsome nearly extinct antelope (*Hippotragus niger*) of eastern and southern Africa that has large curved annulated horns, a tufted tail, and a slight mane and is glossy black in the male except for the white underparts and facial markings — called also *black buck, sable*

sablefish \'≈,≈\ *n* : a large elongated slaty gray to nearly black scorpaenid food fish (*Anoplopoma fimbria*) of the Pacific coast from Alaska to southern California that is a leading market fish usu. sold fresh but sometimes smoked or salted and has a liver rich in vitamins — called also *black cod, blue cod, candlefish*

sa·ble·ness *n* -ES : the quality or state of being sable : BLACKNESS, GLOOMINESS

sa·bly \'sāb(ə)lē\ *adv* [²*sable* + *-ly*] : in a sable manner : BLACKLY, DARKLY

sa·bo·ra \sä'bō(,)rä\ *n, pl* **sabora·im** \,säbō'rä,im\ *often cap* [Aram *sābhōrā*, lit., thinker, fr. *sebhar* to think, intend] : one of the Jewish rabbis active in the Babylonian academies during the 6th century who completed the revision of the Babylonian Talmud — compare AMORA, TANNA

sa·bo·ra·ic \\|säbə\|rāik\ *adj, often cap* : of or relating to the saboraim

sabot \(')sa\|bō, sə'bō, *in sense 1b often* 'sabət\ *n* -s [F, fr. MF, alter. (influenced by *bot, bote* boot) of *savate* old shoe; akin to It *ciabatta* old shoe, Sp *zapato* shoe, OProv *sabata*] **1 a** : a wooden work shoe worn in various European countries (as Germany, France, Belgium, Holland) — compare CLOG **b** (1) *or* **sabot strap** : a strap or wide band of leather or other material fitting across the instep in a shoe esp. of the sandal type (2) : a shoe having a sabot strap **2 a** : a thick circular disk of wood for holding the cartridge bag and projectile of fixed ammunition for smoothbore cannon **b** : a piece of soft metal formerly attached to a projectile for a muzzle-loading rifle to take the grooves of the rifling **c** : a thrust-transmitting light-weight carrier that positions a missile or subcaliber projectile in a tube and is normally discarded when free of the tube

sabot 1 b (2)

¹sab·o·tage \'sabə,täzh, -täj *sometimes* \|j *or* ,≈'≈\ *n* -s [F, fr. *saboter* to botch, do in a clumsy or slipshod way, sabotage (fr. *sabot*) + *-age*] **1** : malicious destruction of or damage to property with the intention of injuring a business or impairing the economic system or weakening a government or nation in time of war or national emergency ⟨a synthetic resin to be used for the ~ of their gasoline supplies in the event the Germans were able to invade Britain —*Current Biog.*⟩: as **a** : destruction of property (as tools of production or materials) or deliberate slowing down of work or interference with production in any way during a labor dispute **b** : the crime in time of war or declared national emergency of willfully injuring or obstructing the U.S. or any nation associated with it in preparing for or carrying on war or national defense **2** : willful effort by indirect means to hinder, prevent, undo, or discredit (as a plan or activity) : deliberate subversion ⟨~ of the project by disgruntled officials⟩; *broadly* : any act or process tending to hamper or hurt ⟨if a racing man can cruise in his boat, if the cruising bug is given a chance to bite him, his racing career is in serious danger of ~ —Peter Heaton⟩

²sabotage \"\ *vt* -ED/-ING/-S : to practice sabotage on : WRECK, DESTROY, DAMAGE ⟨in a war between rival cab companies . . . cabs are *sabotaged* and riders kidnapped —*TV Guide*⟩ ⟨had sought to ~ the meeting by sending misleading telegrams to members —*Call*⟩

sab·o·teur \R \|sabə\|tər (+ *vowel* -\|tər·), -\|tü(ə)r; -R -\|tə, -\|tüə, + *vowel in a word following without pause* -\|tər·, -\|tə, -\|tü(ə)r, -\|tüə *also* -\|tər\ *n* -s [F, fr. *saboter* + *-eur* -or] : one that engages in sabotage ⟨~s . . . plant bombs resembling lumps of coal in our locomotive tenders —*Combat Forces Jour.*⟩ ⟨rain, wind, and sun are not the only ~s . . . which imperil the winning of blue ribbons —D.S.Boyer⟩

sa·bo·tier \,sabə\|tyā\ *n, pl* **sabotiers** \-ā(z)\ [F, fr. MF, *sabot* + *-ier* -eer] : one that makes sabots

sa·bra \'säbrə, -(,)brä\ *n* -s [NHeb *ṣābrāh*] **1** : the reddish prickly edible fruit of various cacti (genus *Opuntia*) growing on the coastal plains of Palestine; *broadly* : INDIAN FIG, PRICKLY PEAR **2** : a native-born Israeli

sabre *var of* SABER

sa·bre·tache \'säbə(r),tash, 'sab-, -taash,-taish\ *n* -s [F, fr. G *säbeltasche*, fr. *säbel* saber (fr. MHG *sabel, sebel*) + *tasche* pocket, fr. OHG *tasca* purse, fr. (assumed) VL *tasca* task, remuneration — more at SABER, TASK] : a flat leather case formerly worn suspended on the left from the saber belt by men of some cavalry units

sa·breur \sə'brər(·), sa'b-\ *n* -s [F, fr. *sabrer* to strike with a saber (fr. *sabre* saber) + *-eur* -or] **1** : one that carries a saber : CAVALRYMAN **2** : one that fences with a saber

sab·u·lous \'sabyələs\ *also* **sab·u·lose** \-,lōs\ *also* **sab·u·line** \-,līn, -lən\ *adj* [*sabulous, sabulose* fr. L *sabulosus*, fr. *sabulum* sand + *-osus* -ose; *sabuline* fr. L *sabulum* + E *-ine* — more at SAND] : SANDY, GRITTY, ARENACEOUS

sa·bur·ra \sə'bərə\ *n* -s [NL, fr. L, sand, ballast; akin to L *sabulum* sand] **1** : SORDES **2** : SAND COLIC — **sa·bur·ral** \-rəl\ *adj*

sa·bu·tan \\|säbə\|tän\ *n* -s [Tag *sabután*] : a coarse fiber or straw from a species of *Pandanus* used in making hats and mats in the Philippines

sab·zi \(,)səb'zē\ *n* -s [Hindi *sabzī*, lit., greenness, fr. Per] **1** *India* : a green vegetable **2** *India* : the larger leaves and the seed capsules of Indian hemp used for making bhang

¹sac \'sak\ *n* -s [F, lit., bag, fr. L *saccus* — more at SACK] **1** : a pouch within an animal or plant; *specif* : a soft-walled cavity usu. having a narrow opening or none at all and containing in many cases a special fluid ⟨a synovial ~⟩ ⟨a lachrymal ~⟩ **2** : SACK 5

²sac *usu cap, var of* SAUK

SAC *abbr* Strategic Air Command

sa·cae \'sā,sē, 'sä,kī\ *n pl, usu cap* [L, fr. Gk *Sakai*] : an ancient people settled in the eastern part of Iran

sa·ca·huis·te \,sakə'wistē, ,säk-\ *also* **sa·ca·huis·ta** \-stə\ *or* **sa·ca·guis·ta** \-kə'wistə\ *n* -s [AmerSp *zacahuiscle*, of AmerInd origin; akin to Nahuatl *zacatl* coarse grass] : a bear grass (*Nolina texana*) having a thick caudex and long linear leaves and used in some areas for forage though reputed to have buds and blossoms that are poisonous to livestock

sac·a·lait \'sakə,lā, ,≈≈'≈\ *n* -s [LaF *sac-à-lait*, by folk etymology (influence of F *sac* bag, F *à* to, for, and F *lait* milk) fr. Choctaw *sakli* trout] **1** : WHITE CRAPPIE **2** : WARMOUTH **3** : KILLIFISH

sac·a·line *also* **sach·a·line** \'sakəlēn, -,lēn\ *n* -s [irreg. fr. *Sakhalin*, island in the Sea of Okhotsk, eastern U.S.S.R.] : a coarse herb (*Polygonum sachalinense*) of Sakhalin and cultivated in the U.S. as forage and for lawn decoration

¹sac·a·ton \'sakə,tōn\ *n* -s [AmerSp *zacatón*, fr. *zacate* coarse grass, fr. Nahuatl *zacatl*] : a coarse perennial grass (*Sporobolus wrightii*) of the southwestern U.S. useful for hay in alkaline regions

²sacaton \"\ *adj, usu cap* [*Sacaton*, town in southern Arizona] : of or belonging to a Hohokam culture in southern Arizona A.D. 900–1150 characterized by rectangular excavated floors with rounded corners, and red-on-buff pottery with intricate fabric design decoration

sacbrood \'≈,≈\ *n* [¹*sac* + *brood*] : a virus disease of the honeybee affecting the larvae and causing them to shrivel and become scalelike

sacc- *or* **sacci-** *or* **sacco-** *comb form* [NL, fr. L *sacc-, sacci-* bag, fr. *saccus*] : sac ⟨*saccate*⟩ ⟨*sacciform*⟩ ⟨*Saccomys*⟩

sac·cade \sa'käd, sə'k-\ *n* -s [F, fr. MF, fr. *saquer, sachier* to pull, draw + *-ade*] : a quick violent check of a horse by a single pull or twitch of the reins

sac·cad·ic \-dik\ *adj* [*saccade* + *-ic*] : of or relating to a sudden movement : JERKY

saccadic movement *n* : the quick movement of the eyes by which the gaze is transferred from one fixation point to another

sac·cam·mi·na \sə'kamənə, sa'k-\ *n, cap* [NL] : a genus of foraminiferans having a thick arenaceous test often in the shape of a pear, spindle, or sphere, having survived from the Ordovician to the present time, and making up with their remains various Carboniferous strata

sac·cate \'sa,kāt\ *adj* [NL *saccatus*, fr. *sacc-* + L *-atus* -ate] **1** : having the form of a sac or pouch **2** : ENCYSTED

sac·cat·ed \-ād·əd\ *adj* [*saccate* + *-ed*] : SACCATE

sacchar- *or* **sacchari-** *or* **saccharo-** *comb form* [L *saccharum*, fr. Gk *sakcharon*, fr. Pali *sakkharā*, fr. Skt *śarkarā* gravel, grit, sugar — more at SUGAR] **1** : sugar ⟨*saccharic*⟩ ⟨*sacchariferous*⟩ ⟨*saccharometer*⟩ **2** : saccharine and ⟨*saccharomucilaginous*⟩

sac·cha·rase \'sakə,rās, -āz\ *n* -s [ISV *sacchar-* + *-ase*] : INVERTASE

sac·cha·rate \-,rāt, -rət\ *n* -s [*saccharic* (in *saccharic acid*) + *-ate*] **1** : a salt or ester of saccharic acid **2** : a metallic derivative of a sugar usu. with a bivalent metal (as calcium, strontium, or barium); *esp* : SUCRATE — not used systematically

sac·cha·rat·ed \-,rād·əd\ *adj* [*sacchar-* + *-ate*, v. suffix + *-ed*] : mixed or combined with sucrose

sac·char·ic \sə'karik, (')sa\|k-\ *adj* [*sacchar-* + *-ic*] : of, relating to, or obtained from saccharine substances

saccharic acid *n* **1** : a deliquescent solid dicarboxylic acid $HOOC(CHOH)_4COOH$ that is obtained by oxidation of glucose or its derivatives (as sucrose) by nitric acid and that readily undergoes inner esterification to a lactone — called also *glucaric acid* **2** : either of two dicarboxylic acids from the other hexoses having the pair of central hydroxyl groups on opposite sides of the molecule similarly to glucose ⟨*manno-saccharic acid*⟩ ⟨*ido-saccharic acid*⟩ — compare MUCIC ACID

sac·cha·ride \'sakə,rīd, -rəd\ *n* -s [ISV *sacchar-* + *-ide*] : a simple sugar, combination of sugars, or polymerized sugar : CARBOHYDRATE — see DISACCHARIDE, MONOSACCHARIDE, OLIGOSACCHARIDE, POLYSACCHARIDE, TRISACCHARIDE

sac·cha·rif·er·ous \\|sakə\|rif(ə)rəs\ *adj* [*sacchar-* + *-ferous*] : producing or containing sugar

sac·chari·fi·ca·tion \sə,karəfə'kāshən, sa,kar-, ,sakər-\ *n* -s [ISV *sacchar-* + *-fication*] : the process of saccharifying

sac·chari·fy \sə'karə,fī, sa'kar-, 'sakər-\ *vt* -ED/-ING/-ES [ISV *sacchar-* + *-fy*] : to hydrolyze (a sugar derivative or complex carbohydrate) into a simple soluble fermentable sugar (as glucose or maltose) — compare DEXTRINIZE

saccharifying enzyme *n* : AMYLASE 2 b

sac·cha·rim·e·ter \,sakə'rimədə(r)\ *n* [ISV *sacchar-* + *-meter*] : a device for measuring the amount of sugar in a solution; *esp* : a polarimeter particularly adapted for distinguishing different kinds of sugar in solution — compare SACCHAROMETER — **sac·chari·met·ric** \\|sakərə\|me·trik, sə\|kar-, sa\|kar-\ *or* **sac·chari·met·ri·cal** \-trəkəl\ *adj* — **sac·cha·rim·e·try** \,sakə'rimə·trē\ *n* -ES

sac·cha·rin \'sak(ə)rən\ *n* -s [ISV *sacchar-* + *-in*] : a crystalline cyclic imide $C_6H_4(CO)(SO_2)NH$ that is remarkable for its sweetness varying from 200 to 700 times that of sucrose in solutions of varying concentration, that is made usu. from the amide of *ortho*-toluenesulfonic acid, and that is used often in the form of its soluble sodium derivative as a sweetening agent (as in cases of diabetes and obesity) but that has no food value — called also *benzosulfimide, gluside*

sac·cha·rin·at·ed \-rə,nād·əd\ *adj* [*saccharine* + *-ate*, v. suffix + *-ed*] : mixed with or containing saccharine matter : SACCHARATED

sac·cha·rine \'sak(ə)rən, -kə,rēn, -kə,rīn\ *adj* [L *saccharum* sugar + E *-ine* — more at SACCHAR-] **1 a** : of, relating to, or of the nature of sugar ⟨~ taste⟩ ⟨~ fermentation⟩ **b** : yielding or containing sugar ⟨~ vegetables⟩ **2** : overly or unpleasantly sweet ⟨~ flavor⟩ **3** : unpleasantly or ingratiatingly pleasant, agreeable, gentle, or friendly ⟨a ~ smile⟩ ⟨~ poetry⟩

sac·cha·rin·ic acid \\|sakə\|rinik-\ *n* [*saccharinic* ISV *saccharin* + *-ic*] : any of several polyhydroxy acids formed from sugars by alkaline treatment as though by internal oxidation and reduction so that one carbon no longer holds an oxygen and in many instances with branching of the carbon skeleton

sac·cha·rin·i·ty \sakə'rinədē\ *n* -ES : the quality or state of being saccharine : SWEETNESS

sac·cha·ro·genesis \,sakərō+\ *n* [*sacchar-* + *genesis*] : the formation of sugar esp. by saccharification

sac·cha·ro·gen·ic \\|sakərō\|jenik\ *adj* [*sacchar-* + *-genic*] : producing sugar — compare DEXTRINOGENIC

¹sac·cha·roid \'sakə,rȯid\ *also* **sac·cha·roi·dal** \\|≈≈\|rȯidᵊl\ *adj* [*saccharoid* ISV *sacchar-* + *-oid*; *saccharoidal* fr. *saccharoid* + *-al*] : CRYSTALLINE, GRANULAR ⟨~ stone⟩

²saccharoid \"\ *n* -s : a saccharoid substance

sac·cha·ro·lyt·ic \\|sakərō\|lid·ik\ *adj* [*sacchar-* + *-lytic*] *of a microorganism* : breaking down sugars as a source of energy in metabolism

sac·cha·rom·e·ter \,sakə'rämədə(r)\ *n* [*sacchar-* + *-meter*] : a device for measuring the amount of sugar in a solution: as **a** : a hydrometer with a special scale (as a Brix scale or Baumé scale) for use where the presence of other dissolved solids does not interfere **b** : a tube arranged for the collection and measurement of the gas evolved in the fermentation of sugars (as in urine) — compare SACCHARIMETER — **sac·cha·ro·met·ric** \\|sakərō\|me·trik, sə\|kar-, sa\|kar-\ *adj* — **sac·cha·rom·e·try** \\|sakə\|rämə·trē\ *n* -ES

sac·cha·ro·my·ces \,sakərō'mī(,)sēz\ *n, cap* [NL *Saccharomycet-, Saccharomyces*, fr. *sacchar-* + *-mycet-, -myces*] : a genus of usu. unicellular yeasts (family Saccharomycetaceae) distinguished by their sparse or absent mycelium and their facility in reproducing asexually by budding — see BREWERS' YEAST, WINE YEAST

sac·cha·ro·my·ce·ta·ce·ae \\|sakərō,mīsə'tāsē,ē\ *n pl, cap* [NL, fr. *Saccharomycet-, Saccharomyces*, type genus + *-aceae*] : a family of ascomycetous fungi (order Endomycetales) comprising the typical yeasts that form asci or reproduce by budding and that typically produce alcoholic fermentations in carbohydrate substrates — **sac·cha·ro·my·ce·ta·ceous** \\|≈≈≈\|≈\|tāshəs\ *adj*

sac·cha·ro·my·ce·ta·les \,≈≈≈,≈'tā(,)lēz\ *n pl, cap* [NL, fr. *Saccharomycet-, Saccharomyces* + *-ales*] *in some classifications* : an order of Fungi comprising the yeasts and various chiefly parasitic molds that are now usu. included in the order Moniliales

sac·cha·ro·my·cete \\|sakərō\|mī,sēt, -,mī\|sēt\ *n* -s [ISV *sacchar-* + *-mycete*] : a yeast fungus — **sac·cha·ro·my·ce·tic** \-ēd·ik\ *adj*

sac·cha·rose \'sakə,rōs *also* -ōz\ *n* -s [ISV *sacchar-* + *-ose*] **1** : SUCROSE — compare SUGAR 1 **2** : any of the compound sugars including the disaccharides and trisaccharides; *esp* : DISACCHARIDE

sac·cha·rum \'sakərəm\ *n* [NL, fr. L, sugar — more at SACCHAR-] **1** *cap* : a genus of large grasses of the Old World tropics resembling reeds and having expanded panicles with very small paired spikelets intermixed with numerous silky hairs — see SUGARCANE **2** -s [L] : SUGAR: as **a** : SUCROSE **b** : INVERT SUGAR

sacci- — see SACC-

sac·ci·form \'sak(s)ə,fȯrm\ *adj* [ISV *sacc-* + *-form*] : resembling a pouch

sacco- — see SACC-

sac·co·branchiata \\|sa(,)kō+\ [NL, fr. *sacc-* + *Branchiata*] *syn of* ASCIDIACEA

sac·co·derm \'sakō,dərm\ *adj* [*sacc-* + Gk *derma* skin — more at DERM-] : having a cell wall consisting of a single piece and lacking vertical pores in the wall — used of desmids of the family Mesotaeniaceae; distinguished from *placoderm*

sac·co·la·bi·um \,sakō'lābēəm\ *n* [NL, fr. *sacc-* + *labium*] **1** *cap* : a genus of epiphytic orchids of the East Indies and the Malay archipelago having racemose flowers with a flat spreading perianth and a lip with a saccate base **2** *pl* **sac·cola·bia** \-ēə\ *or* **saccolabiums** : any plant or flower of the genus *Saccolabium*

sac·co·my·idae \\|sakō'mīə,dē\ [NL, fr. *Saccomys* + *-idae*] *syn of* HETEROMYIDAE

sac·co·my·ina \,sakō,mī'īnə, -,mē'īnə, -,mē'ēnə\ [NL, fr. *Saccomys* + *-ina*] *syn of* GEOMYOIDEA

sac·co·my·oid \\|sakō\|mī,ȯid\ *or* **sac·co·my·oi·de·an** \-ī-\|ȯidēən\ *adj* [*saccomyoid* fr. NL *Saccomyoidea*; *saccomyoidean* fr. NL *Saccomyoidea* + E *-an*] : GEOMYOID

sac·co·my·oi·dea \,≈≈,≈'ȯidēə\ [NL, fr. *Saccomys* + *-oidea*] *syn of* GEOMYOIDEA

sac·co·mys \'sakō,mis\ [NL, fr. *sacc-* + *-mys*] *syn of* HETEROMYS

sac·co·rhi·za \,sakə'rīzə\ *n* [NL, fr. *sacc-* + *-rhiza*] **1** *cap* : a small genus of marine brown algae (family Laminariaceae) having above the holdfast a swelling that resembles a bulb and is formed by whorls of tentacular outgrowths **2** -s : SEA FURBELOW

saccos *var of* SAKKOS

sac·cu·lar \'sakyələ(r)\ *adj* [ISV *saccul-* (fr. NL *sacculus*) + *-ar*] : being like a sac

sac·cu·late \-lət, -,lāt\ *adj* [NL *sacculus* + E *-ate*] : SACCULATED

sac·cu·lat·ed \-,lād·əd\ *adj* [NL *sacculus* + E *-ate* + *-ed*] : furnished with or formed of a sac : having a series of saclike expansions

sac·cu·la·tion \,sakyə'lāshən\ *n* -s [NL *sacculus* + E *-ation*] **1** : the quality or state of being sacculated **2** : the process of developing or segmenting into sacculate structures **3** : a sac or sacculate structure; *esp* : one of a linear series of such structures ⟨intestinal ~s⟩

sac·cule \'sa(,)kyül\ *n* -s [NL *sacculus*, fr. L, small bag, fr. *saccus* bag + *-ulus* — more at SACK] : a little sac; *specif* : the smaller chamber of the membranous labyrinth of the ear — compare UTRICLE

sac·cu·li·na \,sakyə'līnə, -lēnə\ *n* [NL, fr. *sacculus* + *-ina*] **1** *cap* : a genus of parasitic barnacles (order Rhizocephala) **2** -s : any parasite of the genus *Sacculina*

sac·cu·lo·utricular \\|sakyə(,)lō+\ *adj* [*sacculo-* (fr. NL *sacculus*) + *utricular*] : UTRICULOSACCULAR

sac·cu·lus \'sakyələs\ *n, pl* **saccu·li** \-,lī, -,lē\ [NL] : SACCULE

sac·cus \'sakəs\ *n, pl* **sac·ci** \-a,kī, -a(,)kē, -ak,sī\ [NL, fr. L, bag — more at SACK] : SAC

sa·cel·lum \sə'keləm, sa'se-\ *n, pl* **sacel·la** \-lə\ [L, pagan Roman sacellum, dim. of *sacrum* sanctuary, sacred object, fr. neut. of *sacer* sacred] **1** : a small monumental chapel in a church **2** : an unroofed space in an ancient Roman building consecrated to a divinity

sac·er·do·cy \'sasə(r),dōsē, 'sakə-\ *n* -ES [L *sacerdotium*, fr. *sacerdot-, sacerdos* priest] **1** : PRIESTHOOD **2** : priestly office, character, or order

sac·er·do·tal \\|sasə(r)\|dōd·ᵊl, \|sakə-, -ōtᵊl\ *adj* [ME, fr. MF, fr. L *sacerdotalis*, fr. *sacerdot-, sacerdos* priest (fr. *sacer* sacred + *-dot-, -dos* — akin to L *facere* to make, do) + *-alis* -al — more at SACRED, DO] **1 a** : of or relating to priests or a priesthood : PRIESTLY ⟨~ literature⟩ ⟨~ vestments⟩ **b** : belonging to a priesthood ⟨a ~ teacher⟩ **2** : of, relating to, or suggesting sacerdotalism ⟨a ~ emphasis in tribal religions⟩ — **sac·er·do·tal·ly** \-ōd·ᵊlē, -ōtᵊlē, -ᵊli\ *adv*

sac·er·do·tal·ism \,≈≈'≈≈,izəm\ *n* -s [ISV *sacerdotal* + *-ism*] **1** : a belief that assumes a necessity for an authorized priesthood as a mediator between men and their divine needs or aspirations or the doctrine based on such an assumption **2** : undue emphasis on the need for or the authority of a priesthood or of priests

¹sac·er·do·tal·ist \-,əst\ *n* -s [*sacerdotal* + *-ist*] : one who upholds sacerdotalism

²sacerdotalist \\|≈≈\|≈≈≈\ *adj* : of or relating to sacerdotalism

sac·er·do·tal·ize \,≈≈'≈≈,īz\ *vt* -ED/-ING/-S **1** : to make sacerdotal **2** : to subject to sacerdotalism

sac·er·doti·cal \\|≈≈\|dōd·əkəl, -\|däd-\ *adj* [L *sacerdot-, sacerdos* priest + E *-ical*] : SACERDOTAL

sac fry *n* : YOLK FRY

sac fungus *n* [so called fr. the fact that the spores are formed in a sac] : a fungus of the class Ascomycetes : ASCOMYCETE

sachaline *var of* SACALINE

sa·chem \'sāchəm\ *n* -s [Narraganset & Pequot *sachima, sachimau*] **1** : a No. American Indian chief; *specif* : the supreme chief of a confederation among the Algonquian tribes of the north Atlantic coast **2** : the leader of a political party; *specif* : one of the 12 governors of the Tammany Society — **sa·chem·ic** \(')sā\|chemik, 'sāchəm-\ *adj*

sa·chem·ship \'sāchəm,ship\ *n* : the office or authority of a sachem

sa·cher torte \'s\|äkə(r)-, 'z\|\ *n, usu cap S* [G *sachertorte*, fr. *Sacher* (name of a family of 19th and 20th cent. Austrian hotel and restaurant proprietors) + G *torte*] : a torte made of butter, eggs, confectioner's sugar, toasted bread crumbs, chocolate, and spices, baked in layers, put together with apricot jam, and frosted with chocolate — compare LINZER TORTE

sa·chet \(')sa\|shā\ *n* -s [F, fr. OF, dim. of *sac* bag — more at SAC] **1** : a small bag or packet; *esp* : a small bag containing a perfumed powder that is used to scent clothes (as in drawers, closets, trunks) **2** *or* **sachet powder** : a perfumed powder that is often used in small bags

ST

[1]**sack** \ˈsak\ *n* -s [ME *sak* sack, bag, sackcloth, fr. OE *sacc, sæcc;* akin to MD & OHG *sac* sack, bag, ON *sekkr* sack, bag, Goth *sakkus* sackcloth; all fr. a prehistoric Gmc word borrowed fr. L *saccus* sack, bag & LL *saccus* sackcloth; L *saccus* & LL *saccus* both fr. Gk *sakkos* sack, bag, sackcloth, of Sem origin; akin to Heb *śaq* sack, bag, sackcloth] **1 a :** a large usu. rectangular bag of coarse strong material (as canvas or burlap) used to store and ship goods (as grain, fruit, coal) **b :** a small container made of paper, plastic, or other similar material used to contain various kinds of merchandise (as foodstuffs); *specif* **:** a paper bag **c :** a canvas bag for holding mail (as parcel post or second or third class mail) — called also *mail sack* **2** *archaic* **:** SACKCLOTH, SACKING **3 a :** a sack with its contents **b :** the amount contained in a sack; *esp* **:** such an amount as fixed for a certain commodity (as flour, wool) and sometimes used as a unit of measure **4 :** the punishment (as in ancient Rome) whereby an offender is sewn in a sack and drowned — used with *the* **5 a :** a woman's loose-fitting dress; *specif* **:** a gown or overdress of the late 17th and early 18th centuries often made with a Watteau back **b :** a short coat or jacket usu. loose-fitting and made in outdoor and indoor styles for women and children — see DRESSING SACK **c :** SACQUE 2 **d :** SACK COAT **6 a :** DISMISSAL — usu. used with *get* or *give* ⟨an employee who gets the ~⟩ **b :** REJECTION — usu. used with *get* or *give* ⟨she gave the ~ to successive suitors⟩ **7 a :** HAMMOCK, BUNK **b :** BED **8 :** a base in the game of baseball **9 :** SAC 1

sack 1 b

[2]**sack** \ˈ"\ *vt* -ED/-ING/-S [ME *sakken,* fr. *sak,* n.] **1 :** to put or place in a sack (as for storage or shipment) ⟨~ potatoes in the field⟩ ⟨~ corn⟩ **2** *archaic* **:** to kill (as a condemned person) by drowning within a sewn-up sack **3 :** to carry off **:** GAIN ⟨~ an enormous profit⟩ — sometimes used with *up* **4 :** to dismiss (as from employment) esp. summarily ⟨~ a dilatory worker⟩ **syn** see DISMISS — **sack the rear :** to follow a drive in logging and roll in logs that have lodged or grounded — **sack the slide :** to return to a slide logs that have jumped out

[3]**sack** \ˈ"\ *n* -s [modif. of MF *sec* dry (in *vin sec* dry wine), fr. L *siccus;* akin to OE *sīon, sēon* to strain, filter, OHG *sīhan,* ON *sīa* to strain, filter, Gk *hikmas* moisture, Skt *secate* he pours] **:** a usu. dry white wine imported to England from the south of Europe (as from Jerez, Spain, and the Canary islands) during the 16th and 17th centuries

[4]**sack** \ˈ"\ *n* -s [MF *sac,* fr. OIt *sacco,* lit., bag, fr. L *saccus* — more at [1]SACK] **1 :** the plundering or looting of a captured town by its conquerors ⟨a city put to the ~⟩ ⟨the ~ of Rome⟩ **2 :** PLUNDER, LOOT

[5]**sack** \ˈ"\ *vt* -ED/-ING/-S **1 :** to plunder (as a town) after capture **2 :** to strip (as an overpowered person or unprotected building) of valuables **:** LOOT **syn** see RAVAGE

sack·age \ˈsakij\ *n* -s **:** the action of sacking or pillaging

sack–bearer \ˈ≈,≈≈\ *n* **:** any of various caterpillars that are larvae of moths of the family Mimallonidae

sack borer *n* **:** a device used in mining for sinking shafts in soft ground by boring to the full size with a very large tool resembling an auger behind the cutters of which large sacks are attached to catch material as it is removed

sack·but \ˈsak(,)bət\ *n* -s [MF *saquebute, saqueboute,* sackbut, hooked lance, fr. OF, hooked lance, fr. *saquer, sachier* to pull + *bouter* to push, thrust, butt — more at BUTT] **1 a :** the medieval trombone **b :** a player on such a trombone **2** [influenced in meaning by Aram *śabbĕkhā* trigon (in Dan 3:5)] **:** TRIGON

sackcloth \ˈ≈,≈\ *n* [ME *sakcloth,* fr. *sak* sack, bag, sackcloth + *cloth*] **1 :** a coarse cloth made of goat hair or camel hair or of flax, hemp, or cotton and used for sacks or garments **2 :** a garment of sackcloth; *esp* **:** one worn as a sign of mourning, distress, penitence, or protest — **in sackcloth and ashes :** in a spirit of sorrow, repentance, or humility ⟨this, then, is an essay about education by a layman . . . and it is not written *in sackcloth and ashes* —M.B.Smith⟩

sack cloud *n* **:** a well-developed mammatocumulus

sack coat *n* **:** a man's single-breasted or double-breasted jacket with a straight unfitted back

[1]**sack·er** \ˈsakə(r)\ *n* -s [[5]sack + *-er*] **:** one that sacks **:** PILLAGER, LOOTER

[2]**sacker** \ˈ"\ *n* -s [[2]sack + *-er*] **:** one that sacks: as **a :** a device for sacking **b :** BAGGER

[3]**sacker** \ˈ"\ *n* -s [[1]sack + *-er*] **:** a baseball player whose position in the field is one of the three bases **:** BASEMAN — usu. used with *first, second,* or *third* ⟨a hard-hitting first ~⟩

sack·et \ˈsakət\ *n* -s [ME *sakett,* fr. MF *saquet, sachet* small bag — more at SACHET] **1** *Scot* **:** a small sack or wallet **2** *Scot* **:** a small person esp. of a rascally or stupid nature

sack·ful \ˈsak,fu̇l\ *n, pl* **sackfuls** *also* **sacks·ful** \-k,fu̇lz, -ks,fu̇l\ **:** the quantity that fills or would fill a sack

sack in *vi, slang* **:** to go to bed

[1]**sack·ing** \ˈsakiŋ, -kēŋ\ *n* -s [fr. gerund of [5]*sack*] **:** an act or action of plundering or vanquishing; *also* **:** decisive victory

[2]**sacking** \ˈ"\ *n* -s [[1]*sack* + *-ing*] **:** material for sacks; *esp* **:** a coarse fabric (as burlap or gunny)

sack·less \ˈsakləs\ *adj* [ME *sakles,* fr. OE *saclēas,* fr. *sacu* fault, conflict, action at law + *-lēas* -less — more at SAKE] **1** *obs* **:** free from accusation **:** UNMOLESTED **2** *archaic* **:** INNOCENT **3** *chiefly Scot* **a :** WEAK, DISPIRITED **b :** HARMLESS

sack moth *n* **:** the adult of a sack-bearer

sack out *vi, slang* **:** to go to sleep

sack race *n* **:** a race run by persons each with his legs in a sack

sacks *pl of* SACK, *pres 3d sing of* SACK

sack suit *n* **:** a man's suit having a sack coat

sack–winged \ˈ≈,wiŋd\ *adj* **:** having wings resembling or furnished with formations resembling sacks — used esp. of tropical American bats (family Emballonuridae) with a glandular pouch near the front edge of the wing

saclike \ˈ≈,≈\ *adj* **:** having the form of or suggesting a sac

saco·glos·sa \,sakəˈgläsə, ,sāk-, -lȯsə\ *n pl, cap* [NL, fr. *saco-* (fr. Gk *sakos* shield) + *-glossa;* akin to Skt *tvak* skin, hide] *in some classifications* **:** a division of Opisthobranchia including sea slugs (family Elysiidae) that are usu. placed in the suborder Nudibranchia

sacque \ˈsak\ *n* -s [alter. of [1]*sack*] **1 :** SACK 5a, 5b **2 :** a jacket for a small baby

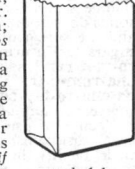

[1]**sacr-** *or* **sacro-** *comb form* [ME *sacr-,* fr. MF & L; MF, fr. L, fr. *sacr-, sacer* — more at SACRED] **1 :** sacred **:** something sacred ⟨*sacral*⟩ **2 :** sacred and ⟨*sacro*pictorial⟩

[2]**sacr-** *or* **sacro-** *comb form* [NL, fr. *sacrum*] **1 :** sacrum ⟨*sacral*⟩ **2 :** sacrum and ⟨*sacro*coccyx⟩ **:** sacral and ⟨*sacro*tuberous⟩

sacque 2

sacra *pl of* SACRUM

sacrad \ˈsa,krad, ˈsakrəd, ˈsā,krad\ *adv* [[2]*sacr-* + *-ad*] **:** toward the sacrum

[1]**sacral** \ˈsakrəl, ˈsāk-\ *adj* [NL *sacralis,* fr. [2]*sacr-* + L *-alis* -al] **:** of, relating to, or lying near the sacrum

[2]**sacral** \ˈ"\ *n* -s **:** a sacral vertebra or sacral nerve

[3]**sacral** \ˈ"\ *adj* [ISV [1]*sacr-* + *-al*] **:** HOLY, SACRED ⟨~ and secular authorities⟩ ⟨~ laws⟩

sacral canal *n* **:** the part of the spinal canal lying in the sacrum

sacral index *n* **:** the ratio of the breadth of the sacrum to its length multiplied by 100

sacral·iza·tion \,sakrələˈzāshən, ,sāk-, -,līˈz-\ *n* -s [ISV [1]*sacral* + *-ization*] **:** incorporation (as of the last lumbar vertebra or any of its parts) into the sacrum; *specif* **:** a congenital anomaly in which the fifth lumbar vertebra is fused to the sacrum in varying degrees

sacral·ize \ˈ≈krə,līz\ *vt* -ED/-ING/-S [[3]*sacral* + *-ize*] **:** to sanctify or make holy by means of a religious sanction ⟨~ a crisis of life⟩

sacral nerve *n* **:** any of the spinal nerves of the sacral region having anterior and posterior branches that pass out through foramina in the sacrum

sacral plexus *n* **:** a nerve plexus supplying the posterior limb and pelvic region and in man being formed by the anterior divisions of the fourth and fifth lumbar and first, second, and third sacral nerves

sacral promontory *n* **:** the inwardly projecting anterior part of the body of the first sacral vertebra

[1]**sac·ra·ment** \ˈsakrəmənt\ *n* -s [ME *sacrement, sacrament,* fr. OF & LL; OF *sacrement, sacrament,* fr. LL *sacramentum,* fr. L, oath of allegiance, solemn obligation, sacramentum, fr. *sacrare* to consecrate + *-mentum* -ment — more at SACRED] **1 :** a religious act, ceremony, or practice that is considered especially sacred as a sign or a symbol of a deeper reality; *esp* **:** one of various Christian acts, ceremonies, or practices distinguished from other Christian rites as having been instituted, observed, or recognized by Jesus Christ **2** *usu cap* **:** the Christian Eucharist, Holy Communion, or Lord's Supper; *specif* **:** the consecrated Host in Roman Catholicism **3 a :** something sacred in character or significance **:** a spiritual sign, seal, or bond (as a covenant held to exist between God and man) **b :** something that has the significance of a deeply religious act or observance

[2]**sac·ra·ment** \-,ment, -mənt — *see* [2]-MENT\ *vt* -ED/-ING/-S **:** to make holy or sacred ⟨a ~*ed* covenant⟩

[1]**sac·ra·men·tal** \ˌsakrəˈmentᵊl\ *adj* [ME, fr. LL *sacramentalis,* fr. *sacramentum* + L *-alis* -al] **1 :** of or relating to sacred rites; *specif* **:** of or relating to the Christian sacraments or one of them (as the Eucharist) **2 :** of the nature of a sacrament **:** characterized by or connected with belief in the sacraments ⟨~ bread⟩ ⟨~ marriage⟩ ⟨~ doctrine⟩ **3 :** solemnly binding, bound, or motivated by or as if by a covenant ⟨a ~ obligation⟩ **4 :** possessed of the dignity or aura of a religious rite **:** SACRED ⟨an almost ~ atmosphere⟩ **5 :** of or relating to a sacramentum — **sac·ra·men·tal·ly** \-ᵊlē, -ᵊli\ *adv*

[2]**sacramental** \ˈ"\ *n* -s **:** a ceremony, action, or sacred object (as in the Roman Catholic Church) resembling or related to a sacrament (as liturgical prayers and holy water) but held to have originated in ecclesiastical custom rather than to have been instituted by Christ

sac·ra·men·ta·lia \,≈≈(,)menˈtālyə, -,mən–, -lēə\ *n pl* [LL, neut. pl. of *sacramentalis*] **:** sacramental things

sac·ra·men·tal·ism \-ˈmentᵊl,izəm\ *n* -s **1 :** the doctrine and use of the sacraments; *esp* **:** the attaching of great importance to sacraments **2 :** the doctrine that sacraments are inherently efficacious and indispensable to salvation and capable of conferring grace on a recipient's soul **3 :** the view that all nature and all life are full of spiritual meaning and symbolic of the unseen and eternal

sac·ra·men·tal·ist \-əst\ *n* -s **1 :** one who holds that the sacraments are inherently efficacious and capable of conferring grace on the recipient's soul **2 :** one versed in or placing great emphasis upon religious ritual and the role and function of sacraments

sac·ra·men·tal·i·ty \,≈≈(,)menˈtaləd·ē, -,mən–\ *n* -ES **:** sacramental nature or quality

sacramental wine *n* **:** wine conforming to prescribed standards of the Christian church and used in its Holy Sacrament

sac·ra·men·tan \,sakrəˈmentᵊn\ *n* -s *cap* [*Sacramento,* California + E *-an*] **:** a native or resident of Sacramento, California

[1]**sac·ra·men·tar·i·an** \,≈≈(,)menˈterēən, -,mən–, -ta(a)r–\ *n* -s [[1]*sacrament* + *-arian*] **1** *usu cap* [trans. of G *sakramenter, sakramentierer*] **:** one who interprets sacraments as visible symbols that are not inherently efficacious or supernaturally potent but of great symbolic significance **2 :** SACRAMENTALIST

[2]**sacramentarian** \ˈ≈≈(,)≈ˈ≈≈≈\ *adj, usu cap* **1 :** of or relating to the Sacramentarians **2 :** of or relating to the sacraments or sacramentalism

sac·ra·men·tar·i·an·ism \-ēə,nizəm\ *n* -s **:** SACRAMENTALISM 2

[1]**sac·ra·men·ta·ry** \,≈≈ˈmentərē\ *n* -ES *usu cap* [[1]*sacrament* + *-ary;* trans. of G *sakramenter, sakramentierer*] **:** SACRAMENTARIAN 1

[2]**sacramentary** \ˈ≈≈ˈ≈≈≈\ *adj* [LL *sacramentarius,* fr. *sacramentum* sacrament + L *-arius* -ary] **1 :** of or relating to a sacrament **:** SACRAMENTAL **2** [[1]*sacramentary*] **:** SACRAMENTARIAN

[3]**sacramentary** \ˈ≈≈ˈ≈≈≈\ *n* -ES [LL *sacramentarium,* fr. neut. of *sacramentarius,* adj.] **:** an early service book of the Western church known in many specific forms and containing typically the celebrant's part of the mass together with prayers for baptisms, ordinations, blessings, and consecrations

sacrament chapel *n* **:** a chapel in which the Eucharistic Host is preserved

sac·ra·men·ter \,≈≈ˈmentə(r)\ *n* -s *usu cap* [G *sakramenter,* fr. *sakrament* sacrament (fr. MHG *sacrament,* fr. LL *sacramentum*) + *-er*] **:** SACRAMENTARIAN

sacrament house *n* **:** an ambry or tabernacle for holding the reserved Eucharist — compare PYX

sac·ra·ment·ism \ˈ≈≈mənt,izəm, -n‧,tizəm\ *n* -s **:** SACRAMENTARIANISM

sac·ra·ment·ize \-nt,īz, -n‧,tīz\ *vi* -ED/-ING/-S **:** to administer the sacraments

sac·ra·men·to \ˌsakrəˈment(,)ō, -n(,)tō\ *adj, usu cap* [fr. *Sacramento,* California] **:** of or from Sacramento, the capital of California ⟨*Sacramento* schools⟩ **:** of the kind or style prevalent in Sacramento

sacramento cat *n, usu cap S* [*Sacramento* river, northwest California] **:** HORNED POUT

sacramento perch *n, usu cap S* **:** a primitive centrarchid sunfish of the Sacramento and San Joaquin river basins that resembles a perch and is the only freshwater percoid fish native to the Pacific coast region of America

sacramento pike *n, usu cap S* **:** SQUAWFISH

sacramento salmon *n, usu cap 1st S* **:** KING SALMON

sacramento sturgeon *n, usu cap 1st S* **:** WHITE STURGEON

sacramento sucker *n, usu cap 1st S* **:** a sucker (*Catostomus occidentalis*) of the streams of California that reaches a length of one foot

sacraments *pl of* SACRAMENT, *pres 3d sing of* SACRAMENT

sacrament sunday *n, usu cap both Ss* **:** a Sunday of the year on which the Lord's Supper is celebrated

sac·ra·men·tum \,sakrəˈmentəm\ *n, pl* **sacramen·ta** \-tə\ [L — more at SACRAMENT] **:** a deposit of money by way of pledge made by each party to a civil action and forfeited to the state by the loser

[1]**sa·crar·i·um** \səˈkra(a)rēəm\ *n, pl* **sacrar·ia** \-ēə\ [ML, fr. L, pagan Roman sacrarium, fr. *sacr-, sacer* sacred + *-arium*] **1 a :** SANCTUARY 1a(2) **b :** SACRISTY **c :** PISCINA 2 **2** [L] **a :** an ancient Roman shrine or sanctuary in a temple or private house holding sacred objects **:** ORATORY, CHAPEL **b :** an ancient Roman building erected for the performance of religious rites by a sacred person

[2]**sacrarium** \ˈ"\ *n, pl* **sacraria** [NL, fr. [2]*sacr-* + *-arium*] **:** SYNSACRUM

sacrary *n* -ES [ME *sacrarie,* fr. MF & ML & L; MF *sacrarie, sacraire* Christian sanctuary, fr. ML *sacrarium,* fr. L, pagan Roman sacrarium, holy place or temple in general] *obs* **:** SACRARIUM

sacrate *vt* -ED/-ING/-S [L *sacratus,* past part. of *sacrare*] *obs* **:** CONSECRATE — **sacration** *n* -s

sacre *vt* -ED/-ING/-S [ME *sacren* to consecrate] **1** *obs* **:** to consecrate as king or bishop **2** *obs* **:** to make holy **:** SANCTIFY **3** *obs* **:** DEDICATE

[1]**sa·cred** \ˈsākrəd\ *adj* [ME, fr. past part. of *sacren* to consecrate, fr. OF *sacrer,* fr. L *sacrare,* fr. *sacr-, sacer* sacred, holy, cursed; akin to L *sancire* to make sacred, Hitt *saklais* rite, custom] **1 :** CONSECRATED ⟨the ~ elements of the Eucharist⟩ **2 a :** dedicated or set apart (as to the honor or veneration of a deity, group, or person) — usu. used with *to* ⟨a tree ~ to Jupiter⟩ **b :** devoted exclusively to the service or use (as of a particular person, purpose, or group) — usu. used with *to* ⟨a fund ~ to charity⟩ ⟨a study ~ to the chairman⟩ **3 a :** holy or hallowed esp. by association with the divine or consecrated **:** worthy of religious veneration ⟨the ~ name of Jesus⟩ ⟨Jerusalem's ~ soil⟩ ⟨a ~ memory⟩ **b :** entitled to reverence and respect **:** VENERABLE ⟨~ old age⟩ **4 :** religious in nature, association, or use **:** not secular or profane ⟨~ vestments⟩ ⟨~ history⟩ **5** *obs* **:** ACCURSED, CONSUMING **6 :** organized around ceremonial and traditionalistic values and patterns to the exclusion of new ones ⟨a ~ society of medieval times⟩ — contrasted with *secular*

[2]**sacred** *n* -s *obs* **:** a sacred rite or oblation

sacred ape *n* **:** SACRED MONKEY

sacred baboon *n* **:** a baboon (*Papio hamadryas*) venerated by the ancient Egyptians

sacred bamboo *n* **:** NANDINA 2

sacred bark *n* **1 :** CASCARA SAGRADA **2 :** CASCARA BUCKTHORN

sacred bean *n* **1 :** seed of the Indian lotus **2 :** INDIAN LOTUS

sacred beetle *n* **:** the scarabaeus which was held sacred by the Egyptians

sacred book *n* **:** any book (as the Bible) regarded by a religious body as an authoritative source or divinely inspired statement of its faith, history, and practices

sacred bo tree *n* **:** PIPAL

sacred cow *n* [so called fr. the veneration of cows in India] **:** a person or thing so well established in and venerated by a society that it seems unreasonably immune from ordinary criticism even of the honest or justified kind

sacred ear *or* **sacred earflower** *n* **:** the fragrant spicy flower of a Mexican and Central American shrub or small tree (*Cymbopetalum penduliflorum*) having the shape of an ear and prized by the Aztecs for flavoring chocolate and for its supposed tonic properties

sacred fig *n* **:** PIPAL

sacred fish *n* **:** any of several fishes of the genus *Mormyrus* (as *M. oxyrhynchus*) that inhabit the river Nile and that were held in veneration by the ancient Egyptians because they were thought to have devoured a part of the body of the god Osiris

sacred girdle *n* **:** the kusti of the Parsis

sacred ibis *n* **:** an ibis (*Threskiornis aethiopica*) common in the Nile basin about two feet long and chiefly white and black with naked head and neck that was venerated by the ancient Egyptians

sacred lotus *n* **:** INDIAN LOTUS

sa·cred·ly *adv* **:** in a sacred manner

sacred monkey *n* **:** any of several monkeys held sacred by natives of the regions they inhabit (as the hanuman, the rhesus monkey, or the sacred baboon)

sacred mushroom *n* **:** MESCAL BUTTON

sa·cred·ness *n* -ES **:** the quality or state of being sacred

sacred order *n* **:** MAJOR ORDER — usu. used in pl.

sacred shirt *n* **:** the shirt worn by Parsis with the kusti which together serve as the distinguishing marks of a Parsi

sacred theology *n* **:** REVEALED THEOLOGY

sacred thread *or* **sacred cord** *n* **:** a cotton thread with which a Hindu youth of the three twice-born castes and some Sudras is invested at the ceremony of initiation (as at the age of from eight to twelve) and which is worn constantly thereafter from the left shoulder across the body to the right

sacred weed *n* **:** a vervain (*Verbena officinalis*)

sacred writ *n, usu cap S&W* **:** SCRIPTURE

sacrifical *adj* [L *sacrificalis,* fr. *sacrificus* sacrificial (fr. *sacri-* — fr. *sacr-, sacer* sacred — + *-ficus* -fic) + *-alis* -al] *obs* **:** SACRIFICIAL

sac·ri·fi·ca·tion \,sakrəfəˈkāshən\ *n* -s [L *sacrification-, sacrificatio,* fr. *sacrificatus* (past part. of *sacrificare* to sacrifice) + *-ion-, -io* -ion] **:** a making of a sacrifice

sac·ri·fi·ca·tor \ˈ≈≈≈,kād·ə(r)\ *n* -s [MF *sacrificateur,* fr. LL *sacrificator,* fr. L *sacrificatus* (past part. of *sacrificare* to sacrifice) + *-or*] **:** SACRIFICER; *esp* **:** PRIEST

sac·rif·i·ca·to·ry \səˈkrifəkə,tōrē, saˈk-; ˈsakrəfək-; *chiefly Brit* ˌsakrəfəˈkātəri, -ātri\ *adj* [L *sacrificatus* (past part. of *sacrificare* to sacrifice, fr. *sacri-* — fr. *sacr-, sacer* sacred — + *-ficare* -fy) + E *-ory*] **:** of or relating to sacrifice esp. of the mass

[1]**sac·ri·fice** \ˈsakrə,fīs *also* -fəs *or* -,fīz *sometimes esp before pl ending* -,fis\ *n* -s [ME *sacrifise, sacrifice,* fr. OF, fr. L *sacrificium,* fr. *sacri-* (fr. *sacr-, sacer* sacred) + *-ficium* (akin to L *-ficare* -fy) — more at SACRED] **1 a :** an act or action of making an offering of animal or vegetable life, of food, drink, or incense, or of some precious object to a deity or spiritual being **b :** something consecrated and offered to God or to a divinity or an immolated victim or an offering of any kind laid on an altar or otherwise presented in the way of religious thanksgiving, atonement, or conciliation **2 a :** the crucifixion of Christ; *specif* **:** the voluntary offering by Christ of himself to reconcile God and man **b** *often cap* **:** the sacramental repetition of Jesus Christ's death on the cross held by some Christians to be Christ's repeatable offering of himself to God on behalf of men ⟨Eastern Orthodoxy's Bloodless *Sacrifice*⟩ **3 a :** destruction or surrender of something for the sake of something else **:** giving up of some desirable thing in behalf of a higher object **b :** something given up or lost ⟨the ~*s* made by parents⟩ **4 a :** LOSS, DEPRIVATION ⟨the ~ of a whole regiment⟩ ⟨flood victims who suffered the ~ of their homes⟩ **b :** financial loss (as incurred from selling goods marked down for immediate sale) **5 :** SACRIFICE HIT

[2]**sac·ri·fice** \-,fīs *also* -,fīz *sometimes* -,fəs *or esp before* əz & iŋ *endings* -,fis\ *vb* -ED/-ING/-S [ME *sacrifisen, sacrificen,* fr. *sacrifise, sacrifice,* n.] *vt* **1 :** to offer (as a sacrificial victim) as a sacrifice **:** make a sacrifice or religious oblation **:** IMMOLATE ⟨Abraham about to ~ Isaac⟩ **2 :** to suffer loss of, give up, renounce, injure, or destroy often for an ideal or belief or for an advantageous or beneficial end ⟨~ lives for the sake of freedom⟩ **3 :** to sell at a loss ⟨the owner ~*ed* his house⟩ **~** *vi* **1 :** to offer up or perform rites of a sacrifice **2 :** to make a sacrifice hit in baseball **syn** see FORGO

sacrifice bunt *n* **:** SACRIFICE HIT

sacrifice fly *n* **:** a fly in baseball that enables a base runner to score after the catch and that gives the batter credit for a run batted in but is not recorded as an official time at bat

sacrifice hit *n* **:** a bunt in baseball laid down with less than two out that enables a base runner to advance a base while the batter is put out at first base and that is not recorded as an official time at bat —abbr. *SH*

sac·ri·fic·er \-ə(r)\ *n* -s **:** one that sacrifices; *specif* **:** a sacrificing priest

sac·ri·fi·cial \ˌsakrəˈfishəl\ *adj* [L *sacrificium* sacrifice + E *-al*] **1 :** of, relating to, of the nature of, or involving sacrifice **2 :** of or relating to the anodes that are consumed in preventing electrolytic corrosion of the metal protected

sac·ri·fi·cial·ly \-shəlē, -li\ *adv* **:** in a sacrificial manner

sacrificial theory *n* **:** a modern theory of the atonement derived from the New Testament epistle to the Hebrews and holding that Christ as both son of God and sinless representative of man has offered on the cross a life of perfect obedience which becomes the expiation cleansing all sin-stained souls — compare SATISFACTION THEORY

sacrificing *adj* **:** SACRIFICIAL

sac·ri·lege \ˈsakrəlij\ *n* -s [ME, fr. OF, fr. L *sacrilegium,* fr. *sacrilegus* one that steals that which is sacred, fr. *sacri-* (fr. *sacr-, sacer* sacred) + *-legus* (fr. *legere* to gather, steal) — more at SACRED, LEGEND] **1 :** the crime of stealing, misusing, violating, or desecrating that which is sacred, holy, or dedicated to sacred uses **2 :** the unworthy or irreverent use of sacred persons, places, or things **:** the profanation of that which is dedicated to God or to sacred purposes **syn** see PROFANATION

sac·ri·le·gious \÷ˌsakrəˈlijəs, -lēj-\ *adj* [*sacrilege* + *-ious*] **:** committing sacrilege **:** characterized by or involving sacrilege **:** polluted with sacrilege ⟨~ robbers⟩ ⟨~ acts⟩ **syn** see IMPIOUS

sac·ri·le·gious·ly *adv* **:** in a sacrilegious manner

sa·cring \ˈsākriŋ\ *n* -s [ME *sacringe,* fr. gerund of *sacren* to consecrate — more at SACRED] **:** the act or action of consecrating: **a** *archaic* **:** the consecration of the eucharistic elements in the service of the mass **b** *archaic* **:** the consecration (as of a king or bishop) to office or orders

sacring bell *n* [ME *sacringe belle,* fr. *sacringe* sacring + *belle* bell] **1 :** a small hand bell made sometimes of silver and rung at the elevation in mass **2 :** the tolling of the church bell announcing the elevation

sacrist \ˈsakrəst, ˈsāk-\ *n* -s [ML *sacrista*] **:** SACRISTAN

sac·ris·tan \ˈsakrəstən\ *n* -s [ME, fr. ML *sacristanus,* fr. *sacrista* (fr. L *sacr-, sacer* sacred + *-ista* -ist) + L *-anus* -an — more at SACRED] **:** an officer of a church in charge of the sacristy, of the utensils or movables, and sometimes of the church in general; *also* **:** SEXTON

sac·ris·ty \-tē, -ti\ *n* -ES [ML *sacristia,* fr. *sacrista* + L *-ia* -y] **:** a room in or attached to a church where the sacred utensils and vestments are kept **:** VESTRY

sacro– — see SACR-

sacro·coccygeus \ˌsa(,)krō *also* ˌsā(-+\ *n* [NL, fr. [2]*sacr-* + *coccygeus*] **:** either the anterior muscle or the posterior muscle extending between the sacrum and coccyx

sacro·coccyx \ˈ"+\ *n* [NL, fr. [2]*sacr-* + *coccyx*] **:** the fused sacrum and coccyx

¹sacro·iliac \¦sakrō¦ilēˌak *also* ¦sāk-\ *adj* [ISV ²*sacr-* + *iliac*] **:** of, relating to, or affecting the sacroiliac ⟨~ distress⟩
²sacroiliac \"\ *n* -s **:** the region of juncture of the sacrum and ilium; *also* **:** the firm fibrocartilage joint between these bones
sacro·lum·balis \ˌ==ˌləmˈbāləs, -bāl-,-bäl-\ *n* -ES [NL, fr. ²*sacr-* + *lumbalis*, adj., lumbar, fr. *lumb-* + L *-alis* -al] **:** ILIOCOSTALIS
sac·ro·sanct \ˈsakrō saŋ(k)t, -rə,s-, -,saiŋ-\ *adj* [L *sacrosanctus*, prob. fr. *sacro* by a sacred rite (abl. of *sacrum* sacred thing, sacred rite, fr. neut. of *sacer* sacred) + *sanctus* (past part. of *sancire* to make sacred) — more at SACRED] **:** most holy or sacred **:** INVIOLABLE; *also* **:** overly or unpleasantly holy or sacred
sac·ro·sanc·ti·ty \¦==¦saŋ(k)təd·ē, -¦saiŋ-, -tətē, -i\ *n* -ES **:** the quality or state of being sacrosanct
sacro·sciatic foramen \¦sa¦(ˌ)krō *also* ¦sā¦+...-\ *n* [*sacrosciatic* prob. fr. (assumed) NL *sacrosciaticus*, fr. NL ²*sacr-* + LL *sciaticus* sciatic] **:** SCIATIC FORAMEN
sacrosciatic notch *n* **:** SCIATIC NOTCH
sacro·spinalis \¦sa(ˌ)krō *also* ¦sā(-+\ *n* [NL, fr. ²*sacr-* + LL *spinalis*, adj., spinal] **:** a muscle extending the length of the back and neck consisting of many distinct parts attached to the crest of the ilium, the vertebrae, and the ribs
sacro·spinous \"+\ *adj* [²*sacr-* + *spinous*] **:** of or relating to a ligament on each side passing from the back of the sacrum to the spine of the ischium and converting the greater sciatic notch of the innominate bone into the greater sciatic foramen
sacro·tuberous \"+\ *adj* [²*sacr-* + *tuberous*] **:** of or relating to a ligament on each side passing from the back of the sacrum to the tuberosity of the ischium and converting the lesser sciatic notch of the innominate bone into the lesser sciatic foramen
sacrum \ˈsakrəm, ˈsāk-\ *n, pl* **sacra** \-rə\ [NL, fr. LL (in *os sacrum* last bone of the spine, trans. of Gk *hieron osteon*), fr. L, neut. of *sacer* sacred] **:** the part of the vertebral column that is directly connected with or forms a part of the pelvis by articulation with the ilia, that consists of a single vertebra or of several more or less consolidated, that has in the transverse processes expanded ends fused into a solid bony mass on each side, and that in man forms the dorsal wall of the pelvis and consists of five united vertebrae diminishing in size to the apex which bears the coccyx — compare SYNSACRUM
sacs *pl of* SAC
¹sad \ˈsad, ˈsaa(ə)d\ *adj* **sadder; saddest** [ME, fr. OE *sæd*; akin to OHG *sat* sated, ON *sathr, saddr*, Goth *sads*, L *satur* sated, *satis* enough, Gk *hadēn* to satiety, enough, Skt *asinva* insatiable] **1 a** *obs* **:** SATED, SATISFIED, SURFEITED **b** *obs* (1) **:** firmly established in status or determination **:** SETTLED, FIXED ⟨settled in his face I see ~ resolution —John Milton⟩ (2) **:** capable of steadfast resistance **:** STOUT, VALIANT **c** *archaic* **:** maturely steady **:** GRAVE, SERIOUS ⟨a *sadder* and a wiser man he rose the morrow morn —S.T.Coleridge⟩ **2 a** *obs* **:** SOLID, COMPACTED **b** *dial Brit, of soil* **:** not friable **c** *chiefly Midland, of food* **:** HEAVY, SOGGY — used esp. of baked goods that do not rise **3 a :** affected with or expressive of grief or unhappiness **:** DOWNCAST, GLOOMY, MOURNFUL ⟨feeling ~ because his pet had died⟩ ⟨a ~ song about his disappointed love⟩ **b** (1) **:** causing or associated with grief or unhappiness **:** DEPRESSING ⟨heard the ~ news of their army's defeat⟩ ⟨gay clothes in ~ weather was sound sense —Audrey Barker⟩ ⟨the long ~ notes of taps —J.M.Virden⟩ (2) **:** giving occasion for regret or dismay **:** DEPLORABLE ⟨those war years were leading to a ~ relaxation of morals —C.W.Cunnington⟩ ⟨~ to say, the funds were exhausted⟩ **c :** of little worth **:** contemptibly bad **:** SORRY, POOR, INFERIOR ⟨some of these stories are good, but many are ~ drivel —Norman Douglas⟩ **4 a** *archaic* **:** DEEP, DARK ⟨a dark greenish color, growing *sadder* . . . as the plant decays, till it approaches a black —Robert Plot⟩ **b :** of a dull somber color or shade **:** DRAB ⟨~ browns and blacks⟩
²sad \"\ *adv, archaic* **:** SADLY ⟨so ~ forlorn —John Keats⟩
sa·dang *or* **sa'·dang** \ˈsäˌdäŋ\ *n* -s *usu cap* **1 :** an Indonesian people inhabiting the mountainous northern part of So. Celebes and sometimes considered a subdivision of the Toradja people **2 :** a member of the Sadang people
sad·den \ˈsadᵊn, ˈsaad-\ *vb* **saddened; saddened; saddening** \-d(ᵊ)niŋ\ **saddens** *vt* **:** to make sad: **a** *dial chiefly Eng* **:** to make firm, solid, or thick **b :** to make gloomy in spirits or appearance **:** DEPRESS ⟨his old age was ~*ed* by the dissoluteness of his eldest son —M.L.Bonham⟩ **c :** to make dark or dull ⟨~ cloth in dyeing⟩ ~ *vi* **1 :** to become or grow sad (as in spirits) **2 :** to make a person or thing sad
sad·den·ing·ly *adv* **:** in a saddening manner
saddhu *var of* SADHU
sad·dish \ˈsa(a)dish\ *adj* **:** somewhat sad
¹sad·dle \ˈsadᵊl\ *n* -s [ME *sadel*, fr. OE *sadol, sadul*; akin to OHG *satul* saddle, ON *söthull*; all fr. a prehistoric Gmc word perh. borrowed fr. an eastern IE word represented by OSlav *sedlo* saddle; akin to L *sedēre* to sit — more at SIT] **1 a** (1) **:** a seat shaped to fit the inside contours of the buttocks of a rider on horseback and made of a leather-covered wooden frame that is padded to comfortably span a horse's back, raised in front and rear, provided with stirrups, and secured by a girth passing under the belly of the horse ⟨a journey of 63 miles in the ~ —*Sacramento (Calif.) Bee*⟩ ⟨few horses are worked under ~ . . . for fear they will break down —A.J.Liebling⟩ — see ENGLISH SADDLE, MCCLELLAN SADDLE, STOCK SADDLE (2) **:** a padded part of a harness centered on a horse's back, fastened with a girth, and used to keep the breeching in place and to carry guides for the reins (3) **:** an adaptation of a riding saddle — see PACKSADDLE **b :** a seat similarly designed to be straddled on a bicycle, tricycle, motorcycle, or similar vehicle — see BICYCLE illustration **c :** the part of a gymnastics side horse between the pommels **2 :** a device mounted as a support and often shaped to fit the object held: as **a :** a hollowed block of wood attached to a spar on a ship as a crutch for another spar **b :** a block over which the cables of a suspension bridge pass or to which they are anchored **c :** the part of a gun carriage that supports the trunnions **d** (1) **:** a sliding carriage for a tool or work-holding table on a machine tool (as a lathe or a milling machine) (2) **:** the part of a binder's sewing machine on which the sections of a book are spread and placed for sewing **e :** CHAIR 5a **f :** a seating for a cylindrical steam boiler **g :** the part of a partial denture that carries an artificial tooth and has connectors for adjacent teeth attached to its ends **h :** a fitting mounted on a pipe (as a gas or sewer main) for attaching a new connection (as a service line) where no branch has been provided and the main is not thick enough for direct connection **i :** a transverse log with a depression cut in it to guide logs along a skid road **j :** a fired clay support for ceramic ware during a glazing fire **3 a** (1) **:** a ridge connecting two higher elevations **:** a low point in the crest line of a ridge (2) **:** COL 2 **b :** SADDLE REEF **c :** a minor upfold along the axis of a syncline **d :** a minor downfold along the axis of an anticline **4 :** a part or marking of an animal suggesting the saddle of a horse in form or position: **a** (1) **:** HINDSADDLE ⟨a ~ of mutton⟩ (2) **:** both sides of the unsplit back of a carcass including both loins **:** the undivided loins prepared for roasting (3) **:** the lower part of the back with the hind legs of a frog **b** (1) **:** a colored marking on the back of an animal (2) **:** a portion of a suture in a cephalopod shell that forms an angle or curve whose convexity is directed toward the orifice of the shell — opposed to *lobe* (3) **:** the rear part of a male fowl's back extending to the tail and covered by long narrow feathers resembling the true hackle — see COCK illustration (4) **:** the clitellum of an earthworm (5) **:** EPHIPPIUM 2 **5 a :** CRICKET 5 **b :** the metal covering of a roll on a metal-covered roof **c** *or* **saddleback** \ˈ==ˌ=\ **:** a ridge that divides a coaling hatch of a ship so that the coal is diverted into the bunkers at each side **6 :** a two-number combination selected to appear among the numbers that will win in a lottery **7 :** a strip of thin board or metal covering the floor joint on the threshold of a door **:** SILL **8 :** a bridging piece between a pair of cylinders in a locomotive **9 :** the central part of the backbone of the binding of a book **10 a :** an ornamental piece or pair of pieces of leather extending across the instep of a shoe and often contrasting in color or design **b :** SADDLE SHOE **11 :** a canvas jacket used on turkey hens to prevent injury during treading **12 :** a folded paper attached over a bag closure to label or strengthen (as for hanging on display) — called also *header* — **in the saddle** *adv* (*or adj*) **1 :** in a position to dictate **:** in control ⟨back *in the saddle* as chairman of the board —Bennett Cerf⟩ **2 :** on top in the act of coitus
²saddle \"\ *vb* **saddled; saddled; saddling** \-d(ᵊ)liŋ\ **saddles** [ME *sadelen, sadlen*, fr. OE *sadelian*; akin to OHG *gisatilen* to saddle, ON *söthla*; denominative fr. the root of OE *sadol* saddle] *vt* **1 :** to put a saddle upon ⟨*saddled* their horses and mounted and rode up to the door —Irving Bacheller⟩ — often used with *up* **2 a :** to place under a burden or encumbrance **:** weigh down with an onerous responsibility or restriction — usu. used with *with* ⟨finds himself *saddled* with a woman he does not want —Vernon Jarratt⟩ ⟨the taxpayers of the nation would be *saddled* with the tremendous burden of the additional costs —*U. S. Code*⟩ ⟨*saddling* the nation with restrictive laws —*New Republic*⟩ **b :** to place (an onerous responsibility, restriction, or reputation) on a person or group — usu. used with *on* ⟨the military attempt to ~ on labor the responsibility for shortages —*Atlantic*⟩ ⟨~ tighter government and military control on the nation —Lindesay Parrott⟩ **3 :** to put in place, support, join, or shape by or as if by means of a saddle **4 :** to put on like a saddle **:** to cause to straddle ⟨barn swallows which . . . *saddled* their nest in the loop of a rope —John Burroughs⟩ ⟨~ the stag's carcass on a pony⟩ **5 :** to send (a horse that one has trained) into a race ⟨the trainer who has *saddled* the greatest number of winners —Harry Disston⟩ ~ *vi* **1 :** to mount a saddled horse **2 :** to put a saddle on an animal ⟨had to ~ for him the first few times⟩ — often used with *up* **syn** see BURDEN
³saddle \"\ *adj* [¹*saddle*] **1 a :** of or attached to a saddle ⟨a ~ holster⟩ **b :** designed for use while riding horseback ⟨a ~ coat⟩ ⟨a ~ rifle⟩ **2 :** ridden with or suitable for riding with a saddle ⟨a ~ pony⟩ ⟨bareback bronc riding and ~ bronc riding⟩ **3 :** caused by riding or by being under a saddle ⟨~ soreness⟩ ⟨a ~ irritation⟩ **4 :** resembling a saddle in shape or position ⟨~ fuel tanks⟩ **5 a :** riding horseback **:** MOUNTED ⟨a ~ preacher⟩ **b :** of or relating to horsemanship with a saddle horse ⟨won the five-gaited ~ championship⟩
¹saddleback \ˈ==ˌ=\ *n* [¹*saddle* + *back*] **1 :** something saddle-backed in outline: as **a** (1) **:** SADDLE ROOF (2) **:** a coping with a slope on the two sides **b :** a hill or ridge having a concave outline at the top **c :** SADDLE OYSTER **d :** two supporting members (as of timber) placed in the form of an inverted V **2 :** an animal having a marking on the back suggesting a saddle: as **a :** the male harp seal **b :** BLACK-BACKED GULL **c :** HOODED CROW **d :** a passerine bird (*Philesturnus carunculatus*) native to New Zealand that is related to the huia and when mature has black plumage with a chestnut-colored band on the back and wings **e** *usu cap* **:** an animal of either of two British breeds (Essex Saddleback and Wessex Saddleback) of medium-sized black swine distinguished by a white band crossing the back at the shoulder and descending on to each forefoot **3** *Brit* **:** a size of wrapping paper measuring 45 by 36 inches
²saddleback \"\ *adj* **:** SADDLE-BACKED
saddleback caterpillar *n* **:** a caterpillar that is the larva of a cup moth (*Sibine stimulea*), has urticating hairs and usu. a green and brown saddle-shaped mark on the back, and feeds on cherry and oak in the southeastern U.S.
saddle-backed \¦==¦=\ *adj* **1 a :** having the outline of the upper part concave **b :** having an upper outline in the form of an arch or an inverted V **2** *of a horse* **:** having a depression behind the withers **3 :** having a marking that suggests a saddle
saddle-backed jackal *n* **:** BLACK-BACKED JACKAL
saddleback roof *n* **:** SADDLE ROOF
saddleback stitch *n* **:** SADDLE STITCH
¹saddlebag \ˈ==ˌ=\ *n* [¹*saddle* + *bag*] **1 a :** a large bag or pouch of leather or a textile fabric carried hanging from one side of a saddle and commonly one of a pair united by a band or strap and so hung that the weight is evenly distributed **b :** one of a pair of similar pouches carried one on each side of the rear wheel of a bicycle or motorcycle **2 :** an upholstering cloth imitating the hand-knotted texture of oriental saddlebags and popular in the late Victorian period **3** *or* **saddlebag house :** a double cabin with two units separated by several feet but covered by one roof
²saddlebag \"\ *vi* **:** to catch on an obstruction and swing around it ⟨a barge that *saddlebagged* on a bridge pier⟩
saddle bar *n* **1 :** one of the slender horizontal iron bars to which the lead panels of a glazed window are secured **2 :** a side bar of the tree of a saddle connecting the pommel and cantle on each side
saddle-bill \ˈ==ˌ=\ *or* **saddle-billed stork** \ˈ==ˌ=-\ *n* **:** a large black-and-white West African stork (*Ephippiorhynchus senegalensis*) having the bill red with a black median band — called also *jabiru*
saddle blanket *n* **:** a blanket folded beneath a saddle to prevent galling the horse
saddle block anesthesia *or* **saddle block** *n* **:** spinal anesthesia confined to the perineal area
saddle board *n* **:** a strip of wood or metal covering the ridge of a roof
saddle boiler *n* **:** a boiler with an arched base serving as a flue
saddlebow \ˈ==ˌ=\ *n* [ME *sadelbowe*, fr. OE *sadulboga*, fr. *sadol, sadul* saddle + *boga* bow] **:** the arch in the front or the pieces forming the front of a saddle
saddle brown *n* **:** SADDLE TAN
saddle-check chair *n* **:** an English wing chair of the 18th century
saddlecloth \ˈ==ˌ=\ *n* [ME *sadylclow*, fr. *sadyl, sadel* saddle + *clow, cloth* cloth] **1 :** a cloth formerly placed under a saddle and extending out behind; *also* **:** HOUSING **2 :** a cloth bearing a racehorse's number and placed over the saddle
saddled *past of* SADDLE
saddle embolus *n* **:** an embolus that straddles the branching of an artery blocking both branches — called also *rider embolus*
saddle flange *n* **:** a pipe flange curved to fit snugly against a cylindrical pipe or tank and used esp. to repair a leak
saddle fungus *n* **:** a fungus of the genus *Helvella* having a saddle-shaped fruiting body
saddle graft *n* **:** a plant graft made by fitting a deep cleft in the end of the scion over a wedge in the end of a stock of similar diameter so that the two cambiums are in contact — see GRAFT illustration
saddle gun *n* **:** a light hand-operated dusting machine designed to be carried on the back of a mule or horse
saddle head *n* **:** a head with a depressed or sunken crown caused by premature closure of the sphenoparietal suture
saddle horn *n* **:** the hornlike prolongation of the pommel of a stock saddle which is usu. made of leather-covered metal and to which the rope or lasso of a cowhand is commonly made fast
saddle horse *n* **1 :** a horse suited for or trained for riding typically with a strong back, well-rounded body with long sloping pasterns and shoulders, a stylish carriage, and several gaits (as the walk, trot, and canter); *specif* **:** AMERICAN SADDLE HORSE — compare HARNESS HORSE, HUNTER, JUMPER **2** *dial* **:** LEAD HORSE
saddle iron *n* **:** a strip of iron used to brace the open bottom of a stage flat (as for a door, arch, or fireplace)
saddle joint *n* **1 :** a joint formed in sheet-metal roofing by bending up the edge of a sheet and folding it downward over the turned-up edge of the next sheet **2 :** a joint in a weathered course of masonry (as a coping or sill) between adjoining stones whose ends are cut higher than the surface of the weathering between **3 :** a joint (as the carpometacarpal of the thumb) with saddle-shaped articular surfaces that are convex in one direction and concave in another and that permit movements in all directions except axial rotation
saddle key *n* **:** a key for securing a member to a machine shaft that fits into a keyway in the secured member and is concave to grip the shaft by friction — compare FLAT KEY, SUNK KEY
saddleleaf \ˈ==ˌ=\ *n* **:** TULIP TREE 1
saddle leather *n* **1 :** vegetable tanned cattlehide usu. tan in color for saddlery **2 :** cattlehide leather for handbags and fancy leather goods colored and finished to resemble saddle leather
sad·dle·less \ˈsadᵊl(l)ə̇s\ *adj* [ME *sadulles*, fr. *sadul, sadel* saddle + *-les* -less] **:** having no saddle
saddlelike \ˈ==ˌ=\ *adj* **:** resembling or suggesting a saddle (as in shape)
saddlemaker \ˈ==ˌ==\ *n* [ME *sadlemaker*, fr. *sadle, sadel* saddle + *maker*] **:** SADDLER 1
saddlenose \ˈ==ˌ=\ *n* **:** a nose marked by depression of the bridge resulting from injury or disease
saddle-notched joint \ˈ==ˌ=-\ *n* **:** a joint made for the overlapping of round logs in log construction by scooped depressions in the members
saddle oyster *n* **1 :** a windowpane oyster (*Placuna sella*) of the Indian and Pacific oceans having a broad arch like a saddle **2 :** a mollusk of *Anomia* or a related genus
saddle pile *n* **:** a sheet pile driven into the ground and made concave on the top edge to support a sewer pipe or the like in soft ground
saddle point *n* **1 :** a point on a curved surface at which the curvatures in two mutually perpendicular planes are of opposite signs — compare ANTICLASTIC **2 :** a value of a function of two variables which is a maximum with respect to one and a minimum with respect to the other
saddle quern *n* **:** METATE
sad·dler \ˈsadlə(r)\ *n* -s [ME *sadelere*, fr. *sadel* saddle + *-ere* -er] **1 :** one that makes, repairs, or sells saddles and other furnishings for saddle horses **2 :** SADDLE HORSE 1 **3 :** the male harp seal **4** [²*saddle* + *-er*] **:** one that saddles
saddle reef *n* **:** one of a nearly vertical succession of saddle-shaped ore deposits straddling anticlinal or synclinal folds
saddle rock \ˈ==ˌ=\ *n* [perh. fr. *Saddle Rock*, rock in Little Neck Bay, Long Island, N.Y.] *Northeast* **:** a large prime oyster
saddle roof *n* **:** a roof (as of a tower) having two gables and one ridge — called also *saddleback, saddleback roof*
sad·dlery \ˈsadlərē, -dᵊlərē, -ri\ *n* -ES **1 :** the skill or employment of a saddler **2 :** saddles and other furnishings for saddle horses **:** TACK **3 :** a place where saddlery is sold or stored
saddles *pl of* SADDLE, *pres 3d sing of* SADDLE
saddle seam *n* **:** a seam used esp. in shoes that is made by sewing together the edges of two pieces of leather placed with their inner sides facing and then opening them out so that the cut edges and stitching show
saddle seat *n* **:** a slightly concave chair seat (as of a Windsor chair) with sometimes a thickened ridge at the center front
saddle-sew \ˈ==ˌ=\ *vt* **:** to fasten together the leaves of (as a book) by a method resembling saddle stitching but using thread instead of wire
saddle-shaped \ˈ==ˌ=\ *adj* **1 :** bent down at the sides so as to give the upper part a rounded form **2 :** having the form of an anticlinal fold
saddle shell *n* **:** JINGLE SHELL
saddle shoe *or* **saddle oxford** *n* **:** an oxford-style shoe having a saddle of a color or leather contrasting with that of the rest of the shoe
saddle skirt *n* **:** the part of a saddle extending down on the flank of a horse — usu. used in pl.
saddle soap *n* **:** a mild soap made with some added unsaponified oil and used in the form of an aqueous paste or bar for cleansing and conditioning leather

saddle shoe

saddlesore \ˈ==ˌ=\ *adj* [¹*saddle* + *sore*, adj.] **:** sore and stiffened from riding
saddle sore *n* [¹*saddle* + *sore*, n.] **1 :** a gall or open sore developing on the back of a horse at points of pressure from an ill-fitting or improperly adjusted saddle **2 :** an irritation or sore on parts of the rider chafed by the saddle
¹saddle stitch *n* **1 :** a stitch made by placing the center of the fold (as of a magazine or pamphlet) across the saddle of the stitcher and driving wire staples through and clinching them on the inside — called also *saddleback stitch, saddle-wire stitch* **2 :** an even or uneven running stitch usu. set in from an edge that is used as a decorative trimming on clothing and leather articles
²saddle stitch *vt* **:** to secure (as a magazine or pamphlet) with a saddle stitch
saddle stone *n* **:** APEX STONE
saddle tan *n* **:** a moderate brown that is redder, lighter, and stronger than coffee, lighter, stronger, and slightly yellower than chestnut brown, and yellower, lighter, and stronger than auburn
saddle tank *n* **:** a water tank straddling the boiler of a locomotive (as a small switch engine) and designed to increase the weight on the drivers
sad·dle·tree \ˈsadᵊl·(ˌ)trē, -ˌtri\ *n* [ME *sadeltre*, fr. *sadel* saddle + *tre, tree* tree] **1 :** the frame of a saddle **2** [¹*saddle* + *tree*; fr. the shape of the leaves] **:** TULIP TREE 1
saddle-wire \ˈ==ˌ=\ *vt* **:** to secure (as a magazine or pamphlet) with a saddle stitch
saddle-wire stitch *n* **:** SADDLE STITCH 1
saddling *pres part of* SADDLE
sad·du·ca·ic \¦sajə¦kāik, ¦sadyə-, -ə¦sā-\ *adj, usu cap* [*sadducee* + *-aic* (as in *pharisaic*)] **:** SADDUCEAN
sad·du·ce·an *or* **sad·du·cae·an** \¦==¦sēən\ *adj, usu cap* [LL *sadducaeus* Sadducee + E *-an*] **:** of, relating to, or characteristic of the Sadducees ⟨the *Sadducean* party⟩ ⟨*Sadducean* materialism⟩
sad·du·cee \ˈ==ˌsē\ *n* -s [ME *saducee*, fr. OE *sadduce*, fr. LL *sadducaeus*, fr. Gk *saddoukaios*, fr. LHeb *ṣăddūqī*, prob. fr. *Ṣadoq* Zadok, high priest of Israel during the reign of King David and supposed founder of the sect] **1** *usu cap* **:** a member of a party or sect among the Jews from the 2d century B.C. to the latter part of the 1st century A.D. consisting largely of the priestly aristocracy, opposing politically and doctrinally the Pharisees, interpreting the law more literally and less strictly than the Pharisees, rejecting the authority of the other parts of Scripture and the rabbinic tradition, and denying the resurrection, personal immortality, retribution in a future life, and the existence of angels, spirits, and demons **2** *often cap* **:** one who denies immortality and tends to materialism or religious indifferentism
sad·du·cee·ism \-ē,izəm\ *n* -s *usu cap* **:** the tenets, disposition, or point of view of the Sadducees
sade \ˈsād\ *vb* -ED/-ING/-s [ME *saden, sadden* to weary, become weary or satiated, fr. OE *sadian* to satiate, become weary or satiated; akin to OHG *satōn* to become satiated; denominative fr. the root of E ¹*sad*] *dial Eng* **:** WEARY
sa·dha·na \ˈsädənə\ *n* -s [Skt *sādhana*; akin to Skt *sādhu* going straight to a goal] **1 :** Hindu religious training or discipline through which an individual attains samadhi **2 :** Hindu or Buddhist spiritual training through which an individual worships a formed image as a mediate step to the worship of a formless deity or principle **3 :** the tantric evocation of a deity by means of spells and ritual for the purpose of getting control of the deity
sa·dhe *also* **sa·de** \ˈsä(ˌ)de, -)dē\ *n* -s [Heb *ṣādhē*] **1 :** the eighteenth letter of the Hebrew alphabet — symbol צ or ץ; see ALPHABET table **2 :** the letter of the Phoenician or of any of various other Semitic alphabets corresponding to Hebrew sadhe
sa·dhu *or* **sad·dhu** \ˈsä(ˌ)dü\ *n* -s [Skt *sādhu*, fr. *sādhu*, adj., straight, going straight to a goal, good; akin to Gk *ithys* straight, direct — more at ATHROGENIC] **:** a Hindu mendicant ascetic claiming great mystic powers, wearing a saffron robe or abjuring all clothing, and often practicing extreme mortification (as burying oneself alive) **:** holy man
sadic \ˈsädik, ˈsad-, -dēk *sometimes* ˈsād- *or* ˈsād-\ *adj* [F *sadique*, fr. Comte de Sade + F *-ique* -ic] **:** SADISTIC

sadiron

sad·iron \ˈsaˌdī(ə)rn, -īən\ *n* [¹*sad* + *iron*; fr. its heaviness and solidity in contrast with a box iron] **:** a flatiron pointed at both ends and having a removable handle
sadism \ˈsäˌdizəm, ˈsaˌd- *sometimes* ˈsā,d- *or* ˈsā,d-\ *n* -s [ISV *sad-* (fr. Comte Donatien Alphonse François de *Sade* †1814 Fr. soldier and pervert) + *-ism*] **1 a :** the

infliction of pain upon a love object as a means of obtaining sexual release — compare MASOCHISM **b** : the satisfaction of outwardly directed destructive impulses as a source of libidinal gratification **2 a** : delight in physical or mental cruelty **b** : excessive cruelty

sadist \'-,dəst\ *n* -s [ISV *sad-* (fr. Comte de *Sade*) + *-ist*] : one who makes a practice of sadism : a sadistic person

sa·dis·tic \sə'distik, -tēk *also* sā'd- *or* sa'd- *sometimes* sä'd- *or* sȧ'd-\ *adj* : of or characterized by sadism ⟨homosexual practices accompanied by strong ~ and masochistic fantasies —Charles Anderson⟩ ⟨a leg . . . sawed off in sections by a ~ surgeon —*New Yorker*⟩ — **sa·dis·ti·cal·ly** \-tək(ə)lē, -tēk-, -li\ *adv*

¹sad·ly \'sadlē, 'saad-, -li\ *adv* [ME, fr. ¹*sad* + *-ly*] : in a sad manner or way: **a** *obs* : in earnest : SERIOUSLY, GRAVELY, SOBERLY **b** : with sorrow or so as to cause sorrow : SORROWFULLY ⟨stood ~ beside the grave⟩ **c** : BADLY, DEPLORABLY ⟨a sedan . . . one of whose fenders is ~ banged up —*New Yorker*⟩

²sadly \"\ *adj, dial Eng* : suffering from poor health : POORLY ⟨the master's well . . . but the missus is very ~ —Samuel Butler †1902⟩

sad·ness *n* -ES [ME *sadnesse* seriousness, firmness, fr. ¹*sad* + *-nesse* -ness] **1** : the quality or state of being sad : SORROWFULNESS, UNHAPPINESS, GLOOMINESS **2** : an instance (as a mood or an appearance) of being sad : something sorrowful, gloomy, or depressing ⟨she talked about death as she spoke . . . of any of the ~*es* of nature —Willa Cather⟩

syn DEPRESSION, MELANCHOLY, MELANCHOLIA, DEJECTION, GLOOM, BLUES, DUMPS: SADNESS is a general term usu. without implications about cause or intensity of unhappy feeling ⟨conscious of a profound *sadness* which was not grief —Arnold Bennett⟩ ⟨a certain sense of desolation and *sadness* —A.C.Benson⟩ DEPRESSION may indicate a brooding, listless, sullen, or despondent condition in which one usu. feels let down, disheartened, enervated, or inadequate ⟨never before, in any mood of *depression*, had she given evidence of suicidal thoughts —Havelock Ellis⟩ ⟨many youngsters are conscious of a vast *depression* when entering the portals of a university; they feel themselves inadequate to cope with the wisdom of the ages garnered in the solid walls —G.D.Brown⟩ MELANCHOLY now is likely to indicate a mood or mental condition marked by sad and serious pensiveness ⟨the wit, the gaiety of spirit tinged with a tender *melancholy* —W.H.Hudson †1922⟩ MELANCHOLIA may indicate a settled deep depression verging on insanity ⟨the excited phase is called mania and its counterpart is known as *melancholia*. In the former there is a slaphappy hilarity and a disregard of the conventional restraints, while the latter phase is marked by mournful and self-accusatory ideas and a countenance disfigured by despair —R.S.Ellery⟩ DEJECTION is close to DEPRESSION but may apply to a more temporary mood and suggest a natural cause or logical reason ⟨it was the last of the regiment's stay in Meryton, and all the young ladies in the neighborhood were drooping apace. The *dejection* was almost universal —Jane Austen⟩ ⟨these notable victories of the mind, from which so much was hoped, have had for result not so much increased happiness as disquiet, have made for *dejection* rather than rejoicing —W.M.Dixon⟩ GLOOM may suggest the dark and dispiriting overall atmosphere or effect of depression or dejection ⟨the leaden *gloom* of one who has lost all that can make life interesting, or even tolerable —Thomas Hardy⟩ ⟨the *gloom* that now lay over it in a dead and menacing quietude and stagnation —Walter de la Mare⟩ BLUES simply indicates low spirits ⟨suffering from a sharp attack of the *blues*. A feeling of depression and foreboding had taken possession of him. The present seemed empty and futile, the future dark with intangible calamity —F.W.Crofts⟩ DUMPS, now usu. used only in the phrase *in the dumps*, may indicate a deeper, more sullen and cheerless state than that indicated by BLUES ⟨in the *dumps* about his stock market losses⟩

sa·do \sä'dō, 'sä(,)dō\ *n* -s [Malay, modif. of F *dos-à-dos*] : a Javanese carriage like the dos-à-dos

sado·masochism \¦sā(,)dō, ¦sa(-, ¦sä(-, ¦sȧ(-+\ *n* [ISV *sadism* + *-o-* + *masochism*] : the derivation of pleasure from the infliction of physical or mental pain either on others or on oneself : sadism and masochism conceived as two aspects of an underlying destructive tendency

sado·masochist \"+\ *n* : one that is given to sadomasochism — **sado·masochistic** \"+\ *adj*

sad sack *n* **1** : a meek inept unmilitary serviceman who blunders his way resignedly finding the odds always against him in military life **2** : a hopelessly inept person : a ludicrous misfit

sadware \'=,=\ *n* ['*sad* + *ware;* fr. its heaviness and solidity] **1** : flat and usu. cold-pressed or hammered pieces (as plates) of fine pewter as distinguished from vessels (as mugs or measures) **2** : LEY PEWTER

sae \(')sā\ *chiefly Scot var of* SO

SAE *abbr* **1** *often not cap* self-addressed envelope **2** standard average European

sae·beins \(')sā¦bēnz, -binz\ *conj* [by alter.] *Scot* : so being

saecular *var of* SECULAR

saec·u·lum \'sekyələm\ *n, pl* **saecu·la** \-lə\ [L, breed, generation, age — more at SECULAR] : a period of long duration : AGE

saeng·er·bund *or* **säng·er·bund** \'zeŋə(r),bůnt, 'se-\ *n* [G *sängerbund*, fr. *sänger* singer (fr. MHG *senger*) + *bund* association, club — more at MINNESINGER, BUND] : a German choral society; *specif* : a choral society having as members chiefly persons of German descent

saeng·er·fest *or* **säng·er·fest** \-,fest\ *n* -s [G *sängerfest*, fr. *sänger* singer + *fest* festival — more at -FEST] : a singing festival of a saengerbund

saennegrass *var of* SENNEGRASS

sae number \,e,sā'ē-\ *n, usu cap S&A&E* [*S*ociety of *A*utomotive *E*ngineers] : a number in a standard series from 10 to 70 for grading lubricating oil as to viscosity ⟨the higher the *SAE number* the greater the viscosity⟩

sa·eta \sä'äd·ə\ *n* -s [Sp, lit., arrow, fr. L *sagitta*] : an unaccompanied partly improvised piercing Andalusian song of lamentation or penitence sung during the religious procession on Good Friday

sae·ter *also* **se·ter** \'sed·ə(r), 'sād-\ *n* -s [Norw *seter, sæter*, fr. ON *setr, sætr;* akin to ON *sitja* to sit — more at SIT] **1** : a pasture high in the mountains of Norway or northern Sweden where herds are kept in summer and butter and cheese are made **2** : a hut built on a saeter as a shelter for the dairymaids and equipment

saf *abbr* safety

SAF *abbr* strategic air force

sa·far \sə'fär\ *n* -s *usu cap* [Ar *ṣafar*] : the second month of the Muhammadan year — see MONTH table

¹sa·fa·ri \sə'färē, -'far-, -ri *also* -'far-\ *n* -s [Swahili, trip, journey, fr. Ar *safarīya*] **1** : the caravan of a hunting or other expedition esp. in East Africa with men, vehicles, animals, and equipment **2 a** : a hunting or other expedition in East Africa esp. on foot **b** : an adventurous expedition elsewhere in the world ⟨arctic ~⟩ **c** : a long carefully planned trip (as a campaign tour or a legislative junket) usu. with a large entourage

²safari \"\ *vi* -ED/-ING/-S : to journey in a safari

safari ant *n* : FORAGING ANT

sa·fa·wid *or* **sa·fa·vid** \sə'fä,wēd\ *also* **sa·fa·vi** \-ä(,)wē\ *n* -s *usu cap* [*Safawid, Safavid* fr. Ar *ṣafawī* descended from *Ṣafī-al-Dīn* (fr. *Ṣafī-al-Dīn* †1334 Persian saint of Arab lineage) + E *-id; Safavi* fr. Ar *ṣafawī*] : a member of a Muhammadan Persian dynasty founded in 1502 by Shah Ismail

¹safe \'sāf\ *adj* -ER/-EST [ME *sauf, saf, save*, fr. OF *salf, sauf, saf, sal*, fr. L *salvus* safe, whole, healthy; akin to L *salus* health, safety, *salubris* healthful, salutary, *solidus* solid, Gk *holos* complete, entire, Skt *sarva* unharmed, entire] **1** : freed from harm, injury, or risk : no longer threatened by danger or injury : UNHARMED, UNHURT ⟨the rocks were to windward on our quarter, and we were ~ —Frederick Marryat⟩ **2** : secure from threat of danger, harm, or loss: as **a** : not exposed to danger ⟨the bullfighters had been developing a technique which simulated this appearance of danger . . . while the bullfighter was really ~ —Ernest Hemingway⟩ ⟨the trees have grown tall enough to be ~ from trampling —*Amer. Guide Series: La.*⟩ **b** (1) : successful in reaching base ⟨the batter was ~ at first on a close play⟩ (2) : enabling a batter in baseball to reach base ⟨a ~ hit to deep short⟩ **c** : secure from loss to the opposition in an election ⟨if a poll shows that a state or district is ~, there may be no reason for spending money . . . for . . . party propaganda —D.D.McKean⟩ **d** : not liable to decipherment ⟨a ~ code⟩ **3** : affording protection from danger : securing from harm ⟨a ~ margin of national revenue must be kept for possible defense needs —*Current Biog.*⟩ ⟨a ~ haven⟩ **4** *obs, of mental or moral faculties* : HEALTHY, SOUND ⟨are his wits ~ —Shak.⟩ **5 a** (1) : not threatening danger : HARMLESS ⟨other animals . . . instinctively realize when a party of lions may be regarded as ~ —James Stevenson-Hamilton⟩ (2) *archaic* : made incapable of doing harm (as by being placed in confinement or under custody) **b** : unlikely to produce controversy or contradiction ⟨the ~, sane, and sanitary cliché —S.H.Adams⟩ ⟨it is *safer* to generalize about institutions than individuals —Harry Levin⟩ **c** : free from contaminating qualities : not liable to corrupt or injure ⟨a ~ vaccine⟩ ⟨a ~ book for young people⟩ **d** *of a part of a file* : left without teeth so that only one surface of an object is cut when filing near a corner or in a narrow slot **6 a** : not liable to take risks : CAUTIOUS ⟨the ~ man usually has been preferred to the audacious —C.E.Silcox⟩ **b** : of known and reliable opinions and actions ⟨a ~ man, unlikely to give trouble —Osbert Sitwell⟩

syn SECURE: SAFE can imply that one has run a risk without incurring harm or damage ⟨to arrive home *safe* after a rough trip⟩ ⟨to see the children *safe* in bed⟩ or can apply to persons or possessions whose situation or position involves no risk ⟨a *safe* place to live⟩ ⟨remain *safe* in an air raid shelter all night⟩, or to such things as bridges, vehicles, or policies so designed or constructed that they expose one to no risk ⟨a bridge not *safe* for heavy trucks⟩ ⟨a *safe* political position⟩ SECURE, sometimes interchangeable with SAFE, usu. implies freedom from anxiety or apprehension of danger and often freedom from all hazards, or it can apply to something conducive to such a frame of mind or such freedom ⟨feel *secure* only among close friends⟩ ⟨a *secure* harbor⟩ ⟨a good bank account often can help make one *secure*⟩ ⟨make your investments *secure*⟩ ⟨a *secure* place for himself in the academic world⟩

²safe \"\ *n* -s [ME *saue*, fr. *sauf, saf*, adj.] **1** : a place or receptacle to keep articles safe: as **a** : a ventilated or refrigerated chest or closet for securing provisions from pests and the effects of weather **b** : a metal box or chest sometimes built into a wall or vault to protect money or other valuables against fire or burglary **2** : a tray under a fixture (as a bath or roof tank) to catch drippings or overflow **3** : CONDOM

safe 1 b

³safe \"\ *adv* -ER/-EST [¹*safe*] : SAFELY, SECURELY ⟨play ~⟩ ⟨hit ~⟩ ⟨land me ~ on Canaan's side —William Williams †1791⟩ — often used in combination ⟨*safe*-hidden⟩ ⟨*safe*-moored⟩

⁴safe *vt* -ED/-ING/-S [¹*safe*] *obs* : to make safe

⁵safe \'sāf\ *Scot var of* SAVE

safe-conduct \'=¦=(,)=\ *n* [ME *sauf conduit, saf conduit*, fr. OF *sauf conduit*, fr. *sauf* safe + *conduit* conduct — more at SAFE, CONDUCT] **1** : a privilege granted by a military or other authority to an enemy, neutral, or other person not otherwise protected to move within or through or perform specified activities within a designated area **2** : a document similar to a passport authorizing safe-conduct

safecracker \'=,==\ *n* : one that breaks open safes to steal

safecracking \'=,==\ *n* : the act or process of breaking into a safe esp. by explosives to burglarize it

safe-deposit \'==¦==\ *adj* : of, providing, or constituting a box or vault for the storage of valuables in safety

safe edge *n* : a smooth uncut edge on a file or rasp

safe-edge file *n* : a file that is left uncut on at least one edge and used for filing near a corner so as not to cut the surface at right angles

¹safeguard \'=,=\ *n* [ME *saufgarde*, fr. MF *salvegarde, saufegarde*, fr. OF, fr. *salve, sauve* (fem. of *salf, sauf* safe) + *garde* guard — more at SAFE, GUARD] **1 a** *obs* : SAFE-CONDUCT 1 **b** : SAFE-CONDUCT 2 **2 a** : a written order issued by a military commander or other authority guaranteeing the safety of specified persons or property **b** : a guard furnished by a military commander or other authority to protect persons or property **3** *archaic* : PROTECTION, DEFENSE ⟨if you do fight in ~ of your wives —Shak.⟩ **4** : a means of protection against something undesirable ⟨necessary ~*s* against the conviction of innocent persons —F.A.Ogg & P.O.Ray⟩ ⟨this diversification is considered a ~ against crises —G.G.Weigend⟩ **5** *archaic* : a protective petticoat worn outside a riding habit

²safeguard \"\ *vt* : to provide a safeguard for : PROTECT ⟨a clause ~*ing* the right of habeas corpus —Irving Brant⟩ ⟨~ the layman against being victimized by quacks —H.G. Rickover⟩ **syn** see DEFEND

safehold \'=,=\ *n* : a refuge esp. from attack

safekeeping \'=¦==\ *n* [ME *safe kepyng*] **1** : the act or process of preserving in safety from injury, loss, or escape ⟨systematic provision is made for the ~ of work slips —*Nat'l Miller*⟩ **2** : the state of being preserved in safety from injury, loss, or escape ⟨had his various business papers and his will in ~ —Glenway Wescott⟩

safelight \'=,=\ *n* **1** : a color filter under which a sensitive paper, plate, or film may be manipulated and developed without danger of fogging and which usu. consists of colored gelatin protected by glass plates or laminated in plastic **2** : a darkroom lamp with its filter

safe·ly *adv* [ME *savely, saufly, safly*, fr. *sauf, saf, save* safe + *-ly* — more at SAFE] : in a safe manner : with safety

saf·en \'sāfən\ *vt* -ED/-ING/-S [¹*safe* + *-en*] : to make safe; *specif* : to reduce the phytotoxic effect of by adding a safener ⟨the use of lime to ~ arsenical sprays⟩

saf·en·er \-f(ə)nə(r)\ *n* -s : a chemical used in an insecticidal or fungicidal spray to prevent damage to trees and foliage by the other ingredients in the spray

safe·ness *n* -ES [ME *savenes, safnes*, fr. *sauf, save, saf* safe + *-nes* -ness] : the quality or state of being safe

safe period *n* : a portion of the human female sexual cycle during which conception is least likely to occur and which usu. includes several days immediately before and after the menstrual period and the period itself — compare RHYTHM METHOD

safe-pledge *n, obs* : a surety for the appearance of a person at a given time

safer *comparative of* SAFE

safes *pl of* SAFE, *pres 3d sing of* SAFE

safest *superlative of* SAFE

¹safe·ty \'sāftē, -ti *sometimes* ÷-fəd- *or* ÷-fət-\ *n* -ES *often attrib* [ME *sauvete, saufte, safte*, fr. MF *salveté, sauveté*, fr. OF, fr. *salve, sauve* (fem. of *salf, sauf* safe) + *-té* -ty — more at SAFE] **1** : the condition of being safe : freedom from exposure to danger : exemption from hurt, injury, or loss ⟨the only ~ against being deceived lies in . . . refusal to bear arms —W.R.Inge⟩ ⟨ferried in ~ across the river⟩ **2** *obs* : CUSTODY ⟨hold him in ~ till the prince come hither —Shak.⟩ **3 a** *archaic* : a means of protection : SAFEGUARD **b** (1) : a locking or interrupting device on a military apparatus (as a mine, missile, weapon) that prevents it from being fired accidentally (2) : the condition of a firearm when the safety is in action ⟨to carry a piece at ~⟩ **c** : a device (as an elevator cable break or a drop hammer trip) applied to equipment to reduce hazard from component failure or personal contact **d** : CONDOM **4 a** : the quality or state of not presenting risks : SAFENESS ⟨people have a tendency to choose the ~ of the middle-ground reply —S.L.Payne⟩ ⟨the captain of an airplane was held responsible for the . . . ~ of his ship —E.K.Gann⟩ **b** : the quality or state of being financially secure ⟨~ of principal⟩ **5** : knowledge of or skill in methods of avoiding accident or disease ⟨an expert in traffic ~⟩ **6** : any of several plays in various sports: **a** : a billiard shot made with no attempt to score and intended to leave the balls in an unfavorable position for the opponent **b** (1) : a football play in which the ball is downed by the offensive team behind its own goal line (2) : a score made by a safety that counts two points for the opposing team — compare TOUCHBACK **c** : BASE HIT **d** : the act of hitting the ball across the back line and not between the goal posts by one of the defending side in a polo match **7** : a member of a defensive backfield in football who occupies the deepest position in order to receive a kick or defend against a pass made by the opposing team or to stop a ballcarrier who has broken away

²safety \"\ *vt* -ED/-ING/-ES : to protect against failure, breakage, or other accident: as **a** : to secure (a nut on an airplane) against loosening by vibration **b** : to engage the safety of (a weapon)

safety arch *n* : an undecorated arch used for purely constructional reasons

safety belt *n* : a belt for fastening a person to some object: as **a** : one used to prevent a person from falling while working at a height **b** : one used in an airplane or vehicle to prevent injury in a crash

safety bicycle *n* : a bicycle made with equal or nearly equal wheels usu. 28 inches in diameter and driven by pedals connected to the rear wheel by a multiplying gear

safety bolt *n* : a bolt to fasten a door or gate; *esp* : a bolt that cannot be moved from the other side of the door or gate

safety button *n* : a medallion worn by nuclear energy workers to warn of excess exposure to radiation

safety cage *n* : a cage for an elevator or mine lift that has appliances to check the fall if the rope breaks

safety catch *n* : a device in an elevator or hoisting appliance to ensure safety from falling in case the mechanism fails to operate properly

safety chain *n* **1 a** : a normally slack chain for preventing excessive movement between a railroad car truck and a car body in sluing **b** : a heavy chain by which railroad cars may be connected to protect against accidental uncoupling **2** : a small chain used as a secondary safeguard on a piece of jewelry (as a watch or bracelet) **3** : a chain formed of sheet metal links with an elongated hole through each broad end and constructed by a repeated series of doubling a link upon itself, slipping the next link through the two now superimposed holes of the first, and doubling it

safety chain 3

safety curtain *n* : an asbestos or metal theater curtain to be lowered in case of fire

safety-deposit *adj* : SAFE-DEPOSIT

safety disk *n* : a thin copper disk over the steam boiler end of an escape pipe designed to break and permit escape of steam under excessive pressure

safety dog *n* : a dog in a lathe equipped with safety setscrews

safety edge *n* : SAFE EDGE

safety explosive *n* : a permissible explosive

safety factor *n* : FACTOR OF SAFETY

safety film *n* : photographic film having a support of cellulose acetate or other somewhat noninflammable material

safety-fund system *n* : a system under which banks are required by law to have or provide a fund (as a common fund provided for by a small tax) as a pledge for the redemption of their circulation

safety fuse *n* **1** : a fuse that burns slowly for communicating fire to a detonator or blasting cap and that consists usu. of a train of fine black powder surrounded by a tight wrapping **2** : CARTRIDGE FUSE

safety glass *n* **1** : LAMINATED GLASS **2** : glass that is strengthened by tempering and that when struck breaks into relatively harmless granules rather than large jagged pieces **3** : WIRE GLASS

safety hanger *n* : a strap or loop under a piece of railroad rolling stock to stop broken rods and other matter from falling on the track

safety hasp *n* : a hasp that is used with a padlock and has a slotted plate fitting over the staple to prevent its removal when locked

safety hat *n* : a shallow domed hat of steel or a similar material worn (as by miners and sandhogs) to protect the top of the head

safety hoist *or* **safety lift** *n* **1** : a hoisting gear that does not overhaul when the tension is released on the fall **2** : a hoisting gear that is provided with a special attachment to prevent overhauling

safety ink *n* : indelible ink

safety island *also* **safety isle** *n* : an area within a roadway from which vehicular traffic is excluded (as by pavement markings or curbing) in order to provide an area of safety for pedestrians or to channel traffic flow

safety lamp *n* : a miner's lamp constructed to avoid explosion in an atmosphere containing inflammable gas usu. by enclosing the flame in fine wire gauze that by its cooling effect prevents the flame from passing

safety link *n* **1** : a device used for the same purpose as a safety chain **2** : a link in a chain designed to fail at rated stress and protect the rest of the links against overstress

safety lock *n* : a lock specially devised to prevent picking

safe·ty·man \-,man, -,maa(ə)n\ *n* : SAFETY 7

safety match *n* : a match capable of being struck and ignited only on a specially prepared friction surface

safety nut *n* : LOCKNUT

safety paper *n* : a paper (as the silk-fibered paper of the U.S. currency or the watermarked paper of Bank of England notes) difficult to duplicate or so made that erasures or changes in matter written or printed on it are readily detectable

safety pin *n* : a pin used esp. for fastening clothes and made in the form of a clasp with a guard covering the point so that it will not prick the wearer

safety pinion *n* : a center pinion gear of a watch that unscrews when the mainspring breaks and relieves the pressure on the delicate train wheel teeth and arbor pivots

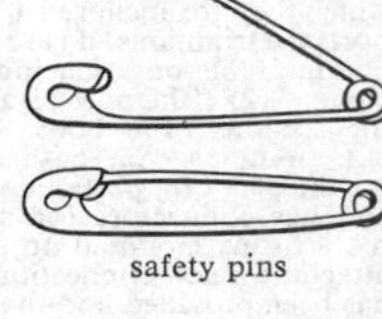

safety pins

safety plug *n* : a fusible metal plug set in a boiler shell to release steam when the plug reaches a predetermined temperature due to excessive pressure in the boiler

safety rail *n* : GUARDRAIL

safety razor *n* : a razor provided with a guard for the blade to prevent deep cuts in the skin — see RAZOR illustration

safety shoe *n* **1** : a shoe with a reinforced toe cap to minimize foot injuries caused by dropped articles **2** : a shoe with a sole of material incapable of sparking for work near combustibles or explosives

safety stop *n* : any of various devices to stop an undesirable motion or action: as **a** : an attachment for an elevator to prevent accidental falling **b** : a device that closes a supply valve and stops an engine in case of accident to the governor belt **c** : a contrivance to prevent a pulley tackle from overhauling **d** : a device in a lathe to prevent a carriage from colliding with the headstock **e** : a system for stopping trains automatically if they try to pass a stop signal **f** : a stop motion for textile machinery

safety straps *n pl* : a harness affixed to the seat of a vehicle and passed over the shoulders or legs; *esp* : one used in an airplane in addition to a safety belt to provide more widely distributed restraint of the body in moments of rapid acceleration or deceleration

safety switch *n* : an electric switch completely enclosed in a metal box with an external control handle and so designed that the box cannot be opened while the switch is closed and the switch cannot be closed while the box is open

safety switchboard *n* : a dead-front switchboard with an enclosure on the back and sides to prevent access to the live parts

safety tread *n* : a surface on a floor or deck (as at the top and bottom of a ladder) designed to prevent slipping

safety tube *n* : a tube to prevent explosion or to control delivery of gases by an automatic valvular connection with the outer air; *esp* : a safety funnel tube — compare FUNNEL TUBE

safety valve *n* **1 a :** an automatic escape or relief valve (as for a steam boiler or hydraulic system) held shut by an arrangement exerting a definite usu. adjustable pressure so that the valve lift and the steam, water, or other contents escape when the pressure exceeds a predetermined amount **b :** a similar valve opening inward to admit air to a vessel in which the pressure is less than that of the atmosphere and prevent collapse **2 :** something that serves as an outlet for an excess or pressure ⟨wit is the best *safety valve* modern man has evolved —A.A.Brill⟩ ⟨emigration can serve as a *safety valve* for transitory problems of critical population pressure —*President's Commission on Immigration & Naturalization*⟩

safety zone *n* **:** a safety island for pedestrians or for street car or bus passengers

saffi *var of* SAPHIE

saf·fi·an \ˈsafēən\ *n* -s [Russ *saf'yan*, fr. Turk *sahtiyan*, fr. Per *sakhtiyān* goatskin, fr. *sakht* hard, strong] **:** a leather made of goatskins or sheepskins tanned with sumac and dyed with bright colors

saf·flor \ˈsa,flȯ(ə)r, ═ˈ═\ *n* -s [fr. *safflor* (safflower)] **:** CARTHAMUS RED

saf·flor·ite \ˈsaflə,rīt\ *n* -s [G *saflorit*, fr. *saflor* zaffer (modif. — influenced by *saflor* safflower — of It *zaffera*) + G *-it* -ite — more at ZAFFER] **:** a mineral $CoAs_2$ that consists of a cobalt arsenide, is isomorphous with loellingite and dimorphous with smaltite, and usu. occurs in tin-white masses

saf·flow·er \ˈsa,flau̇(ə)r, -au̇ə\ *also* **saf·flor** \-lō(ə)r, -ō(ə)\ *n* -s [MF *saffleur*, *safleur*, fr. OIt *saffiore*, *zaffrole*, fr. Ar *aṣfar* yellow, a yellow plant] **1 :** an Old World herb (*Carthamus tinctorius*) that resembles a thistle, is widely grown for its oil, and has large vivid red or orange flower heads **2 :** a dye prepared from the flower heads of the safflower and now used chiefly in the Orient for dyeing silk and cotton light red — see CARTHAMIN **3 :** a drug consisting of the dried florets of the safflower and used in medicine in place of saffron

safflower carmine *n* **:** a commercial preparation of carthamin

safflower oil *n* **:** an edible drying oil obtained from the seeds of the safflower

safflower red *n* **:** CARTHAMUS RED

¹saf·fron \ˈsafrən *sometimes* -fə(r)n\ *n* -s [ME *saffran*, *safroun*, *saffron*, fr. OF *safran*, fr. ML *safranum*, fr. Ar *za'farān*] **1** *or* **saffron crocus :** a crocus (*Crocus sativus*) with purple flowers widely cultivated throughout southern Europe for the drug and dyestuff that it yields **2 :** a deep orange-colored substance consisting of the aromatic pungent dried stigmas of saffron and used to color and flavor foods and formerly as a dyestuff and as a stimulant antispasmodic emmenagogue in medicine **3** *or* **saffron yellow :** a moderate orange to orange yellow — called also *croceus* **4 :** any of several saffron-colored substances used in alchemy **:** CROCUS 2a ⟨antimony ~⟩ **5 :** SAFFLOWER 1, 3 **6** *also* **saffron tree :** SATINLEAF

²saffron \"\ *vt* -ED/-ING/-S **:** to color or flavor with or as if with saffron

saffron plum *n* **:** a buckthorn (*Bumelia angustifolia*) of southern Florida and the West Indies that is a small often shrubby tree with heavy hard close-grained wood and a sweet edible fruit resembling a small plum

saffron thistle *n* **:** SAFFLOWER; *also* **:** a related European herb (*Carthamus lanatus*) with yellow flower heads that is naturalized and a troublesome weed in Australia

saffronwood \ˈ══,═\ *n* **1 :** the yellowish wood of a southern African timber tree (*Elaeodendron croceum*) **2 :** the tree that yields saffronwood

saf·frony \-nē\ *adj* **:** YELLOWISH

safing *pres part of* SAFE

saf·ra·nine *also* **saf·ra·nin** *or* **saf·fra·nine** \ˈsafrə,nēn, -,nən\ *n* -s *sometimes cap* [ISV *safran-* (fr. F or G *safran* saffron) + *-ine*] **:** any of a class of red to blue azine dyes that for the most part are diamino derivatives of *N*-phenylphenazine: as **a :** PHENOSAFRANINE **b** *or* **safranine O** *or* **safranine T :** a basic dye made by oxidation of a mixture of *ortho*-toluidine, *para*-tolylenediamine, and aniline and used chiefly in dyeing paper, as a desensitizer in photography, and as a biological stain — see DYE table I (under *Basic Red 2*)

saf·ra·no·phile \ˈsafrənō,fīl\ *or* **saf·ra·no·phil** \-,fil\ *adj* [*safranine* + *-o-* + *-phile*, *-phil*] *of cells* **:** staining readily with safranine

saf·ra·no pink \ˈsafrə,nō-\ *n* [fr. *Safrano*, a variety of rose, fr. F *safran* saffron] **:** a moderate yellowish pink that is yellower and paler than coral pink and redder and duller than peach pink

saf·role \ˈsa,frōl\ *also* **saf·rol** \-rōl, -rōl\ *n* -s [ISV *safr-* (fr. G *sassafras* sassafras) + *-ole*, *-ol*] **:** a poisonous oily cyclic ether $C_{10}H_{10}O_2$ that is the principal component of sassafras oil and occurs also in other essential oils (as camphor oil) and that is used chiefly for perfuming and flavoring; 4-allyl-1,2-methylenedioxy-benzene — compare ISOSAFROLE

saft \ˈsäft, ˈsaft, ˈsaft\ *chiefly Scot var of* SOFT

¹sag \ˈsag, ˈsaa(ə)g, ˈsaig\ *vb* **sagged; sagged; sagging; sags** [ME *saggen*, prob. of Scand origin; akin to Sw *sacka* to settle, sink down, Norw dial. *sakka* to sink, prob. derivatives fr. the stem of ON *sökkva* to sink — more at SINK] *vi* **1 a :** to sink or settle gradually from an established or normal position ⟨frame store buildings . . . left to ~ and gather cobwebs since lumbering operations stopped —*Amer. Guide Series: Calif.*⟩ **b :** to decline in intensity or vigor ⟨spirits had *sagged* almost to the breaking point —W.H.Waggoner⟩ **c :** to decline from a thriving position ⟨oil shares *sagged* owing to lack of fresh support —*Financial Times (London)*⟩ ⟨cloth output and prices ~ despite the . . . comeback in apparel —*Wall Street Jour.*⟩ **2 a :** to hang loosely **:** lose tautness (as from age or fatigue) ⟨when his face *sagged* like this, worriment claimed it —O.B. Chidsey⟩ **b :** to lie or hang unevenly **:** droop to one side ⟨the chair . . . *sagged* on one rocker —Ellen Glasgow⟩ **c :** to bend downward in the middle under its own or applied pressure ⟨a black reticule that *sagged* under the weight of shapeless objects —Allen Tate⟩ ⟨the clothesline *sagged* between its poles⟩ **d :** to fall from the lack or removal of muscular control ⟨he *sagged* flabbily to his knees —George Orwell⟩ **e :** to flow after application to a vertical or sloping surface and produce irregular films — used of a paint or varnish **3 :** to move ahead at a feeble plodding pace ⟨the depression *sagged* along —Don Baines⟩ **4 :** DRIFT — used chiefly in the phrase *sag to leeward* **5 :** to fail to stimulate or retain interest ⟨his latest picture had *sagged* at the box office —E.L.Acken⟩ ⟨though it ~s in the middle, the novel is readable throughout —Walter Havighurst⟩ ~ *vt* **:** to cause to sag: as **a :** to cause (as a ship or timber) to curve downward in the middle usu. as a result of improper loading or supporting **b :** to leave slack in (an electrical transmission line) to compensate for changes in temperature **syn** see DROOP

²sag \"\ *n* -s **1 :** a tendency to drift (as of a ship to leeward) **:** DRIFT **2 :** a drop or depression below the surrounding area: **a :** a pass or gap in a ridge or mountain range **:** SADDLE **b :** a depression in an otherwise flat or gently sloping land surface **c :** a minor downwarped structure often with faults on one or more sides **d :** a sunken area in a roadbed or pipeline **3 a :** a distortion of an airship in which the center bends down and both ends rise **b :** a bending of an object (as a chain) under its own weight or applied pressure **c :** a curve in the line of chained logs in a log boom caused by wind or current **4 :** a temporary economic decline (as in the price of a particular commodity)

³sag \ˈsag\ *dial Brit var of* SEDGE

⁴sag \"\ *chiefly dial var of* SAW

¹saga *pl of* SAGUM

²sa·ga \ˈsägə, ˈsägə *sometimes* ˈsagə\ *n* -s [ON, story, legend, history, saga — more at SAW] **1 a :** a prose narrative sometimes of legendary content but typically dealing with prominent figures and events of the heroic age in Norway and Iceland esp. as recorded in Icelandic manuscripts of the late 12th and 13th centuries **b :** the saga as a literary genre **2 :** any of various historical or fictional narratives: as **a :** a modern retelling usu. in verse or highly stylized prose of the events of the Icelandic sagas or of similar subjects ⟨I have called it a novel but in fact it is a prose ~ of the wanderings of the Vikings —M.R.Ridley⟩ **b :** an episodic story centering about a usu. heroic figure of earlier ages with factual or fictional details drawn from various sources ⟨one of the old knightly ~s⟩ **c :** a series of legends that embodies in detail the esp. oral history of a people ⟨the great ~ of the patriarchs —A.P. Davies⟩ **d :** a long detailed narrative usu. without psychological or historical depth (as of a particular occupation, area, historical event, period, or person) ⟨a ~ of the Indian Territory at the turn of the nineteenth century —*Current Biog.*⟩ ⟨that ~ of the farm which has occupied so many American novelists —*Times Lit. Supp.*⟩ ⟨the great ~ of the winning of the West⟩ ⟨the ~ of the colonel who piloted the plane that dropped the atomic bomb —John McCarten⟩ **e** *also* **saga novel :** ROMAN-FLEUVE **3 :** an occupation, life, series of events, or location suitable as a subject for a saga ⟨~ of the cattle industry —*Amer. Guide Series: Texas*⟩ **syn** see MYTH

sa·ga·ci·ate \səˈgashē,āt, -gāsh-, -gashə,wāt\ *vi* -ED/-ING/-S [prob. fr. *sagacity* + *-ate*] *chiefly South* **:** to get along **:** THRIVE

sa·ga·cious \səˈgāshəs\ *adj* [L *sagac-*, *sagax* sagacious + E *-ious*; akin to L *sagire* to perceive quickly or keenly — more at SEEK] **1** *obs* **:** quick or keen in sense perceptions ⟨a dog ~ in scent⟩ ⟨~ of his quarry —John Milton⟩ **2 a :** possessing quick intellectual perceptions **:** of keen penetration and judgment **:** discerning and farsighted in judging men and means ⟨a natively ~, intuitively understanding humanitarian —H.F. Wilkins⟩ **b :** caused by keen intellectual perception or penetration **:** indicating acute discernment ⟨a ~ marketing of his product —Lucius Garvin⟩ **syn** see SHREWD

sa·ga·cious·ly *adv* **:** in a sagacious manner

sa·ga·cious·ness *n* -ES **:** SAGACITY

sa·gac·i·ty \səˈgasəd·ē, -ˈgaas-, -ətē, -i\ *n* -ES [MF or L; MF *sagacité*, fr. L *sagacitat-*, *sagacitas*, fr. *sagac-*, *sagax* + *-itat-*, *-itas* -ity] **1 a :** the quality of being sagacious **:** quickness or acuteness of sense perceptions **:** keenness of discernment or penetration with soundness of judgment **:** ability to see what is relevant and significant ⟨a man of exceptional intelligence and unusual political ~ —Brian Crozier⟩ **b :** a sagacious remark or judgment **2** *archaic* **:** acuteness of smell

sa·gai \səˈgī\ *or* **sagai tatar** *n, pl* **sagai** *or* **sagai tatars** *usu cap S&T* **1 :** a group composed of the Beltir, the Koibal, and other peoples on the Abakan river that speak a Turkic dialect **2 :** a member of the Sagai people

sa·gaie \səˈgī\ *n* -s [F *sagaie*, *zagaie* assegai, sagaie, fr. MF *azagaie* assegai — more at ASSEGAI] **:** a Paleolithic bone javelin point

sa·ga·man \ˈsägə,man, -,mən\ *n, pl* **sagamen** [trans. of ON *sögumathr*] **:** a narrator of a saga

sa·ga·mi·te \sə,gäməˈtā\ *n* -s [CanF, of Algonquian origin; akin to Cree *kisāgamitew* the liquid is hot, Nipissing *kijagamite*] **1 :** HULLED CORN **2 :** a thin porridge of hulled corn

sag·a·more \ˈsagə,mō(ə)r, -mȯ(ə)r, -mōə, -mȯ(ə)\ *n* -s [Abnaki *sāgimau*, lit., he prevails over] **1 :** a subordinate or war chief of the Algonquian Indians of the north Atlantic coast **2 :** SACHEM 1

sag and swell *n* **:** an undulating topography (as of a moraine)

sagapen *n* -s [L *sagapenum*] *obs* **:** SAGAPENUM

sag·a·pe·num \,sagəˈpēnəm\ *n* -s [L, fr. Gk *sagapēnon*, a plant (*Ferula persica*), sagapenum] **:** a bitter yellowish or brownish oleo-gum-resin of strong odor derived from plants of the genus *Ferula* in Arabia and Persia and formerly used similarly to asafetida and galbanum

sag·a·thy \ˈsagəthē\ *n* -ES [origin unknown] **:** a fine twilled worsted fabric similar to serge used esp. formerly for clothing and curtains

¹sage \ˈsāj\ *adj* -ER/-EST [ME, fr. OF, fr. (assumed) VL *sapius*, fr. L *sapere* to taste, have good taste, have sense, be wise; akin to OE *sefa* mind, OS *sebo* mind, *afsebbian* to perceive, OHG *antseffen*, *intseffen* to notice, Oscan *sipus* knowing, Arm *ham* juice, taste; basic meaning: to taste] **1 a :** eminent in wisdom **:** wise through reflection and experience **:** prudent and philosophic in judgment and views ⟨the wise reasoning of a certain ~ magistrate —George Berkeley⟩ **b** *archaic* **:** GRAVE, SOLEMN ⟨among the ~ and somber figures that would put his unsophisticated cheerfulness to shame —Nathaniel Hawthorne⟩ **2 :** proceeding from or characterized by wisdom, prudence, and good judgment ⟨providing ~ guidance to nonponderous writing —*Saturday Rev.*⟩ **syn** see WISE

²sage \"\ *n* -s [ME, fr. MF, fr. *sage*, adj.] **1 :** one (as a profound philosopher or eminently wise counselor) distinguished for wisdom ⟨this excellent book considers six ~s . . . whose vision springs from a vivid conception of the principles governing the workings of the world —*Times Lit. Supp.*⟩ **2 :** a mature or venerable man rich in experience and sound in judgment ⟨one of the ancient ~s of our law —B.N.Cardozo⟩ **3** *often cap, Confucianism* **:** a truly natural man who is virtuous and wise and has attained the highest perfection of man

³sage \"\ *n* -s *often attrib* [ME *sauge*, *sage*, fr. MF *saulge*, *sauge*, fr. L *salvia*, fr. *salvus* safe, whole, healthy; fr. its use as a medicinal herb — more at SAFE] **1 a :** a half shrubby mint (*Salvia officinalis*) with grayish green pungent and aromatic leaves that are much used in flavoring foods and as a mild tonic and astringent; *broadly* **:** a plant of the genus *Salvia* — compare BLUE SAGE, CLARY, SCARLET SAGE **b** (1) **:** SAGEBRUSH (2) **:** the sagebrush regions of the western U. S. ⟨~ dog⟩ ⟨~ riders⟩ **c :** any of several plants felt to resemble the true sage — usu. used in combination; see BETHLEHEM SAGE, JERUSALEM SAGE **2 :** SAGE GREEN

SAGE \ˈsāj\ *abbr or n* -s [semiautomatic ground environment] **:** a ground air defense system in which reporting devices feed into a computer that analyzes the air situation and when decision for action is fed into it translates the decision into orders to the various air defense combat units

sage·brush \ˈsāj,brəsh\ *n* [³*sage* + *brush*] **:** any of several No. American hoary undershrubs of the genus *Artemisia*; *esp* **:** a common plant (*A. tridentata*) having a bitter juice and an odor resembling sage and often covering vast tracts of alkaline plains in the western U. S. — called also *big sagebrush*, *blue sage*

sage·brush·er \-shə(r)\ *n* -s [*sagebrush* + *-er*] **:** an inhabitant of or a camper in a sagebrush region of the western U. S.

sagebrush green *n* **:** a dark greenish gray that is yellower and darker than Muscovite and yellower and deeper than castor gray

sagebrush lizard *n* **:** a small variable lizard (*Sceloporus graciosus*) of dry uplands of western No. America

sagebrush rabbit *n* **:** a rather small grayish cottontail (*Sylvilagus nuttallii*) of western No. America

sage cheese *n* **:** a mild cheese similar to cheddar that is flecked with green and flavored with chopped sage leaves or sage extract

sage chippy *or* **sagebrush chippy** *n* **:** BREWER SPARROW

sage cock *n* **:** SAGE GROUSE; *specif* **:** a male sage grouse

sage grass *n* **:** a grass of the genus *Andropogon*

sage gray *n* **1 :** a grayish green **2 :** a light olive gray to light grayish olive that is very slightly greener and deeper than beach

sage green *n* **:** a variable color averaging a grayish yellow green that is greener and deeper than mermaid, stronger and very slightly yellower and lighter than palmetto, and deeper and slightly greener than celadon

sage grouse *n* **:** a very large grouse (*Centrocercus urophasianus*) native to the dry sagebrush plains of western No. America having mottled gray, black, and buff plumage and flesh often poor and bitter from feeding on the buds of the sagebrush

sage hen *n* **1 :** SAGE GROUSE; *specif* **:** the female sage grouse **2** *usu cap S&H* **:** NEVADAN — used as a nickname

sage-king \ˈ═,═\ *n, often cap S&K, Confucianism* **1 :** an ideal ruler of antiquity who by combining the virtue and wisdom of a sage with the power of a king exemplified perfection in government **2 :** an exemplary mythological ruler of prehistoric China

sage·ly *adv* [ME, fr. *sage* + *-ly*] **:** in a sage manner

sage mullein \ˈ═-\ *also* **sageleaf mullein** \ˈ═,═-\ *n* **:** JERUSALEM SAGE

sa·gene \ˈsä,zhen\ *n* -s [Russ *sazhen'*; akin to Russ *syagat'* to reach for, grasp, OSlav *sęgnǫti* to grasp, Latvian *segt* to cover — more at SAGUM] **:** a Russian unit of length equal to 7 feet

sage·ness *n* -ES [¹*sage* + *-ness*] **:** the quality or state of being sage

sag·e·nite \ˈsajə,nīt\ *n* -s [F *sagénite*, fr. L *sagena* large fishing net + F *-ite* — more at SEINE] **:** a mineral consisting of an acicular rutile that occurs in reticulated forms and is often embedded in quartz or other minerals

sag·e·nit·ic \ˌ══ˈnid·ik\ *adj* **:** containing sagenite or similar acicular crystals ⟨~ tourmaline⟩ — used esp. of quartz

sage of bethlehem *usu cap B* [fr. *Bethlehem*, Palestine] **1 :** SPEARMINT **2 :** LUNGWORT 2a

sage oil *n* **:** either of two essential oils from sage: **a :** the yellowish or greenish yellow oil with a penetrating odor of sage obtained from the leaves of the common sage (*Salvia officinalis*) and used chiefly in flavoring **b :** the pale yellow oil with an odor like that of ambergris obtained from the flowers of clary (*Salvia sclarea*) and used chiefly in perfumery — called also *clary sage oil*

sager *comparative of* SAGE

sage rabbit *or* **sage hare** *n* **:** SAGEBRUSH RABBIT

sag·e·re·tia \,sajəˈrēsh(ē)ə, -ēd·ēə\ *n, cap* [NL, fr. Augustin *Sageret* †1852 French agronomist + NL *-ia*] **:** a genus of American and Asiatic shrubs (family Rhamnaceae) having opposite branches, sometimes edible fruit, and opposite leaves that in a Chinese member (*S. theezans*) are used locally as a substitute for tea

sages *pl of* SAGE

sagest *superlative of* SAGE

sage sparrow *n* **:** a sparrow (*Amphispiza belli*) that inhabits esp. sagebrush regions in western No. America

sage tea *n* **:** a beverage prepared by infusion of sage leaves

sage thrasher *n* **:** a thrasher (*Oreoscoptes montanus*) that inhabits sagebrush in western No. America and is pale grayish brown above and white spotted with brownish below

sage willow *n* **:** a willow shrub (*Salix tristis*) of the eastern U.S. growing in dry ground and having linear-oblong leaves that are white-tomentose beneath — called also *dwarf gray willow*

sagey *var of* SAGY

sagged *past of* SAG

¹sag·ger *or* **sag·gar** \ˈsagə(r)\ *n* -s [prob. alter. of ¹*safeguard*] **1 a :** a box made of fire clay in which delicate ceramic pieces are placed while being fired either for biscuit or for glaze **b :** the clay of which saggers are made **2 :** a box in which cast-iron articles are packed in contact with hematite ore or mill scale to be converted to malleable cast iron in an annealing furnace

²sagger \"\ *vt* -ED/-ING/-S **:** to treat (as stoneware) in a sagger

sag·ger·man \ˈ══mən\ *n, pl* **saggermen :** one who forms saggers on a potter's wheel or loads them with pottery to be fired

sagging *n* -s [ME, fr. gerund of *saggen* to sag — more at SAG] **1 :** an arching downward in the middle (as of a ship after being strained) **2 :** a defect in the enamel of a piece of ceramics caused by flow down a vertical surface

¹sag·gy \ˈsagē\ *adj* [³*sag* + *-y*] *chiefly dial* **:** SEDGY

²saggy \"\ *adj* -ER/-EST [¹*sag* + *-y*] **:** characterized or caused by sagging

sagier *comparative of* SAGY

sagiest *superlative of* SAGY

sa·gi·na \səˈjīnə\ *n, cap* [NL, fr. L *sagina* action of stuffing or fattening food, fatness, nourishment; fr. the supposed nutritive value of plants of this genus] **:** a genus of small herbs (family Caryophyllaceae) native to temperate and cool regions that have subulate leaves and small whitish sometimes apetalous flowers with the styles equal in number to the four or five sepals and alternating with them

sag·i·nate \ˈsajə,nāt\ *vt* -ED/-ING/-S [L *saginatus*, past part of *saginare* to fatten, fr. *sagina*] *archaic* **:** FATTEN — **sag·i·na·tion** \ˌ══ˈnāshən\ *n* -s

sa·ging \ˈsä,gēŋ\ *n* -s [Tag] *Philippines* **:** BANANA

sa·git·ta \səˈjid·ə\ *n* [NL, fr. L, arrow, prob. of non-IE origin] **1** -s **:** the distance from the midpoint of an arc to the midpoint of its chord **2** -s **:** the larger of the two large otoliths found in the ear of most fishes **3 a** *cap* **:** the chief genus of Chaetognatha including the largest and several common arrowworms **b** *pl* **sagittas** \-d·əz\ *or* **sagit·tae** \-d·,ē\ **:** any arrowworm of the genus *Sagitta*

sag·it·tal \ˈsajəd·ᵊl, -ətᵊl\ *adj* [L *sagitta* + E *-al*] **1 a :** of or relating to the suture between the parietal bones of the skull **b :** of, relating to, or situated in the median plane of the body or any plane parallel thereto **2 :** of, relating to, or shaped like an arrow or arrowhead — **sag·it·tal·ly** \-ᵊlē\ *adv*

sagittal arc *n* **:** the arc from the nasion to the opisthion along the sagittal line of the skull

sagittal crest *n* **:** an elevated bony ridge that develops along the sagittal suture of many mammals esp. in old age

sagittal diameter *n* **1 :** the distance between the glabella and the opisthocranion **2 :** the distance between the midpoint of the sacral promontory and the midpoint of the posterior ridge of the pubic symphysis

sagittal fontanelle *n* **:** an unossified space in the region of the parietal foramina usu. closed at birth

sagittal sinus *n* **:** either of two venous sinuses of the dura mater: **a :** one passing backward in the convex attached margin of the falx cerebri and ending at the internal occipital protuberance by fusion with the transverse sinus — called also *superior sagittal sinus* **b :** one lying in the posterior two thirds of the concave free margin of the falx cerebri and ending posteriorly by joining the great cerebral vein to form the straight sinus — called also *inferior sagittal sinus*

sagittal suture *n* **:** the deeply serrated articulation between the two parietal bones in the median plane of the top of the head

sag·it·tar·ia \,sajəˈta(a)rēə\ *n, cap* [NL, fr. L *sagitta* + NL *-aria*] **:** a genus of aquatic herbs (family Alismataceae) of temperate and tropical regions having basal often sagittate or hastate leaves and scapose flowers with 3 sepals and 3 deciduous white petals — see ARROWHEAD, WAPATOO

sag·it·tar·i·us \,sajəˈta(a)rēəs, -ter-, -tär-\ *n, pl* **sagittar·ii** \-ē,ī\ [ME, fr. ML, fr. L, a constellation, fr. *sagittarius* archer, fr. *sagitta* arrow + *-arius* -ary] **1** *usu cap* **:** the ninth sign of the zodiac — see SIGN table, ZODIAC illustration **2** [L] **:** ARCHER

sag·it·tary \ˈsajə,terē\ *n* -ES [ME *sagitary*, fr. ML *sagittarius*] **1** *obs* **:** SAGITTARIUS **2 :** CENTAUR

sag·it·tate \ˈsajə,tāt\ *adj* [L *sagitta* arrow + E *-ate*] **1 :** shaped like an arrowhead **2 :** *of a leaf* **:** elongated, triangular, and having the two basal lobes prolonged downward — see LEAF illustration

sa·git·to·cyst \səˈjid·ə,sist, ˈsajəd·ō,-\ *n* [NL *sagitta* + E *-o-* + *cyst*] **:** a capsule having a spindle-shaped needle produced by epidermal cells of certain turbellarians

sag·it·toid \ˈsajə,tȯid\ *adj* [NL *Sagitta* + E *-oid*] **:** of, relating to, or resembling an arrowworm

sag·less \ˈsagləs\ *adj* [²*sag* + *-less*] **:** having no sag

sa·go \ˈsā(,)gō\ *n* -s [Malay *sagu*] **1 :** SAGO PALM **2 :** a dry granulated or powdered starch prepared from the pithy trunks of several tropical palms (as the sago) and used as a thickening agent in foods (as a pudding) and as textile stiffening

sago fern *n* **:** SILVER TREE FERN

sa·goin \səˈgȯin\ *n* -s [F *sagoin*, *sagouin*, fr. Pg *sagüi*, *sagüí*, *sagüim*, fr. Tupi *sagui*, *saguin*, *saguim*] **:** MARMOSET; *esp* **:** one of the genus *Callithrix*

sago palm *n* **1 :** a plant that yields sago: as **a :** any of various lofty pinnate-leaved Indian and Malaysian palms of the genus *Metroxylon* (as *M. laeve* or *M. rumphii*) **b :** a Malaccan palm (*Phoenix farinifera*) **c :** GEBANG PALM **d :** any of several Indian palms: (1) **:** GOMUTI (2) **:** JAGGERY PALM (3) **:** PALMYRA **e :** CABBAGE PALM 1b **2 a :** a cycad (*Cycas revoluta*) with recurved leaves that have revolute edges **b :** COONTIE

sago pondweed *n* **:** a No. American pondweed (*Potamogeton pectinatus*) having sharply acute leaves and seeds that provide feed for wild fowl

sag·o·weer \,sagəˈwi(ə)r\ *n* -s [D *sagoweer*, *saguweer*, fr. Pg *sagüeiro*, fr. *sagu*, *sagú* sago (fr. Malay *sagu*) + *-eiro* -ary (fr. L *-arius*)] **:** GOMUTI

sa·gra \ˈsāgrə, ˈsag-\ *n, cap* [NL] **:** a genus of chrysomelid beetles comprising the kangaroo beetles

sags *pres 3d sing of* SAG, *pl of* SAG

sa·gua·ro \səˈwä(,)rō, -ˈgw-\ *also* **sa·hua·ro** *or* **su·war·ro** *n* -s [MexSp *saguaro*, *sahuaro*, prob. fr. Opata *sahuaro*] **:** an arborescent cactus (*Carnegiea gigantea*) occurring in desert regions of the southwestern U.S. and Mexico, having a tall columnar simple or sparsely branched trunk, attaining a height of 60 feet or more, and bearing white flowers and edible fruit

sa·gum \ˈsāgəm\ *n, pl* **sa·ga** \-gə\ [L, fr. Gaulish; akin to MIr *sēn* snare, W *hoenyn* snare, Latvian *segt* to cover, Skt *sajati* he fastens, sticks; basic meaning: to touch, stick] **:** a square or rectangular cloak made of coarse wool, fastened usu. on the right shoulder, and worn esp. by Gauls, early Germans, and soldiers of ancient Rome

sa·gu·ran \sə'güˌrän\ *n, pl* **sa·gu·ra·nes** \ˌsagü'räˌnās\ [native name in the Philippines] *Philippines* **:** a textile made from the fiber of leaves of the talipot palm and used esp. for packing

sagy *also* **sagey** \'sājē\ *adj* **sagier; sagiest** [³*sage* + *-y*] **:** perfumed or seasoned with sage

sa·haj·da·ri \sə,häj'därē\ *n* -s *usu cap* [native name in India] **:** one of a sect of Sikhs observing many Hindu customs but emphasizing a special regard for Guru Nanak and his teachings

sa·hap·ti·an \sə'haptēən\ *or* **sa·hap·tin** \-tən\ *usu cap, var of* SHAHAPTIAN

¹sa·ha·ra \sə'ha(a)rə, -'herə, -'härə, -'hārə\ *adj, usu cap* [fr. the *Sahara* desert, vast region of wasteland and oases in northern Africa] **:** of or relating to the Sahara desert ⟨a *Sahara* oasis⟩

²sahara \"\ *n* -s [fr. the *Sahara* desert] **1** *usu cap* **:** something regarded as arid, barren, or deserted ⟨the *Sahara* of the early morning streets⟩ ⟨turned bookman and for twenty-one years wandered . . . in the *Sahara* of medieval scholarship —V.L. Parrington⟩ **2** *often cap* **:** SIENNA BROWN

sa·ha·ran \-rən\ *also* **sa·ha·ri·an** \-rēən\ *adj, usu cap* [*Sahara* desert + E *-an, -ian*] **:** of, relating to, characteristic of, or likened to the Sahara desert ⟨a day of *Saharan* temperature⟩ ⟨a *Saharan* landscape of blighted fields⟩

sa·ha·ran·pur \sə'härənˌpu(ə)r\ *adj, usu cap* [fr. *Saharanpur*, India] **:** of or from the city of Saharanpur, India **:** of the kind or style prevalent in Saharanpur

sa·heh·wa·mish \sə'hāwəˌmish\ *n, pl* **sahehwamish** *or* **sahehwamishes** *usu cap* **1 a :** a Salishan people about the inlets at the southern end of Puget Sound, Washington **b :** a member of such people **2 :** a dialect related to Skagit

sa·hib \'sä,(h)ib, 'sȧ,-, -(h)ēb\ *also* **sa·heb** \-ˌ(h)eb\ *n* -s [Hindi *ṣāhib*, lit., master, lord, fr. Ar] **1 :** SIR, MASTER — used as a term of respect esp. among Hindus and Muslims in colonial India when addressing or speaking of a European of some social status and as a general title affixed to the name or official title of a European ⟨colonel-*sahib*⟩ or affixed to the title of a man of rank ⟨raja ~⟩ **2 :** EUROPEAN; *typically* **:** a European official or settler in a largely non-European population ⟨the prewar white ~ sat under a punkah pulled by tireless little Asians —Peggy Durdin⟩

sa·hi·bah *or* **sa·hi·ba** \'sȧēbə\ *n* -s [Hindi *ṣāhiba*, fr. Per, fem. of *ṣāhib* master, lord, fr. Ar] **:** LADY, MISTRESS

sa·hid·ic \sə'hidik\ *n, usu cap* [Ar *ṣa'īdīy* of Upper Egypt, fr. *aṣ-ṣa'īd* Upper Egypt] **:** a Coptic dialect of southern Egypt

sa·hi·wal \'sä(h)əˌväl\ *n* [fr. *Sahiwal*, town in western Pakistan] **1** *usu cap* **:** an Indian breed of humped short-horned solid-colored dairy cattle **2** -s *often cap* **:** any animal of the Sahiwal breed

sah·lin·ite \'säləˌnīt\ *n* -s [prob. fr. Sw *sahlinit*, fr. Carl *Sahlin*, 20th cent. Swed. scientist + Sw *-it* -ite] **:** a mineral $Pb_{14}(AsO_4)_2O_9Cl_4$ composed of an arsenate, oxide, and chloride of lead

sa·ho \'sä(ˌ)hō\ *n, pl* **saho** *or* **sahos** *usu cap* **1 a :** a Hamitic people of northeastern Ethiopia **b :** a member of such people **2 :** the Cushitic language of the Saho people

saib·ling \'zīpliŋ, 'sībl-\ *n* -s [G, fr. G dial. (Bavaria), alter. of *sälmling*, fr. *salm* salmon (fr. OHG *salmo*, fr. L) + *-ling*] **1 :** a char (*Salvelinus alpinus*) of mountain streams of Europe **2 :** SUNAPEE TROUT

sa·ic \sä'ēk, 'säik\ *n* -s [F *saïque*, fr. Turk *şayka*] **:** a ketch common in the Levant

saice \'sīs\ *var of* SYCE

said \'sed\ *adj* [fr. *said*, past part. of *say*] **:** AFOREMENTIONED

saidest \ *or* **saidst** *archaic past of* SAY

sa·if *var of* SEIF

¹sai·ga \'sīgə\ *n* -s [ML] **:** a small silver coin issued under the Merovingians and current in France before the introduction of the denier

²saiga \"\ *n* -s [Russ *saĭga*, fr. Fagatai *saigak*] **:** a sheeplike antelope (*Saiga tartarica*) of Siberia and eastern Russia having the nasal region inflated and the nostrils widely separated and in the male having lyrate annulated horns and tufts of long hair beneath the eyes and ears

sai·gon \(')sī'gän\ *adj, usu cap* [fr. *Saigon*, So. Vietnam] **:** of or from Saigon, the capital of So. Vietnam **:** of the kind or style prevalent in Saigon

saigon cinnamon *n, usu cap S* **:** the bark of an Indo-Chinese tree (*Cinnamomum loureirii*)

¹sail \'sāl, *esp before pause or consonant* -āəl\ *n* -s *see sense 1b* [ME *seil, sail*, fr. OE *segl*; akin to OFris *seil* sail, OS *segel*, OHG *segal*, ON *segl* sail, *sægr* piece torn off of something, strip, *sög* saw — more at SAW] **1 a :** an extent of canvas or other fabric by means of which the wind is used to propel ships through the water; *collectively* **:** the sails of a ship ⟨boats large enough to carry ~ —Thor Heyerdahl⟩ **b** *pl* **usu sail :** SAILING SHIP ⟨saw one ~, a brig —Arnold Bennett⟩ ⟨its mackerel fleet comprised seventy ~ —Elizabeth Coatsworth⟩ ⟨a good many ~*s* in the bay —G.W.Brace⟩ **2 :** an extent of fabric used in propelling a wind-driven vehicle (as an iceboat) **3 :** something that resembles a sail: as **a :** the extended surface of the arm of a windmill **b :** a wing of a bird (as a hawk) **c :** FIN **d :** TENTACLE **e :** a streamlined conning tower on a submarine **4** *Africa* **:** BUCK SAIL **5** [²*sail*] **a** (1) *obs* **:** sailing ability ⟨finding his ship but ill of ~ —William Monson⟩ (2) **:** the handling and navigation of ships under sail as distinct from under steam **b** (1) **:** a passage by a sailing ship **:** CRUISE ⟨a ~ upon the bay⟩ ⟨a ~ around the world⟩ (2) **:** the distance coverable in a specified period of sailing ⟨two days' ~ from port⟩ **c** *obs* **:** a group sailing together ⟨a large ~ of ducks passed here —Jonathan Swift⟩ — **under sail 1 :** in motion with sails set **2 :** propelled by sails

²sail \"\ *vb* -ED/-ING/-S [ME *seilen, sailen*, fr. OE *seglian, seglan*; akin to MLG *segelen* to sail, MHG *segelen, sigelen*, ON *sigla*; denominative fr. the stem of E ¹*sail*] *vi* **1 a** (1) **:** to travel on water in a ship propelled by the wind (2) **:** to travel in a ship propelled by steam or other means ⟨~ down the river by steamer⟩ **b :** to take trips in or manage a sailboat for pleasure **:** YACHT **2 a :** to move forward (as of a ship on water) by the action of wind upon sails **b :** to move forward on water by the action of steam or other motive power **c :** to move without visible effort through or on the water ⟨the swan ~*ing* on the lake⟩ **3 :** to begin a water voyage ⟨~ with the tide⟩ **4 :** to glide through the air without apparent exertion ⟨the white clouds ~*ed* across the sky —William Black⟩ **5 :** to travel or go in any of various manners: as **a :** to stride in a stately, pompous, or proud manner ⟨~*ed* gracefully into the room —L.C.Douglas⟩ **b :** to move without effort ⟨held the door for us and we ~*ed* through —P.E.Deutschman⟩ **c :** to move or arrive so as to attract attention or create a disturbance ⟨~ up in their big new car⟩ **6 a :** to begin vigorously to do something **:** attack with gusto — used with *in* or *into* ⟨coffee and sandwiches, which I ~*ed* into with . . . gratitude —H.A. Chippendale⟩ **b :** to attack a person with words or blows — used with *in* or *into* ⟨with questions and complaints, one after another ~*ed* into him —A.R.Williams⟩ ~ *vt* **1 a :** to move or travel upon (water) by means of sail, steam, or other motive power ⟨trawlers ~*ing* the fishing grounds⟩ ⟨the first man to ~ these waters⟩ **b :** to fly through **:** glide or move smoothly through ⟨gray hawks . . . ~*ing* the sky —J.M.Synge⟩ **2 :** to direct or manage the motion of (a ship or glider) ⟨tugboats and the men who ~ them —*advt*⟩ **3 :** to cause to move smoothly through the air ⟨~ a discus⟩

sail·age \-lij\ *n* -s [¹*sail* + *-age*] **:** the sails of a ship

sail arm *n* **:** WHIP 5

sailboat \'=,=\ *n* **:** a boat usu. propelled by sail

sail burton *n* **:** a top burton with a tail block seized to the lower hook and the hauling part rove through this tail block and thence through a snatch block on deck so that the lead of the hauling part serves to guy a sail clear and keep it from twisting when bending sails

sailcloth \'=,=\ *n* [ME *seilcloth, sailcloth*, fr. *seil, sail* + *cloth*] **1 a :** a strong heavy canvas for sails, tents, or upholstery **b :** a lightweight canvas for clothing or curtains **2 :** a piece of sailcloth

sail·er \-lə(r)\ *n* -s [ME, fr. *seilen, sailen* to sail + *-er* — more at SAIL] **:** a sailing or other ship or a sailboat esp. having specified sailing qualities ⟨failed sadly . . . as a ~ and was shorn of her topmasts —R.B.O'Brien⟩ ⟨a smart ~⟩

sailfin \'=,=\ *or* **sailfin mollie** *n* **:** a topminnow (*Mollienisia latipinna*) of the southern U.S. and Mexico that is predominantly olive green with black markings and fins of lavender, orange, and blue and that has the dorsal fin greatly enlarged in the male

sailfish \'=,=\ *n* **1 :** any of several large pelagic fishes constituting a genus (*Istiophorus*) related to the swordfish but having teeth, scales, pelvic fins of a few rays, and a very large dorsal fin highest at or behind its middle — see ATLANTIC SAILFISH, PACIFIC SAILFISH **2 :** BASKING SHARK

sailflying \'=,==\ *n* **:** the action of flying in a sailplane

sail hook *n* **:** a small hook used to hold cloth while a sail is being made

sailing *n* -s [ME *seiling, sailing*, fr. gerund of *seilen, sailen* to sail — more at SAIL] **1 a :** the technical skill of managing a ship; *esp* **:** the skill of directing a ship to a given place according to the rules of navigation **:** NAVIGATION **b :** the method of determining the course to be followed, the direction and distance to be sailed to reach a given point, and the position of a ship from dead reckoning **2 a** (1) **:** the sport or pastime of navigating or riding in a sailboat (2) **:** the conditions under which one may sail ⟨the ~ was excellent last month⟩ **b :** a trip or voyage in a ship ⟨make a fast ~⟩ **c :** a departure from a port; *esp* **:** a scheduled departure of a liner

sailing boat *n* **:** SAILBOAT

sailing day *n* **1 :** the day of departure of a passenger ship **2 :** the day that cargo will no longer be received on a cargo ship

sailing master *n* **1 :** a ship's officer in charge of navigation **2 :** a warrant officer (as formerly in the U.S. Navy) in charge of navigating a ship and of stowage

sailing ship *n* **:** a ship propelled by sail

sail·less \'sā(ə)lləs\ *adj* **:** having no sail

sail lizard *n* **:** any of several large agamid lizards of the genus *Hydrosaurus* of the Moluccas and the Philippines that have a crested tail

sail loft *n* **:** a loft or room where sails are cut out and made

sailmaker \'=,==\ *n* **:** one who cuts, assembles, and sews sails and canvas parts for ships; *specif* **:** a warrant officer (as formerly in the U.S. Navy) in charge of all sails and articles of canvas

sailmaker's mate *n* **:** a petty officer (as formerly in the U.S. Navy) assisting or acting as a sailmaker and in charge of all canvas (as bags, hammocks, or awnings)

sailmaker's splice *n* **:** a tapered splice joining two ropes of different sizes

sail needle *n* **:** a large needle triangular in section for sewing sailcloth

sail·or \'sālə(r)\ *n* -s [alter. (influenced by *-or*) of *sailer*] **1 a :** one that sails; *esp* **:** one that takes part in or understands the practical operation of a ship **:** MARINER **b :** a member of a ship's crew other than an officer **2** *archaic* **:** SAILER **3 :** a traveler by water ⟨so bad a ~ that he nearly died of seasickness —Robert Graves⟩ **4** *or* **sailor hat :** a man's hat of stiff straw with a low flat crown and a straight circular brim; *also* **:** a woman's hat usu. of straw of somewhat similar shape

sailor 4

sailor blue *n* **:** a moderate purplish blue that is lighter and stronger than marine blue and bluer and duller than average cornflower or gentian blue

sailor collar *n* **:** a broad collar having a square flap across the back and tapering to a V in front

sail·or·ing \-ləriŋ\ *n* -s [*sailor* + *-ing*] **:** the life, occupation, or duties of a sailor **:** SAILORIZING

sail·or·iz·ing \-ləˌrīziŋ\ *n* -s [*sailor* + *-ize* + *-ing*] **:** the practice or act of sailing esp. as a seaman **:** the work of a sailor

sail·or·less \-(r)ləs\ *adj* **:** having no sailor

sail·or·ly *adj* **:** having the characteristics of a sailor

sail·or·man \-(r)mən, -(r)ˌman\ *n, pl* **sailormen :** SAILOR, SEAMAN

sailor's-choice \'=;=;=\ *n, pl* **sailor's-choice :** any of several small grunts of the western Atlantic: as **a :** PINFISH a,b **b :** a pigfish (*Orthopristis chrysopterus*) **c** (1) **:** a ronco (*Haemulon parra*) (2) **:** MARGATE a

sailor's-knot \'=;=;=\ *n, pl* **sailor's-knots :** a wild geranium (*Geranium maculatum*)

sailor's skin *n* **:** skin of exposed portions of the body marked by warty thickening, pigmentation, and presenile keratosis and often considered to be precancerous and to lead to formation of epitheliomas

sailor's-tobacco \'=;=;=(ˌ)=\ *n, pl* **sailor's-tobaccos :** a mugwort (*Artemisia vulgaris*)

sailor suit *n* **:** a boy's outfit of middy blouse and bell-bottom trousers copied from a sailor's uniform

sailor tie *n* **:** a 2-eyelet low shoe with a ribbon tie

sail-over \'=,==\ *n* -s **:** OVERHANG b

¹sailplane \'=,=\ *n* [²*sail* + *plane*] **:** a glider with a wing load small enough to enable it to rise in an upward air current **:** a soaring glider

²sailplane \"\ *vi* **:** to fly in a sailplane

sails *pl of* SAIL; *pres 3d sing of* SAIL

sailship \'=,=\ *n* **:** SAILING SHIP

sail track *n* **:** a track on the afterside of a mast to which the edge of the sail is attached that takes the place of mast hoops

sail yard *n* **:** a yard or spar on which a sail is spread

sailor suit

saim \'sām\ *n* -s [ME *seim, saim*, fr. (assumed) VL *sagimen*, alter. of L *sagina* action of stuffing or fattening, food, fatness] *dial chiefly Brit* **:** animal fat; *specif* **:** LARD

sai·mi·ri \sī'mirē\ *n* [Pg, fr. Guarani *çai miri*, lit., little monkey] **1** -s **:** SQUIRREL MONKEY **2** *cap* [NL, fr. Pg] **:** a genus of small arboreal gregarious So. American monkeys comprising the squirrel monkeys

sain \'sān\ *vt* -ED/-ING/-S [ME *seynen, sainen, senen*, fr. OE *segnian*, fr. LL *signare* — more at SIGN] **1** *dial Brit* **a :** to cross (oneself) esp. as a blessing against evil influence **b :** BLESS **2** *chiefly dial* **:** to save from evil by invocation or blessing

sa·i·ne·te \ˌsīē'nā(ˌ)tā\ *n* -s [Sp, small piece of fat, tidbit, relish, entremés, dim. of *saín* fat, grease, fr. (assumed) VL *saginum*, alter. of L *sagina* action of stuffing or fattening, food, fatness] **:** ENTREMÉS 2

sain·foin \'sānˌfȯin\ *or* **san·foin** \'san-\ *n* -s [F *sainfoin*, fr. MF, fr. *sain* healthy (fr. L *sanus* healthy, sane) + *foin* hay, fr. L *fenum, faenum*; fr. its use as a medicinal herb — more at SANE, FENNEL] **1 :** a Eurasian perennial herb (*Onobrychis viciaefolia*) having pinnate leaves and spicate pink flowers **2 :** an American tick trefoil (*Desmodium canadense*) **3 :** a perennial herb (*Psoralea onobrychis*) of the central U. S.

¹saint \'sānt, *when a name follows* (ˌ)sānt *or* sənt, *when a name follows that begins with a consonant chiefly Brit* sən\ *n* -s [ME, fr. MF, fr. LL *sanctus*, fr. L, sacred, pure, holy, fr. past part. of *sancire* to make sacred, ordain, establish — more at SACRED] **1 a :** one officially recognized or acknowledged as preeminent for consecration, holiness, and piety esp. through canonization by one of the branches of the Christian church ⟨*Saint* Matthew⟩ **b :** an image of a saint ⟨the ~ was cast . . . eighty-two years ago —Norman Douglas⟩ **2 a :** one of the spirits of the departed in heaven **b :** ANGEL ⟨*Saint* Michael the archangel⟩ **3 a :** one of God's chosen people (1) **:** ISRAELITE, JEW; *esp* **:** one who strictly practices his religion ⟨Israel's ~*s* did not defer the day —O.J.Baab⟩ (2) **:** one belonging to the entire company of baptized Christians ⟨with all the ~*s* —2 Cor 1:1 (RSV)⟩ **b** *usu cap* **:** a member of any of various religious bodies ⟨on either side of the preacher several female *Saints* —E.T.Clark⟩: as (1) **:** PURITAN ⟨any news of the *Saints* in Amsterdam —Ben Jonson⟩ (2) **:** LATTER-DAY SAINT **4 a :** a person consecrated or single-heartedly dedicated to holiness, religion, or a religious task **:** a holy or godly person ⟨a great ~ who has given up his life for the sanctification of the Name —Maurice Samuel⟩ ⟨some local ~, a creature who made an annual pilgrimage to some shrine —G.A.Wagner⟩ **b :** one eminent for piety, virtue, or purity of conscience ⟨the calm, serene face of an elderly ~ at a funeral service —A.N. Meckel⟩ **c :** one spiritually reborn and sanctified or undergoing spiritual rebirth ⟨a cry of victory broke through the moaning as a ~ was born —J.C.Brauer⟩ **d :** one slightly or considerably more charitable, self-denying, or virtuous than the average ⟨a reign of the ~*s* which ordinary mortals could not live up to —A.L.Rowse⟩ ⟨the patience of a ~⟩ **5 :** a person honored after death for virtue, piety, or martyrdom ⟨the Muslim ~*s*⟩ **6 :** a member of a 19th century English party zealously advocating emancipation of slaves **7 :** a founder, illustrious example, or benefactor of an art, movement, school, or way of life ⟨became the first precursors of symbolism and were afterwards placed among its ~ —Edmund Wilson⟩

²saint \'sānt\ *vt* -ED/-ING/-S [ME *sainten*, fr. *saint*, n.] **1** *archaic* **:** to make blessed in or as if in heaven **:** BEATIFY **2 :** to recognize or designate as a saint; *specif* **:** to enroll among the saints by an official act **:** CANONIZE **3 :** to make (as a person) an object of veneration or reverence **:** ENSHRINE

saint an·drew \-'an(ˌ)drü\ *n, usu cap S&A* [after *St. Andrew* †60 A.D., one of the twelve apostles, patron saint of Scotland] **:** a Scottish gold coin first issued by Robert III (1390–1406) having a representation of St. Andrew on the reverse and a lion rampant over the shield of Scotland on the obverse — called also *lion*

saint andrew's cross *n, usu cap S&A* [so called fr. the tradition that St. Andrew was crucified on a cross of this type] **1 a :** a figure of a cross having the form of two intersecting oblique bars **:** SALTIRE 2 **b :** such a figure extending to and cut off by the boundaries of the area on which it is depicted — used esp. in describing flags; compare SALTIRE 1 **2 :** CRUX DECUSSATA 1

Saint Andrew's cross

saint-andrew's-cross \(ˌ)=;=;=\ *n, usu cap S&A* [*St. Andrew's cross*] **:** a No. American and West Indian woody plant (*Ascyrum hypericoides*) with petals arranged as a St. Andrew's cross

saint andrew's day *n, usu cap S&A&D* **:** November 30 observed in New Zealand as a statutory bank holiday

saint-ann's-bark \-'anz;-\ *n, usu cap S&A* [after *St. Ann* (Anne), mother of the Virgin Mary] **:** RED BARK

saint an·tho·ny's cross \-'an(t)thənēz-\ *n, usu cap S&A* [after *St. Anthony* †*ab*A.D.350 Egyptian abbot regarded as the founder of Christian monasticism who traditionally wore a tau cross on his cloak] **1 :** a T-shaped cross **:** TAU CROSS 1 **2 :** CRUX COMMISSA 1

saint anthony's fire *n, usu cap S&A* [so called fr. the belief that such diseases could be cured through the intercession of St. Anthony] **:** any of several inflammations or gangrenous conditions (as erysipelas or ergotism) of the skin

saint au·gus·tine grass \-'ȯgəˌstēn-\ *n, usu cap S&A* [after *St. Augustine* — more at AUGUSTINIAN] **1 :** a perennial much-branched creeping grass (*Stenotaphrum secundatum*) of the southern U.S. valuable as a sand binder and sod grass — called also *buffalo grass* **2 :** a grass (*Manisuris rugosa*) similar to St. Augustine grass

saint aus·tin's summer \-'ȯstənz-\ *or* **saint au·gus·tine's summer** \-ȯ'gəstənz-\ *n, usu cap S&A* [after *St. Austin* (*Augustine*); prob. fr. the proximity of his feast day (Aug. 28)] *Brit* **:** Indian summer when occurring in September

saint bar·na·bas' day \-'bärnəbəs(əz)-\ *n, usu cap S&B* [after *St. Barnabas* — more at BARNABY BRIGHT] **:** BARNABY BRIGHT

saint-bar·na·by's-thistle \-ˌbärnəbēz;-\ *n, usu cap S&B* [after *St. Barnabas* — more at BARNABY'S THISTLE] **:** BARNABY'S THISTLE

saint be·noit \-ben'wä\ *n, often cap S&B* [prob. fr. F *St. Benoît*, after *St. Benoît* (Benedict) the Black †1589 Sicilian monk] **:** NEGRO 2

saint ber·nard \-bər'närd, -bə'nȧd\ *n, usu cap S&B* [fr. the hospice of Grand *St. Bernard*, alpine pass between Switzerland and Italy where such dogs were first bred] **1 :** a Swiss alpine breed of powerful tall imposing dogs used esp. formerly in aiding lost travelers and having a massive head, deep stop, short muzzle, large button ears, short and strong neck, sloping shoulders, broad back that slopes gently from the haunches to the rump, well-developed hindquarters, and a long blunt-ended tail **2** *pl* **saint bernards :** any dog of the St. Bernard breed

saint-ber·nard's-lily \-;bərnərdz;-\ *n, usu cap S&B* [prob. after *St. Bernard* of Clairvaux †1153 Fr. ecclesiastic] **:** an Old World herb (*Anthericum liliago*) with long recurved linear leaves commonly cultivated for its racemose greenish white flowers

saint-bru·no's-lily \-;brü(ˌ)nōz;-\ *n, usu cap S&B* [prob. after *St. Bruno* of Querfurt †1009 Ger. archbishop & missionary] **:** a European alpine plant (*Paradisea liliastrum*) of the family Liliaceae resembling the asphodel with fascicled fleshy roots, radical leaves, and funnel-shaped white flowers

saint-cath·er·ine's flower \-'kath(ə)rənz-\ *n, usu cap S&C* [after *St. Catherine* of Alexandria †*ab*307 Christian martyr who was tortured on a spiked wheel] **1** [so called fr. the fancied resemblance of the styles to the spikes on Catherine's wheel] **:** LOVE-IN-A-MIST 1 **2 :** POINSETTIA

saint cuth·bert's beads \-'kəthbə(r)ts-\ *n pl, usu cap S&C* [after *St. Cuthbert* †687 English monk] **:** joints of fossil crinoid stems

saint cuthbert's duck *n, usu cap S&C* **:** EIDER DUCK

saint-dab·e·oc's-heath \-;dabēˌōks;-\ *n, usu cap S&D* [after *St. Dabeoc* (Beoc), 5th or 6th cent. Brit. monk who founded a monastery in Ireland] **:** IRISH HEATH

saint·dom \'sāntdəm\ *n* -s **:** the quality or state of being a saint

sainted *adj* **1 :** of, relating to, befitting, or resembling a saint ⟨the enthron'd gods on ~ seats —John Milton⟩ **2 :** SAINTLY, VIRTUOUS, PIOUS ⟨spiritual and moral stature of their ~ predecessors —K.S.Latourette⟩ **3 :** entered into heaven **:** DEAD ⟨one of our long departed, ~ ministers —Sara King⟩

saint ed·ward's crown \-'edwə(r)dz-\ *n, usu cap S&E* [after *St. Edward* (Edward the Confessor) †1066 king of England] **:** IMPERIAL CROWN 1a

saint elmo's fire *or* **saint elmo's light** \-'el(ˌ)mōz-\ *or* **saint ulmo's fire** *or* **saint ulmo's light** \-'əl(ˌ)mōz-\ *n, usu cap S&E&U* [after *St. Elmo* or *Ulmo* (*Erasmus*) †303 Ital. bishop and martyr, patron saint of sailors] **:** a flaming phenomenon sometimes seen in stormy weather at prominent points on an airplane (as at the wing tips) or ship (as at the masthead or yardarms) and on land (as at the tops of trees or steeples) that is of the nature of a brush discharge of electricity which is reddish when positive and bluish when negative — called also *corposant*

saint-errant \'=;==\ *n, pl* **saints-errant** *or* **saint-errants** [¹*saint* + *errant* (as in *knight-errant*)] **:** a wandering saint **:** a missionary saint

saint-étienne *or* **saint-etienne** \saⁿtātyen\ *adj, usu cap S&E* [fr. *St.-Étienne*, France] **:** of or from the city of St.-Étienne, France **:** of the kind or style prevalent in St.-Étienne

saint·foin \'sāntˌfȯin\ *n* -s [F, alter. of *sainfoin* — more at SAINFOIN] **:** SAINFOIN

saint george's day \-'jȯrjəz-\ *n, usu cap S&G&D* [after *St. George* †*ab*303 Cappadocian Christian martyr, patron saint of England] **:** April 23 observed as a bank holiday in New Zealand

saint george's duck *n, usu cap S&G, Brit* **:** a European sheldrake (*Tadorna tadorna*)

saint george's mushroom *n, usu cap S&G* **:** HORSE MUSHROOM; *also* **:** a related mushroom (*Agaricus gambosus*)

saint george's round *n, usu cap S&G* **:** an archery round of 36 arrows first at 100 yards, 80 yards, and 60 yards respectively

saint he·le·na tea \(ˌ)sānt*ə*'lēnə, -thə'lēnə\ *n, usu cap S&H* [fr. *St. Helena*, island in the south Atlantic ocean] **:** a shrub (*Frankenia portulacifolia*) of St. Helena whose leaves are used as a substitute for tea

saint hel·ens \-'helənz\ *adj, usu cap S&H* [fr. *St. Helens*, England] **:** of or from the county borough of St. Helens,

sails: fore-and-aft and square

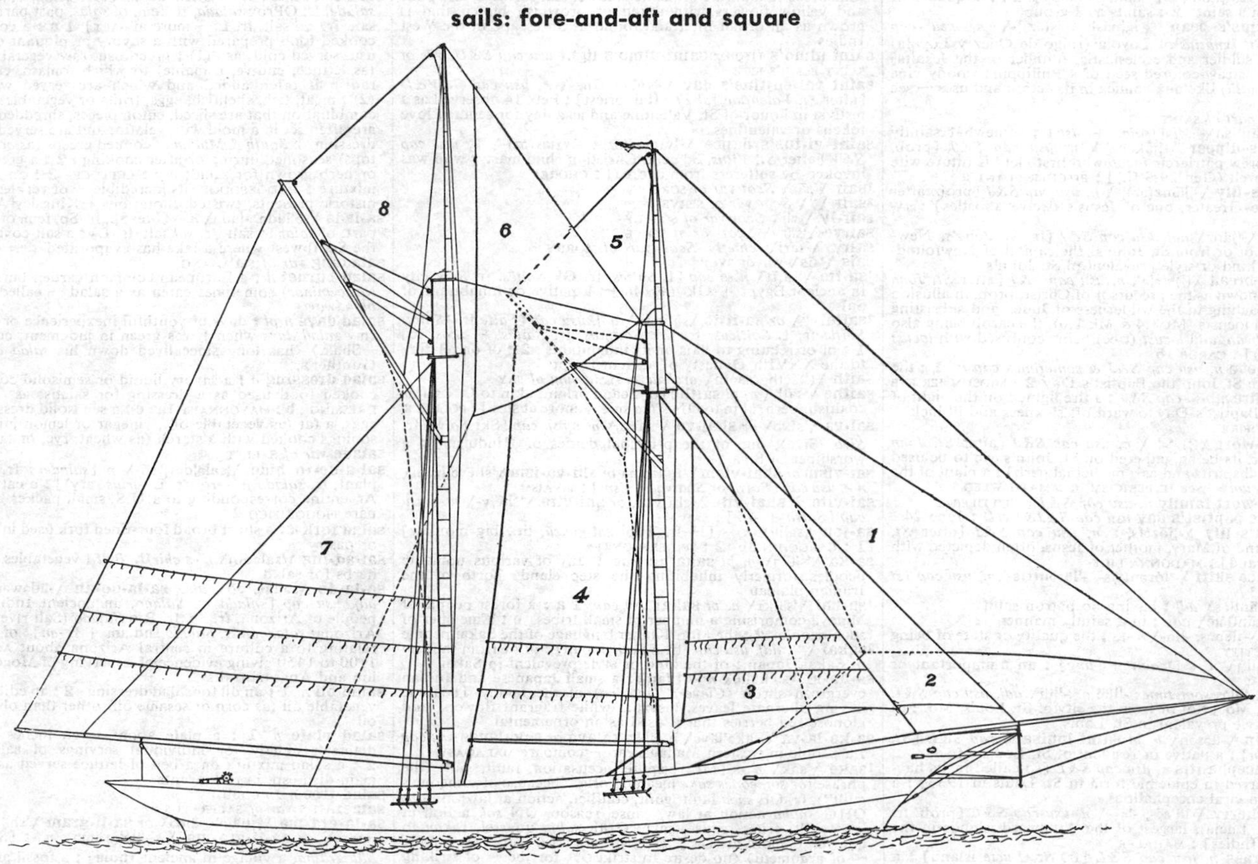

SCHOONER'S SAILS
(an inner and an outer jib are sometimes fitted instead of one jib)
1 flying jib, *2* jib, *3* forestaysail, *4* foresail, *5* fore gaff-topsail, *6* main-topmast staysail, *7* mainsail, *8* main gaff-topsail

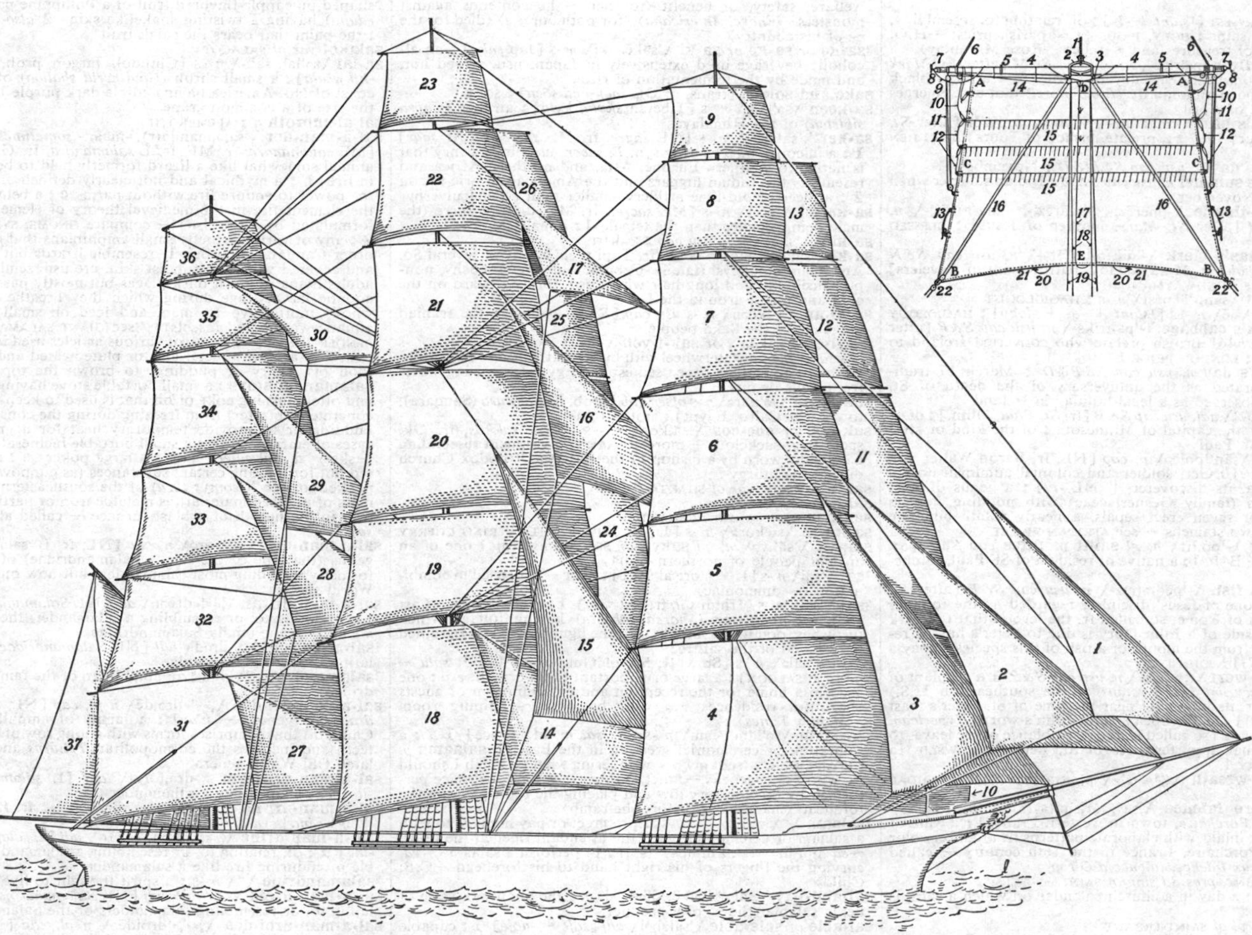

FULL-RIGGED SHIP under ALL PLAIN SAIL to skysails, with all staysails and all port studding sails
(sometimes an inner jib and outer jib are fitted instead of one jib, and also an upper and lower main-topmast staysail instead of one staysail, the upper stay leading just below the foretop; double topgallant sails are sometimes fitted)

1 flying jib, *2* jib, *3* fore-topmast staysail, *4* foresail, *5* lower fore-topsail, *6* upper fore-topsail, *7* fore-topgallant sail, *8* fore-royal, *9* fore-skysail, *10* lower studding sail (never on the main), *11* fore-topmast studding sail, *12* fore-topgallant studding sail, *13* fore-royal studding sail, *14* main staysail, *15* main-topmast staysail, *16* main-topgallant staysail, *17* main-royal staysail, *18* mainsail, *19* lower main topsail, *20* upper main topsail, *21* main-topgallant sail, *22* main royal, *23* main skysail, *24* main-topmast studding sail, *25* main-topgallant studding sail, *26* main-royal studding sail, *27* mizzen staysail, *28* mizzen-topmast staysail, *29* mizzen-topgallant staysail, *30* mizzen-royal staysail, *31* mizzen sail (crossjack), *32* lower mizzen topsail, *33* upper mizzen topsail, *34* mizzen-topgallant sail, *35* mizzen royal, *36* mizzen skysail, *37* spanker

SMALL DIAGRAM: parts of a square sail (topsail) *1* tye, *2* yoke, *3* quarter block, *4* stirrup for footrope, *5* burton bolt, *6* lift, *7* boom ring, *8* pacific iron, *9* Flemish horse, *10* bull earing, *11* reef tackle, *12* reef earing, *13* bowline bridle, *14* footrope, *15* reef point, *16* clew line, *17* bunt whip, *18* topgallant sheet, *19* reef tackle, *20* buntline, *21* buntline toggle, *22* sheet, *A* head-earing cringle, *B* clew, *C* leech, *D* head, *E* foot

Lancashire, England **:** of the kind or style prevalent in St. Helens

saint·hood \ˈsānt,hu̇d\ *n* [¹*saint* + *-hood*] **1 :** the quality or state of being a saint **2 :** saints as a group

saint-ig·na·tius's-bean \-igˈnāsh(ē)əs(əz)ˌ-\ *n, usu cap S&J* [after *St. Ignatius* of Loyola (Iñigo de Oñez y Loyola) †1556 Span. soldier and ecclesiastic, founder of the Jesuits] **:** the greenish straw-colored seed of a Philippine woody vine (*Strychnos ignatii*) like nux vomica in its action and uses — see STRYCHNINE

sainting *pres part of* SAINT

saint·ish \ˈsāntish\ *adj* [¹*saint* + *-ish*] **:** somewhat saintly

saint-ja·cob's-dipper \-ˌjākəbzˌ-\ *n, usu cap S&J* [prob. after the Hebrew patriarch *Jacob* who first met his future wife Rachel by a well (Gen 29:9 ff.)] **:** PITCHER PLANT a

saint-james's-lily \-ˌjāmz(əz)ˌ-\ *n, usu cap S&J* [prob. after *St. James* the Greater, one of Jesus's twelve apostles] **:** JACOBEAN LILY

saint john's \-ˈjänz\ *adj, usu cap S&J* [fr. *St. John's*, Newfoundland] **:** of or from St. John's, the capital of Newfoundland **:** of the kind or style prevalent in St. John's

saint-john's-bread \(ˌ)=ˈ=ˌ=\ *n, usu cap S&J* [after *St. John* the Baptist, known as the precursor of Christ; prob. in allusion to John's preaching in the wilderness of Judea and subsisting on honey and locusts (Mt 3:4 & Mk 1:6), the carob being also called *locust bean*, and *locust* (tree) being confused with *locust* (grasshopper)] **:** CAROB 1b

saint john's eve *n, usu cap S&J & sometimes cap E* **1 :** the evening before St. John the Baptist's Day **2 :** MIDSUMMER EVE

saint john's fire *n, usu cap S&J* **:** a fire lighted on the night of St. John the Baptist's Day to ward off sickness and ill luck — compare NEEDFIRE

saint-john's-wort \(ˌ)=ˈ=ˌ=\ *n, usu cap S&J* [after *St. John* the Baptist; fr. its being gathered on St. John's eve to be used to ward off evil spirits and as a medicinal herb] **:** a plant of the genus *Hypericum* — see HYPERICISM, KLAMATH WEED

saint-john's-wort family *n, usu cap S&J* **:** GUTTIFERAE

saint john the baptist's day *usu cap S&J&B&D* **:** June 24

saint-jo·seph's-lily \-ˌjōzəfsˌ-\ *n, usu cap S&J* [after *St. Joseph*, husband of Mary, mother of Jesus, often depicted with a lily in his hand] **:** MADONNA LILY

saint law·rence skiff \-ˈlȯrən(t)s-, -ˈlärən(t)s-\ *n, usu cap 1st S&L* **:** SKIFF 3

saint·less \ˈsāntləs\ *adj* **:** having no patron saint

saint·li·ly \ˈsāntlə̇lē\ *adv* **:** in a saintly manner

saint·li·ness \-tlēnə̇s, -lin-\ *n* -ES **:** the quality or state of being saintly **:** SANCTITY

saint·ling \-tliŋ\ *n* -S [¹*saint* + *-ling*] **:** an unimportant or young saint

saint lou·is \-ˈlüə̇s *sometimes* -ˈlüē *or* -ˈlüi\ *adj, usu cap S&L* [fr. *St. Louis*, Mo.] **:** of or from the city of St. Louis, Mo. **:** of the kind or style prevalent in St. Louis

saint lou·i·san \-üəsən\ *n, pl* **saint louisans** *cap S&L* [*St. Louis* + E *-an*] **:** a native or resident of St. Louis, Mo.

saint louis encephalitis *n, usu cap S&L* [so called fr. its having first occurred in epidemic form in St. Louis in 1933] **:** a No. American viral encephalitis

saint lu·cie cherry \-lüˈsē-, -ˈ==-\ *n, usu cap S&L* [prob. fr. *St. Lucie* (St. Lucia), largest of the Windward islands in the eastern West Indies] **:** MAHALEB

saint lucie grass *n, usu cap S&L* [fr. *St. Lucie* island] **:** a Bermuda grass that proliferates from aboveground runners

saint lu·cy's day \-ˈlüsēz-\ *n, usu cap S&L* [after *St. Lucy* †303 Sicilian Christian martyr] **:** LUCY LIGHT

saint luke's summer \-ˈlüks-\ *n, usu cap 1st S&L* [after *St. Luke* the Evangelist †*ab*74, whose feast day is Oct. 18] **:** a period of Indian summer weather occurring around St. Luke's Day

saint·ly *adj* -ER/-EST [¹*saint* + *-ly*] **:** of, relating to, resembling, or befitting a saint **:** HOLY, PIOUS ⟨a ~ parish priest —H.O. Taylor⟩ ⟨full of treasures and ~ relics —Rose Macaulay⟩

saint mark's fly \-ˈmärks-\ *n, usu cap S&M* [after *St. Mark* the Evangelist, whose feast day is April 25] **:** a large black angular European bibionid fly (*Bibio marci*) that usu. emerges about the end of April

saint mar·tin's bird \-ˈmärtᵊnz-\ *n, usu cap S&M* [after *St. Martin* of Tours †397 Fr. prelate, bishop of Tours] *Brit* **:** HEN HARRIER

saint martin's day *n, usu cap S&M&D* **:** November 11

saint martin's summer *n, usu cap S&M* **:** Indian summer when occurring in November

saint-mary's-thistle \-ˌmerēzˌ-, -ˌmārēzˌ-, -ˌma(a)rēzˌ-\ *n, usu cap S&M* [after *St. Mary*, mother of Jesus] **:** BLESSED THISTLE

saint nich·o·las's clerk \-ˈnik(ə)ləs(əz)-\ *n, usu cap S&N* [after *St. Nicholas* of Myra †*ab*352, patron saint of travelers] *archaic* **:** THIEF, HIGHWAYMAN

saint·ol·o·gist \sānˈtäləjə̇st\ *n* -S **:** HAGIOLOGIST

saint·ol·o·gy \-jē\ *n* -ES [¹*saint* + *-o-* + *-logy*] **:** HAGIOLOGY

saint-pat·rick's cabbage \-ˈpa·triks-\ *n, usu cap S&P* [after *St. Patrick* †*ab*461 British prelate who converted Ireland to Christianity] **:** LONDON PRIDE 1

saint patrick's day *n, usu cap S&P&D* **:** March 17 traditionally celebrated as the anniversary of the death of St. Patrick and observed as a legal holiday in Ireland

saint paul \-ˈpȯl\ *adj, usu cap S&P* [fr. *St. Paul*, Minn.] **:** of or from St. Paul, the capital of Minnesota **:** of the kind or style prevalent in St. Paul

saint·pau·lia \sāntˈpȯlēə\ *n, cap* [NL, fr. Baron Walter von *Saint Paul* †1910 Ger. soldier and colonial administrator in eastern Africa, its discoverer + NL *-ia*] **:** a genus of East African herbs (family Gesneriaceae) with nodding flowers having five or seven erect sepals, a nearly rotate bilabiate corolla, and two stamens — see AFRICAN VIOLET

saint paul·ite \-ˈpȯ,līt\ *n, pl* **saint paulites** *cap S&P* [*St. Paul*, Minn. + E *-ite*] **:** a native or resident of St. Paul, Minnesota

saint pe·ter's fish \-ˈpēd·ə(r)z-\ *n, usu cap S&P* [after *St. Peter* †*ab*67, one of Jesus' disciples, regarded as the founder of the Church of Rome; so called fr. the legend that the dark spot on each side of a John Dory is due to Peter's having removed a coin from the mouth of a fish of this species to pay a tax (Mt 17:27)] **:** JOHN DORY

saint-peter's-wort \(ˌ)=ˈ=ˌ=\ *n, usu cap S&P* **1 a :** a plant of the genus *Ascyrum* (as *A. stans* of the southeastern U.S.) **b** [so called fr. its blooming near the time of St. Peter's feast day (June 29)] **:** a European Saint-John's-wort (*Hypericum quadrangulum*) **2** [so called fr. the resemblance of the leaves to keys, traditional appurtenances of St. Peter] **:** COWSLIP 1a **3 :** SNOWBERRY 1

saint-peter's-wreath \(ˌ)=ˈ=ˌ=\ *n, usu cap S&P* **:** BRIDAL WREATH 1

saint-porchaire faïence \ˌsaⁿ,pȯrˈsha(a)(ə)r-\ *n, usu cap S&P* [fr. *St.-Porchaire*, town in western France] **:** a ware of pale buff clay inlaid with elaborate patterns in a darker color made at St.-Porchaire, France in the 16th century — called also *Henri Deux faïence, faïence d'Oiron*

saints *pl of* SAINT, *pres 3d sing of* SAINT

saint's day *n* **:** a day in a church calendar on which a saint is commemorated

saints-errant *pl of* SAINT-ERRANT

saint·ship \ˈsānt,ship\ *n* [¹*saint* + *-ship*] **:** the quality or state of being a saint; *specif* **:** the quality or state of being canonized

¹**saint-si·mo·ni·an** \ˌsānt,sīˈmōnēən\ *adj, usu cap both Ss* [Count de *St.-Simon* (Claude Henri de Rouvroy) †1825 Fr. philosopher and social scientist + E *-ian*] **:** of or relating to St.-Simon or Saint-Simonianism

²**saint-simonian** \"\ *n* -S *usu cap both Ss* **:** a follower of St.-Simon or an adherent of Saint-Simonianism

saint-si·mo·ni·an·ism \-ēə,nizəm\ *n* -S *usu cap both Ss* **:** a socialistic system in which the state owns all property and the laborer is entitled to share according to the quality and amount of his work

saint-si·mon·ism \(ˌ)sānˈtsīmə,nizəm\ *n* -S *usu cap both Ss* [Count *St.-Simon* + E *-ism*] **:** SAINT-SIMONIANISM

saint thom·as tree \-ˈtäməs-\ *n, usu cap S & 1st T* [after *St. Thomas*, one of Jesus' disciples; fr. the tradition that the red spots on the flowers were caused by drops of Thomas' blood falling on such a shrub when he was martyred in India] **:** a tropical Asiatic and African shrub (*Bauhinia tomentosa*) with tomentose to glabrate branchlets, lower leaf surfaces, and pods and yellow flowers with a red or brownish blotch that is grown as an ornamental and found as an escape in the West Indies

saint ulmo's fire *or* **saint ulmo's light** *usu cap S&U, var of* SAINT ELMO'S FIRE

saint val·en·tine's day \-ˈvalən,tīnz-\ *n, usu cap S&V&D* [after *St. Valentine* †*ab*270 Ital. priest] **:** Feb. 14 observed as a festival in honor of St. Valentine and as a day for sending love tokens or valentines

saint vi·tus's dance \-ˈvīd·əs(əz)-, -ˈvītəs(əz)-\ *n, usu cap S&V* [after *St. Vitus*, 3d cent. Christian child martyr who was invoked by sufferers from chorea] **:** CHOREA

¹**sair** \ˈsār\ *Scot var of* SORE

²**sair** \"\ *Scot var of* SERVE

sair·ly \-rlī\ *Scot var of* SORELY

sairve \ˈsārv\ *Scot var of* SERVE

sairy \ˈsāri\ *chiefly Scot var of* SORRY

sais \ˈsīs\ *var of* SYCE

¹**sa·ite** \ˈsā,īt\ *n* -S *cap* [L *Saites*, fr. Gk *Saitēs*, fr. *Saïs*, city in ancient Egypt + Gk *-itēs* -ite] **:** a native or inhabitant of Saïs

²**saite** \"\ *or* **sa·it·ic** \sāˈid·ik\ *adj, usu cap* [*Saite* fr. ¹*Saite*; *Saitic* fr. L *Saiticus*, fr. Gk *Saitikos*, fr. *Saitēs* + *-ikos* -ic] **1 :** of or relating to Saïs or its inhabitants **2 :** of or relating to the XXVIth Dynasty of ancient Egypt

saith \(ˈ)seth, ˈsāəth\ *archaic pres 3d sing of* SAY

saithe \ˈsāth\ *n, pl* **saithe** [of Scand origin; akin to ON *seithr* coalfish; perh. akin to ON *sītha* side — more at SIDE] **:** POLLACK

sai·va \ˈsīvə\ *or* **shai·va** \ˈshīvə\ *n* -S *usu cap* [Skt *Śaiva*, fr. *Śiva* (Siva), one of the principal deities of Hinduism] **:** a worshiper of Siva

sai·vism *or* **shai·vism** \-ī,vizəm\ *or* **shi·va·ism** \ˈshēvə,izəm\ *n* -S *usu cap* [*Saiva* or *Shaiva* + *-ism*] **:** SIVAISM

sai·vite *or* **shai·vite** \ˈshī,vīt\ *or* **shi·vite** \ˈshē,v-\ *n* -S *usu cap* [*Saiva* + *-ite*] **:** SAIVA

sa·jou \səˈjü\ *n* -S [F, fr. Tupi *sai-guaçú*, lit., big monkey] **1 :** CAPUCHIN 3b **2 :** SPIDER MONKEY

sa·ka \ˈsäkə\ *n, pl* **saka** *usu cap* **:** any of various nomadic peoples formerly inhabiting the steppelands north of the Iranian plateau

¹**sa·kai** \ˈsä,kī\ *n, pl* **sakai** *usu cap* **1 a :** a forest people of Malaya comprising a number of small tribes **b :** a member of such people **2 :** the Mon-Khmer language of the Sakai people

²**sakai** \"\ *adj, usu cap* [fr. *Sakai*, Japan] **:** of or from the city of Sakai, Japan **:** of the kind or style prevalent in Sakai

sa·ka·ki \səˈkäkē\ *n* -S [Jap] **:** a small Japanese and Indian evergreen shrub (*Cleyera japonica*) of the family Theaceae having alternate leaves, bisexual white fragrant flowers, and globose red berries that is used as an ornamental

sa·ka·la·va \ˌsäkəˈlävə\ *n, pl* **sakalava** *or* **sakalavas** *usu cap* **:** a people in western Madagascar — compare MALAGASY

¹**sake** \ˈsāk\ *n* -S [ME, dispute, accusation, fault, guilt (the phrase *for someones sake* meaning orig. "because of someone's guilt"), fr. OE *sacu* fault, guilt, conflict, action at law; akin to OHG *sahha* action at law, cause, reason, ON *sōk* action at law, guilt, crime, cause, sake, Goth *sakjo* quarrel, *sakan* to quarrel — more at SEEK] **1 :** END, PURPOSE ⟨suppose, for the ~ of argument⟩ ⟨no desire to strike ... for the ~ of striking —*Wall Street Jour.*⟩ **2 a :** the good, advantage, or enhancement of an object, ideal, emotion, or other entity ⟨toil for the ~ of money⟩ ⟨keeps ... its ornate old bar, mostly for sentiment's ~ —Green Peyton⟩ ⟨the highest ends — those to be pursued for their own ~s —Harry Bear⟩ **b :** the good, advantage, or well-being of a person or group **:** personal or social welfare, safety, or benefit ⟨for her ~ he contends against monsters —*Encyc. Americana*⟩ ⟨for both our ~s⟩ ⟨died for the ~ of his country⟩

²**sa·ke** *or* **sa·ké** *or* **sa·ki** \ˈsäkē, -ki\ *n* -S [Jap *sake*] **:** an alcoholic beverage used extensively in Japan, usu. served hot, and made by the fermentation of rice

sake and soke *n* [trans. of OE *sacu ond sōcn*] **:** SOKE

sa·keen \səˈkēn\ *n* -S [Tibetan *skyin, kyin*] **:** an ibex (*Capra sibirica*) of the Himalayas

sa·ker \ˈsākə(r)\ *n* -S [ME *sagre*, fr. MF *sacre*, fr. Ar *ṣaqr*] **1 :** a falcon (*Falco cherrug* syn. *F. sacer*) used in falconry that is native to southern Europe, Asia, and northern Africa and resembles the Indian luggars and the American prairie falcon **2 :** a piece of old-time artillery smaller than a demiculverin

sa·ker·et \-ərə̇t\ *n* -S [ME *sacret*, fr. MF, dim. of *sacre* (the male being smaller than the female)] **:** a male saker

sa·kha \ˈsäkə\ *n* -S *usu cap* **:** YAKUT

sa·ki \ˈsakē, ˈsäkē\ *n* -S [F, fr. Tupi *sagui*] **:** any of several So. American monkeys (family Cebidae) having a bushy nonprehensile tail and long hair which usu. forms a beard on the chin and a ruff around the face

sa·ki·an \ˈsäkēən\ *n* -S *usu cap* [*Saka* + *-ian*] **:** the Iranian language of the Saka people

sak·i·eh \ˈsakē,e\ *or* **sak·i·yeh** \-ē,ye\ *or* **sak·ia** \-ēə\ *n* -S [Ar *sāqiyah*] **:** a waterwheel with buckets attached to its periphery or to an endless rope used esp. in Egypt for raising water from wells or pits

sak·ka·ra \səˈkärə\ *n* -S *often cap* [prob. fr. *Sakkara* (Saqqara), town near Cairo, Egypt] **:** MOUSE GRAY

sak·kos *or* **soc·cos** \ˈsä,kȯs\ *n* -ES [NGk *sakkos*, fr. Gk, sack, bag, sackcloth — more at SACK] **:** a vestment resembling a dalmatic worn by a bishop in the Eastern Orthodox Church during the liturgy

sakta *usu cap, var of* SHAKTA

sakti *var of* SHAKTI

saktism *usu cap, var of* SHAKTISM

sa·ku·ra \səˈkürə\ *n* -S [Jap] **:** JAPANESE FLOWERING CHERRY

sak·ya \ˈsäkyə\ *n, pl* **sakya** *or* **sakyas** *usu cap* **:** one of an ancient people of northern India

¹**sal** \ˈsal\ *n* -S [L — more at SALT] **:** SALT — usu. used in combination ⟨~ ammoniac⟩

²**sal** \ˈsäl\ *n* -S [Hindi *sāl*, fr. Skt *śāla*] **1** *or* **sal tree :** an East Indian timber tree (*Shorea robusta*) having foliage which furnishes food for lac insects **2 :** the light brown close-grained hard wood of the sal tree

sa·la \ˈsälə\ *n* -S [Sp & It; Sp, of Gmc origin like It *sala* — more at SALOON] **:** a large or important room or hall; *esp* **:** one used in a home for the reception and entertainment of guests ⟨beautiful residences ... with balcony, ~, dining room —*Manila Times*⟩

¹**sa·laam** \səˈläm, -lam\ *n* -S [Ar *salām*, lit., peace] **1 a :** a salutation or ceremonial greeting in the East **b salaams** *pl* **:** COMPLIMENTS ⟨sent my ~s, wondering what on earth I should do with the peacocks —Janet Dunbar⟩ **2 :** an obeisance performed by bowing very low and placing the right palm on the forehead ⟨made his ~ before the rajah⟩

²**salaam** \"\ *vb* -ED/-ING/-S *vt* **:** to greet or pay homage to with a salaam or ceremonial bow ⟨the attendant opened the door, ~*ed* him in —J.A.Phillips⟩ ~ *vi* **:** to perform a salaam ⟨~*ed*, curving the fingers of his right hand to his forehead —C.B. Child⟩

sal·abil·i·ty \ˌsāləˈbiləd·ē, -ilətē, -i\ *n* **:** the quality or state of being salable ⟨the ~ of a product⟩

sal·able *or* **sale·able** \ˈsāləbəl\ *adj* [*sale* + *-able*] **1 :** capable of being sold **:** fit to be sold **:** MARKETABLE, VENDIBLE ⟨write a ~ story⟩ ⟨little boys ... find ~ bottles —W.A.White⟩ ⟨develop ~ skills —M.B.Smith⟩ **2** *archaic* **:** susceptible to bribery **:** VENAL — **sal·able·ness** *n* -ES

sa·la·cious \səˈlāshəs\ *adj* [L *salac-, salax* fond of leaping, lustful (fr. *salire* to leap) + E *-ious* — more at SALLY] **1 a** *archaic, of a food* **:** tending to arouse sexual appetite **:** APHRODISIAC **b :** inciting to sexual desire or imagination **:** LASCIVIOUS, OBSCENE ⟨a collection of ~ poems —Malcolm Cowley⟩ **2 :** marked by lecherousness or lewdness **:** LUSTFUL ⟨the ~ rooster⟩ ⟨their erotic skill is emphasized with ~ eagerness —Jack Morpurgo⟩ — **sa·la·cious·ly** *adv* — **sa·la·cious·ness** *n* -ES

sa·lac·i·ty \səˈlasəd·ē, -asətē, -aas-, -i\ *n* -ES [MF or L; MF *salacité*, fr. L *salacitat-, salacitas*, fr. *salac-, salax* + *-itat-, -itas* -ity] **:** the quality or state of being salacious **:** SALACIOUSNESS ⟨handled sex in his novels with a mere suggestion of ~⟩

sal·a·cot *or* **sal·a·kot** \ˈsalə,kät\ *n* -S [Sp & Tag; Sp *salacot*, fr. Tag *salakót*] **:** a broad-brimmed Philippine hat woven from strips of cane or from palm leaves

sal·ad \ˈsaləd\ *n* -S *often attrib* [ME *selad, salade*, fr. MF *salade*, fr. OProv *salada*, fr. fem. of *salat*, past part. of *salar* to salt, fr. *sal* salt, fr. L — more at SALT] **1 a :** a cooked or uncooked food prepared with a savory or piquant dressing and usu. served cold: as (1) **:** green usu. raw vegetables or herbs (as lettuce, endive, romaine) to which tomato, cucumber, or radish is often added and which are served with dressing (2) **:** meat, fish, shellfish, eggs, fruits or vegetables singly or in combination that are sliced, cut in pieces, shredded, or minced, are often set in a mold with gelatin, and are served cold with a dressing **b** *South & Midland* **:** cooked greens (as poke or turnip tops) seasoned during or after cooking **2 :** a green vegetable or herb grown for salad; *esp* **:** LETTUCE **3 :** an incongruous mixture **:** HODGEPODGE ⟨its incredible ~ of verbless sentences, historic presents, twisted quotations —Kingsley Amis⟩

sa·lada \səˈlädə, -ladə\ *n* -S [MexSp, fr. Sp, fem. of *salado*, past part. of *salar* to salt, fr. *sal* salt, fr. L] **:** a salt-covered plain in the Southwest where a lake has evaporated

saladang *var of* SELADANG

salad burnet *n* **:** a European common garden burnet (*Sanguisorba minor*) sometimes eaten as a salad — called also *burnet bloodwort*

salad days *n pl* **:** days of youthful inexperience or indiscretion ⟨my *salad days* when I was green in judgment, cold in blood —Shak.⟩ ⟨has long since lived down his *salad days* —John Gunther⟩

salad dressing *n* **:** a savory liquid or semisolid cooked or uncooked food used as a dressing for salads: as **a :** FRENCH DRESSING **b :** MAYONNAISE 1a **c :** a semisolid dressing made of eggs, a fat (as vegetable oil), vinegar or lemon juice, and seasonings cooked with a starch (as wheat, rye, or tapioca flour)

salade *var of* SALLET

sal·a·de·ro hide \ˌsaləˈde(ˌ)rō-\ *n* [*saladero* fr. Sp, salting plant, fr. *salado* + *-ero* (fr. L *-arius* -ary)] **:** a cattlehide from Argentina corresponding to a U.S. small packer hide — compare FRIGORIFICO 2

salad fork *n* **:** a short broad four-tined fork used in eating salad or pastry

sal·ad·ing \ˈsalədiŋ\ *n* -S *chiefly Brit* **:** vegetables or herbs for salad

sa·la·do \səˈlä(ˌ)dō\ *also* **sa·la·do·an** \-ädəwən\ *adj, usu cap* [*salado* fr. *Salado*, an ancient Indian people of Arizona, fr. Sp, fr. Río *Salado* (Salt river), Arizona; *saladoan* fr. *Salado* Indians + E *-an*] **:** of or relating to a culture in central Arizona about A.D. 1100 to 1450 giving evidence of a merging of Mogollon and Anasazi traits

salad oil *n* **1 :** an oil for salad dressing **2 :** an edible vegetable oil (as corn or sesame oil) other than olive oil

salad plate *n* **1 :** a plate about seven inches in diameter chiefly for individual servings of salad **2 :** a salad mixture on a bed of lettuce served as a main dish esp. in restaurants

salad tree *n* **:** REDBUD

salaeratus *var of* SALERATUS

sa·la·gra·ma \ˌshäləˈgrämə\ *or* **sa·li·gram** \ˈshälə,gram\ *or* **sa·li·gra·ma** \ˌshäləˈgrämə\ *n* -S [Skt *Śālagrāma*, a village in ancient India] **:** a fossil ammonite held by Hindus to be a representative of Vishnu

salad fork

salah *var of* SALAT

sa·lai \səˈlī, ˈsa,lī\ *also* **salai tree** *n* -S [Hindi *śallak, sallak*, fr. Skt *śallakī*] **:** an East Indian tree (*Boswellia serrata*) yielding resin that is used as an incense and as a medicine

sa·lak \səˈlak\ *n* -S [native name in Malaya] **1 :** the pear-shaped pineapple-flavored fruit of a Philippine palm (*Zalacca edulis*) having a twisting snakelike skin **2** *also* **salak palm :** the palm that bears the salak fruit

salakot *var of* SALACOT

sa·lal \səˈlal, saˈl-\ *n* -S [Chinook Jargon, prob. fr. Chinook *-klkwšala*] **:** a small shrub (*Gaultheria shallon*) of the Pacific coast of No. America having edible dark purple berries about the size of a common grape

sal alembroth *n* **:** ALEMBROTH

sal·a·man·der \ˈsalə,mandə(r), -maan- *sometimes* ˌ==ˈ==\ *n* -S [ME *salamandre*, fr. MF, fr. L *salamandra*, fr. Gk] **1 a :** an animal somewhat like a lizard formerly held to be able to live in fire **b :** a mythical and not clearly defined animal having the power to endure fire without harm **c :** a being inhabiting the element fire in the medieval theory of elementals esp. as formulated by Paracelsus — compare GNOME, SYLPH, UNDINE **2 :** any of various chiefly small amphibians that comprise the order Caudata, superficially resemble lizards but are scaleless and covered with a soft moist skin, are usu. semiterrestrial as adults living in moist dark places but mostly pass through an aquatic larval stage during which they breathe by gills, are wholly inoffensive to man, and feed on small animals (as aquatic worms and insects) — see GIANT SALAMANDER, HELLBENDER 1, NEWT **3 :** any of various articles used in connection with fire: as **a :** a metal disk or plate heated and held over a food (as pastry or pudding) to brown the top of it **b** *or* **salamander stove :** a small portable stove having no chimney and often burning coke or oil that is used to keep materials (as concrete or plaster) from freezing during the construction of a building or to provide temporary heat for a greenhouse in cases of emergency **c :** a small portable incinerator (as a wire basket) **d** *dial chiefly Eng* **:** a large poker **e :** an iron used red hot for igniting certain substances (as gunpowder) **4 :** the pocket gopher (*Geomys tuza*) of the southeastern U.S. **5 :** a mass of unfused material (as metallic iron or partially reduced ore) in the hearth of a blast furnace — called also *shadrach, sow*

sal·a·man·dra \ˌ==ˈ=drə\ *n, cap* [NL, fr. L, salamander] **:** a genus (the type of the family Salamandridae) of amphibians formerly including most salamanders but now only a few Old World species

sal·a·man·dri·an \ˌ==ˈ=drēən\ *adj* [NL *Salamandra* + E *-ian*] **:** of, relating to, or resembling a salamander, the genus *Salamandra*, or the family Salamandridae

¹**sal·a·man·drid** \-drə̇d\ *adj* [NL *Salamandridae*] **:** of or relating to the Salamandridae

²**salamandrid** \"\ *n* -S **:** an amphibian of the family Salamandridae

sal·a·man·dri·dae \ˌ==ˈ=drə,dē\ *n pl, cap* [NL, fr. *Salamandra*, type genus + *-idae*] **:** a family of amphibians (order Caudata) that comprises forms with a long row of prevomerine teeth and includes the cosmopolitan *Triturus* and several related Old World genera

sal·a·man·dri·form \-drə,fȯrm\ *adj* [L *salamandra* + E *-iform*] **:** shaped like a salamander

sal·a·man·dri·na \ˌ==ˈ=drīnə, -rēnə\ *n* [NL, fr. L *salamandra* + NL *-ina*] *syn of* MUTABILIA

¹**sal·a·man·drine** \ˌ==ˈ=,drən, -,drīn\ *adj* [L *salamandra* + E *-ine*] **1 :** of, relating to, or resembling a salamander **2 :** capable of enduring fire like a salamander

²**salamandrine** \"\ *n* -S **:** a spirit thought to live in fire

sal·a·man·droid \-,drȯid\ *adj* [NL *Salamandroidea*] **:** of, relating to, or resembling salamanders or the Salamandroidea

sal·a·man·droi·dea \ˌ==,=ˈdrȯidēə\ *n pl, cap* [NL, fr. *Salamandra* + *-oidea*] **:** a suborder of Caudata comprising salamanders of numerous and varied form (as the aquatic newts and the lungless terrestrial plethodonts) that have in common teeth on the roof of the mouth behind the internal openings of the nostrils — compare PLETHODON

sal·am·bao \ˌsaləmˈbau̇\ *n* -S [PhilSp, fr. Tag *salambáw*] **:** a large Philippine fishing net supported by a long bamboo cross-piece mounted on a raft

sa·la·mi \səˈlämē, -lam-, -mi\ *n* -S [It, pl. of *salame* salami, fr. *salare* to salt, fr. *sale* salt, fr. L *sal* — more at SALT] **:** highly seasoned sausage made of pork and beef in various proportions either air-dried, hard, and of good keeping qualities or fresh, soft, and requiring refrigeration until consumed

¹**sal·a·min·i·an** \ˌsaləˈminēən\ *adj, usu cap* [L *Salaminius* Salaminian (fr. Gk *Salaminios*, fr. *Salamin-, Salamis*, city in ancient Cyprus) + E *-an*] **:** of or relating to Salamis, Cyprus

²**salaminian** \"\ *n* -S *cap* **:** a native or inhabitant of ancient Salamis, Cyprus

sal ammoniac *n* [ME *sal armoniak*, fr. L *sal ammoniacus*, fr. *sal* salt + *ammoniacus* of Ammon — more at SALT, AMMONIA] **1 :** ammonium chloride esp. when purified by sublimation **2 :** a mineral NH_4Cl consisting of native ammonium chloride

sal·am·pore *also* **sal·em·pore** \'saləm,pō(ə)r\ *n* -s [origin unknown] **:** a colored cotton cloth with woven stripe and check designs made in India and England usu. for export to Africa and So. America

sal·an·gane \'salən,gan, -gān\ *n* -s [F, fr. Tag & Bisayan *salangan*] **:** any of several swifts producing edible nests — compare EDIBLE BIRD'S NEST

sa·lan·gid \sə'lanjəd\ *n* -s [NL *Salangidae*] **:** a fish of the family Salangidae

sa·lan·gi·dae \-jə,dē\ *n pl, cap* [NL, fr. *Salang-*, *Salanx*, type genus (fr. Gk, a kind of fish) + *-idae*] **:** a family of small slender translucent salmonoid fishes of China and Japan — see ICEFISH

1sa·lar \sə'lär\ *n, pl* **salar** *or* **salars** *usu cap* **1 :** a Moslem people of Chinese Turkestan speaking a Turkic dialect **2 :** a member of the Salar people

2salar \"\ *adj, usu cap* **:** of, relating to, or characteristic of the Salar

3salar \"\ *n* -s [AmerSp, fr. Sp, to salt — more at SALADA] **:** a salt-encrusted depression (as in the nitrate fields of Chile) that may or may not be the basin of an evaporated lake — compare SALADA, SALINA

sa·lar·i·at \sə'la(a)rēət, -ē,at\ *n* -s [F, blend of *salaire* salary (fr. L *salarium*) and *prolétariat* — more at SALARY, PROLETARIAT] **:** the class or body of salaried persons usu. as distinguished from wage earners — compare PROLETARIAT ⟨the wage-labor force and ~ —J.S.Coleman⟩

sal·a·ried \'sal(ə)rēd, -rid\ *adj* **1 :** receiving a salary ⟨the ~ staff⟩ ⟨to point out that the ~ manager of a public or private monopoly is quite unlikely to behave like a Victorian entrepreneur —Peter Wiles⟩ — contrasted with *hourly-rated* **2 :** calling for the payment of a salary ⟨a ~ position⟩

1sal·a·ry \'sal(ə)rē, -ri\ *n* -ES *often attrib* [ME *salarie*, fr. L *salarium* money given to soldiers for salt, pension, stipend, salary, fr. neut. of *salarius* of salt, fr. *sal* salt + *-arius* -ary — more at SALT] **1 :** fixed compensation paid regularly (as by the year, quarter, month, or week) for services **:** STIPEND; *esp* **:** such compensation paid to holders of official, executive, or clerical positions — often distinguished from *wage* **2** *obs* **a :** remuneration for services given **:** FEE, HONORARIUM ⟨why, this is hire and ~, not revenge —Shak.⟩ **b :** REWARD, RECOMPENSE **syn** see WAGE

2salary \"\ *vt* -ED/-ING/-S **1 :** to pay (as a person) for something done **:** RECOMPENSE, REWARD ⟨would string wretched rhymes even when not *salaried* for them —Isaac D'Israeli⟩ **2 a :** to pay a salary to (a person) ⟨the academicians were *salaried* by the Crown —S.F.Mason⟩ **b :** to attach a salary to (a position)

3salary \"\ *dial var of* CELERY

salary savings insurance *or* **salary allotment insurance** *also* **salary deduction insurance** *n* **:** an individual life insurance policy for which the premium is deducted from an employee's pay and remitted by his employer directly to the company

salas *pl of* SALA

1sal·at \'salət\ *archaic & dial var of* SALAD

2sa·lat \sə'lät\ *also* **sa·lah** \-lä\ *n* -s [Ar *ṣalāt*] **:** a ritual prayer of Muslims made five times daily in a standing position alternating with inclinations and prostrations as the worshiper faces toward Mecca

sal·band \'sal,band; 'säl,bänt, 'zäl-\ *n* -s [G, lit., selvage, fr. MHG *selbende*, *selpende*, fr. *selp* self (fr. OHG *selb*) + *ende* end, fr. OHG *enti* — more at SELF, END] **:** the border of an igneous mass (as a dike) usu. characterized by a finer grain or even glassy texture produced by the chilling of the molten rock by the cold country rock

sal·chow \'sal,kōv\ *n* -s *usu cap* [after Ulrich *Salchow*, 20th cent. Swed. skating champion] **:** a figure-skating jump with a takeoff from the back inside edge of one skate followed by a full turn in the air and a landing on the back outside edge of the opposite skate

sal·cio·nal \'salshənᵊl\ *n* -s [by alter.] **:** SALICIONAL

1sal·did \'saldəd\ *adj* [NL *Saldidae*] **:** of or relating to the Saldidae

2saldid \"\ *n* -s **:** a bug of the family Saldidae

sal·di·dae \-ldə,dē\ *n pl, cap* [NL, fr. *Salda*, type genus + *-idae*] **:** a widely distributed family of predacious aquatic bugs

1sale \'sāl, *esp before pause or consonant* -āəl\ *n* -s [ME, fr. OE *sala*, fr. ON — more at SELL] **1 :** the act of selling **:** a contract transferring the absolute or general ownership of property from one person or corporate body to another for a price (as a sum of money or any other consideration); *specif* **:** a present transfer of such ownership of and title to all of or a part interest in personal property (as existing identifiable movable and tangible or fungible goods) under a contract by the seller to the buyer for a price paid or payable in money or other personal property — distinguished from *gift* ⟨arranged the ~ of a large estate to a syndicate of home builders⟩ **2 :** exhibition for selling **:** the status of being purchasable — usu. used in the phrases *for sale* and *on sale* ⟨put a house up for ~⟩ ⟨on ~ at most stationery stores⟩ **3 a :** opportunity of selling or being sold **:** DEMAND, MARKET ⟨counting on a large ~ for their latest publication⟩ **b :** distribution (as of goods or services) by selling ⟨the average total ~ for books in this category —*Saturday Rev.*⟩ **4 :** public disposal to the highest bidder **:** AUCTION ⟨art dealers flocking to the ~ of a famous collection of early Renaissance masters⟩ **5 a :** a selling off of goods (as surplus or shopworn stock) at bargain prices ⟨a clearance ~⟩ ⟨rummage ~⟩ **b :** an advertised disposal of marked-down goods ⟨a dress bought at a department-store ~⟩ **6 sales** *pl* **a :** operations and activities involved in promoting and selling goods or services ⟨a ~*s* department⟩ ⟨vice-president in charge of ~*s*⟩ **b :** gross receipts ⟨~*s* were over five million dollars⟩ — **on sale or return :** on approval

2sale \"\ *adj* [ME, fr. *sale*, n.] **1 :** made for selling rather than home use **:** PURCHASABLE ⟨~ bread⟩ ⟨~ milk⟩ ⟨~ ware⟩ **2 :** produced in large quantities for the trade **:** READY-MADE ⟨~ doors⟩ ⟨~ tools⟩ **3 :** SELLING ⟨special ~ price⟩

saleable *var of* SALABLE

sale–and–leaseback \,==ˈ=,=\ *n* **:** LEASEBACK

sa·lée·ite \sə'lā,īt\ *n* -s [F, fr. A. *Salée*, 20th cent. Frenchman + F *-ite*] **:** a mineral $Mg(UO_2)_2(PO_4)_2.10H_2O$ that is a hydrous phosphate of magnesium and uranium and is isomorphous with autunite and torbernite

sa·le·le \sə'lālē\ *n* -s [Samoan] **:** a small dusky silver or silvery bronze percoid fish (*Dules rupestris*) widely distributed chiefly in fresh or brackish water in the tropical Indo-Pacific area from eastern Africa to Hawaii

1sa·lem \'sāləm\ *adj, usu cap* [fr. *Salem*, Ore.] **:** of or from Salem, the capital of Oregon ⟨a *Salem* lawyer⟩ **:** of the kind or style prevalent in Salem

2salem \"\ *adj, usu cap* [fr. *Salem*, India] **:** of or from the city of Salem, India **:** of the kind or style prevalent in Salem

salem grass \"-\ *n, usu cap S* [prob. fr. *Salem*, Mass.] **:** VELVET GRASS

salempore *var of* SALAMPORE

salem rocker *n, usu cap S* [fr. *Salem*, Mass.] **:** an early 19th century rocking chair with heavy scrolled seat and arms and a back of slender curved spindles and scrolled and often painted and stenciled top rail

sale note *n* **:** a memorandum given by a broker to a buyer or seller of goods stating that the specified goods have been sold by him for the account of a named seller to a named buyer

salep \'saləp, sə'lep\ *also* **saleb** \'saləb, sə'leb\ *n* -s [F or Sp *salep*, fr. Ar *saḥlab*, alter. of *khuṣy ath-tha'lab*, lit., the fox's testicles] **:** the dried tubers of various European orchids (genus *Orchis*) or East Indian orchids (genus *Eulophia*) containing gum and starch and being used for food (as tapioca) and as a demulcent

sal·e·ra·tus *also* **sal·ae·ra·tus** \,salə'rād·əs\ *n* -ES [NL *sal aeratus*, fr. L *sal* salt + *aeratus* aerated, fr. L *aer-* + *-atus* -ate, fr. the carbon dioxide that is evolved upon treatment with acids] **:** either of two salts used as leavening agents: **a :** POTASSIUM BICARBONATE **b :** SODIUM BICARBONATE

sales \'sā(ə)lz\ *adj* [fr. pl. of 1*sale*] **:** of, relating to, or used in selling ⟨~ quota⟩ ⟨~ manager⟩

sales agency *n* **1 :** the commission or authorization of a sales agent **2 :** the place of business of a sales agent

sales agent *n* **:** one who is authorized or appointed by a manufacturer to sell or distribute his products within a given territory but who is in business for himself, takes title to the goods, and does not act as agent for a principal

sales check *n* **:** a strip or piece of paper used by retail stores as a memorandum, record, or receipt of a purchase or sale

salesclerk \'=,=\ *n* **:** a salesman or saleswoman employed in a store

sales engineer *n* **1 :** an engineer who sells equipment and manufactured products by estimating from plans and computing cost of installation and often establishes liaison between designers and contractors for the manufacture of machines and equipment suited to each situation and for efficient operation when installed **2 :** an engineer attached to a sales department to assist salesmen with technical information and advice

salesgirl \'=,=\ *n* **:** SALESWOMAN

1sa·le·sian \sə'lēzhən, -ēsh-\ *adj, usu cap* [St. Francis de *Sales* †1622 Savoyard ecclesiastic + E *-ian*] **1 :** of or relating to St. Francis de Sales **2 :** of or relating to the Salesians

2salesian \"\ *n* -s *cap* **:** a member of the Society of St. Francis de Sales founded as a Roman Catholic religious congregation in the 19th century by St. John Bosco in Turin and devoted chiefly to education

sales·ite \'sāl,zīt\ *n* -s [Reno *Sales* *b*1876 Am. geologist + E *-ite*] **:** a mineral $Cu(IO_3)(OH)$ consisting of a basic copper iodate found at Chuquicamata, Chile

saleslady \'=,==\ *n* **:** SALESWOMAN ⟨*salesladies* will tell you that husbands don't know their wives' fundamental measurements —S.L.Payne⟩

sales·man \'sā(ə)lzmən\ *n, pl* **salesmen :** one that sells: **a :** one employed to sell goods or services either within a given territory or in a store — see SALESCLERK, TRAVELING SALESMAN; compare DETAIL MAN **b :** one who seeks to persuade others to accept or approve an idea, system of thought, or course of action ⟨the new *salesmen* of popular religion —M.W.Straight⟩ ⟨ambassadors in overalls can be the best *salesmen* of democracy —A.E.Stevenson †1965⟩

sales·man·ship \-,ship\ *n* **1 :** the skill or art of selling ⟨a course in ~⟩ **2 :** the act or process of selling ⟨large sums spent in ~⟩ **3 :** ability or effectiveness in selling (as goods) or in presenting persuasively (as ideas) ⟨saw . . . that his tales were not all ~ —Wendell Willkie⟩ ⟨stated that bad ~ . . . was mainly responsible for the party's defeat —Cecil Harden⟩

salespeople \'=,==\ *n pl* **:** persons employed to sell goods or services; *esp* **:** the corps of salesmen and saleswomen of a particular business concern

salesperson \'=,==\ *n* **:** a person employed to sell merchandise to customers in a store; *specif* **:** SALESCLERK

sales promotion *n* **:** activities and devices designed to create goodwill and sell a product; *esp* **:** selling activities (as use of displays, sampling, demonstrations, fashion shows, contests, coupons, premiums, and special sales) that supplement advertising and personal selling, coordinate them, and make them effective

sales register *n* **:** CASH REGISTER

sales representative *n* **:** REPRESENTATIVE 3e

sales resistance *n* **1 :** the power, capacity, or disposition to resist buying goods or services offered for sale ⟨surveys . . . to determine the presumptive *sales resistance* of potential purchasers —Charles Merz⟩ **2 :** disinclination to accept or approve (as new ideas or proposals) ⟨millions were spent . . . to hammer away at the *sales resistance* of voters —*Nation*⟩ ⟨*sales resistance* to the author's ideas is likely to be still more gratuitously stimulated by elementary infelicities of idiom —Randolph Quirk⟩

salesroom *also* **saleroom** \'=,=\ *n* **:** a place where goods are displayed for sale **:** SHOWROOM; *esp* **:** an auction room

sales slip *n* **:** SALES CHECK

sales talk *n* **:** argument often accompanied by demonstration used to persuade others to buy a product or service or to accept an idea or proposal ⟨memorized the *sales talk* he hoped would bring in large orders⟩ ⟨a glib *sales talk* that produced unanimous agreement⟩

sales tax *n* **:** a tax on the privilege or freedom of making sales of tangible personal property that is usu. measured by a percentage (as 3%) of the purchase price, is collected for the government imposing the tax by the seller, and is distinguished from a tax imposed on the property itself

saleswoman \'=,==\ *n, pl* **saleswomen :** a woman employed to sell merchandise esp. in a store

salet *var of* SALLET

saleyard \'=,=\ *n* **:** a yard in which livestock is sold

sal·fern \'salfə(r)n\ *or* **salfern stoneseed** *n* [origin unknown] **:** CORN GROMWELL

sal·ford \'sölfə(r)d\ *adj, usu cap* [fr. *Salford*, Lancashire, England] **:** of or from the county borough of Salford, Lancashire **:** of the kind or style prevalent in Salford

sali- *comb form* [L, fr. *sal* — more at SALT] **:** salt ⟨*sali*ferous⟩ ⟨*sali*meter⟩

1sa·lian \'sālēən, -lyən\ *adj, usu cap* [LL *Salii*, a division of the Franks (fr. the *Sala* — Ijssel — river) + E *-an*] **:** of or relating to a Frankish people dwelling early in the 4th century A.D. on the Ijssel river — see SALIC LAW

2salian \"\ *adj, usu cap* [L *Salii*, priests of Mars in ancient Rome (fr. *salire* to leap) + E *-an* — more at SALLY] **:** of or relating to the Salii of ancient Rome ⟨*Salian* hymns⟩

saliant *var of* SALIENT

salic \'sā|lik, 'sa|, |lēk\ *also* **sa·lique** \", sə|'lēk, sa|\ *adj, usu cap* [MF or ML; MF *salique*, fr. ML *Salicus*, fr. LL *Salii* Salian Franks + L *-icus* -ic] **:** SALIAN

sal·i·ca·ce·ae \,salə'kāsē,ē\ *n pl, cap* [NL, fr. *Salic-*, *Salix*, type genus + *-aceae*] **:** a family of dioecious trees or shrubs (order Salicales) having small apetalous flowers in catkins — see SALIX

sal·i·ca·les \-ā(,)lēz\ *n pl, cap* [NL, fr. *Salic-*, *Salix* + *-ales*] **:** an order of dicotyledonous plants coextensive with the family Salicaceae

salices *pl of* SALIX

sal·i·cet \¦salə¦set\ *n* -s [G, fr. L *salic-*, *salix* willow + F *-et*, dim. suffix — more at SALLOW] **:** a soft-toned labial pipe-organ stop similar to the salicional but of 4-foot or 2-foot pitch

sal·i·ce·tum \,salə'sēd·əm\ *n, pl* **salicetums** \-d·əmz\ *or* **salice·ta** \-d·ə\ [L *salictum*, *salicetum*, fr. *salic-*, *salix* willow] **:** a collection or plantation of living willows

sal·i·cin \'saləsən\ *n* -s [F *salicine*, fr. L *salic-*, *salix* willow + F *-ine* — more at SALLOW] **:** a bitter white crystalline beta-glucoside $C_{13}H_{18}O_7$ esp. in the bark and leaves of several willows and poplars yielding saligenin and glucose on hydrolysis and formerly used in medicine as an antipyretic, antirheumatic, and tonic — compare POPULIN

sa·li·cio·nal \sə'lishənᵊl\ *n* -s [G, fr. *salic-*, *salix* willow + *-ion* + *-al*] **:** a soft-toned labial pipe-organ stop usu. of 8-foot pitch

salic law *or* **salique law** *n, usu cap S* **:** a law or rule held to derive orig. from the legal code of the Salian Franks excluding females from the line of succession to a throne ⟨they would hold up this *Salique law* to bar your Highness claiming from the female —Shak.⟩

sal·i·cor·nia \,salə'kö(r)nēə\ *n* [NL, fr. F *salicorne* glasswort (fr. Catal *salicorn*, fr. *sali-* — fr. L — + *corn* horn, fr. L *cornu*) + NL *-ia* — more at HORN] **1** *cap* **:** a genus of fleshy maritime herbs (family Chenopodiaceae) having thick jointed leafless stems bearing minute flowers in the form of a spike that are succeeded by utricles containing a single seed — see GLASSWORT **2** -s **:** any plant of the genus *Salicornia*

salicyl- *or* **salicylo-** *comb form* [ISV, fr. *salicyl* salicyloyl] **:** related to salicylic acid ⟨*salicyl*amide⟩ ⟨*salicyl*oyl⟩

sal·i·cyl alcohol \'saləsəl-\ *n* [*salicyl* salicyloyl, fr. F *salicyle*, fr. *salicine* + *-yle* -yl] **:** SALIGENIN

sal·i·cyl·aldehyde \¦===+\ *n* [ISV *salicyl-* + *aldehyde*] **:** an oily liquid phenolic aldehyde HOC_6H_4CHO that has a bitter almond odor, that is found esp. in oils from spirea plants but that is usu. made by reaction of phenol, sodium hydroxide, and chloroform, and that is used chiefly in perfumery and in making coumarin; *ortho*-hydroxy-benzaldehyde

sal·i·cyl·amide \,salə'silə,mīd, -məd\ *n* [ISV *salicyl-* + *amide*] **:** the crystalline amide $HOC_6H_4CONH_2$ of salicylic acid made usu. by reaction of methyl salicylate with ammonia and used chiefly as an analgesic, antipyretic, and antirheumatic

sal·i·cyl·anilide \¦saləsəl+\ *n* [ISV *salicyl-* + *anilide*] **:** a crystalline compound $HOC_6H_4CONHC_6H_5$ made usu. by reaction of salicylic acid or methyl salicylate with aniline and used as a fungicidal agent esp. in the external treatment of ringworm of the scalp and in the prevention of mildew in cotton fabrics and cordage

sa·lic·y·late \sə'lisə,lāt, -is(ə)lət, -i,slāt\ *n* -s [ISV *salicyl-* + *-ate*] **:** a salt or ester of salicylic acid; *also* **:** SALICYLIC ACID

sa·lic·y·lat·ed \-ād·əd\ *adj* **:** treated with salicylic acid

sal·i·cyl·ic acid \¦salə¦silik-\ *n* [*salicylic* ISV *salicyl* salicyloyl + *-ic*] **:** a crystalline phenolic acid HOC_6H_4COOH of sweetish acrid taste found in many plants and in most fruits often in the form of its methyl ester but usu. made by reaction of phenol, sodium hydroxide, and carbon dioxide and used chiefly in making pharmaceuticals and dyes, as an antiseptic and disinfectant esp. in treating skin diseases, and in the form of salts and other derivatives as an analgesic and antipyretic and in the treatment of rheumatism; *ortho*-hydroxybenzoic acid — compare ASPIRIN

salicylic aldehyde *n* **:** SALICYLALDEHYDE

sa·lic·y·lide \sə'lisə,līd, -,ləd\ *n* -s [ISV *salicyl-* + *-ide*] **:** any of several anhydrides of salicylic acid; *esp* **:** a crystalline compound $(OC_6H_4CO)_4$ formed by condensation of four molecules of salicylic acid

sal·i·cyl·ism \'saləsə,lizəm, sə'lisə,l-\ *n* -s [ISV *salicyl-* + *-ism*] **:** a toxic condition produced by the excessive intake of salicylic acid or salicylates and marked by ringing in the ears, nausea, and vomiting

sal·i·cyl·iza·tion \,saləsələ'zāshən, -ləsə,lī'z-, -lə,silə'z-; sə,lisələ'z-, -isə,lī'z-\ *n* -s **1 :** the act or process of administering salicylates until a patient is salicylized **2 :** the condition of being salicylized

sal·i·cyl·ize \'saləsə,līz, sə'lisə,l-\ *vt* -ED/-ING/-S [*salicyl-* + *-ize*] **:** to treat (a patient) with salicylic acid or its compounds until physiological effects are produced

sal·i·cyl·o·yl \,salə'silə,wil\ *or* **sa·lic·y·lyl** \sə'lisə,lil\ *n* -s [*salicyl-* + *-yl*] **:** the radical HOC_6H_4CO- of salicylic acid

sal·i·cyl·uric acid \¦saləsəl¦yü|rik-, -ə¦lü|\ *n* [ISV *salicyl-* + *-uric*] **:** a crystalline acid $C_9H_9NO_4$ found in the urine after the administration of salicylic acid or one of its derivatives; *ortho*-hydroxy-hippuric acid

sa·lience \'sālyən(t)s, -lēən- *sometimes* 'sal-\ *or* **sa·lien·cy** \-nsē,-nsi\ *n, pl* **saliences** *also* **saliencies 1 :** the quality or state of being salient: as **a :** physical prominence **:** PROJECTION, PROTRUSION ⟨the ~ of a buttress⟩ **b :** STRIKINGNESS, EMPHASIS ⟨elements of *saliency* and color —Carl Van Doren⟩ ⟨wherever she turned her eyes detail took on an uncanny ~ —Elizabeth Bowen⟩ **2 :** a striking point or feature **:** HIGHLIGHT ⟨seize a ~ of characteristic and . . . present it picturesquely —*Nineteenth Century & After*⟩

1sa·lient \-nt\ *adj* [L *salient-*, *saliens*, pres. part. of *salire* to leap, spring — more at SALLY] **1** *or* **saliant** *heraldry, of a beast* **a :** rampant but leaning forward as if leaping **b :** being in a leaping position with both hind feet on the ground **2 :** moving by leaps or springs **:** JUMPING ⟨a ~ animal⟩ ⟨a ~ fish⟩; *specif* **:** of or relating to the Salientia ⟨a ~ amphibian⟩ **3 :** spouting forth **:** jetting upward ⟨a ~ spring⟩ ⟨a ~ fountain⟩ **4 a :** projecting above or beyond a general line, surface, or level **:** jutting upward or outward **:** PROTUBERANT ⟨his nose was ~ and pointed —Elinor Wylie⟩ ⟨not on the level ground but on a ~ corner . . . of earth —Thomas Hardy⟩ **b :** standing out conspicuously **:** PROMINENT, STRIKING ⟨~ features⟩ ⟨~ traits⟩ ⟨will suffice to give its ~ points only —*Rev. of Religion*⟩ ⟨pick the ~ details out of dull verbiage —J.P.Marquand⟩ **syn** see NOTICEABLE

2salient \"\ *n* -s **1 :** SALIENT ANGLE; *specif* **:** an offensive bulge into enemy-held territory ⟨~*s* . . . so arranged that any one bastion could come to the aid of another by means of cross fire —Lewis Mumford⟩ ⟨a front line . . . has ~*s* and reentrants all along its length, depending on the progress of the fighting at different points —*Infantry Jour.*⟩ **2 :** something (as a promontory or cape along a shoreline or an abrupt change in the profile of a stream course) that projects outward or upward from its surroundings

salient angle *n* **:** an angle pointing outward; *specif* **:** an angle in a fortification (as a bastion) or in a battle line with its apex toward the enemy — opposed to *reentering angle;* see BASTION illustration

sa·li·en·tia \,sālē'ench(ē)ə, ,sal-, -ntēə\ *n pl, cap* [NL, fr. L, neut. pl. of *salient-*, *saliens*] **:** an order of Amphibia comprising the frogs, toads, and tree toads all of which are distinguished by complete absence of a tail in the adult stage and by possession of long strong hind limbs well suited to leaping and swimming

1sa·li·en·tian \¦==¦ench(ē)ən, -¦entēən\ *adj* [NL *Salientia* + E *-an*] **:** of or relating to the Salientia

2salientian \"\ *n* -s **:** an amphibian of the order Salientia

sa·lient·ly *adv* **:** in a salient manner **:** OUTSTANDINGLY, CONSPICUOUSLY ⟨~ characteristic⟩ ⟨~ lacking⟩

salient point *n* **1** *archaic* **:** starting point **:** SOURCE **2 :** a prominent feature or detail

salient pole *n* **:** a magnet pole that projects toward the armature of an electric machine — compare CONSEQUENT POLE

sa·lif·er·ous \sə'lif(ə)rəs, (')sa¦l-\ *adj* [*sali-* + *-ferous*] **:** producing, impregnated with, or containing salt ⟨~ formations⟩

sal·i·fi·able \'salə,fīəbəl, ,=='===\ *adj* **:** capable of being salified

sal·i·fi·ca·tion \,saləfə'kāshən\ *n* -s [prob. fr. F, fr. *sali-* + *-fication*] **1 :** the act, process, or result of salifying **2 :** the state of being salified

sal·i·fy \'salə,fī\ *vt* -ED/-ING/-ES [F *salifier*, fr. *sali-* + *-fier* -fy] **1 :** to combine or impregnate with a salt **:** SALINIZE **2 :** to form a salt with **:** convert into a salt ⟨~ a base by treatment with an acid or an acid by treatment with a base⟩

sal·i·gen·in \,salə'jenən, sə'lijənən\ *n* -s [ISV *sali*cin + *-genin*] **:** a crystalline phenolic alcohol $HOC_6H_4CH_2OH$ that is obtained usu. by hydrolysis of salicin or by reduction of salicylamide or salicylaldehyde and that acts as a local anesthetic; *ortho*-hydroxy-benzyl alcohol — called also *salicyl alcohol*

saligram *or* **saligrama** *var of* SALAGRAMA

sa·lim·e·ter \sə'liməd·ə(r)\ *n* [*sali-* + *-meter*] **:** a hydrometer specially graduated so as to indicate directly the percentage of a salt (as common salt) in a brine or other salt solution

salin- *or* **salini-** *or* **salino-** *comb form* [1*saline*] **1 :** salt **:** saline ⟨*salin*ize⟩ ⟨*salini*form⟩ ⟨*salino*meter⟩ **2 :** saline and ⟨*salino*sulfureous⟩

sa·li·na \sə'lēnə, -līnə\ *n* -s [Sp, fr. L *salinae*, pl., saltworks, salt pits, fr. fem. pl. of *salinus* of salt — more at SALINE] **1 :** a salt-encrusted playa or flat **:** SALADA **2 :** a salt marsh, pond, or lake

sa·li·nan \sə'lēnən\ *n, pl* **salinan** *or* **salinans** *usu cap* [*Salin*as river, western Calif. + E *-an*] **1 a :** an Indian people of southwestern California **b :** a member of such people **2 :** a language of the Salinan people **3 :** a language family of the Hokan stock comprising only the Salinan language

sal·i·nar \¦salə¦när\ *adj, usu cap* [fr. *Salinar*, locality in northern Peru, its type site] **:** of or relating to a culture in northwestern Peru about the 6th century A.D. characterized by irrigated agriculture, use of the llama, weaving and metallurgy, adobe houses, reed-bundle boats, and distinctive pottery

sa·li·na·tion \,salə'nāshən, ,sā-\ *n* -s [*salin-* + *-ation*] **:** treatment with salt or salt solution

1sa·line \'sā,lēn, -līn\ *adj* [ME *salyne*, fr. L *salinus*, fr. *sal* salt + *-inus* -ine — more at SALT] **1 :** consisting of or containing salt **:** SALIFEROUS ⟨~ deposits⟩ ⟨a ~ solution⟩ **2 :** of, relating to, or resembling salt **:** SALTY ⟨a ~ taste⟩ ⟨~ compounds⟩ ⟨the ~ properties of the water —Alice Duncan-Kemp⟩ **3 :** consisting of or relating to the salts of the alkali metals or of magnesium ⟨a ~ cathartic⟩

2sa·line \'sā,lēn, -,līn, *in sense 1 often* sə'lēn\ *n* -s [partly fr. ME *salyne*, fr. L *salinae*, pl., saltworks; partly fr. 1*saline* — more at SALINA] **1 a :** a spring of salt water **b :** a natural deposit of common salt or of any other soluble salt (as left by the evaporation of a lake) **c :** SALINA 2 **2 a** (1) **:** a metallic salt; *esp* **:** a salt of potassium, sodium, or magnesium with a cathartic action (2) **:** an aqueous solution of one or more such salts **b** *also* **sa·lin** \'sālən\ **:** a crude potash obtained from beet residues and similar sources **3 salines** *pl* **:** the naturally occurring soluble salts (as common salt, sodium carbonate, sodium nitrate, potassium salts, borax) **4 :** a saline solution used in physiology; *esp* **:** physiological salt solution for mammals

saline dome *n* **:** SALT DOME

sal·i·nel·la \\,salə'nelə\\ *n, cap* [NL, fr. L *salinus* + NL *-ella;* fr. the fact that it is found in salines and raised in saline aquariums] **:** a genus of minute animals of doubtful relationship having the body composed of a single layer of cells surrounding a central digestive cavity — compare MESOZOA

sal·i·nelle \\,salə'nel\\ *n* -s [F, dim. of *saline* saltworks, fr. L *salinae*, pl., — more at SALINA] **:** a mud volcano that erupts saline mud

sa·line·ness \\'sā,lēnnəs, -līnn-\\ *n* -ES **:** SALINITY

saline soil *n* **:** soil containing enough soluble salts (as 0.2 percent) to interfere with crop growth

saline water *n* **:** water containing salt; *esp* **:** mineral water containing sodium chloride, sodium sulfate, and magnesium sulfate

sa·lin·i·fi·ca·tion \\sə,linəfə'kāshən\\ *n* -s [*salin-* + *-fication*] **:** the act or process of becoming or causing to become saline ⟨the . . . ~ of many agricultural soils —*Science*⟩

sa·lin·i·form \\sə'linə,fȯrm\\ *adj* [*salin-* + *-form*] **:** having the form or qualities of a salt

sal·i·nim·e·ter \\,salə'nimәd·ə(r)\\ *n* [*salin-* + *-meter*] **:** SALINOMETER

sa·lin·i·ty \\sā'linəd·ē, sə'l-, -nətē, -i\\ *n* -ES [¹*saline* + *-ity*] **1 :** the quality or state of being saline **:** SALTINESS **2 :** a concentration (as in a solution) of salt ⟨marine animals . . . adjust themselves to changing *salinities* —R.E.Coker⟩

salinity current *n* **:** an oceanic current the flow of which is caused or controlled by its relatively greater density due to excessive salinity

sa·lin·iza·tion \\,sā,lənə'zāshən, -līn-\\ *n* -s **:** the process by which salts accumulate in soil

sa·lin·ize \\'=,lē,nīz, -,lī,-\\ *vt* -ED/-ING/-s [*salin-* + *-ize*] **:** to impregnate or treat (as a soil) with salt

sa·lin·o·gen·ic \\,sā,lēnə'jenik, -,līn-; sə¦lēn-, -¦līn-\\ *adj* [*salin-* + *-genic*] **:** capable of forming salts ⟨~ dyes⟩

sal·i·nom·e·ter \\salə'nämәd·ə(r)\\ *n* [ISV *salin-* + *-meter*] **:** an instrument for measuring the amount of salt in a solution; *esp* **:** SALIMETER

salique *usu cap, var of* SALIC

salis·bury steak \\'sȯlz,berē-, -b(ə)rē, -ri-\\ *n, usu cap 1st S* [after J. H. *Salisbury*, 19th cent. Eng. physician who advocated dietary reform] **:** ground beef mixed with egg, milk, bread crumbs and seasonings, formed into patties, and broiled, fried, or braised

sa·lish \\'sālish\\ *n* -ES *usu cap* **1 :** a language stock of the Mosan phylum — compare SKAGIT **2 :** the peoples speaking Salish dialects — **salish·an** \\-shən, 'sal-\\ *adj, usu cap*

salite \\'sa,līt, 'sä,-\\ *n* -s [G *salit*, fr. *Sala*, Västmanland, Sweden + G *-it* -ite] **:** a mineral $(Mg,Fe)_2Si_2O_6$ consisting of a diopside with more magnesium than iron

¹**sa·li·va** \\sə'līvə\\ *n* -s [L — more at SALLOW] **:** a viscous colorless somewhat opalescent secretion that is usu. slightly alkaline in reaction, contains water, mucin, protein, salts, and often a starch-splitting enzyme, is secreted into the mouth by salivary glands, and serves to lubricate ingested food and often to begin the breakdown of starches — see PTYALIN

²**sá·li·va** \\'sälәvə\\ *n, pl* **sáliva** *or* **sálivas** *usu cap* [Sp, of AmerInd origin] **1 :** a people of the Orinoco valley, Venezuela **2 :** a member of the Sáliva people

sa·li·val \\sə'līvəl\\ *adj* [ML *salivalis*, fr. L *saliva* + *-alis* -al] **:** SALIVARY

¹**sal·i·vant** \\'saləvənt\\ *adj* [L *salivant-, salivans*, pres. part. of *salivare* to spit out, salivate, fr. *saliva*] **:** causing or increasing the flow of saliva **:** MOUTH-WATERING

²**salivant** \\"\\ *n* -s **:** a salivant drug or agent **:** SIALAGOGUE

sal·i·var·i·um \\,salə'va(a)rēəm\\ *n, pl* **salivar·ia** \\-ēə\\ *or* **salivariums** [NL, fr. L *saliva* + *-arium*] **:** a small pocket within the oral cavity of an insect containing the opening of the salivary duct

sal·i·vary \\'salə,verē, -ri\\ *adj* [L *salivarius* slimy, fr. *saliva* + *-arius* -ary] **:** of or relating to saliva or the glands that secrete it **:** producing or carrying saliva

salivary chromosome *n* **:** one of the very large polytene chromosomal strands made up of many chromatids that are typical of the salivary gland cells of various insects

salivary corpuscles *n pl* **:** degenerating lymphocytes originating in the tonsils and passing into the saliva in the mouth

salivary gland *n* **:** any of various glands discharging a fluid secretion into the mouth cavity that in man comprise the large compound racemose parotid, sublingual, and submaxillary glands and in snakes include the venom glands; *specif* **:** a gland that secretes saliva

sal·i·vate \\'salə,vāt, *usu* -ād·+V\\ *vb* -ED/-ING/-s [L *salivatus*, past part. of *salivare* to spit out, salivate, fr. *saliva*] *vt* **:** to produce an abnormal flow of saliva in **:** produce ptyalism in (as by the use of mercury) ~ *vi* **:** to secrete or have a flow of saliva esp. in excess **:** DRIVEL, DROOL, SLAVER

saliva test *n* **:** a test of a sample of saliva taken from a race horse at the end of a race to determine whether or not the horse is doped

sal·i·va·tion \\,salə'vāshən\\ *n* -s [MF or LL; MF *salivation*, fr. LL *salivation-, salivatio*, fr. L *salivatus* + *-ion-, -io* -ion] **:** the act or process of salivating; *esp* **:** excessive secretion of saliva often accompanied with soreness of the mouth and gums

sa·li·vous \\sə'līvəs\\ *adj* [L *salivosus*, fr. *saliva* + *-osus* -ous] **:** relating to saliva **:** being or made up of saliva ⟨~ discharge⟩

salix \\'sāliks, 'sal-\\ *n* [NL, fr. L, willow — more at SALLOW] **1** *cap* **:** a genus (the type of the family Salicaceae) of shrubs and trees that have the bracts of the ament entire and only 2 to 10 stamens and that are widely distributed in temperate and cold regions — compare OSIER 1, POPULUS, SALLOW, WILLOW **2** *pl* **sali·ces** \\'salə,sēz, 'sāl-\\ **:** any plant of the genus *Salix*

salk vaccine \\'sȯ(l)k-\\ *n, usu cap S* [after Jonas *Salk* *b*1914 Amer. physician and bacteriologist] **:** a vaccine consisting of three strains of poliomyelitis virus grown on embryonated eggs and treated with formaldehyde for inactivation

sall \\sәl, (¦)sal\\ *chiefly dial var of* SHALL

salle \\'sal\\ *n* -s [F, hall, of Gmc origin; akin to OHG *sal* house, hall — more at SALOON] *Brit* **:** a sorting room in a paper mill

sal·lee *or* **sal·ly** \\'salē\\ *n, pl* **sallees** *or* **sallies** [native name in Australia] **1** *Austral* **:** any of several wattles **2** *Austral* **:** BLACK SALLY

sal·lee·man \\'salēmən\\ *also* **sallee-rover** \\-lē,rōvə(r)\\ *n, pl* **salleemen** *also* **sallee-rovers** [*Sallee* (Salé), seaport in Morocco + E *man* or *rover*] **1 :** a Moorish pirate ship **2** *also* **sallyman :** VELELLA

sal·len·ders \\'saləndə(r)z\\ *n pl but usu sing in constr* [origin unknown] **:** an eczematous eruption occurring on the hind leg of a horse in front of the hock — compare MALANDERS

¹**sal·let** *or* **sal·et** \\'salət\\ *or* **sa·lade** \\sə'läd, -lad\\ *n* -s [ME *sallet, salet*, fr. MF *sallade*, prob. fr. OIt *celata*, fr. fem. of *celato* (past part. of *celare* to hide), fr. L *celatus*, past part. of *celare* to conceal, hide — more at HELL] **:** a light helmet common during the 15th century of simple form with or without a visor and with a projection over the neck

sallets

²**sallet** \\"\\ *chiefly dial var of* SALAD

sal·ley \\'salē\\ *chiefly dial var of* ¹SALLOW

¹**sal·low** \\'sa(,)lō, -lə; -,lәw, -,lō+V\\ *n* -s [ME *salwe, sallow*, fr. OE *seal-, sealh;* akin to OHG *salha, salaha* sallow, MLG *salwīde*, ON *selja* sallow, L *salix* willow, MIr *sail* willow, and perh. to OE *salu* dusky, dark — more at ²SALLOW] **1 :** any of various Old World and chiefly Eurasiatic willows having broad leaves and including both shrubs and trees some of which are important sources of charcoal, tanbark, and wood for small implements; *esp* **:** a small northern or alpine Old World shrubby or arborescent much-branched willow (*Salix caprea*) with strongly fissured bark **2 :** a willow twig or shoot

²**sallow** \\"\\ *adj* -ER/-EST [ME *salowe*, fr. OE *salu, salo* dusky, dark, sallow; akin to OE *sōl* dark, dirty, OHG *salo* murky, dirty gray, ON *sölr* dirty, OIr *sal, saile* dirt, L *saliva* spittle, Skt *sāra, sāla* gray; basic meaning: dirty gray] **1 :** having any of several colors averaging a grayish greenish yellow that is paler than the color hay **2 :** of a grayish greenish yellow color suggesting sickliness — usu. used of the skin or complexion

³**sallow** \\"\\ *vt* -ED/-ING/-s **:** to make (as the complexion) sallow ⟨malarial poison had . . . ~*ed* his skin —Irving Bacheller⟩

sal·low·ish \\-ˌlәwish, -ˌlōish\\ *adj* **:** somewhat sallow ⟨a ~ complexion⟩

sal·low·ness *n* -ES **:** the quality or state of being sallow

sallow thorn *n* [¹*sallow*] **:** SEA BUCKTHORN

sal·lowy \\-lәwē, -lōē\\ *adj* [¹*sallow* + *-y*] **:** full of sallows

¹**sal·ly** \\'salē, -li\\ *n* -ES [MF *saillie*, fr. OF, fr. fem. of *sailli*, past part. of *saillir* to jump, rush forward, fr. L *salire* to jump, leap; akin to MIr *saltraid* he tramples, Gk *hallesthai* to leap, Lith *salti* to flow, and perh. to Skt *ucchalati* he jumps up; basic meaning: to jump] **1 a :** an action of rushing or bursting forth; *specif* **:** a sortie of troops from a defensive position to attack the enemy ⟨making a ~ against the besieging force⟩ ⟨sudden *sallies* of solo voices —Irving Kolodin⟩ **b** *dial chiefly Eng* **:** an action of leaping forth **:** BOUND, SPRING ⟨every ~ of the boat —Richard Steele⟩ **2 a :** a brief outbreak into activity or expression (as of affection or temper) **:** OUTBURST ⟨fretted with *sallies* of his mother's kisses —William Wordsworth⟩ ⟨those *sallies* of passion so common in princes —W.H.Prescott⟩ **b :** a boldly witty or imaginative saying (as in conversation or in a written passage) **:** flight of fancy **:** QUIP ⟨the cheap roar which would follow such a . . . ~ —Arnold Bennett⟩ ⟨a volume full of bright and sometimes brilliant *sallies* —*Saturday Rev.*⟩ **3 a :** a venture or excursion usu. off the beaten track **:** JAUNT, TRIP ⟨a ~ into the country⟩ ⟨the first spectacular *sallies* into unknown space —*Swiss Industry & Trade*⟩ **b** *archaic* **:** a bold violation of custom or propriety **:** ESCAPADE ⟨a ~ of youth⟩ **4 :** a projection esp. of a rafter notched to fit over a plate or horizontal beam so as to jut beyond it **5 a :** HANDSTROKE 2 **b :** ²GRIP 6b

²**sally** \\"\\ *vb* -ED/-ING/-s *vi* **1 a :** to leap or rush out **:** burst forth **:** issue suddenly (as troops from a fortified place to attack besiegers) ⟨would ~ out in their canoes and capture passing vessels —*Amer. Guide Series: Mich.*⟩ **b** *archaic* **:** ISSUE, SPURT, JET, SPRING ⟨his warm blood *sallied* from the wound —William Cowper⟩ **2 :** to set out (as from one's home or station) — usu. used with *forth* ⟨tightening the belt of his overcoat, he *sallied* forth —John Galsworthy⟩ ~ *vt* **:** to cause (a ship) to roll by having the crew run or move weights from side to side ⟨bluejackets raced from the port side to the starboard side and back, ~*ing* ship . . . to free her ample bottom from the sucking mud —*Time*⟩

³**sally** \\"\\ *chiefly dial var of* ¹SALLOW

⁴**sally** \\"\\ *n* -ES [prob. fr. the name *Sally*] **1** *Irish* **:** the European house wren **2** *Brit* **:** STONE FLY

⁵**sally** \\"\\ *var of* SALLEE

sally–bloom \\'==,=\\ *n* [³*sally* + *bloom*] **:** FIREWEED b

sally gate *n* [¹*sally*] **:** a minor gate or passage (as in the wall of a fort) used to avoid opening major gates

sal·ly light·foot \\,salē'līt,fu̇t\\ *n, pl* **sally lightfoots** *usu cap S&L* [*sally* fr. the name *Sally*] **:** a common active crab (*Grapsus grapsus*) living among rocks near or below the tide line in the West Indies and adjacent mainland

sally lunn \\-'lən\\ *n, pl* **sally lunns** *usu cap S&L* [after *Sally Lunn*, 18th cent. English baker] **:** a slightly sweetened bread raised with yeast or baking powder, baked as a thin loaf or as muffins, and eaten hot with butter

sally picker \\'==,==\\ *n* [³*sally*] **1 :** CHIFFCHAFF **2 :** WILLOW WREN **3** *Irish* **:** SEDGE WARBLER

sally port *n* [¹*sally*] **1 a :** a large gate or passage in a fortified place suitable for the use of troops making a sortie **b :** a similar passage esp. through the lower story of buildings (as barracks) forming a quadrangle **2** *usu* **sally-port** \\'==,=\\ **a :** a large port on each quarter of a fire ship for escape of the men after the firing of the train **b :** a large port in a three-decker warship

sally saw *n, usu cap 1st S* [prob. fr. ³*sally*] **:** a portable circular saw that consists of a regularly perforated toothed disk power-driven through a gear which engages the perforations

sallywood \\'==,=\\ *n* [³*sally* + *wood*] **1 :** WILLOW WOOD **2 :** MOUNTAIN HOLLY 1

sal·ma·gun·di *also* **sal·ma·gun·dy** \\,salmə'gəndē, -di\\ *n* -ES [F *salmigondis*] **1 :** a salad plate consisting of chopped or sliced meats, anchovies, hard-cooked eggs, pickled vegetables, olives, radishes, endive, and watercress that are arranged in rows for color and flavor contrast and dressed with a salad dressing **2 :** a heterogeneous mixture **:** MEDLEY, POTPOURRI ⟨no ~ made of things, amusements, lust for power, can assuage our gnawing hunger to create —B.I.Bell⟩

sal·ma·naz·ar \\,salmə'nazə(r)\\ *n* -s *usu cap* [after *Salmanasar* IV (Shalmaneser), 8th cent. B.C. king of Assyria mentioned in the Bible (2 Kings 17:3)] **:** an oversize wine bottle holding about 12 quarts ⟨a ~ of champagne⟩

sal·mi *also* **sal·mis** \\'sal(,)mē\\ *n, pl* **salmis** \\-ēz\\ [F *salmis*, short for *salmigondis*] **1 :** a ragout of half roasted game stewed in a rich sauce **2 :** leftover game or domestic duck or goose reheated in a rich brown sauce

sal·mi·ac \\'salmē,ak\\ *n* -s [G *salmiak*, modif. of L *sal ammoniacus* — more at AMMONIA] **:** SAL AMMONIAC

sal·mine \\'sal,mēn\\ *n* -s [ISV *salm-* (fr. NL *Salmo*) + *-ine*] **:** a protamine obtained from the sperm of fishes of the genus *Salmo* and used chiefly in the form of its sulfate to reverse the anticoagulant effect of heparin or as the protamine component of protamine zinc insulin

sal·mo \\'sal(,)mō\\ *n, cap* [NL, fr. L, salmon] **:** a genus of fishes (family Salmonidae) comprising the Atlantic salmon (*S. salar*) and various trouts of Europe and western No. America and formerly the Pacific salmons (genus *Oncorhynchus*) and the European and American chars (genus *Salvelinus*)

salm·on \\'samən *sometimes* 'säm- *or* 'sȧm-\\ *n, pl* **salmon** *also* **salmons** *often attrib* [ME *salmon, samoun*, fr. MF *saumon, samon*, fr. L *salmon-, salmo*] **1 a :** a large isospondylous anadromous game fish (*Salmo salar*) that frequents coastal waters of the northern Atlantic and ascends adjacent streams of Europe and No. America to spawn, is extremely variable in appearance esp. at different ages and under different conditions of life, commonly attains a weight of 15 pounds, and is noted for its gaminess as a sport fish and the quality of its flesh as a table fish — see GRILSE, PARR, SMOLT; LANDLOCKED SALMON, OUANANICHE **b :** any of various other anadromous fishes of the family Salmonidae; *esp* **:** a fish of the genus *Oncorhynchus* that lives in and breeds in rivers tributary to the northern Pacific — often used with a qualifying term; see DOG SALMON, KING SALMON, HUMPBACK SALMON, SILVER SALMON, SOCKEYE **2 :** any of various fishes of families other than Salmonidae having some point of resemblance (as pink flesh) to a true salmon: as **a :** AUSTRALIAN SALMON **b :** BARRAMUNDA a **c :** any of several sciaenid fishes; *esp* **:** GEELBEC 2 **d :** WALLEYED PIKE **3 :** the flesh of a salmon used as food either fresh or cured and smoked **4 :** the variable color of salmon's flesh averaging a strong yellowish pink that is darker and slightly yellower than salmon pink, yellower and deeper than melon, and yellower than peach red

salmonbass \\'==,=\\ *n* **:** KABELJOU

salmonberry \\'==—*see* -BERRY\\ *n* **1 a :** a large red-flowered raspberry (*Rubus spectabilis*) native to the northern Pacific coast **b :** the salmon-colored edible berry of this plant **2 a :** a white-flowered raspberry (*R. parviflorus*) of western No. America that is closely related to the purple-flowering raspberry **b :** the fruit of this plant **3 :** CLOUDBERRY

salmon boat *n* **:** a carvel-built open double-ended cat-rigged sailboat used for fishing on the Columbia river and along the Pacific coast to Alaska

salmon brick *n* **:** an underburned brick

salmon cloud *n* **:** NOAH'S ARK 2

salmon disease *n* **:** a disease of salmon and related fishes and their eggs caused by a water mold of the genus *Saprolegnia*

sal·mo·nel·la \\,salmə'nelə\\ *n* [NL, fr. Daniel E. *Salmon* †1914 American veterinarian + NL *-ella*] **1** *cap* **:** a genus of aerobic gram-negative rod-shaped nonspore-forming usu. motile bacteria (family Enterobacteriaceae) that grow well on artificial media and form acid and gas on many carbohydrates but not on lactose, sucrose, or salicin, that are all pathogenic for man and other warm-blooded animals, and that are chiefly associated with various types of food poisoning, with acute gastrointestinal inflammation, or with diseases of the genital tract — see FOWL TYPHOID, PULLORUM DISEASE, TYPHOID **2** *pl* **salmonellas** \\-ləz\\ *or* **salmonella** \\-lə\\ *also* **salmonellae** \\-(,)lē\\ *sometimes cap* **:** any bacterium of the genus *Salmonella*

sal·mo·nel·lal \\¦==¦neləl\\ *adj* [NL *Salmonella* + E *-al*] **:** of, relating to, or caused by salmonellas

sal·mo·nel·lo·sis \\,salmə,ne'lōsəs\\ *n, pl* **salmonello·ses** \\-ō,sēz\\ [NL, fr. *Salmonella* + *-osis*] **:** infection with or disease caused by bacteria of the genus *Salmonella* typically marked by gastroenteritis but often complicated by septicemia, meningitis, endocarditis, and various focal lesions (as in the kidneys) — compare FOOD POISONING, FOWL TYPHOID, ⁵KEEL, NECROTIC ENTERITIS, PARATYPHOID, PULLORUM DISEASE, TYPHOID

salmonfly \\'==,=\\ *n* **:** any of several stone flies (esp. *Pteronarcys californica*)

salmon grouper *n* **:** any of various reddish rockfishes (as the bocaccio) of the genus *Sebastodes* of the Pacific coast of No. America

salmon gum *n* **1 :** an Australian tree (*Eucalyptus salmonophloia*) with dense hard fine-grained salmon-colored wood **2 :** the wood of the salmon gum tree

salmon herring *n, Austral* **:** MILKFISH 1

¹**salmo·nid** \\'sa(l)mənəd, -,nid *also* 'säm- *or* 'sȧm-\\ *adj* [NL *Salmonidae*] **:** of or relating to the Salmonidae

²**salmonid** \\"\\ *n* -s **:** a fish of the family Salmonidae

sal·mon·i·dae \\sal'mänə,dē\\ *n pl, cap* [NL, fr. *Salmon-, Salmo*, type genus + *-idae*] **:** a family of soft-finned fishes (suborder Salmonoidea) including as generally understood the salmons, trouts, chars, and whitefishes all of which are elongate and typically have the last vertebrae upturned

sal·mon·i·form \\-nə,fȯrm\\ *adj* [*salmon* + *-iform*] **:** resembling a salmon

salmon ladder *or* **salmon leap** *or* **salmon stair :** FISH LADDER

¹**salmo·noid** \\'sa(l)mə,nȯid *also* 'säm- *or* 'sȧm-\\ *adj* [NL *Salmonoidea*] **1 :** like or related to the Salmonidae **2 :** of or relating to Salmonoidea

²**salmonoid** \\"\\ *n* -s **:** a salmonoid fish

sal·mo·noi·dea \\,salmə'nȯidēə\\ *n pl* [NL, fr. *Salmon-, Salmo* + *-oidea* or *-oidei*] **:** a suborder of soft-finned fishes (order Isospondyli) that includes the salmons and trouts and numerous other forms (as the graylings, smelts, and capelins) having an adipose fin

salmon oil *n* **:** a fatty oil obtained usu. from the waste from the canning of salmon and used chiefly in dressing leather and in soap

salmon peal *or* **salmon peel** *n* **:** GRILSE

salmon pink *n* **:** a strong yellowish pink that is yellower and stronger than melon, yellower and lighter than peach red, lighter and much yellower than madder scarlet, and lighter and slightly redder than average salmon

salmon poisoning *also* **salmon disease** *n* **:** a highly fatal febrile disease of dogs and various other fish-eating mammals that resembles canine distemper and is thought due to a rickettsia transmitted by encysted larvae of a fluke (*Troglotrema salmincola*) ingested with the flesh of infested salmon or trout — compare BLACKHEAD 3

salmon shark *n* **:** PORBEAGLE

salm·ons·ite \\'sa(l)mən,zīt\\ *n* -s [Frank A. *Salmons*, 20th cent. Am. mineralogist + E *-ite*] **:** a mineral $Mn_9Fe_2(PO_4)_8 \cdot 14H_2O$(?) consisting of a hydrous manganese iron phosphate occurring in buff-colored cleavable masses (sp. gr. 2.9)

salmon trout *n* **1 a :** a European sea trout (*Salmo trutta*) **b :** LAKE TROUT b **c :** any of numerous large trout of western No. America: as (1) **:** CUTTHROAT TROUT (2) **:** STEELHEAD TROUT **2 :** a half-grown Australian salmon of the size preferred for food

salmon wheel *n* **:** a device for catching salmon in large quantities consisting of a large revolving wheel suspended in the water and turned by the current to which are attached scoop nets that catch the fish passing beneath

sal·mo·per·cae \\,salmō'pər,sē, -r,kē, -r,kī\\ *n pl, cap* [NL, fr. L *salmo* salmon + *percae*, pl. of *perca* perch — more at PERCH] **:** a small order that comprises No. American freshwater fishes in some respects intermediate between the Ostariophysi and the Percomorphi and includes the pirate perch and the trout-perches

salm·wood \\'säm,=\\ *n* [*salm* (origin unknown) + *wood*] **:** PRINCEWOOD 1

salnatron \\=ˈ==\\ *n* [*sal* + *natron*] **:** crude sodium carbonate

sal·oid \\'sa,lȯid\\ *n* -s [*sal* + *-oid*] **:** an insoluble salt of an acidoid in soil

sal·ol \\'sa,lȯl, -lōl\\ *n* -s [fr. *Salol*, a trademark] **:** PHENYL SALICYLATE

sa·lom·e·ter \\sə'lämәd·ə(r)\\ *n* [L *sal* salt + *-o-* + *-meter* — more at SALT] **:** SALIMETER

sa·lo·mó·ni·ca \\,salə'mänəkə\\ *n* -s [Sp, fr. fem. of *salomónico* of Solomon (in the Bible), fr. *Salomón* Solomon + *-ico* -ic; fr. the belief that a similar column in St. Peter's Cathedral in Rome came fr. Solomon's temple — more at SOLOMON] **:** a twisted architectural column

sa·lon \\(')sa¦lōⁿ, sə'län, (')sa¦län *also* sə'lōn *or* (')sa¦lōn *or* (')sa¦lōⁿ *sometimes* (')sa¦läⁿ *or* sə'lōⁿ\\ *n, pl* **salons** \\-ōⁿ(z), -länz, -ōnz, -äⁿ(z)\\ *often attrib* [F — more at SALOON] **1 a :** usu. spacious and elegant apartment or living room (as in a fashionable French home) **2 :** a fashionable assemblage that is held by custom at the home of a usu. socially prominent person and takes its character from the kind of notables (as literary figures, artists, or statesmen) who frequent it ⟨literary ~*s* . . . have flourished in Paris since the days of Louis XIV —Malcolm Cowley⟩ ⟨witty favorite of Society . . . and mistress of a brilliant ~ —*advt*⟩ **3 a :** an apartment or hall for the exhibition of works of art (as paintings and sculptures) **b** *usu cap* (1) **:** an annual exhibition of such works; *esp* **:** one held by a national society of artists (2) **:** an annual exhibition usu. international in scope of outstanding photographs, color slides, and transparencies **4 :** a business establishment or shop having stylishness ⟨a shoe ~⟩ ⟨a beauty ~⟩ ⟨a reducing ~⟩

sa·lon·i·ca *or* **sa·lon·i·ka** \\sə'länəkə *also* ¦salə¦nēkə\\ *adj, usu cap* [fr. *Salonica*, Greece] **:** of or from the city of Salonica, Greece ⟨*Salonica* businessmen⟩ **:** of the kind or style prevalent in Salonica

salon music *n* **:** instrumental music of a light, pleasing, and often sentimental character suitable for the drawing room rather than the concert hall

sa·loon \\sə'lün\\ *n* -s [F *salon*, fr. It *salone*, aug. of *sala* hall, room, of Gmc origin; akin to OE *sele* hall, house, OS *seli*, MD *sale*, OHG *sal*, ON *salr* hall, house, Goth *saljan* to stay at an inn, *salithwos* inn; akin to OSlav *selitva* dwelling, Lith *sala* village] **1 :** a spacious, lofty, and elegant apartment (as in a palace or manor house) for the reception and entertainment of guests **:** a large and elaborate drawing room **:** SALON 1 ⟨the gilden ~*s* in which the first magnates of the realm . . . gave banquets and balls —T.B.Macaulay⟩ **2 :** SALON 2 **3 a :** a usu. elaborately decorated apartment or hall (as a ballroom, gaming room, exhibition room, or a ship's dining hall) **b :** a large cabin for the social use of passengers (as on shipboard) **c :** a business establishment characterized by fanciness (as a shop or an amusement hall) **:** SALON 4 ⟨a shaving ~⟩ ⟨hairdressing ~⟩ ⟨a billiard ~⟩ ⟨a dancing ~⟩ ⟨went out . . . to play at some ice-cream ~ —Betty Smith⟩ **d :** a room or public establishment in which alcoholic beverages are sold and consumed **:** BARROOM, TAPROOM **4** *Brit* **a :** a railroad car approximating the American parlor car in arrangement and function **b :** SEDAN 2a

sa·loon·atic \\sə'lünə,tik\\ *n* -s [blend of *saloon* and *lunatic*] **:** an enthusiastic advocate of saloons and drinking ⟨people who . . . are neither bonehead drys nor ~*s* —*N.Y.Evening Jour.*⟩

saloon deck *n* **:** a deck on which a ship's saloon is located

sa·loon·ist \\sə'lünəst\\ *n* -s **:** SALOONKEEPER

saloonkeeper \\=ˈ=,==\\ *n* **:** a person who owns or manages a saloon

saloon pistol *or* **saloon rifle** *n, Brit* **:** a small light pistol or rifle used chiefly in a shooting gallery

sa·loop \sə'lüp\ *also* **salop** \'saləp, sə'lüp\ *n* -s [modif. of F or Sp *salep* — more at SALEP] **1 :** SALEP **2 :** a common sassafras (*Sassafras albidum molle*) **3 :** a hot drink made from an infusion of powdered salep or sassafras with milk and sugar

sal·op \'saləp\ *adj, usu cap* [fr. county of *Salop*, England] **:** SHROPSHIRE

¹sa·lo·pi·an \sə'lōpēən\ *adj, usu cap* [county of *Salop* + E *-ian*] **:** of or relating to Salop or Shropshire in England

²salopian \"\ *n* -s *cap* **:** a native or inhabitant of Shropshire

salopian ware *n, usu cap S* **1 :** Roman pottery found in Shropshire that is usu. made of red or white clay **2 :** a modern somewhat coarse and opaque porcelaneous Shropshire ware first made toward the end of the 18th century

salp \'salp\ *n* -s [NL *Salpa*] **:** SALPA 2

sal·pa \'salpə\ *n* [NL, fr. L *salpa*, a kind of stockfish, fr. Gk *salpē*] **1** *cap* **:** a genus (the type of the family Salpidae) of transparent barrel-shaped or fusiform free-swimming oceanic tunicates that are abundant in warm seas and that exist in two forms one of which lives solitary and reproduces by budding from an internal organ a series of hermaphroditic individuals of the other kind that are united side by side in a chain or cluster and usu. carry each only a single egg destined to develop into an individual of the solitary kind **2** *pl* **sal·pae** \-(ˌ)pē, -ˌpī\ *or* **salpas :** any tunicate of the genus *Salpa* or family Salpidae

¹sal·pid \'salpəd\ *or* **sal·pid·i·an** \(')sal¦pidēən\ *adj* [*salpid* fr. NL *Salpidae*; *salpidian* fr. NL *Salpidae* + E *-ian*] **:** of or relating to the Salpidae

²salpid \"\ *or* **salpidian** \"\ *n* -s **:** a tunicate of the family Salpidae

sal·pi·dae \'salpəˌdē\ *n pl, cap* [NL, fr. *Salpa*, type genus + *-idae*] **:** a small family of tunicates (order Thaliacea) of which *Salpa* is the chief and in some classifications the sole genus

sal·pi·form \'salpəˌfȯrm\ *adj* [NL *Salpa* + E *-iform*] **:** resembling a salpa

sal·pi·glos·sis \ˌsalpə'gläsəs, -glȯs-\ *n* [NL, irreg. fr. Gk *salpinx* trumpet + *glōssa* tongue — more at GLOSS (explanation)] **1** *cap* **:** a small genus of Chilean herbs (family Solanaceae) having large funnel-shaped variously colored and often showily marked flowers with a tubular 5-cleft calyx **2** -ES **:** any plant of the genus *Salpiglossis*

salping- *or* **salpingo-** *comb form* [NL, fr. *salping-*, *salpinx*] **1 :** salpinx ⟨*salping*ectomy⟩ ⟨*salping*emphraxis⟩ ⟨*salping*itis⟩ **2 :** fallopian tube ⟨*salpingo*tomy⟩ ⟨*salpingo*rrhaphy⟩ **3 a :** fallopian tube and ⟨*salpingo*-oophorectomy⟩ ⟨*salpingo*-uterostomy⟩ **b :** eustachian and ⟨*salpingo*nasal⟩ ⟨*salpingo*palatine⟩ ⟨*salpingo*pharyngeal⟩

sal·pin·gec·to·my \ˌsalpən'jektəmē\ *n* -ES [ISV *salping-* + *-ectomy*] **:** the excision of a salpinx (as a fallopian or eustachian tube)

salpinges *pl of* SALPINX

sal·pin·gi·an \(')sal¦pinjēən\ *adj* [*salping-* + *-ian*] **:** of or relating to a salpinx

sal·pin·gi·on \sal'pinjēˌän\ *n* -s [NL, fr. Gk, tube, dim. of *salping-*, *salpinx* trumpet — more at SALPINX] **:** the apex of the petrous portion of the temporal bone

sal·pin·gi·tis \ˌsalpən'jīd·əs\ *n* -ES [NL, fr. *salping-* + *-itis*] **:** inflammation of a salpinx (as a fallopian or a eustachian tube)

sal·pin·gog·ra·phy \-n'gägrəfē\ *n* -ES [ISV *salping-* + *-graphy*] **:** visualization of a fallopian tube by roentgenography following injection of an opaque medium

salpingo-oophorectomy \sal¦piŋ(ˌ)gō+\ *n* [ISV *salping-* + *oophorectomy*] **:** excision of a fallopian tube and an ovary

sal·pin·go·palatine \"+\ *adj* [*salping-* + *palatine*] **:** of or relating to the eustachian tubes and the palate

sal·pin·go·pharyngeal \"+\ *adj* [*salping-* + *pharyngeal*] **:** of or relating to the eustachian tubes and pharynx

sal·pinx \'sal(ˌ)piŋ(k)s\ *n, pl* **salpin·ges** \sal'pin(ˌ)jēz\ [NL, fr. Gk, trumpet] **1 :** EUSTACHIAN TUBE **2 :** FALLOPIAN TUBE

sal·poid \'salˌpȯid\ *adj* [NL *Salpa* + E *-oid*] **:** of, relating to, or resembling salpae

sal prunella *n* [¹*sal* + *prunella* (angina)] **:** potassium nitrate fused and cast in balls, cakes, or sticks

salps *pl of* SALP

sals *pl of* SAL

salse \'sal(t)s\ *n* -s [F, fr. It *salsa*, lit., sauce, fr. ML *salsa* salty condiment, salt — more at SAUCE] **:** MUD VOLCANO

sal·si·fy \'salsəfē, -ˌfī\ *n* -ES [F *salsifis*, fr. It *salsefica*, *salsefrica*, alter. of *sassefica*, *sassefrica*, fr. LL *saxifrica*, any of various herbs, fr. L *saxum* rock + *-i-* + *-frica* (fr. *fricare* to rub) — more at SAX, FRICTION] **:** a European biennial herb (*Tragopogon porrifolius*) with long-peduncled heads of purple ray flowers and a long fusiform edible root — called also *oyster plant*, *vegetable oyster*

sal·sil·la \sal'silə\ *n* -s [NL *salsilla* (specific epithet of *Bomarea salsilla*), fr. fem. of *salsillus* salty, fr. L *salsus* salted, fr. past part. of *sallere* to salt] **:** a tropical American plant of the genus *Bomarea*; *esp* **:** one (as *B. salsilla* or *B. edulis*) with edible roots that are sometimes boiled and used as a substitute for potatoes

sal soda *n* [¹*sal*] **:** SODIUM CARBONATE a(3)

sal·so·la \sal'sōlə\ *n, cap* [NL, fr. It, a plant of the genus *Salsola*, fr. *salso* salty, fr. L *salsus* — more at SAUCE] **:** a large genus of mostly Old World herbs or shrubs of the family Chenopodiaceae with variously shaped often prickly leaves and small greenish flowers whose 4- to 5-parted perianth remains investing the utricle — see BARILLA, RUSSIAN THISTLE, SALTWORT

sal·so·la·ceous \¦salsə¦lāshəs\ *adj* [NL *Salsola* + E *-aceous*] **:** of, relating to, or resembling the genus *Salsola*

sal·su·gi·nous \(')sal¦süjənəs\ *adj* [L *salsugin-*, *salsugo* saltiness (fr. *salsus* salty) + E *-ous* — more at SAUCE] **:** HALOPHYTIC

¹salt \'sȯlt, *chiefly Brit* 'sält\ *n* -s [ME, fr. OE *sealt*; akin to OFris, OS, ON, & Goth *salt*, OHG *salz*, L *sal* salt, Gk *hals* salt, sea, Arm *al* salt, Skt *salila* sea] **1 a :** a colorless or white crystalline compound NaCl consisting of sodium chloride that occurs abundantly in nature both solid in minerals (as halite) and in solution, that has various uses (as for seasoning food, preserving meat, manufacturing sodium, chlorine, and their compounds, making glass and soap, and refrigerating), that constitutes about 2.6 percent of seawater, is found in small quantities in fresh water, and is present in all animal fluids and esp. in urine, that is obtained commercially from deposits in the earth or by evaporation of natural brines (as seawater), and that in the commercial form usu. contains small quantities of the deliquescent salts magnesium chloride and calcium chloride that cause it to attract moisture — called also *common salt* **b :** any of numerous substances (as sal ammoniac, sal prunella, sal soda) resembling common salt (as in appearance, incombustibility, or taste) **c salts** *pl* (1) **:** a mineral or saline mixture (as Epsom salts, Rochelle salt, or Glauber's salt) used as an aperient or cathartic (2) **:** SMELLING SALTS **d :** one of the three primary elements of matter in alchemy representing in contrast to mercury and sulfur the principle of fixity and solidity **e :** any of a class of compounds typified by common salt that are derived from acids by replacement of part or all of the acid hydrogen by a metal or radical acting like a metal, that may be formed by the reaction of acids with bases either with or without elimination of water, with metallic oxides, or with metals and also in other ways (as by direct union of their elements), that for the most part are dominantly ionic in character and have high melting points, and that in solution or in the fused state conduct an electric current and thereby undergo decomposition ⟨sodium bisulfate and sodium sulfate are sodium ~s of sulfuric acid⟩ — compare ¹ACID 2a(2), ¹BASIC 3c, DOUBLE SALT, ¹NORMAL 10c; -ATE, -IDE, -ITE **2 :** a container for salt at table **:** SALTCELLAR, SALTSHAKER ⟨the roly-poly ~s and peppers that bob right up again if you tip them over —*House Beautiful*⟩ — often used in the phrases *above the salt* and *below the salt* alluding to the former custom of seating persons of higher rank above and those of lower rank below a large saltcellar placed near the middle of a long table **3 :** sustenance or support provided (as by a host or employer) **:** FOOD, HOSPITALITY, KEEP — used often in the phrase *to be worth one's salt* **4 a :** an ingredient or element that gives savor, piquancy, or zest **:** FLAVOR ⟨a people . . . full of life, vigor, and the ~ of personality —Clifton Fadiman⟩ **b :** sharpness of wit **:** PUNGENCY ⟨a wit which has kept something of its ~ —A.T.Quiller-Couch⟩ **c :** COMMON SENSE, EARTHINESS ⟨the speech with the most ~ and the least jargon —Colin Simpson⟩ **d :** corrective allowance **:** RESERVE, SKEPTICISM ⟨take all the political and economic references with a healthy amount of ~ —*New Republic*⟩ — often used in the phrase *take with a grain of salt* **e :** the sprinkling of people thought to set a model of excellence for or to give tone to the rest — usu. used in the phrase the *salt of the earth* ⟨we no longer accept these country gentlemen . . . as the ~ of the earth —W.S.Maugham⟩ **5 a :** SALT MARSH **b salts** *pl, chiefly dial* **:** marshes flooded by the tide **6 :** SAILOR; *esp* **:** an experienced seaman — often used with *old* ⟨a tale worthy of an old ~⟩

²salt \"\ *vt* -ED/-ING/-S [ME *salten*, fr. OE *sealtan*; akin to OHG *salzan* to salt, ON *salta*, Goth *saltan*; all fr. a prehistoric Gmc v. fr. the n. represented by E ¹*salt*] **1 a :** to add salt to **:** sprinkle, rub, impregnate, or season with salt ⟨~ the food⟩ ⟨~ the icy sidewalk⟩ ⟨the spray ~*ing* our faces —Franc Shor⟩ **b :** to preserve (as fish or meat) with salt or in brine ⟨~ mackerel⟩ ⟨~ beef⟩ **2 a :** to give flavor or piquancy to ⟨employs an irreverent humor to ~ her shrewd observations —James Kelly⟩ ⟨~*ed* the work with highly readable case histories —*Saturday Rev.*⟩ **b :** to make bitter ⟨their lives had been ~*ed* by the taste of death —J.P.Bishop⟩ **3 a :** to enrich (as a mine) artificially usu. with fraudulent intent by secretly placing valuable mineral in some of the working places **:** PLANT 4b **b :** to enrich or impoverish either intentionally or accidentally (samples taken from a mine or claim for test purposes) ⟨~*ing* a barren claim . . . thereby setting off a rush that drew 5000 miners into the area on a fruitless search —Oscar Lewis⟩ **c :** to give to (something for sale or upon which a sale is based) an appearance of value, profitableness, or genuineness by fraudulent means ⟨~*ing* the books of a business⟩ **4 :** to supply (as an animal) with salt **:** feed salt to ⟨the field where cattle are ~*ed*⟩ **5 a :** to sprinkle as if with salt ⟨~*ing* clouds with silver iodide crystals⟩ **b :** to intersperse with **:** scatter among ⟨party organizations . . . are heavily ~*ed*, almost inevitably, with men of affairs —W.S.White⟩ **c :** GRAY ⟨experience has . . . ~*ed* his hair —Truman Capote⟩

³salt \"\ *adj* -ER/-EST [ME, fr. OE *sealt* (akin to ON *saltr* salt), fr. *sealt*, n.] **1 a :** full of, impregnated with, or containing salt **:** SALINE, SALTY ⟨~ tears⟩ ⟨~ butter⟩ ⟨a ~ solution⟩ **b :** smelling or tasting of salt ⟨tasted the water, and it was ~*er* than the waters of the sea —Elinor Wylie⟩ ⟨with the sea all around her, and the ~, cold air —William Black⟩ **c :** being or inducing one of the four basic taste sensations — compare BITTER, SOUR, SWEET **2 :** cured or seasoned with salt **:** SALTED ⟨~ beef⟩ **3 a :** overflowed with or impregnated by salt water **b :** growing in or native to a salt marsh **c** *of soil or rock* **:** mixed with salt **:** BARREN **4 a :** SHARP, PUNGENT ⟨a ~ wit —John Buchan⟩ **b :** BITTER ⟨a great and ~ reproach —Stephen Crane⟩

⁴salt \"\ *adj* [by shortening & alter. fr. *assaut*, fr. ME *a sawt*, fr. MF *a saut*, lit., on the jump, fr. *a* at, on + *saut* jump, fr. L *saltus*, fr. *saltus*, past part. of *salire* to jump, leap — more at SALLY] **1** *obs, of a female animal* **:** being in heat **2** *obs, of a person* **:** LUSTFUL, LASCIVIOUS ⟨his ~ and most hidden loose affection —Shak.⟩

sal·ta \'saltə, 'sȯl-\ *n* -s [G, fr. L, jump!, imper. of *saltare* to jump, dance] **:** a game for two played on a board of 100 squares in which the object is to move one's men into the positions orig. occupied by the opponent's men

saltando *adv* (*or adj*) [It, jumping, fr. L *saltandum*, gerund of *saltare* to jump, dance] **:** ARCO SALTANDO

salt-and-pepper \¦=;=¦=\ *adj* **:** PEPPER-AND-SALT

¹sal·tant \'saltᵊnt, 'sȯl-, -ltənt\ *adj* [L *saltant-*, *saltans*, pres. part. of *saltare* to jump, leap, dance, fr. *saltus*, past part. of *salire* to jump, leap — more at SALLY] **:** DANCING, LEAPING

²saltant \"\ *n* -s **:** a mutant individual or strain; *esp* **:** one produced in a fungal or bacterial culture

sal·ta·rel·lo \ˌsaltə're(ˌ)lō, ˌsȯl-\ *also* **sal·ta·rel·la** \-elə\ *n* -s [It *saltarello*, fr. *saltare* to jump, fr. L] **1 :** an Italian dance characterized by a lively hop step at the beginning of each measure **2 :** music for this dance or having its rhythm in quick triple or sextuple time and being characterized typically by skips and dotted triple rhythm **3 :** a jack of a harpsichord

sal·tate \'salˌtāt, 'sȯl-\ *vi* -ED/-ING/-S [L *saltatus*, past part. of *saltare* to jump, leap, dance] **1 :** to move by jumps or leaps **2 :** to undergo or exhibit evolutionary saltation **syn** see JUMP

sal·ta·tion \-'tāshən\ *n* -s [L *saltation-*, *saltatio*, fr. *saltatus* + *-ion-*, *-io* -ion] **1 a :** the action of leaping or jumping ⟨ordained for ~, their hinder legs do far exceed the other —Sir Thomas Browne⟩ **b :** DANCING ⟨continued his ~ without . . . intermission —Sir Walter Scott⟩ **2** *obs* **:** a flow in spurts — used of arterial blood **3 a :** an advance by leaps rather than by continuous gradations **:** a sudden or abrupt change; *specif* **:** the reputed direct transformation of one form into another in the course of evolution **:** DISCONTINUOUS VARIATION, MACROEVOLUTION **b :** the production of saltants **c :** SALTANT **4 :** the transportation of particles by currents of water or air in such a manner that they move along in a series of short intermittent leaps — compare TRACTION TRANSPORT **syn** see JUMP

sal·ta·to \säl'täd·(ˌ)ō\ *adv* (*or adj*) [It (past part. of *saltare* to jump, leap), fr. L *saltatus*, past part. of *saltare* to jump, leap, dance — more at SALTANT] **:** ARCO SALTANDO

sal·ta·tor \sal'tād·ə(r), sȯl-, '=,==\ *n* [NL, fr. L *saltator* dancer, fr. *saltatus* + *-or*] **1** *cap* **:** a large genus of Neotropical birds of relatively large size and plain coloration that are classified with either the finches or the tanagers **2** -s **:** any bird of the genus *Saltator*

sal·ta·to·ria \ˌsaltə'tōrēə, ˌsȯl-\ *n pl, cap* [NL, fr. L, neut. pl. of *saltatorius*] **:** a suborder of Orthoptera that is often considered a separate order, comprises insects with the hind legs usu. adapted for leaping, and includes the grasshoppers, crickets, and related forms — compare CURSORIA

sal·ta·to·ri·al \¦==;==ēəl\ *adj* [L *saltatorius* + E *-al*] **1 :** of, relating to, or marked by leaping or dancing **:** SALTATORY ⟨~ exercises⟩ ⟨the bow's ~ elasticity —Paul Hindemith⟩ **2 :** capable of or adapted for leaping ⟨~ legs⟩

sal·ta·to·ri·an \-ən\ *adj* [L *saltatorius* + E *-an*] **:** SALTATORY 1

sal·ta·to·ry \'==ˌtōrē\ *adj* [L *saltatorius*, fr. *saltatus* + *-orius* -ory] **1 :** of or relating to dancing ⟨the ~ art⟩ **2 :** characterized by movement in leaps and bounds ⟨~ thinking⟩ ⟨~ insects⟩ **3 :** proceeding by leaps rather than by gradual transitions **:** DISCONTINUOUS ⟨a ~ advance⟩ ⟨~ relations between terms⟩ — compare DISCONTINUOUS VARIATION

saltatory evolution *n* **:** evolution by sudden variation or by periods of active variation with intervening inactive periods **:** MACROEVOLUTION — compare SALTATION 3a

salt away *or* **salt down** *vt* **1 :** to prepare (as meat or eggs) with or pack in salt for preserving **2 :** to lay away (as money) **:** invest safely **:** SAVE ⟨*salt away* part of their . . . income each year for retirement —*Wall Street Jour.*⟩ ⟨making quite a little . . . *salting down* my commissions —Elisabeth Thomas⟩

saltbox *or* **saltbox house** *n* **:** a type of frame dwelling much used in colonial New England having two stories in front and one behind and having the roof double-sloping with the longer and lower slope to the rear

saltbox

saltbush \'=,=\ *n* **:** any of various shrubby plants of the family Chenopodiaceae that thrive in dry alkaline soil; *esp* **:** any of numerous oraches that are important browse plants in dry parts of the western U.S., Australia, and southern Africa and are sometimes cultivated for forage and for soil stabilization

salt cake *n* **1 :** anhydrous sodium sulfate Na_2SO_4; *esp* **:** a crude form obtained usu. by reaction in a furnace of sulfuric acid on common salt in the manufacture of hydrochloric acid and used chiefly in the sulfate process for wood pulp and in making glass and chemicals **2 :** a substance made by reaction of soda ash and sulfur and used in the sulfate pulp process

saltcat \'=,kat\ *n* [ME, prob. fr. *salt* + *cat*] **:** a lump of salt; *specif* **:** a mixture chiefly of salt, meal, and lime that is attractive to pigeons

salt cedar *n, Southwest* **:** TAMARIX 2

saltcellar \'=,==\ *n* **:** a vessel usu. of glass or silver used on the table for holding salt

salt-desert cavy *n* **:** a mara (*Dolichotis salinicola*) of the Argentine salt marshes

salt dome *n* **:** a domical anticline in sedimentary rocks having a mass of rock salt as its core and being forced up in plastic form by earth stresses from an underlying bed of salt

sal·teaux \'salˌtō, 'sȯl-\ *n pl but sing or pl in constr, usu cap* [F, irreg. fr. *Sault* Ste. Marie, Ontario] **1 a :** an Algonquian people of the vicinity of Sault Ste. Marie, Ontario **b :** a member of such people **2 :** a dialect of Ojibwa

salted *adj* [fr. past part. of ²*salt*] *of an animal* **:** immune against a contagious disease because of prior infection and recovery from it **:** PREMUNE

salt eel *n* **1** *obs* **:** the end of a rope used as a whip **2** *obs* **:** a flogging with a rope's end

¹salt·er \'sȯltə(r), *chiefly Brit* 'säl-\ *n* -s [ME, fr. OE *sealtere*, fr. *sealt* salt + *-ere* -er — more at SALT] **1 a :** one that manufactures or deals in salt **b** *Brit* **:** DRYSALTER **2** [²*salt* + *-er*] **:** one that salts something (as meat, fish, cheese, hides) to season or preserve it **3 :** a vessel or trough in which meat is salted **4 :** a brook trout (*Salvelinus fontinalis*) that has become catadromous

²salter *comparative of* SALT

sal·tern \'sȯltə(r)n\ *n* -s [OE *sealtern*, fr. *sealt* salt + *ern*, *ærn*, *ren* house — more at SALT, REST] **:** a building or place where salt is made by boiling or evaporation **:** SALTWORKS

salt·ery \'sȯltərē\ *n* -ES [¹*salt* + *-ery*] **1 :** SALTWORKS **2 :** an establishment in which fish are salted for market

saltest *superlative of* SALT

salt·fat \'=,fat\ *also* **salt·foot** \-,fu̇t\ *n* [*saltfat* fr. ME, fr. OE *sealtfæt*, fr. *sealt* salt + *fæt* vat, vessel, jar; *saltfoot* alter. of *saltfat* — more at SALT, VAT] *archaic Scot* **:** SALTCELLAR

salt flat *n* **:** the salt-encrusted bottom of an evaporated lake or pond

salt glaze *n* **:** a stoneware glaze produced by vaporizing common salt in the fire of the kiln at the height of the firing so that the sodium of the salt reacts with silicates of the ware to form a coating of glassy acid-resistant mixed silicate of sodium and aluminum — **salt–glazed** *adj*

salt grass *n* **:** any of various grasses native to salt meadows or other markedly alkaline habitats: as **a :** a rigid erect No. American dioecious perennial grass (*Distichlis spicata*); *broadly* **:** any grass of the genus *Distichlis* **b :** any of several spartinas; *esp* **:** a perennial rhizomatous grass (*Spartina patens*) of wet brackish areas of eastern No. America **c :** FEATHER GRASS 2

salt hay *n* **:** hay made from salt grass or grass growing on tidal marshes; *specif* **:** BLACK GRASS 1

salt horse *n* **:** salted meat (as beef or pork)

¹sal·ti·cid \'saltəsəd, 'sȯl-, -tə,sid\ *adj* [NL *Salticidae*] **:** of or relating to the Salticidae

²salticid \"\ *n* -s **:** a spider of the family Salticidae

sal·tic·i·dae \sal'tisəˌdē, sȯl-\ *n pl, cap* [NL, fr. *Salticus*, type genus (fr. LL *salticus* dancing, fr. L *saltare* to jump, leap, dance + *-icus* -ic) + *-idae* — more at SALTANT] **:** a family of small spiders that stalk and leap upon their prey — see JUMPING SPIDER

¹sal·tier \'sal,ti(ə)r, 'sȯl-, -tī(ə)r\ *archaic var of* SALTIRE

²saltier *comparative of* SALTY

sal·ti·er·ra \ˌsaltē'erə, ˌsȯl-\ *n* -s [Sp, fr. *sal* salt (fr. L) + *tierra* earth, fr. L *terra* — more at SALT, TERRACE] **:** salt left by evaporation of some shallow inland lakes

saltiest *superlative of* SALTY

¹sal·ti·grade \'saltəˌgrād, 'sȯl-\ *adj* [L *saltus* leap + E *-i-* + *-grade* — more at SALT (in heat)] **:** having the feet or legs adapted to leaping — usu. used of spiders (as members of the family Salticidae)

²saltigrade \"\ *n* -s **:** a saltigrade spider

salt·i·ly \'sȯltəlē, -li, *chiefly Brit* 'säl-\ *adv* **:** in a salty manner

sal·tim·ban·co \ˌsaltəm'baŋ(ˌ)kō, ˌsȯl-\ *or* **sal·tim·ban·que** *also* **sal·tim·bank** \'==,baŋk\ *n* -s [F & It; F *saltimbanque*, fr. It *saltimbanco*, lit., one that jumps upon a bench, fr. *saltare* to jump (fr. L) + *in* (fr. L) + *banco* bench, of Gmc origin; akin to OHG *bank* bench — more at SALTANT, IN, BENCH] **:** MOUNTEBANK

sal·tine \(')sȯl¦tēn\ *n* -s [¹*salt* + *-ine*] **:** a thin crisp cracker sprinkled with salt

salt·i·ness \'sȯltēnəs, -tin-, *chiefly Brit* 'säl-\ *n* -ES **:** the quality or state of being salty ⟨the ~ of the sea air⟩ ⟨humor . . . usually flavored late in life with a sardonic ~ —J.C.Fitzpatrick⟩

salt·ing \-tiŋ\ *n* -s [fr. gerund of ²*salt*] *chiefly Brit* **:** land flooded regularly by tides — often distinguished from *salt marsh*; usu. used in pl.

¹sal·tire \'sal,tī(ə)r, 'sȯl-\ *n* -s [ME *sawtuoure*, *sawtire*, fr. MF *saultoir*, *sautoir* X-shaped animal barricade that can be jumped over by people, saltire, fr. *saulter*, *sauter* to jump, fr. L *saltare* — more at SALTANT] **1** *heraldry* **:** an ordinary consisting of a cross formed by a bend dexter and a bend sinister crossing in the center of the field **2 :** an X-shaped cross; *esp* **:** SAINT ANDREW'S CROSS 1 — **in saltire :** in position so as to suggest the form of a saltire: **a** *of a pair of heraldic bearings* **:** one bendwise and the other bendwise sinister so as to cross each other ⟨two crosiers *in saltire*⟩ **b** *of four heraldic bearings* **:** in diagonal position so as to converge toward or meet at a common center ⟨four hands conjoined *in saltire*⟩ **c** *of five or more heraldic bearings* **:** arranged as if along the arms of a saltire ⟨five dice *in saltire* argent⟩ — **per saltire :** divided into four parts by two diagonal lines crossing each other

saltire 1

²saltire \"\ *adj* **:** shaped like an X ⟨a ~ stretcher⟩

saltire cross *n* **:** SALTIRE

sal·tire·wise \-,wīz\ *also* **sal·tire·ways** \-,wāz\ *adv* **1 :** in saltire **2 :** per saltire **3 :** with the arms extending diagonally

salt·ish \'sȯltish, -tēsh, *chiefly Brit* 'säl-\ *adj* [ME, fr. *salt* + *-ish*] **1 :** of, relating to, or impregnated with salt **2 :** somewhat salty — **salt·ish·ly** *adj* — **salt·ish·ness** *n* -ES

salt junk *n* **:** dried salted beef

salt lake *n* **:** an inland body of saline water having no outlet to the sea

salt lake city \¦=,=¦==\ *or* **salt lake** \¦=,=\ *adj, usu cap S&L&C* [fr. *Salt Lake City*, Utah] **:** of or from Salt Lake City, the capital of Utah ⟨a *Salt Lake City* smelter⟩ **:** of the kind or style prevalent in Salt Lake City

salt lak·er \'=,lākə(r)\ *n, cap S&L* [*Salt Lake* (*City*) + E *-er*] **:** a native or resident of Salt Lake City, Utah

salt·less \'=ləs\ *adj* **1 :** having no salt **2 :** lacking liveliness or flavor **:** INSIPID ⟨a dull, ~ life⟩

salt·less·ness *n* -ES **:** the quality or state of being saltless

salt lick *n* **:** LICK 3

saltlike \'=,=\ *adj* **:** resembling a salt esp. in ionic character ⟨~ carbides, hydrides, and nitrides⟩

salt·ly *adv* [³*salt* + *-ly*] **:** in a salty manner ⟨~ bitter⟩

salt·man \'=mən\ *n, pl* **saltmen :** BRINEMAN 2

salt marsh *n* [ME *saltmersh*, fr. *salt* + *mersh* marsh — more at MARSH] **:** flat land that is subject to intermittent or occasional overflow by salt water, contains water that is brackish to strongly saline, and supports a vegetation of halophytic plants usu. consisting chiefly of grasses

salt–marsh caterpillar *n* **:** a hairy caterpillar that is the larva of an American moth (*Estigmene acrea*) of the family Arctiidae and that is destructive to various crop plants

salt–marsh fleabane *n* **:** any of various herbs (genus *Pluchea*) growing chiefly in salt marshes

salt–marsh gerardia *n* **:** SEASIDE GERARDIA

salt–marsh grass *n* **:** SALT GRASS

salt–marsh hen *n* **:** CLAPPER RAIL

salt–marsh mosquito *n* **:** any of various mosquitoes that breed in the brackish water of salt marshes but include some forms (as *Aedes sollicitans*) which migrate inland for miles

salt–marsh moth *n* **:** the moth of the salt-marsh caterpillar

salt–marsh terrapin *n* **:** DIAMONDBACK TERRAPIN

salt meadow *n* **:** a meadow subject to flooding by salt water

salt–meadow grass *n* **:** SALT GRASS

saltmouth \'=,=\ *n* **:** a widemouthed bottle with glass stopper for holding chemicals (as crystallized salts)

salt·ness *n* -ES [ME *saltnesse*, fr. OE *sealtnes*, fr. *sealt* salt + *-nes* -ness — more at SALT] **:** the quality or state of being salt or salty: as **a :** SALINITY ⟨the ~ of the sea water⟩ **b :** PUNGENCY ⟨the ~ of a speech⟩
salt of amber : SUCCINIC ACID
salt of hartshorn 1 : AMMONIUM CHLORIDE **2 :** AMMONIUM CARBONATE c
salt of lemon *or* **salts of lemon :** either of two salts: **a :** POTASSIUM OXALATE b **b :** POTASSIUM TETROXALATE
salt of phosphorus : MICROCOSMIC SALT
salt of saturn *usu cap 2d S* **:** LEAD ACETATE a
salt of soda : SODIUM CARBONATE
salt of sorrel *or* **salts of sorrel :** either of two salts: **a :** POTASSIUM OXALATE b **b :** POTASSIUM TETROXALATE
salt of tartar : POTASSIUM CARBONATE; *esp* **:** a pure form made orig. by heating cream of tartar
salt of vitriol : ZINC SULFATE
salt of wisdom : ALEMBROTH
salt of wormwood : POTASSIUM CARBONATE; *esp* **:** an impure form obtained orig. from the ashes of wormwood (*Artemisia absinthium*)
salt out *vt* **:** to precipitate, coagulate, or separate as a liquid layer or gas (a dissolved substance or lyophilic sol as a soap or protein) from a solution by the addition of salt, esp. common salt; *broadly* **:** to produce similar effects on by the addition usu. of an electrolyte other than a salt ~ *vi* **1** *of a saline solution* **:** to deposit salt **2 :** to become deposited by or separated from a solution ⟨albumin and gelatin both *salt out* reversibly in the presence of high concentrations of the salts —J.W.McBain⟩
salt pan *n* [ME *salt panne*] **1 :** an undrained natural depression in which water gathers and leaves a deposit of salt on evaporation **2 :** a large pan for making salt by evaporation
salt·pe·ter *also* **salt·pe·tre** \ˈsȯlt¦pēd·ə(r), -ētə-, *in rapid speech* -lˈp-; ˈ≈,≈≈\ *n* [alter. (influenced by ¹*salt*) of earlier *salpeter*, fr. ME *salpetre*, *salpeter*, fr. MF *salpetre*, fr. ML *sal petrae*, fr. L *sal* salt + *petrae*, gen. of *petra* rock, fr. Gk] **1 :** POTASSIUM NITRATE **2 :** CHILE SALTPETER **3 :** an efflorescence of salts sometimes formed on the surface of tobacco leaves during curing and fermentation
saltpeter paper *n* **:** TOUCH PAPER
salt·pe·trous \(ˈ)sȯl(t)¦pē·trəs\ *adj* [modif. of F *salpêtreux*, fr. MF *salpetreux*, fr. *salpetre* + *-eux* -ous] **:** relating to, impregnated with, or resembling saltpeter
salt pit *n* [ME *salte pitte*] **:** a pit in which seawater is received and evaporated
salt plug *n* **:** a body of rock salt; *specif* **:** the core of a salt dome
salt–poor diet *n* **:** LOW-SODIUM DIET
salt pork *n* **:** pork cured in salt or brine; *specif* **:** cured pork from the belly, back, or side consisting largely of fat — compare BACON 3, FATBACK, SIDE MEAT, SOWBELLY, WHITE MEAT
salt tree *n* [²*sal*] **:** ²SAL 1
salt reed grass *n* **:** a tall reedlike grass (*Spartina cynosuroides*) common in salt meadows
salt rheum *n* **:** ECZEMA
salt–rheum weed *n* **:** a turtlehead (*Chelone glabra*)
salt–rising bread \ˈ≈,≈≈-\ *n* **:** bread raised by a portion of the sponge of sourdough held over from a previous baking
salt river \ˈ≈ˈ≈≈\ *n, usu cap S&R* [fr. *Salt river*, Ky., that in the early 19th cent. flowed through a region notorious for its backward backwoods quality] **:** a river symbolizing the route to oblivion for defeated political candidates or parties — usu. used in the phrase *row up Salt River*
salts *pl of* SALT, *pres 3d sing of* SALT
saltshaker \ˈ≈,≈≈\ *n* **1 :** a container with a perforated top for sprinkling salt on food **2 :** a pressure-operated microphone that can receive sounds equally well from all directions
salt–sick \ˈ≈,≈\ *also* **salt sickness** *n, South* **:** cobalt deficiency disease of cattle **:** PINE
salt spoon *n* **:** a miniature spoon used with an open saltcellar for individual service
salt stain *n* **:** a mark on leather caused by bacterial action during the process of salting
salt tree *n* **1 :** a small tree (*Halimodendron argenteum*) of the family Leguminosae growing in the Caspian salt plains and Siberia **2 :** an East Indian tamarisk (*Tamarix orientalis*) with frequently salt-encrusted twigs
sal·tus \ˈsaltəs, ˈsȯl-\ *n* -ES [NL, fr. L, leap, jump — more at SALT (in heat)] **:** a break of continuity; *specif* **:** an omission of a necessary step of a proof in logic
salt water *n* [ME] **1 a :** water impregnated with salt; *esp* **:** the water of the ocean and of certain seas and lakes **b :** SEA **2 :** fused sodium sulfate that appears as a layer on top of the melt in glassmaking
saltwater \ˈ≈¦≈≈\ *adj* [*salt water*] **1 :** of or belonging to salt water **:** living in or taken from salt water ⟨~ fish⟩ ⟨~ terrapin⟩ **2 :** consisting of salt as opposed to fresh water ⟨a ~ lake⟩ **3 :** taking place in or on salt water ⟨~ plunge⟩ **4 :** accustomed to navigating in salt waters ⟨~ sailor⟩ **5 :** of or relating to the sea ⟨~ songs⟩
saltwater crocodile *n* **:** a large man-eating crocodile (*Crocodylus porosus*) of East Asia and Indonesia that reputedly attains a length of 30 feet and that is a saltwater or brackish water species common about the outlets of rivers but also encountered far from land — called also *estuarine crocodile*
saltwater muskellunge *or* **saltwater pike** *n* **:** GREAT BARRACUDA
saltwater sheldrake *n* **:** RED-BREASTED MERGANSER
saltwater taffy *n* **:** a pulled candy made from white sugar and variously flavored and colored
saltwater trout *n* **:** either of two weakfishes: **a :** GRAY TROUT 1 **b :** SPOTTED WEAKFISH
saltweed \ˈ≈,≈\ *n* **1 :** TOAD RUSH **2 :** SAMPHIRE 4 **3 :** an annual silvery weed (*Atriplex argentea*) found in various alkaline and dry regions of No. America
salt well *n* **:** a bored or driven well from which brine is obtained
saltworks \ˈ≈,≈\ *n pl but sing or pl in constr* **:** a plant where salt is made on a commercial scale (as by extraction from seawater or the brine of salt springs)
saltwort \ˈ≈,≈\ *n* **1 :** a plant of the genus *Salsola* (as *S. kali*, *S. soda*) used in the manufacture of soda ash — see BARILLA **2 :** GLASSWORT 1 **3 :** a low-growing strong-smelling coastal shrub (*Batis maritima*) of warm parts of the New World
saltwort family *n* **:** BATIDACEAE
salty \ˈsȯltē, -ti, *chiefly Brit* ˈsäl-\ *adj* -ER/-EST [ME, fr. *salt* + *-y*] **1 :** of, seasoned with, or containing salt **:** SALINE ⟨~ tears⟩ ⟨~ butter⟩ ⟨small, ~ bays —*Amer. Guide Series: Md.*⟩ **2 :** smacking of the sea or nautical life ⟨a ~ flavor lent by salvaged anchors . . . and other old marine gear —*Amer. Guide Series: Del.*⟩ **3 a :** engagingly provocative **:** PIQUANT ⟨the *saltiest* . . . autobiography of our time—E.A.Weeks⟩ **b :** EARTHY, RACY ⟨~ . . . talk among men in a livery stable —H.S.Canby⟩ **c :** CAUSTIC ⟨penetrating and ~ in his criticism —August Heckscher⟩ **d :** EXPERIENCED, SOPHISTICATED ⟨trying out his . . . lingo to show us how ~ he was —L.M.Uris⟩ **4** *of a horse* **:** hard to manage **:** INTRACTABLE ⟨able to keep a hot seat on a ~ bronc —F.B.Gipson⟩
sa·lu·bri·ous \səˈlübrēəs\ *adj* [L *salubris* salubrious + E *-ous* — more at SAFE] **1 :** favorable to or promoting health or well-being **:** INVIGORATING ⟨~ food⟩ ⟨a ~ climate⟩ ⟨the ~ mountain air and water —C.B.Davis⟩ **2 a :** spiritually wholesome **:** SALUTARY ⟨brought a ~ excitement . . . to American literary life —Charles Angoff⟩ **b :** conducive to good results **:** BENEFICIAL ⟨has received much publicity as a more ~ environment for the operation of textiles —*Textile Industries*⟩ **syn** see HEALTHFUL
sa·lu·bri·ous·ly *adv* **:** in a salubrious manner **:** with salubrious effects
sa·lu·bri·ous·ness *n* -ES **:** the quality or condition of being salubrious
sa·lu·bri·ty \-brəd·ē\ *n* -ES [ME *salubrite*, fr. L *salubritas*, fr. *salubris* + *-itas* -ity] **:** the quality or state of being salubrious **:** HEALTHFULNESS, WHOLESOMENESS ⟨expatiating on the ~ of the cold bath —Robert Lynd⟩ ⟨the ~ of their walk is sadly tinctured by carbon monoxide —Lewis Mumford⟩
salue *vt* -ED/-ING/-S *obs* [ME *saluen*, fr. OF *saluer*, fr. L *salutare* — more at SALUTE] **:** GREET, SALUTE
sa·lu·ki \səˈlükē\ *n* [Ar *salūqiy* of Saluq, ancient city in southern Arabia, fr. *Salūq* Saluq] **1** *usu cap* **:** an old No. African and Asiatic breed of tall slender swift-footed keen-eyed hunting dogs having long narrow skulls, long silky ears, straight forelegs, strong widely set hind legs, a long well-feathered tail, and a smooth silky coat ranging from white or cream to black or black and tan **2** *or* **sloughi** *or* **slughi** \ˈslügē\ -S *often cap* **:** a dog of the Saluki breed
sa·lung \səˈlən\ *n, pl* **salung** *or* **salungs** [Siamese *salin*] **1 :** an old Siamese silver coin equal to ¼ tical **2 :** the unit of value represented by a silver salung
sal·u·tar·i·ly \ˌsalyə¦terəlē, -li\ *adv* **:** in a salutary manner
sal·u·tar·i·ness \ˈ≈≈,terēnəs, -rin-, ˌ≈≈ˈ≈≈≈\ *n* -ES **:** the quality or state of being salutary
sal·u·tary \ˈsalyə,terē, -ri\ *adj* [modif. (influenced by E *-ary*) of MF *salutaire*, fr. L *salutaris*, fr. *salut-*, *salus* health, safety + *-aris* -ar] **1 :** promoting health **:** CURATIVE, RESTORATIVE ⟨~ exercise⟩ ⟨~ medicine⟩ ⟨the ~ mineral or herb —Walter Pater⟩ **2 :** producing a wholesome, corrective, or ultimately beneficial effect **:** REMEDIAL ⟨~ influence⟩ ⟨a ~ rebuke⟩ ⟨~ suffering⟩ ⟨the ~ discovery that even encyclopedias may disagree —Frances Eldredge⟩ ⟨~ shock to middle-class complacency —Roy Lewis & Angus Maude⟩ **syn** see HEALTHFUL
sal·u·ta·tion \ˌsalyəˈtāshən\ *n* -S [ME *salutacioun*, fr. L *salutation-*, *salutatio*, fr. *salutatus* (past part. of *salutare* to salute) + *-ion-*, *-io* -ion — more at SALUTE] **1 a :** an act or action of saluting (as by expressing goodwill or courtesy) ⟨the polite ~s of the lounging natives —Mary Austin⟩ **b :** a gesture or ceremony (as a bow, kiss, or handshake) of greeting ⟨all classes . . . observe the old forms of ~: men embrace —*Amer. Guide Series: Texas*⟩ **c :** a speech of honor or praise **:** TRIBUTE ⟨the speaker's ~ to the modern dance⟩ **d :** SALUTE 4 ⟨~ to the flag⟩ **e :** the word or phrase (as *Dear Sir* or *Mr. Chairman, Ladies and Gentlemen*) that conventionally comes immediately before the body of a letter or at the opening of a speech and that expresses the writer's or speaker's greeting to the person addressed **2** *archaic* **:** a naval salute (as by the firing of guns or lowering of flags) — **sal·u·ta·tion·al** \ˌ≈≈¦tāshənᵊl, -shnəl\ *adj*
sa·lu·ta·to·ri·an \sə,lüd·əˈtōrēən, -ütə-, -ˈtȯr-\ *n* -S [²*salutatory* + *-an*] **:** the graduating student who is usu. second highest in rank and who in some institutions pronounces the salutatory oration — compare VALEDICTORIAN
sa·lu·ta·to·ri·ly \≈¦≈≈¦rəlē, -li\ *adv* **:** in a salutatory manner
¹sa·lu·ta·to·ry \ˈ≈ˈ≈≈,≈rē, -ri\ *adj* [ML *salutatorius*, fr. L *salutatus* (past part. of *salutare* to salute) + *-orius* -ory] **:** containing or expressing salutations **:** speaking a welcome — used esp. of the oration that often introduces commencement exercises
²salutatory \"\ *n* -ES **:** a salutatory oration delivered at the commencement exercises of an educational institution
¹sa·lute \səˈlüt, *usu* -üd·+V\ *vb* -ED/-ING/-S [ME *saluten*, fr. L *salutare*, fr. L *salut-*, *salus* health, safety, greeting — more at SAFE] *vt* **1 a :** to address with expressions of kind wishes, courtesy, or honor ⟨*saluted* him cheerfully by his name —Charles Dickens⟩ **b** *archaic* **:** to hail with the title or epithet of ⟨*saluted* the fathers of their country —John Milton⟩ **c :** to appear, come forth, or burst into song as if to welcome ⟨the lark ~s the dawn⟩ ⟨the peeping crocus ~s the spring⟩ **d :** to become apparent to (one of the senses) **:** impress itself upon ⟨a moist pungent odor of perfumes *saluted* his nose —James Joyce⟩ **2 a :** to give a sign of respect, courtesy, or goodwill to ⟨*saluted* the old man in the doorway —Kay Boyle⟩ **b :** to compliment by a customary or conventional act of ceremony, ⟨*saluted* her in the style of the French dancing master —Meridel Le Sueur⟩ **c :** to make the sign of formal greeting to (an opponent) in fencing **d :** to bow to (one's partner) in square dancing **:** HONOR 4, ADDRESS 10c **3 a :** to honor (as a person, nation, or event) by a conventional military or naval act or ceremony **b :** to show respect and recognition to (a military superior) by assuming a position prescribed by drill regulations **c :** to express high approval or commendation of **:** PRAISE ⟨~ a tradition of leadership —A.E.Stevenson b.1900⟩ ~ *vi* **:** to make a salute
²salute \"\ *n* -S [ME *salut*, fr. MF, fr. L *salut-*, *salus* health, safety, greeting] **1 :** a speech or gesture expressing welcome, recognition, or courtesy **:** GREETING, SALUTATION ⟨did not return my ~ —L.C.Douglas⟩ ⟨his morning ~ for the tenement mothers —Seamus Brady⟩ **2 :** an old French or Anglo-Gallic gold coin bearing the figure of the Virgin receiving the angel's salutation **3 a :** a sign, token, or ceremony (as a kiss or a bow) expressing goodwill, compliment, or respect ⟨took his ~ on the cheek⟩ ⟨clasped his hands over his head in a prizefighter's ~ —*Time*⟩ ⟨participate in ~ to selling week —*Printers' Ink*⟩ **b :** the formal greeting of fencers about to engage **4 a :** a military or naval token of respect or honor (as presenting arms, discharging cannon, or dipping the colors) for a distinguished or official person, for a foreign vessel or flag, or for some festival or event **b :** a mark of respect and recognition given (as with the hand, rifle, or sword) by military personnel in a manner prescribed by regulations and varying according to circumstances **c :** the position (as of the hand, rifle, or sword) or the entire attitude of a person saluting a superior ⟨stand at ~⟩ **5 :** FIRECRACKER 1 ⟨a string of one-inch ~s —*Time*⟩

salute 4c

salute state *n* **:** a state whose ruler is entitled by treaty with a dominant foreign power to a salute of a specified number of guns
salute to the union : a salute of one gun for each state in the U.S. fired only on Independence Day at noon
sal·u·tif·er·ous \ˌsalyə¦tif(ə)rəs\ *adj* [L *salutifer* salutary (fr. *salut-*, *salus* + *-ifer* -iferous) + E *-ous*] **:** SALUTARY ⟨fell into a ~ sleep —Hugh McCrae⟩
salv *abbr* **1** salvage **2** *often cap* [LL *salvator*] savior
salv·a·ble \ˈsalvəbəl\ *adj* [LL *salvare* to save + E *-able* — more at SAVE] **1 :** capable of being saved **:** admissible to salvation **2 :** SALVAGEABLE
¹sal·va·dor \ˈsalvə,dȯ(ə)r, ˌ≈≈ˈ≈\ *adj, usu cap* [fr. El *Salvador*, republic in Central America] **:** EL SALVADOR
²salvador \"\ *adj, usu cap* [fr. *Salvador*, Brazil] **:** of or from the city of Salvador, Brazil **:** of the kind or style prevalent in Salvador
sal·va·do·ra \ˌsalvəˈdōrə, -dȯrə\ *n, cap* [NL, after Juan *Salvador* †1681 Span. botanist] **:** a genus (the type of the family Salvadoraceae) of trees and shrubs of Africa and southern Asia having opposite leaves and small panicled flowers with a bell-shaped corolla — see TOOTHBRUSH TREE
sal·va·do·ra·ce·ae \ˌsalvə,dəˈrāsē,ē\ *n pl, cap* [NL, fr. *Salvadora*, type genus + *-aceae*] **:** a family (order Primulales) of shrubs and trees related to the Oleaceae but having four stamens and four petals
sal·va·do·ra·ceous \ˌ≈≈≈¦rāshəs\ *adj* [NL *Salvadoraceae* + E *-ous*] **:** of, relating to, or resembling the Salvadoraceae
¹sal·va·dor·an \ˌsalvəˈdōrən, -dȯr-\ *also* **sal·va·dor·ian** \-rēən\ *adj, usu cap* [El *Salvador*, Central America + E *-an* or *-ian*] **1 :** of, relating to, or characteristic of the Central American republic of El Salvador **2 :** of, relating to, or characteristic of Salvadorans
²salvadoran \"\ *also* **salvadorian** \"\ *n* -S *cap* **:** a native or inhabitant of El Salvador
¹sal·vage \ˈsalvij, -vēj\ *archaic var of* SAVAGE
²salvage \"\ *n* -S *often attrib* [F, fr. MF, fr. *salver*, *sauver* to save + *-age* — more at SAVE] **1 a :** the compensation paid for saving a ship or its cargo from the perils of the sea or for the lives and property rescued in a wreck; *specif* **:** the compensation allowed to those who under no duty voluntarily save a ship or lives of those belonging to it from peril ⟨awarded the shipping company a large ~ payment⟩ **b :** the act of saving or rescuing a ship or its cargo; *specif* **:** the act of one or more persons who under no duty voluntarily save a ship or its cargo or wreck or in some cases the lives of persons belonging to it from a marine peril or retake and restore it or its cargo when captured in war — compare MILITARY SALVAGE **c :** the act of saving or rescuing property in danger (as from fire) ⟨had little time for the ~ of his effects⟩ **2 a :** property saved from destruction in a wreck; *specif* **:** the part of the property that survives a marine peril and is saved ⟨~ from the stricken vessel lay on the dock⟩ **b :** something extracted (as from wreckage, ruins, or rubbish) as valuable or having further usefulness ⟨the sale of ~ to the poor⟩; *specif* **:** warehouse grain damaged by fire, smoke, or water **c** (1) **:** insured goods rescued from destruction or loss (2) **:** the value of such goods (3) **:** the proceeds from the sale of such goods **3 :** something (as an organ, tissue, or patient) saved by preventive or therapeutic measures in medicine ⟨fetal ~⟩ ⟨lung ~⟩ ⟨the ~ rate in tuberculosis⟩
³salvage \", *esp in pres part* -vəj\ *vt* -ED/-ING/-S **1 :** to rescue or save esp. from wreckage or ruin ⟨*salvaged* torpedoed vessels —Rachel L. Carson⟩ ⟨materials *salvaged* from crashed airplanes —*Amer. Fabrics*⟩ ⟨expect this teacher . . . to ~ the present or potential hoodlums —A.H.Grommon⟩ ⟨*salvaging* a marriage threatened chiefly by alcohol —J.J.Espey⟩ **2 :** to save (an organ, tissue, or patient) by preventive or therapeutic measures ⟨a *salvaging* operation⟩ ⟨a *salvaged* cancer patient⟩
sal·vage·abil·i·ty \ˌ≈≈əˈbiləd·ē\ *n* **:** the quality or state of being salvageable
sal·vage·able \ˈ≈≈əbəl\ *adj* **:** capable of being salvaged ⟨~ cargo⟩ ⟨a ~ criminal⟩
salvage boat *n* **:** a boat engaged in salvage activities
salvage corps *n* **:** a body of men maintained by fire-insurance companies to protect goods, merchandise, and effects from destruction by fire or from water or chemicals used in fighting fire — called also *fire patrol*
salvage cover *n* **:** a waterproof sheet for protecting goods from damage by water, smoke, or weather during or after a fire
salvage cutting *n* **:** a cutting made to remove injured or killed trees for the primary purpose of recovering usable material before it becomes worthless — compare SANITATION CUTTING
salvage loss *n* **:** the difference between the amount of the proceeds of what is saved after salvage charges have been deducted and the total value of the property loss
salvage man *n* [¹*salvage*] *archaic* **:** one clad in foliage to represent a savage (as in medieval and Renaissance pageantry and mumming)
sal·vag·er \-vijə(r), -vēj-\ *n* -S **:** one that salvages **:** SALVOR
salvage value *n* **:** an amount estimated as expected to be realized or actually realized on sale of a fixed asset at the end of its useful life — used in calculating depreciation
Sal·var·san \ˈsalvə(r),san, -,saa(ə)n\ *trademark* — used for arsphenamine
sal·va·tel·la \ˌsalvəˈtelə\ *n, pl* **salvatel·lae** \-e(,)lē, -e,lī\ [ME, fr. ML, fr. LL *salvatus* (past part. of *salvare* to save) + L *-ella*, dim. suffix] *archaic* **:** a vein on the back of the little finger and hand formerly considered esp. effective for bloodletting
sal·va·tion \salˈvāshən\ *n* -S [ME *salvacioun*, *sauvacioun*, fr. OF *salvation*, *sauvation*, fr. LL *salvation-*, *salvatio*, fr. *salvatus* (past part. of *salvare* to save) + L *-ion-*, *-io* -ion — more at SAVE] **1 :** the saving of man from the power and effects of sin: as **a :** his deliverance from the condition of spiritual isolation and estrangement to a reconciled relationship of community with God and fellowmen **:** redemption from spiritual lostness to religious fulfillment and restoration to the fullness of God's favor **b :** redemption from ultimate damnation through divine agency **c :** the deliverance of the soul from sin or the spiritual consequences of sin **:** the saving of a person's soul from eternal punishment and its admission into heavenly beatitude **2 :** liberation from ignorance or illusion **:** deliverance from clinging to the phenomenal world of appearance and final union with ultimate reality ⟨~ in Hinduism implies deliverance from samsara⟩ **3** *Christian Science* **:** the realization of the supremacy of infinite Mind over all bringing with it the destruction of the illusion of sin, sickness, and death **4 :** preservation esp. from destruction, disintegration, or failure **:** final deliverance esp. from dangers, difficulties, or deficiencies ⟨~ from alcoholism —H.C.Webster⟩ ⟨pursuit of individual ~ through hard work —W.H.Whyte⟩ ⟨seeks in religion ~ from the evils and dangers of the times —H.J.Morgenthau⟩ **5 :** the agent, the means, or the course of spiritual experiences determining the soul's redemption ⟨Christ is our ~⟩ ⟨preach ~⟩ **6 :** something that saves or delivers from danger or difficulty **:** the source, cause, or means of preservation ⟨tourism is their only economic ~ —T.H.Fielding⟩ ⟨arboreal habitat was the evolutionary ~ of the primates —Weston La Barre⟩
sal·va·tion·al \-shənᵊl, -shnəl\ *adj* **:** of, relating to, or conducive to salvation ⟨a ~ religion⟩ ⟨the individual psyche in different stages of its ~ career —Joseph Katz⟩ ⟨elect him back to the ~ office he had resigned —Janet Flanner⟩
sal·va·tion·ism \-shə,nizəm\ *n* -S **1 :** religious teaching in which the saving of the soul is particularly emphasized **2 :** the doctrine of the salvation of the soul esp. as taught by those stressing the need of open conversion **3 a** *usu cap* **:** the doctrine and practices of the Salvation Army organized in the 19th century on military lines as an international evangelistic and philanthropic movement **b :** the zeal of a Salvationist
sal·va·tion·ist \-sh(ə)nəst\ *n* -S *often attrib* **1** *usu cap* **:** a soldier or officer of the Salvation Army ⟨national commander of the *Salvationists*⟩ ⟨posted to *Salvationist* stations⟩ **2 :** an advocate of salvationism ⟨a militant ~⟩ **3 :** EVANGELIST ⟨street-corner ~s⟩
¹salvatory *n* -ES [ML *salvatorium*, any receptacle for keeping property safe, fr. LL *salvare* to save, keep safe + L *-orium* -ory — more at SAVE] *obs* **:** a box or receptacle for ointment
²sal·va·to·ry \ˈsalvə,tōrē\ *adj* [*salvation* + *-ory*] **:** conducive to salvation, saving, or safety ⟨the book . . . was vastly less significant or ~ than the sanctified wafer —H.B.Alexander⟩
sal·va ve·ri·ta·te \ˈsäl,wä,werəˈtäd·ē\ *adv* [L, the truth being safe] **:** in accordance with a principle attributed to Leibniz by which two expressions are said to be synonymous if the substitution of one for the other does not change the truth value or meaning of any context in which either expression appears
¹salve \ˈsav, ˈsaa(ə)v, ˈsaiv, ˈsäv, *Brit sometimes* ˈsälv\ *n* -S [ME *salf*, *salve*, fr. OE *sealf*; akin to OS *salba* salve, MLG & MD *salve*, OHG *salba* salve, Gk *elpos* oil, fat, *elphos* butter, *olpē* oil flask, Skt *sarpis* melted butter, ghee, Alb *gjalpë* butter] **1 :** an unctuous adhesive composition or substance to be applied to wounds or sores **:** a healing ointment **2 :** something likened to a salve: as **a :** something (as an influence, agency, or statement) remedial, comforting, or soothing ⟨a ~ for sin⟩ ⟨a ~ to wounded feelings⟩ **b :** something (as praise or flattery) applied or laid on like a salve **3 :** any ointment or cerate prepared with a base (as of a fat, oil, wool fat, petrolatum, wax, or resin) ⟨a blistering or antiseptic ~⟩
²salve \"\ *vt* -ED/-ING/-S [ME *salven*, fr. OE *sealfian*; akin to OS *salbon* to salve, anoint, MLG & MD *salven*, OHG & Goth *salbōn*; denominative fr. the root of E ¹*salve*] **1** *archaic* **:** to apply salve to (as a wound) **:** ANOINT **2 :** to heal, cure, or soothe (as a disease, sin, grief) with or as if with a salve **:** to provide a remedy or consolation for ⟨the character of the work did not ~ the Prologue's sting —H.O.Taylor⟩ **3** *obs* **:** to cover up (as something festering, ugly, or disgraceful) **:** gloss over **4 :** QUIET, ALLAY, ASSUAGE ⟨did not exacerbate her emotional unfulfillment . . . but *salved* it by writing historical novels —*Times Lit. Supp.*⟩ ⟨give him a raise in salary to ~ his feelings —Upton Sinclair⟩
³salve \ˈsa(l)v, -aa(ə)-,-ai-,-ä-\ *vt* -ED/-ING/-S [ML *salvare*, fr. LL, to save — more at SAVE] **1** *obs* **:** to provide a hypothesis or offer a solution or explanation of **:** SOLVE, RESOLVE ⟨what may we do then to ~ this seeming inconsistence —John Milton⟩ **2** *obs* **:** to make (as a doctrine) capable of a rational or reasonable explanation **:** justify with arguments **:** SUPPORT ⟨lest my liking might too sudden seem, I would have *salved* it with a longer treatise —Shak.⟩ **3** *obs* **:** to save or maintain intact (as one's honor or an oath) **:** preserve the credit or integrity of **:** SAFEGUARD ⟨to ~ his credit . . . still will be tempting him who foils him still —John Milton⟩
⁴salve *n* -S [F — more at SALVO] *obs* **:** SALVO
⁵salve \ˈsalv\ *vt* -ED/-ING/-S [back-formation fr. ²*salvage*] **:** to save (as a ship or its cargo) from destruction or loss **:** SALVAGE ⟨a lifeboat was sent to the wreck . . . and it spent the morning *salving* bedding, crockery, and a small amount of clothing —J.H.Marsh⟩ ⟨the campaign for *salving* and processing kitchen scraps —V.C.Fishwick⟩
salve bug *salve like* ¹SALVE\ *n* [¹*salve*, so called fr. its traditional use by fishermen in preparing a salve] **:** a large stout isopod crustacean (*Aega psora*) parasitic on the halibut and codfish
sal·ve·line \ˈsalvə,līn, -lēn\ *adj* [NL *Salvelinus*] **:** of or relating to the genus *Salvelinus*
sal·ve·li·nus \ˌsalvəˈlīnəs, -lēn-\ *n, cap* [NL, fr. G dial. *sälbling*, a char (*Salvelinus alpinus*), alter. of *sälmling* — more at SAIBLING] **:** a genus of fishes (family Salmonidae) distinguished

chiefly by their small scales and boat-shaped vomer with teeth only at the end and including a common European fish (*S. alpinus*) and the American brook trout and Dolly Varden

salve mull *n* **:** ⁷MULL 2

sal·ver \'salvə(r)\ *n* -s [modif. (influenced by *-er*) of F *salve*, fr. Sp *salva* sampling of food to detect poison, small tray, fr. *salvar* to save, sample food to detect poison, fr. LL *salvare* to save — more at SAVE] **:** a tray of any of a wide range of sizes for a variety of purposes but used esp. for serving food or beverages **:** SERVER, WAITER ⟨pad over the turf to them with a ~ of iced tea —G.A.Wagner⟩ ⟨brought the second post on a silver ~ —Virginia Woolf⟩ ⟨milk and dates were served . . . in great brass ~*s* with decorated conical covers —*N.Y.Times*⟩

sal·ver·form \'salvə(r),fȯrm\ *or* **salver-shaped** \'==,=\ *adj* **:** tubular with a spreading limb — used of a gamopetalous corolla

sal·via \'salvēə\ *n* [NL, fr. L, sage — more at SAGE] **1** *cap* **:** a large and widely distributed genus (family Labiatae) of herbs or shrubs varying greatly in habit and in the size and color of the flowers but having a 2-lipped open calyx and two anthers of which one is erect and perfect and the other spreading and sterile — see ²CLARY, SAGE 1a **2** -s **:** any plant of the genus *Salvia*

salvia blue *n* **:** a strong blue that is redder and less strong than Sèvres and redder and paler than cerulean blue

sal·via·nin \-vēənən, -,nin\ *n* -s [NL *Salvia* + anthocyan*in*] **:** an anthocyanin extracted from salvia and Oswego tea in the form of its chloride $C_{36}H_{38}ClO_{17}$ that yields pelargonidin chloride as one product of hydrolysis

sal·vif·ic \(')sal¦vifik\ *or* **sal·vif·i·cal** \-fəkəl\ *adj, sometimes cap* [*salvific* fr. LL *salvificus*, fr. *salvus* saved (fr. L healthy, safe) + L *-ificus* -ific; *salvifical* fr. LL *salvificus* + E *-al*] **:** having the intent to save or admit to salvation ⟨trusted in the *Salvific* Will —W.H.Gardner⟩ ⟨the ~ life and death of Christ —E.A.Walsh⟩ — **sal·vif·i·cal·ly** \-fək(ə)lē\ *adv*

sal·vin·ia \sal'vinēə\ *n, cap* [NL, fr. Antonio M. *Salvini* †1729 Ital. linguist + NL *-ia*] **:** a small genus (the type of the family Salviniaceae) of widely distributed water ferns having distichous leaves borne mostly on simple stems — see FLOATING MOSS

sal·vin·i·a·ce·ae \(,)sal,vinē'āsē,ē\ *n pl, cap* [NL, fr. *Salvinia*, type genus + *-aceae*] **:** a small family that comprises water ferns with branching stems bearing small leaves and one-celled sporocarps containing either megasporangia or microsporangia and that in some classifications constitutes with the Marsileaceae a distinct order but is usu. included in Filicales

¹**sal·vo** \'sal(,)vō\ *n, pl* **salvos** *or* **salvoes** [modif. of It *salva*, fr. F *salve*, fr. MF, fr. L, imper. (used as a greeting) of *salvēre* to be in good health, fr. *salvus* healthy, safe — more at SAFE] **1 :** a simultaneous discharge of fire weapons: as **a :** a firing of several pieces of artillery all together either in action for increased effect or with blank charges as a salute **b** (1) **:** a simultaneous discharge of two or more guns of the same naval battery at one target (2) **:** a series of shots by an artillery battery with each gun firing one round in turn after a prescribed interval (3) **:** the projectiles so discharged in their flight **c** (1) **:** the release all at one time of a rack of bombs or rockets (as from an airplane) (2) **:** the bombs or rockets so released (3) **:** several bombs or rockets released simultaneously from each of several airplanes — compare STICK 17a, VOLLEY 1a **2 :** SALUTE, TRIBUTE ⟨received ~*s* of praise from three of the four leading . . . critics —Janet Flanner⟩ **3 :** a sudden eruption or explosion (as of laughter, cheers, or handclaps) **:** BURST 2b ⟨laughed heartily, in great ~*s* —S.E.White⟩ ⟨a stirring ~ of applause —*Time*⟩ **4 :** a game for two players in which each has a cross-ruled diagram on which he blacks in groups of squares to represent ships with the object of trying to locate and hit an enemy fleet by calling out numbered squares at random — called also *battleships*

²**salvo** \"\ *vb* -ED/-ING/-S *vt* **:** to release a salvo of ⟨electronic gear . . . automatically ~*s* rockets —*advt*⟩ ~ *vi* **:** to fire a salvo ⟨the rest of the fleet ~*ed* steadily into the jungle —*Sat. Eve. Post*⟩

³**salvo** \"\ *n* -s [L, abl. of *salvus* healthy, safe, intact (as in *salvo jure* with the right intact, saving the right) — more at SAFE] **1 :** a mental reservation **:** PROVISO ⟨a ~ for the rights of their order —David Hume †1776⟩ **2** *archaic* **:** a way out of a difficulty **:** EXPLANATION ⟨we have a ~ for that —Samuel Foote⟩ **3 :** a means of safeguarding (as one's name or honor) or of quieting or allaying (as the conscience) **:** SALVE 2

sal vo·la·ti·le \,salvə'ladᵊl(,)ē\ *n* [NL, lit., volatile salt] **1 :** AMMONIUM CARBONATE c **2 :** an aromatic solution of ammonium carbonate in alcohol or ammonia water or both — compare AROMATIC SPIRIT OF AMMONIA, SMELLING SALTS

sal·vor \'salvər, -vȯ(ə)r\ *n* -s [*salvage* + *-or*] **:** one that engages in salvage **:** SALVAGER ⟨the ~ in offshore work has no time for hesitation . . . as to the salvage method necessary —*Marine Engineering & Shipping Rev.*⟩

salvy *pronunc at* ¹SALVE + ē *or* i\ *adj* -ER/-EST [¹*salve* + *-y*] **:** resembling salve in texture or oiliness ⟨~ butter⟩

Sal·yr·gan \'salə(r),gan\ *trademark* — used for mersalyl

salz·burg \'sȯl¦z,bərg, 'säl¦, 'sal¦, 'säl¦, ¦ts,b-, -bu̇rg, -bōg, -bəig,-bu̇əg, G 'zälts,bu̇rk *or* -rḵ\ *adj, usu cap* [fr. *Salzburg*, Austria] **:** of or from the city of Salzburg, Austria **:** of the kind or style prevalent in Salzburg

salz·git·ter \'zälts,gid·ə(r)\ *adj, usu cap* [fr. *Salzgitter*, Germany] **:** of or from the city of Salzgitter, Germany **:** of the kind or style prevalent in Salzgitter

¹**sam** \'sam\ *dial Brit var of* SAME

²**sam** \"\ *n* -s *usu cap* [fr. *Uncle Sam*, imaginary character supposed to represent the U.S. government] **:** KNOW-NOTHING 2

³**sam** \"\ *or* **samm** *vb* **sammed; sammed; samming; sams** *or* **samms** [perh. fr. E dial. *sam* half-cooked, moist, short for *sam-sodden*] **:** SAMMY

⁴**sam** \"\ *n* -s *often cap* [prob. by shortening and alter. fr. earlier *salmon*, fr. the name *Salomon*, *Solomon* used in oaths] *slang Brit* **:** OATH ⟨swop my solemn ~ —John Masefield⟩

sam- \(¦)sam\ *prefix* [ME, fr. OE; akin to OHG *sāmi-* half — more at SEMI-] *dial Eng* **:** half ⟨*sam*-ripe⟩ ⟨*sam*-sodden⟩

sa·ma \'sämə\ *n* -s [AmerSp] **:** MUTTONFISH 1

sa·mad·era \sə'madərə; ,samə'dirə, -'derə\ *n, cap* [NL, fr. Sinhalese *samadarā*, a tree of Ceylon] **:** a genus of East Indian and African trees (family Simaroubaceae) having flowers with a 3- to 5-parted perianth and 6 to 10 included stamens and a fruit that is a dry drupe — see NIEPA

sa·madh \sə'mäd\ *n* -s [Hindi *samādh*, lit., contemplation, self-immolation, fr. Skt *samādhi* — more at SAMADHI] **:** a tomb built in India over the grave of a holy man

sa·ma·dhi \sə'mädē\ *n* -s [Skt *samādhi*, lit., application, contemplation, fr. *sam* together + *ā* to, towards + *-dhi* (akin to *dadhāti* he puts, places) — more at SAME, ACHARYA, DO] **1** *Hinduism* **a :** a state of deep concentration resulting in union with or absorption into ultimate reality — compare RAJA-YOGA **b :** a religious trance **2** *Buddhism* **:** the meditative concentration that is the final step of the Eightfold Path **3** *Jainism* **:** spiritual self-fulfillment **:** ENLIGHTENMENT

sa·maj \sə'mäj\ *n* -ES *usu cap* [Hindi *samāj* meeting, assembly, fr. Skt *samāja*, fr. *sam* together + *ajati* he drives — more at SAME, AGENT] **:** a Hindu religious association **:** SOCIETY

sa·mal \sə'mäl\ *n, pl* **samal** *or* **samals** *usu cap* [Bisayan] **1 a :** a Moro people inhabiting southwestern Mindanao and the Sulu archipelago **b :** a member of such people **2 :** the Austronesian language of the Samal people

sa·man \sə'män\ *n* -s [Sp *samán*, fr. Carib *zamang*] **:** RAIN TREE

sa·man·du·ra \sə'mandərə, ,samən'du̇rə\ *n* [NL, fr. Sinhalese *samadarā*, *samandarā*, a plant of Ceylon] *syn of* SAMADERA

sa·man·go monkey \sə'maŋ(,)gō-\ *n* [of Bantu origin] **:** a dark-colored forest-dwelling monkey (*Cercopithecus labiatus*) common in parts of southern Africa that resembles but is larger than the vervet

sa·ma·nid \sə'mänəd, 'sämən-\ *n, pl* **samanids** \-dz\ *or* **sama·ni** \-nē\ *usu cap* [*Saman*, eponymous ancestor of the first ruler of the dynasty + E *-id*] **:** a member of a 9th and 10th century Persian dynasty ruling from Bokhara and encouraging literature and art

sa·mar \sə'mär, 'sä,mär\ *n, pl* **samar** [Bengali *chumar*, *chamar*] **:** a caste of tanners among the Hindus of Bengal

sam·a·ra \'samərə, sə'ma(a)rə\ *n* -s [NL, fr. L *samara*, *samera* seed of the elm] **:** a dry indehiscent usu. one-seeded winged fruit (as of an ash or elm tree) — called also *key, key fruit*; see FRUIT illustration

samarang *usu cap, var of* SEMARANG

sam·a·ri·form \'samərə,fȯrm, sə'ma(a)r-\ *adj* [NL *samara* + E *-iform*] **:** having the form of a samara

¹**sa·mar·i·tan** \sə'marətᵊn, -mer-, -rətən,-rəd·ən\ *n* -s [ME, fr. LL *samaritanus*, fr. *samaritanus* of the inhabitants of Samaria, fr. Gk *samaritēs* inhabitant of Samaria (fr. *Samaria*, district of ancient Palestine + Gk *-itēs* -ite) + L *-anus* -an] **1** *cap* **a :** a native or inhabitant of Samaria in ancient Palestine — compare ISRAELITE 1a **b :** the dialect of Hebrew used by the Samaritans **2** *usu cap* **:** a member of a dwindling sect in Nablus similar in doctrine to the Jews except for their centralization of worship at Mount Gerizim and the limitation of their Scriptures to the Pentateuch **3** *often cap* [so called fr. the parable of the good Samaritan, Lk 10: 30–37] **:** a compassionate person **:** one who is ready to help the distressed

²**samaritan** \"\ *adj* [LL *samaritanus* of the inhabitants of Samaria] **1** *usu cap* **:** of or relating to Samaria or the Samaritans **2 :** COMPASSIONATE

sa·mar·i·tan·ism \-ᵊn,izəm, -ə,ni-\ *n* -s [¹*samaritan* + *-ism*] **1** *usu cap* **a :** the religious doctrine of the Samaritans **b :** an expression characteristic of the Samaritan dialect **2** *often cap* **:** a compassionate character or deed

sa·mar·i·um \sə'ma(a)rēəm\ *n* -s [NL, fr. F *samarskite* + NL *-ium* — more at SAMARSKITE] **:** a pale gray lustrous metallic element of the rare-earth group that occurs associated esp. with cerium, yttrium, and neodymium in rare-earth minerals and that is bivalent and trivalent in red-brown and pale yellow compounds respectively — symbol *Sm;* see ELEMENT table

¹**samar·kand** \'samər,kand *also* 'sämər,känd *or* 'sä,mär,kand *sometimes* ¦=(,)=¦=\ *n* -s *usu cap* [fr. *Samarkand*, city or region of Uzbek S.S.R.] **:** a medium-sized oriental rug from Chinese Turkestan usu. tied in Sehna knots and made with a field typically blue, red, or golden brown, often with a fretwork effect and five medallions in the corners and the center, and with Chinese motifs (as dragons or stiff floral forms)

²**samarkand** \"\ *adj, usu cap* [fr. *Samarkand*, city of central Uzbek S.S.R.] **:** of or from the city of Samarkand, U.S.S.R. **:** of the kind or style prevalent in Samarkand

samar-leyte \,sä,mär'lād·ē\ *n, pl* **samar-leyte** *or* **samar-leytes** *usu cap S&L* [fr. *Samar*, island of the Visaya group, central Philippines + *Leyte*, island of the Visaya group] **1 a :** a Bisayan people inhabiting Samar and eastern Leyte, Philippines **b :** a member of such people **2 :** an Austronesian language of the Samar-Leyte people that is often considered a dialect of Bisayan

sa·mar·ra \sə'märə, -marə\ *n* -s [ML, garment worn by those condemned by the Inquisition, fr. OSp *zamarra* sheepskin coat worn by shepherds, prob. of Iberian origin; akin to Basque *zamar* sheepskin] **:** SANBENITO 2

sa·mar·ran \-rən\ *adj, usu cap* [*Samarra*, town of north central Iraq + E *-an*] **:** of or belonging to an aeneolithic culture of Mesopotamia following the Hassunan and characterized by black-on-buff pottery

samar·skite \sə'mär,skīt, 'samər-\ *n* -s [F, fr. Col. von *Samarski* 19th cent. Russ. mine official + F *-ite*] **:** a velvet-black commonly metamict orthorhombic mineral with splendent vitreous or resinous luster consisting of an oxide of rare earths, uranium, iron, lead, thorium, columbium, tantalum, titanium, and tin — compare HJELMITE

samas *pl of* SAMA

¹**sam·ba** \'sämbə, 'sam-,'saam-,'səm-\ *n* -s [Pg, of African origin] **1 a :** a Brazilian dance of African origin characterized by a sprightly step pattern in duple time and by a bouncy dip and spring upward of the torso with a bending of the knee at each beat of the music **b :** music in ²⁄₄ time for dancing the samba **2 a :** a variation of canasta using three decks and six jokers and including in the possible melds a seven-card natural sequence worth 1500 points, game being 10,000 points **b :** a seven-card natural sequence meld in samba **3** [native name in Nigeria] **:** OBECHE

²**samba** \"\ *vi* -ED/-ING/-S **:** to dance the samba ⟨trying to conga, rumba, and ~ —*Time*⟩

¹**sam·bal** \(')säm¦bäl\ *n* -s [Malay] **:** a condiment made typically of peppers, pickles, grated coconut, salt fish, or fish roe and eaten esp. with curry and rice in and around Indonesia and Malaya

²**sam·bal** \"\ *also* **sam·ba·li** \säm'bälē\ *or* **zam·bal** \(')säm-¦bäl\ *n, pl* **sambal** *or* **sambals** *also* **sambali** *or* **sambalis** *or* **zambal** *or* **zambals** *usu cap* [Tag *Sambál, Sambali*] **1 a :** a people of Zambales province, western Luzon, Philippines **b :** a member of such people **2 :** the Austronesian language of the Sambal people

sam·ba·qui \,sambə¦kē\ *n* -s [Pg, fr. Tupi & Guarani *sambaqui, tambaqui*, fr. *tamba* shell + *qui* hill] **:** one of the prehistoric kitchen middens found on the coast of Brazil

sam·bar *or* **sam·bur** *also* **sam·bhar** *or* **sam·bhur** \'sämbə(r), 'sam-\ *n* -s [Hindi *sãbar*, fr. Skt *śambara*] **:** a large Asiatic deer (*Cervus unicolor* or *Rusa unicolor*) having long coarse hair on the throat and the antlers strong and three-pointed; *esp* **:** a dark brown Indian deer (*C. u. unicolor*) — called also *elk*

sam·bho·ga·ka·ya \səm,bōgə'käyə\ *n* -s [Skt *sambhogakāya*, fr. *sambhoga* delight in sexual union (fr. *sam* together + *bhoga* enjoyment, fr. *bhuṅkte, bhuñjati* he enjoys) + *kāya* body; akin to Skt *cinoti* he gathers, heaps up, piles in order — more at SAME, FUNCTION, POET] **:** the body of bliss worshiped as deity in the Buddhist doctrine of trikaya

sam·bo \'sam(,)bō, 'saam-\ *n* -s [AmerSp *zambo* Negro, mulatto, perh. fr. Kongo *nzambu* monkey] **1 :** ZAMBO **2** *often cap* **:** NEGRO — usu. used disparagingly

sam browne belt *or* **sam browne** \,sa|m,braůn-, ,saa|\ *n, usu cap S&1stB* [after Sir *Samuel* James *Browne* †1901 Brit. army officer] **:** a leather belt for a dress uniform supported by a light strap passing over the right shoulder ⟨a Mountie's *Sam Browne* —Andrew Bishop⟩

Sam Browne belt

sam·bu·ca \sam'b(y)ükə\ *n* -s [L, fr. Gk *sambykē*, of Sem origin; akin to Aram *śabbĕkhā* trigon] **:** TRIGON

sam·bu·cus \-kəs\ *n, cap* [NL, fr. L, elder tree] **:** a genus of shrubs, trees, or rarely herbs (family Caprifoliaceae) that are native to temperate regions and have pinnate leaves with serrate or incised leaflets, white or pink flowers in thyrsoid cymes with the corolla regular, rotate, and 3- to 5-lobed and with five stamens, and a black or red berrylike fruit

sam·buk *also* **sam·bouk** *or* **sam·buq** \(')sam¦bük\ *n* -s [Ar *sanbūq*] **:** a small Arab dhow

sam·bul *var of* SUMBUL

sam·bu·nigrin \,samb(y)ə'nīgrən, -nig-\ *n* -s [NL *Sambucus nigra*, species of elder (fr. *Sambucus* + L *nigra*, fem. of *niger* black) + ISV *-in* — more at NEGRO] **:** a crystalline glucoside $C_6H_5CH(CN)OC_6H_{11}O_5$ that occurs esp. in the berries of the common elder, that on complete hydrolysis yields benzaldehyde, hydrocyanic acid, and glucose, and that racemizes in alkaline solution to prulaurasin — compare AMYGDALIN, PRUNASIN

¹**same** \'sām\ *adj* [ME, fr. ON *samr, sami;* akin to OE (*swā*) *same* likewise, OHG & Goth *sama* same, L *similis* like, *semone, simul* together, at the same time, Gk *homos* same, *heis, hen* one, *hama* together, Skt *sama* level, equal, same, *sam* together] **1 a :** resembling in every way **:** not different in relevant essentials at one time ⟨we must not expect to be all happy in the ~ degree —James Boswell⟩ **b :** conforming in every respect — used with *as* ⟨eat the ~ rations as the captain —H.A.Chippendale⟩ ⟨gave him the ~ answer as before⟩ **2 a :** being one without addition, change, or discontinuance **:** having one nature or individuality **:** of like nature or identity **:** IDENTICAL, SELFSAME ⟨you can't do the ~ thing all the time —Jimmy Cannon⟩ ⟨speakers and hearers, who may be one and the ~ persons —Gilbert Ryle⟩ **b :** being the one under discussion or already referred to ⟨the committee backing the fare increase is the ~ committee that recently issued an urgent plea to curb inflation⟩ — often used as an intensive ⟨used six quotations from this ~ book⟩ **3 :** corresponding so closely as to be indistinguishable **:** closely similar **:** COMPARABLE ⟨mother and son have the ~ black eyes⟩ ⟨the way two different drivers treat . . . the ~ sets of tires —R.L.Rosekrans⟩ ⟨the form is diverse; the essence is the ~ —Havelock Ellis⟩

syn SAME, SELFSAME, VERY, IDENTICAL, IDENTIC, EQUIVALENT, EQUAL, and TANTAMOUNT can apply to one thing not different from another or things not differing from each other. SAME may imply, and SELFSAME always implies, that the things under consideration are only one thing ⟨the systems of all three countries conform to the *same* standards of . . . justice and fair play —John Moylan⟩ ⟨in efficiency, one method may be the *same* as another⟩ ⟨each question was directed to the *selfsame* urgent end —E.M.Lustgarten⟩ ⟨voted out of power . . . by the *selfsame* people who had put them into office in the first place —B.F. Fairless⟩ VERY can often be no different from SELFSAME ⟨what others have thought about the *very* problems that face us now —C.F.Strubbe⟩ ⟨here in this *very* town there was once a cafe —Carson McCullers⟩ ⟨the *very* man I was looking for⟩ IDENTICAL implies selfsameness or absolute agreement in all details ⟨consists of several hundred *identical* shacks arranged in rows —*Amer. Guide Series: Pa.*⟩ ⟨we are not *identical* with our former self —Alexis Carrel⟩ IDENTIC is the same as IDENTICAL but has a chiefly diplomatic or governmental provenience ⟨collective or *identic* notes utilized by the powers in making joint representation to a government —G.H.Stuart⟩ ⟨the resolution is *identic* with a resolution enacted last year —*U.S. Code*⟩ ⟨the president in *identic* letters addressed to the attorney general, the secretary of war and the secretary of the navy, notified them of his approval —F.A.Howard⟩ EQUIVALENT applies to things estimated against each other and implies amounting to the same thing ⟨instead of matching it with an *equivalent* folly, we wish to offer an alternative —Herbert Agar⟩ ⟨the voters, who for practical purposes are *equivalent* to the people —W.J.Shepard⟩ ⟨the accumulation of property is therefore *equivalent* to a concentration of power or sovereignty over the lives of those who need the goods owned by others —M.R.Cohen⟩ EQUAL signifies identical in some specific way, as in height, amount, or effectiveness ⟨in many counties cattle and sheep are of almost *equal* importance —*Amer. Guide Series: Nev.*⟩ ⟨when our men have *equal* weapons in their hands —Sir Winston Churchill⟩ ⟨the picture cannot be painted if the significant and the insignificant are given *equal* prominence —B.N.Cardozo⟩ ⟨two boys *equal* in size and age⟩ TANTAMOUNT is the same as EQUIVALENT but applies only to one of two equivalent things, usu. nonmaterial ⟨an article of faith, the denial of which is *tantamount* to treason —Archibald MacLeish⟩ ⟨failure to publish is *tantamount* to suppression —R.H. Rovere⟩ ⟨production of coal is *tantamount* to the destruction of stored energy —W.P.Webb⟩

²**same** \"\ *pron* [ME, fr. ¹*same*] **1 a :** something identical with or similar to another ⟨an actual apple or a picture of the ~ —Einar Haugen⟩ ⟨the rules . . . are the ~ which govern professional big-league play —C.L.Biemiller⟩ ⟨when by sheer luck you strike a wedding . . . and when by more of the ~ you reach Vienna on a feast day —Claudia Cassidy⟩ **b** *obs* **:** something that is a counterpart — used with *that* ⟨such was thy zeal to Israel then, the ~ that now to me —John Milton⟩ **2 :** something that has previously been defined or described ⟨ran up big bills . . . but was not very strong on paying ~ —Bennett Cerf⟩ ⟨each house shall keep a journal of its proceedings, and from time to time publish the ~ —*U.S.Constitution*⟩ ⟨have in his possession gold certificates after ~ had been registered at Washington —F.A.Limpert⟩ — **the same** *adv* **:** in the same manner ⟨*to* and *two* are spelled differently but pronounced *the same*⟩ ⟨a woman's shoulder muscles are not attached *the same* as a man's —Deems Taylor⟩

³**same** \"\ *adv* [¹*same*] **:** in the same manner **:** the same ⟨may be applied with . . . connector strips, ~ as any other wallboard —*Stonewall Board*⟩

same here *adv* **:** similarly with me ⟨said she wanted a soda and I said *same here*⟩

sa·mekh *or* **sa·mech** *also* **sa·mek** \'sä(,)mek, -ek\ *n* -s [Heb *sāmekh*, lit., a support] **1 :** the 15th letter of the Hebrew alphabet — symbol ס; see ALPHABET table **2 :** a letter of the Phoenician or of any of various other Semitic alphabets corresponding to the Hebrew samekh

sam·el *also* **sam·mel** \'saməl\ *adj* [prob. akin to OE *sam-* half and to OE *ǣlan* to burn — more at SAM-, ANNEAL] **:** soft and crumbling — used of bricks that lie outermost in the kiln and are in consequence not thoroughly burned; compare PLACE BRICK

same·ly \'sāmlē\ *adj* [¹*same* + *-ly*] **:** MONOTONOUS, UNVARIED

sam·en \'sāmən\ *adj* [by alter.] *Scot* **:** SAME

same·ness \'sāmnəs\ *n* -ES **1 :** the quality or state of being the same **:** IDENTITY, SIMILARITY ⟨the ~*es*, the traits of mankind which are general —H.W.Taylor⟩ **2 :** unvarying homogeneity **:** MONOTONY, UNIFORMITY ⟨~ of food — oats and hay continuously —Robert Chawner⟩ ⟨the sun-browned ~ of outlying rangelands —*Amer. Guide Series: Texas*⟩

samgha *var of* SANGHA

sa·mhain eve \'saůən-, 'säwən-\ *n, usu cap S&E* [IrGael *samhain* feast of All Saints + E *eve*] **:** HALLOWEEN

sam hill \'sam¦hil\ *n, often cap S&H* [prob. euphemism for *hell*] **:** DEVIL, DEUCE ⟨just what in the *Sam Hill* was he going to do —Norman Mailer⟩

sam·hi·ta \¦səmhi¦tä\ *n* -s *usu cap* [Skt *saṁhitā*, lit., combination, fr. *sam* together + *hita*, past part. of *dadhāti* he puts, places — more at SAME, DO] **:** any of the four basic canonical books of Hindu scriptures comprising hymns, prayers, and liturgical formulas and including the Rig-Veda, the Yajur-Veda, the Sama-Veda, and the Atharva-Veda

sa·mia \'sāmēə\ *n, cap* [NL, fr. L, the Samian goddess (epithet of Juno or Saturnia), fr. fem. of *samius* Samian] **:** a genus of large saturniid moths — see CYNTHIA MOTH

¹**sa·mi·an** \'sāmēən\ *adj, usu cap* [L *samius* Samian (fr. Gk *samios*, fr. *Samos*) + E *-an*] **:** of or relating to the island of Samos in the Aegean sea ⟨fill high the bowl with *Samian* wine —Lord Byron⟩

²**samian** \"\ *n* -s *cap* **:** a native or inhabitant of Samos

samian ware *n, usu cap S* **:** ARRETINE WARE

sam·iel \səm'yel\ *n* -s [Turk *samyeli*, fr. *sam* poisonous + *yel* wind] **:** SIMOOM

sam·i·res·ite \,samə're,sīt, sə'mirə,s-\ *n* -s [F *samirésite*, fr. *Samiresy*, hill near Antsirabe, Madagascar + F *-ite*] **:** BETAFITE

sam·i·sen \'samə,sen\ *also* **sam·si·en** \-msē,en\ *or* **sham·i·sen** \'shamə,sen\ *n, pl* **samisen** *or* **samisens** [Jap *samisen*, fr. Chin (Pek) *san¹ hsien²*, fr. *san¹* three + *hsien²* string] **:** a 3-stringed Japanese musical instrument resembling a banjo

samisen

samite \'sa,mīt, 'sā,-\ *n* -s [ME *samit*, fr. MF, fr. ML *examitum, samitum*, fr. (assumed) MGk *hexamiton* (whence OSlav *oksamitŭ* velvet), fr. Gk, neut. of *hexamitos* of six threads, fr. *hexa-* + *mitos* thread of the warp — more at DIMITY] **:** a rich medieval fabric of silk interwoven sometimes with gold or silver threads and used or worn only by ecclesiastics and nobles ⟨an arm rose up from out the bosom of the lake clothed in white ~, mystic, wonderful —Alfred Tennyson⟩

samkhya *usu cap, var of* SANKHYA

sam·let \'samlət\ *n* -s [irreg. fr. *salmon* + *-let*] **:** a fingerling salmon **:** PARR

samm *var of* SAM

sam·ma \'samə\ *n* -s *usu cap* **:** one of a number of Rajput peoples in the lower Sind in early Indian history

sammarinese *usu cap, var of* SAN MARINESE

sammed *past of* SAM

sammel *var of* SAMEL

sam·mer \'samə(r)\ *n* -s [³*sam* + *-er*] **:** one that sams leather — called also *sammier, sammy man*

sam·mi·er \'samēə(r)\ *n* -s [²*sammy* + *-er*] **:** SAMMER

samming *pres part of* SAM

¹**sam·my** \'samē\ *adj* [perh. alter. of E dial. *sam* half-cooked, moist — more at SAM] **1** *dial* **:** CLAMMY, SODDEN **2** *dial* **:** WATERY

²sammy \"\ *or* **sam·mie** \"\ *vb* **sammied; sammied; sammying** *or* **sammieing; sammies** [alter. of ³*sam*] *vt* : to moisten (leather) before staking : SAM ~ *vi* : to make rough-tanned leather evenly moist throughout

³sammy \"\ *n* -ES [fr. *Sammy*, nickname for *Samuel*] *dial Eng* : SIMPLETON

sammy man *n* [²*sammy*] : SAMMER

sam·na·ni \səmˈnänē\ *n, pl* **samnani** *or* **samnanis** *usu cap* **1 a** : a people of Samnan in north central Iran **b** : a member of such people **2** : the Iranian language of the Samnani people

sam·nite \ˈsam,nīt\ *n* -S *cap* [L *Samnites* (pl.) Samnites, fr. *Samnium*, country in ancient central Italy] **1** : a people of ancient Samnium in central Italy speaking the Oscan language **2** : a gladiator of ancient Rome bearing the arms and oblong shield of the Samnites

¹sa·mo·an \səˈmōən\ *adj, usu cap* [*Samoa*, group of islands in southwest central Pacific ocean + E *-an*] : of or relating to Samoa or the Samoans

²samoan \"\ *n* -S *cap* **1** : a native or inhabitant of Samoa **2** : the Polynesian language of the Samoan people

sam·o·gi·tian \,saməˈgishən, -məˈji-\ *n* -S *cap* **1** : a Lithuanian of the lowlands in the western part of the Kaunas district **2** : the language of the Samogitian people constituting one of the two linguistic divisions of Lithuanian

sa·mo·gon \ˌsäməˌgōn\ *also* **sa·mo·gon·ka** \-ōŋkə\ *n* -S [Russ, prob. fr. *samo-* self (akin to OE *same*) + *peregon*, *peregonka* distillation] : illicitly distilled Russian vodka : HOME BREW

sa·mo·hu \səˈmō(,)hü\ *n* -S [native name in So. America] **1** : FLOSS-SILK TREE **2** : the ashy gray light soft lumber of the floss-silk tree

sam·o·lus \ˈsaməles\ *n, cap* [NL, fr. L, a plant growing in wet places, of Gaulish origin] : a small genus of mainly tropical herbs (family Primulaceae) having small white flowers with a perigynous corolla including five stamens and five staminodia — see BROOKWEED

sa·mos·a·te·nian \sə,mäsəˈtēnēən\ *n* -S *usu cap* [LL Paulus *Samosatenus* Paul of Samosata (fr. Gk *samosatēnos* of Samosata, fr. *Samosata*, city of ancient Syria) + E *-ian*] : PAULIANIST

sam·o·there \ˈsamə,thi(ə)r\ *n* -S [NL *Samotherium*] : an ungulate or fossil of the genus *Samotherium*

sam·o·the·ri·um \,saməˈthirēəm\ *n, cap* [NL, fr. *Samos*, island in the Aegean sea + *-therium*] : a genus of extinct ungulates of the Miocene of Greece related to the giraffe but having a shorter neck and no median frontal knob

¹sam·o·thra·cian \,saməˈthrāshən\ *n* -S *cap* [L *samothracius* of Samothrace (fr. Gk *samothrakios*, fr. *Samothrakē* Samothrace, island in the Aegean sea) + E *-an*] : a native or inhabitant of the Greek island of Samothrace in the Aegean sea

²samothracian \ˌ==ˈ==\ *adj, usu cap* [L *samothracius*] : of, relating to, or constituting the religious cult centering around the Cabiri of ancient Greece

sam·o·var \ˈsamə,vär, -və(r *sometimes* ,==ˈ=\ *n* -S [Russ, fr. *samo-* self (akin to OE *same*) + *varit'* to boil, cook] **1** : a usu. copper urn with a spigot at its base and a central tube for live charcoal used esp. in Russia to boil water for tea **2** : a similar urn of metal or china with an alcohol lamp or other device for heating the contents

samovar 1

¹sam·o·yed *also* **sam·o·yede** \ˈsamə,yed, ˈsa,mói(y)ed, səˈmói(y)əd\ *n* [Russ *samoed*] **1** *pl* **samoyed** *or* **samoyeds** *cap* **a** : a Finno-Asian people of the Nenets district of the Arkhangelsk region of the U.S.S.R. scattered along the coasts and islands from the White sea to the Taimyr peninsula — called also *Nentsi* **b** : a member of such people **2** *also* **sam·o·yed·ic** \,saməˈyedik, ,sa,mói(y)e-\ *n* -S *cap* **a** : a group of Uralic languages spoken by the Samoyed people — see URALIC LANGUAGES table **b** : one of these languages **3 a** *usu cap* : a Siberian breed of medium-sized deep-chested white or cream-colored arctic dogs in coat and proportions much resembling the chow chow and long used by the Samoyeds for herding reindeer and pulling sleds **b** -S *often cap* : a dog of this breed

²samoyed *or* **samoyede** \"\ *also* **samoyedic** \ˌ==ˈ=\ *adj, usu cap* : of or relating to the Samoyeds or their language

samp \ˈsamp\ *n* -S [Narraganset *nasaump* corn mush, soup] : coarse hominy or a boiled cereal made from it

sam·pa·gui·ta \,sampəˈgēd·ə\ *n* -S [PhilSp, fr. Tag *sampaga* Arabian jasmine + Sp *-ita* dim. suffix] *Philippines* : ARABIAN JASMINE

sam·pa·loc \ˈsampə,läk\ *n* -S [Tag *sampalok*] *Philippines* : TAMARIND

sam·pan *also* **san·pan** \ˈsam,pan, ˈsaam,paa(ə)n\ *n* -S [Chin (Pek) *san*¹ *pan*³, fr. *san*¹ three + *pan*³ board, plank] **1 a** : a flat-bottomed wedge-shaped Chinese skiff with low transom bow and rising transom stern with a pronounced rake, usu. having a mat roofing over the cabin, sometimes equipped with a sail but usu. propelled by two short oars in oarlocks consisting of twisted rattan, and used principally for river and harbor traffic **b** : a small open Chinese boat **2** : a Japanese boat with a broad flat keel, a long raking sharp bow and vertical square stern propelled by a single scull or a group of sculls, by square sails on one to three masts, or by an engine **3** *Hawaii* : a boat built on oriental lines, propelled by a diesel motor, and widely used in Hawaiian fishery

sam·phire \ˈsam,fī(ə)r\ *n* -S [alter. (perh. influenced by *camphire*) of earlier *sampere*, *sampiere*, fr. MF (*herbe de*) *Saint Pierre*, lit., St. Peter's herb] **1** : a fleshy European seacoast plant (*Crithmum maritimum*) of the family Umbelliferae that is sometimes pickled **2** : a common glasswort (*Salicornia europaea*) that is sometimes pickled **3** : SEA OXEYE **4** : a tropical American fleshy herb (*Philoxerus vermicularis*) of the family Amaranthaceae with dense heads of white flowers that is common along beaches

¹sam·ple \ˈsampəl, ˈsaam-,ˈsaim-, ˈsȧm-\ *n* -S [ME, fr. MF *essample* — more at EXAMPLE] **1** *obs* : one that is worthy of imitation : EXAMPLE ⟨liv'd in court . . . most prais'd, most lov'd, a ~ to the youngest —Shak.⟩ **2 a** : a representative portion of a whole : a small segment or quantity taken as evidence of the quality or character of the entire group or lot ⟨the ~ of the . . . Nordic race with which he identifies himself —Ruth Benedict⟩ ⟨knowledge of the deep ocean floor comes from . . . bottom ~*s* —F.P.Shepard⟩ **b** : one displaying characteristics typical of its kind : SPECIMEN ⟨the collection of ~*s* for museum displays —R.W.Murray⟩ ⟨molded caps over the windows and the original broad porch make it an excellent ~ of its period —*Amer. Guide Series: Conn.*⟩ **c** (1) : a trial package of a product distributed without cost to potential consumers (2) : a unit of merchandise used for demonstration or display ⟨floor ~⟩ **3** : one that serves to illustrate the full range or scope : INDICATION, INSTANCE ⟨offering listeners ~*s* from the whole tradition of world drama —Leslie Rees⟩ ⟨contrasting ~*s* of church-state policy —Paul Blanshard⟩ **4 a** : a part (as of a population) used for purposes of investigating and comparing properties ⟨poll a national ~ as a means of predicting elections⟩ **b** : SAMPLING ⟨results of the ~ . . . must be translated and interpreted —W.E.Deming⟩ **syn** see INSTANCE

²sample \"\ *vt* **sampled; sampled; sampling** \-p(ə)liŋ\ **samples 1** *obs* **a** : to make comparable to : find a counterpart for : MATCH ⟨she seemed to be *sampled* for him —Henry Lord⟩ ⟨this notion . . . nowhere else *sampled* in any Greek author —Joseph Mede⟩ **b** : SYMBOLIZE ⟨some way ~ that, which no way we can express —Henry Montagu⟩ **c** : COPY ⟨a model . . . must be *sampled* in Jerusalem —Joseph Hall⟩ **2 a** : to take a sample of : assess by examining a small portion : TEST ⟨inspectors . . . ~ a year's output of fifty million parts —Bryan Morgan⟩ ⟨achievement tests . . . each *sampling* a different area —*Univ. of State of N. Y. Bull.*⟩ **b** : to yield in sample ⟨good ore, two feet of which ~*s* more than . . . 30 ounces of silver —*N.Y.Sun*⟩ **c** : to become acquainted with through personal experiment : try out : EXPERIENCE ⟨rail fans will . . . adjust their itineraries this summer to ~ the shiny new equipment —P.J.C.Friedlander⟩ ⟨~ the pleasures of the simple life —Thomas Cadett⟩ **d** : to dip into : glance through : SKIM ⟨~ the literature of social science⟩ ⟨surrounds himself with books . . . and ~*s* them as a dowager might a box of chocolates —*Time*⟩ **3** : to give an impression or show an example of : EXEMPLIFY, REPRESENT ⟨manuscripts are so extensive . . . that it would be a heavy task to undertake even to ~ them adequately —*Times Lit. Supp.*⟩ ⟨denims are *sampled* in red —*Women's Wear Daily*⟩ **4** : to take samples from (a given population) and from them make statistical estimates of the trait or attitude measured ⟨polling organizations *sampled* the electorate at intervals —*Americana Annual*⟩

³sample \"\ *adj* **1** : serving as an illustration or example ⟨~ question⟩ ⟨designed a ~ three-bedroom house —*N.Y.Times*⟩ **2 a** : exemplifying a whole body or lot ⟨~ ore⟩ ⟨~ copy⟩ **b** : making, examining, showing, or distributing samples ⟨~ cutter⟩ ⟨~ tester⟩ ⟨~ card⟩ ⟨~ passer⟩ **3** : of an exploratory nature : EXPERIMENTAL ⟨~ tunnels have already indicated the proximity of fossils —R.W.Murray⟩ **4** : of or relating to a statistical sample ⟨was courteous enough to check his attendances for us during a random ~ week —Ernest & Pearl Beaglehole⟩

sam·ple·ite \-pə,līt\ *n* -S [Mat *Sample* 20th cent. Am. mine superintendent in Chile + *-ite*] : a mineral $NaCaCu_5(PO_4)_4Cl.5H_2O$ consisting of hydrous phosphate and chloride of sodium, calcium, and copper

sam·ple·man \ˈ=pəlmən, -,man\ *n, pl* **samplemen** [¹*sample* + *man*] : a maker, distributor, or tester of samples : SAMPLER

sample post *n* [¹*sample*] : a postal service for international mail provided by Universal Postal Union regulations and allowing special rates on trade samples

¹sam·pler \-plə(r)\ *n* -S [ME, fr. OF *essamplaire*, fr. LL *exemplarium* — more at EXEMPLAR] **1** *obs* : an original model or characteristic sample : ARCHETYPE, EXAMPLE ⟨Christ's baptism was the perfect ~ and pattern of ours —Daniel Featley⟩ **2 a** : a practical example of needlework patterns; *esp* : a piece of cloth with rows of different embroidery stitches worked across it **b** : a decorative square or rectangular piece of needlework typically having the alphabet, numbers, family names and dates, and a motto embroidered on it in various stitches as an example of skill

²sam·pler \-p(ə)lə(r)\ *n* -S [²*sample* + *-er*] **1** : one that collects or examines samples: as **a** (1) : one that determines the quality of a product by testing samples taken from it ⟨cotton ~⟩ ⟨grain ~⟩ (2) : one that prepares samples ⟨the ~ extracts olives from the barrels for the inspector⟩ **b** : a customs inspector who compares samples of merchandise with discharge permits and endorses the permits if there are no discrepancies **c** : a mechanical device for obtaining a small quantity of something for testing or analysis ⟨grab ~*s* . . . are designed to take a surface sample of the bottom —J.D. Isaacs⟩ **2 a** : one that contains representative specimens or selections ⟨a fiction ~ from the work of a notable . . . writer —Harvey Breit⟩ ⟨cities became . . . ~*s* of the past styles of every country but our own —*Amer. Guide Series: Va.*⟩ **b** : a trial package or assortment intended to introduce a product to potential customers ⟨a connoisseur's ~ containing small packets of six choice teas⟩ ⟨each preparation has its . . . niche in the ~ —*Phoenix Flame*⟩ **3** : one engaged in statistical sampling ⟨a ~ of public opinion⟩

sample room *n* [¹*sample*] : a room in which samples are displayed; *esp* : a hotel room in which salesmen display merchandise for the inspection of buyers for retail stores

sampling *n* -S *often attrib* [fr. gerund of ²*sample*] **1 a** : an act or instance of obtaining a sample ⟨improved technic . . . for blood ~ —*advt*⟩ ⟨the purpose of ~ is to determine the average mineral values in the deposit —J.D.Forrester⟩ **b** : assessment of the quality or character of a whole by examination of a sample : TESTING ⟨periodic ~ of the stored grain is necessary to be sure it is not molding⟩ **c** : personal investigation : TRIAL ⟨experimental ~, as with edibles, . . . played a part in the transformation of our material environment —Lewis Mumford⟩ **2** : SAMPLE ⟨those who would like to find out what the French do in commerce and industry can get complete ~*s* at the . . . fair —*N.Y.Times*⟩ ⟨this inventory is far from complete, but it is an adequate ~ —Abram Kardiner⟩ ⟨ask a ~ of people why they didn't buy one client's product —Vance Packard⟩ **3** : the introduction of a product or promotion of its sale by distributing at no cost or at a reduced price a trial package in regular or specially designed smaller size **4** : the act, process, or technique of determining traits or attitudes of a whole population by collecting and analyzing data from a representative segment of it : SURVEY ⟨after allowance has been made for the quantitative and qualitative bias of the ~, series of generalizations are drawn —Sidney Hook⟩

sampling error *n* : the chance difference of a statistic from the corresponding population constant of which it is an estimate

sampling shovel *n* : SPLIT SHOVEL

sampogna *var of* ZAMPOGNA

samps *pl of* SAMP

samp·sae·an \sam(p)ˈsēən\ *n* -S *usu cap* [LGk *sampsaios* + E *-an*] : a member of a branch of the Elkesaites

samp·son fish \ˈsa|m(p)sən-, ˈsaa|, ˈsai|\ *n, usu cap S* [fr. the name *Sampson*] : an Australian fish (*Seriola hippos*) of the family Carangidae

sampson fox *or* **samson fox** \"-\ *n, usu cap S* [prob. after *Samson*, judge of Israel; fr. his tying torches to the tails of foxes to set fire to the grain of the Philistines, Judg 15:4–5] : a red fox having a coat in which the guard hairs are lacking and the under fur is woolly and scorched looking due to genetic variation

sampson snakeroot *or* **sampson's snakeroot** *also* **samson snakeroot** *n, usu cap 1st S* [fr. the name *Sampson* or *Samson*] **1** : an aromatic herb (*Psoralea psoralioides*) of the southeastern U.S. with a root having tonic properties — called also *babroot*, *Congo root* **2** : any of several American gentians of the genus *Dasystephana*

sams *pl of* SAM, *pres 3d sing of* SAM

sam·sa·ra \səmˈsärə\ *also* **sansara** \sənˈ-\ *n* -S [Skt *saṁsāra*, lit., passing through, fr. *sam* together, completely + *sarati* it runs, flows — more at SAME, SERUM] **1** *Hinduism & Buddhism* : the indefinitely repeated cycles of birth, misery, and death caused by karma : TRANSMIGRATION **2** *Hinduism & Buddhism* : ever-changing finite temporal existence : life in society — contrasted with *Nirvana*

sam scratch \ˈsamzˈkrach, -mˈsk-\ *n, usu cap both Ss* : OLD NICK

sam·shu \ˈsam¦shü, -¦syü\ *n* -S [perh. fr. Chin (Pek) *shao*¹ *chiu*³ spirits that will burn, samshu, fr. *shao*¹ to burn + *chiu*³ wine, spirits] : an alcoholic liquor distilled in China usu. from rice or large millet

samsien *var of* SAMISEN

sam·ska·ra \səmzˈkärə, -mˈsk-\ *n* -S [Skt *saṁskāra*, lit., putting together, making perfect, purifying, fr. *sam* together + *karoti* he makes, does — more at SAME, KARMA] **1** : a purificatory Hindu ceremony **2** *Hinduism & Buddhism* : a mental conformation or latent karmic tendency shaping one's present life

sam·skrit *or* **sam·skrt** \ˈsamz,krit, -m,sk-\ *n* -S *cap* [Skt *saṁskṛta* — more at SANSKRIT] : SANSKRIT

sam-sodden \ˈsam,säd³n\ *adj* [fr. (assumed) ME *sam-soden*, fr. OE, fr. *sam-* + *soden*, past part. of *sēothan* to boil — more at SEETHE] *dial Eng* : half cooked

sam·son \ˈsam(p)sən, ˈsaam-,ˈsaim-\ *n* -S [after *Samson*, judge of Israel famed for his strength, Judg 13:24–16:31] **1** *usu cap* : a mighty man ⟨we proclaimed him a *Samson* who might pull down the pillars of our temple —R.H.Jackson⟩ **2** : SAMSON POST

sam·so·ni·an \(ˈ)=ˈsōnēən\ *also* **sam·son·ic** \(ˈ)=ˈsänik\ *adj, usu cap* [*Samson*, judge of Israel + E *-ian*, *-ic*] : of heroic strength or proportions : MIGHTY ⟨a *Samsonian* attempt to demolish the gigantic structure —Douglas Watt⟩

sam·son·ite \ˈ=sə,nīt\ *n* -S [G *samsonit*, fr. the *Samson* mine, Sankt Andreasberg, Harz Mts., Germany + G *-it* -ite] : a mineral $Ag_4MnSb_2S_6$ consisting of a silver manganese antimony sulfide and occurring in steel-black monoclinic prismatic crystals

samson post *n, often cap S* [after *Samson*, judge of Israel; prob. fr. his pulling down the pillars of the palace of the Philistines, Judg 16:25–30] **1 a** : a post resting on the keelson and supporting a deck beam of a ship **b** : a post for use in securing a cable (as the anchor cable) **c** : KING POST **2 2** : an upright post that supports the walking beam in an oil derrick **3** : a heavy timber with a chain and hook used for moving logs

samum *var of* SIMOOM

sa·mu·rai \ˈsam(y)ə,rī, ˈsämə-, ,==ˈ=\ *n, pl* **samurai** *or* **samurais** [Jap] **1 a** : a military retainer of a Japanese daimyo practicing the chivalric code of Bushido, privileged to wear two swords, and having the power of life and death over commoners **b** : the warrior aristocracy of Japan — see SHIZOKU **2** : a professional soldier ⟨used by the militarists to spread the idea of Japan as a nation of ~ —D.C.Buchanan⟩

sam·vat \ˈsəm(,)vət\ *n* -S *usu cap* [Skt *saṁvat* year, short for *saṁvatsara*, fr. *sam* together + *vatsara* year — more at SAME, WETHER] : an era of Hindu chronology used in northern India

¹san \ˈsan\ *n* -S [Gk (Doric), of Sem origin; akin to Heb *sīn* sin] : a sibilant letter of the original Greek alphabet used in numerical notation to represent the numeral 900

²san \ˈsän\ *n pl, usu cap* [Hottentot (Nama dial.)] : BUSHMEN

³san \ˈsan\ *n* -S [by shortening] : SANATORIUM

san *abbr* sanitary; sanitation

sa·n'a \(ˈ)säˈnä\ *adj, usu cap* [fr. *San'a*, city in central Yemen] : of or from San'a, the capital of Yemen : of the kind or style prevalent in San'a

sanable *adj* [L *sanabilis*, fr. *sanare* to cure + *-abilis* -able] *obs* : capable of being healed or cured : susceptible of remedy

san·ad *also* **sun·nud** \ˈsə,nəd\ *n* -S [Ar *sanad* support] **1** : an Indian government charter, warrant, diploma, patent or deed **2** : a letter having the force of an edict or ordinance in India

san an·to·ni·an \,sanən-ˈtōnēən, -nan-, -naan-\ *n* -S *cap S&A* [*San Antonio*, Texas + E *-an*] : a native or resident of San Antonio, Texas

san an·to·nio \ˌ==ˈtōnē,ō *sometimes* -ˈtōn\ *adj, usu cap S&A* [fr. *San Antonio*, city in So. central Texas] : of or from the city of San Antonio, Texas : of the kind or style prevalent in San Antonio ⟨the *San Antonio* climate⟩

san·a·tar·i·um \,sanəˈta(a)rēəm, -ˈter-, -ˈtār-\ *n, pl* **sanatariums** \-mz\ *or* **sanatar·ia** \-ēə\ [NL, alter. (influenced by *sanitarium*) of *sanatorium*] : SANATORIUM

sanation *n* -S [ME *sanacioun*, fr. L *sanation-*, *sanatio*, fr. *sanatus* (past part. of *sanare* to cure) + *-ion-*, *-io* -ion] *obs* : the act or process of healing

san·a·tive \ˈsanəd·iv\ *adj* [ME *sanatif*, fr. MF, fr. LL *sanativus*, fr. L *sanatus* (past part. of *sanare* to cure) + *-ivus* -ive] : having the power to cure or heal : BENEFICIAL, RESTORATIVE ⟨flooded with the bright ~ light of day —C.I.Glicksberg⟩ ⟨a little of the ~ calmness of conservatism —Raymond English⟩

san·a·to·ri·um \,sanəˈtōrēəm, -ˈtȯr-\ *n, pl* **sanatoriums** \-mz\ *or* **sanato·ria** \-ēə\ [NL, fr. LL, neut. of *sanatorius* sanatory] **1** : an establishment that provides therapy by physical agents (as hydrotherapy, light therapy) combined with diet, exercise, and other measures for treatment or rehabilitation **2 a** : an institution for rest and recuperation esp. for invalids and convalescents **b** : an establishment for the treatment of the sick esp. if suffering from chronic disease (as alcoholism, tuberculosis, nervous or mental disease) requiring protracted care

san·a·to·ry \ˈsanə,tōrē\ *adj* [LL *sanatorius*, fr. L *sanatus* (past part. of *sanare* to cure, fr. *sanus* healthy) + *-orius* -ory] : conducive to health : tending to cure : CURATIVE ⟨~ mineral baths at a spa⟩

san·be·ni·to \,sanbəˈnēd·(,)ō\ *n* -S [Sp *sambenito*, fr. *San Benito* St. Benedict †*ab*543 founder of monasticism in western Europe; fr. its resemblance to the scapular believed to have been introduced by St. Benedict] **1** : a sackcloth coat worn by penitents on being reconciled to the church **2** : a Spanish Inquisition garment resembling a scapular and either of yellow with red crosses for the penitent or of black with painted devils and flames for the impenitent condemned to an auto-da-fé

san blas \sanˈblas\ *n, pl* **san blas** *usu cap S&B* [fr. *San Blas* islands, archipelago off the north coast of Panama] **1 a** : a Cunan people of the islands off the north coast of Panama **b** : a member of such people **2** : a Chibchan language of the San Blas people

san·born·ite \ˈsanbə(r),nīt\ *n* -S [Frank *Sanborn* †1945 Am. mineralogist + E *-ite*] : a mineral $BaSi_2O_5$ consisting of a rare triclinic barium silicate

san car·los \sanˈkär,lōs\ *n, pl* **san carlos** *usu cap S&C* [fr. *San Carlos* Reservation, eastern Arizona] **1 a** (1) : a subdivision of the Apache including the Cibecue, the Tonto, and the White Mountain Apaches (2) : a group of Apache bands including the Pinal **b** : a member of such subdivision or group **2** : the language of the San Carlos people

¹san·cho \ˈsaŋ(,)kō\ *n* -S [of African origin; akin to Ewe *sa*ˈ*ngku*³ stringed instrument, guitar, Twi *ō*ˈ*sā*ˈ*ngkū*³ guitar] : a primitive guitar with fiber strings played by both West African and American negroes

²san·cho \ˈsan(,)chō\ *n* -S [Sp *Sancho*, proper name] : the nine of trumps in sancho pedro

san·cho pan·za \ˌsan(,)chōˈpanzə, ˌsän . . . ˈpänzə\ *n, usu cap S&P* [fr. *Sancho Panza*, commonsensical peasant squire of Don Quixote in the satiric novel *Don Quixote de la Mancha* (1605, 1615) by Miguel de Cervantes Saavedra †1616 Span. novelist] : one that occupies a position analogous to the squire of Don Quixote ⟨his realistic colleagues, the *Sancho Panzas* of jurisprudence —M.R.Cohen⟩

sancho pedro *n* : pedro in which the 9 and 5 of trumps are counted at face value and the 10 of trumps counts game — called also *pedro sancho*

san·cord \ˈsan,kȯrd\ *n* -S [Afrik] : a small reddish deep-sea scorpaenid fish (*Helicolenus maculatus*) of southern Africa

sancta *pl of* SANCTUM

sanc·ti·fi·ca·tion \,saŋ(k)təfəˈkāshən, ,saiŋ-\ *n* -S [LL *sanctification-*, *sanctificatio*, fr. *sanctificatus* (past part. of *sanctificare* to make holy) + *-ion-*, *-io* -ion] **1 a** : an act of sanctifying or of being sanctified; *specif* : an act or process of growth in God's grace by which men are set free from the bondage of sin and exalted to a supreme love of God and service to his Kingdom under the inspiration of the Holy Spirit **b** : the state of thus being purified : HOLINESS **2** : development of or increasing adherence to a body of normative rules and standards — contrasted with *secularization*

sanc·ti·fied \ˈsaŋ(k)tə,fīd, ˈsaiŋ-\ *adj* [ME, fr. past part. of *sanctifien* to sanctify] **1 a** : made holy : made free of sin or free from the bondage of sin **b** : set apart to sacred duty or use **2** : made to have the air of sanctity : SANCTIMONIOUS

sanc·ti·fi·er \-ī(ə)r, -īə\ *n* -S [*sanctify* + *-er*] **1** : one that sanctifies **2** : HOLY SPIRIT

sanc·ti·fy \-,fī\ *vt* -ED/-ING/-ES [ME *sanctifien*, *seintifien*, fr. MF *sanctifier*, *saintifier*, fr. LL *sanctificare*, fr. L *sanctus* holy + *-ficare* -fy — more at SAINT] **1** : to make sacred or holy : set apart to a sacred purpose or to religious use : CONSECRATE, HALLOW ⟨God blessed the seventh day and *sanctified* it —Gen 2:3 (AV)⟩ **2** : to make free from sin : cleanse from moral corruption and pollution : PURIFY **3** : to impart or impute sacredness, inviolability, title to reverence, venerability, or respect to : give sanction to ⟨what mankind has *sanctified* with usage —R.M.Weaver⟩ **4** : to make efficient as the means of holiness : make productive of holiness or piety ⟨observe the day of the sabbath, to ~ it —Deut 5:12 (DV)⟩

sanc·ti·mo·ni·al \,saŋ(k)təˈmōnēəl\ *n* -S [LL *sanctimonialis*, fr. *sanctimonialis* holy, pious, fr. L *sanctimonia* sanctimony + *-alis* -al] : NUN

sanc·ti·mo·ni·ous \ˌsaŋ(k)təˈmōnēəs, ˈsaiŋ-, -nyəs\ *adj* [L *sanctimonia* sanctimony + E *-ous*] **1** : affecting piousness : hypocritically devout : displaying high-mindedness with intent to impress ⟨easy to be ~ about loyalty —C.P.Curtis⟩ ⟨a woman who was religious without being ~ —G.S.Stokes⟩ **2** *archaic* : possessing sanctity : HOLY, SACRED **syn** see DEVOUT

sanc·ti·mo·ni·ous·ly *adv* : in a sanctimonious manner ⟨~ criticizing the situation —Chester Bowles⟩

sanc·ti·mo·ni·ous·ness *n* -ES : the quality or state of being sanctimonious ⟨the almost reek of ~ —Kenneth Roberts⟩

sanc·ti·mo·ny \ˈsaŋ(k)tə,mōnē, ˈsaiŋ-, -ni\ *n* -ES [MF *sanctimonie*, fr. L *sanctimonia*, fr. *sanctus* holy] **1** *obs* : devoutness of intent : HOLINESS **2** *obs* : SACREDNESS **3** : outward or artificial saintliness : assumed or pretended holiness : hypocritical devoutness ⟨its religiousness is . . . free of pomp and ~ —*Time*⟩

¹sanc·tion \ˈsaŋ(k)shən, ˈsaiŋ-\ *n* -S [MF or L; MF *sanction*, fr. L *sanction-*, *sanctio*, fr. *sanctus* (past part. of *sancire* to decree, make sacred) + *-ion-*, *-io* -ion — more at SACRED] **1** : a formal decree; *esp* **:** an ecclesiastical decree **2 a** *obs* **:** a solemn agreement **:** OATH **b :** something that makes an oath binding ⟨the solemnity of the administration of the oath with its august ~*s* —L.P.Stryker⟩ **3 :** the detriment, loss of reward, or other coercive intervention that is annexed to a violation of a law as a means of enforcing the law and may consist in the direct infliction of injury or inconvenience (as in the punishments of crime) or in mere coercion, restitution, or undoing of what was wrongly accomplished (as in the judgments of civil actions) or may take the form of a reward which is withheld for failure to comply with the law **4 :** solemn or ceremonious ratification or acceptance ⟨must be divine ~ for all human laws —V.L.Parrington⟩ **5 :** a consideration, principle, or influence (as the findings of conscience or the principle of the golden rule or the goal of perfection) that impels to moral action or determines the moral judgment as valid ⟨the ~ that a religion can add to social ethics —Alfred Cobban⟩ ⟨poetry is one of the ~*s* of life —S.F.Morse⟩ **6 a :** explicit permission or recognition by one in authority that gives validity to the act of another person or body ⟨functioning under the ~ of the state —W.A.Robinson⟩ ⟨so firmly established as not to need the ~ of formal statute —F.B.Simkins⟩ ⟨received his father's ~ and authority —George Meredith⟩ **b :** encouragement or approbation given usu. by an authoritative person, by custom, or by tradition ⟨not as yet received the ~ of tradition —J.L.Lowes⟩ ⟨allows them to become accessories to any crime that has social ~ —Anthony West⟩ **7 :** something that authorizes, confirms, or countenances ⟨their chief ~ was his personal prestige —John Buchan⟩ **8 :** a coercive measure adopted usu. by several nations in concert for forcing a nation violating international law to desist or yield to adjudication esp. by withholding loans or limiting trade relations or by military force or blockade **9 :** a mechanism of social control that punishes deviancy from or rewards conformance to the normative standards of behavior existing in a society ⟨in some societies shame and ridicule may operate as the principal ~⟩ ⟨lives in a world . . . with inescapable pressures in the form of ~*s* —T.D.McCown⟩ **10 :** a restrictive measure used to punish a specific action or to prevent some future activity ⟨establishing ~*s* against the violators of labor legislation —*Current Biog.*⟩

2sanction \"\ *vb* **sanctioned; sanctioned; sanctioning** \-sh(ə)niŋ\ **sanctions** *vt* **1 :** to make valid or binding **:** ratify, confirm, or put into effect typically by decree, fiat, or other formal procedure ⟨the fact . . . would not justify this court in ~*ing* an error —R.B.Taney⟩ ⟨the vicar became reasonable and ~*ed* the marriages —*Amer. Guide Series: Ariz.*⟩ **2 :** to establish, maintain, encourage, or permit usu. by some authoritative approval or consent ⟨~*ed* by his job to drive . . . constantly in an automobile —Bernard De Voto⟩ ⟨use words ~*ed* by long tradition —John Dewey⟩ **3 :** to annex a sanction or penalty to the violation of (as a right, obligation, or command) **4 :** to define as original and fundamental law antecedent to any possible violation, penalty, or sanction — used chiefly in the phrase *sanctioned rights* ~ *vi* **:** to arise as a preventive of violation of a sanctioned right or obligation — used chiefly in the phrase *sanctioning rights* **syn** see APPROVE

sanc·tion·ative \-shə,nād·iv, -,nəd·-\ *adj* [1*sanction* + *-ative*] **:** involving or implying sanction **:** serving or tending to sanction ⟨the functions of the guardian were either administrative or ~ —Edward Poste⟩

sanc·tion·er \-sh(ə)nə(r)\ *n* -s **:** one that sanctions

sanc·ti·tude \'saŋ(k)tə,tüd\ *n* -s [ME *sanctitud*, fr. L *sanctitudo*, fr. *sanctus* holy + *-i-* + *-tudo* -tude] **:** pure and saintly character **:** HOLINESS, SACREDNESS

sanc·ti·ty \'saŋ(k)təd·ē, 'saiŋ-, -ətē, -i\ *n* -ES [ME *saunctite*, *sauntite*, fr. MF *saincteté*, *saintité*, fr. L *sanctitat-*, *sanctitas*, fr. *sanctus* holy + *-itat-*, *-itas* -ity — more at SAINT] **1 a :** holiness of life and character **:** SAINTLINESS, GODLINESS **b sanctities** *pl* **:** sacred excellences or principles ⟨no pretense of *sanctities*⟩ ⟨with no regard for rules or *sanctities* —*Christian Century*⟩ **2 a :** the quality or state of being holy or sacred **:** a religious binding force **:** INVIOLABILITY, SACREDNESS ⟨things whose ~ it would be insane even to question —T.O.Heggen⟩ ⟨the problem of ~ of boundaries —P.C.Nash⟩ **b sanctities** *pl* **:** sacred objects, obligations, or rights

sanc·to·ral \'saŋ(k)tərəl\ *adj* [ML *sanctorale*] **:** of or relating to the sanctorale

sanc·to·ra·le \,saŋ(k)tə'rālē\ *n* -s [ML, fr. neut. of ML *sanctoralis* of saints, fr. *sanctor-* (fr. LL *sanctus* saint, fr. L, holy) + L *-alis* -al] **:** the part of the breviary and missal that contains the offices proper to the saints' days — compare *temporale*

sanc·to·ri·um \,saŋ(k)'tōrēəm\ *n* -s [NL, fr. LL *sanctus* saint + L *-orium* -ory] **:** SHRINE

sanc·tu·ar·ied \'saŋ(k)chə,werēd\ *adj* **:** having or furnishing a sanctuary

sanc·tu·a·rize \'saŋ(k)chəwə,rīz\ *vt* -ED/-ING/-S [1*sanctuary* + *-ize*] **:** to shelter by a sanctuary or sacred privileges ⟨no place indeed should murther ~; revenge should have no bounds —Shak.⟩

1sanc·tu·ary \'saŋ(k)chə,werē, 'saiŋ-, -'ri\ *n* -ES [ME *sanctuarie*, *seintuarie*, fr. MF *sainctuarie*, *saintuarie*, fr. LL *sanctuarium*, fr. L *sanctus* holy + *-arium* -ary] **1 a :** a consecrated place **:** one devoted to the keeping of sacred things: as (1) **:** the temple at Jerusalem or the most retired part of it, in which was kept the ark of the covenant and into which no person was permitted to enter except the high priest and he only once a year to intercede for the people; *also* **:** the most sacred part of the tabernacle — compare HOLY OF HOLIES (2) **:** the most sacred part of any religious building **:** the part of a Christian church in which the altar is placed or the room in which general worship services are held (3) **:** a house consecrated to the worship of God **:** a church, temple, or other building for worship (4) **:** a place consecrated to some god esp. by the ancient Greeks and Romans that might be open (as in a grove) or enclosed and often built around an enclosure containing a temple, shrines, and a theater **b** *obs* **:** HEAVEN **c :** something resembling a sanctuary **:** a place held to be sacrosanct ⟨I hold a ~ in their hearts — Charles Dickens⟩ ⟨this ~ where scrap gold and silver are melted —*Amer. Guide Series: N. Y. City*⟩ **2 a :** a sacred and inviolable asylum; a place of refuge and protection **b :** immunity from law by entering such a place **c :** the right or privilege of conferring such immunity ⟨the ancient privilege of ~ was transferred to the Christian temples —Edward Gibbon⟩ **3 :** a place of resort for those who seek relief **:** a refuge from turmoil and strife **:** HAVEN ⟨her bedroom, that ~ whither she could take refuge in tears —J.C. Snaith⟩ ⟨his quest is the . . . ~ from the modern world —F.R. Leavis⟩ **4 :** a place of refuge for birds or for game or other animals where predatory animals may be controlled and hunting is not allowed — compare PRESERVE 3

2sanctuary \"\ *vt* -ED/-ING/-ES **:** SANCTUARIZE

sanctuary ring *or* **sanctuary knocker** *n* **:** a ring on a church door, ensuring sanctuary to any laying hold of it

sanc·tum \'saŋ(k)təm, 'saiŋ-\ *n, pl* **sanctums** \-mz\ *also* **sanc·ta** \-tə\ [L, neut. of *sanctus* holy] **1 a :** a sacred place **b :** an object of religious regard **:** something hallowed — often used in pl. **2 :** a study, office, or place of retreat where one is free from intrusion ⟨an editor's ~⟩

sanctum sanc·to·rum \-saŋ(k)'tōrəm, -saiŋ-, -'tȯr-\ *n* [LL, trans. of Gk *to hagion tōn hagiōn*, trans. of Heb *qōdhesh haqqōdhāshīm*] **1 :** the most holy place **:** HOLY OF HOLIES **2 :** SANCTUM 2

sanc·tus \'saŋ(k)təs, 'saiŋ-, 'säŋ-\ *n* -ES *often cap* [ME, fr. ML, first word of the conclusion of the eucharistic preface, fr. LL *Sanctus, sanctus, sanctus* Holy, holy, holy, opening of a hymn sung by the angels in Isa 6:3, trans. of Gk *hagios, hagios, hagios*, trans. of Heb *qādhōsh, qādhōsh, qādhōsh*] **:** the last part of the preface of most Christian liturgies commencing with the words *Sanctus, Sanctus, Sanctus* or *Holy, Holy, Holy* — called also *tersanctus*

sanctus bell *n, usu cap S* [ME] **:** a bell rung at the Sanctus in a highly liturgical church service

1sand \'sand, 'saa(ə)nd\ *n* -s [ME *sond*, *sand*, fr. OE; akin to OHG *sant* sand, ON *sandr*, L *sabulum*, Gk *psammos* sand, *psēphos* pebble, *psēn* to rub, Skt *babhasti* he chews] **1 a** (1) **:** a loose material consisting of small but easily distinguishable grains usu. less than two millimeters in diameter, most commonly of quartz resulting from the disintegration of rocks, and commonly used for making mortar and glass, as an abrasive, or for molds in founding (2) **:** a mass of this material esp. on a beach or a desert **b :** a most unstable material or medium that will make futile all effort or endeavor ⟨be like a foolish man who built his house upon the ~ —Mt 7:26 (RSV)⟩ **2 a :** a tract, region, or deposit of sand **:** BEACH, SHORE — often used in pl. ⟨we shall fight them on the ~*s* —Sir Winston Churchill⟩ **b :** a sand bank or sand bar — often used in pl. **c :** a grain of sand — often used in pl. **d :** sandy soil — often used in pl. **3 a :** the sand in an hourglass; *also* **:** a grain of it **b** (1) **:** a moment or interval of time (2) **:** the moments of an existence or a life — usu. used in pl. ⟨the ~*s* of this government run out very rapidly —H.J.Laski⟩ **4 :** a sandstone or unconsolidated sand formation containing oil **:** an oil-producing formation ⟨can produce oil from one ~ and gas from another in the same well —W.F.Cloud⟩ **5 :** firm resolution **:** COURAGE, STAMINA ⟨hasn't got ~ enough to talk back to her⟩ **6 :** a variable color averaging a yellowish gray that is darker and slightly greener and stronger than average natural and redder and deeper than ivory tint **7 :** gritty particles in various body tissues or fluids — compare BRAIN SAND **8 :** tailings esp. from a cyanide mill or stamp mill **9 :** a circular footscraping used as a jazz dance step ⟨doing a slow ~ on the uncarpeted section of the floor —Eugene Brown⟩ **syn** see FORTITUDE

2sand \"\ *vt* -ED/-ING/-S [ME *sanden*, fr. *sand*, n.] **1 :** to sprinkle or powder with or as if with sand ⟨~*ed* the ink to dry it and sealed the letter⟩ ⟨100 miles of public road will remain to be plowed and ~*ed* —David Anderson⟩ ⟨a clear night ~*ed* with stars —R.H.Newman⟩ **2 :** to cover with sand: as **a :** to fill (as harbors) with sand esp. by the action of currents **b :** to treat (as clay soil) with an overspread layer of sand **3 :** to adulterate with sand for purposes of fraud **4 :** to smooth by grinding or rubbing with an abrasive; *specif* **:** to rub or polish with sandpaper ⟨the stain . . . will have to be ~*ed* out —Erle Stanley Gardner⟩

1san·dal \'sandᵊl, 'saan-\ *n* -s [ME *sandalie*, fr. L *sandalium* (pl. *sandalia*), fr. Gk *sandalion* little sandal, dim. of *sandalon* sandal] **1 :** a shoe consisting essentially of a sole fastened to the foot by means of straps or thongs passing over the instep and around the ankle **2 :** a low-cut shoe that is usu. fastened to the foot by means of an ankle strap and has openwork in the upper **3 :** a strap or latchet to hold on a slipper or low shoe by passing across the foot or around the ankle **4 :** a rubber overshoe cut very low either with an entire sole and a strip across the instep or with a sole for the fore part of the foot and a strip back of the heel — compare TOE RUBBER

2sandal \"\ *vt* **sandaled** *or* **sandalled; sandaled** *or* **sandalled; sandaling** \-d(ᵊ)liŋ\ **sandals 1 :** to provide with sandals **:** put sandals on **2 :** to fasten with a sandal

3sandal \"\ *n* -s [ME, fr. MF, fr. ML *sandalum*, *santalum*, fr. LGk *santalon*, *sandanon*, fr. or akin to Skt *candana* sandalwood, of Dravidian origin; akin to Tamil *cāntu* sandal tree] **:** SANDALWOOD 1a

4sandal \"\ *n* -s [Ar *ṣandal*, fr. Per *sandal* skiff] **:** a narrow two-masted boat used on the Barbary coast and on the Nile

sandal brick *n* **:** PLACE BRICK

sandaled *or* **sandalled** *adj* **:** wearing sandals ⟨the measured footfalls of his ~ feet —H.W.Longfellow⟩ ⟨went ~ or even barefoot —David Garnett⟩

sandaling *n* -s [fr. gerund of 2*sandal*] **:** material woven in elastic strips for sandals

sandal tree *also* **sandal** *n* -s [3*sandal*] **1 :** SANTOL **2 :** SANDALWOOD 1a

sandalwood \'⸗,⸗\ *n* [3*sandal* + *wood*] **1 a** (1) **:** a compact close-grained fragrant yellowish wood that is the heartwood of an Indo-Malayan parasitic tree, has insect repelling properties, and is much used for ornamental carving and cabinetwork and esp. for chests and other containers (2) **:** the tree (*Santalum album*) that produces sandalwood **b** (1) **:** any of several other trees of the genus *Santalum* or family Santalaceae (as the Polynesian *S. freycetiarum*, the Hawaiian *S. pyrularium*, or the Australian *Eucarya spicata* and *Exocarpus latifolia*) that have wood similar to or similarly used to the true sandalwood — usu. used with a qualifying term; see SCRUB SANDALWOOD (2) **:** the wood of a tree resembling true sandalwood **2 a :** any of various trees of families other than Santalaceae with usu. fragrant wood that is felt to resemble the true sandalwood: as (1) **:** FALSE SANDALWOOD 1 (2) **:** BASTARD SANDALWOOD 2a(1) (3) **:** PINK MAHOGANY (4) **:** MAIRE a (5) **:** a Russian buckthorn (*Rhamnus dahuriea*) whose wood yields a dye for leather (6) **:** SCENTWOOD **b :** the wood of such a tree; *also* **:** RED SANDALWOOD 1 **3 :** a moderate brown that is lighter and slightly stronger than chestnut brown, yellower, lighter, and less strong than bay, yellower and lighter than auburn, and yellower, less strong, and slightly lighter than toast brown

sandalwood english *n, usu cap S&E* **:** an English-based pidgin language used in the Pacific islands

sandalwood family *n* **:** SANTALACEAE

sandalwood oil *n* **1 :** an essential oil obtained from sandalwood: as **a :** a pale yellow somewhat viscous aromatic liquid obtained from the sandalwood (*Santalum album*) usu. from Mysore, India, and used chiefly in perfumes and soaps and esp. formerly in medicine — called also *East Indian sandalwood oil, santal oil* **b :** a similar oil obtained from a sandalwood (*Eucarya spicata*) in Western Australia — called also *Australian sandalwood oil* **2 :** AMYRIS OIL

san·dan \'sandən\ *n* -s [Nepali *sādan*] **:** an East Indian timber tree (*Ougeinia dalbergioides*) of the family Leguminosae, having hard wood, yielding a valuable red gum, and having bark that is used in various native remedies

san·da·rac *also* **san·da·rach** \'sandə,rak\ *n* -s [L *sandaraca*, *sandaracha* red coloring matter, beebread, fr. Gk *sandarakē*, *sandarachē* realgar, red pigment derived from realgar, beebread; prob. akin to Skt *candana* sandalwood — more at SANDAL] **1 :** REALGAR **2 :** SANDARAC TREE 1 **3 a :** a brittle faintly aromatic translucent resin obtained esp. from the African sandarac tree usu. in the form of small pale yellow dusty tears and used chiefly in making varnish and as incense — compare 6POUNCE 1 **b :** a similar resin from Australian cypress pines

sandarac tree *n* **1 :** a large cypress pine (*Callitris articulata*) of northern Africa that yields a hard durable fragrant wood much used in building (as in the roof of Cordova Cathedral) — see SANDARAC 3, THYINE WOOD **2 :** an Australian cypress pine that yields sandarac

san·da·we \sän'dä(,)we\ *n, pl* **sandawe** *or* **sandawes** *usu cap* **1 a :** a Negro African people of Tanganyika **b :** a member of such people **2 :** the language of the Sandawe people related to Khoisan

sand badger *n* **1** *or* **sand bear :** HOG-NOSED BADGER **2 :** a Japanese badger (*Meles anakuma*)

1sandbag \'⸗,⸗\ *n* [1*sand* + *bag*] **:** a bag filled with sand: as **a :** one used in a pile to form a wall, a revetment, a field fortification, or as a protection for buildings **b :** one used as a weapon swinging at the end of a staff or beam of a quintain or only partially filled for use as a club **c :** one used as ballast in boats and aircraft **d :** one used as a cover for a crevice to exclude drafts **e :** one used to prop a patient in position (as in bed or on an operating table)

2sandbag \"\ *vt* **1 :** to bank, stop up, or weight with sandbags ⟨workers were hurriedly building and *sandbagging* new bomb shelters —*N.Y. Times*⟩ **2 a :** to hit or stun with a sandbag **b :** to coerce by crude means ⟨was really too young to come out but . . . had *sandbagged* her family into it —Al Hine⟩ **3 :** to trap (another poker player) by checking a strong hand and then raising if he bets ~ *vi* **:** to check with a strong hand in a game of poker with intent to raise the ante if another player bets

sand·bag·ger \"+ə(r)\ *n* [*sandbag* + *-er*] **1 a :** one who uses a sandbag; *esp* **:** a robber who stuns his victim with a sandbag **b :** one who uses tactics resembling those of a sandbagger ⟨been one of the best . . . ~*s*, persuading employers to come through with jobs —C.H.Upton⟩ **2 :** a light-draft sailboat with sandbags for ballast **3 :** one that sandbags in poker

sandbank \'⸗,⸗\ *n* [1*sand* + *bank*] **:** a large deposit of sand in a mound, hillside, bar, or shoal

sandbar \'⸗,⸗\ *n* [1*sand* + *bar*] **:** a bar or ridge of sand built up to or near to the surface by currents in a river or in coastal waters

sandbar willow *n* **:** any of various willows that flourish along streams or on alluvial land: as **a :** a much-branched chiefly eastern No. American shrubby willow (*Salix interior*) with lanceolate leaves that are silky when young **b :** a shrubby chiefly western No. American willow (*Salix exigua*) having leaves permanently silky but otherwise resembling the eastern sandbar willow

sand bass *n* **1 a :** a California sea bass (*Paralabrax nebulifer*) that is greenish above and silvery below **b :** KELP BASS **2 a :** GREEN SUNFISH **b :** WHITE BASS 1

sand bath *n* [1*sand* + *bath*] **1 :** a bath of sand in which laboratory vessels to be heated are partly immersed **2 :** a shallow or deep pan usu. of iron for holding the sand

sandbeach grape \'⸗,⸗-\ *n* [*sandbeach* fr. 1*sand* + *beach*] **:** SAND GRAPE

sand bellows *n pl but sing in constr* **:** a blower for sanding surfaces

sand belt *n* **:** a belt surfaced with an abrasive usu. for grinding or polishing

sand–belt machine *n* **:** BELT SANDER

sand·berg bluegrass \'san(d),bərg-\ *n, usu cap S* [after J. H. *Sandberg*, 19th cent. Am. botanist] **:** a densely tufted bluegrass (*Poa secunda*) of No. America esp. of the Northwestern U. S. having slender culms, usu. folded leaf blades, and somewhat appressed branches

sand binder *n* **:** a grass or other plant that grows in sand which it holds in place by its rootstocks and roots

sand bird *n* **:** a shore bird

sand blackberry *n* **:** a stiff thorny blackberry (*Rubus cuneifolius*) of the eastern U. S. having leaves white-tomentose beneath and sweet fruit

1sandblast \'⸗,⸗\ *n* [1*sand* + *blast*] **1 a :** a stream of sand forcibly projected by air or steam usu. for engraving, cutting, or cleaning glass, stone, or other hard materials, for cleaning and sharpening files, or for removing scale from metals **b :** the apparatus used to apply it **2 :** a gust of wind carrying sand **3 :** an irresistible destructive action suggestive of a blast of sand ⟨against ~ of time and spoliation of man —Robert Bridges †1930⟩

2sandblast \"\ *vt* **:** to engrave, cut, or clean with a high⸗velocity stream of sand

sand·blast·er \"+ə(r)\ *n* [*sandblast* + *-er*] **:** one that sandblasts: as **a :** one that cleans objects of metal or similar material with an abrasive blast **b :** one that cleans stone, brick, or metal structures with a spray of sand **c :** one that guided by a stencil cuts lettering and designs on stone monuments or buildings with a blast of sand or shot — called also *blastman* **d :** one that frosts panes of glass by sandblasting one side **e :** one that sandblasts designs onto glass articles (as vases)

sand–blight *n, Austral* **:** BLIGHT 5

sand–blind \'⸗,⸗\ *adj* [ME, prob. by folk etymology fr. (assumed) *samblind*, fr. OE *sam-* half + *blind* — more at SAM-, BLIND] **:** having poor eyesight **:** PURBLIND ⟨are they lazy or *sand-blind* from their own investigations —*Saturday Rev.*⟩ — compare GRAVEL-BLIND

sand block *n* **:** a block to which sandpaper is attached

sandblow \'⸗,⸗\ *n* [1*sand* + *blow*] **:** an area of coarse sandy soil denuded of vegetation by wind action

sand blower *n* **:** SAND BELLOWS

sand bluestem *n* **:** a tall American grass (*Andropogon hallii*) used for forage and in soil conservation having creeping rhizomes and racemes of flowers that are conspicuously villous with grayish to pale golden hairs

sand boa *n* **:** any of various small burrowing boas (genera *Eryx* or *Gongylophis*) of the sandy regions of Africa and Asia having rough keeled scales and a very blunt tail

sandboard \'⸗,⸗\ *n* [1*sand* + *board*] **:** the board that runs over and parallel with the axle of a wagon with the ends resting upon the hounds

sand bobber *n* **:** one who smooths and polishes silverware or jewelry by means of pumice and oil and a leather buffing wheel

sand boil *n* **:** a bubbling spring sometimes several feet in diameter that bursts through the ground at the back of a river levee and is caused by the water in the river at flood stages being forced under the levee through a pervious stratum of sand or silt

sand borer *n* **1 :** a common small Australian anomuran crustacean (*Upogebia simsoni*) that burrows in sandy beaches **2 :** any of several whitings (genus *Sillago*) of the western Pacific ocean

sandbox \'⸗,⸗\ *n* [1*sand* + *box*] **1 :** a box or other receptacle containing loose sand: as **a :** a shaker for sprinkling sand upon wet ink **b :** SAND DOME **c :** a box that is large enough to sit in and contains sand for children to play in **2 :** SAND MOLD **3 a :** SANDBOX TREE **b :** its explosive pod often filled with shot and used as a paperweight

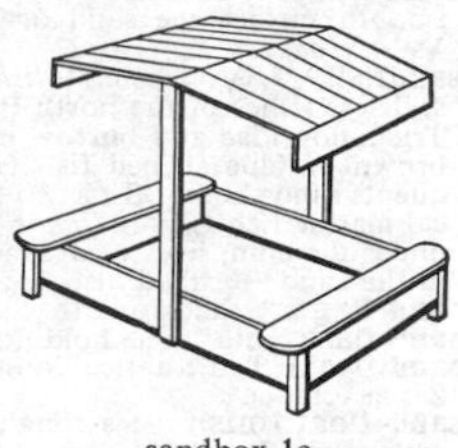
sandbox 1c

sandbox tree *n* **:** a tropical American tree (*Hura crepitans*) having a depressed many-celled woody capsule which when completely dry bursts with a loud report and scatters the seeds — compare YELLOW SANDBOX

sandboy \'⸗,⸗\ *n* [1*sand* + *boy*] **1 :** a peddler of sand at a seashore resort — used chiefly in the phrase *happy as a sandboy* **2 :** any of various hopping insects (as a sand flea) found on sandy beaches **3 a :** one who sprinkles sand on bricks to prevent their sticking together in the kiln **b :** an operator of a machine for separating floor tiles from the sand that held them in the saggers

sand brier *n* **:** HORSE NETTLE

sand bug *n* **:** a common bait bug (*Emerita talpoida*)

sandbur *also* **sandburr** \'⸗,⸗\ *n* [1*sand* + *bur*, *burr*] **:** any of several weeds growing in waste places and having burry fruit: as **a :** BUFFALO BUR **b :** an annual bristly herb (*Franseria acanthicarpa*) of western No. America related to the cocklebur **c** *also* **sandbur grass :** BUR GRASS

sand–burned \'⸗,⸗\ *adj* **:** having a hard skin due to the silica of sand combining with the surface of metal when metal is poured into a mold at too high a temperature — used of a casting

S and C *abbr* **1** shipper and carrier **2** sized and calendered

sand–calcite \'⸗,⸗\ *n* **:** a calcite crystal containing a large proportion of sand grains as inclusions

1sand–cast \'⸗;⸗\ *adj* **:** cast in a mold made of sand

2sand–cast \"\ *vt* **:** to make (a casting) by pouring metal in a sand mold (as in ordinary founding)

sand casting *n* **:** a casting made in a mold of sand

sand cat *n* **:** a desert-dwelling wildcat

sand cay *n* **:** a small sandy island that is not elongate and is parallel with the shore

sand cherry *n* **:** any of several usu. small straggling No. American cherries that grow esp. on dry sandy land: as **a :** a low-growing cherry (*Prunus pumila*) of the northern U. S. and Canada with minute scarcely edible shiny purplish black fruit **b :** a small strongly rooted shrub (*P. cuneata* or *P. susquehanae*) of eastern No. America **c :** WESTERN SAND CHERRY

sand clam *n* **:** SOFT-SHELL CLAM

sand clock *n* **:** SANDGLASS

sand cock *n, Brit* **:** REDSHANK

sand colic *also* **sand disease** *n* **:** distention with resulting catarrh of the stomach and small intestines in horses and cattle caused by the ingestion of sand with feed and water

sand collar *n* **:** the mass of eggs embedded in sand and jellylike matter that is produced by a moon shell and is shaped like a thin collar or bottomless saucer open at one side

sand column *n* **:** DUST DEVIL

sand cone *n* **1 :** a low pinnacle of ice on a glacier protected from melting by a veneer of sand **2 :** a cone-shaped mass of sandy debris deposited esp. in an alluvial cone

sand crab *n* **1 a** (1) **:** LADY CRAB 1 (2) **:** an Australian swimming crab (*Ovalipes bipustulatus*) **b :** a crab of *Ocypode* or a related genus **2 :** BAIT BUG
sand crack *n* **:** a fissure or lesion in the hoof wall of a horse often causing lameness — see QUARTER CRACK, TOE CRACK
sand crater *n* **:** an opening in the earth from which sand and water are erupted during an earthquake
sand cricket *n* **:** any of several large clumsy terrestrial grasshoppers of the genus *Stenopelmatus* (family Stenopelmatidae) that resemble crickets and are found in sandy plains of the western U. S.
sand crystal *n* **:** a large calcite crystal found in sandstone and loaded with inclusions of detrital sand
sandculture \'⸗,⸗⸗\ *n* [¹*sand* + *culture*] **:** hydroponics in which the roots of plants are established in sand
sand cusk *n* **:** CUSK EEL
sand dab *n* **:** any of several flatfishes: as **a :** RUSTY DAB **b :** a fish of the genus *Citharichthys* (family Bothidae) of the Pacific coast of No. America including several small but excellent food fishes
sand darter *n* **:** DARTER; *esp* **:** a small translucent fish (*Ammocrypta beanii*) of the Gulf states
sand dollar *n* **1 :** any of numerous flat circular sea urchins of the order Exocycloida which live on sandy bottoms (as *Echinarachnius parma* of the American coast) **2 :** STAR CACTUS
sand dome *n* **:** the sandbox of a locomotive whose contents are used for sanding the rails to give added friction to the wheels
sand drift *n* **:** an accumulation of sand that drifts down wind in the lee of some obstruction and is usu. smaller than a dune
sand dropseed *n* **:** an erect smooth grass (*Sporobolus cryptandrus*) found in sandy places in eastern No. America
sand drown *n* [so called fr. its occurrence on sandy soils subject to leaching in heavy rainfall areas] **:** a magnesium deficiency disease of tobacco characterized by chlorosis
sand dune *n* **1 :** DUNE 1 **2 :** DRAB 2a
san·de \'sän(,)dā\ *n* -S *usu cap* [Mende *sāne*¹] **:** a Liberia and Sierra Leone secret custom by which young girls are secluded in a separate camp for a variable period of months and trained in the duties and responsibilities of adult society
sanded *adj* [fr. past part. of ²*sand*] **1** *obs* **:** having a sand color **2 a :** formed or composed of sand **:** SANDY ⟨the ~ plains —George Farwell⟩ **b :** sprinkled with sand **3 :** rolled in granulated sugar ⟨~ gumdrops⟩
sanded plaster *n* **:** plaster to which properly graded sand is added at the mill
sand eel *n* **1 :** SAND LAUNCE **2 :** a slender soft-finned fish (*Gonorhynchus gonorhynchus* or *G. grayi*) of the Indo-Pacific having small spiny scales, a single barbel in the produced snout, and the eyes beneath the skin
san·dek \'sän,dek\ *or* **san·dik** \-dēk\ *n* -S [Yiddish *sandik*, fr. LHeb *sandiqōs, sindiqās*, prob. modif. of LGk *synteknos* godfather, fr. Gk, foster brother, fr. *synteknoun* to breed, bring up children together, fr. *syn-* + *teknon* child — more at THANE] **:** a person who holds the Jewish infant on his knees during the circumcision ceremony
san·de·ma·ni·an \,sandə'mānēən\ *n* -S *usu cap* [Robert *Sandeman* †1771 Scot. religious leader + E *-an*] **:** GLASSITE
sand·er \'sandə(r), 'saan-\ *n* -S [²*sand* + *-er*] **:** one that sands: as **a :** a device on a locomotive or electric car operated by a steam or air blast for sanding the rails to give added friction to the driving wheels **b :** SAND BELLOWS **c :** a sand spreader for asphalted or icy roads **d :** SANDING MACHINE **e :** one that by hand or by machine sands surfaces (as of wood, metal, plastic) to smooth, clean, or roughen them in preparation for finishing
sand·er·ling \'sandə(r)liŋ\ *n* -S [¹*sand* + *-erling* (as in *underling*)] **:** a small sandpiper (*Crocethia alba*) that breeds in the arctic regions and migrates south along the coasts of most parts of the world and that has largely gray and white plumage with a reddish breast as a distinction of the adult's summer plumage
san·ders \'sandə(r)z\ *or* **sanderswood** \'⸗⸗,⸗\ *n, pl* **sanderses** *or* **sanderswoods** [*sanders* alter. of earlier *saunders; sanderswood* alter. of *saunderswood* — more at SAUNDERSWOOD] **1** *obs* **:** SANDALWOOD **2 :** RED SANDALWOOD 1a
sander-up \'⸗⸗'⸗\ *n* -S **:** one who beds greenware in sand and clay for firing
san·de·ver *also* **san·di·ver** \'sandəvə(r)\ *n* -S [ME *saundiver*, prob. fr. MF *saïn de voirre* grease of glass] **:** GLASS GALL
S and FA *abbr* shipping and forwarding agent
sand-faced brick \'⸗,⸗-\ *n* **:** a face brick shaped in a mold that has been sprinkled with sand to prevent the clay from sticking to the mold
sand finish *n* **:** a finish of plastering made by rubbing to a smooth surface the sand or mortar coat — **sand-finished** \'⸗;⸗⸗\ *adj*
sandfish \'⸗,⸗\ *n* [¹*sand* + *fish*] **1 :** either of two small silvery scaleless fishes of the north Pacific that constitute the family Trichodontidae and burrow in the sand **2 :** a small grayish brown or blue striped fish (*Diplectrum formosum*) that frequents sand shores **3 :** SAND EEL 2 **4 :** an elongated cylindrical marine fish (genus *Gonorhynchus*) that has a short barbel under the chin, lives over sandy bottoms, and burrows freely in the sand — called also *beaked salmon*
sand flag *n* **:** sandstone that splits up into flagstones
sand flask *n* **:** a frame holding a sand mold
sand flea *n* **1 a :** a flea found in sandy places **b :** CHIGOE **2 :** BEACH FLEA
sand-float finish *n* **:** a rough sand finish made in plastering with a wooden float
sand flotation *n* **:** CHANCE PROCESS
sand flounder *n* **:** any of various flounders frequenting sandy bottom **:** SAND FLUKE; *esp* **:** WINDOWPANE
sand fluke *n* **:** a flounder frequenting a sandy bottom: as **a :** SMEAR DAB **b :** a small flounder (*Hippoglossoides platessoides*) common on both coasts of the north Atlantic
sand fly *n* **:** any of various small biting two-winged flies of the families Psychodidae, Simuliidae, and Ceratopogonidae; *esp* **:** a fly of the genus *Phlebotomus*
sand-fly bush *n* **:** an Australian tree (*Zieria smithii*) of the family Rutaceae that has aromatic foliage and small white flowers in loose cymes and bark which is used for tanning and dyeing
sand-fly fever *n* **:** PHLEBOTOMUS FEVER
sand food *n* **:** a low root-parasitic brownish leguminous herb (*Ammobroma sonorae*) of the Colorado desert having flowers in a saucer-shaped head, all parts but the flower head buried in the sand, and edible stems and tubers resembling sweet potatoes
sand fox *n* **:** any of several small African foxes; *esp* **:** a tawny desert-dwelling No. African fox (*Vulpes rüppelli* syn. *V. pallida*)
sand gall *n* **:** SAND PIPE
sandglass \'⸗,⸗\ *n* [¹*sand* + *glass*] **:** an instrument for measuring time by the running of sand that is similar to an hourglass ⟨three-minute ~*es* . . . to help time our breakfast eggs —A.L. Kroeber⟩
sandgoby \'⸗,⸗⸗\ *n* [¹*sand* + *goby*] **:** any of various sand-dwelling gobies; *esp* **:** a common European fish (*Gobius minutus*) with variable coloration that makes it almost invisible in the sandy tide pools which it frequents
sand grape *n* **:** a shrubby wild grape (*Vitis rupestris*) of the southeastern U. S. having sweet black fruit with or without bloom
sand grass *n* **:** a grass growing in sand: as **a :** a tufted grass (*Triplasis purpurea*) with stiff awl-shaped leaves on the Atlantic coast of the U. S. **b :** a perennial grass (*Calamovilfa longifolia*) **c :** a salt grass (*Distichlis spicata*)
sandgrouse \'⸗,⸗\ *n* [¹*sand* + *grouse*] **:** any of numerous birds constituting the family Pteroclididae, inhabiting arid parts of southern Europe, Asia, and Africa, resembling the related pigeons in structure but having precocial young that are downy and ready to run when hatched, and being strong fliers with long pointed wings and tail — see PAINTED SANDGROUSE, PALLAS'S SANDGROUSE, PIN-TAILED SANDGROUSE
S and H *abbr* Sundays and holidays
san·dhi \'sandē, 'saan-, 'sän-, -di *sometimes* 'sən-\ *n* -S [Skt *saṁdhi*, lit., placing together, fr. *sam* together + *dadhāti* he places — more at SANSKRIT, DO] **:** modification of the sound of a morpheme (as a word or affix) conditioned by the context in which it is uttered (pronunciation of *the* as \thə\ in *the cow* and as \thē\ in *the old cow*, pronunciation of *-ed* as \d\ in *glazed* and as \t\ in *paced*, occurrence of *a* in *a cow* and of *an* in *an old cow*, and occurrence of *'ll* in *he'll go* and of *will* in *he will if he can* are examples of ~) — used orig. of Sanskrit but now of any language
sand hill *n* [ME *sond hylle*, fr. OE *sondhyll*, fr. *sond* sand + *hyll* hill — more at SAND, HILL] **1 :** a natural elevation or ridge of sand **:** DUNE **2 sandhills** *pl* **:** a region of sand hills
sandhill \'⸗,⸗\ *adj* [*sand hill*] **:** of or relating to a region of sand hills ⟨certain types of pines will thrive even in the ~ areas —*Amer. Guide Series: Nebr.*⟩
sandhill crane *n* **1 :** a rare crane (*Grus canadensis*) of eastern and central No. America that is chiefly bluish gray overcast with ocherous **2 :** LITTLE BROWN CRANE
sand·hill·er \"+ə(r)\ *n* -S **:** one that lives in a sandhill region
sandhill rosemary *n* **:** a small aromatic heathlike evergreen shrub (*Ceratiola ericoides*) of the family Empetraceae with reddish whorled axillary flowers
sandhog \'⸗,⸗\ *n* [¹*sand* + *hog*] **:** a laborer who works under compressed air esp. in the driving of tunnels by the pneumatic caisson method
sand hole *n* **1 :** a small hole in a casting **2 :** a water hole in sand
sand hopper *n* **:** BEACH FLEA
¹**san·dia** \sän'dēə\ *n* -S [Sp *sandía*, fr. Ar (*baṭṭīha*) *sindīya* melon of Sind, fr. *baṭṭīha* melon + *sindīya* of Sind, fr. *Sind*, region in the northwestern part of the Indian subcontinent, fr. Hindi; akin to Skt *sindhu* river — more at INDIA] **:** WATERMELON
²**san·dia** \san'dēə, sän-\ *or* **san·di·as** \-əz\ *n, pl* **sandia** *or* **sandias** *usu cap* [fr. *Sandia*, pueblo in central New Mexico] **1 :** a Tanoan people occupying a pueblo in New Mexico **2 :** a member of the Sandia people
³**sandia** \"\ *adj, usu cap* [fr. *Sandia* mountains, east of the Rio Grande, New Mexico, where remains of this culture were found] **:** of or belonging to a pre-Folsom hunting culture in New Mexico characterized by leaf-shaped spear points longer, thicker, and heavier than Folsom points and having a side shoulder at the base as an aid in hafting
sandia man *n, usu cap S* **:** one of a western No. American prehistoric people known only from hearths, flint projectile points, and scrapers and thought to be antecedent to Folsom man
san di·e·gan \,sandē'āgən\ *n* -S *cap S&D* [*San Diego*, Calif. + E *-an*] **:** a native or resident of San Diego, California
san di·e·go \',⸗⸗;ā(,)gō\ *adj, usu cap S&D* [fr. *San Diego*, city in southwestern California] **:** of or from the city of San Diego, Calif. ⟨the *San Diego* fishing fleet⟩ **:** of the kind or style prevalent in San Diego
sandier *comparative of* SANDY
sandies *pl of* SANDY
sandiest *superlative of* SANDY
sandik *var of* SANDEK
sand-in \'⸗;⸗\ *vt* [²*sand*] **:** to use (abrasive paper) to curve the contact face of a dynamo brush to conform to the curvature of the commutator
sand·i·ness \'sandēnəs, 'saand-, -din-\ *n* -ES [¹*sandy* + *-ness*] **:** the quality or state of being sandy
sanding *n* -S [fr. gerund of ²*sand*] **1 :** a sprinkling, covering, or mixing with sand **2 :** a smoothing or polishing esp. with sandpaper **3 :** a fraudulent practice of feeding poultry with a paste of coarse sand to increase the apparent live weight
sanding disk *or* **sanding drum** *n* **:** a disk or drum with an attached abrasive for power tool application in sanding
sanding machine *n* **:** a machine provided with a moving surface coated with abrasive material
sandiver *var of* SANDEVER
san·dix *also* **san·dyx** \'sandiks\ *n* -ES [L *sandix, sandyx* vermilion, fr. Gk *sandyx*; akin to Skt *sindūra* vermilion] **:** any of various red pigments; *esp* **:** ORANGE MINERAL
¹**sand jack** *n* **:** a device consisting essentially of a sandbox and a series of plungers for gradually lowering into position a heavy weight (as a bridge section) supported by the plungers by running out the sand below
²**sand jack** *n* **:** BLUEJACK
sand jet *n* **:** SANDBLAST 1a
sandkey \'⸗,⸗\ *n* [¹*sand* + *key*] **:** SAND CAY
sand·krui·per \'san(d),krōipə(r)\ *n* -S [part trans. of Afrik *zand kruiper*, lit., sand creeper, fr. *zand* sand + *kruiper* creeper, fr. D, fr. *kruipen* to creep, fr. MD *crupen*; akin to ON *krjūpa* to creep — more at CREEP] **:** any of several small So. African viviparous rays (genus *Rhinobatus*) of sandy shallow seas that are considered excellent food fishes
sandlapper \'⸗,⸗⸗\ *n* [¹*sand* + *lapper*] **:** one living in a lowland area esp. in the southeastern U.S.
sand lark *n* **1 :** any of numerous Asiatic larks (genus *Alaudula*) having short toes **2** *Brit* **:** a small sandpiper or plover (as a ring plover, the sanderling, and the common European sandpiper) **3 :** an Australian plover (*Charadrius ruficapillus*)
sand launce *or* **sand lance** *n* **:** any of several small elongate marine teleost fishes of the genus *Ammodytes* (family Ammodytidae) that do not exceed six or eight inches in length, associate in large schools, and remain buried in sandy beaches at ebb tide
sand leaf *n* **:** a small leaf near the base of the tobacco stalk often bearing grains of sand
sand leek *n* **:** ROCAMBOLE
sand lily *n* **:** a spring herb (*Leucocrinum montanum*) native to western No. America and used as an ornamental with narrow linear leaves and fragrant salver-shaped flowers
sand-lime \'⸗;⸗\ *adj* **:** made from mixed sand and lime
sand-lime brick *n* **:** brick made of sand and lime that is pressed into molds and steamed
sand line *n* **:** the rope attached to the bailer in well drilling
sand·ling \'san(d)liŋ\ *n* -S [¹*sand* + *-ling*] **:** a small flounder **:** DAB
sand lizard *n* **1 :** a common and widely distributed European lizard (*Lacerta agilis*) **2 :** RACE RUNNER **3 :** any of several iguanid lizards (as of the genera *Callisaurus, Holbrookia,* or *Uta*) that are common in arid sandy regions
sand lob *n* **:** LUGWORM
¹**sandlot** \'⸗,⸗\ *adj* [¹*sand* + *lot*] **1 :** of or relating to a lot or piece of sandy ground esp. as the scene of unorganized sports for boys from city streets **2** [so called fr. a sandlot laid out for building on the west side of San Francisco where adherents of the movement held meetings] **:** of, relating to, or characteristic of a 19th century workingmen's movement in California opposed esp. to Chinese immigration ⟨people of the ~ type of orators . . . favor the treatment of the Chinese proposed by the legislation —T.J.Geary⟩
²**sandlot** \"\ *n* **:** a vacant lot or piece of ground esp. when used as the scene of unorganized sports for boys from city streets
sand·lot·ter \"+ə(r)\ *n* **:** one who plays on a sandlot **:** one whose training began in the sandlots or something resembling the sandlots
sand lovegrass *n* **:** a fine-stemmed bunch grass (*Eragrostis trichodes*) found native on sandy soils chiefly in the southern Great Plains area of No. America and used as a forage grass
sandman \'⸗,⸗\ *n, pl* **sandmen 1 :** the genie of folklore who makes children sleepy supposedly by sprinkling sand in their eyes **2 :** a worker who screens, mixes, or loads sand **:** one who sands surfaces with an abrasive
sand martin *n, Brit* **:** BANK SWALLOW
sand mason *n* **:** a terebellid worm (*Lanice conchilega*) that builds a dwelling tube of grains of sand
sand mat *n* **:** any of several flat spreading plants of the genus *Euphorbia* that grow in desert areas of the U.S.
sand·mey·er reaction \'san(d),mī(ə)r-\ *n, usu cap S* [after Traugott *Sandmeyer* †1922 Swiss chemist] **:** a reaction for preparing aromatic halides or cyanides from a salt with a cuprous halide or cyanide as catalyst ⟨*ortho*-bromo-toluene can be made from *ortho*-toluene-diazonium bromide by the *Sandmeyer reaction*⟩
sandmite \'⸗,⸗\ *n* [¹*sand* + *mite*] **:** a mite of the genus *Halotydeus*; *esp* **:** a mite (*H. destructor*) that is a serious pest of vegetable crops in Australia and southern Africa
sand mold *n* **:** a mold made of sand and used in sand-casting
sand-molding \'⸗,⸗⸗\ *n* **:** the molding of brick in molds that have been sanded on the inside to prevent sticking in soft-mud process brickmaking — compare SLOP-MOLDING
sand mole *n* **:** MOLE RAT c
sand monitor *n* **:** a large Egyptian lizard (*Varanus griseus*) that inhabits dry localities
sand mullet *n, Austral* **:** either of two mullets: **a :** a sea mullet (*Mugil dobula*) **b :** a small brownish green pink flushed mullet (*Myxus elongatus*) common in warm shallow waters
sand myrtle *n* **:** a highly variable low-branching evergreen shrub (*Leiophyllum buxifolium*) of the family Ericaceae that has coriaceous leaves and small pink or white flowers in terminal clusters and occurs in upland regions of the southeastern U.S.
sand·nat·ter \'san(d),nad·ə(r)\ *n* -S [G, fr. *sand* (fr. OHG *sant* sand) + *natter* adder, fr. OHG *nātara* — more at SAND, ADDER] **1 :** SAND BOA **2 :** SAND VIPER c
sand oat *n* **:** WILD OAT 1a
sand painting *n* **:** a Navaho and Pueblo Indian ceremonial design made of various colored sands, powdered minerals, and vegetable materials upon a flat surface of sand or buckskin and frequently used in healing rites and religious ceremonies — called also *dry painting*
¹**sand·pa·per** \'san(d),pāpə(r), 'saan-\ *n* [¹*sand* + *paper*] **:** paper covered on one side with sand or other abrasive material glued fast and used for smoothing and polishing — compare GARNET PAPER
²**sandpaper** \"\ *vt* **sandpapered; sandpapered; sandpapering** \-āp(ə)riŋ\ **sandpapers :** to rub with or as if with sandpaper ⟨boards are planed and ~*ed* until perfectly smooth —Madge Reese⟩ ⟨the sharp edges of his temper had been ~*ed* down by success —Malcolm Cowley⟩
sand·pa·per·er \-āp(ə)rə(r)\ *n* **:** one that sandpapers
sandpaper fig *n* **:** any of several Australian figs with harsh rough leaves; *esp* **:** PURPLE FIG
sandpaper tree *n* **:** any of several trees having very rough leaves: as **a :** CHAPARRO 3 **b :** a tree (*Dillenia scabrella*) of Asia
sand·pa·pery \-rē\ *adj* [¹*sandpaper* + *-y*] **:** resembling the sound of sandpaper on wood **:** GRATING, HARSH ⟨~ sound of the maracas —Ludwig Bemelmans⟩ ⟨tried to make his ~ voice sound nonchalant —H.N.Hempel⟩
sand partridge *n* **:** any of several small partridges of the genus *Ammoperdix* related to the red-legged partridge, inhabiting southern Asia and northeastern Africa, and frequenting sandy wastes with which its colors harmonize
sand pea *n* **:** BEACH PEA
sand pear *n* **1 :** SNOW PEAR **2 a :** a Chinese pear (*Pyrus pyrifolia*) with large white flowers and in some strains edible fruit that is cultivated as an ornamental, is sometimes used as a stock for grafting horticultural pears, and has been hybridized with the common pear esp. to impart disease resistance **b :** any of various cultivated pears that contain numerous stone cells in the fruit and are usu. hybrids between the common horticultural pears and the Chinese sand pear
sandpeep \'⸗,⸗\ *n* [¹*sand* + *peep* (sandpiper)] **:** a very small sandpiper
sand pig *n* **:** HOG-NOSED BADGER
sand pigeon *n* **:** SANDGROUSE
sand pike *n* **:** SAUGER
sand pile *n* **:** a filling of sand that is rammed hard in a deep round hole, is made by driving and withdrawing a wooden pile, and is sometimes used as a means of preparing foundations in soft soil
sandpile \'⸗,⸗\ *n* [¹*sand* + *pile*] **:** a pile of sand; *esp* **:** sand for children to play in ⟨~ and building blocks —*New Republic*⟩
sand pillar *n* **:** DUST DEVIL
sand pine *n* **1 :** a pine (*Pinus clausa*) common along the coast of Florida and Alabama with smooth bark, leaves in pairs, and spiny-tipped cones **2 :** LODGEPOLE PINE a
sand pink *n* **:** a caespitose herb (*Dianthus armerius*) native to Europe and Asia, having bluish green leaves in spreading mats and flowers with deeply fringed corolla lobes, and widely cultivated as an ornamental
sand pipe *n* **1 :** a pipe containing sand or serving as a channel for sand (as on a locomotive) **2 :** a tubular cavity from a few inches to many feet in depth formed by solution esp. in calcareous rocks and often filled with gravel and sand
sandpiper \'⸗,⸗⸗\ *n* [¹*sand* + *piper*] **1 :** any of numerous small limicoline birds (as the common European sandpiper *Actitis hypoleucos* and the spotted sandpiper of America) that are distinguished from the related plovers chiefly by the bill which is moderately long and often soft and sensitive at the tip but not of the extreme length characteristic of the typical snipe, that have moderately long legs and necks and plumage usu. streaked with brown, gray, or blackish above but more or less extensively white below, and that frequent sandy and muddy shores breeding mostly in the arctic regions but migrating extensively into temperate latitudes — see BAIRD'S SANDPIPER, LEAST SANDPIPER, SEMIPALMATED SANDPIPER, WHITE-RUMPED SANDPIPER **2 :** SAND PRIDE
sandpit \'⸗,⸗\ *n* [ME *sond pitt*, fr. *sond* sand + *pitt* pit — more at SAND, PIT] **:** a pit dug in sandy soil esp. as a place for procuring sand
sand plain *n* **:** an outwash plain usu. of rather small extent composed chiefly of sand deposited by meltwater from a glacier
sand plover *n* **:** RING PLOVER
sand plum *n* **:** a western American variety (*Prunus angustifolia watsonii*) of the Chickasaw plum with thick-skinned fruit
sand pocket mouse *n* **:** a common light-colored pocket mouse (*Perognathus penicillatus pricei*) of the Arizona desert
sand prey *n* **:** SAND PRIDE
sand pride *n* **:** a small European freshwater lamprey (*Petromyzon planeri*)
sand pump *n* **:** a pump for removing wet sand, mud, or silt: as **a :** a centrifugal pump used on a floating dredging machine **b :** a simple plunger pump with a nonreturn valve at the bottom usu. used for cleaning out a borehole
san·dra \'sandrə\ *n* -S [NL (specific epithet of the pike perch *Lucioperca sandra*), fr. G *zander*] **:** ZANDER
sandragon *var of* SANDDRAGON
sand rat *n* **:** any of various rodents native to sandy or desert areas: as **a :** POCKET GOPHER **b :** either of two small nearly naked African mole rats (genus *Heterocephalus*) **c :** any of several African cricetid rodents (genus *Psammomys*) **d :** a southern European rodent (*Meriones longifrons*) related to the typical gerbils
sand reed *n* **1 :** BEACH GRASS **2 :** SAND SEDGE
sand reef *n* **:** a low ridge of sand that borders the shore, is built up by waves and currents, and in many places encloses a lagoon
sand reel *n* **:** a windlass to lower and raise the bailer in a well-boring rig
sandrock \'⸗,⸗\ *n* [¹*sand* + *rock*] **:** SANDSTONE 1
sand rocket *n* **:** a European yellow flowered annual weed (*Diplotaxis muralis*) adventive in No. America
sand roll *n* **1 :** a roll cast in a sand mold **2 :** a take-up roll that guides newly-woven cloth
sand roller *n* **:** TROUT-PERCH
sand runner *n* **1 :** a small plover **:** SANDPIPER **2 :** any of certain freshwater mussels that dig trails at the surface of the sand; *esp* **:** YELLOWBACK
sands *pl of* SAND, *pres 3d sing of* SAND
sand sage *n* **:** a sage (*Artemisia filifolia*) occurring as a troublesome weed on the rangelands of the U.S. and having the leaves 3-parted into filiform segments
sandsailer \'⸗,⸗⸗\ *n* [¹*sand* + *sailer*] **:** a 3-wheeled wind-driven craft that carries two persons, is equipped with a single sail, steered with a tiller over the rear wheel, and is used esp. on firmly packed beach sand — **sandsailing** \'⸗,⸗⸗\ *n*
sand saucer *n* **:** SAND COLLAR
S and SC *abbr* sized and supercalendered
sand screw *n* **:** an amphipod crustacean (*Lepidactylis arenarius*) which burrows in the sandy seabeaches of Europe and America
sand sedge *n* **:** a European maritime sedge (*Carex arenaria*) that is naturalized along the Atlantic coast of the U.S. and has a rootstock with the properties of sarsaparilla
sand shadow *n* **:** SAND DRIFT
sand shark *n* **:** any of numerous elasmobranch fishes native to sandy bottoms and usu. to shallow seas: as **a :** a shark

of the genus *Carcharias* — see NURSE SHARK 3 **b :** a fish of the family Rhinobatidae; *esp* **:** GUITARFISH

sand shell *n* **:** SAND RUNNER 2

sand shilling *n, Austral* **:** SAND DOLLAR

sandshoe \ˈ=,=\ *n* [¹*sand* + *shoe*] **1 :** a shoe designed for wear in sandy ground **2** *Brit* **:** CANVAS SHOE

sand skink *n* **:** any of several Old World lizards of the family Scincidae

sand skipper *n* **:** BEACH FLEA

sand smelt *n* **:** SILVERSIDES 1

sand snake *n* **1 :** SAND BOA **2 :** any snake of an Old World boigid genus (*Psammophis*) with large eyes and variable color pattern common in sandy areas of northern Africa and Asia **3 :** any of a genus (*Chilomeniscus*) of small No. American colubrid burrowing snakes

sand snipe *n* **:** SANDPIPER

sandsoap \ˈ=,=\ *n* [¹*sand* + *soap*] **:** a gritty soap for all-purpose cleaning

sand sole *n* **:** a common brownish speckled flatfish (*Psettichthys melanostictus*) of the Pacific coast of No. America

sandspit \ˈ=,=\ *n* [¹*sand* + *spit*] **:** ¹SPIT 2

sand spout *n* **:** DUST DEVIL

sandspur \ˈ=,=\ *n* [¹*sand* + *spur*] **:** BUR GRASS

sand spurry *or* **sand spurrey** *n* **:** any weed of the genus *Spergularia*: *esp* **:** a Eurasian prostrate herb (*S. rubra*) with tiny pink flowers that is commonly naturalized in eastern No. America

sand squeteague *n* **:** a weakfish (*Cynoscion arenarius*) of the Gulf of Mexico

sand star *n* **:** BRITTLE STAR

sandstay \ˈ=,=\ *n* [¹*sand* + *stay*] **:** SAND BINDER; *specif* **:** an Australian shrub or small tree (*Leptospermum laevigatum*) that is very effective as a sand binder

sandstone \ˈ=,=\ *n* [¹*sand* + *stone*] **1 :** a sedimentary rock made up of sand that usu. consists of quartz more or less firmly united by some cement (as silica, iron oxide, or calcium carbonate) and that varies in color being commonly red, yellow, brown, gray, or white — see GRIT 2, OLD RED SANDSTONE **2 :** a light grayish brown to reddish brown that is lighter and slightly stronger than wood rose and stronger and slightly darker than misty morn — called also *cream beige, tawny birch*

sandstorm \ˈ=,=\ *n* [¹*sand* + *storm*] **:** a storm of wind that drives clouds of sand along a desert

sand-struck brick \ˈ=,=-\ *n* **:** brick made by the sand-molding method of the soft-mud process — compare WATER-STRUCK BRICK

sand sturgeon *n* **:** SHOVELNOSE STURGEON

sand sucker *n* **1 :** CORBINA 1 **2 :** SAND PUMP a

sand swallow *n* **:** BANK SWALLOW

S and T *abbr* supply and transport

sand table *n* **1 a :** a usu. reinforced table with raised edges holding sand for children to mold **b :** a table bearing a relief model of a section of terrain built to scale of hardened sand that usu. reproduces the contours, streams, trees, and buildings for the study of military tactics **2 :** an inclined table used for concentrating ores that typically has the separating surface in motion and a continuous feed and discharge and that uses the motion to separate the ores into layers with the heavy material being shifted for further treatment

sand trap *n* **1 :** a device for separating sand from water **2 :** an artificial hazard on a golf course often near a green consisting of a depression containing sand — see BUNKER

sand trout *n* **:** the sand squeteague or a related weakfish (*Cynoscion nothus*)

sand tube *n* **:** a tube made of sand; *specif* **:** a tubular fulgurite formed in sand

san·dun·ga \sänˈdüŋgə\ *n* -s [MexSp] **:** a Mexican couple dance in which the woman waltzes holding her skirt spread while the man shuffles around her

sand up *vb* [²*sand*] *vt* **:** to choke with sand (as in a well producing sand mixed with oil or gas) ~ *vi* **:** to become choked with sand ⟨the well . . . had *sanded up* —Edwin Corle⟩

san·dust \ˈsan,dəst\ *n* [prob. blend of *sand* and *dust*] **:** a moderate yellowish pink that is much yellower, less strong, and slightly lighter than coral pink, yellower and duller than peach pink, and yellower, less strong, and slightly darker than average peach

sand verbena *n* **:** a western American herb of the genus *Abronia* having flowers resembling the verbena (esp. *A. latifolia* and *A. umbellata* of the Pacific coast)

sand vine *n* **:** a scrambling vine (*Ampelanus albidus*) of the southeastern U.S. related to the milkweeds and having a milky juice, opposite leaves deeply cordate at the base, and small whitish flowers in axillary cymes succeeded by large follicles

sand violet *n* **:** any of several violets found commonly in sandy soil: as **a :** either of two violets (*Viola arenaria* and *V. hirta*) **b :** BIRD'S-FOOT VIOLET

sand viper *n* **:** any of various snakes that burrow into the sand: as **a :** HOGNOSE SNAKE **b :** HORNED VIPER **c :** a common viper (*Vipera ammodytes*) of southeastern Europe

sand wasp *n* **:** any of various wasps that dig burrows in sand; *esp* **:** a wasp of the genus *Bembix*

sand wedge *n* **:** a golfing iron with considerable loft and a wide flange for use in blasting from a sand trap

sandweed \ˈ=,=\ *n* [¹*sand* + *weed*] **1 :** SANDWORT **2 :** SPURRY 1

sandweld \ˈ=,=\ *vt* [¹*sand* + *weld*] **:** to weld with a flux of fused sand which is hammered or squeezed out

sand whiting *n* **:** any of several marine fishes: as **a :** KING WHITING **b :** SAND BORER 2 **c :** an Australian whiting (*Sillago ciliata*)

¹**sand·wich** \ˈsan,(d)wich, ˈsaan- *sometimes esp before a syllable-increasing suffix* -ij\ *n* -ES [after John Montagu, 4th Earl of *Sandwich* †1792 Eng. diplomat] **1 a :** two slices of bread usu. buttered with a thin layer (as of meat, cheese, or savory mixture) spread between them **b :** food consisting of a filling placed upon one slice or between two or more slices of a variety of bread or something that takes the place of bread (as a cracker, cookie, or cake) **2 :** something resembling a sandwich **:** two similar objects enclosing a different one **3 :** composite structural material most commonly consisting of thin high-strength facings bonded to a thicker light low-strength central core

²**sandwich** \ˈ"\ *vt* -ED/-ING/-ES **1 :** to put together like a sandwich ⟨heavy metals (such as lead) and light metals (such as beryllium) are ~*ed* to stop more radiation with less overall weight —*Newsweek*⟩ **2 a :** to insert or place between two or more things ⟨~ the film of metal between two layers of glass —Peter Latham⟩ ⟨song and skit specialties ~*ed* between the longer numbers —*Amer. Guide Series: La.*⟩ **b :** to make a place for **:** CROWD ⟨leisure . . . ~*ed* into the wee hours after an exhausting day —Graenum Berger⟩ ⟨~*es* her writing in with home chores —*Current Biog.*⟩ **3 :** to enclose in the manner of a sandwich ⟨safety spectacles . . . with double lenses ~*ing* a thin layer of the plastic —Harland Manchester⟩

sandwich beam *also* **sandwich girder** *n* **:** FLITCH BEAM

sandwich board *n* **:** two usu. hinged boards designed for hanging from the shoulders with one board before and one behind and used esp. for advertising

sandwich board

sandwich glass *n, usu cap S* [fr. *Sandwich*, Mass.] **:** blown, molded, or pressed glass made by the Boston and Sandwich Glass Company between 1825 and 1886 and now widely collected esp. in some of its lacy pressed forms

sandwich man *n* **:** one who advertises or pickets a place of business by wearing a sandwich board

sandwich panel *n* **:** structural panel material fabricated by bonding several laminations

sandwich tern *n* [*Sandwich*, Kent, England] **:** a rather large tern (*Thalasseus sandvicensis*) that occurs in its typical form in Europe and is represented in No. and Central America by a variety (*T. s. acuflavidus*)

sand widgeon *n, Brit* **:** GADWALL

sand wireworm *n* **:** the larva of an elaterid beetle (*Horistonotus uhlerii*) destructive to corn and cotton in the southern U.S.

sandworm \ˈ=,=\ *n* [¹*sand* + *worm*] **1 :** any of various sand-dwelling polychaete worms: as **a :** CLAM WORM **b :** LUGWORM **c :** a worm (genus *Sabellaria*) that constructs a tube similar to that of the sand mason **2 :** CHIGOE

sandwort \ˈ=,=\ *n* [¹*sand* + *wort*] **1 :** a plant of the genus *Arenaria* growing usu. in dry sandy soil **2 :** a plant of the genus *Moehringia* (esp. *M. lateriflora*)

¹**sandy** \ˈsandē, ˈsaan-, -di\ *adj, usu* -ER/-EST [ME, fr. OE *sandig*, fr. *sand* + *-ig* -y — more at SAND] **1 :** consisting of, abounding in, or containing sand **:** full of sand **:** covered or sprinkled with sand ⟨confined to the rocky region and ~ pools —W.H.Dowdeswell⟩ **2 :** of the color sand ⟨~ hair⟩ **3 :** resembling sand: as **a :** lacking stability **:** being without firmness **:** UNSOUND ⟨the foundation on which to base a friendship was too ~⟩ **b :** lacking interest **:** DRY, STALE ⟨a criticism . . . that it contained long ~ stretches —A.W.Long⟩ **c :** full of pluck **:** possessing grit ⟨the . . . cool and ~ regular army man —A.J.Mekeel⟩ **4** *archaic* **:** of or relating to the time measured by the sand in a sandglass ⟨ere the glass . . . finish the process of his ~ hour —Shak.⟩ **5 a :** that grains like sand — used of varnish, paint, chemicals **b :** containing lactose crystals — used of ice cream

²**sandy** \ˈ"\ *n* -ES [¹*sand* + *-y* (n. suffix)] **1** *Brit* **:** RING PLOVER **2 :** SAND CRAB 1a(2)

³**sandy** \ˈ"\ *n, pl* **sandys** *or* **sandies** *usu cap* [fr. *Sandy*, nickname for *Alexander*, a common Scottish Christian name] **:** SCOTCHMAN

sandy beige *n* **:** SLATE GRAY

sandy blight *n, Austral* **:** BLIGHT 5

sandy·ish \-dēish\ *adj* [¹*sandy* + *-ish*] **:** somewhat sandy

sandy laverock *n* **1** *Scot* **:** RING PLOVER **2 :** the common European sandpiper

sandy loam *n* **:** a loam consisting of less than 7 percent clay, less than 50 percent silt, and between 43 and 50 percent sand

sandy mockingbird *n* **:** BROWN THRASHER

sandyx *var of* SANDIX

¹**sane** \ˈsān\ *adj, usu* -ER/-EST [L *sanus* healthy, sane] **1 :** free from hurt or disease **:** HEALTHY **2 :** mentally sound **:** possessing a rational mind **:** having the mental faculties in such condition as to be able to anticipate and judge of the effect of one's actions **3 :** proceeding from a sound mind **:** being without delusions or prejudice **:** free of ignorance **:** LOGICAL, RATIONAL, SENSIBLE ⟨his . . . school reports were models of ~ educational thinking —Caroline Ticknor⟩ ⟨a more ~ collection of people I have never worked with —Denis Johnston⟩ **syn** see WISE

²**sane** \ˈ"\ *dial var of* SAIN

sane·ly *adv* **:** in a sane manner ⟨speak more ~ about . . . affairs —*Time*⟩

san fe·lipe \,sanfəˈlēpē\ *n, pl* **san felipe** *or* **san felipes** *usu cap S&F* [fr. *San Felipe*, pueblo in north central New Mexico] **1 :** a Keres people occupying a pueblo in New Mexico **2 :** a member of the San Felipe people

sanfoin *var of* SAINFOIN

san·ford's brown \ˈsanfə(r)dz-\ *n, often cap S* [fr. the name *Sanford*] **:** a brownish orange that is stronger than spice or gold pheasant

san fran·cis·can \,sanfrənˈsiskən, ,saan-, -ran-, -raan- *sometimes* -fərn-\ *n* -s *cap S&F* [*San Francisco*, Calif. + E *-an*] **:** a native or resident of San Francisco, Calif.

san fran·cis·co \,==ˈsi(,)skō\ *adj, usu cap S&F* [fr. *San Francisco*, city in western California] **:** of or from the city of San Francisco, Calif. ⟨the *San Francisco* hills⟩ **:** of the kind or style prevalent in San Francisco

¹**sang** [ME, fr. OE] *past of* SING

²**sang** \ˈsaŋ\ *Scot var of* SONG

³**sang** \ˈ"\ *n* -s [F, fr. MF, fr. L *sanguen*, var. of *sanguin-, sanguis* blood] *chiefly Scot* **:** BLOOD — usu. used as a mild oath

⁴**sang** \ˈ"\ *n* -s [by shortening & alter. fr. *ginseng*] *chiefly Midland* **:** a ginseng (*Panax quinquefolium*)

⁵**sang** \ˈsəŋ\ *n* -s [Chin (Pek) *sheng*¹] **1 :** SHENG **2** [Per, prob. fr. Chin *sheng*¹] **:** a Persian harp of the middle ages

san·ga *also* **san·gu** \ˈsaŋgə\ *n* -s [Amharic *sangā*] **:** any of various African cattle: as **a :** an eastern and southern African breed of long-horned small-humped cattle **b :** a western African crossbreed of zebu and native cattle

san·ga·mon \ˈsaŋgəmən\ *also* **san·ga·mo·ni·an** \¦saŋgə¦mōnēən\ *adj, usu cap* [*sangamon* fr. *Sangamon* river & *Sangamon* County, central Illinois; *sangamonian* fr. *Sangamon*, river & county + E *-an*] **:** belonging to the third interglacial interval during the glacial epoch in No. America

san·gar *or* **sun·gar** \ˈsaŋgə(r), ˈsəŋ-\ *n* -s [Hindi *saṅgar*] **1** *also* **san·ger** \ˈ"\ **:** a small breastwork or rifle pit to hold a few men often constructed of boulders around a natural hollow **2 :** a primitive wooden bridge with stone piers

san·ga·ree \,saŋgəˈrē\ *n* -s [Sp *sangría*, lit., action or effect of bleeding, fr. *sangre* blood, modif. of L *sanguin-, sanguis* blood] **:** a tall drink usu. of wine but sometimes of ale, beer, or strong alcoholic liquor that is sweetened, poured into a tumbler of cracked ice, and garnished with nutmeg

san·ga–san·ga \ˈsaŋgəˈsaŋgə\ *n* -s [native name in the Belgian Congo] **:** a tropical African tree (*Ricinodendron africanum*) of the family Euphorbiaceae that has small greenish flowers in dense cymes and nuts that yield an oil

sang de boeuf \säⁿdəbə̄f\ *n* [F, oxblood] **1 :** an opaque claret red to brownish red reduced copper glaze developed in China during the K'ang Hsi period and used chiefly on porcelain wares **2 :** OXBLOOD

sang·dragon \ˈsan,dragən\ *also* **san·drag·on** \ˈsan,-\ *n* [obs. E, dragon's blood, fr. ME *sandragoun*, modif. of MF *sang-dragon*, contr. of *sang-de-dragon*, lit., blood of dragon, fr. *sang* blood + *de* (fr. L, from, away) + *dragon*, fr. OF — more at DE-, DRAGON] **:** AMBOYNA

sängerbund *var of* SAENGERBUND

sängerfest *var of* SAENGERFEST

sang–froid \(ˈ)säŋˈfrwä, (ˈ)säŋ-, (ˈ)säⁿ-, -wäd\ *n* -s [F *sang-froid*, lit., cold blood, fr. MF, fr. *sang* blood + *froid* cold, fr. L *frigidus* — more at SANG, FRIGID] **:** extraordinary often cold-blooded self-possession or imperturbability esp. under strain ⟨with gigantic ~ I performed one of her own dances for her —Agnes de Mille⟩ **syn** see EQUANIMITY

sang·gil *also* **san·gil** \sänˈgēl\ *n* -s *usu cap* **:** SANGIR

sangh \ˈsaŋ, ˈsəŋ\ *n* -s [Hindi *sãg*, lit., association, fr. Skt *saṅga*, fr. *sajati* he adheres to, sticks — more at SAGUM] **:** an association or society having as its object the unification of the different groups in Hinduism and the prevention of the conversion of Hindus to Christianity or Islam

san·gha *also* **sam·gha** \ˈsəŋgə\ *n* -s [Skt *saṅgha*] **1 :** a Buddhist religious community or monastic order **2 :** a Jain monastic community

sang·ir \ˈsäŋ,i(ə)r\ *also* **sang·i·rese** \,säŋəˈrēz, -ēs\ *n, pl* **sangir** *or* **sangirs** *also* **sangirese** *usu cap* **1 a :** a predominantly Muslim people inhabiting the Sangir islands, Indonesia, and the southern coastal regions of Mindanao — called also *Sanggil* **b :** a member of such people **2 :** an Austronesian language of the Sangir people

san·gley \säŋˈglā\ *n* -s [Chin (Pek) *shang*¹*lü*³ merchant guest] **:** a Chinese trader in the Philippines

sang·li·er \ˈsaŋlēə(r)\ *n* -s [ME *singlere*, fr. MF *sengler*, *sanglier*, fr. ML *singularis*, fr. L, single, solitary — more at SINGULAR] **:** a wild boar

san·go \ˈsäŋ(,)gō\ *n* -s *usu cap* **:** a trade language widely used in French Equatorial Africa belonging to the Adamawa-Eastern branch of the Niger-Congo family

san·go·an \ˈsäŋgəwən\ *adj, usu cap* [*Sango* Bay, Uganda, where remains of the culture were found + E *-an*] **:** of or belonging to a modified Acheulean culture of central Africa characterized by a hand-ax altered so that it might be used as a pick

san·gra·do \säŋˈgrä(,)dō\ *n* -ES [after Doctor *Sangrado*, physician (whose panacea was copious bloodletting and drinking of hot water) in the picaresque novel *Gil Blas* (*L'Histoire de Gil Blas de Santillane*, 1715–35) by Alain René Lesage †1747 Fr. novelist and playwright] *archaic* **:** one who pretends to a knowledge of medicine **:** QUACK

san·gree·root \ˈsaŋgrē,-\ *n* [*sangree* (alter. of *snagrel*) + *root*] **:** VIRGINIA SNAKEROOT

sangs *pl of* SANG

sang·sue \ˈsaŋ,sü\ *n* -s [F, fr. L *sanguisuga* bloodsucker, leech, fr. *sanguis* blood + *-suga* (fr. *sugere* to suck) — more at SUCK] **:** ¹LEECH 2 a

sangu *var of* SANGA

sangui- *comb form* [MF, fr. L, fr. *sanguis*] **:** blood ⟨*sanguimotor*⟩

san·guic·o·lous \saŋˈgwikələs\ *adj* [*sangui-* + *-colous*] **:** HEMATOBIC

san·gui·fi·ca·tion \,saŋgwəfəˈkāshən\ *n* -s [MF, fr. L *sangui-* (fr. *sanguis* blood) + MF *-fication*] **:** conversion (as of food) into blood **:** HEMATOPOIESIS

sanguify *vb* -ED/-ING/-ES [*sangui-* + *-fy*] *vi, obs* **:** to produce blood ~ *vt, obs* **:** to change into blood

san·gui·motor \ˈsaŋgwə+\ *adj* [*sangui-* + *motor*] **:** of or relating to the circulation of blood

san·gui·nar·ia \,saŋgwəˈna(a)rēə\ *n* [NL, fr. L, an herb that stanches blood, fr. fem. of *sanguinarius* sanguinary] **1** *cap* **:** a genus of scapose perennial herbs (family Papaveraceae) having reddish juice and capsules that are dehiscent to their base — see BLOODROOT **2** -s **:** the dried rhizome and roots of a plant of the genus *Sanguinaria* used as an expectorant and emetic

san·gui·nar·i·ly \¦saŋgwə¦nerəlē\ *adv* **:** in a sanguinary manner

san·guin·a·rine \saŋˈgwinə,rēn, -,rən\ *n* -s [ISV *sanguinar-* (fr. NL *Sanguinaria*, genus name of the bloodroot *Sanguinaria canadensis*) + *-ine*] **:** a poisonous bitter crystalline alkaloid $C_{20}H_{15}NO_5$ obtained esp. from bloodroot

san·gui·nary \ˈsaŋgwə,nerē, -ri\ *adj* [L *sanguinarius*, fr. *sanguin-*, *sanguis* blood + *-arius* -ary] **1 :** willing or even anxious to shed blood **:** BLOODTHIRSTY, MURDEROUS ⟨went after the collaborators with a ~ fury that drenched the land with blood —G.W.Johnson⟩ **2 :** attended by, prompting, or concerning much bloodshed **:** BLOODY ⟨this bitter and ~ war waged under conditions of incredible hardship —T.H.D. Mahoney⟩ **3 :** consisting of blood ⟨a ~ stream⟩

sanguinary ant *n* **:** a slave-making ant (*Formica sanguinea*) widely distributed over the northern hemisphere

¹**san·guine** \ˈsaŋgwən\ *adj* [ME *sanguin*, fr. MF, fr. L *sanguineus* of blood, bloody, bloodred, fr. *sanguin-, sanguis* blood + *-eus* -eous] **1 a :** red like blood **:** of the color blood red ⟨cedar logs whose ~ color made . . . a fantastic wreath of flames —Elinor Wylie⟩ **b :** of the heraldic color murrey **2 a :** consisting of or relating to blood **b :** SANGUINARY 1 **c** *of the complexion* **:** RUDDY ⟨his complexion was fresh and ~ —Elinor Wylie⟩ **3 a :** having blood as the predominating bodily humor **b :** having the bodily conformation and temperament thought to be characteristic of such predominance and marked by sturdiness, high color, and an appearance of cheerful spiritedness **4 :** anticipating the best **:** marked by eager hopefulness **:** ardently or confidently optimistic ⟨his ~ temper and fearlessness of mind —Jane Austen⟩ ⟨too ~ about success —Ernest Beaglehole⟩ ⟨a ~ happy-go-lucky habit of thought —J.G.Cozzens⟩ **syn** see CONFIDENT

²**sanguine** \ˈ"\ *n* -s **1 a :** BLOOD RED **b :** the heraldic color murrey **2 :** a sanguine humor or temperament ⟨the ~ and melancholic are temperaments of feeling —A.L.Kroeber⟩ **3 a :** a type of red crayon usu. of red hematite **b :** a drawing in red crayon, red chalk, or similar medium

³**sanguine** *vt* -ED/-ING/-S *obs* **:** ENSANGUINE

san·guine·ly *adv* **:** in a sanguine manner

san·guine·ness *n* -ES **:** SANGUINITY

san·guin·e·ous \saŋˈgwinēəs, san'-\ *adj* [L *sanguineus*] **1 :** BLOODRED **2 :** of, relating to, or involving bloodshed **:** BLOODTHIRSTY ⟨~ histories of queens —W.M.Thackeray⟩ **3 a :** of or relating to blood **:** constituting or containing blood **b** *obs, of an animal* **:** having blood or a circulatory system **4 a** *archaic* **:** characterized by a plethora of blood ⟨~ fever⟩ **b :** FULL-BLOODED, SANGUINE 3b ⟨a ~ temperament⟩

sanguini- *comb form* [fr. ¹*sanguine*] **:** SANGUINO- ⟨*sanguinicolous*⟩

sanguinian *n* -s [ME *sanguinien*, fr. MF, fr. *sanguin* sanguine + *-ien* -ian] *obs* **:** one that has a sanguine temperament

sanguinicolous \¦saŋgwə¦nikələs\ *adj* [*sanguini-* + *-colous*] **:** SANGUICOLOUS

san·guin·i·ty \saŋˈgwinəd·ē, san'-, -ətē, -i\ *n* -ES [¹*sanguine* + *-ity*] **:** the quality or state of being sanguine ⟨~ about the financial interests . . . of government officials —*New Republic*⟩

san·gui·niv·o·rous \¦saŋgwə¦niv(ə)rəs\ *adj* [*sanguini-* + *-vorous*] **:** HEMATOPHAGOUS

sanguino- *comb form* [F, fr. *sanguin* sanguine, fr. MF] **:** blood ⟨*sanguinopurulent*⟩

san·guin·o·lent \saŋˈgwinᵊlənt\ *adj* [L *sanguinolentus* bloody, bloodred, fr. *sanguin-, sanguis* blood] **:** of, containing, or tinged with blood ⟨~ sputum⟩

san·gui·no·purulent \¦saŋgwənō+\ *adj* [*sanguino-* + *purulent*] **:** containing blood and pus ⟨~ discharge⟩

san·gui·nous \ˈsaŋgwənəs\ *adj* [L *sanguin-, sanguis* blood + E *-ous*] **:** SANGUINEOUS

san·gui·sor·ba \,saŋgwəˈsȯrbə\ *n, cap* [NL, fr. *sangui-* + *-sorba* (fr. L *sorbēre* to absorb); fr. its styptic quality — more at ABSORB] **:** a small genus of herbs (family Rosaceae) native to temperate regions with odd-pinnate stipulate leaves and small apetalous flowers in dense terminal spikes or clusters — see BURNET 2

san·guiv·o·rous \saŋˈgwiv(ə)rəs\ *adj* [*sangui-* + *-vorous*] **:** feeding on blood

san·he·drin \(ˈ)sanˈhēdrən, sän-, -ˈhed-; ˈsan(h)ē,drin, -nə,-, -,drən\ *or* **san·he·drim** \-rəm, -rim\ *n* -s *usu cap* [Mishnaic Heb *sanhedhrīn* (*gědhōlāh*) (great) Sanhedrin, fr. Gk *synedrion*, lit., council, council chamber, fr. *synedros* sitting in council, fr. *syn-* + *hedra* seat — more at SIT] **1 :** the supreme council and tribunal of the ancient Jewish nation consisting of 70–72 members and having jurisdiction over religious matters and important civil and criminal cases **2 :** one of the provincial councils of the ancient Jews consisting of 23 members and having jurisdiction over minor civil and criminal cases

san hemp \ˈsan-, ˈsən-\ *n* [*san* fr. Hindi, sunn — more at SUNN] **:** SUNN

san·i·cle \ˈsanəkəl\ *n* -s [ME, fr. MF, fr. ML *sanicula*] **:** any of several plants reputed to have healing powers: as **a :** a plant of the genus *Sanicula* having a root that is used esp. in folk medicine as an anodyne or astringent — called also *black snakeroot* **b :** AMERICAN SANICLE **c :** YORKSHIRE SANICLE

sa·nic·u·la \səˈnikyələ\ *n, cap* [NL, fr. ML, sanicle, prob. dim. of L *sanus* healthy] **:** a genus of chiefly American herbs (family Umbelliferae) having palmately compound leaves, unisexual flowers in panicled umbels, and fruit covered with hooked bristles

san·i·dine \ˈsanə,dēn, -,dən\ *n* -s [G *sanidin*, fr. Gk *sanid-*, *sanis* board + G *-in* -ine; fr. its tabular crystals] **:** a variety of orthoclase in often transparent crystals in eruptive rock (as trachyte) that is thought to form at higher temperatures than adularia — called also GLASSY FELDSPAR — **san·i·din·ic** \¦==¦dinik\ *adj*

sa·ni·es \ˈsānē,ēz\ *n, pl* **sanies** [L] **1 :** a thin blood-tinged seropurulent discharge from ulcers or infected wounds — compare ICHOR **2** *archaic* **:** a watery vital bodily fluid; *esp* **:** one comparable to blood

san·i·fi·ca·tion \,sanəfəˈkāshən\ *n* -s [L *sanus* healthy + E *-i-* + *-fication*] **:** the act or process of making sanitary

san·i·fy \ˈsanə,fī\ *vt* -ED/-ING/-ES [L *sanus* healthy + E *-ify*] **:** to make healthful **:** provide with sanitary conditions and equipment

san il·de·fon·so \sa,nildəˈfän(t)(,)sō\ *n, pl* **san ildefonso** *or* **san ildefonsos** *usu cap S&I* [fr. *San Ildefonso*, pueblo in central New Mexico] **1 :** a Tanoan people occupying a pueblo in New Mexico **2 :** a member of the San Ildefonso people

sa·nio's beam \ˈsänē,ōz-\ *n, usu cap S* [prob. after Karl Gustav *Sanio*, 19th cent. Ger. botanist] **:** CRASSULA

sa·ni·ous \ˈsānēəs\ *adj* [L *saniosus*, fr. *sanies* + *-osus* -ose] **:** thin and seropurulent with a slightly bloody tinge ⟨the ~ discharge from an ulcer⟩

¹**san·i·tar·i·an** \,sanəˈta(a)rēən, -ter-, -tār-\ *n* -s [*sanitary* + E *-an* (n. suffix)] **:** one skilled in matters of sanitary science and public health ⟨milk ~⟩

²**sanitarian** \¦==¦===\ *adj* [¹*sanitary* + E *-an* (adj. suffix)] **:** of or relating to sanitary science or public health

san·i·tar·i·ly \¦sanə¦terəlē, -li\ *adv* **:** in a sanitary manner **:** with regard to sanitation ⟨the peculiar, ~ dubious, but often delicious foods —Joseph Alsop⟩

san·i·tar·ium \,sanəˈta(a)rēəm, -ter-, -tār-\ *n, pl* **sanitariums** \-mz\ *also* **sanitar·ia** \-ēə\ [NL, fr. L *sanitat-*, *sanitas* health + *-arium* -ary] **:** SANATORIUM

¹san·i·tary \'sanə,terē, -ri\ *adj* [F *sanitaire*, fr. L *sanitas* health + F *-aire* -ary] **:** of or relating to health **:** for or relating to the preservation or restoration of health **:** occupied with measures or equipment for improving conditions that influence health **:** free from or effective in preventing or checking an agent (as filth or infection) injurious to health **:** HYGIENIC **syn** see HEALTHFUL

²sanitary \"\ *n* -ES **:** a water closet, urinal, or similar equipment fitted with sanitary plumbing

sanitary can *n* **:** PACKER'S CAN

sanitary cordon *n* [trans. of *cordon sanitaire*] **:** CORDON SANITAIRE

sanitary engineer *n* **:** an engineer whose training or occupation is in sanitary engineering

sanitary engineering *n* **:** a branch of civil engineering concerned primarily with the maintenance of environmental conditions (as pure water supply, waste disposal, insect control, nuisance abatement) conducive to public health

sanitary fill *n* **:** the disposition of garbage by spreading in layers and covering with ashes or dirt to a depth sufficient to control rats, flies, and odors

sanitary napkin *n* **:** a disposable absorbent pad of cellulose or similar filler in a gauze covering used to absorb the flow from uterus or vagina during menstruation or postpartum

sanitary sewer *n* **:** a sewer to dispose of sewage but not water from ground, surface, or storm

sanitary ware *n* **:** ceramic plumbing articles (as sinks, baths, lavatories, showers, toilet bowls)

san·i·tate \'sanə,tāt\ *vt* -ED/-ING/-S [back-formation fr. *sanitation*] **:** to make sanitary **:** provide with sanitary appliances

san·i·ta·tion \,sanə'tāshən\ *n* -S [¹*sanitary* + *-ation*] **1 :** the act or process of making sanitary **2 :** the application of measures to make environmental conditions favorable to health **3 :** the maintenance of a healthy population of a wild species by the selective action of predators in removing weak or unfit individuals

sanitation cutting *n* **:** a cutting made to remove trees that have been injured or killed (as by fire or wind) primarily to prevent spread of disease or insects — compare SALVAGE CUTTING

san·i·ta·tion·ist \-sh(ə)nəst\ *n* -S **:** SANITARIAN

san·i·ti·za·tion \,sanədə'zāshən\ *n* -S **:** the act or process of sanitizing

san·i·tize \'sanə,tīz\ *vt* -ED/-ING/-S [L *sanitat-*, *sanitas* health + E *-ize*] **:** to make sanitary (as by cleaning or sterilizing)

san·i·tiz·er \-zə(r)\ *n* -S **:** a sanitizing agent esp. for use in connection with food

san·i·to·ri·um \,sanə'tōrēəm, -tȯr-\ *n, pl* **sanitoriums** \-mz\ *also* **sanito·ria** \-ēə\ [NL, alter. (influenced by *sanitarium*) of *sanatorium*] **:** SANATORIUM

san·i·ty \'sanəd·|ē, -ət|, |i\ *n* -ES [ME *sanite*, fr. L *sanitat-*, *sanitas* health, sanity, fr. *sanus* healthy, sane + *-itat-*, *-itas* -ity] **:** the quality or state of being sane: as **a :** a healthy state of body **b :** soundness or health of mind

san ja·cin·to day \,sanjə'sin(,)tō-\ *n, usu cap S&J&D* [fr. the battle of *San Jacinto*, fr. *San Jacinto*, river in southeastern Texas near the mouth of which Americans under Gen. Sam Houston decisively defeated Mexicans under Santa Anna] **:** April 21 observed as a legal holiday by the state of Texas in commemoration of the battle of San Jacinto in 1836

san·jak \san'jak, '⸗,⸗\ *n* -S [earlier *sangiac*, fr. Turk *sancàk*, lit., flag, standard] **:** a district or subdivision of a vilayet — compare MUTESSARIF

san joa·quin fever \,sanwȯ'kēn-, -wä'-\ *also* **san joaquin valley fever** *n, usu cap S&J&V* [after *San Joaquin* Valley, central California, where it was endemic] **:** COCCIDIOIDOMYCOSIS

san jo·sé *or* **san jo·se** \,san(h)ō'zā, -nə'-\ *adj, usu cap S&J* [fr. *San José*, Costa Rica] **:** of or from San José, the capital of Costa Rica **:** of the kind or style prevalent in San José

san jose scale *n, usu cap 1st S&J* [after *San Jose*, California, where it first appeared in the U.S.] **:** a scale (*Aspidiotus perniciosus*) that is prob. native to eastern Asia but widely distributed in warm and temperate areas, has become one of the most damaging plant pests in the U.S., and is esp. destructive to apple, pear, and other fruit trees

¹san juan \(')san'(h)wän\ *adj, usu cap S&J* [fr. *San Juan*, Puerto Rico] **:** of or from San Juan, the capital of Puerto Rico **:** of the kind or style prevalent in San Juan

²san juan \"\ *n, pl* **san juan** *or* **san juans** *usu cap S&J* [fr. *San Juan*, pueblo in northern New Mexico] **1 :** a Tanoan people occupying a pueblo in New Mexico **2 :** a member of the San Juan people

san jua·ne·ro \,san(h)wə'ne(,)rō\ *n* -S *cap S&J* [AmerSp, fr. *San Juan* + Sp *-ero* (fr. L *-arius* -ary)] **:** a native or resident of San Juan, esp. San Juan, Puerto Rico

san·jua·ni·to \,san(h)wə'nēd·(,)ō\ *n* -S [AmerSp, fr. dim. of *San Juan* St. John] **:** an Ecuadorian couple dance resembling but more melancholy than the marinera of Peru

¹sank [ME, fr. OE *sanc*] *past of* SINK

²sank \'saŋk\ *n* -S [Skt *śaṅkha* — more at CONCH] **:** CHANK

san·khya *also* **sam·khya** \'säŋkyə\ *n* -S *usu cap* [Skt *sāṁkhya*, lit., based on calculation, philosophical method, fr. *saṁkhyā* calculation, number, fr. *saṁkhyāti* he counts up] **:** one of the earliest of the major orthodox systems of Hindu philosophy resting on a metaphysical dualism that exists between the ultimates of prakriti and purusha whose contact produces the phenomenal world and whose disentangling represents the process of individual salvation

san luis po·to·sí *or* **san luis potosi** \sän'lwē,spōd·ə'sē\ *adj, usu cap S&L&P* [fr. *San Luis Potosí*, city in central Mexico] **:** of or from the city of San Luis Potosí, Mexico **:** of the kind or style prevalent in San Luis Potosí

¹san mar·i·nese \(,)san,marə'nēz, -ēs\ *or* **sam·mar·i·nese** \(,)sa(m)¦ma-\ *n, pl* **san marinese** \"\ *or* **san marine·si** \,⸗,⸗⸗'nāzē\ *or* **sammarinese** *or* **sammarinesi** *usu cap S&M* [*San Marino*, republic on the Italian peninsula + E *-ese* (n. suffix)] **:** a native or inhabitant of the Republic of San Marino

²san marinese \"\ *or* **sammarinese** \"\ *adj, usu cap S&M* [*San Marino* + E *-ese* (adj. suffix)] **:** of or relating to San Marino or the San Marinese

san ma·ri·no \¦sanmə¦rē(,)nō\ *adj, usu cap S&M* [fr. *San Marino*, republic on the Italian peninsula in southern Europe] **:** of or from the Republic of San Marino, in Italy **:** of the kind or style prevalent in San Marino

san·mar·tin·ite \san'märtᵊn,īt\ *n* -S [Sp *sanmartinita*, fr. *San Martín*, town in Argentina + Sp *-ita* -ite] **:** a tungstate of zinc, iron, and calcium closely related to wolframite

sann \'san, 'sən\ *n* -S [Hindi *san* — more at SUNN] **:** SUNN

san·na \'sanə\ [by contr. & alter.] *Scot* **:** shall not

sannhemp \'⸗,⸗\ *n* [*sann* + *hemp*] **:** SUNN

san·nup \'sa,nəp\ *n* -S [Abnaki *senanbe*] **:** a married male American Indian — compare SQUAW

sann·ya·si \,sən'yäsē\ *or* **sann·ya·sin** \-sᵊn\ *n* -S [Hindi *sannyāsī*, fr. Skt *saṁnyāsin* abandoning, fr. *sam* together + *ni* down + *asyati* he throws — more at SANSKRIT, NETHER] **:** a wandering mendicant Hindu ascetic **:** a holy man **:** MONK; *specif* **:** one belonging to a Brahman or Jain order comprising men in the fourth ashrama

sanpan *var of* SAMPAN

san pe·dro fish \san'pē(,)drō-, -'pā(,)drō-\ *n, usu cap S&P* [after Point *San Pedro*, Calif.] **:** OPAH

san·poil \'san,pȯil\ *n, pl* **sanpoil** *or* **sanpoils** *usu cap* **1 a :** a Salishan people of northeastern Washington **b :** a member of such people **2 :** a dialect of Okanagon

SANR *abbr, often not cap* subject to approval no risk

san·ron \'sän,rōn\ *n* -S *usu cap* [Jap] **:** a Japanese Buddhist school founded in A.D. 625 and based on Madhyamika principles

¹sans \'sanz, 'saa(ə)nz, 'sänz\ *prep* [ME *saun*, *saunz*, *sans*, fr. MF *san*, *sanz*, *sans*, fr. OF *sen*, *senz*, *sens*, partly fr. L *sine* without, and partly modif. (influenced by L *sine*) of L *absentia* in the absence of, abl. of *absentia* absence — more at SUNDER, ABSENCE] **:** deprived or destitute of **:** WITHOUT ⟨her face seen in repose . . . ~ the liveliness of her eyes revealed her age —Eugene Walter⟩

²sans *pl of* SAN

³sans \'sanz\ *n* -ES [by shortening] **:** SANS SERIF

sansa *var of* ZANZA

san sal·va·dor \san'salvə,dȯ(ə)r\ *adj, usu cap both Ss* [fr. *San Salvador*, El Salvador] **:** of or from San Salvador, the capital of El Salvador **:** of the kind or style prevalent in San Salvador

san·sar \'san(t)sə(r)\ *n* -S [modif. of Ar *ṣarṣar*] **:** SARSAR

sansara *var of* SAMSARA

sans·cu·lotte \,sanzk(y)ə'lät, -nsk-\ *n* -S [F *sans-culotte*, lit., without breeches; prob. fr. the fact that members of the republican party had rejected short breeches as being peculiar to the upper classes and had adopted instead other articles of dress, esp. pantaloons] **1 :** one belonging to the extreme republican party in France at the time of the Revolution **2 :** a political extremist or radical; *esp* **:** one who believes in violence to attain an end

sans·cu·lotte·rie \-ä·trē\ *n* -S [F *sans-culotterie*, fr. *sans-culotte* + *-erie* -ery] **:** SANSCULOTTISM

sans·cu·lot·tic \¦⸗⸗¦läd·ik\ *adj* [*sansculotte* + *-ic*] **:** relating to or involving sansculottism **:** RADICAL, REVOLUTIONARY

sans·cu·lot·tish \-ish\ *adj* [*sansculotte* + *-ish*] **:** SANSCULOTTIC

sans·cu·lot·tism \,⸗⸗'läd·,izəm\ *n* -S [F *sans-culottisme*, fr. *sans-culotte* + *-isme* -ism] **:** extreme republican principles **:** the principles or practice of the sansculottes

sans·cu·lot·tize \-,tīz\ *vb* [*sansculotte* + *-ize*] *vt* **:** to make sansculottic ~ *vi* **:** to uphold radical principles

san se·bas·tián *or* **san se·bas·tian** \,sansə¦bas(h)chən\ *adj, usu cap both Ss* [fr. *San Sebastián*, city in northern Spain] **:** of or from the city of San Sebastián, Spain **:** of the kind or style prevalent in San Sebastián

sans égal \säⁿzā'gȧl\ *n* [F, lit., without equal] **:** bagatelle in which each player uses four balls and another ball is spotted

san·sei \(')sän¦sā\ *n, pl* **sansei** *also* **sanseis** *often cap* [Jap *san* third + *sei* generation] **:** a son or daughter of nisei or kibei parents who is born and educated in America and esp. in the U. S.

san·se·vie·ria \,san(t)sə'virēə\ *n* [NL, fr. Raimondo di Sangro †1774 Ital. scholar and prince of *San Severo* + NL *-ia*] **1** *cap* **:** a genus of tropical chiefly Asiatic and African herbs (family Liliaceae) having sword-shaped leaves which are mottled or striped with various shades of green or yellow, white or yellowish flowers on jointed pedicels, a 3-celled ovary, and a 1- to 3-seeded berry — see BOWSTRING HEMP **2** *or* **san·se·vie·ra** \-rə\ -S **:** any plant of the genus *Sansevieria*

¹san·skrit \'sanz,krit, 'saan-, -n,sk-, *usu* -id·+V\ *n* -S *cap* [Skt *saṁskṛta*, lit., prepared, cultivated, refined, fr. *sam* together (akin to *sama* same) + *karoti* he makes, does — more at SAME, KARMA] **1 :** an ancient Indic language that is the classical language of India and of Hinduism as described by the Indian grammarians (as Panini) — called also *classical Sanskrit* **2 :** classical Sanskrit together with the older Vedic and various later modifications of classical Sanskrit

²sanskrit \"\ *adj, usu cap* **1 :** of, relating to, or written in Sanskrit **2 :** derived from or relating to classical Indian culture

san·skrit·ic \(')sanz¦krid·|ik, (')saan-, -n¦sk-, -it|, |ēk\ *n* -S *usu cap* [*sanskrit* + *-ic*] **1 :** INDIC **2 :** a group of Indic languages developed directly from Sanskrit — see INDO-EUROPEAN LANGUAGES table

san·skrit·ist \'sanz,krid·əst, 'saan-, -n,sk-, -itə-\ *n* -S *usu cap* [ISV *sanskrit* + *-ist*] **:** a specialist in Sanskrit

san·skrit·iza·tion \,sanz,krid·ə'zāshən\ *n* -S *usu cap* [*sanskritize* + *-ation*] **1 :** the assimilation of a language to Sanskrit in vocabulary, syntax, or style **2 :** the assimilation of a culture to that of Brahminical Hinduism

san·skrit·ize \'sanzkrə,tīz\ *vt* -ED/-ING/-S *often cap* [*sanskrit* + *-ize*] **:** to modify (a word, phrase, or language) to conform to characteristics distinctive of Sanskrit ⟨the interpreters' grasp of Hindi is said to be sound but their vocabulary is highly *Sanskritized* —Christopher Rand⟩

sans ser·if \sanz'serəf\ *or* **san·ser·if** \san'-\ *n* [prob. fr. ¹*sans* + modif. of D *schreef* stroke, line — more at SERIF] **:** a letter or typeface with no serifs — called also *Doric*, *gothic*, *grotesque*

¹sant \'sant\ *n* -S [perh. modif. of MF *cent* hundred — more at CENT] **:** a card game similar to piquet and popular in the 15th and 16th centuries **:** CENT

²sant \"\ *vi* [origin unknown] *chiefly Scot* **:** VANISH

³sant *var of* SUNT

san·ta \'santə, 'saan-\ *n* -S *usu cap* [by shortening] **:** SANTA CLAUS

¹san·ta ana \¦santə¦anə\ *n, pl* **santa ana** *or* **santa anas** *usu cap S&A* [fr. *Santa Ana*, pueblo in north central New Mexico] **1 a :** a Keres people occupying a pueblo in New Mexico **b :** a member of such people **2 :** the language of the Santa Ana people

²santa ana \"\ *n, usu cap S&A* [fr. *Santa Ana* mountains, range in southwestern California where the wind is channeled through the Santa Ana canyon whence it spreads over the coastal plain] **:** a strong hot dry foehn wind from the north, northeast, or east in southern California

san·ta cla·ra \¦santə¦kla(a)rə\ *n, pl* **santa clara** *or* **santa claras** *usu cap S&C* [fr. *Santa Clara*, pueblo in northern New Mexico] **1 :** a Tanoan people occupying a pueblo in New Mexico **2 :** a member of the Santa Clara people

san·ta claus \'santə,klȯz, 'saan-, -tē,-\ *n, usu cap S&C* [fr. *Santa Claus*, legendary Christmas figure, modif. of D *Sinterklaas*, alter. of *Sint Nikolaas* St. Nicholas *fl* 4th cent. A.D. bishop of Myra, in Lycia, Asia Minor who is considered as patron saint of children and who is fabled as having provided three maidens with dowry by throwing in at their window purses of gold] **:** the religious and holiday spirit of Christmas personified

san·ta cruz \¦santə¦krüz\ *adj, usu cap S&C* [fr. *Santa Cruz* de Tenerife, Spain] **:** of or from the city of Santa Cruz de Tenerife, in the Canary islands, Spain **:** of the kind or style prevalent in Santa Cruz de Tenerife

san·ta fe \¦santə¦fā, *in sense 2* \¦sän-\ *adj, usu cap S&F* **1** [fr. *Santa Fe*, city in north central New Mexico] **:** of or from Santa Fe, the capital of New Mexico ⟨*Santa Fe* stores⟩ **:** of the kind or style prevalent in Santa Fe **2** [fr. *Santa Fe*, city in east central Argentina] **:** of or from the city of Santa Fe, Argentina **:** of the kind or style prevalent in Santa Fe

san·ta fe·an \-āən\ *n* -S *cap S&F* [*Santa Fe*, New Mexico + E *-an*] **:** a native or resident of Santa Fe, New Mexico

san·ta ger·tru·dis \,santə,gər·'trüdəs\ *n, usu cap S&G* [after *Santa Gertrudis*, section of the King Ranch, Kingsville, Texas] **1 :** a breed of cherry-red beef cattle developed from a Brahman-Shorthorn cross and valuable because of their hardiness in hot climes and their thrifty growth on grass feeding **2 :** an animal of the Santa Gertrudis breed

¹san·tal \'santᵊl\ *n* -S [F, red sandalwood, fr. MF, fr. ML *sandalum*, *santalum* sandalwood — more at SANDAL] **:** a crystalline compound $C_{16}H_{12}O_6$ derived from flavone and obtained from red sandalwood and camwood

²san·tal \,sən·'täl\ *n, pl* **santal** *or* **santals** *usu cap* **:** a member of a Kolarian people in southeastern Bihar and adjacent Bengal

san·ta·la·ce·ae \,santə'lāsē,ē\ *n pl, cap* [NL, fr. *Santalum*, type genus + *-aceae*] **:** a family of mostly tropical herbs, shrubs, or rarely trees (order Santalales) that have clustered apetalous monoecious or dioecious flowers, the ovary partly inferior and the fruit a nut or drupe and that include some members which are stem or root parasites — **san·ta·la·ceous** \¦⸗⸗¦lāshəs\ *adj*

san·ta·la·les \,⸗⸗'lā(,)lēz\ *n pl, cap* [NL, fr. *Santalum* + *-ales*] **:** an order of dicotyledonous plants which are distinguished by having a one-celled inferior ovary and many of which are parasitic or partly parasitic

san·ta·lene \'santə,lēn\ *n* -S [ISV *santal-* (fr. NL *Santalum*) + *-ene*] **:** either of two liquid unsaturated hydrocarbons $C_{15}H_{24}$ occurring in East Indian sandalwood oil: **a :** a tricyclic sesquiterpene — called also *alpha-santalene* **b :** a bicyclic sesquiterpene — called also *beta-santalene*

san·ta·li \,sən·'tälē\ *n* -S *usu cap* **:** the Munda language of the Santal people

san·ta·lin \'santᵊlən\ *n* -S [ISV *santal-* (fr. NL *Santalum*) + *-in*] **:** a red crystalline compound constituting the chief coloring matter in red sandalwood and camwood

santal oil *n* **:** SANDALWOOD OIL 1a

san·ta·lol \'santə,lȯl, -,lōl\ *n* -S [ISV *santal-* (fr. NL *Santalum*) + *-ol*] **:** a mixture of two liquid isomeric sesquiterpene alcohols $C_{15}H_{23}OH$ derived from the santalenes and constituting the chief constituent of sandalwood oil; *also* **:** either of these alcohols distinguished as alpha and beta

san·ta lu·cia fir \¦santəlü¦sēə-\ *n, usu cap S&L* [after *Santa Lucia* range, southwestern California] **:** a pyramidal California evergreen tree (*Abies venusta*) with spiny pointed leaves and cones that have long spines protruding from the scale bracts — called also *bristlecone fir*

san·ta·lum \'santᵊləm\ *n, cap* [NL, fr. ML *sandalum*, *santalum* sandalwood] **:** a small genus (the type of the family Santalaceae) of Indo-Malayan parasitic trees having coriaceous leaves and small perfect flowers in terminal panicles — see SANDALWOOD

santalwood \'⸗⸗,⸗\ *n* [alter. (influenced by ¹*santal*) of *sandalwood*] **:** SANDALWOOD

san·ta ma·ria tree \¦santəmə¦rēə-\ *n, usu cap S&M* [*santa maria* fr. Sp, fr. *Santa María* St. Mary] **:** an evergreen tropical American tree (*Calophyllum calaba*) that yields a durable straight close-grained timber and a fluid balsam like copaiba — called also *calaba*

san·tana \san·'tanə\ *n* -S *usu cap* [by contr.] **:** SANTA ANA

san·tan·der \,san·,tän¦der\ *adj, usu cap* [fr. *Santander*, city in northern Spain] **:** of or from the city of Santander, Spain **:** of the kind or style prevalent in Santander

san·ta·ya·ni·an \¦säntə¦yänēən\ *adj, usu cap* [George *Santayana* †1952 Am. poet and philosopher + E *-an*] **:** of or relating to the philosopher George Santayana or his theories and esp. his realism and separation of essence from existence.

san·tee \san·'tē\ *n, pl* **santee** *or* **santees** *usu cap* **:** either of two Siouan peoples: **a :** a large number of small groups located in the Carolinas **b** (1) **:** a division of the Dakota people (2) **:** a dialect of Dakota

san·tene \'san·,tēn\ *n* -S [ISV *sant-* (fr. NL *Santalum*) + *-ene*] **:** a liquid unsaturated terpene C_9H_{14} derived from norbornane and found esp. in East Indian sandalwood oil and various pine-needle oils

san·te·none \'santə,nōn\ *n* -S [ISV *santene* + *-one*] **:** a crystalline bicyclic ketone $C_9H_{14}O$ that is the lower homolog of camphor and occurs in East Indian sandalwood oil

san·thali \,sən·'tälē\ *n, pl* **santhali** *or* **santhalis :** SANTALI

san·ti·a·go \¦santē¦ä(,)gō\ *adj, usu cap* [fr. *Santiago*, city in central Chile] **1 :** of or from Santiago, the capital of Chile **:** of the kind or style prevalent in Santiago **2** [fr. *Santiago* de Cuba, city on south coast of Cuba] **:** of or from the city of Santiago de Cuba, Cuba **:** of the kind or style prevalent in Santiago de Cuba

san·tims \'säntəmz\ *n, pl* **san·ti·mi** \-təmē\ [Latvian, fr. F *centime* — more at CENTIME] **1 :** a unit of value of Latvia equivalent to 1/100 lat between 1922 and 1940 **2 :** a coin representing one santims

san·tir \san·'ti(ə)r\ *also* **san·tour** \-tů(ə)r\ *n* -S [Ar *sinṭīr*, *sanṭīr*, *sanṭūr*, fr. Gk *psaltērion* psaltery, harp — more at PSALTER] **:** a Persian dulcimer that is played with two curved sticks

santo \'sän·(,)tō\ *n* -S [Sp, fr. LL *sanctus* — more at SAINT] **1 :** SAINT **2 :** a saint's image; *esp* **:** a painted or carved wooden image usu. found in New Mexico ⟨had carved crude ~*s* of the Virgin and St. Joseph and the Child —Ann Ehidester⟩

¹san·to do·min·gan \¦santōdə¦miŋgən\ *adj, usu cap S&D* [*Santo Domingo* (former name of the Dominican Republic) + E *-an*] **:** of or relating to Santo Domingo or the Dominican Republic

²santo domingan \"\ *n, cap S&D* **:** a native or inhabitant of Santo Domingo

san·to do·min·go \-ŋ(,)gō\ *n, pl* **santo domingo** *or* **santo domingos** *usu cap S&D* [fr. *Santo Domingo*, pueblo in central New Mexico] **1 a :** a Keres people occupying a pueblo in New Mexico **b :** a member of such people **2 :** the language of the Santo Domingo people

san·tol \sän·'tōl\ *n* -S [Tag *santól*] **:** an Indo-Malayan tree (*Sandoricum indicum* or *S. koetjape*) of the family Meliaceae that yields a reddish wood and that is sometimes cultivated for its red acid fruits which are used esp. in preserves and pickles

san·to·li·na \,santə'līnə\ *n* [NL, alter. of L *santonica*] **1** *cap* **:** a genus of Mediterranean undershrubs (family Compositae) having dissected leaves resembling those of the yarrow and clustered flower heads that lack ray flowers — see LAVENDER COTTON **2** -S **:** any plant of the genus *Santolina*

¹san·ton \'santᵊn, -tən\ *n* -S [F, fr. Sp *santón*, aug. of *santo* saint] **:** a saint in Muslim countries **:** a dervish regarded by the people as a saint

²san·ton \säⁿtōⁿ\ *n* -S [F, fr. Prov *santoun*, lit., little saint, fr. *sant* saint, fr. LL *sanctus* saint, fr. L, holy — more at SAINT] **:** a small clay image from southern France that is used in a Christmas crèche

san·ton·i·ca \san·'tänəkə\ *n* -S [NL, fr. L (*herba*) *santonica*, an herb, prob. wormwood, fem. of *santonicus* of or belonging to the Santoni, fr. *Santoni* a people of Aquitania + L *-icus* -ic] **1 :** a European wormwood (*Artemisia pauciflora*) **2 :** an anthelmintic drug consisting of the unexpanded dried flower heads of the santonica or a closely related plant (as Levant wormseed)

san·to·nin \'santᵊnən, -tən-\ *n* -S [ISV *santon-* (fr. NL *santonica*) + *-in*] **:** a poisonous slightly bitter crystalline compound $C_{15}H_{18}O_3$ that is a bicyclic sesquiterpenoid ketonic lactone occurring in santonica and in other plants of the genus *Artemisia* and used esp. formerly as an anthelmintic

san·to ni·ño \¦säntō'nēn(,)yō\ *n* [Sp, lit., holy child] **:** an image of the Christ child

san·to·rin earth \¦santə¦rēn-\ *or* **santorin** *n, usu cap S* [fr. *Santorin*, Greek island in the Aegean] **:** a volcanic tuff from the island of Santorin consisting principally of a fine light gray siliceous material used for making cement

san·to·ri·ni's cartilage \¦santə¦rēnēz-, ¦sän-\ *n, usu cap S* [after Giovanni D. *Santorini* †1737? Ital. anatomist] **:** CORNICULATE CARTILAGE

santorini's duct *n, usu cap S* [after Giovanni D. *Santorini* †1737? Ital. anatomist] **:** DUCT OF SANTORINI

¹san·tos \'santəs\ *adj, usu cap* [fr. *Santos*, city in southeastern Brazil] **:** of or from the city of Santos, Brazil **:** of the kind or style prevalent in Santos

²santos \"\ *n* -ES [after *Santos*, Brazil, principal shipping port for coffee in Brazil] **1** *or* **santos coffee** *usu cap S* **:** Brazilian coffee that is produced chiefly in São Paulo and is characterized by moderate body and somewhat acid flavor — see BOURBON 5 **2** *often cap* **:** DARK BEAVER

santour *var of* SANTIR

sants *pl of* SANT, *pres 3d sing of* SANT

san ts'ai \'sän'tsī\ *n* [Chin(Pek) *san¹ ts'ai³* three-color] **:** a 3-color enamel-glazed ceramic ware produced during the Ming dynasty and later

sa·nu·si *also* **se·nus·si** \sə'nüsē\ *n, pl* **sanusi** *or* **sanusis** *also* **senussi** *or* **senussis** *usu cap* [after Muhammad ibn Ali as-*Sanūsī* †1859 Algerian religious leader, founder of the Sanusi brotherhood] **:** a member of a Muslim brotherhood of No. Africa founded in 1837 who observes a strict and ascetic type of Islamic orthodoxy combined with a militant aggressiveness in pursuance of political goals

sa·nu·si·ya *or* **sa·nu·si·yah** \-ē(y)ə\ *n pl, usu cap* [Ar *Sanūsīya*, after Muhammad as-*Sanūsī* †1859] **:** SANUSIS

san·vi·ta·lia \,sanvə'tālēə\ *n* [NL, prob. fr. F. *Sanvitali* †1761 Ital. mathematician (or fr. the *Sanvitali* family, many of whose members were famous) + NL *-ia*] **1** *cap* **:** a small genus of chiefly tropical American annual herbs (family Compositae) having small heads with yellow or white rays, a flat receptacle, and naked or awn-tipped achenes — see CREEPING ZINNIA **2** -S **:** any plant of the genus *Sanvitalia*

san·wa millet \'säŋwə-\ *n* [Hindi *sāwā*, fr. Skt *śyāmāka* millet] **:** JAPANESE MILLET

san·ya \'sänyə\ *n, pl* **sanya** *or* **sanyas** *usu cap* **1 :** a Tlingit people about Cape Fox, Alaska **2 :** a member of the Sanya people

são pau·lo \(')saůⁿ(m)¦paů(,)lü\ *adj, usu cap S&P* [fr. *São Paulo*, Brazil] **:** of or from the city of São Paulo, Brazil **:** of the kind or style prevalent in São Paulo

saora *usu cap, var of* SAURA

sao·shyant \'saůshyənt\ *n* -S *usu cap* [Av, savior] **:** one of three deliverers of later Zoroastrian eschatology appearing at thousand year intervals and each inaugurating a new order of things and a special period of human progress

1sap \'sap\ *n* -s [ME, fr. OE *sæp;* akin to OHG *saf* sap, MD *sap*] **1 a :** the fluid part of a plant; *specif* **:** a watery solution of gases (as carbon dioxide), salts and other materials from the soil, and organic products of metabolism that circulates through the vascular system, carries raw materials to the peripheral chlorophyll-bearing cells, translocates the products of metabolism to other parts of the plant for use or storage, and is a major commercial source of sugar in sugarcane, various palms, and the sugar maple **b** (1) **:** a body fluid (as blood, lymph, saliva, or semen) essential to life or health or characteristic of a healthy, fresh, or vigorous condition (2) **:** bodily health and vigor **:** VITALITY ⟨the ~ of youth, the sapience of age⟩ **c** *chiefly Scot* **:** a beverage taken with solid food **d :** moisture in stone **2 a :** SAPWOOD **b saps** *pl* **:** lumber containing much sapwood and inferior in quality to firsts and seconds **3 a** *Brit* **:** GRIND 3 **b :** a person unusually liable to be taken in (as by his own sentimentality or gullibility or by a deliberate trick) **:** SIMPLETON, FOOL ⟨fleecing one ~ at a time —Alva Johnston⟩ **4 :** outside stone (as in a quarry) softened by weathering **5 :** a blackjack, policeman's club, or other object used as a bludgeon ⟨his ~ made of rocks in a sock —Frank McIntyre⟩

2sap \"\ *n* -s [MF & OIt; MF *sape, sappe* spade, hoe, fr. OIt *zappa,* perh. fr. OIt dial. *zappo* goat] **1 a** *obs* **:** the act or process of undermining an enemy fortification **b :** the act or process of digging a trench from within **c :** the act or process of weakening or destroying by stealth or devious methods ⟨an endeavor by slow ~ to weaken the authority of some of the writers —C.J.Ellicott⟩ **2 a :** a trench prolonged in the desired direction by digging away the earth at its head from within the trench itself and usu. throwing the earth up as a parapet on the exposed flank and on the end as additional protection to the working party — compare FLYING SAP **b :** a trench or gallery dug from an attacker's lines to a point beneath an enemy's fortifications to gain entrance or to destroy them with explosives

3sap \"\ *vb* **sapped; sapped; sapping; saps** [MF *saper, sapper,* prob. fr. OIt *zappare,* fr. *zappa* spade, hoe] *vi* **:** to proceed by or execute a sap ~ *vt* **1 :** to subvert by digging or eroding the substratum or foundation **:** UNDERMINE ⟨the village . . . may be slowly *sapped* away by ants moving blindly over the earth —David Garnett⟩ **2 a :** to diminish gradually the supply or intensity of ⟨his driving ambition . . . was slowly *sapping* away his fundamental decency and idealism —F.G.Slaughter⟩ ⟨old organisms do produce some substance which ~*s* their vigor —Waldemar Kaempffert⟩ **b :** to exhaust the energy or vitality of ⟨it isn't merely danger which ~*s* these young men —Frederic Morton⟩ **3 :** to operate against or pierce by a sap **syn** see WEAKEN

4sap \"\ *vb* **sapped; sapped; sapping; saps** [1*sap*] *vt* **1 a :** to drain or deprive of its sap **b :** to draw off (sap) **2 :** to heat flue-cured tobacco to a high temperature for a short interval after its being hung in a barn to drive off moisture and start the curing **3 :** to knock out with a sap ⟨whether a guy fell or whether he was *sapped —Police Gazette*⟩ ~ *vi, Brit* **:** to act the sap **:** GRIND

sap *abbr* sapwood

SAP *abbr* **1** semi-armor-piercing **2** soon as possible

sa·pa \'sāpə\ *n* -s [L; akin to L *sapere* to taste, have good taste — more at SAGE] **:** grape juice evaporated to a syrupy consistency or to the consistency of honey and used esp. in the 16th century as a cough cure **:** MUST

sap·a·jou \'sapə,jü, ,==ˈzhü\ *n* -s [F, fr. Tupi] **1 :** CAPUCHIN 3b **2 :** SPIDER MONKEY

sa·pan \sə'pan, 'sa,pan\ *n* -s [Malay *sapang*] **:** the heartwood of sappanwood formerly used as an astringent

sapanwood *var of* SAPPANWOOD

sap cavity *n* [1*sap*] **:** VACUOLE

sap chafer *n* **:** any of various sap-feeding flower beetles esp. of the family Cetoniidae

sap–drawer \'=,=(=)\ *n* **:** one of the small lower branches left on a topworked or frameworked tree to nourish the roots until new growth is well established

sa·pe·le mahogany *or* **sapele** *also* **sa·pe·li** \sə'pēlē\ *n* -s [*sapele, sapeli* fr. native name in West Africa] **1 :** MAHOGANY 1b(2) **2 :** a tree (esp. *Entandrophragma cylindricum*) that produces sapele mahogany

sa·peque *also* **sa·pek** \sə'pek\ *n* -s [F *sapèque,* fr. Malay *sa pek, sa pe,* fr. *sa* one + *pek, pe* pie (currency)] **:** 2CASH; *esp* **:** a cash formerly issued by France for use in Indochina

sa·per·da \sə'pərdə\ *n* [NL, prob. fr. Gk *saperdēs,* a fish, prob. perch] **1** *cap* **:** a genus of long-horned beetles containing several whose larvae are destructive borers — see APPLE TREE BORER, LINDEN BORER **2** -s **:** any beetle of the genus *Saperda*

sap flow *n* **:** TRANSPIRATION STREAM

sap·ful \'sapfəl\ *adj* [1*sap* + *-ful*] **:** SAPPY 1a

sap green *n* **1 :** a dull green lake prepared from buckthorn berries — compare LOKAO **2 a :** a strong yellow green **b :** a light olive color that is greener and less strong than citrine and darker than grape green — called also *bladder green, verd vessie*

sap gum *n* **1 :** sapwood from the sweet gum or lumber sawed from it **2 :** SWEET GUM **3 :** lumber sawed from a tree of the genus *Nyssa*

1saphead \'=,=\ *n* [1*sap* + *head*] **:** a weak-minded stupid person **:** SAP 3b

2saphead \"\ *n* [2*sap* + *head*] **:** the end of a sap at which digging is in progress

sa·phe·na \sə'fēnə\ *n* -s *often attrib* [ME, fr. ML, fr. Ar *ṣāfin*] **:** SAPHENOUS VEIN

sa·phe·nous \-nəs\ *adj* [*saphena* + *-ous*] **:** of, relating to, associated with, situated near, or being the two chief superficial veins of the leg ⟨the ~ opening gives passage to the long saphenous vein through the fascia lata⟩

saphenous vein *n* **:** either of two chief superficial veins of the leg: as **a :** one originating in the foot and passing up the medial side of the leg and through the saphenous opening to join the femoral vein — called also *internal saphenous vein, long saphenous vein* **b :** one originating similarly and passing up the back of the leg to join the popliteal at the knee — called also *external saphenous vein, short saphenous vein*

saph·ie *also* **saf·fi** \'safē\ *n* -s [Mandingo *safaye*] **:** a West African talisman, amulet, or charm

sa·phir d'eau \sa'fi(ə)r'dō\ *n, pl* **saphirs d'eau** \-i(ə)r(z)'-\ [F] **:** WATER SAPPHIRE

sa·pi·ao \,säpē'aù\ *or* **sapiao net** *n* -s [native name in the Philippines] **:** a round haul net of the Philippines made of cotton twine and used for catching small pelagic fishes

sap·id \'sapə̇d\ *adj* [L *sapidus* tasty, savory, fr. *sapere* to taste, have good taste — more at SAGE] **1 a :** affecting the organs of taste **:** possessing flavor **b :** having a strong esp. agreeable flavor **:** SAVORY **2 :** agreeable to the mind **syn** see PALATABLE

sa·pid·i·ty \sə'pidəd·ē, -dətē, -i\ *n* -ES **:** the quality or state of being sapid **:** SAVOR, SAVORINESS **syn** see TASTE

sapi·ence \'sāpēən(t)s, 'sap-\ *n* -s [ME, fr. MF, fr. L *sapientia,* fr. *sapient-, sapiens* (pres. part.) + *-ia* -y] **1 a :** the quality of being sapient **:** profound knowledge **:** WISDOM, SAGENESS ⟨the perspective of four or five decades informing his judgment with a clarity and authority which are what we mean by ~ —E.A.Weeks⟩ **b** *obs* **:** wisdom regarding ultimate principles in speculative or theoretical rather than practical knowledge ⟨wisdom . . . may denote either ~, a habit of knowing what is true; or prudence, a disposition of choosing what is good —Isaac Barrow⟩ **2** *obs* **:** exactness and discrimination in expression

sapi·ens \'sapēənz, 'sāp- *also* -ē,enz *or* -ē,en(t)s\ *adj* [NL (specific epithet of *Homo sapiens*), fr. L, knowing] **:** of, relating to, resembling, or being recent man (*Homo sapiens*) as distinguished from various fossil men

1sapi·ent \'sāpēənt, 'sap-\ *adj* [ME, fr. MF, fr. L *sapient-, sapiens,* pres. part. of *sapere* to have sense, be wise — more at SAGE] **:** possessing or expressing great sagacity and discernment **:** SAGE ⟨valuable insights and ~ advice to educators —H.A.Larrabee⟩ ⟨eyes that were ~ and almost ironical —T.W.Duncan⟩ ⟨a ~ author⟩ **syn** see WISE

2sapient \"\ *n, archaic* **:** a sapient person

sapi·en·tial \¦==¦enchəl\ *adj* [ME *sapiencial,* fr. LL *sapientialis,* fr. L *sapientia* wisdom + *-alis* -al] **:** characterized by or peculiar to wisdom ⟨the ~ attitude . . . replaced the imprecatory attitude —Joseph Frank⟩ ⟨attributing a ~ function to prudence —V.J.Bourke⟩

sapiential books *n* **:** the biblical books of Proverbs, Ecclesiastes, Canticle of Canticles, Wisdom, and Ecclesiasticus

sapi·ent·ly *adv* **:** in a sapient manner

sa·pin \sa'paⁿ\ *n* -s [ME, fr. MF, fr. L *sapinus, sappinus,* of Gaulish origin; akin to W *syb-wydd* fir, Corn *sib-nit* silver fir; akin to OSlav *sokŭ* sap] **:** FIR 1

sa·pin·da \sə'pində\ *n* -s [Skt *sapiṇḍa,* lit., having the same lump, fr. *sa-* one and the same (akin to *sama* same) + *piṇḍa* lump of rice offered to deceased ancestors; fr. the fact that the lump is offered to the three nearest ancestors and the crumbs to the next three — more at SAME] **:** a person considered in his relation to any of his three or sometimes six nearest lineal male ancestors or descendants

sap·in·da·ce·ae \,sapən'dāsē,ē\ *n pl, cap* [NL, fr. *Sapindus,* type genus + *-aceae*] **:** a large family of chiefly tropical and predominantly Old World woody plants (order Sapindales) with alternate and usu. pinnate or trifoliolate leaves that lack stipules, small flowers commonly in axillary or terminal panicles, and a fruit that may be capsular, drupaceous, or made up of samaras — **sap·in·da·ceous** \¦==¦dāshəs\ *adj*

sap·in·da·les \,=='dā(,)lēz\ *n pl, cap* [NL, prob. fr. *Sapindus* + *-ales*] **:** an order of dicotyledonous plants having the stamens inserted on a disk and the ovary with one or two ovules in each cell

sa·pin·dus \sə'pindəs\ *n, cap* [NL, prob. fr. L *sapo* soap + *Indus* of India, India, fr. Gk *Indos* — more at SAPONACEOUS, INDIA] **:** a genus of tropical and subtropical trees (family Hippocastanaceae) having simply pinnate leaves, flowers nearly regular, and fruit a globose or 2- to 3-lobed berry — see SOAPBERRY; compare SAPINDACEAE

sa·pit \sä'pēt\ *n* -s [Moro, prob. modif. of E *sailboat*] **:** a decorated sailboat of Sulu Archipelago

sa·pi·um \'sāpēəm\ *n, cap* [NL, prob. fr. L *sapinus* fir] **:** a genus of tropical trees and shrubs (family Euphorbiaceae) having poisonous milky juice, alternate entire leaves and apetalous flowers in spikes — see CHINESE TALLOW TREE

sa·pi·u·tan \¦säpē'ütᵊn\ *n* -s [Malay *sapi hutan* wild cattle, fr. *sapi* cow + *hutan* forest, wild] **:** ANOA

sa·ple \'sāpəl\ *n* -s [by alter.] **:** SABLE

sap·less \'saplə̇s\ *adj* [1*sap* + *-less*] **1 a :** destitute of sap or other vital juices **:** DRY ⟨the wood dry and splintered and dead, the rats and roaches scurrying along the ~ planks —Norman Mailer⟩ **b :** barren and unproductive from lack of moisture ⟨a rock, barren, and herbless, and ~ —E.G.Bulwer-Lytton⟩ **2 :** lacking vitality **:** LIFELESS, FEEBLE ⟨my mother's hair at this time was full of gray and her body looked ~ —Nadine Gordimer⟩ **3 :** being without substantial value **:** INSIPID ⟨a somewhat ~ tale of a poor little rich girl and a rich little poor boy —Florence Bullock⟩ — **sap·less·ness** *n* -ES

sap·ling \'sapliŋ, -lēŋ\ *n* -s [ME, fr. 1*sap* + *-ling*] **1 :** a young tree; *specif* **:** a young forest tree not over four inches in diameter at breast height **2 :** YOUTH ⟨a young foolish ~ —Shak.⟩ **3 :** a greyhound whelped prior to a running season but in the same calendar year

sap·ling·hood \-,hùd\ *n* **:** the state of being a sapling

1sa·po \'sä,pō\ *n* -s [AmerSp, fr. Sp, toad] **:** TOADFISH

2sa·po \'sā,pō\ *n* -s [L] **:** 1SOAP 1; *esp* **:** a sodium soap — compare CASTILE

sap·o·dil·la \,sapə'dilə, -dē(y)ə\ *also* **sap·o·til·la** \-'tilə, -tē(y)ə\ *or* **sap·o·ti·lha** \-'tilyə\ *n* -s [*sapodilla, sapotilla* fr. Sp *zapotillo,* dim. of *zapote* sapodilla plum; *sapotilha* fr. Pg, prob. fr. Sp *zapotillo* — more at SAPOTA] **1 :** a large tree (*Achras zapota*) found throughout tropical No. America but naturalized throughout the tropical world with hard reddish durable wood and handsome evergreen foliage and latex that yields chicle **2** *or* **sapodilla plum :** the fruit of the sapodilla with a rough brownish skin and very sweet brownish pulp — called also *chico, chicozapote, nispero*

sapodilla family *n* **:** SAPOTACEAE

sap·o·gen·in \,sapə'jenə̇n; sə'päjənə̇n, -,nēn\ *n* -s [ISV *saponin* + *-genin*] **:** the nonsugar portion of a saponin obtained by hydrolysis or in a few cases found free in plants and characterized by either a triterpenoid usu. pentacyclic structure (as in quillaic acid) or by a steroid structure usu. having a spiro acetal side chain (as in diosgenin) ⟨interest in the steroidal ~*s* has been increasing in recent years because of their usefulness as starting materials in the synthesis of steroidal hormones —Stephen Kaufmann⟩

sap·o·na·ceous \¦sapə¦nāshəs\ *adj* [NL *saponaceus,* fr. L *sapon-, sapo* soap (of Gmc origin) + *-aceus* -aceous; akin to OE *sāpe* soap — more at SOAP] **1 :** resembling soap **:** having the qualities of soap **:** SOAPY **2 :** liable to slip away **:** ingratiating but evasive **:** ELUSIVE — **sap·o·na·ceous·ness** *n* -ES

sap·o·nar·ia \,=='na(a)rēə\ *n, cap* [NL, fr. ML, fem. of *saponarius* of soap, fr. L *sapon-, sapo* soap + *-arius* -ary] **:** a genus of Old World herbs (family Caryophyllaceae) having large flowers with a tubular or gibbous calyx, five clawed petals, and a 4-valved capsular fruit — see SOAPWORT

sap·o·nary \'==,nerē\ *n* -ES [NL *Saponaria*] **:** SOAPWORT 1

sap·o·nat·ed \¦==¦nād·əd\ *adj* [L *sapon-, sapo* soap + E *-ate* + *-ed*] **:** treated or combined with a soap ⟨~ cresol solution⟩

sa·po·ni \sə'pōnē\ *n, pl* **saponi** *or* **saponis** *usu cap* **1 :** an extinct Siouan people of central Virginia **2 :** a member of the Saponi people

sa·pon·i·fi·able \sə'pänə,fīəbəl, =,=='===\ *adj* **:** capable of being saponified

sa·pon·i·fi·ca·tion \=,==_fə̇'kāshən\ *n* -s [F, fr. *saponifier* to saponify, after such pairs as F *identifier* to identify: *identification*] **1 a :** the act, process, or result of soapmaking **:** conversion into soap **:** the hydrolysis of a fat by alkali with the formation of salts of the fatty acids together with glycerol **b :** the hydrolysis of a fat or wax **2 a :** the hydrolysis esp. by alkali of an ester into the corresponding alcohol and acid or salt of the acid **b :** the hydrolysis of an organic compound esp. by alkali

saponification value *or* **saponification number** *n* **:** a measure of the total free and combined acids esp. in a fat, wax, or resin expressed as the number of milligrams of potassium hydroxide required for the complete saponification of one gram of substance

sa·pon·i·fi·er \sə'pänə,fī(ə)r, -fīə\ *n* -s **:** one that saponifies: as **a :** a reagent used to cause saponification **b :** an apparatus for saponifying fats

sa·pon·i·fy \-,fī\ *vb* -ED/-ING/-ES [F *saponifier,* fr. L *sapon-, sapo* soap + *-ifier* -ify] *vt* **:** to convert (as a fat or fatty acid) into soap **:** subject to saponification ~ *vi* **:** to undergo saponification

sap·o·nin \'sapənə̇n\ *n* -s [F *saponine,* fr. L *sapon-, sapo* soap + *-ine* -in] **1 :** any of numerous glycosides that occur in many plants (as soapbark, soapwort, or sarsaparilla), that are characterized by their properties of foaming in water solution and producing hemolysis when solutions are injected into the bloodstream, and that on hydrolysis yield a triterpenoid or steroid sapogenin and one or more sugars (as glucose, galactose, or xylose) **2 :** a yellowish to white acrid hygroscopic amorphous substance that in powder form causes sneezing, that is extracted esp. from soapbark or soapwort, that contains a triterpenoid saponin as the active ingredient, and that is used chiefly as a foaming and emulsifying agent and detergent

sap·o·nite \-,nīt\ *n* -s [Sw *saponit,* fr. L *sapon-, sapo* soap + Sw *-it* -ite — more at SAPONACEOUS] **:** a mineral consisting of a hydrous magnesium aluminosilicate occurring in soft soapy masses and filling veins and cavities in serpentine, diabase, and other rocks (sp. gr. 2.24–2.30)

sa·por \'sāpə(r)\ *n* -s [ME, fr. L — more at SAVOR] **:** a property (as bitterness) affecting the sense of taste **:** SAVOR, FLAVOR

sap·o·rif·ic \¦sapə¦rifik\ *adj* [NL *saporificus,* fr. L *sapor* savor + *-i-* + *-ficus* -fic] **:** having the power to produce the sensation of taste

sap·o·rous \'sapərəs\ *adj* [LL *saporosus,* fr. L *sapor* savor + *-osus* -ose] **:** of, relating to, or capable of exciting the sensation of taste **:** having flavor; *esp* **:** agreeable in taste **syn** see PALATABLE

sapos *pl of* SAPO

1sa·po·ta \sə'pōd·ə\ [NL, fr. Sp *zapote*] *syn of* ACHRAS

2sapota \"\ *n* -s [earlier *sapote,* fr. Sp *zapote,* fr. Nahuatl *tzapotl*] **:** SAPODILLA

sap·o·ta·ce·ae \,sapə'tāsē,ē\ *n pl, cap* [NL, fr. *Sapota* (syn. of *Achras*) + *-aceae*] **:** a family of trees or shrubs (order Ebenales) that are widely distributed in tropical regions and have milky juice, coriaceous leaves, and axillary flowers with stamens in two or three whorls borne on the corolla and often in alternation with staminodia and a superior 2-celled to many-celled ovary followed by often edible fleshy fruits — **sap·o·ta·ceous** \¦==¦tāshəs\ *adj*

sapota gum *n* **:** chicle obtained from the sapodilla

sa·po·te \sə'pōd·ē\ *or* **za·po·te** \zə-,sə-\ *n* -s [Sp *zapote*] **1 a :** MARMALADE TREE; *also* **:** its fruit **b :** SAPODILLA **2** *Philippines* **:** a date plum (*Diospyros ebenaster*)

sapotilla *or* **sapotilha** *var of* SAPODILLA

sap·o·toxin \,sapə+\ *n* [*saponin* + *toxin*] **:** any of various highly poisonous saponins

sap·pan·wood *or* **sa·pan·wood** \sə'pan,=, 'sa,pan,=\ *also* **sap·pan** *n* -s [*sappanwood, sapanwood* fr. Malay *sapang* + E *wood; sappan* fr. Malay *sapang*] **1 :** a red soluble brazilwood obtained from an East Indian tree (*Caesalpinia sappan*) **2 :** a tree that yields sappanwood

sap·pare \'sa,pa(a)(ə)r, -pe(ə)r\ *n* -s [F, perh. modif. of E *sapphire*] **:** CYANITE

sapped *past of* SAP

1sap·per \'sapə(r)\ *n* -s [3*sap* + *-er*] **:** one that saps: as **a :** a member of a military engineer unit organized, trained, and equipped primarily to execute sapping and other field fortification work **b :** an engineer that lays, detects, and disarms mines

2sapper \"\ *n* -s [4*sap* + *-er*] **:** a sucking insect that punctures plants to feed on the sap (as various bugs or plant lice)

1sap·phic \'safik, -fēk\ *adj* [L *sapphicus,* fr. Gk *sapphikos,* fr. *Sapphō* Sappho *fl ab* 600 B.C. Greek lyric poetess of Lesbos + *-ikos* -ic] **1** *usu cap* **:** of or relating to the Greek lyric poetess Sappho **2** *sometimes cap* [so called fr. the reputed lesbian group associated with Sappho] **:** of or relating to erotic indulgence **3** *sometimes cap* [so called fr. being the verse forms used by Sappho] **:** of, relating to, or consisting of a four line strophe of three primarily trochaic lines made up of five equal beats of which the middle is a dactyl and the others are of two syllables and followed by an adonic

2sapphic \"\ *n* -s *sometimes cap* **1 :** a sapphic strophe **2 :** a line of verse having the metrical pattern of one of the first three lines of a sapphic strophe **3 :** a verse composed of sapphic strophes

1sap·phire \'sa,fī(ə)r, -fīə\ *n* -s [ME *saphir, safir,* fr. OF *safir,* fr. L *sapphirus,* fr. Gk *sappheiros,* fr. Heb *sappīr,* fr. Skt *śanipriya,* lit., dear to the planet Saturn, fr. *Śani* (the planet) Saturn + *priya* dear — more at FREE] **1 a :** a precious stone of transparent rich blue corundum of great value **b** (1) **:** a pure variety of corundum in transparent or translucent crystals used as gems (2) **:** a gem from a corundum crystal **2 a :** a variable color averaging a deep purplish blue that is bluer and deeper than hyacinth blue or Mazarine blue and stronger than cyanine blue (sense 1b) **b :** a dark blue that is greener than Peking blue, greener, lighter, and stronger than Japan blue, and greener and stronger than Flemish blue **3 :** a hummingbird of the genus *Hylocharis* native to So. America and having a bright blue throat and breast

2sapphire \"\ *adj* [ME *saphir,* fr. *saphir,* n., sapphire] **1 :** of or resembling sapphire **2 :** of the color sapphire blue **:** SAPPHIRINE

sapphireberry \'=,=- — *see* BERRY\ *n* **:** ASIATIC SWEETLEAF

sapphire gurnard *n* **:** SAPPHIRINE GURNARD

sapphire quartz *n* **:** a rare blue variety of quartz

sapphirewing \'=,=,=\ *n* **:** a So. American hummingbird (*Pterophanes cyanopterus*) with blue wings

sap·phir·ic \sə'firik\ *adj* **:** having the nature of or resembling a sapphire

1sap·phir·ine \'safərə̇n, -,rīn, -,rēn\ *adj* [ME *saphirin,* fr. L *sapphirinus,* fr. Gk *sappheirinos,* fr. *sappheiros* sapphire + *-inos* -ine] **1 :** made of sapphire **2 :** resembling sapphire esp. in color

2sapphirine \"\ *n* -s [G *saphirin,* fr. *saphir* sapphire (fr. MHG *saphīr,* fr. OIt *saffiro,* fr. L *sapphirus*) + *-in* -ine] **:** a mineral $(MgFe)_{15}(Al,Fe)_{34}Si_7O_{80}$ consisting of a green or pale blue magnesium aluminum iron silicate and oxide and occurring usu. in granular form (hardness 7.5, sp. gr. 3.42–3.48)

sapphirine gurnard *n* **:** a European gurnard (*Trigla hirundo*) having the pectoral fins much blotched with a rich blue

sap·phism \'sa,fizəm\ *n* -s *sometimes cap* [*Sappho fl ab* 600 B.C. Greek poetess of Lesbos + E *-ism;* fr. the belief that Sappho was homosexual] **:** sensual desire of a woman for other women **:** LESBIANISM

sap·phist \-_fə̇st\ *n* -s *sometimes cap* [*Sappho fl ab* 600 B.C. + E *-ist*] **:** LESBIAN 2

sap·pho \'sa,fō\ *n* [NL, after *Sappho fl ab* 600 B.C. Greek lyric poetess, fr. L, fr. Gk *Sapphō*] **1** *cap* **:** a genus of hummingbirds comprising a single So. American showy bird (*S. sparganura*) with a forked tail **2** *also* **sappho comet** -s *usu cap S* **:** any hummingbird of the genus *Sappho*

sap pine *n* **1 :** a pitch pine (*Pinus rigida*) **2 :** LOBLOLLY

sap·pi·ness \'sapēnə̇s, -pin-\ *n* -ES [*sappy* + *-ness*] **1 :** the state of being full of or smelling of sap **2 :** the quality or state of being sappy **:** FOOLISHNESS

sapping *pres part of* SAP

sap·ples \'sapəlz\ *n pl* [prob. dim. (pl.) of E dial. (Sc) *saip* soap, fr. OE *sāpe* — more at SOAP] *Scot* **:** SUDS

sap·po·ro \sə'pōr(,)ō, -pò(,)rō\ *adj, usu cap* [fr. *Sapporo,* Japan] **:** of or from the city of Sapporo, Japan **:** of the kind or style prevalent in Sapporo

sap·py \'sapē, -pi\ *adj* -ER/-EST [ME *sapy,* fr. OE *sæpig,* fr. *sæp* sap + *-ig* -y — more at SAP] **1 a :** abounding with sap **b** *dial* **:** SUCCULENT, JUICY **c** *dial* **:** becoming putrid **:** TAINTED **d** *dial* **:** extremely damp **:** SODDEN **e** *of wool* **:** having a superabundance of yolk **f** *of a feather* **:** immature and with blood in the quill **2 a :** resembling sapwood **b :** consisting largely of sapwood **3 a :** foolishly or immaturely sentimental **:** MAWKISH **b :** lacking in good sense **:** FOOLISH, SILLY **c :** somewhat effeminate **:** FOPPISH **4** *chiefly Scot* **a :** fond of drinking **b :** cheerful as the result of drinking

sappy spot *n* **:** a portion of wood or lumber showing the effects of decay

sapr- *or* **sapro-** *comb form* [Gk, fr. *sapros;* perh. akin to Lith *šupti* to rot] **1 :** rotten **:** putrid ⟨*sapr*emia⟩ ⟨*sapro*stomous⟩ **2 :** dead or decaying organic matter ⟨*sapro*dontia⟩ ⟨*sapro*phyte⟩ **3 :** saprophytic ⟨*Sapro*legnia⟩ **4 :** sapropel ⟨*sapro*coll⟩ ⟨*sapro*dil⟩

sa·pre·mia \sə'prēmēə\ *n* -s [NL, fr. *sapr-* + *-emia*] **:** a toxic state resulting from the presence in the blood of toxic products of putrefactive bacteria and often accompanying gangrene of a part of the body — **sa·pre·mic** \-mik\ *adj*

sap·robe \'sa,prōb\ *or* **sap·ro·bi·ont** \¦sa,prō'bī,änt, sə'prōbē,ä-\ *n* -s [*saprobe* ISV *sapr-* + *-be* (fr. Gk *bios* life); *saprobiont* ISV *sapr-* + *-biont* — more at QUICK] **:** a saprobic organism

sa·probic \sə'prōbik, -präb-\ *adj* [ISV *saprobe* + *-ic*] **:** SAPROPHYTIC; *esp* **:** living in or being an environment rich in organic matter and relatively free from oxygen ⟨~ organisms living in sewage⟩ — compare KATHAROBIC — **sa·probi·cal·ly** \-bə̇k(ə)lē\ *adv*

sap·ro·coll \'saprə,käl\ *n* -s [ISV *sapr-* + *-coll*] **:** gelatinous sapropel

sap·ro·dil \-,dil\ *n* -s [prob. fr. *sapr-* + *-dil* (fr. *dilute*)] **:** a sapropel found in the Tertiary

sap·ro·gen \'saprəjə̇n, -,jen\ *n* -s [ISV *sapr-* + *-gen*] **:** an organism (as a fungus) living upon nonliving organic matter and capable of producing its decay; *also* **:** PERTHOPHYTE

sap·ro·genesis \¦saprə+\ *n* [NL, fr. *sapr-* + *genesis*] **:** a part of the life cycle during which a pathogenic organism is living saprophytically or in a dormant state (as the ascospore stage of the apple scab fungus)

sap·ro·gen·ic \¦==¦jenik\ *adj* [*sapr-* + *-genic*] **1 :** capable of producing decay or putrefaction (as any of various saprophytic bacteria) — compare SAPROPHILOUS **2 a :** of or relating to the production of putrefaction **b :** occurring or produced in or upon putrefying matter

sap·ro·ge·nic·i·ty \,==_jə̇'nisəd·ē\ *n* -ES **:** the capacity for becoming saprogenic

sa·prog·e·nous \sə'präjənəs\ *adj* [*sapr-* + *-genous*] **:** SAPROGENIC

sap·ro·leg·nia \\,saprə'legnēə\\ *n* [NL, fr. *sapr-* + Gk *legnon* border + NL *-ia*] **1** *cap* **:** a genus (the type of the family Saprolegniaceae of the order Saprolegniales) of fungi having a stout tubular multinucleate much-branched thallus without constrictions, producing dimorphic zoospores, growing in water chiefly on plant debris and animal remains, and including one form (*S. ferax*) that attacks living fish, tadpoles, and spawn and causes the white fungus disease **2** -s **:** any fungus of the genus *Saprolegnia*

sap·ro·leg·ni·a·les \\,==,legnē'ā(,)lēz\\ *n pl, cap* [NL, fr. *Saprolegnia* + *-ales*] **:** an order of chiefly aquatic fungi (class Phycomycetes) having a well-developed mycelium, both sexual and asexual reproduction, biflagellate zoospores, and no periplasm in the oogonia and comprising the water molds — see DIPLANETIC — **sap·ro·leg·ni·ous** \\¦==¦legnēəs\\ *adj*

sap·ro·lite \\'saprə,līt\\ *n* -s [*sapr-* + *-lite*] **:** disintegrated somewhat decomposed rock that lies in its original place — compare GEEST, MANTLEROCK — **sap·ro·lit·ic** \\¦==¦lid·ik\\ *adj*

sap·ront \\'sa,pränt\\ *n* -s [contr. of *saprobiont*] **:** SAPROBE

sap·ro·pel \\'saprə,pel\\ *n* -s [ISV *sapr-* + *-pel* (fr. Gk *pēlos* clay, mud) — more at PEL-] **1 :** a slimy sediment of marine, estuarine, or lacustrine deposition consisting largely of organic debris derived from aquatic plants and animals **2 :** KEROGEN

sap·ro·pel·ic \\¦==¦pelik\\ *adj* [ISV *sapropel* + *-ic*] **1 :** living in mud or ooze composed chiefly of decaying organic matter (as various freshwater protozoa) **2 :** of, relating to, or derived from sapropel ⟨the organic carbon may be humic (coaly) or ~ (bituminous) —F.J.Pettijohn⟩

sap·ro·pel·ite \\'==,pe,līt, ,=='=,=\\ *n* -s [*sapropel* + *-ite*] **:** a coal or oil shale formed from sapropel

1**sa·proph·a·gan** \\sə'präfəgən\\ *n* -s [(assumed) NL *saprophagus* + E *-an*] **:** a saprophagous individual

2**saprophagan** \\"\\ *adj* **:** SAPROPHAGOUS

sa·proph·a·gous \\-gəs\\ *adj* [prob. fr. (assumed) NL *saprophagus*, fr. *sapr-* + *-phagus* -phagous] **:** feeding on decaying matter

sa·proph·i·lous \\sə'präfələs\\ *also* **sap·ro·phile** \\'saprə,fīl\\ *adj* [ISV *sapr-* + *-philous* or *-phile*] **:** SAPROPHYTIC; *specif* **:** thriving in decaying matter ⟨~ bacteria⟩

sap·ro·phyte *also* **sap·ro·phite** \\'saprə,fīt\\ *n* -s [ISV *sapr-* + *-phyte, -phite* (alter. of *-phyte*)] **1 :** a plant living on dead or decaying organic matter — compare AUTOPHYTE, PERTHOPHYTE **2 :** an organism engaging in saprophytic nutrition — compare PARASITE

1**sap·ro·phyt·ic** \\¦==¦fid·ik\\ *adj* [*saprophyte* + *-ic*] **:** obtaining food by absorbing dissolved organic material **:** obtaining nourishment osmotically from the products of organic breakdown and decay ⟨~ plants and animals⟩ — compare AUTOTROPHIC, HOLOPHYTIC, HOLOZOIC; see SAPROZOIC — **sap·ro·phyt·i·cal·ly** \\-ək(ə)lē\\ *adv*

2**saprophytic** \\"\\ *n* -s **:** a saprophytic organism

sap·ro·phyt·ism \\'==,fīd·,izəm, -,fī,tiz-\\ *n* -s [*saprophyte* + *-ism*] **:** the condition of feeding saprophytically

sap·ro·spi·ra \\,saprə'spīrə\\ *n, cap* [NL, fr. *sapr-* + L *spira* coil — more at SPIRE] **:** a genus of large free-living or commensal aquatic spirochetes (family Spirochaetaceae) having neither crista nor flagella

sap rot *n* **:** a disintegration (as caused by wood-destroying fungi) of sapwood

sap·ro·zo·ic \\¦saprə¦zōik\\ *adj* [*sapr-* + *-zoic*] **:** SAPROPHYTIC — used of animals (as protozoans) — **sap·ro·zo·on** \\,=='zō,än\\ *n, pl* **sapro·zoa** \\-zōə\\

saps *pl of* SAP, *pres 3d sing of* SAP

sap·sa·go \\sap'sā,gō, 'sapsə,gō\\ *n* -s [modif. of G *schabziger*, fr. *schaben* to scrape (fr. OHG *skaban*) + G dial. *ziger, zieger* whey, whey cheese, fr. MHG *ziger*, prob. fr. a Celt compound whose 1st constituent is akin to OW *dou* two, and whose 2d constituent is akin to MIr *guirim* I warm up; fr. the milk's being heated twice in the cheese-making process; akin to L *duo* two, and to OE *wearm* warm — more at SHAVE, TWO, WARM] **:** a hard green cheese that is made from skim-milk curd, partly ripened, and then mixed with dried powdered leaves of blue melilot for color and flavor

sap·sap \\'säp,säp\\ *n, pl* **sapsap** [native name in the Philippines] **:** any of several small slimy-bodied percoid fishes (genus *Leiognathus*) *esp* **:** a common market fish (*L. equulus*) of the Philippines

sap shield *n* **:** a steel plate used as a shield by a sapper or other advanced worker in places where earth thrown up is inadequate for his defense

sap stain *n* **1 :** a discoloration in sapwood caused by any of various fungi **2 :** a discoloration in newly sawn sapwood due to oxidizing enzymes — compare BLUE STAIN

sapstreak \\'=,=\\ *n* [1*sap* + *streak*] **:** a fungous disease of sugar maple caused by a fungus (*Endoconidiophora virescens*) and characterized by death of the crown from the top down and radial water-soaked reddish or gray streaks across the sapwood

sap stream *n* **:** TRANSPIRATION STREAM

sapsucker \\'=,==\\ *n* [1*sap* + *sucker*] **1 :** any of several small American woodpeckers of the genus *Sphyrapicus; specif* **:** YELLOW-BELLIED SAPSUCKER — see RED-BREASTED SAPSUCKER **2 :** any of various small woodpeckers of genera other than *Sphyrapicus*

sap tie *n* **:** a railroad crosstie having sapwood wider than one-fourth the width of the tie on the top at a point between 20 and 40 inches from the middle of the tie

sap·u·caia *or* **sap·u·ca·ja** *also* **sap·u·ca·ya** \\,sapə'kīə\\ *n* -s [Pg *sapucaia*, fr. Tupi *zabucáya, sapucáya*] **1 :** a tree of the genus *Lecythis* — see SAPUCAIA NUT **2 :** the hard heavy durable timber of various sapucaias that is used for ties, in heavy construction, and to a limited extent in cabinetmaking

sapucaia nut *n* **:** the oily edible seed of various sapucaias esp. of Brazil and British Guiana that resemble but are often considered superior to Brazil nuts and yield a high percentage of oil — compare MONKEY POT

sapucaia–nut family *n* **:** LECYTHIDACEAE

sap·u·cai·nha \\-'kīnyə\\ *n* -s [Pg, dim. of *sapucaia*] **:** a tall central and southern Brazilian tree (*Carpotroche brasiliensis*) of the family Flacourtiaceae with a nut that yields an oil used in the treatment of leprosy

sapwood \\'=,=\\ *n* [1*sap* + *wood*] **:** the younger softer living or physiologically active outer portion of wood that lies between the cambium and the heartwood and is more permeable, less durable, and usu. lighter in color than the heartwood to which it is ultimately converted — called also *alburnum*

sapwood rot *n* **:** SAP ROT

sa·pyg·i·dae \\sə'pijə,dē\\ *n pl, cap* [NL, fr. *Sapyga*, type genus (fr. Gk *saos* whole + *pygē* rump) + *-idae* — more at PYG-] **:** a family of parasitic wasps

SAR *abbr* **1** search and rescue **2** semiautomatic rifle

1**sa·ra** \\'särə\\ *n, pl* **sara** *or* **saras** *usu cap* **1 :** a people on the Shari river in central Africa **2 :** a member of the Sara people

2**sa·ra** \\sə'rȯ\\ *n, pl* **sara** [earlier *Saraw* Cheraw — more at CHERAW] **:** CHERAW

sa·rab·a·ite \\sə'rabə,īt\\ *n* -s *usu cap* [ME *Serabite*, fr. LL *Sarabaïta*] **:** one of various vagrant and independent eastern monks in the early church

1**sar·a·band** *or* **sar·a·bande** \\'sarə,band, -baa(ə)nd *also* 'ser-\\ *n* -s [F *sarabande*, fr. Sp *zarabanda*] **1 :** a stately court dance of the 17th and 18th centuries resembling the minuet and evolved from a quick Spanish dance of oriental origin **2 :** the music for the saraband in slow triple time characterized usu. by an accent on the second beat; *specif* **:** a movement of the classical suite (as of Handel or Bach)

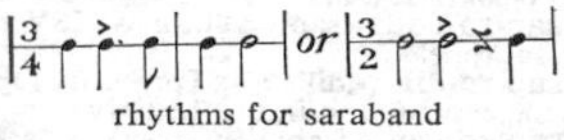

rhythms for saraband

2**saraband** \\" *or* **ser·e·bend** \\'serə,bend\\ *n* -s *usu cap* [fr. *Saravan*, district in Iran] **:** a Persian rug of fairly fine weave and short pile usu. having rows of small cashmere palmettes in delicate hues set in a drop repeat on a mellow red ground

sar·a·cen \\'sarəsən *also* 'ser-\\ *n* -s *usu cap* [ME *Saracen*, fr. LL *Saracenus*, fr. LGk *Sarakēnos*] **1 :** a nomadic people of the deserts between Syria and Arabia — usu. used in pl. ⟨crusaders fighting the *Saracens*⟩ **2 :** a member of the Saracen people; *specif* **:** ARAB

sar·a·cen·ic \\¦==¦senik, -nēk\\ *or* **sar·a·cen** \\'==‿sən\\ *adj, usu cap* [*saracenic* fr. ML *saracenicus*, fr. LL *Saracenus* Saracen + L *-icus* -ic] **:** of, relating to, or having the characteristics of the Saracens

saracenic architecture *n, usu cap S* **:** the architecture of the Muhammadans consisting chiefly of mosques and tombs and characterized by decorated surfaces, bulbous domes, and horseshoe, pointed, and multifoil arches — compare MOORISH ARCHITECTURE

saracen's comfrey *or* **saracen's consound** *n, usu cap S* **:** a ragwort (*Senecio saracenicus*) believed to have been used by the Saracens to heal wounds

saracen's head *n, usu cap S* **:** MOOR'S HEAD 1b

saracen stone *or* **saracen's stone** *n, usu cap 1st S* **:** SARSEN

sa·ra·da \\'shärə,dä, -‿də\\ *n* -s *usu cap* [after *Śāradā* Nandan, said to have first reduced Kashmiri to writing] **:** an older alphabet of Kashmir that is akin to the Devanagari

sar·a·gos·sa \\¦sarə¦gäsə *also* ¦ser- *or* -gȯsə\\ *adj, usu cap* [fr. *Saragossa*, city in northeastern Spain] **:** of or from the city of Saragossa, Spain **:** of the kind or style prevalent in Saragossa

sar·ah *also* **sara** \\'serə, 'sa(a)rə, 'sārə\\ *n* -s *usu cap* [prob. fr. the feminine name *Sarah*] **:** PAINTED TRILLIUM

sa·ra·je·vo *or* **se·ra·je·vo** \\'säraye,vȯ, -yə,-, -vō; ¦särə¦yā(,)vō, ¦sar-, ¦ser-, -ye(-\\ *adj, usu cap* [fr. *Sarajevo*, city in central Yugoslavia] **:** of or from the city of Sarajevo, Yugoslavia **:** of the kind or style prevalent in Sarajevo

sar·a·kolle \\¦sarə¦käl\\ *also* **sar·a·kole** \\-kōl\\ *n, pl* **sarakolle** *or* **sarakolles** *also* **sarakole** *or* **sarakoles** *usu cap* **1 :** a people of the French Sudan claiming descent from light-skinned ancestors of the Ghana empire and speaking a Mandingo dialect **2 :** a member of the Sarakolle people

sar·a·mac·ca \\,sarə'makə\\ *n* -s *usu cap* [fr. *Saramacca*, river and district in central Surinam] **:** an English based Creole language of Surinam

sar·a·mac·can·er \\-nə(r)\\ *n* -s *usu cap* [D, fr. *Saramacca*, river and district in central Surinam] **:** a member of a Negro people living in Surinam

sa·ran \\sə'ran, -raa(ə)n\\ *n* -s [fr. *Saran*, a trademark] **:** a tough flexible thermoplastic made by polymerizing or usu. copolymerizing vinylidene chloride that can be formed into waterproof and chemically resistant filaments, staple fibers, fabrics, pipe, film, molded parts, and protective coatings

sa·rang·ean \\sə'raŋēən\\ *n, pl* **sarangean** *or* **sarangeans** *usu cap* [*Sarang* native name in Seistan + E *-an*] **1 :** an early people inhabiting a region adjacent to the lower Gilmend river in southwestern Afghanistan **2 :** a member of the Sarangean people

sar·an·gous·ty \\,sarən'güstē\\ *n* -ES [Per *sar-angushti* thin paste for painting the tips of fingers, fr. *sari angusht* fingertip, fr. *sar* head + *angusht* finger, toe] **:** stucco made waterproof for protection against dampness

sa·ra·pe *or* **se·ra·pe** \\sə'räpē\\ *n* -s [MexSp *sarape*] **:** a woolen blanket often of bright geometric patterns worn by Spanish-American men as a cloak or poncho

saras *pl of* SARA

sar·a·to·ga \\,sarə'tōgə *also* ,ser-; *attrib* ¦==¦==\\ *n* -s *usu cap* [fr. *Saratoga* Springs, N.Y.] **1 :** a variation of Michigan in which the same number of chips is placed on each boodle card by each player **2 :** SARATOGA TRUNK **3 :** a box or container used in the transfer or temporary storage of tobacco

saratoga chip *or* **saratoga potato** *n, usu cap S* [after *Saratoga* Springs, N.Y.] **:** POTATO CHIP

saratoga chop *n, usu cap S* **:** a boneless shoulder chop of lamb rolled and skewered with the cut surfaces left exposed — see LAMB illustration

saratoga cocktail *n, usu cap S* **:** a cocktail consisting of brandy, sweet vermouth, bitters, and sometimes a fruit juice (as of lemon or pineapple)

saratoga spittlebug *n, usu cap 1st S* **:** a cercopid bug (*Aphrophora saratogensis*) that feeds on pines in northern U.S.

saratoga trunk *n, usu cap S* **:** a large traveling trunk usu. with a rounded top

sar·a·to·gi·an \\,=='tōgēən\\ *n* -s *cap* [*Saratoga* Springs, N.Y. + E *-an*] **:** a native or resident of Saratoga Springs, New York

sa·ra·tov \\sə'räd·əf, -d·əv\\ *adj, usu cap* [fr. *Saratov*, U.S.S.R.] **:** of or from the city of Saratov, U.S.S.R. **:** of the kind or style prevalent in Saratov

sara·wak bean \\sə'räwə(k)-, -ä,wak-, ÷'sarə,vak-\\ *n, usu cap S* [after *Sarawak*, northwestern Borneo] **:** a plant (*Dolichos hosei*) introduced into Australia for forage and hay

sar·ba·cane \\'särbə,kān, -bəkən\\ *also* **sar·bi·can** \\'särbəkən\\ *n* -s [F *sarbacane*, fr. MF, alter. (influenced by *cane* reed, cane) of *sarbatenne*, fr. OSp *cerbatana*, fr. Ar *zarbaṭāna, zabaṭāna* — more at CANE] **:** BLOWGUN 1

sarc- *or* **sarco-** *comb form* [Gk *sark-, sarko-*, fr. *sark-, sarx*] **:** flesh ⟨*sarc*ic⟩ ⟨*sarc*idium⟩ ⟨*sarco*blast⟩ ⟨*sarco*sepsis⟩

-sarc \\,särk, ,sȧk\\ *n comb form* -s [Gk *sark-, sarx* flesh] **:** flesh **:** fleshy material ⟨ecto*sarc*⟩ ⟨peri*sarc*⟩

sar·casm \\'sär,kazəm, 'sȧ,k-\\ *n* -s [F *sarcasme*, fr. LL *sarcasmos*, fr. Gk *sarkasmos*, fr. *sarkazein* to tear flesh like dogs, bite the lips in rage, speak bitterly, sneer, fr. *sark-, sarx* flesh; akin to Av *thwarəs-* to cut] **1 :** a keen or bitter taunt **:** a cutting gibe or rebuke often delivered in a tone of contempt or disgust ⟨speech full of reproachful ~*s*⟩ **2 :** the use of caustic or stinging remarks or language often with inverted or ironical statement on occasion of an offense or shortcoming with intent to wound the feelings **syn** see WIT

sar·cast \\-kast\\ *n* -s [prob. back-formation fr. *sarcastical*] **:** an adept in sarcasm

sar·cas·tic \\(')=¦kastik, -¦kaas-, -tēk\\ *also* **sar·cas·ti·cal** \\-təkəl, -tēk-\\ *adj* [fr. *sarcasm*, after such pairs as E *enthusiasm: enthusiastic, enthusiastical*] **1 :** expressive of or characterized by sarcasm **:** marked by contempt or disgust ⟨made a profound and ~ bow, turned on his heel and left the room —W.H.Hudson †1922⟩ ⟨making the ~ comment that his popularity with his fellow workers depends on his not producing more than they⟩ **2 :** given to the use of sarcasm **:** CAUSTIC ⟨was as a stump speaker ~ . . . as often as he was argumentative —Carl Sandburg⟩

syn SATIRIC, IRONIC or IRONICAL, SARDONIC: SARCASTIC may describe whatever is bitter, cutting, and marked by intent to wound by taunting, mocking, deriding, or making ridiculous ⟨laughed in her face, with a horrid *sarcastic* demoniacal laughter, that almost sent the schoolmistress into fits —W.M.Thackeray⟩ SATIRIC applies to attempts to censure, castigate, or expose to open ridicule weaknesses, faults, or excesses ⟨a *satiric* picture, too, an intermittent glimpse into the smallness of human nature —John Erskine †1951⟩ ⟨the *satiric* theme of the rustic staring wildly about him in the town —G.G.Coulton⟩ IRONIC or IRONICAL applies to amusing, piquant, startling, or surprising difference between what is said and what is intended or between what is given out and accepted and what is really true ⟨it is an *ironic* likelihood that had he written less he would be held in higher esteem —Dorothy S. Davis⟩ ⟨a man so excessively ugly that he went by the *ironical* appellation of "beauty" —Herman Melville⟩ SARDONIC may apply to what manifests scorn, mockery, or derision and arises from disbelief in or doubt about values or motives ⟨continued to grin with a *sardonic* humor, with a cynical mockery and defiance —Jack London⟩ ⟨came to the funeral, full of calm, *sardonic* glee, and without being asked —Arnold Bennett⟩

sar·cas·ti·cal·ly \\-tək(ə)lē, -tēk-, -li\\ *adv* **:** in a sarcastic manner ⟨skilled ability to catalog ~ the interiors of middle-class American homes and offices —*Time*⟩ ⟨you weren't very particular about the roomers you took, we said, ~ —Helen S. Rush & Mary Sherkanowski⟩

sar·cas·tic·ness *or* **sar·cas·ti·cal·ness** *n* -ES [*sarcasticness* fr. *sarcastic* + *-ness; sarcasticalness* fr. *sarcastical* + *-ness*] **:** the quality or state of being sarcastic

sar·cee *also* **sar·see** *or* **sar·ci** *or* **sarsi** \\'särsē\\ *n, pl* **sarcee** *or* **sarcees** *usu cap* [prob. fr. Blackfoot (Siksika) *sa arsi* not good] **1 a :** an Athapaskan people of the upper Saskatchewan and Athabaska river valleys in Alberta, Canada **b :** a member of such people **2 :** the language of the Sarcee people

sar·cel \\'särsəl\\ *n* -s [ME *sercell*, fr. MF *cercel*, fr. L *circellus* small ring, dim. of *circus* ring — more at CIRCLE] **:** a pinion feather of a hawk's wing

sar·celle \\(')sär¦sel\\ *n* -s [ME *sarcell, cercelle*, fr. MF *cercelle*, fr. (assumed) VL *cercedula*, fr. L *querquedula*, a duck, prob. teal, prob. modif. of Gk *kerkithalis* heron; akin to Skt *kṛkara* partridge, Gk *korak-, korax* raven — more at RAVEN] **:** TEAL

sar·cel·ly \\(')sär¦selē\\ *also* **cer·ce·lée** \\", ¦sərsə¦lā\\ *adj* [*sarcelly* modif. of MF *cercelee*, fr. OF, fem. of *cercelé*, past part. of *cerceler* to curl, fr. *cercle* curl, circle — more at CIRCLE] **:** RECERCELLÉE

1**sarce·net** *or* **sarse·net** *also* **sars·net** \\'särsnət\\ *n* -s [ME *sarcenet*, fr. AF *sarzinett*, fr. *Sarzin* Saracen (fr. LL *Saracenus*) + *-ett* (fr. OF *-et*) — more at SARACEN] **:** a soft thin silk of oriental origin made in plain or twill weaves used since the medieval period for dresses, veilings, or trimmings

2**sarcenet** *or* **sarsenet** \\"\\ *adj* **:** like sarcenet in softness **:** TEMPERED ⟨*darn*(*ed*) and *hail Columbia* and *goodness gracious*, and suchlike ~ surety for one's oaths, have largely given way to their undisguised originals —J.W.Clark b. 1907⟩

sar·ci·na \\'särsənə, -rkənə\\ *n* [NL, fr. L, bundle; akin to L *sarcire* to patch, mend — more at EXORCISE] **1** *cap* **:** a genus of bacteria (family Micrococcaceae) that are mostly harmless saprophytes but include a few serious brewery pests and that have cells which under favorable conditions divide in three directions into cubical masses **2** *pl* **sarcinas** *or* **sarci·nae** \\-sə,nē, -kə,nī\\ **:** any bacterium of the genus *Sarcina*

1**sar·cle** \\'särkəl\\ *vt* [MF *sarcler*, fr. LL *sarculare*, fr. L *sarculum* hoe; akin to L *sarire* to hoe, weed — more at ASSART] *obs* **:** to weed or cultivate (crops) with a sarcle

2**sarcle** \\"\\ *n* -s [L *sarculum*] **:** an ancient hoe

sar·cob·a·tus \\sär'käbəd·əs\\ *n, cap* [NL, fr. *sarc-* + Gk *batos* prickly bush] **:** a small genus of branching spiny shrubs (family Chenopodiaceae) that are found on alkali plains and deserts of the western U.S. and have monoecious flowers of which the staminate are borne in aments while the pistillate are solitary and winged fruits containing a single seed — see GREASEWOOD 1

sar·co·carp \\'särkə,kärp\\ *n* -s [F *sarcocarpe*, fr. *sarc-* + *-carpe* -carp] **1 :** MESOCARP; *esp* **:** one that is thickened and fleshy (as in the peach) **2 :** a fleshy fruit

sar·co·cele \\'särkə,sēl\\ *n* -s [NL, fr. Gk *sarkokēlē*, fr. *sark-* sarc- + *kēlē* tumor — more at -CELE] **:** a fleshy swelling of the testicle resembling a tumor

sar·co·ceph·a·lus \\,särkə'sefələs\\ *n, cap* [NL, fr. *sarc-* + *-cephalus*] **:** a genus of tropical trees and shrubs (family Rubiaceae) — see NEGRO PEACH, OPEPE

sar·co·coc·ca \\,särkə'käkə\\ *n, cap* [NL, fr. *sarc-* + *-cocca* (fr. Gk *kokkos* grain, seed)] **:** a small genus of evergreen Asiatic shrubs (family Buxaceae) that are cultivated for their foliage and their black or red showy fruit and have alternate entire leaves and inconspicuous whitish flowers in heads or racemes

sar·co·col \\'särkə,käl\\ *n* -s [ME, fr. L *sarcocolla*] **:** SARCOCOLLA 2

sar·co·col·la \\,särkə'kälə\\ *n* [NL, fr. L, gum of the milk vetch (*Astragalus fasiculifolius*), fr. Gk *sarkokolla*, fr. *sark-* sarc- + *kolla* gum — more at PROTOCOL] **1** *cap* **:** a small genus of shrubs (family Penaeaceae) native to southern Africa and having axillary or spicate red flowers with a long perianth tube and four reflexed lobes **2** -s **:** a gummy exudate believed to be obtained from either of two shrubs of the genus *Penaea* (*P. mucronata* and *P. sarcocolla*) but also held to be obtained from either of two milk vetches (*Astragalus fasiculifolius* and *A. sarcocolla*) and occurring in small yellowish or brownish red grains with a bittersweet and acrid taste

sar·co·cyst \\'särkə,sist\\ *n* [NL *sarcocystis*] **:** SARCOCYSTIS 2; *specif* **:** the large intramuscular cyst of a sarcocystis

sar·co·cys·tid·e·an *or* **sar·co·cys·tid·i·an** \\¦särkəsə¦stidēən\\ *adj or n* [NL *Sarcocystid-, Sarcocystis* + E *-an*] **:** SARCOSPORIDIAN

sar·co·cys·tis \\,särkə'sistəs\\ *n* [NL, fr. *sarc-* + *-cystis*] **1** *cap* **:** the chief and characteristic genus of the order Sarcosporidia **2** *pl* **sarcocystis** *or* **sarcocystises :** any organism of the genus *Sarcocystis; broadly* **:** SARCOSPORIDIAN

1**sar·co·cys·toid** \\¦särkə¦si,stȯid\\ *adj* [NL *Sarcocystis* + E *-oid*] **:** resembling or related to the genus *Sarcocystis*

2**sarcocystoid** \\"\\ *n* -s **:** a sarcocystoid organism

sar·co·cyte \\'särkə,sīt\\ *n* -s [*sarc-* + *-cyte*] **:** the outer clear layer of ectoplasm lying between the myocyte and epicyte or cuticle in gregarines

sar·code \\'sär,kōd\\ *n* -s [F, fr. Gk *sarkōdes* fleshlike substance, fr. neut. of *sarkōdēs* fleshy] **:** PROTOPLASM

sar·cod·ic \\(')sär¦kädik\\ *or* **sar·co·dous** \\-kōdəs\\ *adj* [*sarcodic* ISV *sarcode* + *-ic; sarcodous* fr. *sarcode* + *-ous*] **:** relating to or resembling protoplasm

sar·co·dic·ty·um \\,särkō'diktēəm, -ikshēəm\\ *n* -s [NL, fr. *sarc-* + Gk *diktyon* net — more at DICTY-] **:** a network of protoplasm on the surface of the calymma of a radiolarian

sar·co·di·na \\,särkə'dīnə, -dēnə\\ *n pl, cap* [NL, fr. Gk *sarkōdes* fleshy part, fleshlike substance + NL *-ina*] **:** a class of Protozoa commonly including the subclasses Rhizopoda and Actinopoda and comprising forms whose chief character in common is the formation of pseudopodia that ordinarily serve as the organs for locomotion and for taking food — **sar·co·din·i·an** \\¦==¦dinēən\\ *adj*

sar·coglia \\(')sär¦käglēə, ¦särkə¦glīə\\ *n* -s [NL, fr. *sarc-* + *-glia*] **:** the granular protoplasmic substance marking the junction of a motor nerve and a muscle cell

1**sar·coid** \\'sär,kȯid\\ *adj* [Gk *sarkoeidēs*, fr. *sark-* sarc- + *-oeidēs* -oid] **:** of or resembling flesh

2**sarcoid** \\"\\ *n* -s [ISV *sarc-* + *-oid*] **1 :** a disease of horses and mules characterized by the formation of nodules in the skin **2 :** a nodule characteristic of sarcoid or of sarcoidosis

sar·coid·osis \\,sär,kȯi'dōsəs\\ *n, pl* **sarcoido·ses** \\-ō,sēz\\ [NL, fr. ISV *sarcoid* + NL *-osis*] **:** a chronic disease of unknown cause characterized by the formation of nodules resembling true tubercles in the lymph nodes, lungs, bones, skin and other organs

sar·co·lactic acid \\¦sarkə+ . . . -\\ *n* [*sarcolactic* fr. *sarc-* + *lactic*] **:** the dextrorotatory L-form of lactic acid occurring in muscle

sar·co·lem·ma \\,särkə'lemə\\ *n* [NL, fr. *sarc-* + Gk *lemma* rind, husk — more at LEMMA] **:** the thin transparent homogeneous sheath enclosing a striated muscular fiber — **sar·co·lem·mal** \\¦==¦leməl\\ *adj*

sar·col·o·gy \\sär'käləjē\\ *n* -ES [Gk *sarko-* (fr. *sark-, sarx* flesh) + E *-logy*] **1** *archaic* **:** the anatomy of the soft parts — distinguished from *osteology* **2 :** a theory that a part of the animal body taken into the human system nourishes or affects a corresponding part — compare DOCTRINE OF SIGNATURES, ORGANOTHERAPY

sar·col·y·sis \\sär'käləsəs\\ *n* [NL, fr. *sarc-* + *-lysis*] **:** the lysis of muscular tissue

sar·co·ma \\sär'kōmə, sȧ'k-\\ *n, pl* **sarcomas** \\-məz\\ *or* **sarcoma·ta** \\-məd·ə\\ [NL, fr. Gk *sarkōmat-, sarkōma* fleshy growth, fr. *sarkoun* to grow flesh, become fleshy, fr. *sark-, sarx* flesh — more at SARCASM] **:** a malignant neoplasm arising in connective tissue and esp. in bone, cartilage, or striated muscle that spreads by extension into neighboring tissue or by way of the bloodstream — compare CARCINOMA, TUMOR

sar·co·ma·gen·ic \\=¦==¦jenik\\ *adj* [NL *sarcoma* + E *-genic*] **:** producing sarcoma

sar·co·ma·toid \\='==,tȯid\\ *adj* [NL *sarcomat-, sarcoma* + E *-oid*] **:** resembling a sarcoma

sar·co·ma·to·sis \\(,)=,=='tōsəs\\ *n, pl* **sarcomato·ses** \\-ō,sēz\\ [NL, fr. *sarcomat-, sarcoma* + *-osis*] **:** a disease characterized by the presence and spread of sarcomas

sar·coma·tous \\(')sär¦kämәd·əs, (')sȧ¦k-, -kōm-, -mətəs\\ *adj* [NL *sarcomat-, sarcoma* + E *-ous*] **:** of, relating to, or resembling sarcoma

sar·co·mere \\'särkə,mi(ə)r\\ *n* -s [*sarc-* + *-mere*] **:** a transverse segment of a striated muscle fibril held in some theories to be the fundamental contractile unit

1**sar·coph·a·ga** \\sär'käfəgə\\ *n pl, cap* [NL, fr. *sarc-* + *-phaga*] *in former classifications* **:** an artificial division of marsupials comprising the Didelphidae and Dasyuridae

2**sarcophaga** \\"\\ *n, cap* [NL, fr. fem. of L *sarcophagus* flesh-eating, fr. Gk *sarkophagos*] **:** the type genus of Sarcophagidae comprising typical flesh flies

1**sar·coph·a·gid** \\-fəgəd,-fəjəd\\ *adj* [NL *Sarcophagidae*] **:** of or relating to the Sarcophagidae

2**sarcophagid** \\"\\ *n* -s **:** a two-winged fly of the family Sarcophagidae

sar·co·phag·i·dae \\,särkə'fajə,dē\\ *n pl, cap* [NL, fr. *Sarcophaga*, type genus + *-idae*] **:** a family of two-winged flies (superfamily Muscoidea) that includes flesh flies, some that cause myiases, and others that develop in organic materials (as manure)

sar·coph·a·gine \sär'käfə,gīn, -,jīn\ *adj* [NL *Sarcophagidae* + E *-ine*] : of, like, or relating to the family Sarcophagidae

sar·coph·a·gous \(ˈ)sär¦käfəgəs\ *or* **sar·co·phag·ic** \ˌsärkə¦fajik\ *adj* [*sarcophagous* fr. L *sarcophagus* flesh-eating, fr. Gk *sarkophagos; sarcophagic* fr. L *sarcophagus* + E *-ic*] : CARNIVOROUS

sar·coph·a·gus \sär'käfəgəs, sä'k-\ *n, pl* **sarcopha·gi** \-fə,gī, -fə,jī, -fə,gē\ *also* **sarcophaguses** \-fəgəsəz\ [L *sarcophagus* (*lapis*) limestone used for coffins, fr. Gk (*lithos*) *sarkophagos*, lit., flesh-eating stone, fr. *sark-* sarc- + *-phagos* (fr. *phagein* to eat) — more at BAKSHEESH] **1** *obs* : a limestone used among the Greeks for the construction of coffins and held to disintegrate the flesh of bodies deposited in it **2** [L, fr. Gk *sarkophagos*, fr. *sarkophagos* (*lithos*) limestone used for coffins] : a coffin made of stone, often ornamented with sculpture, and usu. placed in a church, tomb, or vault **3** : a kind of wine cooler forming part of or standing near a sideboard and used chiefly in the 18th century

sar·coph·a·gy \sär'käfəjē\ *n* -ES [Gk *sarkophagia*, fr. *sarkophagos* flesh-eating + *-ia* -y] : the practice of feeding on flesh

sar·co·phile \'särkə,fīl\ *n* -S [*sarc-* + *-phile*] : a carnivorous animal; *esp* : TASMANIAN DEVIL

sar·coph·i·lous \(ˈ)sär¦käfələs\ *adj* [*sarc-* + *-philous*] : fond of flesh

sar·coph·i·lus \s-ˈ==ləs\ *n, cap* [NL, fr. *sarc-* + *-philus*] : a genus of marsupial mammals consisting of the Tasmanian devil

sar·co·plasm \'särkə,plazəm\ *n* [NL *sarcoplasma*] : the hyaline semifluid substance between the fibrils of striated muscular fibers — **sar·co·plas·mic** \ˌ==¦plazmik\ *adj*

sar·co·plas·ma \ˌ==ˈplazmə\ *n, pl* **sarcoplasma·ta** \-məd·ə\ [NL, fr. *sarc-* + *plasma*] : SARCOPLASM

sar·cop·side \sär'käpsəd\ *n* -S [G *sarkopsid*, fr. *sark-* sarc- + Gk *ōps* face, eye + G *-id* -ide; fr. the fleshlike color it exhibits — more at EYE] : a mineral $(Fe,Mn,Ca)_7(PO_4)_4F_2$(?) consisting of a fluoride and phosphate of calcium, manganese, and iron

sar·copsyl·la \ˌsär,käp'silə, -rkō's-\ [NL, fr. *sarc-* + Gk *psylla* flea — more at PSYLLA] *syn of* TUNGA

sar·cop·tes \sär'käp(ˌ)tēz\ *n, cap* [NL, fr. *sarc-* + Gk *koptein* to cut off — more at CAPON] : a genus of itch mites that is the type of the family Sarcoptidae

sar·cop·tic \(ˈ)sär¦käptik\ *adj* [NL *Sarcoptes* + E *-ic*] : of, relating to, or caused by itch mites of the family Sarcoptidae ⟨~ infection⟩

sar·cop·ti·cide \sär'käptə,sīd\ *n* -S [*sarcoptic* + *-cide*] : an agent used for killing itch mites

sarcoptic mange *n* : a mange caused by mites (genus *Sarcoptes*) burrowing in the skin esp. of the head and face — called also *barn itch;* compare CHORIOPTIC MANGE

¹sar·cop·tid \(ˈ)sär¦käptəd\ *adj* [NL *Sarcoptidae*] : of or relating to the Sarcoptidae : SARCOPTIC

²sarcoptid \"\ *n* -S : a mite of the family Sarcoptidae

sar·cop·ti·dae \sär'käptə,dē\ *n pl, cap* [NL, fr. *Sarcoptes*, type genus + *-idae*] : a family of small whitish itch mites that attack the skin of man and other mammals

sar·cop·toid \sär'käp,tȯid\ *adj* [NL *Sarcoptoidea*] : of, relating to, or having the characteristics of the Sarcoptoidea : resembling or related to the Sarcoptidae

sar·cop·toi·dea \ˌsär,käp'tȯidēə\ *n pl, cap* [NL, fr. *Sarcoptes* + *-oidea*] *in some classifications* : a superfamily of mites containing Sarcoptidae and related families

sar·co·ram·phus \ˌsärkə'ram(p)fəs\ *n, cap* [NL, fr. *sarc-* + Gk *rhamphos* beak — more at RHAMPH-] : a genus of vultures including only the king vulture

sar·co·sine \'särkə,sēn, -kəsən\ *n* -S [ISV *sarcos-* (irreg. fr. Gk *sark-*, *sarx* flesh) + *-ine;* orig. formed as G *sarkosin* — more at SARCASM] : a sweetish crystalline amino acid CH_3NHCH_2COOH formed by the decomposition of creatine or made synthetically from methylamine (as by reaction with chloroacetic acid) and used in making an antienzyme agent for toothpaste formulations; *N*-methyl-glycine

sar·co·so·ma \ˌsärkə'sōmə\ *n* -S [NL, fr. *sarc-* + *-soma*] : SARCOSOME 1

sar·co·so·mal \ˌsärkə¦sōməl\ *adj* [NL *sarcosoma* + E *-al*] : of or relating to sarcosomes

sar·co·some \'särkə,sōm\ *n* -S [NL *sarcosoma*] **1** : the fleshy portion of an anthozoan as distinguished from the skeleton **2** : a mitochondrion of a striated muscle fiber

sar·co·spor·i·da \ˌsärkə'spȯrədə\ [NL, fr. *sarc-* + *-spora* + *-ida*] *syn of* SARCOSPORIDIA

sar·co·spo·rid·ia \ˌsär(ˌ)kōspə'ridēə\ *n pl, cap* [NL, fr. *sarc-* + *-sporidia*] : an order of Acnidosporidia comprising imperfectly known parasites of the muscles of vertebrates — see SARCOCYSTIS

¹sar·co·spo·rid·i·an \ˌ=(ˌ)==¦==ən\ *adj* [NL *Sarcosporidia* + E *-an*] : of or relating to the Sarcosporidia

²sarcosporidian \"\ *n* -S : a parasite of the order Sarcosporidia : SARCOCYSTIS

sar·co·spo·rid·i·o·sis \ˌ=(ˌ)==,=dē'ōsəs\ *n, pl* **sarcosporidioses** \-ō,sēz\ [NL, fr. *Sarcosporidia* + *-osis*] : infestation with or disease caused by protozoans of the order Sarcosporidia

sar·co·style \'särkə,stīl\ *n* [*sarc-* + *-style*] **1** : a muscle fibril **2** : the dactylozooid of a calyptoblastic hydroid

sar·co·testa \ˌsärkə+\ *n* [NL, fr. *sarc-* + *testa*] : the outer and usu. soft fleshy part of the testa in various seeds (as of a cycad)

sar·co·theca \"+\ *n* [NL, fr. *sarc-* + *theca*] : the theca of a sarcostyle of a hydrozoan

sar·cous \'särkəs\ *adj* [*sarc-* + *-ous*] : of, relating to, or consisting of muscle tissue : FLESHY

sar·cu·ra \sär'kyu̇rə\ *n pl, cap* [NL, fr. *sarc-* + *-ura*] *in some classifications* : a suborder or other division of rays that have a thick tail, two dorsal fins, and a caudal fin and include the guitarfishes and often the electric rays — compare MASTICURA

¹sard \'särd\ *n* -S [F *sarde*, fr. L *sarda*, prob. modif. of Gk *sardion*, perh. fr. *Sardeis* Sardis, capital of the ancient kingdom of Lydia] : a deep orange-red variety of chalcedony similar to but darker than carnelian and classed by some as a variety of carnelian — called also *sardine, sardius*

²sard \"\ *n* -S *cap* [It *Sardo*, fr. L *Sardus* of Sardinia, Sardinian, fr. Gk *Sardō* Sardinia] : SARDINIAN

sar·da \'särdə\ *n, cap* [NL, fr. L, a fish, perh. sardine] : a genus of marine fishes (family Scombridae) comprising the common bonitos

sar·da·na \sär'dänə\ *n* -S *sometimes cap* [Sp, fr. Catal] **1** : a Catalan dance in which participants form a ring and move alternately to the left and right with long and short steps **2** : the music for the sardana usu. arranged in quick 6/8 time and played on the fife and tabor

sar·da·na·pa·lian \ˌsärdᵊnə¦pālyən, -pāl-, -lēən\ *adj, usu cap* [*Sardanapalus* legendary last king of the Assyrian empire (fr. L, fr. Gk *Sardanapalos*) + E *-an*] : of, relating to, or characterized by the luxuriously sensual nature or way of life attributed to the Assyrian king Sardanapalus

sardar *var of* SIRDAR

sar·delle \sär'delə, (ˈ)sär¦del\ *or* **sar·del** \(ˈ)sär¦del\ *n, pl* **sar·del·len** \-ˈdelən\ *or* **sar·delles** \(ˈ)=¦delz\ *or* **sardels** \(ˈ)=¦delz\ [G *sardelle* & Yiddish *sardel*, fr. It *sardella*, dim. of *sarda* sardine, fr. L] : SARDINE : a fish related to the sardine — compare ANCHOVY

¹sar·di·an \'särdēən\ *adj, usu cap* [L *sardianus*, fr. Gk *sardianos*, fr. *Sardeis* Sardis, capital of the ancient kingdom of Lydia in Asia Minor] **1** : of, relating to, or characteristic of the ancient city of Sardis in Asia Minor **2** : of, relating to, or characteristic of Sardians

²sardian \"\ *n* -S *cap* : a native or resident of ancient Sardis

sardian nut *n, usu cap S* : CHESTNUT 1b

¹sar·dine \'sär,dīn, -dᵊn\ *n* -S [ME, fr. LL (*lapis*) *sardinus* Sardian (stone), fr. Gk *sardinos* (*lithos*), perh. fr. *Sardeis* Sardis, capital of Lydia] : SARD

²sar·dine \(ˈ)sär¦dēn, (ˈ)sä¦d-\ *n, pl* **sardines** *also* **sardine** [ME *sardeine*, fr. MF *sardine*, fr. L *sardina*, prob. fr. Gk *sardinos*] **1 a** : any of several small or immature clupeid fishes: (1) : the young of the European pilchard (*Sardinia pilchardus*) when of a size suitable for preserving for food (2) : any of various similar young of closely related fishes (as *Sardinops caerulea* of the Pacific coast of No. America, *Sardinella anchovia* of the tropical Atlantic and Caribbean area, or *Sardinia neopilchardus* of Australia and New Zealand) (3) : any of various small or immature herrings that resemble or are used similarly to the true sardines — compare BRISLING, SILD **b** : a similar but more distantly related fish (as an anchovy) — not used technically and in some jurisdictions not legally acceptable without a qualifying term **2** *sardines pl but sing in constr* : a game in which one person hides from others who try to find him and the first to do so hides with him, the second hides with the first two, and so on until all are crowded into the hiding spot

sardine oil *n* : a yellow drying oil obtained from sardines and used chiefly as a lubricant, in fat-liquoring leather, and in soap — compare PILCHARD OIL

¹sar·din·i·an \sär'dinēən, sä'd-, -inyən\ *n* -S *cap* [*Sardinia*, island in the Mediterranean west of the Italian peninsula + E *-an*] **1** : a native or inhabitant of Sardinia **2** : the Romance language of central and southern Sardinia

²sardinian \(ˈ)=¦=(=)=\ *adj, usu cap* [in sense 1, alter. (influenced by L *sardinianus* of Sardinia) of *sardonian;* in other senses, fr. L *sardinianus*, fr. *Sardinia* + *-anus* -an] **1** *obs* : SARDONIC ⟨*Sardinian* laughter⟩ **2 a** : of, relating to, or characteristic of the island of Sardinia in the Mediterranean sea **b** : of, relating to, or characteristic of Sardinians **3** : of, relating to, or characteristic of the Sardinian language

sar·di·nier \ˌsär,den¦yā\ *n, pl* **sardiniers** \-ā(z)\ [F, fr. *sardine* (fr. MF) + *-ier* -er] : a boat built for sardine fishing

sar·di·us \'särdēəs\ *n* -ES [LL, fr. (*lapis*) *sardius* Sardian (stone), fr. Gk *sardios* (*lithos*), perh. fr. *Sardeis* Sardis, capital of Lydia] : SARD

sar·do·ni·an \(ˈ)sär¦dōnēən\ *adj* [MF *sardonien*, fr. Gk *sardonios* sardonic + MF *-ien* -ian] *archaic* : SARDONIC

¹sar·don·ic \(ˈ)sär¦dänik, (ˈ)sä¦d-, -nēk\ *also* **sar·don·i·cal** \-nəkəl, -nēk-\ *adj* [*sardonic* fr. F *sardonique*, fr. MF, fr. Gk *sardonios, sardanios* derisive, sardonic + MF *-ique* -ic; *sardonical* fr. F *sardonique* + E *-al;* perh. akin to MBret *huersin* & W *chwarddu* to laugh] : expressive of or characterized by derision or scorn : disdainfully or skeptically humorous : CYNICAL ⟨got a ~ twist to his mouth, the way of a man who feels that the breaks are against him —Mary Austin⟩ ⟨his rebellion is the bitter, ~ laughter of all great satirists —Franz Schoenberner⟩ ⟨with a ~ smile —W.S.Maugham⟩ ⟨predominant mood was reflected in the bright and bitter humor, the ~ portrayal of human futility —D.S.Savage⟩ ⟨the enemy seemed to take a ~ delight in picking Sunday for his most savage forays —Irwin Shaw⟩ ⟨the rather ~ aphorism that there's nothing like a pension to induce longevity —*St. Louis Post-Dispatch*⟩ **syn** see SARCASTIC

²sardonic \"\ *n* -S : a sardonic expression or remark — often used in pl. ⟨laugh ~s about a reprobate —*Time*⟩ ⟨the advertisement — whose impish ~s may be placed in early evidence —K.N.Cameron⟩

sar·don·i·cal·ly \-nək(ə)lē, -nēk-, -li\ *adv* : in a sardonic manner : with a sardonic attitude ⟨some say ~ that combat pay is good and that one can do quite well out of this war —Thomas Griffith⟩ ⟨was heard to say ~ that . . . they preached a good many things they themselves did not believe —A.W.Long⟩

sardonic grin *or* **sardonic laugh** *n* [trans. of NL *risus sardonicus*] : RISUS SARDONICUS

sar·don·i·cism \=ˈ==nə,sizəm\ *n* -S : sardonic quality or humor ⟨speaks her lines with impeccable artifice and gets all the withering ~ out of them —Brooks Atkinson⟩

sar·don·yx \(ˈ)sär¦däniks, (ˈ)sä¦d-, -nēks *sometimes* 'särdᵊniks *or* 'säd-\ *n* -ES [ME *sardonix*, fr. L *sardonyx*, fr. Gk, prob. fr. *sardion* sard + *onyx* onyx, nail — more at SARD, NAIL] : an onyx marked by parallel layers of sard and of mineral of another color

sar·doo·dle·dom \sär'düdᵊldəm\ *n* -S *usu cap* [*Sardoodle-* (blend of Victorien *Sardou* †1908 Fr. playwright criticized by G. B. Shaw †1950 Eng. playwright for the supposed staginess of his plays and E *doodle*) + *-dom*] : mechanically contrived plot structure and stereotyped or unrealistic characterization in drama : STAGINESS, MELODRAMA ⟨the authors of the world's great plays are not mere tricksters in *Sardoodledom* —John Mason Brown⟩

sards *pl of* SARD

sare \'sār\ *chiefly Scot var of* SORE

sa·rep·ta mustard \sə'reptə-\ *n* [after *Sarepta* (former name of Krasnoarmeisk), oblast near Stalingrad, U.S.S.R.] : a Russian mustard (*Brassica besseriana*) grown commercially in No. America as the source of a brownish black mustard

sar·gas·so \sär'ga(ˌ)sō, sä'g-, -gaa(-\ *n* -S [Pg *sargaço*, prob. fr. *sargaço, sargaça* rockrose, perh. fr. L *salicastrum*, a wild vine found in willow-thickets, fr. *salic-, salix* willow — more at SALLOW] **1** *also* **sargasso weed** : a seaweed of the genus *Sargassum* : GULFWEED **2** : a mass of floating vegetation consisting chiefly of sargasso

sargasso weed fish *n, usu cap S* : SARGASSUM FISH

sar·gas·sum \-səm\ *n* [NL, fr. ISV *sargasso*] **1** *cap* : a genus of brown algae that have branching thalli with lateral outgrowths differentiated as leafy segments, air bladders, or spore-bearing structures, that develop initially along tropical shores from which they break away to drift in the open ocean (as the Sargasso sea) and reproduce vegetatively for indefinite periods, and that are usu. placed in the family Fucaceae but are sometimes isolated in a separate family — see GULFWEED **2** -S : any plant of the genus *Sargassum*

sargassum crab *or* **sargasso crab** *n, usu cap S* : GULF-WEED CRAB

sargassum fish *n* : any of several small fantastically formed and colored fishes of genus *Histrio* (family Antennariidae) that float about in the open ocean with the masses of sargassum

sargassum pipefish *n* : a large pipefish (*Syngnathus pelagicus*) that lives among gulfweed

sarge \'särj, 'säj\ *n* -S [by shortening] : SERGEANT

sar·gent cypress \-jənt-\ *also* **sargent's cypress** *n, usu cap S* [prob. after Charles Sprague *Sargent* †1927 Am. dendrologist] : a shrub or bushy tree (*Cupressus sargentii*) of western No. America having dark green acute glandular pitted leaves

sargent juniper *also* **sargent's juniper** *n, usu cap S* [prob. after Charles Sprague *Sargent* †1927] : a low spreading Chinese juniper (*Juniperus chinensis sargentii*) that has needle-pointed leaves on many conspicuous twigs and is used as an ornamental

sar·go \'sär(ˌ)gō\ *n* -S [Sp, fr. L *sargus*, a sea fish, fr. Gk *sargos*] **1** : any of several sparid fishes of *Diplodus* and related genera; *esp* : either of two pinfishes (*D. argenteus* and *Lagodon rhomboides*) **2** : a small silvery grunt (*Anisotremus davidsonii*) of the coast of southern California and adjacent Mexico

sa·ri *or* **sa·ree** \'särē, 'sär-, -ri\ *n* -S [Hindi *sārī*, fr. Skt *śāṭī*] : a garment worn chiefly by Hindu women that consists of a lightweight cloth of 5 to 7 yards in length draped gracefully and loosely so that one end forms a skirt and the other a head or shoulder covering

sa·rin \zä'rēn\ *n* -S [G] : a corrosive organic phosphorus ester $CH_3PFO(OC_3H_7)$ that acts as a nerve gas

sa·rin·da \ˌsärən¦dä\ *n* -S [Hindi *sārindā*] : a bowed stringed musical instrument of India

sark \'särk\ *n* -S [ME (Sc) *serk*, fr. OE *serc, serce;* akin to ON *serkr* shirt and perh. to OHG *saruh* bathtub, cupboard, chest] *dial chiefly Brit* : a body garment for either sex : SHIRT

sark·ful \-ˌfu̇l\ *n* -S [*sark* + *-ful*] *Scot* : a quantity filling or sufficient to fill a shirt

sark·ing \'särkən, -kiŋ\ *n* -S [ME (Sc), fr. gerund of *serken* to clothe in a shirt, sheathe, fr. *serk* shirt] **1** *chiefly Scot* : thin boards for sheathing (as under shingles or slates) **2** *Scot* : linen shirting

sar·ki·nite \'särkə,nīt\ *n* -S [Sw *sarkinit*, fr. *sarkin-* (fr. Gk *sarkinos* fleshlike, fr. *sark-, sarx* flesh) + *-it* -ite — more at SARCASM] : a mineral $Mn_2(AsO_4)(OH)$ consisting of a hydrous manganese arsenate occurring in flesh red greasy monoclinic crystals (hardness 4–5, sp. gr. 4.2)

sark·it \'särkət\ *adj* [fr. past part. of obs. E (Sc) *sark*, v., to clothe in a shirt, fr. ME (Sc) *serken*] *Scot* : provided with a shirt

sar·lak *or* **sar·lyk** \'särlək\ *n* -S [Russ *sarlyk, sarluk*, fr. Mongolian *sarlug*] : YAK

¹sar·ma·tian \(ˈ)sär¦māshən\ *adj, usu cap* [*Sarmatia*, anciently a region north of the Black sea + E *-an*] **1 a** : of, relating to, or characteristic of ancient Sarmatia **b** : of, relating to, or characteristic of the Sarmatians **2** : of, relating to, or characteristic of the Sarmatian language

²sarmatian \"\ *n* -S *cap* [*Sarmatia* + E *-an*, n. suffix] **1** : a native or inhabitant of ancient Sarmatia **2** : the language of the Sarmatians that is now presumed to be Iranian

sar·ma·tier \ˌzärmə¦ti(ə)r, ˌsär-\ *n* -S [G, prob. fr. *Sarmatien* Sarmatia + *tier* animal, beast, fr. OHG *tior* wild animal — more at DEER] : PERWITSKY

sar·ment \'särmənt\ *n* -S [ME, fr. L *sarmentum* twig; akin to L *sarpere* to prune — more at ASSART] **1** : CUTTING, SCION **2** : a slender prostrate running stem : RUNNER

sar·men·ta·ceous \ˌsärmən¦tāshəs\ *adj* [*sarment* + *-aceous*] : SARMENTOSE

sar·men·tif·er·ous \-tif(ə)rəs\ *adj* [*sarment* + *-iferous*] : SARMENTOSE

sar·men·to·cymarin \sär¦mentō+\ *n* [*sarmento-* (fr. NL *sarmentosus* — specific epithet of *Strophanthus sarmentosus* —, fr. L, sarmentose) + *cymarin*] : a crystalline steroid cardiac glycoside $C_{30}H_{46}O_8$ found in the seeds of several plants of the genus *Strophanthus* (as *S. sarmentosus*)

sar·men·to·gen·in \sär,mentō'jenən, ˌsärmən·'täjənən\ *n* -S [*sarmento-* (in *sarmentocymarin*) + *-genin*] : a crystalline steroid lactone $C_{23}H_{34}O_5$ closely related to digitoxigenin, found in several plants of the genus *Strophanthus*, obtained esp. by hydrolysis of sarmentocymarin, and used in a synthesis of cortisone

¹sar·men·tose \sär'ment·,ōs, -n·,tōs, 'särmən·,tōs\ *adj* [L *sarmentosus*, fr. *sarmentum* twig + *-osus* -ose] **1** : producing slender prostrate branches or runners **2** : of the nature of or resembling a sarment

²sarmentose \" *also* -ōz\ *n* -S [*sarment-* (in *sarmentocymarin*) + *-ose*] : a sugar $C_7H_{14}O_4$ that is obtained from sarmentocymarin by hydrolysis and that is stereoisomeric with cymarose and closely related to digitalose

sar·men·tous \(ˈ)sär¦mentəs\ *adj* [L *sarmentosus*] : SARMENTOSE

sar·men·tum \sär'mentəm\ *n, pl* **sarmen·ta** \-tə\ [L, twig] : SARMENT 2

sar·mi·en·tite \ˌsärmē'ent·,īt, -n·,tīt\ *n* -S [Sp *sarmientita*, fr. *Sarmiento*, town in Argentina + Sp *-ita* -ite] : a mineral $Fe_2(AsO_4)(SO_4)(OH).5H_2O$ consisting of a hydrous basic arsenate and sulfate of iron

sa·rod *also* **sa·rode** \sə'rōd\ *n* -S [Hindi *sarod*, fr. Per] : a stringed instrument of India resembling a waisted lute

sa·ron \'sä,rän, sə'rän\ *n* -S [Jav] : a metallophone of seven bronze plates used in the Javanese gamelan

sa·rong \sə'rȯŋ, -räŋ\ *n* -S [Malay (*kain*) *sarong*, fr. *kain* cloth + *sarong* sheath, covering] **1 a** : a loose skirt that is made of a long strip of cloth wrapped around the body and held in place by tucking or rolling at the waist and is worn chiefly by men and women of the Malay archipelago and the Pacific islands **b** : cloth for such garments; *esp* : printed cotton **2** : a close-fitting outer garment or dress copied from the sarong that is worn by western women and usu. draped in the front

sar·os \'sa(ə)ˌräs\ *n* -ES [Gk, fr. Akkadian *sharu* cycle of 3600 years] : a lunar cycle of 6585.32 days at the end of which the centers of sun and moon return so nearly to their relative positions at the beginning that all the eclipses of the period recur approximately as before though in longitudes about 120 degrees west of the regions where they were visible in the saros immediately preceding

saros series *n* : a series of eclipses occurring at intervals of a saros that consists of about 50 lunar eclipses in a period of about 870 years or about 70 solar eclipses in a period of about 1200 years — called also *eclipse series*

sar·o·tham·nus \ˌsarə'thamnəs\ [NL, fr. Gk *saron* brush, broom (fr. *sairein* to sweep) + *thamnos* bush, shrub] *syn of* CYTISUS

sa·roth·rum \sə'rathrəm\ *n* -S [NL, fr. Gk *sarōtron* broom, fr. *saroun* to sweep clean, fr. *saron* broom] : the pollen brush of a bee

sa·rouk *or* **sa·ruk** \sə'rük\ *n* -S *usu cap* [fr. *Saruk, Sarouk*, village near Hamadan, western Iran] : a Persian carpet of fine compact weave, mellow colors, and fluid often medallion designs — compare KASHAN

sar·pler \'särplər\ *or* **sar·pli·er** \-lēər\ *n* -S [ME *sarpler*, fr. MF *sarpilliere*] **1** *obs* : a weight for a bale of wool usu. estimated as 80 tods or 2240 lbs. **2** : a covering or wrapper of coarse cloth (as sackcloth)

sar·ra·ce·nia \ˌsarə'sēnēə\ *n* [NL, fr. Michel *Sarrazin*, †1734 Fr.-Canadian physician and naturalist + NL *-ia*] **1** *cap* : a genus (the type of the family Sarraceniaceae) of American bog herbs having tubular leaves with an arched or hooded flap at the apex and solitary flowers with a style shaped like an umbrella — see PITCHER PLANT a **2** -S : any plant of the genus *Sarracenia*

sar·ra·ce·ni·a·ce·ae \-,sēnē'āsē,ē\ *n pl, cap* [NL, fr. *Sarracenia*, type genus + *-aceae*] : a family of insectivorous plants (order Sarraceniales) having basal tubular leaves with a thin lamina like a wing at the inner margin and a hood or other appendage at the apex and large conspicuous pentamerous flowers — **sar·ra·ce·ni·a·ceous** \ˌ==¦==¦āshəs\ *adj*

sar·ra·ce·ni·al \ˌ==¦sēnēəl\ *adj* [NL *Sarraceniales*] : of, relating to, or having the characteristics of the order Sarraceniales

sar·ra·ce·ni·a·les \ˌ==,=='ā(ˌ)lēz\ *n pl, cap* [NL, fr. *Sarracenia* + *-ales*] : an order of dicotyledonous plants constituting the families Sarraceniaceae, Nepenthaceae, and Droseraceae and having scapose flowers and leaves that secrete a viscous fluid and are variously modified to serve as insect traps

sar·ra·zin \'sarəzən\ *n* -S [F *sarrasin*, fr. (*blé*) *sarrasin* Saracen (wheat), fr. MF, fr. *Sarrasin, Sarrazin* Saracen, fr. LL *Saracenus* — more at SARACEN] : BUCKWHEAT

¹sar·row \'sarə, -a(ˌ)rō\ *also* **sar·ra** \-arə\ *dial Eng var of* SORROW

²sarrow \" *or* **sarra** \"\ *vb* [by alter.] *dial Eng* : SERVE

sar·ruso·phone \sə'rüzə,fōn, -'rasə-\ *n* -S [*Sarrus*, 19th cent. Fr. bandmaster + *-o-* + *-phone*] : a metal wind instrument with a double reed and a tube of wide conical bore played like the bassoon and sometimes used in place of it or a contrabassoon — **sar·ruso·phon·ist** \-nəst\ *n* -S

sar·sa·pa·ril·la \ˌsas(ə)pə'rilə, ˌsaa| *also* ˌsär| *or* ˌsȧ| *or* -¦sprilə *or* -relə, *dial with f instead of p*\ *n* -S [Sp *zarzaparrilla*, fr. *zarza* bush + *parrilla*, dim. of *parra* vine] **1 a** : any of various Mexican, Central American, or So. American plants of the genus *Smilax* (as *S. officinalis, S. papyracea*, and *S. aristolochiaefolia*) **b** : the dried roots of a sarsaparilla plant used as a flavoring or olfactory agent in the form of an infusion, extract, or syrup **2** : any of various plants resembling or used as a substitute for sarsaparilla — see INDIAN SARSAPARILLA, WILD SARSAPARILLA **3** : a sweetened carbonated beverage similar to root beer with the predominant flavor from birch oil and sassafras

sar·sar \'särsər\ *n* -S *usu cap* [Ar *ṣarṣar*] : a whistling violently cold wind

sar·sa·sap·o·gen·in \ˌsasə,sapə'jenən, ˌsärs-, ˌ==ˌsə'päjənən\ *n* -S [*sarsasaponin* + *-genin*] : a crystalline steroid sapogenin $C_{27}H_{44}O_3$ obtained esp. by hydrolysis of sarsasaponin

sarrusophone

sar·sa·sap·o·nin \ˌ==+\ *also* **sar·saponin** \(ˈ)sär, (ˈ)sa+\ *n* [*sarsasaponin* fr. *sarsa* (short for *sarsaparilla*) + *saponin; sarsaponin* blend of *sarsa* and *saponin*] : a saponin $C_{45}H_{74}O_{17}$ obtained from Mexican sarsaparilla root

sarsee *or* **sarsi** *usu cap, var of* SARCEE

sar·sen \'särsᵊn\ *n* -S [short for *sarsen stone*, alter. of *Saracen stone*, i.e., a pagan stone or monument] : a large loose residual mass of stone left after the erosion of a once continuous bed or layer; *specif* : one of the large sandstone blocks scattered over the English chalk downs — called also *druid stone*

sarsenet *also* **sarsnet** *var of* SARCENET

sar·sia \'särsēə, -rshə\ *n, cap* [NL] : a widely distributed genus of small hydrozoan medusae with four tentacles

sar·son \'särs³n\ *n* -s [Hindi *sarsō*, fr. Skt *sarṣapa*] **:** an Indian colza (*Brassica campestris sarson*)

¹sart \'särt\ *adj* [by alter.] *dial Eng* **:** SOFT

²sart \"\ *n, pl* **sart** *or* **sarts** *usu cap* [Kirghiz] **1 :** a trading and town-dwelling people constituting the Iranian populations of central and southwestern Asia **2 :** a member of the Sart people

sar·tain \'särt³n, 'sȧt-\ *dial var of* CERTAIN

sar·to·ri·al \(')sär¦tōrēəl, (')sȧ¦t-, -tȯr-\ *adj* [L *sartor* patcher, tailor + E *-ial*] **1 :** of, relating to, or characteristic of a tailor ⟨sitting in ~ fashion⟩ **2 :** of or relating to dress or to tailored clothes ⟨native sandals, a sport shirt which was whole once upon a time, and an outrageously battered straw sombrero . . . completed a strange ~ picture —Lawrence Dame⟩ ⟨his well-known ~ fancies —Gladwin Hill⟩ ⟨acquired more of the statesman's ~ appearance —*Current Biog.*⟩ ⟨~ elegance⟩ — **sar·to·ri·al·ly** \-əlē,-əli\ *adv*

sar·to·rite \'särd·ə,rīt\ *n* -s [Wolfgang *Sartorius* von Waltershausen †1876 Ger. geologist + E *-ite*] **:** a mineral $PbAs_2S_4$ consisting of a dark gray crystalline compound of lead, arsenic, and sulfur

sar·to·ri·us \sär'tōrēəs\ *n, pl* **sarto·rii** \-ē,ī\ [NL, fr. L *sartor* tailor, fr. *sartus* (past part. of *sarcire* to mend) + *-or* — more at EXORCISE] **:** a muscle that arises from the anterior end of the iliac crest, crosses the front of the thigh obliquely to insert on the upper part of the inner surface of the tibia, assists in rotating the leg to the position assumed in sitting like a tailor, and is the longest muscle in man

sar·tri·an \'sär·trēən\ *adj, usu cap* [Jean Paul *Sartre* b1905 + E *-an*] **:** of, relating to, or characteristic of the French philosopher, novelist, and dramatist Jean Paul Sartre or his existentialist theories

saruk *usu cap, var of* SAROUK

sar·um \'sa(a)rəm\ *adj, usu cap* [fr. *Sarum* (now *Old Sarum*), extinct borough and city near Salisbury in the county of Wiltshire, England] **:** of or relating to Sarum, diocese of Salisbury, England, in the late medieval period ⟨*Sarum* missal⟩ ⟨*Sarum* office⟩ ⟨*Sarum* rubric⟩ ⟨*Sarum* Use⟩

sa·rus \'sȧrəs\ *or* **sarus crane** *n, pl* **saruses** *or* **sarus cranes** [Hindi *sāras*, fr. Skt *sāras*, lit., of a lake, fr. *saras* lake, fr. *sarati* it runs, flows — more at SERUM] **:** a crane (*Grus antigone* or *Antigone antigone*) of the Indian and Malay region

sar·vas·ti·va·din \sə(r),västə'vädən\ *n* -s *usu cap* [Hindi *sarvāstivādin* adherent of a school of Buddhism that flourished in northern India in the 5th cent. B.C., fr. *sarvāstivāda* doctrine that everything exists, fr. *sarva* entire + *asti* is + *vāda* doctrine — more at SAFE, IS] **:** a member of an early realist school of Buddhism that affirms the existence of all material, mental, or other elements of experience

sar·wan \(')sär¦wän\ *n* -s [Per *sārwān*, fr. *sār* camel + *-wān* keeping, guarding] **:** a camel driver

SAS *abbr* sodium aluminum sulfate in the anhydrous form

sa·sak *or* **sas·sak** \'sä,säk, sə'säk\ *n, pl* **sasak** *or* **sasaks** *or* **sassak** *or* **sassaks** *usu cap* [Malay *sasak*] **1 a :** an Indonesian people inhabiting Lombok Island, Indonesia **b :** a member of the Sasak people **2 :** the Austronesian language of the Sasak people

sasanian *usu cap, var of* SASSANIAN

sa·san·qua \sə'säŋkwə\ *n* -s [Jap *sasankwa*] **:** a shrub (*Camellia sasanqua*) of China and Japan often cultivated for its fragrant evergreen leaves and white or red flowers and for seeds that yield tea-seed oil

sa·se·bo \'säsə,bō, sä'sā(,)bō\ *adj, usu cap* [fr. *Sasebo*, Japan] **:** of or from the city of Sasebo, Japan **:** of the kind or style prevalent in Sasebo

¹sash \'sash, -aa(ə)-,-ai-\ *n* -ES [Ar *shāsh* muslin] **1** *obs* **:** an oriental turban **2 :** any of various bands worn about the waist or over one shoulder, fastened with a loop, knot, or bow, and used as an accessory of dress, a symbol of an honorary or military order, or other distinctive badge — see CUMMERBUND

²sash \"\ *n, pl* **sash** *also* **sashes** *often attrib* [prob. modif. of F *châssis* frame, chassis (taken as a pl.) — more at CHASSIS] **1 :** the framework in which panes of glass or other usu. transparent or translucent material are set for installation in a window or door or for covering a hotbed, cold frame, greenhouse, or other glazed enclosure — see CASEMENT 2a; *also* **:** a movable part of a window ⟨raise the ~ for ventilation⟩ **2 :** the frame in which a sash saw or gang saw is stretched or mounted — called also *gate*

³sash \"\ *vt* -ED/-ING/-ES **:** to furnish (as a door or window) with a sash ⟨a door half ~*ed* with glass —Sir Walter Scott⟩

⁴sash \"\ *vt* -ED/-ING/-ES [¹*sash*] **:** to fasten, trim, or adorn with a sash ⟨~*ed* in at the waist —Oliver La Farge⟩

¹sa·shay \(')sa¦shā *also* (')si¦-\ *vi* -ED/-ING/-S [alter. of ²*chassé*] **1 :** CHASSÉ **2 a :** WALK, GLIDE, GO ⟨after the work was through and we all ~*ed* to the chuck wagon —Will James⟩ ⟨~ down to your ship or station library —*All Hands*⟩ ⟨~*s* down the center aisle to the stage —John Kobler⟩ ⟨~*ed* complacently through his duties without any qualms about serious opposition for his job —*Time*⟩ **b :** to strut or move about in an ostentatious or conspicuous manner ⟨putting on a dress that reveals the hidden glories of her shape, and ~*ing* around like a . . . model —Wolcott Gibbs⟩ **c :** to proceed or move in a diagonal or sideways manner ⟨having to ~ from oasis to oasis along the littered sidewalks —*New Yorker*⟩ ⟨the drive ~*s* from one side of a mountain to the other —V.H.Lawn⟩ ⟨~ off to the right and come down on him from that angle —R.G.Hubler & J.A. De Chant⟩

²sashay \"\ *n* -s **1 :** ³CHASSÉ **2 :** TRIP, EXCURSION, VENTURE ⟨a ~ I took with friends —A.B.Guthrie⟩ ⟨scrubbing his own cartridge belt after every ~ in the field —James Jones⟩ ⟨permits himself cautious ~*s* into such subjects as history, education, politics, love —*New Yorker*⟩

sash bar *n* **:** BAR 1d(3)

sash cord *n* **:** the cord used to attach a weight to a window sash

sash house *n* **:** a simple greenhouse made of sash and designed primarily for starting young plants

sa·shi·mi \'säshəmē\ *n* -s [Jap] **:** raw fish served as an appetizer and usu. accompanied by a condiment

sash·less \'sashləs\ *adj* [²*sash* + *-less*] **:** lacking a sash

sash line *n* **:** a rope used in erecting telegraph poles

sa·shoon \(')sa¦shün\ *n* -s [prob. modif. of obs. F *chausson*, fr. F *chausse* tight-fitting breeches, chausses — more at CHAUSSES] **:** a pad worn on the leg under the boot

sash plane *n* **:** a carpenter's plane with a notched cutter esp. suited for trimming the inside of door and sash frames

sash pocket *n* **1 :** the hollow in a pulley stile for a sash weight **2 :** a removable section of a pulley stile giving access to a sash weight and sash cord

sash saw *n* **:** a strip of steel that is toothed on one edge, stretched in a frame, and used for sawing in small water-power mills

sash weight *n* **:** an iron bar or cylinder attached to a window sash as a counterweight

sash window *n* **:** a window consisting of sash usu. double-hung to slide vertically in a window frame — compare CASEMENT WINDOW

sash windows

sasin \'sās³n, 'sas³n\ *n* -s [origin unknown] **:** BLACK BUCK 1

sa·sine \'sāsən\ *n* -s [alter. of *seisin*] **1** *Scots law* **:** the seisin or possession of feudal property; *also* **:** the formality by which it is acquired by the tenant **2 :** the instrument or deed by which the transfer of feudal property is proved

sas·katch·e·wan \sə'skachəwən *also* sa'sk- *or* -,wän\ *adj, usu cap* [fr. *Saskatchewan*, province in western Canada] **:** of or from the province of Saskatchewan **:** of the kind or style prevalent in Saskatchewan

sas·ka·toon \¦saskə¦tün\ *n* -s [fr. *Saskatoon*, city in central Saskatchewan, Canada] **:** JUNEBERRY; *esp* **:** a widely distributed shrubby Juneberry (*Amelanchier alnifolia*) of the northern and western U.S. and adjacent Canada that has leaves like those of an alder and sweet usu. purple fruit

¹sass \'sas, -aa(ə)-,-ai-,-å-\ *n* [alter. of ¹*sauce*] *chiefly Midland* **:** fresh garden vegetables — called also *garden sass*

²sass \"\ *n* [by alter.] *chiefly Midland* **:** ¹SAUCE 5

³sass \"\ *n* -ES [back-formation fr. ¹*sassy*] **:** BACK TALK ⟨takes no ~ from her pupils⟩ ⟨a past master of ~ —*TV Guide*⟩

⁴sass \"\ *vt* -ED/-ING/-ES **:** to talk impudently or disrespectfully to (an elder or superior) ⟨did not yell or ~ their mothers —Sally Carrighar⟩ ⟨call her a bum and she ~*es* them back —Polly Adler⟩

sas·sa·by \'sasəbē\ *or* **tses·se·be** *or* **tses·se·by** \'(t)sesəbē\ *n, pl* **sassabies** *or* **tsessebes** *or* **tsessebies** [Tswana *tshêsêbê*] **:** a large So. African antelope (*Damaliscus lunatus*) similar to the hartebeest that is dark purplish red with the back and face nearly black and has regularly curved horns

sas·sa·fac \'sasə,fak\ *also* **sas·sa·frack** \-frak\ *chiefly Midland var of* SASSAFRAS

sas·sa·fras \'sas(ə),fras, 'saas(ə),fraa(ə)s, 'sais(ə),frais\ *n* [NL, fr. Sp *sasafrás*] **1 a** *cap* **:** a small genus of aromatic No. American and Asiatic trees (family Lauraceae) with soft yellow wood, ovate entire or 1- to 3-lobed leaves, dioecious yellow flowers in umbellate racemes, a 6-lobed perianth, and nine stamens in three rows **b** -ES **:** a tall widely distributed tree (*S. albidum*) of eastern No. America with mucilaginous twigs and leaves — see TREE illustration **2** -ES **:** the dried bark of the root of the American sassafras used as a diaphoretic, a flavoring agent, an aromatic stimulant, or as a source of an aromatic volatile oil used in perfumes **3** -ES **a :** any of several Australian trees of the family Monimiaceae with aromatic bark used esp. for flavoring: as (1) **:** a medium-sized tree (*Atherosperma moschatum*) with soft grayish to nearly black wood used esp. in cabinetry and for carving or turning (2) **:** a tree (*Daphnandra micrantha*) with pale yellowish easily worked wood and a bark rich in physiologically active alkaloids (3) **:** an often large tree (*Doryphora sassafras*) with starry white flowers and bright glossy foliage that yields a yellowish wood suitable for flooring **b :** the bark of any of these trees

sassafras laurel *n* **:** CALIFORNIA LAUREL

sassafras oil *n* **:** a yellow or reddish yellow aromatic essential oil obtained from the roots and stumps of American sassafras and used chiefly in flavoring and perfuming and as a disinfectant — compare OCOTEA CYMBARUM OIL

sassafras pith *or* **sassafras medulla** *n* **:** the dried pith of the American sassafras formerly used in making a mucilage added to eye lotions for its emollient properties

sassafras tea *n* **:** a tea made from the dried bark of roots of the American sassafras

sassak *usu cap, var of* SASAK

¹sas·sa·nian *or* **sa·sa·nian** \sə'sānēən, sa's-, -ānyən\ *adj, usu cap* [*Sassan*, grandfather of Ardashir I *fl ab* A.D. 226 who founded the Sassanid dynasty + E *-an*] **:** of, relating to, or having the characteristics of the Sassanid dynasty of ancient Persia and esp. the art forms or architecture developed during the period of the dynasty

²sassanian *or* **sasanian** \"\ *n* -s *usu cap* **:** SASSANID

¹sas·sanid *also* **sas·sanide** \sə'sänəd, -'san-\ *n, pl* **sassanids** \-dz\ *or* **sassan·i·dae** \-'sanə,dē\ *also* **sassanides** \-'sänədz, -'san-\ *usu cap* [NL *Sassanidae*, pl., Sassanids, fr. *Sassan*, grandfather of Ardashir I + *-idae*] **:** a member of a dynasty of Persian kings succeeding the Arsacids and commencing with Ardashir I in A.D. 226 and ending with Yazdegerd III in the middle of the 7th century

²sassanid \"\ *also* **sassanide** \"\ *adj, usu cap* **:** SASSANIAN

sasse \'sas\ *n* -s [D *sas*] *archaic* **:** SLUICE, LOCK

sas·se·nach \'sas³n,a|k, -³nəl, -³n,ä|, |k\ *n* -s *often cap* [Ir *Sasanach*, of Gmc origin; akin to OE *Seaxan* Saxons] **:** a typical Englishman or something considered typical of England — often used disparagingly by Scots and Irish ⟨a dreadful *Sassenach* concoction —I.A.Bremner⟩

sas·sin·ger \'sasənjə(r)\ *n* -s [by alter.] *dial* **:** SAUSAGE

sas·so·lite \'sasə,līt\ *also* **sas·so·lin** \-,lən\ *n* -s [*sassolite* fr. *Sasso*, Tuscany, Italy + E *-lite*; *sassolin* fr. G, fr. *Sasso*, Italy + connective *-l-* + G *-in* -ine] **:** a mineral $B(OH)_3$ consisting of native boric acid and usu. occurring in small pearly scales as an incrustation

sass·wood \'sa,swůd\ *or* **sas·sy·wood** \'sasē,wůd\ *n* [*sasswood* alter. of *sassywood*; *sassywood* fr. *sassy* (prob. of African origin) + *wood*] **:** a western African tree (*Erythrophloeum guineense*) of the family Leguminosae having a poisonous bark and yielding a hard strong insect-resistant wood

sas·sy \'sa¦sē, 'saa|, 'sai|, 'sȧ|, |si\ *adj* -ER/-EST [alter. of *saucy*] **1 a :** given to back talk **:** FRESH, IMPERTINENT ⟨were polite and . . . not the ~ type —*Boston Herald*⟩ ⟨~ kids —Barbara B. Jamison⟩ **b :** physically vigorous **:** SPIRITED, JAUNTY ⟨the timber mechanic, that fat and ~ plutocrat of the modern logging camps —J.F.Stevens⟩ ⟨feel like I can jump over a six-foot fence and getting very ~ —*Time*⟩ **2 :** distinctively smart or stylish ⟨a ~ black-and-white bow tie —Jean Stafford⟩ ⟨woven into his own nostalgic or ~ musical style —E.T.Canby⟩ ⟨rocketed from a pulp-type blood-and-thunder book to a ~ slick with top-name contributors —*Newsweek*⟩

sassy bark \"+,\ *n* [*sassy* prob. of African origin; akin to Twi *sę̀sę̀* plane tree, Ewe *se³se³wu³* African oak] **:** the bark of the sasswood that is used locally as an ordeal poison

¹sas·te·an \'sastēən\ *n* -s *usu cap* [alter. of *shastan*] **:** a subdivision of the Shastan language family comprising the Shasta language

²sastean \"\ *adj, usu cap* [alter. of *shastan*] **:** SHASTAN

sastra *often cap, var of* SHASTRA

sas·tru·ga *or* **zas·tru·ga** \'s|astrəgə, 'z|, |äs-, -,gä; ·'strügə\ *n, pl* **sastru·gi** *or* **zastru·gi** \-(,)gē\ [Russ *zastruga* groove] **:** a wavelike ridge of hard snow usu. formed on a level surface by the wind parallel to its direction and occurring in great numbers in the snowfields of the arctic and antarctic regions — usu. used in pl. ⟨the crisscrossing and fan-tailed form of the *sastrugi* —R.E.Byrd⟩

¹sat [ME, fr. OE *sæt*] *past of* SIT

²sat \'sȧt\ *Scot var of* SALT

³sat \'sət\ *n* -s [Skt, fr. *sat* being — more at SOOTH] *Hinduism* **:** eternal and immutable existence **:** the pure essence of being

sat *abbr* saturate; saturated; saturation

sa·tan \'sāt³n *also* -tən\ *n* -s *usu cap* [ME *Satan, Sathan*, fr. OE *Satan, Satanas*, fr. LL, fr. Gk, fr. Heb *sāṭān* devil, adversary] **1** *also* **sata·nas** \'sad·ənəs, 'sāt³n-\ **:** ¹DEVIL 1 **2 a** *obs* **:** a minion of the archfiend ⟨the very places from which the *Satans* by transgression fell —John Bunyan⟩ **b :** a wicked person **:** FIEND ⟨that villainous abominable misleader of youth . . . that old white-bearded *Satan* —Shak.⟩

sa·tang \sə'täŋ\ *n, pl* **satang** *or* **satangs** \-ŋz\ [Thai *satāṅ*] **1 :** a monetary unit of Thailand equal to $\frac{1}{100}$ baht — see MONEY table **2 :** a coin representing one satang

sa·tan·ic \sə'tanik, (')sā¦t-, -nēk\ *adj* [LGk *satanikos*, fr. Gk *Satan, Satanas* Satan + *-ikos* -ic] **1** *sometimes cap* **a :** of, relating to, or characteristic of Satan or his minions ⟨in secular history ~ interference is more conspicuous than divine guidance —E.E.Aubrey⟩ ⟨~ pride in the powerful negation of God —E.J.Simmons⟩ **b :** resembling Satan in appearance **:** MEPHISTOPHELIAN, SATURNINE ⟨a pointed ~ face⟩ ⟨herds of ~ black goats —Mollie Panter-Downes⟩ **c :** DERISIVE ⟨the sound of faint ~ mirth —Gordden Link⟩ **2 a :** characterized by extreme cruelty or viciousness **:** DIABOLICAL, FIENDISH ⟨not only the ape and the tiger, but what is far worse — perverted and ~ man —Walter Moberly⟩ **b :** of a hideous or forbidding aspect **:** GHOULISH, INFERNAL ⟨the black ~ landscapes of the Midlands —H.C.Darby⟩ ⟨mills which are dark and ~ with the glare and smoke of the furnaces —Sam Pollock⟩ **c :** of an excruciating nature **:** HELLISH ⟨battle against . . . ~ conditions of climate —J.S.Bradford⟩ **3 :** of a repellent or demented nature **:** AWFUL, DEMONIAC ⟨hoped that his other hat . . . would be smaller and paler than the ~ thing he had always worn pulled down over his eyes —Elinor Wylie⟩ ⟨irreverent, slightly ~, and resolutely bawdy —C.J.Rolo⟩ **4 :** of, relating to, or constituting a group of 19th century writers castigated as immoral by their more pious contemporaries ⟨a ~ spirit of pride and audacious impiety —Robert Southey⟩

sa·tan·i·cal \-nəkəl, -nēk-\ *adj* [*satan* + *-ical*] *archaic* **:** SATANIC

sa·tan·i·cal·ly \-k(ə)lē, -li\ *adv* **:** in a satanic manner **:** to a satanic degree ⟨~ handsome⟩ ⟨~ arrogant⟩

sa·tan·ism \'sāt³n,izəm *also* -tə,ni-\ *n* -s *often cap* [*satan* + *-ism*] **1 :** innate wickedness **:** DIABOLISM ⟨the ~ of Hitlers and Mussolinis —Walter Moberly⟩ **2 :** obsession with or affinity for evil ⟨both in her verse and her one solitary stupendous novel we find . . . this *Satanism* embodied and expressed —J.A. Bramley⟩; *specif* **:** the worship of Satan reputedly practiced by various writers in Paris in the 1890s marked by the travesty of Christian rites ⟨interpretation of *Satanism* as an offshoot of the belief in two coequal and coeternal principles of good and evil . . . deriving ultimately from Zoroastrianism —*Times Lit. Supp.*⟩

sa·tan·ist \-t³nəst, -tən-\ *n* -s *usu cap* [ML *satanista*, fr. LL *Satan, Satanas* + L *-ista* -ist] **1 a** *archaic* **:** one that is regarded as inherently evil ⟨atheistical *Satanists*, or evil-seekers —*Fraser's Mag.*⟩ **b :** EUCHITE **2 :** an adherent of Satan or Satanism **:** DIABOLIST ⟨a *Satanist* . . . contemplating anatomical experiments out of his unique sadism —A.J.Guérard⟩

sa·tan·i·ty \sā'tanəd·ē\ *n* -ES [*satan* + *-ity*] **:** SATANISM

sa·tan·ize \'sāt³n,īz, -tə,nīz\ *vt* -ED/-ING/-S [*satan* + *-ize*] **:** to make satanic ⟨a thirst for blood is the characteristic of . . . *satanized* man —*Dublin Rev.*⟩

satan monkey *n* **:** a small black bearded So. American monkey (*Pithecia satanas*)

sa·tan·o·pho·bia \,sāt³nə'fōbēə, -tən-; sə,tan-, sā,tan-\ *n* [*satan* + *-o-* + *phobia*] **:** abnormal fear of Satan

satan's mushroom *n, usu cap S* **:** a large usu. brownish yellow pore fungus (*Boletus satanus*) that occurs esp. in open woodland and is reputedly somewhat poisonous

SATB *abbr* soprano, alto, tenor, bass

satch·el \'sachəl\ *n* -s [ME *sachel*, fr. MF, fr. L *sacellus*, dim. of *saccus* bag — more at SACK] **1 :** a small bag usu. of leather or canvas with a flat bottom and often having a shoulder strap ⟨the whining schoolboy, with his ~ and shining morning face —Shak.⟩ ⟨people think that the stork brings babies, that the doctor brings the children in his ~ —Morris Fishbein⟩ ⟨picking up . . . the little canvas furlough ~ —James Jones⟩ **2 :** something that resembles a satchel ⟨from above two heavy ~*s* of flesh peered a pair of pale blue, bloodshot eyes —Eric Ambler⟩ ⟨candy ~*s* —*advt*⟩

satchel charge *n* **:** several blocks of explosive usu. taped to a board fitted with a rope or wire loop for use as a handle

sat-chromosome \'sat-; ,e,sā'tē-\ *n, usu cap S & A & T* [*SAT* abbr. of NL *Sine Acido Thymonucleico* without thymonucleic acid] **1 :** a chromosome including the nucleolus organizer **2 :** a chromosome with one or more satellites

satd *abbr* saturated

¹sate [ME, alter. of ¹*sat*] *archaic past of* SIT

²sate \'sāt, *usu* -ād·+V\ *vt* -ED/-ING/-S [prob. short for ²*satiate*] **1 a :** to cloy with overabundance **:** GLUT, SURFEIT ⟨lust, though to a radiant angel link'd, will ~ itself in a celestial bed —Shak.⟩ ⟨engulfed in enough celluloid adventure to ~ any escapist for a decade —John McCarten⟩ **b :** to appease (as a thirst or violent emotion) by indulging to the full ⟨the sort of rage that only the obliteration of a world could ~ —Clellon Holmes⟩ **2 :** SATIATE 1a ⟨~ people's desire to understand the past —J.D.Hart⟩ **3** *obs* **:** SATURATE **syn** see SATIATE

sated *adj* [fr. past part. of ²*sate*] **:** SATIATED

sa·teen *or* **sa·tine** \(')sa¦tēn, sə't-\ *n* -s [alter. (influenced by ¹*-een* & ²*-ine*) of ¹*satin*] **:** a smooth durable lustrous fabric usu. made of cotton in satin weave and in various weights for fine and work clothing, curtains, and linings

sateen weave *n* **:** satin weave used on cotton fabrics

sateenwood \='=,=\ *n* [*sateen* + *wood*] **:** a yellow satiny wood derived from an Amazonian tree (*Euxylophora paraensis*) of the family Rutaceae and widely used in Brazil in combination with acapu for parquetry

sate·less \'sātləs\ *adj* [²*sate* + *-less*] *archaic* **:** INSATIATE

¹sat·el·lite \'sad·³l,īt, -at³l- *sometimes* 'sat,l,īt; *usu* -īd·+V\ *n* -s [MF, fr. L *satellit-, satelles* attendant, bodyguard, prob. of Etruscan origin; akin to the source of L *Satellius*, a Roman name] **1 :** a hired agent or obsequious follower **:** MINION, SYCOPHANT ⟨armed ~*s* of great men, were forced to seek an independent source of livelihood —G.E.Fussell⟩ ⟨no ~ on whom he could bestow recognition with a maestro bow —Marjorie Brace⟩ **2 a :** a celestial body orbiting another of larger size **:** secondary planet **:** MOON ⟨Jupiter has twelve ~*s*, and Saturn probably has millions of them in its rings —*Time*⟩ **b :** a man-made object or vehicle intended to orbit the earth, the moon, or another celestial body and usu. instrumented for the transmission of space data ⟨such far-soaring objects as missiles, ~*s*, and lunar probes —*Newsweek*⟩ ⟨talks of a manned ~ to be used for meteorological observation —J.K. Hutchens⟩ **3 a :** one that resembles a celestial satellite ⟨the central sun he became for a host of surrounding ~*s* —Irving Kolodin⟩ ⟨in both the film and radio firmaments Ireland tends to be a ~ of Great Britain —Paul Blanshard⟩ **b :** one that is subject to external influence: as (1) **:** a political entity within the sphere of influence of a stronger power ⟨when demoralized, disorganized, ideologically confused groups collaborate with a powerful, tightly organized world conspiracy . . . they do not become allies but only ~*s* or puppets —Edmond Taylor⟩ ⟨~*s* have sovereignty, although they lack supremacy —H.D. Lasswell & Abraham Kaplan⟩ ⟨conversion of local regions into federal ~*s* poses a threat deadly to our liberties —D.D.Eisenhower⟩ (2) **:** a subordinate area or suburban community dependent upon a metropolis for economic support ⟨economic activities of the ~ are closely geared to those of the central city —C.D.Harris & E.L.Ullman⟩ (3) **:** an associated or subsidiary enterprise ⟨the hotel moved two blocks away . . . and immediately attracted new shops as ~*s* —Hal Burton⟩ ⟨a main base in the Little America area from which two ~*s* . . . will be supplied —Glen Jacobsen⟩ **4 :** one that is secondary or adjacent: as **a** (1) **:** a short segment separated from the main body of a chromosome by a constriction — called also *trabant* (2) **:** the secondary or later member of a chain of gregarines in syzygy (3) **:** a bodily structure lying near or associated with another (as a vein accompanying an artery) **b :** a smaller lesion accompanying a main one and situated nearby **c :** a spectral line of low intensity having a frequency close to that of another stronger line to which it is closely related (as by having a common energy level) **d :** an auxiliary airfield of limited facilities serving as a dispersal point for a main air base and as a base of operations if the main field is put out of action **5 :** one that accompanies **:** COMPLEMENT ⟨maize and its ~*s* —squashes and beans —A.L.Kroeber⟩

²satellite \"\ *also* **sat·el·lit·ic** \¦sad·³l¦id·|ik, ¦sat³l-, -¦it|, |ēk\ *adj* **1 :** of, relating to, or being a satellite ⟨globular star clusters are ~ systems —G.W.Gray b.1886⟩ ⟨the earth ~ vehicle program —*New Republic*⟩ ⟨the Kremlin could launch four ~ armies against them and still disclaim responsibility —H.F.Armstrong⟩ ⟨T chromosomes are characterized by having a ~ end —Leona Schnell⟩ **2 :** dominated by or dependent upon an external power **:** SUBORDINATE, RELATED ⟨did not take as much as four days . . . to obtain from its vassal ~ regimes acceptance of new measures —W.H.Chamberlin⟩ ⟨a survey of the governmental relationships between that city and its ~ communities —Robert Shaplen⟩ ⟨~ industries which can supply them with parts and components —Darrell Berrigan⟩ **3 a :** being in close proximity or association **:** ADJACENT, ANCILLARY ⟨guarded by a formidable barrier of ~ peaks —*Times Lit. Supp.*⟩ ⟨a large, angry boil . . . surrounded by a crop of what the doctors call ~ boils —S.M.Spencer⟩ ⟨a central library and ~ departmental libraries —*Library Science Abstracts*⟩ **b :** of a correlative nature **:** CONCOMITANT ⟨~ characters . . . correlated with growth —J.W.MacArthur⟩

sat·el·lit·ed \'sad·³l,īd·əd *sometimes* 'sat,lī-\ *adj* [¹*satellite* + *-ed*] **:** having a satellite ⟨a ~ chromosome⟩

satellite sphinx *n* **:** a large handsomely colored sphinx (*Pholus pandorus*) whose larva feeds on the grapevine

sat·el·lit·ism \'sad·³l,īd·,izəm *sometimes* 'sat,lī-\ *n* -s [¹*satellite* + *-ism*] **1 :** the practice of or belief in acquiring political satellites **2 :** the growth of bacteria of one sort in culture about colonies of another sort that supply needed micronutrients or growth factors

sat·el·lit·osis \,sad·³l,īd·'ōsəs, ,sat,lī-\ *n, pl* **satellit·oses** \-ō,sēz\ [NL, fr. ISV *satellite* + NL *-osis*] **:** a condition accompanying degenerative or inflammatory diseases of the central nervous system and characterized by a grouping of satellite cells around ganglocytes in the brain

sa·tem \'säd·əm, -ätəm\ *adj* [Av *satəm* hundred; fr. the fact that the initial sound of Av *satəm* (pronounced approximately \'sätəm\) represents an IE palatal stop; akin to Skt *śatam* hundred — more at HUNDRED] **:** belonging to or constituting a part of the Indo-European language family in which the palatal stops became in prehistoric times palatal or alveolar fricatives — opposed to *centum*

sates *pres 3d sing of* SATE
satg *abbr* saturating
sathan *obs var of* SATAN
sati *var of* SUTTEE
sa·tia·ble \'sāshəbəl *sometimes* -shēəb-\ *adj* [LL *satiabilis* satisfying, fr. L *satiare* to satisfy, satiate + *-abilis* -able] **:** capable of being appeased or satisfied
¹sa·tiate \'sāsh(ē)ət\ *adj* [ME *saciat*, fr. L *satiatus*, past part. of *satiare* to satiate] **:** SATIATED ⟨that ~ moment after dinner —D.L.Morgan⟩
²sa·ti·ate \'sāshē,āt, *usu* -ād.+V\ *vt* -ED/-ING/-S [L *satiatus*, past part. of *satiare* to satiate, fr. *satis* enough — more at SAD] **1 a :** to satisfy (as an appetite or desire) fully ⟨in reviewing a novel, you should try to . . . titillate rather than ~ the reader's interest —Raymond Walters b.1912⟩ **b :** SURFEIT **2** *obs* **:** SATURATE
syn SATE, SURFEIT, CLOY, PALL, GLUT, GORGE: SATIATE is the most general term, referring chiefly to the fact of repletion, without specifying manner or consequence. Both SATIATE and SATE were formerly used in the sense of merely to satisfy completely; both terms, but esp. SATE, now usu. imply overindulgence to the point where there is no longer any pleasure in what once seemed desirable ⟨a vast sameness of sweetness, *satiating* but never satisfying —Winifred Bambrick⟩ ⟨our generation is so overwhelmed by information . . . that curiosity becomes *sated*, discrimination dulled —W.R.Parker⟩ SURFEIT implies feeding, supplying, or indulging to excess, with consequent revulsion or disgust ⟨other poems have other crimes, and long before the reader has finished with them he is *surfeited* —J.G.Southworth⟩ CLOY stresses the aversion resulting from an excess of normally gratifying experience ⟨all breathing human passion far above, that leaves a heart high-sorrowful and *cloy'd* —John Keats⟩ PALL emphasizes loss of power to attract and a consequent waning of interest ⟨the vision *palled*, and Wells, the lifelong Utopian, despaired of man —Karl Meyer⟩ GLUT suggests a full supply or sometimes oversupply not necessarily resulting in extinction of desire; often (except in the economic sense of a *glutted* market) it suggests a constantly renewed greed, limited only by physical necessity ⟨*glutted*, but not sated with blood —Jane Porter⟩ GORGE suggests a greed, whether for material or spiritual goods, that is intensified by gratification and is only abated though not necessarily satisfied when the bursting point is reached ⟨the more she heard, the more she wanted to know; there was no *gorging* her to satiety —Samuel Butler †1902⟩; where food is the object, GORGE may suggest prolonged and unrestrained stuffing ⟨fell upon eggs and bacon and *gorged* till he could *gorge* no more —Rudyard Kipling⟩
satiated *adj* [fr. past part. of ²*satiate*] **:** filled to satiety **:** surfeited to the point of indifference or aversion **:** BORED, GLUTTED ⟨went and went again, never ~ with the theme —R.M.Lovett⟩ ⟨preaching continues until about 9 o'clock at night, when the people, ~ and subdued, begin to leave —*Amer. Guide Series: Tenn.*⟩
sa·ti·a·tion \,sās(h)ē'āshən\ *n* -S [L *satiatus* (past part. of *satiare* to satiate) + E *-ion*] **1 :** the quality or state of being satiated ⟨the fundamental precept of the fight for longevity is avoidance of ~ —A.A.Bogomolets⟩ **2 :** the act or process of achieving gratification ⟨~ of wants⟩
sa·ti·e·ty \sə'tīəd·ē, |t|, |ē *also* 'sāsh(ē)ə|\ *n* -ES [MF *satieté*, fr. L *satietat-, satietas*, fr. *satis* enough] **1 :** the quality or state of being fed to or beyond capacity **:** FULLNESS, SURFEIT ⟨gorged to ~ after a big Thanksgiving dinner⟩ **2 a** *obs* **:** full measure ⟨a ~ of joy, and an uninterrupted happiness —Joseph Addison⟩ **b** *archaic* **:** a completely adequate or more than adequate amount or extent ⟨had miracles even to ~ —J.H.Newman⟩ **3 a :** excessive gratification of a desire ⟨gave one of the soldiers leave to be drunk six weeks, in hopes of curing him by ~ —William Cowper⟩ **b :** the quality or state of being cloyed by overindulgence ⟨when natural pleasures had been indulged in to ~, pleasures . . . were imported from the East to stimulate the exhausted appetite —J.A.Froude⟩
¹sat·in \'sat³n\ *n* -S [ME, fr. MF *satin, satanin, zatanin, zatany*, prob. fr. Ar *zaytūnī*, fr. *Zaytūn*, a seaport in China during the Middle Ages, prob. *Zayton, Zaitun*, described by Marco Polo as one of the great ports of the East in the 13th cent. and usu. identified with *Tsinkiang* (formerly *Chuanchow*), seaport city in Fukien Province, southeastern China] **1 :** a smooth sleek fabric in satin weave with a very lustrous face and a dull back woven of silk and other fibers (as rayon, nylon, cotton) and used in various weights esp. for lingerie, dresses, and upholstery **2 :** something that resembles satin in texture or appearance ⟨parts finished in metallic ~ —*Sweet's Catalog Service*⟩
²satin \"\ *adj* **1 :** made of or covered with satin ⟨~ shoes⟩ ⟨carried the crown on a ~ cushion⟩ **2 :** resembling satin in lustrous finish, smooth appearance, or soft slippery feel ⟨roses break their ~ flake upon my garden floor —Emily Dickinson⟩ ⟨the master bedroom is finished in ~ plywood —*Amer. Builder*⟩
³satin \"\ *vt* -ED/-ING/-S **:** SATINIZE
sat·i·nay \¦sat³n¦ā\ *n* -S [F *satiné* satiny] **:** the wood of an Australian tree (*Syncarpia hillii*) of the family Myrtaceae resembling satiné in color and grain and being used for veneer and fine furniture
satin–back *or* **satin–backed** \'==,=\ *adj* **:** having a satin-weave surface on the back and any of various weaves on the front — used of reversible fabrics
satin bowerbird *or* **satin bird** *n* **:** a bowerbird (*Ptilonorhynchus violaceus*) of southeast Australia having feathered nostrils and being in the fully adult male a glossy violet blue and in the female a light gray green
¹sat·i·né \¦sat³n¦ā\ *n* -S [F, satiny, fr. past part. of *satiner* to satinize, fr. *satin*, n., fr. MF] **1 :** a timber tree (*Brosimum paraense*) of Brazil and the Guianas **2 :** the heavy hard lustrous red wood of satiné used for cabinetwork, veneers and furniture because of its golden sheen
²satine *var of* SATEEN
sat·in·et *also* **sat·in·ette** \¦sat³n¦et\ *n* -S [F *satinet*, fr. *satin*, n. + *-et*] **1 :** a thin silk satin or an imitation satin usu. of silk and cotton or wool and cotton used chiefly for clothing **2 :** a variation of satin weave used in making satinet
satinfin \'==,=\ *or* **satinfin shiner** *n* [²*satin* + *fin*] **:** a common minnow (*Notropis analoctanus*) of the northeastern U.S. or a related fish (*N. spilopterus*) of the eastern and central U.S., both having the lower fins largely white
satinflower \'==,=\ *n* [²*satin* + *flower*] **1 :** HONESTY 3 **2 :** BLUE-EYED GRASS **3 :** COMMON CHICKWEED **4 :** FLANNELFLOWER 3 **5 :** a plant or flower of the genus *Godetia*
satin flycatcher *also* **satin sparrow** *n* **:** a flycatcher (*Myiagra cyanoleuca*) of Tasmania and Australia that in the male is iridescent greenish black above and white below with greenish black throat — called also *shining flycatcher*
sating *pres part of* SATE
satin glass *n* **:** usu. colored or opaque and often cased ornamental glassware given a satinized finish by treatment with hydrofluoric acid vapor
satin grass *n* **:** any of several American grasses of the genus *Muhlenbergia* (as *M. mexicana* and *M. racemosa*)
sat·in·ize \'sat³n,īz\ *vt* -ED/-ING/-S [¹*satin* + *-ize*] **:** to give a satiny finish to ⟨glass . . . *satinized* by plunging in a bath of hydrofluoric acid vapor —C.W.Drepperd⟩
satinleaf \'==,=\ *n* [²*satin* + *leaf*] **:** CAIMITILLO
satin moth *n* **:** a tussock moth (*Stilpnotia salicis*) that is native to Europe but has become established in several parts of the U.S. and Canada whose adults have white satiny wings and whose blackish white-marked larvae feed on the foliage of the poplar and willow
satinpod \'==,=\ *n* [²*satin* + *pod*] **:** HONESTY 3, LUNARIA
satin spar *or* **satin stone** *n* **:** a fine fibrous calcite or gypsum having a satiny luster
satin stitch *n* **:** a padded or nearly alike on broidery stitch that is nearly alike on both sides and worked in various lengths and parallel lines so closely and evenly as to resemble satin fabric

satin stitch

satin walnut *n* **:** SWEET GUM 1
satin weave *n* **:** a weave in which the warp yarns are floated over the weft yarns or the weft over the warp and are interlaced at widely spread regular or irregular intervals thereby forming a smooth compact unbroken surface
satin white *n* **:** a white pigment made usu. by precipitating an aluminum sulfate with calcium hydroxide, consisting essentially of calcium sulfate and aluminum hydroxide and used chiefly in coating paper and as a base for organic pigments
satinwood \'==,=\ *n* [²*satin* + *wood*] **1 a :** an East Indian tree (*Chloroxylon swietenia*) of the family Meliaceae **b :** the very hard yellowish brown wood of this tree which has a satiny luster and is used esp. for fine cabinetwork and farming tools **2 a :** any of several trees with wood felt to resemble the East Indian satinwood: as (1) **:** a rather small yellowwood (*Zanthoxylum coriaceum*) of southern Florida and the West Indies with very heavy pale orange wood used locally for furniture and implements; *also* **:** a similar Australian tree (*Z. brachyacanthum*) with deep yellow wood (2) **:** ORANGE JESSAMINE (3) *Austral* **:** SASSAFRAS 3a(2) **b :** the wood of such a satinwood
sat·iny \'sat³nē, -ni\ *adj* [¹*satin* + *-y*] **1 :** having the soft texture or lustrous smoothness of satin ⟨the acorns . . . were green and ~ —Josephine Johnson⟩ ⟨waters of the harbor were a ~ light blue —Kenneth Roberts⟩ **2 :** richly sensuous ⟨the ~ sandalwood scent that came from the splendid coffin —Thomas Wolfe⟩
sat·ire \'sa,tī(ə)r, -īə\ *n* -S [MF or L; MF, fr. L *satira, satura* satirical poetry, poetic medley, fr. (*lanx*) *satura* full plate, plate filled with fruits, mixture, medley, fr. *lanx* plate + *satura*, fem. of *satur* full of food, sated — more at BALANCE, SAD] **1 a :** an ancient Roman verse commentary on a prevailing vice or folly **b :** a usu. topical literary composition holding up human or individual vices, folly, abuses, or shortcomings to censure by means of ridicule, derision, burlesque, irony, or other method sometimes with an intent to bring about improvement ⟨a farcical ~ about . . . adultery and late-achieved maturity —Orville Prescott⟩ **c :** LAMPOON ⟨diabolically good ~s of single authors —Anthony Boucher⟩ **d :** an expression of satire in another form ⟨dance ~⟩ ⟨visual ~ . . . abetted by hilarious sound effects —M.S.Dworkin⟩ ⟨an ungainly person, whose clothes were a continual ~ on his professional skill —Bayard Taylor⟩ **2 a :** a branch of literature ridiculing vice or folly ⟨~ . . . flourishes in a stable society and presupposes homogeneous moral standards —Evelyn Waugh⟩ ⟨the constructive purpose to which the humor and underlying hopefulness of good ~ give nourishment —J.R.Newman⟩ **b** *obs* **:** SATIRIST **3 :** raillery used to convey rebuke or criticism **:** caustic comment **:** IRONY ⟨into these paragraphs he packed his dry wit and his easy, good-natured ~ on the follies of the day —Eleanor Sickels⟩ ⟨a brilliant writer with a rare talent for corrosive ~ —C.J.Rolo⟩ **syn** see WIT
sa·tir·ic \sə'tirik, -rēk\ *or* **sa·tir·i·cal** \-rəkəl, -rēk-\ *adj* [*satiric* fr. MF *satirique*, fr. LL *satiricus*, fr. L *satira* satire + *-icus* -ic; *satirical* fr. MF *satirique* + E *-al*] **1 :** of, relating to, characterized by, or based on satire ⟨a ~ poet⟩ ⟨~ awareness of the . . . contradictory behavior of the whites —C.I.Glicksberg⟩ ⟨a ~ portrait of a . . . soldier who makes life simple by limiting his horizon —Henry Hewes⟩ ⟨noted for her ~ oils and drawings —*Amer. Guide Series: La.*⟩ **2 :** fond of satire **:** skilled at ironic comment ⟨witty, eloquent, and *satirical* in his sermons —G.H.Genzmer⟩ ⟨a flair for drawing and a nice *satirical* sense —Merle Miller⟩ **3 a :** bearing a device satirizing a political or social issue ⟨*satirical* coin⟩ **b :** circulated for propaganda purposes ⟨*satirical* token⟩ ⟨*satirical* medal⟩ **syn** see SARCASTIC
sa·tir·i·cal·ly \-rək(ə)lē, -rēk-, -li\ *adv* **:** in a satirical manner
sa·tir·i·cal·ness *n* -ES *archaic* **:** the quality or state of being satirical
satirism *n* -S [*satire* + *-ism*] *obs* **:** expression of satire
sat·i·rist \'sad·ərəst, -atə-\ *n* -S [*satire* + *-ist*] **:** one that satirizes; *esp* **:** a satirical writer
sat·i·rize \-,rīz\ *vb* -ED/-ING/-S *see -ize in Explan Notes* [F *satiriser*, fr. MF, fr. *satire* + *-iser* -ize] *vi* **:** to utter or write satires **:** comment satirically esp. in literary form ⟨it is as bad a fault in history to panegyrize, as to ~ without reason — Roger North⟩ ~ *vt* **:** to censure or ridicule by means of satire ⟨makes use of allegory and fantasy to ~ the society of his time —*Amer. Guide Series: N.Y.City*⟩
sat·i·riz·er \-zə(r)\ *n* -S [*satirize* + *-er*] **:** one that satirizes
sat·is·da·tion \,sad·əs'dāshən\ *n* -S [L *satisdation-, satisdatio*, fr. *satisdatus*, past part. of *satisdare* to give security, give enough, fr. *satis* enough + *dare* to give — more at SAD, DATE] *Roman & civil law* **:** the giving of security esp. by a guarantor on behalf of a debtor sometimes in form of a cautio
sat·is·fac·tion \,sad·əs'fakshən, ,satə-\ *n* -S [ME *satisfaccioun*, fr. MF *satisfaction*, fr. LL *satisfaction-, satisfactio* penitence, penance, fr. L, satisfaction, fr. *satisfactus* (past part. of *satisfacere* to satisfy) + *-ion-, -io* -ion — more at SATISFY] **1 a :** reparation for sin made by performing the penance imposed by a confessor ⟨the good works required of penitent sinners in ~ for their offenses —K.S.Latourette⟩ **b :** fulfillment of the demands of divine justice on behalf of mankind ⟨the voluntary death of Christ . . . accomplished this ~ —*Encyc. Americana*⟩ — compare ATONEMENT 2 **2 a :** complete fulfillment of a need or want **:** attainment of a desired end ⟨for this night he entreat you to his bed, give him promise of ~ —Shak.⟩ ⟨primitive art quickly flowers into full ~ of some aesthetic craving —A.N.Whitehead⟩ ⟨when the cause of the arthritis can be definitely determined . . . the condition can be treated with much more ~ —Morris Fishbein⟩ **b :** the quality or state of being satisfied **:** CONTENTMENT, PLEASURE ⟨~ in able work accomplished and recognized —Johnson O'Connor⟩ ⟨derive a melancholy ~ from the conviction that they are on the losing side —Elmer Davis⟩ ⟨the ~ derived from a sense of sharing in creative activities —John Dewey⟩ **c :** a cause or means of enjoyment **:** GRATIFICATION ⟨children . . . found it a novelty and a ~ to work on the soil —Martha Sharp⟩ ⟨journeyed to Kentucky . . . to pay off his debts, an action that gave him one of the greatest ~s of his life —W.J.Ghent⟩ **3 a** (1) **:** compensation for a loss or injury **:** ATONEMENT, RESTITUTION ⟨promised to have the fellows punished, and ~ to be made —Daniel Defoe⟩ (2) *obs* **:** payment for service given ⟨operation of writing, for which it directed the scribe to receive a ~ —William Blackstone⟩ (3) **:** opportunity to vindicate one's honor (as by fighting a duel) ⟨if . . . you will give me your card, I will see that you shall shortly have the ~ you require —Thomas Medwin⟩ **b** (1) **:** the discharge of a legal obligation or settlement of a claim **:** execution of an accord ⟨~ of a mortgage⟩ (2) **:** a legal document showing that such an obligation has been met **c :** fulfillment of an essential condition ⟨~ of the foreign language distribution requirement —*College of William & Mary Cat.*⟩ **4 a :** dissipation of doubt or ignorance **:** CONVICTION, ENLIGHTENMENT ⟨the charge must be proved to the ~ of the court⟩ ⟨for your private ~ . . . I will let you know —Shak.⟩ ⟨this investigation was a legitimate ~ of congressional curiosity —Brian Gilbert⟩ **b** *obs* **:** satisfactory proof ⟨I doubt not but to give you ~ that I am not worthy of this wrong —*Itinerary*⟩
sat·is·fac·tion·al \¦==¦fakshən³l, -shnəl\ *adj* **:** SATISFACTORY
satisfaction piece *n* **:** a formal written acknowledgment by the holder of a mortgage or judgment of its satisfaction with an authorization for its discharge of record
satisfaction theory *n* **:** a theory of the atonement in scholastic theology: according to the requirements of divine justice God and man could not be reconciled until human guilt was punished or acceptable satisfaction was made and Christ made such satisfaction by freely and vicariously suffering and dying — see PENAL THEORY; compare GOVERNMENTAL ATONEMENT, MORAL THEORY, RANSOM THEORY, SACRIFICIAL THEORY
sat·is·fac·to·ri·ly \¦sad·ə¦sfakt(ə)rəlē, ¦satə-, -li\ *adv* **:** in a satisfactory manner
sat·is·fac·to·ri·ness \-rēnəs, -rin-\ *n* -ES **:** the quality or state of being satisfactory
sat·is·fac·to·ry \¦==¦sfakt(ə)rē, -ri\ *adj* [LL *satisfactorius*, fr. L *satisfactus* (past part. of *satisfacere* to satisfy) + *-orius* -ory] **1** *archaic* **:** fulfilling the requirements of divine justice ⟨the ~ . . . and propitiatory sacrifice of Christ Jesus —William Gouge⟩ **2 :** sufficient to meet a condition or obligation ⟨~ scores on the medical college admission test —*Bull. of Meharry Med. Coll.*⟩ **3 :** giving satisfaction: as **a :** capable of dispelling doubt or ignorance **:** CONVINCING, INFORMATIVE ⟨very ~ evidence that around the tenth century A.D. the stories . . . were almost identical —E.R.Leach⟩ ⟨the most ~ and trustworthy . . . book on the subject —Zechariah Chafee⟩ **b :** adequate to meet a need or want ⟨breast milk is the best food for an infant . . . provided the supply is ~ —Morris Fishbein⟩ **c :** producing pleasure or contentment **:** ENJOYABLE, GRATIFYING ⟨a ~ pet is an animal . . . that is not an annoyance to owner or guests —Doris Bryant⟩ ⟨found that . . . the sphere and the cone were ~ objects in themselves —Herbert Read⟩ ⟨particularly ~ are the declines in infantile mortality —R.C. Geary⟩ **d :** having all the necessary qualities for effective use ⟨a number of fountain pens had been patented previously, but to his mind none of them was ~ —C.W.Mitman⟩
sat·is·fi·able \'==,sfīəbəl, ,==¦===\ *adj* [*satisfy* + *-able*] **:** capable of being satisfied
satisfied *adj* [fr. past part. of *satisfy*] **1 :** full of contentment **:** PLEASED, GRATIFIED ⟨a ~ customer⟩ **2 :** paid in full **:** DISCHARGED ⟨a ~ mortgage⟩ **3 :** persuaded by argument or evidence **:** CONVINCED ⟨there is great force in this argument, and the court is not ~ that it has been refuted —John Marshall⟩
sat·is·fi·er \'==,sfī(ə)r, -īə\ *n* -S [*satisfy* + *-er*] **:** one that satisfies
sat·is·fy \'sad·ə,sfī, -atə-\ *vb* -ED/-ING/-ES [ME *satisfien*, fr. MF *satisfier*, modif. (influenced by MF *-fier* -fy) of L *satisfacere*, fr. *satis* enough + *facere* to do, make — more at SAD, DO] *vt* **1 a :** to carry out the terms of (as a contract) **:** DISCHARGE ⟨the property would be insufficient to ~ . . . the lien —G.A.Parks⟩ ⟨helpless to . . . defend a suit because he has no money to ~ court fees —J.M.Maguire⟩ **b :** to meet a financial obligation to (a creditor) ⟨had to sell land . . . to ~ his creditors —T.J. Wertenbaker⟩ **c** *obs* **:** to recompense for services **:** REMUNERATE ⟨not a compositor's duty; especially where he has no expectation of being *satisfied* for it —Philip Luckombe⟩ **2 a** *obs* **:** to serve as compensation for (a loss or injury) **:** AVENGE, REQUITE **b** (1) **:** to do penance for (a sin) (2) **:** to make atonement or reparation to (an injured party) **:** INDEMNIFY ⟨conclude a treaty to ~ Indians deprived of their hereditary lands⟩ **3 a :** to make happy **:** PLEASE ⟨in the position of having to ~ teachers and critics —R.M.Weaver⟩ ⟨farmers . . . were *satisfied* with the administration's flexible farm support program —*Wall Street Jour.*⟩ ⟨a picture, in whatever degree it be realistic or nonrealistic, should . . . ~ the eye —C.W.H.Johnson⟩ **b :** to gratify to the full **:** APPEASE, SATIATE ⟨*satisfied* his omnivorous appetite for reading in the village library —A.C.Cole⟩ ⟨the men in the capital . . . do their utmost to gauge and to ~ the desires of the nation —Lester Markel⟩ **4 a :** to persuade by argument or evidence **:** CONVINCE ⟨took me a long time to ~ them . . . that my engagements prevented me from presiding —O.S.J.Gogarty⟩ ⟨not *satisfied* that I have penetrated this allegory —Paul Pickrel⟩ **b :** to put an end to (doubt or uncertainty) **:** DISPEL ⟨many a world-renowned lecturer came up the Mississippi . . . to ~ his curiosity —*Amer. Guide Series: Minn.*⟩ **c :** to answer or express fully ⟨a question or two in the unquiet heads which nothing can ever ~ —W.L.Sullivan⟩ ⟨cloying repetitions that do not ~ the romantic illusion he has created —I.L.Salomon⟩ **5 a :** to conform to (accepted criteria or requirements) **:** FULFILL, MEET ⟨if a consignment does not ~ all the conditions . . . it is graded down —*Farmer's Weekly (So. Africa)*⟩ ⟨able . . . to ~ the demands of a moral, Victorian society —Ruth R. Chapman⟩ ⟨an explanation which might ~ these statements and be true to the evidence —H.Lovegrove⟩ **b :** to comply with (an academic requirement) ⟨courses . . . taken to ~ the distribution requirements —*Official Register of Harvard Univ.*⟩ **c :** to provide a solution for; *specif* **:** to substitute an expression for an unknown quantity in (an equation) so that the resulting equation is true **d :** to serve as an embodiment of **:** give concrete expression to **:** EXEMPLIFY ⟨the first American foundation which *satisfies* the definition —F.E.Andrews⟩ ⟨a social regime can come into enduring existence only as it *satisfies* some elements of human nature not previously afforded expression —John Dewey⟩ **6 :** to respond to by chemical union ⟨to ~ valences⟩ ~ *vi* **1** *archaic* **:** to do penance **:** ATONE; *specif* **:** to fulfill the requirements of divine justice **2 :** to be a source of pleasure or gratification **:** PLEASE, SUFFICE ⟨where the play seems not to ~ is in the full release of emotions —Leslie Rees⟩
syn CONTENT: SATISFY usu. implies full appeasement of a desire, longing, need, or requirement ⟨*satisfy* curiosity⟩ ⟨*satisfy* an appetite⟩ ⟨*satisfy* the desire for power —W.G. Walter⟩ ⟨the needs which such an effort purports to *satisfy* —Abram Kardiner⟩ CONTENT usu. implies gratification of a desire or longing to the point where one is not disquieted or disturbed even though every wish is not fully realized ⟨must *content* myself with adducing some fresh evidence on the subject —J.G.Frazer⟩ ⟨*contented* with the same food, clothing and lodging which satisfied them in former times —Adam Smith⟩
syn SATISFY, FULFILL, MEET, ANSWER all imply the ability to measure up to a set of criteria or requirements. SATISFY often implies adequacy to a practical extent or for a stated purpose ⟨went a long way toward *satisfying* the long-standing claims of his critics —*Time*⟩ ⟨a culture which will *satisfy* our needs —J. B.Conant⟩ ⟨finding the way to *satisfy* her demands —A.S. Igleheart⟩ FULFILL, when it is not interchangeable with SATISFY, may connote more abundance or richness of qualification ⟨*fulfill* the requirement for graduation⟩ ⟨*fulfill* his greatest need⟩ ⟨*fulfill* all conditions imposed upon a candidate for office⟩ MEET implies an exactness of agreement between a requirement and what is submitted to fill it ⟨the instruments *met* all the criteria with above-average ratings —Helen Vodicka⟩ ⟨the student has not *met* all financial obligations to the University —*Loyola Univ. Bull.*⟩ ⟨the provisions were sufficiently flexible to *meet* the needs of men with very large families —R.A.Billington⟩ ANSWER usu. though not necessarily implies the simple satisfaction of a demand, need, or purpose often in a temporary or expedient manner and may imply some falling short in completeness or fullness of qualification ⟨*answer* a need⟩ ⟨though a sharp knife should be used, a dull one will *answer* the purpose⟩ ⟨*answer* in some way the demands of a growing child for good counseling⟩ **syn** see in addition PAY
satisfying *adj* **:** SATISFACTORY 3 — **sat·is·fy·ing·ly** *adv*
sat·is·fy·ing·ness *n* -ES **:** SATISFACTION
sat·is·pas·sion \,sad·ə'spashən\ *n* [L *satis* enough + E *passion* (sense 1); influenced by ML *satis pati* to suffer enough] **:** penitential suffering
sative *adj* [L *sativus*, fr. *satus* (past part. of *serere* to sow) + *-ivus* -ive — more at SOW] *obs* **:** SOWN, CULTIVATED
satn *abbr* saturation
sa·to·ri \sə'tōrē\ *n* -S [Jap] **:** sudden enlightenment and a state of consciousness attained by intuitive illumination representing the spiritual goal of Zen Buddhism
sa·trae \'sā,trē\ *n pl, usu cap* [NL, fr. Gk *Satrai*] **:** an ancient people of Thrace living on Mount Pangaeus without ever being subjugated by a conqueror
satrap \'sā,trap *also* 'sa,trap, *chiefly Brit* 'sa·trəp\ *n* -S [ME, fr. L *satrapes*, fr. Gk *satrapēs*, fr. OPer *xshathrapāvan*, lit., protector of the dominion, a compound whose first constituent is akin to Skt *kṣatra* might, power, *kṣayati* he rules, and whose second constituent is akin to Skt *pāti* he protects — more at CHECK, FUR] **1 a :** the governor of a province in ancient Persia **b :** the viceroy of a sovereign power ⟨~s who represented the king in Ireland —O.S.J.Gogarty⟩ ⟨Soviet leaders and their East German ~s —*Newsweek*⟩ **2 a :** one having authority ⟨the ~s of Yale University saw nothing wrong in allowing one of its lecture halls to be used —*Amer. Mercury*⟩ **b :** a subordinate often subservient official or supporter **:** HENCHMAN ⟨political ~s who battled for senators in the legislature —W.A.White⟩
satra·py \'sā·trəpē, 'sā,trap-, 'sa·trəp-, 'sa,trap-, -pi\ *n* -ES [F *satrapie*, fr. L *satrapia, satrapea*, fr. Gk *satrapeia*, fr. *satrapēs* satrap + *-ia* -y] **1 a :** a territory governed by a satrap ⟨the Greek city was no mere ~ of a faraway king —C.H.McIlwain⟩ **b :** the sphere of influence of a powerful individual ⟨views . . . unions outside his ~ with the loathing of a high-caste Hindu for an untouchable —Joe Miller⟩ **2 :** a hierarchy of satraps ⟨the most unappetizing man in the Hitler ~ —*New Yorker*⟩
sats *pl of* SAT

sat·sop \ˈsat,säp\ *n, pl* **satsop** *or* **satsops** *usu cap* **1 :** a Salishan people of the Satsop river valley in southwestern Washington **2 :** a member of the Satsop people

sat·su·ma \sat'sümə, ˈsatsəmə\ *n* -s [fr. *Satsuma,* former province in southern Kyushu, Japan] **1** *or* **satsuma ware** *usu cap S* **:** a hard fine-grained buff Japanese pottery first produced about the end of the 16th century, orig. decorated with monochrome glazes, and from the late 18th century finished with increasingly ornate overglaze enamels and gilding **2** *or* **satsuma orange :** any of several cultivated mandarin trees having medium-sized largely seedless fruits with thin smooth skin

sat·ta·gyd·i·an \,sad·əˈjidēən, -ˈgi-\ *n, pl* **sattagydian** *or* **sattagydians** *usu cap* **1 :** an ancient people of the Punjab **2 :** a member of the Sattagydian people

sat·tle \ˈsatᵊl\ *dial Brit var of* SETTLE

satt·va \ˈsətvə\ *n* -s [Skt, lit., existence, fr. *sat, sant* existing, true, good — more at SOOTH] **:** the purity and wisdom constituting one of the three gunas of Sankhya philosophy and leading to true enlightenment — compare RAJAS, TAMAS

sa·tura \ˈsäd·ərə\ *n, pl* **satu·rae** \-,rī\ [L — more at SATIRE] **:** a rudimentary type of stage show with musical accompaniment performed in ancient Rome prior to the introduction of formal Latin comedy

sat·u·ra·ble \ˈsach(ə)rəbəl\ *adj* [LL *saturabilis,* fr. L *saturare* to saturate + *-abilis* -able] **:** capable of being saturated

saturable reactor *also* **saturable core reactor** *n* **:** an AC reactor coil of variable but limited impedance because of magnetic core saturation by means of an auxiliary DC excitation coil — abbr. *SR*

¹sat·u·rant \ˈsachərənt\ *adj* [L *saturant-, saturans,* pres. part. of *saturare* to saturate] **:** impregnating to the full **:** SATURATING

²saturant \"\ *n* -s **:** a substance used to saturate another

¹sat·u·rate \ˈsachə,rāt, *usu* -ād·+V\ *vt* -ED/-ING/-S [L *saturatus,* past part. of *saturare* to fill, saturate, fr. *satur* full of food, satiated — more at SAD] **1 :** to cloy with overabundance **:** SATE, SURFEIT ⟨a surfeit of war and massive injustice have *saturated* our capacity for moral indignation —John Barkham⟩ **2 :** to satisfy the affinity of (a substance) **:** cause to combine till there is no further tendency to combine **:** NEUTRALIZE ⟨~ an acid with an alkali⟩ **3 a :** to infuse thoroughly or cause to be pervaded **:** SOAK, STEEP ⟨~ a sponge with water⟩ ⟨the whole house was *saturated* with the aroma —Ellen Glasgow⟩ ⟨moonglow . . . ~*s* an empty sky —Henry Miller⟩ **b :** to fill completely **:** IMBUE ⟨the novel . . . is *saturated* with individualism and liberal culture —V.S.Pritchett⟩ ⟨this little town with its giant elms is *saturated* with . . . traditions —E.A.Weeks⟩ ⟨literary men ~ themselves in attitudes that have become irrelevant —H.J.Muller⟩ **c :** to load to capacity **:** CROWD, DELUGE ⟨jet operations already ~ all air space between 20,000 ft. and 40,000 ft. —*Time*⟩ ⟨the two-million-dollar . . . campaign, which *saturated* radio and television for two weeks before election day —Robert Bendiner⟩; *specif* **:** to furnish to an amount which meets present and prospective demands at current prices ⟨believed that 8000 machines . . . would about ~ the market —Bryan Morgan⟩ **d** (1) **:** to overwhelm (an air defense system) by sending in so many airplanes in a unit of time that detecting and tracking equipment becomes erratic (2) **:** to blanket (a target area) with bombs or projectiles to the point of utter destruction **4 a :** to impregnate with a vapor to the maximum degree possible at the existing temperature and pressure ⟨~ air with water vapor⟩ **b :** to dissolve in (a solvent) as much of a solute as can be held in solution at the existing temperature and pressure **c :** to magnetize (a substance) until further increase of magnetizing force produces no increase in magnetization **d :** to increase the voltage on (a vacuum tube or other device) until further voltage increase produces no change in current **syn** see PERMEATE

²sat·u·rate \ˈsach(ə)rət, *usu* -əd·+V\ *adj* [L *saturatus,* past part. of *saturare* to saturate] **:** SATURATED ⟨seaweed can loll in the water, buoyed by it and even ~ with it —D.C.Peattie⟩ ⟨words . . . have become enriched by many associations, ~ with many colors —Havelock Ellis⟩ ⟨a ~ solution of silver⟩

³saturate *n* -s **:** a saturated chemical compound

saturated *adj* [fr. past part. of ¹*saturate*] **1 :** brought to a state of full contentment or development **:** SATISFIED, PERFECTED ⟨as well-*saturated* guests, we should . . . willingly recede from the table —Henry More⟩ ⟨exaggerate the differences between . . . ~ and emergent cultures —Edward Sapir⟩ **2 a :** steeped in moisture **:** SOAKED, SOGGY ⟨the top of the ~ zone is called the groundwater table —V.C.Finch & G.T.Trewartha⟩ **b :** completely penetrated **:** ABSORBED, PERVADED ⟨listened to jazz in a smoke-*saturated* room —Molly L. Bar-David⟩ ⟨a ~ knowledge which . . . has entered the very bloodstream of his thought —H.M.Wriston⟩ **3 a** *of a solution* **:** having the greatest concentration that can remain under given conditions (as of temperature and pressure) in the presence of the dissolved substance **b** *of a chemical compound* **:** not tending to form addition products — used esp. of organic compounds containing only single bonds between carbon atoms ⟨paraffin hydrocarbons are ~ compounds⟩ ⟨~ fatty acids⟩ **4 a :** impregnated to the maximum degree ⟨water . . . permanently ~ with oxygen —W.H.Dowdeswell⟩ ⟨a magnetically ~ steel bar⟩ **b :** having high saturation **:** PURE, VIVID — used of a color **c :** containing the greatest possible amount of combined silica — used of a mineral or rock **5 :** filled to capacity **:** fully supplied ⟨500 millions of . . . folk live in a continent which is now essentially ~ —Griffith Taylor⟩ ⟨possible results of such an operation . . . would have but little effect on an already ~ market —*Amer. Guide Series: Wash.*⟩

saturated steam *n* **1 :** water vapor in equilibrium with liquid water at or above the normal boiling point **2 :** WET STEAM

saturated vapor *n* **:** vapor at the temperature of the boiling point corresponding to its pressure and so incapable of being compressed or cooled without condensing — compare EQUILIBRIUM 1c

saturating felt *n* **:** a felt paper for impregnation with asphalt or other waterproofing compound

sat·u·ra·tion \,sachəˈrāshən\ *n* -s *often attrib* [LL *saturation-, saturatio,* fr. L *saturatus* (past part. of *saturare* to saturate) + *-ion-, -io* -ion] **1 :** complete satiety or glut **:** CONTENTMENT, SURFEIT ⟨moving from stable ~ to . . . restlessness, and instability —A.L.Kroeber⟩ ⟨become familiar, to the point of ~ . . . with the subject matter —John Dewey⟩ **2 :** conversion of an unsaturated chemical compound to a saturated one — compare HYDROGENATION a **3 a :** the quality or state of being soaked or steeped **:** PERMEATION ⟨water . . . fills all pores and openings within the zone of ~ —A.M.Bateman⟩ ⟨that ~ with the years that for Europe is synonymous with cultural meaning —Harold Rosenberg⟩ **b :** impregnation to the maximum extent: as (1) **:** the presence in air of as much water vapor per unit volume as possible at a given temperature (2) **:** magnetization to the point beyond which a further increase in the intensity of the magnetizing force will produce no further magnetization and only an equal increase in the magnetic flux density in the body (3) **:** the condition in which all the electrons in an electron tube flow to the plate as fast as they are emitted by the filament, an increase of plate or grid voltage producing no increase of current **c :** the quality or state of being filled to capacity ⟨without drastic regulation of traffic, our streets . . . will reach a point of ~ —Hal Burton⟩ **4 a :** chromatic purity **:** freedom from dilution with white **:** INTENSITY, VIVIDNESS ⟨a dull red lacking in ~⟩ **b** (1) **:** degree of difference from the gray having the same lightness — used of an object color (2) **:** degree of difference from the achromatic light-source color of the same brightness — used of a light-source color **5 a :** the supplying of a market with goods sufficient to meet all present and prospective demands at current prices ⟨falling off of refrigerator sales due to market ~⟩ **b :** widespread coverage of an area (as by personnel or promotional material) ⟨spot announcements used in metropolitan areas in varying degrees of ~⟩ ⟨~ of a tough neighborhood with police patrols⟩ **c :** the ratio of public acceptance ⟨electric cooking . . . has been developed to a ~ of 23 percent —*Electric World*⟩ **d :** the limit of consumer capacity ⟨television set ownership . . . is now less than forty percent short of ~ —Philip Minoff⟩ **6 :** a concentration of military forces or firepower sufficient to overwhelm or completely wipe out enemy defenses ⟨a logical target for quick ~ by parachute troops —George Weller⟩ **7 :** the supposed increased resemblance to the sire of successive offspring of the same parents — compare TELEGONY

saturation bombing *n* **:** AREA BOMBING

saturation current *n* **:** the limiting current through an ionized gas or an electron tube such that further increase of voltage produces no further increase in current

saturation curve *n* **:** a magnetization curve for a process carried to saturation

saturation factor *n* **:** a measure of the saturation of a magnetizable body that is the ratio of a small percentage increase in excitation to the percentage increase in magnetic flux produced thereby and that is usu. applied to the magnetic excitation of dynamoelectric machines at rated speed and voltage

saturation point *n* **:** the point at which saturation is reached: as **a** (1) **:** the limit of response to desire or stimulus ⟨killing . . . reaches a *saturation point* when the hunter ceases to want to hunt —*Nature Mag.*⟩ ⟨the boy has reached the *saturation point* and does not respond to the training school program any longer —Erwin Schepses⟩ (2) **:** the maximum level of provocation or of injurious effect ⟨the mother . . . reached a *saturation point* with the screaming child —Jessie Chamberlin⟩ ⟨a person has . . . reached the *saturation point* of aging between 70 and 80 and, from there on, he will age only very slowly —Martin Gumpert⟩ **b :** a limit of acceptance ⟨immigration . . . has not reached a *saturation point* —D.D.McKean⟩; *specif* **:** the point in a flow of goods or money at which the market will take no more except at a decrease in price ⟨houses will be built until the *saturation point* is reached —Brendon Shea⟩ **c :** the maximum degree of impregnation; *specif* **:** DEW POINT **d :** the maximum number of a kind of organism that can be carried on a particular range under optimum conditions — compare CARRYING CAPACITY

saturation pressure *n* **:** the pressure of a vapor which is in equilibrium with its liquid (as steam with water); *specif* **:** the maximum pressure possible by water vapor at a given temperature

sat·u·ra·tor \ˈsachə,rād·ə(r), -ātə-\ *n* -s [¹*saturate* + *-or*] **:** one that saturates: as **a :** a tank containing sulfuric acid through which vapors are passed in the carbonization of coal to remove ammonia with the formation of ammonium sulfate **b :** HUMIDIFIER 1 **c :** a device for injecting water spray into heated compressed air to cool the air **d :** an operator of a machine for saturating roofing felt with hot asphalt

sat·ur·day \ˈsad·ə(r)dē, -atə-, -(r)(,)dā, *in rapid speech* ˈsaddē *or* ˈsardē *or* ˈsatdē *or* -di\ *n* -s *usu cap* [ME *saterday,* fr. OE *sæterdæg, sæterndæg;* akin to OFris *sāterdei* Saturday, MD *saterdach,* MLG *sāterdach;* all fr. a prehistoric WGmc compound whose first constituent was borrowed fr. L *Saturnus* Saturn and whose second constituent is represented by OE *dæg* day; trans. of L *Saturni dies* — more at DAY] **:** the seventh day of the week **:** the day following Friday

sat·ur·days \-z\ *adv, usu cap* **:** on Saturday repeatedly **:** on any Saturday

sat·u·re·ia \,sachəˈrē(y)ə, ,sad·ə'-\ *n, cap* [NL, fr. L, savory (mint)] **:** a genus of aromatic herbs or shrubs (family Labiatae) that are nearly all native to southern Europe and that have small entire leaves, bracted purple flowers in axillary or terminal clusters, and oblong or oval nutlets — see SAVORY, WILD BASIL, YERBA BUENA

sat·u·re·ja \-ē(y)ə, -ējə\ [NL] *syn of* SATUREIA

sat·urn \ˈsad·ə(r)n, -atə-\ *n* -s *usu cap* [ME *saturne,* fr. ML *saturnus,* fr. L *Saturnus* Saturn (the planet), fr. *Saturnus* Saturn (the god); prob. fr. the sluggishness associated with the planet Saturn by astrologists] *archaic* **:** ⁴LEAD 1a

sat·ur·na·lia \,sad·ə(r)ˈnālyə, ,satə-, -lēə\ *n pl but sing or pl in constr* [L, fr. neut. pl. of *saturnalis* of or relating to Saturn, fr. *Saturnus* Saturn + *-alis* -al] **1** *usu cap* **:** the festival of Saturn in ancient Rome beginning on Dec. 17 and celebrated with feasting, exchange of gifts, and tumultuous revelry and presided over by a king chosen by lot ⟨a survival of the ancient *Saturnalia* of some other pagan rite of orgiastic nature —C.B. Kelland⟩ **2** *sing, pl* **saturnalias** *also* **saturnalia** *sometimes cap* **a :** an unrestrained often licentious celebration or spectacle **:** ORGY ⟨the ~ of an American Legion convention turning Cleveland into Paris for a week —D.W.Brogan⟩ ⟨a ~ of blood and crime in which . . . the guilty are not punished for the most flagrant violation —Sheldon Glueck⟩ ⟨pilferings of . . . rum from her barroom for his noisy ~*s* —Wilmon Menard⟩ **b :** an excess of emotion or immorality ⟨rushed in a ~ of faith to spell out its . . . consequences for the solitary soul —S.E. Whicher⟩ ⟨sacrifice of the state, in a veritable ~ of corruption —C.G.Bowers⟩

sat·ur·na·lian \¦==¦nālyən, -lēən\ *adj* **1** *usu cap* **:** of or relating to the ancient Roman Saturnalia **2** *often cap* **:** characterized by unrestrained emotion or licentious indulgence **:** ORGIASTIC ⟨feast days with their . . . games and merrymakings and their generally *Saturnalian* aspect —Hutton Webster⟩

sat·ur·nals \səˈtərnᵊlz, ˈsad·ər-\ *n pl, usu cap* [L *Saturnalia* + E *-s* (pl. suffix)] *archaic* **:** SATURNALIA

sa·tur·nia \səˈtərnēə\ *n, cap* [NL, fr. L, daughter of the Roman god Saturn (epithet of the goddess Juno), fr. fem. of *saturnius* of Saturn, fr. *Saturnus* Saturn] **:** a genus of wild silk moths that is the type of the family Saturniidae

¹sa·tur·ni·an \səˈtərnēən\ *adj, usu cap* [L *saturnius* Saturnian (fr. *Saturnus* sixth major planet from the sun and the most remote planet known to the ancients, fr. *Saturnus* Roman god connected with the sowing of seed) + E *-an*] **1 :** of, relating to, resembling, or influenced by the planet Saturn **2** *archaic* **:** of or relating to the god Saturn or his flourishing era conceived of as a golden age ⟨a new social order . . . to bring back the ~ era to the world —Thomas Carlyle⟩

²saturnian \"\ *n* -s *usu cap* **1 :** a hypothetical inhabitant of the planet Saturn **2 :** one that has a well-developed Mount of Saturn and a long and large finger of Saturn and that is usu. held by palmists to be characterized by prudence, sobriety, cynicism, and often gloom ⟨the *Saturnian* is predisposed to suicide as an end to his woes —W.G.Benham⟩ **3 :** SATURNIAN VERSE

saturnian verse *n, usu cap S* **:** the ancient Latin verse used before the adoption of Greek verse forms

¹sa·tur·ni·id \səˈtərnēəd\ *adj* [NL *Saturniidae*] **:** of or relating to the Saturniidae

²saturniid \"\ *n* -s **:** a moth of the family Saturniidae

sat·ur·ni·idae \,sad·ərˈnīə,dē\ *n pl, cap* [NL, fr. *Saturnia,* type genus + *-idae*] **:** an important and widely distributed family of moths including some of the largest insects known, having a stout hairy body, strong wide wings, and antennae which are bipectinate to the tip, having larvae which spin silken cocoons, and comprising among others the io, polyphemus, luna, and cecropia moths, the pernyi and tussah silkworms, and the Atlas moth

sat·ur·nine \ˈsad·ə(r),nīn, -atə-\ *adj* [ME, prob. fr. (assumed) ML *saturninus,* fr. L *Saturnus* Saturn + *-inus* -ine; perh. fr. the planet's remoteness from the sun] **1 a** *archaic* **:** born under or influenced astrologically by the planet Saturn **:** SLOW, SLUGGISH ⟨~ heavy-headed blunderers —Thomas Nash⟩ **b :** of a moody or surly character **:** MOROSE, SULLEN ⟨a ~, almost misanthropic young genius —Bruce Bliven b. 1889⟩ ⟨driven to ~ and scornful silence by . . . godless conversation —Elinor Wylie⟩ **c :** having a sardonic aspect **:** DEVILISH, WRY ⟨the face was ~ and swarthy, and the sensual lips . . . twisted with disdain —Oscar Wilde⟩ ⟨~ philosophical laughter —E.K.Brown⟩ **2 a** *archaic* **:** of or relating to lead ⟨acetate of lead and other ~ preparations —A.B.Garrod & E.B.Baxter⟩ **b :** of, relating to, or produced by lead poisoning ⟨victims of ~ poisoning —Thomas Stevenson⟩ **syn** see SULLEN

sat·ur·nin·i·ty \¦==ˈninəd·ē, -ətē, -i\ *n* -ES **:** the quality or state of being saturnine

sat·urn·ism \ˈ==,nizəm\ *n* -s [*saturn* + *-ism*] **:** LEAD POISONING

saturn line *n, usu cap S* **:** LINE OF FATE

saturn red *or* **saturnine red** *n* **:** RED LEAD

saturns *pl of* SATURN

sat·ya·gra·ha \(,)səˈtyägrəhə, (,)sət-ˈy-; ˈsə-tyə,grəhə, ˈsət-y-\ *n* -s *often cap* [Skt *satyāgraha,* lit., insistence on truth, fr. *satya* reality, truth (fr. *sat, sant* existing, true) + *āgraha* clinging to, obstinate inclination for (fr. *ā* to + *grbhnāti* he seizes) — more at SOOTH, ACHARYA, GRAB] **:** reliance on truth **:** the Gandhian method of achieving social and political reform by means of tolerance and active goodwill coupled with a firmness in one's cause expressed through nonviolent passive resistance and noncooperation

sat·ya·gra·hi \-(,)hē\ *n* -s *often cap* [Skt *satyāgrahin,* fr. *satyāgraha*] **:** one that practices satyagraha

satyr \ˈsā¦d·ə(r), ¦tə- *also* ˈsa|\ *n* -s [ME, fr. L *satyrus,* fr. Gk *satyros*] **1 a** *often cap* **:** an ancient Greek sylvan deity often represented as having certain attributes of a horse or goat and having a fondness for Dionysian revelry **b :** ORANGUTAN **c :** a hairy demon of the desert ⟨wild beasts shall meet with hyenas, the ~ shall cry to his fellow —Isa 34:14 (RSV)⟩ **2 :** a lecherous man **:** one having satyriasis ⟨he is neither a eunuch nor a ~ —Raymond Chandler⟩ **3 :** any of numerous butterflies (family Satyridae) that are commonly brown and gray often with ocelli on the wings and have the veins of the fore wings usu. much swollen at the base

saty·ri·a·sis \,sā¦d·əˈrīəsəs, ,sa|, ¦tə-\ *n, pl* **satyria·ses** \-ə,sēz\ [LL, fr. Gk, fr. *satyros* satyr + *-iasis*] **:** excessive or abnormal sexual craving in the male — compare NYMPHOMANIA

sa·tyr·ic \(ˈ)sā¦tirik, səˈt-\ *adj* [F *satyrique,* fr. Gk *satyrikos,* fr. *satyros* satyr + *-ikos* -ic] **:** of, relating to, or having the characteristics of a satyr ⟨the ~ old goat who pursues young girls —*Sat. Eve. Post*⟩

sa·tyr·i·cal \-rəkəl\ *adj* [L *satyrus* satyr + E *-ical*] *archaic* **:** SATYRIC

¹satyr·id \ˈsād·ərəd, ˈsatə-\ *adj* [NL *Satyridae*] **:** of or relating to the Satyridae

²satyrid \"\ *n* -s **:** a butterfly of the family Satyridae

sa·tyr·i·dae \səˈtirə,dē\ *n pl, cap* [NL, fr. *Satyrus,* type genus (fr. L, satyr) + *-idae*] **:** a widely distributed family of butterflies common near the edges of woods

satyr·ine \ˈsād·ə,rīn, ˈsad-\ *adj* [*satyr* + *-ine*] **:** of or relating to the genus *Satyrus*

satyr·ism \-,rizəm\ *n* -s [*satyr* + *-ism*] **:** SATYRIASIS

satyr orchid *n* [so called fr. the ancient Greek and Roman belief that certain kinds of orchids were aphrodisiac] **:** a terrestrial orchid (*Coeloglossum bracteatum*) of the cooler parts of No. America and Europe having broad usu. ovate leaves and long-bracted green very irregular flowers

satyr play *n* **:** an ancient Greek drama usu. composed and performed in conjunction with a trilogy of tragedies but having a less elevated subject and diction and having a chorus representing a ribald band of satyrs

sat-zone \ˈsat,-; ,e,sāˈtē,-\ *n* -s *usu cap S&A&T* [*sat* abbr. of NL *Sine Acido Thymonucleico* without thymonucleic acid] **:** NUCLEOLUS ORGANIZER

sa·u·ba ant \səˈübə-\ *n* [*sauba* fr. Pg *saúba, saúva,* fr. Tupi *saúba, isaúba*] **:** any of several tropical leaf-cutting ants esp. of the genus *Atta* that live in immense subterranean colonies and cultivate a fungus upon leaves and other vegetable material collected by the workers

¹sauce \ˈsós; *usu in senses 4&7, dial in other senses* ˈsas *or* ˈsaa(ə)s *or* ˈsais; *dial* ˈsärs *or* ˈsás\ *n* -s [ME, fr. MF *sauce, sausse,* fr. L *salsa,* fem. of *salsus* salted, fr. past part. of *sallere* to salt, fr. *sal* salt — more at SALT] **1 :** a condiment or composition of condiments and appetizing ingredients eaten with food as a relish ⟨barbecue ~⟩ **2 :** a fluid, semifluid, or sometimes semisolid accompaniment of solid food: **a :** meat or fish stock or milk or cream thickened with flour or other starch, usu. flavored with a concentrate (as from roast meat), seasoned with a variety of condiments or spices, and used for fish, meat, eggs, or vegetables — see ³ALLEMANDE, BÉCHAMEL, BROWN SAUCE, VELOUTÉ **b :** a variously flavored sweetened mixture served as a topping with a dessert: as (1) **:** one composed of water, milk, cream, or fruit juice with sugar and other ingredients added and thickened with flour or other starch or with eggs ⟨butterscotch ~⟩ ⟨lemon ~⟩ ⟨custard ~⟩ (2) **:** one composed of eggs and butter without other liquid **3 :** something that adds zest or piquancy ⟨fame is only one of the ~*s* of life —A.C.Benson⟩ **4 :** vegetables eaten with meat or as a relish **5 :** stewed or canned fruit eaten as an accompaniment with other food or as a dessert ⟨blueberry ~⟩ ⟨cranberry ~⟩ **6 :** a solution used in some manufacturing processes (as moistening layers of tobacco) **:** PICKLE **7 :** pert or insolent language or actions **:** SAUCINESS ⟨it never pays to stand any ~ —Arnold Bennett⟩ **8** *slang* **:** intoxicating drinks **:** LIQUOR ⟨been off the ~ for fourteen months —John O'Hara⟩

²sauce \ˈsós; *usu in sense 4b, dial in other senses* ˈsas *or* ˈsaa(ə)s *or* ˈsais; *dial* ˈsärs *or* ˈsás\ *vt* -ED/-ING/-S [ME *saucen,* fr. *sauce,* n.] **1 :** to dress (food) with something intended to give a higher relish **:** SEASON, FLAVOR **2 a** *archaic* **:** to modify the harsh or unpleasant characteristics of **:** TEMPER ⟨a slice of the densest cloud within his reach, ~*d* with moonshine —Nathaniel Hawthorne⟩ **b :** to add interesting qualities to **:** give zest to **:** make piquant or attractive ⟨technicalities *sauced* and seasoned by songs, recitations, and tales of adventure —Llewellyn Howland⟩ **3** *obs* **:** FLOG **4 a** *dial chiefly Eng* **:** REBUKE **b :** to address in bitter, pert, or tart language **:** be impudent or saucy to

sauce-alone \¦==¦=\ *n* -s **:** GARLIC MUSTARD

sauceboat \ˈ=,=\ *n* **:** GRAVY BOAT

saucebox \ˈ=,=\ *n* **:** a saucy impudent person

saucedish \ˈ=,=\ *n* **:** a small round shallow dish for serving stewed fruit or other food

sauce·less \ˈ=ləs\ *adj* **:** having no sauce

sauce·pan \ˈ=,= *also chiefly Brit* -pən\ *n* [¹*sauce* + *pan*] **:** a deep cooking utensil with a long handle used for stewing or boiling — compare SAUCEPOT

sauce pi·quante \,sóspēˈkänt, ,sōs-, -äⁿt\ *n, pl* **sauces piquantes** \"\ [F] **1 :** PIQUANT SAUCE **2 :** something that stimulates interest or curiosity or intensifies appreciation

saucepot \ˈ=,=\ *n* [¹*sauce* + *pot*] **:** a deep cooking utensil with two hand grips opposite each other used for stewing or boiling — compare SAUCEPAN

saucepot

¹sau·cer \ˈsósə(r), *dial* ˈsas- *or* ˈsaas- *or* ˈsärs- *or* ˈsás-\ *n* -s [ME, fr. MF *saussier,* fr. *sausse* sauce + *-ier* -er] **1** *obs* **:** a dish or plate to contain sauces at table **2 a :** a small shallow dish usu. with a slightly depressed center for holding a cup at table **b :** SAUCEDISH **3 :** something likened to a saucer in shape: as **a :** a saucer-shaped part of a plant **b :** a shallow socket on a capstan **c :** the base of the usual form of chamber used in the manufacture of sulfuric acid turned up round the edges and partly filled with chamber acid into which the dependent side dips to form a seal **d :** a shallow depression in a landscape ⟨a town . . . set in a ~ formed by a range of hills —Hamilton Basso⟩ **e :** FLYING SAUCER

²saucer \"\ *vt* -ED/-ING/-S *dial* **:** to pour into a saucer ⟨~*ed* her coffee and blew on it —H.E.Giles⟩

saucer dome *n* **:** a dome that is less than a hemisphere in form or that shows less than a hemisphere on the exterior

saucer eye *n* **:** a large round staring eye — **saucer-eyed** \¦==¦=\ *adj*

saucer-eye porgy \¦==¦=-\ *n* **:** a porgy (*Calamus calamus*) of the West Indies and southern Florida that is silvery and blue with longitudinal golden-yellow stripes and reaches a length of one foot

saucer·ful \ˈ==,fu̇l\ *n, pl* **saucerfuls** \-(r),fu̇lz\ *also* **saucersful** \-(r)z,fu̇l\ **:** the content of a saucer

sau·cer·iza·tion \,==rəˈzāshən, -,rīˈz-\ *n* -s **:** the operation of saucerizing

sau·cer·ize \ˈ==,rīz\ *vt* -ED/-ING/-S [¹*saucer* + *-ize*] **:** to form a shallow depression by excavation of tissue to promote granulation and healing of (a wound)

sau·cer·less \ˈ==ləs\ *adj* **:** lacking a saucer

saucer magnolia *n* **:** a large shrub or small tree (*Magnolia soulangeana*) native to Asia and Europe and widely used esp. in eastern No. America as a spring-blooming ornamental that bears large open flowers which are purplish or rose-colored on the outside and white within

sauces *pl of* SAUCE, *pres 3d sing of* SAUCE

sau·cier \(ˈ)sōs¦yā, (ˈ)sōs-ˈyā\ *n* -s [F, fr. *sauce* (fr. MF) + *-ier* -er — more at SAUCE] **:** an assistant chef who specializes in preparing sauces and soups

sau·ci·ly \-sə̇lē, -li — *see* SAUCY\ *adv* **:** in a saucy manner

sau·ci·ness \-sēnə̇s, -sin-\ *n* -ES **:** the quality or state of being saucy

saucing *pres part of* SAUCE

sau·cis·son \¦sōsē¦sōⁿ\ *also* **sau·cisse** \sōˈsēs\ *n, pl* **saucissons** \-ōⁿ(z)\ *also* **sau·cisses** \-ēs(əz)\ [*saucisson* fr. F, fr. It *salsiccione,* aug. of *salsiccia* large sausage, powder bag shaped like a sausage, fr. LL *salsicia* sausage; *saucisse* fr. F, fr. LL *salsicia* — more at SAUSAGE] **1 :** a tube of paper or canvas filled with powder and used as a fuse **2 :** a large fascine

sau·con·ite \ˈsȯkəˌnīt\ *n* -s [Upper *Saucon*, Lehigh County, Penn., its locality + E *-ite*] **:** a montmorillonitic mineral $Zn_3Si_4O_{10}(OH)_2.nH_2O$ consisting of a basic hydrous zinc aluminum silicate isomorphous with saponite

saucy \ˈsa|sē, ˈsaa|, ˈsaì| (*usu. in sense 1b*), ˈsȯ|, -si, *dial* ˈsär| *or* ˈsā|\ *adj* -ER/-EST [¹*sauce* + *-y*] **1 a** *archaic* **:** grossly disrespectful ⟨speak to him like a ~ lackey —Shak.⟩ **b :** expressive of or marked by impertinent boldness or forwardness **:** IMPUDENT ⟨sometimes ~, he was by no means an agreeable fellow traveler —S.C.Brownstein & Mitchel Weiner⟩ **c :** amusingly or unobjectionably forward or impertinent **2** *dial chiefly Eng* **:** overly fastidious esp. with regard to food **3** *Scot* **:** DISDAINFUL, SCORNFUL **4 :** SMART, TRIM ⟨a ~ ship⟩ ⟨a ~ automobile⟩

¹**sau·di** \ˈsau̇dē, sä'üdē\ *adj, usu cap* [fr. *Saudi* Arabia, kingdom in southwestern Asia, after Abdul-Aziz Ibn-*Saud* †1953 king of Saudi Arabia who founded the Saudi dynasty] **1 :** SAUDI ARABIAN **2 :** of, relating to, or characteristic of the Saudi dynasty or its supporters

²**saudi** \"\ *n* -s *usu cap* **1 :** SAUDI ARABIAN **2 :** a member or supporter of an Arabian dynasty

saudi ara·bia \-əˈrābēə *also* -byə\ *adj, usu cap S&A* [fr. *Saudi Arabia*, southwestern Asia] **:** of or from the kingdom of Saudi Arabia **:** of the kind or style prevalent in Saudi Arabia **:** SAUDI ARABIAN

¹**saudi arabian** *adj, usu cap S&A* [*Saudi Arabia* + E *-an*] **1 :** of, relating to, or characteristic of Saudi Arabia **2 :** of, relating to, or characteristic of the people of Saudi Arabia

²**saudi arabian** *n, cap S&A* **:** a native or inhabitant of Saudi Arabia

sau·er·bra·ten \ˈsau̇(ə)rˌbrätᵊn, ˈzau̇-\ *n* -s [G, fr. *sauer* sour (fr. OHG *sūr*) + *braten* roast meat, alter. (influenced by *braten* to roast, fr. OHG *brātan*) of MHG *brāte* meat without waste, soft edible meat, fr. OHG *brāto;* akin to OHG *brādam* breath, heat — more at SOUR, BREATH, BRAWN] **:** oven-roasted or pot-roasted beef marinated in a vinegar solution with peppercorns, garlic, onions, and bay leaves before cooking

sauer·kraut *also* **sour·crout** *or* **sour·krout** \ˈsau̇(ə)rˌkrau̇t, -au̇ˌk-, *usu* -rau̇d-+V\ *n* -s [G *sauerkraut*, fr. *sauer* sour (fr. OHG *sūr*) + *kraut* cabbage, fr. OHG *krūt* herb, cabbage; akin to OS *krūd* cabbage, MD *cruut* cabbage, herb, and perh. to Goth *qairu* thorn, L *veru* spit, Gk *bryein* to swell, Av *gravastick* — more at SOUR] **:** cabbage cut fine and allowed to ferment in a brine made of its own juice with salt

sau·ger \ˈsȯgə(r)\ *n* -s [origin unknown] **1 :** a small pike perch (*Stizostedion canadense*) similar to the walleye but without a black blotch on the dorsal fin that is an important food fish in parts of Canada and is distributed from the Hudson Bay drainage east to New Brunswick, west to Montana, and south through much of the Mississippi drainage **2 :** WALLEYE

saugh *or* **sauch** \ˈsau̇k, ˈsȯk, ˈsäk\ *n* -s [ME (Sc) *sauch*, fr. OE *salh*, var. of *sealh* sallow — more at SALLOW] *chiefly Scot* **:** SALLOW

saught \ˈsau̇kt\ *n* -s [ME *saght, saht*, fr. OE *seht, seaht*, fr. or akin to ON *sātt, sætt* agreement, covenant, peace; akin to ON *sækja* to seek — more at SEEK] *archaic* **:** PEACE, QUIET, EASE

sauk \ˈsȯk\ *or* **sac** \", ˈsak\ *n, pl* **sauk** *or* **sauks** *or* **sac** *or* **sacs** *usu cap* [Fox (Sauk dial.) *Osākiwūg*, lit., people of the outlet] **1 a :** an Indian people of the Fox river valley and shores of Green Bay, Wisconsin **b :** a member of such people **2 :** a dialect of Fox

saul \ˈsȯl\ *chiefly dial var of* SOUL

sauld \ˈsȯld\ *Scot past of* SELL

saul·ie \ˈsȯli\ *n* -s [origin unknown] *Scot* **:** a hired mourner

sault *n* -s [ME *saut*, fr. OF, fr. L *saltus*, fr. *saltus*, past part. of *salire* to leap — more at SALLY] **1** *obs* **:** LEAP, JUMP; *specif* **:** a leap in the manege **2** \ˈsü\ **:** a fall or rapid in a river

saul·teur \süˈtər(·)\ *n* -s *usu cap* [F, fr. *Sault* Ste. Marie, city in Ontario, Canada, near which the Salteaux lived in the 17th cent. + F *-eur* -or] **:** a member of the Salteaux people

sau·mont \ˈsȯmənt\ *Scot var of* SALMON

sau·na \ˈsau̇nə\ *n* -s [Finn] **1 :** a Finnish bath in steam from water thrown on heated stones **2 :** a bathhouse designed for a sauna

saun·ders·wood \ˈsȯndə(r)zˌ=, ˈsän-\ *n* [obs. E *saunders* sandalwood (fr. MF *sandre*, alter. of *sandal*) + *wood* — more at SANDAL] **:** SANDALWOOD

¹**saun·ter** \ˈsȯntə(r), ˈsän-, ˈsän-\ *vi* **sauntered; sauntered; sauntering** \-nt(ə)riŋ, -n·triŋ\ **saunters** [prob. fr. ME *santren* to muse, brood] **1 :** to walk about idly and in a leisurely manner ⟨I *~ed* along the docks . . . not knowing what to do or where to go —H.A.Chippendale⟩ **2** *obs* **:** to travel around aimlessly from place to place **3** *archaic* **:** DAWDLE, IDLE

²**saunter** \"\ *n* -s **1 :** a leisurely strolling gait **2 :** an idle aimless walk **:** STROLL

saun·ter·er \-ntərə(r), -n·trə(r)\ *n* -s **:** one that saunters

saun·ter·ing·ly *adv* **:** in a sauntering manner

saur- *or* **sauro-** *comb form* [NL, fr. Gk, fr. *sauros*] **:** lizard

sau·ra *also* **sao·ra** \ˈsau̇rə\ *n, pl* **saura** *also* **saora** *usu cap* **1 :** a forest people of the mountains of the Eastern Ghats, India **2 :** a member of the Saura people

-sau·ra \ˌsȯrə\ *n comb form* [NL, fr. Gk *saura, sauros*] **:** lizard — in generic names ⟨Chamae*saura*⟩

sau·ra·se·ni \ˌsau̇rəˈsānē\ *n* -s *cap* [Skt *Śaurasenī*] **:** the central Prakrit language of northern India

sau·rau·ia \sȯˈrȯyə\ *n, cap* [NL, fr. Count F. J. von *Saurau* †1832 Austrian statesman + NL *-ia*] **:** a genus of trees and shrubs (family Dilleniaceae) with toothed parallel-veined leaves and paniculate pentamerous flowers followed by a baccate fruit that is edible in some Mexican species

sau·rel \ˈsȯrəl\ *n* -s [F, fr. LL *saurus* horse mackerel, fr. Gk *sauros*] **:** any of several elongated compressed fishes (genus *Trachurus*) with a series of bony plates extending the full length of the lateral line: as **a :** a horse mackerel (*Trachurus trachurus*) **b :** JACK MACKEREL a

sau·ria \ˈsȯrēə\ *n pl, cap* [NL, fr. *saurus* lizard (fr. Gk *saura, sauros* horse mackerel, lizard) + *-ia;* akin to Gk *saulos* straddling, waddling, *saukros* delicate, graceful, *psaukros* nimble, *psauein* to touch, graze, and prob. to Gk *psēn* to rub — more at SAND] **1** *in former classifications* **:** a division of Reptilia comprising the lizards, crocodilians, and various extinct elongated limbed reptiles that superficially resemble lizards **2** *in some classifications* **:** a suborder of Squamata coextensive with Lacertilia

-sau·ria \ˈsȯrēə\ *n pl comb form* [NL, fr. *-saurus* + *-ia*] **:** lizards **:** animals resembling lizards — in names of higher taxa ⟨Ptero*sauria*⟩ ⟨Ankylo*sauria*⟩

¹**sau·ri·an** \ˈsȯrēən\ *adj* [NL *Sauria* + E *-an*] **1 :** of or relating to the Sauria **2 :** resembling a lizard

²**saurian** \"\ *n* -s **1 :** a reptile of the group Sauria **2 :** a reptile that resembles a lizard

sauries *pl of* SAURY

sau·rii \ˈsȯrēˌī\ [NL, fr. Gk *saura, sauros* lizard] *syn of* SAURIA

saur·is·chia \sȯˈriskēə\ *n pl, cap* [NL, fr. *saur-* + L *ischium* hip joint + NL *-ia* — more at ISCHIUM] **:** an order of Reptilia including those dinosaurs in which the pelvis is triradiate and the pubes meet in a ventral symphysis — see SAUROPODA, THEROPODA — **saur·is·chi·an** \(ˈ)sȯ¦riskēən\ *adj or n*

¹**sau·ro·dont** \ˈsȯrəˌdänt\ *adj* [NL *Saurodontidae*] **:** of or relating to the Saurodontidae

²**saurodont** \"\ *n* -s **:** a fish of the family Saurodontidae

sau·ro·don·ti·dae \ˌ==ˈdäntəˌdē\ *n pl, cap* [NL, fr. *Saurodont-, Saurodon*, type genus (fr. *saur-* + *-odon*) + *-idae*] **:** a family of extinct Cretaceous clupeoid fishes with powerful jaws and a single row of compressed knifelike teeth

sau·rog·na·thism \sȯˈrägnəˌthizəm\ *n* [*saurognathous* + *-ism*] **:** the quality or state of being saurognathous

sau·rog·na·thous \(ˈ)=¦==thəs\ *adj* [*saur-* + *-gnathous*] **1 :** of, relating to, or being an arrangement of the bones of the palate (as in certain woodpeckers) in which the maxillopalatals are short and the vomer is divided longitudinally and represented by a pair of slender rods **2 :** having a saurognathous palate

¹**sau·roid** \ˈsȯˌrȯid\ *adj* [NL *Sauroidei*] **:** of or relating to the Sauroidei

²**sauroid** \"\ *n* -s **:** a fish of the group Sauroidei

sau·roi·dei \sȯˈrȯidēˌī\ *n pl, cap* [NL, fr. Gk *sauroeidēs* like a lizard, fr. *saur-* + *-oeidēs* -oid] *in former classifications* **:** a group of ganoid fishes having flat rhomboidal scales, reptile-like teeth, and a bony skeleton

sau·roph·a·gous \(ˈ)sȯ¦räfəgəs\ *adj* [*saur-* + *-phagous*] **:** feeding on lizards

¹**sau·ro·pod** \ˈsȯrəˌpäd\ *adj* [NL *Sauropoda*] **:** of or relating to the Sauropoda

²**sauropod** \"\ *n* -s **:** a dinosaur of the suborder Sauropoda

sau·rop·o·da \sȯˈräpədə\ *n pl, cap* [NL, fr. *saur-* + *-poda*] **:** a suborder of Saurischia consisting of herbivorous dinosaurs with a long neck and tail, small head, and more or less plantigrade 5-toed limbs all used in walking, including the most gigantic of land animals of any period, and known from the Middle Jurassic into the Cretaceous — **sau·rop·o·dous** \(ˈ)=¦==dəs\ *adj*

sau·rop·sid \sȯˈräpsəd\ *n* -s [NL *Sauropsida*] **:** a vertebrate of the group Sauropsida

sau·rop·si·da \-psədə\ *n pl, cap* [NL, fr. *saur-* + Gk *opsis* appearance + NL *-ida* — more at OPTIC] *in some esp former classifications* **:** a group of vertebrates comprising the reptiles and birds — compare ICHTHYOPSIDA, MAMMALIA — **sau·rop·si·dan** \(ˈ)=¦=sədən\ *adj or n* — **sau·rop·sid·i·an** \¦=¦=ˈsidēən\ *adj*

sau·rop·te·ryg·ia \sȯˌräptəˈrijēə\ *n pl, cap* [NL, fr. *saur-* + *pteryg-* + *-ia*] **:** an order of Reptilia comprising forms more or less completely adapted to a marine environment and usu. including the suborders Nothosauria and Plesiosauria — **sau·rop·te·ryg·i·an** \=¦==¦rijēən\ *adj or n*

sau·ror·ni·thes \ˌsȯˌrȯ(r)ˈnīˌthēz\ [NL, fr. *saur-* + *-ornithes*] *syn of* ARCHAEORNITHES

sau·ru·ra·ce·ae \ˌsȯrəˈrāsēˌē\ *n pl, cap* [NL, fr. *Saururus*, type genus + *-aceae*] **:** a family of perennial herbs (order Piperales) having small flowers destitute of perianth in terminal spikes and with an ovary of several separate carpels — **sau·ru·ra·ceous** \¦==¦rāshəs\ *adj*

sau·ru·rae \sȯˈrüˌrē\ [NL, fr. *saur-* + *-urae*, fem. pl. of *-urus*] *syn of* ARCHAEORNITHES

sau·ru·rus \-rəs\ *n, cap* [NL, fr. *saur-* + *-urus*] **:** a genus (the type of the family Saururaceae) of herbs having alternate cordate leaves and racemes of white flowers with four to eight stamens and an ovary of four carpels coalescent into a capsule in fruit — see LIZARD'S-TAIL

-sau·rus \ˈsȯrəs\ *n comb form* [NL, fr. Gk *saura, sauros* — more at SAURIA] **:** lizard — in generic names in zoology ⟨Bronto*saurus*⟩ ⟨Icthyo*saurus*⟩

sau·ry \ˈsȯrē, -ri\ *n* -ES [NL *saurus* lizard + E *-y* — more at SAURIA] **1 :** a slender long-beaked fish (*Scombresox saurus*) that is related to the needlefishes, is found in the temperate parts of the Atlantic north to Cape Cod and the French coast, about southern Africa, and possibly off the southern coasts of Australia and New Zealand, reaches a length of 18 inches, swims in large schools, and often leaps from the water when pursued by larger fishes **2 :** a fish (*Cololabis saira*) that is similar to but smaller than the closely related saury and is widely distributed in the Pacific

sau·sage \ˈsȯ|sij, |sēj, *chiefly Brit* ˈsä|, *dial* ˈsa| *or* ˈsā|\ *n* -s [ME *sausige*, fr. ONF *saussiche*, fr. LL *salsicia*, fr. L *salsus* salted — more at SAUCE] **1 a :** highly seasoned finely divided meat that is usu. a mixture (as of beef or pork), is often extended (as with cereal or milk solids), is stuffed in casings of prepared animal intestine or synthetic material which are tied shut at both ends to form a single cylindrical unit or at intervals to form links, and is used either fresh or cured; *also* **:** a single unit of sausage **b :** SAUSAGE MEAT **2 :** SAUCISSON **3** *or* **sausage balloon :** a captive observation or barrage balloon **4 :** GERMAN — usu. used disparagingly **5 :** material (as crude rubber or alumina catalyst) formed in the shape of a sausage

sausage bassoon *n* **:** RACKETT

sausage bull *n* **:** a mature male bovine suitable for producing meat for sausage, bologna, or similar manufactured products

sausage curl *n* **:** a curl shaped like a sausage

sausage meat *n* **:** pork sausage in bulk

sausage tree *n* **:** a tropical African tree (*Kigelia africana*) of the family Bignoniaceae often cultivated in tropical countries for its brownish red bell-shaped flowers and long sausage-shaped fruits

sausage turning *n* **:** a continuous turning used esp. in 19th century American furniture

saus·in·ger \ˈsȯnjə(r)\ *n* [by alter.] *dial* **:** SAUSAGE

saus·su·rea \sȯˈsürēə\ *n, cap* [NL, after H. Bénédict de *Saussure* †1799 and his son N. Théodore de *Saussure* †1845 Swiss naturalists] **:** a genus of herbs (family Compositae) found mostly in temperate and cool regions of Eurasia with heads of blue or purple flowers that resemble thistles — see COSTUSROOT

saus·su·rite \ˈsȯsəˌrīt\ *n* -s [F, fr. H. Bénédict de *Saussure* †1799 + F *-ite*] **:** a mineral consisting of a tough compact substance that is white, greenish, or grayish, is produced in part at least by alteration of feldspar, and consists chiefly of zoisite or epidote — **saus·su·rit·ic** \¦=¦ridik\ *adj*

saus·su·ri·tiza·tion \sȯˈsürəd·əˈzāshən, -dˌīˈz-\ *n* -s [ISV *saussurite* + *-ization*] **:** the process of converting feldspar into saussurite

saus·su·ri·tize \=ˈ=rəˌtīz\ *vt* -ED/-ING/-S [back-formation fr. *saussuritization*] **:** to convert (feldspar) into saussurite

sausage turning

saut \ˈsät, ˈsȯt\ *chiefly Scot var of* SALT

saut de basque \ˌsōdə-\ *n, pl* **sauts de basque** \"\ [F, lit., Basque leap] **:** a jump in ballet in which the dancer turns in the air with the foot of one leg drawn up to the knee of the other

¹**sau·té** \(ˈ)sō¦tā, (ˈ)sȯ¦-\ *n* -s [F, past part. of *sauter* to jump, fr. MF, fr. L *saltare* to dance, freq. of *salire* to leap — more at SALLY] **:** a sautéed dish

²**sauté** *also* **sau·te** \"\ *vt* **sautéed** *or* **sautéd; sautéed** *or* **sautéd; sautéing; sautés :** to fry in very little fat — distinguished from *deep fry*

³**sauté** \(ˈ)=¦=\ *adj* **:** fried in very little fat **:** SAUTÉED

⁴**sauté** \"\ *adj* [F, fr. past part. of *sauter* to jump] *of a ballet step* **:** executed with a jump

sau·te·relle \ˌsōd·əˈrel, sōˈtrel\ *n* -s [F, lit., little jumper, dim. of *sauteur* jumper] **:** an instrument used (as by masons) to trace and form angles

sau·terne \sōˈtərn, sȯ'-, -te(ə)rn\ *n* -s *often cap* [F *sauternes*, fr. *Sauternes*, commune in southwestern France, where it is made] **1 a** *also* **sauternes**, *pl* **sauternes :** a usu. semisweet golden-colored table wine produced from grapes that are allowed to become overripe and modified by a mold (*Botrytis cinerea*) before fermentation **b :** a similar California or New York wine **2 :** a light brown that is redder, stronger, and slightly darker than cork, yellower and deeper than French nude, and yellower and stronger than French beige — called also *Tuscan tan*

sau·teur \(ˈ)sō¦tər\ *n* -s [F, jumper, fr. *sauter* to jump + *-eur* -or] **:** a leatherjacket (*Oligoplites saurus*)

sau·til·lé \ˌsōtēyā\ *adv (or adj)* [F, past part. of *sautiller* to hop, skip, fr. *sauter* to jump] **:** ARCO SALTANDO

sau·toir \sōˈtwär, -wȧ(r, ˈ== *also* -wȯ(ə)r *or* -wȯ(ə)\ *n* -s [F, fr. MF *sautoir, saultoir* saltire — more at SALTIRE] **1 :** a chain, ribbon, or scarf worn about the neck with the ends forming a St. Andrew's cross in front **2 :** a long gold chain often set with precious stones usu. with a pendant hanging from it

sa·u·va ant \saˈüvə-\ *n* [*sauva* fr. Pg *saúba, saúva*, fr. Tupi *saúba, isaúba*] **:** SAUBA ANT

sau·va·ge·sia \ˌsōvəˈjēzēə, -ēzhə\ *n, cap* [NL, fr. Pierre A. Boissier de la Croix de *Sauvages* †1795 Fr. botanist + NL *-ia*] **:** a genus of chiefly tropical American herbs or undershrubs (family Ochnaceae) having alternate leaves, fringed stipules, and small pentamerous flowers with an outer row of staminodia which is filiform and an inner row of staminodia which is petaloid

sauve \ˈsȯv\ *dial Eng var of* SALVE

sauve·garde \ˈsōvˌgärd\ *n* -s [F, lit., safeguard, fr. MF *sauvegarde, salvegarde* — more at SAFEGUARD] **:** MONITOR 3

sauve qui peut \ˌsōvˌkēˈpə, -¦pər(·), -¦pə̄\ *n* [F, save himself who can] **:** a complete rout

sav *abbr* savings

sav·able *or* **save·able** \ˈsāvəbəl\ *adj* [ME *sauvable*, fr. MF, fr. OF *sauver* to save + *-able* — more at SAVE] **:** capable of being saved

¹**sav·age** \ˈsavij, -vēj\ *adj, usu* -ER/-EST [ME *sauvage, savage*, fr. MF *sauvage, salvage*, fr. ML *salvaticus*, alter. of L *silvaticus* of the woods, wild, fr. *silva* wood, grove] **1 a :** not domesticated or under human control **:** UNTAMED ⟨the dog that is kept in a good home is usually watched carefully, kept from contact with ~ dogs —Morris Fishbein⟩ ⟨in time the ~ bull did not bear the yoke —Shak.⟩ **b :** marked by cruelty **:** FEROCIOUS, FIERCE ⟨the victim of a ~ attack that left him crippled⟩ ⟨his tone containing the ~ satisfaction of a cat purring over a freshly caught mouse —Erle Stanley Gardner⟩ **c :** enraged with anger or pain **:** FURIOUS ⟨when I was left at home I was ~ at not being let go —G.B.Shaw⟩ ⟨the mother bird flew about over me, squealing in a very angry, ~ manner —John Burroughs⟩ **d :** violent and extreme in action, manner, or effect **:** DEVASTATING, RELENTLESS ⟨lashed out with all the oratorical fury and ~ invective at his command —Sidney Warren⟩ ⟨what must happen in the *savagest* fury of a hurricane is left to the imagination —T.M.Longstreth⟩ ⟨a ~ flu epidemic —Mollie Panter-Downes⟩ **2 a :** of, relating to, or characteristic of an unsettled and uncultivated place or region **:** RUGGED, WILD ⟨there was something sylvan and ~ in the mountains on the farther side —George Borrow⟩ ⟨seldom have I seen such ~ scenery associated with such placid beauty —Douglas Carruthers⟩ **b** *archaic* **:** growing wild **:** not cultivated ⟨~ berries of the wood —John Dryden⟩ **3 :** BOORISH, RUDE ⟨the ~ bad manners of most motorists —M.P.O'Connor⟩ **4 a :** UNCIVILIZED ⟨think that we have gained much over ~ people in our notion of murder —W.G.Sumner⟩ ⟨civilized countries are more accessible than ~ ones —Elinor Wylie⟩ **b :** of, belonging to, or produced by a primitive or a primitive people ⟨his ~ bones were small and delicate —David Garnett⟩ ⟨in delineation of animal life they are thus superior to modern ~ fine art —*Encyc. Americana*⟩ **syn** see BARBARIAN, FIERCE

²**savage** \"\ *n* -s **1 :** SALVAGE MAN **2 a :** a person living in a primitive state or belonging to a primitive society **:** PRIMITIVE ⟨almost universally the children of *~s* are contented and well behaved —W.D.Wallis⟩ **b :** one who acts with cruelty or ferocity **:** a brutal or inhumane person ⟨a ~ who murdered in cold blood⟩ **c :** a completely undisciplined or unmannerly person ⟨the disagreeable person, however cultured, is a ~ —F.A.Swinnerton⟩ **3 :** a wild or ferocious animal; *esp* **:** a vicious horse

³**savage** \"\ *vt* -ED/-ING/-S **1 :** to make savage ⟨a solvent to the bitterness that had *savaged* him —Angus Mowat⟩ **2 :** to attack or treat violently or brutally ⟨a plump young man whose bare toes in their sandals must have been cruelly *savaged* in the crowd —Alan Moorehead⟩ ⟨the ugly habit of *savaging* mercilessly those who have somehow raised his dander —*Times Lit. Supp.*⟩ **3** *of an animal* **:** to bite or trample furiously ⟨his horse must have gone crazy, thrown him and *savaged* him on the ground —Robert Graves⟩ ⟨set up an irritation which started the dog *savaging* itself —*Veterinary Record*⟩

sav·age·dom \-dəm\ *n* -s [¹*savage* + *-dom*] **:** SAVAGERY

sav·age·ly *adv* [ME *savagelich*, fr. ¹*savage* + *-lich* -ly] **:** in a savage manner ⟨struck her ~⟩ ⟨a ~ funny book⟩

sav·age·ness *n* -ES [ME *savagenes*, fr. ¹*savage* + *-nes* -ness] **:** the quality or state of being savage

sav·age·rous \ˈsavij(ə)rəs, -vēj-\ *adj* [*savagery* + *-ous*] *slang* **:** barbarously savage

sav·age·ry \-j(ə)rē, -ri\ *n* -ES [¹*savage* + *-ry*] **1 a :** the quality of being savage **:** savage disposition or action ⟨this outburst of ~ that was to prove his undoing —Harold Helfer⟩ ⟨the ~ of her methods of warfare —*Times Lit. Supp.*⟩ **b :** an act of cruelty or violence ⟨during the *savageries* of the blitz —Christopher Morley⟩ **2 :** the state or condition of being uncivilized ⟨it is only somewhere between ~ and civilization that love is born —J.W.Krutch⟩ **3 :** WILDNESS ⟨the splendor of the seascape, the ~ of the mountains —Claudia Cassidy⟩

sav·ag·ism \ˈsaviˌjizəm, -vē̦-, -və-\ *n* -s [¹*savage* + *-ism*] **:** SAVAGERY

sa·van \(ˈ)sa¦vä̃, (ˈ)sä¦v-, səˈv-, (ˈ)sä¦v-\ *n* -s [modif. of obs. F *savans*, pl. of F *savant* — more at SAVANT] **:** SAVANT

sav·a·nil·la \ˌsavəˈnilə, -nē(y)ə\ *n* -s [prob. fr. *Savanilla*, former seaport, Colombia] **:** TARPON

savanilla rhatany *n* [after *Savanilla*, former seaport, Colombia] **:** the root of a shrub (*Krameria ixina*) as distinguished from rhatany obtained from other plants of the genus *Krameria*

sa·van·na *or* **sa·van·nah** \səˈvanə\ *n* -s [earlier *zavana*, fr. Sp, fr. Taino *zabana*] **1 :** a treeless plain **:** an open, level region — used esp. of land in the southeastern U.S. **2 :** a tropical or subtropical grassland usu. containing scattered trees or shrubs that develops in areas in which heavy rainfall is interrupted by a distinct dry season, that is often maintained by human action (as of periodic burning or heavy grazing), and that tends to pass on the one hand into steppes and on the other into savanna woodland

savanna blackbird *n* **:** ANI

savanna flower *n* **:** a West Indian plant of the genus *Echites*

sa·van·nah \səˈvanə\ *adj, usu cap* [fr. *Savannah*, Ga.] **:** of or from the city of Savannah, Ga. ⟨the *Savannah* cotton market⟩ **:** of the kind or style prevalent in Savannah

savannah grass *n* **:** a stoloniferous tropical American grass (*Axonopus compressus*) related to carpet grass but with broader leaves and pointed sterile lemmos and sometimes cultivated for pasture

sa·van·nah·ian \-nēən\ *n* -s *cap* [*Savannah*, Ga. + E *-an*] **:** a native or resident of Savannah, Ga.

savannah sparrow *n, cap 1st S* [after *Savannah*, Ga., where it was discovered] **:** a small streaked brown-and-white No. American sparrow (*Passerculus sandwichensis*) inhabiting fields and meadows

savanna woodland *n* **:** a usu. tropical open woodland in which the undergrowth is of the xerophilous type

sa·vant \(ˈ)sa¦vänt, (ˈ)sä¦v-, səˈv-, (ˈ)sä¦v-, -vä̃\; səˈvant, -ˈvaa(ə)nt; ˈsavənt\ *n* -s [F, fr. pres. part. of *savoir* to know, fr. L *sapere* to have sense, be wise — more at SAGE] **:** a man of learning; *esp* **:** a person with detailed knowledge in some specialized field (as of science or literature) **:** SCHOLAR

sav·a·ra \ˈsavərə, ˈsəv-\ *n, pl* **savara** *or* **savaras** *usu cap* **1 a :** a people of northeastern Madras **b :** a member of such people **2 :** the Munda language of the Savara people

sav·a·rin \ˈsavərən\ *n* -s [F, after Anthelme Brillat-*Savarin* †1826 Fr. politician, writer, and gourmet] **:** a brioche baked in a ring mold and covered with nuts and fruit (as almonds and citron)

sa·vate \səˈvat\ *n* -s [F, lit., old shoe, fr. MF — more at SABOT] **:** a form of boxing in which blows are delivered with either the feet or the hands

sav·a·tion \säˈvāshən\ *n* -s [¹*save* + *-ation*] *dial Eng* **:** an act of saving

¹**save** \ˈsāv\ *vb* -ED/-ING/-S [ME *saven*, fr. OF *sauver, salver*, fr. LL *salvare*, fr. L *salvus* safe — more at SAFE] *vt* **1 a :** to deliver from sin **:** rescue from condemnation and spiritual death and bring into spiritual life ⟨Christ Jesus came into the world to ~ sinners —1 Tim 1:15 (RSV)⟩ **b** (1) **:** to rescue or deliver from danger or harm **:** make safe ⟨any human life is to be *saved* if it can be *saved* —Harvey Flack⟩ ⟨risked his life to ~ his friend from drowning⟩ ⟨the retailers who were *saved* by wholesalers during the depression —J.I.Grant⟩ ⟨God ~ the king⟩ — used formerly in phrases of greeting ⟨God ~ you⟩ ⟨~ you⟩ (2) *obs* **:** to spare instead of slaying **:** permit to live **c** (1) **:** to maintain intact **:** PRESERVE, SAFEGUARD ⟨~ his honor⟩ ⟨~ her reputation⟩ ⟨~ his credit⟩ ⟨~ appearances⟩ ⟨~ face⟩ (2) **:** to preserve in a specified state or condition — used esp. in the phrase *save harmless* ⟨agreed to indemnify and ~ harmless the contractor from any and all loss —*Federal Supplement*⟩ **d :** to deliver from an anticipated or likely danger, difficulty, or annoyance ⟨vaccinate children to ~ them from smallpox⟩ ⟨grasped him by the arm to ~ him from falling⟩ **e :** to rescue or deliver from destruction ⟨*saved* the Union⟩ ⟨put out the fire and *saved* the house⟩ **f :** to preserve or guard from injury, destruction, or loss ⟨~ the paint from cracking⟩ ⟨~ the coat from damage by moths⟩ **2 a :** to put by as a store or reserve **:** ACCUMULATE, HOARD ⟨*~s* part of his salary each week⟩ **b** (1) **:** to put aside for a particular purpose or occasion ⟨*~s* his best suit for special dates⟩ ⟨*~s* her best dishes for company⟩ (2) **:** to keep for the

use of another ⟨his outgrown clothing was *saved* for his younger brother⟩ ⟨*saved* a seat for his wife⟩ (3) **:** to keep in reserve **:** hold in abeyance ⟨*saving* him for another spot in this story —Green Peyton⟩ ⟨*saved* his most convincing point for the end of his speech⟩ **c** (1) **:** to keep from being spent, wasted, or lost ⟨walks to work to ~ carfare⟩ ⟨~*s* several dollars a week by careful shopping⟩ ⟨~*s* time by taking a shortcut⟩ (2) **:** to preserve in serviceable condition by careful or sparing use ⟨his youthful hose well *saved* —Shak.⟩ (3) **:** to use or manage with discretion **:** CONSERVE, HUSBAND ⟨cut down on his reading in order to ~ his eyes⟩ ⟨his doctor warned him to ~ his strength⟩ ⟨*saving* himself to become a great pitcher —John Lardner⟩ **3 a :** to make unnecessary **:** enable one to avoid **:** AVOID ⟨it ~*s* a 50-mile detour —*Ford Times*⟩ ⟨*saved* them the trouble of looking for a parking place⟩ **b** (1) **:** to keep from being lost to an opponent ⟨a fine relief pitcher who has *saved* many games⟩ (2) **:** to prevent an opponent from scoring or winning (as a goal, wager, trick, or card) **c** *chiefly Brit* **:** to avoid missing **:** be in time for **:** CATCH ⟨~ the train⟩ ⟨~ the mail⟩ **4** *archaic* **:** to account for **:** EXPLAIN ⟨these were the phenomena which they had to ~ —Benjamin Farrington⟩ **~** *vi* **1 :** to rescue or deliver someone ⟨bow hither out of heaven and see and ~ —A.E.Housman⟩ **2 a :** to accumulate savings **:** put by money ⟨would rather ~ than spend⟩ — often used with *up* ⟨started to ~ up for a trip abroad⟩ **b :** to avoid unnecessary waste or expense **:** ECONOMIZE ⟨~*s* on food by using leftovers⟩ **c :** to last in good condition **:** KEEP ⟨doesn't buy as much bread as she used to, because it doesn't ~ —F.C.Othman⟩ **3 :** to make a save ⟨the visiting goalie went to the ice to ~ —*N. Y. Times*⟩ **syn** see RESCUE — **save ground** *of a racehorse* **:** to run along the inside rail — **save one's bacon :** to preserve or rescue something of vital importance (as one's life, livelihood, or reputation) from loss or harm ⟨the pilots of my section *saved my bacon* many times when I have been attacked from behind —Keith Ayling⟩ ⟨is forced to compromise these beliefs in order to *save his* economic *bacon* —Louis Bromfield⟩

²save \"\ *n* -S **:** the act or an instance of saving ⟨the goalie went down on all fours and smothered the shot to make a honey of a ~ —Cortland Fitzsimmons⟩ ⟨the audience is teased with the hope of a sentimental ~ —*Time*⟩

³save \"\ *prep* [ME *save, sauf, saf, salf,* fr. OF *sauf, saf, salf,* fr. *sauf, saf, salf,* adj., safe — more at SAFE] **1 :** with the exception of **:** BARRING ⟨the two poems have nothing in common ~ the title —T.O.Mabbott⟩ ⟨has a boomtown psychology in every respect ~ zoning —Hal Burton⟩ **2 :** other than **:** BUT, EXCEPT ⟨no question ~ in the minds of prejudiced people⟩ ⟨without duties ~ to eat and sleep⟩ ⟨entirely dark ~ for one light⟩

⁴save \"\ *conj* [ME *save, sauf, saf,* fr. OF *sauf, saf, salf,* fr. *sauf, saf, salf,* adj., safe] **1 :** were it not **:** ONLY — used with *that* ⟨a similar system is followed in the cheese factories, ~ that the farmers usually bring in their own milk —*McGill News*⟩ **2 :** BUT, EXCEPT — used before a word often taken to be the subject of a clause ⟨no one knows about it ~ she⟩ ⟨all the conspirators ~ only he —Shak.⟩ **3 :** UNLESS ⟨~ they could be plucked asunder, all my quest were but in vain —Alfred Tennyson⟩

saveable *var of* SAVABLE

¹save–all \ˈ⸗,⸗\ *n* -S **1 :** something that prevents waste, loss, or damage: as **a :** a device to hold a candle end in a candlestick and permit it to burn to the very end **b** (1) **:** a small sail sometimes set under the foot of another sail or between two sails (2) **:** a net hung between ship and pier for safety purposes **c :** a receptacle for catching waste products for further utilization: as (1) **:** a small sluice used in gold dredging to catch the drippings from the buckets as they go into the well after discharging (2) **:** a device in papermaking that operates on the principle of sedimentation, flotation, or filtration to recover most of the fiber and filler from white water **d** *dial* **:** OVERALLS, PINAFORE **2** *chiefly dial* **:** MISER **3** *chiefly dial* **:** a contribution box or child's bank

²save–all \(ˈ)⸗¦⸗\ *adj* **:** MISERLY

saved \ˈsāvd\ *adj* [ME, fr. past part. of *saven* to save — more at SAVE] **1 :** rescued from eternal punishment ⟨a ~ soul⟩ **2 :** kept unused or unspent **:** HOARDED ⟨~ money⟩ — often used with *up* ⟨*saved*-up scraps of food⟩

sa·ve·lha \səˈvelyə\ *n* -S [Pg, dim. of *savel* shad, prob. of Celt origin; akin to OIr *sam, samrad* summer — more at SUMMER] **1 :** MENHADEN **2 :** a fish (*Brevoortia pectinata*) of the south Atlantic closely related to the menhaden

sav·e·loy \ˈsavə,lȯi, ,⸗⸗ˈ⸗\ *n* -S [modif. of F *cervelas,* fr. obs. F *cervelat,* fr. MF, fr. OIt *cervellata* Milanese sausage, pig's brains, fr. *cervello* brain, fr. L *cerebellum,* dim. of *cerebrum* brain — more at CEREBRAL] *Brit* **:** a cooked dry sausage

sa·vels·berg process \ˈsävəlz,bərg-\ *n, usu cap S* [prob. fr. the name *Savelsberg*] **:** BLAST ROASTING

sav·er \ˈsāvə(r)\ *n* -S [ME, fr. *saven* to save + *-er*] **:** one that saves: as **a :** SAVIOR **b :** one who economizes or hoards **:** one who withholds part of his income from consumption for investment or deposit in a bank **c :** something that prevents loss or waste — often used in combination ⟨labor-*saver*⟩ ⟨money-*saver*⟩ ⟨time-*saver*⟩ **d** *slang* **:** a hedging bet on a horse race **e :** a marginally applied patch to correct an erroneously cut slot in a hand-sorted punch card

saves *pres 3d sing of* SAVE, *pl of* SAVE

sav·in *or* **sav·ine** \ˈsavən\ *n* -S [ME, fr. OE *safine, savine* & OF *savine,* fr. L *sabina*] **1 :** a mostly prostrate Eurasian evergreen juniper (*Juniperus sabina*) with dark foliage and small berries having a glaucous bloom and with bitter acrid tops that are sometimes used in folk medicine (as for amenorrhea or as an abortifacient) — called also *cover-shame, sabina;* see SAVIN OIL **2 a :** CREEPING JUNIPER **2 b :** RED CEDAR 1a **3 :** any of several trees, shrubs, or shrubby herbs somewhat resembling plants of the genus *Juniperus*

¹sav·ing \ˈsāviŋ, -vēŋ\ *n* -S [ME, fr. gerund of *saven* to save — more at SAVE] **1 :** preservation from danger or destruction **:** DELIVERANCE ⟨work's the ~ of mankind —Eden Phillpotts⟩ **2 :** the act or an instance of economizing **:** reduction in cost ⟨a ~ on fuel⟩ ⟨a ~ of ten percent in maintenance costs⟩ **3 a savings** *pl* **:** money put by ⟨keeps her ~*s* under the mattress⟩ ⟨has her ~*s* invested in stocks⟩ **b :** the excess of income over consumption expenditures — often used in pl.

²saving \"\ *prep* [ME, fr. pres. part. of *saven* to save] **1 :** EXCEPT, SAVE **2 :** without disrespect to ⟨there are men in these modern times, ~ your presence, that can't visit a privy without searching out for a meaning behind it —Mary Deasy⟩ ⟨who, ~ your reverence, is the devil himself —Shak.⟩

³saving \"\ *conj* **:** EXCEPT, SAVE

⁴saving \"\ *adj* [fr. pres. part. of ¹*save*] **1 a :** serving to rescue, preserve, or protect; *specif* **:** leading to salvation ⟨a ~ faith⟩ **b :** serving to keep from or compensate for error or weakness **:** REDEEMING ⟨a scholar of vision and insight with a fund of ~ common sense —Geoffrey Bruun⟩ ⟨a ~ sense of humor⟩ **2 :** characterized by thriftiness **:** ECONOMICAL ⟨wealthy by inheritance but ~ by constitution —Ellen Glasgow⟩ **3** *archaic* **:** bringing neither profit nor loss **4 :** embodying or expressing an exception or reservation

saving arch *n* **:** SAFETY ARCH

saving clause *n* **1 :** a clause in an instrument or law exempting something from its operation or providing that the rest of it will stand if part is held invalid **2 :** a statement making a reservation or expressing a condition

saving grace *n* **:** a redeeming quality or factor ⟨shrank at the thought of leaving even a place so austere as this parish house, whose *saving grace* was that he kept busy here —Marcia Davenport⟩

sav·ing·ly *adv* **1 :** in a saving manner **:** FRUGALLY ⟨has few wants and lives ~⟩ **2 :** in a manner that brings salvation **:** so as to redeem

sav·ing·ness *n* -ES **:** the quality or state of being saving **:** FRUGALITY

savings account *n* **:** an account in a savings or interest in a bank on which interest or interest dividends are usu. paid and from which withdrawals can be made usu. only by presentation of a passbook or by written authorization on prescribed forms — distinguished from *checking account*

savings and loan association *n* **:** a cooperative association formed under federal or state law in the U. S. that solicits savings in the form of share capital, invests its funds in mortgages, and permits deposits in and withdrawals from share accounts similar to those allowed for savings accounts in banks — called also *cooperative bank, mutual loan association*

savings bank *n* **:** a banking institution organized to receive savings accounts only on which accrued interest is periodically paid to depositors

savings bank life insurance *n* **:** life insurance sold over the counter by mutual savings banks as authorized by law in some states

savings bond *n* **:** a nontransferable registered U. S. bond issued in denominations of $25 to $1,000

savings deposit *n* **:** a bank deposit usu. of an individual or a nonprofit organization drawing regular interest and payable on 30 days notice

savings stamp *n* **:** a stamp of a small denomination issued by a savings bank or a government to be purchased and accumulated with others (as on a card) for deposit in a bank or exchange for an interest-bearing obligation when a specified amount has been reached

savin oil *n* **:** a pungent essential oil from the tops of a savin (*Juniperus Sabina*) that causes inflammation of the skin and mucous membrane

sav·ior *or* **sav·iour** \ˈsāvyə(r) *also* -,yō(ə)r *or* -ō(ə)\ *n* -S [ME *saviour, saveour,* fr. MF *sauveour, saveour,* fr. LL *salvator,* fr. *salvatus* (past part. of *salvare* to save) + L *-or* — more at SAVE] **1 :** one that preserves or delivers from danger or destruction ⟨this modest leader and ~ died, almost forgotten by the people he had served and saved —Harrison Smith⟩ ⟨atomic energy as a possible ~ of our culture —Waldemar Kaempffert⟩ **2** *usu cap* **:** one who brings salvation ⟨for I am the Lord your God, the Holy One of Israel, your *Savior* —Isa 43:3 (RSV)⟩ ⟨our Lord and *Savior* Jesus Christ⟩

sav·ior·ess \-,yərəs\ *n* -ES [*savior* + *-ess*] **:** a female savior

sav·ior·hood \ˈsāvyə(r),hu̇d\ *n* [*savior* + *-hood*] **:** the quality or state of being a savior

sav·ior·ship \-,ship\ *n* [*savior* + *-ship*] **:** SAVIORHOOD

sa·voir faire \¦sav,wär¦fa(a)(ə)r, -fe|, -wȧ¦f . . . |ə\ *n* [F *savoir-faire,* lit., knowing how to do] **:** a seemingly instinctive ability to act appropriately in a particular situation; *esp* **:** adroitness in social relationships ⟨manifested a deplorable lack of *savoir faire,* and shattered harmony on an occasion on which harmony was above all things to be desired —*Spectator*⟩ **syn** see TACT

savoir vi·vre \-¦vēvr(ᵊ), -v(rə)\ *n* [F *savoir-vivre,* lit., knowing how to live] **:** ability to live elegantly **:** observance of the usages of fashionable society

savona·ro·la chair \,savə|nəˈrōlə-, sə,vä|\ *n, usu cap S* [after Girolamo *Savonarola* †1498 Ital. religious reformer] **:** a folding X-shaped chair of Italian Renaissance style that has interlaced curved slats pivoted at their intersections — called also *scissors chair*

Savonarola chair

sa·vonne·rie \,savənˈrē, ˈ⸗⸗,⸗\ *adj, usu cap* [F (*La*) *Savonnerie,* carpet factory manufacturing Savonnerie carpets established in 1628 on the site of a former soap factory at Chaillot, near the Seine, in Paris, fr. *savonnerie* soap factory, fr. *savonnier* soap maker (fr. *savon* soap — fr. L *sapon-, sapo* — + *-ier* -er) + *-ie* -y — more at SAPONACEOUS] **:** of, relating to, or being a handmade one-piece French carpet with a pile or a similarly woven tapestry

¹sa·vor *also* **sa·vour** \ˈsāvə(r)\ *n* -S [ME *savor, saver, savour,* fr. OF *savor, savour,* fr. L *sapor;* akin to L *sapere* to taste, have good taste — more at SAGE] **1 a :** a quality of something that affects the sense of taste or smell ⟨if the salt have lost his ~, wherewith shall it be salted —Mt 5:13 (AV)⟩ ⟨rosemary and rue; these keep seeming and ~ all the winter long —Shak.⟩ **b :** a particular flavor or smell ⟨described the ~ of the durian as a rich butterlike custard, highly flavored with almonds —V. G. Heiser⟩ ⟨a kettle from which issued the ~ of cooking mutton fat —Willa Cather⟩ **c :** a distinctive quality ⟨an odd blend of bitter naturalism and quiet humor that gives it a ~ quite its own —Anthony Boucher⟩ ⟨contributed their share to the ~ of local life —*Amer. Guide Series: Del.*⟩ **d :** a qualifying flavor **:** SMACK, TINGE ⟨refreshing our minds with a ~ of the antique, primeval world —Laurence Binyon⟩ **2 :** a taste for something **:** RELISH ⟨lost his ~ for food —Rex Ingamells⟩ **3 a :** power to affect the sense of taste or smell ⟨in his illness, food and drink lost their ~ for him⟩ **b :** power to arouse interest or zest ⟨times change, and the sprightliest wit may lose its ~ —V.L.Parrington⟩ **4** *archaic* **:** REPUTATION, REPUTE **5** *obs* **:** CHARACTER, SORT ⟨this admiration . . . is much o' the ~ of other your new pranks —Shak.⟩ **syn** see TASTE

²savor *also* **savour** \"\ *vb* **savored** *also* **savoured; savored** *also* **savoured; savoring** *also* **savouring** \-v(ə)riŋ\ **savors** *also* **savours** [ME *savowren,* fr. OF *savourer, savorer,* fr. LL *saporare,* fr. L *sapor* savor] *vi* **1** *archaic* **:** to be agreeable ⟨what is loathsome to the young ~*s* well to thee and me —Alfred Tennyson⟩ **2 :** to have a specified smell or to smell of a specified substance ⟨the very doors and windows ~ vilely —Shak.⟩ ⟨the solemn vestments, ~*ing* of naphthalene —Norman Douglas⟩ **3 :** to partake of a quality or state **:** indicate a presence or influence **:** SMACK — used with *of* ⟨the argument ~*s* of cynicism —V.L.Parrington⟩ ⟨an intense dislike of anything ~*ing* of regimentation —Chilton Williamson⟩ **~** *vt* **1 a :** to give a salt taste to ⟨the salt that ~*s* the sea —F.K.Lane⟩ **b :** to give flavor to **:** SEASON ⟨the salt of danger ~*ing* nights and days —*Atlantic*⟩ **2 a :** to have experience of **:** TASTE ⟨once before, he had ~*ed* politics —Ellery Sedgwick⟩ **b** *archaic* **:** to be conscious of the odor of **:** SMELL ⟨wisdom and goodness to the vile seem vile, filths ~ but themselves —Shak.⟩ **c :** to taste or smell with pleasure **:** RELISH ⟨~*ing* the succulent watermelon —Jane Nickerson⟩ ⟨walk around . . . ~*ing* the wild roses —Ann Panners⟩ **d :** to take conscious pleasure in **:** appreciate or enjoy with deliberate awareness ⟨this is a book to ~ on leisurely summer days —Pamela Taylor⟩ ⟨he decided to hold it back and thus ~ a little longer the pleasure of the surprise —T.B.Costain⟩ **3** *archaic* **:** to care for **:** LIKE ⟨thou ~*est* not the things that be of God, but those that be of men —Mt 16:23 (AV)⟩

savored *adj* [fr. past part. of ²*savor*] **:** having or indicating a particular savor — usu. used in combination ⟨surrounded by his evil-*savored* companions —Agnes M. Cleaveland⟩

sa·vor·er \ˈsāv(ə)rə(r)\ *n* -S **:** one that savors ⟨a ~, content to taste and retaste what was best or most flavorsome in the volumes he cherished —John Mason Brown⟩

sa·vor·i·ly \-v(ə)rəlē, -li\ *adv* [ME, fr. ¹*savory* + *-ly*] **1 :** in a relishing manner **:** with appetite ⟨would eat our plain food ~ —Charles Lamb⟩ **2 :** in a savory manner **:** APPETIZINGLY ⟨how ~ he described the strawberry —R.L.Cook⟩

sa·vor·i·ness \-v(ə)rēnəs, -rin-\ *n* -ES [ME *saverinesse,* fr. *savery* savory + *-nesse* -ness] **:** the quality or state of being savory

sa·vor·ing·ly *adv* **:** in a relishing manner ⟨get slowly ~ mellow drunk —James Jones⟩

sa·vor·less \ˈsāvə(r)ləs\ *adj* [ME *savourles,* fr. *savour* savor + *-les* — more at SAVOR] **:** lacking savor — **sa·vor·less·ness** *n* -ES

savorly *adv* [ME *saverly,* fr. *saver* savor + *-ly*] *obs* **:** with keen relish, feeling, or understanding

sa·vor·ous \ˈsāv(ə)rəs\ *adj* [ME, fr. MF *savorous, saverous,* fr. LL *saporosus,* fr. L *sapor* savor + *-osus* -ose] **:** having savor **:** FLAVORFUL ⟨written in rich, lusty, ~ English prose —Frances Winwar⟩ — **sa·vor·ous·ly** *adv*

sa·vor·some \-v(ə)rsəm\ *adj* **:** FLAVORSOME

¹sa·vory \ˈsāv(ə)rē, -ri\ *adj* [ME *savory, savery, savure,* fr. OF *savouré,* past part. of *savourer* to savor — more at SAVOR] **1 a :** AGREEABLE, PLEASANT ⟨an exceedingly varied and ~ travel book —*Newsweek*⟩ **b :** morally attractive **:** EDIFYING, WHOLESOME ⟨his fallen partner has proved to be none too ~ a character —John Paterson⟩ ⟨scandals don't make very ~ reading —Green Peyton⟩ **2 a :** agreeable to the taste **:** APPETIZING ⟨fruit more ~ than berries —John Burroughs⟩ **b :** pleasing in smell **:** FRAGRANT ⟨a ~ wooden tray . . . smelling of rich cedarwood and varnish —Elizabeth M. Roberts⟩ **c :** having a stimulating taste ⟨a ~ dish⟩ ⟨~ jelly⟩ **syn** see PALATABLE

²savory \"\ *n* -ES *Brit* **:** a cooked or uncooked dish of stimulating flavor served usu. at the end of dinner but sometimes as an appetizer before the meal

³savory \"\ *n* -ES [ME *saverey,* prob. alter. (influenced by *savery,* adj., savory) of OE *sætherie,* fr. L *satureia*] **:** any of several aromatic mints of the genus *Satureia* — see SUMMER SAVORY, WINTER SAVORY

savour *var of* SAVOR

sa·voy \səˈvȯi *also esp attrib* ˈsa,vȯi\ *n* -S [F (*chou de*) *Savoie* cabbage of Savoy] **1** *also* **savoy cabbage :** a cabbage having a compact head with wrinkled and curled leaves **2 :** a spinach having wrinkled leaves

¹sa·voy·ard \səˈvȯiərd, səˈvȯi,(y)ärd, ¦sa,vȯi,(y)ärd, *F* savȯyȧr *or* savwȧyȧȧr\ *n* -S *cap* [F, fr. *Savoie* Savoy, region in southeastern France + F *-ard*] **:** a native or inhabitant of Savoy

²savoyard \"\ *adj, usu cap* **1 :** of, relating to, or characteristic of Savoy, France **2 :** of, relating to, or characteristic of the people of Savoy

³savoyard \"; *often pronounced in French fashion like the preceding although not from French*\ *n* -S *usu cap* [*Savoy,* theater in London specially built in 1881 by Richard D'Oyly Carte †1901 Eng. operatic impresario for the presentation of the operas of W.S.Gilbert †1911 Eng. playwright and A.S. Sullivan †1900 Eng. composer + E *-ard*] **:** a devotee, performer, or producer of the comic operas of W.S.Gilbert and A.S.Sullivan

savoy cake *n, usu cap S* [fr. *Savoy,* region in France] **1** *or* **savoy finger** *or* **savoy biscuit :** LADYFINGER 2 **2 :** a large sponge cake often baked or cut in fancy shape

savoy disease *n, usu cap S* [so called fr. the resemblance of the leaves to those of savoy cabbage] **:** a virus disease of plants transmitted by a lace bug (*Piesma cinerea*) and marked by wrinkling of leaves

sa·voyed \səˈvȯid *also* ˈsa,vȯid\ *adj* [*savoy* + *-ed*] **:** curled and wrinkled; *specif* **:** abnormally wrinkled as a result of disease (as a virus infection) — used of leaves or plants

sa·voy·ing \səˈvȯi·iŋ, ˈsa,vȯi·-\ *n* -S [*savoy* + *-ing*] **:** a savoyed quality or state

savs *abbr* savings

sav·vi·ness \ˈsavēnəs, -vin-\ *n* -ES **:** the quality or state of being savvy

¹sav·vy \ˈsavē, -vi\ *vb* -ED/-ING/-ES [modif. of Sp *sabe,* 2d pers. (formal) & 3d pers. sing. pres. indic. of *saber* to know, fr. L *sapere* to have sense, be wise — more at SAGE] *vt* **:** COMPREHEND, UNDERSTAND ⟨he *savvied* them, they fitted into his language —Will James⟩ **~** *vi* **:** to understand the meaning or implication of something heard **:** get the point ⟨I take care of myself — ~? —S.V.Benét⟩

²savvy \"\ *n* -ES **:** expertness in a particular field based on experience and native ability **:** practical grasp **:** KNOW-HOW, SHREWDNESS ⟨political ~⟩ ⟨business ~⟩ ⟨baseball ~⟩

³savvy \"\ *adj* [²*savvy*] **:** characterized by shrewdness and practical grasp ⟨most of them are pretty ~ fellows: they know the answers —J.S.Childers⟩

¹saw [ME *saugh* (past sing.), *sawen* (past pl.), fr. OE *seah* (past sing.), *sāwon* (past pl.)] *past or substand past part of* SEE

²saw \ˈsȯ\ *n* -S [ME *sawe,* fr. OE *sagu, sage;* akin to OHG *sega, saga* saw, ON *sǫg* saw, L *secare* to cut, *securis* ax, *secula* sickle, OSlav *sěšti* to cut, *sekyra* ax, Alb *shatë* mattock; basic meaning: to cut] **1 a** (1) **:** a manually operated or power-driven tool used to cut hard material (as wood, metal, or bone) and usu. consisting of a thin flat blade or plate of tempered steel with a continuous series of teeth on the edge and mounted in a handle or frame (2) **:** a saw blade **b :** any of various tools or devices without teeth that cut by wearing out a kerf: as (1) **:** HELICOIDAL SAW (2) **:** a soft steel disk revolved at high speed to cut metal (as armor plate) **c :** a tool or machine having a saw for cutting **2 a :** the ovipositor of a sawfly **b :** the snout of a sawfish

³saw \"\ *vb* **sawed; sawed** \ˈsȯd\ *or* **sawn** \ˈsȯn\ **sawing; saws** [ME *sawen,* fr. *sawe* saw] *vt* **1 a :** to cut with a saw ⟨~ timber⟩ ⟨~ marble⟩ ⟨~ the log in two⟩ **b :** to cut into pieces as if with a saw ⟨about 20 carbines and tommy guns practically ~*ed* him in half —Bill Alcine⟩ **c :** to cut kerfs across (the back of an unbound hand-sewn book) to receive the cords that secure the covers in order to prevent the cords from raising ridges on the covered backbone — usu. used with *in* **2 :** to produce or form by cutting with or as if with a saw ⟨solid wheels ~*ed* from the trunks of cottonwood trees —*Amer. Guide Series: Texas*⟩ **3 a :** to cut through as though using a saw ⟨a fir tree ~*ed* the air with its creaking branches —Elizabeth Taylor⟩ ⟨do not ~ the air too much with your hand —Shak.⟩ **b :** to give the motion of a saw to ⟨~*ing* the towel across his back —A.P.Gaskell⟩ **~** *vi* **1 a :** to use a saw ⟨he ~*s* well⟩ **b :** to cut with or as if with a saw ⟨a machine that can ~ in many patterns⟩ ⟨the river that ~*ed* through the rising mountain barrier —*Amer. Guide Series: Wash.*⟩ **2 :** to admit of being cut with a saw ⟨the timber ~*s* smoothly⟩ **3 a :** to make motions as though using a saw ⟨~*ed* at the reins⟩ **b :** to play on a stringed instrument with a bow ⟨the cellist ~*ed* away⟩ — **saw alive** *or* **saw through and through :** to make all cuts on a log parallel — **saw gourds** *South & Midland* **:** SNORE — **saw wood 1** *slang* **:** to attend to one's affairs **:** mind one's business ⟨said nothing and *sawed wood* and drank his coffee —Helen Reilly⟩ **2** *slang* **:** SNORE

⁴saw \"\ *n* -S [ME *sawe,* fr. OE *sagu* speech, talk, discourse; akin to OHG & ON *saga* tale, saga, account, OE *secgan* to say — more at SAY] **:** a traditional saying **:** MAXIM, PROVERB ⟨the old ~ that ignorance is bliss —M.W.Childs⟩

sa·wah \ˈsäwə\ *n* -S [Malay] **:** a wet or irrigated rice field in Indonesia

sa·wa·li \səˈwälē\ *n* -S [Tag *sawali*] **:** a coarse twilled matting of flattened bamboo strips used in the Philippines for partitions, walling, and baskets

sa·wan \ˈsäwən\ *n* -S *usu cap* [Hindi *sāwan,* fr. Skt *śrāvaṇa*] **:** a month of the Hindu year — see MONTH table

sa·wa·ra cypress \ˈsäwərə\ *n* [Jap *sawara*] **:** a Japanese evergreen tree (*Chamaecyparis pisifera*) used for timber and as the source of many horticultural forms of retinispora

saw arbor *n* **:** MANDREL 4

sawback \ˈ⸗,⸗\ *n* [²*saw* + *back*] **:** something that has a serrate dorsal outline; *specif* **:** a mountain range or crest that has sharp peaks of about equal height

sawbelly \ˈ⸗,⸗⸗\ *n* [²*saw* + *belly*] **1 :** ALEWIFE 1a **2 :** GIZZARD SHAD

sawbill \ˈ⸗,⸗\ *n* [²*saw* + *bill*] **:** a bird with a serrate beak; *esp* **:** MERGANSER

saw bill *n* **:** a list given to a sawyer of sizes to be sawed from logs

saw–billed \ˈ⸗¦⸗\ *adj* **:** having a serrated bill

sawbones \ˈ⸗,⸗\ *n, pl* **sawbones** *or* **sawboneses** [³*saw* + *bones*] *slang* **:** a physician or surgeon ⟨the usual anecdotal memoir churned out by the ~ who takes pen instead of tongue depressor in hand —*Saturday Rev.*⟩

saw brier *n* **:** any of several prickly plants of the genus *Smilax:* as **a :** BULLBRIER **b :** a Bahamian brier (*S. havanensis*) **c :** CATBRIER

sawbuck \ˈ⸗,⸗\ *n* [²*saw* + *buck;* trans. of D *zaagbok*] **1 :** SAWHORSE **2** [prob. so called fr. the Roman numeral X that suggests the crossed ends of a sawhorse] *slang* **:** a 10-dollar bill

sawbuck table *n* **:** a table with X-shaped supports

sawbuck table

saw·bwa \ˈsȯbwə\ *n* -S [Burmese *cdbwā*] **:** the hereditary ruler of a Shan state of Burma

saw cabbage palm *n* **:** SAW PALMETTO b

saw·der \ˈsȯdə(r)\ *vt* -ED/-ING/-S [*soft sawder*] **:** FLATTER

¹saw·dust \ˈsȯ(,)dəst\ *n* [²*saw* + *dust*] **1 a :** dust or small fragments (as of wood or stone) made by a saw in cutting ⟨the floor was covered with ~⟩ **b :** flimsy stuffing ⟨a man made of ~⟩ **2** *or* **sawdust liver :** a cattle abnormality of undetermined cause characterized by the presence of small granular light-colored areas scattered through the liver

2sawdust \"\ *vt* **:** to strew or carpet with sawdust
3sawdust \"\ *adj* **1 :** covered or stuffed with sawdust ⟨the ~ ring⟩ ⟨a ~ doll⟩ **2 :** of, relating to, or connected with an enterprise (as a circus or revival meeting) conducted under a tent ⟨a ~ performer⟩ ⟨a ~ preacher⟩ **3 :** having no real substance **:** not solid ⟨she asks vital questions, but she gives ~ answers —*Saturday Rev.*⟩ ⟨a ~ Caesar⟩
sawdust trail *n* [so called fr. the practice of going down a sawdust-covered aisle to the altar in a revival tent meeting as a sign of repentance or conversion] **1 :** the path of conversion to a gospel or belief ⟨when a notorious grizzled old sinner hits the *sawdust trail*, the hallelujahs shake the tabernacle —Beverly Smith⟩ ⟨drew the students back down the *sawdust trail* to the old-time Congregationalism —*Amer. Guide Series: Conn.*⟩ **2 :** the circuit of revival meetings ⟨five of the biggest attractions on the *sawdust trail* —Furman Bisher⟩
saw·dusty \ˈsȯ(ˌ)dəstē, -ti\ *adj* [1*sawdust* + *-y*] **1 :** filled with, resembling, or smelling of sawdust ⟨the ~, soapy-smelling dark of the shop —Angus Wilson⟩ **2 :** lacking inherent interest or appeal **:** WEARISOME ⟨the old formal, dogmatic, ~ conning of the grammar book —Eric Partridge⟩
sawed *adj* [fr. past part. of 3*saw*] **1 :** cut with a saw ⟨~ boards⟩ ⟨~ bone⟩ **2 :** SERRATE ⟨~ edges⟩
saw–edged \ˈ=ˌ=\ *adj* **:** having a toothed or badly nicked edge
sawed–off \ˈ=ˌ=\ *adj* **1 :** having an end sawed off ⟨a *sawed-off* shotgun⟩ ⟨a *sawed-off* baseball bat which in peaceful times served as a rolling pin —Rose Feld⟩ **2 :** of less than average height **:** PINT-SIZE ⟨a little *sawed-off* mountaineer lugging a rifle longer than he was —F.B.Gipson⟩
saw·er \ˈsȯ(ə)r, -ȯə\ *n* -S [ME, fr. *sawen* to saw + *-er* — more at SAW] **:** one that saws **:** SAWYER
saw fern *n* **:** a widely distributed fern (*Blechnum serrulatum*) with erect stiff fronds that often grows in dense colonies in tropical marshes and is esp. common in Florida and the West Indies
saw file *n* **:** a usu. triangular file for sharpening saw teeth
sawfish \ˈ=ˌ=\ *n* **:** any of several large elongate viviparous fishes constituting the family Pristidae, having a flattened and much elongated snout with a row of stout toothlike structures inserted along each edge, and living in warm shallow seas and about river mouths principally in tropical America and Africa — see PRISTIDAE
sawfly \ˈ=ˌ=\ *n* **1 :** any of numerous hymenopterous insects constituting a superfamily Tenthredinoidea, having the female usu. with a pair of serrated blades in her ovipositor that are used to make the incisions in leaves and stems of plants in which the eggs are laid, developing from larvae that resemble lepidopterous caterpillars but usu. have more numerous prolegs, and including many destructive pests of plants that feed on foliage or mine in leaves and stems **2 :** any of various other hymenopterous insects of similar habits and form
saw gate *or* **saw frame** *n* **:** a stretching frame for a saw or gang of saws
saw gin *n* **:** a cotton gin in which the lint is drawn by the teeth of revolving circular saws through a grating of vertical ribs too closely spaced for the seeds to pass with the lint being removed from the saw teeth by rotating brushes or a blast or air
saw grass *n* **:** any of various sedges having the edges of the leaves set with minute sharp teeth: as **a :** a European sedge (*Cladium mariscus*) **b :** a sedge (*C. jamaicensis*) of southern U.S. and the West Indies — compare RAZOR GRASS
sawhorse \ˈ=ˌ=\ *n* [2*saw* + *horse*] **1 :** a rack shaped like a double St. Andrew's cross that is used to support wood while it is being sawed — called also *buck*, *sawbuck* **2 :** a flat-topped trestle usu. used in pairs to support something (as wood that is being sawed)

sawhorses

sawing *adj* [fr. pres. part. of 3*saw*] **:** having a rasping quality ⟨a ~ sound⟩ ⟨a ~ voice⟩
sawl \ˈsȯl\ *dial chiefly Brit var of* SOUL
sawlike \ˈ=ˌ=\ *adj* **:** resembling a saw or the teeth of a saw ⟨a ~ blade⟩ ⟨~ teeth⟩
sawlog \ˈ=ˌ=\ *n* **:** a log of suitable size for sawing into lumber
saw·man \ˈ=ˌmən\ *n, pl* **sawmen :** one who saws or who repairs saws
sawmill \ˈ=ˌ=\ *n* [2*saw* + *mill*] **1 :** a plant having power-driven machinery for sawing logs **2 :** a machine used for sawing logs
sawmiller \ˈ=ˌ==\ *n* **:** one who operates a sawmill
sawmilling \ˈ=ˌ==\ *n* **:** the process of operating a sawmill
sawn *past part of* SAW
1saw·ney \ˈsȯnē, -ni\ *n* -S [prob. alter. of *zany*] *chiefly Brit* **:** FOOL, SIMPLETON
2sawney \"\ *n* -S *usu cap* [alter. of 3*sandy*] **:** SCOTCHMAN — usu. used disparagingly
3sawney *also* **saw·ny** \"\ *adj* [1*sawney*] *chiefly Brit* **:** naïvely or sentimentally foolish **:** SILLY
saw palmetto *n* **:** any of several palms with spiny-toothed leafstalks: as **a :** a common stemless palm (*Serenoa repens*) of the southern U.S. **b :** a palm (*Paurotis wrightii*) of the West Indies and southern Florida
sawpit \ˈ=ˌ=\ *n* [ME *sawe pitt*, fr. *sawe* saw + *pitt* pit — more at SAW, PIT] **:** a pit over which timber is laid to be sawed with a long two-handled saw operated by two men of whom one stands above the timber and the other below it
saws *pl of* SAW, *pres 3d sing of* SAW
saw–scaled viper \ˈ=ˌ=-\ *n* **:** a small but fierce and aggressive desert-dwelling viper (*Echis carinatus*) found from No. Africa to India, having roughly keeled lateral scales, and being exceedingly venomous and responsible for many deaths esp. in India — called also *kupper*
saw set *n* **:** an instrument used to give set to sawteeth
sawsetter \ˈ=ˌ==\ *n* [2*saw* + *setter*] **:** one that sets the teeth of saws
saw shark *n* **:** any of several small sharks (family Pristiophoridae) found along the shores of southern Africa, eastern Asia, and Australia and having a snout like that of a sawfish but smaller teeth not embedded in sockets and lateral rather than ventral gill openings
saw sharpener *also* **sawsharper** \ˈ=ˌ==\ *n* [so called fr. the grating noise made by the male] **:** GREAT TIT
sawt \ˈsät, ˈsȯt\ *chiefly Scot var of* SALT
saw table *n* **:** an iron or wooden table having a slot in which a circular saw operates **:** a saw bench
sawtimber \ˈ=ˌ==\ *n* **:** timber suitable for sawing into lumber
1sawtooth \ˈ=ˌ=\ *n* [2*saw* + *tooth*] **:** a tooth of a saw or one of the teeth of an animal or machine shaped or arranged like the teeth of a saw
2sawtooth \"\ *adj* **1 :** SAW-TOOTHED **2 :** having a wave form resembling the teeth of a saw and of a quantity that varies periodically either gradually or gradually and abruptly between two peak values — used esp. of voltages and currents
sawtooth building *n* **:** a building having a sawtooth roof
saw–toothed \ˈ=ˌ=\ *adj* **1 :** having teeth like those of a saw **:** having pointed teeth ⟨a *saw-toothed* shark⟩ **2 :** having serrations **:** SERRATE ⟨*saw-toothed* mountains pierced by valleys —*Lamp*⟩
saw–toothed grain beetle *n* **:** a minute widely distributed cucujid beetle (*Oryzaephilus surinamensis*) that feeds esp. on stored cereal products
sawtooth roof *also* **sawtooth** *n* **:** a roof composed of two or more parallel simple roofs resembling in section the teeth of a saw and ordinarily having one slope of each member steeper than the other to receive glazing

sawtooth roof

sawtooth roulette *n* **:** a zigzag stamp roulette that produces a sawtooth pattern on the edge of a detached stamp
saw tree *n* **:** a tree suitable for sawing
sawway \ˈ=ˌ=\ *n* [2*saw* + *way*] **:** the path of a saw in cutting

saw–whet owl \ˈ=ˌ=-\ *also* **saw–whet** *n* **:** a very small No. American owl (*Cryptoglaux acadica*) that is largely dark brown above and white beneath with vertical brown stripes on the breast, has a rasping metallic call suggesting the filing of a saw, and feeds chiefly on small rodents
sawwort \ˈ=ˌ=\ *n* [2*saw* + *wort*] **1 :** any of various plants constituting a genus (*Serratula*) of the family Compositae; *esp* **:** a plant (*S. tinctoria*) the serrate leaves of which yield a yellow dye **2 :** a plant of the genus *Saussurea* **3 :** a button snakeroot (*Liatris spicata*)
saw·yer \ˈsȯyə(r), ˈsȯiə-\ *n* -S [ME *sawier, sawyer*, fr. *sawen* to saw + *-ier* -er — more at SAW] **1 a :** one that saws logs or timber (as in lumbering or in a sawmill) **b :** either of the two men who work together at sawing timber over a sawpit — see BOTTOM SAWYER, TOP SAWYER **c :** one that saws a particular material (as wood, ivory, or metal) esp. for use in manufacturing **2** *or* **sawyer beetle :** any of several large longicorn beetles whose larvae bore large holes in timber or dead wood esp. of various conifers — see PINE SAWYER **3 :** a tree fast in the bed of a stream with its branches projecting to the surface and bobbing up and down with the current — distinguished from *planter*
1sax \ˈsaks\ *or* **seax** \ˈsaəks\ *n* -ES [ME *sexe* knife, short sword, fr. OE *seax, sæx*; akin to OHG *sahs* knife, ON *sax* knife, sword, L *saxum* rock, OE *sagu* saw — more at SAW] **:** a knifelike chopping tool used for trimming the edges of roof slates and having a pointed pick at the back for making nail holes
2sax \ˈsaks\ *dial Brit var of* SIX
3sax \"\ *n* -ES [by shortening] **:** SAXOPHONE
sax·a·tile \ˈsaksəˌtīl\ *adj* [L *saxatilis*, fr. *saxum* rock] **:** SAXICOLOUS
sax·aul \ˈsakˌsȯl\ *n* -S [prob. native name in Turkistan] **:** a leafless xerophytic shrub or tree (*Haloxylon ammondendron*) of the family Chenopodiaceae of Asia that has green or greenish branches and is used for stabilization of desert soils
saxboard \ˈ=ˌ=\ *n* [1*sax* + *board*] **:** the uppermost strake of an open boat
saxe blue \ˈsaks-\ *also* **saxe** *n* -S *often cap S* [F *Saxe* Saxony] **:** a grayish blue that is redder and paler than electric, greener and slightly lighter than copenhagen, redder, lighter, and stronger than Gobelin, and greener, lighter, and stronger than old china
sax·horn \ˈsaks+ˌ-\ *n* [Antoine Joseph (known as Adolphe) *Sax* †1894 Belgian maker of musical instruments, its inventor + E *horn*] **:** one of a complete family of conical-bore brass-wind musical instruments with valves that are characterized by fullness and evenness of tone and large compass and are made in sizes grading from soprano to bass

saxhorn

saxi- *comb form* [L, fr. *saxum*; akin to L *secare* to cut — more at SAW] **:** rock ⟨*saxicolous*⟩
sax·i·ca·vous \ˌsakˈsēˌkāvəs\ *adj* [NL *saxicavus*, fr. *saxi-* + *-cavus* (fr. L *cavare* to make hollow) — more at EXCAVATE] **:** boring in rock — used esp. of a mollusk; compare LITHOPHAGOUS
1sax·ic·o·la \sakˈsikələ\ *n, cap* [NL, fr. *saxi-* + *-cola*] **:** a genus of Old World passerine birds including the whinchat, stonechat, and related birds
2saxicola \"\ [NL] *syn of* 2OENANTHE
sax·ic·o·line \(ˈ)sakˈsikəˌlīn, -ˌlən\ *adj* [NL *Saxicola* + E *-ine*] **:** of or relating to the genus *Saxicola*
sax·ic·o·lous \(ˈ)sakˈsikələs\ *also* **sax·ic·o·line** \-ˌlīn, -lən\ *or* **sax·i·cole** \ˈsaksəˌkōl\ *adj* [*saxi-* + *-colous* or *-coline* or *-cole*] **:** inhabiting or growing among rocks
sax·if·ra·ga \sakˈsifrəgə\ *n, cap* [NL, fr. LL, saxifrage] **:** a genus (the type of the family Saxifragaceae) of usu. perennial herbs of diverse habit of arctic and temperate regions having pentamerous often showy flowers with a 2-celled ovary followed by a 2-beaked follicle and often having basal tufted leaves — see LONDON PRIDE
sax·i·fra·ga·ce·ae \ˌsaksəfrəˈgāsēˌē\ *n pl, cap* [NL, fr. *Saxifraga*, type genus + *-aceae*] **:** a widely distributed family of herbs (order Rosales) of variable habit usu. distinguished by the free ovary with two carpels, by having as many or twice as many stamens as petals, and by the absence of staminodia — **sax·i·fra·ga·ceous** \ˌ===ˈgāshəs\ *adj*
sax·i·frage \ˈsaksəfrij, -rēj\ *n* -S [ME, fr. MF, fr. LL *saxifraga*, fr. L *saxifraga* (*herba*), lit., rock-breaking herb, fr. *saxifraga* (fem. of *saxifragus* rock-breaking, fr. *saxi-* + *-fragus*, fr. *frangere* to break) + *herba* herb; fr. its growing in crevices of rocks — more at BREAK] **1 :** a plant of the genus *Saxifraga*— called also *breakstone* **2 :** any of various plants felt to resemble a saxifrage — usu. used with a qualifying term; see BURNET SAXIFRAGE, GOLDEN SAXIFRAGE
saxifrage family *n* **:** SAXIFRAGACEAE
saxifrage pink *n* **:** a tufted European perennial herb (*Tunica saxifraga*) of the family Caryophyllaceae that has clustered subulate leaves and is adventive in No. America
sax·if·ra·gous \(ˈ)sakˈsifrəgəs\ *adj* [L *saxifragus* rock-breaking] *of a plant* **:** growing in crevices of and promoting splitting of rock
sax·i·frax \ˈsaksəˌfraks\ *n* -ES [modif. (influenced by LL *saxifraga* saxifrage) of Sp *sasafrás* sassafras — more at SAXIFRAGE] **:** SASSAFRAS
sax·ig·e·nous \(ˈ)sakˈsijənəs\ *adj* [LL *saxigenus*, fr. *saxi-* + *-genus* (fr. *gignere* to beget) — more at KIN] **:** SAXICOLOUS
1sax·on \ˈsaksən\ *n* -S [ME, fr. LL *Saxones* Saxons (sing. *Saxo*), of Gmc origin; akin to OE *Seaxe, Seaxan*, pl., Saxons] **1** *cap* **a** (1) **:** a member of a Germanic people entering and conquering England with the Angles and Jutes in the 5th century A.D. and merging with them to form the Anglo-Saxon people (2) **:** an Englishman or Lowlander as distinguished from a Welshman, Irishman, or Highlander — compare SASSENACH **b :** a native or inhabitant of Saxony, Germany **2** *cap* **a :** the Germanic language or dialect of any of the Saxon peoples **b :** the Germanic element in the English language esp. as distinguished from the French and Latin **3** *usu cap* [prob. so called fr. its originating in Saxony] **:** a firework having a brilliant turning fire that produces the appearance of a revolving sun
2saxon \"\ *adj, usu cap* **1 a :** of, relating to, or characteristic of the Anglo-Saxons **:** belonging to the period of English history between the Anglo-Saxon invasions and the Norman Conquest in 1066 **b :** of Anglo-Saxon origin ⟨the *Saxon* words have a simple vigor which no other vocabulary at our disposal could secure —Barrett Wendell⟩ **2 a :** of, relating to, or characteristic of Saxony **b :** of, relating to, or characteristic of the people of Saxony
3saxon \"\ *dial var of* SEXTON
saxon blue *n, usu cap S* **1 :** a dye made by dissolving indigo in sulfuric acid **2** *or* **saxony blue :** SMALT 1
sax·o·nian \(ˈ)sakˈsōnēən, -nyən\ *adj, usu cap* [ML *Saxonia* Saxony (fr. LL *Saxon-, Saxo* Saxon + L *-ia* -y) + E *-an*] **:** SAXON 2 a
sax·on·ic \(ˈ)sakˈsänik\ *adj, usu cap* [1*saxon* + *-ic*] **:** of or relating to the Anglo-Saxons
sax·on·ism \ˈsaksəˌnizəm\ *n* -S *usu cap* [1*saxon* + *-ism*] **:** ANGLO-SAXONISM
sax·on·ist \-nəst\ *n* -S *usu cap* [1*saxon* + *-ist*] **:** a specialist in Old English or in Saxon history or culture
sax·on·ize \-ˌnīz\ *vt* -ED/-ING/-S *sometimes cap* [ML *saxonizare*, fr. LL *Saxon-, Saxo* Saxon + *-izare* -ize] **:** ANGLO-SAXONIZE
sax·on·ly *adv, usu cap* **:** in a Saxon manner
saxon wheel *or* **saxony wheel** *n, usu cap S* [so called fr. its being the invention of a 16th cent. German wood-carver] **:** a flax-spinning treadle machine in which the bobbin lags behind the fly with the spindle giving the twist to the yarn and the difference of speeds of the spindle and bobbin causing the bobbin to be wound
sax·o·ny \ˈsaksənē, -ni\ *n* -ES *often cap* [fr. *Saxony*, former German state in central Germany] **1 a :** any of various fine soft woolen fabrics orig. made in Saxony of merino wool and usu. having a firm texture and small clear patterns **b :** a fine knitting yarn of closely-twisted three-ply wool **2 :** a Wilton jacquard carpet woven with moderately tight twisted pile yarns
saxony green *n, often cap S* **:** COBALT GREEN 2
sax·o·phone \ˈsaksəˌfōn\ *n* [F, fr. Antoine J. (known as Adolphe) *Sax* †1894 Belgian maker of musical instruments, its inventor + F *-phone*] **1 :** a wind instrument that combines the reed mouthpiece of a clarinet with a usu. curved conical metal tube made in various sizes, that is equipped with finger keys, and that is used esp. in military bands and dance orchestras **2 :** a flue or reed pipe-organ stop so constructed as to imitate the saxophone — **sax·o·phon·ic** \ˌ==ˈfänik\ *adj*

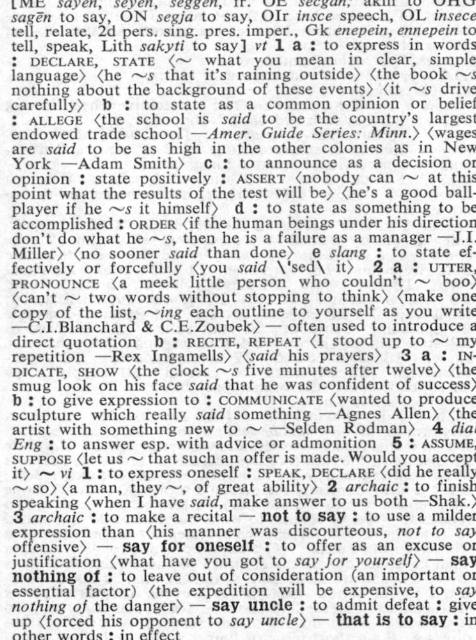

saxophone

sax·o·phon·ist \-ˌfōnəst\ *chiefly Brit* sakˈsäfənəst\ *n* -S **:** a player on the saxophone
sax·tuba \ˈsaks+ˌ-\ *n* [Antoine J. *Sax* †1894 + E *tuba*] **:** a bass saxhorn
1say \(ˈ)sā, *South also* (ˈ)se\ *vb, past* **said** \(ˈ)sed, ˌsəd\ *or archaic* **said·est** \ˈsedəst\ *or* **saidst** \ˈsedzt, -edst, -etst\ *past part* **said**; *pres part* **saying** \ˈsāiŋ\ *pres 1st sing* **say** *or chiefly dial* **says** \(ˈ)sez, ˌsəz\ *2d sing* **say**; *3d sing* **says** \(ˈ)sez, ˌsəz\ *or archaic* **saith** \(ˈ)seth, ˈsā(ə)th\ *pl* **say** [ME *sayen, seyen, seggen*, fr. OE *secgan*; akin to OHG *sagēn* to say, ON *segja* to say, OIr *insce* speech, OL *insece* tell, relate, 2d pers. sing. pres. imper., Gk *enepein, ennepein* to tell, speak, Lith *sakyti* to say] *vt* **1 a :** to express in words **:** DECLARE, STATE ⟨~ what you mean in clear, simple language⟩ ⟨he ~*s* that it's raining outside⟩ ⟨the book ~*s* nothing about the background of these events⟩ ⟨it ~*s* drive carefully⟩ **b :** to state as a common opinion or belief **:** ALLEGE ⟨the school is *said* to be the country's largest endowed trade school —*Amer. Guide Series: Minn.*⟩ ⟨wages are *said* to be as high in the other colonies as in New York —Adam Smith⟩ **c :** to announce as a decision or opinion **:** state positively **:** ASSERT ⟨nobody can ~ at this point what the results of the test will be⟩ ⟨he's a good ballplayer if he ~*s* it himself⟩ **d :** to state as something to be accomplished **:** ORDER ⟨if the human beings under his direction don't do what he ~*s*, then he is a failure as a manager —J.I. Miller⟩ ⟨no sooner *said* than done⟩ **e** *slang* **:** to state effectively or forcefully ⟨you *said* \ˈsed\ it⟩ **2 a :** UTTER, PRONOUNCE ⟨a meek little person who couldn't ~ boo⟩ ⟨can't ~ two words without stopping to think⟩ ⟨make one copy of the list, ~*ing* each outline to yourself as you write —C.I.Blanchard & C.E.Zoubek⟩ — often used to introduce a direct quotation **b :** RECITE, REPEAT ⟨I stood up to ~ my repetition —Rex Ingamells⟩ ⟨*said* his prayers⟩ **3 a :** INDICATE, SHOW ⟨the clock ~*s* five minutes after twelve⟩ ⟨the smug look on his face *said* that he was confident of success⟩ **b :** to give expression to **:** COMMUNICATE ⟨wanted to produce sculpture which really *said* something —Agnes Allen⟩ ⟨the artist with something new to ~ —Selden Rodman⟩ **4** *dial Eng* **:** to answer esp. with advice or admonition **5 :** ASSUME, SUPPOSE ⟨let us ~ that such an offer is made. Would you accept it⟩ ~ *vi* **1 :** to express oneself **:** SPEAK, DECLARE ⟨did he really ~ so⟩ ⟨a man, they ~, of great ability⟩ **2** *archaic* **:** to finish speaking ⟨when I have *said*, make answer to us both —Shak.⟩ **3** *archaic* **:** to make a recital — **not to say :** to use a milder expression than ⟨his manner was discourteous, *not to say* offensive⟩ — **say for oneself :** to offer as an excuse or justification ⟨what have you got to *say for yourself*⟩ — **say nothing of :** to leave out of consideration (an important or essential factor) ⟨the expedition will be expensive, to *say nothing of* the danger⟩ — **say uncle :** to admit defeat **:** give up ⟨forced his opponent to *say uncle*⟩ — **that is to say :** in other words **:** in effect
2say \ˈsā, *South also* ˈse\ *n, pl* **says** \ˈsāz, *South also* ˈsez\ **1** *archaic* **:** something that is said **:** SAYING, STATEMENT ⟨ere the fatal hour I said the ~ that placed me in thy power —W.S.Gilbert⟩ **2 a :** a full expression of opinion **:** all that one wants to say ⟨that gentleman had said his ~ and now chose to be silent —Max Peacock⟩ **b :** an opportunity to express one's views or intentions ⟨feel that if such a person is dissatisfied with the conduct of affairs he should resign before having his ~ —Zechariah Chafee⟩ **3 a :** a right or power to influence action or decision **:** VOICE ⟨had no ~ in the upbringing of his son —W.C.DeVane⟩ ⟨bound-up babies voice complaints but have no ~ about their clothing —*Better Homes & Gardens*⟩ **b :** a right or power of final decision **:** supreme authority — used with *the* ⟨they will have the ~ shortly about what shall be done —E.S.Martin⟩ ⟨he had the ~ over more than $50 billion —*Newsweek*⟩ **4** *chiefly dial* **:** CONVERSATION, TALK
3say \"\ *adv* [fr. imper. of 1*say*] **1 :** ABOUT, APPROXIMATELY ⟨the property is worth, ~, four million dollars⟩ ⟨the car was going, ~, sixty miles an hour⟩ **2 :** for instance **:** by way of example **:** AS ⟨if we compress any gas, ~ oxygen⟩
4say \ˈsā\ *n, pl* **says** \ˈsāz\ [ME *say, saie*, fr. OF *saie*, a cloth, fr. (assumed) VL *sagia*, fr. L *sagum* — more at SAGUM] **1 :** a fine woolen cloth resembling serge formerly worn esp. by Quakers and members of religious orders **2** *obs* **:** SILK
5say \"\ *vb* [ME *sayen*, short for *assayen* to assay — more at ASSAY] *chiefly dial* **:** ASSAY
6say \"\ *n* [ME (Sc dial.), of Scand origin; akin to ON *sār* large vessel, Dan *saa* tub, Sw *så* bucket; akin to OE *sā* tub, bucket] *chiefly Scot* **:** BUCKET
sa·ya \ˈsäyə\ *n* -S [Sp, fr. *saya* man's cloak, sagum, fr. (assumed) VL *sagia*, fr. L *sagum* cloak, sagum] **:** an ankle-length outer skirt tied at the waist that is worn by women in the Philippines and Spanish America
say·able \ˈsāəbəl\ *adj* [1*say* + *-able*] **1 :** capable of being said ⟨what he felt was not easily ~⟩ **2 :** capable of being spoken effectively or easily ⟨the piece is ~ like a speech in a great play —J.M.Barzun⟩
sa·yal brown \säˈyäl-\ *n* [Sp *sayal* sackcloth, fr. *saya* man's cloak, sagum] **:** a light brown that is yellower and deeper than blush and deeper than cork
sa·yan samoyedic \ˈsäyən-\ *n, usu cap both Ss* [fr. *Sayan* mountains, range between the Tuva and Irkutsk regions in Siberia] **:** KAMASIN 2
say blister beetle \ˈsā-\ *n, usu cap S* [after Thomas *Say* †1834 Am. entomologist] **:** a blister beetle (*Pomphopoea sayi*) that is often destructive to apple and other fruit blossoms in parts of northern No. America
say·bolt viscosity \ˈsāˌbōlt-\ *n, usu cap S* [after George M. *Saybolt* †1924 Am. chemist] **:** viscosity as determined by the number of seconds required for an oil heated to 130° F for lighter oils and 210° F for heavier oils to flow through a standard orifice and fill a 60 milliliter flask
say·ee \(ˈ)sāˈē\ *n* -S [1*say* + *-ee*] **:** one to whom something is said ⟨the disaccords between sayer and ~ as to just how much has been said—I.A.Richards⟩
say·er \ˈsāə(r), ˈseə-\ *n* -S [ME, fr. *sayen* to say + *-er* — more at SAY] **1 :** one that says ⟨he is a ~ rather than a doer⟩ **2** *archaic* **:** POET ⟨find some sense which no pen yet from singer, ~, ever has extracted —Robert Browning⟩
say·ing \ˈsāiŋ, -ēŋ\ *n* -S [ME, fr. gerund of *sayen* to say] **1 :** the act of speaking or asserting ⟨he is better at ~ than at doing⟩ **2 :** something that is said: as **a :** a wise or witty statement attributed to a specific usu. well-known person ⟨a collection of the ~*s* of great statesmen⟩ ⟨often quotes the ~*s* of his father⟩ **b :** a commonly repeated statement **:** ADAGE, PROVERB ⟨no ~ was ever more true than the old adage that without his tools the workman is helpless —T.F.McNally⟩
say·nète \(ˈ)sāˈnet\ *n* -S [F, fr. Sp *sainete*, lit., tidbit, delicacy, relish, spice, fr. *sain* grease, fat, fr. (assumed) VL *saginum*, fr. L *sagina* stuffing, food, fatness, fodder] **:** ENTREMÉS 2
sa·yo·na·ra \ˌsīyəˈnärə, ˌsīə-, ˌnäd·ə\ *n* -S [Jap] **:** GOOD-BYE
say over *vt* **:** to repeat from memory ⟨practiced *saying* his speech over until he was letter-perfect⟩
says *pres 3d sing or chiefly dial pres 1st sing of* SAY, *pl of* SAY

say's law \ˈsāz-\ *n, usu cap S & often cap L* [after Jean Baptiste *Say* †1832 Fr. economist] **:** a statement in economics: production creates not only the supply of goods but also the demand for them

say-so \ˈ≈,≈\ *n* -s **1 a :** one's unsupported assertion **:** one's bare word or assurance ⟨you think the jury will find him guilty, just on your *say-so* —H.L.Davis⟩ **b :** an authoritative judgment or pronouncement **:** DICTUM ⟨on the *say-so* of the physicians, the commission granted the extension —Saul Carson⟩ **2 :** a right of final decision **:** AUTHORITY, SAY ⟨the federal government no longer has any *say-so* in the island's internal affairs —*Sat. Eve. Post*⟩

say's phoebe \ˈsāz-\ *n, usu cap S* [after Thomas *Say* †1834 Am. entomologist] **:** a phoebe (*Sayornis saya*) of western No. America that is grayish brown above with cinnamon buff breast and belly, dark brown head, and black tail

say stinkbug *also* **say's stinkbug** *n, usu cap 1st S* [after Thomas *Say* †1834] **:** a common stinkbug (*Chlorochroa sayi*) that is a serious pest esp. on grains in parts of western U. S.

say·yid *also* **sa·yid** *or* **sey·yid** \ˈsī(y)əd, ˈsīd, ˈsā(y)əd, ˈsäd\ *or* **si·di** \ˈsēdē\ *n* -s [Ar *sayyid*] **1 :** an Islamic chief or leader **2 :** LORD, SIR — used as a courtesy title for a Muslim of outstanding achievement or noble lineage

Saz·e·rac \ˈsazə,rak\ *trademark* — used for a cocktail consisting of bourbon, absinthe flavoring, bitters, and sugar stirred with ice, strained, and flavored with a twist of lemon peel when served

sb *abbr* **1** stilb **2** substantive

SB *abbr or n* -s [NL *scientiae baccalaureus*] Bachelor of Science

SB *abbr* **1** sales book **2** savings bank **3** separately binned **4** shipping board **5** short bill **6** signal boatswain **7** simultaneous broadcast **8** small bonds **9** southbound **10** splash block **11** standard bead **12** statement of billing **13** steamboat **14** stolen base **15** stretcher bearer **16** stuffing box **17** switchboard

Sb *symbol* [L *stibium*] antimony

SBA *abbr* standard beam approach

sbj *abbr* subjunctive

s brake *n, cap S* **:** a brake for two consecutive wheels having a brake block at each end of an S-shaped lever

sbrinz \ˈsprints, ˈzbr-\ *n, usu cap* [It *sbrinze, sbrinzo,* fr. *Sbrinze Sbrinzo* Brienz, commune of Bern canton, Switzerland] **:** a hard cheese suitable for grating

sc *abbr* **1** scale **2** scene **3** science **4** scilicet **5** screen **6** screw **7** scruple **8** [L *sculpsit*] he or she carved or engraved it

SC *abbr* **1** salvage charges **2** sanitary corps **3** school certificate **4** security council **5** see copy **6** self-closing **7** self-contained **8** [L *Senatus consulto*] by the decree of the Senate **9** service ceiling **10** sharp cash **11** ship's cook **12** signal corps **13** single case **14** single column **15** single comb **16** *often not cap* single crochet **17** *often not cap* small capital; small capitals **18** special circular **19** special constable **20** spreading coefficient **21** staff college **22** staff corps **23** statement of charges **24** steel casting **25** submarine chaser **26** sugar coated **27** summary court **28** supercalendered **29** superimposed current **30** supply corps **31** supreme court **32** swimming club

Sc *symbol* scandium

¹scab \ˈskab, ˈskaa(ə)b\ *n* -s [ME *scab, scabbe,* of Scand origin; akin to OSw *skabbr* scab; akin to OE *sceabb* scab, L *scabies* mange, *scabere* to scratch — more at SHAVE] **1** *archaic* **:** a disease of the skin forming pustules or scales **2 :** scabies of domestic animals; *esp* **:** PSOROPTIC MANGE **3 :** CRUST 3e(1) **4 a :** a mean contemptible person **:** SCOUNDREL **b** (1) **:** one who refuses to join a union (2) **:** a member of a union who refuses to strike or returns to work before a strike has ended (3) **:** a worker who accepts employment or replaces a union worker during a strike (4) **:** one who works for lower wages than or under other conditions contrary to those prescribed by a union — compare BLACKLEG, STRIKEBREAKER **c :** RAT 2b(1) **5 a :** any of various bacterial or fungous diseases of plants characterized by crustlike spots — see APPLE SCAB, POTATO SCAB, WHEAT SCAB **b :** one of the crusty spots in any of these diseases **6 :** a short piece of timber nailed or bolted to two abutting timbers to splice them together **7 a :** a slight irregular protuberance on a casting caused by a break in the mold **b :** a part of a surface of a wire or strip damaged by an adhesion of scale or other matter **8 :** a defect in enamel resembling a scab on skin **9 :** a piece of a target broken off from the rear opposite the place struck

²scab \ˈ"\ *vb* **scabbed; scabbed; scabbing; scabs** *vi* **1 :** to become covered with a scab **:** form a scab ⟨the wound *scabbed* over⟩ **2 :** to act as a scab ⟨trying to ~ against their own fellow musicians —*Internat'l Musician*⟩ **3 :** to throw off a piece from the rear opposite the place struck ⟨data bearing on the *scabbing* of metals under explosive attack —*Bull. of Amer. Physical Society*⟩ ~ *vt* **1 :** to label or treat (someone) as a scab **:** label (a job or a shop) as such that anyone working will be treated as a scab **2 :** to break off (a piece) from the rear of a target opposite the place struck ⟨bombs *scabbed* the concrete⟩

¹scab·bard \ˈskabə(r)d\ *n* -s [ME *scauberc, scaubert* fr. AF *escaubers, escauberz* (pl.), of Gmc origin, fr. a compound whose first element is akin to OHG *skār* blade and whose second element is akin to OHG *bergan* to shelter, hide — more at SHEAR, BURY] **1 a :** a usu. leather or metal sheath in which the blade of a sword, dagger, bayonet, or other cutting weapon is enclosed when not in use **b :** a sheath for carrying a hand weapon (as a carbine) or a tool (as a saw) for ready use ⟨methods of buckling a ~ to a saddle —William Curtis⟩ ⟨angler's pliers in leather ~ —*advt*⟩ — compare HOLSTER **2** [prob. fr. MLG *schalbort* thin board, fr. *schale* shell + *bort* board; akin to E ¹*scale* and to E *board*] **:** SCALEBOARD

²scabbard \ˈ"\ *vt* -ED/-ING/-s **1 :** to put in a scabbard **2** *archaic* **:** to beat with a scabbard as punishment

scabbard fish *n* **:** a cutlass fish esp. of the genus *Lepidopus; usu* **:** an elongated silvery food fish (*L. caudatus*) that is esp. abundant in southern seas

scab·bard·less \-dləs\ *adj* **:** lacking a scabbard

scabbed \ˈskabəd, -bd\ *adj* [ME, fr. ¹*scab* + *-ed*] **1 :** affected with scab ⟨~ potatoes⟩ **2 :** MEAN, PALTRY — **scabbed·ness** *n* -ES

scab·bi·ly \-bəlē\ *adv* **:** in a scabby manner

scab·bi·ness \-bēnəs\ *n* -ES **:** the condition of being scabby

scab·ble \ˈskabəl\ *or* **scap·ple** \-apəl\ *vt* -ED/-ING/-s [ME *scaplen,* fr. MF *escapler* to dress timber] **1 :** to work or shape roughly (as stone before leaving the quarry) **2 :** to dress (as stone) in any way short of fine tooling or rubbing

scabbled rubble *n* [fr. past part. of *scabble*] **:** undressed stone masonry from which only the roughest irregularities have been removed before laying in a wall

scab·bler \-b(ə)lə(r)\ *or* **scap·pler** \-p(ə)lə(r)\ *n* -s [*scabble* or *scapple* + *-er*] **1 :** a quarryman who scabbles stone slabs to make blocks of uniform size and to reduce shipping weight **2 :** a stonecutter who points blocks to approximate dimensions for finishing

scab·bling \-b(ə)liŋ\ *n* -s [fr. gerund of *scabble*] **:** a fragment or chip of stone

scab·by \ˈskabē, ˈskaab-, -bi\ *adj* -ER/-EST [¹*scab* + *-y*] **1 a :** covered with scabs **:** full of scabs **:** consisting of scabs ⟨~ skin⟩ **b :** affected with scab ⟨a ~ animal⟩ ⟨~ potatoes⟩ **2 :** MEAN, SCURRILOUS, CONTEMPTIBLE ⟨a ~ trick⟩ **3 :** marred with scabs **:** SCALY ⟨temple of brick and rubble and ~ plaster —Aldous Huxley⟩ ⟨wrought-iron gates ~ with rust —Gerald Durrell⟩ ⟨a ~ casting⟩ **4 :** marked by a blotched appearance suggestive of scab ⟨landscape ~ with old mine workings —Sylvia T. Warner⟩ **5 :** like a scab in form or appearance ⟨dark land finally began to wear thin . . . leach white . . . and leave wide ~ places —*Survey Graphic*⟩

scabby mouth *n, Austral & NewZeal* **:** SORE MOUTH

sca·ber·u·lous \skəˈberələs\ *adj* [L *scaber* scabrous + E *-ulous* dim. suffix — more at SCABROUS] **:** minutely scabrous

sca·bia \ˈskābēə\ *n* -s [prob. back-formation fr. ¹*scabious* (taken as a pl.)] *dial Eng* **:** SCABIOUS

sca·bi·ci·dal \ˌskabəˈsīdᵊl\ *adj* [*scabies* + *-cidal*] **1 :** destroying the itch mite causing scabies **2 :** of or relating to a scabicide

sca·bi·cide \ˈskabə,sīd\ *or* **sca·bi·et·i·cide** \ˌskābēˈed·ə,sīd\ *n* -s [*scabicide* fr. *scabies* + *-cide; scabieticide* fr. *scabietic* + *-cide*] **:** a drug that destroys the itch mite causing scabies

sca·bies \ˈskābēz\ *n, pl* **scabies** [L, roughness, scurf, mange, itch; akin to L *scabere* to scratch, scrape — more at SHAVE] **:** itch or mange caused by mites esp. when marked by the formation of exudative crusts

sca·bi·et·ic \ˌskābēˈed·ik\ *also* **sca·bet·ic** \skəˈbed·ik\ *adj* [*scabies* + *-etic*] **:** of, relating to, or infected with scabies **:** MANGY

sca·bi·o·sa \ˌskābēˈōsə, ˌskab-\ *n* [NL, fr. ML, scabious] **1** *cap* **:** a large genus of Old World herbs (family Dipsacaceae) having terminal heads of flowers subtended by a leafy involucre and flowers with a 5-cleft often bilabiate corolla and four stamens **2** -s **:** any plant of the genus *Scabiosa*

¹sca·bi·ous \ˈskābēəs\ *n* -ES [ME *scabiose,* fr. ML *scabiosa* (*herba*), fr. L, fem. of *scabiosus* scabious, mangy; fr. its supposed efficacy in the treatment of scabies] **1 :** a plant of the genus *Scabiosa:* as **a :** SWEET SCABIOUS **b :** FIELD SCABIOUS **2 :** any of several fleabanes (genus *Erigeron*): as **a :** HORSEWEED **1 b :** DAISY FLEABANE **3 :** BLUE SCABIOUS

²scabious \ˈ"\ *adj* [L *scabiosus* scurfy, scabby, mangy, fr. *scabies* + *-osus* -ous] **1 :** consisting of scabs **:** SCABBY **2 :** of, relating to, or like scabies ⟨~ eruptions⟩

scab·ish \ˈskabish\ *n* -ES [alter. of ¹*scabious*] **1 :** FIELD SCABIOUS **2 a :** an evening primrose (*Oenothera biennis*) **b :** either of two sundrops (*O. fruticosa* and *O. glauca*)

scabland \ˈ≈,≈\ *n* [¹*scab* + *land*] **1 :** an elevated tract of bare or shallow-soiled rocky land (as the top of a butte or mesa) in the Northwest caused esp. (as on the Columbia lava plateau) by denudation of the soil mantle or prevention of its formation ⟨gray ~ lifting against the sky —H.L.Davis⟩ — see SCABROCK **2 :** a region characterized by scablands traversed or isolated by postglacial dry stream channels ⟨area of approximately 1,500,000 acres of sage and ~ —*Amer. Guide Series: Wash.*⟩ — often used in pl. ⟨the channeled ~s of eastern Washington⟩

scab mite *n* **:** any of several small mites that cause scab; *esp* **:** one of the genus *Psoroptes*

sca·bres·cent \skəˈbresᵊnt\ *adj* [*scabrous* + *-escent*] **:** becoming minutely scabrous

scab·rid \ˈskabrəd\ *adj* [LL *scabridus,* fr. L *scabrēre* to be rough, be scurfy, fr. *scabr-, scaber* rough, scurfy — more at SCABROUS] **:** somewhat rough in texture — **sca·brid·i·ty** \skəˈbridəd·ē\ *n* -ES

scab·rin \ˈskabrən\ *n* -s [NL *scabra* (specific epithet of *Heliopsis scabra*) (fr. L, fem. of *scaber* rough) + E *-in* — more at SCABROUS] **:** an insecticidal material obtained from the roots of an oxeye (*Heliopsis scabra*) that contains an isobutylamide of a mixture of unsaturated fatty acids

scabrock \ˈ≈,≈\ *n* [¹*scab* + *rock*] **1 :** an area or outcropping of scabland ⟨following the tongues of ~ between the cultivated fields —H.L.Davis⟩ ⟨two-acre patch of ~ —W.M.Mason⟩ **2 :** rock forming or scattered over the surface of scabland

scab·rous \ˈskabrəs *sometimes* ˈskāb-\ *adj* [L *scabr-, scaber* rough, scurfy + E *-ous;* akin to L *scabies* roughness, mange, *scabere* to scratch, scrape — more at SHAVE] **1** *obs* **:** HARSH, UNMUSICAL **2 :** DIFFICULT, KNOTTY ⟨a ~ problem⟩ **3 :** rough to the touch **:** having small raised dots, scales, or points **:** SCALY, PRICKLY, SCURFY, SCABBY ⟨a ~ leaf⟩ ⟨cold sand ~ with cockles —J.M.Brinnin⟩ ⟨patches of darker plaster, of ~ paint —Edith C. Rivett⟩ **4 :** unpleasant, repulsive, or reprehensible in some way: as **a :** dealing with or characterized by suggestive, indecent, or scandalous themes **:** RISQUÉ, SALACIOUS ⟨scandal sheets did their best to improve on a sufficiently ~ text —Simeon Strunsky⟩ ⟨burly, arrogant, swashbuckling toper and ~ gossip —Douglas Bush⟩ ⟨belongs to a ~ genre of writing —Georges Duthuit⟩ ⟨witty, malicious, often ~ character studies —Peter Forster⟩ **b :** inclined to or indicative of licentious or corrupt habits **:** of depraved manners ⟨a ~ resort crowd⟩ ⟨soberest note in this ~, boomtown atmosphere —Davenport Steward⟩ **c :** encrusted or blotched with dirt or other foreign matter **:** FROWZY, GRIMY, SQUALID ⟨shell of the house is ~ with lichen and mildew —James Reynolds⟩ **syn** see ROUGH

scab·rous·ly *adv* **:** in a scabrous manner

scab·rous·ness *n* -ES **:** the quality or state of being scabrous

scabs *pl of* SCAB, *pres 3d sing of* SCAB

scabwort \ˈ≈,≈\ *n* [ME, fr. ¹*scab* + *wort*] **:** ELECAMPANE

scac·chite \ˈska,kīt\ *n* -s [It *scacchite,* fr. Arcangelo *Scacchi* †1894 Ital. mineralogist + It *-ite*] **:** a mineral $MnCl_2$ consisting of native manganese chloride found in volcanic regions

¹scad \ˈskad, ˈskaa(ə)d\ *n, pl* **scad** *also* **scads** [origin unknown] **1 :** any of several carangid fishes: as **a :** BIG-EYED SCAD **b :** MACKEREL SCAD **c :** ROUND SCAD **2 :** CATALUFA

²scad \ˈ"\ *n* [origin unknown] *Scot* **:** a faint gleam of color or light

³scad \ˈskad\ *chiefly Scot var of* SCALD

⁴scad *also* **skad** \ˈskad\ *n* -s [prob. alter. of E dial. *scald,* fr. ²*scald*] **1 a :** a large number or quantity ⟨hooked a ~ of little fish —*Field & Stream*⟩ ⟨costs a ~ of money —Theodore Morrison⟩ **b scads** *pl* **:** a great abundance ⟨~s of money⟩ ⟨~s of guests⟩ ⟨~s of time⟩ ⟨~s of opportunities⟩ **2** *archaic* **:** DOLLAR, COIN — usu. used in pl. ⟨staggerin' along, jinglin' the ~s they had won —Bret Harte⟩

scad·dle *also* **skad·dle** \ˈskadᵊl\ *adj* [alter. of earlier *scathel* harmful, dangerous, of Scand origin; akin to OHG *skadal, skatal* harmful, Goth *skathuls,* OE *sceathian* to injure — more at SCATHE] **1** *dial Eng* **:** FIERCE, WILD **2** *dial Eng, of an animal* **:** badly behaved **:** SKITTISH

scae·na \ˈsēnə\ *n, pl* **scae·nae** \-ē,nē\ [L — more at SCENE] **:** the stage of a Roman theater — compare CAVEA

scae·vo·la \ˈsēvələ\ *n* [NL, after C. Mucius *Scaevola* 6th cent. B.C. Roman hero] **1** *cap* **:** a genus of shrubs (family Goodeniaceae) having flowers with the corolla tube split, anthers free, and an indehiscent succulent drupaceous fruit **2** -s **:** any plant of the genus *Scaevola*

scaf·fie \ˈskafi\ *n* -s [prob. by alter.] *Scot* **:** SCAVENGER

¹scaf·fold \ˈskafəld *also* -a,fōld\ *n* -s [ME, fr. ONF *escafaut,* modif. (perh. influenced by assumed ONF *escache* stilt) of (assumed) VL *catafalicum* — more at SKATE, CATAFALQUE] **1 a** (1) **:** a usu. temporary or movable platform (as a plank) supported by a wood or metal framework, jacks, poles, or brackets or suspended (as by ropes and tackle) and used by workmen (as bricklayers, painters, or miners) to stand or sit on and to support tools and material when working at considerable heights above floor or ground (2) **:** such a platform together with the structure that supports it — compare TRESTLE **b** (1) **:** a platform on which a criminal stands for execution esp. by hanging or beheading (2) **:** the penalty of death by execution esp. by hanging or beheading; *broadly* **:** CAPITAL PUNISHMENT — used with *the* ⟨condemned to the ~⟩ **c** *archaic* **:** a usu. temporary stand on which a public spectacle (as a dramatic performance) is staged **d** *obs* **:** a stand for spectators at a public spectacle (as a tournament or dramatic performance) **e** *chiefly New Eng* **:** a barn loft for storing hay or grain **:** HAYLOFT **1 :** any platform at a considerable height above ground or floor level ⟨~s were used by some American Indians to dispose of the dead⟩ ⟨on the ~ the fishermen kept dip nets for the smaller trout —Julian Dana⟩ **g :** a supporting framework ⟨~ of a ski slide⟩ ⟨plantation bell hanging in a ~ separate and apart from the church —*Amer. Guide Series: La.*⟩ **2 :** an accumulation of adherent partly fused material forming an obstruction above the tuyeres in a blast furnace **3 :** FRAMEWORK 4; *also* **:** SCAFFOLD BRANCH

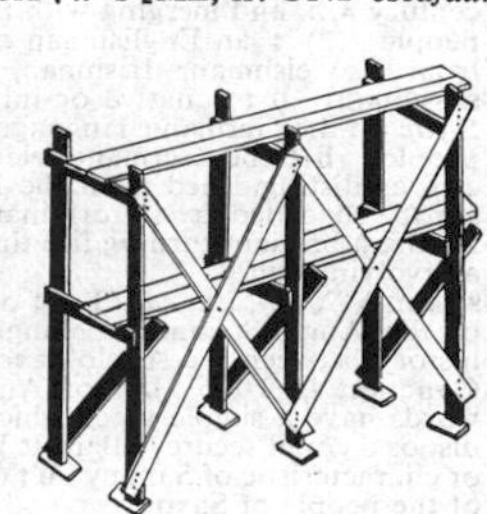

scaffold 1a(2)

²scaffold \ˈ"\ *vb* -ED/-ING/-s *vt* **1 a :** to place on or support by means of a scaffold **b :** to suspend (fresh-cut tobacco plants) upon a portable rack to wilt before hanging in the curing barn **2 a :** to furnish with a scaffold or scaffolding **:** erect scaffolding in front of or against ⟨the opera's ~*ed* shell —Leigh White⟩ **b :** to support (as an argument) by scaffolding ⟨book could well be ~*ed* more strongly with explanation and comment —Roland Mathias⟩ ~ *vi* **:** to form a scaffold esp. in smelting

scaf·fold·age \-dij\ *n* -s [¹*scaffold* + *-age*] **:** SCAFFOLD, SCAFFOLDING

scaffold branch *or* **scaffold limb** *n* [¹*scaffold*] **:** one of the main branches forming the framework of a tree or shrub

scaf·fold·er \-də(r)\ *n* -s [²*scaffold* + *-er*] **:** one who erects scaffolding

scaf·fold·ing \-diŋ, -dēŋ\ *n* -s [ME, fr. ¹*scaffold* + *-ing*] **1 a :** a system of scaffolds ⟨go up ladders and walk about ~s —J.D.Beresford⟩ ⟨erected the steel ~ to support the roof forms —*Civil Engineering*⟩ **b :** materials for scaffolds **2** [fr. gerund of ²*scaffold*] **a :** the construction of scaffolds **b** (1) **:** the formation of a scaffold in the smelting of ores (2) **:** SCAFFOLD 2 **3 a :** a framework serving as a supporting structure, base, or outline for something (as a literary work or a part of an organism) ⟨use of the epic as a ~ for his stories —Robert Halsband⟩ ⟨comprehending the naked ~ of an idea rather than its architectural fulfillment —H.V.Gregory⟩ ⟨cartilaginous skeleton serves as a temporary ~ for a skeleton of much harder material —Norbert Wiener⟩ **b :** evidence or explanatory matter tending to confirm, validate, or bolster something (as an argument) ⟨book . . . a little overequipped with the ~ of research —H.J.Laski⟩

scagl·io·la \skalˈyōlə\ *n* -s [It, lit., little chip, dim. of *scaglia* scale, chip, of Gmc origin; akin to Goth *skalja* tile — more at SHELL] **:** an imitation of ornamental marble consisting of a base of finely ground gypsum mixed with glue, variegated on its surface while soft (as with marble, spar, or granite dust) and subsequently polished, and used for floors, columns, and other ornamental interior work

scaith \ˈskāth\ *dial Brit var of* SCATHE

¹sca·la \ˈskālə\ *n, pl* **sca·lae** \-ā,lē\ [NL, fr. LL, ladder, staircase — more at SCALE] **:** any of the three spiral canals of the cochlea

²scala \ˈ"\ [NL, fr. LL, ladder, staircase; fr. the resemblance of the shell to a spiral staircase] *syn of* EPITONIUM

³scala \ˈ"\ *n* -s [*Scala*] **:** a mollusk of the genus *Epitonium* **:** WENTLETRAP

scal·able \ˈskāləbəl\ *adj* [⁷*scale* + *-able*] **:** capable of being scaled — **scal·able·ness** *n* -ES — **scal·ably** \-blē\ *adv*

sca·lade \skəˈlād\ *or* **sca·la·do** \-ā(,)dō\ *n* -s [obs. It *scalada,* fr. *scalare* to scale (fr. *scala* ladder, staircase, fr. LL) + *-ada* -ade — more at SCALE] *archaic* **:** ESCALADE

scal·age \ˈskālij, -lēj\ *n* -s [⁷*scale* + *-age*] **1 :** an allowance or percentage by which something (as listed weights, bulks, or prices of goods) is scaled down to compensate for loss (as by shrinkage or abrasion) **2 :** the act of scaling in weight, quantity, or dimensions **3 :** the amount that logs or timber scale

scala me·dia \-ˈmēdēə\ *n, pl* **scalae medi·ae** \-dē,ē\ [NL, lit., middle scala] **:** the membranous spiral canal containing the essential organ of hearing — compare COCHLEA

¹sca·lar \ˈskālə(r)\ *adj* [L *scalaris* of a ladder or staircase, fr. *scalae* stairs, ladder — more at SCALE] **1 :** arranged like a ladder **:** having an uninterrupted series of steps **:** GRADUATED, SCALARIFORM ⟨~ chain of authority in business organization⟩ ⟨~ cells⟩ **2** [prob. fr. ⁶*scale* + *-ar*] **:** describable by a number that can be represented by a point on a scale ⟨a ~ quantity⟩

²scalar \ˈ"\ *n* -s **1 a :** an undirected quantity in vector analysis and quaternions **:** a quantity fully described by a number — distinguished from *vector* **b :** a scalar number **2 :** a quantity (as mass or time) that has magnitude but does not involve any concept of direction — compare VECTOR 1b

sca·la·re \skəˈla(a)rē, -lärā\ *n* -s [NL, specific epithet of *Pterophyllum scalare,* fr. L, neut. of *scalaris* of a ladder; fr. the barred pattern on its body] **:** a popular cichlid tropical aquarium fish (*Pterophyllum scalare*) of So. American origin laterally compressed with large pointed fins and strikingly barred with black and silver; *also* **:** a very similar but smaller fish (*P. eimekei*)

sca·lar·ia \skəˈla(a)rēə\ [NL, fr. L *scalaris* of a ladder or staircase + NL *-ia;* fr. the resemblance of the shell to a spiral staircase] *syn of* EPITONIUM

sca·lar·i·an \-ēən\ *adj* [NL *Scalaria* + E *-an*] **:** SCALARIFORM 2

sca·lar·i·form \skəˈla(a)rə,fȯrm\ *adj* [NL *scalariformis,* fr. L *scalaris* of a ladder + *-formis* -form] **1 :** resembling a ladder **:** having transverse bars or markings like the rounds of a ladder ⟨~ cells in plants⟩ **2 :** of or relating to the genus *Epitonium* or related forms — **sca·lar·i·form·ly** \ˌ≈ˈ≈≈,≈lē\ *adv*

scalariform conjugation *n* **:** sexual union between cells in adjacent filaments of an alga — compare LATERAL CONJUGATION

scalariform-pitted tracheid \≈ˈ≈≈,≈,≈≈-\ *n* **:** a tracheid having a ladderlike arrangement of pits

scal·a·ri·idae \ˌskaləˈrīə,dē\ [NL, fr. *Scalaria,* type genus + *-idae*] *syn of* EPITONIIDAE

scalar product *n* **:** the product of two vectors that is obtained by multiplying the product of the magnitudes of the vectors by the cosine of the angle between them — called also *inner product;* compare DOT PRODUCT

sca·la·tion \skāˈlāshən\ *n* -s [⁵*scale* + *-ation*] **:** LEPIDOSIS 2

scala tym·pa·ni \-ˈtimpə,nī, -,nē\ *n, pl* **scalae tym·pa·no·rum** \-,timpəˈnōrəm, -ˈnȯrəm\ [NL, lit., scala of the tympanum] **:** the lymph-filled spiral canal below the scala media in the cochlea of the ear communicating at its upper end with the scala vestibuli and abutting at its lower end upon the secondary tympanic membrane that separates the fenestra cochleae from the middle ear

scala ves·tib·u·li \-veˈstibyə,lī, -,lē\ *n, pl* **scalae ves·tib·u·lo·rum** \-ve,stibyəˈlōrəm, -ˈlȯrəm\ [NL, lit., scala of the vestibule] **:** the lymph-filled spiral canal above the scala media in the cochlea of the ear connecting with the fenestra vestibuli and receiving vibrations from the stapes

scal·a·wag *or* **scal·ly·wag** *also* **scal·la·wag** *or* **skal·a·wag** \ˈskalə,wag, -lē,w-, -waa(ə)g, -waig\ *n* -s [origin unknown] **1 :** RASCAL, ¹SCAMP, REPROBATE ⟨hand a quarter to a bewhiskered old ~ —James Thurber⟩ ⟨something good to say about the worst *scallywag* —John Buchan⟩ **2 :** an animal of little value esp. because of poor feeding, smallness, or age **3 :** a white Southerner who supported reconstruction policies after the Civil War

scal·a·wag·gery \-gərē\ *n* -ES [*scalawag* + *-ery*] **:** the conduct or doings of a scalawag

¹scald \ˈskȯld\ *vb* -ED/-ING/-s [ME *scalden* to burn with hot liquid, fr. ONF *escalder,* fr. LL *excaldare* to wash in warm water, fr. L *ex-* + *calida, calda* warm water, fr. fem. of *calidus, caldus* warm — more at CALDRON] *vt* **1 :** to burn with hot liquid or steam **:** pain or injure by contact with any hot fluid or irritating chemicals **2 a :** to subject to the action of boiling water or steam (as for loosening hair or feathers on a slaughtered animal, for loosening skin of fruits or vegetables, or for stopping enzyme action or bacterial growth) ⟨~ a tomato before peeling it⟩ ⟨~ dishes⟩ — compare BLANCH, PARBOIL **b :** to immerse in a boiling liquid or chemical **c :** to bring (a liquid) to a temperature just below the boiling point ⟨~ milk⟩ **d :** to cook (a slurry of grain meal and water) as the first step in the mashing process by pouring boiling water over the meal or by using live steam to heat the mixture usu. in a pressure cooker **3 :** to affect as painfully as by the application of boiling water ⟨tears that ~ the cheek⟩ **4 :** SCORCH ⟨sun-*scalded* ground —Myrtle R. White⟩ **5** *chiefly Irish* **:** WORRY, TORMENT ⟨it ~s my heart⟩ ~ *vi* **1 :** to produce the effects of boiling water or scorching heat **:** inflict agonizing pain ⟨a desert of dry ~*ing* sand —Daniel Defoe⟩ **2 a :** to suffer the effects of boiling water or scorching heat **b :** to be affected by scald ⟨the apples ~*ed* severely in storage⟩

²scald \ˈ"\ *n* -s **1 :** an injury to the skin or flesh caused by some hot liquid, by steam, or by irritating chemicals ⟨dressed the ~ with carron oil —A.J.Cronin⟩ **2 a :** a process of subjection (as of food or dishes) to scalding **b :** the act of scalding ⟨shorter ~s apparently did not completely inactivate the enzymes —*Biol. Abstracts*⟩ **3** *dial chiefly Eng* **:** the hot bath or solution in which something is or may be scalded **4** *dial chiefly Eng* **:** a piece of land (as part of a larger field) that is prone to scorching and too rapid drying **5 :** any of several plant diseases marked esp. by discoloration suggesting injury by heat: as **a :** CRANBERRY SCALD **b :** a burning and browning of plant tissues resulting from high temperatures or from the combined actions of high temperature and intense light **c :** a browning of bean plants caused by excess of manganese uptake **d :** a storage discoloration of apples or pears due to the volatile products given off by the ripening tissues that is now almost wholly controlled by the use of oiled wrappings which absorb these substances **6 :** a nonspecific inflammation of the feet of sheep often the forerunner of foot rot — **get a good scald on** *dial* **:** to have good success with

³scald \"\ *adj* [*scald* + *-ed*] **1** *archaic* **:** SCABBY, SCURFY ⟨powder or meal was first used . . . to conceal their ~ heads —Tobias Smollett⟩ **2** *archaic* **:** SCURVY, SHABBY, CONTEMPTIBLE ⟨~ rogues⟩

⁴scald *n* -s [alter. (influenced by ³*scald*) of *scall*] **:** scurf on the head **:** a scabby spot or condition caused by disease

⁵scald \ˈskȧd\ *chiefly Scot var of* SCOLD

⁶scald *var of* SKALD

⁷scald \ˈskȯld\ *adj* [by shortening] **:** SCALDED ⟨like coffee covered with ~ cream —Charles Kingsley⟩

scald crow *n* [prob. fr. ³*scald*] *Irish* **:** HOODED CROW

¹scalded *adj* [fr. past part. of ¹*scald*] **1 a :** cooked, burned, or treated with boiling liquid ⟨~ meal⟩ **b :** heated to just below the boiling point ⟨~ milk⟩ **2** *chiefly Austral* **:** composed of hard bare or eroded ground ⟨~ plains⟩

²scalded *adj* [⁴*scald* + *-ed*] **:** affected with scald ⟨~ fruit⟩ ⟨a sheep's ~ foot⟩

¹scald·er \ˈskȯldə(r)\ *n* -s [¹*scald* + *-er*] **:** one that scalds: as **a :** a cannery worker who sterilizes raw fruit by scalding it with lye and water **b :** a machine used for scalding

²scald·er \ˈskȧdə(r)\ *vt* -ED/-ING/-s [prob. freq. of ¹*scald*] *dial Eng* **:** SCALD

³scald·er \ˈskȯldə(r)\ *n* -s [NL, fr. ON *skāld* skald] *archaic* **:** SKALD

scaldfish \ˈ=,=\ *n* [prob. fr. ³*scald*] **:** ²MEGRIM a

scald head *n* [³*scald*] *archaic* **:** any of several diseases of the scalp characterized by falling out of the hair and by pustules the dried discharge of which forms scales

scaldic *var of* SKALDIC

¹scald·ing \ˈskȯldiŋ, -dēŋ\ *n* -s [ME, fr. gerund of *scalden* to scald] **1 :** the act or process of burning or treating with steam or hot liquid (as for cooking, cleansing, bathing, or rinsing) **2 scaldings** *pl, archaic* **:** boiling-hot liquid **3 :** ²SCALD 5 **4 :** a dark discoloration of tobacco leaves resulting from a too rapid increase in temperature during the early stages of curing

²scalding \"\ *adj* [fr. pres. part. of ¹*scald*] **1 :** causing the sensation of scalding or burning ⟨coffee felt ~ all the way down —Wirt Williams⟩ ⟨the ~ pie in my mouth —J.W.Ellison b.1929⟩ **2 :** BOILING ⟨sprayed with ~ water to extract the tanning properties —*Amer. Guide Series: Pa.*⟩ **3 :** SCORCHING, ARDENT ⟨succumb to a dusky oasis from the ~ sun —Claudia Cassidy⟩ **4 :** BITING, STINGING, SCATHING ⟨series of ~ articles —Christopher Isherwood⟩ ⟨a very ~ letter —Virginia D. Dawson & Betty D. Wilson⟩ ⟨a ~ comment on human avarice —*Time*⟩

scalds *pres 3d sing of* SCALD, *pl of* SCALD

¹scale \ˈskāl, *esp before pause or consonant* -āəl\ *n* -s [ME *scale, scole,* fr. ON *skāl* bowl, scale of a balance; akin to OHG *scāla* cup, bowl, *scala* husk, shell — more at SHELL] **1** *dial* **:** a drinking vessel **:** CUP, BOWL ⟨offered him a ~ of beer —Peter Abrahams⟩ **2 a :** either pan or tray of a balance **b :** BALANCE 1a(1)— usu. used in pl. sometimes with *pair* ⟨weighed on the only pair of ~s in the hamlet —Flora Thompson⟩ and sometimes sing. in constr. ⟨weighing something on a big brass ~s —Helen Eustis⟩ **c :** an instrument or machine for weighing ⟨bathroom ~⟩ ⟨counter ~⟩ ⟨livestock ~⟩ — often used in pl. but sometimes sing. in constr.; see COMPUTING SCALE, CYLINDER SCALE, PLATFORM SCALE, SPRING SCALE **3 a :** the position where a grave decision (as for life or death) is called for or a turning point is imminent **:** BALANCE — often used in pl. ⟨you never forget that your life, as well as his, is in the ~s —E.L.Beach⟩ **b :** the process or situation in which something (as a force or set of values) is opposed to or contrasted with other like things or an established or assumed standard for such things ⟨weight of his authority was thrown into the ~ against the teachings —Harvey Graham⟩ — usu. used in pl. ⟨weighed his own life and the life of his neighbors in the ~s —V.L.Parrington⟩ ⟨rig the ~s heavily in favor of the values you see the need of preserving —G.O.Williams⟩ **4 :** WEIGHT, SIZE — used esp. of livestock ⟨new breed is cherry red, possesses lots of ~ —L.M.Winters⟩

counter scale

²scale \"\ *vb* -ED/-ING/-s *vt* **1 a :** to weigh in scales **b** *obs* **:** MEASURE, COMPARE ⟨*scaling* his present bearing with his past —Shak.⟩ **2 :** to make or to lay out so as to be of exact weight, quantity, or dimensions; *specif* **:** to divide into exact parts by weight ⟨~ dough into loaves⟩ **~** *vi* **:** to have a specified weight on scales ⟨at 19 he *scaled* 12 stone —G.E.Odd⟩ ⟨a dog *scaling* 50 pounds⟩ — often used with *in* ⟨man *scaling* in at over 200 pounds⟩

³scale \"\ *n* -s [ME, fr. ON *skāli*; akin to ON *sky̅* cloud — more at SKY] *dial chiefly Eng* **:** HUT

⁴scale \"\ *vb* -ED/-ING/-s [ME *skailen, scalen,* prob. of Scand origin; akin to ON *skilja* to separate, divide — more at SKILL] *vt* **1** *chiefly Scot* **:** DISPERSE, SCATTER ⟨~ a crowd⟩ **2** *chiefly Scot* **:** to spread esp. wastefully **3** *chiefly Scot* **:** SPILL ⟨~ her tea⟩ **~** *vi, chiefly Scot* **:** DISPERSE, SCATTER

⁵scale \"\ *n* -s [ME *scale, skale,* fr. MF *escale,* of Gmc origin; akin to OE *scealu* husk, shell, scale of a balance — more at SHELL] **1 a :** a small, more or less flattened, rigid, and definitely circumscribed plate forming part of the external body covering of an animal, in fishes consisting of dermal bony tissue, in recent forms being commonly in imbricated rows with their posterior edges partly overlapping, and in reptiles and on the legs of birds being horny, circumscribed, and slightly differentiated areas of the epidermis — see FISH illustration **b :** any of various usu. flattened and more or less chitinized outgrowths of the body wall of an insect (as those clothing the wings of most moths and butterflies) **c :** the scaly covering of a scaled animal **:** a coating of scales **d :** a plate of similar structure making up wool fiber and distinguishing it from hair **2 scales** *pl* **:** impediments to seeing rightly ⟨I hope in time the ~s will be taken off the eyes of the landlord —William Ellis⟩ **3 :** a small thin dry lamina shed (as in many skin diseases) from the skin **4 :** a thin outer lamina or layer removable as a peel or in flakes or chips: as **a** (1) **:** a black scaly coating of oxide (as magnetic oxide) forming on the surface of iron when heated for processing (as by hammering or rolling) — called also *iron scale, mill scale;* see HAMMER SCALE (2) **:** a similar coating forming on other metals **b :** a film of tartar encrusting the teeth **c :** a hard incrustation that is deposited esp. on the inside of a vessel (as a boiler) in which water is heated, that in the case of hard water commonly contains calcium sulfate as the principal component, and that is objectionable because it is a nonconductor of heat **5 a :** one of the modified leaves serving in most seed plants to protect a bud before expansion — see BUD SCALE **b :** a thin, membranous, chaffy, or woody bract ⟨the ~ of an alder catkin⟩ ⟨the cone ~ of a pine⟩ **c :** RAMENTUM 2a **d :** the small appendage at the base of the petal in some plants of the family Caryophyllaceae **e :** one of the disklike trichomes making up the characteristic silvery or scurfy pubescence of the foliage in some plants (as Russian olive) **6 a :** one of the small overlapping usu. metal pieces forming the outer surface of scale armor ⟨representations of Byzantine warriors nearly always show corselets of ~s —J.G.Mann⟩ **b :** SCALE ARMOR **7 :** either of the pieces fastened one on each side of the tang of a cutting instrument (as a knife) to form the outside of the handle **8 a** *or* **scale insect** *also* **scale louse** *or* **scale bug :** any of numerous small very prolific insects constituting Coccidae and related families of the suborder Homoptera, having young that suck the juices of plants, adult males that lack mouthparts and do not feed and have a single pair of wings, and adult females that are usu. permanently attached to the host plant, structurally degenerate with most of the external differentiation lost, similar to a scale on the surface of the host, and often obscured by a waxy or powdery secretion that protects the female and her eggs, and including many extremely destructive pests of economic plants as well as a few that yield valuable products — compare COCHINEAL, LAC **b :** infestation with or disease caused by scale insects ⟨our roses are full of ~ this year⟩ ⟨a promising citrus plantation had been destroyed by ~⟩ **9 :** SCALE WAX

⁶scale \"\ *vb* -ED/-ING/-s [ME *scalen,* fr. ⁵*scale*] *vt* **1 a :** to remove the scales from (as by scraping) ⟨~ a fish⟩ **b :** to remove scale from ⟨~ a boiler⟩ **c :** to take off the surface of **:** PEEL, HUSK ⟨~ chestnuts⟩ **d :** to loosen and remove fragments from (as a rock surface) ⟨~ a rock wall after blasting⟩ **2 :** to take off in thin layers or scales **:** remove as if consisting of a scale **:** peel off esp. in pieces ⟨~ tartar from the teeth⟩ — often used with *off* ⟨~ off the bark of a tree⟩ ⟨flames that *scaled* off the soft stone carvings of the interior —F.L.Paxson⟩ **3** *obs* **:** to clean (as the inside of a cannon) by the explosion of a small quantity of powder **4 :** to form scale on **:** cover with scale ⟨water ~s a boiler⟩ **5 :** to throw (as a thin flat stone) so that the edge cuts the air or so that it skips (as on a water surface) **:** SKIM, SAIL ⟨took off his hat, *scaled* it across the room —Burt Arthur⟩ ⟨*scaled* the letter . . . across the broad-topped walnut desk —Don Tracy⟩ ⟨*scaled* the discus 194 feet 6 inches —*N.Y.Times*⟩ **~** *vi* **1 :** to separate and come off in thin layers or laminae **:** FLAKE ⟨some sandstone ~s by exposure⟩ — often used with *off* ⟨bark that ~s off readily⟩ **2 :** to shed scales or fragmentary surface matter **:** EXFOLIATE, SPALL ⟨*scaling* skin⟩ ⟨a *scaling* wall of rock⟩ **3 :** to become encrusted with a hard deposit — used esp. of vessels or pipes containing water or chemical solutions

⁷scale \"\ *n* -s [ME, ladder, staircase, line marked by graduations, fr. LL *scala* ladder, staircase, fr. L *scalae* (pl.) stairs, rungs of a ladder, ladder; akin to L *scandere* to climb — more at SCAN] **1 a** (1) **:** an indication of the relationship between the distances on a map, chart, or plan and the corresponding actual distances usu. in the form of a direct statement (as 1 inch to 1 mile), a representative fraction (as 1/250,000 or 1:250,000), a graphic measure (as a bar or line), or a line subdivided at selected intervals (2) **:** a series of spaces marked off by lines or dots and used for measuring distances, amounts, or quantities **b :** a mathematical instrument consisting of a strip (as of wood, plastic, or metal) with one or more sets of spaces graduated and numbered on its surface and used esp. for measuring or laying off distances and dimensions (as in drawing or plotting) — see ARCHITECTS' SCALE, ENGINEER'S SCALE; compare RULE **c :** a basis for a numeral system ⟨the decimal ~⟩ ⟨the binary ~⟩ **d :** one of the measures on a typewriter by which paper is aligned and centered, margin and tabulator stops set, or characters centered **2 a** *obs* **:** LADDER **b** *obs* **:** a flight of stairs **:** STAIRCASE **c** *archaic* **:** a means of ascending or descending ⟨in th' ascending ~ of heav'n the stars that usher evening rose —John Milton⟩ **3 a :** a graduated series of musical tones ascending or descending in order of pitch according to a specified scheme of their intervals and varying in pitch arrangement and size of intervals according to the number of tones to the octave ⟨descending ~⟩ ⟨minor ~⟩ ⟨major ~⟩ **b :** a scale on a given keynote ⟨the ~ of G⟩ ⟨played the ~ of D minor⟩ **c :** the compass of a voice or instrument **d :** the width of an organ pipe in proportion to its length that may be increased to give full and sonorous tones and decreased to give thin edgy tones **4 :** a graduated or ordered series of degrees, stages, or classes **:** a scheme of comparative rank or order (as of forms of life) ⟨the ~ of being⟩ ⟨a ~ of taxation⟩ ⟨color ~⟩; **a :** a set of graduated wage rates or a wage consistent with such rates ⟨workmen were paid the union ~⟩ **b :** the full range of tones of a photographic material expressed in terms of the brightnesses recorded, the exposure given, or the resultant range of densities **c :** a table for calculating cost based on size ⟨engravers' ~⟩ ⟨electrotypers' ~⟩ **5 a :** relative dimensions without difference in proportion of parts **:** size or degree of the parts or components in any complex thing compared with other like things; *esp* **:** the relative proportion of the linear dimensions of parts (as of a drawing or model) to the dimensions of the corresponding parts of the object that is represented ⟨a map on a ~ of an inch to a mile⟩ **b :** a distinctive relative size, extent, or degree ⟨despite high-*scale* national employment —*Current History*⟩ — often used with *on* ⟨much of the artist's sculpture is on a large ~ —*Current Biog.*⟩ ⟨printing color reproductions on a commercial ~ —*Encyc. Americana*⟩ ⟨gambling on a grand ~⟩ **6 :** a standard for reference in estimating or judging ⟨a ~ to measure degrees of crime⟩ **7 a :** relative size of esp. architectural parts as compared with the whole or with the human figure ⟨importance of ~ and detailing to the layout as a whole —*Architectural Rev.*⟩ ⟨a sense of ~ is produced by introducing into the design some unit which acts as a visual measuring rod —T.F.Hamlin⟩ ⟨harmony of ~ . . . in a room —Mildred J. O'Brien⟩ **b :** proper or intended size, proportion, and relationship with reference to other elements and to the whole or to the setting ⟨the one essential to remember in carrying out the necessary periodic replanting in the park is ~ —S.Lang⟩ ⟨in our time, ~ has survived splendor —Alfred Frankfurter⟩ **8 :** a series of tests graded from easy to difficult or of performances graded from bad to good to be used in rating individual intellectual or emotional behavior or attitudes ⟨rating ~⟩ ⟨intelligence ~⟩ ⟨achievement ~⟩ — **in scale :** in conformity to its due proportion in a fixed scale ⟨a building that is *in scale* with its surroundings⟩ — **out of scale :** not in conformity to its due proportion in a fixed scale — **to scale** *adv* **:** according to the proportions of an established scale of measurement ⟨floor plans drawn *to scale*⟩

⁸scale \"\ *vb* -ED/-ING/-s [ME *scalen,* fr. *scale,* n., ladder] *vt* **1 a :** to attack with or take by means of scaling ladders ⟨~ a castle wall⟩ ⟨~ a walled town⟩ **b :** to climb up or reach by means of a ladder ⟨*scaling* the girl's bedchamber —E.A.Poe⟩ ⟨firemen *scaled* the building⟩ **c :** to ascend or go over by climbing or as if by climbing **:** clamber up ⟨*scaling* the mighty barrier of the Alps —G.F.Maclear⟩ ⟨climbers *scaled* the mountain face⟩ ⟨wildcats might ~ the fence —Zane Grey⟩ **d :** to press one's way up into or over typically with or as if with strong flight ⟨falcon *scaling* the sky⟩ **e :** to reach the highest point of or surmount typically with strong effort ⟨~ the moral and esthetic heights in the novel —Lionel Trilling⟩ **2 :** to treat according to a scale with gradation or in proportion: **a :** to arrange in a graduated series ⟨~ a test⟩ **b :** to measure by or as if by a scale: as (1) **:** to measure (logs) to ascertain the number of board feet (2) **:** to estimate the yield of (standing timber) in board feet **c :** to pattern, make, regulate, set, or estimate according to some proportion, rate, standard, or control **:** increase or reduce according to a fixed ratio ⟨a production schedule *scaled* to actual need⟩ ⟨~ the prices of tickets for a theatrical performance⟩ — often used with *down* or *up* ⟨~ up imports⟩ ⟨~ down the output of a mine⟩ **d :** to crop, reduce, or enlarge (as a pictorial illustration) to fit a given space or layout; *also* **:** to determine the dimensions of (as an illustration) that will result from such scaling **~** *vi* **1 :** to climb by or as if by a ladder ⟨firemen given the command to ~⟩ **2 :** to rise in a graduated series ⟨windows *scaling* beside a stairway⟩ **3 a :** MEASURE ⟨this tree . . . probably ~s no more than about 50 feet —Alexander Tewnion⟩ **b** *of a log, tree, or stand of timber* **:** to yield an estimated number of board feet ⟨growth ~s from forty to sixty thousand board feet an acre —*Nature Mag.*⟩ **4 :** to sing or play a musical scale **:** rise high in pitch ⟨high with the last line *scaled* her voice —Alfred Tennyson⟩ **syn** see ASCEND

⁹scale \"\ *n* -s [⁸*scale*] **1** *obs* **:** ESCALADE **2 :** an estimate of the amount of sound lumber in logs or standing timber

¹⁰scale \"\ *adj* [⁷*scale*] **:** drawn or constructed to scale ⟨~ map⟩ ⟨~ drawing⟩ ⟨~ model of an automobile⟩

¹¹scale *n* -s [F or It; F *escale,* fr. It *scala,* ladder, landing place, fr. LL, ladder, staircase — more at ⁷SCALE] *obs* **:** a landing place **:** PORT

scale armor *n* [⁵*scale*] **:** armor made of small metallic scales overlapping and fastened upon leather or cloth

scaleback \ˈ=,=\ *n* [⁵*scale* + *back*] **:** SCALE WORM

scale bark *n* **1 :** SHAGBARK HICKORY **2 :** RHYTIDOME

scaleboard \ˈ=,=\ *n* [⁵*scale* + *board*] **1** *archaic* **:** thin strips of sheet iron used by printers as leads; *also* **:** thin strips of material (as wood or paperboard) placed in an imposed form before locking up **2 a :** thin wooden boards once used for book covers **b :** a thin leaf of wood used for veneering

scale bug *n* [⁵*scale*] **:** ⁵SCALE 8a

scale carp *n* **:** a normally scaled variety of the common carp — compare LEATHER CARP, MIRROR CARP

scale caterpillar *n* **:** a lepidopterous larva that feeds on scale insects; *esp* **:** the larva of a small moth (*Laetilia coccidivora*) of the family Pyralididae

Sca·le·cide \ˈskāləˌsīd\ *trademark* — used for an agent that destroys scale insects

¹scaled \ˈskāld, *esp before pause or consonant* -āəld\ *adj* [ME, fr. ⁵*scale* + *-ed*] **1 a :** covered with scales or a scalelike structure ⟨~ fish⟩ ⟨~ reptile⟩ ⟨~ moth⟩ or with scalelike parts that overlap in the manner of roof tiles ⟨the ~ bud of a beech tree⟩ **b :** covered with tiles overlapping like scales **c :** having a surface pattern or texture resembling scales ⟨~ jewelry⟩ **2 :** having feathers that in appearance or arrangement somewhat resemble scales — see SCALED DOVE, SCALED QUAIL

²scaled \"\ *adj* [fr. past part. of ⁶*scale*] **:** lacking scales **:** having had the scales removed ⟨~ herring⟩

³scaled \"\ *adj* [⁷*scale* + *-ed*] **:** furnished with or adjusted to a scale ⟨traveled . . . over ~ highways —*From Australia*⟩ ⟨chose delicately ~ antiques —*This Week Mag.*⟩

scaled dove *or* **scale dove** *n* [¹*scaled*] **:** any of several doves (genus *Scardafella*) of tropical America that are pale gray below and usu. light grayish brown above with dark-margined feathers — compare INCA DOVE

¹scale–down \ˈ=,=\ *n* -s [⁸*scale* + *down*] **:** a reduction according to a fixed ratio ⟨a *scale-down* of debts⟩

²scale–down \"\ *adj* **:** characterized by a reduction according to a fixed ratio ⟨*scale-down* investment buying⟩

scaled quail *or* **scaled partridge** *n* [¹*scaled*] **:** a crested partridge (*Callipepla squamata*) of the southwestern U.S. and northern Mexico that is largely grayish brown above with pale bluish gray black-tipped breast feathers — called also *blue quail*

scale duck *n* [⁵*scale*] **1** *dial Brit* **:** SHELDRAKE **2** *dial Brit* **:** MERGANSER

scale effect *n* [⁷*scale*] **:** the correction necessary to apply to measurements made on a model in a wind tunnel in order to deduce corresponding values for the full-sized object

scale fern *n* [⁵*scale*] **:** a small European fern (*Ceterach officinarum*) with chaffy coriaceous fronds

scale fly *n* **:** the winged male of a scale

scale hopper *n* [¹*scale*] **:** a bin mounted on a scale so that its contents can be weighed

scale house *n* **:** a shelter for the beam of an outdoor scale

scale insect *or* **scale louse** *n* [⁵*scale*] **:** ⁵SCALE 8a

scale leaf *n* **:** a scalelike structure that is morphologically a leaf often reduced in size (as a bud scale, various bracts, or the leaves of various conifers)

scale·less \ˈskā(ə)lləs\ *adj* [partly fr. ⁷*scale* + *-less;* partly fr. ⁵*scale* + *-less*] **:** lacking a scale **:** destitute of scales

scalelike \ˈ=,=\ *adj* [⁵*scale* + *like*] **:** resembling a scale ⟨~ design⟩; *specif* **:** reduced to a minute appressed element resembling a scale ⟨~ leaves⟩

scale·man \ˈ=mən\ *n, pl* **scalemen** [¹*scale* + *man*] **1 :** one who repairs scales **2 :** one whose work is weighing goods or ingredients sometimes with automatic scales **3** [⁶*scale* + *man*] **:** a worker who removes scale from newly-processed iron and steel equipment

scale moss *n* **:** LEAFY LIVERWORT

sca·lene \(ˈ)skā¦lēn\ *adj* [LL *scalenus,* fr. Gk *skalēnos* uneven, unequal, scalene; akin to Gk *skolios* crooked — more at CYLINDER] **1** *of a triangle* **:** having the sides unequal — see TRIANGLE illustration **2** [NL *scalenus*] **:** of, relating to, or being a scalenus muscle

sca·le·no·he·dral \skā¦lēnə¦hēdrəl\ *adj* [NL *scalenohedron* + E *-al*] **:** of, relating to, or having the form of a scalenohedron ⟨~ crystal⟩ ⟨~ calcite⟩

sca·le·no·he·dron \=¦==ˈhēdrən\ *n, pl* **scalenohedrons** \-nz\ *or* **scalenohe·dra** \-rə\ [NL, fr. Gk *skalēnos* scalene + NL *-hedron*] **:** a hemihedral form bounded ideally by scalene triangles: **a** *in the hexagonal system* **:** one of 12 faces resembling a double 6-sided pyramid **b** *in the tetragonal system* **:** one of 8 faces somewhat resembling the disphenoid

scalenohedrons: tetragonal, *A;* ditrigonal or hexagonal, *B*

sca·le·nous \skāˈlēnəs\ *adj* [LL *scalēnus*] **:** SCALENE

sca·le·nus \skāˈlēnəs\ *n, pl* **scale·ni** \-ēˌnī, -ēˌnē\ [NL, fr. LL or Gk; LL *scalenus* scalene, fr. Gk *skalēnos* uneven, scalene] **:** any of usu. three deeply situated muscles on each side of the neck each extending from the transverse processes of two or more cervical vertebrae to the first or second rib

scalepan \ˈ=,=\ *n* [¹*scale* + *pan*] **:** a pan of a scale for weighing

¹scal·er \ˈskālə(r)\ *n* -s [⁸*scale* + *-er*] **1 :** one that climbs (as a wall or mountain) or attacks or captures (as a castle) by climbing **2 :** one that measures by means of a scale: as **a :** one that scales logs or standing timber **b :** an electronic device that operates a recorder (as of nuclear disintegrations or cosmic rays) after a specified number of impulses appearing too rapidly for individual recording

²scaler \"\ *n* -s [⁶*scale* + *-er*] **1 :** one that removes scale (as from metal) **2 :** one that removes scales (as from fish)

³scaler \"\ *n* -s [²*scale* + *-er*] **:** one that weighs goods with scales

scale rule *n* [⁷*scale*] **:** a graduated stick having the number of board feet in logs of given diameters and lengths marked upon it and used in scaling logs or timber — compare LOG RULE, LOG SCALE

scales *pl of* SCALE, *pres 3d sing of* SCALE

scales·man \ˈskā(ə)lzmən\ *n, pl* **scalesmen** [¹*scale*] **:** SCALEMAN 2

scaletail \ˈ=,=\ *also* **scale–tailed squirrel** \ˈ=,=-\ *n* [⁵*scale*] **:** a rodent of the genus *Anomalurus* having horny scales under the base of the tail

scale tank *n* [¹*scale*] **:** a tank for spirit mounted on a scale so that the contents can be weighed

¹scale–up \ˈ=,=\ *n* -s [⁸*scale* + *up*] **:** an increase according to a fixed ratio ⟨a *scale-up* of wages⟩

²scale–up \ˈ=,=\ *adj* **:** characterized by an increase according to a fixed ratio ⟨*scale-up* buying in cotton futures⟩

scale wax *n* [⁵*scale*] **:** partly refined paraffin wax obtained by sweating slack wax so that only a small percentage of oil remains — called also *paraffin scale*

scalewing \ˈ=,=\ *n* [⁵*scale* + *wing*] **:** MOTH, BUTTERFLY

scalewise \ˈ=,=\ *adv* (*or adj*) [⁷*scale* + *-wise*] **:** in the manner of a scale ⟨diatonic tones are used ~ —*Down Beat*⟩ ⟨in some of the organ works, he was hypnotized by ~ movement —W.H.Mellers⟩

scale worm *n* [⁵*scale*] **:** any of numerous chaetopod worms of *Polynoe* and related genera that have two rows of large elytra along the back — called also *scaleback*

scaley *var of* SCALY

scalier *comparative of* SCALY

scaliest *superlative of* SCALY

scal·i·ness \ˈskālēnəs, -lin-\ *n* -ES **:** the quality or state of being scaly

¹scaling *n* -s [fr. *gerund of* ⁸*scale*] **1 :** an attack, conquest, or ascent by or as if by means of ladders **2 :** a measurement, arrangement, or adjustment according to a scale **3 :** a system of trading by buying or selling at specified price intervals on a rise or fall in the market in order to average one's costs or profits

²scaling *n* -s [fr. gerund of ⁶*scale*] **1 a :** the act or process of removing scales (as from fish) **b :** the act or process of removing scale (as from the teeth or from metal) **2 a :** deposition of scale (as in steam condensers) **b :** falling scale or fragments of it **3 :** scaly structure, markings, or arrangement **:** LEPIDOSIS

scaling circuit *n* [*scaling* (fr. pres. part. of ⁸*scale*) + *circuit*] **:** ¹SCALER 2b

scall \ˈskȯl\ *n* -s [ME, fr. ON *skalli* bald head; perh. akin to ON *skāl* bowl — more at SCALE] **:** a scurf or scabby disease esp. of the scalp

scallawag *var of* SCALAWAG

scalled \ˈskȯld\ *or* **scall** \ˈskȯl\ *archaic var of* ³SCALD

¹scal·lion \ˈskalyən\ *or* **scul·lion** \ˈskəl-\ *n* -s [ME *scalone, scaloun,* fr. AF *scalun,* fr. (assumed) VL *escalonia,* fr. L *ascalonia* (*caepa*) Ascalonian onion, fr. fem. of *ascalonius* of Ascalon, fr. *Ascalon-, Ascalo* Ascalon, seaport in southern

Palestine] **1 :** SHALLOT **2 :** LEEK **3 :** an onion forming a thick basal portion without a normal bulb as a result of disease, attacks of insects, or unfavorable environmental conditions **4 :** GREEN ONION

[2]scallion \"\ *vi* -ED/-ING/-S *of an onion* **:** to form a scallion

[1]scal·lom \'skaləm\ *n* -S [origin unknown] **:** a straight rod like a stake but usu. thinner with the ends secured by being twisted round another rod used in basketry esp. to serve as a foundation (as for fitching or randing)

[2]scallom \"\ *vt* -ED/-ING/-S **:** to join (as the end of a scallom) to a rod by twisting **:** PLAIT

[1]scal·lop \'skäləp, 'skal-\ *also* **scol·lop** \'skäləp\ *n* -S [ME *scalop*, fr. MF *escalope* shell, of Gmc origin; akin to MD *schelpe* shell — more at SCALP] **1 a :** any of many marine bivalve mollusks of the family Pectinidae that have the shell characteristically radially ribbed and the edge undulated, the mantle edges bearing well-developed ocelli, a single large adductor muscle which is esteemed a great delicacy and is the only part commonly used as food and that usu. do not attach themselves but are able to swim by opening and closing the valves — see BAY SCALLOP, GIANT SCALLOP **b :** the adductor muscle of scallop (as the bay scallop and giant scallop) cooked and served as food — usu. used in pl. **2** *or* **scallop shell a :** one of the valves of the shell of a scallop **b :** an object (as a baking dish) shaped like one of these valves **3 a** (1) **:** one of a usu. continuous series of curves forming an edge or design (as on cloth, leather, or metal) ⟨pillowcases with small ~*s*⟩ ⟨gables trimmed with ~*s*⟩ (2) **:** a small sharply defined curve esp. in a series ⟨sunken road winding in ~*s* —Ellen Glasgow⟩ ⟨cigarettes traced little ~*s* in the darkness —Howard Hunt⟩ ⟨rising and falling ~*s* of the waves —J.E.Macdonnell⟩ **b :** a row or design of scallops **:** SCALLOPING ⟨an edging consisting of small ~*s*⟩ **c :** a decorative motif in the form of a scallop shell **:** ESCALLOP **4** *or* **scallop squash :** CYMLING **5** [F *escalope* — more at SCALLOPINI] **:** a thin slice of boneless meat

scallops 3a(1)

[2]scallop \"\ *also* **scollop** \"\ *vb* -ED/-ING/-S *vt* **1** *or* **escallop** [*escallop* fr. earlier *escallop* scallop shell, alter. (influenced by MF *escalope* shell) of [1]*scallop*] **:** to bake in a sauce usu. covered with seasoned bread or cracker crumbs ⟨~ the potatoes⟩ ⟨oysters ~*ed*⟩ ⟨~*ed* peaches⟩ **2 a :** to shape, cut, or finish an edge or border in scallops **b :** to form scallops in ⟨concentrated settlement ~*s* the eastern border of the country —P.E.James⟩ **~** *vi* **1 :** to cook by scalloping ⟨veal . . . tucked into the oven to ~ —T.H.Fielding⟩ **2 :** to gather or dredge scallops

scallop budding *n* **:** a mode of budding by paring off a strip of bark from the stock and applying the bud with its wood directly to the surface thus formed

scal·loped \-pt\ *adj* [[1]*scallop* + *-ed*] **:** having or forming a wavy edge, border, or design ⟨~ neckline⟩ ⟨battlement-scalloped walls and turrets —Jerome Ellison⟩ ⟨lofty sierra arising from all around the ~ shore —S.E.Morison⟩ — compare INVECTED

scal·lop·er \-pə(r)\ *n* -S [[2]*scallop* + *-er*] **1 a :** one that dredges for or gathers scallops **b** *or* **scallop dragger :** a boat equipped and used to dredge for scallops **2 :** one that finishes cloth (as for awnings, clothing, or embroidery) with scallops or scalloped designs

scalloping *n* -S [fr. gerund of [2]*scallop*] **1 :** the act or work of gathering scallops **2 a :** the act or work of making ornamental scallops **b :** an edge, border, or design of scallops ⟨between an empty sea and a firm ~ of sand —P.H.Newby⟩

scal·lo·pi·ni \,skälə'pēnē\ *n* -S [modif. (influenced by [1]*scallop*) of It *scaloppine*, pl. of *scaloppina*, dim. of *scaloppa* thin slice of meat, fr. F *escalope*, perh. fr. E [1]*scallop*; fr. its being served curled like a shell] **:** thin slices of meat (as veal) sautéed or coated with flour and fried

scallop shell *n* **1 :** SCALLOP 2 **2 :** PILGRIM SCALLOP

scallop-shell moth *n* **:** a yellow-and-brown moth (*Calocalpe undulata*) having wing markings like those on a scallop shell and a caterpillar that feeds esp. on cherry leaves

scalls *pl of* SCALL

scallywag *var of* SCALAWAG

scal·ma \'skalmə\ *n* -S [NL, fr. OHG *scalmo* pestilence] **:** a mild virus disease of the horse marked by inflammation of the pharynx, larynx, and bronchi and by a severe cough

sca·lo·gram \'skālə,gram\ *n* [[6]*scale* + *-o-* + *-gram*] **:** an arrangement of items (as of a psychological or sociological test) in ascending order of difficulty ⟨analysis by ~⟩

sca·lops \'skā,läps\ [NL, fr. Gk *skalops*, mole] *syn of* SCALOPUS

scal·o·pus \'skaləpəs\ *n, cap* [NL, fr. Gk *skalops* mole, lit., digger — more at SHELF] **:** a genus of insectivores including the common mole of the eastern U.S.

[1]scalp \'skalp, 'skaup\ *n* -S [ME, of Scand origin; akin to ON *skālpr* sheath, MD *schelpe* shell, and prob. to OHG *skala* husk, shell — more at SCALE] **1** *chiefly Scot* **:** SKULL, HEAD **2 :** the part of the integument of the human head usu. covered with hair; *broadly* **:** this part including the skin, the dense subcutaneous tissue, the occipitofrontalis muscle with the galea aponeurotica, the loose subaponeurotic tissue, and the cranial periosteum **3 a :** a part of the human scalp with attached hair cut or torn from an enemy as a token of victory by Indian warriors of No. America or their white adversaries **b** (1) **:** an act of capitulation (as a resignation) demanded or obtained (as in retaliation for some act or line of action) ⟨senators clamored for the secretary's ~⟩ ⟨civic airport boosters were calling for ~*s* —Joseph Wechsberg⟩ (2) **:** one whose compliance or defeat is sought or obtained as a means of advancing one's cause or enhancing one's status ⟨a society leader adding ~*s*⟩ (3) **:** something symbolizing the result of punitive action and becoming a tally in a series ⟨boxer who has added four more ~*s* to his belt⟩ **4** *chiefly Scot* **a :** a projecting mass of bare ground or rock ⟨grassy ~ of the hill . . . that stood clear of the . . . pine forest —G.K.Chesterton⟩ **b :** a bank (as a bed of oysters) uncovered by the sea at low tide **5 a :** the part of an animal (as a wolf or a fox) corresponding to the human scalp; *also* **:** the part of a hide (as an ear or tail) surrendered when collecting a bounty whether restricted to this area or not ⟨some country shires pay bonuses on wombat ~*s* —Bill Beatty⟩ **b :** the skin of the head and part of the neck of an animal preserved so as to be suitable for mounting either over the natural skull or an artificial model — compare DOLLYHEAD **c :** the whole upper part of the head of a whale **6 :** a small profit taken by a speculator in a quick transaction **7** [[2]*scalp*] **a :** a sieve or other device for scalping a material (as wheat) **b :** the coarse portion of a material (as wheat) that is removed by scalping

[2]scalp \"\ *vb* -ED/-ING/-S *vt* **1 a :** to deprive of the scalp **:** cut or tear the scalp from the head of **b** (1) **:** to remove a top layer or growth from ⟨seed spots one foot square were ~*ed* free of sod and litter —*Amer. Midland Naturalist*⟩ ⟨most of the land had been ~*ed* for pine lumber —Lenard Kaufman⟩ (2) **:** to cause (as a top layer) to be removed ⟨if sod is heavy, it should be ~*ed* off before planting the shrubs —R.E.Trippensee⟩ ⟨~ weeds⟩ **c :** ROSS ⟨splitting out clapboards and laying them on the ~*ed* joists —Conrad Richter⟩ **d :** to remove a desired constituent from (a material) with the residue left as waste ⟨wasteful refiners ~ petroleum —Lalia P. Boone⟩ **2 :** to screen or sift (as grain, meal, or ore) in order to remove foreign materials or to separate out coarser grades **3 a :** to buy and sell so as to make small quick profits ⟨~ stocks⟩ ⟨~ grain⟩ **b :** to obtain and resell (as theater tickets) at prices usu. greatly above the stated rates without official sanction as a speculation ⟨speculators were ~*ing* tickets at double the going price —Dean Jennings⟩ ⟨possible . . . to ~ tickets even for a free-admission television show —Arthur Godfrey⟩ ⟨newsboys bought copies by the armload, ~*ed* them for as much as $1 each —*Time*⟩ **4 a :** to deprive (as a politician or officeholder) of position or influence **b :** to triumph over esp. in a spectacular fashion ⟨~ a tennis opponent⟩ **c :** to hold up to ridicule **:** polish off **:** HUMILIATE **5 :** to machine the surface from (semifinished metal products) before further fabrication ⟨~ billets⟩ **~** *vi* **1 :** to remove or obtain scalp esp. as tokens of victory **2 a :** to make a small usu. quick profit by slight fluctuations of the market **b :** to scalp tickets

[3]scalp \"\ *vi* -ED/-ING/-S [L *scalpere* to dig, scratch, carve, cut — more at SHELF] *of a horse* **:** to cut the coronary cushion or quarters esp. when traveling at high speed

scalp dance *n* [[1]*scalp*] **:** an American Indian victory dance often by women around a pole with enemy scalps or with scalp-surmounted sticks in hand

[1]scal·pel \'skalpəl, -kaup-, (')skal'pel\ *n* -S [L *scalpellum*, *scalpellus*, dim. of *scalprum*, *scalper* chisel, knife, fr. *scalpere* to carve, cut — more at SHELF] **:** a small straight knife with a thin keen blade used esp. for dissecting; *also* **:** a detachable blade of such a knife

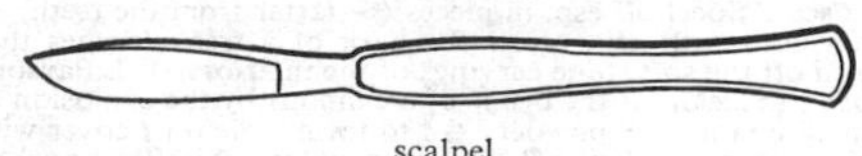

scalpel

[2]scalpel \"\ *vt* **scalpeled** *also* **scalpelled; scalpeled** *also* **scalpelled; scalpeling** *also* **scalpelling; scalpels :** to cut with a scalpel **:** DISSECT

scal·pel·lar \skal'pelə(r)\ *adj* [NL *scalpellum* + E *-ar*] **:** of, relating to, or being a scalpellum

scal·pel·lum \-ləm\ *n, pl* **scalpel·la** \-lə\ [NL, fr. L, scalpel] **:** any of four slender piercing organs in the proboscis of true bugs or bloodsucking two-winged flies corresponding to the mandibles and the first pair of maxillae

[1]scalp·er \'skalpə(r), -kaup-\ *n* -S [[1]*scalp* + *-er*] **:** one that scalps: as **a :** a slaughterhouse worker who skins animals' heads **b :** any of various machines or devices used in scalping grain **c** (1) **:** a speculator who seeks to make small profits on quick transactions (2) **:** a speculator who obtains and resells something (as theater tickets) at prices usu. greatly above the stated rates **d :** ROSSER

[2]scalper \"\ *n* -S [L, chisel, knife — more at SCALPEL] **:** SCORPER

[3]scalper \"\ *also* **scalping boot** *n* -S [*scalper* fr. [3]*scalp* + *-er; scalping* fr. gerund of [3]*scalp*] **:** a light leather or rubber toe boot worn by a horse on the hind foot to prevent scalping

scalp halloo *or* **scalp yell** *n* **:** the shout of an American Indian before, while, or after scalping an enemy

scalping *n* -S [fr. gerund of [2]*scalp*] **1 a :** an act of scalping **b :** the process of scalping **2 scalpings** *pl* **:** foreign matter removed by scalping ⟨oat ~*s* from wheat⟩

scalp·less \-pləs\ *adj* **:** deprived of the scalp

scalp lock *n* **:** a long tuft of hair on the crown of the otherwise shaved head of a warrior of some tribes of American Indians

scal·pri·form \'skalprə,fȯrm\ *adj* [L *scalprum* chisel, knife + E *-iform* — more at SCALPEL] **:** shaped like a chisel ⟨~ incisor⟩

scal·prum \'skalprəm\ *n, pl* **scal·pra** \-rə\ [NL, fr. L, chisel, knife — more at SCALPEL] **:** the front or cutting edge of an incisor tooth

scalps *pl of* SCALP, *pres 3d sing of* SCALP

scaly *also* **scaley** \'skālē, -li\ *adj* **scalier; scaliest** [[4]*scale* + *-y*] **1 a :** covered or abounding with scales ⟨~ fish⟩ ⟨~ trunks of trees⟩ **b :** covered with scale ⟨a ~ boiler⟩ **c :** composed of scales ⟨~ armor⟩; *specif* **:** composed of imbricated scales ⟨a ~ bud⟩ **d :** composed of or forming scale ⟨a ~ encrustation⟩ **e :** cleaving off in flakes at the surface ⟨~ stone⟩ **2 :** consisting of scaly animals **:** being a scaly animal **3 a :** MEAN, DESPICABLE, STINGY ⟨a ~ fellow⟩ **b :** POOR, INFERIOR ⟨a ~ piece of road —Hamlin Garland⟩ **4 :** infested with scale insects ⟨~ fruit⟩

scaly anteater *n* **:** PANGOLIN; *esp* **:** a southern African pangolin (as the Cape armadillo)

scaly bark *n* **1 a** *or* **scaly-bark hickory :** SHAGBARK HICKORY **b :** any of several rough-barked Australian eucalypts; *esp* **:** a rather small tree (*Eucalyptus squamiata*) with dark scaly bark, lanceolate leaves, and coarse reddish wood used chiefly for fuel **2 :** either of two abnormal conditions characterized by roughened scaly bark: **a :** LEPROSIS **b :** PSOROSIS

scaly blazing star *n* **:** a button snakeroot (*Liatris squarrosa*) having purple heads with scaly involucrate bracts

scaly fern *n* **:** SCALE FERN

scaly-finned \'==¦=\ *adj* **:** having scales on the fins — compare SPINY-FINNED

scaly leg *n* **:** a disease of poultry caused by the scaly-leg mite producing an abnormal rough hard scaliness on the featherless parts of the legs — sometimes used in pl. but sing. or pl. in constr.

scaly-leg mite *n* **:** a minute round flattened whitish mite (*Knemidocoptes mutans*) of the family Sarcoptidae that burrows beneath the leg scales of poultry and various other birds

scaly mistletoe *n* **:** a plant of the genus *Arceuthobium*

scaly spleenwort *n* **:** SCALE FERN

scalytail \'==,=\ *n* [*scaly* + *tail*] **:** SCALETAIL

[1]scam·ble \'skambəl\ *vb* **scambled; scambled; scambling** \-b(ə)liŋ\ **scambles** [origin unknown] *vi* **1** *obs* **:** to struggle with others for largess thrown to a crowd; *broadly* **:** to struggle greedily and indecorously for something **2** *chiefly dial* **:** to get on somehow **:** stumble along **3** *dial Eng* **:** to loll around **:** SPRAWL, SHAMBLE **~** *vt* **1** *dial* **:** to scrape together **:** COLLECT **2** *dial Eng* **:** to trample down

[2]scam·ble \'skam(b)əl\ *n* -S *dial Eng* **:** BOTCH, MESS

[3]scamble \"\ *dial Brit var of* SHAMBLE

scam·bler \'skamblər\ *n* -S [origin unknown] *Scot* **:** a mealtime visitor **:** SPONGER

[1]scambling *n* [origin unknown] *dial* **:** a picked up meal

[2]scambling *adj* [fr. pres. part. of [1]*scamble*] **1 :** BRAWLING, QUARRELSOME **2 :** carelessly done **:** MAKESHIFT, SHODDY **3 :** irregularly spread out **:** SCATTERED, RAMBLING ⟨a town ~ in all directions⟩ **4 :** awkwardly formed or executed **:** SHAMBLING ⟨little clean punching and a lot of holding in a ~ bout —*Sunday Independent (Dublin)*⟩

sca·mil·lus \skə'miləs\ *n* -ES [L, lit., little bench, dim. of *scamnum* bench, stool] **:** a second plinth below the base of an Ionic or Corinthian column usu. without moldings and of smaller size horizontally than the pedestal

scam·mo·ni·ate \skə'mōnēət, -ē,āt\ *adj* [NL *scammoniatus*, fr. L *scammonia* + *-atus* -ate] **:** made with scammony

scam·mo·ny \'skamənē\ *n* -ES [ME *scamonie*, fr. L *scammonia*, fr. Gk *skammōnia*] **1 a :** a twining plant (*Convolvulus scammonia*) native to Asia Minor and having a thick root two or three feet long, sagittate leaves, and white flowers **b :** a tropical American morning glory (*Ipomoea orizabensis*) **2 a :** the dried root of scammony **b :** the resin obtained as an exudation from the living root of scammony or prepared by extracting the dried root with alcohol and precipitating with water and used as a drastic cathartic **c :** IPOMOEA 3

scammonyroot \'===,=\ *n* [*scammony* + *root*] **:** MAN-OF-THE-EARTH 1

sca·moz·zi \skə'mȯtsē\ *n* -S *usu cap* [after Vincenzo *Scamozzi* †1616 Ital. architect] **:** a variation of the Ionic order with the volutes of the capital radiating at 45 degrees used esp. in colonial buildings

[1]scamp \'skamp, -aa(ə)mp, -aimp\ *n* -S [obs. *scamp* to roam about idly, perh. short for *scamper*] **1** *archaic* **:** HIGHWAYMAN **2 a :** a scheming person **:** RASCAL, ROGUE ⟨an insincere but ambitious ~ —Lucien Warner⟩ **b :** a usu. young person given to impish playful tricks ⟨a shocking young ~ of a rover —W.S.Gilbert⟩ **3** [so called fr. its ability to steal bait without being caught] **:** a West Indian grouper (*Mycteroperca falcata*) **syn** see VILLAIN

[2]scamp \"\ *vt* -ED/-ING/-S [perh. of Scand origin; akin to ON *skammr* short — more at SCANT] **:** to perform in a hasty, neglectful, or imperfect manner **:** do or make superficially **:** SKIMP, SCANT ⟨the book is brief, but never hurried or ~*ed* —Crane Brinton⟩

[1]scam·per \'skampə(r), -aam-, -aim-\ *vi* -ED/-ING/-S [prob. fr. obs. D *schampen* to flee, fr. MF *escamper*, fr. It *scampare*, fr. (assumed) VL *excampare* to decamp, fr. L *ex-* + *campus* field — more at CAMP] **1 :** to run away **:** FLEE **2 :** to run nimbly and usu. playfully about ⟨a gray squirrel is ~*ing* from limb to limb —D.J.Malcolm⟩

[2]scamper \"\ *n* -S **:** a playful scurrying run

scam·per·er \-p(ə)rə(r)\ *n* -S **:** one that scampers

scamping *n* -S [fr. gerund of [2]*scamp*] **1 :** the intentional failure of an employee to perform his task properly **2 :** the act or practice of an employee in exceeding his usual rate of output for the purpose of gaining a personal advantage over his fellows or contrary to their mutual understanding of a proper rate of production **3 :** the act or practice of an employer in attracting labor from competitors underhandedly

scamp·ish \'skampish\ *adj* [[1]*scamp* + *-ish*] **:** of or like a scamp **:** ROGUISH ⟨~ conduct⟩ — **scamp·ish·ness** *n* -ES

[1]scan \'skan, -aa(ə)n\ *vb* **scanned; scanned; scanning; scans** [ME *scannen*, fr. LL *scandere* to climb, scan verses, fr. L, to climb; akin to Gk *skandalon* trap, stumbling block, offense, Skt *skandati* he leaps, MIr *scendim* I leap] *vt* **1 a :** to analyze (verse) so as to exhibit rhythmic and esp. metrical structure **b :** to indicate rhythmic or metrical structure of (verse) **2** *archaic* **:** to test the correctness, importance, or value of **:** judge critically ⟨know then thyself, presume not God to ~ —Alexander Pope⟩ **3 a** (1) **:** to make an intensive examination of (a small area) ⟨*scanning* each vein of rock for the telltale glint of yellow metal —R.A.Billington⟩ ⟨*scanned* their faces as they passed —Joseph Conrad⟩ ⟨*scanned* closely the claims of individuals as against the state —B.R.Trimble⟩ (2) **:** to check (as a magnetic tape or a punch card) for recorded data by means of a mechanical or electronic device **b :** to make a thorough search of (a wide area) usu. by eye (as by moving one's eyes in repeated sweeping motions from side to side) ⟨*scanning* the forest with binoculars, on the lookout for fire —Isaac Rosenfeld⟩ ⟨~ the field of medicine —Sara Jordan⟩ **c :** to look through or over hastily ⟨read several and ~ the rest —Kermit Ely⟩ ⟨*scanned* the film advertisements —D.M.Davin⟩ **4** *archaic* **:** DISCERN ⟨not wise enough to ~ his best concerns aright —William Cowper⟩ **5** *obs* **:** to explain the meaning of **:** INTERPRET **6 a :** to subject (as an image or picture) to scanning **b :** to cause a narrow beam of light to shine through (a sound track) or to traverse (an object) in order to translate light modulations into a corresponding electrical current **c :** to direct a succession of radar beams so that they traverse (a prescribed area) in searching for a target **~** *vi* **1 :** to scan verse **2 :** to admit of being scanned **:** conform to or reveal a definite metrical pattern **syn** see SCRUTINIZE

[2]scan \"\ *n* -S **1 :** the act or process of scanning **:** a close examination ⟨the captain spins the periscope, making a quick ~ of the situation —E.L.Beach⟩ **2 :** range of vision **:** APPREHENSION ⟨the authors' ~ was limited —*Current Biog.*⟩ **3 :** a radar display

scandahoovian *cap, var of* SCANDIHOOVIAN

[1]scan·dal \'skandᵊl, -aan-\ *n* -S [LL *scandalum* stumbling block, offense, fr. Gk *skandalon* — more at SCAN] **1 a** (1) **:** discredit brought upon religion by unseemly conduct in a religious person (2) **:** offense, doubt, or bewilderment occasioned to a person's religious feelings by another's lapse in ethics or religion ⟨abstained from decorating their private chapels . . . lest ~ should be given to weaker brethren —T.B.Macaulay⟩ (3) **:** conduct that causes or encourages a lapse of faith or of religious obedience in another ⟨his bad example is a constant ~ to all who knew him in the days of his fidelity —D.J.Corrigan⟩ **b :** something that prevents the reception of religious or other faith or serves as justification for a lapse from faith or morals **:** OFFENSE ⟨one ~ of Christendom, the great schism, had indeed been overcome —S.E.Morison & H.S.Commager⟩ ⟨the ~ of the apparent contradiction of reason with itself —Edward Caird⟩ **2 a :** loss of or damage to reputation caused by actual or apparent violation of morality or propriety ⟨a soldier should not bring ~ upon the uniform⟩ **b** *archaic* **:** a disgraceful usu. baseless accusation or imputation ⟨an improbable ~ flung upon the nation by a few bigoted . . . scribblers —Jonathan Swift⟩ **3 a :** a circumstance or action that offends propriety or established moral conceptions or disgraces those associated with or involved in it ⟨the man's life is an open ~ —Willa Cather⟩ ⟨an early history of ~ and mismanagement —*Amer. Guide Series: N.Y. City*⟩ **b :** a person whose conduct offends propriety or morality ⟨under no temptation to nominate men who will be either drones or ~*s* —*Spectator*⟩ **4 :** gossip or utterance of gossip that emphasizes true or false details damaging to another's reputation ⟨the political harridans . . . would attack every possible leader with ~ and abuse and falsehood —H.G.Wells⟩ **5 :** anger, indignation, chagrin, bewilderment, or incredulity brought about by a flagrant violation of morality, propriety, or religious opinion ⟨to the ~ and grief of her sisters, made up her mind not to go to church any more —Margaret Deland⟩ ⟨his marriage would give the gravest ~ to millions —*Manchester Guardian Weekly*⟩ **6 :** something alleged in an equity pleading that is impertinent and is reproachful to a person or derogates from the dignity of the court or is contrary to good manners **:** an immaterial allegation that is slanderous **syn** see DETRACTION

[2]scandal \"\ *vt* -ED/-ING/-S **1** *obs* **:** to bring reproach or scandal upon **:** DISGRACE **2** *chiefly dial* **:** to spread scandal concerning **:** DEFAME, SLANDER

scan·dal·iza·tion \,skandᵊlə'zāshən\ *n* -S **:** the act of scandalizing or the condition of being scandalized

[1]scan·dal·ize \'skandᵊl,īz, -aan-\ *vt* -ED/-ING/-S [partly fr. MF *scandaliser* to cause to stumble, shock, fr. LL *scandalizare* to cause to stumble, fr. Gk *skandalizein*, fr. *skandalon* stumbling block, offense; partly fr. [1]*scandal* + *-ize*] **1 :** to speak falsely or maliciously of **:** DEFAME, MALIGN **2** *archaic* **:** to bring into reproach **:** DISHONOR, DISGRACE **3 :** to offend the feelings, conscience, or propriety of by an action considered immoral, criminal, or unseemly ⟨*scandalized* his brethren by espousing euthanasia, sterilization, easy divorce —*Time*⟩

[2]scandalize \"\ *vt* [alter. of earlier *scantelize* to shorten, curtail, fr. [2]*scantle* + *-ize*] **1 :** to lower the peak and haul up the tack or clew of (a fore-and-aft sail) in order to reduce the size or to spill the sail **2 :** to reduce sail on (a mizzenmast) when before the wind so that the sails on the mainmast may have the full force of the wind

scan·dal·iz·er \-zə(r)\ *n* -S [[1]*scandalize* + *-er*] **:** one that utters scandal

scandalmonger \'==,==\ *n* [[1]*scandal* + *monger*] **:** a person who circulates scandal

scan·dal·ous \'skandᵊləs, -aan-\ *adj* [MF *scandaleux*, fr. ML *scandalosus*, fr. LL *scandalum* stumbling block + L *-osus* -ous] **1 a** *obs* **:** constituting a spiritual or moral lapse endangering by example faith or morals **b** *obs, of a clergyman* **:** endangering faith or morals through conduct or views **2 :** containing shocking or defamatory information **:** LIBELOUS ⟨only read it for the ~ passages —Arnold Bennett⟩ **3 :** offensive to public or individual sense of propriety or morality **:** exciting reprobation ⟨considered the publisher a ~ person, and had refused to meet him —W.B.Yeats⟩ ⟨rumors about the ~ treatment of the native population —H.O.Mackey⟩ — **scan·dal·ous·ly** *adv* — **scan·dal·ous·ness** *n* -ES

scandals *pl of* SCANDAL, *pres 3d sing of* SCANDAL

scandal sheet *n* **:** a newspaper or periodical dealing to a large extent in scandal and gossip

scan·da·lum mag·na·tum \'skandᵊləm,mag'nād·əm\ *n, pl* **scanda·la magnatum** \-ᵊlə,-\ [ML, lit., slander of magnates] **:** a defamatory speech or writing published to the injury of a peer, judge, or other great officer of England

scan·da·roon \,skandə'rün\ *n* -S [fr. *Scandaroon*, now *İskenderon*, seaport of southern Turkey] **:** a long-bodied long-legged domestic pigeon of the carrier type with a curved bill and solid-colored or varied plumage

scan·dent \'skandənt\ *adj* [L *scandent-*, *scandens*, pres. part. of *scandere* to climb — more at SCAN] **:** CLIMBING ⟨plant of a creeping or ~ nature —*Farmer's Weekly (So. Africa)*⟩

[1]scan·di·an \'skandēən\ *adj, usu cap* [L *Scandia*, ancient name of southern Scandinavian peninsula, + E *-an*] **1 a :** of or relating to Scandia **b :** SCANDINAVIAN **2 :** of or relating to the languages of Scandinavia

[2]scandian \"\ *n* -S *cap* **:** SCANDINAVIAN

scan·di·hoo·vi·an *or* **scan·da·hoo·vi·an** \,skandə'hüvēən\ *n* -S *cap* [alter. of *Scandinavian*] **1 :** a Scandinavian individual esp. living in the U. S. — usu. used disparagingly **2 :** a Scandinavian language as spoken in the U. S. esp. by rural people

[1]scan·di·na·vi·an \¦skandə¦nāvēən, -aand-, -vyən\ *adj, usu cap* [*Scandinavia*, ancient name of the country of the Norsemen + E *-an*] **:** of or relating to Scandinavia, its peoples, or languages

[2]scandinavian \"\ *n* -S *cap* **1 a :** a native or inhabitant of

Scandinavia; *esp* **:** a member of the tall blond dolichocephalic dominant race **b :** one that is of Scandinavian descent **2 :** the No. Germanic languages

scan·di·um \'skandēəm\ *n* -s [NL, fr. L *Scandia*, ancient name of southern Scandinavian peninsula + NL *-ium*] **:** a white trivalent metallic element sparsely but widely distributed in combined form in association with the rare-earth metals with which it is sometimes included and found esp. in various Scandinavian minerals (as thortveitite) — symbol *Sc; see* ELEMENT table

scan·dix \'skandiks\ *n, cap* [NL, fr. L, chervil, fr. Gk *skandix*] **:** a small genus of Eurasian herbs (family Umbelliferae) with finely dissected leaves, white flowers, and wingless long-beaked fruit and with obscure oil tubes — see LADY'S COMB

SC and S *abbr* strapped, corded, and sealed

scan·mag \'skan,mag\ *n* -s [*scan*dalum *mag*natum] **:** SCANDAL

scan·na·ble \'skanəbəl\ *adj* [¹*scan* + *-able*] **:** capable of being scanned

scanned *past of* SCAN

scan·ner \'skanə(r), -aan-\ *n* -s **:** one that scans: as **a :** one that scans verse **b :** a device used for scanning (as in television, facsimile, or radar) **c :** a device that automatically checks a process or condition and may initiate a desired corrective action ⟨electronic ~ that can monitor up to 25 different production points, checking such variables as temperature, pressure, liquid level, and rate of flow —*Dun's Rev.*⟩ **d :** a device for sensing recorded data; *esp* **:** such a device that is operated photoelectrically ⟨a punched-card ~⟩

¹scanning *n* -s [ME, fr. gerund of *scannen* to scan] **1 :** SCANSION **2 :** minute, thorough, critical, or judicial examination **3 :** the process of analyzing by means of an electron beam that moves usu. in successive lines the light and dark values that constitute a picture or image and of translating these values into corresponding electrical values for transmission by facsimile or television; *also* **:** the reverse process by means of which a receiver synthesizes the picture or image

²scanning *adj* [fr. pres. part. of ¹*scan*] **:** minutely scrutinizing

scanning disk *n* [²*scanning*] **:** a rotating disk with a number of spirally arranged holes near its edge which permit a light beam to sweep over successive portions of a picture or object

scanning speech *n* **:** speech characterized by regularly recurring pauses between words or syllables

scans *pres 3d sing of* SCAN, *pl of* SCAN

scan·sion \'skanchən, -aan-\ *n* -s [LL *scansion-, scansio*, fr. L, act of climbing, fr. (assumed) L *scansus* (past part. of L *scandere* to climb) + L *-ion-, -io* -ion — more at SCAN] **1 a :** the analysis of a rhythmic structure (as a verse) so as to show the elements or units of which its rhythm is composed and esp. to identify some unifying recurrent element or unit **b :** the division of a rhythmic series into such units; *esp* **:** the division of a metrical series into its component feet **2 :** the product or result of scansion **:** a particular description or representation of a given rhythmic or esp. metrical structure ⟨two possible ~*s* of this verse are printed⟩

scan·sion·ist \-chənəst\ *n* -s [*scansion* + *-ist*] **:** one who practices or is skilled in the art of scansion

scan·so·res \skan'sō,rēz\ *n pl, cap* [NL, lit., climbers, pl. of *scansor*, fr. (assumed) L *scansus* (past. part. of L *scandere* to climb) + L *-or* — more at SCAN] *in former classifications* **:** an order of birds having the toes two before and two behind and including the parrots, woodpeckers, cuckoos, trogons, and toucans

scan·so·ri·al \skan'sōrēəl, -'sȯr-\ *adj* [L *scansorius* (fr. — assumed — L *scansus* + L *-orius* -ory) + E *-al*] **1 :** relating to, capable of, or adapted for climbing **2 :** of or relating to the Scansores

scansorial barbet *n* **:** a barbet of the family Capitonidae

¹scant \'skant, -aa(ə)nt, -aint\ *n* -s [ME, fr. ON *skamt*, fr. neut. of *skammr* short] *chiefly dial* **:** scanty supply **:** SCARCITY

²scant \"\ *adj* -ER/-EST [ME, fr. ON *skamt*, neut. of *skammr* short; akin to OHG *scam* short, L *capon-, capo* capon — more at CAPON] **1 a** *dial* **:** excessively frugal **:** PARSIMONIOUS **b** *dial* **:** wisely sparing **:** not prodigal **:** CHARY ⟨from this time be something ~*er* of your maiden presence —Shak.⟩ **2 a :** barely or scarcely sufficient ⟨likely to pay ~ attention to proportion or design —Ben Riker⟩ ⟨desiccated stalks offer ~ browsing to cattle —*N.Y. Times Mag.*⟩; *specif* **:** lacking a trifle of or not quite coming up to a stated measure ⟨had seen him, three ~ months ago —Donn Byrne⟩ ⟨a ~ chance of one man in ten surviving the torpedoing —*English Digest*⟩ ⟨many insulating boards are cut ~ in width and length —P.D.Close⟩ **b :** lacking in amplitude or quantity **:** MEAGER, SCANTY ⟨amaryllis is tall-stemmed, and has ~ foliage —G.M.Fosler⟩ ⟨a truly ~ black lace underskirt —Lois Long⟩ **3 a :** having a small or insufficient supply ⟨he's fat, and ~ of breath —Shak.⟩ **b :** somewhat wanting or weak in a particular area ⟨this small book . . . is a good bit too ~ in documentation —*New Yorker*⟩ **4** *of a wind* **:** having such a direction or force that a sailing ship can barely hold its course even close-hauled **syn** see MEAGER

³scant \"\ *adv* [ME, fr. ²*scant*] *dial* **:** SCARCELY, HARDLY

⁴scant \"\ *vt* -ED/-ING/-S [²*scant*] **1 :** to provide with a meager or inadequate portion, supply, or allowance ⟨shall not allow myself to be circumscribed and ~*ed* of elbowroom —J.R.Lowell⟩ ⟨~*ed* in my allowance —Clara Reeve⟩ **2 :** to make small, narrow, thin, or meager **:** reduce the size or quantity of ⟨has not hesitated to expand rather than ~ the meaning of the original —*Saturday Rev. (London)*⟩ **3 :** to provide an incomplete supply of **:** fail to give in full **:** WITHHOLD ⟨to ~ one's service was the cardinal sin —V.L.Parrington⟩ **4 :** to give scant attention to **:** SLIGHT ⟨vitally interdependent aims, and neither can be ~*ed* without the other suffering —Fredson Bowers⟩ ⟨a subject ~*ed* in too many grammars —A.F.Hubbell⟩

scant·ies \-tēz\ *n pl* [blend of ²*scant* and *panties*] **:** abbreviated panties for women

scant·i·ly \-tᵊlē, -tᵊli, -təl-\ *adv* [*scanty* + *-ly*] **:** in a scanty manner

scant·i·ness \-tēnəs, -tin-\ *n* -ES **:** the quality or state of being scanty

¹scantle *vt* -ED/-ING/-S [freq. of ⁴*scant*] **1** *obs* **:** to cut down the supply of **2** [prob. back-formation fr. ¹*scantling*] *obs* **:** to adjust to a standard of measure

²scan·tle \'skantᵊl\ *n* -s [prob. fr. ¹*scantle*] **1** *obs* **:** a small portion **:** SCANTLING **2 :** a gage for measuring slates

¹scant·ling \'skantliŋ, -aan-, -lēŋ\ *n* -s [alter. (influenced by *-ling*) of earlier *scantillon* mason's or carpenter's gage, dimension, fr. ME *scantilon*, fr. ONF *escantillon*] **1 a** *obs* **:** the measure or dimension of something (as the caliber of a bullet or shot) **b :** the breadth and thickness of timber and stone used in building **c :** the dimensions of a frame, strake, or other structural part used in shipbuilding **d** *obs* **:** the quantity, amount, or degree of a quality, capacity, or ability **e** *obs* **:** a measure that confines to a comparatively small size or quantity **:** LIMIT, SCOPE ⟨this . . . is to measure truth by a wrong standard, and to circumscribe her by too narrow a ~ —T.P. Blomt⟩ **2 a** *archaic* **:** SPECIMEN, SAMPLE **b** *obs* **:** a rough draft **:** a rude sketch or outline **3 :** something that has a measure or is measured out: as **a :** an allotted portion **b :** a small quantity, amount, or proportion **:** MODICUM ⟨able to devote but a ~ of his philosophical labor to the problem —John Baillie⟩ **c :** a small piece of lumber (as an upright piece in house framing) **d :** a piece of yard lumber that is under 8 inches wide and from 2 inches to 6 inches thick **e :** yellow pine lumber that varies in size from 2 in. x 2 in. to 5 in. x 8 in.

²scantling \"\ *adj* [fr. pres. part. of ¹*scantle*] *archaic* **:** SCANTY

scantling number *or* **scantling numeral** *n* [¹*scantling*] **:** a number variously computed from a ship's dimensions and used in reference to a tabulated scheme specifying the size of structural material required to entitle a ship according to its type to a classification or grading with respect to seaworthiness

scant·ly *adv* [ME, fr. ²*scant* + *-ly*] **1 :** BARELY, SCARCELY **2 :** in small or inadequate measure **:** SCANTILY

scant·ness *n* -ES [ME *scantnesse*, fr. ²*scant* + *-nesse* -ness] **:** the quality or state of being scant **:** INSUFFICIENCY

scant-o-grace \'skantə,grās\ *n* [²*scant* + *o'* + *grace*] *Scot* **:** ROGUE

scanty \'skantē, -aan-, -ain-, -ti\ *adj* -ER/-EST [¹*scant* + *-y*] **1 a :** meager or barely sufficient **:** lacking in amplitude, abundance, or extension ⟨the peasant whose nervous system is best adapted to thrive on ~ nutriment —Brooks Adams⟩ ⟨used to acquire much of his ~ wardrobe by barter —Dwight Macdonald⟩ **b :** somewhat less than is needed **:** INSUFFICIENT, SCANT ⟨his own ~ cavalry . . . would . . . be unequal to the weight which would be thrown on them —J.A.Froude⟩ ⟨issuing bills of credit to supplement the ~ currency —V.L. Parrington⟩ **c :** thinly spread in time or space **:** SPARSE ⟨a desert range with ~ vegetation —G.R.Stewart⟩ ⟨the grass does not renew itself after the rains become ~ —Samuel Van Valkenburg & Ellsworth Huntington⟩ **2 :** giving small portions **:** PARSIMONIOUS **syn** see MEAGER

scap·a·no·rhyn·chus \,skapənō'riŋkəs\ *n, cap* [NL, fr. Gk *skapanē* spade + NL *-o-* + *-rhynchus*; akin to Gk *skaptein* to dig — more at CAPON] **:** a genus of galeoid sharks comprising the goblin sharks and related extinct forms and known from the Lower Cretaceous onward

scap·a·nus \'skapənəs\ *n, cap* [NL, fr. Gk *skapaneus* digger; akin to Gk *skaptein* to dig] **:** a genus of insectivores (family Talpidae) comprising the common mole of the western U. S.

¹scape \'skāp\ *vb* -ED/-ING/-S [ME *scapen*, short for *escapen* — more at ESCAPE] **:** ESCAPE

²scape \"\ *n* -s [ME, fr. *scapen* to scape] **1** *dial* **a :** ESCAPE **b :** a means of escape **2 a** *obs* **:** a breach of morals **:** TRANSGRESSION **b** *obs* **:** an inadvertent error **:** SLIP **3 :** ESCAPEMENT

³scape \"\ *n* -s [L *scapus* shaft of a column, stalk — more at SHAFT] **1 :** a peduncle arising at or beneath the surface of the ground in an acaulescent plant (as the bloodroot, tulip, or primrose); *broadly* **:** a flower stalk **2 a :** the shaft of a column **b :** APOPHYGE **3 :** STEM, SHAFT: as **a :** the basal joint of an insect antenna esp. when longer than the other joints **b :** the shaft of a feather **c :** the peduncle of the balancer of a dipterous insect

⁴scape \"\ *n* -s [back-formation fr. *landscape*] **:** a scenic view (as of sea, land, or sky)

⁵scape \"\ *n* -s [imit.] **1 :** the cry or note of a flushed snipe **2 :** SNIPE

-scape \,skāp\ *n comb form* -s [*landscape*] **:** view **:** pictorial representation of a (specified) type of view ⟨city*scape*⟩ ⟨water*scape*⟩

scapegallows \'=,=(,)=\ *n* [¹*scape* + *gallows*] **:** one who has narrowly escaped the gallows for his crimes

¹scapegoat \'=,=\ *n* [¹*scape* + *goat*; intended as trans. of Heb *'azāzēl* (prob. name of a demon), as if *'ēz 'ōzēl* goat that departs, Lev 16:8 (AV)] **1 :** a goat upon whose head are symbolically placed the sins of the people after which he is suffered to escape into the wilderness as part of the ceremony prescribed by Biblical law for Yom Kippur **2 :** an animal or person to whom sins, ill luck, or other evils are ceremonially attached and who symbolically bears them away by being sacrificed or exiled **3 a :** a person or thing bearing the blame for others ⟨made a ~ and relieved for a failure not his own —H.W.Baldwin⟩ **b :** a person, group, race, or institution against whom is directed the irrational hostility and unrelieved aggression of others ⟨the wholesale hunting for ~*s* at whom all can throw invectives —Walter Coutu⟩

²scapegoat \"\ *vt* -ED/-ING/-S **:** to displace aggression or project guilt upon ⟨the minority groups in the country conveniently ~*ed* —H.H.Long⟩

scape·goat·er \"+ə(r)\ *n* -s [²*scapegoat* + *-er*] **:** one that makes a scapegoat of something or somebody

scape·goat·ism \"+,izəm\ *n* -s [¹*scapegoat* + *-ism*] **:** the casting of blame upon others **:** the attribution of failure to the malign activities of an individual or group

scapegrace \'=,=\ *n* [¹*scape* + *grace*] **:** a reckless unprincipled person **:** REPROBATE

scap·el \'skapəl\ *n* -s [NL *scapellus*, dim. of L *scapus* stalk — more at SHAFT] **:** CAULICLE

scape·less \'skāpləs\ *adj* [³*scape* + *-less*] **:** lacking a scape

scape·ment \'skāpmənt\ *n* -s [¹*scape* + *-ment*] **:** ESCAPEMENT

scape wheel *n* [²*scape*] **:** ESCAPE WHEEL

scaph- *or* **scapho-** *comb form* [*scaphoid*] **1 :** scaphoid ⟨*scapho*cephaly⟩ **2 :** scaphoid and ⟨*scapho*lunar⟩

sca·pha \'skafə\ *n* -s [NL, fr. L, light boat, skiff, fr. Gk *skaphē* trough, bowl, skiff — more at SCAPHOID] **:** an elongated depression of the ear that separates the helix and antihelix

sca·phan·der \skə'fandə(r)\ *n, cap* [NL *Scaphandr-, Scaphander*, fr. *scaph-* + *-ander*] **:** a genus (the type of the family Scaphandridae) of gastropods having an external ovoid shell with a concealed spire

sca·phan·dri·dae \-drə,dē\ *n pl, cap* [NL *Scaphandr-, Scaphander*, type genus + *-idae*] **:** a family of gastropods (suborder Tectibranchia) related to the bubble shells

sca·phi·o·pod·i·dae \,skafēō'pädə,dē\ *n pl, cap* [NL, fr. *Scaphiopod-, Scaphiopus*, type genus, + *-idae*] *in some classifications* **:** a family of toads that comprises the American spadefoot toads and is now usu. included in the cosmopolitan family Pelobatidae

sca·phi·o·pus \skə'fīəpəs\ *n, cap* [NL *Scaphiopod-, Scaphiopus*, fr. Gk *skapheion* spade + NL *-pus*; akin to Gk *skaptein* to dig — more at CAPON] **:** a genus of toads comprising the American spadefoot toads and being placed in the family Pelobatidae or sometimes made the type of Scaphiopodidae

scaph·ite \'ska,fīt\ *n* -s [NL *Scaphites*] **:** a fossil cephalopod of *Scaphites* or a related genus

sca·phi·tes \skə'fīd·(,)ēz\ *n, cap* [NL, fr. *scaph* + *-ites*] **:** a genus (the type of the family Scaphitidae) comprising Cretaceous ammonoid cephalopods that have all the whorls coiled in an involute spiral except the last which is straight for a distance and then bent back toward the coiled part — **scaph·i·toid** \'skafə,tȯid\ *adj*

scaph·o·ce·phal·ic \,skafəsə'falik\ *or* **scaph·o·ceph·a·lous** \¦skafə¦sefələs\ *adj* [ISV *scaph-* + *-cephalic* or *-cephalous*] **:** of, relating to, or exhibiting scaphocephaly

scaph·o·ceph·a·lism \,skafə'sefə,lizəm\ *n* -s [ISV *scaph-* + *-cephalism*] **:** SCAPHOCEPHALY

scaph·o·ceph·a·ly \-fəlē\ *n* -ES [ISV *scaph-* + *-cephaly*] **:** a congenital deformity of the skull in which the vault is narrow, elongated, and boat-shaped because of premature ossification of the sagittal suture

scaph·o·ce·rite \,skafə'si,rīt\ *n* -s [*scaph-* + Gk *keras* horn + E *-ite* — more at HORN] **:** a flattened plate on the second joint of the antennae of many crustaceans — **scaph·o·ce·rit·ic** \¦skafəsə¦rid·ik\ *adj*

sca·phog·na·thite \skə'fägnə,thīt\ *n* [*scaph-* + *gnathite*] **:** a thin leaflike appendage of the second maxilla of decapod crustaceans — **sca·phog·na·thit·ic** \=¦=¦thid·ik\ *adj*

¹scaph·oid \'ska,fȯid\ *adj* [NL *scaphoides*, fr. Gk *skaphoeidēs*, fr. *skaphē* trough, bowl, light boat, skiff + *-oeidēs* -oid; prob. akin to Gk *skaptein* to dig — more at CAPON] **1 :** shaped like a boat **:** NAVICULAR **2 :** characterized by concavity ⟨the ~ abdomen in some serious diseases⟩

²scaphoid \"\ *n* -s [NL *scaphoides*, fr. *scaphoides* boat-shaped] **:** the navicular of the carpus or tarsus

sca·phoi·de·us \skə'fȯidēəs\ *n, cap* [NL, fr. *scaphoides* scaphoid] **:** a genus of leafhoppers including one (*S. luteolus*) that feeds on and transmits phloem necrosis to elm trees

¹scapho·lunar \¦skafə+\ *adj* [*scaph-* + *lunar*] **:** relating to or composed of the navicular and lunar bones of the carpus

²scapholunar \"\ *n* **:** a bone in the carpus of many carnivorous mammals that is made up of the fused navicular and lunar

¹scaph·o·pod \'skafə,päd\ *adj* [NL *Scaphopoda*] **:** of or relating to the Scaphopoda

²scaphopod \"\ *n* -s **:** a mollusk of the class Scaphopoda

sca·phop·o·da \skə'fäpədə\ *n pl, cap* [NL, fr. *scaph-* + *-poda*] **:** a small class of Mollusca comprising bilaterally symmetrical marine forms that have a tapering tubular shell open at both ends, a pointed or spade-shaped foot for burrowing, many long slender prehensile oral tentacles about a mouth containing a radula, a rudimentary heart, no gills, and separate sexes whose reproductive products escape through the right kidney — see TOOTH SHELL; compare GASTROPODA — **sca·phop·o·dous** \-dəs\ *adj*

scapi *pl of* SCAPUS

scapi- *comb form* [L *scapus* shaft of a column, stalk — more at SHAFT] **:** scape **:** stem **:** shaft ⟨*scapi*form⟩ ⟨*scapi*gerous⟩

sca·pi·form \'skāpə,fȯrm, 'skap-\ *adj* [*scapi-* + *-form*] **:** resembling a scape esp. in being a stem without leaves

scap net \'skap-\ *n* [prob. alter. of *scoop net*] **:** a scoop net for catching bait (as fish or shrimp)

sca·poid \'skā,pȯid\ *adj* [L *scapus* shaft, stalk + E *-oid* — more at SHAFT] **:** SCAPIFORM

scap·o·lite \'skapə,līt\ *n* -s [F, fr. L *scapus* shaft + F *-o-* + *-lite*; fr. the prismatic shape of its crystals] **1 :** a mineral of the scapolite group that is intermediate in composition between meionite and marialite, contains 46 to 54 percent of silica, and resembles feldspar when massive but has a fibrous appearance and higher specific gravity (sp. gr. 2.66–2.73) — called also *wernerite* **2 :** a member of the scapolite group

scapolite group *n* **:** a group of minerals crystallizing in the dipyramidal class of the tetragonal system, being white or grayish white in color when pure, and consisting essentially of silicates of aluminum, calcium, and sodium (hardness 5–6.5, sp. gr. 2.5–2.8)

scap·o·lit·iza·tion \,skapə,lid·ə'zāshən\ *n* -s [*scapolite* + *-ization*] **:** the process or state of alteration by which a mineral (as feldspar) is converted into scapolite

sca·pose \'skā,pōs\ *adj* [NL *scapus* + E *-ose*] **:** bearing, resembling, or consisting of a scape

scapple *var of* SCABBLE

scappler *var of* SCABBLER

scapul- *or* **scapulo-** *comb form* [L *scapula*] **1 :** scapula ⟨*scapul*ectomy⟩ ⟨*scapulo*pexy⟩ **2 :** scapular and ⟨*scapulo*axillary⟩

scap·u·la \'skapyələ\ *n, pl* **scapu·lae** \-yə,lē\ *or* **scapulas** [NL, fr. L, shoulder blade, shoulder; prob. akin to Gk *skaptein* to dig — more at CAPON] **1 a :** either of a pair of large essentially flat and triangular bones lying one in each dorsal lateral part of the thorax, forming the principal bone of the corresponding half of the shoulder girdle, divided into unequal parts by an obliquely transverse ridge that terminates in the acromion, providing articulation for the humerus, and articulating with the corresponding clavicle or coracoid — called also *shoulder blade, shoulder bone*; see CORACOID PROCESS, GLENOID CAVITY; BAT illustration **b** (1) **:** HYPERCORACOID (2) **:** SUPRACLAVICLE **2 a :** TEGULA 1a **b :** a pleuron of the mesothorax of an insect **c :** the trochanter of either of the anterior pair of legs of an insect **d :** PATAGIUM 2a

¹scap·u·lar \-lə(r)\ *n* -s [ME *scapulare*, fr. LL, fr. L *scapula* shoulder] **1 a :** a sleeveless outer garment of a monk's habit that falls over the shoulders and down the front and back usu. almost to the feet and may include the cowl **b :** a badge of membership in an order usu. worn over the shoulders **2 a :** SCAPULA **b :** a scapular feather — see BIRD illustration

²scapular \"\ *adj* [NL *scapularis*, fr. *scapula* + L *-aris* -ar] **1 :** of or relating to the shoulder or the scapula **2 :** of, relating to, or constituting the short feathers overlying the base of the wing of a bird

scapular arch *n* **:** PECTORAL GIRDLE

scap·u·la·re \,skapyə'la(a)rē\ *n* -s [NL, fr. neut. of *scapularis* scapular] **1 :** the scapular region of a bird **2 :** POSTTEMPORAL

scapular index *n* **:** the ratio of the length of the scapula to its breadth multiplied by 100

scap·u·lary \'skapyə,lerē\ *n* -ES [ME *scapelarie*, fr. ML *scapularium*, fr. L *scapula* shoulder + *-arium* -ary] **:** SCAPULAR 1

scap·u·late \'skapyələt, -,lāt\ *adj* [*scapul*et + *-ate*] **:** having scapulets

scap·u·lat·ed \-,lād·əd\ *adj* [NL *scapulatus* scapulated (fr. *scapula* + L *-atus* -ate) + E *-ed*] **:** having conspicuous and usu. distinctively colored scapular feathers

scap·u·let *or* **scap·u·lette** \'skapyə,let\ *n* -s [G *scapulette*, fr. NL *scapula* + G *-ette*] **:** a fold at the bases of the lobes of the manubrium of many rhizostomous medusae

scap·u·li·man·cy *also* **scap·u·lo·mancy** \'skapyələ,man(t)sē\ *n* -ES [*scapul-* + *-i-* + *-mancy*] **:** divination by observation of a shoulder blade usu. as blotched or cracked from a fire

sca·pus \'skāpəs\ *n, pl* **sca·pi** \-ā,pī\ [NL, fr. L, shaft of a column, stalk — more at SHAFT] **:** STEM, SHAFT, COLUMN: as **a :** SCAPE 3b **b :** the basal part of a polyp **c :** the main stem of a sea pen

¹scar \'skär, 'skȧ(r\ *n* -s [ME *skerre, skar*, fr. ON *sker* skerry; akin to ON *skera* to cut — more at SHEAR] **1 a :** an isolated or protruding rock **b :** a steep rocky eminence **:** a bare place on the side of a mountain or steep bank of earth **2 :** a hard cinder **:** furnace slag **:** CLINKER

²scar \"\ *n* -s [ME *scar, escare*, fr. MF *escare* scab, fr. LL *eschara*, fr. Gk, hearth, fireplace, scab] **1 :** a mark left in the skin or an internal organ by new connective tissue that replaces tissue injured (as by a burn, ulcer, incision) — compare CICATRIX **2 a** (1) **:** a mark left on a stem or branch by a fallen leaf or harvested fruit or on a seed by separation of the funicle (2) **:** CATFACE **b :** CICATRIX 2 **3 :** a mark or indentation resulting from damage or wear ⟨the ~*s* of bullets on the . . . church door —Kay Boyle⟩ **4 :** a lasting effect of a disturbing experience (as of dishonor, lapse of integrity, or a wound to the feelings by affliction, loss, or disappointment) **:** a remaining painful memory or maladjustment following an emotional or social trauma ⟨one of his men had been killed . . . in a manner that left a ~ upon his mind —H.G.Wells⟩

³scar \"\ *vb* **scarred; scarred; scarring; scars** *vt* **1 :** to mark with a scar **:** MAR, DISFIGURE **2 :** to leave a lasting ill effect on ⟨two events that *scarred* the man — the inquiry into his conduct as governor . . . and the death of his wife —G.W. Johnson⟩ ⟨the weariness, the disdain and passion that *scarred* his mind —Anne D. Sedgwick⟩ ~ *vi* **1 :** to form a scar **2 :** to become scarred

⁴scar \'skär\ *adj* [ON *skjarr*] *chiefly Scot* **:** SCARED, SHY

⁵scar \"\ *dial var of* SCARE

scar·ab \'skarəb *also* -ker-\ *n* -s [MF *scarabée*, fr. L *scarabaeus*; prob. akin to Gk *karabos* horned beetle — more at CARAVEL] **1** *or* **scarab beetle :** any of various usu. rather large beetles that have the clypeus expanded to cover the mouthparts, are typically dung beetles, and constitute the family Scarabaeidae; *esp* **:** SCARABAEUS 1a **2 :** a conventionalized representation of a scarabaeus commonly in stone or faience usu. having an inscription on the flat underside symbolizing the sun-god Khepera and widely used in ancient Egypt as a talisman, an ornament, and a symbol (as on a mummy) of resurrection — called also *scarabaeus*

scar·a·bae·id \,skarə'bēəd\ *adj* [NL *Scarabaeidae*] **:** of or relating to the Scarabaeidae; *broadly* **:** SCARABAEOID

scar·a·bae·i·dae \-ēə,dē\ *n pl, cap* [NL, fr. *Scarabaeus*, type genus + *-idae*] **:** a family of stout-bodied lamellicorn beetles now usu. restricted to beetles (as the tumblebugs or scarabaeus) of subsocial habits that feed on dung but sometimes esp. formerly extended to include the plant-feeding rhinoceros beetles, flower beetles, leaf chafers and others that are usu. placed in separate families — compare CETONIIDAE, DUNG BEETLE, MELOLONTHIDAE, RUTELINIDAE

scar·a·bae·i·doid \¦==¦bēə,dȯid\ *adj* [NL *Scarabaeidae* + E *-oid*] **:** SCARABAEOID

scar·a·bae·i·form \-,fȯrm\ *adj* [NL *scarabaeus* + E *-iform*] **:** resembling a scarabaeid beetle or its larva

¹scar·a·bae·oid \,==¦bē,ȯid\ *n* -s [*scarabaeus* + E *-oid*] **1 :** a beetle of Scarabaeidae or a closely related family **:** SCARABAEUS **2 :** SCARABOID

²scarabaeoid \¦==¦=,=\ *adj* [*scarabaeus* + E *-oid*] **1 :** of, relating to, or constituting the third instar in the development of a blister beetle in which it resembles the larva of a scarabaeid beetle **2 :** of or relating to the Scarabaeoidea

scar·a·bae·oi·dea \,skarəbē'ȯidēə\ *n pl, cap* [NL, fr. *Scarabaeus* + *-oidea*] *in many classifications* **:** a superfamily of Polyphaga that is equivalent to the most inclusive concept of Scarabaeidae or to the superfamily Lamellicornia

scar·a·bae·us \,skarə'bēəs\ *n* [L — more at SCARAB] **1 a** *pl* **scarabaeuses** \-ēəsəz\ *or* **scar·a·baei** \-ē,ī\ **:** a large black or nearly black dung beetle (*Scarabaeus sacer*) of the countries bordering on the Mediterranean that with perhaps also one or more related beetles was regarded by the ancient Egyptians as symbolic of resurrection and immortality **b** *cap* [NL, fr. L, scarab] **:** a genus containing the scarabaeus and related beetles and being the type of the family Scarabaeidae **2** -ES **:** SCARAB 2

scar·a·bee \'skarə,bē\ *n* -s [MF *scarabée* — more at SCARAB] **:** SCARAB 1

scar·a·be·idae \,skarə'bēə,dē\ [NL, fr. *Scarabaeus* + *-idae*] *syn of* SCARABAEIDAE

scarab green *n* **:** a brilliant green that is bluer and stronger than emerald (sense 2a)

[1]**scar·a·boid** \ˈskarə,bȯid\ *n* -s [*scarab* + *-oid*] **:** a gem engraved only on the flat oval base and somewhat rounded on the back but with no imitation of the beetle ⟨a Greek ~ of the late 6th and 5th centuries B.C.⟩

[2]**scaraboid** \"\ *adj* [*scarab* + *-oid*] **1 :** SCARABAEOID **2 :** of or resembling a scarab; *esp* **:** of or forming a scaraboid

scar·a·mouch *or* **scar·a·mouche** \ˈskarə,müsh *also* -ker- *or* -müch\ *n* -s [F *Scaramouche*, fr. It *Scaramuccia*, fr. *scaramuccia* skirmish — more at SKIRMISH] **1** *usu cap* **:** a stock character in the Italian commedia dell' arte characterized orig. in burlesque of a Spanish don by boastfulness and poltroonery **2 a :** a cowardly buffoon **:** NE'ER-DO-WELL **b :** RASCAL, SCAMP

scar·bo·rough lily \ˈskärb(ə)rə-\ *n, usu cap S* [fr. *Scarborough*, municipal borough of Yorkshire, England] **:** a plant (*Vallota speciosa*) of southern Africa resembling the amaryllis and having bright red flowers

scarborough warning *n, usu cap S* [fr. *Scarborough*, Yorkshire, England] *Brit* **:** a very short notice or warning or none at all

scarb–tree \ˈskärb,trē\ *n* [prob. alter. of obs. *scrab-tree*, fr. *scrab* crab apple (prob. of Scand origin) + *tree*] **:** WILDING 1a

[1]**scarce** \ˈske(ə)rs, ˈska(a)(ə)rs, |əs, *dial* ˈski| *or* ˈskərs *or* ˈskəs *or* ˈskās\ *adj* -ER/-EST [ME *scars*, fr. ONF *escars*, *scars*, fr. (assumed) VL *excarpsus*, lit., plucked out, alter. of L *excerptus*, past part. of *excerpere* to pluck out, excerpt — more at EXCERPT] **1 a :** deficient in quantity or number compared with the demand **:** not plentiful or abundant ⟨butter is cheap when it is plentiful, and dear when it is ~ —G.B.Shaw⟩ ⟨snappy looking gals are ~ as hen's teeth out here —*Star Detective*⟩ **:** RARE ⟨collects ~ Japanese prints⟩ **b :** not provided in sufficient abundance to be free **2** *obs* **:** PARSIMONIOUS, STINGY, FRUGAL

[2]**scarce** \"\ *adv* [ME *scars*, fr. *scars*, adj.] **:** SCARCELY, BARELY, HARDLY ⟨would have ~ arrived before she would find some excuse to leave —W.B.Yeats⟩ ⟨cities of the period were ~ more than towns —J.T.Adams⟩

scarce·ly *adv* [ME *scarsly*, fr. *scars* scarce + *-ly*] **1** *obs* **:** in a sparing manner **:** STINGILY **2 :** by a narrow margin (as of quantity, time, or space) **:** only just **:** BARELY ⟨had ~ rung the bell when the door flew open —Agnes S. Turnbull⟩; *also* **:** only just if at all or as much or as many ⟨seemed ~ to notice what passed . . . as if he were in some partial coma —Elizabeth M. Roberts⟩ ⟨~ more than a stone's throw from the square are the great flour mills —*Amer. Guide Series: Minn.*⟩ **:** almost not ⟨~ ever wore this mantle —Arnold Bennett⟩ ⟨~ anything left to sell⟩ ⟨it seemed to the child that it was after midnight . . . but it was ~ eleven o'clock —Margaret Deland⟩ ⟨a guide who knew ~ a word of English⟩ — sometimes used in nonstandard construction with a superfluous negative ⟨wasn't ~ eleven o'clock yet⟩ ⟨ain't ~ 15 years old⟩ **3** *archaic* **:** with difficulty ⟨if the righteous ~ be saved, where shall the . . . sinner appear —1 Pet 4:18 (AV)⟩ **4 a :** certainly not ⟨could ~ interfere between another man and his own beast —Owen Wister⟩ **b :** probably not — used to mitigate the force of the speaker's certainty ⟨there could ~ have been found a leader better equipped for the work —V.L. Parrington⟩

scarce·ment \ˈskersmənt, -ka(a)r-\ *n* -s [obs. *scarce* to diminish (fr. ME *scarsen*, fr. *scars* scarce) + *-ment*] **:** an offset or retreat in the thickness of a wall or bank of earth

scarce·ness *n* -ES [ME *scarsnes*, fr. *scars* scarce + *-nes* -ness] **:** the quality or state of being scarce **:** SCARCITY

scar·ci·ty \ˈske(r)səd·ē, ˈska(a)|, |əs-, -ətē, -i\ *n* -ES [ME *scarsetee*, fr. ONF *escarseté*, fr. *escars* scarce + *-eté* -ity — more at SCARCE] **:** the quality or condition of being scarce: **a** *obs* **:** SPARINGNESS, NIGGARDLINESS, PARSIMONY **b :** smallness of quantity or number in proportion to the wants or demands ⟨a ~ of grain⟩ ⟨the ~ of teachers⟩ **:** very limited supply ⟨the ~ of radium⟩ **c :** lack of provisions for the support of life **:** a period of such want ⟨a drought-struck area suffers ~⟩ **d** *obs* **:** the condition of lacking an adequate supply (as of the necessities of life) **:** PENURY, POVERTY **e** *obs* **:** a state of imperfection **:** INADEQUACY **f :** RARENESS, UNCOMMONNESS ⟨praise . . . owes its value to its ~ —Samuel Johnson⟩

scarcity economics *n pl but usu sing in constr* **:** an economic theory that allegedly justifies limitations of output so as to assure profits

[1]**scare** \ˈske(ə)r, ˈska(a)r, |ə, *dial* ˈski\ *vb* **scared** \|(ə)rd, |əd\ *or dial* **scart** \|(ə)rt, |ət\ **scared** *or dial* **scart; scaring; scares** [ME *skerren*, *skeren*, fr. ON *skirra*, fr. *skjarr* shy, timid] *vt* **1 :** to strike with sudden fear **:** FRIGHTEN, ALARM, PANIC **2 a :** to drive or impel or evoke by fright ⟨rattlesnakes used to ~ me to death —Ben Hogan⟩ ⟨a scream that *scared* away the burglar⟩ ⟨an aloofness that ~*s* off suitors⟩ ⟨~ a confession out of the suspect by threats⟩ ⟨a pet mouse that *scared* the wits out of his mother⟩ **:** cause to become by fright ⟨a wild midnight ride that *scared* him stiff⟩ **b :** to cause (as bird pests) to go away in fright **:** frighten off ⟨from *scaring* birds, the . . . child graduated through the many tasks of mixed farming —*Times Lit. Supp.*⟩ **c :** to frighten (game) from cover — used with *out* or *up* ⟨sent a beater ahead to ~ out the partridge⟩ ~ *vi* **1 :** to become scared **:** take alarm ⟨a woman who ~*s* easily at the sight of a mouse⟩ **2 :** to produce fright **syn** see FRIGHTEN

[2]**scare** \"\ *n* -s [ME *skere*, fr. *skeren* to scare] **1 :** a sensation or state of sudden fear ⟨fired over their heads to throw a ~ into them⟩ **:** an instance of being scared: as **a :** a sudden fright produced by a trifling cause or originating in a mistake ⟨given quite a ~ by hearing the news of a boy's drowning before their son returned⟩ **b :** a widespread state of exaggerated or mistaken alarm **:** PANIC ⟨the frontier situation and British arbitrary naval seizures produced a war ~ in the spring of 1794 —S.F.Bemis⟩ **2 :** something that causes fright ⟨~*s* were made of poles wrapped with reeds hung with potsherds —C.D.Forde⟩

[3]**scare** \"\ *adj* **1 :** tending to cause fright or widespread alarm ⟨~ stories that tuna caught in the Pacific are dangerously radioactive —*U.S. News & World Report*⟩ **2 :** affected by or due to fright or panic ⟨a refuge for ~ money from unsettled parts of the world —*Christian Science Monitor*⟩

scarebabe \ˈ=,=\ *n* [[1]*scare* + *babe*] **:** a thing to scare a baby **:** BOGEY

scarebug *n* [[2]*scare* + *bug*] *obs* **:** BUGBEAR

scare buying *n* **:** buying in advance of need in anticipation of possible shortages (as just after the outbreak of a war)

scarecrow \ˈ=,=\ *n* [[1]*scare* + *crow*] **1 a :** an object typically suggesting a human figure set up to frighten crows or other birds away from crops **b :** something that frightens without harming **2 :** a person whose appearance suggests that of a scarecrow (as in being skinny or ill clad)

scared *adj* -ER/-EST [fr. past part. of [1]*scare*] **:** thrown into or living in a state of fear, fright, or panic ⟨~ that he will fall into the hands of the wrong kind of girl⟩ **:** FRIGHTENED ⟨~ to death of mature responsibilities —*Time*⟩ **syn** see AFRAID

scared·ness *n* -ES **:** the quality or state of being scared

scaredy–cat \ˈskerdē,kat, -ka(a)r-\ *n* [*scared* + *-y* + *cat*] **:** an unduly fearful person

scare·ful \ˈ=fəl\ *or* **scare·some** \ˈ=səm\ *adj* [[2]*scare* + *-ful* or *-some*] *dial* **:** DREADFUL, ALARMING

[1]**scarehead** \ˈ=,=\ *n* [[3]*scare* + *head*] **:** an extraordinarily large or sensational newspaper headline; *esp* **:** one designed to arouse anxiety

[2]**scarehead** \"\ *vt* **:** to provide (a news story) with a scarehead

scare headline *n* [[3]*scare*] **:** SCAREHEAD

scaremonger \ˈ=,==\ *n* [[2]*scare* + *monger*] **:** a person who circulates frightening reports of impending disaster **:** ALARMIST — **scaremongering** \ˈ=,==(=)=\ *n*

scar end *n* [[2]*scar*] **:** the unfinished end of a breakwater or similar structure under construction

scar·er \ˈskerə(r), ˈska(a)r-\ *n* -s **:** one that scares ⟨rooks . . . haunted the newly sown fields, and rose in clouds at the ~'*s* shout —Adrian Bell⟩

scares *pres 3d sing of* SCARE, *pl of* SCARE

scare up *vt* **:** to find by persistent effort **:** bring to light or get together with labor **:** scrape up ⟨managed to *scare up* enough food to fill a freight car —Robert Rice⟩ ⟨*scare up* a light supper for unexpected guests⟩

scarey *var of* SCARY

[1]**scarf** \ˈskärf, ˈskȧf\ *n, pl* **scarves** \|vz, |vz\ *or* **scarfs** [ONF *escarpe* sash, sling, prob. alter. of OF *escrepe* wallet suspended from the shoulder, fr. ML *scrippum* pilgrim's scrip — more at SCRIP] **1 a :** a piece of cloth made in varying widths and lengths and worn for decoration or warmth across the shoulders, around the neck, over the head, or about the waist ⟨a narrow knitted ~ for sports wear and a long lace one for evening wear⟩ **b :** a square or triangle of cloth for similar uses **c :** a fur or set of furs for women's wear **2 a :** a military or official sash usu. indicative of rank **b :** TIPPET 3 **c :** a band of crape worn over the shoulder by mourners at a funeral **3 :** a usu. oblong decorative cloth covering for the top of a table, sideboard, or bureau

[2]**scarf** \"\ *vt* -ED/-ING/-S **1 :** to wrap, cover, or adorn with or as if with a scarf **2 :** to wrap or throw on (a scarf or mantle) loosely

[3]**scarf** *also* **scarph** \ˈskärf, ˈskȧf\ *n* -s [ME *skarf*, prob. of Scand origin; akin to Sw *skarv* seam, scarf, ON *skarfr* scarf — more at SCORPION] **1 :** either of the chamfered or cutaway ends that fit together to form a scarf joint **2 :** SCARF JOINT **3 :** a groove cut along a whale's body preliminary to cutting away the blubber **4 :** the beveled face of a stump or log produced by the undercut in tree felling **5 :** a crease made in a piece of veneer wood or heavy paper to facilitate folding or bending in the making of a plant band

[4]**scarf** *or* **scarph** \"\ *vb* -ED/-ING/-S *vt* **1 :** to unite (as pieces of timber) by a scarf joint **2 :** to form a scarf on esp. for a joint **3 :** FLENSE **4 :** to put a taper in (a leaf spring) ~ *vi* **1 :** to become united by a scarf joint **2 :** to unite members with a scarf joint

[5]**scarf** *or* **scarfe** \ˈskärf\ *n* -s [of Scand origin; akin to ON *skarfr* cormorant] *Scot* **:** CORMORANT

[6]**scarf** \"\ *vb* -ED/-ING/-S [perh. alter. of [2]*scarp*] *vi* **:** to remove defects (as seams, scab, scale) from the surface of unfinished steel (as a bar, ingot, billet, bloom) with oxyacetylene flame or abrasive powder ~ *vt* **:** to smooth by scarfing

scarf cloud *n* [[1]*scarf*] **:** a wispy cloud forming above and later mantling the sides of a rising cumulus

scarfed \ˈskärft\ *or* **scarved** \-rvd\ *adj* [[1]*scarf* + *-ed*] **:** having or wearing a scarf

scarf·er *or* **scarph·er** \ˈskärfə(r)\ *n* -s [[4]*scarf* + *-er*] **:** one that scarfs: as **a :** one that scarfs parts (as of shoes or metal pieces) so that smooth joints may be formed **b :** an operator of a machine for beveling the edges of skelp

scarf joint *n* [[3]*scarf*] **:** a joint made by chamfering, halving, notching, or otherwise cutting away two pieces to correspond to each other and securing them together after overlapping (as by gluing, bolting, riveting, welding, brazing)

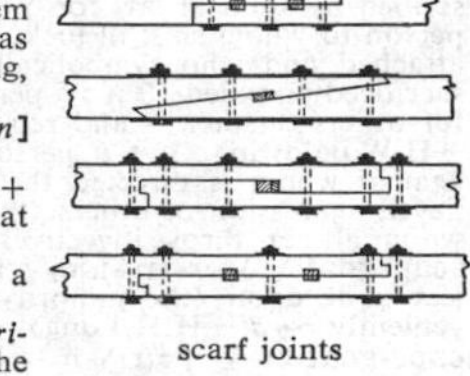

scarf joints

scarfpin \ˈ=,=\ *n* [[1]*scarf* + *pin*] **:** TIEPIN

scarfskin \ˈ=,=\ *n* [[1]*scarf* + *skin*] **:** EPIDERMIS; *esp* **:** that forming the cuticle of a nail

scarfweld *n* [[3]*scarf* + *weld*] **:** a welded scarf joint in metal

[1]**scar·id** \-rəd\ *adj* [NL *Scaridae*] **:** of or relating to the Scaridae

[2]**scarid** \"\ *n* -s **:** a fish of the family Scaridae

Scar·i·dae \ˈskarə,dē\ *n pl, cap* [NL fr. *Scarus*, type genus + *-idae*] **:** a family of marine percoid fishes closely resembling the Labridae but having the teeth of the jaws more or less coalescent and comprising the true parrot fishes

scarier *comparative of* SCARY

scariest *superlative of* SCARY

scar·i·fi·ca·tion \,ska(a)rəfəˈkāshən, ,sker-\ *n* -s [ME, fr. LL *scarification-*, *scarificatio*, fr. *scarificatus* (past part. of *scarificare* to scarify) + L *-ion-*, *-io* -ion] **1 :** the act or process of scarifying **2 :** a mark or group of marks made by scarifying

scar·i·fi·ca·tor \ˈ====,kād·ə(r)\ *n* -s [NL, fr. LL *scarificatus* + L *-or*] **:** an instrument for making superficial cuts in the skin; *esp* **:** one containing several lancets moved by a spring

scar·i·fi·er \ˈska(a)rə,fī(ə)r, ˈsker-, -īə\ *n* -s **:** one that scarifies: as **a :** SCARIFICATOR **b :** a machine that tears up and partially pulverizes surface soil **c :** an implement or machine that tears up the surface of a road prior to resurfacing

[1]**scar·i·fy** \-,fī\ *vb* -ED/-ING/-ES [MF *scarifier*, fr. LL *scarificare*, alter. (influenced by L *-ficare* -fy) of L *scarifare*, fr. Gk *skariphasthai* to scratch an outline, sketch — more at SCRIBE, -FY] *vt* **1 :** to make a number of cuts, scratches, or scars on: as **a :** to make a number of small incisions in (the superficial skin or mucous membrane) with a lancet or scarificator (as for drawing blood or inoculating) **b :** to mark with scars **:** CICATRIZE **2 :** to lacerate the feelings of **:** censure mercilessly **:** FLAY ⟨in a brilliant tirade . . . he denounces, *scarifies*, blasts the pedantic schoolmasters —Gilbert Highet⟩ **3 :** to break up and loosen the surface of (as a field or road) **4 :** to treat (hard-coated seed) by mechanical abrasion or with acid to facilitate water absorption and hasten germination ~ *vi* **1 :** to make cuts, scratches, or scars on skin or mucous membrane **2 :** to subject a person to cutting criticism or some other painful experience **3 :** to break up and loosen a hard surface ⟨if the road has become deeply rutted or pitted it is necessary to ~ at least to the depth of the deepest holes —L.I.Hewes & C.H.Oglesby⟩

[2]**scarify** \"\ *vt* -ED/-ING/-ES [[1]*scare* + *-ify*] *dial* **:** SCARE, FRIGHTEN

scar·i·ly \ˈskerəlē, ˈska(a)r-, -li\ *adv* **:** in a scary manner **:** in a frightened or frightening way

scar·i·ness \-rēn-\ *n* -ES **:** the quality or state of being scary

scaring *pres part of* SCARE

scar·i·ous \ˈska(a)rēəs\ *also* **scar·i·ose** \-ē,ōs\ *adj* [NL *scariosus*] **:** thin and membranous in texture ⟨a ~ bract⟩

scar·la·ti·na \,skärləˈtēnə, -kȧl-\ *n* -s [NL, fr. ML *scarlata*, *scarlatum* piece of cloth, scarlet] **:** SCARLET FEVER — **scar·la·ti·nal** \ˈ==ˈtēnᵊl\ *adj*

scar·la·ti·ni·form \ˈ==ˈtēnə,fȯrm, -tin-\ *adj* [NL *scarlatina* + E *-iform*] **:** resembling the rash of scarlet fever

scar·la·ti·no·gen·ic \-,jenik\ *adj* [NL *scarlatina* + *-o-* + E *-genic*] **:** causing scarlet fever ⟨a ~ streptococcus⟩

scar·la·ti·noid \-ˈtē,nȯid, skärˈlatᵊn,ȯid\ *adj* [NL *scarlatina* + E *-oid*] **:** SCARLATINIFORM

scar·less \ˈskärləs\ *adj* **:** having or leaving no scar

[1]**scar·let** \ˈskärlət, ˈskȧl-, *usu* -əd·+V\ *n* -s [ME *scarlet*, *scarlat*, fr. OF or ML; OF *escarlate*, fr. ML *scarlata*, *scarlatum*, *scarleta*, *scarletum*, fr. Per *saqalāt* kind of rich cloth] **1 a** *obs* (1) **:** a rich cloth of bright color (2) *or* **scarlet in grain** [*scarlet in grain*, ME, fr. *scarlet* + *in grain* — more at GRAIN] **:** a cloth of a fast-dyed red **b :** cloth or clothes of a scarlet color ⟨arrayed in ~⟩; *specif* **:** a costume of scarlet color signifying official or professional rank or worn as a uniform **c :** persons wearing scarlet (as at a fox hunt) **2 a :** any of various bright reds ⟨summer flowers had given place to the ~*s* and mauves of autumn —Frances Towers⟩ **b** *or* **scarlet red :** a vivid red that is yellower and slightly paler than apple red, yellower and lighter than carmine, yellower and duller than Castilian red, yellower and paler than madder crimson, and bluer, less strong, and slightly darker than pimento — called also *French scarlet, Venetian scarlet*

[2]**scarlet** \"\ *adj* [ME, fr. [1]*scarlet*] **1 a :** of the color scarlet **b :** clad in scarlet **c :** having the face reddened by emotion (as embarrassment, anger) **:** RED-FACED ⟨turned ~ with rage⟩ **2** [so called fr. its use in Isa 1:18 and Rev 17:1–6] **a :** glaringly offensive **:** FLAGRANT, HEINOUS ⟨bent upon sinning in flagrant and ~ fashion —G.W.Johnson⟩ **b :** of, characterized by, or associated with sexual immorality; *specif* **:** of or practicing prostitution ⟨in the mining camps . . . the inevitable influx of ~ women who became the hostesses of the gambling dens and night clubs —Mabel Elliott⟩

scarlet admiral *n* **:** RED ADMIRAL

scarlet–berried elder \ˈ==-==-\ *n* **:** RED-BERRIED ELDER

scarletberry \ˈ==- — *see* BERRY\ *n* **1 :** BITTERSWEET 2a **2 :** the fruit of the scarletberry

scarlet bugler *n* **1 :** a pentstemon (*Pentstemon centranthifolius*) native to southwestern No. America, used as an ornamental, and having thick leaves and long tubular scarlet flowers **2 :** a cactus of the genus *Cleistocactus* having long tubular bright-red flowers

scarlet bush *n* **:** SCARLET HAMELIA

scarlet clematis *n* **:** a showy woody vine (*Clematis texensis*) of Texas with solitary nodding scarlet flowers

scarlet cup *n* **:** any of various red fungi of the genus *Peziza*

scarlet–day \ˈ==,=\ *n* **:** a ceremonial occasion at a British university marked by the wearing of official robes of scarlet

scarlet eggplant *n* **:** TOMATO EGGPLANT

scarlet elder *n* **:** RED-BERRIED ELDER

scarlet fever *n* **:** an acute contagious febrile disease caused by a hemolytic streptococcus and characterized by inflammation of the nose, throat, and mouth sometimes with strawberry tongue and a generalized toxemia accompanied by a rash marked by flushing of the skin with red spots and followed in a week or two by desquamation of the affected skin

scarlet fritillary *n* **:** a bulbous herb (*Fritillaria recurva*) with scarlet-and-yellow flowers

scarlet gaura *n* **:** an erect perennial herb (*Gaura coccinea*) of central No. America with alternate lanceolate leaves and rather sparse terminal leafy spikes of bright red flowers

scarlet hamelia *n* **:** a tropical American shrub (*Hamelia erecta*) having edible fruit and often cultivated for its showy scarlet or crimson flowers

scarlet haw *n* **:** any of several hawthorns; *esp* **:** a common American tree or shrub (*Crataegus biltmoriana*) with showy white flowers in corymbs and bright-red fruit

scarlet ibis *n* **:** an ibis (*Eudocimus rubra*) of South and Central America that is an intense scarlet with black-tipped wings

scarlet lake *n* **:** BLOOD RED

scarlet larkspur *n* **:** a perennial herb (*Delphinium cardinale*) of southern California with bright-scarlet flowers

scarlet letter *n* [fr. the novel *The Scarlet Letter* (1850) by Nathaniel Hawthorne †1864 Am. novelist] **:** a scarlet A worn as a punitive mark of adultery

scarlet lightning *n* [by folk etymology fr. *scarlet lychnis*] **:** MALTESE CROSS 2

scarlet lobelia *n* **:** CARDINAL FLOWER

scar·let·ly *adv* **:** in a scarlet manner **:** FLAGRANTLY

scarlet lychnis *n* **:** MALTESE CROSS 2

scarlet macaw *n* **:** a macaw (*Ara macao*) that is the largest and showiest of Mexican parrots and has predominantly scarlet or vermilion plumage with bright yellow wing coverts, deep purplish remiges, and azure blue lower back, rump, and tail coverts

scarlet madder *n* **:** MADDER SCARLET

scarlet maple *n* **:** RED MAPLE

scarlet mite *n* **:** any of numerous bright red carnivorous mites found among grass and weeds including some with young that are parasitic on spiders and insects — compare CHIGGER 2

scarlet monkey flower *n* **:** a perennial herb (*Mimulus cardinalis*) of the western U. S. with showy scarlet 2-lipped flowers

scarlet oak *n* **:** an oak (*Quercus coccinea*) having close-grained wood, deeply 7-lobed leaves that turn scarlet in autumn, and an acorn with a deep cup

scarlet ocher *n* **:** INDIAN RED 2b

[1]**scarlet pimpernel** *n* **:** a common pimpernel (*Anagallis arvensis*) having scarlet, white, or purplish flowers that close at the approach of rainy or cloudy weather — called also *poor man's weatherglass, red pimpernel*

[2]**scarlet pimpernel** *n* [after *The Scarlet Pimpernel*, assumed name of hero of *The Scarlet Pimpernel* (1905), romance by Baroness Emmuska Orczy †1947 Eng. novelist and playwright] **:** a person who rescues others from mortal danger by smuggling them across a border

scarlet plume *n* **:** a Mexican shrub (*Euphorbia fulgens*) often cultivated for its scarlet-bracted flowers

scarlet red *n* **1 :** SCARLET 2b **2** *also* **scarlet red medicinal :** SUDAN IV

scarlet runner *also* **scarlet runner bean** *n* **:** a tropical American high-climbing bean (*Phaseolus coccineus*) with large bright red flowers and red-and-black seeds that is grown widely as an ornamental and is a preferred food bean in Great Britain

scarlets *pl of* SCARLET

scarlet sage *n* **:** any of several red-flowered salvias; *esp* **:** a well-known garden bedding plant (*Salvia splendens*) of Brazil with long racemes of intense scarlet flowers — compare SAGE 1a

scarlet snake *n* **1 :** a small slender colubrid snake (*Cemophora coccinea*) of the southern U. S. having the back transversely striped with black, red, and yellow **2** *also* **scarlet king snake :** a king snake (*Lampropeltis elapsoides*) having marks like those of the scarlet snake

scarlet strawberry *n* **:** VIRGINIA STRAWBERRY

scarlet sumac *n* **:** SMOOTH SUMAC 1

scarlet tanager *n* **:** a common American tanager (*Piranga olivacea*) of which the adult male is scarlet with black wings and tail and the female and young are chiefly olive — called also *redbird, red robin*

scarlet trumpet *n* **:** STANDING CYPRESS

scarlet vermilion *n* **:** a strong reddish orange that is yellower and paler than paprika or poppy, redder and darker than fire red, and less strong and slightly lighter than average coral red

[1]**scarn** \ˈskärn\ *archaic var of* SCORN

[2]**scarn** \"\ *n* -s [of Scand origin; akin to ON *skarn* dung — more at SCAT-] *dial Eng* **:** DUNG

[1]**scar·oid** \ˈska(a),rȯid\ *adj* [NL *Scarus* + E *-oid*] **:** resembling or related to the Scaridae

[2]**scaroid** \"\ *n* -s **:** a scaroid fish

sca·ro·la \skəˈrōlə\ *or* **sca·role** \-ōl\ *n* -s [It *scariola*, *scarola*, fr. OIt *scariola* — more at ESCAROLE] **:** ESCAROLE

[1]**scarp** *or* **scarpe** \ˈskärp\ *n* -s [ONF *escarpe* sash, sling — more at SCARF] *heraldry* **:** a diminutive of the bend sinister half its width

[2]**scarp** \ˈskärp, ˈskȧp\ *n* -s [It *scarpa*, prob. of Gmc origin; akin to OE *scearp* sharp — more at SHARP] **1 :** a nearly vertical sometimes walled side of a ditch below the parapet of a fortification — called also *escarp;* compare COUNTERSCARP **2 a :** a line of cliffs produced by faulting or erosion — see FAULT-LINE SCARP, FAULT SCARP **b :** a low steep slope along a beach caused by wave erosion

[3]**scarp** \"\ *vt* -ED/-ING/-S **:** to cut so as to form a scarp **:** cut down vertically or to a steep slope ⟨~ the face of a ditch⟩ ⟨~ a coast into rugged cliffs⟩

scar·pa's fascia \ˈskärpəz-\ *n, usu cap S* [after Antonio *Scarpa* †1832, Ital. anatomist & surgeon] **:** the superficial fascia of the groin

scarpa's foramen *n, usu cap S* [after Antonio *Scarpa*] **:** either of two canals opening into the incisive foramen in the median plane and transmitting the nasopalatine nerves

scarpa's triangle *also* **scarpa's trigone** *n, usu cap S* [after Antonio *Scarpa*] **:** an area in the upper anterior part of the thigh bounded by Poupart's ligament, the sartorius, and the adductor longus

scarp·er \ˈskäpə(r\ *vi* -ED/-ING/-S [perh. fr. It *scappare* to flee, escape, fr. (assumed) VL *excappare* — more at ESCAPE] *Brit* **:** to run away **:** make off

scarph *var of* SCARF

scarpher *var of* SCARFER

scarp·let \ˈskärplət\ *n* -s [[2]*scarp* + *-let*] **:** a fault scarp only a few inches or at most a few feet high **:** earthquake rent

scarpside \ˈ=,=\ *n* **:** the side of a scarp

scarred *past of* SCAR

scar·rer \ˈskärə(r)\ *n* -s [[2]*scar* + *-er*] **:** one that shaves blemishes from leather

scarring *n* -s [fr. gerund of [3]*scar*] **:** a marking resulting from being scarred

scar·row \ˈska(,)rō\ *n* -s [of Scand origin; akin to ON *skæra* twilight, Gk *skia* shadow — more at SCENE] *Scot* **:** a shadowy or faint light

[1]**scar·ry** \ˈskärē\ *adj* [[1]*scar* + *-y*] **:** characterized by bare and rugged projections of rock ⟨the ~ flank of the mountain⟩

[2]**scarry** \"\ *adj* -ER/-EST [[2]*scar* + *-y*] **:** bearing marks of wounds **:** SCARRED

scars *pl of* SCAR, *pres 3d sing of* SCAR

[1]**scart** \ˈskärt\ *vb* -ED/-ING/-S [ME *skarten*, alter. of *scratten* to scratch] *chiefly Scot* **:** SCRATCH, SCRAPE

[2]**scart** \"\ *n* -s *chiefly Scot* **:** SCRATCH, MARK; *esp* **:** one made in writing

³scart \"\ *or* **scarth** \-rth\ *n* -s [ME *scarth*, of Scand origin; akin to ON *skarfr* cormorant] *chiefly Scot* : CORMORANT
⁴scart *dial past of* SCARE
scarth \'skärth\ *n* -s [of Scand origin; akin to ON *skarth* notch, mountain pass — more at SHARD] *dial Eng* : a bare rough rock
scar tissue *n* : the connective tissue forming a scar and composed chiefly of fibroblasts in recent scars and largely of dense collagenous fibers in old scars
scar·us \'ska(a)rəs\ *n* [L, fr. Gk *skaros*; prob. akin to Gk *skairein* to skip, leap] **1** -ES : a parrot fish (*Sparisoma cretense*) of the Mediterranean of excellent table quality and highly esteemed by the ancient Romans **2** *cap* [NL, fr. L, parrot fish] : the type genus of Scaridae comprising fishes with the teeth completely consolidated so that the jaws have the appearance of a bird's beak — compare PARROT FISH
scarved *var of* SCARFED
scarves *pl of* SCARF
scary *also* **scarey** \'skerē, 'ska(a)r-, -ri, *dial* 'skir-\ *adj* **scarier; scariest** [²*scare* + -*y*] **1** : causing fright : ALARMING ⟨this ... ~ picture story of a jungle tiger who waits to pounce on an unsuspecting camel —Katharine T. Kinkead⟩ **2** : easily scared : TIMID ⟨a sudden movement or sharp noise could cause a stampede in the ~ half-wild cattle⟩ **3** : SCARED, ALARMED, FRIGHTENED ⟨while I'm waiting, I get a little ~ and think I ought to call the cops —Bant Singer⟩
¹scat \'skat\ *n* -s [ON *skattr* tribute — more at SCEAT] : a crown tax in the Shetland and Orkney islands for the use (as for pasturage) of commons
²scat \"\ *n* -s [prob. imit.] **1** *dial Eng* : a sudden shower of rain **2** [perh. fr. ³*scat*] *dial* : SMASH, BANG, SMACK
³scat \"\ *vt* **scat; scat; scatting; scats** [perh. short for ¹*scatter*] **1** *chiefly dial* : SCATTER ⟨~ his bones abroad, so as not one hangs to another —Eden Phillpotts⟩ **2** *chiefly dial* : SMASH, BEAT ⟨~ me across the face with a tar brush —*Manchester Guardian Weekly*⟩
⁴scat \", *usu* -ad·+V\ *vi* **scatted; scatted; scatting; scats** **1** : to go away quickly : leave hurriedly ⟨you just ~ off to bed, young lady —Oakley Hall⟩ — often used interjectionally to drive away an animal (as a cat) **2** : to move with more than ordinary speed ⟨only advertised 125 hp, but the car would ~ in any man's language —*Motor Life*⟩
⁵scat *var of* SKAT
⁶scat *also* **skat** \'skat, *usu* -ad·+V\ *n* -s [Gk *skat-, skōr* excrement — more at SCAT-] : an animal fecal dropping
⁷scat \"\ *n* -s [by shortening fr. NL *Scatophagus*, former generic name, fr. Gk *skatophagos* scatophagous] : ARGUSFISH
⁸scat \"\ *n* -s [perh. imit.] : singing with meaningless syllables instead of words used esp. in jazz for an instrumental effect — compare BOP, RIFF
⁹scat \"\ *vi* **scatted; scatted; scatting; scats** : to improvise or repeat meaningless syllables to a melody : sing scat
scat- *or* **scato-** *comb form* [Gk *skato-*, fr. *skat-, skōr* excrement; akin to OE *scearn* dung, ON *skarn* dung, L *muscerda* mouse dropping, and prob. to Russ *sor* filth] : ordure ⟨*scatology*⟩
scatback \'=,=\ *n* [⁵*scat* + *back*] : a backfield player in football who is an esp. fast and elusive runner
¹scathe \'skāth\ *also* **scath** \'skath\ *n, pl* **scathes** [ME *scath, skathe*, fr. ON *skathi*; akin to OE *sceatha* malefactor, injury, OHG *scado* damage, injury, harm, Goth *skathis*, Gk *askēthēs* unharmed] **1** : HARM, INJURY, DAMAGE ⟨all the British bombers were able to return safely to their base ... without ~ —*Manchester Guardian Weekly*⟩ **2** *chiefly dial* : a source of regret : PITY, MISFORTUNE
²scathe \"\ *also* **scath** \"\ *vt* **scathed; scathed; scathing; scathes** *also* **scaths** [ME *scathen, skathen*, fr. ON *skatha*; akin to OE *sceathian* to injure, OHG *scadōn*; denominative fr. the root of OE *sceatha* injury] **1** : to do harm to : INJURE, DAMAGE; *specif* : to injure by scorching or withering with fire or lightning ⟨a giant oak which heaven's fierce flame had *scathed* —P.B.Shelley⟩ **2** : to assail with withering denunciation ⟨bombarding her with rhetoric and ... *scathing* her with sarcasm —Jean Stafford⟩
scathe·ful \'skāthfəl\ *adj* [¹*scathe* + -*ful*] : HARMFUL, PERNICIOUS
scathe·less \-thləs\ *adj* [ME *scathles*, fr. *scath* scathe + -*les* -less] : being without scathe, injury, or damage : UNHARMED ⟨too excited to stop and shoot, and so they got away ~ —T.E. Lawrence⟩ — **scathe·less·ly** *adv*
scathing *adj* [fr. pres. part. of ²*scathe*] : bitterly severe ⟨silenced him with a ~ look⟩ ⟨braved his ~ scorn⟩ ⟨looked as though he had been through some ~ ordeal —Agnes M. Cleaveland⟩ — **scath·ing·ly** *adv*
scatole *var of* SKATOLE
scat·o·log·i·cal \,skad-ᵊl¦äjəkəl, -atᵊl-, -jēk-\ *also* **scat·o·log·ic** \-jik, -jēk\ *adj* [*scatology* + -*ical*, -*ic*] **1** : of or relating to the study of excrement ⟨~ data⟩ **2** : marked by an interest in excrement or obscenity ⟨of the obscene rhymes contributed by the younger children, the ~ rather than the sexual element prevailed —Brian Sutton-Smith⟩ **3** : of or relating to excrement or excremental functions ⟨~ terms⟩
sca·tol·o·gy *also* **ska·tol·o·gy** \skə'täləjē, ska'- -ji\ *n* -ES [*scatology* fr. *scat-* + -*logy*; *skatology*, alter. (influenced by Gk *skato-* scat-) of *scatology*] **1** : the study of excrement; *specif* : analysis of animal diet by examination of fecal droppings **2** : obscene literature **3** : interest in things filthy or obscene (as in literature)
scat·o·phag·i·dae \,skad-ə'fajə,dē\ *n, cap* [NL, fr. *Scatophaga*, type genus. (fr. Gk *skatophagos* scatophagous) + -*idae*] : a family of round-headed pollinose muscoid flies that comprise the typical dung flies
sca·toph·a·gous \skə'täfəgəs\ *adj* [Gk *skatophagos*, fr. *skat-, skōr* excrement + *phagein* to eat — more at SCAT-, BAKSHEESH] : habitually feeding on dung : COPROPHAGOUS ⟨a ~ beetle⟩
sca·toph·a·gy \-fəjē\ *n* -ES [*scat-* + -*phagy*] : the practice of eating excrement or other filth as a religious ceremonial rite or as a pathological obsession
scats *pl of* SCAT, *pres 3d sing of* SCAT
scatt \'skat\ *n* -s [of Scand origin; akin to ON *skattr* tribute — more at SCEAT] *archaic* : TAX, TRIBUTE ⟨laying waste the kingdom, seizing ~ and treasure —H.W.Longfellow⟩
scatted *past of* SCAT
¹scat·ter \'skad-ə(r), -atə-\ *vb* -ED/-ING/-S [ME *scateren*] *vt* **1** *archaic* : to fling away heedlessly : SQUANDER **2 a** : to cause (a group or collection) to separate into various widely removed parts ⟨approaching cars that ~*ed* the players to both sides of the street⟩ ⟨a gust that ~*ed* the pile of leaves in all directions⟩ ⟨heirs who ~*ed* his library of Colonial history by selling the books when they needed money⟩ **b** : to cause (as a mist) to vanish as if by scattering ⟨combating prejudice and ~*ing* the clouds of ignorance —Julius May⟩ **3** : to place (as buildings) here and there : distribute at irregular and widely separate intervals ⟨~ defense factories instead of concentrating them in a single area easily obliterated by one bombing⟩ ⟨a child who ~*s* his toys all over the house⟩ **4 a** : to spread widely and at random by or as if by throwing : SOW, BROADCAST ⟨plant the seed in rows or ~ it over the plot⟩ : DISSEMINATE ⟨~ tracts from train windows —Roger Pippett⟩ ⟨the editors fled ... ~*ing* flames of discontent along the way —R.A.Billington⟩ : DIFFUSE ⟨the writers have ~*ed* sentiment and glamor over the story with a lavish hand —*Irish Digest*⟩ **b** (1) : to overspread haphazardly with something : SPRINKLE ⟨a battle that ~*ed* the field with dead and wounded⟩ ⟨~*ed* the pages of her book with famous names⟩ (2) : to spread at random over : BESTREW ⟨small floating shapes of paper ... ~*ing* the water like a countless flock of inch-long ducks —William Sansom⟩ **5 a** : to reflect irregularly and diffusely (as from a piece of ground glass) **b** : to diffuse or disperse (a beam of radiation) in a random manner as a result of collision of the particles, photons, or waves with particles of the medium traversed **6** : to divide into ineffectually small portions : make ineffectual by excessive division ⟨was cautious about ~*ing* his strength and frequently had to curb the ambitions of his sons to go into other lines of business —Frank Kent⟩ ~ *vi* **1 a** : to separate and go in various directions ⟨a flock of pigeons feeding that ~*ed* when a dog approached⟩ **b** : to vanish as if by scattering ⟨clouds ~ after a storm⟩ **2** : to occur or fall at irregular widely separated intervals : spread at random over a surface or through a space or substance ⟨that fine chain of lakes which ~ up and down the center of Florida, like bright beads —Marjory S. Douglas⟩ **3** : to cause something to scatter; *esp* : to cause the shot of a shotgun to spread widely when fired

syn SCATTER, DISPERSE, DISSIPATE, and DISPEL can mean in common to cause a group or mass to separate or break up. SCATTER may imply a force which drives, usu. rapidly, in different directions or may imply only throwing so that the units spread out and fall at random ⟨*scatter* a mob with tear gas bombs⟩ ⟨*scatter* seed over a lawn⟩ ⟨the brief yarns *scattered* so profusely through his first novel —Dayton Kohler⟩ ⟨the serious composer must, through necessity, *scatter* his energy and diffuse his efforts by spending innumerable hours in teaching —David Ewen⟩ ⟨a shower of dried mud was *scattered* over her clothes —Ellen Glasgow⟩ DISPERSE usu. implies a wider separation and a complete breaking up of a mass or group ⟨the clouds *dispersed*, driven into fragments by the wind⟩ ⟨the bureau was dismembered, its staff *dispersed* —V.G.Heiser⟩ ⟨when this simple meal was finished, the Webster family *dispersed* to entertain itself —Robertson Davies⟩ ⟨the nature of their employment and adjustment tended to *disperse* the refugees through the whole nation —Oscar Handlin⟩ DISSIPATE stresses the idea of complete disintegration or dissolution, as by evaporation or squandering, and a consequent vanishing ⟨from the far-off wooded hills the haze ... had not yet *dissipated* —D.H.Lawrence⟩ ⟨this hysteria can be *dissipated* —Kenneth Leslie⟩ ⟨other freedoms will be *dissipated* along with that of the press —Hal O'Flaherty⟩ DISPEL stresses the driving away by or as if by scattering, stressing very little the idea of separation of parts ⟨*dispel* all remnants of your influenza —G.B.Shaw⟩ ⟨*dispel* the notion that social life is a peculiarity of the higher organisms —A.N.Whitehead⟩ ⟨truth and frankness *dispel* difficulties —Bertrand Russell⟩ ⟨had not *dispelled* her apprehension and her distrust —Jean Stafford⟩
syn see in addition STREW

²scatter \"\ *n* -s **1** : the act or process of scattering **2** : a small supply or number scattered, irregularly distributed, or carelessly strewn about ⟨there was a ~ of rain on the windows —Dorothy Whipple⟩ ⟨a ~ of applause⟩ **3** : the state or extent of being scattered; *specif* : the dispersion of observations in a frequency distribution measured by the coefficient of variation **4** : SCATTERING 2b
³scatter \"\ *adj* [¹*scatter* & ²*scatter*] **1** : of, characterized by, or effecting scatter ⟨~ analysis⟩ ⟨~ dose⟩ ⟨~ arm⟩ **2** : adapted to being placed here and there
⁴scatter \"\ *n* -s [origin unknown] **1** *slang* : SALOON **2** *slang* : HANGOUT, JOINT
scat·ter·able \-ərəbəl\ *adj* : that can be scattered
scat·ter·ation \,skad-ə'rāshən\ *n* -s [¹*scatter* + -*ation*] **1** : the act or process of scattering ⟨while there are many reasons for the centrifugal whirl of people and business from the older cities, the automobile has been the greatest factor in the ~ —*N.Y.Times*⟩ **2** : the state of being scattered **3** : something scattered ⟨a tract of land, edged on its two coasts with a ~ of islands —Colin Simpson⟩
scatter bomb *n* [³*scatter*] : an incendiary bomb containing a bursting charge that scatters the burning incendiary agent over a considerable area
scatter-bomb \'==,=\ *vb* [*scatter bomb*] *vt* : to bomb with scatter bombs ~ *vi* : to bomb a target so that the bombs land in a loose or random pattern
scatterbrain \'==,=\ *n* [¹*scatter* + *brain*] : a flighty thoughtless person : a person who is incapable of concentration or attention
scatterbrained \'==,=\ *adj* : having the characteristics of a scatterbrain
scatter diagram *n* [³*scatter*] : a two-dimensional graph in rectangular coordinates consisting of points whose coordinates represent corresponding values of two variables whose relationship is being studied — called also *scattergram, scattergraph, scatterplot*
scattered *adj* [fr. past part. of ¹*scatter*] **1 a** : marked by disorganized dispersion : DISUNITED ⟨the growth of modern science from an activity of ~ individuals —John Pfeiffer⟩ **b** : marked by distraction : RAMBLING ⟨~ thoughts⟩ **2 a** : separated by or occurring at wide irregular intervals ⟨only ~ remarks on the subject are to be found in the literature —David Abercrombie⟩ ⟨~ showers⟩ : widely separated ⟨four ~ states — Utah, Texas, Michigan, and New Jersey —Arthur Geddes⟩ **b** : irregular in position : having no fixed or definite arrangement — used of leaves or branches **3** *obs* : negligently tossed aside or dropped ⟨loose now and then a ~ smile —Shak.⟩ **4** : having the parts disorganized or widely separated ⟨a ~ story⟩ : spread over a wide area ⟨a ~ village⟩ ⟨serves the ~ population in this mountain region —*Amer. Guide Series: Tenn.*⟩
scattered clouds *n pl* : clouds covering one tenth to one half of the sky
scat·tered·ly *adv* : in a scattered manner
scat·tered·ness *n* -ES : the quality or state of being scattered
scat·ter·er \'skad-ərə(r), -atər-\ *n* -s : one that scatters
scattergood \'==,=\ *n* [¹*scatter* + *good*] : a wasteful person : SPENDTHRIFT
scat·ter·gram \'skad-ə(r),gram\ *n* [²*scatter* + -*gram*] : SCATTER DIAGRAM
scat·ter·graph \-raf, -räf\ *n* [²*scatter* + -*graph*] : SCATTER DIAGRAM
scatter-gun \'==,=\ *n* [¹*scatter* + *gun*] : SHOTGUN
¹scattering *n* -s [ME *scatering*, fr. *scateren* to scatter + -*ing*] **1** : an act or process in which something scatters or is scattered **2** : something scattered: as **a** : a small number or quantity interspersed here and there ⟨a ~ of visitors⟩ **b** : the random change in direction of a beam or ray due to collision of the particles, photons, or waves constituting the radiation with the particles of the medium traversed
²scattering *adj* [fr. pres. part. of ¹*scatter*] **1** : going in various directions **2** : found or placed far apart and in no order : occurring at irregular intervals ⟨~ shots⟩ **3** : divided among many or several ⟨~ votes⟩ — **scat·ter·ing·ly** *adv*
scattering coefficient *n* : the fractional rate in the transmission of radiation through a scattering medium (as of light through fog) at which the flux density of radiation decreases by scattering in respect to the thickness of the medium traversed
scat·ter·ling \'skad-ə(r)liŋ\ *n* -s [¹*scatter* + -*ling*] *archaic* : VAGRANT
scatter pin *n* [¹*scatter*] : a small pin used as jewelry and worn usu. in groups of two or more on a woman's dress
scatterplot \'==,=\ *n* [³*scatter* + *plot*] : SCATTER DIAGRAM
scatter rug *n* [¹*scatter*] : a rug of such a size that several can be used (as to fill vacant places) in a room
scatters *pres 3d sing of* SCATTER, *pl of* SCATTER
scatter shot *n* : shot loaded for firing in a weapon built to fire a solid projectile through its rifled bore — compare SHOTGUN
scattershot \'==,=\ *adj* [*scatter shot*] : extending over a wide undiscriminating range : broadly haphazard : randomly inclusive : SHOTGUN ⟨~ approaches ... provide services for groups or masses of individuals —R.P.Capes⟩ ⟨disgusted by his ~ accusations⟩
scat·tery \'skad-ərē\ *adj* [¹*scatter* + -*y*] : marked by scattering : SCATTERED
scatting *pres part of* SCAT
scat·ty \'skatī\ *adj* -ER/-EST [prob. fr. *scatterbrain* + -*y*] *Brit* : CRAZY
scat·u·la \'skachələ\ *n, pl* **scatu·lae** \-chə,lē\ [ML] : a flat rectangular box used in dispensing powders and pills
sca·tu·ri·ent \skə'türēənt\ *adj* [L *scaturient-, scaturiens*, fr. pres. part. of *scaturire* to gush out, fr. *scatere* to bubble, gush, be abundant — more at SHAD] : gushing forth : OVERFLOWING, EFFUSIVE
scaud \'skàd, 'skȯd\ *chiefly Scot var of* SCALD
scauld \'skàd\ *Scot var of* SCOLD
scaum \'skàm, 'skȯm\ *vt* -ED/-ING/-S [origin unknown] *chiefly Scot* : BURN, SCORCH
scaup \'skȯp, 'skȯp\ *dial var of* SCALP
scaup duck \'skȯp-\ *or* **scaup** *n, pl* **scaup** *or* **scaups** [*scaup*, perh. alter. of ¹*scalp*; fr. its fondness for shellfish] : any of several ducks of the genus *Aythya*: as **a** : GREATER SCAUP **b** : LESSER SCAUP
scauper *var of* SCORPER
¹scaur \'skär\ *chiefly Scot var of* ⁴SCAR
²scaur \"\ *chiefly Scot var of* ¹SCAR
scav·age \'skavij\ *n* -s [ME *skawage*, fr. ONF *escauwage* inspection, fr. *escauwer* to inspect (of Gmc origin) + -*age*; akin to OE *scēawian* to look at, see, inspect — more at SHOW] : a duty exacted in 14th, 15th, and 16th century England of nonresident merchants by mayors, sheriffs, or corporations on goods shown for sale
scavager *n* -s [ME *skawager*, fr. *skawage* scavage + -*er*; fr. the fact that the official charged with collecting the toll was later made responsible for keeping the streets clean] *obs* : SCAVENGER
scav·enge \'skavənj\ *vb* -ED/-ING/-S [back-formation fr. *scavenger*] *vt* **1 a** (1) : to dislodge or gather and remove (dirt, waste, or impurities) from cast-off matter ⟨sea gulls ... ~ the remains of the daily fish market —Arnold Bennett⟩ (2) : to remove (burned gases) from the cylinder of an internal combustion engine by special means (as a long exhaust pipe or piston-controlled ports in the cylinder wall) **b** (1) : to remove dirt, waste, or impurities from (as a street or chemical solution) (2) : to clean and purify (molten metal) by taking up foreign elements (as oxygen) in chemical union **2 a** : to extract or collect (something for use) from discarded material ⟨with no food, money, or work permits, ... his friends headed south, eating anything they could ~ —*Time*⟩ **b** : to extract or collect usable material from ⟨lighted false beacons for mariners and *scavenged* the wreckage down to the boots of the drowned sailors —Robert Hatch⟩ **3** : to hunt in for wanted or usable material obtainable at no cost ⟨he gathered material for ... settings by *scavenging* museums, textile and rubber factories —Stephen Winship⟩ ~ *vi* **1** : to remove dirt, waste, or impurities from a space or substance **2** : to remove the burned gases from the cylinder of an internal-combustion engine after a working stroke **3** : to extract or collect something for use from material regarded as useless ⟨another way of gathering parts is by *scavenging* off wrecked vehicles —*Infantry Jour.*⟩ : appropriate for use what otherwise would go to waste : exploit leavings **4** : to search about for wanted or usable material usu. obtainable at no cost : HUNT — usu. used with *for* ⟨women who ~ for scrap brass on the artillery range⟩
scavenge pipe *n* : a return pipe for oil from an internal-combustion engine to a tank
¹scav·eng·er \-jə(r)\ *n* -s [alter. of *scavager*] **1** : a former English official charged orig. with the collection of scavage and later with various other duties including that of keeping the streets clean **2** *chiefly Brit* : a person employed to remove dirt and refuse from the streets of a municipality : STREET CLEANER **3** : one that scavenges: as **a** : a garbage collector **b** : JUNKMAN **c** : one that collects the refuse about a logging camp **d** : a chemically active substance either present in or added to a mixture to make innocuous or to remove an undesirable substance ⟨calcium ... is already being used as a ~ in melting steel, copper, nickel, lead —A.M.Bateman⟩ ⟨the tin compound acts also as a ~ for hydrogen chloride —A.S. Kenyon⟩ — compare GETTER **4 a** : an organism that devours refuse, carrion, or matter injurious to the general health **b** : SCAVENGER BEETLE **c** : a small mottled green marine percoid food fish (*Lethrinus nebulosus*) of warm shallow waters of the Indo-Pacific area
²scavenger \"\ *vi* -ED/-ING/-S : to clean up filth (as street refuse)
scavenger beetle *n* [¹*scavenger*] : a beetle (as of the family Hydrophilidae) that feeds on decaying substances
scavenger hunt *n* : a party contest in which couples are sent out with a time limit to acquire without buying one or several articles that are somewhat difficult to obtain
scavenger pump *n* : a pump to return used oil to a tank for cooling, purification, or storage
scavenger roll *n* : a roller in a textile machine for collecting loose fibers or fluff
scav·en·ger's daughter \'skavənjə(r)z-\ *n* [*scavenger's* gen. of ¹*scavenger*, by wordplay fr. Leonard *Skevington* or *Skeffington*, 16th cent. lieutenant of the Tower of London, inventor of the instrument] : an instrument of torture that so compressed the body as to force blood to flow from the nostrils and ears and sometimes from the hands and feet
scav·en·gery \'skavənjərē\ *n* -ES [*scavenger* + -*y*] : the removal of dirt, garbage, and other refuse from streets of a municipality
scavenging *also* **scavenge** *adj* [*scavenging* fr. *scavenging* act of cleaning (fr. gerund of *scavenge* to clean; *scavenge* fr. *scavenge* to clean] : of or relating to the process of removing used oil and waste gases from an engine cylinder ⟨a ~ pump⟩ ⟨the ~ stroke⟩
scaw \'skȯ\ *n* -s [of Scand origin; akin to ON *skagi* headland] *archaic* : HEADLAND, PROMONTORY
scawt·ite \'skȯ,tīt\ *n* -s [*Scawt* Hill, Antrim, Northern Ireland + E -*ite*] : a mineral $Ca_6Si_4O_{11}(CO_3)_3$ consisting of a silicate and carbonate of calcium
sca·zon \'skāzᵊn\ *n* -s [L *scazont-, scazon*, fr. Gk *skazont-, skazōn*, lit., one that limps, fr. pres. part. of *skazein* to limp — more at SHANK] : a classical verse with a limping or halting movement: **a** : CHOLIAMB **b** : a trochaic tetrameter with protraction in the seventh foot : HIPPONACTEAN
sca·zon·tic \skā'zäntik\ *adj* [L *scazont-, scazon* + E -*ic*] : composed in scazons
ScB *abbr or n* -s [NL *scientiae baccalaureus*] Bachelor of Science
scd *abbr* **1** schedule **2** screwed
ScD *abbr or n* -s [NL *scientiae doctor*] : a doctor of science
SCE *abbr* standard calomel electrode
sceat \'sha(ə)t\ *or* **sceat·ta** \-ad-ə\ *or* **skeat** \-a(ə)t\ *n, pl* **sceats** *or* **sceattas** [OE *sceat, sceatt* scat, property, money; akin to OHG *scaz* property, money, ON *skattr* tribute, Goth *skatts* coin] : a small thick Anglo-Saxon coin of silver or rarely of gold or of copper — see STYCA
scel- *or* **scelo-** *comb form* [NL, fr. Gk *skelos* — more at CYLINDER] : leg ⟨*scelalgia*⟩ ⟨*Sceloporus*⟩
scel·er·at \'selə,rat\ *n* -s [F *scélérat*, fr. L *sceleratus*, fr. *sceleratus*, past part. of *scelerare* to pollute, defile, fr. *sceler-, scelus* crime — more at CYLINDER] *archaic* : VILLAIN, ROGUE, CRIMINAL
scelerate *adj* [L *sceleratus*, past part. of *scelerare*] *obs* : notably wicked
sceleton *obs var of* SKELETON
scel·i·do·saur \'selədō,sȯ(ə)r\ *n* -s [NL *Scelidosaurus*] : a dinosaur of the genus *Scelidosaurus*
¹scel·i·do·sau·roid \¦===¦sȯ,rȯid\ *adj* [NL *Scelidosaurus* + E -*oid*] : like or related to the scelidosaurs
²scelidosauroid \"\ *n* -s : a scelidosauroid dinosaur
scel·i·do·sau·rus \,===ˈsȯrəs\ *n, cap* [NL, fr. *scelid-* (fr. Gk *-skelid-, -skelis* leg — as in *periskelid-, periskelis* band worn on the leg, anklet — fr. *skelos* leg) + -*o-* + -*saurus* — more at CYLINDER] : a genus of European Lower Jurassic dinosaurs (suborder Stegosauria) having a dermal armor of longitudinal series of small tubercles and scutes on the back and tail
scel·i·do·the·ri·um \,===ˈthirēəm\ *n, cap* [NL, fr. *scelid-* (fr. Gk *-skelid-, -skelis* leg) + -*o-* + -*therium*] : a genus of extinct Pleistocene four-toed So. American edentates smaller than and intermediate in characters between those of the genera *Megatherium* and *Mylodon*
scel·i·on·i·dae \,selē'änə,dē\ *n pl, cap* [NL, fr. *Scelion-, Scelio*, type genus (prob. fr. L *scelion-, scelio* scoundrel, fr. *scelus* crime) + -*idae*] : a cosmopolitan family of serphoid wasps that are mostly very small, dark, and shining, have elbowed usu. 11-segmented or 12-segmented antennae, and include many economically important parasites of pest insects
scel·i·phron \'selə,frän, sə'lifrən\ *n, cap* [NL, fr. Gk *skeliphron*, neut. of *skeliphros* dry, parched; akin to Gk *skellein* to dry up — more at SKELETON] : a genus of wasps (family Sphecidae) comprising many common mud daubers and having the first segment of the abdomen narrowed into a long smooth round petiole
sce·lop·o·rus \sə'läpərəs\ *n* [NL, fr. *scel-* (fr. Gk *skelos* leg) + -*porous* (fr. Gk *poros* passage, pore); fr. the large femoral pores — more at FARE] **1** *cap* : a large genus of small iguanid lizards of No. and Central America including the pine and sagebrush lizards **2** -ES : any lizard of the genus *Sceloporus*
¹sce·na \'shānə, -(,)nä\ *n* -s [It, fr. L *scaena, scena* stage] **1** : a scene in an opera **2** : an accompanied dramatic recitative usu. followed by one or more sections resembling an aria that

forms a part of an opera or sometimes an independent musical composition

[2]**sce·na** \'sēnə, 'skānə\ *n, pl* **sce·nae** \-ē(,)nē, -ā,nī\ [L *scaena, scena*] : [2]SKENE

sce·nar·io \sə̇'na(a)rē,ō, -ner-, -när-, -nār-, -nȧr- *sometimes* shə̇-\ *n* -s [It, fr. L *scaenarium*, fr. *scaena* stage + *-arium*] **1** *pl also* **sce·nari** \-rē,-ri\ **a :** an outline or synopsis of a play; *esp* : a plot outline used by actors of the commedia dell'arte **b :** the book of an opera **2 a :** SCREENPLAY **b :** SHOOTING SCRIPT

sce·nar·io·ist \-rē,ōə̇st\ *n* -s : SCENARIST

sce·nar·ist \-rə̇st\ *n* -s [ISV *scenar*io + *-ist*] : a writer of scenarios

sce·nar·ize \-,rīz\ *vt* -ED/-ING/-S [*scenar*io + *-ize*] : to make a scenario of (as a story, book)

sce·na·ry \'sēn(ə)rē, -ri\ *n* -ES [It *scenario* scenery, scenario] **1** *obs* : the disposition of the scenes in which the action (as of a play or poem) is laid **2** *archaic* : SCENERY 1, 2

[1]**scend** \'send\ *vi* -ED/-ING/-S [alter. (influenced by *ascend*) of *send*] : to rise or heave upward under the influence of a natural force (as waves in a seaway) — used esp. of a ship; compare PITCH

[2]**scend** \"\ *n* -s **1 :** an upward movement or displacement (as of a ship in a seaway) **2 :** the lift of a wave : SEND

[1]**scene** \'sēn\ *n* -s [MF, stage, fr. L *scaena, scena*, fr. Gk *skēnē* booth, tent, skene, stage; akin to Gk *skia* shadow, Skt *chāyā* color, shadow — more at SHINE] **1 :** one of the subdivisions or units of a dramatic presentation: as **a :** a division of an act during which there is no change of place or lapse of continuity of time; *esp* : a division in a classical Roman or French drama in which there is no change of persons and which ends with the entrance or exit of one or more characters **b :** a part of a drama or narrative featuring a single item (as a situation or dialogue) ⟨a famous mad ~⟩ **c :** [1]SCENA 2 **d** (1) **:** an episode in a motion picture consisting of a shot or a succession of related shots in which a single continuous action is represented (2) **:** a single sequence of continuous action in a television presentation consisting of one or more shots **2 a :** the material objects (as hangings, sets, furnishings) that impart an air of reality to the background of a dramatic representation : stage scenery : STAGE SET ⟨a ~ shifter⟩ — often used in pl. ⟨went back of the ~*s*⟩ **b :** a real or imaginary prospect likened to that presented by stage scenery : VIEW, SIGHT, VISTA ⟨a sylvan ~⟩ ⟨the current ~⟩ **3 a :** the place in which represented action (as in a play or story) is laid : surroundings amid which anything is set before the imagination **b :** the place of occurrence or action : LOCALE ⟨the ~ of a historic event⟩ ⟨the ~ of this disaster⟩ **4 :** the stage on which a play is presented esp. in an ancient Greek or Roman theater **5 a scenes** *pl, obs* : a theatrical presentation : a drama or other play **b** *archaic* : the drama as an art or profession **6 a :** one of a sequence of actions and events esp. as represented in literature or art ⟨~*s* of revelry and despair⟩ ⟨each ~ more stirring than the last⟩ **b :** an episode viewed in real or imagined action ⟨their parting was a sad ~⟩ **7 a :** an exhibition of passionate or explosive and usu. irate emotion (as between individuals) ⟨a tempestuous ~ of tears and remorse⟩ **b :** an affected display of passion or temper ⟨made a ~ to get her own way⟩ — **behind the scenes** *adv* **1 :** in a position to see without being seen : out of public view : in secret ⟨a decision reached *behind the scenes*⟩ **2 :** in a position to see the hidden agencies or workings ⟨made cynical by what went on *behind the scenes*⟩

[2]**scene** \"\ *vt* -ED/-ING/-S : to provide with scenes or scenery

scene cloth *n* : a painted hanging (as a backdrop or drop curtain) for a theatrical stage

scenecraft \'=,=\ *n* : the art of furnishing fitting scenes or stage settings for plays

scene·des·mus \,sēnə'dezməs, ,sen-\ *n, cap* [NL, fr. Gk *skēnē* tent + *desmos* bond, fetter, fr. *dein* to bind — more at SCENE, DIADEM] : a genus (the type of the family Scenedesmaceae of the order Chlorococcales) of colonial green algae having groups of four or eight or rarely sixteen ellipsoid, fusiform, or oblong cells arranged side by side and frequently with more or less conspicuous appendages esp. on the two end cells

scene dock *n* : a space near the stage in a theater where scenery is stored

sceneman *n, pl* **scenemen** *obs* : SCENESHIFTER

scene painter *n* : one that paints scenery: as **a :** a painter of theatrical scenery **b :** an artist specializing in scenic subjects

scene plot *n* : a list and description of the scenes of a play

sce·nery \'sēn(ə)rē, -ri\ *n* -ES [alter. (influenced by *-ery*) of *scenary*] **1 :** the representation of the place of an action or occurrence; *specif* : the representation of the scene of action on a stage consisting usu. of painted scenes or hangings with their accessories **2 :** a view of picturesque spots and expanses esp. in open country : the general aspect of a landscape : the array of impressive natural prospects and imposing features of a particular place ⟨preferred ~ to historical landmarks⟩ ⟨mountain ~⟩ **3 a :** a picturesque view or landscape **b :** a picture representing such a view

sce·nery·less \-lə̇s\ *adj* : lacking scenery ⟨a ~ stage⟩ : presented without the use of scenery ⟨a ~ production of a play⟩

sceneshifter \'=,==\ *n* : a worker who moves the scenes in a theater — called also *grip*

scene-stealer \'=,==\ *n* : an actor who skillfully or ostentatiously diverts attention to himself when he is not intended to be the center of attention

scenewright \'=,=\ *n* [[1]*scene* + *wright*] : a designer and maker of theatrical scenery

[1]**sce·nic** \'sēnik, -nēk *sometimes* 'sen-\ *adj* [L *scaenicus, scenicus*, fr. Gk *skēnikos*, fr. *skēnē* stage + *-ikos* -ic — more at SCENE] **1 a :** of or relating to the stage, a stage setting, or stage representation : of, resembling, or suited to stage representation : DRAMATIC ⟨~ writers⟩ ⟨~ effects⟩ **b :** of, relating to, or concerned with stage scenery ⟨a ~ triumph⟩ ⟨~ carpenters⟩ **2 a :** of or relating to natural scenery ⟨~ beauties⟩ **b :** affording or abounding in attractive scenery ⟨a ~ route⟩ **3 :** representing graphically an action, event, or episode ⟨a ~ bas-relief⟩ ⟨~ wallpapers⟩ — often opposed to *decorative*

[2]**scenic** \"\ *n* -s : something stressing the beauties of nature or naturalistic ornamentation: as **a :** a scenic wallpaper usu. depicting a single continuous scene without repetition **b :** a motion picture the chief interest of which is in the natural scenery depicted **c :** a photograph featuring scenery rather than figures

sce·ni·cal \-nə̇kəl, -nēk-\ *adj* [ME, fr. L *scaenicus, scenicus* scenic + E *-al*] **1 :** SCENIC 1; *esp* : characteristic of or resembling a stage performance ⟨a ~ situation⟩ **2** *obs* : having the illusory quality of a stage scene : IMAGINARY, UNREAL

sce·ni·cal·ly \-k(ə)lē, -li\ *adv* **1 :** in a theatrical manner **2 :** in regard to scenery

scenic artist *n* : SCENE PAINTER

scenic railway *n* : a miniature railway (as in an amusement park) with artificial scenery along the way

sce·nite \'sē,nīt\ *adj or n* [L *scenites*, n., fr. Gk *skēnitēs*, fr. *skēnē* tent + *-itēs* -ite — more at SCENE] *archaic* : NOMAD

sce·no·graph \'sēnə,graf, -ráf\ *n* [back-formation fr. *scenographer, scenographic, scenography*] : a perspective representation of an object

sce·nog·ra·pher \sē'nägrəfə(r)\ *n* -s [LGk *skēnographos* scene painter (fr. Gk *skēno-* — fr. *skēnē* stage — + *-graphos* -grapher) + E *-er*] : a practicer of scenography

sce·no·graph·ic \¦sēnə¦grafik\ *also* **sce·no·graph·i·cal** \fə̇kəl\ *adj* [*scenographic* fr. Gk *skēnographikos*, fr. *skēnographia* + *-ikos* -ic; *scenographical* fr. *scenographic* + *-al*] : of, relating to, or conforming to scenography — **sce·no·graph·i·cal·ly** \-fə̇k(ə)lē\ *adv*

sce·nog·ra·phy \sē'nägrəfē\ *n* -ES [Gk *skēnographia* scene painting, fr. *skēno-* (fr. *skēnē* stage) + *-graphia* -graphy] **1 :** the art or act of representing a body on a perspective plane : representation of an object from a point of view not on a principal axis — compare ORTHOGRAPHIC PROJECTION **2 :** the art of perspective representation applied to the painting of stage scenery (as by the Greeks)

sce·no·pin·i·dae \,sēnə'pinə,dē\ *n pl, cap* [NL, fr. *Scenopinus*, type genus (perh. modif. of Gk *skēnopoios* one that makes tents, fr. *skēno-* — fr. *skēnē* tent — + *poiein* to make) + *-idae* — more at SCENE, POET] : a family of small elongated two-winged flies that sometimes congregate about windows — see WINDOW FLY

[1]**scent** \'sent\ *vb* -ED/-ING/-S [ME *senten*, fr. MF *sentir* to feel, have the odor of, fr. L *sentire* to feel, perceive — more at SENSE] *vt* **1 a :** to perceive by the olfactory organs : SMELL ⟨a hound ~*ing* game⟩ **b :** to get or have an inkling of : detect the existence of ⟨~ a plot⟩ ⟨~ the morning air — Shak.⟩ **2 :** to imbue or fill with odor agreeable or disagreeable ⟨the air ~*ed* with wild thyme⟩ **3 :** to perceive through touch or by the mind ~ *vi* **1 :** to yield an odor of some specified kind ⟨this ~*s* of sulfur⟩; *also* : to bear indication or suggestions — used with *of* ⟨the very air ~*s* of treachery⟩ **2 :** to use the olfactory organ in seeking or tracking prey ⟨dogs ~ after rabbits⟩

[2]**scent** \"\ *n* -s [ME *sent*, fr. *senten*, v.] **1 :** emanations or effluvia from a substance that affect the sense of smell pleasantly or unpleasantly: as **a :** an odor left by an animal on a surface passed over ⟨dogs follow the ~⟩; *also* : a course of pursuit : track of discovery ⟨throw one off the ~⟩ **b :** a characteristic or particular odor; *esp* : one that is agreeable ⟨the ~ of flowers⟩ **2 a** *obs* : perception through touch or by the mind **b :** power of smelling : sense of smell ⟨a keen ~⟩ — used chiefly of a lower animal **c :** power of detection ⟨a ~ for heresy⟩ : NOSE **3 :** a premonitory indication : INKLING, INTIMATION ⟨a ~ of trouble⟩ **4** *chiefly Brit* : PERFUME 2 **5 :** bits of paper dropped by the hares in the game of hare and hounds to mark their course **6 :** a mixture prepared for use as a lure on and around a trap (as for an animal) or in water (as for fish) **syn** see FRAGRANCE, SMELL

scent bag *n* **1 :** a small scented pad or bag; *esp* : SACHET **2 :** a scent gland when pouched in form; *also* : a sac receiving the secretion of a scent gland

scent·ed \¦sentə̇d\ *adj* [partly fr. [2]*scent* + *-ed*, partly fr. past part. of [1]*scent*] : having scent: as **a :** having the sense of smell ⟨a keen-*scented* hound⟩ **b :** PERFUMED ⟨over-*scented* girls⟩ **c :** having or exhaling an odor ⟨a ~ flower⟩ ⟨clean-*scented* laundry⟩

scented fern *n* **1 :** HAY-SCENTED FERN **2 :** a tansy (*Tanacetum vulgare*)

scented satinwood *n* : COACHWOOD 2

scented tea *n* : tea that is fragrant usu. through being packed with or fired with flowers; *esp* : JASMINE TEA

scent·er \-tə(r)\ *n* -s : one that scents

scent gland *n* : a gland (as in the beaver or the civet cat) secreting an odoriferous substance — compare MUSK BAG

scent·less \'sentlə̇s\ *adj* **1 :** lacking the sense of smell **2 :** emitting no odor ⟨~ wisps of straw⟩ **3 a :** holding no scent ⟨a ~ stretch of rocky ground⟩ **b :** yielding no scent ⟨a ~ day⟩ — **scent·less·ness** *n* -ES

scentless camomile *or* **scentless mayweed** *n* : CORN MAYWEED 2

scent scale *n* : ANDROCONIUM

scentwood \'=,=\ *n* : a fragrant Australian and Tasmanian shrub or small tree (*Alyxia buxifolia*) of the family Apocynaceae

scepsis *var of* SKEPSIS

[1]**scep·ter** \'septə(r)\ *n* -s *see -er in Explan Notes* [ME *ceptre, septre, sceptre*, fr. OF *ceptre*, fr. L *sceptrum*, fr. Gk *skēptron* staff, scepter — more at SHAFT] **1 a :** a staff or baton borne by a sovereign as a ceremonial emblem of authority : a royal mace **b :** a representation (as in heraldry) of a scepter **2 :** royal or imperial authority : SOVEREIGNTY

scepter 1a

[2]**scepter** \"\ *vt* -ED/-ING/-S **1 :** to endow with the scepter : invest with royal authority **2 :** to ratify by touching with the scepter

scep·tered \-tə(r)d\ *adj* **1 :** invested with a scepter or sovereign authority **2 :** belonging or relating to a sovereign or to royalty : ROYAL, REGAL

scep·ter·less \-tə(r)lə̇s\ *adj* **1 :** having no scepter **2 :** subject to no royal sovereignty

sceptic *var of* SKEPTIC

scep·tral \'sept(ə)rəl\ *adj* : resembling or relating to a scepter or to royal authority

scerne *vt* [by shortening & alter.] *obs* : DISCERN

sceuo·pho·rion \,skevə'fȯr,yȯn\ *n, pl* **sceuopho·ria** \-_yə\ [MGk *skeuophorion*, fr. Gk, yoke placed over the shoulders for carrying pails, fr. *skeuos* vessel, utensil + *-phorion* (fr. *pherein* to carry) — more at SKEUOMORPH, BEAR] : a receptacle used in the Eastern Orthodox Church and corresponding to the pyx

sceuo·phy·la·cium \,skyüōfə̇'lāsh(ē)əm\ *n* -s [MGk *skeuophylakion*, fr. Gk, storehouse, fr. *skeuos* vessel, utensil + *phylakion, phylakeion* fort, fr. *phylak-, phylax* guard] : a sacristy in the early church and in the Eastern Orthodox Church

sceuo·phy·lax \skyü'äfə,laks, ,skevȯ'fē,läks\ *n* -ES [LGk *skeuophylak-, skeuophylax*, fr. Gk, keeper of a storehouse, fr. *skeuos* vessel, utensil + *phylak-, phylax* guard] : a sacristan in the early church and in the Eastern Orthodox Church

sch *abbr* **1** schedule **2** schilling **3** scholar **4** scholium **5** school **6** schoolhouse **7** schooner

schaap·ste·ker *or* **skaap·ste·ker** \'skäp,stikə(r), -tēk-\ *n* -s [Afrik *skaapsteker*, fr. *skaap* sheep (fr. D *schaap*, fr. MD *schaep*) + *steker* one that stings or pricks, fr. D, fr. *steken* to sting, prick + *-er;* akin to OHG *stehhan* to sting, prick — more at SHEEP, STICK] : any of several inoffensive and generally harmless African back-fanged snakes: as **a :** a snake (*Trimerorhinus rhombeatus*) irregularly marked in shades of brown — called also *spotted schaapsteker* **b :** a related snake (*T. tritaeniatus*) having two or three dark longitudinal bands on the grayish brown back — called also *striped schaapsteker* **c :** a sand snake of the genus *Psammophis*

schab·zie·ger *also* **schab·zi·ger** \'shäp(t),sēgə(r)\ *n* -s *usu cap* [G *schabziger* — more at SAPSAGO] : SAPSAGO

schacht·ism \'shäk,tizəm, -äk,t-\ *also* **schact·ian·ism** \-_tēə,niz-\ *n* -s *usu cap* [*schachtism* fr. Hjalmar *Schacht* *b*1877 Ger. financier + E *-ism; schachtianism* fr. Hjalmar *Schacht* + E *-an* + *-ism;* fr. Schacht's use of such policies as acting minister of national economy in Germany 1934–37] : trade and finance policies including exchange controls, bilateral trade agreements, multiple exchange rates, and other practices designed to benefit one nation at the expense of others

scha·den·freu·de \'shäd^ən,frȯidə\ *n* -s [G, fr. *schaden* damage, injury, harm (fr. OHG *scado*) + *freude* joy, fr. OHG *frewida*, fr. *frō* happy — more at SCATHE, FROLIC] : enjoyment obtained from the mishaps of others

schaef·fe·ria \shā'firēə\ *n* [NL, fr. Jacob Christian *Schäffer* †1790 Ger. naturalist + NL *-ia*] **1** *cap* : a small genus of chiefly tropical American shrubs or occasionally small trees (family Celastraceae) having dioecious tetramerous flowers, coriaceous leaves, dry drupaceous fruits containing two seeds without an aril, and hard fine-grained yellow wood that has been used as a substitute for boxwood **2** -s : any plant of the genus *Schaefferia*

schaef·fer's acid *or* **schäf·fer's acid** \'shāfə(r)z-\ *n, usu cap S* [after L. *Schaeffer*, 19th cent. Ger. chemist] : a crystalline naphtholsulfonic acid $HOC_{10}H_6SO_3H$ used as a dye intermediate; 2-naphthol-6 sulfonic acid

schaeffer's salt *or* **schäffer's salt** *n, usu cap 1st S* : the sodium salt $HOC_{10}H_6SO_3Na$ of Schaeffer's acid

schaer·beek \'skär,bāk\ *adj, usu cap* [fr. *Schaerbeek*, Belgium] : of or from the city of Schaerbeek, Belgium : of the kind or style prevalent in Schaerbeek

scha·far·zik·ite \'shäfə(r),zi,kīt\ *n* -s [G *schafarzikit*, fr. Ferenc *Schafarzik* †1927 Hung. mineralogist + G *-it* -ite] : a mineral $Fe_5Sb_4O_{11}$ consisting of an oxide of iron and antimony and occurring in red to brown prismatic acicular crystals

scha·fer method *or* **schae·fer method** \'shāfə(r)-\ *n, usu cap S* [after Sir Edward A. Sharpey-*Schafer* †1935 Eng. physiologist] : PRONE PRESSURE METHOD

schafs·kopf \'shaf,skȯpf\ *also* **schaf·kopf** \-f,k-\ *n* -s [G, schafskopf, blockhead, sheep's head, fr. *schaf* sheep (fr. OHG *scāf*) + *kopf* head, fr. OHG, drinking vessel — more at SHEEP, CUP] : SHEEPSHEAD 3

schai·rer·ite \'shīrə,rīt\ *n* -s [John F. *Schairer* *b*1904 Am. physical chemist + E *-ite*] : a mineral $Na_3(SO_4)(F,Cl)$ consisting of a rare sodium sulphate with fluorine and chlorine and occurring in colorless rhombohedral crystals

schal·ler·ite \'shalə,rīt\ *n* -s [Waldemar T. *Schaller* *b*1882 Am. mineralogist + E *-ite*] : a mineral $Mn_8Si_6O_{18}(AsO_3)(OH).3\frac{1}{2}H_2O$(?) consisting of a hydrous basic silicate and arsenite of manganese

schal·mei *or* **schal·mey** \(')shäl¦mī\ *n* -s [G *schalmei*, fr. MHG *schalmīe*, fr. OF *chalemie* — more at SHAWM] **1 :** SHAWM **2 :** CHALUMEAU 4

schal·stein \'shäl,s(h)tīn\ *n* -s [G, fr. *schale* husk, shell (fr. OHG *scala*) + *stein* stone, fr. OHG — more at SCALE, STONE] : a slaty rock formed by the compression and metamorphism of basaltic or andesitic tuff or lava : slaty greenstone

schap·bach·ite \'shäp,bä,kīt\ *n* -s [G *schapbachit*, fr. *Schapbach*, Baden, Germany + G *-it* -ite] : MATILDITE; *also* : a high-temperature polymorph of matildite

schap·pe \'shäpə\ *or* **chappe** \'shap\ *n* -s [G dial. (Swiss) *schappe* raw silk waste] : a yarn or fabric of spun silk; *also* : an imitation of it (as in rayon or nylon)

schap·ping \-piŋ\ *n* -s : a European method for fermenting and removing the gum from silk wastes

schap·ska \'shäpskə\ *n* -s [F, modif. of Pol *czapka* cap] : a flat-topped cavalry helmet

schar·ding·er dextrin \'shärdiŋə(r)-\ *n, usu cap S* [after Franz *Schardinger*, 20th cent. Austrian chemist] : any of several nonreducing water soluble low-molecular-weight polysaccharides formed by cultivation of a bacillus (*Bacillus macerans*) upon starch solutions

schardinger enzyme *n, usu cap S* : XANTHINE OXIDASE

scharf \'shärf\ *n* -s [G, fr. *scharf*, adj., sharp, fr. OHG *scarf* — more at SHARP] : a mixture stop in a pipe organ with a bright and penetrating tone

schatchen *var of* SHADCHAN

schechina *usu cap, var of* SHEKINAH

sched *abbr* schedule

schedi·asm \'skēdē,azəm, 'sked-\ *n* -s [Gk *schediasma* caprice, fr. *schediazein* to do offhand, fr. *schedios* temporary, extemporaneous, impromptu; akin to Gk *echein* to have — more at SCHEME] *archaic* : an extemporaneous action (as in writing) : something done offhand

schedi·us \-dēəs\ *n, cap* [NL, perh. fr. Gk *schedios* temporary, extemporaneous, impromptu] : a genus of minute chalcid flies including egg parasites of economic pests (as the gypsy moth)

sched·u·lar \'skejələ(r), -(,)jül-\ *adj* : of or relating to a schedule

[1]**sched·ule** \'ske(,)j|ül, -_j|əl *sometimes* -(,)j|ůl *or* -,j|üəl, *Canadian* " *or* 'she(,)j|, *Brit* 'she(,)dy| *or* 'she(,)j|\ *n* -s [alter. (influenced by LL *schedula*) of earlier *cedule, sedule*, fr. ME, fr. MF, note, slip of paper, fr. LL *schedula* slip of paper, fr. L *scheda, scida* leaf of paper or papyrus (fr. assumed Gk *schidē* split piece of wood, fr. Gk *schizein* to split) + *-ula* — more at SHED] **1 a** *obs* : a piece of written matter : DOCUMENT; *esp* : a supplementary slip appended to a document **b :** an appended statement of supplementary details usu. accompanying a legal or legislative document and often taking the form of a detailed list of relevant matters **2 :** a written or printed formal list (as a catalog or inventory or calendar of events) ⟨a ~ of freight rates⟩ ⟨a ~ of social events⟩: as **a :** a detailed list of a bankrupt's creditors, liabilities, and assets ⟨filed a ~ with his bankruptcy petition⟩ **b :** a transportation timetable **c :** an executive's record of matters (as assignments of subordinate personnel) handled or to be handled **d :** a student's program of studies **e :** a list of questions designed to elicit objective data for a statistical study **3 :** a usu. written plan or proposal for future procedure typically indicating the objective proposed, the time and sequence of each operation, and the materials required ⟨planned a new ~ of operations for the factory⟩ ⟨their ~ allowed for only 50 percent of last year's production⟩ ⟨laid out a ~ for building the new school⟩ **4 :** a body of items requiring to be dealt with usu. at a particular time or within an indicated period ⟨a lecturer with a very heavy ~⟩ ⟨my ~ for tomorrow⟩ — **on schedule :** at the time indicated in a schedule : at the due or proper time ⟨winter arrived *on schedule*⟩ ⟨an *on schedule* presentation⟩

[2]**schedule** \"\ *vt* -ED/-ING/-S **1 a :** to place in a schedule ⟨~ a new train⟩ **b :** to make a schedule of ⟨*scheduled* his income and debts⟩ **2 :** to add in or as a schedule or appendix **3 :** to appoint, assign, or designate to do or receive something at a fixed time in the future ⟨*scheduled* a meeting for the next week⟩

schedule bond *n* : a fidelity bond that covers as principals only those employees specifically designated by name or by position

scheduled caste *or* **scheduled class** *n* : UNTOUCHABLES

scheduled disease *n, Brit* : a notifiable disease

sched·ul·er \-lə(r)\ *n* -s : a preparer of a schedule

schedule rate *n* : an insurance merit rating derived from an analysis of the physical characteristics of a risk according to a schedule of charges and credits

schee·le's green \'shāləz-, -lēz-\ *n* [after Karl W. *Scheele* †1786 Swed. chemist] **1** *usu cap S* : a poisonous yellowish green pigment consisting essentially of a copper arsenite and used esp. formerly in paints **2** *often cap S* : a strong yellow green to yellowish green — called also *English green, Swedish green*

schee·lite \'shā,līt\ *n* -s [G *scheelit*, fr. Karl W. *Scheele* + G *-it* -ite] : a native calcium tungstate $CaWO_4$ that is isomorphous with pomellite, occurs as a white or yellow to brownish when impure tetragonal mineral in tabular and massive forms, and is a commercial source of tungsten and tungsten compounds

schef·fer·ite \'shefə,rīt\ *n* -s [Sw *schefferit*, fr. H. T. *Scheffer* †1759 Swed. chemist + Sw *-it* -ite] : a mineral $(Ca,Mn)(Mg,Fe,Mn)Si_2O_6$ that is a brown to black variety of pyroxene containing manganese and frequently much iron

schef·flera \'sheflərə\ *n* -s [NL *Schefflera*, genus of plants, fr. J. C. *Scheffler*, 18th cent. Ger. botanist] : any of several shrubby tropical plants of the family Araliaceae that are cultivated for their showy digitately compound foliage

sche·her·a·za·di·an \shə̇¦herə¦zädēən, she¦h- *sometimes* -zād-\ *adj* [*Scheherazade*, fictitious queen represented as narrator of the stories in the *Arabian Nights' Entertainments* + E *-an*] : suited to a tale of the fabled queen Scheherazade : strangely fabulous

scheib·ler's reagent \'shīb|lə(r)z-, -īp|\ *n, usu cap S* [after Karl *Scheibler* †1899 Ger. chemist] : a solution of phosphotungstic acid or its sodium salt used as a precipitant for alkaloids

schei·ner speed \'shīnə(r)-\ *n, usu cap 1st S* [after Julius *Scheiner* †1913 Ger. astrophysicist] : the speed of photographic material based on the exposure required to obtain a just-detectable density and indicated by a system of numbers

schel·ling \'skeliŋ\ *n* -s [D, fr. MD *schellinc;* akin to OE *scilling* shilling — more at SHILLING] : an old silver or sometimes billon coin of the Low Countries usu. current at six stivers but varying from five to eight

schel·ling·ian \(')she,liŋēən, shə'l-, -linj(ē)ən\ *adj, usu cap* [Friedrich Wilhelm Joseph von *Schelling* †1854 Ger. philosopher + E *-an*] : of or relating to Schelling or his system of idealism that makes the ego and the world two poles of the Absolute

schel·ly \'sheli\ *n* -s [origin unknown] *dial Eng* : GWYNIAD

schelm \'skelm\ *n* -s [Afrik *skelm*, fr. D *schelm* — more at SKELLUM] *Africa* : ROGUE, RASCAL

schel·orib·a·tes \,skelə'ribə,tēz\ *n, cap* [NL, fr. *schel-* (prob. fr. Gk *schelides* ribs of beef) + *Oribates* (syn. of *Oribata*, type genus of the mite family Oribatidae); akin to Gk *skelos* leg — more at CYLINDER, ORIBATOIDEA] : a genus of oribatid mites containing some that are intermediate hosts of several tapeworms of ruminants

schel·to·pu·sik *or* **shel·to·pu·sic** *or* **shel·to·pu·sick** \¦sheltō¦p(y)üzik\ *n* -s [Russ *zheltopuzik*, fr. *zhelto* yellow (akin to OE *geolu* yellow) + *-puzik* (fr. *puzo* belly) — more at YELLOW] : an anguid lizard (*Ophisaurus apus* or *Pseudopus apus*) chiefly of southeastern Europe and Asia Minor that resembles the glass snake of America

sche·ma \'skēmə\ *n, pl* **schema·ta** \-məd·ə,-mətə\ [G, fr. Gk *schēmat-, schēma* shape, figure, manner — more at SCHEME] **1 :** a general representation produced according to Kantianism by the imagination working with the pure form of time by which the understanding is able to apply a category to particular representations of sense ⟨the universal following in time of something, A, by something else, B, is the ~ of cause and effect⟩ **2 a :** a diagrammatic depiction of a typical or average situation ⟨a ~ of the reflex arc⟩; *broadly* : an abridged or generalized presentation : a framework of reference : OUTLINE, PLAN **b** : a syllogistic figure in logic **3 a** : a nonconscious adjustment of the brain to the afferent impulses indicative of bodily posture that is a prerequisite of appropriate bodily movement and of spatial perception **b** : the organization of experience in the mind or brain

[1]**sche·mat·ic** \(ˈ)skēˌmad·ik, skiˈm-, -at|, |ēk\ *adj* [NL *schematicus*, fr. L *schemat-*, *schema* shape, figure, manner (fr. Gk *schēmat-*, *schēma*) + *-icus* -ic] : of, relating to, or constituting a scheme or schema: as **a** : corresponding to an established or formalized conception ⟨a ~ arrangement⟩ ⟨~ drawing⟩ **b** : showing part for part in a model or diagram ⟨a ~ eye⟩ **c** : employing or constituting a scheme of conventional symbols ⟨a ~ wiring diagram⟩ ⟨using ~ symbols⟩

[2]**schematic** \"\ *n* -s : a schematic drawing or diagram

sche·mat·i·cal·ly \|ək(ə)lē, |ēk-, -li\ *adv* : in a schematic manner

sche·ma·tism \ˈskēməˌtizəm\ *n* -s [NL *schematismus*, fr. Gk *schēmatismos* configuration, assumption of a manner, fr. *schēmatizein* to assume a certain form, put into a systematic arrangement] **1 a** : the disposition of constituents in a pattern or according to a scheme; *also* : a particular systematic disposition of parts **b** : the inclination to arrange or present schematically **2** [G *schematismus*, fr. NL] : the process by which the imagination according to Kantianism mediates between a category or abstract concept of the understanding and a particular content of sense experience by providing a general plan for the application of the concept to the content of sense — compare SCHEMA 1

sche·ma·tist \-mətəst, -məd·ə-\ *n* -s [fr. *schematism*, after such pairs as E *deism: deist*] **1** : one that makes modifications to suit an established or preconceived system **2** *obs* : one given to forming schemes : PROJECTOR, SCHEMER

sche·ma·ti·za·tion \ˌskēmətəˈzāshən, -məd·əˈz-, -məˌtīˈz-\ *n* -s : an act or instance or the product of schematizing

sche·ma·tize \ˈskēməˌtīz\ *vt* -ED/-ING/-S [Gk *schēmatizein* to assume a certain form, put into a systematic arrangement, fr. *schēmat-*, *schēma* shape, figure, manner + *-izein* -ize] **1** : to form or to form into a scheme or schemes : make or put into a systematic arrangement **2** : to express or depict schematically; *usu* : to convert (an art subject) into nonnaturalistic symbols or decorative motifs : STYLIZE, CONVENTIONALIZE

sche·ma·tiz·er \-zə(r)\ *n* -s : one that schematizes

sche·mato·gram \skēˈmad·əˌgram, ˈskēməd·-\ *n* [Gk *schēmat-*, *schēma* shape, figure, manner + E *-o-* + *-gram*] : a tracing made with a schematograph

sche·mato·graph \-raf, -rȧf\ *n* [Gk *schēmat-*, *schēma* shape, figure, manner + E *-o-* + *-graph*] : an apparatus for tracing in reduced form the outline of a person in recording posture

[1]**scheme** \ˈskēm\ *n* -s [L *schemat-*, *schema* shape, figure, manner, figure of speech, fr. Gk *schēmat-*, *schēma*; akin to OE *sigor* victory, OHG *sigu*, ON *sigr*, Goth *sigis* victory, Gk *echein*, *schein* to have, hold, Skt *sahas* strength, victory] **1** *obs* **a** : FIGURE OF SPEECH **b** : FORM, SEMBLANCE **c** : POMP, SHOW **2 a** *archaic* : a mathematical or astronomical diagram; *sometimes* : a representation of the astrological aspects of the planets at a particular time **b** : a graphic sketch, design, or outline : a delineated plan ⟨sketched a small ~ of the watershed⟩ **c** : a diagram or table showing metrical structure or rhyme arrangement (as of a stanza) **3 a** (1) : a concise statement in an outline, table, or list : EPITOME (2) : a preparatory outline or draft **b** : a plan reduced to a precise and definite often tabulated form; *also* : a tabulation of a plan or set of directions **4** : a plan or program of something to be done : a planned undertaking ⟨a business ~⟩ ⟨a new ~ for rural electrification⟩: as **a** : a crafty or unethical project ⟨a ~ to get control of the government⟩ ⟨~s to evade taxes⟩ **b** : a visionary project ⟨a head full of ~s and wild ideas⟩ **c** : a combination of elements (as thoughts, theories, considerations) that are connected, adjusted, and integrated by design : a systematic plan : SYSTEM ⟨worked out a new ~ of philosophical interpretations⟩ ⟨wholly changed his ~ of life⟩ **d** : a planned and often mildly mischievous diversion : LARK, ESCAPADE **e** *chiefly Brit* : a governmental or official plan or project ⟨a contributory pension ~⟩; *also* : the product of such a scheme ⟨obtained their irrigation water from the new ~⟩ **5** : a complexity (as in nature or social institutions) that suggests or reveals systematic design ⟨attain their rightful place in the ~ of things —S.L.A.Marshall⟩ **syn** see PLAN, SYSTEM

[2]**scheme** \"\ *vb* -ED/-ING/-S *vt* **1** : to devise or contrive a scheme for : accomplish by clever contriving : DESIGN, PROJECT, PLOT ⟨*scheming* an escape⟩ — often used with *out* ⟨*schemed* out a plot against the king⟩ **2** : to confine within the arbitrary bounds of a system or formula; *also* : to employ in or under a scheme ~ *vi* : to form plans or designs : devise intrigue **syn** see [1]PLAN

scheme arch \ˈskēm-\ *also* **skeen arch** *or* **skene arch** \ˈskēn-\ *n* [*scheme*, *skeen*, *skene* of unknown origin] : DIMINISHED ARCH

scheme·less \ˈskēmləs\ *adj* : lacking a plan or plot ⟨~ tales⟩

schem·er \-mə(r)\ *n* -s : one that forms schemes (as a plotter or intriguer) : PROJECTOR

sche·mery \ˈskēmərē\ *n* -ES : deceptive contriving : MACHINATION

scheming *adj* : given to forming schemes ⟨a busy ~ brain⟩ : tending to artful contriving : shrewdly devious and intriguing ⟨a ~ wife⟩ — compare DESIGNING — **schem·ing·ly** *adv*

sche·mist \ˈskēməst\ *n* -s : SCHEMER; *also* : an advocate of a particular scheme

sche·moz·zle \shəˈmäzəl\ *n* -s [modif. of Yiddish *shlimazel* bad luck, difficulty, misfortune, fr. *shlim* bad, ill (fr. MHG *slimp* awry, not right) + *mazel* luck, fr. LHeb *mazāl* luck, fate, star — more at SLIM] **1** *slang* : a confused situation or affair : MESS, MUDDLE **2** *slang* : QUARREL, ROW

schemy \ˈskēmē\ *adj* : SCHEMING, ARTFUL

sche·nec·ta·dy putter \skəˈnektədē, -di\ *n*, *usu cap S* [*Schenectady*, city in eastern New York] : a golf putter in which the shaft is fastened near the center of the head

schenk beer \ˈsheŋk-,\ *n* [part trans. of G *schenkbier*, fr. *schenken* to pour out (fr. OHG *skenken*) + *bier* beer; fr. the fact that it is put on draft soon after it is made — more at NUNCHEON] : a beer brewed in the winter by the bottom-fermentation process for immediate consumption and not stored like lager

sche·pel \ˈskāpəl\ *n* -s [D, fr. MD; akin to OHG *sceffil* bushel, *skepfen* form, create — more at SHAPE] **1** *also* **skip·ple** \ˈskipəl\ : an old Dutch unit of dry measure equal to ¼ muid or about ¾ bushel **2** : a modern Dutch unit of capacity equal to one decaliter

sche·pen \ˈskāpə(n)\ *n* -s [D, fr. MD *schepene*; akin to OHG *sceffino* magistrate, *skepfen* to shape, form, create] : a municipal officer in Holland and in Dutch settlements analogous to an English alderman

sche·ring bridge \ˈshe|riŋ-, ˈshā|\ *n*, *usu cap S* [after H. *Schering*, 20th cent. Ger. engineer, the inventor] : an alternating-current bridge used to measure the energy loss in dielectrics and to determine the capacitance of condensers — compare WHEATSTONE BRIDGE

scherm \ˈske(ə)rm, ˈskərm\ *n* -s [Afrik *skerm*, fr. D *scherm* screen, curtain, fr. MD, screen, fence, protection; akin to OHG *skerm*, *skirm* shield, L *corium* skin, hide — more at CUIRASS] *Africa* : SCREEN, FENCE ⟨a brushwood ~⟩; *also* : a plot enclosed by a scherm

[1]**scher·zan·do** \skertˈsän(ˌ)dō, skeat-, -ˈsan-, -ˈsȧn-, -ˈsaan-\ *adj* [It, verbal of *scherzare* to joke, of Gmc origin; akin to MHG *scherzen* to joke, have a good time, leap for joy — more at CARDINAL] : PLAYFUL, JESTING — used as a direction in music indicating style and tempo ⟨allegretto ~⟩

[2]**scherzando** \"\ *n* -s : a passage or movement in scherzando style

scher·zo \ˈskert(ˌ)sō, -eət-\ *n*, *pl* **scherzos** \-ōz\ *also* **scherzi** \-(ˌ)sē\ [It, lit., joke, fr. *scherzare*] : a sprightly humorous instrumental musical composition or movement that is commonly in quick triple time and usu. in ternary form — compare MINUET

scher·zo·so \=ˈsō(ˌ)sō\ *adj* [It, fr. *scherzo* + *-oso* -ose (fr. L *-osus*)] : SCHERZANDO

schesis \ˈskē|səs, -kel\ *n*, *pl* **scheses** \|ˌsēz\ [Gk, condition, quality, relation; akin to Gk *echein*, *schein* to have, hold — more at SCHEME] *obs* : general state or disposition of the body or mind or of one thing with regard to other things : HABITUDE, RELATION

sche·tel·i·gite \shəˈteləˌgīt\ *n* -s [Norw *scheteligit*, fr. Jacob *Schetelig* †1935 Norw. mineralogist + Norw *-it* -ite] : a mineral $(Ca,Y,Sb,Mn)_2(Ti,Ta,Cb)_2O_6(O,OH)$ that is an oxide of calcium, rare earth metals, antimony, manganese, titanium, columbium, and tantalum

scheuch·ze·ria \shȯikˈsirēə\ *n*, *cap* [NL, fr. Johann Jakob *Scheuchzer* †1733 and his brother Johann *Scheuchzer* †1738 Swiss botanists + NL *-ia*] : a monotypic genus (the type of the family Scheuchzeriaceae) of bog herbs that are found throughout the north temperate zone and that have leafy stems with white or greenish racemose flowers, several carpels, and fruits resembling follicles

scheuch·ze·ri·a·ce·ae \(ˌ)shȯikˌsirēˈāsēˌē\ *n pl*, *cap* [NL, fr. *Scheuchzeria*, type genus + *-aceae*] : a family of monocotyledonous plants (order Naiadales) coextensive with the genus *Scheuchzeria*

schia·vo·ne \skyəˈvōnē\ *n* -s [It, lit., Slavonian; fr. its use by the Slavonian guards of the doge of Venice] : a two-edged basket-hilted sword

schick test \ˈshik-\ *n*, *usu cap S* [after Béla *Schick* †1967 Am. pediatrician] : a test for susceptibility to diphtheria performed by injecting a suitable amount of diphtheria toxin into the skin upon which susceptible persons develop an area of redness and slight infiltration followed by some desquamation while immune persons show no reaction

schie·dam \skēˈdam, -ˈdäm, =ˈ=\ *n* -s *sometimes cap* [*Schiedam*, city in southwestern Netherlands, orig. its locality] : a strongly flavored gin

schie·le's pivot \ˈshēlēz-\ *n*, *usu cap S* [after Christian *Schiele*, 19th cent. Eng. engineer] : a pivot having a curved surface which is generated by the revolution of a tractrix about its axis, wearing uniformly, but wasting 50 percent more energy than a flat pivot

schiff base \ˈshif-\ *n*, *usu cap S* [after Hugo *Schiff* †1915 Ger. chemist] : any of a class of bases of the general formula RR′C=NR″ that are obtained typically by condensation of an aldehyde or ketone with a primary amine (as aniline) with elimination of water, that usu. polymerize readily if made from aliphatic aldehydes, and that are used chiefly as intermediates in organic synthesis and in some cases as accelerators of vulcanization and as dyes : AZOMETHINE; *esp* : ANIL — compare ALDIMINE, KETIMINE

schiff·li \ˈshiflē\ *n* -s [G dial. (Swiss), lit., small ship, dim. of G *schiff* ship, fr. OHG *skif*; prob. fr. the shape of its shuttles — more at SHIP] : a complex power machine for working embroidery designs and lace patterns on textiles ⟨~ embroidery⟩

schiff reaction *n*, *usu cap S* : a reaction that is used as a test for aldehydes and consists in the formation by them of a reddish violet color with a solution of fuchsine decolorized with sulfurous acid

schiff reagent *n*, *usu cap S* : a solution of fuchsine decolorized by treatment with sulfur dioxide that gives a useful test for aldehydes because they restore the reddish violet color of the dye — compare FEULGEN REACTION

schih \ˈshē\ *n* -s [native name in northern Africa] : dry grasslands of northern Africa

schill *chiefly Scot var of* SHILL

schil·ler \ˈshilə(r)\ *n* -s [G, play of colors, iridescence, fr. MHG *schilher* iridescent taffeta, fr. *schilhen* to squint, twinkle (fr. OHG *scilihen* to squint) + *-er*; akin to OE *bescȳlan* to look sidelong, MLG *schēlen* to peer out; causative-denominatives fr. the root of OE *sceol* wry, squinting — more at CYLINDER] **1** : the bronzy iridescent luster of a mineral (as hypersthene or schiller spar) due to minute inclusions or cavities in parallel position and sometimes resulting from alteration **2** : lustrously or resplendently iridescent coloration (as of a beetle)

schil·ler·iza·tion \ˌshilərəˈzāshən, -ˌrīˈz-\ *n* -s : the alteration of orthorhombic pyroxene and sometimes diallage in such a way that minute inclusions of secondary minerals are developed that reflect light simultaneously

schil·ler·ize \ˈshiləˌrīz\ *vt* -ED/-ING/-S : to impart a schiller to (a mineral) by the development (as by solution and infiltration) of inclusions or cavities

schiller spar *n* [part trans. of G *schillerspat*, fr. *schiller* play of colors, iridescence + *spat* spar] : an altered enstatite characterized by a schiller on its chief cleavage face, occurring as green or brown foliated masses in igneous rocks, and having a composition approximately that of serpentine

schil·ling \ˈshiliŋ, -lēŋ\ *n* -s [G, fr. OHG *skilling*, a gold coin — more at SHILLING] **1 a** : a subsidiary unit of value formerly used in some of the northern states of Germany **b** : a corresponding coin **2 a** : the basic monetary unit of Austria since 1925 — see MONEY table **b** : a coin representing one schilling

schil·ling index \"-\ *n*, *usu cap S* [after Victor Theodor Adolf Georg *Schilling* b1883 Ger. physician] : an age classification of blood neutrophils into myelocytes, metamyelocytes, stab cells, and mature neutrophils on the basis of increasing irregularity or lobulation of the nucleus — compare ARNETH INDEX

schi·ma \ˈskīmə\ *n*, *cap* [NL, prob. modif. of Gk *skiasma* shadow, fr. *skiazein* to overshadow, fr. *skia* shadow — more at SHINE] : a small genus of East Indian and eastern Asian evergreen trees and shrubs (family Theaceae) that are sometimes cultivated in warm regions for their showy often fragrant white flowers

schim·mel \ˈskiməl\ *n* -s [Afrik *skimmel* gray horse, mildew, fr. D *schimmel*; akin to OHG *scimbalōn* to become moldy, MLG *schimmel* gray horse, mildew, OE *scīnan* to shine — more at SHINE] *chiefly dial* : a gray or grayish horse

schin·dy·le·sis \ˌskindəˈlēsəs\ *n*, *pl* **schindyle·ses** \-ēˌsēz\ [NL, fr. Gk *schindylēsis* act or process of splitting into fragments; akin to Gk *schizein* to split — more at SHED] : an articulation in which one bone is received into a groove or slit in another

schin·dy·let·ic \ˌskindəˈled·ik\ *adj* [fr. *schindylesis*, after such pairs as E *narcosis: narcotic*] : exhibiting or joined in schindylesis

schi·nop·sis \skəˈnäpsəs\ *n*, *cap* [NL, fr. *Schinus* + *-opsis*] : a genus of So. American deciduous to half-evergreen trees (family Anacardiaceae) with extremely hard heavy durable reddish to reddish brown heartwood that is an important source of tannins — see QUEBRACHO 1b

schi·nus \ˈskīnəs\ *n*, *cap* [NL, fr. Gk *schinos* mastic tree] : a genus of tropical American trees (family Anacardiaceae) with odd-pinnate leaves and small dioecious white flowers in panicles — see PEPPER TREE

schip·per·ke \ˈskipə(r)kē, -)kə\ *n* [Flem, dim. of *schipper* boatman, skipper, fr. MD; fr. the use of such dogs as watchdogs on boats — more at SKIPPER] **1** *usu cap* : a Belgian breed of small stocky black dogs with foxy head and erect triangular ears developed originally chiefly for use as a watchdog on canalboats **2** -s : a dog of the Schipperke breed

schir·mer·ite \ˈshərməˌrīt\ *n* -s [J. H. L. *Schirmer*, 19th cent. Am. mint superintendent + E *-ite*] : a mineral $PbAg_4Bi_4S_9$ consisting of a sulfide of bismuth, silver, and lead

schirrhus *var of* SCIRRHUS

schi·san·dra \skəˈzandrə, -ˈsa-\ *n*, *cap* [NL, irreg. fr. *schiz-* + *-andra*] : a genus of aromatic woody vines or shrubs (family Magnoliaceae) including one in No. America and others in eastern Asia and having the leaves often evergreen, unisexual flowers in axillary clusters with the petals and sepals undifferentiated, and a fruit that is an elongated spike crowded with berries

-schi·sis \ˌskəsəs\ *n comb form*, *pl* **-schi·ses** \-skəˌsēz\ *also* **-schi·sis·es** [NL, fr. Gk *schisis* cleavage, fr. *schizein* to split] : breaking up of attachments or adhesions : fissure ⟨gastro*schisis*⟩

schism \ˈsizəm, ÷ˈski-; *among clergymen usu* ˈsi-\ *n* -s [alter. (influenced by LL *schisma*) of earlier *scisme*, fr. ME, fr. MF & LL; MF *cisme*, fr. LL *schismat-*, *schisma*, fr. Gk, cleft, division, fr. *schizein* to split — more at SHED] **1** : DIVISION, SEPARATION; *also* : DISCORD, DISHARMONY ⟨there should be no ~ in the body —1 Cor 12:25 (AV)⟩ **2 a** : formal division or separation in the Christian church or from a church or religious body : breach of unity among people of the same religious faith **b** : the offense of seeking to produce division in a church **c** : a schismatic body or sect **d** *obs* : a schismatic opinion **3 a** *obs* : a condition of disagreement in opinion : mutual hostility **b** : a division of a group into two discordant groups ⟨a ~ in a political party⟩; *also* : a condition of opposition or divergence (as between abstract principles) ⟨the widening ~ between pure and applied science⟩ **4** *archaic* : a tear in fabric (as clothing) **5** *archaic* : FACTION, CLIQUE **syn** see BREACH

schis·ma \ˈskizmə\ *n*, *pl* **schisma·ta** \-məd·ə\ [LL *schismat-*, *schisma* minute interval in music, schism] : the interval between an acoustical pure and an equally tempered fifth — see DIASCHISMA

[1]**schis·mat·ic** \sizˈmad·ik, ÷ski-, -at|, |ēk\ *n* -s [alter. (influenced by LL *schismaticus*) of earlier *scismatyke*, fr. ME *scismatike*, fr. MF *scismatique*, fr. LL *schismaticus*, fr. *schismaticus*, adj.] : one who creates or takes part in schism : one who separates from a church or religious communion on account of a difference of opinion — compare HERETIC

[2]**schismatic** \(ˈ)=¦==\ *adj* [alter. (influenced by LL *schismaticus*) of earlier *scismatyke*, fr. ME *scismatike*, fr. MF *scismatique*, fr. LL *schismaticus*, fr. *schismat-*, *schisma* schism + L *-icus* -ic] : of, relating to, or characteristic of schism : implying schism : having the nature of or tending to schism : separated from some body by schism : guilty of schism ⟨~ opinions⟩ ⟨~ sects⟩

schis·mat·i·cal \|əkəl, |ēk-\ *adj* [alter. (influenced by LL *schismaticus*) of earlier *scismatical*, fr. obs. E *scismatyke*, adj. + E *-al*] : SCHISMATIC — **schis·mat·i·cal·ness** *n* -ES

schis·mat·i·cal·ly \-k(ə)lē, -li\ *adv* [alter. (influenced by LL *schismaticus*) of earlier *scismatically*, fr. obs. E *scismatical* + E *-ly*] : in a schismatic manner : so as to be schismatic

schis·ma·tist \ˈ=mətəst, -məd·ə-\ *n* -s [prob. fr. *schismatize*, after such pairs as E *colonize: colonist*] : SCHISMATIC

schis·ma·tize \-məˌtīz\ *vb* -ED/-ING/-S [prob. fr. [2]*schismatic*, after such pairs as E *harmonic: harmonize*] *vi* : to take part in schism; *esp* : to make a breach of union (as in the church) ~ *vt* : to induce into schism

schismless *adj*, *obs* : free from schismatic disorder

schist *also* **shist** \ˈshist\ *n* -s [F *schiste*, fr. L *schistos*, adj., that splits easily, fr. Gk, divided, divisible, fr. *schizein* to split — more at SHED] : a metamorphic crystalline rock having a closely foliated structure, admitting of division along approximately parallel planes, and differing from gneisses in containing no essential feldspar and usu. in having finer laminations

schis·tic \-tik\ *adj* : SCHISTOSE

schisto- *comb form* [NL, fr. Gk *schistos* divided, divisible] : cleft : divided ⟨*Schisto*cephalus⟩

schis·to·ceph·a·lus \ˌshistəˈsefələs *sometimes* ˌski-\ *n*, *cap* [NL, fr. *schisto-* + *-cephalus*] : a genus of tapeworms closely related to and resembling those of the genus *Ligula* in appearance and behavior

schis·to·cer·ca \-ˈsərkə\ *n*, *cap* [NL, fr. *schisto-* + *-cerca* (fr. Gk *kerkos* tail)] : a genus of large migratory locusts

schis·to·cyte \ˈ==ˌsīt\ *n* -s [ISV *schisto-* + *-cyte*] **1** : a very small red blood cell **2** : a fragmenting red blood cell

schist·oid \ˈshiˌstȯid\ *adj* [ISV *schist* + *-oid*] : resembling schist

schist oil *n* : oil distilled from bituminous schists

schis·tor·rha·chis \shiˈstȯrəkəs *sometimes* ski-\ *n* -ES [NL, fr. *schisto-* + *-rrhachis*] : SPINA BIFIDA

schist·ose *also* **shist·ose** \ˈshiˌstōs *also* -ōz\ *or* **schist·ous** \-stəs\ *adj* [*schistose* fr. *schist* + *-ose*; *schistous* fr. F *schisteux*, fr. *schiste* schist + *-eux* -ous] : of or relating to schist : having the character or structure of a schist

schis·tos·i·ty \shiˈstäsəd·ē\ *n* -ES : the quality or state of being a schist

schis·to·so·ma \ˌshistəˈsōmə *sometimes* ˌski-\ *n* [NL *Schistosomat-*, *Schistosoma*, fr. *schisto-* + *-somat-*, *-soma* -soma] **1** *cap* : the type genus of the family Schistosomatidae comprising digenetic trematodes parasitic in the visceral veins of man and other mammals — see SCHISTOSOMIASIS **2** -s : any worm of the genus *Schistosoma* : SCHISTOSOME

schis·to·so·mat·i·dae \ˌ==ˌsōˈmad·əˌdē\ *n pl*, *cap* [NL, fr. *Schistosomat-*, *Schistosoma*, type genus + *-idae*] : a family of slender elongated digenetic trematodes (superfamily Schistosomatoidea) in which the sexes are separate and marked sexual dimorphism is usu. present — see SCHISTOSOME

schis·to·so·ma·toi·dea \ˌ==ˌsōməˈtȯidēə\ *n pl*, *cap* [NL, fr. *Schistosomat-*, *Schistosoma* + *-oidea*] : a superfamily of digenetic trematodes that lack a metacercaria and have instead a furcocercous cercaria that actively penetrates the skin of a definitive host — compare SCHISTOSOME DERMATITIS

[1]**schis·to·some** \ˈ==ˌsōm\ *adj* [NL *Schistosoma*] : of or relating to the genus *Schistosoma* ⟨~ morphology⟩ : caused by schistosomes

[2]**schistosome** \"\ *n* -s [NL *Schistosoma*] : a trematode of the genus *Schistosoma* or broadly of the family Schistosomatidae — called also *blood fluke*

schistosome dermatitis *n* : an itching inflammation caused by invasion of the skin by furcocercous cercariae of various schistosomes that are not normally parasites of man — called also *swimmer's itch*; see STAGNICOLA

schis·to·so·mi·a·sis \ˌ==ˌsəˈmīəsəs\ *n*, *pl* **schistosomia·ses** \-īəˌsēz\ [NL, fr. *Schistosoma* + *-iasis*] : infestation with or disease caused by schistosomes; *specif* : a severe endemic disease of man in much of Asia, Africa, and So. America that is caused by any of three schistosomes (*Schistosoma haematobium*, *S. mansoni*, and *S. japonicum*) which multiply in snail intermediate hosts and are disseminated into fresh waters as furcocercous cercariae that bore into the body when in contact with infested water, migrate through the tissues to the visceral venous plexuses (as of the bladder or intestine) where they attain maturity, and cause much of their injury through hemorrhage and damage to tissues resulting from the passage of the usu. spined eggs to the intestine and bladder whence they pass out to start a new cycle of infection in snail hosts — compare SCHISTOSOME DERMATITIS

schistosomiasis hae·ma·to·bi·um \-ˌhēməˈtōbēəm\ *n* [*schistosomiasis* + NL *haematobium* (specific epithet of *Schistosoma haematobium*), fr. L *haemat-* hemat- + NL *-bium*, neut. of *-bius* having a (specified) mode of life — more at -BIUS] : schistosomiasis caused by the worm (*Schistosoma haematobium*) occurring over most of Africa and in Asia Minor and predominantly involving infestation of the veins of the urinary bladder

schistosomiasis ja·pon·i·ca \-jəˈpänəkə\ *n* [NL, *schistosomiasis* + *japonica*, fem. of *japonicus* Japanese (of which the neut. *japonicum* is the specific epithet of *Schistosoma japonicum*), fr. *Japonia* Japan, country off the eastern coast of Asia + L *-icus* -ic] : schistosomiasis caused by the worm (*Schistosoma japonicum*) occurring chiefly in eastern Asia and the Pacific islands and predominantly involving infestation of the portal and mesenteric veins

schistosomiasis man·soni \-ˈman(t)səˌnī\ *n* [*schistosomiasis* + NL *mansoni* (specific epithet of *Schistosoma mansoni*), gen. of *Mansonus*, latinization of the name of Sir Patrick *Manson* †1922 Brit. physician and parasitologist] : schistosomiasis caused by the worm (*Schistosoma mansoni*) occurring chiefly in central Africa and eastern So. America and predominantly involving infestation of the mesenteric and portal veins

schis·to·so·moph·o·ra \ˌshistəsəˈmäfərə *sometimes* ˌski-\ *n*, *cap* [NL, fr. *Schistosoma* + *-o-* + *-phora*] : a genus of Oriental freshwater snails (family Bulimidae) including important intermediate hosts of the schistosome (*Schistosoma japonicum*) esp. in the Philippines — compare ONCOMELANIA

schis·to·som·u·lum \ˌ==ˈsämyələm\ *n*, *pl* **schistosomu·la** \-lə\ [NL, fr. *Schistosoma* + *-ulum*] : an immature schistosome in the body of the definitive host

schists *pl of* SCHIST

schiz- *or* **schizo-** *comb form* [NL, fr. Gk *schizo-*, fr. *schizein* to split — more at SHED] **1** : split : cleft : divided ⟨*schiz*axon⟩ **2** : characterized by or involving cleavage ⟨*schizo*genesis⟩ : produced by cleavage ⟨*schizo*coel⟩ **3** : schizophrenia ⟨*schizo*phasia⟩

schi·zaea \skəˈzēə\ *n*, *cap* [NL, irreg. fr. Gk *schizein* to split] : a genus (the type of the family Schizaeaceae) of small leptosporangiate ferns with filiform or linear fronds and the sporangia in close distichous spikes — see CURLY GRASS

schiz·ae·a·ce·ae \ˌskizēˈāsēˌē\ *n pl, cap* [NL, fr. *Schizaea*, type genus + *-aceae*] : a small family of mainly tropical ferns of various habit with simple or pinnate fronds and ovoid sessile sporangia in spikes or panicles — **schiz·ae·a·ceous** \ˌ¦skizē¦āshəs\ *adj*

schiz·af·fin \ˌ¦skitsə¦fēn\ *adj* [ISV *schiz-* + *-affin* (fr. *affinity*)] : ASTHENIC 2

schi·zan·dra \skəˈzandrə\ *syn of* SCHISANDRA

schi·zan·thus \-ˈzan(t)thəs\ *n* [NL, fr. *schiz-* + *-anthus*] **1** *cap* : a genus of Chilean herbs (family Solanaceae) having finely divided leaves and showy variegated flowers with an irregular laciniate corolla and two exserted stamens — see BUTTERFLY FLOWER **2** -ES : any plant of the genus *Schizanthus*

schiz·axon \(ˈ)skiz, skəz+\ *n* [NL, fr. *schiz-* + *axon*] : an axon that splits into nearly equal branches; *esp* : an axon of a sensory neuron entering the spinal cord and being so split

schizo \ˈskit(ˌ)sō *sometimes* -i(d)(ˌ)zō\ *n* -S [short for *schizophrenic*] : a schizophrenic individual

schizo-affective \¦≠(ˌ)≠+\ *adj* [*schiz-* + *affective*] : exhibiting symptoms of both schizophrenia and manic-depressive psychosis

schizo·carp \ˈskizōˌkärp\ *n* -S [ISV *schiz-* + *-carp*] : a dry compound fruit that splits at maturity into several indehiscent one-seeded carpels — see MERICARP; FRUIT illustration — **schizo·car·pic** \¦≠≠¦kärpik\ *adj* — **schizo·car·pous** \-pəs\ *adj*

schizo·coel *also* **schizo·coele** \ˈ≠≠ˌsēl\ *n* -S [*schiz-* + *-coele*] : a perivisceral cavity that arises by the splitting of the mesoblast of the embryo — compare ENTEROCOELE — **schizo·coe·lic** \¦≠≠¦sēlik\ *adj* — **schizo·coe·lous** \-ləs\ *adj*

schizo·din·ic \¦≠≠¦dinik\ *adj* [*schiz-* + Gk *ōdinein* to be in labor + E *-ic*; akin to Gk *odynē* pain — more at ANODYNE] : discharging genital products by rupture

schi·zog·a·my \skəˈzägəmē\ *n* -ES [ISV *schiz-* + *-gamy*] : reproduction involving division of the body into a sexual and an asexual individual (as in some chaetopod worms)

schizo·genesis \ˌskizō+\ *n* [NL, fr. *schiz-* + L *genesis*] : reproduction by fission

schizo·ge·net·ic \¦≠≠jə¦ned·ik\ *or* **schizo·gen·ic** \-¦jenik\ *adj* [*schiz-* + *-genetic* or *-genic*] : SCHIZOGENOUS — **schizo·ge·net·i·cal·ly** \-d·ək(ə)lē\ *adv*

schi·zog·e·nous \skəˈzäjənəs\ *adj* [*schiz-* + *-genous*] : of, relating to, or formed by fission: as **a** : SCHIZOGONOUS **b** : formed by splitting, delamination, or separation of adjacent cell walls ⟨~ intercellular spaces in plants⟩ — compare LYSIGENOUS — **schi·zog·e·nous·ly** *adv*

schi·zog·na·thae \skəˈzägnəˌthē\ *n pl, cap* [NL, fr. *schiz-* + *-gnathae*] *in former classification* : a suborder of carinate birds consisting of those (as the pigeons, gallinaceous birds, penguins, gulls, cranes, shorebirds) with a schizognathous palate

schi·zog·na·thism \-ˌthizəm\ *n* -S [*schizognathous* + *-ism*] : the condition of being schizognathous

schi·zog·na·thous \-thəs\ *adj* [*schiz-* + *-gnathous*] : constituting or having an arrangement of the bones of the palate in which the vomer is narrow and pointed in front and separated by a space on each side from the usu. long narrow maxillopalatals which do not unite with each other or with the vomer — used of birds

schizo·go·ni·a·les \ˌskizəˌgōnēˈā(ˌ)lēz\ *n pl, cap* [NL, fr. *schiz-* + *goni-* + *-ales*] : a monotypic order of green algae (class Chlorophyceae) having a filamentous, flat and expanded, or solid cylindrical body made of uninucleate cells with single stellate chloroplasts

schi·zog·o·nous \skəˈzägənəs\ *also* **schizo·gon·ic** \ˌ¦skizə¦gänik\ *adj* [*schizogonous* fr. *schizogony* + *-ous*; *schizogonic* ISV *schizogon-* (fr. NL *schizogonia*) + *-ic*] : of, relating to, or reproducing by schizogony ⟨~ protozoans⟩

schi·zog·o·ny \skəˈzägənē\ *n* -ES [NL *schizogonia*, fr. *schiz-* + L *-gonia* -gony] : asexual reproduction by multiple segmentation of an enlarged trophozoite that is characteristic of many sporozoans (as the malaria parasite) — compare SPOROGONY

schizo·gregarinae \ˌ¦ski(ˌ)zō+\ [NL, fr. *schiz-* + *Gregarinae*] *syn of* SCHIZOGREGARINARIA

schizo·gregarinaria \"+\ *n pl, cap* [NL, fr. *schiz-* + *Gregarinaria*] : a suborder of Gregarinida comprising sporozoans that possess both sexual reproduction and asexual schizogony — compare EUGREGARININA

schizo·gregarine \"+\ *n* -S [NL *Schizogregarinae*] : a sporozoan of the suborder Schizogregarinaria

schizo·gregarinida \"+\ [NL, fr. *schiz-* + *Gregarinida*] *syn of* SCHIZOGREGARINARIA

¹schiz·oid \ˈskitˌsȯid *sometimes* -i(d),zȯid\ *adj* [ISV *schiz-* + *-oid*] **1** : characterized by, resulting from, or possessed of a split personality **2** : disintegrating into mutually contradictory or antagonistic parts ⟨conflicting values make ours a ~ culture⟩ ⟨a ~ foreign policy⟩

²schizoid \"\ *n* -S : a schizoid individual ⟨extreme devotion to religious pursuits . . . is common among ~*s* —R.S.Banay⟩

schiz·oid·ism \-ˌdizəm\ *n* -S : the state of being split off (as in schizoid personality and schizophrenia) from one's social and vital environment

schizoidmanic \¦≠≠¦≠\ *also* **schizo·manic** \ˌ¦skitsō *sometimes* -i(d)zō-\ *adj* [*schizoidmanic* fr. ¹*schizoid* + *manic*; *schizomanic* fr. *schiz-* + *manic*] : schizo-affective and usu. with predominantly manic features

schizoid personality *n* : a personality disorder characterized by shyness, withdrawal, inhibition of emotional expression, and apparent diminution of affect, displaying an active fantasy life often evidenced by eccentric behavior or by artistic creativeness and sometimes by nomadism or by religiosity but not necessarily going on to intellectual or emotional deterioration or regression, and generally being in actual or potential contact with reality

schiz·o·lite \ˈskizəˌlīt\ *n* -S [Dan *schizolit*, fr. *schiz-* + *-lit* -lite] : a manganese-containing variety of pectolite

schizo·lysigenous \¦skit(ˌ)zō+\ *adj* [blend of *schizogenous* and *lysigenous*] : formed both schizogenously and lysigenously — **schizo·ly·sig·e·nous·ly** *adv*

schiz·o·me·ria \ˌskizəˈmirēə\ *n, cap* [NL, fr. *schiz-* + Gk *meros* part + NL *-ia* — more at MERIT] : a small genus of trees (family Cunoniaceae) of Australia and New Guinea with strong hard wood — see ASH

schizo·my·cete \ˌskizəˈmīˌsēt, -ˌmīˈsēt\ *n* -S [NL *Schizomycetes*] : an organism of the class Schizomycetes : BACTERIUM

schizo·my·ce·tes \-ˌmīˈsēd·ēz\ *n pl, cap* [NL, fr. *schiz-* + *-mycetes*] : a class of unicellular or noncellular organisms lacking true chlorophyll, comprising the bacteria, being classed among the fungi, kept separate, or grouped with the blue-green algae in a distinct division — see PROTOPHYTA, SCHIZOPHYTA; compare BACTERIOCHLOROPHYLL — **schizo·my·cet·ic** \¦≠≠¦mī¦sed·ik\ *adj* — **schizo·my·ce·tous** \-sēd·əs\ *adj*

schizo·my·coph·y·ta \ˌ≠≠ˌmīˈkäfəd·ə\ [NL, fr. *schiz-* + *myc-* + *-phyta*] *syn of* SCHIZOPHYTA

schizo·nemertea \ˌski(ˌ)zō+\ *n pl, cap* [NL, fr. *schiz-* + *Nemertea*] *in some classifications* : a group of nemerteans comprising those having a deep slit along each side of the head and a proboscis devoid of stylets — **schizo·nemertean** \"+\ *or* **schizo·nemertine** \"+\ *adj or n*

schizont \ˈskiˌzänt, -ki,z-\ *n* -S [ISV *schiz-* + *-ont*] : a multinucleate cell in some sporozoans that is formed by the growth of a trophozoite in a cell of the host and that segments directly into merozoites — compare SCHIZOGONY, SPORONT

schi·zon·ti·ci·dal \skəˌzäntəˈsīdᵊl\ *adj* : of or relating to a schizonticide

schi·zon·ti·cide \≠ˈ≠≠ˌsīd\ *n* -S [*schizont* + *-i-* + *-cide*] : an agent selectively destructive of the schizont of a sporozoan parasite (as of malaria)

schiz·o·pel·mous \ˌskizō¦pelməs\ *adj* [*schiz-* + *-pelmous*] : having the two flexor tendons of the toes separate and the flexor of the hallux going to the first toe only

schizo·pet·a·lon \ˌ≠≠ˈped·ᵊlˌän\ *n, cap* [NL, fr. *schiz-* + Gk *petalon* leaf — more at PETAL] : a genus of So. American annual herbs (family Cruciferae) having lobed or sometimes pinnatifid leaves, racemose flowers with unequally cut long-clawed petals, and narrow pods

schizo·pha·sia \ˌskitsōˈfāzh(ē)ə *sometimes* -i(d)zō-\ *n* -S [NL, fr. *schiz-* + *-phasia*] : the disorganized speech characteristic of schizophrenia

schi·zoph·o·ra \skəˈzäfərə\ *n pl, cap* [NL, fr. *schiz-* + *-phora*] : a suborder or other division of Diptera consisting mainly of the Acalyptratae and Calyptratae

schiz·o·phrene \ˈskitsəˌfrēn *sometimes* -i(d)zə-\ *n* -S [ISV, prob. back-formation fr. NL *schizophrenia*] : SCHIZOPHRENIC

schiz·o·phre·nia \ˌskitsəˈfrēnēə *sometimes* -i(d)zəˈf- *or* -fren-\ *n* -S [NL, fr. *schiz-* + *-phrenia*] **1** : a psychotic disorder of unknown commonly etiology that occurs as simple, paranoid, catatonic, or hebephrenic, is characterized by disturbance in thinking involving a distortion of the usual logical relations between ideas, a separation between the intellect and the emotions so that the patient's feelings or their manifestations seem inappropriate to his life situation, and a reduced tolerance for the stress of interpersonal relations so that the patient retreats from social intercourse into his own fantasy life and commonly into delusions and hallucinations, and may when untreated or unsuccessfully treated go on to marked deterioration or regression in the patient's behavior though often unaccompanied by further intellectual loss **2** : SPLIT PERSONALITY — **schiz·o·phre·ni·ac** \-nēˌak\ *n* -S — **schiz·o·phrenic** \¦≠≠¦frenik *also* -rēn- *sometimes* -rin-\ *adj or n*

schizophrenic reaction *n* : SCHIZOPHRENIA 1

schiz·o·phren·i·form \¦≠≠¦frenəˌfȯrm\ *adj* [*schizophreni-* (fr. *schizophrenia*) + *-form*] : similar to schizophrenia in appearance or manifestations

schiz·o·phreno·gen·ic \¦≠≠¦frēnə¦jenik, -ren-\ *adj* [*schizophrenia* + *-o-* + *-genic*] : causative of or tending to produce schizophrenia

schiz·o·phy·ce·ae \ˌskizəˈfīsēˌē\ [NL, fr. *schiz-* + *-phyceae*] *syn of* MYXOPHYCEAE

schi·zoph·y·ta \skəˈzäfəd·ə\ *n pl, cap* [NL, fr. *schiz-* + *-phyta*] *in some classifications* : a division comprising the blue-green algae and bacteria (classes Myxophyceae and Schizomycetes) and characterized by unicellular or loosely colonial and often filamentous organization, by lack of a readily identifiable condensed nucleus, and by reproduction chiefly or wholly by fission — **schizo·phyt·ic** \ˌ¦skizə¦fid·ik\ *adj*

schizo·phyte \ˈskizəˌfīt\ *n* -S [NL *Schizophyta*] : one of the Schizophyta

schizo·pod \ˈskizəˌpäd\ *n* -S [NL *Schizopoda*] : a crustacean of the order Euphausiacea or Mysidacea

schi·zop·o·da \skəˈzäpədə\ *n pl, cap* [NL, fr. *schiz-* + *-poda*] *in former classifications* : an order or other division of Malacostraca that is now divided between the orders Euphausiacea and Mysidacea — **schi·zop·o·dous** \-dəs\ *adj*

schi·zop·o·dal \-dᵊl\ *adj* [NL *Schizopoda* + E *-al*] : having biramous thoracic appendages

schizo·rhinal \ˌskizə¦rīnᵊl\ *adj* [*schiz-* + *rhin-* + *-al*] : having each of the bones forming the posterior contour of the osseous external nares deeply cleft instead of rounded ⟨pigeons, most shore birds, and various other birds are ~⟩ — opposed to *holorhinal*

schizos *pl of* SCHIZO

schizo·saccharomyces \ˌ¦ski(ˌ)zō+\ *n, cap* [NL, fr. *schiz-* + *Saccharomyces*] : a genus (coextensive with the family Schizosaccharomycetaceae of the order Endomycetales) of fungi comprising the fission yeasts and characterized by division of each cell into two daughter cells of similar size — compare BUDDING YEAST

schizo·the·cal \ˌ¦skizə¦thēkəl\ *adj* [*schiz-* + *thec-* + *-al*] : having the horny envelope of the tarsus divided into plates that resemble large firm scales ⟨most birds are ~⟩

schizo·thoracic \ˌ¦ski(ˌ)zō+\ *adj* [*schiz-* + *thorac-* + *-ic*] : having the prothorax large and loosely articulated to the remainder of the thorax ⟨~ insects⟩

schiz·o·thyme \ˈskitsəˌthīm *sometimes* -i(d)zə-\ *n* -S [ISV, prob. back-formation fr. NL *schizothymia*] : an individual exhibiting or characterized by schizothymia

schiz·o·thy·mia \ˌ≠≠ˈthīmēə\ *n* -S [NL, fr. *schiz-* + *-thymia*] : an introvert tendency or temperament that while remaining within the bounds of normality somewhat resembles schizophrenia (as in a tendency to autistic thinking) — opposed to *cyclothymia* — **schiz·o·thy·mic** \¦≠≠¦thīmik\ *also* **schiz·o·thy·mous** \-məs\ *adj*

schiz·o·tryp·a·num \ˌskizōˈtripənəm\ *n, cap* [NL, fr. *schiz-* + Gk *trypanon* anger — more at TRYPAN-] *in some classifications* : a genus of flagellates comprising the trypanosome of Chagas' disease — used when the organism is viewed as generically distinct from *Trypanosoma*

schizo·zo·ite \ˌskizəˈzōˌīt\ *n* -S [*schiz-* + Gk *zōion* animal + E *-ite* — more at ZO-] : MEROZOITE

schl *abbr* school

schlä·ger \ˈshlāgə(r)\ *n, pl* **schläger** [G, lit., one that strikes or beats, fr. *schlagen* to strike, beat (fr. OHG *slahan*) + *-er* — more at SLAY] : a long straight basket-hilted blunt-ended sword that is sharpened only near the end and is used in duels by German university students

schle·miel *or* **schle·mihl** *or* **shle·miel** \shləˈmē(ə)l\ *n* -S [Yiddish *shlumiel*, prob. fr. the name Heb *Shĕlūmīēl* Shelumiel (Num 1:6)] *slang* : an unlucky bungling person : a foolish gullible person : NE'ER-DO-WELL

schlemm's canal \ˈshlemz-\ *n, usu cap S* [after Friedrich S. *Schlemm* †1858 Ger. anatomist] : a circular canal lying in the substance of the sclerocorneal junction of the eye and draining the aqueous humor from the anterior chamber into the anterior ciliary veins

schlen·ter \ˈs(h)lentə(r)\ *n* -S [modif. of Afrik *slenter*, fr. D, trick] *Africa* : IMITATION, FAKE — used esp. of a diamond

schlepp \ˈshlep\ *vb* -ED/-ING/-S [Yiddish *shlepen* to drag, fr. MHG *sleppen*, *slēpen*, fr. MLG *slēpen*; akin to MD *slepen* to drag, OHG *sleifen*; causative fr. the root of MD *slipen* to whet, polish, MLG *slipen* to polish, OHG *slīfan* to slide, whet; akin to OE *slipor* slippery — more at SLIPPERY] *slang* : DRAG, HAUL; *also* : STEAL

schlich \ˈshlik, -ik\ *n* -S [G, slime, mud, fr. MHG *slich* — more at SLICK] : SLIME 2d

schlie·ren \ˈshlirən\ *n pl* [G, fr. G dial. *schlieren*, pl. of *schlier*, lit., ulcer, fr. MHG *slier*, *sliere*; prob. akin to MHG *slier* mud — more at SLUR] **1** : small masses or streaks that differ in mineral composition from the main body of an igneous rock but graduate insensibly into it **2** : regions or streaks in a transparent medium (as a fluid) that have a density and hence a refractive index differing from that of the bulk of the medium and often resulting from pressure or temperature differences and that are detected esp. by photographing the passage of a beam of light (as in the shock waves of a projectile) — **schlie·ric** \-rik\ *adj*

schli·ma·zel *or* **schli·mazl** *or* **shli·ma·zel** *or* **shli·mazl** \shləˈmäzəl\ *n* -S [Yiddish *shlimazel* consistently unlucky person, bad luck, misfortune — more at SCHEMOZZLE] *slang* : a consistently unlucky person

schlip·pe's salt \ˈshlipəz-\ *n, usu cap 1st S* [after Karl Friedrich von *Schlippe* †1867 Ger. chemist] : a crystalline salt $Na_3SbS_4.9H_2O$ used as an intensifier in photography; sodium thioantimonate

schloop \ˈshlüp\ *n* -S [imit.] : a swishing sound ending in a plop

schloss \ˈshlȯs\ *n* -ES [G, castle, lock, fr. MHG *sloz*, fr. OHG, lock, bolt — more at SLOT] : a German castle or manor house

schmaltz *or* **schmalz** \ˈshmȯlts, -mäl-, *in sense 2* -ä-\ *n* -ES [Yiddish *shmalts*, lit., rendered fat, fr. MHG *smalz*, fr. OHG; akin to OHG *smelzan* to melt — more at SMELT] **1 a** : extremely sentimental music **b** : sentimentalism in artistic expression **c** : something notably florid or showy of its kind **2** *slang* : the rendered fat of poultry

schmaltzy *or* **schmalzy** \-tsē\ *adj, sometimes* -ER/-EST : marked by schmaltz : excessively sentimental

schmeiss \ˈshmīs\ *n* -ES [G *schmeissen* to fling, throw away, fr. MHG *smīzen* to stroke, smear, strike, fr. OHG *-smīzan* (in *bismīzan* to defile, stain) — more at SMITE] : a bid in klaberjass that requires the opponent to accept the bidder's trump suit or abandon the hand

schmelz *or* **schmelze** \ˈshmelts\ *n, pl* **schmelz·es** \-tsəz\ [G *schmelz* enamel, fr. OHG *smelzi*; akin to OHG *smelzan* to melt] : any of various decorative glasses; *esp* : a glass colored red with metallic salts and used to flash white glass

schmidt camera \ˈshmit\ *n, usu cap S* [after B. *Schmidt* †1935 Ger. optician] : a camera embodying a Schmidt system and a film or plate holder and used extensively in astronomy and in photofluorography

schmidt system *n, usu cap S* : an optical system that utilizes an objective composed of a concave spherical mirror having in front of it a transparent correction plate carefully figured to offset the spherical aberration of the mirror

schmidt telescope *n, usu cap S* : a photographic astronomical reflecting telescope embodying a Schmidt system so that the curved focal surface is free of significant spherical aberration and coma over a wide angular field

schmier·ka·se \ˈshmi(ə)rˌkäzə\ *n* -S [G *schmierkäse* — more at SMEARCASE] : COTTAGE CHEESE

schmitt box \ˈshmit-\ *n, sometimes cap S* [after P. Jerome *Schmitt* †1904 Am. priest who designed it] : a wooden pest-proof box for storing pinned insects

schmo *or* **schmoe** \ˈshmō\ *n, pl* **schmoes** [prob. modif. of Yiddish *shmok* fool, fr. Slovenian *šmok*] *slang* : JERK 5

¹schmooze *also* **schmoose** \ˈshmüz\ *vi* -ED/-ING/-S [Yiddish *shmuesn* to talk, chat, fr. *shmues* talk, chat, fr. Heb *shĕmū'ōth* news, rumors, reports, pl. of *shĕmū'āh* rumor, report, fr. *shāmō'a* to hear, listen] *slang* : to chatter esp. in jargon or cant

²schmooze \"\ *n* -S [Yiddish *shmues* talk, chat] *slang* : JARGON

schnap·per \ˈshnapə(r)\ *n* -S [alter. (influenced by G *schnapper* snapper, fr. MHG *snapper* gossipy or quarrelsome person, fr. *snappen* to snap + *-er*) of *snapper*] : SNAPPER 3c

schnapps *also* **schnaps** \ˈshnaps\ *n, pl* **schnapps** [G *schnaps*, lit., dram of liquor, fr. LG *snaps* dram, mouthful, fr. *snappen* to snap, fr. MLG — more at SNAP] : any of various distilled liquors; *esp* : strong Holland gin

schnau·zer \ˈshnaüzə(r), -aütsə-\ *n* [G, fr. *schnauze* snout, muzzle + *-er*; fr. the mustache and beard — more at SNOUT] **1** *usu cap* : an old German breed of terriers occurring in three varieties differing only in size that have a long head with small ears and heavy eyebrows, mustache, and beard and a wiry coat of pepper-and-salt, black, or black and tan **2** -S : a dog of this breed

schnec·ke \ˈshnekə\ *n, pl* **schnec·ken** \-kən\ [G, lit., snail, fr. OHG *snecko* — more at SNAIL] : a cinnamon bun made of rich yeast-leavened dough that is rolled up like a jelly roll, cut into crosswise slices, and baked cut side down — usu. used in pl.

¹schnei·der \ˈshnīdə(r)\ *n* -S [G, lit., tailor, fr. MHG *snīdære*, fr. *snīden* to cut (fr. OHG *snīdan*) + *-ære* -er (fr. OHG *-āri*); akin to OE *snīthan* to cut, ON *snītha* to cut, Goth *sneithan* to reap, Czech *snět* bough] **1 a** : the taking of 91 or more points by the bidder in skat or schafskopf or of 90 or more by the opponents **b** : failure of the loser of a game of gin rummy to score any point **c** : the winning of a game of sixty-six by a player before his opponent has scored 33 points **2** : the scoring effect of a schneider (as the doubling of the winner's score)

²schneider \"\ *vt* -ED/-ING/-S : to cause (an opponent) to lose by a schneider

schnei·de·ri·an membrane \(ˈ)shnī¦dirēən-\ *n, usu cap S* [*schneiderian* fr. Conrad Victor *Schneider* †1680 Ger. anatomist + E *-an*] : modified mucous membrane forming the epithelial part of the olfactory organ

schnei·der index \ˈshnīdə(r)-\ *n, usu cap S* [after Edward Christian *Schneider* †1954 Am. biologist] : a measure of comparative circulatory efficiency based on determination of pulse rates under several test conditions (as reclining, standing, or after exercise), time required for rate to alter with change of state, and accompanying variations in systolic pressure

schnell \ˈshnel\ *adv (or adj)* [G, fr. OHG *snel*, adj., strong, bold, agile — more at SNELL] : in a rapid manner : QUICKLY — used as a direction in music

schnitz *or* **snits** *also* **snitz** \ˈshnits\ *n, pl* **schnitz** *or* **snits** *also* **snitz** [PaG, *schnitz*, pl. of *schnutz* section of dried fruit, alter. of G *schnitz* slice, cut, fr. MHG *sniz*; akin to OHG *snīdan* to cut] : sliced dried fruit; *esp* : sliced dried apples

schnitz and knepp \ˌ≠ənkəˈnep, -ənˈknep\ *n* [PaG *gnepp*, pl. of *gnopp* button, lump, fr. MHG dial. *knopp*; akin to OHG *knopf* knot, lump — more at KNOP] : a dish consisting of dried apples and dumplings boiled with or without smoked ham

schnit·zel \ˈshnitsəl\ *n* -S [G, cutlet, shaving, chip, fr. MHG *snitzel* small slice, dim. of *sniz* slice, cut] : a veal cutlet variously seasoned and garnished

schnitz un knepp \ˌshnitsən-\ *n* [PaG *schnitz un gnepp*] : SCHNITZ AND KNEPP

schnook \ˈshnük\ *n* -S [origin unknown] *slang* : a stupid or suggestible person : a person of no importance : DOLT

schnorkel *also* **schnorchel** *var of* SNORKEL

schnor·rer \ˈshnȯrər, -nōr-\ *n* -S [Yiddish *shnorer*, fr. *shnoren* to beg (fr. MHG *snurren* to hum, whir, of imit. origin) + *-er* (fr. MHG *-ære*, fr. OHG *-āri*); fr. the sound of the musical instrument used by strolling beggars] *slang* : BEGGAR

schnoz·zle \ˈshnäzəl\ *n* -S [prob. modif. of Yiddish *shnoitsl*, dim. of *shnoits* snout, fr. G *schnauze* snout, muzzle — more at SNOUT] *slang* : NOSE

schnur·ke·ra·mik \ˈshnü(ə)rkä¦rämik\ *n* -S [G, fr. *schnur* string, cord (fr. OHG *snuor*) + *keramik* ceramics, fr. F *céramique* — more at NARROW, CERAMIC] : a Neolithic pottery decorated by imprints of string or cord

schochet *var of* SHOHET

schoen·feld's purple \ˈshō|nˌfel(d)z-, ˈshə(r)|, -lts-\ *n, often cap S* [prob. fr. the name *Schoenfeld*] : a dark purplish red that is bluer and paler than pansy purple and bluer, lighter, and stronger than raisin, Bokhara, or dahlia purple (sense 1)

schoe·no·cau·lon \ˌskēnəˈkȯˌlän\ *n, cap* [NL, fr. *schoeno-* (fr. Gk *schoinos* rush, reed) + *-caulon* (fr. Gk *kaulos* stem) — more at HOLE] : a genus of bulbous American herbs (family Liliaceae) having linear basal leaves and white flowers with exserted stamens — see SABADILLA

schoe·nus \ˈskēnəs\ *n, cap* [NL, fr. Gk *schoinos* rush, reed] : a genus of stout sedges (family Cyperaceae) chiefly Australasian but including a few from Europe and the warm or tropical parts of No. America and having few-flowered spikelets in a spike or head, flowers without a perianth of bristles, and nutlets lacking a beak

schoep·ite \ˈskeˌpīt, ˈskə(r),p-\ *n* -S [Alfred *Schoep*, 20th cent. Belg. mineralogist + E *-ite*] : a mineral prob. $4UO_3.9H_2O$ that is a hydrous uranium oxide and is found esp. in the Belgian Congo

schoi·nob·a·tes \skȯiˈnäbəˌtēz\ *n, cap* [NL, fr. Gk *schoinobatēs* ropedancer, fr. *schoinos* rush, reed, rope + *-batēs* one that goes (fr. *bainein* to go, walk) — more at COME] : a genus of marsupials comprising the large flying phalangers of Australia

schok·ker \ˈskäkə(r)\ *n* -S [D] : a large Dutch cutter, yawl, or ketch-rigged pleasure boat

scho·la \ˈskōlə\ *n, pl* **scho·lae** \-ˌlē, -ˌlī\ *also* **scholas** [L] **1 a** : an ancient Roman school **b** : a private room in an ancient Roman residence **c** : a lecture hall or meeting room (as of a guild or corporation) **2** [LL, fr. L] : an ancient Roman association of persons (as military men) sharing a common interest or profession

schola can·to·rum \ˌ≠≠ˌkanˈtōrəm\ *n, pl* **scholae cantorum** [ML, school of singers] **1** : a singing school; *specif* : the choir or choir school of a monastery or of a cathedral **2** : the part of an ecclesiastical edifice reserved to the choir

schol·ar \ˈskälə(r)\ *n* -S [ME *scoler*, fr. OE *scolere* & OF *escoler*, fr. ML *scholaris*, fr. LL, adj., of a school, fr. L *schola* school + *-aris* -ar — more at SCHOOL] **1 a** : one who attends a school or studies under a teacher : PUPIL, STUDENT — used esp. in combination ⟨Sunday school ~⟩ **b** : one under the training of a particular master ⟨a ~ of the learned doctor⟩ **2 a** : one who by long systematic study (as in a university) has gained a high degree of mastery in one or more of the academic disciplines; *esp* : one who has engaged in advanced study and acquired the minutiae of knowledge in some special field along with accuracy and skill in investigation and powers of critical analysis in interpretation of such knowledge ⟨a noted Shakespeare ~⟩ ⟨was a ~. He knew the right books, knew them to the core and how to use them —H.S.Canby⟩ **b** : a learned person; *esp* : one who has the attitudes (as curiosity, perseverance, initiative, originality, integrity) considered essential for learning ⟨using the word ~ . . . to include all those . . . endeavoring to be original thinkers in any field of learning —J.B.Conant⟩ ⟨the self-dedication of ~*s* to concerns unrelated to individual profit —Lynn White⟩ **c** *dial* **:** a person knowing how to read and write **3 :** a holder of a scholarship

schol·arch \'skä,lärk\ *n* -s [LGk *scholarchēs*, fr. Gk *scholē* school + *-archēs* -arch — more at SCHOOL] **1 :** the head of a school; *esp* **:** the leader of an Athenian school of philosophy **2** [F *scolarque* & G *scholarch*, fr. LGk *scholarchēs*] *archaic* **:** a school inspector in France or Germany

schol·ar·dom \'skälə(r)dəm\ *n* -s **:** the realm of scholarship **:** the whole body of scholars

scho·lar·i·an \skä'lerēən\ *n* -s [LL *scholarius* scholarian (fr. *schola* ancient Roman association of persons sharing a common interest or profession + L *-arius* -ary) + E *-an*] **:** a member of the Roman imperial guard

schol·ar·ism \'skälə,rizəm\ *n* -s **:** scholastic often pedantic learning

scho·lar·i·ty \skä'larəd·ē\ *n* -ES [ML *scholaritat-*, *scholaritas*, fr. *scholaris* scholar + L *-tat-*, *-tas* -ty] *archaic* **:** status as scholar

schol·ar·less \'skälə(r)ləs\ *adj* **:** lacking students ⟨a ~ tutor⟩

scholarlike \'⸗,⸗\ *adj* **:** SCHOLARLY

schol·ar·li·ly \'skälə(r)lə̇lē, -əli\ *adv* **:** in a scholarly manner **:** so as to be scholarly

schol·ar·li·ness \-)lēnə̇s, -)lin-\ *n* -ES **:** the quality or state of being scholarly

¹schol·ar·ly \'skälə(r)lē, -)li\ *adj*, *sometimes* -ER/-EST [*scholar* + *-ly*, adj. suffix] **:** like, characteristic of, or suitable to a scholar: as **a :** concerned with academic study and esp. with research ⟨contact between the craft and ~ elements of the profession —S.F.Mason⟩ ⟨the author of ~ and reference works —Charlton Laird⟩ **b :** exhibiting the methods and attitudes of a scholar ⟨his method was laborious and ~; it was not exceptional for him to spend three years in research, travel, and sketching, to produce a single canvas —*Amer. Guide Series: Calif.*⟩ **c :** having the manner and appearance of a scholar ⟨never academic — still less pedantic — but always ~; with the effect of profound learning ever so lightly worn —Ronald Storrs⟩

²scholarly \"\ *adv* [*scholar* + *-ly*, adv. suffix] **:** in the manner or character of or as befits a scholar

schol·ar·ship \'skälə(r),ship\ *n* **1 :** a sum of money or its equivalent offered (as by an educational institution, a public agency, or a private organization or foundation) to enable a student to pursue his studies at a school, college, or university — compare FELLOWSHIP **2 :** the character, qualities, or attainments of a scholar: as **a :** scholastic achievement **:** LEARNING ⟨Dante, whose ~ was . . . considerable, appears to have known no more than a word or two of Greek —Gilbert Highet⟩ ⟨devices employed by schools . . . for their supposed influence on ~ are . . . marks on report cards —H.R.Douglass⟩ **b :** methods, attitudes, and traditions characterizing a scholar ⟨if by ~ we mean all of the activities and attitudes encompassed in the sincere search for truth —Hugh & Mabel Smythe⟩ **3 :** the body of learning and esp. of research available in a particular field ⟨acquaint themselves with the actual nature of religious ~ —George Hedley⟩ **syn** see KNOWLEDGE

scho·lasm \'skō,lazəm\ *n* -s [fr. ¹*scholastic*, after such pairs as E *enthusiastic*: *enthusiasm*] **:** a pedantic or academic expression

¹scho·las·tic \skə'lastik -laas-, -tēk *also* skō'l- *or* skä'l-\ *adj* [in sense 1, fr. ML *scholasticus*, fr. L, of a school, fr. Gk *scholastikos* enjoying leisure, devoting one's leisure to learning, academic, fr. (assumed) Gk *scholastos* (verbal of Gk *scholazein* to have leisure, give lectures, keep a school, fr. *scholē* leisure, lecture, school) + Gk *-ikos* -ic; in other senses, fr. L *scholasticus* — more at SCHOOL] **1 a** *often cap* **:** of or relating to the Schoolmen of the medieval period ⟨~ theology⟩ ⟨~ philosophy⟩ **b** (1) **:** characterized by or suggestive of the logic or methods of the medieval Schoolmen (2) **:** characterized by excessive subtlety **:** PEDANTIC, FORMAL **2** *obs* **:** academically trained **:** BOOK-LEARNED **3 a :** of, relating to, or associated with a school ⟨~ standards⟩ ⟨during the ~ holidays⟩ ⟨a sense that ~ teaching is not divorced from the practical world —Bertrand Russell⟩ **b :** having the characteristics of, belonging to, or befitting a scholar **:** SCHOLARLY ⟨a thorough and ~ piece of work⟩ **c :** designed for scholars ⟨an honorary ~ fraternity⟩

²scholastic \"\ *n* -s [ML *scholasticus*, fr. *scholasticus*, adj.] **1 a** *usu cap* **:** a Christian philosopher of the medieval period **:** SCHOOLMAN **b** (1) **:** one who deals with philosophical or theological problems in the spirit of Scholasticism (2) **:** PEDANT, FORMALIST **2** [¹*scholastic*] *obs* **:** SCHOLAR, STUDENT **3** [NL *scholasticus*, fr. L *scholasticus*, adj.] **:** a student in a scholasticate **4** [¹*scholastic*] **:** one who advocates or practices scholastic or traditional methods in art **5 scholastics** *pl* **:** scholastic practices or methods **:** scholastic philosophy or theology; *broadly* **:** PEDANTRY ⟨dry and lifeless ~*s* —P.A. Sorokin⟩

scho·las·ti·cal \-tə̇kəl, -tēk-\ *adj or n* [ML & L *scholasticus* scholastic + E *-al*] *archaic* **:** SCHOLASTIC

scho·las·ti·cal·ly \-k(ə)lē, -li\ *adv* **:** in a scholastic manner **:** in respect to school or scholarship

scho·las·ti·cate \-tə,kāt, -tə̇kə̇t\ *n* -s [NL *scholasticatus*, fr. *scholasticus*, n., scholastic + L *-atus* -ate] **:** a school of general study for those preparing for membership in a Roman Catholic religious order

scho·las·ti·cism \-tə,sizəm\ *n* -s **1** *usu cap* **:** a philosophical movement dominant in western Christian civilization from the Carolingian period in the 9th century until the rise of Cartesianism in the 17th century; *specif* **:** the philosophical systems and speculative tendencies of various medieval Christian thinkers who working on a background of fixed religious dogma sought to solve anew general philosophical problems (as of faith and reason, will and intellect, realism and nominalism, and the provability of the existence of God) initially under the influence of the mystical and intuitional tradition of patristic philosophy and esp. Augustinianism and later under that of Aristotle — compare OCKHAMISM, SCOTISM, THOMISM; see NEO-SCHOLASTICISM **2 :** close adherence to traditional teachings or methods prescribed by schools or sects; *specif* **:** a viewpoint dominated by scholastic modes of thought

scho·las·ti·cize \-tə,sīz\ *vi* -ED/-ING/-s **:** to favor or employ scholastic principles or arguments **:** become influenced by scholasticism

scho·li·ast \'skōlē,ast\ *n* -s [MGk *scholiastēs*, fr. *scholiazein* to write scholia on, fr. Gk *scholion*] **:** a maker of scholia **:** COMMENTATOR, ANNOTATOR — **scho·li·as·tic** \¦⸗⸗¦astik\ *adj*

scho·li·on \'skōlē,än, -ēən\ *n*, *pl* **scho·lia** \-ēə\ *also* **scholions** [Gk] **:** SCHOLIUM

scho·li·um \-ēəm\ *n*, *pl* **scho·lia** \-ēə\ *also* **scholiums** [NL *scholium*, fr. Gk *scholion*, dim. of *scholē* lecture — more at SCHOOL] **1 :** a marginal annotation **:** an explanatory remark or comment (as on the text of a classic by an early grammarian) **2 :** a remark or observation subjoined but not essential to a demonstration or a train of reasoning ⟨explanatory *scholia* inserted by the editors in the text of Euclid's *Elements*⟩

schom·burgk·ia \(')shäm¦bərkēə, -būr-\ *n*, *cap* [NL, fr. Robert H. *Schomburgk* †1865 Brit. traveler and explorer + NL *-ia*] **:** a genus of So. American epiphytic orchids having showy racemose flowers borne either on a scape from pseudobulbs or on a long fleshy stem

schön·fels·ite \'shōn,fel,zīt, 'shə(r)n-\ *n* -s [G *schönfelsit*, fr. *Altschönfels*, Saxony, Germany + G *-it* -ite] **:** a feldspar-free basalt with phenocrysts of olivine and augite in a dense groundmass of titanomagnetite, orthorhombic pyroxene, apatite, interstitial brown glass, and traces of basic plagioclase

¹school \'skül\ *n* -s [ME *scole*, fr. OE *scōl*, fr. L *schola* leisure devoted to learning, lecture, school, fr. Gk *scholē* leisure, learned discussion, lecture, school; akin to Gk *echein*, *schein* to have, hold — more at SCHEME] **1 a** (1) **:** an organized body of scholars and teachers associated for the pursuit and dissemination of knowledge (as in a particular advanced field) and constituting a college esp. of a medieval university (2) **schools** *pl* **:** the academic or learned world **:** UNIVERSITIES — usu. used with the definite article ⟨the view accepted by the ~*s*⟩ (3) *usu cap*, *obs* **:** SCHOOLMEN — usu. used in pl. **b** (1) **:** the body of pupils or students attending a school ⟨the new teacher is liked by the whole ~⟩ (2) **:** the members of a school including both faculty and students ⟨the ~ had a holiday⟩ ⟨the ~ participated in a fire drill⟩ **c** (1) **:** the disciples or followers of a teacher (2) **:** persons who hold a common doctrine or accept the same teachings or follow the same intellectual methods **:** a sect or denomination (as in philosophy, theology, medicine, or politics) ⟨belonged to the radical ~ of economists⟩ (3) **:** people forming a distinguishable group or class and sharing common principles, canons, precepts, or a common body of opinion or practice ⟨a gentleman of the old ~⟩ ⟨other ~*s* of opinion⟩ (4) **:** a group (as of painters, sculptors, or musicians) under a common local or personal influence producing a general similarity in their work ⟨the Wagnerian ~⟩; *also* **:** the artists or art of a country or region ⟨paintings of the Flemish ~⟩ **d** *Brit* **:** a body of gamblers or thieves **:** GANG **2 a :** an organized source of education or training: as (1) **:** an institution for the teaching of children **:** an elementary or secondary school (2) **:** an institution for specialized higher education usu. within a university ⟨the ~ of medicine at the state university⟩ (3) **:** COLLEGE, UNIVERSITY ⟨the excellent east coast ~*s*⟩ (4) **:** an establishment for teaching a particular skill or group of skills ⟨a ~ of design⟩ ⟨a fencing ~⟩ ⟨a beauticians' ~⟩ **b :** a place where instruction is given: (1) **:** a place where lectures are held; *esp* **:** a place for lectures in logic, metaphysics, and theology in the medieval period (2) **:** a building or hall where examinations for degrees and honors are held at an English university (3) **:** a building or group of buildings in which a school is conducted ⟨the new ~ is very elaborate⟩ ⟨the most beautiful ~ in the area⟩ (4) **:** an area (as an enclosure or covered ring) where horses are schooled **:** a riding school **c :** something that is a source of instruction ⟨the ~ of experience⟩ **3 a :** the process of being instructed or educated in institutions for teaching the young ⟨found ~ very difficult⟩ **b :** attendance at a school ⟨he quit ~⟩ ⟨during her last year of ~⟩ **4 :** a session of a school ⟨there will be no ~ on Friday⟩ ⟨late for ~⟩ ⟨kept in after ~⟩ **5 :** an administrative unit in a private school comprising several consecutive grades or forms ⟨a lower ~⟩ ⟨boys in the upper ~⟩ **6 a :** a final examination for the bachelor of arts degree (as at Oxford University) **b :** an honors course (as at Oxford University) **7 a :** a book of instruction (as in a particular system of execution in music) **b :** a system of instruction or execution **8 :** the regulations governing military drill of individuals or of a unit of a given size or kind; *also* **:** the exercises carried out in accordance with such regulations ⟨the ~ of the soldier⟩

²school \"\ *vb* -ED/-ING/-s *vt* **1 :** to educate or provide with education in an institution of learning **:** send to school ⟨the boy was ~*ed* at great cost to his family⟩ **2 :** to give teaching or training to: **a :** to teach or drill in a specific knowledge, attitude, or skill ⟨well ~*ed* in languages⟩ ⟨our parents have ~*ed* us in the principle of the rights of the individual⟩ **b :** to instruct, stabilize, or inure by practice, long or repeated experience, or subjection to systematic discipline — usu. used with *in* ⟨~ oneself in patience⟩ ⟨~*ing* a horse in the five gaits⟩ ⟨~ an athlete in timing⟩ **c :** to make tractable (as by teaching, admonition, or chastisement) **d :** to educate, cultivate, or advance mentally or culturally by formal instruction in or as if in a school ⟨~*ed* his mind with travel and study⟩ **e** (1) *archaic* **:** to reprove for error or fault **:** set right **:** CHIDE, ADMONISH; *also* **:** to dictate to (2) *obs* **:** to punish by way of giving a lesson **~** *vi* **1 :** to go to school **2 :** to ride or course cross-country ⟨~*ing* over meadows and hills⟩ **syn** see TEACH

³school \"\ *adj* **1 :** of or relating to a school ⟨~ traditions⟩ **:** connected with or employed in connection with a school ⟨a ~ library⟩ ⟨the ~ superintendent⟩ **2 a :** of the kind taught in school ⟨~ studies⟩; *sometimes* **:** superficially and incompletely mastered ⟨amateurish ~ French⟩ **b :** of the kind taught or practiced in a school of horsemanship **:** trained in a school of horsemanship **:** SCHOOLED ⟨a ~ gait⟩ **3 a :** of or relating to the Schoolmen ⟨~ theology⟩ **:** of the kind employed by the Schoolmen ⟨~ arguments⟩ **b :** being or involving mere abstractions or quibbling **:** having no practical application or value ⟨~ language⟩ ⟨a ~ name⟩

⁴school \"\ *n* -s [ME *scole*, fr. MD *schole* group esp. of fish or animals of one kind, multitude; akin to OE *scolu* multitude, troop, *sciell* shell — more at SHELL] **1 :** a large number of one kind of fish or other aquatic animals swimming or feeding together ⟨a ~ of dolphins⟩ **2 :** a large group or flock (as of birds or people) ⟨too busy receiving the congratulations of a ~ of admirals for us to buttonhole her —*New Yorker*⟩

⁵school \"\ *vi*, *of fishes* **:** to swim and feed together in large numbers ⟨bluefish are ~*ing*⟩

school·able \'skülәbəl\ *adj* **:** suitable for school or schooling: **a :** sufficiently tractable or intelligent to warrant training ⟨a quiet ~ beast⟩ **b :** of an age to attend school ⟨~ children⟩

school age *n* **:** the period of life during which a child is considered mentally and physically fit to attend school and is commonly required to do so by law — **school–ager** \'skü,läjə(r)\ *n*

schoolbag \'⸗,⸗\ *n* **:** a bag usu. of cloth in which a pupil may carry school books, school supplies, and miscellaneous objects needed at school or for homework

schoolbag

school bass \'⸗¦bas\ *n* **:** a small or immature channel bass

school board *n* **:** a board in charge of local public schools

schoolboy \'⸗,⸗\ *n* **:** a boy attending school

school·boy·ish \'⸗,⸗ish, -ēsh\ *adj* **:** suited to or resembling that of a young boy ⟨an immature ~ laugh⟩

school·boy·ish·ness *n* **:** behavior suited to a young boy **:** immature or childish conduct

school bus *n* **:** a vehicle that is either publicly owned or privately owned and operated for compensation, that is usu. conspicuously marked with the words *school bus*, and that is used for transporting children to or from school or on activities connected with school

school canter *n* **:** a precisely balanced and strongly collected slow canter performed with long clean reaching strides

school certificate *or* **school leaving certificate** *n* **:** a certificate awarded in the British Commonwealth to students 16 years or older who have completed the secondary school course and passed a special examination — called also GENERAL CERTIFICATE OF EDUCATION

schoolchild \'⸗,⸗\ *n*, *pl* **schoolchildren :** a child who attends school

school committee *n* **:** SCHOOL BOARD

schoolcraft \'⸗,⸗\ *n*, *archaic* **:** knowledge purveyed by school

schooldame \'⸗,⸗\ *n* **:** the keeper of a dame school **:** SCHOOLMISTRESS

school district *n* **:** an area within a state sometimes coinciding with a township but having its own board and power of taxation and serving as the smallest unit for administration of a public-school system

school divine *n* **:** SCHOOLMAN 1b

school doctor *n* **1** *obs* **:** SCHOOLMAN 1b **2 :** a physician employed to make periodic examinations of the children of a school or of the schools of a community

school·dom \'sküldəm\ *n* -s **:** school affairs; *also* **:** those concerned with their administration

schooled *past of* SCHOOL

school edition *n* **:** an edition of a book issued esp. for use in schools and usu. differing from the ordinary edition in having a simplified, condensed, or otherwise emended text and glossarial or explanatory matter

school·er \'skül(ə)r\ *n* -s **:** a pupil in school — usu. used in combination

school·ery \'skül(ə)rē\ *n* -ES *archaic* **:** matters taught in or as if in a school **:** SCHOOLING

schoolfellow \'⸗,⸗(,)⸗\ *n* [ME *scollfelau*, fr. *scoll*, *scole* school + *felau*, *felawe* fellow] **:** SCHOOLMATE

school figure *n* **:** one of a progressive series of fundamental figure skating movements that are executed in a prescribed pattern in the form of a 2-lobed or 3-lobed figure eight and constitute a part of championship competition

schoolgirl \'⸗,⸗\ *n* **:** a girl attending school

school·girl·ish \'⸗,⸗ish, -ēsh\ *adj* **:** suited to or resembling that of a young girl ⟨a dress too ~ for office wear⟩ ⟨~ chatter⟩

schoolhouse \'⸗,⸗\ *n* [ME *scolehous*, fr. *scole* school + *hous* house] **1 :** a building used as a school and esp. as an elementary school ⟨little red ~⟩ **2 a :** the headmaster's residence at some British schools **b :** the group of boys boarding in the headmaster's household

schooling *n* -s [ME *scoling*, fr. *scole* school + *-ing*] **1 a :** instruction in or attendance at school ⟨had to interrupt his ~ to go to work⟩ **:** education in an institution of learning ⟨the state now takes responsibility for ~⟩ **b :** training, guidance, or discipline derived from experience or contact with experts ⟨a long and arduous ~ as a performer in several of the best bands —Irving Kolodin⟩ **2** *archaic* **:** chastisement for correction **:** REPROOF, REPRIMAND **3 :** tuition or tuition and maintenance in a school **:** the cost of instruction and maintenance ⟨pay a boy's ~⟩ **4 :** the training of a horse for service ⟨~ a horse to lead⟩ ⟨gave the filly thorough ~ in the gaits⟩: as **a :** the teaching and exercising of horse and rider in the formal techniques of equitation and coordination therein (as in a riding school) **b :** the teaching and exercising of a horse in jumping techniques **c :** the training of a race horse to break from a starting gate

school·ing·ly *adv* [*schooling* (pres. part. of ²*school*) + *-ly*] **:** in a manner intended to teach or admonish

school·ish \-lish,-lēsh\ *adj* **:** characteristic of schools: as **a :** remote from life **:** PEDANTIC **b :** following scholastic traditions **:** ACADEMIC

schoolkeeper \'⸗,⸗\ *n* **:** one that keeps a school: **a :** the proprietor of a private school **b :** a teacher in a school and usu. in a small or elementary school **c** *chiefly Brit* **:** the janitor of a school

school land *n* **:** government lands set aside for the support of public schools — usu. used in pl. ⟨bought up *school lands* in the newly opened area⟩

school leaver *n*, *chiefly Brit* **:** a pupil who has recently left school usu. without completing his course — compare GRADUATE

school·less \'sküllə̇s\ *adj* **:** lacking a school or schooling ⟨~ children⟩

school·man \'skülmən, -,man, -,maa(ə)n\ *n*, *pl* **schoolmen** **1 a :** one skilled in the niceties of academic disputation **b** *usu cap* **:** a philosopher or divine of the schools of the medieval period **:** SCHOLASTIC **2 :** one professionally engaged in education through the schools **:** a teacher or administrative officer of an educational institution **3 a :** an orthodox follower of a school (as of philosophy or politics) **b :** an adherent of neo-scholasticism

school·marm *or* **school·ma'am** *R* '⸗,mä(r)m, *–R* -,mäm, *R* & *–R* -,mam, -,maa(ə)m\ *n* -s **1 :** a woman schoolteacher esp. in an old-type rural or small-town school ⟨the New England ~ of 50 years ago⟩ **2 :** a person either male or female who exhibits characteristics (as pedantry and priggishness) popularly attributed to schoolteachers ⟨the Puritan ~*s* who once kept the tang of the city streets out of our . . . language —Edgar Kemler⟩ **3 a :** a forked tree **b :** a log cut from the fork of such a tree

school·marm·ish \-ish, -ēsh\ *adj* **:** resembling or typical of a schoolmarm

¹schoolmaster \'⸗,⸗⸗\ *n* [ME *scolemaister*, fr. *scole* school + *maister* master] **1 :** a male schoolteacher: as **a :** the teacher of an old-type rural or small-town school ⟨in colonial New England, the ~ was boarded around⟩ **b :** the headmaster of a school **c :** a master or preceptor in a school **d** *obs* **:** a private tutor **2 :** one acting as a teacher or resembling a teacher in effect or behavior: as **a :** one having a guiding or inspiring influence ⟨the ~ of medieval Europe⟩ **b :** one exhibiting the pedantry and despotism popularly attributed to old-time schoolteachers **3 :** a reddish brown edible snapper (*Lutjanus apodus*) of the tropical Atlantic and the Gulf of Mexico with large scales, vertical greenish bars on the sides, and greenish orange fins — called also *black snapper*

²schoolmaster \"\ *vt* **:** to train or instruct in the manner of a schoolmaster; *esp* **:** to force into conformity by constant supervision or faultfinding ⟨the children, obviously much ~*ed*, had lost their natural initiative⟩ ⟨purists who would ~ the language⟩ **~** *vi* **:** to be or act as a schoolmaster **:** teach as a means of livelihood ⟨returned to ~*ing*⟩

³schoolmaster \"\ *n* [⁴*school* + *master*] **:** a member of a school of fishes or whales that appears to be the leader

school·mas·ter·hood \'⸗,⸗⸗,hu̇d\ *n* **:** the position or state of a schoolmaster

school·mas·ter·ish \-ish\ *adj* **:** suggestive of a schoolmaster esp. in pedantry — **school·mas·ter·ish·ly** *adv* — **school·mas·ter·ish·ness** *n* -ES

school·mas·ter·ly \-lē,-li\ *adj* **:** resembling or characteristic of a schoolmaster

school·mas·ter·ship \-,ship\ *n* **:** the status or position of a schoolmaster

school·mas·tery \-ē,-i\ *n* **:** the work or practice of a schoolmaster; *specif* **:** insistence upon obedience to authority even in petty details

schoolmate \'⸗,⸗\ *n* **:** an associate or companion at school

schoolmistress \'⸗,⸗⸗\ *n* [ME *scolemaystress*, fr. *scole* school + *maystress*, *maistresse* mistress] **:** a female schoolteacher

school·mis·tressy \-ē,-i\ *adj* **:** resembling or characteristic of a schoolmistress

school of thought : a group sharing a common point of view in respect to some matter ⟨belongs to the liberal *school of thought*⟩; *also* **:** a point of view recognized as held but not necessarily accepted ⟨there are two *schools of thought* about this question⟩

schoolroom \'⸗,⸗\ *n* **:** a room in which pupils are instructed ⟨the sewing room became a ~ when we were kept home by minor ailments⟩ ⟨the new elementary school has 12 ~*s* together with offices, service rooms, and an auditorium⟩

schools *pl of* SCHOOL, *pres 3d sing of* SCHOOL

school section *n* **:** a section of public land set apart in a surveyed township by the U. S. government for the maintenance of public schools

school shark *n*, *Austral* **:** SOUPFIN SHARK, TOPE

school ship *n* **:** a ship used as a nautical training school for apprentices being educated at public expense

school sister of no·tre dame \-,nōd·ə(r)'däm, -ō·trə'd- *also* -däm *or* -dām *sometimes* -dam *or* -daa(ə)m\ *n*, *usu cap both Ss&N&D* [F *Notre Dame* Our Lady (the Virgin Mary)] **:** a member of a Roman Catholic religious congregation founded in France by St. Peter Fourier in 1597 and devoted chiefly to education

school system *n* **:** the aggregate of the public schools of an area under the administration of an executive officer who represents and is responsible to the board of education for that area

schoolteacher \'⸗,⸗⸗\ *n* **:** a person who teaches in a school

school·teach·er·ish \'⸗,⸗⸗ish\ *adj* **:** resembling a schoolteacher or what a schoolteacher is felt to be; *often* **:** PRISSY, PEDANTIC, FINICKY

school·teach·er·ly \-lē\ *adj* **:** SCHOOLTEACHERY

school·teach·ery \-ē\ *adj* **:** resembling or characteristic of a schoolteacher **:** prim and formal in manner and esp. in speech ⟨admonished them in ~ fashion⟩

schoolteaching *n* **:** the occupation or profession of teaching school

school tie *n* **:** OLD SCHOOL TIE

schooltime \'⸗,⸗\ *n* **1 :** the time for beginning a session of school **:** the time during which school is held **2 :** the period of life spent in school or in study ⟨~ is looked back on as the best part of a life⟩ **3 :** a period of training ⟨this life is our ~⟩ ⟨put in a year's ~ to qualify for his license⟩

¹school·ward \'skülwə(r)d\ *also* **school·wards** \-dz\ *adv* **:** toward school ⟨moving ~ at a snail's pace⟩

²schoolward \"\ *adj* **:** directed or extending toward school ⟨took his ~ way⟩

schoolwork \'⸗,⸗\ *n* **:** matter studied in school or assigned in school to be studied either in or out of school ⟨found her ~ increasingly difficult⟩ — compare HOMEWORK 2a

school year *n* **:** ACADEMIC YEAR

schoo·ner \'skünə(r) *sometimes* -ku̇n-\ *n* -s [origin unknown] **1 :** a fore-and-aft rigged boat having two masts with a smaller sail on the foremast and with the mainmast stepped nearly amidships, sometimes carrying square topsails on one or both masts or even a forecourse, and adapted to sailing close to the wind; *broadly* **:** any of various larger fore-and-aft rigged ships with three to seven masts — see SAIL illustration **2 a :** a large tall drinking glass (as for beer or ale) **b :** a British measure used esp. for beer or ale **3 :** PRAIRIE SCHOONER

schooner rig *n* **:** FORE-AND-AFT RIG — **schooner-rigged** \'==¦=\ *adj*

schoop process \'shōp-\ *n, usu cap S* [after Max Ulrich *Schoop* †1956 Swiss engineer] **:** a process in which objects or surfaces are coated with zinc or other metal by spraying them with the molten metal shot from a nozzle by compressed air

scho·pen·hauerean·ism \¦shōpən¦haůrēə,nizəm, ¦==,haů-'irēə,n-, ¦==,haůə'rēə,n-\ *n* -s *usu cap* **:** SCHOPENHAUERISM

scho·pen·hauerian \¦shōpən¦haůrēən, ¦==,haů¦irēən\ *also* **scho·pen·hauerean** \", ¦==,haůə¦rēən\ *adj, usu cap* [Arthur *Schopenhauer* †1860 Ger. philosopher + E *-an*] **:** of or relating to Schopenhauer or his doctrines

scho·pen·hauer·ism \'==,haů(ə),rizəm\ *n* -s *usu cap* [Arthur *Schopenhauer* + E *-ism*] **:** the philosophy of Arthur Schopenhauer who taught that the essential or absolute reality is a blind and restless will manifesting itself as a will to live and that life is an evil to be cured only by overcoming the will to live — compare VOLUNTARISM

schorl *also* **shorl** \'shȯr(ə)l\ *or* **schorl·ite** \-r,līt\ *n* -s [*schorl, shorl* fr. G *schörl; schorlite* fr. G *schorlit,* irreg. fr. *schörl* + *-it* -ite] **1 :** TOURMALINE; *esp* **:** tourmaline of a common black iron-rich variety **2** *archaic* **:** any of several dark-colored minerals other than tourmaline

schor·la·ceous \(')shȯr¦lāshəs\ *adj* **:** being, containing, or resembling schorl

schor·lo·mite \'shȯrlə,mīt\ *n* -s [*schorl* + Gk *homos* same + E *-ite* — more at SAME] **:** a mineral $Ca_3(Fe,Ti)_2[(Si,Ti)O_4]_3$ consisting of an iron calcium titanate and silicate related to garnet and occurring usu. in black masses with vitreous luster (hardness 7–7.5, sp. gr. 3.81–3.88)

schorly \'shȯrlē\ *adj* **:** containing or mingled with schorl ⟨~ granite⟩

schotten-baumann reaction \¦shät³n¦baůmən-, -,män-\ *n, usu cap S&B* [after Carl *Schotten* †1910 Ger. chemist and *Baumann,* 19th cent. Ger. chemist] **:** acylation (as conversion of an alcohol to an ester, of an amine to an amide, or of hydroxylamine to a hydroxamic acid) by an acid chloride in the presence of alkali

¹schot·tische \'shäd·|ish, -ät|, lēsh, *chiefly Brit* shä'tēsh\ *n* -s [G, fr. *schottische,* weak nom. sing. masc. of *schottisch* Scottish, fr. MHG *schottesch,* fr. *Schotte* Scotchman + *-esch* -ish (fr. OHG *-isc*); akin to OE *Scottas* (pl.) Scotchmen — more at SCOT] **1 :** a round dance in duple measure characterized by gliding and hopping steps and similar to but slower than the polka **2 :** music for the schottische

²schottische \"\ *vi* -ED/-ING/-s **:** to dance a schottische

schott·ky defect \'shätkē-\ *n, usu cap S* [after Walter *Schottky b*1886 Ger. physicist] **:** a defect in a crystal lattice created by removing an ion from its normal site and placing it on the crystal surface

schottky effect *n, usu cap S* **:** the increase of the thermionic current in a vacuum tube with the increase of the applied potential between the cathode and anode due to a lowering of the energy required to remove electrons from the cathode

schout \'skaůt\ *n* -s [D, fr. MD *schoutete* count's or bishop's agent with judicial powers in civil cases; akin to OE *scultheta* bailiff, OHG *sculdheizo* magistrate; all fr. a prehistoric WGmc compound noun whose first constituent is represented by OE *scyld* debt, obligation and whose second constituent is akin to OE *hātan* to command — more at SHALL, HIGHT] **1 :** a Dutch bailiff or sheriff **2 :** a person vested in the former Dutch colonies of America with local judicial functions

schouw \'skaů, 'skōů\ *n* -s [D, schouw, scow — more at SCOW] **:** a light-draft open pleasure boat of the Netherlands

schr *abbr* schooner

schra·dan \'shrā,dan\ *n* -s [Gerhard *Schrader b*1903 Ger. chemist + E *-an*] **:** an almost odorless viscous liquid $\{[(CH_3)_2N]_2PO\}_2O$ made from phosphorus oxychloride, dimethylamine, and sodium ethoxide and used chiefly in emulsions as a systemic insecticide — called also *octamethylpyrophosphoramide, OMPA*

schra·der's bromegrass \'shrādə(r)z-\ *n, usu cap S* [prob. fr. the name *Schrader*] **:** RESCUE GRASS

schre·bera \'shrābərə, shrə'birə\ [NL, fr. J. C. D. von *Schreber* †1810 Ger. botanist] *syn of* HARTOGIA

schrei·ber·site \'shrībə(r),sīt, -,zīt\ *n* -s [G *schreibersit,* irreg. fr. Karl F. A. von *Schreiber* †1852 Austrian museum director + G *-it* -ite] **:** a mineral $(Fe,Ni)_3P$ consisting of a phosphide of iron and nickel and occurring in meteorites

schrei·ner finish \'shrīnə(r)-\ *n, often cap S* [prob. fr. the name *Schreiner*] **:** a finish imparted to cotton fabrics by schreinerizing

schrei·ner·ize \'shrīnə,rīz\ *or* **schrei·ner** \-nə(r)\ *vt* -ED/-ING/-s [*schreinerize* prob. fr. the name *Schreiner* + E *-ize; schreiner* prob. fr. the name *Schreiner*] **:** to calender (cotton fabric) with rollers engraved all over with very fine lines in order to produce a lustrous surface

schrik \'skrik\ *n* -s [Afrik *skrik,* fr. D *schrik,* fr. *schrikken* to be frightened, fr. MD *schricken* to be frightened, stride; akin to OHG *scricken* to jump, MHG *scherzen* to leap for joy — more at CARDINAL] *southern Africa* **:** a sudden fright **:** PANIC

schrö·ding·er atom \'shrā|diŋər-, 'shrə(r)|\ *n, usu cap S* [after Erwin *Schrödinger* †1961 Ger. physicist] **:** a conception of atomic structure in which a nucleus of positive electricity is embedded in and surrounded by concentric spherical shells of diffuse negative electricity

schrödinger equation *also* **schrödinger wave equation** *n, usu cap S* **:** an equation that describes the wave nature of elementary particles and is fundamental to the description of the properties of all matter; *specif* **:** a common formulation of this equation

$$\frac{\delta^2\psi}{\delta x^2} + \frac{\delta^2\psi}{\delta y^2} + \frac{\delta^2\psi}{\delta z^2} + \frac{8\pi^2 m}{h^2}[W - V]\psi = 0$$

where ψ (x, y, z) is the wave function, m is the mass of the elementary particle, h is the Planck constant, W is the total energy, and V is the potential energy

schroec·king·er·ite \'shrekiŋə,rīt, 'shrə(r)k-\ *n* -s [G *schröckingerit,* fr. J. von *Schröckinger,* 19th cent. Austrian mineralogist + G *-it* -ite] **:** a mineral $NaCa_3(UO_2)(CO_3)_3(SO_4)F.10H_2O$ that is a hydrous carbonate, sulfate, and fluoride of calcium, sodium, and uranyl

schro·ther \'shrōd·ə(r), -rāthə(r)\ *n* -s [perh. modif. of G *schröter* one that cuts or chops or crushes, fr. MHG *schrōtære* tailor, mintmaster, fr. *schrōten* to cut, hew, chop (fr. OHG *scrōtan* to cut) + *-ære* -er (fr. OHG *-āri*) — more at SHRED] **:** SHREDDER c

schrund *n* -s [G, crack — more at BERGSCHRUND] **:** BERGSCHRUND

schuet·zen·fest \'shütsən,fest, 'shitsən-, 'shwetsən-\ *n* -s [G *schützenfest,* fr. *schütz, schütze* marksman, archer (fr. OHG *scutzo* archer) + *fest* festival; akin to OE *scytta* archer, ON *skyti* archer, OE *scēotan* to shoot — more at SHOOT, -FEST] **:** a shooting match **:** an entertainment or a picnic where marksmanship is practiced

schuet·zen rifle \-tsən-\ *n, usu cap S* [G *schützen,* pl. of *schütz, schütze* marksman] **:** an extremely accurate single-shot rifle having a heavy barrel, a stock with elaborate butt plate and grip, precision sights, and a palm rest

schuff·ner's dots \'shůfnə(r)z-, 'shül, 'shue|\ *n pl, usu cap S* [prob. after Wilhelm August Paul *Schüffner* †1949 Du. physician] **:** punctate granulations present in red blood cells invaded by the tertian malaria parasite

schuh·platt·ler \'shü,plätlə(r)\ *n* -s *often cap* [G, fr. G dial. *schuochplattlar,* fr. *schuochplattln* to slap the soles of one's shoes (fr. *schuoch* shoe — fr. OHG *scuoh* — + *plattln* to strike two flat objects together, fr. G *platte* slab, fr. OHG *platta* stone slab, fr. ML, flat object, fr. assumed VL, fem. of *plattus* flat) + *-ar* -er (fr. OHG *-āri*) — more at SHOE, PLATE] **:** a Bavarian courtship dance in which before the couple dances together the woman calmly does steps resembling those of a waltz while the man dances vigorously about her swinging his arms and slapping his thighs and the soles of his feet

schul *var of* SHUL

schüller-christian disease *n, usu cap S&C* **:** HAND-SCHÜLLER-CHRISTIAN DISEASE

schul·ten·ite \'shůlt³n,īt\ *n* -s [Baron August B. de *Schulten* †1912 Ger. scientist + E *-ite*] **:** a mineral $PbHAsO_4$ consisting of a lead hydrogen arsenate and occurring in colorless tabular orthorhombic crystals

schultz-dale reaction \'shůlts'dā(ə)l-, 'shül\ *n, usu cap S&D* [after Werner *Schultz b*1878 Ger. physician and Sir Henry Hallett *Dale* †1968 Eng. physiologist] **:** a reaction of anaphylaxis carried out in vitro with isolated tissues (as a guinea pig uterus)

schult·ze powder \'shůltsə-, 'shül\ *n, usu cap S* [after Edward *Schultze,* 19th cent. Ger. chemist who invented it] **:** a propellant of the smokeless powder type consisting essentially of nitrated pellets of wood impregnated with barium nitrate and potassium nitrate

schu·mann region \'shümən-, -,män-\ *n, usu cap S* [after Viktor *Schumann* †1913 Ger. physicist] **:** the portion of the ultraviolet spectrum lying approximately between 1850 and 1200 angstroms

schun·gite \'shůŋ,gīt\ *n* -s [G *schungit,* fr. *Schunga, Shunga,* northwest U.S.S.R. + G *-it* -ite] **:** an amorphous carbon that occurs in schists

¹schuss \'shůs, 'shüs\ *n* -ES [G, lit., shot, fr. OHG *scuz* — more at SHOT] **1 :** a straight high-speed run on skis **2 :** a straightaway skiing course **:** an area in a fall line on which a straight downhill run may be made

²schuss \"\ *vb* -ED/-ING/-ES *vt* **:** to make a schuss over ⟨~ a slope⟩ ~ *vi* **:** to ski directly down a slope

schuyt \'skīt, 'skōit, 'skāt, *D* 'skœiet\ *n* -s [D *schuit,* fr. MD *schute* — more at SCOUT] **:** a bluff-bowed Dutch boat fitted with leeboards, used chiefly on canals and for coasting, and sometimes square-rigged but usu. sloop-rigged

schwa *also* **shwa** \'shwä, |ä *also* 'shf| *or* 'shv| *or* shə'w| *or* shə'v| *or* 'sw| *or* 'sv| *or* 'sf|\ *n* -s [G *schwa,* fr. Heb *shĕwā'*] **1 :** a faint indistinct vowel sound like that of *e* in *quiet* that is indicated in Hebrew by two perpendicular dots (as :) and in transliteration by *ĕ* or by a superior dot or small superior *e* **2 a :** an unstressed mid-central vowel that is the usual sound of the first and last vowels of the English word *America* **b :** the symbol ə commonly used for this vowel and sometimes also for a similarly articulated stressed vowel (as in American English *cut*)

schwann cell \'shw|än-, 'shf|, 'shv|\ *n, usu cap S* [after Theodor Schwann †1882 Ger. naturalist] **:** a cell of the neurilemma of a nerve fiber

schwann·ian \'shwänēən, 'shfä-, 'shvä-\ *adj* [Theodor *Schwann* + E *-an*] **:** of, relating to, or made up of Schwann's cells; *also* **:** NEURILEMMAL

schwan·no·ma \=¦nōmə\ *n, pl* **schwannomas** \-məz\ *or* **schwannoma·ta** \-məd·ə\ [NL, fr. Theodor *Schwann* + NL *-oma*] **:** NEURILEMMOMA

schwann's sheath *or* **schwann tube** *n, usu cap S* **:** NEURILEMMA 1

schwar·me·rei \¦shfermə¦rī, ¦shve-\ *n* -s [G *schwärmerei,* fr. *schwärmen* to be enthusiastic, be fanatical or heretical, swarm (said of bees), fr. MHG *swermen, swarmen* to swarm, fr. *swarm* swarm (of bees), fr. OHG *swaram* — more at SWARM] **:** excessive unbridled enthusiasm or attachment

schwartz·brot *or* **schwarz·brot** \'shfärts,brōt, 'shvä-\ *n* -s [G *schwarzbrot,* fr. *schwarz* black (fr. OHG *swarz*) + *brot* bread, fr. OHG *brōt* — more at SWART, BREAD] **:** BLACK BREAD

schwart·zem·berg·ite \'shwȯrtsəm,bər,gīt\ *n* -s [*Schwartzemberg,* 19th cent. Chilean mineral assayer + E *-ite*] **:** a mineral $Pb_5(IO_3)Cl_3O_3$ that is an iodate, chloride, and oxide of lead

schwarz \'shwȯrts, 'shfärts, 'shvä-\ *n* -ES [G, fr. *schwarz,* adj., black] **:** the winning of all the tricks in skat or schafskopf; *also* **:** the scoring effect of this which adds two multipliers in skat and triples the score in schafskopf

schwed·ler's maple \'shwedlə(r)z-\ *n, usu cap S* [prob. fr. the name *Schwedler*] **:** a commonly cultivated maple that is a variety (*Acer platanoides schwedleri*) of the Norway maple with bronzy red early-spring foliage that later turns green

schwe·gel \'shfāgel, 'shvā-\ *n* -s [G, fr. OHG *swegala;* akin to OE *swegl*horn, a wind instrument, Goth *swiglon* to play the flute] **1 :** WIND INSTRUMENT; *specif* **:** PIPE **2 :** a flue organ pipe

schwein·furt green *or* **schwein·furth green** \'shf|īn,fůrt-, 'shv|\ *n, usu cap S* [*Schweinfurt,* Bavaria, Germany] **:** PARIS GREEN 1

schwei·zer·deutsch \'shfītsə(r),dȯich, 'shvī-\ *n* -ES *usu cap* [G, fr. G *schweizer* of or belonging to Switzerland (fr. *Schweiz* Switzerland, country in central Europe) + *deutsch* German, fr. OHG *thiutisc, diutisc,* fr. *thiutisc, diutisc,* adj., German — more at DUTCH] **:** SCHWYZERTÜTSCH

schwei·zer's reagent *also* **schweit·zer's reagent** \-tsə(r)z-\ *n, usu cap S* [after Matthias E. *Schweitzer* †1860 Ger. chemist] **:** CUPRAMMONIUM SOLUTION

schwenk·feld·er \'shfeŋk,feldə(r), 'shve-\ *n* -s *usu cap* [G, fr. Kaspar *Schwenkfeld* †1561 Ger. Silesian nobleman and Protestant mystic + G *-er*] **:** a follower of Kaspar Schwenkfeld who advanced the cause of the Reformation, encouraged laymen to read the Bible, advocated the separation of church and state, and founded small spiritual communities emphasizing a somewhat mystical interpretation of the Christian faith; *esp* **:** a member of the present-day Schwenkfelder Church located in Pennsylvania and composed principally of descendants of Schwenkfelders from Europe

schwenk·feld·ian \(')=¦=dēən\ *n* -s *usu cap* [Kaspar *Schwenkfeld* + E *-an*] **:** SCHWENKFELDER

schwyz \'shf|ēts, 'shv|, |its\ *also* **schwyz·er** \-tsə(r)\ *n, usu cap* [*schwyz* fr. *Schwyz,* canton in east central Switzerland; *schwyzer* fr. G, one belonging to the canton Schwyz, fr. *Schwyz* + G *-er*] **:** BROWN SWISS

schwyz·er dutsch \'shfētsər,tüēch, 'shvē-\ *n, usu cap S&D* [modif. of G dial. (Swiss) *schwyzertütsch*] **:** SCHWYZERTÜTSCH

schwyz·er·tütsch \-,tüēch\ *n* -ES *usu cap* [G dial. (Swiss), fr. *schwyzer* of or belonging to Switzerland (fr. *Schwyz* Switzerland, country in central Europe) + *tütsch* German, fr. OHG *thiutisc, diutisc*] **:** a dialect of German spoken in Switzerland

sci- *or* **scio-** *also* **scia-** *or* **skia-** *comb form* [NL, fr. Gk *ski-, skio-,* fr. *skia* — more at SCENE] **:** shadow ⟨sciogram⟩ ⟨scioptic⟩ ⟨scialytic⟩ ⟨skiascope⟩

sci *abbr* science; scientific

sci·ae·na \sī'ēnə\ *n, cap* [NL, fr. L, a fish, fr. Gk *skiaina,* a fish, prob. the maigre] **:** the type genus of Sciaenidae comprising somewhat elongated marine fishes with a conical head, terminal or subterminal mouth, and no barbels and including numerous croakers some of which are favored as food or sport fishes — see BLACK CROAKER, MAIGRE, MULLOWAY

¹sci·ae·nid \-nəd\ *adj* [NL *Sciaenidae*] **:** of or relating to the Sciaenidae

²sciaenid \"\ *n* -s **:** a fish of the family Sciaenidae

sci·ae·ni·dae \-nə,dē\ *n pl, cap* [NL, fr. *Sciaena,* type genus + *-idae*] **:** a large, economically important, and widely distributed family of carnivorous percoid fishes comprising the croakers, being nearly all marine along the sandy shores of warm temperate seas, usu. having the air bladder large and complicated and used to produce a sound, and including various large fishes valued as food — see SCIAENA

¹sci·ae·noid \-,noid\ *n* -s [NL *Sciaena* + E *-oid*] **:** a sciaenoid fish

²sciaenoid \"\ *adj* **:** resembling or related to the Sciaenidae

scia·lyt·ic \¦sīə¦lid·ik\ *adj* [*sci-* + *-lytic*] **:** dispersing or dispelling shadows (a ~ lamp)

sci·am·a·chy \sī'aməkē\ *n* -ES [Gk *skiamachia,* fr. *skia* shadow + *-machia* -machy] **1 :** a fighting with a shadow **:** a mock or futile combat (as with an imaginary foe)

sci·an \'shēən\ *adj, usu cap* [It *Scio* Chios, island in the Aegean sea + E *-an*] **:** CHIAN

sciaphilous *var of* SCIOPHILOUS

scia·pod \'sīə,päd\ *also* **skia·pod** \'skī-\ *n* -s [L *Sciapodes* Sciapods, fr. Gk *Skiapodes,* fr. *skia* shadow + *pod-, pous* foot — more at SCENE, FOOT] **:** one of a mythological people having feet big enough for use as sunshades and living according to classic Greek mythology in Libya or according to medieval legend in India where they were one-footed sometimes in India

sci·ap·o·dous \(')sī¦apədəs\ *adj* [L *Sciapodes* + E *-ous*] **:** having very large feet

sci·a·ra \'sīərə\ *n* [NL, fr. Gk *skiaros* shady, dark-colored, fr. *skia* shadow] **1** *cap* **:** a genus (the type of the family Sciaridae) of minute and usu. blackish fungus gnats typically with highly gregarious larvae that are often destructive to mushrooms and seedlings — see ARMYWORM **2** -s **:** any insect of the genus *Sciara*

¹sci·a·rid \-rəd\ *adj* [NL *Sciaridae*] **:** of or relating to the Sciaridae

²sciarid \"\ *n* -s **:** a fly of the family Sciaridae **:** FUNGUS GNAT

sci·ar·i·dae \sī'arə,dē\ *n pl, cap* [NL, fr. *Sciara,* type genus + *-idae*] **:** a family of minute usu. dark or blackish two-winged flies some of which are destructive to mushrooms and to seedlings of higher plants — see FUNGUS GNAT, SCIARA; compare MYCETOPHILIDAE

¹sci·at·ic \(')sī¦ad·|ik, -at|, |ēk\ *adj* [MF *sciatique,* fr. LL *sciaticus,* alter. of L *ischiadicus* of pain in the hip — more at ISCHIADIC] **1 :** of or relating to the hip **:** situated in the region of or affecting the hip **:** ISCHIAL **2 :** of, relating to, or caused by sciatica **:** afflicted with sciatica ⟨~ pains⟩ ⟨a ~ patient⟩

²sciatic \"\ *n* -s **:** a sciatic part (as a nerve or artery)

sci·at·i·ca \sī'ad·əkə, -at|, |ēkə\ *n* -s [ME, fr. ML, fr. fem. of LL *sciaticus* sciatic] **:** pain along the course of a sciatic nerve or its branches and esp. in the leg caused by compression, inflammation, or reflex mechanisms; *broadly* **:** pain in the lower back, buttocks, hips, or adjacent parts — not used technically

sci·at·i·cal \(')=¦=kəl\ *adj* [*sciatica* + *-al*] **:** caused by or affected with sciatica ⟨becoming increasingly ~⟩

sciatic artery *n* **:** the gluteal artery that arises in the ischial region of each side of the body

sciatic foramen *n* **:** either of two foramina on each side leading from the pelvis to the gluteal and peroneal regions and transmitting respectively (1) the sciatic nerve, superior and inferior gluteal, pudendal, and other nerves, associated vessels, and the piriformis muscle and (2) the tendon of the internal obturator muscle and the pudendal vessels and nerve — called also (1) *greater sciatic foramen* (2) *lesser sciatic foramen*

sci·at·icky \sī'ad·əkē\ *adj* [*sciatica* + *-y*] *dial* **:** affected with sciatica

sciatic nerve *n* **:** the largest nerve in the body arising from the sacral plexus on each side and passing out of the pelvis through the greater sciatic foramen and thence down the back of the thigh to its lower third where it divides into the tibial and peroneal nerves

sciatic notch *n* **:** any of four notches on the dorsal border of the innominate bone comprising a greater above and a lesser below the spine of the ischium on each side of the body

sciatic vein *n* **:** any of the veins accompanying the sciatic arteries **:** a gluteal vein

sci·ence \'sīən(t)s, *in rapid speech often* -īn-\ *n* -s [ME, fr. MF, fr. L *scientia* knowledge, science, fr. *scient-, sciens* (pres. part. of *scire* to know) + *-ia* -y; akin to L *scindere* to cut, split — more at SHED] **1 a :** possession of knowledge as distinguished from ignorance or misunderstanding **:** knowledge as a personal attribute ⟨I speak from ~ and the voice is fate —Alexander Pope⟩ **b :** knowledge possessed or attained through study or practice ⟨~ crown my age —Thomas Gray⟩ **2 a :** a branch or department of systematized knowledge that is or can be made a specific object of study ⟨the basic tool ~s of reading, writing, and ciphering⟩ ⟨learned in the ~ of theology⟩ **b :** something (as a sport or technique) that may be studied or learned like systematized knowledge ⟨skilled in the ~ of evading work⟩ ⟨little interested in cards and such like ~⟩: as (1) *obs* **:** a trained skill (as in an occupation) (2) **:** FENCING (3) **:** BOXING **c :** studies mainly in the works of ancient and modern philosophers formerly taught as a group or field of specialization (as at Oxford University) **d :** any of the individual subjects taught at an educational institution in one of the departments of natural science ⟨required to take two ~s to complete a minor⟩ ⟨students majoring in a ~⟩ — compare HUMANITY 3c **3 a :** accumulated and accepted knowledge that has been systematized and formulated with reference to the discovery of general truths or the operation of general laws **:** knowledge classified and made available in work, life, or the search for truth **:** comprehensive, profound, or philosophical knowledge; *esp* **:** knowledge obtained and tested through use of the scientific method **b :** such knowledge concerned with the physical world and its phenomena **:** NATURAL SCIENCE **4 :** a branch of study that is concerned with observation and classification of facts and esp. with the establishment or strictly with the quantitative formulation of verifiable general laws chiefly by induction and hypotheses ⟨mathematical ~⟩ **5 :** a system based or purporting to be based upon scientific principles **:** a method (as of arrangement, functioning) reconciling practical or utilitarian ends with scientific laws ⟨husbandry is a ~⟩ ⟨a student of culinary ~⟩ **6** *usu cap* **:** CHRISTIAN SCIENCE **syn** see KNOWLEDGE

sci·enced \-n(t)st\ *adj, archaic* **:** skilled in science **:** LEARNED

science fiction *n* **:** fiction dealing principally with the impact of actual or imagined science upon society or individuals; *broadly* **:** literary fantasy including a scientific factor as an essential orienting component

science of language : LINGUISTICS

science of religion : the descriptive study of religion that examines all religions phenomenologically, historically, psychologically, and sociologically **:** HISTORY OF RELIGIONS, COMPARATIVE RELIGION

sci·ent \'sīənt\ *adj* [ME, fr. L *scient-, sciens,* pres. part. of *scire* to know] **:** KNOWING, SKILLFUL

¹sci·en·ter \sī'entə(r)\ *adv* [L, fr. *scient-, sciens,* pres. part. of *scire* to know] **:** KNOWINGLY, WILLFULLY

²scienter \"\ *n* -s **1 :** a degree of knowledge that makes an individual legally responsible for the consequences of his act — compare MISTAKE **2 :** an allegation in a legal pleading of such knowledge on the part of the accused or defendant as is necessary to constitute his act a crime or tort

sci·en·tia \skē'entēə, sī'enchēə\ *n, pl* **scienti·ae** \-tē,ī, -chē,ē\ [L] **:** KNOWLEDGE, SCIENCE; *esp* **:** knowledge based on demonstrable and reproducible data

sci·en·tial \(')sī¦enchəl\ *adj* [ME *sciencial,* fr. ML *scientialis,* fr. L *scientia* knowledge + *-alis* -al] **1 :** relating to or producing knowledge or science **2 :** having efficient knowledge **:** CAPABLE

sci·en·tia sci·en·ti·a·rum \skē¦entēəskē,entē'ärəm\ *n* [L, science of sciences] **:** PHILOSOPHY

¹sci·en·tif·ic \¦sīən·¦tifik, -fēk, *in rapid speech often* (')sīn-\ *adj* [ML *scientificus,* fr. L *scient-, sciens* (pres. part. of *scire* to know) + *-i-* + *-ficus* -fic — more at SCIENCE] **1** *obs* **:** yielding knowledge deductively **2 :** concerned with or treating of science **:** devoted to the study or practice of science ⟨a ~ treatise⟩ ⟨~ training⟩ ⟨~ in his interests⟩ **3 :** of, relating to, or used in science or a branch of science ⟨~ apparatus⟩ ⟨a ~ formula⟩ **4 :** agreeing with or conducted or prepared strictly according to the principles and practice of or for the furtherance of exact science **:** skilled in the methods of exact science **:** characteristic or typical of a true scientist esp. in perfect disinterestedness and absolute accuracy ⟨~ research⟩ ⟨a ~ experiment⟩ ⟨the ~ spirit⟩ **5 :** conducted or systematized after the manner of science or according to results of investigation by science **:** practicing thoroughness or systematic methods approximating those of scientists or devised by scientists **:** applying expert knowledge or technical skill (as in sports, warfare, management) ⟨~ advertising⟩ ⟨~ baby care⟩ ⟨a ~ boxer⟩

²scientific \"\ *n* -s **:** SCIENTIST

sci·en·tif·i·cal \-fəkəl, -fēk-\ *adj* [ML *scientificus* + E *-al*] **1** *archaic* **:** SCIENTIFIC **2** *obs* **:** intended to propagate knowledge

sci·en·tif·i·cal·ly \-k(ə)lē, -li\ *adv* **:** in a scientific manner **:** according to the rules or principles of science ⟨a scholar ~ trained in methods of accurate analysis⟩

sci·en·tif·i·cal·ness \-kəlnəs\ *n* -ES **:** scientific quality or nature

scientific empiricism *n* **1 :** a philosophical movement that denies the existence of any ultimate differences in the sciences, strives for unified science through a synthesis of scientific methodologies, comprises in addition to logical positivists thinkers with similar objectives, and is distinguished from earlier empiricism mainly by emphasis upon the analysis of language — called also *unity of science movement* **2 :** the point of view or the theories advocated by scientific empiricism

scientific management *n* **:** planned management of production or other industrial or business activity that is based on the use of codified and verified knowledge of the knowable factors and directed toward the drawing up and carrying out of an overall plan accompanied by detailed instructions for each operation as established from time and motion study standards and research, and that in practice provides for full and effective use of equipment and an incentive system giving adequate compensation to workers
scientific method *n* **:** the principles and procedures used in the systematic pursuit of intersubjectively accessible knowledge and involving as necessary conditions the recognition and formulation of a problem, the collection of data through observation and if possible experiment, the formulation of hypotheses, and the testing and confirmation of the hypotheses formulated
scientific name *n* **:** a taxonomic name **:** TAXON
scientific notation *n* **:** a method of expressing a number by giving only the significant figures within particular limits of accuracy and indicating multiplication by the proper power of 10 (as in 1.591 $(10)^{-20}$)
sci·en·tif·i·co \\,sīən·'tifə,kō\\ *n, pl* **scientificoes** *or* **scientificos** [*scientist* + *-fico* (as in *magnifico*)] **:** a practitioner in some branch of science
scientifico- *comb form* [¹*scientific* + *-o-*] **:** scientific and ⟨*scientifico*romantic⟩ ⟨*scientifico*philosophic⟩
scientific perspective *n* **:** LINEAR PERSPECTIVE
scientific skepticism *n* **:** an impartial attitude of the mind previous to investigation
scientific socialism *n* **:** socialism associated chiefly with Marxians and based principally upon a belief that historical forces (as economic determinism and the class struggle) determine usu. by violent means the achievement of socialist goals — compare UTOPIAN SOCIALISM
scientific stone *n* **:** a synthetic or imitation gemstone (as a ruby or sapphire artificially made of corundum)
sci·en·ti·fiction \\sī¦entə+\\ *n* [blend of ¹*scientific* and *fiction*] **:** SCIENCE FICTION
sci·en·tism \\'sīən·,tizəm\\ *n* -s [*scientist* + *-ism*] **1 :** the methods, mental attitude, doctrines, or modes of expression characteristic or held to be characteristic of scientists **2 :** a thesis that the methods of the natural sciences should be used in all areas of investigation including philosophy, the humanities, and the social sciences **:** a belief that only such methods can fruitfully be used in the pursuit of knowledge
sci·en·tist \\'sīəntəst, *rapid often* 'sīn-\\ *n* -s [L *scientia* science + E *-ist* — more at SCIENCE] **1 :** one learned in science and esp. natural science **:** a scientific investigator ⟨what distinguishes the ~ is his ability to state problems, to frame questions, so that the technicians can make the machines yield facts that are significant —W.A.L.Johnson⟩ ⟨the social ~ is somewhat more handicapped than is the physical or biological ~ in holding extraneous influences constant —A.M.Rose⟩ ⟨put him in the front rank of linguistic ~*s* —Kemp Malone⟩ **2** *usu cap* **:** CHRISTIAN SCIENTIST ⟨the lesson-sermon of the Sunday service is prepared by a committee of *Scientists* —F.S.Mead⟩
sci·en·tis·tic \\¦sīən·¦tistik\\ *adj* **1 :** devoted or pretending to the methods of scientists **:** professedly scientific **2 :** of, relating to, or characterized by scientism — **sci·en·tis·ti·cal·ly** \\-tək(ə)lē\\ *adv*
sci·en·tize \\'sīən·,tīz\\ *vt* -ED/-ING/-S [L *scientia* science + E *-ize*] **:** to apply scientific methods and principles to **:** SYSTEMATIZE ⟨~ a business⟩
sci fa *abbr* scire facias
¹**sci·li·cet** \\'silə,set, 'sīlə,set, 'skēlə,ket\\ *adv* [ME, fr. L, fr. *scire* to know + *licet* it is permitted, 3d pers. sing. pres. indic. of *licēre* to be permitted — more at SCIENCE, LICENSE] **:** to wit **:** NAMELY, VIDELICET — used before a word that is to be supplied or understood (as in completing a text felt to be obscure)
²**scilicet** \\"\\ *n* -s **:** an instance of the use of scilicet or something (as a clause) introduced by it ⟨a text full of ~*s*⟩
scil·la \\'s(k)ilə\\ *n* [NL, fr. L, squill — more at SQUILL] **1 a** *cap* **:** a large genus of Old World bulbous herbs (family Liliaceae) comprising the squills, having narrow basal leaves, pink, blue, or white racemose flowers borne on a naked scape, and a globose 3-lobed capsule, and including several that are cultivated chiefly as ornamentals — see CUBAN LILY, SPANISH JACINTH, WOOD HYACINTH **b** -s **:** any plant, bulb, or flower of the genus *Scilla* **2** -s **:** the sliced bulb of squill
scil·li·ro·side \\-lərō,sīd\\ *n* -s [NL *Scilla* + *-i-* + *-roside* (as in *heteroside*)] **:** a crystalline steroid cardiac glucoside $C_{32}H_{44}O_{12}$ from red squill
scil·li·tan \\'silətən\\ *adj, usu cap* [prob. fr. (assumed) LL *scillitanus*, fr. L *Scillium*, ancient town in Byzacium, Roman province of Africa + LL *-itanus* (as in *metropolitanus* metropolitan)] **:** of or relating to the ancient town of Scillium in Roman Africa
¹**scil·lo·ni·an** \\sə'lōnēən\\ *adj, usu cap* [*Scilly* Isles, group of small islands in southwest England + E *-onian* (as in *Devonian*)] **:** of or relating to the Scilly Isles or their inhabitants
²**scillonian** \\"\\ *n* -s *cap* **:** a native or inhabitant of the Scilly Isles
scim·i·tar \\'siməd·ə(r), -mətə(r) *also* -mə,tär *or* -mə,tä(r\\ *also* **scim·i·ter** \\-əd·ə-,-ətə-\\ *or* **scim·e·tar** *like* SCIMITAR\\ *or* **cim·e·ter** *like* SCIMITER\\ *n* -s [MF *cimeterre*, fr OIt *scimitarra*, perh. fr. Per *shimshīr*] **1 :** a saber having a curved blade with the edge on the convex side that is used chiefly by Arabs and Turks **2 :** something resembling a scimitar (as in sharpness or shape); *esp* **:** a long-handled billhook

scimitar 1

scim·i·tared \\-ə(r)d, -ärd, -ȧd\\ *adj* **:** armed with or shaped like a scimitar
¹**scin·cid** \\'skiŋkəd, 'sinsəd\\ *adj* [NL *Scincidae*] **:** of or relating to the Scincidae
²**scincid** \\"\\ *n* -s **:** a lizard of the family Scincidae
scin·ci·dae \\'skiŋkə,dē, 'sinsə,-\\ *n pl, cap* [NL, fr. *Scincus*, type genus (fr. L, skink) + *-idae* — more at SKINK] **:** a cosmopolitan family of pleurodont lizards (section Scincomorpha) comprising the skinks
scin·ci·doid \\-,dȯid\\ *adj* [NL *Scincidae* + E *-oid*] **:** resembling or related to the Scincidae
scin·coid \\'s(k)iŋ,kȯid\\ *also* **scin·coi·di·an** \\(')ˌ=ˈkȯidēən\\ *adj* [*scincoid* prob. fr. (assumed) NL *scincoīdes* lizard of the family Scincidae, fr. *Scincus*, genus of skinks + L *-oides* -oid; *scincoidian* prob. fr. (assumed) NL *scincoīdes* + E *-an*] **:** of, relating to, or resembling skink
scin·co·mor·pha \\,s(k)iŋkə'mȯrfə\\ *n pl, cap* [NL, fr. *Scincus*, genus of skinks + *-morpha*] **:** a section of the saurian division Autarchoglossa comprising the Scincidae and related families in which the clavicles when present are dilated, the tongue scaly or obliquely plicate, the teeth often perforate and rarely conical or recurved, and the hemipenes usu. laminate
scin·dap·sus \\sin'dapsəs\\ *n, cap* [NL, fr. Gk *skindapsos*, an ivylike tree] **:** a genus of climbing vines (family Araceae) chiefly of eastern Asia and Australasia, having ovate often variegated leaves, sometimes replaced by phyllodia and flowers in a short spadix subtended by a green spathe — compare ANTHURIUM; see IVY-ARUM
scin·iph \\'sinəf\\ *n* -s [LL *sciniphes*, pl., sciniphs, fr. Gk *skniphes*, pl. of *sknips* small woodworm; akin to Gk *knips*, an insect — more at NIP] **:** a stinging or biting insect in Exod 8:17 (DV) or a stand (RSV)
scin·ti·gram \\'sintə,gram\\ *n* [*scintillation* + *-gram*] **:** a picture produced by scintigraphy
scin·tig·ra·phy \\sin·'tigrəfē\\ *n* -ES [*scintillation* + *-graphy*; fr. the scintillation counter used to record gamma radiation on the scintigram] **:** a diagnostic technique in which a two-dimensional picture of a bodily radiation source is obtained by the use of radioisotopes
scin·til \\'sintᵊl\\ *n* -s [L *scintilla*] *archaic* **:** SCINTILLA
scin·til·la \\sin·'tilə\\ *n, pl* **scintillas** \\-ləz\\ *also* **scintil·lae** \\-(,)lē\\ [L] **1 :** a barely perceptible manifestation **:** the slightest particle or trace ⟨not a ~ of evidence⟩ **2 :** a glittering particle
scin·til·lance \\'sintᵊlən(t)s\\ *n* -s **:** a scintillant condition or emission
scin·til·lant \\-nt\\ *adj* [L *scintillant-, scintillans*, pres. part. of *scintillare* to sparkle] **:** emitting sparks or fine igneous particles **:** SCINTILLATING — **scin·til·lant·ly** *adv*
scin·til·lan·te \\,shēn·tə'län·(,)tā\\ *adj (or adv)* [It, fr. pres. part. of *scintillare* to sparkle, fr. L] **:** in a sparkling manner — used as a direction in music
scin·til·late \\'sintᵊl,āt, *usu* -ād.+V\\ *vb* -ED/-ING/-S [L *scintillatus*, past part. of *scintillare* to sparkle, fr. *scintilla* spark, scintilla] *vi* **1 :** to emit sparks **:** SPARK **2 :** to gleam or emit quick flashes as if throwing off sparks ⟨eyes that ~ with fury⟩ ⟨genius that ~*s*⟩; *also* **:** SPARKLE, TWINKLE ⟨fixed stars that ~ in the sky⟩ ~ *vt* **:** to throw off as a spark or as sparkling flashes ⟨~ witticisms⟩
scin·til·lat·ing·ly *adv* **:** in a scintillating manner **:** so as to scintillate
scin·til·la·tion \\,sintᵊl'āshən\\ *n* -s [L *scintillation-, scintillatio*, fr. *scintillatus* (past part.) + *-ion-, -io* -ion] **1 :** an act or instance of scintillating; *esp* **:** rapid changes in the brightness of a celestial body caused by turbulence in the earth's atmosphere **:** TWINKLING **2 a** (1) **:** a spark or flash emitted in scintillating (as from iron exposed to the oxyhydrogen flame) (2) **:** a flash of light produced in a phosphor by an ionizing event (as impingement of an alpha particle) **b :** a scintillating or brilliant outburst (as of thought or genius) **c :** a flash of the eye (as in anger or merriment) **3 :** SCINTILLA
scintillation counter *n* **:** a device for detecting and registering individual scintillations (as due to radioactive emission or cosmic rays)
scintillation spectrometer *n* **:** an apparatus in which mass or energy spectra are observed and their frequency distribution determined by means of a scintillation counter
scin·til·la·tor \\'=ˌ=,lād·ə(r), -ātə-\\ *n* -s **:** one that scintillates: as **a :** a scintillating star **b :** a phosphor in which scintillations occur (as in a scintillation counter) **c :** a person that scintillates (as in conversation) **d** (1) **:** a device for sending out scintillations of light (2) **:** SCINTILLATION COUNTER
scin·til·les·cent \\¦=ˌ=¦esᵊnt\\ *adj* [L *scintillare* to sparkle + E *-escent*] **:** scintillating or twinkling somewhat faintly
scin·til·lom·e·ter \\,=ˌ='ämәd·ə(r)\\ *n* [ISV *scintillo-* (fr. L *scintilla* spark, scintilla) + *-meter*] **1 :** an attachment to a telescope by which the image of a star is made to revolve in a circle to measure the scintillation **2 :** SCINTILLATION COUNTER
scin·til·lo·scope *also* **scin·til·li·scope** \\sin·'tilə,skōp\\ *n* [*scintillo-, scintilli-* (fr. L *scintilla*) + *-scope*] **:** a small instrument similar to the spinthariscope for exhibiting scintillations (as of a radioactive substance) on a sensitive screen
scintle *var of* SKINTLE
scio- — see SCI-
sci·o·lism \\'sīə,lizəm\\ *n* -s [LL *sciolus* sciolist + E *-ism*] **:** superficial knowledge **:** a show of learning without substantial foundation
sci·o·list \\-ləst\\ *n* -s [LL *sciolus* + E *-ist*] **:** one whose knowledge or learning is superficial **:** a pretender to scholarship
sci·o·lis·tic \\¦sīə¦listik\\ *adj* [*sciolist* + *-ic*] **:** of or relating to sciolism or a sciolist **:** partaking of sciolism **:** being or suited to a sciolist ⟨~ arguments⟩ — **sci·o·lis·ti·cal·ly** \\-tək(ə)lē\\ *adv*
sci·o·lous \\'sīələs\\ *adj* [LL *sciolus* sciolist, one having little knowledge, dim. of L *scius* knowing, fr. *scire* to know — more at SCIENCE] **:** knowing superficially or imperfectly **:** SCIOLISTIC
sciol·to \\'shȯl(,)tō\\ *adv (or adj)* [It (past part. of *sciogliere* to loosen), fr. L *exsolutus*, past part. of *exsolvere* to loosen, untie release — more at EXSOLVE] **1 :** with freedom and without strictness — used as a direction in music **2 :** with detachment and without legato in musical performance
sci·o·man·cy \\'sīə,man(t)sē\\ *n* -ES [LL *sciomantia*, fr. LGk *skiomanteia*, fr. Gk *ski-* sci- + *manteia* -mancy] **:** divination by consulting the shades of the dead
sci·o·man·tic \\¦sīə¦mantik\\ *adj* [LL *sciomantia* + E *-ic*] **:** of, relating to, or obtained by means of sciomancy
sci·on *also* **ci·on** \\'sīən *sometimes* -ī,än\\ *n* -s [ME *scion, sioun, ciun*, fr. MF *cion, sion*, of Gmc origin; akin to OHG *kīnan, chīnan* to sprout, OE *cīth* sprout, shoot — more at CHINE] **1 :** a detached living portion (as a year-old shoot) of a plant designed or prepared for union with a stock in grafting and usu. supplying solely or predominantly aerial parts to a graft **2 :** DESCENDANT, CHILD ⟨twelve-year-old . . . ~ of the famous circus family —Henry La Cossitt⟩
scion-rooting \\'=ˌ=ˌ=\\ *adj* **:** developing roots at the point where a scion is inserted into a stock
sci·oph·i·lous \\(')sī¦äfələs\\ *or* **sci·aph·i·lous** \\-¦af-\\ *adj* [*sci-* + *-philous*] *of a plant* **:** thriving in shade
scio·phyte \\'sīə,fīt\\ *n* -s [*sci-* + *-phyte*] **:** a plant that endures or thrives best at lowered light intensity
sci·op·tic \\(')sī¦äptik\\ *adj* [*sci-* + *optic*] **:** of or relating to the formation of images in a darkened room (as in a camera obscura)
sci·op·tics \\-ks\\ *n pl but usu sing in constr* **:** the art or process of exhibiting luminous images (as of external objects) in a darkened room by arrangements of lenses or mirrors
sci·os·o·phist \\sī'äsəfəst\\ *n* -s **:** an accepter or propounder of sciosophy
sci·os·o·phy \\-fē\\ *n* -ES [*sci-* + *-sophy*] **:** pretended knowledge of natural or supernatural forces systematized by tradition or imaginative invention
¹**sci·ot** \\'shē,ät\\ *or* **chi·ot** \\'kīət, 'kēət, -ē,ät\\ *adj, usu cap* [*sciot* modif. (influenced by It *Scio* Chios, island in the Aegean sea) of NGk *Chiōtēs* of Chios, fr. Gk *Chios* Chios + *-ōtēs* -ote; *chiot* fr. NGk *Chiōtēs*] **:** of or relating to the island of Chios
²**sciot** \\"\\ *or* **chiot** \\"\\ *n* -s *cap* **:** a native or inhabitant of Chios
sci·re fa·ci·as \\,sīrē'fāsh(ē)əs, -shē,as; ,skē,rā'fākē,äs\\ *n* [ME, fr. ML, you should cause to know] **1 :** a judicial writ founded upon some matter of record and requiring the party proceeded against to show cause why the record should not be enforced, annulled, or vacated **2 :** a legal proceeding instituted by a scire facias
sci·ren·ga \\sə'reŋgə\\ *n* -s [origin unknown] **:** a West Indian and Mediterranean grouper (*Parepinephelus acutirostris*)
scirocco *var of* SIROCCO
scir·pus \\'s(k)ərpəs, 'skir-\\ *n, cap* [NL, fr. L, rush, bulrush] **:** a large genus of widely distributed annual or perennial sedges (family Cyperaceae) that bear solitary or much-clustered spikelets containing perfect flowers with a perianth of six bristles — see BULRUSH, TULE
scirrhe *obs var of* SCIRRHUS
scir·rhoid \\'s(k)i,rȯid\\ *adj* [NL *scirrhus* + E *-oid*] **:** resembling a scirrhus
scir·rhous \\-irəs\\ *adj* [NL *scirrhosus*, fr. *scirrhus* + L *-osus* -ose] **1 :** of, relating to, or constituting a scirrhus ⟨~ infiltration⟩ **2 :** resembling a scirrhus esp. in being hard or indurated with or as if with fibrous tissue ⟨a ~ carcinoma⟩
scirrhous cord *n* **:** a chronic fibrous enlargement of the cut end of the spermatic cord in a castrated animal caused by bacterial infection
scir·rhus *also* **schir·rhus** \\'s(k)irəs\\ *n, pl* **scir·rhi** \\'s(k)i,rī, 'ski,rē\\ *also* **scirrhus·es** \\'s(k)irəsəz\\ [NL, fr. Gk *skirrhos*, *skiros* hard tumor, fr. *skiros* hard] **1 a** *obs* **:** an indurated organ or part; *esp* **:** an indurated gland **b :** a hard cancerous tumor; *specif* **:** one in which the hardness is due to preponderance of fibrous tissue in the growth **2 :** an abnormal condition characterized by the presence of scirrhi
scis·sel \\'sisəl, -izəl\\ *n* -s [F *cisailles*, pl., scissels, fr. *cisailler* to clip with shears, fr. *cisailles* shears, fr. (assumed) VL *caesaculum*, fr. L *caesus*, past part. of *caedere* to cut, hew] **:** metal scrap clippings left over in various mechanical operations; *esp* **:** the remnants of fillets from which coin blanks have been punched
scis·sile \\"\\ *adj* [F, fr. L *scissilis*, fr. *scissus* (past part. of *scindere* to split) + *-ilis* -ile — more at SHED] **:** capable of being cut smoothly or split easily ⟨the ~ peptide bond —W.N.Lipscomb⟩
scis·sion \\'sizhən, -ish-\\ *n* -s [F, fr. LL *scission-, scissio*, fr. *scissus* (past part. of *scindere* to split) + *-ion-, -io* -ion] **1 :** a division or split in a group or union **:** a state of dissension **:** SCHISM **2 a :** an act of cutting, dividing, or splitting or the state of being cut, divided, or split **:** DIVISION **b :** CLEAVAGE 5 ⟨cracking or carbon-carbon ~⟩
scis·si·par·i·ty \\,sisə'parəd·ē, ,sizə-\\ *n* [L *scissus* (past part.) + E *-i-* + *parity* (parous condition)] **:** SCHIZOGENESIS
¹**scis·sor** \\'sizə(r)\\ *n* -s *often attrib* [ME *sisoure, cisoure*, fr. MF *cisoire*, sing. of *cisoires* scissors] **:** SCISSORS ⟨wore a ~ on her belt⟩
²**scis·sor** \\"\\ *vb* **scissored; scissored; scissoring** \\-z(ə)riŋ\\ **scissors** *vt* **1 a :** to cut, cut up, or cut off with scissors or shears **b** *archaic* **:** to trim (as the beard) with scissors **2 :** to cut out in the form of clippings; *broadly* **:** MINIMIZE, REDUCE, ELIMINATE ⟨items ~*ed* from the budget⟩ **3 a :** to hold or hinge together in a crossed position suggestive of scissors **b :** to move (as one's legs) in a manner suggestive of the snipping of scissors ~ *vi* **:** to move in a manner suggestive of the snipping of scissors ⟨long legs ~*ing* down the street⟩
scissorbill \\'=ˌ=,=\\ *n* [trans. of F *bec-en-ciseaux*] **1 :** SKIMMER 3 **2** *chiefly West* **:** an inferior or stupid person: as **a :** a worker indifferent to the interests of the laboring class (as one unwilling to join a union) **b :** a worker learning to be a railway brakeman
scissorbird \\'=ˌ=,=\\ *n* **:** SCISSORTAIL
scis·sor·er \\-zərə(r)\\ *n* -s **:** one that scissors; *also* **:** COMPILER
scissor jack *n* **:** a powerful lifting jack operated by a screw in horizontal position that lengthens or shortens the horizontal diagonal of a parallelogram consisting of the linkages of the jack
scissorlike \\'=ˌ=,=\\ *adj* **:** resembling a scissors esp. in having crossing parts or motion involving crossing of parts
scis·sors \\'sizə(r)z\\ *n pl but sometimes sing in constr, often attrib* [ME *sisoures, sisours*, fr. MF *cisoires*, fr. (assumed) VL *caesorium* cutting instrument (pl. *caesoria*) — more at CHISEL] **1 :** a cutting instrument consisting of two bevel-edged cutting blades that are connected to handles and that are movable past one another on a pivot by which they are held together **:** a small shears ⟨the ~ are sharp⟩ ⟨took a ~, cut the bedspread, a table scarf, and a plant —Croswell Bowen⟩ ⟨a pair of ~⟩ **2 :** something felt to resemble a pair of scissors (as in movement, form, or cutting ability): as **a :** something that cuts short or makes excisions ⟨use the ~ vigorously on your report⟩ **b :** a gripping contrivance (as a tongs) **c** *usu sing in constr* (1) **:** any of several gymnastic feats (as on the horse and parallel bars) in which the legs are moved in an antero-posterior plane in a manner suggesting the opening and closing of a pair of scissors (2) **:** a wrestling hold in which a contestant locks his legs around the head or body of the opponent (3) **:** a technique of high jumping in which the jumper lifts the leg nearest the bar first so that the body passes over the bar with the buttocks to the bar and the jumper lands first on the leading leg — compare WESTERN ROLL

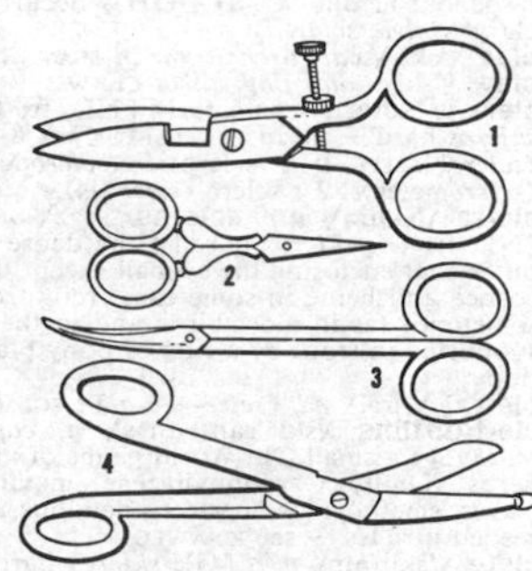

scissors 1: *1* buttonhole, *2* embroidery, *3* manicure, *4* bandage

scissors-and-paste \\¦=ˌ=ˌ=¦=\\ *adj* **:** based on or prepared by compilation **:** lacking in originality or independent thought and investigation ⟨*scissors-and-paste* studies⟩ ⟨a *scissors-and-paste* method⟩
scissorsbill \\'=ˌ=,=\\ *n* [by alter.] **:** SCISSORBILL 2
scissorsbird \\'=ˌ=,=\\ *n* **:** SCISSORTAIL
scissors bridge *or* **scissors-type bridge** *n* **:** a folding light metal bridge that is carried and put in position by a tank
scissors chair *n* **:** SAVONAROLA CHAIR
scissors fault *n* **:** a geological fault in which there is increasing displacement along the strike from an initial point of no displacement
scissors-grinder \\'=ˌ=,=ˌ=\\ *n* **1 :** the common European nightjar **2 :** RESTLESS FLYCATCHER
scissors kick *n* **1 :** a swimming kick used in trudgen strokes and sidestrokes in which, after the upper leg has been swung forward from the hip and the other leg bent backward from the knee, the legs are snapped together **2 :** a dance kick changing legs in the air
scissors step *n* **:** a ballroom dancing step with sudden change of direction
scissorstail \\'=ˌ=,=\\ *n* [by alter.] **:** SCISSORTAIL
scissors truss *n* **:** a roofing truss in which the braces for the rafters cross like the members of a pair of scissors
scissors vault *n* **:** a gymnastic vault similar to the straddle vault but with the legs crossing as the body passes over the apparatus
scissortail \\'=ˌ=,=\\ *or* **scis·sor-tailed flycatcher** \\'=ˌ=¦=-\\ *n* **:** a flycatcher (*Muscivora forficata*) of the southern U.S. and Mexico having a deeply forked tail and being gray above, white beneath, salmon on the sides, and scarlet at the base of the crown feathers

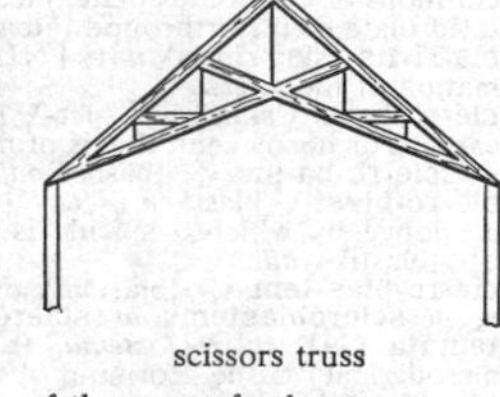
scissors truss

scissor-tailed \\¦=ˌ=¦=\\ *adj* **:** having a deeply forked tail ⟨*scissor-tailed* birds⟩
scissor tooth *n* **:** a cutting tooth **:** CARNASSIAL
scissor truss *n* **:** SCISSORS TRUSS
scis·sure \\'sizhə(r), -ish-\\ *n* -s [ME, fr. L *scissura*, fr. *scissus* (past part. of *scindere* to split) + *-ura* -ure — more at SHED] **1** *archaic* **:** a cleft or elongated opening in a body or surface made by or as if by cutting **:** a cleft separating bodily parts or opening into the body **2** *obs* **:** a split or division in a group or union **:** SCHISM
scis·su·rel·la \\,sizhə'relə, -ish-\\ *n, cap* [NL, fr. L *scissura* scissure + *-ella*] **:** a genus of small marine snails (suborder Rhipidoglossa) having several long ciliated tentacles on each side of the body and a small spiral shell the last whorl of which has a broad fissure or sinus
scit·a·mi·na·les \\,sid·əmə'nā(,)lēz\\ [NL, fr. *Scitamineae* + *-ales*] *syn of* MUSALES
scit·a·min·e·ae \\-'minē,ē\\ [NL, fr. L *scitamenta* delicacies, dainties (fr. *scitus* delicate, dainty — fr. past part. of *sciscere* to approve, accept, inquire, seek to know, incho. of *scire* to know — + *-menta*, pl. of *-mentum* -ment) + *-ineae* — more at SCIENCE] *syn of* MUSALES
scit·a·min·e·ous \\¦=ˌ=¦=nēəs\\ *adj* [NL *Scitamineae* + E *-ous*] **:** of or relating to the Musales
scith·ers \\'sithə(r)z\\ *dial Eng var of* SCISSORS
¹**sci·urid** \\sī'(y)u̇rəd\\ *adj* [NL *Sciuridae*] **:** of or relating to the Sciuridae
²**sciurid** \\"\\ *n* -s **:** a rodent of the family Sciuridae
sci·uri·dae \\-rə,dē\\ *n pl, cap* [NL, fr. *Sciurus*, type genus + *-idae*] **:** a nearly cosmopolitan family of sciuromorph rodents consisting of the true squirrels, ground squirrels, marmots, and related rodents
sci·uroid \\sī'(y)ə,rȯid, 'sī(y)ù,r-\\ *adj* [L *sciurus* squirrel + E *-oid*] **1 a :** resembling a squirrel **b :** resembling the tail of a squirrel — used of the spike of grasses (as barley) **2** [NL *Sciurus* + E *-oid*] **:** related to the Sciuridae
sci·uroi·dea \\,sī(y)ə'rȯidēə\\ *n pl, cap* [NL, fr. *Sciurus* + *-oidea*] *in some classifications* **:** a superfamily coextensive with the family Sciuridae
¹**sci·uro·morph** \\sī'(y)u̇rə,mȯrf\\ *also* **sci·uro·mor·phic** \\¦=¦=ˌ=¦mȯrfik\\ *or* **sci·uro·mor·phous** \\-fəs\\ *adj* [*sciuromorph* fr. NL *Sciuromorpha*; *sciuromorphic*, *sciuromorphous* fr. NL *Sciuromorpha* + *-ic* or *-ous*] **:** of or relating to the Sciuromorpha
²**sciuromorph** \\"\\ *n* **:** a sciuromorph rodent
sci·uro·mor·pha \\ˌ=ˌ=ˌ='mȯrfə\\ *n pl, cap* [NL, fr. Gk *skiouros* squirrel + NL *-morpha* — more at SQUIRREL] **:** a suborder or formerly a superfamily of Rodentia comprising relatively large more or less primitive forms (as the squirrels, marmots,

gophers, beavers, and related rodents) — compare HYSTRICOMORPHA, MYOMORPHA

sci·urop·ter·us \ˌsī(y)əˈräptərəs\ *n, cap* [NL, fr. Gk *skiouros* squirrel + NL *-pterus*] **:** a genus of flying squirrels including only the polatouche of northern Europe and Asia and occurring in several geographic races but formerly including all the smaller Old and New World flying squirrels — compare GLAUCOMYS, PETAURISTA

sci·urus \sīˈ(y)u̇rəs\ *n, cap* [NL, fr. L, squirrel — more at SQUIRREL] **:** the type genus of Sciuridae formerly including all the squirrels but now restricted to a cosmopolitan group of typical moderate sized arboreal squirrels

scive *var of* SKIVE

scivvy *var of* SKIVVY

scl *abbr* scale

SCL *abbr* student of the civil law

[1]**sclaff** \ˈsklaf, -aa(ə)-, -ai-, -ä-\ *n* -s [prob. imit.] **1** *Scot* **:** a slight blow **:** SLAP **2 :** a golf stroke in which the club head strikes the ground behind the ball before contacting the ball

[2]**sclaff** \"\ *vb* -ED/-ING/-s *vi* **1** *Scot* **:** to scuff or shuffle along **2 :** to make a sclaff in golf ~ *vt* **1** *Scot* **:** to strike with something flat **:** SLAP **2 a :** to cause (a golf club) to make a sclaff **b :** to strike (the ground) in making a sclaff

sclar·e·ol \ˈsklə(a)rēˌōl, -ˌȯl\ *n* -s [NL *sclarea* (specific epithet of the clary *Salvia sclarea*) + E *-ol*] **:** a liquid bicyclic diterpenoid alcohol $C_{20}H_{34}(OH)_2$ occurring in the leaves of a clary (*Salvia sclarea*)

sclav \ˈskl-\ *cap, archaic var of* SLAV

sclaw \ˈskl-\ *dial Eng var of* CLAW

scler- *or* **sclero-** *comb form* [NL, fr. Gk *sklēr-, sklēro-*, fr. *sklēros* hard — more at SKELETON] **1 a :** hard **:** dry ⟨*sclerite*⟩ ⟨*sclero*blast⟩ **b :** sclerotic ⟨*sclero*derma⟩ **c :** hardness ⟨*sclero*meter⟩ **2 :** sclera ⟨*scleritis*⟩

scle·ra \ˈsklirə\ *n, pl* **scleras** \-rəz\ *or* **scle·rae** \-ˌirē, -ˌrī\ [NL, fr. Gk *sklēros* hard] **:** the dense fibrous opaque white outer coat enclosing the eyeball except the part covered by the cornea and being in some cases reinforced with cartilage and sometimes (as in most birds and in the extinct ichthyosaurs) supported in front by a ring of bony plates — see EYE illustration

scle·ral \-irəl\ *adj* [*scler-* + *-al*] **:** SCLEROTIC

scle·ran·thus \skləˈran(t)thəs\ *n, cap* [NL, fr. *scler-* + *-anthus*] **:** a small Old World genus of annual weedy prostrate herbs (family Caryophyllaceae) having opposite subulate leaves, small cymose perfect apetalous flowers, and tiny one-seeded utricles — see KNAWEL

sclere \ˈskli(ə)r\ *n* -s [Gk *sklēros* hard] **:** a minute skeletal element (as a spicule of a sponge)

scle·rec·to·my \skləˈrektəmē\ *n* -ES [ISV *scler-* + *-ectomy*] **:** surgical removal of a part of the sclera

scle·re·id \ˈsklirēəd\ *n* -s [ISV *sclere-* (as in *sclerenchyma*) + *-id*] **:** a sclerenchymatous cell of a higher plant distinguished chiefly by having its diameters essentially alike — compare FIBER, STEREID

scle·re·ma ad·ul·to·rum \skləˈrēməˌadᵊlˈtōrəm, -ˌaˌdəl-\ *n* [NL, lit. hardening of the tissues of adults] **:** SCLERODERMA

sclerema neo·na·to·rum \-ˌnēənāˈtōrəm\ *n* [NL, lit., hardening of the tissues of the newborn] **:** hardening of the cutaneous and subcutaneous tissues in newborn infants

scle·ren·chy·ma \skləˈreŋkəmə\ *n, pl* **sclerenchymas** \-məz\ *or* **scle·ren·chym·a·ta** \ˌskliˌrenˈkimədˌə, ˌskleˌr-, -ˌrən-\ [NL, fr. *scler-* + *-enchyma*] **1 :** a protective or supporting tissue in higher plants composed of cells with walls thickened and lignified and often mineralized — compare COLLENCHYMA, FIBER, SCLEREID **2 :** SCLERODERM 2

scle·ren·chym·a·tous \ˌskliˌrenˈkimədˌəs, ˌskleˌr-, -ˌrən-\ *adj* [NL *sclerenchymat-, sclerenchyma* + E *-ous*] **:** constituting or consisting of sclerenchyma

scle·ren·chyme \ˈsklirənˌkīm, ˈskler-\ *n* -s [NL *sclerenchyma*] **:** SCLERENCHYMA

scler·erythrin \skləˈrerəthrən; ˌsklirəˈrith-, -ler-\ *n* -s [*scler-* + *erythrine*] **:** a red or violet coloring matter of ergot

scle·ret·i·nite \skləˈretᵊnˌīt\ *n* -s [*scler-* + Gk *rhētinē* resin + E *-ite*] **:** a mineral resin found in the coal measures of Wigan, England, in the form of reddish-brown to black pellets

scle·ria \ˈsklirēə\ *n, cap* [NL, fr. Gk *sklēria* hardness, fr. *sklēr-* scler- + *-ia* -y] **:** a large and widely distributed genus of sedges (family Cyperaceae) having solitary pistillate flowers and numerous staminate flowers followed by hard shining bony nutlets — see NUT GRASS, RAZOR GRASS

scle·ri·fi·ca·tion \ˌsklirəfəˈkāshən, -ler-\ *n* -s **1 :** the condition of being or becoming sclerified **2 :** an area of sclerified cells or tissue **:** a mass of sclerenchyma

scle·ri·fy \ˈ==ˌfī\ *vt* -ED/-ING/-ES [*scler-* + *-ify*] **:** to become converted into sclerenchyma

scle·rite \ˈskliˌrīt, ˈskleˌr-\ *n* -s [ISV *scler-* + *-ite*] **:** a hard chitinous or calcareous plate, piece, or spicule; *esp* **:** a sclerotized plate of the arthropod integument

scle·ri·tis \skləˈrīdəs\ *n* -ES [NL, fr. *scler-* + *-itis*] **:** inflammation of the sclera

scle·ro·base \ˈsklirōˌbās, -ler-\ *n* [*scler-* + *base*] **:** the calcareous or horny central axis of most compound alcyonarians — **scle·ro·ba·sic** \ˌ==ˈbāsik\ *adj*

scle·ro·blast \-ˌblast\ *n* [*scler-* + *-blast*] **:** one of the cells of a sponge by which a spicule is formed — **scle·ro·blas·tic** \ˌ==ˈblastik\ *adj*

scle·ro·blas·tem \ˌ==ˈblastəm\ *or* **scle·ro·blastema** \ˌ==+\ *n, pl* **scleroblastems** *or* **scleroblastemas** *or* **scleroblastemata** [NL *scleroblastema*, fr. *scler-* + *blastema*] **:** the mesodermal tissue forming bone — **scle·ro·blastemic** \ˌ==+\ *adj*

scle·ro·cau·ly \ˈ==ˌkȯlē\ *n* -ES [*scler-* + *caul-* + *-y*] **:** exceptional development of sclerenchyma in a stem (as of various desert plants) — compare SCLEROPHYLLY

sclero·corneal \ˌ==+\ *adj* [*scler-* + *corneal*] **:** of or involving both sclera and cornea

scle·ro·dac·tyl·ia \ˌ==ˌdakˈtilēə\ *or* **scle·ro·dac·ty·ly** \ˌ==ˈ=ˌtəlē\ *n, pl* **sclerodactylias** *or* **sclerodactylies** [*sclerodactylia* fr. NL, fr. *scler-* + *-dactylia*; *sclerodactyly* fr. *scler-* + *-dactyly*] **:** scleroderma of the fingers and toes

[1]**scle·ro·derm** \ˈ==ˌdərm\ *n* -s [ISV *scler-* + *-derm*] **1 :** TRIGGERFISH, FILEFISH **2 :** the hard tissue of the skeleton of ordinary stony or madreporarian corals

[2]**scleroderm** \"\ *adj* **:** SCLERODERMATOUS

scle·ro·der·ma \ˌ==ˈdərmə\ *n* [NL, fr. *scler-* + *-derma*] **1** *cap* **:** a genus of fungi (family Sclerodermataceae) having hard-skinned fruiting bodies that open irregularly having a single-layered peridium — compare FALSE TRUFFLE **2** *pl* **sclerodermas** \-məz\ *or* **scleroderma·ta** \-mədˌə\ **:** a disease of the skin characterized by thickening and hardening of the subcutaneous tissues and resulting in a rigid hidebound condition

scle·ro·der·ma·ta·ce·ae \ˌ==ˌ=məˈtāsēˌē\ *n pl, cap* [NL, fr. *Sclerodermat-, Scleroderma*, type genus + *-aceae*] **:** a family of basidiomycetous fungi (order Sclerodermatales) that have a single-layered peridium and include the earth-balls — **scle·ro·der·ma·ta·ceous** \ˌ==ˌ==ˈtāshəs\ *adj*

scle·ro·der·ma·ta·les \ˌ==ˌ==ˈtā(ˌ)lēz\ *n pl, cap* [NL, fr. *Sclerodermat-, Scleroderma* + *-ales*] **:** an order of basidiomycetous fungi (subclass Homobasidiomycetes) having closed subterranean or epigeous and sessile or stalked sporocarps with a simple or several-layered peridium surrounding an unchambered or indistinctly chambered gleba — compare LYCOPERDALES

scle·ro·der·ma·tous \ˌ==ˈdərmədˌəs\ *adj* [*scler-* + *-dermatous*] **1 a :** having a hard external covering (as of bony plates or horny scales) **b :** having a skeleton of scleroderm **2** [NL *sclerodermat-, scleroderma* + E *-ous*] **:** of, relating to, or affected with scleroderma

scle·ro·der·mi \ˌ==ˈdərˌmī\ *n pl, cap* [NL, fr. *scler-* + Gk *derma* skin — more at DERM-] *zool, in some classifications* **:** a suborder or other division of Plectognathi, comprising the triggerfishes and filefishes

scle·ro·der·mia \-rmēə\ *n* -s [NL, fr. *scler-* + *-dermia*] **:** SCLERODERMA 2

scle·ro·der·mic \ˌ==ˈ=mik\ *adj* [NL *scleroderma* + E *-ic*] **:** SCLERODERMATOUS 2

scle·ro·der·mite \ˌ==ˈ=ˌmīt\ *n* -s [*scler-* + *derm-* + *-ite*] **:** the hard integument of a segment of an arthropod — **scle·ro·der·mit·ic** \ˌ==ˌdərˈmid·ik\ *adj*

scle·ro·der·mous \ˌ==ˈdərməs\ *adj* [ISV *scler-* + *derm-* + *-ous*] **1 :** SCLERODERMATOUS **2** [NL *Scleroderma* + E *-ous*] **:** of or relating to fungi of the genus *Scleroderma*

scle·ro·gen \ˈsklirəjən, -ler-, -ˌjen\ *n* -s [*scler-* + *-gen*] **:** the lignified and mineralized material of the walls of a brachysclereid

scle·rog·e·nous \skləˈräjənəs, (ˈ)skliˌr-, (ˈ)skleˌr-\ *also* **scle·ro·gen·ic** \ˌsklirəˈjenik, -ler-\ *adj* [ISV *scler-* + *-genous* or *-genic*] **:** making or secreting hard tissue

scle·roid \ˈskliˌrȯid, -leˌr-\ *adj* [ISV *scler-* + *-oid*] **:** HARD, INDURATED ⟨~ tissue cells⟩

scle·ro·ma \skləˈrōmə\ *n, pl* **scleromas** \-məz\ *or* **scle·roma·ta** \-mədˌə\ [NL, fr. Gk *sklērōma*, fr. *sklēroun* to harden (fr. *sklēros* hard) — more at SKELETON] **:** hardening of tissues; *specif* **:** RHINOSCLEROMA

scle·ro·meninx \ˌsklirō, -lerō+\ *n* [NL, fr. *scler-* + *meninx*] **:** DURA MATER

scle·ro·mere \ˈsklirəˌmi(ə)r, -ler-\ *n* -s [*scler-* + *-mere*] **:** a metamere of the skeleton

scle·rom·e·ter \skləˈrämədˌə(r)\ *n* [ISV *scler-* + *-meter*] **:** any of various instruments for determining the relative hardnesses of materials usu. by measuring the pressure necessary to make a scratch or the amount of penetration of a stylus under a given pressure

scle·rop·a·ges \skləˈräpəˌjēz\ *n, cap* [NL, fr. Gk *sklēropagēs* firmly put together, fr. *sklēr-* scler- + *-pagēs* (fr. *pagos* fixed, fastened, fr. *pēgnynai* to fix, fasten together) — more at PACT] **:** a genus of large fishes (family Osteoglossidae) of Australia and Borneo including the barramunda

scle·ro·pa·rei \ˌsklirōpəˈrēˌī, -ler-\ *n pl, cap* [NL, fr. *scler-* + Gk *pareia* cheek] **:** a large and economically important order of spiny-finned fishes comprising the scorpion fishes, greenlings, sculpins, gurnards, and related forms that are distinguished by a process of the third suborbital plate extending backward to or toward the preopercle — compare MAIL-CHEEKED

[1]**scle·ro·phyll** \ˈ==rəˌfil\ *or* **scle·ro·phyl·lous** \ˌ==ˈfiləs\ *adj* [ISV *scler-* + *-phyll* or *-phyllous*] **1 :** of, relating to, or exhibiting sclerophylly ⟨~ plants⟩ ⟨~ characteristics⟩ **2 :** made up of sclerophyll plants ⟨a ~ scrub⟩

[2]**sclerophyll** \"\ *n* -s **:** a sclerophyll plant

scle·ro·phyl·ly \ˈ==ˌfilē\ *n* -ES [*scler-* + *phyll-* + *-y*] **:** exceptional development of sclerenchyma in leaves (as in many desert plants) resulting in thickened hardened foliage resistant to water loss — compare SCLEROCAULY

scle·ro·phyte \-ˌfīt\ *n* -s [*scler-* + *-phyte*] **:** SCLEROPHYLL

scle·ro·protein \ˌsklirō+\ *n* [ISV *scler-* + *protein*] **:** any of a class of fibrous proteins (as collagen, keratin, fibroin) that are usu. insoluble in aqueous solvents and are resistant to chemical reagents — called also *albuminoid*

scle·ro·scope \ˈsklirəˌskōp, -ler-\ *n* [fr. *Scleroscope*, a trademark] **:** a sclerometer devised esp. for use with metals in which the height of rebound of a small standard object dropped from a fixed height onto the surface of a specimen is used as a measure of the hardness of the specimen

scle·rose \skləˈrōs, ˈskliˌr-, ˈskleˌr-, -ōz\ *vb* -ED/-ING/-s [back-formation fr. *sclerosed*] *vt* **:** to cause sclerosis in ⟨chronic infections may ~ kidneys⟩ ~ *vi* **:** to undergo or become affected with sclerosis **:** become sclerotic ⟨arteries of older people often tend to ~⟩

scle·rosed \-ōst, -ōzd\ *adj* [NL *sclerosis* (fr. ML *sclirosis*) + E *-ed*] **1 :** affected with sclerosis **:** HARDENED, INDURATED **2 :** LIGNIFIED; *esp* **:** having thickened pitted walls ⟨sclereids may be interpreted as ~ parenchyma cells⟩

scle·ro·sep·tum \ˌsklirō, -lerō-+\ *n* [NL, fr. *scler-* + *septum*] **:** a calcareous radial septum of a coral

scle·ro·sis \skləˈrōsəs\ *n, pl* **sclero·ses** \-ōˌsēz\ [ME *sclirosis*, fr. ML, fr. Gk *sklērōsis*, fr. *sklēroun* to harden (fr. *sklēros* hard) + *-sis* — more at SKELETON] **1 a :** pathological hardening of tissue produced by overgrowth of fibrous tissue and other changes (as in arteriosclerosis) or by increase in interstitial tissue and other changes (as in multiple sclerosis) **b :** any of various diseases characterized by sclerosis — usu. used in combination; see ARTERIOSCLEROSIS, MULTIPLE SCLEROSIS **2 :** hardening of plant cell walls by thickening or by deposition of lignin

sclero·skeleton \ˌsklirō, -lerō+\ *n* [*scler-* + *skeleton*] **:** the part of the skeleton that is formed by ossifications in tendons, ligaments, and aponeuroses

scle·ros·po·ra *n, cap* [NL, fr. *scler-* + *-spora*] **:** a genus of downy mildews (family Peronosporaceae) parasitic on various grasses and having thick-walled resting spores that are united with the walls of the oogonia

scle·ro·stome \ˈsklirəˌstōm, -ler-\ *n* -s [NL *Sclerostoma*, genus of nematode worms in former classifications, fr. *scler-* + *-stoma*] **:** PALISADE WORM

scle·ro·tal \skləˈrōdᵊl\ *n* -s [NL *sclerotica* + E *-al*] **:** any of the bony plates in the sclerotic of various vertebrates

scle·rote \ˈskliˌrōt, -leˌr-, skləˈrōt\ *n* -s [NL *sclerotium*] **:** SCLEROTIUM

scle·ro·tial \skləˈrōsh(ē)əl\ *adj* [NL *sclerotium* + E *-al*] **1 :** of or relating to a sclerotium **:** bearing sclerotia **2** [NL *Sclerotium* + E *-al*] **:** of or relating to the form genus *Sclerotium*

[1]**scle·rot·ic** \-ˈräd·ik\ *adj* [in sense 1, fr. *scler-* + *-otic*; in other senses, prob. fr. (assumed) ML *scleroticus*, fr. *scler-* + *-oticus* (as in L *exoticus* exotic) — more at EXOTIC] **1 :** HARD, INDURATED: as **a :** being or relating to the sclera **b :** SCLEROSED ⟨a ~ cell wall⟩ ⟨~ patients⟩ ⟨~ arteries⟩ **2 :** of or relating to sclerosis

[2]**sclerotic** \"\ *n* -s [ML *sclerotica*] **:** SCLERA

scle·rot·i·ca \-d·əkə\ *n* -s [ML, prob. fr. fem. of (assumed) ML *scleroticus* sclerotic] **:** SCLERA

sclerotic cell *n* **:** SCLEREID

sclerotic coat *n* **:** SCLERA

scle·ro·tin \ˈsklirətən, -ler-\ *n* -s [ISV *sclerot-* (fr. Gk *sklērotēs* hardness) + *-in*] **:** an insoluble tanned protein permeating and stiffening the chitin of the cuticle of arthropods

scle·ro·tin·ia \ˌ==ˈtinēə\ *n* [NL, fr. *sclerotin-* (irreg. fr. *sclerotium*) + *-ia*] **1** *cap* **:** a large genus of ascomycetous fungi (order Helotiales) having apothecia that arise from a sclerotium and including various destructive plant pathogens — see BROWN ROT **2** -s **:** any fungus of the genus *Sclerotinia* (~ rots) — **scle·ro·tin·i·al** \ˌ==ˈtinēəl\ *adj*

scle·ro·tin·i·ose \-nēˌōs *also* -ōz\ *n* -s [NL *Sclerotinia* + *-ose*] **:** a plant disease caused by a sclerotinia

scle·ro·ti·oid \skləˈrōshēˌȯid\ *also* **scle·ro·toid** \ˈsklirəˌtȯid, -ler-\ *adj* [NL *sclerotium* + E *-oid*] **:** resembling a sclerotium

scle·ro·ti·tis \ˌsklirəˈtīdəs, -ler-\ *n* -ES [NL, fr. ML *sclerotica* sclerotic + NL *-itis*] **:** SCLERITIS

scle·ro·tium \skləˈrōsh(ē)əm\ *n* [NL, fr. Gk *sklērotēs* hardness (fr. *sklēros* hard) + NL *-ium* — more at SKELETON] **1** *pl* **sclero·tia** \-)ə\ **a :** a compact mass of hardened mycelium stored with reserve food material in various true fungi that is usu. dark-colored, often has cells which are short and stout or irregular in shape, and when mature becomes detached and remains dormant until a favorable opportunity for growth when it either sends out hyphae or produces spore fruits ⟨the ergot of rye is a ~⟩ **b :** a waxy mass of protoplasm into which the plasmodium of a myxomycete is transformed during dry seasons **2** *cap* **:** a form genus of sterile fungi (order Mycelia Sterilia) including many that form sclerotia and some that cause blights or rots of plants

sclerotium disease *or* **sclerotium rot** *n* **:** a plant disease caused by fungi of the genus *Sclerotium*; *also* **:** one in which sclerotia are formed

scle·ro·ti·za·tion \ˌsklirətəˈzāshən, -ler-, -ˌtīˈz-\ *n* -s [*sclerotized* + *-ation*] **:** the quality or state of being sclerotized

scle·ro·tized \ˈ==ˌtīzd\ *adj* [[1]*sclerotic* + *-ize* + *-ed*] **:** SCLEROSED; *esp* **:** hardened by substances other than chitin — used chiefly of the cuticle of an insect

scle·ro·tome \-ˌtōm\ *n* -s [*scler-* + *-tome*] **1 :** a fibrous partition separating two myotomes **2 :** the ventromesial portion of a somite that proliferates mesenchyme which migrates about the notochord to form the axial skeleton and ribs — **scle·ro·tomic** \ˌ==ˈtōmik, -ˈtäm-\ *adj*

scle·rot·o·my \skləˈräd·əmē\ *n* -ES [*scler-* + *-tomy*] **:** surgical cutting of the sclera

scle·rous \ˈsklirəs, -ler-\ *adj* [Gk *sklēros*] **:** HARD, INDURATED

sclimb \ˈsklim\ *chiefly Scot var of* CLIMB

ScM *abbr or n* -s [NL *scientiae magister*] Master of Science

SCM *abbr* **1** state certified midwife **2** summary court-martial

scob \ˈskäb\ *n* -s [origin unknown] *dial Brit* **:** a rod or splint of wood; *esp* **:** a thatch peg

scob·by \ˈskäbi\ *n* -ES [origin unknown] *dial Brit* **:** CHAFFINCH

sco·bic·u·lar \skōˈbikyələ(r)\ *adj* [L *scobis* sawdust, filings + E *-icular* (as in *reticular*); akin to L *scabere* to scratch, scrape — more at SHAVE] **:** SCOBIFORM

scob·i·form \ˈskäbəˌfȯrm, ˈskōb-\ *adj* [L *scobis* + E *-form*] **:** resembling sawdust or raspings

scob·i·nate \ˈskäbənət, -ˌnāt\ *adj* [L *scobina* rasp + E *-ate*; akin to L *scabere* to scratch, scrape] **:** NODULATED

scodgy \ˈskäjē\ *n* -ES [origin unknown] *Scot* **:** DRUDGE

[1]**scoff** \ˈskäf, ˈskȯf\ *n* -s [ME *scof*, prob. of Scand origin; akin to obs. Dan *skuf, skof* jest, mockery, deceit, *skuffe* to jest; akin to OFris *skof* mockery, and perh. to OE *scop* poet — more at SCOP] **1 :** SCOFFING, MOCKERY **2 :** a mocking expression of scorn, derision, or contempt **:** GIBE ⟨subject to the ~s and guffaws of his fellows —C.M.Dudley⟩ **3 :** an object of scorn, mockery, or derision ⟨turn the whole matter into a ~ and call it a trifle —*Encore*⟩

[2]**scoff** \"\ *vb* -ED/-ING/-s [ME *scoffen*, fr. *scof*, n.] *vi* **:** to show contempt by derisive acts or language **:** speak contemptuously or with ridicule or mockery ⟨one of those attending the lecture . . . had come to ~, but was converted —Lucile E. Hoyme⟩ — often used with *at* ⟨we may ~ at him in health, but we send for him in pain —B.N.Cardozo⟩ ~ *vt* **:** to treat or address with derision **:** mock at ⟨how I have ~*ed* them in my heart —A.C.Gunter⟩

syn SCOFF, JEER, GIBE, FLEER, GIRD, SNEER, and FLOUT can all mean to show one's contempt in derision or mockery. SCOFF stresses insolence, lack of respect, or incredulity as motivating the derision ⟨in consequence of this illiteracy, he *scoffed* at education and considered the professional scrivener an object of ridicule —L.C.Douglas⟩ ⟨*scoffed* at the idea that modern man might have developed before Neanderthal —L.C.Eiseley⟩ JEER stresses a coarse derisive laughter ⟨before she had yanked me halfway across the floor, men and women were *jeering* at her, calling her a cradle robber —Conrad Richter⟩ ⟨they would laugh at his warning. They would *jeer* him, and, if practicable, pelt him with missiles —Stephen Crane⟩ GIBE stresses taunting whether derisive or good-natured ⟨*gibe* and catcall at a speaker for his political sentiments⟩ ⟨hoot and *gibe* at her —Carl Jonas⟩ FLEER emphasizes derisive grins, grimaces, and laughter rather than utterances ⟨listened with a *fleering* mouth —Joseph Hergesheimer⟩ ⟨saying nothing but *fleering* unpleasantly at any and all remarks⟩ GIRD stresses an attack marked by scoffing, gibing, or jeering ⟨warned us, instead of *girding* at general prejudices, to employ our sagacity in discovering the latent wisdom that commonly exists in them —Walter Moberly⟩ SNEER, of all these terms, carries the strongest implication of ill-natured or caustic contempt, usu. connoting the use of irony or satire augmented by an insultingly contemptuous facial expression, tone of voice, or general manner ⟨his attitude . . . has been often unduly critical, occasionally to the point of *sneering* denunciation —F.E.Hirsch⟩ ⟨they used to *sneer* and to jibe at the Redskin Fife and Drum Ensemble —W.B.Ready⟩ ⟨too many teachers just *sneer* at TV and refuse to look at it —S.H.Horton⟩ FLOUT stresses a contempt of something shown by refusal to heed it or by denial of its truth or force ⟨scorn or neglect of institutions, and characteristic *flouting* or reversing of convention —F.J.Hoffman⟩ ⟨the law of supply and demand cannot be *flouted* indefinitely —C.T. Lanham⟩ ⟨believes that our present immigration laws *flout* fundamental American traditions and ideals —*President's Commission on Immigration & Naturalization*⟩

[3]**scoff** \"\ *vb* -ED/-ING/-s [alter. of earlier *scaff*, of unknown origin] *vt* **1 :** to eat greedily **:** EAT **2 :** PLUNDER, STEAL ~ *vi* **:** to eat greedily **:** EAT ⟨clothes' moth starts ~*ing* the moment she hatches —*Monsanto Mag.*⟩

[4]**scoff** \"\ *n* -s **:** FOOD, MEAL

scoff·er \-fə(r)\ *n* -s [ME, fr. *scoffen* to scoff + *-er*] **:** one that scoffs; *esp* **:** one that scoffs at religion

[1]**scoffing** *n* -s [ME, fr. gerund of *scoffen* to scoff] **:** the act of one who scoffs

[2]**scoffing** *adj* [fr. pres. part. of [2]*scoff*] **:** DERISIVE, CONTEMPTUOUS — **scoff·ing·ly** *adv*

scofflaw \ˈ=ˌ=\ *n* [[2]*scoff* + *law*] **:** a contemptuous lawbreaker; *esp* **:** one who ignores parking tickets

scoffs *pl of* SCOFF, *pres 3d sing of* SCOFF

scog \ˈskäg\ *var of* SCUG

scoggin *n* -s [after John (Thomas?) *Scoggin* (Scogan) *fl* 1480–1500 jester at the court of King Edward IV of England] **:** a coarse or scurrilous jester

scoin·son arch \ˈskȯin(t)sən-\ *n* [*scoinson* alter. (influenced by MF *escoinsson* sconcheon) of *sconcheon*] **:** an arch carrying a part of the thickness of a wall

scoke \ˈskōk\ *n* -s [Massachuset *m'skok*, lit., that which is red] **:** POKEWEED

[1]**scold** \ˈskōld\ *n* -s [ME *scald, scold*, prob. of Scand origin; akin to ON *skald, skāld* poet, skald, Icel *skālda* to make scurrilous or libelous verse; perh. akin to OIr *scél* story, W *chwedl*] **1 a :** one who scolds habitually or persistently ⟨she is an irksome brawling ~ —Shak.⟩ ⟨afraid of going down to posterity as the despised ~ in her husband's life —E.J.Simmons⟩ ⟨scourge of Presidents, constant dissenter and filibustering ~ —L.E.Davies⟩ ⟨has become something of a public ~ against the rebellious young —L.L.King⟩ ⟨only the squirrels, those born ~s, to reprove our indolence —*New Yorker*⟩ **b :** COMMON SCOLD **2 :** a severe reprimand or rebuke **:** SCOLDING ⟨put him in an ill humor by the ~ she gave him —Oliver Goldsmith⟩

[2]**scold** \"\ *vb* -ED/-ING/-s [ME *scalden, scolden*, fr. *scald, scold*, n.] *vi* **1** *obs* **:** to quarrel noisily **:** use harsh or vituperative language **2 :** to find fault usu. noisily or rudely **:** utter harsh rebuke **:** chide sharply and severely — often used with *at* ⟨could come to terms if they came truly to grips instead of ~*ing* at each other over a barrier of misunderstanding —Edward Sapir⟩ ⟨farmers . . . stood up in their wagons and ~*ed* at the horses —Sherwood Anderson⟩ ~ *vt* **1 :** to force by scolding — used esp. with *out of* **2 :** to chide loudly or rudely **:** rebuke or reprove with severity **:** censure severely or angrily ⟨~*ed* the . . . press, not only for undue emphasis on sex and crime but for failure to guess the outcome of elections —*Newsweek*⟩ ⟨~*ed* for attaching too much importance to phonetic similarity —C.E.Bazell⟩ ⟨~ the . . . investor for unwillingness to assume risks —J.F.Rippy⟩ ⟨the younger generation of writers severely for their sins —C.I.Glicksberg⟩

syn SCOLD, UPBRAID, RATE, BERATE, TONGUE-LASH, JAW, BAWL OUT, WIG, RAIL, REVILE, and VITUPERATE mean, in common, to reproach or censure angrily and more or less abusively. SCOLD suggests the censure of a disobedient child by a mother, or implies irritation or ill temper ⟨*scold* a child for getting home late⟩ ⟨one officer who had *scolded* his subordinates for picking apples from trees alongside a road while on a march —Hanama Tasaki⟩ ⟨a catbird . . . flew up on a lilac limb to *scold* us —John Moore⟩ UPBRAID usu. suggests a more or less justifiable anger ⟨the Queen *upbraided* Henry for the scandal he was giving —Francis Hackett⟩ ⟨the scene in which Lincoln *upbraids* his schoolfellows for maltreating a turtle —*Reporter*⟩ RATE and BERATE suggest a more prolonged angry censure and, generally, abusiveness ⟨*rated* himself most severely for this feeling of vengefulness —Howard Nemerov⟩ ⟨*rated* him for his want of tact —Adrian Bell⟩ ⟨*berate* the agent for his ill management of the estates —Pearl Buck⟩ ⟨heatedly *berated* the government's . . . attitude —*Time*⟩ TONGUE-LASH stresses the effect of severe unrestrained censure or berating upon the person berated ⟨*tongue-lashed* them in a way that could be heard blocks off —Howard Fast⟩ ⟨*tongue-lashes* him about the exploitation of the workers —*Time*⟩ The terms JAW, BAWL OUT, and WIG (chiefly British) emphasize the energetic or noisy harangue that usu. characterizes a berating ⟨when we went home late for chores, we got *jawed* some —C.T.Jackson⟩ ⟨a tall, red-headed foreman whose chief asset was *bawling out* his men —H.A.Overstreet⟩ ⟨got a sound *wigging* in the current issue from one of their own and from a pair of practitioners in other fields —*Time*⟩ RAIL, usu. with *at* or *against*, is a strong, more abusive, usu. contemptuous berating ⟨*rail* against humanity for not being abstract perfection —T.L.Peacock⟩ ⟨physicians time and again *rail* at the courts for applying a test of mental responsibility so narrow and inadequate —B.N.

Cardozo⟩ ⟨had called his people lazy louts . . . *railed* against his inclination to dreams —Sherwood Anderson⟩ REVILE puts emphasis upon abusiveness more strongly than any of the others, and usu. implies vilification ⟨had to hear themselves *reviled* as traitors by lesser Americans —Kenneth Roberts⟩ VITUPERATE is interchangeable with REVILE though suggesting even more violence of censure or attack ⟨with his angry face and his trembling hands *vituperating* him —Archibald Marshall⟩ ⟨how the sage reviled and *vituperated* the horrors of city life —A.C.Benson⟩

scol·de·nore \'skōldə,nō(ə)r\ *n* -s [origin unknown] **:** OLD-SQUAW

scold·er \'skōldə(r)\ *n* -s [ME, fr. *scolden* to scold + *-er*] **:** one who scolds

scolding *n* -s [ME, fr. gerund of *scolden* to scold] **1 :** the action of one who scolds **2 :** harsh or severe reproof ⟨he issued a circular . . . that evoked a ~ —F.L.Paxson⟩

scolding locks *n pl, dial* **:** locks of hair usu. curled that do not stay in place

scold·ing·ly *adv* **:** in a scolding manner

scolds *pl of* SCOLD, *pres 3d sing of* SCOLD

scold's bridle *n* **:** BRANK 1a

scolec- *or* **scoleco-** *comb form* [Gk *skōlēk-, skōlēko-*, fr. *skōlēk-, skōlēx* worm, grub — more at SCOLEX] **:** worm ⟨*scolecology*⟩ ⟨*scolecospore*⟩ **:** scolex ⟨*scolecoid*⟩

sco·lec·i·da \skō'lesədə\ *n pl, cap* [NL, fr. *scolec-* + *-ida*] *in some classifications* **:** a phylum or other major division of Metazoa that comprises triploblastic bilaterally symmetrical invertebrate animals lacking a true coelom and having nonstriated musculature, a nonmetameric nervous system, and a primitive or no circulatory system and that includes Platyhelminthes, Nemertea, Acanthocephala, Gastrotricha, Rotifera, Nematoda, Nematomorpha, Kinorhyncha, and Entoprocta — compare ASCHELMINTHES

sco·lec·i·dan \-dᵊn\ *adj* [NL *Scolecida* + E *-an*] **:** of or relating to the Scolecida

scol·e·cite \'skälə,sīt, 'skōl-\ *n* -s [G *skolezit*, fr. *skolez-* scolec- + *-it* -ite] **:** a mineral $CaAl_2Si_3O_{10}·3H_2O$ that is a hydrous calcium aluminum silicate, is a zeolite, occurs in delicate radiating groups of white crystals, in fibrous masses, and in nodules, and in some forms shows a wormlike motion when heated

sco·le·co·dont \skō'lēkə,dänt\ *n* -s [*scolec-* + Gk *odont-, odōn* tooth — more at TOOTH] **:** a fossil worm jaw

sco·le·coid \skō'lē,kȯid, 'skōlə,-\ *adj* [*scolec-* + *-oid*] **:** resembling a scolex or worm

sco·le·co·spore \skō'lēkə,spō(ə)r\ *n* [*scolec-* + *spore*] **:** a slender threadlike spore; *specif* **:** such a spore distinguished from one of another type but both produced by the same fungus (as in the genus *Phomopsis*)

sco·lex \'skō,leks\ *n, pl* **scoli·ces** \skō'lē,sēz\ *also* **scol·e·ces** \'skälə,sēz, 'skōl-\ *or* **scolexes** [NL, fr. Gk *skōlēx* worm, grub; akin to Gk *skelos* leg — more at CYLINDER] **:** the head of a tapeworm either in the larva or adult stage from which the proglottids are produced by budding

-sco·lex \'skō,leks\ *n comb form* [NL, fr. Gk *skōlēx* worm, grub] **:** worm — in generic names ⟨Desmo*scolex*⟩

sco·lia \'skōlēə\ *n, cap* [NL] **:** a genus (the type of the family Scoliidae) of wasps that build or dig no nest but lay their eggs on the bodies of the burrowing larvae of various beetles

¹sco·li·id \-ēəd\ *adj* [NL *Scoliidae*] **:** of or relating to the genus *Scolia* or family Scoliidae

²scoliid \"\ *n* -s **:** a wasp of the genus *Scolia* or family Scoliidae

sco·li·on *also* **sko·li·on** \'skōlē,än\ *n, pl* **sco·lia** \-ēə\ [Gk *skolion*, fr. neut. of *skolios* crooked — more at CYLINDER] **:** an ancient Greek song sung in turn by guests at a banquet and possibly improvised

sco·li·o·sis *also* **sko·li·o·sis** \,skōlē'ōsəs, ,skäl-\ *n, pl* **scolio·ses** \-'ō,sēz\ [NL, fr. Gk *skoliōsis* crookedness, fr. *skolios* + *-ōsis*] **:** a lateral curvature of the spine — **sco·li·ot·ic** \;==;ˈäd·ik\ *adj*

sco·lite \'skō,līt\ *n* -s [Gk *skōlēx* worm, grub + E *-lite* — more at SCOLEX] **:** any of various tubular structures found in rocks and believed to be fossil burrows of marine worms

sco·li·thus \'skōləthəs\ *n* -ES [NL, fr. Gk *skōlēx* + NL *-lithus* -lite] **:** SCOLITE

scollop *var of* SCALLOP

scol·o·pa·ceous \;skälə;pāshəs\ *adj* [LL *scolopac-, scolopax* snipe, woodcock + E *-eous*] **:** resembling a snipe

scol·o·pac·i·dae \,skälə'pasə,dē\ *n pl, cap* [NL, fr. *Scolopac-, Scolopax*, type genus + *-idae*] **:** a family of birds (suborder Charadrii) including the woodcocks, snipes, sandpipers, tattlers, curlews, and godwits — see CHARADRIIDAE

¹scol·o·pa·cine \;==;pā,sīn, -sən\ *adj* [NL *Scolopac-, Scolopax* + E *-ine*] **:** of or relating to the Scolopacidae

²scolopacine \"\ *n* -s **:** a bird of the family Scolopacidae

scol·o·pax \'==,paks\ *n, cap* [NL, fr. LL, woodcock, snipe, fr. Gk] **:** the type genus of Scolopacidae comprising the European woodcock and a few obscure East Indian birds but formerly including several other birds

scol·o·pen·dra \,skälə'pendrə\ *n* [NL, fr. L, a kind of millipede, fr. Gk *skolopendra*] **1** *cap* **:** a widely distributed genus of centipedes that contains some of the largest tropical forms (as the giant red and black centipede, *S. galapagensis* of the Galapagos islands which may reach a foot in length) **2** -s **:** CENTIPEDE

scol·o·pen·drel·la \,==pen'drelə\ *n, cap* [NL, dim. of L *scolopendra*] **:** a genus (the type of the family Scolopendrellidae) of terrestrial arthropods resembling small centipedes with 15 to 24 dorsal scutes and 12 pairs of short legs

scol·o·pen·drel·li·dae \-lə,dē\ *n pl, cap* [NL, fr. *Scolopendrella*, type genus + *-idae*] **:** a family of minute terrestrial arthropods (class Symphyla) with the first pair of legs usu. reduced or imperfect — see SCOLOPENDRELLA

scol·o·pen·drel·loid \;===;dre,lȯid\ *adj* [NL *Scolopendrella* + E *-oid*] **:** resembling or related to the genus *Scolopendrella*

scol·o·pen·dri·dae \,=='pendrə,dē\ *n pl, cap* [NL, fr. *Scolopendra*, type genus + *-idae*] **:** a large cosmopolitan family of centipedes of which *Scolopendra* is the type — **scol·o·pen·drine** \;==;pen,drīn, -drən\ *adj*

scol·o·pen·dri·form \-endrə,fȯrm\ *adj* [NL *Scolopendra* + E *-iform*] **:** resembling a centipede ⟨a ~ beetle larva⟩

scol·o·pen·dri·um \,skälə'pendrēəm\ [NL, fr. LL *scolopendrion*, a kind of fern thought to resemble a millipede, fr. Gk *skolopendrion*, dim. of *skolopendra*] *syn of* PHYLLITIS

scol·o·pid·i·um \,skälə'pidēəm\ *n, pl* **scolopid·ia** \-ēə\ [NL, fr. Gk *skolop-* (fr. *skolops* stake, pale, anything pointed + NL *-idium*; akin to Gk *skalops* mole (animal) — more at HALF] **:** a chordotonal organ

sco·lop·o·phore \skə'läpə,fō(ə)r\ *also* **scol·o·phore** \'skälə,-\ *n* -s [*scolopophore* fr. Gk *skolop-* (fr. *skolop, skolops*) + E *-phore*; *scolophore* contr. of *scolopophore*] **:** an integumentary sense organ in insects believed to be auditory in function — **sco·loph·o·rous** \skə'läf(ə)rəs\ *adj* — **scol·o·poph·o·rous** \;skälə;pä-\ *adj*

scol·y·mus \'skäləməs\ *n, cap* [NL, fr. L *scolymos*, a kind of thistle, fr. Gk *skolymos*] **:** a small genus of thistlelike herbs (family Compositae) of the Mediterranean region having flower heads with only ray flowers — see GOLDEN THISTLE

¹sco·lyt·id \skə'lid·əd\ *adj* [NL *Scolytidae*] **:** of or relating to the Scolytidae

²scolytid \"\ *n* -s **:** a beetle of the family Scolytidae

sco·lyt·i·dae \-d·ə,dē\ *n pl, cap* [NL, fr. *Scolytus*, type genus + *-idae*] **:** a large family of bark-boring or wood-boring rhynchophorous beetles having a very short beak and clubbed antennae and being small but very destructive to forest trees and fruit trees — see BARK BEETLE

scol·y·toid \'skälə,tȯid\ *adj* [NL *Scolytus* + E *-oid*] **1 :** resembling or related to the family Scolytidae **2 :** being or passing through the stage next before the pupa in hypermetamorphic beetles of the family Meloidae

scol·y·tus \-ləd·əs\ *n, cap* [NL, irreg. fr. Gk *skolyptein* to cut short; akin to Gk *kolos* docked, hornless — more at HALT (lame)] **:** the type genus of Scolytidae comprising numerous small bark beetles of which some are destructive to economically important plants and one (*S. multistriatus*) is a vector of the fungus that causes Dutch elm disease

scom·ber \'skämbə(r)\ *n, cap* [NL, fr. L, mackerel, fr. Gk *skombros*] **:** the type genus of Scombridae containing the common Atlantic mackerel

scom·ber·om·o·rus \,skämbə'rämərəs\ *n, cap* [NL, fr. L *scomber* mackerel + Gk *homoros* closely resembling, fr. *homos* same — more at SAME] **:** a genus of elongated compressed fishes (family Scombridae) having the snout long and pointed, the mouth large, and the scales few and rudimentary and including a number of important food and sport fishes

scom·bre·soc·i·dae \,skämbrə'säsə,dē\ *n pl, cap* [NL, fr. *Sombresoc-, Sombresox*, type genus + *-idae*] **:** a family of slender elongate thin-scaled fishes including only the sauries and with the needlefishes (family Belonidae) forming a distinct suborder of the order Synentognathi

scom·bre·sox \'==,säks\ *n, cap* [NL, fr. L *scombr-, scomber* mackerel + *esox* pike — more at ESOX] **:** the type genus of Scombresocidae

¹scom·brid \'skämbrəd\ *adj* [NL *Scombridae*] **:** of or relating to the Scombridae

²scombrid \"\ *n* -s **:** a fish of the family Scombridae

scom·bri·dae \-rə,dē\ *n pl, cap* [NL, fr. *Scombr-, Scomber*, type genus + *-idae*] **:** a family of fishes (suborder Scombroidea) comprising the typical mackerels, the chub mackerels, and a few related forms but formerly including all or nearly all the scombroids

scom·bri·form \-,fȯrm\ *adj* [NL *Scombriformes*] **1 :** of or relating to the Scombriformes **2** [L *scombr-, scomber* mackerel + E *-iform*] **:** resembling mackerel

scom·bri·for·mes \,=='fȯr,mēz\ [NL, fr. L *scombr-, scomber* mackerel + NL *-iformes*] *syn of* SCOMBROIDEA

scom·brine \'skäm,brēn, -,brən\ *n* -s [ISV *scombr-* (fr. L *scombr-, scomber* mackerel) + *-ine*] **:** a protamine obtained from the mackerel

¹scom·broid \'skäm,brȯid\ *adj* [NL *Scombroidea*] **:** resembling or related to the Scombridae **:** of or relating to the Scombroidea

²scombroid \"\ *n* -s **:** a fish of the suborder Scombroidea

scom·broi·dea \skäm'brȯidēə\ *n pl, cap* [NL, fr. *Scombr-, Scomber* + *-oidea*] **:** a suborder of Percomorphi that comprises active streamlined marine fishes having a narrow caudal peduncle, scales absent or small and sometimes spiny, a usu. long dorsal fin without projecting spines but sometimes with finlets, a lunate or forked caudal fin and including numerous oily-fleshed fishes (as mackerels, tunas, albacores, bonitos, and swordfishes) and that are of great economic importance as food fishes

scom·broi·dei \-ē,ī\ [NL, fr. *Scombr-, Scomber* + *-oidei*] *syn of* SCOMBROIDEA

¹sconce \'skän(t)s\ *n* -s [ME *sconse, sconce*, fr. MF *esconse* hiding place, screened lantern with a handle, fr. OF, fr. fem. of *escons*, past part. of *escondre* to hide, fr. L *abscondere* — more at ABSCOND] **1 a** *obs* **:** a screened lantern or candlestick with a handle **b :** a flat candlestick with a handle **2 a :** a bracket candlestick or group of candlesticks projecting or hanging from a plaque and usu. forming an ornamental object secured to a wall **b :** an ornamental electric light fixture for a wall that resembles a bracket candlestick or group of candlesticks **c :** the circular socket of a candlestick into which a candle is inserted esp. when the socket has a brim **3 a :** HEAD, SKULL ⟨knock him about the ~ with a dirty shovel —Shak.⟩ **b :** BRAINS, SENSE

sconce 2a

²sconce \"\ *n* -s [D *schans*, fr. G *schanze*, fr. MHG, fagot, fascine, sconce] **1 :** a detached or isolated defensive work; *specif* **:** a counterfort or redoubt built to defend a particular point **2 :** a protecting cover or screen **:** PROTECTION, SHELTER

³sconce *vt* -ED/-ING/-S *obs* **:** to provide with a sconce **:** ENTRENCH, SHELTER

⁴sconce \'skän(t)s\ *vt* -ED/-ING/-S [origin unknown] **:** FINE

⁵sconce \"\ *n* -s **:** a fine imposed at an English university for a breach of rules or customs

scon·cheon \'skänchən\ *or* **scun·cheon** \'skən-\ *n* -s [ME *scouchon, skonchon, sconcheon*, fr. MF *escoinsson, escouchon, escochon*, fr. *coing, coin* wedge, stamp, corner — more at COIN] **:** the part of the side of an opening from the back of the reveal to the inside face of the wall usu. forming in the masonry a rabbet in which the wooden frame is set

scone *or* **scon** \'skōn, 'skän, 'skən\ *n* -s [perh. fr. D *schoonbrood* fine white bread, fr. MD *schoonbroot*, fr. *schone* bright, clean, beautiful + *broot* bread — more at SHEEN] **1 a :** a quick bread made of oatmeal or barley flour, rolled into a round shape, cut into quarters, and baked on a griddle **b :** a quick bread made of a baking powder dough sometimes enriched with eggs, sugar, and currants, cut into various shapes (as rounds, diamonds, wedges) and usu. baked in an oven **2** *or* **scone cap :** a broad flat bonnet worn by the Lowland Scots

scooch \'sküch\ *vi* -ED/-ING/-ES [origin unknown] *chiefly dial* **:** to crouch esp. in hiding

¹scoop \'sküp\ *n* -s [ME *scope*, fr. MD *schope, schoepe*; akin to MLG *schōpe* scoop, MHG *schuofe* scoop, OHG *skepfen* to form, shape, create, draw up water — more at SHAPE] **1 :** any of various containers or utensils for holding or removing liquid or loose materials: as **a :** a large ladle **:** a vessel with a long handle used for dipping or skimming liquids ⟨a ~ for bailing a rowboat⟩ **b :** a deep shovel or similar but smaller and handheld implement for digging out and dipping or for shoveling ⟨a coal ~⟩ ⟨a flour ~⟩ ⟨a grain ~⟩ ⟨a measuring ~⟩ **c :** a hemispherical utensil with a handle for dipping out soft food (as ice cream or mashed potatoes) **d :** a small utensil often with a spoon-shaped blade for cutting or gouging; *specif* **:** a spoon-shaped surgical instrument used in extracting various materials (as debris, pus, foreign bodies) **e :** a receptacle with high curved sides for holding a loose bulk commodity on a weighing scale **f :** the bucket of a dredging machine or an earth-moving vehicle; *also* **:** an earth-moving vehicle having a bucket **g :** CRANBERRY RAKE **2 a :** the amount contained in a scoop ⟨a ~ of ice cream⟩ **b :** an amount of something obtained in large quantity as if with a scoop (as a large profit in speculation) ⟨had made a huge ~ on the stock exchange —Max Beerbohm⟩ **3 :** SCOOP NET **4 a :** the action of taking with a scoop or ladle **:** a motion with or like that made with a scoop ⟨off these volcanic islands another ~ is made for bait —*Time*⟩ **b :** the act of scooping or the musical effect achieved by it **:** PORTAMENTO ⟨with an occasional hoot and a more than occasional ~ to betray the toll time has taken of her voice —Irving Kolodin⟩ **c** (1) **:** the taking in of all the cards on the table in one play in casino (2) **:** SCOPA **d :** a field hockey stroke executed with the hands apart and the blade of the stick laid back to lift the ball **5 a :** a place hollowed out **:** a basin-shaped cavity **:** HOLLOW ⟨small city rests on a ~ between rocky hills —*Springfield (Mass.) Union*⟩ **b :** a shallow depression in the earth prepared by various birds as a foundation for their nest **c :** a funnel-shaped opening for channeling a fluid (as air or oil) into a desired path — compare AIR SCOOP **d :** a usu. multiple unit and floodlight with a more or less shovel-shaped reflector used esp. in movie and television studios **6 a :** information esp. of immediate interest or significance ⟨you heard the hot ~ —J.A.Michener⟩ ⟨give him the ~ on the identification —J.K.Harris⟩ **b :** an exclusive news report **:** BEAT 10b ⟨the story was a ~ by just a few hours —Stephen Watts⟩ ⟨men whose self-restraint will give way before their desire for a ~ —*Time*⟩ **7 :** a rounded and usu. low-cut neckline on a woman's garment

scoop 1c

²scoop \"\ *vb* -ED/-ING/-S [ME *scopen*, fr. *scope*, n.] *vt* **1 a :** to take out or up with or as if with a scoop **:** DIP ⟨~ sugar out of a barrel⟩ ⟨~ the center out of a melon⟩ ⟨~*ed* up another mug of flip —Kenneth Roberts⟩ ⟨every time she rolled to leeward, she would ~ up the South Atlantic Ocean —H.A.Chippendale⟩ ⟨~*ed* up a handful of the salty earth —Marion Wilhelm⟩ **b :** to gather, take, or get sometimes surreptitiously in a more or less wholesale manner as if with a scoop **:** pick up ⟨~*ed* up a couple of cakes of soap from the hotel —Gilbert Millstein⟩ ⟨~*ing* his books up off the ground —Grace Metalious⟩ **c :** to lift (the ball) into the air with the stick without taking a preliminary swing in field hockey **2 :** to empty by lading ⟨to ~ a boat dry⟩ **3 :** to make hollow **:** dig out **:** EXCAVATE ⟨the earth had been ~*ed* away —Willa Cather⟩ **4 a :** to make or shape by or as if by scooping — often used with *out* ⟨water that by slow attrition had ~*ed* out this wide channel —P.E. More⟩ **b :** to cut (material) away along a curved line; *specif* **:** to make a (garment) with a scoop neck or neckline ⟨a ~*ed* dress⟩ **5 a :** BEAT 4j ⟨let the radio stations consistently ~ the press, or vice versa —Daniel Melcher & Nancy Larrick⟩ **b :** to obtain (a news story) as a beat **c :** to win against **:** BEAT 4d ⟨next film . . . intended to ~ the screen adaptation of the year's biggest stage hit —Lewis Jacobs⟩ **6 :** to glide from (one tone) to another tone esp. in singing so as to sound the intermediate pitches or to begin (a tone) with a slide to the correct pitch ~ *vi* **1 :** to do lading, hollowing, or gathering with or as if with a scoop **2 :** to scoop a tone ⟨the habit of sliding or ~*ing* is another undesirable feature of singing —Sergius Kagen⟩ ⟨she ~*s*, strains for notes —Robert Evett⟩

scoop bonnet *n* **:** a bonnet with a long narrow front shaped somewhat like a scoop and formerly much worn by women

scoop car *n* **:** a railroad car with a scoop for removing obstructions (as snow, rocks, earth slides) from the track

scoop·er \-pə(r)\ *n* -s **1 :** one that uses or works with a scoop (as on a grain unloader or on a centrifugal machine charger) **2 a :** one that scoops **b :** SCORPER **3 a :** AVOCET **b :** SHOVELER 2

scoop·ful \-p,fu̇l\ *n, pl* **scoopfuls** \-lz\ *or* **scoops·ful** \-ps,fu̇l\ **:** SCOOP 2a

scoop net *n* **:** a shallow dip net on a handle used in fishing; *also* **:** a net for sweeping the bottom of a river

scoor \'skü(ə)r\ *chiefly Scot var of* SCOUR

¹scoot \'sküt, *usu* -üd·+V\ *vb* -ED/-ING/-S [prob. of Scand origin; akin to ON *skjōta* to shoot — more at SHOOT] *vi* **1 a :** to go suddenly and swiftly **:** DART, SCUD ⟨cracked the whip over the mare like a rifle shot and she ~*ed* by —H.B.Altuler⟩ ⟨trucks of one of the evening papers ~*ing* around town to deliver the latest editions —Mollie Panter-Downes⟩ ⟨farm prices usu. ~ up and down much faster than the prices of what the farmer buys —*Time*⟩ ⟨~*ed* up the stairs —Richard Burke⟩ **:** go away in haste **:** DECAMP ⟨took his collections and ~*ed* —N.M.Clark⟩ ⟨~*ed* out of the courtroom like the Devil was after her —Eudora Welty⟩ ⟨~ or you will be late⟩ **b :** to slide suddenly or swiftly ⟨~*ed* down a little in his chair —William Brinkley⟩ ⟨placed one hand on his shoulder; the other on the craft's gunwale, raised his feet and ~*ed* overside —K.M. Dodson⟩ **2** *dial chiefly Brit* **:** to shoot or squirt forth ⟨water ~*s* from a hose⟩ ~ *vt* **1 :** to cause to scoot ⟨~*ing* their shoe toes up their calves to restore the shine —Darrell Berrigan⟩ ⟨~*ed* his chair a bit closer —H.O.Yardley⟩ ⟨~*ed* his glass around in large circles —H.D.Skidmore⟩ **2** *chiefly Scot* **:** SQUIRT ⟨~*ing* each other with the hose —Carson McCullers⟩

²scoot \"\ *n* -s **1** *chiefly Scot* **:** a sudden flow (as of water from a hose) **2 :** an act of scooting ⟨its a quick ~ down the sailboat-filled harbor —Pete Barrett⟩ **3 :** a single logging sled **:** DRAY **4 :** a trapshooting game for four-man teams in which the first releases a target with a handtrap, the second man tries to break the target, the third covers for the second and scores if he breaks the target missed by the second, and a fourth acts as scorekeeper, players rotating positions until 20 targets have been thrown **5** *dial* **:** SCOTER

³scoot \"\ *n* -s [origin unknown] **1 :** a piece of hardwood lumber that is inferior to any recognized grade **2 :** a piece of lumber that is very defective and practically worthless

¹scoot·er \'sküd·ə(r), -ütə-\ *n* -s [¹*scoot* + *-er*] **1 :** one that scoots: as **a :** a strongly built sailboat having a flat bottom shod with steel runners and a sharply rising stem for sailing through water or over ice as either is met with **b :** GLIDER 1b **c :** a child's vehicle that consists typically of a narrow footboard mounted between two wheels tandem with an upright handle attached to the front wheel and that is operated by the child placing one foot on the footboard, pushing with the other foot, and steering with the handle **d :** MOTOR SCOOTER **2 :** a plow with a single handle and single shovel used for marking furrows, opening furrows for seed, and breaking up soil between crop rows

scooter 1c

²scooter \"\ *vi* -ED/-ING/-S **:** to go on a scooter esp. with a motor ⟨~*ing* in this country was pretty much started by eggheads, as a hobby or sport —Gene Pavey⟩

³scooter *var of* SCOTER

scoot·er·ist \-ərəst\ *n* -s **:** one that operates a motor scooter

scoot·ers \'sküd·ə(r)z\ *or* **scoots** \'sküts\ *n pl but sing or pl in constr* **:** the barracuda (*Sphyraena argentea*) of the Pacific coast of No. America

scop \'skäp, 'skōp\ *n* -s [OE; akin to OS *skop* poet, OHG *scof* poet, ON *skop, skaup* mockery, and prob. to OE *scūfan, scēofan* to shove — more at SHOVE] **:** an Old English bard or poet ⟨a long way now from the times of oral epic, ~*s*, and ballad singers —Richard Wilbur⟩

scopa \'skōpə\ *n, pl* **sco·pae** \-ō,pē\ *or* **scopas** [NL, fr. L, broom — more at SHAFT] **1 :** a group or arrangement of short stiff hairs on the body surface of an insect that usu. functions like a brush in collecting something (as pollen); *usu* **:** POLLEN BRUSH **2** *pl* **scopas** [It, lit., broom, fr. L] **:** a card game similar to casino

sco·pa·rin \'skōpərən\ *n* -s [ISV *scopar-* (fr. NL *scoparius*, specific epithet of *Cytisus scoparius*) + *-in*] **:** the yellow crystalline coloring matter $C_{22}O_{22}O_{11}$ of the flowers of broom (*Cytisus scoparius*)

sco·par·i·us \skə'pa(a)rēəs\ *n* -ES [NL, fr. *scoparius*, specific epithet of *Cytisus scoparius*, fr. LL, sweeper, fr. L *scopa* broom + *-arius* -ary] **:** the dried tops of the common broom (*Cytisus scoparius*) containing the alkaloid sparteine and formerly used as a diuretic

sco·pate \'skō,pāt\ *adj* [L *scopa* broom + E *-ate*] **:** resembling a brush

¹scope \'skōp\ *n* -s [It *scopo* aim, goal, purpose, object, fr. L *scopus*, fr. Gk *skopos* watcher, goal, purpose, object; akin to Gk *skopein* to view, contemplate, inspect — more at SPY] **1 :** space or opportunity for free and unhampered motion, activity, intention, thought, or vision **:** BREADTH, COMPREHENSIVENESS ⟨full ~ for the exercise of such ability as I had —R.M.Lovett⟩ ⟨a mind remarkable both for its ~ and its mastery over details —John Buchan⟩ **2 a :** an intention in speaking or writing **:** PURPOSE ⟨the author's ~ or aim⟩ **b :** something aimed at or desired **:** OBJECT, END ⟨making religion the main ~ of his life⟩ **c** *obs* **:** a mark aimed at **:** GOAL ⟨arrows speeding to the ~⟩ **3** *chiefly dial* **:** a tract of land esp. when extensive **4 a :** the general range or extent of cognizance, consideration, activity, or influence ⟨the synopsis is a very brief indication of the ~ of the whole argument —Norman Angell⟩ ⟨the ~ of this view — more than 100 miles in all directions —*Amer. Guide Series: Vt.*⟩ ⟨humility . . . a sense of infinite powers beyond our ~ —M.R.Cohen⟩ **b :** the limited field or subject under consideration **:** the range of the matter being treated **:** the marked off area of relevancy ⟨the period of his public career . . . lies outside the ~ of this book —R.W.Southern⟩ ⟨with the extension of the ~ of government to include a wide array of public services —W.J.Shepard⟩ **c :** length of cable or hawser on which a ship rides ⟨pay out more ~, stand by to make sail —S.E.Morison⟩ **5 :** DOMAIN 7 **6 :** the range of operation of a logical operator **:** the part of a statement in the functional calculus that is governed by a quantifier **syn** see RANGE

²scope \"\ *n* -s [*-scope*] **1 :** any of various instruments for viewing or observing: as **a :** BRONCHOSCOPE **b :** GASTROSCOPE **c :** MICROSCOPE **d :** TELESCOPE **e :** TELESCOPE SIGHT **f :** OSCILLOSCOPE **g :** RADARSCOPE **2 :** HOROSCOPE

-scope \ˌskōp\ *n comb form* -s [NL *-scopium*, fr. Gk *-skopion*, fr. *skopein*] **:** a means (as an instrument) for viewing with the eye or observing in any way ⟨*microscope*⟩

scope·less \ˈskōpləs\ *adj* **:** having or affording no scope

sco·pel·i·dae \skəˈpeləˌdē\ [NL, fr. *Scopelus*, type genus (fr. Gk *skopelos* lookout place, promontory, fr. *skopein* to view) + *-idae*] *syn of* MYCTOPHIDAE

scophony \ˈskäfənē\ *n* -ES [prob. blend of Gk *skopein* to view and E *-phony*] **:** a television system in which the scanning is accomplished by the use of mechanical and optical devices rather than a scanning disk or electronic methods

scopi- *comb form* [L *scopa* broom — more at SHAFT] **:** brush ⟨*scopiform*⟩

scop·ic \ˈskäpik\ *adj* [Gk skopein + E *-ic*] **1 :** VISUAL ⟨a ~ method of illustrating a scientific principle⟩ **2 :** having a wide scope **:** COMPREHENSIVE ⟨a ~ subject as the theory of photography —L.E.Varden⟩

-scop·ic \ˈskäpik, -pēk\ *adj comb form* [Gk skopein + E *-ic*] **1 :** looking in a (specified) direction ⟨*basiscopic*⟩ **2 :** viewing or observing ⟨*orthoscopic*⟩ ⟨*nooscopic*⟩

scop·i·dae \ˈskäpəˌdē\ *n pl, cap* [NL, fr. *Scopus*, type genus + *-idae*] **:** a family of African wading birds (suborder Ciconiae) consisting of the hammerkop

sco·pine \ˈskōˌpēn, -ˌpən\ *n* -s [ISV *scopolamine* + *-ine*] **:** a crystalline heterocyclic amino alcohol $C_8H_{13}NO_2$ that is obtained by hydrolysis of scopolamine and that is an epoxy derivative of tropine

sco·pi·ous \ˈskōpēəs\ *adj* [*scope* + *-ious*] **:** having a wide scope **:** SPACIOUS ⟨a theme ~ enough to include a wide variety of characters and incidents —*Times Lit. Supp.*⟩

sco·po·la \ˈskōpələ\ *also* **sco·po·lia** \skəˈpōlēə\ *n* -s [NL *Scopolia*, genus name of *Scopolia carniolica*] **:** the dried rhizome of an herb (*Scopolia carniolica*) of the family Solanaceae that contains the alkaloids scopolamine, atropine, and hyoscyamine and is used as a hypnotic and analgesic

sco·pol·a·mine \skəˈpäləˌmēn, -ˌmən, ˌskōpəˈlamən\ *n* [G *scopolamin*, fr. NL *Scopolia* genus of plants of the family Solanaceae (fr. Giovanni A. *Scopoli* †1788 It. naturalist + NL *-ia*) + G *amin* amine] **:** a poisonous alkaloid $C_{17}H_{21}NO_4$ that is known in three optically isomeric forms of which the syrupy liquid levorotatory isomer occurs in plants of the genus *Scopolia* and other solanaceous plants and is used chiefly in the form of its crystalline hydrobromide as a sedative in connection with morphine or other analgesics in surgery and obstetrics, in the prevention of motion sickness, and as the truth serum in lie detector tests and that is the ester of scopine and tropic acid — called also *hyoscine*

sco·po·le·tin \ˌskōpəˈlētᵊn, skəˈpäləd·ən\ *n* -s [ISV *scopol-* (fr. NL *Scopolia*) + *-et-* + *-in*] **:** a crystalline lactone $C_{10}H_8O_4$ that is found in various solanaceous plants (as members of the genus *Scopolia* or belladonna) and that is a methyl ether of esculetin

sco·po·line \ˈskōpəˌlēn, -lən\ *n* -s [ISV *scopolamine* + *-ine*] **:** a crystalline heterocyclic amino alcohol $C_8H_{13}NO_2$ formed intramolecularly from scopine esp. with an acid or alkali as catalyst and thus usu. formed by hydrolysis of scopolamine

sco·po·ne \skəˈpōnā\ *n* -s [It, aug. of *scopa* — more at SCOPA] **:** a variety of scopa usu. played by four players in two partnerships

sco·po·phil·ia \ˌskōpəˈfilēə\ *or* **scop·to·phil·ia** \ˌskäptə-\ *n* -s [*scopophilia*, NL, fr. Gk *skopein* to view + NL *-o-* + *-philia*; *scoptophilia*, NL, fr. (assumed) Gk *skoptos* (verbal of Gk *skopein*) + NL *-philia* — more at SPY] **:** a desire to look at sexually stimulating scenes esp. as a substitute for actual sexual participation that constitutes a partial or component instinct often sublimated (as in a desire for learning) — **sco·po·phil·i·ac** \ˌ⸗⸗ˈfilēˌak\ *or* **scop·to·phil·i·ac** \ˌ⸗⸗ˈfilēˌak\ *n or adj* — **sco·po·phil·ic** \ˌ⸗⸗ˈfilik\ *or* **scop·to·phil·ic** \ˌ⸗⸗ˈfilik\ *adj*

scop·per·il \ˈskäpərəl\ *n* -s [ME *scoprelle, scoperelle*, perh. of Gmc origin; akin to Icel *skopparakringla* top (toy), *skoppa* to run, jump, spin, OSw *skuppa, skoppa* to run, jump; perh. akin to OE *scūfan, scēofan* to shove — more at SHOVE] **1** *dial chiefly Eng* **:** a spinning top **2** *dial chiefly Eng* **:** a restless active creature

scops *pl of* SCOP

scops owl \ˈskäps-\ *n* [*scops* fr. NL *Scops*, genus of owls, fr. Gk *skōps*, a kind of owl] **:** a small eared owl of *Otus* or a related genus

scoptical *adj* [Gk *skōptikos* scoptical (fr. *skōptein* to mock — prob. fr. *skōps*, a kind of owl — + *-ikos* -ic) + E *-al*] *obs* **:** JESTING, JEERING, SCOFFING — **scoptically** *adv*

scop·u·la \ˈskäpyələ\ *n, pl* **scopulas** \-ləz\ *or* **scopu·lae** \-yəˌlē\ [NL, fr. LL, small broom, dim. of L *scopa* broom — more at SHAFT] **1 a :** a bushy tuft of hairs **:** SCOPA **b :** a tuft of hairs on the feet and chelicerae of spiders that is used in making the web **2 :** an ornamented rhabdus

scop·u·late \-yələt, -yəˌlāt\ *adj* [NL *scopula* + E *-ate*] **:** having scopulae; *also* **:** SCOPATE

scop·u·lite \ˈskäpyəˌlīt\ *n* -s [LL *scopula* small broom + E *-ite*] **:** a crystallite in the form of a stem with a radiating terminal brush or a number of lateral brushes

sco·pus \ˈskōpəs\ *n, cap* [NL, prob. fr. Gk *skopos* watcher — more at SCOPE] **:** the type genus of Scopidae consisting of the umbrette

-sco·pus \skəpəs\ *n comb form* [NL, fr. Gk *skopos*] **:** one that watches — in generic names

-sco·py \skəpē, -pi\ *n comb form* -ES [Gk *-skopia*, fr. *skopein* to view + *-ia* -y — more at SPY] **:** viewing, examination, scrutiny, observation ⟨*fluoroscopy*⟩ ⟨*microscopy*⟩ ⟨*spectroscopy*⟩

scorbute *n* [MF *scorbut*, fr. NL *scorbutus*] *obs* **:** SCURVY

scor·bu·tic \(ˈ)skȯ(r)ˈbyüd·ik, -üt|, |ēk\ *also* **scor·bu·ti·cal** \|əkəl, |ēk-\ *adj* [NL *scorbuticus*, fr. *scorbutus* scurvy (prob. of Gmc origin: akin to OE *scurf, sceorf* scurf) + L *-icus* -ic, *-ical* — more at SCURF] **1 :** of or relating to scurvy **:** having the nature of scurvy **:** diseased with scurvy **2** *obs* **:** ANTISCORBUTIC — **scor·bu·ti·cal·ly** \|ək(ə)lē\ *adv*

scor·bu·ti·gen·ic \skȯ(r)ˈbyüd·əˌjenik\ *adj* [NL *scorbutus* + E *-i-* + *-genic*] **:** causing scurvy ⟨~ diet⟩

scor·bu·tus \skȯ(r)ˈbyüd·əs\ *n* -ES [NL] **:** SCURVY

¹scorch \ˈskȯ(ə)rch, -ȯ(ə)ch\ *vb* -ED/-ING/-ES [ME *scorchen*, alter. of *scorcnen*, prob. of Scand origin; akin to ON *skorpna* to shrivel up (as from heat); akin to OE *scrimman* to dry up — more at SHRIMP] *vt* **1 :** to burn an exposed surface or portion of typically so as to change color and texture or flavor without consuming ⟨a shirt ~*ed* by a careless laundress⟩ ⟨the bottom of the roast ~*ed* by the cook⟩ **2 a :** to burn and shrivel or parch with or as if with unrelieved intense heat ⟨the long drought had ~*ed* the leaves of the trees —Ellen Glasgow⟩ **b :** to burn, excoriate, or otherwise painfully afflict often with or as if with censure or sarcasm ⟨devils in Dante — tearing, mangling . . . ~*ing* demons —Charles Lamb⟩ ⟨~*ed* the court . . . with his acid portrayals of spendthrift profligates —*Time*⟩ **3 a :** to destroy by or as if by fire **:** BURN **b :** to devastate completely esp. before abandoning to the enemy ⟨~*ing* whatever other facilities there were of military value —*Newsweek*⟩ ⟨~*ed* by two wars in a generation —*U.N. World*⟩ — used in the phrase *scorched earth* esp. of property of possible use to an enemy ⟨will resort to mass demolitions — even to a ~*ed* earth policy —P.W.Thompson⟩ ⟨practiced the ~*ed* earth policy by flooding mines, felling fruit trees —Paul Alpert⟩ **4 :** to dry (a newly molded stereotype matrix) in a scorcher **5 :** to cause (a rubber compound) to scorch ~ *vi* **1 a :** to become scorched ⟨cotton and linens may ~ at high temperatures —*Modern Home Laundering*⟩ **b** *of a rubber compound* **:** to undergo vulcanization prematurely (as during mixing or calendering or on standing) **2 :** to burn its way ⟨the scarlet letter, which forthwith seemed to ~ into Hester's breast, as if it had been red hot —Nathaniel Hawthorne⟩ **3 a :** to ride or drive at great usu. excessive speed ⟨~*ing* off on his bicycle —Anne Parrish⟩ ⟨~*ing* by on a motorcycle —Alan Moorehead⟩ **b :** to travel fast ⟨a missile that could . . . ~ off toward a land target —M.G.Miles⟩ ⟨something ~*es* past your face —Fred Majdalany⟩ **syn** see BURN

²scorch \"\ *n* -ES **1 :** a result of scorching **:** a surface burn; *also* **:** heat that scorches **2 :** a browning or scorched appearance of plant tissues that is symptomatic of some diseases or is caused by heat or parasites — called also *scorching*; *see* BARK SCORCH, LEAF SCORCH **3 :** an act of scorching ⟨a play that is all ~ —*Time*⟩ **4 :** a run at high speed (as in a motor vehicle)

³scorch \"\ *vt* [alter. (influenced by ¹*scorch*) of ²*score*] *dial chiefly Eng* **:** CUT, SLASH, SCRATCH

scorched \-cht\ *adj* **:** parched or discolored by or as if by scorching

scorch·er \-chə(r)\ *n* -s **1 a :** something very hot ⟨the day was a ~⟩ **b :** a heating device used for drying newly molded stereotype matrices — called also *roaster* **2 :** something withering or caustic ⟨the rebuke was a ~⟩ **3 a :** one that drives or rides at an excessive rate of speed **b :** a stroke or shot imparting great speed to an object (as a ball or puck) **4 :** one that creates a sensation **:** one that is startling

¹scorching *adj* [fr. pres. part. of ¹*scorch*] **1 :** that scorches **:** BURNING ⟨several days of ~ heat —Allison Danzig & Joe King⟩ **2 :** BLISTERING, SCATHING, STINGING, WITHERING ⟨capable of making ~ retorts when provoked —F.L.Paxson⟩ ⟨~ indictment of the foreign policies —Reinhold Niebuhr⟩ ⟨a ~ message to congress blasting the idle rich —W.A.White⟩ — **scorch·ing·ly** *adv*

²scorching *adv* **:** to a scorching degree ⟨the day was ~ hot —Winston Churchill⟩

³scorching *n* -s [fr. gerund of ¹*scorch*] **1 :** an act of one that scorches **2 :** SCORCH 2

scorchy \-chē\ *adj* -ER/-EST **:** increasing the tendency of a rubber compound to scorch ⟨stronger but less ~ accelerators⟩

scor·da·tu·ra \ˌskȯ(r)dəˈtu̇rə\ *n, pl* **scordatu·re** \-u̇rā\ *or* **scordaturas** [It, fr. *scordato* (past part. of *scordare* to be out of tune, fr. L *discordare* to disagree, be out of tune) + *-ura* -ure (fr. L) — more at DISCORD] **:** an unusual tuning of a stringed musical instrument for some special effect

scor·di·um \ˈskȯ(r)dēəm\ *n* -s [NL, alter. of L *scordion*, fr. Gk *skordion*, dim. of *skorodon, skordon* garlic; akin to Alb *hurdhë* garlic] *archaic* **:** WATER GERMANDER

¹score \ˈskō(ə)r, ˈskȯ(ə)r, -ōə, -ȯ(ə)\ *n* -s *see sense 1a* [ME *score*, fr. ON *skor* notch, tally, twenty; akin to ON *skera* to cut, carve — more at SHEAR] **1 a** *or pl* **score** (1) **:** a sum of twenty **:** TWENTY ⟨more than a ~ of cities⟩ ⟨his paintings have . . . appeared in over a ~ of smaller exhibitions —*Think*⟩ (2) **:** a group of 20 things ⟨a few ~ . . . will be authorized to write and speak —O.T.Mallery⟩ ⟨the flock numbers about two ~⟩ ⟨his years were four ~⟩ (3) **:** a unit of weight esp. for pigs or oxen equal to 20 or 21 pounds (4) *obs* **:** a unit of distance equal to 20 yards **b scores** *pl* **:** a group containing an indefinitely large number ⟨~*s* of lakes⟩ ⟨~*s* of people made homeless by a storm⟩ **2 a :** a line made with or as if with a sharp instrument **:** NOTCH, INCISION, SCRATCH ⟨the ~ should run with the grain whenever possible —*Book Production*⟩ ⟨~*s*, although they do not pass entirely through the skin, are almost as bad as cuts, because they weaken the leather —*Crops in Peace & War*⟩ ⟨a ~ made by a piston on a cylinder wall⟩; *esp* **:** one made as a tally mark **b** (1) **:** a notch (as made in timber) in which another part is fitted (2) **:** the groove cut at the ends and sides of a block to admit the strap **c :** an indented line or partial cut in paper, metal, or other material to aid in folding or tearing **3 a :** a mark used as a starting point or a goal **:** TAW — see CURLING illustration **b :** a mark made on the surface of a pavement by traffic **c :** a mark or line made for the purpose of keeping account **4 a :** an account or reckoning kept by making marks on a tally **b :** ACCOUNT ⟨I keep . . . some sort of log or ~ of what occupies me —Gilbert Ryle⟩ ⟨bade them call at the inn on their way home and drink a pint on his ~ —Adrian Bell⟩ **c :** amount due **:** INDEBTEDNESS ⟨leaving others to pay the ~ —Edith Wharton⟩ **5 :** an obligation or injury kept in mind for requital **:** GRUDGE ⟨took advantage of the meeting to settle old ~*s* —*Amer. Guide Series: La.*⟩ **6 a :** ACCOUNT, REASON, MOTIVE, GROUND ⟨the first airplane was not perfect but it was not chopped up and abandoned on that ~ —H.C.Lodge⟩ ⟨excused himself from the bullring on the ~ of fatigue —Frank Yerby⟩ ⟨his situation was still very desperate; on that ~ he allowed himself no illusions —Rafael Sabatini⟩ **b :** BEHALF, SAKE ⟨ideas on the ~ of feminine loveliness were bounded on all four sides by the golden vision —T.B.Costain⟩ ⟨the droning on that ~ I had to listen to —Learned Hand⟩ **7 a :** the original and entire draft or its transcript of a musical composition or an arrangement with the parts for the different instruments or voices written on staffs one above another — compare REDUCTION, SHORT SCORE ⟨orchestral ~⟩ ⟨piano ~⟩ **b :** a musical composition having parts for different instruments or voices **c :** a complete description of a dance composition in choreographic notation — compare LABAN SYSTEM **8 a :** the number of points gained by contestants in a game or other contest **b :** an account of points made and other specific items in a game or contest; *broadly* **:** total count, SUMMARY ⟨had a ~ of 21 killings —W.J.Ghent⟩ ⟨holds low ~ on reading best sellers —*Current Biog.*⟩ **c :** an act or instance of scoring in a game or contest; *also* **:** a winning point ⟨~*s* are made by carrying or passing the ball over the goal line⟩ **d :** a successful move or stroke **:** HIT ⟨the remark was not intended as a ~ against him⟩ **9 :** a number expressing the degree of success in a psychological or educational test in terms of the amount performed or of the time required or of the difficulty surmounted or of the accuracy and excellence of the performance **10 :** a numerical rating of quality (as of an animal or of butter) that usu. is made on the basis of 100 as a perfect rating and is arrived at by adding numerical values assigned according to some definite scheme to specific significant characteristics (as conformation, condition of coat, aroma) ⟨93 ~ butter⟩ ⟨no animal had a ~ above 80⟩ **11** *slang* **:** a successful theft or its proceeds **12 :** the stark inescapable facts or often the unglossed prospects of a situation ⟨know the ~ on unemployment⟩ ⟨many victims of communism know what the ~ is —*Armed Forces Talk*⟩ — **go off at score 1 a :** to go briskly from the starting mark (as in a walking contest) **b :** to start off briskly **:** proceed without hesitancy or break **2 :** to lose command or control of oneself — **in score :** having all the musical parts arranged and placed one over the other

²score \"\ *vb* -ED/-ING/-S [ME *scoren*, fr. ON *skora*, fr. *skor*, n.] *vt* **1 a :** to keep record or account of by or as if by notches on a tally **:** set down **:** RECORD, CHARGE **b :** to enter a record of the indebtedness of — often used with *up* ⟨*scoring* up the customers⟩ **c :** to enumerate in a record **:** COUNT, LIST, RECKON — often used with *up* ⟨men who would observe and ~ up each point and counterpoint —Osbert Sitwell⟩ ⟨asked to ~ a high rating —*Book Production*⟩ ⟨~*s* him right —J.D.Morris⟩ **2 :** to mark with a line ⟨jet planes ~ the heavens with their vapor trails —Phil Stong⟩: as **a** *obs* **:** to indicate by or as if by lines — used with *out* ⟨to ~ out a path⟩ **b :** to mark with significant lines or notches (as in keeping account of something) ⟨to ~ a tally⟩ ⟨pavements . . . were *scored* with chalk marks for hopscotch —Rebecca West⟩ **c :** to cancel by drawing a line through — often used with *off* or *out* ⟨~*s* through a figure that is wrong —*Seven to Eleven*⟩ ⟨he introduced into his reckoning sets of fixed exceptions, amendments on amendments; then he *scored* them all off —Van Wyck Brooks⟩ **3 :** to cut so as to mark with lines, scratches, or notches **:** NOTCH, SCRATCH, FURROW ⟨~ timber⟩ ⟨the brakedrum surface becomes *scored* when it is worn by braking action —*Principles of Automotive Vehicles*⟩ ⟨the flood has *scored* out a deep channel in the middle of the lane —C.S.Jarvis⟩: as **a :** to cut deeply into or across in less or more parallel lines ⟨~ the flounder diagonally into a diamond pattern nearly to the backbone of the fleshy side —Jan Sebastian⟩ ⟨peels . . . cucumbers, ~*s* them with the tines of a fork —Jane Nickerson⟩ **b :** to abrade in parallel scratches ⟨rock *scored* by a moving glacier⟩ **c :** to crease (as paper or paperboard) so that it will fold easily at a desired line ⟨each form is *scored* without ink in two places across the face to provide a guide and aid for folding —L.B.Gatchell⟩ **d :** to record by cuts or notches — used with *on* or *upon* **4 a :** to lash so as to mark with welts **b :** BERATE, EXCORIATE, SCOLD, CASTIGATE ⟨my predecessors were equally *scored* for expressing personal opinions at variance with the criticism in the magazine —Norman Cousins⟩ ⟨magistrate . . . *scored* the youths, calling them "rough, tough show-offs" . . . —*N.Y. Times*⟩ ⟨much more interesting conversation than the itch to ~ people off —J.C.Powys⟩ **5 a :** to gain (as points or runs in a game) for addition to the score ⟨*scored* a home run⟩ **b :** to make an entry of the score of (a game or contest) **:** keep score in **c :** to have as a value in a game or contest **:** COUNT ⟨a touchdown ~*s* six⟩ **d :** to add to one's score (as in a game or contest) **e :** to cause (a teammate) to make a score ⟨*scored* the man on second⟩ **f :** GAIN, ACHIEVE, WIN ⟨the enemy *scored* a local gain⟩ ⟨~ a victory⟩ ⟨~ a theatrical success⟩ ⟨a reporter *scored* a scoop⟩ ⟨a bomb that ~*s* a direct hit⟩ **6 a :** to determine the merit of **:** GRADE, MARK ⟨~ a test or examination⟩ ⟨~ candidates for a job on the basis of their skill or knowledge⟩ **b :** to determine or judge the score of ⟨butter was *scored* weekly —G.H.Wilster⟩ ⟨dogs were *scored* according to their merits —W.F.Brown b.1903⟩ **7 a :** to orchestrate or arrange (a musical composition) for performance ⟨one refrain takes two and a half hours to ~ and copy —R.R.Bennett⟩ ⟨was originally *scored* for four orchestras —Ralph Hill⟩ **b** (1) **:** to compose a score for (a motion picture) (2) **:** to add music to a motion picture that already has sound effects **8 a :** to bring (as a horse) up to the starting line **b :** to warm up (a trotter or pacer) down the stretch immediately prior to a race ~ *vi* **1** *obs* **:** to run up an account of indebtedness **2 a :** to make marks **b :** to mark lines (as by incision) **c :** CUT **3 :** to keep score in a game or contest **4 :** to make or count a point in or as if in a game or contest **:** TALLY ⟨*scored* in the 7th inning⟩ ⟨a bad throw from the catcher is almost sure to allow the runner to ~ —W.L.Myers⟩ **5 a :** to gain or have the advantage **:** WIN ⟨enjoyed *scoring* over an opponent —Béla Menczer⟩ ⟨nylon also ~*s* over cotton and wool in being resistant to moths —Desmond Reilly⟩ **b :** to make a success ⟨an actor who ~*s* in a play⟩ **c :** RATE ⟨poinsettias have *scored* high, especially at Christmastime —Anne Dorrance⟩ **6 a :** to approach the starting line ready for the start ⟨a horse ~*s* for a race⟩ **b** *of a pack of hounds* **:** to give tongue as a group on finding the scent **7** *slang* **:** to purchase narcotics ⟨told his stories of *scoring* in such places —Clellon Holmes⟩

scoreboard \ˈ⸗ˌ⸗\ *n* **:** a large usu. elevated and often electrically operated board for displaying the score of a game or match and sometimes other pertinent information (as playing time)

scorecard \ˈ⸗ˌ⸗\ *n* **1 :** a card upon which scores are recorded ⟨a golfer's ~⟩ ⟨the judge's ~ at a dog show⟩ **2 :** a card identifying players or contestants, showing their numbers and giving other information about them (as their positions) ⟨a baseball ~⟩

scored *adj* [fr. past part. of ²*score*] **:** marked with lines or grooves ⟨his face was ~ with laughing wrinkles —Elinor Wylie⟩ ⟨~ cylinders may be caused . . . by dirt in oil —A.L. Dyke⟩ ⟨a drug marketed in ~ tablets⟩

scorekeeper \ˈ⸗ˌ⸗⸗\ *n* **:** an official who records the score during the progress of a game or contest

score·less \ˈ⸗ləs\ *adj* **:** having no score; *specif* **:** involving no points ⟨a game that ended in a ~ tie⟩

score off *vt* **:** to get the better of **:** triumph over (as in an argument) ⟨the sissy who ends by *scoring off* the world which has been making fun of him —Edmund Wilson⟩ ⟨*scoring off* an old opponent⟩

scorepad \ˈ⸗ˌ⸗\ *n* **:** a pad of paper printed so that the score of a card or other game may be conveniently recorded

scor·er \ˈskōrə(r), ˈskȯr-\ *n* -s [ME, fr. *scoren* to score + *-er* — more at SCORE] **:** one that scores: as **a :** a logger who marks trees to be felled **b :** an instrument (as a creasing machine or a nib on a woodworking bit) used for scoring **c :** a worker who marks paper for creasing or feeds a creasing machine **d** (1) **:** SCOREKEEPER (2) **:** one that makes a score (as in a game or contest)

scores *pl of* SCORE, *pres 3d sing of* SCORE

sco·ria \ˈskōrēə, ˈskȯr-\ *n, pl* **scori·ae** \-ēˌē\ [ME, fr. L, fr. Gk *skōria*, fr. *skōr* excrement + *-ia* -y — more at SCAT-] **1 a :** the refuse from melting of metals or reduction of ores **:** DROSS, SLAG **b :** a burned clay or clinker deposit characteristic of burned-out coal beds on the western Great Plains **2 :** rough vesicular cindery usu. dark lava developed by the expansion of the enclosed gases in basaltic magma; *also* **:** a piece of such lava

sco·ri·ac \-ēˌak\ *adj* [*scoria* + *-ac* (as in *ammoniac*)] **:** SCORIACEOUS

sco·ri·a·ceous \ˌ⸗⸗ˈāshəs\ *adj* [*scoria* + *-aceous*] **:** having the nature of scoria ⟨~ lava⟩ ⟨~ rock⟩

sco·ri·fi·ca·tion \ˌskōrəfəˈkāshən, ˌskȯr-\ *n* -s [*scoria* + *-fication*] **:** the act, process, or result of scorifying; *specif* **:** a process in assaying that involves the use of a scorifier and consists either of an oxidizing fusion of the ore or other product with lead and borax to produce a slag and leave the gold and silver in a lead button or of such a fusion of the lead button obtained either as above or by fusion in a crucible to reduce its size or purify it for cupellation

sco·ri·fi·er \ˈskōrəˌfī(ə)r, ˈskȯr-, -īə\ *n* -s **1 :** one that scorifies **2 :** a furnace in which sweepings containing waste gold or silver are burnt preparatory to extracting the gold and silver **3 :** a crucible (as of clay) for scorifying a metal

scorifier 3

sco·ri·form \-ˌfȯrm\ *adj* [*scoria* + *form*] **:** having the form of scoria

sco·ri·fy \-ˌfī\ *vt* -ED/-ING/-ES [*scoria* + *-fy*] **:** to reduce to scoria **:** to subject to scorification

scoring *n* -s [fr. gerund of ²*score*] **1 :** the act or process of making a score **2 a :** SCORE ⟨not likely to allow the conductor to alter his ~ —Edward Sackville-West & Desmond Shawe-Taylor⟩ ⟨many pencil-*scorings* against passages he especially hated —H.J.Laski⟩ **b :** SCORES ⟨~ made on rock by glaciers⟩

sco·ri·ous \ˈskōrēəs\ *adj* [*scoria* + *-ous*] **1 :** SCORIACEOUS **2 :** containing scoria

¹scorn \ˈskȯ(ə)rn, -ȯ(ə)n\ *n* -s [ME *scarn, scorn, scharn, schorn*, fr. OF *escarn, escharn, escar, eschar*, of Gmc origin; akin to OHG *scern* jest, joke, trick, *scerōn* to behave in a rowdy manner, MHG *scherzen* to leap for joy, jest — more at CARDINAL] **1 :** an emotion involving both anger and disgust **:** passionate contempt **:** DISDAIN ⟨most of us have such a ~ and loathing of robbery or forgery —B.N.Cardozo⟩ ⟨the public's attitude toward his work changing from ~ to veneration during his lifetime —R.M.Coates⟩ **2 :** an expression of extreme contempt **:** GIBE, FLOUT, TAUNT **3 :** an object of extreme disdain, contempt, or derision ⟨the unfair fighter was the ~ of the spectators⟩

²scorn \"\ *vb* -ED/-ING/-S [ME *scarnen, scornen, schornen*, fr. OF *escarnir, escharnir*, of Gmc origin like *escarn, escharn* — more at ¹SCORN] *vt* **1** *archaic* **:** to treat with extreme contempt **:** make the object of insult **:** scoff at **:** MOCK, DERIDE **2 a :** to hold in or reject with extreme contempt **:** CONTEMN ⟨if one does not work and contribute to the general welfare, he is ~*ed* as a drone —*Amer. Guide Series: Ariz.*⟩ ⟨~*ed* the committee's report⟩ **b :** to be unwilling because of scorn **:** DISDAIN — used with a following infinitive ⟨accepted advertisements which other publishers ~*ed* to print —W.A.Swanberg⟩ ⟨~*ed* to reply in any way —Arnold Bennett⟩ ⟨textbooks . . . published by business men who do not ~ to be educators as well —V.M. Rogers⟩ ~ *vi* **:** to show contumely or derision **:** act disdainfully **:** SCOFF, MOCK ⟨you have ~*ed* at my gifts —Charles Kingsley⟩ ⟨end all patient love with ribald ~*ing* —Donagh MacDonagh⟩ **syn** see DESPISE

scorn·er \-nə(r)\ *n* -s [ME, fr. *scornen* to scorn + *-er*] **:** one that scorns **:** MOCKER

scorn·ful \-nfəl\ *adj* [ME, fr. *scorn* + *-ful*] **1 :** full of scorn **:** contemptuous, disdainful — often used with *of* ⟨a ~ attitude⟩ ⟨a ~ smile⟩ ⟨~ of the conventions that he esteemed —Ellen Glasgow⟩ **2** *obs* **:** treated with scorn **:** exciting scorn — **scorn·ful·ly** \-lē, -li\ *adv* — **scorn·ful·ness** *n* -ES

scor·o·dite \ˈskȯrəˌdīt, ˈskär-\ *n* -s [G *skorodit*, fr. Gk *skorodon, skordon* garlic + G *-it* -ite; fr. its odor when heated — more at SCORDIUM] **:** a leek green or brownish mineral $FeAsO_4.2H_2O$ that is a hydrous ferric arsenate and that is isomorphous with mansfieldite and isostructural and prob. isomorphous with variscite and strengite (hardness 3.5–4, sp. gr. 3.1–3.3)

scor·paena \skȯ(r)ˈpēnə\ *n, cap* [NL, fr. L, a kind of fish, fr. Gk *skorpaina*] **:** the type genus of the family Scorpaenidae

¹scor·pae·nid \-ēnəd\ *or* **scor·pae·noid** \-ēˌnȯid\ *adj* [*scorpaenid* fr. NL *Scorpaenidae*; *scorpaenoid* fr. NL *Scorpaenoidea*] **:** of or relating to the Scorpaenidae

²scorpaenid \"\ *or* **scorpaenoid** \"\ *n* -s **:** a fish of the family Scorpaenidae

scor·pae·ni·dae \-ēnəˌdē\ *n pl, cap* [NL, fr. *Scorpaena*, type genus + *-idae*] **:** a large family of carnivorous usu. bottom-dwelling marine spiny-finned fishes (suborder Scorpaenoidea) having a large head with usu. one or more pairs of spiniferous ridges above, wide gill openings, usu. ctenoid scales, a dorsal fin that is typically supported by strong spines which in some forms have poison glands and inflict severe wounds, occurring in all seas but most abundant in the Pacific, and including numerous forms that are used for food — see ROCKFISH, SCORPION FISH

scor·pae·noi·dea \ˌskȯ(r)pēˈnȯidēə\ *n pl, cap* [NL, fr. *Scorpaena* + *-oidea*] **:** a large suborder of Scleroparei comprising the mail-cheeked fishes (as the scorpion fishes and gurnards) — see SCORPAENIDAE

scor·per \ˈskȯrpər\ *n* -s [alter. of ²*scalper*] **:** a graver with a sharpened square or U-shaped working end: as **1** *or* **scau·per** \ˈskȯpə(r)\ **a :** a flat tool used in wood engraving to clear away the spaces between the lines **b :** a gouge used in line engraving **c :** a tool for leveling the insides of barrel staves **2 :** a jeweler's chisel for engraving, cutting, or piercing metal

scor·pi·dae \ˈskȯ(r)pəˌdē\ [NL, irreg. fr. *Scorpis* + *-idae*] *syn of* SCORPIDIDAE

scor·pid·i·dae \skȯ(r)ˈpidəˌdē\ *n pl, cap* [NL, fr. *Scorpid-, Scorpis*, type genus (fr. Gk *skorpid-, skorpis*, a kind of seafish) + *-idae*] **:** a small family of scaly-finned percoid fishes of the Pacific ocean including the half-moon that have a deep compressed body, well-developed teeth, and a single dorsal fin

scor·pio \ˈskȯ(r)pēˌō\ *n* [L, lit., scorpion — more at SCORPION] **1** -s *usu cap* **:** the 8th sign of the zodiac — see SIGN table, ZODIAC illustration **2** *cap* [NL, fr. L, scorpion] **:** a genus of scorpions formerly including all known forms but now restricted to a few obscure African species

¹**scor·pi·oid** \-ˌȯid\ *adj* [Gk *skorpioeidēs*, fr. *skorpios* scorpion + *-eidēs* -oid — more at SCORPION] **1 a :** resembling a scorpion **b :** of or relating to the Scorpionida **2 :** having a circinate arrangement of parts — used chiefly of inflorescences

²**scorpioid** \"\ *n* -s **:** SCORPION

scorpioid cyme *n* **:** a cyme in which the axis is curved and the flowers arise two-ranked and on alternate sides of the axis (as in the forget-me-not)

scor·pi·oi·dea \ˌ=ˈōidēə\ [NL, fr. *Scorpio* + *-oidea*] *syn of* SCORPIONIDA

scor·pi·on \ˈskȯ(r)pēən\ *n* -s [ME *scorpioun*, fr. OF *scorpion*, fr. L *scorpion-, scorpio*, fr. Gk *skorpios*, akin to OE *scearfian* to cut off, scrape, OHG *scarbōn* to cut into small pieces, ON *skarfr* scarf (of a board), *skera* to cut — more at SHEAR] **1 a :** any of numerous arachnids of most warm and tropical regions that constitute the order Scorpionida, that have an elongated body divided into a cephalothorax and a segmented abdomen whose posterior part forms a narrow segmented tail generally carried curled up over the back and carrying a venomous sting at the tip, that has four pairs of walking legs and in front a pair of limbs with large pinchers and a pair of chelicerae, that breathe by lungs, are viviparous and nocturnal, prey esp. on insects and spiders, sometimes enter houses, sometimes become four or five or even eight or more inches long, and that have a severe sting which is rarely fatal to man — see BOOK SCORPION, WHIP SCORPION **b :** any of various lizards: as (1) **:** BLUE-TAILED SKINK (2) **:** PINE LIZARD **c :** SCORPION FISH; *esp* **:** FORTESCUE **d :** a toadfish (*Opsanus tau*) **2 a :** a scourge prob. studded with metal ⟨my father chastised you with whips, but I will chastise you with ~s —1 Kings 12:11 (RSV)⟩ **3 :** an ancient military engine for throwing missiles (as stones) **:** CATAPULT, ONAGER **4 :** something that incites to action like the severe sting of a scorpion ⟨the ~s of absolute necessity —Arnold Bennett⟩

scorpion bug *n* **:** WATER SCORPION

scor·pi·o·nes \ˌ=ˈōˌnēz\ [NL, fr. pl. of L *scorpion-, scorpio*] *syn of* SCORPIONIDA

scorpion fish *n* **1 :** a fish of the family Scorpaenidae; *esp* **:** one having a venomous spine or spines on the dorsal fin **2 :** the common toadfish (*Opsanus tau*)

scorpion fly *n* **:** an insect of the family Panorpidae; *broadly* **:** any insect of the order Mecoptera

scorpion grass *n* **:** FORGET-ME-NOT 1a

scor·pi·on·ic \ˌskȯ(r)pēˈänik\ *adj* **:** relating to or resembling the scorpion

¹**scor·pi·o·nid** \ˈskȯ(r)pēənəd\ *adj* [NL *Scorpionida*] **:** of or relating to the Scorpionida

²**scorpionid** \"\ *n* -s **:** an arachnid of the order Scorpionida

scor·pi·on·i·da \ˌskȯ(r)pēˈänədə\ *n pl, cap* [NL, fr. *Scorpion-, Scorpio* + *-ida*] **:** an order of Arachnida constituted by the true scorpions

scor·pi·o·nid·ea \ˌskȯ(r)pēəˈnidēə\ [NL, fr. *Scorpion-, Scorpio* + *-idea*] *syn of* SCORPIONIDA

scorpion lobster *n* **:** a slender burrowing crustacean of the subtribe Thalassinidea

scorpion mouse *n* **:** GRASSHOPPER MOUSE

scorpion senna *n* **:** a yellow-flowered shrub (*Coronilla emerus*) of southern Europe having a slender jointed pod that resembles a scorpion's tail

scorpion shell *n* **:** any of numerous tropical marine snails (genus *Lambis*) that as adults have the outer lip of the aperture produced into a series of long curved spines

scorpion spider *n* **:** WHIP SCORPION

scorpion's-tail \ˈ===ˌ=\ *n, pl* **scorpion's-tails :** a plant of the genus *Scorpiurus*

scorpionweed \ˈ===ˌ=\ *n* **:** a plant of the genus *Phacelia*

scorpios *pl of* SCORPIO

scor·pi·u·rus \ˌskȯ(r)pēˈyu̇rəs\ *n, cap* [NL, fr. LL, a kind of heliotrope, fr. L *scorpiuron*, fr. Gk *skorpiouron*, fr. neut. of *skorpiouros* having a tail like that of a scorpion, fr. *skorpios* scorpion + *-ouros* -urous — more at SCORPION] **:** a genus of herbs (family Leguminosae) of the Mediterranean region and the Canary islands having simple leaves, small yellow flowers on naked peduncles, and twisted pods

scorse \ˈskȯ(ə)rs\ *vb* [prob. alter. of ²*corse*] *dial Eng* **:** EXCHANGE, TRADE

scor·za·lite \ˈskȯ(r)zəˌlīt\ *n* -s [Evaristo P. *Scorza* Brazilian mineralogist + E *-lite*] **:** a mineral $FeAl_2(PO_4)_2(OH)_2$ consisting of basic phosphate of iron and aluminum, isomorphous with lazulite

scor·zo·ne·ra \ˌskȯ(r)zəˈnirə\ *n* [NL, fr. Sp *escorzonera* black salsify, fr. Catal *escurçonera*, fr. *escurçó* viper, fr. (assumed) VL *excurtion-, excurtio*, fr. L *ex-* + LL *curtion-, curtio* viper, fr. L *curtus* short + *-ion-, -io* -ion — more at SHEAR] **1** *cap* **:** a large genus of European herbs (family Compositae) having narrow leaves and solitary heads of yellow flowers on long peduncles with plumose pappus and ribbed achenes — see BLACK SALSIFY **2** -s **:** any plant or root of the genus *Scorzonera*

¹**scot** \ˈskät, *usu* -äd.+V\ *n* -s *cap* [ME *Scottes* (pl.) Scotchmen, fr. OE *Scottas* Irishmen, Scotchmen, fr. LL *Scotus, Scottus* Irishman] **1 :** one of a Gaelic people of northern Ireland settling in Scotland about A.D.500 and giving it their name **2 a :** a native or inhabitant of Scotland **b :** one that is of Scotch descent

²**scot** \"\ *n* -s [ME, fr. ON *skot* shot, contribution — more at SHOT] **:** an amount of money assessed or paid

³**scot** \"\ *vt* **scotted; scotted; scotting; scots :** to assess for tax

scot and lot *n* [ME] **1 :** a parish assessment formerly laid on subjects in Great Britain according to their ability to pay **2 :** obligations of all kinds taken as a whole ⟨experienced men of the world know very well that it is best to pay *scot and lot* as they go along —R.W.Emerson⟩

¹**scotch** \ˈskäch\ *vt* -ED/-ING/-ES [ME *scocchen*, prob. fr. AF *escocher* to make an incision, fr. MF *es-* ex- + *coche* notch] **1** *archaic* **:** CUT, GASH, SCORE ⟨he ~*ed* him and notched him like a carbonado —Shak.⟩ **2 :** to injure so as to make temporarily harmless ⟨~*ed* the snake, not killed it —Shak.⟩ ⟨what seemed crushed had only been ~*ed* —*Times Lit. Supp.*⟩ **3 a :** to put a stop to **:** stamp out **:** CRUSH ⟨luckily the mischief was as quickly ~*ed* —Mrs. Humphry Ward⟩ **b :** to end decisively by demonstrating the falsity of ⟨the newspapers ~*ed* reports that four ministers . . . had resigned by publishing a photograph —*N.Y.Times*⟩ ⟨statistics of some accuracy were made available and the depopulation theory was finally ~*ed* —J.H.Plumb⟩

²**scotch** \"\ *n* -ES **1 :** a slight cut **:** SCORE **2 :** one of the lines marked on the ground for hopscotch

³**scotch** \"\ *adj, usu cap* [contr. of ¹*scottish*] **1 a :** of, relating to, or characteristic of Scotland **b :** of, relating to, or characteristic of the inhabitants of Scotland **2 :** of, relating to, or characteristic of the English language of Scotland **3 :** FRUGAL

syn SCOTCH, SCOTTISH, and SCOTS can all apply to what constitutes, belongs to, or derives from the people of Scotland. SCOTCH is most widely used outside Scotland, esp. in the spoken language ⟨the entire *Scotch* people⟩ ⟨the inconvenience of having nothing in England like the *Scotch* one-pound note —J.A.Todd⟩ ⟨a schism in the *Scotch* Church —O.W Holmes †1935⟩ ⟨the overwhelming proportion being English, *Scotch*, or Irish in descent —*Carnegie Mag.*⟩ ⟨a *Scotch* painter⟩ ⟨not all the Scottish names that survive today are truly *Scotch* in origin —H.L.Mencken⟩ SCOTTISH has a more literary, less colloquial flavor and use ⟨the zest, courage, and good humor of the nineteenth-century *Scottish* author are infectious —E.A. Bloom⟩ ⟨she left for Edinburgh the following year to assume the *Scottish* crown —Geoffrey Bruun & H.S.Commager⟩ ⟨the *Scottish* Universities —J.G.Winant⟩ ⟨*Scottish* literature⟩ SCOTS is used in the same way as SCOTTISH ⟨the names of *Scots* and English shipowners —Joseph Conrad⟩ ⟨a *Scots* writer —Howard M. Jones⟩ except that SCOTS is sometimes preferred to SCOTTISH in reference to law and in historical references to money ⟨a pound *Scots*⟩ In Scotland itself SCOTTISH and SCOTS are often preferred to SCOTCH ⟨a delegation of *Scottish* editors —*Scotsman*⟩ ⟨*Scottish* cricket —*Scotsman*⟩ ⟨the *Scots* community in New York —*Scotsman*⟩ ⟨new *Scots* air link —*Scotsman*⟩ but SCOTCH also is used ⟨the signs confirmed my recollection that the *Scotch* Scotch are not ashamed of the word *Scotch* and do not go about protesting that *Scottish* and *Scots* are preferable forms —A.J.Liebling⟩ esp. with regard to the products of Scotland ⟨wool jersey . . . and *Scotch* tweeds are favorite fabrics —*Women's Wear Daily*⟩

⁴**scotch** \"\ *n* -ES *see sense 2* **1** *cap* **:** SCOTS **2** *pl in constr, cap* **:** the people of Scotland **3** *often cap* **a :** SCOTCH WHISKY **b :** a drink of Scotch whisky

⁵**scotch** \"\ *n* -ES [origin unknown] **1 :** a chock placed under a wheel or other curved object to prevent rolling or slipping **2 :** IMPEDIMENT ⟨now there was a ~ in his running with her —D.H.Lawrence⟩

⁶**scotch** \"\ *vb* -ED/-ING/-ES *vi, dial chiefly Eng* **:** to exercise self-control or hesitate before acting ~ *vt* **1 :** to block with a chock to prevent rolling or slipping ⟨~*ed* the back wheels of the wagon with two pieces of wood⟩ **2 :** to put an obstacle in the way of **:** HINDER, THWART ⟨sensible and limited proposals for the reform of spelling and grammar have been ~*ed* —C.P. Barbier⟩ **3 :** to wedge into place ⟨~*ed* a flat stone behind each wheel —E.L.Thomas⟩ ⟨tried to break the slat by ~*ing* it against the wall and hitting it with her foot —H.E.Bates⟩

⁷**scotch** *var of* SCUTCH

Scotch \"\ *trademark* — used for any of numerous adhesive tapes that typically have a tacky coating of a pressure-sensitive adhesive on paper, cloth, or film and can be sealed under slight pressure without heating or moistening: as **a :** a transparent tape with a cellophane or cellulose acetate backing used chiefly for sealing, mending, or attaching **b :** a tape with an impregnated paper backing used as a masking tape (as in painting)

scotch baptist *n, usu cap S&B* [³*scotch*] **:** a member of a Baptist denomination composed chiefly of immigrants from Scotland to northern England uniting with the English Disciples of Christ to form the Churches of Christ

scotch barley *n, usu cap S* **:** HULLED BARLEY

scotch blue *n, often cap S* **:** a dark purplish blue that is slightly stronger and very slightly lighter than homage blue and slightly lighter than national flag blue — called also *infernal blue*

scotch brier *n, usu cap S* **:** any of a race or class of roses developed from the Scotch rose

scotch broom *n, usu cap S* **:** a deciduous erect, spreading, or occas. prostrate broom (*Cytisus scoparius*) that is native to western Europe, is widely cultivated for its bright yellow or sometimes partly red flowers, and has escaped in several areas to become a destructive pest

scotch broth *n, usu cap S* **:** a soup made from beef or mutton and vegetables and thickened with barley

scotch cap *n, usu cap S* **1 :** BONNET 1a **2 :** GLENGARRY

scotch carpet *n, usu cap S* [so called fr. its being made largely in Scotland] **:** KIDDERMINSTER

scotch cart *n, usu cap S* **:** a small two-wheeled cart of southern Africa with a detachable or slanting panel at the back

scotch catch *n, usu cap S* **:** SCOTCH SNAP

scotch collie *n, usu cap S* **:** COLLIE 1

scotch comb *n, usu cap S* **:** a steel comb used to dress the coat of an animal

scotch crocus *n, usu cap S* **:** any of various early-flowering white to lilac or white and lilac cultivated crocuses derived from a species (*Crocus biflorus*) that is native from Italy eastward to Persia

scotch deerhound *n, usu cap S* **:** DEERHOUND

scotch douche *n, usu cap S* **:** a douche with alternate spraying of hot and cold water

scotched *past of* SCOTCH

scotch edge *n, usu cap S* **:** an extension of the outside edge of the outsole of a shoe — called also *spade edge*

scotch elm *n, usu cap S* **:** WYCH ELM

¹**scotch·er** \ˈskächə(r)\ *n* -s **:** one that scotches

²**scotcher** *var of* SCUTCHER

scotches *pres 3d sing of* SCOTCH, *pl of* SCOTCH

scotch fiddle *n, usu cap S* [³*scotch*] **:** ITCH

scotch fingering *n, usu cap S* **:** a loose woolen yarn used in knitting

scotch fir *n, usu cap S* **:** Scotch pine or its wood

scotch foursome *n, usu cap S* **:** FOURSOME 2b

scotch gaelic *n, cap S&G* **:** SCOTTISH GAELIC

scotch gale *n, usu cap S* **:** SWEET GALE

scotch grain *or* **scotch grain leather** *n, usu cap S* **:** a heavy leather marked by a coarse pebbled grain, made usu. of chrome-tanned cowhide, and used esp. for men's shoes

scotch grass *n, usu cap S* **:** PARA GRASS

scotch gray *n, often cap S* **:** a grayish yellow green that is yellower and paler than average sage green or palmetto and greener and duller than mermaid

scotch hands *n pl, usu cap S* **:** a pair of small paddles for working butter

scotch heath *n, usu cap S* **1 :** SCOTCH HEATHER **2 :** TWISTED HEATH

scotch heather *n, usu cap S* **:** a heather (*Calluna vulgaris*)

scotch-hoppers \ˈ=ˌ==\ *n pl but sing in constr, usu cap S* [²*scotch*] **:** HOPSCOTCH

scotch·i·fy \ˈskächəˌfī\ *vt* -ED/-ING/-ES *often cap* **:** to make Scotch

scotch·i·ness \-chēnəs\ *n* -ES *usu cap* **:** the quality or state of being Scotchy

Scotch hands

scotching *n* -s [fr. gerund of ¹*scotch*] **:** the act or process of dressing stone with a pointed instrument (as a pick)

scotch-irish \ˈ=ˈ==\ *adj, usu cap S&I* [³*scotch*] **1 :** of, relating to, or characteristic of the population of northern Ireland that is descended from Scotch settlers **2 :** of, relating to, or characteristic of the people of Scotch descent emigrating from northern Ireland to the U.S. before 1846 or their descendants

scotch kale *n, usu cap S* **:** any of various kales with light green tightly curled leaves

scotch laburnum *n, usu cap S* **:** an ornamental European shrub or tree (*Laburnum alpinum*) having the pod with the upper suture winged

scotch lovage *n, usu cap S* **:** LOVAGE b

scotch·man \ˈskächmən\ *n, pl* **scotchmen 1** *cap* **a :** a man who is a native or inhabitant of Scotland **b :** a man of Scotch descent **2** *sometimes cap* **:** a piece of metal, wood, leather, or canvas used (as over a rope) to prevent chafing **3** *usu cap* **:** a professional golfer **4 :** SCOTSMAN 2

scotch marigold *n, usu cap S* **:** POT MARIGOLD

scotch marriage *n, usu cap S* **:** COMMON-LAW MARRIAGE

scotch mist *n, usu cap S* **1 :** a dense mist mixed with drizzle **2 :** WOOD BEDSTRAW — **scotch-misty** \ˈ=ˈ==\ *adj, usu cap S*

scotch·ness \ˈskächnəs\ *n* -ES *usu cap* **:** the quality or state of being Scotch

scotch nightingale *n, usu cap S* **:** SEDGE WARBLER

scotch pebble *n, usu cap S* **:** a pebble of cryptocrystalline quartz (as agate or chalcedony) found in Scotland and used for ornament after being cut and polished

scotch pine *n, usu cap S* **:** a pine (*Pinus sylvestris*) of northern Europe and Asia with spreading or pendulous branches, short rigid twisted needles, and hard yellow wood that provides valuable timber

scotch rose *n, usu cap S* **:** a thorny Eurasian rose (*Rosa spinosissima*) with small leaflets, pink, white, or yellow flowers, and globose black fruit

scotch snap *n, usu cap S* **:** a rhythmic figure that consists of a sixteenth note on the beat followed by a dotted eighth note

scotch stone *n, usu cap 1st S* **:** AYR STONE

scotch-tape \ˈ=ˈ=\ *vt* **:** to fasten with or apply Scotch tape to ⟨cracked window had been neatly *scotch-taped* —Richard Wormser⟩

scotch terrier *n, usu cap S* **:** SCOTTISH TERRIER

scotch thistle *n, usu cap S* **1 :** any of several European thistles **2** [so called fr. its use as the national emblem of Scotland] **:** COTTON THISTLE

scotch topaz *n, usu cap S* **:** a cairngorm that resembles yellow topaz

scotch verdict *n, usu cap S* **1 :** a verdict of not proven that is allowed by Scottish criminal law in some cases instead of a verdict of not guilty **2 :** an inconclusive decision or pronouncement

scotch whisky *n, usu cap S* **:** whiskey distilled in Scotland in a patent still or a pot still

scotch whist *n, usu cap S* **:** CATCH THE TEN

scotchwoman \ˈ=ˌ==\ *n, pl* **scotchwomen** *cap* **:** a woman of Scotch birth, nationality, or origin

scotch woodcock *n, usu cap S* **:** toast spread with anchovy paste and topped with soft scrambled egg

scotchy \ˈskächē\ *adj* -ER/-EST *usu cap* [³*scotch* + *-y*] **:** having Scotch characteristics

scotch yoke *n, usu cap S* **:** a slotted crosshead used (as in a donkey engine or steam fire engine) in place of a connecting rod

sco·ter \ˈskōd.ə(r), |tə-\ *also* **scoo·ter** \ˈskü|\ *n, pl* **scoters** *or* **scoter** *also* **scooters** [origin unknown] **:** any of several sea ducks constituting the genera *Oidemia* and *Melanitta* that inhabit the northern coasts of Europe and No. America and some larger inland waters

scot-free \ˈ=ˈ=\ *adj* [²*scot* + *free*] **1 :** free from obligation to pay (as a tax, tribute, or bill) ⟨a mere handful may be owners of land and be taxed while many may own their own houses and escape *scot-free* —Brian Chapman⟩ **2 :** completely free of harm ⟨some soul walking *scot-free* in the place of torment —Joseph Conrad⟩ **3 :** completely free of penalty ⟨all his clients were guilty and all of them got off *scot-free* —Norman Douglas⟩

sco·tia \ˈskōsh(ē)ə\ *n* -s [L, fr. Gk *skotia*, darkness, fr. *skotos* darkness; fr. the deep shadow which it casts — more at SHADE] **:** a concave molding used esp. in classical architecture in the bases of columns — see BASE illustration, MOLDING illustration

scot·ic \ˈskäd.ik\ *adj, usu cap* [LL *scoticus, scotticus*, fr. *Scotus, Scottus* Scot + L *-icus* -ic] **:** of or relating to the ancient Scots

scoticism *usu cap, var of* SCOTTICISM

sco·tism \ˈskōˌtizəm\ *n* -s *usu cap* [John Duns *Scotus* †*ab*1308 Scot. scholastic theologian + E *-ism*] **:** the doctrines of the Scholastic Duns Scotus who in his criticism of Thomism proposes a separation of philosophy and theology approaching the conception of twofold truth and is known esp. for his voluntarism, logical realism, and principles of haecceity and the plurality of substantial forms

sco·tist \-ōd.əst\ *n* -s *usu cap* [John Duns *Scotus* + E *-ist*] **:** an adherent of Scotism

sco·tis·tic \skəˈtistik, skōˈ-\ *also* **scotist** *adj, usu cap* **:** of, relating to, or characteristic of Scotism or Scotists

scot·land \ˈskätlənd\ *adj, usu cap* [fr. *Scotland*, northern part of the island of Great Britain] **:** of or from Scotland **:** of the kind or style prevalent in Scotland **:** SCOTCH, SCOTTISH

scoto- *comb form, usu cap* [NL, fr. LL *Scotus* Scot] **1 :** Scotch ⟨*Scoto-Celtic*⟩ **2 :** Scotch and ⟨*Scoto-Irish*⟩

scot·o·din·ia \ˌskäd.əˈdinēə, ˌskōd-\ *n* -s [NL, fr. Gk *skotos* darkness + *dinos* whirling; dizziness + NL *-ia* — more at SHADE, DINO-] **:** dizziness with headache and impairment of sight

scot·o·graph \ˈskäd.əˌgraf, ˈskōd-, -ˌräf\ *n* [Gk *skotos* darkness + E *-graph*] **:** RADIOGRAPH

sco·to·ma \skəˈtōmə, skōˈ-\ *n, pl* **scotomas** \-məz\ *or* **scotomata** \-məd.ə\ [NL *scotomat-, scotoma*, fr. ML, dimness of vision, fr. Gk *skotōmat-, skotōma*, fr. *skotoun* to darken, blind, fr. *skotos* darkness — more at SHADE] **:** a blind or dark spot in the visual field

sco·tom·a·tous \-ˈtäməd.əs\ *adj* [NL *scotomat-, scotoma* + E *-ous*] **:** of, relating to, or affected with scotoma

scotomy *n* -ES [ML *scotomia*, alter. of *scotoma*] *obs* **:** dizziness with dimness of sight

scot·o·pe·lia \ˌskäd.əˈpēlēə, ˌskōd.əˈ-\ *n, cap* [NL, fr. Gk *skotos* darkness + *pelios* livid; akin to Gk *polios* gray — more at SHADOW, FALLOW] **:** a genus of African owls (family Bubonidae) comprising the fish owls

sco·to·pia \skəˈtōpēə, skōˈ-\ *n* -s [NL, fr. Gk *skotos* darkness + NL *-opia*] **:** vision in dim light with dark-adapted eyes believed to be mediated by the rods of the retina — opposed to *photopia* — **sco·top·ic** \-ˈtäpik\ *adj*

¹**scots** \ˈskäts\ *adj, usu cap* [ME *scottis*, alter. of *scottish*] **:** ³SCOTCH 1, 2 **syn** see SCOTCH

²**scots** \"\ *n* -ES *cap* **:** the English language of Scotland

³**scots** *pl of* SCOT, *pres 3d sing of* SCOT

scots broom *n, usu cap S* **:** SCOTCH BROOM

scots elm *n, usu cap S* **:** WYCH ELM

scots grey *n, usu cap S&G* **:** YELLOW-FEVER MOSQUITO

scots·man \ˈskätsmən\ *n, pl* **scotsmen** *see sense 2* [ME *Scottisman*, fr. *Scottis* Scots + *man*] **1** *cap* **:** SCOTCHMAN 1 **2** *or pl* **scotsman :** a brilliantly colored southern African marine percoid food fish (*Polysteganus praeorbitalis*)

scots pine *n, usu cap S* **:** SCOTCH PINE

scots pint *n, usu cap S* **:** an old unit of capacity equivalent to about three imperial pints

scotswoman \ˈ=ˌ==\ *n, pl* **scotswomen** *cap* **:** SCOTCHWOMAN

scott connection *n, usu cap S* [fr. the proper name *Scott*] **:** T CONNECTION

scotted *past of* SCOT

scot·ti·cism \ˈskäd.əˌsizəm, -ätə,-\ *n* -s *usu cap* [LL *scotticus* Scotic + E *-ism*] **1 :** a characteristic feature of Scottish English esp. as contrasted with the standard English of England **2** *or* **scot·i·cism** \"\ **:** predilection for what is Scottish

scot·ti·cize \-ˌsīz\ *vt* -ED/-ING/-S *see -ize in Explan Notes, often cap* [LL *scotticus* + E *-ize*] **1 :** SCOTCHIFY **2 :** to cause to conform with the characteristics of Scottish English ⟨*scotticized* the Latin words without any scruple⟩

scot·tie \ˈskäd.|ē, -ät|, |i\ *n* -s [¹*scot* + *-ie*] **1** *cap* **:** SCOTCHMAN 1 **2** *also* **scot·ty** -ES *often cap* \"\ **:** SCOTTISH TERRIER

scot·ti·fi·ca·tion \ˌskäd.əfəˈkāshən\ *n* -s *often cap* [LL *Scottus* Scot + E *-i-* + *-fication*] **:** the act, action, or product of scotticizing

scot·ti·fy \ˈskäd.əˌfī\ *vt* -ED/-ING/-ES *often cap* [LL *Scottus* Scot + E *-ify*] **:** SCOTTICIZE

scotting *pres part of* SCOT

¹**scot·tish** \ˈskäd.|ish, -ät|, |ēsh\ *adj, usu cap* [ME *scottisc, scottish*, fr. *Scottes* Scotchmen + *-isc, -ish* -ish — more at SCOT] **:** SCOTCH 1, 2 **syn** see SCOTCH

²**scottish** \"\ *n* -ES *cap* **:** SCOTS

scottish asphodel *n, usu cap S* **:** an herb (*Tofieldia palustris*) of the north temperate zone that has a dense raceme of small greenish flowers

scottish blackface *n* **1** *usu cap S&B* **:** a Scottish breed of hardy black-faced long-wooled mutton sheep used esp. in crossbreeding for better meat production **2** *usu cap S & often cap B* **:** a sheep of the Scottish Blackface breed

scottish deerhound *n, usu cap S* **:** DEERHOUND

scottish gaelic *n, cap S&G* **:** the Gaelic language of Scotland — see INDO-EUROPEAN LANGUAGES table

scottish-gaelic *adj, usu cap S&G* [*Scottish Gaelic*] **:** of, relating to, or characteristic of the Gaelic language of Scotland

scot·tish·ly *adv, usu cap* : in a Scottish manner
scot·tish·man \'ˌ==mən\ *n, pl* **scottishmen** *cap* : SCOTCHMAN 1
scot·tish·ness *n* -ES *usu cap* : SCOTCHNESS
scottish philosophy *n, usu cap S* : the natural realism developed by the Scottish school principally in reaction to Berkeleian idealism and Humean skepticism
scottish rite *n, usu cap S & often cap R* **1** : a ceremonial observed by one of the Masonic systems **2** : a system or organization that observes the Scottish rite and confers 33 degrees — compare YORK RITE
scottish terrier *n* **1** *usu cap S&T* : an old Scottish breed of terrier that has short legs, a large head with small prick ears and a powerful muzzle, a broad deep chest, and a very hard coat of wiry hair about two inches long **2** *usu cap S & often cap T* : a dog of the Scottish Terrier breed
scott's spleenwort \'skäts-\ *n, usu cap 1st S* [prob. after D. H. *Scott* †1934 Eng. botanist] : EBONY SPLEENWORT
scouch \'skaůch\ *var of* SCOOCH
¹scoun·drel \'skaůndrəl\ *n* -S [origin unknown] **1** : a bold selfish man that has very low ethical standards **2** : RASCAL **syn** see VILLAIN
²scoundrel \"\ *adj* : SCOUNDRELLY ⟨all sorts of coarse artifices and ~ flatteries —W.M.Thackeray⟩
scoun·drel·dom \-ldəm\ *n* -S [*¹scoundrel* + *-dom*] : scoundrels as a class or as a body
scoun·drel·ism \-rə,lizəm\ *n* -S : the character or behavior of a scoundrel
scoun·drel·ly \-rəlē\ *adj* [*¹scoundrel* + *-ly*] : of, relating to, or having the characteristics of a scoundrel ⟨I will none of his ~ money —Thomas Carlyle⟩ ⟨the tyranny of a ~ aristocracy —W.M.Thackeray⟩
scoup \'sküp\ *vi* [ME *scoupen*, of Scand origin; akin to ON *skopa* to take or run — more at SKIP] *chiefly Scot* : to run with skips and leaps
¹scour \'skaů(ə)r, -aůə\ *vb* -ED/-ING/-S [ME *scuren, scouren*, prob. of Scand origin; akin to Sw *skura* to rush] *vi* **1 a** : to hurry about in search of something ⟨~*ed* over the hillside for kindling⟩ **b** : to move rapidly : RUSH ⟨wild as a hare . . . ~*ed* thro' the heather —Hilary Corke⟩ ⟨~*ed* on my way with more speed than before —George Borrow⟩ **2** *obs* : to roister violently through the streets ~ *vt* **1 a** : to move rapidly through (a region or area) ⟨each bishop was a missionary . . . ~*ing* the surrounding districts —G.G.Coulton⟩ **b** : to range usu. rapidly through (a region or area) in search of something ⟨~*ed* the town in vain for more yellow roses —Edith Wharton⟩ ⟨~*ed* Europe in search of cheap labor —*Amer. Guide Series: Mass.*⟩ **c** : to make a thorough examination or search of ⟨~*ed* all the official documents and wrote his novel⟩ **2** *obs* : to subject to rough treatment while roistering **syn** see SEEK
²scour \"\ *n* -S : rapid motion : RUSH ⟨the white-hot ~ of racing gases —J.N.Leonard⟩
³scour \"\ *vb* -ED/-ING/-S [ME *scouren*, prob. fr. MD *schuren*, fr. OF *escurer*, fr. LL *excurare* to clean off, fr. L *ex-* + *curare* to care for, cleanse — more at CURE] *vt* **1 a** : to rub hard esp. with a rough material for the purpose of cleansing : make clean and bright by friction and washing ⟨~*ed* the pans until they gleamed⟩ **b** : to remove by rubbing hard and washing ⟨~*ed* the stains off with strong soap⟩ **c** : to take the flesh from (a hide) by rubbing **2** *archaic* : to make (a region or area) free (as from undesired occupants) : RID ⟨~ me this famous realm of enemies —Francis Beaumont & John Fletcher⟩ **3** : to clean by purging : PURGE **4** *obs* : BEAT, PUNISH ⟨I will pay the dog, I will ~ him —Henry Fielding⟩ **5** : to clear (as a pipe or ditch) by removing dirt and debris **6** : to cleanse from natural impurities or processing liquids; *esp* : to cleanse (raw wool) by washing **7** *archaic* : to rake with gunfire **8** : to remove as if by rubbing or cleaning; *esp* : to carry off (as by a flood) ⟨the tide enters far up each channel ~*ing* out mud and sand —Charles Lyell⟩ **9 a** : to clear or dig by a powerful current of water ⟨at time of flood the stream may break across and ~ out a channel through the narrow neck between adjacent meanders —C.A.Cotton⟩ **b** : to wear away (as by water, ice, or wind) : ERODE ⟨was born of lean land but raised on newer better soils before they were wracked and ~*ed* —Russell Lord⟩ ⟨the tops of hills and level places where there was only a small amount of mantlerock were ~*ed* by the continental glaciers —E.B. Branson & W.A.Tarr⟩ **10** : to free (grain) from dust, loose bran, and other wastes by blowing while rubbing against a rough surface ~ *vi* **1** : to perform a process of scouring ⟨~*ed* at rusted spots —*Monsanto Mag.*⟩ **2** : to suffer from diarrhea or dysentery : PURGE **3 a** : to pass through the ground in soil tillage without any soil clinging to the smooth blade of the cultivating implement ⟨this plow ~*s* well⟩ **b** : to become polished when in contact with the soil
⁴scour \"\ *n* -S **1** : a place scoured by running water **2 a** : the scouring action of a current of water or a glacier **b** (1) : an artificial current of water that is used to remove mud or other deposit from the bed of a stream (2) : an engineering structure built to produce such a current **3** *Scot* : a hearty swig **4** : DIARRHEA, DYSENTERY — usu. used in pl. but sing. or pl. in constr. **5** : SCOURING
¹scour·er \-aůrə(r)\ *n* -S [*¹scour* + *-er*] : one that scours: as **a** *archaic* : one who roisters violently through the streets **b** : one who ranges far and wide ⟨the relentless boy ~ of Patagonian seas —Bret Harte⟩
²scourer \"\ *n* -S [*³scour* + *-er*] **1** : one whose work consists of scouring: as **a** : one who cleans drains **b** : one who polishes or cleanses by scouring **c** : one who smooths and stretches hides by scraping **d** : one who scours shoe lasts to shape on an abrasive wheel **2** : a machine that scours; *specif* : a machine that scours wheat
¹scourge \'skərj, 'skəj, 'skəij *sometimes* 'skō(ə)rj *or* 'skȯ(ə)rj *or* -ōəj *or* -ȯ(ə)j\ *n* -S [ME, fr. AF *escorge*, fr. (assumed) OF *escorgier* to whip, drive out with a whip (whence OF *escorgiée* whip), fr. OF *es-* ex- (fr. L *ex-*) + L *corrigia* shoelace, strap, whip — more at CORRIGIOLA] **1** : WHIP; *esp* : a whip that is used to inflict pain or punishment **2 a** : one that is an instrument of punishment or severe criticism ⟨can safely ignore it and talk as if he had always been the ~ of reaction —R.H. Rovere⟩ **b** : a cause of widespread or great affliction: as (1) : a person who brings misery ⟨made himself the special ~ of the region —C.L.Jones⟩ (2) : a wasting disease that affects a large area ⟨smallpox finally ceased to be a ~ —*Amer. Guide Series: Mass.*⟩ (3) : a large destructive swarm ⟨a ~ of grasshoppers descended and devoured every sprig of vegetation —*Amer. Guide Series: Texas*⟩ (4) : a social evil ⟨the ~ of recurrent unemployment —Archibald MacLeish⟩
²scourge \"\ *vt* -ED/-ING/-S [ME *scourgen*, fr. *¹scourge*] **1** : to whip severely : LASH, FLOG **2 a** : to punish severely ⟨God had not yet sufficiently *scourged* the city —Daniel Defoe⟩ **b** : to subject to a great affliction : DEVASTATE ⟨barbarians *scourged* the land and destroyed all civilization⟩ ⟨dust storms *scourged* the prairie states —*Newsweek*⟩ **c** : to force into a position as if by the blows of a whip ⟨television . . . is going to ~ the phonies out of politics —Stuart Chase⟩ **d** : to subject to severe criticism or satire ⟨~*s* the schools for their low standards⟩ **3** *Scot* : to cause (as soil) to become exhausted
scourg·er \-jə(r)\ *n* -S : one that scourges; *specif* : a public official charged with scourging
scour·ing \'skaůriŋ, -rēŋ\ *n* -S [ME, fr. *scouren* to scour + *-ing*] **1** : the act or action of one that scours **2** : the process of cleaning raw stock, yarns, or cloth; *specif* : the removal of impurities (as natural grease and foreign substances) from raw wool usu. by a series of washings in soap, alkalies, or chemical solvents **3 a** : material removed by scouring or cleaning : REFUSE ⟨the patients in the pump room don't swallow the ~*s* of the bathers —Tobias Smollett⟩ **b** : the lowest rank of society : SCUM — usu. used in pl. ⟨the associate of the ~*s* of the jail and hulks —Charles Dickens⟩ **4** : the erosion of earth or rock by the action of flowing water or of a glacier
scouring barrel *n* : TUMBLING BARREL
scouring cinder *n* : a basic slag that is produced in an iron blast furnace, is rich in ferrous oxide, and attacks the furnace lining by taking silica from it
scouring rush *n* : a plant of the order Equisetales; *esp* : a widely distributed plant (*Equisetum hyemale*) with strongly siliceous stems formerly used for scouring utensils
scours *pres 3d sing of* SCOUR, *pl of* SCOUR
scourway \'=,=\ *n* [*³scour* + *way*] : a channel formed by a strong current; *esp* : one of the channels of temporary streams associated with margins of Pleistocene ice sheets
scouse \'skaůs\ *n* -S [by shortening] : LOBSCOUSE
¹scout \'skaůt, *usu* -aůd.+V\ *vb* -ED/-ING/-S [ME *scouten*, fr. MF *escouter* to listen, attend to, fr. OF *ascouter*, fr. L *auscultare* to listen — more at AUSCULTATION] *vi* **1** : to explore an area to obtain information (as about an enemy) ⟨~ far and wide into the realm of night —John Milton⟩ **2 a** : to make a search ⟨descended into the basement to ~ around for available lumber —H.A.Overstreet⟩ ⟨began to ~ for a better way to do this —*Linotype News*⟩ **b** : to act as an athletic scout ⟨the jobs of coaching the freshman football team and ~*ing* for the varsity team —*Current Biog.*⟩ **3** *archaic* : to act as a fielder in cricket ~ *vt* **1 a** : to observe in order to obtain information ⟨rode back through the little basin once more carefully ~*ing* the cabin —P.E.Lehman⟩ **b** : to observe (as an athlete or an actor) in order to evaluate ⟨whispered phony rumors to the cast telling them that producers were out front to ~ them —June Allyson⟩ **2** : to explore in order to obtain information : RECONNOITER ⟨had his dragoons to ~ the territory ahead of him —F.V.W.Mason⟩ **3** : to find by making a search ⟨launched the artists he had ~*ed*⟩ ⟨~*s* his own material —Roger Angell⟩ ⟨could ~ up clients and talk up lawsuits —Jackson Burgess⟩
²scout \"\ *n* -S [MF *escoute* act of listening, listener, sentry, fr. *escouter* to listen] **1 a** : the act of scouting ⟨set myself upon the ~ as often as possible —Daniel Defoe⟩ **b** : a scouting expedition : RECONNAISSANCE ⟨set out on foot for a week's rapid ~ in the hope of finding just the right place for a permanent camp —D.C.Worcester⟩ **2 a** : one sent out to obtain and bring back information (as about the position and movements of an enemy) **b** (1) : WATCHMAN, LOOKOUT (2) *archaic* : SPY, SNEAK **c** *archaic* : a reconnoitering party **d** : one employed by a petroleum company to obtain information about prospective oil well locations and operations **3 a** : a ship sent out in war to reconnoiter and obtain information about the position, movements, and strength of the enemy **b** : AIR SCOUT **4** : a servant to a student at Oxford University **5** : a person whose occupation is searching for something rare or difficult to find ⟨the very prince of ~*s* for searching blind alleys, cellars, and stalls for rare volumes —Sir Walter Scott⟩ **6** *archaic* **a** : a fielder in cricket **b** : a boy who chases and returns hit balls in baseball batting practice **7 a** : BOY SCOUT **b** : GIRL SCOUT **8** : FELLOW, GUY — usu. used in the phrase *good scout* **9 a** (1) : a person sent out to secure firsthand information about the style of play, tactics, and strength of a rival in sports (2) : a person sent out by a professional club or by a college to obtain information about players by watching them in action with a view to making recommendations about the acquisition of players **b** : a person sent out to search for talented newcomers to a profession ⟨a ~ for the motion-picture industry⟩
³scout \"\ *n* -S [ME, fr. MD *schute*; akin to ON *skūta* small ship, OE *scēotan* to shoot — more at SHOOT] : SCHUYT
⁴scout \"\ *n* -S [origin unknown] **1** : GUILLEMOT **2** : RAZORBILL
⁵scout \"\ *vb* -ED/-ING/-S [of Scand origin; akin to ON *skūta*, *skūti* taunt — more at SHOUT] *vt* **1** : to make fun of : MOCK, DERIDE ⟨~*ed* the stories as he told them⟩ **2** : to reject scornfully : dismiss as absurd ⟨economists still ~ the idea that the new wave of price hikes spells inflation —*Newsweek*⟩ ~ *vi* : SCOFF — usu. used with *at* ⟨~*ed* at the greenness of the cit who would build his sole piazza to the north —Herman Melville⟩ **syn** see DESPISE
scout car *n* [*¹scout*] **1** : a fast armored military reconnaissance vehicle with a four-wheel drive and an open top **2** : a police patrol car
scoutcraft \'=,=\ *n* [*²scout* + *craft*] : the craft, skill, or practice of a scout
scout·er \'skaůd.ə(r), -aůtə-\ *n* -S **1** : one that scouts **2** : a member of the Boy Scouts of America over 18 years of age
scouth \'sküth\ *n* [origin unknown] **1** *Scot* : ROOM, RANGE, SCOPE **2** *Scot* : PLENTY
scou·ther \'sküthər\ *n* [origin unknown] **1** *dial Scot* : a light shower **2** *dial Scot* : a light fall of snow
scouting *n* -S [in sense 1 fr. *gerund* of *¹scout*; in other senses prob. fr. *²scout* + *-ing*] **1** : the action of one that scouts **2** : the organization, program, activities, and leadership of the various worldwide Boy Scout and Girl Scout movements **3** : SCOUTCRAFT
scout·ing·ly *adv* [*scouting* (fr. pres. part. of *⁵scout*) + *-ly*] : in a scornful manner
scouting plane *n* [*scouting* (fr. pres. part. of *¹scout*) + *plane*] : AIR SCOUT
scoutmaster \'=,==\ *n* [*²scout* + *master*] : the leader of a band of scouts; *specif* : the adult leader of a troop of boy scouts
scouts *pres 3d sing of* SCOUT, *pl of* SCOUT
scove \'skōv\ *vt* -ED/-ING/-S [prob. of Scand origin; akin to ON *skōf* crust on the bottom of a pan, *skafa* to scrape — more at SHAVE] : to cover (the outside exposed surfaces of bricks in a kiln) with a mask of clay in order to save heat
scove kiln *n* : a kiln in which green bricks are stacked, enclosed with burned bricks that are then daubed with clay to reduce the loss of heat, and burned
scov·y \'skōvē\ *adj* [perh. fr. *scove* + *-y*] *dial Eng* : BLOTCHY, SMEARED
¹scow \'skaů\ *n* -S [D *schouw*, fr. MD *schouwe, schoude*; akin to OHG *scalta* cutoff pole, punt pole, *scaltan* to push, shove off, ON *skālda* pole, boat, and prob. to OE *scild, sceld* shield — more at SHIELD] **1** : a large flat-bottomed boat with broad square ends that is used chiefly for transporting sand, gravel, or refuse **2** : a sailboat of very light draft, broad beam, blunt bow, and long overhangs that is used chiefly for racing
²scow \"\ *vt* -ED/-ING/-S : to transport in a scow
³scow \"\ *vt* -ED/-ING/-S [origin unknown] : to fasten (an anchor) by the crown to the end of a cable with a stop on the cable and the ring in such a way that if the anchor fouls the stop breaks and the anchor can be lifted clear by the crown
¹scow·der \'skōdər\ *or* **scou·ther** *or* **scow·ther** \-ōthər\ *vb* -ED/-ING/-S [origin unknown] *chiefly Scot* : SCORCH
²scowder \"\ *or* **scouther** \"\ *n, chiefly Scot* : a slight burning : SCORCHING
¹scowl \'skaůl, *esp before pause or consonant* -aůəl\ *vb* -ED/-ING/-S [ME *skoulen*, prob. of Scand origin; akin to Dan *skule* to scowl] *vi* **1** : to draw down the forehead and make a face in expression of considerable displeasure : frown angrily and threateningly **2** : to exhibit a threatening aspect ⟨the mountain ~*ed* down over the valley⟩ **3** : to express itself in a scowl ⟨a menace ~*ed* upon the brow —Washington Irving⟩ ~ *vt* **1** : to express with a scowl ⟨~*ed* his disappointment at his father⟩
— **scowl·er** \-lə(r)\ *n* -S
²scowl \"\ *n* -S : a facial expression of considerable displeasure : an angry threatening frown
scowl·ing·ly *adv* [*scowling* (fr. pres. part. of *¹scowl*) + *-ly*] : with a scowl
scow·man \'skaůmən\ *n, pl* **scowmen** [*¹scow* + *man*] : one who works on a scow
scp *abbr* **1** scrip **2** script
SCP *abbr, often not cap* spherical candlepower
scr *abbr* **1** screen **2** screw; screwed **3** scrip **4** script **5** scruple
SCR *abbr* senior common room
scrab \'skrab\ *vb* **scrabbed; scrabbed; scrabbing; scrabs** [perh. fr. D *schrabben*, fr. MD] : SCRATCH
¹scrab·ble \'skrabəl\ *vb* **scrabbled; scrabbled; scrabbling** \-b(ə)liŋ\ **scrabbles** [D *schrabbelen* to scratch, paw the ground, fr. MD, freq. of *schrabben* to scratch, perh. alter. of *schrapen* to scrape — more at SCRAPE] *vi* **1** : SCRAWL, SCRIBBLE ⟨*scrabbled* on the doors of the gate —1 Sam 21:13 (AV)⟩ **2 a** : to scratch or claw about clumsily or frantically ⟨fell *scrabbling* in the dirt . . . crying "have mercy" —Rudyard Kipling⟩ **b** : to grope or search hastily or blindly ⟨began to ~ in her handbag for a handkerchief⟩ **3 a** : to struggle for a foothold : SCRAMBLE, CLAMBER ⟨six mules, by hard *scrabbling*, managed to pull the car out of the river —F.B.Gipson⟩ **b** : to struggle by or as if by scraping or scratching ⟨~ for a living on a mountain farm⟩ ~ *vt* **1** : to gather or make hastily by clutching or scraping ⟨*scrabbled* up a supper out of leftovers⟩ ⟨*scrabbled* a living as a part-time teacher and mechanic —*Time*⟩ **2** : to make scratching movements on ⟨hens *scrabbling* the muddy cobbles —Dylan Thomas⟩ or with ⟨heard the dog *scrabbling* his nails on the door⟩ **3** : to mark with irregular lines or letters : SCRIBBLE
²scrabble \"\ *n* -S **1** : something scribbled or scrawled : SCRIBBLE **2** : a repeated scratching or clawing ⟨a ~ of squirrels on the roof⟩ **3** : SCRAMBLE **4** ⟨a ~ for tickets to the game⟩ ⟨a mad ~ up the cliff⟩
Scrabble \"\ *trademark* — used for a board game in which players take turns placing letter tiles each with a count value on squares some of which are marked for extra count to form words with as high a count as possible
scrab·bler \-b(ə)lə(r)\ *n* -S : one that scrabbles
scrab·bly \-lē\ *adj* **1** : SCRATCHY, RASPY ⟨a ~ little scratching sound came out of her throat —Alma Stone⟩ **2** : SPARSE, SCRUBBY ⟨owned a ~ potato patch in Maine —Bennett Cerf⟩
scrabe \'skrāb\ *or* **scra·ber** \-bə(r)\ *n* -S [Dan & Faeroese; Dan *skrabe*, fr. Faeroese *skrāpur*; prob. akin to ON *skrapa* to scrape — more at SCRAPE] **1** : MANX SHEARWATER **2** : BLACK GUILLEMOT
¹scrae \'skrā\ *n* -S [prob. of Scand origin; akin to ON *skrā* dry skin, scroll; akin to OHG *scraz, screz* goblin, ON *skratti* monster, wizard, Lith *skrėsti* to become covered with a dry crust] **1** *Scot* : an old worn-out shoe **2** *Scot* : a thin wizened person
²scrae \"\ *dial var of* SCREE
scraf·fle \'skrafəl\ *vb* -ED/-ING/-S [perh. alter. of *¹scrabble*] *dial Eng* : SCRAMBLE
¹scrag \'skrag, -raa(ə)g, -raig\ *n* -S [perh. alter. of *²crag*] **1 a** : a rawboned or scrawny person or animal **b** *or* **scrag end** : the lean end of a neck of mutton or veal **c** : NECK **2** *Brit* : a rough crooked tree or branch **3** *or* **scrag whale** : any of various small whales with no dorsal fin but with protuberances on the dorsal ridge near the tail usu. regarded as young or abnormal examples of the right whale
²scrag \"\ *vt* **scragged; scragged; scragging; scrags** **1 a** : to execute by hanging or garroting **b** : to wring the neck of ⟨~ a turkey⟩ **2 a** : to seize roughly by the neck : CHOKE, MANHANDLE ⟨*scragged* by the angry mob⟩ ⟨before they *scragged* me and trussed me up —Rose Macaulay⟩ **b** : KILL, MURDER **3** : to bend (as spring steel) for testing
¹scragged *adj* [perh. alter. of *cragged*] *obs* : ROUGH, RUGGED
²scrag·ged \-gəd\ *adj* [*¹scrag* + *-ed*] : LEAN, SCRAWNY ⟨~ neck⟩ — **scrag·ged·ly** *adv* — **scrag·ged·ness** *n* -ES
scrag·ger \-gə(r)\ *n* -S : one that scrags; *esp* : HANGMAN
scrag·gi·ness \-gēnəs, -gin-\ *n* -ES : the quality of being scraggy
scrag·gle \'skragəl, -raig-\ *n* -S [prob. back-formation fr. *scraggled, scraggling, scraggly*] : sparse or ragged growth ⟨~*s* of grass⟩ ⟨~ of fresh beard —Conrad Richter⟩
scrag·gled \-ld\ *adj* [fr. *scraggling*, after such pairs as E *dangling* (pres. part. of *¹dangle*): *dangled* (past part. of *¹dangle*)] : SCRAGGLY
scrag·gling \-g(ə)liŋ\ *adj* [*¹scrag* + *-le* + *-ing*] : SCRAGGLY
scrag·gly \-lē, -li\ *adj* [*scraggl-* (as in *scraggling*) + *-y*] : of rough or irregular outline : RAGGED, UNKEMPT ⟨~ little path to his door —R.M.Coates⟩ : of sparse growth : STRAGGLY ⟨~ beard⟩ ⟨~, frost-heaved lawn —Roger Angell⟩ ⟨two years of ~ border warfare —A.J.Liebling⟩
scrag·gy \'skragē, -raag-, -raig-, -gi\ *adj* -ER/-EST [*¹scrag* + *-y*] **1** : rough with irregular points : RUGGED, JAGGED, KNOTTED ⟨~ cliffs⟩ **2** : lean and thin in body : BONY, MEAGER, SCRAWNY ⟨his sinewy, ~ neck —Sir Walter Scott⟩
scraich \'skrāk\ *Scot var of* SCREECH
¹scram \'skram\ *vt* **scrammed; scrammed; scramming; scrams** [ME *-skramen*] *dial chiefly Eng* : BENUMB, PARALYZE
²scram \"\ *adj, dial Eng* : WITHERED ⟨~ hand⟩
³scram \"\ *dial Eng var of* CRAM
⁴scram \'skram, -aa(ə)m\ *vi* **scrammed; scrammed; scramming; scrams** [short for *¹scramble*] : to go away at once : get out : run away ⟨you're not wanted here, so ~⟩
⁵scram \"\ *n* -S : a sudden or emergency shutting down of a nuclear reactor ⟨leaped for the ~ button⟩
scram·a·sax \'skramə,saks\ *n* -ES [LL *scramasaxus*, fr. (assumed) OFrk *skramasax*, fr. *skrama-* (akin to MHG *schram* gash) + *sax* knife (akin to OE *seax* knife, short sword) — more at CREAM, SAX] : a large knife used by the early Saxons and Franks as a weapon or hunting knife
¹scram·ble \'skrambəl, -aam-\ *vb* **scrambled; scrambled; scrambling** \-b(ə)liŋ\ **scrambles** [perh. alter. of *scrabble*] *vi* **1 a** : to move or climb hastily on all fours ⟨~ over rocks⟩ ⟨~ up a steep bank⟩ **b** : to move with the urgency of or as if of anxiety or panic ⟨*scrambled* into his clothes⟩ ⟨*scrambled* to his feet⟩ **2 a** : to struggle eagerly with others for something on the ground ⟨~ for coins⟩ **b** : to struggle or strive unceremoniously for possession of something ⟨~ for front seats⟩ ⟨all the networks *scrambled* gleefully for the film —*Newsweek*⟩ **c** : to get or gather something with difficulty or in irregular ways ⟨~ for a living⟩ ⟨had to do considerable *scrambling* to get up the tax money —*Newsweek*⟩ **3 a** : to spread or grow irregularly : SPRAWL, RAMBLE, STRAGGLE ⟨*scrambling* frontier town⟩ **b** *of a plant* : to climb upon or over a support — distinguished from *twine* **4** *of an air squadron* : to take off with all speed at the reported approach of hostile or unidentified aircraft ~ *vt* **1** : to collect by scrambling — used with *up* or *together* ⟨~ up a hasty dinner⟩ **2** : to scale or traverse by scrambling ⟨~ a cliff⟩ **3 a** : to toss or mix together in confusion : throw into disorder : JUMBLE ⟨bad weather *scrambled* the air schedules⟩ ⟨trying to collect his *scrambled* wits⟩ ⟨~ the pages of a manuscript⟩ **b** : to prepare (eggs) by stirring during frying **c** : to make (a telephonic or radio message) unintelligible to interceptors by disarranging the frequencies of the transmission **d** : to effect an interdependent combination of (government-owned and privately owned industrial property) ⟨shipyard facilities have been *scrambled* through government building on private land⟩ **4** : to cause or order (a fighter-interceptor group) to take off quickly in response to an alert
²scramble \"\ *n* -S **1** : an act of moving or climbing on all fours ⟨near the top of the hill the climb became a ~⟩ **2 a** : a jostling and pushing for possession ⟨a ~ for places at the rail⟩ **b** : an eager and unceremonious or unscrupulous struggle for possession ⟨unseemly ~ for invitations⟩ ⟨a ~ for scarce raw materials⟩ ⟨the ~ for Africa⟩ **c** : a disorderly or confused progress, race, contest, or proceeding ⟨careful to keep the rapid finale of the symphony from becoming a ~⟩ **3** : a disorderly or jumbled mass ⟨a ~ of tents and huts spread out all over the rocks —*Skyways*⟩ ⟨his plot, which is an improbable ~ of killings —H.A.L.Craig⟩ ⟨when you get your wits working on that crazy ~ of letters . . . sense appears in nonsense —*Cryptogram Bk.*⟩ **4 a** *chiefly Brit* : an engagement with enemy aircraft : DOGFIGHT **b** : an emergency takeoff of fighter-interceptor airplanes in the shortest possible time
scrambled eggs *n pl* **1 a** : eggs whose whites and yolks are stirred together while cooking **b** : eggs beaten slightly usu. with a little milk and stirred while cooking **2 a** : embroidery worn on the cap visors of military officers of the rank of colonel or above or commander or above **b** : officers having such rank
scrambled mitchell *n, usu cap M* [*scrambled* (past part. of *¹scramble*) + *mitchell* (as in *Mitchell movement*)] : a Mitchell movement in which the north-south and east-west pairs exchange compass directions halfway through a bridge game
scramble net *n* : a rope net hung over the side of ship for men to climb up or down
scram·bler \-b(ə)lə(r)\ *n* -S : one that scrambles: as **a** : a plant that scrambles with or without hooks **b** : a device that disarranges the elements of telephone, teletype, facsimile, or television transmissions in order to make them unintelligible to interception
scram·bly \-lē\ *adj* : IRREGULAR, HAPHAZARD
scran \'skran\ *n* -S [origin unknown] : scraps of food : LEFTOVERS; *also* : GRUB, PROVISIONS
scran bag *n* **1** : a bag for leftover food ⟨a beggar's *scran bag*⟩ **2** : a receptacle for articles found lying about on a ship
scranch \'skranch\ *archaic var of* SCRAUNCH
scran·nel \'skranᵊl\ *adj* [origin unknown] **1** : thin and grating on the ears : UNMELODIOUS ⟨their lean and flashy songs grate on their ~ pipes of wretched straw —John Milton⟩ **2** *chiefly dial* : POOR ⟨a ~ crop of winter wheat —Adrian Bell⟩
scran·ton \'skrantᵊn, -aan-\ *adj, usu cap* [*Scranton*, city in northeast Pennsylvania] : of or from the city of Scranton, Pa. ⟨a *Scranton* textile mill⟩ : of the kind or style prevalent in Scranton

scran·to·ni·an \skran'tōnēən\ *n* -s *cap* [*Scranton* + E *-an*] **:** a native or resident of Scranton, Pennsylvania

¹scrap \'skrap\ *n* -s [ME, fr. ON *skrap* scraps, trifles; akin to ON *skrapa* to scrape] **1 scraps** *pl* **:** fragments of discarded or leftover food ⟨fed the dog on ~s⟩ **2 a :** a small detached piece **:** BIT ⟨~ of paper⟩ **b :** a fragment of something written or printed **:** a brief excerpt ⟨read ~s of a letter⟩ **:** a picture cut out or detached from a book or magazine or newspaper for saving in a scrapbook **c :** the least piece ⟨not a ~ of evidence for it⟩ **3 scraps** *pl* **:** the crisp substance that remains after trying out animal fat (as of a whale or fish) **:** CRACKLINGS ⟨pork ~s⟩ **4 a :** small pieces, cuttings, or chips of stock removed in the process of making any product **b :** manufactured articles or parts rejected for imperfection or discarded because of excessive wear or lack of demand and useful only as raw material for reprocessing ⟨metal ~⟩ ⟨rubber ~⟩ **c :** CULLET **5 :** coarsely ground animal waste used as a fertilizer or feed ⟨fish ~⟩ ⟨meat ~⟩ **6 a :** a by-product of the handling of tobacco consisting of loose tangled pieces of leaves, floor sweepings, but no stems **b scraps** *pl* **:** coarsely broken or cut tobacco used for chewing and smoking

²scrap \"\ *vt* **scrapped; scrapped; scrapping; scraps 1 :** to make into scrap **:** dispose of as scrap often for salvage ⟨~ a battleship⟩ **2 :** to abandon or get rid of as no longer of enough worth, merit, use, or effectiveness to retain ⟨by the year 1500 Western civilization was already adapting or trying to ~ its medieval heritage —Stringfellow Barr⟩ **syn** see DISCARD

³scrap \"\ *adj* **1 :** being in the form of scraps or fragments **:** valuable only as raw material ⟨~ metal⟩ **2 :** made up of odds and ends **:** consisting of scraps ⟨~ dinner⟩

⁴scrap \"\ *n* -s [origin unknown] **:** FIGHT, QUARREL ⟨got into a ~ in a barroom⟩ **:** PRIZEFIGHT ⟨the smaller fighter put up a good ~⟩ **syn** see BRAWL

⁵scrap \"\ *vi* **scrapped; scrapped; scrapping; scraps :** SQUABBLE, QUARREL ⟨continually *scrapping* with her sister⟩ **:** FIGHT

scrap basket *n* **:** WASTEBASKET

scrapbook \'ˌ=\ *n* **1 :** a blank book in which miscellaneous items (as newspaper clippings or pictures) may be pasted or inserted **2 :** a book of miscellaneous contents

¹scrape \'skrāp\ *vb* -ED/-ING/-S [ME *scrapen* to scrape, erase, fr. ON *skrapa* to scrape; akin to OE *scrapian* to scrape, MD *schrapen* to scrape, MHG *schreffen* to scratch, L *scrobis* trench, Russ *skorb'* sorrow, grief, Gk *keirein* to cut — more at SHEAR] *vt* **1 :** ERASE, EXPUNGE ⟨~ out a word⟩ **2** *obs* **:** to scratch or dig with the nails **3 a :** to remove (adhering or excrescent matter) from a surface by usu. repeated strokes of an edged instrument drawn or pushed firmly across nearly at right angles to the surface ⟨~ paint off a chair⟩ ⟨~ scales off a fish⟩ ⟨~ mud off shoes⟩ **b** (1) **:** to make (a surface) smooth or clean with strokes of an edged instrument or an abrasive — often used with *down* ⟨*scraped* down and refinished a pine chest⟩ (2) **:** to draw a road grader over **4 a :** to grate harshly over or against ⟨the keel *scraped* the stony bottom⟩ **b :** to damage or injure the surface of by sliding contact with a rough surface ⟨*scraped* his knee on the pavement⟩ ⟨*scraped* a fender in a near collision⟩ **c :** to draw roughly or noisily over a surface ⟨stop *scraping* your feet⟩ ⟨broke the silence by *scraping* a chair on the floor⟩ **5 :** to collect by or as if by scraping **:** gather in small portions by laborious effort — used with *up* or *together* ⟨~ up money for the rent⟩ **6 :** to produce (an engraving) by scraping the previously prepared surface of the plate — compare MEZZOTINT **7 :** to prepare (raw pelts) by removing the flesh and fat and breaking or loosening the fibers to make more flexible by rubbing with a dull-edged instrument — compare FLESH **8 :** to collect scrape from (trees) ~ *vi* **1** *obs* **:** SCRATCH **2 :** to move in sliding contact with a rough surface ⟨*scraped* against the gateposts⟩ **3 :** to accumulate money by small economies ⟨*scraping* and saving to educate their children⟩ **4 :** to bow a stringed instrument; *esp* **:** to play with a rough unmusical tone **5 :** to draw back the foot along the ground in making a bow ⟨bowing and *scraping*⟩ **6 :** to manage to make one's way with difficulty or succeed by a narrow margin ⟨*scraping* along on a small income⟩ ⟨~ through a final examination⟩ — **scrape acquaintance :** to make acquaintance by making advances esp. without an introduction — **scrape a leg :** to make a low bow

²scrape \"\ *n* -s [ME, fr. *scrapen*, v.] **1 a :** the act of scraping ⟨rocks worn by the ~ of glaciers⟩ ⟨took up the remaining mortar with a ~ of his trowel⟩ **b :** a sound made by scraping ⟨rumble and ~ of the wheels of guns and limbers —H.N.Cole⟩ ⟨~ of footsteps up the stairs⟩ **2 a :** SCRAPER; *esp* **:** a dredge for taking crabs or oysters **b :** a bare place, hollow, or heap made by scraping ⟨the tern's nest is a ~ in the sand —C.L. Barrett⟩ **c** *also* **scrape of the pen** *chiefly Scot* **:** a scrap of writing **:** a hasty note ⟨not a ~ from you since your card at Christmas —Michael McLaverty⟩ **3 :** a bow made by drawing back the foot **4 :** a disagreeable predicament **:** an awkward or distressing situation ⟨his brother was continually helping him out of ~s at school⟩; *often* **:** CONFLICT, FIGHT ⟨got into a shooting ~ with a political opponent⟩ **5 :** crude turpentine that collects and hardens on the trunks of turpentined trees and is gathered usu. at the end of the season — compare DIP 6d **syn** see PREDICAMENT

scrape down *vt, chiefly Brit* **:** to silence (a speaker) by scraping the feet ⟨another was coughed and *scraped down* —T.B. Macaulay⟩

scrape-finished \'ˌ=ˌ=\ *adj* **:** finished to a smooth level surface with a scraper ⟨*scrape-finished* lathe bed⟩

scrap·er \'skrāpə(r)\ *n* -s **1 :** a tool for scraping **:** an instrument with which something is scraped: as **a :** an edged blade fixed upright near an entrance for scraping mud off shoes **b :** any of various instruments or tools used esp. in different trades for scraping metal, wood, leather for producing a clean or a smooth finished surface, for cutting grooves, or for shaping objects by scraping away superfluous material **c :** any of various appliances for removing an extraneous coating or layer from something: as (1) **:** a broad hoe for cleaning roads or stables (2) **:** a device for scraping up snow from ice (3) **:** a hoe-shaped implement for raking out ashes **d :** a device armed with curved knives and forced through a pipeline or a flue to clear out obstructions **e :** a curved wooden or metal device for removing the sweat from horses **f :** a 3-sided tool used by engravers to remove lines or burrs **g :** a board or blade whose edge rubs over a tympan sheet to make an impression in an old type of lithographic printing press **h :** ROAD GRADER **i :** a metal scoop with a bail to which motive power is attached for excavating or moving loose or soft material short distances **j :** a contrivance for cleaning out the detritus from a borehole **k :** a power-drawn wheeled self-loading conveyor used to move earth in grading and filling operations **l :** a kitchen tool made of a blade of hard rubber on a wood handle and used to scrape food from dishes or remove batter from mixing bowls **2 a :** one that scrapes money **:** MISER, SKINFLINT **b :** FIDDLER **c :** BARBER **d :** one that cleans, trims, or shapes by scraping **3 :** a bird that scratches the soil **4** *slang* **:** COCKED HAT **5 :** a roughened area on the legs or wings of an insect used in producing sounds

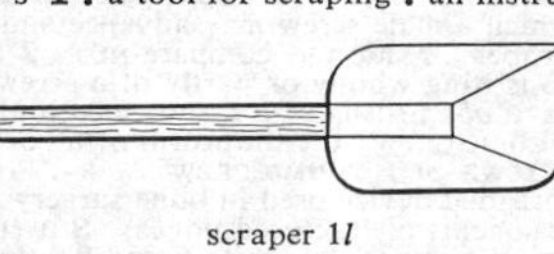
scraper 1*l*

scraperboard \'ˌ=ˌ=\ *n* **1 :** a scratchboard with a smooth finish used to produce drawings usu. in white lines that are incised in a blackened surface **2 a :** the art or practice of using a scraperboard **b :** a product of such art or practice

scraper conveyor *n* **:** DRAG CONVEYOR

scraper ring *n* **:** a piston ring designed to scrape excess oil from the cylinder wall to prevent its entrance into the combustion chamber

scrapes *pres 3d sing of* SCRAPE, *pl of* SCRAPE

scrap heap *n* **1 :** a pile of discarded metal (as iron) **2 :** the place to which useless things are relegated **:** DISCARD, OBLIVION

scrap·i·ana \ˌskrapē'anə\ *n pl* [¹*scrap* + *-ana*] **:** miscellaneous literary scraps

scrap·ie \'skrāpē\ *n* -s [¹*scrape* + *-ie*] **:** a virus disease of sheep characterized by twitching, excitability, intense itching, excessive thirst, emaciation, weakness, and finally paralysis

¹scraping *n* -s [ME *scrapinge* action of one that scrapes, fr. gerund of *scrapen* to scrape] **:** something scraped off, up, or together — usu. used in pl. ⟨street ~s⟩ ⟨fed on pot ~s⟩

²scraping *adj* [fr. pres. part. of ¹*scrape*] **:** that scrapes; *specif* **:** MISERLY — **scrap·ing·ly** *adv*

scrap·ler *or* **scrap·pler** \'skraplə(r)\ *n* -s [by alter. (influence of ¹*scrap*)] **:** SCABBLER

scrap·man \'skrap,man, -,maa(ə)n, -mən\ *n, pl* **scrapmen 1 :** a man dealing in scrap **:** JUNKMAN **2 a :** one who works at disposing of or salvaging scrap **b :** CHIPMAN 1 **3 :** a tobacco worker who blends cigar-filler scrap

scrap·page \'skrapij\ *n* -s **1 :** scrapped material **2 :** the rate of taking articles, buildings, or machinery out of use ⟨prosperity required the ~ and replacement of 4 million cars a year —S.H.Slichter⟩

scrapped *past of* SCRAP

¹scrap·per \'skrapə(r)\ *n* -s [⁵*scrap* + *-er*] **:** QUARRELER, FIGHTER ⟨strong-willed, persistent, and a ~ through and through —*advt.*⟩; *esp* **:** PRIZEFIGHTER

²scrapper \"\ *n* -s [²*scrap* + *-er*] **1 :** one that disposes of scraps **2 :** a worker who knocks off or pulls out the waste parts of scored cardboard box blanks — called also *breaker*

scrap·pi·ly \-pəlē, -li\ *adv* **:** in a scrappy manner

scrap·pi·ness \-pēnəs, -pin-\ *n* -ES **:** the quality or state of being scrappy **:** fragmentary nature **:** DISCONNECTEDNESS

scrapping *pres part of* SCRAP

¹scrap·ple \'skrapəl\ *n* -s [ME *scrapill*, fr. *scrapen* to scrape] *dial Eng* **:** a tool for scraping

²scrapple \"\ *n* -s [dim. of ¹*scrap*] **:** mush containing meat scraps made by boiling cornmeal in the liquor in which bones and meats (as pork) for headcheese and other products have been boiled, seasoned with condiments and herbs, poured into a mold to cool, and served sliced and fried

¹scrap·py \'skrapē, -pi\ *adj* -ER/-EST [¹*scrap* + *-y*] **:** consisting of scraps **:** lacking unity or consistency **:** FRAGMENTARY ⟨~ dinner⟩ ⟨~ narrative⟩ ⟨~ education⟩

²scrappy \"\ *adj* -ER/-EST [⁴*scrap* + *-y*] **1 :** QUARRELSOME **2 :** showing sharp and vigorous attacking qualities and an aggressive and determined spirit ⟨~ football team⟩ ⟨~ admiral⟩

scraps *pl of* SCRAP, *pres 3d sing of* SCRAP

scrap value *n* **:** the value of an item at the time it is discarded **:** the value which it is estimated an item will have at the time it is discarded

scrapy \'skrāpē\ *adj* -ER/-EST [¹*scrape* + *-y*] **:** sounding like scraping **:** produced by scraping ⟨made a small ~ sound in her throat⟩ ⟨~ violin playing⟩

scrapyard \'ˌ=\ *n* **:** a place for receiving or handling scrap **:** JUNKYARD; *broadly* **:** SCRAP HEAP ⟨demanding that every vessel . . . be sent to the ~ —*No. Amer. Rev.*⟩

¹scrat \'skrat\ *vb* **scratted; scratted** *or* **scrat; scratting; scrats** [ME *scratten*] *dial Brit* **:** SCRATCH

²scrat \"\ *n* -s *dial chiefly Eng* **:** a small insignificant thing or amount

³scrat \"\ *n* -s [ME *skratt, scrate*, prob. fr. ON *skratti* monster — more at SCRAE] *chiefly dial* **:** HERMAPHRODITE

¹scratch \'skrach\ *vb* -ED/-ING/-ES [blend of ¹*scrat* and obs. E *cratch* to scratch; obs. E *cratch* fr. ME *cracchen*, prob. fr. MD *cratsen* to scratch, scrape; akin to OHG *krazzōn* to scratch, OSw *kratta* to scratch, Alb *gërruej* I scratch] *vt* **1 :** to scrape with the claws or nails ⟨~*ed* out the eyes of the owl —Ben Jonson⟩ **2 :** to rub and tear or mark the surface of with something sharp or jagged **:** scrape, roughen, or wound slightly by drawing something pointed or rough across ⟨hard enough to ~ glass⟩ ⟨legs ~*ed* by the briers⟩ **3 :** to scrape or rub lightly with something pointed or rough in order to relieve itching ⟨took turns ~*ing* each other's backs⟩ or as a gesture indicating perplexity or hesitation ⟨thoughtfully ~*ing* his jaw⟩ ⟨~*ed* his head in bewilderment⟩ **4 a :** to dig or heap with the claws **b :** to scrape (as money) together **5 a :** to make shallow cuts on the surface of ⟨~*ed* his boot soles to prevent slipping⟩ — often used with *up* ⟨the table was all ~*ed* up by the movers⟩ **b :** to write or draw (as letters, figures) on a surface by such cuts ⟨~*ed* a map on the wet sand⟩ ⟨~*ed* his initials on the silver cover⟩ **c :** to cultivate lightly **:** make shallow furrows in **6 a :** to cancel by drawing a line through **b :** to obliterate with repeated strokes of the pen — used with *out* **c** *obs* **:** to expel or bar from a club **d :** to withdraw (an entry) from competition ⟨his horse was ~*ed* in the third race⟩ **e :** to mark (a ballot) so as to vote for most of the candidates of one party but for some belonging to another party **7 :** to write or draw hastily or roughly **:** SCRIBBLE ⟨~*ed* a note⟩ ⟨~*ed* his signature⟩ **8 :** SCRATCHBRUSH ⟨~ a casting⟩ **9 :** to scrape along a rough surface ⟨~ a match⟩ **10 :** to spur (a horse) by keeping the feet moving in a kicking motion alternately forward and backward ~ *vi* **1 a :** to use the claws in digging, tearing, or wounding ⟨that cat will ~⟩ **b :** to find or make one's way or one's living ⟨turned out at an early age to ~ for themselves⟩ **2 :** to rub oneself with something pointed or rough to relieve itching **3 :** to gather money or get a living by hard work and saving **4 :** to make a thin grating sound ⟨this pen ~*es*⟩ ⟨the dog was ~*ing* lightly at the door⟩ **5 a :** to withdraw from a contest after one's name is listed **b :** to fail to keep a social engagement **6 :** to scratch the name of a candidate on the ticket of one's party or faction **:** split the ticket **7 a :** to make a scratch in billiards or pool **b :** to score by a scratch — **scratch one's back :** to gratify one by favors or flattery esp. in expectation of favors in return ⟨you *scratch my back* and I'll *scratch yours*⟩ — **scratch the surface :** to make a beginning on a project, progress, a solution of a problem, a field of inquiry, or an investigation

²scratch \"\ *n* -ES **1 :** a mark or injury produced by scratching **:** a slight wound ⟨came through the battle without a ~⟩ **2 scratches** *pl but sing or pl in constr* **:** grease heel in its early stages **3 :** a line or furrow that is made in a surface by rasping or rubbing with a pointed or jagged object ⟨her ring left a ~ on the polished table top⟩ ⟨a million years, a mere ~ on the surface of earth's time —W.E.Swinton⟩ **4 :** a written scrawl **:** SCRIBBLE **5 :** a short wig **6 :** the sound made by scratching ⟨~ of a pencil⟩; *esp* **:** noise caused by the friction of a phonograph needle on the surface of a record **7 a :** the line from which contestants start in a race **b :** NOTHING, ZERO ⟨two whole towns have had to be built almost from ~ —Kent Strong⟩ ⟨task of organizing a major institution of learning almost from ~ —William DuBois⟩ **8 a :** a line formerly drawn across a prize ring that a contestant had to approach to begin or continue the fight **b :** a trial or test of courage ⟨imagine myself wanting at the ~ —Henry James †1916⟩ **c :** satisfactory physical condition or standard of performance ⟨bulls . . . that are not up to ~ as to size —*Farmer's Weekly (So. Africa)*⟩ ⟨her acting was right up to ~⟩ ⟨bringing him up to fighting ~ —H.J.Laski⟩ **9 :** the starting time or station or initial score of a competitor who neither is allowed odds nor receives a penalty **10 :** a contestant (as a horse or dog) whose name has been withdrawn from a race in which it was entered ⟨a list of late ~*es*⟩ **11** *also* **scratch feed :** a poultry feed (as mixed grains) scattered on the litter or ground esp. to induce birds to exercise **12 a :** a shot in billiards or pool that fails to comply with some requirement of the game and involves loss of the player's turn; *specif* **:** a pocketing of the cue ball without touching the object ball **b :** a shot that scores by accident **:** FLUKE **c :** SCRATCH HIT **13** *slang* **:** MONEY

³scratch \"\ *adj* **1 :** made as or used for a tentative effort ⟨~ map⟩ **2 :** made or done by chance and not in the way intended ⟨~ shot⟩ **3 :** arranged or put together with little selection of material **:** HAPHAZARD ⟨~ meal⟩ ⟨~ team⟩ **4 :** made up of heterogeneous elements insufficient to be representative ⟨~ vote⟩ **5** *of a contest or a contestant* **:** being without handicap or allowance ⟨~ golfer⟩ ⟨one of the ~ boats in a handicap race⟩ **6 :** CANCELED

scratch·able \-chəbəl\ *adj* **:** capable of being scratched

scratch awl *n* **:** an awl with a sharp point for scratching guidelines on wood or metal **:** SCRIBER

scratchback \'ˌ=\ *n* **:** BACK SCRATCHER

scratchboard *also* **scratchcard** \'ˌ=\ *n* **:** a chalk-covered cardboard often with line or stipple pattern on which an effect resembling block printing or engraving may be achieved by scratching away desired portions (as highlights, shadings, white lines) with a steel tool; *also* **:** the art or practice of using scratchboard

¹scratchbrush \'ˌ=\ *n* [¹*scratch* + *brush*] **:** a stiff wire brush for cleaning metal (as iron castings)

²scratchbrush \"\ *vt* **:** to clean or finish with or as if with a scratchbrush

scratch·brush·er \"+ə(r)\ *n* [²*scratchbrush* + *-er*] **1 :** a machine equipped with scratchbrushes **2 :** a worker who uses a scratchbrush or scratchbrusher

scratch carving *n* **:** furniture carving in which the design is outlined by narrow scratched or incised lines

scratch coat *n* **:** the first coat applied in plastering having lines scratched on its surface to improve the bond with the next coat — called also *first coat*

scratch comma *n* **:** a diagonal formerly used as a comma

scratch dial *n* **:** an early simple sundial formed by lines cut usu. on a church wall

scratch division *n* **:** an old method of division in which the partial products are not set down at all but only the remainders so that it is necessary to scratch out each figure of the dividend from which subtraction is made and place the remainder each time above it — called also *galley method*

scratched *adj* [fr. past part. of ¹*scratch*] **:** CANCELED ⟨8 and 9 are ~ figures⟩

scratch·er \'skrachə(r)\ *n* -s **1 :** one that scratches: as **a :** a workman who uses a tool in scratching or tends a machine which does this work **b :** SCRATCHBRUSHER **c :** one who hand-finishes metal castings to be used as patterns **d :** a rasorial bird **2 a :** a tool used to roughen or scratch the scratch coat of plaster to improve the adhesion between the scratch coat and the brown coat **b :** a tool for corrugating the ends of sewer pipe so that cement will adhere when they are joined **c :** a tool for blazing trees **3** *slang* **:** FORGER 1c

scratches *pres 3d sing of* SCRATCH, *pl of* SCRATCH

scratch–farming \'ˌ=ˌ=\ *n* **:** the growing of crops on land after shallow or indifferent tillage

scratch feed *n* **:** SCRATCH 11

scratch gauge *n* **:** a metalworker's scriber or gauge resembling the carpenter's marking gauge

scratch grass *n* **1 :** TEARTHUMB **2 :** CLEAVERS

scratch hit *n* **:** a batted ball not solidly hit or cleanly fielded yet credited to the batter as a base hit

scratch·i·ly \'skrachəlē\ *adv* **:** in a scratchy manner

scratch·i·ness \-chēnəs\ *n* -ES **:** the quality or state of being scratchy

scratching *pres part of* SCRATCH

scratching post *n* **:** a sturdy wood post or block often covered with carpeting for a cat to scratch its claws on

scratch·ings \'skrachənz, -chiŋz\ *n pl* [pl. of *scratching*, gerund of ¹*scratch*] *dial Eng* **:** CRACKLINGS

scratch·less \'skrachləs\ *adj* **1 :** not marred or wounded **2 :** not likely to scratch ⟨~ vise⟩

scratch line *n* **1 :** a starting line for a race **2 :** a line that marks the extreme limit of the takeoff for a broad jump **3 :** a line from which the javelin is thrown and which must not be overstepped by the thrower

scratch pad *n* **:** a pad of scratch paper

scratch paper *n* **:** any paper that may be used for jottings, memoranda, or other casual writing

scratchproof \'ˌ=ˌ=\ *adj* **:** resistant to scratches

scratch sheet *n* **:** a racing publication listing horses scratched from races and giving the handicapper's grading of the horses in order of winning chances

scratch test *n* **1 :** a test to discover the amount of abrasive material present (as in a paste or powder detergent) or to discover the relative resistance of a surface to abrasive material **2 :** a test for allergy in which scratches are made in the epithelial layer of the skin and the suspected allergen rubbed into the area and which determines a positive reaction by development of redness or a wheal around the scratched part — compare INTRACUTANEOUS TEST, PATCH TEST

scratchweed \'ˌ=\ *n* **:** CLEAVERS

scratch wig *n* **:** a short wig

scratchwork \'ˌ=\ *n* **1 :** SCRATCH COAT **2 :** SGRAFFITO

scratchy \'skrachē, -chi\ *adj* -ER/-EST **1 :** affected with the scratches ⟨horse with ~ feet⟩ **2 :** making a scratching noise ⟨~ tune came from the phonograph⟩ ⟨~ pen⟩ **3 :** marked or made with scratches ⟨~ drawing⟩ ⟨~ handwriting⟩ **4 a :** of sparse or straggly growth ⟨~ mane⟩ **b :** SCANT, MEAGER ⟨made only three hits, two of them ~⟩ **:** RAGGED ⟨played ~ golf through the first nine⟩ **5 :** causing tingling or itching **:** IRRITATING, PRICKLY ⟨~ wool sweater⟩ ⟨~ gas⟩

scrats *pres 3d sing of* SCRAT, *pl of* SCRAT

scratted *past of* SCRAT

scratting *pres part of* SCRAT

scrat·tle \'skratᵊl\ *vi* -ED/-ING/-S [¹*scrat* + *-le*] *dial Eng* **:** SCRATCH, SCRAMBLE

scrat·tling \'skratliŋ\ *adj* **:** BEGGARLY, SCANTY

scraunch \'skrȯnch\ *vb* -ED/-ING/-ES [imit.] *chiefly dial* **:** CRUNCH

scraw \'skrȯ\ *n* -s [IrGael *scraith* & ScGael *sgrath*] *Scot & Irish* **:** a piece of turf **:** SOD ⟨not fit to lift ~s from off the field —Augusta Gregory⟩

scrawk \'skrȯk\ *vi* -ED/-ING/-S [imit.] **1** *dial* **:** SCREECH **2** *dial* **:** SQUAWK

¹scrawl \'skrȯl\ *vb* -ED/-ING/-S [perh. by alter.] *archaic* **:** ¹CRAWL

²scrawl \"\ *vb* -ED/-ING/-S [origin unknown] *vt* **1 :** to write or draw awkwardly and irregularly **:** write hastily and carelessly **:** SCRIBBLE ⟨~ a brief note⟩ ⟨painfully ~*ed* his name⟩ **2 :** to mark or write on with irregular or hasty characters ⟨papers . . . ~*ed* with hieroglyphics —George Borrow⟩ ~ *vi* **:** to write awkwardly or carelessly

³scrawl \"\ *n* -s **1 :** careless, hasty, or irregular writing ⟨eventually deciphered the ~ —Francis King⟩ **2 :** SPRAWL ⟨saw the bright cabins and the ~ of a hidden stream —Bryan MacMahon⟩

scrawl·er \-lə(r)\ *n* -s **1 :** one that scrawls **2 :** a device for marking out fields preparatory to the planting of ridged row crops

scrawl·i·ness \-lēnəs\ *n* -ES **:** the quality of being scrawly

scrawly \-lē, -li\ *adj* -ER/-EST **:** awkwardly or carelessly irregular **:** SPRAWLING ⟨pages covered with ~ figures⟩

scrawm \'skrȯm\ *vi* -ED/-ING/-S [perh. by shortening & alter. fr. ¹SCRAMBLE] *dial Eng* **:** SCRAMBLE, CLAMBER

scrawn·i·ness \'skrȯ|nēnəs, -rä|, |nin-\ *n* -ES **:** the quality or state of being scrawny

scrawny \|nē, |ni\ *adj* -ER/-EST [origin unknown] **:** LEAN, THIN, RAWBONED **:** ill-nourished ⟨~ cattle⟩ ⟨~ bent-over pines⟩ ⟨a ~ ill-favored little girl —Margaret Mead⟩ **syn** see LEAN

¹scray \'skrā\ *n* -s [prob. modif. of D *schraag* trestle, fr. MD *schrage*; akin to MHG *schrage* trestle, Gk *kirkos* ring — more at CIRCLE] **:** a simple container or similar part on a machine where piece goods collect in folds after passing through a machine process

²scray *or* **scraye** \"\ *n* -s [origin unknown] **:** TERN

¹screak *also* **screek** \'skrēk\ *vi* -ED/-ING/-S [of Scand origin; akin to ON *skrækja* to screech — more at SCREAM] **1 :** to emit suddenly a sharp shrill sound **:** SCREECH ⟨~*ed* when she saw the mouse⟩ **2 :** to make a harsh rasping noise **:** GRATE, SQUEAL ⟨that gate ~s when it is opened⟩

²screak *also* **screek** \"\ *n* -s **:** a sound of screaking **:** a harsh rasping noise ⟨the moaning ~ of brakes, and racing, starting motors —Thomas Wolfe⟩ ⟨can remember the ~ on stones of his hoe —Richard Wilbur⟩

screaky \-kē\ *adj* **:** of, making, or resembling a screak **:** very shrill or raspy ⟨bats . . . making their ~ sounds —Eric Knight⟩

¹scream \'skrēm\ *vb* -ED/-ING/-S [ME *scremen*; akin to MD *schreem* screech, Flem *schreemen* to scream, OS *skrikon* to shriek, screech, OS & OHG *scrīan* to scream, yell, ON *skrækja* to shriek, screech, *skraumi* screamer, and perh. to OE *hræfn* raven — more at RAVEN] *vi* **1 a** (1) **:** to voice a sudden sharp loud cry ⟨~*ed* and fainted —Louis Bromfield⟩ ⟨~*ed* with amusement —Marcia Davenport⟩ ⟨children fight and ~ . . . in the streets —Sherwood Anderson⟩ (2) **:** to produce harsh and unpleasant high-pitched musical tones ⟨even a prima donna has been known to ~ occasionally⟩ ⟨horns ~*ed*, and flutes wailed —John Blofeld⟩ **b :** to make an outburst of noise resembling a scream : move with a screaming sound ⟨the wind rose and ~*ed* through the streets —H.E.Rieseberg⟩ ⟨brilliant blue kingfishers ~ at intruders —*Amer. Guide Series: La.*⟩ ⟨a jet ~*ed* out of the cushion of the gray cotton sky —*Saturday Rev.*⟩ **2** : to speak or write with expressions of intense hysterical emotion : make violent protestations or demands ⟨growing industries . . . are ~*ing* for water —*Time*⟩ ⟨travelers . . . ~*ed* loud and long at the shipping lines —*N. Y. Times*⟩ ⟨papers ~ to the heavens about . . . troops along their borders —*Atlantic*⟩ **3** : to produce a vivid, blatant, or startling effect like a scream ⟨framed in garish red, a bold black headline ~*ed* —Paul Hofmann⟩ ⟨the obviousness . . . fairly ~*s* at the reader who is surely ready by now for profounder insights —*New Republic*⟩ ~ *vt* **1 a** : to utter with or as if with a scream ⟨a newsboy in the street below began to ~ an extra —F.V.W. Mason⟩ ⟨~*ed* that she was drowning —George Meredith⟩ **b** : to sing harshly and unpleasantly esp. at high pitch ⟨vocally delivered . . . although some of the second-act music was ~*ed* —*Musical Digest*⟩ **2** : to demand or protest as if in a screaming voice : blare forth ⟨artists . . . write letters to the newspapers ~*ing* that they are being snubbed —Francis Steegmuller⟩ ⟨headlines ~*ed* the news all over the Union —*Atlantic*⟩ ⟨been ~*ing* to go into show business —Myles MacSweeney⟩

[2]scream \"\ *n* -s **1 a** : a sudden loud sharp penetrating cry usu. expressing anger, terror, pain, or sometimes hysterical merriment ⟨her ~*s* filled the air as she turned and fled⟩ **b** : a sound resembling or having the effect of a scream ⟨the crows come flapping with their ~*s* —Thomas Vance⟩ ⟨the shrill ~ of . . . saws and the odor of fresh cedar wood —*Amer. Guide Series: Oregon*⟩ **2** : one that provokes screams of mirth ⟨the instructions are a ~ from start to finish —Margaret Lane⟩ ⟨what a ~ he was on a party —Ring Lardner⟩

scream·er \-mə(r)\ *n* -s **1** : one that screams; *esp* : one that sings in a loud harsh penetrating manner **2** : any of several So. American birds constituting the family Anhimidae — see CRESTED SCREAMER, HORNED SCREAMER **3** *slang* : one that shows remarkable excellence **4** : one (as a play, a comedian) that causes screams usu. either of excitement or mirth **5** : a sensationally large or startling headline **6** *slang* : EXCLAMATION POINT **7** : one engaged to provoke excitement by screaming ⟨began as a publicity stunt with the first swooners and ~*s* —Bruce Bliven b. 1889⟩

screamer bomb *n* : a bomb that has an attachment emitting a penetrating whistle as the bomb falls and that is used to terrify the enemy

[1]screaming *n* -s [ME *skremyng*, fr. gerund of *skremen, scremen* to scream — more at SCREAM] : the act of or sound made by one that screams ⟨a ~ of brakes generally heralded the arrival —Benedict Thielen⟩ ⟨the fog siren began its ~ —John Steinbeck⟩ ⟨distortion of action, harsh ~*s* of the voice . . . are not admissible in the theatric art —Joshua Reynolds⟩

[2]screaming *adj* [fr. pres. part. of [1]*scream*] **1** : uttering screams : emitting or producing sounds resembling screams ⟨snows driven by ~ sea winds —Ann F. Wolfe⟩ ⟨a car rounded the corner with ~ tires —Erle Stanley Gardner⟩ ⟨a ~ jet plane flew overhead —Sam Pollock⟩ ⟨~ hordes of movie fans —Peter Ustinov⟩ **2** : having characteristics similar to a scream : resembling a scream in effect : blatantly arresting : STARTLING ⟨rugs in harsh colors and ~ designs —R.W.Murray⟩ ⟨the papers carried ~ headlines —R.M.Lovett⟩ **3** : evoking screams usu. of raucous mirth ⟨fetched along the book with all those ~ snapshots —Dearing Ward⟩ **4** : EXCELLENT, SPLENDID ⟨within the tradition of the dramatic fiction film, it balances a great weight with ~ finesse —Cecile Starr⟩

scream·ing·ly *adv* : to an extreme degree ⟨thought the whole effort so ~ funny —Joseph Millard⟩

screaming meemies *n pl but sing in constr* [origin unknown] : extreme and intolerable terror or nervous hysteria : JITTERS ⟨about two jumps ahead of the *screaming meemies* —*Time*⟩

screamy \-mē\ *adj* : given to or suggestive of screaming

scree \'skrē\ *n* -s [of Scand origin; akin to ON *skritha* landslide, debris from a landslide, fr. *skrītha* to creep, glide — more at CRISSUM] : a heap of stones or rocky debris lying on a slope or at the base of a cliff : TALUS ⟨the steep *scree*-strewn lower slopes of the mountains —Alistair MacLean⟩

[1]screech \'skrēch\ *vb* -ED/-ING/-ES [alter. of earlier *scritch*, fr. ME *scrichen*; akin to ON *skrækja* to screech — more at SCREAM] *vi* **1** : to utter a high shrill piercing cry : make an outcry usu. in terror or pain **2** : to make a sound resembling a screech ⟨the driver applied his brakes . . . and the car ~*ed* to a standstill —Bruce Marshall⟩ ⟨the gate ~*ed* behind him —Nadine Gordimer⟩ ~ *vt* : to utter with or as if with a screech ⟨their voices ~*ing* out the battle cries —T.B.Costain⟩

[2]screech \"\ *n* -ES **1** : a high very shrill piercing cry usu. expressing extreme pain or terror ⟨the voice was a strident ~ torn from the lungs —Marcia Davenport⟩ **2** : a sound resembling or having the effect of a screech ⟨an earsplitting ~ of brakes —Donald Windham⟩ ⟨the ~ of fire sirens —H.A. Chippendale⟩

screechbird \'=,=\ *also* **screech cock** *or* **screech thrush** *n* : FIELDFARE 1

screech·er \-chə(r)\ *n* -s **1** : one that screeches **2 a** : SWIFT **b** : MISTLE THRUSH

[1]screeching *n* -s [fr. gerund of [1]*screech*] : the act of or sound made by one that screeches ⟨greeted as usual by the . . . ~ of her parrot —Moray Firth⟩ ⟨the chugging of locomotives, the ~ of whistles —*Amer. Guide Series: Pa.*⟩

[2]screeching *adj* [fr. pres. part. of [1]*screech*] : uttering screeches : emitting or producing sounds resembling screeches ⟨a large red cab came to a ~ stop —Reginald Bretnor⟩ ⟨~ seagulls⟩ — **screech·ing·ly** *adv*

screech martin *n* : the common European swift

screech owl *n* **1** : BARN OWL **2** : any of numerous small owls of the genus *Otus* that range from southern Canada to Brazil, are closely related to the Old World scops owls, and have erectile ear tufts and plumage with blackish streaks and vermiculation; *esp* : an eastern No. American owl (*O. asio*) that is represented by several geographical varieties in the west and southwest and that exhibits two distinct phases of coloration consisting of a reddish brown and a gray

screechy \-chē\ *adj* -ER/-EST : given to or suggestive of screeching

[1]screed \'skrēd\ *n* -s [ME *screde*, fr. OE *scrēade* — more at SHRED] **1 a** *dial Brit* : FRAGMENT; *esp* : one torn off a piece of cloth : SHRED **b** *dial Brit* : a strip of land **c** *dial Eng* : a strip or band esp. around the border of a cap **2** *Scot* : RENT, TEAR **3 a** : a lengthy discourse : DIATRIBE **b** : a piece of writing: as (1) : a friendly letter ⟨send me a ~ . . . as often as you can —T.B.Aldrich⟩ (2) : an informal essay, story, or dissertation ⟨wrote a long ~ . . . for the Edinburgh professor —John Buchan⟩ **4 a** *or* **screed strip** : FLOATING SCREED **b** : a strike board usu. used to level up or strike off concrete pavement slabs or to cushion courses for block pavements **5** *Scot* : a drinking bout

[2]screed \"\ *vt* -ED/-ING/-S [ME *screden*, fr. OE *scrēadian* — more at SHRED] **1** *chiefly Scot* : REND, TEAR **2** : to smooth off with a screed ⟨the plaster was laid on very evenly and then ~*ed* off —Katharine S. Woods⟩

screed coat *n* : a layer of plaster laid level with screeds

screek *var of* SCREAK

scree·man \'skrēmən\ *n, pl* **screemen** [alter. of *screenman*] : a coal screener

[1]screen \'skrēn\ *n* -s [ME *screne*, fr. MF *escren, escran*, fr. MD *scherm* screen, shield, protection; akin to OHG *skirm, skerm* shield, screen, MLG *scerm* shield, screen, L *corium* skin, hide — more at CUIRASS] **1** : a device used as a protection from the heat of a fireplace or from drafts or as an ornamental piece: as **a** : a folding temporary partition consisting of hinged leaves usu. made of wood or metal framework covered with cloth, leather, or paper — see FIRE SCREEN **b** : a cloth, paper, or wooden implement with a handle to hold between oneself and the fire **c** : a high-backed settle **2 a** : a nonbearing partition that may be solid or pierced, is often ornamental, and is carried up to a height necessary for separation and protection **b** : a passage screened or partitioned off from the lower end

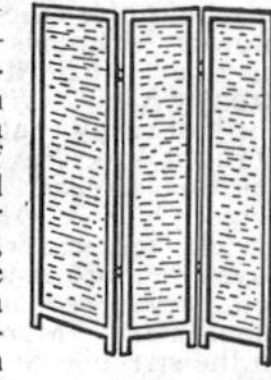

screen 1a

of the hall of a Tudor or Elizabethan house and used to connect the buttery and the kitchen **c** (1) : CHOIR SCREEN (2) : ROOD SCREEN **3** : something that shelters, protects esp. from injury or danger, or conceals from view: as **a** *Scot* : a large head scarf **b** : a natural or cultivated growth of plants ⟨a ~ of ivy across the window⟩ ⟨a ~ of tall pines sheltered the orchard from winter storms⟩ **c** (1) : a body of troops thrown out toward the enemy to protect a command or an area (2) : a formation of light naval vessels (as destroyers or cruisers) about a formation of heavier ships to protect the heavier formation from attack esp. by submarines or aircraft (3) : air patrolling by fighter-interceptors to protect from air attack specific targets (as slower aircraft or surface forces) : air patrolling to defend the entire friendly territory from air incursion (4) : smoke, camouflage, or a natural factor that protects an armed force from observation ⟨misty clouds . . . made such a perfect ~ that the Confederate batteries on top of the mountain could render no effective help —*Amer. Guide Series: Tenn.*⟩ **4 a** : something that guards : a security from possible inconvenience, censorious judgment, or harm ⟨adult care interposes a ~ between the small child and . . . society —Ralph Linton⟩ **b** : a shield for secret sometimes nefarious practices ⟨geniality . . . in our initial sessions was only a ~ —A.H.Vandenberg †1951⟩ ⟨petty larceny . . . only a ~ for something bigger —Claud Cockburn⟩ **5 a** (1) : a perforated plate, cylinder, or similar device or a meshed wire or cloth fabric usu. mounted on a frame and used to separate coarser from finer parts or to allow the passage of smaller portions while preventing that of larger (2) : a continuously operating mechanical straining device for removing knots and coarse foreign matter from paper stock in suspension in water (3) : a device for separating the grain husks from the liquid portion of whole stillage (4) : SILK SCREEN **b** : something that resembles a screen for sifting physical materials; *esp* : a system for examining in order to make a separation into different groups ⟨the new battalion passes through the ~ of officer and instructor observation —*Scientific American*⟩ **6 a** (1) : a flat surface afforded usu. by a curtain, sheet, or wall upon which an image (as a picture) is projected by a lantern, solar microscope, or motion-picture projector (2) : the motion-picture industry **b** : something that resembles a motion-picture screen ⟨a collection of poems . . . provides the reader with that larger ~ on which the poet's essential qualities are thrown —Sara H. Hay⟩ ⟨engrave its picture on the ~ of our mind —Walter Sorell⟩ **7 a** : a part of an instrument or piece of apparatus designed to prevent agencies in one part from affecting other parts ⟨optical ~⟩ ⟨electric ~⟩ ⟨magnetic ~⟩ **b** : a device to prevent radio waves or magnetic or electric fields from crossing a particular area **8** : an erection of white canvas or wood placed near the boundary at both ends of a cricket field in line with the wickets to enable the batsmen to see the ball better **9** : a three-color mosaic of regular pattern used in making the negative and viewing the transparency in the separate screen processes of additive color photography — compare SCREEN PLATE **10 a** : a glass plate ruled with crossing opaque lines through which an image is photographed onto a plate in making a halftone and on which the latticework of the crossed lines produces a dot formation **b** : a unit of measure of the textural fineness of a halftone being the number of dots per linear inch ⟨a coarse 65-*screen* newspaper cut⟩ ⟨a fine 200-*screen* engraving⟩ **11 a** : a frame holding a metallic or textile netting used esp. in a window or door to exclude insects **b** : SCREEN CLOTH **12** : the surface upon which an image or pattern is produced in a television or radar receiver or in a similar apparatus **13** : an act or instance of screening in athletic contests

[2]screen \"\ *vb* -ED/-ING/-S [ME *screanen*, fr. *screne*, n.] *vt* **1 a** : to guard from injury or danger : shield from harm or punishment ⟨the whole village was in a conspiracy to ~ the bandits⟩ **b** : to protect from the attack of an enemy by means of an advance guard (as of fighter aircraft) **2 a** : to give shelter or protection (as from light or wind) to ⟨~*ed* his eyes with his hand⟩ **b** : to shut off by interposing something that resembles a screen ⟨will perhaps try whether the magnetic power is not to be ~*ed* off —John Tyndall⟩ ⟨was ~*ed* by army regulations which forbid his making political speeches —*Time*⟩ **c** : to separate (an opponent in a game) as if with a screen: as (1) : to prevent (an opponent in basketball) from reaching a desired position without causing bodily contact (2) : to prevent (an opponent in soccer) from having a clear view of the ball by standing or moving so as to conceal it (3) : to cover (one's own server) in order to conceal the direction of the serve from opponents in volleyball **3** : to conceal from view or knowledge : HIDE ⟨20 paces of thick falling snow ~*ed* the man from him —Morley Callaghan⟩ ⟨works in a bookshop, her identity ~*ed* from the customers —*Newsweek*⟩ **4 a** (1) : to pass through a screen; *esp* : to pass (as coal, gravel, or paper stock) through a screen in order to separate one part from another (2) : to remove by or as if by a screen — usu. used with *out* ⟨moisture in the air ~*s* out much of the solar heat radiation —Marston Bates⟩ **b** (1) : to examine usu. methodically in order to make a separation into different groups ⟨the students were ~*ed* before leaving their home countries, insuring that no one with false opinions or dangerous attitudes would get through —W.C.Booth⟩ ⟨carefully ~*s* all visa applications —Ralph de Toledano⟩ ⟨industry will be ~*ed* again for the young, healthy, and dispensable —*Newsweek*⟩ ⟨several antibiotics . . . have been ~*ed* for antituberculosis activity —J.F.Bohmfalk⟩ (2) : to examine (an area) in order to remove whatever is undesirable ⟨preceded the diplomats and ~*ed*, made sanitary and reasonably murderproof the area of the conference —H.S.Canby⟩ (3) : to select by a screening process ⟨the colonel had invited 5000 carefully ~*ed* leading citizens to sip punch —*Time*⟩ (4) : to eliminate by or as if by a screening process ⟨the committee should ~ from the material received any items it deems unsuitable —*Accounting Rev.*⟩ — usu. used with *out* ⟨even the best educated . . . are ~*ed* out socially by the policy of white supremacy —Margaret Mackay⟩ (5) : to examine as a censor : CENSOR ⟨passed an ordinance creating a board of review to ~ literature sold in the city —James Rorty⟩ **5** *Brit* : to post on a bulletin board **6 a** : to provide with a screen to keep out insects **b** : to provide (as an electronic device) with a screen to prevent agencies in one part of an apparatus from affecting other parts **7 a** : to project (as a motion-picture film) on a screen ⟨exhibitors were required by law to ~ a short with every feature —Helen Grayson⟩ **b** : to present in a motion picture ⟨~*ed* an abbreviated version of the book⟩ ⟨was ~*ed* in the male leads of several westerns⟩ **8** : SILK-SCREEN ~ *vi* : to appear on a motion-picture screen ⟨he ~*s* well⟩ ⟨sounds a bit more silly and maudlin than it ~*s* —*Newsweek*⟩ **syn** see CONCEAL

[3]screen \"\ *adj* [[1]*screen*] **1** : having a screen to keep out insects ⟨~ door⟩ ⟨~ porch⟩ **2** : of or relating to motion pictures ⟨an actor who became famous as a ~ star⟩ ⟨the novel's ~ potentialities —*Publishers' Weekly*⟩ **3** : SILK-SCREEN

screen·able \-nəbəl\ *adj* : capable of being screened esp. for a motion picture ⟨old-time romances while seldom ~ still furnish plot examples —Louella Parsons⟩

screen analysis *n* : examination of grain meal by passing the particles through screens whose openings gradually decrease in size and by measuring the amount retained on each screen

screen bulkhead *n* : a bulkhead that is dust-tight but not watertight

screen cloth *n* : material for screens; *specif* : a metal or plastic mesh for window and door screens

screen·er \-nə(r)\ *n* -s : one that screens: as **a** : one that puts in screens (as in windows or doors) **b** : SCREENMAN

screen facade *n* : a facade that conceals the form or dimensions of the building to which it is attached (as by exceeding the building in height or width)

screen gate *n* : a screen over the outlet of a drain that blocks entrance but is hinged so as to permit the escape of debris

screen grid *n* : a grid placed between the plate and the control grid of an electron or vacuum tube to eliminate the effect of plate-potential variations on the control grid

screenhouse \'=,=\ *n* : a structure in which berries or other fruits are screened or sorted

screenier *comparative of* SCREENY

screeniest *superlative of* SCREENY

screening *n* -s **1** : the act or action of one that screens: as **a** : the work of a screener **b** : a showing of a motion picture ⟨requested a ~ of his picture —A.D.Roe⟩ **c** : the act of examining in order to make a separation into different groups ⟨sends newly offered finishes through his laboratory for a thorough ~ —R.E.Ellsworth⟩ **2 screenings** *pl but sing or pl in constr* **a** : material that has been passed through a screen: as (1) : the small imperfect grains, weed seeds, and other foreign material having feeding value that are separated in cleaning grain by a screen (2) : fine coal separated from the larger lumps by a screen having holes usu. from slightly more than ½ inch to two inches in diameter — compare SLACK **b** : material retained by a screen: as (1) : the coarse material retained by a screen in the treatment of wood pulp or paper stock (2) : the material removed from sewage by a screen **c** : a coarse wrapping paper made from pulp screenings **3** : a process of stripping a halftone tint film on a transparent area of another negative **4** : SCREEN CLOTH

screenland \'=,=\ *n* : FILMDOM

screen·less \-nləs\ *adj* : having no screen

screenlike \'=,=\ *adj* : resembling a screen

screenman \'skrēnmən\ *n, pl* **screenmen** : a worker who uses or operates screens to clean or size, to sift, to separate, or to strain — called also *screener*

screen memory *n* : an imagined or real recollection of early childhood that is recalled with magnification of importance or other distortion and that aids in the repression of another memory of deep emotional significance

screeno \'skrē(,)nō\ *n* -s *sometimes cap* [[1]*screen* + *-o*] : bingo designed for play by audiences in motion-picture theaters

screen pass *n* : a forward pass play in football in which the receiver is protected by a screen of blockers

screen plate *n* : a photographic plate on which one of the coatings consists of the minute color filters usu. red, green, and blue violet that are necessary for taking and projecting a color image

screenplay \'=,=\ *n* : the written form of a story prepared for motion-picture production including description of characters, details of scenes and settings, dialogue, and stage directions

screen print *n* : a silk-screen print

screen printing *n* : silk-screen printing

screen process *n* **1** : an additive three-color process in which a mosaic screen composed of minute color elements distributed either in an irregular fashion (as in the autochrome) or in a regular order (as in the Finlay process) is so placed that the light during exposure must pass through the screen before it affects a panchromatic emulsion behind it **2** : SILK-SCREEN PROCESS

screens *pl of* SCREEN, *pres 3d sing of* SCREEN

screens·man \'skrēnzmən\ *n, pl* **screensmen** : a tender of a grain-cleaning machine

screen test *n* **1** : a photographic test for estimating the ability of a prospective motion-picture actor **2** : a short film sequence made in order to estimate the ability of a prospective motion-picture actor

screen-test \'=,=\ *vt* [*screen test*] : to subject to a screen test

screen tree *n* : a tree that is left standing in a woodlot to provide shade

screen-wall \'=,=\ *n* : a wall that is erected to conceal or break a view and that supports no vertical weight other than its own weight

screenwell \'=,=\ *n* : a vertical recess for the traveling screen imposed on the cooling-water intake of a steam power plant

screen wiper *n, Brit* : WINDSHIELD WIPER

screenwork \'=,=\ *n* : work that constitutes a screen which sets off or protects : GRILLWORK

screenwriter \'=,==\ *n* : a writer of screenplays

screeny \'skrēnē\ *adj* -ER/-EST : suggestive of a screen

screes *pl of* SCREE

[1]screeve \'skrēv\ *vi* [ME *scryven*, fr. MF *escrever* (3d sing. pres., *escrive, escrieve*), lit., to burst open, fr. OF, fr. *es-* (fr. L *ex-*) + *crever* to burst, fr. L *crepare* to crack — more at RAVEN] *dial Brit* : to exude moisture : OOZE, LEAK

[2]screeve \"\ *n* -s [prob. fr. It *scrivere* to write, fr. L *scribere* — more at SCRIBE] *chiefly Brit* : a piece of writing; *esp* : a begging letter

[3]screeve \"\ *vb* -ED/-ING/-S [prob. fr. It *scrivere* to write] *vt, chiefly Brit* : to write (as a letter) in order to beg ~ *vi, chiefly Brit* : to draw pictures on a sidewalk in order to attract passersby and obtain charity

screev·er \-və(r)\ *n* -s *chiefly Brit* : one who makes a living by drawing pictures on sidewalks in order to obtain charity from passersby : SIDEWALK ARTIST

[1]screw \'skrü\ *n* -s [ME *skrewe*, fr. MF *escroe, escroue* female screw, nut, fr. ML *scrofa*, fr. L, sow] **1 a** : a simple machine of the inclined plane type consisting of a spirally grooved solid cylinder and a correspondingly grooved hollow cylinder of equal dimensions in which the applied force acts in a spiral path along the grooves while the resisting force acts along the axis of the cylinder — compare JACKSCREW **b** : a cylinder with a helical cut groove on the outer surface or a cone with a conical spiral groove used variously (as to fasten, apply pressure, transmit motion, or make adjustments) esp. where a large mechanical advantage and irreversible motion are desired; *specif* : a cylindrical fastener that is usu. pointed, that has a head with a slot or recess, that is helically or spirally threaded, and that is designed for insertion into material by rotating (as with a screwdriver) — compare ARCHIMEDES' SCREW, DIFFERENTIAL SCREW, HINDLEY'S SCREW, INTERRUPTED SCREW, LEFT-HAND SCREW THREAD, MACHINE SCREW, RIGHT-HANDED SCREW, WOOD SCREW, WORM **c** : a hollow cylinder or cone with a spiral groove upon its inner surface into which a male screw may advance and fit when rotated in the proper direction — compare NUT **2** : any of various devices consisting wholly or partly of a screw or possessing a worm: as **a** *obs* : GIMLET **b** : a wormed tool used for pulling; *specif* : CORKSCREW **c** : the worm of a corkscrew or gimlet **d** *usu* **screws** *pl* : THUMBSCREW 2 **e** : SCREW PROPELLER **f** : a threaded device used in bone surgery for fixation of parts (as fragments of fractured bones) **3 a** (1) : a form resembling a screw : SPIRAL ⟨stems thin and lightly twisted — the ~ being communicated to the surface —Albert Hartshorne⟩ (2) : something having a spiral form ⟨scarcely the ~ of his tail to be seen —R.D.Blackmore⟩ (3) : a twisting out of shape : CONTORTION ⟨a kind of ~ in her face and carriage, expressive of suppressed emotion —Charles Dickens⟩ **b** : a spiral twisting motion : a screwing motion ⟨the barber pole rested its stripes from their daily ~ —Herbert Gold⟩ **c** : spiral threading or grooving **d** (1) *Brit* : spin imparted to a cue ball by screwing it (2) *Brit* : a shot made by screwing the cue ball (3) : a similar spin imparted to the ball in various other games (as ping-pong) **4** : a means of applying painful physical, mental, or moral pressure (as for coercion or extortion) ⟨the bookie turns on the ~*s* for his money —*Newsweek*⟩ ⟨they feel the ~: they dread exposure —Henry James †1916⟩ — usu. used in pl. **5 a** : an act of copulation — usu. considered vulgar **b** : a partner in sexual intercourse — usu. considered vulgar **6** : KEY **7** : a worn-out, broken-down, or otherwise unsound horse **8 a** (1) : a prison guard (2) : TURNKEY (3) : POLICEMAN **b** : an extortionate person : a sharp bargainer : SKINFLINT **c** *slang* : FOOL ⟨why, the old ~ took that for a compliment —Joseph Hergesheimer⟩ **d** : COWBOY **9** *chiefly Brit* : a small paper packet wrapped by twisting both ends and often used for small quantities (as of tobacco, salt, pepper) for ready use **10** : SCREW-SHIP **11** *Brit* : SALARY, PAY **12** *Brit* : LOOK, GLANCE ⟨had a ~ at his self in the glass —Richard Llewellyn⟩

[2]screw \"\ *vb* -ED/-ING/-S *vt* **1 a** (1) : to attach or fasten by means of a screw ⟨~ a lock on a door⟩ (2) : to close and seal shut by means of a screw ⟨~*ed* the box top tight⟩ (3) : to unite or separate by means of a screw or a twisting motion ⟨~ the two pieces together⟩ (4) : to press tightly in a device (as a vise) operated by a screw (5) : to operate, tighten, or adjust by means of a screw; *specif* : to tighten or raise the pitch of (a musical string) by turning a screw or key (6) : to torture by means of a thumbscrew (7) : to lace very tight (8) : to cap or uncap by twisting a cover ⟨so clumsy with sleepiness that he could hardly ~ open the toothpaste —Clemence Dane⟩ ⟨~ the jar tight⟩ **b** (1) : to insert (as a spirally grooved object) into a usu. spirally grooved receptacle with a twisting motion ⟨~ one piece of the fishing rod into the other⟩ (2) : to cause to rotate spirally about an axis ⟨the level may be adjusted by ~*ing* the bolt up or down⟩ (3) : to rotate (a receptacle with internal spiral grooves) about a male screw ⟨~ on a nut⟩ **2 a** (1) : to twist (as the face) into strained or contorted configurations ⟨their tanned faces ~*ed* into painful and unaccustomed lines of concentration —E.A.McCourt⟩ ⟨their shoulders ~*ed* up with the cold —Willa Cather⟩ (2) : to partially close or otherwise alter the shape of (an eye) : SQUINT ⟨~*ed* her eyes tight and tried to read the lettering —Mavis Gallant⟩ ⟨~ up one eye into an imaginary monocle —J.P. O'Donnell⟩ (3) : to roll and twist into a shapeless mass : CRUMPLE ⟨with disgust he ~*ed* the sheet up and threw it across the hut —R.E.Robinson⟩ **b** (1) : to cause to move in a spiral, twisting, or tortuous manner (as into or through a narrow opening) ⟨capable of rotating . . . and thus ~*ing* themselves through the water —K.A.Bisset⟩ (2) : to cause (a scrimmage in rugby) to twist round (3) : to cause (a ball) to swerve; *specif, Brit* : to hit (a cue ball) low down and slightly to the side so that it will be deflected in a curve after striking an object ball **c** : to furnish with a spiral groove or ridge : THREAD **3** : to increase the intensity, quantity, or capability of — usu. used with *up* ⟨the speed ~*ed* up exhilaration to a point almost beyond bearing —P.H.Newby⟩ ⟨~ himself up to the talking point —Aldous Huxley⟩ ⟨trying to ~ up courage to confess —Will Scott⟩ **4 a** *obs* : to root deeply (an idea or habit) by insinuation **b** *archaic* : to insinuate (oneself) gradually ⟨~*ed* himself into the partial confidence of the Laird —Sir Walter Scott⟩ **5** : to alter the sense of to suit one's purpose ⟨by jurisprudential construction, ~*ing* up misdemeanors into felonies —Jeremy Bentham⟩ **6 a** : to practice extortion upon : oppress or dispossess by unreasonable or extortionate exactions or conditions ⟨quarrelled with his agents and ~*ed* his tenants —W.M.Thackeray⟩ **b** : to extract by pressure or threat ⟨landlords were ~*ing* the last penny from their poor tenants —Hugh McVeigh⟩ ⟨stayed on for over two months, in order to ~ out of the . . . prime minister a promise —Reader Bullard⟩ **c** : to induce to a reduction in price or rent ⟨~*ed* the landlady down to a shilling —Harry Lauder⟩ **d** *slang* : to deprive of something due : CHEAT ⟨split up the dirty jobs among the deckhands, so nobody got ~*ed* —Richard Bissell⟩ **7** : to copulate with — usu. considered vulgar **8** : to enter for burglary by means of a skeleton key **9** *slang* : to spoil by meddling or incompetence — usu. used with *up* ⟨somebody's ~*ed* things up, we're nowhere near our objective —*Infantry Jour.*⟩ ~ *vi* **1 a** : to rotate or have the ability to rotate like a screw ⟨the nut ~*s* on here⟩ ⟨this piece ~*s* into the other⟩ **b** : to function as a screw **2** : to turn or move with a twisting or writhing motion ⟨~*ing* about to catch a glimpse of that little beauty —Geoff Bingham⟩ **3** : to cause a ball to swerve **4** : to be parsimonious : SCRIMP ⟨must ~ and save in order to pay off the money —W.M.Thackeray⟩ **5** : to move by means of a screw propeller **6** : COPULATE — usu. considered vulgar **7** *slang* : to leave quickly : hurry away ⟨come on, let's ~ out of here —Robert Lowry⟩

³screw \"\ *or* **scrow** \'skrō\ *n* -s [prob. modif. of obs. F *escrouelle* (now *écrouelle*)] : an amphipod crustacean — compare SAND SCREW

screw·able \'skrüəbəl\ *adj* : capable of being screwed

screw anchor *n* **1** : an anchor in the form of a sharp-pointed screw with broad flanges used principally for moorings **2** : an expanding metal shell that wedges itself into a drilled hole upon insertion and is used to retain a screw in material (as concrete, brick, or tile) otherwise unsuitable

screw arbor *n* : an arbor to which a cutter is attached by means of a screw thread

screw around *vi, slang* : to waste or pass time : LOITER ⟨got all night to *screw around* here —Richard Bissell⟩

screw auger *n* **1** : AUGER 1 **2** : a widely distributed ladies'-tresses (*Spiranthes cernua*) having creamy white vanilla-scented flowers and growing esp. in low damp places through much of eastern and central No. America

screw back *vt, Brit* : DRAW 1l

¹screwball \'ₛ,ₛ\ *n* [¹*screw* + *ball*] **1** : a baseball pitch having reverse spin and a break in opposite direction to a curve **2** : one whose ideas, expressions, or actions are considered whimsical, eccentric, dizzily fantastic, or insane

²screwball \"\ *adj* **1** : crazily eccentric or nonsensical : ZANY ⟨carry on a ~ campaign in their editorial columns . . . to undo the work . . . done by their headlines —*Canadian Forum*⟩ ⟨a fantastic ménage characterized by dabbling in the arts, ~ acquaintances drifting in and out, terrible tantrums, and soul-searching —*N. Y. Herald Tribune Bk. Rev.*⟩ **2** : characterized by eccentric or whimsical responses to speech or action upon a pattern of otherwise normal behavior ⟨~ comedy⟩ ⟨~ heroine⟩

screw bean *n* **1** : a shrub or small tree (*Prosopis pubescens*) of the southwestern U. S. — called also *tornillo, screwbean mesquite* **2** : a spirally twisted sweet pod that is the fruit of the screw bean and is used for fodder or ground into meal for use as feed

screw bell *n* : an internally threaded bell-shaped device for recovering tools dropped down a borehole

screw bolt *n* : a bolt having a screw thread on it

screw box *n* **1** : a socket for a screw **2** : a screw plate for cutting wooden screws

screw cap *n* : a cap that screws onto a threaded container finish (as on a bottle or jar)

screw conveyor *n* : CONVEYER 2a(8)

screw coupling *n* : an internally threaded sleeve nut that usu. has right-and-left threads and is used for coupling (as rods or pipes)

screw-cutting lathe \'ₛ,ₛₛ-\ *n* : a slide-rest lathe having a lead screw with a pitch suitable for cutting threads

screw·drive \'skrü,drīv\ *vt* [back-formation fr. *screwdriver*] : to drive in with or as if with a screwdriver

screw·driv·er \-və(r)\ *n* **1** : a tool for turning screws so as to

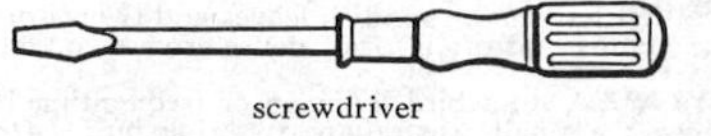

screwdriver

drive them into their place having usu. a thin wedge-shaped end that enters the slot or recess in the head of a screw **2** : a mixture of vodka and orange juice served with ice

screwdriver bit *n* : a brace bit shank with a screwdriver tip

screwed *adj* [fr. past part. of ²*screw*] *Brit* : INTOXICATED

screwed tail *var of* SCREW TAIL

screw·er \'skrüə(r)\ *n* -s : one that screws

screw eye *n* **1** : a wood screw with a head in the form of a closed loop **2** : a long screw with a handle used esp. by stage carpenters

screw fern *n* : EBONY SPLEENWORT

screwfly \'ₛ,ₛ\ *n* : the adult of a screwworm

screw gear *or* **screw gearing** *n* **1** : SCREW WHEEL **2** : gearing composed of or having as a chief essential a worm and worm wheel

screwhead \'ₛ,ₛ\ *n* : the head of a screw

screw hook *n* : a small hook with a threaded shank for screwing into woodwork or paneling

screwier *comparative of* SCREWY

screwiest *superlative of* SCREWY

screw jack *n* : JACKSCREW

screw joint *n* : a rod or pipe joint made with a screw coupling

screw key *n* **1** : a wrench or spanner for turning a screw or nut **2** : a threaded key

screw hooks

screw·less \'skrüləs\ *adj* : having no screw

screw machine *n* : a form of turret lathe usu. having a hollow spindle through which a bar can be fed to be machined into bolts, studs, and other screws or any small repetition work (as handles or spindles)

screw machinery *n* : machinery for making screws; *esp* : semiautomatic machinery for turning out screws in large quantities

screw·man \-ümən\ *n, pl* **screwmen** **1** : one who passes metal through a rolling mill and reduces it to desired thickness by adjusting screws that regulate roller clearance **2** : one who helps to prepare the way for and to set up power shovels and cranes — called also *jackman* **3** : one who loads bales of cotton onto a riverboat

screwnail \'ₛ,ₛ\ *n* **1 a** : WOOD SCREW **b** : DRIVESCREW **2** : a nail with a screw thread to increase its holding power

screw nut *n* : NUT 3

screw peg *n* : a small screw without a head used esp. for fastening boot and shoe soles

screw pile *n* : a usu. hollow and cast iron pile that has a screw flange of usu. from one to two turns and is used in soft mud or other location requiring a large supporting surface at the end of the pile

screw-pile *or* **screw-piled** \'ₛ,ₛ\ *adj* [*screw pile*] : built on screw piles

screw pine *n* : a plant of the genus *Pandanus* including several that are cultivated for their ornamental foliage — see TEXTILE SCREW PINE

screw-pine family *n* : PANDANACEAE

screw-pitch gage *n* : THREAD GAGE

screw plate *n* : a flat metal plate with one or more holes drilled, tapped, and filed with a cutting edge for threading screws, pipes, or rods by hand

screw pod *or* **screw-pod mesquite** *n* : SCREW BEAN

screw press *or* **screw punch** *n* : a press having a ram that is forced downward by the turning of a spindle with a steep-pitched thread

screw propeller *n* : a device consisting of a central hub with two, three, or more similar radiating blades symmetrically placed and twisted so that each forms part of a helical surface like that of a screw thread and used to propel a vehicle (as a steamship, motorboat, or airplane)

screw pump *n* : a pump in which the working pressure is created by means of screw-shaped impellers in the vertical water column

screw rivet *n* : a short bolt threaded throughout its length and riveted over on its ends when in place

screws *pl of* SCREW, *pres 3d sing of* SCREW

screw shell *n* : a long slender spiral gastropod shell (as of a gastropod of *Turritella* or related genera)

screw-ship \'ₛ,ₛ\ *n* : a ship driven by a screw propeller

screw spike *n* : a railroad spike with a screw thread on the upper part of the shank so that the spike can be screwed home after being driven part way in

screw stay *n* : STAY BOLT

screwstem \'ₛ,ₛ\ *n* : a plant of the genus *Bartonia*

screw stud *n* : STUD BOLT

screw surface *n* : a surface resembling a screw in form

screw tail *or* **screwed tail** *n* : a short knotty twisted tail characteristic of the bulldog but abnormal in most other animals

screw tap *n* : TAP 5a

screw thread *n* **1** : the projecting helical rib of a screw **2** : one complete turn of a screw thread — compare PITCH 2b(2); BUTTRESS THREAD, MULTIPLE THREAD, SQUARE THREAD

screw tree *n* : a shrub or tree of the genus *Helicteres; esp* : an East Indian shrub (*H. isora*) sometimes cultivated for its hairy leaves and orange-red flowers

screw up *vt* **1** : to tighten, fasten, or lock by or as by turning a screw **2** : to raise (as a rent) extortionately

screw vault *n* : a vault in gymnastics in which the body is raised sideward to clear the apparatus while making a ¾ turn in the opposite direction around its long axis

screw wheel *n* : a gear wheel with teeth intersecting the pitch surface in helical lines and thus forming parts of the threads of a many-threaded screw : HELICAL GEAR — called also *screw gear*

screwworm \'ₛ,ₛ\ *n* : a grub that is the larva of a two-winged fly (*Callitroga hominivorax*) occurring in the warmer parts of America and sometimes laying its eggs in sores or wounds or in the nostrils of mammals including man, that is armed with rings of small spines, and that bores into the flesh and causes serious or sometimes fatal results; *broadly* : a calliphorid larva that parasitizes the flesh of mammals

screwworm fly *n* : SCREWFLY

screw wrench *or* **screw spanner** *n* : a wrench that has a jaw adjusted by a screw : ADJUSTABLE WRENCH

screwy \'skrüē, -üi\ *adj* -ER/-EST **1** *Brit* : somewhat intoxicated **2** : hard and exacting in selling or renting : NIGGARDLY, MEAN **3** : involuted like a screw : WINDING, SPIRAL ⟨a big-eared head with glasses and ~ hair —Josephine Johnson⟩ **4 a** : crazily absurd, eccentric, or unusual : oddly and often disturbingly different and unfamiliar ⟨unusual chords and odd slips in the tune and ~ forms —Leonard Bernstein⟩ ⟨something is haywire, ~, and badly disrupted —F.A.Johnson⟩ **b** : CRAZY, INSANE ⟨she must have been ~ —Leslie Charteris⟩

scrib·al \'skrībəl\ *adj* [¹*scribe* + *-al*] : of, relating to, or due to a scribe ⟨a ~ error⟩

scrib·bla·tive \'skriblәd·iv\ *adj* [¹*scribble* + *-ative*] : of, relating to, or given to verbose and hastily written writing ⟨the arts babblative and ~ —Robert Southey⟩

¹scrib·ble \'skribəl\ *vb* **scribbled; scribbled; scribbling** \-b(ə)liŋ\ **scribbles** [ME *scriblen*, fr. ML *scribillare*, fr. L *scribere* to write — more at SCRIBE] *vt* **1** : to write hastily or carelessly without regard to legibility, correctness, or considered thought ⟨had to ~ the very first ideas that tinkled in his head —Earle Birney⟩ ⟨just enough time to ~ their own name —H.A.Smith⟩ **2** : to fill or cover with careless or worthless writings ⟨a *scribbled* envelope⟩ ⟨papers . . . *scribbled* over with clues —*English Digest*⟩ ~ *vi* : to write or draw in haste without care as to legibility or value : make indecipherable or meaningless marks

²scribble \"\ *n* -s **1** : a writing of little value; *esp* : a note written without thought **2** : hasty or careless writing or drawing : illegible or random marks written or drawn ⟨these are the fragmentary meanings I contrive to disengage from the ~*s* —Aldous Huxley⟩

³scribble \"\ *vt* -ED/-ING/-S [alter. of earlier *scruble*, prob. fr. D *schrobbelen* to card, freq. of *schrobben* to scrub] : to card (wool fibers) coarsely; *specif* : to perform the preliminary operation of tearing apart

scrib·ble·ment \-bəlmənt\ *n* -s [¹*scribble* + *-ment*] : a scribbled writing : SCRIBBLING

¹scrib·bler \-b(ə)lə(r)\ *n* -s [¹*scribble* + *-er*] : one that scribbles: as **a** : an unknown, minor, or amateur writer ⟨an unimportant ~ whose name does not deserve to be dignified by mention —W.M.Payne⟩ **b** : one that writes rapidly, voluminously, or energetically ⟨I am generally supposed to be a determined and energetic ~ —J.B.Priestley⟩

²scribbler \"\ *n* -s [³*scribble* + *-er*] : a machine that scribbles wool fibers

scrib·bling·ly *adv* [*scribbling* (fr. pres. part. of ¹*scribble*) + *-ly*] : in a scribbling manner

scrib·bly \-b(ə)lē, -li\ *adj* [²*scribble* + *-y*] : covered with or consisting of scribbles

scribbly gum *n* [so-called fr. marks on its bark made by insects] : any of several Australian white ashes (esp. *Eucalyptus rossii* or *E. haemastoma*)

¹scribe \'skrīb\ *n* -s [ME, fr. L *scriba* official writer, fr. *scribere* to write; akin to Gk *skariphasthai* to scratch an outline, sketch, *skariphos* stylus, sketch, *keirein* to cut — more at SHEAR] **1** : one of a class of men devoted to the study and exposition of the law during the Persian and early Greek periods of Jewish history and serving orig. as copyists, editors, and interpreters of Scripture and esp. of the Law and in New Testament times mainly as jurists — called also *sopher;* compare RABBI **2 a** : an official or public writer acting usu. as a clerk or keeper of accounts **b** : one who writes at dictation **c** : an official having secretarial duties; *specif* : the secretary of a girl scout troop **d** : a copier of manuscripts **e** : a skilled penman **3 a** : one who writes : AUTHOR, WRITER; *specif* : JOURNALIST **b** : a paid political writer or journalist

²scribe \"\ *vb* -ED/-ING/-S *vi* : to work as a scribe : WRITE ~ *vt* : to write down : INSCRIBE

³scribe \"\ *vt* -ED/-ING/-S [prob. short for *describe*] **1 a** : to mark (as wood, metal, or brick) by cutting or scratching a line with a pointed instrument (as a scriber or a pair of compasses) **b** : to make (as a line) by cutting or scratching **2** : to cut (an object) to fit closely to a somewhat irregular surface (as a board to the curves of a molding)

⁴scribe \"\ *n* -s **1** *dial Brit* **a** : a written mark **b** : a short piece of writing **2 a** : SCRIBER **b** : a tool used (as in marking survey lines) for cutting marks into wood or bark **c** *also* **scribe saw** : a saw-toothed tool for cutting up beef carcasses

scrib·er \-bə(r)\ *n* -s [³*scribe* + *-er*] **1** : one that scribes; *specif* : a sharp-pointed tool for marking off material (as wood or metal) to be cut — called also *scratch awl* **2** [⁴*scribe* + *-er*] : a slaughterhouse worker using a scribe saw

scribers 1

scribing *n* -s [fr. gerund of ²*scribe*] : an incised or written marking : INSCRIPTION

scribing block *n* : SURFACE GAUGE 1

scribing iron *n* : an iron-pointed instrument for scribing (as on a cask or log)

scrib·ism \'skrī,bizəm\ *n* -s [¹*scribe* + *-ism*] **1** : the doctrines and activities of the Jewish scribes in the time of Christ **2** : internal authoritarianism and literalistic legalism (as in religion)

scried *past of* SCRY

scries *pl of* SCRY, *pres 3d sing of* SCRY

¹scrieve \'skrēv\ *vi* [of Scand origin; akin to ON *skrefa* to stride] *Scot* : to move along swiftly and smoothly

²scrieve \"\ *var of* SCRIVE

scriev·er \'skrēvər\ *Scot var of* SCRIVER 1

¹scrig·gle \'skrigəl\ *vi* -ED/-ING/-S [blend of *squirm* & *wriggle*] : WRIGGLE, TWIST, SQUIRM

²scriggle \"\ *n* -s **1** : the act of wriggling **2** : SQUIGGLE

scrike \'skrīk\ *vi* -ED/-ING/-S [ME *scriken*, of Scand origin; akin to Norw *skrike* to shriek, Dan *skrige*] : SHRIEK

scrim \'skrim\ *n* -s [origin unknown] **1** : a durable plain-woven fabric usu. of cotton woven loosely with fine to coarse meshes and given various finishes for use in clothing, curtains, building trades, and industry **2** : thin canvas glued on the inside of a panel to prevent distortion (as by shrinking or checking) **3** : a transparent theater drop or a transparent section in a drop **4** : a gauze or mesh panel placed outside of the range of a camera to diffuse harsh light

¹scrim·mage \'skrimij, -mēj\ *n* -s [alter. of ¹*skirmish*] **1 a** : a minor battle between small forces of armed men : SKIRMISH **b** : a confused scrambling fight between two or more parties : SCUFFLE, BRAWL ⟨escaped from the ~ minus his hat and with his garments woefully torn —Rachel Henning⟩ **2 a** : SCRUMMAGE **b** : the interplay between two teams in American football that begins with the snap of the ball and continues until the ball is dead **c** : practice play between a team's various squads (as in football) **d** : the first line of scrimmage formed after a kickoff in football ⟨first play from ~⟩

²scrimmage \"\ *vb* -ED/-ING/-S *vi* **1** : to search busily **2** : to take part in a scrimmage ~ *vt* **1** : to throw (a ball) into a scrimmage **2** : to compete against (an opposing team) in a practice football game ⟨~ the junior varsity⟩

scrimmage line *n* : LINE OF SCRIMMAGE

scrim·mag·er \-jə(r)\ *n* -s [²*scrimmage* + *-er*] : a participant in a scrimmage

¹scrimp \'skrimp\ *adj* [perh. of Scand origin; akin to Sw *skrympa* to shrink — more at SHRIMP] : SCANTY, MEAGER

²scrimp \"\ *vb* -ED/-ING/-S *vt* **1** : to be niggardly in providing for : put on short allowance ⟨~*s* his family⟩ **2** : to make too small, short, or scanty : be sparing or niggardly in or with : limit too closely ⟨~ the pattern of a coat⟩ ⟨~ food⟩ **3** : to save slowly and with difficulty by minor economies ⟨here's five bob I've been ~*ing* from the house money —Ruth Park⟩ ~ *vi* : to be frugal or niggardly in economizing ⟨office girls who ~ all year to pay for their vacations —Tibor Koeves⟩ ⟨in restoring the place they ~*ed* on plumbing —W.A.White⟩

scrimp·tion \-m(p)shən\ *n* -s [²*scrimp* + *-tion*] *chiefly dial* : a small amount : PITTANCE

scrimpy \-mpē, -mpi\ *adj* -ER/-EST [*scrimp* + *-y*] **1** : small or barely sufficient in size or quantity : MEAGER, SCANTY ⟨her ~ and short white petticoat —Elizabeth C. Gaskell⟩ **2** : given to scrimping : PARSIMONIOUS **syn** see MEAGER

scrimshander *or* **scrimshandy** *var of* SKRIMSHANDER

scrim·shank \'skrim,shaŋk\ *vi* -ED/-ING/-S [origin unknown] *Brit* : to shirk one's work or obligations

scrim·shank·er \-ŋkə(r)\ *n* -s [*scrimshank* + *-er*] *Brit* : SHIRKER

¹scrim·shaw \'skrim,shȯ\ *n* -s [prob. alter. of *skrimshander*] **1** : any of various carved or engraved useful or decorative articles (as canes, cribbage boards, corset stays, snuff boxes, or small pieces of statuary) sometimes colored by brushing ink into the engraved lines and made esp. by American whalemen esp. from whalebone or whale ivory **2** : scrimshawed work ⟨a large collection of ~⟩ **3** : the art, practice, or technique of producing scrimshaw

²scrimshaw \"\ *vb* -ED/-ING/-S *vt* : to carve or engrave (as a whale's tooth or jawbone) into scrimshaw ~ *vi* : to produce scrimshaw

scri·my \'skrīmē\ *adj* -ER/-EST [origin unknown] **1** : STINGY, NIGGARDLY **2** : DIRTY, DISGUSTING ⟨worry about the gossip, secretiveness, and other ~ sides —Al Hine⟩

scrin \'skrin\ *n* -s [prob. akin to OHG *scrunta* split, crack, *scrintan* to split] *dial Eng* : a small ore vein

scrinch \'skrinch\ *n* -ES [origin unknown] *dial Eng* : a tiny bit : PINCH

¹scringe \'skrinj\ *vi* -ED/-ING/-S [alter. (perh. influenced by *shrink*) of ¹*cringe*] *dial* : CRINGE, FLINCH

²scringe \"\ *vi* [origin unknown] *dial* : to flog the water in fishing

³scringe \"\ *n* -s : a small seine net used in scringing

¹scrip \'skrip\ *n* -s [ME *scrippe*, fr. ML *scrippum* pilgrim's knapsack, perh. fr. L *scirpus* bulrush, reed] *archaic* : a small bag or wallet carried esp. by a pilgrim or shepherd

²scrip \"\ *n* -s [in senses 1 & 2 short for ¹*script;* in senses 3 & 4 prob. short for *subscription receipt*] **1** : a short writing (as a certificate, memorandum, schedule, or list) ⟨call them generally, man by man, according to the ~ —Shak.⟩ **2** : a small piece or scrap (as of paper) **3** : any of various documents used as evidence that the holder or bearer is entitled to receive something either absolutely or conditionally: as **a** : a preliminary certificate issued after an allotment usu. on payment of the first installment to one who has subscribed for stock of a bank, railroad, or other company, for a share of other joint property, or for a loan stating the amount subscribed for, the amount already paid, and the dates when the installments are due ⟨insurance ~⟩ ⟨consol ~⟩ and when all installments are paid exchanged for a bond or share certificate **b** : a certificate for a fractional part of a share of stock or of a bond often issued to bondholders upon reorganization or to a stockholder in lieu of a cash dividend and usu. convertible when presented in an amount equal to the face value of a share or bond **c** : a paper currency or token issued for temporary use in an emergency **d** : a certificate of indebtedness in the form of a promise to pay or a certification good for money or goods receivable from a concern that needs funds or pays wages partly in orders on a company store **e** : a certificate (as issued by a federal or state government) that the holder is entitled to take up or receive an allotment of land **4** : documents issued as scrip

scrip *abbr* scriptural; scripture

scrip dividend *n* [²*scrip*] : a dividend payable in promissory notes instead of cash

scrip·less \'skripləs\ *adj* [¹*scrip* + *-less*] : having no wallet

scrip·page \'skripij\ *n* -s [¹*scrip* + *-age*] : the contents of a scrip

¹script \'skript\ *n* -s [L *scriptum* thing written, fr. neut. of *scriptus*, past part. of *scribere* to write — more at SCRIBE] **1 a** : something written : TEXT ⟨ancient philosophers whose ~*s* they had diligently studied —Erwin Schrödinger⟩ **b** : an original or principal instrument or document (as a will or codicil) when executed with copies or a copy when the original is lost **c** (1) : MANUSCRIPT 2 (2) : the written text of a stage play, screenplay, or radio or television broadcast; *specif* : the typescript or mimeographed or published text of a stage play, screenplay, or radio or television broadcast **2 a** : a printed letter similar to a handwritten letter — sometimes used of letters that join each other and thereby distinguished from *cursive* **b** : written characters : HANDWRITING ⟨drew a sheet of paper to him and began to cover it with his thin irritable ~

—Ngaio Marsh⟩ ⟨some of the letters were printed capitals, others were in ~ —E.D.Radin⟩ **c :** a set of characters used in writing one or more languages **:** ALPHABET ⟨written in a ~ which consists entirely of consonants —T.H.Gaster⟩

²script \"\ *vt* -ED/-ING/-S **1 :** to prepare a script for ⟨has his program ~*ed*, though eventually he plans to work into an ad-lib routine —*Newsweek*⟩ **2 :** to prepare a script from **:** adapt for the stage, screen, or broadcasting ⟨~ a novel into a movie⟩

script *abbr* scriptural; scripture

script editor *or* **script reader** *n* [¹*script*] **:** one that edits radio and television scripts, continuities, and commercials to assure conformity with government regulations and company policy — compare CONTINUITY ACCEPTANCE

script·er \ˈskriptə(r)\ *n* -S [²*script* + *-er*] **:** SCRIPTWRITER

script girl *n* [¹*script*] **:** a secretary to a motion-picture director who records information about the photographing of each scene, prompts actors, and writes a synopsis for advertising the movie

scrip·tio de·fec·ti·va \ˈskriptē,ō,dā,fekˈtēvə\ *n* [NL, lit., defective writing] **:** a writing in a Semitic alphabet that contains no vowel points

scrip·tion \ˈskripshən\ *n* -S [L *scription-, scriptio* act of writing, fr. *scriptus* (past part. of *scribere* to write) + *-ion, -io* -ion — more at SCRIBE] **1** *obs* **:** INSCRIPTION **2 :** style of handwriting **:** HANDWRITING

scrip·tio ple·na \,skriptē,ōˈplānə\ *n* [NL, lit., full writing] **:** a writing in a Semitic alphabet that contains vowel points

script lichen *n* [¹*script*] **:** a letter lichen (*Graphis scripta*)

scriptore *n* -S [alter. (influenced by *scriptory*) of obs. E *scritore* escritoire, modif. of F *escritoire*] *obs* **:** WRITING DESK

scrip·to·ri·al \(ˈ)skripˈtōrēəl\ *adj* [L *scriptorius* of writing + E *-al*] **:** of, relating to, or resembling script

scrip·to·ri·um \skripˈtōrēəm\ *also* **scrip·to·ry** \ˈskriptərē\ *n, pl* **scripto·ria** \skripˈtōrēə\ *also* **scriptories** \ˈskriptərēz\ [ML *scriptorium*, fr. L *scriptus* + *-orium* -ory] **:** a writing room; *specif* **:** a copying room in a medieval monastery set apart for the scribes

scrip·to·ry \ˈskriptərē\ *adj* [L *scriptorius*, fr. *scriptus* (past part. of *scribere* to write) + *-orius* -ory — more at SCRIBE] **:** of, relating to, expressed in, or used in writing

script–scene \ˈ⸗,⸗\ *n* **:** a division of a shooting script or screenplay corresponding to a single shot in a motion picture

scrip·tur·al \ˈskripchərəl, -psh(ə)rəl\ *adj* [*scripture* + *-al*] **1** *sometimes cap* **:** of, relating to, contained in, or according to a sacred writing; *specif* **:** of or relating to the Bible **:** BIBLICAL **2 :** done in or relating to writing

scrip·tur·al·ism \-ə,lizəm\ *n* -S [*scriptural* + *-ism*] **:** literal adherence to a body of scripture

scrip·tur·al·ist \-ələst\ *n* -S *often cap* [*scriptural* + *-ist*] **1 :** one who derives his religious beliefs and general philosophy of life from a body of scripture teaching a single harmonious system of doctrine **2 :** one learned in or a devoted student of a body of scripture **3 :** KITABI

scrip·tu·ral·i·ty \,skripchəˈralədˌē, -pshə-, -lətē, -i\ *n* -ES *sometimes cap* [*scriptural* + *-ity*] **1 :** the quality of being scriptural **2 :** a thing that is scriptural

scrip·tur·al·ly \ˈskripchərəlē, -psh(ə)r-, -li\ *adv* [*scriptural* + *-ly*] **:** in accordance with scripture

scrip·tur·al·ness \-rəlnəs\ *n* -ES **:** the quality or state of being scriptural

scrip·ture \ˈskripchə(r), -psh-\ *n* -S [ME, fr. LL *scriptura*, fr. L, act or product of writing, fr. *scriptus* (past part. of *scribere* to write) + *-ura* -ure — more at SCRIBE] **1 a** (1) *usu cap* **:** the books of the Old and New Testament or of either of them **:** BIBLE ⟨a collection . . . from the various parts of the *Scripture* —J.C.Swaim⟩ — often used in pl. ⟨the demand for the *Scriptures* in a familiar tongue has found expression in a great activity of Bible translation —L.A.Weigle⟩ (2) *usu cap* **:** a passage or text from the Bible ⟨in their case was the *Scripture* fulfilled that the first shall be last and the last first —E.C. Colwell⟩ **b :** sacred writing of a religion ⟨Buddhist ~⟩ **c :** a body of writings considered as authoritative ⟨his critical essays provide the ~ of the movement⟩ or as classically embodying the essence of a way of life, movement, era, or nation — often used in pl. ⟨the American ~*s*, the great books of the eighteen-fifties —Van Wyck Brooks⟩ **2 :** something written **:** a writing or portion of a writing ⟨the primitive man's awe for any ~ —George Santayana⟩

scripturient *adj* [LL *scripturient-, scripturiens*, pres. part. of *scripturire* to desire to write, desiderative of L *scribere*] *obs* **:** having a strong urge to write

scrip·tur·ism \ˈskripchə,rizəm, -psh-\ *n* -S [*scripture* + *-ism*] **1** *sometimes cap* **:** SCRIPTURALISM **2 :** a phrase originating in Scripture

scrip·tur·ist \-pchərəst, -psh(ə)r-\ *n* -S *sometimes cap* [*scripture* + *-ist*] **:** SCRIPTURALIST

scriptwriter \ˈ⸗,⸗⸗\ *n* [¹*script* + *writer*] **:** one that writes screenplays or radio or television programs

scritch \ˈskrich\ *chiefly dial var of* SCREECH

scri·vaille \skrəˈvī\ *n* -S [by alter.] **:** SCRIVELLO

scrivan *or* **scrivano** *n, pl* **scrivans** *or* **scrivani** [It *scrivano*, fr. (assumed) VL *scriban-, scriba* — more at SCRIVENER] **:** SCRIBE

¹scrive \ˈskrīv, -rēv\ *vt* -ED/-ING/-S [ME *scriven*, prob. fr. MF *escrivre*, fr. L *scribere* — more at SCRIBE] *chiefly Scot* **:** WRITE, INSCRIBE

²scrive \"\ *n* -S **1** *chiefly Scot* **:** written matter **2** *chiefly Scot* **:** HANDWRITING

scrive board *n* **:** a platform of well-seasoned boards on which are drawn full-size the lines of the body of a ship to be built — compare BODY PLAN

scri·vel·lo \skrəˈve(,)lō\ *n* -ES [origin unknown] **:** an elephant's tusk of a small size commonly used for making billiard balls

scriv·en \ˈskrivən\ *vt* **scrivened; scrivened; scrivening** \-v(ə)niŋ\ **scrivens** [back-formation fr. *scrivener*] *archaic* **:** to put in writing **:** WRITE ⟨this is the thesis ~*ed* in delight —Wallace Stevens⟩

scriv·en·er \ˈskriv(ə)nə(r)\ *n* -S [ME *scriveiner*, fr. *scrivein* copyist, professional writer (fr. MF *escrivein, escrivain*, fr. — assumed — VL *scriban-, scriba*, fr. L *scriba* scribe) + *-er* — more at SCRIBE] **1 a :** a professional or public copyist or writer **:** SCRIBE **b :** a usu. minor or unknown author ⟨never before had mere ~*s* received weekly salaries in the four-figure bracket —Roger Butterfield & Roland Gelatt⟩ **2 :** one whose occupation is to draw contracts or prepare writings **:** NOTARY **3 :** a former agent receiving money for investment at interest and performing duties now usu. performed by a banker, broker, or lawyer

scrivener's palsy *n* **:** WRITER'S CRAMP

scriv·en·ery \-v(ə)nərē\ *n* -ES [*scrivener* + *-ry*] **:** a scrivener's occupation, writing, or place of work

scrivening *n* -S [fr. gerund of *scriven*] **:** the occupation or product of a scrivener **:** WRITING ⟨editorials and the ~*s* of columnists —R.E.Wolseley⟩

scriv·er \ˈskrīvər, -rēv-\ *n* -S [¹*scrive* + *-er*] **1** *chiefly Scot* **:** WRITER **2 :** PARTING TOOL

scrn *abbr* screen

scrobe \ˈskrōb\ *n* -S [L *scrobis* ditch, trench — more at SCRAPE] **:** a small groove (as at the base of the antenna of a weevil or on the outer surface of a mandible)

scro·bic·u·la \skrōˈbikyələ\ *also* **scrobi·cule** \ˈskrōbə,kyül, -räb-\ *n, pl* **scro·bi·cu·lae** \skrōˈbikyə,lē, -,lī\ *also* **scrobicules** [NL *scrobicula*, alter. of L *scrobiculus* little trench, dim. of *scrobis*] **:** a shallow trench (as one of the smooth depressions surrounding the tubercles of a sea urchin) — **scro·bic·u·lar** \skrōˈbikyələ(r)\ *adj*

scro·bic·u·late \skrōˈbikyələt, -,lāt\ *adj* [L *scrobiculus* + E *-ate*] **:** having numerous shallow grooves or depressions **:** PITTED

scro·bic·u·lus \-ləs\ *n, pl* **scrobicu·li** \-,lī\ [NL, fr. L, small trench] **:** SCROBICULA

¹scrod \ˈskräd\ *or* **es·crod** \əˈskräd\ *n* -S [perh. fr. obs. D *schrood* piece cut off, shred, fr. MD *schrode* — more at SHRED] **1 a :** a young cod (*Gadus morrhua*) **b :** the young of any of several other fishes (as the haddock) **2 a :** a small cod split and boned for cooking **b :** a fillet taken from the thick meat just ahead of the tail of a fish (as a cod, haddock, pollack)

²scrod \"\ *vt* **scrodded; scrodded; scrodding; scrods :** to split or fillet (a fish) for cooking

scroful- *or* **scrofulo-** *comb form* [NL, fr. ML *scrofula*] **1 :** scrofula ⟨*scrofulosis*⟩ **2 :** scrofulous and ⟨*scrofulo*tuberculous⟩

scrof·u·la \ˈskrȯfyələ *also* -räf-\ *n* -S [ML, fr. LL *scrofulae* (pl.) swellings of the lymph glands of the neck, lit., little sows, pl. of *scrofula*, dim of L *scrofa* breeding sow] **:** tuberculosis of lymph glands esp. in the neck

scrofularoot \ˈ⸗⸗⸗,⸗\ *n* [*scrofula* + *root*; fr. its supposed efficacy in the treatment of scrofula] **:** DOGTOOTH VIOLET

scrofulaweed \ˈ⸗⸗⸗,⸗\ *n* [*scrofula* + *weed*; fr. its supposed efficacy in the treatment of scrofula] **:** a rattlesnake plantain (*Goodyera pubescens*)

scrof·u·lo·der·ma \,⸗⸗lōˈdərmə\ *n* -S [NL, fr. *scroful-* + *-derma*] **:** a disease of the skin of tuberculous origin (as an inflammation of the neck from draining tuberculous lymph glands) — **scrof·u·lo·der·mic** \¦⸗⸗⸗¦dərmik\ *adj*

scrof·u·lo·sis \,⸗⸗ˈlōsəs\ *n, pl* **scrofulo·ses** \-ō,sēz\ [NL, fr. *scroful-* + *-osis*] **:** the condition of being scrofulous **:** scrofular diathesis

scrof·u·lous \ˈskrȯfyələs *also* -räf-\ *adj* [*scrofula* + *-ous*] **1** *archaic* **a :** of, relating to, or characteristic of scrofula ⟨a child, full of ~ ulcers —Tobias Smollett⟩ **b :** afflicted with scrofula ⟨handled a ~ Quaker, and made him a healthy man —T.B.Macaulay⟩ **2 a :** having a diseased appearance ⟨our canoe . . . lay with her ~ sides on the shore —Farley Mowat⟩ **b :** morally contaminated ⟨denounce the ~ wealth of the times —J.D.Hart⟩

scrog \ˈskräg\ *n* -S [ME *skrogge, scroge*] **1** *dial Brit* **:** a stunted shrub, bush, or branch **:** SCRUB **2** *dial Brit* **:** scrubby land — usu. used in pl.

¹scroll \ˈskrōl\ *n* -S *often attrib* [ME *scrowle*, alter. (influenced by *rolle* roll) of *scrowe*, fr. MF *escroe, escroue* scrap, strip of parchment, scroll, of Gmc origin; akin to MD *schrode* piece cut off, shred — more at SHRED] **1 a :** a long strip (as of papyrus, leather, or parchment) used as the body of a written document and often having a rod with handles at one or both ends for convenience in rolling and storing it ⟨when parchment became available . . . its greater strength permitted the transcription of the entire book on to one long ~ —A.P. Davies⟩ **b** *archaic* **:** a written message (as a letter) ⟨do not exceed the prescript of this ~ —Shak.⟩ **c :** a roster of names **:** LIST ⟨his name was placed high upon the ~ of the world's great —J.C.Fitzpatrick⟩ **d :** an ornamental riband with rolled ends often inscribed with a motto; *specif* **:** ESCROL **e :** a formal testimonial usu. engraved or hand illuminated on special paper (as parchment or vellum) ⟨the guest of honor received a framed ~ —*Springfield* (*Mass.*) *Union*⟩ **2 a :** something that is likened to a scroll ⟨a great glissando, a ~ from the wind instruments —Sacheverell Sitwell⟩ ⟨history which forms the running ~ of his . . . experience —S.H. Adams⟩ **b :** a crescentic deposit of a meandering stream on a floodplain **3 :** a part or ornament more or less resembling a scroll in shape: as **a :** any of various spiral or convoluted forms in ornamental design derived from the curves of a loosely or partly rolled parchment scroll ⟨an oval mat with a row of ~*s* forming the center —Mabel Roffey & Charlotte Cross⟩ **b** (1) **:** a volute of an Ionic, Corinthian, or composite capital (2) **:** a curved molding common in medieval work **c :** a spiral formation or ornament of furniture — see FLEMISH SCROLL; LEG illustration **d :** the curved head of a bowed stringed musical instrument — see VIOLIN illustration **e :** SCROLLHEAD **f** (1) **:** a spiral-shaped rib or slot for gearing with a slot on a radially moving part (as the jaw of a scroll chuck) (2) **:** a casing for a turbine wheel having a spiral waterway of converging aperture (3) **:** a similar casing on a centrifugal pump or blower (4) **:** a curved portion at the end of a leaf spring (5) **:** a loop or coil of copper tubing inside a still

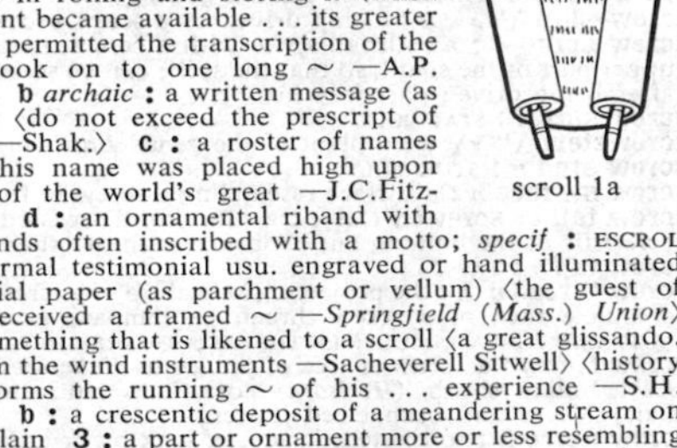

scroll 1a

²scroll \"\ *vb* -ED/-ING/-S *vt* **1 :** to inscribe on or as if on a scroll ⟨the panel on which 38B was delicately ~*ed* —Kay Boyle⟩ **2 :** to form into or adorn with scrolls ⟨the river is ~*ed* in shining bends across the flatlands⟩ ~ *vi* **:** to curl up or roll out like a scroll ⟨bright yellow material, with ~*ing* scarlet roses —H.E.Bates⟩ ⟨the long hourly routine ~*ed* ahead of me —Nathaniel Burt⟩

scroll chuck *n* **:** a universal chuck having jaws moved by a metal scroll that engages slots or threads in the jaws

scroll creeper *n* **:** CROCKET 1

scroll–cut \ˈ⸗,⸗\ *adj* **:** cut in the form of a scroll or with a scroll saw

scrolled \ˈskrōld\ *adj* [¹*scroll* + *-ed*] **1 :** formed into or adorned with scrolls ⟨the dark ~ iron of balustrades —Jack Kerouac⟩ ⟨a boldly ~ tie —Katharine T. Kinkead⟩ **2 :** CURVED, SERPENTINE ⟨the ~ earthworks of the mound builders⟩

scroll·ery \-l(ə)rē, -ri\ *n* -ES [¹*scroll* + *-ery*] **:** SCROLLWORK

scroll foot *n* **:** the foot of a piece of furniture terminating in a downward turning scroll — see FOOT illustration

scroll front *n* **:** the serpentine face of a piece of furniture characteristic esp. of the late Empire style

scroll gear *also* **scroll wheel** *n* **:** a variable gear in the form of a flat scroll having the teeth showing on one face

scrollhead \ˈ⸗,⸗\ *n* **:** an ornamental curved timber at the prow of a ship

scroll lathe *n* **:** a special wood-turning lathe for cutting scrolls and spirals

scroll pediment *n* **:** a broken pediment with raking cornices in the form of reverse curves

scroll saw *n* **1 :** a thin handsaw for cutting curves or irregular designs **2 :** FRETSAW, JIGSAW

scroll–shaped \ˈ⸗,⸗\ *adj* **:** formed in a compound curve

scroll step *n, archit* **:** a curtail step

scrollwork \ˈ⸗,⸗\ *n* **:** ornamentation characterized by scrolls (gilt ~ on hand-painted china); *esp* **:** fancy designs in wood often made with a scroll saw ⟨a wide veranda with ~ along the edge of its roof —Raymond Chandler⟩

scrolly \ˈskrōlē\ *adj, sometimes* -ER/-EST [¹*scroll* + *-y*] **:** full of scrolls or curlicues ⟨fine ~ script⟩ ⟨~ Victorian furniture⟩

scrooch \ˈskrüch *also* -ü·\ *vi* -ED/-ING/-ES [by alter.] **:** CROUCH, HUDDLE — often used with *down* ⟨~*ed* down in the seat and tried to hide —H.E.Giles⟩ ⟨she ~*ed* down in under all the covers —Richard Bissell⟩

scrooge \ˈskrüj\ *n* -S *often cap* [fr. Ebenezer *Scrooge*, chief character in *A Christmas Carol* (1843), story by Charles Dickens †1870 Eng. author] **:** a miserly person ⟨*Scrooges* in the pursuit of the almighty dollar —Warner Olivier⟩

scroonch *var of* SCRUNCH

scroop \ˈskrüp\ *n* -S [imit.] **:** a rasping sound **:** CREAK, SCRAPE; *specif* **:** the crisp rustle of silk or similar cloth that has been treated with dilute acid

scroph·u·lar·ia \,skräfyəˈla(a)rēə, -rȯf-\ *n* [NL, fr. ML *scrofula, scrophula* scrofula + NL *-aria*; fr. the supposed efficacy of such plants in the treatment of scrofula] **1** *cap* **:** a large genus (the type of the family Scrophulariaceae) of coarse often strong-smelling perennial herbs that are native to temperate regions and have terminal clusters of small flowers with a gibbous corolla consisting of four erect lobes and one spreading lip, four anthers, and one staminodium **2** -S **:** any plant or flower of the genus *Scrophularia*

scroph·u·lar·i·a·ce·ae \,⸗⸗,⸗⸗ˈāsē,ē\ *n pl, cap* [NL, fr. *Scrophularia*, type genus + *-aceae*] **:** a widely distributed family of herbs, shrubs, or rarely trees (order Polemoniales) having exstipulate leaves, a more or less irregular bilabiate corolla with four didynamous stamens, and a 2-celled ovary — see FIGWORT — **scroph·u·lar·i·a·ceous** \¦⸗⸗,⸗⸗¦āshəs\ *adj*

scrot- *or* **scroti-** *or* **scroto-** *comb form* [L *scrotum*] **1 :** scrotum ⟨*scroti*form⟩ **2 :** scrotal and ⟨*scroto*femoral⟩

scro·tal \ˈskrōd·ᵊl, -ōtᵊl\ *adj* [NL *scrotalis*, fr. L *scrotum* + *-alis* -al] **1 a :** of or relating to the scrotum ⟨~ testes⟩ or having descended into the scrotum ⟨~ testes⟩ **b :** grooved, furrowed, or fissured like a scrotum ⟨~ tongue⟩ **2 :** having a scrotum ⟨~ mammals⟩

scro·ti·form \ˈ⸗ə,fȯrm\ *adj* [*scrot-* + *-iform*] **:** shaped like a pouch

scro·to·cele \ˈə,sēl\ *n* -S [*scrot-* + *-cele*] **:** a scrotal hernia

scro·tum \ˈskrōd·əm, -ōt-\ *n, pl* **scro·ta** \-ə\ *or* **scrotums** [L; akin to L *scrupus* sharp stone — more at SHRED] **:** the external pouch that in most mammals contains the testes

scrouge \ˈskrüj, -raüj\ *or* **scrooge** \-rüj\ *vb* -ED/-ING/-S [alter. of *scruze*] *chiefly dial* **:** to squeeze together **:** CROWD, PRESS

¹scrounge \ˈskraunj\ *vb* -ED/-ING/-S [alter. of E dial. *scrunge* to wander about idly] *vt* **1 a :** to collect by foraging **:** round up **:** FIND, SALVAGE ⟨~ wood from bombed-out areas —A.W. Bromage⟩ — often used with *up* ⟨manpower might be summoned . . . and feed material *scrounged* up —R.E.Lapp⟩ **b :** to acquire by other expedient means (as by borrowing, stealing, or swapping) ⟨got a shave and a haircut from a fellow prisoner who had *scrounged* a pair of clippers somewhere —E.J.Kahn⟩ ⟨had to ~ water from the engine for their tea —Jack Wadsworth⟩ **2 :** to obtain by persuasion **:** CADGE, WHEEDLE ⟨the more money they can ~ out of local communities, the more projects they can build —*New Republic*⟩ **3** *chiefly dial* **:** SCROUGE ⟨a number of his colleagues . . . are *scrounged* down into two columns under the cartoon —A.J.Liebling⟩ ~ *vi* **1 :** to make a search **:** poke around **:** FORAGE, HUNT ⟨*scrounged* for food in a burned field —*Look*⟩ — often used with *around* ⟨~ around and persuade someone to run off mimeographed copies for you —*Infantry Jour.*⟩ ⟨not ashamed to ~ around at night, picking up useful things —Richard Harrington⟩ **2 :** WHEEDLE ⟨on relief and *scrounging* for more of the city's money than they were entitled to —Harrison Smith⟩

²scrounge \"\ *n* -S **1 :** material acquired by scrounging ⟨decided to improve our surroundings with ~ from neighboring houses —*Infantry Jour.*⟩ **2 :** an act of scrounging

scroung·er \-jə(r)\ *n* -S **:** one that scrounges

scrounging *n* -S [fr. gerund of ¹*scrounge*] **:** the acquisition of goods or services other than by direct purchase ⟨did a little ~ when he was British ambassador to the Porte in 1801, and . . . our possession of these sculptures is due to a mixture of luck and audacity —Elizabeth Montizambert⟩

scrow *var of* SCREW

scroyle \ˈskrȯi(ə)l\ *n* -S [origin unknown] *archaic* **:** GOOD-FOR-NOTHING, SCOUNDREL

¹scrub \ˈskrəb\ *n* -S *often attrib* [ME, alter. of *schrobbe, shrobbe* shrub — more at SHRUB] **1 a :** a stunted tree or shrub ⟨tundra vegetation . . . consists of moss, lichen, dwarf ~*s* and peat moor —W.G.East⟩ **b :** vegetation consisting chiefly of dwarf or stunted trees and shrubs that is often thick and impenetrable and grows in poor soil or in sand ⟨mallee ~⟩ ⟨pine ~⟩ **c :** a tract of country covered with such vegetation (as a palmetto barren of the southern U.S.) **2 a :** a domestic animal of mixed or unknown parentage and usu. without definite type or markings **b :** MONGREL **3 a :** a person of insignificant size or social standing **:** NOBODY, RUNT ⟨some pimpled dirty little ~ in sandals —Virginia Woolf⟩ **b** (1) **:** a person of secondary rank **:** SUBORDINATE ⟨represented in the Far East . . . by incompetents and ~*s* —Richard Watts⟩ (2) **:** a hotel or restaurant worker who substitutes for or assumes part of the responsibility of his superior **4 a :** a sports contest involving random individuals or teams having fewer than the regular number of players; *specif* **:** a softball or baseball game in which players participate as individuals rather than as team members and rotate to new positions as each out is made **b** (1) **:** a player not belonging to the first string (2) **:** a team composed of such players

²scrub \"\ *vb* **scrubbed; scrubbed; scrubbing; scrubs** [of LG or Scand origin; akin to MLG & MD *schrobben, schrubben* to scrub, Sw *skrubba*, Dan *skrubbe*] *vt* **1 a :** to clean with abrasive action (as by using a washboard or a stiff brush) **:** SCOUR ⟨~ clothes⟩ ⟨~ a floor⟩ ⟨we *scrubbed* her with lye and swabbed her down with seawater —Kenneth Roberts⟩ **b :** to subject to friction **:** RUB, SCRATCH ⟨*scrubbed* his eyes in disbelief — *Time*⟩ ⟨rubber tires *scrubbed* the runway —Horace Sutton⟩ **c :** to cleanse and disinfect (the hands and forearms) before participating in surgery **2 a :** to wash (a gas or vapor) with water, a light hydrocarbon oil, or other liquid to remove impurities or recover desired components **b :** to separate from a gas — often with *out* ⟨the light oil *scrubbed* from carbureted water gas⟩ ⟨~ out acetone from tank acetylene⟩ **3 :** to wipe out **:** CANCEL, ELIMINATE ⟨under the tight moon-shooting timetable, a brief delay . . . can ~ the shoot —*Newsweek*⟩ ⟨200 housing units blueprinted for construction there had been *scrubbed* when the . . . budget was reduced —*N.Y.Times*⟩ ~ *vi* **1 :** to do washing and scouring ⟨must ~ and clean for you the rest of my life —W.M.Gallichan⟩ **2 :** to get ready for surgery by scrubbing ⟨the surgeon was preparing to ~ —H.F. & Katharine Pringle⟩

³scrub \"\ *n* -S **1 :** an act or instance of scrubbing; *specif* **:** a surgical scrub-up **2 a :** an implement used for scrubbing **:** BRUSH ⟨churn brushes, deck ~*s* . . . and sundry others —*Country Life*⟩ **b :** something that resembles a scrub brush ⟨a square military ~ of a moustache —William Sansom⟩ **3 :** one that scrubs **:** DRUDGE ⟨hotel ~*s* and chambermaids⟩

scrub·ba·ble \ˈskrəbəbəl\ *adj* **:** capable of being scrubbed

scrubbed *adj* [fr. past part. of ²*scrub*] **1** *archaic* **:** SCRUBBY ⟨a little ~ boy —Shak.⟩ **2 :** made clean by or as if by scrubbing ⟨an immaculate, ~ Scotsman —Eamonn Andrews⟩ ⟨stroll . . . in the ~ Sunday twilight —Alan Schneider⟩

¹scrub·ber \ˈskrəbə(r)\ *n* -S [²*scrub* + *-er*] **:** one that scrubs: as **a :** one that cleans (as floors, clothes, pelts) by scrubbing **b :** ABRASIVE, BRUSH **c :** an apparatus for removing impurities esp. from gases ⟨large exhaust ~*s* . . . filter the exhaust of harmful gases —*Sperryscope*⟩ ⟨ammonia tower ~*s*⟩ ⟨spray ~*s*⟩

²scrubber \"\ *n* -S [¹*scrub* + *-er*] **1 a :** one that inhabits the scrub **b** *Austral* **:** a domestic animal that has run wild **2** *Austral* **:** ¹SCRUB 2

scrubbing *n* -S [fr. gerund of ²*scrub*] **:** a removal of dirt or impurities **:** SCOURING, WASHING ⟨repeated ~*s* have given the wood a silvery sheen —*Amer. Guide Series: Mich.*⟩ ⟨passage of steam through the spray falling from this baffle furnishes additional ~ —*advt*⟩

scrub birch *n* [¹*scrub*] **:** a flat mat-forming or sometimes ascending shrub (*Betula glandulosa*) of arctic and alpine No. America that has small roundish leaves and twigs dotted with resinous glands and often forms dense growths on mountaintops

scrubbird \ˈ⸗,⸗\ *n* **:** a bird living in or frequenting brush or scrub; *esp* **:** a small Australian passerine bird (*Atrichornis rufescens*) related to the lyrebirds, inhabiting dense forests, and having only two pairs of syringeal muscles and rudimentary clavicles

scrubboard \ˈ⸗,⸗\ *n* [²*scrub* + *board*] **:** BASEBOARD

scrub brush *or* **scrubbing brush** *n* **:** a brush with hard bristles for heavy cleaning (as scrubbing floors)

scrub·by \ˈskrəbē, -bi\ *adj* -ER/-EST [¹*scrub* + *-y*] **1 a :** stunted in size **:** meager in quality **:** RUNTY, POOR ⟨jack oak and . . . ~ cut-over pine —W.F.Davis⟩ ⟨stretches of forests, broken . . . by small ~ farms —*Amer. Guide Series: Maine*⟩ **b :** lacking distinction in rank or appearance **:** INFERIOR, SHABBY ⟨~ little shipping clerks —Marguerite Steen⟩ ⟨wears a ~ old tweed coat that has seen better days⟩ **2 :** consisting of scrub **:** covered with stunted vegetation ⟨open ~ forests —P.E.James⟩ ⟨the ~, blotchy land through which he rides —Curtis Dahl⟩ **3 :** being short and bristly ⟨a sandy, ~, wayward little mustache —W.A.White⟩

scrub chestnut oak *n* [¹*scrub*] **:** CHINQUAPIN OAK b

scrub fowl *or* **scrub hen** *n* **:** MEGAPODE

scrub kangaroo *n* **:** GIANT KANGAROO

scrubland \ˈ⸗,⸗\ *n* **:** land covered with scrub

scrub oak *n* **:** any of various chiefly American oaks (as the bear oak, the blackjack, or a chinquapin oak) of small size and usu. shrubby habit that are often a dominant life form on thin dry soils and sometimes form dense thickets of great extent

scrub palmetto *n* **:** any of several low-growing palmettos; *esp* **:** SAW PALMETTO

scrub pine *n* **1 :** a pine of dwarf, straggly, or scrubby growth usu. by reason of environmental conditions **:** a pine tree unsuitable for lumber by reason of inferior or defective growth ⟨much eastern *scrub pine* is Jersey pine while in some western areas it is lodgepole pine⟩ **2 :** BLACK CYPRESS PINE

scrub plane *n* **:** a narrow carpenter's plane with a rounded cutting edge used for the removal of an excessive amount of stock

scrub robin *n* **:** an Australian singing bird of the genus *Drymodes*

scrubs *pl of* SCRUB, *pres 3d sing of* SCRUB
scrub sandalwood *n* **1 :** a small Australian timber tree (*Exocarpus latifolius*) of the family Santalaceae **2 :** the wood of the scrub sandalwood tree
scrub tick *n* **:** an Australian tick (*Ixodes holocyclus*) that attacks mammals and poultry
scrub turkey *n* **:** MEGAPODE; *esp* **:** BRUSH TURKEY
scrub typhus *n* **:** TSUTSUGAMUSHI DISEASE
scrub–up \ˈ=,=\ *n* -S [*³scrub* + *up*] **:** an act or process of scrubbing ⟨the bathroom is equipped with both shower and tub, for quick *scrub-ups* —*Better Homes & Gardens*⟩; *specif* **:** aseptic preparation for surgery
scrub vine *n* [*¹scrub*] **:** a leafless woody vine (*Cassytha melantha*) of Australia
scrub wallaby *n* **:** PADEMELON; *esp* **:** DAMA PADEMELON
scrubwoman \ˈ=,==\ *n, pl* **scrubwomen** [*²scrub* + *woman*] **:** CLEANING WOMAN, CHARWOMAN
scrubwood \ˈ=,=\ *n* [*¹scrub*] **1 :** SCRUB 1b **2 :** GUMWOOD 2
scrub wren *n* **:** a small Australian singing bird of the genus *Sericornis*
¹scruff \ˈskrəf, -rüf-\ *n* -S [alter. of *scurf*] **1** *dial chiefly Eng* **:** DANDRUFF, SCURF **2 :** one that is worthless or contemptible **3 a** *dial chiefly Eng* **:** a thin coating **:** CRUST, FILM **b :** skimmings from tinning pots
²scruff *vt* -ED/-ING/-S *obs* **:** to treat lightly **:** slur over
³scruff \ˈskrəf\ *n* -S [alter. (perh. influenced by *¹scruff*) of *³scuff*] **1 :** the back of the neck **:** NAPE **2 :** a loose part of the clothing (as a coat collar or the seat of the pants)
scruf·fle \ˈskrəfəl, -rüf-\ *dial Eng var of* SCUFFLE
scruff·man \ˈskrəfmən\ *n, pl* **scruffmen** [*¹scruff* + *man*] **:** a smelter who melts tin for use in galvanizing steel in a reverberatory furnace
scruffy \ˈskrəfē\ *adj* -ER/-EST [*¹scruff* + *-y*] **:** of a worthless or slovenly character **:** SHABBY, MISERABLE ⟨a surge of ragged ~ children —Bruce Marshall⟩ ⟨moved to a ~ little coffee bar . . . and sat at a smeared table —Martha Gellhorn⟩ ⟨that ~, sandy waste —Osbert Lancaster⟩
scrum \ˈskrəm\ *or* **scrum·mage** \-mij\ *n* -S [*scrum* short for *scrummage*; *scrummage*, alter. of *scrimmage*] **:** a rugby play in which the forwards of each side crouch side by side typically in 3-2-3 formation and with locked arms, the two front lines meet shoulder to shoulder, and play starts by the placing of the ball between the front lines for the two sides to compete for possession of — called also *tight scrummage*; compare LOOSE SCRUM
scrum half *n* **:** the rugby halfback who places the ball in the scrum
scrum·mage \ˈskrəmij\ *vi* -ED/-ING/-S [*scrummage*, n.] **:** to form a rugby scrum
scrum·mag·er \-jə(r)\ *n* -S **:** one that scrummages
¹scrump \ˈskrəmp, -ü-\ *n* -S [prob. of Scand origin; akin to Sw & Dan *skrumpen* shriveled] *dial Eng* **:** something that is shriveled or cooked to a crisp
²scrump \"\ *vb* -ED/-ING/-S [prob. of Scand origin; akin to Dan *skrumpe* to shrivel] *dial Eng* **:** SHRIVEL, SHRINK
scrump·tious \ˈskrəm(p)shəs\ *adj* [prob. alter. of *sumptuous*] **:** affording keen pleasure **:** exceptionally rich or fine **:** DELIGHTFUL, EXCELLENT ⟨after a ~ lunch they went to a matinee —John Dos Passos⟩ ⟨a brown alligator traveling bag, quite ~ —W.A.White⟩ — **scrump·tious·ly** *adv*
¹scrunch \ˈskrənch, -ü-\ *vb* -ED/-ING/-ES [alter. (perh. influenced by *squeeze*) of *¹crunch*] *vt* **1 :** CRUNCH, CRUSH ⟨a young fox . . . *~ing* the insects up hungrily as he unearthed them —Gerald Durrell⟩ ⟨dropped her half-smoked cigarette to the floor, *~ed* it out with a precise toe —Boyce Eakin⟩ **2 a** *also* **scrooch** \-ü-\ **:** to squeeze together **:** make into a compact mass **:** CONTRACT, HUNCH ⟨*~ed* his eyebrows down again —A.J.Liebling⟩ **b :** CRUMPLE, RUMPLE ⟨~ a paper plate and throw it on the fire⟩ ⟨don't ~ my dress —Lillian Smith⟩ ~ *vi* **1 a :** to make a crunching sound ⟨walked on tiptoe . . . in order that the pebbles might not ~ under my feet —Dwight MacDonald⟩ **b :** to move with a crunching sound ⟨ice *~ed* along the vessel's sides —Frank Hurley⟩ **2** *also* **scrooch** **:** CROUCH, SQUEEZE ⟨*~ed* behind the boxwood hedge and reconnoitered —Al Hine⟩ ⟨we *~ed* together like bulls in a horse trailer —A.J.Liebling⟩ ⟨my bigger brothers had to ~ down to pass for under six —Mary McCarthy⟩
²scrunch \"\ *n* -ES **:** a crunching sound ⟨a ~ of wheels on the gravel outside —Agatha Christie⟩
scrunchy \-chē\ *adj* -ER/-EST [*¹scrunch* + *-y*] **:** CRUNCHY
scrunty \ˈskrəntē\ *adj* [E dial. *scrunt* stunted object or person (prob. blend of *¹scrump* & *runt*) + *-y*] *chiefly dial* **:** STUNTED, RUNTY
¹scru·ple \ˈskrüpəl\ *n* -S [ME *scriple*, fr. L *scrupulus, scripulum*, a unit of weight equal to one twenty-fourth of an ounce, fr. *scrupulus* small sharp stone — more at ²SCRUPLE] **1 a :** a unit of apothecaries' weight equal to 20 grains or ⅓ dram — abbr. *sc;* see MEASURE table **b :** a minute particle or quantity **:** IOTA, JOT ⟨indignant if the old ugly routine . . . is altered by so much as one poor ~ —Margery Bailey⟩ **2** *obs* **:** any of several small units of measure (as a minute of arc or a minute of time) **3 :** a British unit of liquid capacity equal to 20 minims or 0.04166 fluid ounce
²scruple \"\ *n* -S [MF *scrupule*, fr. L *scrupulus* small sharp stone, cause of mental or moral discomfort, scruple, dim. of *scrupus* sharp stone — more at SHRED] **1 a :** an ethical consideration **:** a moral principle that inhibits action ⟨a religious ~ . . . jeopardized his academic career —W.H.Salter⟩ ⟨was not overburdened with constitutional *~s* where measures he favored were concerned —A.H.Meneely⟩ **b :** SCRUPULOUSNESS ⟨the want of ~ or humanity in jockeying for diplomatic advantage —*Times Lit. Supp.*⟩ **c** *archaic* **:** a conscientious excuse or protest **:** APOLOGY, DEMUR ⟨small ~ is made by the authorities in opening private letters —Richard Ford⟩ ⟨made no ~ at taking these goods —Daniel Defoe⟩ **d :** a twinge of conscience **:** mental reservation **:** QUALM ⟨had forgotten his *~s* about accepting lavish hospitalities —Willa Cather⟩ **2** *obs* **:** a lack of certainty **:** DOUBT ⟨hope my innocency will appear beyond a ~ —William Penn⟩
syn COMPUNCTION, QUALM, DEMUR agree with SCRUPLE in denoting restraint upon intended action, usu. self-imposed and arising from a nice sense of what is right or proper; but SCRUPLE is distinguished by the implication that a principle rather than a personal feeling is involved ⟨moral *scruples*⟩ ⟨religious *scruples*⟩ ⟨began to have *scruples*, to feel obligations, to find that veracity and honor were . . . compelling principles —G.B. Shaw⟩ SCRUPLE may sometimes imply undue fastidiousness ⟨overconscientiousness . . . has wrecked many a promising career; I honor *scruples*, but they . . . have their place and should be kept there —Elinor Wylie⟩ COMPUNCTION denotes a spontaneous feeling of personal responsibility often accompanied by compassion for a potential victim ⟨Lady Macbeth . . . had the *compunction* which he lacked — she could not kill . . . the king —S.L.Gulick b.1902⟩ but is now also used of a passing or superficial concern ⟨social *compunction* about occupying so exclusively the attention of the room —Mary Deasy⟩ DEMUR usu. suggests resistance to or protest against an outside influence ⟨fashion is accepted by average people with little *demur* —Edward Sapir⟩ QUALM emphasizes personal aversion to an act offensive to taste or morals ⟨few little girls can squash insects and kill rabbits without a *qualm* —Rose Macaulay⟩ ⟨serious *qualms* were felt by the respectable citizenry . . . at the idea of . . . young women walking unescorted through the town —*Amer. Guide Series: Mass.*⟩
³scruple \"\ *vb* **scrupled; scrupled; scrupling** \-p(ə)liŋ\ **scruples** *vt* **1** *archaic* **a :** to have or raise scruples about **:** boggle at ⟨*scrupled* no means to obtain his ends —Earl of Chesterfield⟩ **b :** to have doubts about **:** QUESTION **2** *obs* **:** to cause to feel scruples **:** TROUBLE ~ *vi* **1 :** to have or raise scruples **:** become worried **:** FRET ⟨knew it was not so, and did not ~ about lying —Irwin Edman⟩ **2 :** to be reluctant on grounds of conscience **:** HESITATE ⟨conspirators will often readily perjure themselves and take the oath, while some conscientious men may ~ to do so —Will Herberg⟩ ⟨when any financial advantage can accrue to us . . . we do not ~ to accept money —Farley Mowat⟩ **syn** see DEMUR
scru·pler \-p(ə)lə(r)\ *n* -S *archaic* **:** one that scruples
scru·pu·list \ˈskrüpyələst\ *n* -S [L *scrupulus* scruple + E *-ist*] *archaic* **:** SCRUPLER
scru·pu·los·i·ty \,==ˈläsəd·ē\ *n* -ES [MF *scrupulosité*, fr. L *scrupulositat-, scrupulositas* scrupulousness, fr. *scrupulosus* scrupulous + *-itat-, -itas* -ity] **1 :** the quality or state of being scrupulous ⟨the classical unities are observed with a ~ rare in modern writers —Oliver Evans⟩ **2 :** SCRUPLE ⟨tied hand and foot by senseless *scrupulosities* —*Reader's Digest*⟩
scru·pu·lous \ˈskrüpyələs\ *adj* [ME, fr. L *scrupulosus*, fr. *scrupulus* scruple + *-osus* -ous] **1 a :** characterized by scruple **:** having moral integrity **:** PRINCIPLED ⟨less ~ producers sent bundles that were deceptive in appearance —*Amer. Guide Series: Md.*⟩ ⟨a more ~ court would disqualify itself —H.L. Ickes⟩ **b :** correct to the smallest detail **:** punctiliously exact **:** PAINSTAKING, PRECISE ⟨the orchestral score . . . was articulated with ~ precision and clarity —*Musical America*⟩ ⟨endeavored to follow the originals with ~ care, even to . . . reproducing mistakes in spelling —M.M.Mathews⟩ ⟨her recoil from her husband's inefficiency was in the direction of a ~ neatness —Ellen Glasgow⟩ **c :** carefully adhering to ethical standards **:** CONSCIENTIOUS, STRICT ⟨it is this ~ honesty toward herself and others that is the redeeming side of her character —Malcolm Cowley⟩ ⟨distinguished for ~ fairness, he was notoriously insusceptible to any political influence —S.H.Adams⟩ **2** *obs* **:** open to question on moral grounds ⟨the justice of that cause ought to be evident; not obscure, not ~ —Francis Bacon⟩ **3 a** *obs* **:** excessively careful **:** CAUTIOUS, WARY ⟨so curious and ~ in many of their cities . . . that they will admit no stranger within the walls —Thomas Coryat⟩ **b** *archaic* **:** hesitant esp. for ethical reasons **:** DOUBTFUL, RELUCTANT ⟨primitive Christians were very ~ of calling the emperors *Dominus* —Edward Stillingfleet⟩ **syn** see CAREFUL, UPRIGHT
scru·pu·lous·ly *adv* **:** in a scrupulous manner **:** CONSCIENTIOUSLY, PAINSTAKINGLY
scru·pu·lous·ness *n* -ES [*scrupulous* + *-ness*] **:** conformity to high standards of ethics or excellence **:** INTEGRITY, PUNCTILIOUSNESS
scrush \ˈskrəsh\ *dial var of* CRUSH
scru·ta·ble \ˈskrüd·əbəl, -ütə-\ *adj* [LL *scrutabilis* searchable, fr. L *scrutari* to search, investigate, examine + *-abilis* -able — more at SCRUTINY] **:** capable of being deciphered **:** COMPREHENSIBLE, LEGIBLE
scru·ta·tor \ˈskrü,tād·ə(r), =ˈ==\ *n* -S [L, fr. *scrutatus* (past part. of *scrutari* to search, examine) + *-or*] **:** OBSERVER, EXAMINER
scru·ti·neer \ˌskrüt³nˈi(ə)r, -iə\ *n* -S [*scrutiny* + *-eer*] **1 :** one that examines **2** *Brit* **:** CANVASSER a
scru·ti·nize *also* **scru·ti·nise** \ˈskrüt³n,īz *also* -üd·ə,nīz *or* -ütə,nīz\ *vb* -ED/-ING/-S [*scrutiny* + *-ize*] *vt* **:** to subject to scrutiny **:** examine closely **:** INSPECT ⟨*scrutinized* the inscription as if it were stubbornly withholding from them some information that they ought to possess —J.B.Benefield⟩ ⟨*scrutinized* herself eagerly and long in her mirror —Robert Grant †1940⟩ ⟨knowledge of one other culture should sharpen our ability to ~ . . . our own —Margaret Mead⟩ ~ *vi* **:** to make a scrutiny ⟨come . . . to perceive and apprehend, or, as critics, to ~ and evaluate —R.W.Stallman⟩
syn SCRUTINIZE, SCAN, INSPECT, EXAMINE, and AUDIT can mean, in common, to look at or look over critically and searchingly. SCRUTINIZE implies close observation and attention to minute detail ⟨the immigration officials carefully *scrutinized* the passengers' entry permits —Robert Sherrod⟩ ⟨manufacturers must *scrutinize* every possible way to lower production costs —*Steel*⟩ SCAN implies a survey from point to point, often suggesting a cursory overall observation ⟨stooping over as he went, his eyes *scanning* every foot of the ground —O.E. Rölvaag⟩ ⟨took his duties seriously, attending meetings and *scanning* reports from every corporation minutely —A.F. Harlow⟩ ⟨had drawn out their telescopes and were *scanning* the mountain above us —H.D.Quillin⟩ ⟨a scheme whereby all journals would be *scanned* and indexed on receipt —*Amer. Documentation*⟩ ⟨to *scan* the headlines over breakfast⟩ INSPECT in general use implies little more than careful observation, but in legal, military, governmental, or industrial use implies a searching scrutiny for errors, defects, or shortcomings ⟨ruefully *inspected* himself after trying on his first white tie and tails —Flora Lewis⟩ ⟨extension of credit is by installments, and projects financed are *inspected* by members of the bank's staff —E.L.Smith⟩ ⟨freshly picked grapes are *inspected* and cleansed before delivery —*Amer. Guide Series: Pa.*⟩ EXAMINE implies a close scrutiny or investigation to determine the facts about or real nature or condition of a thing or to test the thing's quality, truth, validity, and so on ⟨ever bothered to *examine* the serial number on a bank note —*Irish Digest*⟩ ⟨when personality is *examined* as closely and candidly as it has been in the twentieth-century novel —Robert Humphrey⟩ ⟨undying trivialities which the public find romantic without seeking to *examine* them for truth —J.F.Gore⟩ ⟨speakers *examined* great world religions to discover to what extent faith in them encouraged their adherents to escape from life, to exploit life, or to redeem it —Christmas Humphreys⟩ AUDIT applies to a searching examination of accounts to determine their correctness, sometimes extending to any accounting examination ⟨each bank is *audited* annually by a certified public accountant —*Safety for Your Savings*⟩ ⟨*audit* a company's books⟩ ⟨the scandal manages to shake up the other people into *auditing* their close-to-bankrupt lives —*Time*⟩
scru·ti·niz·er *also* **scru·ti·nis·er** \-zə(r)\ *n* -S **:** one that scrutinizes
scru·ti·niz·ing·ly *adv* [*scrutinizing* (fr. pres. part. of *scrutinize*) + *-ly*] **:** in a scrutinizing way **:** ATTENTIVELY
scru·ti·nous \ˈskrüt(³)nəs\ *adj* [*scrutiny* + *-ous*] *archaic* **:** disposed to examine closely **:** INQUISITIVE, SEARCHING — **scrutinously** *adv*
scru·ti·ny \ˈskrüt(³)nē, -ni *also* -üd·ən- *or* -ütən-\ *n* -ES [L *scrutinium* search, investigation, fr. *scrutari* to search, investigate, examine, fr. *scruta* trash, rags; perh. akin to OHG *scrōt* piece cut off — more at SHRED] **1** *archaic* **a :** an act or instance of taking a formal vote by roll call or by secret ballot ⟨the people went to a ~ and began to give their voices —Philemon Holland⟩ **b :** an official examination (as by a committee) of the votes or ballots cast in a parliamentary election **2 a :** a searching study or inquiry **:** close inspection **:** EXAMINATION, INVESTIGATION ⟨fine old houses . . . stand open to the ~ of the tourists —*Monsanto Mag.*⟩ ⟨survived the cold ~ and judicious pruning of the committee —R.S.Churchill⟩ ⟨are . . . diplomats to be terrified by the prospect of future public *scrutinies* staged by politicians —C.L.Sulzberger⟩ **b :** a searching look ⟨took the lynxlike ~ of counsel —L.P.Stryker⟩ **c :** a close watch **:** SURVEILLANCE ⟨keeps public officials under constant public ~ —*Amer. Guide Series: Mass.*⟩ **3 a :** a public examination of catechumens before baptism consisting of catechizings and exorcisms that form a part of the rite of baptism in the Roman Catholic Church **b :** an inquiry and examination preceding elevation to orders **c :** an ecclesiastical method of election by secret written ballot (as in a conclave)
scru·toire \(ˈ)skrüˈtwär\ *n* -S [modif. of F *escritoire*] **:** ESCRITOIRE
scruze \ˈskrüz\ *vt* -ED/-ING/-S [perh. alter. (influenced by *²screw*) of *¹squeeze*] *chiefly dial* **:** SQUEEZE, CRUSH
¹scry \ˈskrī\ *n* -ES [ME *scrye*, short for *ascrye*, fr. *ascryen* to call out, fr. MF *escrier*, fr. OF, fr. *es-* ex- (fr. L *ex-*) + *crier* to cry — more at CRY] *chiefly dial* **:** OUTCRY, SHOUT
²scry \"\ *vb* **scried; scried; scrying; scries** [by shortening] *vt, archaic* **:** DESCRY ~ *vi* **:** to practice crystal gazing
scry·er *also* **skry·er** \-ī(ə)r, -īə\ *n* -S [*²scry* + *-er*] **:** CRYSTAL GAZER, SEER
scrying *n* -S [fr. gerund of *²scry*] **:** CRYSTAL GAZING, DIVINATION
SCS *abbr* superintendent of car service
sct *abbr* scout
sctd *abbr* scattered
sctr *abbr* sector
scu·ba \ˈsk(y)übə\ *n* -S [self-contained *u*nderwater *b*reathing *a*pparatus] **:** an apparatus used for breathing while swimming under water
¹scud \ˈskəd\ *vb* **scudded; scudded; scudding; scuds** [prob. of Scand origin; akin to Norw *skudda* to push, thrust; akin to OE *hūdenian* to shake — more at QUASH] *vi* **1 a :** to move or run swiftly esp. as if driven forward ⟨a brisk wind sending small white clouds *scudding* across the . . . sky —Osbert Lancaster⟩ ⟨freezing weather that sent the delegates and their briefcases *scudding* —Mollie Panter-Downes⟩ **b :** to run before a gale **2** *of an arrow* **:** to fly too high and off the proper course ~ *vt* **1** *archaic* **:** to pass over quickly ⟨the startled red deer *~s* the plain —Sir Walter Scott⟩ **2 :** to cause to scud ⟨*scudded* the jeep back on the paving —S.L.Rubinstein⟩ **3 :** to shake (herring) from a net
²scud \"\ *n* -S **1 :** the act of scudding **:** a driving along **:** RUSH ⟨following her in a ~ came the servants and helpers —Virginia Woolf⟩ **2 a :** loose vapory clouds or fragments of cloud driven swiftly by the wind **b :** something resembling scud: as (1) **:** a slight sudden shower (2) **:** a gust of wind (3) **:** mist, rain, snow, or spray driven by the wind ⟨a strong easterly gale was driving *~s* of rain and torn leaves across the . . . lawns —Margaret Irwin⟩ ⟨a strong wind . . . whipping up a ~ of whitecaps on the bay —Wright Morris⟩ ⟨the air was flecked with a ~ of white specks —Hugh MacLennan⟩ **3 :** an amphipod crustacean (as a beach flea)
³scud \"\ *vt* **scudded; scudded; scudding; scuds** [obs. E *scud* dirt, refuse, prob. blend of E *¹scum* and *¹mud*] **:** to scrape (a depilated and trimmed hide or skin) in order to remove undesirable matter (as remaining hairs or lime)
⁴scud \"\ *n* -S **:** the matter that is worked out of hides or skins in scudding
scud·der \-də(r)\ *n* -S [*³scud* + *-er*] **:** a beamer who scrapes skins by hand or machine
scud·dle \ˈskəd³l\ *vi* [freq. of *¹scud*] **:** HURRY, SCUTTLE
scud·dy \ˈskədi\ *adj* -ER/-EST [origin unknown] *Scot* **:** NAKED
scu·do \ˈskü(,)dō\ *n, pl* **scu·di** \-dē\ [It, lit., shield, fr. L *scutum* shield — more at ESQUIRE] **1 a :** a gold coin first issued in the 15th century or a silver coin first issued in the 16th century and used in Italy to the 19th century approximately equivalent to a dollar **b :** a unit of value equivalent to a scudo **2** [modif. of Sp *escudo* — more at ESCUDO] **:** ESCUDO
¹scuff \ˈskəf\ *vb* -ED/-ING/-S [prob. of Scand origin; akin to Sw *skuffa* to push and perh. to ON *skūfa, skȳfa* to shove — more at SHOVE] *vi* **1 a :** to walk without lifting the feet **:** proceed with a scraping or dragging movement **:** SHUFFLE ⟨peasant girls with . . . their bare feet *~ing* on the flags —Gerald Durrell⟩ **b :** to poke or shuffle a foot in exploration or embarrassment ⟨farmers *~ed* at the powder-dry earth —*Time*⟩ **2 :** to become scratched, chipped, or roughened by wear ⟨a sleek, hard surface that won't dent, crack, or ~ —*advt*⟩ ~ *vt* **1 a** *Scot* **:** to touch lightly in passing **:** GRAZE **b** *Scot* **:** to brush aside **:** wipe off **2 :** to attack or injure with or as if with the fists **:** CUFF, BUFFET ⟨nursing a *~ed* eyelid . . . after the match —*Time*⟩ ⟨a play that has been brutally *~ed* by the critics —Philip Hamburger⟩ **3 a :** to scrape (as the feet) along a surface while walking or back and forth while standing ⟨*~ed* my shoes on a mat —Joseph Wechsberg⟩ **b :** to scatter, tread, or toss aside by or as if by shuffling with the feet ⟨*~ing* the leaves and sniffing the dusty smell of them —John Moore⟩ ⟨the world *~s* them underfoot like dirty snow —*Time*⟩ **c :** to poke at with the toe ⟨mountain people ~ rocks on unpaved Main Street while discussing the weather —Bob Koonce⟩ **4 :** to scratch, gouge, wear away the surface of, or otherwise injure through abrasion or use ⟨a plain pine floor that was very much *~ed* —R.M.Coates⟩ ⟨his cuffs were frayed, his shoes were *~ed* —*New Yorker*⟩
²scuff \"\ *n* -S **1** *Scot* **:** a light glancing blow **:** CUFF **2 :** a noise of or as if of scuffing ⟨the soft ~ of his own footsteps —Leslie Charteris⟩ **3 a :** the act or an instance of scuffing **:** a wearing away or injuring by use or abrasion **b :** a mark, gouge, roughness, or other injury caused by scuffing ⟨shoe leather that resists *~s*⟩ **4 :** a usu. flat-soled house slipper without quarter or counter — compare MULE **5 :** a brush with the heel forward in tap dancing

scuff 4

³scuff \"\ *n* -S [origin unknown] **:** ³SCRUFF 1
scuffed *adj* [fr. past part. of *¹scuff*] **:** shabby from wear
scuff·er \ˈskəfə(r)\ *n* -S [*²scuff* + *-er*] **1 :** SCUFF 4 **2** [by alter.] **:** SCUFFLER
¹scuf·fle \ˈskəfəl\ *vb* **scuffled; scuffled; scuffling** \-f(ə)liŋ\ **scuffles** [prob. of Scand origin; akin to Sw *skuffa* to push — more at SCUFF] *vi* **1 :** to contend with vigor and resolution **2 :** to strive or struggle at close quarters with disorder and confusion **3 a :** to accomplish a task hurriedly, superficially, or haphazardly **b** (1) **:** to make one's way in or as if in a scuffle **:** go in hurry and confusion (2) **:** to move with a quick shuffling gait or sound **:** SCURRY ⟨a mouse ran *scuffling* behind the wainscoting —Oscar Wilde⟩ (3) **:** to move with a shuffling plodding gait ⟨*scuffled* through the four-inch layer of dust —Ben Riker⟩ ~ *vt* **1 :** to poke at or disturb **:** SCUFF ⟨brushed through branches of yew and *scuffled* the gravel —Elizabeth Taylor⟩ ⟨*scuffling* up the dust with long bare feet —Marjorie K. Rawlings⟩ **2 :** to cause to scuff, shuffle, or otherwise move in a confused manner **syn** see WRESTLE
²scuffle \"\ *n* -S **1 a :** a rough haphazard struggle with scrambling and confusion ⟨during the ~ several GI shoes trample his camera underfoot —Ray Duncan⟩ **b :** a verbal conflict usu. involving several sides and with confused claims ⟨without a strong executive the presidential form of government declines into a ~ of local interests —*Times Lit. Supp.*⟩ **2 :** a soft confused shuffling sound ⟨listened to the ~ of children's feet on the great stone floor —Irwin Shaw⟩ **3 :** a brush forward and back in tap dancing
³scuffle \"\ *vt* -ED/-ING/-S [modif. of D *schoffelen* to hoe, scuffle, fr. MD, to shovel, fr. *schoffel, schuffel* shovel] **:** to use a scuffle hoe upon
⁴scuffle \"\ *n* -S [modif. of D *schoffel*, fr. MD *schoffel, schuffel* shovel — more at SHOVEL] **:** SCUFFLE HOE
scuffle hoe *n* **:** a garden hoe with both edges sharpened that can be pushed forward or drawn back — called also *Dutch hoe, push hoe, thrust hoe*
scuf·fler \ˈskəf(ə)lə(r)\ *n* -S [*³scuffle* + *-er*] **:** CULTIVATOR 2; *esp* **:** one drawn by hand or horse and used principally for weed eradication
scuf·fling·ly *adv* **:** in a scuffling manner
scuff plate *n* [*¹scuff*] **:** a protective metal plate; *specif* **:** one fitting over the threshold of the door of an automotive vehicle to cover the flanges of the side body panels

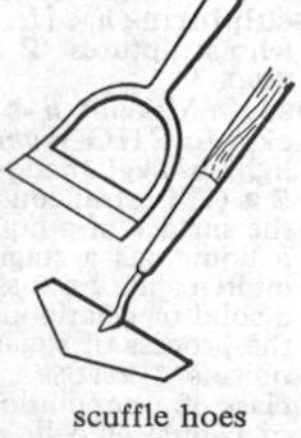
scuffle hoes

scuffs *pres 3d sing of* SCUFF, *pl of* SCUFF
¹scug \ˈskəg\ *n* -S [ON *skuggi* — more at SKY] **1** *Scot* **:** SHADE, SHADOW **2** *Scot* **a :** SHELTER **b :** a sheltered place; *esp* **:** the side of a hill
²scug \"\ *vt* **scugged; scugged; scugging; scugs** **1** *Scot* **:** to screen from view or danger **2** *Scot* **:** to conceal (a sin or wrongdoing) from discovery
³scug \"\ *n* -S [origin unknown] *Brit* **:** a schoolboy without academic or athletic distinction, social grace, or personal attraction; *broadly* **:** an unattractive meanspirited person
sculch \ˈskəlch, -lsh\ *n* -ES [prob. alter. of *culch*] *chiefly dial* **:** TRASH, JUNK, RUBBISH
scul·dud·dery \ˈskəl,dəd(ə)rē, ,=ˈ=(=)=\ *n* -ES [origin unknown] *chiefly dial* **:** shockingly gross or lewd conduct
sculduggery *or* **sculdduggery** *var of* SKULDUGGERY
sculk *var of* SKULK
¹scull *also* **skull** \ˈskəl\ *n* -S [ME *sculle, skulle*] **1 a :** an oar used at the stern of a boat to propel it forward with a thwartwise motion **b :** one of a pair of oars usu. less than 10 feet in length and operated by one person **2 :** a boat usu. for racing propelled by one or sometimes two persons using sculls **3 sculls** *pl* **:** a sculling race **4 :** the act of sculling
²scull *also* **skull** \"\ *vb* -ED/-ING/-S *vt* **1 a :** to propel (a boat) by means of one or more pairs of sculls **b :** to propel (a boat) by means of a large oar resting in a notch in the transom and worked thwartwise with a turning motion **2 :** to convey by sculling ⟨had all he could do to ~ us through the breakers —J.E.H.Nolan⟩ ~ *vi* **1 a :** to scull a boat **b** *of a boat* **:** to admit of being sculled **2 :** to move forward in water by the slow sideways motion of the tail ⟨the sinuous power of the dolphins, whose easy *~ing* imparts such astounding impetus —William Beebe⟩ **3 :** to draw a canoe broadside in the direction

of the paddle by moving the blade in feathered position in the pattern of a figure-eight parallel to the canoe always drawing the blade against the water 4 a : to propel oneself through the water esp. on the back by moving the hands in figure-eight rotations and pressing the palms always away from the direction of movement b : to maintain the body at the surface of the water by moving the hands in a similar pattern with the palms pressing downward

3**scull** \"\ n -s [ScGael or ON; ScGael *sgulan* large wicker basket, fr. ON *skjōla* bucket; akin to ON *skjōl* hiding place, refuge — more at CULET] *Scot* : a large shallow wicker basket often used for produce or fishing tackle

4**scull** n -s [by shortening] *obs* : SCULLION

5**scull** *Scot var of* SKULL

1**scull·er** \ˈskələ(r)\ n -s [1*scull* + -*er*] 1 : one that sculls 2 : a boat rowed by one man with two sculls

2**scull·er** \"\ n -s [*scull* (alter. of *skull*) + -*er*] : a metallurgical workman who removes skull

scul·lery \ˈskəl(ə)rē, -ri\ n -ES [ME, fr. MF *escuelerie*, fr. *escuele, escuelle* bowl, dish (fr. L *scutella* drinking bowl) + -*erie* -ery — more at SCUTTLE] 1 *obs* : a department of a household having charge of the dishes and kitchen utensils 2 : a room near a kitchen for cleaning and storing dishes and culinary utensils, washing vegetables, and similar work

1**scul·lion** \ˈskəlyən\ n -s [ME *sculion*, fr. MF *escouillon* dishcloth, alter. of *escouvillon*, fr. *escouve* broom, fr. L *scopa* broom, twig; akin to L *scapus* shaft, stalk — more at SHAFT] : a kitchen helper

2**scullion** \"\ adj : BASE, MENIAL

3**scullion** *var of* SCALLION

1**sculp** \ˈskəlp\ vt -ED/-ING/-S [L *sculpere* — more at SCULPTURE] 1 *obs* : CARVE, ENGRAVE 2 : SCULPTURE

2**sculp** \"\ vt -ED/-ING/-S [by alter.] : SCALP

3**sculp** \"\ n -s [prob. alter. of 1*scalp*] : the skin or pelt of a seal and esp. of a young seal with the adherent blubber

4**sculp** \"\ vt -ED/-ING/-S : to remove the skin or the skin and blubber of (a seal)

5**sculp** \"\ vt -ED/-ING/-S [alter. of obs. E *scalp*, alter. of E *scapple* — more at SCABBLE] : to break (slate) into slabs suitable for splitting

sculp *abbr* 1 [L *sculpsit*] he or she carved or engraved it 2 sculptor 3 sculptural; sculpture

sculp·er \ˈskəlpə(r)\ n -s [alter. of 2*scalper*] : SCORPER 1

scul·pin \ˈskəlpən\ n, pl **sculpins** *also* **sculpin** [origin unknown] 1 a : any of numerous spiny large-headed broad-mouthed fishes of Cottidae and closely related scorpaenoid families that usu. are scaleless and have scanty and bony flesh b : a dragonet (*Callionymus lyra*) c : a scorpion fish (*Scorpaena guttata*) of the southern California coast esteemed for food and sport 2 : a worthless creature

sculpt \ˈskəlpt\ vb **sculpted** \-ptəd\ **sculpted; sculpting; sculpts** [F *sculpter*, alter. (influenced by *sculpteur* sculptor, fr. L *sculptor*) of obs. F *sculper* to sculp, fr. L *sculpere*] : CARVE, SCULPTURE

sculpt *abbr* 1 [L *sculpsit*] he or she carved or engraved it 2 sculptor 3 sculptural; sculpture 4 [L *sculptus*] carved or engraved

sculp·ti·to·ry \ˈskəlptə,tōrē\ adj [1*sculpture* + -*itory* (as in *auditory*)] : having the characteristics of sculpture

sculp·tor \ˈskəlptə(r)\ n -s [L, fr. *sculptus* (past part. of *sculpere* to carve) + -*or*] : one that sculptures or produces works of sculpture

sculp·tress \-trəs\ n -ES [*sculptor* + -*ess*] : a female sculptor

sculp·tur·al \-pchərəl, -psh(ə)rəl\ adj [1*sculpture* + -*al*] 1 : of, relating to, or consisting of sculpture 2 : resembling sculpture : SCULPTURESQUE — **sculp·tur·al·ly** \-rəlē, -li\ adv

1**sculp·ture** \ˈskəlpchə(r), -psh-\ n -s [ME, fr. L *sculptura*, fr. *sculptus* (past part. of *sculpere* to carve, alter. of *scalpere* to carve, cut) + -*ura* -ure — more at SHELF] 1 a (1) : the act, process, or art of carving, cutting, hewing, molding, welding, or constructing materials into statues, ornaments, or figures (2) : the act, process, or art of producing figures or groups in plastic or hard materials b (1) : work produced by sculpture : the body of primarily three-dimensional works of art ⟨an exhibit of painting and ~⟩ (2) : a carved or molded statue or figure; *broadly* : a nonfunctional work of art whose aesthetic effect depends primarily on three-dimensional relationships ⟨a forged steel ~⟩ 2 *archaic* : an engraved figure or design ⟨published his play with ~s and a preface —Samuel Johnson⟩ 3 : impressed or raised markings or the pattern of such markings on the surface of a plant or animal part 4 : a modification of the forms of the earth's surface by sculpturing

2**sculpture** \"\ vb **sculptured; sculptured; sculpturing** \-pchəriŋ, -psh(ə)r-\ **sculptures** vt 1 a (1) : to form an image or representation of with a chisel or other tool from wood, stone, metal, or other material (2) : to carve, engrave, mold, weld, or construct (plastic or hard materials) into a primarily three-dimensional work of art (3) : to cover or adorn with sculpture or carved work b : to mold or form so as to give the appearance of sculpture or bas relief ⟨a *sculptured* hairdo⟩ ⟨an automobile body of *sculptured* metal⟩ c : to cause (as a line) to flow in the manner of classic sculpture 2 : to develop sculpturesque qualities in (as a musical or literary work or a painting); *specif* : to mold from the basic aesthetic matter rather than adorn by extraneous ornament 3 : to change (the form of the earth's surface) by erosion or by erosion and deposition ⟨the *sculpturing* of a canyon by a river⟩ ~ vi : to work as a sculptor

sculptured adj [fr. past part. of 2*sculpture*] : having raised or impressed markings on the surface ⟨a ~ conch⟩

sculptured glass n : CAMEO GLASS

sculptured rug n : CARVED RUG

sculptured tortoise *or* **sculptured turtle** n : WOOD TORTOISE

sculp·tur·er \-pchərə(r), -pshə-\ n -s : one that sculptures

sculp·tur·esque \ˌ==ˈresk\ adj [1*sculpture* + -*esque*] : done in the manner of or resembling sculpture : resembling a statue in amplitude or clearness of outline — **sculp·tur·esque·ly** adv

sculpturing n -s [fr. gerund of 2*sculpture*] 1 : the action of one who sculptures 2 : the occupation of a sculptor 3 : SCULPTURE 3

1**scum** \ˈskəm\ n -s [ME *scum, scume*, fr. MD *schum, schume*; akin to OHG *scūm* foam, froth and prob. to ON *skūmi* twilight, *skuggi* shadow — more at SKY] 1 *obs* : FOAM, FROTH 2 a (1) : extraneous matter or impurities risen to or formed on the surface of a liquid (2) : a foul filmy covering floating on a liquid (as a stagnant pool) b : the scoria of metals in a molten state : DROSS c : a slimy film formed on the surface of a solid or gelatinous object d : the impurities precipitated in the process of sugar refining 3 a : vile, worthless, or rotten objects : REFUSE b (1) : the lowest and most undesirable class of a population ⟨the social ~, the passively rotting mass of people who lie at the bottom of the social scale —M.D. Geismar⟩ (2) : a rabble made up of low or evil people (3) : a low, evil, or worthless person ⟨he's not a ~⟩

2**scum** \"\ vb **scummed; scummed; scumming; scums** [ME *scumen*, fr. *scum, scume* scum] vt 1 *archaic* : to take the scum from : SKIM 2 *obs* : to range over : SCOUR 3 : to cover with or as if with scum ~ vi : to become covered with or as if with scum

1**scum·ble** \ˈskəmbəl\ vt **scumbled; scumbled; scumbling** \-b(ə)liŋ\ **scumbles** [freq. of 2*scum*] 1 a : to make (color or a painting) less brilliant by covering with a thin coat of opaque or semiopaque color applied with a nearly dry brush b : to apply (a color) in this manner 2 : to soften the lines or colors of (a drawing) by rubbing lightly (as with a stump or a finger) 3 : to paint, draw, or produce by scumbling

2**scumble** \"\ n -s 1 : the act of scumbling 2 : a softened effect produced by scumbling 3 : a material (as paint) used for scumbling

scumbling n -s [fr. gerund of 1*scumble*] : the effect produced by or the color applied in or as if in a scumble

scumboard \ˈ=,=\ n : a device for the removal of scum in sewage-treatment plants

scum·fish \ˈskəm,fish\ vt [by shortening & alter. fr. 1*discomfit*] *dial Brit* : to overpower esp. by suffocation

scum·less \-mləs\ adj : lacking scum

scum·mer \-mə(r)\ n -s [ME, fr. 1*scum* + -*er*] : a utensil for removing scum

scumming n -s [fr. gerund of 2*scum*] 1 : the removal of scum 2 : scum formed on the surface of an object: as a : an imperfection resulting when matter being printed takes ink from a nonprinting area of a printing surface (as a lithographic plate) b (1) : a white or light-colored stain on brick caused by salts in the clay (2) : a defect in enamel characterized by areas of poor gloss

scum·my \ˈskəmē, -mi\ adj -ER/-EST [1*scum* + -*y*] 1 a : covered with scum b : of the nature of or resembling scum 2 : CONTEMPTIBLE, MEAN, SCURVY

scuncheon *var of* SCONCHEON

scun·gil·li *also* **scun·gi·li** \skünˈjēlē, -jilē\ n -s [modif. of It dial. *scunciglio* conch, seashell, prob. alter. of It *conchiglia* seashell, shellfish, fr. L *conchylium* shellfish — more at CONCHYLIUM] 1 : alimentary paste in the shape of conch shells 2 : the meat of a conch cooked and served with a highly seasoned sauce

1**scun·ner** \ˈskənər\ vi -ED/-ING/-S [ME (Sc dial.) *skoneren, skunniren*] *chiefly Scot* : to be in a state of disgusted irritation — usu. used with *at* or *with*

2**scun·ner** \-nə(r)\ n -s 1 : an unreasonable or extremely subjective dislike ⟨took a ~ at his daughter's newest boyfriend⟩ 2 : a unfavorable prejudice ⟨will be accused of having a ~ against the English —J.R.Chamberlain⟩

scup \ˈskəp\ n, pl **scup** *also* **scups** [Narraganset *mishcùp*, fr. *mishe* big + *kuppe* close together; fr. its large, close scales] : either of two sparid fishes (genus *Stenotomus*) of the Atlantic coast of the U. S.: a : a fish (*S. chrysops*) occurring from So. Carolina to Maine and esteemed as a panfish — called also *northern porgy, northern scup* b : a related fish (*S. aculeatus*) of more southerly distribution — called also *southern porgy, southern scup*

scup·paug \(ˈ)skəˈpȯg\ n -s [Narraganset *mishcùppaûog*, pl. of *mishcùp*] : SCUP a

1**scup·per** \ˈskəpə(r)\ n -s [ME *skopper*] 1 a : a drainage opening cut through the side of a ship flush with the deck b : a drain set in the deck of a ship c **scuppers** pl : WATERWAYS 2 a : an opening in the wall of a building to permit water to drain off a floor or flat roof b : a device placed in an opening to facilitate drainage

2**scupper** \"\ vt -ED/-ING/-S [origin unknown] 1 *Brit* : to put or leave in danger or difficulty 2 *Brit* : AMBUSH

scup·per·nong \ˈskəpə(r),nȯŋ, -näŋ\ n -s [fr. *Scuppernong*, small river and lake in Tyrrell county, No. Carolina] 1 a : MUSCADINE 2 b : any of various cultivated muscadines that are derived from wild muscadines, exist as a natural variety, and have yellowish green fruits suggesting a plum in flavor 2 : a white aromatic table wine that is light amber in color, is sweeter and heavier than the average table wine, and is made from the scuppernong

scupper pipe *or* **scupper shoot** n [1*scupper*] : a drainpipe from a deckhouse roof to the scuppers or from the deck to an opening in the side

scup·pit \ˈskəpət, -ku̇p-\ n -s [ME *scopette*, prob. fr. *scope* scoop + -*ette* — more at SCOOP] *dial Eng* : a small shovel

1**scur** \ˈskər(·)\ *var of* SKIRR

2**scur** \"\ n -s [E dial. *scur* scab, scurf, perh. alter. of 1*scurf*] : a small rounded portion of horn tissue attached to the skin of the horn pit of a polled animal

1**scurf** \ˈskərf, -kəf, -kəif\ n -s [ME, of Scand origin; akin to Icel *skurfa* scurf, Dan *skurv*; akin to OE *sceorf* scurf, OHG *scorf* scurf, OE *sceorfan* to gnaw, L *carpere* to pluck — more at HARVEST] 1 : material like bran that becomes detached from the epidermis in thin dry scales esp. in an abnormal skin condition 2 a : anything like flakes or scales adhering to a surface b : the foul remains of anything adherent 3 : the offscourings of society : SCUM 4 : the deposit or covering resembling scales or bran found on some plant parts 5 a : a localized or general darkening and roughening of a smooth plant surface that is usu. more pronounced than russeting b : any of several plant diseases characterized by scurf: as (1) : a disease of sweet potatoes caused by an imperfect fungus (*Monilochaetes infuscans*) (2) : SILVER SCURF

2**scurf** \"\ vt -ED/-ING/-S 1 a : to whiten like scurf b : to cover with or as if with scurf 2 : to remove (as scurf) by scraping, rubbing, or wiping ⟨~*ing* a patch away from the glazed window —Thomas Wolfe⟩; *esp* : to remove deposits of carbon from (as the inner surfaces of coal gas retorts or coke ovens)

scurf·er \-fə(r)\ n -s : a wooden tool coated with coarse emery for smoothing a surface (as of leather) after scraping

scurfy \-fē,-fi\ adj -ER/-EST [ME, fr. 1*scurf* + -*y*] 1 : having or producing scurf : covered with or as if with scurf 2 : resembling or consisting of scurf — compare LEPIDOTE

scurfy bark louse n : SCURFY SCALE

scurfy pea *also* **scurf pea** *or* **scurvy pea** n : any of several plants of the genus *Psoralea*; *esp* : a bushy branched herb (*P. tenuiflora floribunda*) of central No. America with white canescent foliage and purplish flowers in oblong spikes

scurfy scale n : a scale (*Chionaspis furfura*) injurious to trees (as apple or pear)

scurred \ˈskərd\ adj : having scurs

scur·rile \ˈskər·əl, -ə·rəl, -ər·,īl, -ə·,rīl\ *or* **scur·ril** \-ər·əl, -ə·rəl\ adj [MF *scurrile*, fr. L *scurrilis*, fr. *scurra* buffoon, jester + -*ilis* -ile] : SCURRILOUS

scur·ril·i·ty \skəˈriləd·ē, -lətē, -i\ n -ES [MF & LL; MF *scurrilité*, fr. LL *scurrilitat-, scurrilitas*, fr. L *scurrilis* scurrilous + -*itat-, -itas* -ity] 1 : the quality or state of being scurrilous 2 a : scurrilous or abusive language usu. marked by coarse or indecent wording or innuendo, unjust denigration, or clownish jesting ⟨this was the day of journalistic ~ —*Amer. Guide Series: Pa.*⟩ b : an instance of scurrility : a rude or abusive remark **syn** see ABUSE

scur·ri·lous \ˈskər·ələs, -kə·rə-\ adj [L *scurrilis* jeering, scurrilous + E -*ous*] 1 : using or given to using the language of low buffoonery; *broadly* : vulgar and evil in habit or demeanor ⟨~ imposters who used a religious exterior to rob poor people —Edwin Benson⟩ 2 : containing low obscenities or coarse abuse ⟨a ~ collection of highly obscene verses —R.A.Hall b.1911⟩ ⟨a pamphleteering campaign filled with ~ charges and countercharges —A.D.Graeff⟩ — **scur·ri·lous·ly** adv — **scur·ri·lous·ness** n -ES

1**scur·ry** \ˈskər·ē, ˈskə·r\|, \|i\ vb -ED/-ING/-ES [short for *hurry-scurry*] vi 1 : to move in or as if in a brisk rapidly alternating step ⟨~ for miles through inky tunnels —Claudia Cassidy⟩ ⟨*scurried* to a rock for shelter —Audrey Barker⟩ 2 : to circulate in an agitated, confused, or fluttering manner ⟨~*ing* snow whirls —F.V.W.Mason⟩ ⟨a great deal of ~*ing* around, grabbing for slippers or bumping into each other —Gilbert Millstein⟩ ~ vt : to cause to scurry ⟨such a thought might ~ any recalcitrant patient into paying the fee due —W.T.Corlett⟩ ⟨gusty winds *scurried* the crisped and fallen leaves —H.B.Alexander⟩

2**scurry** \"\ n -ES 1 : the act or an instance of scurrying : a hurried or confused movement ⟨the ~ of men mounting in haste —*Blackwood's*⟩ ⟨a little ~ now and then when one cow bumped another —Nancy Hale⟩ 2 : a short run or race 3 : a jumping race in equitation over a series of obstacles with a penalty of one second for each fault 4 : FLURRY ⟨huge snow *scurries* —Robert Payne⟩

s curve n, *cap S* : a curve resembling the letter S

scur·vi·ly \ˈskər·vəlē, -kəv-,-kəiv-, -li\ adv : in a scurvy manner

scur·vi·ness \-vēnəs, -vin-\ n -ES : the quality or state of being scurvy

scur·vish \-vish\ n -ES [alter. of *scabish*] : an evening primrose (*Oenothera biennis*)

1**scur·vy** \ˈskərvē, -kəv-, -kəiv-, -vi\ adj- ER/-EST [1*scurf* + -*y*] 1 : covered or affected with scurf : SCURFY 2 : characterized by meanness and despicableness : CONTEMPTIBLE ⟨went to sea with his ~ crew —C.B.Driscoll⟩ ⟨weather played some ~ tricks⟩ **syn** see CONTEMPTIBLE

2**scurvy** \"\ n -ES : a disease characterized by spongy gums, loosening of the teeth, and a tendency to bleed into the skin and mucous membranes and caused by a dietary deficiency of ascorbic acid ⟨suggested that the anemia of ~ is due to iron deficiency —*Therapeutic Notes*⟩

scurvy grass n 1 : any of several cresses reputed to have value in the treatment or prevention of scurvy: as a : WINTER CRESS b : a widely distributed arctic cress (*Cochlearia officinalis*) 2 *Austral* : DAYFLOWER a

scuse \n ˈskyüs, v -üz\ n or vb [by shortening] : EXCUSE

scus·in \ˈskyüzᵊn\ prep [alter. of *excusing*] *chiefly South & Midland* : EXCEPT

1**scut** \ˈskət\ n -s [origin unknown] : the short erect tail of an animal and esp. of a hare or rabbit

2**scut** \"\ n -s [prob. alter. of obs. E *scout*, fr. ME, prob. of Scand origin; akin to ON *skūta, skūti* taunt — more at SCOUT] : a contemptible fellow

scut- *or* **scuti-** *comb form* [NL, fr. L *scutum* shield] 1 : shield ⟨*scutal*⟩ ⟨*scutella*⟩ ⟨*Scutibranchia*⟩ 2 : scute : scutum ⟨*scutation*⟩ ⟨*scutiped*⟩

scuta *pl of* SCUTUM

scu·tage \ˈskyüd·ij\ n -s [ME, fr. ML *scutagium*, fr. L *scutum* shield + ML -*agium* -age (fr. OF -*age*) — more at ESQUIRE] : an impost tax or fine levied upon a tenant of a knight's fee in commutation for or for default in the render of the military service attached to the fee

scu·tal \ˈskyüd·ᵊl\ adj [*scut-* + -*al*] : of or relating to a shield, scute, or scutum

scu·tate \ˈskyü,tāt\ *or* **scu·tat·ed** \-ād·əd\ adj [*scutate* fr. NL *scutatus*, fr. L, armed with a shield, fr. *scutum* shield + -*atus* -ate; *scutated* fr. NL *scutatus* + E -*ed*] 1 : shaped like a buckler : PELTATE 2 : covered by bony or horny plates or large scales

scu·ta·tion \skyüˈtāshən\ n -s [*scut-* + -*ation*] : the arrangement of scutes

1**scutch** \ˈskəch\ vt -ED/-ING/-ES [obs. F *escoucher* (now *écoucher*), fr. (assumed) VL *excuticare* to beat out, fr. L *excutere* to shake out, beat out, fr. *ex-* 1ex- + *quatere* to shake, strike — more at QUASH] 1 *dial* : WHIP, BEAT 2 *or* **skutch** : to separate the woody fiber from (flax or hemp) by beating 3 *chiefly Brit* : to open (cotton fiber) by beating and form into a lap 4 a : to open (cloth) full width b : DISENTANGLE ⟨~ skeins of yarn⟩

2**scutch** \"\ *or* **scotch** \ˈskäch\ n -ES [obs. F *escouche* (now *écouche*) scutcher, fr. *escoucher* to scutch] 1 : SCUTCHER 2 : a bricklayer's hammer for cutting, trimming, and dressing bricks

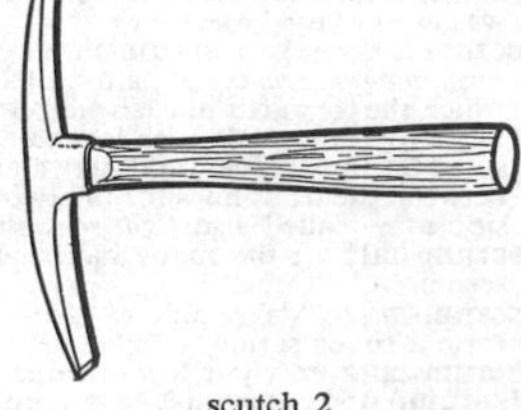

scutch 2

3**scutch** \"\ *or* **scutch grass** n -ES [*scutch* short for *scutch grass*; *scutch grass* alter. of *couch grass*] 1 : COUCH GRASS 1a 2 : BERMUDA GRASS

scutch·eon \ˈskəchən\ n -s [ME *scochon*, fr. MF *escuchon* — more at ESCUTCHEON] 1 : ESCUTCHEON 2 : something shaped like an escutcheon; *specif* : SCUTE

scutch·eoned \-nd\ adj : ESCUTCHEONED

scutch·er \ˈskəchə(r)\ *or* **scotch·er** \-käch-\ n -s [1*scutch* + -*er*] 1 : one whose work is scutching: as a : a mason who cuts with a scutch b : a worker who scutches or tends a machine that does scutching 2 : a machine or device that scutches; *specif* : an implement or machine for scutching flax, cotton, or cloth

scute \ˈsk(y)üt\ n -s [ME, fr. L *scutum* shield; trans. of MF *ecu* ecu, shield — more at ESQUIRE] 1 *archaic* : a coin of small value 2 [NL *scutum*] : an external bony or horny plate : a large scale : SCUTUM: as a : one of the large scales on the head of a snake or other reptile b : one of the broad transverse scales on the belly of a snake c : one of the tergal plates of a myriapod d : ELYTRON 2

scu·tel \(ˈ)skyüˌtel\ n -s [NL *scutellum*] : SCUTELLUM

1**scu·tel·la** \sk(y)üˈtelə\ n, pl **scutel·lae** \-e(,)lē, -e,lī\ [NL, fr. *scut-* + -*ella*] 1 : SCUTELLUM 2b 2 : a very small dermal bone or ossicle : a small scute

2**scutella** *pl of* SCUTELLUM

scu·tel·lar \(ˈ)=ˈtelə(r)\ adj [NL *scutellum* + E -*ar*] 1 : of or relating to a scutellum 2 : having scutella

scu·tel·lar·ia \,sk(y)üd·ᵊlˈa(a)rēə\ n, *cap* [NL, fr. L *scutella* drinking bowl + NL -*aria* — more at SCUTTLE] 1 : a very large widely distributed genus of herbs (family Labiatae) having purple, blue, pink, red, yellow, or white, flowers either axillary or in a terminal raceme and a bilabiate calyx with a scale or a helmetlike appendage above — see SKULLCAP 2 -s : the dried overground portion of the mad-dog skullcap used esp. formerly as a bitter tonic, antispasmodic, and stomachic

scu·tel·larin \sk(y)üˈtelərən, ,sk(y)üd·ᵊlˈa(a)rən\ n -s [ISV *scutellar-* (fr. NL *Scutellaria*) + -*in*] 1 : a resinoid prepared from the root of the mad-dog skullcap and related mints of the genus *Scutellaria* and used esp. formerly as a tonic and nerve sedative 2 : a yellow crystalline compound $C_{21}H_{18}O_{12}$ obtained from the root of the mad-dog skullcap

scu·tel·late \sk(y)üˈtelət, ˈsk(y)üd·ᵊl,āt\ adj [prob. fr. (assumed) NL *scutellatus*, fr. NL *scutellum* + L -*atus* -ate] 1 a : rather flat with a distinct rim and a rounded to oval outline ⟨a fungus with a ~ fruiting body⟩ b : of or resembling a scutellum 2 *or* **scu·tel·lat·ed** \ˈsk(y)üd·ᵊl,ād·əd\ [*scutellated* fr. (assumed) NL *scutellatus* + E -*ed*] a : covered with scales, small plates, or scutella b : faced with a series of broad usu. imbricated plates — used of the tarsus of a bird 3 *or* **scutellated** : having a scutellum — used of an insect (as a beetle)

scu·tel·la·tion \,sk(y)üd·ᵊlˈāshən\ n -s [*scutellate* + -*ion*] : LEPIDOSIS 2

1**scu·tel·ler·id** \sk(y)üˈtelərəd\ adj [NL *Scutelleridae*] : of or relating to the Scutelleridae

2**scutellerid** \"\ n -s : an insect of the family Scutelleridae

scu·tel·ler·i·dae \,sk(y)üd·ᵊlˈerə,dē\ n pl, *cap* [NL, fr. *Scutellera*, type genus (fr. *scutella*) + -*idae*] : a family of broadly oval flattened terrestrial insects (order Hemiptera) having the antennae five-jointed, the legs spineless, and a large scutellum that almost entirely covers the abdomen

scu·tel·li·form \sk(y)üˈtelə,fȯrm\ adj [NL *scutellum* + E -*iform*] : shaped like a scutellum

scu·tel·lig·er·ous \ˌsk(y)üd·ᵊlˈijərəs\ adj [NL *scutellum* + E -*igerous*] : having scutella : SCUTELLATE

scu·tel·li·plantar \sk(y)üˌtelə+\ adj [*scutellate* + -*i-* + *plantar*] : having the tarsi scutellate in front and behind (as some birds) — opposed to *laminiplantar* — **scu·tel·li·plantation** \"+\ n

scu·tel·lum \sk(y)üˈteləm\ n, pl **scutel·la** \-lə\ [NL, fr. *scut-* + -*ellum* (neut. of -*ellus* -el)] 1 a : a rounded apothecium occurring in lichens and having an elevated rim formed of the thallus proper b : the shield-shaped cotyledon of a monocotyledon (as a grass) c : the conical cap of the endosperm in a cycad 2 a : the third of the four pieces forming the upper part of a thoracic segment of an insect situated between the scutum and the postnotum; *specif* : the scutellum of the mesothorax b : one of the transverse scales on the tarsi and toes of birds

scutellum rot n : a molding and rotting seedling disease of germinating maize characterized by and caused by various fungi (esp. of the genera *Rhizopus, Mucor, Penicillium*, and *Fusarium*)

scutes *pl of* SCUTE

scuti- — see SCUT-

scu·ti·branch \ˈsk(y)üd·ə,braŋk\ n -s [NL *Scutibranchia*] : a gastropod of the group Scutibranchia

scu·ti·bran·chia \,==ˈbraŋkēə\ n pl, *cap* [NL, fr. *scut-* + -*branchia*] *in some classifications* : a heterogeneous group of gastropods distinguished by possession of a simple shield-shaped shell and more or less exactly equivalent to Aspidobranchia esp. in modern usage — **scu·ti·bran·chi·an** \,==-ˈbraŋkēən\ adj *or* n — **scu·ti·bran·chi·ate** \-ēət, -ē,āt\ adj *or* n

scu·ti·bran·chi·a·ta \,==,==ˈäd·ə, -ˈād·ə\ n pl, *cap* [NL, fr. *scut-* + *branchiata*] *syn of* SCUTIBRANCHIA

scu·tif·er·ous \(ˈ)sk(y)üˈtif(ə)rəs\ adj [*scut-* + -*ferous*] : bearing scutes

scu·ti·form \ˈsk(y)üd·ə,fȯrm\ adj [NL *scutiformis*, fr. L *scutum* shield + -*iformis* -iform — more at ESQUIRE] : having the shape of a shield : SCUTATE

scu·ti·ger \ˈsk(y)üd·əjə(r)\ n -s [NL *Scutigera*] : a centipede of the genus *Scutigera* — **scu·tig·er·al** \(ˈ)sk(y)üˈtijərəl\ adj

scu·tig·era \sk(y)üˈtijərə\ n, *cap* [NL *scut-* + -*gera* (fr. L *gerere* to bear) — more at CAST] **:** a genus (the type of the family Scutigeridae) of centipedes including the house centipede

scu·tig·er·el·la \(,)sk(y)ü,tijə'relə\ *n, cap* [NL, fr. *Scutigera* + *-ella*] **:** a genus of symphilids that includes the widely distributed garden centipede

scu·tig·er·ous \(')sk(y)ü¦tijərəs\ *adj* [*scut-* + *-gerous*] **:** SCUTIFEROUS

scu·ti·ped \'sk(y)üd-ə,ped\ *adj* [*scut-* + *-ped*] *of a bird* **:** having scutellate tarsi

scuts *pl of* SCUT

¹scut·ter \'skəd-ə(r)\ *vb* -ED/-ING/-S [alter. (prob. influenced by *scatter*) of ²*scuttle*] **:** SCURRY, SCUTTLE

²scutter \"\ *n* -s **1** *chiefly Scot* **:** SCURRY, SCRAMBLE **2** *dial* **:** someone remarkable (as for rascality or excellence)

¹scut·tle \'skəd-ᵊl, -ətᵊl\ *n* -s [ME *scutel*, fr. L *scutella* drinking bowl, tray, dim. of *scutra* flat plate, platter; perh. akin to L *scutum* shield — more at ESQUIRE] **1 :** a shallow open basket of wood or wickerwork for carrying something (as grain or garden produce) **2 :** COAL SCUTTLE **3** *Brit* **:** COWL 3c **4 :** a large glass for beer or ale ⟨~ of suds⟩

²scuttle \"\ *n* -s [ME *skottell*, prob. fr. OSp *escotilla*] **1 :** a small opening in an outside wall or covering furnished with a lid: as **a :** a small opening or hatchway in the deck of a ship large enough to admit a man and with a lid for covering it **b :** a small hole in the side or bottom of a ship furnished with a lid or glazed **c :** an opening in the roof or a floor of a house fitted with a lid **2 :** a lid that covers or closes a scuttle

³scuttle \"\ *vt* **scuttled; scuttled; scuttling** \-d-ᵊliŋ, -t(ᵊ)liŋ\ **scuttles 1 :** to cut a hole through the bottom, deck, or sides of (a ship); *specif* **:** to sink or attempt to sink by making holes through the bottom of **2 a :** to damage severely or destroy completely ⟨war was in full swing, and this effectually *scuttled* my family's travel plans —Polly Adler⟩ **b :** ABANDON ⟨the overtime provisions of the old contract were *scuttled* in the new agreement —*N.Y. Times*⟩

⁴scuttle \"\ *n* -s [alter. of ¹*cuttle*] **1 :** CUTTLEFISH **2 :** OCTOPUS

⁵scuttle \"\ *vi* -ED/-ING/-S [prob. blend of ¹*scud* and *shuttle* v.] **1 :** to move with or as if with short rapidly alternating steps **:** SCURRY ⟨a tiny man came *scuttling* in by another door —Gordon Merrick⟩ ⟨armies of brown fiddler crabs ~ across the road —*Amer. Guide Series: Fla.*⟩ ⟨a little motorcar so small that it *scuttled* up the road . . . with the abruptness of a wound-up toy —Thomas Wolfe⟩ **2 :** to withdraw from or abandon a possession or country once occupied or a policy or obligation in a hasty manner ⟨*scuttling* out of our responsibilities in the Middle East —*New Statesman & Nation*⟩

⁶scuttle \"\ *n* -s **1 a :** a quick shuffling pace ⟨a chimpanzee can easily run away and escape from a man with its half-quadrupedal, half-bipedal ~ —Weston LaBarre⟩ **b :** a short swift run ⟨suddenly made a last frantic ~ —A.J.Cronin⟩ **2 :** hurried withdrawal from occupation or control of a country or area ⟨follow up . . . an electoral reversal by an Imperial ~ —*New Statesman & Nation*⟩

scut·tle·butt \'skəd-ᵊl,bət, -kətᵊl-, *usu* -bəd-+V\ *n* [²*scuttle* + *butt* (cask)] **1 a :** a cask on shipboard to contain fresh water for a day's use **b :** a drinking fountain on a ship or at a naval or marine installation **2 :** RUMOR, GOSSIP ⟨started a round of ~ to the effect that the regiment would arrive soon —H.L. Merillat⟩

scut·tler \'skəd-ᵊlə(r), -kət(ᵊ)l-\ *n* -s [⁵*scuttle* + *-er*] **1 :** one that scuttles **2 :** RACE RUNNER

scu·tu·late \'sk(y)üchə,lāt, -üd-ᵊl,āt\ *also* **scu·tu·lat·ed** \-ād-əd\ *adj* [*scutulate* prob. fr. (assumed) NL *scutulatus*, fr. L *scutulum* small shield + *-atus* -ate; *scutulated* fr. (assumed) NL *scutulatus* + E *-ed*] **:** SCUTELLATE

scu·tu·lum \-chəl|əm, -d-ᵊl|\ *n, pl* **scutu·la** \|ə\ [NL, fr. L, small shield, dim. of *scutum* shield] **:** one of the yellow cup-shaped crusts occurring over hair follicles in favus

scu·tum \'sk(y)üd-əm\ *n, pl* **scu·ta** \-ə\ [NL, fr. L, shield — more at ESQUIRE] **:** a bony, horny, or chitinous plate **:** SCUTE: as **a :** the second and largest of the four parts forming the upper surface of a thoracic segment of an insect between the prescutum and the scutellum **b :** one of the two lower valves of the operculum of a barnacle

scyb·a·lous \'sibələs\ *adj* [NL *scybalum* + E *-ous*] **:** formed of hardened feces

scyb·a·lum \-ləm\ *n, pl* **scyba·la** \-lə\ [NL, fr. LL, dung, fr. Gk *skybalon*] **:** a hardened fecal mass

scyd·mae·ni·dae \sid'mēnə,dē\ *n pl, cap* [NL, fr. *Scydmaenus*, type genus (fr. Gk *skydmainein* to be angry with) + *-idae*] **:** a widely distributed family of very small beetles

scye \'sī\ *n* -s [origin unknown] **:** ARMSCYE

¹scyl·io·rhi·nid \¦silēō¦rīnəd\ *adj* [NL *Scyliorhinidae*] **:** of or relating to the Scyliorhinidae

²scyliorhinid \"\ *n* -s **:** a cat shark of the family Scyliorhinidae

scyl·io·rhin·i·dae \¦==='rinə,dē\ *n pl, cap* [NL, fr. *Scyliorhinus*, type genus (fr. Gk *skylion* dogfish + NL *-rhinus*) + *-idae*] **:** a family of galeoid sharks including the typical cat sharks

scyl·la \'silə\ *n* -s *usu cap* [fr. *Scylla* (now *Scilla*), headland on the Italian coast projecting into the Strait of Messina opposite the whirlpool Charybdis on the Sicilian coast, fr. L, fr. Gk *Skylla*] **:** a destructive peril — usu. used as the alternative to *Charybdis* ⟨the *Scylla* of incomprehensibility and the Charybdis of inaccuracy have both been avoided —*Times Lit. Supp.*⟩

scyl·laea \sə'lēə\ *n, cap* [NL, fr. *Scylla*, in Greco-Roman mythology a female monster who inhabited the rock Scylla on the Italian coast and was a menace to seafarers, fr. L, fr. Gk *Skylla*] **:** a genus (coextensive with the family Scyllaeidae) of pelagic nudibranch mollusks that have small branched gills situated on the upper side of four fleshy lateral lobes and on a median crest on the posterior part of the back and that live among and mimic sargassum and other floating seaweeds

¹scyl·lar·i·an \sə'la(a)rēən\ *adj* [NL *Scyllarus*, genus of crustaceans + E *-an*] **:** of or relating to the Scyllaridae

²scyllarian \"\ *n* -s **:** a crustacean of the family Scyllaridae

scyl·lar·i·dae \sə'larə,dē\ *n pl, cap* [NL, fr. *Scyllarus*, type genus (fr. Gk *skyllaros*, *kyllaros* hermit crab) + *-idae*] **:** a family of marine decapod crustaceans (tribe Palinura) having the body broad and flat, the antennae short and scalelike, and the eyes in sockets in the carapace and living in shallow water buried in mud or sand

scyl·lio·rhin·i·dae [NL] *syn of* SCYLIORHINIDAE

scyl·li·tol \'silə,tōl, -tȯl\ *n* -s [NL *Scyllium*, genus name of the dogfish *Scyllium canicula* (fr. Gk *skylion* dogfish) + ISV *-itol*] **:** an optically inactive sweet crystalline polyhydroxy alcohol $C_6H_6(OH)_6$ that is found esp. in the dogfish, in the leaves of the coconut palm, in flowering dogwood, and in acorns

scyph- *or* **scypho-** *also* **scyphi-** *comb form* [NL, fr. L *scyphus* cup, scyphus — more at SCYPHUS] **:** cup **:** can **:** scyphus ⟨*scyphi*form⟩ ⟨*Scypho*zoa⟩ ⟨*scypho*se⟩

¹scy·pha \'sīfə\ *n, pl* **scyphae** [NL, fr. L *scyphus* cup] **:** SCYPHUS 2

²scypha \"\ *n, cap* [NL, fr. L *scyphus* cup] *in some classifications* **:** a genus equivalent to *Sycon* that is often considered invalid since it was described as a genus of plants

scy·phate \-,fāt\ *adj* [*scyph-* + *-ate*] **:** shaped like a cup

scy·phis·to·ma \sī'fistəmə\ *n, pl* **scyphisto·mae** \-(,)mē\ *also* **scyphistomas** [NL, fr. *scyph-* + *-stoma*] **:** a sexually produced polypoid larva of many scyphozoans that is attached to the substrate, may produce other scyphistomae by budding, but ultimately repeatedly constricts transversely and abscises ephyrae which develop into free-swimming medusae — see STROBILA

scy·pho·medusae \¦sī(,)fō+\ *n* [NL, fr. *scyph-* + *medusae*, pl. of *medusa*] *syn of* SCYPHOZOA

scy·pho·polyp \¦sīfō+\ *n* [*scyph-* + *polyp*] **:** SCYPHISTOMA

scy·phose \'sī,fōs\ *adj* [*scyph-* + *-ose*] **:** having scyphi

scy·pho·zoa \,sīfə'zōə\ *n pl, cap* [NL, fr. *scyph-* + *-zoa*] **:** a class of Coelenterata comprising jellyfishes that have endodermal gastric tentacles, endodermal gonads which discharge their products into the digestive cavity, and usu. tentaculocysts, that lack a true hydroid and have the asexual generation represented by a scyphistoma, and that usu. lack a velum — see CORONATAE, CUBOMEDUSAE, RHIZOSTOMAE, SEMAEOSTOMEAE, STAUROMEDUSAE — **scy·pho·zo·an** \¦sīfə¦zōən\ *adj or n*

scyphu·la \'sīfyələ, 'sif-\ *n, pl* **scyphu·lae** \-,lē\ [NL, fr. *scyph-* + *-ula*] **1 :** SCYPHISTOMA **2 :** a hypothetical ancestral scyphozoan

scyphu·lus \-ləs\ *n, pl* **scyphu·li** \-,lī\ [NL, fr. LL, little cup, dim. of L *scyphus* cup] **:** the vaginula of a liverwort

scy·phus \'sīfəs\ *n, pl* **scy·phi** \-,fī\ [L, fr. Gk *skyphos*] **1** *or* **sky·phos** \'skī,fäs\ *pl* **sky·phoi** \-,fȯi\ **:** a drinking vessel with a deep body, flat bottom, and two small horizontal handles near the rim and used esp. in ancient Greece **2** [NL, fr. L, cup] **:** a cup-shaped enlargement of the podetium in lichens — called also *scypha*

scyt- *or* **scyto-** *comb form* [NL, fr. Gk *skyto-*, fr. *skytos* skin, leather — more at HIDE] **:** skin **:** integument ⟨*scyt*itis⟩ ⟨*scyto*blastema⟩

scyt·a·le \'sid-ᵊl(,)ē\ *n* -s [L *scytale*, *scytala*, *scutula*, fr. Gk *skytalē* staff, cylinder, message] **1 :** a method of cipher writing used esp. by the Spartans in which a narrow strip of parchment was wound on a rod and the message written across the adjoining edges **2 a :** a message written in the scytale cipher **b :** a parchment bearing such a message

scyth \'sith\ *n* -s *usu cap* [ME *Sith*, fr. L *Scytha*, *Scythes*, fr. Gk *Skythēs*] **:** SCYTHIAN

¹scythe \'sīth, ÷'sī, *esp before a voiceless consonant (as in "scythestone")* 'sīth; *absence of* th *or* th *is more common in the plural than in the singular*\ *n* -s [ME *sithe*, fr. OE *sīthe*, *sigthe*; akin to MLG *segede*, *sigde* scythe, MD *sichte*, ON *sigthr* scythe, sickle, OE *sagu*, *sage* saw — more at SAW] **:** an implement used for mowing grass, grain, or other crops and composed of a long curving blade fastened at an angle to a long handle

scythe

²scythe \"\ *vt* -ED/-ING/-S **:** to cut with or as if with a scythe **:** MOW

scythe·less \'sīthləs, ÷'sīl-\ *adj* **:** lacking a scythe

scythe·man \-īthmən, ÷-īm-\ *n, pl* **scythemen :** one who uses a scythe **:** MOWER

scythestone \'=,=\ *n* **:** a whetstone for sharpening a scythe

¹scyth·i·an \'sithēən, -th-\ *adj, usu cap* [L *Scythia* (fr. Gk *Skythia*, fr. *Skythēs* Scythian + *-ia* -y) + E *-an*] **1 a :** of, relating to, or characteristic of Scythia, an ancient country lying partly north and northeast of the Black sea and partly east of the Aral sea **b :** of, relating to, or characteristic of the people of Scythia **2 :** of, relating to, or characteristic of the Scythian language

²scythian \"\ *n* -s *usu cap* [L *Scythes*, *Scytha* Scythian + E *-an*] **1 :** one of an ancient nomadic people inhabiting Scythia **2 :** the Iranian language of the Scythian people

scythian antelope *n, usu cap S* **:** SAIGA

scythian lamb *n, usu cap S* **1 :** an Asiatic tree fern (*Cibotium barometz*) the dense matted hairs of which are sometimes used as a styptic **2 :** COTTON 2

¹scyth·ic \-thik,-th-\ *adj, usu cap* [L *Scythicus*, fr. Gk *Skythikos*, fr. *Skythēs* Scythian + *-ikos* -ic] **:** SCYTHIAN

²scythic \"\ *n* -s **:** SCYTHIAN 2

scyth·ism \-,thizəm, -,th-\ *n* -s *usu cap* [LGk *skythismos*, fr. Gk *Skythēs* Scythian + *-ismos* -ism] *archaic* **:** the paganism developed by the Scythians

scytho- *comb form, usu cap* [L *Scytha* Scythian + E *-o-*]**:** Scythian and ⟨*Scytho*-Aryan⟩ ⟨*Scytho*-Greek⟩

scytho-dravidian \¦si(,)thō, -thō+\ *adj, usu cap S&D* **:** of, relating to, or constituting a mixed racial type found chiefly in Bombay Province, India, and characterized by brachycephaly, medium stature, fair complexion, scanty beard, and well-formed nose

scy·to·dep·sic \¦sīd-ō¦depsik\ *adj* [F *scytodepsique*, fr. Gk *skytodepsikos*, fr. *skytodepsein* to dress leather (fr. *skytos* leather, skin + *depsein* to knead) + *-ikos* -ic — more at HIDE, DIPHTHERIA] **:** of or relating to a tanner or tanning

scy·to·ne·ma·ce·ae \,sīd-ōnə'māsē,ē\ *n pl, cap* [NL, fr. *Scytonema*, type genus (fr. *scyt-* + *-nema*) + *-aceae*] *syn of* SCYTONEMATACEAE

scy·to·nema·ta·ce·ae \,sīd-ō,nēmə'tāsē,ē, -nem-\ *n pl, cap* [NL, fr. *Scytonemat-*, *Scytonema*, type genus (fr. *scyt-* + *-nemat-*, *-nema*) + *-aceae*] **:** a family of filamentous blue-green algae (order Hormogonales) that differ from the Rivulariaceae in having no differentiation in the tips of the filaments and in exhibiting false branching of the filaments — **scy·to·nema·ta·ceous** \¦==,==¦tāshəs\ *adj* — **scy·to·nema·toid** \¦==¦==-,tȯid\ *adj* — **scy·to·nema·tous** \¦==¦=məd-əs\ *adj*

scy·to·pet·a·la·ce·ae \,sīd-ō,ped-ᵊl'āsē,ē\ *n pl, cap* [NL, fr. *Scytopetalum*, type genus (fr. *scyt-* + *petalum* petal) + *-aceae* — more at PETAL] **:** a tropical African family of shrubs and trees (order Malvales) having coriaceous leaves, small clustered flowers with numerous stamens, and woody or drupaceous one-seeded fruits

sd *abbr* **1** said **2** sand **3** seasoned **4** seed **5** sewed **6** signed **7** sound

SD *abbr or n* -s [NL *scientiae doctor*] **:** a doctor of science

SD *abbr* **1** same day **2** sash door **3** saturation deficit **4** sea damage **5** semidiameter **6** senior deacon **7** service dress **8** several dates **9** short delay **10** short delivery **11** sight draft **12** *often not cap* [L *sine dato*] without date **13** *often not cap* [L *sine die*] without day **14** single deck **15** soft drawn **16** solid drawn **17** special delivery **18** special duty **19** specially denatured **20** stage direction **21** standard deviation **22** straight duty **23** supply department; supply depot **24** survival dose

SDA *abbr* specific dynamic action

sdain *or* **sdeign** *vb* -ED/-ING/-S [It *sdegnare*, fr. (assumed) VL *disdignare* — more at DISDAIN] *obs* **:** DISDAIN

SDBL *abbr* sight draft, bill of lading attached

SDD *abbr* store door delivery

sdeignful *adj, obs* **:** DISDAINFUL

sdg *abbr* siding

sdl *abbr* **1** saddle **2** seedling

sdr *abbr* sender

sdruc·cio·la \'zdrüchə,lä\ *adj* [It, fem. of *sdrucciolo* slipping, sliding, having the accent on the antepenult, fr. *sdrucciolare* to slip, slide] **:** being or exhibiting triple rhyme in which the last accent falls on the antepenultimate syllable (as in *femina*, *semina*)

SDT *abbr* shell-destroying tracer

SE *abbr* **1** sanitary engineering **2** *often not cap* second entrance **3** single entry **4** southeast; southeastern **5** standard error **6** starch equivalent **7** stock exchange

Se *symbol* selenium

'se *var of* 's

¹sea \'sē\ *n* -s [ME *see*, fr. OE *sǣ*; akin to OFris *sē* sea, OS & OHG *sē*, *sēo*, ON *sær*, *sjōr*, *sjār*, Goth *saiws*] **1 a :** the great body of salty water that covers much of the earth's surface **:** the oceans of the world with their dependent saline waters; *broadly* **:** the waters of the earth as distinguished from the land and air **b :** a particular part of the sea ⟨southern ~s⟩ ⟨the fair ~ of England⟩ **c :** one of the bodies of salt water of the earth that are secondary in size to oceans **:** a body of salt water of second rank more or less landlocked and generally forming part of, or connecting with an ocean or a larger sea ⟨the Mediterranean ~⟩ **d :** OCEAN — compare HIGH SEA **e :** an inland body of water esp. if large or if salt or brackish ⟨the Caspian ~⟩ ⟨the *Sea* of Aral⟩; *sometimes* **:** a small freshwater lake ⟨the *Sea* of Galilee⟩ **2 a :** surface motion on a large body of water or its direction ⟨the ~ sits southward⟩; *also* **:** rough water **:** a heavy swell or wave ⟨a ~ struck us⟩ ⟨heavy ~s nearly swamped the boat⟩ **b :** the disturbance of the ocean or other body of water due to the wind blowing at the time and place of observation ⟨mild breezes and little ~⟩ **3 :** something (as a vast expanse, an overwhelming flood, or an agitated surface) felt to resemble a sea ⟨saw only an endless ~ of sandy plain⟩ ⟨a ~ of folly⟩ ⟨lost in the ~s of time⟩ **4 :** the expanse of the high seas as a field of life, business, or naval operations **:** voyaging as a livelihood ⟨follow the ~⟩ ⟨retired from the ~⟩ **5 :** SEASHORE, SEASIDE ⟨spent the summer at the ~⟩ **6 :** SEAWATER **7 :** ³MARE — **at sea 1 :** on the sea; *specif* **:** on a sea voyage including for legal purposes the time from the beginning of the voyage till the arrival of the ship at its port of destination or until the intention of proceeding on the voyage is abandoned **2 :** without landmarks for guidance **:** LOST, BEWILDERED — often used with *all* ⟨we were all *at sea* and didn't know what to do next⟩ ⟨*at sea* as to where to turn for help⟩ — **beyond seas** *or* **beyond sea** *or* **beyond the sea** *or* **beyond the seas 1 :** on the farther side of or over the sea **2 :** out of the territory, realm, or jurisdiction of a state — **to sea** *adv* **:** to or upon the open waters of the sea ⟨put *to sea* for a six months cruise⟩

²sea \"\ *adj* **1 :** of, relating to, or characteristic of the sea or a sea ⟨~ arm⟩ ⟨~ smells⟩ **2 :** of or relating to a ship, ship personnel, equipment or related matters **:** of or used by seamen or passengers on a ship ⟨~ discipline⟩ **3 a :** occurring on, upon, or over the waters of the sea or a sea ⟨~ traffic⟩ ⟨~ routes⟩ **b :** of or relating to navigation, shipping, or similar matters ⟨~ charts⟩ ⟨~ terms⟩ **c :** fit for use on the high seas **:** SEAGOING ⟨a ~ yacht⟩ **4 :** of or relating to the navy **:** NAVAL ⟨a ~ engagement⟩ ⟨~ bases⟩ **5 :** having the sea or part of the sea for field, territory, subject, object (as of activity, interest, concern) ⟨~ robber⟩ ⟨a ~ painter⟩ ⟨~ poem⟩ ⟨~ stories⟩ ⟨~ dominion⟩ **6 :** inhabiting the sea or seashore ⟨~ nymphs⟩ ⟨~ dwellers⟩ **7 :** deposited by the sea ⟨~ gravel⟩ **8 :** of, occurring on, or belonging to the seacoast or seashore ⟨~ forts⟩ ⟨~ dunes⟩ **9 :** coming from or showing over the sea or occurring at sea ⟨~ clouds⟩ ⟨the deep ~ roar⟩ **10 :** made, formed, or shaped by the sea or the action of the sea ⟨a ~ frontier⟩ ⟨~ cobbles⟩

sea *abbr* seaman

sea acorn *n* **:** ACORN BARNACLE

sea adder *n* **1 :** a European 15-spined stickleback (*Spinachia spinachia*) **2 :** any of several European pipefishes of the genus *Nerophis*

sea air *n* **:** air (as over the sea and neighboring regions) markedly affected by the evaporation of salt water

sea-air \'=¦=\ *adj* [¹*sea* + *air*] **1 :** concerned with both sea and air ⟨a *sea-air* naval operation⟩ **2 :** occurring between or at the interface of sea and air ⟨a *sea-air* temperature differential⟩

sea anchor *n* **:** a drag typically in the form of an open canvas cone that is thrown overboard to retard the drifting of a ship and to keep its head to the wind **:** DROGUE; *also* **:** a similar device to restrain a seaplane resting on the water

sea anemone *n* **:** any of numerous almost invariably solitary and often large and brilliantly colored polyps of the order Actiniaria that in form, bright and varied colors, and cluster of tentacles surrounding the mouth superficially resemble a flower, that develop no skeleton, that reproduce sexually or rarely by budding or fission, and that prey on small animals which they catch with tentacles armed with stinging cells

sea arrow *n* **:** a squid of the genus *Ommastrephes* or family Ommastrephidae **:** FLYING SQUID

sea arrow grass *n* **:** an arrow grass (*Triglochin maritima*)

sea ash *n* **:** PRICKLY ASH 1

sea aster *n* **:** SEA STARWORT

seabag \'=,=\ *n* **:** a cylindrical canvas bag used esp. by a sailor for clothes and other gear

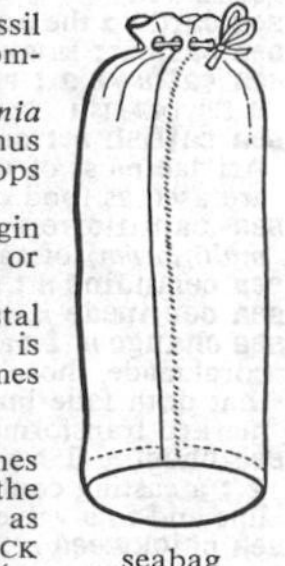

seabag

sea ball *n* **:** a spherical mass of living or fossil vegetation (as algae) produced by the compacting effect of moving shallow waters

sea bamboo *n* **:** a brown alga (*Ecklonia maxima*) that resembles those of the genus *Laminaria* when young but later develops lateral pinnae

sea bank *n* [ME *see bank*] **1 a :** the margin of the sea **:** SEASHORE **b :** a sandbank or dune adjacent to the sea **2 :** SEAWALL

sea barley *n* **:** a European annual coastal squirrel grass (*Hordeum marinum*) that is highly tolerant of saline soil and is sometimes used for pasture

sea basket *n* **:** BASKET STAR

sea bass *n* **1 :** any of numerous marine fishes of the family Serranidae including usu. the smaller more active members of the family as distinguished from the groupers; *esp* **:** BLACK SEA BASS **1 2 :** any of numerous croakers (as the weakfish or the channel bass) — often used with a qualifying term

sea bat *n* **1 :** BATFISH **a 2 :** DEVILFISH 1

seabeach \'=,=\ *n* **:** a beach lying along the sea

seabeach morning-glory *n* **:** GOATSFOOT CONVOLVULUS

seabeach sandwort *n* **:** a perennial succulent herb (*Arenaria peploides*) having decussate leaves and small solitary axillary or terminal flowers

sea bean *n* **1 a :** any of various beans or showy seeds of tropical origin that are frequently carried by ocean currents to remote shores and often used as ornaments: as (1) **:** the large chocolate-colored seed of a snuffbox bean used in poultices and as an emetic (2) **:** OXEYE BEAN (3) **:** NICKER NUT **b :** a plant producing sea beans **2 :** the hard flat rounded calcareous operculum of any of various mollusks (as those of the family Turbinidae)

sea bear *n* **1 :** FUR SEAL **2 :** POLAR BEAR

seabeard \'=,=\ *n* **:** a marine green alga (*Cladophora rupestris*) that grows in dense tufts

sea-beaten \'=,==\ *also* **sea-beat** \'=,=\ *adj* **:** battered or lashed by the sea; *also* **:** worn by life at sea

sea beaver *n* **:** SEA OTTER

seabed \'=,=\ *n* **:** the floor of a sea or ocean **:** land underlying the sea

sea·bee \'sē,bē\ *n* -s *usu cap* [alter. of *cee* + *bee* (letter); fr. the initials of *construction battalion*] **:** a member of one of the construction battalions organized as a volunteer branch of the Civil Engineer Corps of the U.S. Navy for building aviation facilities and naval installations and defending them

sea beef *n* **1 :** beef corned for use at sea **2 :** the flesh of a porpoise or whale used as food **3** *chiefly West Indies* **:** a chiton used as food

sea beet *n* **1 :** a wild Old World beet (*Beta maritima* or *B. vulgaris maritima*) lacking a conspicuously swollen root that is prob. the ancestor of the common garden beets **2 :** SEA LAVENDER

sea bells *n pl but sing or pl in constr* **:** a coastal bindweed (*Convolvulus soldanella*) having pink campanulate flowers

sea belt *n* **:** SEA GIRDLE

sea bent *n* **1 :** BEACH GRASS **2 :** SAND SEDGE

sea-berry \'sē- — *see* BERRY\ *n* **1 :** REDBERRY **1 2 :** either of two Australasian plants of the genus *Haloragis* (*H. alata* and *H. tetragyna*)

sea bindweed *n* **:** SEA BELLS

seabird \'=,=\ *n* **:** any of various birds (as gulls, petrels, shearwaters, albatrosses) frequenting the open ocean

sea biscuit *n* **1 :** hard biscuit or loaf bread prepared for use on shipboard **:** HARDTACK **2 :** HEART URCHIN

sea bladder *n* **:** PORTUGUESE MAN-OF-WAR

sea blite *n* **:** any of various halophile herbs or shrubs of the genus *Suaeda* with fleshy alternate more or less terete leaves; *esp* **:** a plant (*Suaeda maritima*) that grows in salt marshes and has pale green leaves sometimes used as a potherb

sea bloom *or* **sea blossom** *n* **:** a free-floating marine blue-green alga (*Trichodesmium erythraeum*) that has a red pigment in addition to the phycocyanin and sometimes occurs so abundantly in the warmer seas as to color the water red — compare WATER BLOOM

sea blubber *n* **:** JELLYFISH

sea blue *n* **:** a moderate bluish green that is bluer and deeper than porcelain green and greener and deeper than Bremen blue

¹seaboard \'=,=\ *n* [ME *seebord*, fr. *see* sea + *bord* board — more at SEA, BOARD] **1** *obs* **:** the side of a ship toward the sea — used with *a*, *at*, *on*, *or* to **2 :** SEACOAST; *also* **:** the country bordering a seacoast

²seaboard \"\ *adj* **:** bordering on or being near the sea

sea boat *n* **1 :** a boat adapted to the open sea: as **a :** a ship having the power, size, and equipment for maintaining itself on the high seas ⟨these lighter craft cannot be considered *sea boats*⟩ **:** a ship that handles well in heavy seas ⟨the best *sea*

boat we ever owned⟩ **b :** a ship's boat adapted for use at sea **2 :** CHITON 2
sea bob *n* [by folk etymology fr. AmerF *six barbes*, lit., six beards; fr. the appearance of the first long pair of legs together with the antennae and antennules] **:** a small shrimp (*Xiphopenaeus kroyeri*) that has the first pair of legs much elongated and is usu. used dried
sea book *n, archaic* **:** a nautical map
seaboot \'⸗,⸗\ *n* **:** a very high waterproof boot used esp. by sailors and fishermen
sea-born \'⸗,⸗\ *adj* **1 :** born of or in the sea ⟨*sea-born* nymphs⟩ **2 :** originating in or rising from the sea ⟨a *sea-born* isle⟩ ⟨*sea-born* rocks⟩
seaborne \'⸗,⸗\ *adj* **1 :** borne over or upon the sea **:** transported by ship ⟨~ supplies⟩ ⟨a ~ invasion⟩ **2 :** engaged in or carried on by overseas shipping ⟨~ trade⟩
sea bottle *n* **1 :** a marine green alga (*Valonia ventricosa*), whose thallus is a single inflated cell **2 a :** an alga of the genus *Fucus* — usu. used in pl. **b :** one of the swollen vesicles on the thallus of such an alga
seabound \'⸗,⸗\ *adj* **1 :** bounded by the sea **2 :** bound for the sea
sea boy *n* **1 :** SHIP BOY **2 :** a very young sailor
sea brant *n* **1 :** a common brant (*Branta bernicla*) of Europe and eastern No. America **2 :** WHITE-WINGED SCOTER
sea breach *n* **1 a :** a breaking or overflow (as of a bank or dike) by the sea **b** *obs* **:** SEABEACH **2 :** a destructive breaker or series of breakers
sea bread *n* **1 :** HARDTACK **2 :** CRUMB-OF-BREAD SPONGE
sea bream *n* **:** any of numerous marine percoid fishes: as **a :** a fish of the family Sparidae **b :** POMFRET 1; *broadly* **:** a fish of the family Bramidae **c :** any of several grunts (as the pinfish or the pompon)
sea breeze *n* **:** a cooling breeze blowing inland from the sea generally in the daytime
sea brief *n* **:** SEA LETTER
sea buckthorn *n* **:** a Eurasian maritime shrub (*Hippophaë rhamnoides*) of the family Eleagnaceae having silvery leaves and orange-red edible berries and yielding a yellow dye
sea-bull \'⸗,⸗\ *n* [ME *see-bule*, fr. *see* sea + *bule* bull — more at SEA, BULL] **:** a male sea cow
sea bun *n* **:** HEART URCHIN
sea buoy *n* **:** the first buoy at the channel entrance to a harbor from the sea
sea burdock *n* **:** a halophile cocklebur (*Xanthium echinatum*) native to coastal areas of eastern No. America but widely distributed by commerce
sea bush *or* **sea club** *n* **:** GORGONIAN
sea butterfly *n* **:** PTEROPOD
sea cabbage *n* **1 :** SEA KALE **2 :** a European maritime plant (*Brassica oleracea*) from which the cabbage, cauliflower and broccoli have been derived in cultivation
sea cabin *n* **:** an emergency cabin near a ship's bridge for the use of captain and officers
sea calf *n* [ME *see calf*, fr. *see* sea + *calf*] **:** HARBOR SEAL
sea campion *n* **:** a European maritime perennial herb (*Silene maritima*) with bluish gray foliage and showy trusses of usu. white single or double flowers
sea captain *n* **:** the master of a merchant vessel whether active or retired
sea card *n* **:** the card of a mariner's compass
sea carp *n* **:** MORWONG
sea cat *n* **1 a :** FUR SEAL **b :** HARBOR SEAL **2 a :** WEEVER a **b :** WOLFFISH **c :** SEA CATFISH **3** *chiefly Africa* **:** OCTOPUS
sea catfish *n* **:** any of numerous marine fishes of the family Ariidae most of which are mouthbreeders and few of which are used as food
sea cauliflower *n* **:** a multilobed alcyonarian (*Alcyonium multiflorum*) of the No. Atlantic fishing banks
sea celandine *n* **:** HORNED POPPY
sea centipede *n, Austral* **:** any of several marine isopods
sea change *n* **1 :** a change wrought by the sea ⟨of his bones are coral made, those are pearls that were his eyes; nothing of him that doth fade but doth suffer a *sea change* —Shak.⟩ **2 :** a marked transformation (as to something richer or finer)
sea chest *n* **1 :** a sailor's storage chest for personal property **2 :** a casting connected to the side of a ship below the water line and to a valve for obtaining seawater (as for condensers)
sea chickweed *n* **:** SEABEACH SANDWORT
sea clam *n* **:** SURF CLAM
sea cloth *n* **:** a painted cloth representing waves for use on a theatrical stage
sea club rush *n* **:** a common No. American bulrush (*Scirpus robustus*); *also* **:** a closely related Old World bulrush (*S. lacustris*)
sea coal *n* [ME *seecole*, fr. *see* sea + *cole* coal — more at SEA, COAL] **1** *archaic* **:** mineral coal **2 :** pulverized bituminous coal used as a foundry facing
seacoast \'⸗,⸗\ *n* [ME *seecost*, fr. *see* sea + *cost* coast — more at COAST] **:** the shore or border of the land adjacent to the sea
seacoast angelica *n* **:** a stout perennial herb (*Coelopleurum lucidum*) of the family Umbelliferae common in northeastern coastal No. America and having compound leaves on inflated stalks, compound umbels of greenish flowers, and prominently ribbed fruits
seacoast bluestem *n* **:** a bluestem (*Andropogon littoralis*) of beaches and dunes of eastern No. America that is very similar to and often considered a variety of the little bluestem and that is locally valued as a palatable forage grass and as an arrester of wind erosion of sandy soil
seacoast laburnum *n, Austral* **:** LABURNUM 2
sea cock *n* **1 :** a cock or valve close to a ship's hull for opening or closing a pipe which communicates with the sea **2 :** BLACK-BELLIED PLOVER
sea coconut *n* **1** *also* **sea coco a :** a lofty fan palm (*Lodoicea seychellarum*) of the Seychelle islands having leaves that are used for thatching **b :** the fruit of the sea coconut which often weighs 50 pounds and in which are 3 or 4 bilobed nuts with a smooth rind — called also *double coconut* **2 :** the fruit of the bussu
sea cole *n* **:** SEA KALE
sea compass *n* **:** MARINER'S COMPASS
sea coot *n* **1 :** SCOTER **2 :** GUILLEMOT
sea corn *n* **:** the yellow mass of egg capsules produced by some marine snails (as whelks)
sea cow *n* **1 :** SIRENIAN, MANATEE, DUGONG; *esp* **:** STELLER'S SEA COW **2 :** WALRUS 1 **3 :** HIPPOPOTAMUS
sea cradle *n* **:** CHITON 2
seacraft \'⸗,⸗\ *n* **1 :** seagoing ships **2 :** skill in navigation
seacrafty \'⸗,⸗⸗\ *adj* **:** skilled in matters relating to the sea
sea crawfish *or* **sea crayfish** *n* **:** SPINY LOBSTER
sea cress *n* **:** GLASSWORT 1
seacross *n* **:** JELLYFISH; *esp* **:** a jellyfish in which four radial canals appear in the form of a cross
sea crow *n* **1 :** a chough (*Pyrrhocorax pyrrhocorax*) **2 :** CORMORANT **3 :** BLACK-HEADED GULL **4 :** a skua (*Catharacta skua*) **5** *Brit* **:** RAZORBILL **6 :** a coot (*Fulica americana*) **7 :** BLACK SKIMMER **8 :** OYSTER CATCHER
sea cucumber *n* **:** HOLOTHURIAN; *esp* **:** any holothurian whose contracted body suggests a cucumber in form
sea cudweed *n* **:** a hoary European cottonweed (*Diotis maritima*) of the family Compositae
seaculture \'⸗,⸗⸗\ *n* **:** the cultivation of marine life forms (as plankton or fishes) for food
sea·cun·ny \'sē,kənē\ *n* -ES [by folk etymology fr. Per *sukkānī*, fr. *sukkān* rudder, helm, fr. Ar] *India* **:** STEERSMAN, QUARTERMASTER
sea cushion *or* **sea daisy** *n* **:** a thrift (*Armeria maritima*)
sea-cut \'⸗,⸗\ *adj* **:** formed by the erosive action of sea waves **:** WAVE-CUT ⟨a *sea-cut* terrace⟩
sea-daddy \'⸗,⸗⸗\ *n, Brit* **:** a skilled seaman who is detailed to instruct young or green hands
sea daffodil *n* **1 :** a white-flowered bulbous herb (*Pancratium maritimum*) common along the Mediterranean **2 :** a bulbous herb (*Hymenocallis calathina*) of Peru and Bolivia that resembles the Mediterranean sea daffodil
sea dahlia *n* **:** a plant of the genus *Coreopsis* of the Pacific coast of the U.S. with flowers resembling yellow dahlias
sea date *n* **:** any of various bivalves of the genus *Lithophaga* somewhat resembling dates in shape **:** DATE MUSSEL
sea day *n* **:** a period of 24 mean solar hours beginning at local mean noon
sea dayak *or* **sea dyak** *n, usu cap S&D* **:** IBAN 1
sea devil *n* **1 :** DEVILFISH 1 **2 :** MONKFISH 1 **3 :** BLACK SEA DEVIL **4 :** STONEFISH
sea dock *n* **:** a bear's-breech (*Acanthus mollis*)
sea dog *n* **1 a** (1) **:** HARBOR SEAL (2) **:** CAPE SEAL (3) **:** a small sea lion (*Zalophus californianus*) of the California coast **b :** a heraldic representation of a seal with a beaver tail, long back fin, webbed feet, and scaly legs and body **2 :** DOGFISH **3 a :** an experienced sailor **:** one long at sea **b :** PRIVATEER, PIRATE
seadog \'⸗,⸗\ *n* **:** FOGBOW
sea dotterel *n* **1** *dial Eng* **:** TURNSTONE **2** *dial Eng* **:** the common European ring plover (*Charadrius hiaticula*)
sea dove *n* **1 :** DOVEKIE 2 **2 :** BLACK GUILLEMOT
sea dragon *n* **1 :** DRAGONET **2 :** SEA MOTH **3 :** any of several beautifully colored Australian fishes (family Syngnathidae) intermediate between the pipefishes and the sea horses and having many large leaflike appendages on the plates of the body that simulate the seaweed among which they live
sea drake *n* **1 :** CORMORANT **2 :** a male eider
sea·drome \'sē,drōm\ *n* ['sea + -drome] **:** a floating airdrome serving as an intermediate or emergency landing place for airplanes
sea drum *n* **:** BLACK DRUM
sea duck *n* **:** any of various ducks (as the scoters, mergansers, and eiders) that frequent the sea; *esp* **:** EIDER
sea dust *n* **1 :** fine and usu. reddish dust blown to sea by winds from arid lands and when caught in falling raindrops giving rise to blood rain **2** *slang* **:** SALT
sea duty *n* **:** duty in the U. S. Navy performed outside the continental U. S. or specified dependencies thereof
sea eagle *n* **1 a :** any of various eagles that are related to the bald eagle and feed largely on fish — see KAMCHATKAN SEA EAGLE, WHITE-TAILED SEA EAGLE **b :** FISHING EAGLE **b c :** OSPREY **2 :** EAGLE RAY
sea-ear \'⸗,⸗\ *n* **:** ABALONE
sea eel *n* **:** a marine eel (as the conger eel); *also* **:** SEA LAMPREY
sea egg *n* **:** SEA URCHIN; *specif* **:** the bare test of a sea urchin from which the spines have fallen
sea elephant *n* **:** ELEPHANT SEAL
sea explorer *n* **:** a youth at least 14 years old who is enrolled in the sea exploring program of the Boy Scouts of America
sea fan *n* **:** a gorgonian that branches in a fanlike form; *esp* **:** a gorgonian (*Gorgonia flabellum*) of Florida and the West Indies
seafarer \'⸗,⸗⸗\ *n* -s **:** one occupied in or given to seafaring; *specif* **:** MARINER
[1]seafaring \'⸗,⸗⸗\ *adj* ['sea + *faring*, pres. part. of *fare*] **:** of, given to, or engaged in seafaring ⟨~ days⟩ **:** occurring in the course of or concerned with seafaring ⟨a ~ adventure⟩ ⟨~ yarns⟩
[2]seafaring \"\ *n* -s ['sea + *faring*, gerund of *fare*] **:** traveling over the sea as a pursuit or recreation; *esp* **:** the mariner's calling
sea feather *n* **:** a gorgonian that branches in a plumelike form; *esp* **:** SEA PEN
sea fennel *n* **:** SAMPHIRE 1
sea fern *n* **1 :** a gorgonian that branches like a fern **2 :** finely branched and often brightly dyed material resembling a growth of algae, used as an aquarium ornament, and prob. the remains of a marine colonial bryozoan
sea fig *n* **:** BEACH APPLE
sea fight *n* **:** an engagement between ships at sea
sea fir *n* **:** a sertularian hydroid; *esp* **:** a hydroid (*Abietinaria abietina*) common on the British coast that branches like a miniature fir
sea fire *n* **:** marine bioluminescence
sea fisherman *also* **sea fisher** *n* **:** one who fishes esp. as an occupation out in the open sea
sea flea *n* **:** BEACH FLEA
seaflower \'⸗,⸗⸗\ *n* **:** a sea anemone or similar actinozoan
sea-foam \'⸗,⸗\ *n* [ME *seefome*, fr. *see* sea + *fome, fom* foam — more at SEA, FOAM] **1 :** froth on the sea **2** [trans. of G *meerschaum*] **:** MEERSCHAUM 1
seafoam \"\ *n* [*sea-foam*] **:** a brilliant to light green that is very slightly lighter than chrysoprase
seafoam green *n* **:** a pale yellow green that is yellower, lighter, and stronger than smoke gray, yellower and slightly lighter and stronger than oyster gray, and yellower and paler than average Nile
seafoam yellow *n* **:** a pale yellow green that is yellower, lighter, and stronger than smoke gray, yellower, lighter, and slightly stronger than oyster gray, and yellower and paler than average Nile
sea fog *n* **:** a fog drifted onshore or condensed from relatively warm onshore winds
seafolk \'⸗,⸗\ *n* **:** seafaring people **:** MARINERS
seafood \'⸗,⸗\ *n* **:** marine fish and shellfish used as food or of kinds suitable for food
sea·for·thia \sē'fōrthēə\ [NL, fr. Francis Mackenzie Humbertson, Lord *Seaforth* †1815 Eng. nobleman + NL *-ia*] *syn of* PTYCHOSPERMA
seafowl \'⸗,⸗\ *n* **:** a bird (as an auk, gannet, gull, tern, or petrel) that frequents the sea
sea fox *n* **1 :** THRESHER SHARK **2 :** a lanky long-muzzled long-eared more or less rufous jackal (*Canis variegatus*) of the northeastern African seacoast
sea fret *n* [[2]fret] **:** SEA FOG
seafront \'⸗,⸗\ *n* **:** the waterfront of a seaside place; *also* **:** a built-up zone (as of buildings and promenades) along such a front
sea frontage *n* **:** frontage on the sea **:** an extent of seafront
sea frontier *n* **:** a large nonadministrative sea and land area command (as in the U. S. Navy) organized under a district commandant
sea froth *n* **:** SEA-FOAM
sea furbelow *n* **:** a sea tangle (*Laminaria bulbosa*)
sea garfish *n* **:** an Australian pelagic halfbeak (*Hyporhamphus intermedius*)
sea gasket *n* **:** a fixed furling line such as is used at sea
sea-gate \'⸗,⸗\ *n* [[3]gate] **:** a long rolling swell of the sea
sea gate ['gate] *n* **1 :** a way (as a gate, beach, or channel) that gives access to the sea **2 :** a gate that serves as a protection against seas
sea gherkin *n* **:** a small sea cucumber of *Cucumaria* or related genera
sea ginger *n* **:** a hydrocoral (*Millepora alcicornis*) with branching fingerlike processes that much resembles dried gingerroot
sea girdle *n* **1** *or* **sea hanger :** VENUS'S-GIRDLE **2 :** any of various kelps of the genus *Laminaria* (esp. *L. digitata*) with palmately cleft fronds
seagirt \'⸗,⸗\ *adj* **:** surrounded or enclosed by the sea
sea-god \'⸗,⸗\ *n* **:** a deity (as Neptune) held to live in or rule the sea or a part of the sea ⟨the *sea-gods* ride upon the sounding waves —William Hazlitt⟩
seagoer \'⸗,⸗(⸗)\ *n* **:** one that travels by sea **:** SEAFARER
[1]seagoing \'⸗,⸗⸗\ *n* **:** travel by sea **:** SEAFARING
[2]seagoing \"\ *adj* **1 a :** designed or adapted for sailing the open sea in distinction from rivers or harbors ⟨a ~ tug⟩ **b :** fitted to be used on a seagoing vessel ⟨a ~ chronometer⟩ **2 a :** SEAFARING **b :** CATADROMOUS
sea goose *n* **1 :** PHALAROPE **2 :** DOLPHIN
sea gooseberry *n* **:** a ctenophore of *Pleurobrachia* or a related genus **:** a typical ctenophore
sea gown *n, obs* **:** a garment for use at sea ⟨my *sea gown* scarf'd about me —Shak.⟩
sea grape *n* **1 a :** GULFWEED **b :** a tree or shrub of the genus *Coccoloba*; *esp* **:** a variable plant (*C. uvifera*) of sandy shores of Florida and tropical America having rounded leaves with cordate bases and bearing clusters of bluish edible berries **c :** a leafless shrub (*Ephedra distachya*) of southeastern Europe **d :** GLASSWORT **2 sea grapes** *pl* **:** the clusters of gelatinous egg capsules of squids (as those of the genus *Loligo*)
sea grass *n* **1 a :** a tassel grass (*Ruppia maritima*) **b :** a plant of the genus *Salicornia* (esp. *S. europaea*) **c :** THRIFT 6 **d** *or* **sea hay :** EELGRASS 1; *also* **:** its dried stems widely used for stuffing furniture and in making coarse fabrics **2 :** any of several seaweeds; *esp* **:** a green alga (genus *Enteromorpha*) that often causes fouling of the bottoms of ships **3 :** a cirrus cloud of wavy hairlike elements
sea green *n* **1 a :** a moderate green that is bluer and paler than myrtle (sense 3a) and bluer, lighter, and stronger than laurel green (sense 1) — called also *spruce green* **b :** a moderate yellow green that is greener, lighter, and stronger than average moss green, lighter, stronger, and very slightly yellower than average pea green, and stronger than apple green (sense 1) — called also *sea-water green* **c :** SEA BLUE **2 :** land overflowed by the sea in spring tides
sea-green \'⸗,⸗\ *adj* **1 :** green like seawater esp. in waters fathomable with a hand sounding line **2 :** of the color sea green
sea-green incorruptible *n* **:** one utterly, disinterestedly, and rigidly devoted to some ideal or objective esp. in the world of political thought or action
sea gudgeon *n* **:** any of various marine gobies
sea gull *n* **1 :** a gull frequenting the sea; *broadly* **:** GULL **2** *slang* **:** a waterfront prostitute or one chiefly catering to sailors
sea gypsy *n* **:** BAJAU
sea-hair coralline *n* **:** a delicate sertularian hydroid (*Sertularia operculata*)
sea hare *n* **:** any of various large naked mollusks constituting the genus *Tethys*, having arched backs and anterior tentacles that project like ears, and being reputed to attain a length of nearly 2 feet and a weight of over 15 pounds
sea hawk *n* **:** JAEGER, SKUA
sea heath *n* **:** a plant of the genus *Frankenia*
sea-heath family *n* **:** FRANKENIACEAE
sea hedgehog *n* **1 :** SEA URCHIN **2 :** GLOBEFISH
sea hen *n* **1 :** any of several sea birds: as **a :** SKUA **b** *Brit* **:** a common guillemot (*Uria aalge*) **2 :** a lumpsucker (*Cyclopterus lumpus*)
sea hog *n* **:** PORPOISE
sea holly *n* **1 :** a European evergreen herb (*Eryngium maritimum*) formerly used as an aphrodisiac **2 :** a bear's-breech (*Acanthus mollis*)
sea hollyhock *n* **:** a rose mallow (*Hibiscus moscheutos*)
sea horse *n* [ME *sehors*, fr. *se*, *see* sea + *hors* horse — more at SEA, HORSE] **1 a :** WALRUS 1 **b** *obs* **:** HIPPOPOTAMUS **2 :** a fabulous creature half horse and half fish; *also* **:** a heraldic representation of a monster with the forepart of a horse joined to the tail of a fish and with webbed feet **3 a :** any of numerous small fishes (family Syngnathidae) mostly of the genus *Hippocampus* that are related to the pipefishes but of stockier build, have the head and forepart of the body sharply flexed and suggestive of the head and neck of a horse, are covered with rough bony plates and equipped with a prehensile tail and in the male a short broad pouch immediately behind the vent in which the eggs hatch, and occur in most warm and warm-temperate seas **b :** HORSEFISH 1d **4 :** a large whitecap on a wave **5 :** a short-handled clam rake with long prongs

sea horse 3a

seahound \'⸗,⸗\ *n* [ME *seehound*, fr. *see* sea + *hound*] **:** DOGFISH
sea ice *n* **:** ice formed by the freezing of seawater **:** masses of floating ice that have drifted to sea
sea island cotton *also* **sea island** *n, often cap S&I* [fr. *Sea islands*, chain of islands in the Atlantic off the coast of So. Carolina, Georgia, and Florida] **:** a cotton (*Gossypium barbadense*) with unusually long and silky fiber grown esp. in the West Indies and along the coast region of the southeastern U.S. — called also *tree cotton*; see EGYPTIAN COTTON
sea island myrtle *n* **:** GROUNDSEL BUSH
sea jelly *n* **:** JELLYFISH
sea kale *n* **:** a European perennial herb (*Crambe maritima*) that has a fleshy branching rootstalk and is sometimes cultivated for its large ovate long-stalked leaves which are used as a potherb — called also *sea cole*
seakale beet \'⸗,⸗-\ *n* **:** a garden beet grown for its edible foliage and usu. lacking an enlarged root
seakeeping \'⸗,⸗⸗\ *adj* **:** remaining or capable of remaining at sea during severe storms ⟨a ~ ship⟩ ⟨the ~ qualities of a ship design⟩
sea kemp *n* **:** SEA PLANTAIN — usu. used in pl.
sea kidney *n* **:** SEA PANSY
sea-kindliness \'⸗,⸗⸗⸗\ *n* **:** the quality or state of being sea-kindly
sea-kindly \'⸗,⸗⸗\ *adj* **:** well adapted to handling at sea ⟨a *sea-kindly* ship⟩
sea king *n* **1** [trans. of ON *sækonungr*] **:** a Norse pirate chief — compare VIKING **2 :** a prehistoric king in Crete
sea kit·tie \-'kitī\ *n* [*kittie*, short for *kittiwake*] *Brit* **:** KITTIWAKE
[1]seal \'sēl, *esp before pause or consonant* -ēəl\ *n, pl* **seals** *also* **seal** *often attrib* [ME *selch, sele*, fr. OE *sēol-, seolh*; akin to MLG *sel* seal, OHG *selah*, ON *selr* seal, and perh. to OE *sulh* furrow — more at SULCUS] **1 :** any of numerous marine aquatic carnivorous mammals that constitute the families Phocidae and Otariidae, live chiefly near cool seacoasts or on ice floes but crawl ashore to bear young and to breed, feed on fish and other marine animals, have the limbs modified into webbed flippers adapted primarily to swimming, and have been extensively hunted for fur, hides, and oil **:** any pinniped other than a walrus — see EARED SEAL, EARLESS SEAL, ELEPHANT SEAL, FUR SEAL, HAIR SEAL, SEA LION **2 a :** the pelt of a fur seal usu. plucked and dyed for use in garments and often imitated by shearing and dyeing rabbit or muskrat ⟨a ~ coat⟩ **b :** leather made from the skin of a seal — see PIN SEAL **3** *or* **seal brown :** a dark grayish yellowish brown that is less strong and slightly redder than sepia brown and slightly redder and paler than otter
[2]seal \"\ *vi* -ED/-ING/-s **:** to hunt seals
[3]seal \"\ *n* -s [ME *seel*, fr. OF, fr. L *sigillum* small figure, small image, seal, dim. of *signum* sign, mark, figure, image — more at SIGN] **1 a :** something that confirms, ratifies, or makes secure **:** GUARANTEE, ASSURANCE **b** (1) **:** a device (as an emblem, symbol, or word) used to identify or replace the signature of an individual or organization and to authenticate (as under common law) written matter purportedly emanating from such individual or organization (2) **:** a surface (as of a medallion or the face of a ring) bearing such a device incised so as to be reproducible in plastic material (as wax or moist clay); *also* **:** an object (as a ring) bearing such a seal (3) **:** an impression of such a device (as on or attached to a document) in plastic material; *also* **:** a piece of wax, a wafer, or other substance bearing such an impression **c :** an impression, device, sign, or mark given the effect of a common-law seal by statute law or by American local custom recognized by judicial decision ⟨the word "seal" or the letters "L.S." written or printed, or a scroll made with the pen may constitute a ~ within the meaning of the law⟩ **d :** an adhesive stamp bearing a symbolic or pictorial design suggestive of a particular cause and usu. distributed as an appeal for or acknowledgment of a contribution to that cause **2 :** something that firmly closes or secures: as **a :** a piece of material (as sealing wax) placed in such a manner (as on an envelope or a folded document) as to prevent opening without breaking it; *also* **:** any of various closures or fastenings (as on a door, container, or railway car) that cannot be opened without rupture and that serve as a check against tampering or unauthorized opening **b :** something (as a vow) that obliges one to maintain silence **c** (1) **:** a tight and perfect closure (as against the passage of gas or water) ⟨turn the jars upside down to be sure the ~ is tight⟩ ⟨the flashing must make a ~ with the roofing⟩ (2) **:** a device to prevent the passage or return of gas or air into a pipe or container (as by submerging the open end of a pipe in a liquid, by keeping filled with liquid a deep bend in a pipe, or by projecting a partition or gland into a liquid-filled space) ⟨a water ~⟩ ⟨a gland ~⟩ (3) **:** a tight joint formed by the lap or bearing of a valve or similar member beyond the opening or space which the valve closes (4) **:** a cemented stone cover of an altar sepulcher **d :** a sealing coat applied in the finishing of wood **3** *chiefly Brit* **:** an officia seal (as of a chancellor or secretary of state) esp. as a symbo

of official status : an indication or mark of office — usu. used in pl. and with *the* ⟨his majesty ordered the immediate surrender of the ~*s*⟩ **4** *obs* : a ceremony of affixing the great seal to documents **5 a** : something that gives a character to a person such that he may be recognized as belonging to an indicated agent ⟨the Holy Spirit: the ~ of God⟩ **b** : an indication of status and esp. of approved, superior, or desirable status ⟨gave the party the ~ of her approval⟩ — **under seal** *adv* : with an authenticating seal affixed; *esp* : with both signature and seal

⁴seal \ˈ"\ *vb* -ED/-ING/-S [ME *selen*, fr. OF *seeler*, fr. *seel*, n.] *vt* **1** : to confirm or make secure by or as if by a seal : confirm in a particular association — often used in allusion to Rev 7:2–8 (RSV) ⟨God ~*s* His own⟩: as **a** : to give a character to (a person) such that he may be recognized as belonging to an agent — used esp. of God in relation to the faithful **b** : to solemnize for eternity (as a marriage or an adoption of a child) — used by Mormons **2 a** : to set or affix an authenticating seal to; *also* : to formally authenticate : RATIFY **b** : to mark with a stamp usu. as an evidence of standard exactness, legal size, weight, or capacity, or merchantable quality **c** : to give under or as if under seal : grant authentically ⟨now must your conscience my acquittance ~ —Shak.⟩ **d** : to give authenticity to : serve as the seal of ⟨their pleasure ~*s* our satisfaction⟩ **3 a** : to fasten with or as if with a seal to prevent tampering ⟨~ a letter⟩ ⟨the coroner ~*ed* the premises⟩ **b** : to keep shut, enclosed, or confined ⟨lips ~*ed* by a promise⟩ ⟨ice may ~ in the boats as early as September⟩ **c** : to close or fasten by a coating or other fastening that prevents access or leakage ⟨~*ed* the patch in place with strong pitch⟩ ⟨~ each jampot with hot wax⟩; *often* : to make gas or fluid tight by a process of sealing ⟨~*ed* the leak with a blowout patch⟩ ⟨the jars must be perfectly ~*ed* if the food is to keep⟩ **d** : to make fast (as a piece of iron in a wall or a wire in a bulb) with cement, plaster, fusible glass, or other filling : close up chinks, crevices, or breaks in with or as if with plaster ⟨~ a leaky wall⟩; *also* : to close the pores of (a wooden or other porous surface) with a sealer **e** : to complete the movement of (as an electric contactor, switch, or relay) after the contacting parts touch each other **4 a** : to mark or fasten when applied — used esp. of a seal ⟨the new seal ~*ed* it cleanly and without blurring⟩ **b** : to fix firmly or steadily as if fastened **5** : to determine irrevocably or indisputably ⟨this answer ~*ed* our fate⟩ ~ *vi* **1 a** : to affix one's seal or a seal **b** *obs* : to give an assent by or as if by affixing a seal **2** : to perform the act of closing by sealing — **seal a move** : to file a sealed statement of a move to be made on resumption of an adjourned chess game

⁵seal \ˈ"\ *n* -S [ME *sele*, fr. (assumed) ME *selen* to tie up cattle (whence E dial. *seal*), fr. OE *sǣlan* to tie, bind, fr. *sāl* rope — more at SOLE] *chiefly Scot* : a rope or chain used to tie cattle

seal·able \-ləbəl\ *adj* : capable of sealing or being sealed

sea lace *n* : a seaweed (*Chorda filum*) having blackish fronds resembling cords — usu. used in pl. — called also *sea twine*

sea ladder *n* **1** : a rope ladder or set of steps to be lowered over a ship's side for use in coming aboard (as at sea) **2** : SEA STEPS, JACOB'S LADDER

sea lamprey *n* : an anadromous lamprey (*Petromyzon marinus*) of the Atlantic coasts of No. America and Europe that attains a length of about three feet, is sometimes used as food, at maturity ascends streams to breed and then dies, and has recently become a serious pest destructive of native fish fauna in the Great Lakes

sea-lane \ˈ⸗,⸗\ *n* : an established sea route : TRADE ROUTE

sea language *n* : sailors' cant

seal·ant \ˈsēlənt\ *n* -S [⁴*seal* + -*ant*] : a sealing agent ⟨radiator ~⟩

sea lark *n* **1** : ROCK PIPIT **2** *Brit* : any of several small shore birds (as a ringed plover, turnstone, red-backed sandpiper, or sanderling)

sea laurel *n* : a coarse American commercial sponge (*Euspongia dura*)

sea lavender *n* **1** : a plant of the genus *Limonium* **2** : SEA LUNGWORT **3** : a maritime shrub (*Mallotonia gnaphalodes*) of the family Boraginaceae found in subtropical and tropical coastal No. America and having fleshy hairy leaves and white flowers in scorpioid racemes or spikes

sea law *n* : MARITIME LAW; *specif* : any of various compilations of customary maritime laws made in medieval times

sea lawyer *n* **1 a** : GRAY SNAPPER **b** : SHARK **2** : an argumentative captious sailor; *broadly* : a person skilled in the use of red tape and minutiae esp. to avoid unwanted tasks or responsibilities

seal brown *n* [¹*seal*] : SEAL 3

sealch \ˈselk, -lk\ *n* [ME (Sc dial.) *selghe*, fr. OE *seolh* — more at SEAL] *chiefly Scot* : ¹SEAL 1

seal character *n* [³*seal*] : Chinese writing of an early type that is still employed on seals and inscriptions

seal coat *n* [³*seal*] : a final coat of bituminous material applied during construction to a bituminous macadam or concrete for sealing the surface of the pavement

seal cylinder *n* [³*seal*] : CYLINDER SEAL

sea league *n* : MARINE LEAGUE

sealed *adj* [fr. past part. of ⁴*seal*] **1** : unknown or unknowable like a sealed book ⟨a ~ language⟩ **2** : undisclosed at the start like sealed orders ⟨~ handicaps in a race⟩ ⟨a ~ bid⟩

sealed bank bill *n* : BANK BILL 1

sealed-beam \ˈ⸗;⸗\ *adj* : of, relating to, or being an electric light with prefocussed reflector and lens sealed in the lamp vacuum ⟨*sealed-beam* automobile headlights⟩

sealed book *n* : something as inaccessible to the understanding as a book that cannot be opened

sealed orders *n pl* : sealed written directions not to be opened until a specified time; *esp* : such directions given to the captain of a ship whose destination is not to be known until it is at sea

sealed verdict *n* : a written verdict sealed up by the jury prior to leaving their place of confinement and deliberation, delivered to a proper office of the court in the absence of the judge or of the defendant in a criminal case, and not final until read in court with judge, jury and defendant in a criminal case present and then approved by the jury

sealed will *n* : MYSTIC WILL

sea legs *n pl* **1** : adjustment to or ability to move normally in the presence of the rolling or pitching of a ship at sea **2** : freedom from seasickness

sea lemon *n* : any of several nudibranchiate mollusks of the family Dorididae having a smooth convex yellow body

sea lentil *n* : GULFWEED

sea leopard *n* **1 a** : LEOPARD SEAL **b** : WEDDELL SEAL **c** : HARBOR SEAL **2** : leather prepared from the skin of the wolffish

¹seal·er \ˈsēlə(r)\ *n* -S [ME *seler*, fr. *selen* to seal + -*er* — more at SEAL] **1** : one that seals: as **a** : an official who attests or certifies conformity to a standard of correctness or quality ⟨a ~ of weights and measures⟩ ⟨a ~ of leather⟩ **b** : one whose work is sealing containers (as jars, bags, boxes) or articles (as storage batteries, radio tubes); *also* : an operator of a sealing machine **c** : a device or machine that seals ⟨a can ~⟩ **d** : a coat (as of size) applied to prevent subsequent coats of paint or varnish from sinking in **2** : CAPPER 5

²sealer \ˈ"\ *n* -S [²*seal* + -*er*] : a mariner or a ship engaged in hunting seals

sealer's finger *n* : SEAL FINGER

seal·ery \ˈsēlərē\ *n* -ES [¹*seal* + -*ery*] : SEAL FISHERY

sea-less \ˈsēləs\ *adj* [¹*sea* + -*less*] : having no sea

sea letter *n* : a ship's passport issued in time of war to a neutral vessel on leaving a port, entitling the master to sail under the flag and pass of the nation to which it belongs, and specifying its cargo and crew, the names of its captain and owners, place of lading, port of registry, and destination — called also *sea brief*, *sea pass*

sea lettuce *n* : any of various seaweeds (genus *Ulva*) having flat expanded crinkly green fronds sometimes eaten as salad

sea level *n* **1** : the level of the surface of the sea **2** : sea level at its mean position midway between mean high and low water adopted as a standard for the measurement of heights — called also *mean sea level*

seal finger *n* [¹*seal*] : a finger rendered swollen and painful by erysipeloid or a similar infection and occurring esp. in seamen

seal fishery *n* **1** : the act, process, or occupation of taking seals for their oil, skin, or fur **2** : a place (as a rookery) where seals are hunted

sealflower \ˈ⸗,⸗\ *n* [³*seal* + *flower*] : BLEEDING HEART 1

seal hole *n* : a breathing hole made in the ice by a seal

sea light *n* **1** : a light (as a beacon) for guiding ships at sea **2** : the light over or peculiar to the sea

¹sealike \ˈ⸗,⸗\ *adj* [¹*sea* + *like*] : resembling the sea

²sealike \ˈ"\ *adv* : in the manner of the sea

sea lily *n* : CRINOID; *esp* : a stalked crinoid

sea line *n* **1** : a sea outline (as the horizon or coastline) **2** : a line used in the sea (as for sounding or deepwater fishing)

seal·ine \(ˈ)sē¦lēn\ *n* [¹*seal* + -*ine*] : rabbit fur from Australia and New Zealand sheared and dyed to simulate seal

¹sealing *n* -S [fr. gerund of ⁴*seal*] **1 a** : an impression made by a seal **b** : a small piece of clay or other malleable material on which an intaglio seal has been imprinted **2 a** : a thin machine-glazed paper used as a parcel wrapper **b** : a heavy wrapping paper used in covering ream packages of book or writing paper

²sealing *n* -S [fr. gerund of ²*seal*] : the hunting or catching of seals

sealing nut *n* : a nut used in making a seal; *specif* : a nut for sealing the terminal post of a battery at the point where the post leaves the cover of the case

sealing tape *n* : a gummed paper tape used in securing wrapped or boxed packages

sealing wax *n* : a composition that is plastic when warm and is used for sealing (as letters, documents, dry cells, cans) and that in medieval times contained beeswax but now is a resinous composition made usu. by fusing shellac with Venice turpentine and coloring matter

sea lion *n* **1** : any of several large eared seals native to the Pacific ocean related to the fur seals but lacking their valuable coat and including several largely coastal members of the genera *Zalophus* (as the Australian *Z. lobatus* and the Californian *Z. californianus*) and *Otaria* (as the So. American *O. byronia* or *O. jubata*) — see STELLER'S SEA LION **2** : a heraldic representation of a monster having the forepart of a lion with web feet and the tail of a fish

sea lion

sea lizard *n* **1** : an amphibious lizard (*Amblyrhynchus cristatus*) of the Galápagos islands **2** : any of various pelagic nudibranchs that constitute the genus *Glaucus*, are widely distributed in warm seas, and are blue or sometimes white in color

seallike \ˈ⸗,⸗\ *adj* [¹*seal* + *like*] : resembling a marine seal esp. in grace of movement, sleekness, or streamlined form

seal lock *n* [³*seal*] : a lock having a seal (as of glass) that must be broken for the lock to be unlocked

seal maker *n* [³*seal*] : one that makes seals esp. as an occupation

sea-loch \ˈ⸗,⸗\ *n* : an elongated narrow arm of the sea projected into the adjacent land mass

seal off *vt* [⁴*seal*] : to close tightly so as to eliminate ingress or egress ⟨a glass tube *sealed off* by fusing the material together⟩ ⟨*sealed* the airport *off* with a cordon of police⟩

seal oil *n* : a colorless or pale yellow to red-brown unsaturated fatty oil obtained from seal blubber and used chiefly in making soap, in dressing leather and fur, as a lubricant, and formerly as a burning oil

sea lord *n* : one of those lords commissioners of admiralty having direct charge of naval matters under the first lord of the admiralty and including the chief of naval staff with his deputy and assistant, the chief of naval personnel, the controller, and the chief of supplies and transport

sea louse *n* **1** : any of various marine isopods — compare WOOD LOUSE **2** : FISH LOUSE

sea lovage *n* : LOVAGE

seal point *n* : a Siamese cat with cream or fawn-colored body and seal brown points

seal press *n* [³*seal*] : any of various presses having an engraved die in one jaw and used for embossing (as in impressing crests or making seals)

seal record *n* : a record of information about freight car seals made from examinations of the seals at various points en route

seal ring *n* : a ring engraved with a seal, emblem, or monogram or set with a similarly engraved stone : SIGNET RING

seals *pl of* SEAL, *pres 3d sing of* SEAL

sealskin \ˈ⸗,⸗\ *n, often attrib* [ME *seleskin*, fr. *sele* seal + *skin*] **1** : the skin of a seal and esp. of a fur seal **2** : a garment (as a jacket, coat, cape) of sealskin **3** : a strip of sealskin or a coarser fur attachable to the bottom of a ski for preventing slipping backward in uphill climbing — usu. used in pl.

sealstone \ˈ⸗,⸗\ *n* [³*seal* + *stone*] : a stone engraved with a seal and commonly dating from prehistoric times

seal-top spoon *n* [³*seal*] : a silver spoon having a handle with its end in the form of a circular seal and popular in England in the later 16th and 17th centuries

sea lungs *n pl but sing or pl in constr* [trans. of L *pulmo marinus*] *archaic* : JELLYFISH, CTENOPHORE

sea lungwort *n* : a fleshy perennial herb (*Mertensia maritima*) of the northern coasts of both hemispheres with ovate to spatulate leaves and usu. long-stalked rose-pink flowers fading to pale blue or almost white

sealwort \ˈ⸗,⸗\ *n* [³*seal* + *wort*; fr. the markings on the rootstock] **1** : SOLOMON'S SEAL 2a **2** : a pearlwort (*Sagina procumbens*)

sea·ly·ham terrier \ˈsēlē,ham-, -lēəm-\ *n* [fr. *Sealyham*, Pembrokeshire, Wales, where it was developed] **1** *usu cap S&T* : a Welsh breed of long-headed heavy-boned chiefly white terriers with short legs, strong jaws, and long supple body that give it an advantage in tackling the badger underground though it is also used in bolting the fox and the otter **2** *or* **sealyham** -S *usu cap S* : a dog of the Sealyham Terrier breed

sea lyme grass *n* : a grass (*Elymus arenarius*) of the Pacific seacoast that is useful as a sand binder

¹seam \ˈsēm\ *n* -S [ME *sem*, *seem*, fr. OE *sēam*; akin to MD *soom* load of a pack animal, MLG *sōm*, OHG *soum*; all fr. a prehistoric WGmc word borrowed fr. (assumed) VL *sauma* packsaddle (whence ML *sauma*), fr. LL *sagma* — more at SUMPTER] **1** *dial chiefly Eng* : the amount borne by a beast of burden; *esp* : a suitable or standard load for a packhorse **2** *dial chiefly Eng* : any of various units of weight or capacity based on a standard load for a packhorse ⟨a ~ of grain is usu. eight bushels⟩

²seam \ˈ"\ *n* -S [ME *sem*, *seem*, fr. OE *sēam*; akin to OFris *sām* hem, seam, MD *soom*, MLG *sōm*, OHG *soum*, ON *saumr* seam, OE *siwian* to sew — more at SEW] **1 a** : a joining by a line of stitching of two pieces of cloth, leather, or other material usu. near the edge ⟨you must sew more evenly, your ~ is all bumpy⟩ — see FLAT-FELL SEAM, FRENCH SEAM **b** : the line of stitching used in making such a joining **c** : material between the line of stitching and the outer edges of the cloth that is usu. turned to the inside of an article **d** : the slightly⸗indented line on the outside of an article formed when the joining is pressed open or flat **e** : an imitation joining; *esp* : one made in a single piece of material by a full-length tuck on the wrong side or a line of purl or pattern stitches in a knit garment **2** : a crevice or interstice where edges (as of planks or plates) abut; *esp* : the space between adjacent planks or strakes of a ship — usu. used in pl. ⟨the heavy seas opened her ~*s*⟩ **3** : a line of junction (as between metals or plastics) : a line, groove, ridge, or other mark formed by the abutment of edges ⟨~*s* in brickwork⟩: as **a** : SUTURE **b** : a thin layer or stratum (as of rock) between distinctive layers; *also* : a bed of coal or other valuable mineral of any thickness **c** : a line left by a cut or wound; *also* : WRINKLE **4** : a surface defect of limited length in iron or steel caused by a blowhole made visible by working

³seam \ˈ"\ *vb* -ED/-ING/-S *vt* **1 a** (1) : to join (pieces of cloth or other material) by stitching ⟨~ two lengths of carpet together⟩ (2) : to make the seams of (as a garment) ⟨~ up a dress⟩ (3) : to decorate or finish (an article) at the seam or seams or with ornamental seams ⟨~ a slip with faggoting⟩ ⟨stitched and ~*ed* the shoes⟩ **b** : to join as if by sewing (as by the use of welding, riveting, or heat-sealing) **2** : to mark (a surface) with lines suggesting seams : LINE, FURROW, SCAR ⟨a face ~*ed* with saber cuts⟩ ⟨creeks ~ the valley⟩ ~ *vi* : to become fissured or ridgy : crack open ⟨land drying and ~*ing* in the heat⟩

⁴seam \ˈ"\ *var of* SAIM

sea magpie *n*, *Brit* : OYSTER CATCHER

sea-maid \ˈ⸗,⸗\ *also* **sea-maiden** \ˈ⸗,⸗⸗\ *n* : MERMAID; *also* : a goddess or nymph of the sea

sea mail *n* **1** : mail carried over the sea by ship **2** : postal service carrying mail by ship

sea mallow *n* : TREE MALLOW

sea·man \ˈsēmən\ *n*, *pl* **seamen** [ME *seeman*, fr. *see* sea + *man* — more at SEA, MAN] **1 a** : a man whose occupation is concerned with the handling, working, or navigating of ships at sea : a man who follows the sea as a way of life : SAILOR — distinguished from *landsman* **b** : a person other than a master, pilot, or duly indentured and registered apprentice employed or engaged in any capacity on board any ship of the English merchant shipping **c** : a person other than an apprentice employed or engaged in any capacity aboard a U.S. ship : a member of a ship's company; *sometimes* : a worker specifically concerned with the working of a ship as distinguished from either an officer or a worker concerned with the ship's engines and power supply **d** : a naval enlistee or draftee who starts as a seaman recruit, becomes a seaman apprentice upon finishing recruit training, and is then promoted to a rating just below petty officer **2** : MERMAN

seaman apprentice *n* : a naval enlistee or draftee who has completed recruit training and has qualified for the rating of seaman

seaman gunner *n*, *archaic* : an enlisted man (as in the U.S. Navy) passing through courses of instruction in such matters as the construction and handling of ordnance, torpedoes, explosives, or electricity

sea·man·ite \ˈsēmə,nīt\ *n* -S [Arthur E. *Seaman* †1937 Am. geologist + E -*ite*] : a rare mineral $Mn_3(PO_4)(BO_3).3H_2O$ that is a phosphate and borate of manganese and that occurs in pale yellow orthorhombic crystals

seamanlike \ˈ⸗⸗,⸗\ *adj* : characteristic of or befitting a seaman : indicating competent seamanship

sea·man·ly *adj* : SEAMANLIKE

seaman recruit *n* : an enlistee or draftee of the lowest grade in the navy

sea·man·ship \ˈsēmən,ship\ *n* : the art or skill in the art of handling, working, and navigating a ship; *esp* : the principles and practices of ship operation and maintenance within the province of the deck department

sea mantis *n* : SQUILLA

sea marigold *n* : SEA OXEYE

seamark \ˈ⸗,⸗\ *n* [ME *see marke*] **1** : a line on a coast marking the tidal limit; *specif* : FULL SEAMARK **2** : an elevated object discernible at or from sea and serving to guide or warn mariners : BEACON, LANDMARK; *also* : a sign of danger

sea marker *n* : a patch of dye deposited on the sea (as to catch the attention of an airplane's crew)

sea mat *n* : BRYOZOAN; *esp* : an encrusting bryozoan (as of the genus *Flustra*)

sea matweed *n* : BEACH GRASS

seam·berry palm \ˈsēm-. . . — *see* BERRY\ *n* [so called fr. the seamy albumen in the fruit] : a palm of the genus *Coccothrinax*

seam binding *n* : a covering or reinforcement for a seam; *esp* : a narrow strip of fabric in plain weave used (as in garments) to strengthen seams, finish hems, or cover raw edges

seam blasting *n* : the act or process of shattering a boulder by packing a charge of dynamite into a crack or seam in it, tamping clay on top of the charge, and exploding

sea meadow *n* **1** : SALT MARSH **2 sea meadows** *pl* : the upper layers of the open sea that by reason of the abundance of the phytoplankton furnish food for marine animal life

seamed *adj* [fr. past part. of ³*seam*] **1 a** : having a seam **b** : joined by seams **2** : WRINKLED, FURROWED ⟨a ~ face⟩

seam·er \ˈsēmə(r)\ *n* -S [³*seam* + -*er*] : one that seams or makes seams: as **a** : an operator of a seaming machine; *also* : SEAMSTRESS **b** : a worker who removes seams **c** : one whose work is to seam a specified thing or in a specified way — usu. used in combination ⟨a saddle ~⟩ **d** : a machine for sewing seams **e** : a handtool or machine for making joints (as in sheet metal)

seamer man *n* : an operator of a double seamer

sea mew *n* [ME *see mew*, fr. *see* sea + *mew* — more at SEA, MEW] : SEA GULL; *esp* : a European gull (*Larus canus*) resembling the herring gull but smaller

seam face *n* : a face on a building stone formed by a natural seam in the rock

seamier *comparative of* SEAMY

seamiest *superlative of* SEAMY

sea mile *n* : NAUTICAL MILE

sea milkwort *n* : a small fleshy herb (*Glaux maritima*) that is common along northern seashores — called also *sea trifoly*

seam·i·ness \ˈsēmēnəs\ *n* -ES : seamy condition

seam·ing \ˈsēmiŋ, -mēŋ\ *n* -S [ME *semyng*, fr. *sem*, *seem* seam + -*ing* — more at SEAM] **1 a** : the act or process of forming a seam (as by stitching or welding) **b** : a product of seaming **2** *also* **seaming lace** : narrow insertion used for decoration esp. between or over seams

seaming dies *n pl* : a set of shaping dies that press against folded sheet-metal edges and by squeezing the folds together make a seam

sea mink *n* **1** : KING WHITING **2** : NORTHERN WHITING

sea mist *n* **1** : mist from the sea **2** : ART GRAY

seam·less \ˈsēmləs\ *adj* [ME *semlesse*, fr. *sem*, *seem* seam + -*lesse* -less] : having no seam: as **a** : woven full width ⟨a ~ rug⟩ **b** *of a tubular fabric* : woven as a double cloth ⟨~ bagging⟩ **c** : CIRCULAR-KNIT — **seam·less·ly** *adv* — **seam·less·ness** *n* -ES

seamlike \ˈ⸗,⸗\ *adj* : resembling a seam esp. in forming a linear joint or differentiated line

sea·mo·bile \ˈsēmō,bēl\ *n* [¹*sea* + -*mobile*] : a small shallow draft cargo ship driven by automobile-type engines

sea monk *n* : MONK SEAL

sea monster *n* **1** : a large or extraordinary sea animal **2** : a fabulous monster of the sea often represented as man-devouring

sea moss *n* **1** : SEAWEED; *esp* : any of various red algae (as carrageen or dulse) with rose to violet or purple gracefully elaborate fronds **2** : a branched marine bryozoan resembling moss **3 a** : AUCUBA GREEN **b** : PERSIAN GREEN

sea·most \ˈsē,mōst, *esp Brit also* -,məst\ *adj* : situated nearest the sea

sea moth *n* : a fish of the family Pegasidae — called also *sea dragon*

seamount \ˈ⸗,⸗\ *n* : a submarine mountain rising above the deep-sea floor commonly from 3000 to 10,000 feet and having the summit 1000 to 6000 feet below sea level — compare GUYOT

sea mouse *n* **1** : a large broad marine polychaete worm of *Aphrodite* or a related genus having a thick coat of long slender hairlike setae **2 a** *dial Eng* : RED-BACKED SANDPIPER **b** : HARLEQUIN DUCK **3** : a flattened sea urchin (suborder Spatangina) with relatively long spines; *esp* : one belonging to the genus *Lovenia*

seam-rent \ˈ⸗,⸗\ *adj* **1** *archaic* : ripped out at the seams **2** *archaic* : wearing garments that are ripped ⟨poor ~ fellows —Ben Jonson⟩

seam roller *n* : a tool used by a paperhanger to make a seam flat and tight

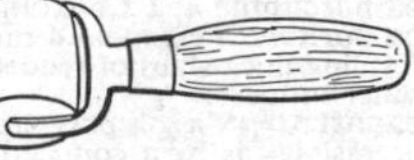

seam roller

seams *pl of* SEAM, *pres 3d sing of* SEAM

seam set *n* : any of various tools for flattening seams (as of metal sheets or leatherwork)

seam squirrel *n* : BODY LOUSE

seam·ster \ˈsēmztə(r), -m(p)st-, *chiefly Brit* ˈsem-\ *also* **semp-**

ster \'sem(p)st-\ *n* -s [ME *semester, semster,* fr. OE *sēamestre* seamstress, tailor, fr. *sēam* seam + *-estre* -ster] **:** a person that is employed at sewing; *usu* **:** a man so employed **:** TAILOR — compare SEAMSTRESS

seam·ster·ing \-t(ə)riŋ\ *n* -s **:** the art or occupation of a seamster

seam strap *also* **seam strip** *n* **:** EDGE STRIP

seam·stress *also* **semp·stress** \-trə̇s\ *n* -ES [*seamster, sempster* + *-ess*] **:** a woman who sews by hand or machine; *esp* **:** one whose occupation is making, altering, or repairing garments, curtains, household linens, or industrial articles of cloth (as airplane covers)

sea mud *or* **sea ooze** *n* **:** mud from the sea; *specif* **:** a slimy deposit along the seashore sometimes used as a manure

sea mugwort *n* **:** SEA RAGWEED

sea mule *n* **:** a boxy steel tug driven by a diesel engine and used esp. for handling pontoons and barges

sea mullet *n* **1 a :** a common bluish green food fish (*Mugil dobula*) of the Australian coasts **b :** a related smaller fish (*Agonostomus forsteri*) often landlocked in Australian lakes **2 :** any of several whitings

seam weld *n* **:** a joint made by seam welding

seam–weld \'=,=\ *vt* [*seam weld*] **:** to unite by a seam weld

seam welding *n* **:** resistance welding in which the weld is made linearly (as between two rollers, a roller and a bar)

seamy \'sēmē, -mi\ *adj* -ER/-EST [²*seam* + *-y*] **1 a** *archaic* **:** having the rough side of the seam showing **b :** less pleasing, less worthy, or less presentable ⟨the ~ side of urban life⟩ **2 :** forming or resembling a seam ⟨a ~ scar⟩; *also* **:** marked by seams **:** SEAMED ⟨an ancient ~ face⟩

sea myrtle *n* **:** GROUNDSEL BUSH

sé·ance \'sā,än(t)s *sometimes* (')sā¦äⁿs\ *n* -s [F, lit., sitting, fr. *seoir* to sit (fr. L *sedēre*) + *-ance* — more at SIT] **:** SITTING: as **a :** a coming together or session (as of a public body, a learned society, a class) for a particular purpose (as deliberation, discussion, recitation) **b :** a meeting for the purpose of receiving spirit communications ⟨the ancestral . . . ghost talked at a ~ —*Times Lit. Supp.*⟩ **c :** a sitting for a portrait

sea necklace *n* **:** a string of disk-shaped egg cases of any of various large whelks of the genus *Busycon* — called also *sea ruffle*

sea nettle *n* **:** a stinging jellyfish (as a siphonophore)

sea oak *n* **1 :** any of various rockweeds (esp. *Fucus vesiculosus* and *F. serratus*) **2** *Brit* **:** a sertularian hydroid (*Dynamena punila*) that forms a small much-branched arborescent colony with a tough horny skeleton into which the polyps can contract

sea oat *n* **1 :** a tall grass (*Uniola paniculata*) that has panicles resembling those of the oat, grows on the coast of the southern U.S., and is useful as a sand binder — usu. used in pl. **2 sea oats** *pl* **:** a cluster of yellowish vase-shaped egg cases of a whelk of the genus *Thais* **:** SEA CORN

sea onion *n* **1 :** a squill (*Urginea maritima*) **2 :** a small delicate European herb (*Scilla verna*) with fragrant blue flowers in clusters that resemble corymbs

sea orach *n* **:** an orach (*Atriplex hastata*) that grows on waste-land esp. near the sea and is used in Europe as a substitute for spinach — compare GARDEN ORACH

sea orange *n* **:** a large American holothurian (*Psolus fabricii*) having an orange-colored convex body

sea otter *n* **1 :** a rare large marine otter (*Enhydra lutris*) of the northern Pacific coasts that attains a maximum length of nearly six feet, has short legs, a blunt cylindrical tail, and larged webbed hind feet, feeds largely on shellfish which it crushes with its broad flat-crowned molars, and produces a pelt which furnishes an extremely valuable fur and consists of rich dark brown underfur with an outer coat of gray-tipped coarser hairs **2 :** the fur or pelt of the sea otter

sea–otter's–cabbage \'=,=='=,=\ *n, pl* **sea–otter's–cabbages :** a gigantic kelp (*Nereocystis lütkeana*) of the northern Pacific in beds of which the sea otter makes its home — called also *bladder kelp*

sea oxeye *n* **:** a plant of the genus *Borrichia; esp* **:** either of two shrubby coastal plants (*B. frutescens* and *B. arborescens*) of the southern U.S. and tropical America with thick fleshy leaves — called also *sea marigold*

sea painter *n* **:** a long strong rope for use on a ship's lifeboat

sea palm *n* **:** an olive-brown kelp (*Postelsia palmaeformis*) of the Pacific coast having an erect stalk resembling a trunk and palmately divided fronds at the apex

sea pansy *n* **:** a showy purple alcyonarian (genus *Renilla*) — called also *sea kidney*

sea parrot *n* **:** PUFFIN

sea parsley *n* **:** LOVAGE a, b

sea parsnip *n* **:** a European plant of the genus *Echinophora* (family Umbelliferae); *esp* **:** a white-flowered prickly-foliaged herb (*E. spinosa*)

sea–partridge \'=,=\ *n* **:** a small variably-colored wrasse (*Ctenolabrus melops*) common along weedy shores of Britain and western Europe

sea pass *n* **:** SEA LETTER

sea pay *n* **:** pay for service on a ship in commission

sea pea *n* **:** BEACH PEA

sea peach *n* **:** an ascidian (*Tethyum pyriformis*) of the coasts of northeastern No. America having the velvety surface and color of a ripe peach

sea pear *n* **:** a stalked ascidian of *Boltenia* or a related genus

sea peat *n* **:** peat formed from seaweeds

sea pen *n* **1 :** any of numerous alcyonarians belonging to *Pennatula* and related genera in which the colony has a feathery form and the stem or shaft of the colony contains a calcareous or horny axis embedded at the lower end in the mud of the sea bottom **2 a :** PEN SHELL **b :** SQUID

sea perch *n* **1 :** any of various sea basses (family Serranidae) **2 :** TRIPLETAIL

sea perils *n pl* **:** PERILS OF THE SEA

sea pheasant *n* **1 :** PINTAIL **2 :** OLD-SQUAW

sea pie *n, chiefly Brit* **:** OYSTER CATCHER

seapiece \'=,=\ *n* **:** a representation of the sea (as in a painting) **:** SEASCAPE

sea pig *n* **1 a :** PORPOISE, DOLPHIN **b :** DUGONG **2 :** a buoy or spar towed by a ship in a fog to guide a following ship

sea pigeon *n* **1 :** a small guillemot of the genus *Cepphus* **:** BLACK GUILLEMOT, PIGEON GUILLEMOT **2** *chiefly Scot* **:** ROCK PIGEON

sea pike *n* **:** any of various marine fishes resembling the true pike in their elongate form and voracity (as garfish or hake); *esp* **:** BARRACUDA

sea pimpernel *n* **:** SEABEACH SANDWORT

sea pine *n* **:** a maritime pine; *esp* **:** CLUSTER PINE

sea pink *n* **1 a :** THRIFT 6 **b :** MARSH PINK **2 :** a strong pink that is yellower and duller than carnation rose, duller and slightly bluer than coral (sense 3b), and bluer and duller than rose d'Althaea

sea plain *n* **:** a plain produced by marine erosion

seaplane \'=,=\ *n* **:** an airplane designed to rise from and land on the water — see FLYING BOAT, FLOATPLANE

sea plantain *n* **:** either of two plantains that grow near the sea: **a :** a perennial usu. glabrous Eurasian plantain (*Plantago maritima*) that thrives along shore and in alpine areas **b :** a perennial plantain (*P. decipiens*) having fleshy leaves and found along the cooler coasts of No. America

sea plume *n* **:** a gorgonian of plumose form (as *Gorgonia acerosa* or *G. setosa*)

sea poacher *also* **sea poker** *n* **:** a fish of the family Agonidae — see POGGE

sea·poose \'sē,püs\ *n* -s [by folk etymology fr. a word of Algonquian origin; akin to Delaware *sepoûs, sepus* small brook, Natick *sepuēse* brook, *sepu* river, Narragansett *sepoēse* little river, *sepe* river] **1 :** a shallow inlet or tidal stream along the Long Island shore **2 :** SEA PUSS

sea poppy *n* **:** HORNED POPPY

sea porcupine *n* **1 :** PORCUPINE FISH **2 :** SEA URCHIN

sea pork *n* **:** a compound tunicate (genus *Amaroucium*) often forming thick slabs of reddish or whitish growth on pilings or other supports

seaport \'=,=\ *n* **:** a port, harbor, or town on the seacoast or accessible (as by a connecting river) to seagoing ships and active in shipping or other marine activities ⟨a ~ with water-front saloons catering to sailors⟩

seapost \'=,=\ *n* **:** SEA MAIL

sea post office *n* **:** a post office maintained on a steamer or packet boat for letters mailed at sea

sea potato *n* **:** an ascidian (*Boltenia rubra*) of the northeastern coast of No. America the body of which is borne on a long stalk and in form resembles a potato

sea power *n* **1 :** a nation having formidable naval strength **2 :** naval strength including those weapons, installations national resources, and geographical circumstances that enable a country to control the sea and the air above it

sea pumpkin *n* **:** HOLOTHURIAN

sea purse *n* **1 :** the horny egg case of skates and of some sharks that is usu. of quadrangular outline with the angles produced into filaments by which it becomes attached (as to seaweeds) and that commonly contains but one egg or embryo **2 :** a coenocytic marine green alga of the genus *Codium* resembling a sponge

sea purslane *n* **1 :** SEABEACH SANDWORT **2 :** any of several plants of the genus *Atriplex* (esp. *A. hastata*) **3 :** a plant of the genus *Sesuvium*

sea puss *or* **sea purse** *n* [by folk etymology fr. the source of *seapoose* — more at SEAPOOSE] **:** a dangerous swirling of undertow due to the combined effect of several breakers; *also* **:** an undertow setting along shore

sea quail *n* **1 :** TURNSTONE **2 :** CASSIN'S AUKLET

sea·quake \'sē,kwāk\ *n* ['*sea* + *-quake* (as in *earthquake*)] **:** a submarine earthquake; *also* **:** a seismic disturbance appreciable at sea

¹**sear** *var of* SERE

²**sear** \'si(ə)r, 'siə\ *vb* -ED/-ING/-S [ME *seren,* fr. OE *sēarian,* fr. *sēar* dry, withered, sere — more at SERE] *vi* **1** *obs* **:** to wither away **:** become sere **2 :** to cause withering or drying ⟨harsh winds that ~ and burn⟩ ~ *vt* **1 :** to make withered and dry **:** DESICCATE, PARCH, SHRIVEL ⟨plants ~*ed* by frost and wind⟩ **2 :** to burn, scorch, or harden (as flesh) with or as if with sudden application of intense heat: as **a :** CAUTERIZE **b :** to injure with or as if with fire ⟨the bullet ~*ed* his leg⟩ ⟨had a bad burn where he was ~*ed* by the soldering iron⟩ **c :** to cook quickly the surface of (a piece of meat) usu. to develop color and flavor **:** brown quickly as a first stage in cooking **syn** see BURN

³**sear** \"\ *n* -s **:** a mark or scar left by searing or by a cautery or branding iron

⁴**sear** \"\ *n* -s [prob. fr. MF *serre* grip, grasp, clip, fr. *serrer* to press, squeeze, grasp, fr. LL *serare* to bolt (a door), fr. L *sera* bar for fastening a door] **1 :** the catch that holds the hammer of a gunlock at cock or half cock **2** *obs* **:** a releasing or yielding point or stage ⟨the clown shall make those laugh whose lungs are tickle o' the ~ —Shak.⟩

sea radish *n* **:** a European wild radish (*Raphanus maritimus*)

sea ragweed *n* **:** a European mostly seaside ragweed (*Ambrosia maritima*) with small heads of green flowers — called also *sea mugwort*

sea ragwort *n* **:** DUSTY MILLER 1a

sea raider *n* **:** one (as a pirate or submarine) that roams the sea preying upon merchant shipping

sea raven *n* **:** a sculpin (*Hemitripterus americanus*) of the northern Atlantic coast of America

¹**searce** \'sərs\ *also* **search** \-rch\ *n, pl* **searces** *also* **searches** [ME *saarce, sarche,* fr. MF *saas* small sieve made of horsehair or bristles, fr. ML *setaceum,* fr. L *seta, saeta* bristle — more at SINEW] *archaic* **:** a fine sieve **:** STRAINER

²**searce** \"\ *vt* -ED/-ING/-S [ME *sarcen,* fr. *saarce, sarche,* n.] *archaic* **:** SIFT, BOLT

searc·er \-sər\ *also* **search·er** \-chə(r)\ *n* -s *archaic* **:** SIEVE

¹**search** \'sərch, 'sēch, 'səich\ *vb* -ED/-ING/-ES [ME *cerchen, serchen,* fr. MF *cerchier* to travel through, traverse, survey, search, fr. LL *circare* to travel through, traverse, fr. L *circum* round about — more at CIRCUM-] *vt* **1 :** to look into or over carefully or thoroughly in an effort to find something: as **a :** to go about or traverse in careful quest ⟨~*ed* the northerly slope of the hill . . . his eyes scanning every foot of the ground —O.E. Rölvaag⟩ ⟨~*ing* the woods for the lost child⟩ **b :** to look into with thorough scrutiny and rigorous objective examination ⟨~ me, O God, and know my heart —Ps. 139: 23(AV)⟩ ⟨~*ing* my conscience while I was compiling these criticisms of others —Elmer Davis⟩ **c :** to look through or explore thoroughly esp. by checking on possible places of concealment or investigating circumstances possibly leading to something being overlooked ⟨~*ing* the apartment building for the suspect⟩ ⟨his hand ~*ing* his pocket for a match —William Faulkner⟩ — often used with *through* ⟨~*ed* through her handbag for a dime⟩ **d :** to peruse thoroughly and usu. with a particular objective **:** subject to a careful check ⟨~ the records of the case⟩ ⟨~*ing* those works for a clue to their authorship⟩ ⟨let him ~ the scriptures for consolation⟩; *esp* **:** to examine a public record or register for information about ⟨~*ing* titles in the courthouse⟩ **e :** to examine (a person) thoroughly to check on whatever articles are carried or concealed ⟨the police ~*ed* the suspect⟩ **f :** to look at fixedly in order to or as if in order to discover true intention, meaning, nature ⟨~*ed* him with a glance —George Meredith⟩ **2 :** to uncover, find, or come to know by diligent persevering inquiry or scrutiny ⟨as if to ~ and value every element in the conflict —Thomas De Quincey⟩ — usu. used with *out* ⟨the broad principle of toleration . . . ~*es* out and lays bare every insincerity —V.L.Parrington⟩ **3 :** to probe or explore with a surgical instrument ⟨doctors ~*ing* the wound⟩ **4 a :** to play upon or surge against or over a particular area as though looking for a weak, vulnerable, or vital point **:** pierce or penetrate at an unprotected point ⟨waves ~ the bases of the cliffs⟩ **b :** to distribute (gunnery fire) over an area; *specif* **:** to distribute (fire) by changes in elevation in gunnery with automatic weapons — compare TRAVERSE ~ *vi* **1 :** to look or inquire diligently and carefully — usu. used with *for* ⟨~*ed* long for the missing papers⟩ **2 :** to examine, investigate, or explore usu. with challenging or rejecting of a superficial or popularly accepted impression ⟨I am a student . . . and ~ into all matters —Edna S. V. Millay⟩ **syn** see SEEK — **search me** — used as a disclaimer of knowledge in response to a question

²**search** \"\ *n* -ES [ME *serche,* fr. MF *cerche,* fr. OF, fr. *cerchier*] **1 a :** an act or the action of searching **:** an endeavor to find, ascertain, recover, or bring into view ⟨a prolonged ~ for a lost will⟩ **b :** pursuit with a view to finding ⟨went south in ~ of health⟩ **c :** a critical scrutiny or survey (as of a ship's cargo or baggage) ⟨a customs ~⟩; *esp* **:** an act of boarding and inspecting a vessel on the high seas in exercise of right of search **d** *obs* **:** an examination of conscience **e** *obs* **:** RESEARCH, INVESTIGATION **2 :** a person or party that searches **3 :** power or range of searching and esp. of penetrating; *also* **:** a penetrating effect

search·able \-chəbəl\ *adj* **:** capable of being searched or of being found by searching

search coil *n* **:** FLIP COIL

search ephemeris *n* **:** an approximate ephemeris for use in locating a returning comet, asteroid, or planet suspected but not yet discovered

search·er \-chə(r)\ *n* -s [ME *serchere,* fr. *serchen* to search + *-ere* -er — more at SEARCH] **1 :** one that searches ⟨a ~ after knowledge⟩ **2 :** a person (as an inspector, looker, tracer) employed to search: as **a :** a guild official formerly functioning as an inspector to maintain standards of workmanship and quality **b :** an officer of the customs who examines (as ships, merchandise, luggage) for dutiable goods or contraband **c** *archaic Brit* **:** CORONER **d** (1) *archaic* **:** a civil officer appointed to observe and report objectionable conduct (2) **:** a minor police officer appointed to search persons arrested **e :** a person employed (as by a title insurance company) to search public records **f :** a kosher examiner who looks for evidence of contamination in freshly killed animals **3 :** an implement (as a probe) used in searching **:** SEEKER **4 :** a large metallic blue-green No. American ground beetle (*Calosoma scrutator*) that feeds on caterpillars

search·ful \-chfəl\ *adj* **:** full of searching **:** INQUIRING; *also* **:** interested or active in searching

search·ing·ly *adv* **:** in a searching manner **:** with searching

search·ing·ness *n* -ES **:** searching quality or state

search lamp *n* **:** SEARCHLIGHT 1a

search·less \-chlə̇s\ *adj* **:** impossible to be searched **:** INSCRUTABLE

searchlight \'=,=\ *n* **1 a :** an apparatus for projecting a powerful beam of light of approximately parallel rays usu. devised so that it can be swiveled about **b :** a beam of light projected by such an apparatus **c :** FLASHLIGHT d **2 :** something that reveals the obscure or concealed in the manner of a searchlight

searchlight lantern *n* **:** a lantern backed by a metal reflector

search warrant *n* **:** a legally issued warrant authorizing an examination or search of a house or other place orig. chiefly for stolen goods but in modern practice under statutory provisions for intoxicating liquors, gambling implements, counterfeiters' or burglars' tools, obscene literature, smuggled goods, or other articles kept or concealed in violation of the law and in some instances for the discovery of persons

sea reach *n* **:** the straight course of a river where it reaches or approaches the sea

seared *past of* SEAR

seared green *n* **:** a moderate yellow green that is paler than average moss green, yellower and less strong than average pea green, and yellower and duller than apple green (sense 1) — called also *glowworm*

¹**searer** *comparative of* SEAR

²**sear·er** \'sirə(r)\ *n* -s [²*sear* + *-er*] **:** one that sears

³**searer** \"\ *n* -s [modif. of Sp *sierra* saw, sawfish, cero — more at SIERRA] **:** CERO

searest *superlative of* SEAR

sea return *n* **:** a radar echo reflected by waves and tending to obscure target indication

sea rim *n* **:** the horizon as seen over the sea

searing *pres part of* SEAR

sear·ing·ly *adv* **:** in a searing manner **:** so as to sear

sea risks *n pl* **:** PERILS OF THE SEA

searles·ite \'sərl,zīt\ *n* -s [John W. *Searles,* 19th cent. Am. settler in California + E *-ite*] **:** a mineral $NaB(SiO_3)_2.H_2O$ consisting of a hydrous sodium borosilicate occurring in small white spherulites

sea road *n* **1 :** a sea route **2 :** ROADSTEAD

sea robber *n* **1 :** a robber at sea; *specif* **:** PIRATE **2 :** JAEGER

sea robin *n* **1 :** any of several gurnards; *esp* **:** an American gurnard of the genus *Prionotus* having more or less red or brown on the body and fins and the first three rays of the pectoral fin separate from the others and used in walking about over the sea bottom **2 :** RED-BREASTED MERGANSER

sea rocket *n* **:** a plant of the genus *Cakile*

sea rod *n* **1 :** a gorgonian with long round branches **2 :** VIRGULARIAN

sea room *n* **1 :** room or space at sea to maneuver without peril of running aground or of collision **2 :** opportunity for freedom (as of action or movement)

sea rover *n* **:** one that roves the sea; *specif* **:** PIRATE

sears *pres 3d sing of* SEAR, *pl of* SEAR

sea ruffle *n* **:** SEA NECKLACE

sea–run \'=,=\ *also* **sea–running** \'=,==\ *adj* **:** having ascended or having the habit of ascending a river from the sea **:** ANADROMOUS ⟨caught a *sea-run* salmon⟩ ⟨*sea-run* races of brook trout⟩

sear up *vt* **:** to close by or as if by searing

sea rush *n* **:** a tall erect perennial rush (*Juncus maritimus*) that is nearly cosmopolitan and often a floral dominant in salt marshes and other moist saline environments

seas *pl of* SEA

sea salt *n* **:** salt resulting from the evaporation of seawater and containing chiefly sodium chloride with small amounts of magnesium chloride, magnesium sulfate, and calcium sulfate

sea–salt \'=,=\ *adj* **:** salty with seawater **:** like sea salt

sea sand *n* [ME *see sond,* fr. *see* sea + *sond* sand — more at SEA, SAND] **1 :** sand of the sea floor or seashore **2 sea sands** *pl* **:** a sandy seabeach

sea sandpiper *n* **:** PURPLE SANDPIPER

sea sand reed *also* **sea sand grass** *n* **:** BEACH GRASS

sea sandwort *n* **:** SEABEACH SANDWORT

sea scallop *n* **:** GIANT SCALLOP

sea·scape \'sē,skāp\ *n* -s ['*sea* + *-scape*] **1 :** a view of or over the sea **2 :** a picture representing a scene at sea — compare LANDSCAPE

sea·scap·ist \-pə̇st\ *n* -s **:** a maker of seascapes

sea scorpion *n* **1 :** SCULPIN; *esp* **:** a common father-lasher (*Cottus scorpius*) **2 :** EURYPTERID

sea sedge *n* **:** any of several maritime sedges; *esp* **:** SAND SEDGE

sea serpent *n* **1 :** a large marine animal more or less resembling a serpent that is often reported to have been seen at sea but is not identifiable with any known animal and that is prob. based on faulty observation of schools of porpoises, various cetaceans, oarfishes, or other large marine animals or on pure fiction **2 :** SEA SNAKE 1 **3 :** OARFISH

sea service *n* **:** service at sea or aboard a seagoing vessel; *sometimes* **:** naval as distinguished from military service

seashell \'=,=\ *n* **:** the shell of a marine animal and esp. of a mollusk (as a whelk, clam, oyster, or scallop)

seashell pink *n* **:** a light to moderate yellowish pink that is less strong and much yellower than Chatenay pink — called also *tussore*

seashine \'=,=\ *n* **:** the shine of the sea; *esp* **:** light reflected off the sea

seashore \'=,=\ *n* **1 :** land adjacent to the sea **:** SEACOAST, SEABEACH **2 :** all the ground between the ordinary high-water and low-water marks **:** FORESHORE

seashore heliotrope *n* **:** SEASIDE HELIOTROPE

seashore lupine *n* **:** a hairy decumbent lupine (*Lupinus littoralis*) that is common on coastal sands of the Pacific coast of No. America and has strong bright yellow roots and blue flowers

sea shrub *n* **:** a shrubby gorgonian

seasick \'=,=\ *adj, sometimes* -ER/-EST ['*sea* + *sick*] **1 :** affected with or suggestive of seasickness **2 :** sick of the sea ⟨thy ~, weary bark —Shak.⟩

sea·sick·ness *n* **:** motion sickness experienced on the water

seaside \'=,=\ *n, often attrib* [ME *seeside,* fr. *see* sea + *side*] **1 :** the district or land bordering the sea **:** country adjacent to the sea **:** SEASHORE **2 :** the side (as of a town) facing the sea

seaside alder *n* **:** a small tree (*Alnus maritima*) of the southeastern U. S. with soft light brown wood

seaside arrowgrass *n* **:** a grassy perennial herb (*Triglochin maritima*) found in salt marshes throughout cooler regions in the north temperate zone and having an erect slender spike of small greenish white flowers

seaside balsam *n* **:** CASCARILLA 2

seaside bean *n* **:** a jack bean (*Canavalia ensiformis*)

seaside bent *n* **:** a coarse seashore grass (*Agrostis maritima*) found along the Atlantic coasts of No. America and northern Europe

seaside crowfoot *n* **:** a widely distributed perennial herb (*Ranunculus cymbalaria*) that is common in saline situations and has mostly basal nearly round or reniform leaves, yellow solitary flowers, and tightly compressed heads of small achenes

seaside daisy *n* **:** a perennial maritime herb (*Erigeron glaucus*) of the Pacific coast with solitary heads of lilac or violet flowers — called also *beach aster*

seaside gerardia *n* **:** a slender annual herb (*Gerardia maritima*) found along the Atlantic coast of the U. S. and having narrow leaves and purple nearly regular flowers

seaside goldenrod *n* **:** a vigorous showy goldenrod (*Solidago sempervirens*) that is common along the eastern and gulf coast of No. America — called also *beach goldenrod*

seaside grape *n* **:** SEA GRAPE 1b

seaside heliotrope *n* **:** a widely distributed tropical annual weed (*Heliotropium curassavicum*) found mostly in saline situations and having one-sided spikes of small white yellow-eyed flowers that become blue on aging — called also *Chinese pusley*

seaside laurel *n* **:** a West Indian plant (*Xylophylla speciosa*) of the family Euphorbiaceae with flattened evergreen branches resembling leaves and whitish flowers

seaside mahoe *n* **:** PORTIA TREE

seaside millet *n* **:** a joint grass (*Paspalum distichum*) used for forage in Australia

seaside morning–glory *n* **:** GOATSFOOT CONVOLVULUS

seaside oat *n* **:** SEA OAT

seaside pea *n* **:** BEACH PEA

seaside pimpernel *n* **:** SEABEACH SANDWORT

seaside pine *n* **:** CLUSTER PINE

seaside plantain *n* **:** SEA PLANTAIN

seaside plum *n* **1 :** MOUNTAIN PLUM **2 :** SEA GRAPE 1b

sea·sid·er \'sē,sīdə(r)\ *n* **:** a seaside resident or frequenter

seaside sandwort *n* **:** a common sand spurry (*Spergularia marina*) found in salt marshes throughout the north temperate zone

seaside sparrow *also* **seaside finch** *n* **:** a salt-marsh sparrow (*Ammospiza maritima*) of the Atlantic and Gulf coasts

seaside spurge *n* **:** a prostrate annual weedy herb (*Euphorbia polygonifolia*) with opposite small linear-oblong leaves and small axillary solitary flowers that is found along the Atlantic coast and shores of the Great Lakes

sea silk *n* **1 :** silky usu. golden yellow fiber obtained from the byssus of mollusks of the genus *Pinna* **2 :** any of various fibers derived from marine algae

Sea Sled *trademark* — used for a gliding shallow-draft high-powered motorboat

sea slope *n* **:** a slope (as of land) toward the sea

sea slug *n* **1 :** HOLOTHURIAN **2 :** a naked marine gastropod; *specif* **:** NUDIBRANCH

sea smoke *n* **:** a fog in arctic regions produced in below-freezing air that lies over a warm sea surface

sea snail *n* **1 :** a creeping marine gastropod mollusk with a spiral shell (as a whelk, triton, or moonshell) **2 :** any of numerous small tadpole-shaped mail-cheeked fishes (family Liparididae) found in cold seas, covered with very lax skin, and usu. having the pelvic fins modified to form a sucker

sea snake *n* **1 :** any of numerous venomous aquatic snakes constituting the family Hydrophidae, having the tail compressed and with small scales on the ventral surface, being usu. viviparous, and with few exceptions living in warm littoral seas and feeding on fish **2 :** SEA SERPENT 1

sea snipe *n* **1 :** PHALAROPE; *broadly* **:** any of various shore birds **2 :** BELLOWS FISH 1

sea soldier *n* **:** MARINE 3

¹sea·son \'sēz°n\ *n* -s [ME *sesoun, seisoun*, fr. OF *saison, seson*, fr. L *sation-, satio* action of sowing, fr. *satus* (past part. of *serere* to sow) + *-ion-, -io* -ion — more at SOW] **1 a :** a time or period of time characterized or made significant by a particular feature, circumstance, or event ⟨during this ~ of sorrow⟩ **b :** a suitable, fitting, or natural time or occasion **:** a proper conjuncture ⟨this is not the ~ for such arguments⟩ ⟨in due ~ you will understand⟩ **c :** a period not specifically limited but usu. of short or moderate duration ⟨agreed to wait for a ~⟩ **d :** a particular point in a period of time or the course of events ⟨at that ~ I could reach no decision⟩ ⟨visitors and interruptions at all ~*s*⟩ **2 :** a particular period of the year: as **a** (1) **:** the annual period during which a plant produces its fruit, flower, or other economic part ⟨the too brief strawberry ~⟩ (2) **:** the annual period in which an animal engages in some activity (as mating or migrating) or is available for hunting or food ⟨during the mating ~ old bucks may be vicious⟩ ⟨the ~ for oysters⟩; *also* **:** ESTRUS, HEAT ⟨a single annual ~⟩ — usu. used with *in* ⟨as heifers come in ~⟩ **b :** the period normally characterized by a particular kind of weather ⟨a long rainy ~⟩ ⟨during the cold ~⟩; *sometimes* **:** inclement weather **:** a spell of damp or rainy weather **c :** the period during which a particular agricultural activity is commonly performed ⟨the planting ~⟩ **d** *archaic* **:** the period in which an organized body (as a court or university) is in session **e :** one of the divisions of the year marked by alterations in the length of day and night or by distinct conditions of temperature and moisture caused mainly by the relative position of the earth's axis with respect to the sun **f :** a period of the year set off or conceived of as set off by a particular and usu. high level of activity in some field (as social, cultural, or business) ⟨a good theatrical ~⟩ ⟨the height of the social ~⟩ ⟨the dull ~ that follows the holidays⟩; *also* **:** the annual period when a place is most frequented for social activities or amusement ⟨the London ~ lasts from May to July⟩ **g** (1) **:** a brief annual period in which a particular holiday occurs; *esp* **:** a period extending from shortly before Christmas through New Year's Day ⟨sent out ~'s greeting⟩ ⟨the busy rush of the holiday ~⟩ (2) **:** any of various periods in the Christian year commemorative chiefly of Christ's life (as Advent, Christmastide, Epiphany, Lent, Eastertide, Ascensiontide, Whitsuntide, Trinity) **3** [ME *sesoun*, fr. *sesounen*, v.] *obs* **:** something that gives relish **:** SEASONING **4** *archaic* **:** a recurrent period in the course of heavenly bodies **5 seasons** *pl* **:** YEARS — used in reckoning age ⟨a boy of seven ~*s*⟩ **6 :** one of eight tiles whose use is optional in a Mah-Jongg game — called also *flower* **7 :** the total schedule of games played or to be played by a sports team during a playing season; *also* **:** the results of such a series of games ⟨an unbeaten ~⟩ — **in season** *adv* **1 :** at the right or fitting time **:** OPPORTUNELY ⟨you will know *in season*⟩; *also* **:** in good time **:** EARLY ⟨arrived *in season*⟩ **2 :** in a state or at the stage of greatest fitness (as for use, marketing, eating) ⟨peaches are *in season*⟩ **3 :** in condition to be hunted or taken and esp. as dictated by law ⟨trout is *in season* for another month⟩ — **in season and out of season :** at all times without regard to season **:** CONTINUOUSLY — **out of season :** not in season; *esp* **:** available or marketed at other than the usual local season ⟨*out of season* fruits⟩ ⟨get tomatoes *out of season*⟩

²season \"\ *vb* **seasoned; seasoned; seasoning** \-z(°)niŋ\ **seasons** [ME *sesounen*, fr. MF *assaisoner* to ripen, make palatable by adding seasoning, fr. OF, fr. *a-* (fr. L *ad-*) + *saison, seson* season] *vt* **1 a :** to give (food) better flavor or more zest by adding seasoning or savory ingredients ⟨likes to ~ the cheese with chives or anchovies —Jane Nickerson⟩; *also* **:** to add seasoning to ⟨~ a dish too highly⟩ **b :** to render more agreeable (as by an addition of something) ⟨~*ing* our thoughts with laughter⟩; *also* **:** to adapt to taste **c** *archaic* (1) **:** to qualify by admixture **:** MODERATE, TEMPER ⟨when mercy ~*s* justice —Shak.⟩ (2) **:** IMBUE, TINGE **2 :** to treat in such a manner or by such a process as will fit best to some end or use ⟨~ a pipe by careful smoking⟩: as **a** *obs* **:** EMBALM **b :** to fit or prepare by time or habit **:** HABITUATE, ACCLIMATIZE **c** *obs* **:** DISCIPLINE, TRAIN **d :** to prepare (lumber) for use by drying in the open air or in a kiln ~ *vi* **1 :** to become seasoned; *esp* **:** to become dry and hard by escape of the natural juices or by being penetrated with other substance ⟨timber that ~*s* well in the open air⟩ **2 :** to flavor food with seasoning or savory ingredients ⟨~ with sliced onions, leeks, tomatoes, paprika—J.D.Vehling⟩; *also* **:** to add seasoning ⟨~ to taste⟩ **syn** see HARDEN

sea·son·able \'sēz(°)nəbəl\ *adj* [ME *sesounable*, fr. *sesoun* season + *-able* — more at SEASON] **1 :** occurring in good or proper time **:** OPPORTUNE ⟨~ advice⟩ ⟨a ~ time for discussion⟩ **2 :** suitable to or in keeping with the season or circumstances **:** TIMELY ⟨a hard but ~ frost⟩ ⟨~ care⟩

syn TIMELY, WELL-TIMED, OPPORTUNE, PAT: SEASONABLE describes what is peculiarly fit or appropriate to the season, occasion, or situation ⟨*seasonable* weather⟩ ⟨*seasonable* clothes⟩ ⟨*seasonable* consolation during his time of trouble⟩ TIMELY refers to whatever occurs or appears at the moment when it is of most use, benefit, or assistance ⟨a *timely* book⟩ ⟨a similar fate for the column on the left bank of the stream was averted by the *timely* arrival of . . . the main army —R.A.Billington⟩ ⟨unfortunate if absorption in affairs at home should cause us to forget that *timely*, well-considered aid now to countries teetering on the verge of economic breakdown and political anarchy would go far to avert the danger of another costly conflict —Vera M. Dean⟩ WELL-TIMED suggests care, forethought, precision, or design in achieving timeliness ⟨the *well-timed* and splendidly executed offensive . . . was a part of the same major strategy —F.D.Roosevelt⟩ OPPORTUNE may describe that which comes at the best possible time, perhaps by accident, and invites being capitalized on ⟨as if this was an encounter which was something more than convenient, something really *opportune* —Rebecca West⟩ ⟨the literary scene was too full of chaotic and short-lived movements to make the launching of a large work *opportune* —J.M.Barzun⟩ PAT applies to that which has happened at the most fit moment or which shows characteristics completely fit or apt for the occasion or often so seemingly apt that it is suspect ⟨one, whose eyes dwelt in a distant void, with spell and omen *pat* upon his lips, and a purse for any crystal prophet ripe —John Drinkwater⟩ ⟨had assuredly the air of a miracle, of something dreamed in a dream, of something pathetically and impossibly appropriate — *pat*, as they say —Arnold Bennett⟩

sea·son·able·ness *n* -ES **:** the quality or state of being seasonable

sea·son·ably \-blē, -li\ *adv* [ME *sesounably*, fr. *sesounable* + *-ly*] **:** in a seasonable manner **:** so as to be seasonable

sea·son·al \'sēz(°)nəl\ *adj* [¹*season* + *-al*] **1 :** of, relating to, or occurring at a particular season ⟨~ rates⟩ ⟨a ~ opportunity⟩ ⟨~ bloom⟩ **2 :** affected by or dependent on a season **:** not continuous (as in activity or availability) ⟨~ employment⟩ ⟨a ~ resort⟩ — **sea·son·al·ly** \-əlē, -əli\ *adv*

sea·son·al·i·ty \,sēz°n'alədē\ *n* -ES **:** the quality or state of being seasonal

season check *n* **:** a longitudinal crack in timber or lumber caused by rapid or uneven seasoning — compare FROST CRACK

season crack *n* **1 :** a crack sometimes occurring in brass or other metal that has been severely strained in rolling or other process of manufacture and left in a condition of internal stress **2 :** SEASON CHECK

season cracking *n* **:** the condition of having season cracks

seasoned *adj* [ME *sesouned*, fr. past part. of *sesounen* to season — more at SEASON] **1 :** made savory with or as if with condiments **2 a :** made fit for use by a process of curing (as by suitable drying and hardening) **b** *of paper* **:** having a moisture content that is uniform and in equilibrium with that of the surrounding atmosphere — compare GREEN **3 a :** made fit by habitude or use ⟨smoking a ~ pipe⟩ **:** HABITUATED, EXPERIENCED ⟨a ~ traveler⟩ **b :** outstanding for a long time and proven in quality by experience — used of securities

sea·soned·ly *adv* **:** in a seasoned manner

sea·son·er \'sēz(°)nə(r)\ *n* -s **:** one that seasons: as **a :** a user of seasonings ⟨a heavy ~⟩ **b :** SEASONING **c :** a worker that seasons hides or leather (as with oil, grease, or tallow) — called also *surfacer*

seasoning *n* -s [fr. gerund of ²*season*] **1 :** something that serves to season: as **a :** an ingredient (as a condiment, spice, or flavoring) added to food primarily for the savor that it imparts **b :** a brightening, stimulating, or enlivening element ⟨wit is the ~ of good conversation⟩ **c :** the diamond dust with which a lapidary's mill is charged **2 :** the process of becoming or making seasoned ⟨the ~ of an executive by responsibility⟩

sea·son·less \'sēz°nləs\ *adj* **:** exhibiting no seasonal changes ⟨the ~ world of the deep sea⟩

seasons *pl of* SEASON, *pres 3d sing of* SEASON

season ticket *n* **:** a ticket giving its holder a privilege (as entrance to all games at an athletic field or daily transportation between two places) for a specified season

sea spider *n* **1 a :** SPIDER CRAB **b :** any of various small marine arthropods constituting the class Pycnogonida **2 :** OCTOPUS **3 :** BASKET STAR

sea squab *n* **:** the tail of a puffer fish when served as food

sea squirt *n* [so called fr. its habit of contracting and squirting out water when disturbed] **:** a simple ascidian

sea staff *n* **:** SEA WAND

sea star *n* **1 :** STARFISH **2 :** MARSH PINK

sea starwort *n* **:** a common European salt-marsh aster (*Aster tripolium*) — called also *sea aster*

sea steps *n pl* **:** projecting metal plates or bars attached to the side of a ship by which it may be boarded — called also *sea ladder*

sea stickleback *n* **:** FIFTEEN-SPINED STICKLEBACK

sea stock *n* **:** provisions for use at sea **:** ship's stores **:** SEA STORES

sea stores *n pl* **:** supplies (as of foodstuffs) laid in before starting on a sea voyage

seastrand \'=,=\ *n* [ME *seestrond, seestrand*, fr. OE *sǣstrand*, fr. *sǣ* sea + *strand* — more at SEA, STRAND] **:** SEASHORE

sea swallow *n* **1 :** TERN; *esp* **:** a common medium-sized tern (*Sterna hirundo*) that is closely related to and much resembles the arctic tern **2 :** STORM PETREL

sea swine *n* [ME *see swine*, fr. *see* sea + *swin, swine* swine] **1 :** PORPOISE **2 :** BALLAN

¹seat \'sēt, *usu* -ēd.+V\ *n* -s [ME *sete*, fr. ON *sæti*, fr. the stem of *sitja* to sit — more at SIT] **1 a :** a special chair (as a throne) of one in eminence; *also* **:** the status of which such chair is an emblem **b :** something (as a chair, stool, bench) intended to be sat in or on **c :** the particular part of something on which one rests in sitting ⟨the ~ of a chair⟩ ⟨a worn trouser ~⟩; *also* **:** the part of the body that bears the weight in sitting **:** the gluteal region **:** BUTTOCKS **d :** FORM 6a **2 a :** the place on or at which one sits or which is available for sitting ⟨rented a block of ~*s* for the season⟩ ⟨a ~ by the fire⟩; *esp* **:** an assigned or regularly assumed sitting place ⟨had a ~ on the aisle⟩ ⟨father's ~ at table⟩ **b :** a right of sitting (as in a deliberative body) ⟨held a ~ in congress for over 20 years⟩ **c :** membership on an exchange **3 :** a place occupied by something **:** a resting place **:** ABODE ⟨starry ~*s* of bliss⟩: as **a :** the see of a bishop **b :** a place (as a city) from which authority is exercised **:** CAPITAL **c :** a bodily part in which some function or condition is centered ⟨the ~ of the pain⟩ ⟨the intestine is the chief ~ of digestion⟩ **d :** the status of an area in respect to factors (as climate) that determine its desirability for a purpose (as habitation) ⟨a home with a charming ~ among gentle wooded slopes⟩ **e :** a place where something specified is prevalent **:** CENTER ⟨the ~ of shoe manufacture in New England⟩ ⟨a ~ of learning⟩ ⟨has long been a ~ of war⟩ **f :** a superior rural residence **:** COUNTRYSEAT **g** *obs* **:** location in space or on the earth's surface **:** geographic location **4** *Scot* **:** COURT OF SESSION **5 :** posture in or way of sitting (as on horseback) ⟨a rider with excellent ~ and hands⟩ **6 a** *obs* **:** a place prepared for the erection of something (as a building) **b :** the part at or forming the base of something ⟨the ~ of a pillar⟩ **c :** a part or surface on which another part or surface rests **:** SEATING ⟨a rubber-cushioned engine ~⟩ ⟨formed a new ~ for the valve⟩ **d :** FLOOR 8 **e :** the part of a shoe sole to which the heel is secured

²seat \"\ *vb* -ED/-ING/-S *vt* **1 a :** to establish or install in a seat of special dignity or office ⟨the queen was ~*ed* the same year⟩ **b** (1) **:** to cause to sit **:** assist in sitting down **:** find a seat for ⟨~*ed* the guests at small tables⟩ (2) **:** to provide seats or seating for ⟨a theater ~*ing* 1000 persons⟩; *also* **:** to provide with seats ⟨~ a church⟩ **c :** to sit (oneself) down ⟨~ yourself by the window and watch the rain⟩ **d :** to put (as oneself) in a sitting position **2 a :** to establish in a place of residence **:** SETTLE **b** *archaic* **:** to provide (as a country) with inhabitants **3 :** to repair the seat of **:** provide a new seat for ⟨~*ed* the chairs with strong cane⟩ **4 :** to adjust on or in relation to a seat **:** fit to or with a seat ⟨~ a valve⟩ ~ *vi* **1** *archaic* **:** to take one's seat or place **2 :** to fit correctly on a seat ⟨the lid must ~ accurately⟩ ⟨this valve does not ~ well⟩

seatang \'=,=\ *n* [¹*sea* + *tang*] **:** ³TANG

sea tangle *n* **:** any of various kelps esp. of the genus *Laminaria* **:** TANG

seat belt *n* **:** an arrangement of straps or webbing designed to hold a person steady in a seat (as during the takeoff of an airplane or in an automobile collision)

seat board *n* **1 :** a board supporting or serving as a seat **2 :** a shelf that supports the movement in a timepiece (as in a long case clock)

seat bone *n* **:** ISCHIUM

seat clip *n* **:** SPRING CLIP 1

seat cut *n* **:** a cut at the outer end of a rafter that adapts it to fit the plate and normally has the form of a right-angled notch — compare PLUMB CUT

seat drop *n* **:** a fundamental trampoline stunt in which the performer drops to a sitting position with his legs straight then rebounds to a standing position

seat·ed \'sēd.əd, -ētəd\ *adj* **1 :** having or equipped with a seat esp. of a specified kind — often used in combination ⟨a soft-*seated* chair⟩ **2 :** settled or established in or as if in a seat **:** SITUATED, LOCATED ⟨deeply ~ disease⟩ **3** *of a horseshoe* **:** having the bearing surface hollowed

seat·er \'sēd.ə(r), -ētə-\ *n* -s **1 a :** one that puts in seats ⟨a chair ~⟩ **b :** a tool or implement for adjusting or fitting something (as a valve) into its seat **2** *archaic* **:** one (as an usher) who apportions seats or assigns persons to seats **3 :** something (as a vehicle) provided with seats esp. of a specified number — usu. used in combination ⟨toured the countryside in a four-*seater*⟩

sea term *n* **:** a seaman's term **:** a nautical word or phrase

sea thief *n* [ME *seethef*, fr. OE *sǣthēof*, fr. *sǣ* sea + *thēof* thief — more at SEA, THIEF] *archaic* **:** SEA ROBBER 1

sea thong *n* **1 :** a brown seaweed (*Himanthalia lorea*) found on the northern coasts of the Atlantic and having a long slender thallus that rises from a top-shaped holdfast **2 :** any of several seaweeds having corded fronds: as **a :** a sea lace (*Chorda filum*) **b :** a member of the genus *Laminaria*

sea thrift *n* **1 :** a thrift (*Armeria maritima*) **2 :** SEA LAVENDER

sea tiger *n* **:** GREAT BARRACUDA

sea time *n* **1 :** time spent at sea **2 :** time as reckoned at sea from noon to noon

seating *n* -s [partly fr. gerund of ²*seat*; partly fr. ¹*seat* + *-ing*] **1 :** the act of providing with seats ⟨the ~ of the crowd took a long time⟩ ⟨in charge of ~⟩ **2 a :** material for covering or upholstering seats ⟨strong cotton ~⟩ **b :** a seat in which something rests ⟨a valve ~⟩

sea titling *n*, *Brit* **:** ROCK PIPIT

seat·less \'sētləs\ *adj* **:** having or requiring no seat ⟨a ~ valve⟩

seat·mate \'=,=\ *n* **:** one with whom one shares a seat (as in a vehicle equipped with double or paired seats)

seat mile *n* **:** PASSENGER-MILE

sea toad *n* **1 :** any of various fishes of heavy or grotesque form: as **a :** SCULPIN **b :** TOADFISH **c :** ANGLER **2 :** an Australian spider crab (*Gonatorhynchus tumidus*) with a rough carapace suggesting the skin of a toad

seat-of-the-pants \'===\ *adj* **:** based on personal experience and appraisal rather than on the use of mechanical aids ⟨*seat-of-the-pants* navigation⟩

sea town *n* **:** a seaside town **:** SEAPORT

seat-pack parachute *n* **:** a parachute that is attached to the harness in such a manner that it may be used by the wearer as a seat cushion

seat-rail \'=,=\ *n* **:** a horizontal member at the front of a seat (as of a chair or sitter)

sea train \'=,=\ *n* **1 :** a seagoing ship equipped for carrying a train of railroad cars **2 :** several army or navy transports forming a convoy at sea

sea tree *n* **:** an arborescent seaweed (as of the genus *Lessonia*)

sea trifoly *n* **:** SEA MILKWORT

seat ring *n* **:** a replaceable ring that forms the seat of a valve

sea·tron \'sē·trən\ *n* -s [blend of *sea* and *citron*] **:** a confection or conserve made from a bladder kelp (*Nereocystis lütkeana*) usu. in syrup

sea trout *n* **1 :** any of various trouts or chars that as adults inhabit the sea but ascend rivers to spawn; *esp* **:** a European fish (*Salmo trutta*) that resembles the salmon but is smaller, weaker, and with smaller scales, that occurs in numerous subspecies in different regions which are sometimes considered separate species, and that may often become landlocked **2 :** any of various marine fishes that more or less resemble trouts: as **a :** WEAKFISH 1 **b :** GREENLING 1 **c :** the queenfish of California

se·at·tle \(')sē¦ad·°l, -¦at°l\ *adj, usu cap* [fr. *Seattle*, Washington] **:** of or from the city of Seattle, Wash. ⟨a *Seattle* shipyard⟩ **:** of the kind or style prevalent in Seattle

se·at·tle·ite \-°l,īt\ *n* -s *cap* [*Seattle*, Wash. + E *-ite*] **:** a native or resident of Seattle

sea turn *n* **:** a breeze or gale from the sea that often brings mist

sea turnip *n* **:** SEA-OTTER'S-CABBAGE

sea turtle *or* **sea tortoise** *n* **:** any of various large turtles having the feet modified into paddles, including the recent leatherback, hawksbill, loggerhead, and green turtles and numerous extinct forms, and being widely distributed in warm seas

sea twine *n* **:** SEA LACE

seatwork \'=,=\ *n* **:** work done at one's seat (as in school)

seatworm *n* **:** the human pinworm

seau \'sō\ *n, pl* **seaux** \'sō(z)\ [F, pail, fr. (assumed) VL *sitellus*, alter. of L *sitella*, a kind of urn, dim. of *situla* bucket, pail, voting urn] **:** a pottery pail that forms a part of the typical 18th century dinner service

sea unicorn *n* **:** NARWHAL

sea urchin *n* **1 :** an echinoderm of the class Echinoidea; *esp* **:** one of somewhat oblate form having a thin brittle shell or test of calcareous plates covered with well-developed and often very sharp movable spines as distinguished from the disk-shaped sand dollars or cake urchins and the heart urchins which also belong to the Echinoidea **2** *Austral* **:** CUSHIONFLOWER

sea urchin cactus *n* **:** any of several cacti (as of the genus *Echinopsis*) that are shaped like a sea urchin

seavalley \'=,==\ *n* **:** a submarine depression having the form of a valley and lacking the steep walls of a submarine canyon

sea valve *n* **:** a valve in the bottom or side of a ship communicating with the sea

sea vampire *n* **:** DEVILFISH 1

seave \'sēv\ *n* -s [ME *seve*, of Scand origin; akin to ON *sef* rush — more at SIEVE] *dial Eng* **:** RUSH

seawall \'=,=\ *n* [ME *seewall*, fr. *see* sea + *wall*] **:** a wall or embankment to resist encroachments of the sea

sea-walled \'=,=\ *adj* **:** provided with or protected by a seawall

sea walnut *n* **:** CTENOPHORE

seawan *or* **seawant** *var of* SEWAN

sea wand *n* **:** a kelp (*Laminaria digitata*) — called also *sea staff*

sea·wan·ha·ka boat \sə'wänəkə-\ *n, usu cap S* [fr. the *Seawanhaka* yacht club, Oyster Bay, Long Island, N.Y.] **:** a flat broad sailboat with centerboard widely used in the U. S.

¹sea·ward \'sēwə(r)d\ *also* **sea·wards** \-dz\ *adv* [*seaward* fr. ME *seeward*, fr. *see* sea + *-ward*; *seawards* fr. *seaward* + *-s*] **:** toward the sea

²seaward \"\ *n* -s **1 :** the direction or side away from land and toward the open sea; *also* **:** a location in this direction ⟨to fly to the ~⟩ **2 :** a service under old English feudal law consisting in guarding or watching against enemies from the sea

³seaward \"\ *adj* **1 :** directed or situated toward the sea **2 :** coming from the sea ⟨a ~ wind⟩

sea·ward·ly *adj* **:** accustomed to looking seaward or traveling at sea ⟨~ eyes⟩

seaware \'=,=\ *n* **:** sea wrack for use as manure

sea-washed \'=,=\ *adj* **:** wet by sea waves

sea wasp *n* **:** any of various cubomedusan jellyfishes that sting virulently

sea watch *n* **:** WATCH 6a(1)

seawater \'=,==\ *n* [ME *seewater*, fr. OE *sǣwæter*, fr. *sǣ* sea + *wæter* water — more at SEA, WATER] **:** water in or from the sea **:** SALT WATER

sea-water green *n* **:** SEA GREEN 1b

sea wax *n* **:** MALTHA

seaway \'=,=\ *n* **1 :** a moderate or rough sea ⟨caught in a ~⟩ **2 :** a ship's headway **3 :** the sea as a route for travel; *also* **:** an ocean traffic lane **4 :** a deep inland waterway that admits ocean shipping

sea-weary \'=,==\ *adj* **:** worn out or wearied by sea voyaging **:** tired by or of the sea

seaweed \'=,=\ *n* **1 :** a mass or growth of marine plants (as algae) **2 :** a plant growing in the sea; *esp* **:** a marine alga (as a kelp, dulse, rockweed, sea lettuce) widely distributed in the ocean, occurring from tide level to considerable depths, floating free or being anchored by specialized holdfasts of the thallus, and including many that are of economic importance (as for food, fertilizer, agar, fiber, potash, or iodine)

seaweed crab *n* **:** any of several common shallow-water Australian spider crabs (genus *Naxia*) that cover the carapace with seaweed

seaweed fern *n* **:** HART'S-TONGUE 1

seaweed glue *n* **:** FUNORI 2

seaweed green *n* **:** a grayish yellow green that is yellower and paler than average sage green and yellower and lighter than palmetto

seaweed marquetry *n* **:** marquetry of Italian origin in the form of conventionalized small-scale foliated or twining forms somewhat resembling seaweed and used esp. in late 17th century England

seaweedy \'=,==\ *adj* **:** characterized by or abounding in seaweeds

sea whip *n* **:** a gorgonian with an elongated flexible unbranched or little-branched axis

sea widgeon *n* **1 :** SCAUP DUCK **2 :** PINTAIL

seawife \'=,=\ *n, pl* **seawives :** either of two European wrasses (*Labrus vetula* and *Acantholabrus yarrelli*) related to the tautog

sea willow *n* **:** a gorgonian with long flexible branches

seawise \ˈ=,=\ *adj* **:** schooled in ways and problems of the sea
sea wolf *n* **1 a** *obs* **:** a fabulous sea beast **b :** any of several voracious marine fishes; *esp* **:** WOLFFISH **c** *archaic* (1) **:** ELEPHANT SEAL (2) **:** SEA LION **2 :** PIRATE, PRIVATEER; *also* **:** SUBMARINE
sea woodcock *n, Brit* **:** BAR-TAILED GODWIT
sea worm *n* **1 :** a marine annelid **2 :** SEA SERPENT 1 **3 :** SHIPWORM
sea wormwood *n* **:** an aromatic somewhat woody chiefly coastal Eurasiatic perennial herb (*Artemisia maritima*) with woolly leaves and racemose panicles of tiny heads of yellowish to reddish hermaphroditic flowers
seaworn \ˈ=,=\ *adj* **1 :** impaired or eaten away by the sea ⟨~ shores⟩ **2 :** SEA-WEARY
sea·wor·thi·ness \ˈsē,wər*th*ēnəs\ *n* **:** the quality or state of being seaworthy; *specif* **:** the fitness of a ship for a particular voyage with reference to the condition of its hull and machinery, the extent of its fuel and provisions supply, the quality of its officers and crew, and its adaptability for the type of voyage proposed
seaworthy \ˈ=,==\ *adj* [¹*sea* + *worthy*] **:** fit for a sea voyage **:** able to stand stormy weather in safety ⟨a ~ ship⟩
sea wrack *n* **1 a :** a growth of seaweed esp. of the large forms (as rockweeds and kelps) **b :** a plant (as the bladder wrack) that tends to form large sea wracks **2 :** EELGRASS 1
seax \ˈsaks\ *var of* SAX
seb·a·cate \ˈsebə,kāt, səˈba,kāt\ *n* -s [ISV *sebacic* (in *sebacic acid*) + *-ate*] **:** a salt or ester of sebacic acid
se·ba·ceous \səˈbāshəs\ *adj* [L *sebaceus* made of tallow, fr. *sebum* tallow, grease + *-aceus* -aceous — more at SOAP] **1 :** relating to, secreting, or composed of fatty matter ⟨the ~ glands of the skin⟩ **2 :** resembling fat in appearance **:** FATTY ⟨~ secretions of some plants⟩
sebaceous cyst *n* **:** a cyst filled with sebaceous matter and formed by distention of a sebaceous gland as a result of obstruction of its excretory duct **:** WEN
sebaceous gland *n* **:** any of the small sacculated glands lodged in the substance of the derma, usu. opening into the hair follicles, and secreting an oily or greasy material composed in great part of fat which softens and lubricates the hair and skin
se·bac·ic acid \səˈbasik-, -bās-\ *n* [*sebacic* ISV *sebac-* (fr. L *sebaceus*) + *-ic*] **:** a crystalline dicarboxylic acid $HOOC(CH_2)_8COOH$ that is made by destructive distillation of a mixture of sodium ricinoleate from castor oil and sodium hydroxide or is obtained as a component of isosebacic acid; decane-dioic acid
se·ba·go salmon \səˈbā(,)gō-\ *n, usu cap 1st S* [*Sebago* Lake, southwestern Maine] **:** LANDLOCKED SALMON 1
se·bala cat \səˈbalə-\ *n* [prob. fr. the name *Sebala*] **:** BLACK-FOOTED CAT
se–baptism \ˈsē;=,=\ *n* [fr. *se-baptist*, after E *baptist: baptism*] **:** the doctrine or practice of baptizing oneself
se–baptist \ˈ=;==\ *n* [L *se* oneself + E *baptist* — more at SUICIDE] **:** one that baptizes himself
se·bas·to·des \səˈbastə(,)dēz\ *n, cap* [NL, fr. *Sebastes*, genus of scorpaenid fish (fr. Gk *sebastos* august, worthy of reverence, fr. *sebesthai* to revere, feel awe) + *-odes*; akin to Skt *tyajati* he leaves, renounces, *tyajate* he shuns] **:** the chief genus of rockfishes (family Scorpaenidae)
se·bas·to·pol goose \səˈvastə,pōl, -aas- *also* ˈ=ˈ==,pōl *sometimes* ˈ=ˈ==,pəl *or* ;sevəˈstōpəl *or* ;==ˈstōpəl\ *n, usu cap S* [*Sebastopol* (*Sevastopol*), city in southwestern U.S.S.R.] **:** a domestic goose having many of its feathers fantastically curled and twisted
sebat *usu cap, var of* SHEBAT
se·bes·ten \səˈbestən\ *n* -s [ME, fr. Ar *sibistān*, fr. Per *segpistān*] **1 a :** an East Indian tree (*Cordia myxa*) with white flowers in loose terminal panicles — called also *Assyrian plum* **b** *or* **sebesten plum :** the fruit of the sebesten used in India for pickles and dried as a demulcent **2 a :** GEIGER TREE **b :** the white edible fruit of the geiger tree
sebi- *or* **sebo-** *comb form* [NL, fr. L *sebum* tallow, grease — more at SOAP] **:** fat **:** grease **:** sebum ⟨*sebific*⟩ ⟨*seborrhea*⟩
se·bif·ic \səˈbifik\ *adj* [*sebi-* + *-fic*] **:** fat-producing **:** FATTY
se·bil·ian \səˈbilyən\ *adj, usu cap* [ISV *sebil-* (fr. *Sebil*, locality in southeastern Egypt) + *-an*] **:** of or relating to a Mesolithic culture of Upper Egypt characterized by microlithic flint tools and composite weapons using microliths
se·bil·la \səˈbilə\ *n* -s [modif. of F *sébile*, prob. fr. Ar *zabīl* date basket, sack] **:** a wooden receptacle used by stonecutters and ore assayers
seb·kha *also* **seb·ka** \ˈsebkə\ *or* **sab·a·kha** \ˈsabəkə\ *or* **sab·kha** \ˈsabkə\ *n* -s [Ar *sabkhah* saline infiltration, shallow lagoon] **:** a smooth flat often saline plain in northern Africa sometimes occupied after a rain by a shallow lake
seb·or·rhea *or* **seb·or·rhoea** \,sebəˈrēə\ *n* -s [NL, fr. *sebi-* + *-rrhea*] **:** a functional disturbance of the sebaceous glands characterized by increased secretion and discharge of sebum that produces an oily appearance of the skin and the formation of greasy scales — **seb·or·rhe·ic** *or* **seb·or·rhoe·ic** \;==-;rēik\ *adj*
se·bright \ˈsē,brīt\ *n* [after Sir John S. *Sebright* †1846 Eng. agriculturist] **1** *usu cap* **:** an old British breed of rose-comb bantam fowls with dark-laced silvery or golden feathers **2** -s *often cap* **:** any bird of the Sebright breed
se·bum \ˈsēbəm\ *n* -s [L, tallow, grease] **:** the material secreted by the sebaceous glands
seb·un·doy \,sebən;dȯi\ *n, pl* **sebundoy** *or* **sebundoys** *usu cap* **1 a :** a people of southern Colombia **b :** a member of such people **2 :** the language of the Sebundoy people
se·bun·dy *also* **se·bun·dee** \səˈbəndē\ *n, pl* **sebundy** *or* **sebundies** [Hindi *sibandī*, fr. Per] **:** irregular native soldiery of the British in India
sec \ˈsek\ *adj* [F, lit., dry — more at SACK] *of champagne* **:** containing three to five percent sugar by volume **:** slightly sweet **:** drier than demi-sec and sweeter than extra sec **:** DRY
sec- *comb form, usu ital* [*secondary*] **:** secondary (sense 2e) — esp. in names of organic chemical radicals ⟨*sec*-butyl⟩
sec *abbr* **1** secant **2** second; secondary **3** secretary; secretariat **4** section **5** sector **6** [L *secundum*] according to **7** secured **8** security
se·ca·le \səˈkā(,)lē\ *n, cap* [NL, fr. L, rye] **:** a genus of cereal grasses having the 2-flowered spikelets in a dense spike, the lemma tipped with a long awn, and the empty glumes one-nerved — see RYE 1
sec·a·lin \ˈsekələn\ *n* -s [ISV *secal-* (fr. NL *Secale*) + *-in*] **1 :** a prolamin obtained from rye **2 :** SECALOSE
sec·a·lose \-,lōs\ *n* -s [NL *Secale* + E *-ose*] **:** a polysaccharide made up of fructose units obtained from green rye and oats or from rye flour
sec·a·mo·ne \,sekəˈmō(,)nē\ *n, cap* [NL, modif. of L *scammonia* scammony] **:** a genus of Old World tropical woody vines (family Asclepiadaceae) bearing flowers with rotate corollas and scales of the crown with distinct tips
¹se·cant \ˈsē,kant, -,kaa(ə)nt, -kənt\ *adj* [L *secant-, secans*, pres. part. of *secare* to cut — more at SAW] **:** CUTTING ⟨a ~ line⟩
²secant \"\ *n* -s [NL *secant-, secans*, fr. L, pres. part. of *secare*] **1 :** a straight line cutting a curve at two or more points **2 a :** a straight line drawn from the center of a circle through one end of a circular arc to a tangent drawn from the other end of the arc **b :** the ratio of this line to the radius of the circle **:** the reciprocal of the cosine — abbr. *sec*
sec art *abbr* [L *secundum artem*] according to art
sec·a·teur \ˈsekə,tə̄(r *also* -,tə(r\ *n* -s [F *sécateur*, fr. L *secare* to cut + F *-ateur* -ator (fr. OF *-atour*)] *chiefly Brit* **:** SCISSORS, SHEARS — usu. used in pl. ⟨roses and other tough flowers are cut with a pair of ~s —*Punch*⟩
¹sec·co \ˈse(,)kō\ *n* -s [It, fr. *secco*, adj., dry, fr. L *siccus* — more at SACK] **:** the art of painting on dry plaster with pigments suspended in a water-thinned binding vehicle — called also *fresco secco*; compare FRESCO 1a(1)
²secco \"\ *adj* (*or adv*) [It, lit., dry] **1 :** short and very staccato — used as a direction in music **2** *of a recitative* **:** accompanied only by the instrument or instruments (as the harpsichord) playing the continuo
Sec·co·tine \ˈsekə,tēn, ;==ˈ=\ *trademark* — used for an adhesive cement
se·cede \səˈsēd, sēˈ-\ *vi* -ED/-ING/-S [L *secedere*, fr. *sed-, se-* apart (fr. *sed, se* without) + *cedere* to go — more at IDIOT, CEDE] **:** to withdraw into isolation **:** leave a group **:** QUIT; *esp* **:** to withdraw from an organization, communion, or federation (as a church or political party) ⟨*seceded* from the conversation —Elizabeth Bowen⟩ ⟨about 10 more deputies have *seceded* from the government majority —*Atlantic*⟩
se·ced·er \-də(r)\ *n* -s **1 :** one that secedes **2** *usu cap* **:** a member of the Secession Church of Scotland or any of its daughter churches
se·cern \səˈsərn,sēˈ-\ *vb* -ED/-ING/-S [L *secernere* to separate, distinguish — more at SECRET] *vt* **1 :** SEPARATE; *esp* **:** to discriminate in thought **:** DISTINGUISH **2** *also* **se·cer·nate** \-,nāt\ [*secernate* fr. *secern* + *-ate*] **:** SECRETE ~ *vi* **:** SEPARATE
se·cern·ent \-_nənt\ *n* -s [*secern* + *-ent*] **:** something that secretes or promotes secretion
se·cern·ment \-nmənt\ *n* -s **:** the act or process of secerning
¹se·cesh \səˈsesh, sēˈ-\ *n, pl* **secesh** [by shortening & alter. fr. *secession & secessionist*] **:** a U. S. secessionist
²secesh \"\ *adj* **:** of or relating to U. S. secessionists or secessionism
secess *n* -ES [L *secessus*, fr. *secessus*, past part. of *secedere*] *obs* **:** RETIREMENT, SECESSION
se·ces·sion \səˈseshən, sēˈ-\ *n* -s [L *secession-, secessio* withdrawal, secession, fr. *secessus* (past part. of *secedere* to withdraw, secede) + *-ion-, -io* -ion — more at SECEDE] **1 :** withdrawal into privacy or solitude **:** RETIREMENT ⟨such *secent* ~ from the trials of the status system —D.B.Meyer⟩ **2 :** formal withdrawal from an organization (as a religious communion or political party or federation) ⟨~ from the union⟩ **3** [trans. of G *sezession*] **:** an Austrian style in art and architecture parallel with French art nouveau and approximately contemporary with it
se·ces·sion·al \-shənᵊl, -shnəl\ *adj* **:** of or relating to secession or to the Secession Church of Scotland
se·ces·sion·ism \-shə,nizəm\ *n* -s **:** the doctrine or policy of secession **:** the tenets of secessionists
se·ces·sion·ist \-sh(ə)nəst\ *n* -s **:** one who joins in a secession or maintains that secession is a right
sech *abbr* hyperbolic secant
sechelt *usu cap, var of* SEECHELT
se·chi·um \ˈsēkēəm\ *n, cap* [NL, perh. irreg. fr. Gk *sikyos* cucumber — more at CUCUMBER] **:** a genus of herbaceous vines (family Cucurbitaceae) having fruit with a single seed and yellow racemose flowers — see CHAYOTE
se·chua·na \,sechəˈwänə, sechˈw-\ *n, pl* **sechuana** *or* **sechuanas** *usu cap* **:** TSWANA
seck \ˈsek\ *dial var of* SACK
se·cle \ˈsekəl\ *n* -s [L *saeculum* generation, age, century — more at SECULAR] *archaic* **:** CENTURY, CYCLE, AGE
sec leg *abbr* [L *secundum legem*] according to law
se·clude \səˈklüd, sēˈ-\ *vt* -ED/-ING/-S [ME *secluden* to keep away, forbid to enter, fr. L *secludere* to confine, separate, seclude, fr. *sed-, se-* apart (fr. *sed, se* without) + *-cludere* (fr. *claudere* to shut, close) — more at IDIOT, CLOSE] **1 a :** to shut up apart **:** confine in a place hard to reach or enter **:** make inaccessible **:** SECRETE, HIDE **b :** to remove or separate (oneself or another) from intercourse or outside influence **:** withdraw into solitude **:** ISOLATE ⟨was accused . . . of an intention to ~ himself in magnificent isolation —Robert Grant †1940⟩ **2** *obs* **a :** to exclude or debar from a privilege, rank, or dignity **:** expel or bar from a membership or office ⟨22 of the old *secluded* members having been at the House door the last week to demand entrance —Samuel Pepys⟩ **b :** to exclude from consideration **c :** to keep out from a place or society **3 :** to shut off **:** PROTECT, SCREEN ⟨a *secluded* spot frequented by those interested in fishing and tramping —*Amer. Guide Series: N.H.*⟩ **4** *obs* **:** to separate by or as if by a barrier **:** keep apart or distinct ⟨nothing but clergy could us two ~ —Andrew Marvell⟩
secluded *adj* **1 :** screened or hidden from view **:** SEQUESTERED ⟨a ~ valley⟩ **2 :** living in seclusion **:** SOLITARY ⟨~ monks⟩ — **se·clud·ed·ly** *adv* — **se·clud·ed·ness** *n* -ES
se·cluse \səˈklüs, sēˈ-\ *adj* [L *seclusus*, past part. of *secludere*] **:** SECLUDED, RETIRED, WITHDRAWN
se·clu·sion \səˈklüzhən, sēˈ-\ *n* -s [ML *seclusion-, seclusio*, fr. L *seclusus* (past part. of *secludere*) + *-ion-, -io* -ion] **1 :** the act of secluding ⟨the ~ of prisoners in cells⟩ **2 :** the condition of being secluded ⟨yellow violets are common . . . in the ~ of damp woods —*Amer. Guide Series: N.H.*⟩ **3 :** a secluded or isolated place **4** *Scots law* **:** the act of keeping out **:** EXCEPTION, EXCLUSION
se·clu·sion·ist \-zh(ə)nəst\ *n* -s **:** one favoring seclusion: as **a :** an advocate of monasticism **b :** one favoring exclusion of immigrants of specified races from his country
se·clu·sive \səˈklüs|iv, sēˈ-, -üz|, |ēv *also* |əv\ *adj* [fr. *seclusion*, after such pairs as E *inclusion: inclusive*] **:** tending or serving to seclude; *esp* **:** inclined to seclude oneself **:** disposed to seek retirement or solitude — **se·clu·sive·ly** \|əvlē, -li\ *adv* — **se·clu·sive·ness** \|ivnəs, |ēv- *also* |əv-\ *n* -ES
sec nat *abbr* [L *secundum naturam*] naturally
seco- *comb form* [L *secare* to cut + E *-o-*] **:** having an opened ring — in names of organic chemical compounds ⟨2,3-*seco*cholestane⟩
sec·o·barbital \,se(,)kō+\ *n* [fr. *Seconal*, a trademark + *barbital*] **:** a barbiturate $C_{12}H_{18}N_2O_3$ used chiefly in the form of its bitter hygroscopic powdery sodium salt as a hypnotic and sedative; 5-allyl-5-(1-methyl-butyl)-barbituric acid
sec·odont \ˈsekə,dänt\ *adj* [ISV *sec-* (fr. L *secare* to cut) + *-odont* — more at SAW] **:** of, relating to, or having teeth adapted for cutting
Sec·o·nal \ˈsekə,nȯl, -,nal, -_nᵊl\ *trademark* — used for secobarbital
¹sec·ond \ˈsekənd, -ənt, *before a consonant often* -kən *sometimes* -kᵊŋ\ *adj* [ME *second, secound*, fr. OF *second*, fr. L *secundus* second, following, favorable, fr. *sequi* to follow — more at SUE] **1 a** (1) **:** being number two in a countable series ⟨the ~ day⟩ — see NUMBER table (2) **:** being a type of grammatical declension or conjugation conventionally placed second in a standard arrangement of the types (3) **:** being the next to the lowest forward gear or speed in an automotive vehicle **b :** next to the first in place or time ⟨~ in line for promotion⟩ **c** (1) **:** next to the first in value, power, excellence, dignity, or degree ⟨her husband was the ~ man in the nation —Martha T. Stephenson⟩ ⟨a ~ car⟩ ⟨the teaching of English as a ~ language —L.L.Rockwell⟩ ⟨production facilities ~ to none —*Punch*⟩ (2) **:** INFERIOR, SUBORDINATE **d :** ranking next below the top of a grade or degree in authority or precedence — used in titles ⟨~ mate⟩ **e :** ALTERNATE, OTHER ⟨every ~ Englishman calls himself shy — *Time*⟩ ⟨elects a mayor every ~ year⟩ **f :** resembling, suggesting, or behaving like a prototype **:** ANOTHER ⟨a ~ Cato⟩ **g :** ingrained by discipline, training, or effort **:** ACQUIRED ⟨~ nature⟩ **2 :** of or relating to a part in concerted or ensemble music typically lower in pitch than the first or to the player or singer performing this part ⟨~ violin⟩ ⟨~ bass⟩ **3 :** being between 1.51 and 2.50 on the magnitude scale — used of the magnitude of a star
²second \"\ *n* -s **1 a :** number two in a countable series ⟨the ~ of the month⟩ **b :** one that is next after the first in rank, position, or any other serial order ⟨the ~ in line⟩ **2 :** one who assists or supports another; *esp* **:** the supporter of a duelist or pugilist ⟨his ~s have to pick him up and yet he's the winner —Charles Oldfather⟩ — compare PRINCIPAL **3 a :** the musical interval embracing two diatonic degrees **b :** a tone at this interval; *specif* **:** the second note or tone of a scale **:** SUPERTONIC **c :** the harmonic combination of two tones a second apart **4 a :** an article of merchandise that is of a grade inferior to the best or that does not conform to a standard grade — usu. used in pl. **b seconds** *pl* **:** tobacco leaves of an inferior quality — compare LEAF 1c(4) **5 a :** SECOND-IN-COMMAND **b :** one having authority or precedence next below that of a person (as a mate or lieutenant) ranking first in a grade or degree ⟨sent the mate ashore to see if he could hire a ~⟩ **6 :** the act or declaration by which a parliamentary motion is seconded ⟨do I hear a ~⟩ **7 a :** a place rated as secondary or inferior to the first (as in an examination, competition, or contest) **:** SECOND CLASS **b :** one obtaining such a place **8 :** SECONDE **9 :** SECOND BASE **10 :** the second gear or speed in an automotive vehicle ⟨the gears locked in ~ —Herbert Passin⟩ **11 :** a playing card that is next under or only a few cards removed from the top card of a pack being dealt and is dealt instead of the top card by card-sharpers or in card tricks — used esp. in the phrase *to deal seconds*; compare BOTTOM DEALER, SECOND DEALER **12 seconds** *pl* **:** a second helping of food ⟨hungry farmhands who called for ~s⟩ **13 :** SECOND PERSON
³second \"\ *adv* [ME *secounde*, fr. *second, secound*, adj.] **1 :** in the second place **:** SECONDLY **2 :** with one exception ⟨the nation's ~ largest city⟩
⁴second \"\ *n* -s [ME *seconde, secunde*, fr. ML *secunda*, fr. L, fem. of *secundus*, adj., second; fr. its being the second sexagesimal division of a unit, as a minute is the first] **1 :** the 60th part of a minute of angular measure ⟨5 minutes and 10 ~s north of this place⟩ — symbol ″ **2 :** the 60th part of a minute of time; *specif* **:** the cgs unit of time **:** 1/86,400 part of the mean solar day — compare SIDEREAL SECOND **3 :** an instant of time **:** MOMENT ⟨said he'd be back in a ~⟩ **4 :** a unit of measure of the Saybolt viscosity of oils equal to one second of time
⁵second \", *in sense 5* səˈkänd\ *vt* -ED/-ING/-S [MF or L; MF *seconder*, fr. L *secundare*, fr. *secundus* favorable — more at ¹SECOND] **1 a :** to give support or encouragement to (a person or his efforts) **:** back up **:** ASSIST ⟨warmly ~*ed* his daughter's efforts toward an education —W.J.Ghent⟩ **b** *obs* **:** to serve as follower or retainer of **:** ATTEND, ACCOMPANY **c** (1) **:** to support (a fighting man or group) in combat **:** bring up reinforcements for **:** act as second to (2) *obs* **:** to take the place of (a fallen fighter) **:** SUCCEED **2 a :** to support or assist (a speaker or a cause) in contention or debate ⟨was ~*ed* in this by the other members of the delegation —Jane Nickerson⟩ **b :** to endorse (a motion or a nomination) so that it may be debated or voted on under parliamentary procedure **c** *obs* **:** to act in support of (an opinion or its holder) **:** CONFIRM, CORROBORATE **3** [¹*second*] **a :** to be second to **:** FOLLOW ⟨lumbering is the leading industry, ~*ed* by agriculture —*Amer. Guide Series: Texas*⟩ **b** *archaic* **:** REPEAT — used esp. of a blow **4** [¹*second*] *obs* **:** to parallel (something) with an equivalent **:** bring forward the equal of **5** [F *second*, n., second position (in the phrase *en second* in second position, subordinate), fr. *second*, adj.] *Brit* **:** to remove (a military officer) temporarily from a regiment or corps for employment on the staff or in some appointment outside a regiment **:** attach temporarily **:** LEND ⟨holds the rank of captain in the Royal Engineers, ~*ed* for special duties —Nevil Shute⟩
second advent *n, usu cap S&A* **:** ADVENT 2b
second adventist *n, usu cap S&A* [*second advent* + *-ist*] **:** ADVENTIST
second angle *n* **:** an angle of the Great Triangle formed on the palm by the intersection of the lines of Life and Mercury that when acute is usu. held by palmists to indicate a weak constitution — called also *lower angle*; compare FIRST ANGLE, THIRD ANGLE
secondar *var of* SECONDER
sec·ond·ar·i·ly \,sekən;derəlē, -li *sometimes* -kᵊŋ;-\ *adv* [ME *secundarily*, fr. *secundarie, secundarie* secondary + *-ly*] **1** *obs* **a** (1) **:** for the second time (2) **:** next in time after the first **b :** as a second consideration **:** SECONDLY **2 :** as an indirect result **:** in consequence of intermediate agents or causes **3 :** in a secondary place, manner, degree, or sense **:** INCIDENTALLY
sec·ond·ar·i·ness \-rēnəs, -rin-\ *n* -ES **:** the quality or state of being secondary
¹sec·ond·ary \ˈsekən,derē, -ri *sometimes* -kᵊŋ,d-\ *adj* [ME *secundarie, secondarie*, fr. L *secundarius*, fr. *secundus* second + *-arius* -ary — more at SECOND] **1 a :** of second rank, importance, or value **:** next below the first in grade or class ⟨~ streets⟩ **b :** of less than first value or importance **:** INFERIOR, SUBORDINATE ⟨everything was ~ to the will to survive —Frank Rounds⟩ **c :** serving to assist or supplement **:** AUXILIARY, SUBSIDIARY ⟨~ boycott⟩ **d :** of, relating to, or constituting the second strongest of the three or four degrees of stress recognized by most linguists ⟨the third syllable of *basketball* carries the ~ stress⟩ ⟨the fourth syllable of *basketball floor* carries the ~ stress⟩ **e :** expressive of past time — used of a grammatical tense ⟨the imperfect, aorist, and pluperfect indicative are the Greek ~ tenses⟩ **2 a :** immediately derived from something original, primary, or basic **:** dependent on or following something fundamental or first **:** having derivative rank, position, or consequence ⟨a ~ producer, manufacturing aluminum alloys into nonfabricated forms from scrap aluminum —*New Republic*⟩; *esp* **:** being a derivative source for scholars ⟨a ~ history or analysis written after study of original material⟩ **b :** derivative from primary qualities — see SECONDARY QUALITY **c :** formed later than and often from the substance of earlier mineral deposits (as by weathering or by groundwater action) **d :** of or relating to the induced current or its circuit in an induction coil or transformer ⟨a ~ coil⟩ ⟨~ voltage⟩ **e :** characterized by replacement in the second degree **:** resulting from the substitution of two atoms or groups in a molecule ⟨a ~ salt⟩ ⟨~ phosphates⟩; *esp* **:** being or characterized by a carbon atom united by two valences to chain or ring members ⟨~ butyl $CH_3CH_2CH(CH_3)$—⟩ — compare PRIMARY 5, TERTIARY **f** (1) **:** not first in order of occurrence or development **:** relating to or derived from a later stage of differentiation or growth (2) **:** produced by activity of formative tissue and esp. cambium other than that at a growing point **g** (1) **:** dependent or consequent on another disease ⟨Bright's disease is often ~ to scarlet fever⟩ (2) **:** occurring or being in the second stage ⟨~ symptoms of syphilis⟩ (3) **:** occurring some time after the original injury ⟨a ~ hemorrhage⟩ **h :** produced by a second process (as by treatment of old metal and alloys, sweepings, or drosses) **:** not obtained directly from ore **3 a :** of or relating to the second order or stage in a series ⟨the stone will be hauled . . . to a ~ and tertiary crusher —*Wall Street Jour.*⟩ **b** *obs* (1) **:** MESOZOIC (2) **:** PALEOZOIC **c :** of, relating to, or being the second segment of the wing of a bird or the quills of this segment **d :** of or relating to a school intermediate between elementary school and college **e :** more advanced than a primary stage **:** next above the first in grade or class
²secondary \"\ *n* -ES [ME *secundarie*, fr. *secundarie, secondarie*, adj.] **1 :** one occupying a subordinate or auxiliary position rather than that of a principal: as **a :** DELEGATE, DEPUTY **b :** a former officer of the corporation of the City of London **c :** a clergyman of second rank on the staff of an English cathedral **2 :** a defensive football backfield — contrasted with *line* **3 a :** the star of lesser mass or brightness in a double-star system **:** COMPANION 4d **b :** SATELLITE **4 :** a secondary electrical circuit or coil **5 a :** a cyclone relatively small in extent but often intense within the outer isobars of an older and larger storm **b :** a small area of low barometric pressure associated with a larger primary one **6 a :** any of the quill feathers arising from the forearm of a bird — see BIRD illustration **b :** one of the hind wings of an insect (as a butterfly or moth) **c :** one of the tubercles on the test of a sea urchin that is noticeably larger than a miliary tubercle but much smaller than a primary; *also* **:** a spine borne by such a tubercle
secondary accent *n* **:** an accent in compound musical measures other than that on the first beat (as on the third beat in 4/4 or on the fourth in 6/8 time)
secondary alcohol *n* **:** an alcohol that is characterized by the group >CHOH consisting of a carbon atom holding the hydroxyl group and one hydrogen atom and attached by its other two valences to other carbon atoms in a chain or ring and that can be oxidized to a ketone
secondary amine *n* **:** an amine (as dimethylamine or piperidine) having two organic substituents attached to the nitrogen atom
secondary axis *n* **:** a line through the center of a thin lens or through the center of curvature of a concave or convex mirror other than the principal axis of the lens or mirror
secondary battery *n* **1 :** STORAGE CELL **2 :** the guns of lesser caliber in a man-of-war having more than one caliber of guns exclusive of antiaircraft guns
secondary body *n* **:** the part of a plant developed from cambial layers — compare PRIMARY BODY
secondary boycott *n* **:** the boycott of an employer by his unionized employees at the instance of another employer's unionized employees in order to induce the first employer to help the cause of the second's employees in a labor dispute usu. by bringing pressure to bear on the second employer
secondary bud *n* **:** ACCESSORY BUD

secondary burial *n* **:** the reburial of human remains or the reburied remains — contrasted with *primary burial*
secondary cambium *n* **:** any of several formative layers that arise after the initial cambial layer in some roots (as of the beet) and produce a ring of tissue
secondary capitulum *n* **:** one of the six small cells surmounting each of the capitula in the antheridium of Characeae
secondary cell *n* **:** STORAGE CELL — compare PRIMARY CELL
secondary circle *n* **:** a great circle through the poles of another great circle and perpendicular to its plane
secondary color *n* **:** a color formed by mixing primary colors in equal or equivalent quantities **:** BINARY COLOR
secondary cortex *n* **:** a phelloderm developed in the cortex
secondary covert *n* **:** a wing covert covering the base of a secondary of a bird
secondary distribution *n* **:** the sale of a large block of an already outstanding stock through dealers but off the floor of an exchange
secondary dormancy *n* **:** dormancy induced in seeds capable of germinating immediately after ripening by the presence of one or more conditions unfavorable to germination
secondary electron *n* **:** an electron belonging to a beam of secondary radiation or emission (as an electron emitted from a metal surface when the surface is bombarded by high speed electrons)
secondary emission *n* **:** the emission of electrons from a surface that is bombarded by electrons or ions from a primary source
secondary enrichment *n* **:** ENRICHMENT 2
secondary evidence *n* **:** legal evidence admitted upon failure to obtain primary evidence (as a copy of a contract when the original is lost)
secondary fermentation *n* **:** the fermentation initiated by the addition of sugar or a sweet syrup to wine (as champagne and other sparkling wines) to induce natural carbonation — see CURÉE; compare DOSAGE
secondary gain *n* **:** pleasure derived from a neurosis primarily necessary to the individual for other reasons
secondary group *n* **:** a social group characterized by conscious collective interest and formal association — contrasted with *primary group;* compare GESELLSCHAFT
secondary growth *n* **:** growth in plants that results from the activity of a cambium producing increase esp. in diameter, is mainly responsible for the bulk of the plant body, and supplies protective, supporting, and conducting tissue — compare PRIMARY GROWTH
secondary host *n* **:** INTERMEDIATE HOST 1
secondary infection *n* **:** infection initiated by spores or other infective bodies produced in a primary infection or another secondary infection
secondary meaning *n* **:** a close and prolonged identification in the public mind of a name, description, or designation of goods, services, or a product that is not in itself susceptible of being a technical trademark with a particular manufacturer or producer who under the law becomes entitled to exclusive use ⟨evidence was insufficient to show that the word had acquired a *secondary meaning* entitling it to protection⟩
secondary meristem *n* **:** a meristem that develops from cells that have differentiated and functioned as part of a mature tissue system and then become meristematic again — compare PRIMARY MERISTEM
secondary minimum *n* **:** a sometimes very slight depression in the light curve of an eclipsing variable that occurs when the fainter of the two stars is eclipsed by the brighter — compare PRIMARY MINIMUM
secondary modern school *n* **:** a British secondary school of a type established since World War I providing a general education — called also *modern school;* compare SECONDARY TECHNICAL SCHOOL
secondary mycelium *n* **:** a dikaryotic mycelium
secondary nucleus *n* **:** PRIMARY ENDOSPERM NUCLEUS
secondary periderm *n* **:** a periderm layer other than the first and outermost layer
secondary phloem *n* **:** phloem produced by the cambium — compare PRIMARY PHLOEM
secondary port *n* **:** a port for which tide tables list differentials from the predictions for a standard port
secondary quality *n* **:** a mode of perception induced by some character of an object that does not coincide with the perception itself ⟨such qualities, which in truth are nothing in the objects themselves, but powers to produce various sensations in us by their primary qualities, i.e. by the bulk, figure, texture, and motion of their insensible parts, as colors, sounds, tastes, etc., these I call *secondary qualities* —John Locke⟩ — contrasted with *primary quality* and *tertiary quality*
secondary radiation *or* **secondary rays** *n* **:** rays (as X rays or beta rays) emitted by molecules or atoms as the result of the incidence of a primary radiation and of the same general nature as the latter
secondary rainbow *n* **:** a rainbow that is concentric with and near but somewhat larger and fainter than a primary rainbow and that differs from it in formation in that there are two internal reflections and the red is seen on the inside edge of the bow
secondary ray *n* **:** a vascular ray formed in the cambium — compare PRIMARY RAY
secondary reserve *n* **:** bank assets (as government securities and bank acceptances) readily convertible into cash to replenish primary reserves
secondary road *n* **1 :** a road not of primary importance whose classification and maintenance vary according to township, county, and state regulations **2 :** FEEDER ROAD
secondary root *n* **1 :** one of the branches of a primary root **2 :** ADVENTITIOUS ROOT
secondary school *n* **:** a school more advanced in grade than an elementary school and offering general, technical, vocational, or college-preparatory courses — compare GYMNASIUM 2, LYCÉE, PUBLIC SCHOOL 1
secondary screwworm *n* **:** a screwworm (*Callitroga Macellaria*)
secondary seventh *n* **:** a seventh chord based on some other tone than the dominant of the key
secondary sex characteristic *or* **secondary sex character** *n* **:** a morphological or psychological peculiarity (as the breasts of a female mammal or the nuptial plumage of a male bird) that becomes differentiated at puberty or in seasonal breeders at the breeding season in members of one sex and that is not directly concerned with reproduction
secondary spectrum *n* **1 :** the spectrum of an element in the molecular state as distinct from its atomic line spectrum **2 :** residual dispersion by a lens that has been corrected as far as possible for chromatic aberration **3 :** the fainter of the two superimposed spectra of a spectroscopic binary star
secondary spermatocyte *n* **:** a spermatocyte that gives rise to spermatids **:** a spermatocyte of the last generation before the spermatozoon — compare PRIMARY SPERMATOCYTE
secondary spore *n* **:** a spore of a basidiomycete other than a basidiospore
secondary substance *n, Aristotelianism* **:** GENUS 2
secondary syphilis *n* **:** the second stage of syphilis appearing from 2 to 6 months after primary infection, marked by lesions esp. in the skin but also in other organs and tissues, and lasting from 3 to 12 weeks
secondary technical school *n* **:** a British secondary school emphasizing technical studies — compare SECONDARY MODERN SCHOOL
secondary triad *n* **:** a musical triad not based on the tonic, dominant, or subdominant of the key — compare PRIMARY TRIAD
secondary twinning *n* **:** the externally caused twinning of crystals (as by pressure in a rock mass after formation of the mineral)
secondary tympanic membrane *n* **:** a membrane closing the cochlear fenestra and separating the scala tympani from the middle ear
secondary use *n, chiefly Eng law* **:** SHIFTING USE
secondary wall *n* **:** the portion of a plant-cell wall formed internal to and subsequent to deposition of the primary wall after the cell has attained its final size and shape usu. constituting most of the cell wall, often being very complex and consisting of several anisotropic layers, and frequently being buttressed internally by or consisting almost entirely of prominent rings, spirals, bars, or reticulations
secondary word *n* **:** a word whose immediate constituents are free forms (as the compound *catfish*) or a free form and a bound form (as the secondary derivative *fisher*)
se·con·da vol·ta \sə͵kōndə'vōltə\ *n* [It, second time] **:** a second ending of a musical section performed only at the repetition of the section and with omission of the first ending
second ballot *n* **:** an electoral system in which the voters choose between the two candidates with the greatest number of votes in an earlier election that fails to produce a majority for any one candidate
second base *n* **1 :** the base that must be touched second by a base runner in baseball **2 :** the player position for defending the area of the baseball infield on the first-base side of second base
second baseman *n* **:** the baseball player stationed at the second-base position — see BASEBALL illustration
second-best \ˈ=ˌ=ˈ=\ *adj* [ME *secunde best,* fr. *second, secound, secunde* second + *best*] **:** next to the best ⟨give unto my wife my *second-best* bed with the furniture —Shak.⟩
[1]**second best** *n* [*second-best*] **:** one that is below or after the best ⟨look upon the president's proposal as a *second best* —*New Republic*⟩
[2]**second best** *adv* [*second-best*] **:** in second place — often used in the phrase *come off second best*
second birth *n* **:** REGENERATION 2
second blessing *n* **:** an experience of sanctification coming sometime after conversion as a second gift (as in holiness churches) of the Holy Spirit and adding to justification the power to live a holy life
second bottom *n* **:** the first terrace above a floodplain
second breath *n* **:** SECOND WIND
second cause *n* **:** a cause caused by something else ⟨a *second cause* through which God, the First Cause, works⟩
second chamber *n* **:** the house in a bicameral legislature that is inferior in status and powers on the ground of constitutional prescription, of custom, or of the locus of responsibility of the ministry, is often orig. designed as a check on the other house, and is often constituted on a different basis (as heredity) from election
second childhood *n* **:** DOTAGE
second class *n* **1 a :** the second and usu. next to highest group in a classification; *specif* **:** the group of persons who have obtained next to highest distinction in an honors course at a British university **b :** a place in or a member of such a group **2 :** a class of accommodations (as on a railroad train) superior to third or tourist class and inferior to first class — compare CABIN CLASS **3 :** a class of U.S. or Canadian mail comprising newspapers and periodicals sent to regular subscribers — see TRANSIENT SECOND CLASS **4 :** the second rank in the rising scale of ranks in the Boy Scouts of America or the Girl Scouts of America — compare FIRST CLASS, TENDERFOOT
[1]**second-class** \ˈ=ˌ=\ *adj* [*second class*] **1 :** of or relating to the next to the highest grade in a series ⟨a *second-class* railway carriage⟩ ⟨a *second-class* honors degree⟩ **2 :** INFERIOR, MEDIOCRE ⟨maybe that is the way to conduct *second-class* works —Virgil Thomson⟩; *esp* **:** socially or economically deprived, suppressed, or limited ⟨racism and its attendant theory of the *second-class* citizen —S.H.Lowell⟩
[2]**second-class** \"\ *adv* **:** by a second-class conveyance **:** with second-class accommodations ⟨travel *second-class*⟩
second classman *n* **:** a third-year cadet or midshipman (as at a military or naval academy) — compare FIRST CLASSMAN, PLEBE
second coming *n, usu cap S&C* **:** ADVENT 2b
second cranial nerve *n* **:** OPTIC NERVE
second crop *n* **1 :** a second harvest from the regrowth or second growth of a crop (as broomcorn) after harvesting earlier in the season **2 :** a crop planted after harvesting another crop on the same land earlier in the season
second crown bud *n* **:** a flower bud (as on the chrysanthemum) that may develop after the first crown bud has been removed
second curvature *n* **:** TORSION 2
second-cut file \ˈ=ˌ=-\ *n* **:** a file of a fineness between bastard and smooth
second day *n, usu cap S* **:** MONDAY — used chiefly by the Friends
second dealer *n* **:** one skilled in dealing the second card from the top of a deck as if it were the first — compare BOTTOM DEALER
second death *n* **:** condemnation to eternal separation from God **:** punishment of the souls of the lost after bodily death
second deck *n* **1 :** the first complete deck of a ship below the main deck **2 :** the main deck on a typical merchant ship — see DECK
second-degree \ˈ=ˌ==ˈ=\ *adj* [fr. the phrase *second degree*] **:** of a degree next to the first; *specif* **:** of a degree of criminal culpability or seriousness next to first-degree ⟨*second-degree* murder⟩
second-degree burn *n* **:** a burn characterized by pain, blistering, and superficial destruction of the dermis accompanied by edema and hyperemia of the tissues beneath the burn
second derivative *n* **:** the derivative of the derivative of a function
second-drawer \ˈ=ˌ=ˈ=(=)\ *adj* [fr. the phrase *second drawer*] **:** of a grade next to the top **:** less than primary or first-rate **:** INFERIOR, MEDIOCRE ⟨preoccupied with money and with quick, *second-drawer* ways of making it —Budd Schulberg⟩
se·conde \sə'känd, -'gä-\ *n* -s [F, fr. fem. of *second,* adj. — more at SECOND] **:** a parry or guard fencing position defending the lower outside right target in which the hand is in a position of pronation, the arm slightly bent, and the tip of the blade directed at the opponent's knee — compare OCTAVE 4
seconded *past of* SECOND
second empire *adj, usu cap S&E* [fr. the noun phrase *Second Empire* (the French empire of 1852–1871 under Napoleon III †1873 emperor of the French), trans. of F *second Empire*] **:** of or relating to a style in furniture and architecture developed in France under Napoleon III and marked by heavy ornate modification of Empire styles
[1]**sec·ond·er** \ˈsekəndə(r)\ *n* -s [[5]*second* + *-er*] **:** one who seconds what another attempts, affirms, moves, or proposes ⟨a most efficient ~ of the department when the House and Administration were harmonious —Allan Nevins⟩
[2]**seconder** *or* **sec·ond·ar** \"\ *n* -s [*seconder* modif. (influenced by [1]*second* and *-er*) of L *secundarius,* adj., secondary; *secondar* modif. (influenced by [1]*second*) of L *secundarius,* adj. — more at SECONDARY] **:** a university student formerly second in social rank to a son of a nobleman — compare TERNAR
second fiddle *n* **:** one who fills a subordinate or secondary role or function — usu. used in the phrase *to play second fiddle* ⟨played *second fiddle* in her own home to her own sister —V.S.Pritchett⟩
second filial generation *n* **:** the second generation from a cross produced by random interbreeding of the first filial generation and resulting in recombination and segregation of the various characters in which the members of the parental generation differ — compare MENDEL'S LAW
second-first \ˈ=ˌ=ˈ=\ *adj* **:** of, relating to, or being the sabbath second between Passover and Pentecost and first after the beginning of the Paschal week
second floor *n* **:** SECOND STORY
second-foot \ˈ=ˌ=ˈ=\ *n* **:** a unit of flow used esp. in connection with the flow of streams that is equal to one cubic foot per second
second-generation \ˈ=ˌ=ˌ==ˈ==\ *adj* [fr. the phrase *second generation*] **1 :** being a member of the second generation of a family to be born in the U.S. **2 :** native-born of foreign or mixed parentage ⟨the *second-generation* girl avoids . . . the feminine alliances that typify the girl of American-born parents —S.G.Dulsky⟩
second growth *n* **:** a growth developing after another growth or on land devoted primarily to some other crop; *specif* **:** forest trees that come up naturally after removal of the first growth by cutting or by fire
second-guess \ˈ=ˌ=ˈ=\ *vt* [fr. the phrase *second guess*] **1 :** to apply hindsight to or to the course of action of **2 a :** OUTGUESS **b :** PREDICT — **second-guesser** \ˈ=ˌ=ˈ==\ *n*
[1]**second hand** *n* [ME *seconde honde,* fr. *seconde, second, secound,* adj., second + *honde, hand* hand] **1 :** an intermediate person or means **:** INTERMEDIARY — usu. used in the phrase *at second hand* ⟨even this historical fact I had only at *second hand,* from my aunt —Ben Riker⟩ **2 :** an assistant foreman esp. in textile industries **3 :** an assistant hand **:** a manual laborer's helper **4 :** the second player to have the right to bid or the second player to play to any trick in bridge
[2]**second hand** *n* [[4]*second* + *hand*] **:** the hand marking seconds on a watch or clock — compare HOUR HAND, MINUTE HAND
[1]**secondhand** \ˈ=ˌ=ˈ=\ *adj* [[1]*second hand*] **1 :** received from or through an intermediary rather than directly from the source **:** BORROWED, DERIVED ⟨this is a ~ account of a memory of something once read, shaky evidence indeed —Ruth P. Randall⟩ **2 a :** used or worn by a previous owner **:** bought or acquired after being used by another **:** not new ⟨~ books⟩ ⟨~ clothing⟩ ⟨a ~ car⟩ **b :** dealing in secondhand merchandise ⟨a ~ bookstore⟩
[2]**secondhand** \"\ *adv* **:** at second hand **:** INDIRECTLY ⟨a region that, like the stars, man must know for the most part ~ —T.A.Manar⟩
secondhanded \ˈ=ˌ=ˈ==\ *adj* [[1]*second hand* + *-ed*] *chiefly dial* **:** SECONDHAND
sec·ond-hand·ed·ness *n* -ES [*secondhanded* + *-ness*] **:** the quality or state of being secondhand **:** JEJUNENESS ⟨actually to have read it all through must remove most *second-handedness* from one's mind —Cyril Connolly⟩
second head *n* **:** broken rice consisting of pieces one-third to three-fourths the size of the rice grains
second-in-command \ˈ=ˌ===ˈ=\ *n, pl* **seconds-in-command** **:** the person ranking next to the head **:** the military officer ranking next below the commanding officer
secondines *var of* SECUNDINES
seconding *pres part of* SECOND
second-in-hand \ˈ=ˌ==ˈ=\ *n* **:** [1]SECOND HAND 4
second injury fund *n* **:** a fund maintained by assessments collected from insurers out of which a worker injured a second time is paid an amount that when added to workmen's compensation benefits brings the total to the amount payable under workmen's compensation for the combined injuries
second intention *n* **1 :** a conception (as species, genus, whiteness) generalized from or formed by reflection on first intention **2 :** the healing of an incised wound by granulations that bridge the gap between skin edges — compare FIRST INTENTION
second inversion *n* **:** a musical chord with its fifth in the bass — see SEVENTH CHORD illustration
second joint *n* **:** the thigh segment of a fowl's leg — compare DRUMSTICK
second law of thermodynamics : LAW OF THERMODYNAMICS 2
second lieutenant *n* **1 :** an army, marine, or air force officer of the lowest commissioned rank **2 :** a Salvation Army officer ranking above a probationary lieutenant and below a first lieutenant
sec·ond·ly *adv* [ME *secoundly,* fr. *second, secound* second + *-ly*] **:** in the second place ⟨firstly it isn't true and ~ it isn't important⟩
second maxilla *n* **:** one of the paired appendages immediately behind the first maxillae of an arthropod that in an insect together form the labium
se·cond·ment \sə'kän(d)mənt\ *n* -s [[5]*second* + *-ment*] **:** the detachment of a person (as a military officer) from his regular organization for temporary assignment elsewhere
second mile *n* [so called fr. the precept of Jesus in Mt 5:41 (RSV) "if any one forces you to go one mile, go with him two miles"] **:** a deed of charity or kindness beyond the demands of duty — used chiefly in the phrase *go the second mile* ⟨employee benefits which go the *second mile* in human relations of this type —*Think*⟩
second mortgage *n* **:** a mortgage the lien of which is subordinate to that of a first mortgage — compare JUNIOR MORTGAGE
second mourning *n* **:** mourning dress of black relieved by white or of dark gray worn for a time after the period of strict mourning
second nature *n* **:** acquired ingrained habits or traits as distinguished from innate or instinctive ones ⟨conformity to the discipline of a small society had become almost his *second nature* —Edith Wharton⟩
second nerve *n* **:** OPTIC NERVE
sec·ond·ness *n* -ES **:** a fundamental category in Peircean philosophy comprising actual facts and expressive of necessity, force, and determination — compare FIRSTNESS, THIRDNESS
se·con·do \sə'kōn(͵)dō, -kän-\ *n, pl* **se·con·di** \-dē\ [It, fr. *secondo,* adj., second, fr. L *secundus* — more at SECOND] **:** the second part in a concerted piece; *esp* **:** the lower part (as in a piano duet) — compare PRIMO
second officer *n* **:** a second mate in the merchant service
second-order reaction \ˈ=ˌ=ˈ=-\ *n* **:** a chemical reaction in which the rate of reaction is proportional to the concentration of each of two reacting molecules — compare ORDER OF A REACTION
second papers *n pl* **:** a petition for citizenship that an alien seeking naturalization must file from two to seven years after his first papers
second person *n* **1 a :** a set of linguistic forms (as verb forms, pronouns, and inflectional affixes) referring to the person or thing addressed in the utterance in which they occur ⟨Latin *videtis* "you see" is in the *second person* plural⟩ ⟨English *you* is a pronoun of the *second person*⟩ **b :** a linguistic form belonging to such a set ⟨Latin *vides* "you see" and *is* "you go" are *second persons*⟩ **2 :** reference of a linguistic form to the person or thing addressed in the utterance in which it occurs ⟨the Latin verb ending *-s* that marks the *second person*⟩
second personal *adj* **:** of or relating to the second person ⟨a *second personal* pronoun⟩
second philosophy *n, Aristotelianism* **:** the special sciences or branches of science (as physics) — distinguished from *First Philosophy;* compare METAPHYSICS
second pointed *adj* **:** DECORATED 2
second public examination *n* **:** the final examination for the B.A. degree (as at Oxford University)
second-rate \ˈ=ˌ=ˈ=\ *adj* [fr. the phrase *second rate*] **:** of second or inferior quality or value **:** lacking excellence **:** MEDIOCRE ⟨will reject this slate of *second-rate* candidates⟩ — **sec·ond-rate·ness** *n* -ES
second-rater \ˈ=ˌ=ˈ==\ *n* **:** one that is second-rate ⟨a team made up of aging *second-raters*⟩
second reader *n, usu cap S&R* **:** a member of a Christian Science church or society chosen for a term of office to assist the First Reader in conducting services by reading aloud selections from the Bible
second reading *n* **1 :** the stage in the British legislative process following the first reading and usu. providing for debate on the principal features of a bill before its submission to a committee for consideration of details **2 :** the stage in the U.S. legislative process that occurs when a bill has been reported back from committee and that provides an opportunity for full debate and amendment before a vote is taken on the question of a third reading of the bill — compare LEGISLATION 1
second run *n* **:** the run of a motion picture under a second release
seconds *pl of* SECOND, *pres 3d sing of* SECOND
second sacker *n* **:** SECOND BASEMAN
second service *n* [so called fr. the fact that it follows Morning Prayer] *Church of England* **:** COMMUNION 2
second sheet *n* **1 :** an often blank sheet of writing paper used for the second and subsequent pages of a letter of which the first sheet bears a letterhead **2 :** a sheet of manifold paper
second sight *n* **:** the capacity to see remote or future objects or events **:** CLAIRVOYANCE, PRECOGNITION
second-sighted \ˈ=ˌ=ˈ==\ *adj* **:** having second sight — **second-sight·ed·ness** *n* -ES
second slip *n* **:** a fielding position in cricket near to and on the off side of first slip; *also* **:** a player fielding in this position — see CRICKET illustration
second sound *n* **:** transfer of heat which is much faster than conduction or convection, which is observed only in helium II, and in which waves of temperature resembling sound waves travel at speeds of about 20 meters per second

seconds pendulum *n* **:** a pendulum requiring exactly one second for each swing in either direction or two seconds for a complete vibration and having a length between centers of suspension and oscillation of 99.353 centimeters at sea level in latitude 45 degrees
second story *n* **1 :** the story just above the ground floor **2** *Brit* **:** the second story above the ground floor
second-story man *n* **:** a burglar who enters a house by an upstairs window **:** CAT BURGLAR
second-string \ˌ=ˌ=ˈ=\ *adj* [fr. the phrase *second string*] **1 :** being a substitute as distinguished from a regular (as on a football team) ⟨went so far as to have his *second-string* catcher . . . play second base in the eighth inning —Roscoe McGowen⟩ ⟨short road tours with *second-string* casts —*Current Biog.*⟩ — compare FIRST-STRING **2 :** being of the second or an inferior order of quality or importance ⟨reporters and *second-string* strategists —R.H.Rovere⟩
second table *n* **1 :** a position of inferiority **2 :** a second setting of tables at a meal partaken of by more persons than can be served at once
second team *n* **:** the members of a squad (as in football or basketball) used chiefly as substitute players
second thigh *n* **:** the part of the hind leg of a quadruped that lies between the stifle joint and the hock
second thought *n* **:** reconsideration after a decision subsequently regarded as impulsive, premature, or otherwise ill-taken ⟨*second thought* became more sober as the days advanced —F.L.Paxson⟩
second touch *n* **:** the second point to which pipe-organ keys or pistons may be moved in a double-touch action
second water *n* **:** the quality or luster next below first water — used of a gem (as a diamond or pearl)
second wind *n* **1 :** recovered full power of respiration after the first exhaustion during exertion due to improved action of the heart **2 :** renewed energy or capacity for effort and endurance ⟨the *second wind* of creative energy which would have carried their early brilliance into ripe maturity —De Lancey Ferguson⟩
se·cours \səˈkü(ə)r\ *n, pl* **secours** \"\ [MF, fr. OF *secors, sucors* — more at SUCCOR] **:** AID, ASSISTANCE, SUCCOR
se·cre·cy \ˈsēkrəsē, -si\ *n* -ES [alter. (influenced by *-cy*) of earlier *secretie*, fr. ME *secretee*, fr. *secre* secret (fr. MF *secré*, fr. L *secretus*) + *-tee, -te* -ty] **1 a :** the habit or practice of keeping secrets or maintaining privacy or concealment **:** SECRETIVENESS ⟨~ is an inherent feature of all governmental administration —C.J.Friedrich⟩ ⟨readily assured her of his ~ —Jane Austen⟩ **b :** the condition of being hidden or concealed ⟨complete ~ surrounded the meeting —*Current History*⟩ **2 :** something concealed or concealing **:** MYSTERY, SECRET ⟨the footsteps . . . sounded peculiarly soft and harmless in the gentle ~ of dusk —Elinor Wylie⟩ **3** *obs* **a :** confidential relationship **:** intimate confidence **:** TRUST **b :** PRIVACY, SECLUSION
sec reg *abbr* [L *secundum regulam*] according to rule
¹se·cret \ˈsēkrət, *usu* -əd·+V\ *adj, sometimes* -ER/-EST [ME, fr. MF, fr. L *secretus*, past part. of *secernere* to separate, distinguish, fr. *sed-, se-* apart (fr. *sed, se* without) + *cernere* to sift — more at IDIOT, CERTAIN] **1 a :** kept from knowledge or view **:** CONCEALED, HIDDEN ⟨advised him, against his own judgment, to keep his mission ~ for a time —W.C.Ford⟩ ⟨the baronage had plunged almost to a man into ~ conspiracies —J.R.Green⟩ **b :** marked by the habit of discretion or faithful concealment **:** loyal to a confidence **:** trustworthy in preserving secrecy **:** CONFIDENTIAL, CLOSEMOUTHED, RETICENT **c :** working with hidden aims or methods **:** UNDERCOVER ⟨a ~ agent⟩ **d :** UNACKNOWLEDGED, UNAVOWED, UNDECLARED ⟨a ~ enemy⟩ ⟨a ~ bride⟩ **2 :** remote from human frequentation or notice **:** RETIRED, SECLUDED ⟨~ harbors —R.W.Hatch⟩ **3 :** known or felt inwardly without avowal ⟨~ alarm⟩ ⟨~ exultation⟩ **:** INMOST ⟨his ~ soul⟩ **4 a :** revealed only to the initiated **:** ESOTERIC, MYSTIC ⟨the ~ learning of the cabalists⟩ **b :** lying beyond ordinary comprehension **:** relating to or dealing with mysteries or occult matters **:** ABSTRUSE, RECONDITE ⟨you ~, black, and midnight hags —Shak.⟩ **5 :** done or undertaken with evident purpose of concealment ⟨we must stand together . . . in ~ alliance —Jack London⟩ **6 :** GENITAL ⟨~ parts⟩ **7 :** constructed so as to elude observation or detection ⟨a ~ panel⟩ ⟨a ~ passage⟩ or to conceal means or mechanics ⟨~ nailing⟩ ⟨a ~ dovetail⟩ **8 :** INVISIBLE, UNSEEN **9 :** classified below top secret but above confidential in a scale rating the value of information to a nation's security — compare CLASSIFICATION 1f
syn COVERT, CLANDESTINE, STEALTHY, SURREPTITIOUS, FURTIVE, UNDERHAND, UNDERHANDED: SECRET is a general term applicable to anything hidden, concealed, known, or known about by a limited few. ⟨seized a lamp . . . and hurried towards the *secret* passage —Horace Walpole⟩ COVERT is the antonym of *overt* or *open;* it stresses the fact of being concealed or veiled ⟨some form of coercion, overt or *covert* —John Dewey⟩ ⟨the meaning of the *covert* addresses of a villain —W.M. Thackeray⟩ CLANDESTINE refers to a situation obtaining, a practice adhered to, a thing made or used in wary or timorous secrecy, often against usage, sanction, or authority ⟨she proposed a *clandestine* marriage, but he swore that when afterwards detected, it would cause his dismissal —Anthony Trollope⟩ ⟨hunted by the gestapo for his anti-Nazi pamphlets and *clandestine* magazine *La Pensée Libre* —*Time*⟩ STEALTHY may suggest slow, wary, sly avoidance of being observed as one proceeds in doing something evil, sinister, or reprehensible ⟨a valet, of *stealthy* step, thence conducted me, in silence, through many dark and intricate passages —E.A.Poe⟩ ⟨comparable to . . . the suffocation of the York princes in the Tower. I'll admit the setting is consonant with that sort of *stealthy*, romantic crime —W.H.Wright⟩ SURREPTITIOUS refers to actions done, emotions cherished, things held or enjoyed secretly, often with opportune cleverness, against usage or authority ⟨enjoying a *surreptitious* cigarette —P.G.Wodehouse⟩ ⟨over the paling of the garden we might obtain an oblique and *surreptitious* view —Henry James †1916⟩ FURTIVE implies sly, wary, slinking caution to escape being perceived, recognized, or apprehended ⟨asked the man, in a *furtive* frightened way —Charles Dickens⟩ ⟨*furtive* shortcuts across the fields of persons who might easily have bawled at me if they had caught sight of me —Siegfried Sassoon⟩ UNDERHAND and UNDERHANDED stress dishonest deception rather than merely the fact of secrecy in itself ⟨whatever scrape he may have been in, I'll warrant there was nothing mean or *underhanded* in his share of it . . . he hasn't a tricky or a dishonest bone in his body —C.B.Nordhoff & J.N.Hall⟩
²secret \"\ *n* -S [ME, fr. MF & L; MF *secret*, fr. L *secretum*, fr. neut. of *secretus*, past part. of *secernere* to separate, distinguish — more at ¹SECRET] **1 a :** something kept hidden **:** an unexplained or inscrutable process or fact (as an operation of God or of nature) **:** MYSTERY ⟨an intimation of the ~ of mysticism —Havelock Ellis⟩ **b :** something kept from the knowledge of others, concealed as one's private knowledge, or shared only confidentially with a few persons **:** information entrusted to one in confidence ⟨a man who knew the ~*s* of one's innermost soul —H.J.Laski⟩ — see TRADE SECRET **c :** a method, formula, or process used in an art or a manufacturing operation and divulged only to those of one's own company or craft ⟨~*s* long cherished by monkish wine makers⟩ **d secrets** *pl* **:** the practices or knowledge making up the shared discipline or culture of an esoteric society ⟨the ~*s* of the ancient Essenes⟩ **2** [ML *secreta*, fr. L, fem. of *secretus*, past part. of *secernere*] **:** a prayer said in a low or inaudible voice by the celebrant just before the preface in the mass **3 :** something taken to be a specific or key to some desired end ⟨called discreet and steady use of whiskey the ~ of his living to the age of a hundred⟩ **4 secrets** *pl* **:** PART 1d(3) **5 :** a coat of mail worn concealed under one's clothing — **in secret** *adv* **:** in a private manner or place **:** in secrecy ⟨already there existed *in secret* . . . a considerable opposition party —J.G.Lockhart⟩
³secret \"\ *adv* [¹secret] *archaic* **:** SECRETLY
⁴secret *vt* -ED/-ING/-S [¹secret] *obs* **:** ²SECRETE
secret- *or* **secreto-** *comb form* [*secretion*] **:** secretion ⟨*secret*in⟩ ⟨*secreto*motor⟩
¹se·cre·ta \səˈkrā(ˌ)tä\ *n, pl* **secre·tae** \-āˌtä\ [ML, fr. L, fem. of *secretus*, past part. of *secernere*] **:** SECRET 2
²secreta *pl of* SECRETUM
³se·cre·ta \səˈkrēd·ə, sēˈ-, -ētə\ *n pl* [NL, fr. L, neut. pl. of *secretus*, past part. of *secernere*] **:** products of secretion
se·cret·age \ˈsēkrəd·ij\ *n* -S [F *secrétage*, fr. *secréter* to carrot + *-age* — more at SECRETE] **:** the carroting of fur
se·cre·ta·gogue *also* **se·cre·to·gogue** \səˈkrēd·əˌgäg, sēˈ- *sometimes* -gōg\ *n* -S [*secretagogue* fr. *secret-* + *-agogue; secretogogue* irreg. (influenced by *-o-*) fr. *secret-* + *-agogue*] **:** a substance that stimulates secretion (as of the stomach or pancreas)
se·cre·taire \ˌsekrəˈta(a)(ə)r, -te(, |ə\ *n* -S [F *secrétaire* escritoire, secretary (person), fr. MF *secretaire* secretary (person), confidant, fr. OF, confidant, fr. ML *secretarius*] **:** ESCRITOIRE, SECRETARY
sec·re·tar·i·al \ˌsekrəˈterēəl, -ta(ə)r-, *in rapid speech* ÷ -kəˈt-\ *adj* **:** of or relating to a secretary or the work of a secretary
sec·re·tar·i·at *also* **sec·re·tar·i·ate** \ˌ==ˈterēət *sometimes* -ta(ə)r- *or* -ēˌat\ *n* -S [*secretariat* fr. F *secrétariat*, fr. ML *secretariatus*, fr. *secretarius* secretary, confidant + L *-atus* -ate; *secretariate* alter. (influenced by *-ate*) of *secretariat*] **1 :** the office or position of a secretary **2 :** a secretarial corps (as in a business office) **:** the working force of secretaries or the clerical staff of an organization **3 a :** the government administrative department presided over by a secretary-general or a cabinet secretary ⟨the ~ of state⟩ ⟨the United Nations ~⟩ **b :** the quarters occupied by a government secretariat **c :** the staff of a secretariat
sec·re·tary \ˈsekrəˌterē, *in rapid speech* ÷-k(ə)ˌt-\ *n* -ES [ME *secretarie*, fr. ML *secretarius* secretary, confidant, fr. L *secretum* secret + *-arius* -ary — more at SECRET] **1** *obs* **a :** one entrusted with the secrets or confidences of a superior **:** ADVISER, CONFIDANT **b :** one considered to understand the secrets of God or of nature or to have penetrated other mysteries **2 :** one employed to handle correspondence and manage routine and detail work for a superior **3 a :** an officer of a business concern who may issue notices and keep records of directors' and stockholders' meetings, oversee and preserve records of stock ownership and transfer and of other company affairs, and cooperate with counsel in supervision of the company's legal interests **b :** an officer of an organization or society responsible for its records and correspondence **4 :** an officer of state who superintends a government administrative department and is usu. a member of the chief executive's cabinet or advisory council ⟨the ~ of the treasury⟩ ⟨the ~ of labor⟩ ⟨foreign ~⟩ **5** [trans. of F *secrétaire*] **a :** WRITING DESK, ESCRITOIRE **b** *or* **secretary bookcase :** a writing desk with a top section for books **6 :** SECRETARY BIRD

secretary 5b

secretary at war : the representative of the army in the British Parliament until 1855
secretary bird *n* [prob. so called fr. the resemblance of the crest to a bunch of quill pens stuck behind the ear] **:** a large long-legged raptorial bird (*Sagittarius serpentarius*) of southern Africa that has a powerful hooked beak, a crest of long feathers, and a long tail, is predominantly blue-gray with black wing quills, thighs, abdomen, and bars on the tail, feeds largely on reptiles, and is often tamed to rid premises of them
secretary-general \ˌ==ˌ==ˌ(=)=ˈ=\ *n, pl* **secretaries-general :** a principal administrative officer ⟨the *secretary-general* of the United Nations⟩ ⟨the *secretary-general* of a political party⟩ ⟨the *secretary-general* to a colonial governor⟩
secretary hand *n* **:** a handwriting style formerly used in engrossing — compare SECRETARY TYPE
secretary of state : the chief officer of a government administrative department: as **a :** any of several British ministers ⟨the *secretary of state* for home affairs⟩ **b :** the head of the U.S. department of state **c :** the head of a department of the government of a U.S. state whose miscellaneous duties include the making and keeping of records
sec·re·tary·ship \-ˌship\ *n* **:** the duties or office of a secretary
secretary type *n* **:** a former black-letter type made to imitate engrossing script — compare SECRETARY HAND
secret ballot *n* **:** AUSTRALIAN BALLOT
¹se·crete \səˈkrēt, sēˈ-, *usu* -rēd·+V\ *vb* -ED/-ING/-S [back-formation fr. *secretion*] *vt* **1 :** to produce and emit (a secretion) from a gland **2 :** to produce or generate in the manner of a gland ⟨to trust . . . to the facts to ~ a purpose of their own —Archibald MacLeish⟩ ~ *vi* **:** to produce and emit a secretion ⟨the mucosa was *secreting* normally⟩
²se·crete \səˈkrē|t, sēˈ-, ˈsēkrə|, *usu* |d·+V\ *vt* -ED/-ING/-S [alter. (influenced by L *secretus*, past part. of *secernere* to separate, distinguish) of ⁴*secret*] **1 :** to deposit or conceal in a hiding place **:** HIDE ⟨he will ~ a small piece of iron about his person —J.G.Frazer⟩ **2 :** to appropriate (another's possessions) secretly **:** ABSTRACT **syn** see CONCEAL
³se·crete \səˈkrēt, sēˈ-, *usu* -rēd·+V\ *vt* -ED/-ING/-S [F *secréter*, fr. *secret*, n.; prob. fr. the fact that the process was originally a trade secret — more at SECRET] **:** ²CARROT
secreter *comparative of* SECRET
secretest *superlative of* SECRET
se·cre·tin \səˈkrēd·ən\ *n* -S [*secret-* + *-in*] **:** a hormone of polypeptide structure that is found in the mucous membrane of the upper intestine and is capable of stimulating the pancreas to secrete its juice and the liver to secrete bile
secret ink *n* **:** a fluid for invisible writing to be made visible afterwards: as **a :** a colorless plant juice that can be made visible by subjecting to heat **b :** one of a pair of water solutions of chemicals that are colorless or nearly so and that when combined form a strongly colored compound **c :** a water solution of a fluorescent substance that is colorless in visible light but leaves characters on paper that fluoresce when exposed to ultraviolet light
se·cre·tion \səˈkrēshən, sēˈ-\ *n* -S [F *sécrétion*, fr. L *secretion-, secretio* separation, fr. *secretus* (past part. of *secernere* to separate, distinguish) + *-ion-, -io* -ion — more at SECRET] **1 a :** the act or process of segregating, elaborating, and releasing some material that is either specialized to perform some function in the organism (as saliva) or is isolated for excretion from the body (as urine) **b :** a product of such secretion formed in the animal or plant body (as the cellulose wall of a plant cell or the pancreatic juice of an animal); *sometimes* **:** any such product that performs a specific useful function in the organism — distinguished from *excretion* **2** [²*secrete* + *-ion*] **:** the act of hiding something **:** CONCEALMENT ⟨thwarted his attempt at ~ of some costly gemstones about his person⟩
se·cre·tion·ary \-shəˌnerē, -ri\ *adj* **:** of or relating to secretion **:** formed by secretion
se·cre·tive *in senses 1 & 2:* ˈsēkrəd·iv, -ətiv; səˈkrēd·|iv, sēˈ-, -ˈkrēt|, |ēv *also* |əv; *in sense 3:* =ˈ==\ *adj* [back-formation fr. *secretiveness*] **1 :** disposed to secrecy **:** given to concealment of one's activities or purposes **:** preferring privacy ⟨the king was a ~ child, and showed little of his mind —Edith Sitwell⟩ **2 :** indicating or betokening a disposition to secrecy ⟨his blue eyes were guarded and ~ —Katherine A. Porter⟩ **3** [*secret-* + *-ive*] **:** SECRETORY **syn** see SILENT
se·cre·tive·ly \-əvlē, -li\ *adv* **:** in a secretive manner
se·cre·tive·ness \-ivnəs, -ēv- *also* -əv-\ *n* -ES [part trans. of F *secrétivité*, fr. *secrétiv-* (fr. *secret*, n. + *-if* -ive) + *-ité* -ity — more at SECRET] **:** the quality or state of being secretive
se·cret·ly *adv* [ME, fr. ¹*secret* + *-ly*] **1 :** in secret **:** in secrecy **:** not openly **2 :** in a low voice **:** INAUDIBLY — used esp. of liturgical prayer
secret mark *n* **:** a minute mark on a stamp or currency note introduced in the die or plate as a distinguishing mark of a particular engraver or of a particular plate or printer rather than as part of the design
se·cret·ness *n* -ES [ME *secretnesse*, fr. ¹*secret* + *-nesse* -ness] **:** the quality or state of being secret
secreto- — see SECRET-
secretogogue *var of* SECRETAGOGUE
se·cre·to·inhibitory \səˈkrēd·ō+\ *adj* [*secret-* + *inhibitory*] **:** checking secretion
sec·re·to·motor \"+\ *adj* [*secret-* + *motor*] **1 :** promoting secretion **2** *of nerves* **:** inducing secretion when stimulated
se·cre·tor \səˈkrēd·ə(r), sēˈ-\ *n* -S [¹*secrete* + *-or*] **:** an individual freely producing and excreting water-soluble group-specific substances in body fluids (as saliva, tears, urine) — compare NONSECRETOR
se·cre·to·ry \səˈkrēd·ərē, sēˈ-, -ētə-, -ri *sometimes* ˈsēkrəˌtōr- *or* -ˌtȯr-\ *adj* [*secret-* + *-ory*] **:** connected with or promoting secretion **:** produced by secretion
secretory duct *n* **:** any of the small ducts within a glandular organ that collect the secretion and convey it to a main duct that carries it from the organ
secret partner *n* **:** a partner whose membership in a partnership is kept secret from the public — called also *silent partner;* compare GENERAL PARTNER, LIMITED PARTNER
secret police *n* **:** a police organization operating for the most part in secrecy and esp. for the political purposes of its government often with terroristic methods — compare POLICE STATE
secret process *n* **:** a process that is a trade secret that would be valuable to competitors but is often protected by rule of court from compulsory disclosure although not protected by patent
secret reserve *n* **:** an amount by which stated net worth is reduced by understatement of asset values or overstatement of liabilities — called also *hidden reserve*
secrets *pl of* SECRET, *pres 3d sing of* SECRET
secret service *n* **1** *archaic* **:** confidential and publicly unacknowledged service to a government **2 :** a government detective or intelligence department ⟨*secret service* men begin to guard a U.S. president as soon as he is known to be elected⟩
secret society *n* **1 :** a society of a kind common among primitive peoples that often exercises magical or religious functions or administers punitive justice **2** *or* **secret order :** any of various modern oath-bound societies usu. devoted to purposes of brotherhood, moral discipline, and mutual assistance
se·cre·tum \səˈkrēd·əm, sēˈ-, -ētəm\ *n, pl* **secre·ta** \-ēd·ə, -ētə\ [ML, fr. L, neut. of *secretus*, past part. of *secernere* to separate, distinguish — more at SECRET] **:** a private seal
sect \ˈsekt\ *n* -S [ME *secte*, fr. MF & LL & L; MF, group, sect, fr. LL *secta* organized ecclesiastical body, fr. L, way of life, school of thought, class of persons, fr. *sequi* to follow — more at SUE] **1 a :** a dissenting religious body; *esp* **:** one that is heretical in the eyes of other members within the same communion **b :** a group within an organized religion whose adherents recognize a special set of teachings or practices ⟨the Pharisees have been called a ~ within Judaism⟩ **c :** an organized ecclesiastical body; *specif* **:** one outside one's own communion ⟨offered religious freedom to all ~*s* except the Roman Catholics⟩ **d :** a comparatively small recently organized exclusive religious body; *esp* **:** one that has parted company with a longer-established communion **2 a** *obs* **:** a class, order, or kind of persons **b** *archaic* **:** a religious order **c** *archaic* **:** SEX ⟨so is all her ~ —Shak.⟩ **3 a :** a separate group adhering to a distinctive doctrine or way of thinking or to a particular leader ⟨fashionable . . . among many different ~*s* of writers —L.S.Woolf⟩ **b :** a school of philosophy or of philosophic opinion ⟨the ~ Epicurean —John Milton⟩ **c :** a group holding similar political, economic, or other views: as (1) **:** PARTY (2) **:** an opinionated faction (as of a party) ⟨Trotskyism . . . and other independent communist ~*s* —Jim Cork⟩ (3) **:** a school of opinion (as in science or medicine) ⟨medical ~*s* in ancient Greece⟩ **4** *obs* **:** a body of followers **:** FOLLOWING **syn** see RELIGION
¹-sect \ˌsekt\ *adj comb form* [L *sectus*, past part. of *secare* to cut, divide — more at SAW] **:** cut **:** divided ⟨pinnati*sect*⟩
²-sect \"\ *vb comb form* -ED/-ING/-S [L *sectus*, past part. of *secare*] **:** cut **:** divide ⟨bi*sect*⟩ ⟨quadri*sect*⟩
sect *abbr* section; sectional
sec·ta \ˈsektə\ *n pl* [ML, fr. L, way of life, school of thought, class of persons] **1 :** the followers or witnesses brought by the plaintiff to support his case in Anglo-Saxon law **2 :** a lawsuit in Anglo-Saxon law
sec·tar·i·al \(ˈ)sekˈta(a)rēəl\ *adj* [¹*sectary* + *-al*] **:** of, relating to, or distinguishing a religious sect in India ⟨a ~ mark⟩
¹sec·tar·i·an \-rēən\ *adj* [¹*sectary* + *-an*] **1 :** of or relating to one or more sectaries; *specif* **:** of or relating to the Independents or another Protestant nonconformist sect (as in 17th century England) **2 :** of, relating to, or having the characteristics of one or more sects esp. of a religious character ⟨~ differences⟩ **3 a :** confined to the limits of one religious group, one school, or one party **:** DENOMINATIONAL, PARTISAN ⟨~ religious training⟩ ⟨the negations of ~ ideology —Sidney Hook⟩ ⟨~ squabbles in psychology —*Times Lit. Supp.*⟩ **b :** limited in character or scope **:** of narrow interests **:** characterized by bigotry **:** PAROCHIAL ⟨a ~ mind⟩ ⟨wishing to avoid a ~ presentation of the matter⟩
²sectarian \"\ *n* -S **1 a :** an adherent of a particular religious sect **b :** DISSENTER 2 **2 :** one characterized by a narrow and bigoted adherence to a sect **:** one limited to narrow and partisan views, interests, or sympathies
sec·tar·i·an·ism \-əˌnizəm\ *n* -S **:** sectarian spirit or beliefs **:** exclusive or narrow-minded attachment to a sect, denomination, party, or school ⟨socialist ~⟩
sec·tar·i·an·ize \-ˌnīz\ *vb* -ED/-ING/-S *vi* **:** to act as sectarians **:** become divided into sects ~ *vt* **:** to make sectarian **:** imbue with sectarian principles or feelings **:** subject to the control of a sect ⟨~ public education⟩
sec·ta·rism \ˈsektəˌrizəm\ *n* -S [¹*sectary* + *-ism*] **:** the spirit, practices, or principles of a religious sect **:** SECTARIANISM
sec·ta·rist \-rəst\ *n* -S [¹*sectary* + *-ist*] *archaic* **:** SECTARY
¹sec·ta·ry \-rē, -ri\ *n* -ES [prob. fr. NL *sectarius*, fr. LL *secta* organized ecclesiastical body + L *-arius* -ary — more at SECT] **1 a :** an adherent of a religious sect held to be heretical or schismatic **b** *sometimes cap* **:** a dissenter from the Church of England; *specif* **:** an Independent or other Protestant nonconformist **2 :** a usu. zealous adherent of a sect ⟨religious or political *sectaries*⟩ **3 a :** a zealous follower, disciple, or partisan (as of a leader, teacher, party, or school) ⟨each old town . . . has its cult of *sectaries*, devotees of its history —Lucien Price⟩ **b :** a votary of a particular study or pursuit ⟨been a ~ astronomical —Shak.⟩ **4** *archaic* **:** SECT
²sectary \"\ *adj, archaic* **:** SECTARIAN
sec·ta·tor \sekˈtād·ə(r)\ *n* -S [MF *sectateur*, fr. L *sectator*, fr. *sectatus* (past part. of *sectari* to follow, accompany, freq. of *sequi* to follow) + *-or* — more at SUE] **:** a usu. devoted follower (as of a teacher or leader) **:** DISCIPLE
sec·tile \ˈsektᵊl, -ˌtīl, -(ˌ)til\ *adj* [L *sectilis*, fr. *sectus* (past part. of *secare* to cut) + *-ilis* -ile] **1 a :** capable of being severed by a knife with a smooth cut but yet pulverizable **b :** cut into small divisions **2 :** constituting a type of mosaic formed of relatively large pieces of marble shaped to fit one another
sec·til·i·ty \sekˈtiləd·ē, -ətē, -i\ *n* -ES **:** the property or condition of being sectile ⟨the ~ of chalcocite⟩
¹sec·tion \ˈsekshən\ *n* -S *often attrib* [L *section-, sectio*, fr. *sectus* (past part. of *secare* to cut) + *-ion-, -io* -ion — more at SAW] **1 a :** the action of cutting or separating by cutting; *esp* **:** the action of dividing (as tissues) surgically ⟨nerve ~⟩ ⟨abdominal ~⟩ ⟨cesarean ~⟩ **b :** an instance of such cutting **2 :** a distinct part or portion of a writing: as **a :** a subdivision of a chapter (as a paragraph or a series of paragraphs not separated by a heading) **b :** a division of a law, statute, or legislative act **c :** a distinct component part of a newspaper ⟨the sports ~⟩ **3 a :** the description or representation of something (as a building, piece of machinery, segment of the earth's crust) as it would appear if cut through by an intersecting plane **:** depiction of what is beyond a plane passing or supposed to pass through an object **:** PROFILE **b :** a diagram showing rock units and structures along a usu. vertical plane below the surface **4 a :** a natural subdivision of a taxonomic group and esp. of a genus but sometimes of a higher group **b :** a tribal segment or a group of segments usu. based on descent, function, or territorial occupancy **5 :** the plane figure resulting from the cutting of a solid by a plane **6 :** the character § commonly used in printing to mark a section or the beginning of a section (as of a statute) and as the fourth in series of the reference marks **7 :** a piece of land one square mile or 640 acres in area forming one of the 36 subdivisions of a township in a U.S. public-land survey **8 a :** a distinct part of a terri-

torial area (as a country or continent) set apart by geographic, economic, cultural, or other distinctive characteristics ⟨the West, the South, and other ~*s* of the U. S.⟩ ⟨the only important grape-growing ~ of Pennsylvania —*Amer. Guide Series: Pa.*⟩ **b** : a usu. distinctive quarter or district (as of a city or town) ⟨the business ~ of the city⟩ **9 a** : a part that is, may be, or is held to be separated : DIVISION, PORTION, SLICE ⟨the southern ~ of the route⟩ ⟨chop the stalks into ~*s* —*Amer. Guide Series: La.*⟩ ⟨an important ~ of the milling industry —*Amer. Guide Series: Minn.*⟩ ⟨a ~ of the task⟩ **b** : one segment of a fruit (as an orange or grapefruit) : CARPEL **c** : one of the parts into which the warp threads are divided during weaving preparation (as warping, beaming, and slashing) **10 a** : a portion of a group of people having or held to have a distinct and separate status usu. by virtue of one or more distinctive characteristics ⟨a cheering ~⟩ ⟨royally entertained by all ~*s* of the local community —Guthrie Moir⟩ ⟨the strongest ~ of the European population —Patrick Smith⟩ **b** : one of the classes formed by dividing a group of students taking a particular course ⟨ten ~*s* of English I⟩ **c** : one of the groups into which a conference of teachers, scholars, or specialists in a given field is divided for discussion purposes **11 a** : a military unit composed of two or more squads **b** : a military unit constituting the basic unit of a larger unit **12 a** : a very thin slice (as of tissue or rock) suitable for microscopic examination **b** : an exposed surface revealing successive geological strata **13 a** : a division of a railroad sleeping car including both an upper and a lower berth or when these are not made up two double seats facing each other **b** : a portion of a permanent railroad way under the care of a particular set of men **c** : one of two or more trains, planes, buses, or similar vehicles which run on the same schedule and for which special signals are usu. shown **14** : one of several component parts that may be assembled or reassembled ⟨a cutter bar with 15 ~*s*⟩ ⟨a bookcase in ~*s*⟩ **15** : one of the frames each made about four inches square, designed to hold about a pound when full, and placed in the super of a hive for bees to store surplus honey in **16** : a profile on a plane perpendicular to the plane of the principal line or trace in fortification **17** : a division of an orchestra composed of one class of instruments ⟨brass ~⟩ ⟨string ~⟩ **18** : SIGNATURE 5b **19** : a subdivision of an office, staff, department, bureau, or other organization ⟨the political ~ of an embassy⟩ ⟨a Communist party ~⟩ ⟨the U. S. ~ of the British Foreign Office⟩ **20** : the sequence of rock units in a given locality or region **syn** see PART — **in section** *adv* : in the view revealed by a section ⟨show a blood vessel *in section*⟩

²section \"\ *vb* **sectioned; sectioned; sectioning** \-sh(ə)niŋ\ **sections** *vt* **1 a** : to cut or separate into sections : make a section of ⟨~ a history class by ability ratings⟩ ⟨~ a rock for examination⟩ **b** (1) : to divide (a body part or organ) surgically ⟨~ a nerve⟩ (2) : to cut (fixed tissue) into thin slices for microscopic examination **2** : to shade (as a part of a mechanical drawing) with crosshatching to indicate a section : to represent in sections ~ *vi* : to form sections : become cut or separated into parts

¹sec·tion·al \-shənᵊl, -shnəl\ *adj* **1 a** : of, relating to, or based upon a section ⟨~ repair of a tire⟩ ⟨a ~ view⟩ ⟨~ drawings⟩ **b** : belonging to a distinct part of a larger body (as a society or population) or territory : local or regional rather than general in character ⟨~ interests⟩ ⟨~ jealousies⟩ ⟨a ~ dialect⟩ — compare PROVINCIAL **2 a** : consisting of or divided into sections ⟨a ~ wire⟩ ⟨~ furniture⟩ **b** : designed for construction by assembling a series of component parts ⟨a ~ garage⟩ — see SECTIONAL BOILER **c** : made up of sections to be added or reduced at will ⟨a ~ bookcase⟩ ⟨a ~ dictionary⟩ ⟨a ~ sofa⟩

²sectional \"\ *n* -s : a piece of furniture made up of modular

sectional

units capable of use separately or in various combinations (as a sectional sofa whose parts may be used as chairs)

sectional boiler *n* : a boiler whose parts are fabricated and shipped in sections and erected in suitable supporting frames and brickwork settings

sectional density *n* : the ratio of the weight of a projectile to the square of its diameter

sec·tion·al·ism \-sh(ə)nə,lizəm\ *n* -s : disproportionate devotion to the interests peculiar to one section (as of a country) : sectional feeling, spirit, or prejudice : consciousness by the people of a section of a common and peculiar set of identifying characteristics (as customs, interests, or social traits) ⟨when ~ exists within a state . . . it may be an upstate versus downstate division —D.D.McKean⟩

sec·tion·al·ist \-ləst\ *n* -s : one characterized by sectionalism : one that advocates sectional interests or aims : one having usu. excessive sectional feeling

sec·tion·al·iza·tion \,seksh(ə)nələ'zāshən, -,lī'z-\ *n* -s : the action of sectionalizing or of becoming sectionalized : the state of being sectionalized

sec·tion·al·ize \'seksh(ə)nə,līz\ *vt* -ED/-ING/-S **1** : to divide into sections : make in sections esp. for later assembly **2** : to divide according to geographical sections or local interests : cause to become characterized by sectionalism

sectional leaf cutting *n* : a section of a leaf (as of a begonia) on which with the proper environment adventitious buds and roots will develop

sec·tion·al·ly \-ᵊlē, -əlī, |i\ *adv* : in a sectional manner : along sectional lines : from a sectional point of view

¹sec·tion·ary \'sekshə,nerē\ *adj* : of or relating to a section : SECTIONAL 1 ⟨~ leaders⟩

²sectionary \"\ *n* -ES : a member or partisan of a sectional group

section bar *n* : a bar of iron or steel rolled so as to have a definite cross section

section boss *n* **1** *or* **section foreman** : the foreman of a section gang **2** : a third hand in a textile mill

section eight *n, pl* **section eights** *usu cap S&E* [*Section VIII*, Army Regulation 615-360, in effect from December 1922 to July 1944] **1** : a discharge from the U. S. Army for military inaptitude or undesirable habits or traits of character **2** : a soldier discharged for military inaptitude or undesirable habits or traits of character ⟨where the *Section Eights* wandered around whimpering all the time —R.O.Bowen⟩

section-eight \'≈≈'≈\ *vt* -ED/-ING/-S *often cap S&E* [*section eight*] : to discharge (a soldier) from the U. S. Army for military inaptitude or undesirable habits or traits of character ⟨until you . . . go crazy and get *section-eighted* —Ernest Hemingway⟩

section gang *also* **section crew** *n* : a gang or crew of trackmen employed to maintain a railroad section

section hand *n* : a laborer belonging to a section gang

section house *n* **1** : a small building for storing tools and equipment needed to maintain a railroad section **2** : a railroad-owned dwelling at or near a railroad section for housing a section boss and his family or the members of a section gang

sec·tion·ize \'sekshə,nīz\ *vt* -ED/-ING/-S : to divide into sections ⟨~ land for disposal to settlers⟩

section line *n* **1** : the boundary line of a section in surveying or land distribution ⟨in eastern Ohio . . . roads followed *section lines* —R.H.Brown⟩ **2** : one of a series of thin parallel lines placed on the cut surfaces of section views (as in an architectural drawing)

section man *n* **1** : SECTION HAND **2** : SECTION BOSS 2

section manager *n* : FLOORWALKER 1

section paper *n, Brit* : GRAPH PAPER

section plane *n* **1** : a surface seen in section (as in cross section) **2** : a hypothetical plane cutting a section

sections *pl of* SECTION, *pres 3d sing of* SECTION

sect·ism \'sek,tizəm\ *n* -s : SECTARIANISM

sect·ist \-təst\ *n* -s *obs* : SECTARIAN 1

¹sec·tor \'sektə(r) *also* -,tȯ(ə)r *or* -ō(ə)\ *n* -s [LL (trans. of Gk *tomeus*), fr. L, cutter, fr. *sectus* (past part. of *secare* to cut) + *-or* — more at SAW] **1 a** : the geometrical figure bounded by two radii and the included arc of a circle **b** (1) : a subdivision of a defensive military position assigned to a commander as an area of responsibility, bounded by arbitrary lines on the sides and rear, and in front extending to the maximum range of the weapons of the garrison — compare ZONE OF ACTION (2) : a portion of a front in military operations **c** : something (as an area or a portion or part of something) resembling or held to resemble a sector : DIVISION, QUARTER, SECTION ⟨the Soviet ~ of Berlin⟩ ⟨a reforested ~ of cutover land —*Amer. Guide Series: Oregon*⟩ **d** : a sociological, economic, or political subdivision of society ⟨maintenance of public order is primarily the responsibility of the public ~ —*Kerner Report*⟩ **2** : a mathematical instrument consisting of two rulers connected at one end by a joint and marked with several scales (as of equal parts chords, sines, or tangents) **3 a** : an astronomical instrument whose limb embraces only a part of a circle and which is used for measuring angles too great for the compass of a micrometer **b** : an arc-shaped attachment to an equatorial mounting often used for communicating slow-motion control of the driving clock to the polar axis **4** : a part of an apparatus whose principal kinematic lines form a sector ⟨an index ~⟩ **syn** see PART

²sector \-tə(r)\ *vb* **sectored; sectored; sectoring** \-t(ə)riŋ\ **sectors** *vt* : to divide into or furnish with sectors ~ *vi* : to form colonies made up of visibly different sectors — used chiefly of bacteria and fungi that form mutant strains early in the colony history

sec·tor·al \'sekt(ə)rəl\ *adj* : of or relating to a sector ⟨~ line⟩

sectored disk \'sektə(r)d-\ *also* **sector disk** *or* **sector wheel** *n* : a disk with alternate opaque and open sectors used in photometers to vary the brightness in a known manner

sector gate *n* : a roller gate in part-circle or sector form for a dam crest

sector gear *n* **1** *or* **sector wheel** : a toothed device resembling a portion of a gear wheel containing the center bearing and a part of the rim with its teeth **2** : a gear having a sector gear as its chief essential feature

¹sec·to·ri·al \(')sek¦tōrēəl, -tȯr-\ *adj* [¹*sector* + *-ial*] **1** : of, relating to, or having the shape of a sector ⟨a ~ box⟩ **2** *of a chimera* : made up of a sector of variant growth involving more than one type of tissue interposed in an otherwise normal body of tissue — compare PERICLINAL

²sectorial \"\ *adj* [NL *sectorius* sectorial (fr. L *sectus* — past part. of *secare* to cut — + *-orius* -ory) + E *-al*] : adapted for cutting : CARNASSIAL ⟨a ~ tooth⟩

sector of a sphere : the solid generated by the revolution of the sector of a circle about one of its radii

sects *pl of* SECT

-sects *pres 3d sing of* -SECT

sectuary *n* -ES [by alter. (influence of such words as *actuary*)] *obs* : SECTARY

secty *abbr* secretary

¹sec·u·lar *also* **saec·u·lar** \'sekyələ(r)\ *adj* [ME, alter. (influenced by LL *saecularis*) of *seculer*, fr. OF, fr. LL *saecularis* secular, worldly, pagan, fr. L, coming or observed once in an age, fr. *saeculum* breed, generation, age + *-aris* -ar; akin to W *hoedl* lifetime, Lith *sėkla* seed, L *serere* to sow — more at SOW] **1 a** : of or relating to the worldly or temporal as distinguished from the spiritual or eternal : not sacred : MUNDANE ⟨~ affairs⟩ ⟨~ occupations⟩ **b** : not overtly or specif. religious ⟨~ rites⟩ ⟨~ music⟩ ⟨~ drama⟩ **c** : of or relating to the state as distinguished from the church : CIVIL ⟨~ courts⟩ ⟨~ jurisdiction⟩ ⟨the champion of the ~ power —A.J.Toynbee⟩ **d** : of or relating to the laity as distinguished from the clergy : NONCLERICAL, LAY ⟨the ~ landowners⟩ ⟨~ benefactors⟩ **e** : not formally related to or controlled by a religious body ⟨the greater number of ~ than denominational schools in the country⟩ **f** : rationally organized around impersonal and utilitarian values and patterns and receptive to new traits ⟨our modern industrialized ~ society⟩ — contrasted with *sacred* **g** : of, relating to, or advocating secularism : SECULARIST ⟨an enlightened ~ humanism —H.N.Fairchild⟩ ⟨the disenchantment of absolute faiths which expresses itself in the ~ outlook of modern man —Louis Wirth⟩ **2 a** : living in the world : not living in a monastery or religious community : not bound by monastic vows or rules ⟨a ~ priest⟩ ⟨the ~ clergy⟩ — opposed to *regular*; compare MONK 1 **b** : of or relating to clergy not bound by monastic vows ⟨~ vestments⟩ **3** [L *saecularis*] **a** : coming or observed once in an age or a century ⟨~ phenomena⟩ **b** : existing or continuing through ages or centuries : AGELONG, CENTURIED, DIUTURNAL ⟨~ oaks⟩ ⟨~ enmities⟩ **c** : of or relating to a long-enduring process ⟨~ change⟩ ⟨regions of the earth's surface where . . . slow ~ movements of the crust are still in progress —*Endeavour*⟩ **d** : taking place within a century ⟨~ fluctuation⟩ ⟨the ~ variation in an astronomical position⟩ **e** : requiring or taking ages (as for operation or completion) ⟨~ forces⟩ ⟨the improvement of man is ~ —John Tyndall⟩ **f** : of or relating to a long term of indefinite duration ⟨the ~ trend of prices⟩ ⟨a ~ increase in the quantity of money is required in a growing economy —Milton Friedman⟩ — compare CYCLICAL 2 **g** : recurring at intervals greater than one year ⟨~ cycles in population pressure⟩ **syn** see PROFANE

²secular \"\ *n* -s [ME *seculer*, fr. OF, fr. *seculer*, adj.] **1** : a secular ecclesiastic (as a parish priest) **2** : LAYMAN

secular arm *n* [ME *seculer arm*, trans. of ML *bracchium saeculare*] : the secular or civil power as distinguished from that of the church

secular canoness *n* : a canoness who is allowed to hold private property and is bound only by vows of celibacy and obedience

secular games *n pl* [trans. of L *ludi saeculares*] : games honoring the gods of ancient Rome, lasting for three days and nights, and celebrated at long irregular intervals with sacrifices, theatrical shows, feasting, and singing of hymns composed for or appropriate to the occasion

secular hymns *n pl* [trans. of L *carmina saecularia*] : hymns composed for or sung at the secular games of ancient Rome

sec·u·lar·ism \'sekyələ,rizəm\ *n* -s : a view of life or of any particular matter based on the premise that religion and religious considerations should be ignored or purposely excluded ⟨a policy of strict ~ in government⟩; *specif* : a system of social ethics based upon a doctrine that ethical standards and conduct should be determined exclusively with reference to the present life and social well-being without reference to religion

¹sec·u·lar·ist \-rəst\ *n* -s : one who advocates secularism ⟨the overemphasis by ~*s* on the scientific —J.L.Teller⟩

²secularist \"\ *or* **sec·u·lar·is·tic** \¦≈≈≈¦ristik, -tēk\ *adj* : of, relating to, or advocating secularism ⟨every philosophy of life is either religious or ~ —Walter Moberly⟩ ⟨the ~ basis of humanism⟩ ⟨that we not transfer our loyalties to hidden ~ presuppositions —J.A.Pike⟩

sec·u·lar·i·ty \,sekyə'larəd·ē, -rətē, -i *also* -'ler-\ *n* -ES [ML *saecularitat-, saecularitas*, fr. LL *saecularis* secular, worldly, pagan + L *-tat-, -tas* -ty — more at SECULAR] **1** : something secular ⟨shunning all *secularities* on the Sabbath⟩ **2** : the quality or state of being secular ⟨prompts them to stress a denominational catholicity if not a candid ~ —W.L.Sperry⟩

sec·u·lar·iza·tion \,sekyələrə'zāshən, -,rī'z-\ *n* -s [F *sécularisation*, fr. MF *secularisation*, fr. *seculariser* + *-ation*] : the act or process of secularizing : the condition of being secularized ⟨demands for ~ of the schools⟩ ⟨the increasing ~ of our culture⟩ — contrasted with *sanctification*

sec·u·lar·ize \'sekyələ,rīz\ *vt* -ED/-ING/-S [F *séculariser*, fr. MF *seculariser*, fr. LL *saecularis* secular, worldly, pagan + MF *-iser* -ize] **1** : to make secular ⟨those centuries *secularized* our belief —Max Lerner⟩ **2** : to transfer from ecclesiastical to civil or lay use, possession, or control ⟨the abbey . . . was *secularized* in 1535 —*Times Lit. Supp.*⟩ **3** : to convert to or imbue with secularism ⟨European civilization became *secularized* —Stringfellow Barr⟩

sec·u·lar·ly *adv* [ME *secularelie*, alter. (influenced by LL *saecularis* secular) of *seculerli*, fr. *seculer*, adj., secular + *-li* -ly] : in a secular manner

secular vicar *n* : CLERK VICAR

secund \'sē,kənd, 'se,-\ *adj* [L *secundus* following] : having some part or element arranged on one side only : UNILATERAL ⟨~ racemes⟩

se·cun·der·a·bad \sə'kəndərə¦bad, -bäd\ *adj, usu cap* [fr. *Secunderabad*, city in south central India] : of or from the city of Secunderabad, India : of the kind or style prevalent in Secunderabad

se·cun·di·grav·id \sə¦kəndē¦gravəd\ *adj* [NL *secundigravida*] : pregnant for the second time

se·cun·di·grav·i·da \≈¦≈≈'≈vədə\ *n* -s [NL, fr. *secundi-* (fr. L *secundus* second, following) + L *gravida* pregnant woman — more at SECOND, GRAVIDA] : a woman in her second pregnancy

secun·dines *or* **secon·dines** \'sekən,dīnz, -,dēnz, sə'kəndənz\ *n pl* [pl. of obs. E *secundine, secondine* afterbirth, fr. ME *secundine*, fr. LL *secundinae* (pl.), fr. L *secundus* second, following + *-inae*, fem. pl. of *-inus* -ine] : AFTERBIRTH

sec·un·dip·a·ra \,sekən'dipərə\ *n* -s [NL, fr. *secundi-* (fr. L *secundus*) + *-para*] : a woman who has borne children in two separate pregnancies

sec·un·dip·a·rous \¦≈≈¦dipərəs\ *adj* [*secundipara* + *-ous*] : of or relating to a secundipara

secund·ly *adv* : in a secund manner : UNILATERALLY

se·cun·do·gen·i·ture \sə,kən(,)dō'jenəchə(r)\ *n* [*secundo-* (fr. L *secundus* second, following) + *geniture*] **1** : the right or system by which inheritance belongs to the second son **2** : a property or possession inherited by secundogeniture

se·cun·dum le·gem \sə'kəndəm 'lē,jem\ *adv* [L] : according to law

se·cur·able \sə'kyu̇rəbəl, sē'-\ *adj* : capable of being secured : OBTAINABLE ⟨fellowships ~ by promising college graduates⟩

se·cur·ance \-rən(t)s\ *n* -s : the act of making secure or of assuring : ASSURANCE ⟨guaranties . . . which are the ~ of freedom —Elisha Mulford⟩

¹se·cure \-kyu̇(ə)r, -ȯə\ *adj, sometimes* -ER/-EST [L *securus* free from care, safe, secure, fr. *sed, se* without + *cura* care — more at IDIOT, CURE] **1 a** *archaic* : unwisely free from fear or distrust : CARELESS, OVERCONFIDENT ⟨went up . . . and smote the host: for the host was ~ —Judg 8:11 (AV)⟩ **b** : free from fear, care, or anxiety : easy in mind : CONFIDENT ⟨~ himself . . . he went out of his way to help others —Vance Palmer⟩ ⟨~ in the knowledge that a nurse is there to take over if necessary —Dorothy Barclay⟩ **c** : assured in opinion or expectation : having no doubt ⟨~ in a belief⟩ ⟨grow to feel too ~ in their power —F.L.Mott⟩ **d** *archaic* : confident of a sure or safe prospect : CERTAIN ⟨~ to be as blest as thou canst bear —Alexander Pope⟩ ⟨when she is ~ of him, there will be leisure for falling in love —Jane Austen⟩ **2 a** : free from danger ⟨the feudal lord and his people were no longer ~ behind their fortifications —Tom Wintringham⟩ — often used with *from* or *against* ⟨~ from harm⟩ ⟨~ against attack⟩ **b** : free from risk of loss ⟨no man's life or fortune was ~ —F. D.Roosevelt⟩ **c** : affording safety : INVIOLABLE ⟨a ~ hideaway⟩ ⟨a ~ telephone line⟩ **d** : TRUSTWORTHY, DEPENDABLE ⟨his judgment on them is not so ~ —Roy Lewis & Angus Maude⟩ ⟨voice under ~ control —John Briggs⟩ **e** : strong, stable, or firm enough to ensure safety : SOLID, UNASSAILABLE ⟨a ~ foundation⟩ ⟨a ~ lock⟩ ⟨made a ~ place for himself in criticism —T.S.Eliot⟩ **3** : capable of being expected or counted on with confidence : ASSURED, SURE ⟨a ~ victory⟩ ⟨~ of an audience that shared his views —C.H.Rickword⟩ **syn** see SAFE

²secure \"\ *vb* -ED/-ING/-S *vt* **1** *obs* : to free (as a person) from care, fear, or anxiety ⟨I came *secured* by her promises —Thomas Fuller⟩ **2 a** : to relieve from exposure to danger : make safe : GUARD ⟨labor's efforts to ~ itself —*New Republic*⟩ — often used with *from* or *against* ⟨~ the country from a repetition of the experience —*Irish Digest*⟩ ⟨~ your own countrymen against brutality —Kenneth Roberts⟩ **b** : to shield or make secure (as a military position or movement) from capture, destruction, or hostile interference ⟨for the time being, the beach was *secured* —Irwin Shaw⟩ **3 a** *archaic* : to give certitude to : ASSURE ⟨finds a way . . . to ~ himself of a powerful advocate —William Broome⟩ **b** : to put beyond hazard of losing or of not receiving : GUARANTEE ⟨~ the blessings of liberty to ourselves and our posterity —*U.S. Constitution*⟩ ⟨*securing* that there are no unfilled gaps —*Lancet*⟩ **c** (1) : to give pledge of payment to (a creditor) (2) : to give pledge or payment of (an obligation) ⟨~ a note by a pledge of collateral security⟩ **4 a** : to seize and confine (a person) : hold fast : PINION ⟨~ a prisoner with handcuffs⟩ ⟨two redcoats quickly *secured* him —Rex Ingamells⟩ **b** : to make fast : tie down : SEAL ⟨~ a door⟩ ⟨~ the hatches of a ship⟩ ⟨~ a letter with a wax seal⟩ **5** *archaic* **a** : to safeguard against (as an evil or danger) : PREVENT ⟨*securing* false and illegal trade —W.S. Perry⟩ **b** : to divert (a person) from a dangerous course ⟨so I may ~ you from acting with . . . rashness —Sir Walter Scott⟩ **6 a** : to come into secure possession of; *esp* : to acquire as the result of effort : PROCURE ⟨~ employment⟩ ⟨~ cooperation⟩ ⟨~ a confession⟩ ⟨the good and rare things, in most countries *secured* and held by the few —Russell Lord⟩ ⟨*secured* an inside room on one of the largest steamers —David Fairchild⟩ **b** : to bring about : EFFECT, PRODUCE ⟨*secured* his ignominious dismissal —T.J.P.Lever⟩ ⟨we *secured* that they remain for some months —Herbert Hoover⟩ ⟨perfect technique will always ~ a finer performance —Warwick Braithwaite⟩ **7** : to release (naval personnel) from work or duty : DISMISS, EXCUSE ⟨~ unnecessary personnel, partly to make it easier on those who still must stay on duty —E.L. Beach⟩ ~ *vi* **1** *of naval personnel* : to stop work : go off duty : knock off ⟨you may ~ now . . . get yourself some eggs and coffee —Herman Wouk⟩ **2** *of a ship* : to tie up : BERTH ⟨she *secured* alongside —Alan Villiers⟩ **syn** see ENSURE, GET

³secure \"\ *n* -s [²*secure*] : a naval signal announcing time to secure

se·cure·ly *adv* : in a secure manner: as **a** *archaic* : without care : TRUSTINGLY ⟨devise not evil against thy neighbor seeing he dwelleth ~ by thee —Prov 3:29 (AV)⟩ **b** : with assurance : SAFELY ⟨she was ~ happy —Ellen Glasgow⟩ ⟨it may ~ be denied —Hilaire Belloc⟩ **c** : without question : CERTAINLY ⟨the shadows of poverty . . . had been ~ dispelled —Osbert Sitwell⟩ **d** : FIRMLY ⟨~ corked⟩ ⟨~ clamped in place⟩ ⟨authority . . . ~ established —B.K.Sandwell⟩

se·cure·ment \-mənt\ *n* -s : the act or process of making secure or of securing: as **a** *obs* : PROTECTION, RELIEF ⟨grew afraid thereof and obtained a ~ from it —Sir Thomas Browne⟩ **b** : ASSURANCE, CERTAINTY ⟨the ~ of maximal clinical control of the . . . infection —*Ciba Clinical Symposia*⟩ **c** : PROCUREMENT ⟨the ~ of an efficient body of public servants —F.W. Taussig⟩

se·cure·ness *n* -ES *archaic* : carefree lack of fear or distrust : TRUSTFULNESS ⟨you think all well; this may be not assurance but ~ —Thomas Adams⟩

sec·u·rif·era \,sekyə'rifərə\ [NL, fr. L *securis* ax, hatchet (fr. *secare* to cut) + *-fera*, neut. pl. of *-fer* -ferous — more at SAW] *syn of* SERRIFERA

¹se·cu·ri·ty \sə'kyu̇rəd·ē, sē'-, -rətē, -i\ *n* -ES *often attrib* [ME *securite*, fr. L *securitat-, securitas*, fr. *securus* free from care, safe, secure + *-itat-, -itas* -ity] **1** : the quality or state of being secure: as **a** : freedom from danger : SAFETY ⟨~ from famine⟩ ⟨~ against aggression⟩ ⟨everyone has the right to life, liberty and ~ of person —*U.N. Declaration of Human Rights*⟩ ⟨seeking after the illusion of certainty . . . in the form of a quest for absolute ~ —E.N.Griswold⟩ **b** *archaic* : carefree or cocky overconfidence ⟨~ is mortals' chiefest enemy —Shak.⟩ **c** : freedom from fear, anxiety, or care ⟨this need for ~ dates back into infancy —K.C.Garrison⟩ ⟨~ . . . thought of as a harmony between internal needs and the social availability of the means for their satisfaction —W.C.Olson⟩ ⟨my one chance of ~ lies in fixing attention solely on the first chapter —Arnold Bennett⟩ **d** (1) : freedom from uncertainty or doubt : CONFIDENCE, ASSURANCE ⟨knowing she still had the ~ of his faithful devotion —Morley Callaghan⟩ ⟨distinguished by a certain ~ of judgment —J.R.Lowell⟩ (2) : sureness of technique ⟨the cellist plays with great ~ but overlooks opportunities to let the sunlight in —Arthur Berger⟩ **e** : basis for confidence : GUARANTEE ⟨our plan gives us no ~ that we shall get the steam engine —G.B.Shaw⟩ **f** : FIRMNESS ⟨~ of attachment⟩ : DEPENDABILITY, STABILITY ⟨the ~ of a knot⟩ ⟨a moral poise, a ~ of values that is very rare in our age —Irving Howe & Eliezer Greenberg⟩ **2 a** : something given, deposited, or pledged to make certain the fulfillment of an obligation (as the payment of a debt) **:** property given or serving to make secure the enjoyment or enforcement of a right **:** GUARANTY, PLEDGE ⟨the ~ is poor⟩ **b :** one who becomes surety for another or engages himself for the performance of another's obligation **:** SURETY ⟨was willing to go ~ for his friend⟩ ⟨fined and ordered to find *securities* for good behavior —Edward Jenks⟩ **3 :** a written obligation, evidence, or document of ownership or creditorship (as a stock, bond, note, debenture, or certificate) giving the holder the right to demand and receive property not in his possession ⟨a government ~⟩ ⟨negotiable *securities*⟩; *specif* **:** one issued to investors to finance a business enterprise **4 :** something that secures **:** DEFENSE, PROTECTION, GUARD ⟨their one source of ~ in a glowering alien climate —A.R.Marcus⟩: as **a :** measures taken (as by a military unit) to ensure against surprise attack ⟨the battalion . . . set up ~ —Walter Bernstein⟩ **b :** measures taken (as by a national government or a governmental unit) to guard against espionage, observation, sabotage, and surprise ⟨~ prevents the reporting of actual production figures —*New Republic*⟩ **c :** protection against economic vicissitudes ⟨government guarantees for old age ~ —T.W.Arnold⟩ ⟨the very heavy emphasis that younger men are now placing on . . . ~ —*Fortune*⟩ **d :** penal custody ⟨the new prison system . . . provides for the care of offenders on the basis of classification as to custody (maximum, medium, and minimum ~) —C.E.Johnson⟩ **5 :** the resistance of a cryptogram to cryptanalysis measured usu. by the time and effort needed to solve it

²security \"\ — an international radiotelephone signal word introducing a safety message

security analysis *n* **:** the work or procedures of the security analyst

security analyst *n* **:** one that studies elements of value and factors affecting future value of securities to appraise their worth in relation to their price

security for costs : an undertaking often required by a court of a nonresident plaintiff to pay the costs of litigation in event of an adverse result

se·cus \ˈsēkəs\ *adv* [L; akin to L *sequi* to follow — more at SUE] *law* **:** to the contrary **:** not so **:** OTHERWISE

secy *abbr* secretary

SED *abbr* skin erythema dose

se·dan \səˈdan, sēˈ-, -aa(ə)n\ *n* -s [origin unknown] **1** *or* **sedan chair a :** a portable chair or covered vehicle for carrying a single person usu. borne on poles by two men **b :** a conveyance borne like a sedan (as a litter or palanquin) **2 a :** an automobile having four or two doors and an enclosed body with permanent top of one compartment seating four to seven persons including the driver **b :** a powerboat having one passenger compartment

sedan 1a

sedan delivery truck *n* **:** a sedan modified for delivery service by replacing the rear seat and tail section with panel sides and a double door at the rear

se·dang \səˈdaŋ, (ˈ)sä¦däŋ\ *n, pl* **sedang** *or* **sedangs** *usu cap* **1 a :** a people related to the Cambodians of the Kontum plateau in central Vietnam **b :** a member of the Sedang people **2 :** the Mon-Khmer language of the Sedang people

sedan landaulet *n* **:** an automobile body similar to the sedan except that the top behind the rear doors is collapsible

sedan limousine *n* **:** a sedan with an adjustable partition behind the front seat

sedarim *pl of* SEDER

¹se·date \səˈdāt, sēˈ-, *usu* -ād.+V\ *adj, usu* -ER/-EST [L *sedatus*, fr. past part. of *sedare* to settle, calm, soothe, appease, caus. of *sedēre* to sit — more at SIT] **1 a :** uninfluenced or not liable to influence by disturbing elements **:** QUIET, DISPASSIONATE ⟨a balance so calm and ~ as to exclude rapture —John Dewey⟩ **b :** of a staid, sober, or grave nature or constitution ⟨the more ~ winter settlers who find antic youth somewhat less attractive than their rocking-chair companions —C.L. Biemiller⟩ **2 :** characteristic of or suitable to sedate persons **:** placid or unobtrusive in appearance or nature ⟨in their ~ beauty of ruby and brown, the trees stretched ahead —T.B. Costain⟩ ⟨a sober brown cover, broken only by a ~ listing of its table of contents —J.D.Adams⟩ **syn** see SERIOUS

²sedate \"\ *vt* -ED/-ING/-S [back-formation fr. *sedative*] **:** to put (a patient) under the influence of a sedative drug

se·date·ly *adv* **:** in a sedate manner

se·date·ness *n* -ES **:** the quality or state of being sedate

se·da·tion \səˈdāshən, sēˈ-\ *n* -s [MF or L; MF *sedation*, fr. L *sedation-*, *sedatio*, fr. *sedatus* (past part. of *sedare* to calm) + *-ion-*, *-io* -ion] **1 :** the inducing of a relaxed easy state esp. by the use of sedatives **2 :** a state resulting from or like that resulting from sedation

¹sed·a·tive \ˈsedəd·iv, -ətiv\ *adj* [F or ML; F *sédatif*, fr. ML *sedativus*, fr. L *sedatus* (past part. of *sedare* to calm) + *-ivus* -ive — more at SEDATE] **:** tending to calm, moderate, or tranquilize; *specif* **:** allaying irritability, nervousness, or excitement

²sedative \"\ *n* -s **:** a sedative agent; *specif* **:** a drug that allays irritability, nervousness, or excitement

sedative salt *n* **:** BORIC ACID

se·dens \ˈseˌdenz\ *n, pl* **se·den·tes** \səˈdenˌtēz\ [NL *sedent-*, *sedens*, fr. L, pres. part. of *sedēre* to sit] **:** a person who remains a resident of the place or region of his birth — compare NOMAD, MIGRANT

se·dent \ˈsēdᵊnt\ *adj* [L *sedent-*, *sedens*, pres. part. of *sedēre* to sit — more at SIT] **:** SITTING — used esp. of a statue

sed·en·tar·ia \ˌsedᵊnˈta(a)rēə\ *n pl, cap* [NL, fr. L, neut. pl. of *sedentarius* sedentary] *in some classifications* **:** a division of Polychaeta comprising sedentary usu. tube-dwelling worms with reduced parapodia and sense organs and typically with highly developed filamentous anterior respiratory organs or gills — compare ERRANTIA, SABELLARIA

sed·en·tar·i·ae \-ēˌē\ *n pl, cap* [NL, fr. L, fem. pl. of *sedentarius* sedentary] *in former classifications* **:** a group including sedentary web-spinning spiders that wait for their prey to become entangled in their snares

sed·en·tar·i·ly \¦sedᵊn¦terəlē\ *adv* **:** in a sedentary manner

sed·en·tar·i·ness \ˈ==ˌterēnəs\ *n* -ES **:** the quality or state of being sedentary

sed·en·tary \-rē, -ri\ *adj* [MF *sedentaire*, fr. L *sedentarius* of one that sits, sedentary, fr. *sedent-*, *sedens* (pres. part. of *sedēre* to sit) + *-arius* -ary — more at SIT] **1 a :** staying in one or the same place **:** not migratory **:** STATIONARY, SETTLED ⟨~ birds⟩ ⟨a ~ tribe⟩ **b :** of, relating to, or characteristic of sedentes ⟨~ culture⟩ **c** *usu cap* **:** of or belonging to a period of development of the Hohokam culture about A.D. 900 to 1000 that precedes the Classic and is characterized by settled villages **2 a :** characterized by or requiring sitting or slight activity ⟨for ~ relaxation he is likely to listen to music —*Current Biog.*⟩ **b :** accustomed to sit much or long ⟨we think of the lawyer, teacher, and bookkeeper as ~ —L.A.Sylvester⟩ **c** *obs* **:** LAZY, INACTIVE **3 :** permanently attached ⟨the ~ oyster⟩ ⟨~ barnacles⟩

sedentary soil *n* **:** soil remaining on the rock from which it has developed

sed·en·ta·tion \ˌsedᵊnˈtāshən\ *n* -s [L or NL *sedent-*, *sedens* + E *-ation*] **:** the adoption of a sedentary mode of life or practices of sedentes

se·der \ˈsādə(r)\ *n, pl* **se·da·rim** \səˈdärəm\ *or* **seders** *often cap* [Heb *sēdher* order, division] **:** a Jewish home or community service and ceremonial dinner held on the first evening of the Passover and repeated on the second by Orthodox Jews except in Israel commemorating chiefly the exodus from Egypt

se·de·runt \səˈdirənt\ *n* -s [L, there sat (the following), 3d pl. perf. indic. of *sedēre* to sit, word used to introduce list of those attending a session — more at SIT] **1 a :** a session of an ecclesiastical assembly or other official body **b :** the persons or a list of persons present at a sederunt **2 :** a prolonged sitting (as for relaxation, reading, or discussion) ⟨the seat under the vine trellis where they had been having their evening ~ —John Buchan⟩

¹sedge \ˈsej\ *n* -s [ME *segge*, fr. OE *secg*; akin to MHG *segge* sedge, OE *sagu*, *sage* saw — more at SAW] **1 a :** a plant of the family Cyperaceae and esp. of the genus *Carex* **b :** SWEET FLAG **c :** YELLOW IRIS **2 a :** any of the caddis flies common along trout streams **b :** an artificial fly imitating a caddis fly **3 :** a grayish brown that is lighter than chestnut, lighter and slightly redder than coconut, and redder and slightly lighter than new cocoa — called also *beach tan, cashew nut, winter leaf*

²sedge *var of* SIEGE

sedge family *n* **:** CYPERACEAE

sedge fly *n* **:** any of several mayflies or caddis flies

sedge grass *n* **1 :** SWEET FLAG **2 :** a broom sedge (*Andropogon virginicus*)

sedge hen *n* **:** CLAPPER RAIL

sedgelike \ˈ=ˌ=\ *adj* **:** resembling or suggesting sedge

sedge root *n* **:** an edible-rooted sedge; *esp* **:** CHUFA

sedge warbler *also* **sedge bird** *or* **sedge wren** *n* **:** a small warbler (*Acrocephalus schoenobaenus*) that breeds among reeds and sedges in Europe and Asia and winters in Africa, is rusty brownish above with dark centers to the feathers and buffy white below, and has a loud sweet song

sedgy \ˈsejē\ *adj* -ER/-EST [¹*sedge* + *-y*] **1 :** of, relating to, or like sedge **2 :** overgrown or bordered with sedge ⟨drainage and steam power have turned ~ marshes into farm and meadow —J.R.Green⟩

se·di·le \səˈdīlē\ *n, pl* **sedil·ia** \-ˈdilēə\ [L, seat, fr. *sedēre* to sit] **:** one of usu. three seats in the chancel of a church near the altar used by officiating clergy during intervals of a service and in an English church usu. placed in a recess in the south wall

¹sed·i·ment \ˈsedəmənt\ *n* -s [MF, fr. L *sedimentum* settling, subsidence, fr. *sedēre* to sit, sink down + *-mentum* -ment — more at SIT] **1 :** the matter that settles to the bottom of a liquid **:** SETTLINGS, LEES, DREGS, FOOTS **2 :** material or a mass of material deposited (as by water, wind, or glaciers)

²sediment \"\ *vb* -ED/-ING/-S *vt* **:** to deposit as sediment **~** *vi* **1 :** to settle to the bottom in a liquid **2 :** to deposit sediment

sed·i·men·tal \¦sedə¦mentᵊl\ *adj* [¹*sediment* + *-al*] **:** formed of or from sediment

sed·i·men·tar·i·ly \¦sedəmən¦terəlē\ *adv* **:** in a sedimentary manner

¹sed·i·men·ta·ry \¦sedə¦mentərē, -n·trē, -ri\ *adj* [¹*sediment* + *-ary*] **1 :** of, relating to, or containing sediment ⟨~ deposits⟩ **2 :** formed by or from deposits of sediment ⟨~ clay⟩

²sedimentary \"\ *n* -ES **:** a sedimentary deposit, rock, or formation

sedimentary rock *n* **:** rock formed of mechanical, chemical, or organic sediment: as **a :** clastic rock (as conglomerate, sandstone, or shale) formed of fragments of other rock transported from its source and deposited in water **b :** rock (as rock salt or gypsum) formed by precipitation from solution **c :** rock (as limestone) formed from secretions of organisms

sed·i·men·tate \ˈsedəmən·ˌtāt, ˌsedəˈmen-\ *vt* -ED/-ING/-S [back-formation fr. *sedimentation*] **:** to cause (as sewage) to deposit sediment

sed·i·men·ta·tion \ˌsedəmənˈtāshən\ *n* -s [¹*sediment* + *-ation*] **:** the action or process of depositing sediment **:** SETTLING; *also* **:** the depositing esp. by mechanical means of matter suspended in a liquid ⟨the ~ of a water supply⟩; *broadly* **:** the movement in any direction of solid particles through a fluid as a result of gravitational or other force — compare CREAMING

sed·i·men·ta·tion·ist \-sh(ə)nəst\ *n* -s **:** one who investigates sedimentation or studies sedimentary processes

sedimentation rate *n* **:** the speed at which red blood cells settle to the bottom of a column of citrated blood and which is used esp. in diagnosing the progress of various abnormal conditions (as chronic infections)

sediment bulb *n* **:** a bulb retaining sediment separated by gravity from liquid in a tank

sed·i·men·to·log·i·cal \¦sedə¦mentᵊl¦äjəkəl\ *adj* **:** of or relating to sedimentology

sed·i·men·tol·o·gist \ˌsedəmənˈtäləjəst\ *n* -s [*sedimentology* + *-ist*] **:** SEDIMENTATIONIST

sed·i·men·tol·o·gy \-jē\ *n* -ES [¹*sediment* + *-o-* + *-logy*] **:** the description, classification, and interpretation of sediments

se·di·tion \səˈdishən, sēˈ-\ *n* -s [ME, fr. MF, fr. L *sedition-*, *seditio* civil discord, faction, lit., separation, fr. *sed-*, *se-* apart (fr. *sed*, *se* without) + *ition-*, *itio* act of going, fr. *itus* (past part. of *ire* to go) + *-ion-*, *-io* -ion — more at IDIOT, ISSUE] **1 :** an insurrection against constituted authority **:** a tumult caused by dissension, partisan hatred, or discontent ⟨by reason of inequalities, cities are filled with ~ —Benjamin Jowett⟩ **2 :** conduct consisting of speaking, writing, or acting against an established government or seeking to overthrow it by unlawful means **:** resistance to lawful authority **:** conduct tending to treason but without an overt act

se·di·tion·ary \-shəˌnerē\ *n* -ES [LL *seditionarius* rebel, revolutionary, fr. L *sedition-*, *seditio* sedition + *-arius* -ary] **:** an inciter or promoter of sedition

se·di·tion·ist \-sh(ə)nəst\ *n* -s [*sedition* + *-ist*] **:** SEDITIONARY

se·di·tious \-shəs\ *adj* [ME, fr. MF *seditieux*, fr. L *seditiosus*, fr. *seditio* sedition + *-osus* -ous] **1 :** disposed to arouse or take part in or guilty of sedition **:** FACTIOUS, TURBULENT ⟨a ~ agitator⟩ **2 :** of, relating to, of the nature of, or tending to excite sedition ⟨the punishment of ~ utterances —J.L.O'Brian⟩ **syn** see INSUBORDINATE

se·dja·deh \səˈjädə\ *n* -s [Turk *seccade*, fr. Ar *sajjādah*, fr. *sajada* to kneel] **:** a small Oriental rug about four feet by six feet

se·do·heptose \¦sēdō+\ *n* [NL *Sedum* + *-o-* + E *heptose*] **:** SEDOHEPTULOSE

se·do·heptulose \"+\ *n* [NL *Sedum* + *-o-* + E *heptulose*] **:** an amorphous ketose sugar $HOCH_2(CHOH)_4COCH_2OH$ of the heptose class that is obtained esp. from the leaves and stems of various stonecrops (as *Sedum spectabile*), that plays a role in carbohydrate metabolism but is not fermented by yeast, and that is a laboratory source of D-altrose and D-ribose — called also *altro-heptulose*

sedra *var of* SIDRA

se·duce \səˈd(y)üs, sēˈ-\ *vt* -ED/-ING/-S [L *seducere* to lead aside, lead away, fr. *se-* apart (fr. *sed*, *se* without) + *ducere* to lead — more at IDIOT, TOW] **1 :** to persuade into disobedience, disloyalty, or desertion ⟨pleaded guilty . . . to the charge of endeavoring to ~ a member of his Majesty's forces from his duty of allegiance —*Manchester Guardian Weekly*⟩ **2 :** to persuade or entice astray in action or belief ⟨employers have tried to ~ union leaders with rewards of money or advancement —Ed Marciniak⟩ ⟨abstract thoughts . . . ~ his mind away from essential experience —J.W.Aldridge⟩ **3 :** to persuade or entice into partnership in sexual intercourse **:** practice seduction upon; *specif* **:** to persuade (a female) to have sexual intercourse for the first time **4 :** to induce or force to come or go ⟨staircases which ~ us upwards to no successful result —Nathaniel Hawthorne⟩ **5 :** to attract or gain by or as if by quiet subtle charm **:** COAX ⟨trying to ~ her back to health with their futile offerings of plums and tangerines —Jean Stafford⟩ ⟨knew how to ~ the interest of his pupils; he did not drive, he led —L.K.Anspacher⟩ ⟨a composer who *seduced* new sounds out of the piano —*Time*⟩ **syn** see LURE

se·duc·ee \sə¦d(y)ü¦sē\ *n* -s [*seduce* + *-ee*] **:** one who is seduced

se·duce·ment \səˈd(y)üsmənt, sēˈ-\ *n* -s [*seduce* + *-ment*] **1 :** SEDUCTION **2** *obs* **:** the quality or state of being seduced **3 :** something that serves to seduce **:** a seductive temptation **:** ENTICEMENT

se·duc·er \-sə(r)\ *n* -s **:** one that seduces; *specif* **:** one that induces a female to surrender her chastity

se·duc·i·ble *also* **se·duce·able** \-səbəl\ *adj* [*seducible* fr. LL *seducibilis*, fr. *seducere* to seduce (fr. L, to lead aside, lead away) + L *-ibilis* -ible; *seduceable* fr. *seduce* + *-able*] **:** capable of being seduced

se·duc·ing·ly *adv* [*seducing* (fr. pres. part. of *seduce*) + *-ly*] **:** in a seductive manner

se·duc·tion \səˈdəkshən, sēˈ-\ *n* -s [MF, fr. LL *seduction-*, *seductio*, fr. L, act of leading aside, fr. *seductus* (past part. of *seducere* to lead aside) + *-ion-*, *-io* -ion] **1 :** the act of seducing esp. to wrong acts or beliefs ⟨the effect of social ~ by public spectacles on an immature mind —Fredric Wertham⟩; *specif* **:** the enticement of a female by some statutes required to be then chaste to unlawful sexual intercourse by promise of marriage or other means of persuasion without use of force **2 :** that which seduces or is adapted to seduce **:** a means of corrupting **3 :** something that entices or influences by attraction or charm ⟨the irresistible ~ of eloquence and literary pursuits —Norman Douglas⟩ ⟨the home carpenter usually succumbs to the ~*s* of the tool catalogs and buys an assortment of power tools —M.I.Zisowitz⟩

se·duc·tive \-ktiv, -tēv *also* -təv\ *adj* [ML, fr. *seductus* (past part. of *seducere* to seduce, fr. L, to lead aside) + L *-ivus* -ive — more at SEDUCE] **:** tending or having the qualities to seduce **:** ALLURING, TEMPTING, ATTRACTIVE ⟨an exceptionally beautiful and ~ woman —*N.Y. Times Bk. Rev.*⟩ ⟨the ~ temptations of a policy of opposition for the sake of opposition —J.G.Colton⟩ — **se·duc·tive·ly** \-tәvlē, -li\ *adv* — **se·duc·tive·ness** \-tivnəs, -tēv- *also* -təv-\ *n* -ES

se·duc·tress \-ktrəs\ *n* -ES [fem. of obs. *seductor* male seducer, fr. LL, fr. *seductus* (past part. of *seducere* to seduce, fr. L, to lead aside) + L *-or*] **:** a female seducer

se·du·li·ty \səˈd(y)üləd·ē\ *n* -ES [L *sedulitat-*, *sedulitas*, fr. *sedulus* sedulous + *-itat-*, *-itas* -ity] **:** sedulous activity **:** DILIGENCE, INDUSTRY

sed·u·lous \ˈsejələs\ *adj* [L *sedulus* diligent, fr. *sedulo* sincerely, on purpose, diligently, fr. *se* without + *dolus* guile, fraud, deceit — more at IDIOT, TALE] **1 :** marked by or accomplished with care and perseverance ⟨his products had . . . the mark of a ~ craftsmanship —H.E.Clurman⟩ ⟨the ~ evasion of racial issues —Oscar Handlin⟩ **2 :** diligent in application or pursuit **:** persevering in endeavors to effect an object **:** steadily industrious ⟨the notes of the great man are gathered together by a ~ devotee —Irwin Edman⟩ **syn** see BUSY

sed·u·lous·ly *adv* **:** in a sedulous manner

sed·u·lous·ness *n* -ES **:** the quality or state of being sedulous

se·dum \ˈsēdəm\ *n* [NL, fr. L, houseleek] **1** *cap* **:** a genus of fleshy widely distributed herbs (family Crassulaceae) having cymose yellow, white, or pink flowers, pellicular fruit, and often tufted stems — see ORPINE, STONECROP **2** -s **:** any plant of the genus *Sedum*

¹see \ˈsē\ *vb* **saw** \ˈsȯ\ *or substand* **seed** \ˈsēd\ *or* **seen** \ˈsēn\ **seen** *or substand* **seed** *or* **saw; seeing; sees** \ˈsēz\ [ME *seen*, *sen*, fr. OE *sēon*; akin to OHG *sehan* to see, ON *sjá*, Goth *saihwan*, OE *secgan* to say — more at SAY] *vt* **1 a :** to perceive by the eye **:** apprehend through sight ⟨opens his eyes to ~ the sunlight coming in through the window⟩ **b :** to perceive as if by sight ⟨it was wonderful what that boy *saw* who was blind —Stuart Cloete⟩ **c :** to detect the presence of ⟨the supersonic streamlining of this vehicle makes it difficult to ~ by radar —L.N.Ridenour⟩ **2 a :** to have experience of **:** UNDERGO ⟨*saw* sea duty on a minesweeper —*Current Biog.*⟩ ⟨if anyone keeps my word, he will never ~ death —Jn 8:51 (RSV)⟩ ⟨opening for keen, practical, final year student to ~ dairy cattle and small-animal practice —*Veterinary Record*⟩ ⟨*seen* better days⟩ ⟨~ life⟩ **b :** to learn or find by observation or experience **:** come to know **:** DISCOVER ⟨a point of view which I have since *seen* cause to modify —John Buchan⟩ **c :** to find out by investigation **:** ASCERTAIN ⟨~ if the hat fits⟩ ⟨~ if the car needs oil⟩ ⟨~ who's at the door⟩ **d :** to give rise to **:** be marked by ⟨the late glacial times *saw* the complete triumph of our ancestral stock —Jacquetta & Christopher Hawkes⟩ **e :** to serve as the setting for **:** be the scene of **:** WITNESS ⟨that house *saw* more worry and unhappiness —Virginia D. Dawson & Betty D. Wilson⟩ **3 a :** to form a mental picture of **:** VISUALIZE ⟨can still ~ her as she was twenty years ago⟩ ⟨*saw* her in his dreams⟩ **b :** to perceive the meaning or importance of **:** COMPREHEND, UNDERSTAND ⟨because the frontier gives shape and life to our national myth, we have preferred to ~ its story in romantic outline —Dayton Kohler⟩ **c :** to be aware of **:** RECOGNIZE ⟨planning to fire you tomorrow, because you just can't ~ a good news story —Sinclair Lewis⟩ ⟨~*s* the folly of further resistance —T.B.Costain⟩ ⟨~*s* only his faults⟩ **d :** to form a conception of **:** imagine as a possibility **:** SUPPOSE ⟨can you ~ me knowing how to furnish a house —Edith Sitwell⟩ ⟨was never whipped . . . she was so dignified and superior you just couldn't ~ her across my mother's lap —Myron Brinig⟩ **e :** to have presented for observation or consideration **:** be made aware of ⟨we *saw*, in the previous lecture, how the problem arose⟩ **f :** to look at from a particular point of view ⟨~ ourselves as others see us —Robert Burns⟩ **g :** to look ahead to **:** FORESEE ⟨can ~ the day when a college will not try to cover the whole field of liberal arts —*Time*⟩ **4 a :** to direct one's attention to **:** put under observation **:** EXAMINE, SCRUTINIZE ⟨want to ~ how he handles the problem⟩ **b** (1) **:** to inspect or read understandingly (something written or printed) ⟨have you *seen* the story of yesterday's game⟩ ⟨let me ~ your pass, soldier⟩ ⟨*seen* and allowed⟩ (2) **:** to read of ⟨I *saw* your appointment in the newspapers⟩ **c :** to refer to ⟨for further information, ~ the documents printed in the appendix⟩ ⟨~ the explanatory notes at the beginning of the book⟩ **d :** to attend or visit as an observer or spectator ⟨~ a parade⟩ ⟨~ a play⟩ ⟨~ the sights of the city⟩ **5 a :** to take care of **:** provide for ⟨would like him to have enough to ~ him easily to the end of his days —T.B.Costain⟩ **b :** to take care or heed **:** make sure ⟨~ thou say nothing to any man —Mk 1:44 (AV)⟩ ⟨~ that your wet umbrella is not placed between your seat and the next —Agnes M. Miall⟩ ⟨will ~ that he is brought up properly⟩ **6 a :** to regard as **:** CONSIDER, JUDGE ⟨the electorate did not ~ fit to ratify the new frame of government —B.W.Bond⟩ ⟨did not ~ it right to ask for special favors⟩ **b :** to prefer to have **:** allow to happen **:** WELCOME ⟨would probably ~ himself shot before he told a deliberate falsehood —J.G.Cozzens⟩ ⟨I'll ~ you dead before I accept your terms⟩ **c :** to regard with approval or liking **:** find acceptable or attractive ⟨still can't ~ the portholes but this is our only complaint in an otherwise clean design —Walt Woron⟩ ⟨hope you'll be able to make her ~ it —W.S.Maugham⟩ ⟨can't understand what he ~*s* in her⟩ **7 a** (1) **:** to make a call upon **:** VISIT ⟨stopped off at the office to ~ his former employer⟩ (2) **:** to call upon or meet with in order to obtain help or advice ⟨~ a doctor⟩ ⟨~ a lawyer⟩ **b** (1) **:** to be in the company of regularly or frequently esp. in courtship or dating ⟨had been ~*ing* each other for a year before they became engaged⟩ (2) **:** to grant an interview to or accept the visit of **:** meet with **:** RECEIVE ⟨the president of the bank will ~ you in a few minutes⟩ ⟨~*s* only a few old friends these days⟩ (3) **:** to meet with for the purpose of influencing esp. by bribery or pressure ⟨charged that the witness had been *seen* by the defense⟩ **8 a :** ACCOMPANY, ESCORT ⟨young men would wait to ~ the young ladies home —Agnes S. Turnbull⟩ **b :** to wait upon **:** be present with ⟨*saw* her onto the plane⟩ ⟨*saw* him off at the station⟩ **c :** to give continued attention, assistance, or guidance to — used with *through* ⟨*saw* a new edition of his book through the press⟩ ⟨the sympathy of his friends *saw* him through this period of grief⟩ **9 :** to meet (a bet) in poker or to equal the bet of (a player) **:** CALL **~** *vi* **1 a :** to give or pay attention ⟨~, the train is coming⟩ **b :** to look about ⟨stood up and fired his pistol in the air, and the naked Indians came out on the shore to ~ —Meridel Le Sueur⟩ **2 a :** to have the power of sight **:** have vision ⟨whereas I was blind, now I ~ —Jn 9:25 (AV)⟩ ⟨he ~*s* poorly with his left eye⟩ **b :** to apprehend objects by sight ⟨it was so foggy that he could hardly ~⟩ **c :** to perceive objects as if by sight ⟨the butterfly lightness that was teaching his fingers to ~ —Marcia Davenport⟩ **3 a :** to grasp something mentally **:** have insight **:** UNDERSTAND ⟨this fundamental bias of all thinking . . . is what enables us to ~, gives thought its real use —H.J.Muller⟩ **b :** to take note ⟨these aren't ordinary trout, you ~ —Corey Ford⟩ **c :** CONSIDER, THINK ⟨when can I finish this — let me ~⟩ **4 a :** to make investigation or inquiry ⟨you'll ~ about the rates, won't you —Agnes S. Turnbull⟩ **b :** to arrive at a conclusion through observation and experience ⟨I can't give you an answer yet, but we shall ~⟩

syn BEHOLD, DESCRY, ESPY, VIEW, SURVEY, OBSERVE, NOTICE, REMARK, NOTE, PERCEIVE, DISCERN: SEE is broad and general and may stand for any of the other words here ⟨I *see* you⟩ ⟨I *see* it⟩ BEHOLD may be used in situations involving awe, grandeur, or dignity, with suggestions of observant, complete vision ⟨it was on a dreary night of November that I *beheld* the accomplishment of my toils —Mary W. Shelley⟩ ⟨Grecian spectators . . . when they *beheld* the innumerable Persian host crossing the Hellespont —George Grote⟩ DESCRY may suggest watchful, careful scanning and observation of the distant or the difficult to view ⟨on a superb day he can *descry* Greenwich, 28 miles away —*New Yorker*⟩ ESPY is similar in suggestion to DESCRY but is more likely to be used to refer to the obscure or covert ⟨flowers we *espy* beside the torrent growing, flowers that peep forth from many a cleft and chink —William Wordsworth⟩ ⟨on these analogies it is not altogether fantastic to *espy* . . . the ghost of a Minoan universal church —A.J. Toynbee⟩ VIEW may designate an overall or comprehensive looking at a subject, often from a specific or particular position or in a specific or peculiar way ⟨the little chapel . . . the white dove . . . green tufted islands . . . the youth had long been *viewing* these pleasant things —John Keats⟩ ⟨the effort is an interesting one if you *view* it in terms of the techniques of political symbolism —Max Lerner⟩ SURVEY, in this sense, may be used in reference to a broad view from a high point or may designate a comprehensive examination of a subject with careful consideration of its salient points ⟨am monarch of all I *survey* —William Cowper⟩ ⟨had plenty of leisure now, day in, day out, to *survey* her life as a tract of country traversed —Victoria Sackville-West⟩ OBSERVE may suggest careful, heedful attention directed and sustained ⟨a genuine scientific process — the play of intellect and imagination around a few fragments of *observed* fact —Havelock Ellis⟩ ⟨the Navy is *observing* the new programs in the Army and Air Force with interest —*Atlantic*⟩ NOTICE may suggest careful observation and intention to record or remember ⟨if we tried to *notice* all the ways in which the idea of beauty has been corrupted —Irving Babbitt⟩ REMARK and NOTE mean to see or sense and to record or make a mental note ⟨I *remarked* their English accents —James Joyce⟩ ⟨believed that the artist should not number the streaks of the tulip but should *remark* general properties and large appearances —F.W.Hilles⟩ ⟨in these brilliant and gifted inhabitants . . . one may *note* a number of characteristics —Geoffrey Bruun⟩ ⟨writers are perhaps the best of travelers, since their sharpened senses seize and *note* impressions —F.B.Millett⟩ PERCEIVE may combine the notions of seeing or sensing and of recognizing and realizing ⟨his lightning dashes from image to image, so quick that we are unable at first to *perceive* the points of contact —C.D.Lewis⟩ ⟨what a great novelist at his best *perceives* in human nature —Bernard De Voto⟩ DISCERN may apply to seeing or perceiving identities or differences which are not immediately obvious ⟨never for a moment *discerned* that there was in him anything out of the ordinary —W.S.Maugham⟩

syn SEE, LOOK, and WATCH can all mean to perceive something by means of the eyes. SEE stresses the reception of the visual impression ⟨*see* clearly with a telescope⟩ ⟨have the power of *seeing*⟩ LOOK stresses the directing of the eyes to something in order to see ⟨*look* and see the man leave⟩ ⟨turn suddenly to *look* at the man⟩ WATCH implies a persistent observing or the following of something with the eyes in order to observe fully ⟨*watch* what a child is up to⟩ ⟨a cat *watching* a mouse⟩
— **see about 1 :** to attend to ⟨I'll *see about* parking if you buy the tickets⟩ **2 :** to think over before deciding ⟨we can't give you an answer now, but we'll *see about* it⟩ — **see after :** to attend to or care for ⟨*see after* the baggage⟩ ⟨*see after* the baby⟩ — **see daylight 1 :** to get over the initial difficulties of a problem or undertaking ⟨after five years of trying, he began to *see daylight*⟩ **2** *slang, of a bronco rider* **:** to bounce high in the saddle so that daylight can be seen between the rider and the saddle — **see for** *dial chiefly Eng* **:** to look for — **see one's way :** to find a course of action possible or reasonable ⟨think I can *see my way* to lending you 10 dollars⟩ — **see red :** to become enraged **:** lose control of oneself ⟨has an insulting manner that makes others *see red*⟩ — **see the elephant** *slang* **:** to gain experience of the world — **see through :** to see the true meaning, nature, or character of ⟨pride themselves on *seeing through* the motives of politicians —*Times Lit. Supp.*⟩ ⟨we have *seen through* the environment theory as we *saw through* the race theory —A.J.Toynbee⟩ — **see to :** to take care of **:** attend to ⟨*saw to* the education of the children —Nancy Mitford⟩ — **see to it :** to make certain by taking necessary or appropriate action ⟨*saw to it* that the men in the armed services received higher pay —*Current Biog.*⟩

²**see** \"\ *n* -s [ME *se, see,* fr. OF *se, sed, sie* seat, throne, see, fr. L *sedes* seat; akin to L *sedēre* to sit — more at SIT] **1 a** *archaic* **:** CATHEDRA **b :** a church containing a cathedra **:** CATHEDRAL **c :** a seat or center of the power or authority of a bishop **:** a diocesan center **2 a :** the rank, office, power, or authority of a bishop ⟨the ~ of Rome⟩ **b :** the jurisdiction (as a diocese or province) of a bishop

see·able \'sēəbəl\ *adj* [ME *seable,* fr. *seen, sen* to see + *-able*] **:** capable of being seen

see·beck effect \'zā,bek-, 'sē,bek-\ *n, usu cap S* [after Thomas J. *Seebeck* †1831 Ger. physicist] **:** the thermoelectromotive force generated in a circuit composed of different metals in successive contact when the junctions are not all at the same temperature; *also* **:** the current resulting from such force when the circuit is closed

see·catch \'sē,kach\ *n, pl* **see·catch·ie** \-chē\ [Russ *sekach*] **:** a grown male Alaskan fur seal

see·chelt *also* **se·chelt** \'sē,shelt\ *n, pl* **seechelt** *or* **seechelts** *usu cap* **1 a :** a Salishan people of southwestern British Columbia **b :** a member of such people **2 :** the language of the Seechelt people

¹**seed** \'sēd\ *n, pl* **seed** *or* **seeds** [ME *sed, seed,* fr. OE *sǣd;* akin to OHG *sāt* seed, ON *sāth,* Goth *manaseths* seed of men, world, OE *sāwan* to sow — more at SOW] **1 a :** something that is sown or to be sown ⟨as he sowed, some ~ fell along the path and the birds came and devoured it —Mk 4:4 (RSV)⟩ **b :** the fertilized and ripened ovule of a seed plant comprising a miniature plant usu. accompanied by a supply of food (as endosperm or perisperm), enclosed in a protective seed coat, often accompanied by auxiliary structures (as an aril or caruncle), and capable under suitable conditions of independent development into a plant similar to the one that produced it — see ENDOCARP illustration **c :** a propagative portion of a plant: as (1) **:** SPORE (2) **:** a dry seedlike fruit (as a caryopsis or seedball) (3) **:** a vegetative reproductive structure (as a bulb, corm, or tuber) **d** (1) **:** MILT, SEMEN, SPERM (2) **:** any of various eggs esp. of insects or other arthropods (3) **:** any of various developmental stages of lower animals suitable for transplanting; *specif* **:** SPAT **e :** the condition or stage of bearing seed ⟨in ~⟩ **2 :** PROGENY ⟨the green turban which proclaimed him to be of the ~ of the Prophet —Lawrence Durrell⟩ **3 :** something from which development or growth takes place **:** a beginning or source **:** GERM ⟨planted a ~ of suspicion in me, which by now has grown to a conviction —Thomas Wood †1950⟩ ⟨the bill had had a far-reaching effect and was the ~ of reform —Roger Burlingame⟩ **4 :** something that resembles a seed in shape or size: as **a :** a small bubble in glass **b :** a small usu. glass and gold or platinum capsule used as a container for a radioactive substance (as radium or radon) to be applied usu. interstitially in the treatment of cancer **5 a** *cap* **:** INNER LIGHT **b :** HOMOEOMERY 1 **6 :** a nucleus in seeding; *esp* **:** a crystal added to a liquid to cause crystallization **7 :** a player who has been seeded in competition — **go to seed** *or* **run to seed 1 :** to develop seed **2 :** to lose vitality or effectiveness **:** DECAY ⟨it is the picture of the idealist *gone to seed,* the sensitive man turned sour —H.E.Clurman⟩ ⟨the eighteenth century upper-class culture was *running to seed* —Roy Lewis & Angus Maude⟩

²**seed** \"\ *vb* -ED/-ING/-S [ME *seden,* fr. *sed* seed] *vi* **1 :** to go to seed **:** grow to maturity and produce seed **2 :** to sow seed **:** PLANT **3 :** to crystallize or form a precipitate or aggregate as the result of seeding **:** GRAIN ~ *vt* **1 a :** to sprinkle with seed **:** plant seeds in **:** sow ⟨~ a plot with barley⟩ **b :** to cause to be filled or furnished with something that grows or stimulates growth or development ⟨a breeder reactor ~*ed* with plutonium —*Time*⟩ **c** (1) **:** to inoculate with microorganisms (2) **:** to inoculate (neighboring or distant tissues) by dispersion from the parent focus — used of bacteria or cancer cells **d :** to supply with nuclei (as of crystallization or condensation) ⟨~ a saturated solution with solid particles of solute⟩; *esp* **:** to treat (a cloud) with solid particles (as silver iodide crystals) for the purpose of converting supercooled water droplets into ice crystals in an attempt to produce precipitation artificially or to dissipate a supercooled cloud **e :** to allow or cause (as lard or syrup) to form granules or crystals by cooling **2 a :** to plant by scattering on or in the soil ⟨~ another crop in the field⟩ ⟨~ beets in the spring⟩ **b :** to distribute at random **:** SCATTER ⟨several hundred bright young intellectuals who were ~*ed* into overseas aid and information programs —Daniel Bell⟩ **3 a :** to extract the seeds from (stone fruit) **b :** ¹RIPPLE 1 **4 :** to give rise to **:** stimulate the development of ⟨although the theory is still not finally proved, it ~*ed* a whole generation of fruitful study —George Gamow⟩ **5 a :** to arrange (the draw in a sports event) so that certain contestants (as those of superior ability or of the same team) will not meet in the early rounds of competition; *also* **:** to arrange the order of competition of (contestants) by seeding **b :** to rank (a contestant) relative to others in a tournament on the basis of previous record

³**seed** \"\ *adj* [¹*seed*] **1 a :** grown or retained for the production of seed ⟨a ~ crop⟩ **b :** selected or used for planting or cultivation to produce a new crop or stock ⟨~ corn⟩ ⟨~ flax⟩ ⟨~ potato⟩ ⟨~ virus⟩ **c :** left or saved for breeding ⟨a ~ population⟩ **2 :** incompletely developed **:** SMALL ⟨the ovaries full of ~ eggs⟩

⁴**seed** *substand past of* SEE

seed·age \-dij\ *n* -s [²*seed* + *-age*] **:** the practice or method of propagating plants by means of seeds or spores

seedball \'=,=\ *n* [¹*seed* + *ball*] **1 :** a rounded and usu. dry or capsular fruit (as of a potato) **2 :** the collection of one-seeded fruits (as utricles) found in various plants (as the beet)

seedbed \'=,=\ *n* **1 :** the soil or forest floor upon which seed becomes bedded: as **a :** the surface soil of cultivated land prepared by tillage for the seeding of a crop **b :** a bed usu. of fine soil for growth of plants from seeds preparatory to transplantation **c :** a subdivision of a tree nursery for raising seedlings **2 :** a place or source of growth or development ⟨must protect and extend our basic research as the ~ of new advances —J.R.Killian⟩

seed beetle *n* **:** a beetle (as a bean weevil or pea weevil) that feeds on the seeds of plants

seedbird \'=,=\ *n* **1 :** ¹MEW **2 :** PIED WAGTAIL

seedbox \'=,=\ *n* **1 :** CAPSULE **2 :** any of various plants of the genus *Ludwigia; esp* **:** a No. American swamp herb (*L. alternifolia*) with yellow flowers and a loosely seeded angled capsule

seedcake \'=,=\ *n* **1 :** a cake or cookie containing aromatic seeds (as sesame or caraway) **2 :** OIL CAKE

seedcase \'=,=\ *n* **:** ²POD 1

seed coat *n* **:** the outer protective covering of a seed that is developed from one or more integuments often in combination with other adherent parts of the ovary (as in a caryopsis)

seed-corn beetle *n* **:** a carabid beetle (*Agonoderus lecontei*) that often feeds on corn seed in the ground

seed-corn maggot *n* **:** a small yellowish grub with a pointed head that is the larva of a grayish brown two-winged fly (*Hylemya platura*), is native to Europe but now widely distributed in No. America, and is typically a destructive borer in seeds and seedlings (as of Indian corn, beans, or melons) but sometimes attacks stems or roots of older plants — called also *corn maggot*

seed cotton *n* **:** the unginned cottonseed with the attached lint

seed down *vt* [²*seed* + *down*] **:** to sow with grass or forage legume seed

seedeater \'=,==\ *n* [¹*seed* + *eater*] **:** any of various birds and esp. finches whose diet consists basically of seeds **:** HARD-BILL: as **a :** any of several southern African finches that resemble and were formerly classified with the canaries **b :** any of numerous tropical American finches of the genus *Sporophila* **c :** GRASSQUIT

seeded *adj* [fr. past part. of ²*seed*] **1 a :** supplied or sprinkled with seed **:** SOWN ⟨a ~ field⟩ **b :** having seeds ⟨a ~ breadfruit⟩; *esp* **:** having a specified kind, number, or quantity of seeds — usu. used in combination ⟨round-*seeded*⟩ ⟨one-*seeded*⟩ ⟨many-*seeded*⟩ **c :** INOCULATED **2 :** run to seed **:** FULL-GROWN, MATURE **3 :** having seeds or seed vessels of specified tincture — used of a heraldic flower **4 :** having the seeds extracted ⟨~ raisins⟩ **5** *of textiles* **:** having flecks or knops ⟨~ yarn⟩

seeded plum *n* **:** PERSIMMON 1a

seedee *var of* SIDI

seed·er \'sēdə(r)\ *n* -s [²*seed* + *-er*] **1 :** an implement used for planting or sowing seeds **2 :** one that seeds fruit ⟨a raisin ~⟩ **3 a :** a plant that produces seed freely **b :** a plant that abnormally produces seed the first season **4 :** one that seeds clouds

seedfall \'=,=\ *n* [¹*seed* + *fall*] **:** the natural dispersal of seed from a plant and esp. from a tree

seed feed cup *n* **:** the seed feed attachment of a cup drill

seed fern *n* **:** a plant or fossil of the order Cycadofilicales **:** PTERIDOSPERM

seed fish *n* **:** a fish full of ripe spawn

seed·ful \'sēdfəl\ *adj* **:** full of seed **:** GENERATIVE ⟨his critical essays are as fruitful — or one might rather call them ~ — as any written in our time —Malcolm Cowley⟩

seedgall \'=,=\ *n* **:** a gall that resembles a seed; *esp* **:** one caused by a phylloxera

seed hair *n* **1 :** KAPOK **2** *or* **seed crown** *or* **seed down :** ²COMA 1c

seedier *comparative of* SEEDY

seediest *superlative of* SEEDY

seed·i·ly \'sēdᵊlē, -dᵊli, -dəl-\ *adv* **:** in a seedy manner

seed·i·ness \-dēnəs, -din-\ *n* -ES **:** the quality or state of being seedy

seeding *n* -s [ME *seding,* fr. gerund of *seden* to seed] **1 a** *archaic* **:** the act or an instance of producing seed **b :** the act or an instance of sowing seed **2 :** SPAWNING ⟨the ~ of spring salmon was fairly satisfactory —*Report: Canadian Fisheries Dept.*⟩ **3 :** the act or an instance of treating a cloud with solid particles **4 :** the act or practice of placing some players in such a position in the draw that they will not meet in the earlier rounds of a tournament; *also* **:** the posted list of such an arrangement

seeding lath *or* **seeding trough** *n* **:** a device used to distribute tree seeds evenly in drills in the seedbed

seeding plow *var of* SEED PLOW

seed lac *n* [¹*seed*] **:** a granular resinous material obtained from stick lac by crushing, cleaning, and washing and further processed to yield shellac

seed leaf *n* **:** COTYLEDON 2

seedleaf \'=,=\ *n* **:** a broadleaf tobacco used in cigars

seed·less \'sēdləs\ *adj* **:** lacking seeds ⟨~ grapefruit⟩ — **seed·less·ness** *n* -ES

seedless orange *n* **:** NAVEL ORANGE

seed·let \-lət\ *n* -s **:** a small seed

seedlike \'=,=\ *adj* **:** resembling a seed

¹**seed·ling** \'sēdliŋ, -lēŋ\ *n* -s [¹*seed* + *-ling*] **1 a :** a plant grown from seed as distinguished from one propagated by a vegetative part (as a cutting or layer) **b** (1) **:** a tree grown from seed as distinguished from one developed as a stump sucker (2) **:** a young tree smaller than a sapling **c :** a nursery plant (as a tree) that has not been transplanted **2 :** a small seed **3 :** a young sponge

²**seedling** \"\ *adj* **1 :** grown or developed from seed **2 :** resembling a small seed **:** existing in an undeveloped form ⟨the poor, rare, struggling, ~ counterpart —A.L.Kroeber⟩

seedling-rooted \'==,==\ *adj, of a tree* **:** developed from grafting or budding on a seedling stock — compare OWN-ROOT

seed·lip \'sēd,lip\ *n* [ME *sedelip,* fr. OE *sǣdlēap,* fr. *sǣd* seed + *lēap* basket — more at SEED, LEAP] *dial chiefly Eng* **:** a basket or other container in which seed to be sowed broadcast is carried

seed·man \'sēdmən\ *n, pl* **seedmen** [¹*seed* + *man*] **:** SEEDSMAN

seedness *n* -ES [¹*seed* + *-ness*] *obs* **:** the act of sowing or the state of being sown ⟨blossoming time that from the ~ the bare fallow brings to teeming foison —Shak.⟩

seed oyster *n* **:** a young oyster after settling and becoming attached to the substrate; *esp* **:** one of a size suitable for transplantation

seed pan *n* **:** a shallow flowerpot used esp. for germinating seeds

seed parent *n* **:** the pistillate parent in plant breeding

seed pearl *n* [³*seed*] **1 a :** a very small and often irregular pearl **b :** minute pearls imbedded in some binding material **2 :** a pale to grayish yellow that is redder and less strong than wine yellow and less strong and slightly redder than Naples yellow — called also *cartridge buff, Spanish flesh*

seed piece *n* **:** any of various parts used in plant propagation: as **a :** a cutting of sugar cane **b :** a piece of a potato tuber including at least one eye

seed plant *n* [¹*seed*] **:** a plant that bears seeds; *specif* **:** a plant of the Spermatophyta

seed planter *n* **:** SEEDER 1

seed plate *n* **:** a round perforated metal plate in the bottom of the hopper of a corn or cotton planter that sorts out and releases the correct amount of seed to be dropped at regular intervals

seed-plot \'=,=\ *n* **:** SEEDBED ⟨its local and national prestige as a *seed-plot* of scholarship —*Dial*⟩

seed plow *or* **seeding plow** *n* **:** a plow equipped with an automatic seeding device

seedpod \'=,=\ *n* **:** ²POD 1

seeds *pl of* SEED, *pres 3d sing of* SEED

seeds hay *n, Brit* **:** hay cut from a temporary or rotation meadow sown not more than 2 to 6 years previously

seeds·man \'sēdzmən\ *n, pl* **seedsmen 1 :** one who sows seed **2 :** one who deals in or handles seed

seed snipe *n* **:** any of several So. American charadriiform birds constituting the family Thinocoridae, related to the sheathbill but resembling quail in general appearance, and mainly frequenting dry inland regions

seedstalk \'=,=\ *n* **:** the fruiting stalk of a flowering plant

seed stitch *n* **1 :** a short straight stitch used for background filling in embroidery **2 :** MOSS STITCH

seed stock *n* **1 :** a supply of seed, tubers, or roots reserved for planting **2 :** the residual population of an animal needed to restock a range (as after hunting); *also* **:** a small population introduced to stock a new or disused range

seed tick *n* **:** the six-legged larva of a tick

seedtime \'=,=\ *n* [ME, fr. ¹*seed* + *time*] **1 :** the season of sowing seeds **2 :** a period of development or preparation

seed treatment *n* **:** the act or process of applying a pesticide to seed

seed tree *n* **:** a tree that bears seed; *specif* **:** a tree left uncut to provide seed for forest reproduction

seed vessel *n* **:** PERICARP

seed weevil *n* **:** any of numerous small weevils that live in seeds

seedy \'sēdē, -di\ *adj, usu* -ER/-EST [¹*seed* + *-y*] **1 a** (1) **:** abounding in seeds **:** bearing or containing seeds (2) **:** run to seed **b** *of a fish* **:** full of spawn **c** *of glass* **:** containing many small bubbles **d** *of bacon* **:** containing granules of melanin **2 a :** shabby or unprepossessing in dress or appearance ⟨a tall ~ man dressed in a frock coat that shone in the sun and looked greenish in the shade —J.B.Priestley⟩ **b :** being in a run-down uncared-for condition **:** DECAYED ⟨a ~ village of long huts with galvanized-iron roofs —John Dos Passos⟩ ⟨an area of ~ houses, industrial plants, and warehouses —*Amer. Guide Series: N.Y. City*⟩ **c :** MEAN, SQUALID ⟨the change in his character from an affluent good fellow to a ~ miser —C.C.Walcutt⟩ **3 :** lacking in vitality or strength **:** under the weather **:** DEBILITATED, SPIRITLESS ⟨have been rather ~ . . . with another cold and coughing at night —O.W.Holmes †1935⟩

seedy buckberry *n* **:** PRIVET ANDROMEDA

seedy toe *n* **:** an abnormality of a horse's foot marked by separation of the wall from the sole in the white line

see-er \'sēə(r)\ *n* -s **:** one who sees ⟨the painter is the *see-er,* he whose trained eye is sensitive —*Scientific Monthly*⟩

see·gar \'sē,gär, =\'=\ *n* -s [Sp *cigarro*] *chiefly dial* **:** CIGAR ⟨with a hitch and sway . . . in the shoulders, and his ~ at a more declarative angle —R.P.Warren⟩

see-ho \sē'hō\ *v imper* [prob. alter. (influenced by *see,* imper. of ¹*see*) of *soho*] — a call to indicate the first sighting of the hare in a hunt

¹**seeing** *n* -s [ME, fr. gerund of *seen, sen* to see] **1 a :** the act of using one's sense of sight ⟨~ is believing⟩ ⟨a sight worth ~⟩ ⟨recounts his ~*s* and doings —Virginia Woolf⟩ **b :** the faculty or power of sight or insight **:** VISION ⟨gain the gift of deeper ~ —Amy Lowell⟩ **2 :** the quality of the images of celestial bodies observed telescopically as determined by the state of turbulence of the parts of the atmosphere through which the light has passed and usu. rated on a scale from 0 for very poor quality to 10 for perfect quality

²**seeing** *adj* [ME, fr. pres. part. of *seen, sen* to see] **:** having the power of sight or insight ⟨if not a blind force but a ~ force runs things —William James⟩ — **see·ing·ly** *adv*

³**seeing** *conj* **:** in view of the fact that **:** inasmuch as **:** CONSIDERING — often used with *that* or *as*

Seeing Eye *trademark* — used for a guide dog trained to lead the blind

seeing glass *n* [¹*seeing*] *dial chiefly Eng* **:** MIRROR

¹**seek** \'sēk\ *vb* **sought** \'sȯt, *usu* -ȯd.+V\ **sought; seeking; seeks** [ME *sechen, seken* (past *soughte,* past part. *sought*), fr. OE *sēcan* (past *sōhte,* past part. *gesōht*); akin to OHG *suohhen* to seek (past *suohta,* past part. *gisuohhit*), ON *sœkja* (past *sōtti,* past part. *sōttr*), Goth *sokjan* to seek (past *sokida,* past part. *sokiths*), *sakan* to quarrel, L *sagire* to perceive keenly, Gk *hēgeisthai* to go ahead, lead] *vt* **1** *obs* **:** to follow or advance against in order to attack **:** PURSUE ⟨of us must Pompey presently be *sought,* or else he ~*s* out us —Shak.⟩ **2 :** to resort to **:** go to ⟨for an hour everyone ~*s* the shade to rest —Richard Roche⟩ ⟨departed for Rome which at that time was *sought* by American painters and sculptors —Charles de Kay⟩ **3 a** (1) **:** to go in search of **:** look for **:** search for ⟨if management does decide to ~ the man within the ranks of the company —Bruce Payne⟩ ⟨~*ing* out keymen and awarding them fellowships —*Bull. of Meharry Med. Coll.*⟩ (2) **:** to move or act so as to reach or arrive at ⟨water ~*s* its own level⟩ ⟨rockets designed to ~ out and destroy with uncanny accuracy enemy bombers —H.W. Baldwin⟩ **b :** to try to discover ⟨not all research is confined to ~*ing* new chemicals —*Monsanto Chemical Co. Annual Report*⟩ ⟨~ the truth⟩ **4 :** to inquire for **:** ask for **:** ENTREAT, REQUEST ⟨his advice was *sought* by many of the party's leaders —H.J.Howland⟩ **5 :** to try to acquire or gain **:** aim at ⟨never held public office, nor did he ever ~ it —W.C.Ford⟩ ⟨teach the child to ~ the good and to avoid the bad —*Better Homes & Gardens*⟩ ⟨~ fame and fortune⟩ **6 :** to make an attempt **:** TRY — used with an infinitive ⟨all governments, of course, ~ to keep the bulk of their people contented —D.M.Potter⟩ **7** *archaic* **:** to look through **:** EXPLORE ⟨have I *sought* every country far and near —Shak.⟩ ~ *vi* **1 :** to make a search or inquiry ⟨~*ing* along the shelf for a volume —G.B.Shaw⟩ **2** *archaic* **:** to pay a visit **:** GO, RESORT ⟨wisdom's self oft ~*s* to sweet retired solitude —John Milton⟩ **3** *archaic* **:** to have recourse **:** make request **:** APPLY ⟨to whom I ~ for my medicine —Geoffrey Chaucer⟩ **4 a :** to be sought or looked for ⟨the connection between dress and war is not far to ~ —Virginia Woolf⟩ **b** *archaic* **:** to be at a loss to know or act ⟨for the details of our itinerary, I am all to ~ —R.L.Stevenson⟩ **c** *archaic* **:** to be at a disadvantage ⟨leave us wholly to ~ in the art of political wagering —Jonathan Swift⟩ **5 :** to retrieve killed game — used chiefly as a command to dogs

syn SEARCH, HUNT, RUMMAGE, RANSACK, SCOUR, COMB, FERRET (*out*): SEEK is a general term meaning to look for; it lacks special connotation but may occas. have a somewhat archaic suggestion ⟨poor health compelled Webb to *seek* some more healthful climate —C.W.Mitman⟩ ⟨the Poles have always *sought* the centers of heavy industry —*Amer. Guide Series: N.Y. State*⟩ ⟨gaze *sought* the horizon —Ellen Glasgow⟩ ⟨those who *seek* the harvest of the sea —Stuart Cloete⟩ ⟨marched out to *seek* battle —C.H.Lanza⟩ SEARCH usu. implies a thorough, careful, sustained seeking or examining of a person, place, or thing ⟨detectives *search* the arrested suspect⟩ ⟨the summer was spent *searching* the Ozark region for the fabled seven cities —R.A.Billington⟩ ⟨*search* the house from top to bottom for a lost ring⟩ HUNT implies a searching or questing after something elusive or well hidden and quite hard to find ⟨*hunt* for a lost collar button⟩ ⟨land speculators . . . reaped a quick fortune, and *hunted* for new bonanzas —*Amer. Guide Series: Minn.*⟩ ⟨the strength to *hunt* out logical difficulties, antinomies, or paradoxes in our own views —M.R.Cohen⟩ RUMMAGE implies the making of a usu. sustained or thorough search or investigation in which things are disarranged, dislodged, or moved around ⟨*rummaged* among the papers that cluttered up the high, old-fashioned desk —Hartley Howard⟩ ⟨*rummaged* in the packs and announced gleefully that their contents were quite dry

—John Buchan⟩ RANSACK suggests a thorough search, esp. of a container, room, or building, often done forcefully and with resulting disorder and sometimes for something stolen or for something to be pillaged or looted ⟨each man *ransacked* his chest or seabag and unearthed trinkets of various kinds —H.A.Chippendale⟩ ⟨St. John's Church . . . was ill-attended in the reaction following the Revolution, and was *ransacked* during the War of 1812 —*Amer. Guide Series: Va.*⟩ SCOUR means to make a very diligent search of (an area) omitting no part or section ⟨*scoured* the coppices and woods and old quarries, so long as a blackberry was to be found —D.H. Lawrence⟩ ⟨while *scouring* the countryside for fresh mounts —*Amer. Guide Series: Ind.*⟩ COMB implies an examination, usu. of territory, as thoroughgoing as the action of a fine comb passing through hair ⟨state policemen *combing* the county for the escaped prisoners⟩ ⟨*comb* London's teeming millions for him —Dorothy Sayers⟩ ⟨*comb* the literature of mythology carefully —Martin Gardner⟩ FERRET (*out*) suggests searching out with keen crafty or shrewd, relentless determination ⟨did remove the bulk of the tribe, but they could not *ferret out* every Indian —A.W.Long⟩ ⟨spent hours trying to *ferret out* the true reasons for the crime⟩

— seek after 1 : to attempt to find, take, or make use of ⟨these marsh buffaloes are much *sought after* —Wilfred Thesiger⟩ **2 :** to desire the presence or companionship of **:** COURT, PURSUE ⟨was much *sought after* on account of his wide reading, charm of manner, and brilliant conversational powers —J.F.Fulton⟩

2seek *n* -s *obs* **:** a hunting signal sounded on a horn

seek·er \-kə(r)\ *n* -s [ME *secher, seker,* fr. *sechen, seken* to seek + *-er*] **:** one that seeks or is used in seeking ⟨a tone more suggestive of the scientific ~ for the truth —B.N.Cardozo⟩: as **a** *usu cap* **:** one of a small group of the English Independents who claimed religious liberty, who professed to seek further revelation as to the true church, ministry, and sacraments, and many of whom joined the Friends **b :** a slender instrument that has a smooth rounded end and is used in dissecting to follow up delicate tubular structures **:** a slender probe **c :** a device in a missile that is attracted to some form of emission (as light, heat, sound, or radio waves); *also* **:** a missile equipped with such a device

seekers b

seek·er·ism \-ə,rizəm\ *n* -s *usu cap* **:** the doctrine or practice of the Seekers

seeking *n* -s [ME *seking,* fr. gerund of *seken* to seek] **:** the act of one who seeks; *specif* **:** one's invitation, search, or choice of action ⟨a misfortune of his own ~⟩

seek·ing·ly *adv* [*seeking* (fr. ME *seking,* fr. pres. part. of *seken* to seek) + *-ly*] **:** in a seeking manner **:** SEARCHINGLY

1seel \'sē(ə)l, 'sā(-\ *var of* SELE

2seel \'sē(ə)l\ *vt* -ED/-ING/-S [alter. of ME *silen,* fr. MF *siller, ciller,* fr. ML *ciliare,* fr. L *cilium* eyelid — more at CILIA] **1 :** to close the eyes of (as a hawk) by drawing threads through the eyelids **2** *archaic* **:** to close up (one's eyes) **:** deprive of sight **:** BLIND ⟨when we in our viciousness grow hard . . . the wise gods ~ our eyes —Shak.⟩

see-low \'sē,lō\ *n* [modif. of Chin (Cant) *sz-ng-lûk,* fr. *sz* four + *ng* five + *lûk* six] **:** FOUR-FIVE-SIX

see·ly \'sēlē\ *adj* [ME *sely* — more at SILLY] **1** *archaic* **a :** blissfully happy **b :** BLESSED **2** *archaic* **:** GOOD **3** *archaic* **a :** INNOCENT **b :** SIMPLE-MINDED **c :** FOOLISH, SILLY **4** *archaic* **a :** pitiable esp. because of weak physical or mental condition **b :** FRAIL

seem \'sēm\ *vi* -ED/-ING/-S [ME *semen,* of Scand origin; akin to ON *sōma* to beseem, befit, *sæmr* becoming, *sæma* to honor, conform, OE *sēman* to reconcile, pacify, Goth *samjan* to please, ON *samr* same — more at SAME] **1** *obs* **:** to be suitable **:** BEFIT **2 a** (1) **:** to be in appearance **:** give the impression of being **:** look to be **:** APPEAR ⟨this officer, who ~*ed* a reasonable human being —Glenway Wescott⟩ ⟨the project had begun to ~ a waste of time —J.G.Cozzens⟩ (2) **:** to pretend to be **:** FEIGN ⟨either you are ignorant, or ~ so craftily —Shak.⟩ **b :** to appear to the observation or understanding ⟨~*ed* to know all of them and to be able to call each one by name —W.A.Slade⟩ ⟨a tiny pebble in the middle of your back ~*s* to grow all night, and by the crack of dawn has grown to boulder size —*Boy Scout Handbook*⟩ **c :** to appear to one's own mind or opinion ⟨~*ed* to leave the café with one or two germs of ideas —Arnold Bennett⟩ ⟨~ to feel no pain⟩ ⟨can't ~ to solve this problem⟩ **d :** to appear according to the known facts ⟨~*s* not to have studied in Europe or to have taken a doctorate —Louise Pound⟩ ⟨~*s* that he began as a painter —Hollis Alpert⟩ ⟨the merger will not take place, it ~*s*⟩ **3 :** to present all the signs of being the case **:** be evidently true **:** be obvious ⟨~*s* to me that he has given up more than he has gained⟩ ⟨would ~ to be a good investment⟩ **4 :** to give evidence of existing or being present ⟨police indicated there ~*ed* nothing in his background that could spawn the brutal attack —*Springfield (Mass.) Daily News*⟩

seem·er \-mə(r)\ *n* -s **:** one who seems; *esp* **:** one who makes a pretense **:** PRETENDER

1seeming *n* -s [ME *seming,* fr. gerund of *semen* to seem] **1 a :** the manner of appearing to sight or mind **:** outward appearance ⟨to all ~ his pious gift was irrevocable —Frederick Pollock & F.W.Maitland⟩ **b :** external appearance as distinguished from true being or character **:** SEMBLANCE ⟨his combination of honest ~ with devilish actuality —F.R. Leavis⟩ **2 :** the form or condition in which a person or thing presents itself **:** LOOK ⟨in the ~ of a rather modest canal —J.B.Cabell & A.J.Hanna⟩

2seeming *adj* [fr. pres. part. of *seem*] **:** apparent on superficial view or examination **:** OSTENSIBLE ⟨the geographic fact of the nation's ~ continental security —Reinhold Niebuhr⟩ **syn** see APPARENT

3seeming *adv* **:** SEEMINGLY ⟨that ~ marble heart —Lord Byron⟩

seem·ing·ly *adv* [*2seeming* + *-ly*] **1** *archaic* **:** BECOMINGLY, SEEMLY **2 a :** so far as can be seen or judged **:** EVIDENTLY ⟨had a marked influence on him and ~ led him into his loved occupation of surveying —C.W.Mitman⟩ **b :** to outward appearance only ⟨~ spontaneous yet carefully devised movements —*Current Biog.*⟩ ⟨two ~ contrasting but naturally allied forces —A.C.Cole⟩

seem·ing·ness *n* -ES [*2seeming* + *-ness*] **:** the quality or state of seeming **:** SEMBLANCE

seem·less \'sēmləs\ *adj* [*seem* + *-less*] *archaic* **:** UNSEEMLY

seem·li·head \'sēmlē,hed\ *n* [ME *semelihed,* fr. *semely* seemly + *-hed* -hood (akin to ME *-hod* -hood)] *archaic* **:** SEEMLINESS

seem·li·ness \'sēmlēnəs, -lin-\ *n* -ES [ME *semelinesse,* fr. *semely* seemly + *-nesse* -ness] **:** the quality or state of being seemly **:** FITNESS, PROPRIETY

1seem·ly \-lē, -li\ *adj, usu* -ER/-EST [ME *semelich, semely,* fr. ON *sæmiligr,* fr. *sæmr* becoming + *-ligr* -ly — more at SEEM] **1 a :** GOOD-LOOKING, HANDSOME ⟨endowed with a delicate physique, a ~ appearance, and a subtle intelligence —Harry Levin⟩ **b :** having properties pleasing to the eye **:** agreeably fashioned or proportioned ⟨the redeveloped city may well be beautiful, but the planners are determined that it shall at least be ~ —S.P.B.Mais⟩ **2 :** conforming to accepted standards of good form or taste **:** PROPER ⟨the company of those whose morals and behavior are less ~ than his own —E.M.Lustgarten⟩ **3 :** suited to the occasion, purpose, or person **:** FIT ⟨a ~ military escort drew near from the direction of the post —Owen Wister⟩ **syn** see DECOROUS

2seemly \"\ *adv, usu* -ER/-EST [ME *semely,* fr. ON *sæmiliga* becomingly, fr. *sæmiligr* becoming] **1** *archaic* **:** in an attractive manner **:** PLEASINGLY **2** *archaic* **:** in a fitting manner **:** APPROPRIATELY, BECOMINGLY

1seen \'sēn\ *adj* [ME *seyn,* fr. past part. of *seen, sen* to see] **1 :** perceived or verified by sight **:** VISIBLE ⟨~ beauty⟩ **2** *archaic* **:** learned in a particular field **:** VERSED ⟨a schoolmaster well ~ in music —Shak.⟩

2seen \"\ [ME *sene, seyn* (past part.), fr. OE *gesegen*] *past part & substand past of* SEE

see·nie bean \'sēnē-\ *n* [alter. of *senvy*] **:** the seed of a yellow-flowered shrub (*Sesbania longiflora*) of southern U.S. and northern Mexico formerly used as a substitute for coffee

see out *vt* ['see] **1 :** to continue with to the end ⟨went back to school determined to *see* his education *out*⟩ **2** *Scot* **:** OUTLIVE

1seep \'sēp\ *vi* -ED/-ING/-S [alter. of *sipe,* fr. ME *sipen,* fr. OE *sipian;* akin to MLG *sipen* to seep] **1 :** to flow or pass slowly through fine pores or small openings **:** OOZE ⟨water had ~*ed* in through a crack in the ceiling⟩ **2 a :** to enter or penetrate slowly ⟨some change gradually ~*ed* into these regions —G.R. Willey⟩ **b :** to become diffused or spread **:** PERMEATE ⟨a sadness ~*ed* through his being —Agnes S. Turnbull⟩ ⟨fear of the plague ~*s* like a miasma through the very air of this story —Jean S. Untermeyer⟩ **3 :** to become lost or dissipated by a gradual process **:** LEAK ⟨speeches and other tokens of immediate vitality ~ away into a colorless feeling of merely belonging —Edward Sapir⟩

2seep \"\ *n* -s **1 a :** a spot where a fluid (as water, oil, or gas) contained in the ground oozes slowly to the surface and often forms a pool **b :** a small spring **2 :** SEEPAGE

3seep \"\ *n* -s [blend of *sea* and *jeep*] **:** an amphibious jeep

seep·age \-pij, -pēj\ *n* -s [*1seep* + *-age*] **1 a :** the act or process of seeping **:** OOZING ⟨many streams lose water by ~ in certain stretches —A.N.Sayre⟩ **b :** a quantity of a fluid that has seeped through porous material (as soil) ⟨~*s* of oil and gas are widely distributed throughout the world —C.G.Lalicker⟩ ⟨families stood barefoot in cellars bailing out ~ —*N.Y. Times*⟩ **2 a :** a draining off by gradual leakage ⟨the unfathomable ~ of all excitement, meaning and potency from so many of our long-cherished values —John Hurkan⟩ **b :** a gradual penetration **:** INFILTRATION ⟨the increasing ~ of gold into certain areas⟩

seepweed \'==,=\ *n* [*2seep* + *weed*] **:** a glabrous undershrub (*Suaeda intermedia*) of alkali plains of western U.S. with narrowly linear leaves that is held to indicate the proximity of groundwater

seepy \'sēpē\ *adj* -ER/-EST [*1seep* + *-y*] **:** full of moisture **:** poorly drained **:** OOZY

1seer \'si(ə)r, 'siə, *esp in sense 1* 'sēə(r)\ *n* -s [ME, fr. *seen, sen* to see + *-er*] **1 :** one who sees ⟨the ~ of visions makes the attempt to humanize —*Times Lit. Supp.*⟩ ⟨she stared and started like a ghost-*seer* —George Eliot⟩ **2 a :** one who predicts events or developments **:** PROPHET ⟨he was the ~ of coming steam engines —Havelock Ellis⟩ ⟨a series of secular ~*s* warned civilized men that civilization was dying —*Time*⟩ **b :** one who has or is thought to have extraordinary intuitive and spiritual insight ⟨the ~'*s* hour of vision is short and rare —R.W.Emerson⟩ **3 :** one who practices divination; *specif* **:** CRYSTAL GAZER

2seer *also* **ser** *or* **sir** \'si(ə)r, 'se(ə)r, 'sər(·)\ *n, pl* **seers** *or* **seer** [Hindi *ser;* perh. akin to Per *sīr*] **1 :** any of various Indian units of weight; *esp* **:** a unit equal to 2.057 pounds **2 :** an Afghan unit of weight equal to 15.6 pounds

3seer \'si(ə)r\ *or* **seerfish** \'=,=\ *also* **seir** \'si(ə)r\ *or* **seirfish** \'=,=\ *n, pl* **seers** *or* **seerfish** *or* **seerfishes** [Pg *serra,* lit., saw, fr. L] **1 :** any of several large fishes (genus *Cybium*) resembling the related mackerels and widely distributed in the tropical Indo-Pacific area and sought for sport and food **2 :** an Indian threadfin (*Polynemus indicus*)

seercraft \'=,=\ *n* [*1seer* + *craft*] **:** the skill or practice of a seer

seer·ess \'sirəs\ *n* -ES [*1seer* + *-ess*] **:** a female seer **:** PROPHETESS

seer·paw \'sir,pȯ\ *n* -s [Hindi *sar-ā-pā* head to foot, fr. Per] **:** KHALAT

seer·ship \'si(ə)r,ship\ *n* [*1seer* + *-ship*] **:** the attributes or function of a seer

seer·suck·er \'sir,səkər, 'siə,səkə(r\ *n* -s [Hindi *śīrśakar,* fr. Per *shīr-o-shakar,* lit., milk and sugar] **:** a durable plainwoven fabric orig. of linen or cotton and now usu. of cotton or rayon, having stripes alternately flat and puckered that are produced by varying the tension in the warp threads, and used for clothing, curtains, bedspreads

sees *pres 3d sing of* SEE, *pl of* SEE

1see·saw \'sē,sȯ\ *n* [prob. redupl. of *3saw*] **1 :** an alternating up-and-down or backward-and-forward motion or movement; *specif* **:** a contest or struggle in which now one side now the other has the lead ⟨warfare . . . has been a continuing ~ between the offensive and the defensive —S.L.A.Marshall⟩ **2 a :** a game in which two children or groups of children ride on opposite ends of a plank or similar piece balanced in the middle so that one end goes up as the other goes down **b :** an apparatus (as a long plank or piece set on a center mount) improvised or manufactured for use in the game of seesaw — called also *teeter-totter*

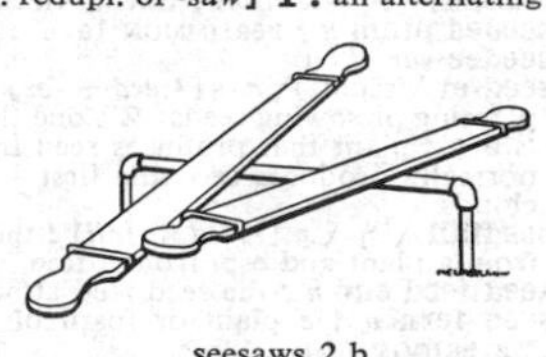

seesaws 2 b

2seesaw \"\ *vi* **1 a :** to move backward and forward or up and down ⟨planes could not land on the ~*ing* box-top flight deck at night —Wirt Williams⟩ **b :** to play at seesaw **2 :** ALTERNATE ⟨it ~*s* between biography and criticism —J.L.Davis⟩ ⟨the lead ~*ed* between the two runners right up to the finish line⟩ ~ *vt* **:** to cause to move in seesaw fashion ⟨~*ed* her skywards —Israel Zangwill⟩

3seesaw \"\ *adj* **:** moving up and down or to and fro **:** having a reciprocating motion **:** RECIPROCAL ⟨the ~ nature of the war during its early stages —Greg MacGregor⟩

see-see \'sē,sē\ *or* **seesee partridge** *n* -s [perh. imit.] **:** a small Asiatic sand partridge (*Ammoperdix griseogularis*)

seet \'sēt\ *chiefly dial var of* SIGHT

1seethe \'sēth\ *vb* **seethed** \-thd\ *or archaic* **sod** \'säd\ **seethed** \-thd\ *or archaic* **sod·den** \-dᵊn\ **seething; seethes** [ME *sethen,* fr. OE *sēothan;* akin to OHG *siodan* to seethe, ON *sjōtha,* Lith *siausti* to rage, Av *hāvayeiti* he stews] *vt* **1 :** to cook in a boiling or simmering liquid **:** BOIL, STEW ⟨allowed to eat anything that is roasted or *seethed* —William Chomsky⟩ ⟨thou shalt not ~ a kid in his mother's milk —Exod. 23:19 (AV)⟩ **2 a :** to soak or saturate in a liquid **:** reduce by soaking or boiling to a flabby lifeless condition **b :** to dull (as the brain or blood) by heat or intoxicating liquor ~ *vi* **1** *archaic* **:** to be cooked by boiling **:** come to a boil **2 a :** to be in a state of rapid and agitated movement ⟨a dark mass in which *seethed* houses, freight cars, trees, and animals —V.G.Heiser⟩ ⟨swarms of flies *seethed* everywhere —Francis Birtles⟩ **b :** to bubble or foam as if boiling **:** BOIL, CHURN ⟨when the surge was *seething* free —Alfred Tennyson⟩ **3 :** to suffer violent internal excitement or commotion **:** be in a state of agitation or turmoil **:** FERMENT ⟨his brain *seethed* with answers, with retorts, with crushing arguments —Francis Hackett⟩ ⟨when the colonies were beginning to ~ with the spirit of revolt —*Nation's Business*⟩

2seethe \"\ *n* -s **:** the act or state of seething **:** EBULLITION ⟨a white ~ of foaming water —F.W.Crofts⟩ ⟨give some outlet to a ~ of violence in his muscles —Leslie Charteris⟩

1seething *adj* [ME *sething,* fr. pres. part. of *sethen* to seethe] **1 :** intensely hot **:** BOILING ⟨a lamp drawn up into the scenery started a blaze, which soon became a ~ inferno —*Amer. Guide Series: Va.*⟩ **2 a :** in constant motion or activity **:** AGITATED ⟨the ~ life that goes on in those brown bamboo and mat huts —Robert Payne⟩ ⟨lovers and madmen have such ~ brains —Shak.⟩ **b :** INTENSE, VIOLENT ⟨had a ~ contempt for mankind —Gordon Merrick⟩ **— seeth·ing·ly** *adv*

2seething *adv* **:** BOILING ⟨~ hot⟩

seewee bean *var of* SIEVA BEAN

sefer torah *usu cap S&T, var of* SEPHER TORAH

1seg *or* **segg** \'seg\ *n* -s [prob. of Scand origin; akin to Dan dial. *seeg, seg* pig castrated at maturity] *dial Brit* **:** an animal (as a bull or boar) when castrated as a mature adult

2seg \"\ *n* -s [of Scand origin; akin to ON *sigg* callus] *dial Eng* **:** CALLUS

seg *abbr* segment

se·gar *var of* CIGAR

se·ger cone \'zāgə(r)-, 'sāgə(r)-\ *n, usu cap S* [after Hermann August *Seger* †1893 Ger. ceramist] **:** PYROMETRIC CONE

seg·e·tal \'sejəd·ᵊl\ *adj* [LL *segetalis,* fr. L *seget-, seges* field of grain, crop] **:** growing in fields of grain

seg·gy \'segi\ *dial Eng var of* SEDGY

1seg·ment \'segmənt\ *n* -s *often attrib* [L *segmentum,* fr. *secare* to cut + *-mentum* -ment — more at SAW] **1 a :** a piece or separate fragment of something **:** PORTION ⟨chopped off the ~ of the line closest to the open hatch —Wirt Williams⟩ ⟨surgeon must remove the affected ~ of the bowel —Greer Williams⟩ ⟨ores of commercial value . . . are found in ~*s* of varying length —*Amer. Guide Series: Nev.*⟩ **b** (1) **:** a portion cut off from a geometrical figure by a line or plane; *esp* **:** the part of a circular area bounded by a chord and an arc of that circle or so much of the area as is cut off by the chord (2) **:** the part of a sphere cut off by a plane or included between two parallel planes (3) **:** the finite part of a line between two points in the line **c :** a portion of an act of speech; *esp* **:** a minimal portion consisting of an item of spoken language that is known as a vowel or a consonant — compare SUPRASEGMENTAL **2 a :** one of the constituent parts into which a body, entity, or quantity is or may be divided **:** SECTION, DIVISION ⟨the canning of juices and ~*s* —*Newsweek*⟩ ⟨calyx of five ~*s,* very deeply cleft —F.E.Hulme⟩ ⟨the concept of fairness toward every ~ of the economy —*Nation's Business*⟩ ⟨the natural gas industry is split into three major ~*s*: producers, pipeliners, and distributors —Walter Goodman⟩ ⟨the ~*s* of a tribe have the same characteristics as a tribe —Audrey Butt⟩ **b :** LOOP 4a **3 a :** a piece or casting (as of a sectional flywheel) in the form of the segment or sometimes the sector of a circle or part of a ring **b :** SEGMENT GEAR **c :** a segmental arch **syn** see PART

2seg·ment \'seg,ment\ *vt* -ED/-ING/-S **1 :** to cause to undergo segmentation by division or multiplication of cells ⟨the new cells which are successively ~*ed* off from the terminal cell —T.H.Huxley & H.N.Martin⟩ **2 :** to separate into segments ⟨the first criteria are linguistic and are used to ~ the poem into manageable units —W.E.Bull⟩ ⟨provides a thoroughness and consistency of instruction lacking in a ~*ed* course of study —J.R.Butler⟩ ⟨the clams are ~*ed* into lineages —Audrey Butt⟩ ⟨the strategy of the police . . . was to keep the demonstration ~*ed* and disorganized —*N.Y. Times*⟩

seg·men·tal \(')seg¦mentᵊl\ *adj* [*1segment* + *-al*] **1 a :** of, relating to, or having the form of the segment or sector of a circle ⟨removable ~ bushings extend across the entire width of the chain —*Modern Industry*⟩ ⟨~ sewer blocks⟩ ⟨~ fanlight⟩ ⟨~ pediment⟩ **b** *of an arch* (1) **:** centered below the springing and having an intrados which forms the segment of a circle (2) **:** drawn from two centers below the springing and having a low pointed intrados **2 a :** of, relating to, or composed of the somites or metameres of a segmented animal; *specif* **:** repeated in successive segments of such an animal **b :** of or relating to the segmental organs **3 :** of or relating to segmentation **:** individualized or isolated in organization or experience **:** SUBSIDIARY ⟨a method of synthesis of ~ data whereby the facts of anthropology, psychology, physiology, biology . . . would be related —*Quarterly Rev. of Biol.*⟩ ⟨religion becomes a ~ experience of no greater value in integrating their lives —Ruth Cavan⟩ ⟨many advertising campaigns, moreover, involve only ~ and not central responses —L.W.Doob⟩ ⟨sets of relationships which . . . will prove to be discontinuous and ~, spanning only part of the way —Oliver Garceau⟩

segmental apparatus *n* [so called fr. the segmental arrangement of the cranial nerves] **:** the brainstem in which the primitive chordate metameric pattern is still perceptible (as by the emergence of cranial nerves) — compare ARCHIPALLIUM, SUPRASEGMENTAL

segmental duct *n* **:** the duct of a segmental organ of a vertebrate embryo; *esp* **:** the duct of the pronephros that persists after the degeneration of the pronephros, receives the tubules of the mesonephros, becomes the mesonephric duct, and in lower vertebrates gives rise to the müllerian duct

segmental interchange *n* **:** RECIPROCAL TRANSLOCATION

seg·men·tal·iza·tion \seg,mentᵊlə'zāshən\ *n* -s **:** the act or process of segmentalizing or the state of being segmentalized

seg·men·tal·ize \seg'mentᵊl,īz\ *vt* -ED/-ING/-S [*segmental* + *-ize*] **:** to divide or separate into segments ⟨our larger *segmentalized* and confused mass society —Kimball Young⟩ ⟨introduces experimentally the concept of wholes in place of *segmentalized* thinking and acting —H.A.Dobbs⟩

seg·men·tal·ly \(')seg¦mentᵊlē\ *adv* **:** in a segmental manner ⟨~ arranged organs⟩ ⟨a detective can identify only casually and ~ with his occupational role —R.N.Denney⟩

segmental organ *n* **1 :** NEPHRIDIUM **2 :** an embryonic excretory organ of a vertebrate whether a pronephros, mesonephros, or metanephros

segmental phoneme *n* **:** one of the phonemes (as \k, a, t\ in *cat, tack, act*) of a language that can be assigned to a relative sequential order of minimal segments — compare SUPRASEGMENTAL PHONEME

segmental resection *n* **:** excision of a segment of an organ; *specif* **:** excision of a portion of a lobe of a lung — compare PNEUMONECTOMY

seg·men·tary \'segmən,terē, -ri\ *adj* [*1segment* + *-ary*] **:** SEGMENTAL

seg·men·tate \-,tāt\ *adj* [*1segment* + *-ate*] **:** composed of segments

seg·men·ta·tion \,segmən'tāshən, -g,men-\ *n* -s [*2segment* + *-ation*] **1 :** the act or process of dividing into segments; *esp* **:** the formation of many cells from a single cell (as in a developing egg) — compare CLEAVAGE **2 :** annular contraction of smooth muscle (as of the intestine) that seems to cut the part affected into segments — compare PERISTALSIS

segmentation cavity *n* **:** BLASTOCOEL

seg·men·tec·to·my \,segmən'tektəmē\ *n* -ES [ISV *1segment* + *-ectomy*] **:** SEGMENTAL RESECTION

segmented seed *n* [fr. past part. of *2segment*] **:** a cut or sheared section of a beet seed ball usu. containing a single seed for planting

seg·ment·er \'seg,mentə(r)\ *n* -s [*2segment* + *-er*] **:** SCHIZONT

segment gear *n* **1 :** SEGMENT RACK **2 :** SECTOR GEAR

segment-headed \¦==¦==\ *adj* **:** topped by a segmental arch ⟨a *segment-headed* window⟩

seg·men·ti·na \,segmən'tīnə\ *n, cap* [NL, fr. L *segmentum* segment + NL *-ina*] **:** a genus of Asiatic freshwater snails (family Planorbidae) of medical importance as intermediate hosts of the intestinal fluke (*Fasciolopsis buski*)

seg·ment·ize \'segmən,tīz\ *vt* -ED/-ING/-S [*1segment* + *-ize*] **:** SEGMENTALIZE ⟨~ production into unit tasks —Jackson Martindell⟩ ⟨sectarian programs ~ the community —H.J. Whiting⟩ ⟨has been so *segmentized* that he has lost the concept of life as a basic unity —Harry Schacter⟩

segment rack *n* **:** a curved rack

segments *pl of* SEGMENT, *pres 3d sing of* SEGMENT

segment saw *n* **:** a saw that consists of a tapered metal flange with several steel segments fastened along its periphery and that is designed for cutting veneer with a small kerf

se·gno \'sā(,)nyō\ *n* -s [It, sign, fr. L *signum* — more at SIGN] **:** a notational sign; *specif* **:** the sign that marks the beginning or end of a musical repeat

se·go lily \'sē(,)gō-\ *also* **sego** *n* -s [Paiute *sego*] **:** a perennial herb (*Calochortus nuttallii*) of western No. America with bell-shaped flowers that are white within and largely green without

se·re·ant \'segrēənt\ *adj* [origin unknown] *heraldry* **:** having the wings expanded — used of a griffin or wyvern which is assumed to be rampant unless preceded by an adjective denoting a different position ⟨a griffin ~⟩ ⟨a griffin passant ~⟩

seg·re·ga·ble \'segrəgəbəl\ *adj* [L *segregare* to segregate + E *-able*] **:** capable of being segregated ⟨these principles involve the concept of ~ units of heredity —H.H.Laughlin⟩

seg·re·gant \-əgənt\ *n* -s [*3segregate* + *-ant*] **:** SEGREGATE

1seg·re·gate \'segrə¦gət, -rē|, ¦gāt, *usu* -ăd·+V\ *adj* [ME, fr. L *segregatus,* past part. of *segregare* to segregate] **:** SEGREGATED ⟨the human animals were immovably ~ —G.B.Shaw⟩

2segregate \"\ *n* -s **1 :** an individual or class of individuals differing in one or more genetic characters from the parental line usu. because of segregation of genes ⟨attempts to develop tomato ~*s* resistant to early blight⟩ **2 :** a taxonomic unit separated out from another of the same rank ⟨~*s* from the old genus *Agromyza*⟩

3seg·re·gate \|,gāt, *usu* -ăd·+V\ *vb* -ED/-ING/-S [L *segregatus,* past part. of *segregare* to set apart, segregate, fr. *se-* apart (fr. *sed, se* without) + *greg-, grex* flock, herd — more at IDIOT, GREGARIOUS] *vt* **1 :** to separate or set apart from others or from the general mass or main body **:** ISOLATE ⟨the scheme . . . to ~ in the foreign-aid bill all capital funds for neutrals —Haldore Hanson⟩ ⟨resumed his research in *segregating* the pure vitamin —*Current Biog.*⟩ ⟨suggestions . . . for tracing and *segregating* the impact of various causal and accentuating factors —Clark Warburton⟩ **2 :** to cause or force the separation of (as races or social classes) from the rest of society or from a larger group ⟨municipal ordinances meant to ~ races were declared void —Paul Hartmann & Morton Puner⟩ ⟨objections were raised to these schools on the ground that they tended to ~ Jewish children —Shlomo Katz⟩ **3 :** to remove nondrying components from (a fatty oil) by winterizing or other methods ~ *vi* **1 :** to separate or withdraw (as from others or from a main body) ⟨observations were made . . . as to whether the solids and the liquid had segregated —R.A.Heindl & W.L.Pendergast⟩ ⟨a community of a million inevitably ~*s* somewhat into classes . . . or castes —A.L. Kroeber⟩ **2 :** to practice or enforce a policy of segregation ⟨railroads admit that they ~ —*Issue*⟩ ⟨unwillingness of prison officials to . . . ~ on an intelligent basis —C.R.Minor⟩ **3 :** to separate during meiosis — used esp. of allelic genes ⟨the two genes at a given locus ~ from one another at meiosis —H.P. Riley⟩

segregated *adj* [fr. past part. of ³*segregate*] **1 a :** set apart or separated from others of the same kind or group ⟨a ~ account in a bank⟩ ⟨consists of a ~ area for absolute beginners —Priscilla Shirley⟩ **b :** divided in facilities or administered separately for members of different groups or esp. races ⟨~ education is . . . provided in the state constitution —*Time*⟩ ⟨the process by which ~ education has come to be accepted doctrine —L.W.Levy⟩ **c :** restricted to members of one group or esp. one race by a policy of segregation ⟨a Negro passenger . . . is placed in a ~ coach —*New Republic*⟩ ⟨~ drinking fountains, rest rooms and restaurants —*Jet*⟩ ⟨state laws requiring ~ schools for Negroes and whites —J.B.Robison⟩ **2 :** practicing or maintaining segregation esp. of races ⟨the inequalities inherent in a ~ economy and status system —M.C. Hill & B.C.McCall⟩ ⟨three . . . were from ~ states —*N.Y. Times*⟩

seg·re·ga·tion \ˌsegrəˈgāshən, -rē'-\ *n* -s *often attrib* [LL *segregation-, segregatio,* fr. L *segregatus* (past part. of *segregare* to segregate) + *-ion-, -io* -ion] **1 a :** the act or process of segregating or the state of being segregated ⟨the attempted ~ of the elements of truth from the picture of an idealized past⟩ ⟨that ~ of the order of grace and the order of nature which . . . others accepted —Douglas Bush⟩ **b** *obs* **:** DISPERSION ⟨a ~ of the Turkish fleet —Shak.⟩ **2 :** the separation or isolation of individuals or groups from a larger group or from society: as **a :** the separation or isolation of a race, class, or ethnic group by enforced or voluntary residence in a restricted area, barriers to social intercourse, divided educational facilities, or other discriminatory means ⟨in only four . . . states where there is educational ~ is a Negro permitted to study law —Henry Wallace⟩ ⟨city-dwelling Southerners have been assured . . . that residential ~ will preserve the separate schools —H.C.Fleming⟩ — see APARTHEID **b :** the separation for special treatment or observation of individuals or items from a larger group ⟨large-scale ~ of gifted children into special classes —H.J.Baker⟩ ⟨~ of extraordinary expenses in the municipal budget⟩ **c :** the separate confinement of individuals or groups (as hardened criminals, perverts, or the mentally deficient) from the rest of the inmate population in an institution ⟨the ~ of the small fraction of incorrigible . . . prisoners —H.E.Barnes⟩ **3 :** the tendency of individuals or units to separate from a larger group or society and associate together on a basis of similar characteristics ⟨industrial areas . . . and financial districts are some examples of industrial and commercial ~ —C.A.Dawson & W.E.Gettys⟩ ⟨~ according to lot size is often a feature of upper-class residential districts⟩ **4 :** a special cell or cellblock for the confinement of persons separated from the rest of the inmate population in an institution ⟨typical action of the adjustment committee includes counseling the offender . . . or placing him in ~ —*Jour. of Social Work Process*⟩ **5 :** the separation of allelic genes that occurs typically during meiosis — see MENDEL'S LAW **6 :** a nonuniform distribution of particles of aggregate throughout a quantity of concrete, mortar, or plaster **7 :** the concentration of alloying elements in specific parts of a metallic alloy

seg·re·ga·tion·ist \-sh(ə)nəst\ *n* -s **:** one that believes in, advocates, or practices segregation ⟨~*s* formed battle lines . . . to preserve the South's traditional color barriers —*United Press*⟩

seg·re·ga·tive \'==ˌgād·|iv, -āt|, |ēv *also* |əv\ *adj* [ML *segregativus,* fr. L *segregatus* + *-ivus* -ive] **1 :** tending to segregate; *esp* **:** inclined to isolate oneself ⟨one man was as ~ as the other was sociable⟩ **2 :** of, relating to, or implementing segregation ⟨restrictive and ~ color policies —John Hughes⟩

segs *pl of* SEG

¹**se·gue** \'sā(ˌ)gwā, 'se(-\ *v imper* [It, there follows, 3d sing. pres. indic. of *seguire* to follow, fr. L *sequi* — more at SUE] **1 :** perform the music that follows at once — compare ATTACCA **2 :** perform the music that follows like that which has preceded

²**segue** \"\ *vi* **segued; segued; segueing; segues :** to proceed without pause from one musical number or theme to another ⟨*segued* into a hot wild . . . chorus —Frederic Wakeman⟩ ⟨~*ing* from one number to the next —Lane Kauffmann⟩

³**segue** \"\ *n* -s **:** a transition from one musical number or sound effect to another

se·gui·di·lla \ˌsāgē'dē(y)ə, ˌseg-, -ēlyə\ *n* -s [Sp, dim. of *seguida,* a dance, lit., sequence, fr. fem. of *seguido,* past part. of *seguir* to follow, fr. L *sequi* — more at SUE] **1 :** a Spanish stanza of four or seven short verses partly assonant **2 a :** a Spanish dance having many regional variations in mood and tempo **b :** music for such a dance in its triple measure usu. performed with guitar and castanets

sehna *usu cap, var of* SENNA

sehna knot *or* **senna knot** *n, usu cap S* **:** a knot used in making carpets and rugs in which the yarn ends appear at the surface with one on each side of the adjacent yarns of warp around which they are twisted — compare GHIORDES KNOT

Sehna knot

sei \'sā\ *also* **sei whale** *n* -s [*sei,* short for *sei whale;* *sei whale,* part trans. of Norw *seihval,* fr. *sei* coalfish (akin to ON *seidhr* coalfish) + *hval* whale; fr. its habit of following the coalfish in search of food — more at SAITHE] **:** a common and widely distributed small white-spotted rorqual (*Balaenopterus borealis*)

sei·cen·to \sā'chen(ˌ)tō\ *n, sometimes cap* [It, lit., six hundred, fr. *sei* six (fr. L *sex*) + *cento* hundred, fr. L *centum* — more at SIX, HUNDRED] **:** the 17th century; *specif* **:** the 17th century period in the literature and art of Italy

seiche \'sāsh\ *n* -s [F] **:** an oscillation of the surface of a lake or landlocked sea that varies in period from a few minutes to several hours and is thought to be initiated chiefly by local variations in atmospheric pressure aided in some instances by winds and tidal currents and that continues for a time after the inequalities of atmospheric pressure have disappeared

se·id \'sāəd\ *n, pl* **seid** *or* **seids** *usu cap* [Ar *sayyid,* lit., lord, prince] **:** a member of a Turkoman people in the Turkmen Soviet Socialist Republic claiming Arab descent

sei·del \'sīdᵊl, 'zīdᵊl\ *n* -s [G, fr. MHG *sīdel,* fr. L *situla* bucket, pail, voting urn] **:** a large glass for beer

seid·litz powders \'sedləts- *sometimes* 'sīdləts-\ *n pl, usu cap S* [fr. *Sedlitz, Sedlice,* town of southwestern Bohemia, Czechoslovakia; fr. the similarity of their effects to those of the water of the town] **:** effervescing salts that consist of two separate powders with one of 40 grains of sodium bicarbonate mixed with 2 drams of Rochelle salt and the other of 35 grains of tartaric acid and that are mixed in water and drunk while effervescing as a mild cathartic — called also *Rochelle powders*

seif *or* **saif** \'sāf, 'sīf\ *n* -s [Ar *saif* sword] **:** a long narrow sand dune or chain of dunes extending in a direction parallel to that of the wind responsible for its construction

sei·gnette salt *or* **seignette's salt** \(')sen¦yet-\ *n, usu cap 1st S* [after Pierre *Seignette* †1719 Fr. apothecary] **:** ROCHELLE SALT

sei·gneur \sān'yər(·)\ *n* -s *often cap* [MF, fr. ML *senior* superior, magnate, lord, fr. L, adj., elder — more at SENIOR] **:** a lord or gentleman: as **a :** a feudal lord ⟨now ~ of the feudal island of Sark —*N.Y. Times*⟩ **b :** a member of the landed gentry of Canada

sei·gneu·ri·al \-'yu̇rēəl\ *adj* [F, fr. MF, fr. *seigneur* + *-ial*] **:** of, relating to, or befitting a seigneur

sei·gneury \'sānyərē\ *n* -ES *sometimes cap* [F *seigneurie,* fr. OF, lit., lordship, fr. *seigneur* + *-ie* -y] **1 a :** the territory under the government of a feudal lord **b :** a landed estate held in Canada by feudal tenure until 1854 **2 :** the manor house of a Canadian seigneur

sei·gnior \'sēnyə(r)\ *n* -s [ME *seignour,* fr. MF *seigneur*] **:** a man of rank or authority; *esp* **:** the feudal lord of a manor

sei·gnior·age *or* **sei·gnor·age** *also* **sei·gneur·age** \-rij, -rēj\ *n* -s [ME *seignorage,* fr. MF, right of the lord, esp. to coin money, fr. *seigneur* + *-age*] **1 :** a government revenue derived from the manufacture of coins that is calculated in the U.S. as the difference between the monetary and the bullion value of the silver contained in silver coins disregarding any alloy metal, all the metals contained in minor coins (as the nickel and the cent), or the silver bullion that is held as backing for silver certificates — compare BRASSAGE **2** *archaic* **:** DOMINION, POWER

sei·gniory *or* **sei·gnory** \'sēnyərē, -ri\ *n* -ES [ME, fr. OF *seigneurie* — more at SEIGNEURY] **1 a :** LORDSHIP, DOMINION; *specif* **:** the power or authority of a feudal lord **b** *also* **seigniory in gross :** a right of feudal superiority annexed to land apart from its ownership and including the rent or services attached thereto **2 :** the territory over which a lord holds jurisdiction **:** MANOR, DOMAIN ⟨their ~ had been broken up during the . . . nineteenth century —Hugh MacLennan⟩ **3 :** SIGNORY

sei·gno·ri·al \sēn'yōrēəl, -'yȯr-\ *also* **sei·gnior·al** \'sēnyərəl\ *or* **sei·gnior·i·al** \sēn'yōrēəl, -'yȯr-\ *or* **sei·gnor·al** \'sēnyərəl\ *adj* [obs. E *seignor* seignior (fr. ME *seignour*) or E *seignior* + *-ial* or *-al*] **:** of, relating to, or befitting a seignior **:** MANORIAL

¹**seine** \'sān\ *also* **seine net** *n* -s *often attrib* [ME, fr. OE *segne;* akin to OHG *segina* seine; both fr. a prehistoric WGmc word borrowed fr. L *sagena* seine, fr. Gk *sagēnē* — more at SUMPTER] **:** a large net having one edge provided with sinkers and the other with floats that hangs vertically in the water and encloses fish when its ends are brought together or drawn ashore — compare POUND NET, PURSE SEINE

seine

²**seine** \"\ *vb* -ED/-ING/-S *vi* **:** to fish with or catch fish with a seine ⟨going to the creek to ~ —Elizabeth M. Roberts⟩ ⟨*seining* for alligators . . . at the edge of the river —Don Brown⟩ ~ *vt* **1 :** to seek or catch with a seine ⟨schooners out *seining* mackerel⟩ **2 :** to fish or seek in (something) with or as if with a seine ⟨the fleet ~*s* the lower river daily⟩ ⟨*seined* such old tomes . . . for obscure facts —*Time*⟩

sein·er \-nə(r)\ *also* **seine–netter** \'=,==\ *n* -s **:** a person or boat that fishes with a seine

seir *or* **seirfish** *var of* SEER

seis *pl of* SEI

seise *var of* SEIZE

sei·sin *or* **sei·zin** \'sēzᵊn\ *n* -s [ME *seisine, sesin,* fr. OF *saisine,* fr. *saisir* to seize — more at SEIZE] **1 :** the possession of land or chattels **:** possession with quiet enjoyment ⟨take ~ of the land⟩ **2 :** the possession of or status with relation to land arising from the completion of feudal investiture by livery of seisin **3 :** the possession of a freehold estate in land by one having title thereto

seism \'sīzəm\ *n* -s [Gk *seismos* — more at SEISMIC] **:** EARTHQUAKE

-seism \ˌsīzəm\ *n comb form* -s [Gk *seismos* earthquake] **:** seismic movement ⟨tachy*seism*⟩

seis·mal \'sīzməl\ *adj* [Gk *seismos* earthquake + E *-al*] **:** SEISMIC

seis·mat·i·cal \sīz'mad·əkəl\ *adj* [Gk *seismat-, seisma* act of shaking (fr. *seiein* to shake) + E *-ical* — more at SEISMIC] **:** of or relating to the study of seismic phenomena

seis·met·ic \-'med·ik\ *adj* [Gk *seismos* + E *-etic*] **:** SEISMIC

seis·mic \'sīzmik, -mēk *also* |sm- *sometimes* 'se| *or* 'sā| *or* 'sē|\ *also* **seis·mi·cal** \-məkəl, -mēk-\ *adj* [Gk *seismos* shock, earthquake (fr. *seiein* to shake, quake) + E *-ic, -ical;* akin to Skt *tveṣati* he is violently moved] **:** of, subject to, or caused by an earthquake or an earth vibration produced artificially (as by an explosion in geophysical prospecting) — **seis·mi·cal·ly** \-mək(ə)lē, -mēk-, -li\ *adv*

seis·mic·i·ty \=ˈmisəd·ē, -ətē, -i\ *n* -ES [ISV *seismic* + *-ity*] **:** the quality or state of being seismic; *specif* **:** the relative frequency and distribution of earthquakes ⟨progress has been made in determining the ~ in a given area —Beno Gutenberg⟩

seismic sea wave *n* **:** one of many gravitational water waves propagated outward in all directions from the epicenter of a submarine earthquake **:** TSUNAMI — compare TIDAL WAVE

seismic vertical *n* **:** the point on the surface of the earth vertically over the focus from which the impulse of an earthquake proceeds; *also* **:** the vertical line joining these two points

seis·mism \'=ˌmizəm\ *n* -s [Gk *seismos* earthquake + E *-ism*] **:** earthquake phenomena **:** seismic activity

seismo- *comb form* [Gk, fr. *seismos* — more at SEISMIC] **:** earthquake **:** vibration ⟨*seismo*meter⟩ ⟨*seismo*tropism⟩

seis·mo·chronograph \¦=mə+\ *n* [*seismo-* + *chronograph*] **:** a chronograph adapted to determining the exact time of earthquake shocks

seis·mo·gram \'sīzməˌgram, -aa(ə)m *also* |sm- *sometimes* 'se| *or* 'sā| *or* 'sē|\ *n* [ISV *seismo-* + *-gram*] **:** the record of an earth tremor made by a seismograph

seis·mo·graph \-raf, -raa(ə)f, -raif, -rȧf\ *n* [ISV *seismo-* + *-graph*] **:** an apparatus of varying type and structure designed to measure and record vibrations within the earth and of the ground (as produced during an earthquake or by artificial explosions or atmospheric conditions)

seis·mog·ra·pher \=ˈmägrəfə(r)\ *n* -s [*seismography* + *-er*] **:** a specialist in seismography **:** SEISMOLOGIST

seis·mo·graph·ic \¦sīzmə¦grafik, -fēk *also* |sm- *sometimes* 'se| *or* 'sā| *or* 'sē|\ *also* **seis·mo·graph·i·cal** \-fəkəl, -fēk-\ *adj* [ISV *seismograph* + *-ic*] **:** of, relating to, or indicated by a seismograph or seismography

seis·mog·ra·phy \=ˈmägrəfē, -fi\ *n* -ES [ISV *seismo-* + *-graphy*] **1 :** the description of earthquakes; *specif* **:** the art of registering the shocks and undulatory movements of earthquakes **2 :** SEISMOLOGY

seis·mo·log·i·cal \¦sīzmə¦läjəkəl, -jek- *also* |sm- *sometimes* ¦se| *or* ¦sā| *or* ¦sē|\ *also* **seis·mo·log·ic** \-jik, -jēk\ *adj* **:** of or relating to seismology — **seis·mo·log·i·cal·ly** \-jək(ə)lē, -jēk-, -li\ *adv*

seis·mol·o·gist \=ˈmäləjəst\ *n* -s **:** a geophysicist who specializes in seismology **:** SEISMOGRAPHER

seis·mo·logue \'=məˌlȯg\ *n* -s [*seismo-* + *catalogue*] **:** a description or catalog of earthquakes

seis·mol·o·gy \sīz'mäləjē, -ji *also* |s'- *sometimes* se| *or* sā| *or* sē|\ *n* -ES [ISV *seismo-* + *-logy*] **:** a science that deals with earthquakes and attendant phenomena including the study of artificially produced elastic waves in earth materials

seis·mom·e·ter \-ˈäməd·ə(r), -mətə-\ *n* [*seismo-* + *-meter*] **:** a seismograph that furnishes data for measuring the actual movements of the ground; *specif* **:** the part of a seismograph assembly that detects the ground movement

seis·mo·met·ric \¦sīzmə¦me·trik, -rēk *also* |sm- *sometimes* ¦se| *or* ¦sā| *or* ¦sē|\ *or* **seis·mo·met·ri·cal** \-rəkəl, -rēk-\ *adj* **:** of or relating to seismometry or a seismometer

seis·mom·e·try \-ˈmämə·trē, -ri\ *n* -ES [ISV *seismo-* + *-metry*] **:** the scientific study of earthquake phenomena esp. by means of the seismometer

seis·mo·nas·tic \¦=mə¦nastik, -aas-, -tēk\ *adj* [ISV *seismonasty* + *-ic*] **:** of or relating to seismonasty

seis·mo·nas·ty \'==ˌnastē, -aas-, -ti\ *n* -ES [ISV *seismo-* + *-nasty*] **:** a nastic movement in plants caused by mechanical shock

seis·mo·scope \'==ˌskōp\ *n* [ISV *seismo-* + *-scope*] **:** an instrument for recording only the time or fact of occurrence of earthquakes — compare SEISMOMETER — **seis·mo·scop·ic** \¦==¦skäpik, -pēk\ *adj*

seis·mo·tectonic \¦=+\ *adj* [*seismo-* + *tectonic*] **:** of, relating to, or designating structural features of the earth which are associated with or revealed by earthquakes

seis·mot·ic \='mäd·|ik, -ät|, |ēk\ *adj* [Gk *seismos* earthquake + E *-otic* — more at SEISMIC] **:** SEISMIC

seisms *pl of* SEISM

-seisms *pl of* -SEISM

sei·so·na·cea \ˌsīsə'nāshēə\ *n pl, cap* [NL, fr. *Seison,* genus of rotifers + *-acea*] **:** a small order of Rotifera comprising elongated rotifers with weakly developed trochal disks that are epizoic on marine crustaceans

sei·so·nid·ea \-'nidēə\ *or* **sei·so·nia** \sī'sōnēə\ [NL, fr. *Seison,* genus of rotifers + *-idea* or *-ia*] *syn of* SEISONACEA

se·i·ty \'sēəd·ē\ *n* -ES [ML *seitat-, seitas,* fr. L *se* oneself + *-itat-, -itas* -ity — more at SUICIDE] **:** a quality peculiar to oneself **:** SELFHOOD, INDIVIDUALITY

Seitz \'zīts\ *trademark* — used for a filter of asbestos fibers compressed into a disk used esp. for sterilizing liquids that cannot be subjected to heat and for other bacteriological proceedings

sei·u·rus \sī'yu̇rəs\ *n, cap* [NL, fr. Gk *seiein* to shake + NL *-urus* — more at SEISMIC] **:** a genus of warblers consisting of the No. American ovenbird and the water thrushes

sei whale *var of* SEI

seize \'sēz\ *vb* -ED/-ING/-S [ME *saisen, seisen, sesen,* fr. OF *saisir,* fr. ML *sacire* to effect legal possession, to assign, of Gmc origin; akin to Goth *satjan* to set — more at SET] *vt* **1 a** *usu* **seise** \"\ **:** to vest ownership of a freehold estate in with or without actual possession ⟨the lord of the manor *seises* his heir in land holdings⟩ ⟨the widow should have the third part of a fief of which her husband was *seised* at the time of their marriage —C.H.McIlwain⟩ **b** (1) *often* **seise :** to put in legal possession of estate or property ⟨we were landowners now, duly *seised* and possessed —Mark Twain⟩ ⟨entitled to inherit the estate of which said deceased died *seized* —*Detroit Law Jour.*⟩ ⟨signed to clear the title to other properties of which her father had died *seized* —G.L.Fake⟩ (2) *often* **seise :** to put in possession of something ⟨temperate men are *seized* of . . . wisdom and knowledge —Richard Carew⟩ ⟨the biographer will be *seized* of all pertinent papers and correspondence⟩ (3) **:** to endow (a governmental agency or deliberative body) with the responsibility for action on a matter by placing it on an agenda ⟨the House when *seized* of the matter either gave its decision forthwith after debate or referred the matter to a select committee —T.E.May⟩ ⟨points out that the Council is still officially *seized* with the dispute eight years after it was settled —*Hadassah Newsletter*⟩ ⟨the Committee may not, however, consider any matter of which the Security Council is *seized* and which the Council has not submitted to the Assembly —*U.N. Dept. of Public Information*⟩ **2 a :** to take possession of **:** CONFISCATE ⟨government *seized* the entire foreign-owned oil industry —R.W. Van Alstyne⟩ ⟨any authorized officer has power to ~ any article of food which appears to him unfit —C.R.A.Martin⟩ **b :** to take possession of (something) after or by a court order, legislative enactment, or other legal process ⟨*seized* control of steel plants to prevent the scheduled walkout —Mary K. Hammond⟩ ⟨ten of the exhibiting artists have had their paintings *seized* —*N.Y. Times*⟩ ⟨authority to ~ and impound the agency's funds⟩ **3 a :** to possess or take by force **:** CAPTURE ⟨the wind ready to ~ the hat off my head —Mary Deasy⟩ ⟨the tremendous riches *seized* in swift attacks on land and water —H.E.Rieseberg⟩ ⟨the military regime which had *seized* power —*Americana Annual*⟩ **b :** to take prisoner **:** ARREST ⟨the three men were *seized* by a large body of Sioux —I.B.Richman⟩ ⟨the determination of the Allied Powers to ~ and punish war criminals —R.G.Neumann⟩ **4 a** (1) **:** to take hold of **:** CLUTCH ⟨ordered his soldiers to shave off their beards so that their enemies might not ~ them —F.J. Haskin⟩ ⟨*seizing* between his teeth the cartilage —G.B.Shaw⟩ (2) **:** to take hold of quickly or eagerly ⟨the hero *seized* her in unaccustomed arms —G.W.Brace⟩ ⟨*seized* pen and paper —John Irwin⟩ **b :** to possess oneself of **:** GRASP ⟨and rise to ~ the everlasting prize —W.W.Walford⟩ ⟨~ the leadership of social reform —*Current Biog.*⟩ ⟨*seized* for the committee the right to report on . . . national finances —Allan Nevins⟩ **c :** to take or use eagerly or quickly often as a rationalization or last resort ⟨*seized* the opportunity to calculate a number of fresh latitudes —Benjamin Farrington⟩ ⟨they'll ~ any excuse to stop work and cut down a tree —Ellen Glasgow⟩ **d :** to understand fully and distinctly **:** APPREHEND ⟨we can only try to ~ the meaning of serfdom —R.W.Southern⟩ ⟨the artist . . . possesses the power of surely and frequently *seizing* reality —Clive Bell⟩ ⟨there's no one now to grasp my half*seized* thought —Donagh MacDonagh⟩ **5** *obs* **:** to fix or establish in a place ⟨the gentleman was *seized* in my country —Thomas Stafford⟩ **6 a :** to attack or overwhelm physically **:** AFFLICT ⟨suddenly *seized* with an acute illness —H.G. Armstrong⟩ ⟨the arthritis which had *seized* him during the summer —Virginia D. Dawson & Betty D. Wilson⟩ **b :** to possess (one's mind) completely or overwhelmingly ⟨he was early *seized* with the idea of building cars —A.F.Harlow⟩ ⟨a kind of panic *seized* her —Mary Austin⟩ ⟨*seized* the popular imagination —Basil Davenport⟩ ⟨conviction *seized* him —Henry Miller⟩ **7 :** to bind or fasten together with a lashing of small stuff (as yarn, marline, or fine wire) ~ *vi* **1 a :** to take possession — usu. used with *on* or *upon* ⟨amassed fortunes, either by *seizing* on their property, or by selling their persons —G.G.Coulton⟩ **b :** to make use often as a last resort — usu. used with *on* or *upon* ⟨*seized* upon business as their sacrificial goat —B.F.Fairless⟩ ⟨~ on any plan, despite its imperfections, hoping for relief —*Dance Observer*⟩ ⟨~ upon the drug as a cure for their real or imaginary ailments —*Irish Digest*⟩ **2 :** to cohere or stick fast to a relatively moving part (as a bearing, a gas-engine piston, or a slide valve) through excessive pressure, temperature, or friction **3** *chiefly Brit* **:** to slow down or proceed with awkwardness or difficulty — usu. used with *up* ⟨the verse *seized* up, sometimes by sheer surfeit of imagery —C.D.Lewis⟩ ⟨compositions for wind alone often *seize* up in the middle parts —Edward Sackville-West⟩ **syn** see TAKE

seiz·er \-zə(r)\ *n* -s **:** one that seizes: as **a :** SEIZOR **b :** a dog trained to seize game

seizin *var of* SEISIN

seizing *n* -s [ME *seising,* fr. gerund of *seisen* to seize] **1 :** the operation of fastening together or lashing with small stuff that is usu. tarred **2 a :** the cord or lashing used in seizing — compare FOX **b :** the fastening so made

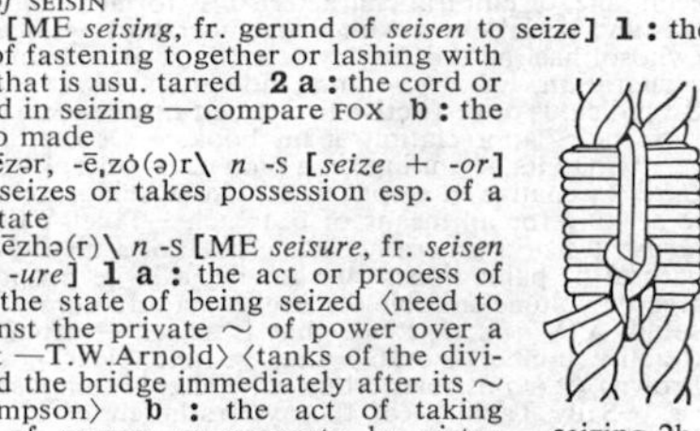

seizing 2b

sei·zor \'sēzər, -ē,zȯ(ə)r\ *n* -s [*seize* + *-or*] **:** one that seizes or takes possession esp. of a freehold estate

sei·zure \'sēzhə(r)\ *n* -s [ME *seisure,* fr. *seisen* to seize + *-ure*] **1 a :** the act or process of seizing or the state of being seized ⟨need to guard against the private ~ of power over a free market —T.W.Arnold⟩ ⟨tanks of the division crossed the bridge immediately after its ~ —P.W.Thompson⟩ **b :** the act of taking possession of person or property by virtue of a warrant or by legal authority **2** *obs* **a :** POSSESSION, OWNERSHIP **b :** HOLD, GRIP **3 :** a sudden attack (as of a disease or sickness) ⟨died of a heart ~⟩ ⟨an epileptic ~⟩

se·jant \'sējənt\ *adj* [modif. of MF *seant,* pres. part. of *seoir* to sit, fr. L *sedēre* — more at SIT] *heraldry* **:** SITTING ⟨a lion ~⟩

se·join \sə'jȯin\ *vt* -ED/-ING/-S [modif. (influenced by ¹*join*) of L *sejungere,* fr. *se-* apart (fr. *sed, se* without) + *jungere* to join — more at IDIOT, YOKE] *archaic* **:** SEPARATE

se·junc·tion \sə'jəŋ(k)shən\ *n* [L *sejunction-, sejunctio,* fr. *sejunctus* (past part. of *sejungere* to sejoin) + *-ion-, -io* -ion] **:** SEPARATION

se·ka·ni \sā'kānē\ *n, pl* **sekani** *or* **sekanis** *usu cap* **1 a :** an Athapaskan people of the upper Peace river drainage, British

Columbia **b :** a member of such people **2 :** the language of the Sekani people — called also *Montagnard*

sek·hwan \'se,kwän\ *n, pl* **sekhwan** *or* **sekhwans** *usu cap* [Chin (Amoy dial.)] **:** one of the distinct aboriginal and agricultural peoples of Formosa

se·kos \'sē,käs\ *n* -ES [Gk *sēkos* pen, sacred enclosure] **:** a sacred enclosure or inner sanctuary of an Egyptian temple

sel \'sel\ *chiefly Scot var of* SELF

sel *abbr* **1** select **2** selected **3** selection **4** selector

se·la \'selə\ *n* -S [native name in Burma] **:** rice that is heated before milling

¹se·la·chi·an \sə'lākēən\ *n* -S [NL *Selachii* + E *-an* (n. suffix)] **:** a fish (as a shark or ray) of the group Selachii

²selachian \"\ *adj* [NL *Selachii* + E *-an* (adj. suffix)] **:** of or relating to the Selachii

se·la·chii \-kē,ī\ *n pl, cap* [NL, irreg. fr. *selachos* cartilaginous fish; akin to Gk *selas* light, brightness — more at SELEN-] *in some classifications* **:** a variously delimited group of elasmobranch fishes: **a :** a primary division of Pisces that includes all the elasmobranchs and is equivalent to Chondrichthyes **b :** a class or subclass that includes all the elasmobranchs except the chimaeras **c :** a subclass or order that includes the existing sharks and rays as distinguished from the extinct Pleuropterygii and Ichthyotomi **d :** a suborder that includes the existing sharks as distinguished from the rays and is equivalent to Pleurotremata

¹sel·a·choid \'selə,kȯid\ *adj* [NL *Selachoidei*] **:** of or relating to the Pleurotremata

²selachoid \"\ *n* -S **:** one of the Pleurotremata

sel·a·choi·dei \,selə'kȯidē,ī\ [NL, fr. *Selachii* + *-oidei*] *syn of* PLEUROTREMATA

sel·a·cho·le·ic acid \¦selə(,)kō¦lēik-, ,==ˈkō,lēik-\ *n* [*selacholeic* fr. Gk *selachos* cartilaginous fish + *oleic*; fr. its being found in some fish-liver oils] **:** NERVONIC ACID

sel·a·cho·stome \'seləkə,stōm, sə'lak-\ *n* -S [NL *Selachostomi*] **:** PADDLEFISH

sel·a·chos·to·mi \,selə'kästə,mī\ *n pl, cap* [NL, fr. Gk *selachos* cartilaginous fish + NL *-stomi*] *in some classifications* **:** an order of ganoid fishes comprising the paddlefishes

sel·a·chos·to·mous \¦selə¦kästəməs\ *adj* [NL *Selachostomi* + E *-ous*] **:** of or relating to the Selachostomi

sel·a·chyl alcohol \'selə,kil-\ *n* [*selachyl* ISV *selach-* (fr. NL *Selachii*) + *-yl*] **:** a liquid unsaturated alcohol $C_{18}H_{35}$-$CH(OH)CH_2OH$ found in the unsaponifiable portion of fish oils (as shark-liver oil); glycerol x-9-octa-decen-yl ether

se·la·dang *or* **sa·la·dang** \sə'lä,däŋ\ *or* **sla·dang** \'släd-\ *n* -S [Malay *sĕladang*] **:** the gaur of the Malay archipelago

seladon green *var of* CELADON GREEN

se·lag·i·na·ce·ae \sə,lajə'nāsē,ē\ [NL, fr. *Selagin-, Selago* + *-aceae*] *syn of* SCROPHULARIACEAE

se·lag·i·nel·la \sə,lajə'nelə\ *n* [NL, fr. L *selagin-, selago*, a plant resembling the savin + *-ella*] **1** *cap* **:** the type and usu. sole genus of the family Selaginellaceae — compare ISOETES **2** -S **:** any plant of the genus *Selaginella*

se·lag·i·nel·la·ce·ae \=,==nə'lāsē,ē\ *n pl, cap* [NL, fr. *Selaginella*, type genus + *-aceae*] **:** a family of terrestrial chiefly tropical plants (order Lycopodiales) that resemble mosses, have branching stems and scalelike leaves which are many-ranked and uniform or 4-ranked and of 2 kinds spreading in 2 planes, and produce 1-celled sporangia which contain both megaspores and microspores — see SELAGINELLA — **se·lag·i·nel·la·ceous** \=¦===¦lāshəs\ *adj*

se·lag·i·nel·la·les \=,==nə'lā(,)lēz\ *n pl, cap* [NL, fr. *Selaginella* + *-ales*] **:** an order of lower vascular plants (subclass Lycopodineae) that are sometimes included among the Lycopodiales from which they differ chiefly in having ligulate leaves, four-sided strobiles, and heterosporous reproduction and that are all placed in the single recent genus *Selaginella*

se·lag·i·nel·li·tes \-'līd·(,)ēz\ *n, cap* [NL, fr. *Selaginella* + *-ites*] **:** a form genus of Paleozoic heterosporous herbaceous plants that suggest and are probably closely related to members of the genus *Selaginella*

se·la·go \sə'lā(,)gō\ *n, cap* [NL, fr. L, a plant resembling the savin] **:** a genus of low African shrubs (family Scrophulariaceae) resembling the heath and having spicate flowers with a nearly regular corolla, four didynamous stamens, a two-celled ovary, and drupaceous or capsular fruit

se·lah \'sēlə, -,lä, sē'lä\ *interj* [Heb *selāh*] — used 71 times in the Psalms and 3 times in Habakkuk probably as an exclamation (as *amen* or *hallelujah*) or possibly as a direction to temple musicians or chorus to lift up music or voices ⟨God will . . . uproot you from the land of the living. *Selah* —Ps 52:5 (RSV)⟩

selas *pl of* SELA

sel·couth \'sel,küth\ *adj* [ME, fr. OE *seldcūth*, fr. *seld-* (fr. *seldan* seldom) + *cūth* familiar, known — more at COUTH] *archaic* **:** UNUSUAL, STRANGE, MARVELOUS ⟨this ~ girl, so rarely fashioned in mind and body —Llewelyn Powys⟩

seld \'seld\ *adv (or adj)* [ME *selde*, back-formation fr. *seldere* (compar. of *selden* seldom) & *seldeste* (superl. of *selden* seldom), fr. OE *seldor* (compar. of *seldan* seldom) & *seldost* (superl. of *seldan* seldom)] *archaic* **:** SELDOM

¹sel·dom \'seldəm\ *adv* [ME *selden, seldom*, fr. OE *seldan, seldon, seldun*; akin to OFris *selden* seldom, OHG *seltan*, ON *sjaldan*, Goth *silda-*; akin to L *sed, se* without, *suus* one's own — more at SUICIDE] **:** in few instances **:** RARELY, INFREQUENTLY — opposed to *often* ⟨he ~ changed a conclusion he had formed —A.H.Tuttle⟩

²seldom \"\ *adj* [ME, fr. *seldom*, adv.] **:** RARE, INFREQUENT ⟨silence was such a ~ thing —R.O.Bowen⟩ ⟨one of those ~ people whom you can love unashamedly —Loudie Claar⟩ ⟨with her small ~ smile —Ethel Wilson⟩

sel·dom·ly *adv* [²*seldom* + *-ly*] *archaic* **:** SELDOM

sel·dom·ness *n* -ES **:** INFREQUENCY, RARENESS

sele \'sē(ə)l, 'sā(-\ *n* [ME, fr. OE *sǣl* happiness, good fortune, sele — more at SILLY] **1** *dial chiefly Brit* **:** good fortune — usu. used in greetings and proverbial expressions **2** *dial chiefly Brit* **:** TIME, OCCASION — used esp. of opportune or favorable times

¹se·lect \sə'lekt\ *adj* [L *selectus*, past part. of *seligere* to separate by picking out, select, fr. *sed-, se-* apart (fr. *sed, se* without) + *legere* to gather, select — more at IDIOT, LEGEND] **1 :** chosen from a number or group by fitness or preference ⟨the valuable ~ bibliography covers 30 pages —R.L.Morton⟩ ⟨with the Bible and Shakespeare in the ~ library to be taken to the proverbial desert island —J.K.M.Rothenstein⟩ **2 a :** of signal value or excellence **:** SUPERIOR, CHOICE ⟨a workshop for a group of young players —*Current Biog.*⟩ ⟨a ~ company of blue-chip shares —Paul Heffernan⟩ ⟨a ~ group of 30 voices which sings for . . . services —*Bull. of Bates Coll.*⟩ **b :** exclusively or fastidiously chosen often with regard to social, economic, or cultural characteristics ⟨formed literary, charitable, and social clubs with ~ memberships —Oscar Handlin⟩ ⟨whoso has passed the system, then, is . . . one of a close corporation, of a ~ and individual few —G.D.Brown⟩ **3 :** judicious or restrictive in choice **:** DISCRIMINATING ⟨pleased with the ~ appreciation of his books —Osbert Sitwell⟩ ⟨university had its beginnings in a pioneer ~ school —*Alfred Univ. Cat.*⟩ ⟨a change in emphasis . . . from being exclusive and ~ to seeking for all means of outreach —Janet Whitney⟩ **4** *of lumber* **a :** of a generally clear grain **:** of a quality suitable for natural or paint finish **b :** having a large proportion of its area or volume suitable for use in manufacture

²select \"\ *n* -S **1 :** one that is select — often used in pl. ⟨quality lumber, notably the ~*s* and clear grades —N.C. Brown⟩ ⟨it is possible to buy ware that is composed wholly of ~*s* —Sally Taylor⟩ ⟨of the oysters he chooses only the ~*s*⟩ **2** *archaic* **:** a select class or group ⟨had his ~ of friends and acquaintance —Roger North⟩

³select \"\ *vb* -ED/-ING/-S [L *selectus*, past part. of *seligere* to select] *vt* **:** to choose from a number or group usu. by fitness, excellence, or other distinguishing feature ⟨the difficult task of ~*ing* a presidential candidate —H.D.Jordan⟩ ⟨farmers ~ their own tracts of ground —*Amer. Guide Series: Fla.*⟩ ⟨content to know only those ~*ed* out for him to meet —H.J.Laski⟩ ~ *vi* **:** to choose something from a number or group **:** to make a selection ⟨has ~*ed* and edited well —Alan Devoe⟩ ⟨whatever the basis, ~ with care and foresight⟩

se·lect·ance \sə'lektən(t)s\ *n* -S [³*select* + *-ance*] **:** the selectivity or discrimination in response to signals of slightly different frequency (as in radio reception)

select committee *n* **:** a legislative committee appointed to inquire into or to consider a particular matter or bill

selected *adj* [fr. past part. of ³*select*] **:** SELECT; *specif* **:** of a higher grade or quality than the ordinary ⟨prefers ~ steel to the mill-run steel⟩

se·lect·ee \sə¦lek¦tē\ *n* -S [³*select* + *-ee*] **:** one inducted into military service under selective service **:** DRAFTEE

se·lec·tion \sə'lekshən\ *n* -S [L *selection-, selectio*, fr. *selectus* (past part. of *seligere* to select) + *-ion-, -io* -ion] **1 :** the act or process of selecting **:** the state of being selected ⟨the ~ of the school he should attend —Sidney Lovett⟩ ⟨pilot ~ in this country . . . is not perfect —H.G.Armstrong⟩ ⟨friends applauding his ~ as president⟩ **2 a :** one that is selected **:** CHOICE ⟨each has been a ~ of one of the major book clubs —*Current Biog.*⟩ ⟨discussed with some of his cabinet ~*s* the ways of increasing pressure —*Nation's Business*⟩ **b :** a composition or passage selected for reading or presentation ⟨included . . . musical comedy ~*s* —*Current Biog.*⟩ ⟨culled and copied ~*s* suitable for coming obituaries —Agnes S. Turnbull⟩ ⟨~*s* from the best writers of the era⟩ **c :** a horse, dog, or other contestant selected usu. by a specialist for betting purposes ⟨the trackman's ~*s* often run in the money⟩ **3 a :** a natural or artificial biological process that results or tends to result in preventing some individuals or groups of organisms from surviving and propagating and in allowing others to do so with the result that particular traits of the latter are given pronounced expression — compare DARWINISM, NATURAL SELECTION **b :** the removal at relatively short intervals of mature timber so that continuous natural reproduction of a forest is encouraged and a stand of uneven age maintained — compare SUSTAINED YIELD **4 a :** the act of selecting land **b :** a piece of land taken up in Australian processes of land settlement ⟨~*s* on which . . . women and children helped to grub the land —E.H.Collis⟩ **5 :** the process by which an insurance company accepts or rejects risks **syn** see CHOICE

selection coefficient *n* **:** a measure of the survival value of a given gene or mutation by comparison of the growth rate of the experimental form with that of the wild type

selection forest *n* **:** a forest in which trees of all age classes are represented

se·lec·tion·ism \-shə,nizəm\ *n* -S [ISV *selection* + *-ism*] **:** a system or theory based on the doctrine of natural, artificial, or social selection

se·lec·tion·ist \-sh(ə)nəst\ *n* -S **:** one who considers natural selection a fundamental factor in evolution

selection pressure *n* **:** the effect of selection on the relative frequency of one or more genes within a population

selection rule *n* **:** a rule that states which of all the conceivable changes in the state of a quantized system (atoms, nuclei, or related entities) are physically possible under specified circumstances usu. in terms of the possible numerical changes in the quantum numbers that characterize the system — compare ALLOWED, FORBIDDEN

selection value *n* **:** the presumed value of a trait or characteristic for the effective operation of the processes of natural selection

se·lec·tive \sə'lektiv, -tēv *also* -təv\ *adj* [L *selectus* (past part. of *seligere* to select) + E *-ive* — more at SELECT] **1 :** of, relating to, or characterized by selection **:** selecting or tending to select ⟨buyers for retail stores have become more and more ~ —Glenn Fowler⟩ ⟨some dyes were highly ~ in their action —S.F.Mason⟩ ⟨monetary controls may be either general or ~ —Jules Backman⟩ ⟨an exceptionally quick and ~ reader —John Mason Brown⟩ **2 :** of, relating to, or constituting the ability of an electrical circuit or apparatus to respond to a specific frequency without interference

selective absorption *n* **:** the absorption by a substance of only certain wavelengths of radiation with the coincident exclusion or transmission of others ⟨*selective absorption* of green⟩

selective assembly *n* **:** the selection from two or more stocks of the particular parts of a mechanism that will fit with the desired degree of clearance when assembled

selective cutting *or* **selective logging** *n* **:** the cutting out of trees that are mature or defective, or of inferior kinds to encourage the growth of the remaining trees in a forest or wood

selective flotation *n* **:** the form of flotation in which only one mineral is floated from an ore pulp containing two or more floatable minerals

se·lec·tive·ly \-təvlē, -li\ *adv* **:** in a selective manner **:** by selection

se·lec·tive·ness \-tivnəs, -tēv- *also* -təv-\ *n* -ES **:** the act or process of being selective

selective radiation *n* **:** the radiation emitted by a surface whose emissivity is distinctly varied for different wavelengths

selective reflection *n* **:** the reflection emitted by a surface that reflects waves of different lengths with varying intensity

selective service *n* **:** a system by which men between specified ages are registered, classified, and called up for military service **:** DRAFT

selective transmission *n* **:** a transmission for automobiles and similar powered vehicles by which the gear can be changed directly from one speed to any other by a single lever

se·lec·tiv·i·ty \sə,lek'tivəd·ē, -vətē, -i *also* (,)sē,l-\ *n* -ES **1 :** the quality or state of being selective ⟨circulation policy which stressed ~ as opposed to mass sales —*Current Biog.*⟩ ⟨the ~ of students in the technical institute —C.V.Newsom⟩ ⟨newer insecticides . . . are tending toward a high degree of ~ —*Industrial & Engineering Chemistry*⟩ **2 a :** the state of possessing or exhibiting selective reflection **b :** a quantitative or qualitative measurement of the degree to which an electrical circuit or apparatus responds to a desired signal and rejects others

se·lect·ly \sə'lektlē, -tli\ *adv* [¹*select* + *-ly*] **:** in a select manner **:** with selectivity

se·lect·man \sə'lek(t)mən, sē'le-,'sle-, -maa(ə)n, (=,)='= *also* (=)'=,mən; 'sē,lek(t)mən, -,lək-, -maa(ə)n, ,=(,)='= *sometimes* 'si(,)=,= *or* ,si(,)='= *or* 'se(,)=,= *or* ,se(,)='=\ *n, pl* **select·men** \-mən *for* -mən *or* -maa(ə)n *in singular*, -mən *for* -mən *in singular*\ [¹*select* + *man*] **:** a person chosen to exercise special powers in a system of government; *esp* **:** one of a board of officers chosen usu. in staggered three-year terms in towns of all the New England states except Rhode Island to transact and administer the general public business of the town

select meeting *n* **:** a meeting of ministers and elders in the Society of Friends

select mortality table *n* **:** a mortality table based on medically selected lives

se·lect·ness \sə'lek(t)nəs\ *n* -ES **:** the quality or state of being select

se·lec·tor \-ktə(r)\ *n* -S [LL, fr. L *selectus* (past part. of *seligere* to select) + *-or*] **:** one that selects: as **a :** a person who selects ⟨~ of All-America teams —*Current Biog.*⟩ ⟨the ~ . . . knows good-looking merchandise —*Women's Wear Daily*⟩ ⟨edited by an expert librarian ~ —*Saturday Rev.*⟩ **b** (1) **:** a person who selects Australian public land to settle on (2) **:** a small farmer of Australia **c :** a mechanical or electrical device for automatically selecting predetermined shapes, sizes, or materials or chosen or actuated for starting or stopping (as an elevator) **d** (1) **:** the element in a transmission gearshift of an automotive vehicle that is guided by the gearshift lever so that the desired gearshift bar is actuated (2) **:** the lever in an automatic gearshift operated by the driver to select the desired speed **e :** a converter with horizontal tuyeres to produce bottoms and a purified copper in one operation **f :** an electric switch mechanism designed to move over a number of terminals and to select a particular one or group in accordance with the signal received **g :** STATION SELECTOR **h :** an apparatus for operating either or any of two or more railroad signals by a single lever so as automatically to connect the particular signal controlling the route or track for which a switch has been set

selector coil *n* **:** an electric coil that when energized will attract and hold in place an armature to permit a predetermined movement of a mechanism

selector switch *n* **:** an electric switch that selects a particular circuit or group of circuits (as on a telephone switchboard)

selects *pl of* SELECT, *pres 3d sing of* SELECT

select school *n* **:** a privately supported and administered elementary or secondary school whose student body is selectively chosen usu. on a sectarian, social, or economic basis ⟨the business of instruction in our universities, colleges, academies, boarding schools, *select schools*, and common schools —*Universal Traveller*⟩

¹selen- *or* **seleno-** *also* **seleni-** *comb form* [L *selen-*, fr. Gk *selēn-*, fr. *selēnē* moon; akin to Gk *selas* light, brightness, L *sol* sun — more at SOLAR] **:** moon **:** crescent-shaped ⟨*seleno*morphic⟩ ⟨*Seleni*cereus⟩ ⟨*Selen*arctos⟩

²selen- *or* **seleni-** *or* **seleno-** *comb form* [Sw, fr. NL *selenium*] **1 :** selenium ⟨*selen*ic⟩ ⟨*seleni*ferous⟩ ⟨*seleno*bismuthite⟩ **2** *usu* *seleno-* **:** containing bivalent selenium usu. in place of oxygen ⟨*seleno*cyanic⟩ — compare THI-

selena- *or* **selen-** *comb form* [ISV, fr. NL *selenium*] **:** containing selenium in place of carbon or regarded as in place of carbon usu. in place of the methylene group $-CH_2-$ ⟨*selena*cyclopentadiene⟩ ⟨*selen*azole⟩ — compare OXA-, THIA-

sel·en·arc·tos \,selən'ärktəs, -,täs\ *n, cap* [NL, fr. ¹*selen-* + Gk *arktos* bear — more at ARCTIC] **:** a genus of mammals (family Ursidae) that includes the Asiatic black bear and is often regarded as indistinguishable from *Ursus*

sel·e·nate \'selə,nāt\ *n* -S [Sw *selenat*, fr. *selen* selenic (fr. NL *selenium*) + *-at* -ate] **:** a salt or ester of selenic acid

se·le·ni·an \sə'lēnēən\ *adj* [¹*selen-* + *-an*] **:** of, relating to, or designating the moon

se·le·ni·ate \-ē,āt\ *n* -S [Sw *seleniat*, fr. *seleni-* (fr. NL *selenium*) + *-at* -ate] **:** SELENATE

¹se·lenic \sə'lenik, -lēn-\ *adj* [¹*selen-* + *-ic*] **:** of, relating to, or like the moon

²selenic \"\ *adj* [Sw *selen* selenic (fr. NL *selenium*) + E *-ic*] **:** of, relating to, or containing selenium — used esp. of compounds in which this element has a higher valence than in selenious compounds

selenic acid *n* **:** a strong acid H_2SeO_4 that is crystalline when pure, that resembles sulfuric acid but is a more powerful oxidizing agent since in hot concentrated form it oxidizes hydrogen chloride and attacks gold and platinum, and that is made by oxidation usu. of selenious acid or selenium dioxide

se·le·ni·cereus \sə¦lēnə+\ *n, cap* [NL, fr. ¹*selen-* + *Cereus*] **:** a genus of mostly epiphytic climbing cacti ranging from southern Texas to Argentina and having ribbed or angled and not very spiny stems and immense white night-blooming flowers that are much prized in northern greenhouses

sel·e·nide \'selə,nīd, -,nəd\ *n* -S [ISV ²*selen-* + *-ide*] **:** a binary compound of selenium usu. with a more electropositive element or radical

sel·e·nif·er·ous \¦selə¦nif(ə)rəs\ *adj* [ISV ²*selen-* + *-ferous*] **:** containing or yielding selenium ⟨~ vegetation⟩

seleniferous plant *n* **:** a plant that absorbs large quantities of selenium from the soil and retains it within the plant tissues

sel·e·nin·ic acid \¦selə¦ninik-\ *n* [ISV ²*selen-* + *-in* + *-ic*] **:** any of a series of organic acids having the general formula $RSeO_2H$ analogous to the sulfinic acids and obtainable by oxidizing diselenides with nitric acid

se·le·ni·ous \sə'lēnēəs\ *also* **sele·nous** \sə'lēnəs, 'selən-\ *adj* [ISV ²*selen-* + *-ious* or *-ous*] **:** of, relating to, or containing selenium — used esp. of compounds in which this element has a lower valence than in selenic compounds

selenious acid *n* **:** a poisonous hygroscopic crystalline acid H_2SeO_3 that is a weaker acid than sulfurous acid, that is an oxidizing agent yielding selenium as it is reduced and that is made by oxidizing selenium with nitric acid or by dissolving selenium dioxide in water

se·le·ni·pe·di·um \sə,lēnə'pēdēəm\ *n, cap* [NL, fr. ¹*selen-* + Gk *pedion* plain, flat surface — more at PEDION] **:** a genus of large reedlike tropical American orchids that is closely related to *Cypripedium* and includes forms with pods used locally as a substitute for vanilla

¹sel·e·nite \'selə,nīt\ *n* -S [L *selenites*, fr. Gk *selēnitēs* (*lithos*), lit., (stone) of the moon, fr. *selēnitēs* of the moon (fr. *selēnē* moon + *-itēs* -ite) + *lithos* stone; fr. the belief that it waxed and waned with the moon — more at SELEN-] **:** a variety of gypsum occurring in transparent crystals or crystalline masses

²selenite \"\ *n* -S [ISV *selen*ious + *-ite*] **:** a salt or ester of selenious acid

¹sel·e·nit·ic \¦selə¦nid·ik\ *also* **sel·e·nit·i·cal** \-d·əkəl\ *adj* [¹*selenite* + *-ic* or *-ical*] **:** of, resembling, or containing selenite

²selenitic \"\ *adj* [Gk *selēnitēs* of the moon + E *-ic*] **:** of, relating to, or influenced by the moon

se·le·ni·um \sə'lēnēəm\ *n* -S [NL, fr. ¹*selen-* + *-ium*; fr. the fact that it is related to an element the name of which (*tellurium*) derives from the Latin word for the planet earth (*tellus*)] **:** a nonmetallic toxic element that is related to sulfur and tellurium and resembles them chemically, that occurs in allotropic forms including an amorphous red powder or black vitreous form, a red crystalline form, and a stable gray metallike form conducting electricity much more readily in the light than in the dark, that is found to a small extent in native sulfur and combined in native sulfides, in a few selenides (as clausthalite), and in various soils and plants, that is obtained usu. as a by-product in the electrolytic refining of copper, and that is used chiefly in photoelectric cells, rectifiers, and other electronic devices, in decolorizing glass, and as a pigment esp. for ruby glass and ceramic glazes and enamels — symbol *Se*; see ELEMENT table

selenium cell *n* **:** an insulated strip of selenium suitably mounted with electrodes, designed for use as a photoconductive element, and commonly used in photometric work

selenium dioxide *n* **:** a poisonous white crystalline compound SeO_2 that sublimes to a yellow-green vapor, that is made by oxidation of selenium with nitric acid or air or by dehydration of selenious acid, and that is used chiefly as a catalyst and an oxidizing agent in organic chemistry (as for oxidizing a methylene group next to a carbonyl group to a second carbonyl group)

selenium oxychloride *n* **:** a vesicant liquid compound $SeOCl_2$ that is made usu. by reaction of selenium dioxide and hydrogen chloride or by chlorination of a mixture of selenium and selenium dioxide, that has a high dielectric constant, and that is used chiefly as a solvent

selenium rectifier *n* **:** a rectifier employing the asymmetrical conductivity characteristic of selenium

selenium red *n* **:** CADMIUM RED 1

sel·e·nized \'selə,nīzd\ *adj* [²*selen-* + *-ize* + *-ed*] **:** containing selenium ⟨~ plants from seleniferous soil⟩ ⟨a ~ animal affected by selenosis⟩

¹seleno- — see ¹SELEN-

²seleno- — see ²SELEN-

sele·no·bismuthite \sə¦lē(,)nō, ¦selə(,)nō+\ *n* [²*selen-* + *bismuth* + *-ite*] **:** a compound containing both selenium and bismuth

sele·no·centric \"+\ *adj* [ISV ¹*selen-* + *-centric*] **:** of or relating to the center of the moon **:** referred to the moon as a center

sele·no·cyanate \"+\ *n* [ISV *selenocyan-* (in *selenocyanic acid*) + *-ate*] **:** a salt or ester of selenocyanic acid

sele·no·cyanic acid \"+...-\ *n* [ISV ²*selen-* + *cyanic*] **:** an acid HSeCN containing selenium analogous to thiocyanic acid

¹se·len·odont \sə'lēnə,dänt, -len-\ *adj* [ISV ¹*selen-* + *-odont*] **:** of, relating to, characteristic of, or being molar teeth with crescentic ridges on the crown ⟨~ artiodactyls⟩

²selenodont \"\ *n* -S **:** a mammal with selenodont teeth

se·len·odon·ta \=¦=='däntə\ *n pl, cap* [NL, fr. ¹*selen-* + *-odonta*] *in some classifications* **:** a group of artiodactyls comprising mammals with selenodont teeth and including the Tylopoda and Pecora

se·len·odon·ty \=¦==,däntē\ *n* -ES [¹*selen-* + *-odonty*] **:** the quality or state of being selenodont

sel·e·nog·ra·pher \,selə'nägrəfə(r)\ *n* -S [*selenography* + *-er*] **:** a specialist in selenography

se·le·no·graph·ic \sə¦lēnə¦grafik\ *also* **se·le·no·graph·i·cal** \-fəkəl\ *adj* [*selenography* + *-ic* or *-ical*] **:** of or relating to selenography — **selenographically** *adv*

selenographic chart *n* **:** a map representing the surface of the moon

sel·e·nog·ra·phy \,selə'nägrəfē\ *n* -ES [¹*selen-* + *-graphy*] **1 :** the science of the physical features of the moon ⟨attention of astronomers was directed to other fields, and ~ . . . made no further progress —R.B.Baldwin⟩ **2 :** the physical geography of the moon ⟨the first major treatise on descriptive ~ to appear in English for a quarter-century —Joseph Ashbrook⟩

se·le·no·lite \sə'lēnᵊl,īt\ *n* -S [²*selen-* + *-lite*] **:** a mineral SeO_2 consisting of native selenium dioxide

se·le·no·log·i·cal \sə¦lēnə¦läjəkəl\ *adj* [ISV *selenology* + *-ical*] : of or relating to selenology — **se·le·no·log·i·cal·ly** \-k(ə)lē\ *adv*

sel·e·nol·o·gist \ˌseləˈnäləjəst\ *n* -s [*selenology* + *-ist*] : a specialist in selenology

sel·e·nol·o·gy \-jē\ *n* -ES [¹*selen-* + *-logy*] : a branch of astronomy that deals with the moon

sel·e·no·ni·um \ˌseləˈnōnēəm\ *n* -s [NL, fr. ²*selen-* + *-onium*] : a univalent cation SeH_3^+ or radical SeH_3 analogous to sulfonium with selenium in place of sulfur

se·le·no·phile \səˈlēnəˌfīl\ *n* -s [²*selen-* + *-phile*] : a plant that when growing in a seleniferous soil tends to take up selenium in quantities greater than can be explained on a basis of chance — **se·le·no·phil·ic** \=ˌ=¦=¦filik\ *adj*

sel·e·no·sis \ˌseləˈnōsəs\ *n* -ES [NL, fr. ²*selen-* + *-osis*] : poisoning of livestock by selenium due to ingestion of plants grown in seleniferous soils characterized in the acute phase by diffuse necrosis and hemorrhage resulting from capillary damage and in chronic poisoning by degenerative and fibrotic changes esp. of the liver and of the skin and its derivatives — called also *alkali disease, blind staggers*

selenous *var of* SELENIOUS

sel·en·sulfur \¦selən+\ *n* [²*selen-* + *sulfur*] : a vitreous brownish red mixture of selenium and sulfur

¹**se·leu·cid** \səˈlüsəd, səlˈyü-\ *n* -s *usu cap* [NL *seleucides*, fr. *Seleucus I* †280 B.C. Macedonian general and founder of the Seleucid dynasty + L *-ides*, masc. patronymic suffix — more at -ID] : a member of a Greek dynasty ruling Syria and at various times other Asian territories from 312 B.C. to 64 B.C.

²**seleucid** \"\ *adj, usu cap* : of or relating to the Seleucids or their era

¹**self** \ˈself, ˈseu̇f, *South often* ˈse(ə)f\ *pron* [ME, fr. OE *self, seolf, sylf*; akin to OFris & OS *self*, OHG *selb*, ON *sjālfr*, Goth *silba*; akin to L *se* oneself — more at SUICIDE] **1** : MYSELF ⟨he died when we — ∼, two brothers, one sister — were very young —*Current Biog.*⟩ **2** : HIMSELF, HERSELF ⟨his family, living in a four-roomed house, consisted of ∼, wife, and six —I.J.C.Brown⟩

²**self** \"\ *adj* [ME, fr. OE *self, seolf, sylf*] **1** *obs* : belonging to oneself : OWN ⟨by ∼ and violent hands took off her life —Shak.⟩ **2** *obs* : IDENTICAL, SAME ⟨that ∼ chain about his neck which he forswore most monstrously to have —Shak.⟩ **3 a** : having a single character or quality throughout : UNIFORM, UNMIXED; *specif* : having one color only : SELF-COLORED ⟨a ∼ flower⟩ **b** *of an archer's bow* : made of a single piece of wood — contrasted with *backed* **c** : of the same kind (as in color, material, or pattern) as something with which it is used ⟨a ∼ belt⟩ ⟨a ∼ trimming⟩

³**self** \"\ *n, pl* **selves** *see sense 6* \ˈselvz, ˈseu̇vz, *South often* ˈse(ə)vz\ [ME, fr. *self*, pron.] **1 a** : the entire person of an individual ⟨his fair daughter's ∼ . . . is my object —Robert Browning⟩ **b** : the realization or embodiment of an abstract quality ⟨she was beauty's ∼ —James Thomson †1748⟩ **2 a** : a personality or mode of behavior regarded as typical of a particular individual ⟨his true ∼ was at last revealed⟩ **b** : an aspect of one's personality predominant at a certain time or under certain conditions ⟨his better ∼⟩ ⟨his weaker ∼⟩ ⟨his reckless ∼⟩ ⟨my clothes keep my various *selves* buttoned up together —L.P.Smith⟩ **c** : a person in his normal state of health or best physical or mental condition ⟨feel like my old ∼ today⟩ ⟨looked like his old ∼ in the ring⟩ **3 a** : the integrated unity of subjective experience specif. including those characteristics and attributes of the experiencing organism of which it is reflexively aware **b** : the internal regulatory system of response and activity tendencies within the organism : the source of social adaptation and growth of the individual personality **c** : the dynamic organization of patterns of behavior acquired through social frustration **4** : personal interest or advantage : SELF-INTEREST ⟨the really successful people in it are those who put service before ∼ —*Farmer's Weekly (So. Africa)*⟩ **5 a** *usu cap, objective idealism* : the supreme self : ABSOLUTE **b** (1) *often cap, Hinduism* : ATMAN (2) *Buddhism* : a dynamic unstable agglomerate of skandhas that in itself possesses no inherent substantiality or enduring quality and that continues in constant flux until final dissolution at death **6** *pl* **selfs** \-fs\ **a** : an individual produced by self-fertilization — distinguished from *crossbred* **b** : a self-colored individual

⁴**self** \"\ *vb* -ED/-ING/-S *vt* **1** : to cause (individuals of the same race or strain) to breed together : INBREED **2** : to pollinate with pollen from the same flower or plant : SELF-FERTILIZE : SELF-POLLINATE ∼ *vi* : to engage in self-pollinating : undergo self-pollination ⟨try to prevent test strains from ∼*ing*⟩

self- *comb form* [ME, fr. OE *self-, seolf-, sylf-*, fr. *self, seolf, sylf*, pron. & adj.] **1 a** : oneself or itself ⟨*self*-asserting⟩ ⟨*self*-loving⟩ **b** : of oneself or itself ⟨*self*-abandonment⟩ ⟨*self*-congratulation⟩ **c** : by oneself or itself : independent : automatic ⟨*self*-rule⟩ ⟨*self*-propelled⟩ ⟨*self*-feeder⟩ ⟨*self*-action⟩ **2 a** : to, with, for, or toward oneself or itself ⟨*self*-consistent⟩ ⟨*self*-concerned⟩ ⟨*self*-addressed⟩ ⟨*self*-love⟩ **b** : of or in oneself or itself inherently ⟨*self*-evident⟩ ⟨*self*-existent⟩ **c** : from or by means of oneself or itself ⟨*self*-fertile⟩ ⟨*self*-fruitful⟩

self-abandoned \¦=÷¦==\ *adj* : abandoned by oneself; *esp* : given up to one's impulses : free from moral restraint : ABANDONED

self-abandonment \¦=÷¦===\ *n* **1** : a surrender of one's selfish interests or desires ⟨the earnest prayer and the complete *self-abandonment* which arise from wise reading and true meditation —Phyllis Hodgson⟩ **2** : a lack of self-restraint ⟨has in its relaxed *self-abandonment* something underbred and ignoble —Matthew Arnold⟩

self-abasement \¦=÷¦==\ *n* : a humiliation of oneself based on feelings of inferiority, guilt, or shame ⟨continual ups and downs of rapture and depression, arrogance and *self-abasement* —Edith Wharton⟩

self-abnegating \(ˈ)=¦==ˌ==\ *adj* : SELF-DENYING

self-abnegation \¦=ˌ==¦==\ *n* : SELF-DENIAL, SELF-SACRIFICE

self-absorbed \¦=(ˌ)=¦=\ *adj* : absorbed in one's own thoughts, activities, or interests

self-absorption \¦=(ˌ)=¦==\ *n* **1** : absorption in oneself : preoccupation with oneself **2** : resonance absorption of part of the radiation emitted by a substance in the outer layers of the emitter itself and esp. noticeable in flame spectra

self-abuse \¦==¦=\ *n* **1** *obs* : SELF-DECEPTION ⟨my strange and *self-abuse* is the initiate fear that wants hard use —Shak.⟩ **2** : reproach of oneself ⟨the *self-abuse* for throwing away his future on the movement for independence —Edward Ryerson⟩ **3** : MASTURBATION

self-accusation \¦=ˌ==¦==\ *n* : the act or an instance of accusing oneself

self-accusatory \¦==¦==ˌ==\ *adj* : SELF-ACCUSING

self-accusing \¦=÷¦==\ *adj* : acting or serving to accuse oneself

self-acquired \¦=÷¦=\ *adj* : acquired by oneself or for one's own use and benefit

self-acting \ˈ=¦==\ *adj* : acting or capable of acting of or by itself : AUTOMATIC

self-action \¦=¦==\ *n* : action not dependent on an external agency or force : independent action

self-active \ˈ=¦==\ *adj* : acting of itself without dependence on an external agency or force

self-activity \¦=¦==\ *n* : SELF-ACTION

self-actor \ˈ=¦=\ *n* : a self-acting machine; *esp* : a self-acting mule

self-addressed \¦==¦=, ˈ=¦=ˌ=\ *adj* : addressed for return to the sender and enclosed or to be enclosed in a communication for the convenience of one making a reply ⟨*self-addressed* envelope⟩

self-adjusting \¦==¦==\ *adj* : adjusting by itself ⟨a *self-adjusting* wrench⟩

self-adjustment \¦==¦==\ *n* : adjustment to oneself or one's environment

self-administered plan \¦==¦===-\ *n* : a pension or retirement plan administered by the employer or by the employer and a trustee jointly — compare INSURED PLAN

self-admiration \¦=ˌ==¦==\ *n* : SELF-CONCEIT

self-affected \¦==¦==\ *adj* : being in love with oneself : CONCEITED

self-affirmation \¦=ˌ==¦==\ *n* **1** : recognition and judgment of the existence of the conscious self **2** *logic* : the character of a truth or proposition that makes it undeniable without inconsistency

self-aggrandizement \¦==¦(ˌ)==, (¦)=¦==¦==\ *n* : the act or process of making oneself greater (as in power or influence)

self-aggrandizing \¦==¦==ˌ==, (ˈ)=¦=ˌ==\ *adj* : acting or seeking to make oneself greater

self-analysis \¦==¦===\ *n* : a systematic attempt by an individual to understand his own personality dynamics without the aid of another person; *specif* : psychoanalysis without transference

self-analytical \¦=¦==¦===\ *adj* : using self-analysis

self-annihilation \¦==ˌ==¦==\ *n* : annihilation of the self (as in mystical contemplation of God)

self-applauding \¦==¦==\ *adj* : applauding oneself : marked by self-applause

self-applause \¦==¦=\ *n* : an expression or feeling of approval of oneself

self-appointed \¦==¦==\ *adj* : appointed or chosen (as to a function or position) by oneself usu. without warrant or qualifications ⟨a *self-appointed* guardian of public morals⟩

self-approbation \¦=ˌ=¦==\ *n* : satisfaction with one's actions and achievements

self-asserting \¦==¦==\ *adj* **1** : asserting oneself or one's own rights or claims **2** : putting oneself forward in a confident or arrogant manner — **self-assert·ing·ly** \¦==¦===\ *adv*

self-assertion \¦==¦==\ *n* **1** : the act of asserting oneself or one's own rights or claims **2** : the act of asserting one's superiority over others esp. by aggressive or inconsiderate behavior

self-assertive \¦==¦==\ *adj* : given to or characterized by self-assertion **syn** see AGGRESSIVE

self-assertively \¦==¦===\ *adv* : in a self-assertive manner

self-assertiveness \¦==¦===\ *n* : the quality or state of being self-assertive

self-assigned \¦==¦=\ *adj* : assigned by oneself

self-assumption \¦==¦==\ *n* : SELF-CONCEIT

self-assurance \¦==¦==\ *n* : assured self-confidence

self-assured \¦==¦=\ *adj* : sure of oneself : SELF-CONFIDENT **syn** see CONFIDENT

self-assuredness \¦==¦===\ *n* : the quality or state of being self-assured

self-awareness \¦==¦==\ *n* : an awareness of one's own personality or individuality

self-baptizer \¦=ˌ=¦==, ˈ=¦=ˌ==\ *n, sometimes cap S&B* : SE-BAPTIST

self-betrayal \¦==¦=(ə)\ *n* : SELF-REVELATION

self-binder \ˈ=¦==\ *n* : BINDER 4b

self-blimped \ˈ=¦=\ *or* **self-blimping** \ˈ=¦==\ *adj, of a motion-picture camera* : sound-insulated by its own housing

self blue *n* : a paper that is derived from blue rag pulp made from indigo-dyed rags and that has a bluish color which is fast to light

self-born \ˈ=¦=\ *adj* : arising within the self ⟨*self-born* sorrows⟩ : springing from a prior self ⟨phoenix rising *self-born* from the fire⟩

self-bounty \ˈ=¦==\ *n, obs* : inherent kindness and benevolence ⟨would not have your free and noble nature, out of *self-bounty*, be abused —Shak.⟩

self-break \ˈ=¦=\ *n* : break of tulips in which the flower turns a darker color or develops darker stripes of the basic color

self-buried \ˈ=¦berēd\ *adj* : buried by natural forces rather than by an intentional act of man ⟨uncovered *self-buried* implements that had sunk into the earth long ago⟩

self-care \ˈ=¦=\ *n* : care for oneself

self-castigation \¦=ˌ==¦==\ *n* : SELF-PUNISHMENT

self-catalysis \¦==¦===\ *n* : catalysis of a chemical reaction without the addition of a special catalyst : AUTOCATALYSIS

self-caused \ˈ=¦=\ *adj* : SELF-CREATED

self-centered \ˈ=¦==\ *adj* **1** : STATIONARY, UNMOVING **2** : not dependent on outside force or influence : SELF-SUFFICIENT ⟨in a world plagued by desperate insecurity, there are still tiny cases of interest that are private, intimate, intensely personal, *self-centered* —J.T.Winterich⟩ **3** : concerned solely with one's own desires, needs, or interests : SELFISH ⟨a *self-centered*, arrogant boy who can't have his own way with life —Jay Williams⟩ — **self-centered·ly** *adv* — **self-centeredness** *n* -ES

self-centering \ˈ=¦=(=)=\ *adj* **1** : centering in or of oneself **2** *of a chuck* : having jaws or dogs that can be made to move with gripping faces always equidistant from the chuck axis

self-charity \(ˈ)=¦===\ *n, obs* : charity toward oneself ⟨unless *self-charity* be sometimes a vice —Shak.⟩

self-closing \¦=¦==\ *adj* : closing or shutting automatically after being opened

self-cocker \ˈ=¦==\ *n* : a self-cocking revolver

self-cocking \¦=¦==\ *adj* : cocked by the operation of some part of the action ⟨*self-cocking* on closing the bolt⟩

self-collected \¦==¦==\ *adj* : SELF-POSSESSED

self-colored \¦=¦==\ *adj* : of a single color — used esp. of a flower, an animal, or textile fabric

self-command \¦==¦=\ *n* : command of oneself : SELF-CONTROL

self-compatible \¦==¦===\ *adj* : capable of effective self-pollination that results in the production of seeds and fruits

self-complacency \¦==¦===\ *n* : SELF-SATISFACTION

self-complacent \¦==¦==\ *adj* : SELF-SATISFIED **syn** see COMPLACENT

self-composed \¦==¦=\ *adj* : having control over one's emotions : CALM, COLLECTED — **self-composedly** \¦==¦===\ *adv* — **self-composedness** \¦==¦=(=)=\ *n* -ES

self-conceit \¦==¦=\ *n* : an exaggerated opinion of one's own qualities or abilities

self-conceited \¦==¦==\ *adj* : marked by self-conceit : VAIN

self-concentered \¦==¦==\ *adj* : concentrated in oneself or itself

self-concern \¦==¦=\ *n* : a selfish or morbid concern for oneself

self-concerned \¦==¦=\ *adj* : marked by self-concern

self-condemnation \¦=ˌ=(ˌ)=¦==\ *n* : condemnation of one's own character or actions

self-condemned \¦==¦=\ *adj* : condemned by oneself

self-conduct \ˈ=¦=(ˌ)=\ *n* : regulation and control of oneself

self-confessed \¦==¦=\ *adj* : openly acknowledged : AVOWED ⟨a *self-confessed* intellectual⟩ ⟨a *self-confessed* gambler⟩

self-confession \¦==¦==\ *n* : AVOWAL

self-confidence \(ˈ)=¦===\ *n* **1** : arrogant or excessive reliance on oneself : COCKINESS, OVERCONFIDENCE ⟨swaggering *self-confidence* and exaggerated efforts to keep up a good front —*Christian Science Monitor*⟩ **2** : confidence in oneself : ASSURANCE ⟨a normal adult manly *self-confidence* —Weston La Barre⟩

self-confident \(ˈ)=¦===\ *adj* **1** : arrogantly overconfident ⟨unruly, impatient of discipline, and too aggressively *self-confident* —Allan Nevins & H.S.Commager⟩ **2** : confident of one's own strength or ability : SELF-RELIANT ⟨looked to be hardly more than a boy, but firm-knit and *self-confident* —S.H.Adams⟩ **syn** see CONFIDENT

self-confidently \(ˈ)=¦====\ *adv* : in a self-confident manner

self-confiding \¦==¦==\ *adj, archaic* : showing self-confidence ⟨free, and fearless, and *self-confiding* —Sir Walter Scott⟩

self-congratulation \¦=ˌ=ˌ==¦==\ *n* : congratulation of oneself; *esp* : a complacent acknowledgment of one's own superiority or good fortune

self-congratulatory \¦==¦===ˌ==\ *adj* : indulging in self-congratulation

self-conscious \ˈ=¦==\ *adj* **1 a** : conscious of one's own acts or states as belonging to or originating in oneself : aware of oneself as an individual that experiences, desires, and acts ⟨not only thinks, but he knows himself as thinking . . . is not only conscious, but he is *self-conscious* —Rufus Jones⟩ **b** : intensely aware of oneself or itself : CONSCIOUS : DELIBERATE ⟨have been very *self-conscious* about their roles as guardians of the social values —D.M.Potter⟩ ⟨this highly *self-conscious* poetical prose —*Times Lit. Supp.*⟩ **2** : uncomfortably conscious of oneself as an object of the observation of others : ill at ease ⟨wondered if there would ever be a time in his life when he could be untidy without being *self-conscious* about it —Jean Stafford⟩ — **self-consciously** \(ˈ)=¦===\ *adv*

self-conscious·ness \ˈ=¦===\ *n* : the quality or state of being self-conscious

self-consequence \(ˈ)=¦==(ˌ)=\ *n* : SELF-IMPORTANCE

self-consistency \¦==¦===\ *n* : the quality or state of being self-consistent

self-consistent \¦==¦==\ *adj* : consistent with oneself or itself : logically consistent throughout : having each part consistent with the rest

self-constituted \(ˈ)=¦==ˌ==\ *adj* : constituted by oneself or itself

self-contained \¦==¦=\ *adj* **1 a** : sufficient in itself : INDEPENDENT ⟨the world of technics is not isolated and *self-contained* —Lewis Mumford⟩ **b** : showing self-command : SELF-CONTROLLED ⟨taller than most of the early frontiersmen . . . more *self-contained* and more dependable —Mari Sandoz⟩ **c** : formal and reserved in manner ⟨cool, composed, indulgent, *self-contained* . . . she watched with sympathy the liberal manners of the new century —Ellen Glasgow⟩ **2 a** : having none of its parts in common with anything surrounding it or adjacent to it : complete in itself ⟨a *self-contained* machine⟩ ⟨small *self-contained* houses, with each its own hedged garden —Mary Baum⟩ **b** *Brit* : including all necessary living facilities and restricted to the use of one family ⟨a *self-contained* house⟩ **c** : having a self-cover — **self-contained·ly** \¦==¦===\ *adv* — **self-contained·ness** \¦==¦=nədnəs\ *n* -ES

self-contained ornament *n* : ornament in which the design is a single complete whole intended to fill a space without being repeated

self-contained ornament

self-containment \¦==¦==\ *n* : a self-contained condition or state

self-contamination \¦==ˌ==¦==\ *n* : contamination by oneself or itself : contamination from within

self-contempt \¦==¦=\ *n* : contempt for oneself

self-content \¦==¦=\ *n* : SELF-SATISFACTION ⟨lived in eminent *self-content*, as one lying on a soft cloud —George Meredith⟩

self-contented \¦==¦==\ *adj* : SELF-SATISFIED — **self-contentedly** \¦==¦===\ *adv* — **self-contentedness** \¦==¦===\ *n* -ES

self-contentment \¦==¦==\ *n* : SELF-SATISFACTION

self-contradiction \¦=ˌ==¦==\ *n* **1** : contradiction of oneself or itself ⟨a person with a poor memory and changeable mind who is given to frequent *self-contradiction*⟩ **2** : a self-contradictory statement or proposition

self-contradictory \¦=ˌ==¦=(=)=\ *adj* : consisting of two members or parts one of which contradicts the other ⟨to be and not to be at the same time is a *self-contradictory* statement⟩

self-control \¦==¦=\ *n* : control of oneself : restraint exercised over one's own impulses, emotions, or desires ⟨his anger blazed out and burned up his *self-control* —H.E.Scudder⟩ ⟨passionate and rebellious, she never learned *self-control* —E.C.Wagenknecht⟩

self-controlled \¦==¦=\ *adj* : manifesting self-control

self-copulation \¦=ˌ==¦==\ *n* : copulation with itself : AUTOCOPULATION

self-correcting \¦==¦==\ *adj* : acting automatically to correct or compensate for (as errors, weaknesses, or imbalances)

self-corrective \¦==¦==\ *adj* : SELF-CORRECTING

self-cover \ˈ=¦==\ *n* : a cover (as of a pamphlet) of the same paper as the inside leaves; *also* : a publication having such a cover — called also *integral cover*

self-created \¦==¦==\ *adj* : created or appointed by oneself

self-critical \(ˈ)=¦===\ *adj* : critical of oneself

self-criticism \(ˈ)=¦==ˌ==\ *n* : the act of or capacity for criticizing one's own faults or shortcomings

self-culture \ˈ=¦==\ *n* : the development of one's mind or capacities through one's own efforts

self-deceit \¦==¦=\ *n* : SELF-DECEPTION

self-deceived \¦==¦=\ *adj* : deceived or misled esp. respecting oneself by one's own mistake

self-deceiver \¦==¦==\ *n* : one who practices self-deception

self-deceiving \¦==¦==\ *adj* : given to self-deception or serving to deceive oneself ⟨a *self-deceiving* hypocrite⟩ ⟨*self-deceiving* excuses⟩

self-deception \¦==¦==\ *n* : the act of deceiving oneself or the state of being deceived by oneself ⟨to presume agreement where none exists is the most dangerous form of *self-deception* —Agnes Repplier⟩

self-deceptive \¦==¦==\ *adj* : SELF-DECEIVING

self-dedication \¦=ˌ==¦==\ *n* : dedication of oneself to a cause or ideal

self-defeating \¦==¦==\ *adj* : acting to defeat its own purpose

self-defense \¦==¦=\ *n* : the act of defending oneself or something that belongs or relates to oneself ⟨the manly art of *self-defense*⟩ ⟨issued a statement in *self-defense* after the newspaper's attack on him⟩; *esp* : a plea of justification for assaulting or killing a human being sustained under very technical rules of law after examining the surrounding circumstances and considering such factors as whether the defendant was the initial aggressor or free from fault, whether he had a reasonable opportunity to retreat to a place of safety, and whether the force used by him was reasonable and used to protect himself or those under his protection

self-defensive \¦==¦==\ *adj* : given to or involving self-defense ⟨a *self-defensive* person⟩ ⟨a *self-defensive* attitude⟩

self-delight \¦==¦=\ *n* : delight in or gratification of oneself

self-deluded \¦==¦==\ *adj* : SELF-DECEIVED

self-delusion \¦==¦==\ *n* : SELF-DECEPTION

self-denial \¦==¦=(ə)\ *n* : denial of oneself : a restraint or limitation of one's own desires or interests ⟨mouth closed tight from . . . disillusion and *self-denial* —D.H.Lawrence⟩

self-denied \¦==¦=\ *adj* : marked by self-denial

self-denier \¦==¦=(ə)\ *n* : one who practices self-denial

self-denying \¦==¦==\ *adj* : forbearing to gratify oneself or advance one's interests : involving or showing self-denial — **self-denyingly** \¦==¦===\ *adv*

self-dependence \¦==¦==\ *n* : dependence on one's own resources or exertions : SELF-RELIANCE

self-dependent \¦==¦==\ *adj* : marked by self-dependence ⟨encourage voluntary *self-dependent* education throughout life —*Amer. Guide Series: Vt.*⟩

self-deprecating \(ˈ)=¦==ˌ==\ *adj* : given to self-depreciation

self-depreciation \¦=ˌ==¦==\ *n* : disparagement or undervaluation of oneself

self-despair \¦==¦=\ *n* : despair of oneself : HOPELESSNESS

self-destroyer \¦==¦=(ə)\ *n* : one who destroys himself

self-destroying \¦==¦==\ *adj* : SELF-DESTRUCTIVE

self-destruction \¦==¦==\ *n* : destruction of oneself or itself; *esp* : SUICIDE

self-destructive \¦==¦==\ *adj* : acting or tending to destroy oneself or itself : SUICIDAL ⟨postulated an innate death instinct to account for aggression and *self-destructive* urges —G.S.Blum⟩ — **self-destructively** \¦==¦===\ *adv*

self-determination \¦=ˌ=ˌ==¦==\ *n* **1** : determination of one's acts or states by oneself without external compulsion **2** : the right of a people to decide its future political status (as with respect to form of government or independence) or its action in so deciding usu. by plebiscite

self-determined \¦==¦==\ *adj* : determined by oneself or itself

self-determining \¦==¦===\ *adj* : capable of determining one's or its own acts ⟨a *self-determining* organism⟩

self-determinism \¦==¦==ˌ==\ *n* : a doctrine that the actions of a self are determined by itself — compare DETERMINISM 1a, INDETERMINISM 1

self-development \¦==¦===\ *n* : development of the capabilities or possibilities of oneself or itself

self-devoted \¦==¦==\ *adj* : characterized by self-devotion — **self-devotedly** \¦==¦===\ *adv* — **self-devotedness** \¦==¦===\ *n*

self-devoting \¦==¦==\ *adj* : SELF-DEVOTED

self-devotion \¦==¦==\ *n* : devotion of oneself esp. in service or sacrifice ⟨his *self-devotion* to science cost him his life⟩

self-devouring \¦==¦==\ *adj* : devouring itself : AUTOPHAGOUS ⟨*self-devouring* cruelty —Philip Sidney⟩

self-differentiation \¦=ˌ==ˌ==¦==\ *n* : differentiation of a structure or tissue due to factors existent in itself and essentially independent of other parts of the developing organism

self-digestion \¦=(ˌ)=¦==\ *n* : the decomposition of plant or animal tissue by internal process : AUTOLYSIS

self-directed \¦=(ˌ)=¦==\ *adj* : directed by oneself or itself : not guided or impelled by an outside force or agency ⟨a *self-directed* personality⟩

self-directing \¦=(ˌ)=¦==\ *adj* **:** directing oneself or itself
self-direction \¦=(ˌ)=¦==\ *n* **:** guidance by oneself or itself
self-discharging \¦==¦==, (ˈ)=¦=ˌ==\ *adj* **:** discharging by itself
self-discipline \(ˈ)=¦==\ *n* **:** the correction or regulation of oneself for the sake of improvement
self-disciplined \(ˈ)=¦=(=)=\ *adj* **:** capable of or subject to self-discipline
self-discovery \¦==¦=(=)=\ *n* **:** the act or process of achieving self-knowledge ⟨sport leads to the most remarkable *self-discovery* of our limitations as well as our abilities —Roger Bannister⟩
self-discrepant \¦==¦==\ *adj* **:** incompatible with self or selfhood
self-distributing \¦==¦===\ *adj* **:** distributing itself automatically
self-distrust \¦==¦=\ *n* **:** a lack of confidence in oneself **:** DIFFIDENCE ⟨he taught self-reliance and felt *self-distrust* —S.E.Whicher⟩
self-distrustful \¦==¦==\ *adj* **:** lacking in self-confidence
self-division \¦==¦==\ *n* **:** division of itself by its own action or process of growth
self·dom *pronunc at* ¹SELF + dəm\ *n* -s [³*self-* + *-dom*] **:** the essence of one's self **:** INDIVIDUALITY
self-doubt \ˈ=¦=\ *n* **:** a lack of faith in oneself **:** a feeling of uncertainty as to the value of one's actions or way of life ⟨all my yearning to live a creative life rushed up and all my characteristic *self-doubt* also —Elise Jerard⟩
self-doubting \¦=¦==\ *adj* **:** given to self-doubt
self-dramatizing \(ˈ)=¦=ˌ=ˌ==\ *adj* **:** seeing and presenting oneself as an actor in a drama **:** giving a false dignity and nobility to one's actions and words ⟨*self-dramatizing*, fraternizing, weak and irresponsible, longing for a literary life —*N.Y. Herald Tribune Bk. Rev.*⟩
self-drive \ˈ=¦=\ *adj, Brit* **:** DRIVE-YOURSELF
self-driven \ˈ=¦==\ *adj* **:** driven by itself **:** AUTOMOTIVE
self-duplicating \(ˈ)=¦=ˌ=ˌ==\ *adj* **:** reproducing itself **:** passing on its characteristics
self-ease \ˈ=¦=\ *n* **:** bodily comfort
selfed *past of* SELF
self-educated \(ˈ)=¦=ˌ=ˌ==\ *adj* **:** educated by one's own efforts without formal instruction
self-education \¦=ˌ==¦==\ *n* **:** education achieved by one's own efforts esp. through reading and informal study
self-effacement \¦==¦==\ *n* **:** effacement of oneself; *specif* **:** the placing or keeping of oneself in the background ⟨Christianity . . . its terms of value all derive from a law of *self-effacement* and of consideration for others —R.M.Weaver⟩
self-effacing \¦==¦==\ *adj* **:** RETIRING ⟨essentially humble, modest, and *self-effacing* —B.K.Malinowski⟩ — **self-effacingly** \¦==¦===\ *adv*
self-elect \¦==¦=\ *or* **self-elected** \¦==¦==\ *adj* **:** chosen or elected by oneself **:** SELF-APPOINTED
self-employed \¦==¦=\ *adj* **:** earning income directly from one's own business, trade, or profession rather than as a specified salary or wages from an employer
self-employment \¦==¦==\ *n* **:** the state of being self-employed
self-endeared \¦==¦=\ *adj* **:** SELF-LOVING ⟨she cannot love . . . she is so *self-endeared* —Shak.⟩
self-energizing brake \(ˈ)=¦=ˌ==-\ *n* **:** a brake that contains within itself some means (as the wrapping action in a band brake) for augmenting the power imparted to it by the pressure on the brake pedal
self-energy \(ˈ)=¦===\ *n* **:** energy that is generated in or by itself
self-enforcing \¦==¦==\ *adj* **:** containing in itself the authority or means to guarantee its enforcement ⟨a *self-enforcing* order⟩
self-enrichment \¦==¦==\ *n* **:** the act or process of increasing one's intellectual or spiritual resources
self-esteem \¦==¦=\ *n* **1 :** a confidence and satisfaction in oneself **:** SELF-RESPECT ⟨worth while to remind ourselves of the reasons that we have for national *self-esteem* —Bertrand Russell⟩ **2 :** one's good opinion of oneself **:** AMOUR PROPRE **:** SELF-CONCEIT ⟨an unfortunate peculiarity of an otherwise admirable personality was his inordinate *self-esteem* —H.W.H. Knott⟩ **syn** see CONCEIT
self-esterification \¦==ˌ===¦==\ *n* **:** the reaction of a compound (as lactic acid or other hydroxy organic acid) with itself to form one or more esters
self-evidence \(ˈ)=¦===\ *n* **1 :** evidence given by itself of its own truth **2 :** the quality or state of being self-evident
self-evidencing \(ˈ)=¦=(ˌ)=ˌ==\ *adj* **:** giving evidence of its own truth — **self-evidencingly** \(ˈ)=¦===\ *adv*
self-evident \(ˈ)=¦=(ˌ)==\ *adj* **:** evident without proof or argument **:** producing conviction on a bare presentation or statement ⟨we hold these truths to be *self-evident* —*U.S. Declaration of Independence*⟩ — **self-evidently** \(ˈ)=¦=(ˌ)==\ *adv*
self-evolution \¦=ˌ==¦==\ *n* **:** development by inherent quality or power
self-exaltation \¦=ˌ=(ˌ)=¦==\ *n* **:** exaltation of oneself **:** VAINGLORY
self-exalting \¦==¦==\ *adj* **:** VAINGLORIOUS — **self-exaltingly** \¦==¦===\ *adv*
self-examination \¦==ˌ=¦==\ *n* **:** INTROSPECTION
self-excite \¦==¦=\ *vt* **:** to excite (the field magnets of a dynamo) by a current produced by the dynamo itself
self-exciter \¦==¦==\ *n* **:** a dynamo whose field magnets are self-excited
self-executing \(ˈ)=¦=ˌ=ˌ==\ *adj* **:** providing for its own execution **:** containing a clause giving effect to its provisions by operation of law on the occurrence of a contemplated event or contingency ⟨a *self-executing* law⟩
self-exiled \ˈ=¦=ˌ=\ *adj* **:** exiled by one's own wish or decision
self-existence \¦==¦==\ *n* **:** the quality or state of being self-existent
self-existent \¦==¦==\ *adj* **:** existing of or by oneself or itself **:** independent of any other being or cause
self-experience \¦==¦===\ *n* **:** one's own experience
self-explaining \¦==¦==\ *adj* **:** SELF-EXPLANATORY
self-explanatory \¦==¦=ˌ===\ *adj* **:** explaining itself **:** capable of being understood without explanation
self-expression \¦==¦==\ *n* **:** the expression of one's own personality **:** the assertion of one's individual traits ⟨*self-expression* is dynamic and ever-changing according to the child's mental and emotional level —W.M.Ivey⟩
self-expressive \¦==¦==\ *adj* **:** given to self-expression or serving as a means of self-expression ⟨a *self-expressive* painter⟩ ⟨*self-expressive* behavior⟩
self-faced \ˈ=¦=\ *adj, of stone* **:** having a natural, broken, or undressed face
self-feed \ˈ=¦=\ *vt* **:** to provide rations to (animals) in bulk so as to permit each animal to select the kind and quantity of food that it wants — compare HAND-FEED
self-feeder \ˈ=¦==\ *n* **:** one that feeds itself automatically; *specif* **:** a device for feeding livestock that is equipped with a feed hopper that automatically supplies a trough below
self-feeling \¦=¦==\ *n* **:** self-centered emotion
self-fertile \ˈ=¦=(ˌ)=\ *adj* **:** fertile by means of its own pollen or sperm — used of either a plant or animal; opposed to *self-sterile*
self-fertility \¦==¦===\ *n* **:** the quality or state of being self-fertile
self-fertilization \¦=ˌ=(ˌ)=¦==\ *n* **:** fertilization effected by pollen or sperm from the same individual
self-fertilized \(ˈ)=¦=ˌ==\ *adj* **:** fertilized by means of one's own pollen or sperm ⟨a *self-fertilized* flower⟩
self-fertilizing \(ˈ)=¦=ˌ==\ *adj* **:** SELF-FERTILIZED
self-flattering \(ˈ)=¦===\ *adj* **:** given to self-flattery
self-flattery \(ˈ)=¦===\ *n* **:** flattery of oneself **:** the glossing over of one's own weaknesses or mistakes or the exaggeration of one's own qualities and achievements
self-forgetful \¦==¦==\ *adj* **:** forgetful of one's own self or selfish interests or marked by forgetfulness of self ⟨absorbed in work of contemplation, *self-forgetful* and lost to consciousness of his surroundings —Laurence Binyon⟩ — **self-forgetfully** \¦==¦===\ *adv* — **self-forgetfulness** \¦==¦===\ *n*
self-forgetting \¦==¦==\ *adj* **:** SELF-FORGETFUL — **self-forgettingly** \¦==¦===\ *adv*
self-formed \ˈ=¦=\ *adj* **:** formed or developed by one's own efforts
self-fruitful \ˈ=¦==\ *adj* **:** capable of setting a crop of self-pollinated fruit without regard to the fertility of the seeds — **self-fruitfulness** \(ˈ)=¦===\ *n*
self-fulfilling \¦==¦==\ *adj* **:** SELF-REALIZING
self-fulfillment \¦==¦==\ *n* **:** fulfillment of oneself
self-generated \(ˈ)=¦=ˌ=ˌ==\ *adj* **:** generated by itself **:** produced by self-generation **:** AUTOGENETIC, AUTOGENOUS
self-generation \¦=ˌ==¦==\ *n* **:** generation independent of external force or agency — called also *autogeny*
self-given \ˈ=¦==\ *adj* **1 :** derived from itself **:** INDEPENDENT ⟨a *self-given* entity⟩ **2 :** given by oneself ⟨the *self-given* role of elder statesman —T.H.White b.1915⟩
self-giving \ˈ=¦==\ *adj* **:** SELF-SACRIFICING, UNSELFISH ⟨*self-giving* creative work without thought of financial compensation —*Key Reporter*⟩
self-glorification \¦==ˌ===¦==\ *n* **:** a feeling or expression of one's superiority to others
self-glorifying \(ˈ)=¦===\ *adj* **:** BOASTFUL
self-glorious \(ˈ)=¦===\ *adj, obs* **:** BOASTFUL, VAIN
self-glory \ˈ=¦==\ *n* **:** personal vanity **:** PRIDE
self-good \ˈ=¦=\ *n* **:** personal advantage
self-governed \ˈ=¦==\ *adj* **1 :** not influenced or controlled by others **2 :** exercising self-control
self-governing \(ˈ)=¦===\ *adj* **:** having control or rule over oneself or itself **:** not subject to outside authority **:** AUTONOMOUS, INDEPENDENT ⟨set up an independent church on a local, *self-governing* basis —V.L.Parrington⟩
self-government \(ˈ)=¦=(=)=\ *n* **1 :** SELF-COMMAND, SELF-CONTROL **2 a :** control of one's or its own affairs **:** AUTONOMY 2a, INDEPENDENCE **b :** government by the joint action of the mass of people constituting a civil body **:** democratic government **:** DEMOCRACY
self-gratification \¦=ˌ===¦==\ *n* **:** the act of pleasing oneself or of satisfying one's desires ⟨the raw human being has unconscious forces that push him crudely toward *self-gratification* —Priscilla Robertson⟩
self-gratulation \¦=ˌ==¦==\ *n* **:** SELF-CONGRATULATION
self-gratulatory \(ˈ)=¦===ˌ==\ *adj* **:** SELF-CONGRATULATORY
self-hardening \(ˈ)=¦=(=)=\ *adj* **:** hardening by itself ⟨*self-hardening* clay⟩
self-hardening steel *n* **:** AIR-HARDENING STEEL
self-hate \ˈ=¦=\ *or* **self-hatred** \ˈ=¦==\ *n* **:** hatred redirected toward one's self rather than toward others
self-hating \ˈ=¦==\ *adj* **:** given to self-hate
self-heal \ˈ=ˌ=\ *n* [ME *selfhele*, fr. *self-* + *hele*, back-formation fr. *helen* to heal — more at HEAL] **:** any of several plants thought to possess healing properties; *esp* **:** a blue-flowered Eurasian mint (*Prunella vulgaris*) naturalized throughout No. America
self-help \ˈ=¦=\ *n* **1 a :** the act or an instance of providing for or helping oneself without dependence on others ⟨the differences between a good refugee camp and a bad refugee camp, particularly from the point of view of *self-help* —Gardner Murphy⟩ **b :** a program of part time usu. domestic or clerical work permitted or made available by a school or college to students to help them defray their expenses **2 :** the act or right of redressing or preventing wrongs by one's own action (as in self-defense, distress, or abatement of a nuisance) without recourse to legal proceedings
self-heterodyne \(ˈ)=¦=(=)=ˌ=\ *n* **:** AUTODYNE
self·hood \ˈselˌfu̇d, ˌfˌhu̇d, ˈseu̇l, ˈse(ə)l\ — *see* ¹SELF\ *n* -s [³*self* + *-hood*; intended as trans. of G *meinheit* (syn. of G *selbheit* selfhood)] **1 a :** the state of possessing an individual identity or the individuality so possessed **:** IPSEITY ⟨the intrinsic ~ of each individual thing in nature —Walker Gibson⟩ **b :** one's own character or personality ⟨the struggle of the partially emancipated woman for ~ —G.J.Becker⟩ **2 :** SELF-CENTEREDNESS, SELFISHNESS ⟨expose the quivering uncleanliness of a festering ~ —Perry Miller⟩
self-humbling \(ˈ)=¦=(=)=\ *adj* **:** acting or serving to humble oneself
self-hunter \ˈ=¦==\ *n* **1 :** a hunting dog who ignores the directions of his master and hunts to suit himself **2 :** a dog who habitually hunts without his master
self-hypnosis \¦=(ˌ)=¦==\ *n* **:** hypnosis of oneself
self-identical \¦=(ˌ)=¦===\ *adj* **:** having self-identity
self-identification \¦=(ˌ)=ˌ===¦==\ *n* **:** identification with someone or something outside oneself ⟨blasphemous in a man's *self-identification* with the deity —H.J.Morgenthau⟩
self-identity \¦=(ˌ)=¦===\ *n* **1 :** the identity of a thing with itself **:** substantial sameness **2 :** identity of subject and object in life and consciousness
self-ignite \¦==¦=\ *vi* **:** to become ignited without flame or spark (as under high compression)
self-ignition \¦==¦==\ *n* **:** ignition without flame or spark
self-image \¦=¦==\ *n* **:** one's conception of oneself or of one's role ⟨changing the *self-image* which many petty offenders have —Irwin Deutscher⟩
self-immolation \¦=ˌ==¦==\ *n* **:** a deliberate and willing sacrifice of oneself ⟨welcoming *self-immolation* to an overwhelming force —Charles Anderson⟩
self-importance \¦==¦==\ *n* **1 :** an exaggerated estimate of one's own importance or merit **:** SELF-CONCEIT **2 :** arrogant or pompous bearing or behavior
self-important \¦==¦==\ *adj* **:** having or showing self-importance **:** arrogant or pompous — **self-importantly** \¦==¦===\ *adv*
self-imposed \¦==¦=\ *adj* **:** imposed by oneself or itself **:** voluntarily assumed ⟨a pity that it should labor under a *self-imposed* handicap —J.L.Lowes⟩
self-impotent \(ˈ)=¦===\ *adj* **:** SELF-STERILE
self-improvement \¦==¦==\ *n* **:** improvement of oneself by one's own actions
self-improving \¦==¦==\ *adj* **:** achieving or aiming at self-improvement
self-inclusive \¦==¦==\ *adj* **:** enclosing itself **:** complete in itself ⟨a *self-inclusive* system⟩
self-incompatibility \¦=ˌ==ˌ=¦===\ *n* **:** the quality or state of being self-incompatible
self-incompatible \¦(ˌ)=¦=ˌ===\ *adj* **:** incapable of effective self-pollination — compare SELF-COMPATIBLE
self-incriminating \¦==¦=ˌ==\ *adj* **:** serving or tending to incriminate oneself
self-incrimination \¦==ˌ=¦==\ *n* **:** incrimination of oneself; *specif* **:** the giving of evidence or answering questions the tendency of which would be to subject one to a criminal prosecution
self-induced \¦==¦=\ *adj* **:** induced by oneself or itself ⟨would wallow in a *self-induced* gloom —Norman Mailer⟩; *specif* **:** existing in a circuit by reason of variation of current in the circuit itself ⟨a *self-induced* voltage⟩
self-inductance \¦==¦==\ *n* **:** INDUCTANCE 1(1)
self-induction \¦==¦==\ *n* **:** induction of an electromotive force in a circuit by a varying current in the same circuit
self-indulged \¦==¦=\ *adj* **:** pampered by oneself
self-indulgence \¦==¦==\ *n* **:** excessive or unrestrained gratification of one's own appetites, desires, or whims **:** irresponsible self-gratification ⟨always fond of the good things of life, he had found . . . increasing opportunity for *self-indulgence* —A.C.Cole⟩
self-indulgent \¦==¦==\ *adj* **:** indulging oneself or marked by self-indulgence ⟨a mild, *self-indulgent* bachelor —G.K. Chesterton⟩ ⟨an easy, *self-indulgent*, dilettante way of looking at life —Havelock Ellis⟩ — **self-indulgently** \¦==¦===\ *adv*
self-inflicted \¦==¦==\ *adj* **1 :** SELF-IMPOSED ⟨*self-inflicted* penance —Lord Byron⟩ **2 :** inflicted by one's own hand ⟨a *self-inflicted* wound⟩
selfing *pres part of* SELF
self-insurance \¦==¦==, ˈ=¦==\ *n* **:** insurance of oneself or of one's own interests by the setting aside of money at regular intervals to provide a fund to cover possible losses (as in the event of fire)
self-insured \¦==¦=\ *adj* **:** insured by oneself
self-insurer \¦==¦==\ *n* **:** one who practices self-insurance
self-interest \(ˈ)=¦=(=)(ˌ)=\ *n* **1 :** one's own interest or advantage ⟨our *self-interest* . . . requires that we do everything in our power to guarantee that the children of Europe grow up strong —George Kent⟩ **2 :** a concern for one's own advantage and material well-being ⟨*self-interest* is regarded as the most, if not the only, reliable motivating force in economic behavior —A.F.Chalk⟩
self-interested \(ˈ)=¦=(=)(ˌ)==\ *adj* **:** characterized or motivated by self-interest — **self-interestedness** \(ˈ)=¦=(=)(ˌ)===\ *n*
self-involution \¦=ˌ==¦==\ *n* **:** SELF-ABSORPTION
self-involved \¦==¦=\ *adj* **:** SELF-ABSORBED
self·ish *pronunc at* ¹SELF + ish *or* ēsh\ *adj* [³*self* + *-ish*] **1 a :** concerned excessively or exclusively with oneself **:** seeking or concentrating on one's own advantage, pleasure, or well-being without regard for others ⟨if he could be proud and patriotic, so too he could be ~ and mean —Francis Parkman⟩ ⟨a formal, greedy, ~ old gentleman —L.P.Smith⟩ ⟨~ ambition⟩ **b :** SELF-CENTERED ⟨the sympathy of children with those who weep is innocently ~ —G.D.Brown⟩ **2 a :** believing or teaching that the chief motives of human action are derived from love of self ⟨the ~ school of philosophers —William Fleming⟩ **b :** performed to benefit oneself esp. in disregard of the welfare of others ⟨a ~ act⟩ — **self·ish·ly** \-əshlē, -li\ *adv*
self·ish·ness \-ishnəs, -ēsh-\ *n* -ES **:** the quality or state of being selfish **:** a concern for one's own welfare or advantage at the expense of or in disregard of others ⟨he was the personification of ~; and as he loved and cared for no one, so did no one love or care for him —George Borrow⟩
self·ism \-ˌfizəm\ *n* -s [³*self* + *-ism*] **1 :** concentration on self-interest **2 :** a system of selfish ethics
self·ist \-fəst\ *n* -s [³*self* + *-ist*] **:** a selfish person
self-justification \¦=ˌ===¦==\ *n* **:** the act or an instance of making excuses for oneself
self-justifying \(ˈ)=¦=ˌ=ˌ==\ *adj* **1 :** seeking to excuse oneself **2 :** automatically justifying itself ⟨a *self-justifying* typewriter⟩
self-killed \ˈ=¦=\ *adj, obs* **:** killed by oneself ⟨liest victorious among thy slain *self-killed* —John Milton⟩
self-knowing \¦=¦==\ *adj* **:** knowing oneself **:** having self-knowledge
self-knowledge \ˈ=¦==\ *n* **:** knowledge of oneself or of one's capabilities **:** understanding of one's own character, feelings, or motivations **:** AUTOGNOSIS ⟨having *self-knowledge* impelled him to start writing —William Saroyan⟩
self-laceration \¦=ˌ=¦==\ *n* **:** laceration of oneself
self-legislating \(ˈ)=¦=ˌ=ˌ==\ *adj* **:** making rules or laws for oneself
self·less *pronunc at* ¹SELF + ləs\ *adj* [³*self* + *-less*] **:** having no concern for self **:** UNSELFISH ⟨~ service to community, state, and nation —*Current Biog.*⟩ — **selflessly** *adv* — **selflessness** *n* -ES
self-life \ˈ=ˌ=\ *n* **1** *obs* **:** SELF-EXISTENCE ⟨who sees God's face, that is *self-life*, must die —John Donne⟩ **2 :** selfish living
self-limitation \¦=ˌ==¦==\ *n* **:** the quality or state of being self-limiting
self-limited \(ˈ)=¦===\ *adj* **:** limited by one's or its own nature; *specif* **:** running a definite and limited course ⟨the disease is *self-limited*, and the prognosis is good —*Science*⟩
self-limiting \(ˈ)=¦===\ *adj* **:** limiting oneself or itself **:** SELF-LIMITED
self-linkage \ˈ=¦==\ *n* **:** linkage of a substance to itself or to others of the same type **:** CATENATION b
self-liquidating \(ˈ)=¦=ˌ=ˌ==\ *adj* **1 :** of or relating to a commercial transaction in which goods are converted into cash in a short time **2 :** generating funds from its own operations to repay the original investment made to create it ⟨a *self-liquidating* housing project⟩
self-liquidating loan *n* **:** a loan having a term approximately equal to the period in which the borrower can complete the transaction financed and use the proceeds to repay the loan
self-loader \ˈ=¦==\ *n* **:** a semiautomatic firearm
self-loading \ˈ=¦==\ *adj, of a firearm* **:** SEMIAUTOMATIC
self-locking \ˈ=¦==\ *adj* **:** locking by its own action
self-lost \ˈ=¦=\ *adj* **:** lost by one's own fault
self-love \ˈ=¦=\ *n* **1 a :** love of oneself **:** AMOUR PROPRE ⟨peevish, proud, idle, made of *self-love* —Shak.⟩ **b :** love redirected toward one's self rather than toward others ⟨return to *self-love* as a consequence of failure to make satisfactory attachments to others —G.S.Blum⟩ **2 :** regard for one's own happiness or advantage **syn** see CONCEIT
self-loved \ˈ=¦=\ *adj, archaic* **:** SELF-LOVING
self-loving \ˈ=¦==\ *adj* **:** characterized by self-love
self-lubricating \(ˈ)=¦=ˌ=ˌ==\ *adj* **:** lubricating itself
self-luminous \(ˈ)=¦===\ *adj* **:** having in itself the property of emitting light
self-made \ˈ=¦=\ *adj* **1 :** made by oneself or itself **2 :** raised from poverty or obscurity by one's own efforts ⟨a *self-made* man⟩
self-mailer \ˈ=ˈ==\ *n* **:** a folder or broadside that can be sent by mail without enclosure in an envelope by use of a gummed sticker or a precanceled stamp to hold the leaves together
self-mailing \ˈ=¦==\ *adj* **:** capable of being mailed without being enclosed in an envelope
self-mastery \(ˈ)=¦=(=)=\ *n* **:** SELF-COMMAND, SELF-CONTROL
self-mate \ˈ=¦=\ *n* **:** SUIMATE
self-mortification \¦=ˌ===¦==\ *n* **:** the infliction of pain or discomfort on oneself
self-motion \ˈ=¦==\ *n* **:** spontaneous or voluntary motion
self-motive \ˈ=¦==\ *adj* **:** having self-motion
self-moved \ˈ=¦=\ *adj* **:** moved by inherent power
self-movement \ˈ=¦==\ *n* **:** SELF-MOTION
self-mover \ˈ=¦==\ *n* **:** one that moves itself **:** AUTOMATON
self-moving \ˈ=¦==\ *adj* **:** capable of moving by itself
self-murder \ˈ=¦==\ *n* **:** SELF-DESTRUCTION, SUICIDE
self-naughting \ˈ=¦==\ *n* **:** SELF-EFFACEMENT
self·ness *n* -ES [³*self* + *-ness*] **1 :** EGOISM, SELFISHNESS **2 :** PERSONALITY, SELFHOOD
self-observation \¦=ˌ==¦==\ *n* **1 :** observation of one's own appearance **2 :** INTROSPECTION, SELF-EXAMINATION
self-operating \(ˈ)=¦=(=)ˌ==\ *or* **self-operative** \(ˈ)=¦=(=)-(ˌ)==\ *adj* **:** SELF-ACTING
self-opinion \¦==¦==\ *n* **:** high or exaggerated estimate of oneself **:** SELF-CONCEIT ⟨if I should ever attain to the degree of *self-opinion* requisite to such an undertaking —William Cowper⟩
self-opinionated \¦==¦=ˌ==\ *adj* **1 :** having a high or exaggerated opinion of oneself or one's own views **2 :** stubbornly holding to one's own opinion **:** OPINIONATED — **self-opinionatedness** *n* -ES \¦==ˌ===\
self-opinionative \¦==¦===\ *adj* **:** SELF-OPINIONATED — **self-opinionativeness** \¦=ˈ=ˌ===\ *n*
self-opinioned \¦==¦==\ *adj* **:** SELF-OPINIONATED — **self-opinionedness** \¦=ˈ==\ *n*
self-organization \¦==(ˌ)=¦==\ *n* **:** organization of oneself; *specif* **:** the act or process of forming or joining a labor union
self-originated \¦==¦=ˌ==\ *adj* **:** originated by oneself or itself
self-originating \¦==¦=ˌ==\ *adj* **:** originating by or from oneself or itself
self-partiality \¦=ˌ=(=)¦===\ *n* **1 :** an excessive estimate of oneself as compared with others **2 :** a prejudice in favor of one's own claims or interests
self-perpetuating \¦==¦=ˌ==\ *adj* **:** capable of continuing or renewing oneself or itself indefinitely ⟨the theoretical fear of a *self-perpetuating* president —J.C.Fitzpatrick⟩ ⟨administered by its own *self-perpetuating* board of trustees —*Current Biog.*⟩
self-perpetuation \¦==ˌ=¦==\ *n* **:** perpetuation of oneself or itself ⟨concerned with *self-perpetuation* in office they too often ignore the public welfare —E.M.Eriksson⟩
self-picture \ˈ=¦==\ *n* **:** SELF-IMAGE
self-pity \ˈ=¦==\ *n* **:** pity for oneself; *esp* **:** a self-indulgent lingering on one's own sorrows or misfortunes ⟨the immensity of her self-love and *self-pity* . . . steeped her pages in an ignoble emotionalism —Agnes Repplier⟩
self-pitying \(ˈ)=¦===\ *adj* **:** given to self-pity — **self-pityingly** \(ˈ)=¦====\ *adv*
self-pleased \ˈ=¦=\ *adj* **:** SELF-COMPLACENT
self-pleasing \ˈ=¦==\ *adj* **:** pleasing to oneself
self-poise \ˈ=¦=\ *n* **:** the quality or state of being self-poised
self-poised \ˈ=¦=\ *adj* **1 :** balanced without support **2 :** having poise by self-command ⟨sturdy moral habit and *self-poised* temperament made him perhaps unduly optimistic —Gamaliel Bradford⟩
self-pollinated \(ˈ)=¦=ˌ=ˌ==\ *adj* **:** subjected to or produced by self-pollination
self-pollination \¦=ˌ==¦==\ *n* **:** the transfer of pollen from the anther of a flower to the stigma of the same flower or sometimes to that of another flower of the same plant or of another plant of the same clone — compare CROSS-POLLINATION
self-portrait \ˈ=¦=(ˌ)=\ *n* **1 :** a portrait of an artist done by him-

self **2 :** a picture of one's character or personality created by oneself ⟨a pleasing *self-portrait* emerges from the letters —Douglas Stewart⟩
self-possessed \ˌ≈≈ˈ≈\ *adj* **:** having or showing self-possession **:** composed in mind or manner **:** CALM ⟨remains strong and *self-possessed* in the face of trouble and strain —James Hewitt⟩ — **self-possessedly** \ˌ≈≈ˈ≈≈\ *adv*
self-possession \ˌ≈≈ˈ≈\ *n* **:** control of one's emotions or reactions **:** presence of mind **:** SELF-COMMAND, COMPOSURE ⟨that carefully cultivated air of quiet *self-possession*, suggesting inner repose and serenity —Harold Strauss⟩
self-potential method \ˌ≈≈ˈ≈-\ *n* **:** a method of electrical prospecting in which the electromotive forces existing in and around an ore body are measured at the surface
self-powered \ˈ≈ˈ≈\ *adj* **:** having its own power or propelling force
self-praise \ˈ≈ˈ≈\ *n* **:** praise of oneself
self-preservation \ˌ≈ˌ≈≈ˈ≈≈\ *n* **1 :** preservation of oneself from destruction or harm ⟨*self-preservation* demands a certain amount of public spirit —S.M.Crothers⟩ **2 :** a natural or instinctive tendency to act so as to preserve one's own existence ⟨man has not only the impulse of *self-preservation*, but also a social impulse —Frank Thilly⟩
self-preservative \ˌ≈≈ˈ≈≈≈\ *adj* **:** tending to self-preservation ⟨*self-preservative* behavior⟩
self-preserving \ˌ≈≈ˈ≈≈\ *adj* **:** acting or tending to preserve oneself or itself
self-pride \ˈ≈ˈ≈\ *n* **:** pride in oneself or in something that belongs or relates to oneself
self-proclaimed \ˌ≈≈ˈ≈\ *adj* **:** based on one's own say-so ⟨a *self-proclaimed* genius⟩
self-produced \ˌ≈≈ˈ≈\ *adj* **:** produced by oneself or itself **:** arising from oneself or itself
self-propelled \ˌ≈≈ˈ≈\ *adj* **1 a** (1) **:** propelled by its own motor ⟨a *self-propelled* vehicle⟩ (2) **:** propelled by its own fuel ⟨a *self-propelled* missile⟩ **b :** moved forward by one's or its own force or momentum ⟨a thundering *self-propelled* egotist —Winthrop Sargeant⟩ ⟨the arms program is now *self-propelled* —*Time*⟩ **2 a :** mounted on or fired from a moving vehicle ⟨a *self-propelled* gun⟩ **b :** serving as a moving carrier for a weapon ⟨a *self-propelled* mount⟩
self-propelling \ˌ≈≈ˈ≈≈\ *adj* **:** SELF-PROPELLED
self-propulsion \ˌ≈≈ˈ≈≈\ *n* **:** propulsion by one's or its own power
self-protection \ˌ≈≈ˈ≈≈\ *n* **:** protection of oneself **:** SELF-DEFENSE ⟨as a measure of *self-protection* against the lawless element —*Blue Bk.*⟩
self-protective \ˌ≈≈ˈ≈≈\ *adj* **:** serving or tending to protect oneself
self-pruning \ˈ≈ˈ≈≈\ *n* **:** NATURAL PRUNING
self-punishment \(ˈ)≈ˈ≈≈≈\ *n* **:** punishment of oneself
self-purification \ˌ≈ˌ≈≈≈ˈ≈≈\ *n* **1 :** purification by natural process ⟨*self-purification* of water⟩ **2 :** purification of oneself ⟨moral *self-purification*⟩
self-quadder \ˈ≈ˈ≈≈\ *n* **:** QUADDER
self-question \ˈ≈ˈ≈≈\ *n* **:** a question put to a person by himself ⟨from the *self-questions* came the self-doubts —Mark Schorer⟩
self-questioning \(ˈ)≈ˈ≈(≈)≈\ *n* **:** the act or process of questioning oneself **:** the examination of one's own actions and motives **:** SELF-SEARCHING ⟨entering a world of imponderables, and at every stage occasions for *self-questioning* arise —Sir Winston Churchill⟩
self-raised \ˈ≈ˈ≈\ *adj* **:** raised by one's or its own power or effort
self-rake \ˈ≈ˈ≈\ *n* **:** a reaper with a rake attachment for sweeping off gavels from the platform
self-rating \ˈ≈ˈ≈≈\ *n* **:** determination of one's own rating with reference to a standard educational scale or other rating device
self-reacting \ˌ≈≈ˈ≈≈\ *adj* **:** automatically compensating or adjusting to changed conditions
self-reading \ˈ≈ˈ≈≈\ *adj* **:** capable of being easily read
self-reading rod *n* **:** a leveling rod with graduations designed to be read directly by the observer
self-realization \ˌ≈ˌ≈(≈)(ˌ)≈ˈ≈≈\ *n* **:** fulfillment by oneself of the possibilities of one's character or personality ⟨has no resource except his impulses and only in improvised and violent action can he attain even an illusion of *self-realization* —A.M. Mizener⟩
self-realizationism \ˌ≈ˌ≈(≈)(ˌ)≈ˈ≈≈ˌ≈≈\ *n* -S **:** the ethical theory that the highest good for man consists in realizing or fulfilling himself usu. on the assumption that he has certain inborn abilities constituting his real or ideal self
self-realizationist \ˌ≈ˌ≈(≈)(ˌ)≈ˈ≈(≈)≈\ *n* -S **:** an advocate of self-realizationism
self-realizing \(ˈ)≈ˈ≈(≈)ˌ≈≈\ *adj* **:** marked by or achieving self-realization
self-recording \ˌ≈≈ˈ≈≈\ *adj* **:** making an automatic record **:** AUTOGRAPHIC ⟨a *self-recording* flowmeter⟩
self-recrimination \ˌ≈≈ˌ≈≈ˈ≈≈\ *n* **:** the act of accusing or blaming oneself
self-rectifying \(ˈ)≈ˈ≈≈ˌ≈≈\ *adj* **:** capable of accomplishing rectification by itself
self-reflection \ˌ≈≈ˈ≈≈\ *n* **:** INTROSPECTION
self-reflective \ˌ≈≈ˈ≈≈\ *adj* **:** INTROSPECTIVE
self-reflexive \ˌ≈≈ˈ≈≈\ *adj* **:** reflecting itself **:** giving back an image of itself — **self-reflexiveness** \ˌ≈≈ˈ≈≈≈\ *n*
self-reform \ˌ≈≈ˈ≈\ *n* **:** reform of oneself
self-regard \ˌ≈≈ˈ≈\ *n* **1 :** consideration of oneself or one's own interests **2 :** SELF-RESPECT
self-regarding \ˌ≈≈ˈ≈≈\ *adj* **:** concerned with oneself or one's own interests ⟨the new generation . . . is iconoclastic, undisciplined, *self-regarding*, violent —*Dial*⟩
self-registering \(ˈ)≈ˈ≈(≈)≈\ *adj* **:** registering automatically ⟨a *self-registering* barometer⟩
self-regulating \(ˈ)≈ˈ≈≈ˌ≈≈\ *adj* **:** regulating oneself or itself ⟨a *self-regulating* community⟩; *specif* **:** AUTOMATIC ⟨a *self-regulating* mechanism⟩
self-regulating currency *n* **:** AUTOMATIC CURRENCY
self-regulation \ˌ≈≈≈ˈ≈≈\ *n* **:** regulation of or by oneself or itself **:** control or supervision from within ⟨*self-regulation* of business⟩
self-regulative \(ˈ)≈ˈ≈≈(ˌ)≈≈\ *or* **self-regulatory** \(ˈ)≈ˈ≈≈≈ˌ≈≈\ *adj* **:** serving or tending to regulate oneself or itself
self-relation \ˌ≈≈ˈ≈≈\ *n* **:** SELF-IDENTITY
self-reliance \ˌ≈≈ˈ≈≈\ *n* **:** reliance upon one's own efforts, judgment, or ability **:** SELF-CONFIDENCE ⟨the people were weathered and bronzed, possessed of a sturdy independence and *self-reliance* —*Amer. Guide Series: N.C.*⟩
self-reliant \ˌ≈≈ˈ≈≈\ *adj* **:** not dependent on others **:** having confidence in and exercising one's own powers or judgment ⟨a mood of fighting men, venturesome, *self-reliant*, proud —J.R. Green⟩
self-renouncing \ˌ≈≈ˈ≈≈\ *adj* **:** marked by self-renunciation
self-renunciation \ˌ≈≈ˌ≈≈ˈ≈≈\ *n* **:** renunciation of one's own wishes, desires, or ambitions
self-repression \ˌ≈≈ˈ≈≈\ *n* **:** the keeping to oneself of one's thoughts, wishes, or feelings ⟨habit of absolute *self-repression*, and of concealment of emotion again prevailed —S.W.Mitchell⟩
self-reproach \ˌ≈≈ˈ≈\ *n* **:** the act or an instance of reproaching oneself **:** SELF-ACCUSATION ⟨felt both *self-reproach* and considerable grief concerning the loss of his friends —Elizabeth Rosenberg⟩
self-reproachful \ˌ≈≈ˈ≈≈\ *adj* **:** reproachful of oneself
self-reproaching \ˌ≈≈ˈ≈≈\ *adj* **:** reproaching oneself — **self-reproachingly** \ˌ≈≈ˈ≈≈≈\ *adv* — **self-reproachingness** \ˌ≈≈ˈ≈≈≈\ *n* -ES
self-reproof \ˌ≈≈ˈ≈\ *n* **:** the act or an instance of reproving oneself **:** censure of oneself
self-reproving \ˌ≈≈ˈ≈≈\ *adj* **:** feeling or expressing self-reproof — **self-reprovingly** \ˌ≈≈ˈ≈≈≈\ *adv*
self-repugnant \ˌ≈≈ˈ≈≈\ *adj* **:** INCONSISTENT, SELF-CONTRADICTORY
self-rescuer \(ˈ)≈ˈ≈(ˌ)≈\ *n* **:** a pocket-size respirator for emergency use that protects the wearer for a period of about one-half hour against atmospheres containing carbon monoxide gas (as in a contaminated mine)
self-respect \ˌ≈≈ˈ≈\ *n* **1 :** an appropriate respect for oneself **:** a confidence in one's own worth as a human being and a concern to maintain it ⟨to cause him to lose his *self-respect*, to make him feel diminished as a person —A.W.Hummel⟩ **2 :** regard for one's or its own standing or position ⟨national *self-respect* demands a high level of education⟩
self-respectful \ˌ≈≈ˈ≈≈\ *adj* **:** SELF-RESPECTING
self-respecting \ˌ≈≈ˈ≈≈\ *adj* **:** having respect for oneself or itself **:** marked by self-respect ⟨every *self-respecting* library should have a copy —M.G.Bishop⟩ ⟨such bargaining seemed unworthy of a *self-respecting* nation —S.E.Morison & H.S. Commager⟩
self-restraining \ˌ≈≈ˈ≈≈\ *adj* **:** marked by self-restraint
self-restraint \ˌ≈≈ˈ≈\ *n* **:** restraint imposed on oneself **:** SELF-CONTROL ⟨enough to tax the *self-restraint* of an exceedingly hot-tempered foster sister —H.G.Wells⟩
self-revealing \ˌ≈≈ˈ≈≈\ *adj* **:** marked by self-revelation **:** serving to reveal oneself ⟨pruned her letters of all that was *self-revealing* —*Spectator*⟩
self-revelation \ˌ≈ˌ≈≈ˈ≈≈\ *n* **:** revelation of one's own thoughts, feelings, and attitudes esp. without deliberate intent ⟨his letters compare more than favorably with any . . . in their *self-revelation*, spontaneity, mother wit —Emily Skeel⟩
self-revelative \ˌ≈ˈ≈≈≈, (ˈ)≈ˈ≈ˌ≈≈\ *or* **self-revelatory** \ˌ≈≈ˈ≈≈ˌ≈≈, (ˈ)≈ˈ≈≈≈ˌ≈≈\ *adj* **:** SELF-REVEALING
self-reversal \ˌ≈≈ˈ≈≈\ *n* **:** transformation due to self-absorption of what should be a brighter spectrum line into a dark one
self-rewarding \ˌ≈≈ˈ≈≈\ *adj* **:** containing or producing its own reward ⟨a *self-rewarding* virtue⟩
self-righteous \ˈ≈ˈ≈≈\ *adj* **:** convinced of one's own righteousness esp. in contrast with the actions and beliefs of others **:** narrowly moralistic and intolerant **:** PHARISAICAL ⟨were altogether very superior, if not stuffy, very much like some smug, *self-righteous* moralists —Edison Marshall⟩ ⟨all the *self-righteous* cruelty of a woman whose happiness has been given up for others —*Time*⟩ — **self-righteously** \(ˈ)≈ˈ≈≈≈\ *adv* — **self-righteousness** \(ˈ)≈ˈ≈≈≈\ *n*
self-righting \ˈ≈ˈ≈≈\ *adj* **:** capable of righting itself when capsized ⟨a *self-righting* boat⟩
self-rising \ˈ≈ˈ≈≈\ *adj* **:** rising or capable of rising by itself
self-rising flour *n* **:** a commercially prepared mixture of flour, salt, and a leavening agent — compare MIX 2a
self-rolled \ˈ≈ˈ≈\ *adj* **:** rolled or coiled upon itself
self-rule \ˈ≈ˈ≈\ *n* **:** independent rule **:** SELF-GOVERNMENT
self-ruling \ˌ≈ˈ≈≈\ *adj* **:** ruling oneself **:** SELF-GOVERNING
selfs *pl of* SELF, *pres 3d sing of* SELF
self-sacrifice \(ˈ)≈ˈ≈≈(ˌ)≈\ *n* **:** sacrifice of oneself or one's interests for others or for some cause or ideal ⟨an act of *self-sacrifice* in giving up a lucrative business career for public service⟩
self-sacrificer \(ˈ)≈ˈ≈≈ˌ≈≈\ *n* **:** one that practices self-sacrifice
self-sacrificing \(ˈ)≈ˈ≈≈ˌ≈≈\ *adj* **:** sacrificing oneself for others or marked by self-sacrifice ⟨a *self-sacrificing* parent⟩ ⟨*self-sacrificing* love⟩ — **self-sacrificingly** \(ˈ)≈ˈ≈≈ˌ≈≈≈\ *adv* — **self-sacrificingness** \(ˈ)≈ˈ≈≈ˌ≈≈≈\ *n*
selfsame \ˈ≈ˌ≈\ *adj* [ME *selve same*, fr. *selve* (var. of [2]*self*) + *same*] **:** precisely the same **:** IDENTICAL ⟨more useful to date by authors than to express the ~ dates in terms of centuries and part centuries —T.E.Hope⟩ **syn** see SAME
self·same·ness \ˈ≈ˌ≈≈, ≈ˈ≈≈\ *n* [*selfsame* + *-ness*] **:** IDENTICALNESS, IDENTITY
self-satisfaction \ˌ≈ˌ≈≈ˈ≈≈\ *n* **:** a usu. smug and complacent satisfaction with oneself or one's position or achievements **:** SELF-COMPLACENCY ⟨have the *self-satisfaction* of courage without the inconvenience of danger —W.S.Maugham⟩
self-satisfied \(ˈ)≈ˈ≈≈ˌ≈\ *adj* **:** marked by self-satisfaction **:** SELF-COMPLACENT ⟨an air of *self-satisfied* dignity⟩ **syn** see COMPLACENT
self-satisfying \(ˈ)≈ˈ≈≈ˌ≈≈\ *adj* **:** giving satisfaction to oneself
self-scrutiny \(ˈ)≈ˈ≈(≈)≈\ *n* **:** INTROSPECTION, SELF-EXAMINATION
self-sealing \ˈ≈ˈ≈≈\ *adj* **:** capable of sealing itself after puncture ⟨a *self-sealing* tire⟩ ⟨a *self-sealing* fuel tank⟩
self-searching \ˈ≈ˈ≈≈\ *adj* **:** SELF-QUESTIONING
self-secure \ˌ≈≈ˈ≈\ *adj* **:** secure of oneself or one's position
self-security \ˌ≈≈ˈ≈≈≈\ *n* **:** security with respect to oneself or one's position
self-seed \ˈ≈ˈ≈\ *vi* **:** SELF-SOW
self-seeker \ˈ≈ˈ≈≈\ *n* **:** one that seeks only or mainly his own advantage or pleasure **:** one that tries to get the most out of something for himself ⟨got into politics, and was victimized by *self-seekers* —*Amer. Guide Series: Minn.*⟩
[1]**self-seeking** \ˈ≈ˈ≈≈\ *n* **:** the act or practice of seeking to advance one's own ends **:** SELFISHNESS
[2]**self-seeking** \"\ *adj* [[1]*self-seeking*] **:** seeking primarily to further one's own interests **:** SELFISH ⟨was no *self-seeking* politician, but a man of vision —V.L.Parrington⟩ — **self-seeking·ness** \(ˈ)≈ˈ≈≈nəs\ *n* -ES
self-selection \ˌ≈≈ˈ≈≈\ *n* **:** selection of goods by retail customers from display racks or counters in a store or department having salespeople available to advise and help the customers in such selection
self-service \ˈ≈ˈ≈≈\ *n* **:** service of customers or patrons by themselves (as in a restaurant, retail food market, or store) with payment usu. made at a designated check-out counter
self-serving \ˈ≈ˈ≈≈\ *adj* **:** serving one's own interests often in disregard of the truth or the reasonable interests of others ⟨a reckless, *self-serving* distortion of facts —M.E.Pew⟩
self-serving declaration *n* **:** a statement made to serve one's own interests; *specif* **:** such a statement made out of court by a party to a legal action and usu. not admissible as evidence
self-slain \ˈ≈ˈ≈\ *adj* **:** killed by oneself
self-slaughter \ˈ≈ˈ≈≈\ *n* **:** SELF-MURDER, SUICIDE ⟨that the Everlasting had not fixed his canon 'gainst *self-slaughter* —Shak.⟩
self-slaughtered \ˈ≈ˈ≈≈\ *adj* **:** killed by oneself
self-slayer \ˈ≈ˈ≈≈\ *n* **:** one that kills himself
self-sounding \ˈ≈ˈ≈≈\ *adj* **:** sounding by itself **:** creating its own sound **:** IDIOPHONIC
self-sow \ˈ≈ˈ≈\ *vi* **:** to sow itself by dropping seeds **:** produce a new generation without human intervention ⟨grasses that *self-sow* and build a firm turf⟩
self-sown *also* **self-sowed** \ˈ≈ˈ≈\ *adj* **:** sown autonomically or by an inanimate agency (as wind or water current)
self-starter \ˈ≈ˈ≈≈\ *n* **1 :** something that actuates itself **:** PERPETUUM MOBILE **2 a :** any of various more or less automatic attachments for starting an internal combustion engine other than the simple starting crank or an auxiliary turning engine **b :** a machine or vehicle equipped with such an attachment **3 :** one that has initiative ⟨the officials associated with its further progress have to be *self-starters* if that progress is to take place —*Atlantic*⟩
self-starting \ˈ≈ˈ≈≈\ *adj* **:** capable of starting by oneself or itself
self-sterile \ˈ≈ˈ≈(ˌ)≈\ *adj* **:** sterile to its own pollen or sperm — used of either a plant or animal; opposed to *self-fertile*
self-sterility \ˌ≈≈ˈ≈≈≈\ *n* **:** the quality or state of being self-sterile
self-study \ˈ≈ˈ≈≈\ *n* **:** study of oneself or itself; *also* **:** a record of observations from such study ⟨recently completed a community *self-study* —Harry Serotkin⟩
self-styled \ˈ≈ˈ≈\ *adj* **:** given a specified designation or title by oneself **:** SOI-DISANT ⟨*self-styled* experts⟩ ⟨the *self-styled* champion⟩
self-subdued \ˌ≈≈ˈ≈\ *adj* **:** subdued by oneself
self-subsistence \ˌ≈≈ˈ≈≈\ *or* **self-subsistency** \ˌ≈≈ˈ≈≈≈\ *n* **:** the quality or state of being self-subsistent
self-subsistent \ˌ≈≈ˈ≈≈\ *adj* **:** subsisting independently of anything external to itself
self-subsisting \ˌ≈≈ˈ≈≈\ *adj* **:** SELF-SUBSISTENT
self-substantial \ˌ≈≈ˈ≈≈\ *adj* **:** of or derived from one's own substance
self-sufficiency \ˌ≈≈ˈ≈≈≈\ *also* **self-sufficience** \ˌ≈≈ˈ≈≈\ *n* **:** the quality or state of being self-sufficient
self-sufficient \ˌ≈≈ˈ≈≈\ *adj* [trans. of Gk *autarkēs*] **1 a** (1) **:** able to maintain oneself or itself without outside aid **:** capable of providing for one's or its own needs **:** SELF-SUPPORTING ⟨organisms are not *self-sufficient*, closed systems —Weston LaBarre⟩ ⟨a rich town, prosperous, clean, self-contained and *self-sufficient* —Arnold Bennett⟩ (2) **:** economically independent **:** not dependent on imports from other countries or regions **:** AUTARKIC **b :** sufficient in or to itself **:** SELF-CONTAINED ⟨these are not essays, it seems, independent and *self-sufficient*, but fragments broken off from some larger book —Virginia Woolf⟩ **2 :** having an extreme confidence in one's own ability or worth **:** HAUGHTY, OVERBEARING ⟨felt *self-sufficient* . . . he acted superior and everyone around the place could hardly stand him —W.J.Reilly⟩ — **self-sufficientness** \ˌ≈≈ˈ≈≈≈\ *n*
self-sufficing \ˌ≈≈ˈ≈≈\ *adj* **:** SELF-SUFFICIENT — **self-sufficingly** \ˌ≈≈ˈ≈≈≈\ *adv* — **self-sufficingness** \ˌ≈≈ˈ≈≈≈\ *n* -ES
self-suggestion \ˌ≈≈ˈ≈≈\ *n* **:** AUTOSUGGESTION
self-suggestive \ˌ≈≈ˈ≈≈\ *adj* **:** AUTOSUGGESTIVE
self-support \ˌ≈≈ˈ≈\ *n* **:** independent support of oneself or itself
self-supported \ˌ≈≈ˈ≈≈\ *adj* **:** supported by oneself or itself
self-supporting \ˌ≈≈ˈ≈≈\ *adj* **:** supporting oneself or itself
self-sure \ˈ≈ˈ≈\ *adj* **:** sure of oneself — **self-sureness** \ˈ≈ˈ≈≈\ *n*
self-surrender \ˌ≈≈ˈ≈≈\ *n* **:** the giving up of oneself or one's will to some feeling or influence ⟨absorption, *self-surrender*, a passing into another world —Charles Morgan⟩
self-sustained \ˌ≈≈ˈ≈\ *adj* **:** sustained by oneself or itself **:** needing no outside support
self-sustaining \ˌ≈≈ˈ≈≈\ *adj* **:** maintaining or capable of maintaining oneself or itself by one's or its independent efforts **:** SELF-SUPPORTING ⟨the individual ranchos had to be *self-sustaining*, for the arrival of the supply ship was uncertain —*Amer. Guide Series: Calif.*⟩ — **self-sustainingly** \ˌ≈≈ˈ≈≈≈\ *adv*
self-tapping screw \ˈ≈ˈ≈≈-\ *n* **:** TAPPING SCREW
self-taught \ˈ≈ˈ≈\ *adj* **1 :** having knowledge or skills acquired by one's own efforts without formal instruction or training ⟨a *self-taught* painter⟩ **2 :** learned or worked out by oneself ⟨*self-taught* instrumentation⟩ ⟨*self-taught* perspective⟩
self-tightening \(ˈ)≈ˈ≈(≈)≈\ *adj* **:** tightening by itself
self-timer \ˈ≈ˈ≈≈\ *n* **:** a delayed-action shutter-tripping device often built into a camera that permits the photographer to be included in a picture
self-toning paper \ˈ≈ˈ≈≈-\ *n* **:** a printing-out paper in which a gold salt incorporated in the emulsion tones the image during fixing
self-torment \ˈ≈ˈ≈(ˌ)≈\ *n* **:** the act or an instance of tormenting oneself — **self-tormentor** \ˌ≈≈ˈ≈≈, (ˈ)≈ˈ≈ˌ≈≈\ *n*
self-tormenting \ˌ≈≈ˈ≈≈, (ˈ)≈ˈ≈ˌ≈≈\ *adj* **:** tormenting oneself or marked by self-torment
self-transcendence \ˌ≈ˌ≈ˈ≈≈\ *n* **:** the capacity to transcend oneself
self-treatment \ˈ≈ˈ≈≈\ *n* **:** AUTOTHERAPY
self-trust \ˈ≈ˈ≈\ *n* **:** SELF-CONFIDENCE
self-understanding \ˌ≈ˌ≈≈ˈ≈≈\ *n* **:** understanding of oneself **:** SELF-KNOWLEDGE
self-unfruitful \ˌ≈ˌ≈ˈ≈≈\ *adj* **:** deficient in self-fertility **:** setting no fruits or a greatly reduced crop of fruits in the absence of cross-pollination ⟨sweet cherries are *self-unfruitful*⟩ — **self-unfruitfulness** \ˌ≈ˌ≈ˈ≈≈≈\ *n*
self-unloader \ˌ≈ˌ≈ˈ≈≈\ *n* **:** a bulk cargo ship used on the Great Lakes that specializes in the hauling of limestone, sand, aggregates, coal, and sometimes grain and that is equipped with swinging booms and endless belt or chain devices permitting independence of harbor facilities
self-validating \(ˈ)≈ˈ≈≈ˌ≈≈\ *adj* **:** validating itself **:** needing no guarantee or judgment of its validity outside of itself
self-violence \(ˈ)≈ˈ≈≈≈\ *n* **:** violence inflicted on oneself; *specif* **:** SELF-MURDER
[1]**self·ward** *pronunc at* [1]SELF +wə(r)d\ *or* **self·wards** \-dz\ *adv* [[3]*self* + *-ward*, *-wards*] **:** toward oneself
[2]**selfward** \"\ *adj* **:** directed or turned toward oneself — **self·ward·ness** *n* -ES
self-will \ˈ≈ˈ≈\ *n* [ME *selfwil*, *self-will*, fr. OE *selfwill*, fr. *self*, pron. & adj. + *will* — more at SELF, WILL] **:** stubborn adherence to one's own desires or ideas esp. in opposition to others **:** OBSTINACY ⟨each of us has his psychopathic streak of *self-will* and rebellion —Weston La Barre⟩
self-willed \ˈ≈ˈ≈\ *adj* [ME, fr. *self-will*, n. + *-ed*] **:** governed by one's own will **:** not yielding to the wishes or opinions of others **:** OBSTINATE ⟨human beings . . . have a way of remaining annoyingly individualistic and *self-willed* —A.M.Schlesinger b.1888⟩ — **self-willed·ly** \ˈ≈ˈ≈≈\ *adv* — **self-willed·ness** \ˈ≈ˈ≈≈\ *n*
self-winding \ˈ≈ˈ≈≈\ *adj* **:** winding itself **:** not needing to be wound by hand ⟨a *self-winding* watch⟩
self-wisdom \ˈ≈ˈ≈≈\ *n* **:** the quality or state of being self-wise
self-wise \ˈ≈ˈ≈\ *adj* **:** wise in one's own estimation
self-worship \ˈ≈ˈ≈≈\ *n* **:** worship of oneself **:** AUTOTHEISM — **self-worshiper** \(ˈ)≈ˈ≈≈≈\ *n*
self-wrong \ˈ≈ˈ≈\ *n* **:** wrong done to oneself
sel·ig·mann·ite \ˈseləgməˌnīt\ *n* -S [G *seligmannit*, fr. Gustav *Seligmann* †1920 Ger. banker and mineral collector + G *-it* -ite] **:** a mineral $PbCuAsS_3$ consisting of a lead and copper arsenic sulfide and occurring in metallic lead-gray orthorhombic crystals
se·li·hoth *or* **se·li·hot** *also* **se·li·choth** *or* **se·li·chot** \səˈlēˌkōt(h), -ōs\ *n pl, sometimes cap* [Heb *sĕlīḥōth*, pl. of *sĕlīḥāh* pardon] **:** liturgical poems recited as prayers of repentance and forgiveness on Jewish fast days and on the days preceding the high holy days
sel·ion \ˈselyən\ *n* -S [ME *sellion*, fr. MF *seillon*, a measure of land, fr. OF *sillon* ridge, furrow] **:** one of the strips or ridges of land allotted for cultivation in the open-field system
[1]**sel·juk** \ˈselˌjük, -ˌju̇k, ≈ˈ≈\ *or* **sel·ju·ki·an** \(ˈ)≈ˈ≈ēən\ *adj, usu cap* [*seljuk* fr. Turk *Selçuk*, eponymous ancestor of the dynasties; *seljukian* fr. Turk *Selçuki* Seljukian, fr. *Selçuk*] **1 :** of or relating to any of several Turkish dynasties that ruled over a great part of western Asia in the 11th, 12th, and 13th centuries **2 :** of, relating to, or characteristic of a Turkish people ruled over by a Seljuk dynasty
[2]**seljuk** \"\ *or* **seljukian** \"\ *n* -S *usu cap* **1 :** a member of a Seljuk dynasty **2 :** a Turk subject to a Seljuk ruler
sel·kirk·shire \ˈsel(ˌ)kərkˌshi(ə)r, -ˌshər\ *or* **selkirk** *adj, usu cap* [fr. *Selkirkshire* or *Selkirk*, Scotland] **:** of or from the county of Selkirk, Scotland **:** of the kind or style prevalent in Selkirk
sel·kirk's violet \ˈselˌkərks-\ *n, usu cap S* [perh. fr. *Selkirk*, range of the Rocky mountains in British Columbia, Canada] **:** an acaulescent violet (*Viola selkirkii*) found in the cooler parts of No. America and in Greenland that has large pale-purple flowers of a pale violet color
sel·kup \ˈsel(ˌ)kəp\ *n* -S *usu cap* **:** OSTYAK SAMOYED
[1]**sell** \ˈsel\ *vb* **sold** \ˈsōld\ **sold; selling; sells** [ME *sellen*, fr. OE *sellan*; akin to OHG *sellen* to sell, ON *selja* to deliver, sell, Goth *saljan* to offer, present; causative-denominative fr. a prehistoric noun represented by OE *salu* sale, OHG *sala* delivery of goods, ON *sal* payment, OSlav *sŭlŭ* deliverer, messenger; akin to Gk *helein* to take, OIr *selb* possession, property] *vt* **1 :** to deliver or give up in violation of duty, trust, or loyalty **:** BETRAY ⟨the puppet who had no compunction over ~*ing* his country —*Times Lit. Supp.*⟩ — often used with *out* ⟨won their confidence to ~ them out⟩ **2 a** (1) **:** to give up (property) to another for money or other valuable consideration **:** hand over or transfer title to (as goods or real estate) for a price ⟨*sold* his books⟩ ⟨*sold* his house⟩ ⟨*sold* his stock⟩ — opposed to *buy* (2) **:** to offer for sale **:** deal in as an article of sale ⟨~*s* home appliances⟩ ⟨~*s* insurance⟩ **b :** to give up in return for something else ⟨~ my title for a glorious grave —Shak.⟩; *esp* **:** to exchange foolishly or dishonorably ⟨*sold* his birthright for a mess of pottage⟩ ⟨*sold* its Puritan heritage for southern trade profits —V.L.Parrington⟩ **c** *Brit* **:** to give up (a military commission or command) by sale under the purchase system formerly in effect **d :** to exact a price for ⟨put up a fierce resistance in his determination to ~ his life dearly⟩ **3 a :** to deliver into slavery for money ⟨*sold* their captives to slave traders⟩ **b :** to give into the power of another ⟨~ his soul to the devil⟩ **c :** to deliver the personal services of for money ⟨noblemen still continued ~*ing* themselves and their soldiers to foreign war lords —J.S.Roucek⟩ ⟨had *sold* her to other rich men —F.M.Ford⟩ **d :** to transfer the contract of for money or other consideration ⟨*sold* their star shortstop for an undisclosed sum⟩ **4 :** to dispose of or manage for profit instead of in accordance with conscience, justice, or duty ⟨even the juries were flagrantly in the business of ~*ing* their verdicts —*Amer. Guide Series: Nev.*⟩ ⟨*sold* his vote to the highest bidder⟩ **5 a :** to develop a belief in the truth, value, or desirability of **:** gain acceptance for ⟨*sold* their

candidate as a true frontiersman and military hero —C.R. Adrian⟩ ⟨trying to ~ his program to Congress —*Kiplinger Washington Letter*⟩ **b :** to persuade or influence to a course of action or to the acceptance of something (as a doctrine, belief, or activity) ⟨after you'd been *sold*, you were to pull the chestnuts out of the fire —Erle Stanley Gardner⟩ ⟨had a tough time ~*ing* her dad on the idea —A.A.Fenton⟩ ⟨~ children on reading⟩ **6 :** to impose upon **:** CHEAT, DECEIVE, TRICK ⟨the belief was profound that America was *sold* in 1917–19 —*New Republic*⟩ ⟨after all my hurry I was *sold*, for the doctor had been called away —Henry Lapham⟩ **7 a :** to cause or promote the sale of ⟨comics ~ newspapers —Coulton Waugh⟩ ⟨his name on the cover ~*s* the book⟩ **b :** to make or attempt to make a sale to ⟨~*s* gift shops⟩ ⟨~*s* druggists⟩ ⟨gives a big dinner party for a prospective customer so he can ~ him —James Jones⟩ **c :** to influence or induce to make a purchase ⟨here are the coats that ~ the whole family —*Women's Wear Daily*⟩ ⟨your product, effectively displayed, will ~ the shopper —*Phoenix Flame*⟩ **~** *vi* **1 a :** to dispose of something by sale **:** make a sale ⟨not allowed to ~ to minors⟩ ⟨must use these next four years to ~, to merchandise our competitive enterprise system —*Printers' Ink*⟩ **b :** to promote sales ⟨the basic purpose of any window or interior display is to ~ —M.S. Hutchins⟩ **2 a :** to achieve a sale **:** find a buyer ⟨fall suits are ~*ing* briskly⟩ **b :** to admit of being sold ⟨the tickets would not ~ —*Amer. Guide Series: N.H.*⟩ ⟨an item that doesn't ~⟩ **3 :** to have a specified price — used with *at* or *for* ⟨~ at three for a dollar⟩ ⟨~ for ten dollars each⟩ — **sell a bill of goods 1 :** to get the better of esp. by fraud **:** DUPE, STICK ⟨a poor sucker who was *sold a bill of goods*⟩ **2 :** to saddle with something disadvantageous ⟨*sold* him *a bill of goods* and got him to buy the tax-ridden property⟩ — **sell short 1 :** to sell something one doesn't own **:** make a short sale ⟨made a fortune on the stock exchange by *selling short*⟩ **2 :** to fail to value properly **:** UNDERESTIMATE ⟨are more inclined to see our world simple and *sell* it *short* —H.J.Muller⟩ ⟨made the mistake of *selling* his rival *short*⟩ — **sell the dummy to :** to deceive (an opponent in rugby) by faking a pass

2sell \"\ *or* **selle** \"\ *n* -S [ME *selle*, fr. MF, fr. L *sella* seat, chair, saddle — more at SETTLE] *archaic* **:** SADDLE

3sell \"\ *chiefly Scot var of* SELF

4sell \"\ *n* -S [1*sell*] **1 :** a deliberate deception **:** CHEAT, HOAX, IMPOSITION ⟨the suspicion is aroused . . . that the principles are fake; and that, in fact, they have been the victims of a ~ —G.E.G.Catlin⟩ **2 a :** the act or an instance of selling **:** SALESMANSHIP ⟨thanks to its chief announcer it was solid ~ for thirty minutes —Goodman Ace⟩ **b :** sales appeal ⟨needed a package with plenty of ~ —*Newsweek*⟩

sel·la \'selə\ *n, pl* **sellas** \-ləz\ *or* **sellae** \-e(,)lē, -e,lī\ [NL, fr. L, seat, saddle] **:** SELLA TURCICA

sell·able \'seləbəl\ *adj* [ME, fr. *sellen* to sell + *-able*] **:** SALABLE

sel·la·ite \'selə,īt\ *n* -S [It *sellaite*, fr. Quintino *Sella* †1884 Ital. mineralogist + It *-ite*] **:** a mineral MgF_2 consisting of magnesium fluoride and occurring in colorless tetragonal prismatic crystals (hardness 5, sp. gr. 3)

sel·lar \'selər, -,lär\ *adj* [ISV *sell-* (fr. NL *sella*) + *-ar*] **:** of, relating to, or involving the sella turcica

sel·late \'se,lāt\ *adj* [L *sella* saddle + E *-ate*] **:** having a saddle — used of the suture of certain cephalopod shells

sel·la tur·ci·ca \,selə'tərkikə, -rsəkə\ *n, pl* **sel·lae tur·ci·cae** \,se,lī'tərki,kī, ,se(,)lē'tərsə,sē\ [NL, lit., Turkish saddle; fr. its shape] **:** a depression in the middle line of the upper surface of the sphenoid bone in which the pituitary body is lodged

sellenders *var of* SALLENDERS

sel·len·ger's round \'selənjə(r)z-\ *n, usu cap S* [*sellenger* prob. alter. of the name *St. Leger*] **:** an English country-dance performed as a round esp. popular in the late 16th century; *also* **:** the music for this dance

sell·er \'selə(r)\ *n* -S [ME, fr. *sellen* to sell + *-er* — more at SELL] **1 :** one that offers for sale ⟨when goods are scarce, the ~ has an advantage over the buyer⟩; *specif* **:** SALESMAN ⟨he is too shy and too reserved to make a real ~ —*English Digest*⟩ **2 :** a product offered for sale and purchased readily or to a specified extent ⟨a poor ~⟩ ⟨a heavy ~⟩ ⟨a popular ~⟩

sel·lers hob \(')selə(r)z-\ *n, usu cap S* [after William *Sellers* †1905 Am. engineer and inventor] **:** a hob designed to be run on centers with the work held against it and fed to it by the motion of the lathe carriage

sellers' market *n* **:** a market in which goods are relatively scarce, buyers have a limited range of choice, and prices are prevailingly high — contrasted with *buyers' market*

seller's option *n* **:** an option allowed to one who contracts to sell stocks to make delivery within a specified period usu. not less than five business days nor more than 60 days after the date of the contract

sellers' thread \'selə(r)z-\ *n, usu cap S* [after William *Sellers* †1905 Am. engineer and inventor] **:** an American standard screw thread with an angle of 60 degrees and flat crests and roots

1selling *n* -S [ME, fr. gerund of *sellen* to sell] **1 :** the act or occupation of one who sells ⟨has been in ~ since he left school⟩ **2 :** the act, process, or art of offering goods for sale **:** SALESMANSHIP ⟨competitive ~⟩ ⟨high-pressure ~⟩

2selling *adj* [fr. pres. part. of 1*sell*] **1 :** readily finding buyers **:** SALABLE ⟨a fast ~ book⟩ **2 :** engaged in selling **:** making a business of selling ⟨maintains at least five ~ crews —*Fortune*⟩ **3 :** of or relating to sale ⟨the ~ price is one dollar⟩

selling agent *n* **:** an agent who sells for a commission the entire output of his principals on a continuing contractual basis, provides them with market information, and often also furnishes financial assistance

selling plate *n* **:** SELLING RACE

selling-plater \'==,plād·ə(r)\ *n* **:** a horse that runs in selling races

selling race *n* **:** a claiming race in which the winning horse is put up for auction

sell off *vt* **:** to dispose of by selling esp. completely ⟨what business firm would seek to improve its position by *selling off* its soundest assets —Bradford Smith⟩ ⟨scraped together all of its assets and *sold* them *off*⟩ **~** *vi* **:** to suffer a drop in selling prices **:** FALL ⟨the market has been *selling off* for six months —*N.Y. Herald Tribune*⟩

sell-off \'=,=\ *n* -S [*sell off*] **:** a decline in prices of stocks or bonds

sell out *vt* **1 :** to part with by sale **:** dispose of entirely ⟨*sold out* their stock within an hour⟩ **2 :** to sell the goods of (a debtor) in order to pay off debts from the proceeds **3 a :** to sell in open market (stocks or commodities) to satisfy an uncovered margin or other unpaid obligation **b :** to sell the stocks or commodities of in such manner **4 :** to prove false to **:** BETRAY ⟨*sold out* his best friend⟩ **~** *vi* **1 :** to dispose of one's goods by sale ⟨had to *sell out* at a loss⟩ **2 :** to betray one's cause or associates ⟨accused him of *selling out*⟩

sellout \'=,=\ *n* -S [*sell out*] **1 :** the act or an instance of betraying one's cause or associates ⟨the cynical ~ of the League's principles by all concerned was the mortal blow to the peace —*New Yorker*⟩ **2 :** a show, exhibition, or contest for which the seats are all sold ⟨every home game has been a ~⟩ **3 :** the exhaustion of the supply of an article of merchandise because of an unusual demand ⟨two stores report ~*s* on lots of snow suits —*Women's Wear Daily*⟩

sells *pres 3d sing of* SELL, *pl of* SELL

sell up *vt* [ME *sellen up*, fr. *sellen* to sell + *up* — more at SELL] *Brit* **:** to sell out ⟨when the hunting box . . . was *sold up* to pay her accumulated feed, farrier, and tack bills —James Reynolds⟩

selsyn \'sel,sin\ *n* -S [*self-synchronous*] **:** a system comprising a generator and a motor connected by a multiple wire circuit of appreciable length, transmitting currents that turn the motor simultaneously to the same relative position as existing or established for the generator, and repeating instrument indications and valve settings remotely — called also *synchro*

selt·zer \'seltsə(r)- *sometimes* -lzə-\ *or* **seltzer water** *or* **sel·ter** \-ltə(r)\ *or* **sel·ters water** \-ltə(r)z-\ *n* -S *sometimes cap S* [modif. of G *selterser (wasser)* water of Nieder Selters, fr. *selterser* of (Nieder) Selters + *wasser* water, fr. OHG *wazzar* — more at WATER] **1 :** a mineral water from Nieder Selters in the district of Wiesbaden, Germany, containing much free carbon dioxide **2 :** SODA WATER 2a

se·lung \sə'lŭŋ\ *n* -S *usu cap* [prob. Burmese] **1 a :** a sea-gypsy people inhabiting the Mergui archipelago and parts of the Malay peninsula **b :** a member of such people **2 :** the Austronesian language of the Selung people

1sel·va \'selvə\ *n* -S [Sp & Pg, forest, fr. L *silva* wood, grove] **:** tropical rain forest

2selva \"\ *n* -S [fr. La *Selva*, estancia near Bogotá, Colombia] **:** OPOSSUM RAT

1sel·vage *or* **sel·vedge** \'selvij, -vēj\ *n* -S [ME *selvage*, prob. fr. MFlem *selvage*, *selvegge*, fr. *selv-* self- + *egge* edge; akin to OE *self-* and to OHG *ecka* edge — more at SELF-, EDGE] **1 a** (1) **:** the edge on either side of a woven or flat-knitted fabric so finished as to prevent raveling; *specif* **:** a narrow border often woven of different or heavier threads than the fabric and sometimes in a different weave — see SPLIT 2e (2) **:** the margin of a sheet or booklet pane of stamps having an outside straight edge as contrasted with the perforated edge of the margin of a single stamp **b :** an edge (as of fabric or paper) meant to be cut off and discarded **:** a waste cutting ⟨begging people to use the ~*s* and scraps of their time —Sinclair Lewis⟩ **2 :** BORDER, EDGE ⟨actually believes it up to the ~ of his consciousness —Rex Stout⟩ ⟨his nondescript, worsted, uncreased trousers, mud-spattered at the ~ —A.J. Cronin⟩ **3 :** a rope or wire selvagee **4 :** GOUGE 4 **5 :** the edge plate of a lock through which the bolt is projected

2selvage *or* **selvedge** \"\ *vt* -ED/-ING/-S **:** to form a border to ⟨all the tiny settlements *selvaging* the desert —*All-Story Weekly*⟩

sel·vaged *or* **sel·vedged** \-jd\ *adj* [fr. past part. of 2*selvage* or *selvedge*] **:** having a selvage

sel·va·gee \'selvə'jē\ *n* -S [prob. fr. 1*selvage* + *-ee*] **1 :** a skein of rope yarns wound round with yarns or marline (as for stoppers or straps) **2 :** a number of parallel wires bound together with a fine wire serving

selves *pl of* SELF

sem *abbr* **1** semble **2** semicolon **3** semimobile **4** seminar; seminary

se·ma \'sēmə\ *n, pl* **sema** *or* **semas** *usu cap* **1 :** a Naga people of Assam related to the Angami **2 :** a member of the Sema people

se·mae·o·sto·ma·ta \sə,mēə'stōməd·ə\ [NL, fr. Gk *sēmaia*, *sēmeia* standard, token (fr. *sēma* sign) + NL *-stomata*] *syn of* SEMAEOSTOMEAE

1se·mae·o·stome \=ˈ==,stōm\ *adj* [NL *Semaeostomeae*] **:** of or relating to the Semaeostomeae

2semaeostome \"\ *n* -S **:** a jellyfish of the order Semaeostomeae

se·mae·o·sto·me·ae \=,=='stōmē,ē\ *n pl, cap* [NL, fr. Gk *sēmaia*, *sēmeia* standard, token + NL *-stomeae* (fr. *-stoma*)] **:** an order of Scyphozoa comprising jellyfishes that have large mouths with four lips and large tentacles at the margin of the umbrella

se·main·ean *or* **se·main·ian** \sə'mānēən, -nyən\ *adj, usu cap* [fr. *Semain*, village in Upper Egypt where remains of the culture were found + E *-an*] **:** of or relating to an Aeneolithic culture of Upper and Middle Egypt forming a branch of Gerzean culture or a survival thereof into early dynastic times

se·mai·nier \sə'men(,)yā\ *n* -S [F, fr. *semaine* week (fr. LL *septimana*, fr. fem. of L *septimanus* of seven, fr. *septem* seven) + *-ier* -er — more at SEVEN] **:** a tall chest with seven drawers for use in a bedroom or dressing room

se·mang \sə'mäŋ\ *n, pl* **semang** *or* **semangs** *usu cap* **1 a :** a Negrito people of Malaya **b :** a member of such people **2 :** the Mon-Khmer language of the Semang people

se·man·teme \sə'man,tēm\ *n* -S [F *sémantème*, fr. *sémant-* (fr. *sémantique* semantic, semantics) + *-ème* -eme] **:** a word (as the noun *dog*, the verb *run*, the adjective *new*, the concrete adverb *fast*) or a base (as Latin *can-* in *canis* "dog", *curr-* in *currere* "to run", *nov-* in *novus* "new") that expresses a definite image or idea — distinguished from *morpheme*

1se·man·tic \sə'mantik, sē'-, -maan-, -tēk\ *also* **se·man·ti·cal** \-tə̇kəl, -tēk-\ *adj* [*semantic* fr. Gk *sēmantikos* significant; *semantical* fr. Gk *sēmantikos* + E *-al*] **1 :** of or relating to meaning in language ⟨English *soon* has undergone ~ change from the Old English meaning of *sōna* "immediately"⟩ — compare FORMAL 1b(2) **2 :** of or relating to differing connotations of words of similar denotative meaning **3 :** of or relating to semantics ⟨a ~ approach to criticism⟩ — **se·man·ti·cal·ly** \-tə̇k(ə)lē, -tēk-, -li\ *adv*

2semantic \"\ *n* -S [F *sémantique*] **:** a system or theory of meaning

semantic aphasia *n* **:** the loss of recognition of the meaning of words and phrases

semantic conception *or* **semantic theory** *n* **:** a rule of translation by which a statement (as "the sentence 'grass is green' is true") in a metalanguage is logically equivalent to a corresponding statement (as "grass is green") in an object language; *also* **:** a theory that defines truth as a logical conjunction of the infinite number of such equivalences

semantic definition *n* **:** DEFINITION 4b(2)

semantic field *n* **:** FIELD 8c

se·man·ti·cian \,sē,man'tishən, -maan-\ *n* -S [*semantics* + *-an*] **:** SEMANTICIST

se·man·ti·cist \sə'mantəsə̇st, sē'-,-maan-\ *n* -S [*semantics* + *-ist*] **:** a specialist in semantics

se·man·ti·cize \-,sīz\ *vt* -ED/-ING/-S [1*semantic* + *-ize*] **1 :** to give a meaning to **2 :** to subject to semantic analysis ⟨~ this difference between knowledge by poetry and knowledge by abstraction out of existence —Archibald MacLeish⟩

se·man·tics \sə'mantiks, sē'-, -maan-, -tēks\ *n pl but usu sing in constr* [F *sémantique*, fr. Gk *sēmantikos* significant, fr. *sēmainein* to signify, show by a sign, indicate, mean, fr. *sēma* sign; akin to Alb *ditme* wisdom, knowledge, Skt *dhyāti* he thinks] **1 :** the study of meanings: **a :** the historical and psychological study and the classification of changes in the signification of words or forms viewed as factors in linguistic development and including such phenomena as specialization and expansion of meaning, meliorative and pejorative tendencies, metaphor, and adaptation **b :** the study dealing with the relations between signs and what they refer to, the relations between the signs of a system, and human behavior in reaction to signs including unconscious attitudes, influences of social institutions, and epistemological and linguistic assumptions **:** SEMIOTIC **c :** a branch of semiotic dealing with the relations between signs and what they refer to and including theories of denotation, extension, naming, and truth — compare PRAGMATICS **d :** the study of the relations of a sign to its referent and to other signs within a system **e :** the study of the connotations and ambiguities of words and their function in communication and propaganda **2 :** GENERAL SEMANTICS **3 a :** the meaning or relationship of meanings of a sign or set of signs ⟨one of the few words in our list to have received close attention as to its ~ —A.H.Schutz⟩ ⟨this lack of understanding has resulted from different terminologies, but the problem is not merely one of ~ —E.L.Kelly⟩; *esp* **:** connotative meaning **b :** the management or exploitation of connotation and ambiguity (as in propaganda) ⟨the dubious ~ of the fascist fanatics⟩

se·man·to·gen·ic \sə'mantə'jenik\ *adj* [*semantics* + *-o-* + *-genic*] **:** arising from impairment in the use of language

se·man·tron \sə'man,trän\ *n* -S [LGk *sēmantron* sign, signal, semantron, fr. Gk, seal, sign, fr. *sēmainein* to signify] **:** a wooden plank or an iron bar that gives a sound like a gong when struck with a mallet and that takes the place of a bell in Eastern Orthodox churches

1sem·a·phore \'semə,fō(ə)r, -fȯ(ə)r, -ōə,-ȯ(ə)\ *n* -S *often attrib* [ISV *sema-* (fr. Gk *sēma* sign) + *-phore*; perh. orig. formed as F *sémaphore*] **1 :** an apparatus for visual signaling (as by the position of one or more movable arms): as **a** *or* **semaphore telegraph :** one of a series of apparatuses on towers used formerly for rapid visual communication by means of code combinations of the positions of orig. movable shutters and later of two movable arms **b :** a mechanical signal for railway traffic consisting of an upright post with an arm moving in a vertical plane for day signals and colored lights for night signals **2 :** a system of visual signaling (as between ships) in which the sender holds a flag in each hand and moves his arms to different positions according to a code alphabet — compare WIGWAG

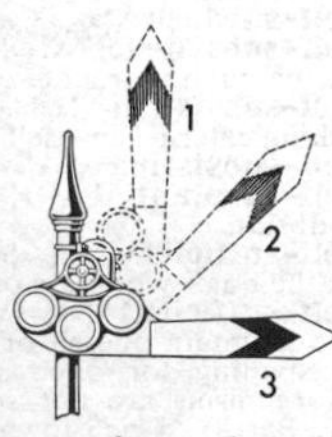

arms of semaphore 1b indicating: *1* clear, *2* caution, *3* stop

2semaphore \"\ *vb* -ED/-ING/-S **:** to signal by or as if by semaphore

semaphore plant *n* **:** TELEGRAPH PLANT

sem·a·phor·ic \'==ˈfȯrik\ *also* **sem·a·phor·i·cal** \-rə̇kəl\ *adj* [Gk *sēma* sign + E *-phoric*] **:** of, relating to, or suggesting a semaphore — **sem·a·phor·i·cal·ly** \-rə̇k(ə)lē\ *adv*

sem·a·phor·ist \'==,fōrə̇st, -fȯr-\ *n* -S [1*semaphore* + *-ist*] **:** one who operates a semaphore or signals by semaphore

se·ma·rang *or* **sa·ma·rang** \sə'mä,räŋ\ *adj, usu cap* [fr. *Semarang*, *Samarang*, Java] **:** of or from the city of Semarang on the island of Java, Indonesia **:** of the kind or style prevalent in Semarang

se·masi·o·log·i·cal \sə̇¦mā|sēə¦läjə̇kəl, sē¦-, -ma|, |zē-, -jēk-\ *adj* [ISV *semasiology* + *-ical*] **:** SEMANTIC — **se·masi·o·log·i·cal·ly** \-jə̇k(ə)lē, -jēk-, -li\ *adv*

se·masi·ol·o·gist \=,=='äləjə̇st\ *n* -S [*semasiology* + *-ist*] **:** SEMANTICIST

se·masi·ol·o·gy \-jē, -ji\ *n* -ES [ISV *semasi-* (fr. Gk *sēmasia* meaning, fr. *sēmainein* to mean) + *-o-* + *-logy*; orig. formed as G *semasiologie*] **:** SEMANTICS 1a, 1b

se·mat·ic \sə'mad·ik\ *adj* [Gk *sēmat-*, *sēma* sign + E *-ic*] **:** serving as a warning of danger — used of conspicuous colors of a poisonous or noxious animal

sem·a·tol·o·gy \,semə'täləjē\ *n* -ES [Gk *sēmat-*, *sēma* sign + E *-o-* + *-logy* — more at SEMANTICS] **:** SEMANTICS

1sem·bla·ble \'sembləbəl\ *adj* [ME, fr. MF, fr. OF, fr. *sembler* to be like, seem + *-able*] **1 :** SIMILAR **2 :** CONFORMABLE, SUITABLE **3 :** APPARENT, OSTENSIBLE, SEEMING — **sem·bla·bly** \-blē\ *adv*

2semblable \"\ *n* -S [ME, fr. MF, fr. *semblable*, adj.] **1** *archaic* **:** something similar **:** the like **2 :** one's fellow — usu. used with a possessive ⟨her ~, . . . like her a seeker after hidden faces —Virginia Woolf⟩

sem·blance \'semblən(t)s\ *n* -S [ME *semblaunce*, fr. MF *semblance*, fr. OF *sembler* to be like, seem + *-ance* — more at RESEMBLE] **1 :** the appearance of a person or thing **:** outward show **:** FORM **2 :** COUNTENANCE, FACE, ASPECT **3 a :** phantasmal form **:** APPARITION **b :** one that resembles another **:** IMAGE, LIKENESS **4 :** actual or apparent resemblance **:** SIMILARITY **5 :** specious appearance **:** mere show ⟨a somewhat different form of protectorate which has the ~ of a pact between equals —*Atlantic*⟩ **6 :** slightest appearance ⟨without the ~ of an excuse⟩ **syn** see APPEARANCE

1semblant *n* -S [ME, fr. OF, fr. pres. part. of *sembler* to be like] *obs* **:** SEMBLANCE; *also* **:** POMP, PRETENSE

2sem·blant \'semblənt\ *adj* [ME, fr. MF, fr. OF, pres. part. of *sembler* to be like] **1** *obs* **:** LIKE, RESEMBLING **2 :** SEEMING, APPARENT

sem·bla·tive \'sembləd·iv\ *adj* [obs. E *semble* to resemble (fr. ME *semblen*, fr. MF *sembler* to be like) + E *-ative*] **:** tending to or characterized by semblance

1sem·ble \'sembəl\ *vt* -ED/-ING/-S [F *sembler* to seem, fr. OF] **1 :** SIMULATE **2 :** to make a representation or likeness of **:** PICTURE

2semble \"\ *vb* -ED/-ING/-S [F, 3d pers. sing. pres. indic. of *sembler* to seem] **:** it seems — used chiefly impersonally in legal reports and judgments to express an obiter dictum

sem·bra·do·ras \,sembrə'dōrəz, -rəs\ *n* -ES [MexSp, fr. Sp, fem. of *sembradores* sowers, pl. of *sembrador* sower, fr. L *seminator*, fr. *seminatus* (past part. of *seminare* to sow, plant) + *-or*] **:** an agricultural dance of Michoacan, Mexico, performed on Candlemas Day by a group of Indian men and women with mime of sowing and harvesting

1se·mé \sə'mā, 'se(,)mā\ *adj* [MF, past part. of *semer* to sow, fr. L *seminare* to sow, plant, fr. *semin-*, *semen* seed — more at SEMEN] **1** *also* **se·méed** \-ād\ [*seméed* fr. F *semée* (fem. of *semé*) + E *-ed*] **:** having an ornamental pattern consisting of usu. regularly disposed separate objects or groups of small figures (as flowers or stars) **:** SOWN, DOTTED ⟨porcelain demitasses . . . ~ with rows of graduated turquoise blue enamel jewels on a gilded ground —*Parke-Bernet Galleries Cat.*⟩ **2** *or* **se·mee** \-ā\ [*semee* fr. F *semée*, fem. of *semé*] *of a heraldic field* **:** having a pattern of small charges **:** POWDERED ⟨azure ~ of five crosslets —Allan Marquand⟩

2semé *also* **semée** \"\ *n* -S **:** a semé pattern ⟨the ~ of slipped trefoils symmetrically disposed around the shield —W. de G. Birch⟩

seme·car·pus \,semə'kärpəs, ,sēm-\ *n, cap* [NL, prob. fr. Gk *sēmeion* mark (fr. *sēma* sign) + NL *-carpus*] **:** a genus of Indo-Malayan trees (family Anacardiaceae) that have coriaceous leaves and small panicled flowers with five petals, five stamens, and three styles followed by a hard nut with a thick black-juiced rind — see ITCHWOOD TREE, MARKING NUT

se·mée-de-lis \sə̇¦mād°l¦ē *sometimes* -ēs\ *adj* [F *semée de (fleurs de) lis*] *heraldry* **:** sprinkled with fleur-de-lis

semei·og·ra·phy *also* **semi·og·ra·phy** \,sē|mī'ägrəfē, ,se|, |,mē'-\ *n* -ES [ISV *semeio-*, *semio-* (fr. Gk *sēmeion* sign) + *-graphy*] **:** a description of the symptoms of disease

semei·o·log·ic \sə̇¦mīə¦läjik; ¦sē|, |,mīə-, ¦se|, |,mēə-\ *or* **se·mei·o·log·i·cal** \-jə̇kəl\ *adj* **:** of or relating to semeiology

se·mei·ol·o·gist \,sē|,mī'äləjə̇st, ,se|, |,mē'-\ *n* -S **:** a specialist in semeiology

se·mei·ol·o·gy *also* **semi·ol·o·gy** \-jē, -ji\ *n* -ES [NL *semaeologia*, fr. Gk *sēmeion* sign + L *-logia* -logy] **:** the study or art of signs: **a :** SEMANTICS 1b **b :** SYMPTOMATOLOGY

se·mei·on \sə'mī,än\ *n, pl* **semeia** \-īə\ [LGk *sēmeion*, fr. Gk, mark, sign, note, fr. *sēma* sign — more at SEMANTICS] **1 :** MORA **2 :** either of the two divisions of a foot; *also* **:** a corresponding division of a measure or colon in Greek and Latin prosody

semei·ot·ic \¦sē|,mī¦äd·ik, ¦se|, |,mē¦-\ *also* **semei·ot·i·cal** \-d·ə̇kəl\ *adj* [*semeiotic* fr. Gk *sēmeiōtikos* observant of signs; *semeiotical* fr. Gk *sēmeiōtikos* + E *-al* — more at SEMIOTIC] **:** of or relating to symptoms of disease

semei·ot·ics \-d·iks, -d·ēks\ *n pl but sing or pl in constr* **:** SYMPTOMATOLOGY

sem·e·le \'semə,lē\ *n* [NL, prob. fr. *Semele*, Greek goddess, fr. L, fr. Gk *Semelē*] **1** *cap* **:** a widely distributed genus of small bivalve mollusks (suborder Tellinacea) with long separate siphons and a thin oval or oblong shell that gapes at the posterior end and is usu. finely striated **2** -S **:** any mollusk of the genus *Semele*

sem·el·fac·tive \'seməl¦faktiv\ *adj* [L *semel* once (akin to L *simul* together, at the same time) + E *factive* — more at SAME] *of a verb form or aspect* **:** expressing action as single in its occurrence without repetition or continuation **:** INSTANTANEOUS, MOMENTARY

sem·eme \'se,mēm\ *n* -S [ISV *sem-* (fr. Gk *sēmainein* to mean) + *-eme* — more at SEMANTICS] **:** the meaning of a morpheme (sense 2)

se·men \'sēmən\ *n, pl* **semi·na** \'semənə *sometimes* 'sēm-\ *or* **semens** [L; akin to OHG & OS *sāmo* seed, OSlav *sěmę* semen, L *serere* to sow — more at SOW] **1 :** SEED 1b — used chiefly in pharmacy and usu. in combination ⟨~ pedicularis, the seed of *Delphinium staphysagra*⟩ **2 a :** a viscid whitish usu. neutral to slightly alkaline fluid produced in the male reproductive tract, consisting of spermatozoa suspended in secretions of accessory glands (as prostate and Cowper's glands), usu. released from the body by ejaculation (as in coitus), and serving as the vehicle in which sperm are maintained in the male genital tract and transferred to that of the female — used esp. of the fluid as characteristically developed in mammals and birds **b :** spermatozoa as released by a male animal together with any accompanying fluid **:** SPERM ⟨fish ~⟩ ⟨worms breaking into a cloud of ~ and eggs⟩

semen con·tra \'==ˈkän·trə\ *or* **semen ci·nae** \-'sī(,)nē\ *n* [*semen contra* fr. NL, short for L *semen contra vermes* seed against worms; fr. its vermicidal action; *semen cinae* fr. NL, lit., santonica seed] **:** SANTONICA

se·men·te·ra \,sāmən'tārə\ *n* -S [Sp, fr. *sementar* to sow, fr. *simiente* seed, fr. L *sementis* sowing, cultivation, fr. *semen* seed] *Philippines* **:** a cultivated field

se·me·os·to·ma \,sēmē'ästəmə\ [NL, fr. Gk *sēmeia* standard, token (fr. *sēma* sign) + NL *-stoma*] *syn of* SEMAEOSTOMEAE

se·mes·ter \sə'mestə(r)\ *n* -s [G, fr. L *semestris* half-yearly, fr. *sex* six + *mensis* month — more at SIX, MOON] **1 :** a half a year : a period of six months **2 :** either of the two periods of instruction commonly 18 weeks in length into which an academic year is usu. divided — compare QUARTER 4b **3 :** any term of instruction : SESSION ⟨the second ~ of summer school⟩

semester hour *n* : a unit of academic credit or load representing an hour a week for an academic semester devoted to class meetings ⟨a course awarding three *semester hours*⟩ — abbr. *SH;* compare QUARTER HOUR

se·mes·tral \-strəl\ *or* **se·mes·tri·al** \-,trēəl\ *adj* [L *semestris* half-yearly + E *-al* or *-ial*] : occurring every six months or within a period of six months : of or relating to a six-month period

¹semi \'semē, -mī\ *n* -ES [NL, short for *semi bejanus* semibejan, fr. L *semi-* + NL *bejanus* bejan] : SEMIBEJAN

²semi \"\ *n* -s [short for *²semidetached*] *chiefly Brit* : one of a pair of semidetached residences

³semi \", 'se,mī\ *n* -s [by shortening] : SEMITRAILER

⁴semi \"\ *n* -s [by shortening] : SEMIFINAL — usu. used in pl.

semi- *in pronunciations below*, ¦=(,)= = ¦semē *or* ¦se,mī *or* ¦semi *or (usu not before vowels)* ¦semə\ *prefix* [ME, fr. L; akin to OE *sam-* half, OHG *sāmi-*, Gk *hēmi-*, Skt *sāmi-*] **1 a :** precisely half of: (1) : forming a bisection of ⟨*semi*ellipse⟩ ⟨*semi*chord⟩ ⟨*semi*cylinder⟩ (2) : being a usu. vertically bisected form of (a specified architectural feature) ⟨*semi*arch⟩ ⟨*semi*bay⟩ ⟨*semi*dome⟩ **b :** half in quantity or value : half of or occurring halfway through (a specified period of time) ⟨*semi*revolution⟩ ⟨*semi*annual⟩ ⟨*semi*centenary⟩ ⟨*semi*phase⟩ — compare BI- **2 a :** to some extent : partly : incompletely ⟨*semi*-independent⟩ ⟨*semi*dry⟩ ⟨*semi*plastic⟩ ⟨*semi*acid⟩ ⟨*semi*-quantitatively⟩ — compare DEMI-, HEMI- **b :** having (a specified characteristic) for half the length or on one side ⟨*semi*pinnate⟩ ⟨*semi*adherent⟩ **3 a :** partial : incomplete ⟨*semi*positivism⟩ ⟨*semi*education⟩ ⟨*semi*adherent⟩ ⟨*semi*-Augustinianism⟩ ⟨*semi*wig⟩ **b :** having some of the characteristics of (a specified class or object) ⟨*semi*luxury⟩ ⟨*semi*campus⟩ ⟨*semi*benzene⟩ ⟨*semi*porcelain⟩ ⟨*semi*citizen⟩ **c :** QUASI- ⟨*semi*-governmental⟩ ⟨*semi*judicial⟩ ⟨*semi*monastic⟩ ⟨*semi*ubiquitous⟩

semi·abstract \¦=(,)= *at* SEMI-+\ *adj* [*semi-* + *abstract*] : having the character of a semiabstraction

semi·abstraction \"+\ *n* [*semi-* + *abstraction*] : a composition or creation (as in painting or sculpture) in which the subject matter is easily recognizable though the form is stylized according to an abstract system or device

semi·aerial \"+\ *adj* [*semi-* + *aerial*] : occurring partially or part of the time in the air

semi·amphibious \"+\ *adj* [*semi-* + *amphibious*] : partially amphibious

semi·annual \"+\ *adj* [*semi-* + *annual*] : occurring, appearing, or being made, done, or acted upon every six months or twice a year

semi·annually \"+\ *adv* : twice a year : every six months

semi·anthracite \"+\ *n* [*semi-* + *anthracite*] : a coal intermediate between anthracite and bituminous coal; *esp* : coal approaching anthracite in nonvolatile character

semi·ape \"+\ *n* [*semi-* + *ape*] : LEMUR

semi·aquatic \"+\ *adj* [*semi-* + *aquatic*] : chiefly aquatic: as **a :** growing indifferently in or adjacent to water (as in moist lowlands) **b :** frequenting but not living wholly in water ⟨mink and other ~ mammals⟩

semi·arboreal \"+\ *adj* [*semi-* + *arboreal*] : often inhabiting or frequenting trees : incompletely arboreal

semi·arch \"+\ *n* [*semi-* + *arch*] : an arch having only one springer and terminating at its highest point : half arch

semi·arian \"+\ *n, usu cap S&A* : one of the Homoiousians led by Basil, 4th-century A.D. bishop of Ancyra

semi·arianism \"+\ *n, usu cap S&A* : the doctrines of the Semi-Arians

semi·arid \"+\ *adj* [*semi-* + *arid*] : characterized by light rainfall and high evaporation, the growth of short grasses, and dry farming of limited yield; *specif* : having from about 10 to 20 inches of annual precipitation

semi·auto \"+\ *adj* [short for *¹semiautomatic*] : SEMIAUTOMATIC b

¹semi·automatic \"+\ *adj* [*semi-* + *automatic*] : not fully automatic: as **a :** operated partly automatically and partly by hand ⟨a lathe that operates automatically after insertion of the rough piece by the operator is ~⟩ **b** *of a firearm* : that employs gas pressure or force of recoil and mechanical spring action in ejecting the empty cartridge case after the first shot and in loading the next cartridge from the magazine but that requires release and another pressure of the trigger for firing each successive shot — compare AUTOMATIC 5 — **semi·automatically** \"+\ *adv*

²semiautomatic \"\ *n* : a semiautomatic device or machine; *esp* : a semiautomatic firearm

semi·autonomous \¦=(,)= *at* SEMI- +\ *adj* [*semi-* + *autonomous*] : largely self-governing (as with respect to local affairs) within a larger political or organizational entity ⟨a federation of ~ states⟩ ⟨a ~ unit within the police agency —D.E.J. MacNamara⟩

semi·bantu \"+\ *n, usu cap S&B* : a group of African languages sharing certain characteristics of the Bantu languages but excluded from them — used sometimes of the Central Branch of the Niger-Congo family exclusive of Bantu and sometimes of all west African languages with noun classes marked by prefixes

semi·basement \"+\ *n* [*semi-* + *basement*] : a basement that is below ground level for only part of its depth

semi·beam \¦=(,)=+,-\ *n* [*semi-* + *beam*] : CANTILEVER

semi·bejan \¦=(,)= *at* SEMI-+\ *n* [NL *semi bejanus*, lit., half a bejan] : a second-year student at some Scottish universities

semi·bituminous \"+\ *adj* [*semi-* + *bituminous*] *of coal* : intermediate between bituminous coal and anthracite and averaging from 10 to 20 percent of volatile matter

semi·breve \¦=(,)= *at* SEMI- +,-\ *n* [*semi-* + *breve*] *chiefly Brit* : WHOLE NOTE — compare CROTCHET, MINIM, QUAVER

-se·mic \¦sēmik\ *adj comb form* [LL *-semus* (fr. Gk *-sēmos*, fr. *sēmeion* unit of time, note, mark, sign) + E *-ic* — more at SEMEION] : having (a specified number of) units of prosodic time ⟨deca*semic*⟩ ⟨icosa*semic*⟩

semi·cadence \¦=(,)= *at* SEMI- +\ *n* [*semi-* + *cadence*] : HALF CADENCE

semi·carbazide \"+\ *n* [ISV *semi-* + *carbazide*] : a crystalline compound $NH_2CONHNH_2$ that is made from hydrazine by reaction with either urea or cyanic acid or from the nitro derivative of urea by reduction and that is used chiefly as a reagent for aldehydes and ketones by the formation of semicarbazones; the hydrazide of carbamic acid

semi·car·ba·zone \"+'kärbə,zōn\ *n* -s [ISV *semicarbazide* + *-one*] : any of a class of usu. well-crystallized compounds having the general formula $RR'C{=}NNHCONH_2$ and formed by the action of semicarbazide on an aldehyde or ketone — compare HYDRAZONE, OXIME

semi·castrate \¦=(,)= *at* SEMI- +\ *vt* [*semi-* + *castrate*] **1 :** to deprive of one testis **2 :** to emasculate partially (as with hormone sprays that do not destroy all pollen) — **semi·castration** \"+\ *n*

semi·cell \¦=(,)=+,-\ *n* [*semi-* + *cell*] : either of the halves of a desmid cell

semi·centenary \¦=(,)= *at* SEMI- +\ *n or adj* [*semi-* + *centenary*] : SEMICENTENNIAL

¹semi·centennial \"+\ *adj* [*semi-* + *centennial*, adj.] : of or relating to a 50th anniversary : occurring in a 50th year

²semicentennial \"\ *n* [*semi-* + *centennial*, n.] : a 50th anniversary or its celebration

semi·ceremonial \¦=(,)= *at* SEMI- +\ *adj* [*semi-* + *ceremonial*] : having some of the characteristics of a ceremony

semicha *also* **semichah** *var of* SEMIKAH

semi·chemical \¦=(,)= *at* SEMI- +\ *adj* [*semi-* + *chemical*] *of wood pulp* : cooked very lightly by any of the chemical processes to give increased yield but less paper fiber

semi·china \"+\ *n* [*semi-* + *china*] : china fired at a low temperature

semi·choric \"+\ *adj* [*semichorus* + *-ic*] **1 :** of or relating to a semichorus **2** [*semi-* + *choric*] : half choral in character; *specif* : half sung and half spoken

semi·chorus \"+\ *n* [*semi-* + *chorus*] : a musical passage to be sung by a selected portion of the voices (as by a few from each part or by either the male or female voices only) in contrast with the full chorus; *also* : the portion of voices or singers that sing such a passage

¹semi·circle \'=(,)=+,-\ *n* [L *semicirculus*, fr. *semi-* + *circulus* circle — more at CIRCLE] **1 a :** the part of a circle from one end of a diameter to the other : an arc equal to one half of a circumference : half circle — called also *semicircumference* **b :** either half of a circular area divided diametrically **2 :** a body, formation, or arrangement of objects in the form of half of a circle or half of a circumference **3 :** an instrument of semicircular form used esp. for measuring angles

²semicircle \"\ *vt* : to form or throw into a semicircle : surround with a semicircle ⟨the port ~*s* a blue bay —Sylvia Martin⟩ ~ *vi* : to become a semicircle : move in a semicircle

semi·circular \¦=(,)= *at* SEMI- +\ *adj* [ML *semicircularis*, fr. L *semicirculus* semicircle + *-aris* -ar] **1 :** having the form of a semicircle **2 :** ROUND 1d — **semi·circularly** \"+\ *adv* — **semi·circularness** \"+\ *n*

semicircular canal *n* : any one of the loop-shaped tubular parts of the membranous labyrinth of the ear that together constitute a sensory organ associated with the maintenance of bodily equilibrium, each canal communicating by either end with the utriculus, having near one end an expanded ampulla that contains an area of sensory epithelium, being enclosed in a corresponding canal of the bony labyrinth, and in all vertebrates above cyclostomes forming one of a group of three in each ear usu. in planes nearly at right angles with one another

semicircular dome *n* : a dome consisting of a half sphere

semicircular vault *n* : BARREL VAULT

semi·circumference \¦=(,)= *at* SEMI- +\ *n* [*semi-* + *circumference*] : SEMICIRCLE 1a

semi·circumferentor \"+\ *n* [*semi-* + *circumferentor*] : a surveyor's instrument used for setting out land or buildings to any angle and in preliminary survey work generally and made up of a horizontal graduated semicircle that surrounds a compass and is attached to a base with fixed vertical sights at each end and of a movable arm with vertical sights at each end that pivots on the center of the base

semi·cirque \¦=(,)=+,-\ *n* [*semi-* + *cirque*] : something (as a hollow among hills) having the shape of a half circle

semi·classic \¦=(,)= *at* SEMI- +\ *n* [*semi-* + *classic*] : a semiclassical work (as of music or literature)

semi·classical \"+\ *or* **semi·classic** \"+\ *adj* [*semi-* + *classical* or *classic*] **1 :** having some of the characteristics (as of traditional style) of the classical: as **a :** of or being a musical composition that acts as a bridge between classical and popular music or jazz : LIGHT **b :** of or being a classical composition that through repeated performance or extraneous association has developed popular appeal **2 :** inferior to the classical in importance or quality : of second rank ⟨a ~ theory in physics⟩

semi·climber \"+\ *n* [*semi-* + *climber*] : a plant that tends to climb or assume a vining habit of growth

semi·climbing \"+\ *adj* [*semi-* + *climbing*] *of a plant* : inclined to climb

semi·coke \"+\ *n* [*semi-* + *coke*] : the solid residue obtained by carbonization esp. of coal at a relatively low temperature (as below 700° C) that is in general softer and more friable than coke from carbonization at higher temperatures, that gives a hot smokeless fire, and that can be used as a domestic fuel

semi·co·lon \'semə,kōlən, -mē,k-\ *n* [*semi-* + *colon*] : a punctuation mark ; that is usu. used to separate the independent clauses of a compound sentence when the clauses are joined by no connective, when the clauses are joined by a conjunctive adverb, or when the clauses are joined by a coordinating conjunction but are long and contain internal punctuation and that is often used to separate long items in a series

semicolon butterfly *n* : VIOLET TIP

semi·colonial \¦=(,)= *at* SEMI- +\ *adj* [*semi-* + *colonial*] **1 :** nominally independent but actually under foreign domination **2 :** dependent on foreign nations to supply manufactured goods needed and to purchase raw materials produced ⟨a ~ economy⟩

semi·colonialism \"+\ *n* [*semi-* + *colonialism*] : the quality or state of being semicolonial

semi·column \"+\ *n* : a half-engaged column

semi·coma \"+\ *n* [*semi-* + *coma*] : a coma from which a person can be aroused

semi·commercial \"+\ *adj* [*semi-* + *commercial*] : of or adapted to limited marketing of an experimental product

semi·compreg \"+\ *n* [*semi-* + *compreg*] : wood that has been impregnated with resin and compressed to a density of less than 1.25

semi·conducting \"+\ *also* **semi·conductive** \"+\ *adj* [*semi-* + *conducting* or *conductive*] : of, relating to, or having the characteristics of a semiconductor

semi·conduction \"+\ *n* [*semi-* + *conduction*] : conduction occurring in a semiconductor

semi·conductor \"+\ *n* [*semi-* + *conductor*] : one of a class of solids (as germanium, silicon) whose feeble electrical conductivity is neither metallic nor electrolytic — compare CONDUCTION

semi·conscious \"+\ *adj* [*semi-* + *conscious*] : half conscious : imperfectly conscious — **semi·consciously** \"+\ *adv* — **semi·consciousness** \"+\ *n*

semi·consonant \"+\ *n* [*semi-* + *consonant*] : SEMIVOWEL — **semi·consonantal** \"+\ *adj*

semi·continuous \"+\ *adj* [*semi-* + *continuous*] : not fully continuous

semi·crisp \"+\ *adj* [*semi-* + *crisp*] : slightly stiff in texture

semi·crustaceous \"+\ *adj* [*semi-* + *crustaceous*] : tending to form a somewhat crisp or brittle layer : imperfectly crustaceous

semi·crystalline \"+\ *adj* [*semi-* + *crystalline*] : HEMICRYSTALLINE

semi·cubical \"+\ *adj* [*semi-* + *cubical*] : characterized by the square root of the cube of a quantity ⟨a ~ parabola⟩

semi·cursive \"+\ *n* [*semi-* + *cursive*] : a Roman minuscule cursive with the principal strokes thickened used as a book hand from about the 5th to the 9th centuries — called also *old Italian book hand*

semi·cyclic \"+\ *adj* [*semi-* + *cyclic*] : half or partly cyclic ⟨a ~ compound containing both a ring and a chain⟩ ⟨a ~ double bond attached to a ring but not a part of it⟩ — **semi·cyclically** \"+\ *adv*

semi·cylinder \"+\ *n* [*semi-* + *cylinder*] : a half of a cylinder divided longitudinally — **semi·cylindrical** \"+\ *adj*

semi·darkness \"+\ *n* [*semi-* + *darkness*] : partial darkness

semi·dehydrated \"+\ *adj* [*semi-* + *dehydrated*] : partially dehydrated

¹semi·desert \"+\ *n* [*semi-* + *desert*] : an area having some of the characteristics of a desert and often lying between a desert and grassland or woodland

²semidesert \"\ *adj* : of or characteristic of a semidesert

¹semi·detached \"+\ *adj* [*semi-* + *detached*] **1 :** intermediate between legato and staccato **2** *of a house* : built with one wall in common with another residence as part of a single building; *specif* : forming one of a pair of residences joined into one building by a common side wall

²semidetached \"\ *n* -s *chiefly Brit* : ²SEMI

semi·diameter \¦=(,)= *at* SEMI- +\ *n* [*semi-* + *diameter*] : the apparent radius of a generally spherical heavenly body ⟨the ~ of the sun is about half a degree⟩

semi·diesel engine \"+-\ *n* : an internal-combustion engine usu. of the two-stroke cycle type and below 50 horsepower that resembles a diesel engine: **a :** an internal-combustion engine of a type resembling the diesel engine in using heavy oil as fuel but employing a lower compression pressure of 100 to 350 pounds per square inch and igniting the charge by spraying it under pressure against an uncooled portion of the combustion chamber, by spraying it into a separate chamber kept above the ignition temperature of the charge by the heat of compression, or by preignition or supercompression of a portion of the charge in a separate member or uncooled portion of the combustion chamber **b :** a true diesel engine using other means of fuel injections than compressed air **c :** a mixed-cycle engine closely resembling a diesel engine

semi·dine \'semə,dīn, -,dēn\ *n* -s [ISV *semi-* + *benzidine*] : any of a group of bases that are ortho and para amino derivatives of diphenylamine and are usu. formed by a molecular rearrangement of hydrazo compounds (as $p\text{-}RC_6H_4\text{-}NHNHC_6H_5 \rightarrow p,p'\text{-}RC_6H_4NHC_6H_4NH_2$)

semi·diurnal \¦=(,)= *at* SEMI- +\ *adj* [*semi-* + *diurnal*] **1 :** relating to or accomplished in half a day **2 :** occurring twice a day **3 :** occurring approximately every half day ⟨the ~ tides⟩

semidiurnal arc *n* : the arc described by a heavenly body (as the sun) between its meridian and its rising or setting

semi·divine \"+\ *adj* [*semi-* + *divine*] : more than mortal but not fully divine : possessing a degree of divine awesomeness or authority

¹semi·documentary \"+\ *n* [*semi-* + *documentary*] : a motion picture that sets a fictional story in a factual background or tells a story true to the type of an actual story or true in outline but not literally true

²semidocumentary \"\ *adj* : of or characteristic of a semidocumentary

semi·dome \'=(,)=+,-\ *n* [*semi-* + *dome*] : a roof or ceiling covering a semicircular or nearly semicircular room or recess and being approximately the quarter of a hollow sphere — compare CUL-DE-FOUR — **semi·domed** \¦=(,)=+-\ *adj*

semi·domesticated \"+\ *or* **semi·domestic** \"+\ *adj* [*semi-* + *domesticated* or *domestic*] : of or living in semidomestication ⟨varieties found only in a ~ state⟩ ⟨~ circus animals⟩

semi·domestication \¦=(,)= *at* SEMI- +\ *n* [*semi-* + *domestication*] : a captive state (as on a fur or game farm or in a zoo) of a wild animal in which its living conditions and often its breeding are controlled and its products or services used by man

semi·dominant \"+\ *n* [*semi-* + *dominant*] : a gene that has a different effect when heterozygous than when homozygous ⟨the yellow lethal gene of mice which mediates yellow coat color when heterozygous but causes death of the embryo when homozygous is a typical ~⟩

semi·dormancy \"+\ *n* : a decrease in rate of growth of a plant that may be seasonal or associated with usu. transitory unfavorable environmental conditions

semi·double \"+\ *adj, of a flower* : having more than the normal number of petals or disk florets though retaining some pollen-bearing stamens or some perfect disk florets

semi–double \"\ *n* [trans. of ML *semiduplex*] : a feast of the Roman Catholic Church marked by omission of part of the antiphon before each psalm in the sacred office and formerly ranked above a simple and below a double but now reduced to the rank of simple

semi·dress \¦=(,)= *at* SEMI-+\ *n* [*semi-* + *dress*] : semiformal dress — **semi·dressy** \"+\ *adj*

semi·dry \"+\ *adj* [*semi-* + *dry*] : moderately dry

semi·drying \"+\ *adj* [*semi-* + *drying*] : that dries imperfectly or slowly — used of fatty oils (as cottonseed oil) intermediate between drying oils like linseed oil and nondrying oils

semi·durables \"+\ *or* **semi·durable goods** \"+-\ *n pl* [*semi-* + *durables, durable goods*] : nondurables (as clothing or house furnishings) whose usefulness diminishes gradually

semi·early \"+\ *adj, of a plant* : intermediate in bloom or maturity between an early and a later variety : MIDSEASON

semi·effigy \"+\ *n* [*semi-* + *effigy*] : a half-length effigy

semi·elastic \"+\ *adj* [*semi-* + *elastic*] **1 :** slightly elastic **2 :** that stretches in only one direction

semi·ellipse \"+\ *n* [*semi-* + *ellipse*] : the part of an ellipse from one end of usu. the transverse diameter to the other : half ellipse

semi·elliptic \"+\ *or* **semi·elliptical** \"+\ *adj* : of, relating to, or forming a semiellipse

semi·erect \"+\ *adj* [*semi-* + *erect*] : imperfectly erect; *specif* : erect for half the length

semies *pl of* SEMI

semi·evergreen \¦=(,)= *at* SEMI-+\ *adj* : HALF-EVERGREEN

¹semi·final \"+\ *adj* [*semi-* + *final*] **1 :** next to the last **2 :** of or participating in a semifinal

²semifinal \"\ *n* : a semifinal round, match, heat, or game: **a :** the next to the last round in an elimination tournament in which four players or teams are paired off in two matches and the winner of each moves on to the final match **b :** a series of contests (as in track and field events) designed to eliminate all but the number designated to participate in the final event

semi·finalist \"+\ *n* [*¹semifinal* + *-ist*] : any of the contestants who meet in the semifinal round or heat of an elimination contest

semi·finished \"+\ *adj* [*semi-* + *finished*] **1 :** partially finished ⟨a ~ nut⟩ **2 :** of or being a material manufactured for use in fabricating finished articles; *specif* : rolled from raw ingots into shapes (as bars, billets, blooms, plates, and rods) ready for further processes ⟨~ steel⟩

semi·fixed \"+\ *adj* [*semi-* + *fixed*] : fixed in some respect or temporarily

semifixed ammunition *n* [*semi-* + *fixed*] : ammunition consisting of complete rounds that can be loaded as a unit but have a cartridge case which is not fixed to the projectile and can be removed in order to remove increments of the propelling charge

semi·flexible \"+\ *adj* [*semi-* + *flexible*] **1 :** somewhat flexible **2** *of a book cover* : consisting of a heavy flexible board under the covering material

semi·floating axle \"+-\ *n* [*semi-* + *floating*] : a live axle for a self-propelled vehicle in which an inner revolving shaft turns the wheels and the weight of the vehicle is carried on the ends of a fixed axle housing attached to the shaft at each end by bearings

semifloating hitch *n* : a hitch allowing limited independent vertical movement of tractor and implement

¹semi·fluid \"+\ *adj* [*semi-* + *fluid*] : having the qualities of both a fluid and a solid but being more closely related to a fluid : imperfectly fluid : VISCOUS ⟨fluid and ~ greases⟩

²semifluid \"\ *n* : a semifluid substance

semi·form \'=(,)=+,-\ *n* [*semi-* + *form*] : a half or imperfect form

semi·formal \¦=(,)= *at* SEMI-+\ *adj* [*semi-* + *formal*] : being or suitable for an occasion of moderate formality or solemnity ⟨a ~ dinner⟩ : formal in some features ⟨a ~ gown for a small wedding⟩

semi·fossil \"+\ *adj* [*semi-* + *fossil*] : incompletely fossilized ⟨~ resins⟩

semi·freestone \"+\ *n* : a peach that is neither completely freestone nor clingstone

semi·girder \"+\ *n* [*semi-* + *girder*] : CANTILEVER

semi·glaze \'=(,)=+,-\ *n* [*semi-* + *glaze*] : a slight glaze

semi·globular \¦=(,)= *at* SEMI- +\ *adj* [*semi-* + *globular*] : having the form of half a sphere

semi·gloss \¦=(,)= *at* SEMI-+\ *adj* : having a low luster; *specif* : having a reflectivity between flat and gloss on a dried surface — used esp. of enamel or paint

semi·governmental \"+\ *adj* [*semi-* + *governmental*] : having some governmental functions and powers ⟨a ~ bank⟩

semi·gregarious \"+\ *adj* [*semi-* + *gregarious*] : partially gregarious : occurring or living usu. in greater proximity than seems likely on the basis of chance ⟨~ predators⟩

semi·hard \"+\ *adj* [*semi-* + *hard*] : moderately hard; *specif* : that can be cut with little difficulty

semi·hardy \"+\ *adj* [*semi-* + *hardy*] : capable of withstanding a moderately low temperature : HALF-HARDY

semi·hexagonal \"+\ *adj* [*semi-* + *hexagonal*] : forming half of a hexagon

semi·holiday \"+\ *n* [*semi-* + *holiday*] : a weekday during a religious festival (as the Passover) on which ceremonial observances continue but activities prohibited on full festival days are permitted though discouraged

semi·hydrate \"+\ *n* [*semi-* + *hydrate*] : HEMIHYDRATE

semi–independent \"+\ *adj* : partially independent; *specif* : SEMIAUTONOMOUS

semi·indirect \"+\ *adj* : using a translucent reflector that transmits some primary light (as to the floor) while reflecting most of it (as to the ceiling) ⟨a *semi-indirect* lamp⟩

semi–infinite \"+\ *adj* **1 :** extending to infinity in one direction or dimension ⟨the propagation of a temperature wave along a *semi-infinite* rod⟩ **2 :** limited only by an infinite plane ⟨a *semi-infinite* metal with a constant flux of heat into its surface —M.L.Storm⟩

semi-ionic \"+\ *adj* : SEMIPOLAR

semi·jobber \"+\ *n* : a merchant doing both wholesale and retail business

se·mi·kah *or* **se·mi·cha** *also* **se·mi·chah** \sə'mēkə\ *n, pl* **semikahs** *or* **semi·koth** \-,kōt(h), -ōs\ *or* **semichas** \-,kəz\ *or* **semi·choth** \-,kōt(h), -ōs\ [LHeb *sĕmīkhāh*, fr. Heb, laying on of hands, leaning on, fr. *sāmakh* to lean on] : rabbinical ordination : the traditional rabbinical degree conferred by Orthodox rabbis

semi·late \¦=(,)= *at* SEMI-+\ *adj, of a plant* : intermediate in season between midseason and late forms

semi·legal \"+\ *adj* [*semi-* + *legal*] : having a broader application than the technical use in law

semi·legendary \"+\ *adj* [*semi-* + *legendary*] : known in legend but historically dubious or unverifiable ⟨~ king⟩

¹semi·liquid \"+\ *adj* [*semi-* + *liquid*] : having the qualities of both a liquid and a solid but being more closely related to a liquid : partially liquid : SEMIFLUID ⟨~ peat⟩

²semiliquid \"\ *n* : a semiliquid substance

semi·literate \¦=(,)= *at* SEMI-+\ *adj* [*semi-* + *literate*] **1** : able to read and write on an elementary level but deficient in learning **2** : able to read but not to write

semi·live skid \"+-\ *n* : a platform skid with two fixed feet and two wheels to facilitate movement

semilive skid

semi·logarithmic \¦==+\ *also* **semi·log** \"+\ *adj* [*semi-* + *logarithmic* or *log* (short for *logarithmic*)] **1** : having one scale logarithmic and the other arithmetic or of uniform spacing — used of graph paper or of a chart or plot made on such paper **2** : being or relating to the relationship of things plotted on semilogarithmic graph paper

semi·looper \¦==+\ *n* [*semi-* + *looper*] : a caterpillar that is the larva of any of various plusiid moths and that moves like a geometrid larva

¹semi·lunar \"+\ *adj* [NL *semilunaris*, fr. L *semi-* + *lunaris* lunar — more at LUNAR] : shaped like a crescent : CRESCENTIC

²semilunar \"\ *also* **semilunar bone** *n* : LUNATUM 1

semilunar fibrocartilage *or* **semilunar cartilage** *n* : one of the crescentic lamellae of fibrocartilage that border and partly cover the articulating surfaces on the head of the tibia : the medial or lateral meniscus

semilunar ganglion *n* **1** : GASSERIAN GANGLION **2** : COELIAC GANGLION

semilunar lobe *n* : either of a pair of rather large crescent-shaped lobes situated one on each side in the posterior and ventral part of the cerebellum

semilunar notch *n* : the deep depression by which the ulna articulates with the humerus at the elbow

semilunar valve *n* : any of the crescentic cusps that occur as a set of three between the heart and the aorta and another of three between the heart and the pulmonary artery, are forced apart by pressure in the ventricles during systole and pushed together by pressure in the arteries during diastole, and prevent regurgitation of blood into the ventricles; *also* : either set of three cusps : an aortic or pulmonary valve

semi·lune \'=(,)=+,-\ *n* [*semi-* + *lune*] : something having the shape of a crescent

semi·lustrous \¦=(,)=+\ *adj* [*semi-* + *lustrous*] : slightly lustrous

semi·machine \"+\ *vt* [*semi-* + *machine*] : to machine partly

semi·magnetic controller \"+-\ *n* : a controller of electric power (as on a motor) that has part of its basic functions performed by electromagnets and part by other means

semi·major axis \"+-\ *n* [*semi-* + *major*] : half the major axis of the elliptical orbit of a celestial body representing the mean or average distance of the body from its primary

semi·manufactures \"+\ *n pl* [*semi-* + *manufactures*] : products (as steel, rubber, newsprint) made from raw materials and used to manufacture finished goods

semi·mat *or* **semi·matt** *or* **semi·matte** \"+\ *adj* [*semi-* + *mat, matt, matte*] : halfway between glossy and mat : having a slight luster ⟨~ photographic paper⟩ ⟨a ~ black glaze⟩

semi·member \"+\ *n* [*semi-* + *member*] : a tie or strut in a frame or truss that ceases to act as such when the stress in it tends to be reversed by variation in the load

semi·mem·bra·no·sus \,semē,membrə'nōsəs\ *n, pl* **semi·membrano·si** \-ō,sī\ [NL, fr. L *semi-* + LL *membranosus* membranous, fr. L *membrana* membrane + *-osus* -ose — more at MEMBRANE] : a large muscle of the inner part and back of the thigh arising by a thick tendon from the back part of the tuberosity of the ischium and inserted into the medial condyle of the tibia

semi·metal \¦=(,)= *at* SEMI-+\ *n* [*semi-* + *metal*] : an element (as arsenic, antimony, tellurium) possessing metallic properties in an inferior degree and not malleable — compare METALLOID 2c — **semi·metallic** \"+\ *adj*

semi·micro \"+\ *adj* [*semimicro-*] : intermediate in size between micro and macro quantities on a scale intermediate between microchemical and macrochemical

semimicro- *comb form* [*semi-* + *micr-*] : of, involving, or for quantities intermediate in size between micro and macro quantities : on a scale intermediate between microchemical and macrochemical ⟨*semimicro*determination⟩

semi·microanalysis \¦=(,)=+\ *n* [*semimicro-* + *analysis*] : chemical analysis (as of quantities of the order of centigrams) on a scale intermediate between macroanalysis and microanalysis

semi·microdetermination \"+\ *n* [*semimicro-* + *determination*] : determination by semimicroanalysis

semi·minim \¦=(,)= *at* SEMI-+\ *n* [*semi-* + *minim*] **1** *also* **semi·minima** \"+-s [*semiminima* fr. NL, fr. L *semi-* + ML *minima* minim — more at MINIM] : a note in mensural notation corresponding to the quarter note **2** : QUARTER NOTE

semi·minor axis \"+-\ *n* [*semi-* + *minor*] : half the minor axis of the elliptical orbit of a celestial body

semi·mobile \"+\ *adj* [*semi-* + *mobile*] **1** : partly equipped with vehicles ⟨a ~ unit⟩ **2** : mobile when partially disassembled ⟨~ artillery⟩

semi·moist \"+\ *adj* [*semi-* + *moist*] : slightly moist

semi·monastic \"+\ *adj* [*semi-* + *monastic*] : having some features like those of a monastic order

semi·monocoque \"+\ *n* [*semi-* + *monocoque*] : a stressed shell structure for airplane fuselages that differs from the monocoque in being reinforced with longitudinal stringers

¹semi·monthly \"+\ *adj* [*semi-* + *monthly*] : occurring, appearing, or being made, done, or acted upon twice a month — compare BIMONTHLY

²semimonthly \"\ *n* : a semimonthly publication

³semimonthly \"\ *adv* : twice a month ⟨paid ~ on the 15th and last days of the month⟩

semi·mystical \¦=(,)= *at* SEMI-+\ *adj* [*semi-* + *mystical*] : having some of the qualities of mysticism : somewhat mystical

semi·nal \'semən°l *also* 'sēm-\ *adj* [ME, fr. MF, fr. L *seminalis*, fr. *semin-*, *semen* seed + *-alis* -al — more at SEMEN] **1** : of, derived from, containing, or consisting of seed or semen ⟨~ vessels⟩ **2** : having the character of an originative power, principle, or source : containing or contributing the seeds of later development : GERMINATIVE, ORIGINAL ⟨existentialism . . . has at least acted as a ~ force, inducing other and perhaps contradictory ideas —Philip Toynbee⟩ ⟨fruitful dialectical interplay between literary history and literary criticism, the ~ ideas of one discipline influencing the growth of the other —C.I.Glicksberg⟩ ⟨one of the great ~ minds of our age, . . . a thinker whose insights have become a part of our cultural heritage —Sidney Ratner⟩

seminal animalcule *or* **seminal filament** *n, archaic* : SPERMATOZOON

seminal duct *n* : a tube or passage serving esp. or exclusively as an efferent duct of the testis and in man being made up of the tubules of the epididymis, the vas deferens, and ejaculatory duct

seminal fluid *n* **1** : SEMEN **2** : the part of semen that is produced by various accessory glands : semen excepting the spermatozoa

sem·i·nal·i·ty \,semə'naləd.ē, -lətē, -i\ *n* -ES **1** : the quality or state of being seminal **2** : a seminal property or particle

semi·nal·ly \'semən°lē *also* 'sēm- *or* -i\ *adv* : in a seminal manner

seminal receptacle *n* : SPERMATHECA — see ECHINOCOCCUS illustration

seminal root *n* : a root that develops from the radicle — compare ADVENTITIOUS ROOT, CORONAL ROOT

seminal vesicle *n* : a pouch on either side of the male reproductive tract that is variously formed in different animals, is connected with the seminal duct, and serves for temporary storage of the semen

sem·i·nar \'semə,när, -nä(r, ,==ˈ=\ *n* -S [G, fr. L *seminarium* seminary] **1** : a group of advanced students studying a subject under a professor, each doing some original research, and all exchanging results by informal lectures, reports, and discussions **2 a** : a course of study pursued by a seminar; *broadly* : an advanced or graduate course **b** : a scheduled meeting of a seminar **c** : a room for such meetings **3** : a meeting for giving and discussing information : a briefing session : CONFERENCE ⟨periodic ~s . . . of the top sales team serves the same end as the summary report —J.K.Blake⟩

sem·i·nar·i·an \,==ˈnerēən, -na(a)r-, -när-\ *or* **sem·i·nar·ist** \ˈ==,nerəst, -,nar-\ *n* -S [ˈ*seminary* + *-an* or *-ist*] **1 a** : a clergyman educated in a seminary **b** : SEMINARY PRIEST **2** : a seminary student

¹sem·i·nary \'semə,nerē, -ri\ *n* -ES *often attrib* [ME, fr. L *seminarium*, fr. neut. of *seminarius* of seed, fr. *semin-*, *semen* seed + *-arius* -ary — more at SEMEN] **1 a** *archaic* : a plot where plants for transplantation are raised from seed **b** *obs* : a stock or breeding place of animals **c** : an environment in which something originates and from which it is propagated : a seed bed producing an often specified class of persons or things ⟨many holy monks from Ireland and Scotland, then *seminaries* of saints —Alban Butler⟩ ⟨the prisons were . . . *seminaries* of every crime and every disease —T.B.Macaulay⟩ **2 a** : an institution of secondary or higher education ⟨by affording aids to *seminaries* of learning already established, by the institution of a national university, or by other expedients —H.L.Wells⟩; *specif* : an academy for girls ⟨the female ~ common in the 19th century⟩ ⟨young English ladies who are being "finished off" in suitable *seminaries* —Cecil Beaton⟩ **b** : an institution for the training of candidates for the priesthood, ministry, or rabbinate: as (1) : a Roman Catholic institution preparing young men for diocesan priesthood or for membership in a religious order and having a course of study comprising typically 12 years of secondary, collegiate, and theological training (2) : a similar Roman Catholic institution having only the final 6-year course of senior college and theological studies — called also *major seminary* (3) : PREPARATORY SEMINARY (4) : a professional school giving training in religion esp. for men preparing for ordination as church pastors, usu. associated with a Protestant denomination, requiring a college degree for entry, and having a three-year course of study leading to a bachelor's degree in theology or divinity **3** *obs* : SEMINARY PRIEST **4** : SEMINAR 1

²seminary \"\ *adj* [L *seminarius*] **1** *obs* : SEMINAL 1 **2** : SEMINAL 2

³seminary *n* -ES *obs* : GERM

seminary priest *n* : a Roman Catholic priest trained and ordained at Douay, France, or some other continental seminary in the 16th and 17th centuries for mission work in England and distinguished in English penal law from a priest ordained in England during the Marian period

sem·i·nate \'semə,nāt\ *vb* -ED/-ING/-S [L *seminatus*, past part. of *seminare* to sow, plant, fr. *semin-*, *semen* seed] : INSEMINATE — **sem·i·na·tion** \,==ˈnāshən\ *n* -S

sem·i·na·tive \'==,nād·iv\ *adj* [L *seminatus* (past part. of *seminare* to sow) + E *-ive*] : propagative by or as if by seed

sem·i·nif·er·ous \¦semə¦nif(ə)rəs\ *also* **sem·i·nif·er·al** \-rəl\ *adj* [*seminiferous* fr. L *semin-*, *semen* seed + E *-iferous*; *seminiferal* fr. L *semin-*, *semen* + *-ifer* -fer + E *-al*] **1** : producing or bearing seed **2** : bearing or producing semen ⟨~ epithelium⟩

seminiferous tubule *n* : any of the coiled threadlike tubules that make up the bulk of a testis and are lined with a germinal epithelium from which the spermatozoa are produced

sem·i·nif·ic \¦semə¦nifik\ *also* **sem·i·nif·i·cal** \-fəkəl\ *adj* [L *semin-*, *semen* + E *-i-* + *-fic* or *-fical* (fr. *-fic* + *-al*)] : forming or producing seed or semen

sem·i·nist \'semənəst\ *n* -S [L *semin-*, *semen* + E *-ist*] : an adherent of the old theory that the offspring is formed by admixture of the seed of the male with the supposed seed of the female — compare OVISM, SPERMISM

sem·i·niv·o·rous \¦==¦nivərəs\ *adj* [prob. fr. (assumed) NL *seminivorus*, fr. L *semin-*, *semen* + *-i-* + *-vorus* -vorous] : feeding on seeds

sem·i·nole \'semə,nōl\ *n, pl* **seminole** *or* **seminoles** *usu cap* [Creek *simanó-li*, *simaló-ni* wild, runaway, escape, Seminole, fr. AmerSp *cimarrón* wild, savage — more at MAROON] **1 a** : a Muskogean people formed from the portions of the Creek Confederacy that separated from the main body and moved into Florida — see MIKASUKI **b** : a member of such people **2** : MUSKOGEE 2

sem·i·no·ma \,==ˈnōmə\ *n, pl* **seminomas** *or* **seminoma·ta** \-məd·ə\ [NL, fr. L *semin-*, *semen* seed, semen + *-oma*] : a malignant tumor of the testis

semi·nomad \¦=(,)= *at* SEMI-+\ *n* [*semi-* + *nomad*] : a member of a people living usu. in portable or temporary dwellings and practicing seasonal migration but having a base camp at which some crops are cultivated — **semi·nomadic** \"+\ *adj*

semi·occasional \"+\ *adj* [*semi-* + *occasional*] : rather rare : occurring once in a while — **semi·occasionally** \"+\ *adv*

semi·occlusive \"+\ *n* [*semi-* + *occlusive*] : AFFRICATE

semi·official \"+\ *adj* [*semi-* + *official*] : having some official authority or importance : half official ⟨a ~ statement⟩ ⟨~ status⟩ — **semi·officially** \"+\ *adv*

semiofficial stamp *n* : a postage stamp authorized by but not issued by a government

semiography *var of* SEMEIOGRAPHY

semiology *var of* SEMEIOLOGY

¹sem·i·o·no·tid \¦semē¦ōnōd·əd\ *adj* [NL *Semionotidae*] : of or relating to the Semionotidae

²semionotid \"\ *n* -S : a fish of the family Semionotidae

sem·i·o·noti·dae \,===ˈnōd·ə,dē, -ˈnäd-\ *n pl, cap* [NL, fr. *Semionotus*, type genus + *-idae*] : a family of extinct Triassic ganoid fishes from America, Europe, and Africa that have a deep body, small mouth with teeth adapted chiefly to grinding or crushing, and rhomboid scales and that are often considered ancestral to the present-day freshwater gars

sem·i·o·no·tus \-ˈnōd·əs\ *n, cap* [NL, fr. Gk *sēmeion* sign + NL *-notus*] : the type genus of the family Semionotidae

semi·opal \¦=(,)= *at* SEMI-+\ *n* [*semi-* + *opal*; trans. of G *halbopal*] : an impure opal

semi·opaque \"+\ *adj* [*semi-* + *opaque*] : nearly opaque

semi·organized \"+\ *adj* [*semi-* + *organized*] : partially organized; *specif* : acting under the direction of a leader

semi·oriental \"+\ *adj* [*semi-* + *oriental*] : somewhat oriental

se·mi·o·sis \,sē,mīˈōsəs, ,se|, |,mē'-\ *n, pl* **semio·ses** \-ō,sēz\ [NL, fr. Gk *sēmeiōsis* observation of signs, examination, fr. *sēmeioun* to observe signs + *-ōsis* -osis] : the process in which something functions as a sign to an organism

¹semi·ot·ic \¦=(,)=¦äd·ik\ *also* **semi·ot·i·cal** \-d·əkəl\ *adj* [*semiotic* fr. Gk *sēmeiōtikos* observant of signs, fr. *sēmeiousthai* to note or interpret signs, fr. *sēmeion* sign, fr. *sēma* sign; *semiotical* fr. Gk *sēmeiōtikos* + E *-al* — more at SEMANTICS] **1** : SEMEIOTIC **2** : of or relating to semiotic

²semiotic \"\ *n, pl* **semiotics** *but sing or pl in constr* : a general philosophical theory of signs and symbols that deals esp. with their function in both artificially constructed and natural languages and comprises the three branches of syntactics, semantics, and pragmatics — **semi·o·ti·cian** \sə,mīəˈtishən, ,sē|,mīə-, ,se|, |mēə-\ *n* -S

semi·oval \¦=(,)= *at* SEMI-+\ *adj* [*semi-* + *oval*] : having the form of a half oval

semi·oviparous \"+\ *adj* [*semi-* + *oviparous*] : bearing imperfectly developed young ⟨a ~ marsupial⟩

semi·pa·la·tinsk \,semə́pəˈläd·,inzk, -in(t)sk\ *adj, usu cap* [fr. *Semipalatinsk*, U. S. S. R.] : of or from Semipalatinsk, U. S. S. R. : of the kind or style prevalent in Semipalatinsk

semi·palmate \¦=(,)= *at* SEMI-+\ *or* **semi·palmated** \"+\ *adj* [*semi-* + *palmate, palmated*] : having the anterior toes joined only part way down with a web

semipalmated plover *n* : a small ring plover (*Charadrius hiaticula semipalmatus*) breeding in arctic America and migrating to So. America that is similar to the common ring plover of Europe but has semipalmate feet

semipalmated sandpiper *n* : a small widely distributed American sandpiper (*Ereunetes pusillus*) slightly larger than the least sandpiper and having semipalmate feet

semipalmated snipe *or* **semipalmated tattler** *n* : WILLET

semi·palmation \"+\ *n* [*semi-* + *palmation*] : the quality or state of being semipalmate : partial webbing

semi·parasite \"+\ *n* [*semi-* + *parasite*] : HEMIPARASITE — **semi·parasitic** \"+\ *adj*

semi·ped \'semə,ped\ *n* -S [L *semiped-*, *semipes*, fr. *semi-* + *ped-*, *pes* foot — more at FOOT] : a metrical half foot — **semi·pedal** \¦==¦ped°l, -pēd-; sə'mipəd-, se'm-\ *adj*

¹semi-pelagian \¦=(,)= *at* SEMI-+\ *n* -S *often cap S & usu cap P* : a person (as a theologian of a 5th or 6th century monastery in Gaul) holding that man requires special help and not merely general guidance from God to overcome original sin, that such help is offered freely to all men, that each man must of his own initiative accept or reject this special divine help, that the individual and not God takes the first step leading to his salvation, and that God's grace toward him is conditioned by his own attitude of acceptance or rejection

²semi-pelagian \"\ *adj, often cap S & usu cap P* : of or relating to semi-Pelagians or semi-Pelagianism

semi-pelagianism \"+\ *often cap S & usu cap P* : the doctrines of semi-Pelagians that were condemned by a synod at Orange in A.D. 529

semi·permanent \"+\ *adj* [*semi-* + *permanent*] **1** : permanent in some respects : partly permanent ⟨a ~ mounting⟩ **2** : lasting for an indefinite time : virtually permanent ⟨a ~ low⟩

semi·permeability \"+\ *n* [*semipermeable* + *-ity*] : the quality or state of being semipermeable

semi·permeable \"+\ *adj* [*semi-* + *permeable*] : partially but not freely or wholly permeable : of or constituting a natural or artificial membrane that is permeable to some usu. small molecules (as of water or inorganic salts) but bars the passage of other usu. larger particles (as protein molecules) ⟨the living cell is enclosed in a ~ membrane and often a rigid permeable cell wall⟩

¹semi·plant \"+\ *n* [*semi-* + *plant*] : SEMIWORKS

²semiplant \"\ *adj* : larger than that of a laboratory or pilot plant but smaller than that of a plant in commercial production ⟨preparation of the new product on a ~ scale⟩

semi·plumaceous \¦=(,)= *at* SEMI-+\ *adj* [*semi-* + *plumaceous*] : having the character of a semiplume

semi·plume \'=(,)=+,-\ *n* [*semi-* + *plume*] : a feather having a plumy or downy web with the shaft of an ordinary feather

semi·pneumatic tire \¦=(,)= *at* SEMI-+-\ *n* : a rubber tire (as for a hand truck, lawnmower, wheelbarrow) having thick completely tubular walls enclosing air not under pressure and having no inner tube and no valve

semi·polar \"+\ *adj* [*semi-* + *polar*] : partly polar — used esp. of chemical bonds and structures regarded as possessing polarity associated with nonpolar covalence (as in an amine oxide $R_3N^+—O^-$)

semipolar bond *or* **semipolar double bond** *n* : COORDINATE BOND

semi·political \"+\ *adj* [*semi-* + *political*] : having some association with politics or involving some political features or activity : slightly political ⟨the work is largely routine and ~, involving the passage of inspection laws and the asking for appropriations —*Science*⟩

semi·porcelain \"+\ *n* [*semi-* + *porcelain*] : any of several ceramic wares resembling or imitative of porcelain: as **a** : a porcelanous stoneware **b** : IRONSTONE CHINA **c** : a relatively high-fired and hard-glazed white earthenware widely used for tablewares

semi·portable \"+\ *adj* [*semi-* + *portable*] : capable of being comparatively easily moved but not designed for ready transportation; *specif* : constituting a steam engine having an attached boiler but not mounted on wheels

semi·postal \"+\ *or* **semipostal stamp** *n* [*semi-* + *postal*] : a postage stamp the price of which goes partly to pay postage and partly to the support of some public expense project (as a charity, a monument, or the restoration of a ruined building) ⟨~s have not been issued in the U. S.⟩

semi·precious \"+\ *adj* [*semi-* + *precious*] *of a gemstone* : of less commercial value than those called precious ⟨such ~ stones as the amethyst, garnet, jade, and tourmaline⟩; *specif* : less than 8 in hardness

semi·privacy \"+\ *n* [*semi-* + *privacy*] : partial privacy

semi·private \"+\ *adj* : of, receiving, or associated with hospital service in which the patient has more privileges than a ward patient but fewer than a private patient (as in having his own doctor, sharing a room with only one other patient)

¹semi·professional \"+\ *or* **semi·pro** \"+\ *adj* [*semiprofessional* fr. *semi-* + *professional*; *semipro* short for *semiprofessional*] **1 a** : engaging in an activity (as a sport) for pay or gain but not as a full-time occupation ⟨amateur and ~ ballplayers⟩ ⟨a ~ actor⟩ **b** : engaged in by semiprofessional players ⟨~ baseball⟩ **2** : being or engaged in work resembling professional work in relating to a broad field of science, learning, or art, but requiring less theoretical knowledge or less creative skill and often less exercise of originality and judgment and typically restricted to the application of technical or mechanical details — **semi·professionally** \"+\ *adv*

²semiprofessional \"\ *or* **semipro** \"\ *n* : a person engaging in an activity (as a sport) semiprofessionally

semi·proof \¦=(,)= *at* SEMI-+\ *n* [*semi-* + *proof*] : evidence from the testimony of a single witness

semi·prostrate \"+\ *adj* [*semi-* + *prostrate*] : imperfectly prostrate ⟨the creeping oxeye, a ~ herb⟩; *specif* : prostrate for half the length

semi·public \"+\ *adj* [*semi-* + *public*] **1** : having some of the features of a public institution; *specif* : maintained as a public service by a private nonprofit organization ⟨a ~ institution⟩ **2** : open to some persons (as the families and guests of members) outside the regular constituency but not to the general public ⟨a ~ meeting⟩

semi·pupa \"+\ *n* [NL, fr. *semi-* + *pupa*] **1** : any of various insects in a developmental stage between the larva and pupa **2** : PSEUDOPUPA — **semi·pupal** \"+\ *adj*

semi·pyramidal \"+\ *adj* [*semi-* + *pyramidal*] : having the form of a half pyramid vertically divided

semi·quantitative \"+\ *adj* [*semi-* + *quantitative*] : approaching or designed to approach the quantitative in precision ⟨a ~ relationship⟩

semi·quaver \"+\ *n* [*semi-* + *quaver*] : SIXTEENTH NOTE

semi·quietism \"+\ *n* [*semi-* + *quietism*] : a moderate form of quietism practiced in France toward the end of the 17th century having none of the antinomianism of pure quietism but placing the essence of the spiritual life in complete surrender to love of God without thought of reward or punishment

semi·quinone \"+\ *n* [*semi-* + *quinone*] : any of a class of free radicals derived from quinones or quinone imines by the addition of a single hydrogen atom to a molecule — compare MERIQUINONE

semi·recondite \"+\ *adj* [*semi-* + *recondite*] : partly concealed; *specif* : half covered by the thorax ⟨an insect with a ~ head⟩

semi·religious \"+\ *adj* [*semi-* + *religious*] : having some association with religion or involving some religious features or activity : somewhat religious in character

semi·respectable \"+\ *adj* [*semi-* + *respectable*] : half respectable

semi·responsible \"+\ *adj* [*semi-* + *responsible*] : having or providing for an executive responsible except in reserved matters to the legislature ⟨a ~ colonial government⟩

semi·rigid \"+\ *adj* [*semi-* + *rigid*] **1** : rigid to some degree or in some parts **2** *of an airship* : having a flexible cylindrical gas container with an attached stiffening keel that carries the load

semi·rimmed \"+\ *adj, of a cartridge case* : having a rim that is only slightly greater in diameter than the body of the case and having a groove immediately forward of the rim for the extractor to engage — compare RIMLESS

semi·ring \ˈ≈(ˌ)≈+ˌ-\ *n* [*semi-* + *ring*] : a partial or incomplete ring; *esp* : HALF RING

semi·rotary \ˌ≈(ˌ)≈ *at* SEMI- +\ *or* **semi·rotative** \"+\ *or* **semi·rotatory** \"+\ *adj* [*semi-* + *rotary* or *rotative* or *rotatory*] : capable of turning or rocking about halfway round ⟨a ~ valve⟩

semi·round \"+\ *adj* [*semi-* + *round*] : round on one side and flat on the other

¹se·mis \ˈsāməs, ˈsēm-\ *n* -ES [L, fr. *semi-* + *as*, a copper coin — more at ACE] : any of three coins of ancient Rome: **a** : a half as of Republican Rome **b** : a half aureus of Imperial Rome **c** : a half solidus under Constantine and later

²se·mis \səˈmē\ *n* -ES [F, act or instance of sowing, fr. *semer* to sow, fr. MF — more at SEMÉ] : a scattering repetition of small design motifs to produce an overall pattern

³sem·is \ˈsemēz, -ˌmīz, -ˌmiz\ *n pl* [by shortening] **1** : SEMI-MANUFACTURES **2** : semifinished metal

⁴semis *pl of* SEMI

semi·sacred \ˌ≈(ˌ)≈ *at* SEMI- +\ *adj* [*semi-* + *sacred*] : SEMI-RELIGIOUS

¹semi·scald \"+\ *vt* [*semi-* + *scald*] : to dip (fowl) for less than a minute in water heated to just below the boiling point

²semiscald \"\ *n* : an act of semiscalding

semi·sedentary \ˌ≈(ˌ)≈ *at* SEMI- +\ *adj* [*semi-* + *sedentary*] : sedentary during part of the year and nomadic otherwise ⟨~ tribespeople⟩

semi·serious \"+\ *adj* [*semi-* + *serious*] : of a light nature but having a possible serious implication or interpretation : partly serious — **semi·seriously** \"+\ *adv* — **semi·seriousness** \"+\ *n*

semi·servile \"+\ *adj* [*semi-* + *servile*] : half servile; *esp* : of or being a class of men (as the Roman colonus or the Welsh aillt) having many rights of freemen but not free in other respects

semi·shrub \"+\ *n* [*semi-* + *shrub*] : SUBSHRUB, UNDERSHRUB — **semi·shrubby** \"+\ *adj*

semi·skilled \"+\ *adj* [*semi-* + *skilled*] : having or requiring less training (as for a few weeks) and the exercise of less independent judgment than skilled labor and more than unskilled labor ⟨while the ~ worker may lack specific experience, he is often used to factory discipline —R.L.Raimon⟩ ⟨machine attendants are typical ~ laborers —J.B.Horton⟩

semi·soft \"+\ *adj* [*semi-* + *soft*] : moderately soft; *specif* : firm but easily cut ⟨a ~ cheese⟩

¹semi·solid \"+\ *n* [*semi-* + *solid*] : having the qualities of both a solid and a liquid but being more closely related to a solid : partly solid : highly viscous ⟨jelly and paste are ~⟩ ⟨the ~ mass becomes semifluid —Morris Fishbein⟩

²semisolid \"\ *n* : a semisolid substance

semi·span \ˌ≈(ˌ)≈ *at* SEMI- +\ *adj* [*semi-* + *span*] : consisting of or incorporating only half of the complete wing or tail of an airplane

semi·sphere \ˈseməˌsfi(ə)r, -iə\ *n* [ML *semisphaera*, fr. L *semi-* + *sphaera* sphere — more at SPHERE] : HEMISPHERE — **semi·spher·ic** \ˌ≈≈ˈsfirik, -fer-, -rēk\ *or* **semi·spher·i·cal** \-rəkəl, -rēk-\ *adj*

semi·spi·na·lis \ˌseməˌspīˈnaləs, -nāl-\ *n, pl* **semispina·les** \-a(ˌ)lēz, -ā(ˌ)lēz\ [NL, fr. *semispinalis*, adj., fr. L *semi-* + LL *spinalis* spinal — more at SPINAL] : a deep layer of muscle of the back on each side of the spinal column extending from the lower dorsal region to the second cervical vertebra, consisting of a number of long slender fasciculi that arise each from the transverse process of one of the lower vertebrae, pass obliquely upward across several vertebrae, and are inserted into the spinous process of a vertebra farther up, and being divided into lower, middle, and upper segments — called also respectively *semispinalis dor·si* \-ˈdȯrˌsī\, *semispinalis cer·vi·cis* \-ˈsərvəsəs\, and *semispinalis ca·pi·tis* \-ˈkapəd·əs\

semi·square \ˌ≈(ˌ)≈ *at* SEMI- +\ *adj* [*semi-* + *square*] : forming half of a square

semi·steel \"+\ *n* [*semi-* + *steel*] : cast iron of low carbon content made by replacing part (as one fourth) of the pig iron in the cupola charge by steel scrap

semi·stock \"+\ *n* [*semi-* + *stock*] : a part or machine that is not carried in stock but can be made up of parts that are carried in stock

semi·subterranean \"+\ *adj* [*semi-* + *subterranean*] : half underground ⟨small, rectangular, single-unit, ~ houses of pole, brush and adobe —R.W.Murray⟩

semi·sul·co·spi·ra \ˌseməˌsəlkəˈspīrə\ *n, cap* [NL, fr. *semi-* + L *sulcus* furrow + NL *-spira* (fr. *spirare* to breathe) — more at SPIRIT] : a genus of freshwater snails (family Thiaridae) of eastern Asia and the Pacific islands where they are sometimes used as food and are of prime medical importance as intermediate hosts of pathogenic trematode worms

semi·sweet \ˌ≈(ˌ)≈ *at* SEMI- +\ *adj* [*semi-* + *sweet*] : slightly sweetened : not very sweet ⟨a ~ cake⟩ ⟨~ chocolate⟩

semi·synthetic \"+\ *adj* [*semi-* + *synthetic*] : partly synthetic : relating to or produced by synthesis from natural starting materials (as cellulose)

sem·ite \ˈseˌmīt, *usu* -īd.+V; *chiefly Brit* ˈsēˌm-\ *n* -S *cap* [F *sémite*, fr. *Sem*, son of Noah, eponymous ancestor of the Semites (Gen 10: 22-31) (fr. LL, fr. Gk *Sēm*, fr. Heb *Shēm*) + F *-ite*] **1** : a member of one of the peoples listed in the Scriptures as descended from Shem. a son of Noah **2** : a member of any of a group of peoples of southwestern Asia speaking Semitic languages and chiefly represented now by the Jews and Arabs but in ancient times also by the Babylonians, Assyrians, Aramaeans, Canaanites, and Phoenicians

sem·i·ten·di·no·sus \ˌsemēˌtendəˈnōsəs\ *n, pl* **semitendi·no·si** \-ōˌsī\ [NL, fr. *semitendinosus*, adj., fr. L *semi-* + NL *tendinosus* tendinous — more at TENDINOUS] : a fusiform muscle of the posterior and inner part of the thigh that arises from the tuberosity of the ischium along with the biceps femoris and is inserted by a remarkably long round tendon which forms part of the inner hamstring into the inner surface of the upper part of the shaft of the tibia

semi·terrestrial \ˌ≈(ˌ)≈ *at* SEMI- +\ *adj* [*semi-* + *terrestrial*] : chiefly terrestrial: as **a** : growing on boggy ground ⟨~ peats⟩ **b** : frequenting but not living wholly on land ⟨~ amphipod⟩

¹se·mit·ic \səˈmid·ik, -mit|, |ēk *also* seˈm-\ *adj, usu cap* [G *semitisch*, fr. *semit*, *semite* Semite (prob. fr. NL *semita*, fr. LL *Sem*, son of Noah + L *-ita* -ite) + *-isch* -ic] : of, relating to, characteristic of, or constituting the Semites or the Semitic languages ⟨*Semitic* peoples⟩ ⟨*Semitic* dialects⟩; *specif* : JEWISH

²semitic \"\ *n* -S *cap* **1 a** : the Semitic languages as a group ⟨discrepancies between structure and function are actually greater in Indo-European than in *Semitic* —*Language*⟩ **b** : one of the Semitic languages ⟨the Babylonians and Assyrians spoke *Semitic* —C.S.Coon⟩ **2** : SEMITE

semitic languages *n pl, cap S* : a branch of the Afro-Asiatic language family including Hebrew, Aramaic, Arabic, Ethiopic — see AFRO-ASIATIC LANGUAGES table

se·mit·ics \-ks\ *n pl but sing in constr, usu cap* [¹*Semitic* + *-s*] : the study of the language, literature, and history of Semitic peoples; *specif* : Semitic philology

sem·i·tism \ˈseməˌtizəm\ *n* -S *usu cap* [*Semite* + *-ism*] **1 a** : Semitic character or qualities **b** : a Semitic idiom or expression (as in Jewish or Christian Greek literature or in versions of the Bible) **2** : policy (as political policy) favorable to Jews : predisposition in favor of Jews

sem·i·tist \-təst\ *also* **se·mit·i·cist** \səˈmid·əsəst, seˈ-\ *n* -S [*semitist* fr. *Semite* + *-ist*; *semiticist* fr. ¹*Semitic* + *-ist*] **1** *usu cap* : a scholar of the Semitic languages, cultures, or histories **2** : a person favoring or disposed to favor the Jews

sem·i·tize \ˈseməˌtīz\ *also* **se·mit·i·cize** \səˈmid·əˌsīz\ *vt* -ED/-ING/-S *often cap* [*semitize* fr. F *sémite* Semite + E *-ize*; *semiticize* fr. ¹*Semitic* + *-ize*] : to make Semitic (as in language)

semito- *comb form, usu cap* [¹*Semitic*] : Semite : Semitic ⟨*Semito*-Hamite⟩ ⟨*Semito*-Hamitic⟩

semi·tonal \ˌ≈(ˌ)≈ *at* SEMI- +\ *adj* [*semitone* + *-al*] : CHROMATIC 3b, SEMITONIC ⟨the ~ scale implies . . . the negation of scale —Gerald Abraham⟩ — **semi·tonally** \"+\ *adv*

semi·tone \ˈ≈(ˌ)≈+ˌ-\ *n* [*semi-* + *tone*] : the tone at a half step; *also* : HALF STEP

semi·tonic \ˌ≈(ˌ)≈+\ *adj* [*semitone* + *-ic*] : of, relating to, or consisting of semitones — **semi·tonically** \"+\ *adv*

semi·trailer \"+\ *n* [*semi-* + *trailer*] **1** : a freight trailer that when attached is supported at its forward end by the fifth wheel device of the truck tractor — compare FULL TRAILER **2** : a trucking rig made up of a tractor and a semitrailer — called also *semi*

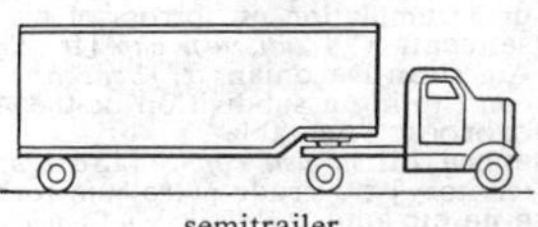

semitrailer

semi·trailing \"+\ *adj* [*semi-* + *trailing*] : imperfectly trailing: *specif* : trailing for half the length

semi·translucent \"+\ *adj* [*semi-* + *translucent*] : somewhat translucent

semi·transparency \"+\ *n* -ES [*semi-* + *transparency*] : the quality or state of being semitransparent

semi·transparent \"+\ *adj* [*semi-* + *transparent*] : imperfectly transparent

semi·tropic \"+\ *or* **semi·tropical** \"+\ *adj* [*semi-* + *tropic* or *tropical*] : SUBTROPICAL

semi·tropics \"+\ *n pl* [*semi-* + *tropics*] : SUBTROPICS

¹semi·uncial \"+\ *adj* [*semi-* + *uncial*] : written in or being half uncial characters

²semiuncial \"\ *n* **1** : HALF UNCIAL **2** : a letter or writing in half uncial

semi·underground \ˌ≈(ˌ)≈ *at* SEMI- +\ *adj* [*semi-* + *underground*] : partially underground

semi·vitreous \"+\ *adj, ceramics* : having not enough glassy phase to reduce porosity below 0.2 percent

semi·vitrification \"+\ *n* [*semi-* + *vitrification*] : half or imperfect vitrification; *also* : a semivitrified substance

semi·vitrified \"+\ *adj* [*semi-* + *vitrified*] : partially vitrified

semi·vocalic \"+\ *adj* [*semi-* + *vocalic*] : of or relating to a semivowel

semi·vowel \"+\ *n* [*semi-* + *vowel*] **1** : any speech sound not a stop, aspirate, or vowel, and not at any stage of the language having a stop as a component — used esp. of ancient Greek (λ, μ, ν, γ nasal, ρ, and σ were ~s) **2** : one of the glides \y\, \w\, \r\ **3** : a letter representing one of these sounds

semi·water gas \"+-\ *n* [*semi-* + *water*] : a producer gas intermediate in composition between water gas and air gas (sense 2) made by blowing a mixture of steam and air into a producer

¹semi·weekly \"+\ *adj* [*semi-* + *weekly*] : occurring, appearing, or being made, done, or acted upon twice a week — compare BIWEEKLY

²semiweekly \"\ *n* -ES : a publication issued twice weekly

³semiweekly \"\ *adv* : twice a week

semi·wildcat \ˌ≈(ˌ)≈ *at* SEMI- +\ *n* [*semi-* + *wildcat*] : an oil well drilled near but not in an established field

semi·woody \"+\ *adj* [*semi-* + *woody*] : somewhat woody : partially lignified ⟨the ~ stem of the milkweed⟩

semi·works \ˈ≈(ˌ)≈+ˌ-\ *n, pl, often attrib* [*semi-* + *works*] : a manufacturing plant operating on a limited commercial scale to provide final tests of a new product or process and to supply market samples

sem·mel \ˈseməl, ˈze-\ *n, pl* **semmels** *or* **semmel** [G, fr. OHG *semala*, *simila* fine wheat flour, fr. L *simila* finest wheat flour — more at SIMNEL] : a bread roll with a crisp crust and a variously shaped top

sem·mit \ˈseməṫ\ *n* -S [origin unknown] *Scot* : UNDERSHIRT

sem·no·pi·the·cus \ˌsem(ˌ)nōpəˈthēkəs, -ˈpithəkəs\ [NL, fr. Gk *semnos* revered, sacred (akin to Gk *sebesthai* to revere, feel awe) + NL *-pithecus* — more at SEBASTODES] *syn of* PRESBYTIS

sem·no·pi·thèque \-pəˈthek\ *n* -S [F *semno-pithèque*, fr. *semno-* (fr. Gk *semnos* revered) + *pithèque* monkey, ape, fr. Gk *pithēkos* — more at BEBUNG] : LANGUR

sem·o·li·na \ˌseməˈlēnə\ *n* -S [modif. of It *semolino*, dim. of *semola* bran, modif. of L *simila* finest wheat flour — more at SIMNEL] **1** : the purified middlings of durum or other hard wheat used for macaroni and other alimentary pastes **2** : coarse middlings used for breakfast cereal, puddings, or polenta

se·mol·o·gy \səˈmäləjē\ *n* -ES [Gk *sēma* sign + E *-o-* + *-logy* — more at SEMANTICS] : SEMANTICS 1a, 1b

se·mos·to·mae \səˈmästəˌmē\ [NL, fr. Gk *sēma* sign + NL *-o-* + *-stomae* (fr. *-stoma*)] *syn of* SEMAEOSTOMEAE

semp *abbr* sempre

sem·per pa·ra·tus \ˌsempə(r)pəˈräd·əs, -räd-\ *n* [L, always ready] : a plea at law by which a defendant in an action of assumpsit alleges that he has always been ready to comply with the demand

sem·per·vi·rent \ˌ≈≈ˈvīrənt\ *adj* [NL *sempervirent-*, *sempervirens*, fr. L *semper* always + *virent-*, *virens*, pres. part. of *virere* to be green] : EVERGREEN

sem·per·vi·rine \ˌ≈≈ˈvīˌrēn, -ˌrən\ *n* -S [ISV *sempervir-* (fr. NL *sempervirens* — specific epithet of the woody vine *Gelsemium sempervirens* —, fr. *sempervirent-*, *sempervirens* evergreen) + *-ine*] : a crystalline alkaloid $C_{19}H_{16}N_2$ obtained from the yellow jessamine shrub

sem·per·vi·vum \ˌ≈≈ˈvīvəm\ *n* [NL, fr. L, neut. of *sempervivus* ever-living, fr. *semper* ever, always + *vivus* alive — more at QUICK] **1** *cap* : a large genus of Old World fleshy often acaulescent herbs (family Crassulaceae) many of which have cymose variously colored flowers with numerous sepals and petals and are cultivated as ornamentals **2** -S : any plant or flower of the genus *Sempervivum*

sem·pi·ter·nal \ˌsempəˈtərnᵊl\ *also* **sem·pi·tern** \ˈ≈≈ˌtərn\ *adj* [*sempiternal* fr. ME, fr. LL *sempiternalis*, fr. L *sempiternus* eternal (fr. *semper* always, fr. *sem-* one + *per* through) + *-alis* -al; *sempitern* fr. ME *sempiterne*, fr. MF, fr. L *sempiternus* — more at SAME, FOR] : of never-ending duration : EVERLASTING, ETERNAL ⟨as they are ubiquitous and ~, war against them must be everlasting —G.W.Johnson⟩ — **sem·pi·ter·nal·ly** \ˌ≈≈ˈtərnᵊlē\ *adv*

sem·pi·ter·ni·ty \ˌ≈≈ˈnəd·ē\ *n* -ES [LL *sempiternitas*, fr. L *sempiternus* eternal + *-itas* -ity] : ETERNITY

sem·ple \ˈsempəl\ *adj* [alter. of *simple*] *Scot* : of humble birth

sem·pli·ce \ˈsempləˌchā\ *adj (or adv)* [It, fr. L *simplic-*, *simplex* simple — more at SIMPLE] : SIMPLE, UNAFFECTED — used as a direction in music

sem·pre \ˈsem(ˌ)prā\ *adv* [It, fr. L *semper*] : ALWAYS — used as a direction in music ⟨~ legato⟩

sempster *var of* SEAMSTER

sempstress *var of* SEAMSTRESS

sems \ˈsemz\ *n, pl* **sems** [prob. fr. *sem* (short for *assembly*) + *-s*] : a fastener assembly consisting of a screw with a washer put on before the threading is cut

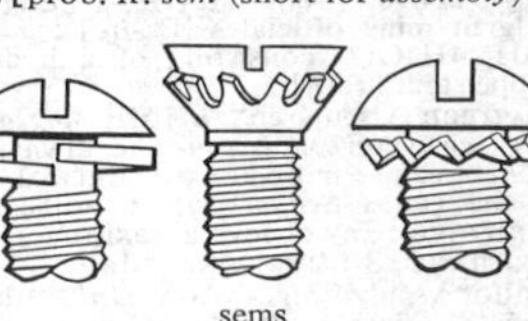

sems

sem·sem \ˈsemˌsem\ *n* -S [Ar *simsim* — more at SESAME] : SESAME

sem·sey·ite \ˈsemˌsēˌīt\ *n* -S [Hung *semseyit*, fr. Andor de *Semsey* †1923 Hung. nobleman + Hung *-it* -ite] : a mineral $Pb_9Sb_8S_{21}$ consisting of a lead antimony sulfide similar in appearance to jamesonite

semul \ˈsēməl, ˈsem-\ *n* -S [Hindi *semal*] : SILK-COTTON TREE

semy \ˈsemē\ *adj* [F *semée*, fem. of *semé* — more at SEMÉ] : SEMÉ 2

¹sen \ˈsen\ *n, pl* **sen** [Jap, fr. Chin *ch'ien*² coin, cash, money] **1** : a Japanese monetary unit equal to 1⁄100 yen — see MONEY table **2** : a coin representing one sen

²sen \"\ *n, pl* **sen** [Indonesian *sén*, prob. fr. E *cent*] **1** : an Indonesian monetary unit equal to 1⁄100 rupiah — see MONEY table **2** : a coin representing one sen

³sen \"\ *n, pl* **sen** [prob. fr. Indonesian *sén*] : a subsidiary unit of value of Cambodia from 1954 equal to 1⁄100 riel

⁴sen \"\ *n, pl* **sen** [prob. fr. Indonesian *sén*] **1** : a monetary unit of Brunei equivalent to 1⁄100 dollar — see MONEY table **2** : a coin representing one sen

⁵sen \"\ *dial Eng var of* SELF

sen *abbr* **1** senate; senator **2** senior **3** [It *senza*] without

sena·ite \ˈsenəˌīt, ˈsān-\ *n* -S [Joachim da Costa *Sena*, 19th cent. Brazilian mineralogist + E *-ite*] : a mineral (Fe,Mn,Pb)-TiO_3 consisting of an oxide of iron, manganese, lead, and titanium occurring in black rounded crystals and fragments in the diamond-bearing sands of Minas Gerais, Brazil

se·nam \səˈnäm\ *n* -S [Ar *sanām* hump, mound] : one of a type of dolmen in Algiers and Tripoli formerly regarded as belonging to the megalithic period but now recognized as the remains of oil presses of the Roman period

se·nar·ius \səˈna(a)rēəs, sēˈ-, -ˈnār-\ *also* **se·nar·i·an** \-rēən\ *n, pl* **se·nar·ii** \-rēˌī\ *also* **senarians** [*senarius* fr. L, fr. *senarius* consisting of six each, fr. *seni* six each (fr. *sex* six) + *-arius* -ary; *senarian* fr. L *senarius* + E *-an* — more at SIX] : a verse of six feet in Latin prosody; *esp* : the classical iambic trimeter

sen·ar·mon·tite \ˌsenə(r)ˈmänˌtīt\ *n* -S [Henri de *Sénarmont* †1862 Fr. mineralogist + E *-ite*] : a colorless or grayish mineral Sb_2O_3 consisting of native antimony trioxide and occurring in octahedral crystals or in masses

¹senary *n* -ES [L *senarius* consisting of six each] *obs* : six or a group of six : something that is constituted of six figures, things, or parts ⟨cold and heat, calm and storm . . . in one ~ of days — John Goad⟩

²sena·ry \ˈsēnərē, ˈsen-, -ri\ *adj* [L *senarius*] : of, based upon or characterized by six : compounded of six things : consisting of six parts : SEXTUPLE ⟨~ scale⟩ ⟨~ division⟩

senat *var of* SENIT

sen·ate \ˈsenəṫ, *usu* -əd.+V\ *n* -S [ME *senat*, fr. OF, fr. L *senatus*, lit., council of elders, fr. *sen-*, *senex* old, old man + *-atus* -ate — more at SENIOR] **1 a** : an assembly or council usu. possessing high deliberative and legislative functions: as (1) : the supreme council of the ancient Roman republic and empire (2) : the governing body in various European free cities ⟨the *Senate* of Frankfort⟩ (3) : the second chamber in the bicameral legislature of a major political unit (as a nation, state, or province) ⟨the *Senate* of the United States shall be composed of two senators from each state —*U.S.Constitution*⟩ ⟨the New York State Legislature consists of an assembly and a ~ —Robert Rienow⟩ **b** : a governing or legislative assembly held to resemble such a senate **2** : the hall or chamber in which a senate meets ⟨the floor of the ~⟩ **3 a** : a governing body of a British university charged with maintaining academic standards and regulations and usu. made up of principal or representative members of the faculty — compare COUNCIL 4c, COURT **b** : a similar body at an American university

sen·a·tor \ˈsenəd·ə(r), -nətə-, *in rapid speech esp before a surname* -nt̬ə- *or* -ndə-; *sometimes* -nəˌtō(ə)r *or* -ō(ə)\ *n* -S [ME *senatour*, fr. OF *senateur*, fr. L *senator*, fr. *senatus* senate + *-or*] **1 a** : a member of a senate ⟨a Roman ~⟩ ⟨the duke and ~s of Venice greet you —Shak.⟩ ⟨U. S. *Senator* from Connecticut⟩ ⟨Canadian ~s are appointed⟩ **b** : a member of a legislative body resembling or held to resemble a senate ⟨most accomplished ~ . . . in either House of Parliament —William King⟩ **2** *or* **senator of the college of justice** : LORD OF COUNCIL AND SESSION **3** : the civil head of the government of the city of Rome under papal administration

sen·a·to·ri·al \ˌsenəˈtōrēəl, -tȯr-\ *adj* [L *senatorius* of a senator (fr. *senator* + *-ius* -y) + E *-al*] **1 a** : of, relating to, or befitting a senator or a senate ⟨~ office⟩ ⟨~ voice⟩ ⟨~ dignity⟩ ⟨~ rank⟩ **b** : composed of senators ⟨the Roman ~ order⟩ **2** : administered by the Roman senate rather than by the emperor ⟨a ~ province⟩

senatorial courtesy *n* : a custom of the U. S. Senate of refusing to confirm a presidential appointment of an official in or from a state when the appointment is opposed by the senators or senior senator of the president's party from that state

senatorial district *n* : a territorial division from which a senator is elected — compare CONGRESSIONAL DISTRICT

sen·a·to·ri·an \-rēən\ *adj* [L *senatorius* senatorial + E *-an*] : SENATORIAL; *specif* : of or relating to the ancient Roman senate ⟨the ~ order⟩

sen·a·tor·ship \ˈ≈≈≈ˌship\ *n* [*senator* + *-ship*] : the office or position of senator

¹senatory *adj* [L *senatorius* — more at SENATORIAL] *obs* : SENATORIAN

²sen·a·to·ry \ˈsenəˌtōrē, -tȯr-, -ri\ *n* -ES [F *sénatorerie*, fr. L *senator* + F *-erie* -ery] : an estate granted to a senator in early 19th century France

se·na·tus aca·de·mi·cus \səˈnād·əˌsakəˈdeməkəs\ *or* **senatus** *n, pl* **senatus academi·ci** \-məˌsī\ *or* **senatus** [NL, academic senate] : the senate in some Scottish universities

senatus con·sul·tum \-əskənˈsəltəm\ *or* **senatus con·sult** \-ˈkänˌsəlt, -ˌkənˈs-\ *n, pl* **senatus consul·ta** \-tə\ *or* **senatus consults** [L *senatus consultum* decree of the senate] **1** : a decree of the ancient Roman senate **2** : a decree of the senate in Napoleonic France

¹send \ˈsend\ *vb* **sent** \ˈsent\ **sent; sending; sends** [ME *senden*, fr. OE *sendan*; akin to OHG *senten*, *sendan* to send, ON *senda*, Goth *sandjan*, OE *sīth* journey, road, OHG *sind*, ON *sinni*, Goth *sinths* going, time, OIr *sēt* road] *vt* **1** : to cause to go by physical means or direct volition: as **a** : to propel or discharge with an aim : throw or direct in a particular direction ⟨~ an arrow⟩ ⟨~ a bullet⟩ ⟨~ a rocket to a distant planet⟩ **b** *obs* : THRUST **c** : DELIVER ⟨*sent* a blow straight to his chin⟩ **d** : DRIVE ⟨*sent* the ball between the goalposts⟩ **2 a** : to cause to happen or come into existence : bestow or grant as a blessing : ordain or inflict as a punishment ⟨God ~s not ill —Alexander Pope⟩ **b** : to grant (as the fulfillment of a hope or a request) to a person ⟨heaven . . . ~ me just thoughts —Charles Dickens⟩ ⟨God ~ your mission may bring back peace —Sir Walter Scott⟩ ⟨God . . . ~ your sleep is light —*N.Y. Times*⟩ **3** : to dispatch by a means of communication (as the post or telegraph) ⟨~ him a letter of appreciation⟩ ⟨~ our compliments⟩ **4 a** : to commission, direct, order, or request (as a person) to go : dispatch on an errand or as a messenger **b** (1) : to dispatch to a specified destination for a course or term (as of residence or employment) ⟨~ a son to college⟩ ⟨~ a representative to Congress⟩ (2) : to permit (a person) to attend a college, school, or other educational institution by paying all or part of the expenses involved ⟨able to ~ both his children to boarding school⟩ **c** : to direct by advice or reference : refer to some person or authority : advise to go to some place or in some direction ⟨*sent* him to the dictionary⟩ ⟨*sent* him to the information desk⟩ **d** : to describe (a person) in narrative as going to a specified place ⟨next he ~s him to Paris⟩ **e** : to cause to enter the world as a gift or on a mission from God ⟨never ceased to hope that they would be *sent* a child⟩ ⟨sincerely believed he had been *sent* to save his people⟩ **f** : to bid to go : cause or order to depart from one : DISMISS ⟨~ him home with a reprimand⟩ ⟨~ him from me⟩ **5 a** : to force or compel to go : DRIVE, IMPEL ⟨~ the rebels flying⟩ ⟨*sent* all the townspeople scuttling out of their houses — Laurence Critchell⟩ **b** : to cause to enter or assume a specified state : drive into a specified condition ⟨~ one mad⟩ ⟨*sent* the household into a frenzy of excitement⟩ **6** : to cause to issue : give forth as a source — usu. used with *forth* or *out*: as **a** : to pour out or discharge (as a liquid) ⟨clouds ~*ing* forth long-needed rain⟩ **b** : to cause to issue in sound : UTTER ⟨~ forth a cry⟩ ⟨*sent* out a bitter bleating⟩ ⟨the steeples *sent* forth a joyous peal —T.B.Macaulay⟩ **c** : to give off or out (as heat or light) : EMIT ⟨tropical flowers *sent* out clouds of warm perfume —Eve Langley⟩ **d** : to throw out (as nerves or stems) in the course of development ⟨each branch and twig began to ~ out clusters of small buds —William Beebe⟩ ⟨an ice cap which . . . ~s out steep glacier tongues to the south —Valter Schytt⟩ **7** : to cause (as a person) to be carried or conducted to a destination; *esp* : to consign or commit to death or a place of punishment ⟨~ a convict to the gallows⟩ **8 a** : to cause (something) to be conveyed or transmitted by an agent to a destination (as a person or place ⟨~ flowers by wire⟩ **b** : to cause (as food or drink) to be brought or served ⟨~ in dinner⟩ **c** : to cause (as a boat or vehicle) to be made available or ready (as at a designated place or time) ⟨asked us to ~ a taxi for him⟩ **9** : to transmit by directing the eyes or the attention : DIRECT ⟨*sent* an inquiring glance at his wife —Laura Krey⟩ **10** : to cause (as music or a cry) to sound through the air ⟨visiting choirs . . . ~ their music through the pine forest —Oscar Schisgall⟩ **11** : to dispatch (a person) in a specified capacity ⟨*sent* him as ambassador to France⟩ **12** : to use force or influence so as to impel : cause to go up or down ⟨~ up a rocket⟩ ⟨*sent* prices down⟩ **13** : to transmit by pulsation ⟨~ a current⟩ ⟨~ blood to the lungs⟩ **14** : to strike or thrust so as to impel violently ⟨~ him sprawling⟩ 15 : to cause to move, travel, or operate usu. in a specified manner ⟨~ the engines full speed ahead⟩ 16 : TRANSMIT 17 : to enthrall, delight, or excite esp. by one's performance or personality ⟨trumpet never failed to ~ his listeners⟩ ~ *vi* 1 : to dispatch an agent or messenger to convey a message or to do an errand : dispatch a messenger or missive ⟨~ to one to come⟩ ⟨*sent* to invite her to supper —C.C.Clarke⟩ — often used with *away, off, out* ⟨~ away to the manufacturer for instructions⟩ ⟨*sent* off for a replacement⟩ ⟨~ out and order some coffee and doughnuts⟩ 2 a : to become carried forward by the impulse of a wave ⟨the ship ~*s* violently⟩ b : SCEND 3 : TRANSMIT 4 : to perform esp. in jazz improvisation in an inspired or admirable way

syn DISPATCH, FORWARD, TRANSMIT, REMIT, ROUTE, SHIP: SEND is a general term meaning to cause to go toward or to reach a given destination; its varying suggestions are indicated by contexts ⟨*send* an order for the supplies⟩ ⟨*send* gifts to the children⟩ ⟨*send* a letter by special delivery⟩ ⟨*send* a murderer to the electric chair⟩ ⟨he *sent* all his children to college⟩ DISPATCH may suggest speed in sending and heighten notions of specific destination or cause ⟨an ambulance and doctor can be *dispatched* within thirty seconds after a call for aid has been received —*Amer. Guide Series: N.Y. City*⟩ ⟨a messenger was *dispatched* with a reprieve but failed to arrive before the soldier had been shot —*Amer. Guide Series: Conn.*⟩ FORWARD indicates a sending on or forward, usu. of something stopped, delayed, or missent ⟨*forward* a letter⟩ ⟨if sent in a commercial code the censor, before passing it, decodes the message and if he considers that the message might contain a hidden meaning, the cable is never *forwarded* —H.O.Yardley⟩ TRANSMIT is likely to be accompanied by an indication of the force or medium involved in sending ⟨a disease *transmitted* by body lice⟩ ⟨a message *transmitted* by shortwave radio⟩ REMIT may mean a sending back, although this is not its most common meaning today ⟨your account is overdue; please *remit*⟩ ⟨the case was *remitted* to the lower court⟩ ⟨to find himself awakened at the small inn to which he had been *remitted* until morning —Charles Dickens⟩ ROUTE suggests a sending along a determined route, course, or itinerary ⟨heavy trucks being *routed* over a detour avoiding the bridge⟩ ⟨when the four railroads to the Pacific coast were completed, all freight from the West was *routed* through what was called the Minnesota Transfer —*Amer. Guide Series: Minn.*⟩ ⟨mail *routed* to the accounting departments⟩ SHIP is sometimes interchangeable with SEND but is likely to suggest carriage in some specific means of transport, as a ship, train, truck, or plane ⟨she was being *shipped* by her father and her mother to marry the youth across the sea —Francis Hackett⟩ ⟨*ship* freight by rail⟩ ⟨orchids *shipped* by plane⟩

— **send about one's business** : to dismiss summarily or peremptorily — **send for 1** : to request by message to come or be brought : SUMMON ⟨*sent for* the child's mother⟩ ⟨*send for* the doctor⟩ : ORDER ⟨*sent for* some stamps on approval⟩ 2 : to summon (a political leader) to the presence of the sovereign as for the purpose of offering the office of prime minister — **send in one's papers** : RESIGN — **send packing** : to send off roughly or in disgrace : DISMISS; *esp* : to dismiss unceremoniously ⟨see that she *sends* this young whippersnapper *packing* —Louis Auchincloss⟩ — **send to the right-about 1** : to cause (as enemy soldiers) to turn and retreat or flee 2 : to dismiss or turn away unceremoniously — **send word** : to dispatch (to a person) a message or notification of information ⟨*sent* me *word* to stay within —Shak.⟩

²**send** \"\ *n* -s 1 a : the impulse of a wave by which a vessel is carried bodily ⟨borne on the ~ of the sea —H.W.Longfellow⟩ b : SCEND 1 2 *archaic* : MESSAGE 3 : an impetus or accelerating impulse

sen·dai \(')sen¦dī\ *adj, usu cap* [fr. *Sendai*, Japan] : of or from the city of Sendai, Japan : of the kind or style prevalent in Sendai

sen·dal *or* **cen·dal** \'sendᵊl\ *n* -s [ME, fr. OF *cendal*, fr. ML *sendallum, cendalum*] : a thin medieval silk of oriental origin used for fine clothing and church vestments

send away *vt* 1 : DISPATCH ⟨*send away* a messenger⟩ ⟨*sent* his application *away* in the evening mail⟩ 2 : to banish from a place ⟨*sent* him *away* for misconduct⟩

send back *vt* : to put out (a batsman in cricket)

send down *vt* [ME *senden doun*, fr. *senden* to send + *doun* down] 1 : to dispatch to a person, body, or place held to be lower (as in rank or status) 2 *Brit* : to suspend or expel (a student) from a university

send·ee \(')sen¦dē\ *n* -s [¹*send* + *-ee*] : the person to whom something is sent

send·er \'sendə(r)\ *n* -s : one that sends ⟨this space for ~'s name and address⟩; *esp* : a telegraph, telephone, or radio transmitter

send forth *vt* 1 : to yield as produce 2 : EXPORT 3 : PUBLISH

send in *vt* 1 : to cause to be delivered (as to some central place) ⟨*sent* his contest entry *in* early⟩ ⟨*send in* a letter of complaint⟩; *specif* : to render (a bill) for payment 2 : to give (one's name or card) to a servant when making a call 3 : to send (a player) into an athletic contest ⟨coach *sent* several substitutes *in*⟩

send·ing \'sendiŋ, -dēŋ\ *n* -s [ME, fr. gerund of *senden* to send] 1 : the action of one that sends; *esp* : transmission by telegraph or radio 2 : something sent (as a message or a visitation of a supernatural power)

sending set *n* : TRANSMITTING SET

sending station *n* : TRANSMITTING STATION

send off *vt* : to cause (as a message or a messenger) to go from one : DISPATCH ⟨were late in *sending* their Christmas packages *off*⟩ ⟨hastily *sent off* two ships laden with coin —Sidney Warren⟩

send-off \'=,=\ *n* -s [*send off*] 1 : a sending off or start given to contestants (as in a race) 2 : a usu. organized demonstration of goodwill and enthusiasm for the beginning of a new venture (as a trip or a new business) ⟨a crowd of friends gave them a fine *send-off*⟩

send on *vt* : to dispatch in advance or from one place to another : FORWARD ⟨readdress a letter and *send* it *on*⟩ ⟨had his baggage *sent on* ahead⟩

send out *vt* [ME *senden out*, fr. *senden* to send + *out*] 1 : ISSUE ⟨had *sent* the wedding invitations *out*⟩ ⟨*sent out* their final decision on all applications⟩ 2 : to dispatch (as an order or shipment) from a store or similar establishment

sendout \'=,=\ *n* -s [*send out*] : the amount sent out or distributed (as by a dealer) ⟨the daily ~ of gas to these cities varies —*Iron Trade*⟩

send over *vt* [ME *senden over*, fr. *senden* to send + *over*] : to dispatch across the sea, through the air, or from one place to another

send round *vt* 1 : CIRCULATE ⟨a circular is being *sent round* to all the members —E.B.Pusey⟩ 2 : to dispatch (as a message or a messenger) for some object or purpose

sends *pres 3d sing of* SEND, *pl of* SEND

send up *vt* 1 : to shoot out or upward : give off : EMIT, VENT ⟨sparks *sent up* by a fire⟩ ⟨the timbers of the drawbridge *sent up* a booming sound —Rafael Sabatini⟩ 2 a : to dispatch to a person, body, or place regarded as higher ⟨the master of the inn . . . *sent up* the bill by the waiter —Frederick Marryat⟩ ⟨a bill . . . having been passed by the Commons and *sent up* to the Lords —Herbert Morrison⟩ ⟨not a single appropriations bill has been *sent up* to the president —*N.Y. Times*⟩ b : to send (as a schoolboy) to the headmaster for punishment or reward 3 : to hoist (as a yard) into place ⟨the night pennant is *sent up* at once —C.D.Lane⟩ 4 : to sentence to imprisonment : send to jail ⟨take his revenge on the marshal . . . who *sent* him *up* —*Time*⟩

¹**sen·e·ca** \'senəkə\ *n, pl* **seneca** *or* **senecas** *usu cap* [D *Sennecaas* (pl.), collective name for the Seneca, Oneida, Onondaga, and Cayuga, fr. Mahican *A'sinnika* Oneida, trans. of Iroquois *Onēyóde'*, lit., standing rock] 1 a : an Iroquoian people of western New York, one of the Five Nations b : a member of such people 2 : the language of the Seneca people

²**seneca** \"\ *var of* SENEGA

seneca grass *n, usu cap S* [¹*Seneca*] : SWEET GRASS 1 b

¹**sen·e·can** \'senəkən\ *adj, usu cap* [Lucius Annaeus *Seneca* †65 A.D. Roman philosopher + E *-an*] : of, relating to, or resembling Seneca, his Stoic philosophy, or of the characteristics of his writings (as the sententiousness of his prose style or the melodrama, high-flown rhetoric, supernatural machinery, or accumulation of horrors of his tragedies)

²**senecan** \"\ *adj, usu cap* [fr. *Senecan*, subdivision of the American Devonian, fr. ¹*Seneca* + E *-an*] : of, relating to, or constituting a subdivision of the American Devonian — see GEOLOGIC TIME table

seneca oil *n, usu cap S* [¹*Seneca*; fr. its discovery in their territory] : a crude petroleum formerly in medicinal use

se·ne·cic acid \sə'nēsik-\ *n* [*senecic* fr. *senec-* fr. NL *Senecio*) + E *-ic*] : an unsaturated hydroxy dicarboxylic acid $HOC_8H_{13}(COOH)_2$ that occurs combined in alkaloids of plants of the genus *Senecio*

se·ne·cio \sə'nēs(h)ē,ō\ *n* [NL, fr. L *senecion-, senecio* old man, groundsel (fr. its hoary pappus), fr. *sen-, senic-, senex* old, old man — more at SENIOR] 1 *cap* : a genus of very widely distributed herbs, shrubs, and trees (family Compositae) that have alternate or basal leaves and heads composed of both tubular and radiate or only tubular flowers, have the rays mostly yellow and pistillate, and have terete achenes crowned by a pappus of soft white hairs — see CINERARIA, ¹GROUNDSEL 2 -s : any plant of the genus *Senecio*

se·ne·ci·o·ic acid \=,==¦ōik-\ *n* [NL *Senecio* + E *-ic*] : a crystalline unsaturated fatty acid $(CH_3)_2C{=}CHCOOH$ found esp. in rhizomes of various plants of the genus *Ligularia* but usu. made from isovaleric acid by bromination and treatment with base; called also β-*methyl-crotonic acid* or β, β-*dimethyl-acrylic acid*

se·ne·ci·oid \=ˈ=ˌ=ˌȯid\ *adj* [NL *Senecio* + E *-oid*] : of, relating to, or resembling plants of the genus *Senecio*

se·ne·ci·o·nine \=ˈ==ə,nēn, -ˌnən\ *n* -s [ISV *senecion-* (fr. NL *Senecion-, Senecio*) + *-ine*] : a poisonous crystalline alkaloid $C_{18}H_{25}NO_5$ in various plants of the genus *Senecio*

se·ne·ci·o·sis \=,==ˈōsəs\ *n, pl* **senecio·ses** \-,sēz\ [NL, fr. *Senecio* + *-osis*] : a frequently fatal intoxication of livestock feeding on ragworts that is marked by intense acute or chronic necrosis and cirrhosis of the liver

se·nec·ti·tude \sə'nektə,tüd, -ə,tyüd\ *n* -s [ML *senectitudin-, senectitudo*, irreg. fr. L *senectus* old age (fr. *sen-, senic-, senex* old, old man) + L *-tudin-, -tudo* -tude — more at SENIOR] : OLD AGE 1 ⟨the mental changes of senescence and ~ —*Science*⟩

sen·e·cu \'senə,kü\ *n, pl* **senecu** *or* **senecus** *usu cap* 1 : a Tanoan people occupying a pueblo in New Mexico 2 : a member of the Senecu people

senecu del sur \-,del'sù(ə)r\ *n, pl* **senecu del sur** *or* **senecus del sur** *usu cap both Ss* [AmerSp, lit., Senecu of the south] 1 : a Tanoan people occupying a pueblo in Chihuahua state, Mexico 2 : a member of the Senecu del Sur people

sen·e·ga \'senəgə\ *or* **sen·e·ca** \-əkə\ *n* -s [*senega root*] 1 : SENEGA ROOT 1 2 a : the dried root of senega root containing an irritating saponin b : the dried root of a related plant (*Polygala alba*) of the central and southern U.S.

sen·e·gal \¦senə¦gȯl, -nē¦g-\ *adj, usu cap* [fr. *Senegal*, state in West Africa] : of or from Senegal : of the kind or style prevalent in Senegal : SENEGALESE

senegal ebony *n, usu cap S* : AFRICAN BLACKWOOD

¹**sen·e·gal·ese** \¦senəgə¦lēz, -,gȯ¦-, -lēs\ *adj, usu cap* [F *sénégalais*, fr. *Sénégal* Senegal, state in West Africa + F *-ais* -ese] 1 : of, relating to, or characteristic of Senegal 2 : of, relating to, or characteristic of the Senegalese

²**senegalese** \"\ *n, pl* **senegalese** *usu cap* : a native or inhabitant of Senegal

senegal gum *n, usu cap S* : gum arabic from the vicinity of the Senegal river

senegal mahogany *n, usu cap S* : MAHOGANY 1b(1)

¹**sen·e·gam·bi·an** \¦senə¦gambēən\ *adj, usu cap* [*Senegambia*, region of the Senegal and Gambia rivers, West Africa + E *-an*] 1 : of, relating to, or characteristic of Senegambia 2 : of, relating to, or characteristic of the Senegambians

²**senegambian** \"\ *n* -s *cap* : a native or inhabitant of the region of Senegambia in West Africa

sen·e·ga root \'senəgə-\ *or* **senega snakeroot** *or* **sen·e·ka root** \-nəkə-\ *or* **seneka snakeroot** *n* [alter. of ¹*Seneca*; fr. its use by the Seneca as a remedy against snakebite] 1 : a No. American milkwort (*Polygala senega*) having tufted leafy stems terminated by small white flowers 2 : SENEGA 2a

sen·e·gin \'senəjən\ *n* -s [G, fr. NL *senega* (specific epithet of *Polygala senega* senega root, fr. E *senega*) + G *-in*] : a saponin obtained from senega root as an amorphous yellow powder

se·nesce \sə'nes\ *vi* -ED/-ING/-S [L *senescere*, incho. of *senēre* to be old, fr. *sen-, senex* old, old man — more at SENIOR] : to grow old : WITHER ⟨growing and *senescing* leaves —J.J.Kennedy⟩

se·nes·cence \sə'nesᵊn(t)s\ *n* -s [fr. *senescent*, after such pairs as E *benevolent: benevolence*] 1 : the quality or state of being senescent ⟨clinical problems of later maturity, ~, and senility —*Therapeutic Notes*⟩ ⟨racial ~⟩ 2 : the phase of plant growth that extends from full maturity to actual death and is characterized by an accumulation of metabolic products, increase in respiratory rate, and a loss in dry weight esp. in leaves and fruits

se·nes·cent \-sᵊnt\ *adj* [L *senescent-, senescens*, pres. part. of *senescere* to grow old] 1 : growing old : AGING ⟨~ persons⟩ ⟨a ~ animal⟩ 2 : of, relating to, or characteristic of one that is aging or obsolescent ⟨~ arthritis⟩ ⟨~ mannerisms⟩ ⟨~ tools⟩ ⟨a ~ industrial system⟩

sen·e·schal \'senəshəl\ *n* -s [ME, fr. MF, of Gmc origin; akin to OHG *senescalh* eldest servant, fr. *sene-* old (akin to Goth *sineigs* old) + *scalh, scalc* servant — more at SENIOR, MARSHAL] 1 : a bailiff, steward, or majordomo of a great medieval lord or king representing the lord (as in the feudal courts, in the management of his estate, and in the superintendence of feasts and domestic ceremonies) and in a royal household often becoming a high officer of state or military commander 2 a : an administrative or judicial officer (as a governor) in a city or province b : a minor judicial officer in Sark

sen·e·schal·ship \-,ship\ *n* [*seneschal* + *-ship*] : SENESCHALSY

sen·e·schal·sy \-,sē, -si\ *n* -ES [ME *seneschalcie*, fr. MF, fr. ML *seneschalcia*, fr. *senescalcus* seneschal (fr. OHG *senescalh*) + *-ia* -y] 1 : a district under a seneschal ⟨the old royal administrative divisions of bailliages and seneschalsies —D.W.S.Lidderdale⟩ 2 : the office of a seneschal

sen·et *or* **sen·net** \'senət\ *n* -s [origin unknown] : any of several barracudas

seng·i·er·ite \'seŋēə,rīt\ *n* -s [Edgard *Sengier*, 20th cent. Belgian mine official + E *-ite*] : a mineral $Cu(UO_2)(VO_4)(OH).4H_2O(?)$ consisting of a hydrous basic vanadate of copper and uranyl

sen·green \'sen,grēn\ *n* [ME *singrene*, fr. OE *singrēne*, fr. *singrēne* evergreen, fr. *sin-* one, always (akin to L *sem-* one) + *grēne* green — more at SAME, GREEN] 1 : any of several plants of the genus *Sedum*; *esp* : HOUSELEEK 2 *also* **sengreen saxifrage** : any of several saxifrages; *esp* : YELLOW MOUNTAIN SAXIFRAGE 3 : ¹PERIWINKLE 1a

se·nhor \sən'yō(ə)r, -'yȯ(-\ *n, pl* **senhors** \-rz\ *or* **senho·res** \-rēs(h)\ [Pg, fr. ML *senior* superior, magnate, lord, fr. L, adj., elder — more at SENIOR] 1 : MISTER — used as a title of courtesy prefixed to the name of a Portuguese or Brazilian man 2 : a Portuguese or Brazilian man

se·nho·ra \-rə\ *n* -s [Pg, fem. of *senhor*] 1 : MISTRESS — used as a title prefixed to the name of a married Portuguese or Brazilian woman 2 : a married Portuguese or Brazilian woman

se·nho·ri·ta \,senyə'rēdə\ *n* -s [Pg, dim. of *senhora*] 1 : MISS — used as a title prefixed to the name of an unmarried Portuguese or Brazilian woman 2 : an unmarried Portuguese or Brazilian woman

sen·i·jex·tee \,senə,jek¦stē\ *n, pl* **senijextee** *or* **senijextees** *usu cap* 1 a : a Salishan people of the Columbia river valley in Washington and British Columbia b : a member of such people 2 : a dialect of Okanagon

¹**senile** \'sē,nīl *also* 'se,- *sometimes* -,nᵊl *or* -(,)nil\ *adj* [L *senilis*, fr. *sen-, senex* old, old man + *-ilis* -ile — more at SENIOR] 1 : of, relating to, or characteristic of old age ⟨~ weakness⟩ ⟨~ decay⟩ ⟨~ wisdom⟩ 2 a : showing the characteristics of old age : AGED ⟨a ~ porter still handling baggage⟩ ⟨shoes that looked positively ~⟩ b : marked by the weakness of old age : DECREPIT ⟨a ~ person⟩ ⟨a ~ empire⟩; *esp* : exhibiting a loss of mental faculties associated with old age : DODDERING ⟨the oldest man and woman of the group are regarded as the ultimate authority, if they are not ~ —E.H. Spicer⟩ 3 : approaching the end of a geological cycle of erosion ⟨a ~ topography⟩ ⟨a ~ river⟩

²**senile** \"\ *n* -s : a senile person : DOTARD 1b

senile atrophy *n* : the atrophy occurring with old age

senile cataract *n* : a cataract of a type that occurs in the aged and is characterized by an initial opacity in the lens, subsequent swelling of the lens, and final shrinkage with complete loss of transparency

senile dementia *n* : SENILE PSYCHOSIS

senile deterioration *n* : SENILE PSYCHOSIS

senile gangrene *n* : gangrene due to lack of blood supply resulting from sclerosis of blood vessels

senile·ly \-(l)lē, -li\ *adv* : in a senile manner ⟨chatters ~ —Rudyard Kipling⟩

senile psychosis *n* : a severe mental disorder of the aged that is manifested by loss of memory, judgment, and moral and aesthetic values, is often accompanied by confusion, irrational ideas, and disturbed emotionality, and commonly results from organic changes in the brain

se·nil·i·ty \sə'niləd·ē, sē'n-, -lətē, -i *also* se'n-\ *n* -ES [¹*senile* + *-ity*] : the quality or state of being senile: as a : OLD AGE b : DOTAGE 1a, SENILE PSYCHOSIS

¹**sen·ior** \'sēnyə(r)\ *n* -s [ME, fr. L, fr. *senior* older, elder] 1 a : an elderly or old person ⟨know how to make us ~*s* very unnecessary —R.W.Emerson⟩ ⟨the ~*s* were active in the local affairs —Roy Lewis & Angus Maude⟩ b : a person accorded distinction or deference in respect for his age : ³ELDER 3 c : one who is older than another ⟨thrown among his ~*s* in the upper grades of the school⟩ d *Brit* : a student in a senior school 2 a : a person holding a position of higher standing in a hierarchy of ranks ⟨as his ~ he would of course command the entire force —H.E.Scudder⟩ b : a senior fellow of a college at an English university; *specif* : a member of a governing council of a college (as at Trinity College, Cambridge) c : HEAD BOY d : a student in his last year before graduating from an educational institution of secondary or higher level ⟨a high school ~⟩ ⟨college ~*s*⟩ ⟨a ~ in law school⟩ 3 : a sexually mature animal 4 : ELDEST HAND; *specif* : the player at the left of the declarer in bridge

²**senior** \"\ *adj* [ME, fr. L, compar. of *sen-, senex* old; akin to Goth *sineigs* old, *sinista* eldest, ON *sina* old grass, Gk *henos* old, Skt *sana*] 1 a : more advanced in age than another : OLDER ⟨~ to her classmate by a full year⟩ ⟨having to support . . . human creatures ~ and junior to themselves —F.L.Allen⟩ — abbr. *Sr* or *sr*; used chiefly and often cap. to distinguish a father with the same given name as his son; opposed to *junior* b : advanced in age ⟨too ~ to begin to try for Cabinet office —John Buchan⟩ c : earliest in date of origin or founding ⟨piracy, one of the ~ sins of the human race —George Woodbury⟩ ⟨the ~ organization of its kind —Thurston Dart⟩ d : ranking above another in length of service ⟨the ~ senator of the state⟩ ⟨the ~ members of the committee⟩; *specif* : having more seniority than another ⟨the most ~ airline pilots flying on the more desirable assignments —H.R.Northrup⟩ 2 a : higher in standing or rank esp. in a hierarchy of ranks : SUPERIOR ⟨the ~ scholars of the university⟩ ⟨lieutenant ~ grade⟩ ⟨~ scientists⟩ ⟨the more ~ the officer, the more time he has —G.S. Patton⟩ ⟨young for so ~ a post —William Ridsdale⟩ b : associated with one or more others in a leading or primary role ⟨~ partner⟩ ⟨~ member of a law firm⟩; *specif* : mentioned first and given major credit among collaborating authors (as of a scientific paper) ⟨the name of the ~ author will be widely recognized —Paul Woodring⟩ 3 : of or relating to seniors in an educational institution ⟨the ~ class⟩ ⟨the ~ prom⟩ 4 a *of a bond* : having a lien preference prior to other bonds b *of a preferred stock* : having a dividend preference prior to other stocks ⟨a ~ security⟩

senior captain *n* [²*senior*] : a Salvationist officer ranking above a captain and below a major

senior chief petty officer *n* : a chief petty officer ranking just below a master chief petty officer and above a chief petty officer

senior classic *n* : a student obtaining the highest honors in the classical tripos at Cambridge University — compare SENIOR MORALIST, SENIOR WRANGLER

senior college *n* [¹*senior*] 1 : a college offering the regular four-year course traditionally required for a bachelor's degree — contrasted with *junior college* 2 : the upper division or last two years of a 4-year college

senior common room *n* : a common room at a British college reserved for the use of fellows and members of the teaching staff

senior girl scout *or* **senior scout** *n* : a girl scout in the age group ranging approximately from 14 through 17 years

senior high school *also* **senior high** *n* : a secondary school usu. public-supported that is organized on a 3-year or a 4-year basis to comprise grades 10 through 12 or grades 9 through 12 and usu. includes several divisions (as college preparatory, commercial, general) — contrasted with *junior high school*

se·nior·i·ty \sēn'yȯrəd·ē, -yär-, -rətē, -i\ *n* -ES *often attrib* [ML *senioritat-, senioritas*, fr. L *senior* + *-itat-, -itas* -ity] 1 : the quality or state of being senior : priority esp. of birth, office, or service ⟨next in ~ of age —Philip O'Connor⟩ ⟨the historical ~ of the experimental field —B.F.Skinner⟩; *specif* : a status attained by length of continuous service (as in a company, institution, or organization or in a department, job, rank, or occupational group) to which are attached by custom or prior collective agreement various rights or privileges (as preference in tenure, priority in promotion, and choice of work or shift) on the basis of ranking relative to others ⟨arguments over the relative weight to be given to ~ and ability —Dale Yoder⟩ ⟨~ system⟩ ⟨~ list⟩ ⟨~ rights⟩ 2 *often cap* : the body of senior fellows of a British college ⟨a matter brought before the ~⟩

seniority rule *n* 1 : a rule in the U.S. Congress by which members have their choice of committee assignments in order of rank based solely on length of service 2 : a rule in the U.S. Congress by which the member of the majority party who has served longest on a committee receives the chairmanship

seniority unit *n* : the unit (as department, plant, company) within which an employee may exercise his seniority rights

senior major *n* [²*senior*] : a Salvationist officer ranking above a major and below a brigadier

senior master sergeant *n* : a noncommissioned officer in the air force rating just below a chief master sergeant and above a master sergeant

senior matriculation *n* [¹*senior*] : a certificate awarded to a high school graduate in Canada for successfully completing at a high school a year of additional studies chiefly of college grade — compare JUNIOR MATRICULATION

senior moralist *n* [²*senior*] : a student obtaining the highest honors in the moral sciences tripos at Cambridge University — compare SENIOR CLASSIC, SENIOR WRANGLER

senior optime *n* : a student in the optime class at Cambridge University

senior school *n* [¹*senior*] : a part of the British school system serving children from 14 to 17 years of age — compare INTERMEDIATE SCHOOL, JUNIOR SCHOOL

senior security *n* [²*senior*] : a security having priority over another ⟨mortgage bonds and preferred stocks are *senior securities* compared to debentures and common stocks respectively⟩

senior soldier *n* : an enrolled member of the Salvation Army aged 14 years or older

senior sophister *n* [¹*senior*] *archaic* : a university student in his last undergraduate year — compare SENIOR 2d

senior wrangler *n* [²*senior*] : a student obtaining the highest honors in the mathematical tripos at Cambridge University and ranking first among the wranglers — compare SENIOR CLASSIC, SENIOR MORALIST

senior yearling *n* : an animal of an age between 18 and 24 months on a specified date of the year (as Aug. 1) established by rules for livestock exhibits of the season

sen·it *also* **sen't** *or* **sen·at** \'senət\ *n* -s [Egypt *snjt*] : a game of ancient Egyptian origin that resembles backgammon

se·ni·um \'sēnēəm\ *n* -s [L, fr. *sen-, senex* old, old man — more at SENIOR] : OLD AGE 1

1sen·na \'senə\ *n* -s [NL, fr. Ar *sanā*] **1 :** a plant of the genus *Cassia; esp* **:** a plant of this genus having medical use **2 :** the dried leaflets of various sennas (esp. *Cassia acutifolia* and *C. angustifolia*) used in medicine as a purgative — see ALEXANDRIA SENNA, TINNEVELLY SENNA

2senna *also* **seh·na** \"\ *n* -s *usu cap* [fr. *Sinneh*, town of northwest Iran] **:** a usu. small Persian rug having a very fine weave with short pile harsh and sandy to the touch and small allover patterns and subdued colors

sennachie *var of* SHANACHIE

senna knot *usu cap S, var of* SEHNA KNOT

senna tree *n* ['senna] **:** a tropical American tree (*Cassia emarginata*) with showy axillary clusters of yellow flowers

sen·ne·grass *also* **saen·ne·grass** \'senə+,-\ *n* [part trans. of Norw *sennegress*] **:** a widely distributed sedge (*Carex vesicaria*) with grasslike leaves that is used by arctic and antarctic explorers as insulating material

1sen·net \'senət\ *or* **sin·net** \'sin-\ *n* -s [prob. alter. of *signet*] **:** a signal call on a trumpet or cornet for entrance or exit on the stage

2sennet *var of* SENIT

sen·nett's oriole \'senəts-\ *or* **sennett's hooded oriole** *n, usu cap S* [after George B. *Sennett* †1900 Am. ornithologist] **:** HOODED ORIOLE

sen·night *also* **se'n·night** \'se,nīt, -,nət\ *n* [ME *sevenight, sennight*, fr. OE *seofon nihta* seven nights] *archaic* **:** the space of seven nights and days **:** WEEK ⟨the rest . . . were to be heard this day *se'nnight* —Samuel Pepys⟩ ⟨on Sunday *se'nnight* . . . died by a fall —Thomas Gray⟩

sen·nit *also* **sen·net** \'senət, *usu* -əd·+V\ *or* **sin·net** \'sin-\ *n* -s [perh. fr. F *coussinet* pad, mat, dim. of *coussin* cushion; fr. its use to protect cables from fraying — more at CUSHION] **1 :** a braided cord or fabric of plaited rope yarns or other small stuff **2 :** a straw or grass braid for hats; *esp* **:** a rice straw braid for men's stiff straw hats

se·no·nian \sə'nōnēən, -nyən\ *adj, usu cap* [F *sénonien*, fr. L *Senones*, ancient people of central Gaul + F *-ien* -ian] **:** of or relating to a subdivision of the European Cretaceous — see GEOLOGIC TIME table

se·nor *or* **se·ñor** \(')sān'yō(ə)r, sēn'y-\ *n, pl* **senors** \-ō(ə)rz\ *or* **señores** \-yō(,)rās, -yō(-\ [Sp, fr. ML *senior* superior, magnate, lord, fr. L, adj., elder — more at SENIOR] **1 :** MISTER — used as a title of courtesy prefixed to the name of a Spanish or Spanish-speaking man **2 :** a Spanish or Spanish-speaking man

se·no·ra *or* **se·ño·ra** \sān'yōrə, sēn-, -yȯrə\ *n* -s [Sp, fem. of *señor*] **1 :** MISTRESS — used as a title prefixed to the name of a married Spanish or Spanish-speaking woman **2 :** a married Spanish or Spanish-speaking woman

se·no·ri·ta *or* **se·ño·ri·ta** \,sānyə'rēd·ə, ,sen-, -ētə\ *n* -s [Sp, dim. of *señora*] **1 a :** MISS — used as a title prefixed to the name of an unmarried Spanish or Spanish-speaking woman **b :** an unmarried Spanish or Spanish-speaking woman **2 :** a slender compressed cream and brown wrasse (*Oxyjulis californica*) of the California coast

senr *abbr* senior

sensa *pl of* SENSUM

1sensate *adj* [LL *sensatus*, fr. L *sensus* sense + *-atus* -ate] **:** endowed with sense or sensation

2sen·sate \'sen,sāt\ *vt* -ED/-ING/-S [back-formation fr. *sensation*] **:** to feel or apprehend through a sense or the senses

3sensate \"\, *usu* -ād·+V\ *adj* [ML *sensatus* perceived by sense, fr. L, endowed with sense] **1 :** felt or apprehended through a sense or the senses **2 :** preoccupied with or exclusively directed toward that which can be experienced through the sense modality **:** MATERIALISTIC — **sen·sate·ly** *adv*

sen·sa·tion \sen'sāshən, sən'-\ *n* -s [ML *sensation-, sensatio*, fr. LL *sensatus* endowed with sense + L *-ion-, -io* -ion] **1 a :** a state of consciousness produced by impingement of an external object or condition upon the body **b :** a mode of mental functioning referable to immediate stimulation of the body from without; *often* **:** such a mode of mental functioning as distinguished from the conscious awareness of the process **c :** the direct, immediate, and not further analyzable awareness (as of heat or pain) resulting from adequate stimulation of a receptor organ in a living organism **d** (1) **:** awareness endopsychic in origin and not the immediate result of sensory stimulation (2) **:** a state of consciousness of a kind usu. caused by physical objects or internal bodily changes but having no physical source **2 a :** a more or less indefinite bodily feeling **b :** a particular emotional feeling **3 a :** an internal organic stimulus **b :** a physical object or something that provides awareness of a physical object **c :** an object (as an afterimage or hallucination) of an endopsychic process of sensation **4 a** (1) **:** a state of excited interest or feeling ⟨his death created quite a ~⟩ (2) **:** the cause of such a state ⟨the new soprano was the ~ of the season⟩ **b :** a vivid emotion or experience attended by excitement **5 :** the use of sensational matter or the evoking of sensational reactions as an effect in art

syn SENSE, FEELING, SENSIBILITY: SENSATION, as here discussed, may center attention on perception through or as if through the sense organs, with or without comprehension, cognition, or other intellectual or emotional reaction ⟨now that he was by her side, she felt his nearness intimately, like a touch. She tried to disregard this *sensation* —Joseph Conrad⟩ ⟨the sweet *sensations* of returning health made me happy for a time; but such *sensations* seldom outlast convalescence —W.H. Hudson †1922⟩ ⟨still he would drink, only instead of port it must be brandy to lash his flagging palate into *sensation* —Virginia Woolf⟩ SENSE may indicate only a sensation or sensory perception; it may indicate a more intellectual cognition marked by full awareness or consciousness ⟨his first consciousness was a *sense* of the light dry wind blowing in through the windows —Willa Cather⟩ ⟨never since the age of seven had he been able to look on feminine beauty without a *sense* of warmth and faint excitement —John Galsworthy⟩ ⟨solaced, even in your chagrin, by a *sense* of injured innocence —B.N.Cardozo⟩ FEELING may indicate the sense of touch, along with awareness to pressure and temperature; it may indicate a complex of sensation, emotion, and thought experienced as a reaction to a situation ⟨some people itch more easily than others because their threshold for *feeling* in the skin is lower than that of other people —Morris Fishbein⟩ ⟨a deep sensation of cold, compounded with deep pressure — in short, a numb *feeling* — persisted even when the skin itself had ceased to deliver the sensation of cold —R.S. Woodworth⟩ ⟨it wasn't raining but there was the *feeling* of its being a rainy night —R.H.Newman⟩ ⟨serious danger that a *feeling* of futility and despair would spread over the continent like a creeping paralysis —Vera M. Dean⟩ SENSIBILITY may suggest power to respond, often a capacity for delicate appreciation or a lively responsiveness to impression, sometimes sentimental, forced, or affected ⟨the extreme *sensibility* to physical suffering which characterizes modern civilization —W.R.Inge⟩ ⟨she was a creature of palpitating *sensibility*, with feelings so delicate that they responded to every breath —S.M.Crothers⟩

sen·sa·tion·al \-shən°l, -shnəl\ *adj* **1 :** of or relating to sensation or the senses **:** having or characterized by sensation **:** involving, depending on, or inducing sensations **2 a :** arousing or suited or designed to arouse a quick, intense, and usu. superficial emotional response ⟨a ~ news report⟩ ⟨a ~ play⟩ ⟨~ crime reporting⟩ **b :** capturing attention or interest **:** ARRESTING, SPECTACULAR ⟨her ~ private life kept her continually before the public —*Amer. Guide Series: La.*⟩ ⟨nothing ~, simply honest building and good stonecutting —Willa Cather⟩ **c :** EXTRAORDINARY, PHENOMENAL ⟨a ~ rookie⟩ ⟨a ~ advancement from major to major general —*Time*⟩ **3 :** of or relating to sensationalism ⟨the ~ school⟩

sen·sa·tion·al·ism \-shən°l,izəm, -shnə,li-\ *n* -s [*sensational* + *-ism*] **1 a :** sensational subject matter or treatment of subject matter or the use of such matter or treatment (as in a literary or dramatic work) ⟨the story is told without swagger or ~ —Margaret Hexter⟩ ⟨the ~ of the daily press⟩ **b :** the effect of such subject matter or treatment ⟨the desire for ~ for its own sake, as sometimes fulfilled in news of sex and crime, must be placed very low in the scale —F.L.Mott⟩ **2 :** a doctrine in ethics that postulates feeling as the sole criterion of good; SENSUALISM **3 :** a doctrine in philosophy that postulates the origin of all our knowledge in sensation or sense perceptions; *also* **:** the view that all knowledge is made up of sense elements — contrasted with *rationalism;* compare ASSOCIATIONISM, EMPIRICISM **4 :** SENSATIONISM 2

sen·sa·tion·al·ist \-ləst\ *n* -s [*sensational* + *-ist*] **1 a :** one who seeks to make sensations **b :** one who practices sensationalism (as in writing) **2 :** an advocate of or believer in ethical or philosophical sensationalism

sen·sa·tion·al·is·tic \¦==shən°l¦istik, -shnə¦l-\ *adj* **:** of or relating to sensationalists or sensationalism

sen·sa·tion·al·ize \=¦=shən°l,īz, -shnə,līz\ *vt* -ED/-ING/-S *see -ize in Explan Notes* [*sensational* + *-ize*] **:** to present in a sensational manner **:** give an effect of sensationalism to ⟨~ a problem⟩

sen·sa·tion·al·ly \-n°lē, -nəlē, -li\ *adv* **:** in a sensational manner

sen·sa·tion·ism \=¦=shə,nizəm\ *n* -s [*sensation* + *-ism*] **1 :** SENSATIONALISM 3 **2 :** a system of psychology based upon sensations as the constituent elements of all conscious experience

1sen·sa·tion·ist \-,nəst\ *n* -s [*sensation* + *-ist*] **:** SENSATIONALIST

2sensationist \"\ *also* **sen·sa·tion·is·tic** \=¦==¦nistik\ *adj* [*sensationist* fr. *1sensationist; sensationistic* fr. *1sensationist* + *-ic*] **:** SENSATIONALISTIC

sen·sa·tion·less \=¦==ləs\ *adj* **:** producing or responding to no sensation

sensation level *n* **:** the range of intensity of sound vibrations in which they are perceived as sound **:** the range between the threshold of audibility and that of feeling usu. expressed in decibels

sensation-monger \=¦==,==\ *n* **:** a purveyor of the sensational (as in literature)

sensations *pl of* SENSATION

sen·sa·to·ry \'sen(t)sə,tōrē, -tȯr-, -ri\ *adj* [*2sensate* + *-ory*] **:** SENSORY

1sense \'sen(t)s\ *n* -s [MF or L; MF *sens*, fr. L *sensus* sensation, feeling, understanding, signification, fr. *sensus*, past part. of *sentire* to perceive, feel, suppose; akin to OHG *sin* mind, sense, *sinnan* to travel, strive after, *sind* journey, road — more at SEND] **1 :** something to be grasped, comprehended, known **:** SIGNIFICATION: as **a :** one of the multifold (as literal, anagogic, allegorical, tropological) meanings considered present in the Bible or in allegorical writings (as the Divine Comedy) **b** (1) **:** the particular meaning intended (as by a writer or speaker) ⟨you miss my ~ —Shak.⟩ ⟨the addition corrupted the ~ of the passage⟩ (2) **:** the one of two or more literal meanings by which a word or passage may rationally be construed in context ⟨there can be but one ~ here⟩ ⟨the context will not admit of such a ~⟩ **c** (1) **:** an interpretation that may be given to a group of words forming a passage **:** the meaning of such a group as a functional unit ⟨I did not understand him in that ~⟩ ⟨learned the speech by heart and missed the ~ entirely⟩ (2) **:** general or essential meaning of an utterance **:** SUBSTANCE, GIST ⟨the ~ of the decision was presented in a summary⟩ ⟨give the ~ of his argument⟩ **d :** the meaning of a word or fixed phrase or one of the distinct meanings that it may bear in diverse situations; *esp* **:** a meaning of a word as segregated in a dictionary or glossary **e :** meaning that is rational or intelligible ⟨he speaks ~ —Shak.⟩ **f :** prose supplied to a student for expression in Greek or Latin verse **2 a :** a mechanism or faculty of perception· (1) **:** the faculty of receiving mental impressions through the action of sense organs of the body or of perceiving changes in the condition of the body — not often used technically (2) **:** any special faculty of sensation ⟨spiritual and occult ~s⟩ (3) **:** a specialized mechanism or function by virtue of which an animal is receptive and responsive to a particular stimulus or class of stimuli either arising externally (as in the case of the senses of sight, hearing, smell, taste, touch, temperature, or pain) or internally (as in the case of the kinesthetic and organic senses) (4) **:** the total function comprising the several sensory mechanisms regarded as a unit distinct from other functions (as of movement or thought) ⟨knowledge derived from ~⟩ ⟨~ experience⟩ **b** *obs* **:** SENSE ORGAN **c :** power or means of perception **:** capacity to perceive and interpret stimuli **:** CONSCIOUSNESS, SANITY — usu. used in pl. ⟨lose her ~s⟩ ⟨his ~s were clear to the last⟩ **d** (1) **:** power of interpolating or deducing from observations or unnoted stimuli in respect to a particular field or relation ⟨a ~ of time⟩ ⟨a good ~ of location⟩ (2) **:** instinctive comprehension (as of fine points) and acuteness or resourcefulness in gaining mastery or success in respect to a particular thing (as an art or a game or medium) ⟨keen musical ~⟩ ⟨a natural language ~⟩ ⟨a born flier with a real air ~⟩ (3) **:** a faculty for intellectual and aesthetic grasp and appreciation ⟨a ~ of beauty⟩ **3 :** awareness or perception arrived at through or as if through interpretation of sensory stimuli: as **a :** perception by means of the intellect **:** understanding or discerning awareness or comprehension **:** APPRECIATION ⟨a good ~ of values⟩ **b** (1) **:** an awareness or feeling of a particular nature resulting from a particular stimulus ⟨a ~ of well-being⟩ ⟨a sudden ~ of warmth on entering the house⟩ (2) **:** a vague and unanalyzable but persistent awareness or feeling ⟨had a ~ that the child was in danger⟩ ⟨a ~ of insecurity⟩ (3) **:** a sensitive and usu. sympathetic or grateful recognition ⟨a ~ of God's mercies⟩ (4) **:** a self-conscious motivating awareness or conviction ⟨a ~ of shame⟩ ⟨tried to control his ~ of injury⟩ (5) **:** a moral awareness or appreciation **:** recognition based on established usage or in accordance with normal behavior ⟨utterly careless and lacking any ~ of responsibility⟩ **c** (1) **:** perception by means of the senses and esp. when aesthetic or emotional in content or orientation ⟨shall reason yield to mere ~⟩ (2) **:** an avenue of sensory perception — usu. used in pl. ⟨feast the ~s on that scene of delight⟩ **4 :** something that is felt or held as a sentiment, view, or opinion — used chiefly of groups of persons ⟨the ~ of the meeting⟩ **5 a :** MIND, SENTIENCE, INTELLIGENCE ⟨as if the steel had ~ —Edmund Spenser⟩ **b :** sound mental capacity often marked by shrewd practical understanding ⟨a man of ~⟩ ⟨had ~ enough to win⟩; *also* **:** something that is based on or typical of such sense **:** a logical, sensible, or practical thing, act, or way of doing ⟨no ~ in waiting⟩ ⟨your decision makes ~⟩ **6** [F *sens*, of Gmc origin; akin to OHG *sinnan* to travel, strive after] **a :** a direction in which something (as motion) takes place or is visualized as taking place **:** TREND, COURSE **b :** one of two opposite directions in which a line, surface, or region may be supposed to be described by the motion of a point, line, or surface — symbolically denoted respectively by + and —

syn COMMON SENSE, GOOD SENSE, HORSE SENSE, JUDGMENT, WISDOM, GUMPTION: SENSE, as herein treated, indicates an accustomed steady ability to judge and decide between possible courses with intelligence and soundness ⟨the only one that has any *sense* in that family —Margaret Deland⟩ ⟨whose practical *sense* equaled his intuitive genius —Henry Adams⟩ COMMON SENSE, GOOD SENSE, and HORSE SENSE add only slight additional suggestions to SENSE, COMMON SENSE suggesting ordinary good judgment and prudence without sophistication, learning, or special knowledge, GOOD SENSE implying an especial perception of circumstances and soundness in analysis, HORSE SENSE connoting a blending of sense with hard, plain, uncultured shrewdness or depth of observation ⟨freedom with *common-sense* regulations that any sensible man may be expected to observe —H.S.Commager⟩ ⟨the main attribute required is a certain balance of experience, prudence and sympathy which is generally called *common sense* —*Economist*⟩ ⟨the tall young king went through the long, intricate, and exhausting service with dignity and *good sense*, and added meaning to much of the symbolism by his understanding of it —*Manchester Guardian Weekly*⟩ ⟨possessed . . . good *horse sense*, which was at times more valuable than the complex conceptions put forth by the party and its leading theoreticians —D.J.Dallin⟩ JUDGMENT involves notions of sense refined and tempered by experience, maturity, training, or discipline to discern coolly and judge soundly in difficult matters ⟨the ultimate test of true worth . . . is the trained *judgment* of the good and sensible man —G. L.Dickinson⟩ ⟨that all shrewdness of speculation had given place to shrewdness of practical *judgment* based on very definite experience —John Galsworthy⟩ WISDOM, of these synonyms the one indicating highest praise, suggests great soundness, sagacity, and insight, the result of blending together common sense, wit, experience, maturity, learning, and understanding ⟨*wisdom*, she saw at last, was knowledge plus vision —Helen Howe⟩ ⟨*wisdom* is a kind of knowledge. It is knowledge of the nature, career and consequences of human values. Since these cannot be separated from the human organism and the social scene, the moral ways of man cannot be understood without knowledge of the ways of things and institutions —Sidney Hook⟩ GUMPTION, like HORSE SENSE in being informal in suggestion, may connote a combination of clever common sense and initiative or drive, especially the latter in today's English ⟨a man's common sense means his good judgment, his freedom from eccentricity, his *gumption* —William James⟩ **syn** see in addition SENSATION

— **in a sense** *adv* **:** according to an interpretation other than the most natural or obvious though possibly admissible under particular circumstances ⟨it was true *in a sense*⟩

2sense \"\ *vt* -ED/-ING/-S **1 a :** to perceive by the senses **b :** to have consciousness of **:** feel the imminence or presence of **:** ANTICIPATE ⟨~ danger⟩ ⟨*sensed* a flaw in the reasoning⟩ **2** *obs* **a :** to give the sense or meaning of **:** EXPOUND **b :** TEST, EXAMINE, ANALYZE **3 :** to get the meaning of **:** GRASP, COMPREHEND, REALIZE ⟨did not ~ his meaning⟩ **4 :** to become aware of without express communication ⟨*sensed* her dislike⟩ **5 :** to estimate the position of burst of (a round or a shot) with reference to a target **6 :** to detect (a symbol) automatically or mechanically ⟨computing machines that ~ the holes in tabulating cards with appropriately spaced steel pins⟩

sense cell *n* **:** a receptor cell of a sense organ; *esp* **:** an isolated cell constituting the receptor mechanism of a sense organ

sensed \'sen(t)st\ *adj* [*1sense* + *-ed*] **:** invested with sense of a specified kind — usu. used in combination ⟨a keen-*sensed* observer⟩

sense-datum \'=¦==\ *n, pl* **sense-data :** an immediate unanalyzable private object of sensation ⟨a sharp pain, an afterimage, or a round coin experienced as an ellipse is a *sense-datum*⟩

sense-datum language *n* **:** a language whose terms refer exclusively to sense-data and their properties or relations — contrasted with *thing-language*

sense finder *n* **:** a portion of a radio direction finder by which the sense of the direction is determined

sense·ful \'=fəl\ *adj* **:** full of sense **:** SIGNIFICANT, JUDICIOUS

sense impression *n* **:** a psychical and physiological effect resulting directly from the excitation of a sense organ **:** SENSATION

1sense·less \'=ləs\ *adj* **:** destitute of, deficient in, or contrary to sense: as **a :** lacking sensibility or feeling **:** INSENSIBLE, UNCONSCIOUS; *also* **:** incapable of sensation or perception **b** *archaic* **:** having no consciousness **c :** deficient in knowledge, appreciation, or reasoning power **:** STUPID **d :** lacking good sense **:** UNWISE, UNREASONABLE, NONSENSICAL **e :** proceeding from or characterized by lack of intelligence or meaning **:** FOOLISH, PURPOSELESS, MEANINGLESS ⟨a ~ custom⟩ — **sense·less·ly** *adv* — **sense·less·ness** *n* -ES

2senseless *adv, obs* **:** SENSELESSLY

sensemaking \'=¦==\ *adj* **:** that makes sense **:** SENSIBLE, REASONABLE, PRACTICABLE ⟨a ~ proposal⟩

sense of humor : the faculty of perceiving and appreciating the humorous; *sometimes* **:** addiction to buffoonery and witticisms ⟨has a great *sense of humor* — always kidding⟩

sense organ *or* **sensory organ** *n* **:** a bodily structure that is affected by a stimulus (as heat or sound waves) in such a manner as to initiate a wave of excitation in associated sensory nerve fibers which conveys specific impulses to the central nervous system where they are interpreted as corresponding sensations (as of warmth or sound) **:** RECEPTOR

sense perception *n* **:** perception by the senses as distinguished from intellectual perception

sense pore *n* **:** a sense organ contained in a cuticular pit of an arthropod

sens·er \'sen(t)sə(r)\ *n* -s **:** one that senses something

sense rod *n* **:** a terminal filament on the sense cell of some insect sense organs

senses *pl of* SENSE, *pres 3d sing of* SENSE

sense stress *n* **:** SENTENCE STRESS

sense-world \'=¦=\ *n* **:** the world as known through the physical senses

sen·si·bil·ia \,sen(t)sə'bilēə, -lyə\ *n pl* [LL, fr. neut. pl. of *sensibilis* capable of being perceived — more at SENSIBLE] **:** what is sensed

sen·si·bil·i·sin \-ləsən\ *n* -s [prob. fr. G, fr. *sensibilisieren* to sensibilize (fr. F *sensibiliser*) + *-in*] **:** ANAPHYLACTIN

sen·si·bil·i·tist \-ləd·əst\ *n* -s [*sensibility* + *-ist*] **:** one having acute sensibility

sen·si·bil·i·ty \-ləd·ē, -ətē, -i\ *n* -ES [ME *sensibilite*, fr. MF *sensibilité*, fr. LL *sensibilitat-, sensibilitas*, fr. *sensibilis* sensible + L *-itat-, -itas* -ity] **1 :** the ability to receive sensation **:** responsiveness to stimuli **:** SENSITIVENESS ⟨tactile ~⟩ **2 :** SENSITIVITY a **3 a :** capacity of emotion or feeling as distinguished from intellect and will **:** peculiar or excessive susceptibility to pleasurable or painful impression **:** acuteness of feeling ⟨great ~ to pain⟩ ⟨~ to praise⟩ — often used in pl. ⟨a man of strong *sensibilities*⟩ **b :** a manifestation of such a capacity ⟨answered the charge with marked ~⟩ **4 :** awareness of and responsive feeling toward something (as emotion in another); *also* **:** an instance or token of this ⟨our ~ of your distress⟩ **5 :** refined sensitiveness in emotion and taste with especial responsiveness to the pathetic ⟨excessive ~ of late 18th century poetry⟩ **6 :** susceptibility to slight or unkindness **syn** see SENSATION

sen·si·bi·lize \'sen(t)səbə,līz\ *vt* -ED/-ING/-S [F *sensibiliser*, fr. *sensible* + *-iser* -ize] **:** SENSITIZE

sen·si·bi·liz·er \-zə(r)\ *n* -s [*sensibilize* + *-er*] **:** SENSITIZER

1sen·si·ble \'sen(t)səbəl\ *adj, sometimes* -ER/-EST [ME, fr. MF, fr. LL *sensibilis* capable of perceiving or being perceived, fr. L, capable of being perceived, fr. *sensus* (past part. of *sentire* to feel, perceive) + *-ibilis* -ible — more at SENSE] **1 a** (1) **:** capable of being perceived by the senses **:** apprehensible through the sense organs ⟨a ~ contact⟩ ⟨~ impressions⟩ (2) **:** perceptible to the mind **:** making an impression upon the sense, reason, or understanding ⟨a warm and clearly ~ affection⟩ ⟨his distress was ~ from his manner⟩ **b :** perceptibly large **:** of a significant size, amount, or degree **:** CONSIDERABLE ⟨a ~ error⟩ **c** (1) **:** readily perceptible by the senses **:** affecting the senses acutely ⟨a ~ odor⟩ (2) *obs* **:** producing a strong impression on the mind (3) *archaic* **:** tending to produce an acute emotional response either positive or negative (4) **:** MATERIAL ⟨waiting to receive more ~ marks of his uncle's approval⟩ **d :** SENSUOUS 1 **2 a :** capable of receiving impressions from external objects through the sense organs **:** liable to be affected by stimuli ⟨the more ~ parts of the skin⟩ ⟨~ to pain⟩ **b :** liable to impression from without **:** easily affected **:** having or exhibiting nice perception or acute feeling ⟨disturbed in the most ~ reaches of his spirit⟩ ⟨with affection wondrous ~ —Shak.⟩ **c** *archaic* **:** capable of reacting readily to an activating force ⟨~ instruments⟩ **3 a :** perceiving or having perception either through the senses or the mind **:** COGNIZANT ⟨made ~ of his mistake⟩ ⟨~ of the gathering storm⟩; *also* **:** perceiving so clearly as to be convinced **:** PERSUADED, SATISFIED ⟨~ of the error in our decision⟩ **b :** perceiving and responding emotionally ⟨~ of his faults⟩ ⟨very ~ of your distress⟩ **4 :** having or containing sense or reason **:** characterized by or resulting from sober serious examination and study **:** INTELLIGENT, REASONABLE ⟨a ~ man⟩ ⟨~ plans⟩ ⟨a ~ answer⟩ **syn** see AWARE, MATERIAL, PERCEPTIBLE, WISE

2sensible \"\ *n* -s **:** something that impresses the senses **:** something perceptible

sensible heat *n* **:** thermal energy whose transfer to or from a substance results in a change of temperature — compare LATENT HEAT

sensible horizon *n* **:** HORIZON 1b(3)

sen·si·ble·ness *n* -ES **:** the quality or state of being sensible

sensible note *or* **sensible tone** *n* [trans. of F *note sensible*] **:** LEADING TONE

sensible species *n, Thomism* **:** an object as apprehended through an act of sensual cognition — contrasted with *intelligible species*

sen·si·bly \'sen(t)səblē, -li\ *adv* [ME, fr. *sensible* + *-ly*] **:** in a sensible manner: as **a :** so as to be perceptible usu. to the senses ⟨became ~ warmer⟩ **b :** APPRECIABLY, SIGNIFICANTLY ⟨~ nearer their goal⟩ **c :** INTELLIGENTLY, DISCREETLY, JUDICIOUSLY ⟨acted ~ in the crisis⟩

sen·sif·ics \sen'sifiks\ *n pl but sing or pl in constr* [¹*sense* + *-ifics* (as in *significs*)] : SIGNIFICS
sen·si·fy \'sen(t)sə,fī\ *vt* -ED/-ING/-ES [¹*sense* + *-ify*] : to make (a stimulus) perceptible as sensation
sen·sile \'sen,sīl, -n(t)səl\ *adj* [L *sensilis*, fr. *sensus* (past part. of *sentire* to feel, perceive) + *-ilis* -ile — more at SENSE] **1** : capable of sensation : SENTIENT **2** : felt or sensed but not registered by an ordinary dry-bulb thermometer ⟨~ temperature changes⟩
sen·sil·lum \sen'siləm\ *n, pl* **sensil·la** \-lə\ [NL, dim. of L *sensus* sense] : a simple epithelial sense organ composed of one or a few cells with a nerve connection and usu. taking the form of a spine, plate, rod, cone, or peg
sensimotor *var of* SENSORIMOTOR
sensing *n* -s [fr. gerund of ²*sense*] : the determination by observation of the location of a gunnery burst or center of impact in relation to a target; *also* : an announcement of such location — often qualified by an indication of direction and amount of deviation from target ⟨~ 200 yards over⟩
sens·ism \'sen,sizəm\ *n* -s [¹*sense* + *-ism*] **1 a** : the philosophic doctrine that sense perceptions furnish the sole data of knowledge **b** : SENSATIONALISM — usu. used disparagingly **2** : hedonistic resort to the sensuous
¹**sen·si·tive** \'sen(t)sə̇d·iv, -n(t)s(ə)tiv *also* -n(t)stəv\ *adj* [ME, fr. MF *sensitif*, fr. ML *sensitivus*, of sensation, receiving sense impressions, irreg. (influenced by LL *intellectivus* intellective) fr. *sensus*, past part. of *sentire* to feel, perceive — more at SENSE] **1** : conveying or receiving sense impressions ⟨~ nerves⟩ **2 a** *obs* : serving to affect the senses : functioning as a sensory stimulus **b** : experienced by means of the senses : SENSUOUS ⟨a ~ pleasure⟩ ⟨~ experience⟩ **3 a** : possessing a capacity for sensation or feeling : receptive to external stimuli **b** *obs* : having capacity to react to stimuli but lacking power to reason **c** : capable of being stimulated or excited by external agents (as light, gravity, contact) functioning as stimuli ⟨~ protoplasm⟩ ⟨~ cells⟩ **d** : exhibiting irritomotility ⟨a ~ compound leaf⟩ **4** : having quick and acute sensibility either to the action of external objects or to impressions upon the mind and feelings : highly susceptible : easily and acutely affected ⟨was too ~ to abuse and calumny —T.B.Macaulay⟩: as **a** : peculiarly or excessively susceptible to the action or effect of a usu. specified factor (as drought, drugs, hypnotism) : HYPERSENSITIVE — usu. used with *to* ⟨~ to moisture⟩ ⟨~ to allergenic pollens⟩ **b** : fluctuating or liable to fluctuation; *esp* : subject to unusual or excessive fluctuations in price and demand ⟨a ~ security⟩ ⟨a ~ market⟩ **c** : abnormally susceptible often because of a specific sensitization ⟨~ to eggs⟩ **d** : having a capacity of being easily affected or moved : capable of indicating minute differences : DELICATE ⟨a ~ thermometer⟩ ⟨~ weighing scales⟩ **e** : readily affected or changed by various agents ⟨photographic paper is ~ to actinic rays⟩ ⟨a ~ explosive is easily exploded by a shock⟩ ⟨a ~ colloid is readily coagulated⟩ — compare PHOTOSENSITIVE **f** : having a higher octane number when tested at specified slower speeds than when tested at specified higher speeds ⟨~ gasolines⟩ **g** : high in radiosensitivity **5** : of or relating to sensation and the senses : SENSORY **6** : indicating by a relatively large angular change any slight movement of the observer toward or away from its center — used esp. in nautical surveying and of a circle passing through two fixed objects and the observer's station so that the angle subtended by the chord joins the objects **7** *of a tree or forest* : marked by unevenness and irregularity in the growth of annual rings that is associated with variations in growing conditions in different years — opposed to *complacent* **8** : concerned with or held vital to the national security by reason of dealing with highly restricted information and materials : demanding or intended to be treated with a high degree of discretion and unquestioned loyalty **syn** see LIABLE
²**sensitive** \"\ *n* -s **1** *obs* : an individual capable of sensory perception **2** : a person having or reputed to have occult or supernormal abilities (as for crystal gazing, clairvoyance, clairaudience, telepathy) **3** : a sensitive person
sensitive brier *n* : any of various trailing prickly perennial herbs constituting the genus *Schrankia* (family Leguminosae) and having twice pinnate leaves which exhibit irritomotility and are divided into numerous leaflets, procumbent stems, and small rosy flowers in round axillary heads
sensitive drill *n* : a drilling machine that responds to delicate adjustments
sensitive fern *n* : a No. American fern (*Onoclea sensibilis*) the leaves of which are notably susceptible to early frosts and when plucked show a slight tendency to fold together
sensitive frog *n* : the plantar cushion of a hoof
sensitive joint vetch *n* : an annual herb (*Aeschynomene virginica*) of the southeastern U. S. and tropical America having foliage sensitive to the touch and jointed pods — called also *curly indigo*
sensitive lamina *n* : LAMINA 2c
sen·si·tive·ly \-ə̇vlē, -li\ *adv* : in a sensitive manner : with sensitivity
sen·si·tive·ness \-ivnə̇s *also* -əv-\ *n* -ES : the quality or state of being sensitive
sensitive paper *n* : paper prepared for photographic purposes by coating or impregnating it with a substance sensitive to light
sensitive pea *n* : any of several herbs of the genus *Cassia* having leaflets somewhat sensitive to the touch; *esp* : either of two No. American plants (*C. fasciculata* and *C. nictitans*)
sensitive plant *n* **1** : any of several plants of the genus *Mimosa* with leaves sensitive to tactile stimulation; *esp* : a tropical American herb (*M. pudica*) that is often cultivated in greenhouses and has palmate leaves the divisions of which are pinnate with many small leaflets and whose leafstalk droops and pinnae and leaflets close tightly when the plant is touched **2** : any of various plants (as a sensitive brier or the sensitive pea) showing motions after irritation
sensitive rose *n* : SENSITIVE BRIER
sensitive shrub *n* : SENSITIVE PLANT 1
sen·si·tiv·i·ty \,sen(t)sə'tivəd·ē, -vətē, -i\ *n* -ES [¹*sensitive* + *-ity*] : the quality or state of being sensitive: as **a** : the rate of displacement of the indicating element with respect to change of the measured quantity — chiefly in technical use ⟨a galvanometer of extreme ~⟩ **b** (1) : the capacity of an organism or of a sense organ to respond to stimulation : IRRITABILITY; *also* : the degree of such responsiveness measured inversely by the weakest stimulus that awakens sensation or other response (2) : the capacity of a person to respond emotionally to changes in his interpersonal or social relationships; *also* : excessive capacity to respond thus **c** : abnormal responsiveness (as to an allergen or parasite) : HYPERSENSITIVITY **d** : the degree to which a radio receiving set responds to incoming waves; *esp* : the quotient of the power or other function of output of the set divided by the power or other function of its input
sensitivity center *n* : a region of a silver halide crystal that increases the photographic sensitivity of the crystal : a region at which latent image material forms or is concentrated
sensitivity speck *n* : a sensitivity center that is considered to constitute a region of impurity (as of silver sulfide) in the silver halide crystal
sen·si·ti·za·tion \,sen(t)səd·ə̇'zāshən, -ə,tī'z-\ *n* -s **1** : the quality or state of being sensitized (as to an antigen) **2** : the act or process of sensitizing
sen·si·tize \'sen(t)sə,tīz\ *vb* -ED/-ING/-S *see -ize in Explan Notes* [¹*sensitive* + *-ize*] *vt* : to cause to become sensitive ~ *vi* : to become sensitive
sen·si·tiz·er \-zə(r)\ *n* -s : one that sensitizes: as **a** : a sensitizing antibody (as a lysin or amboceptor) **b** : an agent that will make a material sensitive to radiation or will increase its sensitivity to radiation **c** : an operator of a machine for sensitizing photographic or blueprint paper
sen·si·tom·e·ter \,sen(t)sə'tämə̇d·ə(r)\ *n* [ISV *sensito-* (fr. *sensitive* + *-o-*) + *-meter*] : an instrument used in the measurement of sensitivity (as of photographic material or of the human eye) by producing upon the sensitive surface a series of known exposures
sen·si·to·metric \¦sen(t)sə̇d·ō+\ *adj* : relating to or used in sensitometry — **sen·si·to·metrically** \"+\ *adv*
sensitometric curve *n* : CHARACTERISTIC CURVE a
sen·si·tom·e·try \,sen(t)sə'tämə·trē\ *n* -ES [ISV *sensito-* (fr. *sensitive* + *-o-*) + *-metry*] : the science, art, or act of measuring sensitivity (as of photographic material or of the human eye)
sen·sive \'sen(t)siv\ *adj* [MF, fr. ML *sensivus*, fr. L *sensus* (past part. of *sentire* to feel, perceive) + *-ivus* -ive — more at SENSE] *archaic* : SENTIENT
sen·so \'sen¦sō\ *n* -s [perh. fr. Chin *shên⁴* kidneys, testes + *su⁴* essence] : a Chinese medicine for dropsy consisting essentially of the dried skin secretion of a native toad and apparently containing appreciable quantities of bufagin
sen·sor \'sen(t)sə(r)\ *n* -s [L *sensus* (past part. of *sentire* to feel, perceive) + E *-or*] : a device designed to respond to a physical stimulus (as heat or cold, light, a particular motion) and transmit a resulting impulse for interpretation or measurement or for operating a control
sensori- *also* **senso-** *comb form* [*sensori-* fr. ²*sensory; senso-* fr. L *sensus* sense] : sensory : sensory and ⟨*senso*paralysis⟩ ⟨*sensori*motor⟩
sen·so·ri·al \(')sen'sōrēəl, -sȯr-\ *adj* [²*sensory* + *-al*] **1** : relating to or concerned in sensation : SENSORY **2** : preoccupied with or primarily responsive to sensations — **sen·so·ri·al·ly** \-ēəlē, -li\ *adv*
sen·so·ri·motor \¦sen(t)s(ə)rē+\ *also* **sen·si·motor** \¦sen(t)sē+\ *or* **sen·so·motor** \¦sen(t)sə+\ *adj* [*sensorimotor, sensomotor,* fr. *sensori-, senso-* + *motor; sensimotor* fr. L *sensus* sense + E *-i-* + *motor*] : of, relating to, concerned with, or functioning in both sensory and motor aspects of bodily activity ⟨~ disturbances⟩ ⟨~ area⟩
sen·so·ri·um \sen'sōrēəm\ *n, pl* **sensoriums** \-ēəmz\ *or* **senso·ria** \-ēə\ [LL, seat or organ of sensation, fr. L *sensus* (past part. of *sentire* to feel, perceive) + *-orium* — more at SENSE] **1 a** *obs* : the brain or a part of the brain regarded as the seat of the mind **b** : BRAIN, MIND — not used technically **2** : the parts of the brain that are concerned with the reception and interpretation of sensory stimuli; *broadly* : the sensory apparatus including receptors, nerves, and central components **3** : a percipient apparatus ⟨existed . . . only as a mechanical ~ and active apparatus —George Santayana⟩ ⟨a social ~ which would serve as the equivalent of the central nervous system —Louis Wirth⟩
¹**sen·so·ry** \'sen(t)s(ə)rē, -ri\ *n* -ES [LL *sensorium*] **1** *obs* : SENSE ORGAN **2** *archaic* : SENSORIUM
²**sensory** \"\ *adj* [L *sensus* (past part. of *sentire* to feel, perceive) + E *-ory* — more at SENSE] **1** : of or relating to sensation or to the senses ⟨~ psychology⟩ ⟨~ data⟩ **2** : conveying nerve impulses from the sense organs to the nerve centers : AFFERENT ⟨~ nerve fibers⟩
sensory aphasia *n* [²*sensory*] : inability to understand spoken, written, or tactile speech symbols that results from a brain lesion
sensory area *n* **1** : an area of the cerebral cortex that receives afferent projection fibers **2** : DERMATOME 2b
sensory cell *n* **1** : a peripheral nerve cell (as an olfactory cell) located at a sensory receiving surface and being the primary receptor of a sensory impulse **2** : a cell of the cerebrospinal nervous system (as a spinal ganglion cell) transmitting sensory impulses
sensory hair *n* : a hair in an arthropod connected basally with a nerve, extending outward through the cuticle, and held to be a receptor of tactile sensation
sensory organ *var of* SENSE ORGAN
sen·su \'sen(,)sü\ *prep* [NL, fr. L, abl. of *sensus* sense] : in the sense of : as understood or defined by — used esp. in technical taxonomic references ⟨*Cortinarius claricolor* ~ Ricken⟩
sen·su·al \'sench(ə)wəl\ *adj* [ME, fr. LL *sensualis*, fr. L *sensus* sense + *-alis* -al] **1** : of, relating to, or affecting the sense organs or senses : perceptible or perceived through the sensory apparatus : SENSORY ⟨~ objects⟩ ⟨~ perception⟩ **2** : relating to or consisting in the gratification of the senses or the indulgence of appetite : CARNAL, FLESHLY **3 a** : devoted to or preoccupied with the senses or appetites ⟨a ~ enjoyment of bodily strength⟩ ⟨the ~ content of a pampered cat⟩ **b** : involving or oriented to the voluptuous or lewd ⟨~ excesses⟩ ⟨a very ~ man⟩ **c** : deficient in moral, spiritual, or intellectual interests : WORLDLY; *esp* : IRRELIGIOUS **4** : MATERIALISTIC ⟨a ~ doctrine⟩ ⟨~ approaches to a problem⟩ **5** : relating to the doctrine of sensationalism **6** : indicative of or affected by sensuality ⟨a ~ age⟩ ⟨~ faces⟩ **syn** see CARNAL, SENSUOUS
sen·su·al·ism \-ə,lizəm\ *n* -s [*sensual* + *-ism*] **1 a** : SENSATIONALISM, SENSISM **b** : stress on the sensuous qualities of an object or on the sensuous as the chief element of beauty as distinguished from ideal and formal qualities and elements **c** : the view in ethics that gratification of the senses is the highest good **2** : preoccupation with sensual matters : persistent or excessive pursuit of sensual pleasures and interests
sen·su·al·ist \-ləst\ *n* -s [*sensual* + *-ist*] : a practicer or adherent of some form of sensualism
sen·su·al·is·tic \¦==¦listik, -tēk\ *adj* [*sensualist* + *-ic*] : relating to or characterized by sensualism
sen·su·al·i·ty \,senchə'waləd·ē, -lətē, -i\ *n* -ES [ME *sensualite*, fr. MF *sensualité*, fr. LL *sensualitat-, sensualitas* capacity for sensation, fr. *sensualis* sensual + L *-itat-, -itas* -ity] **1 a** : the purely animal or physical part of human nature **b** *obs* : the lusts of the flesh **2** : the quality or state of being sensual : devotedness to the gratification of the bodily appetites : free indulgence in carnal or sensual pleasures
sen·su·al·iza·tion \,senchəwələ'zāshən, -ə,lī'z-\ *n* -s : the act of sensualizing or state of being sensualized
sen·su·al·ize \'senchəwə,līz\ *vt* -ED/-ING/-S [*sensual* + *-ize*] : to make sensual: as **a** : to subject to the love of sensual pleasure : debase by carnal gratifications **b** : to represent materialistically **c** : to ascribe to an origin in sensation
sen·su·al·ly \'senchəwəlē, -li\ *adv* : in a sensual manner : so as to be sensual
sen·su·al·ness *n* -ES : the quality or state of being sensual
sensu la·to \-'läd·(,)ō\ *adv* [NL] : in a broad sense — used esp. with names of taxa to indicate that the name is used more inclusively than sanctioned by current practice ⟨*Pyrus sensu lato* includes pear, apple, quince, mountain ash and related forms⟩; compare SENSU STRICTO
sen·sum \'sen(t)səm\ *n, pl* **sen·sa** \-sə\ [NL, fr. L, neut. of *sensus*, past part. of *sentire* to feel, perceive — more at SENSE] : an object of sense or content of sense perception : SENSE-DATUM
sensum theory *n* : a theory in philosophy: sensa are real entities intermediate between the content of perception as such and the ultimate physical reality
sen·su·os·i·ty \,senchə'wäsəd·ē, -sətē, -i\ *n* -ES [fr. *sensuous*, after such pairs as E *pompous: pomposity*] : SENSUOUSNESS
sen·su·ous \'senchəwəs\ *adj* [L *sensus* + E *-ous*] **1** : of or relating to the senses or sensible objects : addressing the senses : suggesting pictures or images of sense ⟨to this poetry would be made precedent, as being less subtle and fine, but more simple, ~, and passionate —John Milton⟩ **2** : characterized by sense impressions or imagery addressing the senses ⟨~ description⟩ ⟨a purely ~ satisfaction⟩ **3** : producing an agreeable effect on the senses : conducive to physical comfort or content ⟨mild ~ breezes⟩ **4** : highly susceptible to influence through the senses
syn SENSUOUS, SENSUAL, LUXURIOUS, VOLUPTUOUS, SYBARITIC, and EPICUREAN can mean, in common, having to do with or providing gratification of the senses. SENSUOUS and SENSUAL, though interchangeable in applying to things of the senses as opposed to spirit or intellect, are often used to carry a distinction: SENSUAL in such case usu. implies gratification in the sense of indulgence of appetite ⟨acute sensitivity to the *sensual* and intellectual pleasures that make life so abundantly worth living —Anthony West⟩ ⟨the richer tobacco enthusiasts want not merely the *sensual* pleasure their pipe brings —*Irish Digest*⟩ ⟨a *sensual* person given to lying on soft couches and overeating⟩ SENSUOUS can imply less an indulgence of appetite than an aesthetic gratification or delight as in beauty of color, sound, or artistic form and usu. carries a weaker overtone of carnality than does SENSUAL ⟨some philosophers insist that most of the arts are *sensuous* and hence that beauty is *sensuous*, but W. T. Stace maintains that . . . beauty must be admitted to display itself in internal percepts —D.H.Rankin⟩ ⟨a *sensuous* love of food and drink and gaiety —William Soskin⟩ ⟨the cat . . . lolling before the fire, stretched in a paroxysm of *sensuous* happiness upon the hearth rug —F.A.Swinnerton⟩ ⟨poetry took on a new and bizarre intricacy of *sensuous* decoration and symbolic metaphor —Douglas Bush⟩ ⟨he eyed the fresh linen laid upon a yellow-painted chair with *sensuous* delight —Elinor Wylie⟩ LUXURIOUS implies indulgence in or provision of either sensual or sensuous pleasures esp. of a kind inducing a pleasant languor, a delightful ease esp. of body, or a grateful peace of mind ⟨in her *luxurious* bed, beneath the satin coverlet, which was scented with lavender —Ellen Glasgow⟩ ⟨sat down to a long, *luxurious* smoke —Rudyard Kipling⟩ ⟨turned his head upon the high cushioned back of his chair and closed his eyes for one *luxurious* instant —Elinor Wylie⟩ VOLUPTUOUS implies a stronger abandonment to sense pleasure esp. for its own sake than does LUXURIOUS ⟨the core of [his] genius is *voluptuous*, surcharged with indolence and passion —Cyril Connolly⟩ ⟨a sullen *voluptuous* mouth —Edmund Wilson⟩ ⟨Cleopatra — fierce, *voluptuous*, passionate, tender, wicked, terrible, and full of poisonous and rapturous enchantment —Nathaniel Hawthorne⟩ SYBARITIC implies luxuriousness and voluptuousness of an extreme, often overrefined sort and esp. indulgence in rare and choice foods and in surroundings calculated to provide a maximum of bodily gratification ⟨a life of pleasure, folly, misfortune, vice, and *sybaritic* elegance —Philip Sherrard⟩ ⟨imagining the feel of the long silky fleece against bare toes makes one shiver with *sybaritic* pleasure —*New Yorker*⟩ ⟨a *sybaritic* banquet of seven courses, each with its own wine or liqueur⟩ EPICUREAN in this context can commonly imply sensuality or voluptuousness or, when nearer to an original sense, a sensuous, often fastidious delight in refined physical pleasures, often of eating or drinking but sometimes in intellectual pleasures ⟨out-of-season delicacies, wines of rare vintage, *epicurean* specialties of a ten-thousand-dollar-a-year chef —J.J.Floherty⟩ ⟨drinking his tea with *epicurean* satisfaction —J.C.Powys⟩
sen·su·ous·ly *adv* : in a sensuous manner : so as to be sensuous ⟨loved ~ the feel of the silk clothes she pressed and folded —Attia S. Hosain⟩
sen·su·ous·ness *n* -ES : the quality or state of being sensuous
sen·sus com·mu·nis \¦sen(t)səskə'myünə̇s\ *n* [L] : a sense held to unite the sensations of all senses in a general sensation or perception
sensu stric·to \-'strik,tō\ *adv* [NL] : in a narrow sense — used esp. with names of taxa to indicate that the name is used in a restricted manner ⟨*Pyrus sensu stricto* includes only the pears⟩; compare SENSU LATO
¹**sent** *past of* SEND
²**sent** \'sent\ *n, pl* **sen·ti** \-(,)tē\ *or* **sents** [Estonian *senti*, prob. fr. Finn *sentti*, fr. L *centum* hundred — more at HUNDRED] **1** : a unit of monetary value in Estonia from 1928–40 equal to ¹⁄₁₀₀ kroon **2** : a coin representing one sent
sent *abbr* sentence
sen't *var of* SENIT
sentd *abbr* sentenced
¹**sen·tence** \'sentᵊn(t)s, -tən-, -nz\ *n* -s *often attrib* [ME, fr. OF, fr. L *sententia* feeling, opinion, expression of opinion, judgment, maxim, fr. (assumed) *sentent-, sentens* (irreg. pres. part. of *sentire* to feel) + *-ia* -y — more at SENSE] **1 a** *obs* : a stated opinion, decision, or judgment; *esp* : a conclusion given on request or reached after deliberation ⟨such applause was heard as Mammon ended, and his ~ pleased, advising peace —John Milton⟩ **b** : a decision or judicial determination of a court or tribunal : DECREE: as (1) : the judgment of a court pronounced in a cause in civil and admiralty law (2) : the judgment passed by a court or judge on a person on trial as a criminal or offender (3) : the order by which a court or judge imposes punishment or penalty upon a person found guilty; *esp* : the punishment or penalty so imposed ⟨the ~ was 10 years and a large fine⟩ **2** : a brief spoken or written passage: as **a** : a short or pithy saying usu. conveying moral instruction : AXIOM, MAXIM, SAW **b** *usu cap* : one of the verses of Scripture with which morning and evening prayers and the burial service commence in churches of the Anglican communion **3** : a grammatically self-contained unit consisting of a word or a syntactically related group of words that expresses an assertion, a question, a command, a wish, or an exclamation, that in writing usu. begins with a capital letter and concludes with appropriate end punctuation, and that in speech is phonetically distinguished by various patterns of stress, pitch, and pauses — compare MINOR SENTENCE, PREDICATION **4** : a complete musical idea usu. consisting of two phrases : PERIOD **5** : a declarative sentence or statement in logic : PROPOSITION
²**sentence** \"\ *vb* -ED/-ING/-S [ME *sentencen*, fr. MF *sentencier*, fr. LL *sententiare*, fr. L *sententia* sentence] *vt* **1** *obs* : to decree, decide, or announce judicially **2 a** : to pronounce sentence on : to condemn to penalty or punishment ⟨the defendant was *sentenced* at the conclusion of the trial⟩ **b** : to prescribe the penalty or punishment of : DOOM — usu. used with *to* ⟨was tried on the charge of inciting to riot and *sentenced* to thirty days in jail —E.S.Bates⟩ **3** : to judge the merits of (as a person or thing) ⟨let us not ~ the play before seeing it⟩ **4** : to cause to suffer or undergo something : DESTINE ⟨elopement *sentenced* her to exile —Ann F. Wolfe⟩ ⟨forces would be *sentenced* to an indefinite and costly stalemate —*Time*⟩ ⟨set down his reactions to the quiet desperation of life they are *sentenced* to endure —W.F.Albright⟩ ~ *vi* **1** *obs* : to give judgment **2** : to pronounce sentence ⟨the judges assemble for *sentencing*⟩
sentence adverb *n* : an adverb that qualifies a sentence as a whole (as *surely* in "surely goodness and mercy shall follow me all the days of my life")
sentence fragment *n* : a word, phrase, or clause usu. having in speech the intonation characteristic of a sentence but lacking the grammatical completeness and independence of a full sentence
sentence sense *n* : the ability to recognize a group of words that forms a written complete sentence as distinguished from a minor sentence or adjacent sentences
sentence stress *also* **sentence accent** *n* : the manner in which stresses are distributed on the syllables of words assembled into sentences — called also *sense stress;* compare WORD STRESS
sen·ten·tia \sen'tenchēə\ *n, pl* **sententi·ae** \-ē,ē\ [L — more at SENTENCE] : an aphorism, maxim, or brief comment on life or living — usu. used in pl. ⟨in 1895 the following *sententiae* on daily life were worth setting forth: . . . never allow yourself to be hurried; do not drink with your mouth full —E.V.Lucas⟩
sen·ten·tial \(')sen¦tenchəl\ *adj* [ME, fr. LL *sententialis*, fr. L *sententia* opinion, judgment, maxim + *-alis* -al] **1** : containing or made up of sentences or maxims ⟨a ~ book⟩ ⟨a collection of ~ sayings⟩ **2** *obs* : of the nature of a judicial sentence **3 a** : of or relating to a sentence or a syntactical sequence ⟨and the sense of the poem as a whole, and of the ~ parts of it —V.C.Aldrich⟩ **b** : PROPOSITIONAL
sentential calculus *n* [trans. of G *satzkalkül*] : PROPOSITIONAL CALCULUS
sentential connective *n* : CONNECTIVE d
sentential function *n* : an expression that contains one or more free variables and becomes a declarative sentence when constants are substituted for the variables (as in *x is green*, *x is taller than y*) — compare PROPOSITION 3a
sen·ten·tial·ly \-əlē, -li\ *adv* [ME, fr. *sentential* + *-ly*] : in a sentential manner
sentential variable *n* : a variable that may be replaced by a declarative sentence
sen·ten·tiary \sen'tenchē,erē\ *n* -ES [ML *sententiarius* theological candidate studying the *Sentences* of Peter Lombard 12th cent. theologian, fr. L *sententiae* sentences] : APHORIST
sen·ten·tious \(')sen¦tenchəs\ *adj* [ME, fr. L *sententiosus*, fr. *sententia* opinion, maxim + *-osus* -ous — more at SENTENCE] **1** *obs* : full of meaning or wisdom ⟨your reasons at dinner have been sharp and ~ —Shak.⟩ **2 a** : terse, aphoristic, or moralistic in expression : PITHY, EPIGRAMMATIC ⟨"contentment breeds happiness" . . . is a proposition with which you can hardly quarrel; ~, sedate, obviously true —A.T.Quiller-Couch⟩ ⟨that ~ brevity which, using not a word to spare, leaves not a moment for inattention —Adrienne Koch⟩ ⟨to push home her ideas on social injustice by ~ precept —Leslie Rees⟩ **b** (1) : given to or abounding in aphoristic expression ⟨"young people often feel they're caged," I said . . . with a

feeling that I was being ~ —Edmund Wilson〉 〈the ~ expression of the middle period of a life that came to late maturity —V.L.Parrington〉 〈there is the type magisterial or imperative; the type laconic or ~ —B.N.Cardozo〉 (2) **:** given to or abounding in excessive moralizing 〈they were verbose, ~, circumlocutious, and grandiloquent —Harold Rosen & H.E. Kiene〉 〈too often the significant episode deteriorates into ~ conversation —Kathleen Barnes〉 **syn** see EXPRESSIVE

sen·ten·tious·ly *adv* **:** in a sententious manner

sen·ten·tious·ness *n* -ES **:** the quality or state of being sententious

senti *pl of* SENT

sen·tience \ˈsench(ē)ən(t)s\ *also* **sen·tien·cy** \-ənsē, -si\ *n*, *pl* **sentiences** *also* **sentiencies** [*sentience* fr. ¹*sentient*, after such pairs as E *intelligent: intelligence; sentiency* fr. ¹*sentient* + *-cy*] **1 :** the readiness to receive sensation, idea, or image **:** unstructured available consciousness 〈then I shall see light . . . and I shall hear the notes of birds; and this ~, this negation of death, will be in itself for me an Easter sermon —Harry Lang〉 **2 :** a state of elementary or undifferentiated consciousness **:** feeling as contrasted with sensation, perception, or ideation 〈gave ~ to slugs and newts —Richard Eberhart〉

sen·ti·en·dum \ˌsentēˈendəm, ˌsenchē-\ *n*, *pl* **sentien·da** \-də\ [NL, fr. L, neut. of *sentiendus*, gerundive of *sentire*] **:** SENSE-DATUM

¹**sen·tient** \ˈsench(ē)ənt\ *adj* [L *sentient-, sentiens*, pres. part. of *sentire* to feel, perceive — more at SENSE] **1 :** capable of sensation and of at least rudimentary consciousness 〈a ~ being〉 〈the conception . . . of impulsive, instinctive, and ~ life —Susanne K. Langer〉 〈these highly ~, motile, instinctive, and often intelligent creatures —D.C.Peattie〉 **2 a :** consciously perceiving **:** AWARE — used with *of* 〈he alone is ~ of the intolerable load —Elinor Wylie〉 〈a boy so ~ of his surroundings —W.A.White〉 **b :** conscious or capable of fine distinctions or perceptions **:** SENSITIVE 〈at its best democracy breeds the ~ person —Elizabeth Bowen〉 〈the problems which confront us all as ~ responsible beings —Randall Stewart〉 **3 :** capable of receiving and reacting to sensory stimuli 〈the ~ cells of the brain〉 **4 :** marked by the stimulation or exercise of the senses or of conscious perception 〈the highly ~ quality in the experiences —G.A.Woods〉 〈her . . . conviction of the tragedy of the ~ life —Hudson Strode〉

²**sentient** \"\ *n* -S **:** a sentient being; *also* **:** the conscious mind

sen·tient·ly *adv* **:** with feeling, consciousness, or perception 〈had ~ been an artist —Janet Flanner〉

sen·ti·ment \ˈsentəmənt\ *n* -S [F or ML; F *sentiment* fr. ML *sentimentum*, fr. L *sentire* to feel, perceive + *-mentum* -ment — more at SENSE] **1 a :** an attitude, thought, or judgment permeated or prompted by feeling **:** a complex of emotion and idea **:** PREDILECTION 〈rising ~ for broadening the tax base —*N. Y. Times*〉 〈public ~ for good roads greatly increased —*Amer. Guide Series: N. C.*〉 〈his own antislavery ~*s* were sincere —Helen C. Boatfield〉 **b :** a specific view or notion **:** OPINION 〈am obliged to differ from nearly every ~ expressed —Gilbert Parker〉 〈share their ~*s* . . . on school problems —Julius May〉 **2 a :** FEELING, EMOTION 〈generated within him a ~ of good will and cooperation —A.L.Funk〉 〈stimulating to the ~*s* and occasionally interesting to the mind —Virgil Thomson〉 **b :** refined feeling **:** keen or delicate sensibility esp. as expressed in a work of art or evinced in conduct 〈a strong, frank, and positive character, of keen wit and generous ~ —E.V.Wilcox〉 〈poems of ~ and reflection —Matthew Arnold〉 〈an almost religious ~ of the dignity of art —Meyer Schapiro〉 **c :** emotional idealism 〈community life in those days was a requisite of survival rather than a matter of ~ —Dana Burnet〉 〈making ~ a substitute for action〉 **d :** a romantic or nostalgic feeling verging on sentimentality 〈still keeps a bartender to preside over its ornate old bar, mostly for ~*'s* sake —Green Peyton〉 〈so much slush and ~ —Jack London〉 〈just the difference between passion and silly ~ —A.T.Quiller-Couch〉 **3 a :** an emotional idea as set forth in literature or art 〈the book expresses the noblest ~*s*〉 **b :** the emotional significance of a passage or expression as distinguished from its verbal context 〈a diplomatic statement is a statement about which everything is true except the ~ which prompts it —Joseph Conrad〉 〈to my thinking the ~*s* of the pledge, properly interpreted, are unexceptionable —W.T. Hastings〉 **c :** an emotionally tinged thought or wish expressed as a maxim, axiom, or epigram 〈cards . . . with appropriate verses and ~*s* —*Bks. of Jewish Interest*〉 〈I'll give you a ~; here's *Success to usury* —R.B.Sheridan〉 **syn** see FEELING, OPINION

¹**sen·ti·men·tal** \ˌsentəˈmentᵊl\ *adj* **1 a :** of, relating to, or characterized by sentiment 〈a scientific as opposed to a ~ appraisal of the situation —*Times Lit. Supp.*〉; *esp* **:** marked or governed by feeling, sensibility, or emotional idealism 〈his sincerely ~ love for children —Sir Winston Churchill〉 〈was profoundly ~; his warm, expansive heart yearned for sympathy —G.S.Haight〉 〈in his earlier days was a ~ liberal —J.T.Farrell〉 **b :** expressive of sentiment or feelings **:** addressed or appealing to the emotions **:** stimulating an emotional response 〈the ~ or sensuous appeal of an art —André Malraux〉 〈was a ~ comedy of love in the modern equivalent of a cottage —*Current Biog.*〉 **c :** resulting from or motivated chiefly by feeling rather than reason or thought 〈many of our old notions . . . are more ~ than accurate —W.H. Whyte〉 〈working-class unity, both for ~ and realistic reasons, has remained an obsession —J.G.Colton〉 **2 a :** having an excess of sentiment or sensibility **:** indulging in feeling to an unwarranted extent **:** affectedly or mawkishly emotional 〈are incurably ~, and take immoderate pleasure in the contemplation of domestic bliss —Eric Linklater〉 〈pity without values is as ~ as if applied to insects —*Accent*〉 〈an age in which the most natural feeling of tenderness, happiness, or sorrow was likely to be called ~ —Randall Jarrell〉 **b :** expressing or stimulating an excessive, affected, or unwarranted emotional indulgence 〈much that is hackneyed, shoddy, and falsely ~ is foisted upon the public under the guise of the Biblical novel —Edmund Fuller〉 〈rant and bombast and ~ cant of politics —Florence Converse〉 〈works of art which have ~ subjects (partings, deaths, waiting for a lover's return, children . . . praying or crying over a hurt pet) —Hunter Mead〉

syn SENTIMENTAL, ROMANTIC, MAWKISH, MAUDLIN, SOPPY, MUSHY, and SLUSHY can mean unduly or affectedly emotional. SENTIMENTAL can apply to anyone strongly and esp. unduly, habitually, or promiscuously affected by the softer, pleasanter, more feminine emotions, or it can apply to anything marked by such an affection, but usu. it suggests a lack of complete genuineness or naturalness, implying that the emotion arises from a factitious situation or out of hyperesthesia, or is purposely evoked for the thrill, as an affectation, or for a given even though often obscure purpose 〈a *sentimental* mother cherishing every memento of the babyhood of her children〉 〈whisky made him somewhat *sentimental* —Sherwood Anderson〉 〈*sentimental* popular songs〉 〈the advertising agent . . . must wax as *sentimental* over one man's soap as over another's laxative —Roger Burlingame〉 〈theological discussion of any kind, as distinct from a loosely *sentimental* religiosity —C.A. Lejeune〉 〈*sentimental* and cheap novels —J.T.Farrell〉 〈compassionate without being *sentimental* —Gertrude Buckman〉 ROMANTIC implies emotion that derives from things not so much as they actually or generally are but as they may be or are imaginatively or ideally conceived, as in literature, drama, or one's waking dreams 〈a *romantic* story of love and adventure in the South Seas〉 〈I am filled with a sense of the French *romantic* spirit. It soars, it expands, it engulfs you with a sweet kind of poetry that is charming, but very unreal —Irving Kolodin〉 〈his idealism — reflected in his *romantic* love of country, hatred of materialism, and concept of the general interest —A.S.Link〉 〈a *romantic* young lady waiting for her Prince Charming to come along〉 MAWKISH suggests a sickening sentimentality marked by gross insincerity or objectionable emotional excess 〈stories simpering with delight and *mawkish* with pathos —J.D.Hart〉 〈his mixture of harshness and *mawkish* sentimentality —Peter Quennell〉 〈murder was punished without *mawkish* concern or delay —C.M.Webster〉 MAUDLIN suggests an excess of emotion or feeling marked by an unwarranted weeping or an inappropriately gushing expression of love, or the like 〈silly *maudlin* ballads of the suicide of young lovers〉 〈the death of a famous actress is the signal, as a rule, for a great deal of *maudlin* excitement —Ben Hecht〉 SOPPY, MUSHY, and SLUSHY are all informal equivalents of MAWKISH, SOPPY, chiefly Brit., often carrying the suggestion of silliness 〈a novel . . . *soppy* with manufactured emotionalism —John Cournos〉 〈a naturally sad but never *soppy* poet —G.S. Fraser〉, MUSHY suggesting a driveling sentimentality 〈the language is *mushy* with sentiment and turgid with rhetoric —C.J.Rolo〉 〈he croons with *mushy* sentimentality over his heroes —Anthony West〉 〈writing *mushy* letters to women admirers —Stanley Walker〉, and SLUSHY applying chiefly to utterances and like MUSHY, suggesting a sentimental or emotional drivel esp. about love 〈*slushy* letters from an adolescent admirer〉 〈*slushy* and woebegone songs〉

²**sentimental** \"\ *n* -S **:** a sentimental person

sentimental comedy *n* **:** comedy that addresses itself to the spectator's love of goodness rather than to his sense of humor and emphasizes the moral aspects of its situations and the virtues of its characters

sen·ti·men·tal·ism \ˌ==ˈ=tᵊlˌizəm\ *n* -S [¹*sentimental* + *-ism*] **1 a :** the quality or state of being sentimental **:** the disposition to favor or indulge in sentiment 〈there was . . . a normal adolescent ~, but none of the turbulence, the storm and stress —H.S.Commager〉 〈rise above the level of gushy ~ —John Dewey〉 〈~ in 19th century art arose . . . largely from the belief that art was a moral agent —Bernard Smith〉 **b :** ROMANTICISM 〈degenerated into a superficial ~, dominated by wishes which were taken for facts —*Time*〉 〈scientific writing that is not accurate . . . can become a kind of sloppy ~ —C.E. Kellogg〉 〈his doctrine was a ~ which tended to present all human instincts as naturally good —L.J.A.Mercier〉 〈the ~ of making our own paltry woes glorious in their bitterness —W.L.Sullivan〉 **2 :** a conception or statement marked by or expressive of sentimentality 〈in this program he was handicapped by various ~*s* —Carl Van Doren〉

sen·ti·men·tal·ist \-tᵊləst\ *n* -S [¹*sentimental* + *-ist*] **:** one disposed to indulge in sensibility or sentimentality **:** ROMANTICIST 〈was essentially a ~ with feelings close to the surface and stirred by the lightest touch —G.S.Haight〉 〈the ~, who lives by illusions, is let down more gently in English fiction than in French —Harry Levin〉 〈the nerveless ~ and dreamer, who spends his life in a weltering sea of sensibility and emotion —William James〉

sen·ti·men·tal·i·ty \ˌ==ˌmenˈtaləd·ē, -ˌmən-ˈ-, -lətē, -i\ *n* -ES [¹*sentimental* + *-ity*] **1 :** the quality or state of being sentimental esp. to excess or in affectation 〈what was respected as honest sentiment is branded as ~, and mocked at, when the emotion which sustained it no longer exists —John Mason Brown〉 〈the indulgence in sentiment that sometimes passes into ~ —N.F.Adkins〉 〈the same objectivity, ruthlessness, and lack of any ~ —Harrison Smith〉 〈culminated in the vapid ~ of a good deal of English romanticism and its steadily more mawkish offshoots —Joseph Frank〉 **2 :** a sentimental idea or its expression 〈is a regular American with *sentimentalities* that are supposed to be sentiments —J.T.Farrell〉

sen·ti·men·tal·iza·tion \ˌ==ˌmentᵊləˈzāshən, -tᵊlˌīˈz-\ *n* -S **:** the act or process of sentimentalizing **:** the state of being sentimentalized

sen·ti·men·tal·ize \ˌ==ˈmentᵊlˌīz\ *vb* -ED/-ING/-S [¹*sentimental* + *-ize*] *vi* **:** to indulge in sentiment **:** ROMANTICIZE 〈it's a waste of breath to go back over the past and ~ —Agatha Christie〉 〈analyzed lust in its crudest form . . . and grieved without *sentimentalizing* over it —Monica Stirling〉 ~ *vt* **:** to look upon or imbue (as a person or thing) with sentiment **:** ROMANTICIZE 〈denounced as a *sentimentalized* Christianity that religious attitude which prefers slavery to war —*Current Biog.*〉 〈the mistake of *sentimentalizing* the politician as a poor abused fellow —John Lodge〉 〈the most insidious vices are those that began as virtues, and have been *sentimentalized* long after they became ugly —Katharine F. Gerould〉

sen·ti·men·tal·ly \ˌsentəˈmentᵊlē, -li\ *adv* **:** in a sentimental manner **:** with sentiment or sentimentality

sen·ti·ment·less \ˈ===ləs\ *adj* **:** that is without sentiment

sentiments *pl of* SENTIMENT

¹**sen·ti·nel** \ˈsent(ᵊ)nᵊl, -tənᵊl\ *n* -S [MF *sentinelle*, fr. OIt *sentinella*, fr. *sentina* vigilance, fr. *sentire* to perceive, fr. L — more at SENSE] **1 :** one that watches or guards **:** SENTRY **2 a** *obs* **:** WATCH, GUARD 〈keep ~〉 **b** *obs* **:** WATCHTOWER **c :** SOLDIER **3 :** an officer of a secret society who is stationed outside the door of a meeting place to prevent unauthorized entry — compare WARDER

²**sentinel** \"\ *vt* **sentineled** *or* **sentinelled; sentineled** *or* **sentinelled; sentineling** *or* **sentinelling; sentinels 1 :** to watch over as a sentinel 〈long lines of shivering poplars that *sentinelled* the meadows —Willa Cather〉 **2 :** to furnish with a sentinel **:** place under the guard of a sentinel or sentinels **3 :** to post as sentinel

sentinel crab *n* **:** a crab (*Podophthalmus vigil*) of the Indian ocean with very long eyestalks

¹**sen·try** \ˈsen·trē, -ri\ *n* -ES [alter. of ME *seintuarie* — more at SANCTUARY] *archaic* **:** SANCTUARY

²**sentry** \"\ *n* -ES [perh. fr. ¹*sentry*] **1** *obs* **:** SENTINEL 2b **2 :** a soldier standing guard (as at a passing point) **3 :** one that guards as a sentry 〈rooks . . . always left a ~ posted on a tree —Adrian Bell〉 **4 :** KITE 7a

³**sentry** \"\ *vb* -ED/-ING/-ES *vt* **:** to guard as a sentry 〈its marble entrance hall sandbagged and *sentried* —R.M.Ingersoll〉 ~ *vi* **:** to stand guard **:** act as a sentry 〈herons had begun ~*ing* up and down, stalking minnows —Edwin Granberry〉

sentry board *n* [²*sentry*] **1 :** a platform for a sentry outside the gangway **2 :** a board hung near a sentry post for posting instructions and orders

sentry box *n* **:** a hut or box to shelter a sentry on his post

sentry go *n* [fr. the phrase *sentry, go*] **1 :** a call for the changing of the guard **2 :** duty as a sentry

sents *pl of* SENT

se·nu·fo \səˈnü(ˌ)fō\ *n*, *pl* **senufo** *or* **senufos** *usu cap* **1 a :** a people of the interior of the Ivory Coast Republic and the Republic of Mali widely known for their wood carving and masks **b :** a member of such people **2 :** a Gur language or the Gur languages of the Senufo people

senussi *usu cap, var of* SANUSI

sen·vy \ˈsenvē\ *n* -ES [ME *senevey, senvey*, fr. MF *senevé*, fr. L *sinapi, sinapis* — more at SINAPIS] **1 :** the mustard plant **2 :** MUSTARD SEED

sen·za rep·li·ca \ˌsentsəˈrepləkə, ˌsenzə-\ *adv* [It, lit., without repetition] **:** without the (normally indicated) repeat — used as a direction in music

seoul \ˈsōl *sometimes* ˈsül *or* ˈsəül *or* seˈül\ *adj, usu cap* [fr. *Seoul*, So. Korea] **:** of or from Seoul, the capital of So. Korea **:** of the kind or style prevalent in Seoul

sep *abbr* **1** sepal **2** separate; separated

sepal \ˈsēpəl *also* ˈsep-\ *n* -S [NL *sepalum*, fr. *sepa* (modif. of Gk *skepas, skepē* covering) + *-lum* (as in *petalum*); akin to Lith *kepùrė* head covering] **:** one of the modified leaves comprising a calyx — compare PETAL; see CARPEL illustration

sepaled *also* **sepalled** \-ld\ *adj* [NL *sepalum* + E *-ed*] **:** having sepals

sepal·ine \ˈsepəˌlīn, ˈsēp-, -ˌlən\ *adj* [NL *sepalinus*, fr. *sepalum* sepal + L *-inus* -ine] **:** SEPALOID

sepa·lo·dy \ˈsepəˌlōdē, ˈsēp-\ *n* -ES [ISV *sepal* + *-ody*] **:** metamorphosis of other floral organs into sepals

sepal·oid \-ˌlȯid\ *adj* [NL *sepaloideus*, fr. *sepalum* + *-oideus* (fr. L *-oides* -oid + *-eus* -eous)] **:** resembling or having the nature of a sepal

-sep·al·ous \ˈsepələs\ *adj comb form* [*sepal* + *-ous*] **:** having sepals 〈gamo*sepalous*〉 〈tetra*sepalous*〉

sep·a·ra·bil·i·ty \ˌsep(ə)rəˈbiləd·ē, -lətē, -i\ *n* [ML *separabilitas*, fr. L *separabilis* separable + *-itas* -ity] **:** the quality or state of being separable 〈~ of the nuclear motion from the electronic motion in molecules —L.M.Branscomb〉 〈consider . . . the ~ of the provision from the remainder of the statute —R.W.Ginnane〉

separability clause *n* **:** a clause often included in a legal document (as a contract) stating that invalidation of some sections or clauses in the document will not affect the validity of the remainder

sep·a·ra·ble \ˈsep(ə)rəbəl\ *adj* [ME *seperable*, fr. L *separabilis*, fr. *separare* to separate + *-abilis* -able] **1 :** capable of being separated or dissociated **:** DISTINGUISHABLE, SEVERABLE **2** *obs* **:** causing separation 〈a ~ spite . . . doth steal sweet hours from love's delight —Shak.〉 — **sep·a·ra·bly** \-blē, -bli\ *adv*

separable attachment plug *n* **:** an attachment plug having a removable cap

sep·a·ra·ble·ness *n* -ES **:** SEPARABILITY

separata *pl of* SEPARATUM

¹**sep·a·rate** \ˈsepəˌrāt *also* -eˌprāt; *usu* -ād+V\ *vb* -ED/-ING/-S [ME *separaten*, fr. L *separatus*, past part. of *separare*, fr. *sed-, se-* apart (fr. *sed, se* without) + *parare* to prepare, procure — more at IDIOT, PARE] *vt* **1 a :** to set or keep apart **:** DETACH 〈two longitudinal valleys ~ the mountains into three high ranges —Samuel Van Valkenburg & Ellsworth Huntington〉 〈a pull on the tab . . . ~*s* seal just below cap —*Modern Packaging*〉 〈~ the white from the yolk of an egg〉 **b :** to make a distinction between **:** DISCRIMINATE, DISTINGUISH 〈how difficult it is to ~ religion from magic in the beliefs . . . of savages —W.R.Inge〉 〈there is usually not much difficulty in ~ a butterfly from a moth —A.D.Imms〉 **c :** SORT 〈~ mail〉 〈~ cards into suits〉 〈parcels fly . . . as clerks ~ them by regions and states —A.C.Fisher〉 **d :** to disperse in space or time **:** SCATTER 〈theaters in Canada are so widely *separated* that the costs of travelling are prohibitive —*Report: (Canadian) Royal Commission on Nat'l Development*〉 **e** *slang* **:** to cause to divest oneself **:** STRIP — used with *from* 〈tricks for *separating* country bumpkins from their bankrolls〉 〈~ them from . . . money to back ventures that never were produced —E.D.Radin〉 **2** *archaic* **:** to set aside for a special purpose **:** CHOOSE, DEDICATE 〈came into existence with the sense of being a "*separated*" nation, which God was using to make a new beginning for mankind —Reinhold Niebuhr〉 **3 :** to part by or as if by a legal separation **: a :** sever conjugal ties with **:** cause to live apart 〈payments made to a divorced or legally *separated* wife —W.C.Warren&S.S.Surrey〉 **b :** to sever contractual relations with **:** DISCHARGE 〈he was *separated* from the service with the rank of captain —E.J.Kahn〉 〈more than 100 employees have been *separated* from the firm in the past six months〉 〈any student who does not remove his probationary status . . . may be *separated* from the institution —*Bull. of Meharry Med. Coll.*〉 **4 :** to block off **:** BAR, SEGREGATE 〈a . . . rood screen ~*s* the nave from the chancel —*Amer. Guide Series: N. Y.*〉 〈the rural worker . . . is not *separated* from the landed aristocracy by racial difference —P.E.James〉 **5 a :** to isolate from a mixture **:** single out **:** EXTRACT 〈~ cream from milk by putting it through a separator〉 〈~ gold from an alloy〉 — often used with *out* 〈by whatever method the smaller organisms are *separated* out —R.E.Coker〉 〈static episodes . . . *separated* out of a larger and more complex historical situation —M.D. Geismar〉 **b** *archaic* **:** to give off **:** SECRETE 〈glands, which ~ a substance that has the smell of musk —Jedidiah Morse〉 ~ *vi* **1 :** to become divided 〈the airflow over the trailing edge of the flap has begun to ~ —*Skyways*〉 〈the Uralian languages . . . ~ into three branches —W.K.Matthews〉 **2 a :** to sever an association **:** become estranged **:** WITHDRAW 〈Puritans . . . unwilling to ~ from the Established Church —*Amer. Guide Series: Mass.*〉 **b :** to cease to live together as man and wife 〈after two stormy years of married life the couple *separated* by mutual consent〉 **3 :** to go in different directions **:** part company **:** DISPERSE 〈after dinner we *separated*, the women to the library —Lucien Price〉 〈thought the House would like to know, before it *separated* —Sir Winston Churchill〉 **4 :** to become isolated from a mixture 〈oil . . . ~*s* readily from water —B.G.A.Skrotzki & W.A.Vopat〉

syn SEPARATE, PART, DIVIDE, SEVER, SUNDER, and DIVORCE can all mean to become or cause to become disunited or disjoined. SEPARATE implies a putting or keeping apart 〈*separate* the sheep from the goats〉 〈the political boundary *separating* this country from Mexico —R.S.Thoman〉 〈the ten centuries which *separated* the reign of Charlemagne and the reign of Napoleon —T.B.Macaulay〉 or a scattering or dispersion of units 〈the war *separated* many families〉 or a removal of one thing from another 〈*separate* a troublesome boy from a group〉 PART suggests the separation, often complete, of two persons or things in close union or association, or of two parts of one thing 〈the two friends did not *part* until they had reached the station〉 〈a man and wife *parted* only by death〉 〈the cable *parted* under the strain〉 DIVIDE commonly stresses the idea of parts, groups, or sections resulting from cutting, breaking, partitioning, or branching 〈*divide* a cake into two pieces〉 〈the land is *divided* by natural boundaries such as streams〉 〈the auditorium proper *divided* into a pit, one or more galleries —C.F.Wittke〉 It can also be used in the sense of SEPARATE, esp. when mutual antagonism or wide separation is suggested 〈the war *divided* many families〉 〈no religious difference arose to *divide* the old inhabitants from the English —G.M.Trevelyan〉 〈the suspicion which the Citizens' Committee predicted would *divide* neighbor from neighbor —David Clinton〉 SEVER often adds the idea of violence, suggesting forced separation, esp. of part from whole or of persons joined in affection, close association, and so on 〈with one stroke he *severed* the head from the body〉 〈man's ancestors later became *severed* from this separate line of evolution —R.W.Murray〉 〈an immense peninsula slightly *severed* from the main mass —Forrest Morgan〉 〈*severs* relations with a hostile nation〉 〈*severed* friend from friend〉 SUNDER implies a violent rending or wrenching apart 〈the *sundered* atom —M.C.Faught〉 〈the dearest ties of friendship and of blood were *sundered* —T.B. Macaulay〉 DIVORCE, in implying the legal dissolution of a marriage, usu. suggests the separation of things so closely associated that they interact, are often regarded as inseparable, or commonly work, often work best, only in union 〈an institution concerned with general education . . . *divorced* from research and education for the professions is admittedly not a university but a college —J.B.Conant〉 〈form in art *divorced* from matter〉 〈*divorce* the worker's income from any dependence on the efforts he makes —*Time*〉 〈his gaiety was as *divorced* from scorn or cynicism as it was wedded to melancholy —John Mason Brown〉

²**sep·a·rate** \ˈsep(ə)rə|t *sometimes* -pər|t; *usu* |d·+V\ *adj* [L *separatus*, past part. of *separare* to separate] **1 a** *archaic* **:** characterized by segregation from other people **:** SOLITARY, SECLUDED 〈the tendency of prolonged ~ confinement is to affect the mind —*Edinburgh Rev.*〉 〈the plan of my bungalow, with all convenience for being ~ and sulky when I please —Sir Walter Scott〉 **b :** having an incorporeal existence **:** DISEMBODIED, IMMATERIAL 〈being . . . is now seen as the nature which constitutes ~ entity —Alan Gewirth〉 **c :** set or kept apart **:** standing alone **:** DETACHED, ISOLATED 〈the more perfect the artist, the more completely ~ in him will be the man who suffers and the mind which creates —T.S.Eliot〉 〈ceremonial chambers . . . were built as ~ units in the central courtyards —*Amer. Guide Series: Ariz.*〉 **2 a :** not shared with another **:** INDIVIDUAL, SINGLE 〈group consciousness . . . makes the individual think lightly of his own ~ interests —M.R.Cohen〉 〈the world's largest city deserves ~ consideration —L.D. Stamp〉 **b** *often cap* **:** estranged from a parent body 〈there were 90 *Separate* churches, with 6,490 members —F.S.Mead〉 **3 a :** existing by itself **:** AUTONOMOUS, INDEPENDENT 〈the partitioning of India created two ~ jute economies —F.F.George〉 〈reorganization of schools into ~ primary and postprimary units —H.C.Dent〉 **b :** dissimilar in nature or identity **:** DISTINCT, DIFFERENT 〈my most recent works, in their ~ ways, embody this tendency —Aaron Copland〉 〈the full bibliography . . . lists 2204 ~ publications —*Geog. Jour.*〉 〈built-in facilities . . . permit cooking in seven ~ ways without the use of additional utensils —*Report of General Motors Corp.*〉 **syn** see DISTINCT, SINGLE

³**separate** \"\ *n* -S **1** *usu cap* **:** NEW LIGHT a; *esp* **:** SEPARATE BAPTIST **2 :** OFFPRINT 〈sent out ~*s* and reprints of his major monographs —J.C.Burnham〉 **3 :** a group of soil particles of a definite size or grade obtained in separation (as in mechanical analysis) **4 separates** *pl* **:** articles of dress designed to be worn interchangeably with others to form various costume combinations

separate baptist *n, usu cap S&B* **:** a member of a Baptist sect organized in 1662 as the English Puritan Separate Baptist Church and migrating to America in 1695, being congregational in polity, and observing open communion, baptism by immersion, and foot washing

separate but equal *adj* **:** of, relating to, or constituting a doctrine of segregation whereby Negroes and whites have equal facilities (as for education or transportation) ⟨the *separate but equal* doctrine has been directly challenged and the Supreme Court has consented to review three cases involving it —Charles Thompson⟩

separated *past of* SEPARATE

separated aggregate *n* [*separated* fr. past part. of ¹*separate*] **:** aggregate for use in concrete that has been separated by the producer into fine and coarse aggregates

separated milk *n* **:** milk left after extraction of the cream

sep·a·ra·tee \ˌsep(ə)rəˈtē\ *n* -s [¹*separate* + *-ee*] **:** an individual in process of separation from active military service

separate estate *n* **:** an estate the ownership and control of which is enjoyed by a person free from any rights or control of others; *esp* **:** an estate enjoyed by a married woman independent of her husband

separate-loading ammunition \ˈ==(=)=ˌ==-\ *n* **:** ammunition in which the projectile, propelling charge, and primer are loaded separately rather than as a unit

sep·a·rate·ly \ˈsep(ə)rətlē, -pərt-, -li\ *adv* **:** in a separate manner **:** INDIVIDUALLY, INDEPENDENTLY

separately excited *adj* **:** having the field magnets excited by a current from a separate source — used of a machine

separate maintenance *n* **:** an allowance made to a wife by her husband under deed of separation or under a court order or decree

sep·a·rate·ness *n* -ES **1 a :** the quality or state of being isolated **:** DETACHMENT, LONELINESS ⟨writing letters . . . to fellow artists in order to counteract the soul-destroying ~ that he felt had caused the poet's death —*New Republic*⟩ **b :** the quality or state of being exclusive or excluded **:** ALOOFNESS, SEGREGATION ⟨the ~ of classes entrenched . . . by the force of law and custom —Oscar Handlin⟩ ⟨~ which denies each group enriching contact with others —C.H.Nichols⟩ **2 :** distinctive character **:** INDIVIDUALITY ⟨it is the ~ of the films that gives the program its strength —Cecile Starr⟩ **3 :** AUTONOMY, INDEPENDENCE ⟨seeking complete political ~ for Lower Canada —B.K.Sandwell⟩

separates *pres 3d sing of* SEPARATE, *pl of* SEPARATE

separate school *n, Canad* **:** a state-supported sectarian school operated outside a local public school system under either Protestant or Catholic control ⟨public, private, and ~ schools⟩

separating *adj* [fr. pres. part. of *separate*] **:** designed or used for or capable of separation

separating funnel *n* **:** SEPARATORY FUNNEL

separating power *n* **:** RESOLVING POWER

sep·a·ra·tio bo·no·rum \ˌsepəˈrād-ē,ōbəˈnōrəm\ *n* [LL, lit., separation of goods] **1** *Roman law* **:** the keeping separate of the estate of a deceased person from that of his heirs or the right of the creditors of the estate to insist on such a separation **2** *Roman law* **:** the estate of an individual at the time of his death together with any subsequent increment

sep·a·ra·tion \ˌsepəˈrāshən\ *n* -s [ME *separacion*, fr. MF *separation*, fr. L *separation-, separatio*, fr. *separatus* (past part. of *separare* to separate) + *-ion-, -io* -ion — more at SEPARATE] **1 a :** an act or instance of dividing **:** DETACHMENT, DISPERSAL ⟨~ of church and state⟩ ⟨shipment of fragile or delicate articles . . . requires ~ and cushioning of items —*Export Packing*⟩ ⟨families . . . would face ~ if they should avail themselves of the provisions of the Refugee Relief Act —D.D.Eisenhower⟩ **b :** arrangement of mail according to destination **:** SORTING ⟨after cancellation . . . trundled the letters on wheeled trays to the next process, ~ —*Nat'l Geographic*⟩ **c :** BURBLE 3 **d :** SEPARATENESS, SEGREGATION ⟨courts and legislature work in ~ and aloofness —B.N.Cardozo⟩ ⟨we can no longer risk letting any large section of the human race live in ~, cut off from . . . the rest —I.A.Richards⟩ **e :** dissimilarity of character **:** DIFFERENCE, DISTINCTION ⟨should not give the impression that there is . . . no great ~ between the ends of Communism and those of the West —D.H.Gillis⟩ **2 a :** an act or instance of parting company ⟨after the ~ of the three boats . . . in the storm —W.J.Ghent⟩ **b (1) :** withdrawal from a parent body **:** SECESSION, SCHISM ⟨personally loyal though he was . . . believed that ~ was inevitable —T.M.Spaulding⟩ **(2)** *usu cap* **:** a body of dissenters esp. from an established church **:** SEPARATISTS ⟨one of the greatest of the early leaders of the *Separation* —George Willison⟩ **3 :** isolation from a mixture **:** EXTRACTION ⟨~ of flour from bran by bolting⟩ **4 a (1) :** cessation of cohabitation between husband and wife by mutual agreement; *esp* **:** JUDICIAL SEPARATION **(2)** *canon law* **:** ANNULMENT **b :** termination of a contractual relationship **:** RESIGNATION, DISCHARGE ⟨~ from the service⟩ ⟨~ from employment⟩ ⟨a serious breach of accepted standards of deportment . . . may be punished by loss of social privileges, probation, or ~ —*College of William & Mary Cat.*⟩ **5 a :** a point or line of division **:** DEMARCATION ⟨recommend that there be a clear line of ~ —J.P.Colbert⟩ **b :** a cause or means of dividing **:** BARRIER, PARTITION; *specif* **:** a compartment in a mail-sorting case ⟨sorted 100 cards to 53 ~s at the rate of 50 per minute —*Postal Service News*⟩ **c :** an intervening space **:** GAP, INTERVAL ⟨the ~ between the spokes of a wheel⟩ **d :** the distance between the two parts of an orig. continuous surface (as the top of a stratum) after dislocation by faulting — compare NORMAL HORIZONTAL SEPARATION, PERPENDICULAR SEPARATION **6 a :** a method or result of dividing: as **a :** the propagation of plants by parts which are naturally or easily removed from the parent plant (as gladiolus corms, lily bulbels) — compare DIVISION 20 **b :** COLOR SEPARATION **c :** a batch of sorted mail

separation disk *n* **:** a biconcave gelatinous layer found between two adjoining vegetative cells in some blue-green algae and associated with hormogonium formation

sep·a·ra·tion·ist \ˌsepəˈrāsh(ə)nəst\ *n* -s **:** one that advocates secession or schism

separation layer *n* **:** a distinct layer within an abscission zone of a plant varying in thickness and composed of cells that are smaller and different in shape from those above and below and contain abundant starch and dense cytoplasm by the disorganization of which abscission is effected — called also *abscission layer*

separation negative *n* **:** a monochrome negative obtained by photographing a subject through a filter and used as one of the component negatives in color printing

separation of powers : the allocation of executive, legislative, and judicial powers to branches of government independent of each other

separation of variables : a regrouping of the terms of a differential equation so that each differential has as a factor a function of the corresponding independent variable

separation point *n* **:** BURBLE POINT

sep·a·rat·ism \ˈsep(ə)rəd-ˌizəm, -əˌti-\ *n* -s [²*separate* + *-ism*] **1 a :** a disposition toward secession or schism ⟨arrest the wave of ~ among the nationalities —Julian Towster⟩; *esp* **:** advocacy of withdrawal from a parent group (as a church) ⟨though a militant Puritan . . . was still opposed to *Separatism* —George Willison⟩ — compare INDIVIDUALISM, ISOLATIONISM **b :** the principles and practices of a separatist ⟨promoters of secession . . . who swept the South into the adventure in ~ —J.G.Randall⟩; *esp, cap* **:** the principles and practices of the Separatists **2 :** social separation **:** EXCLUSIVENESS, SEGREGATION ⟨centuries of class ~ —E.B.George⟩ ⟨various forms and degrees of racial ~ —Sophia McDowell⟩

¹**sep·a·rat·ist** \ˈsep(ə)rəd-əst, -pəˌrā|, |tə-\ *n* -s [²*separate* + *-ist*] **1 :** a dissenter from an established church: as **a** *usu cap* **:** a Congregationalist or English Independent of the 16th and 17th centuries; *esp* **:** one separating from the Church of England **:** NONCONFORMIST ⟨those *Separatists* who founded the Plymouth colony in America⟩ **b :** a member of a congregation of no generally recognized denomination **c :** ZOARITE **2** *archaic, often cap* **:** one that observes strict piety and morality **:** PHARISEE **3** *often cap* **:** an advocate of political autonomy or independence **:** REVOLUTIONARY, SECESSIONIST ⟨sided with Quebec ~s in their struggles against . . . federal usurpation of power —M.S.Stewart⟩ **4 :** an advocate of segregation ⟨~s in the matter of church and state —F.J.B. Flynn⟩ — **sep·a·ra·tis·tic** \ˌsep(ə)rəˈtistik\ *adj*

²**separatist** \"\ *adj, often cap* **1 :** of, relating to, or characteristic of separatists **2 :** advocating separatism

sep·a·ra·tive \ˈsepəˌrād·iv, -p(ə)rəd-·\ *adj* [LL *separativus*, fr. L *separatus* (past part. of *separare* to separate) + *-ivus* -ive — more at SEPARATE] **1 :** tending toward or causing separation ⟨the uniting influence was stronger than the ~ —J.A.Froude⟩ **2 a :** DISTRIBUTIVE 2 **b :** expressive of separation or removal ⟨the ~ genitive⟩ **c :** DISJUNCTIVE 4

sep·a·ra·tor \ˈsepəˌrād·ə(r), -ātə- *also* -eˌprā-\ *n* -s *often attrib* [LL, one that separates, fr. L *separatus* (past part.) + *-or*] **1** *often cap* **:** SEPARATIST **2 :** one that separates a mixture into its constituent elements: as **a :** THRESHING MACHINE **b :** a device for extracting water from steam before it enters a steam engine **c :** a device for separating liquids of different specific gravities (as cream from milk) or liquids from solids; *esp* **:** CENTRIFUGE **d :** a revolving screen or a machine containing a revolving perforated cylinder with beater arms for separating cottonseed meats from the hulls **e (1) :** any of various machines for dressing ore or removing slate from coal **(2) :** an electromagnetic apparatus to separate magnetic ores from rock, sand, or other impurities **3 :** one that divides or serves as a barrier: as **a (1) :** RADDLE 3 **(2) :** a spindle guard that controls the ballooning of yarn — called also *antiballooner* **b :** a device (as of wood or perforated hard-rubber sheets) for preventing metallic contact between the electrodes of opposite polarity within a voltaic cell **c :** a casting for separating the sections of a built-up girder **d :** a dental appliance for separating adjoining teeth to give access to their surfaces **e :** a traffic barrier to discourage or prevent the passage of vehicles from one lane to another **4 :** a worker who separates by hand or machine: as **a :** an operator of a centrifugal machine for reclaiming lubricating oil **b :** one who cuts individual garment parts (as collars, sleeves) from a roll **c :** a classifier of laundry

separator man *n* **:** an operator of a separating apparatus (as a cream separator, a threshing machine)

separator pulp *n* **:** solids remaining after macerated fruit pulp has been centrifuged

sep·a·ra·to·ry \ˈsep(ə)rəˌtōrē\ *adj* [L *separatus* (past part. of *separare* to separate) + E *-ory*] **:** serving to separate **:** used in separating

separatory funnel *n* **:** a funnel usu. in the shape of a globe or cylinder provided with a stopcock for drawing off the lower layer of a mixture of immiscible liquids

separatory funnels

sep·a·ra·trix \ˌsepəˈrā·triks\ *n, pl* **sepa·ratri·ces** \ˌsepəˈrā·trəˌsēz, -ˌrəˈtrī(ˌ)sēz\ *also* **separatrixes** [NL, fr. LL, fem. of *separator*] **1 :** a diagonal or upright stroke used to separate one marginal proof correction from another in the same line **2 :** DIAGONAL 4

sep·a·ra·tum \ˌsepəˈrād·əm\ *n, pl* **sepa·ra·ta** \-d·ə\ [NL, fr. L, neut. of *separatus*, past part. of *separare* to separate] **:** OFFPRINT

sepd *abbr* separated

sepg *abbr* separating

se·phar·di \səˈfärdē, -ˌfärˈdē\ *n, pl* **se·phardim** \-ˈfärdəm, -ˌfärˈdēm\ *also* **se·phardi** *usu cap* [LHeb *sĕphāradhī*, fr. *Sĕphāradh* Spain, fr. Heb, region prob. in northern Asia Minor where Jews were once held in captivity (Obad 20)] **:** a member of the occidental branch of European Jews early settling in Spain and Portugal and later spreading to Greece, the Levant, England, the Netherlands, and the Americas — compare ASHKENAZI

¹**se·phar·dic** \səˈfärdik\ *also* **se·phar·di** \səˈfärdē, -ˌfärˈdē\ *adj, usu cap* [*sephardic* fr. *sephardi*, n. + *-ic*; *sephardi* fr. LHeb *sĕphāradhī*, n. & adj., sephardi, sephardic] **:** of, relating to, or characteristic of the Sephardim — compare ASHKENAZIC

²**sephardic** \"\ *n* -s *cap* [*sephardi*, n. + *-ic*] **:** Hebrew as spoken by the Sephardim

se·pher torah *or* **se·fer torah** \ˌsāfər-\ *n, pl* **si·phrei torah** *or* **si·frei torah** \ˌsi,frā-\ *or* **sepher torahs** *or* **sefer torahs** *usu cap S&T* [Heb *sēpher tōrāh*, lit., book of law] **:** a leather or parchment scroll of the Pentateuch used in a synagogue for liturgical purposes

se·phi·rah \səˈfērə\ *adj* [Heb *sĕphīrāh* counting, fr. *sāphōr* to count; fr. the custom of formally counting the 49 days according to the Commandment in Lev 23:15–16] **:** of, relating to or constituting one of the 49 days of Omer ⟨during the ~ days . . . no marriages may take place —H.E.Goldin⟩

¹**se·pia** \ˈsēpēə\ *n* [NL, fr. L, cuttlefish, fr. Gk *sēpia*; akin to Gk *sēpein* to make putrid, *sapros* rotten, putrid; fr. its inky secretion — more at SAPR-] **1 a cap :** a genus (the type of the family Sepiidae) of oval-bodied cephalopods comprising the cuttlefishes and having narrow fins as long as the body, a large calcareous internal shell, and an ink sac containing a dark fluid used in the preparation of drawing inks and watercolor bister **b** -s **:** the inky secretion of a cuttlefish **2** -s **:** a pigment of rich brown color containing melanin, prepared from the ink of various cuttlefishes, and used in watercolor painting and in ink **3** -s **a :** a drawing executed in sepia or a print or photograph of a brown color resembling sepia **b :** SEPIA PAPER **4** -s **:** a brownish gray to dark olive brown

²**sepia** \"\ *adj* **1 a :** of the color sepia **b :** made of or done in sepia ⟨~ print⟩ **2 :** having brown skin; *specif* **:** NEGRO ⟨the ~ lady with the glittering eyes and mellow singing voice —Brooks Atkinson⟩

sepia brown *n* **:** a dark grayish yellowish brown that is stronger and slightly yellower than seal and stronger and slightly yellower and lighter than otter

sepia paper *n* **:** photographic paper sensitized by a process analogous to kallitype and used esp. for plan copying

se·pi·idae \səˈpīəˌdē\ *n pl, cap* [NL, fr. *Sepia*, type genus + *-idae*] **:** a family of Decapoda comprising the true cuttlefishes

sep·i·ment \ˈsepəmənt\ *n* -s [L *saepimentum*, fr. *saepire* to fence, enclose with a hedge (fr. *saepes* hedge, fence); prob. akin to Gk *haimos* thicket, *haimasia* stone wall] **:** something (as a hedge or fence) that encloses

se·pi·o·la \ˌsēpēˈōlə\ *n, cap* [NL, dim. of *Sepia*] **:** a genus (the type of the family Sepiolidae) of short thick-bodied usu. small squids with a rudimentary internal chitinous shell or none and large rounded lobular fins

se·pi·o·lite \ˈsēpēəˌlīt\ *n* -s [G *sepiolith*, fr. Gk *sēpion* cuttlebone + G *-lith* -lite] **:** MEERSCHAUM 1

se·pi·oph·o·ra \ˌsēpēˈäpərə\ *n pl, cap* [NL, fr. *Sepia* + *-o-* + *-phora*] *in some classifications* **:** a suborder of Decapoda coextensive with the family Sepiidae and comprising the cuttlefishes

se·pi·um \ˈsēpēəm\ *n, pl* **se·pia** \-pēə\ [NL, fr. Gk *sēpion*, fr. *sēpia* cuttlefish] **:** CUTTLEBONE

sepn *abbr* separation

sepose *vt* -ED/-ING/-S [modif. (influenced by ¹*pose* & ¹*suppose*) of L *sepositus*, past part. of *seponere* to set apart, fr. *sed-, se-* apart (fr. *sed, se* without) + *ponere* to place — more at IDIOT, POSITION] *obs* **:** to set aside **:** RESERVE ⟨God *seposed* a seventh of our time for his exterior worship —John Donne⟩

se·poy \ˈsēˌpȯi\ *n* -s [modif. of Pg *sipai, sipaio*, fr. Hindi *sipāhī*, fr. Per, horseman, soldier of the cavalry, fr. *sipāh* army] **:** a native of India employed as a soldier in the service of a European power; *esp* **:** one serving in the British army

sep·pu·ku \seˈpü(ˌ)kü\ *n* -s [Jap, fr. Chin (Pek) *ch'ieh*⁴ to cut + *fu*³ bowels] **:** HARA-KIRI 1

seps \ˈseps\ *n, pl* **seps** [L, fr. Gk *sēps*; akin to Gk *sēpsis* decay] **:** a lizard of an Old World genus (*Chalcides* syn. *Seps*) of the family Scincidae having a snakelike body, very small legs, and smooth overlapping scales, and regarded as poisonous by the ancients

¹**sep·sid** \ˈsepsəd\ *adj* [NL *Sepsidae*] **:** of or relating to the Sepsidae

²**sepsid** \"\ *n* -s **:** a fly of the family Sepsidae

sep·si·dae \ˈsepsəˌdē\ *n pl, cap* [NL, fr. Gk *sēpsis* decay + NL *-idae*] **:** a family of acalyptrate usu. shiny black flies (superfamily Muscoidea) that develop in decaying organic matter or excrement

sep·sis \ˈsepsəs\ *n, pl* **sep·ses** \-pˌsēz\ [NL, fr. Gk *sēpsis* decay; akin to Gk *sēpein* to make putrid — more at SEPIA] **:** a toxic condition resulting from the multiplication of pathogenic bacteria and their products in a region of infection and their absorption into the blood stream; *esp* **:** SEPTICEMIA

¹**sept** \ˈsept\ *n* -s [prob. alter. of *sect*] **:** a branch of a family; *esp* **:** one in which all members are believed to have descended from a single ancestor **:** CLAN, SIB — used esp. of the dependents of a flaith in ancient Ireland

²**sept** \"\ *n* -s [L *septum* — more at SEPTUM] **1** *archaic* **:** an enclosed area (as of a building) set apart for a special purpose **2 :** a partition (as a screen or railing) that marks off a sept

¹**sept-** *or* **septi-** *comb form* [L, fr. *septem* — more at SEVEN] **:** seven ⟨*septinsular*⟩ ⟨*septifolious*⟩ ⟨*septillion*⟩

²**sept-** *or* **septo-** *also* **septi-** *comb form* [NL, fr. *septum* — more at SEPTUM] **:** septum ⟨*septal*⟩ ⟨*septifragal*⟩ ⟨*septocosta*⟩

septa *pl of* SEPTUM

sep·tal \ˈseptəl\ *adj* [²*sept-* + *-al*] **:** of, relating to, or being a part of a septum

septal cartilage *n* **:** the cartilage of the nasal septum

septal cell *n* **:** a small histiocyte characteristic of the lung

septal neck *n* **:** a short tubular prolongation of a septum in a cephalopod shell where it is perforated for the siphon

sep·tan·y·chus \sepˈtanəkəs\ *n, cap* [NL, prob. alter. of *Septonychus*, fr. ¹*sept-* + *-onychus* (fr. Gk *onych-, onyx* nail, claw); fr. the mites being seven-jointed — more at NAIL] **:** a genus of plant-feeding mites

sep·tarch \ˈsepˌtärk\ *adj* [¹*sept-* + *-arch*] **:** having seven protoxylem groups — used of a plant stem

sep·tar·i·an \(ˈ)sepˈta(a)rēən\ *adj* [NL *septarium* + E *-an*] **:** of, relating to, or being a septarium

septarium \=ˈ==əm\ *n, pl* **septar·ia** \-ēə\ [NL, fr. ²*sept-* + L *-arium*] **:** a concretionary nodule usu. of limestone or clay ironstone intersected within by cracks filled with calcite, barite, or other minerals — compare GEODE

sep·tate \ˈsepˌtāt\ *also* **sep·tat·ed** \-ād·əd\ *adj* [*septate* fr. ²*sept-* + *-ate*; *septated* fr. ²*sept-* + *-ate* + *-ed*] **:** divided by or having a septum

sep·ta·tion \sepˈtāshən\ *n* -s [²*sept-* + *-ation*] **1 :** division into parts by a septum **:** the condition of being septate **2 :** SEPTUM

septavalent *var of* SEPTIVALENT

sep·tem·ber \(ˈ)sepˈtembə(r), səpˈt-\ *n* -s *usu cap* [ME *septembre*, fr. OF, fr. L *september* (seventh month), fr. *septem* seven — more at SEVEN] **:** the ninth month of the Gregorian calendar — abbr. *Sept.*; see MONTH table

september elm *n, usu cap S* **:** a tree (*Ulmus serotina*) of the southeastern U.S. that flowers in the autumn — called also *red elm*

sep·tem·brist \=ˈ=brəst\ *n* -s *often cap* [Pg *Setembrista* supporter of the successful revolution of September 1836 in Portugal, fr. *setembro* September (fr. L *september*) + *-ista* -ist] **:** REVOLUTIONARY

septemfluous *adj* [L *septemfluus*, fr. *septem* seven + *-fluus* (fr. *fluere* to flow) — more at FLUID] *obs* **:** flowing in seven streams

sep·tem·vir \sepˈtemvə(r)\ *n, pl* **septemvirs** \-və(r)z\ *also* **septemvi·ri** \-vəˌrī, -vəˌrē\ [L, back-formation fr. *septemviri*, pl., fr. *septem viri* seven men, fr. *septem* seven + *viri*, pl. of *vir* man — more at VIRILE] **:** a member of a ruling body of seven men; *specif* **:** one of seven officiating priests in ancient Rome — compare EPULO

sep·tem·vi·ral \(ˈ)sepˈtemvərəl\ *adj* [L *septemviralis*, fr. *septemvir* + *-alis* -al] **:** of or relating to septemvirs or a septemvirate

sep·tem·vi·rate \=ˈ=vərət, -ˌrāt\ *n* -s [L *septemviratus*, fr. *septemvir* + *-atus* -ate] **1 :** the office or government of septemvirs **2 :** a body of septemvirs

sep·te·nar \sepˈtēnər, ˈseptəˌnär\ *n* -s [L *septenarius*] **:** SEPTENARY 2

sep·te·nar·i·us \ˌseptəˈna(a)rēəs\ *n, pl* **septenar·ii** \-ēˌī\ [L, fr. *septenarius* of or relating to seven] **:** SEPTENARY 2

¹**sep·tenary** \ˈseptəˌnerē, ˈseptəˌnerē, sepˈtenərē\ *n* -ES [L *septenarius*, fr. *septenarius* of or relating to seven] **1** *archaic* **:** a group or set of seven; *specif* **:** SEPTENNIUM **2 :** a fourteener (as the trochaic tetrameter catalectic in medieval Latin verse, the iambic verse of seven and a half feet of Middle English poetry) often printed in two lines — called also *septenar, septenarius*

²**sep·tenary** \(ˈ)sepˈtenərē, ˈseptəˌnerē, (ˈ)sepˈtenərē\ *adj* [L *septenarius*, fr. *septeni* seven each, seven (fr. *septem* seven) + *-arius* -ary] **1 :** of or relating to the number seven or to a septenary **2 :** SEPTUPLE

sep·ten·decillion \ˌsepˌten+\ *n often attrib* [L *septendecim* seventeen + E *-illion* (as in *million*)] — see NUMBER table

sep·ten·decimal \"+\ *adj* [L *septendecim* seventeen (fr. *septem* seven + *decem* ten) + E *-al* — more at SEVEN, TEN] **:** relating to the number 17 **:** based on the number 17

sep·ten·nate \sepˈteˌnāt, -nət; ˈseptəˌnāt\ *n* -s [F *septennat*, fr. *septennal* septennial (fr. LL *septennalis*, fr. L *septennis* of seven years + *-alis* -al) + *-at* -ate] **:** a period of seven years; *esp* **:** a seven-year term of office

sep·ten·nial \(ˈ)sepˈtenēəl, -nyəl\ *adj* [L *septennium* period of seven years (fr. *septennis* of seven years, fr. *septem* seven + *annus* year) + E *-al* — more at ANNUAL] **1 :** occurring, appearing, or being made, done, or acted upon every seven years **2 :** continuing or lasting for seven years ⟨~ parliaments⟩

sep·ten·nial·ly \-əlē, -əli\ *adv* **:** every seven years

sep·ten·ni·um \sepˈtenēəm\ *n, pl* **septenniums** \-ēəmz\ *or* **septen·nia** \-ēə\ [L] **:** a period of seven years

sep·ten·tri·on \sepˈten·trēˌän, -ēən\ *n, pl* **septentrions** \-nz\ *also* **septentrio·nes** \(ˌ)sepˌten·trēˈō(ˌ)nēz\ *often cap* [ME *septemtrioun*, fr. MF *septentrion*, fr. L *septentriones*, pl., the seven stars near the north pole, the northern regions (sing. *septentrio*), fr. *septem* seven + *Triones* Great Bear, Little Bear, fr. *triones* plow oxen, pl. of *trio* plow ox; akin to L *terere* to rub, grind, thresh — more at THROW] *obs* **:** the northern regions **:** NORTH ⟨thou art as opposite to every good . . . as the South to the *Septentrion* —Shak.⟩

sep·ten·tri·o·nal \(ˈ)sepˌten·trēənᵊl\ *adj* [ME, fr. L *septentrionalis*, fr. *septentriones* the northern regions + *-alis* -al] **:** NORTHERN ⟨coldest stretch of ~ weather —Janet Flanner⟩

sep·tet *or* **sep·tette** \(ˈ)sepˈtet\ *n* -s [G *septet*, fr. ¹*sept-* + *-et*] **1 :** a group of seven persons or objects ⟨a ~ of husky linemen⟩ **2 a :** a composition for seven instruments or voices **b :** a performance of such a composition **c :** seven musicians performing such a composition **3 :** a stanza or poem having seven lines — compare RHYME ROYAL

sept·foil \ˈsep(t)ˌfȯil\ *n* [LL *septifolium*, fr. L *sept-* ¹*sept-* + *folium* leaf — more at BLADE] **1 :** TORMENTIL **2 :** an ornamental foliation having seven lobes

septi- — see SEPT-

sep·ti·bran·chia \ˌseptəˈbraŋkēə\ *n pl, cap* [NL, fr. ²*sept-* + *-branchia*] **:** a small order of Lamellibranchia comprising marine bivalves with gills reduced to a horizontal symmetrically fenestrated muscular partition

sep·ti·branchiata \ˌseptə+\ [NL, fr. ²*sept-* + *branchiata*] *syn of* SEPTIBRANCHIA

sep·tic \ˈseptik, -tēk\ *adj* [L *septicus*, fr. Gk *sēptikos*, fr. *sēptos* putrid (verbal of *sēpein* to make putrid) + *-ikos* -ic — more at SEPIA] **1 a :** characterized by or producing bacterial decomposition **:** PUTREFACTIVE ⟨~ sewage⟩ ⟨~ action takes place at the bottom of the tank⟩ **b :** of, relating to, or characteristic of septicemia **:** HECTIC ⟨a ~ temperature curve⟩ **2 :** of an odious or contaminated nature **:** CORRUPT, OBNOXIOUS ⟨a ~ pool of guilt —*Time*⟩ ⟨suffering . . . from a ~ economy —*New Republic*⟩

sep·ti·ce·mia *or* **sep·ti·cae·mia** \ˌseptəˈsēmēə\ *n* -s [NL, fr. L *septicus* septic + NL *-emia, -aemia*] **:** invasion of the blood stream by virulent microorganisms from a focus of infection marked by chills, fever, and prostration and often by the formation of secondary abscesses in various organs — called also *blood poisoning*; compare PYEMIA — **sep·ti·ce·mic** *or* **sep·ti·cae·mic** \ˌseptəˈsēmik\ *adj*

sep·ti·centennial \ˌseptə+\ *n* [¹*sept-* + *centennial*] **:** a 700th anniversary or its celebration

sep·ti·ci·dal \ˌseptəˈsīdᵊl\ *adj* [²*sept-* + *-cidal*] *of a capsular fruit* **:** dehiscent longitudinally at or along a septum — compare LOCULICIDAL; see FRUIT illustration — **sep·ti·ci·dal·ly** \-ᵊlē\ *adv*

sep·ti·ciz·a·tion \ˌseptəsəˈzāshən, -ˌsīˈz-\ *n* -s [*septic* + *-ization*] **:** treatment of sewage by septic action

sep·ti·colored \ˈseptə+ˌ-\ *adj* [¹*sept-* + *colored*] **:** having seven colors

sep·ti·co·pyemia \ˌseptə(ˌ)kō+\ *n* [NL, fr. *septico-* (fr. L *septicus* septic) + *pyemia*] **:** PYEMIA — **sep·ti·co·pyemic** \"+\ *adj*

septic pneumonia *n* **:** hemorrhagic septicemia marked by pneumonia esp. in young animals (as calves)

septic sore throat *n* **:** sore throat characterized by inflammation of the throat and pharynx with associated fever, marked prostration, and other evidences of toxemia and caused by infection with hemolytic streptococci

septic tank *n* **:** a tank in which the organic solid matter of continuously flowing sewage is deposited and retained until it has been disintegrated by anaerobic bacteria

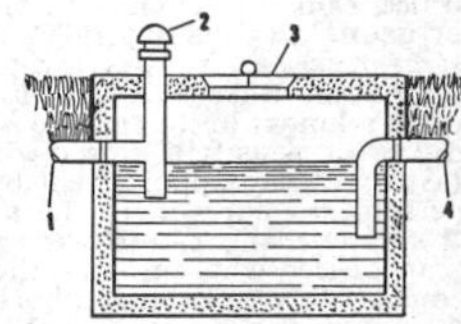

septic tank: *1* inlet, *2* vent cap, *3* manhole, *4* outlet

sep·tième \(ˈ)se·¦tyem\ *n* -s [F, lit., seventh, fr. L *septimus*, fr. *septem* seven — more at SEVEN] **:** a mutation stop of 2⅔ and 1⅓ foot pitch on the manuals and 4⁴⁄₅ foot pitch on the pedals

sep·tier \sə·ˈtyā\ *n* -s [F, alter. of *setier* — more at SETIER] **:** SETIER

sep·tif·ra·gal \(ˈ)sep¦tifrəgəl\ *adj* [*²sept-* + L *frag-* (stem of *frangere* to break) + E *-al* — more at BREAK] **:** breaking from the partitions — used of dehiscence in which the valves of a capsule or pod break away from the dissepiments — **sep·tif·ra·gal·ly** \-əlē\ *adv*

sep·tile \ˈsep,tīl, -təl\ *adj* [ISV *²sept-* + *-ile*; prob. orig. formed in F] **:** of or relating to septa

sep·til·lion \(ˈ)sep¦tilyən\ *n* -s *often attrib* [F, fr. *¹sept-* + *-illion* (as in *million*)] — see NUMBER table

sep·ti·mal \ˈseptəməl\ *adj* [L *septimus* seventh (fr. *septem* seven) + E *-al* — more at SEVEN] **:** based on the number seven

sep·time \ˈseptəm, -,tēm\ *n* -s [L *septima*, fem. of *septimus* seventh; fr. its being the seventh parrying position] **:** a parry or guard position in fencing that defends the lower inside target with the hand to the left in a position of supination and the top of the blade directed at the opponent's knee — compare QUINTE

sep·ti·mole \ˈseptə,mōl\ *also* **sep·tole** \-p,tōl\ *n* -s [*septimole* fr. L *septimus* seventh + E *-ole*; *septole* fr. *¹sept-* + *-ole*] **:** SEPTUPLET

sept·insular \(ˈ)sept+\ *adj, usu cap* [*¹sept-* + *insular*] **:** of, relating to, or consisting of the seven Ionian islands ⟨*Septinsular* Republic⟩

sep·ti·syllabic \¦septə+\ *adj* [*¹sept-* + *syllabic*] **:** consisting of seven syllables

sep·ti·syllable \"+\ *n* [*¹sept-* + *syllable*] **:** a word of seven syllables

sep·ti·valent *also* **sep·ta·valent** \¦septə+\ *adj* [*¹sept-* + *valent*] **:** HEPTAVALENT

septleva *n* -s [F *sept-et-le-va*, lit., seven and the first stake] **:** a sum equal to seven times the amount of the first stake in a game of basset

septo- — see SEPT-

sep·to·basidium \¦sep(,)tō+\ *n, cap* [NL, fr. *²sept-* + *basidium*] **:** a genus (the type of the family Septobasidiaceae) of smooth shelf fungi usu. having a well-developed sometimes thick-walled hypobasidium

sep·to·costa \¦septə+\ *n* [NL, fr. *²sept-* + *costa*] **:** an external costa on the calyx of a coral that marks the position of or is a continuation of a radial septum

sep·to·cylindrical \¦sep(,)tō+\ *adj* [*²sept-* + *cylindrical*] **:** cylindrical with one or more cross septa ⟨the ~ conidia of some fungi⟩

sep·to·gloe·um \,septə'glēəm\ *n, cap* [NL, fr. *²sept-* + *-gloeum* (fr. Gk *gloios* gum) — more at GLOEO-] **:** a form genus of fungi (order Melanconiales) having hyaline two-septate to several-septate and oblong conidia and including one member (*S. profusum*) that causes a leaf spot of elm and hazel

septole *var of* SEPTIMOLE

sep·to·let \¦septə¦let\ *n* -s [alter. (influenced by *-et* as in *septuplet*) of *septole*] **:** SEPTUPLET

sep·to·marginal \¦sep(,)tō+\ *adj* [*²sept-* + *marginal*] **:** of or relating to the margin of a septum

¹sep·to·maxillary \"+\ *adj* [*²sept-* + *maxillary*] **:** of, relating to, or situated in the region of the nasal septum and the maxilla

²septomaxillary \"\ *n* -ES **:** a small bone lying between the nasal septum and the maxilla in many amphibians and reptiles and in some birds

sep·to·nasal \¦sep(,)tō+\ *adj* [*²sept-* + *nasal*] **:** of, relating to, or situated in the region of the nasal septum

sep·to·ria \sep'tōrēə\ *n, cap* [NL, fr. *²sept-* + L *-oria* (fem. of *-orius* -ory)] **:** a form genus of imperfect fungi (family Sphaerioidaceae) having hyaline elongate to threadlike septate spores formed in pycnidia on the leaves of the host and being known in many cases to be the imperfect stages of ascomycetous fungi of the genus *Mycosphaerella* — see HARD ROT

septs *pl of* SEPT

¹sep·tu·age·nar·i·an \(¦)sep¦t(y)üəjə¦nerēən, ¦septəwəj-, ¦sepchəwəj-, ¦septə,waj-, ¦sepchə,waj-, -na(a)r-, -nār-\ *adj* [L *septuagenarius* fr. *septuagenary* + E *-an*] **:** SEPTUAGENARY

²septuagenarian \"\ *n* -s **:** a person who is 70 or more but less than 80 years old

sep·tu·agenary \¦septəwə¦jenərē, -pchəw-, -¦jēn-; -¦wajə,nerē\ *adj* [L *septuagenarius*, fr. *septuageni* seventy each (fr. *septuaginta* seventy) + *-arius* -ary] **1 :** based on the number 70 **2 :** of 70 or between 70 and 80 years old

sep·tu·a·ges·i·ma \,septəwə'jesəmə, -pchəw-, -jāzəmə\ *n* -s [ME *septuagesime, septuagesima*, fr. MF & LL; MF *septuagesime*, fr. LL *septuagesima*, fr. L, fem. of *septuagesimus* seventieth, fr. *septuaginta* seventy] **1** *obs* **:** the period of 70 days extending from the third Sunday before Lent to the Saturday after Easter **2** *or* **septuagesima sunday** *usu cap both Ss* **:** the third Sunday before Lent or the ninth before Easter in the church year observed by various branches of the Christian church

sep·tu·a·gint \ˈsep't(y)üəjənt; ˈseptəwə,jint, -pchəw-\ *n* -s [L *septuaginta* seventy, fr. *septem* seven + *-ginta* (akin to L *-ginti* in *viginti* twenty) — more at SEVEN, VICENARY] **1** *usu cap* **a :** the 70 or 72 Jewish scholars at Alexandria held to have translated the Old Testament into Greek **b** [LL *Septuaginta*, fr. L *septuaginta* seventy] **:** a copy or edition of the Greek translation of the Old Testament including the Apocrypha prepared in the 3d and 2d centuries B.C., constituting the first vernacular translation of the Bible, designed to meet the needs of Greek-speaking Jews of Egypt unable to read their Scriptures in Hebrew, and still used in the Eastern Orthodox Church — symbol *LXX* **2** *sometimes cap* **:** a group of 70

sep·tu·a·gin·tal \(¦)sep¦t(y)üə¦jint°l, ¦septəwə¦-, ¦sepchəwə¦-\ *adj, usu cap* **:** of or relating to the Septuagint

sep·tu·la \ˈseptələ, -pchə-\ *n, pl* **septu·lae** \-,lē, -,lī\ [NL, fr. *²sept-* + *-ula*] **:** one of the small perforations in the walls of the cells between adjacent bryozoan polyps

sep·tu·late \-,lāt, -lət\ *adj* [NL *septulum* + E *-ate*] *bot* **:** having imperfect or spurious septa

sep·tu·lum \-,ləm\ *n, pl* **septu·la** \-lə\ [NL, dim. of *septum*] **:** a small septum

sep·tum \ˈseptəm\ *n, pl* **sep·ta** \-tə\ *or* **septums** [NL, fr. L *septum, saeptum* enclosure, fence, wall, fr. *sepire, saepire* to hedge in, enclose, fr. *sepes, saepes* fence, hedge; akin to Gk *haimos* copse, thicket, *haimasia* stone wall] **1 :** a dividing wall or membrane: as **a :** a wall separating two plant cells or two cavities or masses (as in a compound ovary or fruit) — called also *dissepiment* **b :** NASAL SEPTUM **c :** CRURAL SEPTUM **d :** a narrow dividing layer of rock material separating larger features of the rock fabric **e :** one of the transverse partitions dividing the shell of a cephalopod or a rhizopod into chambers **f :** one of the transverse partitions between the segments of an annelid **2 :** one of the radial calcareous plates projecting into a calyculus of a coral

septum pel·lu·ci·dum \-pə'lüsədəm\ *n, pl* **septa pelluci·da** \-də\ [NL, transparent septum] **:** the thin double partition extending vertically from the lower surface of the corpus callosum to the fornix and neighboring parts, separating the lateral ventricles of the brain, and enclosing the fifth ventricle

septum transversum *n, pl* **septa transversa** [NL, transverse septum] **:** the diaphragm or the embryonic structure from which it in part develops

¹sep·tu·ple \ˈseptəpəl, (ˈ)sep¦t(y)üp-\ *adj* [LL *septuplus*, fr. L *septem* seven + *-uplus* (as in *quadruplus* quadruple) — more at SEVEN] **1 :** consisting of seven **:** being seven times as great or as many **:** SEVENFOLD **2 :** taken by sevens or in groups of seven

²septuple \"\ *n* -s **:** a sum seven times as great as another **:** a sevenfold amount **:** the seventh multiple

³septuple \"\ *vb* **septupled; septupled; septupling** \-p(ə)liŋ\ **septuples** *vt* **:** to make seven times as much or as many **~** *vi* **:** to become seven times as much or as many

sep·tup·let \(ˈ)sep¦təplət, -¦t(y)üp- *sometimes* ˈ≠,təp-\ *n* -s

septuplet 3

[*¹septuple* + *-et*] **1 :** a combination of seven of a kind **2 a :** one of seven offspring born at one birth **b septuplets** *pl* **:** a group of seven such offspring **3 :** a group of seven musical notes to be played in the time of four or six of the same value — called also *septimole, septolet*

¹sep·tu·pli·cate \(ˈ)sep¦t(y)üpləkət, -lēk- *sometimes* -lə,kāt\ *adj* [ML *septuplicatus*, past part. of *septuplicare* to multiply by seven, fr. LL *septuplus* septuple, after such pairs as L *quadruplus* quadruple: *quadruplicare* to quadruple] **:** made in seven identical copies **:** SEVENFOLD

²septuplicate \"\ *n* -s **1 :** a seventh thing like six others of the same kind **2 :** seven copies all alike — used with *in* ⟨typed in ~⟩

³sep·tu·pli·cate \-lə,kāt\ *vt* -ED/-ING/-S **:** to multiply by seven **:** reproduce six times **:** SEPTUPLE; *specif* **:** to make at one time an original and six carbon copies

¹sep·ul·cher *or* **sep·ul·chre** \ˈsepəlkə(r) *archaic* sə'p-\ *n* -s [ME *sepulcre*, fr. OF, fr. L *sepulcrum, sepulchrum*, fr. *sepelire* to bury; akin to Gk *hepein* to care for, prepare, Skt *sapati* he seeks after, courts, honors, *saparyati* he pays homage, worships] **1 a :** a place for the interment of a dead body **:** GRAVE, TOMB **b :** a final end or resting place **:** REPOSITORY, TERMINUS ⟨my heart . . . shall be thy ~ —Shak.⟩ ⟨the ~ of all . . . French hopes —F.L.Schuman⟩ **2 a :** a receptacle for religious relics esp. in an altar **b :** EASTER SEPULCHER 1

²sepulcher *or* **sepulchre** \"\ *vt* -ED/-ING/-S **:** to place or receive in a sepulcher **:** BURY, ENTOMB

se·pul·chral \sə'pəlkrəl, se'p-\ *adj* [L *sepulcralis*, fr. *sepulcrum* sepulcher + *-alis* -al] **1 :** of, relating to, or serving as a sepulcher or a memorial to the dead **:** MORTUARY ⟨~ inscriptions⟩ ⟨the ~ darkness of the catacombs —Nathaniel Hawthorne⟩ ⟨erect ~ monuments in the church —Nikolaus Pevsner⟩ **2 a :** suited to or suggestive of burial rites **:** having a funereal quality ⟨a ~ whisper⟩ ⟨rows of empty benches in the dusk gave the room a somewhat ~ aspect —Hanns Sachs⟩ **b :** emanating from or as if from the tomb ⟨the hollow, ~ tone of editorial comment —G.W.Johnson⟩ — **se·pul·chral·ly** \-əlē\ *adv*

se·pul·tur·al \sə'pəlch(ə)rəl, ¦sepəl¦chürəl\ *adj* [*¹sepulture* + *-al*] *archaic* **:** SEPULCHRAL

¹sep·ul·ture \ˈsepəlchər, -,chü(ə)r\ *n* -s [ME, fr. OF, fr. L *sepultura*, fr. *sepultus* (past part. of *sepelire* to bury) + *-ura* -ure] **1 :** BURIAL **2 :** SEPULCHER

²sepulture \"\ *vt* -ED/-ING/-S **:** to place in or as if in a grave **:** BURY

seq *abbr* **1** sequel **2** sequence **3** [L *sequens, sequentes, sequentia*] the following **4** [L *sequitur*] it follows

seqq *abbr* **1** [L *sequentes, sequentia*] the following **2** [L *sequentibus*] in the following places

sequ *abbr* [L *sequitur*] it follows

se·qua·cious \sə'kwāshəs, sē'k-\ *adj* [L *sequac-, sequax* sequacious (fr. *sequi* to follow) + E *-ious*] **1 a** *archaic* **:** inclined to follow **:** SUBSERVIENT, TRACTABLE **b :** inclined to be servile **:** IMITATIVE, OBSEQUIOUS **2** *obs* **:** characterized by malleability **:** DUCTILE, PLIABLE **3 :** logically sequent

se·qua·cious·ness *n* -ES **:** SEQUACITY

se·quac·i·ty \-wasəd·ē\ *n* -ES [LL *sequacitas*, fr. L *sequac-, sequax* inclined to follow, sequacious + *-itas* -ity] **:** the quality or state of being sequacious **:** disposition to follow

seq·ua·ni \ˈsekwə,nī, -,nē; ˈsākwə,nē\ *n pl, cap* [L] **:** a Celtic people of ancient Gaul inhabiting a region around the sources of the Seine

se·quel \ˈsēkwəl\ *n* -s [ME *sequel, sequele*, fr. MF *sequelle*, fr. L *sequella, sequela*, fr. *sequi* to follow — more at SUE] **1** *obs* **a :** a member of a retinue **:** FOLLOWER, RETAINER — usu. used in pl. ⟨friends, adherents, and ~s, should be comprehended in the truce —John Speed⟩ **b :** SUCCESSION, SERIES ⟨his daughter first; and in ~, all —Shak.⟩ ⟨a ~ of four —Lancelot Andrewes⟩ **2 a :** something that follows naturally from an antecedent cause **:** CONSEQUENCE, RESULT ⟨higher prices as a ~ to rising production costs⟩ **b** *obs* **:** a logical inference ⟨so fareth it with the bodies and by ~ with the souls —Thomas Walkington⟩ **c :** SEQUELA 1 ⟨gangrene is . . . a ~ of wounds —Robert Chawner⟩ **3 a :** the next in an unfolding series (as of events) **:** subsequent development ⟨powered flight as the evolutionary ~ to gliding⟩ **b :** the next installment (as of a speech or narrative) **:** CONTINUATION; *esp* **:** a literary work continuing the course of a narrative begun in a preceding one ⟨the hero performs even more astonishing feats in the ~⟩ **4 :** an allowance of meal or other small perquisite made in thirlage to the servants of the dominant mill for actual or nominal services in grinding — usu. used in pl. **syn** see EFFECT

se·que·la \sə'kwelə, sē'k-,se'k-, -wēlə\ *n, pl* **sequelae** \-(,)lē\ [NL, fr. L, sequel] **1 :** an aftereffect of disease or injury ⟨enteritis . . . as a ~ of indigestion —F.B.Hadley⟩ ⟨the necessity for frequent blood counts to avoid serious *sequelae* —G.F.Dick⟩ **2 :** a secondary result **:** CONSEQUENCE ⟨the poisonous *sequelae* of war —R.M.MacIver⟩

¹se·quence \ˈsēkwən(t)s, -,kwen-\ *n* -s [ME, fr. ML *sequentia*, fr. LL, succession, series, state or fact of following, fr. L *sequent-, sequens* (pres. part. of *sequi* to follow) + *-ia* -y] **1 :** a hymn or rhythm having no regular meter read or sung between the gradual and the Gospel on certain occasions as part of a Christian liturgical service (as in Roman Catholic and Anglican churches) — called also *prose* **2 :** a continuous or connected series: as **a :** a group of similar or related elements ⟨a ~ of market fluctuations⟩ ⟨a photo ~⟩ ⟨bringing . . . a ~ of musicals to Sacramento —*Fortnight*⟩ ⟨the city spreads over a ~ of low hills —*Amer. Guide Series: Texas*⟩; *specif* **:** an extended series of poems united by a single theme ⟨sonnet ~⟩ **b :** three or more playing cards usu. of the same suit in consecutive order of rank (as jack, ten, nine, eight, seven) **c :** a succession of repetitions of a musical phrase each in a new position ⟨rising chromatic ~⟩ — compare ROSALIA **d :** a mathematical aggregate ordered in the same manner as the positive integers — compare SERIES 2 **e :** a planned program of courses ⟨a four-year ~ in social studies —J.B.Conant⟩ **f** *archaeol* (1) **:** a set of components occurring in successive strata, preferably in one site ⟨a local ~⟩ (2) **:** a group of local sequences consolidated into one of larger scope ⟨a cultural ~⟩ **g** (1) **:** a section of a motion picture consisting of a succession of related shots or scenes in which a single subject or a single phase of a story is developed ⟨the . . . roller-coaster ~ in *Cinerama* —Lloyd Shearer⟩ (2) **:** a self-sufficient combination of dance movements permitting of further development, or a movement series with repetition of a theme on an ever lowered or heightened plane of space or dynamic intensity (3) **:** EPISODE ⟨the ~ from which the book takes its title —*Times Lit. Supp.*⟩ ⟨minute rehearsals of each ~ in the coronation ceremony —Blake Ehrlich⟩ **h** (1) **:** an agreed or keyed succession in cryptography (2) **:** KEYING SEQUENCE (3) **:** an arrangement of the alphabet in cryptology **3 a** (1) **:** a chronological succession ⟨birds have no prevision . . . of the ~ of the seasons —E.A.Armstrong⟩ (2) **:** a succession of geologic events, processes, or formations in chronologic order; *esp* **:** STRATIGRAPHIC SEQUENCE **b** (1) **:** a methodical arrangement or consecutive order ⟨a . . . ~ whereby he gets the apartment three days a week, she gets it twice —Lewis Nichols⟩ ⟨the ~ in which one word follows another —Stuart Chase⟩ ⟨paints each little square in ~ —Harland Manchester⟩ (2) **:** a one-dimensional ordering of elements or terms in logic (3) **:** an arrangement of the tenses of successive verbs in a sentence designed to express a coherent interrelationship esp. between main and subordinate verbs (as in indirect discourse, conditional sentences) (4) **:** the order in which portions of a recording are placed on a series of phonograph records — compare AUTOMATIC SEQUENCE **4 a :** a natural result or logical inference **:** SEQUEL ⟨action in ~ to . . . sincere idealism —*Times Lit. Supp.*⟩ ⟨the order of successional stages . . . has been reconstructed by the methods of inference and ~ —*Ecology*⟩ **b :** a subsequent development ⟨everybody was caught up in a succession of ~s —*Time*⟩ **c :** the order in which events are connected or related in time **:** simple succession; *esp* **:** the connection of antecedent and consequent in a temporal series apart from any causal necessity ⟨the reactions of chemical agents may be conceived as merely invariable ~s⟩ **5 :** the quality or state of being sequent **:** continuity between parts **:** CONSECUTIVENESS, PROGRESSION ⟨narrative ~⟩ ⟨formal ~ is useful in the architecture of public buildings because it helps to direct the visitor⟩ ⟨~ in learning depends upon continuity of growth in the learner —Dora Smith⟩

²sequence \"\ *vt* -ED/-ING/-S **:** to arrange in a sequence

se·quenc·er \-ənsə(r), -en(t)s-\ *n* -s [*¹sequence* + *-er*] **1 :** a book of liturgical sequences **2 :** any of various devices for arranging items (as pieces of information or the events in launching a rocket) into or separating items (as amino acids from protein) within a sequence

sequenciary *or* **sequentiary** *n* -ES [ML *sequentiarius*, fr. *sequentia* sequence (sense 1) + L *-arius* -ary] **:** SEQUENCER 1

se·quen·cy \ˈsēkwənsē\ *n* -ES [LL *sequentia*] **:** SEQUENCE

¹se·quent \ˈsēkwənt\ *adj* [L *sequent-, sequens*, pres. part. of *sequi* to follow — more at SUE] **1 :** occurring in sequence **:** ENSUING, CONSECUTIVE **2 :** following as a result **:** CONSEQUENT

²sequent \"\ *n* -s **1** *obs* **:** one of a sequence; *esp* **:** a member of a retinue ⟨a letter to a ~ of the stranger queen's —Shak.⟩ **2 :** CONSEQUENCE, SEQUEL ⟨I adopt the mode of action; and the expected . . . ~ actually follows —C.I.Lewis⟩

se·quen·tial \sə'kwenchəl, (ˈ)sē¦k-\ *adj* [LL *sequentia* sequence + E *-al* — more at SEQUENCE] **1 a :** occurring as a sequela of disease or injury **b :** of, relating to, or forming a sequence **:** CONSECUTIVE, SERIAL ⟨combination of two ~ courses into one —S.L.Pressey⟩ ⟨set forth the essential facts . . . in a well ordered, ~ manner —*N.Y.Herald Tribune*⟩ ⟨the . . . Neolithic setting for which ~ stages have been most fully revealed —H.B.Collins⟩ **c :** having the form or character of a musical sequence ⟨~ arpeggio⟩ **2 a :** occurring without interruption **:** CONTINUOUS **b :** relating to or based on a method of testing a statistical hypothesis that involves examination of a sequence of samples for each of which the decision is made to accept or reject the hypothesis or to continue sampling **3 :** occurring as a result **:** CONSEQUENT — **se·quen·tial·ly** \-ch(ə)lē, -li\ *adv*

sequential system *n* **:** a system of color television based on the successive showing of the three primary colors as dots, lines, or rapidly succeeding whole pictures so that through persistence of vision the colors appear in their proper proportions

¹se·ques·ter \sə'kwestə(r), sē'k-\ *vb* -ED/-ING/-S [ME *sequestren*, fr. MF *sequestrer*, fr. LL *sequestrare* to set aside for safekeeping, surrender, remove, separate, fr. L *sequester* depositary, trustee; akin to L *sequi* to follow — more at SUE] *vt* **1 a :** to set apart **:** separate for a special purpose **:** REMOVE, SEGREGATE ⟨the dentist must ~ with a rubber dam the tooth he is working on —*New Yorker*⟩ **b** *obs* **:** to deprive of membership (as in a church) or of public office or station ⟨was ~*ed* from parliament —David Hume †1776⟩ **c :** to hide from public view **:** withdraw from circulation **:** SECLUDE, SECRETE ⟨old houses . . . ~*ed* under leafy boughs —*Amer. Guide Series: Vt.*⟩ ⟨no crusading idealist . . . ever thought it right to ~ himself in an estate —Norman Thomas⟩ **2 a :** to seize esp. by public authority **:** CONFISCATE ⟨police continued to uncover and ~ . . . arms and ammunition —R.G.Woolbert⟩ **b** (1) **:** to take (property) from the possession of one or more parties to a controversy and put into the possession of a third party until profits have paid an obligation or until the owner has performed a decree of court or clears himself of contempt (2) *international law* **:** to appropriate under the right of preemption **3 :** to bind (as a metal or metal ion) in the form of a soluble complex or chelate by adding a suitable reagent for the purpose of preventing precipitation in water solution by chemical agents that would normally bring it about, of solubilizing precipitants already formed, or of otherwise suppressing undesired chemical or biological activity ⟨~ calcium and magnesium ions in the softening of hard water⟩ **~** *vi* **1** *archaic* **:** to withdraw into seclusion **:** RETIRE **2 :** to disclaim legal responsibility

²sequester \"\ *n* -s [L] **1** *Roman & civil law* **:** a depositary of property pending the settlement of a dispute as to its ownership **:** a receiver appointed by the court **2** [F *séquestre*, fr. L *sequestrum* sequestration, deposit, fr. *sequester* depositary] *obs* **:** SEPARATION ⟨this hand of yours requires a ~ from liberty —Shak.⟩ **3** [NL *sequestrum*] **:** SEQUESTRUM

sequestered *adj* [fr. past part. of *¹sequester*] **1** *obs* **:** cut off from companionship or congenial surroundings **:** ISOLATED, SEGREGATED ⟨a poor ~ stag that from the hunters . . . had taken a hurt —Shak.⟩ **2 a :** CONFISCATED, IMPOUNDED ⟨when the royal officers in Philadelphia seized fifty pipes of Madeira . . . a mob assaulted them and stole the ~ goods —C.A. & Mary Beard⟩ **b** *archaic* **:** deprived of privilege or property **:** DISPOSSESSED **3 a :** withdrawn from public view **:** SHELTERED, SECLUDED ⟨sat close together . . . in the ~ pergola —L.C. Douglas⟩ **b :** living the life of a recluse **:** SOLITARY

sequestra *pl of* SEQUESTRUM

se·ques·tra·ble \-trəbəl\ *adj* [*¹sequester* + *-able*] *archaic* **:** liable to exclusion or seizure

se·ques·trant \-trənt\ *n* -s [*¹sequester* + *-ant*] **:** a sequestering agent (as a sodium phosphate glass, a salt of ethylenediaminetetraacetic acid, or citric acid)

¹seques·trate \sə'kwe,strāt, sē'k-; 'sēkwə,s-, 'sē,kwe,s-; 'sekwə,s-; *usu* -ād·+V\ *adj* [ME, fr. LL *sequestratus*, past part. of *sequestrare* to remove, separate] *archaic* **:** SEQUESTERED

²sequestrate \"\ *vb* -ED/-ING/-S [LL *sequestratus*, past part. of *sequestrare*] *vt* **1 :** SEQUESTER **2 :** to form a sequestrum in **~** *vi* **:** to form a sequestrum

seques·tra·tion \,sēkwə'strāshən, (,)sē,kwe's-, sə,kwe's-, ,sekwə's-\ *n* -s [ME *sequestracion*, fr. LL *sequestration-, sequestratio*, fr. *sequestratus* (past part. of *sequestrare* to remove, separate) + *-ion-, -io* -ion — more at SEQUESTER] **1 a :** an act or instance of cutting off **:** EXCLUSION, SEPARATION ⟨forced into retirement by parliamentary ~ —Douglas Bush⟩ **b :** the quality or state of being sequestered **:** ISOLATION, SECLUSION ⟨lonely ~ on an island —*Time*⟩ **2 :** the separation or removal of property from a person in possession of it in order that the property or the proceeds thereof may be dealt with as a court or other competent authority may direct: as **a :** the authorization of a sheriff or commissioners to take into custody the property of a defendant who is in contempt or its rents and profits until he complies with the orders of a court **b** *English eccl law* **:** an attachment of a vacant benefice usu. granted by a bishop to church wardens for the management of its offices during the vacancy **c** *civil law* **:** a deposit whereby a neutral depositary agrees to hold property in litigation and to restore it to the party to whom it is adjudged to belong **d** *Scots law* **:** the appropriation of the property of a bankrupt in order to divide it among his creditors **e** *international law* **:** the seizure of the property of an individual for use by the state; *esp* **:** the seizure by a belligerent power of debts due from its subjects to the enemy or of property subject to the right of preemption **f** *probate law* **:** the subjection of a renounced interest to judicial management for distribution as the testator would have desired if he had had in mind the renunciation of the interest he tried to create **3 :** a seizure of property esp. by public authority **:** CONFISCATION ⟨the taxation and ~ he suffered during and after the Civil War . . . brought him into debt —J.B.Leishman⟩ **4 :** the formation of a sequestrum **5 :** the process of sequestering or result of being sequestered ⟨in soils various minor elements such as copper, zinc, and manganese are applied in organic complex ~ form so as to be kept from the normal precipitation reaction in soils —M.L. Jackson⟩

seques·tra·tor *pronunc at* SEQUESTRATE +ə(r)\ *n* -s [ML, fr. LL *sequestratus* (past part.) + L *-or*] *law* **:** one that is appointed to receive property in sequestration or to execute a sequestration writ

se·ques·tra·trix \sēkwə'strā·triks, ˌsē,kwe's-, ˌsekwə's-\ *n, pl* **sequestratri·ces** \ˌ-(ˌ)-'strā·trə,sēz; sə,kwestrə·'trī(ˌ)sēz, sē,k-\ [NL, fem. of ML *sequestrator* — more at -TRIX] **:** a female sequestrator

se·ques·trec·to·my \ˌsē,kwe'strektəmē\ *n* -ES [ISV *sequestr-* (fr. NL *sequestrum*) + *-ectomy*] **:** the surgical removal of a sequestrum

se·ques·tree \ˌsē,kwe'strē, sə'kwe,s-\ *n* -S [¹*sequester* + *-ee*] *archaic* **:** SEQUESTRATOR

se·ques·trum \sə'kwestrəm, sē'k-\ *n, pl* **sequestrums** \-rəmz\ *also* **seques·tra** \-rə\ [NL, fr. L, sequestration, deposit, fr. *sequester* depositary — more at SEQUESTER] **:** a fragment of dead bone that becomes detached from the sound portion ⟨necrotic fragments of teeth and bone ~*s* —L.R. Cahn⟩ ⟨an involucrum forms about a ~ in osteomyelitis — C.E.Dunlap⟩ — compare ³SLOUGH 2a

se·quin \'sēkwən\ *n* -S [F, fr. It *zecchino*, fr. *zecca* mint, fr. Ar *sikkah* die, stamp, stamped coin] **1 :** an old gold coin of Italy and Turkey first struck at Venice about the end of the 13th century — called also *chequeen, zecchino, zechin, zequin* **2 :** a small ornament (as a flat disk, star, or other shape) usu. of shiny metal or plastic pierced with a hole for sewing onto cloth in decorative designs **:** SPANGLE

se·quined *or* **se·quinned** \-ənd\ *adj* **:** ornamented with or as if with sequins ⟨separate skirts, ~ and quilted and otherwise bedizened —Lois Long⟩ ⟨petals ~ with dew⟩

sequitur *n* -S [L, it follows, 3d pers. sing. pres. indic. of *sequi* to follow — more at SUE] **:** an inference that follows from a premise ⟨state certain basic postulates and . . . several useful ~*s* —J.B.McMillan⟩ — compare NON SEQUITUR

se·quoia \sə'kwȯi(y)ə, sē'k- *also* -wȯyə\ *n* [NL, after *Sequoya* (George Guess) †1843 Am. Indian scholar] **1** *cap* **:** a genus of coniferous trees (family Taxodiaceae) distinguished by having both linear and awl-shaped decurrent leaves and the winter buds with imbricated scales — see REDWOOD; compare SEQUOIADENDRON **2** -S **:** any tree of the genus *Sequoia* or of the related genus *Sequoiadendron; specif* **:** BIG TREE 1

se·quoia·den·dron \ˌ-ˌ-ˌ-'dendrən\ *n, cap* [NL, fr. *Sequoia* + *-dendron*] **:** a genus of coniferous trees (family Taxodiaceae) sometimes included in the genus *Sequoia* but distinguished by having all the leaves scalelike or awl-shaped and appressed and the winter buds naked — compare SEQUOIA 1

sequoia pitch moth *n* **:** a small clearwing moth (*Vespamima sequoiae*) whose larvae are esp. destructive to lodgepole pine and western yellow pine

ser *var of* SEER

ser *abbr* **1** serial **2** series **3** sermon **4** serve; service; serving

sera *pl of* SERUM

se·rac \sə'rak, (')sā¦rak\ *n* -S [F *sérac* a solid white cheese, serac, fr. ML *seracium* whey, fr. L *serum* whey — more at SERUM] **:** a jagged pinnacle, sharp ridge, or block of ice among the crevasses of a glacier (as in an icefall) — compare NIEVE PENITENTE

se·ra·glio \sə'ral(ˌ)yō, -räl-, -rȧl-\ *n, pl* **seraglios** *also* **sera·gli** \-)yē\ [It *serraglio* enclosure, cage, sultan's palace, harem, partly fr. OIt, fr. ML *serraculum* bar of a door, bolt, fr. (assumed) VL *serrare* to lock up, bolt, fr. LL *serare;* partly fr. Turk *saray* palace — more at SEAR, SERAI] **1 a :** HAREM 1a **b :** a place of licentious pleasure; *esp* **:** BROTHEL **2 :** a palace or residence of a sultan **3** *obs* **a :** CARAVANSARY **b :** WAREHOUSE

se·rai \sə'rī\ *n* -S [Turk & Per; Turk *saray* palace, mansion, fr. Per *sarāī* palace, mansion, inn — more at CARAVANSARY] **1 :** CARAVANSARY **2 :** SERAGLIO 2

se·rail \sə'rī, -rī(ə)l, -rā(ə)l\ *n* -S [MF, fr. OIt *serraglio*] **:** SERAGLIO

serajevo *usu cap, var of* SARAJEVO

ser·al \'sirəl\ *adj* [⁶*sere* + *-al*] **:** of, relating to, or characteristic of an ecological sere ⟨a ~ community of mixed shrubs and trees⟩ ⟨~ stages in community development⟩

ser·and·ite \'serən,dīt\ *n* -S [F *sérandite*, fr. J. M. *Sérand*, 20th cent. West African mineral collector + F *-ite*] **:** a mineral consisting of hydrous silicate of manganese, lime, soda, and potash and occurring in rose-red monoclinic crystals

se·rang \sə'raŋ\ *n* -S [Per *sarhang* commander, boatswain, fr. *sar* chief + *hang* authority] **1 :** BOATSWAIN **2 :** the skipper of a small boat

serape *var of* SARAPE

ser·a·pe·um \ˌserə'pēəm\ *n, pl* **serapeums** \-ēəmz\ *or* **sera·pea** \-ēə\ *usu cap* [LL, fr. Gk *sarapeion, serapeion*, fr. *Sarapis, Serapis*, Egyptian god] **:** a place or building or group of buildings sacred to Serapis

¹**ser·aph** \'serəf\ *also* **ser·a·phim** \-,fim *also* -,fēm *sometimes* ˌ-ˌ-'-\ *n, pl* **seraphim** *or* **seraphs** *also* **seraphims** [LL *seraphim, seraphin* seraphs, fr. Heb *śĕrāphīm*] **1 :** one of an order of fiery six-winged angels who guard God's throne — see CELESTIAL HIERARCHY **2 :** a representation of a seraph often in red symbolizing sacred ardor **3 :** one that is seraphic in character

²**seraph** \"\ *adj* **:** relating to or being a seraph **:** SERAPHIC ⟨the ~ way of those above —Lord Byron⟩ ⟨a ~ wind —G.W. Russell⟩

se·raph·ic \sə'rafik, -fēk\ *also* **se·raph·i·cal** \-fəkəl, -fēk-\ *adj* [*seraphic* fr. ML *seraphicus*, fr. LL *seraphim, seraphin*, seraphs + L *-icus* -ic; *seraphical* fr. ML *seraphicus* + E *-al*] **1 :** of, relating to, or befitting a seraph **:** ANGELIC, SUBLIME, PURE ⟨~ arms and trophies —John Milton⟩ ⟨could have imagined a ~ presence in the room —George Meredith⟩ ⟨his ~ church-offertory style —*N.Y.Times*⟩ **2 :** resembling a seraph esp. in beauty or ecstatic adoration ⟨~ smile⟩ ⟨in appearance he was ~ —E.J.Kahn⟩ — **se·raph·i·cal·ly** \-fək(ə)lē, -fēk-, -li\ *adv* — **se·raph·i·cal·ness** \-kəlnəs\ *n* -ES

ser·a·phim \'serə,fim *also* -,fēm *sometimes* ˌ-ˌ-'-\ *n, pl* **seraphim** [NL, fr. LL, seraphs] **:** a fossil eurypterid (genus *Pterygotus*)

ser·a·phin \-fin, -fēn\ *n* -S [LL, seraphs] *archaic* **:** SERAPH

ser·a·phine \'serə,fēn, ˌ-ˌ-'-\ *also* **ser·a·phi·na** \ˌ-ˌ-'fēnə\ *n* -S [*seraph* + *-ina*] **:** a 19th century English keyboard reed instrument similar to the American organ

seraphlike \'-ˌ-ˌ-\ *adj* **:** resembling a seraph **:** SERAPHIC

se·ra·pi·as \sə'rāpēəs\ [NL, fr. L, an orchid, fr. Gk, fr. *Sarapis, Serapis*, Egyptian god] *syn of* EPIPACTIS

se·raya \sə'rīə\ *n* -S [native name in Borneo] **:** any of several trees of the genus *Shorea*

¹**serb** \'sərb, 'sə̄b, 'səib\ *n* -S *cap* [Serb *Srb*] **1 :** a native or inhabitant of the former kingdom of Serbia or of the federal republic of Serbia in Yugoslavia **2 :** SERBIAN 2

²**serb** \"\ *adj, usu cap* **:** SERBIAN

ser·bi·an \|bēən\ *or* **ser·vi·an** \|vē-\ *n* -S *cap* [*Serbia* (formerly *Servia*), former Balkan kingdom (now a republic of Yugoslavia) + E *-an*] **1 :** SERB 1 **2 a :** the Serbo-Croatian language as spoken in Serbia **b :** a literary form of Serbo-Croatian using the Cyrillic alphabet

²**serbian** \"\ *or* **servian** \"\ *adj, usu cap* [*Serbia, Servia* + E *-an*] **1 a :** of, relating to, or characteristic of Serbia **b :** of, relating to, or characteristic of the Serbs **2 a :** of, relating to, or characteristic of the Serbo-Croatian language as spoken in Serbia **b :** of, relating to, or characteristic of a literary form of Serbo-Croatian using the Cyrillic alphabet

serbian spruce *n, usu cap 1st S* **:** a pyramidal evergreen tree (*Picea omorika*) of southeastern Europe that is widely planted for its rich dark green foliage and brown oblong cones

serbo- *comb form, usu cap* [*serb*] **1 :** Serbian ⟨*Serbophile*⟩ **2 :** Serbian and ⟨*Serbo-Bulgarian*⟩

serbo-croat \ˌ-(ˌ)bō+\ *n or adj, usu cap S&C* [*serbo-* + *croat*] **:** SERBO-CROATIAN

¹**serbo-croatian** \"+\ *n, cap S&C* [*serbo-* + *croatian*] **1 :** the Slavic language of the Serbs and Croats consisting of Serbian written in the Cyrillic alphabet and Croatian written in the Roman alphabet **2 :** one whose native language is Serbo-Croatian

²**serbo-croatian** \"\ *adj, usu cap S&C* **1 :** of, relating to, or characteristic of the Serbo-Croatian language **2 :** of, relating to, or characteristic of the Serbo-Croatians

ser·cial \¦sersē¦al, (')sers¦yal\ *n* -S *usu cap* [F] **:** a dry Madeira wine

ser·dab \sə(r)'dāb\ *n* -S [Ar *sirdāb* cellar, underground vault, fr. Per *sardāb* ice cellar, fr. *sard* cold + *āb* water] **1 :** a narrow chamber of the ancient Egyptian mastaba either concealed or accessible only by a narrow passage and containing a statue of the deceased **2 :** a living room in the basement of a house in the Near East that provides coolness during the summer months

serdar *var of* SIRDAR

¹**sere** *also* **sear** \'si(ə)r, -iə\ *adj* -ER/-EST [ME, fr. OE *sēar;* akin to MLG *sōr* dry, OHG *sōrēn* to wither, L *sudus* dry (of weather), Gk *hauos* dry, *hauein* to parch, dry, Skt *śuṣyati* it dries up, withers] **1 :** dried up **:** WITHERED ⟨rank summer vegetation turns ~ —Marjorie K. Rawlings⟩ ⟨~, cracked mud flats —*Amer. Guide Series: Calif.*⟩ **2** *archaic* **:** worn thin **:** THREADBARE ⟨sails that were so thin and ~ —S.T. Coleridge⟩

²**sere** \"\ *n* -S **1 :** a sere period or condition ⟨the ~ and autumn of the moss animals' year —William Beebe⟩ **2 :** sere vegetation ⟨flame was so swift that it barely singed the green grass among the winter ~ —John Onslow⟩

³**sere** \"\ *n* -S [MF *serre* grip, grasp, clip — more at SEAR (catch of a gunlock)] *archaic* **:** CLAW, TALON

⁴**se·re** \'(t)sā(ˌ)rā\ *n* -S [Heb *ṣĕrē, ṣērī*, lit., perh. a split, opening] **:** a vowel point .. written below its consonant indicating Hebrew close *e* pronounced \ā\

⁵**sere** \'si(ə)r, -iə\ *n* -S [L *series* series] **:** a series of ecological communities that follow one another in the course of the biotic development of an area or formation from pioneer stage to climax — see HYDROSERE, LITHOSERE, PSAMMOSERE, XEROSERE

serebend *var of* SARABAND

¹**se·reh** \sə'rā\ *n* -S [Malay *sĕre, sĕrai*] **:** CITRONELLA GRASS

²**sereh** \"\ *n* -S [¹*sereh*] **:** a destructive East Indian virus disease of sugarcane characterized by necrosis of the phloem, fanlike tops, and general degeneration

se·rein \sə'raⁿ, -ran\ *n* -S [F, fr. MF *serain* evening, nightfall, fr. L *sero* late — more at SOIREE] **1** *archaic* **:** the supposed fall of dew from a clear sky just after sunset **2 :** mist or fine rain falling from an apparently clear sky

se·re·na \sə'rānə\ *n* -S [Prov, poem expressing a lover's longing for evening, fr. *ser* evening, fr. L *sero* late — more at SOIREE] **:** an evening love song — compare ¹ALBA

¹**ser·e·nade** \ˌserə¦nād\ *n* -S [F *sérénade*, fr. It *serenata* (influenced in meaning by *sera* evening, fr. L, fr. fem. of *serus* late), fr. *sereno* clear, calm (of weather), fr. L *serenus* — more at SINCE, SERENE] **1 a :** music sung or played esp. for gallantry in the open air at night **b :** a musical composition suitable for a serenade **c :** the performance of a serenade ⟨a lover's ~ beneath his lady's window⟩ **2 :** SERENATA 2 **3 :** an instrumental composition in several movements, written for a small ensemble and midway in style between the suite and the symphony **4** *dial* **:** SHIVAREE 1 **5 a :** the performance of any music esp. in the open air in compliment to a person or group **b :** the music played at such a performance

²**serenade** \"\ *vb* -ED/-ING/-S *vt* **:** to entertain with or perform a serenade in honor of ⟨singers still gather around your car and ~ you —Green Peyton⟩ ~ *vi* **:** to play a serenade

ser·e·nad·er \-də(r)\ *n* -S **:** one that serenades

ser·e·na·ta \ˌserə'nädə\ *n, pl* **serenatas** \-ädəz\ *also* **serena·te** \-ä(ˌ)tā\ [It, serenade — more at SERENADE] **1 a :** SERENA **b :** SERENADE **2 :** a cantata or secular ode of a pastoral or dramatic character usu. composed in honor of an individual or event

seren·dib·ite \¦serən¦di,bīt, sə'rendə,b-\ *n* -S [fr. *Serendib, Serendip*, former name for Ceylon (fr. Ar *Sarandīb*) + E *-ite*] **:** a mineral $(Ca,Mg)_5Al_5B_2Si_2O_{10}$ consisting of a silicate and borate of calcium, magnesium, and aluminum and occurring in irregular blue grains in Ceylon

ser·en·dip·i·tist \ˌserən'dipəd·əst, -pətə-\ *n* -S [*serendipity* + *-ist*] **:** one who finds valuable or agreeable things not sought for

ser·en·dip·i·tous \¦-ˌ-¦-pəd·əs, -pətəs\ *adj* [*serendipity* + *-ous*] **:** obtained or characterized by serendipity ⟨~ discoveries⟩

ser·en·dip·i·ty \ˌserən'dipəd·ē, -pətē, -i\ *n* -ES [*Serendip, Serendib*, former name for Ceylon (fr. Ar *Sarandīb*) + E *-ity;* fr. the possession of the gift by the heroes of the Persian fairy tale *The Three Princes of Serendip*] **:** an assumed gift for finding valuable or agreeable things not sought for

¹**se·rene** \sə'rēn\ *adj, often* -ER/-EST [L *serenus* clear, fair, calm (of weather), peaceful, cheerful; akin to OHG *serawēn* to become dry, Gk *xeron* dry land, *xēros* dry] **1 a :** completely clear, fine, or balmy **:** suggesting or conducive to calm peacefulness free of storms or unpleasant change ⟨~ weather⟩ ⟨~ skies⟩ ⟨~ will be our days and bright —William Wordsworth⟩ **b :** shining bright and steady and unobscured ⟨elegant contrasts between . . . the ~ shining of the planets and our hot feverish lives —L.P.Smith⟩ **2 :** marked by or suggestive of utter calm and unruffled repose or quietude without suggestions of agitation, trouble, fitful activity, or sudden change ⟨to the end his mind remained ~ and undisturbed —W.S. Maugham⟩ ⟨a ~ expression upon her face —Samuel Butler †1902⟩ ⟨genuine intellectual certainty is generally ~ —Gilbert Murray⟩ ⟨myself sitting all ~ in the rest house —Arthur Grimble⟩ ⟨a ~ lake⟩ **3 :** most high — used as part of a royal style ⟨His *Serene* Highness⟩ **syn** see CALM

²**serene** \"\ *vt* -ED/-ING/-S [L *serenare*, fr. *serenus* serene] *archaic* **:** to make serene **:** TRANQUILIZE

³**serene** \"\ *n* -S [L *serenum*, fr. neut. of *serenus* serene] **1 :** a serene condition or expanse (as of sky, sea, or light) ⟨the blue deep's ~ —Lord Byron⟩ ⟨the day's intense ~ —P.B.Shelley⟩ **2 :** SERENITY, TRANQUILLITY, CALMNESS

⁴**serene** *n* -S [MF *serein* serein, fr. earlier *serain* evening, nightfall — more at SEREIN] *obs* **:** the cool or damp of evening air

se·rene·ly *adv* **:** in a serene manner ⟨~ beautiful⟩

se·rene·ness *n* -ES [¹*serene* + *-ness*] **:** SERENITY

sere·ness *n* -ES [ME *sernesse*, fr. ¹*sere* + *-nesse* -ness] **:** the quality or state of being sere

se·ren·i·ty \sə'renəd·ē, -ətē, -i\ *n* -ES [MF *serenité*, fr. L *serenitat-, serenitas*, fr. *serenus* serene + *-itat-, -itas* -ity] **1 :** the quality or state of being serene **:** CALM, PEACEFULNESS, REPOSE ⟨the ~ of a mind at ease with itself and kindly disposed towards everyone —Jane Austen⟩ **2** *usu cap* **:** a person of honor ⟨Highnesses, *Serenities*, and Excellencies . . . arrived from all quarters—W.M.Thackeray⟩ — used as a title of honor given to reigning princes and other dignitaries ⟨your *Serenity*⟩

sere·noa \sə'rēnəwə, ˌserə'nōə\ *n, cap* [NL, after *Sereno* Watson †1892 Am. botanist] **:** a small genus of nearly stemless fan palms of the southern U. S. having spiny-toothed petioles, nearly round leaves, and ovoid or globose drupes — see SAW PALMETTO

¹**serer** *comparative of* SERE

²**se·rer** \sə're(ə)r\ *n, pl* **serer** *or* **serers** *usu cap* **1 :** a Negro of a people who dwell about Cape Vert, Senegal, and who are among the tallest of Negro peoples **2 :** a West-Atlantic language of the Serer people

¹**se·res** \'si(ə)(ˌ)rēz, 'sē(-\ *n pl, usu cap* [L, fr. Gk *Sēres*] **:** a people of eastern Asia mentioned by Greeks and Romans as making silk fabrics and now usu. identified with the Chinese

²**seres** *pl of* SERE

serest *superlative of* SERE

serf \'sərf, 'səf, 'səif\ *n* -S [F, fr. L *servus* slave, servant, serf — more at SERVE] **1 :** THEOW **2 :** a person (as the English villein of the 12th or 13th century) belonging to any of various grades of the lower class esp. in different feudal systems, bound to the soil and more or less subject to the will of the owner of the soil, and separable from the lord's land by manumission only **3 :** VILLEIN 3 **4 :** any of various unemancipated classes of tillers of the soil (as in Germany, Poland, and Russia) esp. of the 17th and 18th centuries **5 :** SLAVE

serf·age \-fij, -fēj\ *n* -S [*serf* + *-age*] **:** SERFDOM

serf·dom \-fdəm\ *n* -S [*serf* + *-dom*] **:** the quality, state, or fact of being a serf **:** SLAVERY — compare HELOTRY, PEONAGE

serf·hood \-,fu̇d, -ˌf,hu̇d\ *n* [*serf* + *-hood*] **:** SERFDOM

serf·ish \-fish, -fēsh\ *adj* **:** characteristic of a serf — **serf·ish·ness** *n* -ES

serf·ism \-,fizəm\ *n* -S [*serf* + *-ism*] **:** social polity in which serfdom exists

serf·ship \-f,ship\ *n* [*serf* + *-ship*] **:** SERFDOM

serg *abbr, often cap* sergeant

¹**serge** \'sərj, 'səj, 'səij\ *n* -S [ME *sarge*, fr. MF, fr. (assumed) VL *sarica*, fr. L *serica*, fem. of *sericus* of silk — more at SERICEOUS] **:** a durable twilled fabric having a smooth clear face and a pronounced diagonal rib on the front and the back, made in various weights from worsted, wool, cotton, silk, or rayon, and used esp. for suits, coats, and dresses

²**serge** \"\ *vt* -ED/-ING/-S **:** to overcast (raw edges of fabric) usu. with a three-needle machine that forms V-shaped stitches

ser·gean·cy *also* **ser·geant·cy** *or* **ser·jean·cy** \'särjən(t)sē, 'sȧj-, -)si\ *n* -ES [*sergeant* + *-cy*] **:** the function, office, rank, or commission of a sergeant

ser·geant *also* **ser·jeant** \'särjənt, 'sȧj-\ *n* -S [ME, fr. OF *sergent, serjant*, fr. L *servient-, serviens*, pres. part. of *servire* to serve — more at SERVE] **1 a** *obs* **:** SERVANT **b** *obs* **:** an attendant upon a knight in the field **c** *obs* **:** a common soldier **d :** SERGEANT AT ARMS 1 **e** — used with various designations of office (as to indicate appointment by and attendance upon a royal person) ⟨~ surgeon to the king⟩ ⟨~ painter to the court⟩ **2** *usu serjeant* **:** BARRISTER; *esp* **:** SERJEANT-AT-LAW **3 a** *obs* **:** an officer who enforces the judgments of a court or the commands of one in authority **b :** SERGEANT AT ARMS 2 **c :** any of various municipal officers of lower rank (as in the City of London) — see SERGEANT-AT-MACE **d :** an officer in a police force ranking in the U. S. just below captain or sometimes lieutenant and in England just below inspector **4 :** a noncommissioned officer in the army and marine corps rating just below a staff sergeant and above a corporal — see CHEVRON illustration **5 :** SERGEANT FISH **6 a :** a local Salvation Army officer appointed for specific duty **b :** a Salvation Army cadet appointed to assist in the training of officer candidates **7 :** a fire-department officer ranking just below a lieutenant

sergeant at arms [ME] **1 a :** a tenant holding a sergeanty of service as an armed personal attendant for protection of a feudal lord and enforcement of his commands; *esp* **:** such an attendant upon the king or on the king's lord high steward in court to arrest traitors and other offenders **b :** one of two officers who nominally by allowance of the sovereign attend on the houses of Parliament to execute their commands; *also* **:** an officer similarly attending on the Court of Chancery **2 :** an officer of a legislative body, a deliberative or judicial assembly, or other organization (as a fraternal lodge) who attends upon it to execute commands or orders (as in preserving order or arresting offenders)

sergeant-at-law *var of* SERJEANT-AT-LAW

sergeant-at-mace *n, pl* **sergeants-at-mace** \¦-ˌ-ˌ-¦-\ **:** a minor official carrying a mace as his insignia

sergeant ba·ker \ˌ-ˌ-'bākə(r)\ *n, usu cap S&B* [prob. fr. the name *Sergeant Baker*] **:** a brightly colored fish (*Aulopus purpurissatus*) related to the lantern fishes of the Australian coasts and becoming about two feet long

sergeant first class *n* **:** PLATOON SERGEANT

sergeant fish *n* [so called fr. the stripes on the fins] **1 :** COBIA **2 :** SNOOK 1a

sergeant major *n, pl* **sergeants major** *or* **sergeant majors** **1** *obs* **:** a regimental field officer serving either as a major or adjutant **2** *obs* **:** a general officer commanding large bodies of troops **3 a :** a noncommissioned officer in the marine corps ranking above a first sergeant — see RANK table **b :** a noncommissioned officer in the army, air force, or marine corps serving as chief administrative assistant in a headquarters **4 a :** a small deep-bodied compressed damselfish (*Abudefduf marginatus*) bluish green to yellow with black vertical stripes on the sides that is widely distributed in warm seas on both coasts of the Americas **b :** a related fish (*A. saxatilis*) of the western tropical Atlantic **5 :** the chief local officer in a Salvation Army corps who assists the corps officer

sergeant major of the army : a noncommissioned officer of the highest enlisted rank in the army — see RANK table

sergeant major of the marine corps : a noncommissioned officer of the highest enlisted rank in the marine corps — see RANK table

sergeant of the guard : the senior noncommissioned officer of an interior guard

ser·geant·ry *or* **ser·jeant·ry** \'-jəntrē, -ri\ *n* -ES [ME *serjauntrye*, fr. MF *sergenterie*, fr. *sergent* sergeant + *-erie* -ery] **:** SERGEANTY

ser·geant·ship *also* **ser·jeant·ship** \-jənt,ship\ *n* [*sergeant* + *-ship*] **:** the office of a sergeant

ser·geanty *or* **ser·jeanty** \-ntē\ *n* -ES [ME *sergeantie*, fr. MF *sergentie*, fr. *sergent* sergeant + *-ie* -y] **:** any of numerous feudal services of a somewhat personal or menial nature by which an estate is held of the king or other lord distinct from military tenure though it might involve service in war and from socage tenure and varying greatly with different holdings (as steward, marshal, constable, chamberlain, or esquire) — see GRAND SERGEANTY, PETIT SERGEANTY

serg·er \'sərjər\ *n* -S **:** one that serges

serges *pl of* SERGE, *pres 3d sing of* SERGE

serging *n* -S [fr. gerund of ²*serge*] **:** stitching made by serging

sergt *abbr, often cap* sergeant

se·ri \'serē, 'särē\ *n, pl* **seri** *or* **seris** *usu cap* **1 a :** an Indian people of the state of Sonora, Mexico **b :** a member of such people **2 :** the Serian language of the Seri people **3 :** SERIAN

¹**se·ri·al** \'sirēəl, 'sēr-\ *adj* [*series* + *-al*] **1 :** of, relating to, consisting of, or arranged in a series, rank, or row ⟨~ pictures⟩ ⟨~ observations⟩ ⟨a ~ act like walking —A.T.Weaver⟩ **2 :** occurring in regular succession ⟨~ concerts⟩ **3 :** appearing in successive parts or numbers ⟨a ~ story⟩ ⟨a ~ play⟩ ⟨wrote her a ~ account of his adventures —J.W.Krutch⟩ **4 :** belonging to a series; *specif* **:** belonging to a series maturing in installments periodically rather than on a single maturity date ⟨~ bonds⟩ ⟨~ equipment trust certificates⟩ **5 :** causing or producing a series ⟨~ production of a new-model boat⟩ ⟨denies that he is the pursued ~ murderer —Siegfried Kracauer⟩ **6 :** STICHIC **7 :** of or relating to music based on a series of tones in a fixed order without regard to traditional tonality; *esp* **:** TWELVE-TONE

²**serial** \"\ *n* -S **1 a :** a novel or other literary or pictorial work published in sections in successive issues of a publication **b :** a section of such a serial appearing in a single issue of a publication ⟨a cartoon ~ . . . in a boys' magazine —Malcolm Lowry⟩ **2 :** a publication (as a newspaper, journal, yearbook, or bulletin) issued as one of a consecutively numbered and indefinitely continued series **3 a :** a motion picture or radio or television play presented in a number of successive installments or continued indefinitely ⟨soap-opera ~*s*⟩ **b :** a single installment of such a serial ⟨sit through six complete showings of the western and the ~ —William Humphrey⟩ — compare EPISODE 1d **4 :** a subdivision (as of a military force) for movement by marching, by water (as in amphibious operations), or by air ⟨could see shells exploding along the rear of the ~ —*Combat Forces Jour.*⟩ ⟨battalion . . . moving as an independent ~ —P.W.Thompson⟩

serial bond *n* [¹*serial*] **:** one of a series of bonds maturing periodically rather than on a single maturity date

serial homology *n* **:** the resemblance between different members of a single series of structures (as vertebrae) in an organism

se·ri·al·ist \-ələst\ *n* -S [²*serial* + *-ist*] **1 :** a writer of serials **2 :** a composer of serial music

se·ri·al·i·ty \ˌsirē'aləd·ē\ *n* -ES [¹*serial* + *-ity*] **:** serial quality or state

se·ri·al·iza·tion \ˌsirēələ'zāshən, ˌsēr-, -ˌlī'z-\ *n* -S **:** the act or process of serializing; *esp* **:** arrangement and publication in the form of a serial ⟨~ rights to a book⟩

se·ri·al·ize \'-ˌ-ˌ-,līz\ *vt* -ED/-ING/-S *see -ize in Explan Notes* [¹*serial* + *-ize*] **1 :** to arrange in serial form ⟨*serialized* questions save time —S.L.Payne⟩ ⟨some system of concepts mentally classified, *serialized* —William James⟩ **2:** to publish in serial form ⟨~ a novel⟩

se·ri·al·ly \-ēəlē, -li\ *adv* **:** in serial form **:** in sequence ⟨~ numbered brass tags —W.E.Shinn⟩ ⟨school bonds, maturing ~ —*N.Y.Times*⟩

serial number *n* **:** a number indicating place in a series and used as a means of identification ⟨a soldier's *serial number*⟩

se·ri·al·o·graph \ˌ-ˌ-'alə,graf, -räf\ *or* **se·rio·graph** \'-ˌ-ə,g-\ *n* [*serialograph* fr. ¹*serial* + *-o-* + *-graph;* *seriograph* fr. *series* + *-o-* + *-graph*] **:** a device for making a number of radiographs in rapid sequence

serial radiography *n* [¹*serial*] **:** the technique of making radiographs in rapid sequence for the study of high-speed phenomena (as of the flow of blood through an artery)

serial rights *n pl* [²*serial*] **:** a right created by a copyright to publish a manuscript or artistic work or production separately as a serial in a periodical

serial tap *n* [¹*serial*] **:** one of a set of three taps used in succession for forming an internal screw thread first by making a roughing cut, second by cutting the thread a little fuller, and third by smoothing the thread and making it exact

seri·an \'serēən, 'sär-\ *n* -s *usu cap* [*Seri* + E *-an*] **:** a language family of the Hokan stock in Mexico comprising only the Seri language

se·ri·ary \'sirē,erē\ *adj* [*series* + *-ary*] **:** of or relating to a series

¹se·ri·ate \'sirē,ā|t, 'sēr-, -ēə|, *usu* |d·+V\ *adj* [(assumed) NL *seriatus*, fr. L *series* + *-atus* -ate] **1 :** arranged in a series or succession **2 :** characterized by crystals that vary gradually or in a continuous series ⟨granitized rocks have a haphazard, uneven ~ texture —G.E.Goodspeed⟩ — **se·ri·ate·ly** *adv*

²se·ri·ate \-ē,āt, *usu* -ād·+V\ *vt* -ED/-ING/-S [back-formation fr. *seriation*] **:** to arrange in a series ⟨measurements and indices of adults were *seriated* —F.M.Setzler⟩ ⟨rates for all the years covered were *seriated* —P.A.Sorokin⟩

¹se·ri·atim \,==ˈād·əm *also* -ˈad·-\ *adv* [ML, fr. L *series*] **:** in a series **:** SERIALLY ⟨the judges delivered their opinions ~ —*Harvard Law Rev.*⟩ ⟨setting forth ~ the terms of the offer —J.E.Davies⟩

²seriatim \ˈ==ˈ==\ *adj* **:** following seriatim ⟨elaborate ~ opinions —*Harvard Law Rev.*⟩ ⟨turn to the ~ discussion of these six needs —Carlos Baker⟩

se·ri·a·tion \,==ˈāshən\ *n* -s [L *series* + E *-ation*] **1 :** formation, arrangement, succession, or position in a series or orderly sequence **2 :** a method of determining a chronology (as for archaeological material) by a detailed study of a particular style or type (as of potsherds) that reveals an increase or decrease in the popularity of the style giving a tentative scale from early to late

seric \'sirik, 'ser-\ *adj, usu cap* [L *sericus* — more at SERICEOUS] **:** of, relating to, or characteristic of the Seres

sericea lespedeza \sə'rish(ē)ə-\ *or* **sericea** *n* -s [NL *Lespedeza sericea*, fr. *Lespedeza* + *sericea*, fr. LL, fem. of *sericeus* sericeous] **:** a perennial herbaceous lespedeza (*Lespedeza cuneata* syn. *L. sericea*) that is widely planted as a leguminous forage and hay crop esp. on poor soils

sericeo- *comb form* [LL *sericeus* sericeous] **:** sericeous and ⟨*sericeo*tomentose⟩

se·ri·ceous \sə'rishəs\ *adj* [LL *sericeus*, fr. L *sericum* silk, silk garment, fr. neut. of *sericus* of the Seres, silken, fr. Gk *sērikos*, fr. *Sēres* Seres + *-ikos* -ic] **1 :** of or relating to silk **:** consisting of silk **:** SILKY **2 :** PUBESCENT ⟨~ leaf⟩

se·rici·culture \sə'risə,kəlchə(r), 'serəsə-\ *n* [F *sériciculture*, fr. L *sericum* silk + F *culture*, fr. MF — more at SERICEOUS] **:** SERICULTURE

ser·i·cin \'serəsən\ *n* -s [ISV *seric-* (fr. L *sericum* silk) + *-in*] **:** a gelatinous protein that cements the two fibroin filaments in a silk fiber and that can be removed by degumming — called also *silk gum*

ser·i·cite \'serə,sīt\ *n* -s [G *sericit*, fr. L *sericus* silken + G *-it* -ite — more at SERICEOUS] **:** a scaly variety of muscovite having a silky luster and occurring in various metamorphic rocks — **ser·i·cit·ic** \ˈ==ˈsid·ik\ *adj*

ser·i·cit·iza·tion \,serə,sīd·əˈzāshən\ *n* -s [*sericite* + *-ization*] **:** the process or state of alteration by which minerals (as feldspar) are converted into sericite

ser·i·cit·ize \'serə,sīd·,īz\ *vt* -ED/-ING/-S [back-formation fr. *sericitization*] **:** to alter to sericite

ser·i·co·car·pus \,serəkō'kärpəs\ *n, cap* [NL, fr. Gk *sērikos* silken + NL *-carpus* — more at SERICEOUS] **:** a small genus of herbs (family Compositae) of the eastern U. S. having corymbose white-rayed flower heads with an ovoid involucre, squamous bracts, and silky achenes

ser·i·cor·nis \,serə'kȯrnəs\ *n, cap* [NL, fr. Gk *sērikos* + NL *-ornis*] **:** a genus of small noisy semiterrestrial insectivorous warblers (family Sylviidae) of Australia and New Guinea

ser·i·co·sto·mat·i·dae \,serəkōstō'mad·ə,dē\ *n pl, cap* [NL, fr. *Sericostomat-*, *Sericostoma*, type genus (fr. Gk *sērikos* + NL *-stomat-*, *-stoma*) + *-idae*] **:** a large and widely distributed family of caddis flies

ser·ic·te·ri·um \,se(,)rik'tirēəm\ *n, pl* **sericte·ria** \-ēə\ [NL, fr. Gk *sērikon* silk, fr. neut. of *sērikos* silken] **:** SERICTERY

se·ric·tery \sə'riktərē\ *n* -ES [NL *sericterium*] **:** the silk-producing gland of a caterpillar or other insect larva — compare SILK GLAND

seri·cultural \ˈserə+\ *adj* **:** of or relating to sericulture

seri·culture \'serə+,-\ *n* [L *sericum* silk + E *culture* — more at SERICEOUS] **:** the production of raw silk by raising silkworms — **seri·cul·tur·ist** \,serəˈkəlch(ə)rəst\ *n*

ser·i·ema \,sere'ēmə, -'āmə\ *n* -s [Tupi *çariama*, *seriema*, lit., crested] **:** CARIAMA 2

¹se·ries \'si(,)rēz, 'sē(-, -,riz\ *n, pl* **series** [L, fr. *serere* to join, bind together, entwine, link; akin to Gk *eirein* to fasten in rows, string together, *hormos* chain, necklace] **1 :** a group of usu. three or more things or events standing or succeeding in order and having a like relationship to each other **:** a spatial or temporal succession of persons or things **:** a group that has or admits an order of arrangement exhibiting progression ⟨a concert ~⟩ ⟨a TV ~⟩ ⟨a ~ of talks⟩ ⟨a ~ of governors⟩ ⟨a ~ of three European maps —*Nat'l Geographic*⟩ **2 :** the expression obtained from a mathematical sequence by connecting its terms with plus signs **3 a :** the coins or currency of a particular country and period, denomination, or ruler or for a particular purpose considered as a unit for study or collection ⟨ancient Greek ~⟩ ⟨U.S. half-dollar ~⟩ ⟨a commemorative ~⟩ **b :** a group of postage or semipostal stamps in different denominations and for different postal uses issued for a single commemorative or fund-raising purpose or having a common design theme **4 a :** a number of volumes by the same author connected by similarity of subject, grouped usu. under a collective title, and distinguished from his other works **b :** a number of volumes connected by similarity of subject and issued in succession by a single publisher usu. with a collective title and in uniform style **c :** a number of successive parts or volumes of a periodical publication or of writings similar in character or by the same author numbered separately to distinguish them from other similar sequences ⟨second ~⟩ **d :** a number of volumes put out by a single publisher and similar in format and price ⟨a dime-novel ~⟩ ⟨some so-called ~ are nothing more than miscellaneous collections of books published at the same price and in the same style —L.R. McColvin⟩ **5 a :** a succession of sedimentary or igneous rocks either continuously deposited or related in the history of their accumulation **b :** a division of sedimentary formations that are usu. larger than a stage and smaller than a system and are deposited during an epoch ⟨the Niagara ~⟩ ⟨the salt ~ of the Permian basin —H.I.Smith⟩ **6 a :** a group of specimens or types progressively differing from each other in some morphological or physiological attribute ⟨a ~ of fossils⟩ ⟨a ~ of plants⟩ ⟨a ~ of antitoxins⟩ **b :** a category of classification to which various taxonomic ranks have been assigned by different authors **7 a :** a group of chemical compounds related in composition and structure ⟨a homologous ~⟩ **b :** a sequence of chemical elements of increasing atomic numbers (as a period or part of a period in the periodic table) **c :** RADIOACTIVE SERIES **8 :** an arrangement of the parts of or elements in an electric circuit whereby the whole current passes through each part or element without dividing or branching — contrasted with *parallel* **9 :** a set of vowels connected by ablaut (as *i, a, u* in *ring, rang, rung*) — compare GRADE 4 **10 :** a range of printing types of the same name and face but in different sizes ⟨Caslon Old Style ~⟩ ⟨Caslon Old Style italic ~⟩ — compare FAMILY **11 a :** a number of baseball games (as 3 or 4) played on successive days between two league teams **b :** WORLD SERIES **12 :** a group of successive coordinate sentence elements joined together in one or another degree of distinctness represented by separation by commas, separation by commas and connection by *and*'s or *or*'s, separation by commas and connection by *and* or *or* between the last two members, or connection by *and*'s or *or*'s ⟨an a, b, and c ~⟩ **13 :** a rhythmic sequence ordered by continuous repetition of a rhythmic or metrical unit without further organization of the sequence as a whole into some pattern or system based not upon continuous repetition alone but upon other relations and correspondences of elements — compare SYSTEM, STROPHE **14 :** SOIL SERIES **15 :** three consecutive games in bowling **16 :** a classificatory grouping of pottery by similarity of some feature (as shape or design) — **in series :** in a serial arrangement **:** in sequence ⟨water could be raised from great depths by placing several pumps *in series* —S.F.Mason⟩

²series \"\ *adj* **:** of or relating to a series; *specif* **:** having its parts arranged or connected in series ⟨a ~ circuit⟩ **:** being in series with other units **:** SERIES-WOUND ⟨~ motor⟩

series dynamo *n* **1 :** a series-wound generator or motor **2 :** a dynamo running in series with another or others

series limit *n* **:** the position (as of a wavelength, wave number, or frequency) in an atomic line spectrum toward which the series progresses in the ultraviolet direction and which though there is no line at this point corresponds to the limiting value of photon energy characteristic of the series

series parallel *also* **series multiple** *n* **:** an arrangement of cells or circuit elements in which groups of two or more in parallel are connected in series

series resonance *n* **:** electrical resonance accomplished with a capacitance and an inductance in series — **series-resonant** \ˈ=(,)=ˈ=(=)=\ *adj*

series turn *n* **:** one of the turns in a series winding

series winding *n* **1 :** a winding in which the armature coil and the field-magnet coil are in series with the external circuit — opposed to *shunt winding* **2 :** WAVE WINDING

series-wound \ˈ=(,)=ˈ=\ *adj* **:** having the armature coil and the field-magnet coil in series with the external circuit ⟨*series-wound* dynamo⟩

ser·if *also* **ser·iph** *or* **cer·iph** \'serəf\ *n* -s [prob. fr. D *schreef*, stroke, line, fr. MD, fr. *schriven* to write, fr. L *scribere* — more at SCRIBE] **:** any of the short lines stemming from and at an angle to the upper and lower ends of the strokes of a letter — see TYPE illustration

seri·graph \'serə,graf, -rȧf\ *n* [L *sericum* silk + Gk *graphein* to write, draw — more at SERICEOUS, CARVE] **:** an original print produced by serigraphy ⟨there were some 60 ~*s* and other prints on view —*Newsweek*⟩

Serigraph \"\ *trademark* — used for an instrument for testing the breaking strength of materials (as silk)

se·rig·ra·pher \sə'rigrəfə(r)\ *n* -s [*serigraph* + *-er*] **:** one that produces prints by serigraphy

se·rig·ra·phy \-fē\ *n* -ES [L *sericum* + E *-graphy*] **:** the silk-screen process performed by an artist in producing an original print from his own design with color stencils of his own execution

se·rim·pi \sə'rimpē\ *n, pl* **serimpi** *or* **serimpis** [Malay *sĕrimpi*] **1 :** a female choric dancer at a Javanese court **2 :** a court dance performed by four serimpi

se·rin \sə'raⁿ, -an\ *n* -s [F, fr. MF, perh. fr. OProv *serena* bee-eater, fr. L *siren*, *sirena* siren] **:** a small European finch (*Serinus canarius*) related to the canary

ser·ine \'se,rēn, 'si,-, -,rən\ *n* -s [ISV *ser*icin + *-ine*; prob. orig. formed in G] **:** a crystalline amino acid $HOCH_2CH(NH_2)COOH$ known in three optically isomeric forms; *esp* **:** the levorotatory L-form obtained by hydrolysis of many proteins (as sericin, fibroin, or casein) or of various cephalins; β-hydroxy-alanine

ser·i·nette \ˈserəˈnet\ *n* -s [F, fr. *serin*] **:** a small hand organ used in training songbirds

serin finch *n* [NL *Serinus*] **:** a finch of the Old World genus *Serinus*

se·rin·ga \sə'riŋgə\ *n* -s [Pg, fr. syringe, rubber latex (fr. the use of rubber by the Brazilian Indians to make syringes), fr. ML *siringa* syringe] **1 :** MOCK ORANGE 1 **2 :** any of several Brazilian plants of the genus *Hevea* yielding rubber (as *H. brasiliensis*)

se·rin·gal \ˈserənˈgal\ *n* -s [Pg, fr. *seringa* rubber latex] **:** a grove or collection of trees (*Hevea brasiliensis* and possibly other species) yielding rubber

seringe *n* -s [by alter.] *archaic* **:** SYRINGE

ser·in·guei·ro \,serən'gā(,)rü, -)rō\ *n* -s [Pg, fr. *seringa* rubber latex + *-eiro* -er, fr. L *-arius*] **:** a Brazilian rubber gatherer

se·ri·nus \sə'rīnəs, -rēn-\ *n, cap* [NL, fr. F *serin* serin] **:** an Old World genus of finches including the canary, the serin, and related forms

se·rio \'sirē,ō\ *n* -s [by shortening] **:** SERIOCOMIC

serio- *comb form* [*serious*] **1 :** serious ⟨*serio*comedy⟩ **2 :** serious and ⟨*serio*ludicrous⟩

se·rio·comedy \ˈsirē(,)ō+\ *n* [*serio-* + *comedy*] **:** a comedy with serious elements or overtones **:** TRAGICOMEDY

¹se·rio·comic *also* **se·rio·comical** \"+\ *adj* [*serio-* + *comic*, *comical*] **1 :** having a mixture of seriousness and sport **:** serious and comic ⟨a ~ novel⟩ ⟨conducting a ~ feud with certain advertising and network executives —Clifton Fadiman⟩ **2 :** mock serious ⟨a ~ vocalist⟩ — **se·rio·comically** \"+\ *adv*

²seriocomic \"\ *n* **:** a seriocomic performer

seriograph *var of* SERIALOGRAPH

se·ri·o·la \sə'rīələ, -rēə-\ *n* [NL, fr. L, small jar, dim. of *seria* jar] **:** a genus of fishes containing the typical amberfishes and sometimes made type of a separate family but usu. included among the Carangidae — **se·ri·o·line** \-ī ə,līn, -ēə,lēn, -,lən\ *adj*

se·ri·os·i·ty \,sirē'äsəd·ē\ *n* -ES [ML *seriositat-*, *seriositas*, fr. LL *seriosus* serious + L *-itat-*, *-itas* -ity] **:** SERIOUSNESS

se·ri·o·so \ˈsirē'ō(,)sō, ,ser-, -)zō\ *adj* [It, fr. LL *seriosus*] **:** SERIOUS, GRAVE — used as a direction in music

se·ri·ous \'sirēəs, 'sēr-\ *adj* [ME *seryows*, fr. MF or LL; MF *serieux*, fr. LL *seriosus*, alter. (influenced by L *-osus* -ous) of L *serius*; prob. akin to OE *swǣr* heavy, sad, OHG *swār*, *swāri*, ON *svārr*, Goth *swers* respected, Lith *svarus* heavy] **1 :** grave in disposition, appearance, or manner **:** not light, not gay, nor volatile ⟨we were ~ to the point of solemnity —James Joyce⟩ ⟨her habitual expression was sedate and ~ —Eric Linklater⟩ ⟨such a stern and ~ face —Charles Kingsley⟩ ⟨will say facetious things in a most ~ way —Harvey Breit⟩ **2 a :** demanding earnest application **:** requiring considerable care ⟨work which has prevented me from any ~ correspondence —H.J. Laski⟩ ⟨settled down to the ~ study of music —J.T.Howard⟩ **b :** addressed to grave moods — used esp. of literature, drama, and music ⟨~ books⟩ ⟨a ~ play⟩ **c :** demanding or intended to be accepted as sincerely and earnestly motivated ⟨not a good work of art, but it is a ~ work of art —Arnold Bennett⟩ ⟨~ novelists⟩ ⟨~ candidates⟩ **3 a :** being in earnest **:** not jesting, trifling, or deceiving ⟨this observation was not ~. It was merely a trifle of affectionate malicious embroidery —Arnold Bennett⟩ ⟨no ~ antiquarian researches have been carried out —Norman Douglas⟩ ⟨~ conversation⟩ ⟨a ~ question⟩ **b** *archaic* **:** earnest about religious matters **c :** deeply interested **:** DEVOTED ⟨if there are ~ fishermen in your party —Jackson Rivers⟩ ⟨a ~ checker player⟩ ⟨~ drinkers⟩ **4 a :** IMPORTANT, SIGNIFICANT, EMPHATIC ⟨morning was sacred to ~ tasks like sewing —Virginia Woolf⟩ ⟨a drama — on which a ~ amount of care has been spent by many —A.T.Quiller-Couch⟩ ⟨take all the meals that would require any ~ cooking in the nearest restaurant —G.B.Shaw⟩ ⟨took ~ exception to the theory —Irving Babbitt⟩ ⟨the book is a ~ disappointment —*Geog. Jour.*⟩ **b** (1) **:** not easily answered or solved **:** WEIGHTY, DIFFICULT ⟨leaders began to raise ~ objections —C.E.Black & E.C.Helmreich⟩ ⟨a ~ problem⟩ (2) **:** such as to call forth strong measures for combatting or rectifying ⟨most of these systems are in a ~ financial position —*Economist*⟩ ⟨so ~ a lack of knowledge —C.D.Forde⟩ ⟨commodities which are not in ~ competition with our dynamic home industry —R.S.Thoman⟩ **c :** such as to cause considerable distress, anxiety, or inconvenience **:** attended with danger ⟨a ~ injury⟩ ⟨a ~ accident⟩ ⟨~ warfare broke out —R.A.Billington⟩

syn GRAVE, SOLEMN, SOMBER, SEDATE, STAID, SOBER, EARNEST: SERIOUS suggests absorption in, concern about, or inclination to purposive or important work, deep thought, or earnest care rather than frivolity or levity ⟨a *serious* book is one which holds before us some image of society to consider and condemn —Lionel Trilling⟩ ⟨a *serious* student intent on learning⟩ GRAVE may imply both seriousness and dignity, often accompanied by suggestions of weighty interest and responsibilities ⟨the slow, *grave*, simple, convinced tones with which she uttered the things that seemed to her the most worth while in life were more impressive than any arts of the orator —Havelock Ellis⟩ ⟨his *gravest* tone, the one he reserved for his rare appearances in the federal appellate courts —Louis Auchincloss⟩ SOLEMN may indicate deep, serious impressiveness or awesomeness with utter lack of levity ⟨holding the attorney's letter in his hand, and with so *solemn* and important an air that his wife, always ingeniously on the watch for calamity, thought the worst was about to befall —W.M.Thackeray⟩ ⟨Sabbath was made a *solemn* day, meet only for preaching, praying, and Bible reading —C.A. & Mary Beard⟩ SOMBER applies to a melancholy or depressing gravity completely lacking in color, light, or cheer ⟨the Scots, famed for *somber* Calvinism and its intellectual theologizing, did not expect to warm to the enthusiastic kind of religion —P.D.Whitney⟩ ⟨slowly she swept into the *somber* rhythms . . . beginning so softly that the music was scarcely audible, climbing steadily toward a climax —Louis Bromfield⟩ SEDATE implies accustomed, decorous seriousness and studied absence of insouciance or lightness ⟨a professional army man is as *sedate* as a lawyer —Green Peyton⟩ ⟨her habitual expression was *sedate* and serious, a permanent reproof, as it were, to those who were first attracted by the voluptuous quality of her admirable figure —Eric Linklater⟩ STAID indicates a settled, accustomed sedateness and self-restraint ⟨most of the other cults had their public festivals, when the *staid* Roman citizen was repelled by the wild dances and the frenzied paeans —John Buchan⟩ ⟨the older city of *staid* residences, spotless streets, and a homogeneous population, all overhung with a quickly felt aura of contentment and satisfaction —*Amer. Guide Series: Pa.*⟩ SOBER may apply to grave controlling or subduing of emotion or to serious concentrating on purpose ⟨this work is certainly of more *sober* mien than most of its author's others. It is very long and very serious, and both these qualities are certainly deliberate observances —Virgil Thomson⟩ ⟨I never saw a *soberer* holiday crowd . . . it was almost sabbatarian in its decorousness —Robert Lynd⟩ EARNEST suggests steady sincerity and intentness of purpose ⟨an *earnest* student⟩ ⟨many of the *padres* were scholars, and all were *earnest* in their endeavor to convert and civilize the natives —*Amer. Guide Series: Fla.*⟩

se·ri·ous·ly *adv* **:** in a serious manner or vein **:** to a serious extent **:** EARNESTLY, SEVERELY ⟨most of the land . . . is ~ overgrazed —W.W.Beatty⟩ ⟨if we consider his works at all ~ —George Woodcock⟩ ⟨the ~ retarded readers —E.W.Kinne⟩ ⟨could see he was ~ an invalid —Kenneth Roberts⟩

serious-minded \ˈ==ˈ==\ *adj* **:** having a serious disposition or trend of thought — **serious-minded·ly** *adv* — **serious-minded·ness** *n* -ES

se·ri·ous·ness *n* -ES **:** the quality or state of being serious ⟨a lack of solemnity is not necessarily a lack of ~ —Robert Rice⟩ ⟨consider the ~ of the charges⟩

seriph *var of* SERIF

se·rir \sə'ri(ə)r\ *n, pl* **serir :** a pebble-strewn desert in the Libyan Sahara

seris *pl of* SERI

serj *abbr, often cap* serjeant

ser·ja·nia \sə(r)'jānyə, -nēə\ *n, cap* [NL, irreg. fr. Philippe *Serjeant*, 17th cent. Fr. botanist + NL *-ia*] **:** a genus of tropical American woody tendril-bearing vines (family Sapindaceae) having compound leaves, irregular yellow racemose flowers with four petals and five concave sepals, and fruit that is wing-margined

serjeant *var of* SERGEANT

serjeant-at-law \ˈ===ˈ=\ *also* **sergeant-at-law** *n, pl* **serjeants-at-law** *also* **sergeants-at-law :** a barrister of the highest rank answering to the doctor of the civil law, outranking king's counsel socially but in professional rank inferior to them, and until 1846 having the exclusive right to be heard in the Court of Common Pleas

serit *abbr, often cap* serjeant

ser·mo \'se(ə)r(,)mō\ *n, pl* **sermo·nes** \ser'mō(,)nās\ **:** SERMO GENERALIS

sermocination *n* -s [L *sermocination-*, *sermocinatio* conversation, fr. *sermocinatus* (past part. of *sermocinari* to converse, fr. *sermo* speech, conversation) + *-ion-*, *-io* -ion — more at SERMON] **1** *obs* **:** DISCOURSE, SERMON **2** *obs* **:** a form of prosopopoeia in which the speaker answers his own question or remark immediately

sermo co·ti·di·a·nus \-kō,tēdē'ānəs\ *n* [ML, fr. L, everyday speech] **:** Vulgar Latin spoken by the educated class — distinguished from *sermo plebeius*

sermo ge·ne·ra·lis \-,genə'rāləs\ *n, pl* **sermones genera·les** \-ā(,)lās\ [ML, lit., general sermon] **:** AUTO-DA-FÉ

¹ser·mon \'sərmən, 'səm-, 'səim-, *dial* 'särm-, 'sȧm-\ *vb* -ED/-ING/-S [ME *sermonen*, fr. OF *sermoner*, fr. *sermon*] *vt, archaic* **:** to preach to ~ *vi, archaic* **:** PREACH

²sermon \"\ *n* -s [ME, fr. OF, fr. ML *sermon-*, *sermo* speech, conversation, religious discourse, fr. L, speech, conversation, fr. *serere* to join, link together — more at SERIES] **1** *obs* **:** DISCOURSE, TALK **2 a :** a religious discourse delivered in public usu. by a clergyman as a part of a worship service ⟨preached his maiden ~ last Sunday⟩ **b :** a written discourse delivered or intended for delivery as a sermon ⟨a book of ~*s*⟩ **3 a :** a serious address **:** a lecture on conduct or duty **:** HOMILY ⟨going around the country preaching ~*s* on the need of defending the freedom of the mind —Elmer Davis⟩ ⟨the usual ~ by the teacher . . . on "why you should like to go to school" —H.C.McKown⟩ ⟨such little ~*s* on intelligent marketing are part of the instruction —*New Yorker*⟩ **b :** an annoying harangue ⟨didn't ask for a ~ on the subject⟩ **4 :** a person or thing whose nature suggests edifying thoughts ⟨~*s* in stones —Shak.⟩ ⟨her story is a ~ warning men against a devotion to lust —F.N.Magill⟩

ser·mon·ary \-mə,nerē\ *n* -ES [¹*sermon* + *-ary*] **:** a collection of sermons

ser·mon·ette \ˈ==ˈnet\ *n* -s [¹*sermon* + *-ette*] **:** a short sermon ⟨dial a . . . telephone number and receive a two-minute ~ spoken by a minister —Freling Foster⟩

ser·mon·ic \(')=ˈmanik\ *also* **ser·mon·i·cal** \-nəkəl\ *adj* [¹*sermon* + *-ic*, *-ical*] **1 :** of, relating to, resembling, or appropriate to a sermon ⟨devotional and ~ books⟩ ⟨four ~ addresses⟩ ⟨a long ~ essay —Roger Hazelton⟩ **2 :** given to sermonizing **:** DIDACTIC ⟨teachers . . . who are ~ —*Christian Century*⟩ ⟨the *sermonical* turn which I now feel I must take —*Yale Rev.*⟩

ser·mon·ish \ˈ=,mənish\ *adj* [¹*sermon* + *-ish*] **1 :** suggestive of a sermon **2 :** disposed to hear or deliver a sermon

ser·mon·ism \-,nizəm\ *n* -s [L *sermon-*, *sermo* speech, conversation + E *-ism* — more at SERMON] **:** the conceptualism of Abelard

ser·mon·ist \-,nəst\ *n* -s [¹*sermon* + *-ist*] **:** one who writes or delivers sermons

ser·mon·ize \-,nīz\ *vb* -ED/-ING/-S *see -ize in Explan Notes* [¹*sermon* + *-ize*] *vi* **1 a :** to compose, write, or deliver a sermon ⟨listen attentively to the *sermonizing* of the bishop —H.E.Rollins⟩ **b :** to discourse didactically or dogmatically ⟨cannot even enjoy a sunny day without *sermonizing* —*Times Lit. Supp.*⟩ **2 :** to inculcate rigid rules **:** LECTURE, ADMONISH ⟨the film attempts neither to dramatize nor ~ —Arthur Knight⟩ ~ *vt* **1 :** to preach or discourse to or on **:** address at length in a didactic and solemn manner ⟨tries to ~ the government —Isaac Deutscher⟩ ⟨happily does not ~ the gospel of work —Herbert Feinstein⟩ **2 :** to force or put by preaching to ⟨~ one into energy⟩

ser·mon·iz·er \-zə(r)\ *n* -s **:** one that sermonizes **:** PREACHER

ser·mon·less \-mənləs\ *adj* **:** lacking a sermon

ser·mon·ol·o·gy \,=mə'näləjē\ *n* -ES [¹*sermon* + *-o-* + *-logy*] **1 :** knowledge or study of sermons **2 :** the preaching of sermons **3 :** SERMONS

sermo ple·be·ius \ˈ=(,)=plə'bā(y)əs\ *n* [ML, fr. L, speech of the lower classes] **:** Vulgar Latin spoken by the common people — distinguished from *sermo cotidianus*

sero- *comb form* [L *serum* — more at SERUM] **1 :** serum **:** connection with or relation to serum ⟨*sero*diagnosis⟩ **2 :** serous and ⟨*sero*fibrinous⟩

se·ro·diagnosis \ˈsi(,)rō *sometimes* ˈse(-+\ *n* [NL, fr. *sero-* + *diagnosis*] **:** diagnosis by the use of serum (as in the Wassermann and Widal's tests) typically involving either the testing of serum from a patient for its behavior with a known germ or the testing of a germ isolated from a patient against serum from a patient with a known disease

se·ro·diagnostic \"+\ *adj* [*sero-* + *diagnostic*] **:** of or relating to serodiagnosis

se·ro·fibrinous \"+\ *adj* [ISV *sero-* + *fibrinous*] **:** composed of or characterized by serum and fibrin ⟨~ pleurisy⟩

se·ro·log·ic \ˌsirəˈläjik, ˌser-\ *or* **se·ro·log·i·cal** \-jə̇kəl\ *adj* **:** of, relating to, or employing the methods of serology — **se·ro·log·i·cal·ly** \-jə̇k(ə)lē\ *adv*

se·rol·o·gist \sə̇ˈräləjə̇st, seˈr-\ *n* -s **:** a specialist in serology

se·rol·o·gy \-jē\ *n* -ES [ISV *sero-* + *-logy*] **1 :** a science that treats of serums and their reactions and properties esp. concerned with antibodies, antigens, haptens, and complement — compare IMMUNOLOGY **2 a :** serological knowledge in respect to a particular state or disease ⟨the ~ of syphilis⟩ **b :** a serological test ⟨blood ~ was negative⟩

se·ro·mucoid \ˌsi(ˌ)rō *sometimes* ˌse(-+\ *n* [*sero-* + *mucoid*] **:** a glycoprotein of serum that is not coagulated by heat

se·ro·muscular \"+\ *adj* [NL *serosa* + *muscularis*] **:** of combined serosa and muscularis ⟨the ~ layer of the stomach⟩

se·ron \səˈrōn, -rȯn\ *n* -s [MexSp *cerón*] **:** a rather small tropical American tree (*Phyllostylon brasiliensis*) of the family Ulmaceae that yields Santo Domingan boxwood

se·ro·negative \ˌsi(ˌ)rō *sometimes* ˌse(-+\ *adj* [ISV *sero-* + *negative*] **:** having a negative serum reaction ⟨early ~ syphilis⟩

se·ro·negativity \"+\ *n* **:** the state of being seronegative often used as a criterion of the elimination of an infection ⟨after six months' medication complete ~ was attained⟩

se·roon *also* **ce·roon** \səˈrün\ *or* **se·ron** \səˈrōn, -rȯn\ *n* -s [Sp *serón* hamper, crate, aug. of *sera* basket] **:** a bale or package (as of indigo) covered with hide or wood bound with hide

se·root *also* **seroot fly** *or* **se·rut** \səˈrüt(-)\ *n* -s [perh. fr. Ar *surāṭ* sharp like a sword, voracious] **:** a bloodsucking tabanid fly (genus *Pangonia*) that is remarkable for its very long proboscis and is very troublesome to men and animals in southern Egypt and the Republic of the Sudan

se·ro·positive \ˌsi(ˌ)rō *sometimes* ˌse(-+\ *adj* [ISV *sero-* + *positive*] **:** having a positive serum reaction

se·ro·purulent \"+\ *adj* [*sero-* + *purulent*] **:** consisting of a mixture of serum and pus ⟨a ~ exudate⟩

se·ro·reaction \"+\ *n* [ISV *sero-* + *reaction*] **:** a serological reaction

se·ro·resistance \"+\ *n* [*sero-* + *resistance*] **:** failure to attain seronegativity after intensive or prolonged treatment that results in subsidence of clinical symptoms — used chiefly of advanced or congenital syphilis — **se·ro·resistant** \"+\ *adj*

se·ro·sa \sə̇ˈrōsə, -ōzə\ *n, pl* **serosas** \-əz\ *also* **sero·sae** \-ˌsē, -ˌzē\ [NL, fr. fem. of *serosus* serous, fr. L *serum* + *-osus* -ous] **1 a :** CHORION 1 **b :** a comparable membrane of blastodermic origin that encloses the embryo of many insects and other arthropods **2 :** a serous membrane; *specif* **:** the outermost delicate layer of serous connective tissue and mesothelial cells that encloses an organ or lines a bodily cavity

se·ro·sal \-ōsəl, -ōzəl\ *adj* [NL *serosa* + E *-al*] **:** of, relating to, or made up of serosa ⟨the ~ surface of the bowel⟩ ⟨a ~ cyst on the ovary⟩

se·ro·sanguinous *or* **se·ro·sanguineous** \ˌsi(ˌ)rō *sometimes* ˌse(-+\ *adj* [*sero-* + *sanguinous* or *sanguineous*] **:** containing both blood and serous fluid ⟨a ~ discharge⟩

se·ro·si·tis \ˌsirōˈsīd·ə̇s, ˌser-, -ˈzī-\ *n* -ES [NL, fr. *serosa* + *-itis*] **:** inflammation of one or more serous membranes (as the pleura and pericardium)

se·ros·i·ty \sə̇ˈräsəd·ē\ *n* -ES [F *sérosité*, fr. MF, fr. *sereux* serous + *-ité* -ity] **:** the quality or state of being serous

se·ro·therapy \ˌsi(ˌ)rō *sometimes* ˌse(-+\ *n* [ISV *sero-* + *therapy*] **:** the treatment of a disease with specific immune serum

se·rot·i·nal \səˈrätᵊnəl, seˈr-; ˌserəˈtīnᵊl\ *adj* [L *serotinus* coming late + E *-al* — more at SEROTINE] **:** of or relating to the latter and usu. drier part of summer **:** occurring in the latter half of summer ⟨a ~ generation of aphids⟩ ⟨ponds . . . drying up about the beginning of the ~ season —*Ecology*⟩

¹ser·o·tine \ˈserəˌtīn, -tə̇n, -ˌtēn\ *adj* [L *serotinus* coming late, fr. *sero* late — more at SOIREE] **:** late esp. in developing or flowering

²ser·o·tine \-ˌtēn\ *n* -s [F *sérotine*, fr. L *serotina*, fem. of *serotinus* coming late] **:** a common European brown bat (*Eptesicus serotinus*)

se·rot·i·nous \səˈrätᵊnəs, seˈr-\ *adj* [L *serotinus* coming late] **:** SEROTINAL

se·ro·to·nin \ˌsirəˈtōnə̇n, -tän-\ *n* -s [*sero-* + *tonic* + *-in*; fr. its constrictive effect] **:** a crystalline phenolic amine $HOC_8H_5NCH_2CH_2NH_2$ derived from indole that is a powerful vasoconstrictor, that occurs esp. in the blood serum and gastric mucosa of mammals, in small amounts in the brain, and in the secretions of various amphibians and that is formed in animal tissues from tryptophan — called also *5-hydroxytryptamine*

se·ro·type \ˈsirəˌtīp, ˈser-\ *n* [*sero-* + *type*] **:** a group of intimately related microorganisms distinguished by the possession of a common set of antigens; *also* **:** the antigen set characteristic of such a group

se·rous \ˈsirəs, *sometimes* ˈsēr- *or* ˈser-\ *adj* [MF *sereux*, fr. *serum* (fr. L) + *-eux* -ous] **1 :** resembling serum esp. in thin watery constitution ⟨a ~ exudate⟩ ⟨~ fluid⟩ **2 :** of or relating to serum ⟨the ~ fraction of blood⟩

serous gland *n* **:** a gland secreting a serous fluid

serous membrane *n* **:** any of various thin membranes (as the peritoneum, pericardium, or pleurae) that consist of a single layer of thin flat mesothelial cells resting on a connective tissue stroma, secrete a serous fluid, and usu. line bodily cavities or enclose the organs contained in such cavities

se·row \səˈrō\ *n* -s [Lepcha *să-ro* long-haired Tibetan goat] **:** any of several Asiatic goat antelopes of a widely distributed genus (*Capricornis*) related to the gorals and including a large thin-coated maned southern type (*C. sumatraensis*) and a much smaller maneless woolly-coated northern type (*C. crispus*) of Japan and Formosa

serozem *var of* SIEROZEM

se·ro·zyme \ˈsirəˌzīm, ˈser-\ *n* -s [ISV *sero-* + *-zyme*] **:** PROTHROMBIN

¹ser·pent \ˈsərpənt, ˈsə̄p-, ˈsəip-, *dial* ˈsärp- *or* ˈsȧp-\ *n* -s *often attrib* [ME, fr. MF, fr. L *serpent-, serpens*, fr. pres. part. of *serpere* to creep; akin to Gk *herpein* to creep, Skt *sarpati* he creeps, *sarpa* serpent] **1 a** *archaic* **:** a noxious creature (as a snake, crocodile, spider, or toad) that creeps, hisses, or stings **b :** SNAKE; *esp* **:** a large snake **c :** SEA SERPENT **2 :** DEVIL 1 ⟨the great dragon was cast out, that old ~ —Rev 12:9 (AV)⟩ **3 :** a representation of a serpent esp. in the form of an ornament **4 :** a subtle treacherous malicious person or personified quality ⟨a ~ that has betrayed your brother —Liam O'Flaherty⟩ **5 :** a large cannon of the 15th to 17th centuries — compare BOMBARD, ⁵SERPENTINE **6 a :** a firework having a serpentine motion through the air or along the ground **b :** PHARAOH'S SERPENT **7 a :** a bass wind instrument of the trumpet type having a cupped mouthpiece, a long serpentine-twisted conical wooden tube pierced with finger holes, and a strong but coarse tone — compare CORNET 1a **b :** a pipe-organ reed stop with a trombone tone **8 :** a pale green that is bluer and stronger than celadon gray and yellower and darker than spray green

serpent 7a

²serpent \"\ *vi* -ED/-ING/-S [F *serpenter*, fr. MF, fr. *serpent*] **:** to wind or turn like a serpent **:** MEANDER ⟨old rocks want monstrous roots to ~ among them —Robinson Jeffers⟩

ser·pen·tar·ia \ˌsərpənˈta(a)rēə\ *n* -s [LL, snakeroot, fr. L *serpent-, serpens* serpent, snake + *-aria* -ary] **1 :** the dried rhizome and roots of a birthwort (*Aristolochia serpentaria*) **2 :** the dried rhizome and roots of the Texas snakeroot

ser·pen·tar·i·um \-ēəm\ *n, pl* **serpentariums** \-ēəmz\ *or* **serpentar·ia** \-ēə\ [NL, fr. L *serpent-, serpens* + *-arium*] **:** an enclosure in which snakes are kept

ser·pen·tary *also* **serpentary root** \ˈ⸗⸗ˌterē\ *n* -ES [LL *serpentaria*] **:** SERPENTARIA

ser·pent·cleide \ˈ⸗pəntˌklīd\ *n* -s [¹*serpent* + *ophicleide*] **:** a large ophicleide with a wooden tube

serpent cucumber *n* **:** SNAKE MELON

ser·pent d'é·glise \ˌserˌpäⁿdāˈglēz\ *n, pl* **serpents d'église** \"\ [F, lit., church serpent; fr. its being used to accompany the voice in plainchant] **:** SERPENT 7a

serpent eagle *n* **1 :** any of several raptorial birds of the genus *Spilornis* that prey on snakes and inhabit southern Asia and the East Indies **2 :** HARRIER EAGLE

serpent eater *n* **1 :** SECRETARY BIRD **2 :** MARKHOR

serpent eel *n* **:** SNAKE EEL

ser·pen·tes \(ˌ)sərˈpen·(ˌ)tēz\ *n pl, cap* [NL, fr. L, pl. of *serpent-, serpens* serpent] **:** a suborder or other division of Squamata comprising the snakes

serpent fern *n* **:** a tropical often epiphytic American fern (*Phlebodium aureum*) with brown scaly rhizomes often cultivated for its large simple deeply lobed fronds

serpent gourd *n* **:** SNAKE GOURD 2a

serpent grass *n* **:** ALPINE BISTORT

serpenti- *comb form* [L, fr. *serpent-, serpens*] **:** serpent ⟨*serpenti*vorous⟩

ser·pen·ti·form \(ˌ)sərˈpentəˌfȯrm\ *adj* [LL *serpentiformis*, fr. L *serpenti-* + *-formis* -form] **:** having the form of a snake

ser·pen·tile \ˈsərpənˌtīl, -ˌtəl, -(ˌ)til, -ˌtēl\ *adj* [¹*serpent* + *-ile*] **:** resembling a serpent (as in nature or appearance)

¹ser·pen·tine \ˈsərpənˌtēn, -tīn\ *adj* [ME, fr. MF *serpentin*, fr. LL *serpentinus*, fr. L *serpent-, serpens* serpent + *-inus* -ine] **1 :** relating to a serpent **:** resembling a serpent (as in form or movement) ⟨the muscular line moved and swayed in a ~ rhythm —Margaret Long⟩ **2 :** relating to or like the serpent as typifying Satan **:** subtly wily or tempting **:** GUILEFUL, DIABOLIC ⟨the ~ will to power —J.C.Powys⟩ ⟨an inescapable fascination of a ~ kind —Richard Watts⟩ ⟨that ~ plotter —R.B.Morris⟩ **3 :** winding or turning one way and another **:** MEANDERING, SINUOUS ⟨a ~ road⟩ ⟨a ~ wall⟩ ⟨~ braid⟩ ⟨these essays . . . in their intricate and ~ manner —R.W.B. Lewis⟩ **4 :** having a compound curve whose central curve is convex — used esp. of the front of a piece of cabinet furniture; opposed to *oxbow*

²serpentine \"\ *vb* -ED/-ING/-S *vi* **:** to move like a serpent **:** wind along ⟨the trail *serpentining* down —Carl Jonas⟩ ⟨behind them *serpentined* the long line of yoked couples —C.S. Forester⟩ ~ *vt* **:** to take by a serpentine course or serpentine methods **:** INSINUATE

³serpentine \"\ *n* -s **1 :** something (as a line, a wall, or a section of road) that winds sinuously ⟨the cart wheeled round the steep ~*s* —Marcia Davenport⟩; *specif* **:** a file (as of people) moving in a sinuous or winding line ⟨a few minor processions along with any number of spontaneous ~*s* —Ray Duncan⟩ — compare CROCODILE **2 a** *or* **serpentine dance :** a mixed group dance in single file with a leader guiding a wavering snakelike course along the ground — compare FARANDOLE, SNAKE DANCE 2 **b :** a show dance with sinuous manipulation of streamers **3 :** a skating figure in which the skater executes a series of usu. three circles requiring changes of edge **4 :** a light green that is deeper and very slightly bluer than average mint green and bluer and deeper than variscite green — compare SERPENTINE GREEN

⁴serpentine \"\ *n* -s [ME, the rock serpentine, fr. ML *serpentina, serpentinum*, fr. LL, fem. & neut. of *serpentinus* resembling a serpent] **1 :** CHRYSOTILE **2 :** ANTIGORITE **3 :** a rock composed of chrysotile and antigorite often in layers with or without other minerals having usu. a dull green color often with a spotted or mottled appearance or a red or brownish hue due to the presence of iron, occurring in masses (as antigorite) or in fibrous form (as chrysotile), resulting from the alteration of other magnesian minerals (as olivine, amphibole, and pyroxene), and used as an ornamental stone — compare ASBESTOS **4** *or* **serpentine soil :** soil formed by the weathering of serpentine rock

⁵serpentine \"\ *n* -s [ME, fr. MF *serpentin*, fr. *serpentin* resembling a serpent, fr. LL *serpentinus*] **1 :** a cannon of the 15th to 17th centuries of various calibers usu. longer and lighter than a bombard **2 :** a serpentine attachment of a harquebus lock to hold the match

⁶ser·pen·tine \-tēn\ *also* **ser·pen·tin** \-tan\ *n* -s [F *serpentin*, fr. *serpentin* resembling a serpent, fr. MF] **1 :** long narrow strips of rolled colored paper thrown (as at a carnival or party) so as to unroll as streamers ⟨everyone throws ~ and confetti —Bess A. Garner⟩ **2 :** a piece of serpentine ⟨various kinds of noisemakers and ~*s* at each place —*Los Angeles (Calif.) Examiner*⟩

serpentine green *n* [¹*serpentine*] **:** a light olive color that is greener and paler than citrine, redder and deeper than grape green, and redder and paler than old moss green — compare ³SERPENTINE 4

serpentine jade *n* **:** a serpentine that resembles jade

serpentine layerage *n* **:** a method of layering which is used chiefly with woody vines and in which the stem to be propagated is laid on the ground and covered with earth at intervals to induce rooting of the buried sections which are later separated to form new plants

serpentine leaf miner *n* **:** a grub that is the larva of a small fly (*Liriomyza brassicae*) and that eats out slender white winding burrows in the leaves of cabbage and related plants

ser·pen·tine·ly *adv* **:** in a serpentine manner

serpentine roulette *n* **:** a wavy-line stamp roulette that produces scallops on the edge of a detached stamp

serpentine verse *n* [¹*serpentine*; fr. the frequent depiction of serpents with their tails in their mouths] **:** a line of verse beginning and ending with the same word

serpentine ware *n* [⁴*serpentine*] **:** a hard green-spotted or green-veined pottery suggestive of serpentine

ser·pen·tin·ing·ly *adv* [*serpentining* (fr. pres. part. of ²*serpentine*) + *-ly*] **:** in a serpentining manner **:** WINDINGLY

ser·pen·tin·ite \ˈsərpənˌtēˌnīt, -tīˌn-\ *n* -s [ISV ⁴*serpentine* + *-ite*] **:** a rock consisting chiefly of serpentine

ser·pen·tin·iza·tion \ˌ⸗⸗ˌnəˈzāshən, -ˌnīˈz-\ *n* -s [ISV ⁴*serpentine* + *-ization*] **:** the process or state of alteration by which minerals (as olivine) are converted into serpentine

ser·pen·tin·ize \-ˌnīz\ *vt* -ED/-ING/-S [prob. back-formation fr. *serpentinization*] **:** to convert (a magnesian silicate) into serpentine ⟨*serpentinized* dunite⟩

ser·pen·tin·oid \-ˌnȯid\ *adj* [⁴*serpentine* + *-oid*] **:** SERPENTINOUS

ser·pen·ti·nous \-nəs\ *adj* [ISV ⁴*serpentine* + *-ous*] **:** relating to, consisting of, or resembling serpentine ⟨~ rocks⟩ ⟨~ gangue mineral⟩

ser·pent·ize \ˈ⸗pənˌtīz, -ntˌīz\ *vb* -ED/-ING/-S [¹*serpent* + *-ize*] **:** SERPENTINE ⟨the river . . . ~*s* more than you can conceive in the vale —Horace Walpole⟩

serpentlike \ˈ⸗⸗ˌ⸗\ *adj* **:** resembling or felt to resemble a serpent **:** SERPENTINE, SNAKELIKE, TREACHEROUS

ser·pent·ly *adv* [ME, fr. ¹*serpent* + *-ly*] *archaic* **:** in the manner of a serpent

serpent melon *n* **:** SNAKE MELON

serpent radish *n* **:** RAT-TAILED RADISH

ser·pent·ry \ˈsərpəntrē\ *n* -ES [¹*serpent* + *-ry*] **:** SERPENTS

serpents *pl of* SERPENT, *pres 3d sing of* SERPENT

serpent star *n* **:** OPHIUROID

serpent stone *n* **:** ADDER STONE

serpent's–tongue \ˈ⸗⸗ˌ⸗\ *n* **1 :** ADDER'S-TONGUE 1 **2 :** the fossil tooth of a shark

serpentwood \ˈ⸗⸗ˌ⸗\ *n* **1 :** an East Indian shrub (*Rauwolfia serpentina*) the root of which is used as a source of reserpine **2 :** NUX VOMICA 2

serpent worm *n* **:** GUINEA WORM

¹ser·phid \ˈsərfə̇d\ *adj* [NL *Serphidae*] **:** of or relating to the Serphidae

²serphid \"\ *n* -s **:** a wasp of the family Serphidae

Ser·phi·dae \-fəˌdē\ *n pl, cap* [NL, fr. *Serphus*, type genus (fr. Gk *serphos* a small winged insect) + *-idae*] **:** a family of small serphoid wasps having a tubular retractile ovipositor and being parasitic in the eggs and larvae of other insects

¹ser·phoid \-ˌfȯid\ *adj* [NL *Serphoidea*] **:** of or relating to the Serphoidea

²serphoid \"\ *n* -s **:** a wasp of the superfamily Serphoidea

Ser·phoi·dea \(ˌ)sərˈfȯidēə\ *n pl, cap* [NL, fr. *Serphus* + *-oidea*] **:** a superfamily of minute wasps that as larvae are parasites of other insects and sometimes spiders and have females with the usu. tubular ovipositor emerging from the extreme end of the body

ser·pie·rite \ˈsərpēəˌrīt, sərˈpiˌr-\ *n* -s [F *serpiérite*, fr. J. B. *Serpieri*, 19th cent. Ital. engineer, explorer of the ancient silver mines at Laurium + F *-ite*] **:** a mineral $(Cu,Zn,Ca)_5(SO_4)_2(OH)_6 \cdot 3H_2O$ consisting of a hydrous basic sulfate of copper, calcium, and zinc occurring in small tabular bluish green crystals and tufts

ser·pig·i·nous \(ˌ)sərˈpijənəs\ *adj* [ML *serpigin-, serpigo* + E *-ous*] **:** CREEPING, SPREADING ⟨~ ringworm⟩; *broadly* **:** healing over in one portion while continuing to advance in another ⟨~ ulcer⟩ — **ser·pig·i·nous·ly** *adv*

ser·pi·go \(ˌ)sərˈpī(ˌ)gō, -pē(-\ *n, pl* **ser·pig·i·nes** \-pijəˌnēz\ *or* **serpigoes** [ME, fr. ML *serpigin-, serpigo*, fr. L *serpere* to creep — more at SERPENT] *archaic* **:** a creeping or spreading skin disease (as ringworm)

ser·po·let \ˌsərpəˈlet\ *n* -s [F, fr. Prov *serpolet*, dim. of *serpol* wild thyme, fr. L *serpyllum, serpullum*, modif. (influenced by *serpere* to creep) of Gk *herpyllon*, fr. *herpein* to creep — more at SERPENT] **:** WILD THYME

ser·pu·la \ˈsərpyələ\ *n* [NL, fr. L, little snake, fr. *serpere* to creep] **1** *cap* **:** a genus (the type of the family Serpulidae) of small marine polychaete worms having brightly colored gills and constructing and living in contorted calcareous tubes that may be closed with horny opercula **2** *pl* **serpulas** \-ləz\ *or* **serpulae** \-ˌlē, -ˌlī\ **:** any worm of the genus *Serpula* or family Serpulidae

ser·pu·lan \-lən\ *n* [NL *Serpula* + E *-an*] **:** SERPULA 2

¹ser·pu·lid \-lə̇d\ *adj* [NL *Serpulidae*] **:** of or relating to the Serpulidae

²serpulid \"\ *n* -s **:** a worm of the family Serpulidae

Ser·pu·li·dae \(ˌ)sərˈpyüləˌdē\ *n pl, cap* [NL, fr. *Serpula*, type genus + *-idae*] **:** a large family of marine polychaete worms including various cosmopolitan genera — see SERPULA — **ser·pu·li·dan** \-dən\ *adj or n*

ser·pu·line \ˈsərpyəˌlīn, -lən, -ˌlēn\ *adj* [NL *Serpula* + E *-ine*] **:** of or relating to the Serpulidae **:** formed by or composed of the tubes of serpulae

ser·pu·lite \-ˌlīt\ *n* -s [ISV *serpula* + *-ite*] **:** a fossil worm tube — **ser·pu·lit·ic** \ˌ⸗⸗ˈlid·ik\ *adj*

ser·pu·loid \ˈ⸗⸗ˌlȯid\ *adj* [NL *Serpula* + E *-oid*] **:** resembling or related to the Serpulidae

¹ser·ra \ˈserə\ *n, pl* **ser·rae** \-ˌrē, -ˌrī\ [NL, fr. L, saw, sawfish] **1 :** a sawlike organ or part (as the saw of a sawfish or of a sawfly) **2 :** SERRATION

²serra \"\ *n* -s [Pg, saw, serra, fr. L, saw] **:** SIERRA 1a

ser·ra·del·la \ˌserəˈdelə\ *also* **ser·ra·dil·la** \-dilə\ *n* -s [Pg *serradela*, fr. L *serratula* betony, fr. *serratus* serrate] **:** a Eurasian annual herb (*Ornithopus sativus*) of the family Leguminosae with pinnate leaves and long-stalked honey-producing flowers that is used for forage and green manure — called also *bird's-foot*

¹ser·ra·nid \səˈranə̇d, -ran-ˌ-rän-\ *adj* [NL *Serranidae*] **:** of or relating to the Serranidae

²serranid \"\ *n* -s **:** a fish of the family Serranidae

Ser·ran·i·dae \-ranəˌdē\ *n pl, cap* [NL, fr. *Serranus*, type genus + *-idae*] **:** a large and widely distributed family of carnivorous marine percoid fishes having an oblong and more or less compressed body covered with ctenoid scales and including many important food and sport fishes esp. of warm seas — see SEA BASS

ser·ra·no \səˈrä(ˌ)nō\ *n, pl* **serrano** *or* **serranos** *usu cap* [AmerSp, fr. Sp, mountaineer, fr. *sierra* saw, jagged mountain range + *-ano* -an — more at SIERRA] **1 :** a Shoshonean people of southern California **2 :** a member of the Serrano people

¹ser·ra·noid \səˈräˌnȯid, -raˌ-, -rä,-\ *adj* [NL *Serranus* + E *-oid*] **:** resembling or related to the Serranidae

²serranoid \"\ *n* -s **:** a serranoid fish

Ser·ra·nus \-ˈrānəs, -rän-\ *n, cap* [NL, fr. L *serra* saw + *-anus*] **:** a genus (the type of the family Serranidae) of fishes including numerous small Pacific sea basses some of which are regarded as highly toxic

¹ser·ra·sal·mo \ˌserəˈsal(ˌ)mō\ [NL, fr. L *serra* saw + *salmo* salmon] *syn of* SERRASALMUS

²serrasalmo \ˌ⸗⸗ˈ⸗(ˌ)⸗\ *n* -s **:** CARIBE

ser·ra·sal·mus \ˌ⸗⸗ˈ⸗məs\ *n, cap* [NL, fr. L *serra* saw + *salmo* salmon] **:** a genus of So. American characin fishes comprising the caribe

¹ser·rate \ˈseˌrāt, *usu* -ād·+V\ *vt* -ED/-ING/-S [LL *serratus*, past part. of *serrare* to saw, fr. L *serra* saw] **:** to notch or form sawlike teeth on the edge or surface of **:** mark with a serration ⟨~ the ends of a steel shaft⟩ ⟨firs that ~ the long ridge —A.T. Quiller-Couch⟩ ⟨peaks . . . ~ the skyline —*Amer. Guide Series: N.H.*⟩

²ser·rate \-ˌrā\|t, -ˌrə̇\|, *usu* \|d·+V\ *adj* [L *serratus*, fr. *serra* saw + *-atus* -ate] **1 :** notched or toothed on the edge **:** SAW-TOOTHED, SAW-EDGED, DENTICULATE ⟨jagged peaks and ~ ridges —R.F.Flint⟩ — see ANTENNA illustration **2 :** having marginal teeth pointing forward or toward the apex ⟨~ leaf⟩

serrate–ciliate \ˌ⸗(ˌ)⸗+\ *adj* [trans. of NL *serrato-ciliatus*] **:** having fine hairs like eyelashes on the serrations ⟨*serrate-ciliate* leaves⟩

ser·rat·ed \-ˌrād·ə̇d, -ātə̇d\ *adj* [fr. past part. of *serrate*] **:** SERRATE ⟨a ~ wall of high buildings —A.J.Liebling⟩ ⟨a low fence of ~ green —Richard Jefferies⟩ ⟨the lanceolate leaves have a ~ margin —Walter Bally⟩ ⟨a knife with a ~ edge will make cutting easier⟩

serrate–dentate \ˌ⸗(ˌ)⸗+\ *adj* [trans. of NL *serrato-dentatus*] **:** having the margins of the serrations toothed **:** doubly serrate — used of leaves

serrated impulse *n* **:** electronic output chopped into toothlike pulses (as for frame synchronization in television reception)

Ser·ra·tia \səˈrāsh(ē)ə, -räd·ēə\ *n, cap* [NL, fr. Serafino *Serrati*, 19th cent. Ital. entrepreneur + NL *-ia*] **:** a genus of small aerobic saprophytic bacteria (family Enterobacteriaceae) that commonly produce bright red pigments

ser·ra·tion \seˈrāshən\ *n* -s [²*serrate* + *-ion*] **1 :** the condition of being serrate ⟨the continual ~ of the pine forest —John Ruskin⟩ **2 a :** a formation resembling the toothed edge of a saw ⟨mountains receding in ~*s* to the west⟩ **b serrations** *pl* **:** the fine scales projecting from the surface of wool fiber **3 :** one of the teeth in a serrate margin ⟨a dial with two hundred ~*s*⟩

serrato- *comb form* [NL, fr. L *serratus* serrate] **:** serrate and ⟨*serrato*crenate⟩ ⟨*serrato*dentate⟩

Ser·rat·u·la \seˈrachələ\ *n, cap* [NL, fr. L, betony, fr. *serratus* serrate + *-ula*] **:** a genus of Old World perennial herbs (family Compositae) with spirally arranged leaves that are not spiny and solitary or corymbose heads of tubular flowers — compare SANDWORT

ser·ra·ture \ˈserəˌchü(ə)r, -ˌchər\ *n* -s [LL *serratura* act of sawing, fr. *serratus* (past part. of *serrare* to saw) + L *-ura* -ure] **:** SERRATION

ser·ra·tus \seˈrād·əs, -rätəs\ *n, pl* **serra·ti** \-ˌāˌtī, -ˌäˌtē\ [NL, fr. L, serrate] **:** any of several muscles of the trunk having complex origins but chiefly from the ribs or vertebrae that give them a notched appearance and comprising in man (1) a large muscle arising chiefly from the eight upper ribs and inserted into the vertebral border of the scapula, (2) another arising chiefly from the spinous processes of the last two thoracic and two or three upper lumbar vertebrae and inserted into the four lower ribs, and (3) a muscle arising chiefly from the spinous processes of the last cervical and first and two or three additional thoracic vertebrae and inserted into the second, third, fourth, and fifth ribs — called also respectively (1) *serratus mag·nus* \-ˈmagnəs\, *serratus anterior*, (2) *serratus posterior inferior*, (3) *serratus posterior superior*

serre·fine \ˈserəˌfēn, (ˈ)serˈf-\ *n* -s [F *serre-fine*, lit., fine clamp, fr. *serre* grip, clamp + *fine*, fem. of *fin* fine, fr. OF — more at SEAR (catch of a gunlock), FINE] **:** a small forceps for clamping a blood vessel

serrefine

serri- *comb form* **:** saw ⟨*serri*ferous⟩

¹ser·ri·corn \ˈserəˌkȯrn\ *adj* [NL *Serricornia*] **:** of or relating to the Serricornia

²serricorn \"\ *n* -s **:** a beetle of the division Serricornia

Ser·ri·cor·nia \ˌ⸗⸗ˈkȯrnēə\ *n pl, cap* [NL, fr. *serri-* + L *cornu* horn + NL *-ia*] **:** a division of beetles including the Elateridae, Buprestidae, Lampyridae, and related forms in which the antennae are usu. serrate along their inner margin, all the tarsi are usu. pentamerous, and the first ventral abdominal segment is exposed for its entire breadth

ser·ried \'serēd, -rid\ *adj* [fr. past part. of *serry*] **1 :** crowded or pressed together **:** COMPACT, DENSE ⟨the crowd collected in a ~ mass —W.S.Maugham⟩ ⟨a ~ phalanx of reeds —William Beebe⟩ ⟨squat houses huddle, meanly ~ —Laurence Binyon⟩ **2 :** precisely coherent and concise — used of discourse ⟨perorations, but not ~ argument —H.J.Laski⟩ ⟨the reader wading through these solid, ~ pages —*Times Lit. Supp.*⟩ **3** [alter. of [2]*serrate*] **:** marked by ridges or serrations **:** SERRATE ⟨his brow ~ in an inquisitive frown —Harris Downey⟩ ⟨to the south rise the ~ contours of the . . . mountains —*Amer. Guide Series: Oregon*⟩ ⟨to the east headland after headland of the north coast . . . stood out in ~ rank —John Wymer⟩ — **ser·ried·ly** *adv* — **ser·ried·ness** *n* -ES

ser·rif·era \se'rif(ə)rə, sə'r-\ *n pl, cap* [NL, fr. *serri-* + L *-fera*, neut. pl. of *-fer* -ferous] *in some classifications* **:** a division of Hymenoptera including the sawflies and horntails and related forms and being essentially equivalent to Chalastogastra

ser·rif·er·ous \-f(ə)rəs\ *adj* [*serri-* + *-ferous*] **:** having a sawlike organ

ser·ru·la \'ser(y)ələ\ *n* -S [NL, fr. L, small saw, dim. of *serra* saw] **:** a toothed keel; *esp* **:** one on the endite of most spiders that assists in the maceration of prey

ser·ru·late \'ser(y)ələt, -ˌlāt\ *also* **ser·ru·lat·ed** \-ˌlād·əd\ *adj* [NL *serrulatus*, fr. L *serrula* small saw + *-atus* -ate] **:** finely serrate **:** DENTICULATE

ser·ru·la·tion \ˌ==ˈlāshən\ *n* -S [*serrulate* + *-ion*] **1 :** the state of being serrulate **2 :** a serrulate formation

ser·ry \'serē, -ri\ *vb* -ED/-ING/-ES [MF *serré*, past part. of *serrer* to press, crowd — more at SEAR (catch of a gunlock)] *vi, archaic* **:** to press together esp. in ranks **:** CROWD ~ *vt* **:** to close up **:** crowd together

ser·ta \(')ser¦tä\ *also* **ser·to** \-tō\ *n* -S [Syriac *serṭā*, lit., line, writing] **:** the Syriac cursive script characterized by horizontal lines or ligatures uniting the lower portions of the letters

ser·to·li cell \'serd·ᵊlē-, ser'tōlē-\ *also* **sertoli's cell** *n, usu cap S* [after Enrico *Sertoli* †1910 Ital. histologist] **:** one of the elongated striated cells in the tubules of the testis to which the spermatids become attached and from which they apparently derive nourishment

ser·tu·lar·ia \ˌsərchə'la(a)rēə\ *n, cap* [NL, fr. L *sertula* (*campana*) melilot (dim. of *serta*, garland, melilot, fr. fem. of *sertus*, past part. of *serere* to entwine, bind together) + NL *-aria* — more at SERIES] **:** a genus (the type of the family Sertulariidae) of delicate branching calyptoblastic hydroids having small sessile hydrothecae arranged bilaterally along the sides of the branches

[1]**ser·tu·lar·i·an** \¦==¦==ən\ *adj* [NL *Sertularia* + E *-an*] **:** of or relating to the genus *Sertularia* or to the family Sertulariidae

[2]**sertularian** \"\ *n* -S **:** a sertularian hydroid

ser·tu·lar·i·oid \¦==¦==ˌȯid\ *or* **ser·tu·la·roid** \'==ˌləˌrȯid\ *adj* [NL *Sertularia* + E *-oid*] **:** resembling or related to the sertularians

ser·tule \'sər(ˌ)chül\ *n* -S [NL *sertulum*] **:** SERTULUM

ser·tu·lum \'sərchələm\ *n, pl* **sertu·la** \-lə\ [NL, dim. of L *sertum* garland, fr. neut. of *sertus*, past part. of *serere* to entwine, bind together — more at SERIES] **1 :** UMBEL **2** [NL, dim. of *sertum*] **:** a collection of scientifically studied plants

ser·tum \'sərd·əm\ *n, pl* **ser·ta** \-d·ə\ [NL, fr. L, garland] **:** a scientific treatise upon a collection of plants

ser·ule \'ser(ˌ)yül, -e(ˌ)rül\ *n* -S [[5]*sere* + *-ule*] **:** the brief and small sere of a microhabitat

se·rum \'sirəm, *sometimes* 'sēr- *or* 'ser-\ *n, pl* **serums** \-rəmz\ *or* **se·ra** \-rə\ *often attrib* [L, whey, watery fluid, serum; akin to Gk *oros* whey, serum, *hormē* rush, onset, assault, Skt *sarati* it runs, flows] **1 :** the watery portion of an animal fluid remaining after coagulation: **a :** BLOOD SERUM; *esp* **:** immune blood serum that contains specific immune bodies (as antitoxins or agglutinins) ⟨antitoxin ~⟩ — compare VACCINE **b :** WHEY **c :** a normal or pathological serous fluid (as in a blister) **2 :** the watery part of a vegetable fluid; *specif* **:** the watery part of rubber latex on which the rubber floats after coagulation

serum accident *n* **:** an allergic reaction to the injection of a serum to which an individual is hypersensitive

se·rum·al \-rəməl\ *adj* [*serum* + *-al*] **:** belonging to or derived from serum or serous exudations ⟨a ~ calculus at the root of a tooth⟩

serum albumin *n* **:** a crystallizable albumin or mixture of albumins that normally constitutes more than half of the protein in blood serum, blood plasma, and other serous fluids, that can be isolated after precipitation of the globulins or by electrophoresis, that is synthesized in the liver, and that serves to maintain the osmotic pressure of the blood and is used in transfusions for the treatment of shock and other medical and surgical conditions — called also *blood albumin*

serum anaphylaxis *n* **:** anaphylaxis to a foreign serum to which a patient is sensitive (as in the second injection of an antitoxin)

serum globulin *n* **:** a globulin or mixture of globulins occurring with albumin in blood serum, blood plasma, and other serous fluids from which it can be separated by precipitation or by electrophoresis — compare ALPHA GLOBULIN, BETA GLOBULIN, GAMMA GLOBULIN

serum hepatitis *also* **serum jaundice** *n* **:** a sometimes fatal hepatitis caused by a double-stranded DNA virus that tends to persist in the blood serum and is transmitted esp. by contact with infected blood (as by transfusion) or blood products — called also *homologous serum hepatitis*; compare INFECTIOUS HEPATITIS

serum sickness *or* **serum disease** *n* **:** an allergic reaction to the injection of foreign serum (as in serotherapy) manifested by swelling, urticaria, eruption, arthritis, and fever

serum therapy *n* **:** SEROTHERAPY

serut *var of* SEROOT

serv *abbr* **1** [L *serva*] preserve **2** servant **3** service

ser·val \'sərvəl, (ˌ)sər'val\ *n* -S [F, fr. Pg *lobo cerval* lynx, fr. ML *lupus cervalis*, fr. L *lupus* wolf + LL *cervalis* cervine, fr. L *cervus* deer, stag + *-alis* -al — more at WOLF, HART] **1 :** a wildcat (*Felis capensis* or *F. serval*) common in Africa having long legs, large untufted ears, and a tawny coat with black spots and rings **2 :** the pelt of the serval

[1]**ser·va·line** \'sərvəˌlīn, -ˌlən, -ˌlēn\ *adj* [*serval* + *-ine*] **:** of, relating to, or resembling the serval

[2]**servaline** \"\ *also* **servaline cat** *n* -S [NL *servalina* (specific epithet of *Felis servalina*) fr. F *serval* + NL *-ina*] **:** a wildcat (*Felis servalina*) of western Africa resembling the serval but with a more densely spotted coat

[1]**ser·vant** \'sərvənt, 'sə̄v-, 'səiv-, *dial* 'särv- *or* 'såv-\ *n* -S [ME, fr. OF, fr. pres. part. of *servir* to serve — more at SERVE] **1 :** a person bound to do the bidding of a master or superior **:** one that must work for another and obey him: as **a :** one that performs duties about the person or home of a master or employer **:** a personal or domestic attendant **b :** a person in the employ and subject to the direction of an individual or company **:** a wage-earning employee **c :** something (as an animal, tool, or machine) that serves the purposes of another **:** an object or device used as an instrument ⟨organization and machinery, which should be our ~*s* and not our masters, demand we should adapt ourselves to them —J.B.Priestley⟩ ⟨electricity, this marvelous ~ that turns factory wheels —Leonard Engel⟩ ⟨make atomic energy a ~ of man⟩ **2 :** an adherent or agent of a god or of the Deity **3** *obs* **:** an avowed suitor for a woman's affections **:** one that pays court to her or dances attendance on her; *also* **:** PARAMOUR **4 servants** *pl, obs* **:** a troupe of actors under the patronage of an English king or nobleman ⟨his majesty's ~*s*⟩ **5 :** a government official considered as the servant of his sovereign or of the public ⟨a ~ of her majesty the queen⟩ **:** PUBLIC SERVANT — compare CIVIL SERVANT **6 :** SLAVE **7 :** a member of Jehovah's Witnesses who functions in capacities like those of a clergyman

[2]**servant** *vt* -ED/-ING/-S **1** *obs* **:** to make subject **:** SUBORDINATE **2** *obs* **:** to furnish with a servant **3** *obs* **:** to act as servant — used in the phrase *to servant it*

ser·vant·less \-ləs\ *adj* **:** having no servant

ser·vant·ry \-ntrē\ *n* -ES [[1]*servant* + *-ry*] **:** all the servants of one master or house ⟨all the ~ of the dairy were standing in the red-brick entry —Thomas Hardy⟩

ser·vant·ship \-ntˌship\ *n* [[1]*servant* + *-ship*] **:** the place or condition of a servant

[1]**serve** \'sərv, 'sə̄v, 'səiv, *dial* 'särv *or* 'såv\ *vb* -ED/-ING/-S [ME *serven*, fr. OF *servir*, fr. L *servire* to be a slave, serve, be of use, fr. *servus* slave, servant, perh. of Etruscan origin] *vi* **1 a :** to be a servant **:** become employed in domestic service, at manual labor, or upon another's business **:** do menial service ⟨*served* on the staffs of various wealthy households⟩ ⟨so they made the people of Israel ~ with rigor, and made their lives bitter with hard service —Exod 1:13, 14 (RSV)⟩ **b** *obs* **:** to do service (as to God or a feudal superior) — used with *to* ⟨blessed angels he sends to and fro to ~ to wicked man —Edmund Spenser⟩ **c :** to do military or naval service **:** be a soldier or sailor ⟨two of his great-grandfathers *served* in the Revolutionary War —Edna Yost⟩ **2 a :** to perform the duties of a priest or clergyman **:** officiate in a clerical capacity **b :** to assist a celebrant as server at mass **3 a :** to be of use **:** answer a purpose **:** have a function ⟨in a day when few people could write, seals *served* as signatures —Elizabeth W. King⟩ ⟨nothing he had ever experienced *served* to quiet him so much as these end-of-the-week concerts —Edward Bok⟩ ⟨a disused fire station *served* for a clubhouse⟩ **b :** to be favorable, opportune, or convenient ⟨met a tide that *served* for an immediate departure⟩ ⟨told and retold the story wherever occasion *served*⟩ **c :** to be worthy of reliance or trust ⟨it was in the last year of his life, if memory ~*s*⟩ **d :** to hold an office **:** discharge a duty or function **:** act in a capacity ⟨*served* on a jury⟩ ⟨*served* as mayor for several years⟩ **4 a :** to prove adequate or satisfactory **:** SATISFY, SUFFICE ⟨nothing would ~ but she must pack a box for me to take back —John Buchan⟩ **b :** to prove out **:** hold good **:** pass as valid ⟨a safe-conduct that *served* not only for him but for the entire party⟩ **5 :** to help persons to food: as **a :** to wait at table **b :** to set out portions of food or drink **6 :** to wait on customers ⟨~*s* in a grocery store⟩ **7 :** to put the ball in play in any of various games (as tennis or handball) **8** *of a male animal* **:** COPULATE ~ *vt* **1 a :** to be a servant to **:** work for (a master or employer) **:** do tasks set by (a superior) **:** minister to **:** ATTEND ⟨his master shall bore his ear through with an awl; and he shall ~ him for life —Exod 21:6 (RSV)⟩ ⟨*served* several actresses as personal maid⟩ **b :** to give the service and respect due to (a lord, sovereign, or other superior) ⟨several times *served* the queen as prime minister⟩ **c :** to comply with the commands or demands of ⟨*served* the will of venal men⟩ **:** satisfy the needs or wants of **:** GRATIFY **d :** to render military or naval service to **:** fight for **:** be a soldier or sailor of ⟨*served* the nation as a commander in three wars⟩ **e :** to perform the duties of (an office or post) **:** discharge the requirements of **2 :** to offer habitual worship and obedience to (a god or devil) ⟨God whom I ~ with a clear conscience —2 Tim 1:3 (RSV)⟩ **3 a :** to assist (a priest) at mass as server **b :** to act as server at (mass) ⟨*served* mass on Sunday⟩ **c :** to act as pastor to ⟨*served* several large parishes⟩ **4** *archaic* **:** to pay a lover's or suitor's court to (a lady) **5 a :** to work through or perform (a term of service) ⟨had *served* his time as a mate in the merchant marine⟩ ⟨*served* out an apprenticeship⟩ **b :** to put in (a term of imprisonment) **:** SPEND, UNDERGO ⟨felt that anyone who had *served* time was a marked man⟩ ⟨*served* seven years for armed assault⟩ **6 a :** to wait on (one) at table **b :** to bring (food) to a diner — often used with *up* ⟨*served* him up a hearty dinner⟩ **c :** to place food on (the table) **d** *archaic* **:** to put out food for (an animal) **:** FEED **7 a :** to furnish or supply (one) with something needed or desired ⟨a consolidated school *served* the children who had attended the several former one-room schools⟩ **b :** to wait on (a customer) in a store **c :** to provide merchandise serviceable or desirable to (a buyer) ⟨that task has been and continues to be to ~ the American customer well —H.H.Curtice⟩ **d :** to furnish professional service to ⟨a physician who had *served* his community with distinction for nearly half a century⟩ **8 a :** to be of use to or answer the needs of **:** provide for **:** AVAIL ⟨private reservoirs and canals . . . ~ each separate estate —P.E.James⟩ **b :** to be enough for **:** SUFFICE, LAST ⟨the slightest smile would ~ him for encouragement⟩ **c :** to be of help in bringing about **:** contribute to **:** PROMOTE ⟨engaged . . . in *serving* the purposes of the Revolution —Van Wyck Brooks⟩ **9** *obs* **:** ENCOURAGE, PROMPT, PERMIT ⟨certainly my conscience will ~ me to run from this Jew my master —Shak.⟩ **10 :** to treat or act toward in a specified way **:** deal with **:** REQUITE ⟨he *served* me ill⟩ **11 a :** to bring to notice, deliver, or execute actually or constructively as required by law **:** put into effect ⟨to ~ a summons or process is to deliver it, or to read it so as to give due notice, or both⟩ ⟨to ~ an attachment or execution is to levy it by seizure or taking possession⟩ **b :** to make legal service upon (a person named in a writ) **c** *Scots law* **:** to declare (someone) heir to an estate after formal adjudication **12** *archaic* **:** FIT, SUIT **13** *obs* **:** to avail (oneself) of someone or something **:** make use of **14** *archaic* **:** to make convenient opportunity for (one) **:** provide occasion or means for (a person) **:** FAVOR **15 :** to put up or flush game before (a hawk) — used of either the falconer or the dog **16** *of an animal* **:** to copulate with **:** COVER — distinguished from *settle* **17 :** to do (one) a good or bad turn **:** play (one) a trick **:** deal (one) a blow **18 :** to wind spun yarn, canvas, or wire tightly around (a rope or stay) to protect from chafing or from the weather **:** wrap serving around (a bowstring) **19 :** to stand by (one) **:** prove worthy of trust by — used esp. of the memory ⟨that was his last appearance, if memory ~*s* me⟩ **20 :** to provide services that benefit or help ⟨the most distinctive characteristic of a profession — its obligation to ~ society —H.A.Wagner⟩ **21 :** to put (the ball) in play in any of various games (as tennis or handball) **22 :** to keep (artillery or naval guns) in action **:** FIRE **23** *Scot* **a :** to give satisfaction to ⟨heirs were *served*⟩ **b :** prove enough or too much for — **serve one right :** to deal with one as he deserves **:** be the just or fitting return for what one is or does ⟨they *served him right* for his thieving⟩ ⟨felt that his disgrace *served him right*⟩ ⟨it *serves you right* for trying to break into line⟩ — **serve the time** *or* **serve the hour :** to be a timeserver **:** TEMPORIZE

[2]**serve** \"\ *n* -S **:** the act of putting the ball in play in any of various net or court games (as tennis) ⟨won many games with his powerful and accurate ~*s*⟩

served *past of* SERVE

ser·ven·tism \sər'vent·ˌizəm, -n·ˌti-\ *or* **ser·ven·te·ism** \-ntēˌizəm\ *n* -S [(*cavalier*) *servente* + *-ism*] **:** the social convention countenancing the cavalier servente

serve out *vt* **:** to revenge oneself on **:** pay back **:** retaliate against ⟨*served* them *out* royally for their many acts of cruelty⟩

serv·er \'sərvər, 'sə̄və(r, 'səivə(r\ *n* -S [ME, fr. *serven* to serve + *-er*] **1 a :** one that brings food and drink to persons at table **b :** one that dishes up food (as in a cafeteria) **2 :** the player who puts the ball in play in any of various net or court games (as tennis) **3 :** one that assists the celebrant in the Mass, Divine Liturgy, or Holy Communion **:** ACOLYTE **4 :** something used in serving: as **a :** any of various articles of furniture (as a buffet or a wheeled table) from which food may be served **:** CREDENZA, SIDEBOARD, TEA WAGON **b :** a tea or coffee service usu. consisting of pot, sugar bowl, cream pitcher, and tray **c :** a tray, salver, or covered plate used as a serving utensil **d :** any of various special-purpose implements (as salad tongs or a pie lifter) used to serve a particular food **e :** an insulated often decorative vessel for keeping foods hot or cold until served

server 4b

serv·ery \-vərē\ *n* -ES [[1]*serve* + *-ery*] **1 :** BUTLER'S PANTRY **2 :** a service alcove with counter or buffet between dining room and kitchen

serves *pres 3d sing of* SERVE, *pl of* SERVE

ser·ve·tian \¦sər¦vēshən, ˌsər'v-\ *n* -S *usu cap* [Michael *Servet*us †1553 Spanish theologian and physician + E *-ian*] **:** a follower of Michael Servetus who was burned at the stake in Geneva in 1553 for anti-Trinitarianism and antipedobaptism

ser·vette \¦sər¦vet\ *n* -S [[1]*serve*] **:** a small folding table

[1]**servian** *usu cap, var of* SERBIAN

[2]**ser·vi·an** \'sərvēən\ *adj, usu cap* [*Servi*us Tullius + E *-an*] **:** of or relating to Servius Tullius who was the sixth of the legendary kings of Rome 578–534 B.C. ⟨the *Servian* wall⟩

[1]**ser·vice** \'sərvəs, 'sə̄v-, 'səiv- *dial* 'särv- *or* 'såv-\ *n* -S [ME *servise*, *service*, fr. OF, fr. L *servitium* condition of a slave, servitude, body of slaves or servants, fr. *servus* slave + *-itium* -ice — more at SERVE] **1 :** the condition or occupation of a servant **:** the serving of a master: as **a :** the position of a domestic servant ⟨the daughters of yeoman and peasant alike could take ~ with the wife of a squire who had known them all their lives —Roy Lewis & Angus Maude⟩ **b :** the domestic employment of a particular master ⟨entered the ~ of a wealthy townsman⟩ **2 :** the performance of work commanded or paid for by another **:** a servant's duty **:** attendance on a superior ⟨most true, I have lost my teeth in your ~ —Shak.⟩ **3 a :** the employment of a public servant ⟨distinguished himself in his country's ~⟩ **b :** a specified branch or department of government employment or the staff of persons working in it ⟨consular ~⟩ ⟨intelligence ~⟩ **c :** the duties, work, or business performed or discharged by a government official **4 a :** one of a nation's organized fighting forces (as the army, navy, or air force) **b :** the performance of military duty esp. in war **:** COMBAT ⟨saw active ~ in several campaigns⟩ **c :** a particular military operation **:** CAMPAIGN, ENGAGEMENT, EXPEDITION **d :** the profession or career of arms **:** the occupation of a soldier, sailor, or military flier **5 a :** an act done for the benefit or at the command of another ⟨impose some ~ on me for thy love —Shak.⟩ ⟨felt that to avenge his friend's death was the only ~ he could still do him⟩ **b :** the constancy, attentions, or devotion of a lover for his lady **6 a :** the habit or practice of serving God or the acts done with that intention ⟨devoted himself altogether to the ~ of God⟩ **b :** a form or ritual of worship (as public worship) established for customary use, celebration, or observance **c :** the performance of religious worship esp. according to settled public forms or conventions **d :** an assembly or meeting for worship **e :** rites (as religious rites) appropriate to a particular event ⟨a burial ~⟩ ⟨a marriage ~⟩ **f :** a liturgical office set to music **:** a set of such settings esp. of the choral canticles and chants **7 a :** the bringing of food and drink to diners seated at table **:** the work or activity of waiting at table ⟨it was a small place but the ~ was excellent⟩ **b** (1) **:** the food and drink apportioned to one person (2) *obs* **:** COURSE **c :** the dishes, implements, or utensils needed to serve a meal, a specified number of persons, or a particular food or drink ⟨purchased a silver ~ for 12⟩ **d :** a set of vessels used at the altar in celebrating communion ⟨the silver Eucharistic ~ . . . was saved by being hidden in a cistern —*Amer. Guide Series: La.*⟩ **e :** a set of implements and vessels for use in the toilet **:** DRESSER SET **8 :** the return in money, in kind, or in labor owed by a feudal tenant to his lord for the enjoyment of his tenancy **:** RENDER **9 a :** action or use that furthers some end or purpose **:** conduct or performance that assists or benefits someone or something **:** deeds useful or instrumental toward some object ⟨the pioneer-baiters do the country a ~ —Russell Lord⟩ ⟨did me a valuable ~⟩ **b :** professional or other useful ministrations ⟨legal ~*s*⟩ ⟨a bill collection ~⟩ **c :** supply of needs ⟨a vending machine set up for the ~ of casual passersby⟩; *also* **:** UTILITY **10** *archaic* **:** a profession of respect or duty — used in various expressions of courtesy (as in greetings or in toasts) **11 :** the act of putting the ball in play in any of various net or court games (as tennis) **12 :** an act of administering or applying something **13 :** the wrapping or covering of a rope (as with spun yarn, small lines, or canvas) to prevent chafing; *also* **:** the materials used for this purpose **14 a :** useful labor that does not produce a tangible commodity — usu. used in pl. ⟨railroads, telephone companies, and physicians perform ~*s* although they produce no goods⟩ **b :** DEBT SERVICE **c :** a facility or provision for maintenance and repair (as of houses or manufactured articles) ⟨property ~⟩ ⟨radio and television ~⟩ ⟨automobile repair ~⟩ **d :** the provision, organization, or apparatus for conducting a public utility or meeting a general demand ⟨telephone ~⟩ ⟨air freight ~⟩ **15 a :** the act of bringing a legal writ, process, or summons to notice actually or constructively as prescribed by law ⟨accepted ~ of a subpoena⟩ **b :** the carrying into effect or execution of a writ or process (as an attachment by seizing the goods or person attached or an execution by levying it upon the goods or person of the defendant) — compare PERSONAL SERVICE 1, SUBSTITUTED SERVICE **16 :** the act of serving or covering the female — used of a male animal **17 :** a regularly scheduled trip over a public transportation route ⟨three airline ~*s* daily between island and mainland⟩ **18 :** a branch of a hospital medical staff devoted to a particular specialty ⟨obstetric ~⟩ ⟨pediatric ~⟩ **19 a :** a pipe branching from a gas or water main to serve the premises of a user **b :** the lead-in conductors from an electric power or telephone line to a user's premises **20 :** effort inspired by philanthropic motives or directed to human welfare or betterment **syn** see USE — **at one's service :** ready to do one's bidding **:** available for use ⟨assured her that he was entirely *at her service*⟩ ⟨placed a car *at his service*⟩ — **of service :** of use **:** SERVICEABLE, HELPFUL, USEFUL ⟨protested that he was happy to be *of service*⟩

[2]**service** \"\ *adj* **1 a :** of or relating to the armed services or one of them **:** belonging to or used in the army, navy, or air force ⟨a ~ newspaper⟩ **b :** of, relating to, or constituting a branch of an army (as an ordnance department) that exists to serve or supply the army's fighting men **2 :** of or relating to domestic service **:** used in serving or by servants ⟨a ~ hatch⟩ **3 :** worn in or intended for everyday use **:** DURABLE ⟨*service-weight* stockings⟩ **4 a :** providing services rather than tangible goods ⟨transportation and entertainment are ~ industries⟩ **b :** offering a product useful only in making another product or in performing associated tasks or services ⟨diemakers and allied ~ industries —*New Englander*⟩ **c :** offering repair, maintenance, or incidental services

[3]**service** \"\ *vt* -ED/-ING/-S **:** to perform services for **:** meet the needs of **:** SERVE: as **a :** to repair or provide maintenance for ⟨I've had some dealings with them in the *servicing* of my English car —Richard Joseph⟩ **b :** to meet interest and sinking fund payments on (as government debt) **c :** to perform any of the business functions auxiliary to production or distribution of ⟨the accounting department ~*s* the manufacturing and sales programs⟩ **d :** to provide information or other assistance to ⟨for many years the Department of State has *serviced* the press and the scholars interested in foreign affairs —F.H.Russell⟩ **e :** to provide (a philatelic cover) with first-day cancellation or cachet **f :** to copulate with (a female animal) ⟨deer are polygamous and one buck may claim and ~ several does —Lyle St. Amant & Carrol Perkins⟩

[4]**service** \"\ *n* -S [ME *serves*, pl. of *serve* service tree, fruit of the service, fr. OE *syrfe*, fr. (assumed) VL *sorbea*, fr. L *sorbus* service tree, sorb tree] **1 :** SERVICE TREE 1 **2 :** the fruit of a service tree

ser·vice·abil·i·ty \ˌ==ə'biləd·ē, -lətē, -i\ *n* [*serviceable* + *-ity*] **:** fitness to give service **:** usefulness for a purpose **:** wearing quality **:** DURABILITY, SERVICEABLENESS ⟨~ is an essential characteristic of all assets —R.B.Kester⟩

ser·vice·able \'==əbəl\ *adj* [ME *servisable*, fr. MF, fr. OF, fr. *servise*, *service* service + *-able*] **1 :** ready or willing to help **:** disposed to give good offices **:** HELPFUL, USEFUL ⟨a ~ friend⟩ **2 :** fit for use **:** suited for a purpose **:** usable to advantage **:** wearing well in use ⟨a ~ design⟩ ⟨a ~ knife⟩ ⟨~ shoes⟩ ⟨some of the Mound Builders mined copper for ornamental purposes and made ~ pottery —R.W.Murray⟩

ser·vice·able·ness *n* -ES **:** the quality or state of being serviceable

ser·vice·ably \-blē,-bli\ *adv* **:** in a serviceable manner

serviceage *n* -S [[1]*service* + *-age*] *obs* **:** SERVITUDE

ser·vice·ber·ry \'sär|vəs-, 'så|, 'sər|, 'sə̄|, 'səi| — *see* BERRY\ *n* [[4]*service* + *berry*] **:** JUNEBERRY

service book *n* [[1]*service* + *book*] **:** a book setting forth forms of worship used in religious services

service box *n* [[2]*service*] **1 :** a casing or box let in flush with the pavement for access to a corporation cock **2 :** a metal box installed where the electric service wires enter a building to house the main switch with its fuses **3 :** the area in which a player stands while serving in various wall and net games

service brake *n* **:** an automobile brake usu. foot-operated that is used in ordinary driving — compare EMERGENCY BRAKE

service cap *n* **:** a flat-topped visor cap about 3½ inches high worn by officers and men with a military service uniform — compare DRESS CAP

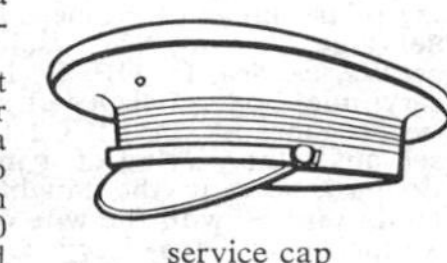
service cap

service ceiling *n* **:** the height above sea level at which under standard air conditions a particular airplane can no longer rise at a rate greater than a small designated rate (as 100 feet per minute in the U.S. and England) — called also *ceiling;* compare ABSOLUTE CEILING
service charge *n* **:** a fee (as an extra fare, a cover charge, or a bank's fee for maintaining an unprofitable checking account) charged for a particular service often in addition to a standard or basic fee
service club *n* **1 :** a club of business and professional men or women concerned esp. with community welfare and usu. forming part of a national or international organization **2 :** a social and recreational club for enlisted men provided by one of the armed services at one of its posts or installations
service company *or* **service battery** *n* **:** an administrative military unit concerned mainly with transportation and supply
service court *n* [¹*service*] **:** a part of the court into which the ball or shuttlecock must be served in any of various court games — see TENNIS illustration
serviced *past of* SERVICE
service door *n* [²*service*] **:** a door intended for the use of servants or to facilitate service (as delivery of goods or removal of waste)
service flag *n* **:** a flag displayed in wartime to show that a member of a family or organization is in active military service or has died in such service
service flat *n, Brit* **:** a flat in which the rental includes housekeeping care and to which prepared meals will be sent if ordered
service hatch *n* **:** an opening in a wall (as between kitchen and dining room) through which dishes may be passed
service life *n* **:** the time during which something can be used economically or the time during which it is used by one owner
service line *n* [¹*service*] **1 a :** a line 21 feet from the net in tennis and parallel to it that marks the rear of a service court — compare FOOT FAULT **b :** a line that is perpendicular to the rear service line and bisects the service court **2 :** a line drawn parallel to a front wall or board in wall games (as handball) to mark a boundary which must not be overstepped in serving
ser·vice·man \ˈ⁼⁼,man, -,mən, -,maa(ə)n\ *n, pl* **servicemen** [²*service* + *man*] **1 :** a male member of the armed forces **2 :** a man employed to repair or maintain equipment
service mark *n* **:** a mark or device used to identify a service (as transportation, dry cleaning, or insurance) offered to customers — compare TRADEMARK
service medal *n* **:** a medal awarded to an individual who does military service in a specified war or campaign — compare DECORATION
service of an heir [¹*service*] *Scots law* **:** a proceeding by inquest of a jury or by publication and proof before a competent officer without a jury to determine the heir of a person deceased
service pipe *n* [²*service*] **:** a pipe connecting a main pipe (as a gas or water main or an electrical conduit) with a building
service plate *n* **:** a large elaborate plate used to indicate a place at table and to serve as an under plate during the first courses
service road *n* **:** FRONTAGE ROAD
services *pl of* SERVICE, *pres 3d sing of* SERVICE
service side *n* [¹*service*] **:** the side of a court-tennis court from which service is made — compare HAZARD SIDE
service speed *n* [²*service*] **:** the average speed maintained by a ship under normal load and weather conditions
service stamp *n* **:** OFFICIAL STAMP
service star *n* **:** a five-pointed gold star worn on a boy scout's uniform and bearing a numeral to indicate years of membership
service state *n* **:** WELFARE STATE ⟨the *service state* . . . takes the whole domain of human welfare for its province and would solve all economic and social ills through its administrative activities —Roscoe Pound⟩
service station *n* **1 :** FILLING STATION **2 :** a depot or place at which some service is offered
service stripe *n* **:** a stripe worn on an enlisted man's left sleeve to indicate three years of service in the army or air force or four years in the navy **:** CHEVRON, HASH MARK
service switch *n* **:** a building's main electric switch usu. located in the service box
service tree *n* [⁴*service*] **1** *or* **service** -s **:** MOUNTAIN ASH 1: as **a :** a medium-sized Old World tree (*Sorbus domestica*) that resembles the common rowan tree but has larger flowers and larger edible fruits containing grit cells **b :** a similar Old World tree (*S. torminalis*) with simple broad ovate and usu. somewhat cordate leaves and small speckled brown fruits — called also *wild service tree* **2 :** JUNEBERRY 1
service uniform *n* [²*service*] **:** a military uniform for routine service — compare DRESS UNIFORM, FULL-DRESS UNIFORM
service wall *n* [¹*service*] **:** the front wall of a court-tennis court
ser·vice·wom·an \ˈ⁼⁼,wu̇mən\ *n, pl* **servicewomen** [²*service* + *woman*] **:** a female member of the armed forces
servicing *n* -s [fr. gerund of ³*service*] **:** the act of providing service
ser·vi·ent \ˈsərvēənt\ *adj* [L *servient-, serviens,* pres. part. of *servire* to serve] **1 a :** doing service **:** SERVING **b :** characteristic of a servant or subordinate **:** INSTRUMENTAL, SERVILE **2 :** subject to some person or thing that dominates, rules, or controls **:** subject to a service, easement, or servitude
ser·vi·ette \¦sərvē¦et\ *n* -s [F, fr. MF, fr. *servir* to serve] *chiefly Brit* **:** a table napkin
ser·vi·grous \sə(r)ˈvīgrəs\ *adj* [alter. (perh. influenced by *vigorous*) of *savagerous*] *South* **:** SAVAGEROUS
¹**ser·vile** \ˈsər\|vəl, ˈsə\|, ˈsəi\|, \|,vīl, \|(,)vil\ *adj* [ME, fr. L *servilis,* fr. *servus* slave, servant + *-ilis* -ile — more at SERVE] **1 a :** of, relating to, or appropriate to slaves ⟨the stigmata . . . of his ~ antecedents —Oscar Handlin⟩ **b :** befitting a slave or servant **:** unsuitable for a free man ⟨the machine increased the servitude of ~ personalities —Lewis Mumford⟩ **c :** held in servitude **:** subject to a master or owner ⟨manors . . . within which both independent farmers and ~ tenants lived —R.B. Morris⟩ **d :** held by or relating to base services or a base as opposed to a free tenure of land under feudal law **2** *Roman Catholicism* **:** of, relating to, or constituting physical or manual as distinguished from mental labor ⟨the first day shall be most solemn unto you, and holy: you shall do no ~ work therein —Lev 23:7 (DV)⟩ **3 :** subject to despotic or tyrannical rule **:** politically oppressed or subjugated ⟨doomed . . . to be destroyed or reduced to a ~ station —Sir Winston Churchill⟩ **4 a :** behaving like a slave **:** lacking spirit or independence **:** ABJECT, SUBMISSIVE ⟨the ~ attitude which he always maintained towards authority in intellectual and religious matters —R.A.Hall b.1911⟩ ⟨leaves a ~ old man in the clutches of his daughter —*Times Lit. Supp.*⟩ ⟨too ~ to the authority of older dictionaries —Louise Pound⟩ **b :** lacking moral worth or dignity **:** IGNOBLE ⟨~ fear⟩ **c :** CONTROLLED, SUBJECT, SUBORDINATE — used with *to* **5 :** slavishly imitative of a model esp. in literature or art **:** lacking independence or originality ⟨could draw inspiration from the past without stooping to ~ imitation —*Amer. Guide Series: N.Y.*⟩ **6 :** of, relating to, or engaged in the work of a servant or menial ⟨if it is used by a ~ class it is avoided by the educated —A.N. Whitehead⟩ **7 a :** of or relating to a derivational, inflectional, or relational element of speech **:** not belonging to the root ⟨~ sounds or letters⟩ ⟨*s* in English *sits, man's, dogs* is ~⟩ **b :** not itself sounded but serving to indicate a long preceding vowel ⟨the *e* in *stone* is ~⟩ **c :** subject to assimilation **8 :** constituting a means rather than an end **:** INSTRUMENTAL ⟨in philosophy itself investigation and reasoning are only preparatory and ~ parts, means to an end —George Santayana⟩ **syn** see SUBSERVIENT
²**servile** \"\ *n* -s **1 :** a servile person **2 :** a servile linguistic element or particle
ser·vile·ly \-əl(l)\|ē, -īll\|, -il(l)\|, \|i\ *adv* **:** in a servile manner, state, or spirit
ser·vil·ism \-ə,lizəm, -ī,l-, -i,l-\ *n* -s [¹*servile* + *-ism*] **1 :** a base or abject servility or obsequiousness **2 :** a doctrine advocating slavery or a system based on slavery
ser·vil·i·ty \(,)sərˈviləd·ē, ,sə'v-, sə̄'v-, səi'v-, -lətē, -i\ *n* -ES [¹*servile* + *-ity*] **1 :** a slave's condition **:** the state of slavery **:** SERVITUDE **2 a :** a mean or cringing submissiveness **:** OBSEQUIOUSNESS ⟨his political advisers flattered him with grotesque ~ —*Times Lit. Supp.*⟩ **b :** lack of independence or spirit **:** undue dependence or deference **3 :** slavish imitation in following a model **:** want of originality, inspiration, or invention
¹**serving** *n* -s [ME, fr. gerund of *serven* to serve] **1 :** the act or function of one that serves ⟨the ~ of a meal⟩ **2 :** a helping of food or drink **3 :** the thread or cord wrapped around the middle of a bowstring to protect it from the nock of the arrow — called also *whipping* **4 :** a layer of protective material (as jute yarn) put on the exterior of an armored or lead-covered electric cable **5 :** SERVICE 13
²**serving** *adj* [ME, fr. pres. part. of *serven* to serve] **1 :** employed or used to serve ⟨a low ~ bench on which are placed four or five pots containing food —Norman Mailer⟩ ⟨~ wench⟩ **2 :** belonging to a military service ⟨a ~ officer in the British army —M.C.A.Henniker⟩
serving board *n* [¹*serving*] **:** a spoon-shaped wooden tool used in putting on service esp. on eye splices
serving mallet *n* **:** a wooden device shaped like a mallet, grooved on the bottom, and used in serving ropes
serv·ing·man \ˈsəviŋ,man\ *n, pl* **servingmen** [ME, fr. ²*serving* + *man*] **:** a male servant
serving stuff *n* [¹*serving*] **:** small lines for serving ropes
serving table *n* **:** a side table used in serving food **:** a small sideboard
servingwoman \ˈ⁼⁼,⁼⁼\ *n, pl* **servingwomen** [ME, fr. ²*serving* + *woman*] **:** a female servant

a serving mallet; *b* mallet in use

ser·vite \ˈsər,vīt\ *n* -s *cap* [ML *Servitae* (pl.), fr. L *servus* slave + *-itae,* pl. of *-ita* -ite] **:** a member of a mendicant order of friars founded at Florence in 1233
ser·vi·tial \(,)sərˈvishəl\ *adj* [ML *servitialis,* fr. LL *servitium* service + L *-alis* -al] **:** of or relating to servitium
ser·vi·ti·um \-shēəm\ *n, pl* **servi·tia** \-shēə\ [LL, fr. L, condition of a slave — more at SERVICE] **:** SERVICE
ser·vi·tor \ˈsərvəd·ər, -və,tȯ(ə)r\ *n* -s [ME *servitour,* fr. MF, fr. LL *servitor,* fr. L *servitus* (past part. of *servire* to serve) + L *-or*] **1 :** a male servant **:** MENIAL; *esp* **:** a table waiter **2** *archaic* **:** one that serves a king esp. as a soldier **3 :** an undergraduate (as at Oxford) acting as servant to the fellows in return for his college expenses under a system now disused — compare EXHIBITIONER, SIZAR **4 :** a member of a chair of glassworkers who shapes the body of the product being made — compare FOOTMAKER, GAFFER
ser·vi·to·ri·al \¦sərvə¦tōrēəl\ *adj* [*servitor* + *-ial*] **:** of, relating to, or resembling a servitor
ser·vi·tor·ship \ˈsərvəd·ər,ship, -və,tȯr,sh-\ *n* [*servitor* + *-ship*] **:** the position or work of a servitor
ser·vi·tress \-və·trəs\ *n* -ES [*servitor* + *-ess*] **:** a woman servant
ser·vi·tude \ˈsərvə,tüd, ˈsə̄v-, ˈsəiv-, -və·,tyüd\ *n* -s [ME, fr. MF, fr. L *servitudin-, servitudo,* fr. *servus* slave, servant + *-tudin-, -tudo* -tude — more at SERVE] **1 :** the condition of a slave or serf **:** a state of subjection to an owner or master **:** BONDAGE, SERFDOM, SLAVERY ⟨neither slavery nor involuntary ~, except as a punishment for crime whereof the party shall have been duly convicted, shall exist within the United States —*U.S.Constitution*⟩ **2 a :** subjection to foreign overlordship or political oppression **:** subjugation by a conqueror or tyrant ⟨society may be expected to disintegrate and fall into ~ when men deny . . . these realities and transcendent obligations —Michael Polanyi⟩ **b :** a particular imposition or term imposed on a defeated or subject people ⟨meant the overthrow of many of the ~s placed upon them by the peace treaties —C.E. Black & E.C.Helmreich⟩ **3 :** a subjection likened to that of slavery **:** an unworthy subservience ⟨by criticizing religion they would attempt to free the religious spirit from its present ~ —Virginia Woolf⟩ **4** *archaic* **:** the state of being a servant (as a domestic servant or an indentured servant) **5** *archaic* **:** the service of an apprentice **:** APPRENTICESHIP **6 :** PENAL SERVITUDE **7 :** a right in respect of an object (as land owned by one person) in virtue of which the object is subject to a specified use or enjoyment by another person or for the benefit of another thing ⟨the common-law easement is a species of ~⟩ — compare NEGATIVE EASEMENT, POSITIVE EASEMENT
ser·vi·tus \ˈsərvə,tüs\ *n, pl* **servitu·tes** \,⁼⁼ˈtü,tās\ [L *servitut-, servitus,* fr. *servus* slave] **1** *Roman law* **:** SERVITUDE, SLAVERY, SUBJECTION **2** *Roman law* **:** EASEMENT
ser·vo \ˈsər(,)vō *sometimes* ˈser-\ *n* -s *often attrib* [by shortening] **1 :** SERVOMOTOR **2 :** SERVOMECHANISM
servo- *comb form, usu cap* [*servian*] **:** SERBO-
servo amplifier *n* **:** a torque-amplifying component of a servomechanism
servo brake *n* **1 :** a multiple-shoe automobile brake in which the action of one part upon another as a result of the forward motion of the vehicle increases the pressure between the second shoe and the brake drum and so increases the brake's effectiveness **2 :** a brake in which pedal or lever power is augmented (as by a servomotor) **:** POWER BRAKE
servo control *n* **:** an auxiliary aeronautical device to reinforce by an aerodynamic or mechanical relay a pilot's effort in operating a control commonly consisting of a small hinged auxiliary airfoil at the trailing edge of an aileron, elevator, or rudder — called also *Flettner control*
ser·vo·mechanism \¦sər(,)vō *sometimes* ¦ser- +\ *n* [*servo-* (as in *servomotor*) + *mechanism*] **:** an automatic device for controlling large amounts of power by means of very small amounts of power and correcting performance of a mechanism to a desired standard by an error-sensing feedback (as in an automatic pilot or a gun-aiming apparatus)
ser·vo·motor \ˈ⁼(,)vō, ˈ⁼,və+,-\ *n* [F *servo-moteur,* fr. L *servus* slave, servant + F *moteur* motor, fr. L *motor* one that moves — more at SERVE, MOTOR] **:** a power-driven mechanism that supplements a primary control operated by a comparatively feeble force (as in a servomechanism)
servo system *n* **:** SERVOMECHANISM
ser·vo·tab \ˈ⁼(,)⁼+,-\ *n* [*servo* + *tab*] **:** SERVO CONTROL
servt *abbr* servant
-ses *pl of* -SIS
ses·a·me \ˈsesəmē, -mi *also* -,mē *sometimes* ˈsezə-\ *n* -s [alter. (influenced by F *sésame,* fr. L *sesamum*) of earlier *sesam, sesama,* fr. L *sesamum, sesama,* fr. Gk *sēsamon, sēsamē,* of Sem origin; akin to Assyr *šamaššamu* sesame, Aram *shūmshĕmā,* Ar *simsim*] **1 :** an East Indian annual erect herb (*Sesamum indicum*) having chiefly rosy or white flowers **2** *or* **sesame seed :** the small obovate flattish seeds of sesame that yield an oil and are used as a flavoring agent — called also *benniseed* **3 :** OPEN SESAME ⟨recognition that wealth, power, fame are not the ~ to happiness —Israel Goldstein⟩
sesame grass *n* **:** GAMA
sesame oil *n* **:** a pale yellow bland semidrying fatty oil obtained from sesame seeds and used chiefly as an edible oil (as in margarine), as a vehicle for various pharmaceuticals, and in cosmetics and soaps — called also *gingelly oil, teel oil* **2 :** CAMELINE OIL
se·sa·mia \sə̇ˈsāmēə, seˈs-\ *n, cap* [NL, fr. L *sesamum* sesame + NL *-ia*] **:** a genus of noctuid moths many of which have larvae that are destructive to maize, sugarcane, rice, and other crop plants
ses·a·min \ˈsesəmə̇n *sometimes* -ezə-\ *n* -s [L *sesamum* sesame + ISV *-in*] **:** a crystalline cyclic ether $C_{20}H_{18}O_6$ that is obtained esp. from sesame oil and is a powerful synergist for pyrethrum insecticides
¹**ses·a·moid** \-,mȯid\ *adj* [Gk *sēsamoeidēs,* lit., resembling sesame seed, fr. *sēsamon* sesame + *-oeidēs* -oid] **:** of, relating to, or being a nodular mass of bone or cartilage in a tendon esp. where the tendon passes over a joint or some bony prominence
²**sesamoid** \"\ *n* -s **:** a sesamoid bone or cartilage
ses·a·moid·itis \,⁼⁼,mȯiˈdīd·əs\ *n* -ES [NL, fr. E ²*sesamoid* + NL *-itis*] **:** inflammation of the navicular bone and adjacent structures in the horse
ses·a·mol \ˈ⁼⁼,mōl, -mȯl\ *n* -s [ISV *sesame* + *-ol*] **:** a crystalline phenolic ether $HOC_6H_3O_2CH_2$ that occurs both free and combined in sesame oil and is an antioxidant for fats and oils; 3,4-methylenedioxy-phenol
ses·a·mo·lin \ˈsesəmə,lin, seˈsamələ̇n\ *n* -s [*sesamol* + *-in*] **:** a crystalline cyclic ether $C_{20}H_{18}O_7$ that is obtained from sesame oil, that is closely related chemically to sesamin, and that is an even more powerful synergist for pyrethrum insecticides
ses·a·mum \ˈsesəməm\ *n* [NL, fr. L, sesame] **1** *cap* **:** a genus of tropical African and Indian herbs (family Pedaliaceae) having entire or divided leaves and irregular campanulate flowers with a curved tube dilated above the base and a 4-angled unarmed capsule — see SESAME **2** -s **:** SESAME
¹**ses·ban** \ˈses,ban\ *n* -s [F, fr. Ar *saisabān,* fr. Per *sīsabān*] **:** either of two East Indian plants of the genus *Sesbania* (*S. aculeata* and *S. aegyptiaca*) — compare DAINCHA
²**sesban** \"\ [NL, fr. F *sesban*] *syn of* SESBANIA
ses·ba·nia \sesˈbānēə\ *n* [NL, fr. F *sesban* + NL *-ia*] **1** *cap* **:** a small genus of chiefly tropical pinnate-leaved herbs, shrubs, or trees (family Leguminosae) usu. having large showy pealike flowers — see COLORADO RIVER HEMP **2** -s **:** any plant of the genus *Sesbania*
ses·cu·ple \(ˈ)ses¦kyüpəl, ˈseskyəp-\ *adj* [L *sescuplus* one and a half times as great, fr. *sesqui-* + *-plus* (as in *duplus* double) — more at DOUBLE] **:** HEMIOLIC
se·se·li \ˈsesəlē\ *n* [NL, fr. L *seselis* seseli, fr. Gk *seselis, seseli,* perh. of Egypt origin] **1** *cap* **:** a large genus of smooth perennial herbs (family Umbelliferae) that are natives of temperate regions of the Old World and have ternately compound leaves, white flowers, and fruit with solitary oil tubes **2** -s **:** any plant of the genus *Seseli*
se·si·idae \sə̇ˈsīə,dē\ [NL, fr. *Sesia* (syn. of *Aegeria*) (fr. Gk *sēs* moth + NL *-ia*) + *-idae*] *syn of* AEGERIIDAE
ses·qui \ˈseskwē\ *n* -s [by shortening] **:** SESQUICENTENNIAL
sesqui- *comb form* [L, one and a half, half again, lit., and a half, fr. *semis* half (fr. *semi-*) + *-que* and (enclitic); akin to Gk *te* and, Skt *ca,* Goth *-h, -uh* — more at SEMI-] **1 :** one and a half times ⟨*sesqui*centennial⟩ **2** *archaic* **:** more than the norm of the type **:** SUPER-, ULTRA- ⟨*sesqui*heretic⟩ **3 :** one and a half times the degree of a (specified) aspect in astrology ⟨*sesqui*quadrate⟩ **4 a :** containing three atoms or equivalents of a (specified) element or radical esp. when combined with two of another ⟨*sesqui*oxide⟩ ⟨*sesqui*sulfide⟩ **b :** intermediate **:** combination — not used systematically ⟨*sesqui*carbonate⟩ ⟨*sesqui*silicate⟩ **c :** containing half again as many atoms ⟨*sesqui*terpene⟩
¹**ses·qui·al·ter** \¦seskwē¦oltə(r), -ē¦al-\ *adj* [L] **:** SESQUIALTERAL
²**sesquialter** \"\ *n* -s **:** SESQUIALTERA
ses·qui·al·tera \,⁼⁼ˈ⁼tərə\ *n* -s [NL, fr. L, fem. of *sesquialter*] **1 :** a musical triplet of three minims in the time of two preceding — compare HEMIOLA **2 :** a mixture pipe-organ stop containing usu. two ranks of pipes that reinforce some high harmonics of ground tone and make the sound more brilliant
ses·qui·al·ter·al \¦⁼⁼¦⁼⁼rəl\ *adj* [L *sesquialter* one and a half times as great (fr. *sesqui-* + *alter* other of two, second) + E *-al* — more at ALTER] **:** one and a half times as great as another **:** having the ratio of one and a half to one
ses·qui·carbonate \¦seskwə̇+\ *n* [*sesqui-* + *carbonate*] **:** a salt that is neither a simple normal carbonate nor a simple bicarbonate but in some cases (as sodium sesquicarbonate) a combination of the two — not used systematically
ses·qui·centenary \"+\ *adj or n* [*sesqui-* + *centenary*] **:** SESQUICENTENNIAL
¹**ses·qui·centennial** \"+\ *n* [*sesqui-* + *centennial*] **:** a 150th anniversary
²**sesquicentennial** \"+\ *adj* **:** of or relating to a 150th anniversary
¹**ses·qui·diploid** \"+\ *n* [*sesqui-* + *diploid*] **:** a triploid produced by a cross between tetraploid and diploid parents
²**sesquidiploid** \"\ *adj* **:** of, relating to, or being a sesquidiploid
sesquih *abbr* [L *sesquihora*] an hour and a half
ses·qui·oxide \¦seskwē+\ *n* [*sesqui-* + *oxide*] **:** an oxide containing three atoms of oxygen combined with two of the other constituent in the molecule ⟨ferric oxide is a ~⟩
ses·quip·e·dal \seˈskwipədᵊl, sə̇ˈs-\ *adj* [L *sesquipedalis*] **:** SESQUIPEDALIAN
ses·qui·pe·da·lia \,seskwə̇pə̇ˈdālyə\ *n pl* [L *sesquipedalia* (*verba*), lit., (words) a foot and a half long] **:** very long words
¹**ses·qui·pe·da·lian** \¦⁼⁼⁼¦dālyən\ *adj* [L *sesquipedalis* a foot and a half long (fr. *sesqui-* + *ped-, pes* foot + *-alis* -al) + E *-an* — more at FOOT] **1 :** having many syllables **:** LONG ⟨simplest language, without any ~ technical terms —J.H.Gottmer⟩ **2 :** given to or characterized by the use of long words ⟨~ orators⟩ ⟨~ style⟩ ⟨this ~ way of saying one has no money —W.F.De Morgan⟩
²**sesquipedalian** \"\ *n* -s **:** a very long word
ses·qui·pe·da·lian·ism \,⁼⁼⁼ˈdālyə,nizəm\ *also* **ses·quip·e·dal·ism** \seˈskwipədᵊl,izəm, sə̇ˈs-\ *n* -s [*sesquipedalian, sesquipedal* + *-ism*] **:** SESQUIPEDALITY
ses·qui·pe·dal·i·ty \se(,)skwipə̇ˈdaləd·ē\ *n* -ES [*sesquipedal* + *-ity*] **1 :** the quality or condition of being sesquipedal **2 a :** the use of sesquipedalian words **b :** a style characterized by the use of sesquipedalian words
ses·qui·plane \ˈseskwə̇+,-\ *n* [*sesqui-* + *plane*] **:** a biplane having one wing of less than half the area of the other
ses·qui·quadrate \¦⁼⁼+\ *n* [fr. (assumed) NL *sesquiquadratus,* fr. L *sesqui-* + *quadrant-, quadrans* quadrant + *-atus* -ate] **:** the astrological aspect of two heavenly bodies when separated by 1½ quadrants
ses·qui·silicate \"+\ *n* [*sesqui-* + *silicate*] **1 :** a silicate (as sodium sesquisilicate) that is intermediate between two silicates **2 :** a mixture of an orthosilicate or metasilicate and a disilicate used esp. in smelting
ses·qui·sulfide \"+\ *n* [*sesqui-* + *sulfide*] **:** a sulfide that contains three atoms of sulfur in the molecule and that may or may not be analogous to a sesquioxide — compare PHOSPHORUS SESQUISULFIDE
ses·qui·terpene \"+\ *n* [ISV *sesqui-* + *terpene*] **:** any of a class of terpenes $C_{15}H_{24}$ containing half again as many atoms in the molecule as monoterpenes; *also* **:** a derivative of such a terpene
¹**ses·qui·ter·pe·noid** \¦seskwə̇¦tərpə,nȯid\ *n* -s [*sesquiterpene* + *-oid*] **:** a sesquiterpene or sesquiterpene derivative (as farnesol or santonin)
²**sesquiterpenoid** \"\ *adj* [*sesquiterpene* + *-oid*] **:** resembling a sesquiterpene in molecular structure
sess *Brit var of* ¹CESS, ²CESS 1a, 1b
sess *abbr* session
ses·sile \ˈsesəl, -e,sīl, -e(,)sil\ *adj* [L *sessilis* of or fit for sitting, low, dwarf (of plants), fr. *sessus* (past part. of *sedēre* to sit) + *-ilis* -ile — more at SIT] **1 a :** attached directly by the base **:** not raised upon a peduncle ⟨~ bubble⟩ ⟨*sessile*-eyed⟩; *specif.* **:** resting on a main stem or branch without an intervening stalk ⟨*sessile*-fruited⟩ ⟨*sessile*-leaved⟩ **b :** attached by a broad base ⟨~ polyp⟩ **2 :** permanently attached **:** not free to move about **:** SEDENTARY ⟨~ marine animals and plants —R.E.Coker⟩ ⟨~ employment⟩ ⟨~ population units⟩ ⟨~ and vulnerable wealth —C.D.Forde⟩ — compare VAGILE
sessile barnacle *n* **:** a barnacle (as the acorn barnacle) of which the calcareous shell is attached directly to the substrate — compare PEDUNCULATE BARNACLE
sessile gonophore *n* **:** a gonophore that never becomes detached
sessile hydatid *n* **:** HYDATID OF MORGAGNI 2
sessile oak *n* **:** DURMAST
ses·sil·i·ty \seˈsiləd·ē\ *n* -ES [*sessile* + *-ity*] **:** the state of being sessile
ses·si·li·ven·tres \,sesələˈven·(,)trēz\ [NL, fr. L *sessilis* sessile (fr. L, of or fit for sitting) + L *ventr-, venter* belly — more at VENTER] *syn of* CHALASTOGASTRA
ses·sion \ˈseshən\ *n* -s [ME, fr. MF, fr. L *session-, sessio* act of sitting, session, fr. *sessus* (past part. of *sedēre* to sit) + *-ion-, -io* -ion — more at SIT] **1 :** an actual or constructive sitting of a body (as a court, council, or legislature); *also*

: the actual or constructive assembly of the members of such a body for the transaction of business ⟨morning ~⟩ ⟨evening ~⟩ ⟨read the letters to the House in secret ~ —C.L.Becker⟩ **2 sessions** *pl* **a** *Eng law* (1) **:** a sitting of justices of the peace in execution of the powers conferred by their commissions — see GENERAL SESSIONS, PETTY SESSIONS, SPECIAL SESSION (2) **:** an English court holding such sessions **b :** any of various courts answering more or less to the English sessions **3** *usu cap, Scots law* **:** COURT OF SESSION **4 :** the time, period, or term during which a body (as a court, council, or legislature) meets regularly for business **:** the space of time between the first meeting and the prorogation or final adjournment ⟨biennial legislative ~s⟩ — see SPECIAL SESSION **5 a :** Jesus Christ's sitting at the right hand of God **b** *archaic* **:** the action of sitting **:** a being seated **6 :** the ruling body of a Presbyterian congregation consisting of the elders in active service moderated by the pastor and exercising the government and discipline of the church and often also direct control of its temporal affairs — compare CONSISTORY, PRESBYTERY **7 a** *chiefly Scot* **:** ACADEMIC YEAR **b :** TERM 4 ⟨summer ~⟩ **c :** the part of the day during which a public school conducts classes ⟨many overcrowded schools have double ~s⟩ **d :** PERIOD 11a **8 :** a group of students in a Salvation Army officers' training school having the same year of graduation **9 :** a period usu. in a series devoted to a particular activity esp. by a group of persons ⟨recording ~⟩ ⟨briefing ~⟩ ⟨were in for a ~ of mental improvement —S.H.Adams⟩ ⟨square dance ~s will be held weekly —Walter Terry⟩ ⟨neglected his tennis ~s —George Sklar⟩ ⟨one ~ with a mop —A.W.Baum⟩ — see BULL SESSION, JAM SESSION

ses·sion·al \ˈseshənᵊl, -shnəl\ *adj* **:** of, relating to, or restricted to a session **:** recurring or renewed at each session ⟨~ program⟩ ⟨~ resolution⟩ ⟨~ allowance⟩

sessional order *or* **sessional rule** *n* **:** an order or rule framed to continue only during the session (as of Parliament) — distinguished from *standing order*

ses·sion·ary \ˈseshəˌnerē\ *adj* [*session* + *-ary*] **:** SESSIONAL

sessioner *n* -s [*session* + *-er*] **1** *obs* **:** a member of a court of session **2** *obs* **:** a member of a kirk session

session laws *n pl* **:** a publication in bound-volume form of all enactments and resolutions of a legislature passed at a particular session, indexed, and numbered usu. in chronological order — distinguished from *code*

session of the peace : a sitting of justices of the peace for the trial of cases or the exercise of other assigned powers — usu. used in pl.

ses·so·blast \ˈsesəˌblast\ *n* [*sessile* + *-o-* + *statoblast*] **:** a bryozoan statoblast that remains fixed to the zooecial wall

sessor *n* -s *obs* **:** one that assesses a tax

ses·terce \ˈseˌ(ˌ)stərs\ *n* -s [L *sestertius*, fr. *sestertius* two and a half times as great (fr. its being equal orig. to two and a half asses), fr. *semis* a half (fr. *semi-*) + *tertius* third — more at SEMI-, THIRD] **1 a :** an ancient Roman coin equal to ¼ denarius **b :** a corresponding unit of value **2 :** SESTERTIUM

ses·ter·tium \-sh(ē)əm\ *n, pl* **sester·tia** \-sh(ē)ə\ [L, fr. gen. pl. of *sestertius* sesterce, in the phrase *milia sestertium* thousands of sesterces] **:** a unit of value in ancient Rome equal to one thousand sesterces

ses·ter·tius \seˈstərsh(ē)əs, səˈs-\ *n, pl* **sester·tii** \-shēˌī\ [L] **:** SESTERCE 1

ses·tet \(ˈ)seˈstet\ *n* -s [It *sestetto*, fr. *sesto* sixth (fr. OIt, fr. L *sextus*) + *-etto* (as in *duetto* duet) — more at SEXT] **1 :** SEXTET 1 **2 :** a stanza or a poem of six lines; *specif* **:** the last six lines of a sonnet of the Italian type — compare OCTAVE 2b

ses·tet·to \seˈsted·(ˌ)ō\ *n* -s [It] **:** SEXTET 1

ses·ti·na \seˈstēnə\ *n* -s [It, fr. OIt, fr. *sesto* sixth] **:** a lyrical form developed before 1200 by Provençal troubadours and now fixed in the form of six 6-line stanzas orig. unrhymed, six end words repeated in different order in each stanza, and a 3-line envoi in which three of these six words occur in the middle and three at the end of the lines

ses·tine \(ˈ)seˈstēn\ *n* -s [MF, fr. OIt *sestina*] **:** SESTINA

ses·tole \ˈseˌstōl\ *or* **ses·to·let** \ˌsestəˈlet\ *n* -s [alter. (influenced by It *sesto* sixth) of *sextole, sextolet*] **:** SEXTUPLET 3

ses·ton \ˈseˌstän\ *n* -s [G, fr. Gk *sēston*, neut. of *sēstos*, verbal of *sēthein* to strain, filter] **:** minute material moving in water and including both living organisms (as plankton and nekton) and nonliving matter (as plant debris or suspended soil particles) — see BIOSESTON; compare TRIPTON — **ses·ton·ic** \(ˈ)seˈstänik\ *adj*

sesunc *abbr* [L *sesuncia*] an ounce and a half

se·su·to \sāˈsüd·(ˌ)ō\ *n* -s *usu cap* **:** SOTHO

se·su·vi·um \səˈsüvēəm\ *n, cap* [NL] **:** a small genus of fleshy maritime herbs (family Aizoaceae) widely distributed esp. in tropical regions and having opposite leaves and reddish flowers with a 5-lobed calyx and five stamens — see SEA PURSLANE

¹set \ˈset, *usu* -ed·+V\ *vb* **set; set; setting; sets** [ME *setten*, fr. OE *settan*; akin to OHG *sezzen* to set, ON *setja*, Goth *satjan*; causative fr. the root of E *sit*] *vt* **1 a :** to cause to sit **:** make assume a sitting position or attitude **b :** to place in or on a seat ⟨~ a man on horseback⟩ ⟨~ a king on a throne⟩ **c** *archaic* **:** to seat in readiness for an activity ⟨were ~ to cards —W.M.Thackeray⟩ ⟨when he was ~, his disciples came unto him —Mt 5:1 (AV)⟩ **2 a :** to put (a fowl) on eggs to hatch them **b :** to put (eggs) into a nest for a fowl to hatch or into an incubator **3 :** to place (oneself) in a position to start running in a race **4** *chiefly Scot* **:** to be becoming to **:** SUIT ⟨this bonnet ~s me —J.M.Barrie⟩ **5 a :** to put to stay in place **:** place with care or deliberate purpose ⟨~ a lamp on the table⟩ ⟨~ a ladder against the wall⟩ ⟨~ a stone on a grave⟩ ⟨~ a figure on a pedestal⟩ **b :** to fix (a plant) in the ground ⟨~ fruit trees⟩ — often used with *out* ⟨~ out seedlings⟩ **c** (1) **:** to put (as a trap or snare) in a proper condition or position to catch prey (2) **:** to force point and barb of (a hook) into the jaw of a fish **d** (1) **:** to put aside (as dough) to rise (2) **:** to fill (a fermenter or yeast tub) with mash, yeast, and other ingredients for distilling and to adjust the contents to the proper temperature for fermentation **e :** to place so as to have relation to something or someone ⟨dainty dish to ~ before a king⟩ ⟨~ a light at each window⟩ **6 :** to direct with fixed attention and preoccupation ⟨had ~ his heart on going with us⟩ ⟨you can solve this problem if you ~ your mind to it⟩ **7 a** *archaic* **:** to fix in writing **:** PHRASE **b :** to place in a particular location or relation in a writing **:** put down **:** ENTER — used with *down* ⟨~ down all the items in one column⟩ ⟨all the happenings ~ down in his diary⟩ **8 :** to cause to assume a specified condition, relation, or occupation ⟨when the slaves were ~ free⟩ ⟨made a raft and ~ it afloat⟩ ⟨~ him over the rest as a foreman⟩ **9 :** to appoint or assign to an office or duty **:** POST, STATION ⟨~ pickets around the camp⟩ ⟨the order to ~ the first watch came at 8 o'clock⟩ **10 :** to cause to assume a specified posture or position ⟨~ the chair back on its feet⟩ ⟨~ the door ajar⟩ ⟨his age ~s him apart from the others⟩ ⟨~ him astride a horse and led him away⟩ **11 a :** to fix as a distinguishing imprint, sign, or appearance ⟨the years have ~ their mark on him⟩ ⟨I do ~ my bow in the cloud —Gen 9:13 (AV)⟩ **b** *archaic* **:** ATTACH ⟨~ feathers to thy heels —Shak.⟩ **c :** AFFIX ⟨my will to which I ~ my hand and seal⟩ **d :** APPLY ⟨~ pen to paper⟩ ⟨~ the horn to his lips⟩ ⟨~ spurs to his horse⟩ ⟨~ a match to the pile of leaves⟩ **12 :** to play (a domino) to begin a game **13 a :** to fix or decide upon as a time, limit, or regulation **:** PRESCRIBE ⟨~ a wedding day⟩ ⟨~ certain conditions as part of the bargain⟩ ⟨~ bounds to ambition⟩ **b :** to lay or mark off (a line) in surveying or drafting **c :** to take the bearings of (as a landfall) ⟨~ a landmark⟩ **d** *obs* **:** to inflict as a burden or penalty **:** IMPOSE **e :** to establish by authority **:** DECREE ⟨once the rules had been ~ there was no changing them⟩ **14** *dial Brit* **:** RENT, LEASE **15** *obs* **:** to put in order **:** SETTLE **16 a :** to establish as the highest level or best performance ⟨~ a record for the half mile⟩ ⟨~s a new record for government spending⟩ **b :** to furnish as a pattern or model ⟨~ an example of generosity⟩ ⟨let another runner ~ the pace⟩ ⟨~ the fashion for epic poems⟩ ⟨preferred to work on lines ~ by his predecessors⟩ **c :** to give a pitch to (a melody) for singing **:** start by fixing the keynote ⟨~ a psalm⟩ **d :** to allot or appoint as a task or portion of work ⟨three books were ~ to be read by the class during the term⟩ ⟨he was ~ the task of finding a way to balance the budget⟩ ⟨the home team was ~ 75 runs to win the cricket match⟩ **17 a :** to put into a desired position, adjustment, or condition ⟨~ a thermostat at 70⟩ ⟨~ the camera lens for a long range shot⟩ ⟨brought the car to a stop and ~ the brake⟩ **b :** to pull (a bell) into the position of standing inverted ready for a full stroke **c :** to fix (a combination of pipe-organ stops) so that the pushing of a piston will throw an entire combination **d :** to restore to normal position or connection when dislocated or fractured ⟨~ a broken bone⟩ **e** *obs* **:** to set up **:** ERECT, RAISE **f :** to spread to the wind ⟨~ the sails of a ship⟩ **g** *obs* **:** to dispose tactically for battle **18 a :** to put in order for immediate use ⟨the table was ~ for three⟩ ⟨~ a place for a guest⟩ ⟨~ a lathe for screw cutting⟩ **b :** to provide (as words, verses) with melody and instrumental accompaniment ⟨~ a sonnet to music⟩; *also* **:** to adapt (a melody) to a text ⟨the same prevailing tunes . . . were customarily ~ to native American folksongs —S.P.Bayard⟩ **c :** to make scenically ready for a performance ⟨~ the scene⟩ ⟨~ the stage⟩ **d** (1) **:** to arrange (type) for printing ⟨~ type by hand⟩ (2) **:** to put into type or typographic characters (as on film) ⟨~ the word in caps⟩ ⟨a book ~ by computer⟩ **e :** to position (an insert) when tipping into the sections of a book usu. so as to correct bad margins **19** *also* **sett** \"\ **:** to determine the fineness of texture of (a fabric) before weaving **20 a :** to put a fine edge on (a cutting blade) by grinding or honing ⟨~ a razor⟩ **b :** to shape (metal) with a set hammer **c :** to bend slightly the tooth points of (a saw) alternately in opposite directions to widen the kerf and so prevent sticking **d :** to adjust (a measuring instrument) to a desired position ⟨~ a pair of calipers to size on a rule⟩ **e :** to fix the iron of (a carpenter's plane) in position so as to take off the desired thickness of shaving **f :** to sink (a nailhead) below the surface **21 :** to dispose (a specimen) for preservation and examination ⟨~ an insect⟩ **22 :** to make (a dye or color) fast **23 :** to put the finishing coat on ⟨plaster, float, and ~ a wall⟩ **24 :** to wave, curl, or arrange (hair) by wetting (as with a wave solution) and drying (as with heat) **25 a :** to cover or border or surround with plants ⟨~ the grounds with trees and bushes⟩ ⟨a parkway ~ with sycamores⟩ **b :** to adorn with something affixed or infixed **:** STUD, DOT ⟨the house was ~ about with fir trees⟩ ⟨clear sky ~ with stars⟩ **c** (1) **:** to fix (as a precious stone) in a border of metal **:** place in a setting ⟨~ a diamond in a ring⟩ (2) **:** to place in or amid something that serves as a setting ⟨~ glass in a sash⟩ (3) **:** to arrange (artificial teeth) upon a plate **26** *obs* **:** to fix upon or watch with a view to theft **27 a :** to hold something in regard or esteem at the rate of — used with *by* ⟨~s a great deal by daily exercise⟩ **b** *obs* **:** ASSUME, SUPPOSE **c :** to place in a relative rank or category ⟨~ duty before pleasure⟩ ⟨justly ~ the gem above the flower —Alexander Pope⟩ **d :** to fix at or adjust to a certain amount ⟨~ bail at $500⟩ ⟨~ the price higher⟩ **e :** WAGER, STAKE ⟨I have ~ my life upon a cast —Shak.⟩ **f :** VALUE, RATE — used with *at* ⟨I do not ~ my life at a pin's fee —Shak.⟩ ⟨his promises were ~ at naught after so many betrayals⟩ **g** *archaic* **:** to rate for assessment ⟨blamed for *setting* so wealthy a man at so low a rate —T.B.Macaulay⟩ **h :** to place as an estimate of something's worth ⟨~ a high value on every man's life⟩ **i :** ESTIMATE ⟨fire losses were ~ at a million dollars⟩ **28 :** to place in relation for comparison or balance ⟨when theory is ~ against practice⟩ ⟨after *setting* our gains against our losses⟩ **29 a :** to direct to action **:** put into activity ⟨~ the children to raking leaves⟩ ⟨~ a thief to catch a thief⟩ ⟨wind the clock and ~ it running⟩ **b :** to incite to attack ⟨~ the dogs on an intruder⟩ or antagonism ⟨war that ~s brother against brother⟩ **30 a :** to place by transporting ⟨~ ashore on the island⟩ ⟨a ferry ~ them across the river⟩ **b :** to put in motion ⟨~ the tongues a-wagging⟩ ⟨~ the bells a-ringing⟩ **c :** to bring by imparting motion ⟨a current ~ us to the northward⟩ ⟨stern started to swing with the tide, *setting* the vessel toward a submerged wreck —*All Hands*⟩ **d :** to put and fix in a direction ⟨~ our faces toward home once more⟩ **e** *of a dog* **:** to point out the seat or position of (as a bird) by holding a fixed attitude **31 :** to adjust in conformity with some standard ⟨~ his watch by the radio time signal⟩ **32 :** to propel (a boat) by poling **33 :** to defeat (an opponent or his contract) in bridge **:** cause to go down **34 a :** to fix firmly **:** make immobile **:** give rigid form or condition to ⟨~ his jaw in renewed determination to win⟩ ⟨~ her lips firmly and shook her head⟩ **b :** to make unyielding or obstinate ⟨~ his mind against all appeals⟩ **35 a** *archaic* **:** to cause or allow to get stuck **b** *dial* **:** to put into a confusing or embarrassing position **:** CHECK, STUMP **36 :** to cause to settle or convert into a solid form ⟨~ milk for cheese⟩ ⟨~ jelly by adding pectin⟩ **37 :** to cause (fruit or seed) to develop ⟨the peaches failed to ~ fruit⟩ ⟨some varieties do not ~ seed under cultivation⟩ **38 a :** to straighten (a bow or arrow) by heating, correcting the deformity, and quickly cooling **b :** to fix (leather) by stretching **39 :** to treat (viscose) so as to cause precipitation of cellulose **40 :** to fix the form or shape of (a synthetic fabric) as with heat or chemicals ~ *vi* **1** *chiefly dial* **:** SIT **2 :** to be becoming **:** be suitable **:** FIT ⟨his behavior does not ~ well with his years⟩ **3** *of a fowl* **:** to cover and warm eggs to hatch them **:** BROOD **4 :** to become lodged or fixed — used with *on* or *upon* ⟨the pudding ~ heavily on his stomach⟩ **5** *of a blossom, fruit, or seed* **:** to adhere to a parent plant and initiate growth or normal development as a result of a stimulus (as pollination) **6 :** to settle and become attached ⟨spawning and *setting* of oysters⟩ **7 a** *of a heavenly body* **:** to pass below the horizon **:** go down **:** DECLINE ⟨the sun ~s later now⟩ — opposed to *rise* **b :** to sink out of sight **:** come to an end **:** pass away **8 :** to place plants or shoots in the ground **:** PLANT ⟨in some cases *setting* is preferable to sowing⟩ **9 a** *obs* **:** to make a stake or wager **:** BET **b :** to make the first play in a game of dominoes **10 a** *chiefly dial* **:** to begin to move **:** set out **:** set forth **b :** to apply oneself to some activity ⟨~ to work to finish the job⟩ **11 a :** to have a specified direction in motion **:** FLOW, TEND ⟨the current ~s to the north⟩ ⟨the wind was *setting* from Pine Hill to the farm —Esther Forbes⟩ **b :** to have a trend **:** gather headway in a definite direction ⟨art is *setting* against modernism⟩ **12** *of a dog* **:** to indicate the position of game by crouching or pointing **13 :** to dance face to face with another in a square dance — used usu. with *to* ⟨~ to your partner and turn⟩ **14 a :** to become fixed or rigid; *specif* **:** to become more solid or hardened (as by chemical action or by cooling or drying) ⟨use up the cement before it ~s⟩ ⟨this ink ~s rapidly⟩ **b** *of cream* **:** to rise and settle at the top **c** *of milk* **:** CURDLE **d** *of a dye or color* **:** to become fast or permanent **15 a** *of a bone* **:** to become whole by knitting **b** *of metal* **:** to acquire a permanent twist or bend from strain **16** *of a balance wheel* **:** to stop swinging

syn PUT, PLACE, LAY, DISPOSE, STOW, DEPOSIT: SET suggests the putting of a person or thing firmly in a specified place, condition, or relationship ⟨bring these fellows into the country, or *set* them aboard ship —R.L.Stevenson⟩ ⟨*set* all her hopes in the son, particularly in her oldest —Franz Alexander⟩ ⟨some new apprentice . . . may turn out in the end to be either a bungler or an enemy, and *set* the whole appliance out of gear —B.N.Cardozo⟩ PUT applies to a motion or action placing a person or thing in an indicated situation or condition ⟨*putting* somebody else in a comfortable chair and making him listen to their efforts —Barrett Wendell⟩ ⟨proceedings in the lower courts were *put* on the same footing as proceedings in the higher ones —B.N.Cardozo⟩ ⟨the Gospels, especially the apocryphal, were *put* into Old French —H.O.Taylor⟩ PLACE may suggest a preciseness or considered intent lacking in PUT ⟨church buildings along Main Street are *placed* some distance back, but the commercial buildings abut the sidewalks —*Amer. Guide Series: N.H.*⟩ ⟨efforts were directed to *placing* his young friend where his talents could find a steady market —H.S.Canby⟩ LAY may convey the notion that the thing moved has been put into a flat position, one compatible with reclining rather than standing ⟨the lacquered services are *laid* upon the matting before them by maidens whose bare feet make no sound —Lafcadio Hearn⟩ ⟨Apollo has not *laid* aside his bow, nor Neptune his trident —William Hazlitt⟩ DISPOSE is likely to suggest considered or calculated placing and arranging ⟨orchids had been conspicuously *disposed* in various receptacles —Edith Wharton⟩ ⟨numerous auxiliary regiments, foot and horse, which were *disposed* over the hill-country —Jacquetta & Christopher Hawkes⟩ STOW is likely to suggest compact or neat and convenient placing, storing, packing ⟨air out the cabin and *stow* away our winter supplies —Willa Cather⟩ ⟨roomy enough for a skillful packer to *stow* a two-week supply of clothes in —*New Yorker*⟩ DEPOSIT may suggest either careful and attentive placing or putting away as in a cache or, in the natural sciences, letting fall to accumulate ⟨two copies of each measure are printed on special vellum . . . to be *deposited* in the Public Record Office —F.A.Ogg & Harold Zink⟩ ⟨took off the silk hat . . . and *deposited* it on the front seat of the cab —Joseph Conrad⟩ ⟨*deposits* more or less of the matter which it holds in suspension —T.H.Huxley⟩

syn FIX, SETTLE, ESTABLISH: SET suggests to put in place, maybe as a definite and final placing, forming, or making ⟨the patristic system of dogma with the antique philosophy *set* the forms of medieval expression —H.O.Taylor⟩ FIX is likely to suggest stability and permanence ⟨his character, his tastes and his private way of life also are during these years pretty well *fixed* —J.W.Krutch⟩ ⟨slowly his place in the McCoy household had been *fixed* —Sherwood Anderson⟩ SETTLE implies finality and permanence ⟨both English and French have been *settled* in their present form roughly since the eighteenth century —*Times Lit. Supp.*⟩ ESTABLISH on the other hand is likely to connote a combination first of placing and forming and second of furthering and fostering until the thing in question is stable and permanent ⟨by distinguishing what the author assumes from what he *establishes* through arguments —M.J.Adler⟩ ⟨enlarging our personality by *establishing* new affinities and sympathies with our fellowmen, with nature, and with God —W.R.Inge⟩

— **set about 1 :** to begin to do or accomplish ⟨had soon *set about* changing the flat tire⟩ ⟨*set about* finding a track into the mountains —Francis Kingdon-Ward⟩ ⟨Arab population suddenly *set about* smashing French shop windows —Claire Sterling⟩ **2 :** to aim at doing **:** ATTEMPT ⟨*sets about* moving the listeners to that position —R.M.Weaver⟩ **3 :** ATTACK — **set abroad** *archaic* **:** to set (a rumor) going **:** put in circulation — **set apart 1 :** to reserve to a particular use **2 :** to make noticeable or outstanding ⟨his enormous strength *set* him *apart* from ordinary men⟩ — **set aside 1 :** to put to one side **:** DISCARD **2 :** to set apart for a purpose **:** RESERVE, SAVE ⟨*set aside* part of the weekly income⟩ ⟨*set* the yolks *aside* to be used later in the sauce⟩ **3 :** to reject from consideration ⟨objections were *set aside* as trivial⟩ **4 :** ANNUL, OVERRULE ⟨the verdict was *set aside* by a higher court⟩ **5 :** EXCLUDE, EXCEPT ⟨*setting aside* the question of financing the project⟩ — **set a sponge :** to make a thin yeast batter which when risen and added to the full amount of flour for bread dough will facilitate fermentation — **set at :** ATTACK, ASSAIL ⟨*set at* the invaders with knives and pitchforks⟩ — **set at defiance :** DEFY — **set at naught :** to treat as of no account **:** DISREGARD, DESPISE — **set by the ears :** to cause to quarrel — **set cock a hoop :** to become reckless **:** act with jubilant abandon **:** CAROUSE — **set eyes on :** to catch sight of **:** BEHOLD, SEE ⟨fell in love the first time he *set eyes on* her⟩ — **set flying :** to set (a sail) without support by spar or stay by hoisting by a halyard until the luff is taut — **set foot in :** ENTER — **set forth 1** *obs* **:** to fit out **:** EQUIP **2** *obs* **:** PUBLISH **3 :** to give an account or statement of **:** present fully and clearly **:** EXPLAIN, DESCRIBE ⟨this ideal . . . is *set forth* with very detailed and precise description —R.A.Hall b. 1911⟩ **4 :** to start out on a journey **:** set out **:** START — **set forward 1 :** to cause or help to advance **:** FURTHER **2 :** to cause (a timepiece) to indicate a later time **3 :** to set out on a journey **:** START — **set home :** to drive (as caulking) into final position — **set light by :** to treat lightly **:** UNDERVALUE, SLIGHT — **set naught by :** to set at naught — **set on** *or* **set upon :** to attack with violence **:** ASSAULT ⟨soldiers were *set upon* by thugs loafing around barracks . . . who knocked down their victims and rifled wallets —Dixon Wecter⟩ — **set one back :** COST ⟨a new suit *set him back* $65⟩ — **set one's cap for :** to try to catch (a man) in marriage — **set one's face against :** to show opposition toward **:** OPPOSE — **set one's hand to :** to set about doing **:** UNDERTAKE — **set on foot :** to begin the development or progress of **:** set in motion ⟨plans were *set on foot* for a very much larger set of negotiations⟩ ⟨sinister rumors were *set on foot* by interested parties⟩ — **set sail :** to begin a voyage **:** start out ⟨we are *setting sail* for England next week⟩ — **set store by :** to consider valuable or trustworthy or worthwhile ⟨*set store by* dieting as a means to health⟩ ⟨convinced that the poorest people *set* the most *store by* family ties —*Irish Digest*⟩ — **set taut :** to take up the slack in running gear preliminary to heaving in on it — **set the palette :** to lay on the palette the required pigments in a special order according to the intended use of them — **set the temperament :** to tune a single octave of a keyboard instrument according to a desired temperament as a standard by which to tune the rest of its scale

²set \"\ *adj* [ME *sett*, fr. past part. of *setten* to set — more at ¹SET] **1 a :** SITUATED, LOCATED ⟨a house ~ on a hilltop⟩ **b :** fixed in place ⟨eyes ~ deep in his head⟩ **2 :** INTENT, DETERMINED — used with *on* or *upon* ⟨~ upon going⟩ ⟨~ on becoming a doctor⟩ **3 :** PITCHED ⟨~ battle⟩ **4 :** fixed by authority or appointment ⟨work at a ~ wage⟩ **:** PRESCRIBED, SPECIFIED ⟨~ forms of worship⟩ ⟨~ hours of study⟩ ⟨~ rules of procedure⟩ **5** *of a style of handwriting* **:** precise, clear, and even ⟨the indictment . . . which in a ~ hand fairly is engrossed —Shak.⟩ **6 :** deliberately conceived, composed, or expressed **:** INTENTIONAL, PREMEDITATED ⟨did it of ~ purpose⟩ ⟨dislike of ~ speeches⟩ ⟨railed on Lady Fortune . . . in good ~ terms —Shak.⟩ **7 :** ASSIGNED, REQUIRED ⟨asked to prepare a talk on a ~ subject⟩ ⟨reading ~ books in preparation for examinations⟩ **8 a :** not open to persuasion or argument **:** reluctant to change **:** OBSTINATE ⟨an old man very ~ in his ways⟩ **b** *chiefly dial* **:** disposed or resolved either by natural inclination or act of will ⟨~ to lead a virgin's life to my death —Philip Sidney⟩ **9 a :** fixed in position or attitude **:** IMMOVABLE, RIGID ⟨~ line of his jaw⟩ ⟨~ frown⟩ ⟨read in measured, ~ tones⟩ **b :** BUILT-IN **10 :** remaining unchanged **:** SETTLED, PERSISTENT ⟨~ defiance⟩ ⟨~ rains⟩ **11 a :** PREPARED, READY ⟨all ~ for an early morning start⟩ ⟨the storm broke before we could get ~ for it⟩ **b :** securely balanced for delivering a blow ⟨continual jabbing kept his opponent from getting ~ for a good punch⟩ ⟨change of pace keeps the batter from getting ~⟩ **c :** poised to start running or to dive in at the instant the signal is given ⟨ready, ~, go⟩

³set \"\ *n* -s [ME *set, sett, sette*, partly fr. *sett*, past part. of *setten* to set; partly fr. *setten* to set; in some senses, fr. or influenced in meaning by obs. *sette* religious body, sect, fr. MF, fr. L *secta* — more at ¹SET, SECT] **1 :** the descent of a heavenly body below the horizon ⟨that will be ere the ~ of sun —Shak.⟩ **2** *or* **sett** \ˈset\ *Scots law* **:** the constitution of a burgh **3** *obs* **:** state of being stopped **:** STANDSTILL, CHECK **4 a :** the first play in the game of dominoes **b :** the first domino played **5 :** an instance of being defeated at a contract in bridge ⟨tried for an overtrick at the risk of a ~⟩ **6 :** DEAD SET **7 a :** the hardening or solidifying of a plastic or liquid substance by chemical action (as of mortar, concrete, cement) or by cooling and drying (as of glue) **b :** the chemical and physical action causing a paint or varnish to become dry and firm **c :** the property of an enamel slip that enables it to form an adherent layer on a metal surface **8 a :** mental inclination, tendency, or habit **:** BENT ⟨a definite ~ toward mathematical reasoning⟩ **b :** a state of preparedness usu. of limited duration for action in response to an anticipated stimulus or situation ⟨mental ~ which functions in blocking all responses except those suited to the occasion —Arthur Weider⟩ ⟨motor ~ produced by lifting a weight⟩ **9 :** direction of flow ⟨against the ~ of the current⟩ ⟨the ~ of public opinion was now strongly toward peace⟩ ⟨the current had a northeasterly ~⟩ **10 :** form or carriage of the body or of its parts ⟨formidable ~ of his shoulders⟩ ⟨graceful ~ of her head⟩ **11 :** the manner of fitting or of being placed or suspended ⟨carefully adjusting the ~ of her hat⟩ **12 a :** amount of deflection from a straight

set 31b

line ⟨~ of an axle⟩ ⟨~ of a saw's teeth⟩ or level position ⟨~ of a gun aimed for distance⟩ **b :** the camber of a curved roofing tile **c :** the camber of a leaf spring **13 :** fixed direction of growth ⟨rubbing against the ~ of the fur⟩ **14 a :** a permanent bend or loss in elasticity ⟨~ in a bow⟩ ⟨~ of a fishing rod⟩ **b :** permanent change of form (as of metal) due to repeated or excessive stress — compare FATIGUE, PERMANENT SET **15 a :** the act of arranging hair by curling or waving when wet with water or wave solution **b :** the result of such arranging **16 :** the act or position of a dog in setting game **17** *also* **sett a :** a young plant or rooted cutting ready for setting out ⟨a ~ of a strawberry⟩ **b :** a small tuber or section of tuber, bulb, or corm ⟨an onion ~⟩ ⟨potato ~⟩ **c :** the amount of bloom produced on a plant **d :** the blossoms of a plant (as a fruit tree) that have set fruit as a result of fertilization of the flowers ⟨heavy ~ of apples⟩ **e :** the attachment of young mollusks (as oysters) to the substrate; *also* **:** the crop set at a particular time **18** *obs* **:** a pleat in a ruff; *also* **:** the manner in which a ruff is pleated **19 :** the burrow of a badger **20 :** a trap or snare placed to catch game ⟨visit each ~ daily⟩ **21** *also* **sett :** SHOT 1d, 4 **22 :** the width of the shank of a piece of type; *also* **:** the overall width of a letter — compare POINT-SET, UNIT-SET; see TYPE illustration **23** *also* **sett a :** a piece placed temporarily upon the head of a pile that cannot be reached directly by the weight or hammer **b :** SET HAMMER **c :** ³PUNCH 1a(3) **d :** SNAP 11a **24 :** the artificially constructed setting in which a stage or television play or motion picture is enacted including decor, properties, and furniture **25** *also* **sett :** a rectangular block of granite or sandstone used for paving streets and truck highways **26 :** SET IRON **27 :** the finishing coat of plaster **28 a :** the contents of a fermenting vat just after all ingredients have been added **b :** the pH value of a freshly filled fermenter **29 :** SET SHOT **30 :** SETUP 6g **31 a :** a unit in a tennis match consisting of a group of games of which one side wins six to opponent's four or less or in case of a deuced score wins two consecutive games **b :** a combination of three or more playing cards of the same rank or of the same suit in sequence **:** MELD **32 :** a number of things naturally connected by location ⟨~ of muscles⟩ ⟨~ of footprints⟩ or formation ⟨~ of teeth⟩ or order in time ⟨~ of temperature readings⟩ **33 :** a collection of books forming a unit: as **a :** the works of one author issued in volumes in uniform style **b :** a file of issues of a periodical **c :** a group of related works on a particular subject or of unrelated volumes printed uniformly and intended to be sold as a group **34 :** a number of associated buildings or rooms ⟨~ of farm buildings⟩ **35 :** the eggs laid by a bird for a single incubation or brood **:** CLUTCH **36 a :** the number of persons necessary for a square dance **b :** the formation assumed by a group of dancers to start a square dance **c :** a balancing step in country-dance usu. done by partners face to face **d :** the music played for a single turn of square, country, or ballroom dancing ⟨between ~s . . . balladeer sings folk songs —*New Yorker*⟩ **37 :** a group of musical compositions forming a whole ⟨~ of dances⟩ **38 :** a team of matched horses **39 a :** a group of articles of uniform design ⟨~ of dining room furniture⟩ ⟨~ of dishes⟩ **b :** the complete apparatus or equipment used in a particular process (as gas manufacture) **c :** an assortment of tools or instruments of identical kind ⟨~ of drill bits in graded sizes⟩ or complementary relationship ⟨~ of drafting tools⟩ ⟨~ of carpenter's tools⟩ ⟨~ of golf clubs⟩ **d :** a complete collection of articles necessary for playing a game ⟨croquet ~⟩ ⟨chess ~⟩ **e** *Brit* **:** a string of railway cars of the same exterior style **f :** a group of pumps that are used for lifting water from one level to another **g :** a group comprising breaker, intermediate, and finisher cards used in wool carding **40 :** a heavy timber frame for supporting the sides of an excavation, shaft, or tunnel **41** *also* **sett :** a standard measurement of the fineness of cloth usu. determined by the number of threads in one inch and the number of threads in each dent of the reed **42 a :** a number of persons associated by custom, occupation, social activity, or age; *collectively* **:** the persons of a specified social type ⟨belonged to the horsy ~⟩ ⟨the younger married ~⟩ **b :** a number of associated workers **:** GANG **c :** a small breeding group of domestic animals; *esp* **:** a gander and one or more geese **43 a :** a series of postage stamps **b :** a group of postage stamps including the lower denominations of a single series **44 a :** a group formed by classification ⟨~ of ideas⟩ ⟨~ of grammatical forms⟩ **b :** a collection of things and esp. mathematical elements (as numbers or points)— called also *class* **45 :** an apparatus of electrical or electronic components assembled so as to function as a unit ⟨radio ~⟩ ⟨television ~⟩ ⟨amplifying ~⟩ ⟨sending ~⟩ **46 :** the chromosome complement of a gamete **47 :** TWELVE-TONE ROW

se·ta \ˈsēd·ə\ *n, pl* **se·tae** \ˈsēd·(ˌ)ē, ˈsē,tē\ [NL, fr. L *seta, saeta* bristle — more at SINEW] **:** any of numerous slender typically rigid or bristly and springy organs or parts of animals or plants: as **a :** one of the hairs of a caterpillar **b :** a slender spine on the carapace of a crustacean **c :** one of the organelles in the form of processes of fused cilia that function in the movement of various ciliated protozoans **d :** the slender stalk of the sporogonium of a bryophyte **e :** one of the stalked glands on plants of the genus *Rubus* **f :** the bristle in the utricle of some plants of the genus *Carex* **g :** one of the chitinous often complex bristles that project from the body wall or from parapodia of chaetopod annelid worms and assist in locomotion **h :** one of the spiny feathers about the base of the bill of various birds **:** rictal bristle **i :** the slender maxilla of various insects with piercing or sucking mouthparts

se·ta·ceous \səˈtāshəs, sēˈ-\ *adj* [L *seta, saeta* bristle + E *-aceous*] **1 :** set with or consisting of bristles **:** BRISTLY **2 :** resembling a bristle in form or texture — see ANTENNA illustration — **se·ta·ceous·ly** *adv*

set acid *n* **:** the titratable acidity of a freshly filled fermenter

se·tal \ˈsēd·ᵊl\ *adj* [NL *seta* + E *-al*] **:** relating to a seta

se·tar·ia \səˈta(a)rēə\ *n* [NL, fr. *seta* + *-aria*] **1 a** *cap* **:** a large and widely distributed genus of annual and perennial grasses having a dense or open cylindrical inflorescence in which the individual spikelets are subtended by one or more bristles that persist after the spikelets fall and including several grasses that yield forage or hay — see FOXTAIL 2a, FOXTAIL MILLET **b** -s **:** any grass of the genus *Setaria* **2** *cap* **:** a genus of filarial worms parasitic as adults in the body cavity of various ungulate mammals and producing larvae that wander in the tissues and occas. invade the eye

se·tar·id \-rəd\ *n* -s [NL *Setaria* + E *-id*] **:** a worm of the genus *Setaria*

se·tar·i·ous \-rēəs\ *adj* [NL *setarius*, fr. L *seta* + *-arius* -ary] **:** resembling a bristle **:** ARISTATE

set-aside \ˈ⸗⸗,⸗\ *n* -s [fr. *set aside*, v.] **:** a required reserving and earmarking of a commodity (as food) up to a specified quantity or percentage of production for a particular purpose esp. by governmental order for the use of the military, for housing, or for veterans; *also* **:** a quantity so set aside

se·ta·tion \səˈtāshən\ *n* -s [NL *seta* + E *-ation*] **:** a covering or growth of setae ⟨the ~ of the hind tarsi⟩

set back *vt* **1 :** HINDER, CHECK, DELAY ⟨the harvest was *set back* by bad weather⟩ **2 :** to cause (a timepiece) to indicate an earlier time ⟨forgot to *set* his watch *back* on his trip west⟩ **3 :** to defeat (an opponent) with the effect that points are subtracted from the opposing score (as in a card game)

setback \ˈ⸗,⸗\ *n* -s [*set back*] **1 :** a checking of progress ⟨~ in steel production occurred this week⟩ ⟨union organization received a ~⟩ **:** a putting in a position less advanced than before ⟨~ in prices⟩ **2 :** DEFEAT, REVERSE ⟨military ~⟩ ⟨diplomatic ~⟩ ⟨baseball team's first ~ of the season⟩ **3 :** BACKSET 2 **4 :** a card game in which points are deducted from a player's score during the play; *esp* **:** AUCTION PITCH **5 a :** OFFSET 3a **b :** a withdrawal of the face of a building to a line some distance to the rear of the building line or to the rear of the wall below in order to reduce the obstruction the upper stories offer to sunlight reaching the streets and the lower stories of adjacent buildings **6 :** the reaction of a mass (as a projectile) to a force producing or tending to produce acceleration (as in ballistics) **7 :** a device for moving over the needles in an annunciator to the normal position after a call

set bar *n* **:** SET IRON

set by *vt* **1** *obs* **:** give up **:** REJECT, DISMISS **2 :** to set apart for future use

set down *vt* **1 :** to cause to sit down **:** SEAT **2 :** to place at rest on a surface or on the ground ⟨I *set* it *down* in this room somewhere and now it's lost⟩ **3** *obs* **:** to place or encamp (an army) so as to besiege **4 :** to suspend (a jockey) from racing because of an offense **5 :** to cause or allow to get off a vehicle ⟨the bus *set* him *down* right before his house⟩ **6 :** to land (an airplane) on the ground or water **7 a :** to lay down **:** ORDAIN, ESTABLISH **b :** to write down **:** record or relate in writing ⟨tried to *set* his thoughts *down* in an orderly way⟩ or in painting ⟨always *set down* exactly what he saw⟩ **8 a :** REGARD, CONSIDER, ESTIMATE ⟨soon *set* him *down* as a liar and a faker⟩ **b :** ATTRIBUTE ⟨let it be *set down* to his credit that he did not retreat⟩ ⟨*set* his success *down* to sheer perseverance⟩ **9 :** to lower the spirit or pride of **:** SNUB, DEFLATE, HUMILIATE **10 a :** to defeat (an opponent) in a game or contest **b :** to prevent (a batter) from reaching base **:** RETIRE ⟨*set* them *down* in order in the last inning⟩ **~** *vi* **1** *archaic* **:** to make up one's mind **2** *archaic* **:** to discharge passengers or occupants ⟨watched the carriages *setting down* for a reception —Osbert Lancaster⟩ **3 :** LAND ⟨time to *set down* and gas up —*Fortune*⟩

setdown \ˈ⸗,⸗\ *n* -s [*set down*] **1** *archaic* **:** a drive in a vehicle **:** TRIP; *also* **:** a lift in a passing vehicle **2 :** an act of humbling or deflating **:** REPROOF, SNUB

se te·nant \sətəˈnäⁿ\ *adj* [F, holding together] *of postage stamps* **:** joined together as in the original sheet **:** not separated

seter *var of* SAETER

set-fair \ˈ⸗;⸗\ *n* -s [fr. the phrase *set fair*] **:** a good troweled surface of plaster; *esp* **:** the coat after roughing-in leveled with the float

setfast *var of* SITFAST

set gage *n* **:** a gage for determining the set of sawteeth

set gun *n* **:** a firearm set as a trap to fire on an intruder or on game when a wire attached to its trigger is disturbed

seth *or* **sett** \ˈsāt\ *n* -s [Hindi *seth*, fr. Skt *śreṣṭha* chief or best person; akin to Gk *kreiōn* noble, master, Skt *śrī* beauty, majesty, power, Av *srī-* beauty] *India* **:** a rich merchant **:** BANKER

set hammer *n* **1 :** a hammer used as a swage or flatter in blacksmithing **2 :** a hammer with a hollowed-out face used as a swage in riveting

set hammer

set-hands dial *n* **:** a small auxiliary dial observable by a person when setting a turret clock or other large clock

sethead \ˈ⸗,⸗\ *n* **:** HEADCAP

set-hedge \ˈ⸗,⸗\ *n* **:** a planted hedge

seth·ite \ˈseˌthīt\ *or* **seth·i·an** \ˈsethēən\ *n* -s *usu cap* [*Sethite* fr. *Seth*, a son of Adam in the Bible + E *-ite*; *Sethian* fr. ML *Sethianus*, fr. LGk *Sēthianos*, fr. *Sēth* Seth + Gk *-ianos* -ian] **:** a member of a Gnostic school of serpent worshipers

set hook *n* **:** a hook on a setline

seti- *comb form* [L *seti-*, *saeti-*, fr. *seta, saeta* — more at SINEW] **:** bristle ⟨*setiferous*⟩

se·tier \səˈtyā\ *n* -s [MF *sestier, setier*, fr. L *sextarius*, a liquid measure, fr. *sextus* sixth + *-arius* -ary — more at SEXT] **:** any of various old French units of capacity or land area

se·ti·fi·ca·tion \ˌsēd·əfəˈkāshən\ *n* -s [*seti-* + *-fication*] **:** the development of setation

se·ti·form \ˈsēd·əˌfȯrm\ *adj* [*seti-* + *-form*] **:** like a bristle

se·ti·ger \ˈsēd·əjə(r)\ *n* -s [NL, fr. L *setiger, saetiger* setigerous] **:** a segment or process bearing bristles

se·tig·er·ous \səˈtijərəs\ *adj* [L *setiger, saetiger* setigerous (fr. *seti-* + *-ger* -gerous) + E *-ous*] **:** bearing or producing setae

set in *vt* **1 :** to put in **:** INSERT; *esp* **:** to stitch (a small part) within a large article ⟨*set in* a sleeve of a dress⟩ ⟨*set in* a belt at the waistline⟩ **2 :** to direct (a ship) towards shore **~** *vi* **1 :** to enter upon a particular state **:** become prevalent or settled ⟨cold weather *set in* before the British could take the forts —E.P.Alexander⟩ **2** *dial* **:** to set to work **:** begin to function **3 :** to blow or flow toward shore ⟨the wind was beginning to *set in*⟩

¹**set-in** \ˈ⸗;⸗\ *adj* [fr. *set in*, past part. of *set in*] **1 :** placed, located, or built as a part of some other construction ⟨*set-in* bookcase⟩ ⟨*set-in* wash basin⟩ **2 :** cut separately and stitched in ⟨*set-in* sleeves⟩ ⟨*set-in* pocket⟩

²**set-in** \ˈ⸗;⸗\ *n* -s [*set in*] **1 :** an instance or time of something setting in ⟨early *set-in* of frosty nights⟩ **2 :** something that is set in **:** INSERT

set iron *n* **:** a flat plate bar of soft iron used in ship construction to transfer the curvature of the frames from the scrive board to the bending slab — called also *set bar*

set kettle *n* **:** SET POT

setline \ˈ⸗,⸗\ *n* **1 :** a long heavy fishline consisting of one or more skates of gear that is anchored at either end and marked with buoys and used chiefly for bottom fishing — called also *groundline* **2 :** TROTLINE

set mark *n* **:** a defect in cloth; *esp* **:** a crosswise streak caused by a loom stoppage or improper setting

set·ness *n* -ES [²*set* + *-ness*] **:** the quality or state of being set **:** FIXITY, RIGIDITY ⟨~ of his gaze showed his fear⟩ ⟨~ of his habits⟩

setnet \ˈ⸗,⸗\ *n* **:** a fishnet that is anchored in position rather than drifted, trawled, or manipulated by hand

set nut *n* **:** LOCK NUT 1

set off *vt* **1** *obs* **:** REMOVE **2 a :** to put in relief **:** show up or intensify by contrast ⟨bright with flowers . . . a sinister brightness . . . *set off* by the blackness of the shadows —William Beebe⟩ **b :** ADORN, EMBELLISH ⟨ribbons and laces to *set off* the faces of pretty young sweethearts —W.S.Gilbert⟩ **c** *obs* **:** to give a flattering description of **d :** to set apart **:** make distinct or outstanding ⟨dramatic fire that generally *sets off* the leaders among men —C.B.Forcey⟩ ⟨*set off* the interjected material with commas⟩ **3 a :** OFFSET, COUNTERBALANCE, COMPENSATE ⟨more variety in the Lancashire weather to *set off* its most disagreeable phases —*Geog. Jour.*⟩ — often used with *against* ⟨strength of the middle classes . . . has been their ability to *set off*, within themselves, intellect against money —Roy Lewis & Angus Maude⟩ **b :** to make a setoff of **:** plead as a setoff **4 a :** to set in motion **:** cause to begin ⟨speculation in stocks often *sets off* speculation in commodities —*Kiplinger Washington Letter*⟩ ⟨sensations of thirst can be shown to be *set off* by dryness of the mouth —F.A.Geldard⟩ **b :** to cause to explode **:** touch off ⟨lightning may *set off* nitroglycerin —Stanley Frank⟩ **5 :** to measure or mark off on a surface **:** lay off **~** *vi* **1 :** to start out on a course or a journey ⟨*set off* for home⟩ ⟨saddled up and *set off* in pursuit⟩ **2 :** to smear the next sheet with ink **:** OFFSET

setoff \ˈ⸗,⸗\ *n* -s [*set off*] **1 :** something that is set off against another thing: **a :** something used to improve the appearance of anything **:** DECORATION, ORNAMENT **b :** COMPENSATION, COUNTERBALANCE **2 :** OFFSET 3a **3 :** the discharge of a debt by setting against it a distinct claim in favor of the debtor; *also* **:** the claim itself — compare COUNTERCLAIM, CROSS CLAIM, RECOUPMENT **4 :** OFFSET 8a **5 :** a railroad car removed from a train to a siding between yards or terminals

set-off man \ˈ⸗,⸗\ *n* **:** FLOORMAN 1b

setoff sheet *n, Brit* **:** SLIP SHEET

set on *vt* **1** *obs* **:** to set on foot **:** PROMOTE **2 :** to urge (as a dog) to attack or pursue **:** UNLEASH **3 :** to incite to action **:** INSTIGATE ⟨*set on* to rebellion by their leaders⟩ **4 :** to set to work **:** set about ⟨an extra gang was *set on* to the job⟩ **~** *vi* **:** to go on **:** ADVANCE

¹**se·ton** \ˈsētᵊn\ *n* -s [ME, fr. ML *seton-, seto*, fr. *seta* silk, fr. L, bristle — more at SINEW] **:** one or more threads or horsehairs or a strip of linen introduced beneath the skin by a knife or needle to form an issue — compare ROWEL **2 :** SUTURE

²**seton** \"\ *vt* -ED/-ING/-S **:** to use a seton on

se·toph·a·ga \səˈtäfəgə\ *n, cap* [NL, fr. Gk *sēto-* (fr. *sēt-*, *sēs* moth, prob. fr. Syr *sāsā*) + NL *-phaga*] **:** a genus of fly-catching warblers consisting of the American redstart and numerous related species of Central and So. America — **se·toph·a·gine** \-fəˌjīn, -jən\ *adj*

se·tose \ˈsēˌtōs\ *also* **se·tous** \ˈsēd·əs\ *adj* [L *setosus, saetosus*, fr. *seta, saeta* bristle + *-osus* -ose, -ous — more at SINEW] **:** BRISTLY, SETACEOUS

set out *vt* **1** *obs* **:** to equip and send out **2 a :** ISSUE, PROMULGATE ⟨this act *sets out* the personnel of a tribunal as follows —F.D.Smith & Barbara Wilcox⟩ **b :** to recite, describe, or state at large ⟨distributed copies of a pamphlet *setting out* his ideas in full —S.F.Mason⟩ **3** *obs* **:** to place in relief **:** set off **4 a :** to arrange and present graphically or systematically ⟨the grammar is well *set out*⟩ ⟨in fig. 67 you will see *set out* the semaphore code —Peter Heaton⟩ **b :** to mark out (as a design) **:** lay out the plan of ⟨*sets out* the wood with square and marking knife, shapes and joints it —*Choice of Careers: Furniture Manufacturing*⟩ **c :** to smooth or flatten (a wet hide or skin) when dressing **5 :** to separate (a railroad car) from a train and place on a siding **6 :** to begin with a definite purpose **:** INTEND, UNDERTAKE ⟨given up the attempt to read poets who *set out* deliberately to mystify him —Douglas Stewart⟩ ⟨necessary for the effect he *set out* to produce —Bernard De Voto⟩ **~** *vi* **:** to start out on a course, a journey, or a career ⟨*set out* across the sea⟩ ⟨*set out* early from his cabin⟩ ⟨the engineering course he had originally *set out* on⟩

setout \ˈ⸗,⸗\ *n* -s [*set out*] **1 a** (1) **:** ARRAY, DISPLAY ⟨complete ~ of dinnerware and glassware⟩ (2) **:** ARRANGEMENT, LAYOUT ⟨in ~ the catalog had the appearance of an ode —Adrian Bell⟩ **b :** BUFFET, SPREAD **c :** TURNOUT 6a **d :** COSTUME, GETUP **e :** OUTFIT, EQUIPMENT ⟨a gambling ~⟩ **2 :** PARTY, ENTERTAINMENT, AFFAIR **3 :** BEGINNING, OUTSET **4 :** the act of taking a car out of a train ⟨average number of ~s for hot boxes per car-mile⟩

setover \ˈ⸗,⸗⸗\ *n* -s [fr. *set over*, v.] **1 :** distance or amount set over **2 :** a device by which a lathe headstock or tailstock can be moved perpendicular to the ways for taper turning

set piece *n* **1 :** a composition of formal pattern in painting, sculpture, music, or literature ⟨an autobiographical *set piece*⟩ ⟨thrilling effect of . . . any of Shakespeare's great *set pieces* —W.S.Maugham⟩ ⟨the *set pieces*, too — the cathedrals and galleries and parks and palaces . . . come alive —Mitchell Goodman⟩ **2 a :** a flat cut to the silhouette of a building, tree, mountain, or some other object required in a stage setting **b :** a piece of constructed scenery **3 :** a framework on which fireworks are so arranged as to form a design on burning **4 :** a precisely planned and conducted military operation

set pin *n* **:** DOWEL

set point *n* **1 :** a point that decides a tennis set if won by the side having an advantage in the score **2 :** a point at which it is desired to have a control system maintain the variable quantity (as of pressure, temperature, relative humidity) **:** SETTING

set pot *n* **:** a vessel usu. of stainless steel heated either directly or indirectly in a fixed location for manufacturing synthetic resins and varnishes — called also *set kettle*

sets *pres 3d sing of* SET, *pl of* SET

set sample *n* **:** a sample taken from a freshly filled fermenter for chemical analyses

setscrew \ˈ⸗,⸗\ *n* **1 :** a machine screw designed to be screwed through a metal part (as a collar) and to jam tightly upon another part (as a shaft) so as to prevent relative movement — compare CLAMP SCREW **2 :** a screw for regulating a valve opening or a spring tension

setscrew wrench *n* **:** ALLEN WRENCH

set shot *n* **:** a two-handed floor shot in basketball from a stationary position

sets·man \ˈsetsmən\ *n, pl* **setsmen :** a workman in a stone quarry who cuts stone paving blocks

set square *n* **1 :** TRIANGLE 3e **2 :** a drafting instrument having a straightedge that may be set at any desired angle with an edge of the drawing board **3 :** a try square with an adjustable sliding head

set-stitched \ˈ⸗;⸗\ *adj* **:** embroidered on tapestry

¹**sett** *var of* SET

²**sett** *var of* SETH

³**sett** \ˈset\ *n* -s [prob. fr. obs. var. of ³*set*] **:** a pattern of a Scottish tartan

set·te·cen·tist \ˌsed·əˈchentəst\ *n, pl* **settecentists** \-sts\ *or* **settecentis·ti** \-ˌchen·ˈtēstē\ [It *settecentista*, fr. *settecento* seven hundred, 18th century (fr. *sette* seven — fr. L *septem* — + *cento* hundred, fr. L *centum*) + *-ista* -ist — more at SEVEN, HUNDRED] **:** an artist, poet, or student of the 18th century period in Italian literature and art

¹**set·tee** \seˈtē\ *n* -s [modif. of It *saettia*, fr. ML *sagittea*, fr. L *sagitta* arrow] **:** a boat with a long sharp prow and single deck fitted with two or three masts with lateen sails and formerly used in the Mediterranean

²**settee** \"\ *n* -s [alter. (influenced by *-ee*) of ¹*settle*] **1 :** a long seat having a back and made to accommodate several at once **2 :** a medium-sized sofa with arms and a back

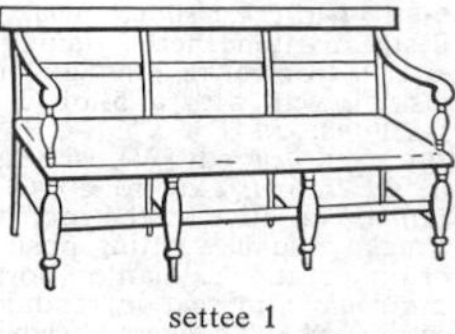
settee 1

settee bed *n* **:** a settee convertible into a bed by turning down or pulling out the seat

settee sail [¹*settee*] *n* **:** a quadrilateral sail on a lateen yard hung obliquely to the mast

set·ter \ˈsed·ə(r), -etə-\ *n* -s [ME, fr. *setten* to set + *-er* — more at SET] **1 :** one that sets ⟨~ of traps⟩ ⟨an accurate ~ of type⟩ ⟨good ~ of fruit⟩ ⟨~ of fashions⟩ — used often in combination ⟨brick*setter*⟩ ⟨tile*setter*⟩ **2 :** a worker who sets something esp. by putting it in readiness for some operation or process or by placing it at a permanent location: as **a :** a sawmill worker who rides on the log carriage of the head saw and adjusts the position of logs so that planks are cut to desired thickness **b :** a textile worker who prepares harnesses for drawing-in **c :** one that places stacks of brick or tile in kilns **d :** one that adjusts paper-cutting machines **e** (1) **:** one that erects stone monuments (2) **:** one that sets stone blocks in a masonry wall **f :** BED SETTER **g :** one that sets stones or seals in jewelry **h :** a leather worker who smooths wrinkles from oiled hides with a dull scraper or by machine — called also *putter-out, setter-out, striker-out* **3 :** one of those who place the cocks beak to beak in a cockfight **4 :** one that sets out plants ⟨tobacco ~⟩ **5** *Scots law* **:** LESSOR **6 :** something used in setting: as **a :** a stone for setting an edge on a tool **b :** a fireclay container to hold a single piece (as a plate or saucer) in the kiln **c :** a low short sawhorse that is placed under the axle of a vehicle after it is raised with a jack and that leaves the wheels free to turn **d :** SAW SET **e :** a device for setting a combination of stops in a pipe organ **7 a :** one that finds and decoys victims for sharpers or thieves **b :** a police spy **:** INFORMER **c :** one employed to run up prices at auctions **8 :** a large bird dog of a type formerly trained to set on finding game but now expected to point — see ENGLISH SETTER, GORDON SETTER, IRISH SETTER; compare POINTER **9 setters** *pl* **:** WOMEN — distinguished from *pointers*

settergrass \ˈ⸗⸗,⸗\ *n* **:** BEAR'S-FOOT

setter-in \ˈ⸗⸗ˈ⸗\ *n, pl* **setters-in** [*set in* + *-er*] **:** a pottery worker who packs ware in saggers and places them in kilns

setter-on \ˈ⸗⸗ˈ⸗\ *n, pl* **setters-on** [*set on* + *-er*] **1 :** one that sets on or attacks **:** ATTACKER **2 :** one that instigates or incites ⟨*setter-on* to treason⟩

setter-out \ˈ⸗⸗ˈ⸗\ *n, pl* **setters-out** [*set out* + *-er*] **1 :** SETTER 2h **2 :** a carpenter or metalworker who lines out the details of the work

setter-to \ˈ⸗⸗ˈ⸗\ *n, pl* **setters-to** [*set to* + *-er*] **:** SETTER 3

setter-up \ˈ⸗⸗ˈ⸗\ *n, pl* **setters-up** [*set up* + *-er*] **:** one that sets something up: as **a :** RAISER 4 **b :** a worker who inserts linings into leather products **c :** a worker who assembles cardboard boxes **d :** one that sets up and sets off fireworks displays **e :** SETTER 2h

setterwort \ˈ⸗⸗,⸗\ *n* [*setter-* (of unknown origin) + *wort*] **:** BEAR'S-FOOT

set theory *n* **:** a branch of mathematical or symbolic logic that deals with the nature and relations of sets — **set theoretic** *adj*

setting *n* -s [ME, fr. gerund of *setten* to set — more at SET] **1 a :** the manner, position, or direction in which something is set ⟨change the ~ of a thermostat⟩ **b :** the numerical reading of a graduated circle or other scale (as in right ascension or declination) by which an instrument is pointed at a celestial body **c :** the placing of a micrometer wire centrally on the image of an object whose position is being measured **d** : the arrangement of spools of colored face yarn for axminster weaving **2** *chiefly Scot* : LEASE **3 a** : the frame or bed in which a gem is set; *also* : style of mounting ⟨marquise ~⟩ **b** : a station, bed, or resting place for a machine **4 a** : the temporal and spatial environment of the action of a narrative ⟨an old plot in a modern ~⟩ **b** : the scenic environment indoors or out including all the physical surroundings (as properties, furniture, buildings) within which a scene of a play or motion picture is enacted **5** : the music composed for a poem, psalm, or other text **6** : the articles of tableware required for setting a table or a place at table ⟨a dining room with ~*s* for 26 —*Time*⟩ ⟨a ~ of sterling flatware⟩ **7** : the mechanism in a timepiece that permits the hands to be manually moved to the correct time **8** : a group of retorts for gas manufacture **9 a** : the area from which logs are skidded by the rigging attached to one spar tree **b** : a site to which grain is hauled for threshing or at which the grain is stacked before the arrival of the thresher **10 a** : the eggs incubated by a fowl at one time **b** : a batch of eggs for incubation **11 a** : the arrangement of individual clichés in a plate or of stamps in a sheet **b** : the arrangement of an overprint on a stamp

setting block *or* **setting board** *n* : a grooved block or board usu. of cork used by entomologists in setting the wings and other parts of insects in the position for drying

setting circle *n* **1** : a graduated scale or wheel on the mounting of an equatorial telescope for indicating right ascension or declination **2** : coordinate scales on any optical pointing instrument (as a surveyor's transit)

setting coat *n* : a finishing coat of plaster

setting dog *n, archaic* : SETTER 8

setting gage *n* : a definite gage used as a standard for testing a limit gage or for setting an adjustable limit gage in size

setting hen *n* : BROODY HEN

setting-out \ˈ⸗⸗ˈ⸗\ *n, pl* **settings-out** [fr. gerund of *set out*] **1** : beginning of a course or journey : DEPARTURE **2** : a bride's trousseau and furniture

setting-out machine *n* : STRIKING-OUT MACHINE

setting point *n* **1** : the temperature at which a liquid changes to a solid or semisolid : FREEZING POINT **2** : a place in a mechanism where adjustments may be made

setting pole *n* : a pole usu. having a steel tip and used for pushing boats along in shallow water

setting punch *n* : a punch used esp. for closing a rivet (as in leatherwork) over a washer — called also *rivet set*

setting room *n, chiefly Midland* : SITTING ROOM

setting rule *n* : COMPOSING RULE

setting stake *n* : a device for setting circular saws that has an adjustable cone center and a hardened revolvable steel anvil beveled at various angles around the edge of its face

setting stick *n* **1** : POKING STICK **2** : DIBBLE **3** : COMPOSING STICK

setting-up exercise \ˈ⸗⸗ˈ⸗-\ *n* : any of a series of gymnastic exercises used to give an erect carriage, supple muscles, and easy control of the limbs

[1]**set·tle** \ˈsed·ᵊl, -etᵊl\ *n* -s [ME *setle, settil, settle*, fr. OE *setl*; akin to OHG *sezzal* seat, chair, Goth *sitls* seat, L *sella* seat, chair, saddle, Gaulish *sedlon* seat, OE *sittan* to sit — more at SIT] **1** *obs* : a place for sitting; *also* : chief place of abode : SEAT **2 a** : a wooden bench with arms, a high solid back sometimes extending to the floor, and often an enclosed foundation serving as a chest whose cover is the seat — see BOX SETTLE, TABLE SETTLE **b** : SETTEE **3** : a raised platform, shelf, or frame; *specif* : a ledge about the lower part of an altar **4** [[2]*settle*] **a** : action or result of settling or sinking ⟨sand boils, bubbles, slides, and ~*s* . . . threaten to wipe out all efforts —*Time*⟩ **b** : the shrinkage measured in height of a kiln of brick when burning

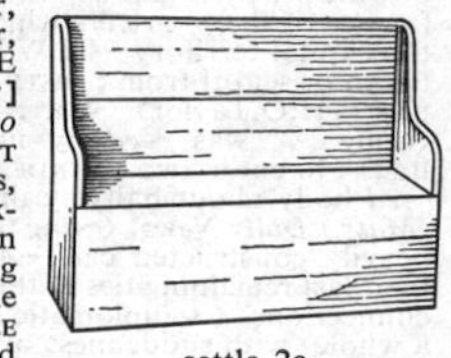
settle 2a

[2]**settle** \"\ *vb* **settled**; **settled**; **settling** \-d·ᵊliŋ, -t(ᵊ)liŋ\ **settles** [ME *setlen, settlen*, fr. OE *setlan*, fr. *setl*, n.] *vt* **1 a** *obs* : to cause to sit : SEAT **b** : to place so as to remain or to be comfortable ⟨*settled* himself in an armchair⟩ ⟨~ a child in its crib⟩ **c** : to direct or apply the attention, will, or effort of (oneself) ⟨the class *settled* itself to work⟩ **2 a** : to establish in residence ⟨~ refugees on farmland⟩ **b** : to furnish with inhabitants : COLONIZE, PLANT ⟨the colony was first *settled* by the Dutch⟩ ⟨a region *settled* by recent emigrants⟩ **c** : to establish (as residence) permanently **d** : to establish in married life ⟨managed to ~ all his daughters⟩ **e** *obs* : to set up (as a business) in a particular place **f** *archaic* : to establish in a pastoral office **3 a** : to make (loose material) compact : CONSOLIDATE ⟨~ the contents of a bag by shaking it⟩ ⟨watering the soil to ~ it as the hole was filled in⟩ **b** : to restore (a road or lawn) or bring to a smooth, dry, or passable condition **c** : to reduce in height or to a lower level ⟨~ a deck⟩ ⟨~ a sail⟩ **d** : to cause (land) to appear lower — opposed to *raise* **e** : to clear of dregs and impurities by causing them to sink : render pure or clear ⟨put eggshells in the coffee to ~ it⟩ **4 a** : to stop by killing or stunning ⟨*settled* his enemy with a single blow⟩ **b** : to reduce to order or to good behavior : SILENCE ⟨a word from his father was enough to ~ him⟩ **5** : to change from disturbance and agitation to repose and tranquillity ⟨a drink to ~ his nerves⟩ ⟨she gave them ten seconds to ~ their faces —Virginia Woolf⟩ ⟨the bump on the head must have *settled* my brain —S.H.Adams⟩ **6 a** : to put in a fixed or permanent state ⟨~ the order of royal succession⟩ : make firm or stable ⟨~ the government on a parliamentary basis⟩ ⟨both English and French have been *settled* in their present form roughly since the eighteenth century —*Times Lit. Supp.*⟩ **b** : to resolve or judge finally : remove from uncertainty, unclarity or dispute ⟨time has *settled* few or none of the essential points of dispute —Henry Adams⟩ **c** : to put in order : ADJUST ⟨*settled* her patient's pillows⟩ ⟨always removed or *settled* their hats with both hands —E.A.Poe⟩ **7 a** : to fix (as a price) by mutual agreement **b** : to conclude (a lawsuit) by agreement between the parties usu. out of court **c** : to close (as an account) by payment : LIQUIDATE; *often* : to close by compromise and payment of less than full amount claimed or due **8** : to secure (a right or an estate) to someone by legal form ⟨*settled* her whole fortune on her nephew⟩ ⟨the family estate is usually *settled* on the eldest son⟩ — compare SETTLEMENT **9 a** : to arrange for proper disposal of on death ⟨~ an estate⟩ **b** : to put in order ⟨*settled* his affairs before entering the army⟩ **10** *of an animal* : to impregnate or cause to conceive — distinguished from *serve* ~ *vi* **1 a** : to come to rest from flight : ALIGHT ⟨the flock *settled* on the meadow⟩ ⟨a fly *settled* on the ceiling⟩ **b** : to descend usu. slowly and stay down or over ⟨mists *settling* in the valley⟩ ⟨dust had *settled* on the furniture⟩ ⟨a pall of silence *settled* over the room⟩ **2 a** : to fall slowly to the bottom ⟨waiting for the coffee grounds to ~⟩ — often used with *out* ⟨suspended pigment . . . is allowed to ~ out —H.J. Wolfe⟩ **b** : to become clear after being turbid or roiled : clarify by depositing sediment or scum ⟨let the wine ~ for a while before pouring⟩ **c** *of ground* : to become firm, dry, and hard after the effects of rain or frost have disappeared **3** : to separate in the soapmaking process into layers of neat soap, nigre, and lye on standing after fitting **4 a** : to sink gradually to a lower level : SUBSIDE ⟨cracks appeared in the walls as the foundations *settled*⟩ **b** *of a ship* : to become steadily more submerged ⟨*settling* fast by the stern⟩ **5 a** : to become established in a fixed location or direction ⟨the wind has *settled* in the east⟩ ⟨a cold *settled* in her chest⟩ **b** : to become fixed or permanent : assume a lasting form or condition ⟨*settling* gracefully into old age⟩ ⟨his mood had *settled* into a dull apathy⟩ ⟨his expression *settled* into a permanent frown⟩ ⟨it is *settling* in to rain now⟩ **6 a** : to establish one's residence — often used with *down* ⟨his sons had married and *settled* down nearby⟩ **b** : to establish an abode or colony abroad ⟨the Germans who *settled* in Pennsylvania⟩ **7 a** : to direct successfully the attention, will, or effort : apply oneself — usu. used with *down* ⟨*settled* down to study⟩ ⟨*settled* down to a steady canter⟩ **b** *of a hunting dog* : to become fixed on a scent **8 a** : to become calm : cease from agitation ⟨~ into a relaxed attitude⟩ ⟨~ into sleep⟩ **b** : to take up an ordered way of life; *esp* : to assume the duties and restrictions of the married state — usu. used with *down* ⟨time to marry and ~ down⟩ **9 a** : to adjust differences or accounts : come to an agreement : COMPOUND ⟨~ with creditors⟩ — often used with *up* ⟨~ up after a poker game⟩ **b** : RESOLVE — used with *on* or *upon* ⟨after much discussion *settled* on the plan originally proposed⟩ ⟨unable to *settle* on which hat to buy⟩ **10** : to become pastor of a church : take over a parish, church, or congregation **11** *of a female animal* : to become pregnant : CONCEIVE **syn** see CALM, DECIDE, SET — **settle accounts** : to make up a quarrel or breach by requital or by agreeing to terms — **settle for** : to content oneself with : be content with ⟨asked an endowment of two million but had to *settle for* one⟩ ⟨would *settle for* a tie score⟩ — **settle halyards** : to slack away on halyards to lower a yard — **settle one's hash** : to give a quietus to : dispose of : SUBDUE, SILENCE — **settle order** : to agree upon or determine a matter (as a court judgment) previously uncertain or in dispute ⟨*settle order* on notice to counsel of the parties⟩ — **settle the stomach** : to remove or relieve the distress or nausea of indigestion in the stomach

set·tle·abil·i·ty \ˌsed·ᵊləˈbiləd·ē\ *n* : the quality or state of being settleable

set·tle·able \ˈsed·ᵊləbəl\ *adj* : capable of removal by settling ⟨~ solids in sewage⟩

settle bed *n* : SETTEE BED

settled *adj* **1 a** : unlikely to change or be changed : FIXED, STABLE, STEADFAST ⟨~ opinion⟩ ⟨~ purpose⟩ ⟨~ habits⟩ **b** : not moving about or wandering ⟨nomads were from time to time absorbed among the ~ people —Owen & Eleanor Lattimore⟩ **2** : established or decided beyond dispute or doubt ⟨~ principles⟩ **3** *of weather* : fair and calm **4** : peopled with settlers : BUILT-UP **5** : secured or held by legal settlement ⟨~ income⟩ — **set·tled·ly** *adv* — **set·tled·ness** *n* -ES

settled charge *n* : an ecclesiastical charge into which a minister is regularly inducted

settle down *vi* **1** : to become established in a dwelling place or in a permanent job, profession, or business : begin to live a normal life **2** : to become inactive or sluggish ⟨liked to *settle down* with the evening paper after dinner⟩ **3** : to make oneself comfortable for rest or sleep ⟨*settled down* for the night⟩

settled production *n* : the production from an oil well after the first abnormally heavy production has steadied down and the flow is not subject to rapid diminution

set·tle·ment \ˈsed·ᵊlmənt, -etᵊl-\ *n* -s [[2]*settle* + *-ment*] **1** : the act of settling or state of being settled **2 a** : fixation in position **b** : a fixed position **c** : establishment in life, in business, in office **d** : ordination or installation as pastor **3 a** : establishment of order : REGULATION **b** : an established order **4 a** : an act of bestowing or giving possession under legal sanction : a formal and permanent grant or conveyance **b** : something that is bestowed formally and permanently : the sum, estate, or income secured to one by a settlement **c** : a disposition of property usu. through the medium of trustees for the benefit of some person or of persons in succession — compare JOINTURE 2 **d** : a provision in addition to salary (as by gift of land or house) made by a congregation for its minister on his installation to help him set up house **5 a** : an act of settling oneself in a position or location ⟨~ of small industries . . . was encouraged —G.W.Hoffman⟩ **b** : legal residence of a person in a particular parish or town that entitles him to maintenance if a pauper and subjects the parish or town to his support **6 a** : occupation by settlers : COLONIZATION ⟨~ preceded survey instead of following it —Arthur Geddes⟩ **b** : a colony newly established : a place or region newly settled **c** : a small village in a sparsely settled region ⟨site of a once prosperous crofting ~ —L.D.Stamp⟩ **d** : an area set apart in eastern countries for the residence of foreigners **e** : a community formed by members of a religious body or faith ⟨Mennonite ~⟩ **f** : a small cluster of houses or huts; *esp* : slave quarters on a plantation **g** : an institution founded and maintained among a congested city population often under the auspices of a church, college, or similar organization to supply various educational, recreational, medical, and other services to the community ⟨social ~⟩ ⟨art ~⟩ — called also *neighborhood house* **7 a** : clarification by deposition of sediment or separation of scum **b** : subsidence of sand or loose earth **c (1)** : the gradual sinking of a structure either by the yielding of the ground under the foundation or by the compression of the joints or the material **(2) settlements** *pl* : fractures or dislocations caused by unequal sinking of a structure **d** : TRANQUILIZATION **8 a** : composure of doubts or differences : ADJUSTMENT ⟨~ of a controversy⟩ ⟨~ of a strike⟩ **b** *India* : the act of arranging between the government and the cultivators the terms and incidence of the land revenue demand over specific areas **9** : payment or adjustment of an account : satisfaction of a claim by agreement often with less than full payment ⟨~ of tax arrears⟩ **10** : the administrative determination pursuant to statute of the amount due under a public contract with the government or a subdivision thereof **11** : an act or process by or the period during which transactions for the account on the London stock exchange are settled by arranging to carry them over or by completing the bargains by payment and delivery

settlement day *n* : the day of settling an account; *specif* : the last day of the settlement upon which payment must be made on any account on a stock exchange except such as are to be carried over to the next settlement — called also *account day, payday, settling day*

settlement house *n* : SETTLEMENT 6g

settlement option *n* **1** : an option giving to an insured or his beneficiary a choice as to how the liability of an insurance company under its policy is to be discharged **2** : an option of an insurer (as in fire insurance) to repair or rebuild instead of paying the loss in cash

settlement sheet *n* : the statement of a bank teller or department summarizing the day's transactions

set·tler \ˈsed·ᵊlə(r), -et(ᵊ)l-\ *n* -s **1** : one that settles ⟨~ of disputes⟩ **2** : a vessel or receptacle in which something is allowed to settle : settling tank : SEPARATOR; *specif* : a forehearth in which the molten furnace products are allowed to settle to separate the lighter from the heavier **3** : one that settles esp. in a new region or a colony : COLONIST ⟨the first ~*s* of New England⟩ **4** : SETTER 3

settler's-clock \ˈ⸗(⸗)⸗ˌ⸗\ *n, pl* **settler's-clocks** : KOOKABURRA

settler's twine *n* : an Australian aroid (*Gymnostachys anceps*); *also* : its coarse fiber

settles *pl of* SETTLE, *pres 3d sing of* SETTLE

[1]**settling** *n* -s [fr. gerund of [2]*settle*] **1** : SUBSIDENCE, SEDIMENTATION **2 settlings** *pl* : matter that settles at the bottom of a liquid : LEES, DREGS

[2]**settling** *adj* [fr. pres. part. of [2]*settle*] : used for holding fluids so that suspended matter may settle out ⟨~ basin⟩ ⟨~ chamber⟩ ⟨~ pond⟩ ⟨~ tank⟩

settling day *n* : a day for settling accounts; *specif* : SETTLEMENT DAY

settling price *n* : an arbitrary price used as the basis for the settlement of contracts through a clearinghouse

settling reservoir *n* : a reservoir consisting of a series of shallow basins arranged in steps with long weirs between so that only the clear upper layer of each will be drawn off

set·tlor \ˈsed·ᵊlə(r), -et(ᵊ)l-\ *n* -s [alter. (influenced by *-or*) of *settler*] : one that makes a settlement or creates a trust of property; *specif* : one that makes a marriage settlement

set to *vi* **1** : to begin actively and earnestly : make an eager or determined start on a job or activity ⟨seized a broom and *set to*⟩ ⟨*set to* with a will on the dinner⟩ **2** : to begin fighting ⟨in the third round stopped sparring and *set to* in earnest⟩

set-to \ˈ⸗ˌ⸗\ *n* -s [*set to*] : a bout of boxing or fighting or arguing : a usu. brief and vigorous contest

set trigger *n* **1** : a trigger on a rifle that may be adjusted for the amount of pressure required to pull it **2** : one of a pair of triggers on some rifles that sets the action so that a very light pull on the second trigger will fire the piece

setts *pl of* SETT

setts·man *or* **sets·man** \ˈsetsmən\ *n, pl* **settsmen** *or* **setsmen** : a maker of paving sets

set tub \ˈ⸗ *sometimes* (ˈ)⸗ˈ⸗\ *n* : LAUNDRY TRAY

set·u·la \ˈsechələ\ *n, pl* **setu·lae** \-ˌlē\ [LL *setula, saetula*, dim. of L *seta, saeta* bristle — more at SINEW] : a small short hair, seta, or bristle

set·ule \ˈseˌchül\ *n* -s [LL *setula, saetula*] : SETULA

set·u·lose \ˈsechəˌlōs\ *or* **set·u·lous** \-ələs\ *adj* [*setula* or *setule* + *-ose* or *-ous*] : having or covered with small hairs or bristles

set up *vt* **1 a** : to raise to and place in a high position ⟨*set up* a mark to shoot at⟩ ⟨*set up* a sail⟩ ⟨*set up* a flag⟩ **b** : to place in view : POST ⟨*set up* a sign⟩ **c** : to put forward (as a plan, a theory) for acceptance **d** *obs* : to put up (as for sale or auction) **2 a** : to make (a loud noise) with the voice ⟨*set up* a fearful bawling⟩ **b** : to cause (a condition) to come into effect ⟨the wind *sets up* a humming in the wires⟩ ⟨the added sugar *sets up* a fermentation⟩ ⟨the splinter *set up* an inflammation⟩ **3 a** : to make taut (a stay, shroud, hawser) **b** : to raise the pitch of (a string) by tightening **c** : to transpose to a higher key ⟨a baritone aria *set up* for a tenor⟩ **d** *obs* : to heighten the brilliance of (a color) **e** : to tighten firmly (as a nut or a pipe joint) **4 a** : to place in power or in office ⟨plotting to *set* him *up* on the throne⟩ ⟨a rival pope was *set up*⟩ **b** : to place in a position of hostility or opposition : OPPOSE ⟨degree of presumption . . . to *set* himself *up* against the authority of so many great men —T.L.Peacock⟩ **c** : to raise from depression : ELATE, GRATIFY ⟨*set up* by unexpected praise from her husband⟩ **d** : to make proud or vain ⟨much *set up* by flattery⟩ **e** : to put forward or extol as a model **f** : to claim (oneself) to be ⟨*sets* himself *up* as an authority on art⟩ or to be capable of ⟨literary journalist . . . seldom *setting up* to pass judgment on major writers —*Brit. Bk. News*⟩ **5 a** : to place upright : ERECT ⟨*set up* a building⟩ ⟨*set up* a post⟩ ⟨*set up* a roadblock⟩ ⟨*set up* a tent⟩ ⟨*set up* a card table⟩ **b** : to assemble the parts of and erect in position for use or operation ⟨*set up* a printing press⟩ **c** : to put (a machine) in readiness or adjustment for a tooling operation **6 a** *archaic* : to put aside and save for future use **b** : to erect (a perpendicular or a figure) on a base in a drawing or diagram **7 a** : FOUND, INSTITUTE, INAUGURATE ⟨*set up* a religious order⟩ ⟨*set up* rules and bylaws for a club⟩ ⟨*set up* a school⟩ ⟨*set up* a regulating committee⟩ **b** : to put (as a way of living or a means of livelihood) in operation esp. for oneself ⟨*set up* housekeeping⟩ ⟨*set up* shop in a new neighborhood⟩ **c** : ESTABLISH 11 **d** : to clear (a route) for the free passage of a train **8 a** : to provide with means or opportunity of making a living ⟨*set* his son-in-law *up* in business⟩ **b** : to place in or restore to comparative prosperity or a chance of success **c** : to bring or restore to normal health and strength **d** : to cause (one) to take on a soldierly or athletic appearance esp. through drill ⟨*set up* recruits⟩ **9 a** : to make carefully worked out plans for ⟨*set up* a bank robbery⟩ : PREARRANGE **b** : to execute one or more plays in preparation for scoring (a goal or touchdown) **10** : to pole (a boat) in hunting waterfowl **11 a** : to pay for (drinks) **b** : to treat (someone) to something ⟨*set* him *up* to a meal and new suit⟩ ~ *vi* **1** : to come into active operation or use **2** : to begin business ⟨saved enough to *set up* for himself as a contractor⟩ **3** : to make pretensions : claim to be or be capable ⟨are you *setting up* for a wit now⟩ **4** : to solidify too rapidly ⟨ways to avoid *setting up* in the cement mixer⟩ — **set up one's staff** : to take up residence : settle down ⟨appeared in London and there *set up their staff* —Anthony Trollope⟩

setup \ˈ⸗ˌ⸗\ *n* -s [*set up*] **1 a** : carriage of the body; *esp* : erect and soldierly bearing **b** : CONSTITUTION, MAKEUP ⟨expert . . . in the determination of the physical and mental ~ required for the combat aviator —H.H.Arnold & I.C.Eaker⟩ **2 a** : the assembly and arrangement of the tools and apparatus required for the performance of an operation **b** : the portion of an operation devoted to preparatory work; *esp* : the preparation and adjustment of machines for an assigned task **3 a** : a restaurant table setting or place setting often including bread and butter **b** : glass, ice, and mixer served to patrons who supply their own liquor in unlicensed premises **4 a** : a camera position from which a scene is filmed; *also* : the footage taken from one camera position **b** : the final arrangement of the set and properties for the filming of a scene **c** : the arrangement of performers, musicians, and broadcasting equipment for a radio or television program **5 a** : the difference in level between the windward and leeward edges of a body of water **b** : the ratio between the strength of the black and the white television signal measured from the blanking signal and usu. expressed as a percent **6 a** : a position of the balls in billiards or pool from which it is easy to score or to make one's play **b** : a task or contest purposely made easy **c** : something easy to get or accomplish **d** : a game or match arranged with an opponent who can easily be defeated **e** : a boxer who engages in a match which he has no chance to win **f** : a ball so played (as in tennis) as to give one's opponent an opportunity for a scoring shot (as a smash return) **g** : a shot in which a volleyball is sent high into the air and close to the net in preparation for a spike by a teammate; *also* : the player who makes such a shot **7 a** : the manner in which the elements or components of a machine, apparatus, or mechanical, electrical, or hydraulic system are arranged, designed, or assembled **b** : the relatively unchanging or dominating patterns within which political, social, or administrative forces operate : customary or established practice **c** : the structure of an organization **d** : facilities and material existing or specially created for a particular goal, service, or task **8** : PROJECT, PLAN, SCHEME

setup box *n* : a rigid container of wood or paperboard that cannot be flattened or folded for shipment to the packers

setup man *n* : one who makes the adjustments for machine tool operations to be performed by one or more routine operators

set·wall \ˈset·ˌwȯl\ *n* -s [ME *sedewale, cetewale, setewale* zedoary, fr. OF *citoual, citoal, citouar*, fr. Per *zadwār*] : GARDEN HELIOTROPE 1

set·wise \ˈset·ˌwīz\ *adv* [[3]*set* + *-wise*] : in the direction of the set — used of printing type ⟨a letter measured ~⟩

setwork \ˈ⸗ˌ⸗\ *n* **1** : embroidery used on tapestry **2** : two-coat plastering on lath **3** : boatbuilding in which abutting strakes are battened inside **4 setworks** *pl* : the mechanism on a sawmill carriage by means of which a log is advanced towards the saw after each cut

seu·dah \ˈsüdə\ *n, pl* **seu·doth** *or* **seu·dot** *or* **seu·dos** \ˈsüˌdōt(h), -ōs\ *or* **seudahs** [Heb *sĕʽūdhāh*] : a Jewish feast or banquet; *esp* : a festive Purim meal

seugh *or* **seuch** \ˈshük\ *n* -s [ME *sough* — more at SOUGH] *chiefly Scot* : an open trench or drainage ditch

sev *abbr* several

se·vas·to·pol \səˈvastəˌpōl, -aas- *also* ⸗ˈ⸗⸗ˌpōl *sometimes* ⸗ˈ⸗⸗ˌpəl *or* ˌsevəˈstōpəl *or* ¦⸗⸗¦stōpəl\ *adj, usu cap* [fr. *Sevastopol*, U.S.S.R.] : of or from the city of Sevastopol, U.S.S.R. : of the kind or style prevalent in Sevastopol

[1]**sev·en** \ˈsevən, ˈsevᵊm, ˈsebᵊm\ *adj* [ME, adj. & pron., fr. OE *seofon*; akin to OHG & Goth *sibun* seven, ON *sjau*, L *septem*, Gk *hepta*, Skt *sapta*] : being one more than six in number ⟨~ years⟩ — see NUMBER table

[2]**seven** \"\ *pron, pl in constr* [ME] : seven countable persons or things not specified but under consideration and being enumerated ⟨~ are here⟩ ⟨~ were found⟩

[3]**seven** \"\ *n* -s [ME, fr. *seven*, adj. & pron.] **1** : one more than six **2 a** : seven units or objects ⟨a total of ~⟩ **b** : a group or set of seven ⟨arranged by ~*s*⟩ **3 a** : the numerable quantity symbolized by the arabic numeral 7 **b** : the figure 7 **4** : seven o'clock — compare BELL table, TIME illustration **5** : a score in a dice game made by throwing with usu. two dice any combination of numbers that totals seven (as 4 and 3, 5 and 2, 6 and 1) ⟨has great luck throwing ~*s*⟩ — see CRAPS **6** : the seventh in a set or series: as **a** : a playing card marked to show that it is seventh in a suit **b** : an article of clothing of the seventh size ⟨wears a ~⟩ **c** : the rower behind the stroke in an 8-oared boat ⟨is a strong ~ on the crew⟩ **7** : something having as an essential feature seven units or members; *esp* : an English trochaic meter with seven syllables

sevens 6a

to the line and typically four lines to the stanza — usu. used in pl. ⟨a poem in ~s⟩

[4]**seven** \"\ *vi* -ED/-ING/-s : to cast a seven in craps ⟨the man ~*ed* —A.B.Guthrie⟩ — often used with *out* ⟨has just ~*ed* out with the dice —Florabel Muir⟩

seven and a half *n* : a card game resembling twenty-one in which face cards count ½ point each and the object is to get a count up to but not exceeding 7½

seven arts *n pl* [trans. of ML *septem artes*] : LIBERAL ARTS 1

sevenbark \'==,=\ *n* **1** : WILD HYDRANGEA 1 **2** : NINEBARK

seven-card stud *n* : stud poker in which each player receives seven cards dealt two facedown and one faceup on the first round, one faceup on each of the next three rounds, and one facedown on the last round with betting following each round and a final showdown in which a player selects five of his cards as his poker hand — called also *seven-toed Pete*

sev·en·er \'sevənə(r)\ *n* -s *usu cap* [[3]*seven* + *-er*] : a member of an Islamic Shi'ite sect that maintains that the seventh imam went into deathless concealment and is to return as the Mahdi — compare TWELVER

seven-eyes *or* **seven-holes** \'==,=\ *n pl but sing in constr* [so called fr. the seven gill holes on each side of the neck] : LAMPERN

[1]**sev·en·fold** \'==¦fōld\ *adj* [ME, fr. OE *seofonfeald*, fr. *seofon* seven + *-feald* -fold] **1** : having seven parts or aspects **2** : being seven times as large, as great, or as many as some understood size, degree, or amount ⟨a ~ increase⟩

[2]**sevenfold** \"\ *adv* [ME, fr. *sevenfold*, adj.] : to seven times as great or as many : by seven times ⟨increased ~⟩

sev·en·fold·ed \¦==¦fōldəd\ *adj* : made of seven parts ⟨~ shield⟩

seven-gilled shark \'==,=-\ *or* **seven-gill shark** *n* : a shark of the genera *Notorynchus* and *Heptranchias*

seven-league \'==¦=\ *adj* : traversing seven leagues at a stride ⟨*seven-league* boots⟩ ⟨a *seven-league* step in the right direction —*Newsweek*⟩

sevens *n pl but sing in constr* : FAN-TAN

seven seas *n pl* : all the waters or oceans of the world ⟨sails the *seven seas*⟩

seven sisters *also* **seven sisters rose** *n, pl* **seven sisters** *also* **seven sisters roses** : a hybrid climbing rose (*Rosa multiflora platyphylla*) that is related to the crimson rambler and has rather large leaves and deep pink flowers in clusters

seven sleeper *n* : FAT DORMOUSE

[1]**sev·en·teen** \'sevən·¦tēn, -evᵊm¦-, -ebᵊm¦-\ *adj* [ME *seventene*, adj. & pron., fr. OE *seofontīene, seofontȳne, seofontēne* (akin to ON *sjautjān, sjautān* seventeen), fr. *seofon* seven + *-tīene, -tȳne, -tēne* (fr. *tien, tȳn, tēn* ten) — more at SEVEN, TEN] : being one more than 16 in number ⟨~ years⟩ — used prepositively to designate various years of the 18th century ⟨the *seventeen*-eighties⟩ ⟨the early *seventeen*-hundreds⟩; see NUMBER table

[2]**seventeen** \"\ *pron, pl in constr* [ME *seventene*] : 17 countable persons or things not specified but under consideration and being enumerated ⟨~ are here⟩ ⟨~ were found⟩

[3]**seventeen** \"\ *n* -s **1** : 10 and seven **2 a** : 17 units or objects ⟨a total of ~⟩ **b** : a group or set of 17 **3** : the numerable quantity symbolized by the arabic numerals 17 **4** : the 17th in a set or series; *esp* : an article of clothing of the 17th size ⟨wears a ~⟩

[1]**sev·en·teenth** \-ēn(t)th\ *adj* [ME *sevententhe*, alter. (influenced by *seventene*) of *seventethe*, fr. OE *seofontēotha* (akin to ON *sjautjāndi, sjautāndi* seventeenth), fr. *seofontiene, seofontȳne, seofontēne* seventeen + *-otha, -tha* -th] **1** : being number 17 in a countable series ⟨the ~ day⟩ — see NUMBER table **2** : being one of 17 equal parts into which something is divisible ⟨a ~ share of the money⟩

[2]**seventeenth** \"\ *n, pl* **seventeenths** **1** : number 17 in a countable series ⟨the ~ of the month⟩ **2** : the quotient of a unit divided by 17 : one of 17 equal parts of something ⟨one ~ of the total⟩ **3 a** : an interval of two octaves and a third **b** : a pipe-organ stop sounding two octaves and a major third above the normal

seventeen-year locust *n* : a cicada (*Magicicada septendecim*) common in eastern parts of the U. S. that has in the north a life of seventeen years and in the south of thirteen years, remains nearly the whole of this time underground in the nymphal condition, and after emerging quickly attains the adult condition in which it lives only a few weeks while it lays its eggs in slits made in the twigs of trees

[1]**sev·enth** \'sevən(t)th, 'sevᵊm-, 'sebᵊm-\ *adj* [ME *seventhe*, alter. (influenced by *seven*) of *sevethe*, fr. OE *seofotha* (akin to OHG *sibunto* seventh, ON *sjaundi, sjundi*), fr. *seofon* seven + *-tha* -th — more at SEVEN] **1** : being number seven in a countable series ⟨the ~ day⟩ — see NUMBER table **2** : being one of seven equal parts into which something is divisible ⟨a ~ share of the money⟩

[2]**seventh** \"\ *n, pl* **sevenths** **1** : number seven in a countable series ⟨the ~ of the month⟩ **2** : the quotient of a unit divided by seven : one of seven equal parts of something ⟨one ~ of the total⟩ **3 a** : a musical interval embracing seven diatonic degrees **b** : a tone at this interval; *specif* : the seventh tone of a scale : LEADING TONE **c** : the harmonic combination of two tones a seventh apart **4** : SEPTIME

[3]**seventh** \"\ *adv* **1** : in the seventh place **2** : with six exceptions ⟨the nation's ~ largest city⟩

seventh chord *n* : a chord comprising a fundamental musical

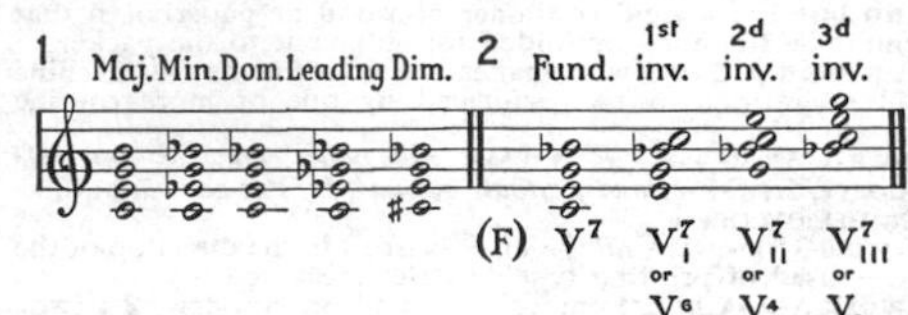

seventh chords: *1* five kinds of seventh chord, *2* dominant seventh chord of key of F and its inversions

note or tone with its third, fifth, and seventh and usu. designated by adding a small *7* to the numerals for triads

seventh cranial nerve *or* **seventh nerve** *n* : FACIAL NERVE

seventh day *n, usu cap S* **1** : SATURDAY — used chiefly by the Friends **2** : the Sabbath of the Jews and some Christian bodies

seventh-day \'==¦=\ *adj* [*seventh day*] **1** : of, relating to, or occurring on the seventh day **2** : advocating or practicing observance of Saturday as the Sabbath

seventh-day adventist *n, usu cap S&A & often cap D* : ADVENTIST

seventh-day baptist *n, usu cap S&D&B* **1** : a member of a Baptist body organized in Rhode Island in 1671 and observing the Sabbath on Saturday **2** : SEVENTH-DAY GERMAN BAPTIST

seventh-day german baptist *n, usu cap S&D&G&B* : a member of a Baptist body founded in Pennsylvania in 1728 whose members observe the seventh day as the Sabbath, live as a monastic religious community, and share goods in common

seventh heaven *n* **1** : the last and highest of the abodes of bliss of the Muslim and of the cabalist systems : the abiding place of supreme rapture **2** : HEAVEN 4a ⟨when I was a kid — it was *seventh heaven* to have my feet wet —Audrey Barker⟩

seventh-inning stretch *n* : a brief period at the beginning of each half of the seventh inning of a baseball game when fans of the team coming to bat customarily stand or move about

sev·enth·ly *adv* : in the seventh place (as in a series of topics)

[1]**sev·en·ti·eth** \'sevən¦tēəth, -vᵊm¦, 'sebᵊm¦, |dē-\ *adj* [ME *seventithe*, fr. OE hund*seofontigotha*, fr. hund*seofontig* seventy + *-otha, -tha* -th — more at SEVENTY] **1** : being number 70 in a countable series ⟨the ~ day⟩ — see NUMBER table **2** : being one of 70 equal parts into which something is divisible ⟨a ~ share of the money⟩

[2]**seventieth** \"\ *n* -s **1** : number 70 in a countable series **2** : the quotient of a unit divided by 70 : one of 70 equal parts of something ⟨one ~ of the total⟩

seven-toed pete \'=,=-\ *n, usu cap P* [*pete* fr. *Pete*, nickname for *Peter*] : SEVEN-CARD STUD

seven-top turnip \'==,=-\ *also* **seventop** \'==,=\ *n* : a stout biennial herb (*Brassica septiceps*) prob. of European origin that produces numerous stems from a woody taproot bearing leaves that are used for greens or in salads — called also *Italian kale*

[1]**sev·en·ty** \'sevən|t|ē, -vᵊm|, 'sebᵊm|, |d|, |i\ *adj* [ME, fr. OE *seofontig*, short for *hundseofontig*, fr. *hundseofontig*, n., group of 70, fr. *hund* 100 + *seofon* seven + *-tig* group of ten — more at HUNDRED, SEVEN, EIGHTY] : being one more than 69 in number ⟨~ years⟩ — see NUMBER table

[2]**seventy** \"\ *pron, pl in constr* [ME, fr. *seventy*, adj.] : 70 countable persons or things not specified but under consideration and being enumerated ⟨~ are here⟩ ⟨~ were found⟩

[3]**seventy** \"\ *n* -es **1** : seven tens : twice 35 : five times 14 **2 a** : 70 units or objects ⟨a total of ~⟩ **b** : a group or set of 70 **3** : the numerable quantity symbolized by the arabic numerals 70 **4** : the 70th in a set or series **5** : something having as an essential feature 70 units or members **6 a** *usu cap* : a group of the traveling elders of the Mormon church who are esp. commissioned by ordination for missionary service and serve under the direction of the apostles **b** : a member of this group ⟨appointed a *Seventy*⟩ **7** **seventies** *pl* **a** : the numbers 70 to 79 inclusive ⟨a golf score in the *seventies*⟩ ⟨all his grades in that subject are in the *seventies*⟩ **b** : the members of a series or set of successive numbers that end in 70 to 79 inclusive ⟨the *seventies* of the preceding century⟩ ⟨lives in the *seventies* in the next block⟩ **c** : the portion of a continuum lying between 70 and 80 on a scale of measurement or segmentation ⟨temperatures in the high *seventies* tomorrow⟩ ⟨a man in his *seventies*⟩ ⟨overcoats selling in the *seventies*⟩

[1]**seventy-eight** \¦===¦=\ *adj* : being one more than 77 in number ⟨*seventy-eight* years⟩ — see NUMBER table

[2]**seventy-eight** \"\ *pron, pl in constr* : 78 countable persons or things not specified but under consideration and being enumerated ⟨*seventy-eight* are here⟩ ⟨*seventy-eight* were found⟩

[3]**seventy-eight** \"\ *n* **1** : eight and 70 : three times 26 : six times 13 **2 a** : 78 units or objects ⟨a total of *seventy-eight*⟩ **b** : a group or set of 78 **3** : the numerable quantity symbolized by the arabic numerals 78 **4** : the 78th in a set or series **5** : a phonograph record designed to be played at 78 revolutions per minute — usu. written 78

[1]**seventy-eighth** \¦===¦=\ *adj* **1** : being number 78 in a countable series ⟨the *seventy-eighth* day⟩ — see NUMBER table **2** : being one of 78 equal parts into which something is divisible ⟨a *seventy-eighth* share of the money⟩

[2]**seventy-eighth** \"\ *n* **1** : number 78 in a countable series **2** : the quotient of a unit divided by 78 : one of 78 equal parts of something ⟨one *seventy-eighth* of the total⟩

[1]**seventy-fifth** \¦===¦=\ *adj* **1** : being number 75 in a countable series ⟨the *seventy-fifth* day⟩ — see NUMBER table **2** : being one of 75 equal parts into which something is divisible ⟨a *seventy-fifth* share of the money⟩

[2]**seventy-fifth** \"\ *n* **1** : number 75 in a countable series **2** : the quotient of a unit divided by 75 : one of 75 equal parts of something ⟨one *seventy-fifth* of the total⟩

[1]**seventy-first** \¦===¦=\ *adj* **1** : being number 71 in a countable series ⟨the *seventy-first* day⟩ — see NUMBER table **2** : being one of 71 equal parts into which something is divisible ⟨a *seventy-first* share of the money⟩

[2]**seventy-first** \"\ *n* **1** : number 71 in a countable series **2** : the quotient of a unit divided by 71 : one of 71 equal parts of something ⟨one *seventy-first* of the total⟩

[1]**seventy-five** \¦===¦=\ *adj* : being one more than 74 in number ⟨*seventy-five* years⟩ — see NUMBER table

[2]**seventy-five** \"\ *pron, pl in constr* : 75 countable persons or things not specified but under consideration and being enumerated ⟨*seventy-five* are here⟩ ⟨*seventy-five* were found⟩

[3]**seventy-five** \"\ *n* **1** : five and 70 : three times 25 : five fifteens **2 a** : 75 units or objects ⟨a total of *seventy-five*⟩ **b** : a group or set of 75 **3** : the numerable quantity symbolized by the arabic numerals 75 **4** : the 75th in a set or series **5** : a 75 millimeter gun; *esp* : the fieldpiece of this caliber used in the armies of France and of the U. S. in World War I — often written 75

[1]**seventy-four** \¦===¦=\ *adj* : being one more than 73 in number ⟨*seventy-four* years⟩ — see NUMBER table

[2]**seventy-four** \"\ *pron, pl in constr* : 74 countable persons or things not specified but under consideration and being enumerated ⟨*seventy-four* are here⟩ ⟨*seventy-four* were found⟩

[3]**seventy-four** \"\ *n* **1** : four and 70 : two times 37 **2 a** : 74 units or objects ⟨a total of *seventy-four*⟩ **b** : a group or set of 74 **3** : the numerable quantity symbolized by the arabic numerals 74 **4** : the 74th in a set or series **5** : an old-time warship rated as carrying 74 guns **6** : a highly regarded southern African sparid food fish (*Polysteganus undulosus*) having a rosy red color above shading to white below with several wavy longitudinal blue streaks along the sides

[1]**seventy-fourth** \¦===¦=\ *adj* **1** : being number 74 in a countable series ⟨the *seventy-fourth* day⟩ — see NUMBER table **2** : being one of 74 equal parts into which something is divisible ⟨a *seventy-fourth* share of the money⟩

[2]**seventy-fourth** \"\ *n* **1** : number 74 in a countable series **2** : the quotient of a unit divided by 74 : one of 74 equal parts of something ⟨one *seventy-fourth* of the total⟩

[1]**seventy-nine** \¦===¦=\ *adj* : being one more than 78 in number ⟨*seventy-nine* years⟩ — see NUMBER table

[2]**seventy-nine** \"\ *pron, pl in constr* : 79 countable persons or things not specified but under consideration and being enumerated ⟨*seventy-nine* are here⟩ ⟨*seventy-nine* were found⟩

[3]**seventy-nine** \"\ *n* **1** : nine and 70 **2 a** : 79 units or objects ⟨a total of *seventy-nine*⟩ **b** : a group or set of 79 **3** : the numerable quantity symbolized by the arabic numerals 79 **4** : the 79th in a set or series

[1]**seventy-ninth** \¦===¦=\ *adj* **1** : being number 79 in a countable series ⟨the *seventy-ninth* day⟩ — see NUMBER table **2** : being one of 79 equal parts into which something is divisible ⟨a *seventy-ninth* share of the money⟩

[2]**seventy-ninth** \"\ *n* **1** : number 79 in a countable series **2** : the quotient of a unit divided by 79 : one of 79 equal parts of something ⟨one *seventy-ninth* of the total⟩

[1]**seventy-one** \¦===¦=\ *adj* : being one more than 70 in number ⟨*seventy-one* years⟩ — see NUMBER table

[2]**seventy-one** \"\ *pron, pl in constr* : 71 countable persons or things not specified but under consideration and being enumerated ⟨*seventy-one* are here⟩ ⟨*seventy-one* were found⟩

[3]**seventy-one** \"\ *n* **1** : one and 70 **2 a** : 71 units or objects ⟨a total of *seventy-one*⟩ **b** : a group or set of 71 **3** : the numerable quantity symbolized by the arabic numerals 71 **4** : the 71st in a set or series

[1]**seventy-second** \¦===¦==\ *adj* **1** : being number 72 in a countable series ⟨the *seventy-second* day⟩ — see NUMBER table **2** : being one of 72 equal parts into which something is divisible ⟨a *seventy-second* share of the money⟩

[2]**seventy-second** \"\ *n* **1** : number 72 in a countable series **2** : the quotient of a unit divided by 72 : one of 72 equal parts of something ⟨one *seventy-second* of the total⟩

[1]**seventy-seven** \¦===¦==\ *adj* : being one more than 76 in number ⟨*seventy-seven* years⟩ — see NUMBER table

[2]**seventy-seven** \"\ *pron, pl in constr* : 77 countable persons or things not specified but under consideration and being enumerated ⟨*seventy-seven* are here⟩ ⟨*seventy-seven* were found⟩

[3]**seventy-seven** \"\ *n* **1** : seven and 70 : seven times 11 **2 a** : 77 units or objects ⟨a total of *seventy-seven*⟩ **b** : a group or set of 77 **3** : the numerable quantity symbolized by the arabic numerals 77 **4** : the 77th in a set or series

[1]**seventy-seventh** \¦===¦==\ *adj* **1** : being number 77 in a countable series ⟨the *seventy-seventh* day⟩ — see NUMBER table **2** : being one of 77 equal parts into which something is divisible ⟨a *seventy-seventh* share of the money⟩

[2]**seventy-seventh** \"\ *n* **1** : number 77 in a countable series **2** : the quotient of a unit divided by 77 : one of 77 equal parts of something ⟨one *seventy-seventh* of the total⟩

[1]**seventy-six** \¦===¦=\ *adj* : being one more than 75 in number ⟨*seventy-six* years⟩ — see NUMBER table

[2]**seventy-six** \"\ *pron, pl in constr* : 76 countable persons or things not specified but under consideration and being enumerated ⟨*seventy-six* are here⟩ ⟨*seventy-six* were found⟩

[3]**seventy-six** \"\ *n* **1** : six and 70 : four times 19 **2 a** : 76 units or objects ⟨a total of *seventy-six*⟩ **b** : a group or set of 76 **3** : the numerable quantity symbolized by the arabic numerals 76 **4** : the 76th in a set or series

[1]**seventy-sixth** \¦===¦=\ *adj* **1** : being number 76 in a countable series ⟨the *seventy-sixth* day⟩ — see NUMBER table **2** : being one of 76 equal parts into which something is divisible ⟨a *seventy-sixth* share of the money⟩

[2]**seventy-sixth** \"\ *n* **1** : number 76 in a countable series **2** : the quotient of a unit divided by 76 : one of 76 equal parts of something ⟨one *seventy-sixth* of the total⟩

[1]**seventy-third** \¦===¦=\ *adj* **1** : being number 73 in a countable series ⟨the *seventy-third* day⟩ — see NUMBER table **2** : being one of 73 equal parts into which something is divisible ⟨a *seventy-third* share of the money⟩

[2]**seventy-third** \"\ *n* **1** : number 73 in a countable series **2** : the quotient of a unit divided by 73 : one of 73 equal parts of something ⟨one *seventy-third* of the total⟩

[1]**seventy-three** \¦===¦=\ *adj* : being one more than 72 in number ⟨*seventy-three* years⟩ — see NUMBER table

[2]**seventy-three** \"\ *pron, pl in constr* : 73 countable persons or things not specified but under consideration and being enumerated ⟨*seventy-three* are here⟩ ⟨*seventy-three* were found⟩

[3]**seventy-three** \"\ *n* **1** : three and 70 **2 a** : 73 units or objects ⟨a total of *seventy-three*⟩ **b** : a group or set of 73 **3** : the numerable quantity symbolized by the arabic numerals 73 **4** : the 73d in a set or series

[1]**seventy-two** \¦===¦=\ *adj* : being one more than 71 in number ⟨*seventy-two* years⟩ — see NUMBER table

[2]**seventy-two** \"\ *pron, pl in constr* : 72 countable persons or things not specified but under consideration and being enumerated ⟨*seventy-two* are here⟩ ⟨*seventy-two* were found⟩

[3]**seventy-two** \"\ *n* **1** : two and 70 : three times 24 : four times 18 : six times 12 : six dozen **2 a** : 72 units or objects ⟨a total of *seventy-two*⟩ **b** : a group or set of 72 **3** : the numerable quantity symbolized by the arabic numerals 72 **4** : the 72d in a set or series

seven-up \'==¦=\ *n* -s : an American variety of all fours in which a turned-up card becomes trump and in which one point is scored in each deal for holding the highest and lowest trumps and the jack of trumps if it is dealt and for winning in tricks the greatest number of high cards or in some variants the ten of trumps with a total of seven points being necessary to win a game — called also *all fours, high-low-jack, old sledge*

seven-year apple *n* **1** : a shrub (*Casasia clusiaefolia*) of Florida and the West Indies having coriaceous leaves, fragrant white flowers, and a fruit similar to the apple **2** : the fruit of the seven-year apple

sev·er \'sevə(r)\ *vb* **severed; severed; severing** \-v(ə)riŋ\ **severs** [ME *severen*, fr. MF *severer, sevrer*, fr. L *separare* — more at SEPARATE] *vt* **1 a** : to put asunder : PART ⟨had been ~*ed* from the case because of illness —Paul Harris⟩ ⟨wean himself from them completely —Samuel Butler †1902⟩ **b** : to disjoin or disunite from one another ⟨will . . . take an opportunity of ~*ing* these young men —Sir Walter Scott⟩ ⟨fighting a war that the parts of the nation might not be ~*ed*⟩ **2** : to keep separate or apart by intervening ⟨a world ~*ed* from . . . downtown by a gap so wide —Louis Auchincloss⟩ ⟨the confluence of the . . . rivers which virtually ~*s* it from the rest of the capital territory —H.W.H.King⟩ **3** : to discriminate between or set off from : DISTINGUISH ⟨~ theology from philosophy —H.O.Taylor⟩ **4 a** : to divide or break up into parts ⟨army . . . was ~*ed* by inroads —Sir Winston Churchill⟩ **b** (1) : to cut in two : SUNDER, CLEAVE ⟨came to a stop with the ~*ed* body about halfway under the locomotive —*Springfield (Mass.) Daily News*⟩ ⟨~*ing* the cable and releasing the flaming, heavily constructed car —*Amer. Guide Series: Minn.*⟩ ⟨~*ed* their last remaining ties to the Old World —Oscar Handlin⟩ ⟨~ connections⟩ ⟨~ diplomatic relations⟩ (2) : to separate (from a whole) with suddenness or force ⟨the guillotine ~*s* the head from the body⟩ **c** : to scatter into parts : DISPERSE ⟨as wild geese that . . ~ themselves and madly sweep the sky —Shak.⟩ **5** : to disunite, disconnect, or divide into independent parts, rights, liabilities, or provisions (as an estate in joint tenancy or a contract or statute) ~ *vi* **1** : to go apart or asunder : to become parted or separated ⟨if from me thou ~ not —John Milton⟩ ⟨in all their lives not to ~⟩ **2** : to become divided or separated into parts ⟨the army must ~ in three parts —Edward Hall⟩ **3** : to act independently or separately in a court of law ⟨claimed the right of ~*ing* in their challenge —T.B. Macaulay⟩ **syn** see SEPARATE

sev·er·abil·i·ty \,sev(ə)rə'biləd·ē\ *n* : the quality or state of being severable

sev·er·able \'sev(ə)rəbəl\ *adj* [*sever* + *-able*] : capable of being severed ⟨grew as a song, never unsung or conceived of as ~ from its melody —H.O.Taylor⟩; *esp* : capable of being divided into legally independent rights or obligations — used of a statute or contract of which the part to be performed consists of distinct items to which the consideration may be apportioned so that the invalidity or failure of performance as to one item does not necessarily affect the others

[1]**sev·er·al** \'sev(ə)rəl, *esp before a vowel* -vərl\ *adj* [ME, fr. AF, fr. ML *separalis*, fr. L *separ* separate (fr. *separare* to separate) + *-alis* -al — more at SEPARATE] **1 a** *archaic* : having a separate existence : SEPARATE, APART ⟨must do it . . . as a person ~ from them —John Milton⟩ **b** (1) *obs* : privately or individually owned or controlled ⟨a ~ plot —Shak.⟩ — opposed to *common* (2) : possessed by or attributed to specified individuals : RESPECTIVE ⟨having thirteen children which somewhat reduced their ~ inheritances —Lucien Price⟩ ⟨will call the members for their ~ opinions —T.R.Ybarra⟩ **c** : being a separate member of a group, class, or series : individually different within a type ⟨elegance of diction was . . . the result of her knowledge of three ~ tongues —Elinor Wylie⟩ **d** (1) : being of different kinds : DIVERSE, VARIOUS ⟨one of the ~ effects of the postwar changes —Taylor Cole⟩ ⟨threw his ~ mercantile ventures into the hands of creditors —Frank Monaghan⟩ (2) *obs* : made up of different elements : diversely composed **e** : of or relating separately to each individual of two or more tenants, persons, or parties involved (as in a contract or a suit) : SEVERABLE ⟨a ~ judgment may be had on a counterclaim . . . when judgment may be rendered for the plaintiff, or all of the plaintiffs, if more than one, or for the defendant, or all of the defendants, if more than one —S.J. Ervin⟩; *specif* : enforceable separately against each party ⟨the contractual liability of each company to insured is ~ and not joint —R.E.Keeton⟩ — compare JOINT 2b(3), JOINT AND SEVERAL **2 a** : more than one **b** : consisting of an indefinite number more than two and fewer than many usu. of the same class or group ⟨were around 75 . . . men present but only ~ women —Linda Braidwood⟩ ⟨a sojourn of ~ months in England —G.H.Genzmer⟩ ⟨have had ~ children —W.J. Ghent⟩ **c** *chiefly dial* : being a good many : MANY ⟨~ young men . . . run into a worse extreme —Jonathan Swift⟩ **syn** see DISTINCT

[2]**several** \"\ *n* -s [ME, fr. AF, fr. *several*, adj.] **1 a** *archaic* : land that is privately owned or controlled; *specif* : an enclosed plot of such land **b** *obs* : private property or ownership **2** *obs* **a** : something that is particular : an individual part : PARTICULAR, DETAIL — usu. used in pl. ⟨the ~*s* and unhidden passages of his true titles —Shak.⟩ **b** **severals** *pl* : individual persons or things **3** **severals** *pl, chiefly dial* : several persons or things — **in several** *adv, archaic* : SEPARATELY, INDIVIDUALLY ⟨compare respectively the greatness of each part of the world *in several* —Philemon Holland⟩

[3]**several** \"\ *adv* [[1]*several*] *archaic* : by itself : SEVERALLY, SEPARATELY

[4]**several** \"\ *pron, pl in constr* [[1]*several*] **1** : an indefinite number more than two and fewer than many ⟨~ of the alumni have served on the board of trustees —*Bull. of Meharry Med. Coll.*⟩ ⟨goes to the store for oranges and purchases ~⟩ **2** *chiefly dial* : a good many : MANY

several fishery *n* : a private fishery founded upon ownership of the underlying soil

[1]**sev·er·al·fold** \¦=(=)=¦fōld\ *adj* [[1]*several* + *-fold*] **1** : having several parts or aspects **2** : being several times as large, as great, or as many as some understood size, degree, or amount

[2]**severalfold** \"\ *adv* : to several times as much or as many : by several times ⟨increased ~⟩

sev·er·al·i·ty \,sevə'raləd·ē\ *n* -ES [alter. of *severalty*] **1** *archaic* : something separate : QUALITY, DETAIL, PART **2** *obs* : the quality or state of being several

sev·er·al·ize \'sev(ə)rə,līz\ *vt* -ED/-ING/-S : DISTINGUISH, SEPARATE

sev·er·al·ly \'sev(ə)rəlē, -li\ *adv* [ME *severally*, fr. *several* + *-ly*] **1** : one at a time : each by itself : SEPARATELY ⟨people would point to . . . herself and Henry, ~, as the perfect wife and husband —Victoria Sackville-West⟩ ⟨premises which are ~ clear, distinct, and certain —A.N.Whitehead⟩ ⟨the strips or lands were not ~ enclosed —G.M.Trevelyan⟩ ⟨the beneficiary to be identified by any of us four jointly or ~ —Geoffrey Household⟩ **2** : apart from others : INDEPENDENTLY ⟨when they were hung ~, they came out . . . smooth and unwrinkled —R.K.Johnson⟩ **3** : RESPECTIVELY **4** *obs* : VARIOUSLY

sev·er·al·ty \'sev(ə)rəltē, -ti\ *n* -ES [ME *severalte*, fr. AF *severalté*, fr. *several* + *-té* -ty] **1** : the quality or state of being several : DISTINCTNESS, SEPARATENESS ⟨things combined may lose their ~⟩ **2 a** : a sole, separate, and exclusive possession, dominion, or ownership : one's own right without a joint interest in any other person — usu. used with *in* ⟨holds an estate in ~⟩ ⟨has tenants in ~⟩; distinguished from *coparcenary, joint tenancy*; opposed to *common* **b** : the quality or state of being individual or particular — usu. used with *in* ⟨treat of each great department of our social life in ~ —H.D. Traill⟩ **3 a** : land owned by individual right ⟨broke up the commons into *severalties*⟩ **b** : the quality or state of being held by individuals ⟨by unanimous vote of the town meeting the common field was converted into ~⟩ **4** *obs* : something separate : QUALITY, DETAIL, PART

sev·er·ance \'sev(ə)rən(t)s, -vərn-\ *n* -S [ME *severaunce*, fr. MF *sevrance, severance*, fr. *sevrer, severer* to sever + *-ance* — more at SEVER] **1 a** : the act or process of severing : the state of being severed ⟨control over native affairs and ~ of the territory —Manfred Nathan⟩ ⟨~ from the authority of traditional organs of government —H.D.Gunn⟩ ⟨the unhappy ~ of the scholar and the man of letters —F.B.Millett⟩ ⟨~ of diplomatic relations —David Lawrence⟩ ⟨~ of the leg below the knee⟩ **b** : DISTINCTION, DIFFERENCE — usu. used with *between* ⟨lines of ~ between truth and falsehood —W.E. Gladstone⟩ **2** : the division of the provisions, rights, liabilities, or similar legal considerations arising under or in something: as **a** : the destruction of the unity of interest in a joint estate **b** : the separation of two or more parties joined in an action so that one may proceed on the other being nonsuited **c** : the separation of two or more codefendants in a criminal prosecution for separate trial **d** : the detachment of fixtures from realty or of crops, fruits, timber, minerals, or related products from the soil **e** : the termination of a contractual association (as employment)

severance contract *n* : an agreement for employment that stipulates certain benefits for the employee at the time of severance

severance pay *n* : an allowance usu. based on length of service that is payable to an employee on severance except usu. in case of disciplinary discharge ⟨provide *severance pay* for officers and enlisted men released from active duty —*Military Rev.*⟩

severance tax *n* : a tax on the taking and use of natural resources imposed at the time the mineral or other product is extracted or severed from the earth

sev·er·a·tion \,sevə'rāshən\ *n* -S [*sever* + *-ation*] : SEVERANCE

se·vere \sə'vi(ə)r, sē'-, -viə\ *adj* -ER/-EST [MF or L; MF, fr. L *severus*, perh. fr. *sed, se* without + *-verus* kindliness, friendliness; akin to L *verus* true — more at IDIOT, VERY] **1 a** : strict or uncompromising in judgment, discipline, or government ⟨parent ~ to the pitch of hostility —H.G.Wells⟩ ⟨the king's temper was arbitrary and ~ —T.B.Macaulay⟩ ⟨did perfect work and was a more ~ taskmistress than the teacher who had sight —Marie A. Kasten⟩ **b** : of a strict or stern bearing or demeanor ⟨her face was composed but not ~ —Archibald Marshall⟩ ⟨her matronly expression became more ~ —Ellen Glasgow⟩ ⟨a hefty six-footer with a rather ~ mien —*Current Biog.*⟩ **2** : absolute or rigorous in restraint, punishment, or requirement : INFLEXIBLE, STRINGENT, RESTRICTIVE ⟨martial law is very ~ in this matter —C.B.Nordhoff & J.N.Hall⟩ ⟨the ~ discipline of military life —John Lodge⟩ ⟨the penalties become more ~ as the bottom is approached —R.A.Hall b.1911⟩ ⟨in connection with phantom circuits, *severer* cross talk requirements have necessitated more precise balances —*Bell System Technical Jour.*⟩ **3** : strongly critical or condemnatory : CENSORIOUS ⟨some voluntary societies have been very ~ about certain films . . . which they consider vague, incoherent, and technically poor —*Report: (Canadian) Royal Commission on Nat'l Development*⟩ ⟨very ~ on the dangers and disease of intoxication —George du Maurier⟩ ⟨delivers ~ remarks against his enemies⟩ **4 a** : establishing or maintaining a scrupulously exacting standard of behavior or self-discipline ⟨there appeared a sounder logic in the ~ decorum and ironbound theology of her youth —Ellen Glasgow⟩ ⟨faults that must seem so black to her, with her simple ~ notions —George Eliot⟩ ⟨one of the *severest* moralists of his times⟩ **b** : establishing or exhibiting scrupulously exacting standards of accuracy and integrity in intellectual processes ⟨models of exact research and ~ scholarship —D.M.Robinson⟩ ⟨the kind of truth demanded by ~ logicians —H.J. Muller⟩ **5** : sober or restrained in decoration or manner : conservatively adorned : AUSTERE, PLAIN ⟨the only decoration to an otherwise ~ facade —*Amer. Guide Series: La.*⟩ ⟨in his ~ black garb —*Amer. Guide Series: Del.*⟩ ⟨in cool, ~ prose —*Amer. Guide Series: Fla.*⟩ **6 a** : inflicting physical discomfort or hardship : INCLEMENT, HARSH ⟨the snows of a ~ New England winter —*Amer. Guide Series: Maine*⟩ ⟨conditions too ~ to effect a rescue either by surf boats or by a breeches buoy —J.P.Baxter b.1893⟩ ⟨growing under ~ alpine conditions —G.R.Stewart⟩ **b** : inflicting pain or distress : AFFLICTIVE, GRIEVOUS ⟨disturbance which may be mild and benign or ~ and malign —*Diseases of the Nervous System*⟩ ⟨the ~ aches connected with muscles —F.A.Geldard⟩ ⟨a ~ wound which . . . cost him a leg —Mary A. Hamilton⟩ ⟨the pain of a badly fitting or too ~ bit is a constant cause of trouble —Beauvoir de Lisle⟩ **7** : requiring great effort : ARDUOUS, DIFFICULT ⟨faces a ~ test of his capacity —*New Statesman & Nation*⟩ ⟨showing, in a ~ physical contest . . . that his bodily strength is not decayed —J.G.Frazer⟩ **8** *chiefly dial* : extremely strong, powerful, or effective ⟨takes a big ~ dog to do that —Horace Kephart⟩ **9** : of a great degree or an undesirable or harmful extent : MARKED, SERIOUS ⟨a ~ economic depression —B.K.Sandwell⟩ ⟨the fight was not ~ for there was only one fatality —*Amer. Guide Series: Calif.*⟩ ⟨~ shortages⟩ ⟨~ difficulties⟩

syn STERN, AUSTERE, ASCETIC: SEVERE implies unsparing adherence to rigorous standards, often those prescribing the hard or plain, enforced without indulgence and sometimes with harshness ⟨a *severe* code of Spartan living⟩ ⟨has high and *severe* standards —C.L.R.James⟩ ⟨was unyielding in his understandable insistence on discipline, was apt to be *severe* —Arthur Berger⟩ STERN may imply inflexible or inexorable severity, often along with a harsh, forbidding, or cold disposition ⟨during 21 *stern* years in the courtroom, Parker sentenced 151 men to the gallows —*Amer. Guide Series: Ark.*⟩ ⟨love indeed they did give, but it was a *stern* and passionless affection —E.T.Thurston⟩ ⟨on its surrender the *stern* justice of Hubert hung the twenty-four knights and their retainers who formed the garrison —J.R.Green⟩ AUSTERE may describe cold, barren, or dispassionate lack of feeling, warmth, color, or animation; it may apply to rigorous and stark restraint, simplicity, or self-denial ⟨*austere*, chill, precise, and dignified, his demeanor made familiarity impossible —Allan Nevins⟩ ⟨banks have sometimes cultivated a cold, *austere* atmosphere, symbolized by hard, cold marble and polished brass —*Banking*⟩ ASCETIC may refer to self-denying abstention, monastic or reminiscent of monasticism, from the pleasurable, easy, or indulgent, or even a courting of the disagreeable and hard in spiritual or intellectual discipline ⟨knowing the *ascetic* measure of his appetites, he was doubly certain that she would not let him starve; crisp drops of spring water and spare and wholesome crusts could never be denied him —Elinor Wylie⟩ ⟨his crabbed style and *ascetic* reasoning —V.L.Parrington⟩ ⟨this intermeddling with worldly business, which the *ascetic* reformer looked upon as the curse that robbed prelates and churchmen of that spiritual authority which could alone meet the vice and suffering of the time —J.R.Green⟩

se·vere·ly *adv* : in a severe manner : with severity

se·vere·ness *n* -ES : SEVERITY

severer *comparative of* SEVERE

severest *superlative of* SEVERE

¹se·ve·ri·an \sə'virēən\ *n* -S *usu cap* [ML *Severianus*, fr. *Severus*, 2d cent. Gnostic + L *-ianus* -ian] : one of a sect of Encratite Gnostics of the 2d century

²severian \"\ *n* -S *usu cap* [*Severus* †538 Pisidian ecclesiastic, bishop of Antioch + E *-ian*] : a follower of the Monophysite patriarch Severus who taught that the body of Christ was subject to corruption prior to his resurrection

severing *pres part of* SEVER

se·ver·i·ty \sə'verəd·ē, sē'-, -ətē, -i *sometimes* -'vir-\ *n* -ES [MF or L; MF *severité*, fr. L *severitat-, severitas*, fr. *severus* severe + *-itat-, -itas* -ity — more at SEVERE] : quality or state of being severe ⟨the ~ of the winter⟩ ⟨the naked *severities* of science —Thomas De Quincey⟩

severity rate *n* : the time lost through injuries as calculated in total days lost per 1000 hours worked

severs *pres 3d sing of* SEVER

sev·ery \'sev(ə)rē\ *n* -ES [ME *severie*, fr. MF *civoire, ciboire* ciborium, severy, fr. ML *ciborium* — more at CIBORIUM] : a section or compartment of a vaulted roof; *esp* : a bay of a Gothic vaulted ceiling

se·vi·che *or* **ce·vi·che** \sə'vē(,)chā, -'vēche\ *n* -S [AmerSp *seviche*] : a dish made of raw fish marinated in lime or lemon juice often with oil, onions, peppers, and seasonings and sometimes served as a snack or appetizer

se·vi·lla·na \,sāvē(l)'yänə\ *n* -S [Sp, fr. fem. of *sevillano* of Seville] : SEGUIDILLA; *esp* : the seguidilla as danced or played in Seville — often used in pl. ⟨all women of Sevilla . . . dance the ~s, a graceful dance —Luis Marden⟩

se·vi·lla·no \-ä(,)nō\ *n* -S *cap* [Sp — more at SEVILLIAN] : SEVILLIAN

se·ville \sə'vil, *chiefly Brit* 'sevəl\ *adj, usu cap* [fr. *Seville*, Spain] : of or from the city of Seville, Spain : of the kind or style prevalent in Seville

seville orange *n* [fr. *Seville*, Spain] **1** *usu cap S* : SOUR ORANGE **2** *often cap S* : a moderate orange that is darker and slightly yellower and less strong than honeydew and redder and duller than Persian orange

¹se·vil·lian \sə'vilyən\ *adj, usu cap* [Sp *sevillano*, adj. & n., fr. *Sevilla* Seville + Sp *-ano* -an] **1** : of, relating to, or characteristic of Seville, Spain **2** : of, relating to, or characteristic of the people of Seville

²sevillian \"\ *n* -S *cap* [Sp *sevillano*] : a native or resident of Seville, Spain

sevl *abbr* several

sè·vres \'sevrə\ *n* [fr. *Sèvres*, France] **1** *usu cap* : a fine often elaborately decorated French porcelain made at the national factory at Sèvres **2** *or* **sèvres blue a** *usu cap S* : a strong blue that is redder and less strong than cerulean blue (sense 1b), redder and paler than cyanine blue (sense 1a), and greener, lighter, and stronger than Victoria blue **b** *usu cap S* (1) : the lighter blue of the Sèvres porcelain esp. of pieces antedating the French Revolution (2) : the darker blue of the Sèvres porcelain — called also *bleu de roi*

se·vum \'sēvəm\ *n* -S [L *sebum, sevum* tallow, grease — more at SOAP] : TALLOW

¹sew \'sō\ *vb* **sewed; sewn** \'sōn\ *or* **sewed; sewing; sews** [ME *sowen, sewen*, fr. OE *sīwian, sēowian, sīwan, sēowan*; akin to OHG *siuwen* to sew, ON *sȳja*, Goth *siujan*, L *suere* to sew, Skt *sīvyati* he sews] *vt* **1 a** : to unite, attach, or fasten by stitches made with a flexible thread or filament ⟨~*ed* and embroidered the clothes and moccasins for the family —Weston La Barre⟩ ⟨long swatches of fur . . . are *sewn* together to make a coat —*Time*⟩ ⟨stand still while mother ~*s* on the button⟩ **b** : to close or enclose by sewing ⟨~ the money in a bag⟩ ⟨with his money ~*ed* into the lining of his coat⟩ — often used with *up* ⟨~*ing* up the tear in his trousers⟩ ⟨orders to ~ up the body in a canvas for the rites at sea⟩ **2** : to secure together (the sections of an assembled book) with thread or wire — distinguished from *stitch* ~ *vi* : to practice or engage in sewing ⟨is learning to ~ in her home science course⟩; *specif* : to work with needle and thread ⟨~*s* to earn extra money⟩

²sew \'sü\ *vb* -ED/-ING/-S [MF *essever, essewer, sewer* to drain — more at SEWER] *vt, chiefly dial* : to drain the water from ~ *vi* **1** *chiefly dial* : to ooze out **2** *or* **sue** *of a ship* : to become grounded

sew·age \'süij, -üēj\ *n* -S [³*sewer* + *-age*] : the contents of a sewer or household drain : refuse liquids or waste matter carried off by sewers

sewage disposal *n* : the process of removing and destroying or converting the noxious substances of sewage esp. by ammonification and nitrification through bacterial action

sewage farm *n* : a farm fertilized and irrigated with raw sewage or sewage liquids

sewage fly *n* : any of several flies of the genus *Psychoda* that breed in sewage or sink drains

sew·all wright effect \'süəl'rīt-\ *n, usu cap S&W* [after *Sewall Wright* b1889 Am. geneticist] : differentiation within a group arising from chance fixation of nonadaptive characters in small isolated populations

se·wan *also* **sea·wan** \'sē,wän\ *or* **sea·want** \-nt\ *n* -S [D (New Amsterdam) *sewan, zeewan, zeewant*, of Algonquian origin; akin to Narraganset *siwân* sewan, Natick *seawan, sewan* loose beads, *seâhham* he scatters] : WAMPUM

sewed shoe *n* [*sewed* fr. past part. of ¹*sew*] : a shoe in which the upper is attached to the sole by stitching

se·wee \'sē,wē\ *n, pl* **sewee** *or* **sewees** *usu cap* **1** : a people on the So. Carolina coast between the Santee and Ashley rivers usu. regarded as Siouan but sometimes considered to be Muskogean **2** : a member of the Sewee people

sewee bean *var of* SIEVA BEAN

se·wel·lel \sə'weləl\ *n* -S [Chinook *šʔulal* blanket of sewellel skins (taken as the name of the animal), fr. dual of *ugwulal* sewellel] : MOUNTAIN BEAVER

sew·en *also* **sew·in** \'süən\ *or* **si·win** \'sēwən\ *n* -S [origin unknown] : the sea trout as found along the west coast of England and Wales and the coasts of Ireland whence it is sometimes regarded as constituting a distinct variety (*Salmo trutta cambricus*)

¹sew·er \'süə(r), 'sü(ə)r, 'süə\ *n* -S [ME, fr. AF *asseour*, fr. OF *asseoir* to seat + AF *-our* -or — more at ASSIZE] : a medieval servant or household officer often of high rank in charge of serving the dishes at table and sometimes of seating and tasting

²sew·er \'sō(ə)r, 'sōə\ *n* -S [ME *sower, sewer*, fr. *sowen, sewen* to sew + *-er* — more at SEW] **1** : one that sews ⟨became an expert textile finishing ~⟩ ⟨fastest shank button ~ ever made —*advt*⟩ **2** : LEAF SEWER

³sew·er \'süə(r), 'sü(ə)r, 'süə\ *n* -S [ME, fr. MF *esseveur, esseweur, seweur*, fr. *essever, essewer, sewer* to drain (fr. — assumed — VL *exaquare*, fr. L *ex-* + *aqua* water) + *-eur* -or — more at ISLAND] **1** : a ditch or surface drain **2** : an artificial usu. subterranean conduit to carry off water and waste matter (as surface water from rainfall, household waste from sinks or baths, or waste water from industrial works)

⁴sewer \"\ *vt* -ED/-ING/-S : to furnish with a system of sewers : drain by sewers ⟨a small proportion of the streets were ~*ed* —*Amer. Jour. of Pub. Health*⟩

sew·er·age \-rij, -rēj\ *n* -S [³*sewer* + *-age*] **1** : SEWAGE **2** : the systematic removal and disposal of sewage and general surface water by sewers **3** *or* **sewerage system** : the system of sewers in a city, town, or locality **4** : unclean thought or language ⟨shocked even his fellow partisans by the ~ he poured forth in an . . . address —C.G.Bowers⟩

sewer brick *n* : a brick made from shale or clay, burned to a greenish blue color in a flame of low oxygen in a kiln, and used in drainage structures for the conveyance of sewage, industrial wastes, and storm water — called also *blue brick*

sewg *abbr* sewing

sew·ing \'sōiŋ, -ōēŋ\ *n* -S [ME *sowing, sewing*, fr. gerund of *sowen, sewen* to sew — more at SEW] **1** : the action or method of one that sews by hand or machine; *also* : the action of a machine that sews **2** : work in progress or products made by a person or machine that sews **3** : the occupation of operating a machine that sews

sewing awl *n* : an awl used (as by a shoemaker) for piercing holes for stitches in leather — see AWL illustration

sewing bird *n* : a clamp usu. fastened to a table edge and having a birdlike beak to hold work to be sewed by hand

sewing bird

sewing cord *n* : material (as hemp) to which book sections are sewn with thread and which is later laced into boards

sewing cotton *n* : hard-twisted cotton thread usu. of three or six plies spooled for home and industrial sewing

sewing machine *n* : any of various machines for stitching material (as cloth, leather, or paper) usu. having a needle and shuttle to carry thread and powered by a treadle or electricity

sewing press *or* **sewing bench** *or* **sewing frame** *n* : a wooden device for bookbinding having a baseboard and two screw-threaded uprights supporting a crossbar from which cords used in hand sewing are stretched to the baseboard

sewing silk *n* : silk thread having two or three yarns tightly twisted together for sewing or loosely twisted together for embroidery

sewn *past part of* SEW

sewround \'≈,≈\ *n* [fr. the phrase *sew round*] : STITCHDOWN

sews *pres 3d sing of* SEW

sew·ster \'sōstə(r)\ *n* -S [ME *sowestre, sewestre*, fr. *sowen, sewen* to sew + *-estre* -ster] *archaic* : SEAMSTRESS

sew up *vt* **1** *Brit* : to wear out : FATIGUE ⟨reclining hopelessly on a settee, already dazed, *sewn up*, exhausted, and knocked out —Herbert Read⟩ **2 a** : to secure or assure exclusive control of (as a business proposition or arrangement) usu. by verbal agreement or contract : MONOPOLIZE ⟨the guilds had *sewed up* such primitive trade and industry as there were —D. C.Coyle⟩ ⟨in a position to *sew up* the preferred time spots —Goodman Ace⟩ **b** : to arrange for exclusive control or use of the services of (a person) : to place under contract ⟨the stars were already *sewed up* in three-year deals by the established hotels —*Time*⟩ ⟨hopes to *sew up* the champion for a 15-round battle⟩ **c** : to obtain or make certain of the support or cooperation of (a person or group) ⟨*sew up* as many . . . delegates as possible —*Newsweek*⟩ ⟨we *sewed up* the women's vote with this one —*Time*⟩ **d** *slang* : to gain exclusive hold on the affection or attention of (a person) ⟨the girl who asked him hadn't been able to *sew up* the captain of the . . . football team —Scott Fitzgerald⟩ **3** : to settle or determine (as the outcome or development) ⟨backstage negotiations have *sewed up* the results in advance —*Newsweek*⟩ ⟨need only one more victory to *sew up* their third straight . . . championship —*Time*⟩ ⟨when he confessed before he died, that *sewed* the whole thing *up* —Hartley Howard⟩

¹sex \'seks\ *n* -ES *often attrib* [ME, fr. L *sexus*; prob. akin to L *secare* to cut — more at SAW] **1** : one of the two divisions of organic esp. human beings respectively designated male or female ⟨a member of the opposite ~⟩ **2** : the sum of the morphological, physiological, and behavioral peculiarities of living beings that subserves biparental reproduction with its concomitant genetic segregation and recombination which underlie most evolutionary change, that in its typical dichotomous occurrence is usu. genetically controlled and associated with special sex chromosomes, and that is typically manifested as maleness and femaleness with one or the other of these being present in most higher animals though both may occur in the same individual in many plants and some invertebrates and though no such distinction can be made in many lower forms (as some fungi, protozoans, and possibly bacteria and viruses) either because males and females are replaced by mating types or because the participants in sexual reproduction are indistinguishable — compare HETEROTHALLIC, HOMOTHALLIC; FERTILIZATION, MEIOSIS, MENDEL'S LAW; FREEMARTIN, HERMAPHRODITE, INTERSEX **3** : the sphere of interpersonal behavior esp. between male and female most directly associated with, leading up to, substituting for, or resulting from genital union ⟨agree that the Christian's attitude toward ~ should not be considered apart from love, marriage, family —M.M.Forney⟩ **4** : the phenomena of sexual instincts and their manifestations ⟨with his customary combination of philosophy, insight, good will toward the world, and entertaining interest in ~ —Allen Drury⟩ ⟨studying and assembling what modern scientists have discovered about ~ —*Time*⟩; *specif* : SEXUAL INTERCOURSE ⟨an old law imposing death for ~ outside marriage —William Empson⟩

²sex \"\ *vt* -ED/-ING/-ES **1** : to determine the sex of (an organic being) ⟨it is difficult to ~ the animals at a distance —E.A.Hooton⟩ — compare AUTOSEXING **2 a** : to increase the sexual appeal or attraction of — usu. used with *up* ⟨titles must be ~*ed* up to attract 56 million customers —*Time*⟩ **b** : to arouse the sexual instincts or desires of — usu. used with *up* ⟨watching you ~*ing* up that bar kitten —Oakley Hall⟩

sex- *or* **sexi-** *comb form* [L *sex* — more at SIX] : six ⟨*sex*annulate⟩ ⟨*sexi*syllable⟩

sex act *n* : SEXUAL INTERCOURSE 1

¹sexa·decimal \¦seksə+\ *adj* [*sexa-* (as in *sexagesimal*) + *decimal*] : of or relating to sixteen or sixteenths : proceeding in computation by sixteens : expressed in the scale of sixteens

²sexadecimal \"\ *n* : a sixteenth part

¹sex·a·ge·nar·i·an \,seksəjə'na(a)rēən, -'ner-, -'nār-\ *n* -S [L *sexagenarius* containing or consisting of sixty + E *-an*, n. suffix] : a person 60 or more and less than 70 years old

²sexagenarian \¦≈≈¦≈≈\ *adj* **1** : 60 or more and less than 70 years old **2** : of or relating to a sexagenarian

sex·a·ge·nar·i·an·ism \,≈≈'≈≈ə,nizəm\ *n* -S : the state of being a sexagenarian

¹sex·ag·e·nary \(')sek¦sajənerē, -ri\ *adj* [L *sexagenarius* containing or consisting of sixty, fr. *sexageni* sixty each (fr. *sexaginta* sixty, irreg. — influence of *quadraginta* forty — fr. *sex* six + *-ginta* — akin to L *-ginti* in *viginti* twenty) + *-arius* -ary — more at QUADRAGESIMAL, SIX, VICENARY] **1** : of, relating to, or based on the number 60 **2** : SEXAGENARIAN

²sexagenary \"\ *n* -ES **1** : SEXAGESIMAL **2** : SEXAGENARIAN

sex·a·ges·i·ma \,seksə'jesəmə, -jäzəmə\ *also* **sexagesima sunday** *n* -S *usu cap both Ss* [LL *sexagesima*, fr. L, fem. of *sexagesimus* sixtieth] : the second Sunday before Lent and the eighth before Easter in the church year as observed by various branches of the Christian church

¹sex·a·ges·i·mal \¦≈≈¦≈≈məl\ *adj* [L *sexagesimus* sixtieth (fr. *sexaginta* sixty) + E *-al*] : SEXAGENARY

²sexagesimal \"\ *n* -S : a sexagesimal fraction

sexagesimal arithmetic : arithmetic in which computation proceeds by sixties

sexagesimal fraction *or* **sexagesimal number** *n* : a fraction whose denominator is some power of 60 (as $\frac{1}{60}$, $\frac{1}{3600}$, $\frac{1}{216000}$)

sex·a·ges·i·mal·ly \-məlē\ *adv* : into or by sixtieths

sexagesimal scale *n* : a scale of numbers that proceeds by sixties (as in degrees or hours, minutes, and seconds)

sex·a·ges·i·mo-quarto \¦seksə¦jesə(,)mō+\ *n* [L *sexagesimo quarto*, abl. of *sexagesimus quartus* sixty-fourth, fr. *sexagesimus* sixtieth + *quartus* fourth — more at QUART] : SIXTY-FOURMO — see BOOK tables

sex·ag·o·nal \(')sek¦sagənᵊl\ *adj* [*sex-* + *-agonal* (as in *hexagonal*)] : HEXAGONAL

sexangled \(')¦≈¦≈≈\ *adj* [*sex-* + *angled*] : HEXAGONAL

sex·an·gu·lar \(')sek¦saŋgyələ(r)\ *adj* [L *sexangulus* hexagonal (fr. *sex* six + *angulus* angle) + E *-ar* — more at SIX, ANGLE] : HEXAGONAL

sex appeal *n* **1** : personal appeal or physical attractiveness for members of the opposite sex ⟨a girl with *sex appeal*⟩ ⟨set the new standard for masculine *sex appeal* —Lloyd Morris⟩ **2** : general appeal or attractiveness ⟨neither of these rates of return has much *sex appeal* —George Shea⟩ ⟨old hands in the Senate knew there was no political *sex appeal* in reorganization —William Benton⟩

sexa·valent \¦seksə+\ *adj* [*sexa-* (as in *sexagesimal*) + *valent*] : HEXAVALENT

sex cell *n* : EGG CELL, SPERM CELL

[1]**sex·cen·te·nary** \ˌsekˌsen·ˈtenərē, (ˈ)sekˈsentᵊnˌerē\ *adj* [L *sescenteni, sexcenteni* six hundred each (fr. *sex* six + *centeni* one hundred each, fr. *centum* hundred) + E *-ary* — more at HUNDRED] **:** relating to the number 600 or a 600th anniversary
[2]**sexcentenary** \"\ *n* **:** a 600th anniversary or its celebration
sex chromosome *n* **:** a chromosome that is inherited differently in the two sexes, that is or is held to be concerned directly with the inheritance of sex, and that is the seat of factors governing the inheritance of various sex-linked and sex-limited characters — called also *idiosome;* opposed to *autosome;* see X CHROMOSOME, Y CHROMOSOME
sex cord *n* **:** SEXUAL CORD
sex·de·cil·lion \ˌseksdə̇ˈsilyən\ *n, often attrib* [L *sesdecim, sexdecim* sixteen (fr. *sex* six + *-decim,* fr. *decem* ten) + E *-illion* (as in *million*) — more at SIX, TEN] — see NUMBER table
sex determination *n* **:** the process of imparting sex and the characteristics distinctive of a sex to a developing organism that results from the interaction of genetic and other factors during ontogeny
sex-digital *or* **sex·digitate** *or* **sex·digitated** \(ˈ)seks+\ *adj* [*sex-* + *digital* or *digitate, digitated*] **:** having six fingers or six toes
sex·dig·it·ism \seksˈdijəˌtizəm\ *n* -s **:** the state of being sexdigital
sexed \ˈsekst\ *adj* [in sense 1, fr. [1]*sex* + *-ed;* in sense 2, fr. past part. of [2]*sex*] **1 :** having sex or sexual instincts ⟨is so urgently ~ as to strain the confines of formal monogamous marriage —Weston La Barre⟩ **2 :** marked by qualities that arouse the sexual instincts **:** having sex appeal ⟨the actual dancing is highly ~ and uninhibited —John Martin⟩
sex·en·ni·al \(ˈ)sekˈsenēəl\ *adj* [L *sexennium* period of six years (fr. *sex* six + *-ennium,* fr. *annus* year) + E *-al* — more at SIX, ANNUAL] **1 :** continuing or lasting six years ⟨a ~ period⟩ **2 :** occurring, appearing, or being made, done, or acted upon every six years — **sex·en·ni·al·ly** \-əlē, -li\ *adv*
sex·er \ˈseksə(r)\ *n* -s [[2]*sex* + *-er*] **:** one that identifies the sex of an animal or other organism; *specif* **:** one that determines the sex of newly hatched chicks by examining the structures associated with the vent
sexes *pl of* SEX, *pres 3d sing of* SEX
sex·foil \ˈseks+ˌ-\ *n* [*sex-* + *foil*] **1 a :** a flower with six perianth segments **b :** a leaf with six leaflets **c :** a group of six leaves **2 :** a figure enclosed by six joined foils; *specif* **:** a 6-lobed foliation in Gothic tracery **3 :** a conventionalized heraldic flower showing six lobe-shaped petals

sexfoil 2

sex gland *n* **:** TESTIS, OVARY
sex·hood \ˈseksˌhu̇d\ *n* **:** the quality or state of being of one sex or the other
sex hormone *n* **:** a hormone having an effect that is usu. stimulatory on the growth or function of the reproductive organs or on the development of secondary sex characters; *esp* **:** one produced in the ovaries or testes ⟨the *sex hormones,* like the adrenal cortical hormones, are all steroids —H.B. MacPhillamy⟩—compare ANDROGEN, ESTROGEN, PROGESTERONE
sexi- — see SEX-
sexier *comparative of* SEXY
sexiest *superlative of* SEXY
sex·i·ness \ˈseksēnə̇s\ *n* -ES **:** the quality or state of being sexy
sex-influenced \ˈ=ˌ==ˌ=\ *adj* **:** acting or occurring as a dominant in one sex and a recessive in the other ⟨*sex-influenced* genes⟩ — compare SEX-LIMITED, SEX-LINKED
sexing *pres part of* SEX
sex-intergrade \ˈ=ˈ==ˌ=\ *n* **:** an individual intermediate in sexual characters **:** INTERSEX
sexi·valent \ˌseksə+\ *adj* [*sex-* + *valent*] **:** HEXAVALENT
sex·less \ˈsekslə̇s\ *adj* **:** lacking sex **:** NEUTER — **sex·less·ly** *adv*
sex·less·ness *n* -ES **:** the quality or state of being sexless
sex-limited \ˈ=ˈ===\ *adj* **:** completely lacking penetrance in one sex ⟨a *sex-limited* character⟩ ⟨*sex-limited* gene⟩ — compare SEX-INFLUENCED, SEX-LINKED
sex-link \ˈ=ˌ=\ *n* **:** an individual having one or more sex-linked characters; *specif* **:** a crossbred fowl having a sex-linked difference in color pattern that makes the hybrid autosexing
sex-linkage \ˈ=ˌ==\ *n* **:** the quality or state of being sex-linked
sex-linked \ˈ=ˌ=\ *adj* **1 :** located in a sex chromosome; *specif* **:** heterozygous in one sex and homozygous in the other ⟨a *sex-linked* gene⟩ **2** *of a heritable character* **:** mediated by a sex-linked gene — compare SEX-INFLUENCED, SEX-LIMITED
sex·o·log·i·cal \ˌseksəˈläjə̇kəl\ *adj* **:** of or relating to sexology
sex·ol·o·gist \sekˈsäləjə̇st\ *n* -s **:** a specialist in sexology
sex·ol·o·gy \-jē, -ji\ *n* -ES [[1]*sex* + *-o-* + *-logy*] **:** the study of sex or of the interaction of the sexes esp. among human beings
sex·os·ti·a·tae \ˌseksˌästēˈād·(ˌ)ē\ *n pl, cap* [NL, fr. *sex-* + *ostium* + L *-atae,* fem. pl. of *-atus* -ate] *in some classifications* **:** a group of spiders distinguished by the presence of six cardiac ostia
sex·os·ti·ate \(ˈ)sekˈsästēət, -ēˌāt\ *adj* [*sex-* + NL *ostium* + E *-ate*] **1 :** having six ostia **2** [NL *Sexostiatae*] **:** of or relating to the Sexostiatae
sex·partite \(ˈ)seks+\ *adj* [*sex-* + *partite*] **1 :** divided into or made up of a combination of six parts **2 :** of or relating to an architectural system (as in the earliest Gothic) in which a vaulting square has two arched subdivisions on each side and one at each end
sex pervert *n* **:** SEXUAL PERVERT
sex play *n* **:** PLAY 1c(2)
sex·pot \ˈseksˌpät\ *n* **:** a conspicuously sexy woman ⟨no lush store beauty she . . . no dished-up ~ —H.E.Clurman⟩
sex ratio *n* **:** the proportion of males to females in a population as expressed by the number of males per hundred females
sex skin *n* **:** areas of skin adjacent to the female external genitals of various lower primates that undergo marked alteration in turgidity and often in color during estrus
sext \ˈsekst\ *n* -s [ME *sexte,* fr. LL *sexta,* fr. L, fem. of *sextus* sixth, fr. *sex* six + *-tus,* adj. suffix used esp. to form ordinal numbers and past participles — more at SIX, -TH] **1** *often cap* **:** the fourth of the seven canonical hours or the sixth hour of the day according to the ancient Roman reckoning **:** 12 o'clock noon; *also* **:** an office recited at this time or in the Roman Catholic Church often somewhat earlier **2** [L *sexta,* fem. of *sextus*] **a :** a musical interval of a sixth **b :** a pipe-organ mixture stop with two ranks of pipes consisting of a twelfth and a seventeenth that sound a sixth apart
sex·tain \ˈsekˌstān\ *n* -s [modif. (influenced by *sex-* and *quatrain*) of obs. F *sestine* — more at SESTINE] **1 :** SESTINA **2 :** a stanza of six lines
sex·tans \ˈsekˌstanz\ *n, pl* **sextans** [L, sixth part of anything, sextans] **:** a bronze coin of the Roman Republic constituting the sixth part of an as
sex·tant \ˈsekstənt\ *n* -s [NL *sextant-, sextans,* fr. L, sixth part of anything, fr. *sextus* sixth + *-ant-, -ans* -ant — more at SEXT] **1 :** the sixth part of a circle **2 :** an instrument for measuring altitudes of celestial bodies from a moving ship or airplane with a maximum angle of 60 degrees between its reflecting mirrors — compare OCTANT
sex·tet *or* **sex·tette** \(ˈ)sekˈstet, *usu* -ed.+V\ *n* -s [alter. of *sestet*] **1 a :** a musical composition in six voice parts or for six voices or instruments **b :** the musicians that perform a sextet **2 :** a 6-line stanza or poem **:** SESTET **3 :** a group or set containing six persons or things; *specif* **:** a team (as a hockey team) composed of six players
sexti- *comb form* [L *sextus* sixth — more at SEXT] **:** six ⟨*sexti*para⟩ ⟨*sexti*polar⟩
[1]**sex·tile** \ˈsekstəl\ *adj* [L *sextilus* sixth, fr. *sextus* sixth + *-ilis* -ile] **:** of, relating to, or measured by 60 degrees
[2]**sextile** \"\ *n* -s **:** the aspect of two heavenly bodies when 60 degrees distant from each other
sex·til·lion \sekˈstilyən\ *n* -s *often attrib* [F, irreg. (influence of *septillion, octillion*) fr. *sex-* + *-illion* (as in *million*)] — see NUMBER table
sex·tip·a·ra \sekˈstipərə\ *n* -s [NL, fr. *sexti-* + *-para*] **:** a woman who has borne children in six pregnancies
sex·ti·polar \ˌsekstə+\ *adj* [*sexti-* + *polar*] **:** having six poles
sex·to \ˈsek(ˌ)stō\ *n* -s [L (*in*) *sexto* in a sixth, fr. abl. of *sextus* sixth — more at SEXT] **:** SIXMO — see BOOK tables
sex·to·dec·i·mo \ˌsekstəˈdesəˌmō\ *n* -s [L, abl. of *sextusdecimus* sixteenth, fr. *sextus* sixth + *decimus* tenth — more at DECIMATE] **:** SIXTEENMO — see BOOK tables
sex·tole \ˈsekˌstōl\ *or* **sex·to·let** \-kstəˌlet\ *n* -s [*sextole* fr. G, fr. L *sextus* sixth + G *-ole* (as in *quintole*); *sextolet* fr. *sextole* + *-et*] **:** SEXTUPLET
sex·ton \ˈsekstən\ *n* -s [ME *secresteyn, sekesteyn, sexteyn, sexten,* fr. MF *secrestain,* fr. ML *sacristanus* — more at SACRISTAN] **:** a church custodian charged with keeping the church and parish buildings prepared for meetings, caring for church equipment, and performing related minor duties
sexton beetle *n* **:** BURYING BEETLE
sex·ton·ess \-nə̇s\ *n* -ES [ME *sexteynesse, sextenesse,* fr. *secresteyn, sekesteyn, sexteyn, sexten* sexton + *-esse* -ess] **:** a female sexton
sex·ton·ship \-nˌship\ *n* **:** the office or position of a sexton
sextry *n* -ES [ME *sextrie,* prob. fr. MF *secresterie,* modif. of ML *sacristia* — more at SACRISTY] *obs* **:** SACRISTY
sextupl *abbr* sextuplicate
[1]**sex·tu·ple** \(ˈ)sekˈst(y)üpəl *also* -təp- *or* ˈsekstəp-\ *adj* [prob. fr. ML *sextuplus,* fr. L *sextus* sixth + *-plus* (as in *duplus* double) — more at DOUBLE] **1 :** consisting of six **:** being six times as great or as many **:** SIXFOLD **2 :** taken by sixes or in groups of six; *specif* **:** having six beats per musical measure **3 :** SEXTUPLEX 2
[2]**sextuple** \"\ *vb* -ED/-ING/-S *vt* **:** to make six times as much or as many ~ *vi* **:** to become six times as much or as many
[3]**sextuple** \"\ *n* -s **:** a sum six times as great as another **:** a sixfold amount **:** the sixth multiple
sex·tup·let \(ˈ)sekˈstəplə̇t, -t(y)üp- *sometimes* ˈsekstəp-\ *n* -s [[1]*sextuple* + *-et*] **1 :** a combination of six of a kind **2 a :** one of six offspring born at one birth **b sextuplets** *pl* **:** a group of six such offspring **3 a :** a group of six equal musical notes to be performed in the time ordinarily given to four of the same value and written in three groups of two **b :** a double triplet with accents on the first and fourth notes

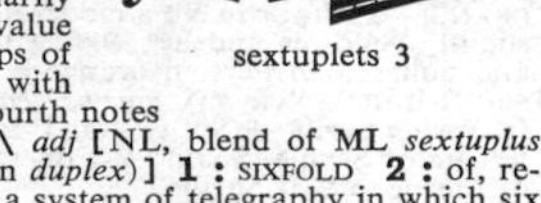

sextuplets 3

sex·tu·plex \ˈsekstəˌpleks\ *adj* [NL, blend of ML *sextuplus* sextuple and L *-plex* (as in *duplex*)] **1 :** SIXFOLD **2 :** of, relating to, or consisting of a system of telegraphy in which six messages with three going each way can be sent simultaneously over one wire
[1]**sex·tu·pli·cate** \(ˈ)sekˈst(y)üplə̇kə̇t, -ləˌkāt\ *adj* [blend of [1]*sextuple* and *-plicate* (as in *duplicate*)] **1 :** repeated six times **:** SIXFOLD **2 :** SIXTH ⟨file the ~ copy⟩
[2]**sextuplicate** \"\ *n* -s **1 :** a sixth thing like five others of the same kind **2 :** six copies all alike — used with *in* ⟨typed in ~⟩
[3]**sex·tu·pli·cate** \-ləˌkāt\ *vt* -ED/-ING/-S **:** to multiply by six **:** SEXTUPLE **:** reproduce five times; *specif* **:** to make at one time an original and five carbon copies
sex·tur \ˈsekˌstu̇(ə)r\ *n* -s [Dan *sekstur,* fr. *seks* six (fr. ON *sex*) + *tur* figure in a dance, fr. F *tour,* lit., turn — more at SIX, TOUR] **:** a Danish clockwise figure dance for six couples
sex type *n* **:** MATING TYPE
sex·u·al \ˈseksh(əw)əl\ *adj* [LL *sexualis,* fr. L *sexus* sex + *-alis* -al — more at SEX] **1 :** of, relating to, or associated with sex as a characteristic of an organic being ⟨~ differentiation⟩ ⟨~ distinctions⟩: **a :** having sex ⟨spores may be ~ or asexual⟩ **b :** involving sex ⟨the conception that bacteria have no ~ mode of reproduction —*Jour. of Bacteriology*⟩ **2 a :** of or relating to the male or female sexes or their distinctive organs or functions ⟨some biologists and anthropologists believe that the origins of art can be discovered in ~ display and ornamentation —Hunter Mead⟩ ⟨~ excitement⟩ ⟨~ compatibility⟩ **b :** of or relating to the sphere of behavior associated with libidinal gratification ⟨decided that the basis of almost all personality conflicts is ~ —*Time*⟩
sexual cell *n* **:** EGG CELL, SPERM CELL
sexual cord *n* **:** one of the cylindrical or band-form masses of mesothelial cells that contain the primitive sexual cells in the developing ovaries and testes of vertebrate embryos and that in the male develop into the seminiferous tubules
sexual cycle *n* **:** a cycle of bodily functional and structural changes associated with sex: **a :** ESTROUS CYCLE **b :** MENSTRUAL CYCLE **c :** a cycle in many males marked by the occurrence of seasonal or annual periods of virility with intervening periods of impotence in which neither sexual impulses nor secretions occur
sexual dimorphism *n* **1 :** a condition of having one of the sexes existing in two forms or varieties **2 :** a condition of having the two sexes markedly dissimilar in appearance (as in various birds)
sex·u·a·le \ˌsekshəˈwālē\ *n* -s [NL, fr. LL, neut. of *sexualis*] **:** a member of the bisexual generation in aphids
sexual generation *n* **:** the generation that reproduces by a sexual process in animals or plants which exhibit alternation of generations — compare ALTERNATION OF GENERATIONS, GAMETOPHYTE
sexual intercourse *n* **1 :** heterosexual intercourse involving penetration of the vagina by the penis **:** COITUS **2 :** intercourse involving genital contact between individuals other than penetration of the vagina by the penis
sex·u·al·ism \ˈseksh(əw)əˌlizəm\ *n* -s **:** emphasis upon sex or sexuality as a major concern
sexual isolation *n* **:** biological isolation in which the isolating mechanism is a psychological inhibition of interbreeding
sex·u·al·ist \-lə̇st\ *n* -s [NL *sexualista,* fr. LL *sexualis* sexual + L *-ista* -ist — more at SEXUAL] **1 :** one who explains phenomena by sexuality **2 :** one who follows the sexual or artificial system of Linnaeus
sex·u·al·i·ty \ˌsekshəˈwalə̇d·ē, -lətē, -i\ *n* -ES **:** the quality or state of being sexual: **a :** the condition of having sex **b :** the condition of having reproductive functions dictated by the union of male and female — compare SEX 2 **c :** the expression of the sex instinct **:** sexual activity ⟨considered ~ as a dissipation of vital forces —Anthony West⟩ **d :** the condition, potential, or state of readiness of the organism with regard to sexual activity ⟨signs of excitation . . . and sometimes increased ~ —H.M.Parshley⟩
sex·u·al·iza·tion \ˌseksh(əw)ələ̇ˈzāshən\ *n* -s **:** the act or process of sexualizing **:** the state of being sexualized ⟨~ may not reach its prepubertal peak until about the ninth or tenth year —L.E.Hinsie⟩
sex·u·al·ize \ˈseksh(əw)əˌlīz\ *vt* -ED/-ING/-S [*sexual* + *-ize*] **1 :** to make sexual **:** to endow with sex ⟨gender does not become *sexualized* until about the fifth or sixth year —L.E. Hinsie⟩ **2 :** to invest with sexual characteristics ⟨love of the child for his mother becomes contaminated with *sexualized* love —Weston La Barre⟩
sex·u·al·ly \-lē, -li\ *adv* **:** in a sexual manner **:** with regard to or by means of sex
sexual organ *n* **:** an organ of the reproductive system; *esp* **:** an external generative organ — often used in pl.; compare GENITALIA
sexual perversion *n* **:** activity (as sodomy, fellatio, bestiality) leading to complete sexual gratification that is preferred by an adult to heterosexual coitus
sexual pervert *or* **sexual deviate** *n* **:** one that practices a sexual perversion
sexual psychopathy *n* **:** the condition of a psychopathic or sociopathic personality manifested by the commission of sexual crimes
sexual relations *n pl* **:** COITUS
sexual selection *n* **:** the choice of a mate on a basis of various attractive characters (as color or bird song)
sexual skin *n* **:** SEX SKIN
sexual spore *n* **:** a spore formed as a result of conjugation of gametes or nuclei (as zygospore, ascospore, basidiospore) of opposite sex
sex·u·pa·ra \sekˈsüpərə\ *also* **sex·u·pare** \ˈseksəˌpa(ə)r\ *n, pl* **sexupa·rae** \-üpəˌrē\ *also* **sexupares** [NL *sexupara,* fr. L *sexus* sex + NL *-para*] **1 :** a parthenogenetic female producing eggs that give rise to males or to females which lay eggs requiring fertilization **2 :** a sexuparous insect
sex·u·pa·rous \-üpərəs\ *adj* [L *sexus* + E *-parous*] **:** producing eggs from which true males and females are hatched — used of various female aphids and phylloxeras
sexy \ˈseksē, -si\ *adj, usu* -ER/-EST **1 :** spicy or racy with references to or portrayals of sexually stimulating matter ⟨the *sexiest,* bawdiest and most outspoken comedy drama —*Ottawa (Canada) Jour.*⟩ ⟨read nothing more than the newspaper or perhaps a sadistic or ~ thriller —Eric Partridge⟩ **2 :** sexually suggestive **:** erotically stimulating ⟨struck ~ poses and smiled for advertising photographs —*Springfield (Mass.) Daily News*⟩ ⟨had a face angelic and ~ —Goodman Ace⟩
sey \ˈsī\ *n* -s [origin unknown] *Scot* **:** a cut of beef — compare BACKSEY, FORESEY
sey·bert·ite \ˈsībə(r)ˌd·ˌīt\ *n* -s [F, fr. Henry *Seybert* †1883 Am. mineralogist + F *-ite*] **:** a basic aluminosilicate $Ca(Mg,Al)_3(Al,Si)_4(O,OH)_{12}$ of the clintonite group consisting of calcium, magnesium, and aluminum, occurring in monoclinic crystals and foliated masses and having a reddish brown, copper red, or yellowish color and submetallic luster (hardness 4–5, sp. gr.3–3.1)
sey·chel·lois \ˌsāshəlˈwä, -ˌshel-\ *n, pl* **seychellois** \-ä(z)\ [(assumed) F, fr. *Seychelles,* group of islands in the Indian ocean + F *-ois* -ese, fr. L *-ensis*] *cap* **:** a native or inhabitant of the Seychelles islands — **seychellois** *adj, usu cap*
sey·me·ria \sēˈmirēə\ *n, cap* [NL, fr. Henry *Seymer,* 19th cent. Eng. naturalist + NL *-ia*] **:** a genus of widely distributed herbs (family Scrophulariaceae) with pinnate leaves and solitary slightly irregular yellow flowers — see MULLEIN FOXGLOVE
[1]**sey·mour·i·a·morph** \sēˈmōrēəˌmȯrf\ *adj* [NL *Seymouriamorpha*] **:** of or relating to the Seymouriamorpha
[2]**seymouriamorph** \"\ *n* -s **:** an amphibian or fossil of the order Seymouriamorpha
sey·mour·i·a·mor·pha \ˌ=ˌ===ˈmȯrfə\ *n pl, cap* [NL, fr. *Seymouria,* genus of Permian Labyrinthodontia (prob. fr. the name *Seymour* + NL *-ia*) + *-morpha*] **:** an order of Permian Labyrinthodontia comprising generalized forms exhibiting a mixture of amphibian and reptilian characters and possibly on the ancestral line of the true reptiles
seyyid *or* **seyid** *var of* SAYYID
sf *abbr* sforzando
SF *abbr* **1** *often not cap* science fiction **2** semifinished **3** senior fellow **4** shipfitter **5** signal-frequency **6** sinking fund **7** spot-faced **8** square foot **9** *often not cap* [L *sub finem*] toward the end **10** *often not cap* surface foot
Sf *symbol* sexagesimo-quarto
SFC *abbr* sergeant first class
sfer·ics *or* **spher·ics** \ˈsfiriks, -fer-, -rēks\ *n pl* [*sferics* by shortening & alter. fr. *atmospherics; spherics* short for *atmospherics*] **1 :** ATMOSPHERICS 1 **2** *sing in constr* **:** an electronic detector of storms using devices for plotting electrical discharges
SFM *abbr, often not cap* surface feet per minute
sfo·ga·to \sfōˈgäd·(ˌ)ō\ *adj* [It, past part. of *sfogare* to exhale, give vent to, fr. *s-* (fr. L *ex-*) + *-fogare* (fr. L *fugare* to put to flight, fr. *fuga* act of running away, flight) — more at FUGUE] **1 :** light and airy in performance — used as a direction in music **2 :** high and thin in tone — used chiefly of a voice in the phrase *soprano sfogato*
[1]**sfor·zan·do** \sfȯ(r)tˈsän(ˌ)dō\ *adj (or adv)* [It, verbal of *sforzare* to force, fr. *s-* (fr. L *ex-*) + *forzare* to force, fr. (assumed) VL *fortiare* to attack, compel — more at FORCE] **:** ACCENTED — used as a direction in music to indicate that a single tone or chord is to be sounded more loudly than the rest of a passage — abbr. *sf, sfz;* symbol >
[2]**sforzando** \"\ *n, pl* **sforzandos** \-dōz\ *or* **sforzan·di** \-dē\ **:** an accented tone or chord
sfor·za·to \-ˈäd·(ˌ)ō\ *adj (or adv)* [It, past part. of *sforzare*] **:** SFORZANDO
SFPM *abbr, often not cap* surface feet per minute
sft *abbr* **1** shaft **2** soft
sftwd *abbr* softwood
sfu·ma·to \sfüˈmä(ˌ)tō\ *n* -s [It, fr. *sfumato,* past part. of *sfumare* to evaporate, shade off into another color, fr. *s-* (fr. L *ex-*) + *fumare* to smoke, fr. L — more at FUME] **:** the definition of form without abrupt outline by delicate gradation from light to shadow producing an atmospheric effect (as in the painting of Leonardo da Vinci) — compare CHIAROSCURO
sfz *abbr* sforzando
sg *abbr* **1** signed **2** singular **3** surgeon
SG *abbr* **1** screen grid **2** secretary-general **3** *often not cap* senior grade **4** solicitor general **5** *often not cap* specific gravity **6** surgeon general
sga·bel·lo \zgäˈbe(ˌ)lō, skä-\ *n* -s [It, fr. L *scabellum* low stool, dim. of *scamnum* bench, stool — more at SHAMBLES] **:** an Italian-Renaissance wooden side chair consisting of a stool or similar form with a simple upright back
sgaw *also* **sgau** \ˈskȯ\ *n, pl* **sgaw** *or* **sgaws** *also* **sgau** *or* **sgaus** *usu cap* **1 a :** a Karen people of Lower Burma **b :** a member of such people **2 :** the language of the Sgaw people
sgd *abbr* signed
sgd *abbr* signatures
sgl *abbr* single
SGO *abbr* **1** squadron gunnery officer **2** surgeon general's office
sgraf·fi·to \zgräˈfē(ˌ)tō, skr-\ *also* **sgraf·fi·a·to** \ˌzgräfēˈä(ˌ)tō, ˌskr-\ *n, pl* **sgraffi·ti** \ˈ=ˈfē(ˌ)tē\ [*sgraffito* fr. It, fr. *sgraffito,* past part. of *sgraffire* to scratch, produce sgraffito, fr. *sgraffio* scratch, sgraffito, fr. *sgraffiare* to scratch, produce sgraffito, fr. *s-* (fr. L *ex-*) + *graffiare* to scratch; *sgraffiato* fr. It, past part. of *sgraffiare* — more at GRAFFITO] **1 :** decoration by cutting away parts of a surface layer (as of clay or plaster) to expose a different colored ground — compare GRAFFITO **2 :** something (as traditional Pennsylvania Dutch pottery) decorated with sgraffito
sgt *abbr, often cap* sergeant
sh \sh *often prolonged*\ *interj* [origin unknown] — often used in prolonged or reduplicated form to enjoin silence or urge moderation of sound
sh *abbr* **1** sash **2** shall **3** share **4** sheep **5** sheet **6** shell **7** shilling **8** shipping **9** shipwright **10** shock **11** shop **12** short **13** show **14** shower **15** shunt
SH *abbr* **1** sacrifice hit **2** schoolhouse **3** *often not cap* semester hour **4** serum hepatitis **5** ship's heading **6** specified hours **7** scrum half
sha \ˈshä, ˈshō\ *n* -s [prob. native name in Ladakh] **:** URIAL
SHA *abbr* sidereal hour angle
sha'ban *also* **shaa·ban** \shəˈbän, shäˈb-,shōˈb-\ *n* -s *usu cap* [Ar *sha'bān*] **:** the 8th month of the Muhammadan year — see MONTH table
shab·bas *or* **shab·bos** \ˈshäbəs\ *n, pl* **sha·bo·sim** \shəˈbōsə̇m\ *usu cap* [Yiddish *shabes,* fr. Heb *shabbāth*] **:** SHABBAT
shabbas goy *or* **shabbos goy** *n, usu cap S* [Yiddish *shabes goy,* fr. *shabes* Sabbath + *goy* gentile, fr. Heb *gōy* people, nation] **:** a non-Jew employed by Orthodox Jews to perform services (as turning lights on and off) which are forbidden to Jews on the Sabbath
shab·bat *or* **shab·bath** \shəˈbät, ˈshäbəs\ *n* -s *usu cap* [Heb *shabbāth* — more at SABBATH] **:** the Jewish Sabbath
shabbathaian *or* **shabbethaian** *usu cap, var of* SABBATIAN
shab·bat shu·bah *or* **shab·bath shu·bah** *or* **shab·bat shu·vah** *or* **shab·bath shu·vah** \ˌshäbəs(h)ˈshüvə\ *n, usu cap both Ss* [LHeb *shabbāth shūbhāh,* lit., Sabbath of return; fr. the fact that Heb *shūbhāh* (return) is the first word of the haftarah read on that day] **:** the Jewish Sabbath that falls between Rosh Hashanah and Yom Kippur
shab·bi·fy \ˈshabəˌfī\ *vt* -ED/-ING/-ES **:** to make shabby
shab·bi·ly \-bə̇lē, -li\ *adv* **:** in a shabby manner
shab·bi·ness \-bēnə̇s, -bin-\ *n* -ES **:** the quality or state of being shabby
shab·by \-bē,-bi\ *adj* -ER/-EST [obs. E *shab* scab + E *-y*] **1 a :** threadbare and faded from wear **:** appearing outworn ⟨~ finery⟩ ⟨saved fragments of lace from her dresses when they became too ~ for use —*Amer. Guide Series: Md.*⟩ **b :** ill kept and worn out **:** POOR, DECAYING, DILAPIDATED, NEGLECTED ⟨~, unpainted shacks, dropping with decay —Van Wyck Brooks⟩ ⟨~ wallpaper⟩ ⟨a ~ neighborhood⟩ **2 :** clothed with worn or seedy garments ⟨an uncommonly comic doctor, ~ alike in dress and ethics —Brooks Atkinson⟩ ⟨when he . . . saw the smartly dressed clerks standing before the stores, he looked at his own ~ person and was ashamed to enter —Sherwood Anderson⟩ **3 a :** MEAN, PALTRY, DESPICABLE ⟨the Nazis,

for all the terrible damage they have done, may turn out to be the *shabbiest* villains in history —*N. Y. Herald Tribune Bk. Rev.*) ⟨all the efforts of propagandists . . . could not make the war anything but ~ in its origin —D.W.Brogan⟩ **b :** UNGENEROUS, UNFAIR, DISHONORABLE ⟨laments the ~ way in which this country often treated a poet so deeply devoted to it —Paul Engle⟩ ⟨concerned both with the dearth of teachers and with the ~ scale on which they are paid —*Pleasures of Publishing*⟩ ⟨the opinions of the man on the street . . . are a motley of hand-me-downs, baggy generalities, and ~ prejudices —H.J.Muller⟩ ⟨both parties played furious and sometimes ~ politics —*Time*⟩ ⟨she drifts into a ~ and then a *shabbier* love —Carl Van Doren⟩ ⟨the explorer's mistress shows up with the ~ truth of the man's life —Henry Hewes⟩ **c :** evincing scant liberality or generosity ⟨a ~ allowance⟩ ⟨a ~ gift⟩ ⟨had paid a very ~ dividend —W.M.Thackeray⟩ **d :** inferior in quality **:** SLOVENLY ⟨a ~ lot of fighting men, as their captured officers contemptuously admitted —*New Yorker*⟩ ⟨a member of a ~ theatrical troupe which tours the provinces —Donald Heiney⟩ ⟨his reasoning is weak, even ~ —J.T.Farrell⟩ **syn** see CONTEMPTIBLE

shab·rack *also* **shab·raque** \'sha,brak\ *n* -s [G & F; F *schabraque*, fr. G *schabracke*, fr. Hung *csáprág*, fr. Turk *çaprak*] **:** a saddlecloth often of goatskin formerly used by European light cavalry

sha·bun·der *also* **sha·ban·dar** \shä'bəndə(r)\ *n* -s [Per *shāhbandar*, fr. *shāh* King + *bandar* city, harbor — more at CHECK] **:** a harbor master formerly the chief official to deal with foreign traders in the East Indies

sha·bu·oth *or* **sha·bu·ot** *or* **sha·vu·oth** *or* **sha·vu·ot** *or* **sha·vu·os** *or* **she·vu·oth** *or* **she·vu·os** \shə'vü,ōt(h), -,ōs, -,əs\ *n, pl* **shabuoths** *or* **shabuots** *or* **shavuoths** *or* **shavuots** \-,ōt(h)s, -,ōs, -,əs\ *or* **shavuos·es** \-,ōsəz, -,əsəz\ *or* **shevuoths** \-,ōt(h)s, -,ōs, -,əs\ *or* **shevuos·es** \-,ōsəz, -əsəz\ *usu cap* [Heb *shābhū'ōth*, pl. of *shābhūa'* week] **:** a Jewish holiday observed on the 6th and 7th of Sivan and commemorating the revelation of the Law at Mt. Sinai and the wheat festival celebrated in biblical times 7 weeks or 50 days after the 16th of Nisan — called also *Feast of Weeks, Pentecost*

shacharit *or* **shacharith** *var of* SHAHARITH

shach·le *also* **shack·le** \'shakəl, 'shäk-\ *vb* -ED/-ING/-S [perh. imit.] *vi, Scot* **:** to walk in a shuffling gate **:** SHAMBLE ~ *vt* **1** *Scot* **:** to wear (shoes) out of shape **2** *Scot* **:** to distort esp. by improper use

¹shack \'shak\ *n* -s [E dial. *shack* to shake, alter. of ¹*shake*] **1** *dial chiefly Eng* **:** grain and stubble left on the field after harvest **2 :** liberty or right of turning pigs or poultry into fields after harvest to feed on the shack; *also* **:** the land so used **3 :** a catch of miscellaneous fish mostly of cheap kinds

²shack \"\ *n* -s [perh. by shortening & alter. fr. *shakerag*] **1** *chiefly dial* **:** a shiftless fellow **:** BUM, TRAMP **2** *slang* **:** a railroad brakeman

³shack \"\ *vi* -ED/-ING/-S **:** to go sluggishly or with a lumbering gait ⟨the old horse ~*ed* along⟩

⁴shack \"\ *n* -s [prob. back-formation fr. *shackly*] **1 :** a small roughly built and often crudely furnished house **:** HUT, SHANTY ⟨a ~ made of old boards and tar paper —C.M.Webster⟩ ⟨found inadequate shelter in a grass ~ —E.E.Shipton⟩ ⟨the camps, with their close-serried ~*s* of tarpaulin, plywood, oilcloth strips, cardboard —Han Suyin⟩ **2 :** a room or similar enclosed structure for a particular person or thing ⟨an ammunition ~⟩ ⟨a cook's ~⟩ ⟨a guard's ~⟩ ⟨the operator's ~ on a crane⟩ ⟨a radio ~⟩

⁵shack \"\ *vi* **1 :** LIVE, DWELL ⟨the schoolhouse had been originally put up for the sawmill hands to ~ in —Clifton Johnson⟩ **2** *slang* **:** SHACK UP

⁶shack \"\ *vt* [perh. alter. of ⁷*shag*] **:** CHASE, RETRIEVE ⟨he'd ~ us away a half-dozen times a night —*Springfield (Mass.) Union*⟩ ⟨~ a baseball⟩

⁷shack \"\ *dial var of* SHUCK

shack·bolt \'shak,bōlt\ *n* [prob. short for *shackle bolt*] **:** a shackle used as a heraldic charge

shack·el *also* **shack·le** \'shakəl\ *n* -s [¹*shackle*] **:** a section of gill net

¹shack·le \'shakəl\ *n* -s [ME *schakel, schakle*, fr. OE *sceacul*; akin to MD *schakel* link of a chain, ON *skǫkull* pole of a cart] **1 :** something that confines the legs or arms so as to prevent their free motion: as **a :** a ring or band enclosing ankle or wrist and fastened to something else (as its mate) by a chain or a strap **:** MANACLE, FETTER **b :** a hobble for a horse **2 :** something that acts like fetters to check or prevent free action — usu. used in pl. ⟨throw off the party ~*s* and do what was best for their country —Elie Abel⟩ ⟨the subtle, intimate, soul-gripping ~*s* of memory and usage that held her by the roots —Timothy Wharton⟩ ⟨free enterprise without the ~*s* of government control —W.M.Blair⟩ ⟨those who have tossed off the ~*s* of illiteracy —Ben Bradford⟩ ⟨must release ourselves from the ~*s* of yesterday's traditions and let our minds be bold —Hubert Humphrey⟩ ⟨want no ~*s* on the mind or the spirit —A.E.Stevenson b.1900⟩ **3 :** any of various devices for making something fast: as **a :** a U-shaped metal fitting with a pin through the ends **:** CLEVIS, COUPLING — compare *anchor shackle* **b :** one of the U-shaped parts that join a spring in a vehicle to its hanger **c :** the link that engages with the staple in a padlock **d :** one of the rope handles for a sea chest **4 :** a length of cable or anchor chain usu. 15 feet

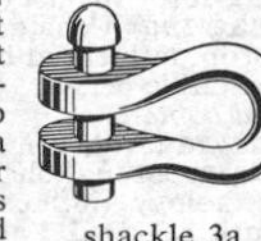
shackle 3a

²shackle \"\ *vb* **shackled; shackled; shackling** \-k(ə)liŋ\ **shackles** [ME *schaklen*, fr. *schakel, schakle*, n.] *vt* **1 a :** to confine the limbs of so as to prevent free motion **:** bind with or as if with shackles **:** FETTER, CHAIN **b :** to make fast with a shackle **:** JOIN, COUPLE ⟨~ each end of a spring to the axle⟩ ⟨got in the port anchor and *shackled* it on the cable —H.A. Chippendale⟩ ⟨*shackled* the policemen together with their own handcuffs —Jan Valtin⟩ **2 a :** to deprive of freedom esp. of action by means of restrictions or handicaps **:** IMPEDE, HAMPER ⟨the illiterate, often with heavy physical and mental handicaps, *shackled* by habits of irritability and poor family background —Dixon Wecter⟩ ⟨*shackled* with precedents⟩ ⟨*shackled* with inherited conventions⟩ ⟨*shackled* by superstition⟩ ⟨people *shackled* by poor leadership⟩ **b :** to tie (a person or thing) to something that is detrimental ⟨the vast resources of the film industry remain predominantly *shackled* to its entertainment deities —E.D.Canham⟩ **syn** see HAMPER

³shackle \"\ *vi* [prob. fr. E dial. *shack* to idle, loaf (fr. E ²*shack*) + E *-le*] *dial* **:** to wander around idly **:** LOAF

shackle bar *n* **1 :** a link coupling formerly used between railroad cars **2 :** a device consisting of an ordinary pinch bar with a hinged shackle near the point for pulling out something (as a driftbolt or railroad spikes)

shackle bolt *n* **1 :** the bolt of a shackle **2 :** a bolt with a shackle

shacklebone \'⸗,⸗\ *n, Scot* **:** WRIST

shackle joint *n* **1 :** a joint consisting of a shackle fitted through a ring **2 :** a joint formed by a bony ring passing through a hole in a bone (as at the base of the spine in some fishes)

shack·ler \'shak(ə)lə(r)\ *n* -s **:** one that shackles **:** COUPLER

shack·ly \-k(ə)lē\ *adj* [prob. fr. E dial. *shackle* to shake, rattle (fr. E dial. *shack* to shake + E *-le*) + E *-y* — more at SHACK] **1** *chiefly dial* **:** RICKETY, RAMSHACKLE **2** *chiefly dial* **:** LOOSE-JOINTED, SHAMBLING

shacks *pl of* SHACK, *pres 3d sing of* SHACK

shacktown \'⸗,⸗\ *n* **:** a group of shacks serving as dwellings ⟨migrant workers have settled by the hundreds and thousands in a gigantic ~ that has grown up in the vicinity —R.H.Fitzgibbon⟩

shack up *vi, slang* **:** to become established in a dwelling or shelter esp. when involving cohabitation **:** spend the night **:** COHABIT — often used with *with* ⟨he *shacked up* with another girl he knew —Wenzell Brown⟩ ~ *vt, slang* **:** to establish in a dwelling or shelter esp. when involving cohabitation ⟨were *shacked up* comfortably inside bamboo huts —*Infantry Jour.*⟩ ⟨the girls get boyfriends who *shack* them *up* for a time —Marya Mannes⟩

shackup \'⸗,⸗\ *n* -s [*shack up*] *slang* **:** the act of shacking up **:** COHABITATION

shacky \'shakē\ *adj* **:** characterized by the presence or semblance of a shack ⟨a ~ settlement near the town dump⟩

shad \'shad, -aa(ə)-\ *n, pl* **shad** *or* **shads** [fr. (assumed) ME *shad*, fr. OE *sceadd*; akin to L *scatēre* to bubble, gush, be abundant, Lith *suskàsti* to leap up] **1 a :** any of several clupeid fishes (genus *Alosa*) that differ from the typical herrings in having a relatively deep body and in being anadromous and that are extremely important food fishes of Europe and No. America; *esp* **:** a common food fish (*A. sapidissima*) of the Atlantic coast of No. America that is naturalized along the Pacific coast and is bluish green above with silvery sides and undersurface — see ALLICE SHAD, RIVER SHAD, TWAITE SHAD **b :** any of several other clupeid fishes (as a menhaden) — usu. used with a qualifying term; see GIZZARD SHAD **2 :** any of various fishes of families other than Clupeidae: as **a :** BROAD SHAD; *also* **:** any of several similar mojarras **b** *southern Africa* **:** BLUE-FISH 1

shad-bellied \'⸗¦⸗⸗\ *adj* **1 :** constituting or resembling a man's coat similar to a cutaway and having the front edges cut on a gradual slant from the front to the tails **2 :** having a thin or flat belly ⟨a *shad-bellied* old man⟩

shadbelly \'⸗,⸗⸗\ *n, pl* **shadbellies 1** *also* **shadbelly coat :** a shad-bellied coat **2 :** a wearer of a shad-bellied coat; *esp* **:** FRIEND 6

shad·ber·ry \'shad-, -aa(ə)d- — *see* BERRY\ *n* **1 :** the fruit of the shadbush **2 :** SHADBUSH

shadbird \'⸗,⸗\ *n* **1** *dial Eng* **:** the common sandpiper **2** *dial* **:** WILSON'S SNIPE

shadblow \'⸗,⸗\ *n* **1** *also* **shadblow serviceberry :** JUNEBERRY 1 **2 :** WHITLOW GRASS a

shadbush \'⸗,⸗\ *n* **:** JUNEBERRY 1

shad·chan *or* **schat·chen** *or* **shad·chen** \'shätkən, -ädk-\ *n, pl* **shad·cho·nim** \-'kōnəm, -nēm\ *or* **shadchans** *or* **schatchens** *or* **shadchens** [Yiddish & MHeb; Yiddish *shadkhn*, fr. MHeb *shadhkhān*, fr. LHeb *shiddēkh* to arrange a marriage] **:** a Jewish marriage broker or a matchmaker

shad·dock \'shadək\ *n* -s [after Captain *Shaddock*, 17th cent. Eng. ship commander who brought the seed from the East Indies to Barbados in 1696] **1 :** a very large thick-rinded typically pear-shaped citrus fruit closely related to the grapefruit but differing esp. in its loose rind and often rather coarse dry pulp — called also *pomelo* **2** *also* **shaddock tree :** a small round-headed citrus tree (*Citrus grandis*) that produces shaddocks and is probably native to southeastern Asia or the Pacific islands but is widespread in warm regions as an escape though largely replaced in cultivation by the grapefruit

¹shade \'shād\ *n* -s *often attrib* [ME, fr. OE *sceadu*; akin to OHG *scato* shadow, Goth *skadus*, OIr *scāth* shadow, Gk *skotos* darkness] **1 a :** comparative darkness or obscurity owing to interception of the rays of light **:** partial or relative darkness caused by the intervention of an opaque body between the space contemplated and the source of light **:** absence of complete illumination **b :** relative obscurity or retirement ⟨the ~ of the convent⟩ ⟨qualities cast in the ~⟩ **2 a :** cover provided by the intervention of an opaque body between the space contemplated and the source of heat or light; *esp* **:** shelter from the sun provided by tree foliage **b** (1) **:** protective foliage (2) **:** PROTECTION **3 a :** a spot not exposed to sunlight **:** a place sheltered from the sun **:** ground overshadowed by foliage ⟨having come . . . to a pleasant ~ near a brook —Cedomilj Mijatovic⟩ **b :** a secluded retreat **:** a retired spot **:** a quiet habitation **:** an abode sheltered from the world ⟨let us seek out some desolate ~ —Shak.⟩ **4 a** *chiefly dial* **:** the figure appearing on the part of a surface from which light is cut off **:** SHADOW **b :** an evanescent or unreal appearance **:** a lingering image of something passing away **:** something that has become reduced almost to nothing **5 shades** *pl* **a :** the shadows which gather as darkness comes on **:** the growing darkness after sunset ⟨the ~*s* of night were falling fast —H.W.Longfellow⟩ **b :** the abode of the dead or of disembodied spirits **:** NETHERWORLD, HADES **6 a :** the soul after its separation from the body **:** the form of a dead person usu. held to be perceptible to the sight although not to the touch **:** a disembodied spirit **:** GHOST ⟨followed . . . by the ~ of their dead relative —J.G.Frazer⟩ **b :** the spirit of a dead or fictional person who would prob. have been startled or horrified by a particular action or situation **7 :** something that shades: as **a :** something that intercepts or shelters from light or the direct rays of the sun **:** something that protects from heat or currents of air **:** SCREEN, SHELTER **b :** a protective cover of glass (as for a clock) **c :** a woman's head scarf or veil usu. of lace and fashionable during the 18th and 19th centuries **d** (1) **:** an appliance of more or less translucent material (as glass, silk, or paper) used chiefly to diminish or to interrupt the flux of a lamp in directions where it is not wanted — compare REFLECTOR (2) **:** an appliance (as a globe) for protecting a flame or arc lamp from air currents **e :** a device or covering designed to protect the eyes from light — see EYESHADE, SUNSHADE **f :** a protective colored or smoked glass interposed between the eye and a bright light (as of the sun) **g :** a flexible screen usu. mounted on a roller and used to obstruct or regulate light passing through a window or to obstruct the view through a window from within or without **h :** a usu. temporary structure open at the sides and providing shelter esp. from the sun **8 a :** the reproduction of the effect of shade in painting or drawing (as by closely repeated lines or by adding a darker or lighter pigment to a given hue or tint) **:** absence of complete illumination as represented pictorially **b :** the part of a picture in which shade is represented **:** the darker color expressing absence of illumination **c** (1) **:** a subdued or somber feature or quality (as of a work of art) — often used in pl. ⟨lights and ~*s* of the work were captured by the pianist⟩ (2) **:** a defect of character ⟨implacable resentment is a ~ in a character —Jane Austen⟩ **9 a :** a color produced by a pigment or dye mixture having some black pigment or dye in it — compare TINT **b :** a color slightly different from the one under consideration **c :** a dye color different from the color under consideration in some way not attributable to variation in strength of the dye used to produce that color **10 a :** a minute difference or variation (as of thought, belief, or expression) **:** NUANCE ⟨leaders of varying ~*s* of political opinion —Drew Middleton⟩ ⟨quibble over ~*s* of meaning —Lewis Nichols⟩ **b :** the quality or degree of something which is distinguished from others of like kind by slight differences **c :** a minute degree or quantity **:** a faint adumbration **:** a minute qualifying infusion **:** TINGE ⟨dropped her voice a ~ —Walter O'Meara⟩ ⟨sung a ~ too loud —Ann M.Lingg⟩ ⟨societies only a ~ less complicated than our own —Ralph Linton⟩ **11** *archaic* **:** SILHOUETTE **12 :** a facial expression of sadness or displeasure **:** CLOUD ⟨a ~ of displeasure on his brow —Sir Walter Scott⟩ ⟨a ~ of disappointment seemed to cross his face —*Yankee*⟩ **13 :** a shutter in the swell box of a pipe organ **syn** see COLOR — **in the shade 1 :** in a shaded place **:** in a position screened from a source of heat or light (as the sun's rays) **2 a :** in retirement or comparative obscurity **b :** in a state of comparative insignificance

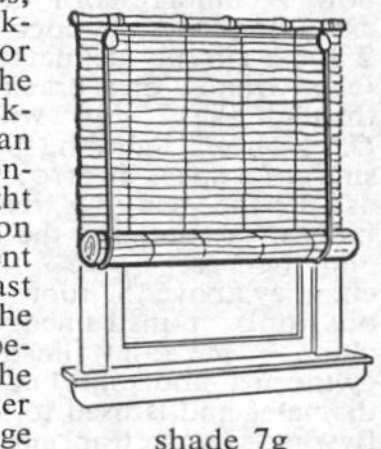
shade 7g

²shade \"\ *vb* -ED/-ING/-S [ME *shaden*, fr. *shade*, n.] *vt* **1 a :** to shelter or screen by intercepting radiated light or heat **:** keep off illumination from **:** protect from glare or heat ⟨deep porches *shaded* with bright awnings —*Amer. Guide Series: Ark.*⟩ ⟨he *shaded* his eyes with his hand⟩ **b** *obs* **:** to place in the shade **:** shelter from light or heat ⟨the cattle . . . lie and ~ themselves under their boughs —William Ellis⟩ **c :** to cover with a shade ⟨~ a lamp⟩ **2 :** to hide partly by or as if by a shadow **:** conceal from view **:** DISGUISE, SCREEN, VEIL **3 :** to darken with or as if with a shadow ⟨a melancholy smile *shaded* his face —Sir Walter Scott⟩ **4 a :** to cast into the shade (as by some exhibition of superiority) **:** surpass by a shade **:** ECLIPSE, OVERSHADOW ⟨a port which is attractive to liners . . . tends to ~ neighboring ports —F.W.Morgan⟩ **b :** to dim the brightness or luster of (as good qualities) **:** OBSCURE **5 a :** to represent the effect of shade or shadow on (an object) **b :** to add shading to (as a drawing or painting) **c :** to color so that the shades pass gradually from one to another **d :** to mark with gradations of light or color **6 :** to change by gradual transition or qualification **7 :** to reduce slightly (as the price of anything) **8 :** to lower the pitch of (an open organ pipe) by an octave by closing its top **9 :** to make (a bid, double, or redouble) in a card game on slightly less than the strength usu. required ~ *vi* **1 :** to pass by slight changes or imperceptible degrees into something else ⟨work and play ~ into each other —H.E. Scudder⟩ ⟨the level . . . cast ~*s* off into the mountains —G.G. Coulton⟩ **2 :** to undergo or exhibit minute difference or variation (as of color, value, meaning, or expression)

³shade \"\ *vt* -ED/-ING/-S [ME (northern dial.) *schaden* to distinguish, fr. OE *scēadan, scādan* to divide, separate — more at SHED] *chiefly Scot* **:** to make a part in (as the hair)

shaded *adj* **1 a :** protected from heat or light (as with shade or shadow) ⟨~ avenues⟩ **b :** having a shade ⟨a ~ lamp⟩ **2 :** covered with shadow ⟨o'er the ~ billows rushed the night —Alexander Pope⟩ **3 :** having colors that shade **:** drawn or painted with shading

shaded-pole motor \'⸗⸗,⸗-\ *n* **:** a single-phase induction motor in small ratings made self-starting by flux displacement derived by means of a permanently short-circuited, high-resistance winding or loop encircling a fraction of the pole pitch or pole piece

shade-grown \'⸗¦⸗\ *adj* **:** grown in the shade; *specif* **:** grown under cloth ⟨*shade-grown* tobacco⟩ — compare SUN-GROWN

shade grown *n, sometimes cap S&G* [*shade-grown*] **:** a tobacco grown under cloth in northern Florida and the Connecticut valley for cigar wrappers

shade·less \'shādləs\ *adj* **:** lacking shade **:** being without shelter from heat or light

shade pine *n* **:** SUGAR PINE

shade plant *n* **1 :** a plant grown to provide shade to various crops (as coffee or vanilla) that require it **2 :** a plant that grows normally in a shaded habitat which it receives only light of low intensity — compare SUN PLANT

shad·er \'shādə(r)\ *n* -s **1 :** one that shades **2 :** one that makes, tests, or colors with shades (as in dyeing and painting) **3 :** one whose work is matching colors or sorting according to colors; *esp* **:** one that selects, grades, or classifies cigars according to their color **4 :** a person who sorts brick as they are taken from a kiln

shade-ripened \'⸗¦⸗⸗\ *adj* **:** ripened in the shade rather than in the sunlight ⟨*shade-ripened* berries⟩

shade roller pin *n* **:** a small metal pin which serves as the axle for the free end of a window shade roller

shades *pl of* SHADE, *pres 3d sing of* SHADE

shadetail \'⸗,⸗\ *n, South* **:** SQUIRREL

shade-tolerant \'⸗,⸗⸗⸗\ *adj* **:** able to grow under shady conditions ⟨a *shade-tolerant* plant⟩

shade tree *n* **:** a tree (as the American elm) grown primarily to produce shade with the flowers being of secondary importance

shadflower \'⸗,⸗\ *n* **1 :** ARBUTUS 3 **2 :** JUNEBERRY 1 **3 :** WHITLOW GRASS a

shad fly *n* **:** any of several insects (as the mayfly) that appear when shad enter the rivers

shad frog *n* **:** LEOPARD FROG

shadier *comparative of* SHADY

shadiest *superlative of* SHADY

shad·i·ly \'shādəlē, -li\ *adv* **:** in a shady manner

shad·i·ness \-dēnəs, -din-\ *n* -ES **:** the quality or state of being shady ⟨~ of a deal⟩ ⟨~ of a woodland grove⟩

shading *n* -s **1 :** a covering or sheltering with shade **:** protection from heat or light **2 :** the filling up within outlines that represents the effect of more or less darkness in a picture or a drawing **3 :** a slight variation (as in color, quality, or class) **:** QUALIFICATION **4 :** a musical effect gained by subtle changes in dynamics as effected by the player **5 :** a process of compensating for unwanted signals in a television picture caused by the scanning process esp. during the trace interval or by inherent characteristics of the picture tube

shading coil *n* **:** a short-circuited coil surrounding part of the pole of an alternating-current magnet to reduce the magnetic flux in that part by currents induced in the coil and used to make single-phase motors self-starting

sha·doof *also* **sha·duf** \shə'düf, (')shä¦d-, (')sha¦d-, -düf\ *n* -s [Ar *shādūf*] **:** a counterpoised sweep used in Egypt and nearby countries for raising water usu. for irrigation purposes

¹shad·ow \'sha(,)dō, -,də; -,dəw, -,dō+V\ *n* -s [ME *shadwe*, fr. OE *sceaduwe, sceadwe*, oblique case form of *sceadu* shade, shadow — more at SHADE] **1 :** comparative darkness or shade within defined bounds **:** partial darkness or obscurity within a part of space from which rays from a source of light are cut off by an interposed opaque body ⟨turned into the ~ of woods —John Buchan⟩ ⟨under the gathering ~ of the dim, purple sky —O.E.Rölvaag⟩ ⟨the grey sagebrush and the blue-grey rock . . . were already in ~ —Willa Cather⟩ **2 a :** a reflected image (as in a mirror or in water) **b :** a colorless or scantily pigmented or stained body (as a degenerate cell or empty membrane) only faintly visible under the microscope **3 :** protecting cover (as of wings) **:** protection from danger **:** shelter from observation ⟨under the ~ of the flag⟩ **4 a :** an imperfect and faint representation **:** an indistinct image **:** a dim or mystical bodying forth **:** ADUMBRATION **b :** an unreal appearance or image **:** an imaginary or delusive vision **:** a vain and unsubstantial object of pursuit **c :** an obscure indication **:** FORESHADOWING, PREFIGURATION, SYMBOL, TYPE **d** *obs* **:** a representation in painting or drama in distinction from the reality portrayed **e :** an imitation of something **:** COPY, COUNTERPART **5 a :** the image made by an obscured space on a surface that cuts across it usu. representing in silhouette the form of the interposed body **:** the dark figure cast upon a surface by a body intercepting the rays from a source of light ⟨the ~ of a man⟩ ⟨the ~ of a tree⟩ **b :** an acoustical phenomenon similar to the optical shadow produced by an obstructing of sound waves or electric waves ⟨the acoustic ~ of an object contains the low-frequency components of the sound —G.A. Miller⟩ **6 :** a spiritual apparition **:** a spectral form **:** PHANTOM ⟨hence, horrible ~ —Shak.⟩ **7 shadows** *pl* **:** shaded parts of sky and landscape merging so as to bring on darkness ⟨night's sable ~*s* from the ocean rise —John Denham⟩ **8 a :** a shaded or darker portion of a picture usu. representing the less illuminated portions of the original **b :** the darkest areas of a photograph corresponding to the lightest areas of a negative of the same subject **9 a :** an attenuated form **:** a vestigial remnant **:** a form from which the substance has departed ⟨reptiles of today are but the veriest ~ of a mighty dynasty —W.E. Swinton⟩ **b :** a person held to resemble a shadow as a result of extreme emaciation or feebleness **10 a :** one that follows or attends like a shadow **:** an inseparable companion or follower ⟨sin and her ~ death —John Milton⟩ **b :** one that shadows as a spy or detective **:** one that follows a person in order to keep watch on his movements **11 :** a small degree or portion **:** a slight or faint appearance **:** TRACE ⟨a meaning . . . for which there is no ~ of justification —Reginald Reynolds⟩ ⟨hasn't really the ~ of a claim on us —Ellen Glasgow⟩ **12 :** a penthouse or roof over the stage of an Elizabethan theater **13** *obs* **:** something (as a veil or canopy) designed to afford shade or protection from light, heat, or observation **14 a :** influence casting a spell, gloom, or unhappiness ⟨love is sunshine, hate is ~ —H.W.Longfellow⟩ **b :** something qualifying adversely a usu. specified state or condition (as happiness, friendship, or fame) **15 a :** an area that is or is held to be within the shadow cast by an object **:** PROXIMITY, VICINITY ⟨the Alamo . . . stands in the ~ of a modern skyscraper —*Amer. Guide Series: Texas*⟩ **b :** the pervasive and dominant influence, power, or reputation of someone or something ⟨reared under the ~ of absolutism —V.L.Parrington⟩ ⟨fallen within the ~ of Roman power —Benjamin Farrington⟩ ⟨a president . . . living in the ~ of his predecessor —H.J.Laski⟩

²shadow \"\ *vb* -ED/-ING/-S [ME *shadwen*, fr. OE *sceadwian*; akin to OHG *biscatwen* to overshadow, Goth *ufarskadwjan*; denominative fr. the root of OE *sceadu* shade, shadow — more at SHADE] *vt* **1** *archaic* **:** to shelter or protect as with covering wings **:** enfold with a beneficent and protecting influence **2 a :** to cast a shadow upon **:** cover or obscure with a shadow **:** overspread with obscurity **:** DARKEN, DIM ⟨the mountains . . . heavily ~*ed* by a storm cloud —G.R.Stewart⟩ ⟨a period of . . . history that is still thickly ~*ed* —*Amer. Guide Series: Ark.*⟩ **b :** to cast a gloom over **:** CLOUD ⟨a glint of displeasure ~*ed* his eyes —Hamilton Basso⟩ ⟨his cheerful face was suddenly ~*ed* —Katharine N. Burt⟩ **3** *obs* **:** to protect or shelter from the sun **4** *obs* **:** to conceal from view or knowledge **:** keep dark

: HIDE ⟨thereby shall we ~ the numbers of our host —Shak.⟩ **5** *obs* **a** : to serve as protection or security for : take under one's protection or patronage ⟨I saw thou wert a coward and *~ed* thee —John Fletcher⟩ **b** : to screen from blame, punishment, or wrong **6** : to represent faintly, mystically, or figuratively : indicate obscurely or in slight outline : ADUMBRATE, BETOKEN, PREFIGURE, TYPIFY ⟨a statement could be delicately *~ed* by an illusion —A.L.Guérard⟩ — often used with *forth* or *out* ⟨my theory of right conduct which these pages ~ forth —Herbert Spencer⟩ ⟨~ forth the doubts that men may have —Sonya Rudikoff⟩ **7** *obs* : to paint the likeness of : DEPICT, PAINT, PORTRAY **8** : to follow like a shadow : attend or follow and watch closely esp. in a secret manner : keep under surveillance : TRAIL ⟨a detective *~ed* the suspect⟩ ⟨the cruiser was *~ed* by a submarine⟩ **9** *archaic* : SHADE 5 ⟨no grays, no tones or softness to ~ the angular blacks —E.L. Wallant⟩ **10** : to produce a shadow of ⟨the light *~ed* him against the side of the tent⟩ **11** : to prevent uniform deposition upon in electroplating — used of an object which by its position interferes with normal current distribution ~ *vi* **1** *archaic* : to cast a shadow ⟨the house *~ed* over them —Richard Llewellyn⟩ **2** *obs* : to become closely alike or verge in color **3** : to pass gradually or by degrees : shade off ⟨the mountains . . . were *~ing* into blackness —Lonnie Coleman⟩ ⟨smooth opal . . . *~ing* to deep jade beneath the rocks —Rose Macaulay⟩ **4** : to become overcast with or as if with shadows : grow dark or gloomy ⟨his eyes *~ed* with doubts —B.A. Williams⟩

³shadow \"\ *adj* [¹*shadow*] **1** : SHADY **2** : having form without substance : DUMMY ⟨a ~ garrison⟩ ⟨the ~ government in exile⟩ **3 a** : having an indistinct pattern; *esp* : having patterns printed on the warp threads before weaving or having the warp threads twisted to produce faint stripes when woven ⟨~ prints⟩ **b** : having a darker section of design usu. in contrast to a sheer background — used esp. of needlework ⟨~ lace⟩ **4** : formulated or constructed in outline so as to be capable of quick completion when needed : inactive but ready to function immediately when the need arises ⟨a ~ factory⟩ ⟨~ army⟩

shadow band *n* : one of a series of darkish narrow parallel bands seen to rush swiftly across the landscape just before or after totality in a solar eclipse probably due to optical effects of the earth's atmosphere

shadow bird *n* : HAMMERKOP

shadow blue *n* : a variable color averaging a grayish blue that is redder and paler than electric, greener and duller than copenhagen, redder and deeper than Gobelin, and greener and deeper than old china

shadow box *n* **1** *or* **shadow box frame** : a shallow enclosing case usu. with a glass front in which something (as a painting, relief, or article of merchandise) is set for protection and display **2 a** : a device built in front of a screen used for daylight projection of motion pictures to shield it from the sun **b** : a partial enclosure on top and side of a screen of a microfilm reader protecting it from extraneous light

shadowbox \'⸗⸗,⸗\ *vi* **1** : to box with an imaginary opponent esp. as a form of training **2** : to deal with an opponent cautiously usu. in order to avoid taking positive or decisive action

shadow cabinet *n* : a group of leaders of the parliamentary opposition who constitute the probable membership of the cabinet when their party is returned to power and who usu. are responsible for formulating party policy and for leading the opposition in parliamentary debate in the fields of their special competence ⟨resigned from Labour's *shadow cabinet*⟩

shadow–casting \'⸗⸗,⸗⸗\ *n* : the production of exaggerated contrast in electron microscopy by irradiating the specimen obliquely with a beam of gold atoms which makes opaque films on the slide in exact imitation of shadows

shadow cone *n* : UMBRA 3a ⟨the *shadow cone* of the moon⟩

shadow dance *n* : a dance shown by throwing the shadows of invisible performers or puppets on a screen

shad·ow·er \'shadəwə(r), -dōə-\ *n* -s : one that shadows

shadow figure *n* : SILHOUETTE

shad·ow·gram \'⸗⸗,gram\ *n* : SKIAGRAM 2

shad·ow·graph \-,graf, -ráf\ *n* **1** : SHADOW PLAY **2** : a photographic image resembling a shadow; *esp* : one made by means of X rays

shad·ow·graph·ic \¦⸗⸗¦grafik\ *adj* : of or relating to shadowgraphs

shad·ow·graph·ist \'⸗⸗,grafəst, -ráf-\ *n* -s : an expert in or practitioner of shadowgraphy

shad·ow·graphy \-rafē\ *n* -ES : the making of shadowgraphs

shadow gray *n* : a brownish gray that is lighter and slightly redder than taupe, paler than chocolate, and redder and lighter than castor

shadow green *n* : a moderate yellow green that is paler than average moss green, yellower and paler than average pea green, and yellower and duller than apple green (sense 1)

shad·ow·i·ly \'shadəwəlē, dōə-, -li\ *adv* : in a shadowy manner : like a shadow ⟨~ visible through the murk⟩

shad·ow·i·ness \-dəw|ēnəs, -dō|, |in-\ *n* -ES : the quality or state of being shadowy ⟨the ~ of night⟩ ⟨that ~ . . . you find in people whose lives are part of the social organism —W.S. Maugham⟩

shadowing *n* -s **1** : the placing or distribution of shadow (as in a scene or painting) : SHADING **2** : a faint, obscure, or mystical representation ⟨in savage theology *~s* . . . of the conception of a Supreme Deity —E.B.Tylor⟩

shadowland \'⸗⸗,⸗\ *n* : the realm peopled by shadows or submerged in shadow: as **a** : the abode of spirits or phantoms **b** : OBSCURITY **c** : the domain of the unconscious

shad·ow·less \'shadōləs, -dəl-\ *adj* : having or casting no shadow

shadowlike \'⸗⸗,⸗\ *adj* : SHADOWY

shadow line *n* **1** : the edge of the shadow of the gnomon of a sundial **2** : a thickened line in a linear drawing of an object supposed to be illuminated by parallel rays of light indicating the edges farthest from the source of light

shad·ow·ly \-dōlē, -dəl-, -li\ *adv* [¹*shadow* + *-ly*] : as a shadow : OBSCURELY ⟨~ lit with indirect lighting —Chandler Brossard⟩

shadow of death [ME *shadwe of deeth*, trans. of LL *umbra mortis*, trans. of Heb *ṣalmāweth*] : deep darkness : GLOOM

shadow play *also* **shadow pantomime** *or* **shadow show** *n* : a drama exhibited by throwing the shadows of invisible puppets or sometimes of living actors on a screen

shadow roll *n* : a thick roll of sheepskin placed across the face of a pacing horse between eyes and nostrils so that he will not look down and be confused by shadows caused by his own movements

shadow roll

shadows *pl of* SHADOW, *pres 3d sing of* SHADOW

shadow stop *n* : the smallest aperture for use in making a halftone negative

shadow striping *n* : obscure striping that gives the effect of shadowing bolder stripes with which it is associated ⟨*shadow striping* in the pattern of a zebra⟩

shadow transit *n* : the passage of the shadow of a satellite across the disk of its primary

shadow welt *n* : a lightweight section of the welt on a stocking

¹shad·owy \'shadəw|ē, -dō|, |i\ *adj* -ER/-EST [ME *shadwy*, fr. *shadwe* shadow + *-y*] **1 a** : of the nature of or resembling a shadow : FLEETING, IMAGINARY, UNSUBSTANTIAL ⟨dim, ~ forms —Bram Stoker⟩ ⟨strange fancies of unreal and ~ worlds —W.A.Butler †1848⟩ ⟨a ~ honor⟩ **b** *obs* : faintly representative : dimly embodying, representing, or foreboding : SYMBOLIC **c** : of or relating to the spirits of the dead : GHOSTLY, SPECTRAL ⟨from the river of death he recalls ~ ghosts —C.S.C. Bowen⟩ **d** : dim as a shadow : faintly perceptible : INDISTINCT VAGUE ⟨the ~ boundaries of a complex government —Edmund Burke⟩ ⟨her tender ~ voice —Elinor Wylie⟩ ⟨the ~ line between reason and faith —H.O.Taylor⟩ ⟨a ~ claim⟩ **2** : full of shade : protected from the sun : in or obscured by shadow ⟨deep ~ interiors⟩ ⟨~ cypress swamps —*Amer. Guide Series: N. C.*⟩ ⟨the wide nave and ~ aisles —Dorothy Sayers⟩ **3** : casting a shadow and affording shade ⟨a broad and ~ hat —Sir Walter Scott⟩

²shadowy \"\ *adv* : as a shadow : DIMLY ⟨in silver mail all ~ pale —Olive Custance⟩

shad porgy *n* : GRASS PORGY

shadrach \'sha,drak *sometimes* 'shā,d-\ *n* -s [after *Shadrach*, one of three loyal Hebrews who according to Dan 3:13–27 were unharmed when cast into a blazing furnace by order of King Nebuchadnezzar] : SALAMANDER 5

shads *pl of* SHAD

shad scale *n* : a scurfy grayish shrub (*Atriplex canescens*) of the western U. S. having a dense cluster of minute greenish flowers

shad tree *n* : JUNEBERRY 1

shad trout *n* : the common weakfish

shaduf *var of* SHADOOF

shady \'shādē, -di\ *adj* -ER/-EST [¹*shade* + *-y*] **1** : producing or affording shade ⟨a ~ hat of natural straw —*Sydney (Australia) Bull.*⟩ ⟨naked trees whose ~ leaves are lost —Edmund Spenser⟩ **2** : sheltered from the glare or heat of the sun's rays : protected by shade : shaded from a source of heat or light : abounding in shade ⟨~ lawns and gardens —*Amer. Guide Series: N. C.*⟩ ⟨~ places⟩ **3** : DARK ⟨the ~ night —A.E.Housman⟩ ⟨her ~ hair —Thomas Hardy⟩ **4** : quiet so as to escape notice or detection — usu. used in the phrase *keep shady* ⟨keep ~ till we want you —Edward Eggleston⟩ **5 a** : equivocal in terms of merit or morality : of questionable merit : UNCERTAIN, UNRELIABLE ⟨what looks very well one way may look very ~ the other —R.S.Surtees⟩ **b** : better kept in darkness : unable to bear investigation : having a disreputable nature or character ⟨politician of large influence but ~ reputation —B.J.Hendrick⟩ ⟨the victim of various ~ speculations —Elinor Wylie⟩ — **on the shady side of** : on the afternoon side of : older than ⟨*on the shady side of* thirty —Washington Irving⟩

shaf·fle \'shafəl\ *vi* -ED/-ING/-S [perh. alter. of *shuffle*] **1** *dial Eng* : SHUFFLE **2** *dial Eng* : LOITER

sha·fi'i \'shafē,ē, 'shäf-\ *n* -s [after al-*Shafi'i* †A.D. 820 Arab scholar and religious leader] *usu cap* **1** : an orthodox school of Muslim jurisprudence predominating in southern Arabia and Indonesia — compare HANAFI, HANBALI, MALIKI **2** *or* **sha·fi·'ite** \-fē,īt\ [*shafi'ite* fr. al-*Shafi'i* + E *-ite*] : a follower of the Shafi'i school

¹shaft \'sha|ft, -aa(ə)|, -ai|, -á|\ *n, pl* **shafts** *see sense 1b* \|f(t)s *or, esp in sense 1b*, |vz\ [ME, fr. OE *sceaft*; akin to OHG *scaft* shaft, spear, ON *skapt* shaft, handle, L *scapus* shaft, stalk, *scopa* broom, Gk *skēptron* staff, Russ *shchepat'* to split — more at CAPON] **1 a** (1) : the long handle of a spear or similar weapon (2) : SPEAR, LANCE **b** *or pl* **shaves** \|vz\ : POLE; *specif* : either of two long pieces of wood between which a horse is hitched to a vehicle **c** (1) : an arrow esp. for a longbow — compare BOLT 1a (2) : the body or stem of an arrow extending from the nock to the head — see ARROW illustration **2 a** : a sharply delineated beam shining through an opening (as a window or a break in a cloud) ⟨*~s* of sunlight pouring through the 75-foot windows —*Amer. Guide Series: N. Y. City*⟩ **b** : a lightning bolt **3** : something suggestive of the shaft of a spear or arrow : a long slender esp. cylindrical part: as **a** : the stem of a tree : TRUNK ⟨straight pine *~s*⟩ **b** : the body of a column : the cylindrical pillar between the capital and the base — see COLUMN illustration **c** : the part of a chimney above the roof **d** : the handle or helve of any of various tools or instruments (as a hammer, whip, pick, or golf club) — see GOLF illustration **e** : a bar that is commonly cylindrical and solid but sometimes hollow esp. when of large diameter and is used to support rotating pieces (as pulleys or flywheels) or to transmit power or motion by rotation — compare AXLE, FLEXIBLE SHAFT, SPINDLE **f** : the stem or midrib of a feather **g** : the narrowed basal part of any stalked structure **h** : the upright member of a cross; *esp* : the portion below the arms **i** : a rod at the end of the heddle of a loom; *also* : one of the series of harness frames on a loom — often used with a prefixed numeral in designating construction of cloth ⟨a 4⸗*shaft* twill⟩ **j** : the cylindrical part of a long bone between the enlarged ends **k** : a small architectural column (as one attached to a pier to support a vault rib or around a doorway or window) **l** : a column, obelisk, or other spire-shaped or columnar monument ⟨a marble ~ commemorates the battle —*Amer. Guide Series: Tenn.*⟩ **m** : the stem of a match **4** : any of various long hollow structures: as **a** (1) : a vertical or inclined opening of uniform and limited cross section made for finding or mining ore, raising water, or ventilating underground workings — compare ADIT (2) : a passage resembling a mine shaft in structure or function (as in a cave or a pyramid) **b** : the chamber of a blast furnace above the bosh **c** : a vertical opening or passage through the floors of a building ⟨air ~⟩ ⟨elevator ~⟩ **5 a** : a projectile (as a dart) thrown like a spear or shot like an arrow **b** : a scornful, satirical, or pithily critical remark : BARB ⟨directs *~s* of ridicule against those who would keep the artist in isolation —L.L.Snyder⟩

²shaft *vb* -ED/-ING/-S *vt* **1** : to fit with a shaft **2** *slang* : to surprise by unfair or unexpectedly harsh treatment ⟨was really *~ed* on that deal⟩ ~ *vi* : to emit or become emitted as a beam of light : BEAM ⟨sunlight *~ed* through the dust —Donald Windham⟩

shaft eye *n* : a transverse hole in a shaft for a bolt or pin

shaft feather *n* : one of the two vanes of an arrow that run on the bow — compare COCK FEATHER

shaft furnace *n* : a furnace of upright form that is charged at the top and tapped at the bottom

shaft grave *or* **shaft tomb** *n* : PIT TOMB

shaft horsepower *n* : horsepower transmitted by an engine shaft : BRAKE HORSEPOWER

shaft house *n* : a structure erected at the top of a shaft to house hoisting machinery

shaft·ing \|ftiŋ, -tēŋ\ *n* -s **1 a** : shafts or material for shafts **b** : a system of connected shafts for communicating motion **2** : a lighter or darker coloring of the shaft of a feather (as of a domestic fowl) compared with that of the web

shaft key *n* : a key fitting in a shaft to secure an operating part fastened in or to the shaft

shaft kiln *n* : a kiln consisting of a steel shell with a vertical axis and a lining of firebrick

shaft·less \|f(t)ləs\ *adj* : having no shaft

shaft louse *n* : a biting louse (*Menopon gallinae*) that commonly infests domestic fowls

shaft·man \|f(t)mən\ *n, pl* **shaftmen** : one who sinks, inspects, or repairs mine shafts

¹shaft·ment \|(t)mənt\ *n* -s [alter. (prob. influenced by *-ment*) of ME *shaftmond*, fr. OE *sceaftmund*, fr. *sceaft* shaft + *mund* hand — more at SHAFT, MANUAL] *archaic* : the distance from the tip of the extended thumb across the breadth of the palm used as a measure equivalent to about six inches : FISTMELE

²shaftment \"\ *n* -s [¹*shaft* + *-ment*] : the part of an arrow on which the crest and feathers are placed

shaft–ring \'⸗,⸗\ *n* : a decorative annulet on the shaft of a column

shafts *pl of* SHAFT, *pres 3d sing of* SHAFT

shaft–straightener \'⸗,⸗(⸗)⸗\ *n* : ARROW STRAIGHTENER

shaft tunnel *or* **shaft alley** *n* : a narrow watertight compartment through which the propeller shaft of a ship passes from the after engine-room bulkhead to the stern tube

shaftway \'⸗,⸗\ *n* : SHAFT 4c

shafty \|ftē\ *adj* -ER/-EST **1** *of wool* : having a close compact free long strong staple **2** *of a feather* : having the shaft lighter or darker than the web

¹shag \'shag, -aa(ə)-,-ai-\ *n* -s [fr. (assumed) ME *shagge*, fr. OE *sceacga*: akin to OE *scēon* to go quickly, happen, OHG *skehan* to befall, happen, ON *skegg* beard, *skaga* to project, OIr *scuchim* I depart, OSlav *skoků* leap; basic meaning: to jump, project] **1 a** : coarse matted wool, hair, or fiber ⟨the ~ of a woolly dog⟩ **b** : a matted or tangled mass of hair or fiber ⟨his great ~ of eyebrow —Eugene Walter⟩ **c** : long nap on cloth or felt ⟨~ rug⟩ **d** : a tangled or matted mass of bushes, trees, or foliage : THICKET **2 a** *archaic* : a worsted or silk cloth with a nap **b** : a shaggy garment or mat **3** : a strong coarse tobacco cut into fine shreds **4** : CORMORANT; *esp* : a European cormorant (*Phalacrocorax aristotelis*) that breeds in Great Britain — called also *green cormorant*

²shag \"\ *adj* : SHAGGY ⟨~ pony⟩

³shag \"\ *vb* **shagged; shagged; shagging; shags** *vi* : to fall or hang in shaggy masses ⟨a mean horse . . . with his head down a little and the mane *shagged* forward between the ears —R.P.Warren⟩ ~ *vt* : to make rough, jagged, or shaggy esp. by covering with shag or shaggy matter ⟨junipers *shagged* with ice —Wallace Stevens⟩ ⟨the long low wagons . . . returning in the evening *shagged* with hay —Virginia Woolf⟩

⁴shag \"\ *vt* [ME *shaggen* to toss about, prob. alter. of *shoggen* to jolt, shake — more at SHOG] *chiefly dial* : TOSS, PEG ⟨~ a stone across a pond⟩

⁵shag \"\ *n* -s [prob. short for ¹*shagrag*] : RASCAL, BLACKGUARD

⁶shag \"\ *n* -s [prob. alter. of ¹*shack*] : refuse barley or other grains

⁷shag \"\ *vt* **shagged; shagged; shagging; shags** [origin unknown] **1 a** : to chase after : chase away ⟨if another dog came in the yard he got *shagged* in a terrible hurry —P.D. Boles⟩ ⟨fields, where you *shagged* flies and slid home with the winning run —Irwin Shaw⟩ **b** : to run an errand after : FETCH **c** : FOLLOW; *specif* : to follow closely and push forward with harassment ⟨~ your crew in here —Allan Bruce⟩ **2** *slang* : to run after with intent to copulate

⁸shag \"\ *vi* **shagged; shagged; shagging; shags** [perh. alter. of ³*shack*] : to move along in a steady easy usu. slow gait : LOPE

⁹shag \"\ *n* -s [prob. fr. ⁸*shag*] : a dance step consisting of a lively hopping on each foot in turn

¹⁰shag \"\ *vi* **shagged; shagged; shagging; shags** : to dance the shag

shag·a·nap·pi \'shagə,napē, ,⸗⸗'⸗⸗\ *n* -s [modif. of Cree *pishaganâbii*, fr. *pishagan* what is flayed, hide + *âbii* cord] : a thread, cord, or thong of rawhide

shagbark \'⸗,⸗\ *n* [²*shag* + *bark*] **1 a** : SHAGBARK HICKORY **b** : a West Indian tree (*Pithecolobium micradenium*) having a contorted pod **2** : ¹THRUSH 4

shagbark hickory *n* : a tall straight erect forest tree (*Carya ovata*) that grows throughout the eastern and central U. S. chiefly in rich moist lowlands, is distinguished by a thick light gray bark which often curls back in large plates from the underlying structure, and yields a sweet edible somewhat aromatic nut — see TREE illustration **2** : a tough strong straight⸗grained light-colored wood yielded by the shagbark hickory and used esp. for implement handles

shag·gi·ly \'shagəlē, -aag-,-aig-, -li\ *adv* : in a shaggy manner

shag·gi·ness \-gēnəs, -gin-\ *n* -ES : the quality or state of being shaggy

shag·gy \-gē, -gi\ *adj* -ER/-EST [¹*shag* + *-y*] **1 a** : covered with, possessing, or consisting of usu. long, coarse, or matted hair ⟨his face was ~ with a sprouting black beard —G.R.Stewart⟩ ⟨an extraordinary growth of ~ hair on his chest —Frank Sargeson⟩ **b** : covered with or consisting of thick, tangled, or unkempt vegetation ⟨cedar, spruce, pine, and balsam find a precarious foothold on the ~ cliffs —*Amer. Guide Series: Minn.*⟩ ⟨~ garden hedges —F.G.Turnbull⟩ **c** : having a rough nap, texture, or surface ⟨a ~, cream-colored sports coat —Raymond Chandler⟩ ⟨twisted, ~ tamarisk trees —Phyllis Pearsall⟩ **d** : having hairlike processes ⟨~ tongue⟩ **2 a** : unkempt or casual in appearance or action ⟨a sad, shabby, *shaggy*-looking lot —Peter Taylor⟩ **b** : RUDE, UNPOLISHED ⟨the rough ~ boy who had lived so much in the woods —S.V. Benét⟩ **c** : casually eccentric, vague, and individualistic **3** : confused and unclear in outline, conception, or thinking ⟨a young novelist . . . under the spell of . . . the *shaggier* manuals of psychoanalysis —Sinclair Lewis⟩ ⟨thoughts without words are vague and ~ —Carl Van Doren⟩

shaggy cap *n* : SHAGGYMANE

shaggy–dog story \,⸗⸗'⸗-\ *n* **1 a** : a long-drawn-out circumstantial story concerning an inconsequential happening that impresses the teller as humorous but the hearer as boresome and pointless **b** : a similar humorous story whose humor lies in the pointlessness or irrelevance of the punch line **2** : a humorous anecdote involving a talking animal (as a horse or dog)

shaggymane \'⸗⸗,⸗\ *or* **shaggymane mushroom** *n* : a common edible mushroom (*Coprinus comatus*) having an elongated shaggy white pileus and black spores

shag hair *n* : a branched and often arborescent hair on a plant

sha·gia \shə'gēə\ *n, pl* **shagia** *or* **shagias** *usu cap* : a nomadic people of mixed Semitic origin inhabiting both sides of the Nile near the Third Cataract, speaking Arabic, and prob. descended from invaders from Arabia about the 7th century

shag·let \'shaglət\ *n* -s : a young cormorant

¹shag·rag \'sha,grag, 'shaa,graa(ə)g, 'shai,graig\ *n* [alter. (prob. influenced by ²*shag*) of *shakerag*] **1** : a ragged or contemptible person **2** : RAGTAG 1 — used in the phrase *shagrag and bobtail*

²shagrag \"\ *adj, archaic* : SHAGGY, RAGGED, UNKEMPT

¹sha·green \(')sha¦grēn, -aa¦g-, -ai¦g-, shə'g-\ *n* -s [by folk etymology (influence of ¹*shag* and *green*) fr. F *chagrin*, fr. Turk *çagri*] **1** : an untanned leather prepared from the skins of horses, asses, camels, and other animals, covered with small round granulations by pressing small seeds into the grain or hair side when moist, scraping off the roughness when dry, and soaking to cause the compressed or indented portions of the skin to swell up into relief, and dyed a bright color usu. green **2** : the rough skin of various sharks and rays when covered with small close-set tubercles

²shagreen \"\ *or* **sha·greened** \-nd\ *adj* [*shagreen* fr. ¹*shagreen*; *shagreened* fr. ¹*shagreen* + *-ed*] : made of, covered with, or resembling the surface of shagreen

shags *pl of* SHAG, *pres 3d sing of* SHAG

shah \'shä, 'shò, 'shä\ *n* -s *often cap* [Per *shāh* king — more at CHECK] : the sovereign of Iran

sha·hap·ti·an \shə'haptēən\ *or* **sa·hap·tin** \sə'haptən\ *or* **sa·hap·ti·an** \-tēən\ *n, pl* **shahaptian** *or* **shahaptians** *or* **sahaptin** *or* **sahaptins** *or* **sahaptian** *or* **sahaptians** *usu cap* **1 a** : an Indian people of a large territory along the Columbia river and its tributaries in Oregon, Washington, and northern Idaho **b** : a member of such people **2** : the language of the Shahaptian people including Nez Percé and Yakima

sha·hara \shə'ha(a)rə, -hàrə\ *n, pl* **shahara** *or* **shaharas** *usu cap* **1** : a non-Arabic-speaking people inhabiting the region between Hadhramaut and Oman **2** : a member of the Shahara people

sha·ha·rith *or* **sha·ha·rit** *or* **sha·cha·rit** *or* **sha·cha·rith** \'shäkris\ *n* -s [Heb *shaḥărīth* morning] : the daily morning liturgy of the Jews — compare MAARIB, MINHAH, MUSAF

shah·dom \'shädəm, -shòd-, 'shäd-\ *n* -s **1** : the state or territory ruled by a shah **2** : the rank or dignity of a shah

sha·hi *also* **sha·hee** *or* **cha·hi** \(')shä¦hē, (')shò¦-, (')shä¦-\ *n* -s [Per *shāhī*, fr. *shāhī* royal, fr. *shāh* king] : a former Persian unit of value equal to $\frac{1}{20}$ silver kran; *also* : a corresponding coin of silver or copper or nickel

sha·hi·di \shä hēdē\ *n* -s *usu cap* [Hindi *shāhidī*, fr. Per, witness, testimony, fr. *shāhid* one who bears witness, fr. Ar] : AKALI

sha·hin *or* **sha·heen** \shä'hēn\ *n* -s [Per *shāhīn*, fr. *shāh* king] : an Indian falcon (*Falco peregrinus peregrinator*) having the underparts of a plain unbarred ferruginous color, being related to the peregrine falcon, and used in falconry

shah·ja·han·pur \¦shäjə¦hän,pu̇r(ə)r\ *adj, usu cap* [fr. *Shahjahanpur*, city in northern India] : of or from the city of Shahjahanpur India : of the kind or style prevalent in Shahjahanpur

shah·za·da *or* **shah·za·dah** \¦shäzä¦dä\ *n* -s *often cap* [Hindi *shāh-zāda*, fr. Per, fr. *shāh* king + *zāda* son] : the son of a shah

shaikh *var of* SHEIKH

shaikh al–islam \¦shā,kalə'slām, ¦shī,k-\ *or* **sheikh ul islam** \-kůl-\ *n, usu cap S&I* [Ar *shaykh al-islām*] : the chief judge of any of various large Muslim cities; *esp* : the grand mufti of Constantinople

shai·khi *or* **shay·khi** \(')shä¦kē, (')shī¦-\ *n* -s *cap* [Ar *shaykhī*, fr. *Shaikh* Ahmad †1826 Shi'ite religious teacher] **1** : a Shi'ite sect emphasizing the mystical doctrine of a hidden imam as a living channel of communication **2** : a member of the Shaikhi sect

shai·tan *also* **shei·tan** \(')shā¦tän, (')shī¦-\ *n* -s [Ar *shayṭān*] : an evil spirit; *specif* : one of the rebellious jinn that lead men astray

shaiva *usu cap, var of* SAIVA

shakable *or* **shakeable** \'shākəbəl\ *adj* : capable of being shaken

sha·kal·sha \shə'kalshə\ *n, pl* **shakalsha** *or* **shakalshas** *usu cap* **1** : a people emigrating from Phrygia and colonizing Sicily in early times **2** : a member of the Shakalsha people

¹shake \'shāk\ *vb* **shook** \'shu̇k, *dial* 'shək\ *or chiefly dial* **shaked** \'shākt\ *or dial* **shaken**; **shak·en** \'shākən\ *or chiefly dial* **shaked** *or* **shook**; **shaking**; **shakes** [ME *shaken*, fr. OE *sceacan*; akin to OS *skakan* to depart, ON *skaka* to shake, Skt *khajati* he churns, agitates, and prob. to ON *skaga* to project — more at SHAG] *vi* **1** : to move to and fro : QUIVER, FLUTTER ⟨the long light ~*s* across the lakes —Alfred Tennyson⟩ ⟨sails *shaking* in the wind⟩ **2** : to undergo vibration esp. as the result of a blow or shock ⟨the earth itself seemed to ~ beneath my feet —W.H.Hudson †1922⟩ ⟨felt the ship ~ and toss⟩ **3 a** : to tremble as a result of physical or emotional disturbance ⟨felt his heart *shaking* within him —Marguerite Young⟩ ⟨his voice *shook* and became shrill —Kenneth Roberts⟩ ⟨were *shaking* in their shoes⟩ **b** : to become convulsed with laughter **4** : to experience a state of instability ⟨the economy was still *shaking* from the inflationary impact of the minimum wage decree —*Time*⟩ **5** : to move something to and fro, up and down, or from side to side in a brisk manner esp. in order to bring about mixing ⟨~ well before using⟩ **6** : to clasp hands ⟨agreed to ~ and be friends⟩ **7** : TRILL **8** : to form a crack by a separation between growth rings : SPLIT **9** *dial chiefly Brit* : FALL — usu. used of grain or fruit ~ *vt* **1 a** : to brandish, wave, or flourish often in a threatening manner ⟨people passing by . . . ~ their fists and curse —A.E. Housman⟩ ⟨the lightly clenched hand and fist *shaken* vigorously in the direction of the players concerned —Warwick Braithwaite⟩ **b** : to wave in farewell ⟨*shaking* her fingers playfully in the direction of the vehicle —W.M.Thackeray⟩ **2 a** : to cause to move in a quick jerky manner ⟨~ their heads like angry bulls —Goddard Lieberson⟩ ⟨rattling and *shaking* the latch —Dorothy C. Fisher⟩ **b** : to cause to be moved briskly in order to remove what adheres or is contained ⟨*shook* the dustcloth out the window⟩ ⟨*shook* the tree to get some apples⟩ **c** : to cause to be moved to and fro, up and down, or from side to side esp. in order to bring about mixing ⟨the vial is half filled and *shaken* vigorously —*Jour. of Economic Entomology*⟩ — often used with *up* **d** : to move (a part of the body) rhythmically in dancing ⟨resolved to ~ their heels . . . in jigs and Highland reels —David Grant⟩ **3 a** : to cause to quake, quiver, or vibrate ⟨the earthquake . . . *shook* all that coast —James Courage⟩ ⟨thunder that *shook* the tropical foliage —Allen Churchill⟩ ⟨the boom of a football rally ~*s* the night air —Corey Ford⟩ **b** : to cause to tremble ⟨a shudder *shook* the long emaciated frame —T.B.Costain⟩ ⟨toward afternoon another chill began to ~ her —Laura Krey⟩ **c** : to cause to become convulsed with laughter **4 a** : to take hold and move vigorously to and fro ⟨*shook* the boy until his teeth chattered⟩ ⟨*shook* him by the shoulder to wake him up⟩ **b** : WORRY 2 **5 a** : to free oneself from : cast off ⟨had *shaken* his bad habits and was firmly launched on his career —*Quick*⟩ ⟨have been disappointed so often that they cannot ~ their despair —M.H.Rubin⟩ — often used with *off* ⟨find it hard to ~ off these tentacles of organized crime —R.E.Merriam⟩ **b** : to get away from : get rid of ⟨can you ~ your friend? I want to talk to you alone —Elmer Davis⟩ ⟨the enemy gunboat has far too good a contact to be *shaken* so easily —E.L. Beach⟩ — often used with *off* ⟨there was no *shaking* off the press —Polly Adler⟩ **6 a** : to lessen the stability of : cause to waver : WEAKEN ⟨ignored any book that could ~ your faith —Virginia Woolf⟩ ⟨nothing that the emperor said or did could ~ him —Douglas Stewart⟩ **b** : to bring about an impairment of ⟨her mind had been *shaken* . . . by the cruelty of her husband —Mary H. Vorse⟩ **7 a** : to bring to a specified condition by or as if by repeated quick jerky movements ⟨the roads are so bad that we nearly get *shaken* to pieces —Rachel Henning⟩ ⟨*shook* his coat into place as he bent forward —Marguerite Steen⟩ **b** : to bring (oneself) to a specified state by or as if by a shake ⟨*shook* himself loose from the man's grasp⟩ **c** : to arouse (oneself) to or as if to activity ⟨~ thyself from the dust; arise —Isa 52:2 (AV)⟩ **8 a** : to distribute with or as if with a shake : SPRINKLE ⟨*shook* salt and pepper over the potatoes⟩ **b** *obs* : to cast down : SCATTER ⟨confounds thy fame as whirlwinds ~ fair buds —Shak.⟩ **9** *chiefly Austral* : ROB, STEAL **10** : to dislodge or eject by or as if by quick jerky movements of the support or container ⟨~ the quarry from the limb —*Amer. Guide Series: Tenn.*⟩ ⟨*shook* the sand from his shoes⟩ **11 a** : to clasp (hands) in greeting or farewell or as a sign of good will or agreement **b** : GRASP ⟨*shook* him by the hand at parting —Joseph Addison⟩ **12** : to stir the feelings of : UPSET ⟨the appalling nature of the disaster . . . *shook* her very much —Nevil Shute⟩ — often used with *up* ⟨you were all *shaken* up inside —R.H.Newman⟩ **13** : TRILL ⟨~ a note in music⟩ **14** : to cause a shake in (lumber) **15 a** : to separate the staves of (a cask) **b** : to disassemble (a cask) and bind into a shook

syn AGITATE, ROCK, CONVULSE: SHAKE means to move up and down or to and fro, usu. with sharp violence, or occas. to strike with jarring, unsettling impact ⟨as there is a high wind blowing nearly all the time, the nests are continually *shaken* to and fro —John Seago⟩ ⟨this social upheaval is *shaking* the underdeveloped parts of the world —A.H.Hansen⟩ AGITATE may suggest continued strong tossing or violent stirring or stirring up with commotion and disturbance ⟨the leaves on the trees were *agitated* as if by a high wind —W.H.Hudson †1922⟩ ⟨the water became *agitated* with the flapping of countless fins —Tom Marvel⟩ ⟨the physician interposes, frightens the family, *agitates* the patient to the utmost —H.A.Overstreet⟩ ROCK suggests a swinging back and forth, a violent swaying, or a violent impact bringing about or threatening a fall or collapse ⟨*rock* a child to sleep⟩ ⟨the road was rough and twisting, and the ambulance *rocked* a great deal —Fred Majdalany⟩ ⟨family life *rocked* with the rise in the divorce rate and the new liberty in sexual matters —Oscar Handlin⟩ CONVULSE suggests the violent, disturbed, wild motion of a spasm or paroxysm ⟨*convulsed* on the carpet in the paroxysms of an epileptic seizure —Thomas Hardy⟩ ⟨earthquakes *convulsing* the island⟩ ⟨*convulsed* with terror of hellfire —*Amer. Guide Series: Mass.*⟩ **syn** see in addition SWING

— **be shook on** *chiefly Austral* : to be infatuated with ⟨*was shook on* a big canecutter with more hair on his chest than a goat —D'Arcy Niland⟩ — **shake a leg 1** : DANCE ⟨*shaking a leg* at junketings and fairs —Siegfried Sassoon⟩ **2** : to hurry up : move quickly ⟨if you *shake a leg* and somebody doesn't get in ahead of you —John Dos Passos⟩ — **shake one's head** : to move the head from side to side esp. as an expression of disagreement, disapproval, or doubt

²shake \"\ *n* -s **1** : an act of shaking: as **a** : an act of shaking hands ⟨welcomed the visitor with a hearty ~⟩ **b** : an act of shaking oneself ⟨now lapdogs give themselves the rousing ~ —Alexander Pope⟩ **2 a** : a blow or shock that upsets the equilibrium or disturbs the balance of something ⟨the rude ~*s* which science has given to . . . their cherished convictions —Herbert Spencer⟩ **b** : EARTHQUAKE **3 a** : nervous agitation resulting esp. from fear — usu. used in pl. ⟨I don't think I got over the ~*s* for two hours —Brad Sebstad⟩ **b** : a condition or disease accompanied by marked trembling — usu. used in pl. ⟨nobody has a hangover and . . . nobody has the ~*s* —Mary McCarthy⟩ **c shakes** *pl* : MALARIA 2a ⟨the ~*s* . . . supposed to be the result of a miasma emanating from the spring plowing of wild ground —Edna Ferber⟩ **d** : an attack of the shakes **4** : something produced by or as if by shaking; as **a** (1) : a fissure or crack between and parallel to the annual rings of growth in timber usu. caused by wind or frost — compare CHECK 14a(1) (2) : a longitudinal crack in an archery bow **b** : a fissure in strata : a cleft in rock **c** : MILK SHAKE ⟨a chocolate ~⟩ **5** : a wavering, quivering, or alternating motion caused by or as if by a blow or shock **6** : TRILL **7 a** : a very brief period of time : INSTANT ⟨for a ~ they had stood there and looked at each other —Conrad Richter⟩ **b** : a unit of time used in nuclear physics and related fields that constitutes one hundredth of a microsecond **8 shakes** *pl* : one of importance or ability — usu. used in the phrase *no great shakes* ⟨no great ~*s* as a philosopher —Wanda Neff⟩ **9a** (1) : STAVE 2a (2) : SHOOK 1a **b** : a shingle split from a piece of log usu. three or four feet long **10** : ³DEAL 2b ⟨the honest merchants who gave baffled marines a square ~ —L. M.Uris⟩ **11** : DISMISSAL ⟨they all give him the cold ~ —Mark Twain⟩ **12** : the mechanism that shakes the wet end of a fourdrinier paper machine sideways and thereby causes the fibers to felt together as they settle through the water **13** *Brit* : a slur or mackle in printing **14** : BACKLASH **15** : SHAKE CULTURE **16 a** : the distance between the fork and a roller in a watch while at the lock position **b** : the space between the let-off of an escape-wheel tooth and pallet stone in a watch while at the lock position **c** : the end play of arbors in a watch

shake·able *var of* SHAKABLE

shake-bag \'-,-\ *n* **1** *archaic* : a cock turned out of a bag to fight **2** *archaic* : a rascally or roguish person

shake-bolt \'-,-\ *n* : a bolt of timber used in making shakes

shake-cabin \'-,--\ *n* [²*shake* (shingle) + *cabin*] : a cabin for temporary lodging

shake culture *n* : a deep culture of agar or gelatin through which the inoculum is evenly distributed by shaking before the medium is solidified and which is used chiefly for the demonstration of anaerobic colonies

shaked *chiefly dial past of* SHAKE

¹shakedown \'-,-\ *n* -s [partly fr. the phrase *shake down*; partly fr. *shake down*, v.] **1** : an improvised bed; *specif* : one made up on the floor **2** : a boisterous dance **3** : an act or instance of obtaining money in a dishonest or illegal manner; *esp* : EXTORTION ⟨an unparalleled opportunity for ~ and blackmail —Morris Ploscowe⟩ **4** : a thorough search ⟨a ~ that didn't leave a tent fold unexplored —F.B.Gipson⟩ **5** : an act or process of bringing to a more satisfactory state : ADJUSTMENT ⟨the economic ~ which the industry has experienced —*Financial World*⟩

²shakedown \"\ *adj* : designed to test a new ship or airplane under operating conditions and to familiarize the crew with it ⟨~ cruise⟩ ⟨~ flight⟩

shake down *vb* [¹*shake* + *down*, adv.] *vi* **1 a** : to take up temporary quarters ⟨a good plan for me to *shake down* in New York alone . . . before you join me —Margaret A. Barnes⟩ **b** : to occupy an improvised or hastily prepared bed ⟨had to be content to *shake down* with blankets in the inn parlor —B.L.K. Henderson⟩ **2 a** : to become accustomed or conditioned esp. to new surroundings or new duties ⟨four months . . . was long enough for a new man to *shake down* —Edwards Park⟩ **b** : to undergo a period of adjustment : settle down ⟨until the whole entertainment business *shakes down* and new patterns have been established —*Publishers' Weekly*⟩ **3** : to become reduced ⟨the fighting *shook down* to a straight infantry battle —*Newsweek*⟩ ~ *vt* **1** : to obtain money from in a dishonest or illegal manner (as under pretense of official authority or under promise of protection) ⟨impostors . . . *shook down* soldiers by pretending to arrest them —Dixon Wecter⟩ **2** : to make a thorough search of ⟨decided to *shake down* the inmates to make sure nothing had been smuggled into the jail —*Police Detective*⟩ **3** : to bring about a reduction of ⟨ordered . . . to *shake down* the hundreds of duplicating and overlapping service boards —*Time*⟩ **4** : to test on a shakedown cruise ⟨the work . . . included training men and *shaking down* the ships for the Pacific theater —Walter Karig⟩

shake flask *n* : a culture flask (as for molds) in which the medium is kept uniform by constant agitation during incubation

shakefork \'-,-\ *n* [ME *schakforke*, fr. *schaken*, *shaken* to shake + *forke* fork] **1** *chiefly dial* : a fork for shaking hay or straw **2** : a heraldic ordinary or charge having the form of a Y with couped and pointed ends — compare PAIRLE

shakefork 2

shake-hand \'-,-, -'-\ *n* : a token payment consisting of goods or money given an African tribal landowner for the use of his land

shake-hands \'-,-, -'-\ *n pl but usu sing in constr* : HANDSHAKE

shaken [ME, fr. OE *scacen*] *dial past of* SHAKE, *past part of* SHAKE

shake-off \'-,-\ *n* -s [fr. the phrase *shake off*] : an act or instance of getting rid of what is unpleasant, undesirable, or unwanted

shake off *vt* [¹*shake* + *off*, adv.] *of a baseball pitcher* : to express disagreement with (as a catcher's sign) by a negative gesture

shake out *vt* [ME *shaken out* to remove with or as if with a shake, fr. *shaken* to shake + *out*, adv.] **1** : to let out with or as if with a shake ⟨took that whip from his saddle horn and *shook it out* —H.G.Evarts⟩ **2** : to drive (weak speculators) from the market by increasing margin requirements or causing prices to move adversely

shake-out \'-,-\ *n* -s [*shake out*] **1** : an act or process of shaking out **2** : severe liquidation in a market at declining prices usu. with much forced or frightened selling **b** : a moderate slowing down of commercial and industrial activity and decrease in prices and employment after a protracted period of inflation **3** : the removal of metal castings from a mold

shakeproof \'-,-\ *adj* : capable of withstanding vibration

shak·er \'shākə(r)\ *n* -s [ME *schakare*, fr. *schaken*, *shaken* to shake + ME *-er*, *-ere*, *-are* -er] **1 a** : one that shakes ⟨thou mighty ~ of the earth —George Chapman⟩; *specif* : a worker who shakes things by hand or by machine to clean, separate, size, settle, loosen, or dry them **b** : any of various utensils or machines used in shaking: as (1) : a conveyor on which materials (as coal) are shaken to and fro by an eccentric or similar action (2) : a reciprocating rack in a thresher or combine that sifts grain and chaff from the straw (3) : a vibrating screen used in a distillery to clean grain; *also* : a similar screen used to separate spent beer into thick stillage and thin stillage (4) : a container with perforated top from which something (as salt) is shaken (5) : a utensil in which the ingredients of a mixed drink are prepared by shaking or stirring **2** *usu cap* : a member of any of several religious groups: as **a** [so called fr. a former practice of performing a dance with shaking movements as a part of worship] : a member of a communal and celibate religious body originating in England in the mid 18th century and brought to the U.S. in 1774, holding that God is both male and female, and stressing the obligation of living a simple and strict life under the guidance of the Holy Spirit **b** : a member of a Northwest Indian religious group founded in the late 19th century that combines traditional Christian beliefs with indigenous elements **3** *archaic* : FANTAIL 2a

shaker 1b(5)

shakerag \'-,-\ *n* [¹*shake* + *rag*, n.] *archaic* : an unkempt disreputable person

shak·er·ess \'shākərəs\ *n* -ES *usu cap* : a Shaker woman

shak·er·ful \'shākə(r),fu̇l\ *n* -s : as much as a shaker will hold ⟨a ~ of salt⟩

shaker furniture *n*, *usu cap S* : wooden furniture made in the U.S. in the late 18th and early 19th centuries by the Shakers and characterized by simplicity and purity of design, sound construction, and complete practicality

shak·er·ism \'shākə,rizəm\ *n* -s *usu cap* : the beliefs and practices of the Shakers

shaker knit *adj* : coarse flat-knit

shaker tumbler *n* : a machine for untangling damp flat pieces of laundry and preparing them for ironing

shakes *pres 3d sing of* SHAKE, *pl of* SHAKE

¹shake·spear·ean *or* **shake·spear·ian** *also* **shak·sper·ean** *or* **shak·sper·ian** \(')shāk¦spirēən\ *adj*, *usu cap* [William *Shakespeare* (or *Shakspere*) †1616 Eng. dramatist and poet + E *-an*] : of, relating to, or having the characteristics of Shakespeare or his writings

²shakespearean *or* **shakespearian** *also* **shaksperean** *or* **shaksperian** \"\ *n* -s *usu cap* : an authority on or devotee of Shakespeare; *specif* : a specialist in the works of Shakespeare

shake·spear·eana *or* **shake·spear·iana** \(,)shāk,spirē'anə, -'änə, -'ānə *also* -'anə\ *n pl*, *usu cap* [William *Shakespeare* + E *-ana*] : collected items by, about, or relating to Shakespeare

shake·spear·ean·ize \'-'--ə,nīz\ *vt* -ED/-ING/-S *often cap* : to treat in the manner of Shakespeare

shakespearean sonnet *n*, *usu cap 1st S* : ENGLISH SONNET

shake up *vt* **1** *obs* : to denounce or chide vehemently ⟨go apart . . . and thou shalt hear how he will *shake me up* —Shak.⟩ **2 a** : to loosen with or as if with a shake ⟨*shook up* and arranged my pillows —Anne Marsh⟩ **b** : to arouse with or as if with a shake ⟨headed for the chart house to *shake up* the radar crew —K.M.Dodson⟩ **3** : to jar by or as if by a physical shock ⟨the collision *shook up* the drivers of the two cars⟩ **4** : HURRY — usu. used in the phrase *shake it up* ⟨*shake it up*, you fellows . . . we don't have all day —Ralph Ellison⟩ **5** : to effect an extensive and often drastic rearrangement or reorganization of ⟨a trend that has *shaken up* the marketing notions of manufacturers —*Monsanto Mag.*⟩ ⟨the detective force was *shaken up* —Allan Nevins⟩

shake-up \'-,-\ *n* -s [*shake up*] **1** : MAKESHIFT; *specif* : a hastily constructed building **2** : an act or instance of shaking up; *specif* : an extensive and often drastic rearrangement or reorganization ⟨is expected to result in personnel ~*s* in Soviet embassies —*N.Y.Times*⟩

shake wave *n* : a seismic disturbance in which the motion of particles is perpendicular to the direction of the wave's propagation — compare LOVE WAVE

shakh·ty \'shäktē\ *adj*, *usu cap* [fr. *Shakhty*, city in southwest U.S.S.R.] : of or from the city of Shakhty, U.S.S.R. : of the kind or style prevalent in Shakhty

shak·i·ly \'shākəlē, -li\ *adv* : in a shaky manner

shak·i·ness \-kēnəs, -kin-\ *n* -ES : the quality or state of being shaky

shaking *n* -s [ME, fr. gerund of *shaken* to shake] **1** : something that is shaken down, out, or off — usu. used in pl. **2 shakings** *pl* : odds and ends of waste rope, canvas, and small stuff used esp. in making oakum

shaking chill *n* : a chill of severe degree

shaking grate *n* : a grate that can be shaken to drop ashes accumulated at the base of the bed of coals

shak·ing·ly *adv* : in a shaking manner

shaking palsy *n* : PARALYSIS AGITANS

shaking prairie *n* : a plain of delta land (as in Louisiana) with a soil of matted vegetable mold resting upon water, peat, or quicksands and vibrating to the tread

shaking quaker *n*, *usu cap S&Q* : SHAKER 2a

shaking table *n* : a table used for concentrating ores — compare WILFLEY TABLE

shako \'sha(,)kō, 'shā(-, 'shä(-\ *n*, *pl* **shakos** *or* **shakoes** [F *shako*, *schako*, fr. Hung *csákó*, prob. fr. G *zacke*, *zacken* peak, point, fr. MHG *zacke*, modif. of MLG *tacke* pointed instrument, sharp point — more at TACK] : a stiff military headdress with a metal plate in front, a high crown, and a plume

shako

shaksperean *or* **shaksperian** *usu cap*, *var of* SHAKESPEAREAN

shak·ta *or* **sak·ta** \'shäktə\ *n* -s *usu cap* [Skt *śākta* related to Shakti, fr. *Śakti*] : a worshiper of Shakti as a goddess

shak·ti *or* **sak·ti** \-tē\ *n* -s [Skt *śakti*, *Śakti*, fr. *śaknoti* he is strong, is able; akin to OIr *cēcht* power, Toch A *kākmart* lordship] **1** : the creative energy of nature : life force **2** *usu cap* : the dynamic energy of a Hindu god (as Siva) personified as his female consort

shak·tism *or* **sak·tism** \-,tizəm\ *n* -s *usu cap* : a sect comprising the worshipers of Shakti under various names (as Kali, Durga) divided into a mother cult of devotion through contemplation and pure humble activity and a tantric cult with magical orgiastic rites involving the use of wine, meat, fish, grain, and sexual intercourse — called also respectively *right-hand Shaktism*, *left-hand Shaktism*

sha·ku \'shä(,)kü\ *n*, *pl* **shaku** [Jap] : a Japanese unit of length equal to 11.93 inches

shaky \'shākē, -ki\ *adj* -ER/-EST **1** : characterized by shakes ⟨~ timber⟩ **2 a** : marked by insecurity or instability : likely to fall or be overthrown : PRECARIOUS ⟨extremism will wreck the present ~ center government —A.E.Stevenson b.1900⟩ ⟨the ~ market for cars and other durable goods —George Soule⟩ **b** : lacking in firmness of beliefs, principles, or allegiance : UNSETTLED ⟨this loyalty . . . does not become ~ or dubious as the years pass —D.F.Miller⟩ ⟨came to college with ~ religious foundations —W.J.Whalen⟩ **c** : lacking in authority, correctness, or reliability : QUESTIONABLE, UNTRUSTWORTHY ⟨studies . . . based on extremely ~ experimental methods —Martin Gardner⟩ ⟨was still ~ in English grammar —John Buchan⟩ ⟨in making such judgments . . . I am on ~ ground —S.L.Payne⟩ **3 a** : somewhat unsound in health ⟨am rather ~ just now —Charles Dickens⟩ **b** : characterized by shaking : TREMBLING, TREMULOUS ⟨lit a cigarette with ~ fingers —J.C.Powys⟩ ⟨a hoarse and ~ voice —Sinclair Lewis⟩ **4** : easily shaken : likely to give way or break down : RICKETY ⟨a ~ chair⟩ **5** : marked by or giving rise to jolting : BUMPY ⟨a ~ ride through the fields in a cart⟩

sha·lach mo·nos *or* **shalach ma·noth** \,shä,läk'mō,nōs, -,nəs\ *n* [*shalach monos* fr. Yiddish *shlakh mones*, fr. Heb *mishlōaḥ mānōth* sending of portions; *shalach manoth* fr. NHeb *shālaḥ mānōth*, alter. of Heb *mishlōaḥ mānōth*] **1** : the exchange of gifts or the sending of gifts to the poor at the time of the Purim festival **2** : a Purim gift consisting typically of cakes, confections, fruit, wine, or money

sha·la·ko \shə'lä(,)kō\ *n* -s *usu cap* [Zuñi] **1** *or* **shalako dancer** : one of the dancers impersonating a Zuñi mythical being of extraordinary stature **2** : a Zuñi ceremony in which Shalakos play a central role and which celebrates the advent or departure of the kachinas

¹shale \'shāl, *esp before pause or consonant* -āəl\ *n* -s *often attrib* [ME, fr. OE *scalu*, *scealu* — more at SCALE] **1** *obs* : SHELL, HUSK **2** *dial chiefly Eng* : SCALE **3** *dial chiefly Eng* : a mesh of a net **4** : a fissile rock that is formed by the consolidation of clay, mud, or silt, has a finely stratified or laminated structure parallel to the bedding, and is composed of minerals that have been essentially unaltered since deposition

²shale *vt* -ED/-ING/-S [ME *shalen*, fr. *shale*, n.] *obs* : to remove the shell from

³shale *same as* ¹SHALE\ *vi* -ED/-ING/-S [ME *schaylen*] *chiefly dial* : SHUFFLE

shale clay *n* : a clay produced by grinding shale and used for brick, tile, and pottery

shale green *n* : MALACHITE GREEN 3

shale naphtha *or* **shale spirit** *n* : naphtha obtained by refining shale oil

shale oil *n* : an oil obtained from oil shale by heating usu. in retorts : the crude dark green to brown oil from the first distillation that on refining yields liquid fuels and other useful products

shaley *var of* SHALY

shalier *comparative of* SHALY

shaliest *superlative of* SHALY

shall \shəl, (¦)shal\ *vb*, *past* **should** \shəd, (¦)shu̇d\ *or archaic 2d sing* **shouldst** \shə(d)dzt, (¦)shu̇|, |dst, |tst\ *or* **should·est** \¦shu̇dəst\ *pres sing & pl* **shall** *or archaic 2d sing* **shalt** \shəlt, (¦)shalt\ [ME *shal* owe, owes, ought to, must, am going to, is going to (1st & 3d sing. pres. indic., past *sholde*), fr. OE *sceal* owe, owes, ought to, must (past *sceolde*); akin to OHG *scal* owe, owes, ought to, must (infin. *scolan*), ON *skal* must (infin. *skulu*), Goth *skal* owe, owes, ought to, must, OE *scyld* debt, obligation, OHG *sculd*, ON *skuld*, Lith *skolà* debt] *verbal auxiliary* **1** *archaic* **a** : will have to : MUST ⟨he that parts us ~ bring a brand from heaven —Shak.⟩ **b** : will be able to : CAN ⟨how with this rage ~ beauty hold a plea —Shak.⟩ **2 a** — used to express a command or exhortation ⟨you ~ not kill —Exod 20:13 (RSV)⟩ ⟨ye ~ pray for the president of these United States —*Bk. of Com. Prayer*⟩ ⟨thou *shalt* let her go whither she will —Deut 21:14 (AV)⟩ **b** — used in laws, regulations, or directives to express what is mandatory ⟨a vessel when under way ~ carry at her stern a white light —*U.S.Code*⟩ ⟨it ~ be unlawful for any person to keep any wild animal in captivity —*Maine Hunting & Trapping Laws*⟩ **3 a** — used to express what is inevitable or what seems to be fated or decreed or likely to happen in the future ⟨cherubim and seraphim falling down before Thee, which wert and art and evermore ~ be —Reginald Heber⟩ ⟨those who can best bear taxation ~ have to do it —Francis Downing⟩ ⟨what-e'er ~ be, don't let anyone bomb me —John Betjeman⟩ **b** — used to express simple futurity ⟨when ~ we three meet again —Shak.⟩ ⟨I ~ just put these papers together . . . and send them off by the morning mail —A.J.Coutts⟩ ⟨even if you are too stingy to buy a guide book you ~ not remain uninstructed —Douglas Goldring⟩ ⟨~ you want to see me often —Arnold Bennett⟩ ⟨no young man believes he ~ ever die —William Hazlitt⟩ ⟨again ~ pleasure overflow thy cup with sweetness —Robert Bridges †1930⟩ ⟨~ he chat in an amiable way about things in general —Walter Goodman⟩ ⟨a brief story ~ suffice —C.H.Grandgent⟩ ⟨in the following chapter . . . the reader ~ be presented with examples —W.H.Mallock⟩ ⟨we have . . . agreed that they ~ publish their document and we ours —Sir Winston Churchill⟩ ⟨and all ~ come out right —John Galsworthy⟩ **4** — used to express determination ⟨one of the principal reasons why I have been against commercial gambling . . . and why I always ~ be —*New Republic*⟩ ⟨I came through and I ~ return —Douglas MacArthur⟩ ⟨the stone belongs to Scotland . . . we ~ get it back —Wendy Wood⟩ ⟨say what ye will I ~ deny no more —P.B.Shelley⟩ ⟨it ~ never break my heart I promise you —R.B.Sheridan⟩ **~ *vi* :** will go ⟨he to England ~ along with you —Shak.⟩

shal·lon \ˈshalən\ *n* -s [of AmerInd origin; akin to Chinook *-klkwšala* salal] **1 :** SALAL **2 :** the fruit of the salal

shal·loon \shəˈlün\ *n* -s [*Châlons*-sur-Marne, northeast France] **:** a lightweight twilled fabric of wool or worsted used chiefly for linings of coats and uniforms

shal·lop \ˈshaləp\ *n* -s [MF *chaloupe* — more at CHALOUPE] **1 :** a usu. 2-masted ship with lugsails **2 :** a small open boat propelled by oars or sails and used chiefly in shallow waters

shal·lot \shəˈlät, *usu* -äd·+V\ *n* -s [modif. of F *échalote*, fr. MF *eschalotte*, alter. of *eschaloigne*, fr. (assumed) VL *escalonia* — more at SCALLION] **1 a :** a bulbous perennial herb (*Allium ascalonicum*) that resembles an onion and produces small clustered bulbs used in seasoning **b :** GREEN ONION **2 :** a thin metal tube in an organ reed pipe against which the reed or tongue is placed

¹shal·low \ˈsha(ˌ)lō, -lə; -ləw, -lō+V\ *adj* -ER/-EST [ME *schalowe*; prob. akin to OE *sceald* shallow, Gk *skellein* to dry up — more at SKELETON] **1 a :** having little depth **:** not deep ⟨~ water⟩ ⟨a ~ dish⟩ ⟨~ wells⟩ ⟨a ~ grave⟩ ⟨~ valleys⟩ **b** *of soil* **:** forming a thin layer over rock **c :** departing from the horizontal by only a few degrees — used of an airplane dive, glide, or climb **2 a :** having little extension inward or backward ⟨the broad flight of ~ steps —Charles Dickens⟩ ⟨office buildings have taken the form of ~ slabs —Lewis Mumford⟩ ⟨a ~ bridgehead had been established —P.W. Thompson⟩ **b** *of a lens* **:** slightly convex or concave **3 a :** not penetrating farther than the easily or quickly apprehended **:** markedly obvious or apparent ⟨will not bare my soul to their ~ prying eyes —Oscar Wilde⟩ ⟨his short book is repetitious, untidy in form, ~ in characterization —Charles Lee⟩ ⟨offhand sayings, flippant judgments, and ~ generalizations —J.H.Newman⟩ **b :** lacking in depth of knowledge, thought, or feeling **:** SUPERFICIAL ⟨the general rule that specialists must be narrow and generalists ~ —W.B.Fagg⟩ ⟨a ~ demagogue who incited the mob —V.L.Parrington⟩ **4** *of musical tone* **:** lacking resonance **:** THIN **5** *of breathing* **:** displacing comparatively little air **:** WEAK

²shallow \"\ *vb* -ED/-ING/-S *vt* **:** to make shallow ⟨the slow current of the silt-laden water ~*ed* the canal —E.L.Sabin⟩ **~** *vi* **:** to become shallow ⟨the creek gully ~*ed* and widened —H.L.Davis⟩

³shallow \"\ *n* -s **1 :** a shallow place or area in a body of water — usu. used in pl. but sometimes sing. in constr. ⟨wading in the rocky ~*s* of the river —Marcia Davenport⟩ ⟨the sloop . . . skimming a clear glass-green ~*s* —Nelson Hayes⟩ **2 :** a low-crowned hat worn by men in the late 18th and early 19th centuries **3** *Brit* **:** a basket, tray, or cart used by street peddlers

⁴shallow \"\ *adv* **:** to or at a slight depth

shal·low·ish \ˈshaləwish, -lōi-\ *adj* **:** somewhat shallow

shal·low·ly *adv* **:** in a shallow manner

shal·low·ness *n* -ES **:** the quality or state of being shallow

shallow-pate \ˈ=(ˌ)=ˌ=\ *n, archaic* **:** a person of superficial intellectual achievements or abilities

shal·lu \ˈshaˌlü\ *n* -s [Marathi *śāḷū*] **:** any of various grain sorghums usu. held to constitute a distinct variety (*Sorghum vulgare roxburghii*), introduced into the U.S. from India, and having slender dry stalks, large open pale yellow heads, and small hard seeds that are exposed at maturity

shalm *var of* SHAWM

sha·lom *or* **sho·lom** \shäˈlōm\ *interj* [Heb *shālōm* well-being, peace] — used as a Jewish greeting and farewell

shalom ale·chem *or* **sholom alei·chem** *or* **sholom alei·chem** \ˈshōləməˈläkəm\ *interj* [Heb *shālōm ʿalēkhem* peace unto you] — used as a traditional Jewish greeting

sha·losh seu·doth *or* **shalosh seu·dot** *or* **shalosh seu·dos** \ˈshä,lō(sh)ˈsü,dōt(h), -ˌdōs, ˈshäl ə(sh)ˈsüdəs\ *n* [Yiddish & LHeb; Yiddish *shalesh seudes*, fr. LHeb *shālōsh sĕʿūdhōth* 3 meals] **:** the 3d meal eaten on the Sabbath as ordained in the Talmud and usu. served as light refreshments accompanied by songs and ceremonies late in the afternoon following the minhah service in the synagogue

shalt *archaic pres 2d sing of* SHALL

shaltie \ˈshalti, ˈshäl-\ *Scot var of* SHELTY

shaly *or* **shaley** \ˈshālē, -li\ *adj* **shalier; shaliest** [ˈ*shale* + *-y*] **:** of, containing, or resembling shale

¹sham \ˈsham, -aa(ə)m\ *n* -s [perh. fr. E dial. *sham* shame, alter. of E ¹*shame*] **1 :** a trick that deludes **:** HOAX ⟨the so-called sale of stocks was a mere ~⟩ **2 :** cheap falseness **:** HYPOCRISY, DECEITFULNESS ⟨saw through the hollowness, the ~, the silliness of the empty pageant —Oscar Wilde⟩ **3 :** a decorative piece of cloth that is made to simulate an article of personal or household linen and is used in place of it or over it; *specif* **:** PILLOW SHAM **4 :** a fraudulent imitation **:** a counterfeit purporting to be genuine ⟨has reduced national sovereignty to a ~ although it has left its outward symbols intact —Isaac Deutscher⟩ **5 :** a person who shams **syn** see IMPOSTURE

²sham \"\ *vb* **shammed; shammed; shamming; shams** *vt* **1** *archaic* **:** TRICK, DECEIVE, CHEAT **2 :** to put (as into a desirable position) by fraud ⟨*shammed* herself into favor at court⟩ **3** *obs* **:** to get rid of by fraud **:** pass off **4 :** to go through the external motions necessary to counterfeit ⟨have *shammed* headache and have the garden all to myself —G.B.Shaw⟩ **~** *vi* **1 :** to act intentionally so as to give a false impression **:** FAKE ⟨decided she was not sick but only *shamming*⟩ **2 :** to pretend to be ⟨if you want me for a friend you must not ~ stupid —George Meredith⟩ **syn** see ASSUME — **sham abraham** *usu cap A* [*Abraham*, Biblical patriarch of the Jews; prob. fr. the use of the term *abraham-man* to denote a beggar feigning lunacy] **:** to feign sickness **:** MALINGER

³sham \"\ *adj* **:** marked by falseness: as **a :** not genuine ⟨the reaction of a terribly sincere spirit to something he believes to be ~ and sophisticated —Herbert Read⟩ ⟨fought ~ battles while waiting for the real thing⟩ ⟨~ pearls⟩ **b :** having such poor quality as to seem false **:** ADULTERATED ⟨~ tea, ~ jam, processed butter, gray bread scorched into toast —Wyndham Lewis⟩ **syn** see COUNTERFEIT

sha·ma \ˈshämə\ *n* -s [Hindi *śāmā*] **:** an Indian thrush (*Copsychus malabaricus*) that is noted for its song

sha·mal *or* **shi·mal** \shəˈmäl\ *n* -s [Ar *shamāl, shimāl*] **:** a northwesterly wind of Iraq and the Persian gulf

sha·ma millet \ˈshämə-\ *n* [Hindi *sāmā, śāmā*, fr. Skt *śyāmāka* millet] **:** a tropical Asiatic grass (*Echinochloa colona*) whose seeds are used as food in India

¹sha·man \ˈshämən, ˈshā-, ˈsha-, ˈshā-, shəˈmän, -əˈmän\ *n* -s [Russ or Tungus; Russ, fr. Tungus *šaman* shaman, Buddhist monk, fr. Pali *samaṇa* Buddhist monk, fr. Skt *śramaṇa* Buddhist monk, ascetic, fr. *śrama* fatigue, exertion, religious exercise — more at ASHRAM] **:** a priest-doctor who uses magic to cure the sick, to divine the hidden, and to control events that affect the welfare of the people

²shaman \"\ *adj* **:** SHAMANISTIC

sha·man·ic \shəˈmanik, -män-, -män\ *adj* **:** SHAMANISTIC

sha·man·ism \ˈshäməˌnizəm, ˈshā-, ˈsha-\ *n* -s **1 :** a religion of the Ural-Altaic peoples of northern Asia and Europe that is characterized by the belief that the unseen world of gods, demons, and ancestral spirits is responsive only to the shamans **2 :** religious practices similar to the shamanism of the Ural-Altaic peoples of northern Asia and Europe followed esp. among Indians of No. America and characterized by use of the mediumistic trance

sha·man·ist \-ˌnəst\ *n* -s **:** one who believes in or practices shamanism

sha·man·is·tic \ˌ==ˈristik, -tēk\ *or* **shamanist** *adj* **:** of, relating to, or characteristic of shamanism or shamanists

shamanistic dance *n* **:** a frenzied trance dance that is the climax of a shaman's ritual for cure or divination

sha·man·ize \ˈ==ˌnīz\ *vi* -ED/-ING/-S **:** to perform the functions of a shaman

shamas *or* **shamash** *var of* SHAMMASH

sham·ba \ˈshämbə\ *n* -s [Swahili, plantation] **1** *Africa* **:** a piece of ground under cultivation **:** GARDEN **2** *Africa* **:** PLANTATION

sham·ba·la \shämˈbälə\ *n, pl* **shambala** *or* **shambalas** *usu cap* **1 a :** a Bantu people of eastern Tanganyika **b :** a member of such people **2 :** the language of the Shambala people

¹sham·ble \ˈshambəl, -aam-\ *vt* -ED/-ING/-S [fr. *shambles*] **:** SLAUGHTER

²shamble \"\ *adj* [fr. obs. E *shamble* table for the exhibition of meat for sale, fr. ME *shamel*; fr. the use of the expression *shamble legs* to refer to a person's legs resembling those of such a table] **:** BOWED, MALFORMED ⟨hobbled along on his ~ legs⟩

³shamble \"\ *vi* **shambled; shambled; shambling** \-b(ə)liŋ\ **shambles 1 :** to walk awkwardly with dragging feet **:** SHUFFLE **2 :** to move awkwardly ⟨a crab *shambled* across the uneven bottom of the pool⟩ ⟨exercised a style that *shambled* and wobbled self-consciously in a welter of qualifications —Van Wyck Brooks⟩

⁴shamble \"\ *n* -s [³*shamble*] **:** a shambling gait

sham·bles \-lz\ *n pl but usu sing in constr, also* **shamble** [*shambles* fr. pl. of *shamble* meat market (also obs. E *shamble* table for the exhibition of meat for sale), fr. ME *shamel* table for the exhibition of meat for sale, shop counter, footstool, fr. OE *scamul, sceamul* money changer's table, stool; akin to MD *schamel* footstool, OHG *scamal*; all fr. a prehistoric WGmc word borrowed fr. (assumed) VL *scamellus* small bench, dim. of L *scamnum* bench, stool; akin to Skt *skabhnoti* he supports] **1** *archaic* **:** a meat market **2 :** SLAUGHTERHOUSE **2 3 a :** a place of mass slaughter or bloodshed ⟨the bridge instantly became a ~, every officer and man on that key position being either killed or wounded —Russell Grenfell⟩ **b (1) :** a scene of great destruction ⟨the imposing entrance . . . is a ~ and inside the quadrangle the great aula is demolished from a direct bomb hit —J.G.Gray⟩ **(2) :** the result of great destruction **:** WRECKAGE, WRECK ⟨have not cleaned up the ~ of bombing —Ruth Benedict⟩ ⟨this buxom ball of fire makes a ~ of decorum —Irving Kolodin⟩ **(3) :** the state of being wrecked ⟨the bombers left the city in ~⟩ **c (1) :** a scene of great disorder ⟨the apartment became a ~ —S.J.Perelman⟩ ⟨conference this year was an utter ~ chaired by an elderly lawyer who apparently could neither speak nor hear —A.F.Buchan⟩ **(2) :** great confusion **:** MESS ⟨their ideals are vanity and illusion and their pretended moralities a ~ —Irwin Edman⟩

shambling *adj* [fr. pres. part. of ³*shamble*] **:** characterized by slow awkward movement ⟨a ~ village in which little happened⟩

sham·bling·ly *adv* **:** in a shambling manner

¹shame \ˈshām\ *n* -s [ME, fr. OE *scamu, sceamu*; akin to OHG *scama* shame, ON *skömm*] **1 a :** a painful emotion caused by consciousness of guilt, shortcoming, or impropriety in one's own behavior or position or in the behavior or position of a closely associated person or group ⟨she felt no ~, no remorse, seeing the death as purely accidental —Arnold Bennett⟩ **b :** the susceptibility to such emotion ⟨was not upset because she had no ~⟩ **2 a (1) :** the condition of one that is in disgrace **:** IGNOMINY ⟨free from these slanders and this open ~ —Shak.⟩ ⟨put his father to ~ by his dishonest acts⟩ **(2) :** an instance of dishonor ⟨let his ~*s* quickly drive him to Rome —Shak.⟩ **b** *archaic* **:** dishonor from loss of chastity or illegitimacy of birth ⟨every woe a tear can claim except an erring sister's ~ —Lord Byron⟩ **3 a :** something worthy of strong censure ⟨it were ~ to our profession were we to suffer it —Sir Walter Scott⟩ — often used interjectionally ⟨interrupted the speech by calling out ~⟩ **b :** a cause of feeling shame ⟨put out of human reach to be a warning and a ~ —Sacheverell Sitwell⟩ **c** *archaic* **:** the external genitalia **syn** see DISHONOR — **in shame of** *prep, obs* **:** in order to bring shame upon ⟨the gods do this in *shame of* cowardice —Shak.⟩

²shame \"\ *vb* -ED/-ING/-S [ME *shamen*, fr. OE *scamian*; akin to MD *schamen* to feel shame, be ashamed, OHG *scamōn*; denominative fr. the root of OE *scamu, sceamu*, n.] *vi, chiefly dial* **:** to feel shame ⟨I do ~ to think of it —Shak.⟩ **~** *vt* **1 :** to bring shame to **:** cover with contempt **:** DISHONOR, DISGRACE ⟨public opinion tolerant to a degree which ~*s* the prejudice of other peoples —W.C.Brownell⟩ **2** *archaic* **:** to shun from shame ⟨she *shamed* his fond embrace —Robert Bridges †1930⟩ **3 :** to put to shame by outrivaling ⟨the urge to self-preservation among politicians ~*s* that among the beasts of jungle and tundra —R.L.Neuberger⟩ **4 :** to cause to feel shame **:** make ashamed ⟨his father had *shamed* him for playing with dolls —John Dollard⟩ **5 :** to force by shame ⟨*shamed* him into action by running the gauntlet of the forts in his own small vessel —*Amer. Guide Series: La.*⟩ — **shame the devil :** to tell the truth

shamed *adj* **1 :** ASHAMED ⟨was rather ~ to be traveling first-class in front of them all —Bruce Marshall⟩ **2 :** marked by shame ⟨made a ~ supplicating gesture —Harriet La Barre⟩

shamed·ly \ˈshām(ə)dlē, -li\ *adv* **:** in a shamed manner

shameface \ˈ=ˌ=\ *n* [back-formation fr. *shamefaced*] **1 :** a shamefaced aspect **2 :** a wild geranium (*Geranium maculatum*) of eastern No. America

shame·faced \ˈshāmˌfāst\ *adj* [alter. (influenced by *faced*) of *shamefast*] **1 :** marked by modesty **:** BASHFUL ⟨cheerfully bearing reproaches but ~ at praise —H.O.Taylor⟩ **2 :** marked by shame **:** ASHAMED ⟨the weary, hangdog, and ~ air of the retreating enemy —Eric Linklater⟩ — **shame·faced·ly** \-ˈfāsədlē, -fāstlē, -li\ *adv* — **shame·faced·ness** \-nəs\ *n* -ES

shamefaced crab *n* **:** BOX CRAB

shame·fast \ˈ=ˌfast\ *adj* [ME, fr. OE *scamfæst*, fr. *scamu, sceamu* shame + *fæst* firmly fixed — more at SHAME, FAST] **:** SHAMEFACED — **shame·fast·ly** *adv* — **shame·fast·ness** *n* -ES

shame·ful \ˈshāmfəl\ *adj* [ME, bringing shame, modest, fr. OE *scamful* modest, fr. *scamu, sceamu* shame + *-ful*] **1 a :** bringing shame **:** injurious to reputation **:** DISGRACEFUL ⟨the wicked rascally ~ conduct of the bankrupt —W.M.Thackeray⟩ **b :** arousing the feeling of shame **:** INDECENT ⟨that indecent exposure of teeth that became even more ~ when one realized the teeth were his own —Douglas Woolf⟩ **2** *archaic* **:** full of the feeling of shame **:** ASHAMED ⟨one of the most penitent and ~ offenders —John Keble⟩ — **shame·ful·ly** \-fəlē, -li\ *adv* — **shame·ful·ness** \-fəlnəs\ *n* -ES

shame·less \ˈ=ləs\ *adj* [ME *shameles*, fr. OE *scamlēas*, fr. *scamu, sceamu* shame + *-lēas* -less] **1 :** devoid of shame **:** insensible to disgrace **:** UNSCRUPULOUS ⟨fiend and ~ courtesan —Shak.⟩ ⟨a ~ exploiter of the native workmen⟩ **2 :** showing lack of shame on the part of the agent **:** DISGRACEFUL ⟨a ~ betrayal of principle —Rebecca West⟩ ⟨there was something ~ and indecent about not singing true —Willa Cather⟩

syn SHAMELESS, BRAZEN, BAREFACED, BRASH, and IMPUDENT, applying in common to persons or acts that defy the accepted moral of social code, mean, in this application, bold or lacking a sense of shame. SHAMELESS implies a lack in modesty, decency, respect for others, or so on ⟨makes such *shameless* use of patriotic feelings to advertise his product —Virgil Thomson⟩ ⟨a *shameless* display of arrogance⟩ ⟨a *shameless* and brutal treatment of relatives⟩ BRAZEN adds to *shameless* the idea of hardness and insolence ⟨hip movements and more or less *brazen* imitations of the sexual embrace —Samuel Putnam⟩ ⟨solicited praise and power with the *brazen*, businesslike air of a streetwalker on the prowl for clients —R.H.Rovere⟩ BAREFACED suggests an extreme and brazen effrontery ⟨the whole deal was a *barefaced* double cross —*Time*⟩ ⟨so *barefaced* a swindle —Arnold Bennett⟩ ⟨a *barefaced* lie⟩ BRASH stresses rather a heedlessness, implying a shamelessness that is largely callowness ⟨not like the other girls who were boisterous and *brash*, liking to walk loudly in their high heels across the drug store's tiled floor —Jean Stafford⟩ ⟨an all-too-intimate revue, it bawls out *brash* ditties, featured loud-colored, low-cut skits, winks its eye and wiggles its hips —*Time*⟩ ⟨*brash* college graduates of recent vintage who claimed to know almost everything —R.F.Scholz⟩ IMPUDENT, now rare in this sense, implies bold and cocky defiance of modesty or decency ⟨conduct so sordidly unladylike that even the most *impudent* woman would not dare do it openly —G.B.Shaw⟩

shame·less·ly *adv* **:** in a shameless manner

shame·less·ness *n* -ES **:** the quality or state of being shameless

¹shames *pl of* SHAME, *pres 3d sing of* SHAME

²shames *var of* SHAMMASH

shame vine *or* **shame brier** *n* **:** SENSITIVE BRIER

sham-feed \ˈ=ˌ=\ *vt* **:** to give food to (an experimental animal) and recover it (as from a gastric fistula) before it has been wholly altered by digestive processes

sha·mi·a·na *or* **sha·mi·a·nah** \ˌshämēˈänə\ *n* -s [Hindi *shāmiyāna*, fr. Per *shāmyānah*] *India* **:** a cloth canopy

sham·ing·ly *adv* [*shaming* (pres. part. of ²*shame*) + *-ly*] **:** in a shameful or disgraceful manner

sha·mir \shəˈmi(ə)r, ˈshä,m-\ *n* -s [Heb *shāmīr*] **1 :** a very hard precious stone believed to have been used in building Solomon's temple **2 :** a tiny worm believed capable of splitting the hardest stone

shamisen *var of* SAMISEN

sham·ma·ite \ˈshamə,īt\ *n* -s *usu cap* [*Shammai*, 1st cent. B.C. Jewish teacher + E *-ite*] **:** an adherent of the rigorous and often literal interpretation of the Jewish law taught by Shammai as opposed to the more liberal interpretation of the contemporary Hillelites

sham·mar \ˈshamär\ *n, pl* **shammar** *or* **shammars** *usu cap* **1 :** a bedouin nomadic people of Arabia **2 :** a member of the Shammar people

sham·mash *or* **sha·mash** *or* **sham·mas** *or* **sha·mas** *or* **sham·mes** *or* **sha·mes** *or* **sham·mos** *or* **sha·mus** \ˈshäməs\ *n, pl* **sham·ma·shim** *or* **sha·ma·shim** *or* **sham·ma·sim** *or* **sha·ma·sim** *or* **sham·mo·sim** *or* **sha·mo·sim** \shäˈmōsəm, -səm\ [Yiddish & MHeb; Yiddish *shames*, fr. MHeb *shāmmāsh*, fr. Aram *shĕmmāsh* to serve] **1 :** the sexton of a synagogue **2 :** the candle or taper used to light the other candles in a Hanukkah menorah

shammed *past of* SHAM

sham·mer \ˈshamə(r)\ *n* -s **:** one that shams

shamming *pres part of* SHAM

sham·mock \ˈshamək\ *vi* -ED/-ING/-S [perh. alter. of ³*shamble*] *chiefly dial* **:** to go around idly **:** LOAF, DAWDLE, SLOUCH

¹shammy *or* **shamoy** *var of* CHAMOIS

²sham·my \ˈshamē, -mi\ *n* -ES **:** a chamois bag used by Australian miners as a container for gold dust

¹sham·poo \(ˈ)shamˈpü\ *vt* -ED/-ING/-S [Hindi *cāpo*, imper. of *cāpnā* to press, knead, shampoo] **1** *archaic* **:** MASSAGE **2 a :** to wash (the hair and scalp) with soap and water or a specially prepared shampoo **b :** to wash the hair of (a person) **c :** to wash or clean (as a rug or upholstery) with soap and water or with a dry-cleaning preparation

²shampoo \"\ *n* -s **1 :** an act or instance of shampooing **2 :** a preparation (as a soap solution, dry powder, or chemical solvent) used in shampooing

sham·poo·er \-üə(r)\ *n* -s **:** one that shampoos; *specif* **:** a hairdresser who washes hair

sham·rock \ˈshamˌräk *sometimes* -ˌrək\ *n* -s [IrGael *seamrōg*, dim. of *seamar* trefoil, clover, honeysuckle] **1 :** any of several trifoliolate plants used as a floral emblem of the Irish: as **a :** a hop clover (*Trifolium dubium*) occurring naturally in Ireland and often regarded as the true or original shamrock **b :** a wood sorrel (*Oxalis acetosella*) **c :** WHITE CLOVER **a d :** BLACK MEDIC **2** *or* **shamrock green :** a strong yellowish green that is greener and darker than Cyprus green and lighter, stronger, and slightly yellower than emerald (sense 2b)

shamrock pea *n* **:** a trailing trifoliolate Asiatic and African herb (*Parochetus communis*) of the family Leguminosae having inconspicuous pale purple cleistogamous flowers

shams *pl of* SHAM, *pres 3d sing of* SHAM

¹shamus *var of* SHAMMASH

²sha·mus \ˈshäməs, ˈshā-\ *n* -ES [prob. fr. ¹*shamus*; prob. fr. a jocular suggestion of similarity between the duties of a sexton and those of a house detective in a department store] **1** *slang* **:** POLICEMAN **2** *slang* **:** PRIVATE DETECTIVE

shan \ˈshän, ˈshan\ *n, pl* **shan** *or* **shans** *usu cap* **1 a :** a group of Mongoloid peoples of the Tai stock of southern China, Assam, Burma, and Thailand who vary in civilization from savagery to a Buddhistic culture equal to that of the Thai **b :** a member of such people **2 :** the Thai language of the Shan people

shan·a·chie \ˈshanəˌkē\ *n* -s [IrGael *seanchaidhe* antiquary, historian] *Irish* **:** a teller of old tales or legends

¹shan·de·an *also* **shan·de·ian** \ˈshandēən, =ˈ==\ *or* **shan·dy·an** \ˈshandēən\ *adj, usu cap* [*shandean, shandyan* fr. *Tristram Shandy* (1760–67), novel by Laurence Sterne †1768 Brit. novelist + E *-an*; *shandeian* irreg. fr. *Tristram Shandy* + E *-an*] **:** of, relating to, or characteristic of *Tristram Shandy* by Laurence Sterne

²shandean *also* **shandeian** \"\ *or* **shandyan** \"\ *n* -s *usu cap* **:** one who has the spirit of *Tristram Shandy*

shan·de·ism *also* **shan·dy·ism** \ˈshandēˌizəm\ *n* -s *usu cap* [*shandeism* irreg. fr. *Tristram Shandy* + E *-ism*; *shandyism* fr. *Tristram Shandy* + E *-ism*] **:** the philosophy of *Tristram Shandy*

shand·ite \ˈshanˌdīt\ *n* -s [James S. *Shand* †1957 Brit. geologist + E *-ite*] **:** a mineral $Ni_3Pb_2S_2$ consisting of sulfide of nickel and lead and occurring in rhombohedral crystals near Trial Harbour, Tasmania

shan·dry \ˈshandrē\ *n* -ES [origin unknown] **:** a light carriage on springs

shan·dry·dan \-drēˌdan\ *also* **shan·dra·dan** \-drə,-\ *n* -s [origin unknown] **1 :** a chaise with a hood **2 :** a rickety vehicle ⟨saw a car moving up the road, not a decayed ~ like the other, but a new and powerful car —John Buchan⟩

¹shan·dy \ˈshandē\ *adj* [origin unknown] *dial chiefly Eng* **:** wild and inclined to irresponsible ideas

²shandy \"\ *n* -ES [short for *shandygaff*] **1 :** SHANDYGAFF **2 :** a drink consisting of lemonade and light ale

shan·dy·gaff \-ˌgaf\ *n* -s [origin unknown] **:** a drink consisting of beer and ginger beer or ginger ale

shang \ˈshäŋ\ *adj, usu cap* [*Shang*, Chin. dynasty (1766–1122 B.C.)] **:** of, relating to, or having the characteristics of the period of the Shang dynasty

shan·gal·la \shäŋˈgälə\ *or* **shan·kal·la** \-ˈkälə\ *n, pl* **shangalla** *or* **shangallas** *or* **shankalla** *or* **shankallas** *usu cap* [Amharic *khānqellā* Negro] **1 :** any of the peoples living in western Ethiopia and in the eastern part of the Republic of the Sudan that are not of Ethiopian or of Arab origin **2 :** a member of any of the Shangalla peoples

shan·gan \ˈshaŋən\ *n* -s [ScGael *seangan*] *chiefly Scot* **:** a cleft stick to fasten to the tail of a dog

¹shang·hai \(ˈ)shaŋˈhī, -aiŋ(ˌ)-\ *adj, usu cap* [fr. *Shanghai*, city in eastern China] **:** of or from the city of Shanghai, China **:** of the kind or style prevalent in Shanghai

²shanghai \"\ *n* -s *usu cap* **:** a tall long-legged red and black domestic fowl held to have been imported from the Orient

³shanghai \"\ *vt* **shanghaied; shanghaied; shanghaiing; shanghais** [fr. *Shanghai*, China; fr. the formerly widespread use of unscrupulous means to procure sailors for voyages to the Orient] **1 a :** to put aboard a ship by force often with the help of liquor or a drug ⟨was notorious as a hell ship whose sailors were usually ~*ed* —*Amer. Guide Series: Wash.*⟩ **b :** to put by force or a threat of force into or as if into a place of detention ⟨prisoners of war, ~*ed* laborers, forcibly displaced people and other uprooted men —*Jour. Amer. Med. Assoc.*⟩ ⟨~*ed* by a white slaver while on her way home from choir practice —Polly Adler⟩ **2 :** to put by trickery into an undesirable position ⟨no other agent in this patriotic traffic has ~*ed* more unwary industrialists —E.J.Kahn⟩ — **shanghai·er** \-hī(ə)r, -īə\ *n* -s

⁴shanghai \"\ *n* -s [perh. alter. (influenced by *Shanghai*, China) of *shangan*] *Austral* **:** SLINGSHOT

shang·hai·land·er \=ˈ=ləndə(r)\ *n* -s *cap* [*Shanghai*, China + E *-lander* (as in *highlander*)] **:** a native or resident of Shanghai, China

shan·go \shäŋˈgō\ *adj, often cap* [fr. *Shango*, Yoruba god of thunder and fertility] **:** of or relating to the worship of Shango by the Yoruba people and by Negroes in Brazil and Trinidad

shangri-la \ˌshaŋgrēˈlä, -aiŋ-, -rə-, -lä\ *n* -s *usu cap S & often cap L* [fr. *Shangri-La*, imaginary mountain land depicted as a utopia in the novel *Lost Horizon* (1933) by James Hilton †1954 Eng. novelist] **1 :** a remote beautiful imaginary place where life approaches perfection : UTOPIA **2 a** : a remote usu. beautiful and delightful place ⟨by those familiar with these *Shangri-las* of the Atlantic coast its locale is readily identifiable —J.D.Adams⟩ **b** : a place whose name is not known or not given ⟨will fly in huge flocks from 100 unnameable *Shangri-las* to destinations which the Axis wishes it could guess —*Science News Letter*⟩

shan-jen \ˈshänˈrən\ *n, pl* **shan-jen** *or* **shan-jens** *usu cap* S&J [Chin (Pek) *shan*¹ *jen*², fr. *shan*¹ mountain, hill + *jen*² man, person, people] : any of several hill tribes (as the Lisu, the Chingpaw, or the Lashi) generally of Tibeto-Burman stock of the west Yunnan frontier region

¹**shank** \ˈshaŋk, -aiŋk\ *n* -S [ME *shanke*, fr. OE *scanca*; akin to MLG *schenke* leg, shank, Sw *skank* leg, shank, ON *skakkr* crooked, askew, Gk *skazein* to limp, and perh. Skt *sakthi* thigh] **1 a** : the lower part of the leg: (1) : the part between the knee and the ankle in man (2) : the corresponding part in various other vertebrates; *specif* : the part between the fetlock and the joint above (3) : TARSOMETATARSUS (4) : TIBIA **b** : the entire leg in man ⟨sat down to rest his weary ~*s*⟩ **c** : a cut of beef, veal, mutton, or lamb from the upper or the lower part of the leg : SHIN — see BEEF illustration, LAMB illustration **d** : the part of a hide that comes from the leg of an animal **2** : a straight narrow usu. essential part of an object: as **a** : the straight part of a nail or pin **b** : a straight part of a plant : STEM, STALK; *specif* : the stalk to which an ear of Indian corn is attached **c** : the part of an anchor that is between the ring and the crown — see ANCHOR illustration **d** : the stem of a goblet or other glass with a stem **e** : the part of a fishhook that is between the eye and the bend **f** : the smooth part of a screw between the thread and the head **g** : the part of a key that is between the handle and the bit **h** (1) : the stem of a tobacco pipe (2) : the part of a tobacco pipe that is between the stem and the bowl **i** : the tang of a hoe, rake, knife, or other instrument with a handle **j** : each of the two parts of a pair of scissors between the joint and the bows **k** (1) : the narrow part of the sole of a shoe beneath the instep — see SHOE illustration (2) : SHANKPIECE **3 a** *Scot* : STOCKING **b shanks** *pl, dial* : LEGGINGS **4** *chiefly Scot* : a ridge joining a hill to the plain **5** : a part of an object by which it can be attached: as **a** (1) : a projection (as a loop or an eye) on the back of a solid button by which it is attached to the cloth (2) : a short bar of thread that holds a sewn button away from the cloth so that it can be buttoned and unbuttoned easily **b** : the projecting part of a knob handle that contains the spindle socket **c** : the end (as of a drill, milling cutter, or lathe center) that is gripped in a chuck **6** : ¹BODY 10a **7** : the part of a finger ring that encircles the finger excluding the bezel and engraving **8 a** : a short rope or chain **b** : a tie strap of a halter **9** : the space between two channels of the Doric triglyph **10 a** : the latter part of a period of time ⟨along in the ~ of the afternoon —J.F.Dobie⟩ **b** : the early or main part of a period of time ⟨don't go yet; it is just the ~ of the evening —J.B.Weston⟩ **11 a** : a long-handled ladle for molten metal for use by two or more men **b** : a handle by which a ladle of molten metal can be carried by one or more men **12** : the curved iron bar that connects a cultivator shovel to the beam **13** : a device for locking inserted teeth in a circular saw **14** [²*shank*] : an act or instance of shanking a golf ball **15** *slang* : KNIFE

shank 5a(1)

²**shank** \ˈ"\ *vb* -ED/-ING/-S *vi* **1** *chiefly Scot* : to go on foot : WALK **2** : to decay at the footstalk; *specif* : to suffer from shanking ~ *vt* **1** *chiefly Scot* **a** : to cause to go on foot **b** : to traverse on foot **2** : to form a shank on **3** : to hit (a golf ball) with the extreme heel of the club so that the ball goes sharply to the right **4** : to cut (a person) deeply with a knife

shankalla *usu cap, var of* SHANGALLA

shank bone *n* [ME *shanke bon*, fr. *shanke* shank + *boon*, *bon* bone] : TIBIA 1a

shank cutter *n* **1** : END MILL **2** : a device for trimming the edges of outsoles in the shank of a shoe

shanked \ˈshaŋkt, -aiŋ-\ *adj* **1** : having a shank **2** : having such or so many shanks — usu. used in combination ⟨long-*shanked*⟩ ⟨two-*shanked*⟩

shank·er \ˈshaŋkə(r), -aiŋ-\ *n* -S **1** : one whose work consists of making or fastening on shanks **2** : SHAFTMAN

shanking *also* **shanking disease** *n* -S [*shanking* fr. gerund of ²*shank*] **1** : a disease of tulips caused by a fungus (*Phytophthora erythroseptica*) and characterized by rot of the flower stalk base **2** : a disease of onions and shallots caused by a fungus of the genus *Phytophthora*

shank mill *n* : an end mill that is formed solid with the shank

shank painter *n* [ME *shankpayntor*, fr. *shank*, *shanke* shank + *payntor*, *paynter* painter] : a short rope or chain that holds the shank of an anchor near the flukes against the vessel esp. on the billboard to a toe of the tumbler arm

shankpiece \ˈ=,=\ *n* : a piece of metal or other material inserted in the shank of a shoe to support the arch of the foot

shanks *pl of* SHANK, *pres 3d sing of* SHANK

shanks·man \ˈshaŋksmən, -aiŋ-\ *n, pl* **shanksmen** [*shank's* (gen. of ¹*shank*) + *man*] : SHAFTMAN

shanks' mare *also* **shank's mare** *or* **shanks' pony** *or* **shank's pony** *n* : one's own legs ⟨just moseyed along mostly traveling by *shanks' mare* —Helen Eustis⟩

shan·na \ˈshanə\ [Sc *shan-* (fr. E *shall*) + *na*] *Scot* : shall not

¹**shan·ny** \ˈshanī\ *adj* [prob. alter. of ¹*shandy*] *dial Eng* **1** : SILLY, GIDDY **2** : SHY

²**shan·ny** \ˈshanē\ *n* -ES [origin unknown] : a small European blenny (*Blennius pholis*) that is olive green with irregular dark spots and has no appendages on the head

shans *usu cap, pl of* SHAN

shant \ˈshant, -aa(ə)nt, -aint\ *n* -S [origin unknown] *slang* : a large stein : POT

shan't \ˈshant, -aa(ə)-, -ai-, -á-, -ä-\ [by contr.] : shall not

shantey *or* **shanty** *var of* CHANTEY

shan·tung \(ˈ)shan;ˈtəŋ\ *n* -S *sometimes cap* [fr. *Shantung*, province in northeast China] : a fabric in plain weave characterized by a slightly irregular surface that is due to the uneven slubbed filling yarns of wild silk or other fibers

shantung straw *also* **shantung** *n* -S *sometimes cap Shantung* : a fine smooth hat straw woven from buntal

¹**shan·ty** \ˈshantē, -aan-, -ain-, -án-, -ti\ *n* -ES [CanF *chantier* hut in a lumber camp, shack, fr. F, lumberyard, shipyard, gantry, fr. OF, gantry, fr. L *cantherius* trellis, rafter, gelding — more at GANTRY] **1** : a small poorly built dwelling usu. made of wood : SHACK **2** : a small crude building for temporary use **3** *Austral* : BAR, PUB

²**shanty** \ˈ"\ *vi* -ED/-ING/-ES : to live in a shanty

³**shanty** \ˈ"\ *adj* **1 a** : constituting a shanty ⟨rough ~ roadside restaurants —A.L.Himbert⟩ **b** : consisting of shanties ⟨a ~ native village⟩ **2** : living or having lived in a shanty : of a low social class ⟨the lower-lower class, the ~ Irish, not the lace-curtain Irish —J.P.Marquand⟩

shantyboat \ˈ==,=\ *n* : a small crude houseboat

shantyboater \ˈ==,==\ *n* : one who lives on a shantyboat

shanty boss *n* : BULL COOK

shantyboy \ˈ==,=\ *n* : LOGGER

¹**shan·ty·man** \ˈ==mən\ *n, pl* **shantymen** **1** : one who lives in a shanty; *specif* : LOGGER **2** : SHANTYBOATER

²**shantyman** *also* **shanteyman** *var of* CHANTEYMAN

shantytown \ˈ==,=\ *n* **1** : a section of a city or town in which the houses are shanties **2** : an entire town consisting mostly of shanties; *esp* : a poor suburb inhabited by Negroes in South Africa

shao·hing \(ˈ)shau̇ˈshiŋ\ *adj, usu cap* [fr. *Shaohing*, city in eastern China] : of or from the city of Shaohing, China : of the kind or style prevalent in Shaohing

shap·able *or* **shape·able** \ˈshāpəbəl\ *adj* **1** *usu shapeable* : capable of being shaped **2** *usu shapable* : SHAPELY

¹**shape** \ˈshāp\ *vb* **shaped**; **shaped** *or archaic* **shap·en** \-pən\ **shaping**; **shapes** [ME *shapen*, alter. of OE *sceppan*, *scyppan*; akin to OHG *skepfen* to shape, form, create, ON *skepja*, Goth *gaskapjan* to create, and perh. to L *scabere* to scratch, scrape — more at SHAVE] *vt* **1** : FORM, CREATE; *esp* : to give a particular or proper form to by or as if by molding or modeling from an undifferentiated mass **2** : to give definite or finished shape to esp. by altering a prior shape ⟨*shaping* rolls from dough⟩ ⟨*shaped* a sturdy mortar from the log⟩ **3** *obs* : ORDAIN, DECREE, DESTINE, APPOINT ⟨there's a divinity that ~*s* our ends, roughhew them how we will —Shak.⟩ **4 a** : to alter or manipulate so as to give a particular form or produce a particular object — usu. used with *into* ⟨*shaping* the seasoned lumber into a sturdy frame⟩ ⟨~*s* the clay into bricks⟩ ⟨heat and ~ the iron⟩ **b** *obs* : to change in form : METAMORPHOSE **c** *archaic* : to cut out and fashion (as a garment) **d** : to adapt in shape usu. so as to fit neatly and closely — usu. used with *to* ⟨a dress *shaped* to her figure⟩ **e** : to fashion (a knitted garment) by decreasing or increasing according to pattern **f** : to style (hair) by thinning and tapering esp. to the contour of the head **5 a** : to marshal facts and present them by way of (answer) ⟨~*s* an earnest answer to the accusation⟩ **b** : to give a particular form or direction to : DEVISE, PLAN ⟨together *shaped* a dark conspiracy⟩ **c** : to embody in definite or definitive form ⟨*shaping* a folktale into an epic⟩ — often used with *up* ⟨*shaping* up a set of notes for publication⟩ **6** *archaic* : to bring about : CONTRIVE **7 a** : to make fit for (as a particular use or purpose) : ADAPT, REGULATE, ADJUST ⟨*shaping* a character to future responsibilities⟩ **b** : to determine or direct the course of (as conduct, life, history) ⟨*shaping* our plans for a happy holiday⟩ **8** : to produce a plane surface on (work) by means of a tool that moves to and fro — compare MILL, PLANE ~ *vi* **1** : to come to pass usu. in a particular way : HAPPEN, BEFALL ⟨if things ~ right⟩ **2** *archaic* : to cut out and fashion clothing **3** *obs* : SUIT, CONFORM **4 a** : to take on or approach a mature form — often used with *up* **b** : to develop to or toward a definitive form (as in character, proficiency, or excellence) : show promise — often used with *up* **syn** see MAKE — **shape one's course** : to direct one's way

²**shape** \ˈ"\ *n* -S [ME *shap*, fr. OE *gesceap*, fr. *ge-* (perfective, associative, and collective prefix) + *-sceap* (akin to OE *sceppan*, *scyppan* to shape, form, create) — more at CO-] **1 a** : the visible makeup characteristic of a particular item or kind of item : characteristic appearance or visible form ⟨a demon appearing in the ~ of a man⟩ **b** (1) : spatial form or contour that is usu. fixed by a relatively constant spatial relation between the parts of the periphery or surface ⟨water takes the ~ of its container⟩ ⟨a common ~ of glass⟩ ⟨the ~ of a jellyfish⟩ (2) : any of numerous standardized or universally recognized and usu. basically geometric spatial forms or contours ⟨squares, diamonds, and other ~*s*⟩ ⟨a hill of perfect cone ~⟩ **c** : phonetic composition or structure or a representation thereof ⟨emphatic *of* has the ~ \ˈəv\ or \ˈäv\, unemphatic *of* usually has the ~ \əv\⟩ **2** : the appearance of the body usu. as distinguished from that of the face : bodily contour esp. with respect to beauty : FIGURE ⟨bathing beauties showing their ~*s*⟩ ⟨your whole ~ shows when you stand against the light⟩ **3** [ME *shap* male or female sex organ, fr. OE *sceap*; akin to OE *sceppan*, *scyppan*] *dial chiefly Eng* : the female pudenda **4 a** *dial chiefly Eng* : a represented form (as a painting or photograph) **b** : PHANTOM, APPARITION **c** : assumed appearance : GUISE, LIKENESS ⟨our troubles started in the ~ of a helpful neighbor⟩ **d** (1) *obs* : a theatrical role or its makeup (2) : a stage costume **5** : form of embodiment (as in words) : form (as of thought) that is relatively definite and organized ⟨a plan was beginning to take ~ as they argued⟩ ⟨whipping his speech into ~⟩ **6** : a mode of existence or form of being having identifying or individuating features ⟨the first ~ of an essay⟩ ⟨the final ~ of a society⟩ **7** : something having a particular form ⟨a hatter's ~⟩ ⟨a metal ~ for holding flowers⟩: as **a** : a mold for imparting a shape to a food (as a jelly or blancmange); *also* : a dish molded in a shape **b** (1) : a length of metal (as a bar or beam) having a constant cross section; *also* : one with a cross section other than square, rectangular, round, or hexagonal (2) : a piece roughly forged to approximately the final form **c** : a cone, ball, or drum of light metal or canvas hoisted in making signals on a ship **d** : a gaming die with one or more faces rounded so that it is more likely to fall one way than another **e** : the bend of a fishhook **8** *dial chiefly Eng* : bodily posture : ATTITUDE **9 a** : condition in which someone or something exists at a particular time usu. as compared with a more general state or that of the same item at other occasions or on the average ⟨in excellent ~ for his age⟩ ⟨the market has been in poor ~ lately⟩ **b** : good condition (as for sports) **syn** see FORM — **in no shape** *adv* : NOWISE — **in shape** *adv* : in the original, normal, or fit condition ⟨exercises to keep *in shape*⟩ : in the best condition possible under the circumstances ⟨getting the property *in shape* for sale⟩

shapeable *var of* SHAPABLE

shaped \ˈshāpt\ *adj* **1 a** : having or fashioned to a particular form — often used in combination ⟨a V-*shaped* notch⟩ **b** : designed to conform to the contours of something ⟨a ~ coat⟩ **2** : formed by or as if by altering the shape of a plastic or pliable mass ⟨~ steel plates⟩ **3** : given direction or plan ⟨a carefully ~ course⟩

shaped charge *n* : an explosive charge the energy of which is focused in one direction; *esp* : a charge in a projectile so packed that an empty cone is left in the nose in which the force of the explosion on impact is directed largely to the front with armor-penetrating effect

shaped note *n* : SHAPE NOTE

shape forth *vt* : to picture or outline in visible or understandable form ⟨*shaping forth* his plan for their approval⟩

shape·ful \ˈshāpfəl\ *adj* : SHAPELY

shape–knife \ˈ=,=\ *n* : a knife on which shapes for heels are cut out

shape·less \ˈ=ləs\ *adj* [ME *scapless*, fr. *scap*, *shap* shape + *-less*, *-les* -less] **1** : destitute of regularity or fixity of shape ⟨a ~ blob of protoplasm⟩ **2 a** : deprived of usual or normal shape : MISSHAPEN ⟨a ~ old hat⟩ **b** : lacking the structural qualities that impart elegance and grace ⟨straight ~ garments⟩ ⟨a ~ young girl⟩ **3** : lacking direction or purpose — **shape·less·ly** *adv* — **shape·less·ness** *n* -ES

shape·li·ness \ˈshāplēnəs, -lin-\ *n* -ES [ME *shaplynesse*, fr. *shaply* shapely + *-nesse* -ness] : the quality or state of being shapely

shape·ly *adj* -ER/-EST [ME *shaply*, fr. *shap* shape + *-ly*] **1** : having a regular or pleasing shape : well formed : SYMMETRICAL **2** : having definiteness of form : orderly in arrangement or plan ⟨a ~ conception⟩

shap·en \ˈshāpən\ *adj* [ME, fr. past part. of *shapen* to shape] : fashioned to or provided with a definite shape — usu. used in combination ⟨an ill-*shapen* body⟩

shape note *n* : one of a system of seven notes showing the

1 2 3 4 5 6 7 8

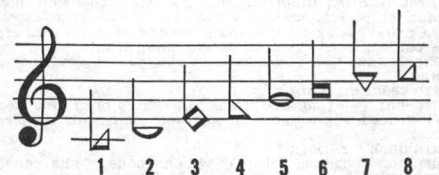

shape notes: *1* do, *2* re, *3* mi, *4* fa, *5* sol, *6* la, *7* ti, *8* do

musical scale degree by the shape of the note head — called also *buckwheat note*, *character note*, *patent note*

shap·er \ˈshāpə(r)\ *n* -S [ME, fr. *shapen* to shape + *-er*] : one that shapes: as **a** : one whose work is the shaping of articles (as of wood, metal, or cloth) either by hand or machine **b** : POET; *esp* : a bard who reworks old matter in fresh language **c** (1) : a machine tool for shaping metal or sometimes other materials (2) : a woodworking machine with one or two cutters mounted on vertical revolving spindles and projecting above a flat table for cutting irregular outlines (as of moldings) (3) : any of various tools or machines (as a swage for shaping saw teeth, for stamping or pressing sheet metal) (4) : a machine for blocking hats

shapes *pres 3d sing of* SHAPE, *pl of* SHAPE

shapeshifter \ˈ=,==\ *n* : an individual (as a werewolf) able or held to be able to change form esp. at will

shape–shifting \ˈ=ˈ==\ *n* [*shifting* fr. gerund of *shift*] : a change of physical form brought about by or as if by supernatural means

shape target *n* : a railroad target conveying meaning by shape

shape–up \ˈ=,=\ *n* -S [*shape up*] : a system of hiring longshoremen by having applicants gather usu. in a semicircle at least once a day for selection by a union-appointed hiring boss of those to work on that day or shift; *also* : an instance of such hiring practice — compare HIRING HALL

¹**shap·ing** \ˈshāpiŋ, -pēŋ\ *n* -S [ME *shapinge*, fr. gerund of *shapen* to shape] **1** : the act of one that shapes **2** : a thing created or shaped : CREATURE, CREATION

²**shaping** \ˈ"\ *adj* [ME *shapinge*, fr. pres. part. of *shapen* to shape] : that shapes or is designed to shape — **shap·ing·ly** *adv*

shaping dies *n pl* : a set of dies that bends, presses, draws, or hammers a material to a required form in a press or hammer — compare COINING DIE, SEAMING DIES, SPLIT DIE, WIRING DIES

shaping planer *n* : a planer (as a crank planer) with a shaper drive

sha·po \ˈshä(,)pō\ *or* **sha·poo** \-pü\ *n* -S [Tibetan *shabo*] : a wild sheep of Kashmir and Tibet that is a variety of the urial

shap·om·e·ter \shäˈpämədə(r)\ *n* [²*shape* + *-o-* + *-meter*] : a device for measuring the shapes of pebbles

shaps *var of* CHAPS

shap·wai·lu·tan \,shap,wīˈlütᵊn\ *n, usu cap* [*shahaptian* + *wailatpuan* + *lutuamian* + *-an*] : a language stock of Washington, Oregon, and Idaho comprising Shahaptian, Wailatpuan, and Lutuamian

shar' *or* **shar** *often cap, var of* SHARI'A

sharable *var of* SHAREABLE

¹**shard** \ˈshärd, ˈshȧd\ *also* **sherd** \ˈshərd, -ōd, -əid\ *n* -S [ME, fr. OE *sceard*; akin to MHG *scharte* notch, nick, ON *skarth* notch, mountain pass, OE *sceran*, *scieran* to cut, shear — more at SHEAR] **1 a** : a piece or fragment of a brittle substance (as of an earthen vessel); *broadly* : a small piece : RESIDUE, REMAINS **b** : SHELL, SCALE; *esp* : an elytron of a beetle **c** *usu sherd* : fragments of pottery vessels found on sites and in refuse deposits where pottery-making peoples have lived and regarded as one of the best indexes of time differences in culture — compare STRATIGRAPHY **d** : highly angular curved glass fragments of tuffaceous sediments **2 a** : a notch or gap (as in a hedge or bank) **b** *obs* : a separating body of water

²**shard** \ˈ"\ *vb* -ED/-ING/-S *vt* : to break shards from : break into shards ~ *vi* : to shed bark in shards

³**shard** \ˈ"\ *n* -S [prob. alter. (influenced by ¹*shard*) of *sharn*] *chiefly dial* : a dropping of cow dung

⁴**shard** \ˈ"\ *archaic var of* CHARD

shar·da·na \shärˈdänə\ *n, pl* **shardana** *usu cap* : one of a group of early mercenary warriors from the eastern Mediterranean and prob. from Lydia and first fighting for Egypt then against it

shard beetle *n* [³*shard*] : a dung beetle of the genus *Geotrupes*

shard–born \ˈ=;=\ *adj* [³*shard*] *archaic, of a beetle* : born in dung

shard–borne \ˈ=;=\ *adj* [¹*shard*] *archaic* : borne on scaly wing cases ⟨*shard-borne* beetles⟩

¹**sharded** *adj* [³*shard* + *-ed*] *obs, of a beetle* : dwelling in dung

²**shard·ed** \ˈshärdəd, ˈshȧd-\ *adj* [¹*shard* + *-ed*] *obs* : having elytra or scales

¹**share** \ˈshe(ə)r, ˈsha(ə)r, |ə\ *n* -S [ME, pubic region, due portion, share, fr. OE *scearu* tonsure, pubic region; akin to OHG *skara* troop, ON *skǫr* hair, rim, OE *sceran*, *scieran* to cut, shear — more at SHEAR] **1** *obs* **a** : the bony pubis or the pubic region **b** (1) : the fork of the human body (2) : PRIVATE 3 **2 a** : a portion belonging to, due to, or contributed by an individual ⟨his ~ in his father's estate⟩ ⟨put up his ~ of the cost⟩ **b** : one's full or fair portion ⟨had his ~ of luck⟩ **c** (1) : the part allotted or belonging to one of a number owning together any property or interest : the undivided interest of any one of a number owning jointly or in common : an apportioned lot : ALLOTMENT, DIVIDEND (2) : any of the equal portions into which any property or invested capital is divided ⟨a ship owned in 64 ~*s*⟩; *usu* : any of the equal interests or rights into which the entire capital stock of a corporation is divided : any of a number of equal indivisible rights or interests in the management, profits, and ultimate assets of a corporation constituting the property of those who own it and being regularly evidenced by one or more certificates — compare PREFERRED STOCK (3) **shares** *pl, chiefly Brit* : STOCK 28a **3** *archaic* : SEGMENT, PIECE, DIVISION: as **a** *obs* : a portion of land assigned to a particular holder **b** *obs* : a part cut off : CUT, SECTION — **for one's share** : for one's part — **on shares** : on the basis of sharing in the risks and profits (as in fishery or farming)

²**share** \ˈ"\ *vb* -ED/-ING/-S *vt* **1** : to divide and distribute in portions : APPORTION, DIVIDE ⟨~ one's estate between one's heirs⟩ — usu. followed by *out* or *with* ⟨*shared* out the proceeds of the sale⟩ **2** : to partake of, use, experience, or enjoy with others : have a portion of ⟨~ a room⟩ **3** : to grant or be granted a share in ⟨~ one's gains with another⟩ ⟨*shared* their crops in season⟩ **4** : to participate in, take, possess, or undergo in common ⟨~ danger⟩ ⟨*sharing* a common responsibility⟩ **5** *archaic* : to allot as one's share **6** *obs* : to receive, take, or possess as one's share ~ *vi* **1** : to have a share : take part — used with *in* ⟨all may ~ in these pleasures⟩ ⟨willing to ~ in the work⟩ **2** : to apportion and take shares of something ⟨the robbers *shared* and fled separately⟩ — **share and share alike** **1** : to be held in equal shares as tenants in common rather than in joint tenancy with a per capita rather than a per stirpes distribution or ownership **2** : to be distributed in severalty in equal shares

syn SHARE, PARTICIPATE, and PARTAKE can mean to have, use, exercise, experience, or engage in something in common with another or others. SHARE implies that one as original owner or holder grants to another the partial use, enjoyment, or possession of a thing ⟨*share* your lunch with a friend⟩ ⟨*share* one's enjoyment with another⟩ ⟨none has *shared* so generously with the reader her personal passion for the stuffs, jewels and decorations that made the palace a wonder —*Time*⟩ ⟨to *share* surpluses is not really to *share* at all —H.S. Truman⟩ or, often with *in*, that one as receiver accepts the partial use, enjoyment, or possession of something belonging to or held by another ⟨ask a neighbor to *share* in a Thanksgiving dinner⟩ ⟨*share* in another's joy⟩ ⟨*share* another's disgust at losing an important golf game⟩ ⟨those who do not *share* his faith in the sufficiency of empirical science —J.E. Smith⟩ or it can merely imply a mutual use, enjoyment, or possession of something ⟨the few artists or writers who have *shared* the tastes of the average man —Roger Fry⟩ ⟨diseases which man *shares* with animals —*Time*⟩ PARTICIPATE implies a having or taking of a part of or a share in a thing, as an experience, work, or an enterprise ⟨the citizens refused to *participate* in any further elections under this law —*Amer. Guide Series: Mich.*⟩ ⟨she did not *participate* in the inheritance of the husband after they were married —Ralph Linton⟩ ⟨a citizen of one state has no right to *participate* in the government of another —R.B.Taney⟩ ⟨invited to *participate* in the discussion —L.M.Goodrich⟩ PARTAKE, often used with *of* and sometimes with *in*, implies an accepting, taking, or acquiring a share of something, esp. food, drink, or a pleasure, often in extension signifying merely to consume ⟨he had *partaken* of as much as a pint daily of alcohol for years —*Jour. Amer. Med. Assoc.*⟩ ⟨the story itself ceases to be merely melodramatic, and *partakes* of true drama —T.S.Eliot⟩ ⟨they unconsciously *partake* in his imagery —E.H.Erikson⟩

³**share** \ˈ"\ *n* -S [ME *shaar*, fr. OE *scear*; akin to MLG *schār*, *schāre* plowshare, OHG *scaro* plowshare, OE *sceran*, *scieran* to cut, shear] : PLOWSHARE — see PLOW illustration

⁴**share** *vt* [alter. of ¹*shear*] *obs* : CUT, SHEAR, CLEAVE, DIVIDE; *also* : to form by cutting

share·abil·i·ty \,sherəˈbilədē, ,sha(a)r-, -lətē, -i\ *n* : the quality or state of being shareable

share·able *or* **shar·able** \ˈ==bəl\ *adj* : capable of being shared ⟨~ experience⟩

sharebone \ˈ=,=\ *n, archaic* : PUBIS

sharebroker \ˈ=,==\ *n, chiefly Brit* : STOCKBROKER

sharecrop \ˈ=,=\ *vb* [back-formation fr. *sharecropper*] *vi* : to farm as a sharecropper ~ *vt* : to farm (land) or produce (a

particular crop) as a sharecropper ⟨*sharecropped* 100 acres⟩ ⟨*sharecropping* tobacco⟩
sharecropper \ˈ=,==\ *n* [*share-crop* (in the phrase *share-crop system*, fr. earlier *share of the crop system*) + *-er*] **:** a tenant farmer esp. in the southern U.S. who works the land, receives from the landlord seed, tools, stock, and usu. living quarters and credit for food and other necessities consumed prior to harvesting, and is paid a specified share of the crop from which deductions to cover advances (as for drainage and fencing) or for credit advanced may be made — compare SHAREMAN
shared *past of* SHARE
shareef *var of* SHARIF
shareholder \ˈ=,==\ *n* **:** one that holds or owns a share in a joint fund or property; *esp* **:** STOCKHOLDER
share·man \ˈ=₋mən\ *n, pl* **sharemen** **1 :** SHARESMAN **2 :** a farmer who farms on shares in respect to both expenses and product and who usu. has his own farming equipment — compare SHARECROPPER
share out *vt* **:** to divide and assign in portions ⟨the executor *shared out* the estate⟩ **~** *vi* **:** to earn or produce shares (as of profits) ⟨some small cooperative enterprises *share out* very well⟩
share-out \ˈ=,=\ *n* -s [*share out*] **:** an act or instance of distributing in shares
shareowner \ˈ=,==\ *n* **:** an owner of a share or shares; *esp* **:** STOCKHOLDER
sharepusher \ˈ=,==\ *n, Brit* **:** a high-pressure salesman of often inferior securities
shar·er \ˈsherə(r), ˈsha(a)r-\ *n* -s **:** one that shares: as **a** *obs* **:** a member of a theatrical company who shares in the expenses and profits **b** *obs* **:** SHAREHOLDER **c :** PARTICIPATOR, PARTAKER **d :** DIVIDER, DISTRIBUTOR
share rent *n* **:** a rent for farm land in the form of an agreed or customary fractional part of a crop grown thereon — compare SHARE-TENANT
shares *pl of* SHARE, *pres 3d sing of* SHARE
shares·man \ˈsherzmən, ˈsha(a)rz-\ *n, pl* **sharesmen** [*share's* (gen. of ¹*share*) + *man*] **:** a member of a fishing crew who shares the risk and profits of a voyage or season
share-tenant \ˈ=,==\ *also* **share-renter** \ˈ=,==\ *n* **:** one who operates a farm owned by another, pays a share of the crop as rent, and provides labor, power and implements, and usu. his share of seed and fertilizer — compare SHARECROPPER
share warrant *n, Brit* **:** a freely transferable certificate indicating that the bearer is entitled to specified shares of stock
shar·gar *also* **shar·ger** \ˈshärgər\ *n* -s [ScGael *seargaire*] *Scot* **:** a lean, faded, or stunted person or animal **:** STARVELING, RUNT
sha·ri'a *or* **sha·ria** \shəˈrēə\ *also* **sha·ri·at** \-ēət\ *or* **shar'** *or* **shar** \ˈshär\ *or* **she·ri** \shəˈrē\ *or* **she·ria** \shəˈrēə\ *or* **she·ri·at** \-ēət\ *n* -s *often cap* [Ar *sharīʻah*] **:** the body of formally established sacred law in Islam based primarily on Allah's commandments found in the Koran and revealed through the sunna of Muhammad, governing in theory not only religious matters but regulating as well political, economic, civil, criminal, ethical, social, and domestic affairs in Muslim countries, and commonly in practice being supplemented by the customary law of a region — compare ADAT
sha·rif *or* **she·rif** *also* **sha·reef** *or* **she·reef** \shəˈrēf\ *n, pl* **sharifs** *or* **sherifs** \-fs\ *also* **ash·raf** \ashˈrāf\ [Ar *sharīf* (pl. *ashrāf*), lit., noble, illustrious] **:** a descendant of the prophet Muhammad through his daughter Fatima; *broadly* **:** one of noble ancestry or religious preeminence in Islam — used chiefly as a title
sha·ri·fa *or* **she·ri·fa** \-ˈrēfə\ *n* -s [Ar *sharīfah*, fem. of *sharīf*] **:** the wife of a sharif
sha·rif·ian *or* **she·rif·ian** *or* **she·reef·ian** \shəˈrēfēən\ *adj* **:** of or relating to a sharif
sharing *n* -s [fr. gerund of ²*share*] **:** mutual confession practiced in group meetings by the Oxford Group movement
¹**shark** \ˈshärk, ˈshȧk\ *n* -s [origin unknown] **1 a :** any of numerous elasmobranch fishes that conform more or less nearly to the ordinary fishes in the fusiform shape of the body and lateral position of the gill clefts as distinguished from the greatly flattened rays and the grotesquely shaped chimaeras, that are mostly marine and though widely distributed most abundant in warm seas, that are usu. of medium or large size including the largest existing fishes, that have a tough, usu. dull gray, and sometimes conspicuously spotted skin which is roughened by minute tubercles, strongly heterocercal tail, and a snout produced beyond the mouth, that may be active, voracious, and rapacious predators including some which are dangerous to man or sluggish bottom dwellers feeding chiefly on mollusks, and that are of economic importance for their flesh which is in some cases used as food, for their large livers which are a source of oil, and for their hides from which leather is made — see BASKING SHARK, BLUE SHARK, DOGFISH, HAMMERHEAD, MAN-EATER, PORBEAGLE; compare CHONDRICHTHYES, SELACHII **b :** a living or extinct elasmobranch other than a skate or ray **2 :** any of several large voracious fishes (as the goonch) **3 :** a synchronized swimming stunt in which the body while lying on one side parallel to the surface with the back arched and the top arm extended overhead in line with the body is propelled in a circle headfirst by the action of the bottom arm
²**shark** \ˈ"\ *vi* -ED/-ING/-S **1 :** to fish for sharks **2 :** to prey or swim like a shark
³**shark** \ˈ"\ *n* -s [prob. modif. (influenced in form and meaning by ¹*shark*) of G *schurke* scoundrel] **1** *obs* **:** PARASITE, SPONGE, SHARPER **2 :** a rapacious crafty person who gains by usury, extortion, swindling, or trickery ⟨a mortgage ~⟩ ⟨~*s* of the poolroom and racetrack⟩ **3** *slang Brit* **:** a customs officer **4 :** one who excels greatly esp. in a particular line **:** an exceptionally capable or brilliant person
⁴**shark** \ˈ"\ *vb* [¹*shark* & ³*shark*] *vt, archaic* **:** to get or gather together rapaciously or by fraud, trickery, or other irregular means **:** get by playing the shark **~** *vi* **1 :** to play the sharper **:** practice fraud or trickery **2 :** to live by shifts and stratagems — **shark on** *or* **shark upon** *obs* **:** to sponge upon **:** SWINDLE
sharker *n, obs* **:** one that lives by sharking others **:** SHARPER
shar·ki \ˈshərkē\ *n* -s [Ar *sharqīy*, lit., eastern, fr. *sharq* east] **:** a southeasterly wind of the Persian gulf
shark·ish \ˈshärkish, ˈshȧk-, -kēsh\ *adj* **:** resembling or suggestive of a shark esp. in appearance, habits, rapacity, or fierceness
shark·let \-lət\ *n* -s **:** a small or young shark
shark·like \ˈ=,līk\ *adj* **:** resembling a shark; *esp* **:** having the streamlined elongate form of a typical shark
shark-liver oil \ˈ=ˈ==-\ *also* **shark oil** *n* **:** a yellow to red-brown fatty oil obtained from the livers of various sharks (as the soupfin shark or various dogfishes) and used chiefly as a source of vitamin A and as a leather dressing
shark moth *n* **:** any of various noctuid moths (genus *Cucullia*) with larvae that feed mainly on flowers
shark pilot *or* **shark's pilot** \ˈ=,==\ *n* **1 a :** PILOT FISH 1 **b :** BANDED RUDDERFISH **2 :** REMORA
shark ray *n* **:** MONKFISH
sharkskin \ˈ=,=\ *n* **1 :** the hide of a shark or leather made from it — compare SHAGREEN 2 **2 a :** a smooth durable woolen or worsted suiting made in twill or basket weave with small woven designs in two tones or colors **b :** a smooth crisp fabric with a dull finish made usu. of rayon in basket weave and used esp. for dresses or sportswear
shark's mouth *n* **:** an opening in a boat awning in the wake of a mast, stay, or other rigging
shark's-tooth \ˈ=ˈ=\ *or* **shark's-teeth** \ˈ=ˈ=\ *adj* **:** of, resembling, or armed with the teeth of sharks ⟨a *shark's-tooth* sword⟩
shark sucker *n* **:** REMORA 1a
sharky \ˈshärkē, ˈshȧk-, -ki\ *adj* -ER/-EST [¹*shark* + *-y*] **:** infested with sharks
sharn \ˈshärn, ˈshȧn\ *n* -s [ME, fr. OE *scearn* — more at SCAT-] *dial chiefly Eng* **:** DUNG
sharny \-ni\ *adj, chiefly Scot* **:** befouled with dung
¹**sharp** \ˈshärp, ˈshȧp\ *adj* -ER/-EST [ME, fr. OE *scearp*; akin to OHG *scarf* sharp, ON *skarpr*, MIr *cerb* sharp, Russ *shcherba* notch, Gk *keirein* to cut — more at SHEAR] **1 :** adapted to cutting or piercing: as **a** (1) **:** having a thin keen edge ⟨a ~ sword⟩ (2) **:** of such thinness and keenness as to facilitate cutting ⟨an axe with a ~ edge⟩ **b** (1) **:** tapering to a fine point ⟨a ~ needle⟩ (2) **:** of such tapered fineness as to facilitate piercing ⟨a pin with a ~ point⟩ **c :** beset with prickles **:** PRICKLY ⟨~ brambles and thorns⟩ **d :** briskly or bitingly cold **:** NIPPING, RAW ⟨a ~ wind⟩ ⟨several ~ frosts⟩ **e :** composed of hard angular particles **:** GRITTY ⟨~ sand⟩ **2 a :** keen in intellect **:** mentally alert and able **:** QUICK-WITTED **b :** keen in perception **:** efficient in sensory function ⟨a ~ ear⟩ ⟨~ sight⟩ **c :** keen in attention **:** VIGILANT ⟨a ~ lookout⟩ ⟨kept a ~ watch on the market⟩ **d** (1) *obs* **:** DISCRIMINATING, SAGACIOUS (2) **:** cleverly biting **:** aptly witty ⟨~ bits of whimsy⟩ **e :** keen in attention to one's own interest **:** unduly smart or shrewd in practical matters sometimes to the point of being unethical ⟨a ~ trader⟩ ⟨sometimes the customer may be ~*er* than the dealer⟩ **3 :** keen in spirit or action **:** VIOLENT, IMPETUOUS: as **a :** conducted with eagerness or fierceness **:** FIERY, FURIOUS ⟨a ~ military engagement⟩ **b :** closely or keenly contested ⟨a ~ run⟩; *also* **:** full of activity or energy **:** BRISK ⟨~ blows⟩ ⟨a ~ young runner⟩ ⟨hounds in ~ condition⟩ **c** (1) *of a hawk* **:** urgent for prey or food (2) **:** impatient for gratification **:** demanding or requiring to be sated ⟨a ~ appetite⟩ **d :** capable of acting or reacting strongly **:** very active in some particular way; *esp* **:** CAUSTIC ⟨a ~ lime liquor for removing hair from hides⟩ ⟨a ~ soap rich in free alkali⟩ **4 :** SEVERE, HARSH, MERCILESS: as **a :** inclined to or marked by intense irritability or anger **:** IRASCIBLE ⟨a ~ temper⟩ **b :** very trying to the feelings or spirit **:** causing intense mental or physical distress ⟨a ~ pain⟩ ⟨in ~*est* distress⟩ **c :** cutting in language or import **:** conveying or intended to convey rebuke, anger, or satire ⟨~ words⟩ ⟨a ~ rebuke⟩ **d** *obs* **:** AUSTERE **e** (1) *archaic* **:** flowing rapidly or turbulently — used of a stream of water (2) **:** marked by sudden brusque distention of the artery **:** JERKY ⟨a ~ pulse⟩ **5 :** affecting the senses or sense organs intensely: as **a** (1) **:** having a characteristic strong and usu. pungent or acid odor or flavor ⟨~ cheese⟩ (2) **:** ACRID ⟨a ~ odor⟩ **b :** having a characteristic strong and usu. piercing or shrill sound ⟨a ~ whistle⟩ ⟨a ~ clap of thunder⟩ **c :** having the effect of or involving a sudden brilliant display of light ⟨a ~ flash⟩ **6 a :** terminating in a point or edge **:** not smoothly obtuse or rounded **:** PEAKED, RIDGED, ANGULAR ⟨~ features⟩ ⟨a ~ hill⟩ **b** (1) *of an angle* **:** ACUTE (2) **:** requiring or involving an abrupt change of direction **:** formed about an acute angle ⟨a ~ turn⟩ (3) **:** involving marked change and usu. increase of gradient ⟨a ~ climb⟩ ⟨a ~ dip in the road⟩ **c :** appearing as if cut off clean **:** clear in outline or detail **:** DISTINCT ⟨figures standing out ~ against the sky⟩ ⟨a ~ photographic negative⟩ **d :** set forth with clarity and distinctness and usu. with marked contrast between elements **:** free from shading or transition ⟨a ~ line of demarcation⟩ ⟨in ~ contrast with modern methods⟩ **e :** FINE, NARROW — used esp. of the bows of a ship **7 a :** having a high pitch ⟨a *sharp*-toned musical instrument⟩ **b** *of a musical note or tone* **:** raised a half step in pitch ⟨a ~ fourth⟩ **c :** higher than the true pitch of a musical tone ⟨sang ~ all evening⟩ **d :** MAJOR, AUGMENTED — used of an interval in music **e :** having a sharp in the signature ⟨played in the key of F ~⟩ **8 :** STYLISH, ELEGANT, DRESSY ⟨a ~ suit⟩ **9** *of a radio circuit* **:** having a rapidly varying response to different frequencies — opposed to *broad*
syn KEEN, ACUTE: SHARP, in reference to things, may refer either to fine edges making cutting easy or to fine points facilitating piercing ⟨a *sharp* knife⟩ ⟨*sharp* as a needle⟩ and in reference to persons may indicate quick accurate perception or analysis, general cleverness and resourcefulness, or tricky, sometimes questionable cunning ⟨a cold and analytical mind, as *sharp* in criticism and often as bitter as has appeared —*Irish Digest*⟩ ⟨lying was not high diplomacy, nor *sharp* practices good commerce —Haldane Macfall⟩ KEEN may describe quite sharp cutting edges ⟨a *keen* knife⟩ In reference to persons it implies perceptiveness, clear-sightedness, skill in quick analysis, and overall mental readiness ⟨skillfully and pleasantly written, it was in effect a *keen* attack upon the English Church and its clergy —H.E.Starr⟩ ⟨his teaching was remarkable for a variety of qualities: swift and *keen* generalization, ready control of the background of ideas —C.N. Greenough⟩ ACUTE is likely to refer to angles; in reference to people it may suggest discrimination and analytical penetration equipping one to solve more knotty problems ⟨it was very *acute* . . . to spot such a deep game —Joseph Conrad⟩ ⟨as the *acute* reader will not have failed to note —Havelock Ellis⟩
²**sharp** \ˈ"\ *vb* -ED/-ING/-S [ME *sharpen*, fr. OE *scerpan, scyrpan*; akin to MHG *scherpfen* to sharpen, Icel *skerpa*; causative fr. the root of E ¹*sharp*] *vt* **1** *dial* **:** SHARPEN **2 :** to raise (as a musical tone) in pitch; *esp* **:** to raise in pitch by a half step **3** *archaic* **:** to obtain by trickery or swindling **:** PILFER **~** *vi* **1 :** to sing or play above the true pitch **2** *archaic* **:** to act the sharper
³**sharp** \ˈ"\ *adv* -ER/-EST [ME *sharpe*, fr. OE *scearpe*, fr. *scearp*, adj. — more at ¹SHARP] **:** in a sharp manner **:** SHARPLY: as **a** *obs* **:** SHRILLY **b :** to a point or edge **c :** close to the wind ⟨a ship braced ~ up⟩ **d :** higher than the true or accepted musical pitch ⟨sang ~⟩ **e :** ABRUPTLY, QUICKLY, BRISKLY **f :** PRECISELY, EXACTLY ⟨an appointment at one o'clock ~⟩ **g :** ACUTELY — often used in combination ⟨*sharp*-angled⟩ **h :** in a trim well-turned-out manner or style **:** so as to be notable for style or dressiness ⟨looking ~ in a new tweed⟩
⁴**sharp** \ˈ"\ *n* -s [ME, fr. *sharp*, adj. — more at ¹SHARP] **:** one that is sharp: as **a :** a sharp edge or point **b** *archaic* **:** a sharp weapon **c** (1) **:** a musical note or tone one half step higher than a note or tone named ⟨C sharp is the ~ of C⟩ (2) **:** a character ♯ on a line or space of the musical staff indicating a pitch a half step higher than the degree would indicate without it (3) **:** the key next to the right of any given key on a keyboard musical instrument **d sharps** *pl, chiefly Brit* **:** MIDDLING 1b **e :** a long needle with sharp point for general sewing **f :** a real or self-styled expert; *also* **:** SHARPER **g :** a thin sharp piece of diamond used esp. for cutting, for cleaving, or for engraving gems

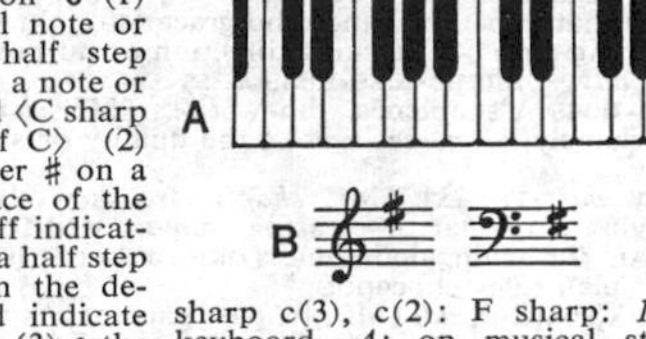

sharp c(3), c(2): F sharp: *1* on a keyboard, *A;* on musical staff, *B*

sharp-beaked \ˈ=ˈ=\ *adj* **:** having a pointed elongated beak or snout
sharp cedar *n* **:** ⁴CADE
sharp-cut \ˈ=ˈ=\ *adj* **:** cut so as to be sharp or make a clear well-defined impression ⟨an engraved plate with *sharp-cut* lines⟩
sharp dock *n* **:** ¹DOCK 1
sharp·en \ˈshärpən, ˈshȧp-\ *vb* **sharpened; sharpened; sharpening** \-p(ə)niŋ\ **sharpens** [ME *sharpenen*, fr. ¹*sharp* + *-enen, -nen -en*] *vt* **1 :** to make sharp **:** give a keen edge or fine point to ⟨~ an ax⟩ **2 :** to make sharper: as **a :** to make quicker or more acute in perception or ready in action **b :** to make more eager **c :** to make (as a law) more severe **d :** to make more intense ⟨~ a pain⟩ **e :** to make (as one's speech) biting, sarcastic, or harsh **f :** to make shriller or more piercing **g :** to make more tart or pungent ⟨the rays of the sun ~ vinegar⟩ ⟨cheese ~*ed* by ripening⟩ **h :** to make thinner or emaciated **i :** to make distinct in outline **j :** to increase the activity of (lime liquors used in removing hair from hides) usu. by adding sodium sulfide **3** *chiefly Brit* **:** SHARP *vt* 2 **4 :** to brace up sharp **~** *vi* **1 :** to grow or become sharp **2** *chiefly Brit* **:** SHARP *vi* 1 — **sharpen one's knife :** to be ready or preparing to punish or attack — usu. used with *for* ⟨*sharpening my knife* for the fellow that told that lie⟩
sharp·en·er \ˈshärp(ə)nər, ˈshȧp(ə)nə(r\ *n* -s **:** one that sharpens something (as tools or gears): as **a :** PENCIL SHARPENER **b :** one that sharpens the saws of linter machines
sharpening stone *n* **:** a hand sharpening device (as a whetstone)
sharp·er \ˈshärpər, ˈshȧpə(r\ *n* -s [¹*sharp* + *-er*] **1 :** an unduly sharp or canny person: as **a :** a cheater in bargains **b :** SWINDLER **c :** a cheating gamester **:** CARDSHARPER **2** *chiefly South* **:** an oyster having a thin sharp edge
sharpest *superlative of* SHARP
sharp-eyed \ˈ=ˈ=\ *adj* **:** having keen sight; *also* **:** keen in observing or penetrating
shar·pey's fiber \ˈshärpēz-, ˈshȧp-\ *n, usu cap S* **:** FIBER OF SHARPEY
sharp-fanged \ˈ=ˈ=\ *adj* **:** having sharp teeth **:** BITING, SARCASTIC
sharp-freeze \ˈ=ˈ=\ *vt* **:** QUICK-FREEZE
sharp-heeled \ˈ=ˈ=\ *adj* **:** having a sharp or pointed heel; *specif* **:** armed with spurs — used chiefly of a gamecock
sharp·ie *or* **sharpy** \ˈshärpē, ˈshȧpē, -pi\ *n, pl* **sharpies** [¹*sharp* + *-ie*] **1 :** a long rather narrow shallow-draft boat with flat or slightly V-shaped bottom and one or two masts that bear a triangular sail **2 a :** SHARPER 1 **b :** an exceptionally keen alert person

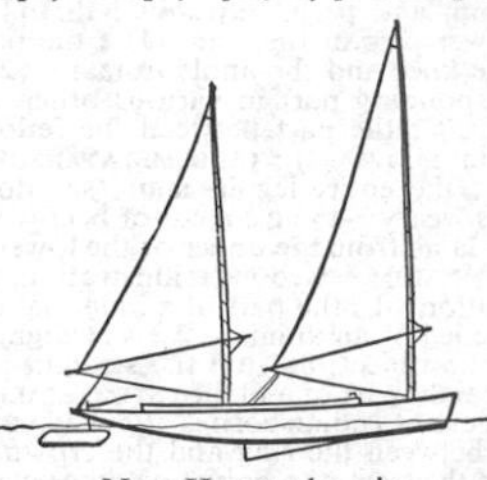
New Haven sharpie

sharping *pres part of* SHARP
sharp iron *n* [trans. of G *scharfeisen*] **:** a tool for opening seams (as in a wooden ship) into which caulking material is to be thrust
sharp·ish \ˈshärpish, ˈshȧp-, -pēsh\ *adj* **:** somewhat sharp
sharp·ite \-,pīt\ *n* -s [F, fr. R.R.*Sharp*, 20th cent. Brit. army officer + F *-ite*] **:** a mineral $(UO_2)_6(CO_3)_5(OH)_2 \cdot 6H_2O(?)$ consisting of a hydrous basic carbonate of uranyl found with other uranium minerals
sharp·ly *adv* [ME, fr. OE *scearplīce*, adv. of *scearplīc* sharp, severe, fr. *scearp* sharp + *-līc* -ly] **:** in a sharp manner **:** so as to be or appear sharp — often used as an intensifier ⟨distribution is to be ~ limited⟩
sharp mixture *n* **:** ACUTE MIXTURE
sharp·ness *n* -ES [ME *sharpnesse*, fr. OE *scearpnes*, fr. *scearp* sharp + *-nes* -ness] **:** the quality or state of being sharp
sharp-nosed \ˈ=ˈnōzd\ *adj* **1 :** having a pointed nose or snout ⟨a *sharp-nosed* beetle⟩ **2 :** keen of scent ⟨*sharp-nosed* still-trailing hounds⟩ — **sharp-nosed·ly** \-nōz(ə)dlē, -li\ *adv* — **sharp-nosed·ness** \-nəs\ *n* -ES
sharp-nosed crab *n* **:** a rough pear-shaped shallow-water spider crab (*Scyra acutifrons*) having the rostrum prolonged in two hornlike points and being common along the Pacific coast of No. America
sharp-nosed shark *or* **sharpnose shark** \ˈ=ˈ=-\ *n* **:** a small gray or brown shark (*Scoliodon terrae-novae*) of both coasts of the Atlantic and esp. abundant in the Caribbean area; *also* **:** a closely related slaty or bluish gray shark (*S. longurio*) of the Pacific coast of Mexico and southern California
sharp practice *n* **:** dealing in which advantage is taken or sought unscrupulously; *also* **:** a particular piece of or custom involving such dealing ⟨determined to put down *sharp practices* in his department⟩
sharps *pl of* SHARP, *pres 3d sing of* SHARP
sharp sand *n* **:** a sand with angular grains that is nearly or wholly free from foreign particles (as of clay or loam)
sharps and flats *n pl* **1 :** keys of a keyboard musical instrument other than the ones in the natural scale of C major **2 :** ACCIDENTALS ⟨the piece is full of *sharps and flats*⟩
sharp-set \ˈ=ˈ=\ *adj* **1 :** set at a sharp angle **:** set so as to present a sharp edge **2 :** eager in appetite or desire of gratification; *usu* **:** very hungry **:** RAVENOUS — **sharp-set·ness** *n* -ES
sharpshin \ˈ=,=\ *n, archaic* **:** a piece of cut money
sharp-shinned hawk \ˈ=ˈ=-\ *also* **sharpshin** *n* [*sharp-shinned* fr. ¹*sharp* + *-shinned* (fr. *shin*, n. + *-ed*)] **:** a common widely distributed No. American hawk (*Accipiter striatus velox*) having the upper parts ashy gray, the underparts white barred with rufous, and the rather long tail barred with blackish and tipped with white, being scarcely larger than the American sparrow hawk, noted for its dash and spirit, and often attacking poultry
sharpshod \ˈ=ˈ=\ *adj, of a horse* **:** shod with sharp calks
sharpshooter \ˈ=,==\ *n* [trans. of G *scharfschütze*] **1 a :** one skilled in shooting **:** a good marksman: as (1) **:** a member of a military unit employed primarily in skirmishing or on outposts (2) **:** a member of an armed force who has formally qualified in marksmanship according to a prescribed standard with a rating below expert but above marksman; *also* **:** the rating of such a qualified person **b :** a player in a sport whose aim is consistently accurate ⟨a basketball ~⟩ **c :** a person whose aim is to win without regard to equity or scruples **:** one who seeks to make an inordinate immediate profit without thought of building up a continuing business relationship **2 :** any of numerous leafhoppers that have sharply conical heads and include various economically important pests some of which puncture and damage young cotton bolls **3 :** the person in charge of explosives in an oil-well drilling operation **4 :** a sailboat common around the Bahamas islands and having the form of a rather deep sharp-keeled catboat **5 :** a usu. narrow-bladed spade

sharpshooter 4

sharpshooting \ˈ=,==\ *n* -s [fr. *sharpshooter*, after E *shooter: shooting*] **1 :** shooting with great precision **2 :** accurate and usu. unexpected attack (as in words) **:** SNIPING
sharp-shot \ˈ=,=\ *n* **:** BALL CARTRIDGE
sharp-sighted \ˈ=ˈ==\ *adj* **1 :** having quick or acute sight **2 :** mentally keen or alert — **sharp-sight·ed·ly** *adv* — **sharp-sight·ed·ness** *n* -ES
sharp·ster \ˈshärpstər, ˈshȧpstə(r\ *n* -s **:** SHARPER
sharptail \ˈ=,=\ *n* **:** any of several birds with a pointed tail (as a sharp-tailed grouse, duck, or sparrow)
sharp-tailed \ˈ=ˈ=\ *adj* [ME *sharpe tayled*, fr. *sharpe, sharp*, adj., sharp + *tayled, tailed* tailed] **1 :** having a pointed tail **2 :** having acuminate tail feathers
sharp-tailed duck *n* **1** *chiefly Brit* **:** OLD-SQUAW **2 :** PINTAILED DUCK
sharp-tailed grouse *n* **:** a large grouse (*Pedioecetes phasianellus*) of the western U.S. and Canada that inhabits open prairies and foothills mostly farther west than the true prairie chicken with which it is often confused, that is light buff in color and barred and mottled with blackish, and that has the head slightly crested and the middle tail feathers somewhat elongated
sharp-tailed sandpiper *n* **:** a sandpiper (*Erdia acuminata*) similar to the pectoral sandpiper that breeds in eastern Siberia and winters as far south as Australia and New Zealand
sharp-tailed sparrow *or* **sharp-tailed finch** *n* **:** a No. American sparrow (*Ammospiza caudacuta*) having narrow pointed tail feathers and inhabiting salt marshes
sharp-tongued \ˈ=ˈ=\ *adj* **:** having a sharp tongue **:** harsh or bitter of speech
sharp-toothed \ˈ=ˈ=\ *adj* **:** having sharp teeth **:** ready to use the teeth (as in rending or tearing)
sharp tuning *n* **:** radio tuning such that the current in the receiving apparatus is changed materially by a slight change in the frequency of the received waves — compare FLAT TUNING
sharpware \ˈ=,=\ *n* **:** EDGE TOOLS
sharp-witted \ˈ=ˈ==\ *adj* **:** having an acute or a quickly or nicely discerning mind — **sharp-wit·ted·ly** *adv* — **sharp-wit·ted·ness** *n* -ES
sharpy *var of* SHARPIE
shar·ra \ˈshärə\ *n, pl* **sharra** *usu cap* **1 :** one of a Mongol people of Outer Mongolia who with the Kalmucks are the

most typical of the Mongols **2 :** the dialect of Mongolian spoken by the Sharra people

shas *pl of* SHA

shash·lik *also* **shash·lick** *or* **shas·lik** \(')shäs(h)¦lik\ *n* -s [Russ *shashlyk*, of Turkic origin; akin to Kazan Tatar *šyšlyk* kabob] **:** KABOB

sha·si \(')shä¦sē\ *adj, usu cap* [fr. *Shasi*, city in east central China] **:** of or from the city of Shasi, China **:** of the kind or style prevalent in Shasi

shas·ta \'shastə\ *n, pl* **shasta** *or* **shastas** *usu cap* **1 a :** an Indian people of northern California and southern Oregon **b :** a member of such people **2 :** a Shastan language of the Shasta people **3 :** SHASTAN

shasta cypress *n, usu cap S* [fr. Mt. *Shasta*, northern California] **:** MACNAB CYPRESS

shasta daisy *n, usu cap S* **:** a large-flowered garden daisy that is a variety of a Pyrenean perennial herb (*Chrysanthemum maximum*) and resembles the common oxeye daisy

[1]**shas·tan** \'shastən\ *n* -s *usu cap* [*Shasta* + *-an*, n. suffix] **:** a language family of the Hokan stock in northern California and southern Oregon comprising Achomawi, Atsugewi, and Shasta

[2]**shastan** \"\ *adj, usu cap* [*Shasta* + *-an*, adj. suffix] **:** of or relating to the Shasta people or their language

shasta red fir *also* **shasta fir** *n, usu cap S* [fr. Mt. *Shasta*] **:** an immense evergreen tree (*Abies magnifica shastensis*) of the Pacific coast of No. America closely related to the California red fir but less hardy in cultivation

shasta sam *n, usu cap both Ss* [fr. *Sam*, nickname fr. the name *Samuel*] **:** a card game like California Jack except that the pack drawn from is turned face down

shas·tra *or* **sas·tra** \'shästrə\ *n* -s *often cap* [Skt *śāstra*, lit., instruction, fr. *śāsti* he punishes, instructs; akin to Av *sāsti* he teaches] **:** the sacred scriptures of Hinduism consisting of four categories of text, the sruti, smriti, purana, and tantra — **shas·tra·ic** \(')shä¦strāik\ *adj, often cap*

[1]**shat** *past of* SHIT

[2]**shat** \'shat, *usu* -ad·+V\ *also* **shat·ter** \-ad·ə(r), -atə\ *n* -s *chiefly Midland* [*shat* prob. alter. of [1]*chat; shatter* prob. alter. (infl. by [2]*shatter*) of [1]*chat*] **:** PINE NEEDLE — usu. used in pl.

shath·mont \'shath,mänt\ *Scot var of* SHAFTMENT

[1]**shat·ter** \'shad·ə(r), -atə-\ *vb* -ED/-ING/-S [ME *schateren*; perh. akin to MLG *schāteren* to explode, Gk *skedannynai* to scatter, Lith *skedervà* splinter] *vt* **1 :** to cause to drop or be dispersed **:** SCATTER ⟨with a measured tap of his forefinger he ~*ed* the ash from his cigar —Hamilton Basso⟩ ⟨the slightest jar ~*s* the petals of a full-blown rose⟩ ⟨wind could ~ out wheat —A.B.Guthrie⟩ **2 a :** to splinter with or as if with a blow **:** reduce to fragments **:** FRACTURE, SMASH ⟨fifty windowpanes were ~*ed* by the missiles —*Amer. Guide Series: Conn.*⟩ ⟨amethysts caught the light, ~*ing* it and sending it forth again in a thousand fragments —Louis Bromfield⟩ **b :** to damage badly **:** RUIN, WRECK ⟨men whose faces had been ~*ed* on the Italian fronts —James Stern⟩ ⟨rough weather . . . ~*ed* the mainmast —C.O.Paullin⟩ **3 a :** to cause the disruption or annihilation of **:** DISINTEGRATE, DEMOLISH ⟨riflemen . . . ~*ed* each wave of attackers before it could come within volleying distance —*Amer. Guide Series: Tenn.*⟩ ⟨one cold puff of piety . . . ~*ed* the warm colorful world of romance —Osbert Lancaster⟩ ⟨the legend of Rome's invincibility had been ~*ed* —John Buchan⟩ **b :** to cause to break down **:** IMPAIR, DESTROY ⟨his health was ~*ed* . . . by the war —V.H.Paltsits⟩ ⟨people collide with harsh experience and are ~*ed* —Paul Engle⟩ ⟨nothing but death was strong enough to ~ that inherited restraint —Ellen Glasgow⟩ **4 :** to separate (a flower) into clusters of petals which are then wired or taped ⟨her wrist corsage was of ~*ed* yellow carnations —*Springfield (Mass.) Daily News*⟩ ~ *vi* **1 :** to make a rattling sound **:** CLATTER ⟨rain . . . ~*s* at the windowpane —Maurice Hewlett⟩ **2 :** to break apart **:** become shattered **:** SHIVER, DISINTEGRATE ⟨turned back . . . to see the laboratory window ~ —W.N. Marsh⟩ ⟨the Empire of the Incas . . . ~*ed* at Pizarro's touch —Bernard De Voto⟩ **3 :** to drop or scatter leaves, petals, fruit (as kernels of ripe grain or the berries of grapes) ⟨the wheat ~*ed* in the field before harvest⟩ **syn** see BREAK

[2]**shatter** \"\ *n* -s **1 :** FRAGMENT, SHRED — usu. used in pl. ⟨the plate was in ~*s* on the floor⟩ **2 :** an act of shattering or state of being shattered; *specif* **:** a plant disease characterized by premature dropping or dehiscence ⟨studies on the ~ of grapes —L.P.Miller⟩ **3 :** a result of shattering **:** SHOWER, SPATTER ⟨sunlight broke . . . painfully in his eyes like a ~ of gold glass —David Beaty⟩

shat·ter·able \-rəbəl\ *adj* **:** capable of being shattered

shatterbrain \'==,=\ *n, archaic* **:** SCATTERBRAIN — **shatter-brained** \¦==¦=\ *adj, archaic*

shatter crack *n* **:** a minute crack which sometimes develops in the head of a rail usu. half an inch or more beneath the surface owing to defective forging

shat·ter·er \'shad·ərə(r), -atərə-\ *n* -s **:** one that shatters

[1]**shattering** *adj* [fr. pres. part. of [1]*shatter*] **1 :** causing deterioration or breakdown **:** DESTRUCTIVE, DEMORALIZING ⟨the ~ action of frost —R.F.Flint⟩ ⟨somehow we staggered through that ~ heat —A.E. Stevenson †1965⟩ ⟨the economic collapse of the thirties was a ~ thing, a nightmare that still haunts us —Lester Markel⟩ **2 :** having tremendous impact **:** TERRIFIC, OVERPOWERING ⟨the giants of our past, their ~ words, their stunning achievements —Jerome Weidman⟩ ⟨a ~ display of technical knowledge —Lennox Robinson⟩ ⟨the ~ tones of an enormous carillon reverberating through a tower room —Arthur Knight⟩ — **shat·ter·ing·ly** *adv*

[2]**shattering** *n* -s [fr. gerund of [1]*shatter*] **1 :** an act or result of breaking down **2** *dial Eng* **:** a small quantity **:** SPRINKLING

shatterpated \¦==¦==\ *adj* **:** SCATTERBRAINED

shatterproof \¦==¦=\ *adj* **:** proof against shattering ⟨transparent, ~ acrylic plastic —W.A.Hamor⟩

shatterproof glass *n* **:** LAMINATED GLASS

shatters *pres 3d sing of* SHATTER, *pl of* SHATTER

shat·tery \'shad·ərē, -atərē, -ri\ *adj* **:** easily shattered

shat·tuck·ite \'shad·ə,kīt\ *n* -s [*Shattuck* Denn Mine, near Douglas, Arizona + E *-ite*] **:** a mineral $2CuSiO_3.H_2O$ consisting of a massive fibrous blue hydrous copper silicate (sp. gr. 3.8)

shauch·le \'shäkəl\ *var of* SHACHLE

shaugh \'shäk\ *var of* SHOCH

shaugh·nes·sy playoff \'shȯnəsē-, -si-\ *n, usu cap S* [after Francis J. *Shaughnessy*, *b* 1883 Am. baseball official] **:** a playoff among the top four teams of a league (as in minor league baseball and ice hockey) in which team one usu. plays team three, team two plays team four, and the two winners play each other

sha·van·te \shə'vantē\ *n, pl* **shavante** *or* **shavantes** *usu cap* **1 :** any of several not clearly identifiable peoples of Brazil **2 :** a member of any of the Shavante peoples

[1]**shave** \'shāv\ *vb* **shaved; shaved** *or* **shav·en** \'shāvən\ **shaving; shaves** [ME *shaven*, fr. OE *scafan*; akin to OHG *skaban* to scrape, ON *skafa* to scrape, shave, Goth *skaban* to shave, shear, L *scabere* to scratch, scrape, Russ *skobel'* adz, plane, Gk *skaptein* to dig — more at CAPON] *vt* **1 a :** to remove a thin layer from **:** PARE, SCRAPE ⟨showed him how to trim, ~ and properly soften a new and playable reed —Harold Sinclair⟩ ⟨the rims are delicately *shaved* by steam power —Lois I. Woodville⟩ **b :** to cut off in thin layers or shreds **:** SLICE, SLIVER ⟨a red-hot mass which a steel cutting machine was *shaving*, as though it were cheese —W.J.Locke⟩ ⟨maple sugar . . . in a bricklike cake which can be readily grated or *shaved* —*House Beautiful*⟩; *specif* **:** to trim slightly (as the edge of a book page) ⟨the paper of the MS has been *shaved* at the bottom —Sydney Race⟩ **c :** to reduce or make uniform the thickness of (a hide) by cutting away a portion from the flesh side — compare SKIVE **d :** to cut off closely **:** CROP, DENUDE ⟨a smooth *shaven* lawn⟩ ⟨a frontier that has been *shaved* of all trees and shrubbery —Claire Sterling⟩ **2 a :** to sever the hair from (the head or another part of the body) close to the roots ⟨*shaving* . . . part of the scalp on aesthetic grounds or to denote a certain rank —A.G.Petitpierre⟩ ⟨~ a patient for surgery⟩; *specif* **:** TONSURE ⟨~ the crown of a monk⟩ **b :** to remove beard from (the face or neck) with a razor ⟨hire a ballplayer to ~ himself on a TV commercial⟩ **c :** to cut off (hair or beard) close to the skin ⟨~*s* the hair off her legs⟩ ⟨got him to ~ off his beard⟩ **3 a** *chiefly dial* **:** [2]FLEECE 2 **b :** to discount (a note) at an exorbitant rate — compare NOTE SHAVER **c :** to subtract or make smaller **:** DEDUCT, REDUCE ⟨new procedures ~ . . . minutes from the unloading process —*N. Y. Times*⟩ ⟨imports must be cut, armed forces *shaved*, food rations trimmed —Arthur Hepner⟩ **4 :** to come close to or touch lightly in passing **:** CLIP, GRAZE ⟨set the buoy rocking . . . as she *shaved* it close —Llewellyn Howland⟩ ~ *vi* **1 :** to cut off hair or beard close to the skin ⟨~*s* with an electric razor⟩ ⟨borrowed a friend's room so that he could ~ that morning —Russell Lord⟩ **2 :** to proceed with difficulty **:** SCRAPE ⟨*shaved* through the gap with inches to spare —C.S.Forester⟩

[2]**shave** \"\ *n* -s *often attrib* [in sense 1, fr. ME *shave*, fr. OE *scafa*; in other senses, fr. [1]*shave*; OE *scafa* akin to OHG *scaba* scraper, plane, Icel *skafa*; derivative fr. the root of [1]*shave*] **1 :** SHAVER 3: as **a :** SPOKESHAVE **b :** DRAWKNIFE **c :** a tool through which basketwork splits are drawn to remove the pith and make them uniform in width **2 :** SHAVING ⟨took real pride in cutting delicate ~*s* of cold beef —Katherine Mansfield⟩ **3 a :** an act or process of shaving ⟨felt fresh from his ~ and shower —Hamilton Basso⟩ **b :** a result of shaving ⟨got a ~ and a haircut⟩ **4 :** CLOSE SHAVE ⟨it was a ~ but we made it⟩ ⟨all-around sportsman — had gone after big game all over the world and had a good many narrow ~*s* —Max Beerbohm⟩ **5** *archaic* **:** SWINDLE

shaved *adj* **1 :** finely sliced or shredded **:** CHIPPED ⟨~ beef⟩ ⟨~ ice⟩ **2 a :** having the hair or beard cut off close to the root ⟨a clean-*shaved* man⟩; *specif* **:** TONSURED ⟨monk with a ~ head⟩ **b :** TRIMMED, CROPPED ⟨a ~ hide⟩

shave grass *also* **shave rush** *n* [*shave grass* fr. ME *schavegres*, fr. *schaven*, *shaven* to shave + *gres*, *gras* grass; *shave rush* fr. [1]*shave* + *rush*] **:** SCOURING RUSH

shave hook *n* [ME *shave hok*, fr. *shaven* to shave + *hok* hook] **:** a tool consisting of a sharp-edged steel plate set transversely at the end of a shank fixed in a handle and used esp. by plumbers and metalworkers for scraping metals

shave hook

shave·ling \'shāvliŋ, -lēŋ\ *n* -s **1 :** a tonsured clergyman **:** PRIEST — usu. used disparagingly **2 :** STRIPLING

shav·en \¦shāvən\ *adj* [ME *shaven*, fr. past part. of *shaven* to shave] **:** SHAVED

shav·er \'shāvə(r)\ *n* -s [ME, fr. *shaven* to shave + *-er*] **1 a :** one that shaves with a razor; *specif* **:** BARBER **b :** one that slices, trims, or crops: as (1) **:** an operator of a machine for shaving fur from skins (2) **:** a workman who shaves hides to reduce them to even thickness or to remove rough spots (3) **:** one who trims the edges of granite blocks with a circular saw (4) **:** an operator of a machine for shaving split rattan to proper thickness and width for basketry **2 a** *archaic* **:** SWINDLER, EXTORTIONER **b :** NOTE SHAVER **3 :** a tool or machine for shaving ⟨took off the rough corners of the plank with a ~⟩ ⟨pull an ice ~ over the rink after each of the many skating sessions —Melvin Beck⟩ ⟨the transcribing machine; and the ~ —H.D.Fasnacht⟩; *specif* **:** an electric-powered razor for removing a beard ⟨a ~ is simpler to use than the old-fashioned hand razor⟩ **4 :** a little child **:** BOY, YOUNGSTER ⟨a little ~ . . . wanted to be a doctor just like his daddy —*My Baby*⟩ ⟨tried to remember those ragged days when he was only a ~ —J.T.Farrell⟩

shaves *pl of* SHAVE *or of* SHAFT, *pres 3d sing of* SHAVE

shavetail \'=,=\ *n* [[1]*shave* + *tail*; fr. the custom of shaving the tails of mules when they are broken in so that they can be easily distinguished from the untrained ones] **1 :** a pack mule esp. when newly broken in **2 :** a newly commissioned officer **:** SECOND LIEUTENANT — usu. used disparagingly ⟨hell hath no fury like a ~ scorned —Harold Fleming⟩

[1]**sha·vi·an** \'shāvēən, -vyən\ *n* -s *usu cap* [*Shavius* (latinized form of the name of George Bernard *Shaw* †1950 Brit. playwright, novelist, and critic) + E *-an*, n. suffix] **:** an admirer or devotee of G. B. Shaw, his writings, or his theory of social and political organization

[2]**shavian** \"\ *adj, usu cap* [*Shavius* + E *-an*, adj. suffix] **:** of, relating to, or characteristic of G. B. Shaw or his writings ⟨*Shavian* wit⟩ ⟨this gem of *Shavian* perspicacity —*Newsweek*⟩ ⟨a fresh setting, a *Shavian* philosophy and a modern meaning —Hesketh Pearson⟩

sha·vi·ana \,shāvē'anə, -änə, -ānə *also* -'ānə\ *n pl, usu cap* [*Shavius* + E *-ana*] **:** memorabilia concerning G. B. Shaw ⟨has just given Yale University his entire collection of *Shaviana* —*N.Y.Times*⟩

sha·vian·ism \'shāvēə,nizəm, -vyə,-\ *n* -s *usu cap* **1 :** an attitude or utterance of or characteristic of G. B. Shaw **2 :** devotion to the writings or social theories of G. B. Shaw

shav·ie \'shāvi\ *n* -s [perh. fr. [2]*shave* + *-ie*] *Scot* **:** PRACTICAL JOKE, PRANK

shav·ing \'shāviŋ, -vēŋ\ *n* -s [ME, fr. gerund of *shaven* to shave] **1 :** an act or process of trimming or cutting closely: as **a :** the removal of hair or beard with a razor ⟨~ with an electric razor takes him about five minutes⟩ **b :** the removal of excess material with a cutting tool ⟨~ is now the most widely used productive method of finishing . . . gear teeth —R.S. Kegg⟩ **c :** the scraping of old material from the surface of a recording medium (as a cylinder) to obtain a new recording surface **2 :** a slice or fragment produced by a shaver: as **a :** a thin strip of wood pared off by a plane — usu. used in pl. ⟨fragrant boards and ~*s* —G.W.Brace⟩ **b shavings** *pl* **:** the strips trimmed from either side of a paper web or from a pile of sheets **c :** FLAKE, CHIP ⟨the roll is then dusted with cocoa and decorated with ~*s* of bitter chocolate —*New Yorker*⟩ **3 a :** the discounting of a note at an exorbitant rate **b :** a reduction in amount ⟨some price ~*s* were announced —*Dun's Rev.*⟩

shaving board *n* **:** a small slanted beam on which barrel hoops are shaved

shaving brush *n* **:** a brush used to lather the face preparatory to shaving — see BRUSH illustration

shaving cream *n* **:** an emollient paste made usu. of soap and free fatty acid (as stearic acid) that forms a mild firm lather for softening the beard before shaving

shaving die *n* **:** a cutting die for shaving a thin finishing cut from work previously blanked or pierced nearly to size

shaving horse *n* **1 :** a bench astride which a workman sits while shaving down work (as with a drawknife) **2 :** a sloping frame having two wooden clamps to hold material being shaved

shaving machine *n* **:** a machine with a high speed revolving spiral knife for smoothing off the flesh side of a hide

shav·ings \'shāviŋz, -vēŋz\ *n pl but sing or pl in constr* **:** FRINGE TREE

shaving soap *n* **:** a soap made from either a soda or potash base to which is added a relatively large amount of free fatty acid (as palmitic acid or stearic acid) to decrease the customary alkalinity of the soap and produce a thick lather for shaving

shavuoth *or* **shavuot** *or* **shavuos** *usu cap, var of* SHABUOTH

[1]**shaw** \'shȯ, 'shä\ *n* -s [ME *shawe*, fr. OE *scaga*, *sceaga*; akin to ON *skagi* promontory, *skaga* to project — more at SHAG] *dial* **:** a small grove of trees **:** COPPICE, THICKET ⟨scattered through the ~ —C.S.Coon⟩; *esp* **:** a strip of woods forming the boundary of a field

[2]**shaw** \'shȯ\ *chiefly dial var of* SHOW

[3]**shaw** \"\ *n* -s [prob. fr. [2]*shaw*] *chiefly Brit* **:** the tops and stalks of a cultivated crop (as potatoes or turnips) ⟨heavy-yielding . . . potato, with great ~*s* that protected the tubers from the hot sun —Paul de Kruif⟩

shawabti *var of* USHABTI

shaw·a·nese salad \¦shȯ(w)ə¦nēz-, -ēs-\ *n, usu cap 1st S* [*shawanese* fr. obs. E *Shawanese* Shawnee, Shawnees — more at SHAWNEE] **:** VIRGINIA WATERLEAF

shawfowl \'=,=\ *n* [perh. fr. [2]*shaw* + *fowl*] *obs* **:** SCARECROW

[1]**shawl** \'shȯl\ *n* -s *often attrib* [Per *shāl*] **1 :** a simple garment or wrapper usu. made of a square or oblong piece of fabric (as wool) and used esp. as a covering for the head or shoulders or as a light blanket **2 :** something that resembles a shawl; *specif* **:** a section of window glass cut from a glass cylinder and split lengthwise preparatory to flattening

[2]**shawl** \"\ *vt* -ED/-ING/-S **:** to wrap in or as if in a shawl ⟨little convoys of overloaded donkeys and gaily ~*ed* women —John Masters⟩ ⟨eucalypt forests ~*ed* the quiet earth —June Hartnett⟩ ⟨nobility . . . carefully ~*ed* under her function as hostess —Elizabeth M. Roberts⟩

shawl collar *n* **:** an attached collar rolled back in a continuous tapering line that follows the surplice neckline of a garment

shawl collar

shawl goat *n* [so called fr. the use of its fur in weaving shawls] **:** KASHMIR GOAT

shawl·less \'shȯlləs\ *adj* **:** lacking a shawl

shawl pattern *n* **:** a pattern copied from a cashmere shawl and usu. made with bright-colored leaf or petal motifs — compare CASHMERE 2a

shawl strap *n* **:** a holder made of two or more straps attached to a handle and used for compactly carrying a shawl, steamer rug, or baggage roll

shawl tongue *n* **1 :** a long tongue of a shoe, slashed at the loose end and folded over at the instep to conceal the lacing of the shoe **2 :** KILTIE 2a

shawm *also* **shalm** \'shȯm\ *n* -s [ME *schalme*, *shalmye*, fr. MF *chalemie*, fr. OF, alter. of *chalemel*, fr. LL *calamellus* small reed, dim. of L *calamus* reed, fr. Gk *kalamos* — more at HAULM] **:** one of a family of early double-reed straight-bodied woodwind instruments preceding the oboe family — compare BOMBARD, BOMBARDON

shaw·nee \(')shȯ¦nē, (')shä¦-\ *also* **shaw·a·nee** \¦shȯ(w)ə¦nē\ *or* **shaw·a·no** \-nō\ *n, pl* **shawnee** *or* **shawnees** *usu cap* [*Shawnee*, *Shawanee* back-formation fr. obs. E *Shawnese*, *Shawanese* Shawnee, Shawnees, fr. Shawnee *Shaawanwaaki*, pl., lit., those in the south (fr. *shaawanawa* south) + E *-ese*; *Shawano* modif. of Shawnee *Shaawanwaaki*] **1 a :** an Indian people of the Cumberland river valley, Tenn., but ranging through most of the states east of the Mississippi and south of the Great Lakes **b :** a member of such people **2 :** an Algonquian language of the Shawnee people

shawnee salad *n, usu cap 1st S* **:** VIRGINIA WATERLEAF

shawneewood \(')=¦=,=\ *n* **:** WESTERN CATALPA

shaw·ny \'shȯnē, 'shän-, -ni\ *n* -ES [alter. of *shawnee salad*] **:** VIRGINIA WATERLEAF

shaws *pl of* SHAW

shaw·wal \shə'wäl\ *n* -s *usu cap* [Ar *shawwāl*] **:** the 10th month of the Muhammadan year — see MONTH table

shay \'shā\ *n* -s [back-formation fr. *chaise*, taken as pl.] **1** *chiefly dial* **:** CHAISE 1 **2 :** a slow wood-burning geared locomotive used esp. for hauling logs to a mill

shaykh *var of* SHEIKH

shaykhi *cap, var of* SHAIKHI

shays·ite \'shā,zīt\ *n* -s *usu cap* [Daniel *Shays* †1825 Am. Revolutionary officer and insurrectionary leader + E *-ite*] **:** a sympathizer with or participant in Shays' Rebellion of 1786–87 in Massachusetts brought on by business depression and heavy taxes

shcher·ba·kov \¦shcherbə¦kȯf\ *adj, usu cap* [fr. *Shcherbakov*, city in north central European Russia, U. S. S. R.] **:** of or from the city of Shcherbakov, U. S. S. R. **:** of the kind or style prevalent in Shcherbakov

shd *abbr* should

[1]**she** \(')shē, shi\ *pron* [ME *she*, *sho*, prob. alter. of *hye*, *hyo*, alter. of OE *hīe*, *hīo*, *hēo* — more at HE] **1 :** that female one ⟨~ is now the wife of Marcus Antonius —Shak.⟩ **:** that one regarded as feminine (as by personification) ⟨if Nature . . . refused to reproduce the effect he wanted, he would patiently return, evening after evening, until ~ did —Hesketh Pearson⟩ ⟨I bought a motorcycle . . . and ~ was a dandy —Burl Ives⟩ — used as nominative feminine pronoun of the third person singular usu. in reference to a previously specified subject or to someone identified by an accompanying relative clause or prepositional phrase; usu. considered impolite when used in reference to a woman or girl who has not previously been mentioned by name or referred to by means of an identifying noun; sometimes in poetry and in substandard speech used pleonastically together with a noun as subject of a verb ⟨the Liner ~'s a lady —Rudyard Kipling⟩; see [1]HER, [3]HER, [1]HERS; compare HE, IT, THEY **2** *Scot* **:** I, YOU, HE — used esp. in literary representations of the English spoken by Scottish Highlanders **3 :** YOU ⟨did ~ bump her little head⟩ — compare [1]HE 4 **4 a** *substand* **:** HER — used in a compound object ⟨between the boy and ~⟩ **b** *dial chiefly Brit* **:** HER — used emphatically as object of a verb or preposition ⟨the earth hath swallow'd all my hopes but ~ —Shak.⟩ ⟨no fit place for ~ —James Spilling⟩

[2]**she** \'shē\ *n* -s *often attrib* [ME, fr. *she*, pron.] **1 :** a female person or animal ⟨you are the cruelest ~ alive —Shak.⟩ — often used in compounds ⟨*she*-cat⟩ ⟨*she*-cousin⟩ **2 a :** one that is feminine in composition or characteristics — used in compounds ⟨*she*-poetry⟩ ⟨*she*-society⟩ **b :** a plant that resembles one of a different species that is regarded as better — used in compounds ⟨*she*-balsam⟩ ⟨*she*-oak⟩

[3]**she** \"\ *n, pl* **she** *or* **shes** *usu cap* **1 :** a people inhabiting the mountains in the interior borderland between Chekiang and Fukien provinces of China **2 :** a member of the She people

shea butter \'shē-, 'shā-\ *n* **:** a solid grayish, yellowish, or whitish fat obtained from the seeds of the shea tree and used chiefly as a food, in soap, and in candles

shea butter tree *or* **shea** *var of* SHEA TREE

shead·ing \'shēdiŋ\ *n* -s [ME *sheding* separation, division — more at SHEDDING] **:** any of the six divisions into which the Isle of Man is divided for the purposes of civil jurisdiction and over which there is a coroner or chief constable appointed by the governor

[1]**sheaf** \'shēf\ *n, pl* **sheaves** \-ēvz\ *also* **sheafs** [ME *sheef*, fr. OE *sceāf*; akin to OHG *scoub* sheaf, ON *skauf* fox's tail, Russ *chub* forelock] **1 a :** a quantity of the stalks and ears of wheat, rye, or other grain bound together **:** a bundle of grain or straw **b :** a bundle of other plant stalks or flowers bound together ⟨the altar banked with *sheaves* of lilies⟩ **2 :** something resembling or likened to a sheaf of grain: as **a :** a collection of things bound together **:** BUNDLE **b :** a quantity of arrows sufficient to fill a quiver; *also* **:** the allowance of arrows (as 24) allotted to each archer **c :** a cluster of similar items associated but not bound together ⟨a ~ of letters in her hand⟩ **d :** a representation of a sheaf (as of arrows) used as a crest **e :** planes of gunnery fire of two or more pieces of a battery as a group ⟨a converged ~⟩ ⟨parallel ~⟩ **3** *sheaves pl* **:** a large number or quantity

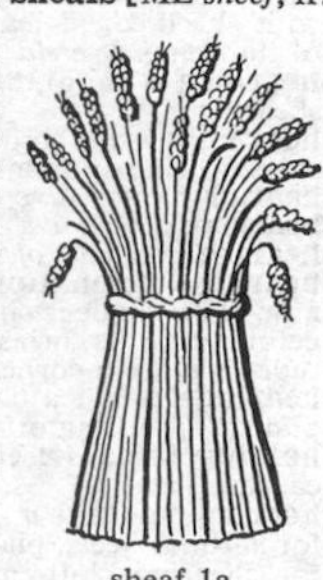
sheaf 1a

[2]**sheaf** *var of* SHEAVE

[3]**sheaf** \'shēf\ *n, pl* **sheaves** \-ēvz\ [by alter.] **:** SHEATH ⟨had another knife with a blade better than this, a leather ~ to keep it in —Donald Windham⟩

sheaf arrow *n* [ME *shefe arow*, fr. *shefe*, *sheef* sheaf + *arow*, *arewe* arrow] **:** an ancient English military arrow having a long and heavy stele, full fletching, and a narrow head with or without barbs

sheaf catalog *n* **:** a loose-leaf catalog

sheaflike \'=,=\ *adj* **:** resembling a bundle of sheaved grain

sheafy \'shēfē\ *adj* **:** of, resembling, or forming a sheaf ⟨~ crystalline needles⟩

[1]**sheal** \'shē(ə)l\ *var of* SHIEL

[2]**sheal** \"\ *vt* [ME *schelen*, *schyllen*; akin to OE *scealu* shell, husk — more at SHELL] *dial chiefly Eng* **:** SHELL

sheal·ing *or* **sheel·ing** \'shēliŋ\ *also* **shil·ing** \'shiliŋ\ *n* -s [ME *schyllinge* action of removing shells, fr. gerund of *schelen*, *schyllen*] **:** husked grain — usu. used in pl.

[2]**sheal·ing** \'shēliŋ\ *var of* SHIELING

shea nut *n* **:** the seed of the shea tree

shea–nut oil *n* **:** SHEA BUTTER

shea–oak *var of* SHE-OAK

[1]**shear** \'shi(ə)r, -iə\ *vb* **sheared** \-i(ə)rd, -iəd\ *or chiefly dial* **shore** \'shō(ə)r, 'shȯ(ə)r, -ōə, -ȯ(ə)\ **sheared** \'shi(ə)rd, -iəd\ *or* **shorn** \'shō(ə)rn, -ȯ(ə)n\ **shearing; shears** [ME *sheren*, fr. OE *sceran*, *scieran*; akin to OHG *skeran* to shear,

ON *skera* to cut, L *cernere* to separate, sift, *curtus* shortened, Gk *keirein* to cut, Skt *kartati* he cuts] *vt* **1 a** (1) **:** to cut off the hair from ⟨with crown *shorn*⟩; *also* **:** to cut off or cut short (hair) by or as if by the use of shears ⟨~*ed* the baby curls away⟩ (2) *obs* **:** TONSURE **b :** to cut, clip, or sever from something (as wool from sheep or superfluous nap from cloth) with or as if with shears ⟨~*ed* 100 bales of wool⟩ ⟨a hidden rock ~*ed* the keel from the ship⟩; *also* **:** to cut something from ⟨*shorn* sheep⟩ ⟨a ~*ed* velvet⟩ ⟨~ a lawn⟩ **c** *chiefly Scot* **:** to reap (as hay or grain) with a sickle **d :** to cut superfluous material from (a woody plant); *esp* **:** to prune (a hedge) with shears or other implement that cuts to a smooth even contour **e :** to cut (as metal or glass) with shears or a similar instrument **2 a :** to cut with something sharp ⟨~*ing* the hawser asunder⟩ **b** *obs* **:** to injure or separate into pieces by or as if by cutting **3 :** to traverse by or as if by cleaving ⟨a ship ~*ing* the sea⟩ ⟨a swallow that ~*s* the summer sky⟩ **4 :** to deprive of something as if by cutting **:** STRIP, DIVEST ⟨his recent ill-health had *shorn* him of strength⟩ ⟨has been *shorn* of his authority⟩ **5 a :** to subject to a shear (sense 5a) **b :** to cause (as a rockface) to move along a surface of shear ~ *vi* **1 :** to cut through something with or as if with a sharp instrument or shears **:** cleave a way ⟨birds ~*ing* through the air⟩ **2** *chiefly Scot* **:** to reap crops with a sickle **:** use a sickle in reaping **3** *chiefly Scot* **:** to split and then continue in different directions — used chiefly in the phrase *where wind and water shears* **4 :** to become more or less completely divided under the action of a shear ⟨the bolt may ~ off⟩ **5 :** to cut a vertical groove in a face in mining coal

²shear \"\ *n* -s *often attrib* [in sense 1, fr. ME *shere,* fr. OE *scēara* (pl.); in other senses, fr. ¹*shear;* OE *scēara* akin to OHG *skār* blade, ON *skæri* pair of shears, OE *sceran, scieran* to shear] **1 a** (1) **:** a cutting implement similar or identical to a pair of scissors but typically larger ⟨a ~ blade⟩ — usu. used in pl. ⟨trim a hedge with ~*s*⟩ (2) **:** one element or one blade of a pair of shears **b :** an instrument whose blades are connected at one end by a curved spring and which is used esp. for shearing sheep or skins — usu. used in pl. **c :** any of various cutting tools or machines operating by the action of opposed cutting edges of metal: as (1) **:** a machine for shearing metal and esp. in sheets; *esp* **:** ROTARY SHEARS — usu. used in pl. (2) **shears** *pl* **:** a power or hand-operated machine that cuts by means of a blade or a set of blades working against a resisting edge with the material to be sheared being between the two — see GUILLOTINE SHEARS, LEVER SHEARS (3) **:** a tool for cutting a gob of glass from the punty or a feeder (4) **:** SHEARING MACHINE 2 **d :** something felt to resemble a shear or a pair of shears: as (1) *obs* **:** WING (2) **:** a hoisting apparatus consisting of two or sometimes more spars fastened together at their upper ends, resting on their spread heels, secured or steadied by a guy or guys, and provided with tackle for masting or dismasting ships or lifting guns or other heavy loads — usu. used in pl. but sing. or pl. in constr. ⟨rigged a ~*s* to handle the timbers⟩; called also *hoisting shears, shear legs* **e :** the bed piece of a machine tool on which a table or slide rest is secured **:** WAY — often used in pl. **2** *chiefly Brit* **:** SHEARING — used in combination to indicate the approximate age of sheep in terms of shearings undergone ⟨a flock of healthy three-*shears*⟩ **3** *chiefly dial* **:** a crop that has been mowed or harvested **4 :** something (as an animal, a fleece, or an edge) that is shorn **5 a :** a strain resulting from applied forces that cause or tend to cause contiguous parts of a body to slide relatively to each other in a direction parallel to their plane of contact; *specif* **:** the ratio of the relative displacement of these parts to the distance between them **b :** the stress giving rise to this strain — see SHEARING STRESS **6 :** the sliding of a part of a rock body past another part along a fracture **syn** see STRESS — **off shears** *Austral, of a sheep* **:** recently shorn

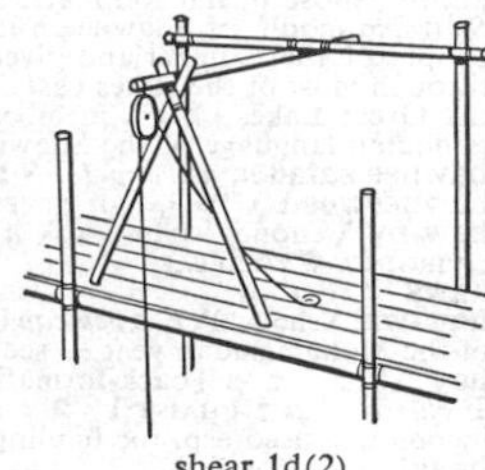
shear 1d(2)

³shear \"\ *dial var of* SHARE

shear·bill \'shi(ə)r,bil\ *n* [trans. of F *bec-en-ciseaux*] **:** BLACK SKIMMER

shear boom *n* [alter. (influenced by ²*shear*) of *sheer boom*] **:** a boom designed to guide floating logs in a desired direction

shear boy *n* **:** a worker in the glass industry who oils cutting shears and the funnels through which molten glass passes

sheard \'shärd\ *chiefly dial var of* SHARD

sheared *adj* **:** formed or finished by shearing ⟨a ~ border⟩; *esp* **:** cut to uniform length esp. to improve the appearance ⟨~ beaver⟩ ⟨~ raccoon⟩ ⟨a ~ hedge⟩

shear·er \'shirə(r)\ *n* -s [ME *sherer,* fr. *sheren* to shear + *-er*] **1 :** one that shears: as **a :** one that shears sheep **b :** a worker who uses shears on metal, textiles, leather, or other materials **c :** a machine that shears **d :** an operator of a machine for shearing out a channel down the working face of coal prior to blasting **2 :** one (as an animal) that is fit or ready for shearing or that yields a product (as fleece) to shearing ⟨sheep that are good ~*s*⟩

shear fracture *n* **:** a fracture produced in rocks by shear — compare GASH FRACTURE

sheargrass \'≈,≈\ *n* [ME *scheregresse,* fr. *scheren, sheren* to shear + *gresse, gras* grass] **:** any of various grasses or sedges with sharp-edged leaves: as **a :** SAW GRASS **b :** a plant of the genus *Leersia* **c :** COUCH GRASS 1a

shear·hog \'shi(ə),räg\ *n, dial Eng* **:** a sheep after the first shearing

shear hulk *n* **:** a ship unfit for other service that is fitted with shears for hoisting masts and other heavy articles

shearier *comparative of* SHEARY

sheariest *superlative of* SHEARY

shearing *pres part of* SHEAR

shearing deformation *n* **:** detrusion or deformation by which a small rectangle is changed into a parallelogram and in which deformation is measured as the total angular change in radians at each corner

shearing die *n* **:** a cutting die having a matrix and shearing punch for cutting off work from stock

shearing force *n* **:** either of a pair of equal opposed forces causing shear

shearing machine *n* **1 :** a machine with blades or rotary disks for cutting sheets, plates, or bars (as of metal) **2 :** a machine for shearing cloth usu. consisting of a roller with cutters operating against a ledger blade **3 :** a machine for shearing sheep

shearing punch *n* **:** a mechanical punch designed to act by shearing with little or no crushing

shearing strain *n* **:** SHEAR 5a

shearing stress *n* **:** a stress that results from the shear of an elastic solid and is measured by the force per unit area exerted by adjacent mutually displaced layers upon each other in the plane common to both

shearing tool *n* **:** a cutting tool (as a lathe tool) ground with considerable top rake

shear joint *n* **:** a crack produced in a rock body by compression **:** an incipient shear plane

shear legs *n pl but sing or pl in constr* **:** SHEAR 1d(2)

shear·less \'shi(ə)rləs\ *adj* **:** free from shear **:** having no shears

shear·ling \'shi(ə)rliŋ\ *n* -s [ME *scherling,* fr. *scheren, sheren* to shear + *-ling*] **1** *chiefly Brit* **:** a sheep that has produced one crop of wool **:** a one-year-old sheep **2 a :** sheepskin or lambskin taken from recently sheared sheep; *esp* **:** such skin tanned and dressed with the wool on **b shearlings** *pl* **:** short wool obtained by plucking from shearling skins

shear·man \'shi(ə)rmən\ *n, pl* **shearmen** [ME *sherman, shereman,* fr. *sheren* to shear + *man*] **:** one whose occupation is to shear something (as wool, cloth, or metal)

shear mark *n* **:** a mark or crease in pressed glass resulting from the local chilling action of the shears in cutting off the piece of glass for pressing

shear modulus *n* **:** the ratio of the shearing stress in a body to the corresponding shearing strain

shear·mouse \'shi(ə)r,maůs\ *n, pl* **shear·mice** \-mīs\ *dial chiefly Eng* **:** FIELD MOUSE

shear pin *n* **:** an easily replaceable pin (as the pin fixing the propeller to an outboard motor shaft) inserted at a critical point in a machine and designed to shear when subjected to excess stress — called also *break pin*

shear plane *or* **shearing plane** *n* **:** a plane or other surface along which rocks are ruptured by compressive stress

shears *pl of* SHEAR, *pres 3d sing of* SHEAR

shear skid *n* **:** FENDER SKID

shears·man \'shi(ə)rzmən\ *n, pl* **shearsmen** [by alter. (influence of *shears*)] **:** SHEARMAN

shear steel *n* **:** a steel produced by heating blister steel sheared into short lengths to a high heat, welding by hammering or rolling or both, and finally finishing under the hammer at the same or a slightly greater heat — called also *single-shear steel;* compare DOUBLE-SHEAR STEEL

shear strength *n* **:** capacity of a material or a union to resist shear

shear stress *n* **:** SHEARING STRESS

shear structure *n* **:** a local geologic structure resulting from the relief of earth stresses by the formation of a multitude of minute closely spaced fractures with slight slipping or faulting along each

sheartail \'≈,≈\ *n* **:** any of various hummingbirds with long forked tails

¹shearwater \'≈,≈\ *n* [¹*shear* + *water,* n.] **1 :** any of numerous oceanic birds chiefly of the genus *Puffinus* varying in size from that of a pigeon to that of a large gull, having like the related petrels and albatrosses tubular nostrils and long wings, and in their flight usu. skimming close to the waves **2 :** SKIMMER 3

²shearwater \"\ *n* [¹*shear* + *water,* n.] **:** a line of chained logs across the entrance of a bay or inlet to keep logs out

shear wave *n* **:** a wave in which the propagated disturbance is a shear strain in an elastic medium

sheary \'shirē\ *adj* -ER/-EST [perh. blend of *shiny* and *smeary*] **:** having a gloss that lacks uniformity ⟨a ~ painted surface⟩

shear zone *n* **:** a zone of shear structure or of closely spaced approximately parallel faults that often becomes a channel for underground solutions and the seat of ore deposition

she-ass \'≈,≈\ *n* [ME *she asse,* fr. ²*she* + *asse* ass] **:** a female donkey **:** JENNIE

sheat·fish \'shēt,fish\ *n* [alter. (perh. influenced by G *schaid* sheatfish, fr. OHG *sceida* sheatfish, sheath) of *sheathfish*] **:** a large elongated catfish (*Silurus glanis*) of central and eastern European rivers that may attain a length of 10 feet and a weight of 400 pounds and that lacks an adipose fin and has the long anal nearly confluent with the caudal; *broadly* **:** any of several large catfishes

sheath \'shēth\ *n, pl* **sheaths** \-ēthz, -ēths\ [ME *shethe,* fr. OE *scēath, scǣth;* akin to OHG *sceida* sheath, separation, ON *skeithir* sheath, OE *scēadan, scādan* to divide, separate — more at SHED] **1 :** a case for the blade of a sword, hunting knife, or other instrument to which it fits closely — compare SCABBARD **2 :** an investing cover or case of a plant or animal body or body part: as **a** (1) **:** the tubular fold of skin into which the penis of many mammals is retracted (2) **:** the connective tissue of an organ or part that binds together its component elements and holds it in place (3) **:** the lorica of a protozoan or rotifer **b** (1) **:** the lower part of a leaf (as of a grass) that more or less completely surrounds the stem (2) **:** an ensheathing spathe (3) **:** OCREA **3 :** any of various covering or supporting structures that are applied like or felt to resemble the sheath of a blade: as **a** *dial Brit* **:** a covering for holding and supporting a needle while knitting **b :** SHEATHING 2 **c :** a bar connecting the beam and sole in front in an old-time plow **d :** a thin metal plate having its edges bent over to hold a sheet of photographic film or a plate during exposure **e :** CONDOM **f :** a woman's close-fitting dress having narrow straight unbroken lines and usu. worn without a belt **g :** a portion of an electric discharge through a gas in which the positive and negative ion densities differ so much as to result in an appreciable space charge — compare PLASMA

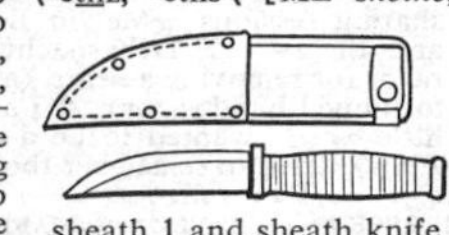
sheath 1 and sheath knife

sheathbill \'≈,≈\ *n* **:** any of several white shorebirds constituting the family Chionididae that are confined to the colder parts of the southern hemisphere, have a saddle-shaped horny sheath over the base of the upper mandible and a blunt carpal spur on the wing, and are in many characters intermediate between the gulls and plovers but suggest the pigeons in general appearance

sheathe \'shēth\ *also* **sheath** \-ēth\ *vt* **sheathed; sheathed; sheathing; sheathes** *also* **sheaths** [ME *shethen,* fr. *shethe* sheath] **1 :** to put into a sheath **:** enclose or cover with or as if with a sheath **2 a :** to plunge or bury (as a sword or tusk) in flesh **b :** to withdraw (a claw) into a sheath **3 :** to fit or furnish with or as if with a sheath **4 :** to case or cover with something (as thin boards or sheets of metal) that protects **:** cover with sheathing ⟨~ a ship's bottom with copper⟩ ⟨~ in the frame of a house⟩ **5 :** to make less noticeable: as **a** *archaic* **:** to render less acrid or pungent **b :** BLUNT, DULL

¹sheath·er \'shēthə(r)\ *n* -s [ME *shether,* fr. *shethe* sheath + *-er*] **:** a maker of sheaths

²sheath·er \'shēthə(r), -ēthə-\ *n* -s [*sheathe* + *-er*] **:** one that sheathes; *esp* **:** a worker who applies sheathing

sheathfish \'≈,≈\ *n* [*sheath* + *fish;* prob. intended as approximate trans. of G *schaid*] **:** SHEATFISH

¹sheathing *n* -s [fr. gerund of *sheathe*] **1 :** the action of one that sheathes something **2 :** material used to sheathe something ⟨no. 1 tongue-and-groove ~⟩ **:** a protective or ornamental cover ⟨~ of copper⟩ ⟨waterproof ~⟩; *esp* **:** the first covering of boards or of waterproof material on the outside wall of a frame house or on a timber roof

²sheathing *adj* [fr. pres. part. of *sheathe*] **:** enclosing or investing as or with a sheath

sheathing board *n* **:** a composition board (as fiber board or gypsum plaster board) used to take the place of wood sheathing for buildings

sheathing paper *n* **:** a building paper of a heavier and better than usual grade

sheath knife \'shēth\ *n* **:** a knife having a fixed blade and designed to be carried in a sheath — see SHEATH illustration

sheath·less \'shēthləs\ *adj* **:** lacking a sheath **:** UNSHEATHED

sheathlike \'≈,≈\ *adj* **:** resembling or functioning like a sheath

sheath moth *n* **:** any of several moths whose larvae eat the sheaths of sugarcane and corn

sheath of hen·le \-'henlē, -lə\ *usu cap H* [after Friedrich Gustav Jacob *Henle* †1885 Ger. anatomist] **:** the attenuated extremely delicate prolongation of the perineurium at the peripheral ends of a nerve fiber

sheath of schwann \-'shwän, -'shvän\ *usu cap 2d S* [after Theodor *Schwann* †1882 Ger. naturalist] **:** NEURILEMMA 1

sheaths *pl of* SHEATH, *pres 3d sing of* SHEATHE

sheath-tailed bat \'≈,≈-\ *n* **:** any of numerous chiefly tropical bats (family Emballonuridae) distinguished by rather long slender tails free of the uropatagium

sheath-winged \'≈;≈\ *adj* **:** having the wings covered by sheaths **:** having elytra or wing cases ⟨beetles are *sheath-winged* insects⟩

sheathy \'shēthē, -ethē\ *adj* -ER/-EST **:** resembling or having the form of a sheath ⟨a ~ skirt⟩ ⟨the ~ silhouette registers strongly in the sportswear market —*Women's Wear Daily*⟩

shea tree \'shē-, 'shā-\ *or* **shea butter tree** *or* **shea** *n* -s [*shea* fr. Bambara *si*] **:** a rough-barked tropical African tree (*Butyrospermum parkii*) of the family Sapotaceae having round to elongate fruits that usu. contain a single fatty nut and very hard heavy dark red wood used locally for fuel and construction — see SHEA BUTTER

¹sheave \'shiv, 'shēv\ *n* -s [ME *sheve, shive* sheave, slice; akin to OHG *sciba* disk, Icel *skīfa* disk, L *scipio* staff, Gk *skipōn* staff, OE *scēadan, scādan* to divide, separate — more at SHED] **1** *also* **sheeve** \"\ **a :** the grooved wheel or pulley of a pulley block or any of several such wheels **b :** any grooved wheel or pulley **c :** the eccentric disk of an eccentric **2** *archaic* **:** SLICE

²sheave \'shēv\ *or* **sheaf** \-ēf\ *vt* -ED/-ING/-S [*sheave* fr. ¹*sheaf,* after such pairs as E *grief: grieve; sheaf* fr. ¹*sheaf*] **:** to gather and bind into a sheaf

³sheave \'shēv\ *vi* -ED/-ING/-S [perh. fr. ME *scheven* to shove, fr. OE *scēofan,* alter. of *scūfan* — more at SHOVE] **:** to reverse the action of the oars in rowing a boat **:** BACKWATER

sheaved \'shivd, 'shēvd\ *adj* **:** having a specified number or kind of sheaves ⟨a double-*sheaved* pulley block⟩ ⟨a thin-*sheaved* block⟩

sheave·less *adj* **:** having no sheave

sheave·man \'≈mən\ *n, pl* **sheavemen :** a worker who greases and repairs sheaves

sheaves *pl of* SHEAF *or of* SHEAVE, *pres 3d sing of* SHEAVE

she·ba \'shēbə\ *n* -s [*Sheba,* ancient country in southern Arabia; fr. the Biblical account (1 Kings 10:1–13) of the Queen of Sheba's visit to Solomon] **:** an attractive and often flirtatious or giddy young woman

she-balsam \'≈,≈≈\ *n* [²*she* (plant) + *balsam*] **:** FRASER FIR

she·bang \shə'baŋ, shē'-, -aiŋ\ *n* -s [perh. alter. of *shebeen*] **1 :** a crude or primitive dwelling **:** HUT **2 :** ESTABLISHMENT, CONTRIVANCE, AFFAIR, CONCERN, THING ⟨put on a stylish ~⟩ — usu. used with *whole* ⟨blew up the whole ~⟩

she·bat *or* **se·bat** *also* **she·vat** \shə'bät, -'vät\ *or* **shvat** \'shvät\ *n* -s *usu cap* [Heb *shĕbhāt,* fr. Assyr-Bab *shabāṭu*] **:** the 5th month of the civil year or the 11th month of the ecclesiastical year in the Jewish calendar — see MONTH table

she-beech \'≈,≈\ *n* [²*she* (plant) + *beech*] **1 :** an Australian timber tree (*Cryptocarya obovata*) with close-grained aromatic wood **2 :** BOLLY GUM

she·been \shə'bēn\ *n* -s [IrGael *sībīn* bad ale] *chiefly Irish* **:** an unlicensed or illegally operated drinking establishment **:** SPEAKEASY

she·bek \(')shä;bek\ *n, pl* **shebek** *or* **shebeks** *usu cap* **1 :** a people inhabiting the Mosul region of Iraq **2 :** a member of the Shebek people

she·chem·ite \'shēkə,mīt\ *n* -s *cap* [*Shechem,* ancient city in north central Palestine + E *-ite*] **:** a native or inhabitant of the ancient city of Shechem, Palestine

shechina *or* **schechinah** *usu cap, var of* SHEKINAH

shechita *or* **shechitah** *var of* SHEHITAH

¹shed \'shed\ *vb* **shed; shed; shedding; sheds** [ME *sheden* to divide, separate, shed, fr. OE *scēadan, scādan* to divide, separate; akin to OHG *skeidan* to separate, Goth *skaidan* to separate, L *scindere* to cut, split, Gk *schizein* to split, Skt *chinatti* he splits] *vt* **1 a** *chiefly dial* **:** to cause to separate from something **:** divide or draft off usu. from a larger group or body **:** set apart **:** SEGREGATE ⟨*shedding* off the best lambs for market⟩ ⟨~ the cattle into two groups⟩ **b** *archaic* **:** to divide (as hair or wool) by a part **:** PART **c :** to divide (the warp) in weaving so as to form a shed **2 a** *obs* **:** to distribute (as seed) abroad **:** SOW **b** *obs* **:** to cause (as mist) to break up or dissipate **c :** to cause to be dispersed without penetrating **:** throw off by repelling ⟨the duck's oily plumage ~*s* water⟩ **3 a :** to cause (blood) to flow by cutting or wounding **b :** to pour forth or down in drops ⟨*shedding* tears of remorse⟩ **c :** to give off in or as if in a stream **:** pour forth ⟨fishes *shedding* their eggs in spawning⟩; *also* **:** to give off or out **:** IMPART, RELEASE, DIFFUSE ⟨*shedding* kindness on all she met⟩ ⟨to ~ abroad such power may be dangerous⟩ ⟨the sun ~*s* warmth over the earth⟩ **4 :** to make disposal of or separate from (some natural part) in the normal course of life: as **a :** to cast off (as a hairy, chitinous, or other body covering) **:** MOLT ⟨caterpillars ~ their skins repeatedly⟩ ⟨the cat ~ hair over his trousers⟩ **b :** to be affected by a dropping of (as leaves or other parts) **c :** to eject (as seed or spores) from a natural receptacle ⟨a puffball *shedding* its spores⟩ ~ *vi* **1** *obs* **:** to become separated or divided **:** come apart **:** DIVIDE, DEPART **2** *dial chiefly Brit* **a :** FALL, DROP, DESCEND **b :** to pour out **:** SPILL **c :** to be dispersed **:** SCATTER **3 :** to separate off some natural covering (as of hair or skin) or part (as leaves or twigs) usu. in the normal course of life ⟨the dog is *shedding* badly⟩ ⟨some oats shatter and ~ more readily than others⟩ **syn** see DISCARD — **shed blood :** to cause death by bloodshed or violence

²shed \"\ *n* -s [ME *shed,* fr. OE *gescēad, gescād,* fr. *ge-* (perfective, associative, and collective prefix) + *-scēad, -scād* (fr. *scēadan, scādan* to divide, separate) — more at CO-] **1** *obs* **:** a separation of one thing from another; *also* **:** DISTINCTION, DIFFERENCE **2 a** *chiefly dial* **:** the part of one's hair **b :** a similar parting in the wool of a sheep **3 a** *obs* **:** a part broken away **:** FRAGMENT, CLOT **b :** something (as a cocoon or the skin of a snake) that is discarded in shedding **4 :** a divide of land — compare WATERSHED **5 :** a passageway between the threads of a warp which is made by raising and lowering the alternate or selected ends to form a narrow diamond-shaped opening and through which the shuttle is thrown in weaving

³shed \"\ *adj* [ME *sched* separated, fr. past part. of *scheden, sheden* to divide, separate, shed] **1 :** fallen off or out **:** let fall **:** SPILLED ⟨~ blood⟩ ⟨a mass of ~ hair⟩ **2** [prob. alter. (influenced by ³*shut*) of ³*shut*] *dial* **:** FREE, RID — usu. used with *of* ⟨couldn't get ~ of the old cat⟩

⁴shed \"\ *n* -s [alter. of earlier *shadde,* prob. fr. ME *shad, shade* shade — more at SHADE] **1 a :** a slight structure (as a penthouse, lean-to, or partially open separate building) built primarily for shelter or storage **:** OUTBUILDING; *esp* **:** a single-storied building with one or more sides unenclosed **b :** any of various buildings felt to resemble a shed (as in openness of structure, in use, or in having a pent roof): as (1) **:** WOODSHED (2) **:** a covered structure for housing aerostats **2** *archaic* **:** a place of shelter: **a :** an inferior dwelling or humble domicile **:** HUT **b :** the hiding or resting place of an animal **:** DEN, LAIR, NEST

⁵shed \"\ *vt* **shedded; shedded; shedding; sheds :** to put or house in a shed ⟨~ tobacco for curing⟩ ⟨the added cost of *shedding* cattle in cold weather⟩

⁶shed \"\ *Scot var of* SHADE

shed-builder ant *n* **:** any of various ants (as of the genus *Cremastogaster*) that build carton nests attached to trees or bushes

shed burn *n* **:** POLE ROT

shed·der \'shedə(r)\ *n* -s [ME *scheder,* fr. *scheden, sheden* to shed + *-er*] **1 :** one that sheds something ⟨a ~ of blood⟩: as **a** (1) **:** a crab or lobster about to begin to molt its shell **:** PEELER (2) **:** a crab that has just shed its shell **b :** a female salmon after spawning **c :** a spring device to eject a blank from a die **d :** an individual that sheds agents of infection (as through feces or other body discharges) — compare CARRIER **2 :** a fruit that has fallen from a tree

¹shed·ding \'shediŋ, -dēŋ\ *n* -s [ME *sheding,* fr. gerund of *sheden* to shed] **1 :** an act or the process by which things are shed **:** PARTING, DIVISION, SEPARATION **2 :** something that is shed off — usu. used in pl. **3 :** a nutritional disturbance in cotton resulting in the premature dropping of bolls

²shedding \"\ *adj* [fr. pres. part. of ¹*shed*] **:** that sheds or is shed ⟨~ rose petals⟩

³shedding \"\ *n* -s [⁴*shed* + *-ing*] **:** SHEDS; *esp* **:** storage or other facilities provided in the form of sheds

shedding box *or* **shedding float** *n* **:** a crab float in which crabs are held until they shed and emerge as marketable soft-shelled crabs

shed dormer *n* **:** a dormer window with a horizontal eave line as distinguished from a gabled dormer

shed dormer

she·der \'shēdə(r)\ *n* -s [prob. fr. ²*she* + *deer* (animal)] *dial Eng* **:** a female sheep; *specif* **:** one past eight or nine months that has not yet been sheared

she-devil \'≈;≈≈\ *n* **:** a woman that is like a devil (as in harshness toward or torment of others)

shedhand \'≈,≈\ *n* **:** a workman employed in an Australian woolshed

shedlike \'≈,≈\ *adj* **:** resembling a shed

shed·man \'≈mən\ *n, pl* **shedmen :** one who works in a shed: as **a :** one who stacks lumber in a shed **b :** a cannery worker who sorts food products according to size or grade and removes defective ones

shed roof *n* **:** PENT ROOF

sheds *pres 3d sing of* SHED, *pl of* SHED

she·du \ˈshā(ˌ)dü\ *n, pl* **she·dim** \-ädəm\ [Assyr-Bab *shēdu*] **1** *usu cap* **:** one of various semidivine beings represented by ancient Assyrian sculptors as colossal human-headed bulls or lions **2** [Heb *shēdh*, fr. Assyr-Bab *shēdu*] **:** a traditional Jewish evil demon

shee *var of* SIDHE

shee·fish \ˈshēˌfish\ *n* [*shee* (prob. native name in Alaska or northwest Canada) + *fish*] **:** INCONNU

sheel \ˈshē(ə)l\ *var of* SHEAL

¹sheeling *var of* SHEALING

²sheel·ing \ˈshēliŋ\ *var of* SHIELING

¹sheen \ˈshēn\ *adj* [ME *shene*, fr. OE *scēne, sciene;* akin to MD *schone* bright, clean, beautiful, OHG *skōni* bright, beautiful, Goth *skauns* beautiful, OE *scēawian* to look — more at SHOW] **:** BEAUTIFUL, SPLENDID, RESPLENDENT, BRIGHT, GLITTERING, RADIANT

²sheen \ˈ"\ *adv* [ME *shene*, fr. *shene*, adj.] *archaic* **:** BEAUTIFULLY, BRIGHTLY

³sheen \ˈ"\ *vi* -ED/-ING/-S [ME (northern dial.) *shenen* to shine, fr. ME *shene*, adj.] **:** to be bright **:** show a sheen **:** SHINE

⁴sheen \ˈ"\ *n* -S [¹*sheen*] **1 a :** a bright or shining condition **:** BRIGHTNESS **b :** a subdued and often iridescent or metallic glitter that approaches but is just short of optical reflection **:** a surface luster (as of a mineral cleavage surface or of a dark feather) **c :** a lustrous surface ranging from dull to brilliant imparted to textiles through finishing processes or use of shiny yarns (as rayon) **2 :** something marked by surface brilliance: as **a :** bright or showy clothing **:** splendid raiment **b** *slang* **:** counterfeit coin **c :** a textile exhibiting notable sheen

⁵sheen \ˈ"\ *archaic pl of* SHOE

sheen·ful \-nfəl\ *adj* **:** exhibiting or characterized by sheen

sheen·less \-nləs\ *adj* **:** lacking sheen **:** having no surface luster or glitter **:** DULL

sheen·ly *adv* [ME *scheenely*, fr. *scheene, shene*, adj., sheen + *-ly*] **:** BRIGHTLY

¹sheeny \ˈshēnē, -ni\ *adj* -ER/-EST [⁴*sheen* + *-y*] **:** lustrous with sheen **:** SHINING, RADIANT

²shee·ny *or* **shee·nie** *also* **shee·ney** \ˈ"\ *n, pl* **sheenies** *also* **sheeneys** [origin unknown] **:** JEW — usu. taken to be offensive

¹sheep \ˈshēp\ *n, pl* **sheep** *often attrib* [ME, fr. OE *scēap, scēp;* akin to MD *schaep* sheep, OHG *scāf*] **1 :** any of numerous ruminant mammals (genus *Ovis*) native to upland regions of the northern hemisphere and related to the goats from which they may usu. be distinguished by a stockier build, absence of a beard in the male, and horns that when present are more divergent and in older males often coiled into flattened lateral spirals; *specif* **:** a mammal (*O. aries*) long domesticated for its flesh, specialized hair or wool, and other products and differentiated through continued selection into many breeds some of which are notable for meat production, others for wool, and a few for fur or milk — see EWE, LAMB, RAM; MUTTON; KARAKUL **2 :** one that is like a sheep (as in being a defenseless innocent creature or in being readily preyed upon or shorn): as **a :** mankind or a group of people under the shepherding care of God or Christ; *also* **:** a group under the charge of a pastor or similar director **b :** a stupid docile person **:** a silly bashful fellow **c** *obs* **:** a biddable kindly woman — often opposed to *shrew* **3 :** leather prepared from the skins of sheep **:** SHEEPSKIN

²sheep \ˈ"\ *vt* -ED/-ING/-S **:** to graze or pasture (as land or crops) by sheep — often used with *off* or *down* ⟨~*ing* off the grass⟩

sheepback \ˈ=ˌ=\ *n* **:** ROCHE MOUTONNÉE

sheep·berry \ˈshēp- — *see* BERRY\ *n* **1 a :** a No. American shrub or small tree (*Viburnum lentago*) having white flowers in flat cymes **b :** the black edible berrylike drupe of this plant **2 :** BLACK HAW 1

sheepbine \ˈ=ˌ=\ *n* **:** FIELD BINDWEED

sheepbiter *n* **1** *obs* **:** one that practices petty thefts **2** *obs* **:** PHILANDERER

sheep biting louse *n* **:** SHEEP LOUSE 1

sheep blowfly *n* **:** any of several blowflies that attack sheep

sheep bot *n* **:** the larva of the sheep botfly

sheep botfly *or* **sheep gadfly** *n* **:** a botfly (*Oestrus ovis*) whose larvae parasitize sheep and lodge esp. in the nasal passages, frontal sinuses, and throat

sheep bur *n* **:** any of several plants whose fruits or seeds tend to lodge in sheep's wool: as **a :** an annual composite weed (*Acanthospermum australe*) of the southern U.S. and tropical regions with a prickly fruit shaped like a starfish **b :** COCKLEBUR **c :** STICKSEED

sheep·cote \ˈshēpˌkōt\ *also* **sheep·cot** \-ˌkät\ *n* -S [ME *shepcote, schepcott*, fr. *shep, schep, sheep* sheep + *cote* shed for small domestic animals, small house & *cot* small house — more at COTE, COT] *chiefly Brit* **:** SHEEPFOLD, SHEEPHOUSE

sheep crab *n* **:** a large rough spider crab (*Loxorhynchus grandis*) living in shallow water along the California coast

sheepcrook \ˈ=ˌ=\ *n* [ME *shepe-crook*, fr. *shepe, sheep* sheep + *crook, crok* crook] **:** a shepherd's crook

sheep-dip \ˈ=ˌ=\ *n* **1 :** a liquid preparation of toxic chemicals into which sheep are plunged esp. to destroy parasitic arthropods (as lice, mites, keds, ticks) **2 :** a coal-tar disinfectant for use about farms or on animals' wounds

sheep dog *n* **:** a dog used to tend, drive, or guard sheep — compare OLD ENGLISH SHEEPDOG

sheep eater *n, usu cap S&E* **:** one of a band of Shoshone Indians in the neighborhood of Yellowstone Park

sheep·faced \ˈshēpˌfāst\ *adj* **:** BASHFUL, SHY, SHEEPISH — **sheep·faced·ly** \-sədlē, -stlē, -li\ *adv* — **sheep·faced·ness** \-sədnəs, -s(t)nəs\ *n* -ES

sheep fescue *or* **sheep's fescue** *n* **:** a hardy European perennial fescue grass (*Festuca ovina*) that is widely cultivated for sheep pasturage in upland situations, is used as a lawn grass, and has densely tufted erect stems and very fine foliage

sheep flake *n, dial Brit* **:** a rack or open wicker cage for carrying fodder to sheep in winter

sheep fly *n* **:** any of several flies (superfamily Muscoidea) having larvae that live in the wool of sheep and feed on the flesh beneath and are particularly destructive in arid regions

sheepfold \ˈ=ˌ=\ *n* [ME *sheep fold*, fr. ¹*sheep* + *fold*] **1 :** a pen or shelter for sheep **2 :** a source or center of security (as a church or sanctuary)

sheepfoot \ˈ=ˌ=\ *n, pl* **sheepfoots :** BIRD'S-FOOT TREFOIL 1a

¹sheepgate \ˈ=ˌ=\ *n* [¹*sheep* + *gate* (opening)] **:** a gate for the passage of sheep **:** a hurdle for enclosing sheep

²sheepgate \ˈ"\ *n* [¹*sheep* + *gate* (pasturage)] **:** pasturage for sheep; *also* **:** the cost of such pasturage

sheep grass *n* **:** BERMUDA GRASS

sheephead *var of* SHEEPSHEAD

sheepheaded \ˈ=ˌ==\ *adj* **:** SILLY, SIMPLEMINDED, STUPID

sheepherder \ˈ=ˌ==\ *n* **:** a worker in charge of a band of sheep esp. on open range **:** SHEPHERD

sheepherding \ˈ=ˌ==\ *n* **:** the business of a sheepherder

sheephook \ˈ=ˌ=\ *n* [ME *shephoke*, fr. *shep, sheep* sheep + *hoke, hok* hook] **:** a shepherd's crook

sheephouse \ˈ=ˌ=\ *n* [ME *shephous*, fr. *shep, sheep* sheep + *hous* house] **:** a covered enclosure for housing sheep

sheepier *comparative of* SHEEPY

sheepiest *superlative of* SHEEPY

sheeping *pres part of* SHEEP

sheep·ish \ˈshēpish, -pēsh\ *adj* [ME *shepish*, fr. *shep, sheep* sheep + *-ish*] **1** *archaic* **:** of or relating to sheep **2 :** like a sheep in some quality (as meekness, stupidity, timidity): as **a :** meanly or foolishly diffident **:** timorous to excess **:** BASHFUL **b :** embarrassed by consciousness of a fault — **sheep·ish·ly** *adv* — **sheep·ish·ness** *n* -ES

sheep ked *n* **:** a wingless bloodsucking hippoboscid fly (*Melophagus ovinus*) that feeds chiefly on sheep and is a vector of sheep trypanosomiasis — called also *sheep tick*

sheepkill \ˈ=ˌ=\ *n* **:** SHEEP LAUREL

sheep-kneed \ˈ=ˌ=\ *adj* **:** having knees like those of a sheep — used of a horse when the foreleg below the knee deviates slightly forward

sheep laurel *n* **:** a No. American dwarf shrub (*Kalmia angustifolia*) that is poisonous to young stock and that resembles mountain laurel but has narrower leaves and smaller bright red flowers

sheep·less \ˈshēpləs\ *adj* **:** having no sheep

sheep-lice \ˈ=ˌ=\ *n pl but sing or pl in constr* **:** HOUND'S-TONGUE 1

sheeplike \ˈ=ˌ=\ *adj* (*or adv*) **:** like a sheep esp. in meekness, docility, or stupidity

sheep loco *n* **:** LOCOWEED; *esp* **:** any plant of the genus *Astragalus*

sheep louse *n* [ME *scheplows*, fr. *schep, sheep* sheep + *lows, lous* louse] **1 :** a biting louse (*Bovicola ovis*) that infests sheep and feeds on the wool **2 :** SHEEP KED

sheep maggot *n* **:** the larva of a sheep fly

sheep·man \ˈshēpmən, -ˌman, -ˌmaa(ə)n\ *n, pl* **sheepmen :** a man engaged in the handling, raising, or breeding of sheep: as **a** *obs* **:** SHEPHERD, SHEEPHERDER **b :** an owner or rancher of sheep esp. when specializing in sheep to the exclusion of other activities

sheepmaster \ˈ=ˌ==\ *n, chiefly Brit* **:** SHEEPMAN b

sheep measles *n pl but sing or pl in constr* **:** infestation of the muscles of sheep with cysticerci of a dog tapeworm (*Taenia ovis*)

sheepmint \ˈ=ˌ=\ *n* **:** FIELD BALM 1

sheep nasal fly *or* **sheep nostril fly** *n* **:** any of several oestrid flies having larvae that live as parasites in the nasal cavities of sheep and occas. goats; *esp* **:** SHEEP BOTFLY

sheepnose \ˈ=ˌ=\ *n* **:** any of several apples that have rather long fruit with four decided prominences at the blossom end

sheepnut \ˈ=ˌ=\ *n* **:** JOJOBA

sheep plant *n* **:** any of several New Zealand plants of the genus *Raoulia* (as *R. eximia, R. lutescens*, and *R. mammillaris*) with white woolly tufted foliage that when viewed from a distance suggests the form of a sheep — called also *vegetable sheep*

sheep-pod \ˈ=ˌ=\ *n* **:** any of several western No. American locoweeds of the genus *Astragalus*

sheep poison *n* **1 :** SHEEP LAUREL **2 :** a California lupine (*Lupinus densiflorus*) **3 :** a common yellow-flowered wood sorrel (*Oxalis stricta*)

sheep pox *n* **:** a virus disease of sheep and possibly goats that is related to smallpox and was formerly epizootic in warmer Old World areas, is marked by formation of vesicles or pocks esp. on the bare or thinly wooled areas of the body, and is frequently complicated by secondary septic infection

sheep rack *n* **:** a rack for feed for sheep

sheep rot *n* **1** *dial Eng* **a :** MARSH PENNYWORT **b :** BUTTERWORT **2 :** liver rot of sheep

sheeps *pres 3d sing of* SHEEP

sheep saffron *n* **:** SHEEP SORREL 1

sheep's-bane \ˈ=ˌ=\ *n, pl* **sheep's-banes :** MARSH PENNYWORT

sheep's-bit \ˈ=ˌ=\ *n, pl* **sheep's-bits :** a European herb (*Jasione montana*) that is adventive in the eastern U.S. and has blue flowers somewhat resembling those of scabious

sheep scab *n* **:** mange (as psoroptic mange) of sheep — compare HEAD SCAB

sheep's eye *n* **:** a shy longing and usu. amorous glance — usu. used in pl. ⟨cast *sheep's eyes* at someone⟩

sheep's fescue *var of* SHEEP FESCUE

sheep's-foot \ˈ=ˌ=\ *n, pl* **sheep's-foots :** a metal bar formed into a hammer head at one end and a claw at the other and used as a lever and hammer esp. by printers

sheepsfoot roller \ˈ=ˌ=-\ *or* **sheepsfoot tamper** *also* **sheepsfoot** *n, pl* **sheepsfoots :** a roller for earth or pavement with spikes inserted to compact, pre-rotate, or scarify the rolled surface

sheep's-gowan \ˈ=ˌ==\ *n, pl* **sheep's-gowans :** WHITE CLOVER a

sheepshank \ˈ=ˌ=\ *n* **1 :** a knot for shortening a line **2** *Scot* **:** something of no worth or importance

sheepshead *or* **sheephead** \ˈ=ˌ=\ *n* **1** *archaic* **:** a silly or stupid person **2 a :** a sparid food fish (*Archosargus probatocephalus*) of the Atlantic and Gulf coasts of the U.S. with broad incisor teeth suggesting those of a sheep and a compressed black-banded body **b :** FRESHWATER DRUM **c :** a common California wrasse (*Pimelometopon pulcher*) that in the males is black more or less marked with crimson and in the females and young uniformly rose-colored **3** [trans. of G *schafskopf, schafkopf*] **:** a simple form of skat — called also *schafskopf*

sheep's-head clock \ˈ=ˌ=-\ *or* **sheep's-head** *n, pl* **sheep's-heads :** a lantern clock with one hand and a crown escapement and large dials that overlap the movement

sheepshead porgy *n* **:** a small fish (*Calamus penna*) of the family Sparidae found from Florida to Brazil

sheepshearer \ˈ=ˌ==\ *n* **1 :** a person that shears sheep by hand or machine **2 :** a machine for shearing sheep

sheepshearing \ˈ=ˌ==\ *n* **1 :** the act of shearing sheep **2 :** the time or season at which sheep are sheared; *also* **:** a festival held at or about this time

sheep shears *n pl but sing or pl in constr* **:** a shears with broad flat blades forming the two ends of an elastic steel bow by means of which they open automatically when released from the closing pressure of the hand

sheep shears

sheep-sick \ˈ=ˌ=\ *adj, of soil or pasture* **:** heavily infested with parasitic worm eggs following prolonged or excessive pasturage of sheep; *broadly* **:** incapable of supporting sheep

sheepskin \ˈ=ˌ=\ *n* [ME *shepskyn*, fr. *shep, sheep* sheep + *skyn, skin* skin] **1 a :** the skin of a sheep; *also* **:** leather prepared from it **b :** PARCHMENT **c :** a garment (as a jacket) made of or lined with sheepskin and usu. having the wool on the inside **2 :** DIPLOMA **3 :** MOTH GRAY

sheep sorrel *n* **1** *also* **sheep's sorrel :** a small herb (*Rumex acetosella*) common esp. in dry places and having pleasantly acid-tasting auricled leaves **2 :** SORREL b

sheep's-parsley \ˈ=ˌ==\ *n, pl* **sheep's-parsleys** *dial Eng* **:** WILD CHERVIL 1; *also* **:** a related annual weedy herb (*Chaerophyllum temulum*)

sheepsplit \ˈ=ˌ=\ *n* **:** a split of a sheepskin **:** a thin section made by splitting a sheepskin with a cutting knife or machine

sheepswool \ˈ=ˌ=\ *also* **sheepswool sponge** *n* **:** WOOL SPONGE

sheep tansy *n* **:** FIDDLE-NECK 1

sheep tick *n* [ME *scheptyke*, fr. *schep, sheep* sheep + *tyke* tick] **1 :** SHEEP KED **2 :** CASTOR-BEAN TICK

sheep vault *n* **:** a gymnastic vault similar to a squat vault executed with the back arched and the knees flexed but with the thighs extended

sheep wagon *n* **:** an enclosed covered wagon fitted up as living accommodations for a sheepherder on the range

sheepwalk \ˈ=ˌ=\ *n, chiefly Brit* **:** a pasture or range for sheep; *also* **:** a property devoted solely or primarily to sheep culture

sheep wash *n* **1 :** a place where sheep are washed **2** *chiefly Brit* **:** SHEEP-DIP

sheepweed \ˈ=ˌ=\ *n* **1 :** SOAPWORT 1 **2 :** an Indian mallow (*Abutilon theophrasti*) **3 :** a butterwort (*Pinguicula vulgaris*)

sheepy \ˈshēpē\ *adj* -ER/-EST [ME *shepy*, fr. *shep, sheep* sheep + *-y*] **:** of, relating to, or suggestive of sheep ⟨a ~ odor⟩

sheepyard \ˈ=ˌ=\ *n, Austral* **:** a place where sheep are yarded — compare STOCKYARD

¹sheer \ˈshi(ə)r, -iə\ *adj* -ER/-EST [ME *schere* acquitted, purged of sin or guilt, prob. alter. (influenced by ME *shire, shir* bright, pure, unmixed, fr. OE *scīr*) of *skere* purged of sin or guilt, unharmed, fr. ON *skǣrr* bright, pure; akin to OE *scīr* bright, pure, unmixed, MHG *schīr*, ON *skīrr* bright, pure, Goth *skeirs* clear, OE *scīnan* to shine — more at SHINE] **1** *obs* **:** BRIGHT, FAIR, SHINING **2 :** of very thin or transparent texture **:** fine and light in weight **:** DIAPHANOUS ⟨~ woolens⟩ ⟨a ~ summer dress⟩ **3 a :** being wholly as indicated or implied **:** belonging to such a kind or category and no other **:** unqualifiedly such **:** UTTER, ABSOLUTE ⟨frightened by the ~ immensity of the place⟩ ⟨~ folly⟩ **b :** being free from any adulterant or diluent **:** PURE, UNMIXED ⟨a layer of ~ sand provided drainage⟩ ⟨~ ale⟩ **c :** viewed or acting in dissociation from other matters **:** stressed or functioning to the exclusion of other factors ⟨the power of ~ mind⟩ ⟨won through by ~ determination⟩ **4 :** marked by great and unrelieved steepness **:** PRECIPITOUS ⟨a ~ drop⟩ **syn** see PURE, STEEP

²sheer \ˈ"\ *adv* **1 :** ALTOGETHER, COMPLETELY, DIRECTLY, QUITE ⟨fell ~ into the water⟩ **2 :** straight up or down without a break **:** PERPENDICULARLY

³sheer \ˈ"\ *n* -S **1 :** a sheer fabric (as chiffon, organdy, ninon); *also* **:** an article (as a dress) of such a fabric **2 :** PRECIPICE

⁴sheer \ˈ"\ *chiefly dial var of* SHEAR

⁵sheer \ˈ"\ *dial Eng var of* SHIRE

⁶sheer \ˈ"\ *vb* -ED/-ING/-S [perh. alter. of ¹*shear*] *vi* **:** to deviate from a course **:** turn aside to or as if to avoid collision **:** SWERVE — usu. used with an adverb of direction (as *off, away, up, in*) **~** *vt* **:** to cause to sheer ⟨~ a car around a puddle⟩ ⟨~ away the brunt of wind-driven tides —Walter Fountain⟩ **syn** see TURN

⁷sheer \ˈ"\ *n* -S **1 :** a turn, deviation, or change in a course (as of a ship) **:** SWERVE **2 :** the position of a ship riding to a single anchor and heading toward it

⁸sheer \ˈ"\ *n* [perh. alter. of ²*shear*] **1 :** the fore-and-aft curvature from bow to stern of a ship's deck as shown in side elevation **2 :** SHEER STRAKE

sheer batten *n* **:** a long strip of wood to guide carpenters in following the sheer plan in shipbuilding; *also* **:** SHEER POLE

sheer boom *n* [⁷*sheer*] **:** SHEAR BOOM

sheer draft *n, archaic* **:** SHEER PLAN

sheered \ˈshi(ə)rd\ *adj* [⁸*sheer* + *-ed*] *of a ship* **:** built with a specified sheer

sheer hook *n* [ME *sherhok*, fr. *sheren* to shear + *hok* hook] **:** an arrangement of heavy hooks usu. on a pole and with the inner surfaces sharpened formerly used to seize and cut an enemy ship's rigging

sheer leg *n* **:** one of two spars secured together at the head to form shears

sheerlegs \ˈ=ˌ=\ *n pl but sing or pl in constr* **:** SHEAR 1d(2)

sheer line *n* [⁷*sheer*] **:** the stretched rope of a trail bridge to which a boat or raft is attached and along which it passes

sheer·ly *adv* **1 :** PURELY, SOLELY; *also* **:** ABSOLUTELY, QUITE, UTTERLY **2 :** SHARPLY, DIRECTLY **3 :** PERPENDICULARLY, VERTICALLY, PRECIPITOUSLY

sheer·ness *n* -ES **:** the quality or state of being sheer

sheer-off \ˈ=ˌ=\ *n* -S [fr. the phrase *sheer off*] **:** an act or instance of sheering off

sheer plan *n* **:** a drawing of the profile or side elevation of a ship's form

¹sheer pole *n* [⁴*sheer* + *pole*] **:** SHEAR 1d(2)

²sheer pole *n* [⁸*sheer* + *pole;* fr. its position parallel to the sheer of the ship] **:** a pole seized to the shrouds of a ship just above the deadeyes and forming the first ratline — see SHIP illustration

sheer ratline *n* [⁸*sheer*] **:** every fifth ratline of the rigging of a ship extending to the swifters, after shrouds, and backstays

sheers *pl of* SHEER, *pres 3d sing of* SHEER

sheer strake *n* **:** the upper strake of shell plating at the main deck in a steel ship or the top line of planking in a wooden ship — see SHIP illustration

sheer thursday *n, usu cap S&T* [ME *scherethursday*, fr. *schere* purged of sin or guilt + *thursday;* prob. fr. the practice of confessing one's sins on Maundy Thursday — more at SHEER] **:** MAUNDY THURSDAY

¹sheet \ˈshēt, *usu* -ēd·+V\ *n* -S [ME *shete*, fr. OE *scēte, scȳte;* akin to OE *scēat* corner, region, napkin, fold, lap, OHG *scōz* coattail, lap, bosom, ON *skaut* corner, coattail, bosom, sheet (rope regulating a sail), Goth *skaut* edge (of a garment), OE *scēotan* to shoot — more at SHOOT] **1 a :** a piece of cloth (as a towel or napkin) — obs. except in specific applications **b :** WINDING-SHEET **c :** an oblong of usu. linen or cotton cloth used in pairs as an article of bedding and placed one immediately under and one immediately over the person ⟨fresh ~s each week⟩ **d :** a piece of cloth used as a covering or wrapping (as for a horse); *esp* **:** DUST COVER 1 **e :** SAIL 1 **2 :** a usu. oblong or square piece of paper esp. in one of the various sizes in which paper is made according to the uses to which it is to be put ⟨brown wrapping paper in separate ~s⟩ ⟨box of writing paper containing 24 ~s and 12 envelopes⟩ ⟨500-*sheet* roll of toilet paper⟩: as **a :** a piece of paper of a size suitable for printing esp. of books or other matter of which the page is a subdivision of a larger area — often distinguished from *reel* and *web;* compare SIGNATURE **b :** a printed signature for a book esp. before it has been folded, cut, or bound — usu. used in pl. ⟨a book in ~s⟩ **c :** a piece of paper comprising one unit of a larger printed whole ⟨a poster in 24 ~s⟩ **d :** a newspaper, periodical, or occasional publication; *often* **:** one of a scandalous or scurrilous nature ⟨a hate ~⟩ ⟨a scandal ~⟩ **e :** printed or duplicated matter for reference or instruction (as in an office, shop, or factory) and often in pamphlet form ⟨an 8vo style ~ of 64 pages⟩ **f** (1) **:** the unseparated postage stamps printed by one impression of a plate on a single piece of paper (2) **:** a quarter or half section of a sheet of stamps **:** PANE — called also *post-office sheet* (3) **:** one of the primary sections into which a reel of stamps printed by a rotary press is cut for shipment to post offices **:** MINIATURE SHEET, SOUVENIR SHEET **3 a :** a broad stretch or surface of something that is usu. thin in comparison to its length and breadth or that presents a white, bright, or glistening surface ⟨hills covered with a ~ of ice⟩ ⟨whole ~s of daisies deck the meadows⟩ ⟨a broad ~ of hardened lava⟩ **b :** the expanse of ice on which a curling match is played **4 a :** a suspended or moving expanse (as of fire, lightning, rain, or mist) ⟨rain came down in ~s⟩ ⟨~s of flame and smoke were driven by the wind⟩ ⟨a ~ of fog rolled in from the sea⟩ **b :** a thin flat current of compressed air striking the lip of a flue pipe in a pipe organ **5 :** a broad thinly expanded portion of metal or other substance: as **a :** a plate forming part of a tank or boiler regardless of thickness **b :** a portion of metal less than about a quarter or sometimes an eighth of an inch in thickness — distinguished from *plate;* compare LEAF 2d(2) **c :** SHEET RUBBER **d** (1) **:** a large shallow baking pan; *esp* **:** a flat baking utensil of tinned metal usu. with a lip on the front edge for handling — see COOKIE SHEET (2) **:** cake or bread baked in one piece in a large shallow pan ⟨a ~ of gingerbread⟩ **6 :** all of a surface so connected that it is possible to pass from any one point of it to any other without leaving the surface — **between the sheets :** in bed

²sheet \ˈ"\ *vb* -ED/-ING/-S *vt* **1 a :** to wrap in a sheet **:** cover with or as if with a sheet **:** SHROUD ⟨floors ~*ed* with dust⟩ **b :** to cover in a sheet or layer ⟨mist ~*s* the valleys⟩ **2 :** to furnish (as a bed) with sheets ⟨a freshly-*sheeted* couch⟩ **3 :** to form into sheets: as **a :** to convert rubber to sheet form by calendering **b** (1) **:** to cut (a roll of paper) into sheets (2) **:** to run (pulp) into a sheet (as on a paper machine) **4 :** SLIP-SHEET **~** *vi* **1 :** to fall, spread, or flow in or as if in a sheet ⟨fog ~*ing* in from the sea⟩ **2 :** to partially set and slip from a spoon in a sheet when poured after slight cooling — used of a test sample of jelly taken from a boiling mass ⟨bottle the jelly as soon as it ~*s*⟩

³sheet \ˈ"\ *adj* **1 :** rolled or spread out in a sheet ⟨~ copper⟩ **2 :** of, relating to, or concerned with the making of sheet metal ⟨a ~ mill⟩ ⟨~ rollers⟩

⁴sheet \ˈ"\ *n* -S [ME *shete*, fr. OE *scēata* corner, lap, lower corner of a sail; akin to MLG *schōte* sheet (rope regulating a sail), OE *scēat* corner, lap — more at ¹SHEET] **1 :** a rope or chain that regulates the angle at which a sail is set in relation to the wind — see MAINSHEET, WEATHER SHEET; compare TACK; see SAIL illustration **2 sheets** *pl* **:** the spaces at either end of an open boat not occupied by thwarts **:** foresheets and stern sheets together — **sheet in the wind** *or* **sheet to the wind :** a disordered state caused by drinking **:** INTOXICATION — usu. used with *have* or *be* and often qualified quantitatively ⟨he was three *sheets in the wind* by then⟩ ⟨already had a *sheet in the wind*⟩

⁵sheet \ˈ"\ *vt* -ED/-ING/-S **:** SHEET HOME 1

⁶sheet \ˈ"\ *n* -S [by shortening] **:** SHEET ANCHOR

sheet·age \ˈshēd·ij\ *n* -S **:** the total surface area of a paperboard esp. as contrasted with its weight ⟨a high-*sheetage* boxboard high in bulk and low in weight⟩

sheet anchor *n* [alter. (prob. influenced by ⁴*sheet*) of earlier *shoot anchor*, fr. ME *shute anker*, perh. fr. *shute, shutte* sheet (rope regulating a sail) (fr. MLG *schōte*) + *anker* anchor] **1 :** a large strong anchor carried in the waist of a ship — called also *waist anchor* **2 :** something that constitutes a main support or dependence in danger **:** the best or surest hope, reliance, or refuge

sheet bend

sheet bend *n* **:** a bend or hitch used for temporarily fastening a rope to the bight of another rope or to an eye — called also *becket bend, mesh knot, netting knot, swab hitch, weaver's knot*

sheet–block \'ˌ=,=\ n : one of the blocks used to sheet sails home
sheet cable n : the cable of a sheet anchor
sheet chain n : a sheet cable of chain
sheet composting n : the incorporation (as by plowing under) of large quantities of organic residue in the soil usu. accompanied by the addition of extra nitrogen to speed decomposition
sheet deposit n : a mineral deposit (as a lode or bed) that is extended in length and breadth, has relatively small thickness, and is typically approximately horizontal
sheet·ed \'shēd·əd\ adj [¹sheet + -ed] **1** : covered with or wrapped in a sheet or sheets **2** : moving or driving in sheets ⟨a ~ rain⟩ **3** dial Eng : belted with white ⟨a ~ cow⟩ **4** : consisting of so many sheets — usu. used in combination ⟨a 2-sheeted hyperboloid⟩
sheet·er \'shēd·ə(r)\ n -s **1** : a worker that prepares or attends to sheets (as in metallurgy or papermaking) **2** : a machine that makes sheets
sheet erosion n : erosion that removes surface material more or less evenly from an extensive area as contrasted with erosion along well-defined drainage lines that produces or enlarges gullies or ravines
sheet–fed \'=,=\ adj [fed fr. past part. of feed] **1** : designed to print sheets — used of a printing press; compare WEB-FED **2** : printed by a sheet-fed press ⟨sheet-fed gravure⟩
sheet film n : photographic film cut into sheets of various sizes for individual exposure when held in suitable holders in a camera
sheetflood \'=,=\ n : an expanse of moving water into which the transient streams of arid regions spread out as they issue from the mountains upon the plains
sheet·ful \'shēt,fu̇l\ n -s : a quantity sufficient to fill a sheet ⟨a ~ of equations⟩ ⟨crammed home a ~ of nuts and apples⟩
sheet glass n : glass made in large sheets by the drawing process or esp. formerly by the cylinder glass process
sheet home vb [⁵sheet + home, adv.] vt **1** : to extend (a sail) by hauling upon the sheets until it is set as flat as possible ⟨sheeted the topsail home⟩ **2** : to fix the responsibility for : bring home to one ~ vi : to extend a sail by sheeting it home
sheet ice n : ice formed by the freezing of the surface layer of the sea or other water body
sheet imposition n : a process of imposition used when the front of a sheet is to be printed from one form and the back from another form — compare HALF SHEET, WORK AND TURN
¹**sheet·ing** \'shēd·iŋ, -ēt|, |ēŋ\ n -s [¹sheet + -ing] **1** : material in the form of sheets or suitable for forming into sheets: as **a** : a sturdy cloth usu. plainwoven of cotton or linen, made full width on a broad loom, and used esp. for bed sheets **b** : material (as a plastic) in the form of a continuous film ⟨some beautiful ~s that are resistant to moisture, oils, greases and chemicals —Steelways⟩ **2 a** : a lining of planks or boards used for supporting an embankment, trench, or cofferdam and usu. placed vertically and supported by horizontal wales that are in turn supported by braces or piles **b** : a structure produced in rock by the formation of numerous closely spaced parallel fractures that divide the rock into plates or sheets
²**sheeting** \"\ n -s [fr. gerund of ²sheet] : the act or process of forming into, disposing in, or covering with sheets
sheeting pile n : SHEET PILE
sheet·less \'shētləs\ adj : lacking a sheet
sheet·let \-lət\ n -s : a small sheet; esp : a tabloid publication
sheet lightning n : lightning in diffused or sheet form due to reflection and diffusion by the clouds and sky
sheetlike \'=,=\ adj : resembling a sheet esp. in flatness and broad expansion
sheet line n : the edge of a longitudinal seam of shell plating visible from inside of a ship
sheet metal n : metal in the form of a sheet
sheet metal screw n : TAPPING SCREW
sheet mill n : a mill in which metal sheets esp. of steel are rolled
sheet mold n : a mold (as Fusarium javanicum or any of several penicillia) growing on sheet rubber
sheet music n : music printed on large unbound sheets of paper
sheet pavement n : an asphalt pavement
sheet pile n : any of various thick boards or planks that are wedge-shaped at the lower end and sometimes tongued on one edge and grooved on the other and are driven into the ground close together between gauged piles to form walls (as of a cofferdam); also : a rolled steel member used for the same purpose and so designed that each pile interlocks along its edges with the adjacent piles
sheetpiling \'=,==\ n : a row or wall of sheet piles
Sheetrock \'=,=\ trademark — used for a plasterboard formed of gypsum between two surfaces of tough paper
sheet rubber n : freshly coagulated latex rolled into smooth or ribbed sheets — compare SMOKED SHEET
sheets pl of SHEET, pres 3d sing of SHEET
sheet–silicate \'=,=(,)=\ n : PHYLLOSILICATE
sheetwash \'=,=\ n **1** : SHEETFLOOD **2** : detritus transported and deposited by the water of a sheetflood
sheet watermark n : a watermark on a stamp that is a portion of a large design covering the entire sheet — called also overall watermark
sheet web n : a more or less extended tissue of web woven irregularly but largely in a single plane by various arachnomorph spiders — compare ORB WEB
sheetwise \'=,=\ adv (or adj) : by sheet imposition ⟨a signature run ~⟩ ⟨printed by the ~ method⟩
sheetwork \'=,=\ n **1** : printing done by sheet imposition **2** : bookbinders' work including all of the operations from handling flat printed sheets, inserts, and maps to sewing the sections together — compare ³CASE vt 1d, FORWARD vt 3
sheet writer n : a bookmaker's clerk who records odds and other racing information (as on sheets affixed to walls or on blackboards) and cashes winning tickets
sheety \'shēd·ē\ adj -ER/-EST [¹sheet + -y] **1** : resembling a sheet esp. in forming a broad expanse **2** : having a sheeting structure ⟨~ rock formations⟩
sheeve var of SHEAVE
shef·fer's stroke \'shefə(r)z-\ n, usu cap 1st S [after Henry M. Sheffer †1964 Am. philosopher] **1** : JOINT DENIAL **2** : ALTERNATIVE DENIAL
shef·field \'she,fēld\ adj, usu cap [fr. Sheffield, city in northern England] : of or from the city of Sheffield, England ⟨Sheffield cutlery⟩ : of the kind or style prevalent in Sheffield
sheffield plate n, usu cap S : a clad plate made by rolling and fusing a thin covering of silver on either side of a copper sheet
she·getz \'shāgəts\ n, pl **shkot·zim** \'shkōtsəm\ [Yiddish sheykets, sheygets, fr. Heb sheqeṣ blemish, abomination] **1** : a non-Jewish boy or youth — often used disparagingly **2** : a Jewish boy who does not observe Jewish precepts — used esp. by Jews
she·he·he·ya·nu or **she·he·che·ya·nu** \,she(h)ekə'yä(,)nü\ n -s [Heb sheheḥeyānū, lit., who has kept us alive; fr. the seventh word of the blessing] : a blessing pronounced by Jews on joyful occasions (as on the first night of a festival, at the first eating of a new fruit, on donning new clothes)
she·hi·tah or **she·hi·ta** or **she·chi·tah** or **she·chi·ta** \shə'kētə\ n [Heb shĕḥīṭāh slaughter] : the slaughtering of animals for food in accordance with rabbinic law
sheikh or **sheik** also **sheykh** or **shaikh** or **shaykh** \'shēk, 'shāk, 'shīk, in sense 2 'shek\ n -s [Ar shaykh] **1 a** : the head of an Arab family, clan, tribe, or village : an Arab chief — often used as a title or form of respectful address **b** : a governor or prince among peoples of Arabian or Muslim descent **c** : a Muslim religious leader or scholar **2** usu sheik : a man supposed to be endowed with an irresistible fascination in the eyes of romantic young women
sheikh·dom or **sheik·dom** \-kdəm\ n -s : a region under the governance of a sheikh
sheikh·ly or **sheik·ly** adj : of, relating to, or suggestive of a sheikh
sheikh ul islam usu cap S&I, var of SHAIKH AL-ISLAM
shei·la \'shēlə\ n -s [alter. (influenced by the name Sheila) of E (slang) shaler] Austral : a young woman : GIRL
sheiling \'shēliŋ\ var of SHIELING
she–ironbark \'=,==,=\ n [²she (plant) + ironbark] : any of several Australian eucalypts (esp. Eucalyptus boormani)
sheitan var of SHAITAN

shei·tel \'shāt°l\ n -s [Yiddish sheytl, fr. MHG scheitel crown of the head, fr. OHG skeitila; akin to MLG schēdele crown of the head, OE scēadan, scādan to divide, separate — more at SHED] : a wig worn by some Orthodox Jewish matrons in accordance with the tradition of covering the hair as a sign of modesty
she·kar \shə'kär\ var of SHIKAR
shek·el \'shekəl\ n, pl **shekels** \-lz\ or **she·ka·lim** \shə'käləm\ [Heb sheqel (pl. sheqālīm)] **1 a** : any of various ancient units of weight (as of the Babylonians, Hebrews, and Syrians) equivalent to a small fraction (as $\frac{1}{50}$ or $\frac{1}{60}$) of a mina; esp : a Hebrew unit equal to about 252 grains troy **b** : a unit of value based on the value of a shekel weight of gold or silver **2 a** : a coin weighing one shekel (as a Tyrian or Phoenician coin or a Hebrew coin of the period between the 2d century B.C. and the 2d century A.D.) **b** shekels pl : MONEY, CASH **3** : a small annual fee payable by a Zionist into the general fund of the World Zionist Organization entitling the payer to vote for delegates to the Zionist congress **4** : the basic monetary unit of Israel — see MONEY table
she·ki·nah also **she·ki·na** or **she·chi·na** or **she·chi·nah** or **sche·chi·na** \shə'kēnə, -'kēnə, -'kīnə\ n, usu cap [Heb shĕkhīnāh] : the presence of God in the world conceived by Jewish and later by Christian theologians as manifested in natural and esp. supernatural phenomena (as the burning bush or the cloud on Sinai's summit) or as manifested in history through a mystical as opposed to revelational intervention in human affairs or as manifested in a sense of mystic personal communion with God felt by man
sheld·fowl \'shel(d)ˌ=\ n [sheld- (as in sheldrake) + fowl] dial Eng : SHELDRAKE
shel·drake \'shel,drāk\ n, pl **sheldrakes** also **sheldrake** [ME sheldedrake, sheldrake, fr. shelde-, sheld- (akin to MD schillede particolored, variegated, piebald) + drake; akin to G schillern to be iridescent, and perh. to MHG schilhen to wink, squint, OE sceol wry, squinting — more at CYLINDER] **1** : a duck of the Old World genus Tadorna; esp : a common European duck (T. tadorna) that is slightly larger than the mallard, frequents coast regions and nests in burrows, and is chiefly black and white with the head and neck greenish, the lower breast broadly chestnut, the speculum green, and the bill with its frontal knob red **2** : MERGANSER
shel·duck \'shel,dək\ n [sheld- (as in sheldrake) + duck] **1** : SHELDRAKE **2** : the female of the sheldrake
¹**shelf** \'shelf, 'sheu̇|\ n, pl **shelves** \|vz\ often attrib [ME shelfe, shelf, prob. fr. OE scylfe deck of a ship, shelf; akin to OE scylf pinnacle, crag, ledge, MLG schelf frame, rack, MD schelve hayrick, haystack, ON skjölf bench (in Hlithskjölf, Odin's throne), L scalpere, sculpere to dig, scratch, carve, cut, Gk skalops mole (animal), OE sciell shell — more at SHELL] **1 a** : a thin flat usu. long and narrow piece of wood or other material fastened horizontally at a distance from the floor (as on a wall or in a frame) to hold objects **b** : one of several similar pieces in a closet, bookcase, cabinet or similar structure **c** : the books or other contents of a shelf : a number of items constituting or held to constitute the contents of a shelf **2** : something resembling a shelf in form or position: as **a** : a sandbank in a river or the sea : a rock or ledge of rocks usu. partially submerged : REEF, SHOAL **b** : a stratum with a shelf-like surface : bedrock under alluvial soil **c** : a flat projecting layer of rock **d** : the submerged border of a continent or of an island extending from the shoreline to the depth at which the sea floor begins to descend steeply toward the bottom of the ocean basin — see CONTINENTAL SHELF **3** : a longitudinal member of a wooden vessel extending the entire length immediately below the deck beams which rest on and are fastened to it **4** : the upper edge of the bow hand on which an arrow rests when the bow is drawn — **on the shelf** adv (or adj) **1** : in a state of inactivity or uselessness : out of the way ⟨a querulous old man who refuses to be put on the shelf —James Kelly⟩ **2** : without matrimonial prospects — used of a woman
²**shelf** \"\ vt -ED/-ING/-S : to put on the shelf : SHELVE 3a ⟨brigadiers ~ed as principals of colleges —Charles Kingsley⟩
shelf angle n : an angle iron attached to an I beam to provide support for the ends of joists
shelfback \'=,=\ n : BACKBONE 3
shelf·ful \'shelf,fu̇l, -eu̇f,f-\ n -s : a quantity sufficient to fill a shelf : the contents of a shelf
shelf fungus n : BRACKET FUNGUS — compare POLYPORACEAE
shelf ice n : an extensive ice sheet originating on land but continuing out to sea beyond the depths at which it rests on the sea bottom : BARRIER ICE
shelf ladder n : a tall ladder run on wheels for access to high shelves (as in a library or store)
shelf life n : the period of time during which a material may be stored and remain suitable for sale — called also storage life
shelflike \'=,=\ adj : resembling or held to resemble a shelf ⟨long ~ wooden tables —Rufus Jarman⟩
¹**shelflist** \'=,=\ n [¹shelf + list] : a record kept on cards of the books and other materials in a library in the order in which they stand on the shelves
²**shelflist** \"\ vt : to enter in a shelflist
shelf mark n : a character from a library's system of book arrangement usu. appearing at the base of the spine of a book and used to indicate the shelf in a fixed location or the relative position of the book to others of its class in an expansive classification
shelfpiece \'=,=\ n : SHELF 3 — see SHIP illustration
shelf register n, Brit : SHELFLIST
shelf rest n : an angle bracket for supporting adjustable-height cabinet shelves and having a plug extension on the side angle that is inserted in a hole in the side of the cabinet

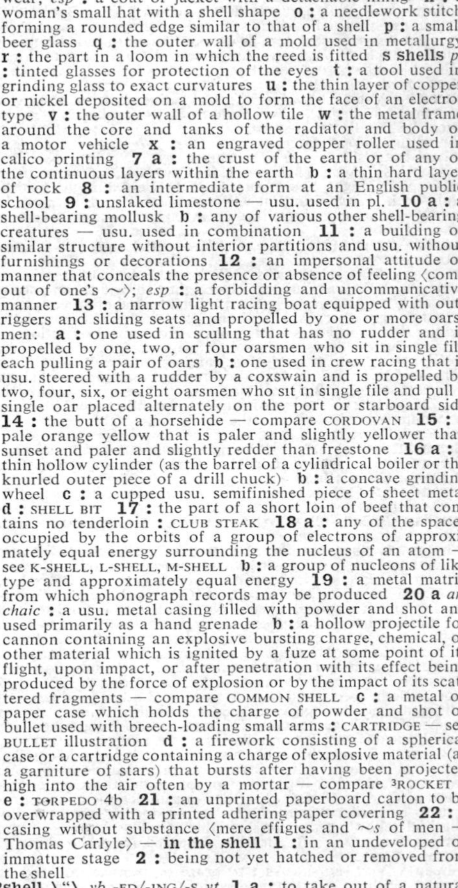
shelf rest

shelf sea n : the part of a sea or ocean which is on a continental or insular shelf : an epicontinental sea
shelfy \'shelfē, -eu̇f-, -fi\ adj -ER/-EST : abounding in shelves: **a** : full of sandbanks or dangerous shallows **b** : full of ledges or flat projecting layers of rock
¹**shell** \'shel\ n -s [ME schell, shell, fr. OE sciell; akin to OE scealu shell, husk, MLG schelle shell, husk, scale on a fish, OHG scala shell, husk, ON skel shell, Goth skalja tile, L silex pebble, flint, siliqua pod, Gk skallein to hoe, Lith skelti to split, Skt kalā small part; basic meaning: to cut] **1 a** : a hard rigid covering of an animal that is commonly largely calcareous but in some cases is chiefly or partly chitinous, horny, or siliceous — see CLAM illustration **b** : the hard or tough outer covering of an egg esp. of a bird — see EGG illustration **c** obs : a scale of a fish or reptile **2 a** : the covering or outside part of a fruit or seed esp. when hard or fibrous : NUTSHELL, POD, HUSK ⟨the hazelnut ~⟩ ⟨the fiber-covered ~ of the coconut⟩ — compare PERICARP **b** usu pl : COCOA SHELLS **3** : a seashell used for some purpose (as for a target or for drinking or sounding) : CONCH **4** archaic : OSTRACON **5** : shell material or a quantity of shells esp. of mollusks, turtles, or tortoises **6** : something that resembles or is held to resemble a shell: as **a** : a hollow structure usu. of a spherical, hemispherical, or domed shape **b** : a slight hollow structure : a framework or exterior structure that is frail in construction or has had its interior removed or destroyed or is regarded as not complete or filled in ⟨the ~ of a house⟩ **c** : a semicircular or nearly semicircular guard plate sometimes of openwork attached to the cross guard on either side of a European sword of the 15th century and later : COQUILLE **d** archaic : LYRE **e** : the external case or outside covering of something : HUSK ⟨the ~ of a ship⟩ ⟨the ~ of religion⟩ **f** : the outer frame or case of a pulley block **g** (1) : a rough or temporary wooden coffin (2) : a thin interior coffin enclosed in a more substantial one **h** : CONCHA 2b(1) **i** (1) : something shaped like a scallop shell; esp : a household utensil for cooking or serving (2) : an edible case for holding a filling **j** : a hollow cabochon **k** : a reinforced concrete arched or domed roof that is used primarily over large unpartitioned areas, is comparatively thin esp. at the crown of the arch, and carries no loads other than its own weight **l** : a prepared and usu. hollow counterpart of an object that is secretly substituted by a magician for the article itself **m** : an unlined article of outerwear; esp : a coat or jacket with a detachable lining **n** : a woman's small hat with a shell shape **o** : a needlework stitch forming a rounded edge similar to that of a shell **p** : a small beer glass **q** : the outer wall of a mold used in metallurgy **r** : the part in a loom in which the reed is fitted **s** shells pl : tinted glasses for protection of the eyes **t** : a tool used in grinding glass to exact curvatures **u** : the thin layer of copper or nickel deposited on a mold to form the face of an electrotype **v** : the outer wall of a hollow tile **w** : the metal frame around the core and tanks of the radiator and body of a motor vehicle **x** : an engraved copper roller used in calico printing **7 a** : the crust of the earth or of any of the continuous layers within the earth **b** : a thin hard layer of rock **8** : an intermediate form at an English public school **9** : unslaked limestone — usu. used in pl. **10 a** : a shell-bearing mollusk **b** : any of various other shell-bearing creatures — usu. used in combination **11** : a building or similar structure without interior partitions and usu. without furnishings or decorations **12** : an impersonal attitude or manner that conceals the presence or absence of feeling ⟨come out of one's ~⟩; esp : a forbidding and uncommunicative manner **13** : a narrow light racing boat equipped with outriggers and sliding seats and propelled by one or more oarsmen: **a** : one used in sculling that has no rudder and is propelled by one, two, or four oarsmen who sit in single file each pulling a pair of oars **b** : one used in crew racing that is usu. steered with a rudder by a coxswain and is propelled by two, four, six, or eight oarsmen who sit in single file and pull a single oar placed alternately on the port or starboard side **14** : the butt of a horsehide — compare CORDOVAN **15** : a pale orange yellow that is paler and slightly yellower than sunset and paler and slightly redder than freestone **16 a** : a thin hollow cylinder (as the barrel of a cylindrical boiler or the knurled outer piece of a drill chuck) **b** : a concave grinding wheel **c** : a cupped usu. semifinished piece of sheet metal **d** : SHELL BIT **17** : the part of a short loin of beef that contains no tenderloin : CLUB STEAK **18 a** : any of the spaces occupied by the orbits of a group of electrons of approximately equal energy surrounding the nucleus of an atom — see K-SHELL, L-SHELL, M-SHELL **b** : a group of nucleons of like type and approximately equal energy **19** : a metal matrix from which phonograph records may be produced **20 a** archaic : a usu. metal casing filled with powder and shot and used primarily as a hand grenade **b** : a hollow projectile for cannon containing an explosive bursting charge, chemical, or other material which is ignited by a fuze at some point of its flight, upon impact, or after penetration with its effect being produced by the force of explosion or by the impact of its scattered fragments — compare COMMON SHELL **c** : a metal or paper case which holds the charge of powder and shot or bullet used with breech-loading small arms : CARTRIDGE — see BULLET illustration **d** : a firework consisting of a spherical case or a cartridge containing a charge of explosive material (as a garniture of stars) that bursts after having been projected high into the air often by a mortar — compare ³ROCKET 1 **e** : TORPEDO 4b **21** : an unprinted paperboard carton to be overwrapped with a printed adhering paper covering **22** : a casing without substance ⟨mere effigies and ~s of men —Thomas Carlyle⟩ — **in the shell 1** : in an undeveloped or immature stage **2** : being not yet hatched or removed from the shell
²**shell** \"\ vb -ED/-ING/-S vt **1 a** : to take out of a natural enclosing cover (as a shell, husk, pod, capsule) : strip, break off, or remove the shell of : SHUCK ⟨~ nuts or peas⟩ ⟨~ oysters⟩ **b** : to separate the kernels of (as an ear of Indian corn, wheat, or oats) from the cob, ear, or husk **2** : to encase in or as if in a shell **3** : to throw shells at, upon, or into : BOMBARD ⟨~ a town⟩ ⟨~ an enemy position or fortification⟩ **4** : to cover (a surface) with shells ⟨~ an oyster bed⟩ ~ vi **1** : to fall or scale off in the manner of a shell, crust, or outer coat : come off in thin pieces **2** : to cast the shell or exterior covering : fall out of the pod or husk ⟨nuts ~ in falling⟩ : become disengaged from the ear or husk ⟨wheat or rye ~s in reaping⟩ **3** : to gather shells (as from a beach) : collect shells **4** : to form a shell of a solution (as on the inner surface of the container in freeze-drying)
³**shell** \"\ adj **1** : having a shell ⟨a ~ animal or fruit⟩ **2** : consisting of or containing shells and esp. seashells ⟨a ~ bluff⟩ ⟨~ marl⟩ ⟨~ concrete⟩ **3 a** : made from or ornamented with shells ⟨~ earrings⟩ ⟨~ belt⟩ ⟨~ workbox⟩ **b** : made of tortoise shell ⟨~ comb⟩ **4** : resembling a shell in shape or pattern ⟨a ~ roof⟩ — used esp. of a carved decoration on furniture of the period 1720–80 ⟨a ~ chair⟩ ⟨~ trimmings⟩ **5** : having a through longitudinal hole to receive a bar which is pushed through it and fastened in position — used of a tool
¹**shel·lac** also **shel·lack** \shə'lak\ n -s [¹shell + lac, lack; trans. of F laque en écailles] **1** : purified lac that is prepared in the form of thin orange or yellow flakes usu. by heating and filtering seed lac and is often bleached white and that is used chiefly in varnishes, polishing and sealing waxes, binding agents, stiffening agents (as for felt hats), electric insulators, phonograph records, and other molded products **2** : a preparation of lac dissolved usu. in alcohol and used chiefly in filling wood and as a varnish — compare LACQUER 1a **3 a** : a composition containing shellac used for pressing phonograph records **b** : an old 78 rpm phonograph record ⟨a ~ containing only two songs —Thomas Lask⟩
²**shellac** \"\ vt **shellacked** also **shellaced** \-kt\ **shellacked** also **shellaced**; **shellacking** also **shellacing** \-kiŋ\ **shellacs 1** : to coat or otherwise treat with shellac or a shellac varnish **2** : to defeat decisively or ignominiously : administer a beating to : DRUB ⟨played truant and got soundly ~ed for it when he was found out —William Irish⟩
shel·lack·ing \shə'lakiŋ\ n -s [fr. gerund of ²shellac] : a decisive or ignominious defeat : BEATING, DRUBBING ⟨a ~ he received that made him hors de combat after nine rounds —Nat Fleischer⟩ ⟨took a ~ in the fall election⟩ ⟨worst ~ in their military history —Richard Joseph⟩
shellac wax n : a hard wax separated from shellac (as by its insolubility in alcohol) and used chiefly in polishes and insulating materials
shell·ap·ple \'she,lapəl\ n [alter. of earlier sheldapple, prob. fr. obs. E sheld particolored, variegated + dapple; akin to MD schillede particolored, variegated — more at SHELDRAKE] **1** dial Eng : CHAFFINCH **2** dial Eng : CROSSBILL
shellback \'=,=\ n **1** : an old or veteran sailor : OLD SALT **2** : one who has crossed the equator and been initiated in the traditional ceremony — compare POLLIWOG 2
shellbark \'=,=\ or **shellbark hickory** n **1** : SHAGBARK HICKORY **2** : BIG SHELLBARK
shell bark n **1** : a disease of lemon trees caused by a fungus (Phomopsis californica) and characterized by scaling or sloughing of the bark — called also decorticosis; see DRY BARK **2** : RHYTIDOME
shell–barked \'=,bärkt\ adj : having a rhytidome
shell bean n **1** : a bean grown primarily for its edible seeds — compare SNAP BEAN **2** : the edible seed of any bean and esp. of a shell bean
shell bit n : a boring tool shaped like a gouge and used with a brace
shell cooling n : a method of storing potatoes in bins having tight sides and floors with air circulated around and under the bins by gravity or by power-operated blowers
shellcracker \'=,==\ n : REDEAR
shell crest n : a rounded crest on the head (as of various pigeons) — distinguished from peak crest
shell dove n : SCALED DOVE
shell·drake n, pl **shelldrake** or **shelldrakes** [by alter.] : SHELDRAKE
shell drill n : a short 4-fluted drill mounted on an arbor and used for rough reaming — compare AUGER, ¹BIT 3a, CROSS BIT
shell·duck n [by alter.] : SHELDUCK
shelleater \'=,==\ n : OPENBILL
shelled \'sheld\ adj [in sense 1, fr. ¹shell + -ed; in sense 2, fr. past part. of ²shell] **1 a** : having a shell **b** : covered or paved with shells ⟨a ~ road⟩ **c** : encased in a shell **2 a** : taken from the shell ⟨~ nuts⟩ ⟨~ oysters⟩ **b** : removed from the cob ⟨~ corn⟩
shell egg n : an egg in the shell as distinguished from a dried or powdered egg

shell·er \'shelə(r)\ *n* -s **:** one that shells: **a :** a worker who shells (as peas, nuts, grain, or bivalves) **:** an operator of a shelling machine **b :** a machine or device that shells ⟨a nut ~⟩

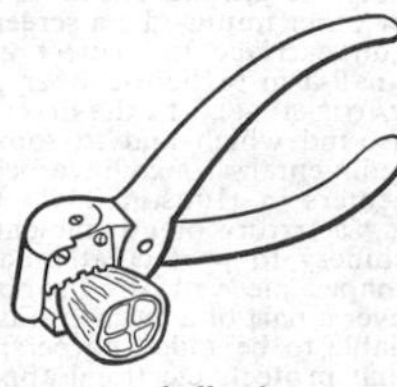
sheller b

shell expansion *n* **:** a drawing showing the shell plating of a ship and giving the size, shape, and weight of the plates and their connections

¹shel·ley·an *also* **shel·le·ian** \'shelēən, ±'±±\ *adj, usu cap* [Percy Bysshe *Shelley* †1822 Eng. poet + E *-an*] **:** of, relating to, or having the characteristics of the poet Shelley or his writings

²shelleyan \"\ *n* -s *usu cap* **:** a follower or admirer of the poet Shelley

shell eye *n* **:** any of numerous pigmented spots in the shell of chitons that are sensitive to light and to disturbances in the water and that sometimes develop a retina

shel·ley·esque \¦shelē¦esk\ *adj, usu cap* [Percy Bysshe *Shelley* + E *-esque*] **:** of, relating to, or characteristic of the poet Shelley or his writings ⟨such romantic and *Shelleyesque* claims for him —Kimon Friar⟩

shell fire *n, dial Eng* **:** phosphorescence from decaying matter

shellfire \'±,±\ *n* **:** firing or shooting of shells **:** the explosions from shells

shellfish \'±,±\ *n* [ME, fr. OE *scielfisc,* fr. *sciell* shell + *fisc* fish — more at SHELL, FISH] **1 :** an aquatic invertebrate animal having a shell: **a :** an oyster, clam, or other mollusk **b :** a lobster or other crustacean **2 :** BOXFISH

shell·fish·ery \'±,fish(ə)rē\ *n* **1 :** the production or catching of shellfish **2 :** the study of shellfish from the economic point of view

shellflower \'±,±\ *n* **1 :** MOLUCCA BALM **2 :** TURTLEHEAD **3 :** a showy East Indian herb (*Languas speciosa*) of the family Zingiberaceae commonly cultivated for its shining oblong leaves, bracted white flowers with shell-pink shading, and crisped yellow magenta-variegated lip

shell game *n* **:** a gambling game derived from the earlier thimblerig and in which a person by sleight-of-hand manipulates a pea or similar pellet and three half walnut shells or similar cuplike objects so that a spectator can seldom know surely under which shell the pea rests and then invites bets on the location of the pea ⟨the *shell game* is so often played dishonestly that its name has become symbolic of chicanery⟩ — compare THREE-CARD MONTE

shell ginger *n* **:** a large ornamental herb (*Alpinia speciosa*) from eastern Asia having clusters of irregularly bell-shaped flowers that are white marked with red and yellow and that bend downward from the tip of leafy arching stems which are 5 to 12 feet high

shell gland *n* **1 :** a looped tubular excretory organ of an entomostracan or the young of many other crustaceans that ends blindly at one extremity and opens to the exterior on or near the second maxilla **2 :** a glandular organ in the embryo of many mollusks that secretes the embryonic shell **3 :** a specialized glandular part of the oviduct of many animals that forms the egg's shell

shell gray *n* **:** a yellowish gray to light slightly yellowish gray that is duller than sand or natural — called also *plaza gray*

shell heap *or* **shell midden** *or* **shell mound** *n* **:** KITCHEN MIDDEN

shell hole *n* **:** the cavity made by the explosion of an artillery shell

shell ibis *n* **:** OPENBILL

shell ice *n* **:** ice orig. formed on a sheet of water but no longer resting on it because the water has been withdrawn — called also *cat ice*

shellier *comparative of* SHELLY

shelliest *superlative of* SHELLY

shel·ligs \'sheligz\ *n, pl* **shelligs** [origin unknown] **:** a large green crab (*Callinectes ornatus*) brightly marked with yellow, white, and red living in moderately deep water from New Jersey to Brazil

shelling *n* -s [fr. gerund of ²*shell*] **1 a :** hulled oats or other grain **b :** the husks or chaff from such grain **2 :** the action of one that shells: as **a :** the removal of the shell (as from nuts, peas, or oysters) **b :** the action of fertilizing with shells **c :** bombardment with shells **d :** the action of collecting shells esp. along the sea **3 :** a disease of the grape of uncertain origin causing the immature fruit to drop

shell jacket *n* **1 :** a short tight military jacket worn buttoned up the front **2 :** MESS JACKET

shell landings *n pl* **:** marks made on a ship's frames to show the location of the edges of the shell plates

shell-less \'shelləs\ *adj* **:** having no shell **:** lacking shells

shell-like \'shel,līk\ *adj* **:** resembling a shell (as in form or composition)

shell·man \'shelmən, -,man\ *n, pl* **shellmen :** JACKMAN 1

shell membrane *n* **:** the tough membraneous covering of an egg immediately within the shell

shell money *n* **:** a medium of exchange consisting of shells — compare COWRIE, WAMPUM

¹shell out *vb* [²*shell* + *out*] *vt* **1 :** to hand out or over (as money) demanded or needed **:** pay out **:** CONTRIBUTE, DISBURSE, PRODUCE ⟨known for his reluctance to *shell out* money —Barry Bingham⟩ **2 :** to remove entire by separation from its environment (as by the use of blunt instruments) ⟨*shell out* a tumor⟩ **~** *vi* **:** to furnish the money needed or called for **:** pay up ⟨makes it unnecessary to *shell out* to . . . racketeers —J.F.McDonald⟩

²shell out *n* **:** a pocket billiards game played with 15 object balls by three or more players with a stake being received by a player from his opponents each time a red ball is pocketed

shell parrakeet *or* **shell parrot** *n* **:** BUDGERIGAR

shell pink *n* **1 :** a variable color averaging a light yellowish pink that is yellower and slightly stronger than petal pink and slightly lighter and stronger than opera pink **2** *of textiles* **:** a strong yellowish pink

shell plating *n* **:** the plates covering over the frames of a steel ship and corresponding to the planking of a wooden ship

shellproof \'±¦±\ *adj* **:** capable of resisting shells or bombs **:** BOMBPROOF

shell pump *n* **:** a simple form of sand pump or sludger consisting of a hollow cylinder with a ball or clack valve at the bottom and used with a flush of water to remove detritus

shell quail *n* **:** SCALED QUAIL

shell reamer *n* **:** a hollow reamer that when used is fitted to a suitable shank made usu. of less expensive metal

shell reducer *n* **:** a thin metal shell or liner inserted into the force-feed shell of a grain drill to decrease the rate of planting of small seeds (as flaxseed)

shell road *n* **:** a road having a surface built of marine shells

shell roof *n* **:** a roof of relatively large expanse (as of a hangar or arena) composed of concrete panels curved cylindrically or spherically for strength

shells *pl of* SHELL, *pres 3d sing of* SHELL

shellshake \'±,±\ *n* **:** RING SHAKE

shell shock *n* **:** any of numerous psychoneurotic conditions akin to hysteria and anxiety neurosis appearing in soldiers exposed to modern warfare — compare COMBAT FATIGUE

shell-shock \'±,±\ *vt* [*shell shock*] **:** to affect with shell shock ⟨were gassed and wounded and *shell-shocked*⟩

shell socket *n* **:** TAPER REDUCER SLEEVE

shell strake *n* **:** a strake running the length of the hull of a ship

shell tint *n* **:** a variable color averaging a yellowish white that is stronger and slightly redder and darker than milk white — called also *pearl*

shell turtle *n* **:** HAWKSBILL TURTLE

shell-vault \'±,±\ *n* **:** a structure of thin material gaining its rigidity through its calculated shape rather than through bulk and strength

shellwork \'±,±\ *n* **:** work composed of a pattern of shells or adorned with shells

shelly \'shelē, -li\ *adj* -ER/-EST **1 a :** abounding in or covered with shells, esp. seashells ⟨a ~ shore⟩ ⟨~ ground⟩ **b :** consisting of shells or of a shell ⟨the hermit crab in his ~ cave⟩ **2 a :** of, relating to, or of the nature of a shell **:** CHITINOUS, SILICEOUS, TESTACEOUS **b :** of, relating to, or constituting fractured coal that breaks up easily into small pieces **3 :** having a shell **4 :** like a shell esp. in being hollow, frail, or easily breakable: as **a** *of a dog* **:** having a narrow weedy body **b** *of market livestock* **:** thin, gaunt, and ill-nourished (as from age) **c** *of a hoof* **:** thin and brittle and with the horny matter ridged

shellycoat \'±±,±\ *n* [*shelly* + *coat*] *Scot* **:** a water sprite wearing a coat made of shells

shelly rail *n* **:** a rail in which small shell-like pieces have become detached from the top surface or side of the railhead

shel·ta \'sheltə\ *n* -s *usu cap* [origin unknown] **:** a secret jargon of the tinkers and kindred groups still spoken to some extent in Great Britain and Ireland and consisting chiefly of a systematic deformation of Irish Gaelic and Scottish Gaelic

¹shel·ter \'sheltə(r)\ *n* -s *often attrib* [origin unknown] **1 a :** something that covers or affords protection esp. from the elements **:** something that provides refuge or defense (as from injury, exposure, observation, attack, pursuit, danger, or annoyance) **:** a means or place of protection **:** an area of safety **:** REFUGE, SCREEN **b :** a structure (as a small building in a park) used as a refuge in bad weather **c :** a structure or dugout affording protection to troops in the field **d :** an area or a specially constructed structure for refuge and protection from bombs, radiation, and other features of air attack ⟨an air raid ~⟩ ⟨bomb ~s⟩ **e :** HOUSING 3; *esp* **:** temporary housing **f :** a covering (as a box or cage) used to protect an object ⟨instrument ~⟩ **g :** an establishment to shelter the homeless: as (1) **:** a Salvationist institution operated for the homeless (2) **:** an institutional home (as for delinquent or neglected children or unmarried mothers) **h :** protection from bad weather (as by trees or walls) ⟨the trees afforded shade and ~ —Willa Cather⟩ **2 :** the state of being covered and protected (as from the elements) **:** PROTECTION ⟨I took ~ under a shed —Nora Waln⟩ ⟨the witness refuses to answer under the ~ of the Fifth Amendment —E.N.Griswold⟩

²shelter \"\ *vb* **sheltered; sheltered; sheltering** \-lt(ə)riŋ, -l·tr-\ **shelters** *vt* **1 :** to constitute or provide a shelter for: as **a :** to screen or protect from the elements ⟨the pedimented facade ~s a niched figure —*Amer. Guide Series: Md.*⟩ ⟨a light awning . . . to ~ the observer from the wind —*Topographic Surveying*⟩ **b :** to afford protection from something held to resemble unfavorable weather **:** shield from injury, attack, pursuit, annoyance, censure, punishment, or notice ⟨the defenders were . . . ~*ed* by the walls —Tom Wintringham⟩ ⟨women are ~*ed* . . . by the men of their families —Lois Long⟩ ⟨a ~*ed* life⟩ **c :** to provide with a home, security, refuge, temporary accommodation, or protection **:** HARBOR ⟨building that ~s the rare and extensive . . . collection —*Amer. Guide Series: Oregon*⟩ ⟨no other small community . . . has ~*ed* so many noteworthy American writers —*Amer. Guide Series: N.H.*⟩ **2 :** to place under shelter or protection **:** betake to cover or refuge **:** take to a safe place ⟨~ myself in the crannies of the rocks —Margaret A. Barnes⟩ ⟨every American political party . . . has ~*ed* itself behind the Supreme Court —Felix Frankfurter⟩ **~** *vi* **:** to take shelter **:** find refuge or cover ⟨if you must ~ under a tree —G.H.T.Kimble⟩ ⟨refugees . . . came here to ~ from trouble —Han Suyin⟩ ⟨a long annex . . . in which the animals ~ at night —Wilfred Thesiger⟩

shelterbelt \'±±,±\ *n* **:** a natural or planted barrier of trees or shrubs primarily for protection of soil and crop fields from wind and storm and for lessening erosion — compare WINDBREAK

shelter deck *n* **:** a continuous deck of light construction above the principal deck of a ship and usu. covering a full-length superstructure or space not permanently closed against the weather — see DECK illustration

sheltered *adj* **1 :** protected from competition esp. from abroad ⟨~ trades⟩ ⟨a ~ industry⟩ ⟨~ domestic markets⟩ **2 :** protected from risks or from burdens (as taxes) ⟨a tax-sheltered investment in municipal bonds⟩ **3 :** providing a noncompetitive environment for the useful occupation and training of persons (as the physically disabled, the aged, or emotionally disturbed or handicapped children) in order to promote their adjustment and rehabilitation ⟨~ workshop⟩ ⟨~ employment⟩

shel·ter·er \-ltərə(r)\ *n* -s **1 :** one that takes shelter **2 :** one that provides shelter

shelter foot *n* **:** immersion foot from long exposure to cold and damp without actual immersion in water

shelter half *n* **:** one of the interchangeable halves of a two-man shelter tent

shelter leg *n* **:** SHELTER FOOT

shel·ter·less \'sheltə(r)ləs\ *adj* **1 :** destitute of shelter or protection **:** having no covering **2 :** affording no shelter

shelter tent *n* **1 :** a small tent usu. composed of two or more pieces of waterproof cotton duck fixed for buttoning or tying with accessory cords and poles and in military service divided into usu. interchangeable parts some of which will be carried by each soldier as part of his field equipment **2 :** a tent erected with two poles and a ridge rope with the roof sloping to the rear only often with a perpendicular drop, the sides perpendicular, and the front closed by a hanging flap that can be raised as an awning

shelter trench *n* **:** a trench hastily constructed to secure shelter from direct fire that is usu. first dug as a shallow excavation with the dirt thrown up as a parapet in front to shelter a man lying down and then if time permits is deepened as rapidly as possible until it will shelter a man standing

shelterwood method \'±±,±-\ *n* [¹*shelter* + *wood*] **:** a method of securing natural tree reproduction under the shelter of old trees which are removed by successive cuttings to admit to the seedlings a gradually increasing amount of light

shel·tery \'sheltərē, -l·trē\ *adj* **:** affording shelter ⟨sitting in a ~ nook —Patrick Kennedy⟩

sheltopusic *or* **sheltopusick** *var of* SCHELTOPUSIK

shel·ty *or* **shel·tie** \'sheltē\ *n, pl* **shelties** [prob. fr. Scand origin; akin to ON *Hjalti* Shetlander] **1 :** SHETLAND PONY **2 :** SHETLAND SHEEPDOG

¹shelve \'shelv, -eùv\ *vb* -ED/-ING/-S [fr. *shelves,* pl. of ¹*shelf*] *vt* **1 :** to furnish with shelves ⟨~ a closet⟩ ⟨~ a library⟩ ⟨a *shelved* table⟩ **2 :** to place on a shelf **:** arrange or store upon shelves ⟨~ books⟩ ⟨many libraries ~ recent fiction by itself —W.H.Jesse⟩ **3 :** to put on the shelf: as **a :** remove from active service **:** DISMISS ⟨~ an army officer⟩ **b :** to put aside (as from consideration) **:** put off indefinitely ⟨the dangerous inclination of . . . politicans to ~ thorny problems —Henri Peyre⟩ ⟨~ a project⟩ ⟨~ a bill⟩ **~** *vi* **:** to slope in a formation like a shelf **:** INCLINE — often used with an adverb of direction ⟨the mountains ~ off into the mesa country —*Amer. Guide Series: Colo.*⟩ ⟨the ground ~s steeply toward the north —James Whyle⟩ ⟨a grassy plain . . . ~s out into a clean white beach —George Tichenor⟩

²shelve \"\ *n* -s [back-formation fr. *shelves,* pl. of ¹*shelf*] **1** *archaic* **:** SHELF 2a **2 :** SHELF 2c

shelv·er \və(r)\ *n* -s **:** one that shelves (as books in a library)

shelves *pl of* SHELF *or of* SHELVE, *pres 3d sing of* SHELVE

¹shelv·ing \-viŋ\ *n* -s [fr. gerund of ¹*shelve*] **1 :** the state or degree of sloping **2 :** a sloping surface or place

²shelving \"\ *n* -s [²*shelve* + *-ing*] **1 :** material for shelves **2 :** a number or quantity of shelves; *esp* **:** the shelves inside a closet or fitted to a wall

shelvy \'shelvē, -eùvē\ *adj* -ER/-EST [²*shelve* + *-y*] **:** sloping or inclining in the manner of a geologic shelf ⟨the shore was ~ and shallow —Shak.⟩

she·mi·ni a·tze·reth *or* **shemini a·tze·ret** *or* **shemini a·ze·ret** \shə'mē,nēä'tse(,)ret(h), -res\ *n, usu cap S&A* [LHeb *shĕmīnī 'ăṣereth,* fr. Heb *shĕmīnī* eighth + *'ăṣereth* assembly, convocation] **:** a Jewish festival observed on the 22d day of Tishri, following the 7th day of Sukkoth proper, and marked by a memorial service and a special prayer for seasonal rain

shem·ite \'she,mīt\ *n* -s *usu cap* [*Shem* (Sem), son of Noah and eponymous ancestor of the Semites (Gen 10:22–31) + E *-ite*] **:** SEMITE

she·mit·ic \shə'mid·ik, she'm-\ *adj, usu cap* **:** SEMITIC

shem·it·ish \'she,mīd·ish\ *adj, usu cap* **:** SEMITIC

she·mit·tah \shə'mētə\ *n, pl* **shemit·tot** *or* **shemi·toth** \-,tōt(h), -ōs\ [Heb *shĕmiṭṭāh,* lit., remission, release] **:** SABBATICAL YEAR

she·moz·zle *var of* SCHEMOZZLE

shen·a·chie \¦shenə¦kē\ *var of* SHANACHIE

she·nan·go \shə'naŋ(,)gō\ *n, pl* **shenangoes** *also* **shenangos** [prob. fr. the *Chenango* river and *Chenango* canal in south-central N. Y. state] **:** a casually employed dock worker

she·nan·i·gan \shə'nanəgən, -anēg-\ *n* -s [origin unknown] **1 a :** an often devious trick used esp. to divert attention for an underhand purpose **:** DECEPTION, STRATAGEM, FAST ONE ⟨a scamp who had pinched pennies out of the teacups of the poor by various ~s —W.A.White⟩ **b :** any act that is high-spirited, daring, or mischievous **:** PRANK, ESCAPADE ⟨boys up to some ~ or other⟩ **2 a :** tricky or questionable practices or conduct **:** HUMBUG, FAKERY ⟨febrile prosperity . . . founded on ~ —*Yale Rev.*⟩ ⟨the simplest business transaction today is enveloped in such a mantle of idiotic ~ —*Amer. Mercury*⟩ ⟨revealed certain indications of ~ on the part of these judges —*N.Y.Sun*⟩ — usu. used in pl. ⟨symbol of all the fraud and force and ~s and duress —W.A.White⟩ ⟨unfair ~s by a competitor —M.T.Bloom⟩ **b :** any high-spirited, daring, or mischievous activity **:** GOINGS-ON, HIGH JINKS, MONKEY BUSINESS — usu. used in pl. ⟨the ~s attending a supercolossal film production —Ilka Chase⟩ ⟨as soon as the usual parade ~s were over —Saul Bellow⟩ ⟨the raiders, after an hour or two of highly diverting ~s . . . during which they drew the wildest kind of inaccurate fire, retired —Walter Karig⟩

¹shend \'shend\ *vt* **shent** \-nt\ **shent; shending; shends** [ME *shenden,* fr. OE *scendan;* akin to OFris *skenda* to shame, disgrace, OS *skendian,* OHG *scenten;* causative-denominative fr. the root of OE *scand* shame, disgrace, OFris *skande,* OHG *scanta,* Goth *skanda;* akin to OE *scamu* shame — more at SHAME] **1** *archaic* **a :** to confuse, confound, or put to shame esp. by superiority ⟨Cynthia doth ~ the lesser stars —Edmund Spenser⟩ **b :** to get the better of (as in battle or argument) **:** DISCOMFIT **2** *archaic* **:** to subject to reproach **:** REPROVE, REVILE ⟨I am *shent* for speaking to you —Shak.⟩ **3** *chiefly dial* **a :** INJURE, MAR, HARM **b :** RUIN, DESTROY ⟨the withered crown will soon slide down a skull all bleached and *shent* —G.M.Hopkins⟩

²shend *vt* [perh. alter. (influenced by ¹*shend*) of ²*shield*] *obs* **:** PROTECT, SHIELD, DEFEND

sheng *also* **shing** *or* **cheng** \'s(h)əŋ, 'chəŋ, 'jiŋ\ *n, pl* **sheng** *or* **shengs** [Chin (Pek) *sheng*¹] **:** a Chinese unit of liquid capacity equal to 1.094 quarts or 1.035 liters according to the 1914 standard or 1.057 quarts or 1 liter according to the 1929 standard

shen·zi \'shen(,)zē\ *n, pl* **shenzi** *or* **shenzis** [Swahili] **:** an uncivilized African tribesman

she-oak \'±¦±\ *n* [²*she* (plant) + *oak*] **1 :** any of several Australian trees of the genus *Casuarina* — compare BEEFWOOD 2a **2** [so called fr. its having been first applied to a kind of cheap beer regarded as inferior to good beer as the she-oak is inferior to the oak] *slang Austral* **:** BEER

she·ol \shē'ōl, shə'ōl, 'shē,ōl\ *n, usu cap* [Heb *Shĕ'ōl*] **:** the subterranean world of darkness that in early Hebrew thought resembled the Greek Hades in being an underworld abode where all spirits of the dead were assumed to live a shadowy existence involving neither punishment nor joy, was later conceived of as the intermediate realm of departed spirits where the wicked were punished and the good awaited resurrection to a blessed reward, and was still later conceived of as a place where the wicked were tortured and tormented — compare GEHENNA, HELL, NETHERWORLD

¹shep·herd \'shepə(r)d\ *n* -s [ME *sheephirde, sheepherde, shephirde, shepherde,* fr. OE *scēaphyrde,* fr. *scēap* sheep + *hyrde* herdsman — more at SHEEP, HERD] **1 :** a man employed in tending, feeding, and guarding sheep, esp. in a flock that is grazing **2 :** one charged with the religious care and guidance of others **:** PASTOR **3 :** a dog used as or considered suitable for use as a sheep dog; *esp* **:** one of any of several breeds having *shepherd* as part of their name ⟨toy ~⟩ — see GERMAN SHEPHERD **4 :** SHEPHERD KING

²shepherd \"\ *vt* -ED/-ING/-S **1 :** to tend as a shepherd **2 :** to gather, guard, herd, lead, or drive in the manner of a shepherd **:** ESCORT, CONDUCT ⟨a lawyer friend ~*ed* her into investment in two houses —Rex Ingamells⟩ ⟨gray ships, ~*ed* by sleek naval craft, off-loaded —A.H.Brown⟩ ⟨officers started ~*ing* the wounded aboard the hospital train —Fred Majdalany⟩ ⟨parents . . . ~*ing* a good-sized group of youngsters on an excursion —Dorothy Barclay⟩ **3 :** to give spiritual guidance to ⟨four missionaries . . . hurried back to bury the dead and ~ the living —W.C.Fairfield⟩

shepherd dog *or* **shepherd's dog** *n* [ME *scheperd dog, scheperdys dogge*] **:** SHEEP DOG

shep·herd·ess \-dəs\ *n* -ES [ME *shepherdesse,* fr. *shepherde* + *-esse* -ess] **1 :** a woman or girl who tends sheep **:** a female shepherd **2 :** a rural lass

shep·her·dia \she'pərdēə, -ep'hə-\ *n, cap* [NL, fr. John *Shepherd* †1836 Eng. botanist + NL *-ia*] **:** a genus of American shrubs (family Elaeagnaceae) with silvery or scurfy opposite leaves, small dioecious flowers with eight stamens and baccate fruit — see BUFFALO BERRY

shepherd king *n, usu cap S* [trans. of Gk *basileus poimēn;* trans. of Egypt *ḥqꜣ šꜣsw*] **:** one of the Hyksos kings

shep·herd·less \'shepə(r)dləs\ *adj* **:** lacking a shepherd or guide

shepherdlike \'±±,±\ *adj* **:** resembling or characteristic of a shepherd ⟨~ care of the needy —*Atlantic*⟩

shep·herd·ly \-pə(r)dlē\ *adj* **:** of, relating to, or having the characteristics of a shepherd **:** PASTORAL

shepherd's bag *n* [ME *schepherdes bagge*] **:** SHEPHERD'S PURSE

shepherd's check *or* **shepherd check** *or* **shepherd's plaid** *or* **shepherd plaid** *n* **1 :** a pattern of small even black-and-white checks **2 :** a fabric woven in shepherd's check pattern

shepherd's check

shepherd's clock *n* **1** *or* **shepherd's weatherglass :** SCARLET PIMPERNEL **2 :** SALSIFY

shepherd's club *n* **:** a common mullein (*Verbascum thapsus*)

shepherd's coffin *n* **:** RATTLE 3a

shepherd's companion *n* **:** a fantail flycatcher (*Rhipidura leucophrys*) of Australia

shepherd's cress *n* **:** a small European annual herb (*Teesdalia nudicaulis*) of the family Cruciferae having a rosette of pinnatifid leaves and small white flowers in racemes

shep·herd·ship \'shepə(r)d,ship\ *n* **:** the position, duty, or occupation of a shepherd

shepherd's hourglass *n* **:** WOOD PIMPERNEL

shepherd's needle *n* **:** LADY'S-COMB

shepherd spider *n* **:** HARVESTMAN 2

shepherd's pie *n* **:** a savory mixture of leftover meat baked in a crust of mashed potatoes

shepherd's pipe *n* [ME *scheperdys pype*] **1 :** FLAGEOLET 1 **2 :** MUSETTE

shepherd's pouch *n* **:** SHEPHERD'S PURSE

shepherd's purse *n* [ME *shepherdys purs*] **:** a white-flowered annual European herb (*Capsella bursa-pastoris*) that is nearly cosmopolitan as an introduced weed and bears triangular notched pods

shepherd's thyme *n* **:** WILD THYME

shepherdy *n* -ES [¹*shepherd* + *-y*] *obs* **:** the position or occupation of a shepherd

she-pine \'±¦±\ *n* [²*she* (plant) + *pine*] **1 :** an Australian timber tree (*Podocarpus elata*) the yellow durable wood of which is used for spars and masts **2** *also* **she pitch pine :** CARIBBEAN PINE

shep·pey argentine \'shepē-\ *n, usu cap S* [*Sheppey,* island at the mouth of the Thames, Eng. + *argentine*] **:** PEARLSIDES

shep·stare \'shepstər, -,sta(ə)(r)\ *or* **shep·star·ling** \'shep-,±±\ *or* **shep·ster** \'shepstər\ *n* -s [*shep-* (as in *shepherd*) + *stare* (starling) *or starling*] *dial Eng* **:** the common starling

she·ra·ni *or* **shi·ra·ni** \shə'rānē\ *n, pl* **sherani** *or* **sheranis** *or* **shirani** *or* **shiranis** *usu cap* **1 :** a chiefly agricultural people of northwestern Pakistan belonging to the Pathan group and being short in stature and slim in body **2 :** a member of the Sherani people

sherard·ize \shə'rär,dīz, 'sherər,d-\ *vt* -ED/-ING/-S *see -ize in Explan Notes* [*Sherard* O. Cowper-Coles †1936 Eng. inventor + E *-ize*] **:** to coat (an article of iron or steel) with zinc by covering with commercial zinc dust in a tightly closed drum and heating for several hours at 300° to 420° C so that a zinc-iron alloy is formed at the surface through the action of zinc vapor — **sherard·iz·er** \-zər\ *n* -S

sher·a·ton \'sherət°n, -rəd·ən,nətən\ *adj, usu cap* [after Thomas *Sheraton* †1806 Eng. furniture maker and designer, its inventor] **:** of, relating to, or closely imitating a style of furniture originating around 1800 in England and marked by straight lines and graceful proportions, delicate and often ingenious construction, much inlay esp. of satinwood, and as a rule sparing use of carving except in the characteristic reeding of tapering legs

sher·bet \'shərbət, 'shəb-,'shəib-, *usu* -əd·+V\ *also* **sher·bert** \-bə(r)t, *usu* -)d·+V\ *n* -S [Turk & Per; Turk *şerbet*, fr. Per *sharbat*, fr. Ar *sharbah* drink, fr. *shariba* to drink] **1 :** a cooling drink made of sweetened and diluted fruit juice **2** *or* **sherbet powder :** a variously flavored preparation esp. of sodium bicarbonate, tartaric acid, and sugar for making an effervescent drink **3 :** a water ice to which milk, egg white, or gelatin is added before freezing **4** *or* **sherbet glass :** a footed glass cup for serving frozen or unfrozen desserts

sherbet 4

sherd *var of* SHARD

shereef *var of* SHARIF

sheri *or* **sheria** *or* **sheriat** *often cap, var of* SHARI'A

sher·i·dan·ite \'sherədᵊn,īt\ *n* -S [*Sheridan* county, Wyo., its locality + E *-ite*] **:** a mineral $(Mg_9Al_3)(Al_3Si_5)O_{20}(OH)_{16}$ of the chlorite group consisting of pale greenish colorless basic silicate of magnesium and aluminum

sherif *var of* SHARIF

sherifa *var of* SHARIFA

sher·iff \'sherəf, *dial or in rapid speech* 'sherf, *dial* 'shər(·ə)f\ *n* -S [ME *shirreve, sherreve, shiref, sheref, shreve*, fr. OE *scīrgerēfa*, fr. *scīr* district, shire + *gerēfa* reeve — more at SHIRE, REEVE] **1 :** the chief executive officer of a shire or county in Britain holding office usu. by royal appointment but sometimes formerly by inheritance and having duties and powers varying from time to time and from place to place (as in England, Scotland, Ireland) but typically being charged with the duty of superintending parliamentary elections, returning juries in criminal cases, attending the judges, holding certain courts, and executing the orders and processes of the courts and judges — see DEPUTY SHERIFF, POCKET SHERIFF, UNDERSHERIFF **2 :** an important county officer in the U. S. who is usu. elected by the people of the county as the chief executive officer of the courts of superior jurisdiction therein and is charged with the duty of attending these courts and executing their orders and processes through deputies appointed by him, has charge of the county jail and other penal institutions and the prisoners therein awaiting trial or under sentence, has the duty of preserving the peace and quelling riots with the power to deputize posses to apprehend criminals, has the duty of transferring prisoners sentenced to state prisons and patients committed to state institutions, and often has the power to summon jurors as well as other powers granted by statute **3 :** any officer (as a deputy sheriff or constable) performing duties relating to the office of sheriff

sher·iff·al·ty \-fəlte\ *n* -ES [by alter. (influence of *sheriff*)] **:** SHRIEVALTY

sher·iff·cy \-fsē\ *n* -ES [*sheriff* + *-cy*] **:** SHRIEVALTY

sheriff depute *n, Scots law* **:** a lawyer designated to perform the judicial duties of a sheriff

sher·iff·dom \-fdəm\ *n* -S [ME *shirrevedom, sherrevedom, shirefdom, sherefdom*, fr. *shirreve, sherreve, shiref, sheref* sheriff + *-dom*] **:** SHRIEVALTY

sheriff–pink \'==(,)=\ *n* **:** DAISY 1b

sheriff's court *n* **1** *Eng law* **:** a court held by a sheriff or an undersheriff with a jury and authorized to assess damages in undefended and in compulsory taking-of-land cases, to find the value of defendants' lands taken on executions, and formerly to try other issues of fact sent to it by courts of superior jurisdiction **2** *Scots law* **:** a court presided over by a sheriff depute or a sheriff substitute trained in law that is the ordinary and the small debt court and a criminal court and since 1913 has jurisdiction in practically all civil actions with the principal exceptions of actions involving the status of marriage, divorce, or legitimacy, reductions, winding-up of companies where paid-up capital exceeds £10,000, and actions to prove the text of lost documents but cannot sentence to more than two years' imprisonment

sheriff substitute *n, Scots law* **:** an undersheriff who usu. hears cases in the first instance

sheriffwick \'==,=\ *n* [ME *shirrefwyke*, fr. *shirref, shirreve* sheriff + *wyke, wik* wick — more at WICK] **:** SHRIEVALTY

¹sherifian *var of* SHARIFIAN

²she·rif·ian \shə'rēfēən\ *adj, usu cap* **:** of or relating to the Sherifian Empire

she·ris·ta·dar \shə'ristə,där\ *n* -S [Hindi *sarrishtadār*, fr. Per *sarrishta* record office + *dār* having] *India* **:** RECORDER, REGISTRAR, SECRETARY

¹sher·lock \'shər,läk, 'shə̄,l-, 'shəi,l- *sometimes* 'sher,l- *or* 'sheə,l- *or* -lək\ *vb* -ED/-ING/-S [after *Sherlock* Holmes] *vt* **:** to observe and infer in the manner of Sherlock Holmes ~ *vi* **:** to act as a detective

²sherlock \"\ *n* -S *often cap* [after *Sherlock* Holmes] **:** SHERLOCK HOLMES

sherlock holmes \,=(,)='hōmz *also* -ōlmz\ *n, pl* **sherlock holmeses** *usu cap S&H* [after *Sherlock Holmes*, detective par excellence in short stories and novels by Sir Arthur Conan Doyle †1930 Brit. writer] **1 :** DETECTIVE; *esp* **:** one having remarkable powers of deduction **2 :** a person exhibiting unusual powers of deduction in solving any problem

sher·lock·ian \(;)=¦läkēən\ *adj, usu cap* [*Sherlock* Holmes + E *-ian*] **:** of or resembling the fictional detective Sherlock Holmes esp. in the exercise of unusual powers of deduction ⟨solved the mystery with *Sherlockian* ease⟩ ⟨could almost see the *Sherlockian* glitter in the doctor's eyes —Philip Wheelwright⟩

sher·pa \'sherpə, 'shər-\ *n, pl* **sherpa** *or* **sherpas** *usu cap* **1 :** a Tibetan people living on the high southern slopes of the Himalayas and skilled in mountain climbing **2 :** a member of the Sherpa people

sher·ra \'sherə\ *Scot var of* SHERIFF

sher·ra·moor \'sherə,mu̇(ə)r, 'shər-\ *n* -S *usu cap* [alter. of *Sheriffmuir*, site of the battlefield in Perth county, Scotland, where on Nov. 13, 1715 the Jacobites were defeated by the Royalists and their rebellion checked] *Scot* **:** TUMULT, ROW

sher·ried \'sherēd, -rid\ *adj* [*sherry* + *-ed*] **:** flavored with sherry wine ⟨~ trifle⟩ ⟨~ lobster⟩

sher·ris \'sherə̇s\ *archaic var of* SHERRY

sherris–sack *n, obs* **:** sack imported into England from Jerez, Spain

sher·ry \'sherē, -ri\ *n* -ES [alter. of earlier *sherris* (taken as pl.), fr. *Xeres* (now *Jerez*), town near Cádiz, Spain] **1 a :** a fortified wine of Spanish origin ranging from pale to dark amber in color and from very dry to sweet in taste with typically a distinctive nutty flavor — see AMONTILLADO, FINO, OLOROSO **b :** a wine with characteristics similar to those of true Spanish sherry but produced elsewhere (as in the U. S. in New York and California) **2** *or* **sherry brown :** a moderate brown that is yellower and lighter than bay, yellower and duller than toast brown, and lighter, stronger, and slightly yellower than chestnut brown — called also *clove, Manchu, manganese brown, mineral bister, Rangoon*

sher·ry·val·lies \¦sherē¦valēz\ *n pl* [modif. of Pol *szarawary*, fr. Russ *sharavary*, fr. Gk *sarabara* loose trousers, prob. of Iranian origin; akin to Per *shalwār, shulwār* loose trousers] **:** overalls or protective leggings of thick cloth or leather formerly worn for riding on horseback

sher·wa·ni \shə(r)'wänē\ *n* -S [Hindi *śērwānī*] **:** a long-sleeved close-fitting knee-length coat with a stand-up collar worn by men of India and Pakistan

shes *pl of* SHE

shetadlan *var of* SHTADLAN

she teak *n* [²*she* (plant)] **:** NATIVE TEAK a

sheth \'sheth\ *n* -S [ME; akin to OE *scēath* sheath — more at SHEATH] **1 :** a number of rows (as of galleries in a mine or furrows in a field) at right angles to similar rows which they intersect or adjoin **2 :** one of the bars forming a framework (as of a wagon) **3 :** SHEATH 2a(2), 3c

sheth of boards : a group of cross workings in a mine

¹shet·land \'shetlənd\ *adj, usu cap* [fr. the *Shetland* islands, archipelago off northern Scotland] **:** of or from the Shetland islands constituting the county of Shetland, officially Zetland, in Scotland **:** of the kind or style prevalent in Shetland **:** SHETLANDIC

²shetland \"\ *n* -S **1** *usu cap* **:** an animal of a breed or type native to or developed in the Shetland islands: as **a :** SHETLAND PONY **b :** SHETLAND SHEEPDOG **2** *sometimes cap* **a :** a lightweight loosely twisted yarn of Shetland wool used for knitting and weaving **b :** a soft napped fabric loosely woven of Shetland wool

shetland argus *n, usu cap S&A* **:** a basket star (*Gorgonocephalus Linckii*)

shet·land·er \'shetləndə(r)\ *n* -S [*Shetland* islands + E *-er*] **1** *cap* **:** a native or inhabitant of Shetland **2** *usu cap* **:** SHETLAND PONY

shet·lan·dic \(')shet¦landik\ *adj, usu cap* [*Shetland* islands + E *-ic*] **:** of, relating to, or characteristic of Shetland

shetland pony *n* **1** *usu cap S&P* **:** a breed of small, stocky, hardy ponies with a long rough coat and long mane and tail that originated in the Shetland islands **2** *usu cap S* **:** a pony of the Shetland pony breed

shetland sheepdog *n* **1** *usu cap both Ss* **:** a breed of small dogs resembling miniature collies with profuse double coats and developed in the Shetland islands presumably by interbreeding collies with smaller long-haired dogs native to the area and possibly with Pomeranians **2** *usu cap 1st S* **:** a dog of the Shetland sheep dog breed

shetland wool *n, usu cap S* **1 :** the fine undercoat hand-plucked from sheep raised in the Shetland islands **2 :** yarn hand-spun from Shetland wool

¹sheugh *also* **sheuch** \'shük\ *n* -S [ME *sough* — more at SOUGH] **1** *chiefly Scot* **:** a small ravine or gully; *sometimes* **:** one with water running through it **2** *chiefly Scot* **:** a man-made ditch or trench

²sheugh \"\ *vt* -ED/-ING/-S **1** *chiefly Scot* **:** to make ditches or drains in ⟨~ a marsh⟩ **2** *chiefly Scot* **:** to cover over **:** heel in

she·va *n* -S [Heb *shĕwā'*] **:** SCHWA

shevat *usu cap, var of* SHEBAT

shev·eled *or* **shev·elled** \'shevəld\ *adj* [by shortening] **:** DISHEVELED

shevuoth *or* **shevuos** *usu cap, var of* SHABUOTH

shew \'shō\ *archaic var of* SHOW

she·wa *n* -S [Heb *shĕwā'*] **:** SCHWA

shewbread *or* **showbread** \'=,=\ *n, pl* **shewbread** *also* **shewbreads** *or* **showbread** *also* **showbreads** [trans. of G *schaubrot*] **:** any of the 12 loaves of consecrated unleavened bread ritually placed by the Jewish priests on a table in the sanctuary of the Tabernacle on the Sabbath as an expression of the belief that Yahweh is the source of every material blessing and as an expression of gratitude

shew·el \'shüəl\ *n* -S [back-formation fr. ME *sheules, sheweles*; akin to MLG *schūwelse* scarecrow, MHG *schiusel* scarecrow, OHG *sciuhen* to scare off, OE *scēoh* shy — more at SHY] *archaic* **:** SCARECROW; *esp* **:** one made of feathers tied to a string

shew·er \'shō(ə)r\ *archaic var of* SHOWER

she–woman \'=¦==\ *n, pl* **she–women :** a woman abundantly endowed with obviously or pronouncedly feminine qualities

sheykh *var of* SHEIKH

sheyle \'shā(ə)l\ *vi* -ED/-ING/-S [akin to MHG *schilhen* to wink, squint, OE *sceol* wry, squinting — more at CYLINDER] *chiefly Scot* **:** to look cross-eyed **:** SQUINT

SHF *abbr, often not cap* superhigh frequency

shg *abbr* shipping

shi'a *or* **shia** *or* **shiah** \'shē(,)ä, -ēə\ *n* -S *usu cap* [Ar *shī'ah* following, sect — more at SHI'ITE] **1 :** the Muslims comprising one of the two major branches of Islam originating as a legitimist party rejecting the first three caliphs and holding Ali the son-in-law of Muhammad as the legitimate successor of the Prophet, established as the national faith of Persia since 1500, and comprising many diverse sects — compare SUNNI **2 :** SHI'ITE **3 :** the branch of Islam formed by the Shi'a

shi·bah *or* **shi·vah** *or* **shi·va** \'shivə\ *n* -S [Heb *shibh'āh* seven (days)] **:** a traditional 7-day period of mourning that follows the funeral of a close relative and is observed in the home by Jews ⟨the family will sit ~ until Friday⟩

shib·bo·leth \'shibələth *sometimes* -,leth\ *n* -S [Heb *shibbōleth* ear of grain, stream, flood; fr. the use of this word as a test to distinguish Gileadites from Ephraimites, who pronounced it *sibbōleth* (Judges 12:6)] **1 a :** a sound or a word containing a sound whose proper articulation is difficult for and whose mispronunciation is regarded as reliably indicating or betraying a speaker who is not native or whose speech has been influenced by early acquaintance with another language **b :** a custom or usage regarded as a criterion for distinguishing members of one group (as a social class) from those of another ⟨for most of the well-to-do in the town, dinner was a ~, its hour dividing mankind —Osbert Sitwell⟩ **2 a :** a word or saying characteristically used by the adherents of a party, sect, or belief and usu. regarded as empty of real meaning **:** CATCHWORD, SLOGAN ⟨the criticism of liberal and radical thought wherever it deteriorated to ~ and dogma —Lionel Trilling⟩ **b :** a use of language regarded as distinctive of a particular class, profession, or group of persons ⟨our listeners type us — stereotype us — according to the impression they gain from our verbal habits . . . every word we speak is a ~ —G.A.Miller⟩ **c :** a commonplace saying or idea **:** PLATITUDE, TRUISM ⟨some truth in the ~ that crime does not pay —Lee Rogow⟩

¹shib·i·lant \'shibələnt\ *adj* [alter. (influenced by the digraph *sh*, representing the sound \sh\) of *sibilant*] **:** pronounced or containing the sound \sh\ or \zh\ ⟨\ch\ (=t+sh) and \j\ (=d+zh) are ~ affricates⟩

²shibilant \"\ *n* -S **:** a shibilant sound

shi·bu·ichi \¦shēbəwə¦chē, ,==¦wēchē\ *n* -S [Jap, fr. *shi* four + *bu* part, parts + *ichi* one] **:** an orig. Japanese alloy that consists of one part of silver to three parts of copper and that assumes a silvery gray patina when properly treated

shi·cer \'shīsə(r)\ *n* -S [G *scheisser* one that defecates, contemptible person, fr. *scheissen* to defecate (fr. OHG *schīzan*) + *-er* — more at SHIT] *Austral* **:** an unproductive mine

shick \'shik\ *adj* [Yiddish *shiker*] *Austral* **:** DRUNK

¹shick·er \'shikə(r)\ *or* **shick·ered** \-d\ *adj* [*shicker* fr. Yiddish *shiker*, fr. Heb *shikkōr*, fr. *shikhar* to be drunk; *shickered* fr. Yiddish *shiker* + E *-ed*] *slang* **:** DRUNK

²shicker \"\ *n* -S [Yiddish *shiker*, fr. Heb *shikkōr*, fr. *shikkōr*, adj.] *slang* **:** DRUNKARD

shicksa *var of* SHIKSA

shied *past of* SHY

shiel \'shē(ə)l\ *n* -S [ME (northern dial.) *schele, shale*; prob. akin to OFris *skūl* hiding place, *skūle* stable, MLG *schūle* hiding place, ON *skjōl* shelter, cover, *skāli* hut, room, OE *hȳd* hide, skin — more at HIDE] *chiefly Scot* **:** SHIELING

¹shield \'shē(ə)ld\ *n* -S [ME *sheld, shild*, fr. OE *scield, sceld, scyld, scild*; akin to OHG *scilt* shield, ON *skjöldr*, Goth *skildus* shield, OE *sciell* shell — more at SHELL] **1 a :** a broad piece of defensive armor (as of metal, wood, or leather) carried on the arm or held in the hand by a handle and formerly in general use for the protection of the body (as from spears, arrows, or sword thrusts) in battle or individual combat **b :** a means or method of defense ⟨a fighter ~ for their war industries —*Manchester Guardian Weekly*⟩ ⟨understanding . . . that the haughtiness was a ~ —Anne D. Sedgwick⟩ **c :** the field on which the bearings in coats of arms are placed **:** ESCUTCHEON **2 :** a structure, device, or part that serves as a protective cover or barrier: as **a :** the hard horny skin of a boar's flank or neck **b :** a protective structure on an animal (as a large scale, carapace, or lorica); *usu* **:** any of the large scales on the head of a snake or lizard or the horny plates of a turtle's shell **c :** an iron or steel framework moved forward at the end of a tunnel or adit in process of excavation to support the ground ahead of the concrete, cast iron, brickwork, or other lining **d :** a screen of armor plate usu. attached to a gun carriage to protect an otherwise exposed gun against small-arm or light-caliber projectiles or shrapnel **e :** CULTIVATOR SHIELD **f :** the Precambrian nuclear mass of a continent around which and to some extent upon which the younger sedimentary rocks have been deposited ⟨the Canadian ~ . . . centers in Hudson Bay —C.O.Dunbar⟩ — compare CRATON **g :** a fixture or attachment placed over moving parts of machinery to protect attendants or others from injury **h :** a shaped piece of often rubberized cloth that is worn inside or over a part of a garment (as the underarm of a dress or blouse) liable to be soiled by perspiration **i** (1) **:** a screen or device that protects electrical apparatus from being affected by outside electrostatic or magnetic influences (2) **:** a wall, screen, housing, or other device that protects against radiation ⟨a lead ~⟩ **3 :** something that has the shape of a shield or is thought to resemble a shield: as **a** (1) **:** APOTHECIUM (2) **:** one of the eight wall cells of the antheridium of a stonewort **b :** a bodily marking or otherwise differentiated area of an animal resembling a shield **c :** a policeman's badge ⟨turned in his ~ and applied for retirement⟩ **d :** a decorative or identifying emblem (as of a state, club, or organization) ⟨these cars will carry no state ~ —*Springfield (Mass.) Daily News*⟩

²shield \"\ *vb* -ED/-ING/-S [ME *shelden, shilden*, fr. OE *scieldan, scildan, scyldan*, fr. *scield, sceld, scyld, scild*, n.] *vt* **1 a :** to protect with or as if with a shield **:** give cover to **:** DEFEND ⟨~*ing* his eyes from the light —John Seago⟩ ⟨have your work to retire into, your ideas to ~ you —Aldous Huxley⟩ **b :** to cut off from observation **:** CONCEAL, HIDE ⟨usually work in gangs, clustering about exhibits in such a manner as to ~ their activities —*Irish Digest*⟩ ⟨the act of concealment and the reasons for it are themselves ~*ed* from public observation —J.G.Palfrey⟩ **2** *obs* **:** AVERT, FORBID — used in the phrase *God shield* ⟨God ~ I should disturb devotion —Shak.⟩ **3 :** to ward off **:** keep off or out — often used with *off* ⟨their own messes and own company to ~ off loneliness —*Time*⟩ ~ *vi* **:** to serve as a shield **:** DEFEND, PROTECT ⟨a desire to ~ and save —Lord Byron⟩ **syn** see DEFEND

shield–back chair \'=,=-\ *n* **:** a Hepplewhite chair that has a back whose short side posts support a shield-shaped framework

shield–backed bug \'=,=-\ *n* **:** SHIELD BUG

shield bearer *n* **1 :** an attendant who carries a warrior's shield — compare SQUIRE **2 :** any of various small moths constituting a genus (*Coptodisca*) and having larvae that cut out an oval bit of leaf to form a case

shield budding *n* **:** plant budding in which an oval to shield-shaped piece of bark bearing a scion bud is fitted into an approximately T-shaped opening in the bark of the stock

shield bug *n* **:** a bug of the family Pentatomidae characterized by a very large scutellum suggesting a shield **:** STINKBUG

shield cell *n* **:** SHIELD 3a(2)

shield cone *or* **shield dome** *n* **:** a conical or domical shield volcano

shield·er \-ēldə(r)\ *n* -S **:** one that shields

shield fern *n* **:** any of various ferns (as of the genera *Dryopteris* and *Polystichum*) having more or less shield-shaped indusia — called also BUCKLER FERN

shield fungus *n* **:** a fungus of the family Microthyriaceae

shield graft *n* **:** a side graft in which a scion with a wedge-shaped base is inserted in a T-shaped cut in the side of the stock

shielding *n* -S **1 :** the act or process of protecting or supplying with a protective device or screen ⟨the problems the engineers solve in their bunker are complex exercises in ~ —*Newsweek*⟩ **2 :** something that protects; *specif* **:** a device or screen that protects against radiation ⟨the radioactive metals must be treated behind heavy ~ by remote control —Leon Svirsky⟩

shield·less \-ē(ə)ldləs\ *adj* **:** having no shield

shield–maid \'=,=\ *or* **shield–maiden** \'=,==\ *n* [trans. of ON *skjaldmær*] **:** a woman warrior **:** VALKYRIE

shieldmay \'=,=\ *n* [¹*shield* + *may* (maiden); trans. of ON *skjaldmær*] **:** SHIELD-MAID

shield of arms : a coat of arms carried or displayed on a shield or shield-shaped object or design

shield of brawn : a piece of a boar's shield stuffed with meat and cooked

shield of da·vid \-'dāvə̇d\ *usu cap S&D* [trans. of Heb *māghēn Dāwīdh*] **:** MAGEN DAVID

shield of pretense : a small shield of arms carried within another shield of arms

shields *pl of* SHIELD, *pres 3d sing of* SHIELD

shield scale *or* **shield louse** *n* **:** ARMORED SCALE

shield–shaped \'=,=\ *adj* **:** having the shape of a shield; *specif* **:** PELTATE

shieldtail \'=,=\ *n* **:** a small Oriental burrowing snake of the family Uropeltidae having a large scute on the tail

shield volcano *n* **:** a volcano built up by successive outpourings of lava with little or no fragmental material and consequently having a diameter at its base many times as great as its height — contrasted with *stratovolcano*; compare BASALT DOME

shiel·ing \'shēliŋ\ *n* -S [*shiel* + *-ing*] **1** *dial Brit* **:** a hut or small cottage in the hills or mountains that is used as a shelter by shepherds **2** *dial Brit* **:** a summer pasture in the mountains

¹shi·er \'shī(ə)r, -īə\ *comparative of* SHY

²shier \"\ *also* **shy·er** \"\ *n* -S [²*shy* + *-er*] **:** a horse given to shying

³shier \"\ *n* -S [⁴*shy* + *-er*] **:** one that shies a missile

shies *pres 3d sing of* SHY, *pl of* SHY

shiest *superlative of* SHY

¹shift \'shift\ *vb* -ED/-ING/-S [ME *shiften* (also, to arrange, order), fr. OE *sciftan*; akin to OFris *skifta, skiffa* to decide, determine, test, MLG *schiften, schichten* to decide, separate, arrange, order, MD *schichten* to arrange, order, ON *skipta* to divide, change, be of importance, OE *scēadan* to divide, separate — more at SHED] *vt* **1** *chiefly dial* **:** to apportion into shares **:** DISTRIBUTE, DIVIDE **2 a :** to exchange for or replace by another of the same category **:** CHANGE ⟨~ tasks to vary the monotony —Stuart Chase⟩ ⟨the clouds . . . were actually beginning to form very rapidly, and to ~ shape from moment to moment —G.R.Stewart⟩ ⟨~ his clothes⟩ ⟨~ the scenery⟩ **b** *chiefly dial* **:** to change the clothes of **3 a** (1) **:** to change the place, position, or direction of **:** MOVE, TRANSFER ⟨move everything on deck had to be ~*ed* to put the bow down —D.B. Putnam⟩ ⟨~*ed* his head round again to glance at her —Walter de la Mare⟩ ⟨the weight of the mammoth building was ~*ed* to new foundations —*Amer. Guide Series: Pa.*⟩ ⟨went forward to ~ the jib —Peter Heaton⟩ (2) **:** TRANSPLANT (3) **:** to cause (the printing position of a typewriter character) to be changed so that the character on the upper half of the key will print **b :** to make a change in (position or place) ⟨the shortstop ~*ed* his position as the next batter came up⟩ ⟨unto Southampton do we ~ our scene —Shak.⟩ **4 a :** to change the form or condition of **:** TRANSFORM ⟨different curtains and chairs — we can ~ the house all around —Marcia Davenport⟩ **b :** to change phonetically esp. in accordance with Grimm's law **5** *archaic* **:** AVOID, ESCAPE **6 :** to get rid of **:** DISLODGE ⟨nothing less than a hot shower will ~ the dirt that has caked on my skin —O.E.Middleton⟩ **7 :** to put away (food or drink) **:** CONSUME ⟨I've ~*ed* a lot in the last twenty years . . . not real heavy drinking —Geoffrey Household⟩ ~ *vi* **1 a :** to change place, location, or residence ⟨actual farm migrants, up against it, ~ from one place to another —Russell Lord⟩ **b :** to change position **:** move about ⟨interrupted her by ~*ing* heavily in his chair —Scott Fitzgerald⟩ **c :** to change direction ⟨the trail twisted and ~*ed* —Philip Rooney⟩ ⟨the wind ~*ed* to the east⟩ **d :** to make a shift on a stringed musical instrument **e :** to raise the carriage or lower the typebar segment of a typewriter by pressing a special key so that the character on the upper half of any typeface will print **f :** to shift gears **2 a** (1) **:** to manage by or for oneself **:** get along ⟨left the cadets to ~ for their own maintenance on their monthly pay of ten dollars —Herman Beukema⟩ ⟨his uncle died a year later so he was obliged to ~ for himself —W.R.Steiner⟩ (2) **:** to get along badly or with difficulty **:** make shift ⟨go around looking for worries to take up from other people, while their own house ~*s* along the best way it can —Mary Deasy⟩ **b :** to resort to evasions or fraud **:** make use of expedients ⟨prompts him to ~ and dissimulate —H.L.Mencken⟩ **3** *archaic* **:** to go away **:** DEPART, WITHDRAW ⟨let us not be dainty of leave-taking, but ~ away —Shak.⟩ **4 a :** to go through a change (as in form, character, or condition) **:** become transformed ⟨a voice deep, yet *~ing* easily to falsetto quavers —William Beebe⟩ ⟨the situation *~ed*⟩ **b :** to change one's clothes ⟨taught me to ~ into a madman's rags —Shak.⟩ **c :** to become changed phonetically esp. in accordance with Grimm's law **syn** see MOVE — **shift gears 1 :** to change the gear rotating the transmission shaft of an automobile **2 :** to make a change from one method, tempo, or approach to another ⟨*shifted gears* in the middle of his speech⟩ — **shift the helm :** to put the tiller of a boat from starboard to port or vice versa and usu. from hard over one way to hard over the other

²shift \"\ *n* -s **1 a :** a means or device for effecting an end ⟨an index may or may not be a trustworthy ~ for finding something —Joshua Whatmough⟩ — compare MAKESHIFT **b** *archaic* **:** ability to contrive **:** RESOURCEFULNESS **c** (1) **:** a deceitful or underhand scheme **:** DODGE, FRAUD, TRICK ⟨not amused by her *~s* and her shameful deceit —C.B.Tinker⟩ (2) **:** an effort or expedient exerted or tried in difficult circumstances **:** EXTREMITY — usu. used in pl. ⟨during the air raids the staff were put to extraordinary *~s* to keep the programs on the air at all —T.O.Beachcroft⟩ **2 :** the act of putting one thing in place of another **:** something put in place of another **:** SUBSTITUTION: as **a** (1) *chiefly dial* **:** a change of clothes (2) *chiefly dial* **:** SHIRT; *specif* **:** a long undershirt (3) **:** a woman's slip or chemise **b** (1) **:** a group of people who work or occupy themselves in turn with other groups ⟨three *~s* of little citizens go to school in the same classroom each day —W.E.Goslin⟩ (2) **:** a change of one group of people (as workers or students) for another in regular alternation **:** a scheduled period of work or duty ⟨in a department working on *~s*, the morning ~ started at 6:00 A.M. —B.B.Gardner⟩ ⟨nurses leaving their *~s* at night —J.P.Browne⟩ **c :** one of the land units or successive crops in a crop rotation **d :** a change in emphasis, judgment, or attitude ⟨small or larger *~s* in fashion are a commonplace of the literary scene —Bernard De Voto⟩ ⟨a sudden ~ in values⟩ **e :** CONSONANT SHIFT **f :** a bid in bridge in a suit other than the suit one's partner has bid **g :** the transposition of two portions of a pack of cards in a manner designed to escape detection by an observer **h :** the character on the upper half of a typewriter type bar ⟨the underscore is the ~ of the 6⟩ **3 :** a change in direction ⟨a ~ in the wind⟩ **4 :** a change in place or position ⟨he hesitated and I heard the slight sound of his ~ of weight —R.P.Warren⟩: as **a** (1) **:** a change in the position of the hand on the fingerboard in playing the violin or a similar musical instrument (2) **:** a change in position of the movable slide of a trombone (3) **:** the movement of the entire key action in a grand piano by the operation of the soft pedal so that the hammers strike only one or two strings instead of two or three **b** (1) **:** a dislocation of a mine vein or seam **:** FAULT (2) **:** the relative displacement of rock masses on opposite sides of a fault or fault zone and far enough away to be unaffected by bending or other local distortion along the zone of dislocation — compare SLIP **c :** the disposition of members in a structure (as a building or boat) so as to separate the joints and secure strength by overlapping **d** *dial Eng* **:** a change of residence **e** (1) **:** a simultaneous change of position in football esp. from one side of the line to the other made by two or more players of the side in possession of the ball just before the ball is snapped (2) **:** a change in position (as to the right or left) by one or more players on a baseball field for better defense against a particular hitter **f :** a change in frequency resulting in a change in position of a spectral line or band — see DOPPLER SHIFT, RED SHIFT **5 :** a removal from one person or thing to another **:** TRANSFER ⟨a ~ of responsibility⟩ ⟨a ~ of interest from natural philosophy to politics and ethics —Benjamin Farrington⟩ **6 :** GEARSHIFT **syn** see RESOURCE

shift·abil·i·ty \ˌshiftəˈbilədˌē\ *n* **:** the quality or state of being shiftable

shift·able \ˈshiftəbəl\ *adj* **:** capable of being shifted; *esp* **:** capable of being transferred from one holder or owner to another ⟨a ~ asset⟩

shift bid *n* **1 :** a deliberately unsound bid in bridge from which the bidder expects to rescue himself if he is doubled **2 :** SHIFT 2g

shift boss *n* **1 :** a foreman in charge of the workers of a particular shift **2 :** a foreman in charge of workers in a particular section of a metal mine — compare PIT BOSS

shifted *past of* SHIFT

shift·er \ˈshiftə(r)\ *n* -s **1 :** one that resorts to evasion in reasoning **2 :** one that shifts; *esp* **:** a worker whose job is to shift a specified thing ⟨bobbin ~⟩ ⟨stone ~⟩ **3 a :** a shift boss in a metal mine **b :** one that works in a coal mine assisting workers other than those who do the actual mining **4 :** any of various devices for shifting something: as **a :** BELT SHIFTER **b :** a wire for changing a loop from one needle to another (as in narrowing)

shifter fork *n* **:** a belt-shifter fork between whose prongs a belt runs and moves laterally (as from a loose to a tight pulley) in response to pressure from either prong

shift·ful \ˈshiftfəl\ *adj* **:** TRICKY

shiftier *comparative of* SHIFTY

shiftiest *superlative of* SHIFTY

shift·i·ly \ˈshiftəlē, -li\ *adv* **:** in a shifty manner

shift·i·ness \-tēnəs, -tin-\ *n* -ES **:** the quality or state of being shifty **:** TRICKINESS ⟨a look of ~ and hardness, a mixture of prison and the boxing ring —John Masefield⟩

shifting *pres part of* SHIFT

shifting accent *n* **:** SHIFTING STRESS

shifting backstay *n* **:** a permanent stay so rigged as to be set up or cast off as the working of a ship requires

shifting boards *n pl* **:** boards placed fore-and-aft in the hold of a ship to prevent bulk cargoes (as grain) from shifting

shifting executory devise *n* **:** a shifting use created by will

shifting pedal *n* **:** SOFT PEDAL 1

shifting stress *n* **:** stress that is not the same for a particular speech item with all speakers or in all occurrences or environments

shifting use *n* **:** a use that takes effect in derogation of some other estate and is expressly limited by the deed or may be created on a certain contingency by a person named in the deed

shift joint *n* **:** a vertical building joint so placed as to come above a solid member of the course below; *also* **:** the process of forming such a joint

shift key *n* **:** a typewriter key used for shifting

shift·less \ˈshiftləs, *in rapid speech* -fl-\ *adj* **1 a :** lacking in ability or resourcefulness **:** INEFFICIENT ⟨is not being backward or ~ when he clears a patch, burns the trees, cultivates it for a few years, and then abandons the area —W.H.Camp⟩ **b :** lacking in ambition or incentive **:** IDLE, LAZY ⟨caused many who were once proud, industrious, property-owning people to become indifferent, ~, languid and sickly —A.C. Chandler⟩ **2 :** marked by lack of ambition, energy, or purpose ⟨living there in a ~ way, without any serious purpose —Ellen Glasgow⟩ ⟨flabby, ~ writing —Whitney Balliett⟩ — **shift·less·ly** *adv* — **shift·less·ness** *n* -ES

shift lock *n* **:** a typewriter key that when depressed locks the carriage or typebars into shifted position

shift·man \ˈ=mən, -ˌman\ *n, pl* **shiftmen :** SHIFT BOSS

shift of butts : an arrangement of butts of planks or plates in a ship

shifts *pres 3d sing of* SHIFT, *pl of* SHIFT

shift to the left : alteration of an Arneth index by an increase of immature leukocytes in the circulating blood

shift to the right : alteration of an Arneth index by an increase in mature or overaged leukocytes in the circulating blood

shifty \ˈshiftē, -ti\ *adj, usu* -ER/-EST **1 :** full of expedients **:** capable of meeting situations **:** RESOURCEFUL ⟨the exigencies of a new country made them quick-witted and ~ —Edward Eggleston⟩ **2 a :** given to deception, evasion, or fraud **:** SLIPPERY, TRICKY ⟨the ~ little men whose craftiness for once would fail them —A.P.Davies⟩ **b :** capable of evasive movement **:** ELUSIVE ⟨a small, ~ back who's tough to nail with a low tackle —Eugene Hopper⟩ **3 :** indicative or characteristic of a deceitful or untrustworthy person **:** FURTIVE ⟨the ~ eyes above the lying mouth would peer and probe —G.D.Brown⟩ **4 :** not fixed **:** CHANGEABLE, UNSTABLE ⟨grammatical phenomena are extremely numerous, extremely varied, and bafflingly ~ —Charlton Laird⟩ **5 :** shifting or tending to shift in position or direction ⟨if the ~ election-year winds should blow the nomination into his lap —*Newsweek*⟩

shi·ga bacillus \ˈshēgə-, -(ˌ)gä-\ *also* **shiga dysentery bacillus** *n, usu cap S* [after Kiyoshi *Shiga*] **:** a widely distributed but chiefly tropical bacillus (*Shigella dysenteriae*) that causes dysentery in man and monkeys

shi·gel·la \shəˈgelə\ *n* [NL, fr. Kiyoshi *Shiga* †1957 Jap. bacteriologist + NL *-ella*] **1** *cap* **:** a genus of nonmotile aerobic bacteria (family Enterobacteriaceae) that form acid but no gas on many carbohydrates and do not form acetylmethylcarbinol and that cause dysenteries in man and other animals **2** *pl* **shigel·lae** \-(ˌ)lē, -ˌlī\ *also* **shigellas** *sometimes cap* **:** any bacterium of the genus *Shigella*

shig·el·lo·sis \ˌshigəˈlōsəs\ *n, pl* **shigello·ses** \-ōˌsēz\ [NL, fr. *Shigella* + *-osis*] **:** infection with or dysentery caused by bacteria of the genus *Shigella*

shi'i \ˈshēˈē, ˈ=ˌ=\ *n* -s *usu cap* [Ar *shiyaʻīy*] **:** SHI'ITE

shi'·ism *or* **shi·ism** \ˈshēˌizəm\ *n* -s *usu cap* [*shi'a* + *-ism*] **:** the religious system or distinctive tenets of the Shi'a

shi'·ite *or* **shi·ite** \-ˌīt\ *n* -s *usu cap* [Ar *shiyaʻīy* partisan, Shi'ite, fr. *shīʻah* following, sect, fr. *shāʻa* to accompany] **:** a Muslim belonging to the Shi'a branch of Islam

shik \ˈshik\ *n, pl* **shik** *or* **shiks** *usu cap* **1 :** a people of the Turkmen Soviet Socialist Republic that is regarded as of Arabian origin but has become assimilated to the Turkoman people **2 :** a member of the Shik people

¹shi·kar \shəˈkär\ *n* -s [Hindi *śikār*, fr. Per *shikār*, MPer *shkār*] *India* **:** HUNTING, SPORT

²shikar \"\ *vb* **shikarred; shikarred; shikarring; shikars** *vi, India* **:** to hunt game ~ *vt, India* **:** to hunt (animals) for sport

shi·ka·ra \ˈshikərə\ *or* **sik·ar** \ˈshikə(r)\ *or* **si·kha·ra** \-kərə\ *n* -s [Skt *śikhara*] **1 :** the tower or spire of a medieval Indian temple; *esp* **:** a curvilinear spire in the northern style surmounted by an amalaka **2 :** a Kashmirian boat resembling a gondola

shi·kar·gah \shəˈkär(ˌ)gä\ *n* -s [Hindi *śikārgāh*, fr. Per *shikārgāh*, fr. *shikār* hunting + *-gāh* place — more at IDGAH] *India* **:** a game preserve

shi·ka·ri *also* **shi·ka·ree** \shəˈkärē, -karē\ *n* -s [Hindi *śikārī*, fr. Per *shikārī*, fr. *shikār* hunting] *India* **:** a big game hunter; *esp* **:** a professional hunter or guide

shi·kas·ta \shəˈkastə\ *n* -s [Per *shikasta* broken, fr. *shikastan* to break, fr. MPer *shkastan*] **:** the broken or current Persian hand in which correspondence and sometimes manuscripts are written

shike·poke \ˈshīkˌpōk\ *n* [euphemism] **:** SHITEPOKE

shik·ii \ˈshi(ˌ)kē\ *n* -s [Jap] **1 :** coarse rough silk filling **2 :** a heavy silk or rayon fabric with a texture similar to that of shantung

shi·kim·ic acid \shəˈkimik-\ *n* [Jap *shikimi* star anise + E *-ic*] **:** a crystalline acid $C_6H_6(OH)_3COOH$ that is obtained esp. from the fruit of the Japanese star anise and is formed as a precursor in the biosynthesis of aromatic amino acids and of lignin; 2,3,4,5-tetrahydro-gallic acid

shik·ken \(ˈ)shiˈken\ *n* -s [Jap] **:** a chief executive officer and later a virtual regent under the Japanese shoguns during the period from 1192 to 1333

shikker *var of* SHICKER

¹shi·ko \shiˈkō, ˈ=(ˌ)=\ *vi* -ED/-ING/-S [Burmese *śikhō* (written *hrikhō*)] **:** to assume the shiko ⟨she *~ed* to him as though he had been royalty —F. Tennyson Jesse⟩

²shiko \"\ *n* -s **:** a Burmese posture of kneeling with joined hands and bowed head before a superior ⟨bowing, touching the floor with her forehead in the full ~ of utter abasement —George Orwell⟩

shik·ra \ˈshikrə\ *n* -s [Hindi *śikra*, fr. Per *shikara* bird trained to hunt, fr. *shikār* hunting] **:** a small Indian hawk (*Accipiter badius*) sometimes used in falconry

shik·sa *or* **shik·se** *or* **shick·sa** \ˈshiksə\ *n* -s [Yiddish *shikse*, fem. of *sheykets*, *sheygets* shegetz — more at SHEGETZ] **1 :** a non-Jewish girl — often used disparagingly ⟨goy and ~ were not words for such as her —Stanley Sultan⟩ **2 :** a Jewish girl who does not observe Jewish precepts — used esp. by Jews

shil·fa \ˈshil,fä\ *n* -s [origin unknown] *chiefly Scot* **:** CHAFFINCH

shilha *usu cap, var of* SHLUH

shilingol *usu cap, var of* SILINGAL

¹shill \ˈshil\ *adj* [ME, fr. OE *sciell*, *scyl*; akin to OE *sciellan*, *scyllan* to resound, sound loudly, D *schel* shrill, strident, OHG *scellan* to resound, sound, ring, ON *skjallr* loud, shrill, *skjalla* to clash, clatter, Lith *skalyti* to bark for a long period of time, and perh. to OE *hlōwan* to low (like a cow) — more at LOW] *archaic chiefly Scot* **:** SHRILL, SONOROUS

²shill \"\ *var of* SHEAL

³shill \"\ *n* -s [prob. short for *shillaber*] **:** one who acts as a decoy or steerer: as **a :** one who is employed by an amusement enterprise (as a circus or carnival) to get the sale of tickets started after the barker has finished his spiel **b :** one who is employed by a pitchman to pose as a member of the audience and make the first purchase **c :** one who is employed by a gambling house to pose as a customer and keep action going **d :** one who poses as an innocent bystander to help a confidence man win over a prospective victim

⁴shill \"\ *vi* -ED/-ING/-S **:** to act as a shill

shil·la·ber \ˈshiləbə(r)\ *n* -s [origin unknown] **:** SHILL

shil·le·lagh *also* **shil·la·lah** \shəˈlālē, -ālì *sometimes* -ālə\ *n* -s [fr. *Shillelagh*, town in County Wicklow, Ireland] *chiefly Irish* **:** CUDGEL; *specif* **:** one cut from an oak or blackthorn sapling

shil·let \ˈshələt, ˈshil-\ *n* -s [prob. fr. ²*shill* + *-et*] *dial Eng* **:** SHALE

shil·li·beer \ˈshilə,bi(ə)r\ *n* -s [after George *Shillibeer* †1866 Eng. coach proprietor] **1 :** a horse-drawn omnibus **2 :** a horse-drawn hearse with seats for mourners

¹shil·ling \ˈshiliŋ, -lēŋ\ *n* -s *often attrib* [ME, fr. OE *scilling*; akin to OHG *skilling*, a gold coin, ON *skillingr*, Goth *skillings*; all fr. a prehistoric Gmc compound whose first constituent is represented by E ¹*shield* and whose second is represented by E *-ling*] **1 a :** a British monetary unit since the Norman conquest equal to twelve pence or ¹⁄₂₀ pound — see MONEY table **b :** a coin representing one shilling first issued under Henry VII and coined in silver until 1946 when it was changed to cupronickel **2 a :** a unit of value and corresponding coin of Scotland before 1707 that by the 17th century had depreciated to the value of one English penny **b** (1) **:** a unit of value equal to ¹⁄₂₀ pound in any of several countries in or formerly in the British Commonwealth (as Australia, New Zealand, Union of South Africa, Ireland) — see MONEY table (2) **:** a coin representing this unit **3 a :** any of several early American coins or tokens (as of Maryland or Massachusetts) **b :** any of numerous fluctuating units of value used in the U.S. in colonial times and later after the use of shilling coins had ceased ⟨New York ~⟩ ⟨Connecticut ~⟩ **c :** any of several units or coins (as the schilling or the skilling) of the Continent related to the English shilling **4 a :** the basic monetary unit of British East Africa **b :** a coin representing this unit **5 :** a measure of weight for arrows equal to 87¼ grains

shillelagh

²shilling *var of* SHEALING

shil·ling·less \-ŋləs\ *adj* **:** being without a shilling

shilling shocker *n* **1 :** a novel of crime or violence esp. popular in late Victorian England and costing orig. one shilling — compare DIME NOVEL, PENNY DREADFUL **2 :** a usu. short novel that is characterized by sensational incidents and lurid writing

shil·lings·worth \-ŋzˌ=\ *n* **:** the worth of a shilling **:** the amount that a shilling buys

shilluh *usu cap, var of* SHLUH

shil·luk \shəˈlük\ *n, pl* **shilluk** *or* **shilluks** *usu cap* **1 a :** a Nilotic Negro people of the Sudan dwelling mainly on the west bank of the White Nile **b :** a member of such people **2 :** a Nilotic language of the Shilluk people

¹shilly-shally \ˈshilēˌshalē, -ilìˌshali\ *adv* [redupl. of *shall I*] **:** in an irresolute, undecided, or hesitating manner

²shilly-shally \"\ *adj* **:** showing or marked by indecisiveness **:** IRRESOLUTE, VACILLATING ⟨a *shilly-shally* person⟩ ⟨this man's *shilly-shally* temporizing —*Atlantic*⟩

³shilly-shally \"\ *n* -ES **1 :** INDECISION, IRRESOLUTION, VACILLATION ⟨one can hardly say suddenly after four years of *shilly-shally* —Janet Flanner⟩ **2 :** SHILLYSHALLYER

⁴shilly-shally \"\ *vi* **shilly-shallied; shilly-shallied; shilly-shallying; shilly-shallies 1 :** to fail to act **:** show hesitation or lack of resolution ⟨having reached a decision, I did not *shilly-shally* about the affair —*Harper's*⟩ **2 :** to alternate between two attitudes or courses of action **:** back and fill ⟨never took a stand but *shilly-shallied* on all sides of it —C.W.M.Hart⟩ **3 :** to waste time **:** DAWDLE ⟨twenty people for supper . . . and thee *shilly-shallying* in thy shirttail at six in the morning —Jessamyn West⟩

shilly·shally·er \-ə(r)\ *n* -s **:** one that shilly-shallies ⟨a ~ who can't make up her mind —John McCarten⟩

shi·lo·nite \ˈshī(ˌ)lōˌnīt\ *n* -s *cap* [irreg. (influence of LL *Silonita* Shilonite) fr. *Shiloh*, town of ancient Palestine + E *-ite*] **:** a native or inhabitant of the town of Shiloh in ancient Palestine

shil·pit \ˈshilpət\ *adj* [origin unknown] **1** *Scot* **:** having a pinched and starved appearance **:** PUNY **2** *Scot* **:** WEAK, INSIPID, FLAT ⟨pronounced the claret ~ —Sir Walter Scott⟩

shily *var of* SHYLY

¹shim \ˈshim\ *n* -s [prob. akin to OE *scima* twilight, gloom, *scīma* ray, light, brightness, OS *skimo* shadow, OS & OHG *skīmo* brightness, ON *skimi* brightness, Goth *skeima* lantern, OE *scīnan* to shine — more at SHINE] **1** *dial Eng* **:** a white streak on a horse's face **2** *dial Eng* **:** a fleeting glimpse

²shim \"\ *n* -s [origin unknown] **1 :** a horizontal knife attachment to a cultivator used for surface scraping between crop rows and for weed removal **2 :** a thin piece or slip usu. of wood, metal, or stone that is often tapered, is used to fill in (as in leveling a stone in building or a railroad tie or rail), or is designed to be removed to take up wear (as in a bearing) **3 :** a shingle with sides not equally thick **4 :** a thin strip usu. of brass used to separate parts in making a piece mold

³shim \"\ *vt* **shimmed; shimmed; shimming; shims 1 :** to hoe or weed with a shim **2 a :** to fill out or level up to a desired height or a true surface by the use of a shim **b :** to fill up (cracks or joints) usu. with putty

shimal *var of* SHAMAL

¹shim·mer \ˈshimə(r)\ *vb* **shimmered; shimmered; shimmering** \-m(ə)riŋ\ **shimmers** [ME *shimeren*, *schemeren*, fr. OE *scimerian*; akin to MLG *schēmeren* to get dark, G *schimmern* to glimmer, OE *scīmian* to shine, grow dark, *scīma* ray, light, brightness — more at SHIM] *vi* **1 :** to shine with a tremulous or fitful light **:** gleam faintly **:** GLIMMER ⟨the street lights *~ed* behind the veil of snow —Morley Callaghan⟩ ⟨by moonlight its powdery sands ~ like snow —D.L.Graham⟩ **2 :** to reflect a wavering sometimes distorted visual image ⟨heat waves *~ed* before our eyes —F.P. Conant⟩ ~ *vt* **:** to cause to shimmer ⟨the night breeze . . . stirred the leaves on trees, *~ing* them in the moonlight —Stuart Cloete⟩

²shimmer \"\ *n* -s **1 :** a fitful, tremulous light **:** GLIMMER **:** a subdued sparkle or sheen **:** a scintillating effect ⟨the faint ~ of heat lightning —R.P.Warren⟩ ⟨the ~ of young foliage —L.P.Smith⟩ ⟨enough to give a ~ of danger to the atmosphere —Ellery Sedgwick⟩ **2 :** a wavering sometimes distorted visual image usu. produced by a reflection from heat waves ⟨the slate roofs sent *~s* up . . . in the glare —Elizabeth Bowen⟩ ⟨a constant ~ of heat over wide concrete highways —S.W.Matthews⟩

³shimmer \"\ *vt* -ED/-ING/-S [²*shim* + *-er* (freq. suffix)] **1 :** SHIM 1 **2 :** to fit a shim between surfaces of (work)

⁴shimmer \"\ *n* -s [³*shim* + *-er* (n. suffix)] **1 a :** one that shims **b :** SHIM **2 :** one that inserts shims

¹shimmering *adj* [ME *schimering*, fr. pres. part. of *schimeren* to shimmer] **:** tremulously shining **:** having a subdued but often tantalizing sparkle or sheen **:** producing a scintillating effect ⟨~ chandeliers and deep carpets —Catherine Paul⟩ ⟨low emerald islands in a ~ painted sea —*Amer. Guide Series: Fla.*⟩ ⟨wore a gown of ~ satin⟩ ⟨~ sounds and sights and delights —Vicki Baum⟩ ⟨an easy style, a ~ humor —James Kelly⟩ — **shim·mer·ing·ly** *adv*

²shimmering *n* -s [ME *schimering*, *schemering*, fr. gerund of *schimeren*, *schemeren* to shimmer] **:** SHIMMER

shim·mery \ˈshim(ə)rē\ *adj* [¹*shimmer* + *-y*] **:** SHIMMERING ⟨black ~ velvet curtains —Rudyard Kipling⟩

¹shim·my \ˈshimē, -mi\ *n* -s [alter. of *chemise*] **1 :** CHEMISE **2** [short for *shimmy-shake* & *shimmy shiver*] **:** a jazz dance popular after World War I and similar in form and function to the cooch but probably of Negro origin and characterized by a shaking of the body from the shoulders down **3 :** an abnormal oscillation esp. in the front wheels of a motor vehicle reinforced by resonance at critical speeds

²shimmy \"\ *vi* -ED/-ING/-S **1 :** to shake, quiver, or tremble in or as if in dancing a shimmy **2 :** to oscillate abnormally — used esp. of automobiles

³shimmy \"\ *n* -ES [by folk etymology] *slang* **:** CHEMIN DE FER

shimmy shirt *n* **:** SHIMMY 1

shim·o·no·se·ki \ˌshimənōˈsekē, -ˈsekē; -ˈnōsəkē\ *adj, usu cap* [fr. *Shimonoseki*, Japan] **:** of or from the city of Shimonoseki, Japan **:** of the kind or style prevalent in Shimonoseki

shi·mo·se \shəˈmōsə\ *also* **shimose powder** *n* -s [after Masachika *Shimose* †1911 Jap. naval engineer, its inventor] **:** a Japanese explosive composed chiefly of picric acid

shim·per \ˈshimpə(r)\ *vi* -ED/-ING/-S [by alter.] **:** SHIMMER

shim plow *n* [²*shim*] **:** ²SHIM 1

shims *pl of* SHIM, *pres 3d sing of* SHIM

shim-sham shimmy \ˈshim,sham-\ *n* [redupl. of ¹*shimmy*] **:** a swing step with stamps, heel-beats, and runs

¹shin \ˈshin\ *n* -s [ME *shine*, fr. OE *scinu*; akin to MD *schene* shin, OHG *scina* shin, needle, Sw dial. *skener* iceskate, Norw dial. *skina* thin plate or disk, OE *scēadan* to divide, separate — more at SHED] **1 a** (1) **:** the front part of the vertebrate leg below the knee (2) **:** the front edge of the tibia (3) **:** the lower part of the leg **b :** the lower part of the foreleg in beef cattle; *specif* **:** a cut of meat consisting of a cross section of lower-leg bone and muscle used for boiling or braising **c :** TIBIA 1b **2** *archaic* **:** the ridge of a hill **3 :** the lower forward corner of a plow moldboard

²shin \"\ *vb* **shinned; shinned; shinning; shins** *vi* **1 :** to use the shins in climbing **:** climb (as a mast, tree, rope) by embracing alternately with the arms or hands and legs without help (as of steps or spurs) ⟨*shinned* down a drainpipe —Frank O'Connor⟩ ⟨still building bridges, but was not *shinning* up cables —Allan Seager⟩ **2 :** to move forward rapidly on foot ⟨was up in a second and *shinning* down the hill —Mark Twain⟩ ~ *vt* **1 :** to kick or strike on the shins ⟨been well *shinned* half a dozen times in scrimmages at football —Samuel Butler †1902⟩ **2 :** to climb up or down by shinning ⟨reached the open window by *shinning* the tree⟩

³shin \", ˈshēn\ *n* -s *cap* [Jap, lit., belief, faith] **:** a major Japanese Buddhist sect growing out of Jodo that emphasizes salvation by faith alone, has a married clergy, and holds to the exclusive worship of Amida Buddha — called also *Shin-shu*

⁴shin \ˈshēn *also* ˈshin\ *n* -s [Heb *shīn*, lit., tooth] **1 :** the 22d letter of the Hebrew alphabet — symbol ש; see ALPHABET table **2 :** the letter corresponding to Hebrew shin in the Phoenician or in any of various other Semitic alphabets

shi·na \ˈshēnə\ *n* -s *usu cap* **:** the Dard language of Gilgit in northern Kashmir

shi·nar·ump \shəˈnarəmp\ *n* -s [origin unknown] *Southwest* **:** agatized wood

shinbone \ˈ=ˌ=\ *n* [ME *shinbon*, fr. OE *scinbān*, fr. *scinu* shin + *bān* bone — more at SHIN, BONE] **:** the anterior bone of the lower leg **:** TIBIA 1a

shin·dig \ˈshinˌdig\ *n* -s [prob. alter. (influenced by *shin* & *dig*) of *shindy*] **1 :** a festive occasion: as **a :** a social gathering often with dancing ⟨every community has its weekly ~ in some farm home —*Amer. Guide Series: Okla.*⟩ **b :** a usu. large often overly lavish party ⟨coming-out party . . . was the gaudiest ~ since the war —*Time*⟩ **c :** an elaborate celebration often commemorating some special event and involving extensive planning ⟨to mark the day with the largest peace-time parade . . . I had drawn the assignment of assembling and staging this enormous ~ —Frank Zachary⟩ **2 :** SHINDY 2 ⟨touched off the whole bloody ~ that raged for years —Alan Devoe⟩

shin·dy \ˈshindē, -di\ *n, pl* **shindys** *or* **shindies** [prob. alter. of *shinny*] **1 :** SHINDIG 1 ⟨the summer tourist season . . . is marked by galas, festivals, and other ~*s* —*Holiday*⟩ **2 :** a general commotion : noisy row : FRACAS, UPROAR ⟨created a ~, saying that they were already an oppressed class —F.A.Swinnerton⟩ ⟨it must look bad after that ~ I had with the director —C.D.Lewis⟩

¹shine \ˈshīn\ *vb* **shone** \ˈshōn *also* ˈshän *sometimes* ˈshən *or* ˈshȯn\ *or* **shined; shined; shining; shines** [ME *shinen*, fr. OE *scīnan*; akin to OHG *skīnan* to shine, ON *skīna*, Goth *skeinan* to shine, Gk *skia* shadow, *skēnē* tent, stage, Skt *chāyā* shadow, reflection, OSlav *sijati* to shine, get bright] *vi* **1 :** to emit rays of light : give light : beam with steady radiance ⟨the stars ~ with a brilliance never seen down in valleys —G.W.Gray b.1886⟩ ⟨the points of light were . . . *shining* with a greenish luster —Ambrose Bierce⟩ **2 :** to be bright by reflection of light : GLEAM, GLISTEN : be glossy ⟨the berries . . . decorated with sunlight and dew *shone* like black-purple glass —G.S.Perry⟩ ⟨the air was bright and the water *shone* like dark silk —G.A.Wagner⟩ **3 :** to be eminent, conspicuous, or distinguished : exhibit brilliant talent or intellectual powers ⟨restrained any inclination to ~ or push himself forward —H.R.Warfel⟩ ⟨acquiring those graces which would enable him to ~ at dinner parties —E.J. Simmons⟩ **4 :** to have a bright glowing appearance : give the effect of radiance : display or show beauty or splendor ⟨as he talked his eyes began to ~ —Sherwood Anderson⟩ ⟨his withered face *shone* with a spiritual power —Liam O'Flaherty⟩ **5 :** to be conspicuously evident : be clearly apparent ⟨the courage and ability which ~ brightly in adversity —A.M.Young⟩ ⟨the glory of Greece ~*s* not only in her antiquity —Sir Winston Churchill⟩ ⟨human feeling ~*s* through all her books —S.T.Williams⟩ **6** *archaic* **:** to be sunny : DAWN **7 :** to cast an auspicious or favoring light ⟨the light which *shined* to him was the single divine light —V.L.Parrington⟩ — often used with *upon* **8 :** to sparkle or glow with cleanliness ⟨though the furnishings may be modest . . . her home fairly ~*s* —*Amer. Guide Series: La.*⟩ ~ *vt* **1 a** (1) : to cause to emit light (2) : to send forth like light ⟨the hardest thing . . . for one human being to ~ into another human being the glow that burned within himself —Bruce Marshall⟩ **b :** to throw or flash the light of ⟨stood there and *shined* our flashlights on the deck —Richard Bissell⟩ **2 :** to make bright by polishing ⟨was not going to ~ shoes longer than he had to —H.A.Sinclair⟩ ⟨*shined* his brass buttons —Robert Hazel⟩ **3 :** to throw light into (as the eyes of an animal) while hunting for the purpose of attracting the attention of and getting an opportunity to kill the prey

²shine \ˈ"\ *n* -s **1 a** (1) : brightness caused by the emission of light : ILLUMINATION, RADIANCE ⟨the ~ of a lantern signaled the approach of a sentry⟩ ⟨the windows gleamed gold in the ~ of the setting sun⟩ (2) *obs* : a beam of light : NIMBUS **b** (1) : a brilliance of quality or appearance : SPLENDOR ⟨a magazine with a high literary ~ —Norman Cousins⟩ ⟨grand opera . . . that has kept its ~ for 200 years —*Time*⟩ (2) : an ostentatious display : SHOW ⟨celebrate the nuptials with due ~ and celebration —Thomas Carlyle⟩ **2 a :** brightness caused by the reflection of light : LUSTER, SHEEN ⟨on the black ~ of boulevard the buses plowed up and down —Bruce Marshall⟩ **b :** brightness usu. of countenance reflected from an inner quality of spirit ⟨the sort of ~ you want . . . does come from the heart that is gay —Constance Foster⟩ ⟨exuding modesty, humility and the ~ of honesty —*Time*⟩ **3 :** fair weather : SUNSHINE ⟨will go rain or ~⟩ **4 a :** a stupid trick : silly caper : PRANK — usu. used in pl. ⟨figured you never would try to pull any ~*s* —R.P.Warren⟩ **b** *dial chiefly Eng* **:** a meeting or gathering that is noisy and disorderly **5 :** a sudden fancy : LIKING ⟨if she takes a ~ to you she'll treat you all right —H.A.Sinclair⟩ **6 a :** a polish or gloss given to shoes **b :** a single polishing of a pair of shoes **7 :** NEGRO — usu. taken to be offensive **8 :** MOONSHINE 3

³shine *adj* [alter. (influenced by ¹*shine*) of ¹*sheen*] *obs* **:** SHINING

shine ball *n* **1 :** a baseball polished on one side against the pitcher's uniform and rubbed with dirt or powder on the other side to obtain more curve when pitched **2 :** the pitch of a shine ball

shin·er \ˈshīnə(r)\ *n* -s **1 :** one that shines: as **a :** STAR **b :** DIAMOND **2 :** a bright piece of money **3** *slang* **:** a card-sharper's mirror used to reflect the cards in his opponent's hand **4 :** any of numerous small silvery freshwater American cyprinid fishes of *Notropis* and closely related genera: as **a :** a small blunt-nosed fish (*Notropis atherinoides*) of the Great Lakes region and Mississippi valley with a metallic greenish luster — called also *emerald shiner* **b :** GOLDEN SHINER **c :** SPOTTAIL SHINER **d :** REDFIN a,b **5 :** any of various silvery fishes: as **a :** DOLLARFISH **b :** MENHADEN **c :** SILVERFISH **6 a :** a shiny streak in a fabric (as rayon) produced by overstretched yarns **b :** a shiny spot in paper caused by calendering a lump of fiber, filler, or starch **c :** a gloss spot appearing on a flat or semigloss paint finish **7 :** BLACK EYE 1a **8 :** MOONSHINER

shine up *vi* **:** to pay marked attention esp. to one of the opposite sex — usu. used with *to* ⟨*shined up* to all the pretty girls⟩

shing *var of* SHENG

¹shin·gle \ˈshiŋgəl\ *n* -s [ME *scincle, schingel*, prob. fr. L *scindula*, alter. of *scandula*; akin to ON *skinn* skin — more at SKIN] **1 a :** a small thin piece of building material (as wood or asbestos) often with one end thicker than the other laid in overlapping rows as a covering for the roof or sides of a building **b :** a piece of wood similar in shape to a roofing shingle but larger and usu. from ⅞ to 1¼ inches thick at the butt and applied to the ordinarily flat bottom of a racing motorboat to form a series of small steps **2 :** a small signboard — usu. used with *hang out* ⟨hung out a ~ and worked up a nice medical practice —R.L.Taylor⟩ **3 :** a woman's haircut with the hair trimmed short from the back of the head to the nape

²shingle \ˈ"\ *vt* **shingled; shingled; shingling** \ g(ə)liŋ\ **shingles 1 :** to cover with or as if with shingles ⟨helped his neighbor to ~ his roof⟩ **2 :** to bob and shape (the hair) by cutting close at the nape of the neck and gradually longer up the back of the head **3 :** to lay or dispose so as to overlap ⟨bacon for this package is stacked rather than *shingled* —*Meat Mag.*⟩ **4 a :** to overlap or duplicate one's own claims on land **b :** to encroach knowingly upon the lawful claims of others

³shingle \ˈ"\ *n* -s [prob. of Scand origin; akin to Norw & Sw *singel* coarse gravel (esp. on the seashore); akin to MLG *singele* gravely bank] **1 :** coarse rounded detritus or alluvial material esp. on the seashore differing from ordinary gravel only in the size of the stones which may be as large as a man's head **2 :** a place (as a beach) strewn with shingle

⁴shingle \ˈ"\ *vt* -ED/-ING/-s [F dial. (Picardy) *chingler*, lit., to whip, fr. MF dial., fr. *chingle* strap, belt, fr. L *cingula* — more at CINGLE] **:** to subject (as a mass of iron from the puddling furnace) to the process of expelling cinder and impurities by hammering and squeezing

shingle-back \ˈ≈,≈\ *n* [¹*shingle*] **:** STUMP-TAIL

shingle bolt *n* [¹*shingle*] **:** ¹BOLT 7a

¹shin·gled \-gəld\ *adj* [ME *schyngled*, fr. *scincle, schingel* shingle + *-ed*] **1 :** covered, roofed, or sheathed with shingles **2** *of hair* **:** cut in a shingle

²shingled \ˈ"\ *adj* [³*shingle* + *-ed*] **:** covered with shingle or coarse rounded detritus

shingle lap *n* [¹*shingle*] **:** a lap joint (as for a sheet-metal stack) in which the sections joined are tapered so that the bottom of each section fits over the top of the section below it

shingle nail *n* [ME *schingelneil*, fr. *schingel* shingle + *neil* nail] **:** a usu. galvanized nail used in applying shingles to a house

shingle oak *n* [¹*shingle*] **1 :** an American oak (*Quercus imbricaria*) with shining leaves resembling laurel and wood that is used in western states for shingles **2 :** SHE-OAK

shin·gler \-g(ə)lə(r)\ *n* -s [ME *shyngeler*, fr. *shyngel, schingel* shingle + *-er*] **:** one that shingles: as **a :** one who shingles esp. roofs **b :** a man or a machine that makes shingles **c :** a workman who tends a shingling machine or hammer **d :** a machine for shingling puddled iron

shin·gles \ˈshiŋgəlz\ *n pl but sing in constr* [ME *schingles*, by folk etymology fr. ML *cingulus*, fr. L *cingulum* girdle; trans. of Gk *zōnē* girdle, shingles — more at CINGULUM, ZONE] **:** HERPES ZOSTER

shingle tow *n* [¹*shingle*] **:** shredded wood resulting from the manufacture of shingles; *broadly* **:** wood shavings

shingle tree *n* [¹*shingle*] **:** an East Indian timber tree (*Acrocarpus fraxinifolius*) of the family Leguminosae with hard durable wood used esp. for tea boxes

shingle weaver *n* [¹*shingle*] **:** one that makes, trims, or packs shingles

shin·gling \ˈshiŋ(g)(ə)liŋ\ *n* -s [³*shingle* + *-ing*] **:** the arrangement of pebbles by currents so that they slope in the same direction and overlap like shingles on a roof

shingling hatchet *n* **:** a hatchet usu. with a notch in the blade for extracting nails and a hammerhead opposite the cutting edge

shingling hatchet

shin·gly \ˈshiŋg(ə)lē\ *adj* [³*shingle* + *-y*] **:** composed of or abounding in shingle ⟨landed at a ~ little beach —D.B.Putnam⟩

shin·gon \ˈshin,gän\ *n* -s *cap* [Jap, lit., true word] **:** a Japanese Buddhist sect that emphasizes a mystical symbolism of mantras and mudras together with an esoteric doctrine centered around the Buddha's ideal which is held to be essentially inexpressible

shin guard *n* **:** a protective covering for the shin that is usu. of stiffened canvas or leather and is used in various sports

shinier *comparative of* SHINY

shiniest *superlative of* SHINY

shin·i·ness \ˈshīnēnəs, -īnin-\ *n* -ES **:** the quality or state of being shiny ⟨hard days . . . have taken off the ~ of youth —Mary Deasy⟩

shining *adj* [ME, fr. pres. part. of *shinen* to shine — more at SHINE] **1 :** emitting light : shedding radiance : GLOWING ⟨one ~ morning —John Muir †1914⟩ ⟨gazed up at the ~ heavens⟩ **2 a :** reflecting light : GLEAMING, LUSTROUS ⟨its ~ white church and background of fir and spruce —*Amer. Guide Series: Maine*⟩ ⟨covered with ~ enamel —*Victorian Naturalist*⟩ **b :** reflecting an inner spirit often of radiance or joy ⟨essentially unsophisticated . . . with ~ eyes —Donald Foley⟩ **3 :** bright often splendid in appearance or aspect : RESPLENDENT ⟨its shape was destroyed, its ~ newness a bruised memory —Henry LaCossitt⟩ ⟨a warm and ~ company of friends —*Newsweek*⟩ **4 :** possessing a distinguished quality : marked by illustrious eminence or exceptional merit ⟨her sharp and ~ prose —Carl Van Doren⟩ ⟨had ~ virtues and few faults —Richard Garnett †1906⟩ ⟨singled out . . . as the ~ example of his tribe —C.R.Anderson⟩ **5 :** full of sunshine ⟨a wiser . . . way to improve the ~ hours —L.P.Smith⟩ ⟨have had my fair share of ~ hours —R.F.Wagner⟩ **6 :** unusually clean and bright ⟨the men and boys with ~ faces and in Sunday suits —Flora Thompson⟩

shining flycatcher *n* **1 :** SATIN FLYCATCHER **2 :** PHAINOPEPLA

shining gum *n* **:** an Australian gum tree (*Eucalyptus nitens*) with shiny often ribbony bark

shin·ing·ly *adv* [ME, fr. *shining* + *-ly*] **:** in a shining manner ⟨genius manifests itself most ~ —C.J.Rolo⟩

shin·ing·ness *n* -ES **:** a shining quality : BRILLIANCE ⟨the medals . . . in their rich ~ seemed to belong there —F.K.Kelly⟩

shining sumac *n* **:** DWARF SUMAC

shining willow *n* **:** a common No. American shrub (*Salix lucida*) with lanceolate shiny leaves

shinleaf \ˈ≈,≈\ *n, pl* **shinleafs** [prob. so called fr. its use in plasters to treat sore legs] **:** an American wintergreen of the genus *Pyrola*; *esp* **:** WILD LILY OF THE VALLEY 3

shinned *past of* SHIN

shin·nery \ˈshinərē, -ri\ *n* -ES [modif. of AmerF (La.) *chênière* chenier — more at CHENIER] **:** a dense growth of small trees; *esp* **:** a thick interlacing growth of scrub oak in the West and Southwest

shinnery oak *n* **:** any of several small shrubby oaks that tend to form thickets; *esp* **:** a low shrub (*Quercus havardii*) that spreads by underground suckers to form dense thickets, produces large sweet acorns, and grows on dry sandy land of the southwestern U.S.

shinning *pres part of* SHIN

¹shin·ny *also* **shin·ney** \ˈshinē, -ni\ *n* -ES [perh. fr. ¹*shin* + *-y*; fr. the damage done to shins by the sticks] **1 a :** the game of hockey as informally played with a curved stick and usu. a ball or block of wood by schoolboys **b :** the curved stick used in the game **2 :** ice hockey poorly played and usu. without benefit of proper equipment or officials

²shinny \ˈ"\ *vi* -ED/-ING/-s [alter. of ²*shin*] **:** SHIN 1

shin oak \ˈshin;≈\ *n* [prob. alter. of *shinnery oak*] **:** any of various scrub oaks (esp. *Quercus mohriana* and *Q. undulata*) chiefly of the southern and western U.S.

shinplaster \ˈ≈,≈≈\ *n* [fr. obs. *shinplaster*, a plaster used to treat sore legs, fr. ¹*shin* + *plaster*] **1 :** a piece of privately≈ issued paper currency; *esp* **:** one poorly secured and depreciated in value **2 :** FRACTIONAL NOTE

shins *pl of* SHIN, *pres 3d sing of* SHIN

shin-shu *n, cap 1st S* [Jap *shinshū*] **:** ³SHIN

shin splints *n pl but sing in constr* **:** injury to and inflammation of the tibial and toe extensor muscles or their fasciae characterized by tenderness over the anterior surface of the lower and middle thirds of the tibia and fibula, caused by repeated minimal traumas (as by running on a wood or cement floor), and seen esp. in track athletes but sometimes also in football or basketball players

shin·tai \ˈshin,tī\ *n, pl* **shintai** *or* **shintais** [Jap] **:** an object believed to contain the spirit of a kami : a Shinto fetish most frequently housed in a shrine

¹shin·to \ˈshin,tō\ *n* -s *cap* [Jap *shintō*] **:** the indigenous religion and former ethnic cult of Japan characterized by the reverence of kami, deified nature spirits, and spirits of ancestors and its great antiquity but lack of an historical founder or organized teachings

²shinto \ˈ"\ *adj, usu cap* **:** SHINTOISTIC

shin·to·ism \-ō,izəm\ *n* -s *cap* **:** SHINTO

shin·to·ist \-ōəst\ *n* -s *usu cap* **:** an adherent of Shinto

shin·to·is·tic \ˌ≈≈ˈistik\ *adj, usu cap* **:** of, relating to, or characteristic of Shinto

shin·ty \ˈshinti\ *n* -ES [by alter.] *Brit* **:** SHINNY 1a

shin·wa·ri \shinˈwärē\ *n, pl* **shinwari** *or* **shinwaris** *usu cap* **:** a member of a nomadic Afghan people inhabiting the valleys of the Safed Koh range and south of Jalalabad

shinwood \ˈ≈,≈\ *n* **:** a ground hemlock (*Taxus canadensis*)

¹shiny \ˈshīnē, -ni\ *adj* -ER/-EST [¹*shine* + *-y*] **1 a :** SUNSHINY ⟨only when it is warm and ~ —Andrew Young⟩ **b :** filled with light : GLISTENING ⟨a ~ night —*Blackwood's*⟩ **2 :** having a bright appearance, aspect, or exterior : GLITTERING, POLISHED ⟨*shiniest* show place on the whole summer coast —*Holiday*⟩ ⟨seen in the ~ magazines —*Times Lit. Supp.*⟩ ⟨the taxi takes you past the rich ~ buildings —Bernard Gutteridge⟩ **3 :** rubbed or worn smooth ⟨clad in ~ rags that were in their time smart suits —C.P.Rodocanachi⟩ **4 :** scrubbed clean; *esp* **:** lacking face powder ⟨none likes a ~ nose⟩

²shiny \ˈ"\ *adv* **:** with a shiny surface or appearance

shiny willow *n* **:** SHINING WILLOW

¹ship \ˈship\ *n* -s *often attrib* [ME *schip, ship*, fr. OE *scip*; akin to OHG *skif* ship, boat, vessel for liquids, ON & Goth *skip* ship, boat, OE *scēadan* to divide, separate — more at SHED] **1 a :** any large seagoing boat **b :** a sailing boat having a bowsprit and usu. a square-rigged foremast, mainmast, and mizzenmast each composed of a lower mast, a topmast, a topgallant mast, and sometimes higher masts **2 a :** a boat intended or used for navigation and propelled by power or sail **b :** a boat or structure used for purposes of navigation or intended or used for transportation on a river, sea, ocean, or other navigable water without regard to its form or means of propulsion **3 :** a ship's company or crew ⟨the whole ~ cheering the captain⟩ **4 :** an incense vessel or boat **5 :** one's affairs or good fortune ⟨when his ~ comes in he will pay his debts⟩ **6 :** AIRSHIP, AIRPLANE **7 :** a part used to move something from one place to another ⟨the ~*s* of scissors⟩ **8 a :** a unit of at least five sea explorers of the Boy Scouts of America under the leadership of a skipper **b :** a senior girl scout mariner troop

²ship \ˈ"\ *vb* **shipped; shipped; shipping; ships** [ME *schippen, shippen*, fr. *schip, ship*, n.] *vt* **1 a :** to place or receive on board of a ship for transportation by water : cause to embark ⟨kept busy . . . *shipping* mackerel and cod —Cid R. Sumner⟩ **b** (1) : to cause to be transported ⟨~*s* hundreds of carloads annually —*Amer. Guide Series: Md.*⟩ ⟨was *shipped* off to do five months in jail —H.D.Quillin⟩ (2) : to transport or cause to be transported under military orders ⟨was *shipped* overseas as an infantry replacement —Gordon Harrison⟩ — often used with out ⟨recruits are *shipped* out as soon as they can be processed⟩ **2** *obs* **:** to provide with a ship **3 :** to put in place for use ⟨~ the tiller⟩ ⟨~ the mast⟩ ⟨lights should be *shipped* and in working order —*Manual of Seamanship*⟩ **4 :** to take into a ship or boat ⟨*shipped* his dripping paddle into the rented canoe —Erle Stanley Gardner⟩ ⟨when the oars are *shipped* they should be laid in the boat —H.A.Calahan⟩ **5 :** to engage or secure for service on a ship ⟨*shipping* 10 extra hands for the voyage⟩ **6 :** to take (as water) over the side ⟨had *shipped* a good amount of water —Alexander MacDonald⟩ ⟨~*s* up to 500 tons of ice topside —*Time*⟩ **7 :** to put or take on (as clothing or a burden) ⟨*shipped* the pack onto his back⟩ **8 :** to move (something) from one place or position to another : SHIFT ⟨*shipped* the gun to his shoulder and . . . fired both barrels —Gerald Durrell⟩ ~ *vi* **1 :** to embark on a ship : BOARD ⟨travelers to the Pacific ~ at a western port⟩ **2 a :** to go or travel by ship ⟨*shipped* to America in 1819 —W.A. Swanberg⟩ — often used with *out* ⟨might even ~ out on a tramp . . . and go to Mexico —James Jones⟩ **b :** to proceed by ship or other means under military orders ⟨had a letter . . . with a San Francisco A.P.O. number, and knew that Dennis had *shipped* overseas —C.O.Gorham⟩ — often used with *out* ⟨is now on a nine day leave before *shipping* out for overseas duty —*Manteca (Calif.) Bull.*⟩ **3 a :** to engage to serve on board of a vessel ⟨ran away from home and *shipped* before the mast —H.O.Brundidge⟩ **b :** to reenlist for navy or marine service — usu. used with *over* ⟨I mean when I finish this last hitch, not to ~ over —Martin Dibner⟩ **4 :** to rest or have its position when ready for use — used with *in* ⟨the lower end of a sprit ~*s* in a grommet⟩ **syn** see SEND — **ship a sea :** to have a wave come over the side

³ship \ˈ"\ *chiefly dial var of* SHEEP

⁴ship \ˈ"\ *n* -s [by shortening] *Brit* **:** COMPANIONSHIP

ship *abbr* **1** shipment **2** shipping

-ship \,ship\ *n suffix* -s [ME *-schipe, -shipe, -ship*, fr. OE *-scipe*; akin to OFris *-skip, -skipi* -ship, OS *-skap, -skepi, -skipi*, OHG *-scaf, -scaft*, ON *-skapr*; all fr. a prehistoric Gmc word represented by OHG *scaf* nature, condition, quality; akin to OE *sceppan, scyppan* to shape — more at SHAPE] **1 :** state : condition : quality ⟨son*ship*⟩ ⟨friend*ship*⟩ ⟨scholar*ship*⟩ **2 :** office : dignity : profession ⟨clerk*ship*⟩ ⟨chancellor*ship*⟩ ⟨lord*ship*⟩ ⟨author*ship*⟩ **3 :** art : skill ⟨horseman*ship*⟩ ⟨marksman*ship*⟩ ⟨seaman*ship*⟩ **4 :** something showing, exhibiting, or embodying a quality or state ⟨town*ship*⟩ ⟨fellow*ship*⟩ ⟨court*ship*⟩ **5 :** one entitled to a (specified) rank, title, or appellation — used with possessive pronouns ⟨his Lord*ship*⟩

ship auger *n* **:** an auger having a simple spiral body and a single cutting edge with or without a screw on the end of it and without a spur at the outer end of the cutting edge

shi·pau·lo·vi \shəˈpōləvē, -pau̇l-\ *n, pl* **shipaulovi** *or* **shipaulovis** *usu cap* **1 :** a Shoshonean people occupying a pueblo in northeastern Arizona **2 :** a member of the Shipaulovi people

ship biscuit *also* **ship bread** *n* **:** HARDTACK

shipboard \ˈ≈,≈\ *n* [ME *schipbord, shipbord*, fr. *schip, ship* + *bord* board — more at BOARD] **1 :** the side of a ship **2 :** SHIP — used chiefly in adverbial phrases ⟨prepared for storage on ~⟩ ⟨tipped a shilling simply because it was on ~ —Richard Joseph⟩

ship borer *n* **:** SHIPWORM

shipborne \ˈ≈,≈\ *adj* **:** transported or designed to be transported by ship ⟨~ expeditions prowled among the antarctic icebergs —*Time*⟩ ⟨~ aircraft⟩

shipbound \ˈ≈,≈\ *adj* **:** confined to a ship

shipboy *also* **ship's boy** \ˈ≈,≈\ *n* **:** a boy who serves in a ship usu. as a cabin attendant

ship-breaker \ˈ≈,≈≈\ *n* **:** one who breaks up vessels unfit for further use and deals in their materials

shipbreaking \ˈ≈,≈≈\ *n* **1 :** the occupation or business of a ship-breaker **2 :** the offense of breaking into a ship to commit there a criminal offense

shipbroken \ˈ≈,≈≈\ *adj* [ME *schipbroken*, fr. *schip* ship + *broken*] **:** destitute because of shipwreck : SHIPWRECKED

ship broker *n* **1 :** a mercantile agent employed in buying and selling ships **2 :** a representative acting in behalf of the ship owner in obtaining cargo and often in arranging such port activities of a vessel as the discharge and loading of cargo, clearance, and insurance

shipbuilding \ˈ≈,≈≈\ *n* **:** the occupation or business of constructing ships

ship canal *n* **:** a canal large enough for seagoing ships

ship carpenter *n* **:** SHIPWRIGHT

ship chandler *n* **:** a dealer in supplies and equipment for ships

ship·en·tine \ˈshipən,tēn\ *n* -s [¹*ship* + *-entine* (as in *barkentine*)] **:** FOUR-MASTED BARK

ship fever *n* **:** TYPHUS 1a

shipfitter \ˈ≈,≈≈\ *n* **1 :** one that fits together the structural members of ships and puts them into position for riveting or welding **2 :** a naval enlisted man who works in sheet metal and performs the work of a plumber aboard ship

ship-holder \ˈ≈,≈≈\ *n* **:** REMORA

shi·pi·bo \shəˈpē(,)bō\ *n, pl* **shipibo** *or* **shipibos** *usu cap* **1 a :** a Panoan people dwelling in the middle Ucayali river valley of Peru **b :** a member of such people **2 :** the language of the Shipibo people

ship joiner *n* **:** a joiner who constructs the woodwork in a ship

shipkeeper \ˈ≈,≈≈\ *n* **1 :** a watchman in charge of a ship in the absence of officers and crew **2 :** the one left in charge of a whaling ship when the captain's boat is lowered

¹shiplap \ˈ≈,≈\ *n* [¹*ship* + *lap*] **1 a** (1) : wooden sheathing in which the boards are rabbeted so that the lower edge of each board overlaps the upper edge of the next (2) : boards rabbeted for such sheathing **b :** a shiplapped joint **2 :** the lapping of two steel plates (as in the hull plating of a ship)

²shiplap \ˈ"\ *vt* **1 a :** to work (as lumber) to a shiplap pattern **b :** to furnish with shiplap sheathing ⟨the house is *shiplapped*⟩ **2 :** to install in the manner of shiplap (as steel plates or planks on the side or deck of a ship)

ship·less \ˈshipləs\ *adj* **:** lacking a ship

ship letter *n* **1 :** a letter conveyed by a ship that is not a mail ship **2 :** a letter sent by a person on shipboard

shipload \ˈ≈,≈\ *n* **1 :** the load or cargo of a ship **2 :** as much as will fill or load a ship; *specif* **:** an indefinitely large amount ⟨~*s* of excellent gentlemen were driven from their firesides —V.L. Parrington⟩ ⟨~*s* of merchandise —H.R.Warfel⟩

ship·man \ˈshipmən\ *n, pl* **shipmen** [ME *schipman, shipman*, fr. OE *scipman*, fr. *scip* ship + *man*] **1 :** SEAMAN, SAILOR **2 :** SHIPMASTER

shipman's card *n* **:** COMPASS CARD

shipmaster \ˈ≈,≈≈\ *n* [ME *schipmaster*, fr. *schip* + *master*] **1** *obs* **:** STEERSMAN, PILOT **2 :** the master or commander of a ship other than a warship

shipmast locust \ˈ≈,≈-\ *n* **:** a locust that forms a variety (*Robinia pseudoacacia rectissima*) of the black locust, is native to Long Island, and has an erect stem and wood of great strength and durability

shipmate \ˈ≈,≈\ *n* **:** one who serves on board the same ship with another : a fellow sailor

ship·ment \ˈshipmənt\ *n* -s [²*ship* + *-ment*] **1 :** the act or process of shipping : the delivery of goods to a carrier for transportation **2 :** a commodity, consignment, or cargo shipped — compare UNLOAD

ship money *n* **:** an impost levied at various times on the ports, towns, or shires of England to provide ships for the national defense

ship: principal ropes, spars, parts of hull

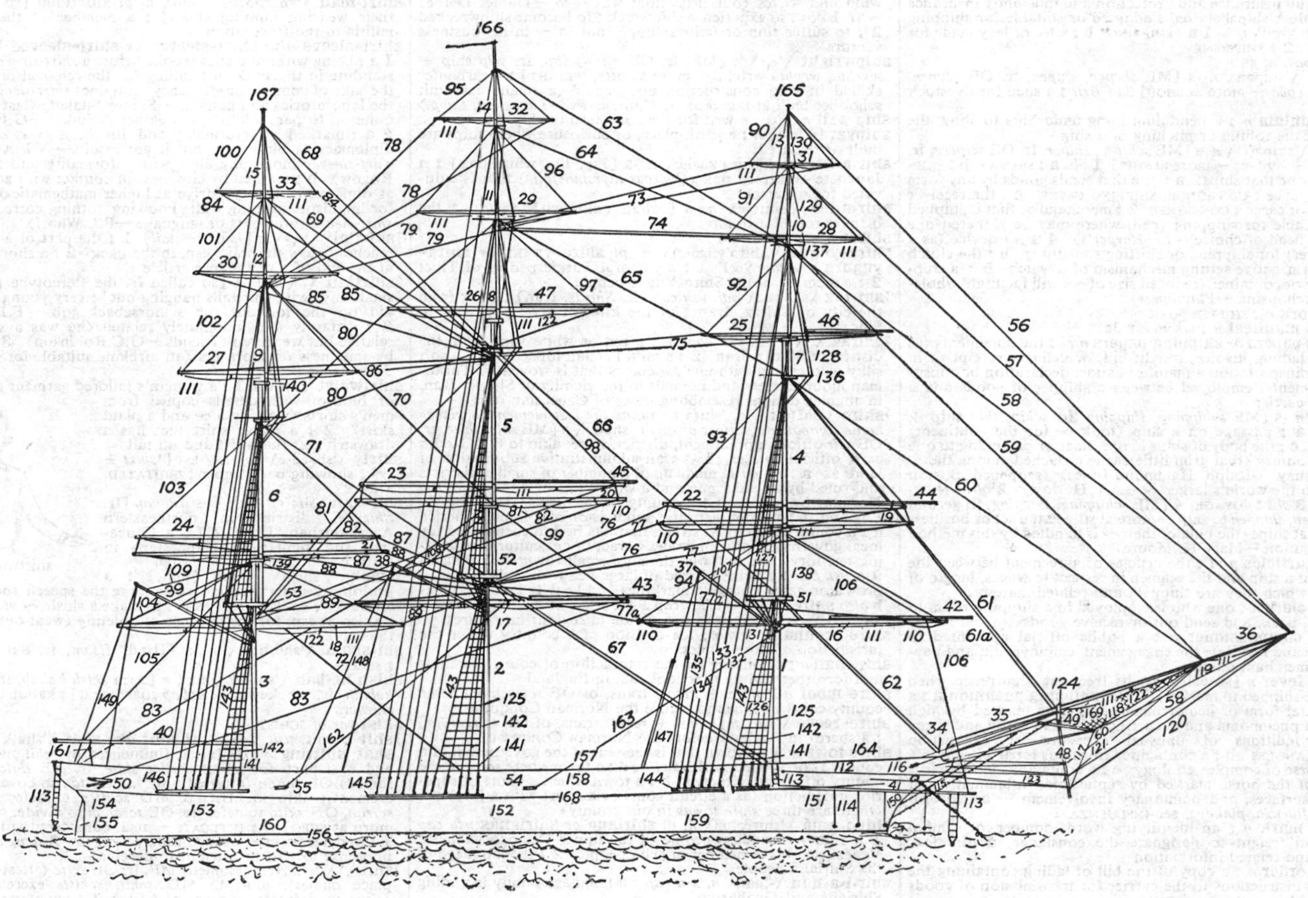

SHIP: PRINCIPAL ROPES, SPARS

1 foremast, *2* mainmast, *3* mizzenmast, *4* fore-topmast, *5* main-topmast, *6* mizzen-topmast, *7* fore-topgallant mast (at the doubling), *8* main-topgallant mast, *9* mizzen-topgallant mast, *10* fore-royal mast (sometimes not a part of the topgallant mast), *11* main-royal mast, *12* mizzen-royal mast, *13* fore-skysail pole, *14* main-skysail pole, *15* mizzen-skysail pole, *16* foreyard (at the quarter), *17* main yard (at the slings), *18* crossjack yard, *19* lower fore-topsail yard (at yardarm), *20* lower main-topsail yard, *21* lower mizzen-topsail yard, *22* upper fore-topsail yard, *23* upper main-topsail yard, *24* upper mizzen-topsail yard, *25* fore-topgallant yard, *26* main-topgallant yard, *27* mizzen-topgallant yard, *28* foreroyal yard, *29* main-royal yard, *30* mizzen-royal yard, *31* fore-skysail yard, *32* main-skysail yard, *33* mizzen-skysail yard, *34* bowsprit, *35* jibboom, *36* flying jibboom (sometimes in a separate piece), *37* fore-trysail gaff, *38* main-trysail gaft, *39* spanker gaff, *40* spanker boom, *41* lower boom, *42* fore-topmast-studding-sail boom, *43* main-topmast-studding-sail boom, *44* fore-topgallant-studding-sail boom, *45* main-topgallant-studding-sail boom, *46* fore-royal-studding-sail boom, *47* main-royal-studding-sail boom, *48* dolphin striker, *49* whisker boom, *50* main-brace bumpkin, *51* foretop, *52* maintop, *53* mizzen top, *54* foresheet sheave hole, *55* mainsheet sheave hole, *56* fore-skysail stay, *57* foreroyal stay, *58* flying-jib stay, *59* fore-topgallant stay, *60* jibstay, *61* fore-topmast stay, *61a* fore-topmast staysail-stay, *62* forestays, *63* main-skysail stay, *64* main-royal stay, *65* main-topgallant stay, *66* main-topmast stay, *67* mainstays, *68* mizzen-skysail stay, *69* mizzen-royal stay, *70* mizzen-topgallant stay, *71* mizzen-topmast stay, *72* mizzen stay, *73* fore-skysail braces, *74* fore-royal braces, *75* fore-topgallant braces, *76* upper fore-topsail braces, *77* lower fore-topsail braces, *77a* forebraces, *78* main-skysail braces, *79* main-royal braces, *80* main-topgallant braces, *81* upper main-topsail braces, *82* lower main-topsail braces, *83* main braces, *84* mizzen-skysail braces, *85* mizzen-royal braces, *86* mizzen-topgallant braces, *87* upper mizzen-topsail braces, *88* lower mizzen-topsail braces, *89* cross-jack braces, *90* port fore-skysail lift, *91* port foreroyal lift, *92* port fore-topgallant lift, *93* port fore-topsail lift, *94* port fore lift, *95* port main-skysail lift, *96* starboard main-royal lift, *97* starboard main-topgallant lift, *98* starboard main-topsail lift, *99* starboard main lift, *100* port mizzen-skysail lift, *101* port mizzen-royal lift, *102* port mizzen-topgallant lift, *103* port mizzen-topsail lift, *104* port crossjack lift, *105* spanker-boom topping lift, *106* lower-boom topping lift, *107* fore-trysail peak halyards, *108* main-trysail peak halyards, *109* spanker peak halyards, *110* Flemish horses, *111* footropes, *112* lifeline, *113* Jacob's ladders, *114* mooring pendants, *115* bobstays, *116* bowsprit shrouds, *117* whisker jumper, *118* jib guy, *119* flying jib guy, *120* flying jib martingale, *121* jib martingale, *122* stirrups, *123* backropes, *124* bowsprit cap, *125* ratlines, *126* fore rigging, *127* fore-topmast rigging, *128* fore-topgallant shrouds, *129* fore-royal shrouds, *130* fore-skysail shroud, *131* futtock shrouds, *132* fore-topmast backstays, *133* fore-topgallant backstays, *134* fore-royal backstay, *135* fore-skysail backstay, *136* fore-topmast crosstrees, *137* fore jack, *138* doubling of the masts, *139* mizzen cap (lower), *140* mizzen-topmast cap, *141* sheer poles, *142* swifters, *143* after shrouds, *144* fore-chains, *145* main chains, *146* mizzen chains, *147* foretrysail vangs, *148* main-trysail vangs, *149* spanker vangs, *150* cutwater, *151* starboard bow, *152* starboard beam, *153* starboard quarter, *154* starboard counter, *155* rudder, *156* waterline, *157* rail, *158* bulwarks, *159* entrance, *160* run, *161* spanker sheets, *162* starboard mainsheet, *163* starboard foresheet, *164* nameboard, *165* fore truck, *166* main truck and pennant, *167* mizzen truck, *168* sheer strake, *169* jib netting

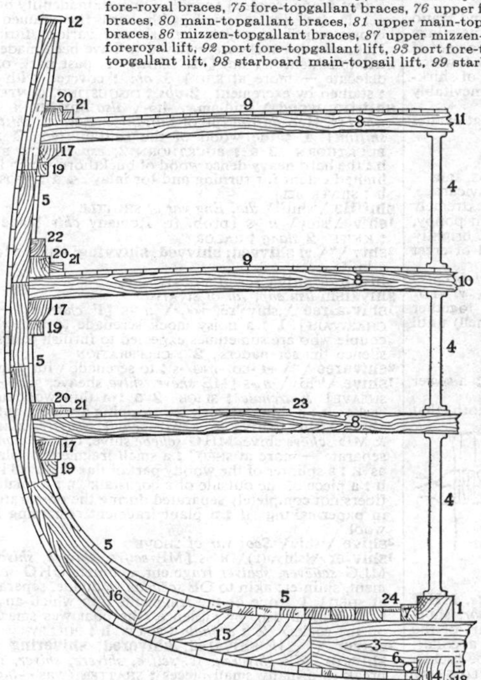

WOODEN SHIP: PRINCIPAL PARTS OF THE HULL

1 keelson, *2* garboard, *3* floor *or* floor timber, *4* stanchion, *5* ceiling, *6* limber hole, *7* side keelson, *8* beam, *9* deck planking, *10* main deck, *11* upper deck, *12* rail, *13* false keel, *14* keel, *15*, *16* first and second futtock forming the frame, *17* shelfpiece, *18* rabbet of the keel, *19* beam clamp, *20* waterway, *21* inner waterway, *22* spirketing, *23* partial hold deck, the planking extending as far as the figure 23, *24* limber board

STEEL SHIP: PRINCIPAL PARTS OF THE HULL

1 keelson, *2* garboard, *3* floor *or* floor plate, *4* stanchion, *5* ceiling, *6* limber hole, *7* side keelson, *8* beam, *9* deck planking, *10* main deck, *11* upper deck, *12* rail, *13* frame angle iron, *14* reverse-frame angle iron, *15* bar keel, *16* intercostal plate of first longitudinal or side keelson, *17* bilge keelson *or* hold stringer, *18*, *19* plating, *20* bilge keel, *21* bracket plate, *22* stringer, *23* batten, *24* steel deck, *25* stringer angle irons, *26* tie plate, *27* stringer plate

ship of state : the affairs of a state symbolized as a ship on a course

ship of the line : a ship of war large enough to have a place in the line of battle **:** a ship superior to a frigate and usu. a 74-gun or three-decker ship — called also *line-of-battle ship*

ship of war [ME *schep of warr*] **:** WARSHIP

shipowner \ˈ=,==\ *n* **:** an owner of a ship or of a share in a ship

shipowners' club *n* **:** a mutual association of shipowners operating ordinarily on an assessment basis and organized for writing hull insurance and protection and indemnity insurance

ship·pa·ble \ˈshipəbəl\ *adj* **:** adapted or suitable for shipping

ship·page \-pij\ *n* -s **1 a :** SHIPPING **b :** a fee or levy made for shipping **2 :** SHIPMENT

shipped *past of* SHIP

ship·pen \ˈshipən\ *n* -s [ME *shepen, shipen,* fr. OE *scypen, scipen, scepen* — more at SHOP] *dial Brit* **:** a shed for livestock (as cows)

ship pendulum *n* **:** a pendulum hung amidships to show the extent of the rolling or pitching of a ship

ship·per \ˈshipə(r)\ *n* -s [ME *schiper, shiper,* fr. OE *scipere,* fr. *scip* ship + *-ere* -er — more at SHIP] **1** *obs* **a :** SEAMAN **b :** SKIPPER **2 :** one that ships: **a :** one that sends goods by any form of conveyance **:** CONSIGNOR, SHIPPING CLERK **b :** the receiver of goods or cargo **:** CONSIGNEE **3 :** merchandise that is shipped or is suitable for shipping ⟨pen, where may be gathered one hundred head of choice ~*s* —*Harper's*⟩ **4 a :** a device (as a belt shifter) for shipping or shifting something **b :** the clutch lever in a negative setting mechanism of a watch **5 :** a shipping case or container ⟨reduced size of ~*s* will facilitate wholesaler warehousing —*Playthings*⟩

shipper fork *n* **:** SHIFTER FORK

shipper's manifest *n* **:** MANIFEST 3a

shipper's papers *or* **shipping papers** *n pl* **:** the documents (as a bill of lading, invoice, freight bill, or delivery receipt or in marine transportation a manifest export declaration or consular documents) employed between a shipper of goods and a common carrier

shipping *n* -s [ME *schipping, shipping,* fr. *schip, ship* ship + *-ing*] **1 a :** passage on a ship ⟨took ~ for the continent⟩ **b :** SHIPS **c :** the body of ships in one place or belonging to one port or country ⟨that grim little castle crouched among the ~ at the quay —Ralph Hammond-Innes⟩ ⟨reopened Boston harbor to the world's larger ~ —A.F.Harlow⟩ **2** *obs* **:** NAVIGATION **3** *obs* **:** VOYAGE **4** [ME *schipping, shipping,* fr. gerund of *schippen, shippen* to ship — more at SHIP] **:** the act or business of one that ships ⟨the bulk of their ~ is handled by this method of distribution —Mary K. Moore⟩

shipping articles *n pl* **:** the articles of agreement between the captain of a ship and the seamen in respect to wages, length of time for which they are shipped, and related matters

shipping clerk *n* **:** one who is employed in a shipping room to assemble, pack, and send out or receive goods

shipping commissioner *n* **:** a public official appointed to supervise and facilitate the engagement, employment, and payment of merchant seamen

shipping fever *n* [so called fr. its frequent occurrence when cattle are shipped to market] **1** *also* **shipping pneumonia :** a highly fatal form of hemorrhagic septicemia marked by high fever and pneumonia and occurring chiefly in cattle and sheep under conditions of unusual exposure or exhaustion **2 a :** STRANGLES **b :** a contagious fibrinous lobar pneumonia of the horse of complex etiology **c :** a contagious febrile virus disease of the horse marked by septicemia, inflammation of mucous surfaces, and pulmonary involvement — called also *equine influenza, pinkeye;* see INFLUENZA 2

shipping mark *n* **:** an identifying word, number, or symbol placed on freight to designate the consignee, destination, weight, and related information

shipping order *n* **:** a copy of the bill of lading containing the shipper's instructions to the carrier for transmission of goods

ship·pon \ˈshipən\ *var of* SHIPPEN

ship railway *n* **1 :** an inclined railway running into the water with a car on which a ship may be drawn out on land for repairs or storage **2 :** a railway on which to transport ships overland between bodies of water

ship rat *n* **:** the common brown rat or the roof rat that frequently infests ships

ship-rigged \ˈ=;=\ *adj* **:** SQUARE-RIGGED

ship rigger *n* **:** a worker who takes care of a ship and its rigging while in port

ships *pl of* SHIP, *pres 3d sing of* SHIP

ship's articles *n pl* **:** SHIPPING ARTICLES

ship's bell *n* **1 :** a bell used on shipboard to strike each half hour of a watch **2 :** SHIP'S CLOCK

ship's boy *var of* SHIPBOY

ship's clerk *n* **1 :** CLERK 3b(2) **2 :** a warrant officer in the U. S. Navy whose specialty is the supervision of records, reports, correspondence and related matters

ship's clock *n* **:** a clock that measures time in ship's bells

ship's company *n* **:** COMPANY 2d

ship's corporal *n* **:** CORPORAL 1b

ship's days *n pl* **:** the days allowed a ship for loading or unloading

ship·shape \ˈship¦shāp\ *adj* [short for earlier *shipshapen,* fr. ¹*ship* + *shapen,* archaic past part. of ¹*shape*] **:** arranged in a manner befitting a ship **:** TRIM, TIDY, ORDERLY ⟨it was a ~ job — stoutly built, weatherproof, and sightly with its bright new thatch —C.B.Nordhoff & J.N.Hall⟩ **syn** see NEAT

²**shipshape** \ˈ"\ *n* [¹*ship* + ²*shape*] **:** the quality or state of being shipshape, prepared, or organized — usu. used with *in* ⟨sail a boat and keep it in ~ —*advt*⟩ ⟨spend millions to get their dock facilities in ~ —*Newsweek*⟩ ⟨everything was in ~ tonight for the big rowing finale —*N.Y. Herald Tribune*⟩

ship's husband *n* **:** an agent on land representing the owners of a ship who attends to its provisioning, repairing, and general management

¹**shipside** \ˈ=,=\ *n* [ME *shippe syde*] **:** the area adjacent to shipping that is used for storage and loading of freight and passengers **:** DOCK ⟨maintain a uniform flow of all models of vehicles from factory to ~ —*New Yorker*⟩ ⟨failed to arrive at ~ on time —C.L.Walker⟩

²**shipside** \ˈ"\ *adj* **:** located alongside a ship **:** being within reach of the ship's tackle ⟨has two railroad tracks and direct ~ access —*Ships and the Sea*⟩ ⟨~ permits may be granted —*Port of Manila Yr. Bk.*⟩

ship's option *n* **:** the privilege of computing freight charges for a particular commodity on either a weight or a space basis

ship's papers *n pl* **:** the papers with which a ship is required to be provided for due inspection under the law including the certificate of enrollment or registry, the license, crew list, shipping articles, clearance, and passenger list required by the country to which the ship belongs and the sea letter, proofs of ownership, bills of lading, invoices, manifest, muster roll, log book, and bill of health required of neutral vessels by the law of nations

ship's passport *n* **:** SEA LETTER

ship splice *n* **:** SCARF JOINT

ship's service *n* **:** a ship or navy post exchange — called also *navy exchange*

ship's stores *n pl* **:** the supplies and equipment required for the operation and upkeep of a ship

ship's time *n* **:** the local mean time of the meridian where a ship is located

ship stuff *n* **1 :** a low-grade wheat flour with high bran content **2 :** wheat offals that are used as a stock feed

shipt *abbr* shipment

shipway \ˈ=,=\ *n* **1 :** the ways on which a ship is built **2 :** the supports used under a ship in dry dock **3 :** a channel for ships **:** SHIP CANAL

shipworm \ˈ=,=\ *n* **:** any of various elongated marine clams mostly of the family Teredinidae that resemble worms, burrow in submerged wood, and are very destructive to piles of wharves or wooden ships — compare BANKIA

¹**ship·wreck** \ˈshi,prek\ *n* [alter. (influenced by *wreck*) of earlier *shipwrack,* fr. ME *schipwrak,* fr. OE *scipwræc,* fr. *scip* ship + *wræc* something driven by the sea — more at SHIP, WRACK] **1 :** a wrecked ship or its parts **:** WRECKAGE **2 :** the destruction or loss (as by sinking or being cast ashore or driven against rocks or shoals) of a ship **3 :** an irretrievable loss or failure **:** RUIN, DESTRUCTION ⟨the conference nearly ended in ~ —*New Statesman & Nation*⟩ ⟨the ~ of her marriage —Judith Heller⟩ ⟨the ~ of our hopes —Harrison Smith⟩

²**shipwreck** \ˈ"\ *vt* **1 a :** to cause (as sailors or passengers) to experience shipwreck ⟨they too were ~*ed* in another great mystery of the sea —W.E.Swinton⟩ **b :** to afflict with disaster or loss **:** RUIN ⟨~*ed* his career —C.L.Jones⟩ ⟨the human animal, nearly ~*ed,* will turn toward some means to save itself —J.S.Collis⟩ **2 :** to destroy (a ship) by driving ashore or upon rocks or sandbanks or causing to founder by the force of wind and waves ⟨our little float was ~*ed* —Daniel Defoe⟩ ~ *vi* **1** *obs* **:** to experience shipwreck **:** to become shipwrecked **2 :** to suffer ruin or failure ⟨hopes not to ~ in his business venture⟩

shipwright \ˈ=,=\ *n* [ME, fr. OE *scipwyrhta,* fr. *scip* ship + *wyrhta, wryhta* wright — more at SHIP, WRIGHT] **:** a carpenter skilled in ship construction and repair ⟨a small teak-built schooner built at Bangkok by Chinese ~*s* —*Times Lit. Supp.*⟩

ship writ *n, obs* **:** a writ for the collection of ship money

shipyard \ˈ=,=\ *n* **:** a yard, place, or enclosure where ships are built or repaired

shir·a·ka·shi \,shirəˈkäshē\ *n* -s [Jap, lit., white oak] **:** a Japanese evergreen oak (*Quercus myrsinaefolia*) that is cultivated for ornament

shir·a·lee \ˈshirəlē\ *n* -s [origin unknown] *Austral* **:** the blanket roll of a tramp

shirani *var of* SHERANI

shira-yugur \,shirəˈyügə(r)\ *n, pl* **shira-yugur** *or* **shira-yugurs** *usu cap S&Y* **1 :** a pastoral Turkic people of Tibet **2 :** a member of the Shira-Yugur people

¹**shi·raz** \shəˈräz\ *adj, usu cap* [fr. *Shiraz, Iran*] **:** of or from the city of Shiraz, Iran **:** of the kind or style prevalent in Shiraz

²**shiraz** \ˈ"\ *n* -ES *usu cap* **1 :** a red or white wine from the district of Shiraz, Iran **2 :** a mild Persian tobacco **3 :** a soft silky woolen rug with mellow colors that is woven by Turkoman mountaineers and nomads in the vicinity of Shiraz, Iran, in angular designs resembling those of Caucasian rugs

¹**shire** \ˈshī(ə)r, -īə, ˈshi(ə)r, -iə, *as the last element in place-name compounds* ,shi(ə)r *or* -iə *or* ,shə(r)\ *n* [ME *shir, shire,* fr. OE *scīr* office, appointment, district, shire; akin to OHG *scīra* care, official charge] **1** -s **:** an administrative subdivision of land: as **a :** a district made up of a number of smaller districts and ruled by an alderman and a sheriff in England before the Norman Conquest **b :** a county in the British Isles esp. in England **c :** an administrative subdivision of colonial America **d :** a country area in Australia that has been incorporated for local government and embraces a tract of agricultural or grazing territory including one or more small towns and villages **2 a** *usu cap* **:** a British breed of large heavy draft horses usu. brown or bay with white markings and heavily feathered legs **b** *also* **shire horse** -s *often cap S* **:** a horse of the Shire breed

²**shire** \ˈ"\ *vt* -ED/-ING/-S **:** to divide (a region) into shires

shire ground *n, archaic* **:** a division of a country under the jurisdiction of shire officers

shire hall *n* **:** a building for the transaction of county business and for other county functions esp. in England

shire moot *n* [¹*shire* + *moot;* trans. of OE *scīrgemōt*] **:** the county court in England before the Norman Conquest

shire-reeve \ˈ=,=\ *n* [¹*shire* + *reeve;* trans. of OE *scīrgerēfa*] **:** a sheriff in England before the Norman Conquest

shire town *n* **1 :** a town that is the seat of the government of a county **:** COUNTY SEAT **2** *NewEng* **a :** a town where some of the county offices are situated **b :** a town where a court of superior jurisdiction (as a circuit court or a court with a jury) sits ⟨there are three *shire towns* in our county⟩

shir·i·a·ná \,shirēə¦nä\ *n, pl* **shirianá** *or* **shirianás** *usu cap* **1 a :** an Amerindian people of the upper Orinoco valley in Venezuela **b :** a member of such people **2 :** the language of the Shirianá people

shir·i·a·nan \-ˈnän\ *n, usu cap* **:** a language family including Shirianá and Guaharibo

¹**shirk** \ˈshərk, ˈshə̄k, ˈshəik\ *vb* -ED/-ING/-S [origin unknown] *vi* **1 a** *obs* **:** to live by trickery and fraud **:** SHARK, SPONGE **b** *chiefly dial* **:** to take care of oneself under somewhat difficult circumstances **:** FEND, SHIFT **2 :** to go stealthily **:** SNEAK ⟨obliged to ~ on board by night to escape from their wives —W.M.Thackeray⟩ **3 a :** to withdraw because of lack of courage ⟨one of the cities ~*ed* from the league —Lord Byron⟩ **b :** to evade the performance of an obligation because of laziness or fear ⟨the timid flee, the lazy ~ —H.A.Overstreet⟩ ~ *vt* **1 a :** to avoid (as a disagreeable task) because of laziness, lack of courage, or distaste ⟨he had of course ~*ed* telling her that no marriage would occur that day —Arnold Bennett⟩ **b :** to evade meeting (as a person) **:** DODGE ⟨~*ed* his gaze⟩ **2 :** to shift (as a responsibility) elsewhere ⟨if he could ~ off the work upon the others he would —Nathaniel Hawthorne⟩ **syn** see DODGE

²**shirk** \ˈ"\ *n* -s **1** *obs* **:** one who lives by trickery and fraud **:** SHARK **2 :** one who shirks work or obligations ⟨was a lazy bum, a no-good, and a ~ —*American Songbag*⟩ **3 a :** an act of shirking ⟨saw the many ~*s* from doing his duty of which Hamlet was guilty —F.J.Furnivall⟩ **b :** the practice of shirking ⟨work that is not needed and whose spirit of ~ inevitably demoralizes men —C.H.Rowell⟩

shirk·er \-kə(r)\ *n* -s **:** one that shirks; *esp* **:** one that evades duty

shirky \-kē\ *adj* -ER/-EST **:** disposed to shirk

¹**shirl** \ˈshər(-ə)l\ *dial var of* SHRILL

²**shirl** \ˈ"\ *vi* [origin unknown] *dial Eng* **:** SLIDE, GLIDE, SLIP

shir·ley poppy \ˈshərlē-\ *n, usu cap S* [fr. *Shirley* vicarage, Croydon, Eng., where it was developed] **:** an extremely variable annual garden poppy derived from the corn poppy, typically forming a branched plant, and bearing usu. brightly colored solitary single or double flowers at the end of erect scapes — compare ICELAND POPPY

¹**shirr** *R* ˈshər, + *vowel* -ər·; *-R* -ə̄, + *suffixal vowel* -ər· *also* -ə̄r, + *vowel in a following word* -ər· *or* -ə *also* -ə̄r\ *vt* -ED/-ING/-S [origin unknown] **1 :** to draw (as cloth) together in a shirring **2 :** to bake (eggs removed from the shell) until set

²**shirr** \ˈ"\ *n* -s **:** SHIRRING

shir·ra \ˈshirə\ *Scot var of* SHERIFF

shirr·er *R* ˈshər·ər, *-R* ˈshər·ə(r *also* ˈshə̄rə(r\ *n* -s **:** a sewer who does shirring

shirring *n* -s **:** a decorative gathering of material (as cloth) that is made by drawing up the material along two or more parallel lines of stitching or encased cords, by stitching it with elastic thread, or by weaving rubber threads under tension into it

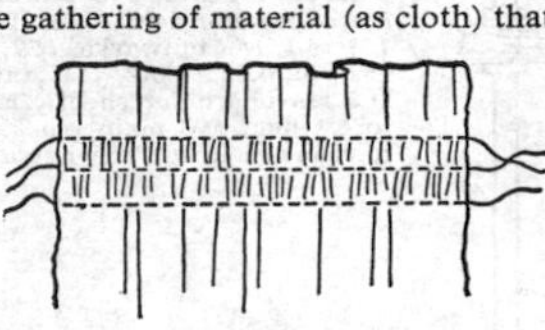

shirring

¹**shirt** \ˈshər|t, ˈshə̄|, ˈshəi|, *usu* |d·+V\ *n* -s [ME *shirte, sherte,* fr. OE *scyrte;* akin to MD *schorte* apron, MLG *schörte,* MHG *schurz* apron, ON *skyrta* shirt, kirtle, OE *scort, sceort* short — more at SHORT] **1 :** a garment for the upper part of the body: as **a :** a loose cloth garment usu. having a collar, sleeves, a front opening, and a tail long enough to be tucked inside the waistband of trousers or a skirt **b :** POLO SHIRT **c :** JERSEY **d :** UNDERSHIRT **2 a :** a loose garment that reaches to the thighs or lower ⟨a white ~ reached almost to his ankles —Humayun Kabir⟩ **b :** NIGHTSHIRT **3 :** all or a large part of one's possessions ⟨lost her ~ in the war —T.H.Fielding⟩ ⟨put his ~ on the favorite only to see a rank outsider about to nip him at the post —F.J.Warburg⟩ **4** *Austral* **:** a thin calico bag in which frozen carcasses are shipped **5 :** a member of a political organization that uses a colored shirt as its badge

²**shirt** \ˈ"\ *vt* -ED/-ING/-S **:** to clothe with a shirt

shirtband \ˈ=,=\ *n* **:** the neckband of a shirt

shirtfront \ˈ=,=\ *n* **1 :** the front of a shirt: as **a :** the part of a man's shirt that is not covered by his coat or vest **b :** the usu. starched, pleated, or ruffled front of a man's dress shirt **2 :** DICKEY

shirtfront wicket *n* **:** a cricket wicket esp. of turf that is in perfect condition

shirt·ing \ˈshərd·|iŋ, -ə̄|, -əi|, |t|, |ēŋ\ *n* -s [¹*shirt* + *-ing*] **:** any of various fabrics (as fine lightweight cotton) suitable for men's shirts

shirt·less \-|tləs\ *adj* **:** being without a shirt — **shirt·less·ness** *n* -ES

shirtlike \ˈ=,=\ *adj* **:** resembling a shirt

shirtmaker \ˈ=,==\ *n* **1 :** one that makes shirts **2 :** a woman's tailored garment (as a dress or blouse) with details copied from a man's shirt

shirt·man \ˈshərtmən, -,man\ *n, pl* **shirtmen** [so called fr. their wearing hunting shirts] **:** a member of the Virginia militia in the Revolution

shirt-sleeve *also* **shirt-sleeves** *or* **shirt-sleeved** \ˈ=;=\ *adj* **1 a :** being without a coat ⟨spoke before a *shirt-sleeve* audience standing in the sun⟩ **b :** calling for the removal of coats for the sake of comfort or efficiency ⟨still does *shirt-sleeve* work in the laboratories and hangars —Sidney Shalett⟩ ⟨last week was quite up to par, *shirt-sleeve* weather included —G.F.T.Ryall⟩ **2 a :** marked by informality and directness ⟨was *shirt-sleeve* diplomacy, a bit rough, but it got results —V.L.Albjerg⟩ ⟨a *shirt-sleeves* biography alive with informality and fun —Lee Rogow⟩ **b :** marked by closeness of contact with actual facts as opposed to theory ⟨strive at higher mathematical formulas for linguistic meaning while knowing nothing correctly of the *shirt-sleeve* rudiments of language —B.L.Whorf⟩

¹**shirttail** \ˈ=,=\ *n* [¹*shirt* + *tail*] **1 :** the part of a shirt that reaches below the waist esp. in the back **2 :** a short addition at the end of a newspaper article

²**shirttail** \ˈ"\ *adj* **1** [so called fr. the stereotype picture of small boys with shirttails hanging out] **:** very young ⟨just a ~ kid on the lookout for a horseback job —F.B.Gipson⟩ **2 :** distantly and indefinitely related ⟨he was a sort of ~ relative but we weren't friends —G.C.Robinson⟩ **3 :** marked by smallness or shortness ⟨an airplane suitable for ~ runs of 50 to 100 miles⟩

shirtwaist \ˈ=,=\ *n* **1 :** a woman's tailored garment (as a dress or blouse) with details copied from men's shirts ⟨wearing a ~ and a plaid skirt⟩ **2 :** a man's shirt that has a drawstring at the waist and no tail

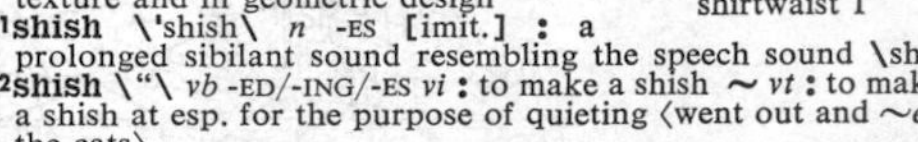

shirtwaist 1

shirty \ˈshərd·ē\ *adj* -ER/-EST [¹*shirt* + *-y*] **:** showing bad temper **:** IRRITATED, ANGRY

shir·van \shə(r)ˈvän\ *n* -s *usu cap* [fr. *Shirvan,* district in northeastern Azerbaidzhan, U.S.S.R.] **:** a Caucasian rug similar to Daghestans in texture and in geometric design

¹**shish** \ˈshish\ *n* -ES [imit.] **:** a prolonged sibilant sound resembling the speech sound \sh\

²**shish** \ˈ"\ *vb* -ED/-ING/-ES *vi* **:** to make a shish ~ *vt* **:** to make a shish at esp. for the purpose of quieting ⟨went out and ~*ed* the cats⟩

shi·sham \ˈshēshəm\ *n* -s [Hindi *śīśam,* fr. Skt *śiṁśapā*] **:** SISSOO

shish ke·bab \ˈshishkə,bäb\ *n* [Arm *shish kabab,* fr. Turk *şiş kebabı,* fr. *şiş* skewer + *kebap* roast meat] **:** kabob broiled on skewers

shist *var of* SCHIST

¹**shit** \ˈshi|t, *usu* |d·+V\ *vb* **shit** *also* **shat** \ˈsha|\ **shit** *also* **shat; shitting; shits** [alter. (influenced by ²*shit* and the past and past part. forms) of earlier *shite,* fr. ME *shiten,* fr. (assumed) OE *scītan* (attested only in *bescītan* to cover with excrement); akin to MLG & MD *schiten* to defecate, OHG *scīzan,* ON *skīta* to defecate, OE *scēadan* to divide, separate — more at SHED] *vi* **:** DEFECATE — usu. considered vulgar ~ *vt* **1 :** to defecate in — usu. considered vulgar **2** *slang* **a :** to talk nonsense to **b :** to attempt to deceive

²**shit** \ˈ"\ *n* -s [fr. (assumed) ME, fr. OE *scite* (attested only in place names); akin to MD *schit, schitte* excrement, OE *scītan* to defecate — more at ¹SHIT] **1 :** EXCREMENT — usu. considered vulgar **2 :** an act of defecation — usu. considered vulgar **3** *slang* **a :** NONSENSE, FOOLISHNESS **b :** something of little value ⟨didn't give a ~⟩ ⟨not worth a ~⟩ **c :** trivial and usu. boastful or inaccurate talk **4** *slang* **:** a contemptible person **5 shits** *pl but sing or pl in constr* [ME *schyt,* fr. OE *scitte;* akin to OE *scītan* to defecate] **:** DIARRHEA — used with *the;* usu. considered vulgar

shite \ˈshīt\ *obs var of* SHIT

shite·poke \ˈshīt,pōk, -īd,p-, -īk,p-\ *n* [*shite* + *poke;* fr. its traditional habit of defecating when flushed] **:** any of various herons: as **a :** GREEN HERON **b :** NIGHT HERON

shith·er \ˈshithə(r)\ *vi* [perh. alter. of *shudder*] *dial Eng* **:** SHIVER

shit·tah \ˈshid·ə, -itə\ *or* **shittah tree** *n, pl* **shittahs** *or* **shit·tim** \-id·əm, -itəm\ *or* **shittah trees** [Heb *shiṭṭāh,* fr. Egypt *šanḏa, šanḏat*] **:** a tree of uncertain identity but prob. an acacia (as *Acacia seyal*) with hard fine-grained yellowish brown wood of which the ark and various fittings of the Hebrew tabernacle are believed to have been made

shit·ten \ˈshitᵊn\ *adj* [ME *shiten,* fr. past part. of *shiten* to defecate — more at SHIT] **1** *obs* **:** covered with excrement **:** stained by excrement **2** *obs* **:** DISGUSTING, CONTEMPTIBLE

shit·tim·wood \ˈshid·əm,=, -itə-\ *also* **shittim** *n* -s [*shittim-wood* fr. Heb *shittīm* (pl. of *shiṭṭāh*) + E *wood; shittim* fr. Heb *shiṭṭīm*] **1 :** the wood of the shittah tree **2 :** CASCARA BUCKTHORN **3 a :** BUCKTHORN 2; *esp* **:** FALSE BUCKTHORN **b :** the hard heavy dense wood of buckthorn which is used to a limited extent for turning and for inlay **4 a :** OPOSSUM WOOD **b :** SILVER BELL

shit·tle \ˈshitᵊl\ *dial Eng var of* SHUTTLE

¹**shiv** \ˈshiv\ *n* -s [prob. fr. Romany *chiv* blade] **1** *slang* **:** KNIFE **2** *slang* **:** RAZOR

²**shiv** \ˈ"\ *vt* **shivved; shivved; shivving; shivs :** to stab with a knife

shivah *or* **shiva** *var of* SHIBAH

shivaism *usu cap, var of* SIVAISM

¹**shiv·a·ree** \,shivəˈrē, ˈ=,=\ *n* -s [F *charivari* — more at CHARIVARI] **1 :** a noisy mock serenade to a newly married couple who are sometimes expected to furnish refreshments to silence the serenaders **2 :** CELEBRATION

²**shivaree** \ˈ"\ *vt* -ED/-ING/-S **:** to serenade with a shivaree

¹**shive** \ˈshīv\ *n* -s [ME *sheve, shive* sheave, slice — more at SHEAVE] **1** *archaic* **:** SLICE **2 a :** a thin wooden bung for casks **b :** a thin flat cork for stopping a wide-mouthed bottle

²**shive** \ˈshiv, ˈshīv\ *n* -s [ME *schyfe, schyffe;* akin to MLG & MD *schēve* shive, MHG *schebe* shive, OE *scēadan* to divide, separate — more at SHED] **:** a small fragment of plant matter: as **a :** a splinter of the woody part of flax removed in breaking **b :** a piece of the outside of a cornstalk **c :** a small bundle of fibers not completely separated during the preparation of pulp in papermaking **d :** a plant fragment remaining in scoured wool

³**shive** \ˈshiv\ *Scot var of* SHOVE

¹**shiv·er** \ˈshivə(r)\ *n* -s [ME *scifre, shivere, shiver;* akin to MLG *schēver, schiver* fragment, splinter, OHG *scivaro* fragment, splinter; akin to OE *scēadan* to divide, separate — more at SHED] **1 :** one of the fragments into which an object has been broken usu. by violence ⟨the boat was smashed to ~*s* on the rocks⟩ **2 a** *archaic* **:** SLICE **b :** PULLEY

²**shiver** \ˈ"\ *vb* **shivered; shivered; shivering** \-v(ə)riŋ\ **shivers** [ME *shiveren,* fr. *scifre, shivere, shiver,* n.] *vt* **:** to break into many small pieces **:** SHATTER ⟨was ~*ing* his lance against it in vain —A.W.Long⟩ ~ *vi* **:** to fall apart into many small pieces ⟨his statue fell and ~*ed* on the stones —J.A. Froude⟩ **syn** see BREAK

³**shiver** \ˈ"\ *vb* **shivered; shivered; shivering** \-v(ə)riŋ\ **shivers** [ME *shiveren,* alter. (influenced by *shiveren* to shatter) of *chiveren*] *vi* **:** to undergo trembling (as from cold, fear, or the application of a physical force) **:** SHAKE, QUIVER, VIBRATE ⟨in spite of the heat of the room he ~*ed* —Victor Canning⟩ ⟨crystal chandeliers ~*ed* when he sang —George Jellinek⟩; *specif* **:** to tremble in the wind as it strikes first one and then the other side — used of a sail ~ *vt* **1 :** to cause to shiver ⟨another jerk ~*ed* her body —Olive H. Prouty⟩; *specif* **:** to cause (a sail) to shiver by steering close to the wind **2 :** to produce with or as if with a shiver ⟨the sweet heaven-bird ~*ed* out his song above him —George Meredith⟩

⁴**shiver** \ˈ"\ *n* -s **1 :** an instance of shivering **:** TREMBLE ⟨a ~ ran down my spine —Helen Eustis⟩ ⟨a momentary ~ of leaves

drew our eyes to the left —William Beebe⟩ **2 shivers** *pl* **:** an attack of shivering; *specif* **:** AGUE — usu. used with preceding *the*

shiv·er·eens \ˌshivəˈrēnz\ *n pl* [¹*shiver* + *-eens* (as in *smithereens*)] *dial Brit* **:** SMITHEREENS

shiv·er·er \ˈshivərə(r)\ *n* -s **:** one that shivers

¹shivering *n* -s [ME, fr. gerund of *shiveren* to shiver (tremble) — more at SHIVER] **1 :** an act or action of one that trembles **2 :** a constant abnormal twitching of various muscles in the horse that is prob. due to sensory nerve derangement

²shivering *n* -s [ME, fr. gerund of *shiveren* to shiver (shatter) — more at SHIVER] **1 :** an act or action of one that breaks into fragments **2 :** the cracking and scaling of a glaze on pottery caused by unequal contractions between the materials as they cool

shiv·er·ing·ly *adv* **:** in a shivering manner

shivering owl *n* **:** SCREECH OWL

shiv·er·some \ˈshivə(r)səm\ *adj* **:** productive of shivers

shiver spar *n* [¹*shiver;* intended as trans. of G *schieferspar,* fr. *schiefer* slate + *spar*] **:** a calcite with a slaty structure

shiverweed \ˈ==,=\ *n* [³*shiver* + *weed*] *Austral* **:** CORN WOUNDWORT

¹shiv·ery \ˈshiv(ə)rē\ *adj* [²*shiver* + *-y*] **:** inclined to break into flakes **:** BRITTLE, FLAKY

²shivery \"\ *adj* [³*shiver* + *-y*] **1 :** characterized by shivers **:** TREMULOUS ⟨awoke sweating, cold, and ~ —Richard Sale⟩ ⟨thatched with ~ grasses —Ethel Anderson⟩ **2 :** causing shivers: as **a :** CHILLING, COLD ⟨a ~ January day⟩ **b :** frightening enough to cause trembling ⟨had the right uninhibited reactions to all the ~ threats —John Mason Brown⟩

shives *pl of* SHIVE

shivite *usu cap, var of* SAIVITE

shi·voo \shəˈvü\ *n* -s [origin unknown] *Austral* **:** a boisterous social gathering

shivs *pl of* SHIV, *pres 3d sing of* SHIV

shivved *past of* SHIV

shivving *pres part of* SHIV

shiv·wits \ˈshiv,wits\ *n, pl* **shivwits** *or* **shivwitses** *usu cap* **1 :** a band of Paiute Indians of southern Utah **2 :** a member of the Shivwits band

shivy *or* **shiv·ey** \ˈshivē, -īvē\ *adj* [²*shive* + *-y*] **:** containing shives ⟨~ wool⟩ ⟨~ paper⟩

shi·zo·ku \ˈshēzō,kü, shēˈzō(,)kü\ *n, pl* **shizoku** [Jap] **:** the Japanese social class consisting of the old samurai and their families and descendants as distinguished from the heimin and the kwazoku

shi·zu·o·ka \shēˈzüə,kä\ *adj, usu cap* [fr. *Shizuoka,* Japan] **:** of or from the city of Shizuoka, Japan **:** of the kind or style prevalent in Shizuoka

shkotzim *pl of* SHEGETZ

shl *abbr* **1** shell **2** shoal

shld *abbr* **1** shield **2** shoulder

shlemiel *var of* SCHLEMIEL

shlimazel *or* **shlimazl** *var of* SCHLIMAZEL

shlp *abbr* shiplap

shltr *abbr* shelter

shluh \shəˈlü, ˈshlü\ *or* **shil·ha** \-lä\ *or* **shil·luh** \-lü\ *n, pl* **shluh** *or* **shluhs** *or* **shilha** *or* **shilhas** *or* **shilluh** *or* **shilluhs** *usu cap* **1 a :** a Berber people of southern Morocco **b :** a member of the Shluh people **2 :** a Berber language of the Shluh people

shlw *abbr* shallow

SHM *abbr* simple harmonic motion

shmo *var of* SCHMO

shmoos *var of* SCHMOOZE

shnook *var of* SCHNOOK

shoad \ˈshōd\ *n* -s [origin unknown] *dial Eng* **:** a fragment of vein material removed by natural agencies from an outcrop and lying in the surface soil or debris; *specif* **:** ¹FLOAT 7a

¹shoal \ˈshōl\ *adj* -ER/-EST [alter. of earlier *shold, shoald,* fr. ME *sheld, shald, shold,* fr. OE *sceald* — more at SHALLOW] **:** having little depth **:** SHALLOW

²shoal \"\ *n* -s [alter. of earlier *shold, shoald,* fr. ME *sheld, shald, shold,* fr. *sheld, shald, shold,* adj.] **1 :** a place where a sea, river, or other body of water is shallow **:** SHALLOW **2 :** a sandbank or sandbar which makes the water shoal; *specif* **:** an elevation or knoll which is not rocky and on which there is a depth of water of six fathoms or less — compare BANK, REEF **3 :** a rocky area on the sea bottom within soundings esp. where fish abound

³shoal \"\ *vb* -ED/-ING/-S [alter. of earlier *shold, shoald,* fr. *shold, shoald,* adj.] *vi* **:** to become shallow ⟨the loch ~*s* badly within three cables of its outer points —C.K.Finlay⟩ ~ *vt* **1 a :** to come to a shallow or less deep part of ⟨the ship ~*s* her water⟩ **b :** to cause to become shallow or less deep **c :** to fill up or block off with a shoal ⟨the inlet is continually ~*ed*⟩ **2 :** to drive (an otter) to shallow water

⁴shoal \"\ *adv* [¹*shoal*] **:** to or at a shallow depth

⁵shoal \"\ *n* -s [fr. (assumed) ME *shole,* fr. OE *scolu* multitude, troop — more at SCHOOL] **:** a great number thronged together or considered as a group ⟨herring ~*s*⟩ ⟨the ~ of congratulatory letters he received —*Times Lit. Supp.*⟩ ⟨students left in ~*s* to answer the call to arms —A.W.Long⟩

⁶shoal \"\ *vi* -ED/-ING/-S **:** to assemble in a large group **:** THRONG, SCHOOL ⟨why the shrimp ~ furiously off the ocean inlets is a mystery —V.O.Williams⟩

shoal duck *n* [²*shoal*] *NewEng* **:** EIDER DUCK

shoalgrass \ˈ=,=\ *n* [²*shoal* + *grass*] **:** a submerged herb (*Halodule wrightii*) of the family Potamogetonaceae that is native to the southeastern coastal U. S., has flat linear leaves and flowers with anthers unequally attached to the filament, and is an important food for wild fowl

shoal·i·ness \ˈshōlēnəs\ *n* -ES **1 :** the state of being shoal **2 :** the condition of being filled with shoals

shoal·ness *n* -ES **:** the state of being shallow **:** SHALLOWNESS

shoaly \-lē\ *adj* -ER/-EST [²*shoal* + *-y*] **:** full of shoals

shoat *also* **shote** \ˈshōt\ *or* **shott** \ˈshät\ *n* -s [ME *schoyth, shote;* akin to Flem *schote* shoat] **:** a young hog of either sex and esp. less than one year old — compare BARROW, GILT

shoch \ˈshäk\ *n* -s [IrGael *seach* (*tobac*), fr. *seach* turn, quantity taken at a time + *tobac* tobacco] *Irish* **:** a draw at a pipe of tobacco

shochet *var of* SHOHET

¹shock \ˈshäk\ *n* -s [ME; akin to MD *schoc, schocke* heap, pile, group of sixty, MLG *schok* shock, group of sixty, OS *scok* group of sixty, MHG *schoc* heap, pile, group of sixty, *schoche* haystack, G dial. (Switzerland) *hock* heap, pile, OE *hēah* high — more at HIGH] **1 a :** a pile or assemblage of usu. 8 to 16 sheaves of grain (as wheat) set up in a field with the butt ends down and one or two of the sheaves often broken to serve as a cap to protect the tops from weather — called also *stook* **b :** a somewhat conical stack of separate stalks of corn **c** *chiefly dial* **:** a pile of hay **:** HAYCOCK **2** [prob. fr. MD *schoc, schocke* or MLG *schok*] *archaic* **:** a group or lot of 60 pieces

²shock \"\ *vb* -ED/-ING/-S [ME *schocken,* fr. *schock,* n.] *vt* **:** to collect or make up into a shock ⟨on vacations he ~*ed* wheat and had other jobs —*Current Biog.*⟩ ~ *vi* **:** to build shocks

³shock \"\ *n* -s *often attrib* [MF *choc,* fr. *choquer* to strike against, shock — more at ⁴SHOCK] **1 a :** the impact or encounter of individuals or groups in a battle, charge, or joust **b :** the concentration of effort upon the force of impact in a battle (as in an armored or cavalry attack or close personal contact in an assault) ⟨the lack of tanks deprives the airborne force of one of its major means of ~ action —H.A.Jordan⟩ ⟨the defenders created small ~ . . . groups for the house-to-house fighting required there —*Infantry Jour.*⟩ **c :** the bringing to bear of concentrated effort upon a special objective ⟨~ workers whose output is very high and who develop new speed production methods —T.P.Whitney⟩ **2 a** (1) **:** a violent shake or jar **:** BLOW, COLLISION, CONCUSSION ⟨the ~ of tides that fall upon a crumbling shore —Francis Stuart⟩ ⟨banging the door with a ~ that made the house rattle —Arnold Bennett⟩ (2) **:** an oscillation, loss of equilibrium, or other effect of such violence **b** (1) **:** EARTHQUAKE (2) **:** the impact of an earth vibration (as an earthquake) **3 a** (1) **:** a disturbance in the equilibrium or permanence of an institution or organized entity ⟨the transition from the roles of childhood to those of adult life is accomplished with little ~ to the personality —Ralph Linton⟩ (2) **:** a sudden or violent disturbance in the mental or emotional faculties ⟨the ~ and elation of victory and defeat —Oscar Handlin⟩ ⟨fresh ~*s* of wonder at the unaccountable apparition —George Meredith⟩ (3) **:** a sense of outrage to one's convictions esp. of morality or propriety ⟨terms that in better districts would have caused disgust and ~ —Ruth Park⟩ **b :** something that causes outrage, horror, stupefaction, or disturbance or agitation in an institution, person, or organized system ⟨the further ~ of weaning —Henry Wynmalen⟩ ⟨he was liable not only to the ~ of outward circumstance but of inward impulses —Havelock Ellis⟩ ⟨ready the nation for that economic ~ —*New Republic*⟩ **4 a :** a state of profound depression of the vital processes of the body characterized by pallor, rapid but weak pulse, rapid and shallow respiration, restlessness, anxiety or mental dullness, nausea or vomiting associated with reduced total blood volume and low blood pressure and subnormal temperature resulting from severe esp. crushing injuries, hemorrhage, burns, major surgery, or other causes ⟨the patient was admitted to the hospital in ~⟩ **b :** a state induced for therapeutic purposes (as by the injection of a drug) ⟨insulin ~⟩ — compare SHOCK THERAPY **5 :** sudden stimulation of the nerves or convulsive contraction of the muscles accompanied by a feeling of concussion that is caused by the discharge through the animal body of electricity from a charged body — compare ELECTROSHOCK THERAPY **6 a :** a stroke of paralysis **:** APOPLEXY **b :** a condition resulting from or associated with myocardial infarction; *specif* **:** CORONARY THROMBOSIS **7 :** an acute disturbance of the physiology of a plant caused by extremes of temperature or moisture or by parasitic organisms or viruses and often marked or followed by reduction of yield or loss of leaves and fruit **8 :** SHOCK ABSORBER **syn** see IMPACT

⁴shock \"\ *vb* -ED/-ING/-S [MF *choquer,* fr. OF *choquier, chuquier,* prob. of Gmc origin; akin to MD *schocken* to shake, jolt, *schocke* swing, OS *skogka,* MHG *schoc, schocke*] *vt* **1 a** *obs* **:** to disorganize or cause to waver by a sudden violent attack **b** *obs* **:** to charge or assault suddenly and violently **:** ASSAIL **2 a :** to strike with surprise, terror, horror, or disgust **:** strongly affect **:** OFFEND, ASTONISH, SCANDALIZE ⟨the individual who may be ~*ed* by the expression of an unfamiliar or unpopular opinion —*Saturday Rev.*⟩ ⟨many audiences are ~*ed* by the sounds of new compositions —Goddard Lieberson⟩ **b :** to cause to undergo a physical or nervous shock **c :** to subject (the body or a body part) to the action of an electrical discharge so as to cause a more or less violent nervous and muscular response **3 a :** to cause to disappear or depart by or as if by a shock ⟨his sense of humor was ~*ed* out of him for the moment —Archibald Marshall⟩ **b :** to drive by or as if by a shock ⟨a way of ~*ing* the reader into realizing that both sides . . . have gone all-out in their savagery —Bruce Bliven b. 1916⟩ ~ *vi* **1 :** to meet with a shock **:** come together in violent encounter **:** COLLIDE ⟨her teeth ~*ed* against each other —Dorothy Baker⟩ **2 :** to cause or arouse astonishment, offense, horror, or fear ⟨the subject is meant to ~ rather than attract —Herbert Read⟩

⁵shock \"\ *n* -s [perh. fr. ¹*shock*] **1** *or* **shock dog :** a dog with long coarse hair **2 :** a thick bushy mass ⟨an untidy ~ of thick gray hair —Hamilton Basso⟩

⁶shock \"\ *adj* **:** BUSHY, SHAGGY ⟨the ~ headdress of hair besmeared with mutton fat —C.G.Seligman⟩

⁷shock \"\ *chiefly dial var of* SHUCK

⁸shock \"\ *n* -s [origin unknown] **:** a silvered pane of window glass ⟨~ mirror⟩

shock absorbent watch *n* [³*shock*] **:** a wristwatch having the balance pivot jewel bearings set into resilient housings to decrease the possibility of breakage due to a fall or shock

shock absorber *n* **1 :** any of several devices for absorbing the energy of sudden impulses or shocks: as **a :** a spring, pneumatic, or hydraulic device used on an automobile in addition to the regular springs to lessen the shocks from unevenness of the road **b :** a spring or damped elastic device interposed between the wheels, floats, or tail skid and the rest of an airplane to secure resiliency in landing and taxiing **2 :** something that acts as a buffer esp. against disturbing economic forces ⟨the private consumption sector and especially agriculture serve as *shock absorbers* with reference to labor —Naum Jasny⟩

shock bump *n* **:** an earth tremor resulting from the sudden collapse of rock over a subsidence cavity and usu. causing a heavy blow to a mine roof

shock cord *n* **:** a cord made of rubber strands bound in woven casing and used as landing shock absorbers on small airplanes, as supports for rotor blades, and as a tow for launching gliders

shock damper *n, Brit* **:** SHOCK ABSORBER

shock disease *n* [³*shock*] **:** an acute fatal hypoglycemia of wild hares and rabbits associated with degenerative changes of the liver and believed to be a factor in cyclic decline of the animals

shocked *past of* SHOCK

¹shock·er \ˈshäkə(r)\ *n* -s [⁴*shock* + *-er*] **1 a :** one that shocks **:** something horrifying, startling, astonishing, frightening, or offensive ⟨our verbal taboos are being shattered by the hundred, with the resulting ~*s* sometimes disguised by giving only initials —D.W.Maurer⟩ **b :** a work of fiction or drama designed to shock the moral sensibilities esp. by the use of sordid detail or to hold interest by the use of a high proportion of suspense, intrigue or sensational matter (as crime or violence) ⟨classy ~*s* of the hard-boiled school —C.J.Rolo⟩ — compare DREADFUL **2 :** an instrument for producing an electric shock

²shocker \"\ *n* -s [²*shock* + *-er*] **:** one that puts grain into shocks

shock excitation *n* [³*shock*] **:** IMPULSE EXCITATION

shock-head \ˈ=,=\ *n* [⁶*shock*] **:** a head with a shock of hair

¹shocking *adj* [fr. pres. part. of ⁴*shock*] **1 :** causing to shake or tremble **:** STUNNING ⟨repeated ~ blows to the head —W.A.D. Anderson⟩ **2 :** extremely startling and offensive **:** novel and distasteful through being or appearing immoral, horrifying, immoderate, reprehensible ⟨persons of old-fashioned views might regard this as a very ~ admission —Rebecca West⟩ ⟨solecism of this kind . . . would have seemed a ~ thing to so accurate a scholar —L.P.Smith⟩ **3 :** having a color tone that is striking, vivid, bright, or intense ⟨~ pink⟩ **syn** see FEARFUL

²shocking \"\ *adv* **:** SHOCKINGLY ⟨a ~ bad orator and altogether deficient in humanity —Norman Douglas⟩

shock·ing·ly *adv* **:** in a shocking manner

shock·ing·ness *n* -ES **:** the quality or state of being shocking

shock mount *n* [³*shock*] **:** a resilient mounting as for delicate instruments to absorb shock

shocks *pl of* SHOCK, *pres 3d sing of* SHOCK

shock stall *n* **:** a stall induced by separation of flow caused by pressure changes resulting from shock waves

shock therapy *or* **shock treatment** *n* **:** the treatment of mental disorder by the artificial induction of coma or convulsions through use of drugs or electricity

shock troops *n pl* **:** troops esp. suited and chosen for offensive work because of their high morale, training, and discipline

shock tube *n* **:** a long closed tube of uniform cross section used for studying the transient effects of a shock wave usu. produced when a diaphragm dividing the tube into two chambers containing gas at different pressures is ruptured

shock wave *n* **1 :** BLAST 5b **2 :** a compressional wave formed whenever the speed of a body relative to a medium exceeds that at which the medium can transmit sound and characterized by a disturbed region of small but finite thickness within which very abrupt changes occur in the pressure, density, and velocity of the medium ⟨passage of a *shock wave* (from an explosion . . . or from the leading wing edge of a supersonic airplane) through a compressible fluid such as air —*Fortune*⟩

shod \ˈshäd\ *adj* [ME, fr. past part. of *shoen* to shoe — more at SHOE] **1 a :** wearing shoes **b :** equipped with tires **2 :** furnished or equipped with a shoe (as of metal) — often used in combination

shodden *adj* [fr. past part. of ²*shoe*] *dial* **:** SHOD

shod·di·ly \ˈshädᵊlē, -dəlē\ *adv* **:** in a shoddy manner

shod·di·ness \-dēnəs\ *n* -ES **:** the quality or state of being shoddy

¹shod·dy \ˈshädē, -di\ *n* -ES [origin unknown] **1 a :** wool of better quality and longer staple than mungo reclaimed from unfelted materials, rags, or waste and usu. mixed with new wool before reusing **b :** a fabric often of inferior quality manufactured in whole or in part from reclaimed wool (as shoddy) **2 a :** refuse, inferior, imitation, or pretentiously vulgar articles or matter ⟨cheap ~ for oak and mahogany —H.J.Massingham⟩ ⟨show up a younger generation of writers as the blunted manufacturers of ~ they are —*Times Lit. Supp.*⟩ **b :** a pretentious vulgarity in way of life esp. from the exploitation of newly or underhandedly acquired wealth ⟨preserved itself inviolate from respectability and ~ and the invasions of twentieth-century commonplaceness —Robert Lynd⟩ **3 :** reclaimed rubber

²shoddy \"\ *adj* -ER/-EST **1 :** made wholly or in part of shoddy ⟨~ cloth⟩ ⟨a ~ uniform⟩ **2 a :** falsely claiming moral worth and social status ⟨~ aristocracy⟩ **b :** cheaply imitative or vulgarly pretentious ⟨antique metalware is sold here as well as the *shoddiest* machine-made articles —*Amer. Guide Series: N.Y. City*⟩ ⟨a great deal of distinctly ~ veneered furniture was turned out —S.F.Horn⟩ **c :** employing, consisting of, or made by hasty, scamping, or unsound methods ⟨had done as cheap and ~ a job as he could do —Thomas Wolfe⟩ ⟨the construction of the shattered dam had been ~ —Louis Bromfield⟩ **d :** appearing sordid or squalid esp. through wear or use **:** SHABBY, RUN-DOWN ⟨sitting on a couch in the ~ hotel lobby —Knox Burger⟩ ⟨~ second-hand clothes⟩ **e :** vaguely reprehensible **:** DISREPUTABLE ⟨a ~ military adventurer had plunged his country into civil war —Anthony West⟩ ⟨the whole ~ fraud was disclosed —R.L.Riggs⟩

shode *var of* SHOAD

sho·der \ˈshōdə(r)\ *n* -s [modif. of F *chauderet, chaudret,* alter. of *chaucheret,* fr. obs. *chaucher* to press, fr. L *calcare* to tread on, trample, press, fr. *calc-, calx* heel — more at CALK] **:** a package of goldbeater's skins in which gold leaf is beaten the second time — compare ²CUTCH

¹shoe \ˈshü\ *n, pl* **shoes** \-üz\ *often attrib* [ME *sho, shoo,* fr. OE *scōh;* akin to OHG *scuoh* shoe, ON *skōr,* Goth *skohs* shoe, OE *hȳd* hide, skin — more at HIDE] **1 a :** an outer covering for the human foot usu. made of leather, with a thick or stiff sole and an attached heel: as (1) **:** an outer foot covering reaching to the ankle or thereabouts (2) **:** a low-cut outer foot covering — compare BOOT, OXFORD (3) **:** a foot covering with a leather sole and heel and an upper covering at least the instep for wear outdoors — compare OVERSHOE, SLIPPER **b :** a metal plate or rim usu. made of iron and nailed to the hoof of an animal to protect it from injury or to assist it in obtaining a foothold; *specif* **:** HORSESHOE **2 :** an object or device placed at the bottom, foot, or end of or beneath an object: as **a :** a socket or ferrule of iron or other material to protect the point of a wooden pile, pole, cane, or staff **b :** a metal socket or plate to take a thrust (as of a strut, rafter, or jack) **c :** a band of iron or steel or a slip of wood fastened to the bottom of the runner of a vehicle (as a sleigh) that slides on the snow or ice **d :** the removable iron or steel tip of a stamp in a set of stamps for crushing ore **e :** a steel cutting edge attached to the bottom of a caisson or lining in sinking a drop shaft **f :** the part of a bridge supporting the superstructure and bearing on a bearing plate or roller nest upon the supporting pier or abutment **g :** a small molding or strip placed in the angle between a baseboard and the floor of a room **h** (1) **:** an often disk-shaped turned or shaped termination on furniture legs used esp. during the 17th and early 18th centuries (2) **:** a metal, glass, or rubber cap or cup placed upon or under a furniture leg for protection or ornament **i :** a strong piece of paper or paperboard upon which standing type matter is sometimes placed for storage **j :** a wooden block or other device placed under an object to steady or support it or provide traction ⟨ladder ~⟩ **k :** a ground plate that forms or is attached to a link of a traction belt on a caterpillar tractor **3 shoes** *pl* **:** economic, social, or hierarchical status or position or a vantage point for regarding events or circumstances in a particular perspective ⟨next in line of succession for my boss's ~*s* —F.S.Mitchell⟩ — usu. used in such phrases as *in another's shoes* ⟨had never taken even two minutes to try to put himself in a woman's ~*s* —Louis Auchincloss⟩ **4 :** a device serving as a trough or spout: as **a :** a trough or spout for conveying grain from a hopper to the eye of a millstone **b :** a trough-shaped or spout-shaped member at the foot of a water leader that directs the water outward **c :** an inclined trough in an ore-crushing mill to secure steady feeding **5 :** a device covering or jacketing an object (as for protection) ⟨propeller ~*s* for ice protection —*Flying*⟩: as **a :** a steel strip on the bottom of the keel of a boat **b :** TIRE **6 :** a gold or usu. silver ingot suggestive of a Chinese shoe in shape formerly used in China as money **:** a piece of sycee **7 :** a device that retards, stops, or controls the motion of an object ⟨the friction ~*s* engage the inner surface of the flywheel —*Mech. Engineering*⟩ ⟨clutch ~⟩: as **a :** DRAG 3a(2) **b :** the part of a brake that presses on the wheel of a wagon or other vehicle to retard its motion **c :** one of usu. two metal pieces lined with a frictional material that press upon a brake drum to retard its motion — see HYDRAULIC BRAKE illustration **8 :** any of various devices, members, or attachments that are inserted in or run along a track, channel, or groove to guide a movement, provide a contact or friction grip, or protect against wear, damage, or slipping: as **a :** a runner in the sash channel of a window or at the base of a door (as a metal fire door) **b :** the sliding contact member of a current collector ⟨a third-rail ~ of a subway car⟩ **c :** GIB 1 **d :** a track or pad that positions or otherwise influences (as by friction) the movement of a strip of photographic film or paper in its passage through a projector (as a camera or printer) **9 :** a wedge-shaped furrow opener used on some grain drills and on corn and cotton planters **10 :** the end of a dynamo pole usu. curved to conform to the arc of the armature and shaped to distribute the flux peripherally **11 :** a flat metal plate in a pressing machine or a concave metal plate in a mangle that is usu. heated by electricity and pressed against the buck or roller **12 :** a case designed to hold three or more packs of cards so that the top card may be pulled out singly and used in baccarat or chemin de fer

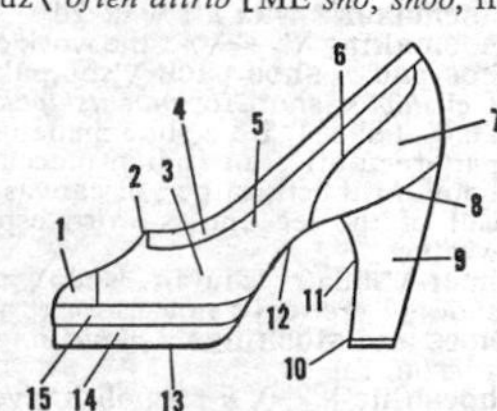

parts of shoe 1a: *1* tip, *2* throat, *3* vamp, *4* collar, *5* arch, *6* foxing, *7* quarter, *8* heel seat, *9* heel, *10* top lift, *11* breasting, *12* shank, *13* sole, *14* platform, *15* mudguard

²shoe \"\ *vt* **shod** \ˈshäd\ *also* **shoed; shod** \ˈshäd\ *also* **shoed** \ˈshüd\ *or* **shod·den** \ˈshädᵊn\ **shoeing; shoes** [ME *shoen, shooen,* fr. OE *scōgian, scōgan, scōan,* fr. *scōh,* n.] **1 :** to put a shoe on **:** furnish with a shoe ⟨who will ~ your pretty little foot⟩ ⟨mules were much easier *shod* —W.F.Harris⟩ **2 :** to cover for protection, strength, or ornament with harder or handsomer material ⟨a pole *shod* with an iron tip —K.A. Henderson⟩ **3 :** to cover with or as if with a shoe ⟨fragments of hard rock with which the glacier was *shod* —W.J.Miller⟩ **4 :** to fit a tire to (a wheel of a vehicle)

shoebill *also* **shoebird** \ˈ=,=\ *n* **:** a large wading bird (*Balaeniceps rex*) that is related to the storks and herons, inhabits the valley of the White Nile, is chiefly ashy gray with blackish wings and tail, and has a much widened bill

shoeblack \ˈ=,=\ *n* [¹*shoe* + *black* (v.)] **:** BOOTBLACK

shoeblack plant *n* **:** CHINA ROSE 2

shoe block *n* **:** a block with two sheaves one above the other and at right angles to each other

shoe board *n* **:** a hard board of highly compressed wood pulp and leather clippings used in making soles and heels of shoes

shoe boil *n* **:** a soft swelling on the elbow of a horse caused by irritation (as from bruising in lying or by clipping with a heel calk)

shoe bolt *n* **:** a bolt with a long unslotted countersunk head for fastening a shoe on a sleigh runner

shoe button *n* **:** an often black, glossy, and globe-shaped button used in fastening a shoe

shoe-button spider *n* **:** BLACK WIDOW

shoecraft \ˈ=,=\ *n* **:** the art of designing and making shoes

shoe drill *n* **:** a grain drill with shoe furrow openers

shoeflower \ˈ=,=\ *n* **:** CHINA ROSE 2

¹shoehorn \'⸗,⸗\ *n* [¹*shoe* + *horn*] **:** a curved piece (as of horn, wood, or metal) to aid in slipping on a shoe

²shoehorn \"\ *vt* **1 :** to force (something unwanted) to be accepted or admitted **:** FOIST ⟨tried to ~ the cooperative societies . . . into the international alliance —*Time*⟩ **2 :** to force into a small, narrow, or insufficient space **:** SQUEEZE ⟨papa, mama and children . . . would be ~*ed* into the family car —Rafe Gibbs⟩

shoehorn

shoe·ing \'shüiŋ, -üēŋ\ *n* -s [ME *shoing;* partly fr. gerund of *shoen, shooen* to shoe; partly fr. *sho, shoo* shoe + *-ing* — more at SHOE] **1 :** the act of one who shoes **2 a :** covering for the feet **:** SHOES **b :** a protective or supporting covering or band ⟨the ~ of the runner —J.S.Mutch⟩

shoeing-horn \'⸗⸗,⸗\ *n* [ME *schoynge horne*] **1 :** SHOEHORN **2** *archaic* **:** APPETIZER **3 a :** something that facilitates a transaction or passage ⟨the best *shoeing-horn* for drawing on a sound sleep —Sir Walter Scott⟩ **b** *archaic* **:** someone that acts for another (as a go-between or decoy)

shoeingsmith \'⸗⸗,⸗\ *n* **:** FARRIER

shoelace \'⸗,⸗\ *n* **:** a thin cord or strip of material (as of fabric) used for lacing together the sides of a shoe upper over the arch

shoe·less \'shüləs\ *adj* **:** having no shoe

shoemake \'⸗,⸗\ *n* -s [by folk etymology fr. *sumac*] **:** SUMAC; *esp* **:** SMOOTH SUMAC

shoemaker \'⸗,⸗⸗\ *n* [ME *shomaker,* fr. *sho* shoe + *maker*] **1 a :** one that makes shoes **b :** a shopkeeper whose business is selling or repairing shoes **2 a :** THREADFISH **b :** RAINBOW RUNNER

shoemaker's wax *n* **:** WAX 2d

shoemaking \'⸗,⸗⸗\ *n* **:** the work or occupation of a shoemaker

shoe·pac *or* **shoe·pack** \'shü,pak\ *n* -s [by folk etymology fr. Del *shipak,* short for *machtshipak,* fr. *machtshi* bad + *paku,* a kind of shoe] **1 :** a shoe made usu. of oil-tanned leather and patterned after an Indian moccasin **2 :** a waterproof laced boot of rubber, leather, or canvas that usu. extends well up the calf of the leg and is worn esp. over heavy socks in cold weather

shoer \'shüə(r) 'shü(ə)r, 'shüə\ *n* -s [ME *schoere,* fr. *shoen* to shoe + *-ere* -er] **:** HORSESHOER

shoes and stockings *n pl but sing or pl in constr* **:** BIRD'S-FOOT TREFOIL 1a

shoeshine \'⸗,⸗\ *n* **:** a polish given to shoes

shoespoon \'⸗,⸗\ *n* **:** SHOEHORN

shoe stone *n* **1 :** a whetstone used by shoemakers and other workers in leather **2 :** a sharp-gritted sandstone used esp. for making shoe stones

¹shoestring \'⸗,⸗\ *n* [¹*shoe* + *string*] **1 :** SHOELACE **2** [so called fr. shoestrings' being a typical item sold by itinerant vendors] **:** a small sum of money **:** capital inadequate or barely adequate to the needs of a transaction ⟨many eminently successful men started business on a ~ —J.R.Sprague⟩ **3 a :** TRUMPET CREEPER **b :** the long slender tough root of a leadplant (*Amorpha canescens*) **4** *also* **shoestring disease :** a plant disease that is characterized by slender growth of leaves; *esp* **:** a disease of tomatoes caused by the cucumber mosaic virus **5 :** SHOESTRING FUNGUS

²shoestring \"\ *adj* **1 :** narrow and elongated as a shoestring ⟨~ tie⟩ **2 a :** operating on, accomplished with, or consisting of little or no capital or backing ⟨efforts of a ~ producer to raise money for a theatrical venture —Henry Hewes⟩ ⟨~ financing —H.E.Hoagland⟩ **b :** small in conception, operation, or scope **:** MINOR, PETTY ⟨in amphibious warfare . . . the first landings are of a ~ character compared with the power the enemy might assemble —W.V.Pratt⟩

shoestring catch *n* **:** a catch (as in baseball) made while running and with the hands held close to the ground

shoestring district *n* **:** an election district gerrymandered into a long narrow strip

shoestringer \'⸗,⸗⸗\ *n* **:** a person that operates on a shoestring ⟨couldn't afford the performers and studios needed for . . . standard recorded fare, but he was a resourceful ~ —Daniel Lang⟩

shoestring fern *n* **:** GRASS FERN

shoestring fungus *n* **:** a fungus (esp. *Armillaria mellea*) that forms brown stringy rhizomorphs and causes destructive rot of the roots of trees (as apples or maples)

shoestring potato *n* **:** a long slender strip cut from a raw potato and fried in deep fat — usu. used in pl.

shoestring root rot *n* **:** a root rot disease of trees caused by the shoestring fungus

shoestring sand *or* **shoestring sandstone** *n* **:** a very long narrow body of sand or sandstone in the midst of mud or shale

shoestring tackle *n* **:** a football tackle made at or near the ankles

shoe tree *n* **1 :** a foot-shaped form over which a completed shoe is placed for finishing and dressing the upper **2 :** a foot-shaped device for inserting in a shoe to preserve its shape

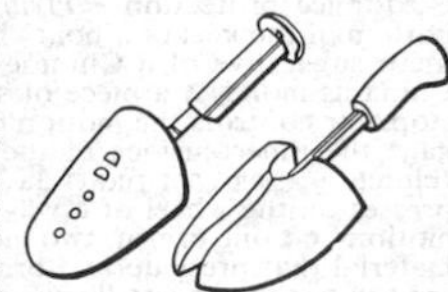

shoe trees 2

sho·far *also* **sho·phar** \'shō,fär, -ōfər\ *n, pl* **shof·roth** *also* **shoph·roth** \shō'frōt(h)\ [Heb *shōphār*] **:** a ram's horn blown as a trumpet by the ancient Hebrews as a signal in battle and in high religious observances and used at present in synagogues before and during Rosh Hashanah and at the conclusion of Yom Kippur

¹shog \'shäg\ *vb* **shogged; shogged; shogging; shogs** [ME *shoggen;* prob. akin to MD *schocken* to shake, jolt — more at SHOCK (disorganize)] *vt* **1** *chiefly dial* **:** JOLT, SHAKE, JOSTLE **2** *chiefly dial* **:** to push aside **:** SHOVE **3** *chiefly dial* **:** RACK 6 ~ *vi, chiefly dial* **:** to move along

²shog \"\ *n* -s *chiefly dial* **:** SHAKE, JOG

sho·ga·ol \'shōgə,ōl, -,ōl\ *n* -s [ISV *shoga-* (fr. Jap *shōga* ginger) + *-ol*] **:** a liquid unsaturated phenolic ketone $C_{17}H_{24}O_3$ that constitutes one of the pungent principles of ginger and is synthesized by condensation of zingerone and hexanal

shog·gie \'shägi\ *vb* [¹*shog* + Sc *-ie,* freq. suffix] *chiefly Scot* **:** SWAY, SWING

shog·gle \'shägəl\ *vb* -ED/-ING/-S [freq. of ¹*shog*] **1** *dial Eng* **:** JOGGLE **2** *dial Eng* **:** DANGLE

shog·gly \-g(ə)lē\ *adj* [*shoggle* + *-y*] *chiefly dial* **:** LOOSE, SHAKY

sho·gi \'shōgē\ *n* -s [Jap *shōgi*] **:** Japanese chess played on a board of 81 squares with 40 pieces to the set

sho·go·in turnip \'shōgəwən-\ *n* [*shogoin* of unknown origin] **:** a turnip that is prob. of Japanese origin and is cultivated chiefly for its green-topped leaves which are used as a potherb

sho·gun \'shō(,)gən\ *n* -s [Jap *shōgun* general, fr. Chin (Pek) *chiang⁴ chün¹*] **:** a military governor of Japan before the mid-19th century revolution with power exceeding the emperor's — called also *tycoon*

sho·gun·ate \'shōgənət, -,nāt\ *n* -s **:** the office, dignity, or government of a shogun

sho·het *or* **sho·chet** \'shōkət\ *n, pl* **sho·he·tim** *or* **sho·che·tim** \-kətēm\ *or* **shoch·tim** \-ktēm\ *also* **shohets** *or* **sho·chets** \-kəts\ *or* **sho·ha·tim** \-kətēm\ [Heb *shōḥēṭ* slaughterer] **:** a person officially licensed by rabbinic authority as slaughterer of animals and poultry for use as food in accordance with Jewish laws

sho·ji \'shōjē\ *or* **shoji screen** *n, pl* **shoji** *also* **shojis** [Jap *shōji*] **:** a paper screen serving as a wall, partition, or sliding door

sho·la·pur \'shōlə'pù(ə)r\ *adj, usu cap* [fr. *Sholapur,* India] **:** of or from the city of Sholapur, India **:** of the kind or style prevalent in Sholapur

shole \'shōl\ *n* -s [origin unknown] **:** a plank or plate placed beneath an object (as a shore) to give increased bearing surface or to act as a protection

sholom *var of* SHALOM

sho·mer \'shō,mer\ *n, pl* **shom·rim** \-ōmrəm\ [Heb *shōmēr,* fr. *shēmōr* to watch] **:** GUARDIAN, WATCHMAN; *specif* **:** a mounted guard of the Palestinian Jewish colonies

shom pen \'shäm'pen\ *n, pl* **shom pen** *usu cap S&P* **1 :** a subdivision of the Nicobarese of Great Nicobar Island **2 :** a member of the Shom Pen people

sho·na \'shänə, 'shōnə\ *n, pl* **shona** *or* **shonas** *usu cap* **1 a :** a group of Bantu peoples of eastern Rhodesia south of the Zambesi river **b :** a member of any of the Shona peoples **2 a :** a Bantu language or group of closely related languages used by the Shona peoples **3 :** a written language, designed consciously to serve as a literary medium for the whole Shona group — called also *Union Shona*

shone [ME *shoon,* fr. OE *scān*] *past of* SHINE

sho·neen \shō'nēn, '⸗,⸗\ *n* -s [IrGael *seoinín,* dim. of *Seon* John, fr. E *John*] *Irish* **:** a would-be gentleman who puts on pretentious airs

shon·gop·o·vi \(,)shəŋ'gäpəvē\ *n, pl* **shongopovi** *or* **shongopovis** *usu cap* **1 :** a Shoshonean people occupying a pueblo in northeastern Arizona **2 :** a member of the Shongopovi people

shon·kin·ite \'shäŋkə,nīt\ *n* -s [*Shonkin* (Highwood mountains, Montana), its locality + E *-ite*] **:** a dark granular igneous rock consisting of augite with subordinate orthoclase and smaller amounts of olivine, biotite, nephelite, sodalite, and plagioclase

¹shoo \'shü\ *interj* [ME *schowe*] — used in frightening away an animal (as a hen)

²shoo \"\ *vb* -ED/-ING/-S *vt* **1 :** to scare or drive away (as birds) by or in the manner of one crying *shoo* ⟨~*ing* out a parcel of hens —Ida Treat⟩ ⟨like a fly . . . settling whenever the hand ceased to ~ it away —Robert DeVries⟩ **2 a :** to send or cause to move away or along esp. by urging gently with words or gestures suggestive of the shooing of fowls ⟨were ~*ing* the passengers off a country bus —Mollie Panter-Downes⟩ ⟨~*ed* them off for their walk —Ann Bridge⟩ **b :** to drive out **:** chase away **:** DISPEL ⟨softened her, ~*ing* away the madness —Adria L. Langley⟩ ⟨~ away the memory —D.B.Chidsey⟩ ~ *vi* **1 :** to make the sounds or gestures of one shooing fowls ⟨~*ing* at them with her umbrella —Elizabeth Taylor⟩ **2 :** to go away or along at or as if at the cry of *shoo* ⟨the fly ~*ed* —Danforth Ross⟩

shood *or* **shude** \'shüd\ *n* -s [akin to MLG *schōde* covering, pod, OHG *scōta,* OE *hȳd* skin, hide — more at HIDE] **1** *dial Eng* **:** the husk of oats after threshing **2 :** rice husks or similar refuse used in adulterating linseed cake

shoofly \'⸗,⸗\ *n* [¹*shoo* + *fly*] **1 :** a child's rocker having the seat built on or usu. between supports representing an animal figure (as of a duck or swans) ⟨a swan ~⟩ ⟨a ~ hobby horse⟩ **2 a :** a wild indigo (*Baptisia tinctoria*) **b :** FLOWER-OF-AN-HOUR **c :** APPLE OF PERU **3 a :** a temporary track laid on the ground or on cribwork at one side of a railroad line to permit trains to pass an obstruction in that line **b :** a temporary road (as an access road) used during completion of a construction project **4 a :** a policeman usu. in plain clothes detailed to watch or investigate other policemen ⟨~ squad⟩ **b :** a foreman in the postal service who checks on carriers and drivers **5 :** a long-fingered device in some cylinder presses for freeing the printed sheet from the cylinder for delivery

shoofly pie *also* **shoofly cake** *n* [¹*shoo* + *fly*] **:** a sticky dessert made by pouring a mixture of molasses, hot water, and soda into a pastry-lined pan, adding crumbs made by mixing flour, butter, and sugar, and baking till the molasses bubbles up through the layer of crumbs in dark syrupy veins

shoog·le \'shügəl\ *var of* SHOGGLE

shoo–in \'⸗,⸗\ *n* -s [fr. *shoo in,* v.] **:** one that is a certain and easy winner (as among candidates for an office or contestants in a race) **:** one that is bound to be successful **:** SURE THING ⟨figures as a *shoo-in* again⟩ ⟨seems to be a *shoo-in* for a second term —*Newsweek*⟩ ⟨ants, another supposed *shoo-in* to supplant mankind —*New Yorker*⟩

¹shook [ME *shook* (past), fr. OE *scōc*] *past or chiefly dial past part of* SHAKE

²shook \'shùk\ *n* -s [origin unknown] **1 a :** a set of staves and headings for one hogshead, cask, or barrel trimmed and bound together compactly **b** (1) **:** a bundle or set of tops, bottoms, sides, and ends of boxes ready to be put together (2) **:** a veneer of wood out of which boxes (as wire-bound boxes) are made **c :** the parts of a piece of house furniture (as a bedstead) packed together **2 :** a shock of sheaves ⟨broad fields covered with wheat in ~*s* —F.M.Ford⟩ ⟨rows of wigwam-shaped ~*s* —John Dos Passos⟩

³shook \"\ *vt* -ED/-ING/-S **:** to pack (as staves) in a shook

s hook *n, cap S* **:** an S-shaped hook

shook-up \'⸗'⸗\ *also* **shook** *adj* [*shook-up* fr. *shook up,* chiefly dial. past part. of *shake up; shook* fr. chiefly dial. past part. of *shake*] **:** SHAKEN; *esp* **:** suffering under or showing the effects of great emotional disturbance or disorganization **:** UNNERVED ⟨a *shook-up* generation⟩ ⟨had had it — he was *shook-up*⟩

S hooks

¹shool \'shül\ *vi* -ED/-ING/-S [origin unknown] **1** *chiefly dial* **:** to drag or scrape along **:** SHAMBLE, SHUFFLE **2 :** to loaf or idle about begging **:** LOITER, SAUNTER

²shool \"\ *dial var of* SHOVEL

shoon \'shün\ *chiefly dial pl of* SHOE

shoop \'shüp\ *n* -s [ME *schowpe,* of Scand origin; akin to Norw dial. *hjupa* hip of a rose — more at HIP] *dial Eng* **:** HIP

shoor \'shù(ə)r\ *chiefly Scot var of* SHOWER

shoos *pres 3d sing of* SHOO

shoosh \'shùsh\ *vt* -ED/-ING/-ES [imit.] **:** SHUSH ⟨would . . . put his finger to his lips and ~ her right back —William Humphrey⟩

¹shoot \'shüt, *usu* -üd.+V\ *vb* **shot; shot** \'shät, *usu* -äd.+V\ *also chiefly dial* **shot·ten** \'shät³n\ **shooting; shoots** [ME *sheten, shoten, shuten,* fr. OE *scēotan;* akin to OHG *skiozzan* to shoot, ON *skjōta* to shoot, Crimean Goth *schieten* to shoot an arrow, Lith *skudrus* quick, agile, Skt *codati* he incites, *skundate* he hurries] *vt* **1 a** (1) **:** to let fly or cause to be driven forward with force (as an arrow, bolt, stone, bullet) from a bow, sling, or similar device or from a firearm ⟨~ an arrow into the air⟩ ⟨~ six bullets after a fleeing burglar⟩ ⟨were ~*ing* off live ammunition⟩ (2) *of a device* **:** to send forth or be capable of sending forth ⟨automatically ~*s* one bullet per second⟩ ⟨~ a line to a ship for hauling in a breeches buoy⟩; *use* or accommodate as its proper charge or missile ⟨a target pistol that ~*s* lead pellets⟩ ⟨this bow ~*s* standard arrows⟩ (3) **:** to cause a missile to be driven forth from (as a bow, sling, gun) **:** DISCHARGE ⟨expert at ~*ing* a pistol⟩ — often used with *off* ⟨was a grown man when he first *shot* off a gun⟩ ⟨the sound of rifles being *shot off*⟩; *also* **:** to set off the explosive charge in (a gun) ⟨~*ing* pistols loaded with blank cartridges⟩ **b :** to send forth in a manner suggestive esp. in suddenness or intensity of one discharging a missile from a bow or gun **:** DART ⟨the porcupine . . . does not, as commonly supposed, ~ his spines at an enemy —*Amer. Guide Series: Minn.*⟩ ⟨*shot* uneasy glances over their shoulders —Kenneth Roberts⟩ ⟨*shot* a long-toothed smile —Earle Birney⟩ ⟨*shot* at him a look of amazement⟩ **c :** to let fly or send forth in a manner suggestive esp. in the course taken of the flight of something shot: as (1) **:** to let fly (as a marble, a pellet) by propelling from the forefinger with the thumb ⟨*shot* a spitball across the room⟩ (2) **:** to send forth or drive along by a finger-tip flicked across the thumb ⟨*shot* a crumb off his sleeve⟩ ⟨~ a poker chip across a table⟩ (3) **:** to send forth (as a ball or puck) in a game esp. toward or at a particular objective (as a goal, net, pocket, another player) by propelling with the hands or feet or with an implement ⟨~*ing* fouls with his left hand —Stanley Frank⟩ ⟨swung his mallet and *shot* the ball into the goal⟩ ⟨~ the eight ball into the side pocket⟩ ⟨scooped up the ball and *shot* it to second⟩; *also* **:** to score by so doing ⟨~ a basket⟩ ⟨~ the winning goal⟩ ⟨*shot* a hole in one⟩ ⟨~*s* an 80 on the home links⟩ **2 a :** to strike with something shot **:** hit with a missile esp. from a bow or gun; *esp* **:** to wound or kill with a missile discharged from a firearm ⟨~ a rabbit⟩ ⟨try to ~ a fleeing burglar⟩ ⟨was accidentally *shot*⟩ ⟨*shot* him dead⟩ ⟨*shot* him through the heart⟩ ⟨*shot* himself in the leg⟩ **b** (1) **:** to remove or destroy by means of something shot or by shooting ⟨set about ~*ing* it to bits⟩ ⟨had *shot* every building into rubble⟩ — often used with *away, off, out* ⟨*shot* away her masts⟩ ⟨had his hand *shot* off⟩ ⟨~ off the lock⟩ ⟨~ every window in the building out⟩ ⟨*shot* out the light⟩ (2) **:** to destroy as completely as something shot to pieces **:** RUIN, WRECK ⟨an occasional ~*ing* of the mood is a minor complaint of modern U.S. poets —*Reporter*⟩ ⟨a delicate mechanism *shot* by prolonged misuse⟩ **:** EXPLODE ⟨seems to ~ the theory that she was specially detailed to work on me —L.C.Stevens⟩ **c :** to put to death by a missile discharged from a firearm esp. as a penalty ⟨was sentenced to be *shot* as a spy⟩ ⟨that scoundrel ought to be taken out and *shot*⟩ ⟨we don't ~ traitors, we hang them⟩ **d** (1) **:** to engage in the practice of killing (as birds, game) with firearms esp. as a sport ⟨goes south every year to ~ quail⟩ ⟨preferred ~*ing* small game⟩ (2) **:** to do shooting for game in or on **:** hunt over ⟨had *shot* the surrounding country many times⟩ ⟨~ a tract of woodland⟩ ⟨allowed no one to ~ his land⟩ **3 a :** to push or slide (as the bolt of a door or a lock) into or out of a fastening ⟨slammed the iron door and *shot* the bolts —R.M.Stern⟩ ⟨a few minutes manipulation with a bunch of skeleton keys sufficed to ~ back the bolt —F.W.Crofts⟩ **b :** to pass (a shuttle or filling thread) through the warp threads in weaving **4 a :** to throw or cast suddenly esp. with force **:** FLING, PRECIPITATE ⟨*shot* his rider over his head⟩ ⟨the pilot must be *shot* from his cockpit to clear the tail —*Time*⟩ ⟨grabbed the troublemakers and *shot* them out the door⟩ **b :** to discharge, dump, or empty esp. by overturning, upending, or directing into a slide ⟨~ the flour into the bins⟩ ⟨*shot* 10 tons of coal through the cellar window⟩ ⟨a pit into which the dead carts had nightly *shot* corpses by scores —T.B. Macaulay⟩ **c :** to deal with or dispose of as if throwing away or casting aside: as (1) **:** to toss or thrust hurriedly or carelessly ⟨~ the dishes into the sink⟩ ⟨*shot* the letter under the blotter as the door opened⟩ ⟨*shot* his hat and coat into the closet and dashed upstairs⟩ (2) *slang* **:** to get rid of **:** give up **:** DISCARD, QUIT (3) **:** to spend esp. extravagantly ⟨~ 1000 francs on a dinner for four —*Sat. Eve. Post*⟩ **:** use up **:** EXHAUST ⟨had *shot* his roll⟩ **d :** to throw out (dice) for inspection esp. in craps **:** CAST; *also* **:** to place or offer (a bet) on the result of such casting ⟨~ five dollars⟩ **e** *of a crab or lobster* **:** to drop or cast off (a limb) **5 a :** to push or thrust forward **:** stick out **:** PROJECT, PROTRUDE ⟨*shot* his finger at my father's nose —Alan Harrington⟩ — usu. used with *out* ⟨~ out a hand in greeting⟩ ⟨tiny lizards ~*ing* out their tongues⟩ ⟨weather had warped and separated some of the clapboards, ~*ing* the nails —Thomas Williams⟩ **b :** to put forth (a growth) **:** send out **:** EXTRUDE — usu. used with *out* or *forth* ⟨plants ~*ing* out buds⟩ ⟨~ out long thin hairs that act not only as organs of defense but as anchors —W.E.Swinton⟩ ⟨*shot* forth a thick growth of new branches⟩ **6 a** (1) **:** to utter (as words, sounds) rapidly or suddenly or with force ⟨his stomach tightened as he heard . . . ~ the next question —Erle Stanley Gardner⟩ ⟨*shot* out some angry words⟩ ⟨*shot* back a simple and satisfactory answer instantly —J.D.Hart⟩ ⟨*shot* everything out in one sentence⟩ ⟨*shot* out a snort of disbelief⟩ (2) **:** to engage in (aimless talk) often as a means of passing the time ⟨sit around ~*ing* the bull⟩ **b :** to emit (as light, flame, fumes) suddenly or rapidly ⟨the clanking tractor monster . . . ~*ing* smoke and fumes out of its belly —A.R.Williams⟩ ⟨a small window *shot* an oblique square of whiter light —Stephen Crane⟩ **c :** to eject or discharge from within the body ⟨spitting snakes that are popularly supposed to ~ their venom⟩ ⟨the archerfish can ~ a drop of water six feet or more —Bill Beatty⟩ ⟨stepped to the rail and *shot* a stream of tobacco juice down into the water —Erle Stanley Gardner⟩: (1) *obs* **:** to discharge (excreta) from the bowels; *also* **:** to empty (as the bowels, the body) of wastes (2) *of a fish* **:** to make a deposit of (spawn) (3) *of a spider* **:** to spin out (thread) (4) **:** VOMIT ⟨*shot* his lunch⟩ **7 a :** to place or bring in position by sudden motion (as in launching, casting anchor, seining) ⟨when the net is *shot* the wind is brought abeam —G.S.L. Clowes⟩ ⟨*shot* the trawl over the starboard side —Robert Gibbings⟩; *specif* **:** to release (a fishing line) in casting **b** (1) **:** to cause (as a boat) to move suddenly or swiftly forward (2) **:** to urge (as a horse) swiftly forward **c :** to send or carry in haste or swiftly (as on an errand or to a destination) **:** DISPATCH ⟨elevators ~ us to appointments on the fiftieth floor —Katharine F. Gerould⟩ ⟨a giant air bubble that *shot* him to the surface —*Newsweek*⟩ ⟨~ him over to that Tactical Air Force —J.G.Cozzens⟩ **d** *slang* **:** PASS ⟨~ the salt⟩ **8 a :** to variegate by or as if by sprinkling or intermingling color in streaks, flecks, or patches — usu. used with *with* and often with *through* ⟨hair was *shot* with gray —Will Cook⟩ ⟨the Holy War had *shot* her earliest landscapes with a valiant blood-red —Francis Hackett⟩ ⟨descending through clouds *shot* with sunlight —Rex Ingamells⟩ ⟨like night, ~ through with star beams —Esther Carlson⟩ ⟨a most accomplished work . . . *shot* through with the reflections of a thoughtful man of action —William Clark⟩ ⟨level tones . . . faintly *shot* with irony —E.M.Lustgarten⟩ **b :** to subject to admixture in excessive amounts or of an undesirable kind — usu. used with *through* ⟨interpretation . . . *shot* through with partisan feeling —V.L.Parrington⟩ ⟨is *shot* through with restraints of trade —T.W. Arnold⟩ **9 a :** to pass swiftly along by going down ⟨~*ing* terrific rapids⟩ or by or past ⟨the London cabdriver will not ~ the traffic lights —Charles Roetter⟩ or under ⟨*shot* bridge after bridge —C.S.Forester⟩ or over ⟨have *shot* this reef many times —Ernest Beaglehole⟩ **b :** to dash by (a competitor) in a race **10 :** to form by crystallization or similar physical change ⟨rock *shot* into figures⟩ **11 :** to plane (as the edge of a board) straight or true **:** fit by planing **12 :** to engage in a game of **:** PLAY ⟨~ craps⟩ ⟨~ marbles⟩ ⟨~ a round of golf⟩ ⟨~ a little pool with some of the boys⟩ **13 a :** to cause (as a blast) to explode **:** DETONATE, IGNITE **:** set off ⟨~ a charge of dynamite⟩ ⟨~*ing* off firecrackers⟩ **b :** to effect by blasting: (1) **:** to mine (coal) by blasting without previous undercutting or shearing ⟨~ off the solid⟩ (2) **:** to break up oil-retaining rock formation in (an oil well) by exploding nitroglycerin (3) **:** to remove (as a tree stump) by blasting **14 :** to expose to or make the subject of an operation employing a device suggestive of a bow or gun (as in being trained on a distant object by aiming or sighting or in propelling a charge): as **a :** to take the altitude of ⟨I pick up my sextant and ~ the star Arcturus —C.F.Blair⟩ ⟨the optical, hand-held sextant which has *shot* the sun for mariners for centuries —*Think*⟩ **b :** to photograph with a motion-picture camera or with a still camera **:** take a picture of **:** FILM ⟨were ~*ing* a western⟩ ⟨*shot* her from various angles⟩ ⟨had to ~ several scenes over again⟩ ⟨techniques for ~*ing* sports⟩ **c :** to give an injection to esp. for inoculation against disease ⟨had the children *shot* for diphtheria⟩ ⟨all calves TB and Bang tested and *shot* for shipment fever —*Nat'l Live Stock Producer*⟩ ~ *vi* **1 a :** to go or pass with the sudden swiftness of something shot **:** move rapidly and precipitately **:** dart or rush as if propelled or driven forcefully **:** precipitate oneself or be precipitated ⟨hoping to see a star ~⟩ — usu. used with an adverb or an adverbial phrase esp. of direction ⟨the bow twanged and the arrow *shot* across the narrow space —T.B.Costain⟩ ⟨far, far below him . . . *shot* the crystal Meramec —Winston Churchill⟩ ⟨the car had *shot* forward again with a jerk —Aldous Huxley⟩ ⟨elevator *shot* upward⟩ ⟨felt his feet ~ out from under him⟩ ⟨~ into the stream of traffic —Paul Bowles⟩ ⟨great fists, left and right, *shot* into his face —Arthur Morrison⟩ ⟨dragonflies *shot* at tangents through our rigging —H.M.Tomlinson⟩ ⟨bundles of sawn lumber should begin to ~ down the flume —S.E.White⟩ ⟨steam ~*s* from a high-pressure nozzle —Waldemar Kaempffert⟩ ⟨a wild idea *shot* into her mind —Ellen Glasgow⟩ ⟨businessman who had *shot* into new prominence —F.L. Allen⟩ ⟨~ out the door⟩ ⟨*shot* from his chair with a yell⟩ ⟨soon *shot* ahead of his classmates⟩ ⟨~*ing* to the surface to breathe⟩ ⟨*shot* back into the living room again —*Irish Digest*⟩ ⟨his horse, covered with foam, *shot* down the road over a bridge —H.E.Scudder⟩ ⟨in ~*s* a breathless towheaded twelve-year-old —Blanche E. Baughan⟩ ⟨*shot* along with a shriek that meant business —E.K.Brown⟩ ⟨the thought of that lifeless immobility *shot* through my joy with a kind of benumbing dread —P.E.More⟩ ⟨lifted his hand in parting and *shot* away —Marjorie K. Rawlings⟩ ⟨river ~*s* over the cliffs in a dazzling waterfall —*Amer. Guide Series: Minn.*⟩ **b** (1) **:** to move ahead by force of momentum ⟨a sailboat ~*s* when the helm is put hard alee⟩ ⟨a heavy boat will ~ much further than a light one —C.D.Lane⟩ (2) *of a bowled ball in cricket* **:** to travel fast and close to or along the ground after pitching

c : to stream out suddenly **:** SPURT ⟨blood *shot* from the wound at a frightening rate⟩ ⟨felt the tears ~*ing* from his eyes⟩ **d :** to dart in or as if in rays **:** appear suddenly from or as if from a source of light ⟨the clouds split and a ray of pure sunlight *shot* through the clear air —William Beebe⟩ ⟨from her black eyes there *shot* a magnificent look of defiance —Winston Churchill⟩ ⟨a glint of humor *shot* into his eyes —Laura Krey⟩ **2 a :** to dart with a piercing sensation ⟨pain *shot* through the Negro bullfighter —F.B.Gipson⟩ **b :** to throb in pain ⟨waiting for the tooth to ~ again⟩ **3 a :** to cause an engine or weapon to discharge a missile ⟨they *shot* at a target⟩ ⟨tripped and fell just as he turned to ~⟩ **b :** to practice the sport of hunting or of target firing with a gun ⟨~*s* better than he rides⟩ ⟨has *shot* from childhood⟩ **c :** to practice archery **d** (1) **:** to become discharged **:** go off ⟨~*s* at the touch of a trigger⟩ (2) **:** to propel a missile ⟨guns that ~ many miles⟩ ⟨a rifle that ~*s* accurately⟩ **4 :** PROTRUDE, PROJECT, EXTEND ⟨the land ~*s* into a promontory⟩ ⟨trees ~*ing* up against the sky⟩ ⟨Broadway, coming in from the south, ~*s* north and west from Union Square —*Amer. Guide Series: N.Y. City*⟩ **5 a** (1) **:** GROW, SPROUT ⟨grass beginning to ~⟩ ⟨plant life ~*ing* up on all sides⟩ (2) **:** to put forth shoots **:** BUD, GERMINATE (3) **:** to put out limbs — used of an animal **b :** DEVELOP, MATURE ⟨teach the young idea how to ~ —James Thomson †1748⟩ **6 :** to spring up or grow rapidly **:** advance to maturity — usu. used with *up* ⟨~*s* up to twice its length⟩ ⟨now he was ~*ing* up with the promise of attaining a man's proper stature after all —T.B.Costain⟩ ⟨had *shot* up to be a tall lad for his slender fourteen years —Waldo Frank⟩ **7 :** to solidify so as to form spicules or crystals **8 :** to play by propelling a ball or other object esp. in a particular way: as **a :** to kick the ball at goal in soccer **b :** to throw the ball at a basket in basketball **c :** to propel a ball to make a hit in croquet **d :** to drive the ball at goal in hockey or lacrosse **e :** to propel a golf ball toward a green or a cup **f :** to cast dice **9 :** to slide into or out of a fastening ⟨something wrong with the way this bolt ~*s*⟩ ⟨a bolt that ~*s* in either direction⟩ **10 :** to begin to speak **:** speak out **:** say what one has to say — usu. used as an imperative ⟨all right, ~ and ~ quick. What's happened —J.M.Cain⟩ **11 a :** to photograph a scene esp. of a moving picture **b :** to operate a camera or set cameras in operation **:** take a photograph **12 :** to explode a charge of dynamite to produce vibrations in the ground esp. in seismic prospecting **:** explore a region by means of portable seismographs **syn** see RUSH — **shoot at** *or* **shoot for :** to have in mind or in view as a goal **:** aim at **:** strive for ⟨when it is achieved there will be other goals for them to *shoot at* —Bernard De Voto⟩ ⟨all stores are *shooting for* sales gains —*Women's Wear Daily*⟩ ⟨a definite plan to *shoot at* —*N.Y.Times*⟩ ⟨*shot for* immortality —Barnaby Conrad⟩ — **shoot off one's mouth** *or* **shoot off one's face :** to talk freely often abusively regardless of the effect — **shoot one's bolt :** to do all within one's power **:** exhaust one's capabilities and resources ⟨had *shot his bolt* and had no more to say⟩ — **shoot one's cuffs** *also* **shoot one's linen :** to pull one's shirt cuffs below those of one's coat esp. as a gesture of self-importance or uneasiness — **shoot one's way :** to gain (an objective) by war or threat of war or by resort to other forms of force or intimidation — **shoot straight** *also* **shoot square :** to speak and deal honestly — **shoot the chutes :** to slide down a steep incline on a special type of toboggan or boat — **shoot the moon** *slang Brit* **:** to move one's goods by night to avoid foreclosure or seizure for overdue rent — **shoot the red** *Brit, of a young turkey* **:** to develop adult plumage and the red carunculated skin about head and neck that is characteristic of adulthood — **shoot the works 1 :** to play for the highest stake permitted **:** venture all one's capital on one play **2 :** to put forth all one's efforts **:** to do something without restraint

[2]shoot \"\ *n* -s [ME *schoyte*, fr. *shoten* to shoot] **1 :** a sending out of new growth (as by sprouting, budding) or the new growth or amount of new growth sent out: as **a** (1) **:** the aerial part of a plant **:** a stem with its leaves and other appendages in contrast to the root (2) **:** a branch or portion of plant growth developed from a bud and not yet mature **b :** a growth from a main stem or stock **:** OFFSHOOT ⟨was an easily identifiable ~ on such a family tree —Helen Howe⟩ ⟨a ~ of the oldest New England —Van Wyck Brooks⟩ ⟨turnpike . . . may someday send ~*s* south to the Dayton-Columbus area —Richard Thruelsen⟩ **c :** a budding horn or antler **d :** a similar formation of crystal **e :** the part of an oyster shell between two yearly rings **2 a :** an act of shooting (as with a bow or a firearm) **:** discharge of a missile: (1) **:** SHOT ⟨hoped to get a ~ at a deer⟩ ⟨a wild ~ into the treetops⟩ (2) **:** the firing of a missile or a group of missiles during a limited period of time esp. by artillery ⟨a tremendous predawn artillery ~ —*Time*⟩ ⟨many of our ~*s* have been wild —H.W.Baldwin⟩ **b** *obs* **:** the reach of a shot **:** shooting distance **:** RANGE **c** (1) **:** a hunting trip ⟨a duck ~⟩ ⟨autumn ~*s* over the rough bogs —James Reynolds⟩ ⟨invited some of his friends down for a winter ~ —*Newsweek*⟩ (2) **:** the game shot on a hunting trip (3) **:** the right to shoot game in a particular area (4) **:** a piece of usu. privately owned land used and often reserved and specially kept up for shooting game ⟨a 5000-acre ~⟩ ⟨a walk around the ~ with dogs at heel —*Bk. of the Dog*⟩ (5) **:** a group of persons taking part in a hunting trip **:** shooting party ⟨was invited to be one of a small ~⟩ **d** (1) **:** SHOOTING MATCH ⟨horseshoe pitching and bow-and-arrow and gun ~*s* —*Amer. Guide Series: Tenn.*⟩ ⟨a tournament ~⟩ ⟨a skeet ~⟩ ⟨celebration will get into action again with a muzzle-loading rifle ~ —Warren Weaver⟩; *specif* **:** a prescribed form of competition at archery ⟨a wand ~⟩ ⟨a clout ~⟩ (2) **:** a round of shots in a shooting match **e :** any of various acts or actions suggestive of the discharge of a missile from a bow or firearm: as (1) **:** a cast of a fishnet (2) **:** the action of shooting (as a scene, a subject) with a camera (3) **:** a launching of a rocket device or a guided missile esp. experimentally ⟨space-shooting timetable averaging one big ~ a month —Edwin Diamond⟩ ⟨has been . . . to Las Cruces to see a rocket ~ —Bruce Bliven b.1916⟩ ⟨a moon ~⟩ **3 a :** a motion or movement resembling or suggesting that of something shot **:** a movement of rapid thrusting ⟨a quick outward ~ of his arms⟩ or the space or distance traversed by such a movement: as (1) **:** a sudden or rapid advance ⟨the lift, ~, and swing of the seas —W.H.Taylor⟩ ⟨a ~ of lightning crossed the horizon —Theodora Keogh⟩ (2) [perh. by folk etymology fr. F *chute* — more at CHUTE] **:** a rush of water down a steep or rapid (3) **:** a momentary darting sensation **:** THRILL, TWINGE ⟨between ~*s* of pain⟩ ⟨there was no padding . . . of familiarity to deaden the ~*s* of delight that I felt —*Times Lit. Supp.*⟩ (4) **:** THRUST 3b (5) **:** a falling of a detached mass of earth or ice (6) **:** the pace between strokes in rowing **b :** something having or seeming to have such a motion: as (1) **:** a bar of rays **:** BEAM, SHAFT ⟨a ~ of sunlight⟩ ⟨the ~ of a flashlight⟩ ⟨came all together like a dust ~ —Joyce Cary⟩ (2) **:** an inshoot or outshoot in baseball **4** [prob. by folk etymology fr. F *chute* — more at CHUTE] **:** CHUTE: as **a :** a place whether natural or artificial where a stream runs or descends swiftly **b :** any of various natural or artificial inclined passages, channels, or troughs through which something (as water, logs, grain, ore) is moved (as by sliding) from one place to another on a lower level **c :** a narrow high-walled passageway for moving cattle or sheep (as to or from a pen) **5** *also* **shute** \"\ **:** a throw of the shuttle in weaving; *also* **:** the filling thread thus laid through the shed **6 :** ORE SHOOT **7 :** a place for dumping rubbish (as by shooting or tipping from a receptacle) **8 :** AGGREGATE, LOT — used in the phrase *the whole shoot* ⟨fed up with the whole ~ and no heart for nothing —Richard Llewelyn⟩

[3]shoot \'shüt\ *dial Eng var of* SHOUT

[4]shoot \"\ *Brit var of* SHOAT

[5]shoot \", *usu* -üd·+V\ *interj* [euphemism for [1]*shit*] — an exclamation expressing annoyance

shoot·able \'shüd·əbəl\ *adj* **:** that may be shot **:** suitable for shooting ⟨get within range . . . of a ~ stag —C.E.Hare⟩ ⟨such a day could not be blank even if one never saw a ~ beast, or missed him when seen —John Buchan⟩

shoot apex *n* **:** GROWING POINT

shootboard \'=,=\ *n* **:** SHOOTING BOARD

shoot down *vt* **:** to bring down by shooting: as **a :** to kill or incapacitate with a shot; *esp* **:** to kill (a person) by shooting mercilessly or in cold blood ⟨warned that anyone who tried to escape would be *shot down*⟩ ⟨*shot* him *down* without a qualm⟩ **b :** to cause (as an airplane) to fall to earth by shooting ⟨four of our planes were *shot down* in flames⟩ ⟨*shot* his first plane *down* at the age of eighteen⟩

shoot·ee \(')shüd·¦ē\ *n* -s [[1]*shoot* + *-ee*] **:** one that is shot or shot at

shoot·er \'shüd·ə(r), -ütə-\ *n* -s [ME *sheter*, *shoter*, *shuter*, fr. *sheten*, *shoten*, *shuten* to shoot + *-er* — more at SHOOT] **1 a :** a person (as an archer, gunner, sharpshooter, hunter) that shoots a missile-discharging device esp. for sport ⟨a well-known skeet ~⟩ **b** *archaic* **:** a guard on a horse-drawn coach **c :** a person that sets off explosives esp. as an occupation **:** BLASTER; *specif* **:** one that sets off explosives in oil wells to start the flow of oil **2 :** something that shoots: as **a :** SHOOTING STAR **b :** a plant of very rapid growth **c :** a cricket ball that on bouncing keeps very close to the ground **3 :** something that is shot or is used in shooting: as **a :** a marble shot from the hand **:** TAW **b :** FIREARM; *esp* **:** a repeating pistol — used chiefly in combination ⟨six-*shooter*⟩ ⟨five-*shooter*⟩ **4 :** one that casts or launches: as **a :** one that casts the net in seining **b :** one that moves or transfers something (as a commodity) by directing into or through a chute **c :** the player who is shooting the dice in a crap game **5 :** a printer's shooting stick

shoo·ther \'shüthə(r)\ *dial Brit var of* SHOULDER

shoot·ing \'shüd·|iŋ, -üt|, |ēŋ\ *n* -s [ME *sheting*, *shoting*, *shuting*, fr. gerund of *sheten*, *shoten*, *shuten* to shoot] **1 a :** the act or practice or a performance of one that shoots ⟨expert rifle ~⟩ ⟨best in the league at foul ~⟩ **b :** a wounding or killing with a firearm ⟨a mysterious ~ at a summer resort⟩; *specif* **:** the killing of game with a gun **:** HUNTING **c** *chiefly Brit* (1) **:** the right to shoot game in a given area (2) **:** the area designated **2 :** a sensation of darting pain **3 a :** sprouting or rapid growth (as of a plant); *also* **:** a shoot or cluster of shoots **b :** the period in the growth of various plants (as grasses and cereal grains) when the flowering and fruiting stem develops **4 :** the issue of spicules in crystallization **5 :** BLASTING

shooting board *n* **1 :** a fixture used as a guide in planing or shooting the edge of a board when greater accuracy is required than can be obtained with the miter box — called also *miter shooting board* **2 :** a metal table equipped with a plane for trimming, squaring, and sometimes beveling metal printing plates (as electrotypes)

shooting box *or* **shooting lodge** *n, chiefly Brit* **:** a cabin or small house in the country for use in the shooting season

shooting brake *n, Brit* **:** STATION WAGON

shooting fields *n* **:** a group of adjoining archery fields containing rovers at ranges of 140 to 360 yards

shooting fish *n* **:** ARCHERFISH

shooting gallery *n* **1 :** a range usu. covered and equipped with targets for practice or competition with firearms **2** *slang* **:** a place where an injection of a narcotic can be bought

shooting glove *n* **:** an archer's glove for protecting the fingers in drawing the bow

shooting iron *n* **:** FIREARM; *esp* **:** HANDGUN

shooting line *n* **:** a line that an archer must straddle when shooting at a target

shooting match *n* **1 :** a competitive test in shooting **:** competition in marksmanship **2 :** a collection or aggregate of persons or things **:** LOT; *also* **:** the entire affair or matter **:** CONCERN, BUSINESS — used chiefly in the phrase *the whole shooting match* ⟨sick and tired of the whole *shooting match*⟩ ⟨rich enough to buy the whole *shooting match*⟩

shooting script *n* **1 :** the final completely detailed version of a motion picture script in which scenes are grouped in the order most convenient for shooting and without regard to plot sequence **2 :** the final version of a television script used in the production of a program

shooting star *n* **1 :** a visual meteor appearing as a temporary streak of light in the night sky **:** FIREBALL **2 :** a plant of the genus *Dodecatheon; esp* **:** a No. American perennial herb (*D. meadia*) with entire oblong leaves and showy umbellate, purple, pink or white flowers — called also *American cowslip, bird bills, cowslip*

shooting stick *n* **1 :** a spiked stick with a top that opens into a seat typically used at a hunting stand or at races **2 :** a short wooden or iron bar often with a notched end used by printers for loosening and tightening wooden quoins

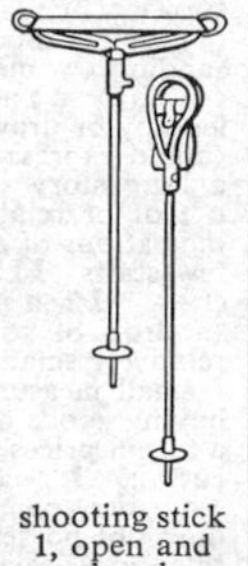

shooting stick 1, open and closed

shooting tab *n* **:** a flat piece of leather worn on the fingers used in shooting a bow

shooting time *n* **:** the period of elongation of the flower stem of a plant (as a hardy bulb) that is being forced

shooting war *n* **:** a war or warfare involving military operations and actual conflict between armed forces — compare COLD WAR, WAR OF NERVES

shoot·ist \'shüd·əst\ *n* -s [[1]*shoot* + *-ist*] **:** one who shoots; *esp* **:** MARKSMAN

shoot·man \'shütmən\ *n, pl* **shootmen** [[2]*shoot* (chute) + *man*] **1** *Austral* **:** a workman who stacks sawn timber **2** *Brit* **:** a coal teemer

shoot moth *n* **:** any of several moths of the family Olethreutidae whose larvae burrow in developing shoots of conifers

shoot off *vi* **1 :** to participate in a shoot-off **2 :** to talk too freely or unwisely **:** shoot off one's mouth ⟨*shot off* in Spain about atomic bombs —Drew Pearson⟩

shoot-off \'=,=\ *n* -s [*shoot off*] **:** a final shoot (as in a trapshooting or rifle-shooting contest) to determine the winner among two or more competitors that have tied in prior contests

shoot out *vt* **:** to settle by shooting ⟨to talk things out, no matter how inconclusively, rather than to *shoot* them *out* —A.H.Vandenberg †1951⟩ — often used with *it* ⟨tried to *shoot it out* with the cops —Mickey Spillane⟩

shoot-out \'=,=\ *n* -s [*shoot out*] **:** an exchange of shots resorted to as a means of settling a dispute or determining superiority; *esp* **:** a fight to the finish between gunfighters

shoot-root ratio *n* **:** the quotient of the dry weight of the shoots produced during a given growth period divided by the dry weight of the roots esp. for crop plants

shoots *pres 3d sing of* SHOOT, *pl of* SHOOT

shoot-the-chutes \'=='=\ *n pl but sing or pl in constr* **:** an amusement ride consisting of a steep incline down which toboggans or flatbottomed boats slide usu. to continue across a body of water at the bottom

shoot up *vi* **1 :** to rise sharply ⟨*shoots up* forty-one stories unrelieved and formidable —*Amer. Guide Series: N.Y.City*⟩ ⟨prices *shot up*⟩ ⟨corn *shot up* to seventy-three cents a bushel —John Bird⟩ ⟨hope *shot up* within me —Kenneth Roberts⟩ ⟨*shot up* to colonel —Green Peyton⟩ **2** *slang* **:** to take an injection of a narcotic **~** *vt* **:** to shoot or shoot at esp. promiscuously ⟨*shot up* a crowd of striking miners —*Atlantic*⟩ ⟨met a Russian patrol and *shot* them *up* —R.H.Newman⟩; *esp* **:** to pass through (as a town) shooting recklessly in all directions ⟨one of the factional leaders . . . *shot up* the town —F.L.Paxson⟩ ⟨*shoots up* the countryside periodically —Henry Cavendish⟩

[1]shop \'shäp\ *n* -s *often attrib* [ME *shoppe*, fr. OE *sceoppa* booth; akin to MD *schoppe* booth, OHG *scopf* shed, OE *scypen*, *scepen*, *scipen* cowshed, and prob. to OE *scēaf* sheaf — more at SHEAF] **1 a :** a handicraft establishment **:** ATELIER, STUDIO ⟨three ~*s* exclusively devoted to the hand-hammering of gold leaf —*Amer. Guide Series: N.J.*⟩ **b :** a team of glassworkers usu. consisting of a gatherer, blower, and servitor **:** CHAIR ⟨one . . . ~ of men worked at each glory hole —Freda Diamond⟩ **2 a :** a building or room stocked with merchandise for sale **:** STORE ⟨the ~*s* offer plenty of food and consumers' goods —Drew Middleton⟩ **b** *or* **shoppe** \"\ (1) **:** a small retail establishment or a department in a large one offering a specified line of goods or services ⟨gift ~⟩ ⟨sport ~⟩ ⟨beauty ~⟩ (2) **:** a small retail establishment concentrating on exclusive or top quality merchandise **:** a specialty shop **c :** something that resembles a shop ⟨Paris University was the great thinking-*shop*, the main European market of theologico-philosophical ideas —G.G.Coulton⟩ **d** (1) **:** a center of operations ⟨sets up ~ on the tailboard of a station wagon —J.S.Redding⟩ ⟨set up ~ in the area . . . and handled over half a million refugees before the exodus was stopped —*New Yorker*⟩ (2) **:** functional activity ⟨sets up ~ as the local commissar —*Time*⟩ ⟨the city shuts up ~ for a week —Ray Duncan⟩ **e :** a source of supply ⟨he's come to the wrong ~ for that —Charles Dickens⟩ **3 a :** a commercial establishment for the making or repairing of goods or machinery ⟨blacksmith's ~⟩ ⟨machine ~⟩ ⟨casting ~*s* and rolling mills —*Amer. Guide Series: Conn.*⟩ ⟨at the San Francisco yard . . . one steel ~ covers almost five acres —*All Hands*⟩ **b** *obs* **:** something that resembles a workshop ⟨the liver . . . the ~ and source of the blood —James Howell⟩ **c :** a home workshop ⟨spends every spare minute in his ~ making model airplanes⟩ **d** (1) **:** a laboratory in an elementary or secondary school equipped for instruction in manual arts ⟨the general ~ may provide facilities for work in metals, electricity, and transportation —L.V.Newkirk⟩ (2) **:** the art or science of working with tools and machinery ⟨there will be one exception, perhaps . . . one boy out of twenty who does badly in English and well in ~ —C.D.Green⟩ ⟨made bookends for his mother as a project in ~⟩ **4 a :** a business establishment **:** place of employment ⟨print ~⟩; *esp* **:** OFFICE ⟨it had been a battle to get them into the ~ and behind their typewriters or drawing boards before 9:30 —*Advertising Age*⟩ — compare UNION SHOP **b :** a gathering place **:** center of activity ⟨farmers filled the front of the ~, leaning against the bar —Sigerson Clifford⟩ **c :** JOB; *esp* **:** a theatrical engagement ⟨now she would be out of a ~ all through the autumn —Leonard Merrick⟩ **d :** SHOPTALK ⟨safety-conscious young men who could talk intelligent ~ with any engineer in Detroit —*Time*⟩ ⟨summarized a good deal of dead musical ~ in smaller type —*New Statesman & Nation*⟩ ⟨talk golf-*shop* in season and out of season — Andrew Lang⟩

[2]shop \"\ *vb* **shopped**; **shopped**; **shopping**; **shops** *vt* **1** *dial* **a :** ARREST, IMPRISON **b :** to inform on **:** BETRAY ⟨she had *shopped* him to the police —*Manchester Guardian Weekly*⟩ **2** *archaic* **:** to take to market **:** put on sale **3 a** (1) **:** to look over (available goods or services) with an eye to purchase ⟨~ our quality collection of . . . mink capes —*advt*⟩ (2) **:** to examine the stock of ⟨get back in time to ~ the curio stores along the bay front —*Holiday*⟩ (3) **:** BUY ⟨~ me a couple of those little . . . figurines —Lawrence Durrell⟩ **b :** to scan (as a newspaper) for information about available goods or services ⟨make a habit of *shopping* the catalogs —F.F.Rockwell⟩ **4 :** to send to a repair shop ⟨~ a railroad car for periodic maintenance⟩ **~** *vi* **1 a :** to examine goods and services with intent to buy ⟨~ for groceries⟩ ⟨~ for clothes⟩ — compare WINDOW-SHOP **b :** to probe a market in search of the best buy ⟨exhibitors were kept busy . . . booking orders, despite the tendency to ~ on opening day —*Women's Wear Daily*⟩ — usu. used with *around* ⟨after you've decided on a brand, ~ around — there is more than one dealer for each make of car —*Motor Trend*⟩ **c :** to look something over ⟨went to his gage panel and *shopped* over it with his eyes —Joseph Whitehill⟩ **2 :** to make a search **:** HUNT ⟨two very similar parties each *shopping* for winning ideas —F.L.Allen⟩ — often used with *around* ⟨students . . . *shopping* around for something consoling to believe —Sidney Hook⟩

shop assistant *n, Brit* **:** a clerk in a retail store

shopboard \'=,=\ *n* **1** *archaic* **:** a counter or table for the display of merchandise **2** *archaic* **:** a table or platform on which a tailor sits to sew

shopbreaker \'=,==\ *n* **:** one that breaks into a shop or breaks out after having committed a crime therein

shopbreaking \'=,==\ *n* **:** the act of a shopbreaker

shop card *n* **:** a card posted by a union as evidence that the shop in which it is displayed is operating under a union contract

shop coat *n* **:** a priming coat applied in a manufacturing plant

shop committee *n* **:** a committee elected by workers in a plant to represent them in discussing grievances with the management

shop drawing *n* **:** WORKING DRAWING

shope papilloma \'shōp-\ *also* **shope's papilloma** *n, usu cap S* [after Richard E. *Shope* †1966 Am. physician] **:** a transmissible fibrous tumor of cottontail rabbits of which the transmitting agent is believed to be a specific nucleoprotein that behaves as a pathogenic virus in wild rabbits but an innocuous plasmagene in domestic ones — compare TUMOR VIRUS

shop·ful \'shäp,fu̇l\ *n* -s **:** as many as a shop will contain ⟨a ~ of customers⟩ ⟨pick your way through ~*s* of . . . trinkets —*Mademoiselle*⟩

shopgirl \'=,=\ *n* **:** SALESWOMAN

shophar *var of* SHOFAR

shopkeeper \'=,==\ *n* **:** the proprietor of a retail store **:** STOREKEEPER

shopkeeping \'=,==\ *n* -s **:** the occupation of a shopkeeper

shop·lift \'shäp,lift\ *vb* [back-formation fr. *shoplifter* and *shoplifting*] *vt* **:** to steal (goods that are on display) from a store ⟨bought a nickel sack of tobacco and ~*ed* a bag of flour —Russell Lord⟩ **~** *vi* **:** to steal displayed merchandise from a store ⟨diagnosis of the mental quirk that led them to ~ —Dwight Macdonald⟩

shop·lift·er \-tə(r)\ *n* [[1]*shop* + *lifter*] **:** a thief that steals merchandise on display in stores

shop·lift·ing \-tiŋ, -tēŋ\ *n* -s [[1]*shop* + *lifting*] **:** the stealing of goods on display in a store

shop lumber *n* **:** FACTORY LUMBER

shop·man \'shäpmən\ *n, pl* **shopmen 1** *chiefly Brit* **:** a clerk in a retail store **2 :** a workman in a shop **:** a mechanic who assists with repairs

shopmark \'=,=\ *n* **:** HALLMARK 1c

shop mileage *n* **:** the mileage potentiality of a steam locomotive after undergoing general repairs

shop paper *n* **:** thin wrapping paper

shoppe *var of* SHOP

shopped *past of* SHOP

shop·per \'shäpə(r)\ *n* -s **1 :** one that shops for goods or services esp. in a store **:** CUSTOMER, PURCHASER ⟨~*s* were three deep at the bargain counter⟩ ⟨~*s*, going from one community agency to another —H.A.Rusk⟩ **2 :** one whose occupation is shopping as an agent for customers or for an employer — see COMPARISON SHOPPER, PERSONAL SHOPPER

shopping *n* -s [fr. gerund of [2]*shop*] **1 :** searching for, inspecting, or buying available goods or services ⟨~ not only was keener . . . but selling was more satisfactory —*Retailing Daily*⟩ ⟨does her weekly ~ at the supermarket⟩ **2 :** overhauling in a repair shop ⟨modern steam locomotives require ~ after 200,000 to 275,000 miles —*Scientific American*⟩

shopping center *n* **:** a concentration of retail stores and service establishments in a suburban area usu. with generous parking space and usu. planned to serve a community or neighborhood

shopping goods *n pl* **:** consumer goods that are usu. purchased only after the customer has compared price, quality, and style in more than one store — compare CONVENIENCE GOODS, SPECIALTY 2a(4)

shop right *n* **:** the right of an employer to use without payment of any royalty his employee's invention developed in the course of his employment

shop rivet *n* **:** a rivet driven in place in a shop — opposed to *field rivet*

shops *pl of* SHOP, *pres 3d sing of* SHOP

shop steward *or* **shop chairman** *n* **:** a union member elected by the employees in a shop, department, or plant to serve as the representative of the union and charged mainly with negotiating adjustment of grievances of employees with the employer usu. through the foreman — called also *committeeman*

shoptalk \'=,=\ *n* **:** the jargon or subject matter peculiar to an occupation or a special area of interest ⟨graduate students . . . talking their highly specialized ~ —Dorothy Baker⟩

shopwalker \'=,==\ *n, Brit* **:** FLOORWALKER

shopwindow \'=¦=(,)=\ *n* [ME] **1 :** a display window of a store ⟨new spring prints brighten winter ~*s*⟩ **2 :** something that serves as a showcase ⟨film festivals . . . recognized in recent years as a sort of international ~ —Arthur Knight⟩

shopwork \'=,=\ *n* **:** mechanical work (as carpentry, patternmaking, molding, machining, forging) done in a shop

shopworker \'=,==\ *n* **:** one who works in a shop

shopworn \'=,=\ *adj* **1 :** faded, soiled, or otherwise impaired by remaining too long on display in a store ⟨sell ~ merchandise at a sizeable discount⟩ **2 :** deprived of freshness or effectiveness by continuous use or exposure to detrimental influences **:** BEDRAGGLED, JADED ⟨half-melted glaciers of a rather ~ kind, looking like . . . dirty corn snow —Christopher Rand⟩ ⟨this figure astonishes even a ~ newspaperman —G.W. Johnson⟩ ⟨the tendency to use ~ clichés —Helen Mustard⟩ **syn** see TRITE

shor \'shȯ(ə)r\ *n* -s [Russ, of Altaic origin; akin to Kalmuck & Mongolian *šor* salt, Turk *şūre* brackish soil] **:** a salt lake in Turkestan **:** SALINA

sho·ran \'shōr,an, 'shȯ,ran, ˌ=ˈ=\ *n* -s [*sho*rt-*ra*nge *n*avigation] **:** a system of short-range navigation in which two radar signals transmitted by an airplane are intercepted and rebroadcast to the airplane by two ground stations of known position with the time that the signals take for their round trips indicating the distance to each station and thus the position of the airplane

¹shore [alter. (influenced by *shorn*) of *sheared*] *chiefly dial past of* SHEAR

²shore \'shō(ə)r, 'shȯ(ə)r, -ōə, -ȯ(ə)\ *n* -s *often attrib* [ME *shor, shore,* fr. (assumed) OE *scor, scora* (attested only in place names); akin to Fris *skoarre* shoal, alluvial land outside a dike, MD *schor, schore, schorre* shoal, alluvial land, MLG *schōr* foreland, foreshore, *schār* shore, OHG *scorra* steep cliff, OE *sceran, scieran* to cut — more at SHEAR] **1 a :** the land bordering a usu. large body of water; *specif* **:** the land bordering the sea **:** COAST **b :** FORESHORE 2 **2 :** a boundary or the country or place that it bounds ⟨hold him accountable for difficulties beyond our ~*s* that he could do nothing about —Dorothy Fosdick⟩ **3 :** land as distinguished from the sea

³shore \"\ *vt* -ED/-ING/-S **1 :** to set ashore **:** LAND **2 :** to serve as a shore to **:** BORDER ⟨a sand river, half a mile wide, of golden-colored sand, *shored* by green trees —Ernest Hemingway⟩

⁴shore \'shü̇ər, 'shō(ə)r\ *vt* -ED/-ING/-S [ME *schoren*] **1** *chiefly Scot* **:** to scold with a warning of punishment **:** THREATEN **2** *chiefly Scot* **:** OFFER

⁵shore \'shō(ə)r, 'shȯ(ə)r, -ōə, -ȯ(ə)\ *vt* -ED/-ING/-S [ME *shoren;* akin to Fris *skoarje* to support, brace up, MD *schooren,* ON *skortha* to support, brace up, ME *shore,* n. — more at ⁶SHORE] **1 :** to support by a shore **:** PROP — often used with *up* ⟨dug into hedgerows, which they *shored* up with timbers —*Infantry Jour.*⟩ **2 :** to give support to **:** BRACE ⟨a tunnel which is electrically lit and *shored* with concrete —Ralph Hammond-Innes⟩ — often used with *up* ⟨*shoring* up farm prices —W.S.White⟩

⁶shore \"\ *n* -s [ME; akin to Fris *skoarre* prop, stay, support, MD *schore, schoor,* MLG *schōre, schāre,* ON *skortha* prop, stay, support, and prob. to OE *sceran, scieran* to cut — more at SHEAR] **:** a prop (as a timber) placed against the side of a structure **:** a prop (as a beam) placed beneath something to prevent sinking or sagging

shores supporting a ship

⁷shore \'shü̇ər, 'shō(ə)r\ *n* -s [prob. alter. of ³*sewer*] *dial chiefly Brit* **:** an open sewer or drainage ditch

sho·rea \'shōrēə\ *n, cap* [NL, after John *Shore,* Lord Teignmouth †1834 governor general of India] **:** a genus of Indo-Malayan timber trees (family Dipterocarpaceae) that are rich in resin, have flowers with twisted petals, a very short calyx tube, and sepals which become enlarged and winglike in fruit, and that include forms yielding valuable lumber — see RED LAUAN, SAL

shorebird \'=,=\ *n* **:** a bird of the suborder Charadrii (as a plover, snipe, or sandpiper) chiefly found along the seashore

shore boat *n* **:** a boat plying from shore to ship

shore cod *n* **:** cod caught off the New England coast — called also *native cod*

shore cover *n* **:** an extension of the coverage under a marine insurance policy to include risks to goods while in the custody of land transportation companies or while located at docks, wharves, or piers

shore crab *n* **:** any of numerous crabs living between the tide-marks: as **a :** GREEN CRAB **b :** a spider crab of the genus *Libinia* common along the eastern coast of the U.S. **c :** any of several grapsoid crabs of the western coast of No. America — usu. used with a qualifying term; see PURPLE SHORE CRAB, STRIPED SHORE CRAB, YELLOW SHORE CRAB **d :** a common So. Australian grapsoid crab (*Leptograpsus variegatus*)

shore current *n* **:** a current in water adjacent to a shoreline and often moving in a direction more or less parallel to it

shored *past of* SHORE

shore dinner *n* **:** a usu. full course dinner consisting mainly of seafood

shore drift *n* **:** material moving in or deposited by waves and currents along a shore

shoreface \'=,=\ *n* **:** the narrow zone seaward or lakeward from the low watermark in which sand and gravel are moved by waves and currents

shore fast *n* **:** any of the lines securing a vessel to a pier or the shore

shorefish \'=,=\ *n* **:** a sea fish living near shore; *broadly* **:** any marine fish not living in the depths of the ocean

shore fly *n* **:** a fly of the family Ephydridae

shoregoing \'=,==\ *adj* **1 :** living on shore **2 :** used for or suitable for going ashore

shore grape *n* **:** SEA GRAPE

shore grass *n* **:** SHOREWEED

shore hardness \'shō(ə)r-, 'shȯ(ə)r-\ *n, usu cap S* [after Albert F. *Shore,* 20th cent. Am. manufacturer] **:** hardness of metal or other material as measured by a Shore scleroscope

shore juniper *n* **:** a low mat-forming Japanese shrub (*Juniperus conferta*) used as an ornamental and having needlelike leaves in whorls of three

shoreland \'=,=\ *n* **:** land along a shore

shore lark *n* **:** HORNED LARK

shore leave *n* **:** a leave of absence to go on shore granted to a sailor or naval officer

shore·less \'=ləs\ *adj* **1 :** having no shore ⟨the sea beats against a ~ cliff⟩ **2 :** of indefinite or unlimited extent **:** BOUNDLESS ⟨a great expanse of ~ water —H.L.Bridgman⟩

shoreline \'=,=\ *n* **:** the outline of the shore **:** the zone of contact of a body of water with the land

shore·man \'=mən\ *n, pl* **shoremen 1 :** one who dwells on a shore or on shore **2 :** SHORESMAN

shore onion *n* **:** CHIVE

shore party *n* **:** a task organization formed to provide logistic support for a landing force during early phases of an amphibious military operation ⟨detailed a *shore party* to stockpile gasoline drums on the beachhead⟩

shore patrol *n* **1 :** an organized naval unit that has duties similar to those of the military police **2 :** a member of a shore patrol — abbr. *SP*

shore pine *n* **:** LODGEPOLE PINE a

shore pipit *n* **:** ROCK PIPIT

shore plate *n* **:** a blue plate consisting mainly of seafood

shor·er \'shōrə(r), 'shȯr-\ *n* -s [ME, fr. *shoren* to shore + *-er* — more at SHORE (to prop)] **:** one that shores up; *specif* **:** one that builds cribbing which will serve as a retaining wall to support the sides of an open excavation — called also *bracer, cribber*

shores *pl of* SHORE, *pres 3d sing of* SHORE

shore scleroscope *n, usu cap 1st S* [after Albert F. *Shore,* 20th cent. Am. manufacturer] **:** SCLEROSCOPE

¹shoreside \'=,=\ *n* [²*shore* + *side*] **:** the margin of the shore

²shoreside \"\ *adj* **:** ONSHORE

shores·man \'=mən\ *n, pl* **shoresmen :** one who works on shore in connection with a maritime business or enterprise (as a fishery)

shore snipe *n* **1 :** SANDPIPER **2 :** SHOREBIRD

shore spurge *n* **:** SEASIDE SPURGE

shore terrace *n* **:** a coastal terrace that is cut in rock or built up of gravel or sand

¹shore·ward \'shōr,wərd, 'shȯ(ə)-\ *or* **shore·wards** \-dz\ *adv* [²*shore* + *-ward, -wards*] **:** toward the shore

²shoreward \"\ *adj* **:** facing or moving toward the shore

shoreweed \'=,=\ *n* **:** an aquatic weed (*Littorella uniflora*) of the family Plantaginaceae that has few flowered scapes and flowers with a one-celled ovary — called also *plantain shoreweed*

shor·ey·er \'shō,rī(ə)r\ *n* -s [perh. fr. ²*shore* + *eyer,* alter. of *eider*] **:** EIDER

shoring *n* -s [fr. gerund of ⁵*shore*] **1 :** the act of supporting or strengthening with or as if with a prop **2 :** a system or group of shores

shoring 2

shorl *var of* SCHORL

¹shorn *past part of* SHEAR

²shorn *n* -s [¹*shorn*] **:** a market sheep offered for sale after shearing

shors *pl of* SHOR

¹short \'shȯ(ə)r|t, -ȯ(ə)|, *usu* |d.+V\ *adj* -ER/-EST [ME *short, shert,* fr. OE *scort, sceort;* akin to OHG *scurz* short, ON *skort, skortr* lack, *skorta* to be lacking, *skera* to cut — more at SHEAR] **1 a :** having little length **:** not extending far from end to end ⟨the big guns pointed ~, ugly snouts seaward —Bill Davidson⟩ ⟨~ pouting lips —William Empson⟩ **b :** having little height **:** not tall **:** LOW ⟨a ~ man⟩ ⟨of ~ stature⟩ ⟨a ~ smokestack⟩ **2 a :** not extended in time **:** of brief duration **:** lasting a little while only ⟨a diversion which brought him ~ periods of physical peace —Louis Bromfield⟩ ⟨a ~ life⟩ ⟨a ~ season⟩ **b :** not retentive for more than a brief period ⟨a ~ memory⟩ **c :** EXPEDITIOUS, QUICK ⟨wished to make ~ work of the business —H.E. Scudder⟩ **d :** seeming to pass quickly ⟨in the space of a few ~ years made terrifying headway —R.K.Carr⟩ **e :** allowing or requiring little time for preparation or action ⟨~ notice⟩ **3 a** *of a speech sound* **:** having a relatively short duration ⟨the vowel of *dock* is ~*er* than the vowel of *dark* when the *r* is not pronounced⟩ **b :** indicating the member of a pair of similarly spelled vowel or partly vowel sounds that is descended from a durationally short vowel but that now is not durationally short or does not have duration as its chief distinguishing feature ⟨~ *a* in *fat*⟩ ⟨~ *e* in *equity*⟩ ⟨~ *i* in *sin*⟩ ⟨~ *o* in *odd*⟩ ⟨~ *u* in *fuss*⟩ **c** (1) *of a syllable in Greek or Latin verse* **:** of relatively brief duration (2) *of a syllable in English verse* **:** UNSTRESSED **4 a :** limited in vision or range ⟨the windows on to the outer world were few, and the view from them was ~ and uninviting —R.W.Southern⟩ **b :** limited in distance **:** not covering much ground or space ⟨a ~ walk⟩ ⟨a ~ trip⟩ ⟨a ~ flight⟩ **c** *archaic* **:** traveling only a few miles — used of a train or train passenger **5 a :** not coming up to a measure, standard, or requirement ⟨eliminate adulteration, ~ weights and measures —V.S.Alanne⟩ **:** not sufficient in quantity **:** INADEQUATE, INSUFFICIENT, SCANTY ⟨stockpile critical materials in ~ supply —J.M.Minifie⟩ ⟨on ~ rations then, trying to live on a dollar a day —R.B. Gehman⟩ **b :** not extending, reaching, or traveling far enough ⟨the coat is ~ on him⟩ ⟨the page is two lines ~⟩ ⟨his throw was ~⟩ **c :** having an insufficient supply **:** lacking a needed article or amount — usu. used with *of* or *in* ⟨~ of cash at the end of the month⟩ ⟨five dollars ~ in his accounts⟩ ⟨somebody might marry her and leave him ~ a cook —H.G.Evarts⟩ **d :** enduring privation **:** doing without ⟨local settler families . . . who may be temporarily ~ as a result of a poor harvest or bad planning —J.B.Watson⟩ **e :** inherently or basically weak in — used with *on* ⟨long on ambition but ~ on brains⟩ ⟨long on ideas but ~ on knowledge⟩ **6 a :** ABRUPT, CURT, UNCEREMONIOUS ⟨the service is rendered in a blunt, impersonal, irritated, or ~ manner —Lou Smyth⟩ ⟨was less ~ with her at such moments than usual —David Walden⟩ **b :** quick to respond to provocation **:** easily aroused ⟨tempers are ~ in the morning —W.S.Gilbert⟩ **7 a :** recurring quickly in succession — used of recurrent bodily phenomena (as breaths or pulse beats) **b :** having waves that break in quick succession **:** CHOPPY ⟨their swift currents and steep, ~ seas —*Amer. Guide Series: Mass.*⟩ **8 a** *archaic* **:** not distant in time **:** near at hand **b :** payable at an early date **9 a :** easily broken **:** crumbling readily (as from shortening content) **:** CRISP, FRIABLE ⟨~ pastry⟩ **b** (1) *of metal* **:** brittle under certain conditions — compare COLD-SHORT, HOT-SHORT, RED-SHORT (2) **:** lacking tensile strength (as through desiccation) ⟨~ lumber stock⟩ (3) **:** difficult to spread because of excess sanding ⟨~ mortar⟩ (4) **:** defective in tenacity or plasticity ⟨~ clay⟩ **c :** not flowing readily **:** STICKY ⟨~ ink⟩ **10 a :** not lengthy or drawn out in content or style **:** CONCISE, SUCCINCT ⟨could express my faith in ~*er* terms —John Adams⟩ ⟨make a long story ~⟩ **b :** ABBREVIATED ⟨*doc* is ~ for *doctor*⟩ **c :** of or relating to a musical score having the notes and indications of essential parts of a full score condensed onto a few staffs **11 :** consisting of or containing chopped or cut straw **12 a :** consisting of undiluted liquor **:** STRAIGHT ⟨a drop of something ~⟩ **b** *of a beverage* **:** served in a relatively small glass usu. of five ounces or less **:** constituting a small measure ⟨a ~ beer⟩ ⟨a ~ rum punch⟩ **13 a :** not having goods or property that one has sold in anticipation of a fall in prices — usu. used with *of* or *in* ⟨~ of wheat⟩ ⟨~ in cotton⟩ **b :** consisting of, relating to or involving a sale of securities, commodities, or foreign exchange that the seller does not possess or has not contracted for at the time of the sale ⟨a ~ sale⟩ ⟨~ contracts⟩ **14 :** having or containing fewer than the average number of cards in a particular suit; *specif* **:** having or containing fewer than three cards in a particular suit in bridge **15 a :** pitched at a spot too near the bowling end to be considered of good length — used of a bowled ball in cricket **b :** placed relatively close to the batsman's wicket — used of a fielder or fielding position ⟨~ slip⟩ ⟨~ mid on⟩ **syn** see BRIEF — **in short order** *adv* **:** with dispatch **:** EXPEDITIOUSLY ⟨disposed of the piles of correspondence *in short order*⟩

²short \"\ *adv* -ER/-EST [ME, fr. *short,* adj.] **1 :** in a curt manner ⟨always going about in his apron and talking ~ with everyone —W.D.Steele⟩ **2 :** for or during a brief time — used in combination (*short*-lasting) (*short*-living) **3 :** TIGHTLY ⟨caught him up ~ by his coat lapels —Barnaby Conrad⟩ **4 :** at a disadvantage **:** ABACK, UNAWARES ⟨caught ~⟩ ⟨taken ~⟩ **5 :** so as to interrupt ⟨took him up ~ before he could continue⟩ **6 :** ABRUPTLY, SUDDENLY ⟨would halt ~, order everybody to be still, and insist that she had heard something —H.L.Davis⟩ **7 :** at some point or distance before a goal or limit aimed at or approached ⟨his throw fell five yards ~⟩ ⟨the shells dropped ~⟩ **8 :** clean across ⟨the axle was snapped ~⟩ **9 :** by or as if by a short sale — compare SELL SHORT

³short \"\ *n* -s [¹*short*] **1 :** the sum and substance **:** UPSHOT — usu. used with *the* ⟨the ~ of it is, in my judgment —A.E. Stevenson †1965⟩ **2 a :** a short musical note **b :** a short syllable **c :** a short sound or signal (as in Morse code) ⟨the buzzer sounded in the hall: three longs and a ~ —Harold Brodkey⟩ **3 shorts** *pl* **a :** a by-product of wheat milling that includes the germ, fine bran, and a small amount of flour **b :** refuse, clippings, or trimmings, discarded in various manufacturing processes **4 :** straight liquor **5 shorts** *pl* **a :** SMALLCLOTHES 1 **b :** knee-length or less than knee-length trousers made in various styles for informal wear or sports-wear **c :** short drawers **6 a :** one who purchases or operates on the short side of the market — compare ¹BEAR 3b **b shorts** *pl* **:** short-term bonds **7 shorts** *pl* **:** items that are lacking to make up a quantity or total **:** DEFICIENCIES; *specif* **:** the copies of different printed sheets needed to complete an imperfect edition **8 :** something of less than a full or required length: as **a shorts** *pl* **:** lumber of less than standard length **b :** a fish or lobster of less than the length required for legal catching **c :** a clothing size for short men **d :** one of the smaller standard firearm cartridges **e :** a short often documentary or educational film shown with a full-length feature or as part of a program of short films **f :** a brief news story or feature item in a newspaper or periodical **9 :** something that falls short; *specif* **:** a shot that strikes or bursts short of the target **10 :** SHORT CIRCUIT **11 a :** SHORTSTOP ⟨plays a fine ~⟩ **b :** SHORT FIELD ⟨hit the ball to deep ~⟩ — **for short** *adv* **:** by way of abbreviation — **in short** *adv* **1 :** by way of summary **:** in brief **:** BRIEFLY **2 :** in an inner column in a statement of figures in accounting — **the short and long** *or* **the short and the long :** the whole story **:** the long and short **:** GIST

⁴short \"\ *vt* -ED/-ING/-S [¹*short*] **1 :** to supply with less than is customary, needed, or expected ⟨~*ed* him on his favorite hog jowl and turnip greens —*Time*⟩ **2 :** SHORTCHANGE, CHEAT ⟨slugged a . . . weighman who was ~*ing* him at the scales —*Irish Digest*⟩ **3 :** SHORT-CIRCUIT

short account *n* **1 :** the account of a short seller **2 :** the total of open short sales in a given subject of trade or in the market as a whole

short·age \'shȯr|d·|ij, -ȯ(ə)|, |t|, |ēj\ *n* -s **:** a deficiency in an amount required **:** DEFICIT ⟨a ~ in petty cash⟩ ⟨a ~ of trained teachers⟩ ⟨a ~ of oil⟩ — opposed to *overage*

short and *n* **:** AMPERSAND

short and sweet *adj* **:** brief and to the point

short appoggiatura *n* **:** a grace note performed very quickly, played either on the beat or before the beat, and symbolized by a small note with a stroke through the stem — see APPOGGIATURA illustration

short arm *n* **:** HANDGUN

short arm inspection *also* **short arm** *n* **:** an examination of the penis for venereal disease or other abnormal condition

short ballot *n* **:** a ballot limiting the number of elective offices to the most important legislative and executive posts and leaving minor positions to be filled by appointment — compare BLANKET BALLOT

short bill *n* **:** a bill of exchange maturing in 30 days or less and sometimes in ten days or less — compare LONG BILL

short-billed marsh wren \'=,=-\ *n* **:** a marsh wren (*Cistothorus stellaris*) of No. America that resembles the long-billed marsh wren but is smaller, has a bill much shorter than its head, and has fine whitish streaks along its upper parts

shortbread \'=,=\ *n* **:** a thick cookie traditionally made of flour, a small amount of sugar, and a proportionately large amount of butter or other shortening

short-breathed \'=ˈ=\ *adj* **1 :** breathing with quick shallow respirations **2 :** of brief duration or limited breadth ⟨the poems of the later years being obviously more fragmentary and *short-breathed* —Irving Howe⟩

short buchu *n* **:** BUCHU 1a

shortcake \'=,=\ *n* **1 :** a cake rich in shortening; *specif* **:** a crisp and often unsweetened biscuit, cookie, or teacake with the texture of pastry **2 a :** a dessert made of very short baking-powder-biscuit dough typically cooked in a large cake and served hot after being split, buttered, and spread with sweetened esp. fresh fruit (as strawberries or peaches) **b :** a sweet but not necessarily short cake spread with fruit and served cold **3 :** a luncheon dish consisting of a rich biscuit split and covered with a meat mixture (as of chicken)

short change *n* **:** an amount of change less than the amount due

shortchange \(')=ˈ=\ *vt* [*short change*] **1 :** to give less than the correct amount of change to ⟨charged that the cashier had *shortchanged* him⟩ **2 :** to deprive of something due or to give less than the due amount of to **:** CHEAT ⟨most people ~ themselves on the good things of life —*House Beautiful*⟩

short-change \'=ˈ=\ *adj* [*short change*] **:** of or relating to cheating ⟨a *short-change* artist⟩ ⟨a *short-change* racket⟩

shortchanger \(')=ˈ==\ *n* **:** one that shortchanges

short circuit *n* **1 :** a conductor of comparatively low resistance that is accidentally or intentionally connected between points on a circuit between which the resistance is normally much greater; *also* **:** direct contact between such points that makes the resistance zero **2 :** something that interrupts, cuts off, or bypasses ⟨the extent to which *short circuits* may be developing in the system of internal check —*Jour. of Accountancy*⟩; *specif* **:** an artificial communication established surgically between two parts (as of the alimentary canal) to enable the contents to pass around an intervening obstruction

short-circuit \(')=ˈ==\ *vt* [*short circuit*] **1 :** to apply a short circuit to or establish a short circuit in **2 a :** to jump over or detour around **:** BYPASS ⟨*short-circuiting* the judgment and appealing directly to the emotions —Louise Young⟩ **b :** to create (a short circuit) by surgery **3 :** to interfere with or put out of action **:** FRUSTRATE, IMPEDE ⟨nothing can more quickly *short-circuit* friendly feelings —F.M.Keesing⟩ ⟨would *short-circuit* the country's rapid development —Welles Hangen⟩ **~** *vi* **:** to become shunted by a short circuit

short-circuit·er \"+ə(r)\ *n* **:** something that short-circuits; *specif* **:** a device operated by centrifugal force that actuates the mechanism which short-circuits the commutator bars or raises the brushes from the commutator in some forms of single-phase motors

shortclothes \'=,=\ *n pl* **:** SMALLCLOTHES 1

shortcoat \'=,=\ *vt* [fr. the phrase *short coat*] **:** to put (a child) into its first smallclothes ⟨think o' that boy, ~*ed* but yesterday —Eden Phillpotts⟩

shortcoming \(')=ˈ==\ *n* [¹*short* + *coming* (after the phrase *come short*)] **:** the condition or fact of failing to reach an expected or required standard of character or performance **:** DEFECT, IMPERFECTION ⟨guilt feeling may exist from a sense of personal ~ —R.L.Jenkins⟩ ⟨management ~*s* in one form or another cause most business failures —*Nation's Business*⟩

short corner *n* **:** PENALTY CORNER

short count *n, often cap S&C* **:** a system of dating in the Maya calendar according to the current katun or series of katuns — compare LONG COUNT

short covering *n* **:** buying in securities or other property to terminate or close out a short sale

¹shortcut \'=,=\ *n* [¹*short* + *cut* (easy passage)] **1 :** a route more direct or more quickly traveled than the one ordinarily taken **2 :** a method of doing or achieving something more directly and quickly than by ordinary procedure ⟨the ~*s* which we have worked out to make the work simple and easy —Tom Marvel⟩ ⟨no panaceas or ~*s* to peace or stability —S.K.Padover⟩ **3** *usu* **short cut :** something cut into short parts; *specif* **:** tobacco cut in short bits instead of in long shreds

²shortcut \"\ *adj* [²*short* + *cut,* past part. of *cut*] **1** *usu* **short-cut** \'=ˈ=\ **:** cut so as to be short **2 :** affording or constituting a shortcut

short-cut \'=,=\ *vb* [¹*shortcut*] *vt* **:** to shorten by use of a shortcut **~** *vi* **:** to take or use a shortcut

short-cycled *also* **short-cycle** \'=ˈ==\ *adj* **:** lacking an aecial or uredinial stage or both and sometimes also a pycnial (*short-cycled* rusts) — opposed to *long-cycled*

short-dated \'=ˈ==\ *adj* **:** having little time to run after date — used of a bill or note

short-day \'=ˈ=\ *adj* **:** responding to a short photoperiod — used esp. of a plant

short deck *n* **:** a pack of cards having fewer than the prescribed number

short division *n* **:** mathematical division in which the successive steps are performed without writing out the remainders

short-eared hare \'=,=-\ *n* **:** a hare (*Nesolagus netscheri*) of Sumatra that has short ears and fur and whose color shades from grayish yellow on the foreparts to mahogany-brown on the haunches with black bands on back, sides, face, and hind feet

short-eared harvest mouse *n* **:** a common harvest mouse (*Reithrodontomys humilis*) of the eastern U.S.

short-eared owl *n* **:** a medium-sized nearly cosmopolitan owl (*Asio flammeus*) that frequents seacoasts and grassy marshes, commonly nests on the ground, is dark brown above and buff below streaked with brown, and has very short ear tufts

shorted *past of* SHORT

short·en \'shȯrtᵊn, -ȯ(ə)tᵊn\ *vb* **shortened; shortened; shortening** \-t(ᵊ)niŋ\ **shortens** [¹*short* + *-en*] *vt* **1 a :** to make short or shorter **:** reduce the length or duration of ⟨~ the roads that lead to a profession —J.B.Conant⟩ ⟨voted to ~ the firm name —*Wall Street Jour.*⟩ ⟨~ a dangerous and costly war —D.H.McLachlan⟩ **b :** to cause to seem short ⟨have tried to ~ or to enliven the tedium of waiting —C.E. Montague⟩ ⟨many a long night he ~*ed* for us with his stories and songs —Michael O'Reilly⟩ **c :** to cut down in amount or extent **:** LESSEN ⟨found their pleasures ~*ed* by emptiness of purse —J.A.Froude⟩ **d :** to cut back (a shoot) in pruning **2 a :** to reduce in power or efficiency ⟨is my hand ~*ed,* that it cannot redeem —Isa 50:2 (RSV)⟩ **b** *obs* **:** to deprive of effect ⟨to be known ~*s* my made intent —Shak.⟩ **c :** to prevent from securing **3 :** to get a closer grip on **:** grasp nearer the middle ⟨~*ed* his bat⟩ **4 :** to put into smallclothes **5 :** to make crumbly ⟨~ pastry with butter⟩ **~** *vi* **1 :** to become short or shorter ⟨when the early summer days begin to cool and ~ —Hugh Cave⟩ **2** *of betting odds* **:** DECREASE, LOWER

⟨looked quickly at the betting . . . six to one, ~*ing* to eleven to two —Robert Westerby⟩

syn CURTAIL, ABBREVIATE, ABRIDGE, RETRENCH: these verbs have in common the sense of to reduce in extent, esp. by cutting. SHORTEN commonly implies reduction in length or duration ⟨*shorten* a rope⟩ ⟨*shorten* a war⟩ ⟨*shorten* the pain by administering drugs⟩ ⟨*shorten* a life⟩ CURTAIL generally adds to SHORTEN the idea of docking, a cutting that in some way deprives of completeness ⟨emergency orders drastically *curtailing* the use of fuel —*Current Biog.*⟩ ⟨the country editor *curtailed* his contributions on large issues —*Amer. Guide Series: Minn.*⟩ ABBREVIATE implies a making shorter usually by omitting some part or cutting off some normally following part; thus, one *abbreviates* a word or phrase by cutting out or cutting off letters in such a way that the remaining part stands for the whole ⟨*abbreviate* the name *Shakespeare* to *Shak.*⟩ ⟨a . . . man of great physical strength and energy, though of *abbreviated* intelligence —W.L.Shirer⟩ ABRIDGE, sometimes interchangeable with SHORTEN and CURTAIL ⟨*abridge* visiting hours at the hospital during the epidemic⟩ ⟨*abridge* freedom of speech⟩ generally suggests reduction in extent, compass, or scope but usu. implies the retention of the essential elements and a relative completeness in the result ⟨so fearful of being detected . . . that I must *abridge* this narrative —Charles Dickens⟩ ⟨*abridge* the large volume so that it can be read in one evening⟩ RETRENCH puts stress upon reduction in extent or costs of something felt to be in excess ⟨must *retrench* on the expenses of her household —Edith Sitwell⟩ ⟨in keeping with the austerity drive the school administration *retrenched* on our coal supply —Maria Yen⟩ — **shorten sail** : to reduce the extent of sail (as by reefing or furling)

short end *n* **1** : the inferior or losing end **2** : the side receiving odds in a bet

shorten down *vi* : to shorten sail ⟨the wind came ripping out of the west, and for the first time we *shortened down* to less than working canvas —A.F.Loomis⟩

short·en·er \-t(ᵊ)nə(r)\ *n* -s : one that shortens

shorten in *vt* **1** : to take in the slack of (a rope) **2** : to heave in the cable

shortening *n* -s [fr. gerund of *shorten*] **1** : the action or process of making or becoming short; *specif* : the dropping of the latter part of a word so as to produce a new and shorter word of the same meaning **2** : an edible fat used to shorten baked goods (as pastry or cookies)

shorter *comparative of* SHORT

short ess *var of* SHORT S

shortest *superlative of* SHORT

shortfall \ˈ⸗ˌ⸗\ *n* [¹*short* + *fall* (after the phrase *fall short*)] : the act or an instance of falling short or the amount by which something falls short : DEFICIT, SHORTAGE ⟨standing useless because of a ~ in traversing mechanisms —*Time*⟩ ⟨the ~ will amount to $4 to $5 billion —*Newsweek*⟩

short-fed \ˈ⸗¦⸗\ *adj, of cattle* : kept on a fattening ration for a period of three months or less — compare LONG-FED

short field *n* : the area of a baseball infield to the left of second base

short-focus lens \ˈ⸗ˌ⸗⸗-\ *n* : a camera lens having a focal length substantially less than that of the lens normally supplied with a particular type of camera

short game *n* **1** : the phase of golf in which accuracy of direction and control of limited distance (as in approach play or putting) are factors of first importance — compare LONG GAME **2** : a card game in which not all the cards are dealt

short gown *n* [ME *short goun*] **1** : NIGHTGOWN **2** : a short-skirted dress

short grain *adj* : having the machine direction running the short way of the sheet ⟨*short grain* paper⟩

short-grained \ˈ⸗¦⸗\ *adj* : having a short fiber — used chiefly of wood and bone

shortgrass \ˈ⸗ˌ⸗\ *n* : any of various grasses that are characterized by short stature and marked drought tolerance, form the dominant feature of dry upland plains (as those just east of the Rocky mountains), and include important range grasses of such lands — compare MIDGRASS, TALLGRASS

shorthair \ˈ⸗ˌ⸗\ *also* **short-haired cat** \ˈ⸗ˌ⸗-\ *n* : a domestic cat with a relatively short close coat in which the guard hairs are not notably elongated — compare LONG HAIR

¹**shorthand** \ˈ⸗ˌ⸗\ *n* [¹*short* + *hand*] **1** : a method of writing rapidly by substituting characters, abbreviations, or symbols for letters, words, or phrases : STENOGRAPHY — compare LONGHAND **2** : a system or instance of rapid or abbreviated communication or notation ⟨could converse in a joking verbal ~, which meant little to anyone else —Robert Graves⟩ ⟨a master of visual ~ . . . could capture in a few light strokes the elusive passing moment —*Fortnight*⟩

²**shorthand** \"\ *adj* **1 a** : using shorthand ⟨a ~ reporter⟩ **b** : written in shorthand ⟨a ~ report⟩ **2** : of, relating to, or involving an abbreviated or symbolic method of communication or expression ⟨one of those rare watercolorists who work from nature in quick ~ notes —L.S.Reiss⟩ ⟨this ~ historical chronicle —Nancy Ross⟩ **3** : resembling shorthand : ABRIDGED, CONDENSED ⟨the committee majority type of ~ mathematics —R.M.Blough⟩

shorthanded \ˈ⸗¦⸗⸗\ *adj* **1** : short of the regular or necessary number of people : inadequately staffed : UNDERMANNED ⟨passed shells to the ~ mortar crew —*Time*⟩ **2** : having short hands — **short·hand·ed·ness** *n* -ES

short haul *n* **1** : transportation of goods or passengers for a short distance **2** : a comparatively brief period of time — used with *the* ⟨to achieve this, Americans must work for the long pull — not the *short haul* —Earl Bunting⟩

short-haul \ˈ⸗¦⸗\ *adj* [*short haul*] **1** : traveling or involving a short distance ⟨a *short-haul* bus⟩ ⟨*short-haul* flights⟩ **2** : of, relating to, or lasting for a short period ⟨*short-haul* attractions such as the glitter of a fraternity —C.E.Lovejoy⟩

shorthead \ˈ⸗ˌ⸗\ *n* : a brachycephalic individual : ROUNDHEAD

short head *n, Brit* : a margin of victory in a horse race of less than the length of a horse's head

short-headed \ˈ⸗¦⸗⸗\ *adj* : BRACHYCEPHALIC — **short-head·ed·ness** *n* -ES

shorthorn \ˈ⸗ˌ⸗\ *n* **1** *usu cap* : a breed of red, roan, or white beef cattle originating in the north of England and including good milk-producing strains from which the Milking Shorthorn breed has been evolved — called also *Durham* **2** -s *often cap* **a** : an animal of the Shorthorn breed **b** : any of various small African cattle with short horns and a high resistance to trypanosome infections **3** -s *slang* : TENDERFOOT

short-horned buffalo \ˈ⸗ˌ⸗-\ *n* : a small reddish or blackish West African buffalo that is a variety of the Cape buffalo distinguished by short upwardly curved horns and fringed ears

short-horned grasshopper *n* : a grasshopper of the family Acrididae

short hundredweight *n* : HUNDREDWEIGHT a — see MEASURE table

shor·tia \ˈshȯ(r)d·ēə\ *n* [NL, fr. Charles Wilkins *Short* †1863 Am. physician and botanist + NL *-ia*] **1** *cap* : a genus of perennial herbs (family Diapensiaceae) having smooth coriaceous basal leaves and long-stalked showy white and solitary flowers with campanulate corollas — see OCONEE BELLS **2** -s : any plant of the genus *Shortia*

shortie *var of* SHORTY

shorting *pres part of* SHORT

short interest *n* : the sum of securities or commodities sold short as of a given date — called also *short position*

short iron *n* **1** : a golf iron (as a No. 7, No. 8, or No. 9 iron) that has a short shaft and relatively great loft and is used for hitting a ball near the green **2** : a shot or stroke made with a short iron — compare LONG IRON

short·ish \ˈshȯrd·ish\ *adj* : somewhat short

short·ite \ˈshȯrd·ˌīt\ *n* -s [Maxwell N. *Short* †1952 Am. mineralogist + E *-ite*] : a mineral $Na_2Ca_2(CO_3)_3$ consisting of a carbonate of sodium and calcium

short jenny *n* : a losing hazard in English billiards in which the ball is played in a middle pocket of the table — compare LONG JENNY

short-jointed \ˈ⸗¦⸗⸗\ *adj* : having short intervals between the joints

short-laid \ˈ⸗¦⸗\ *adj* : HARD-LAID

shortleaf pine \ˈ⸗ˌ⸗-\ *n* **1** *also* **shortleaf yellow pine** **a** : a pine (*Pinus echinata*) of the southern U. S. that has short flexible leaves and cinnamon-colored bark **b** : the yellow wood of the shortleaf pine **2** : LOBLOLLY PINE 1

short-leaved pine \ˈ⸗¦⸗-\ *n* : SHORTLEAF PINE

short leet *n, Scot* : a select list; *esp* : a limited list of candidates submitted to an elective or appointive authority

short leg *n* : a fielding position in cricket on the leg side relatively close to the batsman; *also* : a player fielding in this position — compare LONG LEG; see CRICKET illustration

short line *n* **1** : the railroad or combination of railroads having the shortest mileage between two points **2** : a transportation system (as a railroad or bus line) operating over a relatively short distance

short-lived \ˈ⸗¦līvd, -livd\ *adj* [²*short* + *lived*] **1** : having a short life ⟨men are *short-lived* in comparison with women⟩ **2** : lasting only a short time ⟨*short-lived* joy⟩ ⟨*short-lived* interest⟩ **syn** see TRANSIENT

short-lived·ness *n* -ES : the quality or state of being short-lived

short loin *n* : the portion of a hindquarter of beef which starts behind the ribs and from which club, T-bone, and porterhouse steaks are cut — see BEEF illustration

short·ly *adv* [ME, fr. OE *scortlice*, fr. *scortlic* brief, fr. *scort* short + *-lic* -ly — more at SHORT] **1 a** : in a few words : BRIEFLY ⟨may be described ~⟩ ⟨to put it ~⟩ **b** : in an abrupt manner : CURTLY, HARSHLY ⟨said ~ that they looked all right, his antagonism beginning to rise —Archibald Marshall⟩ **2 a** : in a short time : PRESENTLY, SOON ⟨the two concluding volumes which will appear ~ —P.H.Douglas⟩ **b** : at a short interval of time ⟨the glacial action which ~ preceded man's arrival in America —R.W.Murray⟩ ⟨~ before⟩ ⟨~ after⟩ **c** : for a short time **3** : at or for no great distance : not far ⟨~ beyond this site —*Amer. Guide Series: Vt.*⟩ ⟨an apron that fell from her waist to ~ below her knees —*Newsweek*⟩

short mark *n* : BREVE 2a

short meter *n* **1** *also* **short measure** : a quatrain of which the first, second, and fourth lines are in iambic trimeter and the third in iambic tetrameter : a poulter's measure written as a quatrain — abbr. *S.M.* **2 a** : quick work ⟨make *short meter* of the job⟩ **b** : a short time ⟨finished the job in *short meter*⟩

short-natured \ˈ⸗¦⸗⸗\ *adj, of glass* : having a short temperature range within which easy working or shaping is possible : setting quickly — contrasted with *good-natured*

short·ness *n* -ES [ME *shortnesse*, fr. *short* + *-nesse* -ness] **1** : the quality or state of being short in length, distance, or duration : BREVITY ⟨the ~ of his fingers⟩ ⟨the ~ of the trip⟩ ⟨the ~ of the days in winter⟩ **2 a** *obs* : CONCISENESS ⟨your plainness and your ~ please me well —Shak.⟩ **b** : ABRUPTNESS, CURTNESS ⟨our anger changed to glumness and ~ with each other —A.R.Matthews⟩ **3** : defectiveness of range or vision ⟨the ~ of his sight⟩ **4** *of metals* : BRITTLENESS **5** : DEFICIENCY, SCANTINESS ⟨the ~ of provisions⟩ ⟨hampered by a ~ of money⟩

short-nosed cattle louse \ˈ⸗ˌ⸗-\ *n* : a large bluish broad-bodied and short-headed sucking louse (*Haematopinus eurysternus*) that attacks domestic cattle

shortnose gar *also* **short-nosed gar** *or* **short-nosed garfish** \ˈ⸗ˌ⸗-\ *n* : a gar of the family Lepisosteidae

short oat *n* : an oat (*Avena brevis*) cultivated in mountainous parts of Europe for its grain

short octave *n* : an incomplete lowest octave in an organ or keyboard musical instrument having certain seldom used tones omitted and tuned according to those tones most frequently used — called also *broken octave*

short of *prep* **1** : not reaching to : on this side of : up to ⟨possesses a meticulous memory just *short of* total recall —Robert Cantwell⟩ ⟨took all measures *short of* war⟩ ⟨a talent little *short of* genius⟩ **2** : with the exclusion or exception of : except for ⟨*short of* a new fight by the senators on the patent or power provisions, the bill may soon be law —*New Republic*⟩

short-oil \ˈ⸗¦⸗\ *adj* : containing a relatively low proportion of drying oil to resin ⟨*short-oil* varnishes are very hard, brittle and glossy⟩ — compare OIL LENGTH

short·om·e·ter \shȯ(r)d·ˈäməd·ə(r)\ *n* [*shortening* + *-o-* + *-meter*] : a device used by commercial bakers for testing the shortening power of various fats in dough

short order *n* : an order for food that can be quickly cooked

short-paid \ˈ⸗¦⸗\ *adj* **1** : bearing less than the required amount of stamps : having insufficient postage ⟨*short-paid* airmail letter⟩ **2** : paid short of the legal requirement ⟨*short-paid* postage⟩

short paint *n* : a stiff paint that has poor flowing properties

short pair *n* : a pair short of opening requirements in poker jackpots : a pair ranking lower than a pair of jacks

short particular meter *n* : a six-line hymn stanza of which the first, second, and fifth lines are iambic trimeter and the third, fourth, and sixth are iambic tetrameter

shortpath distillation \ˈ⸗ˌ⸗-\ *n* : MOLECULAR DISTILLATION

short-period comet *n* : one of numerous periodic comets whose times of revolution around the sun range from 3.3 years (as for Encke's comet) to a few dozen years

short-period variable *n* : a variable star whose regular cycle of light fluctuations has a length of a few hours, days, or weeks

short plate *n* : the shortest leaf of a leaf spring

short position *n* : SHORT INTEREST

short-range \ˈ⸗¦⸗\ *adj* : having a short range : of or relating to a short distance or a short period of time ⟨*short-range* navigation⟩ ⟨a *short-range* policy⟩

short rate *n* : an insurance premium charge for less than a year of coverage that is more than a pro rata part of the annual premium

short ribs *n pl* : a cut of beef consisting of rib ends between the rib roast and the plate — see BEEF illustration

short run *n* **1** : a period during which the factors in a situation remain relatively stable **2** : a run in cricket that is invalidated by the failure of a batsman to touch the ground inside the popping crease at one end before he starts to run to the other end; *also* : a run made from a hit that sends the ball a very short distance

short-run \ˈ⸗¦⸗\ *adj* [*short run*] **1** : of or relating to a relatively brief period of time ⟨*short-run* planning⟩ ⟨*short-run* thinking⟩ **2** : only partially filled with molten metal — used of a mold or casting

shorts *pl of* SHORT, *pres 3d sing of* SHORT

short s *or* **short ess** *n* : the ordinary written or printed lowercase form of the letter s — compare LONG S

short·schat \ˈshȯrt,shat\ *or* **shortschat pine** *also* **short·shat** \"\ *or* **shortshat pine** *n* -s [¹*short* + *shat*] **1** : SHORTLEAF PINE 1 **2** : a scrub pine (*Pinus virginiana*)

short score *n* : a condensed orchestral score with the less important parts omitted — called also *compressed score*

short-sea \ˈ⸗¦⸗\ *adj* : moving or carried on between ports relatively close to each other ⟨*short-sea* traffic⟩ ⟨*short-sea* trade⟩ — compare COASTWISE

short seller *n* [¹*short* + *seller* (after *sell short*)] : one who makes a short sale

short selling *n* [¹*short* + *selling* (after *sell short*)] : the act or practice of making a short sale

short service line *n* : a line 6½ feet behind the net that marks the point beyond which a serve in badminton must travel

short session *n* : a session of a U. S. Congress before 1934 beginning in December of an even-numbered year following an election and terminating on March 3 of the next year — compare LAME DUCK

short sheet *n* : a sheet leading from the inner clew of a topmast studding sail into the top

short-sheet \ˈ⸗¦⸗\ *vt* : to make up (a bed) in such a way that a person cannot get in under the covers

short-short \ˈ⸗¦⸗\ *n* : an extremely brief short story usu. seeking an effect of shock or surprise

short shrift *n* **1** : a brief respite from death ⟨taken thus with but *short shrift*, the young Pharaoh hesitated not a moment in attempting to cut his way out —J.H.Breasted⟩ **2 a** : summary treatment : little consideration ⟨this kind of talk, however good, gets *short shrift* from me —M.D.Armstrong⟩ ⟨unfortunately, little care is given *short shrift* —R.K.Beardsley⟩ **b** : quick work ⟨of this breed we can make *short shrift* —Lucius Garvin⟩

short-shucks \ˈshȯrt,shəks\ *n pl but sing or pl in constr* : SHORTSCHAT 2

short sight *n* : MYOPIA

shortsighted \ˈ⸗¦⸗⸗\ *adj* **1** : not able to see far : NEARSIGHTED, MYOPIC **2 a** (1) : not looking ahead : not anticipating or planning for the future : lacking foresight ⟨became the object of widespread derision by ~ critics —*Amer. Guide Series: Minn.*⟩ (2) : characterized by lack of foresight ⟨~ policies⟩ ⟨~ investments⟩ **b** : concerned with immediate advantage only ⟨a ~ rush for quick profits —P.E.James⟩ — **short·sight·ed·ly** *adv*

short·sight·ed·ness *n* -ES : the quality or state of being shortsighted

short snorter *n* [*short snort* quick drink + *-er*] **1** : a member of an informal club for which a pilot, crew member, or passenger who has made a transoceanic flight is eligible **2** : a piece of paper money (as a dollar bill) endorsed by short snorters as a membership certificate for a new member

short·some \ˈshärtsəm\ *adj* [¹*short* + *-some*] *Scot* : making time seem short : DIVERTING, ENTERTAINING

short splice *n* : a splice using less material than the long splice but increasing the circumference

short splice

short-spoken \ˈ⸗¦⸗\ *adj* : not given to wasting words : CURT

short-staple \ˈ⸗-\ *adj* : having relatively short fibers

¹**shortstop** \ˈ⸗ˌ⸗\ *n* [¹*short* + *stop* (after the phrase *stop short*)] **1** : a workman at a rod mill who diverts the rod for winding in a coil **2 a** : the player position in baseball for defending the infield area to the third-base side of second base — see BASEBALL illustration **b** : the player stationed in the shortstop position **3** : an agent that interrupts at some desired stage a polymerization reaction proceeding by way of radicals

²**shortstop** \"\ *vt* : to cause (a polymerization reaction) to stop by adding a suitable chemical

short-stop \ˈ⸗ˌ⸗\ *or* **short-stop bath** *n* [¹*short* + *stop* (after the phrase *stop short*)] : STOP BATH

short story *n* **1** : a relatively brief invented prose narrative that typically deals with a limited group of characters involved in a single action, usu. aims at unity of effect, and often concentrates on the creation of mood rather than the telling of a story **2** *slang* : a forged check

short-story writer *n, slang* : a check forger

short subject *n* : a short film

short sweetening *n, South & Midland* : SUGAR — compare LONG SWEETENING

short-swing \ˈ⸗ˌ⸗\ *adj* : tending to close out commitments quickly ⟨*short-swing* traders⟩; *also* : SHORT-TERM 2b

shortswing \ˈ⸗ˌ⸗\ *n* [trans. of G *kurzschwung*] : a skiing technique developed for maximum speed esp. in slalom racing and based on sideslipping, heel thrusting, and keeping the ski edges parallel

shorttail \ˈ⸗ˌ⸗\ *n* : a snake of the family Aniliidae

short-tailed albatross \ˈ⸗ˌ⸗-\ *n* : a large and chiefly white albatross (*Diomedea albatrus*) found in the northern Pacific ocean

short-tailed mealybug *n* : a mealybug having short terminal filaments

short-tailed shrew *n* : any of several No. American shrews of *Blarina* or a related genus with dense usu. gray or dark brown fur, a tail less than half the body length, often a toxic saliva, and in some cases scent glands on the sides which release a noxious secretion

short-tailed wallaby *n* : QUOKKA

shortt clock \ˈshȯ(ə)rt-\ *n, usu cap S* [after William H. *Shortt*, 20th cent. Eng. inventor] : an accurate clock having an improved free pendulum

short-tempered \ˈ⸗¦⸗⸗\ *adj* : having a quick temper

short-term \ˈ⸗¦⸗\ *adj* **1** : occurring over or involving a relatively short period of time — opposed to *long-term* **2 a** : of or relating to a financial transaction based on a term usu. of less than a year **b** : of or relating to capital assets held for less than six months

short-term·er \"+ə(r)\ *n* [fr. the phrase *short term* + *-er*] : a person serving a short prison sentence

short-term note *n* : a financial obligation that generally runs for less than two years

short-term paper *n* : a negotiable paper (as a note or bill) that matures within a three to six months period

short time *n* : a reduced working period

short-time \ˈ⸗¦⸗\ *adj* [fr. the phrase *short time*] : of, relating to, or limited to a short period of time

short-tim·er \"+ə(r)\ *n* [fr. the phrase *short time* + *-er*] : one that serves for a short time; *esp* : SHORT-TERMER

short title *n* : an abbreviated form of entry for a book in a list or catalog that usu. gives only the author's name, the title in brief, the date and place of publication, and the publisher's or printer's name

short-toed eagle \ˈ⸗ˌ⸗-\ *n* : HARRIER EAGLE

short ton *n* : TON 1b — see MEASURE table

¹**shortwave** \ˈ⸗¦⸗\ *n, often attrib* [¹*short* + *wave*] **1** : an electromagnetic or radio wave having a wavelength of between 10 and 100 meters **2** : a radio transmitter using shortwaves

²**shortwave** \ˈ⸗ˈ⸗\ *vt* : to transmit by radio using shortwaves

shortwave therapy *n* : medical diathermy in which wavelengths of about 11 meters are employed

short weight *n* : weight less than the stated weight : UNDERWEIGHT

short-weight \ˈ⸗ˈ⸗\ *vt* [*short weight*] : to defraud with short weight

short whist *n* : whist played under the rule that five points constitute a game

short-winded \ˈ⸗¦⸗⸗\ *adj* [ME, fr. *short* + *winded*] **1** : affected with or characterized by shortness of breath : easily put out of breath **2 a** : BRIEF ⟨the most sensible, sympathetic, scholarly, and *short-winded* exposition —*Times Lit. Supp.*⟩ **b** : broken up into short units : DISCONNECTED ⟨an especially bumpy kind of *short-winded* prose —S.E.Fitzgerald⟩

¹**short-wool** *or* **short-wooled** \ˈ⸗¦⸗\ *adj* [¹*short* + *wool* or *wooled*, fr. *wool* + *-ed*] : of, relating to, or being domestic sheep that have short but fine wool ⟨Southdown, Shropshire, and Suffolk are breeds of *short-wooled* sheep⟩

²**short-wool** \ˈ⸗ˌ⸗\ *n* : a short-wool sheep

shorty *or* **short·ie** \ˈshȯr|d·ē, -ȯ(ə)|, |t|, |i\ *n, pl* **short·ies** : one that is short: as **a** : a person of less than average height **b** : a garment of less than average length

short yard rope *n* : a rope hooked to the slings of a topgallant or royal yard and used with a purchase whose fall leads to the deck to hoist the yard

short yearling *n* : a young beef animal approaching one year in age; *esp* : one between 9 and 12 months old

shor·tzy \ˈshȯrtsē\ *n, pl* **shortzy** *or* **shortzies** *usu cap* **1** : a mixed nomadic Tatar people of western Siberia **2** : a member of the Shortzy people

sho·sho·ko \shəˈshō(ˌ)kō, shōˈ-\ *n, pl* **shoshokoes** *or* **shoshokos** *usu cap* [Shoshoni, lit., walker] **1** : a Shoshonean people of southern Utah and neighboring states **2** : any member of the Shoshoko people

sho·sho·ne·an \shəˈshōnēən, shōˈ-, ¦shōshə¦nēən\ *n, pl* **shoshonean** *or* **shoshoneans** *usu cap* [*Shoshone* + *-an*] **1** : a language family of the Uto-Aztecan phylum comprising the languages of most of the Uto-Aztecan peoples in the U. S. **2 a** : any of the Indian peoples whose language is Shoshonean **b** : a member of any such peoples

sho·sho·ni *also* **sho·sho·nee** \shəˈshōnē, shōˈ-, -ni\ *n, pl* **shoshoni** *or* **shoshonis** *also* **shoshone** *or* **shoshones** *or* **shoshonee** *or* **shoshonees** *usu cap* **1 a** : a group of Shoshonean peoples in California, Colorado, Idaho, Nevada, Utah, and Wyoming **b** : a member of such group of peoples **2** : the language of the Shoshoni people

¹**shot** \ˈshät, *usu* -ăd.+V\ *n* -s [ME, fr. OE *scot*, *sceot*; akin to OFris & ON *skot* action of throwing, missile, shot, OHG *scoz* missile, *scuz* shot, *skiozzan* to shoot — more at SHOOT] **1 a** : an action of shooting : RUSH, FLASH ⟨a ~ of lightning⟩ ⟨heard the ~ of the bolt on the front door⟩ **b** : a directed propelling of a missile (as an arrow, stone, rocket) ⟨took a ~ at the hat with his snowball⟩ ⟨fired a second rocket ~ at the

moon); *specif* **:** a directed discharge of a firearm ⟨heard three ~s fired in rapid succession⟩ ⟨exchanged ~s but no one was hit⟩ ⟨a bad ~ that missed by a mile⟩ **c** (1) **:** a stroke in a game (as billiards, golf, or tennis) (2) **:** a scoring stroke or throw (as in cricket, curling) (3) **:** a try for goal (as in basketball, hockey, lacrosse, soccer) **d :** a single cast and haul of a fishing net or set of nets **e :** one throw of the shuttle in weaving **:** ⁵PICK 2a **f :** the act of estimating distance or altitude by means of an instrument (as a sextant, transit) **g :** a setting off of a charge of explosives **:** BLAST ⟨the fifth ~ of the 1955 nuclear test series —*N. Y. Times*⟩ **h :** an injection of a drug, immunizing substance, nutrient, or medicament ⟨got a ~ for the pain⟩ ⟨gave himself a second ~ of the narcotic⟩ **2 a** *pl* **shot :** material propelled by shooting: as (1) **:** large solid or nearly solid projectiles (as for a cannon) with no bursting charge ⟨heaps of shells, scrap iron, and solid ~ were placed on top of the gunpowder —C.S.Forester⟩ ⟨granite ~ was used for guns . . . in the sixteenth century —E.E.Evans⟩ ⟨the ~ and shell of an election year —*Time*⟩ (2) **:** small lead or steel pellets of any of various sizes for ammunition of which a quantity usu. loaded in a cartridge forms a charge for a shotgun — see BB, BIRD SHOT, BUCKSHOT; CARTRIDGE illustration (3) **:** a single projectile of such shot ⟨load another ~⟩ ⟨BB ~ are a poor goose load —Elmer Keith⟩ **b :** a metal sphere of iron or brass usu. weighing 16 pounds for men's events or 8 pounds for women's events which is put for distance **c** *pl* **shot** (1) **:** metal in small pellets for use as an abrasive (as for blast cleaning of castings, core drilling, and sawing, grinding, and polishing stone), for peening, and for other industrial or craft use — compare GRIT (2) **:** a single pellet of such shot ⟨a cracked ~⟩ ⟨~ are soldered to metal parts —A.F.Rose & Antonio Cirino⟩ **3 :** one of the forged lengths of chain usu. 15 fathoms long and joined by shackles to form an anchor cable **4 a :** a place or spot for setting nets **b :** a single catch of fish **5 a :** the distance that a missile is or can be thrown ⟨lying a cannon ~ apart⟩ **b :** the distance within which something is effective **:** RANGE, REACH ⟨out of the ~ and danger of desire —Shak.⟩ **6 :** a charge to be paid (as at a tavern) **:** SCOT, BILL **7** *dial Eng* **:** FURLONG 2a **8 :** one that shoots: **a** *obs* **:** a soldier with a firearm; *also* **:** a group of such soldiers **b :** MARKSMAN ⟨policemen who are all good ~s with a pistol⟩ **9 a** (1) **:** an effort designed to accomplish a definite end **:** ATTEMPT, TRY, GO ⟨his first ~ at saying anything —P.G.Wodehouse⟩ — often used in the phrase *have a shot at* ⟨sent for the village priest to have a ~ at reforming him —*Calgary (Canada) Herald*⟩ (2) **:** an exchange in checkers that is advantageous to the side that forces it **b :** GUESS, CONJECTURE ⟨made rather random ~s in identifying the men . . . cantering up and down —William Black⟩ ⟨dating on stylistic grounds alone is but a ~ in the dark because too often we lack the proper elements of comparison —Maurice Vieyra⟩ **c :** a chance at odds ⟨a horse that left the gate as a 12 to 1 ~⟩ ⟨it's a 10 to 1 ~ that he'll be on time⟩ **d :** a chance to do something **:** OPPORTUNITY ⟨give you a ~ at the property first —Sinclair Lewis⟩ **e :** a single appearance as an entertainer ⟨was offered a guest ~ on a television program⟩ **10** *dial Brit* **:** a creature of little value (as an animal culled from a herd or a young or stunted animal) **11 :** a remark so directed as to have telling effect ⟨"you're finished in New York . . ." was his parting ~ —Polly Adler⟩ **12 a :** a single photographic exposure; *esp* **:** SNAPSHOT **b :** a single sequence of a motion picture or a television program shot by one camera without interruption **:** a continuous view produced from one camera angle or by panning or dollying ⟨a moving ~⟩ ⟨a head-on ~⟩ ⟨an action ~⟩ — see CLOSE SHOT, LONG SHOT, MEDIUM SHOT, PROCESS SHOT, TRAVEL SHOT **13 a :** a weft thread shot through the shed in one throw of a weaving shuttle **:** ⁵PICK 2b **b :** the number of filling yarns to each row of tufts in carpet manufacture ⟨two-*shot* carpet⟩ **14 :** a charge of explosives ⟨a ~ of nitroglycerine⟩ **15 a :** a quantity (as of a drug) for injection **b :** a single drink of liquor **:** a serving (as of whiskey) that can be drunk in one swallow; *esp* **:** a jigger of spirits taken undiluted **c :** a small amount applied at one time **:** DOSE ⟨sometimes, in flight, the pilot may want a momentary ~ of oxygen —*Popular Science Monthly*⟩ ⟨a dramatist could inject a ~ of colloquialism into a tragic aria —Kenneth Tynan⟩ **16 :** the quantity (as of plastic) injected into a mold at one time — **like a shot** *adv* **1 :** QUICKLY, INSTANTANEOUSLY ⟨the dog lunged against the opening, came through *like a shot* . . . and tore out of the house —Erle Stanley Gardner⟩ **2 :** without hesitation **:** WILLINGLY ⟨if we could do anything in return, then we would *like a shot* —D.G. Mackail⟩ — **shot in the arm :** STIMULUS, BOOST ⟨possible for such inspirational or emotional *shots in the arm* to hop us up and give us temporary relief —W.J.Reilly⟩ ⟨machine tool industry will get a $100 million *shot in the arm* —*Time*⟩ — **shot in the locker 1 :** a shot left in a war vessel's shot locker **2 :** a remnant or reserve of money or supplies **:** a last resource

²shot \"\ *adj* [partly fr. ¹*shot,* partly fr. *shot* (past part. of *shoot*), fr. ME *shoten, shot* — more at SHOTTEN] **1 :** of, relating to, or used with ordnance or firearms shot ⟨~ hoist⟩ **2 a :** of contrasting and changeable color effects in fabrics produced by weaving warp and weft threads of different colors or by dyeing a fabric made of two fibers (as cotton and nylon) that react to dyes in varying manner **:** IRIDESCENT ⟨~ silk⟩ **:** VARIEGATED ⟨black cloth ~ with silver thread⟩ **b :** suffused or streaked with a color ⟨the sky was a cold gray, ~ over with a coppery light —T.B.Costain⟩ ⟨his hair was ~ with gray —Erle Stanley Gardner⟩ **c :** interpenetrated with an often contrasting quality or element **:** INFUSED, PERMEATED ⟨full of robust satire, ~ with gleams of tenderness —John Squire⟩ ⟨an outdated, feudalistic upper class, ~ through with quislings and collaborators —Bernard Seeman⟩ **3 :** having the form of pellets resembling shot ⟨~ clay soil⟩ ⟨~ copper⟩ ⟨~ ore⟩ **4 :** WELDED ⟨~ scissors⟩ **5 a** (1) **:** hit by a discharged missile ⟨the birds swallow lead pellets picked up . . . in heavily ~ areas —*Texas Game & Fish*⟩ (2) **:** reduced to a state of ruin, prostration, or uselessness ⟨went to a doctor because his nerves were ~⟩ **:** washed up **:** FINISHED ⟨a strike that left the bus line's business all ~⟩ **:** worn out ⟨replace the faucets that are pretty well ~ with some of the new type⟩ **b** *slang* **:** INTOXICATED ⟨killed the bottle and got ~⟩ **c :** used up ⟨my stock of adjectives is really ~, though, this late in the game —Richard Joseph⟩ **6 :** bleached or otherwise injured by excessive moisture ⟨~ wheat⟩

³shot \"\ *vb* **shotted; shotted; shotting; shots** [¹*shot*] *vt* **1 :** to subject to or form by the shotting process **2 :** to form into small round particles (as by spraying) ~ *vi* **:** to form into granules

⁴shot \"\ *chiefly dial var of* SHUT

shot bag *n* **:** a bag designed for carrying pellets of shot for a gun ⟨keeps his money in a *shot bag*⟩

shot berry *n* **:** a small imperfectly developed berry in a grape cluster

shot blade *n* [²*shot*] **:** the part of a grain stalk that encloses the developing head

¹shotblast \ˈ=,=\ *n* [¹*shot* + *blast*] **:** a stream of shot forcibly projected against a surface by air or steam (as for removing scale from oxidized metal)

²shotblast \"\ *vt* **:** to clean or descale with a shotblast

shotblaster \ˈ=,==\ *n* **:** one that does the work of a sandblaster using fine steel shot instead of sand

shot borer *n* **:** SHOT-HOLE BORER

shotbush \ˈ=,=\ *n* [¹*shot;* fr. the shape of the fruit] **1 :** HERCULES'-CLUB 3 **2 :** WILD SARSAPARILLA 1

shot cartridge *n* **:** a cartridge loaded with a charge of shot rather than a solid projectile

shot-clog *also* **shot-log** *n, obs* **:** a bore tolerated only because he pays the shot

¹shot·crete \ˈshät,krēt\ *n* -s [²*shot* + *concrete*] **:** a Gunite mixture

²shotcrete \"\ *vb* -ED/-ING/-S **:** GUNITE

shot drill *n* **:** a rotary rock drill using chilled steel shot as an abradant — compare CORE DRILL

shote *var of* SHOAT

shot effect *n* [trans. of G *schroteffekt*] **:** random fluctuations in the number of thermions per second emitted from the filament of a valve (as a vacuum tube) that give rise to sputtering or popping noises in the amplifier — compare THERMAL NOISE

shot-firer \ˈ=,==\ *n* **:** a miner who loads and fires drill holes

shot-free \ˈ=ˈ=\ *adj* [¹*shot* + *free*] **1** *archaic* **:** safe from being shot **2 :** SCOT-FREE

shot glass *n* **:** a glass holding one shot (as of whiskey)

¹shotgun \ˈ=,=\ *n* [¹*shot* + *gun*] **1 :** an often double-barreled smoothbore shoulder weapon for firing shot at short ranges — see GAUGE table; compare PUMP GUN **2 :** a variety of draw poker in which there is betting after each round of cards is dealt (as in stud poker)

²shotgun \"\ *adj* **1 :** of, relating to, or using a shotgun ⟨a ~ shell⟩ ⟨~ hunting⟩ **2 :** involving coercion (as by the threat of arms) **:** obtained, enforced, or marked by duress ⟨a ~ title⟩ ⟨a ~ quarantine⟩ ⟨a ~ agreement⟩ ⟨a ~ merger⟩ **3 a :** containing many ingredients or features of which one is expected to prove efficacious ⟨a ~ prescription⟩ ⟨~ therapy⟩ **b :** applied to a whole group or class without consideration of individual circumstances **:** covering a wide field with hit-or-miss effectiveness **:** inclusive but random ⟨~ propaganda mailed to all boxholders⟩ ⟨pledge themselves to selective, not ~, investigations —*New Republic*⟩ ⟨rely on direct controls, and . . . use a rifle not a ~ technique —*Fortune*⟩ **4** *South & Midland* **:** of or being a shotgun house ⟨a shack of ~ construction⟩

³shotgun \"\ *vt* **1 :** to shoot with a shotgun ⟨an enemy who *shotgunned* him from ambush⟩ **2 :** to compel as if with a shotgun **:** force by duress ⟨~ western Europe into federal unity —Andrew Roth⟩

shotgun can *n* **:** a tall narrow milk can holding about four gallons (as for setting)

shotgun can

shotgun feed *n* **:** a steam-driven feed for the log carriage of a sawmill

shotgun house *n, South & Midland* **:** a house in which all the rooms are in direct line with each other usu. front to back

shotgun marriage *or* **shotgun wedding** *n* **1 :** a marriage forced or required because of pregnancy **2 :** a forced union or accord between two groups or elements

shotgun messenger *n* **:** an armed guard on a stagecoach

shot hole *n* **1 :** a drilled hole in which a charge of dynamite is exploded in mining or to produce artificial earth vibrations in seismic prospecting for oil **2 :** a hole made in wood by a boring insect **3 a** *also* **shot-holing** \ˈ=,==\ **:** the dropping out of small rounded fragments of leaves because of parasitic action or other causes with a resultant shot-riddled appearance — compare CHERRY LEAF SPOT **b :** one of the perforations so formed

shot-hole borer *n* **:** a small bark beetle (*Scolytus rugulosus*) that attacks orchard fruit trees and kills the bark of small branches and twigs; *broadly* **:** any of several other beetles of the family Scolytidae attacking trees or shrubs (as the beetle *Xyleborus fornicatus* that attacks the tea plant)

shot·less \ˈshätləs\ *adj* **:** having no shot

shot lighter *n* **:** BLASTER

shotlike \ˈ=,=\ *adj* **:** resembling pellets of shot in shape or size

shot line *n* **:** a light line attached to a projectile and used with a Lyle or other line-throwing gun (as to pass a cable to a wrecked vessel)

shotmaker \ˈ=,==\ *n* **:** one that makes shots ⟨a left-handed ~ who because of his ability to shoot from any angle plays right wing —*Newsweek*⟩

shot·man \ˈshätmən\ *also* **shots·man** \-tsm-\ *n, pl* **shotmen** *also* **shotsmen :** BLASTER

shot metal *n* **:** an alloy of 98 percent lead and 2 percent arsenic for making small shot

shot noise *n* **:** a sputtering or popping produced (as in a radio) by shot effect

shot plant *n* **:** an Indian shot (*Canna indica*)

shot point *n* **:** the place at which an explosion generates vibrations in the ground (as in seismic prospecting)

shot put *n* [¹*shot* + *put* (after the phrase *put the shot*)] **1 :** a field event consisting in putting the shot for distance from a circle 7 feet in diameter **2 :** a throw of the shot in the shot put

shot-putter \ˈ=,==\ *n* [¹*shot* + *putter* (after the phrase *put the shot*)] **:** one who puts the shot in a field event

shot-putting \ˈ=,==\ *n* [¹*shot* + *putting* (after the phrase *put the shot*)] **:** the act or practice of putting the shot in a field event

shot rock *n* **:** the stone that is nearest the center of the rings in curling

shot rope *n* **:** a guide rope used in deep-sea diving that is attached to the ship near the ladder and has a sinker on the lower end

shots *pl of* SHOT, *pres 3d sing of* SHOT

shot samples *n* **:** samples taken for assay from molten metal by pouring a portion into water to granulate it

shotshell \ˈ=,=\ *n* **:** a shotgun cartridge loaded with shot — compare RIFLED SLUG

shotstar \ˈ=,=\ *n* [²*shot* + *star*] **1** *archaic* **:** METEOR **2 :** an alga (*Nostoc commune*)

¹shott \ˈshät\ *dial Brit var of* ¹SHOT 10

²shott *var of* CHOTT

³shott *var of* SHOAT

shot·ted \ˈshäd·əd\ *adj* [¹*shot* + *-ed*] **1 :** loaded with a shot — used esp. of a cannon not loaded with a blank charge (as for saluting, giving warning) **2 :** weighted down with shot ⟨a ~ tennis skirt⟩

shot·ten \ˈshätᵊn\ *adj* [ME *shotyn,* fr. *shoten, shotyn* (past part. of *sheten, shoten, shuten* to shoot), fr. OE *gescoten*] **1 a :** having ejected the spawn and so of inferior food value ⟨full or ~ herrings⟩ ⟨lean as a ~ herring⟩ **b** *dial* (1) **:** WEAKENED, DISPIRITED (2) **:** GOOD-FOR-NOTHING **2** *obs* **:** shot out of its socket ⟨swayed in the back and shoulder ~ —Shak.⟩

shotting *n* -s [fr. gerund of ³*shot*] **1 :** a process for producing metal shot or powders by dropping molten metal (as lead) through small openings from a height (as in a shot tower) so that the metal forms spherical drops in the descent that are received in water or other liquid **2 :** an operation in a process of producing wrought iron in which molten pig iron is poured into a ladle of molten slag at a temperature below the freezing point of the iron so that small globules of iron are formed, the slag absorbs the gases, and on cooling a porous ball of wrought iron forms — compare PUDDLING

shot to pieces *adj* **:** ²SHOT 5a(2)

shot tower *n* **:** a tower about 200 feet high for making shot by the shotting process

shot·ty \ˈshäd·ē\ *adj* -ER/-EST [¹*shot* + *-y*] **:** hard and round like a pellet of shot ⟨~ lymph nodes⟩

shot window *n* [ME *shotwyndowe,* fr. *shot* + *wyndowe, windowe* window] **:** a small casement window often with little or no glass formerly common in Scotland

shou \ˈshō\ *n* -s [Chin (Pek) *shou*⁴] **:** a Chinese character signifying longevity and often used in decoration

¹shough *n* -s [origin unknown] *obs* **:** a curly-haired lapdog believed to come orig. from Iceland

²shough \ˈshük\ *var of* SHEUGH

should [ME *sholde,* fr. OE *sceolde, scolde;* akin to OHG *scolta* owed, was obliged to, had to, ON *skylda* had to, Goth *skulda* owed, was obliged to, had to — more at SHALL] *past of* SHALL **1** — used in auxiliary function to express condition ⟨if he ~ call, I'm out⟩ ⟨for if he ~ leave his father, his father would die —Gen 44:22 (RSV)⟩ ⟨if I ~ die, think only this of me —Rupert Brooke⟩ ⟨~ Naples be captured . . . we shall have a first-rate port —Sir Winston Churchill⟩ ⟨as if the atom bomb ~ find a benevolent use —Herbert Kupferberg⟩ ⟨I ~ not allow anyone to inconvenience me if I could hinder it —Emily Brontë⟩ ⟨they can very easily be ennobled ~ they wish it —Nancy Mitford⟩ **2** — used in auxiliary function to express duty, obligation, necessity, propriety, or expediency ⟨for 'tis commanded I ~ do so —Shak.⟩ ⟨but now he is dead, why ~ I fast —2 Sam 12:23 (RSV)⟩ ⟨the law was then passed . . . that every senator ~ take an oath —J.A.Froude⟩ ⟨in such cases the officer ~ first give notice to those in the house —Paul Wilson⟩ ⟨and this is as it ~ be —H.L.Savage⟩ ⟨was determined that his son ~ have a good education⟩ ⟨you ~ brush your teeth after each meal⟩ **3** — used in auxiliary function to express futurity from a point of view in the past ⟨she realized that she ~ have to do most of her farm work before sunrise —Ellen Glasgow⟩ ⟨had expected that he ~ be able to press forward —T.B.Macaulay⟩ **4** *archaic* **:** MIGHT, COULD ⟨may have wondered what this present distress ~ mean —John Keble⟩ **5** — used in auxiliary function to express what is probable or expected ⟨this year's treasury deficit ~ be $6 billion or more —T.R.Ybarra⟩ ⟨effects of the trends cited above ~ not be felt . . . for another decade —A.W.Griswold⟩ ⟨it ~ be child's play for the three of us —John Buchan⟩ ⟨recordings which ~ confuse even the most ingenuous listener —Robert Evett⟩ ⟨with an early start, they ~ be here by noon⟩ **6** — used in auxiliary function to express a desire or request in a polite or unemphatic manner or to tone down a direct or blunt statement ⟨one aspect of his critical work to which I ~ like to call attention —Malcolm Cowley⟩ ⟨I ~ suggest that a guide to available materials is the first essential —L.D.Reddick⟩ ⟨~ you wish to look at it —O.Henry⟩ ⟨in general I ~ say that the salaries . . . make up very nearly two thirds of the budget —Deems Taylor⟩ **syn** see OUGHT

should-be \ˈ=,=\ *adj* [fr. the phrase *should be*] **:** that ought to be ⟨looking out for his *should-be* guardian⟩

¹shoul·der \ˈshōldə(r)\ *n* -s *often attrib* [ME *shulder, sholder,* fr. OE *sculdor;* akin to OFris *skuldere* shoulder, MLG *schulder,* MD *schouder,* OHG *scultra, sculterra* shoulder, OE *sciell* shell — more at SHELL] **1 a :** the laterally projecting part of the human body on each side of the base of the neck that is formed of the bones and joints by which the arm is connected with the trunk and the muscles covering them **b :** the corresponding but usu. less projecting region of the body of a lower vertebrate **:** the structures connecting the forelimb with the trunk **c :** the bend of the wing of a bird — not used technically; see GOOSE illustration **2 a :** the two shoulders and the upper part of the back forming together the part of the human frame on which it is most easy to carry a heavy burden — usu. used in pl. ⟨his ~s bowed with age⟩ **b shoulders** *pl* **:** capacity for bearing a task or blame **:** the seat of responsibility ⟨the task of conservation farming rests squarely on the ~s of the farmer —*Farmer's Weekly (So. Africa)*⟩ ⟨placed the guilt on the ~s of the planters —*Amer. Guide Series: Fla.*⟩ **3 a :** the upper joint of the foreleg and adjacent parts of an animal dressed for market including more or less of the neck and chest ⟨a ~ of mutton⟩ — see LAMB illustration **b :** the part of a leather hide between the butt and the cheeks and head — see HIDE illustration **4 :** the part of a garment at the wearer's shoulder **5 :** a part suggesting a human shoulder in shape, position, or function: as **a :** an angle or curve in the outline of an object (as between the body and the neck of a bottle) and often also the parts adjacent to it ⟨overloading causes . . . excessive strain of the fabric of the sidewalls and ~s of the tire —L.W.Mason⟩ ⟨a bolt threaded up to the ~⟩ ⟨the northwest ~ of Europe⟩ **b :** an abrupt projection that forms an abutment on an object or limits motion (as the projection around a tenon, the ring next to the wheel on an axle) **c :** an abutting projection between a blade and a tang (as of a knife or chisel) **d :** the flat top of the body of a piece of printing type from which the bevel rises to join the face; *sometimes* **:** the part of this area at the belly and back ends — compare SIDE BEARING; see TYPE illustration **e** (1) **:** the part of a hill or mountain near the top **:** the slope below the summit ⟨a road along the ~ of the mountain⟩ (2) **:** a lateral protrusion or extension of a hill or mountain ⟨from valley to intermediate ~s and crags, to a secondary and thence to the highest point —W.O.Douglas⟩ **f** (1) **:** the part of a railroad ballast between the end of the tie and the edge of the ballast slope (2) **:** the part of the railroad subgrade between the edge of the ballast and the ditch in cuts or between the edge of the ballast and the top of a slope on an embankment (3) **:** either edge of a roadway; *specif* **:** the part of a roadway outside of the traveled way on which vehicles may be parked in an emergency **g** (1) **:** a rough edge or ridge left beside a line or dot on a photoengraved plate (2) **:** a beveled edge around a printing plate by which the plate can be fastened to a base **h :** RIDGE 6 **i :** the section of a finger ring on either side of the central ornament or bezel **j :** the part of a flat key between the bow and the blade **6 :** HALF SOLE — **from the shoulder** *adv* **:** in a direct or outspoken manner of telling **:** without holding anything back ⟨tell them straight *from the shoulder* . . . that we intend to stay until someone kicks us out —O.E.Rölvaag⟩ — **shoulder to shoulder** *adv* **1 :** in close proximity **:** side by side ⟨soldiers fighting *shoulder to shoulder*⟩ ⟨old brick houses standing *shoulder to shoulder* against the sidewalk⟩ **2 :** in close cooperation ⟨work *shoulder to shoulder* in the common cause⟩

²shoulder \"\ *vb* **shouldered; shouldered; shouldering** \-d(ə)riŋ\ **shoulders** [ME *shulderen, sholderen,* fr. *shulder, sholder,* n.] *vt* **1 :** to push or thrust with or as if with the shoulder **:** JOSTLE ⟨~s his way through the crowd⟩ ⟨in China . . . the Dutch ~*ed* other European competitors aside —Stringfellow Barr⟩ **2 a :** to provide with a shoulder **:** form a shoulder on (as a casting) **b :** to fill or pad out as a shoulder (as ballast on the sides of a railroad track or mortar under the edge of a roofing slate) **3 a :** to place or bear on the shoulder ⟨~ a basket⟩; *specif* **:** to place (as a rifle) aslant on the shoulder **b :** to assume the burden or responsibility of ⟨~*ing* the burden of preparing these two books for publication —*Geog. Jour.*⟩ ⟨called to ~ the great responsibilities of high office —Clement Attlee⟩ ⟨~ the blame⟩ ⟨~ the costs of the war⟩ **4 :** to stand close beside ⟨old frame buildings ~ modern masonry structures in the business center —*Amer. Guide Series: Oreg.*⟩ ~ *vi* **1 :** to push with or as if with the shoulders **:** make one's way (as through a crowd) in an aggressive manner ⟨the mules ~ up to the trough —Christopher Rand⟩ ⟨the Scandinavians . . . who are trying to ~ into their sacred, ancient Yankee caste —Sinclair Lewis⟩ **2 :** to rise or protrude in a manner suggesting a shoulder ⟨the ridge that ~*ed* to the sky —J.H.Stuart⟩ ⟨a particularly dilapidated building that ~*ed* alarmingly out to one side —W.O.Mitchell⟩ **3 :** to move side by side ⟨a yoke of the great sulky white bullocks . . . came ~*ing* along together —Rudyard Kipling⟩

shoulder arm *n* **:** SHOULDER WEAPON

shoulder bag *n* **:** a woman's handbag that can be worn suspended by a shoulder strap

shoulder belt *n* **:** a belt passing over the shoulder — compare BANDOLIER

shoulder blade *n* [ME *shulder blade*] **:** SCAPULA 1a

shoulder block *n* **:** a block with a projection near the upper end so that it can rest against a spar without jamming the rope

shoulder board *n* **:** one of a pair of broad pieces of stiffened cloth worn on the shoulders of a military uniform and carrying insignia of rank; *specif* **:** SHOULDER MARK

shoulder bone *n* [ME *shulderbon, sholderbon*] **:** SCAPULA 1a

shoulder-clapper \ˈ==,==\ *n* -s *archaic* **:** BAILIFF

shouldered arch *n* **:** a spanning member consisting of a straight lintel carried on corbels projecting into the opening and usu. cut into hollow curves under their projecting ends

should·er·er \ˈshōld(ə)rə(r)\ *n* -s **:** one that shoulders

shoul·der·ette \ˌshōldəˈret\ *n* -s [¹*shoulder* + *-ette*] **:** a woman's light shawl with ends formed into sleeves

shoulderette

shoulder girdle *n* **:** PECTORAL GIRDLE; *esp* **:** a pectoral girdle that is complex and highly developed (as in most quadrupeds or in man)

shoulder-hand syndrome *n* **:** pain in and stiffening of the shoulder followed by swelling and stiffening of the hand and fingers often associated with or following myocardial infarction

shoulder head *n* **:** a printed head or subhead set flush with the left margin

shoulder-high \ˈ=ˈ=,=\ *adv (or adj)* **:** as high as or up to one's shoulder ⟨carried him *shoulder-high*⟩ ⟨a *shoulder-high* shelf⟩

shoulder-hitter \ˈ==,==\ *n* **:** ROWDY

shoul·der·ing \ˈshōld(ə)riŋ\ *n* -s [¹*shoulder* + *-ing*] **:** a projecting or supporting part: as **a :** the mortar under the edge of roofing slates **b :** SHOULDER 5f

shoulder knot *n* **1 :** an ornamental knot of ribbon or lace worn on the shoulder in the 17th and 18th centuries (as by

men of fashion, liveried servants) **2 :** a detachable ornament consisting of braided wire cord and worn on the shoulders of a uniform of ceremony by a commissioned officer
shoulder loop *n* **:** a flap on each shoulder of a service uniform

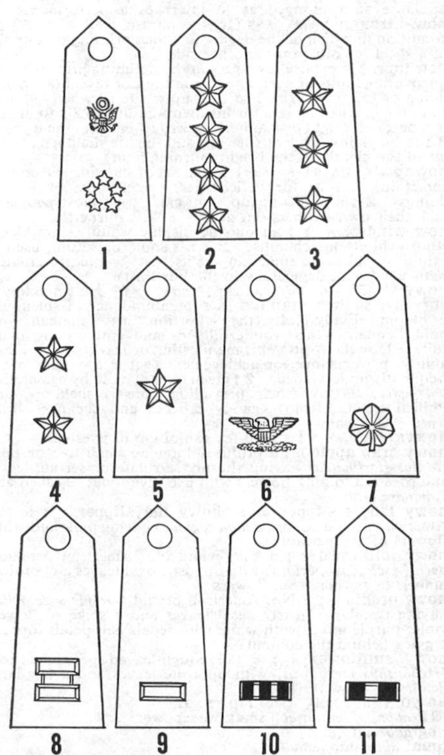

shoulder loops of United States Army: *1* general of the army, *2* general, *3* lieutenant general, *4* major general, *5* brigadier general, *6* colonel, *7* lieutenant colonel (silver oak leaf) and major (gold oak leaf) *8* captain, *9* first lieutenant (silver bar) and second lieutenant (gold bar) *10* chief warrant officer, grade IV (silver bar) and chief warrant officer, grade II (gold bar) *11* chief warrant officer, grade III (silver bar) and warrant officer (gold bar)

(as of the U.S. Air Force, Army, or Marine Corps) which extends inward from the sleeve seam and fastens by a button at the edge of the collar and on which an officer wears metal insignia of rank
shoulder mark *n* **:** one of a pair of nearly rectangular pieces

1 2 3 4 5
6 7 8 9 10

shoulder marks of United States Navy: *1* fleet admiral, *2* admiral, *3* vice-admiral, *4* rear admiral, *5* captain, *6* commander, *7* lieutenant commander, *8* lieutenant, *9* lieutenant junior grade, *10* ensign

of stiffened cloth worn parallel to the shoulder seam of some uniforms of U.S. Navy officers, bearing embroidered or gold lace or black braid insignia of rank and line or corps devices, and secured at the inner triangular end by a gilt button — called also *shoulder board*
shoulder note *n, printing* **:** a note at the top outer corner of a page
shoulder–of–mutton sail \ˈ===ˈ==-\ *n* **:** LEG-OF-MUTTON SAIL
shoulder patch *n* **:** a cloth patch bearing an identifying mark and worn on one sleeve of a uniform below the shoulder; *specif* **:** SHOULDER SLEEVE INSIGNIA
shoulder pitch *or* **shoulder point** *n, archaic* **:** ACROMION
shoulders *pl of* SHOULDER, *pres 3d sing of* SHOULDER
shoulder screw *n* **:** a screw having an unthreaded shoulder below the head to act as a fulcrum for a lever pivoted on it
shoulder sleeve insignia *n* **:** a distinctive cloth patch worn on the left sleeve of a uniform just below the shoulder seam by individuals assigned to Army divisions, corps, and armies, to Air Force wings, and to other specifically authorized organizations and also worn on the right sleeve by individuals to indicate overseas service with certain units during periods of active operations — called also *shoulder patch*
shoulder strap *n* **1 :** a strap or one of two straps that pass across the shoulder or shoulders and hold up an article or garment **2 a :** one of a pair of narrow rectangular pieces of cloth worn parallel to the shoulder seams of a military dress uniform, bearing the wearer's insignia of rank embroidered in gold or silver, being of the color of his branch (as dark blue for a general officer, red for an artillery officer), bordered with gold bullion, and now replaced in the U.S. Navy by shoulder marks and worn in the U.S. Army only on the blue dress coat **b :** SHOULDER LOOP
shoulder–striker \ˈ==,==\ *n* **:** ROWDY
shoulder tuft *n* **:** TEGULA
shoulder weapon *or* **shoulder gun** *n* **:** a firearm that is normally fired while held in the hands and braced against or upon the shoulder — called also *shoulder arm*
shoud·na \ˈshüdnə\ *Scot* **:** should not
shouldn't \ˈshu̇dᵊnt\ [by contr.] **:** should not
shouldst *or* **shouldest** *archaic past 2d sing of* SHALL
shous *pl of* SHOU
¹shout \ˈshau̇t, *usu* -au̇d·+V\ *vb* -ED/-ING/-S [ME *shouten;* prob. akin to ON *skūta, skūti* taunt, *skjōta* to shoot — more at SHOOT] *vi* **1 a :** to utter a sudden loud cry (as to express joy or triumph or to attract attention) ⟨the crowd . . . *~ed* with delight —Sherwood Anderson⟩ ⟨like any grief-stricken peasant, *~ing* against the misery of death —Robert Payne⟩ ⟨a crowd quickly gathered and *~ed* for a speech —*Amer. Guide Series: Md.*⟩ **b :** to speak in a loud voice ⟨can't hear even when people ~ in her ear⟩ ⟨became angry and began *~ing* at each other⟩ **c** *of a bird* **:** to utter a cry or song ⟨the cuckoo *~s* all day at nothing —A.E.Housman⟩ **2 a :** to command attention as if by shouting **:** be conspicuous (as in appearance) ⟨girls whose lips *~ed* with red⟩ ⟨*~ing* needs⟩ **b :** to issue publicity (as in praise or protest) **:** make a great to-do ⟨natural beauties that give the chamber of commerce plenty to ~ about⟩ **3** *Austral* **:** to treat a person to a drink, refreshments, or entertainment **:** stand treat ⟨now I'm going to stand treat; you've *~ed* for us already —Henry Lapham⟩ **4 :** to give expression to religious ecstasy often in vigorous rhythmic movements (as shuffling, jumping, jerking); *specif* **:** to take part in a ring shout **5 :** to render the words of a song (as a blues song) in a vigorous rhythmic recitative manner **~** *vt* **1 a :** to utter in a loud voice ⟨*~ed* insults at each other across the street⟩ ⟨*~ed* out the names on the list⟩ ⟨*~ed* "Hallelujah!" and "Amen!" throughout the preacher's exhortation⟩ **b** *archaic* **:** to acclaim with a shout **c :** to make public announcement of in a loud voice ⟨the peddlers . . . ~ their wares with a cry which is like the howl of a wolf —Erle Stanley Gardner⟩ ⟨listened for the conductor to ~ the stations⟩ **d :** to cause to be, come, or go by or as if by shouting ⟨~ himself hoarse⟩ ⟨had to ~ up a clerk from the back room to wait on him⟩ ⟨~ the runners on to the finish line⟩ ⟨a number of newspapers, all strident in upholding their own views and in *~ing* down rival opinion —H.L.Smith b.1906⟩ **2** *Austral* **a :** to treat a person to (as a drink) ⟨I had to go in and have a drink with them, and ~ one in return —Nevil Shute⟩ **b :** to treat (a person) to a drink or some other refreshment ⟨came in considerably the worse for Saint Patrick's Day, for he had been *~ed* by more than one of his friends —Ruth Park⟩
²shout \"\ *n* -S [ME; akin to ME, *shouten* to shout] **1 :** a loud burst of voice **:** a vehement and sudden outcry (as to attract attention); *esp* **:** the outcry of a crowd expressing joy, triumph, rage, or other strong emotion ⟨~ of welcome⟩ ⟨drew a loud ~ of laughter from the audience⟩ **2** *Austral* **a :** a free drink **:** TREAT **b :** one's turn to order (as a round of drinks) **3 a :** RING SHOUT **b :** a religious gathering (as in a praise house) marked by a ring shout **c :** SHOUT SONG **4** *slang* **:** EXCLAMATION POINT
shout·er \ˈshau̇d·ə(r), -au̇tə-\ *n* -S **1 :** one that shouts **2** *usu cap* **:** a member of a religious sect found among Negroes in the West Indies and marked by the use of ceremonies resembling African rituals
shou·ther \ˈshüthə(r)\ *chiefly Scot var of* SHOULDER
shouting distance *n* **:** easy reach — usu. used with *within* ⟨a barber's shop within *shouting distance* of the Cotton Exchange —Constance Foley⟩ ⟨from just under $200,000,000 in 1939 to within *shouting distance* of the billion mark —*Monsanto Mag.*⟩
shout·ing·ly *adv* **:** in a shouting manner
shout song *n* **1 :** a strongly rhythmic religious song used by Negroes in the South, associated with a ring shout, and characterized by responsive singing or shouting between a leader and the congregation **2 :** any song delivered in a responsive or shouting manner
¹shove \ˈshəv\ *vb* -ED/-ING/-S [ME *shuven, shouven, shoven,* fr. OE *scūfan;* akin to OHG *scioban* to push, shove, ON *skūfa, skȳfa* to push, shove, Goth *afskiuban* to reject, cast off, Lith *skùbti* to hurry, OSlav *skubati* to pluck, tear] *vt* **1** *archaic* **:** to thrust or cast violently away **2 :** to cause to go by the application of force: as **a :** to move forcibly by the direct and continuous application of strength **:** DRIVE ⟨more than forty steamboats . . ., piece by piece, had been *shoved* and pulled from the lower river on makeshift rollers —Tom Marvel⟩ **b :** to push or put in a rough, careless, or hasty manner **:** THRUST ⟨~ the smaller children out of the way and take over the swings⟩ ⟨*shoved* the papers into his bag and ran for the bus⟩ **c :** to force by other than physical means **:** COMPEL ⟨the vigilance committee . . . may ~ aside police and courts —B.N.Cardozo⟩ ⟨~ the bill through the legislature⟩ ⟨a surplus that will ~ the price down from a dollar to 60 cents⟩ ⟨felt he was being *shoved* around by his boss and should show his independence⟩ **3 a :** to dispose of to advantage by passing ⟨*shoving* the boring jobs off onto other people —Ann Bridge⟩ ⟨~ counterfeit money⟩ **b :** engage in the sale of (narcotics) **:** PEDDLE ⟨~ dope⟩ **~** *vi* **1 :** to move by forcing a way ⟨glaciers that ~ seaward⟩ ⟨bargain hunters ~ up to the counter⟩ **2 a :** to move something by exerting force ⟨boarded the boat and *shoved* off from the dock⟩ **b :** to go away from a place **:** LEAVE ⟨put on his hat and *shoved* off for home⟩ ⟨let's have one for the road and ~ out of this rathole —Maritta Wolff⟩ ⟨saw the cops coming and said it was time to ~⟩ **3** *of bituminous paving* **:** to form surface waves under traffic when softened by heat **syn** see PUSH
²shove \"\ *n* -S [ME *shov,* fr. *shuven, shouven, shoven,* v.] **1 :** an act or instance of shoving **:** a forcible push ⟨gave him a ~ that sent him reeling⟩ ⟨gave the project the ~ it needed to succeed⟩ **2 :** STRIKE SLIP
³shove \ˈshōv\ *n* -S [by alter.] **:** SHIVE a,b
shoved joint *also* **shove joint** *n* **:** PUSH JOINT
shovegroat \ˈ==,=\ *n* [ME *shove grote,* fr. *shoven* to shove + *grote* groat] **:** SHOVE-HALFPENNY
shove–halfpenny *or* **shove–ha'penny** \ˈ=ˈ=(=)=\ *n* [¹*shove* + *halfpenny* or *ha'penny*] **:** a game played on a special board in which players drive coins or other disks with the thumb or palm from the edge of the board into scoring beds at the other end
¹shov·el \ˈshəvəl\ *n* -S *often attrib* [ME, fr. OE *scofl;* akin to MLG *schūfle, schuffele* shovel, OHG *scūfla, scūvala,* OSw *skofl* shovel, OE *scūfan* to shove — more at SHOVE] **1 a :** a hand implement consisting of a broad scoop or a more or less hollowed out blade with a handle used to lift and throw material (as earth, coal, grain) **b :** a working part in an implement or machine resembling a shovel in shape or use: as (1) **:** a working point in a cultivator (2) **:** the share of a shovel plow — compare TWISTED SHOVEL (3) **:** SPADE **c :** an excavating machine **2 :** SHOVEL HAT **3 :** SHOVELFUL **4 :** a cue used in shuffleboard (sense 2a) **5 :** a small abrasive or polishing hand lap used in conjunction with a watchmaker's lathe to finish cylindrical surfaces **6 :** the upcurved forward tip of a ski

shovels 1a

²shovel \"\ *vb* **shoveled** *or* **shovelled; shoveled** *or* **shovelled; shoveling** *or* **shov·elling** \-v(ə)liŋ\ **shovels** [ME *shovelen,* fr. *shovel,* n.] *vt* **1 :** to take up and throw with a shovel **:** turn with a shovel **2 :** to dig or clean out (as a ditch) with a shovel **3 :** to throw or convey roughly or in the mass as if with a shovel ⟨*shoveled* his food into his mouth⟩ **~** *vi* **:** to take up and cast something with a shovel
³shovel \"\ *vi* -ED/-ING/-S [ME *shovelen,* freq. of *shuven, shoven* to shove — more at SHOVE] **:** SHUFFLE
shovelbill \ˈ==,=\ *n* **:** SHOVELER 2
shovelboard \ˈ==,=\ *n* [alter. (influenced by ¹*shovel*) of obs. E *shove-board,* fr. ¹*shove* + *board*] **1** *archaic* **:** SHOVE-HALFPENNY, *also* **:** a coin or table used in playing shove-halfpenny **2 :** SHUFFLEBOARD 2
shovel cultivator *n* **:** a mechanical cultivator with flat triangular blades for use with row crops
shov·el·er *or* **shov·el·ler** \ˈshəv(ə)lə(r)\ *n* -S [ME *shoveler;* in sense 1, fr. *shovelen* to shovel + *-er;* in sense 2, fr. *shovel,* n. + *-er*] **1 :** one that shovels; *esp* **:** SHOVELMAN **2 :** any of several river ducks (genus *Anas*) having a large and very broad bill; *esp* **:** a widely distributed duck (*A. clypeata*) that in the male has the head and neck blackish green and the abdomen chestnut
shovelfish \ˈ==,=\ *n* [so called fr. the shape of its head] **:** PADDLEFISH
shov·el·ful \ˈshəvəl,fu̇l\ *n, pl* **shovelfuls** *or* **shovelsful :** the quantity that a shovel contains
shovel hat *n* **:** a shallow-crowned hat with a wide brim curved up at the sides that is worn by some clergymen
shovelhead \ˈ==,=\ *n* **1** *or* **shovelhead shark :** BONNETHEAD **2** *also* **shovelhead cat** *or* **shovelhead catfish :** FLATHEAD CATFISH
shovellike \ˈ==,=\ *adj* **:** resembling a shovel (as in being broad and flat in the forward part or in curving up at the sides)
shov·el·man \ˈshəvəl,man, -lmən\ *n, pl* **shovelmen :** one who works with a hand or power shovel
shovelnose \ˈ==,=\ *n* **:** any of various shovel-nosed animals: as **a :** SHOVELER 2 **b :** SHOVEL-NOSED RAY **c :** SHOVELNOSE SHARK **d :** SHOVELNOSE STURGEON **e :** GUITARFISH
shovel–nosed \ˈ==,=\ *adj* **:** having a broad flat head, nose, or beak
shovel–nosed duck *n* **:** SHOVELER 2
shovel–nosed ray *n* **:** an Australian guitarfish (*Rhinobatos banksii*) that reaches a length of about four feet
shovelnose shark *or* **shovel–nosed shark** *n* **1 :** COW SHARK; *esp* **:** a large dark cow shark (*Hexanchus corinus*) of the Pacific coast of No. America **2 :** GUITARFISH **3 :** a hammerhead shark or a closely related shark
shovelnose sturgeon *n* **1 :** a small sturgeon (*Scaphirhynchus platorhynchus*) of the Mississippi valley that has a broad flattened snout — called also *hackleback* **2 :** a light-colored sturgeon (*Parascaphirhynchus albus*) of the Mississippi river
shovel pass *n* **:** a short forward pass thrown underhand
shovel plow *n* **:** a plow having a triangular share and used for cultivating
shovel–tusker \ˈ==,==\ *n* **:** any of several Miocene and Pliocene mastodons with the lower tusks broadened and flattened into a large structure suggesting a shovel
shovelweed \ˈ==,=\ *n* [so called fr. the shape of the pods] **:** SHEPHERD'S PURSE
shove net *n* [ME *shofnet,* fr. *shuven, shoven* to shove + *net* — more at SHOVE, NET] **:** a fishing net attached to a hoop on a handle
¹shov·er \ˈshəvə(r)\ *n* -S [¹*shove* + *-er*] **:** one that shoves: as **a :** an aggressive person **b :** a passer of counterfeit money **c :** a slaughterhouse worker who pushes carcasses and cuts from place to place on an overhead conveyor
²shov·er \ˈshəvə(r\ *n* -S [by alter.] *slang Brit* **:** CHAUFFEUR
shoves *pres 3d sing of* SHOVE, *pl of* SHOVE
shoving *pres part of* SHOVE
¹show \ˈshō\ *vb* **showed; shown** \ˈshōn *sometimes* ˈshōən\ *or* **showed; showing; shows** [ME *shewen, showen* (also, to look at), fr. OE *scēawian* to look, see, look at; akin to OFris *skāwia, skōwia* to look, see, look at, OS *skauwon,* OHG *scouwōn* to look, see, look at, L *cavēre* to be on one's guard — more at HEAR] *vt* **1 :** to cause or permit to be seen: as **a :** to put on view ⟨would have *~ed* us their sacristy —Thomas Gray⟩ ⟨had *shown* his strength, the power of reason over panic —Victor Canning⟩ **b :** to present (as oneself) to public notice in a personal appearance ⟨*~ed* himself in public places to quiet rumors that he was ill⟩ **c :** to hold (a light) in the dark or as a signal **d :** to present (as a sign or indication) to view or observation ⟨*~ed* every mark of extreme agitation⟩ **2 a :** to offer for inspection ⟨*~ed* his ticket at the gate⟩ ⟨had to ~ their passports⟩ **b :** to set out for sale **:** place on view for customers **:** OFFER ⟨stores were *~ing* luxury goods of every kind⟩ ⟨*~ing* new spring suits⟩ **3 :** to make evident or apparent **:** serve as the means to reveal or make visible ⟨a style that *~ed* a lovely figure to perfection⟩ ⟨a basement window *~ed* him just the feet of passersby⟩ **4 :** to wear (colors) in indication of loyalty **:** hang out or carry (a flag) ⟨openly *~ed* royalist colors⟩ **5 :** to present as a public spectacle **:** PERFORM ⟨a play that had been *shown* in every town hall and opera house⟩ **6 :** to make deliberate or conscious display of for the notice or admiration of others ⟨*~ed* the trimmest of well-turned ankles and the demurest of pert smiles⟩ **7 :** to present (a part or aspect) to view **:** make (a particular appearance) noticeable ⟨trees were *~ing* the first light shimmer of green⟩ ⟨a rundown house *~ed* a blind and vacant face to the street⟩ **8 :** to offer to the sight of eye or mind **:** present for consideration or reflection ⟨lies in a valley as beautiful as France can ~ —A.B.Osborne⟩ ⟨attractions for tourists such as only a metropolis can ~⟩ **9 :** to reveal (something) by one's condition or nature **:** make conspicuous ⟨a light-colored overcoat that *~ed* soil readily⟩ **10 a :** to give a reading of **:** INDICATE ⟨a lighted tower clock *~ed* the time to be 2:15⟩ ⟨speedometer *~ed* 70⟩ **b :** to exhibit when counted, recorded, or reported ⟨utilities *~ed* slight gains in generally erratic trading⟩ ⟨major crops continued to ~ a surplus⟩ ⟨*~ed* a loss for the first time in several years⟩ **11 a :** to point out (as an object, a place) to someone **:** conduct (as a person, a group) to or about a place or thing **:** act as cicerone or conductor in guiding or exhibiting ⟨*~ed* him the house and grounds⟩ ⟨~ the view of the distant mountaintops to his companion⟩ ⟨*~ed* them around the city⟩ **b :** ESCORT, USHER ⟨*~ed* me to an aisle seat⟩ ⟨*~ed* him to his room⟩ ⟨*~ed* him over the property⟩ **12 a :** to reveal or display (an inward disposition, feeling, or trait) by appearance or behavior ⟨his speech and bearing *~ed* a mind at ease⟩ ⟨*~ed* the generosity and freedom of gentle breeding⟩ **b :** to prove (oneself) to be of a particular disposition or kidney ⟨*~ed* himself kind no less than brave⟩ **c :** to make (itself) evident, apparent, or manifest — used of a condition or trait ⟨a strange deviousness *~ed* itself in everything he did⟩ **13 :** to accord (favor) to **:** do (kindness) to **:** exhibit (a disposition) toward ⟨render true judgments, ~ kindness and mercy each to his brother —Zech 7:9 (RSV)⟩ **14 a :** to set forth in a statement, account, or description **:** make evident or clear **:** ASSERT, DECLARE ⟨presented a carefully worked out report *~ing* the benefits to be expected from a system of expressways⟩ ⟨a composition that *~s* predominantly classical influences⟩ **b** *archaic* **:** ANNOUNCE, COMMUNICATE, TELL **c :** ALLEGE, PLEAD, PRESENT — used esp. in law ⟨~ cause why judgment should not be entered⟩ **15 a :** to demonstrate or establish by argument or reasoning **:** PROVE ⟨~ . . . that the method of knowledge-by-definition is and long has been in standard use —Vilhjalmur Stefansson⟩ ⟨~s the futility of many accepted inferences⟩ ⟨this is *shown* by every test of reason and tradition⟩ **b :** to constitute evidence of **:** amount to proof of **:** establish by inference ⟨uneven inking *~s* carelessness in the pressroom⟩ ⟨this habit *~s* that discipline has been long continued⟩ **c :** to give an explanation of **:** TEACH, INFORM, INSTRUCT ⟨*~ed* me how to solve the problem⟩ **16 :** to present the image or likeness of ⟨a photograph *~ing* his whole family⟩ ⟨a painting that *~s* the author as a young man⟩ **17 :** to claim (points won) in cribbage ⟨*~ed* eight and won the game⟩ **~** *vi* **1 a :** to be or come in view **:** be visible ⟨the lovely peaks . . . *~ed* for a while as spectral shapes above the tree tops —E.E.Shipton⟩ **b :** to put in an appearance **:** join a gathering **:** appear in company ⟨the guest of honor failed to ~ —*Newsweek*⟩ **c :** to come as expected **:** be on hand **:** turn up ⟨I'm glad you *~ed,* kid —H.A.Sinclair⟩ ⟨shad have begun to ~ at the dam⟩ **2 a :** to give a particular appearance **:** have a particular look or quality ⟨his nature *~ed* strong in adversity⟩ **b :** to appear in a particular way or manner — used with an adverb ⟨slackness among civilians . . . *~ed* plainly in public life —Dixon Wecter⟩ **c** *obs* **:** to have an appearance implying or suggesting something not actually so or not known to be so — used with *as if* **3 :** to give a theatrical performance ⟨a tough town to ~ in⟩ **4 :** to appear as a contestant (as in entering a prize ring) **5 :** to finish third or at least third esp. in a horse race **6 :** to indicate and claim cribbage points for the combinations in one's hand and crib after the play
syn EVINCE, MANIFEST, EVIDENCE, DEMONSTRATE: in this series SHOW is a general term, usu. interchangeable with any of the others, for indicating, revealing, displaying ⟨in this decision he *showed* his capacity for extreme boldness —John Buchan⟩ EVINCE in today's English may designate revealing, or making perceptible, for inspection or consideration ⟨the two phases seem to draw apart, or at least to *evince* themselves in distinct expression —H.O.Taylor⟩ ⟨proposal *evinces* a change of attitude —*New Republic*⟩ MANIFEST may designate fuller, plainer, or more obvious revelation or indication requiring no examination or attention for perception ⟨a wealth of creative design as is *manifested* in these prints —Laurence Binyon⟩ ⟨the power the Western democracies can wield is greater than that which Soviet Communism can *manifest* in aggression —Sumner Welles⟩ EVIDENCE may occas. suggest indication or display which on consideration could serve as valid evidence ⟨she was a good business woman, as is *evidenced* by the success

of her petition, November 4, 1779, to the General Assembly —R.W.Thorp⟩ ⟨retains a strong appreciation of its history, *evidenced* in the collections of antiquities —*Amer. Guide Series: N.H.*⟩ DEMONSTRATE may indicate most obvious revelation or indication, either full and orderly or marked and palpable ⟨undertook both to *demonstrate* and popularize the Copernican hypothesis —Stringfellow Barr⟩ ⟨one whose entire life had *demonstrated* an inability to grapple successfully with business and financial problems —Edna Yost⟩

syn EXHIBIT, DISPLAY, PARADE, FLAUNT, EXPOSE: SHOW is the general term for presenting in such way as to invite notice. EXHIBIT applies to putting forward prominently, openly, or conspicuously to attract rather than merely permit attention and inspection ⟨he *exhibited* with peculiar pride two cream-colored mules —Willa Cather⟩ ⟨we are sure that she would like to hurl the prayer book, *exhibited* so ostentatiously before the dowagers, in the face of the congregation —E.K.Brown⟩ ⟨can *exhibit* a contempt of death because of the exaltation of her faith —F.R.Leavis⟩ DISPLAY may indicate an unfolding, stretching out, spreading out, or otherwise showing in full detail or to best advantage ⟨*displaying* the new fabrics to the buyers⟩ ⟨certain events considered important were *displayed* under six-column headlines —Jacques Kayser⟩ PARADE suggests sustained ostentatious, arrogant, or defiant display ⟨he did not *parade* his knowledge. Indeed he seemed honestly apologetic because he knew so little —L.C.Douglas⟩ ⟨they could not *parade* their virtue. They had lost, and that was the end —Irving Stone⟩ FLAUNT, a close synonym of PARADE, may suggest ostentatious challenging, boasting, or mocking ⟨ladies of the bluest blood and the highest social rating flippantly *flaunted* their lovers and their husbands made no secret of their mistresses —C.G.Bowers⟩ ⟨the grandees no longer *flaunted* their wealth in exotic entertainments, for most were dead or bankrupt —John Buchan⟩ ⟨and ye vaunted your fathomless power, and ye *flaunted* your iron pride —Rudyard Kipling⟩ EXPOSE may indicate a displaying after being brought out of concealment or from under cover or being discovered or unmasked ⟨he . . . looked me over as though I had been *exposed* for sale —Joseph Conrad⟩ ⟨he shrinks from *exposing* his mind. He is bashful, constrained, often resentful —H.A.Overstreet⟩ ⟨a vitriolic joy in *exposing* their pretentions and their hypocrisy —Van Wyck Brooks⟩
— **show one's hand 1 :** to display one's cards faceup **2 :** to declare one's intentions or reveal one's resources — **show one's heels to :** OUTRUN, OUTSTRIP — **show the door :** to tell (a person) to get out (as from a house or a room) : turn out : send packing

²**show** \"\ *n* -S *often attrib* [ME *shewe*, fr. *shewen, showen*, v.] **1 :** an exhibition or display intended as a demonstration of strength (as of military power) ⟨sent a squadron to make a ~ of force⟩ **2 a** *archaic* **:** outward appearance ⟨command him in ~ at least —Robert Burton⟩ **b :** a vain or empty semblance or pretense or one intended to deceive ⟨made a plausible ~ of being a man of means and position⟩ **c :** an appearance or semblance more or less consonant with reality, fact, or substance ⟨seemed to be acting with some ~ of reason⟩ **d :** an appearance or suggestion of a particular kind ⟨the place made a poor ~ of domestic comfort and warmth⟩ ⟨carefully tended shrubs and flowers made a striking ~⟩ **e :** a display meant to impress others : OSTENTATION, PARADE ⟨in moments of introspection, when there is no longer a necessity of putting off with a ~ of wisdom the uninitiated interlocutor —B.N. Cardozo⟩ **3 :** a favorable opportunity (as to prove oneself) : CHANCE, PROBABILITY ⟨his background was irregular but they gave him a ~⟩ ⟨do you see any ~ of discovering who fired the gun⟩ **4 :** something or someone exhibited or proposed for regard of any kind (as wonder or ridicule) : CYNOSURE, SPECTACLE ⟨she was a boast, a marvel, and a ~ —Lord Byron⟩ ⟨between the cliffs it booms, a mighty ~, then softly laps the shore —P.A.Cole⟩ **5** *obs* **:** the apparition either of beings held to be supernatural or of visions seeming to present such beings **6 :** a large display arranged or organized to arouse interest or enthusiasm or to stimulate sales : EXPOSITION ⟨a state flower ~⟩ ⟨the national motorboat ~⟩ **7 a :** a theatrical presentation (as a play or motion picture) ⟨significant steps forward in the development of the musical ~ in this country from . . . operetta —H.W.Wind⟩ ⟨~ people are a hardy and resilient lot⟩ **b :** a dramatic or other radio or television program ⟨hundreds of cowboy movies and television ~s are watched . . . by millions of Americans —D.B.Davis⟩ ⟨top-drawer radio ~s began to be presented from recordings⟩ **c :** an act by singers, dancers, instrumentalists, or other performers presented as entertainment in a nightclub or cabaret or the entire program of such acts given at one time **d :** a pageant, contest, or other large spectacular presentation intended to amuse or inform large numbers of people ⟨the Romans had some success in low comedy . . . but their instinct turned to ~s and circuses —T.S. Eliot⟩ ⟨you get more free ~s in Britain than anywhere else on earth —Anthony Day⟩ **e :** a circus or carnival or any of its acts or sideshows — compare RIDE **8 :** a public art exhibition (as of paintings or sculpture) in a museum or gallery intended to display an artist's work or promote its sale ⟨a sidewalk ~ of watercolors⟩ **9 a :** a military operation or engagement : ACTION ⟨pilots . . . who had not gone out with us were pretty peeved to think that they had missed the ~ —*McGill News*⟩ ⟨that battle was the fleet's big ~⟩ **b :** a unit or group engaged in a military operation or mission ⟨the other member of my ~ rode at my wing tip, a big black shape, sinister in the half-light —J.L.Rhys⟩ **10 a :** an event or performance regarded as carried off well or esp. as visually or theatrically satisfying ⟨the first stake race of the season was a good ~ —G.F.T.Ryall⟩ **b :** personal or group conduct regarded as meeting or falling short of some test or standard or as meriting praise or blame ⟨good ~, his flying that old crate to get here when you were ill⟩ ⟨the department had been drained of morale and pride and was putting on a pretty poor ~⟩ **11 :** an effort or operation (as a business enterprise) taken as a whole or regarded as to its success or prospects ⟨a new president who tried at first to run the whole ~ in all its details himself⟩ ⟨logging proved a poor ~ that winter⟩ **12 :** a trace or indication showing that a mine contains metal or a well gas or oil ⟨widely used to test cores, samples, and drilling mud for oil ~s —C.G.Lalicker⟩ **13 a :** a discharge of mucus streaked with blood from the vagina at the onset of labor **b :** the first appearance of blood in a menstrual period **14 :** ¹CAP 9 **15 :** third place at the finish of a horse race ⟨paid $2.60 for ~⟩ — compare WIN, PLACE

show·able \ˈshōəbəl\ *adj* **:** capable of being shown

show bill *n* **:** an advertising poster

show biz \-ˈbiz\ *n* [by shortening & alter.] **:** SHOW BUSINESS

showboard \ˈ=,=\ *n* **:** a small billboard for outdoor advertising

showboat \ˈ=,=\ *n* **:** a river steamship containing a theater and carrying a troupe of actors to give plays at river communities

show box *n* **:** a box for a peep show

showbread *var of* SHEWBREAD

show business *n* **:** the amusement arts, occupations, and businesses (as theater, motion pictures, circus, radio, and television)

show card *n* **:** an advertising placard or display card

show card color *n* **:** POSTER COLOR

¹**showcase** \ˈ=,=\ *n* [²*show* + *case*] **1 :** a glazed case, box, or cabinet to display and protect wares in a store or articles in a museum **2 a :** a setting or framework for exhibiting something esp. at its best ⟨after the run . . . a proud ~ of the legitimate theater will close its doors —*N.Y.Times*⟩ **b :** a medium or vehicle for exhibiting a tentative offering or tryout of something ⟨a program that has consistently been a ~ for rising talent⟩

²**showcase** \"\ *vt* **:** EXHIBIT ⟨network radio alone programs some six hours a week of regularly scheduled shows that ~ the candidates —*Newsweek*⟩

show cause order *n, law* **:** an order from a court or judge to a litigant ordering him to appear at a stated time to give a good reason why a conditional order should not be made absolute or why something should not be permitted or done in the case

show dahlia *n* **:** any of various dahlias having much doubled flower heads with closely packed ray florets

showdown \ˈ=,=\ *n* [fr. *show down* to display one's hand at poker] **1 a :** the placing of poker hands faceup on the table to determine the winner of a pot **b :** COLD HANDS **2 :** the final settlement of a contested issue or the test of strength by which it is settled ⟨emerged on the winning end of a 257–26 ~ in the House of Commons —*Wall Street Jour.*⟩

showdown inspection *n* **:** a detailed inspection of the clothing and equipment of each individual in a military unit for completeness and serviceability

showed *past of* SHOW

¹**show·er** \ˈshau̇(ə)r, -au̇ə, *esp in the southern US* -au̇wə(r\ *n* -S [ME *shur, shour, showre*, fr. OE *scūr*; akin to OHG *scūr* shower, storm, ON *skūr* shower, Goth *skūra* (*windis*) windstorm, L *caurus, corus* northwest wind, Lith *šiaurỹs* northwind, OSlav *sěverŭ* north, Arm *curt* cold, shower; basic meaning: north, northwind] **1 a :** a fall of rain that is of short duration or rapidly varying intensity over a limited area with drops usu. about 1/25 inch in diameter and a velocity of from 10 to 25 feet per second — compare DRIZZLE **b :** a like fall of sleet, hail, or snow **c :** a shower of meteors **d :** COSMIC-RAY SHOWER **2 :** something likened to a rain shower: as **a :** a spray of water (as from a hose or waterfall) **b :** a rain of sparks **c :** a dense fall of bullets or other missiles ⟨the whole target area was left ablaze and cratered with huge bomb holes from a ~ of incendiary and high-explosive missiles —*Springfield (Mass.) Union*⟩ **d :** a firework for producing a brilliant shower (as of slow-burning stars) **3 :** something that comes in large and concentrated numbers or quantity ⟨walked down from the aircraft in a ~ of applause —*N.Y.Times*⟩ ⟨brought down on his head a ~ of reproaches —A.P.Ryan⟩ ⟨organized a postcard ~ to cheer him up after the accident⟩ **4 :** a party given by friends or well-wishers who bring gifts often of a particular kind ⟨the bride was given linen and kitchen ~s⟩ ⟨got up a stork ~ for her when her baby was expected⟩ **5 :** SHOWER BATH ⟨felt fresh from his shave and ~ —Hamilton Basso⟩ **6 a :** one of the individual flowers or small bouquets that hang by ribbons from a shower bouquet **b :** a ribbon used in a shower bouquet

²**shower** \"\ *vb* -ED/-ING/-S *vi* **1 :** to rain or fall in or as if in a shower ⟨it had ~ed off and on all day⟩ ⟨letters ~ed on him in praise and in protest⟩ **2 :** to bathe in a shower bath ⟨~ed and changed to clean clothes —James Jones⟩ ~ *vt* **1 a :** to pour down on in or as if in showers (as of rain, spray, or drops) **b :** to wet with rain showers, water spray, or other liquid **c :** to spray or bedew : pour on like a shower ⟨the wind veered and ~ed a fishing boat with radioactive ash⟩ ⟨factory chimneys ~ the district with soot⟩ ⟨gusts were ~ing dust and bits of paper and other small debris on our yard⟩ **2 :** to bestow liberally : give in abundance : RAIN ⟨~ed invitations on him⟩; *also* **:** to cover as if with a shower of rain ⟨~ed him with honors⟩

³**show·er** \ˈshō(ə)r, -ōə\ *n* -S [ME *shewer, shoer*, fr. *shewen, showen* to show + *-er* — more at SHOW] **:** one that shows : EXHIBITOR

shower bath *n* **1 :** a bath in which water is showered on the person **2 :** the apparatus including a finely perforated nozzle that provides a shower bath

shower bouquet *n* **:** a large bouquet from which many small bouquets or individual flowers hang by ribbons of various lengths ⟨the maid of honor and flower girl carried *shower bouquets* of pink sweetheart roses and ivy —*New Orleans (La.) Times-Picayune*⟩

shower of gold : YELLOW ELDER

showerproof \ˈ=,=,=\ *adj* **:** treated so as to shed or resist slight wetting (as from a shower) — used of a fabric; compare RAINPROOF, WATERPROOF

show·ery \ˈshau̇(ə)rē, -ri, *esp in the southern US* -au̇wər-\ *adj* **1 :** raining in showers : abounding with frequent showers of rain **2 :** of, relating to, or resembling a shower **3 :** producing, produced by, or falling in showers

show fever *n* **:** PANLEUCOPENIA

showfolk \ˈ=,=\ *n pl* **:** the performers in any kind of show business

show geranium *n* **:** MARTHA WASHINGTON GERANIUM

show girl *n* **:** a chorus girl in a musical comedy or nightclub show; *esp* **:** one who performs or poses in elaborate costumes

show glass *n, Brit* **:** SHOWCASE

showgoer \ˈ=,==\ *n* **:** one who habitually attends shows

showground \ˈ=,=\ *n* **1 :** the site of a circus, fair, or exposition

showhouse \ˈ=,=\ *n* **1 :** THEATER **2 :** a greenhouse (as in a park, a botanical garden, or on a private estate) used primarily for display

show-how \ˈ=,=\ *n* -S [fr. the phrase *show how*] **:** a demonstration esp. of technical method or procedure — compare KNOW-HOW

show·i·ly \ˈshōəlē, -li\ *adv* **:** in a showy manner

show·i·ness \ˈshōēnəs, -ōin-\ *n* -ES **:** the quality or state of being showy

show·ing \ˈshōiŋ, -ōēŋ\ *n* -S [ME *shewing*, fr. gerund of *shewen* to show — more at SHOW] **1 :** an act of putting something on view (as a play or motion picture, the work of an artist, new merchandise) : DISPLAY, EXHIBITION ⟨a ~ of new-model cars⟩ **2 :** performance in a test of skill or power or of comparative effectiveness : RECORD ⟨made a good ~ in competition with acknowledged front-runners⟩ **3 a :** a statement or presentation of a case or an interpretation of a set of facts ⟨it is, on the treasury's own ~, impossible . . . to sustain a boom on this basis —*New Statesman & Nation*⟩ **b :** APPEARANCE, EVIDENCE ⟨on present ~, this industry seems to have little future⟩ **4 :** ²SHOW 12 ⟨a number of wells . . . had reported ~s of oil and gas —A.I.Levorsen⟩ **5 :** proof or prima facie proof of a matter of fact or law **6 a :** an advertising poster : BILLBOARD **b showings** *pl* **:** a group of posters or billboards sold as a unit designed to provide adequate coverage of a market

showish *adj, obs* **:** SHOWY

show·man \ˈshōmən\ *n, pl* **showmen 1 :** the producer of a play or other theatrical show ⟨one of the great *showmen* whose reading of human nature has passed the test of time —*Times Lit. Supp.*⟩ **2 :** a person having a sense or knack for dramatization or visual effectiveness ⟨some young American musicians who have established themselves in the first rank are excellent *showmen* —Robert Evett⟩

show·man·ly *adj* **:** characteristic of or befitting a showman

show·man·ship \-n,ship\ *n* **1 :** the art or skill of a showman : the capacity for effective or spectacular display esp. in the theater **2 :** the ability to present a person or thing in a favorable light (as to win support or favor or to promote sales)

show-me \ˈ=,=\ *adj* [fr. the phrase *show me*] **:** insistent on proof or evidence : SKEPTICAL, INCREDULOUS ⟨faced popular enthusiasms with a questioning, *show-me* attitude⟩

shown *past part of* SHOW

show off *vt* **:** to display with ostentation or pride ⟨wanted to *show* his new car *off*⟩ ~ *vi* **1 :** to seek to attract attention by conspicuous behavior : display strength, adroitness, or other attraction in order to be noticed ⟨was *showing off* for the girls⟩ **2 :** to begin sparring in a round of boxing

show-off \ˈ=,=\ *n* -S [*show off*] **1 :** the act of showing off : conspicuous or ostentatious display **2 :** one that shows off : EXHIBITIONIST ⟨some nasty little high-I.Q. *show-off* —J.D. Salinger⟩

show of hands : a display of raised hands expressing the vote of a group ⟨voted overwhelmingly by a *show of hands* to have a picnic⟩

showpiece \ˈ=,=\ *n* **:** a prime or outstanding example used for exhibition ⟨the ship was a ~ of advanced nautical design —James Dugan⟩

show pipe *n* **:** a pipe that forms part of the case of a pipe organ

showplace \ˈ=,=\ *n* **1 :** a place where plays or theatrical or other spectacles are shown or where exhibitions are held ⟨New York . . . is the ~ of change —*Time*⟩ **2 :** a place (as an estate or building) that is frequently exhibited or is regarded as an example of beauty or excellence ⟨the rambling stone mansion . . . is one of the ~s of the state —*Amer. Guide Series: Md.*⟩

show-ring \ˈ=,=\ *n* **:** a ring (as at a cattle show) where animals are displayed

showroom \ˈ=,=\ *n* **1 :** a room where merchandise is exposed for sale or where samples are displayed **2 :** a room where a show is exhibited

shows *pres 3d sing of* SHOW, *pl of* SHOW

showshop \ˈ=,=\ *n* **1 :** a shop where salable wares are displayed **2 :** THEATER ⟨the realm of the ~s . . . where a hummable melody . . . is apt to be the highest musical expectation —John Mason Brown⟩ ⟨a fairly clever farce-melodrama . . . not without its entertaining moments, its ~ shrewdness —*New Republic*⟩

show stone *n* **:** a crystal gazer's glass

showstopper \ˈ=,==\ *n* **:** an act, song, or performer that wins applause so prolonged as to interrupt a performance

show-through \ˈ=,=\ *n* -S [fr. the phrase *show through*] **:** a condition in which or the degree to which printing on one side of a sheet is visible on the other side

show up *vt* **:** to expose (as a person) by deflating pretensions or uncovering faults or misdoings : point out or reveal (as wrongdoing or folly) ~ *vi* **1 :** to turn up where or when expected : ARRIVE ⟨*showed up* late for his own wedding⟩ **2 :** to appear in a particular light or manner ⟨*showed up* badly in the tryouts⟩ **3 :** to be plainly evident ⟨her age and the life she'd led *showed up* all too clearly in the bright morning light⟩

showup \ˈ=,=\ *n* -S [*show up*] **1 :** an act of showing someone or something up (as for deficiencies, pretensions, or wrongdoings) **2 :** a police lineup ⟨you can't trust most people to pick their own mothers out at a ~ —W.R.Burnett⟩

show window *n* **1 :** an outside display window in which a store exhibits merchandise **2 :** a sample or setting used to exhibit or illustrate something at its best ⟨wanted to create a *show window* of democracy in the Far East⟩

showy \ˈshōē, -ōi\ *adj* -ER/-EST [²*show* + *-y*] **1 a :** making an attractive show : STRIKING ⟨a superabundance of splendidly ~ bloom —Emily Holt⟩ ⟨the ~ portions of the chateau —Arnold Bennett⟩ ⟨this wonderfully ~ and entertaining ballet suite —Douglas Watt⟩ **b :** manifesting or marked by brilliant ability, performance, or achievement ⟨wit is a ~ gift that is frequently undervalued⟩ **2 :** given to or marked by ostentation : FLASHY, GAUDY ⟨their prevailing note is slick, ~, and Philistine —C.J.Rolo⟩ ⟨gaudy calicoes and cheap ~ brass ware —G.B.Shaw⟩

showyard \ˈ=,=\ *n* **:** a yard for exhibition of livestock

showy crab apple *n* **:** a profuse-blooming small tree or bush (*Malus floribunda*) having sharply serrulate or serrate leaves and rose-red to pink flowers with usu. five styles — called also *Japanese crab*

showy lady's-slipper *also* **showy ladyslipper** *n* **:** a No. American orchid (*Cypripedium reginae*) having pink-and-white flowers of great beauty

showy milkweed *n* **:** a silky-white No. American perennial herb (*Asclepias speciosa*) with opposite oval leaves and profuse umbels of purple-green flowers

showy orchis *n* **:** a No. American orchid (*Orchis spectabilis*) having two large nearly basal leaves and a spike of flowers violet-purple mixed with white with sepals and petals forming a galea behind the column

showy sunflower *n* **:** a tall rough-leaved perennial herb (*Helianthus laetiflorus*) with opposite leaves and a few large heads of yellow flowers

sho·yu \ˈshō(,)yü\ *n* -S [Jap] **:** SOY

SHP *abbr, often not cap* shaft horsepower

shpg *abbr* shipping

shpmt *abbr* shipment

shpt *abbr* shipment

SHQ *abbr* station headquarters

shr *abbr* share

shrab \ˈshräb, -rȯb\ *n* -S [Hindi *sharāb*, fr. Ar — more at SYRUP] *India & Pakistan* **:** any plain or mixed drink containing alcohol

shraddha *var of* SRADDHA

shrammed \ˈs(h)ramd, -aa(ə)md\ *adj* [prob. alter. of *scrammed*, past part. of ¹*scram*] *dial Eng* **:** shriveled and benumbed with cold

shrank [ME *schrank*, fr. OE *scranc*] *past of* SHRINK

shrap·nel \ˈshrapnəl, *esp South* ˈsra-, *dial* ˈswa-\ *n, pl* **shrapnel** [after Henry *Shrapnel* †1842 Eng. artillery officer] **1 :** a projectile consisting of a case provided with a powder charge and a large number of usu. lead balls packed in resin or a smoke-producing substance that are discharged with increased energy over an area when the projectile is exploded in flight by a time fuse — compare SHELL **2 :** bomb, mine, or shell fragments

shrap·nell's membrane \-nəlz-\ *n, usu cap S* [after Henry J. *Shrapnell fl*1832 Eng. anatomist] **:** a triangular flaccid part of the tympanic membrane of the ear

shra·van \ˈshrävən\ *n* -S *usu cap* [Skt *śrāvana*] **:** SAWAN

shread·head \ˈs(h)red,hed\ *n* [perh fr. obs. E *shread* shred (fr. ME *shrede*) + E *head*] **:** JERKINHEAD

¹**shred** \ˈshred, *esp South* ˈsred, *dial* ˈswed\ *n* -S [ME *shrede*, fr. OE *scrēade*; akin to MD *schrode* piece cut off, shred, OHG *scrōt* piece cut off, ON *skrjōthr* old worn-out book, L *scrupus* sharp stone, OE *sceran, scieran* to shear — more at SHEAR] **1 a :** a long narrow piece usu. cut or torn off something : STRIP ⟨a ~ of ground⟩ ⟨~s of paper⟩ **b :** a very thin shaving or paring ⟨~s of bark⟩ ⟨~s of celery⟩ **2 a :** a threadlike or stringy piece : WISP ⟨whole wheat ~s⟩ ⟨~s of fog —Herman Melville⟩ **b :** a ragged scrap of cloth : TATTER ⟨~s of canvas —John Hunt & Edmund Hillary⟩ **3 :** a very small fragment or bit of something immaterial : PARTICLE, SCRAP ⟨a successful novelist without a ~ of common sense —H.A. Smith⟩ **4 :** a small nodule-shaped piece of light-sensitive photographic emulsion produced by pressing the chilled emulsion through holes in a metal plate in a hydraulic press

²**shred** \"\ *vb* **shredded** *also* **shred; shredded** *or* **shred; shredding; shreds** [ME *shreden*, fr. OE *scrēadian*; akin to MD *schroden* to cut up, grind into coarse meal, OHG *scrōtan* to cut, OE *scrēade*, n., shred] *vt* **1** *archaic* **a :** to cut or lop (as a branch, bodily part, or lock of hair) ⟨scythe blades which ~ off the unwary passenger's limb —Sir Walter Scott⟩ **b :** PRUNE **2 :** to cut or tear into shreds : rip up ⟨*shredded* streamers hung . . . from the roof —D.C.Loughlin⟩ ⟨sharks . . . *shredded* the great fish —J.D.Adams⟩; *specif* **:** to cut (food) into shreds ⟨sugarcane *shredded* by machine⟩ ⟨a dish of *shredded* cabbage⟩ ⟨a frosting with *shredded* coconut⟩ **3 :** to press and break up (photographic emulsion) into shreds ⟨the emulsion . . . is *shredded* and thoroughly washed to remove water-soluble salts —*Complete Photographer*⟩ ~ *vi* **:** to come apart in or break up into shreds ⟨one of the yellow tearoses had *shredded* —Stephen Longstreet⟩ — **shred out :** to subdivide (a project) usu. for handling by persons not fully trained

shred·cock \ˈs(h)red,käk\ *n, dial Eng* **:** FIELDFARE

shred·der \ˈshredə(r), *esp South* ˈsre-, *dial* ˈswe-\ *n* -S **:** one that shreds: as **a :** any of various utensils, implements, or machines for cutting, scraping, or tearing something (as corn, sugarcane, wheat, vegetables, wastepaper) into shreds **b :** HUSKER-SHREDDER **c :** an operator of a machine for flaking scrap metal for use in polishing powder — called also *schrother*

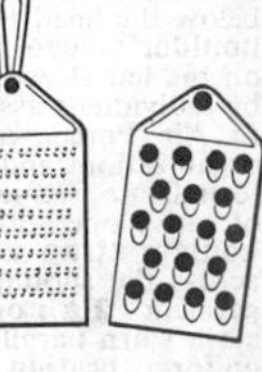

shredders for vegetables

shred·ding \-diŋ, -dēŋ\ *n* -S [ME *schredynge* action of pruning, fr. OE *scrēadung* action of pruning, shred, fr. *scrēadian* to lop off + *-ung* -ing] **:** a strip or piece shredded off something : SHRED ⟨sewn together . . . with ~s of warmed saplings —J.M.Cooper⟩

shred·dy \-dē, -di\ *adj* -ER/-EST **:** consisting of or resembling shreds : RAGGED ⟨a ~ garment⟩

shredout \ˈ=,=\ *n* -S [fr. the phrase *shred out*] **:** a division or analysis of a project (as a job, piece of work, course of study) into subunits usu. so that it can be carried out by persons not fully trained — compare BREAKDOWN 7a

shreeve \ˈs(h)rēv\ *archaic var of* SHERIFF

shrend \ˈs(h)rend\ *vi* -ED/-ING/-S [prob. fr. G dial. *schrinden*, fr. OHG *scrintan* to crack open — more at BERGSCHRUND] **:** to break into shivers as a result of internal stresses — used of glass not properly tempered or annealed

shreve·port \ˈshrēv,pō(ə)r|t, -ȯ(ə)r|, -ōə|, -ȯə|, *usu* |d.+V; *esp South* ˈsrē-, *dial* ˈswē-\ *adj, usu cap* [fr. *Shreveport*, city in northwest Louisiana] **:** of or from the city of Shreveport, La. **:** of the kind or style prevalent in Shreveport

shreve·port·er \|d.ə(r)\ *n* -S *cap* **:** a native or resident of Shreveport, Louisiana

1**shrew** \'shrü, *esp South* 'srü, *dial* 'swü\ *n* -s [ME *shrewe* evil person, scolding person, scolding woman, fr. OE *scrēawa* shrew (small mammal)] **1 :** any of numerous small mouselike chiefly nocturnal mammals of the family Soricidae which are most closely related to the moles, have a long pointed snout, very small eyes, and velvety fur, feed mainly on worms and insects, and of which most U. S. forms belong in two genera (*Sorex* and *Blarina*) — see ELEPHANT SHREW, LONG-TAILED SHREW, SHORT-TAILED SHREW, TREE SHREW, WATER SHREW **2** *obs* **:** a wicked or evil person **:** SCOUNDREL **3 :** a vexatious, scolding, or brawling woman **:** SCOLD, TERMAGANT ⟨a ~, a woman with the temper of a fiend —C.S.Forester⟩ ⟨~ berating her unemployed husband for not supporting her —John McCarten⟩ — often opposed to *sheep*

2**shrew** \"\ *vt* -ED/-ING/-S [ME *shrewen*, fr. *shrewe*, n.] **1** *obs* **:** CURSE ⟨~ me if I would lose it —Shak.⟩ **2 :** to treat with shrewish abuse ⟨a wicked woman to ~ his splendid features out of shape —Randall Jarrell⟩

shrewd \'shrüd, *esp South* 'srüd, *dial* 'swüd\ *adj* -ER/-EST [ME *shrewed*, fr. *shrewe* + *-ed*] **1 a** *archaic* **:** causing trouble **:** MISCHIEVOUS, NAUGHTY ⟨a ~ and knavish spirit called Robin Goodfellow —Shak.⟩ **b** *obs* **:** causing injury **:** HURTFUL ⟨an ant . . . is a ~ thing in an orchard —Francis Bacon⟩ **2** *obs* **:** marked by bad temper **:** SHREWISH, ABUSIVE ⟨~ words . . . improved into smart blows —Thomas Fuller⟩ ⟨thou wilt never get thee a husband if thou be so ~ of thy tongue —Shak.⟩ **3 a** *obs* **:** tending to disadvantage **:** OMINOUS, UNFORTUNATE **b :** beset with hardships or difficulties **:** DANGEROUS, DISTRESSING ⟨the ordeal of a situation ~ as any that can happen to her sex in civilized life —George Meredith⟩ **4 a :** SEVERE, HARD ⟨a ~ knock⟩ ⟨gives out ~ galvanic shocks —R.L.Stevenson⟩ ⟨give you a ~ kick in the wind —*Punch*⟩ **b :** BITING, PIERCING ⟨a ~ wind⟩ ⟨the first ~ gust of a storm —S.H.Adams⟩ **5 a :** marked by cleverness, discernment, or sagacity **:** ASTUTE, KEEN ⟨~ observer⟩ ⟨~ design⟩ ⟨~ reply⟩ ⟨~ business sense⟩ ⟨~ appraisal of political maneuvers —W.A.Swanberg⟩ **b :** marked by artfulness or trickiness **:** WILY ⟨a ~ operator —Irving Bacheller⟩ **c :** penetrating near the truth **:** KNOWING ⟨~ guess⟩ ⟨~ suspicion⟩ ⟨had a very ~ idea where to look for her —Margery Allingham⟩ **d :** sharp and searching ⟨a ~ eye⟩ ⟨an inspection of the ~*est* sort —Sarah O. Jewett⟩

syn SAGACIOUS, PERSPICACIOUS, ASTUTE: SHREWD may describe a blended practical, hardheaded cleverness, judgment, and acute perception ⟨could on occasions be surprisingly *shrewd* — she had a habit of seeing through people's words right down into their motives —Victoria Sackville-West⟩ ⟨he is *shrewd*, sharp, hard and acute, and he is, one believes, the greatest master of the art of publicity and propaganda to arise in this generation —Sidney Hyman⟩ SAGACIOUS may connote wisdom, penetration, discernment, farsightedness and, above all, keen mature judgment ⟨his strength was in his *sagacious* sifting of practical ideas from the mass of suggestions proffered by his contemporaries —T.D.McCormick⟩ ⟨a strategical withdrawal might have been *sagacious* here —C.H.Sykes⟩ PERSPICACIOUS may indicate unusual power to perceive or understand what is obscure or mysterious ⟨these were the fundamental difficulties, but few men were *perspicacious* enough to appreciate them —Allan Nevins & H.S.Commager⟩ ⟨those blind spots which are found in the most *perspicacious* mortals —L.P.Smith⟩ ASTUTE may indicate mature shrewd perspicacity with esp. careful discretion, wise diplomacy, and calculated discernment ⟨a masterpiece of calculated cajolery from an *astute* adventuress —J.C.Powys⟩ ⟨*astute* financiers who see in the large organization an easier mechanism for their manipulations of credit, for their inflation of capital values, for their monopolistic controls —Lewis Mumford⟩

shrewd·ly *adv* [ME *shrewedly*, fr. *shrewed* shrewd + *-ly*] **:** in a shrewd manner: as **a :** HURTFULLY, SEVERELY ⟨gore him ~ in the exposed flank —James Stevenson-Hamilton⟩ **b :** INTENSELY ⟨hated each other ~ —H.O.Taylor⟩ **c :** ASTUTELY, KNOWINGLY ⟨~ estimating his son as a man of very mediocre parts —Herman Wouk⟩ ⟨her eyes followed him ~ —Liam O'Flaherty⟩

shrewd·ness *n* -ES [ME *shrewednesse*, fr. *shrewed* shrewd + *-nesse* -ness] **:** the quality or state of being shrewd: as **a :** sagacity in practical affairs ⟨the political ~ that characterized his later career —Carol L. Thompson⟩ **b :** keenness of discernment **:** ACUMEN ⟨the tradition of rural ~ —Malcolm Cowley⟩

shrewdy \-dē, -di\ *n* -ES *slang* **:** a shrewd person

shrew·ish \'shrüish, -üēsh, *esp South* 'srü-, *dial* 'swü-\ *adj* **:** resembling or having the characteristics of a shrew **:** ILL-TEMPERED, INTRACTABLE ⟨a small, ~ woman with . . . eyes which boded temper —Dorothy Sayers⟩ ⟨her ~ tongue —Peggy Durdin⟩ ⟨the ~ river —Murray Schumach⟩

shrew·ish·ly *adv* **:** in a shrewish manner

shrew·ish·ness *n* -ES **:** the quality or state of being shrewish

shrewlike \'=,=\ *adj* **:** resembling a shrew

shrew·ly *adv* [obs. E *shrew*, adj., evil, malicious (fr. ME *shrewe*, fr. *shrewe*, n., evil person) + E *-ly* — more at SHREW] **:** SHREWDLY

shrew mole *n* **:** any of numerous relatively slender moles that somewhat resemble shrews: as **a :** a mole of an Asiatic genus (*Uropsilus*) **b :** one of a No. American genus (*Neurotrichus*)

shrewmouse \'=,=\ *n*, *pl* **shrewmice :** SHREW 1

shrews *pl of* SHREW, *pres 3d sing of* SHREW

shrews·bury cake \'sh(r)ü|zb(ə)rē-, 'sh(r)ō|, -,berē-, -ri- *sometimes by r-dissimilation* 'shü| *or* |'shō|\ *n*, *usu cap S* [fr. *Shrewsbury*, city in western England] **:** a short sweet biscuit baked in wafers

shri *var of* SRI

1**shriek** \'shrēk, *esp South* 'srēk, *dial* 'swēk\ *vb* -ED/-ING/-S [prob. irreg. fr. ME *shriken* to shriek; akin to ON *skrækja* to screech — more at SCREAM] *vi* **1 a :** to utter a sharp shrill sound (as of some birds and animals) ⟨hear . . . an old hare —G.G.Carter⟩ **b :** to cry out in a high-pitched voice **:** SCREECH ⟨the ladies ~*ed* at the sight of the skull —T.L.Peacock⟩ ⟨a tangle of hysterical girls . . . sweeping down the main street, ~*ing* —Jean Stafford⟩ **2 a :** to make a sound resembling a shriek ⟨keep the siren ~*ing* —*Amer. Guide Series: Minn.*⟩ ⟨the wind . . . ~*ing* like ten thousand devils —P.B.Cronk⟩ **b :** to suggest such a sound (as by vividness of expression) ⟨yellow landscape print that ~*ed* from the flowered wallpaper —Margaret Long⟩ ~ *vt* **1 :** to utter or sound forth with a shriek or sharply and shrilly ⟨~ an alarm⟩ ⟨the sirens ~*ed* their warning —*Rotarian*⟩ **2 :** to express in a manner suggestive of a shriek ⟨headlines ~*ing* their sensational news of the murder⟩

2**shriek** \"\ *n* -s **1 :** a shrill usu. wild or involuntary cry (as of sudden or extreme terror or pain or of violent laughter) ⟨a starling . . . gave a piercing ~ —*Time*⟩ ⟨the agonizing ~*s* of the wounded —Charles Lever⟩ ⟨~*s* of mirth —R.B.D. French⟩ **2 :** a sound resembling a shriek ⟨the sudden ~ of chalk on a blackboard —Earle Birney⟩

shriek·ing·ly *adv* **:** with a shriek ⟨~ the timber cracks —George Meredith⟩

shriek owl *n* **1 a** *archaic* **:** SCREECH OWL **b** *dial Eng* **:** BARN OWL **2** *dial Eng* **:** SWIFT

shrieky \-kē, -ki\ *adj* -ER/-EST **:** resembling a shriek **:** HIGH-PITCHED, HYSTERICAL ⟨a ~ voice⟩

shriev·al \'shrēvəl, *esp South* 'srē-, *dial* 'swē-\ *adj* [*shrieve* + *-al*] **:** of or relating to a sheriff ⟨~ badge⟩ ⟨the functions of his ~ office⟩

shriev·al·ty \-ltē, -ti\ *n* -ES [*shrieve* + *-alty* (as in *royalty*)] *chiefly Brit* **1 :** the office of a sheriff ⟨the honor of the ~⟩ **2 :** the term of office of a sheriff ⟨the events of his ~⟩ **3 :** the jurisdiction of a sheriff ⟨the sheriff has publicly admitted that there are . . . milk bars in his ~ —H.F.Ellis⟩

1**shrieve** \'s(h)rēv\ *archaic var of* SHERIFF

2**shrieve** \"\ *archaic var of* SHRIVE

1**shrift** \'shrift, *esp South* 'sri-, *dial* 'swi-\ *n* -s [ME *shrift*, *shrifte*, fr. OE *scrift*, fr. *scrīfan* to shrive — more at SHRIVE] **1** *archaic* **a :** the act of shriving **:** confession of one's sins esp. to a priest in the sacrament of penance **b :** ABSOLUTION 3a **2 :** acknowledgment or disclosure (as of guilt, wrongdoing, something secret) to someone ⟨those . . . who have made ~ of love —Sebastian Evans⟩ **3** *obs* **:** CONFESSIONAL ⟨his bed shall seem a school, his board a ~ —Shak.⟩

2**shrift** \"\ *vt* -ED/-ING/-S *archaic* **:** SHRIVE

shriftfather \'=,==\ *n* [ME *shriftfader*, fr. *shrift*, *shrifte* shrift + *fader* father] *archaic* **:** FATHER CONFESSOR

1**shrike** \'shrīk, *esp South* 'srīk, *dial* 'swīk\ *chiefly dial var of* SHRIEK

2**shrike** \"\ *n* -s [perh. fr. (assumed) ME *shrik*, fr. OE *scrīc* thrush; akin to ME *shriken* to shriek — more at SHRIEK] **1 :** any of numerous oscine birds of the family Laniidae and esp. of the genus *Lanius* that have a strong notched bill hooked at the tip, feed chiefly on insects and often impale their prey on thorns, and generally have the plumage predominantly gray or brownish with the wings and tail black marked with white — see BUTCHER-BIRD, LOGGERHEAD SHRIKE, MIGRANT SHRIKE, NORTHERN SHRIKE, RED-BACKED SHRIKE, WHITE-RUMPED SHRIKE **2 :** any of various birds felt to resemble or formerly classified with the Laniidae (as an antbird or drongo) — usu. used with a qualifying term; see ANTSHRIKE, CUCKOO SHRIKE, WOOD SHRIKE

shrike thrush *n* **1 :** an Indian timaliine bird of the genus *Gampsorhynchus* **2 :** any of several Australian singing birds of the genus *Colluricincla* that resemble the shrike

shrike tit *n* **1 :** any of several species of Australian birds of the genus *Falcunculus* that have a strong toothed bill and sharp claws and that creep over the bark of trees like titmice in search of insects **2 :** HILL TIT **3 :** FALCONET 3

1**shrill** \'shril, *esp South* 'sril, *dial* 'swil\ *vb* -ED/-ING/-S [ME *shrillen*; prob. akin to OE *scralletan* to resound loudly, OSw *skrælla* to rattle, bang] *vi* **:** to utter or emit an acute, piercing sound **:** produce a sharp shrill sound **:** SCREECH, SCREAM ⟨in the trees outside the cicadas were ~*ing* —Lucien Price⟩ ⟨the loudspeaker ~*ed* with the noise —C.S.Forester⟩ ~ *vt* **:** to utter or express (as a sound or words) in a shrill tone ⟨~*ed* orders and then fell with a scream —F.V.W.Mason⟩ ⟨headlines have ~*ed* disquieting news —Dorothy Barclay⟩

2**shrill** \"\ *adj* -ER/-EST [ME *shrille*, fr. *shrillen*, v.] **1 a :** having or emitting a sharp high-pitched tone or sound **:** PIERCING, PENETRATING ⟨a ~ whistle⟩ ⟨the ~ music of the calliope —*Amer. Guide Series: Tenn.*⟩ **b :** accompanied by sharp high-pitched sounds or cries ⟨make ~, hysterical little sorties around the shops after lunch —C.G.Glover⟩ **2 :** having an intense, sharp, or vivid effect on the senses **:** KEEN, PUNGENT ⟨arc lamps bathed the occasion in ~ blue light —Noel Coward⟩ ⟨everything looked different: the outlines were ~*er* —Elizabeth Pollet⟩ **3 a :** marked by a sharp insistence on being heard **:** ILL-TEMPERED, STRIDENT ⟨criticism . . . so ~ and partisan that it has provoked resistance and resentment —R.K. Carr⟩ **b :** marked by a lack of restraint or emotional control **:** INTEMPERATE, EXTRAVAGANT ⟨with every look his wrath became ~*er*, narrower, more personal —Max Lerner⟩

3**shrill** \"\ *adv* [ME *shrille*, fr. *shrille*, adj.] *archaic* **:** SHRILLY ⟨through the high wood echoing ~ —John Milton⟩

4**shrill** \"\ *n* -s [1*shrill*] **:** a shrill sound ⟨the ~ of a ship's whistle⟩ ⟨the ~ of crickets —F.D.Ommanney⟩

shrilling *n* -s [fr. gerund of 1*shrill*] **:** a more or less continued shrill noise or cry ⟨the clash of swords and ~ of trumpets —P.J.Searles⟩; *esp* **:** STRIDULATION ⟨the slow ~ of the field cricket in the grass —Sidney Lanier⟩

shrill·ness *n* -ES **:** the quality or state of being shrill ⟨the voice of woman . . . stretched into unnatural ~ by anger and impatience —T.L.Peacock⟩ ⟨the ~ of the . . . electoral campaign —*Foreign Affairs*⟩

1**shril·ly** \-il(l)ē, -li\ *adv* [2*shrill* + *-ly*] **:** in a shrill manner: as **a :** in a high-pitched voice ⟨the medics were whistling ~ —R.O.Bowen⟩ **b :** in a high-strung, sharply insistent manner ⟨protests a little too ~ —Robert Payne⟩

2**shrilly** \-ilē, -li\ *adj* [2*shrill* + *-y*] **:** somewhat shrill ⟨a ~ sound⟩ ⟨parrots of ~ green —W.W.Gibson⟩

1**shrimp** \'shrimp, *esp South* 'sri-, *dial* 'swi-\ *n*, *pl* **shrimps** *also* **shrimp** [ME *shrimpe* shrimp (crustacean), puny person; akin to MHG *schrimpf* scratch, slight wound, *schrimpfen* to wrinkle, Sw *skrympa* to shrink, L *curvus* curved — more at CROWN] **1 a :** any of numerous relatively small mostly marine decapod crustaceans (suborder Natantia) having a slender elongated body with a laterally compressed abdomen, long legs, and a long, more or less spiny rostrum **b :** any of various small crustaceans (as mysids, euphausids, amphipods, and branchiopods) that resemble the true shrimps — often used with a qualifying term — see BRINE SHRIMP, FAIRY SHRIMP; compare PRAWN **2 :** a very small or puny person or thing — usu. used disparagingly ⟨an unimposing little ~ of a man —*Living Age*⟩ **3** *or* **shrimp pink** *or* **shrimp red :** a variable color averaging a deep pink that is bluer, lighter, and stronger than average coral and stronger and slightly yellower and lighter than fiesta

2**shrimp** \"\ *vi* -ED/-ING/-S **:** to fish for or catch shrimps ⟨~*ing* further offshore —*Fishing Gazette*⟩

shrimp·er \-pə(r)\ *n* -s **:** one that shrimps: **a :** a shrimp fisherman **b :** a boat engaged in shrimping

shrimpfish \'=,=\ *n* **:** any of numerous small compressed East Indian marine fishes of the family Centriscidae that are related to the bellows fish and have a tubular snout and the body covered with an armor of transparent bony plates which is fused with the endoskeleton, extends over and beyond the down-turned dorsal and caudal fins, and terminates in a long spine

shrimp·ish \-pish, -pēsh\ *adj* **:** somewhat diminutive **:** PUNY ⟨tied the apron around his ~ person —Christopher Morley⟩

shrimp plant *n* **:** a widely cultivated tropical American shrubby plant (*Beloperone guttata*) of the family Acanthaceae having whitish flowers borne in spikes and protruding from overlapping broadly ovate reddish brown bracts

shrimpy \-pē, -pi\ *adj* -ER/-EST **:** **1** full of shrimp ⟨a ~ bay⟩ **2 :** DIMINUTIVE ⟨a ~ child —Doris Peel⟩ ⟨~ rosebuds —*Harper's*⟩

1**shrine** \'shrīn, *esp South* 'srīn, *dial* 'swīn\ *n* -s [ME *shrin*, *shrine*, fr. OE *scrīn*, fr. L *scrinium* case, chest, box; perh. akin to Russ *krivoĭ* crooked, L *curvus* curved — more at CROWN] **1 :** a case, box, or receptacle; *esp* **:** one in which sacred relics (as the bones of a saint) are deposited **:** RELIQUARY **2 :** a receptacle (as a casket or tomb) for the dead; *esp* **:** the tomb of one considered holy or of hallowed memory **3 a :** a place or object hallowed or honored from its history or associations ⟨a small country township . . . famous to tourists as the ~ of a late-Victorian novelist —*Sydney* (*Australia*) *Bull.*⟩ **b :** an object, structure, or place that is considered sacred by a religious group and that serves as the focus of the performance of some ritual **:** SANCTUARY

2**shrine** \"\ *vt* -ED/-ING/-S [ME *shrinen*, fr. *shrin*, *shrine*, n.] **1** *archaic* **:** to place in or provide with a shrine ⟨a goddess *shrined* in every tree —Alexander Pope⟩ **2 :** to enclose as if in a shrine **:** ENSHRINE ⟨has the feeling of truth already *shrined* in his own breast —William Hazlitt⟩

shrin·er \-nə(r)\ *n* -s *usu cap* [*Shrine* (in the name *Order of the Mystic Shrine*) + *-er*] **:** a member of a secret fraternal society called the Order of the Mystic Shrine that is non-Masonic but admits only Knights Templars and 32d-degree Masons to membership

1**shrink** \'shr|iŋk, *esp South* 'sr|, *dial* 'sw|\ *vb* **shrank** \|aŋk, |aiŋk\ *also* **shrunk** \|əŋk\ **shrunk** *or esp in adjectival use* **shrunk·en** \-kən *sometimes* -kᵊŋ\ **shrinking; shrinks** [ME *shrinken*, fr. OE *scrincan*; akin to MD *schrinken* to draw back, shrink back, OSw *skrunkin* shrunken, L *curvus* curved — more at CROWN] *vi* **1 :** to contract or curl up the body or part of it usu. because of physical stress, fear, or revulsion **:** HUDDLE, COWER ⟨~ with cold⟩ ⟨~ in horror⟩ ⟨seemed to ~ into himself —Gordon Merrick⟩ ⟨found the atmosphere . . . so oppressive that he was glad to ~ out of sight —Samuel Butler †1902⟩ **2 a :** to contract to a less extent or compass ⟨the black peaty earth *shrank* as soon as it was dry —G.M.Trevelyan⟩ **b :** to become smaller or more compacted (as from heat or wetting) ⟨*shrank* over 30% after five launderings —*For Instance*⟩ **c :** to contract after the release of tension ⟨nylon yarn, when wound off a package into skein form, ~*s* . . . as much as 2.8% —W.E. Shinn⟩ **d :** to lose substance or weight (as in cooking) ⟨meat ~*s* in cooking by losing water and fat⟩ **e :** to lessen in value **:** DWINDLE ⟨seeing their earnings ~ as overtime gave way to shorter work weeks —J.A.Lack⟩ **3 a :** to draw back **:** retire to shelter ⟨*shrank* toward a doorway some few yards on —Arthur Morrison⟩ **b** (1) **:** to withdraw to avoid encounter **:** slink away ⟨turns and ~*s* from the room —Sidney Howard⟩ (2) **:** FLINCH ⟨refused to ~ from a . . . thrusting knife —Ward Moore⟩ **c :** to hold back (as from an action or responsibility) esp. because of fear or distaste **:** RECOIL ⟨a very formidable deed, but he was determined not to ~ from it —Eden Phillpotts⟩ ~ *vt* **1** *obs* **:** to draw back or in (as a horn) **:** RETRACT ⟨make the Sun ~ in his beam —Edward Young⟩ **2 a** *archaic* **:** to reduce (as the body) to smaller compass ⟨her body huge she *shrank* —William Morris⟩ **b :** to cause to contract or shrink ⟨human heads *shrunk* to orange-size —J.H.Cutler⟩ **c :** to compact (cloth) by causing to contract when subjected to washing, boiling, steaming, or other processes **d :** to make smaller or less significant ⟨~*ing* the office to the holder's ability⟩ **3 a** *archaic* **:** to draw or move out of the way (a part of the body) ⟨she *shrank* her hand back —George Meredith⟩ **b** *obs* **:** SHRUG ⟨he *shrunk* up his shoulders at it —Daniel Defoe⟩ **syn** see CONTRACT, RECOIL — **shrink on :** to cause (as a metal ring or hoop) to become fixed tightly around another object by heating sufficiently to slip into place while expanded and then allowing to cool and contract — **shrink out :** to remove (fullness) in tailoring esp. woolen fabrics by steam pressing

2**shrink** \"\ *n* -s **1 :** the act of shrinking **:** WITHDRAWAL, RECOIL ⟨the shiver and ~ with which the sitter caught sight of him —Lew Wallace⟩ **2 :** SHRINKAGE

shrink·able \-kəbəl\ *adj* **:** capable of being shrunk ⟨a ~ fabric⟩

shrink·age \-kij, -kēj\ *n* -s **1 :** the act or process of shrinking: as **a :** the contraction of metal when cooled **b :** the reduction in volume of excavated earth when compacted in the fill **c :** the loss in weight of livestock during shipment and in the process of preparing the meat for consumption **d :** the loss in weight of meat during cooking **e :** DRY SHRINKAGE **f :** reduction in number or value ⟨a deplorable ~ in the number of qualified teachers —Douglas Bush⟩ ⟨a ~ in the public budget will depress . . . economic activity —R.A.Musgrave⟩ **2 :** the amount of contraction, reduction or depreciation ⟨suffered a 10% ~ in transit⟩

shrinkage rule *or* **shrink rule** *n* **:** CONTRACTION RULE

shrinkage stope *n* **:** an overhand stope without timbering in which the broken ore is stored as a filling to support the workings and form a working floor

shrink·er \-kə(r)\ *n* -s **:** one that shrinks: as **a :** one that puts articles (as textiles) through a shrinking process **b :** one that shrinks on a metal part **c :** a device for reducing the diameter of a metal tire while hot

shrinkhead \'=,=\ *also* **shrinking head** *n* **:** FEEDHEAD

shrinking *pres part of* SHRINK

shrink·ing·ly *adv* **:** in a frightened or withdrawing manner **:** SHYLY ⟨staring ~ at you as you pass —G.W.Cable⟩

shrinking violet *n* **:** a bashful or retiring person ⟨no *shrinking violet* when it comes to telling the umpires off —*Springfield* (*Mass.*) *Daily News*⟩; *esp* **:** one who shrinks from public recognition of his merit

shrink link *n* **:** PRISONER 2b

shrink–mixed concrete \'=¦=-\ *n* **:** concrete that is partially mixed in a stationary mixer before being finally mixed in a truck mixer

shrink ring *n* **:** a ring shrunk on in order to hold assembled parts (as the commutator bars of a dynamo) in fixed relative position

shrinks *pres 3d sing of* SHRINK, *pl of* SHRINK

shrite \'s(h)rīt\ *n* -s [prob. alter. of 2*shrike*] *dial Eng* **:** MISTLE THRUSH

shrive \'shr|īv, *esp South* 'sr|, *dial* 'sw|\ *vb* **shrived** \|īvd\ *or* **shrove** \|ōv\ **shriv·en** \|ivən *also* ivᵊm *or* ibᵊm\ *or* **shrived; shriving; shrives** [ME *shriven*, fr. OE *scrīfan* to shrive, prescribe; akin to OFris *skrīva* to shrive, write, OHG *scrīban* to write; all fr. a prehistoric WGmc word borrowed fr. L *scribere* to write — more at SCRIBE] *vt* **1 :** to hear the confession of, impose penance on, and give absolution to (a person) in the sacrament of penance ⟨the resident parson . . . would sing his daily Mass and come in to ~ the sick —G.G.Coulton⟩ **2 :** to free from guilt **:** PARDON, PURGE ⟨~*s* his burdened mind —Robert Trumbull⟩ ~ *vi* **1** *archaic* **:** to hear confessions, to impose penance, and to give absolution in performance of the ecclesiastical office of confessor ⟨priests were praying, preaching, *shriving* —T.B.Macaulay⟩ **2 :** to confess one's sins esp. to a priest ⟨mocked at the priest when he called her to ~ —Elizabeth B. Browning⟩

1**shriv·el** \'shrivəl, *esp South* 'sri-, *dial* 'swi-\ *vb* **shriveled** *or* **shrivelled; shriveled** *or* **shrivelled; shriveling** *or* **shrivelling** \-v(ə)liŋ\ **shrivels** [origin unknown] *vi* **1 :** to draw or be drawn into wrinkles **:** shrink and form corrugations ⟨the skin ~*s* with age⟩ ⟨the expanding economy would ~ like a pricked balloon —*Lamp*⟩ — often used with *up* ⟨a leaf ~*s* up in the hot sun⟩ **2 :** to become reduced to inanition, helplessness, or inefficiency ⟨all their vain terrors ~*ing* up like ghosts at sunrise —Edith Wharton⟩ ~ *vt* **:** to cause to shrivel **:** SHRINK, WITHER ⟨one blazing weekend can ~ the receipts for the stoutest hit —Richard Maney⟩ ⟨filmy clouds which do not always disperse until the sun has risen and *shrivelled* them —Mary S. Broome⟩

2**shrivel** \"\ *n* -s **:** something (as a withered nut or fruit) that is shriveled

1**shroff** \'shräf\ *n* -s [Hindi *ṣarrāf*, fr. Ar] **:** a banker or money changer in the Far East; *esp* **:** one who tests and determines the worth of coin

2**shroff** \"\ *vb* -ED/-ING/-S *vt* **:** to inspect and sort (coins) and separate out bad pieces ~ *vi* **:** to act as a shroff

shroff·age \-fij, -fēj\ *n* -s [1*shroff* + *-age*] **:** the commission charged for shroffing

shrogs \'s(h)rägz\ *n pl* [ME *shrogys*, pl. of *shrog*, perh. alter. of *skrogge* stunted shrub or branch] *dial Eng* **:** BRUSHWOOD

1**shrop·shire** \'s(h)räp,shi(ə)r, -iə, -pshə(r)\ *adj*, *usu cap* [fr. *Shropshire*, county in western England] **:** of or from Shropshire, England **:** of the kind or style prevalent in Shropshire **:** SALOPIAN

2**shropshire** \"\ *n*, *usu cap* **:** a widely distributed English breed of dark-faced hornless mutton-type sheep that are similar to the Southdown but larger and that produce a heavy well-crimped fleece of medium fineness and length

1**shroud** \'shraůd, *esp South* 'sraůd, *dial* 'swaůd\ *n* -s [ME, fr. OE *scrūd*; akin to ON *skrūth* shrouds of a ship, cloth, OE *scrēade* shred — more at SHRED] **1 a** *obs* **:** a covering for the body **:** GARMENT **b :** burial garment **:** WINDING-SHEET, CEREMENT **2 a** *obs* **:** a covered place (as a cave or den) used as a retreat or shelter **b shrouds** *pl*, *archaic* **:** an underground chapel (as the chapel of St. Faith's under St. Paul's Cathedral in London) **c** *obs* **:** PROTECTION ⟨put yourself under his ~, the universal landlord —Shak.⟩ **d** *archaic* **:** the overspreading foliage of a tree ⟨a cedar . . . with fair branches, and with a shadowing ~ —Ezek 31:3 (AV)⟩ **3 :** something that covers, screens, or guards ⟨a ~ of secrecy⟩ ⟨a ~ of dust hanging over the city⟩: as **a :** the metal piece between the hood and the cowl on an automobile body **b** *or* **shroud plate :** one of the two annular plates at either side at the periphery of a waterwheel that form the sides of the buckets **c :** one of two similarly placed flanges forming part of the wheel casting to strengthen the teeth of a gear wheel or peripheral support to turbine or fan bedding **d :** the disk ends of lantern clock pinions into which the pins are set **e :** the muslin cloth put on dressed beef for protection and cleanliness **f :** a sheet-metal guard protecting an airplane fuselage from exhaust heat **4 a :** one of the ropes of hemp or wire leading usu. in pairs from a ship's mastheads to give lateral support to the masts — see SHIP illustration **b** *also* **shroud line :** one of the cords that suspend the harness of a parachute from the canopy

2**shroud** \"\ *vb* -ED/-ING/-S [ME *shrouden*, fr. *shroud*, n.] *vt* **1 a** *archaic* **:** to cover (as a person) for protection **:** SHELTER ⟨~ these weaklings from blows —Nathaniel Fairfax⟩ **b** *obs* **:** to conceal (as a person) in a secret or hidden place ⟨I have been closely ~*ed* in this bush —Shak.⟩ **2 a :** to cut off from view **:** SCREEN ⟨trees ~*ed* in a heavy mist⟩ **b :** to veil under another appearance (as by obscuring or disguising) ⟨~*ed* in cipher⟩ ⟨uncertainty . . . ~*s* the identity of the early peoples —*Amer. Guide Series: Ind.*⟩ **3 :** to cover with a shroud; *esp* **:** to enclose in a winding sheet **:** dress for burial **4 :** to cover (sides of beef) with muslin **5 :** TRIM, LOP ⟨climb up . . . and ~ off the lower boughs —Thomas Hardy⟩ ~ *vi*, *archaic* **:** to take or seek shelter ⟨wilt thou ~ in haunted cell —William Collins †1759⟩

shrouding *n* -s **:** the shrouds on a water wheel, gear wheel, fan wheel, or propeller

shroud knot *n* **:** a knot for fastening together a parted ship's shroud
shroud–laid \ˈ=,=\ *adj, of a rope* **:** composed of four strands and laid right-handed with a heart or core
shroud·less \ˈ=,ləs\ *adj* **:** having no shroud or winding-sheet ⟨~ dead on their rocky beds —Jane Wilde⟩
shroud·man \ˈ=mən\ *n, pl* **shroudmen :** a worker who assembles the sheet-metal guards that protect airplane fuselages from exhaust heat
shroud plate *n* **1 :** a chain plate to which a ship's shrouds are fastened **2 :** SHROUD 3b
¹shrove [ME *shroof*, fr. OE *scrāf*] *past of* SHRIVE
²shrove *vi* -ED/-ING/-S [fr. *shrove-* (in *shrovetide*)] *obs* **:** to make merry ⟨went a-*shroving* through the city —John Fletcher⟩; *esp* **:** to join in the festivities of Shrovetide
³shrove \ˈshrōv, *esp South* ˈsrōv, *dial* ˈswōv\ *n* -S *usu cap* **:** SHROVETIDE
shrove monday *n, usu cap S&M* [ME *shrovemonday*, fr. *shrove-*, *schrof-* (as in *schroftyde* Shrovetide) + *monday*] **:** the Monday before Ash Wednesday
shrove sunday *n, usu cap both Ss* [ME *shrofsunday*, fr. *shrof-*, *schrof-* (as in *schroftyde* Shrovetide) + *sunday*] **:** the Sunday before Ash Wednesday **:** QUINQUAGESIMA

shroud knot

shrovetide \ˈ=,=\ *n, usu cap* [ME *schroftyde*, fr. *schrof-* (fr. *shriven* to shrive) + *tyde*, *tide* time — more at SHRIVE, TIDE] **:** the period usu. of three days immediately preceding Ash Wednesday
shrove tuesday *n, usu cap S&T* [ME *chroftetewesday*, fr. *chrofte-*, *schrof-* (as in *schroftyde* Shrovetide) + *tewesday*, *tuesday* Tuesday] **:** the Tuesday immediately before Ash Wednesday — called also *Pancake Day*
¹shrub \ˈshrəb, *esp South* ˈsrəb, *dial* ˈswəb\ *n* -S [ME *schrubbe*, *schrobbe*, *shrobbe*, fr. OE *scrybb* brushwood; akin to Norw *skrubbebær* dwarf cornel] **1 :** a low usu. several-stemmed woody plant — compare HERB, TREE **2 :** CAROLINA ALLSPICE
²shrub \"\ *vt* **shrubbed; shrubbed; shrubbing; shrubs 1 :** to clear (ground) of shrubs **2 :** LOP, PRUNE ⟨~ a tree⟩ ⟨~ a branch⟩ **3 :** to plant (as a lawn) with shrubs
³shrub \"\ *n* -S [Ar *sharāb* alcoholic drink, beverage — more at SYRUP] **1 :** a beverage that consists of an alcoholic liquor, fruit juice, fruit rind, and sugar aged in crockery, glass, or wood and then strained and that is usu. served iced and diluted with water and soda ⟨rum ~⟩ **2 :** a beverage made by adding acidulated fruit juice to iced water ⟨raspberry ~⟩
shrubbed \-bd\ *adj* [¹*shrub* + *-ed*] **:** SHRUBBY
shrub·ber·ied \-b(ə)rēd, -rid\ *adj* **:** bordered with shrubbery
shrub·bery \-b(ə)rē, -ri\ *n* -ES **1 :** a plantation of shrubs **:** HEDGE ⟨driving her opponent's croquet ball into a ~ —C.D. Lewis⟩ ⟨a huge gaunt house ... asleep in its *shrubberies* —H.V.Morton⟩ **2 :** a growth or group of shrubs ⟨planned to trim the ~ after lunch⟩ ⟨hills covered only with kunai grass or an occasional grove of ~ —Norman Mailer⟩
shrub·bi·ness \-bēnəs, -be'n-\ *n* -ES **:** the quality or state of being shrubby
shrub·by \-bē, -bi\ *adj* -ER/-EST [¹*shrub* + *-y*] **1 :** consisting of or covered with shrubs ⟨every ~ field was alive with butterflies —William Beebe⟩ **2 :** resembling a shrub (as in size, habit, or growth) **:** SCRUBBY ⟨a subalpine species, usually ~ or prostrate in habit —William Dallimore & A.B.Jackson⟩
shrubby althaea *or* **shrubby althea** *also* **shrub althaea** *or* **shrub althea** *n* **:** ROSE OF SHARON 3
shrubby bittersweet *n* **:** BITTERSWEET 2b
shrubby cinquefoil *n* **:** a much-branched low shrub (*Potentilla fruticosa*) with pinnately compound leaves and yellow solitary or cymose flowers — called also *golden hardhack*, *hardhack*
shrubby fern *n* **:** SWEET FERN 2
shrubby horsetail *n* **:** any joint fir of the genus *Ephedra*
shrubby st.–john's–wort *n, usu cap 2d S&J* **:** a stiff shrub or woody herb (*Hypericum spathulatum*) having oblong entire leaves and dense cymes of yellow flowers with numerous stamens
shrubby trefoil *n* **:** HOP TREE
shrub garden *n* **:** a planting of shrubs in garden style
shrub layer *or* **shrub stratum** *n* **:** the undergrowth of a forest consisting usu. of plants from 3 to about 15 feet in height and including both shrubby and seedling trees
shrub·let \ˈshrəblət, *esp South* ˈsrə-, *dial* ˈswə-\ *n* -S **:** a small shrub
shrub mallow *n* **:** ROSE OF SHARON 3
shrub oak *n* **:** SCRUB OAK
shrubs *pl of* SHRUB, *pres 3d sing of* SHRUB
shrubwood \ˈ=,=\ *n* **:** a woodland in which shrubs predominate
shrub yellowroot *n* **:** a half-shrubby plant (*Xanthorhiza apiifolia*) of the family Ranunculaceae with large pinnate or bipinnate leaves and small brownish racemose flowers
shruff \ˈs(h)rəf\ *n* -S [perh. fr. ME *schroff* rubbish; prob. akin to OE *sceorf* scurf — more at SCURF] **:** dross of metals
¹shrug \ˈshrəg, *esp South* ˈsrəg, *dial* ˈswəg\ *vb* **shrugged; shrugged; shrugging; shrugs** [ME *schruggen* to shiver, shrug] *vi* **1** *obs* **:** to shudder with cold or nervousness **:** SHIVER ⟨it makes me ~ when I call to mind the agonies which he suffered —Samuel Parker †1730⟩ **2 :** to raise or draw in the shoulders esp. as an expression of indifference, aloofness, or aversion ⟨the ordinary citizen has no defense against incredible and unwelcome statements other than to ~, turn the page, forget it —Russell Lord⟩ **3** *obs* **a :** to move the body sidewise as in expressing uneasiness or complacency **:** FIDGET **b :** SHRINK, COWER ~ *vt* **1 :** to lift or contract (the shoulders) esp. by way of expressing lack of interest, aloofness, or dislike **2 :** to express by a shrug ⟨*shrugged* his low opinion of the occupant of the room —T.B.Costain⟩ **3 a :** to draw together or bunch up (as the body) in putting on a garment ⟨took out her own serviceable blue coat ... *shrugged* herself into it —Shirley Jackson⟩ **b :** to pull or work (as a garment or covering) into place ⟨*shrugging* the clothes together upon his body —Pearl Buck⟩
²shrug \"\ *n* -S **1 :** a drawing up of the shoulders usu. to express indifference **2 :** a woman's small waist-length or shorter jacket that is easily slipped on and off and often has a one-button closing
shrug away *vt* **:** to get rid of **:** throw off **:** DISREGARD ⟨*shrugged away* her annoyance —Mary Jane Rolfs⟩
shrug·ging·ly *adv* **:** with a shrug **:** INDIFFERENTLY
shrug off *vt* **1 :** to brush aside **:** MINIMIZE, EVADE ⟨*shrug off* this whole problem —C.D.Lewis⟩ **2 :** to shake off ⟨the continent, which is *shrugging off* the sleep of centuries —*Atlantic*⟩ **3 :** to remove (a garment) by wriggling out of it ⟨she *shrugged* it *off*, draped it over the electric jigsaw —John Updike⟩

shrug 2

shrunk [ME *shronk* (past), *shronken* (past part.), fr. OE *scruncon* (past pl.), *gescruncen* (past part.)] *past of* SHRINK
shrunken [ME *shronken*, fr. OE *gescruncen*] *past part of* SHRINK
shruti *var of* SRUTI
sht *abbr* sheet
shtad·lan *also* **she·tad·lan** \ˈshtäd(,)län\ *n, pl* **shtad·la·nim** *also* **she·tad·la·nim** \=ˈlōnəm, -nēm\ [Yiddish & MHeb; Yiddish *shtadlen*, fr. MHeb *shtādlān*] **:** a person appointed by a Jewish community to represent Jewish interests (as before a government or ruler)
shtetl *also* **shtet·el** \ˈshtet°l\ *n, pl* **shtet·lach** \-tläk, -lək\ [Yiddish *shtetl*, fr. MHG *stetel* small place, small town, dim. of *stat* place, town, city, fr. OHG, place — more at STEAD] **:** a Jewish small town or small-town community in Eastern Europe
shtg *abbr* shortage
shthg *abbr* sheathing
shu \ˈshü\ *n* -S [Chin (Pek) *shu*⁴] *Confucianism* **:** reciprocity or mutual considerateness in all actions
shua *usu cap, var of* SHUWA
shu·ba \ˈshübə\ *n* -S [Russ, fr. MHG *schūbe* outer garment, fr. OIt *giubba* jacket, fr. Ar *jubbah*] **:** a Russian fur or fur-lined overcoat or cloak
shu·bun·kin \ˈshübən,kin, shüˈbuŋkən\ *n* -S [Jap] **:** a goldfish of a breed having transparent scales covering a mottled skin and slightly lengthened fins
¹shuck *vi* -ED/-ING/-S [origin unknown] *obs* **:** to shrink back **:** RECOIL ⟨bitter pills, at which we so wince and ~ —John Bunyan⟩
²shuck \ˈshək\ *n* -S [origin unknown] **1 :** an outer covering **:** HUSK, SHELL, POD: as **a :** the husk of Indian corn **b :** the outer covering of a nut (as the walnut, peanut, chestnut) **c :** the shell of an oyster or clam **d :** the dried calyx of the peach flower usu. pushed off by the expanding fruit **e :** the nymphal cuticle cast off by a subimago mayfly **2 :** a cigarette or cigar rolled in corn shucks **3 :** something of little value — usu. used in the pl. often interjectionally ⟨not worth ~s⟩ ⟨don't care ~s about it⟩ ⟨can't sing for ~s⟩ ⟨no great ~s for looks⟩ ⟨~s, that's not worth talking about⟩
³shuck \"\ *vb* -ED/-ING/-S *vt* **1 :** to strip the shucks or husks from ⟨~ corn⟩ ⟨~ peas⟩ **2 :** to remove (as an oyster) from the shell **3 a :** to peel off or remove (as clothing) — often used with *off* ⟨~*ed off* his clothes and slid between the sheets — Clements Ripley⟩ **b :** to lay aside **:** slough off **:** DISCARD — usu. used with *off* ⟨some of the bad habits are being ~*ed off* — A.W.Smith⟩ ~ *vi* **:** to take off or slip out of a covering (as clothes) — usu. used with *out of* ⟨went to my room and ~*ed* out of my soaked clothes —J.R.Phillips⟩
⁴shuck \"\ *n* -S [origin unknown] *dial Eng* **:** a spectral hound whose appearance is held to presage a calamity
shuck–bottom \ˈ=,==\ *or* **shuck–bottomed** \ˈ=,==\ *adj* [*shuck-bottom* fr. ²*shuck* + *bottom*, n.; *shuck-bottomed* fr. ²*shuck* + *bottomed* (past part. of *bottom*, v.)] **:** having a seat of interwoven maize husks ⟨a *shuck-bottomed* chair⟩
shuck bottom *n* [²*shuck* + *bottom*, n.] **:** a shuck-bottom chair
shuck·er \ˈshəkə(r)\ *n* -S **:** one that shucks: as **a :** a worker who shucks something (as oysters) for a livelihood **b :** a shucking machine
shucking *n* -S **:** CORNHUSKING, HUSKING BEE
shuck–split \ˈ=,=\ *adj* **:** of or relating to the growth stage when the dry calyxes of peach flowers split
shuck spray *n* **:** CALYX SPRAY
shuckworm \ˈ=,=\ *n* **:** HICKORY SHUCKWORM
shucky bean \ˈshəkē-, -ki-\ *n* [*shucky* fr. ²*shuck* + *-y*] **:** a shell bean dried in the pod
¹shud·der \ˈshədə(r)\ *vb* **shuddered; shuddered; shuddering** \-d(ə)riŋ\ **shudders** [ME *shoddren*; akin to MLG *schodderen* to shudder, OFris *skedda* to shake, OHG *skutten* to shake, Lith *kutėti* to shake up, arouse] *vi* **1 :** to tremble convulsively **:** shake with fear, horror, or aversion **:** shiver with cold **:** QUAKE ⟨~*ed* constantly in the chill air⟩ ⟨~ at the thought of contamination with persons ... lower in the social scale — L.C.Douglas⟩ **2 :** to move as if with a shudder **:** QUIVER ⟨a rumbling roar ... the windows rattle and the floor ~s sickeningly —Michael Allen⟩ ⟨the train slowed, ~*ed*, halted, the air brakes panting —Marc Brandel⟩ ~ *vt* **:** to cause to shudder **:** SHAKE ⟨the chill of an age-old recognition ~*ed* my spine — Arthur Miller⟩
²shudder \"\ *n* -S **1 :** an act or instance of shuddering **:** TREMOR ⟨a ~ of alarm ran ... through the senate house — J.A.Froude⟩ ⟨the ... ~ of the ship as her screw comes above the surface —F.A.Swinnerton⟩ **2 a :** an involuntary tremor of the body (as from fear, horror, or cold) ⟨shrank back with a strong ~ —Zane Grey⟩ **b shudders** *pl* **:** a fit of shuddering — usu. used with *the*
shuddering *adj* **1 :** moving with a shudder **:** FEARFUL, TREMBLING ⟨delicate ~ introverts —J.B.Priestley⟩ **2 :** marked by or producing a shudder ⟨a ~ sense of chill and desolation — Alfred Buchanan⟩ ⟨~ slums —J.P.O'Donnell⟩
shud·der·ing·ly *adv* **:** with a shudder or in such a manner as to produce a shudder ⟨~ sensational plots —Carl Van Doren⟩
shud·der·some \ˈshədə(r)səm\ *adj* **:** marked by or producing shudders ⟨the crime story and the unexpected and ~ ending — *Encore*⟩
shud·dery \ˈshəd(ə)rē, -ri\ *adj* **:** SHUDDERSOME ⟨the most terrible and ~ of all tales of murder and revenge —John Mason Brown⟩
shude *var of* SHOOD
shudra *usu cap, var of* SUDRA
¹shuf·fle \ˈshəfəl\ *vb* **shuffled; shuffled; shuffling** \-f(ə)liŋ\ **shuffles** [perh. irreg. fr. ¹*shove* + *-le*] *vt* **1 a :** to mix in a mass confusedly **:** throw into disorder **:** JUMBLE ⟨war has ... *shuffled* our population —Lucien Price⟩ **b :** to cause to mingle indiscriminately — usu. used with *among* or *with* ⟨*shuffled* first offenders in with hardened criminals⟩ **2 a :** to introduce into trickily **:** smuggle in ⟨contrived by your enemies and *shuffled* into the papers that were seized —John Dryden⟩ **b :** to put or thrust aside or under cover ⟨*shuffled* the whole matter out of his mind⟩ ⟨*shuffling* the letter out of sight as someone entered⟩ **3 a :** to manipulate (as a group of playing cards or tiles) with the real or ostensible purpose of causing a later appearance in random order (as in dealing or drawing) **b :** to push or move about, back and forth, or from one place to another **:** SHIFT ⟨~ funds among various accounts⟩ ⟨pulled all the drawers open to ~ his belongings more handily —Josephine Pinckney⟩ ⟨dispatchers had godlike ... power to ~ us to and fro —Christopher Morley⟩ **4 a :** to move (as the feet) by sliding along or back and forth without lifting ⟨*shuffled* his feet nervously as he waited⟩ ⟨*shuffled* his slippers over the floor⟩ **b :** to perform (as a dance) with a dragging, sliding step ⟨~ a saraband⟩ ~ *vi* **1 :** to work into or out of trickily **:** WORM — usu. used with *in, into,* or *out of* ⟨managed to ~ in with his betters⟩ ⟨*shuffled* out of the difficulty somehow⟩ **2 :** to act or speak in a shifty or evasive manner **:** EQUIVOCATE ⟨the more the cardinals *shuffled*, the more furiously the mob raged —G.G.Coulton⟩ ⟨without *shuffling* for a moment about his past errors —J.M.Barzun⟩ **3 a :** to move or walk in a sliding, dragging manner without lifting the feet **:** SCUFF, SCUFFLE ⟨saw a bear *shuffling* along⟩ ⟨boxers *shuffling* around in the ring⟩ ⟨saw him *shuffling* through the streets in his battered carpet slippers —Van Wyck Brooks⟩ **b :** to dance in a lazy nonchalant manner with sliding and tapping motions of the feet **c :** to execute in a perfunctory or clumsy manner — usu. used with *through* ⟨allowed to ~ through his lessons —George Eliot⟩ **d :** to get into or out of shoes or clothing awkwardly or fumblingly — usu. used with *into, off, on,* or *out of* ⟨began to ~ on his fur jacket and his moccasins —Willa Cather⟩ ⟨watched him ~ gloomily into his overcoat —William DuBois⟩ **4 :** to mix playing cards or counters (as dominoes or tiles) by shuffling **5 :** to attack with the spurs in cock fighting
²shuffle \"\ *n* -S **1 :** an evasion of the issue **:** EQUIVOCATION ⟨answer it now, yes or no, plain word and no ~ —Max Pemberton⟩ **2 a :** an act of shuffling (as of cards or playing counters) ⟨after the ~ the players select tiles in turn⟩ **b :** a right or turn to shuffle ⟨reminded sharply that it was his ~⟩ **c :** a confused mass **:** JUMBLE ⟨a desk with a ~ of papers on it —Adrian Bell⟩ ⟨the goal of training good teachers had been lost in the ~ of educational trappings —Benjamin Fine⟩ **3 a :** a dragging sliding walk **:** SCUFFLE ⟨the ... ~ of the man's feet across the dusty floor —Victor Canning⟩ **b** (1) **:** a sliding or scraping step in dancing (2) **:** a dance characterized by such a step ⟨dancing a sailor's ~⟩ ⟨the double ~⟩
shuffleboard \ˈ=,=,=\ *n* [alter. (influenced by ¹*shuffle*) of obs. E

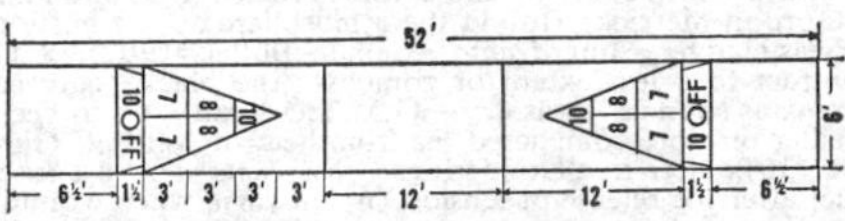

shuffleboard 2b

shove-board, fr. E ¹*shove* + *board*] **1 :** SHOVELBOARD 1 **2 a :** a game in which players use long-handled cues to shove wooden disks into scoring beds of a diagram marked on a smooth surface **b :** the diagram on which this game is played
shufflecap \ˈ=,=\ *n* **:** a game in which the stake is money shaken in a hat or cap
shuffle dance *n* **:** an Iroquois women's round dance marked by a gliding sideward twist of the foot
shuffle off *vt* **:** to get rid of **:** push away **:** SHIRK ⟨when we have *shuffled off* this mortal coil —Shak.⟩ ⟨*shuffle off* the heavy burden of our guilt —Richard Chase⟩ ⟨teachers cannot ... *shuffle off* their responsibility —C.I.Glicksberg⟩ ~ *vi* **:** to be on one's way **:** mosey along ⟨let him *shuffle off* to the wilderness —J.B.Priestley⟩
shuf·fler \ˈshəf(ə)lə(r)\ *n* -S **1 :** one that shuffles; *esp* **:** one that shuffles cards or whose turn it is to do so **2 :** SCAUP DUCK
shuffle walk *n* **:** a step-drag used in square dancing
shufflewing \ˈ=,=\ *n, dial Brit* **:** HEDGE SPARROW
shuffling *adj* **:** disposed to shuffle: as **a :** moving with a shuffle ⟨a ~ dancer⟩ **b :** EVASIVE, OPPORTUNISTIC ⟨a ~ politician⟩ — **shuf·fling·ly** *adv*
shug \ˈshəg, ˈshüg\ *var of* SHOG
shug·ni \ˈshügnē\ *n, pl* **shugni** *or* **shugnis** *usu cap* **1 :** an Iranian people of the western Pamirs **2 :** a member of the Shugni people
shu·kria \shüˈkrēə\ *n, pl* **shukria** *or* **shukrias** *usu cap* **1 :** a nomadic Arabic-speaking people of the region between the Blue Nile and the Atbara river in northeastern Africa **2 :** a member of the Shukria people
shul *also* **schul** \ˈshül *sometimes* ˈshül\ *n* -S [Yiddish *shul*, fr. MHG *schuol*, *schuole*, lit., school, fr. OHG *scuola*, fr. L *schola* — more at SCHOOL] **:** SYNAGOGUE
shumac *var of* SUMAC
shu·mard oak \(ˈ)shü¦märd-\ *also* **shumard red oak** *n, usu cap S* [after Benjamin F. *Shumard* †1869 Am. geologist] **:** a large red oak (*Quercus shumardii*) of the southern and eastern U. S. that grows chiefly over limestone and has dark shiny elliptical leaves divided into 7 to 9 lobes, medium to very large acorns, and coarse-grained wood of medium hardness and weight
shummick *South & Midland var of* SHAMMOCK
shun \ˈshən\ *vt* **shunned; shunned; shunning; shuns** [ME *shunnen*, *shunen*, fr. OE *scunian*] **1 :** to avoid deliberately and esp. habitually **:** keep clear of **:** shy away from **:** ESCHEW ⟨~ temptation⟩ ⟨~ publicity⟩ ⟨was *shunned* by his former friends⟩ ⟨lived alone, *shunning* all community activities⟩ ⟨~s pure theory and sticks to ascertainable facts —J.H.Powers⟩ **2** *archaic* **:** to escape from **:** EVADE ⟨no man of woman born ... can ~ his destiny —W.C.Bryant⟩ **3** *archaic* **:** PREVENT ⟨wish you may be able to ~ for us this war —Thomas Jefferson⟩ **syn** see ESCAPE
shu·nam·mite \ˈshünə,mīt\ *n* -S *cap* [modif. (influenced by *-ite*) of Heb *shūnammīth*, fr. *Shūnēm* Shunem, town in ancient Palestine] **:** a native or inhabitant of the town of Shunem north of Mt. Gilboa in ancient Palestine
shune \ˈshün\ *chiefly dial pl of* SHOE
shun·less \ˈshənləs\ *adj* **:** UNAVOIDABLE ⟨with ~ destiny —Shak.⟩
shunning *n* -S [fr. gerund of *shun*] **:** a Mennonite practice of excluding from any social interaction with other members of a congregation a church member who has been censured for some serious infraction
shunpike \ˈ=,=\ *n* **:** a side road used to avoid toll on a turnpike
¹shunt \ˈshənt\ *vb* -ED/-ING/-S [ME *shunten* to flinch, shy, run away, perh. fr. *shunen* to shun] *vt* **1 :** to shove or put aside or out of the way **:** SIDETRACK ⟨didn't want to feel ~*ed* —Peggy Bennett⟩ ⟨the manufacturer had been ~*ed* aside —*Advertising Age*⟩ **2 :** to turn off to one side **:** SHIFT ⟨~ cattle into a corral⟩; *specif* **:** to turn off (as a car or train) from one track to another **:** SWITCH ⟨the train was ~*ed* to a siding⟩ **3 a :** to provide with or divert by means of a shunt **b :** to interrupt (the flow of an electrical circuit in a railroad track) and so cause the signals in the block affected to change their aspect automatically ⟨the circuit is ~*ed* by the wheels of a train, the opening of a switch, or the breaking of a rail⟩ **c :** to divert (blood) from one part to another by surgical creation of a shunt ~ *vi* **1 :** to move to the side **:** turn off from a course being followed ⟨~*ed* from his main interest to a profitable sideline⟩; *specif* **:** to move onto a sidetrack ⟨one of the standard goods engines ... was ~*ing* at the time —O.S.Nock⟩ **2 :** to travel back and forth **:** SHUTTLE ⟨~s between the two towns⟩
²shunt \"\ *n* -S **:** a means or mechanism for turning or thrusting aside: as **a** *chiefly Brit* **:** a railroad switch **b** (1) **:** a conductor joining two points in an electrical circuit so as to form a parallel or alternative path through which a portion of the current may pass (as for the purpose of regulating the amount passing in the main circuit) (2) **:** a conductor providing a low-resistance path for the flow of current ⟨a brush ~⟩ (3) **:** DIVERTOR **c :** a vascular passage by which blood is diverted from its usual or normal circulatory path ⟨an arteriovenous ~⟩; *esp* **:** a surgical passage created between two blood vessels to divert blood from one part to another ⟨portacaval ~⟩
shunt dynamo *or* **shunt motor** *n* **:** a shunt-wound generator or motor
shunt·er \ˈshəntə(r)\ *n* -S **1 :** one that shunts: as **a** *Brit* **:** SWITCHMAN **b** *Brit* **:** a locomotive used in a railroad yard for switching **2** *Brit* **:** ARBITRAGER
shunt excitation *n* **:** excitation by shunt winding
shunting *n* -S [fr. gerund of ¹*shunt*] *Brit* **:** arbitrage conducted between certain local markets without the necessity of the exchange involved in foreign arbitrage
shunt valve *n* **:** a valve permitting a fluid under pressure an easier avenue of escape than normally; *specif* **:** a valve actuated by the governor and used in one system of marine-engine governing to connect both ends of the low-pressure cylinder as a supplementary control
shunt winding *n* **:** a winding so arranged as to divide the armature current and lead a portion of it around the field-magnet coils — opposed to *series winding*
shunt–wound \ˈ=,=\ *adj* **:** wound so that the armature winding and field winding are in parallel ⟨a *shunt-wound* direct-current generator⟩
shus *pl of* SHU
¹shush \ˈshəsh\ *n* -ES [imit.] **:** a sibilant sound uttered to enjoin silence ⟨listeners who break into a spontaneous handclap or two are immediately shamed with pious ~*es* —Winthrop Sargeant⟩
²shush \"\ *vb* -ED/-ING/-ES *vt* **1 :** to urge quiet upon (as by making the sound "sh" and holding an index finger before the lips) **:** repress the agitation or clamor of **:** HUSH, SILENCE ⟨made animal noises until he was ~*ed* —John McDonald⟩ ⟨applauded happily but was ~*ed* by my neighbors —Hyman Toldberg⟩ ⟨the policeman ~*ed* him with his hand —Claud Cockburn⟩ **2 :** to restrain from a desired course or action **:** SUPPRESS ⟨those ... who demurred and privately pressed for a changed policy were ~*ed* by the functionaries —Frank Tollman⟩ ~ *vi* **:** to become silent **:** grow still **:** HUSH — used in the imperative to urge cessation of talk or moderation of sound ⟨~ now, let's be quiet enough to hear a pin drop⟩
shu·swap \ˈshü,swäp\ *n, pl* **shuswap** *or* **shuswaps** *usu cap* **1 a :** a Salishan people of the Fraser and Columbia river valleys in British Columbia **b :** a member of such people **2 :** a language of the Shuswap people
¹shut \ˈshət, *dial* ˈshet; *usu* |d·+V\ *vb* **shut; shut; shutting; shuts** [ME *shutten*, *shetten*, *shitten*, fr. OE *scyttan*; akin to MD *schutten* to shut in, hinder, OE *scēotan* to shoot — more at SHOOT] *vt* **1** *obs* **:** to move (as a bolt) so as to fasten something (as a door, window) **2 a :** to move (as a door, window, gate) into position to close an opening ⟨~ the lid⟩ ⟨leads us to ~ the gates of mercy —M.R.Cohen⟩ ⟨~ his door against his enemies⟩ — often used with *up* ⟨~ up his windows and closed the shop⟩ or *down* ⟨~ all the windows down⟩ ⟨~s the top down and locks it⟩ **b :** to prevent passage to or from by closing doors or openings **:** CLOSE ⟨~ the cottage for the winter⟩ — often used with *up* ⟨~ up the house and set off for Europe⟩ **c :** to close (as an opening, a passage) by an obstacle or barrier ⟨the enemy ~ every pass through the mountains⟩ — often used with *up* or *in* ⟨another upland valley ~ in by the easy slope of wooded hills —*Amer. Guide Series: Vt.*⟩ **d :** to close (as the mind) to ideas and other influences from without ⟨prejudice ~s the mind tighter than illiteracy —Bice Clemow⟩ — often used with *up* **3 :** to confine by or as if by enclosure or by closing a means of escape ⟨~ him in the closet⟩ ⟨was ~ in prison⟩ — usu. used with *up* ⟨~ up with him in the ... chill smoky carriage —Anne D. Sedgwick⟩ ⟨food and muskets and gunpowder to stand by their own army ~ up in Boston — Dorothy C. Fisher⟩ ⟨~ up in an acquired intellectual pride — V.S.Pritchett⟩ **4 :** to fasten with a lock or bolt ⟨buys a lock to ~ his chest⟩ **5 :** to close by bringing enclosing or covering

parts together ⟨~ the eyes⟩ ⟨~ the mouth⟩ ⟨~ the fist⟩ ⟨~ a book⟩ ⟨~ a locket⟩ — often used with *up* ⟨~ up the piano⟩ **6 :** to cause to cease or suspend operation or business — often used with *down* ⟨obliged the administration to ~ down the university for the remainder of the spring term —R.G.Woolbert⟩ **7 :** WELD **~** *vi* **1 :** to close itself or become closed ⟨door ~ with a slam⟩ ⟨flowers ~ at night⟩ ⟨the seams worked . . . opening and *shutting* as the ship strained on the waves —C.S. Forester⟩ — often used with *down* ⟨the lid ~*s* down to keep the dust out⟩ **2 :** to become visually continuous without a perceptible break ⟨earth and the sky and the sky and the sea, seem *shutting* together as a book that is read —Joaquin Miller⟩ **3 :** to close in ⟨and soon evening will ~ —A.E.Housman⟩ — often used with *in* ⟨observing the sunshine beginning to ~ in —Samuel Richardson⟩ **4 :** to cease or suspend an operation or business **:** CLOSE ⟨cafés and bars which never seemed to ~ while I was there —James Reach⟩ — often used with *up* ⟨all my kids . . . were reporting for the parade, so I thought we'd ~ up early —J.G.Cozzens⟩ or *down* ⟨plants cut down the number of their employees and in many cases ~ down entirely —*Amer. Guide Series: N.H.*⟩ ⟨force newspapers to accept censorship or ~ down —*Time*⟩ — **shut one's eyes :** to pretend not to see **:** IGNORE ⟨*shut their eyes* to crime in which they did not themselves participate —George Horne b.1902⟩ — **shut one's face** *or* **shut one's head** *slang* **:** to shut one's mouth ⟨when, she asked herself angrily, would she learn to *shut her face* —Margaret Long⟩ — **shut one's mouth :** to stop or refrain from speaking ⟨our first barbaric impulse is to *shut* the *mouth* of any man or woman who says anything that might offend . . . tribal customs —Manus O'Neill⟩ ⟨if you *shut your mouth*, you have your choice —Scott Fitzgerald⟩ — **shut the door :** to exclude from participation or consideration **:** cut off ⟨cannot afford to *shut the door* on any honest speculator —Elmer Davis⟩ ⟨it *shut the door* upon all democratic aspiration —V.L.Parrington⟩ — **shut up shop :** to cease or suspend an operation or activity ⟨the committee decided to *shut up shop*, at least for the present —*Atlantic*⟩ ⟨even the city's criminals seem to have *shut up shop* for the occasion —S.E.Hyman⟩

[2]shut \"\ *n* -S [ME *schett*, fr. *shutten, shetten, shitten*, v. — more at [1]SHUT] **1 :** a device used in shutting or closing: **a** *archaic* **:** BOLT, BAR **b** *chiefly dial* **:** SHUTTER **c :** a door or plate used to close an opening **2 :** the act or time of shutting ⟨at ~ of evening⟩ **3 :** the line or place of union at a welded joint **4 :** COLD SHUT

[3]shut \"\ *adj* [fr. past part. of [1]*shut*] **1 :** closed, fastened, or folded together ⟨the ~ door was blank against the summer sunlight —Elizabeth M. Roberts⟩ ⟨listened with ~ eyes⟩ ⟨has her mind ~ against all other civilizations —Nora Waln⟩ ⟨a terrible, white ~ face —S.V.Benét⟩ **2 :** RID, CLEAR, FREE — usu. used with *of* ⟨I thought I'd never get ~ of him⟩ ⟨would soon be ~ of them all —Hervey Allen⟩

[4]shut \'shət, 'shüt, 'shet\ *chiefly dial var of* SHOOT

shut away *vt* **:** to remove or isolate from others ⟨in order to escape from the prison where society *shut* her *away* —H.M. Parshley⟩ ⟨I *shut* myself *away* for two hours —R.G.G.Price⟩

shut down *vi* **:** to settle so as to obscure vision **:** close in ⟨the rain mists *shut down* like stained rolls of wool —Marjory S. Douglas⟩ ⟨the night *shut down* early⟩

shutdown \'=,=\ *n* -S [*shut down*] **:** the cessation or suspension of an activity or function: as **a :** a usu. temporary stoppage of work in a factory, mine, or other business enterprise (as because of a strike, lockout, installation or repair of equipment, vacation, or lack of orders or materials) ⟨workers were threatening a total ~ —Ida A.R. Wylie⟩ ⟨increasing the efficiency . . . and decreasing maintenance ~*s* —H.W.Iversen⟩ ⟨trains . . . resumed operating this morning after a 24-hour ~ —*N.Y.Times*⟩ **b :** the stopping of a machine or engine that activates itself ⟨the ~ . . . of generating equipment in 17 industrial plants —*Ohio Edison Co. Report*⟩ ⟨permitting escape of neutrons and causing a ~ of the chain reaction —J.L. Collins⟩ **c :** the discontinuance of a physical function (as of an organ) ⟨to prevent kidney ~ —*Anesthesia Digest*⟩

[1]shute *var of* SHOOT

[2]shute *var of* CHUTE

shut-eye \'=,=\ *n* [[3]*shut* + *eye*] *slang* **:** SLEEP ⟨when he awakes . . . he makes no attempt to fall back on the pillow and catch a little more *shut-eye* —Philip Hamburger⟩

shut in *vt* [ME *shetten in*, fr. *shutten, shetten, shitten* to shut + *in*, adv.] **1 :** CONFINE, ENCLOSE ⟨*shut* himself *in* for days on end⟩ ⟨had been *shut in* by illness during much of the winter⟩ **2 :** to prevent production of (oil) by closing down a well

[1]shut-in \'=¦=\ *adj* [fr. past part. of *shut in*] **1 :** confined to one's home or an institution by illness or incapacity ⟨made more than 7000 home visits to *shut-in* boys and girls —Dorothy Barclay⟩ **2 :** so encompassed as to be confined or cut off ⟨thickly wooded foothills, broken knob country, and narrow valleys have made it . . . the most *shut-in* section of the state —*Amer. Guide Series: Tenn.*⟩ **3 a :** closed in **:** BROODING, SECRETIVE ⟨twisted, sad, with a bitter, *shut-in* face —Claudia Cassidy⟩ ⟨assumed the proud, *shut-in* look with which he guarded himself from doubt —Gordon Merrick⟩ **b :** tending to avoid social contact **:** WITHDRAWN ⟨diagnostic and prognostic significance of the *shut-in* personality type —S.K. Weinberg⟩

[2]shut-in \'=,=\ *n* -S **1 :** an invalid or incapacitated person who is confined to his home, a room, or his bed ⟨through your love of music and your skill you can bring happiness to *shut-ins* —*Girl Scout Handbk.*⟩ **2 :** a narrow gorge-shaped part of an otherwise wide valley **3 :** available oil or gas which is not being produced from an existing well

shut-mouthed \'=¦=\ *adj* **:** CLOSEMOUTHED, SECRETIVE ⟨didn't want people to know about it . . . decided to keep *shut-mouthed* —F.B.Gipson⟩

shut·ness *n* -ES **:** the quality or state of being shut ⟨against the Spanish ~ . . . I lacked energy to battle —Rose Macaulay⟩

shut off *vt* **1 a :** to cut off (as a flow or passage or something flowing or passing) **:** STOP ⟨*shut* the steam *off*⟩ ⟨would require *shutting off* the patient's circulation during part of the operation —Ben & Marie Pearse⟩ ⟨*shut off* the flow of visitors —*Amer. Guide Series: Ark.*⟩ **b :** to stop the operation of (as a machine) ⟨*shuts off* his motor —P.B.Kyne⟩ ⟨*shuts* the machine *off* when a full package of yarn is completed —V.A.Schiffer⟩ ⟨*shut* the radiator *off*⟩ **c :** to block or terminate the operation or activity of ⟨*shut off* the supply of new three percent savings bonds —Harold Wincott⟩ ⟨*shut off* its high-powered . . . recruiting campaign —*Newsweek*⟩ ⟨*shut off* this racket by scowling at him —L.C.Douglas⟩ **2 :** to close off **:** SEPARATE — usu. used with *from* ⟨would have *shut* Guatemala *off* from the Atlantic coast —C.L.Jones⟩ ⟨long arms of the ridge *shut* us *off* from the world —Elyne Mitchell⟩ ⟨*shut off* from most of the activities and pleasures of normal children —W.E.Clark⟩ **~** *vi* **:** to cease operating **:** STOP ⟨the generator *shuts off* automatically⟩

shutoff \'=,=\ *n* -S [*shut off*] **1 a :** something that shuts off **:** VALVE, STOPPER ⟨must build a cement ~ to plug the leaking well casing⟩ ⟨~ is located in the cellar⟩ **b** *or* **shutoff nozzle :** a fire hose nozzle designed to control the flow of water as it leaves the hose **2 :** the act of shutting off ⟨a ~ of blood flow to the brain would be required for the type of operation —Ben & Marie Pearse⟩ **3 :** a closed season for game

shut out *vt* [ME *shetten out*, fr. *shutten, shetten, shitten* to shut + *out*, adv.] **1 :** to keep or force out ⟨branches meet . . . *shutting out* the sunlight —*Amer. Guide Series: Mich.*⟩ ⟨his nostrils clenched as if to *shut out* the evil and moldy smell of the room —Marcia Davenport⟩ ⟨not to know . . . was to be *shut out* of his life completely —Morley Callaghan⟩ — sometimes used with *from* ⟨began to talk French, *shutting out* the mulatto woman from their conversation —Louis Bromfield⟩ ⟨*shutting out* from his thoughts any thought that disturbs him —Morris Fishbein⟩ **2 :** to hide from sight ⟨clouds *shut* the sun *out*⟩ ⟨as we rounded the point the peninsula *shut out* the bay⟩ **3 a :** to prevent (an opponent) from scoring in a game or contest ⟨*shut* them *out* with two hits⟩ ⟨*shut* them *out* 1–0⟩ ⟨a fisherman . . . was *shut out* the first two days and boated only two on the lush last day —*Newsweek*⟩ **b :** to forestall the bidding of (one's opponents in bridge) by making a high or preemptive bid ⟨*shut* the opposition *out* with a bid of five hearts⟩ **syn** see EXCLUDE

shutout \'=,=\ *n* -S [in sense 1, fr. *shut out;* in sense 2, fr. past part. of *shut out*] **1 a :** a game or contest in which one side fails to score ⟨punched out a three-touchdown ~ 20–0 —*Newsweek*⟩ ⟨had a six-hit ~ going into the 9th inning —Roscoe McGowen⟩ **b :** a preemptive bid in bridge **c :** the presence of sufficient men on a player's inner table in backgammon to prevent entrance to the table by the opponent's men **2 :** one that is shut out ⟨was a shut-in within a paralyzed body and a *shutout* from the world outside —*Jour. Amer. Med. Assoc.*⟩

shuts *pres 3d sing of* SHUT, *pl of* SHUT

shut·tance \'shət[ə]n(t)s, 'shüt-\ *n* [[1]*shut* + *-ance*] *dial Eng* **:** RIDDANCE

shut·ten \'shət[ə]n, 'shüt-\ *dial past part of* SHUT

[1]shut·ter \'shəd·ə(r), -ətə-\ *n* -S *often attrib* **1 :** one that shuts **2 a :** a usu. movable cover or screen for a window or door (as to shut out the light or obstruct the view) — compare BLIND, JALOUSIE, LOUVER **b :** such a cover or screen for a picture or altarpiece **3 a :** a mechanical device of various forms (as the rotary, iris diaphragm, or focal-plane shutter) attached to a camera to expose the film or plate by opening and closing an aperture **b :** a usu. rotating element that obscures the light in the optical path of a motion-picture mechanism at a predetermined interval **4 :** a removable cover, lid, or gate for closing an aperture (as the passageway through which molten iron flows from a ladle) **5 :** the movable louvers in a pipe organ by which the swell box is opened and which are manipulated by means of the swell pedal

shutters 2a

[2]shutter \"\ *vb* **shuttered; shuttered; shuttering** \-d·əriŋ, -ətər-, -ə·tr-\ **shutters** *vt* **1 :** to close with or by shutters ⟨saw us looking out the windows and came up and ~*ed* them —Rumer Godden⟩ ⟨the gate was ~*ed* —Anne Green⟩ ⟨during the heat of the day, houses are ~*ed* —*Amer. Guide Series: Fla.*⟩ **2 :** to close (an establishment) to business by or as if by closing shutters ⟨suppressed their dances, banned movies, ~*ed* nightclubs —*Time*⟩ ⟨a ~*ed* butcher's shop —Lionel Shapiro⟩ **3 :** to close (the eyes) as if with shutters ⟨death in his ~*ed* eyes —Dorothy Hewett⟩ **~** *vi* **1 :** to close to business by or as if by closing shutters ⟨the bars in the village ~ at midnight —Leslie Waller⟩ ⟨many operators will ~ rather than take continuous gambles —*Billboard*⟩ **2 :** to close as if with shutters ⟨eyes that ~ — too quick — when someone speaks —Jennette Yeotman⟩

shutter box *n* **:** a recess at the side of a window to receive an inside shutter when opened

shutterbug \'==,=\ *n* **:** a photography enthusiast ⟨you will find other ~*s* if you are a camera fiend —Christina Kirk⟩

shutter dam *or* **shutter weir** *n* **:** a dam formerly consisting of one or more simple shutters or gates turning on a horizontal axis near the top and now consisting of a series of short pieces that revolve on their horizontal axes and are lowered to rest flatwise on the sill

shut·tered \'shəd·ə(r)d, -ətə-\ *adj* [[1]*shutter* + *-ed*] **:** provided with shutters ⟨a church with a ~ belfry and spire⟩

shut·ter·ing \-d·əriŋ, -ətər-, -ə·tr-, -rēŋ\ *n* -S [[1]*shutter* + *-ing*] **1 a :** material for making shutters **b :** SHUTTERS **2 :** FORMWORK

shut·ter·less \'==ləs\ *adj* **:** without shutters

shut·ting \'shəd·|iŋ, 'shət|, |ēŋ\ *n* -S [ME *shutyng, schettyng, shitting*, fr. gerund of *shutten, shetten, shitten* to shut] **:** the act or process of one that shuts; *specif* **:** WELDING

shutting post *n* **:** GATEPOST

shutting stile *n* **:** the stile of a hinged door which strikes the rabbet of the jamb when the door is shut and on which the fastenings are secured — compare HANGING STILE

[1]shut·tle \'shəd·[ə]l, -ət[ə]l\ *n* -S *often attrib* [ME *schutylle, schetylle, shittle*, prob. fr. OE *scytel, scytels* bar, bolt; akin to ON *skutill* bar, bolt, Dan *skyttel* shuttle, OE *scēotan* to shoot — more at SHOOT] **1 a :** any of various types of slender pointed wooden devices used in weaving for passing or shooting the thread of the woof between the threads of the warp from one side of the cloth to the other **b :** a spindle-shaped device holding the thread that one manipulates in tatting, knotting, or netting **c** (1) **:** any of various sliding thread holders for the lower thread of a sewing machine that carry the lower thread through a loop of the upper thread to make a stitch (2) **:** a sewing-machine bobbin **2 :** SHUTTLECOCK **3 :** a sliding shutter (as for a sluiceway) **4** *dial chiefly Brit* **:** a small drawer (as for odds and ends); *sometimes* **:** a drawer for money **5** [[3]*shuttle*] **a :** a going back and forth over a specified route or path at regular intervals; *esp* **:** such a plying by any of various vehicles (as planes, automobiles, trains, ships) ⟨in addition to planes that fly direct to Bermuda and return in a ~, some flights continue to England —*Skyways*⟩ ⟨kept up a round-the-clock ~ delivering a truckload of coral every 40 seconds —*Time*⟩ **b :** an established or specified route used in a shuttle ⟨carted paratroopers across the short ~ from Denmark to Norway —Richard Thruelsen & Elliott Arnold⟩ **c :** a vehicle used in a shuttle ⟨took the ~ across the city⟩ **6 :** CLAW 4f

[2]shut·tle \'shə|d·[ə]l, 'shů|, |t[ə]l\ *adj* [ME *schyttyl*, fr. *schutylle, schetylle, shittle*, n.] *chiefly dial* **:** WAVERING, UNSETTLED

[3]shut·tle \'shəd·[ə]l, -ət[ə]l\ *vb* **shuttled; shuttled; shuttling** \-d·[ə]liŋ, -t([ə])liŋ\ **shuttles** [[1]*shuttle*] *vt* **1 :** to cause to move around or back and forth frequently ⟨was *shuttled* from one unsympathetic relative to another —Ruth & Edward Brecher⟩ ⟨reserves to be *shuttled* between branches to meet varying . . . needs —*Investor's Reader*⟩ **2 :** to move or transport in, by, or as if by a shuttle ⟨crews were to be *shuttled* from their ships to the gun-carrying ships before landing —*Coast Artillery Jour.*⟩ ⟨dual drive tractors ~ eight 35-foot insulated trailers between the eastern and western terminals —*Motor Transportation in the West*⟩ ⟨keeps *shuttling* substitutes in and out with instructions to run until they tire, then signal for relief —*Time*⟩ **~** *vi* **1 :** to move or travel around or back and forth frequently ⟨continued feverishly to ~ between sidewalk and stairs —H.J.Kaplan⟩ ⟨tangled with red tape, they have *shuttled* from bureau to bureau —*Newsweek*⟩ ⟨the book ~*s* from one locale to another —*Time*⟩ **2 :** to move or travel in, by, or as if by a shuttle ⟨every type of landing craft *shuttling* continuously between the tumultuous beaches and the scores of cargo vessels —E.L.Jones⟩ ⟨bombed it and *shuttled* to Africa —Tex McCrary & D.E.Scherman⟩ ⟨*shuttled* over to Milwaukee —L.E.Arndt⟩ ⟨has *shuttled* back and forth across the years —Pamela Taylor⟩

shuttle armature *n* **:** an armature shaped like an elongated shuttle with wires that run longitudinally in grooves

shuttle bone *n* **:** the navicular of the foot of a horse

shuttle box *n* **1 :** a case at either end of the lay of a loom to receive the shuttle after its passage through the shed **2 :** any of various compartments containing additional shuttles with different colored threads to be brought into action as the pattern requires

[1]shuttlecock \'==,=\ *n* [[1]*shuttle* + *cock* (bird)] **1 a :** a feathered object with a rounded base that is volleyed back and forth with rackets in badminton and battledore and shuttlecock — called also *bird, shuttle* **b :** BATTLEDORE AND SHUTTLECOCK **2 :** GADWALL

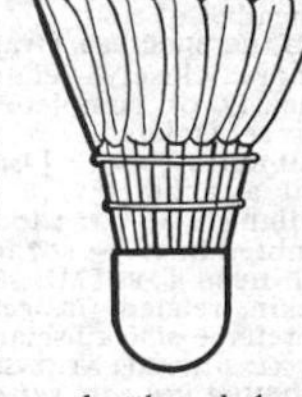

shuttlecock 1a

[2]shuttlecock \"\ *vt* **:** to send or toss to and fro **:** BANDY ⟨they just go on ~*ing* letters —Israel Zangwill⟩ ⟨I waver and am lost: ~*ed* between the opinions of others —*Good Housekeeping* (*London*)⟩ **~** *vi* **:** to go to and fro ⟨was ~*ing* up and down behind the zinc counter dolloping out cups of coffee —Bruce Marshall⟩

[3]shuttlecock \"\ *adj* **:** bandied here and there or back and forth **:** VARIABLE

shut·tle·man \'==‚mən\ *n, pl* **shuttlemen 1 :** a worker who inspects and repairs loom shuttles **2 :** an operator of a locomotive for shuttling supplies in a mine yard

shuttle mark *n* **:** a fabric defect resulting from injury of the warp threads by the shuttle

shut·tler \'shəd·[ə]lə(r), -ət([ə])l-\ *n* -S [[1]*shuttle* + *-er*] **:** a textile worker who replaces the empty shuttles

shuttle race *n* **1 :** a relay race which is run back and forth over a straight course with the first and third runners of a team running in one direction and the second and fourth runners running in the opposite direction **2 :** LAY RACE

shuttle shell *n* **:** any of several cowries having a smooth spindle-shaped shell (as the egg cowry)

shuttle train *n* **:** a train running back and forth over a short route

shut up *vb* [ME *shutten up*, fr. *shutten, shetten, shitten* to shut + *up*, adv.] *vt* **1** *archaic* **:** to finish up **:** TERMINATE, CONCLUDE ⟨will *shut up* this melancholy subject with part of a letter —John Wesley⟩ **2 :** to cause or force (a person) to stop talking ⟨couldn't *shut* him *up* or keep him talking in a straight line —W.F.Davis⟩ **~** *vi* **:** to cease writing or speaking ⟨want this to sail tomorrow . . . and so must *shut up* in a minute —O.W. Holmes †1935⟩ ⟨you would be wise to *shut up* —Marcia Davenport⟩ ⟨sit down and *shut up* —Erle Stanley Gardner⟩

shu·wa *also* **shua** \'shü(w)ə\ *n, pl* **shuwa** *or* **shuwas** *usu cap* **1 :** a negroid Arabic-speaking nomadic or seminomadic pastoral people of the Lake Chad region of western Africa **2 :** a member of the Shuwa people

SHV *abbr, often not cap* [L *sub hac voce* or *sub hoc verbo*] under this word

shvat *usu cap, var of* SHEBAT

shwa *var of* SCHWA

shwr *abbr* shower

[1]shy \'shī\ *adj, usu* **shi·er** *or* **shy·er** \-ī(ə)r, -īə\ *usu* **shi·est** *or* **shy·est** \-īəst\ [ME *schey*, fr. OE *scēoh;* akin to MHG *schiech* shy, OHG *sciuhen* to frighten off, make timid, Sw *skygg* shy, OSlav *ščuti* to chase] **1 a :** easily frightened **:** SKITTISH, TIMID ⟨a diminutive mouse deer, *shiest* of them all —Virginia Hamilton⟩ **b :** expressive of fear or timidity ⟨fled down the forest glade with ~ and subtle steps —Elinor Wylie⟩ **2 :** disposed to avoid a person or thing **:** CAUTIOUS, DISTRUSTFUL, SUSPICIOUS ⟨the gorilla is sullen, untamable and ferocious, ~, wary, and slow-moving —Weston La Barre⟩ ⟨a boy is ~ of a girl who does not have these proofs of efficiency —Margaret Mead⟩ **3 a :** hesitant or chary in committing oneself in action or belief **:** RELUCTANT, CIRCUMSPECT ⟨not in the least ~ about disclosing the secrets of their craft to the uninstructed —*Listener*⟩ ⟨travellers were very ~ of being confidential on a short notice —Charles Dickens⟩ ⟨~ of assuming the moral attitude —W.S.Maugham⟩ **b :** disinclined to discuss or admit to consideration ⟨may well be rather ~ of reverting to topics that are not . . . yet exhausted —F.R.Leavis⟩ ⟨very ~ about the actual condition and number of the . . . navy —G.M.Dallas⟩ ⟨scholars had been ~ of these documents, for fear of their destroying the authority of the . . . text —Edmund Wilson⟩ **4 a :** sensitively diffident or retiring **:** RESERVED, BASHFUL ⟨~ in the presence of strangers and bold with people she knew well —Sherwood Anderson⟩ ⟨the boy ~ and sidelong with adolescence's indecisive shames and inferiorities —Ruth Park⟩ ⟨of a ~ modesty and excessive fear of intrusion which often obscured his real . . . worth —H.E.Starr⟩ **b :** expressive of such reticence or bashfulness ⟨spoke in a ~, delicate voice, hushed and bookish —Irwin Shaw⟩ ⟨remembered her childlike look . . . and ~ tremulous grace —Oscar Wilde⟩ **5 :** withdrawn from view or notice **:** HIDDEN, SECLUDED ⟨the ~ recesses of the woodland —George Meredith⟩ ⟨the ~, almost sly, processes of evolution —Holbrook Jackson⟩ ⟨some ~ intuition on the edge of consciousness that would disappear if looked at directly —F.R.Leavis⟩ **6 a :** meager in growth or reproduction **:** UNPRODUCTIVE ⟨sells off his ~ breeders annually⟩ ⟨is a ~ bloomer in the house —Bessie Buxton⟩ ⟨the greengage . . . is a ~ bearer —F.D.Smith & Barbara Wilcox⟩ **b** (1) **:** having less than the full or a specified amount or number **:** SCANT, LACKING, SHORT ⟨looks about 10 years ~ of his 62 —E.P.Snow⟩ ⟨could get $2000 on a GI loan but would still be $6000 ~ —N.M.Clark⟩ (2) having less money at stake than required in a game; *esp* **:** indebted to the pot (as in poker) **7 :** of a disreputable character or type ⟨gambling hells and ~ saloons —*Blackwood's*⟩

syn BASHFUL, DIFFIDENT, MODEST, COY: SHY applies to a reserved or timid tendency to be unobtrusive, to avoid familiarity or contact with others, or to shun participation in group activity ⟨a *shy* youth, uneasy with girls⟩ ⟨the young people seemed *shy*, almost apprehensive. None stepped forward to greet the stranger; they seemed rather to shrink from him, whispering together in little groups —C.B.Nordhoff & J.N. Hall⟩ BASHFUL implies a frightened or hesitant shyness, often characteristic of childhood or awkward adolescence ⟨he became increasingly *bashful*, and he never had a close friend of either sex —R.J.Donovan⟩ ⟨*bashful* children afraid of the guests⟩ DIFFIDENT may apply to a shyness arising from lack of confidence or distrust in one's ability or personality ⟨a small-town youth, unsure, *diffident*, reaching toward friendship with noble minds, and then drawing back with an unmannerly shrug —H.S.Canby⟩ ⟨too *diffident* a man to have much truck with girls —Nevil Shute⟩ MODEST may indicate absence of any undue self-confidence or conceit ⟨the board in its report cautions scientists to be *modest* and restrained when they step beyond their special fields in expression of opinions as citizens —Vannevar Bush⟩ ⟨the *modest* procedure is not to avow loudly, not to protest too much, our love of truth —G.W. Sherburn⟩ COY may suggest an artful or coquettish affectation of shyness and hesitation ⟨*coy*, like the no's of a woman who has decided in advance to yield —James Burnham⟩ ⟨the ladies of the chansons are not *coy*, and often make the first advances. Such natural lusty love is not romantic —H.O.Taylor⟩

[2]shy \"\ *vb* **shied; shied; shying; shies** *vi* **1 :** to develop or exhibit a sudden antipathy **:** SHRINK, RECOIL ⟨here an old liberal should begin to ~; to halt and wonder —Ernest Barker⟩ — often used with *at* or *from* ⟨*shied* at the publicity guns trained on him —Eloise Hazard⟩ ⟨the conservative court . . . had *shied* from the idea of encouraging revolutionaries —Oscar Handlin⟩ **2 :** to start suddenly aside through fright or alarm ⟨always *shied* at this particular spot —Laura Krey⟩ ⟨falls that thump the ~*ing* trout —Allen Tate⟩ ⟨seemed to ~, white-eyed, from the figure . . . on the kitchen floor —Kenneth Roberts⟩ **3 :** to move or dodge to evade a person or thing — usu. used with *away* or *off* ⟨does not come near to touching this point, but *shies* away into . . . misleading examples —*Times Lit. Supp.*⟩ ⟨candidates *shied* away as soon as they heard the old pastor had not been paid —R.C.Wood⟩ ⟨you ~ off me because I am not your sort —Elizabeth Bowen⟩ and sometimes with *clear* ⟨always *shied* clear of publicity —*Fortune*⟩ **~** *vt* **:** to fight shy of **:** AVOID, SHUN ⟨in trade it is a dangerous thing to ~ danger —Isak Dinesen⟩ **syn** see DEMUR

[3]shy \"\ *n* -ES [[2]*shy*] **:** a sudden start aside (as from fright) ⟨thrown by the horse's unexpected ~⟩

[4]shy \"\ *vb* **shied; shied; shying; shies** [perh. fr. [1]*shy;* fr. the once popular amusement of throwing sticks or stones at cocks specially trained in wariness and ability to dodge] *vt* **:** to throw (an object) with a jerk **:** FLING ⟨boys who delighted in ~*ing* stones at her fowls —H.A.Overstreet⟩ **~** *vi* **:** to make a sudden throw ⟨young men . . . ~*ing* for coconuts —Adrian Bell⟩

[5]shy \"\ *n* -ES **1 :** the act of shying **:** TOSS, THROW **2 :** a verbal fling ⟨took a few *shies* at the integrity of his opponent⟩ **3 :** an experimental attempt **:** TRY ⟨made a few *shies* at orchestral recording —Roland Gelatt⟩ **4 :** COCKSHY 1a, 2a

shy·ish \'shīish, -ēsh\ *adj* **:** rather shy **:** inclined to be shy

[1]shy·lock \'shī,läk\ *n* -S *usu cap* [after *Shylock*, merciless moneylender portrayed in *The Merchant of Venice* (1596) by William Shakespeare †1616 Eng. dramatist and poet] **:** an extortionate creditor or moneylender ⟨an international spider web of *Shylocks* squeezing the heart of hungry multitudes —D.L.Molinari⟩

[2]shylock \"\ *vi* -ED/-ING/-S **:** to lend money at high rates of interest ⟨expose of systematic thievery . . . ~*ing*, and murder —*Current Biog.*⟩

shy·ly *also* **shily** *adv* **:** in a shy manner ⟨blinking ~ before the press cameras —J.B.Boothroyd⟩ ⟨listened ~ to the stranger —H.A.Sinclair⟩ ⟨spring steals in ~ —D.C.Peattie⟩

shy·ness *n* -ES **:** the quality or state of being shy **:** TIMIDITY

1**shy·ster** \'shīstə(r)\ *n* -s [prob. alter. of earlier *shicer* contemptible fellow, fr. G *scheisser*, lit., one that defecates] **:** one who is professionally unscrupulous esp. in the practice of law or politics **:** PETTIFOGGER ⟨has observed too many ~*s*, too many ambulance chasers, too many political confidence men, too many blackmailers —Stanley Walker⟩ ⟨there are tyrants and ~*s* in all positions, and especially those dressed in subordinate authority —Walt Whitman⟩

2**shyster** \"\ *vi* **shystered; shystered; shystering** \-t(ə)riŋ\ **shysters :** to deal as a shyster

si \'sē\ *n* -s [It] **1 :** the tone *B* in the fixed-do system of solmization **2 :** the seventh tone of the diatonic scale in solmization

SI *abbr* silent

SI *abbr* **1** *often not cap* short interest **2** staff inspector

Si *symbol* silicon

sia \'sēə\ *or* **zia** \'zēə, '(t)sēə\ *n, pl* **sia** *or* **sias** *or* **zia** *or* **zias** *usu cap* **1 a :** a Keres people occupying a pueblo in northwestern New Mexico **b :** a member of such people **2 :** the language of the Sia people

sia·fu \sēˈä(,)fü\ *n* -s [Swahili] **:** an African driver ant esp. of the genus *Anomma*

si·al \'sī,al\ *n* -s [G, fr. NL *silicium* + *aluminium*] **1 :** siliceous or acid igneous rock whether solid or molten **2 :** the lighter outer portion of the earth composed mainly of solid or molten rocks rich in silica and alumina — compare SIMA

sial- *or* **sialo-** *comb form* [NL, fr. Gk, fr. *sialon;* akin to L *spuere* to spit — more at SPEW] **:** saliva ⟨*sialolith*⟩

si·al·a·gog·ic \(,)sī¦alə¦gäjik, -gägik\ *adj* [*sialagogue* + *-ic*] **:** promoting the flow of saliva

si·al·a·gogue \sīˈalə,gäg\ *n* -s [NL *sialagogum*, neut. of *sialagogus* inducing flow of saliva, fr. *sial-* + LL *-agogus*] **:** an agent which promotes the flow of saliva

si·a·lia \sīˈālēə\ *n, cap* [NL, fr. Gk *sialis*, a bird + NL *-ia*] **:** a genus of singing birds (family Turdidae) comprising the American bluebirds

1**si·al·ic** \(ˈ)sī¦alik\ *adj* [*sial-* + *-ic*] **:** of or relating to the saliva **:** SALIVARY

2**sialic** \"\ *adj* [ISV *sial* + *-ic*] **:** of or relating to the sial ⟨~ rocks⟩ ⟨the basic substratum, in which the ~ continents float —*Jour. of Geol.*⟩

sialic acid *n* **:** any of a group of crystalline reducing amido acids of carbohydrate character that are acyl (as acetyl or glycolyl) derivatives of neuraminic acid and that are found esp. as components of various gangliosides, blood glycoproteins and mucoproteins

1**si·a·lid** \'sīələd\ *also* **si·al·i·dan** \(ˈ)sī¦alədən\ *adj* [*sialid* fr. NL *Sialidae; sialidan* fr. NL *Sialidae* + E *-an*] **:** of or relating to the Sialidae

2**sialid** \"\ *also* **sialidan** \"\ *n* -s **:** an insect of the family Sialidae

si·al·i·dae \sīˈalə,dē\ *n pl, cap* [NL, fr. *Sialis*, type genus + *-idae*] **:** a family of usu. large insects (order Megaloptera) including the hellgrammite, alderflies, and related forms and having the hind wings broad at the base with their anal angle folding in plaits

si·a·lis \'sīələs\ *n, cap* [NL, fr. Gk, a bird] **:** a genus (the type of the family Sialidae) of insects

si·al·kot \sēˈäl,kōt\ *adj, usu cap* [fr. *Sialkot*, Pakistan] **:** of or from the city of Sialkot, Pakistan **:** of the kind or style prevalent in Sialkot

sialogogue *n* -s [by alter.] **:** SIALAGOGUE

si·al·o·gram \sīˈalə,gram\ *n* [*sial-* + *-gram*] **:** a roentgenogram of the salivary tract made by sialography

si·a·log·ra·phy \,sīəˈlägrəfē\ *n* -ES [*sial-* + *-graphy*] **:** roentgenography of the salivary tract after injection of a radiopaque substance

si·a·loid \'sīə,lȯid\ *adj* [*sial-* + *-oid*] **:** resembling saliva

si·al·o·lith \sīˈalə,lith\ *n* -s [ISV *sial-* + *-lith*] **:** a salivary calculus

si·al·o·li·thi·a·sis \sī¦alə+\ *n* [NL, fr. *sial-* + *lithiasis*] **:** the condition of having one or more salivary calculi

si·al·or·rhea *also* **si·al·or·rhoea** \(,)sī,aləˈrēə\ *n* -s [NL, fr. *sial-* + *-rrhea, -rrhoea*] **:** SALIVATION

si·am \(ˈ)sī¦am, -¦a(ə)m\ *adj, usu cap* [fr. *Siam* (Thailand), country in southeastern Asia] **:** THAILAND

si·a·mang \'sēə,maŋ, -mäŋ\ *n* -s [Malay] **:** a black gibbon of the genus *Symphalangus* (*S. syndactylus*) of Sumatra and the Malay peninsula that is the largest of the gibbons and has the second and third toes partially united by a web

1**si·a·mese** \¦sīə¦mēz, -ēs\ *adj* [*Siam* (Thailand) + E *-ese* (adj. suffix)] **1** *usu cap* **:** THAILAND **2** *usu cap* [fr. *siamese* (*twin*)] **:** exhibiting great resemblance **:** very like — compare SIAMESE TWIN **3** [fr. *siamese* (*twin*)] **a :** serving to connect two or more pipes or hose so as to permit discharge in a single stream ⟨~ connection⟩ ⟨~ joint⟩ **b :** having a siamese connection ⟨~ fire-hose lines⟩

2**siamese** \"\ *n, pl* **siamese** [*Siam* (Thailand), country in southeastern Asia + E *-ese* (n. suffix)] **1** *cap* **:** THAI 1 **2** *cap* **:** THAI 2 **3** *usu cap* [1*siamese*] **:** SIAMESE CAT **4** [1*siamese*] **:** a siamese connection or joint

3**siamese** \"\ *vt* -ED/-ING/-S *sometimes cap* [fr. *siamese* (*twin*)] **:** to unite in a manner suggestive of Siamese twins; *esp* **:** to unite (as pipes) by the use of a siamese connection

siamese cat *n, usu cap S* **:** a slender blue-eyed short-haired domestic cat of a breed of oriental origin having the body fawn or pale gray and the ears, paws, tail, and face darker brown or gray

siamese fighting fish *n, usu cap S* **:** BETTA 2

siamese twin *n, usu cap S* [so called after Chang †1874 and Eng †1874 congenitally united twins born in Meklong, Siam, of Chinese parentage] **1 a :** one of a pair of congenitally united twins in man or animals — compare CRANIOPAGUS, THORACOPAGUS, XIPHOPAGUS **b :** a double monster (as a conjoined fruit) **2 :** one of two persons or things that are closely or indissolubly associated ⟨distribution (the *Siamese twin* of production) —Lewis Galantiere⟩

si·an \(ˈ)shē¦än\ *adj, usu cap* [fr. *Sian*, China] **:** of or from the city of Sian, China **:** of the kind or style prevalent in Sian

si·a·po \sēˈä(,)pō\ *n* -s [Samoan] *in Samoa* **:** TAPA

sias *pl of* SIA

1**sib** \'sib\ *n* -s [ME *sib, sibbe*, fr. OE *sibb;* akin to OHG *sippa, sippea* kinship, family, ON *sifjar*, pl., Goth *sibja* and prob. to Skt *sabhā* assembly; akin to L *suus* one's own — more at SUICIDE] **:** KINSHIP

2**sib** \"\ *adj* [ME *sib, sibbe*, fr. OE *sibb*, fr. *sibb*, n., kinship] **1 :** related by blood **:** AKIN — usu. used with *to* ⟨owners of the neighborhood, ~ to English squire or Scots laird —Mary Johnston⟩ **2** *chiefly dial* **:** on good or intimate terms — usu. used with *to* ⟨~ to the ladies⟩ ⟨this ethereal quality of hers was always ~ to the earth —Llewelyn Powys⟩ **3** *dial* **:** WELL-DISPOSED, CONGENIAL — usu. used with *to*

3**sib** \"\ *n* -s [ME *sib, sibbe*, fr. OE *sibb*, fr. *sibb*, adj., related] **1 a :** KINDRED, RELATIVES **b :** a blood relation **:** KINSMAN **2 a :** a brother or sister considered irrespective of sex **:** SIBLING 1a **b :** a plant or animal having the same degree of relation to another as human siblings **3 :** a group consisting of all persons unilaterally descended from a real or supposed ancestor

sib·bal·di·us \səˈbaldēəs, -bȯl-\ [NL, fr. Sir Robert *Sibbald* †1722 Scot. scientist] *syn of* SIBBALDUS

sib·bald's rorqual \'sibəl(d)z-\ *n, usu cap S* [after Sir Robert *Sibbald* †1722] **:** BLUE WHALE

sib·bal·dus \səˈbaldəs, -bȯl-\ *n, cap* [NL, fr. Sir Robert *Sibbald* †1722 Scot. scientist] **:** a genus of marine cetaceans including solely the blue whale and being often included in the genus *Balaenoptera*

sib·bing \'sibiŋ\ *n* -s [3*sib* + *-ing*] **:** the process of pollinating (as in corn breeding) an emasculated plant with pollen from a sister plant — compare SELF-POLLINATION

si·be·ria \(ˈ)sī¦birēə, -bēr-\ *adj, usu cap* [fr. *Siberia*, region of the U.S.S.R. in Asia] **:** of or from Siberia **:** of the kind or style prevalent in Siberia **:** SIBERIAN

1**si·be·ri·an** \-ēən\ *adj, usu cap* [*Siberia*, region of the U.S.S.R. extending from the Ural mountains to the Pacific ocean in northern Asia (fr. NL, fr. Russ *Sibir'* — fr. *Sibir'*, first Tatar fort in the region conquered by Cossacks in 1581 — + NL *-ia*) + E *-an* (adj. suffix)] **1 :** of, relating to, or characteristic of Siberia **2 :** of, relating to, or characteristic of the Siberians

2**siberian** \"\ *n* -s [*Siberia* + E *-an* (n. suffix)] **1** *cap* **:** a native or inhabitant of Siberia **2** *usu cap* [by shortening] **:** SIBERIAN HUSKY 2

siberian brown *n, often cap S* **:** a moderate olive brown that is stronger and very slightly darker than olive brown and redder and paler than average mustard brown (sense 1)

siberian cedar *n, usu cap S* **:** SWISS PINE

siberian chipmunk *n, usu cap S* **:** BARONDUKI

siberian crab *also* **siberian crab apple** *n, usu cap S* **:** an Asian wild crab apple (*Malus baccata*) that is an ancestor of cultivated forms and has small yellow or red very hard fruits — called also *cherry apple, cherry crab*

siberian cranesbill *n, usu cap S* **:** an Asian annual weed (*Geranium sibiricum*) that is adventive in the eastern U. S. and has deeply parted leaves and showy nearly white flowers

siberian dogwood *n, usu cap S* **:** a shrubby Siberian dogwood (*Cornus alba sibirica*) having brilliant red stems and used as an ornamental

siberian elm *n, usu cap S* **:** a rapid-growing small to medium often shrubby Asian tree (*Ulmus pumila*) naturalized in the U. S., planted for shelter or ornament, and having rough bark, rounded crown, and glabrous branchlets — called also *Chinese elm, dwarf elm*

siberian fir *n, usu cap S* **:** an ornamental evergreen tree (*Abies sibirica*) of eastern Asia that is often cultivated for its bright green foliage and handsome bluish cones

siberian fir-needle oil *or* **siberian pine-needle oil** *n, usu cap S* **:** PINE-NEEDLE OIL b

siberian flax *n, usu cap S* **:** FIREWEED b

siberian gray owl *n, usu cap S* **:** a large owl (*Scotiaptex nebulosa barbata*) related to the great gray owl and occurring in eastern Siberia and casually in Alaska

siberian husky *n* **1** *usu cap S&H* **:** a breed of medium-sized compact dogs developed as sled dogs in northeastern Siberia, having a coat of white, gray, black, or some combination of these with a very dense undercoat, and in general resembling the larger Alaskan malamute **2** *usu cap S & often cap H* **:** a dog of the Siberian Husky breed

siberian ibex *n, usu cap S* **:** a large-horned Siberian wild goat

siberian iris *n, usu cap S* **:** any of various beardless irises that have lilac, blue, or white rather small flowers borne on stiffly erect stalks and are mostly hybrids between two Old World species (*Iris sibirica* and *I. sanguinea*)

siberian larch *n, usu cap S* **:** a larch (*Larix sibirica*) of northeastern Russia and Siberia used in cultivation and having leaves two inches or more in length and cone scales slightly incurved at the apex

siberian millet *n, usu cap S* **:** a foxtail millet (*Setaria italica rubrofructa*) having orange to reddish fruits in long spikes beset with purple bristles — compare GERMAN MILLET

siberian oilseed *n, usu cap S* **:** GOLD-OF-PLEASURE

siberian pea tree *n, usu cap S* **:** a small spiny tree or shrub (*Caragana arborescens*) of eastern Asia with yellow flowers that is often cultivated in shelterbelts and hedges

siberian pine *n, usu cap S* **:** SWISS PINE

siberian sable *n, usu cap 1st S* **:** SABLE 2a(1); *also* **:** its fur

siberian snow hare *n, usu cap 1st S* **:** any of several large active northern Asian hares that constitute distinct races of the common hare (*Lepus timidus*) and that turn white in winter

siberian spruce *n, usu cap 1st S* **:** a tall evergreen tree of northern Europe and Asia that is considered a variety of the Norway spruce or assigned to a separate species (*Picea obovata*) and that has brownish branchlets and bluish green leaves

siberian squill *n, usu cap 1st S* **:** a Eurasian blue-flowered herb (*Scilla sibirica*) cultivated as a spring-blooming bulb

siberian squirrel *n, usu cap 1st S* **:** any of several northern and eastern Old World squirrels which constitute varieties of the common squirrel (*Sciurus vulgaris*) and whose soft fur is used for linings and trimmings

siberian wallflower *n, usu cap S* **:** a showy erect biennial or short-lived perennial cruciferous herb (*Cheiranthus* × *allionii*) that is often cultivated for its terminal racemes of bright orange-yellow flowers with the claws of the petals exceeding the calyx in length

si·be·rite \sīˈbi,rīt, 'sībə,r-\ *n* -s [F *sibérite*, fr. *Sibérie* Siberia + *-ite*] **:** rubellite from Siberia

si·ber·ski \səˈbirskē, sīˈb-\ *n, pl* **siberski** *or* **siberskis** *usu cap* [Russ *sibirskiĭ*, fr. *Sibir'* Siberia + *-skiĭ* (adj. & n. suffix denoting a person or thing originating from or connected with a specified place)] **:** a Siberian settler from European Russia; *esp* **:** one long settled in Siberia or born of earlier Siberian settlers — called also *Siberyak*

siber·yak *or* **siber·iak** *also* **sibir·yak** *or* **sibir·iak** \¦sībər¦yak, ¦sib-, -bir-\ *n, pl* **siberyaks** \-ks\ *or* **siber·yaki** \,=(,)=ˈyakē\ *or* **siberiaks** *or* **siber·iaki** *usu cap* [Russ *sibiryak*, fr. *Sibir'* Siberia + *-yak* (n. suffix denoting a person connected with something specified)] **:** SIBERSKI

sib·i·lance \'sibələn(t)s\ *n* -s **1 :** an *s*-like or sibilant quality ⟨sudden silence, broken only by the ~ of mass sniffing —C.B. Kelland⟩ **2 :** an utterance characterized by sibilance ⟨the courtroom buzzed with a sudden ~ of whispered comment —Erle Stanley Gardner⟩

sib·i·lan·cy \-nsē, -nsi\ *n* -ES **1 :** SIBILANCE **2 :** high content of sibilant sounds

1**sib·i·lant** \-nt\ *adj* [L *sibilant-, sibilans*, pres. part. of *sibilare* to hiss, whistle; of imit. origin like Gk *sizein* to hiss, Goth *swiglon* to blow the flute, whistle, OHG *sweglōn* to blow the flute, W *chwythu* to blow an instrument, OSlav *svistati, zvizdati* to hiss, whistle, Skt *kṣvedati* he whistles, roars, hums, hisses] **:** having, containing, or producing the sound of or a sound resembling that of the *s* or the *sh* in *sash* ⟨a ~ affricate⟩ ⟨a ~ snake⟩ — compare SHIBILANT — **sib·i·lant·ly** *adv*

2**sibilant** \"\ *n* -s **:** a sibilant speech sound (as English \s\, \z\, \sh\, \zh\, \ch(=tsh)\, or \j(=dzh)\)

sib·i·late *also* **sib·il·late** \'sibə,lāt\ *vb* -ED/-ING/-S [L *sibilatus*, past part. of *sibilare* to hiss, whistle] *vi* **1 :** HISS **2 :** to utter an initial sibilant **:** prefix an \s\-sound ~ *vt* **1 :** HISS **2 :** to pronounce with an initial sibilant **:** prefix an \s\-sound to

sib·i·lat·ing·ly *adv* **:** in a sibilating manner

sib·i·la·tion \,sibəˈlāshən\ *n* -s [LL *sibilation-, sibilatio*, fr. L *sibilatus* (past part.) + *-ion-, -io -ion*] **1 :** the action of sibilating **2 :** a sibilated utterance

sib·i·la·tor \-,lād·ə(r)\ *n* -s [*sibilate* + *-or*] **:** one that sibilates

sib·i·la·to·ry \'sibələ,tōrē\ *adj* [*sibilate* + *-ory*] **:** hissing or characterized by hissing **:** SIBILANT

sib·i·lous \'sibələs\ *adj* [L *sibilus*, fr. *sibilus* act of hissing, act of whistling, fr. *sibilare* to hiss, whistle] *archaic* **:** SIBILANT

si·bir·ic \(ˈ)sī¦birik, səˈb-\ *adj, usu cap* [Russ *Sibir'* Siberia + E *-ic*] **:** relating to or resembling the peoples of Siberia (as the Tungus, Mongols, and Tatars)

sib·ley stove \'siblē-\ *n, usu cap 1st S* [after Henry Hopkins *Sibley* †1886 Am. army officer] **:** a simple heating stove for a tent consisting of a sheet-iron cone with a small stovepipe attached extending outside the tent

sibley tent *n, usu cap S* [after Henry Hopkins *Sibley* †1886] **:** a light tent of conical shape erected on a tripod with a ventilating device at the top and sometimes with a vertical drop near the bottom

sib·ling \'sibliŋ, -lēŋ\ *n* -s [3*sib* + *-ling*] **1 a :** one of two or more persons who have the same parents but are not necessarily of the same birth; *sometimes* **:** one of two or more persons having one common parent ⟨~ rivalry⟩ **b :** SIB 2b **2 :** a member of a sib

sibling species *n* [trans. of G *geschwisterarten*] **:** one of two or more closely related species that are morphologically nearly or completely indistinguishable but are reproductively isolated

1**sibmate** \'=,=\ *n* [3*sib* + *mate*] **:** one that belongs to the same sib as another

2**sibmate** \"\ *vi* **:** to interbreed sibs esp. in the production of inbred lines ~ *vt* **:** to produce by sibmating

sib·ness *n* -ES [ME *sibnesse*, prob. fr. OE *gesibness*, fr. *gesibb* akin, related (fr. *ge-*, perfective, associative, and collective prefix + *sibb* kinsman, sib) + *-ness* — more at CO-, SIB] *archaic* **:** KINSHIP, RELATIONSHIP, CONNECTION

siboney *usu cap, var of* CIBONEY

sib·ret *or* **sib·rit** \'sibrət\ *n* -s [ME *sibred, sibrede*, fr. *sibred, sibrede* kinship, consanguinity, fr. OE *sibrǣden*, fr. *sibb*, adj., sib + *rǣden* condition; prob. fr. the mention in the banns of certain forms of kinship as impediments to marriage — more at SIB, KINDRED] *dial Eng* **:** BANNS 1 — often used in pl.

sibs *pl of* SIB

sib·ship \'sib,ship\ *n* [3*sib* + *-ship*] **1 :** the quality or state of being a sib or a member of a sib **2 a :** SIB 3; *broadly* **:** KINDRED **b :** a group of sibs **:** KINSHIP ⟨of 16 ~ groups, 13 consisted of two and 3 of three siblings each —J.H.Conn & Leo Kanner⟩

sib test *n* **:** a test of the desirability of individuals as breeders based on the performance of their brothers or sisters and serving as an indirect test of prepotency — compare PROGENY TEST

si·bu·cao \¦sēbə¦kaů\ *n* -s [Tag *sibukáw*] **:** SAPPANWOOD

sib·yl *also* **syb·il** \'sibəl\ *n* -s *often cap* [ME *sibile, Sybylle*, fr. MF *Sibile, Sebile*, fr. L *Sibylla*, fr. Gk] **1 :** any of several prophetesses usu. accepted as 10 in number and credited to widely separate parts of the ancient world (as Babylonia, Egypt, Greece, and Italy) **2 a :** a female prophet **b :** FORTUNE-TELLER

si·byl·la \səˈbilə\ *n, pl* **sibyl·lae** \-i(,)lē, -i,lī\ *usu cap* [L] **:** SIBYL

si·byl·lic \-ilik\ *adj* [L *Sibylla* + E *-ic*] **:** SIBYLLINE

sib·yl·line *also* **syb·il·line** \'sibə,līn, -,lēn, -lən\ *adj* [L *sibyllinus*, fr. *Sibylla* sibyl + *-inus* -ine] **1** *often cap* **a :** of, relating to, resembling, or characteristic of a sibyl **:** PROPHETIC ⟨the novelist . . . growing a little ~ in her success —Lionel Trilling⟩ **b :** uttered or written in or as if in prophecy ⟨a kind of Sibylline book in which ready and infallible answers will be found to problems —*Times Lit. Supp.*⟩ **2 a :** MYSTERIOUS, CRYPTIC, OCCULT ⟨thoroughly ~ in most of his pronouncements —John Gunther⟩ **b :** AMBIGUOUS, EQUIVOCAL ⟨utterances remained ~ —A.R.E.Pinchot⟩

sib·yl·list \-,ləst\ *n* -s *usu cap* [LGk *sibyllistēs* interpreter of the Sibylline Oracles, fr. Gk *Sibylla* sibyl + *-istēs* -ist] **:** one who believes in sibylline prophecies

1**sic** \(ˈ)sik\ *chiefly Scot var of* SUCH

2**sic** *or* **sick** \'sik\ *vt* **sicced** *or* **sicked** \-kt\ **sicced** *or* **sicked; siccing** *or* **sicking; sics** *or* **sicks** [alter. of 1*seek*] **1 :** SEEK, CHASE, ATTACK — usu. used as an imperative esp. to a dog ⟨~ 'em⟩ **2 :** to incite or urge to an attack, to pursuit, or to harassment **:** SET ⟨tried to ~ his old feist dog on us —Walter Karig⟩ ⟨had to ~ her lawyer on him first —John Dos Passos⟩

syn see URGE

3**sic** \'sik, 'sēk\ *adv* [L, thus; akin to L *si* if, OL *soc* so, OE *swā* — more at SO] **:** intentionally so written — used after a printed word or passage to indicate that it is intended exactly as printed ⟨it is better to say . . . *Tuesday* (~) than *Choosdy* —R.S.Bridges⟩ or to indicate that it exactly reproduces an original ⟨all that glisters [~] is not gold⟩

SIC *abbr, often not cap* specific inductive capacity

si·ca·na \səˈkānə\ *n, cap* [NL, fr. native name in Peru] **:** a genus of tendril-bearing herbaceous vines (family Cucurbitaceae) found in tropical America with angled stems, large roundish leaves, solitary yellow monoecious flowers, and bright-colored aromatic fruit

si·car·i·us \səˈka(a)rēəs\ *n, pl* **sicar·ii** \-ē,ī\ *often cap* [L, assassin, murderer, fr. *sica* dagger; akin to L *secare* to cut — more at SAW] **:** one of a party of Zealots and terrorists resorting to murder in attempting to expel the Romans from Palestine A.D. 52–60

sic·car *chiefly Scot var of* 1SICKER, 3SICKER

sic·ca rupee \¦sikə-\ *n* [Hindi *sikkā rupiyā, sikka rūpaiya*, fr. Ar *sikkah* die, stamp, stamped coin + Hindi *rupiyā, rūpaia* rupee — more at RUPEE] **1 :** a newly coined or unworn rupee **2 :** a rupee issued in Bengal before 1836 weighing more than the rupee of the British East India Company

1**sic·ca·tive** \'sikəd·iv, -ətiv\ *adj* [LL *siccativus*, fr. L *siccatus* (past part. of *siccare* to dry, fr. *siccus* dry) + *-ivus* -ive — more at SACK] **:** causing to dry **:** promoting the action of drying

2**siccative** \"\ *n* -s **:** that which promotes drying; *esp* **:** DRIER 2

1**sice** \'sīs, 'sīz\ *n* -s [ME *sice, sis*, fr. MF *sis*, fr. L *sex* six — more at SIX] *archaic* **:** the number six on a die **:** a throw of six in dice

2**sice** *var of* SYCE

sic·el \'sikəl, -isəl\ *n, usu cap* [Gk *Sikelos*] **1 :** one of the Siculi **2 :** the Italic language of the Siculi

si·cel·i·ot \səˈkelēət, səˈse-, -ē,ät\ *or* **si·kel·i·ot** \səˈk-\ *n* -s *cap* [Gk *Sikeliōtēs*, fr. *Sikelia* Sicily + *-ōtēs* -ote] **:** one of the ancient Greeks colonized in Sicily

si·chom·o·vi \səˈchəməvē, -chäm-\ *n, pl* **sichomovi** *or* **sichomovis** *usu cap* **1 :** a Shoshonean people occupying a pueblo in northeastern Arizona **2 :** a member of the Sichomovi people

sicht \'sikt\ *Scot var of* SIGHT

1**si·cil·ian** \səˈsilyən, -lēən\ *n* -s *cap* [L *Sicilia* Sicily, island in the Mediterranean sea west of the Italian peninsula (fr. Gk *Sikelia*, fr. *Sikelos* Sicel + *-ia* -y) + E *-an* (n. suffix)] **1 :** a native or inhabitant of Sicily **2 :** the Italian language as spoken in Sicily

2**sicilian** \"\ *adj, usu cap* [L *Sicilia* Sicily + E *-an* (adj. suffix)] **1 a :** of, relating to, or characteristic of Sicily **b :** of, relating to, or characteristic of the people of Sicily **2 :** of, relating to, or characteristic of the Sicilian dialects of Italian

sicilian circle *n, usu cap S* **:** a blend of square and round dance with an indefinite number of couples who meet in figures and proceed to other vis-a-vis couples

si·cil·ian·ism \-ə,nizəm\ *n* -s *usu cap* [ISV *sicilian* + *-ism;* prob. orig. formed as It *sicilianismo*] **:** a word or phrase peculiar to the dialects of Sicily

si·cil·i·a·no \sə,silēˈä(,)nō, sə,chi-\ *or* **si·cil·i·a·na** \-,nə\ *or* **si·cil·i·enne** \sə¦silē¦en\ *n* -s [*siciliano* modif. (influenced by It *siciliano* Sicilian) of It *siciliana; siciliana* fr. It, fr. fem. of *siciliano* Sicilian, fr. *Sicilia* Sicily (fr. L) + *-ano* -an (fr. L *-anus*); *sicilienne* fr. F, fr. It *siciliana*] **1 :** a graceful Sicilian rustic dance in which the partners are joined with handkerchiefs **2 :** the music for the siciliano in 6/8 or 12/8 time characterized by a lyrical melody with dotted rhythm and similar to the pastorale

sicilian octave *n, usu cap S* **:** a stanza or poem having eight iambic pentameters rhyming *abababab*

sicilian sumac *n, usu cap S* **:** TANNER'S SUMAC

sicilian umber *n, usu cap S* **:** RAW UMBER

sicilo- *comb form, usu cap* [L *Sicilia* Sicily] **:** SICULO- ⟨*Sicilo-Norman*⟩ ⟨*Sicilo-Muslim*⟩

1**sick** \'sik\ *adj, usu* -ER/-EST [ME *sik, sek, seke*, fr. OE *sēoc;* akin to MD *siec* sick, OHG *sioh*, *siuh* sick, ON *sjūkr* sick, distressed, Goth *siuks* sick, MIr *socht* depression, silence] **1 a** (1) **:** affected with disease **:** not well or healthy **:** ILL, AILING, INDISPOSED ⟨lay ~ of a fever —Mk 1:30 (AV)⟩ ⟨fell ~ of an obscure depressing fever —Frank Outram & G.E.Fane⟩ ⟨took ~ this morning⟩ (2) **:** accompanying, indicating, or suggestive of sickness **:** SICKLY ⟨the ~ smell of age and medicine —Irwin Shaw⟩ (3) **:** designed for or put to the use or service of a sick person ⟨~ chair⟩ ⟨~ lamp⟩ ⟨~ ward⟩ (4) **:** relating to the sick ⟨~ benefit⟩ ⟨~ insurance⟩ ⟨~ pay⟩ **b :** affected with or attended by nausea **:** inclined to vomit or being in the act of vomiting **:** QUEASY — used with *stomach* with *at, to, in,* or *on* ⟨felt ~ at his stomach —Ernest Hemingway⟩; compare AIRSICK, CARSICK, SEASICK **c** *chiefly dial* **:** confined in childbed **d :** MENSTRUATING **2 :** spiritually or morally unsound or corrupt ⟨and heal my soul diseased and ~ —John Wesley⟩ **3 a :** affected by some strong emotion (as shame, horror, fear, or envy) to the degree that one feels nauseated or faint ⟨~ with fear⟩ ⟨worried ~ by repeated failures⟩ **b :** having a strong distaste from surfeit **:** SATIATED — used with *of* ⟨~ of flattery⟩ ⟨~ of a task⟩ ⟨~ of the noise and the smoke —William Black⟩ **c :** DISGUSTED, CHAGRINED ⟨gossip that makes one ~⟩ **d :** depressed and longing for something ⟨~ for one's home⟩ **4 a :** mentally or emotionally unsound or disordered **:** MORBID, UNWHOLESOME ⟨a ~ personality⟩ ⟨~ thoughts⟩ **b :** dealing with unpleasant or macabre subjects ⟨~ jokes⟩ **5 :** requiring repair or replacement **:** DEFECTIVE, FAULTY ⟨a ~ locomotive⟩ **6 :** weak during molting — used of a bird's feathers **7 a :** pale or sickly in appearance or tone **:** SALLOW, WAN ⟨a ~ skin —John Updike⟩ ⟨light from my torch showed his heavy square face a ~ yellow —Marcia Davenport⟩ **b** (1) **:** lacking vigor **:** subnormal in growth or development ⟨a ~ tree⟩ (2) *of grain* **:** low in viability and deteriorated in milling quality due to slightly excessive moisture content at the time of storing ⟨~ wheat⟩ **c :** SICKLY 5a(2) ⟨said . . . finally, in a ~ whisper

—T.B.Costain⟩ **d :** badly outclassed **:** POOR — usu. used with *look* ⟨observers racked up 141 species, making their previous record of 113 look ~ —*Time*⟩ ⟨a girl won . . . and made the speedsters look very ~ —*Irish Digest*⟩ **8 :** SPAWNING; *broadly* **:** POOR, WATERY ⟨~ fish⟩ ⟨~ oysters⟩ **9 :** being in a declining or inactive state esp. after a period of excessive speculation ⟨a ~ market⟩ ⟨~ commodities⟩ ⟨a ~ economy⟩ **10 :** incapable of producing profitable yields of a crop because infested with disease organisms ⟨clover ~ soils⟩ ⟨ground that gets ~ to melons —*Market Growers Jour.*⟩ ⟨~ valleys across the land —R.G.Struble⟩ **11** *of glass* **:** having a cloudy appearance caused esp. by impurities — **sick to death :** extremely fatigued or bored — **sick unto death 1 :** mortally ill **2 :** sick to death ⟨*sick unto death* of the violent partisanship —Inez Robb⟩

[2]**sick** \"\ *n* [ME *sik, sek,* fr. OE *sēoc,* fr. *sēoc,* adj., sick] **1** *pl* **sick :** a sick person ⟨then saith he to the ~ of the palsy —Mt 9:6 (AV)⟩ — usu. used collectively ⟨the number of absentees and ~ has risen —*Time*⟩ **2** -S **a :** SICKNESS **b** *chiefly Brit* **:** VOMIT ⟨a room smelling rather of ~ —Elizabeth Taylor⟩

[3]**sick** *vb* -ED/-ING/-S [ME *siken, seken,* fr. *sik, sek,* adj., sick] *vi* **1** *obs* **:** to become ill **:** fall sick **2 :** VOMIT — often used with *up* ~ *vt, obs* **:** to cause to be ill **:** make sick

[4]**sick** \(ˈ)sik\ *dial Brit var of* SUCH

[5]**sick** *var of* SIC

[1]**sick-abed** \ˈ≈≈,≈\ *adj* [fr. the phrase *sick abed*] **:** confined to bed by illness ⟨*sick-abed* youngsters —*Playthings*⟩

[2]**sick-abed** \"\ *n* -S **:** one confined to bed by illness ⟨an ideal gift for the *sick-abed* —Rosemary Benét⟩

sick and tired *adj* **:** thoroughly fatigued or bored ⟨*sick and tired* of so much idle talk⟩

sick bay *or* **sick berth** *n* **1 :** a compartment in a ship (as a warship or transport) used as a dispensary and hospital **2 :** a place (as a ward in a hospital or the infirmary of a school) restricted to the care of the sick or injured ⟨opened *sick bays* and dispensaries in the refugee camps —*Picture Post*⟩ ⟨got him back to the palm shack we used as *sick bay* —J.F.Regan⟩

sickbed \ˈ≈,≈\ *n* [ME *seke bed,* fr. *seke* sick + *bed* — more at SICK, BED] **:** the bed upon which one lies sick ⟨forced to direct operations from a ~ —*Current Biog.*⟩

sick book *n* **:** a book in which are entered the names of all individuals esp. in a military unit who require medical attention

sick call *n* **1 a :** a usu. daily formation at which individuals report as sick to the medical officer ⟨the attendance at *sick call* would vary —T.O.Heggen⟩ ⟨missed our duty formation and I thought I would cover up by going on *sick call* —Joseph Grant⟩ **b :** the period during which sick call is held **2 :** a visit (as by clergyman or physician) to a sick person ⟨the doctor on his round of *sick calls*⟩

sicked *past of* SIC *or of* SICK

sick·en \ˈsikən\ *vb* **sickened; sickened; sickening** \-k(ə)niŋ\ **sickens** [ME *seknen,* fr. *sek,* adj., sick + *-nen* -en — more at SICK] *vt* **1 :** to make sick **:** DISEASE, NAUSEATE ⟨the fogs have settled . . . thousands of persons have been ~*ed* —*N.Y. Times*⟩ **2 a :** to cause revulsion as a result of weariness or satiety ⟨the growing pile of cakes on the scrubbed table ~*ed* him —John Morrison⟩ **b :** to make nauseated or faint from some strong feeling (as fear, disgust, envy) ⟨feel more ~*ed* than stimulated by the public admiration —T.E.Lawrence⟩ ⟨others, ~*ed* by conditions under which they lived —Sinclair Lewis⟩ ⟨~*ed* by the sight of blood⟩ **3 :** to make sickly **:** IMPAIR, WEAKEN, IMPOVERISH ⟨land ~*ed* by overgrazing⟩ ~ *vi* **1 :** to become sick **:** fall into disease ⟨a hummingbird which had apparently been hurt or had ~*ed* —B.A.Williams⟩ **2 a :** to become faint or nauseated as a result of being affected by some strong emotion (as fear, horror, or desire) ⟨his heart ~*ed* at the thought of this brutal indignity —F.V.W.Mason⟩ — often used with *of* ⟨when the expected excesses began he speedily ~*ed* of the spectacle —J.C.Fitzpatrick⟩ **b :** to become weary or satiated — often used with *of* ⟨voters might ~ of political bickering —W.J.Jorden⟩ **3 :** to become weak or faded **:** DECAY, DECLINE, DETERIORATE ⟨his self-esteem ~*ed* —Maurice Hewlett⟩ ⟨became plain my story was ~*ing* from surfeit of material —Catherine D. Bowen⟩ **4** *chiefly Brit* **:** to undergo the preliminary symptoms — used with *for* ⟨he was ~*ing* for mumps⟩ ⟨pig that looked as though it were ~*ing* for a disease —Pearl Buck⟩ **syn** see DISGUST

sick·en·er \-k(ə)nə(r)\ *n* -S **:** something that tends to sicken or disgust **:** a sickening blow **:** OVERDOSE

sick·en·ing·ly *adv* **:** in a manner or to a degree that sickens ⟨a ~ unctuous person⟩ ⟨a ~ sweet syrup⟩

[1]**sick·er** \ˈsikər\ *adj* [ME *siker,* fr. OE *sicor;* akin to OFris *sikur* safe, secure, OS *sikor,* OHG *sichur, sichor;* all fr. a prehistoric WGmc word borrowed fr. L *securus* free from care — more at SECURE] **1** *chiefly Scot* **:** SECURE, SAFE ⟨a ~ road⟩ **2** *chiefly Scot* **:** TRUSTWORTHY, DEPENDABLE ⟨a ~ man⟩ **3** *chiefly Scot* **:** CONFIDENT, ASSURED **4** *chiefly Scot* **:** firm and well-established

[2]**sicker** \"\ *vi* -ED/-ING/-S [ME *sikeren,* fr. OE *sicerian;* akin to LG *sikern* to trickle, froth, drizzle, and prob. to OHG *sīhan* to filter — more at SACK] *chiefly dial* **:** TRICKLE, OOZE

[3]**sicker** \"\ *adv* [ME *siker,* fr. *siker,* adj., safe] **1** *chiefly Scot* **:** SECURELY, SAFELY **2** *chiefly Scot* **:** ASSUREDLY, CERTAINLY

[4]**sicker** \"\ *vt* -ED/-ING/-S [ME *sikeren,* fr. *siker* safe] *archaic* **:** ASSURE, SECURE, PLEDGE

[5]**sicker** *comparative of* SICK

sick·er·ly *adv* [ME *sikerly, sikerlich,* fr. *siker* safe + *-ly, -lich* -ly] *chiefly Scot* **:** SICKER

sickest *superlative of* SICK

sick flag *n* **:** QUARANTINE FLAG

sick headache *n* **:** MIGRAINE

sick house *n* [ME *sekehous,* fr. *seke* sick + *hous* house — more at SICK, HOUSE] **:** HOSPITAL, INFIRMARY ⟨convalescing after measles in the *sick house* —C.G.Chenevix-Trench⟩

sicking *pres part of* SIC *or of* SICK

sic·king·ia \siˈkiŋēə\ *n, cap* [NL, prob. fr. Franz von *Sickingen* †1523 Ger. knight + NL *-ia*] **:** a genus of small or medium-sized Central and So. American trees (family Rubiaceae) of which some yield usable timber and some are a source of red dyes and extracts of repute in local folk medicine esp. as febrifuges and purgatives — see ARARIBA

sick·ish \ˈsikish\ *adj* [[1]*sick* + *-ish*] **1** *archaic* **:** somewhat ill **:** SICKLY **2 :** somewhat nauseated **:** somewhat qualmish ⟨made her feel ~ the way she felt from the ether —Josephine Pinckney⟩ **3 :** somewhat sickening ⟨a ~ odor⟩ ⟨a *sickish*-sweet taste⟩ ⟨disperse the ~ fog of sentimentality that has clouded man's knowledge of himself —J.L.Liebman⟩ — **sick·ish·ly** *adv* — **sick·ish·ness** *n* -ES

sicklaemia *var of* SICKLEMIA

[1]**sick·le** \ˈsikəl\ *n* -S [ME *sikel,* fr. OE *sicol, sicel;* akin to OHG *sichila* sickle, MD *sekele;* all fr. a prehistoric WGmc word borrowed fr. L *secula* sickle — more at SAW] **1 a :** an agricultural implement consisting of a hook-shaped metal blade with a short handle fitted on a tang **b** (1) **:** the cutting mechanism of a binder, reaper, combine, or header consisting of a flat bar to which are riveted a head and a series of sharp serrated 5-sided cutting blades (2) **:** the knife with smooth sections used on a mower **2 :** any of a series of sickle-shaped arms in a spinning mule to guide the thread **3 :** SICKLE FEATHER **4 :** something that is suggestive of a sickle in shape or use **:** CRESCENT ⟨this ~ of sand which encloses one of the finest harbors —Mary H. Vorse⟩

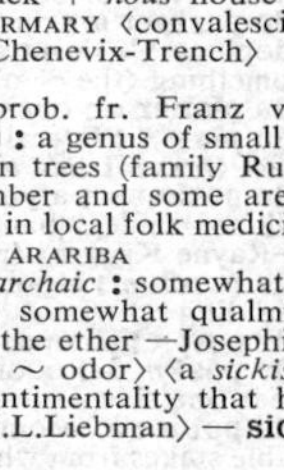

sickle 1a

[2]**sickle** \"\ *vb* **sickled; sickled; sickling** \-k(ə)liŋ\ **sickles** *vt* **1 :** to mow or reap with a sickle ⟨~ down the weeds along the wall —Rumer Godden⟩ **2 :** to form (a red blood cell) into a crescent ~ *vi* **1 :** to move in a curving line suggestive of that of a sickle ⟨children . . . would ~ quietly back like boomerangs along the soundless lawn —Ray Bradbury⟩ **2 :** to form into a crescent ⟨the ability of red blood cells to ~⟩

[3]**sickle** \"\ *adj* **:** having the form of a sickle blade **:** having a curve similar to that of a sickle blade ⟨the ~ moon⟩ ⟨a ~ beach⟩

sickle alfalfa *also* **sickle lucerne** *or* **sickle medick** *n* **:** a European medic (*Medicago falcata*) naturalized in No. America and having yellow flowers and falcate or nearly straight pods

sickle and hammer *n, sometimes cap S&H* **:** HAMMER AND SICKLE

sick leave *n* **1 :** a period of absence from duty due to illness or other disability ⟨the foreign secretary was on *sick leave* when the decisions were taken —*New Statesmen & Nation*⟩ ⟨ill health required several *sick leaves* —C.D.Rhodes⟩ **2 :** an allowance of paid leave specified in days or hours per month or year that is granted to employees or salaried personnel for absence due to illness or other disability ⟨entitled to 40 hours' *sick leave* each calendar year —*New South Wales Industrial Gazette*⟩ ⟨as a rule, *sick leave* accumulates at the same rate, namely eighteen days each year —*Employment Opportunities in the Civil Service (Canada)*⟩ **3 :** SICK PAY ⟨paid us *sick leave* for the six weeks Jack was in hospital —*Sat. Eve. Post*⟩

sickle bar *n* **1 :** CUTTER BAR **2 :** the complete cutting mechanism of any grain harvester consisting of the sickle, the guards and ledger plates, and the bar to which they are attached

sicklebill \ˈ≈≈,≈\ *n* [[3]*sickle* + *bill*] **:** any of various birds with a strongly curved bill: as **a :** CURLEW; *specif* **:** HEN CURLEW **b :** any of several thrashers; *esp* **:** CALIFORNIA THRASHER **c :** a bird of paradise of the genus *Drepanornis* **d :** a saberbill of the genus *Campylorhamphus* **e :** any of several Hawaiian birds of the family Drepanididae and esp. of the genus *Drepanis* **f :** a So. and Central American hummingbird of the genus *Eutoxeres*

sickle-billed \ˈ≈≈;≈\ *adj* **:** having a bill curved like a sickle

sickle cell *n* **:** an abnormal red blood cell of crescent shape

sickle-cell anemia *or* **sickle-cell disease** *n* **:** a chronic familial anemia in which a large proportion or the majority of the red cells in the blood are sickle cells and which occurs mainly in persons of Negro blood

sickle-cell trait *n* **:** an inherited blood condition in which some red blood cells tend to sickle but usu. not enough to produce anemia, which occurs primarily in individuals of Negro ancestry, and which is held to result from heterozygosity for a semidominant gene — called also *sicklemia*

sick·led \ˈsikəld\ *adj* [[1]*sickle* + *-ed*] **:** furnished with a sickle or sickles ⟨the ~ tail of chanticleer⟩

sickle feather *n* **:** one of the long curved tail feathers of a cock; *esp* **:** one of the middle or upper pair — see COCK illustration

sickle-grass \ˈ≈≈,≈\ *n* **1 :** a stout 3-angled sedge (*Carex crinita*) of eastern No. America with dense drooping sickle-shaped spikes **2 :** a tearthumb (*Polygonum arifolium*)

sickle ham *n* **:** SICKLE HOCK — **sickle-hammed** \ˈ≈≈;≈\ *adj*

sickle hock *n* **:** a hock (as of a horse) that is much flexed with the foot far under the body — **sickle-hocked** \ˈ≈≈;≈\ *adj*

sicklelike \ˈ≈≈,≈\ *adj* **:** resembling or suggesting a sickle

sick·le·man \ˈsikəlmən\ *n, pl* **sicklemen :** one who uses a sickle **:** REAPER

sick·le·mia *also* **sick·lae·mia** \,sikəˈlēmēə, siˈklē-\ *n* -S [NL, fr. E [3]*sickle* + NL *-emia*] **:** SICKLE-CELL TRAIT — **sick·le·mic** \,sikəˈlēmik, (ˈ)siˈklē-\ *adj*

sicklepod \ˈ≈≈,≈\ *n* [[3]*sickle* + *pod*] **1 :** a No. American rock cress (*Arabis canadensis*) having very long curved pods **2 :** a cosmopolitan tropical weed (*Cassia tora*) with yellow flowers and slender curved pods

sick·ler \ˈsik(ə)lə(r)\ *n* -S [[1]*sickle* + *-er*] **:** one that uses a sickle **:** SICKLEMAN

sick·ler·ite \ˈsikləˌrīt\ *n* -S [*Sickler* family of Pala, San Diego county, Calif. + E *-ite*] **:** a mineral (Li,Mn)(PO_4) consisting of a hydrous lithium manganese phosphate and occurring in dark brown cleavable masses and isomorphous with ferrisicklerite (sp. gr. 3.4)

sickles *pl of* SICKLE, *pres 3d sing of* SICKLE

sickle senna *n* **:** SICKLEPOD 2

sickle tail *n* **:** a tail (as of a dog) that curves upward and over the back

sickle-tailed \ˈ≈≈;≈\ *adj* **:** having a tail carried curved like a sickle

sicklewort \ˈ≈≈,≈\ *n* [ME *sikelwert,* fr. *sikel* sickle + *wert* wort — more at SICKLE, WORT] **:** a yellow-flowered European vetch (*Coronilla scorpioides*) with curved pods

sick·li·ly \ˈsikləlē, -əli\ *adv* **:** in a sickly manner

sick·li·ness \-klēnəs, -klin-\ *n* -ES **:** the quality or state of being sickly

sickling *pres part of* SICKLE

sick list *n* **:** a list containing the names of the sick — **on the sick list :** ILL, INDISPOSED

sick·lo·cyte \ˈsik(ə)ləˌsīt\ *n* -S [[3]*sickle* + *-o-* + *-cyte*] **:** SICKLE CELL

[1]**sick·ly** \ˈsiklē, -li\ *adj* -ER/-EST [ME *siklich, sekly,* fr. *sik, sek* sick + *-lich, -ly* -ly — more at SICK] **1 :** somewhat sick **:** disposed to illness **:** habitually ailing ⟨a ~ body⟩ ⟨~ children⟩ **2 a :** produced by or associated with sickness ⟨a ~ complexion⟩ ⟨a ~ appetite⟩ **b** *archaic* **:** of or relating to a sick person or to sickness **3 :** characterized by the presence of sickness **:** attended with disease ⟨a ~ place⟩ ⟨a ~ season⟩ ⟨the ~ aims, the false ideals, of our age —Oscar Wilde⟩ **4 :** producing or tending to disease **:** UNHEALTHY ⟨a ~ climate⟩ **5 a** (1) **:** appearing as if sick **:** WEAK, LANGUID, PALE ⟨uneasy influence of that ~ moonlight —David Kidd⟩ ⟨lamp burning with a ~ flame⟩ (2) **:** WRETCHED, UNHAPPY, UNEASY ⟨a ~ smile⟩ ⟨a ~ attempt at humor⟩ ⟨shared their ~ social unease —Herbert Gold⟩ **b :** resembling in state a sickly person ⟨a ~ plant⟩ ⟨a ~ mind⟩ ⟨~ beer⟩ **6 a :** tending to produce nausea ⟨the air was ~ with the odor of locust beans —Norman Lewis⟩ **b :** disgusting or repelling by reason of being weak, silly, or sentimental **:** MAWKISH ⟨why do they want to play those ~ waltzes —Winifred Bambrick⟩ **syn** see UNWHOLESOME

[2]**sickly** \"\ *vt* -ED/-ING/-ES **:** to make sick or sickly (as in hue) — usu. used with *over* ⟨*sicklied* o'er with the pale cast of thought —Shak.⟩ ⟨an era which has been *sicklied* over with doubt —John Lodge⟩

[3]**sickly** \"\ *adv* [[1]*sick* + *-ly*] **:** in a sick manner or condition **:** ILL ⟨heart lurched ~ as the footsteps attacked the stairs —Marcia Davenport⟩

sick·ness *n* -ES [ME *siknesse, seknesse,* fr. OE *sēocnesse,* fr. *sēoc* sick + *-nesse* -ness — more at SICK] **1 a :** the condition of being ill **:** ill health **:** ILLNESS **b :** a disordered, weakened, or unsound condition ⟨a ~ of judgment would seem to be easily recognizable —*Cross Currents*⟩ **2 a :** a form of disease **:** MALADY **b :** MENSES **3 a :** NAUSEA, QUEASINESS ⟨~ of stomach⟩ — see MOTION SICKNESS **b :** VOMIT

sick nurse *n* **:** a nurse who tends the sick

sick pay *n* **:** salary or wages paid to an employee while on sick leave

sickroom \ˈ≈,≈\ *n* [[1]*sick* + *room*] **:** a room in which a person is confined by sickness

sicks *pres 3d sing of* SIC *or of* SICK, *pl of* SICK

siclike \ˈsi,klīk\ *chiefly Scot var of* SUCHLIKE

sic passim \ˈsik-, ˈsēk-\ *adv* [L] **:** so throughout — used esp. to indicate that something (as a word or idea) is to be found at various places throughout a book or writer's work

sics *pres 3d sing of* SIC

si·cu *also* **si·ku** \ˈsē(,)kü\ *n* -S [native name in Bolivia] **:** the Bolivian panpipe

sic·u·la \ˈsikyələ\ *n, pl* **sicu·lae** \-,lē\ [NL, fr. L, small dagger, dim. of *sica* dagger — more at SICARIUS] **:** the conical chitinous skeleton of the initial zooid of a colony of graptolites — **sic·u·lar** \-lə(r)\ *adj*

[1]**sic·u·lan** \ˈsikyələn\ *adj, usu cap* [L *siculus* siculan (fr. *Siculus* Sicel, fr. Gk *Sikelos*) + E *-an* (adj. suffix)] **:** of, relating to, or characteristic of the Siculi

[2]**siculan** \"\ *n* -S *cap* [L *Siculus* Sicel + E *-an* (n. suffix)] **:** one of the Siculi

sic·u·li \ˈsikyə,lī\ *n pl, cap* [L, fr. Gk *Sikeloi*] **:** an ancient people occupying part of the island of Sicily — **si·cu·li·an** \ˈsiˈkyülēən\ *adj or n, usu cap*

siculo- *comb form, usu cap* [L *siculus* siculan] **:** Sicilian and ⟨*Siculo*-Arabian⟩ ⟨*Siculo*-Norman⟩

[1]**sic·y·o·nian** \ˌsisēˈōnyən, -ikē-, -ōnēən\ *adj, usu cap* [L *sicyonius* of Sicyon (fr. Gk *sikyōnios,* fr. *Sikyōn* Sicyon) + E *-an* (adj. suffix)] **1 :** of, relating to, or characteristic of the ancient city of Sicyon in the Peloponnesus or the surrounding district Sicyonia **2 :** of, relating to, or characteristic of the people of Sicyon or Sicyonia

[2]**sicyonian** \"\ *n* -S *cap* [L *Sicyonii,* pl., Sicyonians (fr. *sicyonius* of Sicyon) + E *-an* (n. suffix)] **:** a native or inhabitant of Sicyon or Sicyonia

sic·y·os \ˈsisēəs, -ikē-, -ē,äs\ *n, cap* [NL, fr. Gk *sikyos* cucumber — more at CUCUMBER] **:** a genus of annual herbaceous vines (family Cucurbitaceae) found in the New World and Australasia with branched tendrils, angled or lobed leaves, small greenish white monoecious flowers, and spiny indehiscent fruit

sid \ˈsid\ *n* -S [perh. alter. of [1]*seed*] *Brit* **:** an inner husk of a grain

si·da \ˈsīdə\ *n* [NL, fr. Gk *sidē,* a water plant] **1** *cap* **:** a very large genus of tropical herbs or shrubs (family Malvaceae) having usu. small white or yellow flowers followed by five or more schizocarps with solitary pendulous ovules and including forms that yield useful fibers or mucilaginous substances — see INDIAN MALLOW, QUEENSLAND HEMP **2** -S **:** any plant of the genus *Sida*

si·dal·cea \sīˈdalshēə, səˈ-\ *n, cap* [NL, fr. *Sida* + *Alcea,* genus of mallows, fr. L *alcea* mallow, fr. Gk *alkaia*] **:** a genus of often showy herbs (family Malvaceae) confined to western No. America and having palmately cleft leaves, variously colored spicate or racemose flowers, and 5 to 9 suculate schizocarps

[1]**sid·dha** \ˈsidə\ *n* -S *usu cap* [Skt, lit., successful, fr. *sidhyati* he goes straight to a goal, succeeds; akin to Skt *sādhati* he comes to his goal — more at ATHROGENIC] *Jainism & Hinduism* **:** one who has attained perfection esp. as shown by occult powers

[2]**siddha** \"\ *n* -S [native name in Bengal] **:** rice that is soaked in water and then boiled before milling

sid·dur \ˈsi,dů(ə)r, -üə, -də(r)\ *n, pl* **sid·du·rim** \sə'důrəm\ *also* **siddurs** [MHeb *siddūr,* lit., order, arrangement, short for Heb *sēder tĕfillōth* order of prayers] **:** a Jewish prayer book containing both Hebrew and Aramaic prayers used chiefly in the daily liturgy — compare MAHZOR

[1]**side** \ˈsīd\ *n* -S [ME, fr. OE *sīde;* akin to OS *sīda* side, OHG *sīta,* ON *sītha;* derivative fr. a prehistoric adj. represented by OFris *side* low, wide, OE *sīd* long, large, wide, OHG *sīto,* adv., weakly, loose, ON *sīthr* long, pendulous; akin to OE *sāwan* to sow — more at SOW] **1 a :** the right or left lateral part of the wall or trunk of the body ⟨a pain in the ~⟩ **b** *archaic* **:** the female seat of generation or birth **c :** the area in which is felt the exertion produced by speaking or by boisterous laughter ⟨split his ~*s* with laughing —Charles Dickens⟩ **2 :** a place, space, or direction with respect to a center or to a line of division (as of an aisle, river, or street) ⟨found on all ~*s*⟩ ⟨on this ~⟩ **3 :** one of the surfaces or surface parts of an object which are distinguished from the ends as being longer and from the front or back as being more or less perpendicular to the observer ⟨tacking . . . bunting to the front and ~*s* of the platform —John Updike⟩ — often used in combination ⟨be*side*⟩ ⟨fore*side*⟩ ⟨in*side*⟩ ⟨top*side*⟩ ⟨up*side*⟩ **4 a :** a bounding line of a geometrical figure ⟨the ~ of the road⟩ ⟨the ~ of a triangle⟩ **b :** one of the surfaces and esp. one of the longer surfaces that define or limit a solid **:** a part (as a wall of a room) connecting the extremities of the top and bottom **:** FACE ⟨the ~ of a box⟩ ⟨the ~ of a prism⟩ **c** (1) **:** either of the two surfaces of a thin object (as a sheet, disk, slice, or partition) ⟨the other ~ of the coin⟩ (2) **:** the inner or outer aspect of something **d :** one of the surfaces serving to enclose or bound a space ⟨the ~ of a pool⟩ ⟨~ of a valley⟩ ⟨~*s* of a cave⟩ **e :** a line joining two consecutive vertices of a polygon **f** (1) **:** one playing surface of a phonograph record (2) **:** a single recorded selection **5 :** the space immediately beside or in close proximity to someone ⟨never from thy ~ henceforth to stray —John Milton⟩ **6 a :** the outer surface of a ship on either side above the waterline **b :** the portion of the outer surface below the main deck — distinguished from *topside* **7 a :** an outer portion of something held to face in a particular direction ⟨the upper ~ of a sphere⟩ **b :** an aspect or part of something held to be contrasted with some other aspect or part ⟨the better ~ of his nature⟩ ⟨try to find the brighter ~ of the tragedy⟩ **8 a :** a slope or declivity (as of a hill or bank) considered as opposed to another slope over the ridge ⟨along the ~ of yon small hill —John Milton⟩ — often used in combination ⟨hill*side*⟩ ⟨mountain*side*⟩ **b** *obs* **:** the outskirts of a grove or city **c :** land bordering a body of water **:** BANK, SHORE — often used in combination ⟨lake*side*⟩ ⟨river*side*⟩ ⟨sea*side*⟩ **9 :** the attitude or action of one person or group with respect to another **:** PART **10 :** a position viewed as opposite to or contrasted with another ⟨balanced on both ~*s*⟩ ⟨there are two ~*s* to every question⟩ **11 a :** the position of a person or party regarded as opposed to another person or party whether as a rival or a foe ⟨God on our ~, doubt not of victory —Shak.⟩ **b :** the interest or cause which one maintains against another **:** a doctrine or cause opposed to another **12 a :** one of the halves of the body of an animal or man on either side of the mesial plane ⟨a ~ of beef⟩ **b :** a cut of meat including that about the ribs of one lateral half of the body — used chiefly of smoked pork products ⟨a well-cured ~⟩; see PORK illustration **13 a :** one of the parties in a transaction, battle, or debate **:** a body of advocates or partisans **:** a political party or faction ⟨a victory for neither ~⟩ **b :** one of the contesting parties in a game or sport **c :** a group of players in a card game who are partners **d** *Brit* **:** TEAM ⟨a soccer ~⟩ ⟨a match is played between two ~*s* of eleven players each —*Laws of Cricket*⟩ **14 :** a line of descent traced through one parent ⟨the grandfather on one's mother's ~⟩ ⟨of Irish ancestry on his father's ~ —*Current Biog.*⟩ **15 a :** a part (as of a place or thing) located in a particular direction from a center or line of division ⟨on one ~ of the church⟩ ⟨this ~ of the city⟩ **b** (1) **:** a geographical region or district (2) **:** the inhabitants of such a region — usu. used in combination ⟨country*side*⟩ **16 :** one page of a book or writing **:** one side of a sheet of paper ⟨a man might blur ten ~*s* of paper in attempting a defense —Charles Lamb⟩ **17 :** a position, movement, or inclination away from a central line or point ⟨to one ~⟩ ⟨on one ~⟩ **18 :** one half of a hide divided along the backbone for use in leather manufacturing **19 :** sideways spin imparted to a billiard ball — compare ENGLISH 5 **20 a :** a sheet containing the lines and cues for a single theatrical role and used in learning a role **b :** a speech in a play ⟨she knew all her ~*s* after only a few rehearsals⟩ **21 :** the front or back cover of a book **22 :** the aspect and the functioning of a court in some distinct portion of its general jurisdiction ⟨the criminal-law ~ of the English High Court of Justice⟩ ⟨the admiralty ~ of a U.S. district court⟩ ⟨the equity ~ of a state court⟩ **23 :** the surface of a screw thread that joins a crest with a root **24 :** the men and equipment engaged in the removal of a section of timber in logging **25 :** the area outside the center in craps or an imaginary area outside the layout in banking games where bets are held to be placed by players among themselves rather than against the shooter or house ⟨place a bet on the ~⟩ — see SIDE BET **syn** see PHASE — **at side :** running with its dam and nursing without restriction — used of a young domestic mammal ⟨a heifer with bull calf *at side*⟩ ⟨ewes with lambs *at side*⟩ — **on the side** *adv* **1 :** in addition to the regular or main portion ⟨a hamburger with onions *on the side*⟩ **2 :** in addition to a regular or principal occupation or pursuit ⟨took a night job *on the side*⟩ ⟨bet a dollar *on the side*⟩ — **over the side** *adv* **1 :** from outside a ship on to its deck (as in arriving on board) **2 :** from the deck of a ship to its outside (as in leaving) — **this side :** short of **:** not beyond ⟨that's all we may expect of man *this side* the grave —Robert Browning⟩ — **through one's sides** *archaic* **:** through one as if by transfixing **:** indirectly through one ⟨attacked him, *through my sides,* in a pamphlet —James Boswell⟩

[2]**side** \"\ *adj* [ME, fr. *side,* n.] **1 :** of, relating to, or used on the side (as of a person) ⟨~ armor⟩ ⟨a ~ sore⟩ **2 a :** directed toward or from the side ⟨a ~ blow⟩ ⟨~ thrust⟩ **b :** held to be directed toward or from the side **:** COLLATERAL, INCIDENTAL, INDIRECT ⟨a ~ issue⟩ ⟨a ~ view⟩ ⟨a ~ remark⟩ **c :** made on the side (as a side agreement between member A and member B may . . . prevent general agreement —Harold Stein⟩ ⟨~ money⟩ ⟨~ payment⟩ **d :** additional to the regular or main portion or order ⟨a ~ order of french fries⟩ **3 a :** located at or towards the side (as of a building, structure, or thoroughfare) ⟨~ window⟩ ⟨~ room⟩ ⟨~ path⟩ **b :** having the principal part (as the blade or head) located on one side rather than on the end ⟨~ chisel⟩ ⟨~ hammer⟩ ⟨~ plane⟩ — see SIDE TOOL **c :** used at the side ⟨~ screen⟩ ⟨~ hook⟩ **d :** of, relating to, or

used on the side of a boat ⟨~ guy⟩ ⟨~ plates⟩ **e** : growing to or from one side ⟨a ~ branch⟩ ⟨~ shoot⟩ **4** : blowing at right angles to a line from the mark to an archer ⟨a ~ wind⟩

3side \"\ *adv* [ME, fr. *side*, n.] : to, at, by, or from one side ⟨~ launched them for use as cargo barges —K.M.Dodson⟩ — usu. used in combination ⟨*side*cast⟩ ⟨*side*-hanging⟩

4side \"\ *vb* -ED/-ING/-S [ME *siden*, fr. *side*, n.] *vt* **1** *archaic* : to cut or carve (as a haddock) into sides **2** : to be or range oneself on the side with : agree with : SUPPORT ⟨not a fighting friend left to ~ him —F.B.Gipson⟩ **3** : to range (as oneself) on or with one of two contesting sides **4** : to be, go, or stand at the side of : come to the side of : walk by the side of : be side by side with **5** : to work (as a timber or rib) to a specified thickness by trimming the sides **6** *dial* **a** : to put (as a room) in order : clean or tidy up (as a table) : ARRANGE — often used with *up* **b** : to place at one side : set or put aside : clear away : REMOVE ⟨~ dishes⟩ **7** : to furnish with sides or siding ⟨~ a house⟩ **8** : to draw (as a rope) toward the side : draw over or out **9** : to apply covers of cloth or other material to the boards of (as a book or case) after the backbone and corners have been affixed — often used with *up* ~ *vi* **1** : to embrace the opinions of one party or engage in its interest in opposition to another party : take sides : join or form sides ⟨all ~ in parties and begin the attack —Alexander Pope⟩ — usu. used with *with* or *against* ⟨the local justice of the peace *sided* with the squatters —*Amer. Guide Series: Pa.*⟩ ⟨*sided* against the Administration on most issues⟩ **2** : to move, turn, or bend sideways **3** *chiefly dial* : to stand or move to one side

5side \"\ *adj* [ME, long, large, wide, fr. OE *sīd* — more at SIDE (n.)] *chiefly Scot* : WIDE, CAPACIOUS, FLOWING — used esp. of a garment

6side \"\ *n* -S [obs. E *side* proud, boastful, fr. ME, wide, capacious] : swaggering manner : arrogant behavior : CONCEIT, PRETENTIOUSNESS

side action *n* : SIDE EFFECT ⟨some *side actions* may be alleviated by symptomatic therapy —*Therapeutic Notes*⟩

side aisle *n* : one of the lateral aisles of a building (as a church, basilica, or theater) as distinguished from the central aisle or nave

side arm *n* : a weapon worn at the side or in the belt (as a sword, revolver, or bayonet)

1sidearm \ˈ⸗,⸗\ *adj* [*1side* + *arm*] **1** : of, relating to, or constituting a style of pitching or throwing (as in baseball) in which the arm is not raised above the shoulder and the ball is delivered with a sideways sweep of the arm across the body between the shoulder and the hip ⟨~ delivery⟩ **2** : of, relating to, or constituting a device with outlet on the side (as a gas-fired heater for connection to a water tank)

2sidearm \"\ *adv* : in a sidearm manner or style : with a sidearm delivery ⟨he pitched ~⟩

side ax *n* : an ax having the handle bent to one side

side band *n* : the band of radio frequencies on either side of the carrier frequency produced by the process of modulation — compare SIDE FREQUENCY

side-band transmission *n* : CARRIER SUPPRESSION

sidebar \ˈ⸗,⸗\ *n* [*1side* + *bar*] **1 a** : either of a pair of longitudinal elastic wooden bars on which the bodies of buggies and other light vehicles are sometimes suspended **b** : either of two plates uniting the pommel and cantle of a saddle **c** : either of the outside plates located one on each side of the lower part of a side-bar keel **2** : a short news story designed to accompany a major news story and present sidelights (as personalities or human interest aspects) of the major story ⟨a ~ on the crime investigation⟩

side-bar keel *n* : a bar keel formed in three thicknesses

side-bar rule *n* [so called fr. its being formerly moved for by the attorneys within a bar on the side of the court in Westminster Hall, former chief law court of England] : an English legal rule authorized by the court to be granted by the clerk of the rules upon a praecipe as a matter of course without formal application being made to the court

side beam *n* : a walking beam of a side-lever engine

side-beam engine *n* : SIDE-LEVER ENGINE

side bearing *n* : the part of the shoulder of a piece of printing type at the right and left sides of the face

side bench *n* : the seat along the side of a small boat; *esp* : the fore-and-aft planking over the air tanks in a small boat fitted with air tanks that is available as a seat

side bet *n* **1** : a bet made with a player other than a house that customarily books all bets or other than with the shooter (as in craps) **2** : a bet made by the shooter in craps on any event other than the outcome of his center bets **3** : a bet (as on whose hand holds the highest spade) made on an event not integral to the game being played **4** : a bet with another player in a game additional to the regular stakes for which the game (as in bridge or golf) is being played

sideboard \ˈ⸗,⸗\ *n* [ME *side-bord*, fr. *1side* + *bord* board — more at BOARD] **1** : a table at the side of the dining hall or room: as **a** *obs* : a side table as distinguished from the head table **b** : a heavy open cupboard or dresser (as of oak) for dishes or wines common in the 16th and 17th centuries : CREDENCE **c** (1) : a serving table with drawers and cupboards beneath its tabletop developed by Georgian designers (2) : a combination serving table and dresser often with a mirror developed in the 19th century — compare BUFFET **2 a** : a board forming a side or part of a side of a structure (as of a crib or hospital bed) **b** : an additional removable board fitted on the side of a vehicle (as a wagon or cart) to increase the carrying capacity **3** : a piece of dining-room furniture having compartments and shelves for holding articles of table service **4 sideboards** *pl* : SIDE-WHISKERS

sideboard-table \ˈ⸗,⸗,⸗⸗\ *n* : a serving table usu. with a marble top and often having one or two narrow drawers in the apron

sidebone \ˈ⸗,⸗\ *n* **1** : the lateral part of the hipbone of a fowl easily separable from the backbone in carving **2 a** *also* **sidebones** *pl but sing in constr* : abnormal ossification of the cartilages in the lateral posterior part of a horse's hoof (as of a forefoot) often causing lameness **b** : one of the bony structures so caused

side-box \ˈ⸗,⸗\ *n* : a box or enclosed seat on the side of a theater

side boy *n* : one of from two to eight members of the crew of a ship who are detailed to stand at the gangway as a mark of respect to a person arriving or departing

side·burned \ˈsīd,bərnd, -bə̄nd, -bəind\ *adj* [*sideburns* + *-ed*] : having or characterized by sideburns ⟨lavishly ~ lotharios —G.A.Wagner⟩

side·burns \-nz\ *n pl* [anagram of *burnsides*] **1** : SIDE-WHISKERS; *esp* : short side-whiskers worn with a smooth chin **2** : continuations of the hairline in front of the ears whether the hair is worn long or clipped short

side by side *adv* [ME] **1** : beside one another with bodies in line ⟨walked *side by side* down the aisle⟩ **2** : in the same place, time, or circumstances ⟨lived peacefully *side by side* in the same village —Philip Mason⟩

1side-by-side \ˌ⸗⸗ˈ⸗\ *adj* : standing or situated next to one another

2side-by-side \"\ *n* : a double-barreled shotgun having the barrels mounted on the frame in a horizontally side-by-side position — compare OVER-AND-UNDER

sidecar \ˈ⸗,⸗\ *n* [*1side* + *car*] **1** : JAUNTING CAR **2** : a car attached to a motorcycle for the accommodation of a passenger seated abreast of the cyclist and usu. supported by a single third wheel **3** : WING CAR **4** : a cocktail consisting of an orange flavored liqueur, lemon juice, and brandy shaken in cracked ice and served strained and garnished with a twist of lemon peel

side card *n* : an unmatched card other than part of a pair or of three or four of a kind in a poker hand

side-centered \ˈ⸗;⸗⸗\ *adj* : centered on the side faces only — used of crystals

side chain *n* **1** : one of the two chains passing over the pinions on the countershaft and the gears on the driving wheels in a chain final drive on automotive vehicles **2** : a branched chain of atoms attached to the principal chain or to a ring in a molecule ⟨aromatic hydrocarbons with paraffinic *side chains*⟩

side-chain theory *n* : a largely displaced theory of the chemical basis of immunological phenomena: living organisms are complex aggregations of complex molecules capable of reacting with one another through some of their side chains when these side chains have a definite correspondence in structure exemplified by various outlying cell receptors that can combine with foreign molecules (as of food or toxins), and stimulate the cell to the production of other like receptors some of which may become detached from the cell and function as antibodies

side chair *n* : a chair without arms used esp. in the dining room — see WINDSOR CHAIR illustration

side chapel *n* : a small chapel within a church usu. at the side or back of the choir or chancel — compare LADY CHAPEL

sidecheck \ˈ⸗,⸗\ *n* : a checkrein carried at the side of a horse's head — compare OVERCHECK

side clearance *n* : BACKLASH 1b

side-close \ˈ⸗,⸗\ *n* -S : a ballroom step in which a dancer places one foot to the side and brings the other to it

side-coat \ˈ⸗,⸗\ *n* [ME *side cote*, fr. *side*, adj., long, large, wide + *cote* coat — more at SIDE, COAT] *archaic* : GREATCOAT 1

side comb *n* : a short slightly-curved comb for holding a woman's hair in place esp. at the side of the head

side construction *n* : hollow structural blocks or tiles laid with the cells running horizontally — compare END CONSTRUCTION

side couple *n* : the couple at right angles to the head couple in a square dance set

side curtain *n* **1** : a curtain attached or fitted so as to be attached at the side of something (as a vehicle, window, or building) ⟨the *side curtains* of an automobile⟩ ⟨canvas *side curtains* for a tent⟩ **2 a** : one of several canvas weather cloths rigged vertically between the deck or the bulwarks and the ridgerope of a ship **b** : one of several similar cloths used to close the openings between the hull and the canopy of a small boat

1side cut *n* : an intersecting way (as a road, path, or canal) branching out from the main one

2side cut *n* : BREAKDOWN 5

side-cut \ˈ⸗,⸗\ *adj* : containing no pith — used of pieces of timber and lumber

side-cut brick *n* : wire-cut brick having the bed surfaces wire cut — compare END-CUT BRICK

side cutting *n* : material excavated outside the established slopes required for a roadbed

sid·ed \ˈsīdəd\ *adj* [ME, fr. *1side* + *-ed*] **1** : having or provided with sides ⟨a salad bowl ~ with fruit sections⟩ **2** : having sides of a specified number or of a specified kind or quality — used in combination ⟨steep-*sided*, sharp-peaked mountains —Joaquin Noval⟩ ⟨an open-*sided* structure . . . resembling an airplane hangar —*Amer. Guide Series: La.*⟩ ⟨a shingle-*sided* house⟩ — see MANY-SIDED, ONE-SIDED **3** : having a specified siding — used in shipbuilding

side degree *n* : one of various Masonic degrees conferred in the Cryptic rite

side-delivery rake *n* : a hay rake carrying teeth usu. on a reel that lift and push the hay to the side into a windrow at right angles to the forward path of the rake

side dish *n* : one of the foods subordinate to the main course of a meal

sid·ed·ness *n* -ES **1** : the quality or state of being sided in a specified way — usu. used in combination ⟨one-*sidedness*⟩ **2** : a tendency to functional dominance of complementary organs (as the hands or eyes) of one side of the body

side door *n* **1** : a door in one side of a structure or of a main door ⟨the large *side doors* were thrown open towards the sun to admit a bountiful light —Thomas Hardy⟩ **2** : an indirect or less conspicuous means of entrance ⟨trying to get religion back by the *side door* of the new physics —H.J.Laski⟩

side draft *n* **1** : the tendency of a tillage implement (as a plow) to move or be forced in a direction at right angles to the direction of its forward motion **2** : the amount of the force applied to overcome the direction of a side draft

side draw *n* : a ballroom step in which a dancer places one foot to the side and slides the other to it

side-dress \ˈ⸗,⸗\ *vi* : to place plant nutrients on or in the soil near the roots of a growing crop usu. beside each row and often by means of a cultivator having a fertilizer-distributing attachment ~ *vt* : to place plant nutrients on or in the soil near the roots of ⟨*side-dress* a crop⟩

side-dressing \ˈ⸗,⸗⸗\ *n* : the plant nutrients (as fertilizer) used to side-dress a crop

side drum *n* : SNARE DRUM

side effect *n* : an effect of a drug other than the one it was administered to evoke ⟨a fall in blood pressure often is a *side effect* of spinal anesthesia⟩ ⟨a *side effect* of drowsiness caused by antihistamines⟩ ⟨a *side effect* of chloroform may be damage to the liver⟩

side-end lines \ˈ⸗;⸗-\ *n pl* : the sidelines of a mining claim that are considered as end lines (as for determining extralateral rights)

side-eyed \ˈ⸗;⸗\ *adj* : having the eyes placed well to the sides of the head — used of a mammal (as a deer or rabbit) that depends much on visual acuity to escape danger

side face *n* : a face or a representation of a face seen in profile

side fender *n* : a fender constituted by fore-and-aft timbers faced with steel fastened on the outside of a ship's hull for protection

sideflash \ˈ⸗,⸗\ *n* [*1side* + *flash*] : a disruptive discharge between a conductor traversed by an oscillatory current of high frequency (as lightning) and neighboring masses of metal or between different parts of the same conductor

side frame *n* : either of the longitudinal side members of the frame of an automotive vehicle

side frequency *n* : any of the frequencies in the side band

side-glance \ˈ⸗,⸗\ *n* **1** : a glance directed to the side ⟨she shot an impatient *side-glance* at him —S.H.Adams⟩ **2** : a passing allusion : an indirect or slight reference : a cursory examination ⟨a rather suspicious *side-glance* at poetry —W.R.Benét⟩

side graft *n* : a plant graft in which the scion is inserted into the side of the stock and the aerial head of the stock permitted to grow until union is established between stock and scion — see PEG GRAFT

sidehall \ˈ⸗,⸗\ *adj* [*1side* + *hall*] : designed with an entrance to one side rather than at the center ⟨~ layout⟩ ⟨~ brick residence⟩

sidehead \ˈ⸗,⸗\ *n* [*1side* + *head*] **1** : an additional slide rest on a planer **2** : a subhead placed at or in the side of printed matter; *esp* : one placed in the left side of the first line of a paragraph in bookwork

1sidehill \ˈ⸗,⸗\ *n* [*1side* + *hill*] : HILLSIDE ⟨horses grazing up the ~ —H.L.Davis⟩

2sidehill \"\ *adj* **1** : used on or designed for sidehills ⟨a ~ attachment for farm machinery⟩ **2** : located on a sidehill ⟨a ~ road⟩ ⟨~ village⟩ ⟨~ land⟩

sidehill plow *n* : a reversible or two-way plow for turning all furrows to the lower side of the slope

sidehold \ˈ⸗,⸗\ *n* **1** : a hold in mountain climbing in which the edge or point of a projecting rock is grasped with the hand turned sideways **2** : a hold in wrestling in which each wrestler places his right arm around the opponent's waist and with the left hand grasps the opponent's right elbow

side horse *n* : a piece of apparatus made with a leather-covered cylindrical body having two pommels on top near the center, held parallel to the floor by two uprights attached to a steel frame and adjustable in height, and used in gymnastics esp. for vaulting — called also *horse;* compare LONG HORSE

side horse

side issue *n* : an issue apart from the main point : something of subordinate or incidental importance

side judge *n* : a judge seated at the side of the chief or presiding judge : an associate judge of a court

side keelson *n* : a reinforcing keelson between the main keelson and the commencement of the bilge curvature — called also *sister keelson;* see SHIP illustration

sidekick \ˈ⸗,⸗\ *also* **sidekicker** \ˈ⸗,⸗⸗\ *n* [*1side* + *kick* or *kicker*] : a person closely associated with another esp. in a subordinate capacity : ASSISTANT, PAL, PARTNER

side lamp *n* : a lighting unit on either side of a vehicle to indicate its location

side leather *n* : leather used generally for shoe uppers and made from cattlehide divided in the tanning process into two sides

side·less \ˈsīdləs\ *adj* : having no sides : open at the sides

side lever *n* : SIDE BEAM

sidelight \ˈ⸗,⸗\ *n* **1 a** *or* **side lighting** : light coming or produced from the side **b** (1) : incidental light or information upon a subject ⟨fragments of information and of ~ —Helen Macafee⟩ ⟨it throws so much ~ upon that rationalistic temper —William James⟩ (2) : a means of such incidental illustration or illumination ⟨curious ~*s* thrown upon the politics of appointments —*Saturday Rev.*⟩ ⟨throws many interesting ~*s* upon the Russian character —*Dial*⟩ ⟨giving humorous ~*s* on misadventures —*English Jour.*⟩ **2** : a narrow window flanking a door or larger window ⟨the paneled doorway is flanked by fluted columns and ~*s* —*Amer. Guide Series: La.*⟩ **3** : the red light on the port bow or the green light on the starboard bow carried by ships under way at night **4** : SIDE LAMP **5** : the thick glass covering of a ship's porthole

1sideline \ˈ⸗,⸗\ *n* **1** : a line extending along or marking the side of something; *esp* : a line running usu. at right angles to a goal line or end line and marking a side of an area (as a court or field of play) used for sports — see FIELD HOCKEY illustration **2 a** : a line of goods sold in addition to one's principal articles of trade **b** (1) : a course of business or activity pursued aside from one's regular occupation ⟨a farmer who had taken to writing as a ~ —A.J.P.Taylor⟩ (2) : something subsidiary to the principal subject considered ⟨his pursuit . . . took him into many interesting ~*s* —*Current Biog.*⟩ **3 a** : the space immediately outside the lines along either side of an athletic field or court — usu. used in pl. **b** : the standpoint of persons not immediately participating (as in an athletic contest) — usu. used in pl. — **on the sidelines** : out of action : confined to or choosing the role of a spectator rather than a participant ⟨when he was forbidden to play . . . fretted through a winter *on the sidelines* —W.B.Furlong⟩

2sideline \"\ *vt* [*1sideline*] **1** *West* : to restrain or hobble (an animal) by tying together the front and hind leg on the same side of the body **2** : to prevent (as a player) from taking part in a game or other activity ⟨a sore shoulder *sidelined* him⟩ ⟨has been *sidelined* with a broken arm⟩

side·lin·er \"+ə(r)\ *n* **1** : one that remains on the sidelines during an activity : one that does not participate **2** : SIDEWINDER 2

1side·ling *or* **sid·ling** \ˈsīdliŋ, -lēŋ\ *adv* [ME, fr. *1side* + *-ling*] **1** : in a sidelong direction : with a sideward movement : OBLIQUELY, SIDEWAYS **2** *obs* : on a sidesaddle

2sideling *or* **sidling** \"\ *adj* **1** : directed or moving toward one side : OBLIQUE ⟨with a ~ motion of the head —Hall Caine⟩ ⟨a ~ glance⟩ **2** : having an inclination : inclining or sloping to one side : STEEP ⟨~ hill⟩ ⟨~ ground⟩

3sideling \"\ *n* -S *chiefly dial* : SLOPE

side·lings \ˈsīd·lənz, -liŋz\ *also* **side·lins** \-lənz\ *adv* [ME *sidelinges*, fr. *1side* + *-linges* -lings] **1** *dial Brit* : SIDEWAYS **2** *dial Brit* : ALONGSIDE **3** *dial Brit* : FURTIVELY, STEALTHILY

sidelock \ˈ⸗,⸗\ *n* : a lock of hair falling at the side of the face and often worn as a distinguishing mark esp. by some Jews and by children in some cultures ⟨an old Jew . . . with a beard and ~*s* —Walter Sorell & Denver Lindley⟩ ⟨wearing the ~ of youth⟩

1sidelong \ˈ⸗,⸗\ *adv* [*1side* + *long*] **1** : in the direction of or along the side : LATERALLY, OBLIQUELY, SIDEWAYS ⟨darting eyes looking ~ out of a wizened face —*Irish Digest*⟩ ⟨glanced at them ~ —*Hearst's*⟩ **2** : with the side toward someone or something ⟨seated . . . ~ to the window —Nathaniel Hawthorne⟩ **3** : on the side : with one side to the ground or floor ⟨~ the plow beside the field-gate lay —William Morris⟩

2sidelong \"\ *adj* **1** : having a slanting direction or a sloping position : lying on or inclining to one side ⟨moved downwards in a ~ way —Bram Stoker⟩ ⟨~ country⟩ **2 a** : directed to one side or sideways ⟨the bashful virgin's ~ looks of love —Oliver Goldsmith⟩ ⟨~ glances⟩ **b** : moving or extending sideways ⟨shot out ~ boughs —Alfred Tennyson⟩ **c** : indirect rather than straightforward or open ⟨a ~ hope that there will be . . . reward in it —Frances Keene⟩

side-look \ˈ⸗,⸗\ *n* : a look or glance to one side : an oblique look ⟨a *side-look* from the girl was enough —Eden Phillpotts⟩

sideman \ˈ⸗,⸗\ *n, pl* **sidemen 1** *obs* : SIDESMAN 1 **2** : a member of a band or orchestra or of a section of a band or orchestra esp. a jazz or swing orchestra; *specif* : a supporting instrumentalist

side meat *n, chiefly South & Midland* : salt pork or bacon usu. from the sides of a hog

side milling *n* : the process of milling surfaces that are at right angles to the axis of rotation of the cutter with a side milling cutter

side milling cutter *n* : a cylindrical milling cutter with teeth on the circumferential surface and on both sides — see MILLING CUTTER illustration

side money *n* : the chips or money in a side pot in a poker game

side-necked \ˈ⸗;⸗\ *adj* : capable of bending the neck sideways but not of retracting it — used of turtles; compare PLEURODIRA

sidenote \ˈ⸗,⸗\ *n* : a note of reference that is set in the side margin of a page usu. in smaller type than the text

side oat *n* : an oat (*Avena orientalis*) in which the panicle usu. droops and the branches are on one side — usu. used in pl.

side oats grama *n* : a forage grass (*Bouteloua curtipendula*) of the southern U. S. having loosely flowered second racemes

side-on \ˈ⸗;⸗\ *adv* : with one side facing in a given direction esp. toward the observer

side out *n* : the termination of a team's right to serve (as in volleyball)

side paper *n* : plain or patterned paper used on the front and back covers of books

side partner *n* : one that works closely with another

sidepiece \ˈ⸗,⸗\ *n* : a piece forming or contained in the side of something ⟨the ~ of a window⟩ ⟨the ~ of a carriage⟩

side planer *n* : OPENSIDE PLANER

side play *n* : lateral freedom of motion in a moving machine part ⟨prevent *side play* in gears —*Motor Transportation*⟩

side pocket *n* : a pocket in or at one side (as of a garment or billiard table) ⟨hands in the *side pockets* of his . . . jacket —Rayne Kruger⟩ ⟨put the eight ball in the *side pocket*⟩

side porch *n* : a porch or the part of a porch at one side of a building

side port *n* : an opening in the side of a ship for handling cargo

side post *n* **1** : DOORJAMB **2** : a post supporting a roof at or near one side

side pot *n* : a second or subsequent pot in poker played with table stakes from which is excluded any player who has bet his entire table stake in a previous pot

1sider *n* -S [*4side* + *-er*] *obs* : one that takes a side : an adherent of a person : a partisan of a cause

2sid·er \ˈsīdə(r)\ *n* -S [*1side* + *-er*] : one placed or living in a usu. specified side (as an area or section of a city) — used in combination ⟨an east-*sider*⟩

sider- *or* **sidero-** *comb form* [MF, fr. L, fr. Gk *sidēr-*, *sidēro-*, fr. *sidēros*] : iron ⟨*sidero*lite⟩ ⟨*sidero*sis⟩

sideraerolite *var of* SIDEROLITE

side rail *n* : one of the long narrow members connecting the headboard and footboard of a bed

side rake *n* : the angle of deviation of a side of a cutting tool from a specified reference plane (as a plane normal to the surface of the work and parallel to the line of relative motion of tool and work)

sid·er·al \ˈsidərəl\ *adj* [MF, fr. L *sideralis*, fr. *sider-*, *sidus* star, constellation + *-alis* -al] **1** : SIDEREAL **2** *archaic* : emanating from the stars and esp. from stars held to be malefic : BALEFUL

siderate *vt* -ED/-ING/-S [L *sideratus*, past part. of *siderari* to be struck by a star, be sunstruck, fr. *sider-*, *sidus* star] *obs* : to blast or strike down (as with lightning)

sid·er·az·ot *or* **sid·er·az·ote** \ˌsidəˈra,zōt, -ərəˈzōt\ *n* -S [*sider-* + *azote*] : a mineral Fe_5N_2 consisting of a nitride of iron and found about Vesuvius and Etna volcanoes after various eruptions

side reaction *n* **1** : a less important reaction of two or more chemical reactions occurring at the same time ⟨undesirable complex *side reactions*⟩ — compare SIMULTANEOUS REACTION **2** : SIDE EFFECT

si·de·re·al \sīˈdirēəl\ *adj* [L *sidere*us sidereal (fr. *sider-*, *sidus* star, constellation + *-eus* -eous) + E *-al;* akin to Lith *svidus* shining and prob. to OHG *swīdan* to burn, ON *svītha* to burn, OE *swathul* smoke] **1 :** of or relating to stars or constellations ⟨~ system⟩ ⟨~ bodies⟩ **2 :** expressed in relation to the heavens above — see SIDEREAL TIME

sidereal astronomy *n* **:** a branch of astronomy that treats of the origin, nature, and relationship of the stars including the nebulas

sidereal clock *n* **:** an astronomical clock regulated to sidereal time

sidereal day *n* **:** the interval between two successive transits of the March equinox over the upper meridian of a place that is equal to 23 hours, 56 minutes, 4.09 seconds of mean solar time — compare SIDEREAL MIDNIGHT

sidereal hour *n* **:** the twenty-fourth part of a sidereal day

sidereal hour angle *n* **:** a coordinate in the equator system of coordinates used by navigators in place of right ascension, measured westward from the March equinox, and expressed in degrees up to 360°

sidereal midnight *n* **:** the instant when the March equinox crosses the lower meridian of a place — compare SIDEREAL DAY

sidereal minute *n* **:** the sixtieth part of a sidereal hour

sidereal month *n* **:** the mean time of the moon's revolution in its orbit from a star back to the same star **:** 27 days, 7 hours, 43 minutes, 11.5 seconds of mean solar time

sidereal noon *n* **:** the instant when the March equinox crosses the upper meridian of a place

sidereal period *or* **sidereal revolution** *n* **:** the time in which a planet or satellite completes one revolution round its primary as referred to a star seen from the primary

sidereal second *n* **:** the sixtieth part of a sidereal minute — compare SECOND 2

sidereal time *n* **1 :** time based on the sidereal day consisting of 24 hours of sidereal minutes and seconds **2 :** the hour angle of the March equinox at a place

sidereal year *n* **:** the time in which the earth completes one revolution in its orbit around the sun measured with respect to the fixed stars **:** 365 days, 6 hours, 9 minutes, and 9.54 seconds of solar time

side relief angle *n* **:** the angle between the part of the flanks of a cutting tool below the cutting edge and a plane perpendicular to the base

sid·er·in yellow \ˈsidərən-\ *n* [*sider-* + *-in*] **1 :** a pale yellow pigment consisting of a basic iron chromate, used esp. mixed with water glass and giving a very durable paint **2 :** MARS YELLOW 2

sid·er·ism \ˈsidə,rizəm\ *n* -s [NL *siderismus*, fr. *sider-* + L *-ismus* -ism] **:** a phenomenon similar to animal magnetism formerly supposed to result from the bringing of iron or other inorganic bodies into connection with the human body

¹sid·er·ite \ˈsidə,rīt, *usu* -īd +V\ *n* -s [*sider-* + *-ite*] **1 a** *archaic* **:** PHARMACOSIDERITE **b** *archaic* **:** HORNBLENDE **c** *archaic* **:** SAPPHIRE QUARTZ **d** *obs* **:** LAZULITE **e :** HOLOSIDERITE **2 :** a nickel-iron meteorite

²siderite \"\ *n* -s [G *siderit*, fr. *sider-* + *-it* -ite] **:** a native ferrous carbonate $FeCO_3$ that occurs in rhombohedral crystals often with curved faces, in cleavable or granular masses, and in botryoid and globular forms, that may also contain manganese and magnesium, that is usu. light yellowish brown but is sometimes white or gray, that contains 48.2 percent of iron when pure, and that is a valuable iron ore — called also *chalybite, sparry iron, spathic iron*

sid·er·it·ic \ˌsidəˈrid·ik\ *adj* [¹*siderite* + *-ic*] **:** of, relating to, or containing siderite ⟨~ limestone⟩

sid·er·i·tis \ˌsidəˈrīd·əs\ *n, cap* [NL, fr. L, ironwort, fr. Gk *sidēritis*, fr. fem. of *sidēritēs* of iron, fr. *sidēr-* + *-itēs* -ite] **:** a genus of European woolly mints having small flowers with the corolla included in the calyx

¹sidero- — see SIDER-

²sidero- *comb form* [L *sider-, sidus* star, constellation — more at SIDEREAL] **1 :** star ⟨*sidero*mancy⟩ ⟨*sidero*stat⟩ **2 :** sidereal ⟨*sidero*graph⟩

side road *n* **:** a road off a main road **:** a feeder or branch road

sid·er·o·cyte \ˈsidərə,sīt\ *n* -s [*sider-* + *-cyte*] **:** an atypical red blood cell containing iron not bound in hemoglobin

side rod *n* **1 :** either of the rods connecting the piston-rod crosshead with the side levers in a side-lever engine **2 :** a steel rod connecting the crankpins of any two adjoining driving wheels on the same side of a locomotive to distribute power from the main rod to each of the driving wheels **:** COUPLING ROD

sid·er·o·graph \ˈsidərə,graf, -rȧf\ *n* [²*sidero-* + *-graph*] **:** a combination clock and navigation device that keeps the sidereal time of the Greenwich meridian of longitude

sid·er·og·ra·pher \ˌsidəˈrägrəfə(r)\ *n* -s [ISV *sider-* + *-grapher*] **:** one that makes steel plate engravings

sid·er·o·graph·ic \ˌsidərəˈgrafik\ *adj* [ISV *sider-* + *-graphic*] **:** of, relating to, or executed by siderography ⟨~ art⟩ ⟨~ impressions⟩

sid·er·og·ra·phy \ˌsidəˈrägrəfē\ *n* -ES [ISV *sider-* + *-graphy*] **:** the art of engraving steel; *esp* **:** a process of multiplying facsimiles of an engraved steel plate by rolling over it when hardened a soft steel cylinder and then rolling the cylinder when hardened over a soft steel plate

sid·er·o·lite \ˈsidərə,līt\ *or* **sid·er·aerolite** \ˌsidə(r)+\ *n* -s [*siderolite* fr. *sider-* + *-lite*; *sideraerolite* fr. *sider-* + *aerolite*] **:** a stony iron meteorite **:** one containing at least 25 percent of both metal and stone

sid·er·o·mel·ane \ˌsidərəˈme,lān\ *n* -s [G *sideromelan*, fr. *sider-* + *-melan* -melane] **:** OBSIDIAN

sid·er·o·na·trite \ˌsidərəˈnā,trīt\ *n* -s [It, fr. *sider-* + *natr-* + *-ite*] **:** a mineral $Na_2Fe(SO_4)_2(OH).3H_2O$ consisting of a basic hydrous sulfate of sodium and iron occurring in fibrous yellow masses

sid·er·o·phile \ˈsidərə,fīl\ *adj* [ISV *sider-* + *-phile*] **:** having so little affinity for oxygen and sulfur that in a molten mass the greatest concentration (as of an element) would be found in the metallic phase (as in the iron of a blast furnace) — compare CHALCOPHILE, OXYPHILE

sid·er·oph·i·lin \ˌsidəˈräfələn\ *n* -s [*sider-* + *-phil* + *-in*] **:** TRANSFERRIN

sid·er·ose \ˈsidə,rōs\ *adv* [ISV *sider-* + *-ose*] **:** full of or like iron

sid·er·o·sis \ˌsidəˈrōsəs\ *n* -ES [NL, fr. *sider-* + *-osis*] **1 :** pneumoconiosis occurring in iron workers from inhalation of particles of iron **2 :** deposit of iron pigment in a tissue

sid·er·o·stat \ˈsidərə,stat\ *n* -s [ISV ²*sidero-* + *-stat*] **:** an equatorially mounted mirror moved by clockwork to reflect the rays of a celestial body observed in a constant usu. horizontal direction — compare HELIOSTAT

sid·er·o·stat·ic \ˌ==ˈstad·ik\ *adj* **:** of, relating to, or consisting of a siderostat

sid·er·ot·ic \ˌsidəˈräd·ik\ *adj* [*sider-* + *-otic*] **:** of or relating to siderosis

sid·er·o·til \ˈsidərə,til\ *n* -s [G *siderotyl*, fr. *sider-* + *-tyl* (irreg. fr. Gk *tilos* anything plucked, fiber, fr. *tillein* to pluck)] **:** a mineral $FeSO_4.5H_2O$ consisting of hydrous ferrous sulfate

sid·er·ous \ˈsidərəs\ *adj* [*sider-* + *-ous*] **:** FERROUS

sid·er·ox·y·lon \ˌsidəˈräksə,län\ *n, cap* [NL, fr. *sider-* + *-xylon*] **:** a large genus of tropical trees (family Sapotaceae) having very hard wood and somewhat bell-shaped regular pentamerous flowers and round few-seeded berries — compare IRONWOOD

side run *n* **:** paper made to utilize the full width of the paper machine wire but differing in width from the main portion of the run

sides *pl of* SIDE, *pres 3d sing of* SIDE

¹sidesaddle \ˈ=,==\ *n* [ME *sid saddil*, fr. *sid*, side side + *saddil*, *sadel* saddle — more at SIDE, SADDLE] **:** a saddle for women in which the rider sits with both legs on the same side of the horse

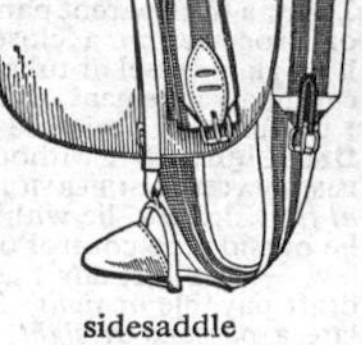

sidesaddle

²sidesaddle \"\ *adv* **:** on or as if on a sidesaddle ⟨the girl rode ~⟩

sidesaddle flower *also* **sidesaddle** *n* **1 :** a common pitcher plant (*Sarracenia purpurea*) **2 :** the flower of the sidesaddle flower

side scene *n* **1 a :** a wing in a theater **b :** a movable piece of stage scenery **2 :** a dramatic scene occurring to one side of the main action

sidescraper \ˈ=,==\ *n* [¹*side* + *scraper*] **:** a prehistoric flint scraper having a curved scraping edge on one side

side-sew \ˈ=,=\ *vt* **:** to fasten (as a book or magazine) with a side stitch usu. of thread

sideshake \ˈ=,=\ *n* [¹*side* + *shake*] **1 :** a shake or play from side to side **2 a :** the free space between a timepiece pivot and the inside surface of its bearing **b :** the distance of this space

side shot *n* **:** a survey reading to locate a point off the traverse

sideshow \ˈ=,=\ *n* **1 :** a subsidiary show accompanying or part of a main exhibition (as of a circus) **:** a minor attraction **2 :** an incidental diversion ⟨the constant danger of dispersing military strength on ~s —J.P.Marquand⟩ ⟨comedy admits of interludes and ~s —James Smith⟩ ⟨regarding student activities as a sort of educational ~ —D.D.Feder⟩

side shuffle *n* **:** an American Indian round dance step consisting of a sideward shuffling with flexible knees

¹sideslip \ˈ=,=\ *vi* [³*side* + *slip*] **:** to slip or skid sideways: as **a :** to skid sideways — used esp. of an automobile or cycle **b :** to slide sideways through the air in a downward direction along an inclined lateral axis; *esp* **:** to slide in such a manner while turning — used of something (as an airplane) in flight **c :** to slide sideways in a downward direction in skiing (as by slightly advancing one ski and edging both skiis slightly for retardation)

²sideslip \"\ *n* **1 :** the action of sideslipping **2 :** an instance of sideslipping

sides·man \ˈsīdzmən\ *n, pl* **sidesmen** [*sides* (poss. of ¹*side*) + *man*] **1 :** an assistant to the churchwarden of a parish **2 :** one who directs shunting in collieries

sidespin \ˈ=,=\ *n* [¹*side* + *spin*] **:** a rotary motion that causes a ball to revolve horizontally

sidesplitter \ˈ=,==\ *n* **:** one that is sidesplitting; *specif* **:** an exceedingly funny story or joke

sidesplitting \ˈ=,==\ *adj* **:** affecting the sides convulsively (as with laughter) ⟨a ~ yarn⟩

side sprig *n* **:** a lateral growth on the comb of a fowl that is considered a defect in an exhibition bird

side step *n* **1 a :** a step aside (as in boxing to avoid a blow) **b :** a step taken sideways (as when climbing on skis) **2 :** a step attached at the side of something ⟨climbed the *side steps* to the porch⟩

sidestep \ˈ=,=\ *vb* [³*side* + *step*] *vi* **1 :** to take a side step **2 :** to avoid meeting an issue, taking a stand, or making a decision ⟨men who know how to dodge, trim, and ~ —C.M. Fassett⟩ ~ *vt* **1 :** to avoid (as a blow) esp. by moving to one side **2 :** to avoid as if by physical movement **:** EVADE ⟨~ issues⟩ ⟨~ responsibility⟩ ⟨~ a question⟩ **syn** see DODGE

sidestepper \ˈ=,==\ *n* **:** one that sidesteps

sidestick \ˈ=,=\ *n* **:** a wooden or metal strip that when wedged with quoins secures one side of a locked-up type page in printing

side stitch *or* **side-thread stitch** *n* **:** a stitch made by passing thread or wire from side to side through a complete book or magazine before covering — called also *side-wire stitch*

sidestitch \ˈ=,=\ *vt* [*side stitch*] **:** to fasten by means of side stitches

side strap *n* **:** a strap attached to or fitted to be attached to the side of an object (as in harness)

side street *n* **:** a street joining and terminated by a main thoroughfare — compare BACK STREET, CROSS STREET

side stringer *n* **:** a structure similar to a keelson between the turn of the bilge and the lowest deck beams of a ship

side-striped jackal \ˈ=,=-\ *n* **:** a common African jackal (*Canis adustus*)

¹sidestroke \ˈ=,=\ *n* **:** a stroke made by a swimmer while lying on his side in which the arms are alternately worked forward and backward without breaking water, and the legs execute a scissors kick

²sidestroke \"\ *vi* [¹*sidestroke*] **:** to swim by using a sidestroke

side suit *n* **1 :** a suit other than the trump suit in a card game (as bridge) **2 :** a long suit held in addition to trumps

sidesway \ˈ=,=\ *n* [¹*side* + *sway*] **:** the action of swaying from side to side — used esp. of an automotive vehicle ⟨a good car should . . . take curves without excessive ~ —*advt*⟩

sideswept \ˈ=,=\ *adj* [¹*side* + *swept*] **:** pulled or arranged to one side — used esp. of an asymmetrical clothing design or a hairdo

¹sideswipe \ˈ=,=\ *vt* [prob. fr. ³*side* + *swipe*] **1 :** to strike with a glancing blow along the side ⟨*sideswiped* a parked car⟩ ⟨the derailed cars were *sideswiped* by an express train⟩ **2 :** to block (an opponent in football) by throwing one's body across the legs from the side

²sideswipe \"\ *n* **1 a :** the action of sideswiping **b :** an instance of sideswiping **:** a glancing blow **2 :** a criticism made in passing **:** an incidental deprecatory remark, allusion, or reference ⟨the author takes some well-aimed ~s at our foreign policy —*New Yorker*⟩

side table *n* [ME] **1 :** a table (as a console table or pier table) designed to be placed against a wall **2 :** a table placed at the side of or apart from the main table **:** a table set at or toward one side of a room **3 :** a usu. large table used as a sideboard until near the 19th century

sidetone \ˈ=,=\ *n* **1 :** the sound heard in a telephone receiver originating in signals being picked up by the associated transmitter **2 :** the sound of a speaker's voice as received at his own ears

side tool *n* **:** a tool with its principal cutting edge on one side rather than on the end

¹sidetrack \ˈ=,=\ *n* [¹*side* + *track*] **1 :** SIDING **2 :** a position or condition of secondary importance to which one may be diverted

²sidetrack \"\ *vt* **1 :** to transfer to a railroad siding from a main line ⟨the president's special train was ~*ed* to clear the main line —*Spokane (Wash.) Spokesman-Rev.*⟩ **2 a :** to turn aside from a purpose **:** divert (as from the main subject or principal trend of action) into another and usu. less important channel ⟨~ a person⟩ **b :** to divert to a position that is relatively secondary (as in activity, importance, or effectiveness) **:** reduce to a subordinate condition **:** prevent action upon by diversionary tactics ⟨~ an issue⟩ ⟨~ a question⟩ ⟨~ a problem⟩

side trip *n* **:** an excursion incidental to a trip

side vault *n* **:** FLANK VAULT

side view *n* **1 :** a view from the side **:** a view apart from the main view **2 :** a view of a person or object presenting a side instead of a front toward the observer or camera **:** a profile view

sidewalk \ˈ=,=\ *n* **:** a walk for foot passengers usu. at the side of a street or roadway **:** a foot pavement

sidewalk artist *n* **:** an artist who makes drawings usu. with chalk directly on the sidewalk to obtain money from passersby

sidewalk bike *n* **:** a child's bicycle having a usu. detachable extra wheel placed on either side of the rear wheel to serve as support and guidance for a child learning to ride a bicycle

sidewalk bike

sidewalk bridge *n* **:** a temporary bridge over an excavation or obstruction in the area of a sidewalk

sidewalk door *n* **:** a cellar door opening out of a sidewalk and lying flush with the sidewalk when closed

sidewalk elevator *n* **:** an elevator or lift operating through a sidewalk esp. for the handling of goods or refuse

sidewalk superintendent *n* **:** one that watches demolition or construction work in progress

sidewall \ˈ=,=\ *n* [ME *side-wall*, fr. ¹*side* + *wall*] **:** a wall forming the side of something: as **a :** FOURCHETTE 2 **b :** the side of an automotive tire between the tread shoulder and the rim bead

¹side·ward \ˈsīdwə(r)d\ *or* **side·wards** \-dz\ *adv* [*sideward* fr. ME *side-warde*, fr. ¹*side* + *-warde* -ward; *sidewards* fr. ¹*side* + *-wards*] **:** toward the side **:** to one side or the other ⟨turning a figure ~ —Kenneth Croft⟩ ⟨the craft can be flown . . . *sidewards* —S.A.Constantino⟩

²sideward \"\ *or* **sidewards** \"\ *adj* **:** moving, directed, or tending toward one side ⟨a soulful ~ glance —James Lord⟩ ⟨the extreme end of its *sidewards* journey —B.E.Ellis⟩

sidewash \ˈ=,=\ *n* [¹*side* + *wash*] **:** the lateral flow of the air about an airfoil or airplane

¹sideway \ˈ=,=\ *n* **1 :** a way (as a road or path) lying to the side of or diverging from a main road **:** BYWAY **2 :** a roadside path **:** SIDEWALK

²sideway \"\ *adv (or adj)* [¹*side* + *way*] **:** SIDEWAYS

¹side·ways \ˈsīd,wāz\ *adv* [¹*side* + *-ways*] **1 :** from the side ⟨the scenes are viewed ~ —*Eastman Kodak Monthly Abstract Bull.*⟩ **2 :** with one side to the front or in advance **:** with the side rather than the face, front, or end presented to view **:** with the side foremost **:** in a position so as to offer one side ⟨lie ~⟩ ⟨turn ~⟩ **3 a :** to, toward, or at one side horizontally **:** in a lateral or sideward direction **:** OBLIQUELY ⟨slip ~⟩ ⟨glance ~⟩ ⟨swim ~⟩ **b :** downward on one side **:** with an inclination downward and to one side ⟨leaning ~⟩ **c :** with a slighting, scornful, or flirting glance ⟨look ~ at someone⟩

²sideways \"\ *adj* **:** moving, directed, or tending toward one side **:** INDIRECT ⟨~ glances⟩ ⟨a ~ movement⟩

side-wedge graft *n* **:** PEG GRAFT

side-wheel \ˈ=,=\ *adj* **:** of, relating to, or constituting a steamer having a paddle wheel on each side

side-wheeler \ˈ=,==\ *n* **1 :** a side-wheel steamer **2 :** PACER 1b **3 :** a left-handed baseball pitcher **:** SOUTHPAW

side whip graft *n* **:** a whip graft in which the scion is placed on the side of the stock

side-whiskered \ˈ=,==\ *adj* [*side-whiskers* + *-ed*] **:** having or characterized by side-whiskers ⟨a *side-whiskered* old gentleman⟩

side-whiskers \ˈ=,==\ *n pl* **:** whiskers on the side of the face usu. worn long

side wind *n* [ME] **1 :** a wind from or on one side **2 :** an indirect attack, means, method, or manner

side-wind \ˈ=,=\ *adj* [*side wind*] **1 :** INDIRECT **2 :** ILLEGITIMATE

sidewinder \ˈ=,==\ *n* [¹*side* + *winder*] **1 :** a heavy swinging blow from the side **2 :** a small pale-colored desert rattlesnake (*Crotalus cerastes*) of the southwestern U.S. that does not crawl but moves by throwing the body forward in a series of loops — called also *horned rattlesnake* **3 a :** a falling tree that upon hitting another tree rolls on its axis **b :** a tree knocked down by a falling tree

side-wire \ˈ=,=\ *vt* **:** to fasten (as a book or magazine) with a side stitch

side-wire stitch *n* **:** SIDE STITCH

sidewise \ˈ=,=\ *adv (or adj)* **:** SIDEWAYS

side yard *n* **:** an area adjoining one side of a house or other building

sidhe *also* **shee** \ˈshē\ *n, pl* **sidhe** *or* **sidhes** [partly fr. Ir *sīdh* fairy hill; partly fr. Ir *sīdhe* fairy folk] **1** *pl* **sidhes :** an underground fort or palace in which fairies in Gaelic folklore are held to live **2 a** *sidhe pl* **:** the fairy folk of Ireland in Gaelic folklore **b :** a member of the sidhe **:** a fairy in Gaelic folklore — compare BANSHEE

¹si·di \ˈsēdē\ *n* -s [Ar (in India and Africa) *sīdī*, fr. *sayyidī* my lord, fr. *sayyid* lord] **1 :** an African Muslim holding a high position under a King of the Deccan — used as a title of respect **2** *India & East Africa* **a :** ETHIOPIAN **b :** NEGRO

²sidi *var of* SAYYID

siding *n* -s [fr. gerund of ⁴*side*] **1** *archaic* **:** the action of taking sides (as in a debate or conflict) **:** attachment to a party **:** PARTISANSHIP ⟨seriously religious without any taint of ~ or faction —Richard Baxter⟩ **2 :** the dimensions of a ship's timber measured parallel to the center line — opposed to *molding* **3** *or* **siding track a :** a short railroad track connected by switches or points at one or more places with the main track and used esp. to enable trains to pass each other or to provide a storage place for temporarily idle cars — called also *sidetrack* **b :** a short track connecting a railroad directly with the premises of a business concern **4 :** material (as boards or metal sections) of special design usu. nailed horizontally to vertical studs with or without intervening sheathing to form the exposed surface of outside walls of frame buildings — see BEVEL SIDING, DROP SIDING **5 :** a passing place for ships in a canal **6 :** a board cut from the outer portion of a log of which the central portion becomes a timber — compare SLAB

siding tool *n* **:** SIDE TOOL

¹si·dle \ˈsīdᵊl\ *vb* **sidled; sidled; sidling** \-d(ᵊ)liŋ\ **sidles** [prob. back-formation fr. ¹*sideling*] *vi* **:** to go or move with one side foremost **:** move sideways esp. in a furtive advance **:** advance obliquely in an unobtrusive manner ⟨when a seedy-looking man ~s up to you —T.H.Fielding⟩ ⟨edgewise I *sidled* through the narrow aperture —*Pall Mall Mag.*⟩ ⟨the little ship slowly *sidled* away from her sister craft —L.C. Douglas⟩ ~ *vt* **:** to cause to move or turn sideways **:** direct sideways ⟨*sidled* his horse back along the wagon —Jackson Burgess⟩ ⟨the pilot *sidled* the boat up to the dock⟩

²sidle \"\ *n* -s **:** the act or action of sidling

sidling *var of* SIDELING

¹si·do·ni·an \sīˈdōnēən\ *n* -s *cap* [LL *Sidonii*, pl., Sidonians (fr. L, fr. Gk *Sidōnioi*, fr. *Sidōn* Sidon, fr. Heb *Ṣīdōn*) + E *-an*] **:** a native or inhabitant of Sidon

²sidonian \"\ *adj, usu cap* [L *sidonius* (fr. Gk *sidōnios*, fr. *Ṣīdōn*) + E *-an*] **:** of or relating to the ancient seaport Sidon in Phoenicia

si·dot blende \səˈdō-\ *n, usu cap S* [ISV, after T. *Sidot*, 19th cent. Fr. chemist] **:** a synthetic highly phosphorescent crystalline zinc sulfide

sid·ra \ˈsidrə\ *or* **sed·ra** \ˈsed-\ *n, pl* **sidras** \ˈsidrəz\ *or* **sid·roth** *or* **sid·rot** \ˈsi,drōt(h)\ *or* **sedras** \ˈsedrəz\ *or* **sed·roth** *or* **sed·rot** \ˈse,drōt(h)\ [LHeb *sidrāh*, lit., order, arrangement, fr. Heb *sēder* order] **:** a weekly portion of the Pentateuch read in the synagogue on the Sabbath

sids *pl of* SID

sie \ˈsī\ *vb* [ME *sien, syen* to strain, fr. OE *sīon, sēon* to strain, filter — more at SACK] *vt, chiefly Scot* **:** STRAIN ~ *vi, dial Brit* **:** DROP, DRIP

sieg·bahn unit \ˈsēg,bän-\ *n, usu cap S* [after Karl Manne Georg *Siegbahn* b1886 Swed. physicist] **:** X UNIT

¹siege \ˈsēj\ *n* -s *often attrib* [ME *sege*, fr. OF, seat, act of sitting, act or instance of settling, siege, fr. (assumed) VL *sedicum*, fr. *sedicare* to sit, settle, fr. L *sedēre* to sit — more at SIT] **1** *obs* **a :** a seat usu. of distinction (as in a theater) for a knight **b :** THRONE **2** *obs* **:** a center of power or authority **:** SEE, SEAT **3 a :** the operations of an army around or before a fortified place for the purpose of compelling its surrender or of reducing it by assault after systematic blockade, advances, and bombardment; *broadly* **:** BESIEGING, BELEAGUERING ⟨the battlement on which 15 Americans were to withstand . . . an arm's length ~ by a force tenfold their strength —S.L.A.Marshall⟩ ⟨a weapon designed to conduct ~ operations —*Time*⟩ **b :** a persistent attack (as of illness or other misfortune) ⟨a ~ of typhoid fever⟩ ⟨the ~ of age-old fears —Francis Ratcliffe⟩ **c :** a period of time esp. when trying ⟨a ~ in the territorial prison and also a term in the insane asylum —D.D.Martin⟩ ⟨your ~ in the hospital —Louis Auchincloss⟩ **d :** a large amount **:** QUANTITY ⟨didn't get around much because of having such a ~ of work to be done —Eugene Walter⟩ ⟨after a ~ of persuasion agreed to visit the recruiting station —*Springfield (Mass.) Union*⟩ **4** *obs* **a :** PRIVY **b :** evacuation of the bowels **c :** fecal matter **d** (1) **:** ANUS (2) **:** RECTUM **5** *or* **sedge** \ˈsej\ **:** a flock or brood of birds (as herons or bitterns); *also* **:** the station of a heron on the lookout for prey **6 :** the floor of a glass furnace **7 :** a hewer's workbench — **lay siege to 1 :** to besiege militarily ⟨*laid siege to* the town⟩ **2 :** to pursue diligently or persistently **:** BESIEGE ⟨*lays siege to* Anastasie and is making excellent progress until he ventures a clumsy reference to her father —E.K.Brown⟩ ⟨*laid* diplomatic *siege to* the Greeks —Alexander Kendrick⟩

²siege \"\ *vt* -ED/-ING/-S [ME *segen*, fr. *sege*, n., siege] **:** BESIEGE ⟨mankind is sorely *sieged* by hate's black hordes —E.P.Fewster⟩

siege coin *or* **siege piece** *n* **:** a coin issued for use during a siege

sie·gen·ite \ˈsēgə,nīt, ˈzē-\ *n* -s [*Siegen*, city in western Germany, its locality + E *-ite*] **:** a mineral $(Co,Ni)_3S_4$ consisting of sulfide of nickel and cobalt isomorphous with linnaeite, violarite, carrollite, and polydymite

sieg·er \'sējə(r)\ *n* -s [²*siege* + *-er*] : BESIEGER

siege tower *n* : TOWER 1d

sie·mens's law \'sēmənz(əz)-, 'zē-\ *n, usu cap S* [after Werner von *Siemens* †1892 Ger. electrical engineer and inventor, its formulator] : a statement in electricity: the greater the ratio of counter electromotive force to impressed electromotive force in a motor, the greater is its efficiency

si·ena \sē'enə\ *n* -s *often cap* [after *Siena,* city in central Italy] : VENETIAN RED 2a

¹si·en·ese *also* **si·en·nese** \ˌsēə'nēz, -ˈnēs\ *n, pl* **sienese** *cap* [*sienese* fr. It, fr. *Siena,* city in central Italy + It *-ese; siennese* fr. *Sienna, Siena,* Italy + E *-ese*] : a native or resident of Siena

²sienese *also* **siennese** \"\ *adj, usu cap* [*sienese* fr. It, fr. *Siena,* Italy + It *-ese* (adj. & n. suffix); *siennese* fr. *Sienna, Siena,* Italy + E *-ese* (adj. & n. suffix)] **1 :** of or relating to Siena, Italy; *also* : characteristic of Siena or the Sienese **2 :** being in or following a style of art ascribed traditionally to Siena and marked by a decorative surface treatment, delicate painting, and a conservative approach to religious iconography — compare FLORENTINE

si·en·na \sē'enə\ *n* -s [short for earlier *terra-sienna,* modif. of It *terra di Siena* earth of Siena, fr. *terra* earth (fr. L) + *di* of (fr. L *de* from, away) + *Siena,* Italy — more at DE-, TERRACE] : any of various earthy substances that are brownish yellow when raw and orange red to reddish brown when burnt, that in general are darker in color and more transparent in oils than ochers, that occur in limonites, and that are used as pigments for oil stains as well as paints — compare IRON OXIDE, UMBER

sienna brown *n* : a moderate brown that is deeper than auburn and redder and deeper than chestnut brown — called also *teak*

siennese drab *n, often cap S* : a light grayish brown to reddish brown that is duller than sandstone and paler than wood rose

sien–pi \'syen'pē\ *n, pl* **sien–pi** *or* **sien–pis** *usu cap* **1 :** a Tartar people orig. of Mongolia and later of northern Korea **2 :** a member of the Sien-pi people

si·er·o·zem \sē'erəˌzem\ *or* **ser·o·zem** \ˈser-\ *n* -s [Russ *serozem,* fr. *seryĭ* gray + *zemlya* earth; akin to Lith *žemė* earth, L *humus* — more at HUMBLE] : any of a group of zonal soils that are brownish gray at the surface and lighter colored below, based in a carbonate layer or a hardpan layer, and characteristic of temperate to cool arid regions with mixed shrub vegetation

¹si·er·ra \sē'erə\ *n* -s [Sp, lit., saw, fr. L *serra* saw] **1 a :** a range of mountains esp. with a serrated or irregular outline ⟨the wild ~ overhead, the desert's death below —J.G.Whittier⟩ — often used in pl. ⟨never lost sight of the towering ~*s* —*Library of Congress Information Bull.*⟩ ⟨north of Lake Tahoe the ~*s* are divided —W.W.Atwood †1949⟩ **b :** a mountainous region ⟨in the ~, the prevailing pattern among the Indian population is subsistence farming —*Internat'l Reference Service*⟩ ⟨the southern ~ fairly bristles with distinguished art —*Scientific Monthly*⟩ **2 :** any of various large fishes (genus *Scomberomorus*) that resemble mackerel: as **a :** CERO **b :** either of two common Spanish mackerel (*S. maculatus* and *S. sierra*) **3** *often cap* : VENETIAN RED 2a

²sierra \"\ *usu cap* — a communications code word for the letter *s*

sierra brownbark pine *n* : PONDEROSA PINE

sierra juniper *n* : WESTERN CEDAR 1

sier·ra le·one \sēˌerəlē'ōn, *chiefly Brit* ˌsirə-\ *adj, usu cap S & L* [fr. *Sierra Leone,* West Africa] : of or from Sierra Leone : of the kind or style prevalent in Sierra Leone

¹sier·ra le·on·e·an \sēˌerəlē'ōnēən, ˌsirə-\ *adj, usu cap S&L* [*Sierra Leone,* West Africa + E *-an* (adj. suffix)] **1 :** of, relating to, or characteristic of Sierra Leone, West Africa **2 :** of, relating to, or characteristic of Sierra Leoneans

²sierra leonean \"\ *n, pl* **sierra leoneans** *cap S&L* [*Sierra Leone,* West Africa + E *-an* (n. suffix)] : a native or resident of Sierra Leone; *esp* : a native of Sierra Leone claiming no tribal affiliation

sierra leone peach *n, usu cap S&L* : COUNTRY FIG 1

¹si·er·ran \sē'erən\ *adj* [¹*sierra* + *-an*] **1 :** of or relating to a sierra, the region around it, or its inhabitants **2** *usu cap* : of or relating to the Sierra Nevada mountains of the western U.S. ⟨the Rocky and *Sierran* mountain systems —A.C.Kinsey⟩ ⟨darkness had accompanied a *Sierran* stagecoach toward the summit —Bret Harte⟩

²sierran \"\ *n* -s *cap* [*Sierra* Nevada, mountain range in eastern Calif. + E *-an*] : a native or inhabitant of the region around the Sierra Nevada mountains ⟨about one hundred . . . Appalachians and *Sierrans* were gathered around a campfire —*Out West*⟩

sierra plum *n* : a shrub or small tree (*Prunus subcordata*) of the Pacific coast of the U.S. with somewhat spinescent branches and small red insipid fruit

sierra redbark pine *n* : JEFFREY PINE

sierra shrew *n, usu cap 1st S* : a small upland shrew (*Sorex vagrans amoenus*) of the western U.S.

-sies *pl of* -SY

¹si·es·ta \sē'estə\ *n* -s [Sp, fr. L *sexta* (*hora*) sixth (hour) (i.e., after sunrise), noon, fr. *sexta,* fem. of *sextus* sixth + *hora* hour — more at SEXT, HOUR] : an afternoon nap or rest in some usu. Latin countries and esp. formerly so customary that business is usu. suspended daily to allow for it ⟨when he slept his ~ (as the Spaniard calls it) —James Howell⟩ ⟨the honored Italian ~ —*Time*⟩; *also* : a short sleep or rest ⟨about nine or ten in the morning the sheep settle down to a ~⟩ ⟨take a ~ for twenty minutes or so —Anita Colby⟩ — sometimes used without the article ⟨the hour of ~⟩ ⟨roused the . . . museum guardian from ~ —Claudia Cassidy⟩

²siesta \"\ *vi* -ED/-ING/-S : to take a siesta : NAP ⟨could not ~ with the argument going on —Gerald Durrell⟩

sie·va bean \'sēvə-\ *also* **see·wee bean** *or* **se·wee bean** \'sēwē-\ *n* [*sieva, seewee, sewee* of unknown origin] **1 :** any of several bush or weakly vining beans that are derived from a tropical American annual species (*Phaseolus lunatus*), are closely related to and sometimes classed as lima beans, and are cultivated esp. in the southern U.S. for their small flat edible seeds — compare JAVA BEAN **2 :** the seed of a sieva bean — called also *butter bean*

¹sieve \'siv\ *n* -s [ME *sive, seve,* fr. OE *sife;* akin to MD *seve* sieve, OHG *sib* sieve, ON *sef* rush (plant), Serb *sipiti* to drizzle; basic meaning: drip, trickle] **1 a :** a meshed or perforated device or utensil through which dry loose material (as flour or ashes) is winnowed or refined, material containing liquid is strained, and soft solids (as hard-boiled eggs) are comminuted by forcing (as with a pestle); *sometimes* : SIFTER **b :** material meshed or perforated like a sieve ⟨strips of ~⟩ **2 :** a meshed or perforated sheet (as of metal or cloth) with apertures of uniform size used to separate powdered or granulated material according to the size of its particles as: **a :** one woven from wire cloth having square apertures and used chiefly in a chemistry laboratory **b :** a rectangular wooden frame covered with wire screen on one side and silk cloth on the other and used in a flour-milling sifter **3 :** GOSSIP ⟨the ~ of a patron let it out —Lord Byron⟩ **4** *slang* : a body riddled by bullets ⟨made a mistake trying to kill his ex-wife's new husband — ending up a ~ —Bill O'Rourke⟩ **5 :** SIEVE OF ERATOSTHENES — usu. used with *the* ⟨first proposed by the ancient Greek philosopher and mathematician Eratosthenes and . . . usually known as the ~ —George Gamow⟩

sieve 1a with pestle

²sieve \"\ *vb* -ED/-ING/-S *vt* **1 a :** to put through a sieve or sifter or meshed material ⟨*sieved* avocado⟩ ⟨~ the cocoa with the flour⟩ ⟨the oxide catalyst is . . . crushed and *sieved* to give granules of uniform size —E.R.Riegel⟩ **b :** to separate or separate out by putting through a sieve or sifter or meshed material ⟨~ the juice from the pulp⟩ — usu. used with *out* ⟨~ out the finer grains⟩ **2 a :** to study (a whole) carefully for the purpose of extracting a part : SCREEN ⟨a hundred candidates must be *sieved* to find one who knows the score —H.M. Silver⟩ **b :** to separate by a process of careful study or by trial : WINNOW — usu. used with *out* ⟨~ out inessentials⟩ ⟨the test *sieved* out several of the candidates⟩ ⟨in order to identify the essence of a national style one must ~ out the radical evidence —Harvey Breit⟩ **3 :** PERFORATE ⟨the ceiling . . . *sieved* with millions of pinpoint holes for ventilation —*New Republic*⟩ ~ *vi* **1 :** to use a sieve or sifter : do sieving **2 :** to pass through or as if through a sieve or sifter or meshed material ⟨the dust from the ashes *sieved* through⟩ ⟨her mother's voice . . . *sieved* through the screen . . . out of the lighted kitchen —John Hermann⟩ — compare SIFT

sieve analysis *n* : a grading by size of particles of powdered or granulated material done with a sieve

sieve and shears *n pl but sing in constr* : divination (as for guilt or a marriage partner) by observation of the motion of a sieve suspended from the points of an open pair of shears : COSCINOMANCY — called also *riddle and shears*

sieve area *also* **sieve field** *n* : an area in the wall of a sieve-tube element, sieve cell, or parenchyma cell in which are clustered pores through which cytoplasmic connections pass to adjoining cells and which in sieve-tube elements are typically most highly developed on the end walls between adjacent elements where they constitute sieve plates

sieve cell *n* : an elongated tapering cell characteristic of the phloem of gymnosperms and lower vascular plants that is basically similar in form, function, and relationships to a sieve-tube element but distinguished by rather uniformly distinguished sieve areas which are not aggregated into sieve plates — compare TRACHEID

sieve element *n* : a transport element of phloem whether taking the form of a sieve cell or a sieve-tube element

sievelike \'ˌ=ˌ=\ *adj* : resembling a sieve in appearance or function

sieve of er·a·tos·the·nes \-ˌerə'tästhəˌnēz\ *usu cap E* [after *Eratosthenes fl* 3d cent. B.C. Greek astronomer and geographer] : a device for finding prime numbers consisting of the writing down of the odd numbers from 3 up in succession and of erasing every third number after 3, every fifth after 5, every seventh after 7, and so on, the numbers remaining being prime

sieve pit *n* : one of the fine perforations that occur in a sieve plate

sieve plate *or* **sieve disk** *n* : a wall or portion of a wall between sieve-tube elements containing one or more sieve areas — compare COMPOUND SIEVE PLATE, SIEVE TUBE

siev·er \'sivə(r)\ *n* -s [¹*sieve* + *-er*] **1 :** one that makes sieves **2 :** one that sieves : SIFTER

si·e·ver·sia \sēˈvərsēə\ *n, cap* [NL, fr. J. *Sievers,* 18th cent. Ger. botanist + NL *-ia*] *in some classifications* : a genus of perennial herbs that includes the prairie smoke and is usu. made a subgenus of *Geum*

sieves *pl of* SIEVE, *pres 3d sing of* SIEVE

sieve tissue *n* : PHLOEM

sieve tube *n* : a tube consisting of an end to end series of thin-walled living cells characteristic of the phloem, having no nucleus when mature, and believed to function chiefly in translocation of organic solutes — compare COMPANION CELL, SIEVE CELL, SIEVE PLATE

sieve–tube element *or* **sieve–tube member** *n* : a thin-walled elongated living cell that has no nucleus at maturity, is continuous with other similar cells by protoplasmic strands which pass through the perforations of specialized sieve plates, prob. functions primarily in the translocation of organic solutes, and is the basic element of the sieve tube — compare SIEVE CELL

sieving *n* -s [fr. gerund of ²*sieve*] **1 :** the act or process of sieving **2 :** the work of a sieve **3 sievings** *pl* : sieved material **4 :** a turn through a sieve ⟨give the flour two ~*s*⟩; *also* : the amount resulting from a turn through a sieve ⟨a shovelful and a ~⟩

si·faka \sə'fakə\ *also* **si·fac** \'sēˌfak\ *n* -s [Malagasy] : any of several diurnal lemurs of the genus *Propithecus* that have a long tail and silky fur and that are of a usu. black and white color

si·fat·ite \sə'fädˌīt\ *n* -s *usu cap* [Ar *Ṣifātī* (fr. *ṣifāt* attributes) + E *-ite*] : one of an early Muslim school holding to a literal interpretation of the Koran and to an anthropomorphic interpretation of the attributes of Allah

sife \'sīf\ *dial Eng var of* SIGH

sif·fi·late \'sifəˌlāt\ *vb* -ED/-ING/-S [modif. (influenced by *sibilate*) of F *siffler* to whistle, fr. MF] : WHISPER

sif·fle \'sifəl\ *vi* -ED/-ING/-S [ME *siflen,* fr. MF *siffler, sifler,* fr. (assumed) VL *sifilare,* fr. L *sibilare* to hiss, whistle — more at SIBILANT] : to blow or speak with a sibilant sound : WHISTLE, HISS

sif·fleur *R* sē'flœr, +V -lər·; -*R* -lə̄, + *vowel in a word following without pause* -lər· *or* -lə̄ *also* -lər\ *n* -s [F, fr. *siffler* to whistle + *-eur* -or] : WHISTLER; *esp* : an animal (as the whistling marmot) that makes a whistling noise

sif·flöt \'sifˌflət\ *n* -s [G, prob. modif. (influenced by *flöte* flute) of F *sifflet* whistle, fr. MF, fr. *siffler* to whistle + *-et* — more at BLOCKFLÖTE] **1 :** a whistle flute **2 :** a small flute organ stop with a whistling tone

sifrei torah *pl of* SEPHER TORAH

¹sift \'sift\ *vb* -ED/-ING/-S [ME *siften,* fr. OE *siftan;* akin to MLG *siften* to sift, OE *sife* sieve — more at SIEVE] *vt* **1 a :** to put through a sifter or sieve or meshed material ⟨~ flour⟩ ⟨~*ed* through coarse screens to remove matter larger than the wheat kernels —*Studies for Flour Salesmen*⟩ ⟨grinding granulated sugar and ~*ing* through silk or nylon cloth —L.A.Wills⟩ **b :** to separate or separate out by putting through a sifter or sieve or meshed material ⟨~ the fine grains from the coarse⟩ — often used with *out* ⟨~ out the powdered portion⟩ **2 a :** to study or examine carefully and extract the good, essential, or desirable (as that which falls in a class) : SCREEN ⟨knowing where to get information is of little importance unless you know how to ~ and evaluate it —*Armed Forces Talk*⟩ ⟨offer, ~, and pass as many basic laws as came from the first two sessions —F.L.Paxson⟩ ⟨~ the men who enter the armed forces⟩ **b :** to separate or separate out by a process of careful study or examination or by trial : WINNOW ⟨~ propaganda from fact —Karl Baehr⟩ ⟨~*ing* Ph.D. candidates who are a drain on faculty time —S.E.Harris⟩ — often used with *out* ⟨~ out the fact from the theory —C.I.Glicksberg⟩ ⟨a training process which ~*s* out . . . the students with a natural aptitude in our direction —H.D.Gideonse⟩ **c :** to study or investigate thoroughly : PROBE ⟨will ~ this matter to the uttermost —Sir Walter Scott⟩ ⟨~ a family pretty thoroughly before turning a . . . dog over to them —Arthur Mayse⟩ **d :** to subject to close questioning ⟨multiplied his questions and ~*ed* me thoroughly —Jonathan Swift⟩ **3 :** to scatter by or as if by passing through a sieve ⟨~ sugar on a cake⟩ **4 :** to run one's fingers through ⟨the barber was lifting and ~*ing* her tresses —P.H. Newby⟩ ~ *vi* **1 :** to use a sifter or sieve : do sifting **2 :** to pass through or as if through a sifter or sieve or meshed material : SIEVE : FILTER ⟨the flour ~*ed* through⟩ ⟨snow ~*ing* in around the sashes —Dixon Wecter⟩ ⟨men ~*ed* in along the border —Oscar Handlin⟩ ⟨bags sewn with a close stitch to minimize ~*ing*⟩ **3 a :** to study or examine something carefully and extract from it the good, essential, or desirable (as something that falls in a class) : SCREEN ⟨in working through the documents he was constantly ~*ing*⟩ **b :** to separate something out by sifting : WINNOW : SELECT ⟨in all his people . . . he is ~*ing* until he comes down to the infinitesimal deposit of humanity —V.S.Pritchett⟩ **c :** to study or investigate something thoroughly : PROBE ⟨the mind unwilling to be rushed to conclusions, the ~*ing,* scientific mind —H.A.Overstreet⟩ — compare SIEVE — **sift through** : to work through by sifting ⟨has *sifted through* some of the material used in the monumental project —R.D.Gardner⟩ ⟨*sift through* them for the one that best suits his purpose —Shirley A. Briggs⟩

²sift \"\ *n* -s : that which is sifted ⟨acres . . . when their toughness is reduced by winter frosts to a rich ~, as of molehills —Adrian Bell⟩

sift·age \-tij\ *n* -s **1 :** SIFT ⟨pulling asunder the fibrous clods, but not reducing them to ~ —R.D.Blackmore⟩ **2 :** the action of sifting ⟨a small sleeve and large valve prevent ~ —*Modern Packaging*⟩

sift·er \-tə(r)\ *n* -s : one that sifts: as **a :** a device or utensil like a sieve but usu. of finer mesh for winnowing or refining powdered or granulated substances (as flour) and more often with a contrivance (as a rotator) to aid the action of sifting; *sometimes* : SIEVE **b :** SHAKER; *also* : the perforated top of a shaker **c :** a machine used in flour milling to separate particles of ground grain according to size by running them through sieves of increasing degrees of fineness arranged one above the other so that the coarsest is on top **d :** a worker who sifts cut tobacco on a riddle

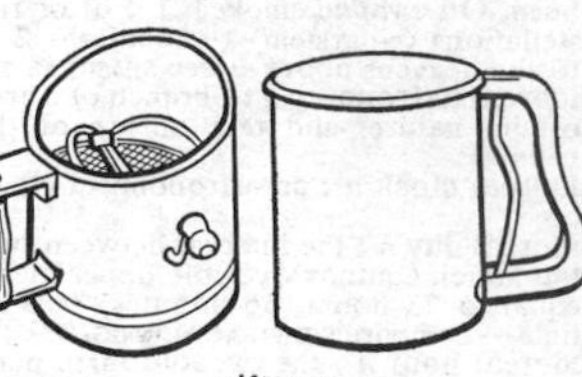

sifters a

sifting *n* -s [ME, fr. gerund of *siften* to sift] **1 :** the act or process of sifting **2 :** the work of a sifter **3 siftings** *pl* : sifted material ⟨bran mixed with ~*s*⟩ **4 :** a turn through a sifter ⟨give the flour a ~⟩; *also* : the amount resulting from a turn through a sifter ⟨the farmer has no time to weigh and measure; he speaks to his men of double handfuls, ~*s,* forkfuls —Adrian Bell⟩

sig \'sig\ *n* -s [abbr. of *signature*] : SIGNATURE: as **a :** the logotype of a newspaper **b :** the identifying music that closes a broadcast program or commercial

sig *abbr* **1** signal; signaller; signalman **2** signature **3** signifying **4** *often cap* signor

si·ganid \sə'ganəd, -gān-\ *adj* [NL *Siganidae*] : of or relating to the Siganidae

si·gan·i·dae \-ganəˌdē\ *n pl, cap* [NL, fr. *Siganus,* type genus + *-idae*] : a small family of compressed ovate-bodied herbivorous fishes having minute scales concealed in slippery skin and strong fin spines capable of inflicting painful wounds that is usu. isolated in a special suborder of the order Percomorphi and is widely distributed in the tropical Indo-Pacific

si·ga·nus \sə'gānəs\ *n, cap* [NL, fr. Ar *sijān* rabbitfish] : the type genus of Siganidae comprising the rabbitfishes

sig·a·to·ka \ˌsigə'tōkə\ *n* -s [fr. *Sigatoka,* district and river in the Fiji islands] : a serious leaf spot disease of bananas occurring esp. in tropical America and caused by a sooty mold (*Cercospora musae*)

sigg *abbr* signatures

¹sigh \'sī\ *vb* -ED/-ING/-S [ME *sihen, sighen* (past *sihte, sighte*), prob. alter. (after such pairs as ME *techen* to teach: *tahte, taghte* taught) of *sichen,* fr. OE *sīcan;* akin to MD *versiken* to sigh] *vi* **1 :** to let out slowly and audibly a deeply drawn breath esp. as the involuntary expression of weariness, dejection, grief, regret, longing, yearning, relief **2 :** to make a sound like sighing ⟨wind ~*ing* in the branches⟩ ⟨the sails did ~ like sedge —S.T.Coleridge⟩ **3 :** LAMENT, GRIEVE, YEARN — used often with *for* ⟨~*ing* for the days of his youth⟩ ~ *vt* **1 a :** to express by sighs : utter in or with sighs ⟨~*ed* out her grief⟩ ⟨poor shawled woman ~*ing* her prayers —Sean O'Faolain⟩ **b :** to breathe out in sighs ⟨drove his blade . . . to the bull's heart . . . as the wild life ~*ed* itself out, and vanished —C.G.D. Roberts⟩ **2** *archaic* : to utter sighs over : MOURN ⟨shall bless her name, and ~ her fate —Matthew Prior⟩ **3 :** to spend or waste in sighing ⟨~*ing* away his days⟩ **4 :** to bring by sighs into a particular state ⟨~*ed* himself to sleep⟩

²sigh \"\ *n* -s [ME *sihe, sighe,* fr. *sihen, sighen,* v.] **1 :** an act of sighing : a deep and prolonged audible inspiration and expiration of air esp. when involuntary and expressing some emotion or feeling (as grief, yearning, weariness, or relief) ⟨~*s* of parting⟩ **2 :** the sound of gently moving or escaping air ⟨~ of the summer breeze⟩ ⟨the engine stopped with a ~⟩

sigh·er \'sī(ə)r, -īə\ *n* -s : one that sighs

sigh·ful \'sīfəl\ *adj* : full of sighs : MOURNFUL

sigh·ing·ly *adv* [ME, fr. *sihing, sighing* (pres. part. of *sihen, sighen* to sigh) + *-ly*] : in a sighing manner : with sighing

¹sight \'sīt, *usu* -īd·+V\ *n* -s [ME *sighth, sith, siht, sight,* fr. OE *sihth, gesihth, gesiht;* akin to MLG & MD *sicht* sight, OHG *siht;* derivative fr. the root of E *see*] **1 a :** something that is seen or beheld : SPECTACLE, SHOW ⟨a ~ more familiar to our forefathers than to us —Dana Burnet⟩ **b** *obs* : VISION 1 **2 a :** a thing regarded as worth seeing — used usu. in pl. ⟨a tour of the ~*s* of the city⟩ **b :** something ludicrous, surprising, shocking, or disorderly in appearance ⟨he had fallen in a puddle and his clothes were a ~⟩ ⟨you must get some sleep, you look a ~⟩ **c** *obs* : ASPECT, APPEARANCE ⟨in ~ like unto an emerald —Rev 4:3 (AV)⟩ **3 a** *chiefly dial* : a great number or quantity ⟨a ~ of old women in decent shawls —Mary Webb⟩ ⟨~ of cows to feed —Jean Stafford⟩ **b** *chiefly dial* : a great deal : LOT ⟨thought a ~ of you all my life and . . . tried to make you happy —J.C.Lincoln⟩ **4** *dial* : a straight uninterrupted stretch (as of a road) **5 a :** the process, power, or function of seeing : the animal sense whose end organ is the eye by which the position, shape, and color of objects are perceived or received as stimuli through the medium of light proceeding from them : EYESIGHT, VISION **b :** faculty of mental or spiritual perception resembling vision ⟨truth as it appeared to his inward ~⟩ — compare SECOND SIGHT **c :** mental view : VIEWPOINT, OPINION, JUDGMENT ⟨abomination in the ~ of God —Lk 16:15 (AV)⟩ **d :** power of seeing exercised by a particular individual ⟨made my pledge in the cathedral in the ~ of God —Frank Yerby⟩ **6 a :** act of looking at or beholding ⟨always fainted at the ~ of blood⟩ ⟨I know him only by ~, not intimately⟩ **b** *archaic* : GLANCE, LOOK **c :** INSPECTION, PERUSAL ⟨this letter is intended for your ~ only⟩ **d :** VIEW, GLIMPSE ⟨window cartons giving a ~ of their contents —L.A.Lewinton⟩ **e :** an observation taken for determining direction or position ⟨when the . . . mate gets another ~ this afternoon that'll give us a good fix of the ship's position —N.D.Ford⟩ **7 a :** perception of an object by the eye : presence in the field of vision ⟨caught ~ of the fox⟩ ⟨lost ~ of the plane in the clouds⟩ **b :** the space through which the power of vision extends : range of view ⟨a ship came into ~ over the horizon⟩ **c :** position affording a view ⟨came within ~ of the mountains⟩ **d :** presentation of a note or draft to the maker or draftee : DEMAND 1b **8 :** opportunity of seeing, examining or investigating: as **a :** the right to a showdown in a poker game **b :** a viewing of goods arranged for prospective buyers ⟨the diamond buyers of the world come to the monthly ~ —Russell Chappell & E.W.Griffiths⟩ **9** *dial* **a :** EYE **b :** the pupil of the eye **c sights** *pl* : SPECTACLES **10 a** *obs* : VISOR **b sights** *pl* : the eye slits in a helmet or in the visor of a helmet ⟨their eyes of fire, sparkling through ~*s* of steel —Shak.⟩ **11 a** (1) : a device for guiding the eye in aiming a firearm that consists of a small often beaded projection (as a blade or a post) placed on top of the muzzle end of the barrel (2) : a transverse bar or leaf fixed near the breech and having a notch or a hole that allows alignment with a projection at the muzzle end and is often adjustable for changes in range or direction — usu. used in pl. and often with *pair* ⟨a pair of ~*s*⟩; see OPEN SIGHT, PANORAMIC SIGHT, PEEP SIGHT, TELESCOPE SIGHT **b :** a device with a small aperture through which objects are to be seen and by which their direction is settled or ascertained ⟨the ~ of a quadrant⟩ **c :** BOW SIGHT **d sights** *pl* : AIM, GOAL, ASPIRATION ⟨plenty of time for adjusting the business ~*s* upward —*Kiplinger Washington Letter*⟩ ⟨set its ~*s* high for the 1949 March of Dimes —Basil O'Connor⟩ **12 a :** a transparent pane or window through which substances or processes in a closed chamber or flue can be observed **b :** a glass vessel or tube for exhibiting the flow of oil in a lubricating arrangement **13 :** the opening in a picture frame; *also* : the part of a picture exposed to view within a frame — **at first sight** *adv* : without investigation or analysis : OFFHAND, IMMEDIATELY, SUPERFICIALLY ⟨though these problems appear, *at first sight,* to lie within the agricultural industry, they often lie outside the control of the individual farmer —G.P.Wibberley⟩ — **at sight** *adv* : as soon as seen or presented to view ⟨a draft payable *at sight*⟩ ⟨play a piece of music *at sight*⟩ ⟨translate a passage *at sight*⟩ ⟨vowed to shoot his enemy *at sight*⟩ — **in sight** : at or within a reasonable distance away in space or time ⟨able to keep the quarry *in sight*⟩ ⟨the end of our troubles is now *in sight*⟩ ⟨victory is *in sight*⟩ ⟨a girl who hasn't a man *in sight* by the time she is 20 —Sidonie M. Gruenberg⟩ — **on sight** *adv* : at sight — **out of sight 1** : beyond comparison ⟨*out of sight* the best thing he has written⟩ **2** : beyond all expectation or reason; *esp* : excessively high ⟨butter . . . went almost *out of sight* when price ceilings . . . were removed —*New Republic*⟩ — **sight for sore eyes** : one whose appearance or arrival is an occasion for joy or relief : a gladdening or heartening sight

²sight \"\ *adj* **1** : calling for or based on recognition or comprehension without previous study or recourse to notes, reference books, or other aid ⟨a ~ translation⟩ ⟨teachers should build up the ~ vocabulary of children⟩ **2** : payable on presentation ⟨~ draft⟩ ⟨~ exchange⟩

³sight \"\ *vb* -ED/-ING/-S *vt* **1** *obs* : INSPECT, SCRUTINIZE **2** : to get or catch sight of : see for the first time ⟨~ a star⟩ ⟨several whales were ~*ed*⟩ ⟨more than merely ~*ing* a familiar face in a crowd —Irving Kolodin⟩ ⟨~*ed* land soon after sunrise⟩ **3** : to look at through or as if through a sight; *esp* : to test for straightness or trueness by looking along the length of ⟨~ a rifle⟩ **4 a** : to aim (a firearm) by means of sights **b** : to aim at (a target) **c** : to sight in **5 a** : to equip with sights **b** : to adjust the sights of ⟨the rifle was ~*ed* to 1000 yards⟩ **6** : to present (as a bill) for payment ~ *vi* **1** : to take aim ⟨hard to ~ for the center of the greatly narrowed channel —C.S.Forester⟩ **2** : to look carefully in a certain direction ⟨~ down the edge of a board⟩ ⟨~ down a gun barrel⟩ — **sight the anchor** : to haul up an anchor enough to see whether it is fouled or clear

sight board *n* : SCREEN 8

sight draft *n* : a draft payable on presentation

sight·ed \ˈsīd·əd, -ītəd\ *adj* [¹*sight* + *-ed*] **1** : having the use of one's sight : SEEING ⟨to the ~, loss of vision seems the most hopeless and pitiable . . . —P.A.Zahl⟩ ⟨son who was partially ~ —Alice Lake⟩ **2** : having a specified kind of sight — usu. used in combination ⟨clear-*sighted*⟩ ⟨quick-*sighted*⟩

sight edge *n* : the edge of an overlapping or outer strake of the shell plating of a ship

sight·er \ˈsīd·ə(r), -ītə-\ *n* -S **1** : one who tests the accuracy of sights on small arms — called also *aligner, targeteer* **2** : SIGHTING SHOT

sight-feed \ˈ=,=\ *adj* : of or belonging to a feed-pipe fitting, device, or system arranged so that the flowing liquid may be observed through a transparent section of a tube or wall ⟨*sight-feed* oil cup⟩

sight gag *n* : a comic bit or episode achieved by pantomime or camera shot rather than words

sight glass *n* : a transparent section in a pipe or tank wall for giving visual indication of level or flow of liquids

sight in *vt* : to adjust the sights of (a gun) so that at a selected range the missile will strike the point aimed at

sighting *n* -S : an act of one who sights ⟨no further ~*s* of the enemy were made⟩

sighting angle *n* : RANGE ANGLE

sighting hood *n* : a raised hood with slits or peepholes in the sides mounted on top of a gun turret

sighting shot *n* : a shot made to test the adjustment of the sights of a firearm

sight·less \ˈsītləs\ *adj* [ME *sightles*, fr. *sight* + *-les* -less] **1** : lacking sight : being without sight : BLIND **2 a** : INVISIBLE **b** *obs* : UNSIGHTLY **c** : UNSEEN — **sight·less·ly** *adv* — **sight·less·ness** *n* -ES

sight line *n* : a straight line extending from the eye of a spectator to an object or area (as of a stage) to be viewed : one of the lines that define an unimpeded field of vision ⟨the complications of providing good *sight lines* increase proportionately with the numbers to be seated —*Architect & Building News*⟩

sight·li·ness \ˈsītlēnəs, -lin-\ *n* -ES : the quality or state of being sightly

¹sight·ly \-lē,-li\ *adj* -ER/-EST [¹*sight* + *-ly*] **1** *obs* : CONSPICUOUS, VISIBLE **2** : acceptable or pleasing to the sight : decent in appearance ⟨~ building⟩ ⟨~ typography⟩ **3** : affording a fine view ⟨homes . . . enjoying a ~ location overlooking the river —*Springfield (Mass.) Union*⟩

²sightly \"\ *adv* : in a sightly manner

sight·me·ter \ˈsīt,mēd·ə(r)\ *n* : a light meter that indicates in foot-candles relative visibilities of illuminated surfaces or positions

sight picture *n* : the alignment of the sights of a firearm with the target as seen by the firer

sightproof \ˈ=,=\ *adj* : impenetrable to sight ⟨~ hedge six feet high⟩

sight radius *n* : the distance between the front and rear sights of a firearm

sight-read \ˈ=,=\ *vb* [back-formation fr. *sight reading* & *sight reader*] *vt* : to read (as a foreign language) or perform (music) without previous preparation or study ~ *vi* : to read something at sight; *esp* : to play or sing music at sight

sight reader *n* : one who reads at sight something that ordinarily requires previous study; *specif* : a musician who can read or perform music at first sight of the score

sight-reading \ˈ=,==\ *n* **1 a** : the action or an instance of reading at sight **b** : the ability to read at sight **2** : material for reading at sight

sight rhyme *n* : EYE RHYME

sights *pl of* SIGHT, *pres 3d sing of* SIGHT

sight-see \ˈ=,=\ *vi* [back-formation fr. *sight-seeing*] : to go about seeing sights of interest

¹sight-seeing \ˈ=,==\ *adj* [¹*sight* + *seeing*, pres. part. of *see* (after the phrase *see the sights*)] : engaged in, devoted to, or used for seeing sights ⟨~ trip⟩ ⟨~ buses⟩

²sight-seeing \"\ *n* [¹*sight* + *seeing*, gerund of *see* (after the phrase *see the sights*)] : the act or pastime of seeing sights

sightseer \ˈ=,==\ *n* -S : one that visits places of interest : one that goes about in search of novelty or picturesque sights or scenery

sight-shot \ˈ=,=\ *n* : EYESHOT

sightsinging \ˈ=,==\ *n* : the sight reading of vocal music

sight tree *n* : LINE TREE

sight unseen *adv* : without inspection or opportunity of appraisal ⟨can't expect him to buy such an expensive place *sight unseen*⟩

sightworthy \ˈ=,==\ *adj* : worth seeing

sig·il \ˈsijəl\ *n* -S [L *sigillum* — more at SEAL] **1** : SEAL, SIGNET **2** : a sign, word, or device of supposed occult power in astrology or magic **3** : a coded bibliographical reference consisting typically of letters and numerals representing respectively date, name of publication, volume, page, and article

sigill *abbr* [L *sigillum*] seal

sig·il·lar·ia \,sijəˈla(a)rēə\ *n, cap* [NL, fr. L *sigillum* seal + NL *-aria*; fr. the leaf scars that resemble seals] : a genus (the type of the family Sigillariaceae) of fossil arborescent club mosses of the Middle Carboniferous — **sig·il·lar·id** \¦==¦=rəd\ *n or adj*

sig·il·lar·i·a·ce·ae \,==,=rēˈāsē,ē\ *n pl, cap* [NL, fr. *Sigillaria*, type genus + *-aceae*] : a family of arborescent Carboniferous club mosses (order Lepidodendrales) that have the trunks marked with vertical rows of leaf scars suggesting seals — **sig·il·lar·i·a·ce·ous** \¦==,==¦āshəs\ *adj*

sig·il·lar·i·os·tro·bus \,==,=rēˈästrəbəs\ *n, cap* [NL, fr. *Sigillaria* + *-o-* + Gk *strobos, strombos* top, ball; akin to Gk *strephein* to turn — more at STROPHE] : a form genus based on lepidodendrid cones believed to belong to plants of the genus *Sigillaria*

¹sig·il·late \ˈsijə,lāt\ *vt* -ED/-ING/-S [L *sigillatus*, past part. of *sigillare*, fr. *sigillum* seal — more at SEAL] : to close by or as if by a seal : SEAL

²sigil·late \ˈsijə,lāt, səˈjilət\ *or* **sig·il·lat·ed** \ˈsijə,lād·əd\ *adj* [*sigillate* fr. L *sigillatus*, fr. *sigillum* + *-atus* -ate; *sigillated* fr. L *sigillatus* + E *-ed*] **1** : decorated by means of stamped-on patterns or motifs — used esp. of ancient Roman ware **2** : having markings like seals ⟨~ rootstock⟩

sig·il·la·tion \,sijəˈlāshən\ *n* -S [ML *sigillation-, sigillatio*, fr. L *sigillatus* (past part. of *sigillare* to seal) + *-ion-, -io* -ion] **1** : impression of or by a seal **2** : the mark of a cicatrix **3** : decoration (as of pottery) by means of stamped designs

sig·il·log·ra·phy \,==ˈlägrəfē\ *n* -ES [F *sigillographie*, fr. L *sigillum* seal + F *-o-* + *-graphie* -graphy] : the study of seals : SPHRAGISTICS

si·glar·i·an \siˈgla(a)rēən\ *adj* [*siglum* + *-ary* + *-an*] : of or relating to sigla

sig·los \ˈsi,gläs\ *n, pl* **si·gloi** \-lȯi\ [Gk *siglos, siklos*, of Sem origin; akin to Heb *sheqel* shekel] : a silver coin of ancient Persia equal to $\frac{1}{20}$ daric and weighing about 5.6 grams

sig·lum \ˈsigləm\ *n, pl* **sig·la** \-lə\ [L, dim. of *signum* sign, mark, figure, image — more at SIGN] **1** : a sign, abbreviation, letter, or character standing for words in ancient manuscripts or on coins or medals **2** : a letter used to indicate manuscript or other source of an edited text

sig·ma \ˈsigmə\ *n* -S [Gk, of Sem origin; akin to Heb *sāmekh* samekh] **1** : the 18th letter of the Greek alphabet — symbol Σ or σ or ς; see ALPHABET tables; compare LUNAR SIGMA **2** : the thousandth part of a second : MILLISECOND **3 a** : STANDARD DEVIATION — symbol σ **b** : the sum of — symbol Σ **4** : a C-shaped sponge spicule

sig·ma·spire \-,spī(ə)r\ *n* [*sigma* + *spire*] : an S-shaped sponge spicule : a sigma twisted spirally

¹sig·mate \ˈsig,māt\ *vt* -ED/-ING/-S [*sigma* + *-ate* (v. suffix)] : to affix a sigma or *s* to (a root) in forming a tense or a plural

²sigmate \"\ *adj* [*sigma* + *-ate* (adj. suffix)] **1** : having the shape or form of the Greek sigma or the letter S **2** *of a sponge spicule* : C-SHAPED

sig·mat·ic \(ˈ)sigˈmad·ik\ *adj* [ISV *sigmat-* (fr. Gk, fr. *sigma*) + *-ic*] *of a tense* : characterized by the addition of *s* to the root in forming the tense stem — used esp. of an aorist and a future in Greek and of corresponding forms in other Indo-European languages; opposed to *asigmatic*

sig·ma·tion \sigˈmāshən\ *n* -S : the addition of a sigma or *s* to a root

sig·ma·tism \ˈsigmə,tizəm\ *n* -S [ISV *sigmat-* (fr. Gk) + *-ism*] : faulty articulation of sibilants

sig·mo·don \ˈsigmə,dän\ *n, cap* [NL, fr. Gk *sigma* + NL *-odon*] : a genus of cricetid rodents including the American cotton rats

sig·mo·dont \-nt\ *adj* [*sigma* + *-odont*] : having bituberculate molars — used of a rodent

sig·mo·don·tes \,==ˈdän·(,)tēz\ *n pl, cap* [NL, fr. pl. of *Sigmodon*] *in former classifications* : a group of New World rodents approximately equal to the typical subfamily of Cricetidae

¹sig·moid \ˈsig,mȯid\ *also* **sig·moi·dal** \(ˈ)sigˈmȯidᵊl\ *adj* [*sigmoid* fr. Gk *sigmoeidēs*, fr. *sigma* + *-oeidēs* -oid; *sigmoidal* fr. Gk *sigmoeidēs* + E *-al*] **1 a** : curved like the letter C **b** : curved in two directions like the letter S **2** : relating to the sigmoid flexure of the intestine ⟨the ~ artery branches from the inferior mesenteric⟩ — **sig·moi·dal·ly** \-ᵊlē\ *adv*

²sigmoid \"\ *n* -S : a sigmoid bodily part; *esp* : SIGMOID FLEXURE

sigmoid cavity *n* : either of two articulatory surfaces in the elbow: **a** : SEMILUNAR NOTCH — called also *greater sigmoid cavity* **b** : a surface on the inner side of the distal end of the radius for articulation with the ulna — called also *lesser sigmoid cavity*

sig·moid·ec·to·my \,sig,mȯiˈdektəmē\ *n* -ES [²*sigmoid* + *-ectomy*] : surgical removal of part of the sigmoid flexure

sigmoid flexure *n* **1** : an S-shaped curve (as in the neck of a bird or turtle) **2** *or* **sigmoid colon** : the contracted and crooked part of the intestine between the descending colon and the rectum terminating in the latter at the brim of the true pelvis — see DIGESTION illustration

sig·moid·itis \-ˈdīd·əs\ *n* -ES [NL, fr. ISV ²*sigmoid* + NL *-itis*] : inflammation of the sigmoid flexure of the colon

sigmoid notch *n* : a curved depression on the upper border of the lower jaw between the coronoid process and the articulatory condyle absent in lower primates and some extinct men

sig·moid·o·scope \sigˈmȯidə,skōp\ *n* [²*sigmoid* + *-o-* + *-scope*] : a long hollow tubular instrument designed to be passed into the sigmoid colon through the anus and to permit inspection, diagnosis, treatment, and photography — **sig·moid·o·scop·ic** \¦=¦==ˈskäpik\ *adj* — **sig·moid·os·co·py** \,sig,mȯiˈdäskəpē\ *n* -ES

sig·moid·os·to·my \,sig,mȯiˈdästəmē\ *n* -ES [ISV ²*sigmoid* + *-o-* + *-stomy*] : transabdominal formation of an artificial anus in the sigmoid by means of surgery

sigmoid valve *n* : SEMILUNAR VALVE

¹sign \ˈsīn\ *n* -S *see sense 10b* [ME *signe*, fr. OF, fr. L *signum* sign, mark, figure, image; perh. akin to L *secare* to cut — more at SAW] **1 a** : a motion, gesture, or bodily action by which a thought is expressed or a command or a wish is made known **b** : SIGNAL 3a **c** : a unit of language (as a word) that means, stands for, designates, or denotes something to an interpreter — compare ICON, INDEX, SYMBOL **d** : one of the members of a methodical set of gestures used to represent language directly word by word or letter by letter — compare DACTYLOLOGY **2 a** : a conventional mark or device having a recognized particular meaning and used in place of words **b** : an ideographic mark, figure, or picture conventionally used in writing or printing to represent a usu. technical term or conception ⟨brackets are frequently used in bibliographical work as a ~ of inference —Fredson Bowers⟩ **c** : a character standing for a number or a contraction in braille or other system of writing for the blind **3** : one of the 12 divisions of the zodiac that are marked by the positions of the 12 zodiacal constellations beginning at the point of intersection of the ecliptic and the equator and reckoning eastward each being now because of the precession of the equinoxes displaced 30 degrees to the west of the constellation bearing its name

THE SIGNS OF THE ZODIAC

NUMBER	NAME	SYMBOL	SUN ENTERS
1	Aries the Ram	♈	March 21
2	Taurus the Bull	♉	April 20
3	Gemini the Twins	♊	May 21
4	Cancer the Crab	♋	June 22
5	Leo the Lion	♌	July 23
6	Virgo the Virgin	♍	August 23
7	Libra the Balance	♎	September 23
8	Scorpio the Scorpion	♏	October 24
9	Sagittarius the Archer	♐	November 22
10	Capricorn the Goat	♑	December 22
11	Aquarius the Water Bearer	♒	January 20
12	Pisces the Fishes	♓	February 19

4 a : a character (as a flat, sharp) used in musical notation; *specif* : SEGNO **b** : a character indicating a relation between quantities (as + addition, = equality) or an operation performed (as the radical √, integral ∫, factorial !); *also* : a character that forms part of a representation of a number (as — in −4) **5** *archaic* **a** : a heraldic or military device (as on a banner or a shield) **b** : STANDARD, BANNER, ENSIGN **c signs** *pl, obs* : INSIGNIA **d** *obs* : an attesting mark (as on a seal) **e** *obs* : EFFIGY, IMAGE, IMPRINT **6 a** : a lettered board or other public display placed on or before a building, room, shop, or office to advertise the business there transacted or the name of the person or firm conducting it **b** : a conspicuously placed word or legend (as on a board or placard) of direction, warning, identification, or other information of general concern ⟨ignoring the Danger Keep Out ~ he opened the gate and entered⟩ ⟨looking for street ~*s*⟩ **c** : SIGNBOARD **7 a** : something material or external that stands for or signifies something spiritual — compare SACRAMENT 1 **b** : something that serves to indicate the presence or existence of a thing or quality or condition : TOKEN ⟨removed their hats as a ~ of respect⟩ ⟨all the ~*s* point to him as the guilty one⟩ ⟨~*s* of suffering in his drawn face and tightened mouth⟩ **c** : PRESAGE, PORTENT ⟨~*s* of an early spring⟩ ⟨the wind changed, a ~ of coming rain⟩ **d** (1) : an objective evidence of disease esp. as observed and interpreted by the physician rather than by the patient or lay observer ⟨narrow retinal vessels are a ~ of arteriosclerosis⟩ — contrasted with *symptom*; see PHYSICAL SIGN (2) : an indication of disease (as spores of the pathogen, gummy exudate) other than the reaction of the plant itself — contrasted with *symptom* **8** : a remarkable event believed to indicate the will or power of a deity : MIRACLE, WONDER, PRODIGY, OMEN ⟨what things I have wrought in Egypt, and my ~*s* which I have done among them, that ye may know how that I am the Lord —Exod 10:2 (AV)⟩ **9** : a grammatical inflection characteristic of a mood, tense or number ⟨*to* is traditionally the ~ of the infinitive in English⟩ ⟨*s* is the usual plural ~⟩ **10 a** : remaining evidence : VESTIGE — used chiefly in negative construction ⟨no ~ of human habitation⟩ ⟨not a ~ of remorse⟩ ⟨not a sound, not a ~ of life anywhere⟩ **b** *pl usu* **sign** : traces (as footprints, droppings) left by a wild animal ⟨we found plenty of bear ~ about but never saw a bear⟩ **11** *obs* : SEMBLANCE, PRETENSE

syn MARK, TOKEN, BADGE, NOTE, SYMPTOM: SIGN is a very general term for any indication to be perceived by the senses or reason ⟨the *sign* of the cross⟩ ⟨suicide is a *sign* of failure, misery, and despair —Havelock Ellis⟩ ⟨the *signs* of her fate in a footprint here, a broken twig there, a trinket dropped by the way —Joseph Conrad⟩ ⟨a patient showing *signs* of improvement⟩ ⟨highway *signs*⟩ MARK may more strongly indicate some indication deeply impressed, inherently characteristic, or properly affixed ⟨the bitter experience left its *marks* on him⟩ ⟨the *mark* of a gentleman⟩ ⟨the *mark* of Cain on their foreheads, which sets them visibly apart from the rest of humanity before they have committed their crime —H.J.Morgenthau⟩ ⟨a flood's *marks*⟩ ⟨making his *mark* on the paper⟩ TOKEN may refer to a sign expressive of something intangible ⟨he wears a silver ring on his ankle as a *token* of his dignity —J.G. Frazer⟩ ⟨marriage if you do not regard it as a sacrament — as no doubt it ought to be regarded — was nothing more than a *token* that a couple intended to stick to each other —F.M. Ford⟩ BADGE designates a distinctive emblem or an accoutrement or a characteristic serving as an emblem to indicate a belonging or being part of ⟨a policeman's *badge*⟩ ⟨to wear a leopard's skin (the *badge* of royalty) —J.G.Frazer⟩ ⟨the diplomat wearing his *badge* of office, the Homburg hat —Tom Siler⟩ ⟨essentially we were taught to regard culture as a veneer, a *badge* of class distinction —Malcolm Cowley⟩ NOTE may indicate any distinguishing mark; it may suggest something that seems to emanate from a thing as an indication of its true, inherent nature ⟨tolerance, moderation, and pity are the abiding *notes* which help to keep Chaucer's poetry level with life —H.S.Bennett⟩ ⟨the genteel poverty which was the *note* of his grandfather's house —Archibald Marshall⟩ SYMPTOM may indicate a sign of some change, new development or old condition not thoroughly perceived ⟨the *symptoms* of disease⟩ ⟨the decadence of the walls was a *symptom* of the decline of that intense civic patriotism which had inspired medieval townsfolk —G.M.Trevelyan⟩ ⟨every *symptom* of being hopelessly in love —W.S.Gilbert⟩ **syn** see in addition CHARACTER — **at the sign of** : at the inn or tavern or shop having the sign specified ⟨an appointment to meet . . . *at the sign of* the griffin —Sir Walter Scott⟩

²sign \"\ *vb* -ED/-ING/-S [ME *signen*, fr. MF *signer*, fr. L *signare* to mark, seal, fr. *signum* sign, mark, figure, image — more at ¹SIGN] *vt* **1 a** : to place a sign upon : consecrate, bless, or mark esp. with the sign of the cross **b** : CROSS 3a **c** : to represent or indicate by a sign **2 a** : to affix a signature to : ratify or attest by hand or seal ⟨~ a legislative bill into law⟩ : subscribe in one's own handwriting ⟨confession was typed out and read to the prisoner, who then ~*ed* it⟩ **b** : to write down (one's name) ⟨~*ed* his name with a flourish⟩ **c** : to identify (a printed signature) with a symbol at the bottom of the first page **3 a** : to assign or convey formally ⟨~*ed* away his rights in the invention⟩ ⟨~*ed* over the property to his brother⟩ **b** : to accept as a professional obligation : agree to perform or carry out ⟨~*ed* to direct two plays for the newly formed company⟩ **4** : to communicate by making a sign ⟨~*ed* that he was ready to leave, glancing toward the door⟩ : signify or express in signs or a sign language **5** : to engage or hire by securing the signature of ⟨~*ed* to act in a movie⟩ ⟨the club has ~*ed* two new pitchers⟩ **6** : to place signs on or along ⟨~ a street⟩ ⟨~ a highway intersection⟩ ~ *vi* **1** : to write one's name esp. as a token of assent, responsibility, or obligation **2** : to make a sign or signal : communicate or converse by signs or a sign language **3** *obs* : to be an omen or portent : BODE ⟨music in the air . . . it ~*s* well, does it not —Shak.⟩ **4** : to place signs (as along a highway)

signa *pl of* SIGNUM

sign·able \ˈsīnəbəl\ *adj* **1** : suitable to be signed **2** : requiring signature

¹sig·nal \ˈsignəl, -nᵊl\ *n* -S [ME, fr. MF *seignal, segnel, signal*, fr. ML *signale*, fr. LL, neut. of *signalis* of a sign, fr. L *signum* sign + *-alis* -al — more at SIGN] **1** *obs* : EMBLEM, SYMBOL **2** *archaic* : TOKEN, INDICATION ⟨in ~ of my love to thee —Shak.⟩ **3 a** : an act, event, or watchword that has been agreed upon as the occasion of concerted action ⟨~ fires of rebellion⟩ **b** : something that incites to action : an immediate cause or impulse ⟨his remark was the ~ for a storm of weeping⟩ **4 a** : a sound or gesture made to give warning or command ⟨~ that warns of an air raid⟩ ⟨waiting for the ~ to open fire⟩ **b** : an object placed to convey notice or warning: as (1) : a device (as a colored light) for regulating vehicular or pedestrian traffic (2) : a device used to warn trainmen or persons approaching a railroad of danger or to convey orders or information to a train crew **5** : an object (as a flag on a pole) centered over a point so as to be observed from other positions in surveying **6 a** : an identifying tab (as of a thumb index) fastened to a book leaf at its fore edge **b** : a small projecting tab that attaches to the edge of a card or folder as an aid in filing or indexing **7** : a play indicating to one's partner in a card game that one holds certain cards or desires a certain play **8** : the beam of light reflected from the face of a crystal rotated into a particular position in a goniometer **9 a** : an object used to transmit or convey information beyond the range of human voice ⟨flying a flag as a distress ~⟩ **b** : the intelligence, message, sound, or image conveyed in telegraphy, telephony, radio, radar, or television **c** : a detectable physical quantity or impulse (as a voltage, current, magnetic field strength) by which messages or information can be transmitted **10** : a speech sound or form or combination of sounds and forms that communicates a meaning or a difference in meaning — compare MORPHEME, PHONEME

²signal \"\ *vb* **signaled** *or* **signalled**; **signaled** *or* **signalled**; **signaling** *or* **signalling**; **signals** *vt* **1** : to notify by a signal : make a signal to ⟨~*ed* his wife to leave the room⟩ ⟨~*ed* the fleet to turn back⟩ **2 a** : to communicate (a message) by signals ⟨~ orders to a field unit⟩ **b** : announce by signal ⟨the ship ~*ed* her departure with warning blasts on the whistle⟩ **c** : to determine or fix (meaning) in a speech utterance ⟨the kind of sentence . . . is ~*ed* by special contrastive patterns in the arrangement of . . . parts of speech —C.C.Fries⟩ : constitute a characteristic feature of (a meaningful linguistic form) ⟨plurality is usually ~*ed* by *s*⟩ **3** : SIGNALIZE ⟨waiter with tray ~*s* a café —*Nat'l Geographic*⟩ ~ *vi* : to make or send a signal ⟨frantically ~*ing* with both arms⟩

³signal \"\ *adj* [modif. of F *signalé*, past part. of *signaler* to distinguish, fr. OIt *segnalare* to signal, distinguish, fr. *segnale* signal, fr. ML *signale*] **1** : distinguished from what is ordinary : NOTICEABLE, OUTSTANDING ⟨~ achievement⟩ ⟨students of ~ promise⟩ ⟨~ experience⟩ **2** : SIGNIFICATIVE, DISTINCTIVE ⟨~ markings⟩ **3** : employed or used in signaling ⟨~ beacon⟩ ⟨~ flags⟩ ⟨~ corps⟩ **syn** see NOTICEABLE

signal board *n* : a board on which signals are recorded; *esp* : such a board with electrical connections for indicating the source of a signal : ANNUNCIATOR

signal box *n, Brit* : SIGNAL TOWER

signal bridge *n* **1** : BRIDGE 3 1 **2** : an open platform near the navigating bridge of a warship for the use of signalmen

sig·nal·er *or* **sig·nal·ler** \-ə(r)\ *n* -S **1** : one that signals : a signaling device or mechanism **2** : SIGNALMAN

signal halyard *or* **signal halliard** *n* : a woven cotton line used for halyards on signal yards because free from kinking

sig·nal·i·ty \sigˈnaləd·ē\ *n* -ES [³*signal* + *-ity*] : the quality or state of being notable or outstanding : SIGNIFICANCE

sig·nal·iza·tion \,signələˈzāshən, -nᵊlə-, -nə,līˈz-, -nᵊl,īˈz-\ *n* -S **1** : the act of signalizing **2** : the act of equipping with signals ⟨parking restrictions . . . and improved ~ —Robert Moses⟩

sig·nal·ize \ˈ⸗nə,līz, -nᵊl,īz\ *vb* -ED/-ING/-S *see -ize in Explan Notes* [³*signal* + *-ize*] *vt* **1 :** to make conspicuous **:** make known **:** MARK, DISTINGUISH ⟨conform to some ceremonial prescribed to ~ loyalty —G.W.Johnson⟩ ⟨~ their product by a distinctive name or label —D.M.Potter⟩ **:** CELEBRATE ⟨~ an anniversary⟩ **2 :** to point out carefully or distinctly **:** draw attention to ⟨to ~ the extension of an idea, *moreover* is usually more appropriate than *also* —R.M.Weaver⟩ **3 a :** to make signals to **:** SIGNAL ⟨~ an approaching ship⟩ **b :** to announce or indicate by a signal ⟨stood up to ~ the departure of the ladies —J.W.Krutch⟩ **4 :** to place traffic signals at or on ⟨~ an intersection⟩ ~ *vi* **:** to send or exchange signals **:** converse by means of signals

sig·nal·ly \-nəlē, -nᵊl\|, \|i\ *adv* **1 :** in a signal manner **:** NOTABLY, UNMISTAKABLY, REMARKABLY ⟨~ undiplomatic methods of dealing with those . . . in a position to help them —R.D.Altick⟩ **2 :** by way of a signal ⟨a term which is used symbolically and not ~ —Susanne K. Langer⟩

sig·nal·man \\|mən\ *n, pl* **signalmen 1 :** one who inspects and maintains railroad signals **2 a** *Brit* **:** one who sets railroad signals **b :** a logger who signals orders from the yard boss to the yarder engineer **c :** a member of a construction crew who signals operators of power hoisting equipment — called also *highballer* **3 :** a petty officer esp. qualified in visual⸗ signal duties

sig·nal·ment \\|mənt\ *n* -S [F *signalement,* fr. *signaler* to distinguish, mark out, describe + *-ment* — more at SIGNAL] **:** description by peculiar, appropriate, or characteristic marks; *specif* **:** the systematic description of a person for purposes of identification — compare BERTILLON SYSTEM; DACTYLOGRAPHY, DACTYLOSCOPY

signal noise ratio *n* **:** the ratio of radio field intensity to noise field intensity; *also* **:** the ratio of the signal transmitted through a piece of radio equipment to the noise generated within the equipment itself

signal number *n* **:** a naval officer's numerical order on the official seniority list

signal oil *n* **:** a petroleum distillate that burns slowly and cleanly and is used in signal lanterns

signal plate *n* **:** an element of a television camera tube from which the electrical signal is obtained for transmission into the television system

signal red *n* **:** CHINESE VERMILION

signals *pl of* SIGNAL, *pres 3d sing of* SIGNAL

signal tower *n* **:** an enclosed or armored elevated structure from which signals are displayed or controlled; *specif* **:** a switch tower for a system of railroad signals

sig·na·ry \ˈsignərē\ *n* -ES [L *signum* sign + E *-ary*] **:** a system or list of syllabic or alphabetic signs of a language or an ancient script ⟨hieroglyphic ~⟩

sig·na·tary \ˈsignə,terē\ *n* -ES [L *signatus* (past part. of *signare* to mark, seal) + E *-ary* — more at SIGN] **:** SIGNATORY

sig·nate \ˈsig,nāt, -,nət\ *adj* [L *signatus,* past part. of *signare* to mark, seal, designate — more at SIGN] **1 :** DESIGNATED, IDENTIFIED **2 :** having markings like letters

signate matter *n* **:** matter that is numerically distinct in different individuals but is the same in quality or character for cognition

sig·na·tion \sigˈnāshən\ *n* -S [LL *signation-, signatio,* fr. *signatus* (past part. of *signare* to make the sign of the cross, fr. L, to mark, seal) + L *-ion-, -io* -ion] **1 :** the act of making the sign of the cross **2** *obs* **:** a distinguishing mark

¹sig·na·to·ry \ˈsignə,tōrē, -tȯr-, -ri\ *adj* [L *signatorius* of sealing, fr. *signatus* + *-orius* -ory] **1** *obs* **:** relating to a seal **:** used in sealing **2 :** joining or sharing in a signature **:** bound by the terms of a signed agreement

²signatory \"\ *n* -ES **:** a signer with another; *specif* **:** a government bound with others to the terms of a signed convention

sig·na·tur·al \-nə,chürəl\ *adj* **:** of or relating to a signature

¹sig·na·ture \ˈsignə,chü(ə)r, -üə, -nəchə(r), -nēchə(r) *also* -nə,tü(ə)r *or* -nə-,tyü- *or* -üə\ *n* -S [MF or ML; MF, fr. ML *signatura,* fr. L *signatus* (past part. of *signare* to mark, seal) + *-ura* -ure — more at SIGN] **1** *Scots law* **:** a writing prepared to be signed or sealed as a warrant for a proposed royal grant or charter **2 a :** the name of a person written with his own hand to signify that the writing which precedes accords with his wishes or intentions **b :** the act of signing one's name ⟨letters waiting for his ~⟩ ⟨witnesses to the ~⟩ **3 :** a feature in the appearance or qualities of a natural object (as a plant) formerly held to indicate its utility in medicine either because of a fancied resemblance to a body part (as a heart-shaped leaf indicating utility in heart disease) or because of a presumed relation to some phase of a disease (as the prickly nature of thistle indicating utility in case of a stitch in the side) **4 a** *obs* **:** STAMP, IMPRESSION **b :** a distinguishing or identifying mark, feature, or quality ⟨a clear little eye in her center, the ~ of a hurricane —*Time*⟩ ⟨the ~ of the Church is legible enough on the houses and streets of Oxford —P.E.More⟩ **5 a :** a letter or figure placed usu. at the bottom of the first page on each sheet of printed pages (as of a book) as a direction to the binder in arranging and gathering the sheets **b :** the sheet itself which when folded becomes one unit of the book — compare GATHERING, QUIRE **6 a** *obs* **:** natural markings forming an image or figure **b** *obs* **:** BIRTHMARK **7 a :** KEY SIGNATURE **b :** TIME SIGNATURE **8 :** the part of a medical prescription which contains the directions to the patient — abbr. *s, Sig.* **9 :** a tune, sound effect, or pictorial device used to identify a program, entertainer, or orchestra

²signature \"\ *vt* -ED/-ING/-S **1** *obs* **:** DESIGNATE **2 :** to subscribe to or authenticate with one's signature

signature by mark : an indication usu. in the presence of witnesses by a distinctive sign or mark (as an X) of acquiescence in or assent to the content of a document by one unable to write

sig·na·ture·less \-ləs\ *adj* **:** lacking a signature **:** UNSIGNED

signature loan *n* **:** a loan granted without security

signature tune *n* **:** a melody, passage, or song chosen by an orchestra or musical entertainer as a means of identification and played at the opening or close or both of each program

sig·na·tur·ist \-ürəst, -chərə-\ *n* -S **:** one who holds to belief in signatures of healing agents

signboard \ˈ⸗,⸗\ *n* **1 :** a board bearing a notice or sign — compare BILLBOARD **2 :** a conspicuous indication or warning

signed *past of* SIGN

signed number *n* **:** one of a system of numbers represented by a sign + or — prefixed to a digit or other numeral such that the sum of two numbers with unlike signs and like numerical elements is 0

sign·ee \(ˈ)sīˈnē\ *n* -S [²*sign* + *-ee*] **:** SIGNATORY

sign·er \ˈsīnə(r)\ *n* -S **1 :** one that signs **:** SIGNATORY **2 :** one who uses sign language

¹sig·net \ˈsignət, *usu* -əd·+V\ *n* -S [ME, fr. MF, dim. of *signe* sign, seal — more at SIGN] **1 :** a seal used officially to give personal authority to a document in lieu of signature: **a :** the seal used formerly by the sovereign of England in sealing private letters and grants prior to the affixing of the great seal **b :** the seal used formerly in Scotland to authenticate royal warrants connected with administration of justice **2 a :** the impression made by or as if by a signet **b :** an identifying or authenticating mark or stamp **3 a :** a small intaglio seal (as in a finger ring) **b :** SIGNET RING

²signet \"\ *vt* -ED/-ING/-S [ME (Sc dial.) *signeten,* fr. *signet,* n.] **:** to stamp or authenticate with a signet

signet ring *n* **1 :** a finger ring having a bezel engraved with a signet, seal, or monogram or bearing a stone so engraved **:** SEAL RING **2 :** something shaped like a signet ring; *esp* **:** a malaria parasite in an intracellular developmental stage in which the nucleus is peripheral and the cytoplasm somewhat attenuated and annular

sig·ni·fer \ˈsignəfə(r)\ *n* -S [L, fr. *signifer,* adj., bearing a sign, bearing the heavenly signs, fr. *signum* sign + *-i-* + *-fer* -ferous — more at SIGN] **1** *obs* **:** ZODIAC **2 :** STANDARD-BEARER

sig·ni·fi·able \ˈsignə,fīəbəl, ,⸗⸗ˈ⸗⸗⸗\ *adj* **:** capable of being represented by a sign or symbol

sig·ni·fi·ant \ˈ⸗⸗,fīənt\ *n* -S [F, fr. pres. part. of *signifier* to signify — more at SIGNIFY] **:** SIGNIFICANT, SIGN

sig·nif·ic \(ˈ)sigˈnifik\ *adj* [*signify* + *-ic*] **:** acting as a sign or signal ⟨argues that the expression of ideas may be through a symbolic function, not a ~ function —L.W.Elder⟩

sig·nif·i·cance \sigˈnifəkən(t)s, -fēk-\ *n* -S [ME *significaunce,* fr. L *significantia,* fr. *significant-, significans* + *-ia* -y] **1 a :** something signified **:** IMPORT, MEANING, BEARING ⟨a familiar sight even though it broke upon her now with a new ~ —Thomas Hardy⟩ ⟨having cosmic ~*s,* which I never suspected, extracted from my work —T.S.Eliot⟩ ⟨apt to read ~ into every casual remark⟩ **b :** the quality of conveying or implying **:** SUGGESTIVENESS ⟨the young gentleman uttered this exultant sound with mysterious ~ —Charles Dickens⟩ **2 a :** the quality of being important **:** CONSEQUENCE, MOMENT ⟨knack for discovering the ordinary and investing it with warmth and ~ —Arthur Knight⟩ ⟨the industrial ~ of coal⟩ **b :** the quality of being statistically significant **syn** see IMPORTANCE

sig·nif·i·can·cy \-kənsē, -si\ *n* -ES [L *significantia*] **1 :** the quality or state of being significant **:** EXPRESSIVENESS **2 :** SIGNIFICANCE

¹sig·nif·i·cant \-kənt\ *adj* [L *significant-, significans,* pres. part. of *significare* to signify — more at SIGNIFY] **1 :** having meaning; *esp* **:** full of import **:** SUGGESTIVE, EXPRESSIVE ⟨the painter's task to pick out the ~ details —Herbert Read⟩ ⟨~ anecdote⟩ **2 a :** suggesting or containing some concealed, disguised, or special meaning **:** standing as a sign or token ⟨perhaps her glance was ~⟩ **b :** INDICATIVE ⟨his actions were more ~ of his real purpose than were his words⟩ **3 a :** having or likely to have influence or effect **:** deserving to be considered **:** IMPORTANT, WEIGHTY, NOTABLE ⟨even though the individual results may seem small, the total of them is ~ —F. D.Roosevelt⟩ **b :** characterized by conveyance of an idea, thought, or feeling ⟨transform what would otherwise be meaningless juxtapositions or sequences of sensations into ~ entities —Vernon Lee⟩ **c :** probably caused by something other than mere chance ⟨~ decrease in average yearly growth⟩ ⟨statistically ~ correlation between vitamin deficiency and disease⟩ **d :** characteristic and essential to the determination of some larger element of a language **:** DISTINCTIVE ⟨a ~ grammatical form⟩ ⟨every language . . . moves within a clearly definable range of ~ speech sounds —R.A.Hall b.1911⟩ ⟨the difference between the initial sounds of *keel* and *cool* is not ~ in English⟩ **syn** see EXPRESSIVE

²significant \"\ *n* -S **:** something that has or conveys significance **:** SIGN, TOKEN, SYMBOL

significant figures *n pl* **:** figures of a number that begin with the first figure to the left that is not zero and that end with the last figure to the right that is not zero or is a zero that is considered to be correct

sig·nif·i·cant·ly *adv* **:** in a significant manner ⟨mentioned ~ that he was very short of money⟩ **:** to a significant degree ⟨~ large number of exceptions⟩ ⟨men made ~ higher scores than the women⟩

sig·nif·i·cate \-kət, -fə,kāt\ *n* -S [ME *significat,* fr. L *significatum,* fr. neut. of *significatus,* past part. of *significare*] **1 a :** thing that is signified or indicated **2 :** one of several characters or instances signified by a common term

sig·ni·fi·ca·tion \,signəfəˈkāshən\ *n* -S [ME *significacioun,* fr. OF *signification,* fr. L *signification-, significatio,* fr. *significatus* (past part. of *significare* to signify) + *-ion-, -io* -ion — more at SIGNIFY] **1 a :** the act of signifying **:** a making known (as a choice, intent, decision) by signs or other means **b :** a formal notification ⟨~ of a judicial decree⟩ **2 a :** IMPORT, SIGNIFICANCY ⟨few of our poets have responded to its beauty and ~ —Norman Douglas⟩ **b :** the meaning that a sign, character, or token is intended to convey **:** SENSE ⟨using the word in its ordinary ~⟩ **c** *obs* **:** TOKEN, INDICATION **3** *chiefly dial* **:** IMPORTANCE, CONSEQUENCE **4 a :** the connotation or comprehension of a term or the implications of a proposition **b :** the process of designating — compare DESIGNATION 6

¹sig·nif·i·ca·tive \sigˈnifə,kā\|d·\|iv, -,kəl, \|t\|, \|ēv *also* \|əv\ *adj* [ME, fr. MF *significatif,* fr. LL *significativus,* fr. L *significatus* + *-ivus* -ive] **1 :** pointing out or representing by an external sign **:** serving as a sign **:** INDICATIVE **2 :** having signification or meaning **:** expressive of a usu. concealed meaning **:** SIGNIFICANT, SUGGESTIVE **3 :** of or relating to signification (sense 4) **:** DESIGNATIVE ⟨in the proposition "she is a beauty" *beauty* is a ~ term⟩ — **sig·nif·i·ca·tive·ly** \\|əvlē, -li\ *adv* — **sig·nif·i·ca·tive·ness** \\|ivnəs, \|ēv- *also* \|əv-\ *n* -ES

²significative \"\ *n* -S **:** a significative thing or term

sig·nif·i·ca·tor \-,kād·ə(r), -ātə-\ *n* -S [LL, fr. L *significatus* + *-or*] **:** one that signifies or foreshows; *specif* **:** a planet that rules a house in a horoscope

significator of life : ASCENDANT 1

sig·nif·i·ca·to·ry \-,kə,tōrē\ *adj* [LL *significatorius,* fr. L *significatus* + *-orius* -ory] **:** SIGNIFICATIVE ⟨names of deities are often ~ of their special powers⟩

sig·nif·i·ca·tum \(,)sig,nifəˈkäd·əm, -kād-\ *n, pl* **significa·ta** \-d·ə\ [L — more at SIGNIFICATE] **:** something that a sign intensionally signifies **:** SIGNIFICATION

sig·nif·i·ca·vit \-kāvət, -kāv-\ *n* -S [ME, fr. L, he has signified (the first word in the writ), 3d per. sing. perf. ind. of *significare*] **1 a :** a bishop's certificate that a person has been in a state of excommunication for 40 days **b :** a resulting chancery writ ordering the recalcitrant's imprisonment until submission to the church **2 :** a writ commanding a stay of a suit because of plaintiff's excommunication

sig·nif·ics \sigˈnifiks\ *n pl but sing or pl in constr* [*signify* + *-ics*] **:** SEMIOTIC, SEMANTICS

si·gni·fié \sēnyəfˈyā\ *n* -S [F, fr. past part. of *signifier*] **:** SIGNIFICATUM

sig·ni·fi·er \ˈsignə,fī(ə)r, -īə\ *n* -S **:** one that signifies **:** SIGN

sig·ni·fy \-ī\ *vb* -ED/-ING/-ES [ME *signifien,* fr. OF *signifier,* fr. L *significare,* fr. *signum* sign, mark + *-i-* + *-ficare* -fy — more at SIGN] *vt* **1 a :** to be a sign of **:** MEAN, DENOTE ⟨a well⸗ proportioned voice that *signified* a sense of justice and compassion —Osbert Sitwell⟩ ⟨sentences ~ propositions⟩ ⟨perfection . . . *signifies* the approaching end of an epoch —A.N. Whitehead⟩ ⟨the name is derived from the Celtic *alb,* which by some is made to ~ white, by others height —Marrion Wilcox⟩ **b :** to bear as an inference or logical consequence **:** IMPLY ⟨machinery *signifies* urgency —David Sylvester⟩ **2 a :** to show or make known esp. by a conventional token (as word, signal, gesture) ⟨*signified* his desire for another slice⟩ **b :** ANNOUNCE, INTIMATE ⟨*signified* his willingness to run for the office⟩ **3** *obs* **:** INFORM ~ *vi* **:** to have meaning or significance **:** be of consequence **:** MATTER ⟨according to this interpretation, only economic relations ~ —*Times Lit. Supp.*⟩ ⟨never mind, it doesn't ~⟩ ⟨married to Vulcan or married to Mars, what does it ~ —W.S.Gilbert⟩ **syn** see MEAN

sign in *vi* **:** to make a record of arrival by signing a register or punching a time clock ~ *vt* **:** to record arrival of (a person) or receipt of (an article) by signing

signing *pres part of* SIGN

sign·ist \ˈsīnəst\ *n* -S [¹*sign* + *-ist*] **1 :** SIGN PAINTER **2 :** one who believes in the exclusive use of signs for teaching the deaf

sign language *n* **1 :** a method of communicating by means of systematic conventionalized chiefly manual gestures used by the deaf or by people speaking different languages ⟨*sign language* of the American Plains Indians⟩ **2 :** DACTYLOLOGY

sign·less \ˈsīnləs\ *adj* **:** having no algebraic sign

sign·man \-mən\ *n, pl* **signmen :** SIGN PAINTER

sign manual *n, pl* **signs manual 1 a :** SIGNATURE; *specif* **:** the king's signature on a royal grant or charter placed at the top of the document **b :** an identifying mark or device **2 :** a hand gesture for conveying a command or message

sign of aggregation : any of various conventional devices used in mathematics to indicate that two or more terms are to be treated as one quantity — compare BRACE, BRACKET, PARENTHESIS, VINCULUM

sign off *vi* **1 :** to withdraw from an engagement or association **2 :** to make a sign-off bid ⟨partner *signed off* with four spades⟩ **3 a :** to announce the end of a message, program, or broadcast and discontinue transmitting **b :** to end a speech or a conversation **:** fall silent **c :** to cease or withdraw from an activity **:** QUIT

sign-off \ˈ⸗,⸗\ *n* -S [*sign off*] **:** the act of signing off; *specif* **:** a bid in contract conventionally urging one's partner to pass

sign of inequality : a sign (as ≠ or ≑) indicating that one quantity is not equal to another

sign of summation : the Greek character Σ placed before a general term to indicate the sum of all terms of which it is the type

sign of the cross : a gesture of the hand forming a cross; *esp* **:** such a motion from one's forehead to the breast and from the left to the right shoulder in the Roman Catholic Church or from the right to the left shoulder in the Eastern Orthodox Church

sign on *vi* **:** to engage oneself for duty by signature or agreement **:** ENLIST ⟨*signed on* as a member of the crew⟩ ⟨*signed on* for another six years⟩ ~ *vt* **:** to secure the signature of **:** sign up **:** EMPLOY

si·gnor *also* **si·gnior** \(ˈ)sēnˈyō(ə)r, -yō(-\ *n, pl* **signors** \-rz\ *or* **si·gno·ri** \⸗ˈyōr(,)ē, -ō(,)rē\ [It *signor* (when followed by a name), *signore,* fr. ML *senior* superior, magnate, lord, fr. L, adj., elder — more at SENIOR] **1 :** a usu. Italian man of rank or gentility **2 :** MISTER — used as a title of courtesy prefixed to the name of an Italian man

si·gno·ra \(ˈ)sēnˈyōrə, -yȯrə\ *n, pl* **signoras** \-rəz\ *or* **si·gno·re** \-ōr(,)ā, -ō(,)rā\ [It, fem. of *signore*] **1 :** an Italian married woman usu. of rank or gentility **2 :** MISTRESS — used as a title prefixed to the name of an Italian married woman

si·gno·re \-ōr(,)ā, -ō(,)r\|\ *n, pl* **signo·ri** \\|ē\ [It] **:** SIGNOR 1

si·gno·ria \,sēnyəˈrēə\ *n* -S [It, fr. *signore* + *-ia* -y (fr. L)] **:** SIGNORY

si·gno·ri·al \(ˈ)sēnˈyōrēəl, -yȯr-; ˈsēnyəˈrē-\ *adj* **:** relating or belonging to a signory or a lord ⟨~ privilege⟩ ⟨~ courts⟩

si·gno·ri·na \ˌsēnyəˈrēnə\ *n, pl* **signorinas** \-rēnəz\ *or* **signori·ne** \-rē(,)nā\ [It, dim. of *signora*] **1 :** an unmarried Italian woman **2 :** MISS — used as a title prefixed to the name of an unmarried Italian woman

¹si·gno·ry *or* **si·gnio·ry** \ˈsēnyərē\ *n* -ES [ME *signerie, signorie,* fr. MF *seigneurie, signerie, signorie* — more at SEIGNEURY] **:** SEIGNIORY

²signory \"\ *n* -ES [It *signoria*] **:** the chief executive body of a medieval Italian city (as Venice)

sign out *vi* **:** to indicate departure by signing a register ⟨*signed out* of her dormitory for the evening⟩ ⟨*sign out* of a hospital⟩ or by punching a time clock ~ *vt* **:** to record or approve the release or departure of ⟨*sign* books *out* of a library⟩

sign painter *n* **:** one who paints signs, notices, billboards, posters

¹signpost \ˈ⸗,⸗\ *n* [¹*sign* + *post*] **1 :** a post bearing a sign or signs; *specif* **:** a guidepost at a crossroad **2 :** GUIDE, BEACON ⟨~*s* which, in a well-regulated market, show the way along which savings ought to move —W.T.C.King⟩

²signpost \"\ *vt* **:** to provide with signposts or guides ⟨statistics and endpaper maps to ~ the reader —Grace Banyard⟩

signs *pl of* SIGN, *pres 3d sing of* SIGN

sig·num \ˈsignəm\ *n, pl* **sig·na** \-nə\ [L — more at SIGN] **1 :** something that marks or identifies or represents **:** SIGN, SIGNATURE **2** [ML, fr. LL, ringing of a bell, fr. L, sign] **:** a tower bell large enough to serve as a signal

sign up *vi* **:** to join a working force or an organization or scheme or accept an obligation by signing a contract **:** CONTRACT ⟨*sign up* for a set of reference volumes⟩ ~ *vt* **:** to induce to sign a contract **:** contract with ⟨*sign* a customer *up* for a new car⟩

sign vehicle *n* **:** a particular event (as a sound or gesture) or object (as a written character or word) that acts as a sign

signwriter \ˈ⸗,⸗⸗\ *n* **:** one that letters signs (as for advertising)

sigs *pl of* SIG

si·gua \ˈsē(,)(g)wä\ *n, pl* **sigua** *or* **siguas** *usu cap* [Sp, of AmerInd origin] **1 :** a Nahuatlan people on the Atlantic coast of Panama **2 :** a member of the Sigua people

si·ha·sa·pa \sə̇ˈhäsəpə\ *n, pl* **sihasapa** *or* **sihasapas** *usu cap* **1 :** SIKSIKA **2 :** a people of the western plains constituting a division of the Teton Dakotas

¹si·ka \ˈsēkə\ *n* -S [Jap *shika*] **1 :** JAPANESE DEER **2 :** any of several deers of the eastern Asiatic mainland closely related to the Japanese deer

²sika \ˈsikə\ *n* -S [of Cariban origin; akin to Galibi *chico* chigoe] **:** CHIGOE

sikar *or* **sikhara** *var of* SHIKARA

sike \ˈsīk\ *n* -S [ME *syke, sike,* fr. OE *sīc;* akin to OHG *seih* urine, ON *sīk* small stream, ditch, OE *sīcerian* to trickle — more at SICKER] **1** *dial chiefly Brit* **:** a small stream; *esp* **:** one that dries up in summer **:** BROOK, GUTTER **2** *dial chiefly Brit* **:** DITCH, TRENCH, DRAIN

si·kel·i·an \sə̇ˈkelēən\ *n* -S [Gk *sikeloi* Sicels + E *-ian*] **:** SICEL

sikeliot *cap, var of* SICELIOT

sik·er \ˈsikə(r)\ *chiefly Scot var of* ¹SICKER

¹sikh \ˈsēk\ *n* -S *usu cap* [Hindi, lit., disciple, fr. Skt *śikṣati* he studies, desiderative of *śaknoti* he is strong, is able — more at SHAKTI] **:** an adherent of Sikhism

²sikh \"\ *adj, usu cap* **1 :** of, relating to, or characteristic of Sikhism **2 :** of, relating to, or characteristic of the Sikhs

sikh·ism \ˈsē,kizəm\ *n* -S *cap* [¹*sikh* + *-ism*] **:** a radically monotheistic religion of India founded about 1500 in the Punjab and characterized by its worship of one deity, by its allegiance to sacred scriptures, and by its witness to a line of 10 personal gurus until the guruship was transferred in 1708 — compare KHALSA 2, NANAKPANTHI

si·kin·nis \sə̇ˈkinəs\ *n* -ES [Gk, of Thraco-Phrygian origin] **:** a grotesque orgiastic dance of ancient Greece associated with the satyric drama

sik·kim·ese \ˌsikəˈmēz, -ēs\ *n, pl* **sikkimese** *cap* [*Sikkim* + E *-ese*] **:** a native or inhabitant of the territory of Sikkim in northeastern India

sik·si·ka \ˈsiksəkə\ *n, pl* **siksika** *or* **siksikas** *usu cap* [Blackfoot, fr. *siksinam* black + *oqkatsh* foot] **1 a :** an Algonquian people of Montana and southern Alberta and Saskatchewan, Canada **b :** a member of such people **2 a :** ¹BLACKFOOT 1a **b :** ¹BLACKFOOT 1b

siku *var of* SICU

sil \ˈsil\ *n* -S [L] **:** YELLOW OCHER 1

sil- *comb form* [*silicon*] **:** containing or derived from silicon ⟨*silane*⟩ — compare SILIC-

sil *abbr* **1** silence **2** silver

sila- *or* **sil-** *comb form* [ISV, fr. *sil-* + *-a-*] **:** containing silicon esp. in place of carbon ⟨*sila*cyclohexane C_5SiH_{12}⟩

¹si·lage \ˈsīlij, -lēj\ *n* -S [short for ¹*ensilage*] **:** fodder (as of field corn, sorghum, grass, or clover) either green or mature converted into succulent winter feed for livestock through processes of fermentation usu. by being cut fine and blown into an airtight chamber (as a silo) where it is compressed to exclude air and where it undergoes an acid fermentation that retards spoiling — called also *ensilage*

²silage \"\ *vt* -ED/-ING/-S **:** ENSILE

silage cutter *n* **1 :** a stationary machine for chopping forage for silage and delivering it into the silo **2** *or* **silage harvester :** FIELD CHOPPER

sil·ane \ˈsi,lān\ *n* -S [ISV *sil-* + meth*ane*] **:** any of several silicon hydrides having the general formula Si_nH_{2n+2} analogous to that of hydrocarbons of the methane series; *esp* **:** MONOSILANE — compare CHLOROSILANE, DISILANE

sil·crete \ˈsil,krēt\ *n* -S [*silica* + ²*concrete*] **:** a superficial quartzite formed by the cementation of rock fragments (as soil, sand, or gravel) by silica

sild \ˈsil\ *n, pl* **sild** *or* **silds** [Norw, herring; akin to ON *sīld, sild* herring and perh. to ON *sā* to sow — more at SOW] **:** a young herring other than a brisling that is canned as a sardine in Norway

¹sile \ˈsī(ə)l\ *n* -S [ME, perh. fr. OE *sȳl* pillar, column; akin to OHG *sūl* pillar, ON *sūl, sūla,* Goth *sauls*] *Scot* **:** BEAM, RAFTER

²sile \"\ *vi* -ED/-ING/-S [ME] *dial chiefly Brit* **:** to move esp. downward with a flowing or gliding motion ⟨the rain *siled* down⟩

³sile \"\ *vt* -ED/-ING/-S [ME *silen,* of Scand origin; akin to Sw *sila* to strain, *sil* strainer, Norw *sile* to strain, *sil* strainer] *dial Brit* **:** STRAIN, FILTER ⟨~ milk⟩

⁴sile \"\ *n* -S [ME, of Scand origin; akin to Sw & Norw *sil* strainer] *dial Brit* **:** STRAINER, SIEVE

⁵sile \"\ *dial var of* SOIL

⁶sile \"\ *n* -S [of Scand origin; akin to ON *sīld* herring — more at SILD] *dial Brit* **:** spawn or fry of fish (as herring)

si·len \ˈsīlən\ *n* -S [L *silenus* — more at SILENUS] **:** SILENUS

¹si·lence \ˈsīlən(t)s\ *n* -S [ME, fr. OF, fr. L *silentium,* fr. *silent-, silens* silent] **1 :** the state of keeping or being silent **:** forbearance from speech or noise **:** MUTENESS ⟨that ~ in the kitchen when, on a drowsy afternoon, the ticking of the clock would stop —Carson McCullers⟩ ⟨sat close together smoking contentedly and in ~ —Fred Majdalany⟩ ⟨complete radio ~ guarded whereabouts of the . . . powerful task force —K.M. Dodson⟩ — often used interjectionally **2 a :** absence of sound **:** absence of noise ⟨~ of midnight⟩ **b :** a general stillness **:** a relative stillness in which particular sounds may be distinctly heard ⟨rooster would crow lingeringly in the sunny ~ —Marjory S. Douglas⟩ ⟨starlings chattered in a rural ~ —Aldous Huxley⟩ **3 :** absence of mention: **a :** OBLIVION, OBSCURITY ⟨wrote it in the thirties of last century and after seventy years of ~ someone gave it forth again —H.J.Laski⟩ **b** (1) **:** failure to make something known **:** tacit omission ⟨in the ~ of any positive rule it would be presumed that foreign corporations were by comity permitted to make contracts —Charles Fairman⟩ ⟨took advantage of the fundamental law's ~ to twist it to their own purposes —F.A.Ogg & Harold Zink⟩ ⟨the studied ~*s* of the document as to the existence of God —W.L.Sperry⟩ (2) **:** SECRECY ⟨broke the ~ which has shrouded use of radar for aircraft navigation by the armed forces —David Mannheimer⟩ **c :** withholding from written communication ⟨a decade of ~ on the part of such a writer —M.D.Geismar⟩; *broadly* **:** cessation of any state of communicativeness or productivity ⟨producing sculptors of this authority after so long and heavy a ~ —J.T.Soby⟩ **4 a :** a period of being silent **:** a space of time marked by the cessation or absence of speech or of noises ⟨a movie of waiting and of ~*s* at the pithead and in the pit as the rescuers work their way toward the trapped men —*Time*⟩; *specif* **:** such a period observed in commemoration **b :** REST 5 ⟨elegiac meter of the poems (in which a ~ takes the place of the last foot of the distich) —Madeleine S. & J.L.Miller⟩ **5 a** *usu cap* **:** the state beyond death **b :** DEATH **6 :** lack of flavor or odor in distilled spirits **:** FLATNESS

²silence \"\ *vb* -ED/-ING/-S *vt* **1 :** to compel or reduce to silence **:** cause to be still **:** stop the noise of **:** STILL ⟨whatever specious arguments would ~ an opponent —John Dewey⟩ ⟨the air intake must be *silenced* to some degree —R.L.Boyer⟩ **2 a :** to restrain from the exercise of any function involving the expression of opinion; *esp* **:** to restrain from the act of preaching **b :** to put down **:** REPRESS, SUPPRESS ⟨violent means were used to ~ unwelcome opinions —R.P.Ludlum⟩ ⟨a nation that ~*s* or intimidates original minds —H.S. Commager⟩ **3 :** to cause to cease hostile firing by return fire or bombing ⟨~ the batteries of an enemy⟩ ⟨*silenced* the guns with hand grenades —P.W.Thompson⟩ **~** *vi* **1 :** to become silent **2 :** to cause silence ⟨the common denominator ~*s* and satisfies —B.N.Cardozo⟩

silence cloth *n* **:** a pad (as of flannel or felt) used under a tablecloth

silenced *adj* [fr. past part. of ²*silence*] **:** reduced to silence

si·lenc·er \-nsə(r)\ *n* -s **:** one that silences: as **a :** a device that when applied to exhaust or suction lines absorbs or silences the sound waves which produce undesirable noises **b** *chiefly Brit* **:** the muffler of an internal-combustion engine **c :** a silencing device for small arms that permits the exit of the projectile but reduces the noise without materially impeding the escape of the exploding gases **d :** a device for silencing or reducing noise ⟨door ~⟩

si·le·ne \sī'lēnē\ *n* [NL, prob. fr. L *silenus* silenus] **1** *cap* **:** a very large and widely distributed genus of plants (family Caryophyllaceae) having mostly showy flowers of various colors with a 10-nerved 5-toothed calyx and 3 styles and fruit with a capsule opening by 3 or 6 teeth — see BLADDER CAMPION, CATCHFLY, MOSS CAMPION, WILD PINK; compare LYCHNIS **2** -s **:** any plant of the genus *Silene*

si·le·nic \sī'lēnik\ *adj, sometimes cap* [*silenus* + *-ic*] **:** of, relating to, or characteristic of Silenus or the sileni

¹si·lent \'sīlənt\ *adj, often* -ER/-EST [L *silent-, silens,* fr. pres. part. of *silēre* to be silent; akin to Goth *anasilan* to subside, abate (of wind), L *sinere* to leave, let go, lay — more at SITE] **1 :** making no utterance: **a :** unable to speak **:** MUTE, TONGUE-TIED, AWESTRUCK ⟨stared at the Pacific . . . ~, upon a peak in Darien —John Keats⟩ **b :** unaccustomed or indisposed to speak **:** not conversing or answering **:** resolved not to speak ⟨he laughed and chattered, but she was ~, seeming to brood over something —D.H.Lawrence⟩ ⟨the ~ suspect, refusing to answer the police⟩ **2 :** free from sound or noise **:** making no sound or noise **:** perfectly quiet **:** NOISELESS, STILL ⟨a ~ room⟩ ⟨a ~ audience⟩ ⟨a ~ forest⟩ **3 a :** conducted, performed, enjoyed, or borne without spoken word or utterance **:** UNSPOKEN, TACIT ⟨the banquet, at first so ~, slowly changes to a merry tumult —Lafcadio Hearn⟩ ⟨~ protest must at length come to words —Thomas Carlyle⟩ ⟨~ reading⟩ ⟨~ prayer⟩ **b :** not expressed in words **:** felt or experienced without expression in words or vocal utterance ⟨suffering in ~ grief⟩ **4 a :** making no mention or account **:** omitting explanation and leaving questions unanswered ⟨on the crucial point of enforcement methods the assembly resolution is ~ —Ruth Lawson⟩ ⟨did not tell us that logic is to be ignored when experience is ~ —B.N.Cardozo⟩ ⟨remained ~ on the reasons for the change⟩ **b :** not recorded **:** not mentioned, explained, or referred to ⟨the secretary's ~ role in the conspiracy⟩ **c :** not known or not generally known **:** unnoticed and therefore not appreciated ⟨the railways might well be said to render a ~ service —O.S.Nock⟩ ⟨new ways of life developing under the ~ pressure of a freer environment —V.L.Parrington⟩ **d :** taking no active part in the conduct of a business ⟨a ~ member of a firm⟩ — compare SILENT PARTNER **e :** unresponsive esp. from lack of feeling or understanding ⟨this humbug of the judge as a soulless automaton whose mind and heart are ~ when he performs his operations —H.J.Laski⟩ **5 :** being an orthographic letter or letter combination which if removed from a word would still leave letters enough to account for the pronunciation of the word ⟨~ *b* in *doubt*⟩ ⟨~ *ph* in *phthisis*⟩ or which serves as a conventional indicator of the quality of another letter without itself being pronounced ⟨~ *e* in *pine* shows that the *i* has the value \ī\ rather than the value \i\ in *pin*⟩ **6 a :** maintaining a state of inactivity ⟨a ~ volcano⟩ **b** (1) **:** not exhibiting the usual evidences (as signs or symptoms) of presence ⟨a ~ bone fracture⟩ ⟨~ heat in cattle⟩ **:** causing no symptoms ⟨~ gallstones⟩ ⟨~ tuberculosis⟩ (2) **:** characterized by such a silent state ⟨the ~ phase of a tumor⟩ (3) **:** yielding no detectable response to stimulation — used esp. of an association area of the brain **7 :** FLAVORLESS, FLAT — used of distilled spirits esp. when rectified for use in the arts **8 a :** lacking spoken dialogue **b :** of or relating to silent motion pictures ⟨the ~ screen⟩ ⟨Hollywood in the great days of the ~ stars —Budd Schulberg⟩ **9 :** inaudible to the human ear because outside its frequency range ⟨a ~ dog whistle⟩

syn RETICENT, RESERVED, TACITURN, UNCOMMUNICATIVE, CLOSE, CLOSE-MOUTHED, CLOSE-LIPPED, TIGHT-LIPPED, SECRETIVE: as here discussed, SILENT may refer to a disposition to speak rather little or to a determination not to speak ⟨a *silent* man with a great sense of his personal worth which made his speeches guarded —Joseph Conrad⟩ ⟨was very *silent* during the speech and . . . had listened attentively —George Meredith⟩ RETICENT indicates reluctance to speak out induced either by cautious discreetness or by shy lack of assertiveness ⟨almost *reticent* in his stingy use of words exactly chiseled out of the moment's need —W.A.White⟩ ⟨about his own experiences . . . was inclined to be *reticent* . . . because he considered them, as he put it, uninteresting —Kenneth Roberts⟩ RESERVED describes speaking or acting under the restraining influence of caution or formality checking easy unguarded expression ⟨I wished that she had told me frankly . . . Jane was always so *reserved* —Rose Macaulay⟩ ⟨even the *reserved* Washington wrote caustically of their bad manners —Allan Nevins & H.S. Commager⟩ TACITURN suggests a deep and accustomed disinclination to talk much; it may connote the unsociable or the laconic ⟨he had become more and more gloomy and *taciturn*. Mills tried in vain to draw him into talk —C.B.Nordhoff & J.N.Hall⟩ ⟨always *taciturn*, he now hardly spoke at all —Stuart Cloete⟩ UNCOMMUNICATIVE indicates an unwillingness to impart information ⟨an atomic scientist quite *uncommunicative* about his work⟩ CLOSE indicates a general disposition to keep information from being revealed ⟨will confide in nobody . . . every one feels that he is emphatically *close* —J.H.Newman⟩ ⟨you're a *close* one, but you give yourself away sometimes —Willa Cather⟩ CLOSE-MOUTHED and CLOSE-LIPPED have about the same suggestions as CLOSE, although they are more likely to be used in reference to matters confidential or secret ⟨a millionaire's *close-mouthed* confidential secretary⟩ ⟨a duke's *close-lipped* adviser⟩ TIGHT-LIPPED may suggest resolute or determined silence about a specific matter ⟨company officials, all *tight-lipped* about the uranium thefts⟩ SECRETIVE suggests either a disposition towards carefully guarding secrets or undue caution or concealment about less important matters ⟨you're so excessively *secretive* that I can't help being curious —Dashiell Hammett⟩

²silent \"\ *n* -s **1** *obs* **:** a time of silence ⟨the ~ of the night —Shak.⟩ **2 silents** *pl* **:** motion pictures without spoken dialogue ⟨some primitive Western of the ~*s*, at which you were supposed to laugh —Edmund Wilson⟩ ⟨in the days of the ~*s* —Alfred Kazin⟩

silent area *n* [so called fr. the comparative absence of symptoms when it is injured] **:** an association area of the cerebral cortex

silent barter *or* **silent trade** *n* **:** DUMB BARTER

silent butler *n* **:** a small portable receptacle with projecting handle and hinged lid for gathering up table crumbs and the contents of ash trays

silent butler

silent cop *n* **:** a device usu. equipped with lights and signs and placed at the center of a crossroads to replace an officer directing traffic

silent gerrymander *n* **:** a gerrymander that has been developed through failure of a legislature to revise election district boundaries in accord with population shifts usu. with benefit to one political party over its opponents

si·len·tial \sī'lenchəl\ *adj* [L *silentium* silence + E *-al*] **:** conducted in silence **:** SILENT

si·len·ti·ary \sī'lenchē,erē\ *n* -ES [L *silentiarius* slave charged with maintaining silence among the domestic staff, fr. *silentium* silence + *-arius* -ary] **1 :** an advocate of silence esp. as a religious observance **2 :** one of various court officials of the later Roman Empire sworn not to divulge secrets of state **3 :** one appointed to keep silence and order (as in a court of law or a public assembly)

si·len·tious \sī'lenchəs\ *adj* [L *silentiosus,* fr. *silentium* + *-osus* -ous] **:** habitually silent **:** TACITURN, RETICENT

si·lent·ly *adv* **:** in a silent manner **:** in silence **:** without speaking **:** NOISELESSLY

si·lent·ness *n* -ES **:** the quality or state of being or keeping silent **:** NOISELESSNESS, SPEECHLESSNESS

silent partner *n* **1 :** a partner who has no voice in the firm business as between partners **2 :** SECRET PARTNER

silent service *n* **1 :** NAVY — used with *the* **2 :** the submarine service — used with *the*

silent system *n* **:** a system of penal discipline that forbids conversation among prisoners ⟨subjected to a *silent system* . . . for infraction of rules —L.E.Lawes⟩

silent treatment *n* **:** an act of completely ignoring a person or thing by resort to silence esp. as a means of expressing contempt or disapproval ⟨too often, the most forthright speakers were given the *silent treatment* —Saul Carson⟩

silent vote *n* **:** the vote of those whose choice is not publicly known ⟨it's feared the *silent vote* is going to go against the administration —*Newsweek*⟩

si·le·nus \sī'lēnəs\ *n, pl* **sile·ni** \-ē,nī\ *often cap* [L, fr. Gk *silēnos,* fr. *Silēnos* Silenus, foster father and companion of Dionysus] **:** a minor woodland deity of ancient Greek mythology having usu. human form but with a horse's ears and tail and occas. with the legs of a horse or goat and being one of the companions of Dionysus but usu. distinguished from a satyr by being always old, frequently bald, and always bearded

siles *pl of* SILE, *pres 3d sing of* SILE

si·le·sia \sī'lēzh(ē)ə, sə'-, -ēsh(ē)ə\ *n* -s [fr. *Silesia,* former Prussian province] **1** *archaic* **:** a linen cloth of Silesian origin **2 :** a soft sturdy lightweight cotton with a lustrous finish that is closely woven in twill weave and used esp. for linings and pockets

¹si·le·sian \-(ē)ən\ *adj, usu cap* [*Silesia,* region of central Europe formerly partly in Prussia & partly in Poland + E *-an*] **1 :** of, relating to, or characteristic of Silesia **2 :** of, relating to, or characteristic of the people of Silesia

²silesian \"\ *n* -s *cap* **:** a native or inhabitant of Silesia; *esp* **:** a German native of Silesia

si·letz \sī'lets, sə'-\ *n, pl* **siletz** *or* **siletzes** *usu cap* **1 a :** a Salishan people of the Oregon coast **b :** a member of such people **2 :** a language of the Siletz people

si·lex \'sī,leks\ *n* -ES [L *silic-, silex,* hard stone, flint, quartz — more at SHELL] **1 :** SILICA; *esp* **:** a pure form (as finely ground quartz or flint) for use as a filler in paints or wood or as a dental material **2 :** siliceous powders (as tripoli) for uses similar to those of silex

Silex \"\ *trademark* — used for a vacuum coffee maker

si·lex·ite \'sī,lek,sīt\ *n* -s [L *silex* + E *-ite*] **:** an igneous rock composed essentially of quartz, occurring in dikes, and representing the end members of the pegmatitic intrusions

¹sil·hou·ette \¦silə¦wet, *usu* -ed·+V\ *n* -s [F, after Étienne de *Silhouette* †1767 Fr. controller general of finances; fr. his parsimony and petty economies] **1 a :** a representation of the outlines of an object filled in with black or some other uniform color ⟨~*s* cut from paper⟩ ⟨a book illustrated with ~*s*⟩ **b :** a style of representation in which outlines are filled in with black or some other uniform color **:** OUTLINE 2a ⟨illustrations done in ~⟩ **2 :** the outline or a delineation of the outline of a person or thing esp. when used as a means of characterizing or identifying ⟨learn to identify ships or planes by their varying ~*s*⟩ ⟨the ~ of a new-model automobile⟩ ⟨the robin's handsome ~ —Morris Gilbert⟩ ⟨for a moment they were in ~ against a morning sky —Ross Santee⟩; *specif* **:** the outline or contour of a fashionable costume or part of such a costume varying from year to year and period to period ⟨this year's full-skirted ~⟩ ⟨an hourglass ~ in women's clothes⟩ **3 :** a photograph of essentially only two tones showing the subject against a light background **4 :** a halftone with background dots etched or cut away **5 :** a target shaped to approximate the silhouette of a man **6 :** the visible outline of the body in a movement of action in the dance **syn** see OUTLINE

silhouette 1a

²silhouette \"\ *vb* **silhouetted; silhouetted; silhouetting; silhouettes** *vt* **1 :** to represent by a silhouette **:** project upon a background like a silhouette ⟨the line of the dune *silhouetted* against the sky —W.T.Scott⟩ ⟨deep off-white color which does not ~ the pictures like the more glaring whites —J.T.Soby⟩ ⟨attack with the moon *silhouetting* the targets —E.L.Beach⟩ ⟨a flock of roosting vultures, *silhouetted* on the sky —G.W. Cable⟩ **2 :** to etch or cut away background dots of (a halftone) **~** *vi* **:** to appear in profile like a silhouette

sil·hou·et·tist \-ed·əst\ *n* -s [¹*silhouette* + *-ist*] **:** one who makes silhouettes

silic- *or* **silico-** *comb form* [*silicon* or *silicium*] **1 :** relating to or containing silicon or its compounds ⟨*silicone*⟩ ⟨*silicofluoride*⟩ ⟨*silicochloroform*⟩ — compare SIL-, SILA- **2 :** silicic and ⟨*silicalkaline*⟩ **3 :** silicosis and ⟨*silicotuberculosis*⟩

sil·i·ca \'siləkə, -lēkə\ *n* -s [NL, fr. L *silic-, silex* hard stone, flint, quartz — more at SHELL] **:** the chemically resistant dioxide SiO_2 of silicon that occurs naturally in the three crystalline modifications of quartz, tridymite, and cristobalite, in amorphous and hydrated forms (as opal), and in less pure forms (as sand, diatomite, tripoli) and combined in silicates, that can be prepared artificially as a fine white powder from water glass or other soluble silicates and also in colloidal form, and that is used chiefly in making glass, ceramic products, and refractories, in producing elemental silicon, its alloys, and compounds, and as an abrasive, adsorbent, and filler

silica aerogel *n* **:** colloidal silica in the form of a fine lightweight powder with grains having minute pores that is made from silica gel and used chiefly as thermal insulation esp. at low temperatures (as in refrigerators)

silica brick *n* **:** brick made from crushed quartzite bonded with milk of lime and used as a high-grade refractory

silica cement *n* **:** a refractory mortar suitable for laying silica brick

silica gel *n* **:** colloidal silica resembling coarse white sand in appearance but possessing many fine pores and therefore extremely adsorbent that is made by coagulation of hydrated silica and is used chiefly as a selective adsorbent and as a catalyst or catalyst carrier

silica glass *n* **:** VITREOUS SILICA

sil·i·cane \'silə,kān\ *n* -s [*silic-* + meth*ane*] **:** MONOSILANE

¹sil·i·cate \'silə,kāt\ *vt* -ED/-ING/-S [NL *silica* + E *-ate*] **:** to combine with silica or silicates **:** coat or impregnate with silica or silicates

²silicate \", -ləkət, *usu* -d·+V\ *n* -s [NL *silica* + E *-ate*] **1 :** a salt or ester derived from a silicic acid; *esp* **:** ORTHOSILICATE **2 :** any of numerous insoluble often complex metal salts that contain silicon and oxygen in the anion, that constitute the largest chemical group of minerals and with quartz make up the greater part of the earth's crust (as in rocks, soils, and clays) and building materials such as cement, concrete, bricks, and glass, and that have crystal structures characterized by fundamental units of SiO_4 tetrahedrons consisting of one silicon atom surrounded by four oxygen atoms either as independent groups (as in nesosilicates) or linked by sharing of one or more oxygen atoms — compare ALUMINOSILICATE, CYCLOSILICATE, INOSILICATE, PHYLLOSILICATE, SOROSILICATE, TECTOSILICATE

silicate bond *n* [²*silicate*] **:** a water-glass binder for abrasive particles (as in grinding wheels and sanding disks)

silicate cotton *n* **:** MINERAL WOOL

silicate of soda : SODIUM SILICATE — not used systematically

silicate paint *n* **:** a paint the vehicle of which consists chiefly of water glass and which is used esp. for painting on mortar

sil·i·ca·tion \,silə'kāshən\ *n* -s [¹*silicate* + *-ion*] **:** the act or process of silicating; *specif* **:** the development of silicates in rocks (as carbonates) orig. poor in them

sil·i·ca·ti·za·tion \,silə,kād·ə'zāshən\ *n* -s [²*silicate* + *-ization*] **:** SILICIFICATION

sil·i·ca·tor \'silə,kād·ə(r)\ *n* -s [¹*silicate* + *-or*] **:** one that puts a coat of sodium silicate on the inside of steel drums that are to be used for shipping caustic soda

silica ware *n* **:** ware consisting of silica usu. in the form of pure sand partly or wholly fused and shaped into tubes, dishes, and beakers for use as scientific apparatus

si·li·cea \sə'lishēə\ [NL, fr. L, neut. pl. of *siliceus* siliceous] *syn of* NONCALCAREA

siliceo- *comb form* [L *siliceus* siliceous] **:** siliceous and ⟨*siliceo*calcareous⟩ ⟨*siliceo*feldspathic⟩

si·li·ceous *also* **si·li·cious** \sə'lishəs\ *adj* [L *siliceus* of flint, fr. *silic-, silex* flint, quartz — more at SHELL] **1 :** of, relating to, or derived from silica **:** containing or resembling silica or a silicate **:** SILICIC ⟨~ limestone⟩ **2 :** SILICICOLOUS

siliceous sinter *n* **:** sinter formed by evaporation of the water of hot siliceous springs or geysers

siliceous sponge *n* **:** a sponge having a siliceous skeleton

silici- *comb form* [NL *silica*] **1 :** silex **:** silica ⟨*silici*ferous⟩ **2 :** siliceous and ⟨*silici*calcareous⟩

si·lic·ic \sə'lisik, -sēk\ *adj* [*silica* or *silicium* + *-ic*] **:** of, relating to, or derived from silica or silicon ⟨highly ~ rocks, such as normal granite —A.M.Bateman⟩

silicic acid *n* **:** any of various weakly acid substances formed in dilute solution or as gelatinous masses by treating soluble silicates with acids or obtained in the form of salts or esters; *esp* **:** ORTHOSILICIC ACID — compare METASILICIC ACID, SILICA GEL

sil·i·cic·o·lous \¦silə¦sikələs\ *adj* [*silici-* + *-colous*] **:** growing or thriving in siliceous soil ⟨~ plants⟩

sil·i·cide \'silə,sīd, -sə̇d\ *n* -s [ISV *silic-* + *-ide*] **:** a binary compound of silicon usu. with a more electropositive element or radical

si·li·ci·dize \sə'lisə,dīz\ *vt* -ED/-ING/-S [*silicide* + *-ize*] **:** to convert into a silicide

sil·i·cif·er·ous \¦silə¦sif(ə)rəs\ *adj* [*silici-* + *-ferous*] **:** producing, containing, or united with silica

si·lic·i·fi·ca·tion \sə,lisəfə'kāshən\ *n* -s [*silici-* + *-fication*] **:** the act or process of silicifying **:** the state of being silicified; *specif* **:** the development of silica minerals (as quartz and chert) by metasomatic action

silicified wood *n* [fr. past part. of *silicify*] **:** chalcedony in the form of petrified wood often preserving even microscopic details of the replaced wood

si·lic·i·fy \sə'lisə,fī\ *vb* -ED/-ING/-ES [*silici-* + *-fy*] *vt* **:** to convert into or impregnate with silica or siliceous material commonly in the form of quartz **~** *vi* **:** to become silicified

si·lic·i·o·phite \sə'lisēə,fīt\ *n* [*silici-* + *ophite*] **:** serpentine penetrated by opal

sil·i·ci·sponge \'siləsə,spənj, sə'lisə,-\ *n* [NL *Silicispongiae*] **:** a sponge of the class Noncalcarea

sil·i·ci·spon·gi·ae \,siləsə'spənjə,ē, sə,lisə'-, -pən-\ [NL, fr. *silici-* + *-spongiae*] *syn of* NONCALCAREA

si·li·ci·um \sə'lishēəm, -isēəm\ *n* -s [NL, fr. *silica* + *-ium*] **:** SILICON

sil·i·cize \'silə,sīz\ *vt* -ED/-ING/-S [*silic-* + *-ize*] **:** to treat with silicon or silica

sil·i·cle \'siləkəl\ *n* -s [L *silicula,* dim. of *siliqua* pod, husk — more at SHELL] **:** a silique of nearly equal length and width

silico- — see SILIC-

sil·i·co·aluminate \¦silə(,)kō+\ *n* [*silic-* + *aluminate*] **:** ALUMINOSILICATE

sil·i·co·chloroform \"+\ *n* [*silic-* + *chloroform*] **:** TRICHLOROSILANE

sil·i·co·flagellata \"+\ *n pl, cap* [NL, fr. *silic-* + *flagellata,* neut. pl. of *flagellatus* flagellate] *in some classifications* **:** a group of marine flagellates formerly classified among the radiolarians but now usu. constituting a family of the order Chrysomonadina and having one or two flagella, a definite nucleus, and a spiny siliceous skeleton like that of a radiolarian — **sil·i·co·flagellate** \"+\ *n*

sil·i·co·flagellatae \"+\ [NL, fr. *silic-* + *flagellatae,* fem. pl. of *flagellatus*] *syn of* SILICOFLAGELLATA

sil·i·co·fluoride \"+\ *n* [*silic-* + *fluoride*] **:** FLUOSILICATE — not used systematically

sil·i·co·mag·ne·sio·flu·o·rite \,silə̇kōmag,nēshō'flü(ə),rīt\ *n* -s [*silic-* + *magnesio-* + *fluor-* + *-ite*] **:** a mineral $Ca_4Mg_3Si_2O_5(OH)_2F_{10}$ consisting of a basic fluoride and silicate of calcium and magnesium

sil·i·co·manganese \¦silə(,)kō+\ *n* [*silic-* + *manganese*] **:** a crude alloy of silicon and manganese and some iron used esp. in the manufacture of alloy steel

sil·i·con \'siləkən, -lēkən, -lə,kän\ *n* -s [*silica* + *-on* (as in *carbon*)] **:** a tetravalent nonmetallic element that occurs in combined form as the most abundant element next to oxygen in the earth's crust, that can be obtained as brittle hard lustrous gray crystals with the lattice structure of diamond, as a glistening black graphitic form, or as a dark brown powder, that is usu. prepared by reducing silica with carbon in an electric furnace, and that is used chiefly in the form of alloys (as ferrosilicon), in combination with ceramic materials in cermets, and as a semiconductor (as in transistors) and element in photovoltaic cells ⟨~ plays an important part in the inorganic world, similar to that played by carbon in the organic world —Linus Pauling⟩ — symbol *Si*; see ELEMENT table

silicon bronze *n* **:** an alloy of copper and usu. 1.5 or 3 percent silicon with small amounts of various third elements (as zinc, tin, or manganese)

silicon carbide *n* **:** a compound SiC of silicon and carbon that is obtained as brittle crystals next to diamond and boron carbide in hardness and often dark bluish black and iridescent, that is made by heating sand and coke together in an electric resistance furnace, and that is used chiefly in crushed form as an abrasive esp. for grinding hard materials of low tensile strength (as cast iron or marble) and materials needing sharp cutting (as fiber, rubber, or aluminum), as a refractory, and in electric resistors

silicon chloride *n* **:** a chloride of silicon; *esp* **:** SILICON TETRACHLORIDE

silicon copper *n* **:** an alloy of 80 to 70 percent copper and 20 to 30 percent silicon used as an ingredient to free molten copper or brass from oxygen

silicon dioxide *n* **:** SILICA

sil·i·cone \'silə,kōn\ *n* -S [*silic-* + *-one*] **1 a :** an organic compound R_2SiO analogous to a ketone **b :** an organic siloxane; *esp* **:** any of a large group of polymerized organic siloxanes that are unusually stable over a wide temperature range, that are obtained as oily fluids, resins, and elastomers convertible into greases and other compounds, coatings, and rubbers, and that are used chiefly in waterproofing, lubrication, and electric insulation — see BOUNCING PUTTY **2 :** an organosilicon compound in which silicon is attached directly to carbon — used chiefly commercially

silicone rubber *n* **:** rubber made from silicone elastomers and characterized by its retention of flexibility, resilience, and tensile strength over a wide temperature range (as from −100° to +500°F) and its resistance to weathering, the electric arc, and many chemicals

silicon fluoride *n* **:** a fluoride of silicon; *esp* **:** SILICON TETRAFLUORIDE

silicon hydride *n* **:** a compound of silicon with hydrogen — see SILANE

sil·i·con·iza·tion \,silәkənə'zāshən\ *n* -S **:** the process of siliconizing

sil·i·con·ize \'silәkə,nīz\ *vt* -ED/-ING/-S [*silicon* + *-ize*] **1 :** to combine or impregnate with silicon; *specif* **:** to treat (a metal) with silicon or a silicon compound to form a protective surface alloy ⟨~ steel⟩ **2 :** to treat or coat (as a lens) with a silicone

silicon oxide *n* **:** an oxide of silicon; *esp* **:** SILICA

silicon spiegel *n* **:** a spiegeleisen containing 15 to 20 percent of manganese and 8 to 15 percent of silicon and used in making certain special steels

silicon tetrachloride *n* **:** a colorless fuming corrosive liquid $SiCl_4$ made usu. by heating silicon or silicon carbide with chlorine and used chiefly for smoke screens and in making chlorosilanes, silicones, and other organic derivatives of silicon

silicon tetrafluoride *n* **:** a colorless fuming suffocating gas SiF_4 made by the action of fluorine on silicon or of hydrofluoric acid on silica or silicates (as glass) and used chiefly in making fluosilicic acid and fluosilicates

sil·i·co·sis \,silə'kōsəs\ *n, pl* **silico·ses** \-ō,sēz\ [NL, fr. *silic-* + *-osis*] **:** a condition of massive fibrosis of the lungs marked by shortness of breath and resulting from prolonged inhalation of silica dusts by those (as stonecutters, asbestos workers, miners) regularly exposed to such dusts — compare [13]CON b

sil·i·co·thermic \,silə(,)kō+\ *adj* [*silic-* + *thermic*] **:** of or relating to a method of producing heat and chemical reduction by oxidizing finely crushed silicon or ferrosilicon with oxygen taken from another metal (as chromium)

[1]**sil·i·cot·ic** \,silə'käd·ik\ *adj* [*silic-* + *-otic*] **:** relating to, caused by, or affected with silicosis

[2]**silicotic** \"\ *n* -S **:** a person affected with silicosis

sil·i·co·titanate \,silə(,)kō+\ *n* [*silic-* + *titanate*] **:** a combined silicate and titanate

sil·i·co·tuberculosis \"+\ *n* [NL, fr. *silic-* + *tuberculosis*] **:** silicosis and tuberculosis in the same lung

sil·i·co·tungstate \"+\ *n* [*silic-* + *tungstate*] **:** a salt of a silicotungstic acid — called also *tungstosilicate*

sil·i·co·tungstic acid \"+ . . . -\ *n* [*silic-* + *tungstic*] **:** any of several heteropoly acids of silicon and tungsten; *esp* **:** a pale yellow crystalline acid $H_4SiW_{12}O_{40}.xH_2O$ containing 12 atoms of tungsten in the molecule, obtainable by acid hydrolysis of a mixture of sodium tungstate and sodium silicate, and used chiefly as a precipitant for alkaloids — called also *tungstosilicic acid*

si·lic·u·la \sə'likyələ\ *n, pl* **silicu·lae** \-yə,lē\ [NL, fr. L, dim. of *siliqua* pod, husk — more at SHELL] **:** SILICLE

si·lic·u·lar \-lə(r)\ *adj* [NL *silicula* + E *-ar*] **:** having the form or appearance of a silicle

sil·i·cule \'silə,kyül\ *n* -S [NL *silicula*] **:** SILICLE

si·lic·u·lose \sə'likyə,lōs\ *adj* [NL *siliculosus*, fr. *silicula* + L *-osus* -ose, -ous] **1 :** bearing silicles **2 :** of the form or appearance of a silicle **:** SILICULAR

si·lic·u·lous \-yələs\ *adj* [NL *siliculosus*] **:** SILICULOSE

siling *pres part of* SILE

silin·gal \sə'liŋgəl\ *or* **shilin·gol** \shə'-\ *n, pl* **silingal** *or* **silingals** *or* **shilingol** *or* **shilingols** *usu cap* **1 :** a branch of the East Mongols living in Inner Mongolia **2 :** a member of the Silingal people

sil·i·qua \'siləkwə\ *n, pl* **sili·quae** \-lə,kwē\ [NL, fr. L, pod, husk, a small weight, coin worth 1/24 solidus — more at SHELL] **1 :** SILIQUE **2** [L] **:** a Roman silver coin first issued by Constantine the Great **:** the 1/24 solidus or later the half miliarensis — **sil·i·qua·ceous** \,silə'kwāshəs\ *adj*

sil·i·qua·ria \,silə'kwa(a)rēə\ *n, cap* [NL, fr. L *siliqua* pod, husk + NL *-aria*] **:** a genus of worm shells (family Vermetidae) sometimes placed in a separate family and comprising forms that differ from those of the genus *Vermetus* in having a continuous slit or row of clefts or pores throughout the whorls of the shell

si·lique \sə'lēk, 'silik\ *n* -S [F, fr. NL *siliqua*, fr. L, pod, husk — more at SHELL] **:** a narrow elongated usu. many-seeded capsule that is characteristic of the family Cruciferae, consists of two valves with a false dissepiment, opens by sutures at either margin, and has the seeds attached to two parietal placentas

siliqui- *comb form* [NL *siliqua*] **:** siliqua ⟨*siliqui*ferous⟩ ⟨*siliqui*form⟩

sil·i·quose \'silə,kwōs\ *or* **sil·i·quous** \-kwəs\ *adj* [NL *siliquosus*, fr. *siliqua* + L *-osus* -ose, -ous] **:** bearing or having the form of a silique

[1]**silk** \'silk, 'siu̇k\ *n* -S [ME *selk*, *silk*, fr. OE *sioloc*, *seolc*, prob. of Baltic or Slav origin; akin to OPruss *silkas* silk, OSlav *shelkŭ*] **1 :** a fine continuous protein fiber produced by various insect larvae usu. for cocoons; *esp* **:** the lustrous tough elastic hygroscopic fiber that is produced by silkworms by secreting from two glands viscous fluid in the form of two filaments consisting principally of fibroin cemented into a single strand by sericin and solidifying in air, that is capable of being reeled in a single strand from the cocoon, and that with or without boiling off the sericin is used for textiles **2 a :** thread, yarn, or fabric made from silk filaments — see SPUN SILK **b :** strands of silk thread of various thicknesses and plain or braided used as suture material in surgery ⟨surgical ~⟩ ⟨~ technique⟩ **3 a :** a garment (as a dress) of silk **:** silk apparel ⟨a crowd dressed in ~⟩ ⟨printed ~*s* on sale today⟩ ⟨wear ~⟩ **b** (1) **:** a gown worn by a King's or Queen's Counsel or barrister of high rank appointed by the lord chancellor (2) **:** a King's or Queen's Counsel (3) **:** the rank or persons entitled to such a gown — see SILK GOWN **c silks** *pl* **:** the colored cap and blouse of a jockey or harness horse driver made in the registered racing color of the stable for which he is riding or driving in a particular race **4 a :** a filament resembling silk but produced by some other organism: as (1) **:** the filament produced by various spiders esp. in building their webs and used for cloth and telescopic sights (2) **:** the byssal thread of a mollusk of the genus *Pinna* **b :** a thread of such material or of wire (as used in a sieve of a sifter in flour milling) **5 a :** CORN SILK **b :** a style of corn silk — compare [1]TASSEL 2a **6 :** inclusions of minute crystals that impart a silky luster to a gem (as a ruby) **7 :** SILK SPONGE **8 :** PARACHUTE ⟨pack the ~⟩ ⟨the ~ opened⟩

[2]**silk** \"\ *adj* [ME, fr. [1]*silk*] **1 :** relating to or made of silk **:** SILKEN ⟨a ~ ribbon⟩ **2 :** resembling silk

[3]**silk** \"\ *vb* -ED/-ING/-S [[1]*silk*] *vt* **1 :** to fashion of or cover with silk **2 :** to strip (an ear of corn) of silk ~ *vi* **1 :** BLOSSOM — used of corn ⟨inbred lines were pollinated at successive intervals after ~*ing* —R.H.Andrew⟩ **2 :** to develop a striated appearance and luster suggestive of silk cloth — used of varnish and enamels

silk·a·line *or* **silk·o·line** *also* **silk·o·lene** \,silkə'lēn -iu̇k-\ *n* -S [*silkaline*, *silkolene*, fr. *silk* + *-aline*, *-olene*, alter. of *-oline* (as in *crinoline*); *silkoline* fr. *silk* + *-oline*] **:** a soft light cotton fabric in plain weave with a smooth lustrous finish similar to silk used plain or printed esp. for curtains and linings

silk cotton *n* **:** a cottony substance enveloping the seeds of any of various trees of the family Bombacaceae; *esp* **:** KAPOK — compare VEGETABLE SILK

silk-cotton family *n* [*silk cotton*] **:** BOMBACACEAE

silk-cotton tree *n* **:** a tree of the family Bombacaceae that produces silk cotton: as **a :** CEIBA 2a **b :** SIMAL

silk crab *n* **:** a mature female crab

silked \'silkt\ *adj* [[1]*silk* + *-ed*] **:** dressed in or covered with silk

[1]**silk·en** \'silkən, 'siu̇k-\ *adj* [ME, fr. OE *seolcen*, fr. *seolc* silk + *-en*] **1 :** made of silk **:** consisting of silk ⟨~ threads⟩ ⟨a ~ veil⟩ ⟨in certain spiders the female carries the eggs about with her in a ~ case —H.M.Parshley⟩ **2 :** resembling silk: as **a :** SOFT, LUSTROUS ⟨her ability to look gracefully ~ on occasion —Adrian Bell⟩ **b** (1) **:** agreeably smooth **:** HARMONIOUS ⟨~ voices⟩ ⟨the ~ sonority of the strings —Virgil Thomson⟩ ⟨doesn't hold with the ~ and the silver epithet —Josephine Miles⟩ (2) **:** INGRATIATING, INSINUATING ⟨said . . . in the ~ town voice —Paul Bowles⟩ **c :** DELICATE, TENDER, GENTLE ⟨~ slumbers⟩ ⟨a ~ touch⟩ **d :** LOW, EVEN ⟨a ~ sound⟩ **e :** extremely graceful **:** LITHE ⟨whirled upon him with the ~ savagery of a little panther —Elinor Wylie⟩ **3 :** furnished with silk **:** producing silk ⟨from ~ Samarcand —John Keats⟩ ⟨~ chambers⟩ **4 a :** dressed in silk ⟨~ ankles⟩ **b :** LUXURIOUS ⟨~ young gallants —F.X.Braun⟩ ⟨reading public is preoccupied with murder, mayhem, and ~ dalliance —*Police Rev.*⟩ **c :** EFFEMINATE ⟨~ sons of pride —Van Wyck Brooks⟩

[2]**silken** \"\ *vt* -ED/-ING/-S **1 :** to make silken or silklike ⟨a shampoo that ~*s* your hair —*advt*⟩ ⟨the new ~*ed* worsted —*N. Y. Times Mag.*⟩ **2 :** to cover with or as if with silk **:** dress in silk ⟨smiles and graces of ~*ed* beauty —George Catlin⟩

silk·en·ly *adv* **:** in a silken manner

silk·er \'silkə(r)\ *n* -S [[1]*silk* + *-er*] **:** one that works with silk or silk thread; *esp* **:** POINTER 1a(2)

silk floss *n* **:** KAPOK

silk fowl *n* **:** SILKY

silk gland *n* **:** a gland that produces a viscid fluid which is extruded in filaments and on exposure to air hardens into silk: as **a :** either of a pair of greatly enlarged modified salivary glands of an insect larva that extend backward along the sides of the body and produce a compound filament from which is spun a larval or pupal cover (as a cocoon) **b :** any of two or more abdominal glands of a spider that open through spinnerets and produce a filament used chiefly in the spinning of webs

silk gown *n* **1 :** the distinctive robe of a King's or Queen's Counsel — compare STUFF GOWN **2 :** a King's or Queen's Counsel

silk grass *n* **1 a :** a needlegrass (*Stipa comata*) **b :** a mountain rice (*Oryzopsis hymenoides*) with long awns **c** *Austral* **:** ROUGH BENT **2 :** any of several fiber plants esp. of *Agave* or the related genus *Nidularium* (family Bromeliaceae) **3 :** any of several commercial fibers from plants of the family Bromeliaceae: as **a :** a fine flexible lustrous strong fiber obtained from the pineapple and used for textiles **b :** a similar fiber from a karatas (*Karatas plumieri*)

silk green *n* **:** DEEP CHROME GREEN

silkgrower \'ₛ,ₛₛ\ *n* [[1]*silk* + *grower*] **:** one that raises silkworms for their silk

silk gum *or* **silk glue** *n* **:** SERICIN

silk gut *n* **:** a strong gut used for fishing tackle and surgery and made from the silk gland of the silkworm — called also *silkworm gut*

silk hat *n* **:** a hat with a tall cylindrical crown usu. made with a silk-plush finish and worn by men as a dress hat and sometimes by women as a riding hat

silk hat

silkie *var of* SILKY

silkier *comparative of* SILKY

silkiest *superlative of* SILKY

silk·i·ly \'silkəlē, 'siu̇k-, -li\ *adv* **:** in a silky manner ⟨the young wheat shone ~ —D.H.Lawrence⟩

silk·i·ness \-kēnəs, -kin-\ *n* -ES **:** the quality or state of being silky

silking *pres part of* SILK

silking machine *n* [fr. gerund of [3]*silk*] **:** a machine for removing the silk from the ears of fresh sweet corn being processed

silklike \'ₛ,ₛ\ *adj* **:** resembling silk in softness, fineness, or luster

silklined \'ₛ'ₛ\ *adj* **:** lined with silk

silkman \'ₛmən\ *n, pl* **silkmen** [[1]*silk* + *man*] **1 :** one who makes silks **2 :** one who sells silks

silk moth *n* **:** a silkworm moth

silk oak *or* **silky oak** *n* **:** any of various Australian timber trees of the family Proteaceae (as of the genus *Grevillea*) having fernlike foliage and attractively mottled wood that is used in cabinetry and veneering; *specif* **:** a medium to large tree (*Grevillea robusta*) with feathery bipinnate leaves that are silvery white below and orange-red flowers

silkoline *also* **silkolene** *var of* SILKALINE

silk paper *n* **1 :** a paper similar to granite paper but having only a very few silk fibers scattered in the tissue **2 :** a safety paper sometimes used in printing postage and revenue stamps

silk plant *or* **silk plantain** *n* **:** RUGEL'S PLANTAIN

silks *pl of* SILK, *pres 3d sing of* SILK

silk screen *n* **1 :** a screen usu. of silk or organdy used in a silk-screen process **2 :** SILK-SCREEN PROCESS

[1]**silk-screen** \'ₛ;ₛ\ *adj* [*silk screen*] **:** of, made or done by, or using a silk-screen process ⟨*silk-screen* printing⟩ ⟨*silk-screen* method⟩ ⟨*silk-screen* color⟩

[2]**silk-screen** \'ₛ,ₛ\ *vt* [*silk screen*] **:** to produce, reproduce, or print by a silk-screen process

silk-screen process *n* **:** a stencil process in which coloring matter (as ink, paint, or dye) is forced with a squeegee onto the material to be printed through the meshes of a silk or organdy screen so prepared (as by blocking out with tusche and glue) as to have pervious printing areas and impervious nonprinting areas — compare SERIGRAPHY

silk snapper *n* **:** a medium-sized West Indian snapper (*Lutjanus vivanus*) similar to the red snapper

silk spider *n* **:** a large spider (*Nephila clavipes*) native to the southern U. S. and remarkable for its large webs composed of strong silk; *broadly* **:** any of several related spiders that produce unusually heavy silk

silk sponge *n* **:** a very fine-textured soft close-grained Old World commercial sponge

silk-stocking \'ₛ;ₛₛ\ *adj* [[2]*silk* + *stocking*] **1 :** elegantly or richly dressed **:** LUXURIOUS ⟨a *silk-stocking* audience⟩ **2 :** ARISTOCRATIC, EXCLUSIVE, WEALTHY ⟨*silk-stocking* politicos —H.R. Cayton⟩ **3 :** of or relating to the American Federalist party **4 :** of or relating to the silk-stocking district of a city ⟨lost the *silk-stocking* and middle-class precincts —W.G.Carleton⟩

silk stocking *n* [*silk-stocking*] **1 :** an elegantly dressed person **2 :** an aristocratic or wealthy person ⟨they know who the *silk stockings* are —August Hollingshead⟩ **3 :** FEDERALIST 2

silk-stocking district *n* **:** a part of a city in which the aristocratic or wealthy class is politically influential or active

silk-stockinged \'ₛ;ₛₛ\ *adj* **:** SILK-STOCKING

silk system *n* **:** a warping system in which sections of the warp are wound separately on a reel and then simultaneously rewound on a loom beam

silktail \'ₛ,ₛ\ *n* [[2]*silk* + *tail*] *dial Brit* **:** BOHEMIAN WAXWING

silk-tassel tree *also* **silk tassel** *n* **:** a plant of the genus *Garrya*; *esp* **:** an evergreen shrub or small tree (*G. elliptica*) of western Oregon and California with inconspicuous flowers in silky drooping racemes

silk throwster *or* **silk thrower** *n* **:** THROWSTER

silk tree *n* **:** an Asiatic tree (*Albizzia julibrissin*) having flowers with long silky stamens

silk vine *n* **:** a Eurasian woody nearly evergreen vine (*Periploca graeca*) with silky seeds

silkweed \'ₛ,ₛ\ *n* **1 :** MILKWEED **2 :** any of several filamentous smooth algae

silk wire *n* **:** silk-covered wire

silkwoman \'ₛ,ₛₛ\ *n, pl* **silkwomen** [ME, fr. [1]*silk* + *woman*] *archaic* **:** a woman who makes, sells, or sews silk

silkwood \'ₛ,ₛ\ *n* **:** any of several trees with lustrous wood: as **a :** CALABUR TREE **b :** FLINDERSIA 2

silkworm \'ₛ,ₛ\ *n* [ME, fr. OE *seolcwyrm*, fr. *seolc* silk + *wyrm* worm] **:** a moth larva that spins a large amount of strong silk in constructing its cocoon before changing to a pupa: as **a :** a rough wrinkled hairless whitish caterpillar that is the larva of a stocky creamy white Asiatic moth (*Bombyx mori*), feeds chiefly on the leaves of white and black mulberry, is found almost entirely under human care and has been reared in China since the dawn of recorded history, and matures in about 45 days to pupate in a thick oval white or yellowish cocoon which is the source of most of the silk of commerce **b :** the larva of any of various moths of the family Saturniidae (as the ailanthus silkworm, the pernyi silkworm, the tussah silkworm, and the yamamai silkworm) — called also *giant silkworm*, *wild silkworm*

silkworm gut *n* **:** SILK GUT

silkworm jaundice *n* **:** polyhedrosis of the silkworm

silkworm rot *n* **:** CALCINO

silkworm seed *n* **:** the eggs of the silkworm

[1]**silky** \'silkē, 'siu̇k-, -ki\ *adj, usu* -ER/-EST [[1]*silk* + *-y*] **1 a :** consisting of silk **b** (1) **:** like silk in appearance, feel, or sound **:** SOFT, SMOOTH, GLOSSY, SLEEK ⟨~ printed cottons —Lois Long⟩ ⟨velvet that feels almost as thick and ~ as fur —*New Yorker*⟩ ⟨commonest of these ~ quartzes is tigereye —*Jewelers' Circular-Keystone*⟩ ⟨faint, ~ cirrus wisps —John Muir †1914⟩ ⟨hear the ~ swish of a hurled spear —Charles Lee⟩ (2) **:** INGRATIATING ⟨~ insinuations⟩ ⟨a ~ voice⟩ ⟨names that have a ~ sound to them —John McNulty⟩ **2 :** having or covered with fine soft hairs, plumes, or scales

[2]**silky** *or* **silk·ie** \"\ *n, pl* **silkies** [[1]*silky*] **1 :** a bird of a breed of small five-toed crested domestic fowls having soft white webless feathers and the ear lobes and the lumpy rose comb purple **2 :** a mutation of the domestic fowl in which the barbs of the feathers are not linked together to form a web

silky anteater *n* **:** a squirrel-sized So. American arboreal anteater (*Cyclopes didactylus*) distinguished by very beautiful long silky golden fur — called also *two-toed anteater*

silky ash *n* **:** an Australian timber tree (*Ehretia acuminata*) with lustrous tough firm light wood that works well

silky beech *n* **:** an Australian evergreen tree (*Villaresia moorei*) of the family Icacinaceae with hard lustrous grayish wood that is used esp. for cabinetwork and interior joinery

silky bent grass *n* **:** a stout leafy European grass (*Agrostis spica-venti*) occas. naturalized in the eastern U. S.

silky camellia *n* **:** a shrub or small tree (*Stewartia malachodendron*) of the southeastern U.S. often cultivated as an ornamental and having white flowers with blue anthers and dark purple filaments

silky cornel *or* **silky dogwood** *n* **:** either of two No. American shrubs: **a :** a shrub (*Cornus amomum*) with purplish twigs, finely pubescent leaves, and blue fruit — called also *kinnikinnick* **b :** a closely related and very similar shrub (*C. obliqua*)

silky marmoset *n* **1 :** a tawny Brazilian marmoset (*Callithrix chrysoleucos*) with long silky fur **2 :** SILKY TAMARIN

silky oak *var of* SILK OAK

silky swallowwort *n* **:** a common milkweed (*Asclepias syriaca*)

silky tamarin *n* **:** a golden yellow So. American lion monkey (*Leontocebus rosalia*) having long soft hair forming a mane

silky wallaby *n* **:** NAIL-TAILED WALLABY

silky willow *n* **1 :** WHITE WILLOW **2 :** a No. American willow (*Salix sericea*) with silky-pubescent leaves that usu. blacken in drying **3 :** SITKA WILLOW

silky wisteria *n* **:** a Chinese wisteria (*Wisteria venusta*) widely cultivated as an ornamental vine and having white flowers and leaves that are pubescent at maturity

[1]**sill** *also* **cill** \'sil\ *n* -S [ME *sille*, *selle*, fr. OE *syll*; akin to OHG *swelli* beam, threshold, ON *svill*, *syll* sill, Gk *selis* crossbeam, rower's bench, *selma* deck, rower's bench] **1 a :** a horizontal piece (as a timber) that forms the lowest member or one of the lowest members of a framework or supporting structure (as of a house, a bridge, a loom, a mine set, or a truck body) — compare MUDSILL **b :** the horizontal member or structure (as of wood, stone, or brick) at the base of a window opening serving esp. to cover the wall at the base of the opening **:** WINDOWSILL **c :** the timber or stone at the foot of a door **:** THRESHOLD **d :** a piece of timber across the bottom of an entrance to a dock or a canal lock for the gates to shut against **e** (1) **:** the inner lower edge of an embrasure of a fortification (2) **:** one of the horizontal timbers forming the upper and lower boundaries of a gun port (as on an old warship) **2 :** the floor of a coal seam **3 :** a tabular body of igneous rock injected while molten between sedimentary or volcanic beds or along foliation planes of metamorphic rocks **4 :** an elevation (as a low ridge between mountains) separating two valleys or basins; *esp* **:** a submerged ridge at relatively shallow depth separating the basins of two bodies of water **5 :** the top surface of a usu. low or normally submerged dam

[2]**sill** \"\ *vt* -ED/-ING/-S **:** to provide with a sill

[3]**sill** \"\ *n* -S [by alter.] *archaic* **:** THILL

sillabub *var of* SYLLABUB

sil·la·gin·i·dae \,silə'jinə,dē\ *n pl, cap* [NL, fr. *Sillagin-*, *Sillago*, type genus + *-idae*] **:** a small family of elongate percoid fishes of the shallow waters of the tropical Indo-Pacific that though small are excellent food fishes

[1]**sil·lag·i·noid** \sə'lajə,nȯid\ *adj* [NL *Sillagin-*, *Sillago* + E *-oid*] **:** resembling or related to the Sillaginidae

[2]**sillaginoid** \"\ *n* -S **:** a sillaginoid fish

sil·la·go \sə'lā(,)gō\ *n, cap* [NL *Sillagin-*, *Sillago*] **:** a genus (the type of the family Sillaginidae) of percoid fishes — see WHITING

si·llar \sēl'yär\ *n, pl* **silla·res** \-ä,rās\ [Sp, ashlar, fr. *silla* seat, chair (fr. L *sella*) + *-ar* (fr. L *-aris*) — more at SETTLE] **:** building material consisting of large blocks cut from a natural deposit (as of lava, tuff, limestone, or compact clay)

sill cock *n* **:** a water faucet placed at about sill height on the outside of a building and usu. threaded for attaching a hose — called also *hose cock*

sill course *n* **:** a course at the level of a windowsill

sil·len·ite \'silə,nīt\ *n* -S [L. G. *Sillén*, 20th cent. Swed. mineralogist + E *-ite*] **:** a mineral Bi_2O_3 that consists of a native bismuth oxide in earthy masses and that is polymorphous with bismite

sil·ler \'silə(r)\ *chiefly dial var of* SILVER

sill floor *n* **:** the bottom floor of a stope in the square-set system of mining

sillibub *var of* SYLLABUB

sil·li·ly \'silәlē, -li\ *adv* **:** in a silly manner

sil·li·man·ite \'siləmə,nīt\ *n* -S [Benjamin *Silliman* †1864 Am. chemist and geologist + E *-ite*] **:** a brown, grayish, or pale green mineral Al_2SiO_5 that consists of an aluminum silicate in orthorhombic crystals often occurring in fibrous or columnar forms and that is polymorphous with cyanite and andalusite — called also *fibrolite*; see SILLIMANITE GROUP

sillimanite group *n* **:** the group of minerals comprising sillimanite, cyanite, andalusite, dumortierite, topaz, and mullite

sil·li·ness \'silēnəs, -lin-\ *n* -ES **1 :** the quality or state of being silly **2 :** a silly practice

silling *pres part of* SILL

sill man *n* **:** a worker who replaces rotten sills of lead-lined copper-refining tanks

sil·lock \'silək\ *n* -S [Sc *sill* young herring (of Scand origin; akin to Norw *sild* herring) + *-ock* — more at SILD] *Scot* **:** a young pollack

sil·log·ra·pher \sə'lägrəfə(r)\ *n* -S [Gk *sillographos*, fr. *sillos* satirical poem + *-graphos* writer, fr. *graphein* to write — more at CARVE] **:** a writer of satires

sills *pl of* SILL, *pres 3d sing of* SILL

[1]**sil·ly** \'silē, -li\ *adj* -ER/-EST [ME *sely*, *silly* happy, blessed, innocent, pitiable, feeble, fr. (assumed) OE *sǣlig*, fr. OE *sǣl* happiness + *-ig* -y; akin to OHG *sālig* happy, ON *sæla* happiness, Goth *selei* kindness, L *solari* to console, comfort, Gk *hilaros* cheerful] **1 a :** needing compassion or sympathy **:** PATHETIC **b :** helpless against attack **:** DEFENSELESS — usu. used of sheep **c :** WEAK, SICKLY **d** *obs* **:** MEAGER, PALTRY, SCANTY **2 a :** RUSTIC, SIMPLE, PLAIN ⟨~ buckets on the deck —S.T. Coleridge⟩ ⟨a sound peaceful and ~ as any cowbell heard in the Alps —Osbert Sitwell⟩ **b** *obs* **:** lowly in station **:** HUMBLE **3 a :** weak in intellect **:** destitute of ordinary strength of mind ⟨a child who was rather ~⟩ **b :** exhibiting a lack of judgment or intelligence **:** FOOLISH, INANE, VACUOUS ⟨although we maintained a blackout at night, we felt ~ about it —A.J.Liebling⟩ ⟨the ~ air of one who does not understand fear —Arnold Bennett⟩ **c :** contrary to reason **:** ABSURD, RIDICULOUS, IRRATIONAL ⟨the question is as ~ as it sounds —Telford Taylor⟩ ⟨always making ~ remarks⟩ **d :** lacking importance or serious meaning **:** TRIVIAL, TRIFLING, FRIVOLOUS ⟨written in a facetious strain that accords with the rather ~ title —*Times Lit. Supp.*⟩ ⟨if we tend to regard the pursuit of the new as necessarily ~ and modish —E.R.Bentley⟩ ⟨passed the time by telling ~ stories⟩ **4 :** DAZED, STUNNED, STUPEFIED — used postpositively ⟨was knocked ~ by the blow⟩ ⟨would slap me ~ —J.H.Burns⟩

⟨bored ~ by the unwonted inactivity⟩ **5 :** very close to the batsman — used of a fielding position in cricket or the player in it ⟨~ point⟩ ⟨~ mid on⟩ ⟨~ leg⟩ **syn** see FOOLISH, SIMPLE

²silly \"\ *adv* **:** SILLILY ⟨behave ~⟩

³silly \"\ *n* -ES **:** one who is silly ⟨am very likely a ~ — meeting trouble half-way —D.H.Lawrence⟩ ⟨well then, ~, why not stay! —Edna Ferber⟩

⁴silly \"\ *vb* -ED/-ING/-ES *vt, chiefly dial* **:** to make silly ~ *vi, chiefly dial* **:** to be or act silly

silly billy *n, usu cap B* [¹*silly* + *Billy*, nickname for William; prob. after William IV †1837, king of England] **:** a foolish person

sillyhow \'==,=\ *n* [¹*silly* + *how* (caul)] *chiefly Scot* **:** a caul on a newborn infant

silly season *n* **:** a period (as late summer) when newspapers must resort to minor or fantastic matters for lack of major news stories

¹si·lo \'sī(,)lō\ *n* -S [Sp, perh. of Celtic origin; akin to OIr *sil* seed; akin to OE *sāwan* to sow — more at SOW] **1 :** a trench, pit, or typically cylindrical structure usu. sealed (as with earth, heavy paper, or plastic) when full to exclude air and used for storing silage **2** *chiefly Brit* **:** a tall usu. cylindrical bin for grain storage esp. as part of a grain elevator; *also* **:** ELEVATOR 1c **3 a :** a deep usu. cylindrical bin either aboveground or belowground for storing material (as cement or coal) **b :** an underground structure for storing a guided missile in readiness for firing

²silo \"\ *vt* -ED/-ING/-ES **:** to place (as fodder) in a silo **:** ENSILE

silo filler *n* **:** a machine for blowing, elevating or unloading chopped fodder into a silo **:** SILAGE CUTTER

si·lox·ane \sə'läk,sān\ *n* -S [blend of *silane* and *oxygen*] **:** any of a class of compounds that contain alternate silicon and oxygen atoms in either a linear structure [as $H_3Si(OSiH_2)_nOSiH_3$] or a cyclic structure [as $(H_2SiO)_n$] and that in many cases contain methyl, phenyl, or other organic radicals in place of some or all of the hydrogen atoms and are made by hydrolysis of chlorosilanes or alkoxy-silanes — see SILICONE

sil·pha \'silfə\ *n, cap* [NL, fr. Gk *silphē* cockroach, bookworm] **:** a genus (the type of the family Silphidae) of clavicorn beetles

¹sil·phid \-fəd\ *adj* [NL *Silphidae*] **:** of or relating to the Silphidae

²silphid \"\ *n* -S **:** a beetle of the family Silphidae

sil·phi·dae \-fə,dē\ *n pl, cap* [NL, fr. *Silpha*, type genus + *-idae*] **:** a widely distributed family of clavicorn beetles comprising the burying beetles, carrion beetles, and related forms

sil·phi·um \'silfēəm\ *n* [L, fr. Gk *silphion*; of North African origin] **1** *pl* **sil·phia** \-ēə\ **:** an extinct umbelliferous plant of the genus *Ferula* not definitely identifiable as to species but well known to the ancient Greeks and used by them medicinally **2** *cap* [NL, fr. L] **:** a large genus of tall No. American perennial herbs (family Compositae) having coarse heads of yellow flowers with fertile rays and broad flat winged achenes — see CUP PLANT

sils *pl of* SIL

¹silt \'silt\ *n* -S [ME *cylte*, prob. of Scand origin; akin to Dan & Norw *sylt* salt marsh, Sw dial. *sylta*; akin to OHG *sulza* salt marsh, OE *sealt* salt — more at SALT] **1 a :** unconsolidated or loose sedimentary material whose constituent rock particles are finer than grains of sand and larger than clay particles; *specif* **:** material consisting of mineral soil particles ranging in diameter from 0.02 to 0.002 millimeters **b :** sedimentary material consisting esp. of mineral particles intermediate in size between those of sand and clay suspended in running or standing water **c :** a deposit of sediment (as by a river) **d :** a material that is similar to silt in particle size and consistency **:** FINES ⟨coal ~⟩ **2 :** SCUM, DREGS, RESIDUE ⟨chocolate . . . covered with tobacco grains from the ~ of his pockets —Norman Mailer⟩

²silt \"\ *vb* -ED/-ING/-S *vi* **1 :** to become choked or obstructed with silt — often used with *up* ⟨the channel ~*ed up*⟩ **2 :** to flow as silt **:** PERCOLATE, DRIFT ⟨sand ~*ed* over wheat fields —*Lamp*⟩ ~ *vt* **:** to choke, fill, cover, or obstruct with silt or mud ⟨the beaver had ~*ed* the creek —Hugh Fosburgh⟩ — often used with *up* ⟨its harbor is now entirely ~*ed* up —L.R. Colcord⟩

silt·age \-tij\ *n* -S [²*silt* + *-age*] **:** a mass of silt

sil·ta·tion \sil'tāshən\ *n* -S [²*silt* + *-ation*] **:** the deposition or accumulation of silt ⟨since ~ has been negligible, the lake is clear —W.H.Thompson & Don Hutson⟩

silting *n* -S [fr. gerund of ²*silt*] **1 :** the process by which a stream deposits silt behind a dam or other place of retarded flow **:** SILTATION **2 :** the act of filling old mine workings hydraulically with fine waste material

silt loam *n* [¹*silt*] **:** soil containing not less than 70 percent silt and clay and not less than 20 percent sand

silt soil *n* **:** soil containing not less than 80 percent silt and not more than 12 percent sand

siltstone \'=,=\ *n* **:** a rock composed chiefly of indurated silt

silty \'siltē, -ti\ *adj* -ER/-EST **:** full of silt **:** of, like, or suggestive of silt ⟨~ soil⟩

silty clay *n* **:** a clay soil containing from 50 to 70 percent silt

silty clay loam *n* **:** soil containing from 50 to 80 percent silt

sil·u·res \'silyə,rēz\ *n pl, usu cap* [L] **:** a people of ancient Britain described by Tacitus as occupying chiefly southern Wales

¹si·lu·ri·an \sə'lu̇rēən, sī'-\ *adj, usu cap* [L *Silures* + E *-ian*] **1 :** of or relating to the Silures or their place of habitation **2 :** of or relating to the part of the Paleozoic era between the Ordovician and Devonian characterized by the flourishing of invertebrate marine life, the beginning of coral-reef building, and the appearance of some great crustaceans — see GEOLOGIC TIME table

²silurian \"\ *n* -S *usu cap* **1 :** one of the Silures **2 :** the Silurian period or system of rocks

silurian gray *n, often cap S* **:** a pale yellow green that is yellower, stronger, and slightly lighter than smoke gray, stronger than oyster gray, and yellower and slightly lighter than average Nile

¹si·lu·rid \sə'lu̇rəd, sī'-\ *adj* [NL *Siluridae*] **:** of or relating to the Siluridae

²silurid \"\ *n* -S **:** a catfish of the family Siluridae

si·lu·ri·dae \-rə,dē\ *n pl, cap* [NL, fr. *Silurus*, type genus + *-idae*] **:** a family of catfishes formerly comprising most of the catfishes but now usu. restricted to various freshwater fishes of Europe and Asia that differ from No. American catfishes in having the adipose dorsal fin rudimentary or lacking and in having the anal fin long and more or less confluent with the eellike caudal fin

sil·u·rist \'silyərəst\ *n* -S *usu cap* [L *Silures* + E *-ist*] **:** a native of Brecknockshire in Wales

¹si·lu·roid \-ü,rȯid\ *adj* [NL *Siluroidea*] **:** of or relating to the Siluroidea

²siluroid \"\ *n* -S **:** a fish of the suborder Siluroidea **:** CATFISH

sil·u·roi·dea \,silyə'rȯidēə\ *n pl, cap* [NL *Silurus* + *-oidea*] **:** a suborder of the order Ostariophysi comprising the catfishes

si·lu·roi·dei \-ē,ī\ [NL *Silurus* + *-oidei*] *syn of* SILUROIDEA

si·lu·rus \sə'lu̇rəs, sī'-\ *n* [NL, fr. L, a large river fish, fr. Gk *silouros*, fr. *sil-* (of unknown origin) + *oura* tail; akin to Gk *orrhos* buttocks — more at ASS] **1** *cap* **:** the type genus of Siluridae containing the sheatfish and several other Old World catfishes **2** -ES **:** any fish of the genus *Silurus*

sil·va \'silvə\ *n, pl* **silvas** \-vəz\ *or* **sil·vae** \-l,vē\ [NL, fr. L, wood, forest] **1 a :** the forest trees of a region or country **b :** a description of or treatise on the trees of a region **2 :** ¹SELVA

¹silvan *var of* SYLVAN

²sil·van *or* **syl·van** \'silvən\ *adj* [NL *silva* + E *-an*] **:** of or relating to a silva

silvanite *var of* SYLVANITE

¹sil·ver \'silvə(r)\ *n* -S [ME, fr. OE *seolfor*; akin to OHG *silabar*, *silbar* silver, ON *silfr*, Goth *silubr*; all fr. a prehistoric Gmc word borrowed fr. an Asiatic source] **1 :** a white metallic element that is sonorous, ductile, very malleable, capable of a high degree of polish, and chiefly univalent in compounds, that has the highest thermal and electric conductivity of any substance, that is found native and also combined (as in stephanite, argentite, proustite, pyrargyrite, cerargyrite), that is obtained as the main product and as a by-product in copper and lead smelting, that is one of the noble metals in view of its resistance to oxidation or corrosion except tarnishing by combination with sulfur, that is usu. alloyed with copper to increase its hardness, and that is used for coinage, tableware, jewelry, plate, and a great variety of articles, in photography, in electrical contacts, and as a catalyst — symbol *Ag*; see COIN SILVER, ELEMENT table **2 :** silver as a commodity ⟨the value of ~ has risen⟩ **3 :** coin made of silver **:** silver money **:** MONEY ⟨cross my palm with ~⟩ ⟨customers . . . came now with cold hard ~ —Nelson Algren⟩ ⟨this I do for you and not for ~ —Pearl Buck⟩ **4 a :** flatware used at table and made of a variety of materials including sterling or plated silver ⟨her ~ is of stainless steel⟩ **b :** hollow ware made of silver or other metal and usu. used at table **5 :** ¹ARGENT 3 **6 a :** something having the luster or appearance of silver: as (1) **:** SILVER FOX (2) **:** SILVER SALMON **b :** a nearly neutral slightly brownish medium gray — called also *argent*

²silver \"\ *adj* [ME, fr. ¹*silver*] **1 :** made of silver ⟨polished ~ candlesticks⟩ **2 :** resembling silver: as **a :** having a white lustrous sheen **:** silvery in appearance ⟨a land of ~ rivers where the salmon leap —*Holiday*⟩ ⟨balloons waved slowly . . . looking like huge fat ~ sausages —Upton Sinclair⟩ ⟨her ~ head was held erect in spite of the years⟩ **b :** having or producing a clear resonant sound **:** dulcet in tone ⟨the ~ sound of the river over the pebbles —Winston Churchill⟩ **c :** eloquently persuasive ⟨whose . . . ~ tongue was heard in every movement of reform —Meridel Le Sueur⟩ **3** *obs* **:** sweetly gentle **:** PEACEFUL **4 a :** ARGENTIFEROUS **b :** partly composed of silver **5 :** of, relating to, or characteristic of silver ⟨the ~ legislation of 1873⟩ ⟨~ wagons headed down from the mines⟩ **6 :** of or relating to a silver age ⟨great periods of golden and ~ Latin —T. H. Savory⟩ **7 :** advocating the adoption of silver as a standard of currency **8 :** mounted, coated, or plated with silver **9 :** ARGENT 3 **10** [so called fr. the practice during the construction of the Panama canal of paying skilled white labor in gold and unskilled colored labor in silver] **:** of or for the Negro population in the Panama Canal Zone — compare GOLD 5

³silver \"\ *vb* **silvered; silvered; silvering** \-v(ə)riŋ\ **silvers** [ME *silveren*, fr. ¹*silver*] *vt* **1 a :** to cover with silver (as by electroplating) **b :** to coat with a substance (as a metal) resembling silver ⟨~ a glass with an amalgam of tin and mercury⟩ **2 a :** to give a silvery luster to ⟨daylight fails and the moon ~*s* your way —Dorothy P. Richards⟩ **b :** to make white like silver ⟨time had ~*ed* her hair⟩ ~ *vi* **1 :** to move like a stream of silver **2 :** to acquire a silvery color ⟨light ~*ed* on windshields and fenders where cars were parked —Richard Llewellyn⟩

silver age *n* [²*silver*] **:** an historical period of successful achievement but falling short of the highest ideals and goals — compare GOLDEN AGE

silver anniversary *n* **:** a 25th anniversary

silver ash *n* **:** any of various trees of the genus *Flindersia*; *esp* **:** BUNJI-BUNJI

silver aster *n* **:** an aster (*Chrysopsis graminifolia*) with silvery pubescent leaves

silver award *n* **:** the highest of three ranks in the exploring program of the Boy Scouts of America

silverback \'==,=\ *n, NewEng* **:** ³KNOT b

silver-backed fox \'==-=-\ *n* **:** CAAMA 1

silver bal·li \-'balē\ *n* [alter. of *siruaballi*] **1 :** any of several timber trees of the genera *Nectandra, Ocotea* and *Aniba* of northern So. America with yellowish or brown wood **2 :** the wood of a silver balli

silver bass *n* **1 :** WHITE PERCH 1 **2 :** FRESHWATER DRUM **3 :** WHITE BASS 1

silver bath *n* **:** a bath of dissolved silver salt

silver beard grass *n* **:** a tropical American grass (*Andropogon saccharoides*) established in No. America and having a dense panicle made up of several short clusters on an elongate axis with the pedicels and rachis joints being long-villous

silverbeater \'==,==\ *n* [¹*silver* + *beater*] **:** one that beats silver into leaf or foil

silver beech *n* [²*silver*] **:** a New Zealand tree of the genus *Nothofagus* (esp. *N. Menziesii*)

silver beet *n, Austral & NewZeal* **:** CHARD

silver bell *also* **silver-bell tree** *n* **:** a medium sized tree (*Halesia carolina*) of the southeastern U.S. often cultivated for its showy bell-shaped white flowers — called also *opossum wood*

sil·ver·bel·ly \'silvə(r),belē\ *also* **sil·ver·bid·dy** \-,bidē\ *n* [*silverbelly* fr. ²*silver* + *belly*; *silverbiddy*, alter. of *silverbelly*] *Austral & NewZeal* **:** a fish of the family Gerridae

sil·ver·ber·ry \'silvə(r)- — *see* BERRY\ *n* [²*silver* + *berry*] **:** a silvery No. American shrub (*Elaeagnus commutata*)

silverberry family *n* **:** ELAEAGNACEAE

silverbill \'==,=\ *n* [²*silver* + *bill*] **:** a weaverbird of the genus *Lonchura*

silver birch *n* **1 :** PAPER BIRCH **2 :** YELLOW BIRCH **3 :** a British birch (*Betula verrucosa*) having a trunk that is black and fissured below but silvery white above

silver-black fox *n* **:** SILVER FOX 1a

silver blight *n* **:** SILVERLEAF 2

sil·ver·blu \'silvə(r),blü\ *adj* [²*silver* + *blu*, alter. of *blue*] **:** a silvery gray-blue variety of mutation mink

silver bream *n* **:** any of several silvery fishes: as **a :** a large sea bream (*Rhabdosargus sarba*) of the tropical Indo-Pacific; *broadly* **:** any of several fishes of the genus *Rhabdosargus* (as the white stumpnose) **b :** TREVALLY 1

silver bromide *n* [¹*silver*] **:** a compound AgBr that occurs naturally as bromyrite and is obtained synthetically as a white to yellowish curdy precipitate when aqueous solutions of a silver salt and a bromide are mixed and that is extremely sensitive to light and is much used in photography in the preparation of sensitive emulsion coatings for film, plates, and paper

silverbush \'==,=\ *n* [²*silver* + *bush*] **1 :** JUPITER'S-BEARD 2 **2 :** SILVERBERRY

silver button *n* **:** PEARLY EVERLASTING

silver cape *n, usu cap C* **:** a Cape diamond having a very slight yellow tint

silver carp *n* **1 :** the common carpsucker (*Carpiodes carpio*) **2 :** CARP 1a

silver cedar *n* **:** ROCKY MOUNTAIN JUNIPER

silver certificate *n* **:** a paper certificate issued by a government against silver deposited with it to a specified amount and payable to the bearer on demand; *specif* **:** a certificate issued against the deposit of silver coin that is legal tender for all public and private debts and for public charges, taxes, duties, and dues in the U.S. and its possessions — compare GOLD CERTIFICATE, TREASURY NOTE

silver chain *n* **:** LOCUST 3a(2)

silver chickweed *n* **:** a small silvery leaved perennial herb (*Paronychia argyrocoma*) of the southeastern U.S.

silver china grass *n* **:** RAMIE 1

silver chloride *n* [¹*silver*] **:** a compound AgCl that occurs naturally as cerargyrite and is obtained synthetically as a white curdy precipitate when aqueous solutions of a silver salt and a chloride are mixed, that is sensitive to light becoming violet and finally black, and that is used chiefly in photography esp. for papers

silver cloth *n* [²*silver*] **1 :** CLOTH OF SILVER **2 :** LAMÉ

silver-copper glance *n* **:** STROMEYERITE

silver cord *n* **1 :** UMBILICAL CORD **2 :** the emotional tie between mother and child

silver cyanide *n* [¹*silver*] **:** a poisonous compound AgCN or $Ag_2(CN)_2$ that is obtained as a white curdy precipitate when a soluble cyanide is added to aqueous solutions of a silver salt and that readily forms complex cyanides (as potassium argentocyanide $KAg(CN)_2$) used in silver plating

silver deposit *n* **:** silver electroplated often in intricate designs to glass

silvered *adj* [fr. past part. of ³*silver*] **1 a :** covered, adorned, or dressed with or as if with silver **b :** backed with quicksilver and tinfoil and thus made into a mirror **2 :** having a silvery sheen, luster, or color ⟨~ furs⟩ ⟨~ gray hair⟩ **3 :** affected with silverleaf

silvered glass *n* **:** MERCURY GLASS

silver eel *n* [²*silver*] **1** *South* **:** CUTLASS FISH **2 :** an eel just attained to sexual maturity, characterized by a silvery color, and about to return to the ocean to breed

sil·ver·er \'silvərə(r)\ *n* -S **:** one that silvers: as **a :** ELECTROPLATER **b :** a worker who silvers mirror glass **c :** a device used for silvering

silvereye \'==,=\ *n* [²*silver* + *eye*] **:** any of several small Old World singing birds of *Zosterops* or related genera (as *Z. palpebroso* of India or *Z. lateralis* of Australia and New Zealand) having the eyes encircled by a ring of white feathers — called also *white-eye*

silver fern *n* **:** any of various ferns (as of the genera *Gleichenia, Notholaena*, and *Pityrogramma*) having the lower surface of the fronds silvery white

silverfin \'==,=\ *n* [²*silver* + *fin*] **1 :** SATINFIN **2 :** SPOTTAIL SHINER

silver fir *n* **:** any of various true firs having leaves white or silvery white beneath: as **a :** a valuable European timber tree (*Abies alba*) yielding Burgundy pitch and Strasbourg turpentine **b :** AMABILIS FIR **c :** WHITE FIR 1a (1) **d :** BALSAM FIR

silverfish \'==,=\ *n, pl* **silverfish** *or* **silverfishes** **1 :** any of various silvery fishes: as **a :** TARPON **b :** a white or silvery variety of the goldfish **c :** SILVERSIDES **d :** GOLDEN SHINER **e :** SILVER HAKE **f :** CUTLASS FISH **g :** any of several fishes of the family Denticidae; *esp* **:** an important So. African food fish (*Argyrozona*, or *Dentex, argyrozona*) **2** *pl* **silverfish :** any of various small wingless silvery insects of the order Thysanura; *esp* **:** an insect (*Lepisma saccharina*) found about houses and sometimes injurious to sized papers or starched clothes — called also *fish moth*

silver fizz *n* **:** a fizz made from lemon juice, gin, and white of egg

silver foil *n* [ME *silverfoile*, fr. ²*silver* + *foile* foil] **:** silver or other metal of a similar color (as aluminum) in very thin sheets

silver fox *n* **1 a :** a color phase of the red fox in which the pelt is black and more or less tipped with white and which apparently represents a genetic variant that can be induced to breed true under controlled conditions **b :** CAAMA 1 **c :** BLACK-BACKED JACKAL **2** *usu cap* **:** an American breed of rabbits with white hairs scattered among the jet black fur

silver fulminate *n* [¹*silver*] **:** a white crystalline compound AgONC similar to mercury fulminate but more violently explosive

silver gar *n* [²*silver*] **:** NEEDLEFISH 1

silver gibbon *n* **:** an ashy gray gibbon (*Hylobates moloch*) of Java and Borneo

silver gilt *n* [ME, fr. ¹*silver* + *gilt*, adj.] **:** gilded silver ⟨the coronets are of *silver gilt* —H.S.London⟩

silver glance *n* [²*silver*] **:** ARGENTITE

silver grain *n* **:** the lines or figures of the medullary rays on various woods (as oak or bird's-eye maple) in longitudinal or tangential sections

silver-grained \'=;=;=\ *adj* **:** QUARTER-SAWED

silver grass *n* **:** any of several grasses or grasslike plants having silvery pubescence: as **a :** RIBBON GRASS **b :** a plant of the genera *Danthonia, Deschampsia*, and *Festuca* of Australia and New Zealand **c :** a golden aster (*Chrysopsis graminifolia*) of southern U.S. with silvery grasslike foliage

silver gray *n* **:** a light brownish gray that is yellower, lighter, and slightly less strong than slate gray and yellower and lighter than ashes

silver-gray fox *n* **:** SILVER FOX

silver green *n* **:** a grayish yellow green that is yellower and paler than average sage green and yellower, lighter, and stronger than palmetto

silver-haired bat \'==,=-\ *n* **:** a No. American vespertilionid bat (*Lasionycteris noctivagans*) that is blackish brown with the hairs tipped with silvery white

silver hake *n* **:** a common hake (*Merluccius bilinearis*) of the northern New England coast that is important as a food fish

silver halide *n* [¹*silver*] **:** a halide of silver; *esp* **:** one used in photography — see PHOTOHALIDE; compare SILVER BROMIDE, SILVER CHLORIDE, SILVER IODIDE

silverhead \'==,=\ *n* [²*silver* + *head*] **:** SILVER CHICKWEED

silver herring *n* **:** the menhaden esp. when processed and canned for food

sil·ver·i·ness \'silv(ə)rēnəs\ *n* -ES **:** the quality or state of being silvery

silvering *n* -S [fr. gerund of ³*silver*] **1 a :** the silver or a film resembling silver on a silvered object **b :** the act or process of covering with silver **2 :** a silvery appearance **3 :** a sprinkling of white or light hairs in the coat of a mammal

silver iodide *n* [¹*silver*] **:** a compound AgI occurring naturally as iodyrite and obtained synthetically as a yellow curdy precipitate when aqueous solutions of a silver salt and an iodide are mixed that darkens on exposure to light, and that is used chiefly in photography, in rainmaking, and in medicine in colloidal form in treatment of infections of mucous membranes

sil·ver·ite \'silvə,rīt\ *n* -S [¹*silver* + *-ite*] **:** one favoring use or establishment of silver as a monetary standard

sil·ver·ize \-īz\ *vt* -ED/-ING/-S [¹*silver* + *-ize*] **:** to cover or treat with silver **:** make silvery

silver jackal *n* [²*silver*] **1 :** BLACK-BACKED JACKAL **2 :** CAAMA 1

silver jenny *n, pl* **silver jennies** **:** a small mojarra (*Eucinostomus gula*) of the Atlantic coast from Cape Cod to Rio de Janeiro

silver jubilee *n* **:** SILVER ANNIVERSARY

silver king *n* **:** TARPON

silver lace *n* **:** lace or braid formerly made of silver wire but now made of threads or cords with a silver color or with a covering of silver threads and used for uniforms or official robes as an indication of rank

silver-laced \'=;=;=\ *adj* [*silver lace* + *-ed*] **:** adorned with silver lace

silver-lace vine *n* **:** a twining perennial (*Polygonum aubertii*) of China having racemes of fragrant greenish flowers

silver-lead \'==,=\ *adj* [¹*silver* + *lead*] **:** containing silver and lead ⟨*silver-lead* ore⟩

silver leaf *n* **:** very thin silver foil

silverleaf \'==,=\ *n* [²*silver* + *leaf*] **1 :** any of several plants having silvery leaves: as **a :** BUFFALO BERRY **b :** a hydrangea (*Hydrangea radiata*) with white tomentum on the lower leaf surfaces **c :** QUEEN'S-DELIGHT **d :** WHITE POPLAR 1a **e :** JEWELWEED **f :** HARDHACK 1 **g :** HONESTY 3 **h :** PEARLY EVERLASTING **2** *also* **silver leaf disease :** a disease of shrubs and trees caused by a basidiomycete (*Stereum purpureum*) and characterized by the peculiar silvery appearance of the leaves; *also* **:** a similar symptom of various other diseases — called also *silver blight*

silverleaf nightshade *also* **silver-leaved nightshade** \'==,=-\ *n* **:** TROMPILLO

silverleaf oak *n* **:** a small to medium-sized oak (*Quercus hypoleuca*) of the southwestern U.S. and adjacent Mexico having silvery white tomentum on the lower surfaces of the slender lanceolate leaves — called also *whiteleaf oak*

silver linden *n* **1 :** WHITE BASSWOOD **2 :** a basswood (*Tilia tomentosa*) that is native to eastern Europe and Asia Minor but widely cultivated as an ornamental and that has leaves with a white tomentum on their lower surfaces

silverline system \'==,=-\ *n* [²*silver* + *line*] **:** a series of superficial lines in many protozoans that stain intensely with silver impregnation techniques and are variously regarded as supporting or coordinating organelles or as pellicular striations and sculpturings

sil·ver·ling \'silvə(r)liŋ\ *n* -S [G *silberling*, fr. OHG *silabarling*, fr. *silabar* silver + *-ing* — more at SILVER] **:** a small silver coin

silver lining *n* [²*silver*] **1 :** a white edge on a cloud **2 :** a consoling or hopeful prospect

silver lip *n* **:** a pearl oyster that is specif. identical with the gold lip but has the inner shell margin white or silvery

silver louse *n* **:** SILVERFISH 2

silver lunge *n* **:** LAKE TROUT b

silver lupine *n* **:** SILVERY LUPINE

sil·ver·ly *adv* [²*silver* + *-ly*] **:** with silvery appearance or sound ⟨Venus brooding ~ above a line of pale green sky —Edith Wharton⟩

silver-mail \'==,=\ *n* [²*silver* + *mail* (payment)] **:** WHITE RENT

silver maple *n* **1 :** a common No. American maple (*Acer saccharinum*) with deeply cut leaves that are light green above and silvery white beneath **2 :** the hard close-grained but brittle light brown wood of the silver maple

silver marlin *n* **:** a silvery blue marlin of the Pacific ocean sometimes recognized as a distinct variety (*Makaira nigricans tahitiensis*)

silver mite *n* **:** RUST MITE

silver moth *n* **:** SILVERFISH 2

sil·vern \ˈsilvə(r)n\ *adj* [ME *silveren, selvern,* fr. OE *seolfren, seolfern,* fr. *seolfor* silver + *-en*] **1 :** made of silver **2 :** resembling or characteristic of silver **:** SILVERY ⟨the soft ~ voice . . . quickened the place —W.A.White⟩

sil·ver·ness *n* -ES **:** the quality or state of being silver

silver nitrate *n* [¹*silver*] **:** a poisonous irritant crystalline soluble salt $AgNO_3$ obtained by the action of nitric acid on silver that blackens on contact with organic matter, that is used chiefly in making silver halides for photography, in silvering (as glass for mirrors), as a chemical reagent in indelible inks and hair dyes, and in medicine externally as an astringent, antiseptic, and germicide — see LUNAR CAUSTIC

silver oak *n* [²*silver*] **1 :** FLANNELBUSH **2 :** SILK OAK

silver owl *n* **:** BARN OWL

silver oxide *n* [¹*silver*] **:** an oxide of silver; *esp* **:** the compound Ag_2O obtained as a dark-brown amorphous precipitate when an aqueous solution of a silver salt is treated with a caustic alkali, that reacts as a hydroxide if moist, that dissolves in ammonia water, and that oxidizes aldehydes to acids

silver palm *n* [²*silver*] **:** a fan palm (*Coccothrinax argentata*) of Florida and the West Indies, with leaves brilliantly white on the underside — called also *silver thatch, silvertop*

silver paper *n* **1 :** a fine white tissue paper; *esp* **:** tissue paper free from acids and sulfur used as a wrapping for silverware — called also *silver tissue* **2 :** a metallic paper with a coating or lamination resembling silver — called also *tinfoil*

silver-penciled \ˈ==ˌ=\ *adj* **1 :** penciled in silver **2** *of feathers* **:** penciled with white

silver perch *n* **:** any of various somewhat silvery fishes that resemble perch: as **a :** a silvery brown-dotted Australian freshwater grunt (*Therapon bidyana*) or a related fish esteemed for food and sport **b :** a mademoiselle (*Bairdiella chrysura*) **c :** WHITE PERCH 1 **d :** CRAPPIE **e :** any of several mojarras

silver pheasant *n* **1 a :** a large long-tailed pheasant (*Lophura nycthemera* or *Gennaeus nycthemerus*) of southern China that is often reared in Europe and America, has in the male a naked red face, a flowing bluish black crest, white tail, upper parts lightly penciled with black, and bluish black underparts, and is in the female chiefly mottled brownish **b :** any of various other pheasants of the same genus **2 :** any of several of the eared pheasants

silver picrate *n* [¹*silver*] **:** a poisonous explosive yellow crystalline salt $(O_2N)_3C_6H_2OAg.H_2O$ used as an antiseptic esp. in vaginitis and urethritis

silver pine *n* [²*silver*] **1 :** WESTERN WHITE PINE 1 **2 :** PONDEROSA PINE 1 **3 :** BALSAM FIR 1 **4 :** any of several evergreen timber trees of the genus *Dacrydium* (esp. *D. colensoi*) having shiny white wood

silver plate *n* **1 :** a plating of silver **2 :** domestic flatware and hollow ware made of silver or of a silver-plated base metal

silver-plate \ˈ==ˌ=\ *vt* [*silver plate*] **:** to electroplate with silver

silver plover *n, Scot* **:** ³KNOT

silverpoint \ˈ==ˌ=\ *n* [²*silver* + *point*] **1 :** the process of drawing with a pencil of silver usu. on paper or parchment which has been specially prepared (as with a wash of Chinese white) **2 :** a drawing made by this process

silver point *n* [¹*silver*] **:** the melting point of silver that is 960.8°C and that is used as one of the fixed points of the international temperature scale

silver poplar *n* [²*silver*] **:** WHITE POPLAR 1a

silver print *n* **1 :** a photographic print on a surface sensitized with silver salts or formerly on albumen printing-out paper **2 :** a print made by silver printing

silver-print drawing *n* **:** a pen drawing that is made over the photographic image of a light-sensitive paper after which the silver print is bleached out leaving the traced drawing and that is used frequently for changing a photograph into a line drawing

silver printing *n* **:** printing in silver usu. by using size instead of ink and dusting over with silver bronze

silver protein *n* [¹*silver*] **:** any of several colloidal light-sensitive preparations of silver and protein used in aqueous solution on mucous membranes as antiseptics and classified by their efficacy and irritant properties: as **a :** a preparation containing 19 to 23 percent of silver and consisting of dark brown or almost black shining scales or granules — called also *mild silver protein* **b :** a more irritant preparation containing 7.5 to 8.5 percent of silver and consisting of a pale yellowish orange to brownish black powder — called also *strong silver protein*

silver quandong *n* [²*silver*] **:** BRISBANE QUANDONG

silverrod \ˈ==ˌ=\ *n* **1 :** a European asphodel (*Asphodelus ramosus*) with paniculate white flowers **2 :** a white-rayed goldenrod (as *Solidago bicolor*)

silvers *pl of* SILVER, *pres 3d sing of* SILVER

silver sage *n* **:** any of several sages having silvery foliage: as **a :** PURPLE SAGE **b :** SILVER SAGEBRUSH

silver sagebrush *n* **:** a usu. low and much-branched perennial sagebrush (*Artemisia cana*) of the western U.S. that has silvery entire leaves and is an important browse and shelter plant — called also *gray sage*

silver salmon *n* **1 :** a rather small salmon (*Oncorhynchus kisutch*) that has flesh which is very light-colored but of good flavor and that is a native of both coasts of the No. Pacific **2 :** KING SALMON

silver salt *n* [in sense 1, fr. ¹*silver;* in sense 2, fr. ²*silver*] **1 :** a salt of silver **2 :** a silvery crystalline salt $C_{14}H_7O_2SO_3Na$ used in dye manufacture **:** the sodium salt of anthraquinone-2-sulfonic acid

silverscale \ˈ==ˌ=\ *n* [²*silver* + *scale*] **:** a bushy annual saltbush (*Atriplex argentea*) that has scurfy gray foliage and is widespread on alkaline soils of the western U.S.

silver screen *n* **1 :** a motion-picture screen **2 :** MOTION PICTURES ⟨my favorite heroine of the *silver screen* —Richard Bissell⟩

silver scurf *also* **silver scab** *n* **1 :** a disease of potato tubers caused by a fungus (*Spondylocladium atrovirens*) and characterized by silvery patches on the skin **2 :** a silvering of citrus fruits caused by thrips

silverside \ˈ==ˌ=\ *n* [²*silver* + *side*] *Brit* **:** top of a round of beef

silversides \ˈ==, sīdz\ *n pl but sing or pl in constr, also* **silverside** \-d\ [²*silver* + *sides, side*] **1 :** any of various small fishes of the family Atherinidae that have a silvery stripe along each side of the body and are related to the gray mullets; *esp* **:** a fish (*Menidia notata*) that is very abundant on the American Atlantic coast **2 :** any of various freshwater minnows of *Notropis* and related genera **3 :** SILVER SALMON

silverskin \ˈ==ˌ=\ *n* [²*silver* + *skin*] **:** a thin papery layer that surrounds a coffee bean immediately inside the parchment

silversmith \ˈ==ˌ=\ *n* [ME, fr. OE *seolforsmith,* fr. *seolfor* silver + *smith*] **1 :** an artisan who makes vessels, jewelry, or other articles of silver **2 :** a manufacturer of or dealer in silver or silverware

silversmith·ing \"+iŋ\ *n* [*silversmith* + *-ing*] **:** the work of a silversmith

silver snake *n* [²*silver*] **:** RUBBER BOA

silver solder *n* **:** any of various solders containing silver

silver spoon *n* [fr. the phrase *born with a silver spoon in one's mouth* (born wealthy)] **:** WEALTH; *esp* **:** inherited wealth ⟨endowed with a *silver spoon* or burdened with poverty —P.A. Sorokin⟩ ⟨social grace is acquired more easily by those who grow up with *silver spoons* in their mouths —C.J.Friedrich⟩

silver-spoon \ˈ==ˌ=\ *adj* [*silver spoon*] **:** having a prosperous background **:** of a well-to-do family environment ⟨you might from a hint of courtliness . . . think he's a *silver-spoon* man —Anita Brenner⟩

silverspot \ˈ==ˌ=\ *n* [²*silver* + *spot*] **:** a butterfly of *Speyeria* or a related genus having silvery spots on the underside of the hind wings

silver spruce *n* **:** any of several spruces of western No. America with pale or glaucous leaves: as **a :** COLORADO SPRUCE **b :** SITKA SPRUCE **c :** ENGELMANN SPRUCE

silver squeteague *n* **:** a common weakfish (*Cynoscion nothus*) of the Atlantic coast of No. America that is tan above and silvery below

silver stain *n* **:** a transparent yellow enamel used upon the glass of decorative windows and esp. prominent in windows of the sixteenth century

silver standard *n* [¹*silver*] **:** a monetary standard under which the basic unit of currency is defined by a stated quantity of silver and which is usu. characterized by the coinage and circulation of silver, unrestricted convertibility of other money into silver, and the free import and export of silver for the settlement of international obligations

silver stick *n* [²*silver*] **1 :** a silver-headed staff presented by the British sovereign to a field officer of the Life Guardsmen **2** *usu cap both Ss* **:** one entitled to carry the silver stick on state occasions

silversword \ˈ==ˌ=\ *n* [²*silver* + *sword*] **:** a low growing plant (*Argyroxiphium sandwichense*) of the family Compositae that is found only in craters in Hawaii and has narrow pointed silver green leaves in rosettes and clusters of purplish flower heads

silvertail \ˈ==ˌ=\ *n* [²*silver* + *tail*] **:** SILVERFISH 2

silver tea *n* [¹*silver*] **:** a tea at which voluntary contributions of money are given usu. for special fund-raising or charitable purposes

silver teal *n* [²*silver*] **:** CINNAMON TEAL

silver tetra *n* **:** a small silvery compressed So. American characin fish (*Ctenobrycon spilurus*) often kept in the tropical aquarium

silver thatch *n* **:** any of several thatch palms with silvery leaves: as **a :** SILVER PALM **b :** SILVERTOP 2a **c :** a palm (*Thrinax parviflora* syn. *T. keyensis*) of southern Florida and the West Indies that is closely related to and much resembles the common silvertop but has leaves somewhat bluish green at maturity

silver thaw *n* **1** *or* **silver storm :** a coating of ice on trees and other exposed objects **:** GLAZE **2 :** RIME

silver thistle *n* **:** COTTON THISTLE

silvertip \ˈ==ˌ=\ *n* [²*silver* + *tip*] **:** a grizzly bear having the hairs whitish at the tips

silver tissue *n* **:** SILVER PAPER 1

silver-tongue \ˈ==ˌ=\ *n* [²*silver* + *tongue*] **1 :** a silver-tongued person **2 :** SONG SPARROW

silver-tongued \ˈ==ˈ=\ *adj* **:** possessed of agreeable persuasive speech **:** ELOQUENT

silvertop \ˈ==ˌ=\ *n* -S **1 :** an abnormal condition of various plants marked by whitened patches on the leaves and distortion and dwarfing of growing parts and caused by the feeding of insects or mites: as **a :** such a condition of cereal and other grasses caused usu. by a mite (*Sitopteres graminum*) **b :** a widespread condition of onions caused by the onion thrips **2** *or* **silvertop palmetto a :** a rather small stocky fan palm (*Thrinax microcarpa*) of southernmost Florida and Cuba that has broad fan-shaped long-petioled leaves pale green above and whitish and tomentose below — called also *silver thatch* **b :** any of various usu. low-growing and silvery-leaved palms (as a silver palm) of southern Florida or the West Indies that resemble or are related to the common silvertop **3 :** any of several eucalypts: as **a :** SHINING GUM **b :** SPOTTED GUM

silver torch *or* **silver torch cactus** *n* **:** a cylindrical cactus (*Cleistocactus strausii*) of the family Cactaceae having numerous hairlike white spines and red flowers

silver tree *n* **1 :** a So. African tree (*Leucadendron argenteum*) commonly cultivated for its long silvery silky leaves **2 :** an Australian timber tree (*Tarrietia argyrodendron*) of the family Sterculiaceae **3 :** SILVER BELL

silver tree fern *n* **:** a showy New Zealand tree fern (*Cyathea medullaris*) frequently cultivated for its handsome crown of much-pinnate fronds which are whitish on the underside

silver trout *n* **:** any of several silvery fishes: as **a :** a trout that is a silvery variety of the cutthroat trout and is native to Lake Tahoe and adjacent waters **b :** a salmon that is a small landlocked variety of the sockeye salmon **c :** a trout that is a silvery variety of the brook trout and is known only from Monadnock Lake

silver twig *n* **:** a diseased condition of smooth-barked twigs in which the epidermis is lifted up causing a silvery appearance

silvervine \ˈ==ˌ=\ *n* **1 :** a climbing Indo-Malayan aroid (*Scindapsus pictus argyraeus*) often cultivated for its white-mottled foliage **2 :** an ornamental dioecious woody vine (*Actinidia polygama*) of eastern Asia that has edible fruits and is very attractive to cats

silverware \ˈ==ˌ=\ *n* **:** SILVER PLATE; *esp* **:** table knives, forks, and spoons usu. of silver, a silver-plated base metal, or stainless steel

silver wattle *n* **:** any of several plants of the genus *Acacia:* as **a :** a shrub or small tree (*Acacia dealbata*) with white or silvery bark and young foliage **b :** LIGHTWOOD 2a

silver wedding *n* **:** a silver anniversary of a wedding

silverweed \ˈ==ˌ=\ *n* **:** any of various somewhat silvery plants: as **a :** a European perennial cinquefoil (*Potentilla anserina*) with leaves silvery white beneath that is naturalized in the eastern U.S. **b :** an East Indian shrub of the genus *Argyreia* (family Convolvulaceae) **c :** JEWELWEED b **d :** TALL MEADOW RUE **e :** HARDHACK 1

silver white *n* **1 :** WHITE 1c **2 :** any of various white pigments (as flake white)

silver whiting *n* **:** a dull silvery whiting (*Menticirrhus littoralis*) marked with oblique dusky bars that is common along the south Atlantic and Gulf coasts of the U.S.

silver whitlowwort *n* **:** SILVER CHICKWEED

silver willow *n* **:** any of several willows having silvery leaves; *esp* **:** a pussy willow (*Salix discolor*)

silverwing \ˈ==ˌ=\ *n* **:** CINDER GRAY

silver witch *n* **:** SILVERFISH 2

silverwork \ˈ==ˌ=\ *n* **:** work in silver **:** a piece of work made of silver esp. when ornamental or decorative **:** the work of the silversmith

sil·very \ˈsilv(ə)rē, -ri\ *adj* [¹*silver* + *-y*] **1 :** having the clear musical tone of silver **:** RESONANT **:** soft and clear in sound ⟨the clarinet's . . . tone will be muted and ~ —Roland Gelatt⟩ ⟨the ~ tinkling of his spurs as he moved —Zane Grey⟩ **2 :** resembling or having the luster of silver ⟨repeated scrubbings have given the wood a ~ sheen —*Amer. Guide Series: Mich.*⟩ ⟨a mop of ~ curls —Thomas Wood †1950⟩ **3 :** full of, containing, or made of silver or something resembling silver

silvery anchovy *n* **:** any of numerous small fishes of *Anchoviella* or related genera of the family Engraulidae having a silvery stripe along the side

silvery cinquefoil *n* **:** a prostrate cinquefoil (*Potentilla argentea*) of the north temperate zone with small yellow flowers and 5-foliolate to many-foliolate leaves that are densely white-tomentose beneath — called also *hoary cinquefoil*

silvery gibbon *n* **:** SILVER GIBBON

silvery-haired bat \ˈ=(=)=ˌ=-\ *n* **:** SILVER-HAIRED BAT

silvery hair grass *n* **:** a hair grass (*Aira caryophyllea*) with silvery shining panicles

silvery iron *n* **:** a peculiar light-gray fine-grained variety of cast iron of high silicon content

silvery lupine *n* **:** either of two silvery-pubescent herbs of the western U.S. with blue or purple flowers: **a :** an herb (*Lupinus argenteus*) that has foliage poisonous to sheep **b :** an herb (*L. caudatus*) that is common on well-drained land

silvery minnow *n* **:** a cyprinoid fish (*Hybognathus nuchalis*) that is common in the rivers of the eastern, central, and southern U.S., *also* **:** any of several related fishes

silver y moth *n, cap Y* [²*silver* + *y* + *moth*] **:** a moth of the genus *Plusia* having a silvery Y on the fore wings; *esp* **:** GAMMA MOTH

silvery sage *n* **:** SILVER SAGEBRUSH

silvery spleenwort *n* **:** a fern (*Athyrium thelypterioides*) with elongate silvery indusia

sil·ves·ter method \silˈvestə(r)-\ *or* **sil·ves·ter's method** \-ə(r)z-\ *n, usu cap S* [after Henry Robert *Silvester* †1908 Eng. physician] **:** a method of artificial respiration in which the subject is laid on his back and air is expelled from his lungs by pressing his arms over his chest and fresh air drawn in by pulling them above his head

sil·vi·cal \ˈsilvəkəl\ *adj* [*silvics* + *-al*] **:** of or relating to silvics

sil·vic·o·lous \silˈvikələs\ *adj* [L *silvicola* inhabitant of a wood (fr. *silva* wood + *-i-* + *-cola* — fr. *colere* to inhabit) + E *-ous* — more at WHEEL] **:** living in or inhabiting woodlands

sil·vics *or* **syl·vics** \ˈsilviks\ *n pl but sing in constr* [NL *silva, sylva* + E *-ics*] **:** the study of the life history and characteristics of forest trees esp. as they occur in stands and with particular reference to environmental influences

sil·vi·cul·tur·al \ˌsilvəˈkəlch(ə)rəl\ *adj* **:** of or relating to silviculture — **sil·vi·cul·tur·al·ly** \-rəlē\ *adv*

sil·vi·cul·ture *or* **syl·vi·cul·ture** \ˈ==ˌkəlchə(r)\ *n* [F, fr. L *silva, sylva* wood, forest + *-i-* + F *culture,* fr. L *cultura*] **:** a phase of forestry that deals with the establishment, development, reproduction, and care of forest trees — compare ARBORICULTURE

sil·vi·cul·tur·ist \ˌ==ˈkəlch(ə)rəst\ *n* **:** a forester who specializes in silviculture

sil·yl \ˈsiləl\ *n* -S [*sil-* + *-yl*] **:** the univalent radical SiH_3 derived from monosilane by removal of one hydrogen atom

sim *abbr* **1** similar **2** simile

SIM *abbr* sergeant instructor of musketry

¹**si·ma** \ˈsīmə\ *var of* CYMA

²**sima** \"\ *n* -S [G, fr. *si*licium + *ma*gnesium] **:** basic igneous rock whether solid or molten — compare SIAL — **si·mat·ic** \(ˈ)sīˈmad·ik\ *adj*

si·ma·ba \səˈmäbə\ *n, cap* [NL, fr. native name in Guiana] **:** a genus of tropical So. American trees (family Simaroubaceae) having pinnate leaves and panicles of small flowers with 5 imbricated sepals, 5 petals, and 10 stamens — see CEDRON

si·mal \ˈsēməl\ *n* -S [Hindi *semal*] **1 :** an East Indian silk-cotton tree (*Bombax malabarica*) that yields a fiber inferior to kapok **2 :** the fiber of the simal tree — called also *red silk cotton*

si·mar *or* **sy·mar** \səˈmär\ *n* -S [F *simarre,* fr. It *zimarra,* fr. Sp *zamarra,* prob. fr. Basque *zamar* sheepskin] **1** *archaic* **a** *or* **si·marre** \"\ **:** a flowing coat dress with a full skirt and train worn by women during the Renaissance **b** *or* **cy·mar** \"\ **:** a light undergarment **:** SHIFT **2 :** ZIMARRA

sim·a·rou·ba \ˌsiməˈrübə\ *n, cap* [NL, fr. F, fr. Galibi *simaruba*] **:** a genus (the type of the family Simaroubaceae) of tropical American shrubs and trees with odd-pinnate leaves, pale light soft wood, bitter bark sometimes used medicinally, and clustered thin-fleshed drupes — see MARUPA, PARADISE TREE

sim·a·rou·ba·ce·ae \ˌ==(ˌ)=ˈbāsēˌē\ *n pl, cap* [NL, fr. *Simarouba,* type genus + *-aceae*] **:** a family of chiefly tropical trees and shrubs (order Geraniales) having bitter bark, mainly pinnate leaves, small 3-merous to 5-merous flowers with a prominent disk that are succeeded by a drupe, berry, or samara — see AILANTHUS, SIMAROUBA — **sim·a·rou·ba·ceous** \ˌ==(ˌ)=ˈbāshəs\ *adj*

sim·a·ru·ba \ˌsiməˈrübə\ [NL, fr. Galibi] *syn of* SIMAROUBA

sim·e·on·ism \ˈsimēəˌnizəm\ *n* -S *usu cap* [Charles *Simeon* †1836 Eng. evangelical preacher + E *-ism*] **:** the principles and practices of the Simeonites

¹**sim·e·on·ite** \-ˌnīt\ *n* -S *usu cap* [LL *Simeonitae* Simeonites, fr. *Simeon,* second son of the patriarch Jacob + L *-itae,* pl. of *-ita* -ite] **:** a member of the Hebrew tribe of Simeon

²**simeonite** \"\ *n* -S *usu cap* [Charles *Simeon* †1836 + E *-ite*] **1 :** a follower of the clerical leader Charles Simeon of the Evangelical Revival in the Church of England and founder of a trust for purchasing advowsons for Low Churchmen **2 :** LOW CHURCHMAN

sim·fer·o·pol \ˌsim(p)fəˈrōpəl, -rōp-\ *adj, usu cap* [fr. *Simferopol,* city of Crimea Region, U.S.S.R.] **:** of or from the city of Simferopol, U.S.S.R. **:** of the kind or style prevalent in Simferopol

sim·hah *or* **sim·cha** \ˈsimkə\ *n, pl* **sim·hoth** *or* **sim·hot** \-ˌkōt(h), -ōs\ *or* **sim·has** \-kəz\ *or* **sim·choth** *or* **sim·chot** \-ˌkōt(h), -ōs\ *or* **sim·chas** \-kəz\ [Heb *śimḥāh* rejoicing, mirth] **:** a happy occasion **:** a joyous celebration (as a bar mitzvah) ⟨the neighbors were guests at the family ~⟩

sim·hath to·rah *or* **sim·hat to·rah** *or* **sim·chas to·rah** *or* **sim·chath to·rah** *or* **sim·chat to·rah** \ˈsimkäˈstōrə\ *n, usu cap S&T* [Heb *śimḥath tōrāh* rejoicing of the Torah] **:** a festival observed on the 23d of Tishri in celebration of the completion of the Pentateuchal readings in the annual cycle

sim·ia \ˈsimēə\ *n, cap* [NL, fr. L, ape — more at SIMIAN] **:** a Linnaean genus of primates orig. including most of the apes and monkeys, subsequently restricted to the orang, later transferred to the chimpanzee and still later to the Barbary ape, and finally suppressed by international agreement to avoid confusion

sim·i·al \-ēəl\ *adj* [L *simia* ape + E *-al*] *archaic* **:** SIMIAN

¹**sim·i·an** \-mēən, -myən\ *adj* [L *simia* ape (fr. *simus* snub-nosed, fr. Gk *simos*) + E *-an;* prob. akin to OHG *swīnan* to vanish, subside, ON *svina*] **:** of, relating to, characteristic of, or resembling monkeys or apes

²**simian** \"\ *n* -S **:** MONKEY, APE; *esp* **:** ANTHROPOID 2

sim·i·an·i·ty \ˌsimēˈanəd·ē\ *n* -ES **:** the quality or state of being simian

simian shelf *n* **:** a bony ledge on the inside of the mandible characteristic of the anthropoid apes

sim·i·as \ˈsimēəs\ *n, cap* [NL, fr. L *simia* ape] **:** a genus including solely the pig-tailed langur

¹**sim·i·id** \-ēəd\ *adj* [NL *Simiidae*] **:** of or relating to the Pongidae

²**simiid** \"\ *n* -S **:** an ape of the family Pongidae

si·mi·i·dae \səˈmīəˌdē\ [NL, fr. *Simia* + *-idae*] *syn of* PONGIDAE

¹**sim·i·lar** \ˈsimələ(r) *also* -ml-, *substand* -myəl-\ *adj* [F *similaire,* fr. MF, fr. L *similis* like, similar + OF *-aire* -ary — more at SAME] **1 :** having characteristics in common **:** very much alike **:** COMPARABLE ⟨for shaping slots, keyways . . . or ~ cuts —H.D.Burghardt & Aaron Axelrod⟩ ⟨instruction for children in daily ethics, religion . . . and ~ subjects —S.P.Chase & J.K.Snyder⟩ ⟨extremists of the right — so ~ in so many ways to the extremists of the left —J.B.Oakes⟩ **2 :** alike in substance or essentials **:** CORRESPONDING ⟨no two animal habitats are exactly ~ —W.H.Dowdeswell⟩ **3 a :** having the same shape **:** differing only in size and position — used of geometrical figures **b :** moving in the same direction in relation to pitch — used of the motion of two or more voice parts in a musical progression **syn** see LIKE

²**similar** \"\ *n* -S **:** one that resembles another **:** COUNTERPART, LIKE

sim·i·lar·i·ty \ˌsiməˈlarəd·ē, -myə-, -rətē, -i *also* -ler-\ *n* -ES **1 :** the quality or state of being similar **:** RESEMBLANCE, CONFORMITY ⟨the ~ between cougars and jaguars⟩ ⟨the dangerous ~ of a mushroom to a toadstool⟩ ⟨~ of tastes among teen-agers⟩ ⟨of association by contiguity, by ~ and by contrast —R.S.Woodworth⟩ **2 :** a comparable aspect **:** ANALOGY, CORRESPONDENCE ⟨has a better eye for *similarities* among cultures than for diversities —Raphael Demos⟩

sim·i·lar·ly *adv* [¹*similar* + *-ly*] **:** in the same or a comparable manner **:** CORRESPONDINGLY, LIKEWISE ⟨suffered less from declining . . . production than most ~ situated communities —*Amer. Guide Series: Texas*⟩ ⟨~, the political and economic background of the conspiracy is inadequately treated —Nathan Schachner⟩

similarly placed *adj* **:** having the corresponding sides parallel and directed in the same sense

¹**sim·i·la·tive** \ˈsiməˌlād·iv, -ləd-\ *adj* [L *similis* similar + E *-ative*] **:** expressing similarity

²**similative** \"\ *n* -S **:** something expressing similarity

¹**sim·i·le** \ˈsimə(ˌ)lē, -li\ *n* -S [L, fr. neut. of *similis* like, similar] **1 :** a figure of speech comparing two essentially unlike things and often introduced by *like* or *as* (as in *cheeks like roses, a heart as hard as flint*) — compare METAPHOR **2 :** SIMILARITY ⟨a close ~ between the conditions of occurrence of the disease and those of certain other virus diseases —*Veterinary Record*⟩

²**si·mi·le** \ˈsēməˌlā\ *adj* [It, fr. L *similis*] **:** LIKE, SIMILAR — used as a direction in music to continue the same phrasing, use of pedals, or whatever has been previously directed

³**simile** \"\ *or* **simile mark** *n, pl* **simi·li** \(ˌ)lē\ [It *simile*] **:** a printed sign (as ʻ/⁄.) indicating that a musical figure or measure is to be repeated as often as the mark occurs

¹**si·mil·i·ter** \səˈmiləd·ə(r)\ *n* -S [L, in like manner, fr. *similis* like] **:** a reply by which the pleader in a common law pleading concurs with the other party in requesting trial by jury

²**similiter** \"\ *adv* [L] **:** in like manner

si·mil·i·tude \səˈmiləˌtüd, -əˌtyüd\ *n* -S [ME, fr. MF, likeness, resemblance, fr. L *similitudin-, similitudo,* fr. *similis* similar + *-tudin-, -tudo* -tude] **1 a :** COUNTERPART, DOUBLE ⟨met my own ~ —Agnes Repplier⟩ **b :** a visible likeness

: IMAGE, SEMBLANCE ⟨a spirit or devil in the ~ and proportion of a man —Margaret A. Murray⟩ **2** : an imaginative comparison : ALLEGORY, SIMILE ⟨London is often likened to Babylon; but the ~ is . . . unjust —Arthur Helps⟩ **3 a** : RESEMBLANCE, UNIFORMITY ⟨~ of specimens and test conditions was maintained —*Technical News Bull.*⟩ **b** : a point of comparison ⟨all medieval variances of thought show common ~s —H.O. Taylor⟩ **4** : maximal similarity of adjacent phonemes because of use of maximally similar allophones

sim·i·lize \'simə,līz\ *vt* -ED/-ING/-S [*simile* + *-ize*] : LIKEN, COMPARE; *esp* : to express in simile

sim·i·ous \'simēəs\ *adj* [L *simia* ape + E *-ous* — more at SIMIAN] : SIMIAN

sim·lin \'simlən\ *also* **sim·ling** \-liŋ\ *n* -S [prob. alter. of *simnel*] *chiefly South & Midland* : CYMLING

sim·men·tal *also* **sim·men·thal** \'zimən,täl\ *or* **sim·men·tha·ler** \-lə(r)\ *n* [*Simmental, Simmenthal* fr. *Simmental*, valley of the Simme river in central Switzerland; *Simmenthaler* fr. G *Simmentaler* of Simmental, fr. *Simmental*] **1** *usu cap* : a Swiss breed of large buff or dull red and white cattle used widely in Europe for meat, milk, and draft **2** -S *sometimes cap* : an animal of the Simmental breed

¹sim·mer \'simə(r)\ *vb* **simmered; simmered; simmering** \-m(ə)riŋ\ **simmers** [alter. of ¹*simper*, fr. ME *simperen*, of imit. origin] *vi* **1** : to stew gently with a bubbling sound below or just at the boiling point ⟨cover with water and let ~ four hours⟩ ⟨an iron pot . . . ~*ing* in one corner —*Amer. Guide Series: Tenn.*⟩ **2 a** : to be in a state of incipient development : FERMENT ⟨manages to keep about four plots constantly ~*ing* —Martin Levin⟩ ⟨a crisis began to ~ a fortnight ago —*Time*⟩ **b** : to be in inward turmoil : SEETHE ⟨this family . . . ~s with hostilities —Brooks Atkinson⟩ ⟨underneath these well-mannered exchanges there will continue to ~ a deeply felt . . . irritation —H.G.Nicholas⟩ ~ *vt* : to cook slowly in a liquid at a uniform heat just below the boiling point ⟨~ the meat until tender⟩ ⟨fruits which are to be kept whole should be ~*ed* —Marjorie M. Heseltine & Ula M. Dow⟩

²simmer \"\ *n* -S **1** : a condition approaching a boil ⟨the bubble and ~ of a stew⟩ ⟨crowded tenement houses, always on the ~ with crime —*Fortnight*⟩ **2** : a degree of heat that produces simmering ⟨electric ranges now can be adjusted for . . . degrees of heat, from ~ to superhot —*House Beautiful*⟩ ⟨that ~ of sun —Ira Wolfert⟩

³sim·mer \'simər\ *Scot var of* SUMMER

simmer down *vi* [¹*simmer*] **1** : to become reduced by or as if by simmering ⟨let the broth *simmer down* to a rich stock⟩ ⟨it . . . all *simmers down* to a matter of design —E.B.White⟩ **2** : to become calm or peaceful : QUIET, RELAX ⟨protests angrily but soon *simmers down*⟩ ⟨time would have elapsed for things to *simmer down* —Nevil Shute⟩ ⟨early May days find social activities *simmering down* a bit —Alice Dameron⟩

sim·mon \'simən\ *n* -S [by shortening] : PERSIMMON

sim·monds' disease \'simən(d)z-\ *n, usu cap S* [after Morris *Simmonds* †1925 Ger. physician] : a disease characterized by extreme and progressive emaciation with atrophy of internal organs, loss of body hair, evidences of premature aging and caused by atrophy or destruction of the anterior lobe of the pituitary gland

sim·nel \'simnəl\ *n* -S [ME *simenel*, fr. OF, fr. L *simila* finest wheaten flour, prob. of Sem origin like Gk *semidalis* finest wheaten flour; akin to Assyr *samīdu* fine meal, Syr *sĕmīdā*] **1** *or* **simnel bread** : a bun or bread made of the finest wheat flour **2** *or* **simnel cake** *Brit* **a** : a fruited cake resembling a plum pudding that is covered with a flour paste and first boiled, then baked, and traditionally eaten on Mothering Sunday **b** : a rich fruit cake sometimes coated with almond paste and baked for mid-Lent, Easter, and Christmas

si·mo·leon \sə'mōlēən, -lyən\ *n* -S [perh. alter. (influenced by *napoleon*) of earlier *simon*, of unknown origin] *slang* : DOLLAR

¹si·mo·ni·ac \sī'mōnē,ak, sə'm-\ *n* -S [ME, fr. MF or ML; MF *simoniaque*, fr. ML *simoniacus*, fr. *simoniacus* of simony, fr. LL *simonia* simony] : one who practices simony

²simoniac \"\ *or* **si·mo·ni·a·cal** \¦sīmə¦nīəkəl, ¦sim-\ *adj* : of, relating to, or characterized by simony — **si·mo·ni·a·cal·ly** \-k(ə)lē, -li\ *adv*

¹si·mo·ni·an \sī'mōnēən\ *n* -S *usu cap* [LGk *simōnianoi* followers of Simon Magus, fr. pl. of *simōnianos* of Simon, fr. *Simōn*, personal name of Simon Magus, 1st cent. Samaritan sorcerer] : a follower of Simon Magus : a member of any of various early gnostic sects reputed to follow his teachings

²simonian \"\ *adj, usu cap* : of, relating to, or characteristic of Simon Magus or the Simonians

si·mo·nian·ism \-ə,nizəm\ *n* -S *usu cap* : the doctrines and practices of Simonians

si·mo·ni·ous \sī'mōnēəs, sə'm-\ *adj* [*simony* + *-ous*] *archaic* : SIMONIAC

simo·nist \'sīmənəst, 'sim-\ *n* -S : one who practices or defends simony

si·mo·nize \'sīmə,nīz\ *vt* -ED/-ING/-S [fr. *Simoniz*, a trademark] : to polish with or as if with wax ⟨the children had been bathed, brushed and scrubbed till they looked sullen but *simonized* —Peter De Vries⟩

si·mon le·gree \'sīmənlə'grē\ *n, pl* **simon legrees** *usu cap S&L* [after *Simon Legree*, cruel slave dealer in *Uncle Tom's Cabin* (1852), novel by Harriet Beecher Stowe †1896, Am. author] : a cruel taskmaster

¹simon-pure \¦==¦=\ *adj* [fr. the phrase *the real Simon Pure*, alluding to a character impersonated by another in the play *A Bold Stroke for a Wife* (1718) by Susanna Centlivre †1723 Eng. dramatist and actress] **1** : of unqualified authenticity : GENUINE, UNADULTERATED ⟨remained during the thirties a *simon-pure*, uncompromising Marxist —C.I.Glicksberg⟩ **2** : untainted by bribery ⟨fight to make U.S. college football a *simon-pure* amateur game —*Time*⟩

²simon-pure \"\ *n* -S : a legitimate amateur ⟨was a professional until his reinstatement as a *simon-pure* —*Newsweek*⟩

simo·ny \'sīmənē, 'sim-, -ni\ *n* -ES [LL *simonia*, fr. *Simon* Magus, 1st cent. Samaritan sorcerer rebuked by Peter for offering money to purchase the power of giving the Holy Ghost, Acts 8: 9–24 + L *-ia* -y] : the buying or selling of a church office or ecclesiastical preferment

si·moom \sə'müm, sī'müm\ *also* **si·moon** \-ün\ *or* **sa·mum** \sə'müm\ *n* -S [Ar *samūm*] : a hot dry violent wind laden with dust from Asian and African deserts — called also *samiel*

simorg *or* **simorgh** *var of* SIMURGH

simous *adj* [L *simus* snub-nosed — more at SIMIAN] *obs* : flat or curving in : CONCAVE, SNUB ⟨a ~ nose⟩ ⟨~ beak⟩

simp \'simp\ *n* -S [by shortening] : SIMPLETON

sim·pai \'sim,pī\ *n* -S [Malay] : a highly colored Sumatran langur (*Presbytis melalopha*) having a narrow blackish crest, the forehead, cheeks, and underparts yellowish, the upper parts brown and reddish — called also *black-crested monkey*

sim·pati·co \sim'päd·ə,kō, -pad-\ *adj* [It *simpatico* (fr. *simpatia* sympathy, congeniality — fr. L *sympathia* sympathy — + *-ico* -ic, fr. L *-icus*) & Sp *simpático*, fr. *simpatia* (fr. L *sympathia*) + *-ico*, fr. L *-icus* — more at SYMPATHY] **1** : possessing attractive qualities : APPEALING, LIKABLE ⟨a bull I liked — a ~, noble animal —Barnaby Conrad⟩ **2** : exhibiting or inclined toward harmony : CONGENIAL, SYMPATHETIC ⟨buildings . . . ~ with the early Spanish and Indian motif —Conrad Richter⟩

¹sim·per \'simpə(r)\ *vi* **simpered; simpered; simpering** \-p(ə)riŋ\ **simpers** *dial Eng* : SIMMER

²simper \"\ *vb* -ED/-ING/-S [perh. of Scand origin; akin to Norw *semper* fine, smart, Dan dial. *semper, simper* affected, coy] *vi* **1** : to smile fatuously : SMIRK ⟨a two-fisted writer . . . does look out of place ~*ing* over a cup of tea —Jeann Beattie⟩ **2** *dial Eng* : WHIMPER ~ *vt* : to say with a simper

³simper \"\ *n* -S : an inane self-conscious smile : vacuous grin : SMIRK

sim·per·er \-p(ə)rə(r)\ *n* -S : one that simpers

simpering *adj* [fr. pres. part. of ²*simper*] : marked by insipidity : COY, PUSILLANIMOUS ⟨in a rather ~ voice —J.B.S.Haldane⟩ ⟨chocolate boxes flaunting their ~ inanity —Albert Dasnoy⟩ — **sim·per·ing·ly** *adv*

¹sim·ple \'simpəl\ *adj* **simpler** \-p(ə)lə(r)\ **simplest** \-p(ə)ləst\ [ME, fr. OF, plain, uncomplicated, artless, fr. L *simplus* or *simplex*; L *simplus* fr. *sem-, sim-* one + *-plus* multiplied by; L *simplic-, simplex* fr. *sem-, sim-* + *-plic-, -plex* -fold; akin to Gk *diplak-, diplax* twofold, double, and perh. to L *plaga* surface, region — more at SAME, DOUBLE, FLAKE] **1** : free from guile : INNOCENT, ARTLESS ⟨children grow up in ~ beauty around his table —*Irish Digest*⟩ **2 a** : free from vanity or conceit : MODEST, UNASSUMING ⟨his ~ manners and unaffected friendliness —A.W.Long⟩ **b** : free from ostentation or display : PLAIN, UNADORNED ⟨her black dress, ~ to austerity —W.S.Maugham⟩ ⟨a ~ rectangular brick building —*Amer. Guide Series: Va.*⟩ ⟨his home ~, his possessions few —P.E.James⟩ ⟨love of the ~ life, of trees and small animals —B.M.Woodbridge⟩ **3 a** : of humble origin : COMMON ⟨found it easier to proclaim himself a prophet than in his home city, where everyone had known him as a ~ camel driver —H.W. Van Loon⟩ **b** *archaic* : lacking special distinction : ORDINARY ⟨this change affected . . . only the ~ barons —William Stubbs⟩ **c** *archaic* : wanting in power or importance : FEEBLE, INSIGNIFICANT ⟨a ~ woman, much too weak to oppose your cunning —Shak.⟩ ⟨scoffed at . . . this high quest as at a ~ thing —Alfred Tennyson⟩ **4 a** : lacking in knowledge or scholarly finesse : UNEDUCATED, INEXPERT ⟨a ~ amateur . . . or a serious scholar —Denys Sutton⟩ ⟨show my mind, according to my shallow ~ skill —Shak.⟩ **b** (1) : mentally retarded : STUPID, HALF-WITTED ⟨one of the girls is ~, the other works as a domestic —J.M.Mogey⟩ (2) : easily deceived : CREDULOUS, GULLIBLE ⟨the whole town was baited with . . . trickery to catch the ~ cowhand and remove his cash —S.H.Holbrook⟩ **c** : being at a relatively low cultural level : NAÏVE, UNSOPHISTICATED ⟨the worldwide story of the conquest of ~ peoples and their homelands by the civilization, arms, and diseases of a more dominant race —*Amer. Guide Series: Minn.*⟩ **5 a** : lacking admixture or qualification : PURE, SHEER ⟨~ honesty requires us to admit that none of our creeds are entirely free from guesswork —M.R.Cohen⟩ ⟨a net rusher pure and ~ lacking a really powerful serve —*Sydney (Australia) Bull.*⟩ ⟨in no case may a warrant be issued for a ~ exploratory search —Paul Wilson⟩ ⟨ratification of treaties by a ~ majority —Vera M. Dean⟩ **b** (1) : free of secondary complications ⟨a ~ fracture⟩ (2) : containing or consisting of elementary ingredients ⟨her cures were ~ . . . usually very sensible —Mary Webb⟩ **c** : consisting of or constituting a basic element : FUNDAMENTAL, UNCOMPOUNDED ⟨one of those ~ and profound experiences . . . which people seem always to have known when it happens to them —Thomas Wolfe⟩ ⟨even under the most uniform laboratory conditions, a ~ color will be complex to the extent of having a bluish edge —John Dewey⟩; *specif* : ELEMENTAL 2a(2) **d** (1) : having a relatively small and uncomplicated molecule : not complex (2) : made up of essentially similar constituents ⟨a ~ compound⟩ : characterized by the same groups, radicals, or ions ⟨triacetin is a ~ glyceride⟩ — opposed to *mixed* **e** : admitting of no analysis into parts — opposed to *complex* **f** : having the least possible scoring value in its class **6 a** : grammatically uncomplicated: as (1) : having no subsidiary components (as suffixes or combining forms) : being a simplex ⟨a ~ word⟩ — contrasted with *complex, compound* (2) : having only one main clause and no subordinate clauses ⟨"let's go for a walk" is a ~ sentence⟩ — contrasted with *complex, compound* (3) : having no modifiers, complements, or objects ⟨in the sentence "birds fly" *birds* is the ~ subject and *fly* the ~ predicate⟩ — compare COMPLETE (4) : formed without the use of an auxiliary verb ⟨~ tense⟩ — opposed to *compound* **b** (1) : having two, three, or four basic rhythmic units to the musical measure (as ²⁄₄, ³⁄₂, ⁶⁄₈) ⟨~ time⟩ ⟨~ meter⟩ — compare COMPOUND (2) : free from elaboration or figuration ⟨~ harmony⟩ ⟨~ counterpoint⟩ — contrasted with *figurate* (3) : not greater than the octave ⟨~ interval⟩ **c** : not complex or compound ⟨~ fractions⟩ ⟨~ magnitudes⟩ ⟨~ operations⟩ ⟨~ equations⟩ ⟨~ interest⟩ **d** (1) : not subdivided into branches ⟨~ stem⟩ (2) : MONOCARPELLARY (3) : consisting of cells of a similar structure and function ⟨~ tissue⟩ (4) : developing from a single ovary ⟨~ fruit⟩ **e** : uncomplicated in structure ⟨a ~ lens⟩ ⟨a ~ democracy in which the heads of families met fortnightly to consult about . . . matters —*Amer. Guide Series: R.I.*⟩ **f** : apparently dependent on the action of a single gene ⟨~ inherited characters⟩ **g** (1) : HOMOGENEOUS 2a ⟨a ~ mineral⟩ (2) : PRIMITIVE 1c — compare SPACE LATTICE **7 a** : oral or written but not under seal or of record ⟨~ contract⟩ **b** : unaccompanied by complicating factors (as violence) **c** : having no limitation or restrictions : ABSOLUTE, UNCONDITIONAL ⟨~ obligation⟩ — compare FEE SIMPLE **8** : readily understood or performed : causing little difficulty : EASY, STRAIGHTFORWARD ⟨our mother . . . was as complex as our father was ~ —L.C.Powys⟩ ⟨the causes . . . lie deep, and to explain them is not ~ —William Petersen⟩ ⟨nontechnical, clear-cut, easily understandable, ~ step-by-step . . . rules which could be used by the average person —W.J.Reilly⟩

syn FOOLISH, SILLY, FATUOUS, ASININE: SIMPLE in this sense may imply either a degree of intelligence inadequate to cope with anything complex, a more definite feeblemindedness, or, in relation to persons of normal capacity, a failure to use one's intelligence ⟨she's rather *simple*, poor dear, and she thinks we're all wonderful —W.S.Maugham⟩ ⟨you are fretting about General Tilucy, and that is very *simple* of you —Jane Austen⟩ FOOLISH may indicate a mere lack of judgment or discretion or capricious failure to employ good sense and seriousness ⟨virtuous or vicious, thrifty or careless, wise or *foolish* —G.B. Shaw⟩ ⟨but *foolish* man foregoes his proper bliss —William Cowper⟩ SILLY may describe gross lack of judgment; it may connote folly, inanity, or nonsense ⟨the cut of her chiffon dress hinted that she had a *silly* conception of romance —Rebecca West⟩ ⟨the vapid and *silly* chatter of ordinary sociability —J.C.Powys⟩ FATUOUS is likely to involve fond, delusive, obtuse foolishness and disregard of reality ⟨with *fatuous* beaming he described a night at Barney's; without any success whatever, he tried to be funny —Sinclair Lewis⟩ ⟨her haughtiness in the day of glory was simply *fatuous*, based on stupidity —Arnold Bennett⟩ ⟨a number of *fatuous* theories about the connection of Central American culture with that of the Old World have been broached —Edward Clodd⟩ ASININE describes utter failure to exercise normal intelligence, rationality, or perception ⟨his reply was simply contemptuous . . . "What an *asinine* question!" —Bram Stoker⟩ ⟨their cumulative efforts have resulted in the most *asinine* and inept movie that has come out of Hollywood in years —John McCarten⟩ **syn** see in addition EASY, NATURAL, PLAIN, PURE

²simple \"\ *n* -S [ME, fr. ¹*simple*] **1 a** : a person of humble birth : COMMONER ⟨thought very little of anybody, ~s or gentry —Virginia Woolf⟩ **b** (1) : an uneducated or unduly credulous person : IGNORAMUS, GULL ⟨universal education destroyed the advantage which the shrewd had over the ~ —Reinhold Niebuhr⟩ (2) : a mentally retarded person : SIMPLETON ⟨buffoons . . . were usually ~s or hunchbacks —J.S.Clarke⟩ **2 a** : a plant used for its supposed medicinal properties ⟨the herb garden and barn redolent with drying bunches of ~s —Lucy Embury⟩ **b** : a vegetable drug or medicinal preparation having only one ingredient ⟨herbs for their homely ~s —Flora Thompson⟩ **3** : a single element : one component of a complex; *specif* : an unanalyzable constituent **4 simples** *pl, dial chiefly Eng* : foolish behavior : SILLINESS ⟨you should be cut for the ~s this morning —Jonathan Swift⟩ **5** : a set of cords for raising the heddles of a drawloom **6** : a feast of the lowest liturgical order of precedence in the Roman Catholic Church — compare DOUBLE 1b

³simple \"\ *adv* **1** *obs* : in an unassuming manner : HUMBLY, MODESTLY ⟨as ~ as I stand here —Ben Jonson⟩ **2** *dial* : in a silly manner : FOOLISHLY

⁴simple \"\ *vb* **simpled; simpled; simpling** \-p(ə)liŋ\ **simples** *vi* [²*simple*] *obs* : to gather herbs for simples ~ *vt* [¹*simple*] : to cause (a compound steam engine) to work like a simple engine by admitting live steam directly from the boiler to the low-pressure cylinder ⟨~ the engine in starting a heavy freight train⟩

simple beam *n* [¹*simple*] : a structural beam that rests on a support at each end

simple bitters *n pl* : bitters containing practically no aromatic oils or tannin

simple bond *n* : a bond without conditions

simple bud *n* : a bud that produces either a vegetative leaf-bearing shoot or a flower but not both — compare MIXED BUD

simple consequence *n* : IMMEDIATE INFERENCE 1

simple contract *n* : PAROL CONTRACT

simple conversion *n* : the transposing of the subject and predicate of a proposition without altering the quantity or quality ⟨"no P is S" becomes "no S is P" by *simple conversion*⟩

simple curve *n* : a circular arc (as of railroad track) joining two tangents — compare COMPOUND CURVE

simple engine *n* **1** : an engine (as a steam engine) in which the expansion is completed in a single phase and exhausted to atmosphere or condenses after a single stroke of the piston — compare COMPOUND ENGINE **2** : a steam engine in which the live steam is fed directly to the cylinders and after a single use of its expansive force is allowed to escape through the exhaust — contrasted with *compound engine*

simple equation *n* : LINEAR EQUATION

simple eye *n* : an eye having a single lens — compare COMPOUND EYE; see INSECT illustration

simple-faced \¦==¦=\ *adj* [¹*simple* + *faced*] : having no nasal appendages — used of vespertilionid bats

simple fraction *n* : a fraction having whole numbers for the numerator and denominator — compare COMPLEX FRACTION

simple harmonic motion *n* : a harmonic motion of constant amplitude in which the acceleration is proportional and oppositely directed to the displacement of the body from a position of equilibrium : the projection on any diameter of a point in uniform motion around a circle

simplehearted \¦==¦==\ *adj* [¹*simple* + *hearted*] : having a simple nature : ARTLESS, UNSOPHISTICATED

simple honors *n pl* : three trump honors or three aces at a no-trump contract in bridge held by the same side

simple idea *n* : an idea of an unanalyzable quality : an immediate object of sensation or reflection

simple immersion *n* : immersion of a metal in an electroplating solution without the application of an external electromotive force

simple interest *n* : interest paid or computed on the original principal only of a loan or on the amount of an account often on the assumption that each day is ¹⁄₃₆₀ of a year — compare COMPOUND INTEREST

simple interval *n* : a musical interval of an octave or less — compare COMPOUND INTERVAL

simple knot *n* : OVERHAND KNOT

simple larceny *n* : larceny that is not accompanied by special aggravating circumstances

simple leaf *n* : a leaf whose blade is not divided to the midrib even though lobed — compare COMPOUND LEAF

simple machine *n* : any of various elementary mechanisms having the elements of which all machines are composed and including the lever, the wheel and axle, the pulley, the inclined plane, the wedge, and the screw

simpleminded \¦==¦==\ *adj* [¹*simple* + *minded*] **1** : characterized by simplicity : devoid of subtlety : CANDID, UNSOPHISTICATED ⟨~ in the fashion that only geniuses can be —Irving Kristol⟩ ⟨terrors which the religious belief in demons . . . aroused in the daily lives of ~ men and women —M.R.Cohen⟩ **2** : lacking in education or mental capacity : FEEBLEMINDED, SLOW ⟨palming off paper imitations of . . . valuables on the ~ ghosts and gods, who take them in all good faith for the genuine articles —J.G.Frazer⟩ **3** : marked by foolishness or frivolity : STUPID, NONSENSICAL ⟨a ~ mistake⟩ ⟨~ games, like scattering beans on the floor and handing out straws for the guests to draw them up —*Fortune*⟩ — **sim·ple·mind·ed·ly** *adv* — **sim·ple·mind·ed·ness** *n* -ES

simple mode *n, Lockeanism* : a mode resulting from the combination of simple ideas of the same kind (as a dozen or a score) — contrasted with *mixed mode*

simple motion *n* : a motion in a straight line, circle or circular arc, or helix ⟨*simple motion* of a clock pendulum⟩

sim·ple·ness *n* -ES [ME *simplenesse*, fr. ¹*simple* + *-nesse* -ness] **1** *archaic* : SIMPLICITY **2** *obs* : irresponsible behavior : FOOLISHNESS ⟨what ~ is this —Shak.⟩

simple ointment *n* : an ointment consisting of 5 percent white wax and 95 percent white petrolatum

simple ore *n* : an ore yielding only one metal

simple pendulum *n* : an ideal pendulum consisting of a point mass suspended by a weightless inextensible perfectly flexible thread and free to vibrate without friction — distinguished from *physical pendulum*

simple pit *n* : a plant cell pit lacking a prominent overarching margin — compare BORDERED PIT

simple prebend *n* : a prebend having no parish responsibility for cure of souls attached to it

simple proposition *n* **1** : CATEGORICAL PROPOSITION **2** : a proposition not resolvable into separate statements : an atomic proposition

simple protein *n* : a protein (as an albumin or globulin) that yields amino acids as the chief or only products of complete hydrolysis — distinguished from *conjugated protein*

¹simpler *comparative of* SIMPLE

²sim·pler \'simp(ə)lə(r)\ *n* -S [²*simple* + *-er*] *archaic* : HERBALIST 1a

simple reaction time *n* : the time required for a subject to initiate a prearranged response to a defined stimulus

simpler's-joy \'==¦=\ *n* [²*simpler*] : BLUE VERVAIN

simples *pl of* SIMPLE, *pres 3d sing of* SIMPLE

simplest *superlative of* SIMPLE

simple stress *n* : stress consisting either of tension or compression but not both

simple substitution *n* : MONOALPHABETIC SUBSTITUTION

simple syllogism *n* **1** : CATEGORICAL SYLLOGISM **2** : a syllogism not resolvable into other syllogisms

simple tide *n* : a tide theoretically resulting from the influence of the sun and the moon if moving in circular orbits in the plane of the equator — see TIDAL CONSTANT

sim·ple·ton \'simpəltᵊn, -tən\ *n* -S [¹*simple* + *-ton*, as in *skimmington*] : a simpleminded person **syn** see FOOL

simple tone *n* : PURE TONE

simple vault *n* : a vault having a smooth intrados without ribs or cross arches

simple vow *n* : a public vow taken by a religious in the Roman Catholic Church under which retention of property by the individual is permitted and marriage though regarded as a sin is valid under canon law — compare SOLEMN VOW

simple watermark *n* : UNIT WATERMARK

¹sim·plex \'sim,pleks\ *adj* [L *simplic-, simplex* — more at SIMPLE] **1** : SIMPLE, SINGLE **2 a** : having one representative of a given dominant gene — used esp. of an autotetraploid; compare DUPLEX 2 **b** : having the gametic or haploid number of chromosomes **3** : allowing telecommunication in only one direction at a time ⟨~ system⟩ — compare DUPLEX 3

²simplex \"\ *n* -ES **1** *or pl* **sim·pli·ces** \-plə,sēz\ *or* **sim·pli·cia** \sim'plish(ē)ə\ : a simple word — contrasted with *complex* **2** : a method of telecommunication employing only one direction of transmission at any one time **3** : a spatial configuration of *n*-dimensions determined by *n* + 1 points in a space of dimension equal to or greater than *n*

³simplex \"\ *vt* -ED/-ING/-ES : to make simplex

simplex machine *n* [¹*simplex*] : a warp knitting machine that resembles a tricot machine but has two sets of needles and produces a double fabric

simplex ob·li·ga·tio \-,äblə'gäd·ē,ō\ *n* [NL, lit., simple obligation] : an unconditional bond — compare ¹SIMPLE 7c

simplex pile *n* [¹*simplex*] : a bearing pile formed by driving a steel shell with a specially designed point into the ground and filling the hole with concrete as the shell is withdrawn

simplex pump *n* : a pump having one steam and one water cylinder

simplex winding *n* : an armature winding that has only two paths from a brush of one polarity to another of opposite polarity

sim·pli·cial \sim'plishəl\ *adj* [*simplicia* + *-al*] : of or relating to simplexes ⟨~ mapping⟩

sim·pli·ci·den·ta·ta \sim,plisə,den·'täd·ə, -tād·ə\ *n pl, cap* [NL, fr. L *simplic-, simplex* simple + *-i-* + *dentata*, neut. pl. of *dentatus* toothed — more at DENTATE] *in former classifications* : a suborder of Rodentia coextensive with the order as now limited — compare LAGOMORPHA

sim·pli·cist \'simpləsəst\ *n* -S [L *simplic-, simplex* simple + E *-ist*] : an advocate or practitioner of simplism — **sim·pli·cis·tic** \¦==¦sistik, -tēk\ *adj*

sim·pli·ci·ter \sim'plisəd·ə(r)\ *adv* [L, simply, fr. *simplic-, simplex* simple] **1** : in or by itself : SIMPLY **2** *chiefly Scots law* : of its own nature : UNQUALIFIEDLY, UNCONDITIONALLY

sim·plic·i·ty \sim'plisəd·ē, -sətē, -i\ *n* -ES [ME *simplicite*, fr. MF, fr. L *simplicitat-, simplicitas*, fr. *simplic-, simplex* simple + *-itat-, -itas* -ity] **1 a :** absence of complexity in form or structure ⟨the ~ of a tulip⟩ ⟨the ~ of the circular zonation within the city —H.W.H.King⟩ **b :** an irreducible element **:** FUNDAMENTAL ⟨people seeking the basic *simplicities* of life —T.J.Panter⟩ **c :** organic unity ⟨the multiplicity . . . of our environment seems suddenly to attain clarification, ~, and homogeneity —Hunter Mead⟩ **2 :** lack of knowledge or good judgment **:** IGNORANCE, STUPIDITY ⟨because of his relative political ~ . . . can still be the prey of extremists —Ignazio Silone⟩ ⟨to save his contemptible life . . . dared to practice on our credulous ~ —W.S.Gilbert⟩ **3 a :** ingenuousness of spirit **:** freedom from vanity or guile **:** HUMILITY, CANDOR ⟨retained a great ~ and kindliness of character, was always easily approachable —Martha Gruening⟩ ⟨wish to appear all innocence and ~, and they full of malice and deceit all the time —George Borrow⟩ **b :** unaffected naturalness **:** freedom from artificiality or display **:** GENUINENESS, PLAINNESS ⟨the peace and ~ of natural surroundings —J.L.Phelan⟩ ⟨the almost bare ~ of life in his grandfather's house —Archibald Marshall⟩ **c :** INNOCENCE, NAÏVETÉ ⟨the combination of great intellect with childlike ~ —Bertrand Russell⟩ **4 a :** directness of expression **:** absence of ambiguity or overrefinement **:** CLARITY, INTELLIGIBILITY ⟨pleased the general reader by the smoothness and ~ of her verse —Bertha Stearns⟩ ⟨sang with feeling and ~ —T.L.Peacock⟩ **b :** limitation in the use of ornament **:** AUSTERITY, RESTRAINT ⟨all garments were white . . . and of the utmost ~ in cut and material —*Amer. Guide Series: Pa.*⟩ ⟨the dignity and ~ of colonial architecture⟩ **5 a :** a simple act, idea, or characteristic ⟨reverence for the *simplicities* of . . . rural and village America —Bernard De Voto⟩ ⟨the *simplicities* and certainties of 1914 had given way to . . . confusions —*Times Lit. Supp.*⟩ **b :** an instance or epitome of something simple ⟨the average transatlantic flight is ~ itself —Richard Joseph⟩

sim·pli·fi·ca·tion \,simpləfə'kāshən\ *n* -S [ML *simplificatus* (past part. of *simplificare*) + E *-ion*] **:** an act, process, or result of simplifying: as **a :** the elimination of superfluous detail in art **:** ABSTRACTION, GENERALIZATION ⟨the public understands . . . his subtle and beautiful ~s down to essential form as part of the great tradition of sculpture —Aline B. Saarinen⟩ **b :** the reduction or elimination of complexity or multiplicity **:** STREAMLINING ⟨~ of the control panel of an airplane⟩ ⟨product-line ~ is equally applicable to wholesale and retail businesses⟩ **c (1) :** the reduction of a double consonant to a single one (as in Latin *vacilo* for *vacillo*) **(2) :** the elision of silent letters (as in *gram* for *gramme*) — compare CONTRACTION 4 **d :** SIMPLISM

simplified *adj* [fr. past part. of *simplify*] **:** made simple **:** reduced in complexity

simplified spelling *n* **:** REFORMED SPELLING

sim·pli·fi·er \'simplə,fī(ə)r, -īə\ *n* -S **:** one that simplifies

sim·pli·fy \-,fī\ *vt* -ED/-ING/-ES [F *simplifier*, fr. ML *simplificare*, fr. L *simplus* simple + *-ificare* -ify] **:** to make simple or simpler: as **a :** to reduce to basic essentials **:** divest of superfluous elements ⟨hooded fishermen whose forms are *simplified* to black silhouettes —Stewart Beach⟩ **b :** to diminish in scope or complexity **:** ABRIDGE, STREAMLINE ⟨~ an application form⟩ ⟨~ a manufacturing process⟩ **c :** to make more intelligible **:** CLARIFY, EXPLAIN ⟨*simplifies* the issue for his hearers⟩ **d :** OVERSIMPLIFY ⟨there are too many people in this country who go after a slogan, who ~ things down —F.D.Roosevelt⟩

simpling *pres part of* SIMPLE

sim·plism \'sim,plizəm\ *n* -S [F *simplisme*, fr. *simple* simple, single + *-isme* -ism] **:** OVERSIMPLIFICATION; *esp* **:** the tendency to concentrate on a single aspect (as of a problem) to the exclusion of all complicating factors ⟨division of mankind into workingmen and capitalists suffers from the fallacy of ~ —M.R.Cohen⟩

sim·plis·tic \(')sim¦plistik, -tēk\ *adj* **:** of, relating to, or characterized by simplism — **sim·plis·ti·cal·ly** \-tək(ə)lē, -tēk-, -li\ *adv*

sim·ply \'simplē, -li, *in senses 1 & 2 sometimes* -pəl-\ *adv* [ME *simplely, simply*, fr. ¹*simple* + *-ly*] **1 :** in a straightforward manner **:** MODESTLY, SINCERELY ⟨behaved so ~ and magnificently that even his enemies found themselves won over —C.L.Carmer⟩ **2 a :** without ambiguity **:** INTELLIGIBLY, CLEARLY ⟨let the narrative unfold ~ and objectively —R.A. Cordell⟩ **b :** without extravagance or embellishment **:** PLAINLY ⟨within the range of the ~ educated —J.H.Plumb⟩ ⟨a graceful structure, built ~ when simplicity was not considered a virtue —*Amer. Guide Series: Minn.*⟩ **c :** without complexity or subterfuge **:** DIRECTLY, CANDIDLY ⟨everything . . . came to happen as ~ and as naturally and as gradually as a season coming on —R.P.Warren⟩ ⟨this she said as ~ as a child recites a tale —Pearl Buck⟩ **3 a** *obs* **:** ABSOLUTELY, CATEGORICALLY ⟨that they have any being, purely and ~, I deny —R.G.Preston⟩ **b :** in or of itself **:** without augmentation **:** MERELY, SOLELY ⟨readers who read books ~ to finish them —James Thurber⟩ ⟨in this chapter . . . we ~ note the principal characteristics of the period —Tom Wintringham⟩ ⟨she was ~ and solely a beautiful woman —Jean Stafford⟩ **c :** in actual fact **:** LITERALLY, REALLY ⟨there ~ is not enough work to go around —Hamilton Basso⟩ — often used as an intensive ⟨you ~ must wear a British bowler —John McCaffrey⟩ **4** *archaic* **:** IGNORANTLY, FOOLISHLY ⟨got money from various ~ disposed persons, under pretence of getting them confidential appointments —W.M.Thackeray⟩

simps *pl of* SIMP

simp·son·ite \'sim(p)sᵊn,īt\ *n* -S [Edward S. *Simpson* †1939 Australian mineralogist + E *-ite*] **:** a mineral $AlTaO_4$ consisting of an oxide of aluminum and tantalum in short hexagonal crystals

simp·son's honey-plant \'sim(p)sᵊnz-\ *n, usu cap S* [perh. after Sir George *Simpson* †1860 Canadian explorer] **:** a figwort (*Scrophularia marylandica*)

simpson's rule *n, usu cap S* [after Thomas *Simpson* †1761 Eng. mathematician] **:** a method used esp. by naval architects for computing the approximate area bounded by a curve by adding the areas of a series of figures formed from an odd number of equally spaced ordinates to the curve and parabolas drawn through the points where these ordinates cut the curve

sim·sim \'sim,sim\ *n* -S [Ar; akin to Assyr *šamaššamu* sesame — more at SESAME] **:** SESAME

sim·son \'sim(p)sᵊn\ *n* -S [alter. of earlier *sinsion*, fr. ME *synchon*, fr. MF *senechion*, fr. L *senecion-, senecio* — more at SENECIO] **:** GROUNDSEL

simson line *n, usu cap S* [after Robert *Simson* †1768 Scot. mathematician] **:** the line joining the feet of the perpendiculars let fall from any point on the circumcircle of a triangle upon the sides of the triangle

sims system \'simz-\ *n, usu cap 1st S* [after Philip H. *Sims* †1949 Amer. bridge expert] **:** a system of bidding at contract bridge characterized by notably strong opening bids by first or second hand, weaker opening bids by third or fourth hand, and very strong opening no-trump bids

sim·u·la·cre \'simyə,lākə(r)\ *n* -S [ME, fr. MF, fr. L *simulacrum*] *archaic* **:** SIMULACRUM

sim·u·la·crum \,==¦'lākrəm, -'lak-\ *n, pl* **simula·cra** \-rə\ *also* **simulacrums** [L, fr. *simulare* to imitate, represent — more at SIMULATE] **1 :** a representation of something **:** IMAGE, EFFIGY ⟨after the doge's death, a wax figure, his ~, was laid out in the chamber —Mary McCarthy⟩ ⟨only . . . tireless interworking of sources could have produced this vibrant ~ of a period —Marianne Moore⟩ **2 a :** something having the form but not the substance of a material object **:** IMITATION, SHAM ⟨moved silently away in the night, . . . leaving an exact ~ of its tanks, where it had been, and proceeded to its points of attack —Sir Winston Churchill⟩ **b :** a superficial likeness **:** APPEARANCE, SEMBLANCE ⟨was glad to have his presence and that of his weapon justified by some ~ of fear and trouble —C.E.Craddock⟩ **syn** see IMPOSTURE

¹**sim·u·lar** \-lə(r)\ *n* -S [irreg. fr. L *simulare* + E *-ar*] *archaic* **:** DISSEMBLER

²**simular** \"\ *adj* [L *simulare* + E *-ar*] *archaic* **:** COUNTERFEIT, IMITATIVE

¹**sim·u·late** \-lət, -,lāt, *usu* -d·+V\ *adj* [ME, fr. L *simulatus*, past part. of *simulare*] *archaic* **:** SIMULATED

²**sim·u·late** \-,lāt, *usu* -ād·+V\ *vb* -ED/-ING/-S [L *simulatus*, past part. of *simulare* to imitate, represent, feign, fr. *similis* like, similar — more at SAME] *vt* **1 :** to give the appearance or effect of **:** FEIGN, IMITATE ⟨felt obliged to ~ reluctance, and the air of having had her hand forced —Edith Wharton⟩ ⟨to ~ real mink, the muskrat pelts are let out —Pete Barrett⟩ ⟨pegs in the oak flooring further ~ pioneer construction —*Amer. Guide Series: Ark.*⟩ **2 :** to have the characteristics of **:** RESEMBLE ⟨the raised forelegs of the praying mantis ~ the attitude of a man at prayer⟩ ⟨mycoses . . . which may involve the lungs and ~ tuberculosis —J.B.Amberson⟩ **~** *vi* **:** to make believe **:** PRETEND ⟨while the unseen musician plays, the actor ~s⟩ **syn** see ASSUME

simulated *adj* [fr. past part. of ²*simulate*] **:** of a feigned or imitative character **:** MOCK, SHAM ⟨a large scale experimental parachute drop . . . under ~ combat conditions —J.G. Cozzens⟩ ⟨the handles are handsome, ~ stag or mother-of-pearl —*N.Y. Times*⟩

simulated pearl *n* **:** a bead made to resemble a pearl ⟨mock-jeweled trim of *simulated pearls* and glass beads —*Sears, Roebuck Cat.*⟩ — contrasted with *cultured pearl*

simulated rank *n* **:** a civilian status equated to a military rank ⟨the chief of research had the *simulated rank* of colonel⟩

sim·u·la·tion \,simyə'lāshən\ *n* -S [ME *simulacion*, fr. MF, fr. L *simulation-, simulatio*, fr. *simulare* to simulate + *-ion-, -io* -ion] **1 a :** the act or process of simulating **:** IMITATION, PRETENSE ⟨the ~ of tigers by the rainmakers at the grave may be intended to intimidate the dead man —J.G.Frazer⟩ ⟨flung her arms around his neck with an almost perfect ~ of surprise and spontaneity —Louis Auchincloss⟩ **b :** a sham object **:** COUNTERFEIT ⟨bogus gilt dadoes . . . and other ~s —Janet Flanner⟩ **2 :** willful deception **:** COLLUSION, MISREPRESENTATION **3 :** one that shows a superficial resemblance **:** ANALOGUE ⟨the ~ of a black mask on the face of a raccoon⟩ ⟨a shabby room that still gave a ~ of elegance⟩

sim·u·la·tor \'==,lād·ə(r), -ātə-\ *n* -S [L, fr. *simulatus* (past part. of *simulare*) + *-or*] **:** one that simulates; *specif* **:** a device in a laboratory that enables the operator to reproduce under test conditions phenomena likely to occur in actual performance

¹**si·mul·cast** \'siməl,kast, -aa(ə)st, -aist, -àst\ *vb* [*simul*taneous + broad*cast*] **:** to broadcast by radio and television simultaneously

²**simulcast** \"\ *n* -S **:** a simultaneous transmission over radio and television

¹**si·mu·li·id** \sə'myülēəd\ *adj* [NL *Simuliidae*] **:** of or relating to the Simuliidae

²**simuliid** \"\ *n* -S **:** a fly of the family Simuliidae

sim·u·li·i·dae \,simyə'līə,dē\ *n pl, cap* [NL, fr. *Simulium*, type genus + *-idae*] **:** a family of small biting two-winged flies including the blackflies and related pests and having larvae that usu. live in rapidly flowing water — see SIMULIUM

si·mu·li·um \sə'myülēəm\ *n, cap* [NL, fr. L *simulare* to simulate] **:** the type genus of Simuliidae comprising dark-colored biting flies of which some are vectors of onchocerciasis or of protozoan diseases of birds

simul·ta·ne·i·ty \,sīməltə'nēəd·ē, ,sim-, -ēətē, -i\ *n* -ES [ML *simultaneitas*, fr. (assumed) ML *simultaneus* + L *-itas* -ity] **:** the quality or state or an instance of being simultaneous ⟨the ~ of these events has been exaggerated —G.G.Simpson⟩; *specif* **:** the presentation of different views of the same object (as a profile and full view of a face) in one work of art ⟨~ . . . in Egyptian painting —Helen Gardner⟩

simul·ta·neous \,sīməl¦tānēəs, ,sim-, -nyəs\ *adj* [fr. (assumed) ML *simultaneus* (whence *simultaneitas* simultaneity), fr. L *simul* at the same time (fr. *similis* same, similar) + ML *-taneus* (fr. LL *momentaneus* momentary) — more at SAME, MOMENTANEOUS] **1 :** existing or occurring at the same time **:** COINCIDENT, CONCURRENT ⟨~ fixing of prices of commodities affecting each other . . . as maize and dairy or pig products —*Farmer's Weekly (So. Africa)*⟩ ⟨just by twisting a dial, visitors to the U.N. General Assembly can hear ~ interpretations of what the speaker is saying in any of the five official languages⟩ **2 :** satisfied by the same values of the variables ⟨~ equations⟩ **syn** see CONTEMPORARY

simultaneous contrast *n* **:** the tendency of a color to induce its opposite in hue, value and intensity upon an adjacent color and be mutually affected in return ⟨by the law of *simultaneous contrast* a light, dull red will make an adjacent dark, bright yellow seem darker, brighter and greener; in turn, the former will appear lighter, duller and bluer⟩

simultaneous death act *n* **:** a statute prescribing the rules of inheritance applicable when two or more persons die at the same time or from the same accident or event, or within a specified short period

simul·ta·neous·ly *adv* **:** in a simultaneous manner **:** at the same time **:** CONCURRENTLY

simul·ta·neous·ness *n* -ES [*simultaneous* + *-ness*] **:** SIMULTANEITY

simultaneous reaction *n* **:** any of two or more chemical reactions occurring at the same time in the same system — compare SIDE REACTION

si·murgh *or* **si·murg** \sē'mu̇(ə)rg, '=,=\ *also* **si·morg** *or* **si·morgh** \-mo̊(ə)rg\ *n* -S [Per *sīmurgh*, fr. MPer *sēnmurv*; akin to Av *mərəghō saēnō*, fr. *mərəgha-* bird + *saēna-* eagle] **:** a huge ancient bird of Persian legend credited with possessing great wisdom — compare ROC

¹**sin** \'sin\ *n* -S [ME *sinne*, fr. OE *synn, syn*; akin to OFris *sende sin*, OS *sundia*, OHG *sunta, suntea* and perh. to L *sont-, sons* guilty; prob. akin to L *est* is —more at IS] **1 a :** a transgression of religious law **:** an offense against God ⟨making her dream . . . of the ~ which he resolved to allure her to commit —Daniel Defoe⟩ **b :** a serious offense **:** a violation of propriety ⟨colleges which glorify research and publication . . . are guilty of a grave and perhaps irreparable ~ against civilization —Millicent McIntosh⟩ ⟨the rhetorical ~ of the meaningless variation —Lewis Mumford⟩ **c :** a serious shortcoming **:** FAULT ⟨the English ~ has always been . . . a lack of social coherence —Herbert Read⟩ **2 :** violation of religious law **:** disregard of God's will ⟨thought about the nature of ~ in general —H.E.Fosdick⟩; *specif* **:** violation of proscription of fornication ⟨accused . . . of living in ~ with her fiancé —Leslie Rees⟩ — see ACTUAL SIN, DEADLY SIN, MORTAL SIN, ORIGINAL SIN, VENIAL SIN

²**sin** \"\ *vb* **sinned; sinned; sinning; sins** [ME *sinnen, singen*, fr. OE *syngian*; akin to MD *sondigen* to sin, ON *syndga*; denominative fr. the root of E ¹*sin*] *vi* **1 :** to violate religious law **:** commit an offense against God; *specif* **:** FORNICATE **2 :** to commit an offense ⟨critics often *sinned* against good critical sense —C.I.Glicksberg⟩ **~** *vt* **1 :** to perform sinfully ⟨there remains so much to be *sinned* and suffered in the world —Nathaniel Hawthorne⟩ **2** *archaic* **:** to drive by sinning ⟨we have *sinned* him hence —John Dryden⟩ — **sin one's mercies :** to show ingratitude

³**sin** *var of* SYNE

⁴**sin** \'sēn *also* 'sin\ *n* -S [Heb *śīn*] **1 :** the 21st letter of the Hebrew alphabet — symbol שׂ; see ALPHABET table **2 :** the letter corresponding to Hebrew sin in the Phoenician or in any of various other Semitic alphabets

sin *abbr* **1** sine **2** [L *sinistra*] left hand

si·na·gua \sə'nä(g)wə\ *adj, usu cap* [fr. *Sinagua*, village in northern Arizona where remains of the culture were found] **:** of or relating to a people living in northern Arizona from about A.D. 600 to about 1400 whose culture is characterized by rectangular pit houses entered through a hole in the roof, by pueblo structures on high land, by pottery shaped with paddle and anvil and fired in an oxidizing atmosphere, ball courts, and extended burial with offerings

si·na·ite \'sīnə,īt\ *n* -S [F, fr. *Sinai*, peninsula in Egypt + F *-ite*; fr. its being the type of rock found in the Gebel Musa group of mountains in the Sinai peninsula] **:** SYENITE

si·na·it·ic \'=¦=¦id·ik\ *adj, usu cap* [NL *sinaiticus*, fr. *Sinai*, mountain prob. of the Gebel Musa group in So. Sinai peninsula from which according to Exod 19:20 God gave the Ten Commandments to the Israelites and *Sinai*, peninsula in northeastern Egypt at the north end of the Red sea (fr. LL, fr. Heb *Sīnai*) + L *-iticus* -itic] **1 :** of or relating to Mount Sinai **2 :** of or relating to the Sinai peninsula

sinaitic alphabet *n, usu cap S* **:** an alphabet found in inscriptions in Sinaitic mines that forms a link between the Egyptian hieroglyphs and the Phoenician alphabet

si·nal \'sīnᵊl\ *adj* [NL *sinus* + E *-al*] **:** of, relating to, or coming from a sinus ⟨a ~ discharge⟩

sinalagmatic *var of* SYNALLAGMATIC

sin·al·bin \sə'nalbən\ *n* -S [ISV *sin-* (fr. L *sinapis* mustard) + L *alba* (fem. of *albus* white) + ISV *-in* — more at ELF] **:** a bitter crystalline glucoside $C_{30}H_{42}N_2O_{15}S_2$ in white mustard seeds that on hydrolysis by myrosin yields glucose, sinapine hydrogen sulfate, and the yellow irritant mustard oil *para-*hydroxy-benzyl isothiocyanate

sina·may \,sēnə'mī, 'sinə,mī\ *n* -S [Tag *sinamáy*] **:** a stiff coarse open textile woven in the Philippines chiefly from abaca

sin·an·thro·pus \sə'nan(t)thrəpəs, ,si,nan'thrōpəs\ *n* [NL, fr. LL *Sinae*, pl., Chinese + NL *-anthropus* — more at SINOLOGUE] **1** *cap* **:** a genus of fossil primitive men that includes the Peking man and is often considered generically inseparable on the one hand from *Pithecanthropus* and on the other from *Homo* **2** -ES **:** PEKING MAN

sin·a·pate \'sinə,pāt\ *n* -S [ISV *sinap-* (in *sinapic acid*) + *-ate*] **:** a salt or ester of sinapic acid

si·nap·ic acid \sə'napik-\ *n* [ISV *sinap-* (in *sinapine*) + *-ic*] **:** a yellow crystalline phenolic unsaturated acid $HO(CH_3O)_2$-$C_6H_2CH{=}CHCOOH$ that is related structurally both to cinnamic acid and to pyrogallol and obtained by hydrolysis of sinalbin

sin·a·pine \'sinə,pīn, -,pən\ *n* -S [ISV *sinap-* (fr. L *sinapis* mustard) + *-ine*; orig. formed as G *sinapin*] **:** an alkaloid $C_{16}H_{25}NO_6$ in black mustard seeds that is an unstable ester of choline and sinapic acid — see SINALBIN

si·na·pis \sə'nāpəs\ *n* [NL, fr. L *sinapi, sinapis* mustard, fr. Gk] **1** *cap, in some classifications* **:** a genus comprising cruciferous herbs with a long beak on the tip of the seedpod and being now usu. included as a section in the genus *Brassica* **2** -ES **:** MUSTARD

sin·a·pism \'sinə,pizəm\ *n* -S [LL *sinapismus*, fr. Gk *sinapismos* act of using mustard plaster, fr. *sinapizein* to apply mustard plaster, fr. *sinapi, sinapis* mustard] **:** MUSTARD PLASTER

sin·ar·quism \'si,när,kizəm, sə'n-\ *or* **sin·ar·quis·mo** \,si,när'kiz(,)mō\ *also* **sin·ar·chism** *or* **syn·ar·chism** \'=,=,kizəm\ *n* -S *usu cap* [MexSp *sinanarquismo*, fr. Sp *sin* without (fr. L *sine*) + *anarquismo*, fr. *anarquia* anarchy (fr. Gk *anarchia*) + *-ismo* -ism (fr. L *-ismus*) — more at SUNDER, ANARCHY] **:** a Mexican counterrevolutionary movement embracing chiefly peasants and workers under secret leaders that seeks restoration of an early Christian social order, favors hispanidad, and opposes communism, Pan-Americanism, labor unionism, and military conscription

¹**sin·ar·quis·ta** \,si,när'kēstə\ *also* **sin·ar·quist** *or* **syn·ar·chist** \'=,=,kəst\ *n* -S *usu cap* [MexSp *sinarquista*, fr. *sinarquismo*, after Sp *anarquismo* anarchism: *anarquista* anarchist] **:** an adherent of Sinarquism

²**sinarquista** \"\ *also* **sinarquist** *or* **sin·ar·chist** *or* **synarchist** \"\ *adj, usu cap* [MexSp *sinarquista*] **:** of, relating to, or characteristic of Sinarquism

si·nay bean \(')sē¦nī-\ *n* [Ilocano *sinay*] **:** RICE BEAN

sincamas *var of* SINGKAMAS

¹**since** \(¦)sin(t)s, ,sən-, *chiefly dial* (¦)sen-\ *adv* [ME *sins, sinnes* afterwards, since, contr. of *sithens, sithenes*, adv. & prep., since, fr. *sithen* (fr. OE *siththan*, contr. of *sith tham* afterwards, since that, fr. *sith*, adv. & prep., since + *tham*, dat. of *thæt* that) + *-s, -es* -s; akin to OHG *sīd* since, ON *sīth*, adv., late, Goth *seithu*, neut. adj., late, OIr *sīr* long-lasting, L *serus* late, *serere* to sow — more at THAT, SOW] **1 :** continuously from a time in the past until the present ⟨established in 1935 . . . it has ~ been the majority party —*Current Biog.*⟩ — often used with *ever* ⟨went abroad eight years ago and has stayed there ever ~⟩ **2 :** before the present time **:** AGO ⟨that wood fire he let out of hand some time ~ —J.H.Powers⟩ — often used with *long* ⟨a bachelor's degree has long ~ lost any meaning —J.B.Conant⟩ **3 :** after a time in the past **:** SUBSEQUENTLY ⟨in 1719 a brick wall, ~ removed, was ordered built around the churchyard —*Amer. Guide Series: Va.*⟩ ⟨settled in what has ~ become South Carolina —*Current Biog.*⟩

²**since** \(¦)sin(t)s, *chiefly dial* (¦)sen-\ *prep* **1 :** in the period after a specified time in the past ⟨a few improvements have been made ~ the beginning of the century⟩ **2 :** continuously from a specified time in the past ⟨~ that time the two groups have opposed each other —Cecil Hobbs⟩

³**since** \'sin(t)s, *chiefly dial* 'sen-\ *adj, archaic* **:** occurring or existing after ⟨my ~ experience of Sunday evenings —J.A. Froude⟩

⁴**since** \(¦)sin(t)s, *chiefly dial* (¦)sen-\ *conj* [ME *sinnes*, fr. *sins, sinnes*, adv.] **1 :** after the time in the past when ⟨the building has been razed ~ I visited the city⟩ ⟨it has been 20 years ~ he was first elected⟩ **2** *obs* **:** the time in the past when **:** WHEN ⟨thou remembrest ~ once I sat upon a promontory —Shak.⟩ **3 :** up to the present time from the time in the past when ⟨has known him ever ~ he was a child⟩ **4 :** for the reason that **:** because of the fact that ⟨~ it was raining he wore a hat⟩

sin·cere \(')sin¦si(ə)r, ,sən's-, -iə\ *adj, usu* -ER/-EST [MF, fr. L *sincerus*, prob. fr. *sem-* one + *-cerus* (fr. *creare* to create) — more at SAME, CRESCENT] **1 :** marked by genuineness: as **a :** free of dissimulation **:** not hypocritical **:** REAL, TRUE, HONEST ⟨the missionaries were prompted by a ~ desire for good —Herman Melville⟩ ⟨was above all ~ and detested any form of pretense or affectation —Terry de Valera⟩ **b (1) :** free from adulteration **:** not mixed ⟨to find and isolate Nazism in its pure ~ form proved extremely difficult —J.C.Harsch⟩ **(2) :** not containing any foreign element **:** PURE ⟨wood is cheap and wine ~ outside the city gate —Robert Browning⟩ **c :** marked by truth **:** GENUINE ⟨the only ~ glimpse that we get of the living breathing word-compelling Dante —J.R.Lowell⟩ **d :** motivated by a desire for meaningful expression ⟨the emotional substratum which we feel to be inseparable from a truly great and ~ work of musical art —Edward Sapir⟩ **2** *archaic* **:** DEVOID ⟨air ~ of ceremonious haze —J.R.Lowell⟩ **3 :** characterized by firm belief in the validity of one's own opinions ⟨an entirely ~ and cruel tyrant⟩

syn WHOLEHEARTED, WHOLE-SOULED, HEARTFELT, HEARTY, UNFEIGNED: SINCERE suggests absence of hypocrisy, dissimulation, falsification, feigning, or embellishment and consequent honest genuineness ⟨too *sincere* for dissimulation —Ellen Glasgow⟩ ⟨individuals are considered *sincere* when there is little or no discrepancy between the goals they seek and those they claim to be seeking —L.W.Doob⟩ WHOLEHEARTED and WHOLE-SOULED stress lack of reservation or misgiving and may suggest devotion, zeal, and sincerity ⟨writes himself down a frank and *wholehearted* Tory —V.L.Parrington⟩ ⟨who could help liking her? her generous nature, her gift for appreciation, her *wholehearted*, fervid enthusiasm —L.P.Smith⟩ ⟨men whose dedication to their country was *whole-souled*, nevertheless, and for whom the supreme frustration of personal ambition never deflected them away from public services of a monumental nature —Eric Sevareid⟩ HEARTFELT suggests a genuine stirring of innermost feelings and usu. contrasts with formal, conventional, outwardly indicated, more or less factitious manifestation ⟨our sympathy for you therefore is *heartfelt*, for we are sharing the same sufferings —Sir Winston Churchill⟩ ⟨if ever men have offered *heartfelt* thanks to God for deliverance from the perils of the sea, surely we were those men —C.B.Nordhoff & J.N.Hall⟩ HEARTY may suggest vigorous manifestations like notable warmth and robust exuberance ⟨infuriated elderly traveling salesmen were backslapped all day long by *hearty* and powerful unknown persons —Sinclair Lewis⟩ ⟨a courtier's laugh, decorous, brief and not too *hearty* —J.H.Wheelwright⟩ UNFEIGNED may stress spontaneity and absence of simulation ⟨I confess to *unfeigned* delight in the insurgent propaganda —J.L.Lowes⟩

sin·cere·ly *adv* **:** in a sincere manner — often used as a complimentary close often followed by *yours*

sin·cere·ness *n* -ES **:** SINCERITY 1

sin·cer·i·ty \sən'serəd·ē, -'sir-, -rətē, -i\ *n* -ES [MF *sincerité*, fr. L *sinceritat-, sinceritas*, fr. *sincerus* sincere + *-itat-, -itas* -ity] **1 :** the quality or state of being sincere ⟨the passionate ~ of artists and other intellectuals may still be warped by wishful preferences —H.J.Muller⟩ **2 a :** a sincere feeling ⟨grounded not on garnitures and semblances but on realities and *sincerities* —Thomas Carlyle⟩ **b :** an expression of a sincere feeling ⟨his voice altered and ceased to sing its pleasantly tuned *sincerities* —Nancy Keesing⟩

sinch *var of* CINCH

sin·cip·i·tal \(')sin¦sipəd·ᵊl\ *adj* [L *sincipit-*, *sinciput* + E *-al*] **:** of or relating to the sinciput

sin·ci·put \'sin(t)sə(,)pət, *usu* -əd.+V\ *n, pl* **sinciputs** \-ts\ *or* **sin·cip·i·ta** \sin'sipəd·ə\ [L, fr. *semi-* + *caput* head — more at HEAD] **:** a part of the head: **a :** FOREHEAD **b :** the whole upper half of the skull **:** CALVA **c :** the forepart of the head of a bird from the base of the bill to the crown **d :** the part of the head of an insect and esp. of a beetle between the vertex and the clypeus

sin·cos·ite \'siŋkə,sīt\ *n* -s [*Sincos*, Peru, where it was discovered + E *-ite*] **:** a mineral $Ca(VO)_2(PO_4)_2.5H_2O$ consisting of hydrous calcium vanadyl phosphate and occurring in thin tetragonal scales or plates

sind \'sin(d), 'sīn\ *vt* [ME (Sc & northern dial.) *sinden*] *chiefly Scot* **1 :** to rinse out **2 :** to wash down (food)

sin·der \'sində(r), 'sinər\ *chiefly Scot var of* SUNDER

sin·dhi \'sindē\ *n* [Ar *Sindi*, fr. *Sind* Sind, Sindh, region in the northwestern part of the Indian subcontinent, fr. Hindi; akin to Skt *sindhu* river — more at INDIA] **1** *also* **sin·di** \"\ *pl* **sindhi** *or* **sindhis** *also* **sindi** *or* **sindis** *usu cap* **a :** a Scytho-Dravidian mostly Muslim people of Sind **b :** a member of such people **2** *pl* **sindhi** *or* **sindhis** *usu cap* **:** the Indic language of Sind **3 a** *usu cap* **:** an Indian breed of dark red short-horned humped dairy cattle that is widely distributed and much used for crossbreeding in warm regions **b** *pl* **sindhi** *or* **sindhis** *often cap* **:** an animal of the Sindhi breed

sind ibex \'sind-\ *n, usu cap S* [*sind* fr. *Sind*, region in the northwestern part of the Indian subcontinent] **:** a wild goat (*Capra hircus blythi*) of Sind and Baluchistan

sin·di·co \'sēndə,kō\ *n* -s [Sp, fr. LL *syndicus* — more at SYNDIC] **:** SYNDIC

sin·don \'sindən\ *n* -s [ME, fr. L, fr. Gk *sindōn*] **1** *archaic* **:** a fine fabric esp. of linen **2** *archaic* **:** a covering made of sindon: as **a :** SHROUD ⟨Christ's ~⟩ **b :** ¹CORPORAL

sin·dry \sindri\ *chiefly Scot var of* SUNDRY

sine \'sīn\ *n* -s [ML *sinus* (intended, under influence of Ar *jaib* curve, as trans. of Ar *jība* sine, fr. Skt *jīva* bowstring, chord of an arc), fr. L, curve, fold — more at SINUS] **:** the *y* coordinate of any point except the vertex on the terminal side of an angle divided by the distance between the vertex and the point, the vertex coinciding with the origin of a plane rectangular coordinate system and the initial side of the angle coinciding with the positive x-axis

sin–eater \'=,==\ *n* **:** a person formerly hired to assume the sins of a dead person by eating food placed near the corpse

sin–eating \'=,==\ *n* **:** the act or practice of a sin-eater

sine bar *n* **:** a device that consists of a steel straightedge at whose extremities buttons are attached with their centers equidistant from the straightedge and that is used to locate work at desired angles on angle plates

¹si·ne·cure \'sīnə,kyů(ə)r, 'sin-, -nē,-, -ùə\ *n* -s [ML (*beneficium*) *sine cura* (benefice) without cure of souls] **1 :** an ecclesiastical benefice without cure of souls **2 :** an office or position that requires little or no work and that usu. provides an income

²sinecure \"\ *adj* **:** having the characteristics of a sinecure ⟨a practically ~ office —Valentine Heywood⟩

sine·cur·ism \-,rizəm\ *n* -s **:** the practice of granting sinecures

sine·cur·ist \-,rəst\ *n* -s **:** one who has a sinecure

sine curve *n* **:** the graph in rectangular coordinates of the equation $y = a \sin bx$ where *a* and *b* are constants that when *a* = 1 and *b* = 1 passes through the origin and all points on the x-axis where the abscissas are multiples of *π* radians, is concave towards the x-axis, and has maximum and minimum ordinate values of +1 and −1

¹sine die \,sīnē'dī,ē, -nə'd-, ÷ -dī *also* ,sin-; ,si\(,)nā'dē,ā, ,sē, \nē'd-, \nə'd-, -di,ā\ *adv* [L] **:** without any future date being designated (as for resumption) **:** INDEFINITELY ⟨declared the House adjourned *sine die* —Hodding Carter⟩

²sine die \"\ *adj* **:** made without any future date being designated (as for resumption) **:** INDEFINITE ⟨favored an adjournment *sine die* of Congress⟩

sine law *n* **:** LAW OF SINES

sine plate *n* **:** a block or plate for holding parts for machining at desired angles

sine pro·le \,sīnē'prō,lā, ,sin-, -nə'p-; ,si\(,)nā'prō(,)lā, ,sē, \nē'p-, \nə'p-\ *adv* [L] **:** without issue ⟨died *sine prole* in his 80th year⟩

¹sine qua non \,si\(,)nā,kwä'nōn, ,sē, \nēk-, \nək-, -'nän; ,sīnē,kwā'nän, -īnə,k- *also* ,sin-\ *n, pl* **sine qua nons** [LL, lit., without which not] **1 :** the one thing that is absolutely essential ⟨the *sine qua non* . . . is that the star shall appear bright enough to give a measurable spectrum —Herbert Dingle⟩ **2 :** something that is considered essential ⟨this book is a *sine qua non* for Mill scholars —W.D.Templeman⟩

²sine qua non \"\ *adj* **:** absolutely necessary **:** ESSENTIAL, INDISPENSABLE ⟨wider spaced patterns are . . . *sine qua non* in men's wardrobes —*N.Y.Times*⟩ ⟨it's the *sine qua non* sense —Amy Lowell⟩

sinetic *usu cap, var of* SINITIC

¹sin·ew \'si(,)nyü *also* ÷ 'si(,)nü\ *n* -s [ME *sinwe*, *senewe*, fr. OE *sinu*, *seonu*; akin to MD *senewe* sinew, OHG *senawa*, ON *sin* sinew, MIr *sīn* chain, L *seta*, *saeta* bristle, Gk *himas* leather strap, thong, Skt *syati*, *sinati* he binds, straps] **1 :** TENDON; *esp* **:** one dressed for use as a cord or thread ⟨his linden cradle . . . safely bound with reindeer ~s —H.W.Longfellow⟩ **2** *obs* **:** NERVE **3 a :** solid resilient strength **:** POWER, FORCE ⟨to espouse democratic government demands intellectual and moral ~ as well as armies and good feeling —G.K.Chalmers⟩ ⟨a solidly constructed novel, a tale with thews and ~s —William McFee⟩ **b :** the chief supporting force **:** MAINSTAY — usu. used in pl. ⟨equipment . . . providing the ~s of better living —Sam Pollock⟩ **c :** financial or material resources — usu. used in the phrase *sinews of war*

²sinew \"\ *vt* -ED/-ING/-S **1 :** to run through as if with sinews in order to make strong ⟨no ordinary belt . . . because it is ~ed with finely stranded airplane-type steel cables —*Newsweek*⟩ **2 :** to give force or solidity to **:** STRENGTHEN ⟨serve to ~ the state in times of danger —Oliver Goldsmith⟩

sine wave *n* **:** a fundamental form of wave (as in one of the sound waves giving rise to a pure tone or in a wave of alternating current) that represents periodic oscillations in which the amplitude of displacement at each point is proportional to the sine of the phase angle of the displacement and that is visualized as a sine curve

sinew–backed bow \'=(,)=¦=-\ *n* **:** REINFORCED BOW

sin·ewed \'si(,)nyüd *also* ÷ 'si(,)nüd\ *adj* [¹*sinew* + *-ed*] **:** having sinews **:** SINEWY

sin·ew·i·ness \'sin(y)əwēnəs, -win-\ *n* -ES **:** the state or quality of being sinewy

sin·ew·less \'=(,)=ləs\ *adj* **:** having no sinews

sin·ew·ous \'sin(y)əwəs\ *adj* **:** SINEWY

sin·ewy \-(y)əwē, -wi\ *adj* [ME *senewy*, fr. *senewe* sinew + *-y*] **1 :** having sinews: **a :** full of sinews **:** TENDINOUS ⟨the ~ parts of a cut of meat⟩ **b :** marked by strong or prominent sinews ⟨~ arms rising and falling in tireless unison —T.B. Costain⟩ **2 :** marked by the strength of sinews **:** strong and firm **:** TOUGH ⟨putting down the sum of his experience in his rich ~ prose —Cyril Connolly⟩ ⟨bitter and ~ intellectuality —Robert Halsband⟩

sin·fo·nia \,sinfə'nēə\ *n, pl* **sinfo·nie** \-ē,ā\ [It, symphony, sinfonia, fr. L *symphonia* — more at SYMPHONY] **1 :** an orchestral musical composition of Italian origin found in 18th century opera or other vocal composition **:** OVERTURE **2 :** SYMPHONY 2

sin·fo·nie \'zinfə¦nē, ¦si-\ *n, pl* **sinfoni·en** \,==='nēən\ *usu cap* [G, fr. It *sinfonia*] **:** SYMPHONY

sin·fo·niet·ta \,sinfən'yed·ə, -fōn-, -etə\ *n* -s [It, dim. of *sinfonia* symphony] **1 :** a symphony of less than standard length or for fewer instruments **2 :** a small symphony orchestra; *esp* **:** an orchestra of strings only

sin·ful \'sinfəl\ *adj* [ME, fr. OE *synfull*, fr. *syn* sin + *-full* -ful — more at SIN] **1 :** tainted with or full of sin **:** WICKED, INIQUITOUS ⟨~ men⟩ **2 :** marked by or involving sin ⟨~ thoughts⟩ ⟨~ practices⟩ **3 :** highly culpable ⟨a ~ waste in a world that lacks a sufficiency of food —Lionel Trilling⟩

sin·ful·ly \-fəlē, -li\ *adv* [ME, fr. *sinful* + *-ly*] **1 :** in a sinful manner **:** WICKEDLY **2 :** CULPABLY, UNREASONABLY ⟨cars can be hired at a ~ high price —T.H.Fielding⟩

sin·ful·ness \-lnəs\ *n* -ES [ME *sinfulnesse*, fr. *sinful* + *-nesse* -ness] **:** the quality or state of being sinful ⟨man of moderate intelligence and normal ~ —R.H.Rovere⟩

¹sing \'siŋ\ *vb* **sang** \'saŋ, -aiŋ\ *or* **sung** \'səŋ\ **sung** *also* **sang; singing; sings** [ME *singen*, fr. OE *singan*; akin to OHG *singan* to sing, ON *syngja*, Goth *singwan* to sing, MW *deongl* to explain, Gk *omphē* voice, oracle and prob. to Prakrit *saṃghai* to say, teach] *vi* **1 a :** to produce musical tones by means of the voice **b :** to utter words in musical tones and with musical inflections and modulations ⟨to ~ at one's work⟩ ⟨children that dance and ~⟩ **c :** to produce in a proper or skilled manner tones generated by vibrations of the vocal cords and resonated by the various oral cavities; *also* **:** to deliver songs, arias, or other compositions in the character of a trained or professional singer ⟨~ extremely well⟩ ⟨~ for charity or in opera⟩ **2 :** to make a shrill whining or whistling sound ⟨a kettle ~*ing* on the hearth —Elizabeth Goudge⟩ ⟨the high overtone of the saw . . . ~*ing* when it runs free —*Amer. Guide Series: Ark.*⟩ ⟨bullets hit the road surface and *sung* off —Ernest Hemingway⟩ **3 a :** to relate, describe, or celebrate something in verse ⟨~*s* of Arthur and his Knights of the Round Table⟩ ⟨poets *sang* of the natural man —*Amer. Guide Series: Minn.*⟩ ⟨gave substance and reality to the beauty of which he *sang* —H.M.Reynolds⟩ **b :** to compose poetry **:** make verse ⟨it was in blank verse that she *sang* —Virginia Woolf⟩ **c :** to convey in or through words a feeling or sense of rhythm ⟨writes a prose remarkable for its live and lyric qualities; she makes the language ~ —Charles Lee⟩ ⟨the second means of writing prose that ~*s* is to train yourself to feel the cadence of words —Grace Fletcher⟩ ⟨his lyrics ~ and flow, with simple, fresh imagery, with delicacy and often humor —Eleanor Sickels⟩ **4 a :** to produce musical or harmonious sounds ⟨grasshoppers chirping and birds ~*ing* —G.B.Shaw⟩ ⟨frogs and crickets *sang* —Rex Ingamells⟩ ⟨most mysterious thing about a pack of hounds is the way they ~ or . . . chime —Thurstan Holland-Hibbert⟩ **b :** to give forth such sounds when played ⟨when the violin *sang* —J.D.Carr⟩ ⟨to hear the heavy tuba ~ sweetly —Arthur Berger⟩ **5** *obs* **:** to chant or intone a religious observance ⟨sad and solemn priests still ~ for Richard's soul —Shak.⟩ **6 a :** to be filled with a humming or buzzing **:** RING ⟨next moment her ears were ~*ing* —Audrey Barker⟩ **b :** to be heard repetitively in the imagination **:** ECHO ⟨their murmured words of farewell *sang* in my ears —Eula Long⟩ ⟨voice saying, Remember my party, Remember my party, *sang* in his ears —Virginia Woolf⟩ **7 :** to be fit or apt for vocal rendition ⟨thinks *Medea* ~*s* as well as any concert work she knows —*Time*⟩ ⟨any translation would be something of a pity when it ~*s* so well in French —Douglas Watt⟩ **8 :** to make a cry **:** CALL — usu. used with *out* ⟨heard the captain of his escort ~ out to him in the darkness —Winston Churchill⟩ ⟨"You don't feel weak, or anything?" she *sung* out at me —Mary R. Rinehart⟩ **9 :** to give evidence or information ⟨is tough enough to have his goons dispatch anyone who dares to ~ to a crime commission —A.H.Weiler⟩ ⟨*sang* to a grand jury in return for a promise of leniency —*Time*⟩ ⟨don't let him know we *sung* on him —Priest Collins⟩ ~ *vt* **1 a :** to utter with musical inflections; *esp* **:** to interpret in musical tones produced by the voice ⟨~ a tune⟩ ⟨~ the tenor part⟩ **b :** to produce vocally the musical tones of ⟨~ G⟩ **2 a :** to relate, describe, or celebrate (something) in verse ⟨~*ing* the beauties of the garden and of simplicity —John Ciardi⟩ ⟨in antique style it ~*s* the loss of friends and fields —H.O.Taylor⟩ ⟨as men have loved their lovers . . . and *sung* their wit, their virtue, and their grace —Edna S. V. Millay⟩ **b :** to announce or proclaim in a clear or resonant manner ⟨stationmaster ~*ing* the stops to the west coast⟩ — often used with *out* ⟨the bell ~*ing* out the hour of midnight⟩ **3 :** CHANT, INTONE ⟨a high mass of requiem . . . will be *sung* —*N.Y.Times*⟩ **4 a :** to bring or accompany to a place or state by singing ⟨~*s* the child to sleep⟩ ⟨his blithe and cheerful verse *sang* itself into the memory —Brander Matthews⟩ **b :** to move or drive by singing ⟨hopes to ~ away his troubles⟩ — **sing one's praises :** to laud a person or thing vigorously and openly ⟨the west country thereafter is the richer for one more pen to *sing its praises* —*Times Lit. Supp.*⟩ ⟨parents *singing his praises* after the award⟩ — **sing the blues :** to express a pessimistic or discouraged attitude **:** COMPLAIN ⟨called me every now and then to *sing the blues* about her troubles —Polly Adler⟩

²sing \"\ *n* -s **:** the act of singing: as **a :** a singing esp. in company ⟨an all-night gospel ~ down South —Furman Bisher⟩ **b :** a ritualistic ceremony of a primitive society consisting largely of chanting ⟨without instruction the Navajo chorus at a ~ provides a moving choral performance —Joyce R. Muench⟩

sing *abbr* **1** single **2** singular **3** [L *singulorum*] of each

sing·able \'siŋəbəl\ *adj* [ME *singabil* (part trans. of LL *cantabilis*) fr. *singen* to sing + L *-abilis* -able] **:** apt or suitable for singing ⟨every word is ~ and modestly poetic —Winthrop Sargeant⟩ ⟨agrees that ~ melody is the essence of music —Winthrop Sargeant⟩

singa·pore \'siŋ(g)ə,pō(ə)r, -ō(ə)r, -ōə, -ó(ə) *also* ,==¦=\ *adj, usu cap* [fr. *Singapore*, Asia] **:** of or from the city or the country of Singapore **:** of the kind or style prevalent in Singapore

¹singa·po·re·an \,==¦pōrēən, -pór-\ *adj, usu cap* [*Singapore*, country and its capital off the south end of the Malay peninsula (fr. Malay *Singapura*, fr. Skt *Siṁhapura*, lit., lion city, fr. *siṁha* lion + *pura* city) + E *-an*] **1 :** of, relating to, or characteristic of Singapore, southeast Asia **2 :** of, relating to, or characteristic of the people of Singapore

²singaporean \"\ *n* -s *cap* **:** a native or resident of Singapore

singapore sling *n, usu cap 1st S* **:** a sling in which cherry brandy and sometimes Benedictine are added to the usual gin base

¹singe \'sinj\ *vt* **singed; singed; singeing; singes** [ME *sengen*, fr. OE *sengan*; akin to OHG *bisengan* to singe, OFris *sendza* to singe off, scorch, MD *sengen* to singe, MHG *senge* dryness, Sw dial. *sjängla* to singe, OSlav *isočiti* to dry] **1 :** to burn (something) superficially or lightly **:** SCORCH: as **a :** to remove the hair or down from (an animal or fowl) by passing over a flame **b :** to remove projecting fibers and fuzz from (thread, yarn, or cloth) by passing rapidly over a gas flame or heated rollers **2 :** to cause (a person) unexpected trouble, distress, or embarrassment (as for an injudicious interference or venture) ⟨after being *singed* once or twice, I gave up on direct haggling —C.W.Morton⟩ **syn** see BURN

²singe \"\ *n* -s **:** a slight burn **:** SCORCH

³singe *obs var of* SIGN

singed \'sinjd\ *adj* [ME *senged*, fr. past part. of *sengen* to singe] **1 :** that has undergone singeing **2** *of fur* **:** having dried or curled over guard hairs caused by an animal's rubbing or inferior processing

singed cat *n* **:** one that is of better quality than appearance indicates ⟨had an instinctive sympathy for underpups and *singed cats* and the courage to champion their causes —I.S. Cobb⟩

¹sing·er \'siŋə(r)\ *n* -s [ME, fr. *singen* to sing + *-er* — more at SING] **:** one that sings: as **a :** one whose profession is to sing **:** vocal artist **b :** POET ⟨the sweet ~ of Avon⟩ **c :** a bird with a natural or acquired ability to sing **:** SONGBIRD **d :** one of an order of officials managing and taking part in the psalmody in the early Christian church **e :** a primitive medicine man who cures sickness and gets rid of evil influences by means of a chanted ritual

²sing·er \'sinjə(r)\ *n* -s [¹*singe* + *-er*] **:** one that singes: as **a :** a textile worker who singes cloth **b :** one that singes surplus threads from shoe uppers with a gas flame or torch **c :** a slaughterhouse worker who removes hair from hog carcasses with a singeing torch

sin·ge·rie \(')saⁿzh¦rē, ¦saⁿzhə¦rē\ *n* -s [F, fr. *singe* ape (fr. L *simius*, *simia*) + *-erie* -ery — more at SIMIAN] **:** a picture, decoration, or design in which monkeys are depicted

sing·er's node \'siŋə(r)z-\ *n* **:** a thickening of tissue on a vocal cord resulting from excessive or incorrect use of the voice

singh \'siŋ\ *n* -s [Hindi *siṅgh*, lit., lion, fr. Skt *siṁha*] **:** a member of one of the warrior castes of northern India; *specif* **:** a Sikh baptized into the Khalsa

singhalese *or* **singalese** *usu cap, var of* SINHALESE

singing *n* -s [ME, fr. gerund of *singen* to sing] **1 :** the act or sound of one that sings **2 :** SING a — often used in pl. ⟨Sunday night ~*s* for the young people —J.W.Frey⟩ **3 :** a whining, whistling, or humming sound as if from something in vibration ⟨the ~ of crosscut saws —*Amer. Guide Series: Mich.*⟩ ⟨the strange high ~ of some aeroplane overhead —Virginia Woolf⟩; *specif* **:** a humming or ringing in one's ears

singing arc *n* **:** a direct current arc in parallel with which is a local circuit containing a condenser and inductance in series where oscillations take place according to the tuning and cause the arc to emit a musical note — compare POULSEN ARC

singing bird *n* **1 :** SONGBIRD **2 :** a passerine bird

singing canary *n* **:** BELUGA 2

singing falcon *or* **singing hawk** *n* **:** CHANTING FALCON

singing fish *n* **:** the midshipman (*Porichthys notatus*) or a related toadfish that makes a humming sound by vibration of the air bladder

singing flame *n* **:** MUSICAL FLAME

singing game *n* **1 :** a game (as *Farmer in the Dell* or *London Bridge*) in which the players accompany their actions with the singing of a narrative song **2 :** SWINGING PLAY

singing gibbon *n* **:** SILVER GIBBON

sing·ing·ly *adj* **:** in a singing manner **:** LYRICALLY

singing muscle *n* **:** an intrinsic syringeal muscle in a bird

sing·ka·mas *also* **sincamas** \,seŋkä'mäs\ *n* -ES [Tag, fr. MexSp *jicama*, fr. Nahuatl *xicama*] **:** YAM BEAN

¹sin·gle \'siŋgəl\ *adj* [ME *single*, *sengle*, fr. MF, fr. L *singulus* one only, individual; akin to L *sem-* one — more at SAME] **1 a :** living in an unmarried state **:** CELIBATE ⟨take anything she can get in the way of a husband rather than face penury as a ~ woman —G.B.Shaw⟩ **b :** of or relating to celibacy ⟨prefers the ~ state⟩ **2 :** unattended or unaccompanied by others **:** SOLITARY ⟨he is left alone, ~ and unsupported, like a leafless trunk —*Mirror*⟩ **3 a** (1) **:** consisting of or having only one part, feature, or portion as opposed to or contrasted with double or complex ⟨double consonants are often used in place of ~ consonants⟩ ⟨binocular ~ vision was tested —H.G. Armstrong⟩ (2) **:** consisting of one as opposed to or in contrast with many **:** UNIFORM ⟨undertaking to justify a ~ scale of rates for the entire country —W.M.W.Splawn⟩ ⟨the states sought a ~ type of automobile plate⟩ (3) **:** consisting of only one in number ⟨a ~ anchor holds the boat⟩ ⟨holds to a ~ ideal⟩ — often used with *not* ⟨not a ~ opponent of statehood appeared before the committee —*Midwest Jour.*⟩ ⟨has not made one ~ concession to any other quarter —R.T.H.Fletcher⟩ **b :** having only the normal number of petals or rays **:** not double — used esp. of a horticultural plant ⟨a ~ rose⟩ **4 a :** of or relating to a particular member or part **:** INDIVIDUAL ⟨when nature is so careless of the ~ life, why should we coddle ourselves —R.L.Stevenson⟩ ⟨each ~ citizen is an important part of the community⟩ **b :** of, relating to, or involving only one person ⟨check his ~ judgments against a larger conception or in a perspective of the whole —Meyer Schapiro⟩ ⟨will try his ~ strength against all the world⟩ **5 a** *obs* **:** lacking qualification or addition **:** PLAIN **b** *archaic* **:** of poor quality **:** WEAK ⟨drank his ~ ale⟩ **6 :** taken by itself apart from its group or constituency **:** DISTINCT, SEPARATE ⟨every ~ minute I kept wishing —Agnes S. Turnbull⟩ ⟨the most important ~ resource —B.B.Jennings⟩ ⟨more than any other ~ influence of their period —*Amer. Guide Series: Texas*⟩ ⟨the largest ~ agency providing assistance —Shlomo Katz⟩ **7 a :** free from duplicity or insincerity **:** FRANK, HONEST, OPEN ⟨the willingness of the incumbent . . . to devote himself with a ~ mind to the public good —R.M.Dawson⟩ ⟨jealousy is the flaw in the ~ heart —Ellen Glasgow⟩ ⟨keep your eye ~ and your hands clean —Charles Kingsley⟩ **b :** exclusively concerned or attentive — usu. used of an eye ⟨lives with an eye ~ to his own advantage —*New Republic*⟩ ⟨everything in this line has been procured . . . with an eye ~ to the taste of his numerous patrons —D.D.Martin⟩ **8 :** consisting of a whole **:** UNBROKEN, UNDIVIDED ⟨science and speed have made our world into a ~ neighborhood —Barbara Ward⟩ ⟨the great cause was the same; the source of all the movements was elemental, natural, and ~ —J.L.Motley⟩ **9 :** having one on each side **:** man to man ⟨who now defies thee thrice to ~ fight —John Milton⟩ **10 :** having no equal or like **:** UNUSUAL, SINGULAR ⟨was that rare critic, perhaps even that unique and ~ critic —J.C.Ransom⟩ ⟨~ among his fellows⟩ **11 :** ONLY, SOLE ⟨his ~ speech, that of January 31, 1861, received high praise —W.C.Ford⟩ ⟨his ~ intent was to speak a word of sympathy —A.T.Quiller-Couch⟩ ⟨the ~ piece of evidence⟩ **12 :** having the added musical part lying uniformly above or below the cantus firmus in two-part counterpoint **13 :** designed for the use of one person or family only ⟨a ~ room⟩ ⟨a ~ house⟩

syn SOLE, UNIQUE, LONE, SOLITARY, SEPARATE, PARTICULAR: SINGLE applies to that consisting of one alone and not capable of being felt as accompanied by or joined with another ⟨a *single* instance⟩ ⟨a *single* currency system⟩ ⟨Maine . . . is the only one adjoined by but a single sister state —*Amer. Guide Series: Maine*⟩ ⟨the lover imagines but a *single* joy; to be master of his love in body and soul —George Santayana⟩ SOLE may intensify the notion that what is under consideration is the only one ⟨the *sole* lien to the estate⟩ ⟨the *sole* product of his factory⟩ ⟨invention is almost never the *sole* work of a single inventor —Lewis Mumford⟩ ⟨buy out his partners . . . and thus become *sole* stockholder —*Current Biog.*⟩ ⟨the *sole* casualty of the battle . . . was one cow —R.W.Hatch⟩ UNIQUE in reference to things like manuscripts and coins designates the only one extant; in other uses it indicates that which stands alone because of its unusual character ⟨the manuscript of Beowulf is *unique*⟩ ⟨the *unique* character of the English conquest of Britain needs special emphasis —Kemp Malone⟩ ⟨a *unique* combination of warm and relatively sunny winters, and a summer without excessively high temperatures —E.L.Ullman⟩ LONE and SOLITARY may suggest both single and isolated ⟨who in cells deep and *lone* have languished —P.B.Shelley⟩ ⟨the ambitious Aaron Burr who played a *lone* hand against the field —V.L.Parrington⟩ ⟨the *solitary* sin of an otherwise blameless character⟩ ⟨a sentry kept *solitary* vigil —J.H. Cutler⟩ SEPARATE stresses lack of connection with others; it indicates discreteness rather than singleness ⟨there was no *separate* church, in our sense of the term, as an independent organism within the state —G.L.Dickinson⟩ ⟨given in two *separate* and distinct sections of the constitution —John Marshall⟩ PARTICULAR in this sense stresses the fact of being regarded as distinct ⟨we shall venture beyond the *particular* book in search of qualities that group books together —Virginia Woolf⟩ ⟨some *particular* achievement of modern technology, like an electric shaver or the automobile —D.W. Brogan⟩

²single \"\ *n* -s [ME *sengle*, fr. *sengle*, adj., single] **1 a :** a claw of a hawk or falcon **b :** the tail of a deer **2 a :** a separate individual person ⟨the guests arrive in ~*s* and pairs⟩ **b :** a separate individual member of a large class of similar or identical objects: as (1) **:** a one-dollar bill ⟨flashing a big bankroll, generally a wad of ~*s* wrapped up in a hundred-dollar bill —*Police Gazette*⟩ (2) **:** a phonograph record usu. with not over five minutes of recording on each side ⟨will release the sides both as ~*s* and as an . . . LP record —*Down Beat*⟩ (3) **:** a piece or section of sheet metal over ¹⁄₃₂ of an inch in thickness — used in pl. **c :** a modification of the coursing order in change ringing consisting of holding one bell in place through several changes **3 singles** *pl* **:** change ringing as performed on four bells **4 a :** a continuous strand of reeled or spun silk **b :** a thread or yarn of any fiber that is twisted or thrown — often used in pl. **5 a :** a hit for one run in the game of cricket **b :** ONE-BASE HIT **6 singles** *pl* **a :** a tennis match or similar game with one player on each side ⟨we play ~*s* or doubles⟩ **b :** a golf match between two players — distinguished from *foursome* **7 :** a boat or shell propelled by one oarsman **8 a :** a performance or entertainment by only one person ⟨offers to do ~*s* on other shows and in some clubs —*Newsweek*⟩ **b :** a person who does a single ⟨started hiring out as a ~ at lodge dances —*Time*⟩ **9 :** a flower having the normal number of petals or ray florets typical of the species **10 :** a room, apartment, or house designed to accommodate one person or one family ⟨the apartment is a ~⟩ ⟨small ~*s* of five and six rooms —Brendon Shea⟩

³single \"\ *vb* **singled; singled; singling** \-g(ə)liŋ\ **singles** [¹*single*] *vt* **1 a** *archaic* **:** to move asunder **:** PART, SEPARATE **b :** to separate (an animal) from a herd in order to chase or hunt separately ⟨~ out a young cow⟩ **2** *obs* **:** to lead aside **:** SEQUESTER, WITHDRAW ⟨I have ~*ed* thee alone —Shak.⟩ **3 a :** to select or distinguish (a person or thing) from a number or group ⟨walks up to the line and ~*s* every 10th man⟩ — usu. used with *out* ⟨~*s* out for special praise the guidebook to Wells cathedral —Pyke Johnson⟩ **b :** to select or distinguish (a person or thing) for especial attention or comment — usu. used with *out* ⟨something about his person that *singled* him out from the rest of the punctual moving crowd —E.V. Lucas⟩ ⟨had *singled* him out as his successor —John Buchan⟩ ⟨all I can do is to ~ out a few of the basic ideas —A.W. Hummel⟩ **4** *Brit* **:** to thin (seedlings) so as to leave space between the plants **5 a** *archaic* **:** to reduce to only one **:** CONCENTRATE **b :** to reduce (as a doubled rope) from a number of parts to one **6 a :** to advance (a base runner) by a one-base hit ⟨*singled* him to third base⟩ **b :** to bring about the scoring of (a run) by a one-base hit ~ *vi* **1** *archaic* **:** to separate oneself from others **:** proceed alone **2 :** to thin out seedlings **3 :** to take in all bights of mooring lines on a ship except single lines preparatory to getting under way — usu. used with *up* **4 :** to make a one-base hit ⟨*singled* to center and knocked in two more runs —James Thurber⟩ ⟨*singled* behind his catcher —John Drebinger⟩

[4]**single** \"\ *adv* **:** SINGLY

single-acting \ˈ==ˈ==\ *adj* **:** acting in one direction only ⟨a *single-acting* plunger⟩

single-action \ˈ==ˈ==\ *adj* **1 :** SINGLE-ACTING **2** *of a firearm* **:** that requires cocking before each shot

single-banked \ˈ==ˈbaŋkt, -aiŋ-\ *adj* **:** having a single bank or row: as **a :** having a single row of oarsmen or one on each thwart with the oars alternating on each side **b :** having but one tier of oarsmen (as a unireme) — compare DOUBLE-BANKED

singlebar \ˈ==,=\ *n* [[1]*single* + *bar*] **:** SINGLETREE

single-barrel \ˈ==ˈ=-\ *n* **:** a single-barreled gun

single-barreled \ˈ==ˈbarəld *also* -ber-\ *adj, of a gun* **:** having one barrel

single-base powder \ˈ==ˈ=-\ *n* **:** an explosive powder or propellant that contains nitrocellulose as the only essential component — compare DOUBLE-BASE POWDER

single bill *or* **single bond** *n* **1 :** a bill or bond for the future payment of money with no annexed condition **2 :** a bill on which a single party is to be heard in a judicial proceeding

single bond *n* **:** SIMPLE BOND

single-breasted \ˈ==ˈ==\ *adj, of a coat or jacket* **:** having a center closing with one row of buttons and no lap — compare DOUBLE-BREASTED

single brilliant *n* **:** a brilliant with 16 facets above the girdle and 12 or 16 facets below

single-chamber \ˈ==ˈ==\ *adj* **:** having a single chamber **:** UNICAMERAL ⟨a *single-chamber* legislature⟩

single-coat·ed \ˈ==ˈkōd·əd\ *adj, of paper or board* **:** coated only once on one or both sides

single comb *n* **:** a comb on a fowl having the form of an erect or pendant median serrated crest — see COMB illustration

single corner *n* **:** one of the two diagonally opposed corners of a checkerboard that have a single dark or playing square

single counterpoint *n* **:** counterpoint in which the added part lies uniformly above or below the cantus firmus

single-crop \ˈ==ˈ=\ *vi* **:** to practice one-crop farming **:** grow a single crop on the same land repeatedly ~ *vt* **:** to use (land) in a one-crop system ⟨*single-cropping* their lands with wheat —*Rev. of Reviews*⟩

single cross *n* **:** the heterotic first generation hybrid between two selected and usu. inbred lines ⟨many commercial hybrid seeds are *single crosses*⟩ — compare DOUBLE CROSS, HETEROSIS, TOPCROSS

single cut *n* **:** a simplified brilliant cut used on small stones — see CUT illustration

single-cut file \ˈ==ˈ=-\ *n* **:** a file having a single parallel series of diagonal cuts across its face

single doubler *n* **:** DOUBLER 2a

single-end·ed \ˈ==ˈendəd\ *adj* **:** having the principal or working portion at one end only ⟨a *single-ended* boiler⟩

single entry *n* **:** a method or system of bookkeeping that recognizes only one side of a business transaction and usu. consists only of a record of cash and personal accounts with debtors and creditors — compare DOUBLE ENTRY

single-entry table *n* **:** a mathematical table in which a tabulated function depends on but one independent variable

single escheat *n, Scots law* **:** escheat to the crown of one's movable estate

single-eye \ˈ==ˈ=\ *adj* **:** having only one bud ⟨a *single-eye* cutting⟩

single-eyed \ˈ==ˈ=\ *adj* **1 :** having a clear honest eye **:** SINGLE **2 :** having but one eye or the sight of one eye

[1]**single file** *n* **:** a line of persons, animals, or things moving one behind another; *also* **:** a single row — called also *Indian file* ⟨marching in *single file*⟩

[2]**single file** *adv* **:** in a single line ⟨traffic is slowed by having to crawl *single file* through the doors in the . . . barricades —Mollie Panter-Downes⟩

single-file \ˈ==ˈ=\ *vi* [fr. *single file*, n.] **:** to walk or move in single file ⟨all *single-filed* past the . . . bed —J.D.Salinger⟩ ⟨*single-filing* down the St. George's channel to Liverpool —Gordon Webber⟩

single fish *n* **:** a single fish joint

[1]**single-foot** \ˈ==,=\ *n, pl* **single-foots :** [7]RACK b

[2]**single-foot** \"\ *vi, of a horse* **:** to go at a rack ⟨has seen him *single-foot* up to a wall and go over clear —Allan Forbes & R.M.Eastman⟩ — **single-footer** \ˈ==,==\ *n*

single-framed roof \ˈ==ˈ=-\ *n* **:** a roof in which opposite rafters are tied together by the upper floor frame or by boards nailed across horizontally

single-gear \ˈ==ˈ=\ *vt* **:** to gear directly (as by belting or a single pair or train of gear wheels) without the use of any additional speed-reducing mechanism

[1]**single-handed** \ˈ==ˈ==\ *also* **single-hand** \ˈ==ˈ=\ *adj* **1 :** managed or done by one person or with one on a side ⟨account of his *single-handed* journeys in the sixties —*Brit. Bk. News*⟩ ⟨a cannon used . . . in his *single-handed* defense of the local coastline —*Amer. Guide Series: Conn.*⟩ ⟨fighting in *single-handed* combat⟩ **2 :** working alone or unassisted by others ⟨reference book . . . for the *single-handed* cook with a family to feed —Margaret Lane⟩ ⟨people who are *single-handed* or too old to manage holdings —A.D.Rees⟩ **3 :** used or adapted for using with one hand ⟨*single-handed* fishing rod⟩ **4 :** having or using only one hand ⟨a *single-handed* billiard player⟩ — **single-hand·ed·ness** *n* -ES

[2]**single-handed** \"\ *adv* **:** with or by oneself or without assistance ⟨fought his own cause in both war and politics *single-handed* —*advt*⟩ ⟨had to build his little log hut *single-handed* —A.F.Harlow⟩

single-hand·ed·ly *adv* **:** in a single-handed manner ⟨undertook the superhuman task of *single-handedly* creating a historical dictionary —Robert Pick⟩

single-hearted \ˈ==ˈ==\ *adj* **1 :** SINGLE 7a ⟨the perfect, *single-hearted*, crusading knight —H.O.Taylor⟩ **2 :** characterized by or resulting from sincerity and unity of purpose or dedication ⟨such a task requires an expenditure of time and energy, a *single-hearted* consecration —B.N.Cardozo⟩ ⟨the man who seizes on one deep-reaching idea . . . and with *single-hearted* fervor forces it upon the world —P.E.More⟩ ⟨her lifelong, *single-hearted*, and unshakable conviction —Albert Lynd⟩

single-heart·ed·ly *adv* **:** in a single-hearted manner ⟨works nobly and *single-heartedly*⟩

single-heart·ed·ness *n* -ES **:** the quality or state of being single-hearted ⟨fervent saint who sang because he suffered, and whose mysticism was tinged with kindly *single-heartedness* —Frances P. Keyes⟩

single jack *n* **:** a short-handled hammer weighing about four pounds and used in hand drilling

single jacker *n* **:** a miner using a single jack

single knot *n* **:** OVERHAND KNOT

single-leaf \ˈ==,=\ *or* **single-leaf pine** *or* **single-leaf pinyon** *n* **:** PIÑON

single-leaf ash *also* **single-leaved ash** *n* **:** a unifoliolate or rarely bifoliolate or trifoliolate ash (*Fraxinus anomala*) of the western U.S.

single-line \ˈ==ˈ=\ *adj* **:** confining commercial activity to one line of goods ⟨a *single-line* manufacturer⟩ ⟨a *single-line* representative⟩

single-loader \ˈ==ˈlōdə(r)\ *n* **:** a firearm in which each charge is inserted separately

single man *n* **:** a checker that may be moved only forward — compare KING

single-member district \ˈ==ˈ==-\ *also* **single-member constituency** *n* **:** an electoral district or constituency having a single representative in a legislative body rather than two or more — compare LIST SYSTEM, PROPORTIONAL REPRESENTATION

single-minded \ˈ==ˈ==\ *adj* **1 :** SINGLE 7a ⟨a dedicated, *single-minded* man —*Time*⟩ ⟨an honest, farsighted, *single-minded* and liberal statesman —J.F.Gore⟩ — opposed to *double-minded* **2 :** SINGLE-HEARTED 2 ⟨his *single-minded*, selfless devotion to the liberation of his country —H.H. Fisher⟩ ⟨had a *single-minded* love of God and a catholic love of humanity —W.L.Sperry⟩ **3 :** having one unifying purpose ⟨with all the emotional ferocity and energy of genius, was *single-minded* for victory —J.H.Plumb⟩ ⟨his *single-minded* concern with the political dimension —Martin Price⟩ ⟨affable manner covered a *single-minded* ruthlessness —*Time*⟩

single-mind·ed·ly *adv* **:** in a single-minded manner

single-mind·ed·ness *n* -ES **:** the quality or state of being single-minded ⟨had a passionate *single-mindedness* which their divided minds and loyalties lacked —W.L.Sperry⟩

single money *n, obs* **:** small currency **:** SMALL CHANGE

single-name paper \ˈ==ˈ=-\ *n* **:** a promissory note with no endorsement other than the signature of the maker

sin·gle·ness *n* -ES [[1]*single* + *-ness*] **1 :** sincerity and honesty in design or intent **:** STRAIGHTFORWARDNESS ⟨a man the ~ of whose motives could not be questioned —Winston Churchill⟩ ⟨those who with ~ of mind try to do God's will —*Interpreter's Bible*⟩ **2 :** the state of being unmarried **:** CELIBACY ⟨traces the trends in nuptiality and ~ —*Population Index*⟩ **3 :** the fact of being single or one of a kind or group **:** ONENESS ⟨the ~ of a small operation . . . lost in the confusion of dozens of outfits —H.D.Skidmore⟩ **4 :** the condition of standing or remaining alone or apart ⟨the vulnerability of ~ will disappear before unity of effort —Douglas MacArthur⟩ **5 :** the quality of concentrating on one central objective ⟨the ~ of our aim generates a tremendous sense of solidarity —F.A. Perry⟩

single nickel salt *n* **:** NICKEL SULFATE

single-nose \ˈ==ˈ=\ *adj* **:** having only one growing point and usu. producing a single flower stalk ⟨a *single-nose* narcissus bulb⟩ — compare DOUBLE-NOSE

single-pass \ˈ==ˈ=\ *vt* **:** to pass (gases) once across the tubes of a boiler

single-phase \ˈ==ˈ=\ *adj* **:** of or relating to a circuit energized by a single alternating electromotive force with the currents in the two wires differing in phase by 180 degrees or a half cycle

single-phaser \ˈ==ˈ==\ *n* **:** a single-phase machine

single-phasing \ˈ==ˈ==\ *n* -S **:** the operation of a polyphase motor on single-phase supply

single-pole switch \ˈ=ˈ=-\ *n* **:** an electric switch having only one blade and one contact

single premium *n* **:** the sum that would meet in a single payment the cost of a life insurance policy for the entire policy term

single-punch \ˈ==ˈ=\ *vt* **:** to punch one hole at a time in

single-rail crane \ˈ=ˈ=-\ *n* **:** WALKING CRANE

single-rail track circuit *n* **:** a track circuit comprising two running rails with one divided into sections by insulated joints and the other used as a common return

single rhyme *n* **:** a monosyllabic rhyme

single-rivet \ˈ==ˈ==\ *vt* **:** to secure (a joint) by a single row of rivets or by a single row on each side of the seam of a butt joint

singles *pl of* SINGLE, *pres 3d sing of* SINGLE

singles court *n* **:** a court (as for tennis) laid out for only two players

single-screw \ˈ==ˈ=\ *adj* **:** having one screw propeller ⟨a *single-screw* ship⟩ — compare TWIN-SCREW

single-seater \ˈ==ˈ==\ *n* **:** a vehicle (as an airplane) with a single seat

single-seed cucumber \ˈ==ˈ=-\ *n* **:** STAR CUCUMBER

single shear *n* **:** shear along one surface only

single-shear steel *n* **:** SHEAR STEEL

single-shot \ˈ==ˈ=\ *adj* **:** capable of firing only one shot without reloading

single-shot pistol *n* **:** a pistol that can be loaded with only one cartridge at a time and that is used chiefly in target practice — compare AUTOMATIC PISTOL

single-side-band modulation \ˈ==ˈ=ˈ=-\ *n* **:** a modulation used in a radio or telephone carrier in which the normal carrier signal is eliminated and one of the two modulation side bands is removed usu. by filtering

single-side-band transmission *n* **:** carrier suppression in which the power associated essentially with one side band is not transmitted

single-space \ˈ==ˈ=\ *vt* **:** to type (copy) leaving no blank line spaces ⟨*single-space* the list of services, but leave a double space both before and after —D.D.Lessenberry & T.J.Crawford⟩ ~ *vi* **:** to type on every line space

single spanish burton *n, usu cap 2d S* **:** a tackle with two single blocks

single spruce *n* **:** WHITE SPRUCE 1a

single-stage \ˈ==ˈ=\ *adj* **:** of one stage only **:** complete in one rather than in two or more operations ⟨*single-stage* turbine⟩ ⟨*single-stage* rocket⟩ ⟨*single-stage* trigger⟩

single standard *n* **1 :** MONOMETALLISM **2 :** a set of principles that apply equally to all members of a group; *specif* **:** a code of morals that applies the same standards of sexual behavior to both men and women — compare DOUBLE STANDARD

singlestick \ˈ==,=\ *n* [[1]*single* + *stick*] **1 :** fighting or fencing with a one-handed wooden stick or sword ⟨the crisp click of sportsmen at ~ —Lawrence Durrell⟩ **2 :** the weapon used in singlestick combat

singlesticker \ˈ==,==\ *n* [[1]*single* + *stick* + *-er*] **:** a single-masted vessel **:** SLOOP, CUTTER

single stitch *n* **:** a bookbinder's stitch made by passing a single loop through the center of the matter to be secured and tying

single-surfaced \ˈ==ˈ==\ *adj* **:** having one finished surface ⟨*single-surfaced* airplane wing⟩

sin·glet \ˈsiŋglət, *usu* -əd.+V\ *n* -S [[1]*single* + *-et*] **1 a** *dial chiefly Brit* **:** an unlined waistcoat **b** *chiefly Brit* **:** an undershirt or athletic jersey ⟨his coppery-brown torso that was only partly covered by the torn ~ —Vance Palmer⟩ ⟨athletes, stripped to their ~*s* and shorts, raced, cycled and pole-jumped —H.V.Morton⟩ **2 a :** an atomic, molecular, or nuclear energy level with a spin of zero **b :** a spectrum line that is not resolved into components by even the highest dispersion

single-tap r \ˈ==ˈ=-\ *n* **:** a trilled *r* made by a single flip of the point of the tongue against the teethridge (as in the southern British pronunciation of *very* sometimes spelled *veddy*)

sin·gle·tary pea \ˈsiŋgəl,terē-\ *n* [*singletary* prob. fr. [1]*single* + *-tary* (as in *solitary*); fr. its being an escape] **:** a weak-stemmed and usu. decumbent winter annual legume (*Lathyrus hirsutus*) native to the Mediterranean region but long established as an escape in the southern U.S. and more recently cultivated as a cover and pasture crop — called also *Caley pea, rough pea, wild winterpea*

single tax *n* **:** a tax to be levied on a single object as the sole source of public revenue esp. by taking the entire economic rent of land

single taxer *n* **:** an advocate of a single-tax system

single-throw switch \ˈ==ˈ=-\ *n* **:** a switch (as on an electrical switchboard) that by one operation engages a set of fixed contacts

sin·gle·ton \ˈsiŋgəltən, -tᵊn\ *n* -S [F, fr. E [1]*single* + F *-eton* (dim. suffix)] **1 :** a card (as in bridge) that is the only one of its suit orig. held in a hand — compare DOUBLETON **2 :** an individual member or thing distinct from others grouped with it ⟨a quatrain consisting of a triplet and a ~⟩ ⟨the birds scattered . . . and the ~*s* were easy to pick up one by one —Thomas Barbour⟩; *specif* **:** a single offspring ⟨in May or June the spotted fawns are born, usually ~*s*, but rarely twins —W.A.Weber⟩

single-tongue \ˈ==ˈ=\ *vi* [[4]*single* + *tongue*, v.] **:** to articulate notes on a wind instrument by repeated single articulations (as *t*, *t*) — compare DOUBLE-TONGUE

single-track \ˈ==ˈ=\ *adj* **1 :** having but one track ⟨a *single-track* railroad⟩ **2 :** lacking intellectual range, receptiveness, or flexibility **:** ONE-TRACK ⟨with a *single-track* mind devoted solely to his duty —Leo Crane⟩

single transferable vote *n* **:** a vote on a ballot that can be transferred from a candidate of first choice who has already obtained the necessary quota of votes for election to a candidate marked by the voter as second or third choice in order that every vote may count toward the election of a candidate — compare HARE SYSTEM

sin·gle·tree \ˈsiŋgəl·(,)trē, -l·tri\ *n* [[1]*single* + *tree*] **1 :** WHIFFLETREE **2 :** a heavy horizontal bar sometimes used to spread the loop of a hoisting chain to prevent crushing the load

single-valued \ˈ==ˈ(,)=\ *adj* **:** having only one value for any one value of the argument ⟨a *single-valued* function⟩

single vote *or* **single nontransferable vote** *n* **:** a simple form of proportional representation by which each voter casts his ballot for one candidate only

single whip *n* **:** a purchase consisting of a single block and a small rope for lifting light articles — compare DOUBLE WHIP

single wicket *n* **:** a variation of cricket that is played on a pitch with a single batting end having three stumps and a bowling end usu. marked by one stump with all bowling being done from the same end and but one batsman being in at a time

single wingback formation *or* **single wing** *n* **:** an offensive football formation to the left or right in which a back plays just outside of and a yard behind one of the ends, the blocking back is on the same side of the center and usu. a yard behind the guard, and the two other backs are four or five yards behind a balanced or unbalanced line and in a position to receive a direct snap from the center

singling *n* -S [fr. gerund of [3]*single*] **1 :** the act or process of one that singles **2 singlings** *pl* **:** the crude product that first passes over in distilling **:** the low wine that is usu. redistilled at a lower temperature **3 :** a defect in the plying of yarns caused by the omission of one or more strands

sin·gly \ˈsiŋg(ə)lē, -li\ *adv* [ME *senglely*, fr. *sengle* single + *-ly* — more at SINGLE] **1 a :** by or with oneself **:** as an individual person or thing **:** SEPARATELY ⟨they come ~ or in scattered groups —*Amer. Guide Series: Pa.*⟩ ⟨the tree-living primate mother and her ~ born infant —Weston La Barre⟩ **b :** without the assistance or support of others **:** SINGLE-HANDEDLY ⟨either ~ or in cooperation, have carried on noteworthy educational activities —*Amer. Guide Series: Oregon*⟩ ⟨~ and successfully opposed the . . . proposal for a drastic shortening of hours in industry —*Current Biog.*⟩ **2** *archaic* **:** as or by a single unit **:** EXCLUSIVELY, SOLELY **3 :** STRAIGHTFORWARDLY, HONESTLY, SINCERELY ⟨having its accomplishment ~ in mind —F.J.Haskin⟩

sing·pho \ˈsiŋ,pō\ *n, pl* **singpho** *or* **singphos** *usu cap* **:** CHINGPAW

sings *pres 3d sing of* SING, *pl of* SING

[1]**sing-sing** \ˈsiŋ,siŋ\ *n* -S [Malinke *si-nsing* antelope] **:** a West African waterbuck (*Kobus defassa unctuosus*) distinguished by rather long sandy brown distinctly greasy hair

[2]**sing-sing** \"\ *n* [redupl. of [1]*sing*] **:** an Oceanian ceremony of singing and dancing

[1]**singsong** \ˈ=,=\ *n* [[1]*sing* + *song*] **1 a :** a verse selection with marked and regular rhythm and rhyme **:** a jingling song or ballad **b :** verse of such characteristics ⟨the ~ of the epic, its repetitious phrases and familiar story —*College English*⟩ **2** *chiefly Brit* **:** SING 1a ⟨food, refreshments, entertainment, and a ~ combined to make it a highly enjoyable evening —*Crows-nest*⟩ **3 :** a voice delivery characterized by a narrow range of pitch or a mechanically repetitious pitch variation ⟨began in the ~ of a professional guide —Donn Byrne⟩ ⟨the ~ of . . . campaign oratory —Max Ascoli⟩ ⟨the auctioneer with his rapid ~ —*Amer. Guide Series: Tenn.*⟩ ⟨speaking English in a Welsh ~ —John Barkham⟩

[2]**singsong** \"\ *adj* **1 :** making or delivering singsong ⟨is known as a ~ poet⟩ **2 :** characterized by the light or trivial usu. monotonously expressed ⟨writes ~ verse⟩ ⟨cases of long-windedness, foggy meanings, clichés, and ~ phrases —Stuart Chase⟩ **3 :** having a monotonous cadence or rhythm **:** marked by a singsong ⟨story in a deliberately rhythmical, ~ prose —*New Yorker*⟩ ⟨cultivated a ~ manner of speaking —Thomas Pyles⟩ ⟨the ~ orchestration from a loud radio sawed the air —Kathryn Grondahl⟩

[3]**singsong** \"\ *vb* -ED/-ING/-S *vt* **1 :** to move by or as if by means of a singsong or chant ⟨watched coolies ~ a dismantled truck up the cliff —*Time*⟩ **2 :** to speak, chant, or declaim in singsong ⟨the class ~*ing* the number tables⟩ ⟨~*ed* her way through Shakespeare with a . . . native-born inflection —Joan Comay⟩ ~ *vi* **:** to speak, chant, or sing in a singsong manner ⟨droning on and on, his voice ~*ing* almost unrecognizably —Norman Mailer⟩ ⟨vendors ~*ed* up and down the platform —Jobo Nakamura⟩

singsong girl *n* **:** a Chinese girl engaged in professional entertainment similar to that performed by the geisha

sing·songy \ˈ=,sȯŋē, -ŋi *also* -,säŋ-\ *adj* [[1]*singsong* + *-y*] **:** suggestive of singsong

sing·spiel \ˈsiŋ,spēl, ˈziŋ,shpēl\ *n, usu cap* [G, fr. *singen* to sing (fr. OHG *singan*) + *spiel* play, fr. OHG *spil* — more at SING, SPIEL] **:** a somewhat dramatic musical work popular in Germany esp. in the latter part of the 18th century, usu. comic in nature, and characterized by spoken dialogue interspersed with popular or folk songs — compare BALLAD OPERA

sing·spi·ra·tion \,siŋspəˈrāshən\ *n* -S [[1]*sing* + *inspiration*] **:** a song service featuring the group singing of hymns conducted esp. by revivalistic churches and often followed by a sermon

[1]**sin·gu·lar** \ˈsiŋgyələ(r)\ *adj* [ME *singuler*, fr. MF *singuler*, *singulier*, fr. L *singularis* single, solitary, singular, fr. *singulus* one only, individual + *-aris* -ar — more at SINGLE] **1 a :** of or relating to a separate person or thing **:** INDIVIDUAL ⟨every fact in the world might be ~, that is, unlike any other fact and sole of its kind —William James⟩ ⟨assumption that the ~ person can be understood apart from his culture —*Amer. Polit. Sci. Rev.*⟩ ⟨saw that each weed was a ~ knife —Stephen Crane⟩ ⟨to all and ~ to whom these presents shall come, greetings⟩ **b :** of, relating to, or being a word form denoting one person, thing, or instance ⟨one subject usually takes a ~ verb⟩ — opposed to *plural;* compare DUAL **c :** of or relating to a single instance or to something considered by itself **:** applied to only one individual ⟨a ~ term⟩ ⟨a ~ proposition⟩ — opposed to *general* **d** (1) **:** of or relating to a single or individual unit ⟨convey several parcels of land all and ~⟩ (2) **:** of, relating to, or affecting a particular property or one or more separate interests or rights in property as distinguished from the entire body of a decedent's estate or any interest or right in property acquired otherwise than by inheritance — compare SINGULAR SUCCESSION **2 a** *obs* **:** set apart or distinguished by superiority **:** EMINENT **b :** of considerable extent or worth **:** EXTRAORDINARY, EXCEPTIONAL ⟨achieved a ~ mechanical triumph that won him wide renown —Sherwood Anderson⟩ ⟨a ~ poetic achievement —H. W.V.Lange⟩ ⟨holds a ~ regard for his people⟩ ⟨his death is a ~ loss⟩ **c** *obs* **:** especially helpful or efficacious **:** BENEFICIAL **3** *archaic* **a :** consisting of one only **b :** having but one on each side ⟨those in his high place fight no ~ combats —Sir Walter Scott⟩ **4 a :** of unusual quality **:** UNCOMMON, UNIQUE ⟨various speculations put forward in explanation of the ~ phenomena of this remarkable place —Harry Luke⟩ ⟨a work of ~ originality and analytical power —*Economica*⟩ ⟨that woman of ~ mystery, the Mona Lisa —Elizabeth Janeway⟩ **b :** RARE, VALUABLE ⟨a man of ~ charm and sterling character —D.S. Muzzey⟩ ⟨an effect of ~ grace and delicacy —*Amer. Guide Series: Maine*⟩ ⟨of ~ and exquisite workmanship⟩ **5 a :** being at variance with others **:** DIFFERING, CONTRARY ⟨am not ~ in the opinion that much of the disease which does prevail might be avoided —Charles Dickens⟩ ⟨nor are we ~ in our judgment —Aldous Huxley⟩ **b :** departing from general usage or expectation **:** PECULIAR, ECCENTRIC ⟨a ~

dog . . . of the color of chocolate —Arnold Bennett⟩ ⟨~ to say, the one dangerous and objectionable feature in this little volume preserved it from limbo —George Meredith⟩ ⟨hit upon the ~ expedient of diminishing the quality of their justice in order to reduce the demand for it —T.F.T.Plucknett⟩ **c :** possessing various unique mathematical properties ⟨a ~ point or integral in a differential equation⟩ **syn** see STRANGE

²singular \"\ *n* -s [L *singularis*, fr. *singularis*, adj., single] **1 :** the singular number, the inflectional form denoting it, or a word in that form ⟨that the human mind has to think in terms of ~ and plural —Weston La Barre⟩ ⟨*he* is the ~ of *they*⟩ **2 a** *archaic* **:** a single person, instance, or thing **:** INDIVIDUAL ⟨eloquence would be but a poor thing, if we should converse only with ~s —Ben Jonson⟩ **b :** something that is considered by itself or as a single term; *also* **:** SINGULAR PROPOSITION — usu. used in pl. ⟨experiences might all have been ~s, no one of them occurring twice —William James⟩ ⟨an accepted principle in the middle ages that reason or intellect and science are of universals, whereas the senses are of ~s —G.P.Klubertanz⟩ **c** (1) *obs* **:** an adult wild boar (2) **:** a company of wild boars

singular integral *n* **:** SINGULAR SOLUTION

sin·gu·lar·ism \ˈsiŋgyələ͵rizəm\ *n* -s **:** any philosophy that derives the universe from a single principle — contrasted with *pluralism;* compare MONISM

sin·gu·lar·i·ty \͵==ˈlarəd·ē, -rətē, -i *also* -ler-\ *n* -ES [ME *singularite*, fr. MF *singularité*, fr. LL *singularitat-, singularitas*, fr. L *singularis* single, singular + *-itat-, -itas* -ity — more at SINGULAR] **1 :** something that is separate or singular **:** UNIT ⟨for the Aristotelian, knowledge of universals proceeds from experience with *singularities*⟩ **2 a :** an unusual manifestation or eccentricity in manner or behavior ⟨*singularities* of dress and speech make life a burden for their unfortunate possessors —Sacheverell Sitwell⟩ ⟨even our faults have some attractiveness for us . . . as if they were pleasant *singularities* —F.A. Swinnerton⟩ **b :** a unique or remarkable characteristic or development ⟨some natural productions require such a ~ of soil and situation —Adam Smith⟩ **c :** an odd or peculiar feature or characteristic ⟨forgotten habits, uses that are now lost to memory, significances once powerful . . . all of these things and many more *singularities* are recalled to the student of plant names —*Notes & Queries*⟩ **3 :** the quality or state of being singular ⟨the amount of ~ one finds among the people of the country —*New Republic*⟩ ⟨personality . . . expresses its ~ even in handwriting —O.W.Holmes †1935⟩ ⟨as individuality approaches ~, it . . . isolates itself —J.L.Lowes⟩ ⟨the ~ of an analytic function⟩

sin·gu·lar·iza·tion \͵==͵lərəˈzāshən, -͵rīˈz-\ *n* -s **:** the act or process of singularizing **:** the state of being singularized

sin·gu·lar·ize \ˈ==lə͵rīz\ *vt* -ED/-ING/-S [*singular* + *-ize*] **:** to make singular: as **a :** DISTINGUISH, SIGNALIZE ⟨observes the rule that never by display of peculiarity, or even by a display of brave or noble behavior, must she ~ herself by standing out —Albert Hubbell⟩ **b :** to make single ⟨in this people that we place our confidence — in the specific and *singularized* vocation of each one of its members —*Commonweal*⟩

sin·gu·lar·ly *adv* [ME *singulerly*, fr. *singuler* singular + *-ly* — more at SINGULAR] **:** in a singular manner ⟨potash, a ~ effective component of these fertilizers —*advt*⟩ ⟨a woman of ~ frank temperament —Robert Hichens⟩ ⟨a ~ charming woman —Rudyard Kipling⟩ ⟨had first stood there so ~, and vanished at the approach of strangers —Thomas Hardy⟩ ⟨majority of these high altitude birds are ~ voiceless —Douglas Carruthers⟩

sin·gu·lar·ness *n* -ES **:** SINGULARITY

singular point *n* **:** a point of the curve f(x, y)=0 where both partial derivatives are zero

singular proposition *n* **:** a proposition having as its subject a proper name or a descriptive phrase which applies only to one individual

singular solution *n* **:** a mathematical solution that contains no arbitrary constant and is not a particular solution — called also *singular integral*

singular square matrix *n* **:** a square matrix whose determinant is zero

singular statement *n* **:** a statement that contains only constants and no variables — contrasted with *general statement*

singular succession *n, chiefly Scots law* **:** the succession to a particular object or property — distinguished from *universal succession*

singular syllogism *n* **:** a syllogism whose middle term is a singular term

singular universal *n* **:** CONCRETE UNIVERSAL

sin·gu·li in so·li·dum \ˈsiŋgyə͵lī̇n ˈsäləd̮əm, -gə͵lēin-\ *adj* [L, singly for the whole] **:** singly liable for a whole amount due

sin·gult \ˈsiŋ͵gəlt\ *n* -s [L *singultus*] *archaic* **:** SOB ⟨heart=thrilling cries, with sobs and ~s sore —Gilbert West⟩ — usu. used in pl.

sin·gul·ti·ent \siŋˈgəltēənt\ *adj* [L *singultient-, singultiens*, pres. part. of *singultire* to sob, hiccup, fr. *singultus* sob, hiccup] *archaic* **:** SOBBING ⟨wakes with a deep-drawn ~ breath —Lewis Morris⟩

sin·gul·tus \-ltəs\ *n* -ES [L] **:** HICCUP

sinh *abbr* [*sine* + *hyperbolic*] hyperbolic sine

¹sin·ha·lese \͵sin(h)əˈlēz, -ēs\ *also* **sin·gha·lese** \͵siŋgə-, -iŋ(h)ə-\ *or* **sin·ga·lese** \-iŋ(g)ə-\ *or* **cin·ga·lese** \͵siŋ(g)ə-\ *or* **cin·gha·lese** \-iŋgə-, -iŋ(h)ə-\ *adj, usu cap* [Skt *Siṁhala* Sri Lanka, island in the Indian ocean south of the Indian subcontinent + E *-ese* (adj. suffix)] **1 :** of, relating to, or characteristic of the Sinhalese **2 :** of, relating to, or characteristic of the Sinhalese language

²sinhalese \"\ *also* **singhalese** \"\ *or* **singalese** \"\ *or* **cingalese** \"\ *or* **cinghalese** \"\ *n, pl* **sinhalese** *cap* [Skt *Siṁhala* Sri Lanka + E *-ese* (n. suffix)] **1 a :** a people inhabiting the island of Sri Lanka and forming a major portion of its population **b :** a member of such people **2 :** the Indic language of the Sinhalese people which is the leading language of Sri Lanka

sin·ha·lite \ˈsin(h)ə͵līt\ *n* -s [*sinhal-* (as in *sinhalese*) + *-ite;* fr. the fact that the gemstones identified as sinhalite came from Sri Lanka] **:** a mineral consisting of a magnesium aluminum borate that is structurally related to olivine and is occas. used as a gem

sin·ha·san \sinˈhäsᵊn, -ˈhəs-\ *n* -s [Skt *siṁhasana*, lit., lion's seat] **:** a throne often depicted in sculpture with legs in the shape of lions and designed as a seat for the figure of a deity

sin·ic \ˈsinik, -nēk\ *adj, usu cap* [ML *sinicus*, fr. LL *Sinae*, pl., Chinese + L *-icus* -ic — more at SINOLOGUE] **:** CHINESE, SINITIC

sin·i·cism \ˈsinə͵sizəm\ *n* -s *usu cap* [*sinic* + *-ism*] **:** something (as a manner or custom) peculiar to the Chinese

sin·i·ci·za·tion \͵==səˈzāshən, -͵sīˈz-\ *n* -s *usu cap* **:** the act or process of sinicizing **:** the state of being sinicized

sin·i·cize \ˈ==͵sīz\ *vt* -ED/-ING/-S *often cap* [*sinic* + *-ize*] **:** to modify by Chinese influence ⟨came of a wholly *sinicized* Mongol family —*Times Lit. Supp.*⟩

sinico- *comb form, usu cap* [*sinic* + *-o-*] **:** Chinese and ⟨*Sinico*=Japanese⟩ ⟨*Sinico*=Russian⟩

sin·i·co-japanese \͵sinə͵kō-, -nē͵kō-\ *n, cap S&J* **1 :** Chinese as adapted and used in Japanese **2 :** a style of writing in Japanese modeled on the Chinese classics and containing many Chinese words and idioms

sin·i·fi·ca·tion \͵sinəfəˈkāshən\ *n* -s *usu cap* [LL *Sinae* + E *-i-* + *-fication*] **:** SINICIZATION

sin·i·fy \ˈ==͵fī\ *vt* -ED/-ING/-ES *often cap* [LL *Sinae*, pl., Chinese + E *-ify*] **:** SINICIZE ⟨writers popularized the foreign-style novel and short story by ~*ing* it —*Times Lit. Supp.*⟩

sin·i·grin \ˈsinəgrən\ *n* -s [ISV *sinigr-* (fr. NL *Sinapis nigra*, genus of black mustard seed) + *-in*] **:** a crystalline glucoside $CH_2{=}CHCH_2C(SC_6H_{11}O_5){=}NOSO_3K$ found in the seeds of black mustard (*Brassica nigra*) and other brassicas that on enzymatic hydrolysis by myrosin yields glucose, potassium hydrogen sulfate, and allyl isothiocyanate by Lossen rearrangement — compare MUSTARD OIL

¹sin·is·ter \ˈsinəstə(r), *chiefly archaic* səˈnis-\ *adj* [ME *sinistre*, fr. L *sinister* left, on the left side, awkward, injurious, evil, unlucky, inauspicious] **1** *archaic* **:** ominous of evil or wrong-doing **:** UNFAVORABLE, PREJUDICIAL **2** *obs* **:** conveying misleading or detrimental opinion or advice ⟨the ~ application of the malicious, ignorant, and base interpreter —Ben Jonson⟩ **3** *archaic* **:** dishonestly underhanded **:** FRAUDULENT ⟨nimble and ~ tricks and shifts —Francis Bacon⟩ **4 :** evil or productive of evil **:** BAD, CORRUPTIVE ⟨the ~ character of the early factory system —Walter Lippmann⟩ ⟨emotions long repressed sometimes find ~ outlets —V.L.Parrington⟩ ⟨the scheme of some ~ intelligence bent on punishing him —Thomas Hardy⟩ ⟨critics who . . . exaggerate the ~ influence of a kind of underworld of economic werewolves —F.L.Mott⟩ ⟨denouncing the ~ aims and wicked conduct of those in high places —C.L. Becker⟩ **5 a :** of, relating to, or situated to the left or on the left side of something ⟨was placed on . . . the ~ side of the church —J.A.Davison⟩ ⟨on a helmet, a wreath with the crest, a dexter and a ~ hand proper, grasping a two-handed sword argent —F.W.Steer⟩; *specif* **:** of or relating to the side of a heraldic shield or escutcheon at the left of the bearer ⟨a theory that the bearings of a person who fled . . . could be assumed and borne in a ~ quarter —F.P.Barnard⟩ **b :** of ill omen by reason of being on the left ⟨the victor eagle, whose ~ flight retards our host —Alexander Pope⟩ **6 :** presaging ill fortune or trouble **:** PORTENTOUS, OMINOUS ⟨everything in the room had a new significance, a ~ meaning —G.D. Brown⟩ ⟨something devilish and ~ about the whole business —Lewis Mumford⟩ ⟨or, more ~ still, the black fog full of birds —*Listener*⟩ ⟨a ~ brightness — a poisonous, threatening flash of pigment, set off by the blackness of the shadows —William Beebe⟩ ⟨with a somewhat ~ haircut, a unique black beard that would mark him as a dangerous man —Harrison Smith⟩ **7 :** accompanied by or leading to disaster or unfavorable developments ⟨expressed their alarm over the ~ results that had followed —W.H.Lawrence⟩ ⟨was a ~ idea from the beginning, a surefire recipe for civil war —Edmond Taylor⟩

²sinister \"\ *adv* **:** to or toward the left ⟨the flag was criticized because the eagle faced ~, that is, to its own left —Elizabeth W. King⟩

sinister base point *n* **:** the lower sinister part of the field of an escutcheon — see POINT illustration

sinister chief point *n* **:** the upper sinister part of the field of an escutcheon — see POINT illustration

sin·is·ter·i·ty \͵sinəˈsterəd·ē, -rətē, -i\ *n* -ES [L *sinisteritas*, fr. *sinister* left + *-itas* -ity] **:** SINISTERNESS

sin·is·ter·ly *adv* [ME *sinistrely*, fr. *sinistre* sinister + *-ly*] **:** in a sinister manner ⟨rolled his yellow eyes ~ —Earle Birney⟩ ⟨a ~ mature concealment of evil —R.B.Heilman⟩ ⟨its water . . . was ~ opaque —Anthony West⟩ ⟨vultures . . . coasted ~ away into the mist —Dan Wickenden⟩

sin·is·ter·ness *n* -ES **:** the quality or state of being sinister ⟨among the club names collected the predominant connotations are of power, speed, and aggressiveness, with ~ as a muted countermelody —Arthur Minton⟩

sinistr- *or* **sinistro-** *comb form* [ML, fr. L *sinistr-, sinister* left, on the left side] **1 a :** left ⟨*sinistr*ad⟩ **b :** better developed in or using preferentially the left ⟨*sinistro*cular⟩ **2 :** levorotatory ⟨*sinistr*in⟩

si·ni·stra \səˈnēstrə\ *n* -s [It, fr. L, fr. fem. of *sinister* left] **:** the left hand — used as a direction in music to play a note or passage with this hand

sinis·trad \ˈsinə͵strad, səˈni͵s-\ *adv* [*sinistr-* + *-ad*] **:** toward the left side **:** SINISTRALLY

¹sinis·tral \ˈsinəstrəl, səˈnis-\ *adj* [ML *sinistralis*, fr. L *sinistr-, sinister* left + *-alis* -al] **:** of or relating to the left **:** inclined to the left: as **a :** LEFT-HANDED **b** *of a flatfish* **:** having the left side turned uppermost — opposed to *dextral* **c** *of a gastropod shell* **:** having the whorls coiling counterclockwise down the spire when viewed with the apex toward the observer and having the aperture situated on the left of the axis when held with the spire uppermost and with the aperture opening toward the observer

²sinistral \"\ *n* -s **:** a person exhibiting dominance of the left hand and eye **:** a typical left-handed individual ⟨if you are left-handed and also definitely left-eyed . . . you are classified as a straight ~ —Bob Nichols⟩

sin·is·tral·i·ty \͵sinəˈstraləd·ē, -lətē, -i\ *n* -ES **1 :** the quality or state of having the left side or one or more of its parts (as the hand or eye) different from and usu. more efficient than the right or its corresponding parts; *also* **:** LEFT=HANDEDNESS ⟨dental societies don't keep track of ~ among their members —*New Yorker*⟩ **2 :** the condition of being sinistral — used esp. of a mollusk shell

sinis·tral·ly \ˈsinəstrəlē, səˈnis-, -li\ *adv* **:** toward the left ⟨recross ~ his legs —V.V.Nabokov⟩

sin·is·tra·tion \͵sinəˈstrāshən\ *n* -s [¹*sinistral* + *-ation*] **:** the quality or state of being sinistral

sinis·trin \ˈsinəstrən, səˈnis-\ *n* -s [ISV *sinistr-* + *-in*] **:** a levorotatory polysaccharide $(C_6H_{10}O_5)_x$ derived from squill and constituted of repeating fructose units

sin·is·troc·u·lar \͵sinəˈsträkyələ(r)\ *adj* [*sinistr-* + *ocular*] **:** using the left eye habitually or more effectively than the right — **sin·is·troc·u·lar·i·ty** \͵==͵==ˈlarəd·ē\ *n* -ES

sinis·trorse \͵sinəˈstrȯ(ə)rs, səˈni͵s-\ *also* **sin·is·tror·sal** \͵sinəˈstrȯrsəl\ *adj* [*sinistrorse* fr. NL *sinistrorsus*, fr. L *sinistrorsum, sinistrorsus* toward the left side, fr. *sinistr-, sinister* left, fr. *sinister* left + *versus*, past part. of *vertere* to turn; *sinistrorsal* fr. NL *sinistrorsus* + E *-al* — more at WORTH] **1** *of a plant* **:** twining spirally upward around an axis from right to left: **a :** twining counterclockwise when the observer's point of view is within or above the spiral **b :** twining clockwise when the observer's point of view is outside the spiral — compare DEXTRORSE **2 :** SINISTRAL c — **sinis·trorse·ly** \-slē\ *also* **sinis·tror·sal·ly** \-sələ\ *adv*

sinis·trous \ˈsinəstrəs, səˈnis-\ *adj* [L *sinistr-, sinister* + E *-ous*] **:** SINISTER — **sin·is·trous·ly** *adv*

si·nit·ic \səˈnid·ik, (ˈ)sī¦n-\ *also* **si·net·ic** \-ned-\ *adj, usu cap* [LL *Sinae*, pl., Chinese + E *-itic* or *-etic* — more at SINOLOGUE] **:** of or relating to the Chinese or the Chinese language or culture

¹sink \ˈsiŋk\ *vb* **sank** \-aŋk, -aiŋk\ *or* **sunk; sunk** \-əŋk\ *or* **sunk·en** \-kən\ **sinking; sinks** [ME *sinken*, fr. OE *sincan;* akin to OHG *sinkan* to sink, ON *sökkva*, Goth *sinqan* to sink, Gk *heaphthē* clung, sank, Arm *ankanim* I fall, yield] *vi* **1 a :** to become submerged **:** go to the bottom **:** SUBMERGE ⟨the Atago ~s in 19 minutes —H.W.Baldwin⟩ ⟨the overloaded raft *sank* below the surface⟩ **b :** to become partly buried or submerged (as in mud) ⟨~*ing* up to his hips in the snow⟩ ⟨must ~ deeper into the morass before we again emerge onto firm ground —Vannevar Bush⟩ **c :** to descend into or become engulfed by the earth ⟨whole towns ~*ing* as the earth opens great cracks⟩ **2 a** (1) **:** to fall or drop to a lower place or level ⟨letting his head ~ to his chest⟩ ⟨peeled off and *sank* into a cloud layer —W.F.Jenkins⟩ ⟨the hand opens out fully and . . . quietly ~s down below the waist —Warwick Braithwaite⟩ (2) **:** to flow at a lower depth or level ⟨water . . . ~s down in the sandstone and finds its way extremely slowly north —K.S.Sandford⟩ ⟨after the spring floods the brooks ~⟩ (3) **:** to burn with lower intensity **:** die down ⟨watching the flames ~ and the coals begin to glow⟩ (4) **:** to fall to a lower pitch or tone **:** become fainter ⟨in the general hush his voice *sank* to a whisper —Waldo Frank⟩ ⟨sounds of voices ~*ing* in the distance⟩ **b :** to subside gradually **:** SETTLE ⟨some parts of the mainland are slowly ~*ing* and some rising as time works its changes —*Amer. Guide Series: Texas*⟩ **c :** to move or go out of sight **:** disappear from view ⟨riding on, he looked back to see the workers ~ below the tops of the hedgerows⟩ **d :** to move down in the sky toward or at the horizon ⟨the sun *sank* below the western rim of the prairies —F.B.Gipson⟩ ⟨though sun is *sunk* and darkness near —R.P.Warren⟩ ⟨to follow knowledge like a ~*ing* star —Alfred Tennyson⟩ **e :** to decline or slope gradually **:** DIP ⟨a spur of hills ~*ing* into the opalescence of the far seas —Osbert Sitwell⟩ ⟨ahead of her the road *sank* between the autumn fields and the brilliant patches of woods —Ellen Glasgow⟩ **3 a :** to become lost or absorbed **:** PENETRATE ⟨the river seems literally to ~ into the earth before the hills on the horizon —Tom Marvel⟩ ⟨the ink quickly ~s in the blotting paper⟩ ⟨the kind of psychological poison which ~s so deeply into our system —H.A.Overstreet⟩ **b :** to become impressively known or felt or comprehended — usu. used with *in* or *into* ⟨the lesson of inflation had not *sunk* in —Roy Lewis & Angus Maude⟩ ⟨the gloomy truth has *sunk* in that the buffalo no longer fill the prairies —D.W.Brogan⟩ ⟨any abstract pattern . . . may in this way ~ into the mind —Herbert Read⟩ ⟨for any picture really to ~ into your imagination . . . it is necessary to carry the feeling of the picture away with you —J.C.Powys⟩ **4 :** to become deeply absorbed or immersed **:** FALL — usu. used with *in* or *into* ⟨drew thoughtfully at his pipe and *sank* into a reverie —Dorothy Sayers⟩ ⟨had *sunk* morosely into thought —Berton Roueché⟩ ⟨overcome by exhaustion she *sank* quietly into sleep —Louis Bromfield⟩ **5 a :** to go downward or deteriorate in quality, state, or condition **:** DEGENERATE, RETROGRESS — usu. used with *into* or *to* ⟨the old aristocracy *sank* in wealth and prestige —F.J.Mather⟩ ⟨architectural training and taste had *sunk* back into a period of chaos —J.E.Gloag⟩ ⟨should ~ back into another Dark Age —Lindsay Rogers⟩ ⟨~ into decay and eventual ruin —Ivor Bulmer-Thomas⟩ ⟨causes the world of custom to ~ into its deserved oblivion —C.S.Kilby⟩ ⟨if the writer of fiction turns from this task he will ~ deservedly to the level of formalistic entertainer —Elizabeth Janeway⟩ **b :** to grow less in amount **:** diminish in worth **:** DECLINE ⟨the population . . . *sank* from about 20 millions to about 9 —Herbert Agar⟩ ⟨support from public funds had *sunk* to the vanishing point —C.L.Jones⟩ ⟨real estate values *sank* to a new low —*Amer. Guide Series: N.Y.City*⟩ **c :** to fall in reputation or standing **:** lower oneself ⟨I had *sunk* considerably in her estimation —Norman Douglas⟩ ⟨no medieval artist ~s so low —G.G.Coulton⟩ ⟨she'd die rather than ~ to such a deed —Eden Phillpotts⟩ **6 a :** to fall or drop slowly for lack of strength **:** give way **:** COLLAPSE ⟨nearly *sank* to the ground through languor and extreme weakness —Mary W. Shelley⟩ ⟨rose and *sank* upon her seat . . . fainting, praying, raving, despairing —Thomas De Quincey⟩ ⟨his legs ~ beneath him⟩ **b :** to move oneself gradually to a lower position ⟨he *sank* down on the steps —Laura Krey⟩ ⟨his body crouched almost as if he were going to ~ upon all fours —Edith Sitwell⟩ ⟨widows, bachelors, and old folk would ~ back in their chairs with a nostalgic look —Charles Ruffing⟩ **7 a :** to become borne down by misfortune or the pressure of events or difficulties ⟨in imminent danger of ~*ing* under the tyranny of a succession of small men —T.B.Macaulay⟩ **b :** to become depressed, discouraged, or sorrowful ⟨studied this fresh proof of poverty with a ~*ing* heart —T.B.Costain⟩ ⟨sometimes his heart *sank* when he asked himself whether he and his family were withstanding it —Glenway Wescott⟩ ⟨his courage *sank*⟩ **c :** to fail in health or strength ⟨the frail system had been shattered, and all around saw that she was slowly ~*ing* —William Black⟩ ⟨his frame soon *sank* under the effects of study, toil, and persecution —T.B.Macaulay⟩ ⟨were chasing a ~*ing* fox and babbling for the kill —G.S.Patton⟩ ~ *vt* **1 a :** to cause or allow (something) to go or drop to a lower point or level ⟨could have *sunk* the gun down the after hatch —Nevil Shute⟩ ⟨*sank* his chin on his hands —Christine Weston⟩ **b :** to force or send down esp. below the earth's surface ⟨the iron clothes post Burton had *sunk* for her . . . near the fence —Minnie H. Moody⟩ ⟨framed their rude huts with pairs of light poles *sunk* in the ground —*Amer. Guide Series: N.Y.*⟩ ⟨he had been *sunken* into his grave —Marguerite Young⟩ **c :** to cause (something) to become embedded **:** DRIVE, THRUST ⟨saw the hideous creature . . . as it prepared to ~ its proboscis —William Beebe⟩ ⟨*sank* the dagger up to its hilt⟩ — often used with *into* ⟨*sank* her nails into the palms of her hands —John Dos Passos⟩ **2 a :** to cause (a ship or other object) to go under the water or to the bottom ⟨estuaries were cluttered with *sunken* shipping —*Current Biog.*⟩ ⟨*sank* his colors in the Rio Grande and led the remnant of his command into Mexico —B.I.Wiley⟩ **b :** to place or force beneath the water **:** SUBMERGE ⟨caissons had been *sunk* to keep out the water —*Amer. Guide Series: Vt.*⟩ ⟨men . . . *sunk* a grappling hook into position —Erle Stanley Gardner⟩ **c :** to engage deeply **:** engross the attention of **:** IMMERSE — usu. used with *in* or *into* ⟨a wish to ~ my mind into everything I saw and did and to absorb it all —Elyne Mitchell⟩ ⟨described the scientist aptly by saying . . . that he ~s himself in the object —H.A.Overstreet⟩ ⟨some producers can't bear the idea of ~*ing* their own individualities in that of a man perhaps long since dead —Warwick Braithwaite⟩ ⟨*sunk* in a sea of mystery —W.L.Sullivan⟩ **3 a :** to dig or bore (a well or shaft) in the earth **:** EXCAVATE ⟨this mine had been *sunk* to the tenth level —*Amer. Guide Series: Minn.*⟩ ⟨hopes . . . to ~ a shaft on the north side of the pyramid —Patrick Smith⟩ ⟨water wells are *sunk* in various ways —W.J.Miller⟩ ⟨*sank* a trial pit —O.M.Marashian⟩ **b** (1) **:** to form (a hole or depression) by cutting or excising ⟨~ words in stone⟩ (2) **:** to permit ingress or insertion of (something) by such sinking ⟨~ the screwhead level with the wood⟩ ⟨a new kind of pottery . . . with loop handles *sunk* in the body on either side —Jacquetta & Christopher Hawkes⟩ **4 :** to cast down or bring to a low condition or state **:** OVERWHELM, RUIN, DEFEAT ⟨fighting gallantly under odds which would ~ a less courageous . . . people —T.H.Fielding⟩ ⟨*sunk* to the hovels though he was, he had the rags of a finer past about him —Robert Lynd⟩ ⟨we've got to watch our step clear through . . . or we're *sunk* —Christopher Isherwood⟩ — sometimes used as an imprecation ⟨~ me, mister, but ye gave me a turn! I never heard ye open the door —Max Peacock⟩ **5 a :** to lower in standing or reputation **:** ABASE ⟨my motive . . . will not ~ me in your esteem —Jane Austen⟩ ⟨his prestige in society was *sunk* —Virginia Woolf⟩ **b** *archaic* **:** to set or consider as being at a low state or level **:** DEGRADE **6 a** *obs* **:** to cause (as water) to subside **:** LOWER **b :** to make (something) disappear by moving or sailing away ⟨the ship gradually *sank* the coast⟩ **7 a** *archaic* **:** to cause (a person) to become depressed or dejected **b** (1) **:** to weaken physically **:** DEBILITATE ⟨trouble enough to ~ a much younger man⟩ ⟨seemed too *sunken* under the heat to take any notice of who took their passports —Dan Jacobson⟩ (2) **:** to weaken or reduce the strength of (a bow) ⟨~ your bow with repeated flexings⟩ **8 a** *archaic* **:** to lessen in value or amount **:** cause (as prices) to decline **b :** to lower or soften (the voice) in speaking **:** MODULATE ⟨he went on, ~*ing* his voice —Hugh Walpole⟩ **9 a :** to stop using **:** ABANDON ⟨*sank* his old name when he got his title⟩ **b** (1) **:** to avoid mention of or reference to (a matter or fact) ⟨has a habit of ~*ing* unpleasant truths⟩ (2) **:** to conceal (a card or combination) by not melding (as in calling a trio when one holds quatorze at piquet) **c :** to set aside (the weight of the offal) when weighing meat **d** (1) **:** to set aside **:** RESTRAIN, SUPPRESS ⟨so to ~ our personality as to be ready to drift with every current of opinion —S.J.Brown⟩ ⟨men are able to ~ passions for the good of the race —Waldemar Kaempffert⟩ ⟨~s her pride and approaches the despised neighbor —Richard Harrison⟩ (2) **:** to exclude from consideration **:** SUBORDINATE ⟨induce rival groups to ~ their differences in the face of common danger —C.L.Jones⟩ ⟨was ready to ~ his republicanism so long as the nation was made —*Times Lit. Supp.*⟩ **10** *archaic* **:** to take or assume (as money) for personal use **:** APPROPRIATE **11 :** to pay off (as a debt) **:** LIQUIDATE **12 a :** to invest (capital or labor) in a holding or development with intent to gain income or other receipts ⟨no government could take land away from settlers who have *sunk* skill and capital in it for 50 years —Elspeth Huxley⟩ ⟨will ~ something over a million dollars into this plant just as a starter —Green Peyton⟩ **b :** to invest or spend (money) unprofitably or without hope of financial return ⟨were more inclined to hurry past a town where they had *sunk* money that would never come back —Willa Cather⟩ ⟨in undertaking to make this a sylvan retreat he *sunk* a large part of his patrimony —I.J.Cox⟩ **13 :** to place (as the heading of a section of a book) below the level of the top line of the full text page ⟨~ *preface* four picas⟩ **14 :** to cause (a ball or other object) to go in or through a receptacle or hole in a game ⟨~s foul shots consistently⟩ ⟨*sank* the eight ball in the corner pocket⟩ ⟨always ~s his putts⟩ **syn** see FALL — **sink one's teeth 1 :** BITE ⟨pleasure of *sinking one's teeth* into a succulent apple —W.F.Hambly⟩ **2 :** to deal directly with as a reality or a concrete matter explicitly set forth **:** to treat with as something substantial — usu. used with *into* ⟨stories such as a man can *sink his teeth* into —Richard Joseph⟩ ⟨approach that can change an ethereal abstraction into meat and potatoes that people can *sink their teeth* into —S.L.Payne⟩ — **sink or swim 1 :** to drown unless one swims ⟨if he fall in, good night, or *sink or swim* —Shak.⟩ **2 :** to fail or perish unless one exerts oneself ⟨sending him out on his own to *sink or swim*⟩

[2]sink \"\ n -s [ME *sinke*, fr. *sinken* to sink — more at [1]SINK] **1 a** (1) **:** a pool or sand-filled pit for the deposit of waste or sewage **:** CESSPOOL (2) **:** a container for foul matter or waste ⟨the sea is the ~ of the earth⟩ ⟨making ~*s* of our rivers⟩ **b :** a ditch, drainpipe, or vaulted tunnel for carrying off sewage **:** SEWER **c :** a stationary basin or a cabinet with a basin connected with a drain and usu. a water supply for washing and drainage **2 a :** a place where vice, corruption, or evil collects or gathers **:** DEN ⟨came to be a ~ of debauchery, vice, and crime —R.A.Hall b.1911⟩ ⟨will seem to him a ~ of mediocrity and human indecency —V.S. Pritchett⟩ ⟨known as a ~ of iniquity⟩ **b :** a place where such evil breeds and spreads ⟨from this ~ of sin and bawdy carousal issued murderers, sneak thieves, footpads, burglars, harlots, arsonites, and swindlers of every variety —Herbert Asbury⟩ **3** *obs* **:** the vicious, corrupt, or evil persons of a place **4 :** a preliminary excavation or pit to be enlarged until it is a full-sized shaft **:** SUMP **5 a :** a depression in the land surface; *esp* **:** one having a central playa or saline lake with no outlet **b :** a hollow in a limestone region communicating with a cavern or subterranean passage so that waters running into it disappear — called also *sinkhole, swallow* **6** *obs* **:** WELL 3a **7** *archaic* **:** a place where things disappear or are engulfed **8 :** a depression made in a flat surface (as in the face of a time-piece) **9 :** a part of the printing area of a plate (as an electrotype) that is too low to print properly **10 :** a body or substance used for the disposal of a fluid or heat in the course of a hydrodynamic or a thermodynamic process (as the condenser of a steam engine)

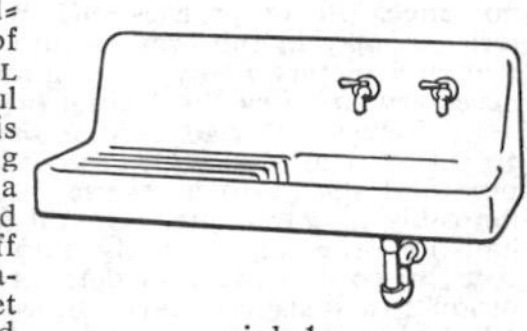
sink 1c

sink·able \'siŋkəbəl\ *adj* **:** capable of being sunk

sink·age \-kij, -kēj\ n -s **1 :** the act, process, or degree of sinking ⟨important in view of ~, heel, and change of trim that might ensue after damage —E.L.Attwood⟩ ⟨the creek . . . disappeared through ~ and evaporation —Rex Ingamells⟩ **2 :** SINKING, DEPRESSION ⟨a square block on which was carved a rosette set in a small ~ —A.S.Whiton⟩ **3 :** the distance from the level of the top line of a full text page to the first line of sunk matter **4 :** SHRINKAGE

sinkapace *n* [by alter.] *obs* **:** CINQUEPACE

sinkbox \'=,=\ *or* **sinkboat** \'=,=\ *n* [[2]*sink* + *box* or *boat*] **:** a device used in hunting wild fowl consisting of a raft or broad low float having a rectangular depression in which a hunter may conceal himself — called also *battery*

sink·er \'siŋkə(r)\ n -s [[1]*sink* + *-er*] **1 :** one that sinks: as **a** (1) **:** one who sinks mine shafts and puts in supporting timber or concrete (2) **:** SINKER DRILL (3) **:** SINKING PUMP **b :** any of several devices in knitting machines for depressing the loops upon or between the needles **c** (1) **:** a weight (as a piece of lead or a stone) that is used to sink a fishline or sounding line below the surface or to the bottom (2) **:** a large weight of metal, concrete, or other material for sinking or holding in position the mooring line of a ship, mine, buoy, or other floating object **2** *slang* **a :** base coin **b :** a silver dollar **3 a :** doughy muffin; *also* **:** DOUGHNUT **4 a :** HAUSTORIUM **b :** DROPPER **3 5 :** a slender wire nail **:** COOLER NAIL **6 a :** a ball pitched in baseball that sinks or drops when it reaches the batter **:** DROP 2a(3) **b :** a fly ball that sinks rapidly as it approaches a fielder **7 :** DEADHEAD **2 8 :** a small square or rectangle in a woven design that usu. indicates where the warp passes under the filling — compare RISER 8

sinker bar *n* **:** a short bar or stem placed above the drill jars to give force to the upward jar in well drilling with cable tools

sinker drill *n* **:** a rock drill of the jackhammer type commonly used in shaft sinking — called also *sinker*

sink·er·less \'==ləs\ *adj* **:** having no sinker

sinker wood *n* **:** lumber sawed from deadheads or other heavy wet logs

sinkfield \'=,=\ *n* [by folk etymology] **:** CINQUEFOIL 1

sinkhead \'=,=\ *or* **sinking head** *n* **:** FEEDHEAD

sinkhole \'=,=\ *n* [ME *sinke holl*, fr. *sinke* sink + *holl* hole] **1 a :** a hollow place or depression where drainage or waste collects or is deposited **:** CESSPOOL **b :** the outlet or drain of a sink **2 :** a place or center for the gathering, accumulation, or concentration of undesirable or evil things ⟨during the thirties it was a ~ of depression and unemployment —J.V.Kelleher⟩ ⟨surroundings he considered the ~ of culture —Harry Hansen⟩ ⟨a wild and pagan ~ —Harrison Smith⟩ ⟨that infamous ~ of fever and death —*Dial*⟩ **3 :** SINK 5 **4 :** an unprofitable enterprise in which money is repeatedly sunk

sinking *pres part of* SINK

sinking fund *n* **:** a fund set up and accumulated by usu. regular payments or interest-earning deposits for paying off the principal of a debt when it falls due — compare AMORTIZATION

sinking-fund bond *n* **:** a bond issued with a provision that a specified amount or percentage of the issuer's income will be paid annually into a sinking fund set up to retire the bond issue

sinking pump *n* **:** a pump esp. designed for use in shaft sinking — called also *sinker*

sinking speed *n* **:** the rate of vertical descent of an airplane in a steady glide

sinking spell *n* **:** a short-lived decline in prices ⟨stocks suffered a *sinking spell*⟩

sin·ki·use \siŋ'kī(,)(y)üs\ *n, pl* **sinkiuse** *or* **sinkiuses** *usu cap* **:** COLUMBIA

sinks *pres 3d sing of* SINK, *pl of* SINK

sin·ky·one \'siŋke,ōn\ *n, pl* **sinkyone** *or* **sinkyones** *usu cap* **1 :** an Athapaskan people of northwestern California **2 :** a member of the Sinkyone people

sin·less \'sinləs\ *adj* [ME *sinnelesse*, fr. OE *synlēas*, fr. *syn* sin + *-lēas* -less — more at SIN] **:** free from sin **:** IMPECCABLE, HOLY — **sin·less·ly** *adv* — **sin·less·ness** *n* -ES

sin money *n* [trans. of LL *pecunia pro peccatis*, trans. of Heb *keseph hakippūrīm*] **:** money offered in expiation of sin

sinned *past of* SIN

sin·ner \'sinə(r)\ n -s [ME, fr. *sinne* sin + *-er* — more at SIN] **1 a :** one that sins; *esp* **:** one that sins without repenting **b :** a persistent and incorrigible transgressor **:** one condemned by the law of God **2 a :** OFFENDER, REPROBATE, SCAMP **b** *chiefly dial* **:** FELLOW, PERSON

sinnet *var of* SENNIT

sinn fein·ism \¦shin'fā,nizəm\ n -s *usu cap S&F* [*Sinn Fein*, national Irish society founded about 1905 (fr. IrGael *sinn féin* we ourselves) + E *-ism*] **1 :** the doctrines, policies, or practices of Sinn Fein **2 :** a movement based on the doctrines of Sinn Fein

sinning *pres part of* SIN

sin·nin·gia \sə'ninjēə\ *n, cap* [NL, fr. Wilhelm *Sinning* †1874 Ger. horticulturist + NL *-ia*] **:** a genus of Brazilian tuberous herbs (family Gesneriaceae) having large petioled leaves and large flowers with a turbinate calyx and irregular bell-shaped 5-lobed corolla — see GLOXINIA 2

sin·ning·ly *adv* **:** in a sinning manner

sin·ning·ness *n* -ES **:** a tendency to sin

[1]sino- *comb form, usu cap* [F, fr. LL *Sinae* — more at SINOLOGUE] **1 :** Chinese ⟨*Sino*gram⟩ **2 :** Chinese and ⟨*Sino*-American⟩ ⟨*Sino*-Japanese⟩ — compare [1]CHINO-

[2]sino- *or* **sinu-** *comb form* [NL *sinus*] **1 :** relating to the sinus and ⟨*sino*respiratory⟩ **2 :** relating to the sinus venosus and ⟨*sinu*ventricular⟩

si·no·atrial \¦sī(,)nō+\ *also* **si·nu·atrial** \¦sī(,)n(y)ü+\ *adj* [[2]*sino-* + *atrial*] **1 :** of or relating to the sinus venosus and the right auricle of the heart **2 :** of, involving, or being the sinoatrial node

sinoatrial node *n* **:** a small mass of tissue made up of Purkinje fibers, ganglion cells, and nerve fibers, embedded in the musculature of the right auricle of higher vertebrates, representing the remains of the sinus venosus of lower forms, serving as a pacemaker to the heart, and transmitting the impulse to beat by way of the Purkinje's network to the auricles, the atrioventricular node and bundles, and the ventricles — called also *sinus node*

si·no·auricular \"+\ *or* **si·nu·auricular** \"+\ *adj* [[2]*sino-* + *auricular*] **:** SINOATRIAL

sin offering *n* [prob. trans. of G *sündopfer*, trans. of Heb *ḥaṭṭā'th*] **:** a sacrifice for sin **:** something offered as an expiation for sin; *specif* **:** an animal sacrifice in ancient Jewish religious ceremony in which the blood is smeared on the altar, the choice and fat parts are burned there, and the remainder is burned outside the sanctuary

sino·gram \'sīnō,gram *sometimes* 'sinō *or* 'sēnō-\ *n, usu cap* [[1]*sino-* + *-gram*] **:** a Chinese phonogram or other written character

sino–japanese \¦sī(,)nō *sometimes* ¦si(,)nō *or* ¦sē(,)nō+\ *n, cap S&J* **:** the Japanese language as strongly affected by Chinese

sino·log·i·cal \¦==¦läjəkəl\ *also* **sino·log·ic** \-jik\ *adj, sometimes cap* [*sinological* fr. *sinologue* + *-ical*; *sinologic* prob. fr. F *sinologique*, fr. *sinologie* + *-ique* -ic] **:** of, relating to, or characteristic of the Chinese culture, language, or literature

si·nol·o·gist \sī'näləjəst, sə'-, sē'n-\ *n* -s *sometimes cap* [prob. fr. F *sinologie* sinology + E *-ist*] **:** SINOLOGUE

sino·logue *also* **sino·log** \'sīnə,lȯg, 'sin-, 'sēn- *also* -läg\ *n* -s [F *sinologue*, fr. *sino-* (fr. LL *Sinae*, pl., Chinese, fr. Gk *Sinai*, fr. Ar *Sīn* China, prob. fr. Chin *Ch'in²*, feudal state in China during 897–221 B.C. that established the Ch'in dynasty in the 3d century B.C.) + *-logue*] **:** a specialist in sinology

si·nol·o·gy \sī'näləjē, sə'n-, -ji\ *n* -ES *sometimes cap* [prob. fr. F *sinologie*, fr. *sino-* [1]sino- + *-logie* -logy] **:** the study of the Chinese esp. with reference to their language, literature, history, and culture

si·nom·e·nine \sə'nämə,nēn, -,nən\ *n* -s [*sinomen-* (fr. NL *Sinomenium*, genus name of the woody vine *Sinomenium acutum*) + *-ine*] **:** a crystalline alkaloid $C_{19}H_{23}NO_4$ structurally related to thebaine but obtained from various eastern Asiatic plants (as *Sinomenium acutum*) of the family Menispermaceae

si·non \'sī,nän\ *n* -s *usu cap* [fr. *Sinon*, a relative of Odysseus described in the *Aeneid* (epic poem by Vergil †19 B.C. Roman poet) as the Greek who by a false tale induced the Trojans to drag the wooden horse into Troy, fr. L, fr. Gk *Sinōn*] **:** one who deceives and betrays by false tales **:** one guilty of perfidy

sin·o·per \'sinəpə(r)\ *n* -s [MF *sinopre*, *sinople* sinople] *archaic* **:** SINOPLE

[1]sino·phile \'sīnə,fīl, 'sin-, 'sēn- *also* **sino·phil** \-,fil\ *adj, often cap* [[1]*sino-* + *-phile*, *-phil*] **:** approving or favoring the Chinese or their policy or characteristics

[2]sinophile \"\ *also* **sinophil** \"\ *n* -s *sometimes cap* **:** one partial to or esp. fond of Chinese culture or characteristics

si·no·pia \sə'nōpēə\ *or* **si·no·pis** \-pəs\ *n, pl* **sinopias** *or* **sinopises** [*sinopia* fr. NL, fr. L *sinopis* sinopite + *-ia*; *sinopis* fr. NL, fr. L, sinopite] **:** a red pigment made from sinopite

si·nop·ic \(')sī¦näpik, sə'n-, -näp-\ *adj, usu cap* [L *sinopicus*, fr. Gk *sinōpikos*, fr. *Sinōpē* Sinope + Gk *-ikos* -ic] **1 :** of, relating to, or characteristic of the ancient city of Sinope in Asia Minor **2 :** of, relating to, or characteristic of the natives or inhabitants of Sinope

sin·o·pite \'sinə,pīt\ *n* -s [G *sinopit*, fr. L *sinopis* + G *-it* -ite] **:** a brick-red ferruginous clay used by the ancients as a paint

sin·o·ple \'sinəpəl\ *n* -s [MF *sinople*, *sinopre*, fr. L *sinopis* sinopite, fr. Gk *sinōpis*, fr. *Sinōpē* Sinope, ancient seaport on the Black sea in Asia Minor] **:** ferruginous quartz that is blood-red or brownish red sometimes with a tinge of yellow

si·no·respiratory \¦sī(,)nō+\ *adj* [[2]*sino-* + *respiratory*] **:** of, relating to, or affecting both the sinuses and the respiratory tract ⟨~ symptoms⟩

sino–tibetan \¦sī(,)nō *sometimes* ¦si(,)nō *or* ¦sē(,)nō+\ *n, cap S&T* **:** a language group comprising Tibeto-Burman and Chinese and sometimes considered to include Thai

si·no·ventricular \¦sī(,)nō+\ *also* **si·nu·ventricular** \¦sī(,)n(y)ü+\ *adj* [[2]*sino-* + *ventricular*] **1 :** of or relating to the sinus venosus and the ventricles of the heart **2 :** of, involving, or being the sinoventricular system

sinoventricular system *n* **:** the system of modified muscle fibers that regulates the beat of the heart — compare PURKINJE'S NETWORK, SINOATRIAL NODE

sins *pl of* SIN, *pres 3d sing of* SIN

sins·ring \'sins,riŋ\ *n* -s [Jav] **:** TREE SHREW

sin·syne \'sin,sīn\ *adv* [ME (Sc) *sensyne*, fr. (Sc) *sen*, prep., from, since (contr. of *sethen*, *sithen*, adv. & prep., since) + (Sc) *syne*, adv., since — more at SINCE, SYNE] *chiefly Scot* **:** since that time **:** AGO

[1]sin·ter \'sintə(r)\ *n* -s [G, fr. OHG *sintar* dross, slag — more at CINDER] **1 :** a deposit formed by the evaporation of spring or lake water — see SILICEOUS SINTER; compare GEYSERITE, TRAVERTINE **2 :** the product of sintering

[2]sinter \"\ *vb* **sintered**; **sintered**; **sintering** \-ntəriŋ, -n·triŋ\ **sinters** *vt* **:** to cause to become a coherent mass by heating without melting — used of powdered or earthy substances ~ *vi* **:** to become a coherent mass from heating without melting — **sin·ter·er** \-ntərə(r)\ *n* -s

sinu- — see SINO-

[1]sin·u·ate \'sinyəwət, -,wāt, *usu* -d·+V\ *adj* [L *sinuatus*, past part. of *sinuare* to curve, bend, fr. *sinus* curve, fold — more at SINUS] **1 :** SINUOUS, WAVY, TORTUOUS **2 :** having the margin wavy with strong indentations ⟨~ leaves⟩ — compare UNDULATE — **sin·u·ate·ly** *adv*

[2]sinuate \-,wāt, *usu* -ād·+V\ *vi* -ED/-ING/-s [L *sinuatus*, past part. of *sinuare* to curve, bend] **:** to bend or curve in and out **:** be sinuous **:** WIND ⟨saw the river *sinuating* toward the sea —Anais Nin⟩

sin·u·at·ed \'sinyə¦wād·əd, -ātəd\ *adj* [L *sinuatus* (past part.) + E *-ed*] **:** SINUATE

sinuate–dentate \¦==(,)=¦=,=\ *adj* **:** varying between sinuate and dentate

sin·u·a·tion \,sinyə'wāshən\ *n* -s [LL *sinuation-*, *sinuatio*, fr. L *sinuatus* (past part. of *sinuare* to curve, bend) + *-ion-*, *-io* -ion] **:** a winding or bending in and out

sinuatrial *var of* SINOATRIAL

sinuauricular *var of* SINOAURICULAR

sin·u·ose \'sinyə,wōs\ *adj* [L *sinuosus*] **:** SINUOUS — **sin·u·ose·ly** *adv*

sin·u·os·i·ty \,==¦wäsəd·ē, -sətē, -i\ *n* -ES [ML *sinuositas*, fr. L *sinuosus* sinuous + *-itas* -ity] **1 :** the quality or state of being sinuous ⟨the flexible ~ of a serpent —J.C.Powys⟩ **2 :** that which is sinuous: as **a :** BEND, WINDING, CURVE ⟨the *sinuosities* of the canyon —E.L.Ullman⟩ **b :** INTRICACY ⟨the *sinuosities* of a murder-mystery plot⟩ **c :** sinuous movement ⟨the dancer's *sinuosities*⟩

sin·u·ous \'sinyəwəs\ *adj* [L *sinuosus*, fr. *sinus* curve, fold + *-osus* -ose] **1 a :** bending in and out **:** of a serpentine or wavy form **:** WINDING ⟨the lava cascade glows as a ~ ribbon —*Endeavour*⟩ ⟨great ~ vines —Bill Beatty⟩ **b :** marked by strong lithe movements ⟨a ~ grace of movement —Francis King⟩ **2 a :** INTRICATE, COMPLEX ⟨a ~ system of canals —W.E. Rudolph⟩ **b :** deviating esp. morally ⟨~ arguments⟩ **3 :** SINUATE — **sin·u·ous·ly** *adv* — **sin·u·ous·ness** *n* -ES

si·nus \'sīnəs\ *n* -ES [NL, fr. L, curve, fold, hollow, bay; prob. akin to Alb *gjiri* bosom, lap, Serb *zaošijati* to bend] **:** CAVITY, HOLLOW, RECESS: as **a :** a narrow elongated cavity or tract which extends from a focus of suppuration or other inflammatory softening to a free surface and through which pus discharges ⟨a tuberculous ~ leading to the skin surface from a tuberculous bone or abscess⟩ — compare FISTULA **2 b :** a cavity, recess, or depression that forms part of an animal body: (1) **:** a cavity in the substance of a bone of the skull that usu. communicates with the nostrils and contains air ⟨the frontal ~⟩ (2) **:** one of the broad channels the outer coats of which are formed by the dura mater and which conduct blood from the brain (3) **:** one of the spaces among the muscles and viscera of various invertebrates through which blood returns to the heart (4) **:** a dilatation in a canal or vessel (as at the commencement of the internal jugular vein) (5) **:** PALLIAL SINUS (6) **:** a moderately deep indentation in the outer lip of the aperture of a univalve shell (as of a member of the genus *Scissurella*) that is progressively filled in as the shell grows and forms a distinct band **c** (1) *archaic* **:** a hole in the earth (2) **:** a bay of the sea ⟨the deep ~ of the Norwegian trench —A.H.W. Robinson⟩ **d :** a cleft or indentation between adjoining lobes (as of a leaf or corolla) **e :** the folds of the drapery of a toga covering the left arm and serving as a pocket

sinus gland *n* **:** a small glandular mass in the eyestalk of a crustacean having an endocrine function and being in some respects analogous to the neurohypophysis of the vertebrates

si·nus·i·tis \,sīnə'sīd·əs, -ītəs\ *n* -ES [NL, fr. *sinus* + *-itis*] **:** inflammation of a sinus

sinus node *n* **:** SINOATRIAL NODE

sinus of mor·ga·gni \-mȯr'gänyē\ *usu cap M* [after Giovanni B. *Morgagni* †1771 Ital. anatomist] **:** a space at the upper back part of each side of the pharynx where the walls are deficient in muscular fibers and closed by the aponeurosis only

sinus of val·sal·va \-väl'sälvə\ *usu cap V* [after Antonio M. *Valsalva* †1723 Ital. anatomist] **:** any one of the pouches of the aorta and pulmonary artery which are located behind the flaps of the semilunar valves and into which the blood in its regurgitation toward the heart enters and thereby closes the valves

si·nus·oid \'sīnə,sȯid\ *n* -s [ISV *sinus* + *-oid*] **1 :** the curve whose ordinates are proportional to the sines of the abscissas with the equation $y = a \sin x$ **2 :** a minute endothelium-lined space or passage for blood in the tissues of an organ (as the liver)

si·nus·oi·dal \¦==¦sȯid°l\ *adj* [ISV *sinusoid* + *-al*; orig. formed in F] **:** of or relating to a sinusoid — **si·nus·oi·dal·ly** \-d°lē, -d°li\ *adv*

sinusoidal projection *n* **:** an equal-area map projection capable of showing the entire surface of the earth with all parallels as straight lines evenly spaced, the central meridian as one half the length of the equator, and all other meridians as curved lines

sinus rhom·boi·da·lis \-,räm,bȯi'dāləs\ *n* [NL, rhomboidal sinus] **:** the posterior expanded and for a long time incompletely closed part of the medullary canal of vertebrate embryos; *also* **:** an expansion of the central canal in the sacral region derived from it

sinus ve·no·sus \-və'nōsəs\ *n* [NL, venous sinus] **1 :** a distinct chamber of the heart formed by the union of the large systemic veins and opening into the auricle in lower vertebrates and the embryos of higher forms **2 :** the main cavity of either auricle esp. of the human heart **3 :** the part of the right auricle between the openings of the venae cavae

sinuventricular *var of* SINOVENTRICULAR

sin·ward \'sinwə(r)d\ *adv* **:** toward sin

sion *usu cap, var of* ZION

siou·an \'süən\ *n, pl* **siouan** *or* **siouans** *usu cap* [*Sioux* + *-an*] **1 :** a language stock of central and eastern No. America including Crow, Hidatsa, Dakota, Chiwere, Winnebago, Dhegiha, Ofo, Biloxi, Tutelo, Catawba **2 a :** a group of peoples speaking Siouan languages — called also *Sioux* **b :** a member of such peoples — called also *Sioux*

sioux \'sü\ *n, pl* **sioux** *usu cap* [F, Dakota, short for *Nadowessioux*, fr. Ojibwa *Nadoweisiw*, lit., little snake, enemy] **1 :** DAKOTA **2 :** SIOUAN

[1]sip \'sip\ *vb* **sipped**; **sipped**; **sipping**; **sips** [ME *sippen*; akin to LG *sippen* to sip] *vi* **:** to drink a small quantity esp. repeatedly with the lips **:** take a sip of something ⟨*sipped* delicately at the bottle like effete bees —John Steinbeck⟩ ⟨*sipped* at the fragrant steaming liquid —*Chatelaine*⟩ ⟨listeners understood, after one fleeting hearing, what the composer intended for slow *sipping* —P.H.Lang⟩ ~ *vt* **1 :** to take into the mouth in small drafts ⟨~ tea⟩ **:** drink in small quantities ⟨she has *sipped* excitement experimentally, the way people ~ a drink —Sally Benson⟩ **2 :** to take sips from ⟨~ a flower⟩ **:** TASTE **3 :** to bring to a specified condition by sipping ⟨*sipped* the glass dry⟩

[2]sip \"\ *n* -s **1 :** the act of sipping **2 :** a small draft taken with the lips **:** a slight taste ⟨a ~ . . . from reservoirs of abstract philosophy —Thomas De Quincey⟩

SIP *abbr* **1** standard inspection procedure **2** step in place

si·pa·pu \'sē,pä(,)pü\ *n* -s [Hopi *sïipaapu*] **:** a hole in the floor of a Pueblo Indian kiva symbolizing the place where the mythical tribal ancestors first emerged from the primordial underworld regions into the earthly realm

[1]sipe \'sēp, *Brit usu* 'sīp\ *vi* [ME *sipen*, fr. OE *sipian* — more at SEEP] *chiefly dial* **:** SEEP, PERCOLATE

[2]sipe \"\ *n* -s [[1]*sipe*; fr. its wiping the road surface dry] **:** any of the small often hook-shaped or bracket-shaped grooves in the tread of an automobile tire for providing extra traction and preventing skids

[1]si·phon *also* **sy·phon** \'sīfən *sometimes* -,fän\ *n* -s [F *siphon*, fr. L *sipho*, *siphon* tube, pipe, siphon, fr. Gk *siphōn*; prob. akin to L *tibia* shinbone] **1 a :** a tube bent to form two branches of unequal effective length by which a liquid can be transferred to a lower level over an intermediate elevation by the pressure of the atmosphere in forcing the liquid up the shorter branch of the tube immersed in it while the excess of weight of the liquid in the longer branch when once filled causes a continuous flow that takes place only when the discharging extremity is lower than the liquid surface and when no part of the tube is higher above that surface than the same liquid will rise by atmospheric pressure **b :** a channel through which water passes as if in a siphon **c :** INVERTED SIPHON **d** *usu* **syphon :** a bottle for holding aerated water that is driven out through a bent tube in its neck by the pressure of the gas when a valve in the tube is opened ⟨a soda water *syphon*⟩ **e :** any of several small reservoirs placed at certain points in a gas main to drain off condensed water **2 a :** either of a pair of posteriorly extending tubes in many bivalve mollusks formed by the coalescence and extension of the edges of the mantle lobes of each side of the body and commonly more or less united externally though their passages are separate: (1) **:** a ventral tube that conducts water to the mouth and gills (2) **:** a dorsal tube that carries away waste water — see CLAM illustration **b :** an anterior channel-shaped prolongation of the mantle in many gastropods serving to conduct water to the gills and often being protected by a grooved extension of the margin of the shell — see SNAIL illustration **c :** the swimming funnel of a cephalopod **d :** the membranous siphuncle of a shelled cephalopod **e :** the sucking proboscis of various arthropods **f :** the cornicle of an aphid **g :** a tubular anal respiratory organ in a bug of the family Nepidae consisting of two grooved filaments **h :** the branchial or atrial orifice in an ascidian esp. when borne on a more or less produced tube

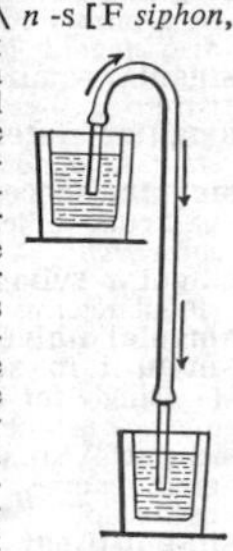
siphon 1a

[2]siphon *also* **syphon** \"\ *vb* **siphoned**; **siphoned**; **siphoning** \-f(ə)niŋ, -,fän-\ **siphons** *vt* **1 :** to convey, draw off, or empty by or as if by a siphon ⟨~ gasoline from a tank⟩ ⟨a dredge ~*ing* up bay bottom —George Bourke⟩ **2 :** to divert for a special purpose **:** WITHDRAW ⟨an expressway to ~ motor traffic from the crowded downtown area —J.H.Fenton⟩ ⟨irresponsible ~*ing* of skilled farm labor by the Selective Service —Louis Bromfield⟩ — often used with *off* ⟨the federal government is ~*ing* off their wealth to support itself —D.L.Hamilton⟩ ⟨heavy taxes ~ off the huge profits —*N.Y. Times*⟩ ~ *vi* **:** to pass or become conveyed by or as if by a siphon ⟨a fine spray of gasoline was still ~*ing* from three of the holes —E.K.Gann⟩

siphon- *or* **siphono-** *also* **siphoni-** *comb form* [NL, fr. Gk *siphōn-*, *siphōno-*, fr. *siphōn*] **1 :** siphon **:** tube **:** pipe ⟨*Siphon*aptera⟩ ⟨*Siphono*phora⟩ ⟨*Siphoni*ata⟩ ⟨*siphon*ate⟩ **2 :** Siphonophora ⟨*siphono*some⟩ ⟨*siphono*zooid⟩

si·phon·aceous \¦sīfə¦nāshəs\ *adj* [*siphon-* + *-aceous*] **1 :** resembling a siphon esp. in forming a continuous protoplasmic column or tube ⟨lower fungi with ~ mycelia⟩ **2 :** having a siphon or group of siphons ⟨~ mollusks⟩

si·phon·age \'sīf(ə)nij\ *n* -s [*siphon* + *-age*] **:** the action or use of a siphon

si·phon·al \-fən°l\ *adj* [*siphon-* + *-al*] **:** of, relating to, or resembling a siphon

si·phon·ales \¦sīfə'nā(,)lēz\ *n pl, cap* [NL, fr. *siphon-* + *-ales*] **:** an order of marine and freshwater green algae (class Chlorophyceae) whose filaments consist essentially of a large multinucleate cell with cross walls rare and usu. only adjacent to reproductive organs — compare CODIUM, SIPHONOCLADALES

si·phon·anth \'sīfə,nan(t)th\ *n* -s [back-formation fr. obs. E *siphonanthous* of or belonging to the siphonophoran suborder Siphonanthae, fr. NL *Siphonanthae* (fr. *siphon-* + *-anthae* — fem. pl. of *-anthus*) + E *-ous*] **:** a feeding zooid of a compound siphonophore

si·phon·aptera \¦sīfən+\ *n pl, cap* [NL, fr. *siphon-* + *Aptera*; fr. the piercing and sucking mouthparts] **:** an order of insects consisting of the fleas — **si·phon·apterous** \"+\ *adj*

si·phon·ap·ter·ol·o·gy \ˌsīfəˌnaptəˈräləjē\ *n* -ES [NL *Siphonaptera* + E *-logy*] **:** a branch of entomology concerned with the fleas

si·pho·nar·ia \ˌsīfəˈna(a)rēə\ *n, cap* [NL, fr. *siphon-* + *-aria*] **:** the type genus of Siphonariidae

si·pho·na·ri·idae \ˌsīfənəˈrīəˌdē\ *n pl, cap* [NL, fr. *Siphonaria*, type genus + *-idae*] **:** a family of littoral gastropod mollusks (order Opisthobranchia) that cling to rocks along seacoasts, resemble limpets, and have both gills and a pulmonary sac

si·pho·na·ta \ˌsīfəˈnādə, -nädə\ *n pl, cap* [NL, fr. *siphon-* + *-ata*] *in some classifications* **:** a division formerly ranked as a suborder of bivalve mollusks including all having siphons

si·phon·ate \ˈsīfənət, -ˌnāt\ *adj* [*siphon-* + *-ate*] **:** having a siphon ⟨the aperture of the shell is said to be entire or ∼ —Nellie Eales⟩

siphon barometer *n* **:** a J-shaped mercury barometer having the longer leg closed at the top and the other exposed to the air

si·pho·ne·ae \sīˈfōnēˌē\ *n pl, cap* [NL, fr. fem. pl. of *siphoneus* siphoneous] *in some classifications* **:** a class of algae approximately equivalent to the Siphonales

siphoned *past of* SIPHON

si·pho·ne·ous \(ˈ)sīˈfōnēəs\ *adj* [NL *siphoneus*, fr. *siphon-* + L *-eus* -eous] **:** SIPHONACEOUS

si·phon·et \ˌsīfəˈnet\ *n* -S [*siphon-* + *-et*] **:** a honey tube of an aphid

siphoni- — see SIPHON-

si·pho·ni·a·ta \(ˌ)sīˌfōnēˈādə, -ˈädə\ [NL, fr. *siphon-* + *-ata*] *syn of* SIPHONATA

si·phon·ic \(ˈ)sīˈfänik\ *adj* [*siphon-* + *-ic*] **1 :** of or relating to a siphon **2 :** characterized by siphonage

si·pho·nif·era \ˌsīfəˈnif(ə)rə\ [NL, fr. neut. pl. of *siphonifer* one of the Siphonifera, fr. *siphon-* + *-fer*] *syn of* TETRABRANCHIA

siphoning *pres part of* SIPHON

si·pho·ni·um \sīˈfōnēəm\ *n, pl* **sipho·nia** \-ēə\ [NL, fr. Gk *siphōnion*, dim. of *siphōn* tube, siphon — more at SIPHON] **:** a bony tube in some birds connecting the tympanum with the air chambers of the articular piece of the mandible

si·phon·less \ˈsīfənləs\ *adj* [*siphon-* + *-less*] **:** having no siphon

siphono- — see SIPHON-

si·pho·no·branchiata \ˌsīfə(ˌ)nō+\ *n pl, cap* [NL, fr. *siphon-* + *branchiata*] *in former classifications* **:** a group of gastropods having the margin of the mantle produced into a siphon — **si·pho·no·branchiate** \"+\ *adj or n*

si·pho·noc·la·da·les \ˌsīfəˌnäkləˈdā(ˌ)lēz\ *n pl, cap* [NL, fr. *Siphonocladus*, type genus (fr. *siphon-* + Gk *klados* branch, sprout) + *-ales* — more at GLADIATOR] **:** an order of green algae (class Chlorophyceae) originally including all multinucleate members of the class capable of vegetative division but now usu. restricted to those that are apparently derived from the Siphonales and are nonseptate when young (as in the families Valoniaceae and Dasycladaceae)

si·pho·no·cla·di·a·les \ˌsīfə(ˌ)nōˌklādēˈā(ˌ)lēz\ [NL] *syn of* SIPHONOCLADALES

si·pho·nog·a·ma \ˌsīfəˈnägəmə\ [NL, fr. *siphon-* + Gk *gamos* marriage — more at BIGAMY] *syn of* SPERMATOPHYTA

si·pho·nog·a·mous \ˌsīfəˈnägəməs\ *adj* [*siphon-* + *-gamous*] **:** accomplishing fertilization by means of a pollen tube ⟨most seed plants are ∼⟩ — **si·pho·nog·a·my** \ˌ≈≈ˈ≈≈mē\ *n* -ES

si·phono·glyph \sīˈfänəˌglif, ˈsīfənō,g-\ *also* **si·pho·nog·ly·phe** \ˌsīfəˈnägləˌ(ˌ)fē\ *n* -S [*siphon-* + Gk *glyphē* carved work — more at GLYPH] **:** a special groove leading down into the gullet from a corner of the mouth in many anthozoans

si·pho·noph·o·ra \ˌsīfəˈnäfərə\ *n pl, cap* [NL, fr. *siphon-* + *-phora*; prob. fr. the hollow float] **:** an order of Hydrozoa consisting of various free-swimming or floating pelagic mostly delicate transparent and often showily colored forms that are usu. regarded as compound animals composed of zooids modified to perform various functions for the colony (as feeding, defense, locomotion), that sometimes have two or more zooids in the form of a bell which by their contractions cause the colony to swim, and that often have a hollow float which keeps the colony afloat — compare DIPHYES, PORPITA, PORTUGUESE MAN-OF-WAR, VELELLA — **si·pho·noph·o·ran** \ˌ≈≈ˈ≈≈rən\ *adj or n* — **si·phono·phore** \sīˈfänəˌfō(ə)r, ˈsīfənə,f-\ *n* -S — **si·pho·noph·o·rous** \ˌsīfəˈnäfərəs\ *adj*

si·phono·plax \sīˈfänəˌplaks, ˈsīfənō,p-\ *n* -ES [NL, fr. *siphon-* + Gk *plax* flat surface, tablet — more at PLEASE] **:** one of the calcareous plates that protect the siphon of various boring mollusks

si·pho·no·rhi·nal \ˌsīfənōˈrīnᵊl\ *or* **si·phono·rhine** \sīˈfänəˌrīn, ˈsīfənō,r-\ *adj* [*siphon-* + *rhinal* or *-rhine*] **:** SIPHORHINAL

si·phono·some \sīˈfänəˌsōm, ˈsīfənə,s-\ *n* -S [*siphon-* + *-some*] **:** the part of the stock of a siphonophore bearing the nutritive and reproductive zooids

si·phono·stele \sīˈfänəˌstēl, ˈsīfənō,s- *also* ˌsīfənōˈstēlē\ *n* [*siphon-* + *stele*] **:** a stele consisting of vascular tissue surrounding a central core of pith parenchyma — compare PROTOSTELE — **si·phono·ste·lic** \ˌsīfənōˈstēlik, sīˌfänə's-\ *adj* — **si·phono·ste·ly** \ˈsīfənōˌstēlē, sīˈfänə,s-\ *n* -ES

si·pho·no·sto·ma·ta \ˌsīfənōˈstōmədə\ *n pl, cap* [NL, fr. *siphon-* + *stomata*] **1** *in some classifications* **:** a tribe of parasitic copepod crustaceans including many parasites of fishes (as the lernaeans) that have a mouth adapted to suck blood **2** *in former classifications* **:** an artificial group of marine snails possessing a canal for the passage of the siphon at the base of the aperture — **si·phono·stome** \sīˈfänəˌstōm, ˈsīfən-\ *n* -S

si·pho·no·stoma·tous \ˌsīfənōˈstōmədəs, -ˈtäm-\ *adj* [*siphon-* + *-stomatous*] **1 :** having the front edge of the aperture of the shell prolonged in the shape of a channel for the protection of the siphon — used of various marine snails **2 :** having a tubular mouth **3** [NL *Siphonostomata* + E *-ous*] **:** of or relating to the Siphonostomata

si·pho·no·zooid \ˌsīfənə+\ *n* [*siphon-* + *zooid*] **:** one of various degenerate zooids of some alcyonarians supposed to serve to regulate the water supply of the colony

siphon recorder *n* **:** a sensitive recorder which is used in submarine telegraphy and the record of which is an irregular line made by ink discharged from a small siphon

siphons *pl of* SIPHON, *pres 3d sing of* SIPHON

siphon spillway *n* **:** a spillway that siphons water from a reservoir when a predetermined head is reached

si·phon·u·la \sīˈfänyələ\ *n, pl* **siphonu·lae** \-ˌlē, -ˌlī\ [NL, fr. *siphon-* + *-ula*] **:** a bilaterally symmetrical larva of various siphonophores

si·pho·rhi·nal \ˌsīfəˈrīnᵊl\ *also* **si·pho·rhin·i·an** \-rinēən\ *adj* [L *sipho* siphon + E *rhinal* or *-rhinian* (fr. *-rhine* + *-ian*)] **:** having tubular nostrils ⟨petrels are ∼⟩

si·pho·some \ˈsīfəˌsōm\ *n* -S [L *sipho* siphon + E *-some*] **:** SIPHONOSOME

siphrei torah *pl of* SEPHER TORAH

si·phun·cle \ˈsīˌfəŋkəl\ *n* -S [NL *siphunculus*, fr. L, little pipe, dim. of *sipho*, *siphon* siphon — more at SIPHON] **1 a :** a membranous tubular extension of the mantle which runs through the partitions of the chambers to the apex of a shelled cephalopod **:** SIPHON **b :** the shelly structures that are usu. funnel-shaped or tubular processes of the septa and that ensheathe and support the cephalopod siphuncle **2 :** a cornicle of an aphid

si·phun·cled \-ld\ *adj* [*siphuncle* + *-ed*] **:** SIPHUNCULATE

si·phun·cu·lar \(ˈ)sīˈfəŋkyələ(r)\ *adj* [NL *siphunculus* + E *-ar*] **:** of, relating to, or of the nature of a siphuncle

si·phun·cu·la·ta \(ˌ)sīˌfəŋkyəˈlādə, -ˈlädə\ *n pl, cap* [NL, fr. *siphunculus* siphuncle + *-ata*] *syn of* ANOPLURA

si·phun·cu·late \(ˈ)sīˈfəŋkyələt\ *or* **si·phun·cu·lat·ed** \-ˌlādəd\ *adj* [NL *siphunculus* + E *-ate* or *-ated* (fr. *-ate* + *-ed*)] **:** having a siphuncle

sip·id \ˈsipəd\ *adj* [back-formation fr. ¹*insipid*] **:** SAPID — **si·pid·i·ty** \səˈpidəd·ē\ *n* -ES

si·po \ˈsē(ˌ)pō\ *also* **sipo mahogany** *n* -S [*sipo* native name in the Cameroons] **:** a very large African mahogany (*Entandrophragma utile*) that occurs chiefly in the Cameroons and Ivory Coast and that yields an attractively banded moderately hard and heavy light to dark red or reddish brown scented wood which is sometimes exported in quantity

sipped *past of* SIP

sip·per \ˈsipə(r)\ *n* -S [¹*sip* + *-er*] **1 :** one that sips **2 :** BIBBER, TOPER **3** [fr. *Sipper*, a trademark] **:** a device (as a straw or a paper or plastic cylinder) adapted for sipping liquid

sip·pet \ˈsipət\ *n* -S [*sip* (alter. — influenced by ¹*sip* — of ¹*sop*) + *-et*] **1 :** a small bit or piece of toast soaked in milk or broth **:** a small piece of toasted or fried bread for garnishing **2 :** a small piece **:** tiny bit **:** FRAGMENT

sipping *pres part of* SIP

sip·pio \ˈsipēˌō\ *n* -S [origin unknown] **:** a game of the bagatelle kind played with eight object balls and a cue ball on a table having fifteen numbered holes into which the balls are driven

sip·ple \ˈsipəl\ *vb* [¹*sip* + *-le*] *Scot* **:** TIPPLE

sip·py diet \ˈsipē-\ *or* **sippy regimen** *n, usu cap S* [after Bertram W. *Sippy* †1924 Am. physician] **:** a bland diet for the treatment of peptic ulcer consisting mainly of measured amounts of milk and cream, farina, and egg taken at regular hourly intervals for a specified period of time

sips *pres 3d sing of* SIP, *pl of* SIP

si·pun·cu·la·cea \(ˌ)sīˌpəŋkyəˈlāshēə\ [NL, fr. *Sipunculus*, genus of marine worms + *-acea*] *syn of* SIPUNCULOIDEA

¹**si·pun·cu·lid** \(ˈ)sīˈpəŋkyələd\ *or* **si·pun·cu·loid** \-ˌlȯid\ *adj* [*sipunculid* fr. NL *Sipunculida*; *sipunculoid* fr. NL *Sipunculoidea*] **:** of or relating to the Sipunculoidea

²**sipunculid** \"\ *or* **sipunculoid** \"\ *n* -S **:** a sipunculid worm

si·pun·cu·li·da \ˌsīˌpəŋˈkyüləda\ [NL, fr. *Sipunculus*, genus of marine worms + *-ida*] *syn of* SIPUNCULOIDEA

si·pun·cu·loi·dea \(ˌ)sīˌpəŋkyəˈlȯidēə\ *n pl, cap* [NL, fr. *Sipunculus*, genus of marine worms (fr. L *sipunculus*, *siphunculus* little pipe) + *-oidea* — more at SIPHUNCLE] **1 :** a group of marine worms of obscure systematic position that are commonly classed as a division of Gephyrea and that lack setae and have the mouth at the end of a retractile introvert similar to a proboscis and usu. provided with tentacles and the anus anterior and dorsal **2** *in some classifications* **a :** a group coextensive with Gephyrea **b :** a class or other group comprising Sipunculoidea (sense 1) and Priapuloidea

¹**sir** *R* ˌsər, ˈsər, + *vowel* ˈsər·; *-R* ˌsə, (ˈ)sə, *South often* ˈsə + *suffixal vowel* ˈsər· *also* ˈsər, + *vowel in a following word* ˌsə(r) *or* ˈsər· *or* (ˈ)sə *or* ˈsə *also* (ˈ)sər\ *n* -S *often cap* [ME, fr. *sire* — more at SIRE] **1 a :** a man of rank or position **:** GENTLEMAN, LORD ⟨some ∼ of note —Shak.⟩ ⟨a very . . . petulant hot little ∼ —*Saturday Rev.*⟩ **b :** a man entitled to be addressed as *sir* **:** KNIGHT ⟨the proprietor was now a ∼ —Max Beerbohm⟩ — used as a title of honor before the given name of a knight or baronet ⟨*Sir* Charles⟩ ⟨*Sir* William Smith, Bart.⟩; formerly sometimes used as a title of honor before the names of historical or legendary figures ⟨*Sir* Pandarus of Troy⟩ and as a title of respect before the given name of a priest ⟨*Sir* Robert, the parish priest⟩ ⟨the medieval custom of calling any priest *Sir* John⟩ **2** *obs* — used often disparagingly as a form of address before a common noun (as of rank or occupation) ⟨I am *Sir* Oracle —Shak.⟩ **3** *obs* — used in a British university before the surname of a bachelor of arts **4** — used as a usu. respectful form of address (as to an older person, a superior, or the presiding officer of a legislative assembly) ⟨your car is ready, ∼⟩ ⟨I'd be very grateful, ∼, for your advice⟩ ⟨I rise, ∼, to a point of personal privilege⟩ **5** — used as a conventional form of address in the salutation of a letter ⟨Dear *Sir*⟩

²**sir** *stressed forms at* ¹SIR\ *vt* **sirred; sirred; sirring; sirs :** to address as *sir* ⟨thinks good discipline means *sirring* officers —A.C.Fields⟩

³**sir** *var of* SEER

si·rat \səˈrät\ *n* -S *usu cap* [Ar *ṣirāṭ* road] **:** a bridge in Muslim eschatology which spans the chasm of hell and connects this world with paradise and over which according to tradition only the righteous can cross while the unrighteous fall to a flaming punishment — called also *al sirat*

sir·car *or* **sir·kar** *also* **cir·car** \ˈsərˌkär, (ˌ)sərˈk-\ *n* -S *often cap* [Hindi *sarkār*, fr. Per] **1 :** a district or province in India under the Mogul empire **2** *India* **a :** the supreme authority **:** GOVERNMENT **b :** MASTER — used also as a title of respect **3** *Bengal* **a :** a domestic servant having the functions of a steward **b :** PURCHASING AGENT, ACCOUNTANT

sir·dar \ˈsərˌdär, (ˌ)sərˈd-\ *or* **sar·dar** *or* **ser·dar** *n* -S [Hindi *sardār*, fr. Per] **1 a :** a person of high rank (as an hereditary noble, a chieftain, or a high military officer) in India, Pakistan, or Afghanistan **b :** a commander in chief esp. in Turkey or Egypt **2 :** one holding a position of some responsibility in India: as **a** *or* **sirdar bearer :** a head palanquin bearer **b :** VALET **c :** FOREMAN, STEWARD **d :** TENANT FARMER

¹**sire** \ˈsī(ə)r, -īə\ *n* -S [ME, fr. OF, fr. L *senior* older, elder — more at SENIOR] **1 a :** a male parent **:** FATHER ⟨carried almost as many business burdens as his ∼ —R.J.Purcell⟩ **b** *archaic* **:** male ancestor **:** FOREFATHER ⟨we are wiser than our ∼s —Alfred Tennyson⟩ **c :** one that produces or originates something; *specif* **:** AUTHOR ⟨the ∼ of an immortal strain —P.B.Shelley⟩ **2 a** *archaic* **:** a man of rank, station, or authority; *esp* **:** one who holds the lordship of a domain or realm **:** LORD, MASTER — used formerly as a form of address and as a title (as of the king of France) **b** *obs* **:** an elderly man **:** SENIOR ⟨an aged ∼, all hoary gray —Edmund Spenser⟩ **3 a :** the male parent of an animal and esp. of a domesticated mammal or bird — compare DAM **b :** a stallion having at least one colt who has won a race

²**sire** \"\ *vt* -ED/-ING/-S **1 :** to make oneself the father of **:** FATHER, BEGET, PROCREATE ⟨*sired* seven children —Green Peyton⟩ — used esp. of domestic animals ⟨was mated with 25 ewes and *sired* 18 lambs —*Fla. Agric. Experimental Station Bull.*⟩ **2 a :** to bring into being **:** GENERATE, ORIGINATE ⟨motion picture industry, *sired* and nourished by private enterprise —W.H.Hays⟩ **b :** to be the author of (a literary work) ⟨*sired* another play —E.L.Wallant⟩

si·re·don \sīˈrēˌdän, -ēdᵊn\ *n, cap* [NL, fr. Gk *seirēdōn* siren] *in some classifications* **:** a genus of salamanders comprising members of the genus *Ambystoma* that normally continue as axolotls throughout life

siree *var of* SIRREE

sire index *n* **:** a measure of the prepotency and quality of a sire in terms of the production of his offspring and esp. in respect to characteristics (as egg or milk production) that he cannot himself exhibit — compare PROGENY TEST

sire·less \ˈsī(ə)rləs, -īəl-\ *adj* [¹*sire* + *-less*] **:** FATHERLESS

¹**si·ren** \ˈsīrən *sometimes* ˈsī(ə)rn, *in sense 3* " *or* ÷(ˈ)sīˈrēn\ *n* [ME *serein*, *siren*, fr. MF *sereine* & L *siren*; MF *sereine*, fr. LL *sirena*, fr. L *siren*, fr. Gk *seirēn*, *seirēdōn*] **1** -S *often cap* **a :** one of a group of creatures in Greek mythology having the heads and sometimes the breasts and arms of women but otherwise the forms of birds that were believed to lure mariners to destruction by their singing **b** *obs* **:** MERMAID **2** -S **a :** a woman who sings with bewitching sweetness **:** SONGBIRD **b :** an alluringly beautiful woman ⟨so young and delicious a ∼ —Ben Hecht⟩; *esp* **:** one who is usu. insidiously or deceptively enticing or seductive to men **:** TEMPTRESS, FEMME FATALE ⟨the slinky ∼ of the silent screen⟩ ⟨while constantly emanating sex, she lacked the graceful presence, the subtlety of manner, the mysterious reticence of a real ∼ —Carey McWilliams⟩ **3** -S [F *sirène*, lit., siren (sense 1), fr. MF *sereine*; fr. its property of producing sounds in water] **a :** an apparatus producing musical tones esp. in acoustical studies by the rapid interruption of a current of air, steam, or fluid by a perforated rotating disk **b :** a similar device often electrically operated for producing a penetrating warning sound ⟨fire ∼⟩ ⟨ambulance ∼⟩ ⟨the three-minute warbling sound of the air-raid ∼s —*N.Y. Times*⟩ **4 a** *cap* [NL, fr. L] **:** a genus of elongated amphibians (family Sirenidae) having small forelimbs but lacking hind legs and pelvis and having permanent external gills as well as lungs **b** -S **:** any amphibian of the genus *Siren* or of the family Sirenidae **5** -S **:** SIRENOMELUS **6** -S **:** SEA COW 1

²**si·ren** \ˈsīrən *sometimes* ˈsī(ə)rn\ *adj* **:** of or relating to a siren **:** ENTICING, BEWITCHING, BEGUILING ⟨a ∼ song⟩ ⟨listening intently to the ∼ voice⟩ ⟨the ∼ call of modern materialism —George Thomas⟩

³**siren** *like* ¹SIREN\ *vi* -ED/-ING/-S **:** to proceed with siren sounding to clear the way ⟨fire trucks ∼*ed* to the scene from two miles away —*Time*⟩

si·re·nia \sīˈrēnēə\ *n pl, cap* [NL, fr. L *siren* + NL *-ia*] **:** an order of large aquatic herbivorous mammals including the manatee, dugong, Steller's sea cow, and several fossil forms that have the tail horizontally flattened and expanded into a broad rounded or bilobed fin, the hind limbs rudimentary or wanting and the front ones paddle-shaped, and jaws with horny plates on the front part and usu. numerous flat-crowned molar teeth

¹**si·re·ni·an** \(ˈ)sīˈrēnēən\ *adj* [NL *Sirenia* + E *-an* (adj. suffix)] **:** of or relating to the Sirenia

²**sirenian** \"\ *n* -S [NL *Sirenia* + E *-an* (n. suffix)] **:** a mammal of the order Sirenia

si·ren·ic \(ˈ)sīˈrenik\ *or* **si·ren·i·cal** \-nəkəl\ *adj* [¹*siren* + *-ic* or *-ical*] **:** of, resembling, or suited to a siren **:** MELODIOUS, ALLURING, DECEPTIVE ⟨∼ song⟩ ⟨∼ enchantments⟩ — **si·ren·i·cal·ly** \-nək(ə)lē\ *adv*

si·ren·i·dae \sīˈrenəˌdē\ *n pl, cap* [NL, fr. *Siren*, type genus + *-idae*] **:** a family of eel-shaped amphibians comprising the sirens (genera *Siren* and *Pseudobranchus*) of the southern U. S.

¹**si·ren·oid** \ˈsīrəˌnȯid\ *adj* [NL *Sirenoidei*] **1 :** resembling or related to the Sirenoidei **2** [¹*siren* + *-oid*] **:** of, relating to, or resembling a siren or sirenomelus

²**sirenoid** \"\ *n* -S **1 :** a lungfish of the group Sirenoidei **2 :** SIRENOMELUS

si·ren·oi·dei \ˌsīrəˈnȯidēˌī\ *also* **si·ren·oi·dea** \-ēə\ *n pl, cap* [NL, fr. L *siren* + NL *-oidei*, *-oidea*] *in some classifications* **:** a group of lungfishes containing the genera *Neoceratodus* and *Lepidosiren* and some extinct forms from the Mesozoic

si·re·nom·e·lus \ˌsīrəˈnäməlәs\ *n, pl* **sirenome·li** \-ˌlī\ [NL, fr. *siren* mermaid (fr. L, siren) + *-o-* + *-melus*] **:** a congenital malformation in which the lower limbs are fused

siren song *n* **:** an alluring utterance or appeal; *esp* **:** one that is seductive or deceptive ⟨the *siren song* of the metropolis⟩ ⟨the *siren song* of the advertising man —H.H.Martin⟩ ⟨follow the *siren song* of printing more money —W.M.Martin b.1906⟩

sires *pl of* SIRE, *pres 3d sing of* SIRE

si·rex \ˈsīˌreks\ *n* [NL, irreg. fr. L *siren* — more at SIREN] **1** *cap* **:** the type genus of the family Siricidae including various horntails that are destructive pests of unseasoned lumber from coniferous trees **2** -ES **:** any horntail of the genus *Sirex*

sir galahad *n, usu cap S&G* **:** GALAHAD

sir·gang \ˈsərˌgaŋ\ *n* -S [prob. fr. native name in Ceylon and Sumatra] **:** a predominantly pale green crested cissa (*Kitta chinensis*) that has largely maroon-red wings and black markings from bill to nape, on the wings, and across the tail and that occurs from the Himalayas through southeastern Asia and into the Pacific islands

siri *or* **sir·ih** \ˈsirē\ *n* -S [Malay *sireh*] **:** BETEL

sir·i·an \ˈsirēən\ *adj, usu cap* [*Sirius*, star of the constellation Canis Major that is the brightest in the sky (fr. ME, fr. L, fr. Gk *Seirios*, fr. *seirios* glowing, burning) + E *-an*] **:** of, relating to, or resembling (as in spectrum) the star Sirius

si·ri·a·sis \səˈrīəsəs\ *n, pl* **siria·ses** \-əˌsēz\ [L, fr. Gk *seiriasis*, fr. *seirian* to be hot, be scorching (fr. *seirios* glowing, burning) + *-sis*; akin to Gk *seiein* to shake, quake — more at SEISMIC] **:** SUNSTROKE

¹**si·ric·id** \səˈrisəd, ˈsirəsəd\ *adj* [NL *Siricidae*] **:** of or relating to the Siricidae

²**siricid** \"\ *n* -S **:** a wasp of the family Siricidae

si·ric·i·dae \səˈrisəˌdē\ *n pl, cap* [NL, fr. *Siric-*, *Sirex*, type genus + *-idae*] **:** a family of hymenopterous insects comprising the horntails and having larvae that are wood borers and female adults with a stout hornlike ovipositor for inserting the eggs in wood

siring *pres part of* SIRE

sir·i·o·no \ˌsirēˈō(ˌ)nō\ *or* **sir·i·o·ne** \-ˈ(ˌ)nā\ *n, pl* **siriono** *or* **sirionos** *or* **sirione** *or* **siriones** *usu cap* **1 a :** a Guaranian people of eastern Bolivia **b :** a member of such people **2 :** the language of the Siriono people

si·ris \səˈrēs\ *n* -ES [Hindi *siris*, fr. Skt *śirīṣa*, prob. of Dravidian origin; akin to Tamil *uriñcil*, Kanarese *sirsala*] **:** any of several trees of the genus *Albizzia*: as **a :** LEBBEK **b :** SILK TREE

sirkar *var of* SIRCAR

sir·keer \ˈsərˌki(ə)r, sərˈk-\ *n* -S [perh. fr. Hindi *sarkīr*, fr. *sar* head + *kīr* parrot] **:** a large Indian cuckoo (*Taccocua leschenaultii*)

sir·ki \ˈsirkē, sirˈkē\ *also* **sir·ky** \ˈsirkē\ *n, pl* **sirkis** *or* **sirkies** [Hindi *sirkī*] **1 :** the culms of munj **2 :** a matting or thatch made of the upper part of the flower stalks of munj

sir knight \ˈ≈ˌ≈\ *n* **:** a member of a fraternal society styling itself an order of knighthood (as the Knights Templar)

sir·loin \ˈsərˌlȯin, ˈsə̄l-, ˈsəi,l-\ *n* [alter. (influenced by ¹*sir*) of earlier *surloin*, modif. (influenced by *loin*) of MF *surlonge*, fr. *sur* over, above (fr. L *super*) + *longe*, alter. of *loigne* loin — more at OVER, LOIN] **:** a cut of meat and esp. of beef taken from the hindquarter usu. from between the porterhouse and the round — see BEEF illustration, LAMB illustration

sirmark *var of* SURMARK

sir·mi·an \ˈsərmēən\ *adj, usu cap* [*Sirmium* + E *-an*] **:** of or relating to the city of Sirmium in the eastern and now Yugoslav part of the Roman province of Pannonia; *esp* **:** of or relating to any of four councils held there in the fourth century or to the Arian creeds issued by them

sir·muel·lera \(ˌ)sərˈmyülərə, -mil-\ [NL, after *Sir* Ferdinand von *Müller* †1896 Australian naturalist born in Germany] *syn of* BANKSIA

siro·ba·sid·i·a·ce·ae \ˌsī(-)rōbəˌsidēˈāsēˌē, ˌsī(-\ *n pl, cap* [NL, fr. *Sirobasidium*, type genus (fr. Gk *seira* cord, rope + NL *basidium*) + *-aceae* — more at QUARTZ] **:** a family of jelly fungi (order Tremellales) with the basidia borne in chains

si·roc \ˈsīˌräk, səˈr-\ *n* -S [prob. fr. obs. F *siroch* (now *siroc*, *siroco*), fr. It *sirocco*, *scirocco*] **:** SIROCCO

si·roc·co \səˈrä(ˌ)kō\ *also* **sci·roc·co** \shə-\ *n* -S [It *sirocco*, *scirocco*, fr. Ar *sharq* east] **1 a :** a hot oppressive dust-laden wind from the Libyan deserts that blows on the northern Mediterranean coast chiefly in Italy, Malta, and Sicily **b :** a warm moist oppressive southeast wind in the same regions **2 :** a hot or warm wind of cyclonic origin (as the harmattan of the west coast of Africa, the hot winds of Kansas and Texas, the khamsin of Egypt) blowing from an arid or heated region

s-iron \ˈ≈ˌ≈(≈)\ *n, cap S* **:** an S-shaped iron driven into and across the end of a railroad tie to prevent splitting

si·rop \səˈrō\ *n* -S [F, syrup, fr. MF — more at SYRUP] **:** a syrup of concentrated fruit juice, sugar, and water ⟨a kiosk that sold ices and ∼s —Rumer Godden⟩

sir·rah *also* **sir·ra** \ˈsirə\ *n* -S [alter. of ¹*sir*] *obs* — used as a form of address implying inferiority and often used in anger, contempt, or disrespectful familiarity ⟨go to, ∼! leave your jesting and tell us where he is —Christopher Marlowe⟩

sirred *past of* SIR

sir·ree *also* **sir·ee** \səˈrē, ˌsərˈē *also* sə̄ˈrē\ *n* -S [by alter.] **:** SIR 4 — used as an emphatic form usu. after *yes* or *no* ⟨no, ∼, you'll never see me there⟩

sir-reverence \ˌ≈ˈ≈(≈)≈\ *n* [prob. alter. (influenced by ¹*sir*) of *sa-reverence*, contr. of *save-reverence*, trans. of L *salva reverentia* saving (your) reverence] **1** *obs* — used as an expression of apology before a statement that might be taken as presumptuous or offensive ⟨such a one as a man may not speak of without he say *sir-reverence* —Shak.⟩ — compare ²SAVING 2 **2** *archaic* **a :** human excrement **:** FECES 2 ⟨a pan of *sir-reverence* —Tobias Smollett⟩ **b :** a lump of human excrement ⟨a ponderous *sir-reverence* —J.H.Frere⟩

sirring *pres part of* SIR

sir rog·er de cov·er·ley \-ˌräjə(r)dəˈkəvə(r)lē\ *or* **sir roger** *n, usu cap S&R&C* [*sir roger de coverley* alter. (influenced by *Sir Roger de Coverley*, fictitious country gentleman appearing in many of the *Spectator* papers by Joseph Addison †1719 and Sir Richard Steele †1729 Eng. essayists, fr. *roger of coverley*) of *roger of coverley*, prob. fr. *Roger* (the name) + *of* + *Coverley* (a fictitious place name); *sir roger* short for *sir roger de coverley*] **:** an English country-dance in compound triple measure performed longways by an indefinite number — compare VIRGINIA REEL

sirs *pl of* SIR, *pres 3d sing of* SIR

sir·ua·bal·li \ˌs(h)irəwəˈbalē\ *n* -S [Arawak, fr. *sirua*, a tree of the genus *Nectandra* + *balli* similar] **:** SILVER BALLI

sirup *var of* SYRUP

sir·vente \(ˌ)sərˈvent, sirˈvänt\ *or* **sir·ven·tes** \sərˈventəs\ *also* **sir·vent** \(ˌ)sərˈvent, sirˈvänt\ *n, pl* **sir·ventes** \-t(ə)s\ *also* **sir·vents** \-ts\ [F *sirvente*, fr. Prov *sirventes*, lit., servant's song, fr. *sirvent*, *servent* servant (fr. L *servient-*, *serviens*, pres. part. of *servire* to serve) + *-es* -ese (prob. fr. L *-ensis*) — more at SERVE] **:** a usu. moral or religious song of the Provençal troubadours satirizing social vices

¹sis *pl of* SI

²sis \'sis\ *n* -ES [by shortening] **:** SISTER

-sis \sə̇s\ *n suffix, pl* **-ses** [L, fr. Gk, fem. suffix of action] **1 :** process **:** action **:** -ING ⟨analy*sis*⟩ ⟨peristal*sis*⟩ ⟨ar*sis*⟩ **2 :** diseased state **:** disease produced by ⟨stephanofilaria*sis*⟩

si·sal \'sīsəl, 'sīzəl *also* sə̇'säl *or* 'sēsəl *or* 'sēzəl *or* 'sisəl\ *n* -S [MexSp, fr. *Sisal*, Yucatán, Mexico] **1 a** *also* **sisal hemp :** a strong durable white fiber that is three to five feet long and is used for hard fiber cordage and for binder twine **b :** a West Indian agave (*Agave sisalana*) whose leaves yield sisal for which it is widely cultivated (as in Java, East Africa, the Bahama islands, and Mexico) **2 :** a fiber derived from any of various plants (as henequen, false sisal) related to sisal

si·sa·la·na \,sīsə'lānə, ,sīzə-, ,sēs-, ,sēz-, -lanə, -lānə\ *n* -S [NL (specific epithet of *Agave sisalana*), fr. MexSp *sisal* + NL *-ana* (fr. L, neut. pl. of *-anus* -an)] **:** SISAL 1a

sisal rug *n* **:** a summer rug of sisal yarn

sis·co·wet \'siskə,wet\ *n* -S [CanF *ciscoette*, fr. Ojibway *pemitewiskawet* fish with oily flesh] **:** a large lake trout (*Salvelinus namaycush siscowet*) found in the deeper parts of Lake Superior and some of the other Great Lakes

sisel \'sisəl, 'sēs-\ *n* -S [G *ziesel*, fr. MHG *zisel*, of Slav origin; akin to Czech *sysel* suslik, Pol *susel*, Russ *suslik*] **:** SUSLIK

sis·er·ara \,sisə'ra(a)rə\ *or* **sis·er·ary** \-)rē\ *n, pl* **siseraras** *or* **siseraries** [obs. E *siserari*, *sasarara* certiorari, fr. ME *sesserary*, modif. of L *certiorari* — more at CERTIORARI] **1** *chiefly dial* **:** a severe blow or attack **2** *chiefly dial* **:** a violent scolding — **with a siserary** *adv, chiefly dial* **:** with a vengeance

siser·skite \'sisər,skīt, sə̇'sər-\ *n* -S [G *sisserskit*, fr. *Syssertsk*, Sverdlovsk region, U.S.S.R. + G *-it* -ite] **:** a mineral consisting of a natural alloy of osmium and iridium with the latter ranging from 20 to 50 percent — compare IRIDOSMINE

sish \'sish\ *n* -ES [prob. alter. of *slush*] **:** fine slushy ice **:** new and thin ice

si·si \sə̇'sē\ *n* -S [AmerSp *sesi*] **:** PORKFISH

sisith *var of* ZIZITH

sis·kin \'siskə̇n\ *n* -S [G dial. *sisschen*, dim. of MHG *zīse*, *zīsic* siskin, of Slav origin; akin to Czech *číž*, *čížek* siskin, Pol *czyż*, Russ *chizh*; all of imit. origin] **1 :** a small sharp-billed chiefly greenish and yellowish finch (*Spinus spinus*) of temperate Europe and Asia related to the goldfinch **2 :** any of various small birds resembling the siskin — usu. used in combination; see RED SISKIN

siss \'sis\ *vi* -ED/-ING/-ES [ME *sissen*, *cissen*, of imit. origin] **:** HISS

sis·se·ton \'sisət°n\ *n, pl* **sisseton** *or* **sissetons** *usu cap* [Dakota *sisitoṅwaṅ*, fr. *sisiṅ*, *siṅsiṅ* besmeared, slimy + *toṅwaṅyaṅ* to make a village, dwell at a place] **:** a member of a Dakota people of the northern Mississippi valley

sis·si·fied \'sisə,fīd\ *adj* [¹*sissy* + *-fy* + *-ed*] **:** SISSY

sis·si·ness \'sisēnə̇s, -isin-\ *n* -ES **:** the quality or state of being sissy

sis·sle \'sisəl\ *dial Eng var of* SIZZLE

sis·sonne *or* **sis·sone** \sə̇'sän, -'sȯn, -'sōn\ *n* -S [after François César de Roussy, count of *Sissonne*, 17th cent. Fr. nobleman credited with the invention of the step] **:** a ballet step in which the legs are spread in the air and closed on the descent

sis·soo *also* **sis·su** \'si(,)sü\ *n* -S [Hindi *sīso*, fr. Skt *śiṁśapā*] **1 :** any of several trees of the genus *Dalbergia*; *esp* **:** an East Indian tree (*D. sissoo*) whose leaves are used as fodder **2 :** the dark brown compact and durable timber of the sissoo tree used esp. in shipbuilding and for making railroad ties

¹sis·sy \'sisē, -isi\ *n* -ES [*sis* + *-y*] **1 :** SISTER **2 a :** an effeminate man or boy **b :** a timid or cowardly person ⟨one old lady . . . didn't want to be a ~ —Robert Rice⟩

²sissy \"\ *adj* -ER/-EST **:** of, relating to, or having the characteristics of a sissy ⟨no longer think it ~ to give or carry flowers —*Amer. Quarterly*⟩ ⟨a ~ boy with nastily damp hands and white eyelashes —Jean Stafford⟩

sissy-pants \'==,=\ *or* **sissy-britches** \'==,==\ *n pl but sing or pl in constr* **:** SISSY 2

¹sist \'sist\ *vt* [L *sistere* to cause to stand, stop; akin to L *stare* to stand — more at STAND] **1** *chiefly Scot* **:** to bring into court **:** SUMMON **2** *chiefly Scot* **:** to stay by judicial decree

²sist \"\ *n* -S *chiefly Scot* **:** a stay or suspension of legal proceedings; *also* **:** an order for a stay of proceedings

sist *abbr* sister

sis·ta·ni \sə̇'stänē\ *n, pl* **sistani** *or* **sistanis** *usu cap* **1 :** a people of southwestern Afghanistan **2 :** a member of the Sistani people

sis·ten \'si,sten\ *or* **sistens** \-nz\ *n, pl* **sistens** \-nz\ *or* **sisten·tes** \sə̇'stent·(,)ēz\ [NL *sistent-*, *sistens*, fr. L, pres. part. of *sistere* to stand still, cause to stand] **:** a wingless parthenogenetic form of a plant louse

¹sis·ter \'sistə(r)\ *n* -S *often attrib* [ME *sister*, *suster*, *soster*, partly fr. OE *sweostor* and partly of Scand origin; akin to ON *systir* sister; akin to OHG *swester* sister, Goth *swistar*, L *soror*, OSlav *sestra*, Skt *svasṛ*] **1 a** (1) **:** a female human being related to another person having the same parents (2) **:** HALF SISTER (3) **:** SISTER-IN-LAW **b** (1) **:** a kinswoman by blood (2) **:** a female member of the same family, clan, or line **c :** a girl or woman felt to be a sister ⟨she was a ~ to the homeless child⟩ **d :** a female of a lower animal in relation to another having a common parent **2** *often cap* **a :** a member of a religious sisterhood **b :** a female member of a Christian church — often used with a surname or given name **3 a :** a woman related or linked to another by a common tie or interest ⟨she has ~*s* in graciousness over all the world —William Beebe⟩; *esp* **:** a female human being sharing a common national or racial origin with another ⟨the brightness . . . of their Irish, Danish, and French ~*s* —T.H.Fielding⟩ **b :** one having similar characteristics to another ⟨the sonata is a thing . . . without ~*s* in more familiar musical literature —David Hebb⟩ **4** *chiefly Brit* **:** a head nurse in a hospital ward or clinic; *broadly* **:** NURSE **5** *slang* **a :** GIRL, WOMAN — often used in direct address ⟨get going, ~, while you're able —Erskine Caldwell⟩ **b :** PERSON — usu. used in the phrase *weak sister* ⟨a subject introduced into the curriculum for the benefit of the weaker ~*s* —Kemp Malone⟩

²sister \"\ *vt* **sistered; sistered; sistering** \-t(ə)riŋ\ **sisters 1 :** to stand in the relationship of a sister to **:** treat in the manner of a sister ⟨her art ~*s* the natural roses —Shak.⟩ **2 :** to address by the name of sister

sister block *n* **:** a tackle block having two sheaves of the same size one above the other

sister-german \'==,==\ *n, pl* **sisters-german** [ME *sister germain*, part. trans. of MF *sœur germaine*, fr. *sœur* sister + *germaine*, fem. of *germain* having the same parents — more at GERMAN] **:** a sister through both father and mother **:** a full sister — compare HALF SISTER

sis·ter·hood \'sistə(r),hu̇d\ *n* [ME *sosterhode*, fr. *soster* sister + *-hode* -hood] **1 a :** the state of being a sister **b :** sisterly relationship ⟨the dark shades of her ~ —Virginia Woolf⟩ **2 :** a community or society of sisters; *specif* **:** a community or society of women religious **3 :** a group associated by common characteristics ⟨joined the ~ of nations⟩ ⟨resists the Hollywood ~'s best efforts —*Time*⟩

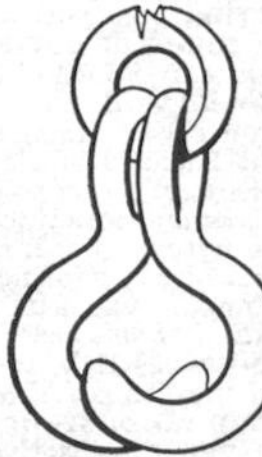
sister hooks

sister hook *n* **:** either of a pair of hooks fitted together so that the shank of each forms a mousing for the other; *also* **:** a pair of such hooks — called also *clip hook*, *clove hook*

sistering *adj* [fr. pres. part. of ²*sister*] **:** close by **:** CONTIGUOUS

sister-in-law \'sistə(r)ə̇n,lȯ, -trən-, -tə(r)n-\ *n, pl* **sisters-in-law** \-tə(r)zə̇n-\ [ME *suster-in-lawe*; prob. fr. the fact that the canon law forbids marriage with one's spouse's sister or brother] **1 :** the sister of one's spouse **2 a :** the wife of one's brother **b :** the wife of one's spouse's brother

sister keelson *n* **:** SIDE KEELSON

sis·ter·less \'sistə(r)lə̇s\ *adj* **:** having no sister

¹sisterlike \'==,=\ *adv* [¹*sister* + *like*] **:** in the manner of sisters

²sisterlike \"\ *adj* **:** SISTERLY

sister line *n* **:** a line on the palm running parallel to another and more important line and usu. held by palmists to add strength to it

sis·ter·li·ness \'sistə(r)lēnə̇s, -lin-\ *n* -ES **:** the quality or state of being sisterly

¹sis·ter·ly \-lē,-li\ *adj* [¹*sister* + *-ly* (adj. suffix)] **:** of, relating to, or having the characteristics of a sister; *specif* **:** AFFECTIONATE ⟨~ kindness⟩

²sisterly \"\ *adv* [¹*sister* + *-ly* (adv. suffix)] **:** in a sisterly manner ⟨a kiss sagely and ~ administered —Robert Browning⟩

sis·tern \-tə(r)n\ *chiefly dial pl of* SISTER

sister of charity *usu cap S&C* [trans. of F *sœur de charité*] **:** a member of a Roman Catholic sisterhood founded in France by St. Vincent de Paul in 1634 for nursing the sick

sister of charity of montreal *usu cap S&C&M* **:** a nun of a Roman Catholic community established in Montreal in 1745 and devoted esp. to the service of the suffering

sister of lo·ret·to \-lə'red·(,)ō\ *usu cap S&L* **:** a member of a Roman Catholic community of nuns founded in 1812 at Loretto, Kentucky, and devoted to educational work and the care of orphans

sister of mercy *usu cap S&M* **:** a member of a Roman Catholic congregation founded in 1827 by Catherine McAuley in Dublin and devoted to works of charity and education

sister of no·tre dame de na·mur \-,nōd·ər'dämdənä'mü(ə)r, -ō·trə'd-, -dənə'm- *also* -däm- *or* -dȧm- *sometimes* -dam- *or* -daam-\ *usu cap S & both Ns & 1st D* [part. trans. of F *sœur de Notre Dame de Namur*, after *Notre Dame de Namur* Our Lady of Namur, patron saint of Namur, province in southern Belgium] **:** a member of a Roman Catholic community founded in 1803 and devoted chiefly to teaching

sister of providence *usu cap S&P* [part. trans. of F *sœur de providence*] **1 :** a member of a Roman Catholic teaching order founded in France in 1806 **2 :** a member of a Roman Catholic congregation founded in Montreal in 1843 and devoted to teaching and charitable works

sister of st. jo·seph \-sānt'jōzə̇f, -sənt- *also* -ōsə̇f\ *usu cap both Ss&J* [trans. of F *sœur de Saint-Joseph* (*du Puy*), after *Joseph*, husband of Mary, mother of Jesus] **:** a member of a Roman Catholic congregation established in Le Puy, France, in 1650 and devoted to teaching and charitable works

sister of saint vin·cent \-'vin(t)sənt\ *usu cap both Ss&V* [trans. of F *sœur de Saint-Vincent* (*de-Paul*), after *Saint Vincent de Paul* †1660 Fr. Roman Catholic priest who founded the sisterhood] **:** SISTER OF CHARITY

sister of the good shepherd *usu cap both Ss&G* [trans. of F *sœur du Bon Pasteur*] **:** a member of a cloistered Roman Catholic order established at Caen, France, in 1641 and devoted esp. to the shelter and rehabilitation of girls and women

sister of the holy cross *usu cap S&H&C* [trans. of F *sœur de la Sainte Croix*] **:** a member of a Roman Catholic sisterhood founded at Le Mans, France, in 1841 and devoted to teaching and charitable works

sister of the holy names of jesus and mary *usu cap S&H &N&J&M* [after *Jesus* Christ and *Mary*, mother of Jesus] **:** a member of a Roman Catholic congregation founded in Canada in 1843 and devoted to teaching

sister of the immaculate heart of mary *usu cap S&I&H&M* [after *Mary*, mother of Jesus] **:** a member of a Roman Catholic teaching sisterhood founded at Monroe, Michigan, in 1845

sisters *pl of* SISTER, *pres 3d sing of* SISTER

sis·ter·ship \'sistə(r),ship\ *n* **:** SISTERHOOD

sister ship *n* **:** one of two or more essentially similar ships usu. built from the same general plans

sister superior *n, pl* **sister superiors** *also* **sisters superior :** MOTHER SUPERIOR

¹sis·tine \'si,stēn *sometimes* sə̇'stēn, *chiefly Brit* 'si,stīn\ *or* **six·tine** \'sik,stīn, -,stēn, -,stən\ *adj, usu cap* [*sistine* fr. It *sistino*, fr. NL *sixtinus*, fr. L *sextus* sixth + *-inus* -ine; *sixtine* fr. NL *sixtinus* — more at SEXT] **1 :** of or relating to any of the popes named Sixtus ⟨the *Sistine* edition of the Vulgate⟩ **2** [so called fr. its having been built by Pope Sixtus IV †1484] **:** of or relating to the Sistine chapel in the Vatican ⟨the *Sistine* choir⟩

²sistine \"\ *n, often cap* [after the *Sistine* chapel in the Vatican, noted for its famous paintings esp. the frescoes on its ceilings painted by Michelangelo Buonarroti †1564 Ital. sculptor, painter, architect, and poet of the High Renaissance] **:** a pale blue that is redder and deeper than average powder blue, greener and stronger than average cadet gray, redder and stronger than old blue, and greener and darker than average Wedgwood blue (sense 1)

sis·tren \'sistrə̇n, -tə(r)n\ *chiefly dial pl of* SISTER

sis·trum \'sistrəm\ *n, pl* **sistrums** \-rəmz\ *or* **sis·tra** \-rə\ [ME, fr. L, fr. Gk *seistron*, fr. *seiein* to shake — more at SEISMIC] **1 :** an ancient Egyptian percussion instrument consisting of a thin metal frame with numerous metal rods or loops that jingle when shaken **2 :** any of various musical instruments played like a rattle

sis·tru·rus \sə̇'strürəs\ *n, cap* [NL, fr. L *sistrum* rattling instrument, sistrum + NL *-urus*] **:** a genus of small rattlesnakes (family Crotalidae) having the top of the head covered with plates — see MASSASAUGA

sists *pl of* SIST

si·sym·bri·um \sə̇'simbrēəm\ *n* [L, a fragrant herb, perh. mint, fr. Gk *sisymbrion* bergamot, watercress] **1** *cap* **:** a genus of annual or biennial herbs (family Cruciferae) having a pubescence of simple unbranched hairs, lyrate pinnatifid leaves, and terete stems and comprising the hedge mustards — see DESCURAINIA **2** -S **:** any plant of the genus *Sisymbrium*

sis·y·phe·an \,sisə'fēən\ *or* **si·syph·i·an** \sə̇'sifēən\ *adj, usu cap* [L *sisypheius*, *sisyphius* sisyphean (fr. Gk *sisypheios*, *sisyphios*, fr. *Sisyphos* Sisyphus, in Greco-Roman mythology the cruel king of Corinth whose punishment in Hades was to roll up a hill a heavy stone that constantly rolled down again) + E *-an*] **:** of, relating to, or suggestive of the labors of Sisyphus; *specif* **:** requiring continual and often ineffective effort ⟨would go back to the National Assembly for rereading and repassage, a *Sisyphean* task —Janet Flanner⟩

si·syr·i·dae \sə̇'sirə,dē\ *n pl, cap* [NL, fr. Gk *sisyra* fur, goat's hair + NL *-idae*; fr. the hairy covering of the body and wings] **:** a family of neuropterous insects having larvae that feed on freshwater sponges

sis·y·rin·chi·um \,sisə'riŋkēəm\ *n* [NL, fr. Gk *sisyrinchion* sisyrinchium] **1** *cap* **:** a genus of chiefly No. American grasslike mostly blue-flowered herbs (family Iridaceae) having mostly basal leaves and several 6-parted flowers usu. from a single spathe **2** -S **:** any plant of the genus *Sisyrinchium*

¹sit \(')sit, *usu* -id.+V; *before a vowel-initial adverb with primary stress often* ,səd· *or* ,sət; *before "down" often* ,sə *or* (')si\ *vb* **sat** \(')sat, -ad·, *before "down" often* (')sa\ *also chiefly dial* **sot** \(')sä|t, |d·\ *or archaic* **sate** \(')sä|t, (')sa|, |d·\ **sat** *also chiefly dial* **sot** \(')sä|t, |d·\ *or archaic* **sit·ten** \'sit°n\ **sitting; sits** [ME *sitten*, fr. OE *sittan*; akin to OHG *sizzen* to sit, ON *sitja*, Goth *sitan*, L *sedēre*, Gk *hezesthai* to sit, *hedra* seat, Skt *sīdati* he sits] *vi* **1 :** to rest in a position in which the body is essentially vertical and supported or balanced chiefly on the buttocks or thighs or both ⟨~ on a stool⟩ ⟨~ in a chair⟩ ⟨~ cross-legged⟩ **2 a** *obs* **:** KNEEL **b** *of an animal* **:** to assume a position with the hindquarters at rest on a supporting surface ⟨a dog trained to stand and ~ at command⟩ **c** *of a bird* **:** to perch or rest esp. with the feet drawn up close or with the body touching the ground **3 :** to occupy a place as a member of an official body ⟨~ in Congress⟩ ⟨~ on the board of directors⟩ ⟨~ as a member of a committee⟩ **4 :** to hold a session **:** be in session for official business ⟨magistrate . . . may ~ in any place convenient —F.T.Giles⟩ ⟨the legislature is still *sitting*⟩ ⟨official committee . . . *sitting* on the question of the ultimate size and organization —Roy Lewis & Angus Maude⟩ **5 :** to have or continue in an occupation or function ⟨gamblers dealt or *sat* lookout with their sombreros on —W.N.Burns⟩ **6** *of a hen* **:** to cover eggs for hatching **:** BROOD, SET **7 a :** to take a position for having one's portrait painted or for being photographed ⟨~ for a painter⟩ **b :** to serve as the original of a painted or sculptured figure or of a fictional character **8 a** *archaic* **:** to have one's dwelling place **:** DWELL **b** *obs* **:** to remain as a tenant **9 :** to lie in wait ⟨anyone *sitting* at the entrance to the pass, they'll see us if we go through the field —Norman Mailer⟩ **10 a** *of clothing* **:** to lie or hang relative to the wearer ⟨the collar *sits* awkwardly at the back⟩ ⟨trying to see how the new coat ~*s* behind⟩ **b :** LIE, REST — used with *on* or *upon* ⟨author's assumed regionalism ~*s* uneasily on his verse —W.M.Maidment⟩ ⟨great triumvirate of Edwardian novelists . . . that label ~*s* comfortably on these three —P.M.Fulcher⟩ **c :** to affect one with or as if with a certain weight **:** PRESS, WEIGH ⟨her years *sat* lightly upon her⟩ ⟨the pie *sat* heavily on his stomach⟩ **11 :** to float in a specified manner ⟨load so that the ship ~*s* several feet deeper in the water aft⟩ ⟨the boat ~*s* practically on top of the water⟩ **12 a :** to have a location ⟨thy rapt soul *sitting* in thine eyes —John Milton⟩ ⟨cottage *sitting* on the edge of a cliff⟩ ⟨house ~*s* well back from the road⟩ **b** *of wind* **:** to blow from a certain direction ⟨when the wind ~*s* one way I can hear the steam train —Christopher Morley⟩ ⟨always rains when the wind ~*s* in the west⟩ **13 :** to please or agree with one — used with *with* and an adverb ⟨setting an example that may not ~ well with the more obedient Communist leaders —*N.Y. Times*⟩ **14 :** to remain in the same state ⟨left the dishes *sitting* on the table⟩ **:** remain inactive or quiescent ⟨the car ~*s* in the garage unused all week⟩ ⟨do something, don't just ~ there⟩ ⟨*sitting* behind prison bars⟩ **15 :** to be a candidate for a degree, certificate, or award **:** take or prepare to take an examination — used with *for* ⟨was *sitting* for a scholarship at Newton College —Angela Thirkell⟩ ⟨*sat* for his examinations . . . as a river pilot —*N.Y. Herald Tribune*⟩ **16 :** to act as a relief for a parent or nurse in watching over a child or an invalid ⟨~ with a friend's baby⟩ **~** *vt* **1 :** to cause (oneself) to be seated — usu. used with *down* ⟨*sat* him down to write a letter⟩ **2 :** to cause to be seated **:** place on or in a seat **:** put in a sitting position ⟨let me ~ you on the sofa . . . and talk over small matters —F.D.Roosevelt⟩ ⟨a story that *sat* me up straight —S.H.Holbrook⟩ **3** *of a hen* **:** to sit upon (eggs) **4 a :** to keep one's seat upon ⟨~ a horse⟩ **b :** to trim (a boat) by the poise of the body or by the use of oars **5** *chiefly dial* **:** SUIT, BECOME, BEFIT **6 :** to provide seats or seating room for ⟨the car will ~ six people comfortably⟩ **7** *Brit* **:** to answer the questions of (an examination) in writing — **sit at one's feet :** to listen to or follow as a pupil, disciple, or admirer — **sit at table :** to be at table for eating **:** DINE — **sit loose :** to be heedless or indifferent ⟨scholars . . . who *sit loose* to the obligations and responsibilities of church membership —Alan Richardson⟩ — **sit on 1 :** to hold deliberations concerning ⟨several judges have *sat on* this case⟩ **2 :** REPRESS, SQUELCH **3 :** to delay action or decision concerning **:** keep quiet or out of sight **:** SUPPRESS ⟨he had *sat on* stories before, like some other newsmen —*Time*⟩ ⟨*sat on* appropriations plans until they were certain which way winds . . . were blowing —*Newsweek*⟩ — **sit on one's hands 1 :** to withhold applause **:** fail to show approval or enthusiasm **2 :** to fail to take expected or appropriate action **:** sit by — **sit on the lid :** to keep down agitation **:** hold in check forces of protest or rebellion — **sit on the splice** *cricket* **:** STONEWALL — contrasted with *lay on the wood* — **sit on the throne :** REIGN — **sit pretty :** to be in a highly favorable situation ⟨*sitting pretty* with a full house against a flush and a straight⟩ ⟨Americans . . . had a virtual monopoly of piston-engined air transports, and they were *sitting pretty* —Charles Gardner⟩ — **sit tight 1 :** to maintain one's position without change ⟨preferred to *sit tight* with his present investments⟩ ⟨colonel decided to *sit tight* and send out patrols —Walter Bernstein⟩ **2 :** to remain quiet in or as if in hiding — **sit under :** to attend religious service under the instruction or ministrations of; *also* **:** to attend the classes or lectures of (a teacher)

²sit \'sit, *usu* -id.+V\ *n* -S **1 :** an act or period of sitting ⟨a long ~ at the station between trains⟩ **2 :** the manner in which a garment fits ⟨~ of a coat around the shoulders⟩ **3 :** a settling or falling of the roof of a mine — usu. used in pl. **4 :** an entire mature celery plant

sit *abbr* situation

SIT *abbr* **1** spontaneous ignition temperature **2** stopping or storage in transit

si·tao \sə̇'tau̇\ *n* -S [Tag *sitaw*] **:** a long-podded cowpea of the Philippines

si·tar *also* **sit·tar** \sə̇'tär\ *n* -S [Hindi *sitār*, fr. Per, a three-stringed guitar, fr. *sih* three + *tār* string, thread] **:** a Hindu lute with a long broad neck and a varying number of strings

sit around *vi* **:** to be idle **:** LOAF ⟨had to *sit around* until they got orders —Ira Wolfert⟩

si·ta·tun·ga *or* **sit·u·tun·ga** \,sid·ə'tu̇ŋgə\ *n, pl* **sitatungas** *or* **sitatunga** *or* **situtungas** *or* **situtunga** [Subiya & Tonga] **:** an antelope (*Strepsiceros spekei*) of the central African swampland that is nearly related to the harnessed antelope but shows white striping only when young

sit back *vi* **:** to rest or withdraw from work or active participation ⟨*sit back* in indifference or in helpless bewilderment⟩

sit by *vi* **:** to assume an attitude of indifference or passivity or restraint ⟨we see nothing . . . that compels the government to *sit by* while a food supply is cut off —O.W.Holmes †1935⟩

sit down \see ¹SIT\ *vi* [ME *sitten doun*, fr. *sitten* to sit + *doun* down — more at SIT, DOWN] **1 a :** to lower oneself to a sitting position **:** take a seat **b :** to fall on the buttocks ⟨suddenly *sat down* on the ice⟩ **c :** to pause from activity through fatigue or complacency **d :** to establish a residence **:** settle down **2 :** to begin a siege **:** ENCAMP **3 :** to enter into conference, negotiation, or consultation ⟨if we could *sit down* together and straighten out our differences peaceably⟩ **4 :** ALIGHT, LAND ⟨a field big enough for a bomber to *sit down* on safely⟩ — **sit down on :** REPRIMAND, SQUELCH

¹sit-down \'=,=\ — *see* ¹SIT\ *n* [fr. *sit down*, v.] **1 a :** act or place of sitting down ⟨a nice quiet *sit-down* by the fire —Elizabeth Taylor⟩ **b** *or* **sit-down strike :** a cessation of work by employees while maintaining continuous occupation of shop, plant, or like place of employment as a protest and means toward forcing compliance with demands — called also *sit-in*; compare STAY-IN STRIKE **2 :** a meal taken sitting down — compare BUFFET, HANDOUT

²sit-down \"\ *adj* **:** that one sits or settles down to ⟨a *sit-down* lunch⟩ **:** performed in a sitting position ⟨*sit-down* dance⟩

sit-down·er \'=,==(r)\ *n* -S **:** a worker engaged in a sit-down strike

¹site \'sīt, *usu* -īd.+V\ *n* -S [ME, fr. MF or L; MF *site*, fr. L *situs* position, place, site, fr. *situs*, past part. of *sinere* to leave, let go, lay, place; akin to L *serere* to plant, sow — more at SOW] **1 a** *obs* **:** the original or fixed position of a thing ⟨wisdom of God in the ~ and motion of the sun —Sir Thomas Browne⟩ **b** *obs* **:** ATTITUDE, POSTURE ⟨fixed in melancholy ~, with head declined —James Thomson †1748⟩ **2 a :** the local position of building, town, monument, or similar work either constructed or to be constructed esp. in connection with its surroundings ⟨how Oxford and Cambridge in particular came to be chosen for ~*s* —A.T.Quiller-Couch⟩ ⟨suitable ~ for a factory⟩ ⟨his structural solutions and his great sense of ~ —Lincoln Kirstein⟩ **b :** a space of ground occupied or to be occupied by a building ⟨offered the city a library . . . if the city would provide a ~ —*Amer. Guide Series: Md.*⟩ **c :** land made suitable for building purposes by dividing into lots, laying out streets, and providing facilities (as water, sewers, power supply) ⟨desirable corner ~*s* are available⟩ ⟨waterfront ~*s* for summer cottages⟩ **3 :** the scene of an action ⟨battle ~⟩ ⟨~ of the murder⟩ ⟨~ of an auto collision⟩ or specified activity ⟨mining ~⟩ ⟨picnic ~⟩ ⟨launching ~ for a rocket⟩ ⟨choosing a ~ for a convention⟩ ⟨~ of a bone fracture⟩ **4 :** a place where a group of remains of prehistoric human occupation is or has been located ⟨a burial ~⟩ ⟨a village ~⟩ ⟨excavations at a ~⟩ **5 :** the situation of a growing plant with respect to all the environmental factors (as climate, soil, drainage, other plant and animal life) affecting growth **6 :** the angle between the horizontal and a line joining the base of a target and a firing piece

²site \"\ *vt* -ED/-ING/-S **1 :** to provide with a site **:** LOCATE ⟨hotel magnificently *sited* on a headland —Mitchell Goodman⟩ ⟨the camp kitchen should be *sited* so that the breeze will not blow smoke into the cook's face —R.H.Graves⟩ **2 :** to put (artillery) in position so as to be able to perform a specific mission ⟨∼ a machine gun⟩

site index *n* **:** a measure of the worth of a particular area as a habitat for forest usu. given as the average height in feet of the dominant and codominant trees at a given age (as 50 or 100 years)

1sitfast *or* **setfast** \ˈ≈,≈\ *n* -s [1*sit* or 1*set* + *fast* (after the phrase *sit fast, set fast*)] **:** a callosity with inflamed edges formed on a horse's back by the chafing of the saddle — compare SADDLE SORE

2sitfast \"\ *adj* [1*sit* + *fast* (after *sit fast*, v.)] *chiefly dial* **:** FIXED, STATIONARY, IMMOVABLE

sith \(ˈ)sith\ *or* **sith·ence** \ˈsithən(t)s\ *or* **sith·ens** \-nz\ *archaic var of* SINCE

sith·cund \ˈsēth,kůnd\ *n* -s [by shortening] **:** GESITHCUND

sithe \ˈsīth, -th\ *dial var of* SIGH

sit in *vi* **1 :** to take a hand in a card game **2 :** to take part in or be present at a session (of music, discussion) as a visitor ⟨*sit in* with a dance band⟩ — usu. used with *on* ⟨invited to *sit in* on a rehearsal⟩ ⟨*sat in* on some of the board's policy-making meetings⟩ **3** *Brit* **:** BABY-SIT **4** *Brit* **:** to sit down at table

sit-in \ˈ≈,≈\ *n* -s **1 :** SIT-DOWN 1b **2 a :** an act of occupying seats in a racially segregated establishment as an organized protest against discrimination **b :** an act of sitting in the seats or on the floor of an establishment as a means of organized protest

si·tio \ˈsēd·ē,ō\ *n* -s [Sp, place, prob. modif. of L *situs* site — more at SITE] **:** a hamlet or subdivision of a barrio in the Philippines

sit·ka \ˈsitkə\ *n, pl* **sitka** *or* **sitkas** *usu cap* [Tlingit, lit., behind on Shi (native name of Baranof Island)] **1 :** a Tlingit people on Baranof and Chichagof Islands, Alaska **2 :** a member of the Sitka people

sitka alder \ˈ≈≈-\ *n, usu cap S* [fr. *Sitka*, town in Baranof Island, prob. fr. Tlingit *Sitka*] **:** a shrub or small tree (*Alnus sinuata*) ranging from Alaska to California and having oval bright green leaves and clustered catkins

sitka crab *n, usu cap S* **:** a small anomuran crustacean (*Cryptolithodes sitchensis*) that resembles a crab with a domed carapace bright red in the male, rosy gray in the female and lives among rocks near the tide line from Alaska to California

sitka cypress *n, usu cap S* **:** YELLOW CEDAR 1a

sit·kan \ˈsitkən\ *n* -s *cap* [*Sitka*, Baranof Island, Alaska + E *-an*] **:** a native or resident of Sitka, Alaska

sitka spruce *n, usu cap 1st S* **:** a tall spruce (*Picea sitchensis*) of the northern Pacific coast having loosely scaled thin reddish brown bark and flat needles

sitka spruce beetle *n, usu cap 1st S* **:** a bark beetle (*Dendroctonus obesus*) the larva of which is a serious pest on Sitka spruce in northwestern No. America

sitka spruce weevil *n, usu cap 1st S* **:** a curculionid weevil (*Pissodes sitchensis*) that is very destructive to Sitka spruce

sitka willow *n, usu cap S* **:** a tree (*Salix sitchensis*) ranging from Alaska to Oregon and having oblong leaves often with glandular-toothed margins

sito- *comb form* [Gk, fr. *sitos*] **1 :** grain ⟨*Sito*philus⟩ ⟨*sito*sterol⟩ **2 :** food ⟨*sito*logy⟩

si·tol·o·gy \sīˈtäləjē, sə̇ˈt-\ *n* -ES [ISV *sito-* + *-logy*] **:** the science of nutrition and dietetics

si·to·na \sə̇ˈtōnə\ *n, cap* [NL, prob. fr. LL, grain buyer, fr. Gk *sitōnes*, fr. *sitos* grain] **:** a genus of weevils including some that are injurious to various crop plants — see SWEETCLOVER WEEVIL

si·toph·i·lus \sīˈtäfələs, sə̇ˈt-\ *n, cap* [NL, fr. *sito-* + *-philus*] **:** a widely distributed genus of weevils containing two (*S. granarius* and *S. oryzae*) that are highly destructive to grain

si·to·sterol \ˌsīd·(ˌ)ō+\ *n* [*sito-* + *sterol*] **:** any of several widely occurring sterols or a mixture of such sterols useful as a starting material for the synthesis of steroid hormones: as **a :** a crystalline secondary alcohol $C_{29}H_{49}OH$ obtained esp. from cottonseed oil, tall oil, wheat-germ oil, or cinchona bark or synthetically from stigmasterol by hydrogenation — called also *beta-sitosterol* **b :** a crystalline alcohol $C_{29}H_{49}OH$ that is stereoisomeric with beta-sitosterol, that is the principal sterol of soybean oil, and that is also found in several invertebrates — called also *gamma-sitosterol*

sit out *vt* **1 :** to remain to the end of ⟨*sit out* a dull speech⟩ **2 :** to outstay in a social call ⟨determined to *sit* his rival *out*⟩ **3 a :** to remain seated during (a dance) **b :** to fail to take part in **:** stay aloof from ⟨believe we would find it impossible to *sit out* any war in Europe —Elmo Roper⟩ **4 :** to stretch the back of (a skirt) by wearing while sitting

sit over *vi* **:** to move sideways on a seat or along a row of seats to make room

sit·rep \ˈsit·,rep\ *n* -s [*sit*uation *rep*ort] **:** a periodic report of the current military situation

sits *pres 3d sing of* SIT, *pl of* SIT

sit spin *n* **:** a spin in figure skating executed on one foot in a sitting position with the other leg extended forward — called also *Jackson Haines*

sit·ta \ˈsid·ə\ *n, cap* [NL, fr. Gk *sittē* nuthatch] **:** the type genus of Sittidae comprising various typical nuthatches

sit·ta·ble \ˈsid·əbəl\ *adj* [1*sit* + *-able*] **:** suitable for sitting on ⟨∼ chairs⟩ or sitting through ⟨a movie of ∼ length⟩

sittar *var of* SITAR

sit·tee \(ˈ)sidˌ|ē\ *n* -s [1*sit* + *-ee*] **:** one occupying a seat

sitten *archaic past part of* SIT

sit·ter \ˈsid·ə(r), -itə-\ *n* -s [ME, fr. *sitten* to sit + *-er* — more at SIT] **1 :** one that sits: as **a** *obs* **:** RIDER **b :** a broody hen **c :** one who sits for a portrait or a bust **d :** one who has a seance with a psychic **e** [by shortening] **:** BABY-SITTER **f :** B-GIRL **2 a :** an easy target ⟨∼ for enemy submarines⟩ **b :** an easy scoring or fielding chance **:** SETUP **3** *Brit* **:** SITTING ROOM

sitter-by \ˌ≈≈ˈ≈\ *n, pl* **sitters-by :** one who sits near or apart

sitter-in \ˌ≈≈ˈ≈\ *n, pl* **sitters-in** *chiefly Brit* **:** BABY-SITTER

sit through *vt* **:** to watch or listen to without enjoyment **:** sit out ⟨conscientiously *sitting through* the movies which it is one of his official duties to censor —Edmund Wilson⟩

sit·ti·dae \ˈsid·ə,dē\ *n pl, cap* [NL, fr. *Sitta*, type genus + *-idae*] **:** a family of passerine birds consisting of the nuthatches and formerly regarded as a subfamily of Paridae or of Certhiidae

sit·tine \ˈsi,tīn\ *adj* [NL *Sitta* + E *-ine*] **:** of or relating to the nuthatches

1sitting *n* -s [ME, fr. gerund of *sitten* to sit] **1 :** an act of one that sits; *esp* **:** a single occasion of continuous sitting ⟨read a book at one ∼⟩ ⟨finished the portrait in three ∼*s*⟩ ⟨turkey supper at the church . . . with ∼*s* at 5:30 and 6:30 —*Springfield (Mass.) Daily News*⟩ **2 a :** a brooding over or time or season for brooding over eggs for hatching **b :** SETTING 10 **3 :** the actual presence or meeting of a body of persons in their seats with authority to transact business **:** SESSION ⟨a ∼ of a court⟩ ⟨∼ of the legislature⟩ — often used in pl. **4 :** a space occupied by or allotted for one person (as in a church or theater) ⟨a space of 18 in. in the length of the pew is considered a ∼ —J.H.Frank⟩ **5 :** SÉANCE b

2sitting *adj* [ME, fr. pres. part. of *sitten* to sit] **1 :** that is setting ⟨∼ hen⟩ **2 :** occupying a judicial or legislative seat **:** being in office ⟨the first business of any ∼ politician is, naturally, to be reelected —W.S.White⟩ **3** *Brit* **:** being in occupancy **:** holding tenancy ⟨prices to ∼ tenants are often very favorable —*advt*⟩ **4 :** easily hit or played ⟨∼ target⟩ ⟨∼ game in spades⟩

sitting duck *n* **:** an easy or defenseless target for attack ⟨the tanks ran out of gas and became *sitting ducks* for enemy artillery⟩ or criticism or sharp practice ⟨Eliot's intellectual and mystic snobbishness puts him in the unfortunate position of a *sitting duck* —C.B.Davis⟩ ⟨an alien may be a *sitting duck* for extortioners —*New Republic*⟩

sitting height *n* **:** the distance from the vertex of the head to the supporting surface on which a person is sitting erect

sitting room *n* **1 :** a room for sitting in; *esp* **:** a room provided in addition to the bedroom of a private suite ⟨had a bedroom and *sitting room* on the same floor of a small private hotel —Nevil Shute⟩ **2 :** LIVING ROOM 1

sitting shot *n* **:** a shot made while in a sitting position

sitting trot *n* **:** a slow trot in which a rider does not post

sit·trin·gee \sə̇ˈtrinjē\ *n* -s [Per *shatranjī*, lit., checkered, fr. *shatranj, shatrang* chessboard, chess, fr. Skt *caturaṅga*, lit., four limbs, fr. *catur* four + *aṅga* limb — more at FOUR, ANKLE] *India* **:** a carpet of striped or checkered cotton

sit·u·al \ˈsichəwəl\ *adj* [ML *situalis*, fr. L *situs* site, position + *-alis* -al] **:** POSITIONAL — **sit·u·al·ly** \-wəlē\ *adv*

1sit·u·ate \ˈsichəwə̇t, -,wāt, *usu* |d.+V\ *adj* [ML *situatus*, past part. of *situare* to place] **:** having its site **:** LOCATED ⟨parcel of land ∼ in the village of Riverview —*Detroit Law Jour.*⟩

2sit·u·ate \-,wāt, *usu* -ād.+V\ *vt* -ED/-ING/-S [ML *situatus*, past part. of *situare* to place, fr. *situs* place, position, site — more at SITE] **1 :** to place in a site **:** LOCATE **2 :** to place in a situation **:** give a place to ⟨∼ the reader in the main currents of the life of a dynamic society —*New Republic*⟩ **3 :** to assign to a category or particular set of associations **:** LOCALIZE ⟨study that tries to ∼ the particular thinker and his thought in their proper place in man's ever growing consciousness —J.W. Evans⟩ ⟨liberalism alone does not create . . . it does not ∼ truth —H.E.Clurman⟩

situated *adj* [fr. past part. of 2*situate*] **1 :** having a site, situation, or location **:** LOCATED ⟨a town ∼ on a hill⟩ **2 :** CIRCUMSTANCED ⟨his family, while not rich, were comfortably ∼⟩

sit·u·a·tion \ˌsichəˈwāshən\ *n* -s [MF or ML; MF, fr. ML *situation-, situatio*, fr. *situatus* (past part. of *situare* to place) + L *-ion-, -io* -ion] **1 a :** the way in which something is placed in relation to its surroundings ⟨its insular ∼ made it readily accessible —Kemp Malone⟩ ⟨in some spelling ∼*s* letters represent no sounds —*ABC Language Arts Bull.*⟩ **b :** SITE ⟨so uneasy . . . that we thought of removing our ∼ —Daniel Defoe⟩ **c** *archaic* **:** LOCALITY, SPOT ⟨small rancho in a lonely spot . . . the ∼ was also wild and solitary —W.H.Hudson †1922⟩ **2** *obs* **:** act of situating, settling, or occupying **3 a** *archaic* **:** state of health ⟨the flesh of the bear in this ∼ . . . is inferior —E.H.Criswell⟩ **b :** state of pregnancy ⟨the woman should have concealed her ∼ —Sir Walter Scott⟩ **4 a :** position or place of employment **:** POST, JOB ⟨rise in help, ∼ wanted ads —*Nation's Business*⟩ **b :** position in life **:** STATUS ⟨striving to better his ∼⟩ **5 a :** position with respect to conditions and circumstances ⟨the rebels' military ∼ appeared to be hopeless⟩ ⟨in the unpleasant ∼ of having to choose between two evils⟩ **b :** the sum total of internal and external stimuli that act upon an organism within a given time interval **c :** the total set of physical, social, and psychocultural factors that act upon an individual in orienting and conditioning his behavior **6 a :** relative position or combination of circumstances at a given moment ⟨how to behave in unexpected ∼*s*⟩ ⟨daily reports on the ∼ at each stage of the campaign⟩ ⟨the ∼ seemed to call for a general retreat⟩ ⟨a ∼ map attached to the report⟩ **b :** a critical, trying, or unusual state of affairs ⟨in the event of a recession . . . to arouse the people to the need of using their own ingenuity to meet the ∼ —Paul Wooton⟩; *often* **:** PROBLEM ⟨no human ∼ is simple, has one cause and one cure —D.W.Brogan⟩ **c :** a particular or striking complex of affairs at a stage in the action of a narrative or drama **:** CRISIS, CLIMAX ⟨highly contrived and implausible ∼*s*⟩

syn see STATE

sit·u·a·tion·al \ˌ≈≈ˈwāshənᵊl, -shnəl\ *adj* **1 :** relating to or caused by a situation ⟨elaborate ∼ plot of a novel⟩ ⟨∼ testing of officer candidates⟩ **2 a :** produced or conditioned by a specific set of social or interpersonal circumstances ⟨delinquency due to family ∼ factors⟩ ⟨∼ drinker⟩ **b :** dealing with the total situation as determining the individual's behavior ⟨a ∼ analysis of prejudice⟩ — **sit·u·a·tion·al·ly** \-ᵊlē, -əl|, |i\ *adv*

situational neurosis *n* **:** a reactive neurosis

sit·u·a·tion·ism \ˌ≈≈ˈwāshə,nizəm\ *n* -s **:** a theory viewing human personality as a function of response to situations

sit·u·a·tion·ist \-sh(ə)nə̇st\ *n* -s **:** one who holds a theory of situationism

sit·u·la \ˈsichələ, -id·ᵊlə\ *n, pl* **situ·lae** \-chə,lē, -d·ᵊl,ī\ [L] **:** an ancient vessel shaped like a bucket usu. of decorated bronze and found in Italy and other parts of Europe

sit up *vi* [ME *sitten up*, fr. *sitten* to sit + *up* — more at SIT, UP] **1 :** to rise from a lying to a sitting position **:** sit with the body erect ⟨able to *sit up* and take nourishment⟩ **2 :** to show interest or alertness or surprise ⟨we *sit up* with pleasure when he suddenly lashes out at some literary stuffed shirt —Alfred Kazin⟩ **3 :** to stay up after the usual time for going to bed ⟨*sit up* with a sick child⟩ ⟨a late movie not worth *sitting up* for⟩ — **sit up and take notice :** to show a lively interest or apprehension

sit-up \ˈ≈,≈\ *n* -s [*sit up*] **:** a conditioning exercise consisting of raising the trunk to a sitting position from a supine position with the legs remaining straight

sit-upon \ˈ≈≈,≈\ *n* -s [fr. *sit upon*, v.] **1 :** BUTTOCKS **2 :** a square of waterproof cloth carried by hikers and campers for sitting on wet ground

si·tus \ˈsīd·əs, ˈsē|\ *n* -ES [L, place, site — more at SITE] **1 :** the place where something exists or originates ⟨∼ of a bodily function⟩ ⟨∼ of an inflammation⟩ ⟨∼ and quantity of the local water supplies —P.A.Rollins⟩ ⟨Palestine as . . . the ∼ of their Semitic ancestry —B.A.Javits⟩ **2 :** the place to which an intangible right or property is deemed to belong for purposes of taxation or legal jurisdiction ⟨∼ of a corporation⟩ ⟨a taxpayer's ∼ of income⟩

situs in·ver·sus \-inˈvərsəs\ *n* [NL, lit., inverted position] **:** a congenital abnormality characterized by lateral transposition of the viscera (as of the heart or the liver)

situtunga *var of* SITATUNGA

sitz bath \ˈsits-\ *n* [part trans. of G *sitzbad*, fr. *sitz* act of sitting (fr. MHG *siz*, fr. *sitzen* to sit, fr. OHG *sizzen*) + *bad* bath — more at SIT] **1 :** a tub in which one bathes in a sitting posture **2 :** a bath used esp. in postoperative cases in which the hips and thighs of the patient are immersed in hot water for the therapeutic effect of the moist heat in the perineal and anal regions

sitz bath 2

sitz·krieg \ˈsits,krēg, ˈzi-\ *n* -s [G *sitz* act of sitting + *krieg* war] **:** static warfare — contrasted with *blitzkrieg*

sitz·mark \-t,smärk\ *n* [part trans. of G *sitzmarke*, fr. *sitz* act of sitting + *marke* mark, sign] **:** a depression left in the snow by a skier falling backward

si·u·ai \sēˈ(y)ü,ī\ *n, pl* **siuai** *or* **siuais** *usu cap* **1 :** a Papuan people inhabiting a section of southwestern Bougainville Island **2 :** a member of the Siuai people

si·um \ˈsīəm\ *n, cap* [NL, fr. Gk *sion*, a marsh plant, perh. the water parsnip or marshwort] **:** a small genus of herbs (family Umbelliferae) that are natives of the north temperate zone and of southern Africa and have pinnate leaves, white flowers, and fruit with prominent ribs bearing oil tubes in the intervals

si·u·si \sēˈ(y)üsē\ *n, pl* **siusi** *or* **siusis** *usu cap* **1 a :** an Arawakan people of the Içana river valley in northwestern Brazil **b :** a member of such people **2 :** the language of the Siusi people

si·u·slaw \sēˈ(y)ü(,)slȯ\ *n, pl* **siuslaw** *or* **siuslaws** *usu cap* [Siuslaw *šayušta*] **1 a :** an Indian people of the Pacific coast of Oregon **b :** a member of such people **2 :** a Yakonan language of the Siuslaw and Kuitsh peoples

si·va \ˈsēvə\ *n* -s [Samoan] **1 :** a western Polynesian gesture dance with vocal accompaniment **2 :** a gathering at which the siva is danced

si·va·ism \ˈsēvə,izəm\ *or* **shi·va·ism** \ˈshē-\ *n* -s *usu cap* [*Siva, Shiva*, supreme god of many Hindu sects (fr. Skt *Śiva*, lit., friendly, auspicious) + E *-ism*; akin to OE *hīwan*, pl., members of a household — more at HOME] **:** a sect comprising the worshipers of the god Siva

si·va·ite *or* **shi·va·ite** \-və,īt\ *n* -s *usu cap* [*Siva, Shiva*, supreme god of many Hindu sects + E *-ite*] **:** SAIVA

si·van *or* **si·wan** \ˈsivən\ *n* -s *usu cap* [Heb *Sīwān*, fr. Assyr-Bab *Simānu*] **:** the 9th month of the civil year or the 3d month of the ecclesiastical year in the Jewish calendar — see MONTH table

si·va·pithe·cus \ˌsēvəpə̇ˈthēkəs, -ˈpithə̇k-\ *n, cap* [NL, fr. *Siva* (fr. Skt *Śiva*) + *-pithecus*] **:** a genus of generalized Lower Pliocene Indian apes related to *Dryopithecus* and exhibiting resemblances to the orangutan

siva snake *n* **:** KING COBRA

1si·va·there \ˈsēvə,thi(ə)r\ *adj* [NL *Sivatherium*] **:** of or relating to *Sivatherium*

2sivathere \"\ *n* -s [NL *Sivatherium*] **:** a mammal or fossil of the genus *Sivatherium*

si·va·the·ri·oid \ˌ≈≈ˈthirē,ȯid\ *adj* [NL *Sivatherium* + E *-oid*] **:** resembling or related to the genus *Sivatherium*

si·va·the·ri·um \ˌ≈≈ˈ≈əm\ *n, cap* [NL, fr. *Siva*, supreme god of many Hindu sects (fr. Skt *Śiva*) + *-therium*] **:** a genus that comprises very large mammals from the Pliocene of India with two pairs of horns of which the posterior are large and somewhat palmated and a muzzle probably fleshy or dilated like that of the saiga antelope and that is placed in the same family as the giraffe or sometimes made the type of a distinct family

si·va·ti \sə̇ˈväd·ē\ *n, pl* **sivati** *or* **sivatis** *usu cap* **1 :** a Pathan people of the Afghan-Pakistan frontier **2 :** a member of the Sivati people

siv·vy bean \ˈsivē-, -vi-\ *n* [by alter.] *chiefly South* **:** SIEVA BEAN

SIW *abbr* self-inflicted wound

si·wan \ˈsēwən\ *adj, usu cap* [*Siwa*, oasis in northwestern Egypt + E *-an*] **1 :** of, relating to, or characteristic of the Egyptian oasis Siwa **2 :** of, relating to, or characteristic of the people of Siwa

1si·wash \ˈsī,wȯsh, -wäsh\ *n* -ES *usu cap* [Chinook Jargon, fr. F *sauvage* savage, fr. MF — more at SAVAGE] **1** *Northwest* **:** AMERICAN INDIAN — usu. used disparagingly **2 :** the jargon used by and in talking with Siwashes

2siwash \"\ *vb* -ED/-ING/-ES *sometimes cap, vi* **1** *Northwest* **:** to live or do things like a Siwash — often used with *it* ⟨∼ it in some cabin up on the flats⟩ **2** *Northwest* **:** to camp or travel with little or no equipment **:** rough it ⟨∼*ing* up there by the head of the ravine —*Alaska Sportsman*⟩ — often used with *it* ∼ *vt* **:** to do (something) in a slipshod manner; *esp* **:** to haul (logs) so as to sideswipe trees and stumps

3siwash \"\ *n* -ES *usu cap* [fr. *Siwash*, fictional college in stories by George Fitch †1915 Am. author] **:** a small usu. inland college that is notably provincial in outlook

siwin *var of* SEWEN

1six \ˈsiks\ *adj* [ME *six, sex*, adj. & pron., fr. OE *six, siex, seox*; akin to OHG *sehs* six, ON *sex*, Goth *saihs*, L *sex*, Gk *hex*, Skt *ṣaṣ*] **:** being one more than five in number ⟨∼ years⟩ — see NUMBER table

2six \"\ *pron, pl in constr* [ME] **:** six countable persons or things not specified but under consideration and being enumerated ⟨∼ are here⟩ ⟨∼ were found⟩

3six \"\ *n* -ES [ME, fr. *six*, adj. & pron.] **1 :** twice three **:** three times two **2 a :** six units or objects ⟨a total of ∼⟩ **b :** a group or set of six ⟨arranged by ∼*es*⟩ **3 a :** the numerable quantity symbolized by the arabic numeral 6 **b :** the figure 6 **4 :** six o'clock — compare BELL table, TIME illustration **5 a :** a playing card marked to show that it is sixth in a suit **b :** a domino with six spots on one of its halves **c :** a die with six spots on the uppermost side **d :** an article of clothing of the sixth size ⟨wears a ∼⟩ **6** *cricket* **:** a hit that counts six runs (as by crossing the boundary before touching the ground); *also* **:** one from which six runs are scored **7 a :** a playing team of six members (as in ice hockey) **b** (1) **:** a boat rowed by six oars (2) **:** a crew of six oarsmen (3) **sixes** *pl* **:** races for 6-oared boats **8 a :** an internal-combustion engine having six cylinders **b :** an automobile powered with a six-cylinder engine **9 :** the subdivision of six girls in a brownie scout pack in the Girl Guide movement in Britain, Canada, and various other countries — **at sixes and sevens** *also* **at six and seven :** in disorder **:** CONFUSED ⟨the house is rather *at sixes and sevens* —Arnold Bennett⟩ ⟨far from being the only authorities who are *at sixes and sevens* on this problem —R.S.Churchill⟩

six-ace flats *n pl* **:** a pair of dice so shaped as to produce a disproportionate frequency of appearance of the numbers 6, 2, and 12, and so to increase the likelihood of the shooter's losing in craps

six·ain \sə̇ˈzān, (ˈ)sikˌsān\ *n* -s [F, fr. OF *sisain*, fr. *sis* six, fr. L *sex*] **:** a stanza of six lines **:** SEXTAIN

six-banded armadillo \ˈ≈,≈≈-\ *n* **:** PELUDO 1

six-bid solo *n* **:** a card game resembling frog

six-by-six \ˈ≈ˌbaˈ≈\ *n* **:** a six-wheeled motor vehicle with six driving wheels

six-coupled locomotive \ˈ≈,≈≈-\ *n* **:** a locomotive with three pairs of driving wheels connected together by coupling rods

six-day bicycle race *n* **:** an endurance race usu. held on an indoor track between teams of two cyclists who ride alternately for a total of 144 hours

six-day disease *n* **:** a highly fatal nutritional deficiency disease of very young chicks marked by extreme thirst, incoordination, collapse, and death

six-eared barley \ˈ≈,≈-\ *n* **:** SIX-ROWED BARLEY

six·er \ˈsiksə(r)\ *n* -s **:** a leader of a six in a pack of brownie scouts in the Girl Guide movement in Britain, Canada, and various other countries

six·ern \ˈsiksərn\ *n* -s [Norw *seksæring, seksring*, fr. ON *sexæringr*, fr. *sex* six + *ār* oar + *-ingr* -ing; akin to OE *ār* oar — more at SIX] **:** a long Scottish fishing boat propelled by six oars and used esp. in the Shetland islands

six·foil \ˈsik,sfȯil\ *n* [by alter.] **:** SEXFOIL

1six·fold \ˈsikˌsfōld\ *adj* [ME *sexfold*, fr. OE *sixfeald*, fr. *six* + *-feald* -fold] **1 :** having six parts or aspects **2 :** being six times as large, as great, or as many as some understood size, degree, or amount ⟨a ∼ increase⟩

2sixfold \"\ *adv* **:** to six times as much or as many **:** by six times ⟨increased ∼⟩

six-gilled shark *also* **sixgill shark** \ˈ≈,≈-\ *n* **:** a cowshark (genus *Hexanchus*) having six gill slits; *esp* **:** a common dusky Pacific shark (*H. griseus*) — compare HEXANCHIDAE

six-gun \ˈ≈,≈\ *n* **:** a 6-chambered revolver

six-man football *n* **:** football retaining the basic features of the American game and played on a modified field between six-man teams

six-mast·er \ˈ≈ˈ≈ə(r)\ *n* **:** a 6-masted ship

six·mo \ˈsik(ˌ)smō\ *n* -s [*six* + *-mo*] **:** the size of a piece of paper cut six from a sheet; *also* **:** paper or a page of this size — abbr. *6mo*; symbol 6° ; see BOOK tables

six-o-six *or* **606** \ˌsikˌsōˈsiks\ *n* [so called fr. its having been the 606th compound tested and introduced by Paul Ehrlich †1915 Ger. bacteriologist] **:** ARSPHENAMINE

six-pack \ˈ≈,≈\ *n* **1 :** a container for six bottles or cans purchased together **2 :** the contents of a six-pack

six-pack

six-pack bezique *n* **:** rubicon bezique played with six packs of cards shuffled together — called also *Chinese bezique*

six·pence \ˈsikspən(t)s *or* -k,spen-; *Brit* ˈsikspən(t)s\ *n, pl* **sixpence** *or* **sixpences** [ME *sixe pens*, fr. *sex* six + *pans* pence, pl. of *peny* penny — more at SIX, PENNY] **1 a :** the sum of six usu. British pennies **b :** a coin representing six pennies or half a shilling **2 :** FIPPENNY BIT

six·pen·ny \-nē, -ni\ *adj* [ME *sixpeny*, fr. 1*six* + *peny* penny] **1 :** of the value of or costing sixpence ⟨a ∼ thriller⟩ **2 :** of trifling worth **:** CHEAP, TRASHY

sixpenny bit *n* **:** SIXPENCE

sixpenny nail *n* [ME *sixpeny nail* nail costing sixpence per hundred, fr. *sixpeny* sixpenny + *nail*] **:** a nail about 2 inches long

six·pen·ny·worth \(ˈ)sikˈspeni,wōth, (ˈ)sikˈspenəth, ˈsikspəni,wōth\ *n* [ME *sixe peny worthe*] **:** amount purchasable with or valued at sixpence

six-principle baptist *n, usu cap S&P&B* **:** a member of a Baptist denomination organized in Providence, R.I., in 1653 and distinguished generally by the acceptance of six foundational principles of repentance, baptism, faith, laying on of hands, resurrection of the dead, and eternal judgment drawn from Hebrews 6:1–2

six-rowed barley \ˈ≈,≈-\ *n* **:** a barley having the three spikelets of each cluster fertile so that the spike is six-rowed — compare FOUR-ROWED BARLEY

six-shafted bird of paradise \ˈ≈,≈≈-\ **:** a bird of paradise (*Parotia sefilata*) having three long spatulate feathers on each side of the head

six-shooter \ˈ≈ˌ≈≈\ *n* **:** SIX-GUN

six·some \'siksəm\ *n* -s **:** a group of six persons or things esp. when playing together

six-spotted leafhopper \'⸗,⸗⸗-\ *n* **:** a leafhopper (*Macrosteles fascifrons*) that feeds on various crop plants and transmits several virus diseases of plants

six-spotted mite *n* **:** a plant-feeding mite (*Eotetranychus sexmaculatus*) that causes injury to citrus and other fruit trees

six-square \'⸗¦⸗\ *adj* **1 :** HEXAGONAL **2 :** CUBICAL

sixte \'sikst\ *n* -s [F, lit., sixth, fr. L *sextus;* fr. its being the sixth parrying position — more at SEXT] **:** a fencing parry or guard position defending the upper outside right target in which the hand is to the right at breast height in a position of supination and the tip of the blade is directed at the opponent's eyes — compare TIERCE

1six·teen \(')sik¦stēn\ *adj* [ME *sixtene*, adj. & n., fr. OE *sixtȳne* (akin to OHG *sehszehan*, ON *sextān*), fr. *six* + *-tȳne* (fr. *tȳn* ten) — more at SIX, TEN] **:** being one more than 15 in number ⟨~ years⟩ — see NUMBER table; used prepositively to designate specified years of the 17th century ⟨the *sixteen⸗*eighties⟩ ⟨the early *sixteen*-hundreds⟩

2sixteen \"\ *pron, pl in constr* [ME *sixtene*, fr. *sixtene*, n. & adj.] **:** 16 countable persons or things not specified but under consideration and being enumerated ⟨~ are here⟩ ⟨~ were found⟩

3sixteen \"\ *n* -s [ME *sixtene*, fr. OE *sixtȳne*] **1 :** 10 and six **:** twice eight **:** eight times two **:** four fours **:** the square of four **2 a :** 16 units or objects ⟨a total of ~⟩ **b :** a group or set of 16 **3 :** the numerable quantity symbolized by the arabic numerals 16 **4 :** the 16th in a set or series; *esp* **:** an article of clothing of the 16th size ⟨wears a ~⟩ **5 sixteens** *pl* **:** SIXTEENMO

sixteen-foot octave *n* **:** CONTRAOCTAVE

sixteen-foot pitch *n* **:** the pitch of a 16-foot stop on a pipe organ

sixteen-foot stop *n* **:** a pipe-organ stop sounding pitches an octave lower than the notes indicate — compare EIGHT-FOOT STOP

six·teen·mo \⸗'⸗,mō\ *n* -s [*sixteen* + *-mo*] **:** the size of a piece of paper cut 16 from a sheet; *also* **:** paper or a page of this size — abbr. *16mo;* symbol *16°;* see BOOK tables

sixteen-penny nail \'⸗,⸗,penē-, ⸗'⸗,⸗⸗-\ *n* **:** a nail about 3½ inches long

1six·teenth \(')sik¦stēn(t)th\ *adj* [ME *sixtenthe*, alter. (influenced by *sixtene* sixteen) of *sixtethe*, fr. OE *sixtēotha* (akin to MHG *sehzehende*, ON *sextāndi*) fr. *sixtȳne* sixteen + *-otha*, *-tha* -th] **1 :** being number 16 in a countable series ⟨the ~ day⟩ — see NUMBER table **2 :** being one of 16 equal parts into which something is divisible ⟨a ~ share of the money⟩

2sixteenth \"\ *n, pl* **sixteenths** \-n(t)s, -n(t)ths\ **1 :** number 16 in a countable series ⟨the ~ of the month⟩ **2 :** the quotient of a unit divided by 16 **:** one of 16 equal parts of something ⟨one ~ of the total⟩ **3 a :** a musical interval comprising two octaves and a second **b :** SIXTEENTH NOTE

sixteenth note *n* **:** a musical note with the time value of one sixteenth of a whole note — called also *semiquaver*

sixteenth rest *n* **:** a musical rest corresponding in time value to the sixteenth note

sixteenth notes

1sixth \'siks(t)th, -kst\ *adj* [ME *sixte*, *sexte*, fr. OE *sixta*, *siexta* (akin to OHG *sehto*, *sehsto*, ON *sētti*, Goth *saihsta*), fr. *six*, *siex* six + *-ta* (fr. *-otha*, *-tha* -th)] **1 :** being number six in a countable series ⟨the ~ day⟩ — see NUMBER table **2 :** being one of six equal parts into which something is divisible ⟨a ~ share of the money⟩

2sixth \"\ *n, pl* **sixths** \-ks(ts), -ks(t)ths\ **1 :** number six in a countable series ⟨the ~ of the month⟩ **2 :** the quotient of a unit divided by six **:** one of six equal parts of something ⟨one ~ of the total⟩ **3 a :** a musical interval embracing six diatonic degrees **b :** a tone at this interval; *specif* **:** the sixth note or tone of a scale **:** SUBMEDIANT **c :** the harmonic combination of two tones a sixth apart **4 :** SIXTE

3sixth \"\ *adv* **1 :** in the sixth place **2 :** with five exceptions ⟨the nation's ~ largest city⟩

sixth chord *n* **:** a musical chord consisting of a tone with its third and its sixth above and usu. being the first inversion of a triad

sixth column *n* **1 :** the aggregate of persons in a country at war who assist the subversive activities of the fifth column by defeatist talk, the spreading of rumors, and other activities that weaken resistance or appease the enemy **2 :** a group organized to combat the fifth column

sixth columnist *n* **:** a member of a sixth column

sixth cranial nerve *or* **sixth nerve** *n* **:** ABDUCENS NERVE

sixth day *n, usu cap S* **:** FRIDAY — used chiefly by the Friends

sixth form *n* **:** the highest form of a British secondary school traditionally representing the moral and intellectual leadership of the school

sixth·ly *adv* **:** in the sixth place

six-three-three \'⸗,⸗'⸗\ *adj* **:** of or relating to a plan of school organization with six grades for the elementary school and three each for the junior and senior high schools — compare EIGHT-FOUR

sixth sense *n* **:** a power of perception like but not one of the five senses **:** a special ability to perceive or comprehend **:** a keen intuitive power ⟨journalists who have a *sixth sense* of news —R.S.Simpson⟩

1six·ti·eth \'sikstēəth, -tiə\ *adj* [ME *sixtithe*, fr. OE *sixtigotha* (akin to ON *sextugandi*), fr. *sixtig* sixty + *-otha*, *-tha* -th] **1 :** being number 60 in a countable series ⟨the ~ day⟩ — see NUMBER table **2 :** being one of 60 equal parts into which something is divisible ⟨a ~ share of the money⟩

2sixtieth \"\ *n* -s **1 :** number 60 in a countable series **2 :** the quotient of a unit divided by 60 **:** one of 60 equal parts of something ⟨one ~ of the total⟩

sixtine *usu cap, var of* SISTINE

1six·ty \'sikstē\ *adj* [ME, fr. OE *sixtig*, *siextig*, n., group of 60, fr. *six*, *siex* six + *-tig* group of ten — more at SIX, EIGHTY] **:** being one more than 59 in number ⟨~ years⟩ — see NUMBER table

2sixty \"\ *pron, pl in constr* **:** 60 countable persons or things not specified but under consideration and being enumerated ⟨~ are here⟩ ⟨~ were found⟩

3sixty \"\ *n* -ES [ME, fr. *sixty*, adj.] **1 :** six tens **:** twice 30 **:** 12 fives **:** four fifteens **:** three twenties **:** three score **:** five dozen **2 a :** 60 units or objects ⟨a total of ~⟩ **b :** a group or set of 60 **3 :** the numerable quantity symbolized by the arabic numerals 60 **4 :** the 60th in a set or series; *esp* **:** an article of clothing of the 60th size **5 :** something having as an essential feature 60 units or members **6 sixties** *pl* **a :** the numbers 60 to 69 inclusive ⟨a golf score in the *sixties*⟩ ⟨all his grades in that subject are in the *sixties*⟩ **b :** the members of a series or set of successive numbers that end in 60 to 69 inclusive ⟨the *sixties* of the preceding century⟩ ⟨lives in the *sixties* in the next block⟩ **c :** the portion of a continuum lying between 60 and 70 on a scale of measure or segmentation ⟨temperatures in the high *sixties* tomorrow⟩ ⟨a man in his *sixties*⟩ ⟨overcoats selling in the *sixties*⟩ — **like sixty :** with great speed, ease, or force ⟨run *like sixty*⟩ ⟨reading a book and chewing gum *like sixty* —Jean Stafford⟩ ⟨it was raining *like sixty* —Mark Twain⟩

1sixty-eight \¦⸗⸗¦⸗\ *adj* **:** being one more than 67 in number ⟨*sixty-eight* years⟩ — see NUMBER table

2sixty-eight \"\ *pron, pl in constr* **:** 68 countable persons or things not specified but under consideration and being enumerated ⟨*sixty-eight* are here⟩ ⟨*sixty-eight* were found⟩

3sixty-eight \"\ *n* **1 :** eight and 60 **:** four times 17 **2 a :** 68 units or objects ⟨a total of *sixty-eight*⟩ **b :** a group or set of 68 **3 :** the numerable quantity symbolized by the arabic numerals 68 **4 :** the 68th in a set or series

1sixty-eighth \¦⸗⸗¦⸗\ *adj* **1 :** being number 68 in a countable series ⟨the *sixty-eighth* day⟩ — see NUMBER table **2 :** being one of 68 equal parts into which something is divisible ⟨a *sixty⸗eighth* share of the money⟩

2sixty-eighth \"\ *n* **1 :** number 68 in a countable series **2 :** the quotient of a unit divided by 68 **:** one of 68 equal parts of something ⟨one *sixty-eighth* of the total⟩

1sixty-fifth \¦⸗⸗¦⸗\ *adj* **1 :** being number 65 in a countable series ⟨the *sixty-fifth* day⟩ — see NUMBER table **2 :** being one of 65 equal parts into which something is divisible ⟨a *sixty⸗fifth* share of the money⟩

2sixty-fifth \"\ *n* **1 :** number 65 in a countable series **2 :** the quotient of a unit divided by 65 **:** one of 65 equal parts of something ⟨one *sixty-fifth* of the total⟩

1sixty-first \¦⸗⸗¦⸗\ *adj* **1 :** being number 61 in a countable series ⟨the *sixty-first* day⟩ — see NUMBER table **2 :** being one of 61 equal parts into which something is divisible ⟨a *sixty⸗first* share of the money⟩

2sixty-first \"\ *n* **1 :** number 61 in a countable series **2 :** the quotient of a unit divided by 61 **:** one of 61 equal parts of something ⟨one *sixty-first* of the total⟩

1sixty-five \¦⸗⸗¦⸗\ *adj* **:** being one more than 64 in number ⟨*sixty-five* years⟩ — see NUMBER table

2sixty-five \"\ *pron, pl in constr* **:** 65 countable persons or things not specified but under consideration and being enumerated ⟨*sixty-five* are here⟩ ⟨*sixty-five* were found⟩

3sixty-five \"\ *n* **1 :** five and 60 **:** five times 13 **2 a :** 65 units or objects ⟨a total of *sixty-five*⟩ **b :** a group or set of 65 **3 :** the numerable quantity symbolized by the arabic numerals 65 **4 :** the 65th in a set or series

1six·ty·fold \¦⸗⸗¦fōld\ *adj* [ME, fr. OE *sixtigfeald*, fr. *sixtig* sixty + *-feald* -fold — more at SIXTY] **1 :** having 60 parts or aspects **2 :** being 60 times as large, as great, or as many as some understood size, degree, or amount ⟨a ~ increase⟩

2sixtyfold \"\ *adv* **:** to 60 times as much or as many **:** by 60 times ⟨brought forth fruit, some an hundredfold, some ~, some thirtyfold —Mt 13: 8 (AV)⟩

1sixty-four \¦⸗⸗¦⸗\ *adj* **:** being one more than 63 in number ⟨*sixty-four* years⟩ — see NUMBER table

2sixty-four \"\ *pron, pl in constr* **:** 64 countable persons or things not specified but under consideration and being enumerated ⟨*sixty-four* are here⟩ ⟨*sixty-four* were found⟩

3sixty-four \"\ *n* **1 :** four and 60 **:** four times 16 **:** the square of 8 **:** the cube of 4 **2 a :** 64 units or objects ⟨a total of *sixty⸗four*⟩ **b :** a group or set of 64 **3 :** the numerable quantity symbolized by the arabic numerals 64 **4 :** the 64th in a set or series

sixty-four-dollar question *n* [so called fr. the fact that $64 was the highest award in the CBS radio quiz show "Take It or Leave It" (1941–48)] **:** a crucial question expressing the basic issue on a problematical subject

sixty-four·mo \,⸗⸗'⸗,mō\ *n* -s [*sixty-four* + *-mo*] **:** the size of a piece of paper cut 64 from a sheet; *also* **:** paper or a page of this size — abbr. *64mo;* symbol *64°;* see BOOK tables

1sixty-fourth \¦⸗⸗¦⸗\ *adj* **1 :** being number 64 in a countable series ⟨the *sixty-fourth* day⟩ — see NUMBER table **2 :** being one of 64 equal parts into which something is divisible ⟨a *sixty⸗fourth* share of the money⟩

2sixty-fourth \"\ *n* **1 :** number 64 in a countable series **2 :** the quotient of a unit divided by 64 **:** one of 64 equal parts of something ⟨one *sixty-fourth* of the total⟩

sixty-fourth note *n* **:** a musical note with half the time value of a thirty-second note

sixty-fourth rest *n* **:** a musical rest corresponding in time value to the sixty-fourth note

sixty-fourth notes

six·ty·ish \'sikstēish, -ti·ish\ *adj* **:** approaching or being about 60 years old ⟨a tall thin ~ man⟩

1sixty-nine \¦⸗⸗¦⸗\ *adj* **:** being one more than 68 in number ⟨*sixty⸗nine* years⟩ — see NUMBER table

2sixty-nine \"\ *pron, pl in constr* **:** 69 countable persons or things not specified but under consideration and being enumerated ⟨*sixty-nine* are here⟩ ⟨*sixty⸗nine* were found⟩

3sixty-nine \"\ *n* **1 :** nine and 60 **:** three times 23 **2 a :** 69 units or objects ⟨a total of *sixty-nine*⟩ **b :** a group or set of 69 **3 :** the numerable quantity symbolized by the arabic numerals 69 **4 :** the 69th in a set or series **5 :** SOIXANTE-NEUF

1sixty-ninth \¦⸗⸗¦⸗\ *adj* **1 :** being number 69 in a countable series ⟨the *sixty-ninth* day⟩ — see NUMBER table **2 :** being one of 69 equal parts into which something is divisible ⟨a *sixty⸗ninth* share of the money⟩

2sixty-ninth \"\ *n* **1 :** number 69 in a countable series **2 :** the quotient of a unit divided by 69 **:** one of 69 equal parts of something ⟨one *sixty-ninth* of the total⟩

1sixty-one \¦⸗⸗¦⸗\ *adj* **:** being one more than 60 in number ⟨*sixty-one* years⟩ — see NUMBER table

2sixty-one \"\ *pron, pl in constr* **:** 61 countable persons or things not specified but under consideration and being enumerated ⟨*sixty-one* are here⟩ ⟨*sixty-one* were found⟩

3sixty-one \"\ *n* **1 :** one and 60 **2 a :** 61 units or objects ⟨a total of *sixty-one*⟩ **b :** a group or set of 61 **3 :** the numerable quantity symbolized by the arabic numerals 61 **4 :** the 61st in a set or series

six·ty·pen·ny nail \'⸗⸗,penē-\ *n* **:** a nail about 6 inches long

1sixty-second \¦⸗⸗¦⸗⸗\ *adj* **1 :** being number 62 in a countable series ⟨the *sixty-second* day⟩ — see NUMBER table **2 :** being one of 62 equal parts into which something is divisible ⟨a *sixty-second* share of the money⟩

2sixty-second \"\ *n* **1 :** number 62 in a countable series **2 :** the quotient of a unit divided by 62 **:** one of 62 equal parts of something ⟨one *sixty-second* of the total⟩

1sixty-seven \¦⸗⸗¦⸗⸗\ *adj* **:** being one more than 66 in number ⟨*sixty-seven* years⟩ — see NUMBER table

2sixty-seven \"\ *pron, pl in constr* **:** 67 countable persons or things not specified but under consideration and being enumerated ⟨*sixty-seven* are here⟩ ⟨*sixty-seven* were found⟩

3sixty-seven \"\ *n* **1 :** seven and 60 **2 a :** 67 units or objects ⟨a total of *sixty-seven*⟩ **b :** a group or set of 67 **3 :** the numerable quantity symbolized by the arabic numerals 67 **4 :** the 67th in a set or series

1sixty-seventh \¦⸗⸗¦⸗⸗\ *adj* **1 :** being number 67 in a countable series ⟨the *sixty-seventh* day⟩ — see NUMBER table **2 :** being one of 67 equal parts into which something is divisible ⟨a *sixty-seventh* share of the money⟩

2sixty-seventh \"\ *n* **1 :** number 67 in a countable series **2 :** the quotient of a unit divided by 67 **:** one of 67 equal parts of something ⟨one *sixty-seventh* of the total⟩

1sixty-six \¦⸗⸗¦⸗\ *adj* **:** being one more than 65 in number ⟨*sixty-six* years⟩ — see NUMBER table

2sixty-six \"\ *pron, pl in constr* **:** 66 countable persons or things not specified but under consideration and being enumerated ⟨*sixty-six* are here⟩ ⟨*sixty-six* were found⟩

3sixty-six \"\ *n* **1 :** six and 60 **:** three times 22 **:** six times 11 **2 a :** 66 units or objects ⟨a total of *sixty-six*⟩ **b :** a group or set of 66 **3 :** the numerable quantity symbolized by the arabic numerals 66 **4 :** the 66th in a set or series **5 :** a two-hand card game played with a 24-card pack in which the object is to score 66 of a possible 130 points

1sixty-sixth \¦⸗⸗¦⸗\ *adj* **1 :** being number 66 in a countable series ⟨the *sixty-sixth* day⟩ — see NUMBER table **2 :** being one of 66 equal parts into which something is divisible ⟨a *sixty⸗sixth* share of the money⟩

2sixty-sixth \"\ *n* **1 :** number 66 in a countable series **2 :** the quotient of a unit divided by 66 **:** one of 66 equal parts of something ⟨one *sixty-sixth* of the total⟩

1sixty-third \¦⸗⸗¦⸗\ *adj* **1 :** being number 63 in a countable series ⟨the *sixty-third* day⟩ — see NUMBER table **2 :** being one of 63 equal parts into which something is divisible ⟨a *sixty⸗third* share of the money⟩

2sixty-third \"\ *n* **1 :** number 63 in a countable series **2 :** the quotient of a unit divided by 63 **:** one of 63 equal parts of something ⟨one *sixty-third* of the total⟩

1sixty-three \¦⸗⸗¦⸗\ *adj* **:** being one more than 62 in number ⟨*sixty-three* years⟩ — see NUMBER table

2sixty-three \"\ *pron, pl in constr* **:** 63 countable persons or things not specified but under consideration and being enumerated ⟨*sixty-three* are here⟩ ⟨*sixty-three* were found⟩

3sixty-three \"\ *n* **1 :** three and 60 **:** three times 21 **:** seven times nine **2 a :** 63 units or objects ⟨a total of *sixty-three*⟩ **b :** a group or set of 63 **3 :** the numerable quantity symbolized by the arabic numerals 63 **4 :** the 63d in a set or series

1sixty-two \¦⸗⸗¦⸗\ *adj* **:** being one more than 61 in number ⟨*sixty-two* years⟩ — see NUMBER table

2sixty-two \"\ *pron, pl in constr* **:** 62 countable persons or things not specified but under consideration and being enumerated ⟨*sixty-two* are here⟩ ⟨*sixty-two* were found⟩

3sixty-two \"\ *n* **1 :** two and 60 **:** 31 times two **2 a :** 62 units or objects ⟨a total of *sixty-two*⟩ **b :** a group or set of 62 **3 :** the numerable quantity symbolized by the arabic numerals 62 **4 :** the 62d in a set or series

six-weeks grama *or* **six week grama** *n* [so called fr. its rapid growth] **:** any of various grama grasses (as *Bouteloua barbata*) of the western and southwestern U.S.

six-weeks grass *n* **:** any of several low quick-growing annual grasses (as *Poa annua*)

six-wheel·er \'⸗¦⸗ə(r)\ *n* **:** a vehicle (as a motor truck) with six wheels

si·yakh·push \sē'(y)äk,pu̇sh\ *n, pl* **siyakhpush** *or* **siyakhpushes** *usu cap* **:** one of an early people of the southwestern Pamir region of Central Asia

siz·able *or* **size·able** \'sīzəbəl\ *adj* [2*size* + *-able*] **1 :** of reasonable or suitable size or bulk **:** fairly large **:** CONSIDERABLE ⟨the settlement soon grew into a ~ community —Ray Millholland⟩ ⟨a ~ mud puddle —Ring Lardner⟩ **2 :** LARGE ⟨a ~ man⟩ ⟨a pretty ~ chunk of votes —*Emporia* (*Kans.*) *Gazette*⟩

siz·able·ness *n* -ES **:** the quality or state of being sizable

siz·ably \-blē,-bli\ *adv* [*sizable* + *-ly*] **:** in a sizable manner **:** to a sizable degree

si·zal \'sīzəl\ *n* -s [alter. of *sisal*] **:** SISAL HEMP

siz·ar *also* **siz·er** \'sīzə(r)\ *n* -s [*sizar* alter. of *sizer; sizer* fr. 1*size* (sense 2) + *-er*] **:** a student (as in the universities of Cambridge and Dublin) who receives orig. in return for acting as a servant to other students an allowance toward his college expenses — compare SERVITOR

siz·ar·ship \-,ship\ *n* **:** the position or standing of a sizar

1size \'sīz\ *n* -s [ME *sise*, fr. MF, fr. OF, short for *assise* — more at ASSIZE] **1** *dial Brit* **:** ASSIZE 5a — usu. used in pl. **2 a** *obs* **:** ASSIZE 3 **b** *archaic* **:** a fixed portion of food or drink allowed esp. to a university student **3 a** (1) **:** physical magnitude, extent, or bulk **:** the actual, characteristic, normal, or relative proportion of a thing **:** relative or proportionate dimensions ⟨measure the ~ of a box⟩ ⟨trees of all ~*s*⟩ ⟨attain full ~⟩ (2) **:** equal magnitude ⟨boys all of a ~⟩ **b :** relative aggregate amount ⟨the ~ of an order⟩ ⟨the ~ of her bank account⟩ **c :** considerable amount, proportions, volume, character, or importance **:** BIGNESS ⟨few of the fish attain any ~⟩ ⟨we saw no inhabited place of any ~ —Heinrich Harrer⟩ ⟨every town of ~ in the Balkans —*Christian Science Monitor*⟩ **4 a :** one of a series of graduated measures esp. of manufactured articles (as of clothing) conventionally identified by numbers or letters each representing a particular dimension or set of dimensions ⟨a ~ 7 hat⟩ ⟨a shoe of ~ 4A⟩ ⟨~ B pajamas⟩ ⟨khaki breeches about two ~*s* too big —Danforth Ross⟩ ⟨book ~*s*⟩ ⟨rope ~*s*⟩ **b** (1) **:** an article of a particular size ⟨just fills this ~ of glass⟩ ⟨I prefer this ~⟩ (2) **:** one of a series of articles of graduated size ⟨shoe manufacturers make 72 ~*s* —*Women's Wear Daily*⟩ **c :** 2COUNT 8a **5 :** character, quality, or status of a person or thing esp. with reference to importance, relative merit, or correspondence to needs ⟨the office demands a man of larger ~⟩ **6 a :** actual state of affairs **:** true condition ⟨that's about the ~ of it⟩ **b :** true character or significance — used with *down* and *to* and usu. with *cut* or *chop* ⟨cut his opponent down to ~ by skillful questioning⟩

syn SIZE, DIMENSIONS, AREA, EXTENT, MAGNITUDE, VOLUME can signify, in common, the amount of space or, sometimes, time or energy occupied or used. SIZE usu. applies to things having length, width, and depth or height whether involving accurate measurements or merely a general impression of smallness or largeness; it often applies to things computed in terms of the individuals comprising them or the space occupied by the individuals or to things having qualities conceived of in terms of largeness or smallness (as a voice) ⟨a box two feet by three in *size*⟩ ⟨a house of small *size*⟩ ⟨the increase in the *size* of the reading public —Helen Sullivan⟩ ⟨his company . . . has expanded under his management thus far to twice its original *size* in the number of its employees —*Current Biog.*⟩ ⟨the *size* of its power and potentialities —Rupert Emerson⟩ ⟨her remarkably clear and sweet voice is not of great *size* —*New Yorker*⟩ DIMENSIONS (pl. of dimension, a measurement in a single direction, as in width) is a close synonym of SIZE usu., however, implying more frequently an accurate measurement ⟨compute the exact *dimensions* of a building lot⟩ ⟨this book suggests the *dimensions* of the modern tasks of the federal government and of its chief executive —J.M.Blum⟩ ⟨the *dimensions* of the artist's genius —Herbert Read⟩ AREA applies to things measurable in two dimensions or directions only, for example, length and breadth (as of the surface of the ground or a floor) ⟨a parking lot with an *area* of 1500 square yards⟩ ⟨other lakes . . . have an *area* of more than 10,000 acres —*Amer. Guide Series: Minn.*⟩ ⟨a relatively small population compared with the vast *area* served —*Canada Yr. Bk.*⟩ EXTENT chiefly applies to the measurement in one direction, usu. length (as of a driveway), often applying to something conceived of as if it had length; sometimes, however, it is used interchangeably with AREA or SIZE ⟨estimate to the *extent* of the territory from east to west⟩ ⟨the full *extent* of its extreme northern boundary —*Amer. Guide Series: Ariz.*⟩ ⟨a wide *extent* of territory —C.D.Forde⟩ ⟨the *extent* of his vocabulary —C.D.Lewis⟩ ⟨underestimate the *extent* of an enemy's vindictiveness⟩ MAGNITUDE, largely a mathematical and scientific term, may refer to size or two-dimensional extent or to something whose quantity, extent, or degree are expressible chiefly in mathematical figures ⟨a star of small *magnitude*⟩ ⟨an earthquake of sizable *magnitude* —Mary W. Shelley⟩ ⟨a European catastrophe of a *magnitude* so appalling, and a scope so unpredictable —G.B.Shaw⟩ VOLUME, though sometimes close in meaning to SIZE, usu. refers to anything that can be measured in cubic measurements (as cubic feet) or is thought of in terms of cubic size ⟨the expanding air increased considerably the *volume* of the balloon⟩ ⟨the *volume* of the box⟩ ⟨a voice of small *volume*⟩ ⟨the *volume* of bank reserves —G.L.Harrison⟩ ⟨a much greater *volume* of credit —Rafael De Haro⟩ ⟨the *volume* of commercial airline passenger traffic —H.G.Armstrong⟩

— **for size 1 :** for the purpose of determining adequacy or proper fit — usu. used with *try* ⟨try on a hat *for size*⟩ ⟨try a dramatic role *for size*⟩ **2 :** according to the various sizes ⟨these things are going to have to be separated *for size* —James Jones⟩ — **of a size :** of similar size ⟨the robin and the bluejay are much *of a size*⟩

2size \"\ *vb* -ED/-ING/-S [ME *sisen*, fr. *sise*, n.] *vt* **1** *archaic* **:** to fix the standard (as of weight, measure, or capacity) of **:** conform (something) to standard **2** *archaic* **:** to record (a portion of food or drink) as a financial obligation of a university student usu. by an appropriate entry in an account book **:** CHARGE **3 a :** to make a particular size **:** bring to proper or suitable size ⟨systems . . . *sized* to fit anybody's living room —*advt*⟩ ⟨these cars are *sized* to the human frame, not to the human ego —Lewis Mumford⟩ ⟨they're *sized* for bill enclosure use —*Jewelers' Circular-Keystone*⟩ ⟨they ~ clothes to fit, not for children to grow into —Mary B. Picken⟩ ⟨chutes for dropping supplies are *sized* according to the weight of the load they are meant to carry —O.J.Mink⟩ **b :** COIN 1c **4 a :** to arrange, grade, or classify according to size or bulk ⟨copper and nickel powders . . . were *sized* by screening into the four ranges —*Symposium on Powder Metallurgy*⟩ **b :** to make in a series of graduated sizes conventionally identified by numbers or letters each representing a particular dimension or set of dimensions **:** grade (as clothing patterns) according to a set of specified measurements ⟨women's rings may be *sized* to 10; men's to 14 —*Sears, Roebuck Cat.*⟩ ⟨sport shirts *sized* to fit —*G. Fox & Co. Cat.*⟩ **c :** to check (as clothing) against patterns during manufacture **5 :** to arrange (men) in units or formations according to stature ⟨first to ~ the corps of cadets —W.H. Baumer⟩ **6 :** to size up ⟨could feel her listening, *sizing* me —Joseph Hitrec⟩ ~ *vi* **1** *archaic* **:** to order an allowance of food or drink from the buttery esp. of a university college **2 :** to be equal in size, quality, power, or other particular characteristic **:** COMPARE — usu. used with *up* and often with *to* or *with* ⟨a yield that *sized* up very well with last year's⟩ **3 :** to increase in size

3size \"\ *n* -s [ME *sise*, prob. fr. MF, setting, fixing, fr. OF, settlement, assize — more at ASSIZE] **1 a :** any of various glutinous materials (as preparations of glue, flour, varnish, or resins) used for filling the pores in surfaces (as of paper, textiles, leather, or plaster) or in bookbinding for applying color or leaf to book edges or covers — compare GLAIR, GOLD SIZE

b : any material used in papermaking to prevent or retard the penetration of liquids **c :** the adhesive used in coating paper **2 :** a sticky substance used in place of ink when the printing is to be dusted with metallic powder

⁴size \"\ *vt* -ED/-ING/-S **1 :** to cover, stiffen, or glaze with or as if with size **:** treat with size **2 :** to compact (felt) by means of moisture, heat, and pressure esp. in hat making

⁵size *var of* SICE

⁶size \ˈsīz\ *adj* [¹*size*] **:** SIZED 1 — usu. used in combination ⟨has only a pond-*size* harbor —Christopher Rand⟩ ⟨conventional-*size* midtown blocks —Lewis Mumford⟩ ⟨the large economy-*size* box of a breakfast cereal⟩ ⟨bite-*size* candies⟩

sizeable *var of* SIZABLE

size block *n* **:** GAGE BLOCK

size bone *n* **:** a whalebone measuring six feet or more

sized \ˈsīzd\ *adj* [partly fr. ¹*size* + *-ed;* partly fr. past part. of ²*size*] **1 :** having a specified size or bulk — usu. used in combination ⟨a small-*sized* house⟩ ⟨a family-*sized* car⟩ ⟨a fair-*sized* crowd⟩ **2 :** arranged or adjusted according to size **3 a :** being up to standard in size **b :** of the same size

size down *vt* **:** to gradate or arrange from larger to smaller ⟨*size down* roofing slates from the eaves to the ridge⟩

size·man \ˈsīzmən\ *n, pl* **sizemen** [³*size* + *man*] **1 :** one who puts size on leather **2 :** a papermill worker who makes size

¹sizer *var of* SIZAR

²siz·er \ˈsīzə(r)\ *n* -S [²*size* + *-er*] **1 :** one that determines or sorts by sizes or checks for size ⟨an orange ~⟩ **2 :** one that shapes or surfaces articles to the required size ⟨timber ~⟩ **3 :** CLOCKER

³sizer \"\ *n* -S [⁴*size* + *-er*] **1 :** one that applies size **2 :** one that sizes felt hat bodies

sizer die *also* **sizing die** *n* **:** a die to finish threaded work to standard size

sizes *pl of* SIZE, *pres 3d sing of* SIZE

size stick *n* **:** a measuring stick or mechanical device used by shoe fitters to measure a wearer's foot from heel to toe or from heel to ball and the width of the foot at its widest point

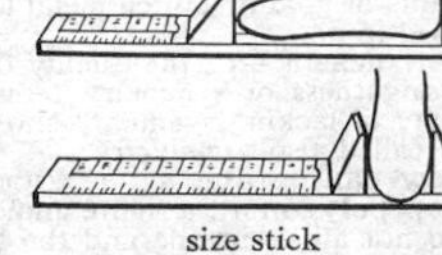

size stick

size up *vt* **:** to estimate or ascertain the character and ability of (a person) **:** form an opinion or judgment (as of a situation) ⟨*sizes up* the candidate quickly —W.L.Gresham⟩ ⟨at the stockyards the steers were *sized up* by two kinds of buyers —*advt*⟩ ⟨the power to *size up* a new problem —H.A. Overstreet⟩ **~** *vi* **:** to appear or be known as a result of being sized up ⟨here's the way the situation *sizes up* in key fields —*Newsweek*⟩ ⟨as the outlook *sizes up* . . . at this time —*U.S. News & World Report*⟩

size–up \ˈ=,=\ *n* -S [*size up*] **1 :** the action of sizing up (a person or thing) ⟨preventing a quick *size-up* of existing conditions —J.J.McCarthy⟩ **2 :** an evaluation arrived at by sizing up ⟨give a *size-up* of the applicants⟩

siz·i·ness \ˈsīzēnəs, -zin-\ *n* -ES *archaic* **:** the quality or state of being sizy **:** VISCOUSNESS

¹sizing *n* -S [fr. gerund of ²*size*] **1 :** the act or process of one that sizes **2 :** a fixed portion of food or drink ordered from the kitchen of an English university **3 sizings** *pl* **:** the coarsest particles of wheat endosperm broken out in the milling process **:** coarse middlings

²sizing *n* -S [fr. gerund of ⁴*size*] **:** ³SIZE

sizing tool *or* **sizing chisel** *n* **:** a wood-turning tool with a gauge clamped to it to determine the size of the wood turned

sizy \ˈsīzē, -zi\ *adj* -ER/-EST [³*size* + *-y*] *archaic* **:** VISCOUS, GLUTINOUS

¹sizz \ˈsiz\ *vi* -ED/-ING/-ES [prob. back-formation fr. ¹*sizzle*] **:** to hiss or to move with a hissing sound ⟨the bumblebee ~*ed* right under his straw hat —Feike Feikema⟩

²sizz \"\ *n* -ES **:** a hissing sound

¹siz·zle \ˈsizəl\ *vb* **sizzled; sizzled; sizzling** \-z(ə)liŋ\ **sizzles** [perh. freq. of *siss*] *vt* **1 :** to burn up or sear with scorching heat typically so as to produce a hissing sound ⟨the sun was beginning to ~ the whole wide valley —Richard Bissell⟩ **2 :** to affect painfully by heated language ⟨speakers *sizzled* the opposition⟩ **~** *vi* **1 a :** to make a hissing sound ⟨a dish of *sizzling* fat —Richard Llewellyn⟩ ⟨oil lamp which *sizzled* softly on his table —R.P.Warren⟩ ⟨powdery snow *sizzled* under their skis —Aldous Huxley⟩ ⟨only the desultory *sizzling* of some little bird —D.C.Peattie⟩ **b :** to produce the effect of making a hissing sound ⟨ink that ~s on the page —*Rotarian*⟩ ⟨everyone *sizzling* with enthusiasm —W.A.White⟩ ⟨the town *sizzled* with the news —Dorothy Parker⟩ **2 :** to move with or as if with a hissing sound ⟨lava *sizzling* down the snowy mountainside⟩ ⟨cars *sizzled* past us on the highway⟩ **3 :** to be in a state of partially repressed agitation caused esp. by deep anger or resentment ⟨*sizzling* because of the unsupported allegations⟩ **4 :** to perform or become performed at top form or in a noticeably improved manner ⟨the champion *sizzled* on the course today⟩ ⟨sales immediately began to ~⟩

²sizzle \"\ *n* -S **:** a hissing sound (as of something frying over a fire) ⟨there trailed in her wake a ~ of gossip —Marcia Davenport⟩

siz·zler \-z(ə)lə(r)\ *n* -S **:** one that sizzles; *esp* **:** SCORCHER

¹sizzling *adj* **:** that sizzles ⟨~ steaks⟩ ⟨a ~ commentary on investor psychology —Felix Belair⟩ ⟨~ political issues —J.A. Mayer⟩ **:** very hot ⟨a ~ spell of weather⟩ — **siz·zling·ly** *adv*

²sizzling *adv* **:** to a sizzling degree ⟨~ hot steaks⟩

sizzling heat *n* **:** a degree of heat (as about 400 to 450° F) that is approximately that of iron just hot enough to hiss when touched with a moistened finger

SJ *abbr, often not cap* [L *sub judice*] under consideration

sjam·bok \(ˈ)shamˌbäk, -ˌbək\ *n* -S [Afrik *sambok*, fr. Malay *cambok* large whip, fr. Hindi *cābuk* — more at CHAWBUCK] *southern Africa* **:** a heavy leather whip often of rhinoceros hide

SJC *abbr* Supreme Judicial Court

SJD \ˌesˌjāˈdē\ *abbr or n* -S [NL *scientiae juridicae doctor*] **:** a doctor of juridical science

sjo·gren·ite \ˈshōgrəˌnīt, ˈshə(r)g-\ *n* -S [Sw *sjögrenit*, fr. Hjalmar *Sjögren* †1922 Swed. mineralogist + Sw *-it* -ite] **:** a mineral $Mg_6Fe_2(OH)_{16}(CO_3).4H_2O$ consisting of a hydrous hydroxide and carbonate of magnesium and iron isomorphous with manasseite and barbertonite

sjt *abbr, often cap* serjeant

sk *abbr* **1** sack **2** sick **3** sink; sinking **4** sketch **5** skewbald **6** skewness **7** skip

SK *abbr* storekeeper

skaam·oog \ˈskäˌmōg\ *n* -S [Afrik, fr. *skaam* to be ashamed (fr. D *schamen*, fr. MD) + *oog* eye, fr. D, fr. MD *oge;* prob. fr. the habit of folding the tail over the head when caught; akin to OHG *ouga* eye — more at SHAME, EYE] *southern Africa* **:** a cat shark of the family Scyliorhinidae

skaapsteker *var of* SCHAAPSTEKER

skad *var of* SCAD

¹skaddle *var of* SCADDLE

²skad·dle \ˈskadᵊl\ *vi* -ED/-ING/-S [by alter.] *dial* **:** SKEDADDLE

skaff·ie \ˈskafi\ *n* -S [E dial. *skaff* light boat, skiff (fr. ME *skaf*, fr. MF *scaphe, escaffe*, fr. L *scapha*, fr. Gk *skaphē*) + E *-ie* — more at SCAPHOID] **:** a Scottish fishing boat having the stem raked and rounding and the stern raked and usu. main and mizzen dipping lugsails

¹skag *var of* SKEG

²skag \ˈskag, -aa(ə)g, -aig\ *n* -S [origin unknown] *slang* **:** CIGARETTE

skag·it \ˈskajət\ *n, pl* **skagit** *or* **skagits** *usu cap* **1 a :** a Salishan people of the Skagit and Stillaguamish river valleys, northwestern Washington **b :** a member of such people **2 :** a Salishan dialect often taken as representative of a group of dialects that includes also Nisqualli, Puyallup, Snoqualmie, Suquamish, and Swinomish

skaif *var of* SKEIF

skail *chiefly Scot var of* ⁴SCALE

skain *var of* SKEIN 1

skair \ˈskär\ *chiefly Scot var of* SCARE

skait \ˈskāt\ *archaic var of* ²SKATE, ³SKATE

skaith \ˈskāth\ *dial var of* SCATHE

skalawag *var of* SCALAWAG

skald *or* **scald** \ˈskȯld, ˈskäld\ *n* -S [ON *skāld* — more at SCOLD] **1 :** one of the ancient Scandinavian poets and historiographers **:** a Norse reciter and singer esp. of heroic poems and eulogies **2 :** a bard of an ancient Teutonic tribe

skald·ic *or* **scald·ic** \-dik, -dēk\ *adj* **:** of or relating to the Norse skalds or their poetry

skan·dhas \ˈskändəs\ *n pl* [Skt *skandha*] *Buddhism* **:** the five transitory personal elements of body, perception, conception, volition, and consciousness whose temporary concatenation forms the individual self

skarn \ˈskärn, kȧn\ *n* -S [Sw, lit., filth; akin to ON *skarn* dirt, dung — more at SCAT-] **:** contact metamorphic rock rich in iron

skart *var of* SCART

¹skat *or* **scat** \ˈskät, *usu* -äd·+V\ *n* -S [G, modif. of It *scarto* discard, fr. *scartare* to discard, fr. *s-* (fr. L *ex-*) + *-cartare* (fr. *carta* card) — more at CARD] **1 :** a three-handed card game played with 32 cards in which players bid for the privilege of attempting any of several contracts and value their hands according to the contract played, trump suit, points taken, and number of matadors **2 :** a widow of two cards in skat that may be used by the winner of the bid when various contracts are undertaken

²skat *var of* SCAT

¹skate \ˈskāt, *usu* -ād·+V\ *n, pl* **skates** *also* **skate** [ME *scate*, fr. ON *skata*] **1 :** any of numerous rays of *Raja* and related genera of the family Rajidae that have the pectoral fins greatly developed giving the animal a rhomboidal shape and that include the common gray skate (*Raja batis*) of Europe which sometimes weighs over 100 pounds and is extensively used as food, the barn-door skate, the little skate, and the thornback **2 a :** SKATE BOTTOM **b :** one of the units of gear making up a setline esp. in Pacific coast fisheries and consisting of several hundred fathoms of groundline with gangions and hooks attached — compare TUB

²skate \"\ *n* -S [modif. of D *schaats* skate, stilt, fr. MD *schaetse* stilt, fr. (assumed) ONF *escache* (akin to OF *eschace* stilt), perh. of Gmc origin; akin to OS *skakan* to depart — more at SHAKE] **1 a :** one of a pair of devices worn on the feet for skating on ice: as (1) **:** a shoe with a metal runner fastened to the sole — called also *ice skate;* see FIGURE SKATE, HOCKEY SKATE, RACING SKATE (2) **:** DOUBLE-RUNNER **b :** ROLLER SKATE **2** [³*skate*] **:** a period of skating ⟨went for a ~ on the pond⟩ **3 :** a sliding shoe fitting over a rail (as in a classification yard) to stop railroad cars not being retarded by brakes **4 :** a vertical fender (as a curved steel skid) fastened to the side of a ship's boat to fend it clear of the ship's side while lowering from davits on the high side of a listing ship

³skate \"\ *vb* -ED/-ING/-S *vi* **1 a :** to glide along on skates propelled by the alternate action of the legs **b :** to compete in a skating match ⟨picked to ~ against the visiting team⟩ **2 :** to slip or glide as if on skates ⟨bugs that ~ on top of the creek⟩ **3 :** to proceed in a superficial or venturesome manner (as over a dangerous subject) **:** pass lightly ⟨his ability deftly to ~ over subjects which Americans find unfit for mixed society — Ernest Beaglehole⟩ **~** *vt* **:** to go along or through by skating ⟨watched him ~ the length of the rink⟩ ⟨merely ~s the surface of the difficulties involved —*New Republic*⟩

⁴skate \"\ *n* -S [prob. alter. of ³*skite*] **1 :** a contemptible person ⟨these shyster ~s . . . just slip in like the boll weevil —*Tourist News*⟩ **2 :** a thin awkward-looking or decrepit horse **:** NAG **3 :** FELLOW ⟨the baseball throng beams upon the president and agrees that he is a pretty good ~ after all —*Los Angeles (Calif.) Examiner*⟩

skate·able \ˈskād·əbəl\ *adj* **:** suitable to skate on

skate barrow *n* **:** the egg case of a skate

skate bottom *n* **:** a square of canvas with a length of rope attached to each corner for storing a coiled skate of setline

skate machine *n* **:** a mechanism electrically controlled and electrically or pneumatically operated for placing a skate on or removing it from the rail

skate·mo·bile \ˈskātmōˌbēl\ *n* -S **:** a child's vehicle similar to a scooter moving on skates or skate wheels

skatemobile

skat·er \ˈskād·ə(r), -ātə-\ *n* -S **1 :** one that skates **2 :** WATER STRIDER

skate sailing *n* **:** the sport of sailing on ice skates using a large sail attached to crossed sticks and held on the shoulders at an angle to the wind

skating *adj* **:** that is being skated upon or weighted ⟨the ~ foot⟩; *also* **:** that is on the same side of the body as the foot on which one is skating ⟨the ~ shoulder⟩ ⟨the ~ arm⟩

skating position *n* **:** a figure skating and folk dancing position in which partners are side by side with arms crossed in front and identical hands clasped

skat·ole *also* **skat·ol** *or* **scat·ole** \ˈskaˌtōl, -tȯl\ *n* -S [ISV *scat-* + *-ole*] **:** a crystalline compound C_9H_9N that has a disagreeable odor unless much diluted, that is found along with indole in the intestines and feces and also occurs in civet and several plants, but is usu. synthesized from propionaldehyde phenylhydrazone, and that is used in perfumes chiefly as a fixative; 3-methyl-indole

skatology *var of* SCATOLOGY

skaw *var of* SCAW

¹skean *or* **skeen** *or* **skene** *also* **skhian** \ˈs(h)kē(ə)n\ *n* -S [IrGael *scian* & ScGael *sgian;* ScGael *sgian* akin to IrGael *scian;* IrGael *scian* fr. MIr, knife; akin to OE *scēadan, scādan* to divide, separate — more at SHED] **:** DAGGER, DIRK: **a :** a bronze double-edged dagger anciently used in Ireland **b :** SKEAN DHU

²skean *or* **skeane** *var of* SKEIN

skean dhu \-ˈthü\ *n, pl* **skean dhus** [ScGael *sgian dubh*, lit., black skean] **:** a dagger worn by Scottish Highlanders in full dress

skean·ock·le *also* **skene·oc·cle** \ˈskēˌnäkəl\ *n* -S [ScGael *sgian-achlais*, fr. *sgian* skean + *achlais* armpit; akin to L *axilla* armpit — more at AXIS] *Scot* **:** a small dirk

skeat *var of* SCEAT

¹sked \ˈsked\ *n* -S [by shortening & alter.] **:** SCHEDULE

²sked \"\ *vt* **skedded; skedded; skedding; skeds** [by shortening & alter.] **:** SCHEDULE — **sked·der** \-də(r)\ *n* -S

¹ske·dad·dle \skəˈdadᵊl, skēˈ-\ *vi* **skedaddled; skedaddled; skedaddling** \-d(ᵊ)liŋ\ **skedaddles** [origin unknown] **:** to run away **:** leave hastily; *specif* **:** to take flight in a panic — **ske·dad·dler** \-d(ᵊ)lə(r)\ *n* -S

²skedaddle \"\ *n* -S **:** the act of skedaddling

skedge \ˈskej\ *also* **skedge·with** \-ˌwith\ *n* -S [Corn *skeswedhen, skeswȳth*, lit., shade tree, fr. *skēs* shade + *gwedhen, gwȳth* tree; akin to OIr *scāth* shadow and to OIr *fid* tree — more at SHADE, WOOD] **:** PRIVET 1a(1)

sked·lock \ˈskedˌläk, -dlək\ *n* [alter. of Sc *skeldock*] **:** JOINTED CHARLOCK

skee *var of* SKI

Skee–Ball \ˈ=,=\ *trademark* — used for an indoor target game in which a series of hard rubber balls are rolled along a slightly inclined wooden alley whose far end is curved upward so as to project the ball up and backward into one of several concentric circular scoring troughs whose score values increase as the circles decrease in size

skeel \ˈskēl, *esp before pause or consonant* -ēəl\ *n* -S [ME *skele*, of Scand origin; akin to ON *skjōla* pail, bucket; akin to OFris *skūl* hiding place — more at SHIEL] *dial chiefly Brit* **:** a wooden pail, bucket, or tub usu. having handles formed by staves extending above the rim

skeel·ing \ˈskēlən, -liŋ\ *or* **skil·ling** \ˈskil-\ *n* -S [ME *skelyng*, fr. *skel-* (of Scand origin; akin to ON *skjōl* shelter, cover) + *-inge, -ing, -yng* -ing — more at SHIEL] *dial Brit* **:** an outbuilding attached like a lean-to to another

skeely \ˈskēlē\ *archaic var of* SKILLY

skeen *var of* SKEAN

skeen arch *var of* SCHEME ARCH

¹skeet \ˈskēt, *usu* -ēd·+V\ *n* -S [ME *skete*] **:** a scoop on the end of a long pole formerly used for throwing water on the sails of a ship to tighten the canvas

²skeet \"\ *vb* -ED/-ING/-S [prob. alter. of ¹*scoot*] *vi* **1** *dial* **:** to move along quickly **:** SCOOT ⟨when you ~*ed* across the field — P.E.Green⟩ **2** *dial* **:** to cause a liquid to squirt **~** *vt, dial* **:** to cause to move along quickly or squirt ⟨you ~*ed* the water right in my ear —Carson McCullers⟩

³skeet \"\ *or* **skeet shooting** *n* -S [modif. of ON *skjōta* to shoot — more at SHOOT] **:** trapshooting in which clay targets are thrown in such a way as to simulate the angles of flight found in wing shooting

⁴skeet \"\ *n* -S [origin unknown] **:** a special hand recognized in some poker games that is composed of 9, 5, 2, and two other cards below the ten in rank (as 9, 6, 5, 3, 2) and no pair and that beats three of a kind but loses to a straight — called also *kilter, pelter*

¹skeet·er \ˈskēd·ə(r), -ētə-\ *n* -S [by shortening & alter.] **1 :** MOSQUITO **2 :** a small iceboat approximately 16 feet in length equipped with a single sail, a single steering runner in the front, and two runners in the rear

²skeeter \"\ *n* -S [³*skeet* + *-er*] **:** a skeet shooter

skee trap *n* [perh. so called fr. the resemblance of the trajectories of the targets to those of ski jumpers] **:** a trap used in trap and skeet shooting that is mounted in such a way as to make possible its inclination at any desired horizontal or vertical angle before the target is thrown — called also *joker trap*

skee·zicks *or* **skee·sicks** *or* **skee·zix** \ˈskēziks\ *n* -ES [origin unknown] **:** RASCAL ⟨you little ~⟩

skeg \ˈskeg\ *also* **skag** \ˈskag, -aa(ə)g, -aig\ *n* -S [D *scheg, schegge;* akin to ON *skaga* to project — more at SHAG] **1 :** the afterpart of the keel of a vessel near the sternpost or a part in extension of the keel upon which the rudder rests; *esp* **:** the part connecting the keel with the bottom of the rudderpost in a single-screw vessel **2 :** the vertical triangular piece taking the place of the afterpart of a keel in a flat-bottomed boat **3 :** a protecting part that projects below the propeller of an outboard motor

skeg·ger \ˈskegə(r)\ *n* -S [origin unknown] **:** a young salmon

skeif *also* **skaif** \ˈskīf, -kāf\ *n* -S [D *schijf* skeif, disk; akin to OHG *sciba* disk — more at SHEAVE] **:** a diamond cutter's polishing wheel

skeigh \ˈskēk\ *adj* [perh. of Scand origin; akin to Sw *skygg* shy — more at SHY] *chiefly Scot* **:** proudly spirited **:** SKITTISH — often used of a horse or a woman

skeily *var of* SKILLY

¹skein \ˈskān\ *n* -S [ME *skeyne, skayne*, fr. MF *escaigne*] **1** *or* **skean** *or* **skeane** \"\ **:** a loosely coiled length of yarn or thread wound on a reel in lengths suitable for a manufacturing process (as dyeing) or for sale as knitting wool or embroidery floss; *also* **:** such a bundle containing a given amount — compare HANK **2 :** something suggesting the twistings and contortions of a skein ⟨unravel the tangled ~ of evidence⟩ **3 :** a flock of wild fowl (as geese or ducks) in flight — compare GAGGLE **4 :** SPIREME

²skein \"\ *vt* -ED/-ING/-S **:** to wind into skeins

³skein \ˈskān\ *n* -S [D *scheen* narrow strip, shin, fr. MD *schene* — more at SHIN] **1** *also* **skain** \"\ **:** a trimmed strip of osier made from splits for basketwork **2 :** a metal thimble on an axletree arm

skein·er \ˈskānə(r)\ *n* -S **:** one that skeins: as **a :** an operator of a machine for winding thread, yarn, or twine into skeins **b :** a worker who winds unfinished cloth into skein form for boiling off

skel·der \ˈskeldə(r)\ *vb* -ED/-ING/-S [origin unknown] *vi, archaic* **:** to live by begging **:** BEG **~** *vt* **1** *archaic* **:** to obtain money from by fraud **:** CHEAT **2** *archaic* **:** to obtain (money) dishonestly

skel·et \ˈskelət\ *n* -S [Gk *skeletos*, fr. *skeletos*, adj.] *archaic* **:** SKELETON

skelet- *or* **skeleto-** *comb form* [NL, fr. *skeleton*] **1 :** skeleton ⟨*skelet*al⟩ ⟨*skeleto*logy⟩ **2 :** skeletal and ⟨*skeleto*muscular⟩

skel·e·tal \ˈskeləd·ᵊl, -lətᵊl\ *adj* [*skelet-* + *-al*] **1 :** of or relating to a skeleton ⟨~ material of the mound builders is abundant in many localities —Thomas Barbour⟩ **2 :** having the character of a skeleton, framework, or outline **:** SKELETON ⟨a large red and green buoy, with a ~ body like a derrick —Wirt Williams⟩ ⟨no more than a ~ survey of the life of the university —F.C.James⟩ **3 :** resembling a skeleton; *esp* **:** EMACIATED ⟨a nightmare population of gaunt men and ~ boys —Sydney Alexander⟩ **4** *of a soil* **:** belonging to the lithosol group and composed chiefly of rock fragments — **skel·e·tal·ly** \-ᵊlē, -ᵊli\ *adv*

skeletal muscle *n* **:** a muscle attached to the skeleton — distinguished from *smooth muscle* and *cardiac muscle*

skel·e·tog·e·nous \ˌskeləˈtäjənəs\ *adj* [*skelet-* + *-genous*] **:** forming skeletal tissue **:** OSTEOGENIC

skel·e·to·muscular \ˌskeləd·(ˌ)ō, -ə(ˌ)tō+\ *adj* [*skelet-* + *muscular*] **:** constituting, belonging to, or dependent upon the skeleton and the muscles that move it ⟨~ activity⟩ ⟨~ structures⟩

¹skel·e·ton \ˈskelətᵊn\ *n* -S [NL, fr. Gk, neut. of *skeletos* dried up, withered; akin to OE *scealdi* shallow, *hellheort* terrified, MLG *schal* dull, clouded, insipid, MHG *hel* weak, Sw *skäll* watery, ON *hallæri* bad season, famine, Gk *skellein* to dry up, *sklēros* hard, harsh, stiff] **1 :** a supportive or protective structure or framework of an animal, a plant, or a part of an animal or plant: as **a :** the bones of a human being or other vertebrate; *broadly* **:** the bony or more or less cartilaginous framework supporting the soft tissues and protecting the internal organs **b :** any of various analogous structures in an invertebrate (as the mesh of spicules of a sponge, the shell of a brachiopod or mollusk, or the chitinous or partially calcareous covering of an arthropod) — see ENDOSKELETON, EXOSKELETON **c :** a rigid protective covering of a lower plant (as the frustule of a diatom) **d :** the vascular system of a vascular plant and esp. of an herbaceous plant or leaf in which it is a framework readily separable (as by weathering or retting) ⟨the lacy ~ of a leaf⟩ **2 :** something reduced to its minimum form or essential parts **3 :** an emaciated person or animal **4 :** something forming a structural framework: as **a :** the basic structure of a creative work (as a play) **b :** a written plan for a literary work having headings for main divisions **:** OUTLINE **c :** a rigidly connected frame of steel or reinforced concrete used in the construction of tall buildings that supports the external wall and distributes all loads and stresses to the foundation **d :** the framework of a molecular structure comprising a straight or branched chain or ring of atoms to which other atoms may be attached — compare NUCLEUS 2j, RING SYSTEM ⟨the carbon ~ of isoleucine⟩ **5 :** something shameful and kept secret (as in a family) — often used in the phrases *skeleton in the closet, skeleton in the cupboard* **6 :** a heavy steel-runnered sled capable of great speed and steered only by dragging the feet and shifting one's weight and used by Alpine tobogganers **7 :** the disposition of the pawns in a chess position — **skeleton at the feast :** someone or something that serves to bring unpleasant memories or prospects to the minds of pleasure-seekers

²skeleton \"\ *vt* -ED/-ING/-S **:** SKELETONIZE

³skeleton \"\ *adj* **1 :** of or having the character of a skeleton ⟨a ~ hand⟩; *specif* **:** having only the minimum form or essential parts ⟨a ~ plan⟩ ⟨a ~ wagon⟩ **2 :** consisting of the smallest number of persons who can care for an establishment and do essential work ⟨a ~ crew⟩ ⟨a ~ staff⟩ **3 :** of a structure having open interior parts ⟨a ~ spade⟩; *specif* **:** of or being a movement, dial, or timepiece with all but essential metal framework removed in order to allow the works to be observed **4** *of clothing* **:** PARTIAL ⟨a ~ lining⟩

skeleton chase *n* **:** a large narrow-framed printer's chase with no crossbars or slots for crossbars

skeleton construction *n* **:** a method of constructing high buildings in which the chief horizontal and vertical members are of rolled steel and the walls are for the most part supported at the floor levels by the steel frame itself

skeleton crystal *n* **:** an imperfect crystal arrested in development after the forming of the outline but before the filling in of the faces

skeleton dance *n* **:** a ceremonial dance in which dancers are costumed to represent skeletons or death; *also* **:** the dance of death in European folklore

skeleton form *n* **1 :** a form with limited printing areas (as used in printing blankbooks) **2 :** a form with scattered printing areas for printing a second color

skel·e·ton·ic \¦skelə¦tänik\ *adj* **:** resembling or resembling that of a skeleton

skel·e·ton·iza·tion \ˌ⸗⸗tᵊnə'zāshən, -tᵊn,ī'z-\ *n* -S **:** the act or process of skeletonizing

skel·e·ton·ize \'⸗⸗tᵊn,īz\ *vb* -ED/-ING/-S *vt* **:** to produce in or reduce to skeleton form or strength ⟨~ a leaf⟩: as **a** (1) **:** to produce or reproduce in brief outline ⟨~ the plot of a novel in one paragraph⟩ (2) **:** to shorten (newspaper copy) for cable or headline purposes by eliminating nonessential words (as articles, personal pronouns) **b :** to reduce (as a regiment) to a number of men and officers far below the complement ⟨machinery was put in motion to bring men home early for discharge, to start *skeletonizing* units —T.R.Phillips⟩ **c :** to break up for colors ~ *vi* **1 :** to produce or reproduce something in skeleton form **2 :** to become a skeleton or like a skeleton

skel·e·ton·iz·er \-zə(r)\ *n* -S **:** one that skeletonizes; *specif* **:** any of various lepidopterous larvae that eat the parenchyma of leaves leaving the skeleton of veins and the upper or lower epidermis

skeleton key *n* **:** a key with a large part of the bit filed away so as to avoid the wards and thus enable it to open a low quality lock by manipulation

skel·e·ton·less \'⸗⸗⸗ˌləs\ *adj* **:** having no skeleton

skeleton pattern *n* **:** a pattern constructed in skeleton form in whose open spaces sand is inserted

skeleton proof *n* **:** a proof of a print or engraving with the inscription in hair strokes only

skeleton keys

skeletons *pl of* SKELETON, *pres 3d sing of* SKELETON

skeleton shrimp *n* **:** an amphipod crustacean of *Caprella* or a related genus

skeleton suit *n* **:** a boy's tight-fitting suit with the trousers buttoned to the jacket worn in the 19th century

skeleton weed *n* **1 :** GUM SUCCORY **2 a :** a central No. American perennial composite weed (*Lygodesmia pincea*) with rosy purple flower heads on leafless rushlike stems that rise from a basal tufted rosette of elongated leaves — called also *purple skeleton weed* **b :** any of several other plants of the genus *Lygodesmia*

skel·e·tony \'skelətᵊnē\ *adj* **:** SKELETONIC

skelets *pl of* SKELET

¹**skelf** \'skelf\ *Scot var of* SHELF

²**skelf** \"\ *n* [perh. fr. ScGael *sgealb*] *Scot* **:** SLIVER, SPLINTER

skelic index \'skelik-\ *n* [*skelic* fr. Gk *skelos* leg + E *-ic* — more at CYLINDER] **:** an anthropometric index consisting of the ratio of the length of the leg to the length of the trunk multiplied by 100

skel·lat \'skelət\ *n* [ME (northern dial.) *skellet*, fr. ONF *escalete*, fr. *esquelle* small bell (of Gmc origin; akin to OHG *scella* small bell) + OF *-ete* -ette; akin to OHG *scellan* to resound, ring — more at SHILL] **1** *Scot* **:** a small bell; *esp* **:** HANDBELL **2** *Scot* **:** a shrewish woman

skel·ling·ton \'skeliŋtən\ *n* -S [by alter. (influence of names such as *Washington, Uffington*)] **:** SKELETON

¹**skel·loch** \'skelək\ *n* [prob. imit.] *Scot* **:** SCREECH, SCREAM

²**skelloch** \"\ *vi* -ED/-ING/-S *Scot* **:** SCREAM

skel·lum \'skeləm\ *n* -S [D *schelm*, fr. LG, fr. MLG, scoundrel, corpse, carrion; akin to OHG *skelmo* person deserving death, *scalmo* pestilence, corpse, and prob. to Lith *skelti* to split — more at SHELL] *chiefly Scot* **:** SCOUNDREL, SCAMP, RASCAL ⟨that ~ of a boy⟩

skel·ly \'skelī\ *n* -ES [prob. of Scand origin; akin to ON *skjalgr* wry, squinting — more at CYLINDER] *chiefly dial* **:** SQUINT

¹**skelp** \'skelp\ *vb* **skelped** \-pt\ *also* **skel·pit** \-pət\ **skelped** *also* **skelpit; skelping; skelps** [ME *skelpen*, prob. of imit. origin] *vt* **1** *dial Brit* **:** STRIKE, SLAP, BEAT **2** *dial Brit* **:** to drive with blows **3** *dial Brit* **:** to perform or accomplish in a brisk and lively fashion ~ *vi* **:** to walk in a brisk and lively manner **:** HUSTLE

²**skelp** \"\ *n* -S [ME, fr. *skelpen*, v.] *dial Brit* **:** a smart blow; *esp* **:** a slap with the palm of the hand

³**skelp** \"\ *n* -S [perh. fr. ScGael *sgealb* splinter, strip of wood] **:** a strip of metal (as wrought iron, steel) for making a hollow cylindrical piece or tube by bending it round longitudinally or helically and welding

⁴**skelp** \"\ *vt* -ED/-ING/-S **1 :** to form (as a plate or bar of iron) into a skelp by rolling **2 :** to bend round (a skelp) in tube making

⁵**skelp** \"\ *dial var of* SCALP

skelp·er \-pə(r)\ *n* -S **:** one that skelps

¹**skelping** *adj* [fr. pres. part. of ¹*skelp*] *chiefly Scot* **:** unusually large or outstanding of its kind

²**skelping** \"\ *n* -S [fr. gerund of ¹*skelp*] *dial* **:** WHIPPING, BEATING

¹**skel·ter** \'skeltə(r)\ *vi* -ED/-ING/-S [fr. *-skelter* (in *helter-skelter*)] **:** to run helter-skelter **:** SCURRY

²**skelter** \"\ *n* -S *chiefly dial* **:** a bustling rush

skel·to·nian \(')skel¦tōnēən, -nyən\ *adj, usu cap* [John *Skelton* †1529 Eng. poet + E *-an*] **:** SKELTONIC

skel·ton·ic \(')skel¦tänik\ *or* **skel·ton·i·cal** \-nəkəl\ *adj, usu cap* [John *Skelton* + E *-ic* or *-ical*] **:** of, relating to, or characteristic of the English poet John Skelton, his writings, or Skeltonics

skel·ton·ics \skel'täniks\ *n pl, usu cap* **:** short verses of an irregular meter much used by John Skelton having two or three stresses arranged sometimes in falling and sometimes in rising rhythm and usu. rhymed in couplets

sken \'sken\ *vi* **skenned; skenned; skenning; skens** [origin unknown] *dial Eng* **:** SQUINT

¹**skene** *var of* SKEAN

²**ske·ne** \'skē(ˌ)nē\ *n, pl* **ske·nai** \-ˌnī\ [Gk *skēnē* — more at SCENE] **:** the structure in an ancient Greek theater behind the orchestra facing the cavea and being often of stone and of two stories of which the lower projects toward the orchestra, forms the proscenium, and serves as a background to the play — compare SCENE 4; see THEATER illustration

skene arch *var of* SCHEME ARCH

skeneoccle *var of* SKEANOCKLE

skeo \'skyō\ *n* -S [of Scand origin; akin to Norw *skjå* shed; akin to ON *skjōl* shelter, cover — more at SHIEL] **:** a shed of loose stones formerly used in the Shetland and Orkney islands for drying fish and meat

skep \'skep\ *n* -S [ME *skeppe* skep, skepful, fr. OE *sceppe* skepful, fr. ON *skeppa* bushel; akin to OHG *sceffil* bushel — more at SCHEPEL] **1 a :** a coarse round farm basket **b** *or* **skep·ful** \-fəl\ (1) **:** the quantity held by a skep (2) **:** any of various old units of capacity based on this quantity **2 :** BEEHIVE; *esp* **:** a domed hive made of twisted straw

skep·sis *also* **scep·sis** \'skepsəs\ *n* -ES [NL, fr. Gk *skepsis* examination, doubt, skeptical philosophy, fr. *skeptesthai* to look, consider] **:** philosophic doubt as to the objective reality of phenomena; *broadly* **:** a skeptical outlook or attitude

skep·tic *or* **scep·tic** \'skeptik, -tēk\ *n* -S [L or Gk; L *scepticus*, fr. Gk *skeptikos*, fr. *skeptikos* thoughtful, reflective, fr. (assumed) Gk *skeptos* (verbal of Gk *skeptesthai* to look, consider) + Gk *-ikos* -ic — more at SPY] **1 a :** one who believes the doctrine of skepticism or employs skepticism as a method **b** *usu cap* **:** a member of one of the ancient schools (as the Sophists) teaching skepticism **2 :** one who is disposed to or is in a state of skepticism **:** a doubting or incredulous person **3 :** a person marked by skepticism regarding religion or religious principles

skep·ti·cal *or* **scep·ti·cal** \-tәkәl, -tēk-\ *adj* **1 :** of, relating to, or characteristic of a skeptic or skepticism ⟨~ arguments⟩ **2 :** characterized by skepticism ⟨a ~ listener⟩ ⟨a ~ look⟩ — **skep·ti·cal·ly** \-tәk(ә)lē, -tēk-, li\ *adv* — **skep·ti·cal·ness** \-kәlnәs\ *n* -ES

skep·ti·cism *or* **scep·ti·cism** \-tә,sizәm\ *n* -S [NL *scepticismus*, fr. L *scepticus* skeptic + *-ismus* -ism] **1 a :** the doctrine that any true knowledge is impossible or that all knowledge is uncertain **:** a position that no fact or truth can be established on philosophical grounds ⟨total or radical ~⟩ **b :** a viewpoint that universally reliable knowledge is unattainable in particular areas of investigation ⟨theoretical or scientific ~⟩ ⟨moral ~⟩ ⟨metaphysical ~⟩ ⟨religious ~⟩ **c :** the method of suspended judgment, systematic doubt, or destructive criticism characteristic of skeptics — compare DOGMATISM, HUMISM, SOPHISM **2 :** an attitude of doubt or disposition toward incredulity in general or in regard to something particular (as a supposed fact) **3 :** doubt concerning but not necessarily denial of the basic religious principles (as immortality, providence, revelation) **:** FREETHINKING — compare AGNOSTICISM **syn** see UNCERTAINTY

skep·ti·cize \-ˌsīz\ *vi* -ED/-ING/-S **:** to indulge in skepticism

sker·rick \'skerik\ *n* -S [perh. irreg. fr. ¹*scar* (clinker)] *chiefly Austral* **:** the least bit **:** SEMBLANCE, TRACE ⟨not a ~ of food left over⟩

¹**sker·ry** \'skerē\ *n* -ES [origin unknown] *archaic* **:** a punt seating two

²**skerry** \"\ *n* -ES [of Scand origin; akin to ON *sker* skerry and to ON *ey* island — more at SCAR, ISLAND] **:** an insular rock or reef (as along the coast of Scotland or Scandinavia) **:** a rocky isle

¹**sketch** \'skech\ *n* -ES [D *schets*, fr. It *schizzo* sketch, splash, fr. *schizzare* to splash, squirt, prob. of imit. origin] **1 a :** a rough drawing representing the chief features of an object or scene and often made as a preliminary study **b :** a tentative draft or preliminary study (as for a literary work or musical composition) **2 :** a brief description (as of a person) or outline ⟨his ~ of the little born flirt devastating the hearts of the male cherubs at a children's ball —C.E.Montague⟩ ⟨a ~ of the rise of human culture —Benjamin Farrington⟩ **3 :** a short or slight creative work: **a :** a short literary composition somewhat resembling the short story and the essay but less formal and more simple in design, usu. intentionally slight in treatment, discursive in style, and familiar in tone **b :** a short instrumental composition usu. for piano **c :** a slight theatrical piece having a single scene; *esp* **:** a comic often burlesque variety or vaudeville act typically developed around a mishap or misunderstanding and involving a small cast or a single performer **4 :** a person peculiar or amusing in his actions or speech **syn** see COMPENDIUM

²**sketch** \"\ *vb* -ED/-ING/-ES *vt* **1 :** to draw, describe, or outline the chief features of **:** make a sketch of **:** ROUGH ⟨can ~ the look and attitude of a man in a few pithy sentences —Harry Hansen⟩ — often used with *in* or *out* ⟨the background is rapidly ~*ed* in, and only enough of it to serve as setting for the story itself —R.A.Hall b.1911⟩ ⟨it is the purpose of this paper to ~ out the broad outline of some of the areas within which research is under way —D.P.Cartwright⟩ **2 :** to execute in a superficial manner **:** do or make sketchily **:** SIMULATE ⟨his mother ~*ed* a hurried, amazed sign of the cross over her breast —Kay Cicellis⟩ ~ *vi* **1 :** to draw or paint a sketch ⟨docks where artists come to ~⟩ **2 :** to act in or as if in a theatrical sketch

sketchbook \'⸗,⸗\ *n* **1 :** a published collection of literary sketches **2 :** a book containing drawing paper for sketches **3 :** a notebook of preliminary sketches

sketch·er \'skechə(r)\ *n* -S **1 :** one that sketches; *specif* **:** one that sketches designs for stage sets **2 :** LETTERER d

sketch·i·ly \-chəlē, -li\ *adv* **:** in a sketchy manner ⟨the spoon . . . having been only ~ washed —David Fairchild⟩

sketch·i·ness \-chēnəs, -chin-\ *n* -ES **:** the quality or state of being sketchy ⟨alarmed at the ~ of . . . security measures —Christopher Rand⟩

sketch map *n* **:** an outline map drawn from observation rather than from exact survey measurements and showing only the main features of the area

sketchmaster \'⸗,⸗⸗\ *n* **:** an instrument operating on the principle of the camera lucida and used for superimposing an image of an aerial photograph on a map

sketch plan *n* **:** a preliminary plan that is less detailed than a working drawing

sketch plate *n* **:** a plate of steel or iron of nonstandard shape used in building a ship and ordered from the rolling mill according to a dimensioned sketch

sketchy \'skechē, -chi\ *adj* -ER/-EST **1 :** depicting or describing in outline with little detail **:** of the nature of a sketch **:** roughly outlined **2 :** wanting in completeness, clearness, or substance **:** SLIGHT, SUPERFICIAL ⟨gulped a ~ breakfast and rushed to catch the train⟩ ⟨found only the *sketchiest* records for the early period⟩

ske·te \skə'tē\ *n* -S [NGk *skētē*, fr. LGk *Skitis, Skētis*, desert in northern Egypt once famous for its many hermitages] **:** a settlement of Eastern Orthodox monks inhabiting a group of small cottages around a church and dependent upon a parent monastery

skeu·o·morph \'skyüə,mȯrf\ *n* -S [Gk *skeuos* vessel, implement + E *-morph*; akin to OE *hēgan* to perform, achieve, ON *heyja* to perform, and prob. to Russ *kutit'* to carouse] **:** an ornament or design representing a utensil or implement — **skeu·o·mor·phic** \¦⸗⸗¦mȯrfik\ *adj*

skev·ish \'skevish\ *n* -ES [origin unknown] **:** a No. American fleabane (*Erigeron philadelphicus*) with a hairy stem, spatulate toothed leaves, and corymbose or paniculate heads of showy pinkish purple flowers — called also *Philadelphia fleabane*

¹**skew** \'skyü\ *n* -S [ME, coping stone on a masonry gable, fr. AF *escu*, fr. OF, shield — more at ECU] *chiefly Scot* **:** a coping or coping stone on a masonry gable

²**skew** \"\ *vb* -ED/-ING/-S [ME *skewen* to skew, escape, fr. ONF *escuer* to shun, avoid, of Gmc origin; akin to OHG *sciuhen* to frighten off, make timid — more at SHY] *vi* **1 :** to take an oblique direction or course **:** move or turn aside **:** TWIST, SWERVE ⟨~*s* around in his chair⟩ **2 :** to look sideways or askance ~ *vt* **1 :** to make, set, or cut on the skew **:** turn or place at an angle **2 :** to give a bias or disproportionate weight to **:** DISTORT ⟨the list is badly ~*ed* in favor of the subjects with which I myself feel most at home —Bonaro W. Overstreet⟩ **3 :** to cause (a frequency distribution or its graphic curve) to lack symmetry

³**skew** \"\ *adj* **1 :** deviating from a straight line **:** set, placed, or running obliquely **:** DISTORTED, SLANTING **2 :** more developed on one side or in one direction than another; *specif* **:** lacking statistical symmetry ⟨for a symmetrical distribution the median is identical with the arithmetic mean, but for a ~ distribution it is not —*Statistical Methods in Research & Production*⟩

⁴**skew** \"\ *n* -S **1 :** a deviation from a straight line **:** an oblique course or direction **:** SLANT ⟨wearing her hat on the ~⟩ **2 :** deviation from rectangularity ⟨detects the ~ in cloth and controls the operation which straightens it —*Newsweek*⟩

⁵**skew** \"\ *vt* -ED/-ING/-S [origin unknown] **:** to remove loose particles of gold or silver leaf from with a soft brush

⁶**skew** \"\ *n* [origin unknown] *dial Eng* **:** a sudden gusty drizzle of rain

skew aileron *or* **skewed aileron** *n* **:** an aileron whose hinge line is set at an angle to the lateral axis of the airplane

skew arch *n* **:** an arch whose jambs are not at right angles with the face

skewback \'⸗,⸗\ *n* -S **1 :** a course of masonry, a stone, or an iron plate having an inclined face against which the voussoirs of a segmental arch abut **2 :** a plate, cap, or shoe with an inclined face to receive the nut of a diagonal brace or rod in a truss or frame

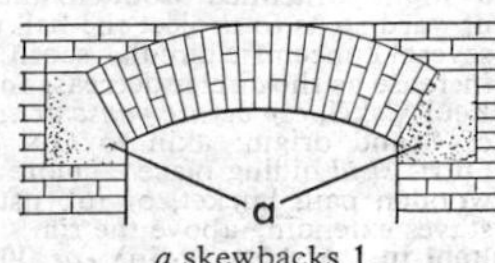

a skewbacks 1

¹**skew·bald** \'skyü¦,⸗\ *adj* [*skew-* (fr. *skewed*) + *bald*] *of an animal* **:** marked with spots and patches of white and some other color — used esp. of horses and sometimes distinguished from *piebald* when the latter is restricted to cases in which the colors are white and black **syn** see VARIEGATED

²**skewbald** \"\ *n* -S **:** a skewbald horse

skew bevel gear *or* **skew gear** *n* **:** a bevel gear in which the axes lie in different planes

skew bridge *n* **:** a bridge built obliquely from bank to bank

skew chisel *n* **:** a turning chisel with a straight cutting edge at an angle to the shank

skew curve *n* **:** SPACE CURVE

skew distribution *n* **:** an unsymmetrical frequency distribution having the mode at a different value from the mean

skewed \'skyüd\ *adj* [ME, prob. fr. *skew, skewe* cloud, sky (of Scand origin; akin to ON *skȳ* cloud) + *-ed* — more at SKY] **:** SKEWBALD

¹**skew·er** \'skyüə(r), -yü(ə)r, -üə\ *n* -S [prob. alter. of ¹*skiver*] **1 :** a pin of wood or metal for fastening meat to keep in form while roasting or to hold small pieces of meat and vegetables for broiling ⟨shish kebab served on ~*s*⟩ **2 :** any of various things shaped or used like a meat skewer: as **a :** an ornamental pin used to secure clothing or hair **b :** a pointed wooden rod at each end of a bobbin creel (as on a roving machine) on which the creel runs **c :** a pointed rod formed with a loop for a handle and used to secure a loose piece while ramming a mold **d :** a long slender bone artifact found in Hopewell archaeological sites and thought to have been used to pin matting or hides to the ground

²**skewer** \"\ *vt* -ED/-ING/-S **1 :** to fasten or pierce with a skewer ⟨~ a roast⟩ **2 :** to fasten or pierce as if with a skewer **:** TRANSFIX ⟨accidentally ~*ed* in the rear by the bayonet of another recruit —Earle Birney⟩ ⟨~*s* both the dunderheads of the fun-and-games department and the sacred cows in the newspaper hierarchy —W.W.Smith⟩ **3 :** to cause to penetrate like a skewer ⟨~*s* his criticism home⟩ — **skew·er·er** *n* -S

skew·er·ing \-riŋ, -rēŋ\ *n* -S **:** the act or process of cooking food on skewers

skewerwood \'⸗⸗,⸗\ *n* **1** *dial Eng* **:** a spindle tree (*Euonymus europaeus*) **2** *dial Eng* **:** RED DOGWOOD

skew facet *n* **:** one of the broad triangular facets which abut in pairs on the girdle of a brilliant between each pair of skill facets — called also *cross facet*

skew-gee \(')skyü¦jē\ *adv* (*or adj*) [perh. irreg. fr. ²*skew* + *gee* (to jibe)] **:** ASKEW

skew hinge *n* **:** a hinge with oblique knuckle joints (as a common rising hinge)

¹**skewing** *pres part of* SKEW

²**skewing** *n* -S **:** waste portions of gold leaf for remelting or remnants of gold or Dutch metal leaf available for reusing — usu. used in pl.

skew·ness *n* -ES **:** the quality or state of being skew **:** lack of straightness or symmetry **:** DISTORTION; *esp* **:** the quality or state of lacking symmetry shown by a frequency distribution — called also *asymmetry*

skew pantograph *n* **:** PLAGIOGRAPH

skew polygon *n* **:** a figure analogous to a polygon whose sides do not all lie in one and the same plane

skew putt *n* [¹*skew* + Sc *put* buttress, prob. fr. E *put* (throw, thrust)] **:** a stone at the foot of the slope of a masonry gable cut with a sloping surface and with a check to hold the coping stones

skew ray *n* **1 :** a ray in a symmetrical optical system that is neither parallel to nor intersecting the axis **2 :** a ray of a prism not perpendicular to the edge

skews *pl of* SKEW, *pres 3d sing of* SKEW

skew-symmetric \¦⸗⸗¦⸗⸗\ *adj, of a matrix* **:** such that the element in the *r*th row and *s*th column is the negative of the element in the *s*th row and *r*th column

skew-symmetric determinant *n* **:** a determinant whose matrix is skew-symmetric

skewwhiff \'⸗,⸗\ *adj* (*or adv*) [perh. irreg. fr. ²*skew* + *whiff*, v.] *dial Eng* **:** ASKEW, AWRY ⟨put a patch on . . . pants without getting it ~ —Ruth Park⟩

skey \'skā\ *n* -S [Afrik *skei*, fr. D *schei*, fr. MD *scheide* dividing place, crossroads; akin to OHG *sceida* sheath, separation — more at SHEATH] **:** one of four slightly wedge-shaped bars that pass down through an ox yoke one on each side of the neck of an ox to hold the yoke in place and that are notched at the bottom for the riem

skhian *var of* SKEAN

skhul man \'skül-\ *n, usu cap S* [Mugharet es-*Skhul*, cave on Mount Carmel, Palestine] **:** a strain of Palestine man showing distinct resemblances to Upper Paleolithic neanthropic man but retaining strongly developed brow ridges and associated with an early Mousterian type of culture

¹**ski** *also* **skee** \'skē *sometimes chiefly Brit* shē\ *n, pl* **skis** *or* **ski** *also* **skies** *or* **skiis** *or* **skees** *or* **skee** [Norw *ski*, fr. ON *skīth* stick of wood; akin to OE *scīd* stick of wood, OHG *skīt* stick of wood, OE *scēadan, scādan* to divide, separate — more at SHED] **1 a :** one of a pair of narrow strips of wood, metal, or plastic of varying length and width and curving upward in front that are used esp. for gliding over snow **b :** a piece of material similar to a ski used as a runner on a vehicle **2 :** WATER SKI

²**ski** \"\ *also* **skee** *vb* **skied; skied; skiing; skis** *vi* **:** to glide on skis in travel or as a sport ~ *vt* **:** to travel or pass over on skis ⟨the trail . . . can only be ~*ed* when snow and weather conditions are favorable —*Amer. Guide Series: N.H.*⟩

skia- — see SCI-

ski·able \'skēəbəl *sometimes chiefly Brit* 'shē-\ *adj* **:** passable on skis **:** suitable for skiing ⟨spectators donned their skis and broke the heavy crust to make the slope ~ —*Springfield (Mass.) Union*⟩

ski·a·gram \'skīə,gram\ *n* [ISV *sci-* + *-gram*] **1 :** a figure formed by shading in the outline of the shadow cast by an object **2 :** a shadowgraph made by X rays **:** an X-ray photograph **:** RADIOGRAPH

ski·a·graph \-,graf\ *n* [*sci-* + *-graph*] **:** SKIAGRAM

ski·ag·ra·pher \skī'agrəfə(r)\ *n* -S [*skiagraph* + *-er*] **:** RADIOGRAPHER

ski·ag·ra·phy \-fē\ *n* -ES [ISV *sci-* + *-graphy*] **:** the art, science, or act of depicting or projecting shadows **:** the making of skiagrams esp. by means of X rays

ski·am·e·try \⸗'amə·trē\ *n* -ES [*sci-* + *-metry*] *med* **:** the measurement of shadows: as **a :** the measurement of their movement in skiascopy **b :** the measurement of their intensity in X-ray photography

skiapod *var of* SCIAPOD

ski·a·scope \'skīə,skōp\ *n* [*sci-* + *-scope*] **:** a device for determining the refractive state of the eye by observing the movements of the retinal lights and shadows

ski·as·co·py \skī'askəpē\ *n* -ES [ISV *sci-* + *-scopy*] **1 :** RETINOSCOPY **2 :** FLUOROSCOPY

skib·by \'skibē, -bi\ *n* -ES [E dial. (western U. S.) *skibby* Japanese prostitute, prob. fr. Jap *sukebei* lewdness] **:** JAPANESE — usu. taken to be offensive

ski boot *n* **:** a rigid padded shoe that is usu. made of leather or plastic, extends just above the ankle, is securely fastened to the foot by various means (as laces, buckles, or hinges), and has a sole, heel, and toe that are locked into position in a ski binding

ski boots

skice \'skīs\ *vi* -ED/-ING/-S [Corn *scüsy*] *dial Eng* **:** to scurry about

¹**skid** \'skid\ *n* -S [perh. of Scand origin; akin to ON *skīth* stick of wood — more at SKI] **1 :** one of a group of objects (as planks or logs) used to support or elevate a structure or object ⟨commodities which are particularly susceptible to water damage should be on ~*s*, pallets or elevated platforms —*Nat'l Fire Codes*⟩: as **a :** one of a number of beams on which a small ship is constructed or repaired ⟨two landing craft which had come to grief on the coral were in the ~*s* —K.M.Dodson⟩ **b :** one of a number of beams on which a boat is elevated above a ship's deck **2 a :** a wooden fender hung over a ship's side to protect it in handling cargo — usu. used in pl. **3 a :** a usu. iron shoe or clog attached to a chain and placed under a wheel to prevent its turning when descending a steep hill **:** DRAG **b :** a hook attached to a chain and used by catching round a spoke for the same purpose **c :** a brake for a power machine (as a crane) **4 :** a timber, bar, rail, pole, or log used in pairs or sets to form a slideway (as for an incline from a truck to the sidewalk) or such a set fastened temporarily or permanently to the bottom of a machine or structure to be slid ⟨gas-turbine power plants . . . may be

mounted on ~s and moved from place to place —*Modern Industry*); *specif* : one of the logs forming a skid road **5** [*2skid*] : the act of skidding : SLIP, SIDESLIP **6** : a runner used as a member of the landing gear of an airplane or helicopter — see TAIL SKID, WING SKID **7 skids** *pl* : a route to defeat, downfall, failure, destruction, or other disastrous situation ⟨a celebrated matador who has been on the ~s for some time —*New Yorker*⟩ ⟨will have to put the ~s under the pressure-groups who are trying to keep up the price of whatever they have to sell —*Sydney (Australia) Bull.*⟩ **8 a** *or* **skid platform** : a low platform of wood or metal mounted on wheels, legs, runners, or combinations thereof on which material is mounted for handling and moving (as by a fork truck) **b** : a varying quantity (as no more than 3000 pounds of paper) packed on a skid

2skid \"\ *vb* **skidded; skidded; skidding; skids** *vt* **1** : to apply a brake or skid to : slow or halt by a skid ⟨the guard got down to ~ the wheel for the descent —Charles Dickens⟩ **2 a** : to drag (logs) from the stump to a landing, skidway, or mill : YARD **b** : to haul along or slide on skids ⟨the new span will be *skidded* to the river by high powered winch equipment over heavily greased rails —*Windsor Star (Canada)*⟩ **c** : to raise, hoist, or store upon skids ⟨contents . . . should be *skidded* at least 4 inches above the floor level —*Nat'l Fire Codes*⟩ **d** : to package (as paper) on a skid **3** : to reinforce or repair (a road) with logs or poles **4** : to cause to skid ⟨*skidded* his car on an icy pavement —F.B.Gipson⟩ ~ *vi* **1** : to slide without rotating (as a wheel held from turning while a vehicle moves onward) **2 a** : to fail to grip the roadway; *specif* : to slip sideways on the road ⟨the truck *skidded* on the wet road⟩ **b** *of an airplane* : to slide sidewise away from the center of curvature when turning — compare SIDESLIP **c** : to cross an esp. slippery surface without effort or fall or nearly fall through loss of balance : SLIDE, SLIP ⟨*skidding* clumsily across the ice —Arthur Knight⟩ ⟨both horses *skidding* in the mud at every step —H.L.Davis⟩ **3** : to fall rapidly, steeply, or far ⟨sales of new models have *skidded* 60 percent —*Newsweek*⟩

skid box *or* **skid bin** *n* : a box mounted on skids

skid chain *n* : TIRE CHAIN

skidded *adj* : having skids or runners attached to facilitate handling ⟨~ freight⟩

skid·der \'skidə(r)\ *n* -s : one that skids or uses a skid: as **a** : a worker who skids logs **b** : an engine for hauling the cable used in skidding logs **c** : BUMMER 3

skid·ding \-diŋ, -dēŋ\ *n* -s [*1skid* + *-ing*] : skids or material for skids

skidding hooks *or* **skidding tongs** *n pl* [*skidding* fr. gerund of *2skid*] : tongs used in skidding logs; *specif* : a pair of hooks attached to a ring

skid·ding·ly *adv* [*skidding* (pres. part. of *2skid*) + *-ly*] : in a skidding manner

skidding trail *n* [*skidding* fr. gerund of *2skid*] : the path of a log being skidded

skid·dles \'skidᵊlz\ *n pl but sing in constr* [prob. blend of *2skid* and *skittles* (pl. of *1skittle*)] : a game in which sticks are thrown at pins of different score value set up as the corners and center of a diamond — called also *stick bowling*

skid·doo *or* **ski·doo** \ski'dü\ *vi* -ED/-ING/-S [prob. alter. of *1skedaddle*] : to go away : DEPART

skid·dy \'skidē, -di\ *adj* -ER/-EST : likely to skid or cause skidding ⟨cars and trucks littering the ~ roads —Noel Barber⟩

skidegate *usu cap, var of* SKITTAGET

skid engine *n* **1** : SKIDDER b **2** : an engine mounted on skids

skid fin *n* : a fore-and-aft vertical surface usu. placed above the upper wing of a biplane and designed to provide the vertical keel surface required for lateral stability

ski·di \'skēdē\ *n, pl* **skidi** *or* **skidis** *usu cap* **1** : a people of the Pawnee confederacy **2** : a member of the Skidi people

skidpan \'=,=\ *n, Brit* : DRAG 3a(2)

skid road *n* **1** : a road along which logs are dragged to a skidway or landing often over heavy logs partly sunken at intervals of about five feet — called also *travois* **2 a** *West* : the part of a town frequented by loggers **b** : SKID ROW

skid row *n* [alter. (influenced by *row*) of *skid road*] : a district of cheap saloons, beaneries, flophouses, and employment agencies frequented largely by migrant workers, vagrants, and alcoholics

skidway \'=,=\ *n* **1** : a usu. inclined platform on which logs are piled for loading or sawing **2** : a road or way formed of skids or along which objects are skidded

skie *obs var of* SKY

1skied *past of* SKY

2skied *past of* SKI

ski·er *also* **skii·er** \'skēə(r) *sometimes chiefly Brit* 'shē-\ *n* -s [*skier* fr. *2ski* + *-er*; *skiier* fr. *skii-* (as in *skiing*) + *-er*] : one that skis

1skies *pl of* SKY, *pres 3d sing of* SKY

2skies *pl of* SKI, *pres 3d sing of* SKI

skiey *var of* SKYEY

1skiff \'skif\ *n* -s [MF or OIt; MF *esquif*, fr. OIt *schifo*, of Gmc origin; akin to OHG *skif* ship — more at SHIP] **1** : a small light sailing ship **2** : a light rowboat **3** : a boat with centerboard and spritsail light enough to be rowed and sometimes steered by an occupant's shifting his weight — called also *St. Lawrence skiff* **4** : a small fast powerboat

2skiff \"\ *vi* -ED/-ING/-S : to navigate in a skiff

3skiff \"\ *vb* -ED/-ING/-S [prob. alter. of *1skift*] *vi, Scot* : SKIM, FLIT ~ *vt, Scot* : to touch lightly

skiff·less \'=ləs\ *adj* : having no skiff

skif·fling \'skifliŋ, -lēŋ\ *n* -s [prob. alter. of *scabbling*, gerund of *scabble*] : rough dressing of stone by knocking off projections

1skift \'skift\ *vb* -ED/-ING/-S [ME *skiften* to shift, divide, fr. ON *skipta* to divide, change, be of importance — more at SHIFT] *dial Brit* : SHIFT

2skift \"\ *or* **skiff** \'skif\ *n* -s *dial* : something that is light: as **a** : a light fall of snow or rain **b** : WISP

3skift \'skift\ *dial var of* 1SKIFF

ski·ing \'skēiŋ, -ē·ēŋ *sometimes esp Brit* 'shē-\ *n* -s : the art or sport of sliding and jumping on skis

skiis *pl of* SKI

ski·jor·ing \'skē,jōriŋ, =ˈ==\ *or* **ski·ör·ing** \"; '=,(y)ər-iŋ, =ˈ(y)ər-iŋ\ *n* -s [modif. of Norw *skikjøring*, fr. *ski* + *kjøring* driving, fr. *kjøre* to drive; akin to ON *keyra* to drive and perh. to Skt *javate* he hurries on] : a winter sport in which a person wearing skis is drawn over snow or ice by a horse or vehicle

1ski jump *n* **1** : a steeply inclined artificial course or track leveled off at its lower end and built at or near the top of a natural slope from which a skier makes a takeoff through the air **2** : the act or instance of a skier taking off from a ski jump esp. in competition

2ski jump *vi* : to jump on skis from a ski jump

skil \'skil\ *or* **skil·fish** \'=,=\ *n, pl* **skils** *or* **skilfish** *or* **skilfishes** [Haida *sqil*] : SABLEFISH

skilful *var of* SKILLFUL

ski lift *n* : a power-driven conveyor for transporting skiers or sightseers up a long slope or mountainside and consisting usu. of a series of seats suspended from a motor-driven overhead endless cable

1skill \'skil\ *n* -s *see sense 4* [ME *skile, skil*, fr. ON *skil* distinction, discernment, knowledge; akin to OE *scylian* to separate, part, MLG *schēlen* to distinguish, ON *skilja* to separate, divide, Goth *skilja* butcher, Lith *skélti* to split — more at SHELL] **1** *obs* : CAUSE, REASON ⟨you have as little ~ to fear as I have purpose to put you to't —Shak.⟩ **2 a** (1) : knowledge of the means or methods of accomplishing a task ⟨~s disappear . . . when we fail to put them to work —T.W.Arnold⟩ (2) : the ability to use one's knowledge effectively and readily in execution or performance : technical expertness : PROFICIENCY ⟨revealed considerable ~ in the practice of law —Carol L. Thompson⟩ ⟨sufficient political ~ to govern wisely —J.G.Colton⟩ **b** : dexterity, fluency, or coordination in the execution of learned physical or mental tasks ⟨loss of motor ~ in the use of the hands —C.D.Martz & Frances Ekstam⟩; *specif* : technical competence without insight or understanding or the ability for further elaboration or development ⟨a volume of verses which show some ~ in versification, but little originality in thought or form —H.E.Starr⟩ ⟨frequently a person acquires certain reading ~s but never understands what he has read —John Haverstick⟩ **3 a** : a learned power of doing a thing competently : a developed or acquired aptitude or ability ⟨because of the influence which the language ~s exert on each other, the present trend is to teach them together —*Education Digest*⟩ ⟨the endless ~s the human hand is capable of developing —Abram Kardiner⟩ **b** : a craft requiring the use of related skills ⟨practiced the ~ of a carpenter⟩ **c** : a coordinated set of actions become smooth and integrated through practice ⟨thought canoeing was not a difficult sport or ~ —Ernest Beaglehole⟩ **4** *pl* **skill** : a skilled person ⟨immigration of ~ is . . . welcomed in all undeveloped areas —E.P.Hutchinson & W.E.Moore⟩ **5** *dial Brit* : discriminating taste : LIKING — usu. used with *of* ⟨he has a ~ of good wines⟩ **syn** see ART

2skill \"\ *vb* -ED/-ING/-S [ME *skilen*, fr. ON *skilja* to separate, divide] *vi* **1 a** : to make a difference : MATTER ⟨perhaps she was a soprano . . . it ~s not —Thomas Wolfe⟩ **b** : to be of help : AVAIL **2 a** *obs* : to have practical skill : be dexterous or competent **b** *archaic* : to have understanding : be knowing ~ *vi, dial Eng* : UNDERSTAND, COMPREHEND

skilled \'skild\ *adj* [*1skill* + *-ed*] **1** : having skill : EXPERT, SKILLFUL ⟨one ~ in the science of mechanics —B.N.Cardozo⟩ **2** : of, relating to, consisting of, or requiring workers or labor with skill and training in a particular occupation, craft, or trade and full competence for a task ⟨a craft for those who wish to become ~ artisans —Maurice Graney⟩ ⟨a ~ electrician⟩ ⟨a far greater proportion of the population is engaged in ~ work in a truly mechanized society —David Goldknopf⟩ **syn** see PROFICIENT

1skil·let \'skilət, *usu* -əd·+V\ *n* -s [ME *skelet*, prob. fr. *skele* pail + *-et* — more at SKEEL] **1 a** *chiefly Brit* : a small kettle or pot usu. having three or four often long feet and used for cooking on the hearth in front of an open fire **b** : FRYING PAN **2** : a flat mold in which a precious metal is cast for sale as bullion

2skillet \"\ *n* -s [origin unknown] : a thin veneer of wood used esp. in making matchboxes

skill facet *n* [so called fr. the skill required in placing such a facet correctly] : one of the narrow triangular facets that abut in pairs on the girdle of a brilliant at the corners of the stone

skill·ful *or* **skil·ful** \'skilfəl\ *adj* [ME *skilful*, fr. *skile, skil* skill + *-ful*] **1** : possessed of or displaying skill : having knowledge, readiness, and ability : well versed ⟨a ~ observer whose skill depended upon both native capacity and long practice —G.K.Chesterton⟩ ⟨one of the most ~ debaters and men of business in the kingdom —T.B.Macaulay⟩ **2** : accomplished with skill : done with trained proficiency ⟨~ use of precedent —G.W.Johnson⟩ ⟨less ~ efforts at perspective representation are not rare —Franz Boas⟩ **syn** see PROFICIENT

skill·ful·ly \-fəlē, -li\ *adv* : in a skillful manner

skill·ful·ness \-lnəs\ *n* -ES : the quality or state of being skillful

skil·li·ga·lee \'skiləgə,lē\ *n* -s [origin unknown] *chiefly Brit* : a thin broth or porridge usu. of oatmeal

skil·li·gil·lee *or* **skil·ly·goel·le** \"\ *n* -s [perh. alter. of *skilligalee*] : MARLIN

1skilling *var of* SKEELING

2skil·ling \'skiliŋ, 'shi-\ *n* -s [Sw, Norw, & Dan, fr. ON *skillingr*, a gold coin — more at SHILLING] : any of various old Scandinavian units of value equal to some small fraction of the Swedish, Norwegian, or Danish rix-dollars; *also* : any of the small coins representing one skilling unit

skil·lion \'skilyən\ *n* -s [alter. of *skeeling*] *Austral* : LEAN-TO

skill-less *or* **skil·less** \'skilləs\ *adj* **1** *archaic* : having no knowledge **2** : having no skill — **skill-less·ness** *n* -ES

skills *pl of* SKILL, *pres 3d sing of* SKILL

1skilly \'skili\ *adj* -ER/-EST [*1skill* + *-y*] *dial Brit* : SKILLFUL, SKILLED ⟨and the ~ use of words had not forsaken him —Maurice Walsh⟩

2skil·ly \'skilē, -li\ *n* -ES [by shortening & alter.] : SKILLIGALEE

skilo *or* **ski·lo** \'ski(,)lō\ *n* -s [*skilo* alter. of *skillo*, fr. *1skill* + *-o*] : a game of rolling balls into depressions in a grid based on the cards used at bingo with the object of getting five balls in a row

skils *pl of* SKIL

1skim \'skim\ *vb* **skimmed; skimmed; skimming; skims** [ME *skimmen*, prob. alter. of *scumen* — more at SCUM] *vt* **1 a** (1) : to clear (a liquid) of scum or floating substance ⟨~ boiling syrup⟩ (2) : to remove scum or floating matter from the contents of **b** : to remove (as film or scum) from the surface of a liquid ⟨foam rises as the liquid boils, and is *skimmed* off —*Amer. Guide Series: Tenn.*⟩ **c** (1) : to remove cream from (milk) by skimming (2) : to remove (cream) from milk by skimming **d** : to remove foreign particles from the surface of molten glass (in a pot or tank) ⟨*skimming* a glass pot before pouring —C.J.Phillips⟩ **e** : TOP 1f **f** (1) : to remove from the surface of a solid ⟨the dust could be *skimmed* from the cooking food —Russell Lord⟩ (2) : to remove a substance from the surface of (a solid body) ⟨then came a wind, *skimming* straw from the stacks —Adrian Bell⟩; *specif* : to remove roughnesses or irregularities from the surface of (a solid body) ⟨valve seats should be very lightly *skimmed* with a cutter —B.C.MacDonald⟩ **g** (1) : to remove the best or easiest obtainable contents from ⟨forests whose treasury of bird and beast and insect secrets had been only *skimmed* —William Beebe⟩ (2) : to take away (the most valuable or easiest obtainable contents) ⟨ore beds were *skimmed* and abandoned for richer deposits —D.A.Shepard⟩ ⟨nimble searchers after profits . . . ~ the cream off markets —Hartley Withers⟩ **2** : to read, study, deal with, or examine superficially and rapidly ⟨~s American poetry of the period —*College English*⟩; *specif* : to glance through (as a book) for the chief ideas or the plot ⟨the habit of *skimming* volumes in bookshops —*Time Lit. Supp.*⟩ **3** : to throw in a gliding path ⟨~ a hat across the room⟩; *specif* : to throw so as to ricochet along the surface of water ⟨taking a slate from the low wall and *skimming* it across the pond —Robert Graves⟩ **4 a** : to cover with or as if with a film or scum ⟨the standing water . . . was *skimmed* with ice —William Faulkner⟩ **b** : to put a finishing coat of plaster on **5** : to pass swiftly or lightly over : touch lightly, barely miss, or glide along in passing ⟨kingfishers . . . darted across the water, their wings just *skimming* the surface —David Walden⟩ ⟨~ the shores —Claudia Cassidy⟩ ~ *vi* **1 a** : to pass lightly or hastily : glide or skip along, above, or near a surface ⟨the plane ~s 200 feet above ground —A.C.Fisher⟩ ⟨*skimming* along the high road —D.S.Boyer⟩ **b** : to give a cursory glance or consideration ⟨*skimmed* through the overseer's report book —Eve Langley⟩ ⟨a flow of racy comment, *skimming* from one topic to another —Rose Macaulay⟩ — distinguished from *dip* **2** : to become coated with a thin layer of film or scum ⟨during the cold night the puddles *skimmed* over⟩ **3** : to put on a finishing coat of plaster

2skim \"\ *n* -s **1** : a thin layer, coating, or film ⟨bread with a ~ of jam on it —Anthony West⟩ ⟨a little ~ of ice in the ruts —William Faulkner⟩ **2** : the act of skimming ⟨the ~ of the swallows over the grass —Virginia Woolf⟩ **3** : something skimmed; *specif* : SKIM MILK **4** : a streak of dense seeds in glass

3skim \"\ *adj* **1** : that skims or is used for skimming ⟨~ net⟩ **2 a** : SKIMMED **b** : made of skim milk ⟨~ cheese⟩

skimback \'=,=\ *n* [so called fr. its habit of skimming the water as it swims] : QUILLBACK 1

1skim·ble-skam·ble \'skim(b)əl'skam(b)əl\ *adj* [redupl. of *1scamble*] : RAMBLING, UNCONNECTED, SENSELESS ⟨such a deal of *skimble-skamble* stuff as puts me from my faith —Shak.⟩

2skimble-skamble \"\ *n* -s : meaningless discourse : NONSENSE

skim coat *n* : FINISHING COAT 1

skim colter *n* : JOINTER c

skimeister \'=,==\ *n* -s [part trans. of G *skimeister*, fr. *ski* + *meister* master, fr. OHG *meistar*, fr. L *magister* — more at MASTER] **1** : a skier with the best all-around performance in downhill, slalom, cross-country, and jumping competition **2** : a professional skier or skiing instructor

skim gate *or* **skimming gate** *n* : a gate or runner having a bridge to arrest the flow of slag

skimmed-milk white \'=ˌ=-\ *n* : a light bluish gray to light gray that is greener and lighter than glaucous gray or cinerous — compare MILK WHITE

skim·mel·ton \'skiməltən\ *or* **skim·mer·ton** \-mə(r)t-\ *n* -s [alter. of *skimmington*] *North* : SHIVAREE 1

1skim·mer \'skimə(r)\ *n* -s [ME, alter. (influenced by *-er*) of *skymour*, fr. MF *escumoir*, fr. *escumer* to skim, fr. *escume* scum + *-oir*, *-our* -or] **1** : a utensil or implement used for skimming: as **a** : a flat perforated scoop or spoon used for skimming cooking liquids or lifting ripened cream from milk **b** : a broad-bladed jointer **c** : an implement to prevent dross or slag from running over with the molten metal from a ladle to a mold **d** : a device similar to a power shovel for skimming off the surface of the ground in grading **e** : a perforated shovel used in lifting salt out of an evaporating pan **2 a** : one that skims ⟨the structure of the modern news story is suited to the ~ —F.L.Mott⟩ **b** : one whose work is skimming (as dirt from the surface of a vat of oysters or slag from molten metal) **c** : a worker who sprinkles flux on molten magnesium to keep it from igniting when it is poured into molds **3** : any of several long-winged littoral marine birds of the genus *Rynchops* that are related to the terns, have the lower mandible compressed like a knife blade and much longer than the upper, fly rapidly along the surface of the water with the lower mandible immersed to skim out small marine animals **4 a** : WATER STRIDER **b** : a dragonfly of the genus *Libellula* **5** : a usu. straw flat-crowned hat with a wide straight brim

skimmer 1a

2skimmer \" *dial Brit var of* SHIMMER

skim·mia \'skimēə\ *n, cap* [NL] : a small genus of evergreen shrubs (family Rutaceae) of eastern Asia having small tetramerous flowers with a 2-celled to 5-celled ovary and red drupes

skim milk *also* **skimmed milk** *n* : milk from which the cream has been taken

skim·ming \'skimiŋ, -mēŋ\ *n* -s [ME *skemmyng*, fr. gerund of *skemmen, skimmen* to skim] **1** : that which is skimmed from a liquid ⟨do not add drosses, sweepings, or ~s —*Lubrication Engineering*⟩ **2** : the act or process of one that skims

skimming back *n* : a vat in which surplus yeast is skimmed from beer after the first fermentation

skimming dish *n* : a utensil for skimming : SKIMMER 1

skim·ming·ly *adv* [*skimming* (pres. part. of *1skim*) + *-ly*] : in a skimming manner

skim·ming·ton \'skimiŋtən\ *n* -s [*skimming* (fr. gerund of *1skim*) + *-ton* (as in surnames such as *Washington*); fr. the practice of representing the woman as beating her husband with a skimming ladle] **1** : one publicly impersonating and ridiculing a henpecked or cuckolded husband or his shrewish or unfaithful wife **2** *dial Eng* : a boisterous procession intended to ridicule an unfaithful spouse or a shrewish wife often with effigies and a mock serenade

skim·mi·ty \'skiməd·ē, -mətē, -i\ *or* **skimmity ride** *n* -ES [*skimmity* alter. of *skimmington*] : SKIMMINGTON 2

1skimp \'skimp\ *adj* [perh. alter. of *1scrimp*] : barely sufficient : SCANTY, MEAGER ⟨a thin woman whose ~ dress hung flat —Elizabeth M. Roberts⟩

2skimp \"\ *vb* -ED/-ING/-S *vt* : to give insufficient or barely sufficient attention or effort to or funds for : SCAMP ⟨their homes are all facade — ~*ed* under the superficial show —F.A. Swinnerton⟩ ~ *vi* : to save by or as if by skimping : SCRIMP ⟨we build schools without libraries, ~ on new-book budgets —Bice Clemow⟩ ⟨the two-dollar entry fee must have required a little ~*ing* —Dixon Wecter⟩

skimp·i·ly \-pəlē, -li\ *adv* : in a skimpy manner

skimp·i·ness \-pēnəs, -pin-\ *n* -ES : the quality or state of being skimpy

skimp·ing·ly *adv* : in a skimping manner

skimpy \'skimpē, -pi\ *adj* -ER/-EST : deficient in supply or execution esp. through skimping ⟨a ~ and inadequate training —Elspeth Mosscrop⟩ **syn** see MEAGER

skims *pres 3d sing of* SKIM, *pl of* SKIM

1skin \'skin\ *n* -s *often attrib* [ME, fr. ON *skinn*; akin to OE *scinn* skin, MHG *schint* peel of a fruit, ON *skān* crust, W *ysgythru* to cut, scratch, and prob. to L *secare* to cut — more at SAW] **1 a** : the integument of an animal separated from the body with or without hair whether green, dry, tanned, or dressed; *specif* : that of a small animal (as a calf, sheep, or goat) as distinguished from the hide of a large animal **b** : the hide or pelt of a game animal and esp. of one to be hunted **c** (1) : the pelt of an animal prepared for use as a trimming or in a garment ⟨her neckpiece of four ~s⟩ ⟨it takes forty ~s to make a coat⟩ (2) : a sheet of parchment or vellum made from the whole or part of a hide (3) : BOTTLE 1b (4) : SEALSKIN 3; *also* : a plush covering for a ski used like a sealskin — usu. used in pl. **2 a** : the external limiting layer of an animal body esp. when forming a tough but flexible cover relatively impermeable from without while intact: as (1) : the 2-layered covering of the vertebrate body sometimes modified by the presence of bony plates (as in an armadillo) or scales (as in most fishes and reptiles) and consisting of an outer ectodermal epidermis that is more or less cornified and penetrated by the openings of various glands (as sweat and sebaceous glands in man) and an inner mesodermal dermis that is composed largely of connective tissue and is richly supplied with blood vessels and nerves (2) : the hypodermis and the overlying cuticle that it secretes in many invertebrates — compare EXOSKELETON, MUCOUS MEMBRANE **b** : an outer covering of a fruit or seed (as a rind, husk, or peel) ⟨a black eye caused by a swiftly hurled orange —*Amer. Guide Series: N.C.*⟩ **c** : the epidermis of a plant **d** (1) : a membranous film or scum (as on boiling milk or on the surface of paints or varnishes) : PELLICLE ⟨how cold the gravy was getting — a ~ was forming on it —Agatha Christie⟩ (2) : a thin frozen coating ⟨a ~ of ice⟩ **e** (1) : an outermost layer or surface of an object ⟨the ~ of a casting⟩ ⟨the ~ of a diamond⟩ ⟨the ~ of an electric conductor⟩ (2) : a layer and esp. the outermost layer of nacreous matter composing a pearl (3) : the surface of a bituminous pavement **f** : the part of a furled sail that is on the outside and covers the whole **g** : a casing for sausage **h** : the rind of ham or bacon **3** : the life or physical well-being of a person ⟨when the troopship went down he took care that if anybody's ~ was saved it should be his —Peter Forster⟩ **4** : a sheathing or casing forming the outside surface of a structure ⟨steel for auto ~s —A.G.Tombs⟩: as **a** : a covering of planking or metal plates outside the framing that forms the sides and bottom of a ship : SHELL **b** : an exterior wall of a building: (1) : either of two panels that enclose a hollow space containing the framework ⟨external walls are of 11-inch cavity brickwork, with inner ~s of cellular flettons —*Architectural Rev.*⟩ (2) : thin weather-resistant stainless steel, aluminum, or other metal used alone or in combination with glass and other material to form a curtain wall **c** : an outer sheet covering of an airplane, missile, or satellite that is in an airplane usu. made of metal and designed to carry a portion of the stress **5** : PURSE, POCKETBOOK **6** : a contemptible person: as **a** : MISER, SKINFLINT **b** : one given to cheating : SWINDLER, SHARPER **7** : MADE-BEAVER **8** *slang* : DRUM **9** : SKINBALL **10** [short for *frog-skin*] *slang* : DOLLAR **11** *slang* : HORSE **12** [*2skin*] *slang* : an unfavorable report or a reprimand — **in a whole skin** *or* **with a whole skin** : without bodily harm : safe and sound — **in one's skin** : wearing no clothes : NAKED ⟨in every section a man stood *in his skin* while a doctor examined his teeth or palpated his chest —Robert Lynd⟩ — **out of one's skin** : in or into unrestrained expression of joy, enthusiasm, vigor, surprise, or other emotion : EXCITEDLY ⟨people . . . always jump *out of their skins* when they hear our own artillery —R.M.Ingersoll⟩ — **the skin of one's teeth** : a very narrow margin ⟨escaped by *the skin of my teeth* —Job 19:20 (RSV)⟩ — **under one's skin** : beneath one's surface powers of resistance to emotional or intellectual excitation : so deeply penetrative as to irritate, stimulate, provoke thought, or otherwise excite ⟨that last had got *under his skin* a little . . . he lost his good humor —Mary Deasy⟩ — **under the skin** : beneath apparent or surface differences : at heart ⟨determined to confirm that women are all sisters *under the skin* —Elizabeth Taylor⟩

2skin \"\ *vb* **skinned** *or dial* **skun** \'skən\ **skinned** *or dial*

skun; skinning; skins *vt* **1 a :** to cover with or as if with skin ⟨fuselages and wings will be *skinned* with steel . . . or titanium alloys —Wernher Von Braun⟩ **b :** to heal over with skin **2 a :** to strip, scrape, or rub off the skin, peel, rind, or other outer covering of **:** remove a surface layer from ⟨huge catfish are *skinned* and dressed by hand —*Amer. Guide Series: La.*⟩ ⟨*skinning* out a moose —F.C.Craighead b.1916 & J.J. Craighead⟩ ⟨~ the Bermuda onion —Dione Lucas⟩ **b :** to remove (skin or outer covering) from an object **:** pull or strip off ⟨too late to ~ out the hide that night —Corey Ford⟩ ⟨and amiably *skinned* off his coat to help —R.V.Mills⟩ ⟨~ the insulation from the wire⟩ **c** (1) **:** to chip, cut, or damage the surface of ⟨*skinned* his hand on the rough rock⟩ ⟨saw the *skinned* fender⟩ (2) **:** to remove (a portion of a surface) by wearing, chipping, or cutting away from a body ⟨the movers *skinned* the paint off the front steps —Virginia D. Dawson & Betty D. Wilson⟩ **d** (1) **:** to slide (a single card) from the top of a pack in dealing (as in faro) (2) **:** to slide the cards off the top of (a pack) one by one **e** (1) **:** to peel a thin layer of paper from ⟨~ an album page⟩ (2) **:** to peel (a thin layer of paper) from a surface ⟨~ a stamp from an envelope⟩ **f :** to remove the patina from (a painting) in the process of restoration **3 a :** to strip of money or property **:** FLEECE ⟨determined to collect his army bounty from a town selectman who . . . had been trying to ~ him —Dixon Wecter⟩ **b :** to outdistance or defeat in a race or contest **c** (1) **:** to criticize, satirize, or otherwise unfavorably comment upon ⟨had once *skinned* me because . . . I seemed unable to take literature seriously —Bernard De Voto⟩ (2) *slang* **:** to administer a reprimand to or report a deficiency in ⟨he was *skinned* for dirty boots⟩ **4 :** to exhaust by excessive cultivation or exploitation **:** despoil of natural resources ⟨during the grain rush of the war years this raw new stretch . . . of farms was horribly *skinned* —Russell Lord⟩ **5 a :** to urge on and direct the course of (a draft animal) ⟨one talent he could turn to a profit — mules, *skinning* mules —H.G.Evarts⟩ **b :** to act as operator of (a caterpillar tractor) **6 :** to equalize the thickness of adhesive on (a pasted or glued surface) by placing a sheet of wastepaper over it and rapidly rubbing or pressing **~** *vi* **1 :** to become covered with or as if with skin ⟨these inks won't dry on the press . . . nor will they ~ in the can —*Graphic Arts Monthly*⟩ — usu. used with *over* **2 a :** to climb or descend — used with *up* or *down* ⟨when you leave you ~ up the rope —C.E.Rose⟩ ⟨*skinned* down inside ladders from the bridge deck —K.M.Dodson⟩ **b** (1) **:** to pass with scant room to spare **:** traverse a narrow opening — used with *through* or *by* ⟨the big ship barely *skinned* through the open draw⟩ (2) **:** to succeed or qualify by a narrow margin — used with *through* or *by* **c :** to pass or go hurriedly **:** SCURRY ⟨*skinned* . . . out the gate before she even had time to think —Helen Eustis⟩

syn SKIN, DECORTICATE, PEEL, PARE, and FLAY agree in meaning to divest of skin or an outer covering. SKIN can apply to any animal or to a vegetable or fruit ⟨*skin* a bear⟩ ⟨*skin* an orange⟩ DECORTICATE applies to the stripping of the bark of a tree, the husk of a seed, or the rind of a fruit ⟨cut down and *decorticate* a birch tree⟩ ⟨for the production of the best quality oil . . . the seeds are *decorticated* before being expressed in the cold —J.F.Thorpe & Martha Whiteley⟩ PEEL and PARE are usu. interchangeable but PEEL more generally applies when the skin or outer covering can be removed by stripping, PARE when cutting is necessary ⟨*peel* an orange⟩ ⟨*pare* an apple⟩ FLAY applies largely to persons or animals and implies a skinning under torture or by scourging ⟨a man nearly *flayed* alive for criminal attack upon a tribesman⟩

— **skin a flint :** to make a gain by the most disreputable means — **skin alive :** to torture or fleece callously or mercilessly — **skin the cat :** to grasp a horizontal bar, raise the feet and legs up under the bar, and turn over backward or forward

skin and bones *n* **1 :** a condition of extreme emaciation **2 :** excessive thinness

skinball \ˈ=,=\ *n* [²*skin* + *ball;* fr. the fact that the cards are skinned from the top of the pack] **:** a card game similar to faro in which players bet on which of certain cards will win or lose — called also *skin game, skinning*

skin beetle *n* **:** any of several beetles esp. of the genera *Trox* and *Dermestes* whose larvae feed on leather or hides

skin boat *n* **:** a boat made of skins stretched over a frame

skinch \ˈskinch\ *vb* -ED/-ING/-S [origin unknown] *vt, dial Brit* **:** to be stingy or niggardly in respect to (material or a person) **~** *vi* **:** to be sparing — usu. used with *on* ⟨tried to ~ on the food⟩

skin–deep \ˈ=ˈ=\ *adj* **1 :** as deep as the skin ⟨the cut was ~⟩ **2 :** not thorough or lasting in impression **:** SUPERFICIAL ⟨discovered . . . that love is more than *skin-deep* —W.L.Gresham⟩

skin dive *vi* **1 :** to swim beneath the surface of water esp. at considerable depth without a diving helmet and suit, with a face mask and flippers, and with or without a portable breathing device **2 :** GOGGLE 3

skin diver *n* **:** one that engages in skin diving esp. as a sport

skin effect *n* **:** an effect characteristic of current distribution in a conductor at high frequencies by virtue of which the current is greater near the surface of the conductor than in its interior resulting in an increase of resistance with increasing frequency

skinflint \ˈ=,=\ *n* [²*skin* + *flint*, n.] **1 :** a person who would save, gain, or extort money by any means **:** MISER, NIGGARD **2 :** an old or worn-out horse **:** PLUG, SKATE

skin–food \ˈ=,=\ *n* **:** any of various cosmetics (as creams) for improving the condition and appearance of facial skin

skin friction *n* **1 :** friction between a fluid and the surface of a solid moving through it or between a moving fluid and its enclosing surface **2 :** the part of the drag of an airplane or of the head resistance of a ship due to the friction of air or of air and water

skin·ful \ˈ=,fu̇l\ *n* -S **1 a :** the flesh and bones within a skin **:** BODY **b :** the contents of a skin bottle **2 a :** a large or satisfying quantity ⟨a proper ~ of food —Joseph Hergesheimer⟩ **b :** an intoxicating amount of alcohol ⟨roar in pubs with a ~ —R.P.Warren⟩

skin game *n* [²*skin*] **1 :** a swindling game or trick ⟨*skin games* running to fleece you as fast as you can get your money to the center —Andy Adams⟩ **2 :** SKINBALL

1skin graft *vt* **:** to graft skin to

2skin graft *n* **:** a piece of skin of variable size and thickness cut from a donor area and transferred to the place to be repaired

skinhead \ˈ=,=\ *n, slang* **:** a person with a bald or close shaven head; *specif* **:** a marine boot

skin in *vt* **:** to apply a first coat of French polish to (furniture or woodwork)

1skink \ˈskiŋk\ *vt* -ED/-ING/-S [ME *skinken*, fr. MD *schenken, schinken;* akin to OE *scencan* to pour out drink, give to drink — more at NUNCHEON] *chiefly dial* **:** to draw, pour out, or serve (drink)

2skink \"\ *n* -S [perh. fr. obs. D *schenk, schink* shank of an animal, ham; akin to OHG *scinka* shank, MLG *schenke, schinke* leg, shank — more at SHANK] **:** a soup made of the shin or hock of beef

3skink \"\ *n* -S [L *scincus*, fr. Gk *skinkos*] **:** any of numerous lizards that constitute the family Scincidae, usu. live in dry sandy places where they often burrow in the sand, and are typically small with small scales, a slightly notched tail covered with scaly papillae, and usu. well developed but sometimes reduced or wanting limbs

4skink \"\ *archaic var of* SKUNK

skink·er \-kə(r)\ *n* -S **1 :** one that serves liquor **:** TAPSTER **2** *obs* **:** a drinking vessel

1skin·kle \ˈskiŋkəl\ *vi* -ED/-ING/-S [perh. blend of ²*skimmer* and *twinkle*] *chiefly Scot* **:** SPARKLE, GLITTER

2skinkle \"\ *vt* -ED/-ING/-S [perh. fr. ¹*skink* + *-le*] *chiefly Scot* **:** to scatter piecemeal **:** SPRINKLE

skin·less \ˈ=ləs\ *adj* [ME *skinles*, fr. ¹*skin* + *-les* -less] **1 :** having no skin or casing ⟨a ~ hot dog⟩ **2 :** easily moved **:** SENSITIVE ⟨that . . . defenseless ~ creature —Evelyn Whitehead⟩

skin maggot *n* **:** a maggot that is the larva of the tumbu fly

skin man *n* **:** one who covers the skeleton work of airplanes with sheet metal or plywood — called also *skinner*

1skinned \ˈskind\ *adj* [ME *skynned*, fr. *skyn, skin* skin + *-ed*] **:** having a skin — often used in combination ⟨dark*skinned*⟩

2skinned *adj* [fr. past part. of ²*skin*] **:** having no turf ⟨~ infield⟩ ⟨~ racetrack⟩

skin·ner \ˈskinə(r)\ *n* -S [ME *skynner*, fr. *skyn, skin* skin + *-er*] **1 a :** one that deals in skins, pelts, or hides **b :** one that removes, cures, or dresses skins **2 :** one of a band of guerillas and irregular cavalry claiming attachment to either the British or American troops and operating in Westchester county in New York during the American Revolution — compare COWBOY 2a **3 a :** one that swindles, cheats, or engages in sharp bargaining **b :** a bet won at long odds **4 a :** a driver of draft animals **:** TEAMSTER ⟨~*s* driving six- and eight-horse teams —*Amer. Guide Series: Mont.*⟩ **b :** an operator of a large piece of construction equipment ⟨steam-shovel ~*s* —Clark Craig⟩ **5 :** SKIN MAN

skinner box *n, usu cap S* [after Burrhus F. *Skinner* b1904 Am. psychologist] **:** a laboratory apparatus in which an animal is caged for experiments in operant conditioning typically containing a lever that must be pressed by the animal to gain reward or avoid punishment

skin·nery \ˈskin(ə)rē\ *n* -ES [ME *skynnery*, fr. *skyn, skin* skin + *-ery, -erie* -ery] **:** a skinner's workshop or place of business

skin·ni·ness \ˈskinēnəs, -nin-\ *n* -ES **:** the quality or state of being skinny

skinning *n* -S [fr. gerund of ²*skin*] **:** SKINBALL

skinning loam *n* [*skinning* fr. gerund of ²*skin*] **:** a fine loam that is used for the last coating and forms the skin of a mold in founding

skin·ny \ˈskinē, -ni\ *adj* -ER/-EST **1 :** of the nature of or like skin **:** MEMBRANOUS **2 a :** thin and lacking flesh (as from emaciation) ⟨a ~ little guy, kind of funny, kind of sad —Barbara B. Jamison⟩ ⟨those ~ hands of his, withered beyond their years —Rex Ingamells⟩ **b :** lacking usual or desirable bulk, quantity, qualities, or significance ⟨a ~ old spirea bush —John Moore⟩ ⟨~ unimaginative settings —Whitney Balliett⟩ **3 :** of the nature of a skinflint **:** NIGGARDLY, STINGY **syn** see LEAN

skin on *vt* **:** to apply (as paint or varnish) in an excessively thin coat

skins *pl of* SKIN, *pres 3d sing of* SKIN

skin spot *n* **:** a disease of potato tubers caused by a fungus (*Oospora pustulans*) and characterized by circular spots that on coarse-skinned varieties resemble pimples and are similar in color to normal skin and on smooth-skinned varieties are dark and sunken with raised centers

skin test *n* **:** a test for susceptibility performed on the skin of the patient and used in detecting allergic hypersensitivity (as to pollens or foods) and in diagnosing infection (past or present) with diseases that produce local hypersensitivity — compare COCCIDIOIDIN, INTRACUTANEOUS TEST, PATCH TEST, SCRATCH TEST, TUBERCULIN TEST

1skintight \ˈ=ˈ=\ *adj* **:** closely fitted to the figure ⟨playing tennis in ~ green shorts —*Sydney (Australia) Bull.*⟩

2skintight \"\ *n* -S **:** a skintight garment

skin·tle *also* **scin·tle** \ˈskintᵊl\ *vt* -ED/-ING/-S [origin unknown] **1 :** to stack (molded brick) with spaces between to allow ventilation for drying **2 :** to set (bricks) in a wall irregularly so that the bricks are out of line with the face of the wall ⅛ to ¼ inch or more

skin wool *n* **:** an inferior scoured wool obtained from sheep after death **:** PULLED WOOL

skinworm \ˈ=,=\ *n* **1 :** a caterpillar that is the larva of a moth (*Archips franciscana*) of the family Tortricidae that burrows beneath the skin of apples in the western U. S. **2 :** a grub that is the larva of a skin beetle

sköring *var of* SKIJORING

1skip \ˈskip\ *vb* **skipped; skipped; skipping; skips** [ME *skippen*, perh. of Scand origin; akin to ON *skopa* to take a run, Sw dial. *skopa* to hop, dance; prob. akin to OS *skop* poet — more at SCOP] *vi* **1 a** (1) **:** to move or proceed with a skip **:** move with leaps and bounds **:** move in a light dancing motion **:** CAPER, GAMBOL ⟨can ~ and frisk about with wonderful agility —William Cowper⟩ (2) **:** to move by bounding off one point after another **:** RICOCHET ⟨*skipping* across the surface of the water like a flung stone —C.L.Biemiller⟩ (3) **:** to proceed as if by exaggerated bounds ⟨the shock wave, which often ~*s* erratically, was felt . . . some 130 miles distant —*N.Y. Times*⟩ **:** HOP ⟨~ along the Florida coast towns in a . . . helicopter —Horace Sutton⟩ **b :** to move quickly, easily, and usu. blithely ⟨*skipped* happily to his hotel to interview him —Sinclair Lewis⟩ ⟨small yachts *skipped* here and there —Alan Villiers⟩ ⟨the opening chapters alternately plod and ~ along —Jay Leyda⟩ **c :** to leave hurriedly ⟨cut poles for a corral and put a couple of horses in it so we could ~ pretty fast —Bruce Siberts⟩ ⟨a warrant of arrest . . . was never served because the person *skipped* out —Erle Stanley Gardner⟩ esp. after getting funds by fraud or dishonest means ⟨the teller *skipped* with the till⟩ or to avoid paying a debt ⟨guests who ~ on their bills —Horace Sutton⟩ **d :** to move erratically or at random ⟨*skipping* through the country from one town to another⟩ **e :** to discuss or investigate quickly **:** SKIM ⟨bought the paper, calmly *skipped* through the interview —H.Ledig-Rowohlt⟩ **2 a :** to pass over or omit a topic, section, or line **:** move from one point to another by omitting or disregarding the intervals ⟨you may ~ through a book, reading only those passages here and there which concern you —L.R.McColvin⟩ ⟨a little bored by the passage . . . he ~*s* over it —Bernard De Voto⟩ ⟨the biography ~*s* from his infancy to his graduation from law school⟩ **b :** to pass from one grade in school to the next but one without going through the intermediate grade **c :** to leave out a step in a progression or series ⟨his heart *skipped* in terror⟩; *specif* **:** MISFIRE 1 — used of an internal combustion engine **d :** JUMP *vi* 3a(5) **~** *vt* **1 a :** to pass over without notice, mention, or attention **:** omit in reading, investigation, or discussion ⟨to ~ the old guard . . . two writers with definite talent must be noted —Richard Plant⟩ ⟨the scientists should ~ that part of the book —*London Calling*⟩ ⟨it ~*s* and dodges all the real questions —A.H.Vandenberg b. 1907⟩ **b :** to pass over (a step or stage in development or time) ⟨when an adjustment for the superior child is attempted, it sometimes takes the form of *skipping* a grade —J.D.Russell & C.H.Judd⟩ ⟨the festival concerts ~ a day —Claudia Cassidy⟩ **:** fail to participate in or do (a normal or regular function) ⟨the president *skipped* his regular Thursday press conference —*Newsweek*⟩ ⟨the three of us *skipped* chow and lit for town —Len Zinberg⟩ **c :** to pass over or by (a point, space, or area) ⟨separate related groups of paragraphs by *skipping* four blank lines —W.R. Parker⟩ ⟨they plan to ~ the larger cities on their trip⟩ **d :** to pass by or leave out (a step in a progression or series) ⟨~*s* every third line⟩ ⟨makes the strongest pulse beat faster and the weakest to ~ many beats —L.P.Stryker⟩ ⟨the tune ~*s* a note⟩ **e :** to fail or neglect to take, accept, order, or give ⟨if I've only stayed overnight and he has done nothing for me, I ~ the tip —Richard Joseph⟩ **2 a :** to cause to skip ⟨parents want their daughter or son . . . *skipped* to second grade the day he enters school —Caroline Tryon⟩ ⟨looking for flat stones to ~ in the sea —*Tomorrow*⟩ **b :** to drop (a bomb) in skip bombing ⟨*skipped* heavy bombs into their railroad-tunnel lairs —F.G.Vosburgh⟩ **3 :** to leap over lightly and with agility ⟨*skipped* the hedge and the wall⟩ **4 a :** to depart from quickly and secretly esp. under suspicion or after a misdemeanor ⟨built up a big load of debts, then *skipped* town with all his merchandise —J.P.Blank⟩ **b :** to stay away from without permission ⟨~ school⟩ ⟨*skipped* the staff meeting again⟩ — **skip bail :** to jump bail — **skip rope :** to jump rope

2skip \"\ *n* -S [ME *skippe*, fr. *skippen*, v.] **1 :** an act or instance of skipping: as **a :** a light blithe bounding step ⟨the ~ of the lamb and the caper of the kid —Douglas Kennedy⟩ **b :** a gait composed of alternating hops and steps **c :** a dance step consisting of a hop taking off and landing on the same foot with the free foot raised slightly in front or back **2 a :** a deliberate or accidental passing over or omission ⟨read the book without a ~⟩; *specif* **:** a melodic musical progression from one note to another at an interval greater than one scale step **b :** something skipped or to be skipped: as (1) **:** a small isolated spot or area left unintentionally when painting (2) **:** a depression in the surface of a board missed by the planer or finisher **c :** a small spot in planted ground where a crop fails to establish itself ⟨the seeder left many ~*s*⟩ **d :** SKIP STRAIGHT **3 a** [short for *skipkennel*] **:** FOOTMAN, LACKEY — compare SCOUT 4 **b :** a debtor who attempts to avoid paying by moving away without leaving a forwarding address

3skip \"\ *n* -S [alter. of *skep*] **1 a :** SKEP **b :** a basket, bucket, or open car mounted on wheels, rails, or vertical shafts for carrying men and materials (as in mining, quarrying, or manufacturing) **:** GUNBOAT 2 **c :** the container on a concrete mixer that receives the charge of aggregate and cement and is hoisted to discharge these materials into the drum **2 :** a slab of coal cut from a pillar or breast **3 skips** *pl* **:** thin brown papers of a grade suitable for lining containers (as for textiles)

4skip \"\ *n* -S [short for ²*skipper*] **1 :** the captain of a side in a game (as curling or lawn bowling) who advises his men as to the play and controls the action **2 :** SKIPPER

5skip \"\ *vt* **skipped; skipped; skipping; skips :** to act as skipper of (a curling or lawn bowling team)

ski pants *n pl* **:** pants worn for skiing that are ribbed or close-fitted at the ankle

ski pants

skip bomb *vt* **:** to attack by releasing delayed-action bombs from a low flying airplane near and parallel to the surface esp. so that they skip along the surface and strike the target

skipdent \ˈ=,=\ *n* [*skip* + *dent*] **:** an openwork fabric woven by skipping selected dents when drawing in the warp in the loom reed

skip distance *n* **:** the outer limit of the skip zone beyond which high-frequency radio signals are received satisfactorily

skip·e·tar \ˈskipə,tär, ,==ˈ=\ *n* -S *cap* [Alb *Shqiptarë*] **:** ALBANIAN 1

skip hoist *or* **skip elevator** *n* **:** ³SKIP 1b

skipjack \ˈ=,=\ *n see sense 2* **1 a :** a young conceited fop **b** *obs* **:** JOCKEY **2** *or pl* **skipjack :** any of various fishes that jump above or play at the surface of the water: as **a** (1) **:** any of various bonitos (as the Chile bonito or frigate mackerel) (2) *or* **skipjack tuna :** a rather small large-eyed fish (*Katsuwonus pelamis*) that is bluish above and silvery below with a series of dark stripes on sides and belly and with a series of small finlets following both dorsal and anal fins, that is widely distributed in warm seas, and that is an important food and sport fish — called also *oceanic bonito* **b :** TENPOUNDER **c :** RAINBOW RUNNER **d :** a common freshwater herring (*Pomolobus chrysochloris*) of eastern No. America; *also* **:** any of several related fishes (as an alewife or gizzard shad) **e :** BLUEFISH **f :** a small freshwater silversides (*Labidesthes sicculus*) of the southern U. S. **g :** a large pale green Australian percoid food fish (*Temnodon saltator*) **3 :** CLICK BEETLE **4 :** a small sailboat with bottom similar to a flat V and the sides vertical or nearly so

skipkennel \ˈ=,==\ *n* [¹*skip* + *kennel* (gutter)] **:** LACKEY, FOOTBOY

ski–plane \ˈ=,=\ *n* **:** a land-based airplane equipped with landing skis

skip mackerel *n* **:** BLUEFISH

skip·man \ˈ=mən\ *n, pl* **skipmen :** a worker who loads, unloads, or tends a skip

ski pole *n* **:** a metal-pointed pole or stick, made of steel or cane, fitted with a handstrap at the top and an encircling disk set a little above the point to keep it from sinking into deep snow, and used as an aid in skiing — called also *ski stick*

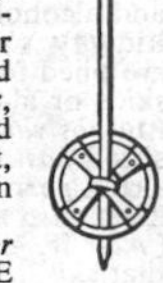

ski pole

skip·pable \ˈskipəbəl\ *adj* **1 :** capable of being skipped **2 :** liable to cause skipping ⟨the world's most ~ novel —*Times Lit. Supp.*⟩

skipped *past of* SKIP

1skip·per \ˈskipə(r)\ *n* -S [ME *skippere* erratically active insect, one that skips, fr. *skippen* to skip + *-er, -ere* -er] **1 :** any of various erratically active insects: as **a :** CHEESE SKIPPER **b :** CLICK BEETLE **c** *South* **:** a maggot infesting meat **d :** WATER STRIDER **2 a :** one that skips ⟨the best readers are those that know how to skip, and I'm a good ~ —Meredith Nicholson⟩ **b :** a young thoughtless person **:** SKIPJACK **3 a :** the Atlantic saury (*Scombresox saurus*) or a related fish that jumps freely above the water **b :** LONG TOM 2b **4 :** any of numerous small stout-bodied lepidopterous insects of the superfamily Hesperioidea that differ from the typical butterflies in wing venation and the form of the antennae, are usu. somber in color, and have comparatively small wings, thickened antennae usu. hooked at the tip, a short swift flight, and larvae that usu. make a rudimentary cocoon **5 :** SKIP STRAIGHT

2skipper \"\ *n* -S [ME *skypper*, fr. MD *schipper* boatman, skipper, fr. *schip* ship + *-er;* akin to OE *scip* ship — more at SHIP] **1 a :** the master of a ship; *esp* **:** the master of a fishing, small trading, or pleasure boat **b :** the commander of a military or naval installation or unit **c :** the captain or first pilot of an airplane **2 a :** the captain of an athletic team **b :** the manager or coach of an athletic team (as a baseball team) **3 :** the conductor of a train **4 :** the adult leader of a sea explorer ship in the Boy Scouts of America **5 :** a dull blue

3skipper \"\ *vt* -ED/-ING/-S **1 :** to act as skipper or master of (a boat) **2 :** to act as coach or captain of (a team)

4skipper \"\ *n* -S [³*skip* + *-er*] **:** a skipman in a metal mine

skip·pered \-pə(r)d\ *adj* **:** infested with maggots

skip·per·ship \-pə(r),ship\ *n* **:** the position, duties, or skill of a skipper

skip·pery \-p(ə)rē, -ri\ *adj* [¹*skipper* + *-y*] **:** containing cheese skippers — used of cheese and meat

1skip·pet \ˈskipət, *usu* -əd.+V\ *n* -S [ME *skipet* small receptacle, perh. fr. *skeppe, skippe* skep + *-et*] **:** a small box for covering and preserving a seal (as for a document)

2skippet *n* -S [perh. irreg. fr. ¹*skiff* + *-et*] *obs* **:** a small boat **:** SKIFF

skipping *pres part of* SKIP

skip·ping·ly *adv* [*skipping* (pres. part. of ¹*skip*) + *-ly*] **:** in a skipping manner

skipping rope *or* **skip rope** *n* [*skipping* fr. gerund of ¹*skip*] **:** JUMP ROPE

skipple *var of* SCHEPEL

skips *pres 3d sing of* SKIP, *pl of* SKIP

skip–stop \ˈ=,=\ *n* **:** the omission of intermediate vehicular stops (as of a bus or elevator) for operating advantage or emergency

skip straight *n* **:** a special hand recognized in some poker games that is composed of five cards in alternate sequence (as 3, 5, 7, 9, and jack) and beats two pairs but loses to three of a kind — called also *alternate straight, dutch straight, skip, skipper*

skiptail \ˈ=,=\ *n* **:** SPRINGTAIL

skip tender *n* [³*skip*] **:** CAGER 1a

skip tracer *n* **:** a person employed (as by an insurance company) to locate persons who disappear leaving unpaid bills

skip zone *n* **:** the area around a high-frequency radio transmitting station between the outer effective range of ground wave transmission and the inner limit of transmission by means of signals reflected from the ionosphere in which little or no signal reception is possible

skire thursday *n, usu cap S&T* [ME *skire thursday* (trans. of ON *skíri-thōrsdagr*), fr. *skir, skire* bright, pure (fr. ON *skírr*) + *thursday* Thursday; prob. fr. the practice of confessing one's sins on Maundy Thursday — more at SHEER] *obs* **:** MAUNDY THURSDAY

1skirl *R* ˈskərl, *chiefly before pause or consonant* ˈskər·əl; *–R* ˈskəl *or* ˈskəil; *Scot usu* ˈskirl\ *vb* -ED/-ING/-S [ME (Sc) *skirlen, skrillen*, of Scand origin; akin to OSw *skrælla* to rattle, bang — more at SHRILL] *vi* **1 :** to utter or emit a shrill tone **:** SHRIEK **2 a** *of a bagpipe* **:** to emit the high shrill tone of the chanter; *also* **:** to give forth music **b :** to play the bagpipe **~** *vt* **1 :** to give forth (a shrill sound) **2 :** to play (music) on the bagpipe

2skirl \"\ *n* -S **1 :** a shrieking sound **:** SCREAM ⟨the ~ of a curlew —Vance Palmer⟩ **2 :** a high shrill sound produced by the chanter of a bagpipe

3skirl \"\ *vi* -ED/-ING/-S [origin unknown] **:** to fly or sweep in a whirl : move or become moved in a twisting, curving, or flurrying path ⟨newspapers and old sacks ~*ed* a little in the gutters —P.D.Boles⟩

⁴**skirl** \"\ *n* -s : something that skirls, is skirled, or is formed by skirling ⟨~*s* of dust and wind and crumpled newspapers —Thomas Wolfe⟩

¹**skir·mish** \'skərmish, 'skə̄m-, 'skəim-, -mēsh\ *n* -ES [ME *skyrmissh*, alter. (influenced by ME *skirmysshen* to fence, brandish a sword, fr. MF *eskermiss-*, *escremiss-*, stem of *eskermir*, *escremir* to fence, of Gmc origin; akin to OHG *skirmen* to defend) of *skarmish*, *scarmuch*, fr. MF *escarmouche*, fr. OIt *scaramuccia*, of Gmc origin; akin to OHG *skirmen* to defend, *skerm*, *skirm* shield — more at SCHERM] **1** : a minor engagement in war usu. incidental to larger movements : combat between detached and small bodies of troops — distinguished from *pitched battle* **2** : a minor dispute or contest between opposing parties : a brisk preliminary conflict ⟨this verbal ~ is viewed here as the opening round in negotiations scheduled to start next Tuesday —*N.Y. Times*⟩

²**skirmish** \", *chiefly in pres part* -məsh\ *vi* -ED/-ING/-ES [ME *skyrmysshen*, alter. (influenced by ME *skirmysshen* to fence, brandish a sword) of *scarmysshen*, *scarmuchen*, fr. MF *escarmouchier*, fr. OIt *scaramucciare*, fr. *scaramuccia*, n.] **1 a** : to fight as skirmishers : engage in a skirmish **b** : to engage in a minor or preliminary argument ⟨would prevent the many would-be presidential candidates within the party from ~*ing* among themselves —*Newsweek*⟩ **2** : to search about (as for supplies) : scout around : SCRIMMAGE, RUMMAGE

skir·mish·er \-shə(r)\ *n* -s : one of a group of soldiers deployed in extended order as an advanced guard, a small independent attack force, or as cover for the front and flanks of a column

skirmish line *n* : a line of skirmishers; *esp* : the skirmishers in advance of a line of battle

¹**skirr** *also* **scur** \'skər(·)\ *vb* -ED/-ING/-s [perh. alter. of ¹*scour*] *vi* **1** : to leave hastily : FLEE ⟨birds ~*ed* off from the bushes —D.H.Lawrence⟩ **2** : to run, fly, sail, or otherwise move rapidly ~ *vt* **1** : to search about in ⟨~ the country round —Shak.⟩ **2 a** : to pass rapidly over : SKIM **b** *dial* : to cause to skim ⟨~ a stone⟩

²**skirr** \"\ *n* -s [prob. imit.] : a whirring, rasping, or roaring sound ⟨the ~ of a bird⟩ ⟨the occasional ~ of an automobile starting —*Harper's*⟩

skir·reh \'skirə\ *n* -s [origin unknown] : a cord used by masons in keeping brickwork or foundations straight and by surveyors and excavators in marking out sites

skir·ret \'skirət, *usu* -əd·+V\ *n* -s [ME *skirwhit*, by folk etymology (influence of ME *skir*, *skire* bright, pure and ME *whit* white) fr. MF *eschervi*, prob. modif. of Ar *karawyā* skirret, caraway — more at CARAWAY, SKIRE THURSDAY, WHITE] : an Asiatic herb (*Sium sisarum*) cultivated in Europe for its sweet edible tuberous roots

¹**skirt** \'skərt, 'skə̄t, 'skəit, *usu* -d·+V\ *n* -s [ME, fr. ON *skyrta* shirt, kirtle — more at SHIRT] **1 a** (1) : the part of an outer garment or undergarment extending from the waist down that has a free hanging lower edge and is cut in one with the upper part of the garment or attached at the waistline ⟨the ~ of a jacket⟩ ⟨the sweeping ~ of a ball gown⟩ — often used in pl. ⟨gathered up her ~*s* and ran away⟩ (2) : a separate outer garment or undergarment for women and girls covering the body from the waist down **b** : either of two usu. leather flaps on a saddle covering the bars on which the stirrups are hung — see STOCK SADDLE illustration **c** : a cloth facing hanging loosely and usu. in folds or pleats from the bottom edge or across the front of a piece of furniture ⟨dressing table ~⟩ ⟨chair ~⟩ **d** : the outer part of a parachute canopy **e** : the lower branches of a tree when near the ground **2 a** : the rim, periphery, or environs of an area, territorial division, or natural feature ⟨the long white ~ of the salt desert lay awash —Dean Jennings⟩ — often used in pl. **b skirts** *pl* : the outlying parts of a town or city : OUTSKIRTS, SUBURBS ⟨unfenced pastures on the ~*s* of the village —Joseph Mitchell⟩ **3** : a part or attachment serving as a rim, border, edging, or endpiece of an object: as **a** : the lip of a bell **b** : an apron piece or border in a building (as a baseboard or the molded piece under a window stool) **c** : a decorative piece on furniture connecting the legs along the lower edge of the table top, chair seat, or base **d** : a protective guard or plating on machinery and appliances **e** : a sheet metal covering for the wheels and other working parts of a locomotive **f** : FENDER SKIRT **g** : the bottom portion of the vertical wall of a screw-on jar cap; *also* : the vertical portion of a can wall attached to the cap of a key-opened can **4** : the final portions of a period of time **5 a** : the diaphragm or midriff of an animal used as edible meat **b** *Brit* : a flank of beef **6** *slang* : GIRL, WOMAN ⟨the American soldiers' . . . reputation as perhaps the most tireless ~ chasers of all time and all peoples —D.L.Cohn⟩ **7** : the bearing surface of a piston consisting of the plain cylindrical portion below the ring ⟨neither the cylinder bore nor the piston ~ is perfectly stiff —H.F.Blanchard & Ralph Ritchen⟩ **8** : SKIRTING 3

²**skirt** \"\ *vb* -ED/-ING/-s *vt* **1** : to form the border or edge of : run along the edge of : BORDER ⟨the shell of mountains that ~*s* the southeast coast —W.B.Furlong⟩ ⟨~*ed* by a lofty iron railing —John Godley⟩ **2 a** : to provide a skirt for ⟨an old-fashioned full-*skirted* frock coat —O.S.J.Gogarty⟩ **b** : to furnish a border or guard for ⟨machines ~*ed* and fendered —*Newsweek*⟩ **3 a** : to go or proceed closely around or about : follow the outskirts of ⟨set out to ~ the marshes that lay between them and the fort —Kenneth Roberts⟩ ⟨the dusty path that ~*ed* the field —Ellen Glasgow⟩; *specif* : to go around or keep away from in order to avoid danger or discovery ⟨sent back word to ~ the frowning walls and make no contacts with the inhabitants —J.R.Perkins⟩ ⟨the friendly neighborhood cop whom everybody knows and the criminal ~*s* —George Barrett⟩ ⟨~*ed* right end on a 7-yard touchdown run —*N.Y. Times*⟩ **b** : to avoid (as a topic or question) because of difficulty, complexity, danger, or fear of controversy ⟨both candidates were seen as ~*ing* the referendums —*Current Biog.*⟩ **c** : to escape (as danger, death, or error) though coming very close : evade or miss by a very narrow margin ⟨an empiricist has to seek the justification . . . in the motivational make-up of man . . . yet to ~ the naturalistic fallacy —P.B.Rice⟩ ⟨unaware of having ~*ed* disaster —Edith Wharton⟩ **4** : to remove the skirtings from (a fleece of wool) ~ *vi* **1** : to be, lie, or move along an edge, border, or margin : follow a roundabout path ⟨the tanker . . . was expected to ~ around submerged obstacles —*N.Y. Times*⟩ **2** *of a hound* : to cut corners rather than follow the actual path of a fox

³**skirt** \'skirt, 'skərt\ *vi* -ED/-ING/-s [origin unknown] *Scot* : to hurry away

skirtboard \'=,=\ *n* **1** : BASEBOARD **2** : a side plate to protect conveyor chains and increase the capacity of a conveyor or sitting spillage or redirect it to the conveyor belt

skirt cassock *n* : CASSOCK 2c

skirt-dance \'=,=\ *vi* [¹*skirt* + *dance*, v.] : to execute a skirt dance — **skirt-dancer** \'=,=\ *n*

skirt dance *n* [¹*skirt* + *dance*, n.] **1** : a ballet dance popular in the 19th century distinguished by the dancer's manipulations of her long flowing and varicolored skirts or drapery **2** : a folk dance (as the chiapanecas) accompanied by the manipulation of full skirts or drapery

skirt·er \'skər|d·ə(r), 'skə̄|, 'skəi|, |t|\ *n* -s : one that skirts: as **a** : a hunter or hound that tends to go around rather than over obstacles; *also* : a dog that runs wide of the pack **b** : one that removes skirtings from fleeces

skirting *n* -s [fr. gerund of ²*skirt*] **1** : something that skirts: as **a** : BORDER, EDGING, ENCLOSURE; *specif* : SKIRT 3c **b** *or* **skirting board** *Brit* : BASEBOARD **2** : fabric (as wool) suitable for skirts **3 skirtings** *pl* : inferior or soiled wool trimmed from the edges of a fleece **4** : the act or process of one that skirts

skirting leather *n* : a leather used in the manufacture of saddles and bridles

skirt·ing·ly *adv* [*skirting* (pres. part. of ²*skirt*) + -*ly*] : in a skirting manner

skirt·less \'=ləs\ *adj* : having no skirt

skirtlike \'=,=\ *adj* : resembling a skirt esp. in forming an enveloping dependent covering for the lower part of something ⟨the ~ indusium of a fungus⟩

skirt-roof \'=,=\ *n* : a small usu. false portion of roofing between the stories of a building

skirt-roof

skirts *pl of* SKIRT, *pres 3d sing of* SKIRT

skirty \'skər|d·|ē, 'skə̄|, 'skəi|, |t|, |i\ *adj* [*skirtings* + -*y*] *of wool* : containing excessive skirtings

ski run *n* : a slope or trail suitable for skiing

skis *pl of* SKI, *pres 3d sing of* SKI

skish \'skish\ *n* -ES [prob. blend of ³*skeet* and *fish*] : a target game for fishermen in which a small lead weight is cast at a set of targets placed flat on the surface of the water or sometimes on the ground

ski stick *n* : SKI POLE

ski suit *n* : a warm outfit for winter sports and play made in one-piece or two-piece style with a jacket top and pants usu. having ribbed cuffs

ski suit

¹**skit** \'skit, *usu* -id·+V\ *n* -s [ME *skytte*, of Scand origin; akin to Icel *skita* diarrhea; akin to ON *skīta* to defecate — more at SHIT] : SCOURS

²**skit** \"\ *vi* **skitted**; **skitted**; **skitting**; **skits** [prob. back-formation fr. *skittish*] **1** : to leap or start aside or away : be skittish : SHY **2** : to dance or jump about : CAPER, FLOUNCE

³**skit** \"\ *n* -s [perh. fr. ²*skit*] **1** : a jeering or satirical remark : JIBE, TAUNT **2 a** : a satirical or humorous story or sketch often outwardly serious; *esp* : PARODY ⟨a sophisticated and stylish ~ on typical review material —Barry Carman⟩ **b** (1) : a brief burlesque or comic sketch included in a dramatic performance (as a revue) (2) : a short serious dramatic piece included in a review or given separately; *esp* : one written, produced, and performed by amateurs ⟨the program . . . featured ~*s* by four church families on the ways religion can be brought into modern home life —*Springfield (Mass.) Union*⟩ **3** *dial Eng* : a sudden sharp shower or gust of rain

⁴**skit** \"\ *vb* **skitted**; **skitted**; **skitting**; **skits** *vi* : to make a jibe : make satirical remarks — used with *at* ~ *vt* : to satirize or caricature by means of a skit

¹**skite** \'skīt, *usu* -īd·+V\ *vi* -ED/-ING/-s [prob. of Scand origin; akin to ON *skjōta* to shoot — more at SHOOT] **1** *chiefly dial* : to move quickly or hurriedly ⟨now ~ along to school⟩ **2** *chiefly Scot* : to strike an object with a glancing blow : RICOCHET, SKIP

²**skite** \"\ *n* -s **1** *chiefly dial* : a sudden glancing blow or impact **2** *dial* : TRICK, PRANK

³**skite** \"\ *n* -s [prob. fr. E dial. *skite* to defecate, fr. ME *skyten*, fr. ON *skīta*] *dial* : a disagreeable offensive person

⁴**skite** \"\ *vi* -ED/-ING/-s [prob. fr. E dial. *skite* to defecate] *chiefly Austral* : BOAST, BRAG

⁵**skite** \" *or* **skit·er** \-d·ə(r)\ *n* -s [*skite* fr. ⁴*skite*; *skiter* fr. ⁴*skite* + -*er*] *chiefly Austral* : BRAGGART, BOASTER

ski tow *n* **1** : a power-driven conveyor for pulling skiers to the top of a slope consisting usu. of an endless motor-driven moving rope which the skier grasps **2** : SKI LIFT

ski trooper *n* : a member of the ski troops

ski troops *n pl* : troops trained and equipped to maneuver and fight on skis

skit·swish \'skit,swish\ *n, pl* **skitswish** *usu cap* : COEUR D'ALENE

skit·ta·get \'skid·əgət, -d·ə,get\ *or* **skid·e·gate** \'skidəgət, -də,gāt\ *n, pl* **skittaget** *or* **skittagets** *or* **skidegate** *or* **skidegates** *usu cap* : HAIDA

skit·ta·getan \,==ˈgētᵊn, -'getᵊn\ *n, pl* **skittagetan** *or* **skittagetans** *usu cap* : HAIDA 3

¹**skit·ter** \'skid·ə(r), -itə-\ *vb* -ED/-ING/-s [prob. freq. of ¹*skite*] *vi* **1** : to pass or glide lightly or hurriedly: as **a** : to skip along a surface ⟨~*ing* across the ice on belly or back —S.H.Adams⟩ **b** : to skim along or scamper with bobbing motions : SCURRY, SKIP ⟨watch a rabbit ~ off into the woods —Grace Metalious⟩ **2** : to draw the hook of a fishing line through or along the surface of water with a twitching or quivering motion ~ *vt* : to cause to skitter ⟨~ stones across the pond⟩; *specif* : to impart a twitching motion to (a fish-hook) when drawing through or along the surface of the water

²**skitter** \"\ *n* -s **1** : a light gliding or bobbing motion : SCURRYING, SCAMPER **2** : a sound of skittering : RUSTLE

skit·tery \-ərē, -ri\ *adj* -ER/-EST [¹*skitter* + -*y*] : SKITTISH

skit·tish \'skid·|ish, -it|, |ēsh\ *adj, sometimes* -ER/-EST [ME, fr. *skit-* (perh. of Scand origin; akin to ON *skjōta* to shoot) + -*ish* — more at SHOOT] **1 a** : excessively lively or frivolous in nature or action : CAPRICIOUS, IRRESPONSIBLE ⟨felt that for a minister the pastime was unduly ~ —Jean Stafford⟩ **b** : given to marked or rapid fluctuations : VARIABLE, UNSTABLE ⟨the ~ fads of musical fashion —Winthrop Sargeant⟩ **2** : easily frightened or agitated : given to shying : RESTIVE — used chiefly of horses **3 a** : COY, BASHFUL, SHY **b** : marked by extreme caution : FEARFUL, WARY ⟨old wooden bridges that were a nightmare for ~ drivers —Jack Westeyn⟩ — **skit·tish·ly** *adv* — **skit·tish·ness** *n* -ES

¹**skit·tle** \'skid·ᵊl, -itᵊl\ *n* -s [perh. of Scand origin; akin to Dan *skyttel* shuttle — more at SHUTTLE] **1 a skittles** *pl but sing in constr* : English ninepins played by pitching or sliding a wooden disk or rolling a wooden ball to knock down pins **b** : one of the pins used in skittles **2 skittles** *pl* : PLAY, ENJOYMENT — used chiefly in the phrase *beer and skittles* **3 skittles** *pl but sing in constr* : rapid informal play at chess with nothing at stake; *also* : a game so played

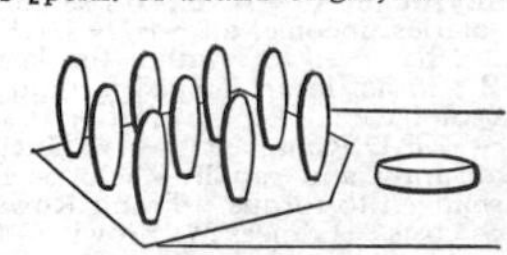

skittles 1b with disk

²**skittle** \"\ *vb* **skittled**; **skittled**; **skittling** \-itliŋ, -id·ᵊl-, -itᵊl-\ **skittles** *vi* : to play skittles ~ *vt* : to put out (several batsmen) easily in cricket — usu. used with *out*

skittle ball *n* : a heavy wooden disk used in skittles — called also *cheese*

skittle pool *n* : a game played on a billiard table with two white balls, a red ball, and a number of black and white pins in which counts are made by knocking down any of the white pins with the cue ball after contact with an object ball but if a black pin is knocked down the striker loses his entire score and must start anew

skit·tler \'skid·ᵊlə(r), -it(ᵊ)l-\ *n* -s : one that skittles

¹**skive** *or* **scive** \'skīv\ *vt* **skived** *or* **scived**; **skived** *or* **scived**; **skiving** *or* **sciving**; **skives** *or* **scives** [of Scand origin; akin to ON *skīfa* to slice, Icel *skīfa* disk — more at SHEAVE] : to cut off (as leather or rubber) in thin layers or pieces : SHAVE, PARE

²**skive** \"\ *n* -s : a skived or beveled part of a leather (as a shoe upper where it is seamed together)

³**skive** \"\ *n* -s [modif. of D *schijf* — more at SKEIF] : a diamond wheel : SKEIF

⁴**skive** \"\ *vi* -ED/-ING/-s [origin unknown] **1** *chiefly dial* : to dart or skim lightly and rapidly **2** *chiefly dial* : to depart in a hurry

¹**ski·ver** \'skivə(r)\ *n* -s [origin unknown] *dial* : SKEWER

²**ski·ver** \"\ *vt* -ED/-ING/-s : SKEWER, IMPALE

³**ski·ver** \'skīvə(r)\ *n* -s [¹*skive* + -*er*] **1** : a thin soft leather made of the grain side of a split sheepskin, usu. tanned in sumac and dyed, and used for hat linings, pocketbooks, and bookbindings **2** : one that skives: as **a** : a cutting tool a machine uses in splitting leather or skins **b** : a workman who bevels or pares leather, rubber, or fiber parts so that they will form a smooth joint

skiv·vy \'skivī\ *n* -ES [origin unknown] *Brit* : a female domestic servant

sklent \'sklent\ *vb* -ED/-ING/-s [ME *sclenten* to strike obliquely, alter. of *slenten* — more at SLANT] *vi* **1** *chiefly Scot* : to glance sideways : look askance **2** *chiefly Scot* : to cast aspersions ~ *vt, Scot* : to direct sideways : SLANT

sklim \'sklim\ *vb* [origin unknown] *Scot* : CLIMB

sklo·dow·skite \sklə'dóf,skīt\ *n* -s [F, fr. Marja *Skłodowska* Curie †1934 Pol. born Fr. chemist + F -*ite*] : a mineral $Mg(UO_2)_2Si_2O_7.6H_2O$ consisting of a hydrous magnesium uranyl silicate that is isomorphous with uranophane

¹**skoal** \'skōl\ *n* -s [Dan *skål*, lit., bowl, cup; akin to ON *skāl* bowl — more at SCALE] : a toast to someone's health, well-being, or prosperity — often used interjectionally

²**skoal** \"\ *vi* -ED/-ING/-s : to drink an alcoholic beverage usu. as a toast

sko·be·loff green \'skōbə,lóf-\ *n, often cap S* [prob. fr. the name *Skobeloff*] : a moderate bluish green that is greener, lighter, and stronger than porcelain green or sea blue

skoi·no·lon \'skóinə,län\ [NL, perh. irreg. fr. Gk *schoinos* rush, reed] *syn of* SCHOENOCAULON

sko·ko·mish \skō'kōmish, skə'-, -mēsh\ *n, pl* **skokomish** *or* **skokomishes** *usu cap* **1** : a Salishan people of western Washington **2** : a member of the Skokomish people

skolion *var of* SCOLION

skoliosis *var of* SCOLIOSIS

skol·ly \'skälē, -li\ *n* -ES [prob. modif. of Afrik *skorrimorrie* rascal, riffraff, fr. D *schorrimorrie*, *schorremorrie* riffraff, perh. modif. of Yiddish *soyrer-umoyre* rogue, good-for-nothing, hoodlum, fr. Heb *sorēr ūmōreh* stubborn and rebellious] *chiefly southern Africa* : a young hoodlum

¹**skoo·kum** \'skükəm\ *n* -s [Chinook jargon, powerful, evil spirit, fr. Chehalis *skukm*] : an evil spirit

²**skookum** \"\ *adj* [Chinook jargon] **1** : marked by strength or power ⟨was a ~ eater most times, but he pushed his bowl away —Arthur Mayse⟩ **2** : marked by excellent quality : FIRST-RATE ⟨as handsome and healthy as ~ apples —*Time*⟩

skookum-house \'==,=\ *n* : JAIL ⟨had recently been arrested . . . put in the *skookum-house* . . . and fined —*Century Mag.*⟩

skop·lje \'skóp,lā, -p,yā\ *adj, usu cap* [fr. *Skoplje*, city in southern Yugoslavia] : of or from the city of Skoplje, Yugoslavia : of the kind or style prevalent in Skoplje

skop·tsy \(,)skäpt'sē\ *n pl, usu cap* [Russ, pl. of *skopets*, lit., eunuch; akin to OSlav *skopiti* to castrate — more at CAPON] : members of an ascetic religious sect of dissenters from the Russian Orthodox Church dating prob. from the 18th century and stressing sexual abstinence

skraup synthesis \'skraüp-\ *n, usu cap 1st S* [after Zdenko H. *Skraup* †1910 Czechoslovak chemist] : the production of quinoline by heating aniline, glycerol, and sulfuric acid with an oxidizing agent (as nitrobenzene); *also* : any of various similar syntheses performed with aromatic amino compounds other than aniline

skreak *or* **skreek** \'skrēk\ *chiefly dial var of* SCREECH

skreich \'skrēk\ *chiefly Scot var of* SCREECH

skriegh \'skrēk\ *chiefly Scot var of* SCREECH

¹**skrim·shan·der** *or* **scrim·shan·der** \(ˈ)skim'shandə(r)\ *or* **scrim·shan·dy** \-dē, -di\ *n, pl* **skrimshanders** *or* **scrimshanders** *or* **scrimshandies** [origin unknown] : SCRIMSHAW ⟨young seamen . . . examining . . . divers specimens of ~ —Herman Melville⟩

²**skrimshander** \"\ *vb* -ED/-ING/-s : SCRIMSHAW

skrimshank *var of* SCRIMSHANK

skryer *var of* SCRYER

skua \'skyüə\ *also* **skua gull** *n* -s [*skua* fr. NL, fr. Faeroese *skūgvur*; akin to ON *skūfr* skua, tassel, OE *scēaf* sheaf — more at SHEAF] : JAEGER 3; *esp* : a jaeger of the genus *Catharacta* — see GREAT SKUA

skul·dug·gery *or* **skull·dug·gery** *also* **scul·dug·gery** *or* **scull·dug·gery** \,skəl'dəg(ə)rē, -ri *also* '=,=(=)=\ *n* -ES [alter. of *sculduddery*] **1 a** : dishonest, underhanded, unfair, or unscrupulous behavior or activity ⟨suspects ~ in death of Londoner —*Saturday Rev.*⟩ ⟨counterfeiting is a prehistoric form of gainful ~ —St. Clair McKelway⟩ ⟨some alleged ~ in the state department —Elmer Davis⟩ ⟨won over to producing his major shows on the rival chain only by ~ —Herman Wouk⟩ **b** : proficiency in or a tendency toward such behavior or activity ⟨with such skill and ~ that nothing was suspected —*Time*⟩ ⟨the ~ in human nature —John Cournos⟩ **2** : an instance of skulduggery ⟨a stranger to those *skulduggeries* which have brought politics into disrepute —*New Republic*⟩

¹**skulk** *also* **sculk** \'skəlk\ *vb* -ED/-ING/-s [ME *skulken*, of Scand origin; akin to Dan *skulke* to shirk, play truant, Norw *skulka*, Sw *skolka*] *vi* **1** : to move in or as if in a stealthy, furtive, or cautious manner : SNEAK ⟨Indians ~*ing* through the tall sage —*Amer. Guide Series: Nev.*⟩ ⟨~ up and down with the air of a charity-boy, a bastard, or an interloper —R.W. Emerson⟩ **2 a** : to hide or conceal oneself often from cowardice or fear or sometimes with sinister intent ⟨children with ice-cream cones ~*ed* in the doorways, like abused cats —Jean Stafford⟩ ⟨scrambling over fence rails and ~*ing* in thickets —D.C.Peattie⟩ ⟨what bedevilled idiocy ~*s* behind that arrogant mask —Herbert Read⟩ **b** *chiefly Brit* : to avoid duty : MALINGER ~ *vt* : to avoid in a furtive or cowardly manner ⟨~ our obligation to our country⟩ **syn** see LURK

²**skulk** \"\ *n* -s [ME *skulke*, fr. *skulken*, v.] **1** *of foxes* : PACK, GROUP **2** : SKULKER

skulk·er \-kə(r)\ *n* -s [ME, fr. *skulken* to skulk + -*er*] : one that skulks

¹**skull** \'skəl\ *n* -s [ME *skulle*, of Scand origin; akin to Sw *skulle* skull; prob. akin to OHG *scollo* clod, lump, *scala* shell, husk — more at SHELL] **1 a** : the skeleton of the head of a vertebrate : the bony or cartilaginous case or framework that encloses and protects the brain and chief sense organs, supports the jaws, is cartilaginous in primitive forms (as cyclostomes and elasmobranchs) and in the embryos of all forms, but in higher vertebrates has the cartilage usu. replaced by bone and the structure made more complete by the union with it of other bones developed in membrane, and consists of the cranium, the bony capsules of the nose, ear, and eye, and the jaws **b** : the cranium together with those bones that are immovably fused with it (as the mammalian upper jaw) **2** : the seat of understanding or intelligence : MIND ⟨it penetrated his thick ~ what had happened —*Storyteller Weekly*⟩ ⟨a multitude of things that the ordinary sealed ~ rejects —J.M.Barzun⟩ **3 a** : the crown of the head ⟨an unattractive old man, with a bald yellow ~ —Ellen Glasgow⟩ **b** (1) : SKULLCAP 1b (2) : the top of a helmet ⟨the sides of the helmet were commonly hinged to the ~ —Christopher & Adrian Lynch-Robinson⟩ **4** : DEATH'S-HEAD **5** : a crust of solidified material (as metal, matte, or slag) that forms on the walls of a ladle or other vessel containing this material in the molten state — often used in pl.

²**skull** *var of* SCULL

skull and crossbones *n, pl* **skulls and crossbones** : a representation of a human skull over crossbones usu. used as a warning of danger ⟨stamped a *skull and crossbones* on the labels of poisonous drugs⟩

skullcap \'=,=\ *n* **1 a** : any of various close-fitting brimless cloth caps for indoor or outdoor wear — compare BEANIE, CALOT, YARMULKE, ZUCCHETTO **b** : a close-fitting steel or iron helmet **2** : a plant of the genus *Scutellaria* having a calyx that when inverted resembles a helmet with the visor raised **3** : a domed capping layer (as of rock) **4** : the top of the skull : CALVARIUM

skullcap speedwell *n* : MARSH SPEEDWELL

skull coral *n* : any of several bulky corals having closely set polyps and resembling the brain corals

skull cracker *n* : a heavy iron or steel ball swung or dropped by a derrick to demolish old buildings or compact bulky scrap for shipment — called also *ball breaker*, *wrecking ball*

skullduggery *var of* SKULDUGGERY

skulled \,skəld\ *adj* : having a skull — usu. used in combination ⟨long-*skulled*⟩ ⟨broad-*skulled*⟩

skullfish \'=,=\ *n* : a whale more than two years old

skullguard \'=,=\ *n* : a helmet worn by workers for protection against head injuries from falling objects

skull-pan \'=,=\ *n* : SKULLCAP 4

skull practice *or* **skull session** *n* **1** : a training class held by an athletic coach for planning strategy and diagramming plays ⟨hold *skull practice* an hour before school each morning —J.M.Blount⟩ **2 a** : a meeting for consultation, discussion, or the interchange of ideas or information ⟨just got through having a *skull session* with the county leaders —*New Yorker*⟩ **b** : intellectual exercise ⟨the product of intellectuals interested

in experiment, abstractions, erudite allusions and other *skull practice* —C.B.Taylor⟩
skun \ˈskən\ *dial past of* SKIN
¹skunk \ˈskəŋk\ *n, pl* **skunks** *also* **skunk** [of Algonquian origin; akin to Abnaki *segākw* skunk] **1 a** (1) **:** any of various common omnivorous New World mammals forming a subfamily of Mustelidae, showing typical warning coloration of brilliantly patterned black and white, and possessing a pair of muscular-walled perineal glands from which an intensely malodorous secretion is ejected when the animal is startled or in danger — see CONEPATUS, MEPHITIS, SPILOGALE; HOG-NOSED SKUNK, LITTLE SPOTTED SKUNK, STRIPED SKUNK (2) **:** any of various offensive-smelling Old World animals (as the teledu or the zoril) **b :** the fur of a skunk **2 :** a contemptible ill-mannered person — used as a generalized term of abuse ⟨you're a low-down, foul-mouthed, impertinent ~ —Sinclair Lewis⟩ **3 :** an unidentified surface target detected visually or by radar — compare BOGEY
²skunk \"\ *vt* -ED/-ING/-S **1 a :** to subject to defeat **:** inflict defeat upon ⟨~*ed* the other candidate by a wide margin of votes⟩ **b :** to shut out (an opponent) in a game — compare ⁴LURCH **2 a :** to fail to pay (as a bill or a creditor) ⟨made a practice of ~*ing* hotels⟩ **b :** to deprive by or as if by cheating ⟨a man . . . who has been ~*ed* out of a summer vacation —Horace Sutton⟩
³skunk \"\ *n* -S [²*skunk*] **:** SHUTOUT
skunk bear *n* **:** WOLVERINE
skunkbill \ˈ=,=\ *n* **:** SURF SCOTER
skunk bird *or* **skunk blackbird** *n* [so called fr. the coloring of the male] **:** BOBOLINK
skunkbrush \ˈ=,=\ *also* **skunkbush** \ˈ=,=\ *n* **:** any of various shrubs having an offensive odor: as **a :** BEAR BRUSH **b :** SQUAWBUSH
skunk cabbage *n* **1 a :** a perennial herb (*Symplocarpus foetidus*) of the family Araceae of eastern No. America and Asia that sends up in early spring an offensive-smelling cowl-shaped brownish purple spathe that is followed in summer by a tuft of broad leaves **b :** a similar and related plant (*Lysichiton camstchatcense*) of the U. S. Pacific coast **2 :** PITCHER PLANT a
skunk currant *n* **:** a wild currant (*Ribes glandulosum*) native to the eastern U. S. that bears offensive-smelling red fruit
skunk·ery \ˈskəŋkərē, -ri\ *n* -ES **:** a place where skunks are bred and raised usu. for commercial purposes
skunk grass *n* [so called fr. its odor] **:** a grass of the genus *Eragrostis*
skunk porpoise *n* **:** SPECTACLED DOLPHIN
skunk spruce *n* **:** WHITE SPRUCE 1a
skunktail \ˈ=,=\ *also* **skunktail grass** *n* **:** SQUIRRELTAIL
skunk turtle *n* **:** MUSK TURTLE
skunkweed \ˈ=,=\ *n* **:** any of several offensive-smelling herbs: as **a :** SKUNK CABBAGE **b :** an annual Californian weed (*Gilia squarrosa*) **c :** a Rocky Mountain sticky-leaved herb (*Polemonium viscosum*) **d :** JOE-PYE WEED
skunky \ˈskəŋkē, -ki\ *adj* -ER/-EST **:** of, relating to, or having the characteristics of a skunk
skur·ry \ˈskər|ē, ˈskə·r|, |i\ *chiefly Brit var of* SCURRY
skutch *var of* SCUTCH
skut·te·rud·ite \ˈskəd·ə,rə,dīt\ *n* -S [G *skutterudit*, fr. *Skutterud*, near Drammen, southern Norway + G *-it* -ite] **:** a mineral $(Co,Ni)As_3$ that consists of a native arsenide of cobalt and nickel and is isomorphous with smaltite, nickel-skutterudite, and chloanthite
¹sky \ˈskī\ *n* -ES *often attrib* [ME, cloud, sky, fr. ON *ský* cloud; akin to OE *scēo* cloud, *scua* shadow, OHG *scuwo*, ON *skuggi* shadow, Goth *skuggwa* mirror, Skt *skunāti* he covers — more at HIDE] **1 a :** the expanse of space surrounding the earth **:** the upper atmosphere — usu. used in pl. ⟨lifted his tiny hands to the *skies* —Sherwood Anderson⟩ **b :** the expanse appearing as a great vault or arch over the earth **:** FIRMAMENT ⟨the ~ was a cold stone-grey —Pearl Buck⟩ ⟨the daughter of earth and water, and the nursling of the ~ —P.B.Shelley⟩ ⟨behold a rainbow in the ~ —William Wordsworth⟩ ⟨a blue ~ of spring —William Allingham⟩ ⟨the infinitely perilous night ~ —V.V.Nabokov⟩ — often used in pl. ⟨promise in the *skies* neither of sun nor of snow —Jean Stafford⟩ ⟨the *skies* they were ashen and sober —E.A.Poe⟩ **2 :** HEAVEN 2 ⟨fate snatch'd her early to the pitying ~ —Alexander Pope⟩ — often used in pl. ⟨he rais'd a mortal to the *skies* —John Dryden⟩ **3 a :** meteorological conditions as manifested in the upper atmospheric regions — usu. used in pl. ⟨stormy *skies*⟩ ⟨the papers forecast clear *skies* tomorrow⟩ **b :** CLIMATE — usu. used in pl. ⟨our temperate English *skies* —G.G.Coulton⟩ ⟨creatures from neighboring fields and *skies* —R.W.Murray⟩ **4 :** SKY BLUE **5 :** an unrestricted or indefinite amount or degree of something — used in the phrase *the sky is the limit* — **to the sky** *or* **to the skies** *adv* **:** in an enthusiastic manner **:** EXTRAVAGANTLY ⟨praising positive thinking *to the sky* —Bernard Kalb⟩
²sky \"\ *vb* **skied** *or* **skyed; skied** *or* **skyed; skying; skies** *vt* **1** *chiefly Brit* **:** to toss up (a coin) **:** FLIP ⟨*skied* a copper for heads or tails —S.H.Adams⟩ **2 a :** to hang (as a painting) above the line of vision ⟨have been *skied* or placed in obscure corners —*Carnegie Mag.*⟩ **b :** to place (as a person) in an inconveniently high place ⟨the world's press, *skied* up in the gallery —Mollie Panter-Downes⟩ **3 :** to hit (a ball) high into the air ⟨*skied* his simple pitch a full 40 yards short of the green —H.W.Wind⟩ **4 :** to pass (as cotton cloth) in dyeing through air on rollers (as for oxidizing the reduced form of a vat dye) ~ *vi* **1 :** to hit a ball high into the air ⟨the batter *skied* to the center fielder⟩ **2 :** to rise precipitously ⟨a way to keep insurance rates from *skying* —*Wall Street Jour.*⟩
sky·bal *or* **sky·bald** \ˈskībəl\ *n* -S [origin unknown] *dial Brit* **:** one that is worthless **:** GOOD-FOR-NOTHING
sky-blue \ˈ=¦=\ *adj* [¹*sky* + *blue*, adj.] **:** of the color sky blue **:** AZURE, CERULEAN
sky blue *n* [*sky-blue*] **:** a variable color averaging a pale to light blue — called also *celestial, ethereal blue*
skyborne \ˈ=,=\ *adj* **:** AIRBORNE ⟨~ troops⟩
skycap \ˈ=,=\ *n* [¹*sky* + *-cap* (as in *redcap*)] **:** one who is employed to carry hand luggage at an airport — compare REDCAP
sky cavalry *n* **:** a lightplane reconnaissance unit often functionally integrated with surface cavalry units
skycoach \ˈ=,=\ *n* **:** a commercial airplane that provides low-cost transportation without sleeping accommodations or other special services
sky compass *n* **:** a device used by navigators for estimating the position of the sun when it is a few degrees below the horizon (as during long polar twilights)
sky control *n* **:** a gunnery control station aloft on a naval vessel
sky cover *n* **:** the extent to which the sky is obscured by clouds
sky-dome *n* **:** a dome that curves around and over the stage of a theater and represents the sky — compare CYCLORAMA
sky·er \ˈskī(ə)r, -īə\ *n* -S [²*sky* + *-er*] **:** a bowled ball that is skied by a batsman in cricket
skye terrier \ˈskī-\ *n* [*Skye*, island of the Inner Hebrides, northwest Scotland] **1** *usu cap S&T* **:** a Scottish breed of terrier having a long head with prick or pendent ears and close-set hazel eyes, a long low body with a short soft woolly inner coat and a long hard straight outer coat, a tail about 9 inches long, and short straight legs **2** *also* **skye** *usu cap S & often cap T* **:** a dog of the Skye terrier breed
sky·ey *or* **ski·ey** \ˈskīē\ *adj* [¹*sky* + *-y*] **:** of, relating to, or having the characteristics of the sky **:** EXALTED, LOFTY ⟨bright, ~ distances —Clara Laidlaw⟩ ⟨~ worlds of general principles —Ernest Barker⟩
sky father *n, often cap S&F* **:** the sky viewed (as in primitive theology) as the male member or masculine principle of the primordial parents — compare EARTH MOTHER
sky-flower \ˈ=,=\ *n* **:** GOLDEN DEWDROP
sky fog *n* **:** the fogging of a plate exposed for astronomical photography at night caused by the general light of the sky
sky·ful *also* **sky·full** \ˈskī,fu̇l\ *n* -S **:** as much or as many as the sky can accommodate ⟨chaotic ~ of crowding flakes —Thomas Hardy⟩ ⟨~ of bombers —Donald Armstrong⟩
sky-gazer \ˈ=,==\ *n* **:** a triangular skysail used esp. on clipper ships
sky glow *n* **:** a glow in the night sky deriving from an artificial source (as the lights of a city)
sky gray *n* **:** a light bluish gray that is redder and paler than chicory
sky green *n* **:** a light yellow green that is greener and deeper than glass green and greener and stronger than reed green

¹sky-high \ˈ=¦=\ *adv* [¹*sky* + *high*, adv.] **1 a :** high into the air ⟨men on the upper deck were flung *sky-high* —J.E.Macdonnell⟩ **b :** to an unusually or unprecedentedly high level ⟨raising taxes *sky-high* —Laura Krey⟩ ⟨lifted my spirit *sky-high* —Elmer Morriss⟩ **2 :** in an enthusiastic manner ⟨extolling the virtues of the crew *sky-high* —Frederick Way⟩ **3 :** to pieces **:** APART ⟨the thesis . . . was blown *sky-high* —*Times Lit. Supp.*⟩ ⟨blasted another popular myth *sky-high*⟩
²sky-high \"\ *adj* [¹*sky* + *high*, adj.] **:** excessively expensive **:** EXORBITANT ⟨spend *sky-high* sums —Norman Cousins⟩ ⟨top restaurants are often *sky-high* —T.H.Fielding⟩
skyhook \ˈ=,=\ *n* [¹*sky* + *hook*, n.] **1 :** a hook conceived as being suspended from the sky ⟨the nearest thing to hanging a roof from ~*s* and leaving out the walls entirely —*Popular Science Monthly*⟩ **2 :** a self-propelled carriage suspended from two or more cables and used for high-line hauling logs esp. in logging **3 :** SKYHOOK BALLOON
sky hook *vt* [*skyhook*] **:** to reinforce (a mine ceiling) by inserting bolts vertically into the secure rock above
skyhook balloon *n* **:** a large semitransparent helium-filled high-altitude plastic balloon used to carry instruments aloft for the study of cosmic rays
sky hooker *n* [¹*sky* + *hooker*] **:** TOP LOADER
sky·hoot \(ˈ)skī¦hüt\ *vi* [by alter.] **:** SCOOT — often used in the phrase *go skyhooting*
skying *pres part of* SKY
sky·ish \ˈskīish, -ēsh\ *adj* **:** SKYEY
sky·ko·mish \skīˈkōmish, -mēsh\ *n, pl* **skykomish** *or* **skykomishes** *usu cap* **1 :** an Indian people of the Skykomish river valley in Washington **2 :** a member of the Skykomish people
¹skylark \ˈ=,=\ *n* **1 :** a common Old World lark (*Alauda arvensis*) with dark brown upper parts, a buff throat and breast streaked with brown, and creamy white abdomen that inhabits chiefly open country and is noted for its song esp. as uttered in vertical flight **2 :** any of various birds (as Sprague's pipit) that resemble the skylark
²skylark \"\ *vi* **1 :** to run up and down the rigging of a ship in sport **2 :** to frolic in a playful or boisterous manner **:** fool around ⟨were ~*ing* on the hike —L.M.Uris⟩
³skylark \"\ *n* [²*skylark*] **:** ⁴LARK 1 ⟨full of gusto, and to him everything is a ~ —John Hersey⟩
sky·less \ˈ=,ləs\ *adj* **:** having the sky obscured by clouds
¹skylight \ˈ=,=\ *n* **1 a :** the diffused and reflected light of the sky ⟨the flux density due to sunlight and ~ —H.G.Houghton⟩ **b :** the general background of illumination of the nighttime sky that includes light from both natural and artificial sources **:** AIRGLOW **2 :** an opening in a roof or a deck of a ship covered with translucent or transparent material (as glass or plastic) and designed for the admission of light

skylight 2

²skylight \"\ *vt* **:** to light (as a room) by a skylight
¹skyline \ˈ=,=\ *n* **1 :** an apparent line in the landscape at the juncture of earth and sky **:** HORIZON ⟨towers . . . rising above the ~ —A.B.Osborne⟩ **2 :** an outline (as of buildings or a mountain range) against the background of the sky ⟨the newer skyscrapers . . . along the ~ of New York —*Irish Statesman*⟩ ⟨the waving ~ of the foothills —C.W.Gordon⟩ **3 :** a cable stretched taut between two spar trees and used as a track along which logs are hauled — compare SLACKLINE **syn** see OUTLINE
²skyline \"\ *vt* **:** to outline against the sky ⟨let us be . . . *skylined* on earth's highest hill —Sean O'Casey⟩
skyline logging *n* **:** HIGH-LINE LOGGING
skyliner \ˈ=,==\ *n* [¹*sky* + *liner*] **:** AIRLINER
skylook \ˈ=,=\ *vt* **:** to survey (timber) from a position aloft
sky·man \ˈ=,mən\ *n, pl* **skymen** *slang* **:** PARATROOPER
sky map *n* **1 :** a chart showing the positions of celestial bodies **:** STAR CHART **2 :** a pattern of varying degrees of glare on the underside of a cloud area caused by reflected light from the earth's surface
skymark \ˈ=,=\ *n* **:** an object appearing against the background of the sky ⟨the tower clock . . . is a familiar ~ —*Amer. Guide Series: N.Y.City*⟩
sky parlor *n* **:** a room at the top of a house ⟨sat hungry and cold in their *sky parlor*, looking down on a bystreet in the city — *N. Y. Herald Tribune*⟩
skyphos *var of* SCYPHUS
sky pilot *n* **:** CLERGYMAN; *specif* **:** CHAPLAIN
sky pipit *n* **:** SPRAGUE'S PIPIT
skyport \ˈ=,=\ *n* **:** HELIPORT
skyr \ˈskir\ *n* -S [Icel, fr. ON; akin to ON *skera* to cut — more at SHEAR] **1 :** sour curdled milk **2 :** a dessert prepared from sweet and sour cream with sugar
skyre \ˈskī(ə)r\ *vi* [prob. fr. obs. E *skyre, skire*, adj., bright, fr. ME *skir, skire* — more at SKIRE THURSDAY] *chiefly Scot* **:** to shine in a gaudy manner **:** GLITTER
sky-rider \ˈ=,==\ *n* **:** one who travels in or flies an airplane
¹skyrocket \ˈ=,==\ *n* **1 :** ³ROCKET 1 **2** *or* **skyrocket gilia :** a No. American biennial or perennial herb (*Gilia aggregata*) having flowers with linear reflexed lobes and often cultivated as an ornamental
²skyrocket \"\ *vi* **1 :** to rise abruptly and rapidly ⟨expenses, salaries, income, all ~*ed* —J.T.Farrell⟩ ⟨national advertising . . . has ~*ed* . . . within the last few years —F.W.Doepke⟩ **2 :** to act in an impulsive, thoughtless, or irrational manner ⟨you have . . . kept my feet on the ground when I was about to ~ —F.D.Roosevelt⟩ ~ *vt* **1 :** to cause to rise or increase abruptly and rapidly ⟨help ~ horsepower but add only a smidgen to torque —Frank Rowsome⟩ ⟨lavish touches which ~ costs —Frances W. Brown⟩ **2 :** to bring about the rapid and unexpected elevation of ⟨won instant success and ~*ed* its author to fame —Fanny K. Wister⟩
sky·rock·ety \-ˌkəd·ē, -ətē, -i\ *adj* **:** resembling a skyrocket
sky·sail \ˈskī,sāl, -ˈīsəl\ *n* **:** a sail set immediately above the royal — see SAIL illustration
skysail pole *n* **:** the part of the royal mast above the shoulder when skysails are carried — see SHIP illustration
skysail-yarder \ˈ=(,)=,==\ *n* [*skysail yard* + *-er*] **:** a ship having skysail yards
sky·scape \ˈskī,skāp\ *n* -S **1 :** a part of the sky with outlined terrestrial objects that can be comprehended in a single view ⟨gaps between the fluffy white mountains of the ~ —*McGill News*⟩ **2 :** a picture that includes an extensive view of the sky
sky·scrape \ˈ=,skrāp\ *vi* [back-formation fr. *skyscraper*] **:** to build a skyscraper ⟨city ruling . . . limits *skyscraping* to about twenty-two stories —*New Yorker*⟩
sky·scrap·er \-pə(r)\ *n* [¹*sky* + *scraper*] **1 :** a triangular skysail used on a clipper ship **2 :** one that is unusually tall ⟨that vegetable ~, the giant cactus —D.C.Peattie⟩; *esp* **:** a many-storied building ⟨a typical American ~, tall and narrow, with a spire and beacon —*Amer. Guide Series: Mich.*⟩
sky·scrap·ered \ˈ=¦=pə(r)d\ *adj* **:** having or marked by skyscrapers ⟨~ cities⟩
skyscraping \ˈ=,==\ *adj* [fr. *skyscraper*, after E *scraper: scraping*] **:** of, relating to, or having the characteristics of a skyscraper **:** very high ⟨a ~ building⟩
sky shade *n* **:** a screen that is usu. attached to the shutter or lens tube of a camera and is used for reducing the light from the sky
sky sign *n* **:** a usu. electric display sign on top of a building
skystone \ˈ=,=\ *n* **:** METEORITE
skysweeper \ˈ=,==\ *n* **:** a 75 millimeter antiaircraft gun that automatically locates and aims at a target and fires up to 45 rounds a minute by means of radar
sky train *n* **:** an airplane that has one or more unpowered aircraft (as gliders) in tow — called also *air train*
skytrooper \ˈ=,==\ *n* **:** PARATROOPER
skytroops \ˈ=,=\ *n pl* **:** PARATROOPS
sky truck *n* **:** a transport plane used for carrying heavy and bulky loads
sky·ward \ˈ=wə(r)d\ *also* **sky·wards** \-dz\ *adv* **1 :** to or toward the sky ⟨gaze ~⟩ **2 :** UPWARD ⟨spending by all consuming units shot ~ —E.W.Swanson⟩
sky wave *n* **:** a radio wave that is propagated by means of the ionosphere

skyway \ˈ=,=\ *n* **1 :** a route used by airplanes **:** AIRLANE, AIRWAY 2 **2 :** an elevated highway
skywrite \ˈ=,=\ *vi* **:** to engage in skywriting ⟨~ in long, slim letters —*Popular Science Monthly*⟩ ~ *vt* **1 :** to produce by means of skywriting ⟨~ a slogan⟩ **2 :** to give wide publicity to ⟨~ some of the ugly, underground truths of racial intolerance —John Mason Brown⟩
skywriter \ˈ=,==\ *n* **:** one that skywrites
skywriting \ˈ=,==\ *n* **:** writing formed in the sky by means of smoke or other visible substance emitted from an airplane
sl *abbr* **1** slate **2** slide **3** slip **4** slow
SL *abbr* **1** salvage loss **2** sea level **3** searchlight **4** [L *secundum legem*] according to law **5** seditious libeler **6** sergeant-at-law **7** *often not cap* [L *sine loco*] without place **8** single line **9** solicitor-at-law **10** sound locator **11** south latitude **12** squadron leader **13** stock length **14** streamline **15** sub-lieutenant **16** *often not cap* [L *suo loco*] in its place
sla \ˈslā\ *archaic var of* SLOE
¹slab \ˈslab, -lah(ə)b\ *n* -S [ME *slabbe, sclabbe*] **1 :** a comparatively thick plate or slice of something (as of metal, stone, wood, or food) ⟨a ~ of bread⟩ ⟨cut the marble into ~*s*⟩: as **a** (1) **:** the irregular outside piece cut from a log in squaring it or preparing it for being sawed into boards (2) *Austral & Africa* **:** a thick roughhewn plank (3) **:** a thin piece cut from a board in resawing (as for box making) **b :** a flat substantial piece of timber or stone forming the top of a table or counter **c :** a rectangular piece of iron or steel made by rolling an ingot so that the width of the section is at least twice the thickness — compare BLOOM **d :** PLATE 1h(2) **e :** a flat piece (as of stone, glass, or porcelain) on which drugs or colors are ground, printing ink distributed, or various substances (as ointments) are mixed **f :** concrete pavement (as of a road); *specif* **:** a strip of concrete pavement laid as a single unjointed piece **g :** a sheet of crystallized sugar before it is cut into cubes **h slabs** *pl* **:** fruit halves (as of apricots, peaches) flattened and matted together during drying **i** (1) **:** a flat rectangular architectural element that is usu. formed of a single piece or mass ⟨the use of a concrete foundation ~ in modern small houses⟩ ⟨the park included a dance ~⟩ — see SLAB BRIDGE (2) **:** a rectangular building having small depth in comparison with its length and usu. height and designed to provide optimum light and air distribution to the inside **2 :** firewood cut from lumber waste (as edgings) ⟨burned ~ except in the coldest weather⟩ **3 :** an offset of a bulb and esp. of a narcissus bulb
²slab \"\ *vb* **slabbed; slabbed; slabbing; slabs** *vt* **1 a :** to saw, divide, or form into slabs **b :** to remove an outer slab from (as a log) **2 a :** to cover (as a roadbed or roof) with slabs **b :** to support (as the sides of a shaft or well) with slabs **3 :** to put or stick on in slabs **:** apply thickly ⟨*slabbed* butter on the bread⟩ ⟨enjoyed *slabbing* paint onto the wall⟩ ~ *vi* **:** to prepare or form slabs **:** slab something esp. as an occupation ⟨spent the winter *slabbing* at the mill⟩
³slab \"\ *adj* [prob. of Scand origin; akin to obs. Dan *slab* slippery and prob. to Dan *slab* slime] **1** *dial chiefly Eng* **:** THICK, SLIMY, VISCID **2 :** sloppily sentimental; *also* **:** put on thickly **:** using profuse and exaggerated language ⟨prose too thick and ~⟩
⁴slab \"\ *n* -S [of Scand origin; akin to Sw dial. *slabb* slime, mud, *slabba* to roll in mud — more at SLAVER] *chiefly dial* **:** SLIME, MUD
⁵slab \"\ *n* -S [prob. short for *slab line*] **:** the slack part of a sail
slabbed tie *n* [*slabbed* fr. past part. of ²*slab*] **:** a railroad tie sawed to provide flat surfaces on the top and bottom only — called also *pole tie*
¹slab·ber \ˈslabə(r)\ *vb* -ED/-ING/-S [prob. fr. D *slabberen*, freq. of *slabben* to slaver, fr. MD — more at SLAVER] **1 :** SLOBBER, DROOL; *also* **:** DRIVEL **2 :** GORGE, BOLT
²slabber \"\ *n* -S **:** SLOBBER, SLAVER
³slab·ber \ˈslabə(r), -laab-\ *n* -S [²*slab* + *-er*] **:** one that slabs: as **a :** a saw for slabbing logs **b :** a machine for cutting soap into slabs **c :** MILLING MACHINE; *esp* **:** PLANOMILLER **d :** a person that forms slabs (as by cutting) or fixes slabs in place (as by cementing) **e :** an operator of any slabber
slab·ber·er \-labərə(r)\ *n* -S **:** one that slabbers
slab·bery \-bərē\ *adj* **:** like or covered with slabber **:** SLIPPERY, SLOPPY
slab·bi·ly \-bəlē\ *adv* [¹*slabby* + *-ly*] **:** in a slabby manner **:** as if made of something slabby
slab·bing \ˈslabiŋ, -laab-\ *n* -S [in sense 1, fr. ¹*slab* + *-ing*; in other senses, fr. gerund of ²*slab*] **1 :** SLABS **2 :** the cutting of a skip from the side of a pillar or face of coal **3 :** lamination of clay wares caused by rapid firing
slabbing cutter *n* **:** a plain milling cutter esp. when having a broad face
slabbing machine *n* **:** PLANOMILLER
slabbing mill *n* **:** a steel rolling mill that produces slabs
slab bridge *n* **:** a short-span bridge consisting of a reinforced-concrete slab resting on abutments
¹slab·by \ˈslabē\ *adj* -ER/-EST [prob. of Scand origin; akin to Sw dial. *slabb* slime, mud — more at SLAB] **1** *archaic* **:** WET, SLOPPY, MUDDY, MIRY **2 :** VISCOUS, JELLYLIKE
²slab·by \ˈslabē, -laabē\ *adj* [¹*slab* + *-y*] **1 :** covered or paved with slabs **2 :** made up of slabs **:** having the form of slabs ⟨~ fragments of rock⟩
slab door *n* **1 :** a rude door (as of a log cabin) made from rough slabbing **2 :** a door without panels and with a continuous smooth surface on both sides **:** FLUSH DOOR
slab house *n* **:** a pit house lined with stone slabs
slab line \ˈslab-, -laab-\ *n* [earlier *slabline*, part modif., part trans. of D *slaplijn*, fr. *slap* slack + *lijn* line] **:** a line or small rope by which seamen haul up the body of a course or topsail
slab·man \ˈslabmən, -laab-\ *n, pl* **slabmen 1 :** a worker who cuts or piles up slabs (as of lumber) **2 :** ANGLESMITH 2 **3 :** a worker who prepares hard candy mixture and pulls it to proper consistency for use
slab mill *n* **:** SLABBING CUTTER
slab-on-ground \ˈ=,=¦=\ *adj* **:** marked by construction in which a foundation slab is laid directly on the ground without a basement ⟨*slab-on-ground* houses⟩
slab reef *n* **:** a small reef between tack and clew on the foot of a sail by which the sail may be made flatter
slabs *pl of* SLAB, *pres 3d sing of* SLAB
slab-sided \ˈ=¦==\ *adj* **:** having the rib cage narrow from side to side with flat sides and the ribs deficient in lateral curvature ⟨a *slab-sided* horse⟩; *also* **:** giving an effect of such a condition by reason of leanness or slenderness ⟨an airplane with a *slab-sided* fuselage⟩ ⟨*slab-sided* cheeks⟩
slabstone \ˈ=,=\ *n* **:** ³FLAG 3
slab tie *n* **:** a railroad tie made from the outside cut of a log
slab-top \ˈ=,=\ *adj* **:** having a cover in the form of a slab (as of reinforced concrete) ⟨a *slab-top* culvert⟩
slabwood \ˈ=,=\ *n* [¹*slab* + *wood*] **:** SLAB 2
¹slack \ˈslak\ *adj* -ER/-EST [ME *slak*, fr. OE *sleac;* akin to OS *slak* slack, OHG *slah*, ON *slakr* slack, L *laxus* slack, loose, spacious, *languēre* to be languid, Gk *lēgein* to leave off, stop, Skt *langa* lame] **1 :** not using due diligence, care, or dispatch **:** REMISS, INATTENTIVE, NEGLIGENT ⟨~ in service⟩ **2 a :** characterized by slowness, sluggishness, or lack of energy **:** wanting in life, vigor, or strength ⟨a ~ pace⟩ ⟨a very ~ performance⟩ **b :** moderate in some quality; *esp* **:** moderately warm ⟨a ~ oven⟩ **c :** blowing or flowing at low speed — used esp. of wind or tide **3 a :** not tight **:** not tense or taut **:** LOOSE, RELAXED ⟨a ~ rope⟩ **b :** lacking in firmness **:** WEAK, SOFT, UNSTEADY ⟨a ~ hand⟩ ⟨~ control⟩ **c** *of one edge of a roll of paper* **:** not wound as tightly as the other edge **4 a :** wanting in activity **:** not busy **:** DULL ⟨fall is our ~ season⟩ **b :** marked by a low level of activity **:** reduced below a desired, normal, or usual level ⟨employment is very ~⟩ **5 :** lacking in completeness, finish, or perfection ⟨the finish was much ~*er* than the design⟩ **6 a :** made with joints sufficiently tight for packing dried materials but not watertight ⟨~ cooperage⟩ **b :** concerned with or engaged in the making of slack cooperage **syn** see NEGLIGENT
²slack \"\ *vb* -ED/-ING/-S *vt* **1 a :** to be slack, inattentive, or negligent in performing, executing, or completing ⟨~ one's vigilance⟩ **b** *archaic* **:** to fail to take advantage of (as an opportunity) or use to advantage (as time) **c :** to moderate or slacken deliberately by or as if by relaxing one's energy, zeal,

grip, or other controlling factor : cause to lessen (as in speed, vigor, violence, fervor) ⟨~*ed* his pace as the sun grew hot⟩ — often used with *up* ⟨~ up one's effort⟩ **2** : to cause to be relaxed, loose, or otherwise free from tension : LOOSEN ⟨~ the girth while the horse is cooling⟩ ⟨~ a line⟩ — often used with an adverb (as *off, out*) ⟨~ off the sail⟩ **3 a** : to cause to abate : SLAKE 2 **b** : SLAKE 4 ~ *vi* **1 a** : to be or become slack : decline in some effort (as in speed, force, activity) : slow up : relax tension ⟨the wind ~*ed*⟩ **b** : to approach an end (as of activity) : cease to progress : ⟨our enthusiasm ~*ed off*⟩ ⟨retail business ~*s* down when employment drops⟩ **2** : to shirk or evade work or obligations : be or become a slacker, idler, or shirker **3** : SLAKE 3

³**slack** \"\ *adv* : SLACKLY

⁴**slack** \"\ *n* -s [ME *slak*, fr. ON *slakki*] **1** *dial Eng* : a pass between hills : GLEN **2** *dial Brit* **a** : a pool of water **b** : MARSH

⁵**slack** \"\ *n* -s [ME *sleck*, prob. fr. MD *slecke, slacke* slag, slack; perh. akin to MLG *slagge* slag — more at SLAG] : the finest screenings of coal produced at a mine and often containing slate and dirt that make it undesirable for fuel unless cleaned — called also *coom, culm*

⁶**slack** \"\ *n* -s [¹*slack*] **1** : cessation in movement or flow; *specif* : SLACK WATER **2** : a part of something that hangs loose without strain ⟨take up the ~ of a rope⟩ **3 a** : TROUSERS **b** : long pants for casual wear often of a looser cut than suit trousers and with pleats at the waist — usu. used in pl. but sometimes sing. in constr. **4** : a lull in activity : a dull season or period **5** : looseness of fit (as of a part in a mechanism) : BACKLASH **6** : the weak or stressless element in a rhythmic unit or foot : UNSTRESS

slacks 3b

⁷**slack** \"\ *n* [prob. short for *slack jaw*] *dial Eng* : impudent talk

⁸**slack** \"\ *n* -s [ME *slak* — more at SLAKE] : ³SLAKE

slack·age \'slakij\ *n* -s : amount of slack : SLACKENING

slack–baked \'⸗ˌ⸗\ *adj* : inadequately or badly baked; *also* : imperfectly made or finished

slack coal *n* : ⁵SLACK

¹**slack·en** \'slakən\ *vb* **slackened; slackened; slackening** \-k(ə)niŋ\ **slackens** *vt* **1** : to render less active : hold back ⟨~ a flow of water⟩ ⟨~ one's interest⟩ : slow up : ABATE, MODERATE, RETARD ⟨~ one's speed⟩ **2** : to render slack (as by lessening tension, tautness, firmness) : LOOSEN ⟨~ sail⟩ ~ *vi* **1** : to become slack or slow or negligent : slow down ⟨determined not to ~ as a correspondent —Jane Austen⟩ **2** : to become less active : SLACK **syn** see DELAY

²**slack·en** *also* **slak·in** \'slakən\ *n* -s [modif. of obs. G *schlacken* (now *schlacke*), fr. or akin to MLG *slagge* slag — more at SLAG] : slag mixed with ores in smelting to promote their fusion

slack·en·er \-k(ə)nə(r)\ *n* -s : one that slackens

slackening *n* -s [fr. gerund of ¹*slacken*] : DECLINE, MODERATION

slack·er \'slakə(r)\ *n* -s : one that slacks: as **a** : a drawgate in a sluice **b** : a person who shirks work, responsibility, or an obligation; *esp* : one that evades military service in time of war

slack·er·ism \-kəˌrizəm\ *n* -s : the behavior of a slacker

slackest *superlative of* SLACK

slack–filled \'⸗ˌ⸗\ *adj* [³*slack*] : incompletely or deceptively packed : abnormally or excessively loose-packed ⟨a *slack-filled* carton⟩

slack ice *n* : broken ice floating on quiet or slowly moving water

slacking *pres part of* SLACK

slack in stays *adj, of a ship* : slow in going about

slack jaw *n* : wearisome or impudent talk

slack–jawed \'⸗ˌ⸗\ *adj* [³*slack*] : having the lower jaw dropped esp. as indicating amazement or stupidity ⟨*slack-jawed* yokels⟩ ⟨stood *slack-jawed* with surprise⟩

slackline \'⸗ˌ⸗\ *n* **1** : a cable (as in a lumbering operation) suspended slackly between spar trees and adapted esp. to yarding downhill or across steep-sided canyons or gullies — compare SKYLINE **2** : a hoist that lowers an empty bucket by gravity with a slackline and applies cable tension to lift the loaded bucket on the return

slack·ly *adv* [ME *slackely*, fr. OE *sleaclīce*, fr. *sleac* slack + *-līce* -ly — more at SLACK] : in a slack manner : LOOSELY, CARELESSLY, INADEQUATELY

slack·ness *n* -ES [ME *slaknesse*, fr. OE *sleacness*, fr. *sleac* slack + *-ness*] **1** : the quality or state of being slack or behaving slackly **2** : something that is slack

slack rope *n* : a loosely stretched rope used by some rope-walkers and acrobats — compare TIGHTROPE

slacks *pres 3d sing of* SLACK, *pl of* SLACK

slack–sized \'⸗ˌ⸗\ *adj, of paper* : so lightly sized as to be permeable to water with relative ease — compare HARD-SIZED

slack–spined \'⸗ˌ⸗\ *adj* : WEAK, INEFFECTIVE ⟨*slack-spined* heedless leaders⟩

slack suit *n* : a comfortable man's or woman's suit for casual or sports wear or lounging consisting of a pair of slacks and jacket top or sport shirt often of the same material and color

slack–twisted \'⸗ˌ⸗⸗\ *adj* : lacking in firmness of fiber : weak in character or energy ⟨wanted no part of such a *slack-twisted* fellow⟩

slack water *n* **1** *or* **slack tide** : the period at the turn of the tide when there is little or no horizontal motion of tidal water **2** : a slowly moving or still body of water (as in a stream above a dam) **3** : ocean water marked by virtual absence of current **4** : a slackening of the current of a stream resulting from a log-jam

¹**slack–water** \'⸗ˌ⸗⸗\ *adj* [*slack water*] **1** : marked by slack water ⟨a *slack-water* period⟩ **2** : carried on in slack water produced artificially (as by a lock or dam) ⟨*slack-water* navigation⟩

²**slack–water** \"\ *vt* : to produce slack water in (as a river) by a construction (as a dam, lock, or jetty)

slack wax *n* : yellow to dark-colored crude paraffin wax that is separated from part of the oil in paraffin distillate by chilling and pressing or by use of a solvent and that contains considerable residual oil — compare SCALE WAX

slack wire *n* : a wire slack rope

sladang *var of* SELADANG

¹**slade** \'slād\ *n* -s [ME, fr. OE *slæd*] **1** *dial chiefly Eng* : a little valley : RAVINE, GLEN — often used in place names **2** *dial chiefly Eng* : GLADE 1 **3** *dial chiefly Eng* : HILLSIDE

²**slade** \"\ *n* [origin unknown] **1** : the sole of a plow **2** : PEAT SPADE

slae \'slā\ *chiefly Scot var of* SLOE

¹**slag** \'slag, -aa(ə)-, -ai-\ *n* -s [MLG *slagge*; prob. akin to MHG *slage* hammer, tool for striking, OE *slēan* to strike; prob. fr. the dross resulting from hammering or forging — more at SLAY] **1 a** : the dross of a metal; *specif* : a product of smelting containing mostly as silicates the substances not sought to be produced as matte or metal and having a lower specific gravity than the latter — called also *cinder* **b** : a similar substance that floats on molten impure steel during refining, protects the metal from oxidation, and removes unwanted substances chemically **2** : scoriaceous lava from a volcano **3** : a fused or partly fused and usu. glassy mass resulting from contact of bases with silica or silicates at high temperatures and often deliberately developed in enameling and glazing **4** : worthless matter : DEBRIS ⟨~ accumulations in the bottom of a wash tank⟩ ⟨nothing like a brisk walk to drag the ~ from your head⟩

²**slag** \"\ *vt* **slagged; slagged; slagging; slags** : to free from or convert into slag

slag block *n* : a masonry structural unit made from slag concrete

slag cement *n* : a pozzolana cement using slag as the pozzolana material

slag concrete *n* : concrete in which blast-furnace slag is used as the aggregate

slag furnace *or* **slag hearth** *n* : a metallurgical furnace in which lead ore is smelted and slagged for further treatment

slag·ger \-gə(r)\ *n* -s : a worker who removes slag from furnaces

slagging hole *n* : CINDER NOTCH

slag glass *n* : an opaque marbled glass

slag·gy \-gē,-gi\ *adj* -ER/-EST : of, relating to, containing, or resembling slag ⟨~ cobalt⟩ ⟨a ~ coal⟩

slag·less \-gləs\ *adj* : containing no slag — **slag·less·ness** *n* -ES

slag·man \-gmən\ *n, pl* **slagmen** : SLAGGER

slag sand *n* : slag crushed into fine particles and used esp. in mortar or concrete

slag–tap furnace *n* : a blast furnace or pulverized-fuel furnace with a tap opening in the bottom for removal of slag

slag wool *n* : a mineral wool made usu. from molten blast-furnace slag by the action of jets of steam under high pressure

slain *past part of* SLAY

slain·te \'slō(i)ntə\ *interj* [Ir *slāinte* health] *Irish* — used as a salutation or toast

¹**slais·ter** \'slāstə(r)\ *vi* -ED/-ING/-S [origin unknown] *dial Brit* : to be occupied with dirty, gooey, or messy materials : slop around

²**slaister** \"\ *n* -s *chiefly Scot* : a sloppy mess

slak·able *or* **slake·able** \'slākəbəl, -lak-\ *adj* : capable of being slaked

¹**slake** \'slāk, *in senses vi 3 & vt 4* " *or* 'slak; *chiefly dial in other senses* 'slak\ *vb* -ED/-ING/-S [ME *slaken*, fr. OE *slacian, sleacian*, fr. *sleac* slack — more at SLACK] *vi* **1** *obs* : to slacken one's efforts : FLAG, SLACK 1a **2** *archaic* : to become less violent, intense, or severe : grow less : ABATE, MODERATE ⟨no flood by raining *slaketh* —Shak.⟩ **3** : to become slaked : CRUMBLE, DISINTEGRATE ⟨lime may ~ spontaneously in moist air⟩ ~ *vt* **1** *obs* : SLACK 2 **2 a** *obs* : to make less : reduce in quantity or size : DIMINISH **b** *archaic* : to cause to be less acute : EASE, MITIGATE **c** : to cause to lessen (as in vigor, speed, force) : lessen the violence or fury of : MODERATE ⟨unwilling to ~ his anger⟩ **3 a** : to bring (as thirst) to an end with or as if with refreshing drink : SATISFY, ALLAY ⟨*slaked* our curiosity with an account of the night's happenings⟩; *also* : to make moist : WET ⟨land *slaked* with blood⟩ ⟨*slaking* our dry throats with melted snow⟩ **b** : to put out (as a fire) or cause to burn less strongly : DEADEN ⟨*slaking* all earthly desires⟩ **4 a** : to cause (as lime) to heat and crumble by treatment with water : HYDRATE **b** : to alter (as lime) by exposure to air with conversion at least in part to a carbonate : AIR-SLAKE

²**slake** \'slāk, 'slak — *see* ¹SLAKE\ *n* -s [ME *slak*, fr. *slaken* to slake] : an act or an instance of slaking

³**slake** \'slāk\ *also* **slake kale** *n* -s [*slake* fr. ME *slak*, alter. of *slauk*, prob. fr. MIr *sleabhac* edible seaweed, slake] *Brit* : SLOKE 1; *also* : any of various confervoid freshwater algae

⁴**slake** \'slāk\ *vt* [alter. of earlier *slaik* to lick, daub, of Scand origin; akin to OSw *slekja* to lick, ON *sleikja* — more at LICK] *chiefly Scot* : DAUB, BESMEAR

⁵**slake** \'slāk\ *n* -s [by alter.] : ⁵SLACK

slaked lime \'slāk(t)-, 'slak(t)-\ *n* : HYDRATED LIME

slake·less \-kləs\ *adj* : not capable of being slaked

slak·er \-kə(r)\ *n* -s : one that slakes: as **a** : a piece of equipment for slaking lime ⟨horizontal rotary ~*s*⟩ **b** : a worker who makes hydrated lime

slake trough *n* : a blacksmith's water tank for cooling forgings or tools

slakin *var of* SLACKEN

slaky \'slākē\ *adj* -ER/-EST [obs. E dial. *slake* mud, mire + E *-y*] : MIRY, MUDDY

sla·lom \'släləm *also* 'slāl- *or* -ˌlōm *or* -ˌlōm; *also* 'slaləm *sometimes* 'slāləm\ *n* -s [Norw, lit., sloping track] : skiing in a zigzag or wavy course between upright obstacles (as flags); *also* : a race against time over such a course

¹**slam** \'slam, -laa(ə)m\ *n* -s [origin unknown] : a winning of all the tricks or points of a deal in a game of cards — see GRAND SLAM, LITTLE SLAM

²**slam** \"\ *n* -s [prob. of Scand origin; akin to Icel *slæma* to slam] **1** : a heavy blow or impact **2 a** : a noisy violent closing (as of a door) **b** : a banging noise; *esp* : one made by the slam of a door **3** : a cutting or violent criticism

³**slam** \"\ *vb* **slammed; slammed; slamming; slams** [of Scand origin; akin to Sw dial. *slämma* to slam, Norw *slemba, slemma*, Icel *slæma* and prob. to ON *slambra* to strike at something] *vt* **1** : to strike or beat vigorously or thoroughly : hit strongly : KNOCK ⟨*slammed* him about the head with a stick⟩ **2** : to shut forcibly and noisily : BANG ⟨wind often ~*s* the shutter⟩ **3 a** : to put in place with undue force or noise or in a great hurry : push, move, activate, or throw with impetuosity ⟨*slamming* the lid of the trunk⟩ ⟨~ home the bolt⟩ — often used with an adverb of direction ⟨*slammed* on the brake⟩ ⟨~ the window down⟩ **b** : to cause to occur through vigorous or impetuous action ⟨the batter *slammed* out a homer⟩ ⟨the committee determined to ~ through a new appropriation⟩ **4** : to criticize vigorously, brutally, or recklessly : abuse verbally ~ *vi* **1** : to make a banging noise **2** : to function (as in moving or working) with obvious and usu. noisy vigor ⟨ready to ~ into his chores⟩ ⟨a football player *slamming* into the line⟩ **3** : to utter verbal abuse — **slam the door** : to repel communication or contact usu. brusquely or arrogantly : refuse discussion or consideration ⟨*slammed the door* on the best chance of a peaceful settlement⟩ — **slam the door in one's face** : to refuse one entry or hearing

⁴**slam** \"\ *adv* **1** : with a slam ⟨~ went the doors⟩ **2** *dial* : CLEAR, COMPLETELY ⟨~ across the road⟩

¹**slam–bang** \(ˈ)⸗ˌ⸗\ *vi* : to behave boisterously ~ *vt* : BELABOR

²**slam–bang** \"\ *adv* **1** : with violence and noise **2** : without due thought or care : RECKLESSLY **3** : SLAM 2

¹**slambang** \"\ *adj* [*slam-bang*] **1** : unduly loud or violent ⟨a ~ clatter⟩ **2 a** : notably vigorous ⟨made a ~ effort to win⟩ **b** : exceptionally good : OUTSTANDING ⟨a ~ address that greatly impressed his auditors⟩

²**slambang** \"\ *n* : noisy clatter

slam·mock \'slamək\ *var of* SLOMMACK

SLAN *abbr, often not cap* [L *sine loco, anno, (vel) nomine*] without place, year, (or) name

slanch·wise \'slanchˌwīz\ *or* **slanch·ways** \-ˌwāz\ *adv* [*slanchwise* alter. of *slantwise; slanchways* alter. of *slantways*] : diagonally and usu. so as to face something ⟨turned ~ to watch the clouds⟩

SL and C *abbr* shipper's load and count

¹**slan·der** \'slandə(r), -laan-,-lān-\ *n* -s [ME *slaundre, sclaundre, sclandre*, fr. OF *esclandre, esclande, escandle* scandal, slander, fr. LL *scandalum* stumbling block, offense — more at SCANDAL] **1** : utterance of false charges or misrepresentations which defame and damage reputation **2** : a false tale or report maliciously uttered orally, tending to injure the reputation of another, and constituting a legal tort : a malicious oral utterance of false defamatory reports : malicious publication by speech of false tales or suggestions to the injury of another — compare LIBEL **3** *obs* : disgrace, shame, or reproach that falls on one usu. by reason of personal acts or character ⟨thou ~ of thy mother's heavy womb —Shak.⟩ **4** *obs* : a cause of sin : an obstacle to virtue **5** *obs* : one that is a disgrace or discredit to a body of which he is a part **syn** see DETRACTION

²**slander** \"\ *vb* **slandered; slandered; slandering** \-d(ə)riŋ\ **slanders** [ME *slaunderen, slaundren, sclaunderen, sclaundren*, fr. MF *esclandrer, esclander*, fr. OF, fr. *esclandre, esclande* slander] *vt* **1** : to hurt the reputation of by malicious utterance containing a false or injurious representation : utter slander against : DEFAME **2** *obs* : to bring shame or discredit to : DISGRACE **3** *obs* : to accuse unjustly : CHARGE, BLAME ~ *vi* : to utter or spread slander **syn** see MALIGN

slan·der·er \-dərə(r)\ *n* -s [ME *sclaunderer*, fr. *sclaunderen* to slander + *-er*] : one that utters or spreads slander

slanderful *adj* [ME *sclandirful*, fr. *sclandre* slander + *-ful*] *obs* : SLANDEROUS — **slanderfully** *adv*

slander of title : a false and malicious statement disparaging a person's title to property to his special damage; *broadly* : a disparagement of the property of a person by false and malicious statements to his special damage

slan·der·ous \-d(ə)rəs\ *adj* [ME *sclaundrous*, fr. *sclaundre* slander + *-ous*] **1** *obs* : being a source or occasion of scandal or disgrace **2** : containing or constituting slander : CALUMNIOUS ⟨a ~ utterance⟩ **3** : given to or uttering slander ⟨a ~ tongue⟩ — **slan·der·ous·ly** *adv* — **slan·der·ous·ness** *n* -ES

SL and T *abbr* shipper's load and tally

slane \'slān\ *n* -s [IrGael *sleaghān*] : PEAT SPADE

¹**slang** *chiefly dial past of* SLING

²**slang** \'slaŋ, -laiŋ-\ *n* -s [origin unknown] *dial Eng* : a narrow strip of land

³**slang** \"\ *n* -s [origin unknown] **1** : language peculiar to a particular group: as **a** : the special and often secret vocabulary used by a class (as thieves, beggars) and usu. felt to be vulgar or inferior : ARGOT **b** : the jargon used by or associated with a particular trade, profession, or field of activity **2** : a nonstandard vocabulary composed of words and senses characterized primarily by connotations of extreme informality and usu. a currency not limited to a particular region and composed typically of coinages or arbitrarily changed words, clipped or shortened forms, extravagant, forced, or facetious figures of speech, or verbal novelties usu. experiencing quick popularity and relatively rapid decline into disuse **syn** see DIALECT

⁴**slang** \"\ *adj* **1** : of, constituting, or expressed in slang **2** : SLANGY, VULGAR, RAKISH

⁵**slang** \"\ *vb* -ED/-ING/-S *vt* **1** *slang, Brit* : CHEAT, SWINDLE, DUPE **2** *chiefly Brit* : to abuse with words : censure abusively or with harsh or coarse language ~ *vi* : to use slang or vulgar abuse : talk in a slangy manner

slang·i·ly \-ŋəlē, -li\ *adv* : in a slangy manner

slang·i·ness \-ŋēnəs, -ŋin-\ *n* -ES : the quality or state of being slangy

slang·ish \-ŋish, -ŋēsh\ *adj* : somewhat slangy — **slang·ish·ly** *adv*

slang·ism \-ŋˌizəm\ *n* -s : a slangy word or expression : slangy language

slang·kop \'slaŋˌkäp\ *n* -s [Afrik, fr. D *slang* snake (fr. MD *slange*) + *kop* head, cup (fr. MD *coppe* drinking vessel); akin to OHG *slango* snake, *slingan* to wind, twist — more at SLING, CUP] : either of two southern African plants whose foliage is poisonous to cattle: **a** : a squill (*Urginea burkei*) **b** : a bulbous herb (*Ornithoglossum glaucum*) of the family Liliaceae

slang·ster \'slaŋztə(r), -aiŋ-, -ŋ(k)st-\ *n* -s [³*slang* + *-ster*] : a user of slang

slan·guage \'slaŋgwij, -laiŋ-, -wē| *sometimes* -ŋw-\ *n* -s [blend of ³*slang* and *language*] : slangy speech or writing

slangy \'slaŋē, -laiŋ-, -ŋi\ *adj* -ER/-EST **1** : given to vulgarity or flashiness **2 a** : of, relating to, or constituting slang **b** : containing or addicted to slang

slank *archaic past of* SLINK

¹**slant** \'slant, -aa(ə)-, -ai-, -ā-\ *adv* [ME *slonte*, short for *aslonte* aslant — more at ASLANT] : ASLANT, OBLIQUELY

²**slant** \"\ *vb* -ED/-ING/-S [alter. of *slent*, fr. ME *slenten*, of Scand origin; akin to Sw *slinta* to slide, ON *sletta*; akin to MHG *sliten* to slide — more at SLIDE] *vi* **1** : to hit or strike obliquely : GLANCE — used with *against, on,* or *upon* **2** : to turn or incline from a right line or a level : lie or fall obliquely to a horizontal or perpendicular line : SLOPE ⟨the roof ~*s*⟩ ⟨where the field ~*s* to the river⟩ **3** : to take a diagonal course, direction, or path ⟨we ~*ed* across the river⟩ **4** : to have an inclination : TREND — used with *toward* ~ *vt* **1** : to cut or strike (something) obliquely : cut across at a sharp angle ⟨shafts of sunlight ~*ing* the earth —Carl Sandburg⟩ **2** : to turn from a direct line : give an oblique or sloping direction to ⟨~ a line⟩ **3** : to bend or incline (one) by training, urging, or similar effort **4** : to direct (written or spoken matter) to the interests of a particular audience or according to a particular interpretation : ANGLE ⟨a magazine ~*ed* for farm readers⟩; *specif* : to warp from objective presentation so as to favor a particular bias ⟨~ the news⟩

³**slant** \"\ *adj* **1 a** : inclined from a direct line whether horizontal or perpendicular : SLOPING ⟨a ~ line⟩ **b** : moving in an oblique path ⟨a ~ ray of light⟩ **2** : BIASED — used of a person or his faculties

⁴**slant** \"\ *n* -s [prob. alter. (influenced by ²*slant*) of *slent*, fr. ME, of Scand origin; akin to Sw *slänt* slope, slant, *slinta* to slide] **1** : a slanting direction, line, or plane : SLOPE, INCLINATION ⟨the east slope has a sharp ~⟩ ⟨sits at a ~⟩ ⟨lay a cloth on the ~⟩ **2** : something (as a slope or a shaft of light) that slants ⟨a ~ of sunlight fell between the branches⟩ ⟨puffing up the steep ~ and onto the highway⟩: as **a** : a short inclined passageway in a coal mine the course of which is diagonal to the main workings **b** : a slab with slanting depressions for artists' colors **c** : a sewer pipe that has one end beveled and is used for making a connection to a sewer **d** (1) : a culture medium solidified obliquely in a tube so as to increase the surface area ⟨a blood-agar ~⟩ — compare STAB 5a (2) : SLANT CULTURE **e** *or* **slant line** : DIAGONAL 4 **f** : a football running play in which the ball carrier moves obliquely toward the line of scrimmage **3** *chiefly dial* : an oblique or sarcastic remark : TAUNT **4 a** : a view from a particular angle : a peculiar or personal point of view, attitude, or opinion ⟨considered from a new ~⟩ ⟨you have a wrong ~ on the problem⟩ **b** : a slanting view : GLANCE ⟨take a ~ at him⟩

⁵**slant** \"\ *n* -s [alter. of earlier *slent* slant, spell (of weather), fr. ME, sprinkling, splash] : a light or brief breeze esp. over water : GUST

slant·able \-təbəl\ *adj* : capable of being slanted; *esp* : subject to biased interpretation

slant culture *n* : a culture (as of bacteria) made by inoculating the surface of a slant

slant dam *n* : RAFTER DAM

slant drilling *n* : drilling for oil or gas in other than a vertical direction

¹**slant·er** \-tə(r)\ *n* -s [²*slant* + *-er*] : one that slants something (as a person with a decidedly sloping handwriting)

²**slan·ter** \"\ *adj* [prob. modif. of D *slenter* trick, lie, shift, slow pace, loitering gait, fr. *slenteren* to saunter, loiter; akin to Sw *slinta* to slide — more at SLANT] *Austral* : TRICKY, UNFAIR, UNTRUTHFUL

slant–eye \'⸗ˌ⸗\ *n* [back-formation fr. *slant-eyed*] : a person with slanting eyes; *esp* : one of Mongoloid ancestry — usu. taken to be offensive

slant–eyed \'⸗ˌ⸗\ *adj* : having slanting eyes; *specif* : MONGOLOID

slant–front \'⸗ˌ⸗\ *adj* : SLANT-TOP

slant height *n* **1** : the segment of a generating line of a right half cone lying between the vertex and the base **2** : the altitude of a side of a regular pyramid

slant·in·dic·u·lar \ˌ⸗ˈnˌdikyələ(r)\ *adj* [blend of *slanting* and *perpendicular*] : somewhat oblique

slanting eye *n* : an eye with an epicanthic fold

slant·ing·ly *adv* : in a slanting manner : with a slant

slant·ing·ness *n* -ES : the quality or state of being or having a slant

slant·ing·ways \'⸗⸗ˌwāz\ *or* **slant·ing·wise** \-ˌwīz\ *adv* : SLANTWISE

slant line *n* : SLANT 2e

slant·ly *adv* [³*slant* + *-ly*] : SLANTINGLY, SLOPINGLY

slant of wind : a local or passing variation of the wind from its general direction; *esp* : such a variation favoring a sailing vessel

slants *pres 3d sing of* SLANT, *pl of* SLANT

slant–top \'⸗ˌ⸗\ *adj* : having a drop-front cover that lies at a slant when closed — used esp. of a desk

slant·ways \'⸗ˌwāz\ *adv* : SLANTWISE

slantwise \'⸗ˌ⸗\ *adv (or adj)* : at a slant : moving or directed in a slanting position or direction

¹**slap** \'slap\ *n* -s [ME *slop*, fr. MD; akin to MHG *slupf* place to slip into, hiding place, sling, OHG *slupfen* to slip, slide, MD *slippen* to slip — more at SLIP] **1** *dial Brit* : a pass or notch between hills **2** *dial Brit* : OPENING, BREACH ⟨a ~ in the fence⟩

²**slap** \"\ *n* -s [LG *slapp*, of imit. origin] **1 a** : a quick sharp blow with the open hand ⟨a ~ on the cheek⟩ **b** : a quick sharp blow : SMACK ⟨used by hunters to protect their arm from the ~ of the bowstring —J.H.Howard⟩ **2** : a sharp noise like that produced by a slap ⟨listening . . . to the ~ and plunge of people in the water —Nadine Gordimer⟩ ⟨noise of construction — crashing slides of stone, whang of hammers, ~ of plaster —Ruth Adams⟩; *specif* : a noise resulting from play or slackness between parts of a machine (as in transmission gears) ⟨a bad piston ~⟩ **3 a** : REBUFF, INSULT ⟨words of praise like this are generally preliminary to a ~ —Erle Stanley Gardner⟩ — often used with *at* ⟨a ~ not only at this country but at all Asia —Robert Trumbull⟩ **b** : a sudden calamity : BLOW ⟨loyalty splintered under the ~ of a moderate economic setback —Samuel Lubell⟩ **4** : a quick try : GO — used with *at* ⟨have a ~ at the rabbits —F.E.Smedley⟩ **5** : an emphasized

brush of the foot usu. backward in tap dancing — **slap in the face** : a direct sharp insult or rebuff ⟨comfortable officers' clubs were, naturally, a *slap in the face* for enlisted men —*Tomorrow*⟩ — **slap on the wrist** : a gentle usu. ineffectual reprimand ⟨punishment will be more than just a *slap on the wrist* and will discourage recurring violations —Arthur Herrick⟩

³slap \"\ *vb* **slapped; slapped; slapping; slaps** [prob. fr. ²*slap*] *vt* **1** : to strike usu. quickly and sharply with the open hand ⟨~ a child's face⟩ ⟨he ~*s* his knee⟩ ⟨~ the table⟩ **2 a** : to strike with a motion or sound like that of a blow with the open hand ⟨a pinch hitter *slapped* the ball —Vic Wall⟩ ⟨clothes *slapped* warm and dry with wind and sun —Janet Frame⟩ ⟨a *slapped* bull fiddle⟩ **b** : to cause to strike with a motion or sound like that of a blow with the open hand ⟨~ your feet on the floor⟩ ⟨women washing clothes in the canal ~ them . . . against stones —Christopher Rand⟩ **c** : to actuate (a trigger) with a sudden sharp pull rather than a slow squeeze **3** : to place summarily and often carelessly ⟨carved a . . . bun into three horizontal slices, *slapped* two beef patties between them —*Time*⟩ ⟨little hats *slapped* against the back of the head —Lois Long⟩ — often used with *on* ⟨~ paint on a wall⟩ ⟨*slapping* new taxes on farm cooperatives —G.E.Cruikshank⟩ ⟨~ a quota restriction on foreign imports of fur —*New Republic*⟩ ⟨~ an additional fine on the violator —J.M. Flagler⟩ **4** : CENSURE, REPRIMAND ⟨~ certain academic critics —Dudley Fitts⟩ ⟨*slapped* the workers who had gone on strike —Walter Sullivan⟩ **5** : to take legal action against : SERVE ⟨~ him with a summons⟩ ~ *vi* **1** : to strike usu. sharply with the open hand ⟨he ~*ed* with the palm of his hand on the table⟩ **2** : to make a motion or sound similar to that of a blow with the open hand ⟨heelless slippers *slapping* on the stones —Claud Cockburn⟩ ⟨rain *slapped* at the stained-glass window —Berton Roueché⟩ ⟨the steady one, two, three, four beat of the *slapping* drums —*New Yorker*⟩ **syn** see STRIKE — **slap in the face** : INSULT, HUMILIATE ⟨*slapped in the face* by not being invited to the party⟩ ⟨*slapped* his own board *in the face* with a public statement —Irving Stone⟩ — **slap on the back** : BACKSLAP — **slap on the wrist** *or* **slap the wrist of** *or* **slap one's wrist** : to reprimand gently and usu. ineffectually ⟨*slapped on the wrist* for composing in too urbanized a manner —*Time*⟩ ⟨*slapped the wrists of* missionaries who demanded a show of forceful aid —D.L.Oliver⟩ ⟨*slapped his wrist* for reporting the story falsely⟩ — **slap together** : to construct or produce by constructing hastily and carelessly ⟨rude shanties *slapped together* —*Amer. Guide Series: Pa.*⟩ ⟨*slapped* the movie *together* in a month⟩

⁴slap \"\ *adv* [prob. fr. LG *slapp* with a sudden blow, suddenly, instantly, of imit. origin] **1** : DIRECTLY, RIGHT, PLUMP, SMACK ⟨we hadn't sighted a thing . . . and then we ran ~ into her —Hugh MacLennan⟩ ⟨houses are ~ on the street; no sidewalk — not so much as a curb —Faubion Bowers⟩ **2** *dial* : COMPLETELY, ABSOLUTELY ⟨she was ~ out of black sewing cotton —Frances Gaither⟩

slap around *vt* **1** : BUFFET, MANHANDLE ⟨drunks . . . have a way of becoming much less troublesome if they are *slapped around* a little —*Time*⟩ **2** : to treat roughly, overbearingly, or harshly ⟨critics really *slapped* the play *around*⟩

¹slap-bang \ˈ=,=\ *adj* [²*slap*] : marked by roughness and impetuousness of manner or method ⟨businessmen of the *slap-bang*, horn-blowing, bluff, good-natured . . . kind —Edna Ferber⟩ ⟨*slap-bang* . . . production methods —K.B.Butler⟩

²slap-bang \"\ *adv* : with excessive force, haste, and usu. noise : PRECIPITATELY ⟨yachts and . . . chasers ran *slap-bang* at 16 knots into a convoy —*Springfield (Mass.) Republican*⟩

slapdab \ˈ=,=\ *adv* [⁴*slap* + *dab*] *chiefly South & Midland* : EXACTLY, RIGHT ⟨~ in the middle⟩

¹slapdash \ˈ=,=\ *adv* [⁴*slap* + *dash*] **1** : in a slapdash manner ⟨the house was put together ~⟩ **2** : DIRECTLY, RIGHT, SMACK ⟨with a picture . . . ~ on the middle of it —Ward Moore⟩

²slapdash \"\ *adj* : HAPHAZARD, SLIPSHOD, SLOPPY ⟨the overture emerged as a ~ affair, marred not only by a rough and uncalculated style but by technical inaccuracies —Winthrop Sargeant⟩ ⟨a ~ excursion which fails to do justice to the abilities of any of its three authors —D.L.Olmsted⟩

³slapdash \"\ *n* : SLAPDASHNESS ⟨the case is being built carefully, not with ~ —*Kiplinger Washington Letter*⟩

slap·dash·ery \ˈ=,=ərē\ *n* -ES [²*slapdash* + *-ery*] : SLAPDASHNESS ⟨~ of the London slums —*Newsweek*⟩

slap·dash·ness \ˈ=,=nəs\ *n* -ES : the quality or state of being slapdash : HAPHAZARDNESS, SLOPPINESS ⟨has amazing defects, flippancy, ~ —H.J.Laski⟩

slap down *vt* **1** : to prohibit or restrain (a person or group) usu. abruptly and with censure from acting in a specified way : SQUELCH ⟨were *slapped down* with the . . . law regulating railroads —W.A.Lydgate⟩ **2** : to put an abrupt stop to : SUPPRESS ⟨*slapped down* a Labor attempt to censure his government —*Time*⟩ ⟨open criticism of the regime is quickly *slapped down* by the police —Richard Mowrer⟩

¹slape \ˈslāp\ *adj* [ME, fr. ON *sleipr* — more at SLIP] *dial Eng* : SLIPPERY, SMOOTH

²slape \"\ *chiefly dial var of* SLEEP

slape end *n* : the end of a leaf in a leaf spring that is sharply bent back on itself to form a bearing surface to slide on a casting provided on the vehicle frame

slap·hap·pi·ness \ˈ=,==nəs\ *n, slang* : the quality or state of being slaphappy

slaphappy \ˈ=,==\ *adj* [²*slap* + *happy*] *slang* : PUNCH-DRUNK, WITLESS ⟨~ with exhaustion —Ned Calmer⟩ ⟨it's driving me ~. In fact, I'm getting whacky —William Kozlenko⟩; *also* : buoyantly carefree : deliriously irrational : CRAZY ⟨~ abandon with which members . . . have been prying state secrets out of the administration —*New Yorker*⟩

slap in *vt* : to put in place hastily and usu. carelessly ⟨*slapped in* a new set of lyrics and put it to work as a singing commercial —*Time*⟩ ⟨new owners broke it and *slapped in* row crops —Russell Lord⟩

slap·jack \ˈslap,jak\ *n* [³*slap* + *jack* (as in *flapjack*)] **1** : PANCAKE, FLAPJACK **2** : a game in which playing cards are turned up one by one on a pile with the first player to slap his hand on any jack that appears acquiring the pile and the player who acquires the most cards winning

slap on *vt* : to put into effect usu. suddenly and decisively ⟨*slap on* the death penalty for narcotics smugglers —*Time*⟩ ⟨*slapped on* a hard money policy —T.R.Ybarra⟩

slapped *past of* SLAP

slap·per \ˈslapə(r)\ *n* -S : one that slaps; *specif* : a device that consists of two strips of canvas attached to a handle and is used for driving and directing cattle esp. in stockyards

slapping *adj* [fr. pres. part. of ³*slap*] **1** : very rapid : RATTLING ⟨away we went at a ~ pace —T.C.Haliburton⟩ **2** : very large : STRAPPING ⟨a ~ horse⟩

slap·py \ˈslapē\ *adj* -ER/-EST [³*slap* + *-y*] : marked by or productive of slapping ⟨~ tone-production marred what might otherwise have been one of the season's musical treats —Virgil Thomson⟩ ⟨thunderstorm suddenly gets ~ and twisty —*Flying*⟩

slaps *pl of* SLAP, *pres 3d sing of* SLAP

¹slapstick \ˈ=,=\ *n* [²*slap* + *stick*] **1 a** : a device consisting of two flat pieces of wood fastened together at one end but loose at the other and sometimes used by an actor in farce to make a loud noise in simulation of a severe blow **b** : any of several similar devices: as (1) : two flat pieces of leather sewed together, weighted at the hitting end, and used as a club (2) : a stick hinged on one side to the top of a slate and clapped against the top to mark on a sound track the beginning of a movie take **2 a** : comedy that depends for its effect on fast, boisterous, and zany physical activity and horseplay (as the throwing of pies, the whacking of posteriors with a slapstick, chases, mugging) often accompanied by broad obvious rowdy verbal humor ⟨relies heavily on ~. Rosalind is trapped in the slats of a venetian blind, spanked by an exploding engine part in a hot-rod race, nearly strangled in an electric fan —*Time*⟩ ⟨the extravagant ~ comedy used by English pantomimists —M.E.McIntosh⟩ **b** : humor, language, or activity like that in slapstick comedy ⟨humor that ranges from arrant ~ to satire —*Newsweek*⟩ ⟨an exuberance and colloquial vigor that often only just stop short of ~ —F.W. Bateson⟩ **3** : a flat strip of wood upon which an abrasive (as a piece of emery paper) is fixed for use in polishing or finishing work

²slapstick \"\ *adj* : of, relating to, or having the characteristics of slapstick ⟨~ comedy⟩ ⟨~ humor⟩ ⟨a ~ style⟩ ⟨his extravagant ~ English —B.D.Wolfe⟩

slap-up \ˈ=,=\ *adj* [⁴*slap*] *chiefly Brit* : FIRST-RATE, FINE, EXCELLENT; *also* : ELEGANT, FANCY ⟨a *slap-up* feed — complete with sherry wine —C.G.Glover⟩ ⟨lured into the middle of a *slap-up* garden party —Christopher Isherwood⟩

slare \ˈsla(a)(ə)r\ *vi* [origin unknown] **1** *dial Eng* : to scuff the feet **2** *dial Eng* : SMEAR

slar·gan·do \slärˈgän(,)dō\ *adj* (*or adv*) [It, making slow, widening, verbal of *slargare* to make slow, widen, fr. *s-* (fr. L *ex-*) + *largare* to widen, loosen, fr. L *largus* abundant, generous — more at LARD] : ALLARGANDO — used as a direction in music

¹slash \ˈslash, -aa(ə)-, -ai-\ *vb* -ED/-ING/-ES [ME *slaschen*, prob. fr. MF *eslachier* to break] *vt* **1** : to cut with sweeping strokes that are typically rapid and forceful or savage with or as if with a blade producing long cuts or slits and usu. without careful aim ⟨when our tools are blasted and our canvases ~*ed* —E.M.Forster⟩ ⟨the dog managed to ~ both his opponents severely —C.G.D.Roberts⟩ **2** : to hit with a stroke like that used in slashing: as **a** : LASH, WHIP ⟨~ him with bridle reins and dog whips —Sir Walter Scott⟩ **b** : to strike swiftly and forcibly : DRIVE ⟨~*ed* the ball across the court⟩ **3** : to wield with movements like those used in slashing ⟨~*ing* his bright sword somewhat aimlessly about —Evangeline Davis⟩; *esp* : CRACK ⟨~*ing* his whip so near the horse that the creature was frightened —Harriet B. Stowe⟩ **4 a** : to reduce to slash ⟨the growth has been ~*ed* by . . . scrub-cutting gangs —K.B. Cumberland⟩ **b** : to clear (land) by slashing down trees and bushes ⟨~*ed* fifty acres⟩ **5 a** : to advance (a thing) by or as if by slashing the obstacles in the way ⟨~*ed* his way through the Oregon wilderness —*Amer. Guide Series: Oregon*⟩ **b** : to move (a thing) swiftly and forcefully ⟨~*ed* the curtain across the light —Morley Callaghan⟩ **6 a** : to cut slits in (as a garment) so as to insert or expose an underlying contrasting color ⟨~*ed* cuff with inset bands of contrast —*Women's Wear Daily*⟩ **b** : to mark as if by slashing in such a manner : STREAK ⟨brown iris . . . ~*ed* with yellow —Willa Cather⟩ ⟨this gloom ~*ed* by a few bands of bright light —John Cheever⟩ ⟨great yellow flashes ~ the night —Guthrie Wilson⟩ **7** : to criticize cuttingly and sweepingly : censure unsparingly ⟨~*ed* the administration for its policies⟩ **8 a** : to reduce sharply (as in amount or extent) : CUT ⟨~ the cost of fashion on every item in the store —*advt*⟩ ⟨would personally like to see the tax on corporations not just cut, but ~*ed* —*Wall Street Jour.*⟩ ⟨incidence of major crime in that area was ~*ed* by almost 50 percent —George Barrett⟩ **b** : to reduce the length of : SHORTEN ⟨editing would have ~*ed* this volume to half its size —Wayne Andrews⟩ **c** : to delete usu. by crossing out : EXPUNGE ⟨~*ed* many pages out of the typescript —F.A.Swinnerton⟩ **d** : remove by or as if by cutting : EXCISE ⟨~ twenty minutes out of the first act —Clemence Dane⟩ **9** : to size (yarn) with a slasher ~ *vi* **1** : to cut recklessly or savagely with or as if with a sword, knife, or razor ⟨these lads hacked and ~*ed* with the same tremendous spirit —Mark Twain⟩ **2** : to fall, move, or advance with a sweeping cutting motion like that used in slashing : PELT, DASH, DRIVE ⟨a pouring night late in March, and the rain ~*ed* against the windows —Laura Krey⟩ ⟨the winds ~ before them —Marjory S. Douglas⟩ ⟨the rockets ~ groundward —*advt*⟩ **3 a** : to use unnecessary roughness in striking with one's stick at an opponent's stick in lacrosse **b** : to use unnecessary force when swinging the stick in playing the puck in ice hockey **syn** see CUT — **slash at 1** : to attack swiftly and forcefully ⟨roar off runways . . . at minute intervals to *slash at* the communications of the . . . army —*Current History*⟩ **2** : to censure unsparingly : EXCORIATE ⟨when you *slash at* my things —Dorothy C. Fisher⟩

²slash \"\ *n* -ES **1 a** : a long cut made by slashing : GASH **b** : a stroke or blow delivered with a slashing motion ⟨two revengeful ~*es* —H.G.Wells⟩ **2** : an ornamental slit esp. for showing a lining, underlayer, or insertion in a contrasting color ⟨his paned hose were of velvet lined with purple silk, which garniture appeared at the ~*es* —Sir Walter Scott⟩ ⟨~*es* in the glaze to show the beige pottery beneath —*New Yorker*⟩ **3** : a line or band of vivid or flashing color or light : STREAK ⟨peeping in yellow ~*es* through the trees —C.E.W. Bean⟩ ⟨~*es* of sunlight —Sylvia T. Warner⟩ **4 a** : an open tract in a forest strewn with debris (as logs, chunks of wood, bark, branches) from logging, wind, or fire **b** : the debris in such a tract **5** *also* **slash mark** : DIAGONAL 4 **6** : a long straight cut or mark that is made in a garment or pattern and that usu. indicates or serves as the base for an opening or placket **7** : REDUCTION, CUT ⟨5 to 10 percent price ~ in new cars —*Christian Science Monitor*⟩ ⟨substantial ~*es* in this year's defense outlays —Felix Belair⟩

³slash \"\ *n* -ES [prob. alter. (influenced by ¹*slush*) of ¹*plash*] : a low swampy area often overgrown with bushes : MARSH

slash-and-burn \ˈ=ˈ=ˈ=\ *adj* : characterized or developed by felling and girdling trees and then burning them to make land arable usu. for temporary purposes ⟨the *slash-and-burn* method of agriculture⟩

slashed *past of* SLASH

slash·er \-shə(r)\ *n* -S : one that slashes: as **a** : one that uses a slashing implement or weapon (1) : a bully esp. when boastfully wielding a weapon (as a sword or knife) : a slashing fellow : SWASHBUCKLER (2) : a prowler or other evildoer who uses a slashing instrument (as a knife or blade) as a weapon (3) : SWORDSMAN (4) : one that cuts down timber esp. in a wasteful or destructive manner (5) : one that tends an implement that slashes **b** : a weapon, implement, or machine that slashes: as (1) : SWORD (2) : KNIFE (3) : RAZOR (4) *dial Eng* : BILLHOOK (5) : an implement with an iron blade used in brickmaking to prod or slash the clay to detect stones (6) : a machine fitted with one or more coarse circular saws and used in lumbering for sawing logs, slabs, and scrap wood into pieces suitable for laths, pulpwood, or firewood or for transportation to the refuse burner (7) : a machine to apply size to warp yarns (8) : a cockfighting gaff with razor-edged sides and a sharpened tip

slashes *pres 3d sing of* SLASH, *pl of* SLASH

slash grain *n* : a grain produced by sawing wood so that the annual rings are parallel with the surface

¹slashing *n* -S [fr. gerund of ¹*slash*] **1** : the act or process of slashing : the work of a slasher: as **a** : the illegal use of a slashing weapon (as a blade or knife) ⟨a three month sentence for ~ —*Springfield (Mass.) Union*⟩ **b** : the sizing of yarn by a slasher ⟨yarn sizing or ~ has become a fine art —H.R. Mauersberger⟩ **2 a** : an insert or underlayer of contrasting color revealed by a slash (as in a garment) ⟨the pink with the chocolate ~ in the skirt —R.P.Warren⟩ **b** : the slash that reveals such an insert or underlayer ⟨a different material being sewn under the ~*s* —Sophia Caulfeild & Blanche Saward⟩ **3 a** : an open tract of forest land covered with slash ⟨less forest and more open, hot, shadeless, weed-grown ~ —Ernest Hemingway⟩ **b** : the slash in such a tract ⟨dug out stumps, cut ~ —*Amer. Guide Series: Oregon*⟩ — usu. used in pl. ⟨using a power saw to salvage worthless pine ~*s* —Frank Cameron⟩ ⟨flinging aside the ~*s* —J.S.Qualey⟩

²slashing *adj* [fr. pres. part. of ¹*slash*] **1** : incisively satiric : unsparingly critical or censorious ⟨his terrible ~ wit, his fine scorn of stupidity —John Reed⟩ ⟨a ~ attack on religious hypocrisy and scientific nonsense —R.A.Cordell⟩ **2** : DASHING, SPIRITED, VIGOROUS ⟨a ~ fellow⟩ **3** : HUGE, IMMENSE, SPLENDID ⟨a ~ fortune at her disposal —Charles Dickens⟩ **4** : that strikes with a blow or a succession of blows like those used in slashing : PELTING, DRIVING, BITING ⟨~ southeaster⟩ **5** : VIVID, BRILLIANT, FLASHING ⟨~ juxtapositions of blacks and whites —R.M.Coates⟩ ⟨bold ~ green canvas —*Sydney (Australia) Bull.*⟩ — **slash·ing·ly** *adv*

slash pine *n* [³*slash*; fr. the fact that caribbean pine esp. in Florida grows in slashes] **1 a** : CARIBBEAN PINE **b** : the strong hard heavy coarse-grained orange wood of the Caribbean pine **2** : any of several pines (as the loblolly or longleaf pine) that grow in similar situations to or are used like the slash pine and esp. that are sources of turpentine and lumber in the southern U.S.

slash pocket *n* : a pocket suspended on the wrong side of a garment from a finished slit on the right side that serves as its opening

¹slat \ˈslat, *usu* -ad.+V\ *n* -S [ME *slat*, *sclat*, fr. MF *esclat* fragment, splinter, fr. OF — more at ÉCLAT] **1** *chiefly dial* : a piece of slate : SLATE **2** : a thin narrow flat strip esp. of wood or metal: as **a** : LATH **b** : LOUVER **c** : STAVE **d** : a piece of wood about the length and half the diameter of a pencil that has been planed and grooved preparatory to receiving the lead in pencil manufacturing **e** : one of the thin flat members in the back of a slat-back chair **3** : a sheepskin from which all or most of the wool has been removed and which has been air dried to preserve it for tanning **4 slats** *pl, slang* **a** : BUTTOCKS **b** : RIBS **5** : an auxiliary airfoil at the leading edge of the wing of an airplane that is normally closed to form part of the regular contour of the wing but that may be opened to form a slot when flight conditions require it

²slat \"\ *adj* [ME *sclat*, fr. *sclat*, n., slat] : having or made of slats ⟨the ~ seat of the garden swing —Saul Bellow⟩ ⟨protected from the sun by ~ roofs —*Amer. Guide Series: Fla.*⟩

³slat \"\ *vt* **slatted; slatted; slatting; slats** [ME *slatten*, fr. *slat*, *sclat*, n., slat] **1 a** : to make or equip with slats ⟨small *slatted* houses over tombs —*Amer. Guide Series: La.*⟩ **b** : to stripe or bar as if with slats ⟨a single spread of green *slatted* with watercourses —Sheila Kaye-Smith⟩ **2** : to close the slats of ⟨~ the Venetian blinds against the blaze of noon —Christopher Morley⟩

⁴slat \"\ *vb* **slatted; slatted; slatting; slats** [prob. of Scand origin; akin to ON *sletta* to slap, splash, throw, *sletta* to slide — more at SLANT] *vt* **1** *dial Eng* : to hurl or throw smartly against something else : toss or cast with force and vehemence **2** *dial Eng* : STRIKE, BEAT, PUMMEL ~ *vi* **1** : to flap violently ⟨sails that ~ and belly in the wind —Hamilton Basso⟩ **2** : to move with a motion or sound like that of a violently flapping sail ⟨the calms, with their exasperating rolling and *slatting* —W.H.Taylor⟩ ⟨rain . . . came in gusts, *slatting* and spattering against the rocky slopes —B.A.Williams⟩ ⟨boxcars *slatting* past at fifty miles an hour —Thomas Wolfe⟩

⁵slat \"\ *vt* [obs. F *esclater* (now *éclater*), fr. OF, to splinter, burst — more at ÉCLAT] *dial Eng* : SPLIT, CRACK

⁶slat \"\ *n* -S [IrGael] *Brit* : ¹KELT

slat-back \ˈ=,=\ *adj* : having two or more horizontal or vertical slats; *esp* : LADDER-BACK — used of the back of a chair

slat bonnet *n* : a sunbonnet with a stitched brim stiffened by cardboard or wooden inserts

slatch \ˈslach\ *n* -ES [alter. of ¹*slack*] **1** : a transitory breeze or its duration **2** : an interval of fair weather ⟨a ~ in the storm —*Time*⟩ **3** : a calm between breaking waves ⟨big waves generally come in groups of three, and between them there is a ~ —Hickman Powell⟩ **4** : the loose or slack part of a rope

slat bonnet

slat conveyor *n* : a conveyor consisting of one or more endless chains to which horizontal spaced slats are attached to form a moving support for the objects being conveyed

¹slate \ˈslāt, *usu* -ād.+V\ *n* -S [ME *slate*, *sclate*, fr. MF *esclate*, fr. OF, fem. of *esclat* fragment, splinter — more at ÉCLAT] **1 a** : a thin flat slab, piece, or layer of laminated rock (as slate); *sometimes* : ¹BONE 8b **b** : a piece of slate or other construction material prepared in the shape of a shingle and used esp. for roofing and siding : TILE, SHINGLE ⟨roofing ~*s*⟩ ⟨roofs are covered with asbestos cement ~*s* —H.M.Dunnett⟩ ⟨roofing ~ is manufactured by a hand method and by a mill method —J.H.Bateman⟩ **2** : a dense fine-grained rock produced by the compression of clays, shales, and various other rocks that develops a characteristic cleavage which may be at any angle with the original bedding plane and consisting essentially of sericite and quartz with biotite, chlorite, and hematite as principal accessories; *also* : a cleavable rock that resembles slate **3 a** : a tablet of slate or slatelike material used esp. by children for writing on usu. with chalk **b** : a tablet usu. of slate bearing take and scene numbers, date, director's name, or similar identifying data and photographed at the beginning or end of a movie take — compare SLAPSTICK 1b(2) **c** *Brit* : a slate on which a compositor in a piecework shop writes his name when he runs out of copy to set **d** : a hand instrument for writing braille consisting of a metal plate pitted with the six points of the braille cell and another metal plate above it with openings through which a stylus is pressed down into the pits one at a time to emboss points in desired position on paper placed between the two plates — called also *braille slate* **4 a** : a written or unwritten record of deeds or events ⟨leaving evaluation of the rest of the . . . ~ to history —*New Republic*⟩ ⟨wiped the ~ clean of past mistakes —R.G.Woolbert⟩ **b** (1) : a list prepared in advance of candidates for appointment, nomination, or election (as to political or corporation office) ⟨the 10,000 names needed to put an independent ~ on the ballot —H.H.Martin⟩ ⟨the committee presents one ~ to be voted upon at the annual . . . meeting —*Saturday Rev.*⟩ (2) : the group of persons proposed for appointment, nomination, or election ⟨install a new ~ of officers for the coming year —*Springfield (Mass.) Daily News*⟩ **c** : a list of entrants in a horse race with the betting odds offered posted by a bookmaker **d** : a schedule of sports events ⟨the thirteen-game ~ includes home-and-home contests —*N.Y.Times*⟩ **5 a** : a dark purplish gray that is bluer and deeper than pigeon, redder, lighter, and stronger than charcoal, and bluer and darker than taupe gray **b** : any of various grays similar in color to common roofing slates — **clean slate** : a record unblemished by discreditable acts or measures ⟨left a *clean slate* for his successor in office⟩ — **have a slate loose** *chiefly Brit* : to be slightly defective mentally — **on the slate** *adv* (*or adj*) **1** *slang* : on credit : on a charge account ⟨give me another beer and put it *on the slate* —J.A.Lee⟩ **2** *Brit, of a compositor* : with one's name on the slate : without copy to set ⟨about one fourth of the time . . . is spent compulsorily *on the slate*, for which the compositor receives no remuneration —G. E.Rowles⟩

²slate \"\ *adj* [ME *sclate*, fr. *sclate*, n., slate] **1** : made of slate ⟨a ~ roof⟩ **2** : of the color slate : slate-colored ⟨a ~ dress⟩ **3** : containing slate ⟨an Ordovician ~ belt⟩

³slate \"\ *vb* -ED/-ING/-S [¹*slate*] *vt* **1** : to cover with slate or a slatelike substance ⟨~ a house⟩ ⟨the roof was *slated* instead of being thatched —C.K.Finlay⟩ **2 a** : to register or record the name of (a person or event) on a slate or in a schedule ⟨the party *slated* its candidates⟩ ⟨~ the game⟩ **b** : to schedule for or to schedule to occur or materialize at a specified time or in a specified place ⟨conclave is *slated* Sunday through next Thursday —*Sacramento (Calif.) Bee*⟩ ⟨elections *slated* in Japan next Sunday —*Newsweek*⟩ — usu. used with *for* ⟨market had been *slated* for Jan. 24–28 —*Retailing Daily*⟩ ⟨elections *slated* for July 1–2 —R.J.Kerner⟩ ⟨new ammonia plant is *slated* for the Midwest —*Wall Street Jour.*⟩ ⟨thunderstorms are *slated* for the northern Appalachians —*New Orleans (La.) Times-Picayune*⟩ **c** : to designate (a person or thing) for a specified function or purpose : act or be acted upon in a specified way at some time in the future : SCHEDULE, APPOINT ⟨*slated* for a prominent role in these plans —*Printers' Ink*⟩ ⟨John had been *slated* to start the game —Roscoe McGowen⟩ ⟨bill S246 *slated* for passage —W.A.Wittich⟩ ⟨work is *slated* to start shortly —P.S.Nathan⟩ ⟨*slated* to be converted into a . . . hospital —E.J.Kahn⟩ **d** : DESTINE, PREDESTINE, FOREORDAIN ⟨everything is . . . *slated* to fulfill a rational end —Harry Bear⟩ ⟨by aptitude, personality, and work he is obviously *slated* to go up —E.J. Fitzgerald⟩ **3** : to flesh (hides) with a slater ~ *vi* **1** : to make slates **2** : to lay slates **3** : to flesh hides with a slater

⁴slate \"\ *vt* -ED/-ING/-S [ME *slaiten*, irreg. fr. or akin to OE *slǣtan* to bait; akin to OHG *sleizen* to split, OE *slītan* to slit, tear — more at SLIT] *dial Brit* : to set a dog on : HOUND

⁵slate \"\ *vt* -ED/-ING/-S [prob. alter. of ⁴*slat*] **1** : to thrash or pummel severely **2** *chiefly Brit* : to criticize or censure severely : BERATE ⟨*slated* him years later for having a part in the vilification —W.T.Scott⟩ ⟨severely *slated* for his pedantry, literary arrogance —R.G.Howarth⟩

slate black *n* **1** : a nearly neutral slightly purplish black that is very slightly bluer and darker than sooty black and slightly redder and darker than neutral tint (sense 2) **2** : a black pigment made by grinding black slate — compare MINERAL BLACK a

slate blue *n* **:** a variable color averaging a grayish blue that is redder and paler than electric, greener and less strong than copenhagen, redder, stronger, and slightly lighter than Gobelin, and greener and slightly paler than old china — called also *blue slate*
slate club *n, Brit* **:** a group of persons who save money in a common fund for a specified purpose (as distribution at Christmas)
slate-colored junco *also* **slate-colored snowbird** \ˈ=ˌ==-\ *n* **:** a common junco (*Junco hiemalis*) of northeastern No. America that is dark slaty gray above with white underparts and outer tail feathers
slated *adj* [fr. past part. of ³*slate*] **:** SLATY 1 ⟨dark ~ clouds —Norman Mailer⟩
slate flour *or* **slate powder** *n* **:** a finely ground mineral that is obtained from slate and used esp. in the manufacture of gray paints
slate gray *n* **:** a light olive gray to medium gray — called also *oriental pearl, Russian gray*
slate green *n* **:** a grayish green that is yellower and duller than average bayberry or blue spruce (sense 2a)
slatelike \ˈ=ˌ=\ *adj* **:** resembling slate (as in form, texture, composition, or color)
slate·man \ˈslātmən\ *n, pl* **slatemen :** a mine worker who handles rock or slate instead of coal — called also *rockman*
slate olive *n* **:** a dark greenish gray that is paler than sagebrush green and yellower and paler than muscovite
slate pencil *n* **:** a pencil of soft slate or of soapstone used for writing on a slate
slate-pencil sea urchin *n* **:** a large purple sea urchin (*Heterocentrotus mammillatus*) having stout heavy spines that resemble slate pencils
slate picker *n* **:** a person or a machine that picks slate and bone coal from coal
slate purple *n* **:** a dark grayish to dark reddish purple
¹**slat·er** \ˈslādə(r), -ātə-\ *n* -s [ME *sclater*, fr. *sclate* slate + *-er* — more at SLATE] **1 :** one that slates; *esp* **:** a tool or machine with a blade of slate or similar stone used for fleshing hides **2 :** SLATE PICKER **3 a :** WOOD LOUSE 1 **b :** any of various marine isopods — called also *sea slater*
²**slat·er** \"\ *n* -s [⁵*slate* + *-er*] *chiefly Brit* **:** one that censures sweepingly and violently **:** a severe critic
slaters' felt *n* **:** a tarred building paper used esp. under slate roofing
slates *pl of* SLATE, *pres 3d sing of* SLATE
slate tan *n* **:** a light olive gray that is deeper than piping rock and deeper and slightly redder than average covert gray
slate violet *n* **:** a grayish red that is bluer, less strong, and slightly darker than bois de rose, yellower and duller than appleblossom, and bluer and duller than Pompeian red
slate writer *n* **:** one that does slate writing
slate writing *n* **:** a spiritualistic or conjuring performance in which writing is mysteriously done upon a slate
slatey *var of* SLATY
slath \ˈslath, -ȧ-\ *n* -s [perh. of Scand origin; akin to Norw dial. *slōda*, a basket used in fishing] **:** the center of the bottom of a basket where the weaving is begun that is formed by crossing sticks at right angles and binding them
¹**slath·er** \ˈslath̲ə(r)\ *n* -s [origin unknown] **:** a great quantity **:** a lavish amount ⟨seems to be a ~ of public and private money available —Lee Rogow⟩ — often used in pl. ⟨~s of friends⟩ ⟨~s of luck⟩ — **open slather** *Austral* **:** FREE REIN ⟨asking to be allowed an *open slather* at an essential public service without being challenged —John Morrison⟩
²**slather** \"\ *vt* **slathered; slathered; slathering** \-th̲(ə)riŋ\ **slathers 1 a :** to spread thickly or lavishly — usu. used with *on* ⟨grabbed some bread and ~*ed* jam on it —P.E.Stevenson⟩ **b :** to spread thickly or lavishly on — usu. used with *with* ⟨~*ing* the cars with paint⟩ **2 :** to use or spend in a wasteful or lavish manner **:** SQUANDER ⟨~*ed* money on ice cream —Dorothy C. Fisher⟩
slatier *comparative of* SLATY
slatiest *superlative of* SLATY
¹**slating** *n* -s [fr. gerund of ³*slate*] **1 :** the work of a slater **2 :** material used for slating **:** SLATE ⟨ordered ~ for the roof⟩ **3 :** the movie-making process of preparing and photographing a slate ⟨original photography is often identified by ~ —W.H. Offenhauser⟩
²**slating** *n* -s [fr. gerund of ⁵*slate*] **:** a verbal or written lashing **:** a severely critical or censorious attack ⟨a hearty *slating* always does me good —H.L.Mencken⟩
slating nail *n* **:** a nail for use in nailing down slate roofing
slat·ish \ˈslād·ish\ *adj* [¹*slate* + *-ish*] **:** somewhat slate-colored ⟨the clouds . . . had taken a ~ tinge —Clark Russell⟩
slats *pl of* SLAT, *pres 3d sing of* SLAT
slatted *adj* [fr. past part. of ³*slat*] **:** having or made of slats ⟨a ~ blind⟩ ⟨~ crates⟩
slat·ter \ˈslad·ə(r)\ *n* -s [ME *sclatter*, fr. *sclat* slat + *-er* — more at SLAT] **1** *dial chiefly Eng* **:** SLATER **2 :** a worker who removes slabs of soap from the frames in which they are formed
¹**slat·tern** \ˈslad·ə(r)n, -atə-\ *n* -s [prob. modif. of G *schlottern* to hang loosely, waddle, slouch (taken as a n.), fr. MHG *slottern, slattern, sluttern*; akin to D *slodderen* to hang loosely, *slodder* slovenly person, slut, Icel *sludda* clod of spittle, *slydda* sleet, slush, MHG *slote* mud, slime, *sloten* to stagger, shake, ON *slothra* to drag oneself forward, Goth *afslauthjan* to be anguished, shaken and prob. to ME *sloor* mud — more at SLUR] **1 :** a person who is negligent of his appearance or surroundings; *esp* **:** an untidy slovenly woman ⟨two blowzy waitresses . . . ~s whose off-white aprons blended perfectly with their pasty cheeks —John Wain⟩ **2 :** SLUT, PROSTITUTE ⟨there was a ~ or two . . . ladies of the profession —Bruce Marshall⟩
²**slattern** \"\ *adj* **:** SLATTERNLY ⟨~ hovels⟩ ⟨their gray ~ bodies —Liam O'Flaherty⟩
³**slattern** \"\ *vb* -ED/-ING/-S *vt* **:** to fritter away **:** WASTE — usu. used with *away* ⟨every fool who ~s away his whole time in nothings —Earl of Chesterfield⟩ ~ *vi* **:** to move or act in a slatternly manner
slat·tern·li·ness \-lēnəs, -lin-\ *n* -ES **:** the quality, state, or condition of being slatternly ⟨the room was . . . depressing from its ~ —Samuel Butler †1902⟩
¹**slat·tern·ly** \-lē, -li\ *adj* [¹*slattern* + *-ly* (adj. suffix)] **1 :** untidy and usu. dirty through habitual neglect **:** SLOVENLY, UNKEMPT ⟨tatterdemalion, ~, slipshod women —E.C.Clayton⟩ ⟨streets terribly shabby and ~ and badly paved —Arnold Bennett⟩; *also* **:** CARELESS, DISORDERLY ⟨I am . . . ~; I seldom put, and never keep things in order; I am careless —Charlotte Brontë⟩ **2 :** of, relating to, or characteristic of a slut or harlot
syn DOWDY, FROWSY, BLOWSY: SLATTERNLY stresses notions of slovenliness, unkemptness, and sordidness ⟨a small, *slatternly* looking craft, her hull and spars a dingy black, rigging all slack and bleached nearly white, and every thing denoting an ill state of affairs aboard —Herman Melville⟩ ⟨lived with them, in the *slatternly* apartment among the unwashed dishes in the sink and on the table, the odor of stale tobacco smoke, the dirty shirts and underwear piled in corners —R.P.Warren⟩ DOWDY may apply to a complete lack of taste typically marked by a blend of the untidy, unfit, or either drab or tawdry ⟨her shoes were bought a long time ago and have no relation to the dress, and the belt of her dress has become untied and is hanging down. She looks clean and *dowdy* —Lillian Hellman⟩ ⟨so dreadfully *dowdy* that she reminded one of a badly bound hymnbook —Oscar Wilde⟩ FROWSY suggests a lazy lack of neatness, order, and cleanliness ⟨a dumpy, *frowsy* woman, clad in old dress and apron —A.J.Coutts⟩ ⟨if a fully fed, presentably clothed, decently housed, fairly literate and cultivated and gently mannered family is not better than a half-starved, ragged, *frowsy*, overcrowded one, there is no meaning in words —G.B.Shaw⟩ BLOWSY suggests rude, loud, florid coarseness and lack of refinement ⟨a big *blowsy* Jezebel from the docks —Bruce Marshall⟩ ⟨the fat and *blowsy* wife bowed in an exaggerated fashion, never stopping the while to fan her red face vigorously —Louis Bromfield⟩
²**slatternly** \"\ *adv* [¹*slattern* + *-ly* (adv. suffix)] **:** in a slatternly manner
slat·tery \ˈslatəri\ *adj* [E dial. *slatter* to spill, splash, slop (perh. of Scand origin) + E *-y* (adj. suffix); akin to ON *sletta* to slap, splash — more at SLAT (throw)] *dial Eng* **:** RAINY, WET, SLOPPY
slatting *n* -s [fr. gerund of ³*slat*] **1 :** SLATS **2 :** the material from which slats are made
slaty *also* **slat·ey** \ˈslād·|ē, -āt|, |i\ *adj* [¹*slate* + *-y*] **1 :** of the nature or composition of, containing, or characteristic of slate ⟨a ~ texture⟩ ⟨a ~ cleavage⟩; *esp* **:** of a grayish cast suggestive of slate ⟨the ~ sky of dawn —Ethel Wilson⟩ ⟨house had a ~ impoverished look —Viola Meynell⟩ **2 :** having mineral grains that are extremely small — used of rock foliation ⟨those with a ~ foliation have a very smooth cleaved surface —D.O.Woolf⟩
slaty gray aphid *n* **:** a plant louse (*Brevicoryne brassicae*) that infests various crop plants in New So. Wales
slaty gum *n* **:** any of several Australian eucalypts (as *Eucalyptus polyanthemos*) with slate-colored bark
¹**slaugh·ter** \ˈslȯd·ə(r), -ȯtə-\ *n* -s [ME *slauhter, slaughter*, of Scand origin; akin to ON *slātr* butcher's meat, *slātra* to slaughter; akin to OE *sleaht* slaughter, OHG *slahta*, Goth *slauhts*; derivative fr. the root of E ¹*slay*] **1 a :** the killing of animals ⟨the ~ of a hundred lions afforded him no recreation —Agnes Repplier⟩; *esp* **:** the butchery of cattle for market **b :** the killing of a person esp. in a bloody or barbarous manner ⟨was marked for ~ but escaped death and became the leader of the minority —E.E.Dale⟩ **2 a :** mass killing and bloodshed (as in war) **:** wholesale carnage **:** MASSACRE ⟨hoped that after the ~ it would be possible really to create . . . one world in peace —Alva Myrdal⟩ **b :** wanton destruction ⟨notwithstanding this wholesale ~, bird life is still plentiful —*Amer. Guide Series: Tenn.*⟩ ⟨half a century of . . . insensate ~ sufficed to destroy the magnificent forest —M.M.Quaife⟩ **c** *obs* **:** carnage personified ⟨besmeared and overstained with ~'s pencil —Shak.⟩ **3 :** an act or instance of utter annihilation or defeat ⟨it was no longer a battle but a ~ —Robert Graves⟩ ⟨ended the ~ with a par 4 on the tenth hole to win by the awful margin of 9 and 8 —*New Yorker*⟩
²**slaughter** \"\ *vt* **slaughtered; slaughtered; slaughtering** \-ȯd·əriŋ, -ȯtər- *also* -ȯ·tr-\ **slaughters 1 :** to kill (animals) for food; *esp* **:** BUTCHER **2 a :** to kill (a person) esp. in a bloody or barbarous manner **:** SLAY ⟨five men in a stolen car ~*ed* a paymaster and a factory guard —Phil Stong⟩ ⟨the number of people ~*ed* annually by cars —F.L.Allen⟩ **b :** to discredit or demolish completely ⟨tears through our literature ~*ing* Emerson, Thoreau, Melville, and Hawthorne —S.E.Hyman⟩ ⟨his team was . . . ~*ed* by Oklahoma —Eddie Beachler⟩ **c** *slang* **:** to make an irresistible impression on ⟨~*ing* them at the box office —*Metronome*⟩ **3 a :** to kill (people) in large numbers **:** MASSACRE ⟨overwhelming automatic firepower . . . proved too much for them, and 700 were ~*ed* in one day —Barrett McGurn⟩ **b :** to destroy in large quantities ⟨~*ed* fish in astronomical numbers —Henry LaCossitt⟩ ⟨timber was ~*ed* —Russell Lord⟩ **4 :** to sell (securities) at a sacrifice
slaugh·ter·er \-ȯd·ərə(r), -ȯtər-\ *n* -s **:** one that slaughters: as **a :** KILLER **b :** BUTCHER, MEAT-PACKER — called also *slaughterman*
slaughterhouse \ˈ==ˌ=\ *n* [ME *slaughterhous*, fr. *slaughter* + *hous* house — more at HOUSE] **1 :** an establishment where animals are butchered for market **:** ABATTOIR — called also *meatworks* **2 :** something that resembles a slaughterhouse ⟨a political campaign is a ~ for issues and reputations —Norman Cousins⟩
slaughterhouse case *n* [so called fr. the fact that the matter at issue was the right of the city of New Orleans to regulate by law the carrying on of the butchering industry in that city] **:** one of a group of cases decided by the Supreme Court of the U.S. establishing that the police power of the states is not impaired by the fourteenth amendment to the Constitution
slaughtering *n* -s [fr. gerund of ²*slaughter*] **:** the butchering of animals for food ⟨custom ~ usu. includes the weighing of dressed carcasses —L.E.Zraick⟩
slaugh·ter·man \ˈslȯd·ə(r)mən, -ȯtə-\ *n, pl* **slaughtermen** [ME] **1** *archaic* **:** EXECUTIONER, SLAYER **2 :** SLAUGHTERER b
slaugh·ter·ous \-ȯd·ərəs, -ȯtər- *also* -ȯ·tr-\ *adj* **:** of, relating to, or characterized by slaughter — **slaugh·ter·ous·ly** *adv*
slaugh·tery \-ȯd·ərē,-ȯtərē,-ȯtrē\ *n* -ES [¹*slaughter* + *-y* (n. suffix)] **1 :** KILLING, SLAUGHTER **2 :** ABATTOIR
slaunch·ways \ˈslȯnch,wāz, -län-\ *adv* [alter. of *slantways*] *Midland* **:** DIAGONALLY, SLANTWAYS
slav \ˈsläv, -a-, -ȧ-\ *n* -s *usu cap* [ME *Sclav*, fr. ML *Sclavus, sclavus* Slav, Slav held in servitude, slave] **:** a person speaking a Slavic language as his native tongue — see INDO-EUROPEAN LANGUAGES table
slav·dom \-vdəm\ *n* -s *usu cap* [*slav* + *-dom*] **1 :** the whole body of Slavs **2 :** the area inhabited by or under the influence of Slavs
¹**slave** \ˈslāv\ *n* -s [ME *sclave*, fr. OF or ML; OF *esclave* slave, fr. ML *Sclavus, sclavus* Slav, Slav held in servitude, slave, fr. LGk *Sklabos* Slav, fr. *Sklabēnos* of or relating to the Slavs, fr. *Sklabēnoi*, pl., Slavs, of Slav origin; akin to OBulg *Slověne*, a Slavic group of people in the area of Thessalonike, ORuss *Slověne*, an East-Slavic group of people near Novgorod, *Slovutich* Dnieper river, Serb *Slavnica*, a river] **1 a :** a person held in servitude **:** one that is the chattel of another **:** BONDMAN, THRALL ⟨plantation life with ~s, indentured servants, or tenants —W.M.Kollmorgen⟩ ⟨begins her career as a ~, a pretty child bought from miserably poor parents under a contract —Lafcadio Hearn⟩ **b** *archaic* **:** a despicable person ⟨the . . . atheist, if earth bear so base a ~ —William Cowper⟩ **c** *obs* **:** an inconsequential person **:** FELLOW, JOKER ⟨oh ~s, I can tell you news, news you rascals —Shak.⟩ **2 a :** a servile or submissive follower **:** LACKEY ⟨his father's most abject ~ —Abram Kardiner⟩ **b :** a person completely subservient to a dominating influence **:** one who has surrendered control of himself ⟨all his life he had been a ~ to the land, harnessed to the elemental forces —Ellen Glasgow⟩ ⟨spineless ~s of tradition —Bennett Cerf⟩ **c :** one that labors for another **:** SERVANT ⟨a civilization in which machines are ~s, and all men may be free —W.H.Camp⟩ **d** (1) **:** a mechanical device that is directly responsive to another (as an electronic device for firing auxiliary flash bulbs); *esp* **:** a remote-control device for handling radioactive materials (2) **:** SLAVE STATION **3 :** a toiler at hard monotonous work **:** DRUDGE ⟨~s in the Pentagon worked nights and through the holidays to revamp the budget —T.R.Phillips⟩ **4 :** SLAVE ANT
²**slave** \"\ *vb* **slaved; slaved; slaving; slaves** *vt* **1 a** *archaic* **:** to reduce to bondage **:** ENSLAVE ⟨thou canst not ~ or banish me —John Marston⟩ **b :** to make directly responsive to another mechanism ⟨the gyro unit is continuously *slaved* to a compass —C.G.Yates⟩ **2 a** *archaic* **:** to employ at hard labor ⟨Egyptian kings built them monuments, wherein they *slaved* their whole nation —Martin Lister⟩ **b :** to wear out by hard work ⟨bullied . . . and *slaved* her half to death —H.G. Evarts⟩ ~ *vi* **1 :** to work like a slave **:** TOIL, DRUDGE ⟨*slaved* sixteen hours a day for money to buy food —*Irish Digest*⟩ ⟨had to ~ so hard to make . . . a showing at his school work —Archibald Marshall⟩ **2 :** to traffic in slaves ⟨*slaving* was still active and profitable, in spite of the best efforts of the missionaries —A.W.Smith⟩
³**slave** \"\ *adj* **1 :** held in servitude **:** ENSLAVED ⟨born of ~ parents⟩ ⟨activity to liberate ~ peoples in eastern Europe —Quincy Wright⟩ **2 a :** of, relating to, involving, or characteristic of slaves ⟨~ auction⟩ ⟨~ owner⟩ ⟨~ question⟩ ⟨with true ~ mentality . . . sacrifices himself to the group —Priscilla Robertson⟩ **b :** used for or restricted to the use of slaves ⟨~ ship⟩ ⟨~ quarters⟩ ⟨a ~ gallery extends across the . . . end of the nave —*Amer. Guide Series: N.C.*⟩ **c :** concerned with or dealing in slaves ⟨~ voyage⟩ ⟨~ trader⟩ **d** (1) **:** favoring or legally permitting slavery ⟨~ territory⟩ (2) **:** based on or characterized by slavery ⟨~ economy⟩ **3 :** activated by remote control ⟨the device now tucked away behind the dials isn't properly a clockwork but a . . . ~ unit activated by an electric clock inside the bank —*New Yorker*⟩; *specif* **:** responding to manipulation of the master-end of the apparatus ⟨scientists manipulate radioactive material with intricate ~ hands —*Time*⟩
⁴**slave** \ˈsläv, -a-, -ȧ-\ *archaic var of* SLAV
⁵**slave** \ˈslāv\ *n* -s *usu cap* **1 a :** an Athapaskan people living between the Rocky mountains and the Great Slave lake in the Northwest Territories of Canada — called also *Slavey* **b :** a member of such people **2 :** the language of the Slave people
slave ant *n* **:** an ant enslaved by a slave-making ant
slave bracelet *n* **:** a chain-link bracelet often having a plain plaque or nameplate and often worn around the ankle — compare IDENTIFICATION BRACELET
slave clock *n* **:** the auxiliary apparatus of a precision astronomical clock that relieves the latter of nearly all the work and thus assures uniformity of performance
slave-drive \ˈ=ˌ=\ *vt* [back-formation fr. *slave driver*] **:** to coerce relentlessly to action
slave driver *n* **1 :** a supervisor of slaves at work **2 :** a person in authority (as a foreman) who exacts extreme effort from his subordinates **:** RAWHIDER, SIMON LEGREE
slaveholder \ˈ=ˌ==\ *n* **:** one that holds slaves
slaveholding \ˈ=ˌ==\ *adj* **:** allowing slavery or inhabited by slaveholders ⟨the ~ South⟩ ⟨~ states⟩
slave labor *n* **1 :** labor performed by slaves **2 :** forced labor performed under duress ⟨deporting Belgian civilians into Germany for what amounted to *slave labor* —J.L.O'Brian⟩
slave·less \ˈslāvləs\ *adj* **:** being without slaves
slave·ling \-liŋ\ *n* -s [¹*slave* + *-ling*] **:** ¹SLAVE 2a
slave-making ant \ˈ=ˌ==-\ *or* **slave maker** *n* **:** an ant (as the Amazon ant or the sanguinary ant) that attacks the colonies of ants of other species and carries off the larvae and pupae to be reared in its own nest as slaves
slave market *n* **1 :** a market where slaves are exhibited and sold **2 :** something that resembles a slave market ⟨imprisoned the free development of ideas almost to the point that we have . . . created an intellectual *slave market* —J.A.Brandt⟩; *specif* **:** EMPLOYMENT AGENCY
slaveocracy *var of* SLAVOCRACY
¹**slaver** \ˈslavə(r), -lāv-, -läv-, -lȧv-\ *vb* **slavered; slavered; slavering** \-v(ə)riŋ\ **slavers** [ME *slaveren*, of Scand origin; akin to ON *slafra* to slaver, Norw dial. *slevja*; akin to MD *slabben* to dirty, lap, slaver, Sw dial. *slabba* to roll in mud, G *schlabbern* to slaver, ON *slafast* to droop, slacken, Lith *slōbti* to grow weak, L *labi* to glide, slide — more at SLEEP] *vi* **1 a :** to let saliva dribble from the mouth **:** DROOL, SLOBBER ⟨a dog ~s over his food⟩ **b :** to have a craving **:** go in eager pursuit ⟨were ~*ing* after that small fortune —W.B.Mowery⟩ **2 :** to voice elaborate praise or servile flattery **:** FAWN, ECSTASIZE ⟨spent years ~*ing* before the idol of American efficiency —*Times Lit. Supp.*⟩ ~ *vt* **1** *archaic* **:** to smear with or as if with saliva **2** *archaic* **:** to truckle to **:** FLATTER
²**slaver** \"\ *n* -s [ME, fr. *slaveren* to slaver] **1 :** saliva dribbling from the mouth **2** *archaic* **:** effusive commendation or flattery **:** DRIVEL
³**slav·er** \ˈslāvə(r)\ *n* -s [¹*slave* + *-er*] **1 :** one that is engaged in the slave trade ⟨warships, whalers, sealers and ~s . . . sailed from New England to the ends of the earth —Dana Burnet⟩ ⟨tough, cruel but desperately brave Arab ~s . . . rule the land —Rodney Gilbert⟩ **2 :** WHITE SLAVER
¹**slavery** \ˈslav(ə)rē, -lāv-, -läv-, -lȧv-, -ri\ *adj* [ME, fr. ²*slaver* + *-y*] *archaic* **:** SLOBBERY, DRIVELING
²**slav·ery** \ˈslāv(ə)rē, -ri\ *n* -ES [¹*slave* + *-ery*] **1 :** hard work **:** DRUDGERY, LABOR ⟨I never rowed — about the most awful form of ~ which mankind knows —A.P.Herbert⟩ **2 a :** submissiveness to a dominating influence **:** SUBSERVIENCE ⟨~ to habit⟩ ⟨deliverance of mankind from the long ~ of want, fear and cruelty —Leslie Rees⟩ **b :** control by imposed authority **:** SUBJECTION ⟨the . . . ~ of soldiers on the march —W.R.Inge⟩ ⟨all government without the consent of the governed is . . . ~ —Jonathan Swift⟩ **3 :** the quality or state of being a slave **:** the practice or institution of keeping slaves **:** BONDAGE, SERVITUDE ⟨no one shall be held in ~ or servitude —*U.N. Declaration of Human Rights*⟩ ⟨neither ~ nor involuntary servitude, except as a punishment for crime . . . shall exist within the United States or any place subject to their jurisdiction —*U.S.Constitution*⟩ ⟨the inhuman exploitation of chattel ~ —Lewis Mumford⟩
slaves *pl of* SLAVE, *pres 3d sing of* SLAVE
slave state *n* **1 :** a state of the U.S. in which Negro slavery was legal until the Civil War — compare FREE SOIL **2 :** a nation subjected to totalitarian rule
slave station *n* **:** a transmitter in an electronic communication system (as in radio navigation) operated by remote control — compare MASTER STATION
slave trade *n* **:** traffic in slaves; *esp* **:** the buying and selling of Negroes for profit prior to the American Civil War
slav·ey \ˈslāvē, -vi\ *n* -s [¹*slave* + *-y* (dim. suffix)] **1 :** DRUDGE; *esp* **:** a maid of all work **2** *usu cap* [⁵*slave* + *-y*] **:** ⁵SLAVE 1a
¹**slav·ic** \ˈslavik, -läv-, -lȧv-, -vēk\ *adj, usu cap* [*slav* + *-ic*] **:** of or relating to the Slavs or their languages
²**slavic** \"\ *n* -s *cap* **:** a branch of the Indo-European language family containing Belorussian, Bulgarian, Czech, Polish, Serbo-Croatian, Slovene, Russian, and Ukrainian — see INDO-EUROPEAN LANGUAGES table
slav·i·cist \-vəsəst\ *or* **slav·ist** \-lävəst, -lav-, -lȧv-\ *n* -s *usu cap* [*slavicist* fr. ²*slavic* + *-ist*; *slavist* ISV *slav* + *-ist*] **:** a specialist in the Slavic languages or literatures
slav·i·cize \ˈslavəˌsīz, -läv-, -lȧv- *or* **slav·ize** \-läˌvīz, -la,v-, -lȧ,v-\ *also* **slav·o·nize** \-lavə,nīz\ *or* **sla·vo·ni·cize** \slə-ˈvänəˌsīz, slaˈv-\ *vt* -ED/-ING/-S *often cap* [*slavicize* fr. ¹*slavic* + *-ize*; *slavize* fr. *slav* + *-ize*; *slavonize* fr. obs. E *slavon* slavonian (fr. ML *Slavonia* land of the Slavs) + E *-ize*; *slavonicize* fr. ¹*slavonic* + *-ize*] **1 :** to make Slavic in quality or characteristics **:** cause to become adapted to Slavism ⟨a *slavicized* German⟩ ⟨the region was *slavicized* within a few centuries⟩ **2 :** to adapt to Slavic usage **:** alter to a characteristically Slavic form
slav·ik·ite \ˈslavəˌkīt\ *n* -s [Czech *slavíkite*, fr. František *Slavík* †1957 Czech mineralogist + Czech *-ite*] **:** a mineral $(Na, K)_2Fe_{10}(OH)_6(SO_4)_{13}.63H_2O(?)$ consisting of a hydrous basic sodium ferric sulfate and occurring as small greenish yellow rhombohedral crystals on weathered shales from Bohemia
slaving *pres part of* SLAVE
slav·ish \ˈslāvish, -vēsh *sometimes* ÷ -lav-\ *adj* [¹*slave* + *-ish*] **1 a** *archaic* **:** SLAVE 2a **b :** requiring hard work **:** LABORIOUS ⟨~ attention and practice were required —Richard Hayward⟩ **2 a :** resembling or characteristic of a slave **:** SPINELESS, SUBMISSIVE ⟨a ~ yes-man to the party bosses —S.H.Adams⟩ **b** *archaic* **:** of a despicable nature **:** CONTEMPTIBLE, LOW ⟨to lie is a ~ vice —James Astry⟩ **3** *archaic* **:** of a despotic nature **:** OPPRESSIVE ⟨shake off our ~ yoke —Shak.⟩ **4 :** copying obsequiously or without originality **:** IMITATIVE ⟨out of the realm of mere ~ imitation of nature —Aldous Huxley⟩
syn see SUBSERVIENT
slav·ish·ly *adv* **:** in a slavish manner **:** SUBSERVIENTLY ⟨~ accepted the viewpoints of foreign scientists —Martin Gardner⟩ ⟨did not copy too ~ the designs of his predecessors —Edith Diehl⟩
slav·ish·ness *n* -ES **:** the quality or state of being slavish
slav·ism \ˈslä,vizəm, -la,v-, -lȧ,v-\ *also* **slav·i·cism** \-lavə-ˌsizəm, -läv-, -lȧv-\ *n* -s *usu cap* [*slavism* ISV *slav* + *-ism*; *slavicism* fr. ¹*slavic* + *-ism*] **1 a :** Slavic traits or attitudes **b :** SLAVOPHILISM **2 :** a characteristically Slavic word or expression occurring in another language
slav·oc·ra·cy \slāˈväkrəsē\ *n* -ES [¹*slave* + *-o-* + *-cracy*] *also* **slave·o·c·ra·cy :** a powerful faction of slave-owners and advocates of slavery in the South before the Civil War
slav·o·crat \ˈslāvəˌkrat\ *n* -s [fr. *slavocracy*, after such pairs as E *democracy*: *democrat*] **:** a member of the slavocracy — compare DOUGHFACE 2a
¹**sla·vo·nian** \sləˈvōnēən, slaˈv-, -ōnyən\ *n* -s *cap* [ML *Slavonia, Sclavonia* land of the Slavs, Slavonia (fr. *Slavus, Sclavus* Slav) + E *-an* (n. suffix) — more at SLAVE] **:** SLOVENE 1b
²**slavonian** \"\ *adj, usu cap* [ML *Slavonia* + E *-an* (adj. suffix)] **1 :** SLOVENE **2** *archaic* **:** SLAVIC
slavonian grebe *n, usu cap S* **:** HORNED GREBE
¹**sla·von·ic** \sləˈvänik, slaˈv-, -nēk\ *adj, usu cap* [NL *slavonicus*, fr. ML *Slavonia* + *-icus* -ic] **:** SLAVIC
²**slavonic** \"\ *n* -s *usu cap* **1 :** SLAVIC **2 :** OLD CHURCH SLAVONIC
slav·o·phile \ˈslavəˌfīl, -läv-,-lȧv-\ *or* **slav·o·phil** \-ˌfil\ *n* -s *usu cap* [*slav* + *-o-* + *-phile, -phil*] **:** an advocate of Slavophilism

slav·oph·i·lism \slä'väfə,lizəm\ *n* -s *usu cap* [*slavophil* + *-ism*] **1 :** advocacy of Slavic and specif. Russian culture over that of the West esp. as practiced by some members of the Russian intelligentsia in the middle 19th century **2 :** PAN-SLAVISM
¹**slaw** \'slȯ\ *dial Brit var of* SLOW
²**slaw** \"\ *n* -s [by shortening] **:** COLESLAW
¹**slay** \'slā\ *vb* **slew** \-lü\ **slain** \-lān\ **slaying; slays** [ME *slan, slen,* fr. OE *slēan* to strike, beat, slay; akin to OHG *slahan* to strike, beat, ON *slā,* Goth *slahan* to strike, beat, MIr *slacaim* I beat] *vt* **1 a :** to deprive of life by force **:** put (a person) to death violently **:** MURDER ⟨began to throttle his enemy, meaning . . . to ~ him —Rudyard Kipling⟩ **b :** to strike down **:** KILL ⟨gradually they were eliminated, slaughtered by bullets or *slain* by disease —Philip Mason⟩ **2 :** to put (an animal) to death esp. for food or as a sacrifice **:** SLAUGHTER ⟨growers *slew* laying hens when poultryless Thursday depressed prices —*advt*⟩ **3 :** to stifle or destroy completely **:** ERADICATE, SUPPRESS ⟨these semiautomatic words and phrases should be *slain* —J.E.Gloag⟩ ⟨the great love she . . . had she was *~ing* —Rose Macaulay⟩ **4 :** to affect overpoweringly **:** OVERWHELM ⟨used to ~ myself with exhaustion —Eve Langley⟩ ⟨*~s* the girls with his rugged virility —C.J.Rolo⟩ ~ *vi* **:** to cause death **:** KILL ⟨no other infection so quickly *~s* —*Jour. Amer. Med. Assoc.*⟩ **syn** see KILL
²**slay** *var of* SLEY
slay·er \'slāə(r), -le(ə)r, -leə\ *n* -s [ME *sleer,* fr. *slen* to slay + *-er*] **:** one that slays **:** KILLER
SLC *abbr, often not cap* straight-line capacitance
sld *abbr* **1** sailed **2** sealed **3** solder
slead \'slēd, -lăd\ *n* -s [ME *slede,* fr. MD or MLG; — more at SLED] *chiefly dial* **:** SLED
¹**sleave** \'slēv\ *vb* -ED/-ING/-S [fr. (assumed) ME *sleven,* fr. (assumed) OE *slǣfan* to cut (whence *tōslǣfan* to cut up); akin to OE *tōslīfan* to split — more at SLIVE] *vt, obs* **:** to separate (silk thread) into filaments ~ *vi* **:** to separate into filaments ⟨the hair had *sleaved* out thin and fine —Aldous Huxley⟩
²**sleave** \"\ *n* -s **1** *obs* **:** ¹FLOSS 1 **2 :** SKEIN ⟨sleep that knits up the raveled ~ of care —Shak.⟩
sleave silk *n, obs* **:** floss silk that is easily separated into filaments for embroidery
slea·zi·ly \'slēzəlē, -əli *also* 'slāz-\ *adv* **:** in a sleazy manner
slea·zi·ness \-zēnəs, -zin-\ *n* -ES **:** the state or quality of being sleazy
slea·zy \-zē,-zi\ *or* **slee·zy** \-lēz-\ *adj* -ER/-EST [origin unknown] **1 a :** lacking firmness of texture **:** having little substance **:** FLIMSY ⟨wore a ~ yellow coat and cheap high-heeled shoes —Wenzell Brown⟩ **b** (1) **:** carelessly made of inferior materials **:** SHODDY ⟨~ new apartment blocks, their broken rubble-salvaged brick unfaced —Flora Lewis⟩ (2) **:** marked by disrepair and cheapness **:** SHABBY ⟨a ~ rooming house sadly in need of paint⟩ **2 a :** marked by slightness **:** UNSUBSTANTIAL ⟨the series as a whole is ~ as history though frequently helpful as criticism —G.H.Genzmer⟩ **b :** marked by cheapness of character or atmosphere ⟨a ~ little gold digger —*New Republic*⟩ ⟨the ~ submerged seldom glimpsed underworld —J.B.Martin⟩ **c :** marked by low ethical standards ⟨outlaws about a dozen of the *sleazier* forms of competition —*Fortune*⟩ ⟨a ~ maneuver —H.C.Lodge⟩ **d :** marked by low artistic quality ⟨too many ~ spy stories —*Harper's*⟩
¹**sled** \'sled\ *n* -s [ME *sledde,* fr. MD; akin to MD & MLG *slede* sled, OHG *slito, slita,* ON *slethi,* OE *slīdan* to slide — more at SLIDE] **1 :** a vehicle that moves by sliding usu. on a pair of runners esp. over snow or ice: as **a :** SLEDGE **b** *archaic* **:** SLEIGH **c :** a small sled designed to be used by children for coasting down snow-covered hills **d :** ROCKET SLED **2 :** COTTON SLED **3 :** the sliding contact of an underground trolley system that is drawn under the car

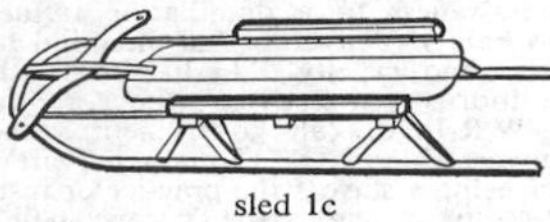
sled 1c

²**sled** \"\ *vb* **sledded; sledded; sledding; sleds** *vt* **1 :** SLEDGE ⟨contraband goods were *sledded* over the ice —*Amer. Guide Series: Vt.*⟩ **2 :** to harvest with a cotton sled ~ *vi* **1 :** to ride on a sled ⟨a celebrated place for the boys in winter to ~ —J.F.Watson⟩ **2** *archaic* **:** to ride in a sleigh **3 :** SLEDGE 2 ⟨*sledded* 70 miles up the Yukon —Jack London⟩
sled corrugator *n* **:** a device with sharp runners for opening small furrows for irrigation of cultivated fields
sled cultivator *n* **:** GO-DEVIL
sled·der \'sledə(r)\ *n* -s **:** one that sleds
sledding *n* -s [¹*sled* + *-ing*] **1 a :** the use of a sled ⟨enough snow for good ~⟩ **b :** the conditions under which one may use a sled ⟨the ~ last winter was exceptionally fine⟩ **2 :** GOING 5 ⟨the appliance tax slash faces tough ~ in the final House-Senate conference —*Wall Street Jour.*⟩ ⟨envisioned easy ~ ahead —Ralph Cokain⟩ **3 :** the action of harvesting with a cotton sled
sled dog *n* **:** a dog trained to draw a sledge esp. in the Arctic regions
¹**sledge** \'slej\ *n* -s [ME *slegge, slege,* fr. OE *slecg;* akin to MD *slegge* sledgehammer, ON *sleggja,* OE *slēan* to beat, slay — more at SLAY] **:** SLEDGEHAMMER
²**sledge** \"\ *vb* -ED/-ING/-S **:** SLEDGEHAMMER ⟨was *sledging* in the quarry⟩ ⟨were *sledging* out the wall —*Newsweek*⟩
³**sledge** \"\ *n* -s [D dial. *sleedse;* akin to MD *sledde, slede, sled* — more at SLED] **1** *Brit* **:** SLEIGH **2 :** a vehicle with low runners that is used for transporting loads esp. over snow or ice **3 a :** a frame formerly used for stretching the yarns in the manufacture of rope **b :** a platform on runners that is weighted to maintain tension on rope while it is being laid
⁴**sledge** \"\ *vb* -ED/-ING/-S *vi* **1** *Brit* **:** to ride in a sleigh **2 :** to travel with a loaded sledge esp. over snow or ice ⟨a small antarctic expedition . . . on which we would ~ and map the coastline —Finn Ronne⟩ ~ *vt* **:** to transport on a sledge ⟨millstones had been cut and laboriously *sledged* down the rough mountainsides —E.E.Evans⟩
sledge dog *n* [³*sledge*] **:** SLED DOG
¹**sledgehammer** \'=,=\ *n* [ME *slege hamer,* fr. *slege* sledge + *hamer* hammer] **:** a large heavy hammer that is usu. wielded with both hands and used esp. for driving stakes and breaking stone
²**sledgehammer** \"\ *vt* **:** to strike with or as if with a sledgehammer ⟨stills are officially *~ed* at intervals —*Amer. Guide Series: Ind.*⟩ ⟨have been today *~ing* your idea . . . into a sermon —Richard Whately⟩ ~ *vi* **:** to strike blows with or as if with a sledgehammer ⟨a racket of riveting and *~ing* —Emily Hahn⟩ ⟨kept *~ing* away on a procedural point —*Time*⟩

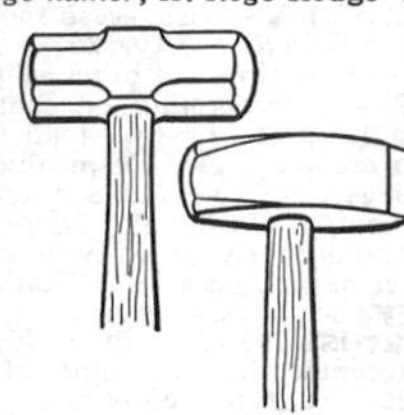
sledgehammers

³**sledgehammer** \"\ *adj* **:** marked by heavy-handed directness or the unsubtle use of force **:** BLUNT ⟨a plain direct ~ method —J.C.Powys⟩ ⟨trusting in ~ warfare —C.J.Rolo⟩
¹**sledg·er** \'slejə(r)\ *n* -s [³*sledge* + *-er*] **:** one that drives a sledge
²**sledger** \"\ *n* -s [¹*sledge* + *-er*] **1 :** a strip mine worker who digs out coal, rock, or dirt with a sledge **2 :** a worker who breaks up large stone into usable pieces with a sledge
sled harvester *n* [¹*sled*] **:** a wide flat horse-drawn implement equipped at its front end with a V-shaped knife that cuts cornstalks close to the ground
sled-length \'=,=\ *adv* **:** all out ⟨said he would join me *sled-length* in declining to yield —A.H.Vandenberg †1951⟩
sled lister cultivator *n* **:** a cultivator that has lister cultivating devices behind sled runners and a cultivator shield and that is used for cultivating row crops planted in furrows
sled marker *n* **:** a crop row marker consisting essentially of short sled runners and a platform from which a pipe rod with a small blade at the end extends to the side and makes a mark for the marker to follow on the return trip across a field
sleds *pl of* SLED, *pres 3d sing of* SLED
slee \'slē\ *dial Brit var of* SLY
sleech \'slēch\ *n* -ES [ME *sliche;* akin to MHG *slīch* shine — more at SLICK] *dial Brit* **:** ooze deposited by the sea or a river
sleechy \-chi\ *adj* [*sleech* + *-y*] *dial Brit* **:** OOZY, SLIMY
¹**sleek** \'slēk\ *vb* -ED/-ING/-S [ME *sleken,* alter. of *sliken* to slick] *vt* **1 :** SLICK 1a, 1b, 2 **2 :** to cover up **:** gloss over ⟨*~ed* over . . . his agitated expression —J.C.Powys⟩ ~ *vi* **:** SLICK
²**sleek** \"\ *adj* -ER/-EST [alter. of ²*slick*] **1 a :** smooth and shining usu. from good health or attentive care ⟨his ~ coat gleaming like mirror velvet —Alice Duncan-Kemp⟩; *also* **:** having sleek hair or fur ⟨steer and heifer calves — some of them so ~ and beefy that they had won blue ribbons —Lewis Nordyke⟩ **b :** being in a flourishing condition from or as if from attentive care ⟨animally alive, his naked brown body so ~ with health —Christopher Isherwood⟩ **2 a :** having a smooth or polished surface ⟨the metal felt ~ and warm to his touch —Stuart Cloete⟩ **b :** being wet and slippery ⟨cobbles were ~ with mud —Marguerite Steen⟩ **3 :** disagreeably ingratiating or fawning **:** UNCTUOUS ⟨novels . . . in which every young man is ~ and feverish for an unattainable success —Marjory S. Douglas⟩ **4 a :** gracefully proportioned **:** SLENDER ⟨a ~ brunette in a green dress and fur jacket —J.J. Godwin⟩ ⟨the early engines, ~ and graceful —C.J.Allen⟩ **b :** fashionably or luxuriously trim or elegant ⟨~ figures in expensive clothes —Green Peyton⟩ ⟨~ establishments specializing in Peking duck —Jane Nickerson⟩ **c :** superficially stylish or elegant **:** FLASHY ⟨radiated merely the ~ and obvious aspects —J.S.Bowman⟩ **d :** having slender graceful lines **:** STREAMLINED ⟨a long ~ car gliding away —Andrew Buchanan⟩
³**sleek** \"\ *adv* **:** SLEEKLY
⁴**sleek** \"\ *n* -s **:** SLICK 1,2
sleek·en \'slēkən\ *vt* **sleekened; sleekened; sleekening** \-k(ə)niŋ\ **sleekens** [²*sleek* + *-en*] **:** to make sleek
sleek·er \-kə(r)\ *n* -s [¹*sleek* + *-er*] **:** SLICKER
sleek·it \'slēkət\ *adj* [Sc, fr. past part. of ¹*sleek*] **1** *chiefly Scot* **:** SLEEK, SMOOTH **2** *chiefly Scot* **:** CRAFTY, DECEITFUL
sleek-leaf \'=,=\ *n* [²*sleek* + *leaf*] **:** SAND MYRTLE
sleek·ly *adv* **:** in a sleek manner
sleek·ness *n* -ES **:** the quality or state of being sleek
sleekstone *n* [ME *slekstone,* fr. *sleken* to sleek + *stone*] *obs* **:** a stone for smoothing or polishing
sleek sumac *n* [²*sleek*] **:** SMOOTH SUMAC
sleeky \'slēkē, -ki\ *adj* -ER/-EST [²*sleek* + *-y*] **1 :** SLEEK **2** *chiefly Scot* **:** having a fawning and deceitful character or quality
¹**sleep** \'slēp\ *n* -s [ME *slep, slepe,* fr. OE *slǣp;* akin to OHG *slāf* sleep, Goth *sleps,* OE *slǣpan* to sleep] **1 a :** the natural usu. regular suspension of consciousness during which the powers of the body are restored **b :** the suspension of consciousness caused by an abnormal physical condition or by artificial means ⟨the medium speaking for the first time . . . out of his mesmeric ~ —W.B.Yeats⟩ **2 :** a state resembling sleep: as **a :** a state marked by inactivity or lack of awareness **:** TORPOR ⟨the depressed fellaheen who likewise are rousing from their centuries of ~ —D.M.Friedenberg⟩ **b :** DEATH **c :** a condition in plants that is marked by the closing of leaves or petals esp. at night **d :** complete quiet ⟨the ~ that is among the lonely hills —William Wordsworth⟩ **e :** a state marked by a diminution of feeling followed by tingling caused by pressure on a part of the body ⟨my foot has gone to ~⟩ **f :** the state of an animal during hibernation ⟨the ground hog's winter ~⟩ **3 :** a period of sleep ⟨hoped for late morning *~s* in his new home —Dorothy C. Fisher⟩ **4 a :** NIGHT ⟨not ten *~s* have passed since the last of our fighting men returned —Mary Austin⟩ **b :** a unit of measurement indicating the distance that can be traversed in a period including a specified number of nights ⟨one of the Indian discoverers . . . said only that the mine was two *~s* from the post —*Amer. Guide Series: Mont.*⟩ **5 :** the signs of sleep **:** SLEEPINESS ⟨eyes heavy with ~⟩
²**sleep** \"\ *vb* **slept** \-lept, *esp before a consonant* -p\ **slept; sleeping; sleeps** [ME *slepen,* fr. OE *slǣpan;* akin to OHG *slāfan* to sleep, Goth *slepan,* L *labi* to slide, slip, sink, fall, and perh. to Gk *lobos* pod of a vegetable, lobe of the ear or other bodily organ; basic meaning: to hang loose] *vi* **1 :** to rest in a state of sleep **:** be asleep ⟨is able to relax and always *~s* well —C.B.Palmer b.1910⟩ ⟨*slept* at the club last night⟩ **2 :** to be in a state resembling sleep: as **a** (1) **:** to lack awareness ⟨his judgment could neither ~ nor be softened —W.B.Yeats⟩; *specif* **:** to lack awareness and fail to take advantage (as of one's rights) ⟨the bill would favor claimants who have been *~ing* on their rights —*U.S.Code*⟩ (2) **:** to lie dormant or inactive ⟨the ancestral idealism . . . that *slept* uneasily under the spell of middle-class ambitions —V.L.Parrington⟩ ⟨the seasons when nature *~s* in seeds —Alan Devoe⟩ (3) **:** to remain quiet or motionless ⟨the day, immeasurably long, *~s* over the broad hills —R.W.Emerson⟩ **b :** to lie dead ⟨two of them still ~ in an old graveyard —Dana Burnet⟩ **c** *archaic* **:** to have a diminution of feeling followed by tingling due to pressure on a part of the body **d :** to have the leaves or petals closed esp. at night **3 :** to have sexual relations ⟨a lovely aristocratic woman who wants to ~ with him —H.C.Webster⟩ ⟨must have *slept* around —A.O.Myrer⟩ **4 :** to wait until the next day before making a decision — usu. used with *on* ⟨said he would like to ~ on the proposition⟩ **5** *Scots law* **:** to lie over without being prosecuted for such a period as to become abeyant ~ *vt* **1 :** to be slumbering in ⟨*slept* the sleep of the dead⟩ **2** *archaic* **:** to disregard because of indifference ⟨extraordinary that any body of men . . . should ~ obedience —Thomas Paine⟩ **3 :** to get rid of by sleeping — used with *off* or *away* ⟨curls up along the base of the stone wall to ~ off his orgy of eating —Doris Cochran⟩ ⟨your oversize . . . berth is an airfoam invitation to ~ away business cares —*Wall Street Jour.*⟩ **4 :** to spend in sleep — used with *away* or *out* ⟨if he is not doped to make him ~ away the hours of travel, he is shivering with fear —S.J.G.Ervine⟩ **5 :** to bring (oneself) to a specified condition by sleeping ⟨retreated down to his own den . . . to ~ himself sober —Sir Walter Scott⟩ **6 :** to provide with a place to sleep ⟨the place *~s* 18 besides the servants —John Selby⟩
syn SLUMBER, DROWSE, DOZE, NAP, SNOOZE: SLEEP is the general term, applying to periodical repose with lack of consciousness; it lacks the connotations of the following. SLUMBER often applies to a light sleep; the word may sound somewhat literary ⟨the cradle of the *slumbering* babe —William Wordsworth⟩ DROWSE may suggest a dull or listless inactivity in which one may drift off to sleep ⟨quaint Spanish towns, with adobe houses and wide squares, sunk in their noonday sleep, — beautiful senoritas *drowsing* away the afternoon in hammocks —S.B.Leacock⟩ DOZE, close to DROWSE, may differ in applying to a deeper degree of sleep or sleepiness ⟨we laughed and *dozed,* then roused and read again —Vachel Lindsay⟩ As a verb NAP often applies to a sleeping or dozing when one should be alert and vigilant ⟨he *napped* again and when he opened his eyes he knew the sun was shining. He jumped out of bed, wondering about the time —Cortland Fitzsimmons⟩ ⟨caught *napping*⟩ SNOOZE may apply to a pleasant comfortable sleep between times ⟨having nothing to do, read a little Shakespeare and *snooze* —O.W.Holmes †1935⟩
sleepcoat \'=,=\ *n* **:** a man's knee-length coat with a tie belt similar in style to a pajama jacket
¹**sleep·er** \'slēpə(r)\ *n* -s *often attrib* [ME *sleper,* fr. *slepen* to sleep + *-er*] **1 :** one that sleeps: as **a :** one that is inclined to sleep a great deal ⟨a great ~ and fond of his bed —W.M. Thackeray⟩ **b :** one that is asleep ⟨at such a distance from the ~ that their low words could hardly disturb her —Anthony Trollope⟩ **2 :** a strong piece of wood or other material used as a support: as **a** (1) **:** a horizontal beam placed on or near the ground to support a floor or superstructure (2) **:** one of the heavy strips of wood that are set in or on a concrete floor base so that a wooden floor can be nailed down over the concrete base **b :** one of the knees that connect the transoms to the after timbers on a ship's quarter **c** *archaic* **:** the rafter of a roof valley **d** *chiefly Brit* **:** a railroad tie **e :** one of the longitudinal beams in a wooden bridge on which the transverse logs or planks are laid **3 :** DORMOUSE **4 a :** a fish of the family Eleotridae **b :** GREENLAND SHARK **5 a :** a bet that is accidentally left standing on the layout of a gambling game **b :** a bet on a dead card in faro **6 :** something (as a vehicle) that provides accommodation for sleeping: as **a :** SLEEPING CAR **b :** a truck with a sleeping compartment **7 :** one that has no apparent importance and remains unnoticed for some time before becoming very important: as **a :** a racehorse that wins after a series of poor performances **b :** an article of merchandise having a value that is much greater than its recognized worth **c :** a book that sells well year after year without being advertised **d :** a movie whose box-office returns are out of proportion to the cost of its production and publicity and far exceed the expectations of the producers **e :** a piece of music that unexpectedly becomes a hit **f :** a provision, clause, or amendment inconspicuously introduced into legislation in the hope that it will be adopted without consideration before its actual intent or force is recognized by potential opponents **g :** a security apparently overlooked by investors and therefore selling too low in relation to the market as a whole **8 :** a calf that has been earmarked but not branded **9 a :** RUDDY DUCK **b :** DOWITCHER **10 :** a sleeping garment esp. for children: as **a :** pajamas often with feet **b :** a sleeping bag for babies **11 :** an article of merchandise that sells slowly ⟨his unerring sense of what to buy, rarely gets stuck with *~s* —E.O.Hauser⟩ **12 :** a foal that is born comatose and usu. dies within a few days of birth due to intrauterine septicemic infection with one of the organisms (*Shigella equirulis* or *S. equuli*) commonly associated with navel ill **13 :** a bowling pin that cannot be seen easily because it is directly behind another pin

sleeper 10a

²**sleeper** \"\ *vt* -ED/-ING/-S **:** to earmark (a calf) so as to give the appearance of having been branded
sleep·ered \-pə(r)d\ *adj* [¹*sleeper* + *-ed*] **:** provided with sleepers
sleeper fire *n* **:** a forest fire that smolders for some time before bursting into a blaze
sleeper shark *n* **:** GREENLAND SHARK
sleep·ful \-pfəl\ *adj* [¹*sleep* + *-ful*] **:** marked by sleep ⟨a ~ night⟩ — **sleep·ful·ness** *n* -ES
sleepier *comparative of* SLEEPY
sleepiest *superlative of* SLEEPY
sleep·ify \'slēpə,fī\ *vt* -ED/-ING/-ES [*sleepy* + *-fy*] **:** to make sleepy
sleep·i·ly \-pəlē, -li\ *adv* **:** in a sleepy manner
sleep in *vi* **1 :** to sleep where one is employed ⟨two maids who *sleep in*⟩ **2 a :** OVERSLEEP **b :** to sleep late intentionally ⟨was up too late and decided to *sleep in* the next morning⟩
sleep-in \'=,=\ *adj* [*sleep in*] **:** that sleeps at the place of employment ⟨five *sleep-in* servants —*New Yorker*⟩
sleep·i·ness \'slēpēnəs, -pin-\ *n* -ES **1 :** the quality or state of being sleepy **2 :** an abnormal condition in flowers (as carnations or snapdragons) marked by a partial closing of the petals
sleeping *pres part of* SLEEP
sleeping bag *n* **1 :** a bag usu. of canvas or waterproof material and often warmly lined or padded in which one may sleep esp. outdoors **2 :** a baby's sleeping garment resembling a bag with sleeves and a zipper closing
sleeping bag
sleeping beauty *also* **sleeping clover** *n* **:** a wood sorrel (*Oxalis acetosella*)
sleeping car *n* **:** a railroad passenger car having berths for sleeping
sleeping carriage *n, Brit* **:** SLEEPING CAR
sleeping lizard *n* **:** STUMP-TAIL
sleep·ing·ly *adv* [*sleeping* (pres. part. of ²*sleep*) + *-ly*] **:** SLEEPILY
sleeping partner *n* **:** a partner who takes no active part in the partnership to which he belongs and whose existence is often not known to the public
sleeping porch *n* **:** a porch or room having open sides or many windows arranged to permit sleeping in the open air
sleeping rent *n* **:** a fixed rent **:** a rent that is not determined by the amount of profits
sleeping sickness *n* **1 :** a serious disease prevalent in much of tropical Africa that is characterized by fever, protracted lethargy, tremors, and loss of weight, is caused by either of two trypanosomes (*Trypanosoma gambiense* and *T. rhodesiense*), and is transmitted by tsetse flies — called also *African sleeping sickness, African trypanosomiasis* **2 :** any of various viral encephalitides or encephalomyelitides of which lethargy or somnolence is a prominent feature; *esp* **:** EQUINE ENCEPHALOMYELITIS **3** *also* **sleeping disease :** SLEEPY DISEASE
sleeping suit *n* **:** ¹SLEEPER 10a
sleeping table *n* **:** a stationary buddle that is neither rotated nor shaken during the washing of the ore
sleep·less \'slēpləs\ *adj* [ME *slepeles,* fr. *slep* sleep + *-les* -less] **1 :** not able to sleep **:** INSOMNIAC ⟨lay all that night ~ and yearning to go home —W.M.Thackeray⟩ **2 a :** affording no sleep ⟨troubles, cares, and ~ nights to him who wears the royal diadem —John Milton⟩ **b :** marked by absence of sleep ⟨the ~ sobriety of the drinker who has tried to go to sleep without drinks —Edmund Wilson⟩ **3 :** unceasingly active ⟨the ~ ocean murmurs for all ears —William Wordsworth⟩ ⟨~ conserves the attention of every American citizen and the ~ concern of the responsible agencies of government —A.E. Stevenson b.1900⟩ — **sleep·less·ly** *adv* — **sleep·less·ness** *n* -ES
sleep movements *n pl* **:** movements (as nyctinasty or nyctitropism) in plants in which leaves or other organs assume positions suggestive of sleep
sleep out *vi* **1 :** to sleep outdoors **2 :** to go home at night from one's place of employment ⟨a cook who *sleeps out*⟩ **3 :** to sleep away from home ⟨you can't *sleep out* . . . simply anything might happen to you —Edith Sitwell⟩
¹**sleep-out** \'=,=\ *n* -s [*sleep out*] **1** *Austral* **:** a place for sleeping outdoors; *esp* **:** SLEEPING PORCH **2 :** an outing on which the participants sleep outdoors
²**sleep-out** \"\ *adj* [*sleep out*] **:** that sleeps at home rather than at the place of employment ⟨the *sleep-out* cooks and maids were coming to work —*New Yorker*⟩
sleep paralysis *n* **:** a complete temporary paralysis occurring in connection with sleep
sleeps *pl of* SLEEP, *pres 3d sing of* SLEEP
¹**sleepwalk** \'=,=\ *vi* [back-formation fr. *sleepwalking*] **:** to walk in one's sleep
²**sleepwalk** \"\ *n* **:** a walk taken in one's sleep
sleepwalker \'=,==\ *n* [¹*sleep* + *walker*] **:** SOMNAMBULIST
sleepwalking \'=,==\ *n* [¹*sleep* + *walking,* gerund of *walk*] **:** walking in one's sleep **:** SOMNAMBULISM
sleepwear \'=,=\ *n* **:** NIGHTCLOTHES 1
sleepy \'slēpē, -pi\ *adj* -ER/-EST [ME *slepy,* fr. *slep* sleep + *-y*] **1 a** (1) **:** having an inclination to sleep **:** ready to fall asleep **:** DROWSY ⟨is ~ and wants to go to bed⟩ (2) **:** inclined to sleep more than is usual for most people ⟨a ~ boy who is always late to school⟩ **b :** of, relating to, or characteristic of sleep ⟨has a ~ look on his face —Morris Fishbein⟩ **2 :** marked by a state resembling sleep: as **a :** lacking alertness **:** SLUGGISH, LETHARGIC ⟨amateurs with a ~ sense of what is really at stake in the critic's business —R.E.Garis⟩ **b :** having little activity **:** quietly slow-moving ⟨this ~ little city lost among the gentle hills —Arnaldo Cortesi⟩ ⟨~ rivers lined with sycamores —*Amer. Guide Series: Ind.*⟩ **c :** having a dull glow rather than a sparkle ⟨even the best zircon is a bit ~ —F.B.Wade⟩ **3 :** tending to induce sleep **:** SOPORIFIC ⟨will give you ~ drinks —Shak.⟩ ⟨the yellowhammer trills his ~ song in the noonday heat —L.P.Smith⟩ **4 :** beginning to rot ⟨expect her to drop every minute like an overripe ~ pear —Frederick Marryat⟩
sleepy catchfly *n* **:** a No. American catchfly (*Silene antirrhina*) with small pink diurnal flowers
sleepy coot *n* **:** RUDDY DUCK
sleepy dick \'==,dik\ *n* [*sleepy* + *Dick,* nickname for *Richard*] **:** STAR-OF-BETHLEHEM
sleepy disease *n* **:** any of several wilt diseases of plants; *esp* **:** a tomato wilt caused by either of two fungi (*Fusarium lycopersici* and *Verticillium alboatrum*)
sleepy grass *n* **:** a tall coarse grass (*Stipa robusta*) of the southwestern U.S. and northern Mexico that causes a deep sleep in horses or sheep that feed on it
sleepyhead \'===,=\ *n* **1 :** a sleepy person **2 :** RUDDY DUCK

sleepy hollow chair \ˌ≈≈ˈ≈≈-\ *n, usu cap S&H* [fr. *Sleepy Hollow*, valley near Tarrytown, N.Y.] **:** a deep upholstered chair designed for comfort

Sleepy Hollow chair

sleepy lizard *n* **:** STUMP-TAIL

sleepy sickness *n* **1** *Brit* **:** SLEEPING SICKNESS 1 **2** *Brit* **:** ENCEPHALITIS LETHARGICA **3** *NewZeal* **:** pregnancy disease of sheep

sleepy staggers *n pl* **:** FORAGE POISONING

sleer \ˈsli(ə)r\ *vi* -ED/-ING/-S [alter. (perh. influenced by ³*slur*) of *sneer*] *dial Eng* **:** MOCK, SNEER

¹**sleet** \ˈslēt, *usu* -ēd·+V\ *n* -s [ME *slete;* akin to MHG *slōz, slōze* hailstone, ON *slota* to hang down, ME *sloor* mud — more at SLUR] **1 :** precipitation in the form of frozen or partly frozen rain **:** fine driving icy particles **2 :** GLAZE 1a **3 :** a mixture or combination of rain and snow

²**sleet** \"\ *vi* -ED/-ING/-S [ME *sleten,* fr. *slete* sleet] **:** to shower sleet

sleety \ˈslēd·|ē, -ēt|, |i\ *adj* -ER/-EST [¹*sleet* + -*y*] **:** consisting of, accompanied by, or of the nature of sleet

¹**sleeve** \ˈslēv\ *n* -s *often attrib* [ME *slefe, sleve,* fr. OE *sliefe;* akin to OE *slēfan* to slip (clothes) on, MD *slove* covering, apron, OE *slūpan* to slip, OHG *sliofan,* Goth *sliupan* to slip in, L *lubricus* slippery] **1 a :** a part of a garment covering an arm sometimes tied on at the shoulder or usu. set in by stitching at the armscye or cut with a body section of the garment (as a raglan or kimono sleeve) **b :** SLEEVELET ⟨postmistress in her brown paper ~*s* —James Stern⟩ **2 a :** a tubular part designed to fit over another part: as (1) *or* **sleeve axle :** a hollow axle or quill having relative movement to a shaft inside it (2) **:** a long bushing or thimble (3) *or* **sleeve coupling :** a piece of pipe or a thimble for covering a joint or for coupling two lengths of piping (4) **:** a longitudinally split quill or hollow mandrel for temporarily gripping a part (5) **:** a double tube of copper having a cross section like a figure 8 into which the ends of bare wires are pushed so that when the tube is twisted an electrical connection is made (6) **:** a pronged tubular spring used in a watch with a negative setting mechanism to set the stem in position (7) **:** a collar of coarse mesh wire screening placed around the base of a young tree or shrub to prevent injury by rodents (8) **:** a collar usu. of heavy paper placed around the base of a young plant (as a tomato) to prevent injury by grubs or cutworms **b :** an open-ended flat or tubular packaging or cover ⟨light bulbs in a ~⟩: as (1) **:** JACKET 3f (4) (2) **:** a protective cover usu. made of paper, cloth, or leather over board and slipped over a book to cover all but the fore edge and backbone **3 :** MANTLE 7a **4 :** SLEEVE TARGET — **up one's sleeve :** held secretly in reserve ⟨has an emergency plan *up his sleeve*⟩

²**sleeve** \"\ *vt* -ED/-ING/-S [ME *sleven,* fr. *sleve* sleeve] **1 a :** to furnish, cover, or surround with a sleeve **b :** to place (a part) as a sleeve upon another **2 :** to wipe off or away with the sleeve ⟨*sleeving* the sweat off his face —N.C.McDonald⟩

sleeve bearing *n* **:** a machine bearing in which the axle or shaft turns in a sleeve that is often grooved to facilitate distribution of lubricant to the bearing

sleeveboard \ˈ≈,≈\ *n* **:** a small ironing board for pressing sleeves

sleeveboard

sleeve brick *n* **:** a tubular firebrick used to line slag vents

sleeve button *n* **:** a button for fastening a cuff; *esp* **:** CUFF LINK

sleeved \ˈslēvd\ *adj* [¹*sleeve* + -*ed*] **1 :** made with sleeves ⟨~ garments⟩ **2 :** having sleeves of a particular type — usu. used in combination ⟨short-*sleeved*⟩ ⟨puff-*sleeved*⟩ ⟨long-*sleeved*⟩

sleeve dam *n* **:** a canvas dam for diverting part of the water from an irrigation ditch while the remainder flows through a sleeve whose opening can be regulated

sleeve dog *n* **:** a dog (as a Pekingese) small enough to carry inside the sleeve or in a muff

sleeve garter *n* **:** GARTER 1c

sleevehand *n, obs* **:** CUFF

sleeve·less \ˈslēvləs\ *adj* [ME *sleveles,* fr. OE *sliefléas,* fr. *sliefe* sleeve + -*lēas* -less] **1 :** having no sleeve **2 a :** PROFITLESS, FUTILE ⟨the errand they were on was ~ —Virginia Peterson⟩ **b** *Brit* **:** PETTY, FRIVOLOUS ⟨the ~ butterfly world —Llewelyn Powys⟩ — **sleeve·less·ness** *n* -ES

sleeve·let \-lət\ *n* -s [¹*sleeve* + -*let*] **:** a fitted covering for the forearm worn for protection or warmth

sleevelike \ˈ≈,≈\ *adj* **:** resembling a sleeve

sleeve link *n* **:** CUFF LINK

sleeve nut *n* **:** a right-and-left nut

sleev·er \ˈslēvə(r)\ *n* -s [¹*sleeve* + -*er*] **1 a :** a garment worker who sews in sleeves **b :** a laundry worker who presses sleeves and neckbands of shirts on heated forms **2 :** a worker who reinforces the pouring openings of paper bags

sleeve target *n* **:** a tubular cloth target towed by an airplane for use in air and ground antiaircraft gunnery practice

sleeve valve *n* **:** an admission and exhaust valve on an internal-combustion engine that consists of one or two hollow sleeves fitting around the interior of the cylinder and moving as the piston moves so that openings in them come into line with inlet and exhaust ports in the cylinder at proper stages in the cycle

sleev·ing \ˈslēviŋ\ *n* -s [¹*sleeve* + -*ing*] **:** a braided, knitted, woven, or extruded tube used to slip over bare or weakly insulated conductors in an electronic assembly — called also *spaghetti*

sleezy *var of* SLEAZY

sleided *adj* [alter. (prob. influenced by *sleyed,* past part. of ²*sley*) of *sleaved,* past part. of ¹*sleave*] *obs, of silk* **:** UNTWISTED

¹**sleigh** \ˈslā\ *n* -s [D *slee,* alter. of *slede,* fr. MD — more at SLED] **1 a :** a vehicle on runners used for transporting persons or goods on snow or ice — called also *sledge* **b** *dial* **:** a child's sled **2 :** the part of a gun carriage that supports the cannon, recoils with it, and guides it along the slides upon which the cannon moves in recoil

²**sleigh** \"\ *vi* -ED/-ING/-S **:** to drive or travel in a sleigh

³**sleigh** *var of* SLEY

sleigh bed *n* [¹*sleigh*] **:** a bed common esp. in the first half of the 19th century having a headboard and footboard that are solid and roll outward at the top

sleigh bell *n* **:** any of various bells commonly attached to a sleigh or to the harness of a horse drawing a sleigh: as **a :** CASCABEL 3 **b :** a hemispherical bell with an attached clapper often attached in series to a leather or metal strap fastened to a harness or sleigh

sleigh·er \ˈslāə(r), -le(ə)r, -leə\ *n* -s [²*sleigh* + -*er*] **:** one that sleighs

¹**sleight** \ˈslīt, *usu* -īd·+V\ *n* -s [ME *sleght, sleight,* fr. ON *slægth,* fr. *slægr* sly, crafty — more at SLY] **1 a :** deceitful craftiness **:** CUNNING, TRICKERY ⟨every interest did by right, or might, or ~, get represented —R.W.Emerson⟩ **b** (1) **:** mental or manual skill in making or performing **:** DEXTERITY, DEFTNESS ⟨a new ~ in the reading of poetry —R.P.Blackmur⟩ (2) **:** skill in a particular task **:** KNACK (3) *archaic* **:** SLEIGHT OF HAND 1 (4) **:** mental or physical quickness or agility **:** NIMBLENESS ⟨brilliant intuitions . . . and speculative hypotheses derived by ~ of mind from a fairly small number of works of the imagination —R.G.Davis⟩ **2 a :** a sly artifice **:** STRATAGEM, TRICK, SHIFT ⟨watching closely to discover by what mental artful ~ he would accomplish the miracle —Archibald Rutledge⟩ ⟨a wicked ~ that causes the assailant to put out his own shoulder —Lafcadio Hearn⟩; *specif* **:** SLEIGHT OF HAND 2 **b** *obs* **:** a skillfully executed pattern

²**sleight** *obs var of* SLIGHT

sleight of hand [¹*sleight*] **1 a :** expertness and adroitness in manual manipulation **:** manual dexterity **b :** skill and dexterity in the performance of juggling or conjuring tricks ⟨the simplest card trick defeats me if it demands *sleight of hand* —Geoffrey Household⟩ **c :** adroitness and cleverness in accomplishing a deception ⟨verbal *sleight of hand* —Marjorie Grene⟩ ⟨music that is free of self-conscious formulas and tricks of stylistic *sleight of hand* —Winthrop Sargeant⟩ **2 a :** a trick of conjuring or juggling requiring sleight of hand **b :** a cleverly executed trick or deception ⟨the *sleight of hand* by which a faction of the people as voters is invested with the authority of the people —Walter Lippmann⟩

sleighty \ˈslīd·ē\ *adj* [ME, fr. ¹*sleight* + -*y*] **1** *obs* **:** CUNNING, SLY, CRAFTY **2** *dial* **:** DEXTEROUS, SKILLFUL

slen·dang \ˈslen,daŋ, -dăŋ\ *n* -s [Malay *sĕlendang*] **:** a long narrow scarf worn esp. by Indonesian women

slen·der \ˈslendə(r)\ *adj, usu* -ER/-EST [ME *slendre, sclendre*] **1 a** (1) **:** spare in frame or flesh **:** not fleshy or large of bone ⟨a man of ~ build, being only five feet, five inches in height, and weighing less than one hundred pounds —D.Y.Thomas⟩; *esp* **:** gracefully slight ⟨she was like a feather in my arms, so ~, so ethereal —Jack London⟩ (2) **:** not robust **:** FRAIL ⟨as boy and girl neighbors, each of ~ health, they had enjoyed . . . playing the piano together —M.A.D.Howe⟩ **b** (1) **:** thin or insubstantial in proportion to breadth ⟨a ~ volume . . . of twenty-one pages —V.L.Parrington⟩ ⟨a ~ partition wall⟩ (2) **:** small or narrow in circumference or width in proportion to the length or height ⟨a ~ perpendicular steel framework tower —*Amer. Guide Series: Oregon*⟩; *esp* **:** delicately elongated in pleasing proportions ⟨a graceful portico of ~ columns —*Amer. Guide Series: N.C.*⟩ (3) **:** excessively thin and elongated **:** TENUOUS ⟨the new arrivals took over the defensive sector south of the airfield where the ~ line . . . had been punctured —H.L.Merillat⟩ **c :** limited in extent, size, quantity, capacity, or scope ⟨published a ~ list of generalized headings —John Lawler⟩ ⟨his critical powers were very ~ —G.C.Sellery⟩ **2 a** (1) **:** inadequate or barely adequate in quantity or supply **:** SCANTY, MEAGER ⟨compelled by ~ family finances to leave school early —E.M.Lustgarten⟩ (2) **:** barely adequate in dimensions or scope **:** NARROW, SCANT ⟨elected by a ~ margin⟩ ⟨a few attempts had been made to deepen and embank the natural streams, but with ~ success —T.B.Macaulay⟩ **b** (1) **:** inadequate to justify an inference, opinion, or action ⟨tended to start from some observation . . . and then elaborate on this ~ foundation a theory of the universe —Benjamin Farrington⟩ (2) **:** having slight or inadequate grounds or justification ⟨a ~ hope⟩ **c :** slight in significance, seriousness, or complexity ⟨the material is slighter, the texture more ~, and the formal exigencies shorter than the full-size sonata —Norman Demuth⟩ **3 a** (1) **:** FRONT — used of a vowel in some Celtic languages (2) **:** having the allophone that characterizes it when it is pronounced with a front vowel — used of a consonant in some Celtic languages **b :** characterized by or consisting of a tone that lacks fullness or volume ⟨fortunate in his recordings, for his rather ~ voice reproduces exceptionally well —P.L.Miller⟩ **syn** see THIN

slender aster *n* **:** an annual aster (*Aster exilis*) of the southwestern U. S. having usu. simple stems and thin linear upper leaves

slender bent grass *n* **:** ROUGH BENT

slender blue flag *n* **:** either of two irises: **a :** a dwarf iris (*Iris verna*) **b :** an eastern No. American iris (*Iris prismatica*) with stout ropy stolons and an acutely angled seed pod

slender deutzia *n* **:** JAPANESE SNOWFLOWER

slender foxtail *n* **:** a Eurasian annual weedy grass (*Alopecurus myosuroides*) that is locally established (as about seaports) in No. America

slender gooseberry *n* **:** MISSOURI GOOSEBERRY

slender grama *n* **:** a tufted perennial grama (*Bouteloua filiformis*) of Texas, Arizona, Mexico, and Panama having erect or spreading sparingly branched culms

slen·der·ish \-dərish\ *adj* **:** somewhat slender

slen·der·ize \-də,rīz\ *vt* -ED/-ING/-S **1 :** to make slender **2 :** to cause to appear slender

slender loris *n* **:** LORIS 1a

slen·der·ly *adv* [*slender* + -*ly*] **1 :** to a small degree **:** SLIGHTLY, SPARSELY ⟨~ endowed with natural resources —W.B.Fisher⟩ **2 :** in a slender manner ⟨a ~ built man⟩

slen·der·ness *n* -ES **:** the quality or state of being slender

slenderness ratio *n* **:** the ratio of the length of a structural member (as a column) to its least radius of gyration

slender rush *n* **:** a tufted wiry rush (*Juncus tenuis*) of wide distribution

slender vetch *n* **:** a Eurasian vetch (*Vicia tetrasperma*) with blue or purple flowers that is naturalized in eastern No. America — called also *lentil tare*

slender wheat grass *n* **:** a No. American grass (*Agropyron trachycaulum*) cultivated in the western U. S. for its excellent forage

¹**slent** \ˈslent\ *n* -s [ME — more at SLANT] *chiefly Scot* **:** SLOPE, PITCH, DECLIVITY

²**slent** \"\ *vi* -ED/-ING/-S [ME *slenten* — more at SLANT] **1** *dial Brit* **:** SLANT, SLOPE **2** *dial Brit* **:** to move or glance sideways

³**slent** \"\ *vt* -ED/-ING/-S [origin unknown] *archaic* **:** TEAR, SPLIT

slen·tan·do \slen·ˈtän(,)dō\ *adv (or adj)* [It, fr. verbal of *slentare* to slow down, fr. *s-* away, off (fr. L *dis-* or *ex-*) + *lento* slow, fr. L *lentus* pliant, tough, slow — more at LITHE] **:** gradually decreasing in tempo — used as a direction in music

sle·pez \slāˈpets\ *n* -ES [Russ *slepets,* lit., blind one, fr. *slepoi* blind] **:** a mole rat (*Spalax typhus*)

slept *past of* SLEEP

sleugh \ˈslü\ *Brit var of* ¹SLOUGH 1b

¹**sleuth** \ˈslüth\ *or* **sleuthhound** \ˈ≈,≈\ *n* -s [*sleuth,* short for *sleuthhound,* fr. ME, fr. *sloth, sleuth* track of a person or animal (fr. ON *slōth*) + *hound*] **1 :** a hound that tracks by the scent; *specif* **:** BLOODHOUND **2 :** DETECTIVE; *broadly* **:** one that searches out and investigates obscure information, facts or phenomena ⟨been a good ~ and critic in assembling the text —T.D.Clark⟩

²**sleuth** \"\ *vb* -ED/-ING/-S *vi* **:** to act as a detective or investigator **:** follow a track, trace, or clue **:** search for information or facts ⟨assigned eleven reporters and five lawyers to ~ out the facts —*Time*⟩ ~ *vt* **:** to search into the affairs or follow the trail of (a person)

¹**slew** *past of* SLAY

²**slew** *var of* SLOUGH

³**slew** *var of* SLUE

⁴**slew** *also* **slue** \ˈslü\ *n* -s [IrGael *sluagh*] **:** a large number or quantity **:** LOT ⟨a whole ~ of uptown rowdies —Paul Gallico⟩ ⟨had ~*s* of work —Conrad Richter⟩

⁵**slew** \"\ *n* -s [origin unknown] **:** filling consisting of usu. three rods worked together — see BASKET illustration

¹**slewed** \-üd\ *adj* [fr. past part. of ³*slew* (to twist)] **:** somewhat intoxicated **:** TIPSY

²**slewed** \"\ *adj* [⁵*slew* + -*ed*] *of a basket* **:** filled in with slews woven around the stakes and by-stakes

slew·ing \ˈslüiŋ\ *n* -s [⁵*slew* + -*ing*] **1 :** the act of filling in in basketmaking with two or more rods worked together **2 :** SLEWS

¹**sley** *or* **slay** *or* **sleigh** \ˈslā\ *n* -s [ME *sleye, slay,* fr. OE *slege,* lit., act of beating, stroke; akin to OHG *slag* blow, ON *slagr,* OE *slēan* to strike, beat, slay — more at SLAY] **1 a :** a weaver's reed **b :** a movable frame in a loom that carries the reed **2 :** a guideway in a knitting machine **3 :** the number of warp ends per inch in a cloth **4 :** a device in a lace machine that contains small holes through which some warp ends pass and is used in selecting the pattern

²**sley** \"\ *vt* -ED/-ING/-S **:** to separate and arrange in a reed the threads of (the warp) — **sley·er** \-lāə(r), -le(ə)r, -leə\ *n* -s

sleyb *usu cap, pl of* SLUBBI

slg *abbr* sailing

slibbersauce *or* **slibber-slabber** *n* -s [*slibbersauce,* prob. fr. MLG *slibber, slipper* slippery (akin to OE *slipor* slippery) + *E sauce; slibber-slabber,* perh. redupl. of ¹*slabber* — more at SLIPPERY, SLABBER] *obs* **:** a sloppy or nauseating concoction used as food or medicine or as a cosmetic

¹**slice** \ˈslīs\ *n* -s [ME *sklise, slice,* fr. MF *esclice, esclisse* splinter, thin piece of wood, fr. OF, fr. *esclicier* to splinter — more at ²SLICE] **1 a :** a thin flat portion that is cut from something ⟨a ~ of bread⟩ ⟨a ~ of roast beef⟩ **b :** ¹CHIP 1i **c :** something that resembles a slice ⟨looked . . . through the narrow ~ of window in the tower room —Kay Boyle⟩ **2 a** *obs* **:** a spatula or paddle used esp. for mixing or spreading medical compounds **b :** a knife with a broad or wedge-shaped blade used esp. for serving food ⟨a fish ~⟩ **c** *archaic* **:** an iron bar flattened at one end for use as a fire shovel **d :** a tool with a flat blade for scraping or stripping (as for flensing a whale); *specif* **:** SLICE BAR **e** (1) **:** the removable sliding bottom of a printer's slice galley (2) **:** INK KNIFE **3 :** a part separated from the whole **:** SEGMENT, SHARE ⟨territorial claims to ~*s* of Antarctica —J.D.M.Blyth⟩ ⟨make a bid for a ~ of the . . . prize money —H.W.Young⟩ ⟨for plot must be substituted the reality of a ~ of life —F.B.Millett⟩

²**slice** \"\ *vb* -ED/-ING/-S [ME *sklicen,* fr. MF *esclicier, esclissier* to splinter, fr. OF, of Gmc origin; akin to OHG *slīzan* to tear apart — more at SLIT] *vt* **1 a :** to cut with or as if with a knife ⟨~ bread⟩ ⟨~ a melon in two⟩ ⟨~ hickory sapwood for chair-bottom splints —*Amer. Guide Series: Ark.*⟩ ⟨jets ~ the air like giant scythes —Claudia Cassidy⟩ ⟨production would be *sliced* by more than half —*Newsweek*⟩ **b :** to divide into segments as if by cutting ⟨the chimney's shade . . . ~*s* the glistening roof —Thomas Vance⟩ ⟨the data . . . have not been *sliced* in all the ways that they might —R.M.Goldman⟩ **2 a :** to cut off cleanly with or as if with a knife ⟨this machine ~*s* off a narrow edge from each envelope —J.R.Gregg⟩ ⟨the industry will be able to ~ $30,000,000 from its . . . annual fuel bill —D.C.Spaulding⟩ **b** (1) **:** to cut a passage through ⟨expressways . . . ~ our parks —Joseph Hudnut⟩ (2) **:** to make by or as if by slicing ⟨~ an opening in a wall⟩ ⟨troops . . . *sliced* their way through the crumpled resistance —*Police Gazette*⟩ **3 :** to stir, spread, or clear with a slice ⟨~ printer's ink⟩ ⟨~ a grate⟩ **4 :** to hit (as a golf ball or tennis ball) so that a slice results — distinguished from *drive;* compare ²HOOK 6b ~ *vi* **1 :** to cut or seem to cut cleanly ⟨the turbine blade . . . *sliced* into the fuel line —J.A.Michener⟩ ⟨wind . . . *slicing* through his overcoat as though it were the thinnest cotton —Irwin Shaw⟩ **2 a :** to move with a cutting action often on the diagonal ⟨the planes *sliced* on over —James Jones⟩ ⟨the luxury liner . . . *sliced* through the Atlantic today in quest of a speed record —*New Orleans States*⟩ ⟨the bull's horn *slicing* by his shoulder —Barnaby Conrad⟩ **b :** to hew a passage ⟨a four-lane superhighway . . . ~*s* through the craggy sierra —*Lamp*⟩ **3 a :** to put a slice on a stroke or ball **b** *of a ball* **:** to curve in flight in the direction of a slice

³**slice** \"\ *n* -s **:** a flight of a ball (as in golf, tennis, volley ball) that deflects to the right of a right-handed player or to the left of a left-handed player usu. as a result of being hit across its center line; *also* **:** a ball following such a course — compare HOOK, SPIN

slice·able \-səbəl\ *adj* **:** capable of being sliced

slice bar *n* [²*slice* + *bar*] **:** a steel bar with a broad flat blade for chipping or scraping operations (as breaking up clinkers or removing excess dirt from a trench wall)

sliced veneer *n* [fr. past part. of ²*slice*] **:** veneer that is sheared from the flat surface of a flitch or squared log

slice galley *n* [¹*slice*] **:** an old form of printer's galley having a sliding bottom for handling heavy forms

slice-of-life \ˈ≈≈ˈ≈\ *adj* [fr. the noun phrase *slice of life,* trans. of F *tranche de vie*] **:** of, relating to, or marked by the accurate transcription into drama or another art form of a segment of actual experience ⟨in these *slice-of-life* literary times, the novel that analyzes life at more than one level is somewhat of a rarity —Benjamin Appel⟩

slic·er \ˈslīsə(r)\ *n* -s [²*slice* + -*er*] **1 :** an implement designed for cutting: as **a :** a piece of cutlery for slicing food by hand ⟨roast ~⟩ ⟨fruit ~⟩ ⟨cheese ~⟩ **b :** a mechanically operated device usu. employing a revolving disk for slicing ⟨food ~⟩ ⟨veneer ~⟩ ⟨~ for sugar beets⟩ **c :** a lapidary's slitter **d :** CLIPPER 2b **2 :** a person using a cutting implement: as **a :** one that cuts materials (as butter, bread, fruit) by hand or by machine **b :** a worker who cuts slits in turpentine trees for the insertion of gutters

slicers 1a: *1* fruit, *2* cheese

slicht \ˈslikt\ *Scot var of* SLIGHT

¹**slicing** *n* -s [fr. gerund of ²*slice*] **:** the act or process or a result of cutting; *specif* **:** TOP SLICING

²**slicing** *adj* **:** of, relating to, or adapted for cutting ⟨~ blade⟩ ⟨~ method⟩

¹**slick** \ˈslik\ *vb* -ED/-ING/-S [ME *sliken;* akin to OE *nigslycod* newly smoothed, glossy, OHG *slīhhan* to glide — more at ²SLICK] *vt* **1 a :** to make (a surface) flat or slippery **:** LEVEL, POLISH ⟨a spatula is used to ~ . . . the flour on a board —*Correspondence Course in Flour Milling*⟩ ⟨men . . . were ~*ing* the skids with grease —James Dugan⟩ **b :** to give an elegant finish to **:** REFINE, SMARTEN ⟨~*ed* up and sentimentalized the . . . rough-hewn original story —*Time*⟩ ⟨called in a decorator to ~ it up, turning the . . . café into a restaurant de luxe —A.J.Liebling⟩ **c :** SLEEK 2 **2 a :** to give a smooth and glossy appearance to (the hair) esp. by combing with water or pomade **:** PLASTER ⟨hair ~*ed* down and then brushed up in a barber's curl above his left eye —B.A.Williams⟩ **b :** to make presentable **:** spruce up ⟨dress as if they were ~*ed* up for Saturday night in town —J.H.Jackson⟩ ⟨Mother was . . . a great one for keepin' things ~*ed* up —J.C.Lincoln⟩ ~ *vi* **1 :** to spruce up **:** make oneself presentable ⟨he ~*ed* up and courted her in the regular way —Helen Rich⟩ **2 :** to glide smoothly **:** SLIP ⟨the logs ~*ed* along without jamming or stranding —Hugh Fosburgh⟩

²**slick** \"\ *adj* -ER/-EST [ME *slike,* akin to MHG *slīch* slime, OHG *slīhhan* to glide, ON *slīkr* smooth, Gk *ligdēn* grazing the surface, *leios* smooth — more at LIME] **1 a :** having a glassy surface **:** SMOOTH, SLIPPERY ⟨waters ~ with oil —*Time*⟩ ⟨the grass was ~ from the night's dew, and the men slipped frequently as they moved downhill —Norman Mailer⟩ **b :** having surface glitter **:** polished but not profound **:** GLIB, GLOSSY ⟨an entertaining job of ~ writing, all surface and no depth —B.R.Redman⟩ ⟨turned out ~ and sound conventional likenesses in the best School of Fine Arts manner —*Time*⟩ **c :** lacking in complexity or originality **:** OBVIOUS, CONTRIVED ⟨the young gentlemen are altogether too pat, and the adventures which befall them altogether too ~ —Virginia Woolf⟩ ⟨neatly plotted story of the ~ variety, easily read, soon forgotten —Jerome Stone⟩ ⟨no ~ solutions, no easy cures are peddled —R.J.McCracken⟩ **2** *archaic* **:** SLEEK 1 ⟨fattens all their beasts of war, and makes them ~ and fine —John Fryer⟩ **3 a :** characterized by subtlety or nimble wit **:** CLEVER, INGRATIATING ⟨this ~ type of youngster anticipates exactly how adults will react to him and plays on their sensibilities —Agnes Meyer⟩ ⟨a good many ~ sales tricks —J.M. Guilfoyle⟩ ⟨approached this problem in . . . too unctuous and ~ a mood —A.M.Schlesinger b.1917⟩; *esp* **:** WILY ⟨a pair of ~ operators had given the district a bad name by salting a barren claim —Oscar Lewis⟩ **b :** characterized by expert proficiency **:** DEFT, SKILLFUL ⟨a notable level of ~ technical perfection in every department —Arthur Knight⟩ ⟨smooth ground attack and incredibly ~ passing attack —*New Yorker*⟩ **4 :** extremely good **:** FIRST-RATE **5 :** lacking identification marks **:** UNBRANDED—used of livestock on the range **6 a :** SLEEK 3 **b** *or* **slick-paper** \ˈ≈,≈\ **:** of, relating to, being, or conforming to the standards of a slick ⟨~ fiction⟩ ⟨nationally circulated ~ and quality magazines —Paul Roberts⟩ ⟨appeals to the *slick-paper* or carriage trade —Rosemary Benét⟩

³**slick** \"\ *adv* **:** CLEVERLY, SMOOTHLY

⁴**slick** \"\ *n* -s **1 a :** something that is smooth or slippery ⟨snow left an icy ~ on the roads⟩; *esp* **:** a smooth patch of water often covered with a film of oil ⟨band ~*s* on the sea surface . . . are commonly seen along the shore when the wind is a light breeze —G.C. Ewing⟩ ⟨searchers spotted an oil ~ . . . and what might be the wreckage of a plane —*N.Y. Times*⟩ **b :** a film of oil ⟨an oily ~ drifted away from our boat —*Field & Stream*⟩ **2 :** an

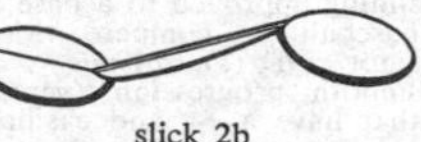
slick 2b

implement for producing a slick surface: as **a** : a flat paddle now usu. of steel for smoothing a sample of flour **b** : a foundry tool for smoothing the surface of a sand mold or unbaked core **3** : an unbranded range animal ⟨all of them added to their herds by branding ~*s* —Bruce Siberts⟩ — compare SLICK-EAR **4** : a shrewd or untrustworthy operator ⟨~*s* . . . exploited the plight of their brothers to ease their own paths —H.W.Baldwin⟩ **5** *chiefly Midland* : a treeless area in the southern Appalachians covered by a dense shrubby tangle usu. of rhododendron or mountain laurel **6** : a large-circulation consumer magazine printed on coated stock and usu. characterized by articles chosen for popular appeal and fiction limited to formulized stories with happy endings ⟨calculating editors of the ~*s*, who design moonshine to suit popular taste —Leo Marx⟩ — compare PULP 5a

⁵slick \" *or* **slick·er** \-kə(r)\ *vt* -ED/-ING/-S [*slick* fr. *²slick; slicker* fr. *slicker*, n.] : to defraud cleverly : OUTSMART, TRICK ⟨explanations . . . only tended to confirm them in the notion that they were being ~*ed* —R.W.Riis & Webb Waldron⟩

slick–ear \ˈ=,=\ *n* [*²slick* + *ear*] : a range animal lacking an earmark : MAVERICK — compare SLEEPER 8, SLICK 3

slick·en \ˈslikən\ *vt* -ED/-ING/-S [*²slick* + *-en*] *chiefly dial* : to make slick

slick·ens \ˈslikənz\ *n pl* [prob. irreg. fr. *slick* finely pounded ore, fr. G *schlich* slime — more at SCHLICH] **1 a** : the thin layer of extremely fine silt sometimes deposited by flood waters of a stream **b** : finely pulverized material from a quartz mill or washings of lighter earth sluiced away in hydraulic mining **2** : SLICKENSIDE

¹slick·en·side \ˈslikən,sīd\ *n* [E dial. *slicken* smooth (alter. of *²slick*) + *side*] : a smooth striated polished surface produced on rock by movement along a fault, a subsidiary fracture, a bedding plane, or at the bottom of a landslide — usu. used in pl. ⟨interpretation of the relative age of the faulting, on the basis of ~*s* alone, is difficult —J.D.Forrester⟩

²slickenside \"\ *vt* -ED/-ING/-S : to form slickensides upon

slick·er \ˈslikə(r)\ *n* -S [*¹slick* + *-er*] **1** : one that slicks: as **a** : a sharp-edged two-handled tool used for removing a thin layer of leather from hides to smooth them and reduce them to proper thickness **b** (1) : FLOAT 5d(1) (2) : GOOSENECK SLICKER **c** : a leather worker who uses a slicker **d** : a worker who lures hats **2** [*²slick* + *-er*] **a** : a bright yellow oilskin of loose full cut often worn with a matching sou'wester; *broadly* : RAINCOAT **b** : something that resembles an oilskin in style or smooth waterproof texture **3** [*⁵slick* + *-er*] **a** : a clever crook : SWINDLER, CHEAT; *sometimes* : a professional gambler **b** : a city dweller esp. of natty appearance or sophisticated mannerisms **4** [prob. fr. *¹slick* + *-er*] : SILVERFISH 2

slickest *superlative of* SLICK

slicking *n* -S [fr. gerund of *¹slick*] **1** : an act or process of making slick; *specif* : smoothing fine leathers by hand after setting by machine **2 slickings** *pl* : narrow veins of ore

slick·ly *adv* : in a slick manner : DEFTLY, SMOOTHLY

slick·ness *n* -ES : the quality or state of being slick

slickrock \ˈ=,=\ *n* [*²slick* + *rock*] : smooth slippery rock ⟨rough going over sand and ~ —S.W.Taylor⟩

slicks *pres 3d sing of* SLICK, *pl of* SLICK

slick spot *n* : an area usu. of a B horizon soil containing enough exchangeable sodium to interfere with the growth of most crops

slick·ster \ˈslikstə(r)\ *n* [*⁵slick* + *-ster*] : SLICK 4

slickstone \ˈ=,=\ *n* [ME *slikestone*, fr. *slike* slick + *stone*] *archaic* : a stone for smoothing or polishing

slid \ˈslid\ *adj* [prob. short for earlier *slidder* slippery, fr. ME, fr. OE *slidor;* akin to OE *slidrian* to slidder] *Scot* : SLIPPERY

slid·able *also* **slide·able** \ˈslīdəbəl\ *adj* [*¹slide* + *-able*] : capable of sliding or of being slid — **slid·ably** *or* **slide·ably** \-blē\ *adv*

slid·age \ˈslīdij\ *n* -S [*¹slide* + *-age*] : the charge for using a log slide

slid·der \ˈslidə(r)\ *vi* -ED/-ING/-S [ME *slideren* — more at SLITHER] **1** *chiefly dial* : SLIDE, SLIP **2** *chiefly dial* : SLITHER

slid·dery \ˈslidərē\ *adj* [ME *slidery*, fr. *slideren* to slidder + *-y*] **1** *chiefly dial* : offering insecure footing : SLIPPERY, SLICK **2** *dial Brit* : TRICKY, UNTRUSTWORTHY

¹slide \ˈslīd\ *vb* **slid** \ˈslid\ *or dial* **slod** \ˈsläd\ *or archaic* **slided; slid** *or archaic* **slid·den** \ˈslidᵊn\ **sliding; slides** [ME *sliden*, fr. OE *slīdan* to glide, slip, backslide; akin to MHG *sliten* to slide, Gk *olisthanein* to slip, glide, fall, Skt *sredhati* he errs, blunders, Gk *leios* smooth — more at LIME] *vi* **1 a** : to go with a smooth continuous motion : GLIDE ⟨fishes . . . *sliding* swiftly from your boat —*Amer. Guide Series: Fla.*⟩ ⟨a little red convertible *slid* up the . . . driveway —S.A.Offit⟩ ⟨shadows *slid* along the huge wooden tables —Sinclair Lewis⟩ **b** : to coast over a surface (as snow or ice) by means of gravity or momentum ⟨a startled dog ~*s* toward the skaters on all four feet⟩ ⟨~ downhill on a toboggan⟩ ⟨when the glacier *slid* down across New England —L.K.Porritt⟩ **c** : to drop down and approach a base in baseball along the ground usu. feet first with the weight of the body carried on one hip ⟨*slid* safely into third base ahead of the catcher's throw⟩ **2 a** (1) : to suffer a moral relapse : BACKSLIDE ⟨lead me in all thy righteous ways, nor suffer me to ~ —Charles Wesley⟩ (2) : to take a downward turn ⟨if the readjustment . . . ~*s* into a recession —*Fortune*⟩ **b** : to slip or fall by loss of footing ⟨stumbled over a log and *slid* down the slope⟩ **c** : to change position or become dislocated : SHIFT, SLIP ⟨the packages ~ from her arms⟩ ⟨rain *slid* off the smooth hide of the mountains —G.T.Nunn⟩ **3** : to become dissipated : VANISH ⟨it was inevitable that existentialism should ~ out of men's minds —Norman Cousins⟩ **4 a** : to slither along the ground : CRAWL, WRIGGLE ⟨began their advance, one *sliding* forward on his stomach —Georg Meyers⟩ **b** : to stream along : FLOW, POUR ⟨walked . . . along the dark *sliding* river —Irwin Shaw⟩ **5 a** : to pass effortlessly or unobserved : DRIFT — used of time ⟨how happily must my old age ~ away —Henry Fielding⟩ **b** : to become readily transferred or diverted ⟨his eye ~*s* from the printed page to the wonderful world outdoors⟩ **c** : to take a natural course ⟨finds it easier to let things ~ than to insist on strict observance of the rules⟩ **d** : to get along with a minimum of effort ⟨this means doing your best, not just *sliding* through —*Boy Scout Handbk.*⟩ **6 a** : to move softly or unobtrusively : disappear surreptitiously : SNEAK, STEAL ⟨*slid* behind the bole of a fir tree —F.V.W.Mason⟩ ⟨after playing to empty benches for two nights, they *slid* out of town —*Amer. Guide Series: Wash.*⟩ **b** : to pass easily or gradually ⟨~ into a reverie —John Masters⟩ **c** : to become gradually transformed ⟨may not godly authority imperceptibly ~ over into plain tyranny —V.L.Parrington⟩ **d** : to pass by gradations from one pitch to another without cessation of sound ⟨*sliding* . . . is another undesirable feature of singing —Sergius Kagen⟩ ~ *vt* **1 a** : to cause to glide or slip ⟨*slid* the car to the curb —Erle Stanley Gardner⟩ ⟨~ the left ski forward, then the right⟩ **b** : to traverse in a sliding manner ⟨firemen ~ the poles to the street floor⟩ **2** : to put or introduce surreptitiously ⟨*slid* the gun out of sight under his coat —Raymond Chandler⟩ ⟨the danger of . . . getting an emperor or a king or a dictator *slid* over on them —Dorothy C. Fisher⟩ **3** : to place (as an alphabetic sequence) beside another sequence in various juxtapositions at each of which the letters of one correspond one-to-one to those of the other

²slide \"\ *n* -S **1 a** : an act or instance of sliding: as (1) : a transit over a slippery surface ⟨a skier's hunger for more ~*s* . . . per weekend —William Gilman⟩ (2) : CHASSÉ (3) : the distance the fork moves after drop lock in a lever-escapement watch to reach the banking pin (4) : a sliding approach to a base in baseball — compare HOOK SLIDE **b** (1) *archaic* : a smooth progression ⟨verses, that have a ~, and easiness —Francis Bacon⟩ (2) : a lapse in morals or fortunes ⟨if he should . . . discover a bit of backward ~ in himself —H.A.Overstreet⟩ (3) : a downward turn ⟨action to halt the economic ~ —S.H. Slichter⟩ **c** (1) : a musical grace consisting of two or more small notes moving by adjacent degrees and leading to a principal note either above or below (2) : PORTAMENTO **2** : a sliding part or mechanism: as **a** : any of various clothing ornaments that slide on and hold by gripping ⟨tie ~⟩ ⟨belt ~⟩ **b** (1) : a U-shaped section of tube in the trombone that is pushed out and in to produce the tones between the fundamental and its harmonics (2) : a short tube that is used in most metal wind instruments to adjust the pitch **c** (1) : a moving piece (as the ram of a punch press) that is guided by a part along which it slides ⟨~ valve⟩ (2) : a guiding surface (as a feeding mechanism) along which something slides — compare CROSS SLIDE **d** : SLIDING SEAT **e** : a small runner to which something is attached to guide it along a track ⟨the luff of the sail . . . is sewn on to ~*s* which run in a metal track along the after side of the mast —F.E.Dodman⟩ **f** (1) : the knee of a composing stick (2) : a slugcasting-machine matrix for casting rules or borders **g** : a cryptographical device resembling a slide rule with a fixed member usu. carrying one alphabetic sequence and a double-length sliding member another one repeated **3 a** (1) : the descent of a mass (as of earth, rock, or snow) down a hill or mountainside ⟨a ~ of rock⟩ — used chiefly in combination ⟨land*slide*⟩ ⟨snow*slide*⟩ (2) : the track left by a slide (3) : a mass of debris deposited by a slide **b** : a dislocation in which one rock mass in a mining lode has slid on another : FAULT **4** : a drag or sledge for transporting heavy loads over a relatively smooth surface ⟨cut the last of the crop and . . . hauled it on a ~ to the tobacco barn —Elizabeth M. Roberts⟩ — called also *slider* **5 a** (1) : a slippery surface for coasting or sliding ⟨ski ~⟩ ⟨toboggan ~⟩ (2) : a chute with a flat polished bed sloping down from the top of a mounting ladder ⟨playground ~⟩ ⟨gave him a ~ for his swimming pool —*Brit. Books of the Month*⟩ **b** : a channel or track on which something is slid ⟨pushed the heavy door on the ~ and . . . followed him into the barn —Astrid Peters⟩ **c** : a sloping trough down which objects are carried by gravity ⟨log ~⟩ **d** : an inclined plane on moist soil adjoining water and smoothed by otters or occas. other aquatic mammals at play **e** *or* **slide stacker** : an inclined plane up which hay is drawn for stacking **6 a** : a usu. rectangular piece of glass on which an object is mounted for microscopic examination **b** (1) : a photographic transparency on a small plate or film suitably protected for projection — see FILM-SLIDE, LANTERN SLIDE (2) : DARK SLIDE **7** : SCUFF 4

slide 5a (2)

slide–action \ˈ=,==\ *adj* : PUMP-ACTION

slide caliper *n* : CALIPER SQUARE

slide detector fence *n* : an electrically charged fence along a railroad track that when broken by a rock or earth slide automatically sets signals to halt trains from either direction until the obstruction is cleared

slide fastener *n* : ZIPPER

slidefilm \ˈ=,=\ *n* [*²slide* + *film*] : FILMSTRIP

slide–off \ˈ=,=\ *n* -S : SLIDE 1b (3)

slide pole *n* : POLE 2d

slid·er \ˈslīdə(r)\ *n* -S [*¹slide* + *-er*] **1** : one that uses or operates a slide: as **a** : a person that coasts over a slippery surface ⟨the hill was swarming with ~*s*⟩ **b** : a worker who slides covers onto commodities (as matches, tobacco) packed in slide-top boxes **2** : SLIDE 4 **3** : a sliding part or device; *esp* : a zipper pull ⟨the annoyance of a zipper that pops open behind the ~ —*N.Y. Times Mag.*⟩ **4** : any of various No. American freshwater edible turtles esp. of the genus *Pseudemys* **5** : a pitch in baseball that looks like a fast ball but curves slightly

slide rest *n* : an attachment for a machine tool (as a lathe or planing machine) designed to hold the tool or cutter firmly and to give it motion — compare FEED SCREW

slide–rock \ˈ=,=\ *n* **1** : SLIDE 3a (1) **2** : rock shards in talus

slide rule *n* : an instrument consisting in its simple form of a ruler and a medial slide that are graduated with similar logarithmic scales labeled with the corresponding antilogarithms and used for rapid calculation

slide rule

slides *pres 3d sing of* SLIDE, *pl of* SLIDE

slide stacker *n* : ²SLIDE 5e

slide valve *n* : a valve that opens and closes a passageway by sliding over a port; *specif* : such a valve often used in steam engines for admitting steam to the piston and releasing it and having a cuplike cavity in its face through which the exhaust passes

slideway \ˈ=,=\ *n* [*¹slide* + *way*] : a way along which something slides : GUIDEWAY, SLIDE

slide–wire \ˈ=,=\ *n* : a resistance-measuring device used as part of a Wheatstone bridge and consisting essentially of a straight or spiral wire divided by a sliding contact into two parts forming the whole or known portions of adjacent arms of the bridge

¹slid·ing \ˈslīdiŋ, -dēŋ\ *n* -S [ME, fr. gerund of *sliden* to slide] : the act of one that slides

²sliding \"\ *adj* [ME, fr. pres. part. of *sliden* to slide] **1 a** *obs* : PASSING, TRANSITORY **b** : of an unreliable nature : SHIFTY ⟨the gentleman with the ~ smile —John Galsworthy⟩ **2 a** : going with a smooth continuous motion : SLIPPING, GLIDING ⟨a ~ avalanche⟩ ⟨a ~ snake⟩ **b** *archaic* : moving smoothly : FLOWING ⟨naturalize the ~ rhymes . . . in English —J.R. Lowell⟩ **3 a** : designed to slip along the cord around which it is made : RUNNING ⟨~ knot⟩ **b** : adjusted by sliding ⟨the ~ fan windows are unusual —*Amer. Guide Series: La.*⟩ **c** : equipped with or characterized by a sliding part or mechanism ⟨a ~ piston⟩ ⟨~ calipers⟩ **4** : rising or falling in accordance with a standard of comparison ⟨rent is charged . . . in a ~ ratio to the wages of the tenant —Hewlett Johnson⟩ ⟨~ definition of an old man as anyone who is fifteen years older than you are —Alan Gregg⟩ — **slid·ing·ly** *adv*

sliding board *n* [*¹sliding*] : a playground slide

sliding bow *n* [*²sliding*] : a metal framework mounted on an electric locomotive or trolley car to connect with the overhead wire

sliding fit *n* [*¹sliding*] : a fit for mechanical parts that slide on one another

sliding friction *n* : the friction between two bodies that are in sliding contact — called also *kinetic friction*

sliding gear *n* [*²sliding*] : a change gear in which speed changes are made by sliding gear wheels along their axes so as to place them in or out of mesh

sliding–gear trans·mission *n* : a power-transmission system in which any given pair of gears is engaged by sliding one axially into mesh with the other

sliding growth *n* : GLIDING GROWTH

sliding gunter *n* : GUNTER RIG

sliding hinge *n* : a hinge that permits a sliding as well as a rotary movement (as of a door) — compare CLEANING HINGE

sliding keel *n* : CENTERBOARD

sliding microtome *n* : a microtome in which the object to be cut is fixed and the knife is carried obliquely across it — compare ROTARY MICROTOME

sliding rule *n, archaic* : SLIDE RULE

sliding scale *n* **1** : a wage scale geared to the selling price of the product or to the cost-of-living index but usu. assuring the worker a minimum rate **2 a** : a system for raising or lowering tariffs in proportion to the fall or rise of prices **b** : a flexible scale (as of fees or subsidies) adjusted to the needs or income of the individual ⟨the *sliding scale* of medical fees making it . . . possible to balance the losses with large fees from wealthy patients —Milton Terris⟩ ⟨advocate of a *sliding scale* for farm support prices —*Newsweek*⟩

sliding seat *n* : a rower's seat (as in a racing shell) that slides fore and aft — called also *slide*

sliding tumbler *n* : an internal member of a lock usu. of flat sheet metal that is adapted to slide in a guiding slot or groove in the lock as it is operated upon by the key — called also *plate tumbler;* compare LEVER TUMBLER

sliding ways *n pl* : the lower part of the cradle on which a ship is built and which slides down the ground ways with it when it is launched

slid·om·e·ter \slīˈdämədˌə(r)\ *n* [*¹slide* + *-o-* + *-meter*] : an instrument for indicating and recording shocks to railroad cars occasioned by sudden stopping

slied *past of* SLY

slier *comparative of* SLY

slies *pres 3d sing of* SLY

sliest *superlative of* SLY

slif·ter \ˈsliftə(r)\ *n* -S [origin unknown] *dial Eng* : a crack in the surface of the earth : CREVICE

¹slight \ˈslīt, *usu* -īd.+V\ *adj* -ER/-EST [ME *sleght, slight*, prob. fr. MD *slecht, slicht* smooth, simple, of slight measure; akin to OE eorth*slihtes* level with the ground, ON *slēttr* smooth, OHG *sleht*, Goth *slaihts*, ON *slīkr* smooth — more at SLICK] **1** *chiefly dial* : SMOOTH, CALM, SLEEK ⟨a ~ sea⟩ **2 a** : having a slim or delicate build : not stout or massive in body ⟨a ~ girl⟩ **b** : lacking in strength or substance : FLIMSY, FRAIL ⟨a ~ temporary construction⟩ **c** : deficient in weight, solidity, gravity, importance, or other esteemed quality : TRIVIAL, PALTRY, SUPERFICIAL ⟨a ~ argument⟩ ⟨a ~ attack of indigestion⟩ **3** *of persons* : of low rank : HUMBLE, MEAN **4** : small of its kind or in amount : SCANTY, MEAGER ⟨the rewards were ~⟩ ⟨a ~ odor of gas⟩ **syn** see THIN

²slight *n* -S *obs* : something (as an amount, quantity, or matter) that is slight or insignificant

³slight \ˈslīt, *usu* -īd.+V\ *adv* -ER/-EST **1** *obs* **a** : in small or slight degree : POORLY **b** : to a small degree : SOMEWHAT **2** : in a light or slender manner — usu. used in combination ⟨*slight*-built shapely persons⟩

⁴slight \"\ *vt* -ED/-ING/-S [ME *slighten*, fr. *¹slight*] **1** *obs* : to make smooth or level; *also* : to level with the earth : OVERTHROW, RAZE **2** *obs* : to throw heedlessly or contemptuously **3 a** : to treat as slight or unimportant : disregard the significance of : make light of ⟨~ divine commands⟩ — sometimes used with *over* ⟨~*ed* his request over⟩ **b** : to treat with disdain or indifference : ignore discourteously ⟨~ a guest⟩ ⟨feel ~*ed*⟩ **c** : to perform or attend to carelessly and inadequately ⟨~ one's work⟩ **d** : ¹SLUR 4 **syn** see NEGLECT

⁵slight \"\ *n* -S **1** : an act or an instance of slighting **2** : an instance of being slighted or treated indifferently or superciliously : a humiliating discourtesy : an affront to one's dignity

slight·er \-īd.ə(r)\ *n* -S : one that slights

slight falcon *n* [*¹slight*] : FALCON-GENTLE

slighting *adj* [fr. pres. part. of *⁴slight*] : characterized by disregard or disrespect : DISPARAGING ⟨a ~ remark⟩ — **slight·ing·ly** *adv*

slight·ish \ˈslīd.ish\ *adj* [*¹slight* + *-ish*] : rather slight

slight·ly *adv* : in a slight manner or degree : SLENDERLY, LIGHTLY, CARELESSLY ⟨~ built⟩ ⟨touch ~⟩

slight negligence *n* [*¹slight*] : failure to exercise the great degree of care commonly exercised by an extraordinarily prudent person — compare GROSS NEGLIGENCE, ORDINARY NEGLIGENCE

slight·ness *n* -ES : the quality or state of being slight ⟨the ~ of the charge⟩ ⟨the ~ of her build⟩

slighty \ˈslīd.ē\ *adj* -ER/-EST [*¹slight* + *-y*] *chiefly dial* : SLIGHT

sli·go \ˈslī(,)gō\ *adj, usu cap* [fr. *Sligo*, county of Ireland] : of or from County Sligo, Ireland : of the kind or style prevalent in County Sligo

slily *var of* SLYLY

¹slim \ˈslim\ *adj* **slimmer; slimmest** [D, bad, inferior, crafty, fr. MD *slim, slimp* slanting, crooked, bad; akin to MHG *slimp* slanting, awry] **1** : of small diameter or thickness in proportion to the height or length : SLENDER ⟨a ~ person⟩ **2 a** : MEAN, WORTHLESS **b** : somewhat crafty : CLEVER, ADROIT ⟨a ~ rascal never at a loss for an answer⟩ **3 a** : inferior in substance, structure, quality, amount : SLIGHT ⟨a volume of ~ verse⟩ **b** : SCANTY, SMALL, SPARE ⟨a very ~ audience⟩ **syn** see THIN

²slim \"\ *vb* **slimmed; slimmed; slimming; slims** *vt* **1** *chiefly dial* : to do (as a task) carelessly or half-heartedly; *also* : to fail to make good use of (time) : LOAF **2** : to make slender or less : give an appearance of slimness to ⟨princess lines that ~ the waist⟩ ⟨~ your demands down⟩ ~ *vi* : to become slender

slim cake *n* : a plain Irish cake

¹slime \ˈslīm\ *n* -S [ME *slim, slime*, fr. OE *slīm;* akin to MHG & ON *slīm* slime, OHG *slīmen* to make smooth, L *lima* instrument for smoothing, file — more at LIME] **1** : soft moist earth or clay : viscous mud **2** : a viscous and usu. dirty or offensive substance : something felt to resemble viscous mud: as **a** : the original substance (as earth or clay) of the human body; *also* : a human being **b** *archaic* : BITUMEN **c** : a mucous or mucoid secretion of the skin of various animals (as slugs, land snails, hagfishes, catfishes) **d** : a product of wet crushing, consisting of ore ground so fine as to pass a 200-mesh screen — often used in pl. **e** : very wet inferior mortar **f** : a mass or coating of bacteria or algae growing in paper stock

²slime \"\ *vb* -ED/-ING/-S *vt* **1** : to smear or cover with slime : make slimy **2** : to remove slime from (as fish for canning) **3** : to crush or grind (ore) to a slime ~ *vi* : to become slimy

slime bacterium *n* : MYXOBACTERIUM

slimeball \ˈ=,=\ *n* [*¹slime* + *ball*] : a mass of cercariae enveloped in clear gelatinous material that constitutes the form in which some larval trematodes characteristically leave the snail host

slime body *n* : one of the discrete bodies of variable form, number, and distinctness that occur in a developing sieve-tube element, fuse prior to disintegration of the nucleus and form a viscous mass in the vacuole of the element, and are demonstrable after killing and fixing as a slime plug

slime disease *or* **slime sickness** *n* : any of several bacterial diseases of plants marked by slimy rot; *esp* : a destructive disease of tobacco caused by a bacterium (*Pseudomonas solanacearum*) and usu. contracted in the seedbed

slime flux *n* : a fluid or semifluid outflow from the bark or wood of a deciduous tree that is indicative of injury or disease

slime head *n* : a fish of the family Trachichthyidae

slime mold *also* **slime fungus** *n* : a plant of the class Myxomycetes

slime pit *n* : a pit yielding bitumen; *also* : a pit in which ore slimes are deposited

slime plug *n* : one of the funnel-shaped masses on each side of a sieve plate formed by aggregation of slime bodies (as in an injured sieve tube element)

slim·er \ˈslīmə(r)\ *n* -S [*¹slime* + *-er*] **1** : TOADFISH **2** : any of various devices (as a buddle or shaking table) for concentrating ore slime **3** [*²slime* + *-er*] : a worker who slimes something: as **a** : a cannery worker who cleans fish by hand **b** : a slaughterhouse worker who ties intestines into hanks and cleans them before they go individually to the casing-cleaning machine

slimesick \ˈ=,=\ *adj* : heavily populated with organisms capable of causing slime disease ⟨a ~ soil⟩

slime sponge *or* **slimy sponge** *n* : any of several marine encrusting sponges (class Demospongiae) lacking any form of skeleton

slime spot *n* : a colored or translucent spot in paper caused by a lump of slime in the stock that has been crushed in calendering

slime table *n* : SLIMER 2

slime thickening *n* : the thickening of an ore slime by the removal of clear water

slim file *n* : a file very narrow in proportion to its length

sli·mi·cide \ˈslīmə,sīd\ *n* -S [*¹slime* + *-i-* + *-cide*] : a chemical that prevents the growth of slime in paper stock

slim·i·ly \ˈslīməlē, -li\ *adv* : in a slimy manner : so as to be slimy

slim·i·ness \-mēnəs, -min-\ *n* -ES : the quality or state of being slimy

slim–jim \ˈslimˈjim\ *n* -S [*¹slim* + *Jim*, nickname for *James*] : something (as a person) that is notably slender

slimline \ˈ=,=\ *adj* [*¹slim* + *line*] : of, relating to, or being a long small-diameter fluorescent lamp used esp. in a concealed location (as for showcase illumination)

slim·ly *adv* **:** in a slim manner
slimmed *past of* SLIM
slimmer *comparative of* SLIM
slimmest *superlative of* SLIM
1slimming *adj* [fr. pres. part. of 2*slim*] **:** giving an effect of slenderness ⟨a dress with ~ hipline⟩
2slimming *n* -s [fr. gerund of 2*slim*] **:** the following of a regime (as of diet and exercise) designed to reduce the body weight
slim·mish \'slimish\ *adj* [1*slim* + -*ish*] **:** somewhat slight or slender ⟨~ evidence⟩
slim·ness *n* -ES **:** the quality or state of being slim
slim pickings *n pl* **:** little to be had or gained ⟨had *slim pickings* for supper⟩
slimp·sy \'slimpsē\ *adj* [alter. (influenced by 3*limp*) of *slimsy*] **:** lacking in substance or sturdiness: as **a :** SLIMSY **b :** being in poor health **:** FEEBLE, PEAKED **c :** hanging limply **:** DROOPING
slims *pres 3d sing of* SLIM
slim·sy \'slimzē, -zi\ *adj* [blend of 1*slim* and 1*flimsy*] *of cloth* **:** lacking wearing qualities **:** FLIMSY, FRAIL
slimy \'slīmē, -mi\ *adj* -ER/-EST [ME, fr. 1*slime* + -*y*] **1 :** of, relating to, resembling, or being slime **:** VISCOUS, GLUTINOUS; *also* **:** covered with or yielding slime **2 :** of such a character as to be highly distasteful **:** VILE, OFFENSIVE, VULGAR ⟨inexcusably ~ language⟩ ⟨a ~ traitor⟩ ⟨such ~ trickery⟩
slimy-backed \ˌ=ˌ=ˈ=\ *adj* **:** having a slimy back or surface
slimy salamander *n* **:** a No. American salamander (*Plethodon glutinosus*) secreting quantities of mucus from the body surface
1sling \'sliŋ\ *vb* **slung** \'sləŋ\ *or chiefly dial* **slang** \'slaŋ\ **slung; slinging; slings** [ME *slingen*, prob. fr. ON *slyngva* to hurl; akin to OE & OHG *slingan* to creep, wind, Lith *slinkti*] *vt* **1 :** to cast forcibly and usu. suddenly **:** HURL, FLING ⟨*sling* the net out to dry⟩ ⟨~ your coat over your shoulder⟩ **2 :** to throw (as a stone) with a sling **~** *vi* **1 :** to hurl missiles with a sling **2 :** to move with vigor as if slung ⟨~*ing* angrily out of the room⟩; *esp* **:** to stride along purposefully **:** SWING **syn** see THROW — **sling ink** *slang* **:** to write for publication — **sling one's hook** *Brit* **:** to go away **:** move on
2sling \"\ *n* -s **1 :** a slinging or hurling of or as if of a missile **:** a violent blow ⟨the ~*s* and arrows of outrageous fortune —Shak.⟩ **2 :** a fault in badminton committed when the racket makes a sliding contact with the shuttlecock
3sling \"\ *n* -s [ME, perh. fr. MLG *slinge*; akin to OHG *slinga* sling, *slingan* to creep, twist] **1 a :** an instrument for throwing stones or other missiles that usu. consists of a short strap with two strings fastened to its ends or with a string fastened to one end and a light stick to the other and that is used by whirling round until on losing one end the missile is let fly with centrifugal force **b :** SLINGSHOT **2** *obs* **:** a small cannon **:** CULVERIN **3 a :** a usu. looped line (as of strap, chain, rope) used to hold securely something to be hoisted, lowered, carried, or suspended: as (1) **:** a strap forming a loop (as on a rifle, a pack, or a woman's purse) and used esp. to suspend the burden over the shoulder (2) **:** a hanging bandage suspended from the neck to support an arm or hand (3) **:** a strip of the upper of a shoe having a cutout back part that forms a strap fitting over the wearer's heel and holding the shoe in place **b :** a device based on or substituted for such a looped line and usu. fitted with hooks or tackles: as (1) **:** a chain or rope attached to a lower yard at the middle and passing around a mast near the masthead to support a yard — usu. used in pl.; see SHIP illustration (2) **:** a chain hooked at the bow and stern of a boat to hook the tackles to when it is lowered or hoisted aboard ship; *also* **:** a group of three or four wire legs spliced to a ring, fitted with shackles at their outer ends, and used for hoisting a man-of-war's boats with a crane (3) **:** BUTT SLING (4) **:** a harness esp. constructed for supporting a sick animal in a standing position (5) **:** a device (as a rope net) for actually enclosing material to be hoisted or lowered by a tackle or crane (6) **:** the skeleton supporting frame of an elevator car and its attached guide shoes and cable beam **4 slings** *pl* **:** the middle part of a ship's yard **5 :** a piece of wire with a handle at each end used for cutting potter's clay
4sling \"\ *vt* **slung; slung; slinging; slings 1 a :** to place in a sling for hoisting or lowering ⟨the load must be carefully *slung* if it is to be safely hoisted⟩ **b :** to move by slings ⟨~ a cask⟩ **2 :** to suspend by or as if by a sling ⟨~ a scaffold from a roof⟩ **3 :** to cut (clay for potting) with a sling **4 :** to suspend (a yard) from the masthead of an old-time war vessel by extra chains on going into action
5sling \"\ *adj* **1 :** attached to or suspended in or from a sling ⟨a ~ wagon⟩ ⟨wearing an alligator ~ bag over her shoulder⟩ **2 :** designed to be worn thrown loosely over the shoulders ⟨a ~ cape⟩
6sling \"\ *n* -s [origin unknown] **:** an alcoholic drink usu. made of whiskey, brandy, or esp. gin with plain or carbonated water, sugar, and sometimes bitters and often garnished with lemon or lime peel if cold or dusted with nutmeg if hot ⟨gin ~⟩ ⟨rum ~⟩
7sling \"\ *vi* **:** to drink slings
8sling \"\ *n* [fr. native name in Tibet, prob. modif. of *Sining*, *Hsining*, city of west central China, important trade station on route to Lhasa] **:** an Indian cloth of fine goat's wool
slingball \'=ˌ=\ *n* [3*sling*] **:** a missile hurled from a sling
slingboard \'=ˌ=\ *n* [3*sling*] **:** a strong wood floor to which ropes are attached at the corners so that it can be lifted by a ship's winch in handling cargo
sling cart *n* [3*sling*] **:** a cart to transport heavy loads in which the load is suspended by a chain attached to the axletree
sling chair *n* [3*sling*] **:** a chair formed of a metal or wooden frame to which a piece of canvas, leather, or other flexible material is loosely fitted

sling chair

sling dogs *n pl* [3*sling*] **:** a pair of dogs (sense 3b) or crampons with the attached chain or rope
slinge \'slinj\ *vi* -ED/-ING/-S [origin unknown] *dial Brit* **:** to hang around **:** LOAF
1sling·er \'sliŋə(r)\ *n* -s [ME, fr. *slingen* to sling, hurl + -*er*] **:** one that slings or uses a sling as a weapon; *esp* **:** a soldier of former times armed with a sling
2slinger \"\ *n* [4*sling* + -*er*] **1 :** one that uses a sling (as to support, hoist, or carry); *esp* **:** a workman that attaches slings to articles for hoisting **:** RIGGER **2 :** a device for centrifugally throwing oil into a bearing and usu. also for keeping dirt from getting into it
slinger ring *n* [2*slinger*] **:** a tubular ring fitted round the propeller hub of an airplane through which a spray of antifreeze solution is spread by centrifugal force over the propeller blades to prevent formation of ice
slinging *n* -s [fr. gerund of 4*sling*] **:** a charge for attaching slings to a cargo
sling·man \'sliŋmən\ *n, pl* **slingmen** [3*sling* + *man*] **1** *archaic* **:** SLINGER **2 :** CRANE FOLLOWER
sling psychrometer *n* [3*sling*] **:** a psychrometer that can be whirled in the air until the reading of the wet-bulb thermometer reaches a constant value
sling pump *or* **sling-back pump** *also* **sling** *n* -s **:** a woman's shoe with a sling across the back and usu. an open toe
sling rope *n* **:** a rope used in fastening the pack on a pack animal
slings *pres 3d sing of* SLING, *pl of* SLING
slingshot \'=ˌ=\ *n* [1*sling* + *shot*] **1 :** a forked stick with an elastic band attached that shoots small pellets (as pebbles or beans) and is used esp. by small boys in play and hunting **2 :** SLING 1a

sling pump

slings·man \'sliŋzmən\ *n, pl* **slingsmen** [*sling's* (poss. of 3*sling*) + *man*] **:** SLINGER
sling stay *n* [3*sling*] **:** any of the stay rods from which a crown bar of a steam boiler is suspended
slingstone \'=ˌ=\ *n* [ME, fr. 3*sling* + *stone*] **:** a stone to be thrown from a sling
sling strap *n* [3*sling*] **1 :** any of several long straps attached to a packsaddle for fastening the pack **2 :** SLING 3a (3)
sling unloader *n* **:** a hay unloader consisting of a rope sling which is laid on a wagon rack in advance, on which the hay is placed, and the ends of which in unloading are pulled together so that the entire load of hay may be lifted and transported (as by block and tackle) to the mow or stack
1slink \'sliŋk\ *vb* **slunk** \'sləŋk\ *or chiefly dial* **slinked** *or archaic* **slank** \'slaŋk\ **slunk; slinking; slinks** [ME *slinken*, fr. OE *slincan* to creep, crawl; akin to OSw *slinka* to creep, slink, MD *slinken* to sag, OE *slingan* to creep — more at SLING] *vi* **:** to go or move stealthily or furtively (as in fear, shame, sneaking) **:** creep or steal along or away **:** retire ignominiously ⟨~ behind an enemy⟩ ⟨*slunk* into a corner⟩ **~** *vt* **1 :** to give premature birth to — used esp. of a domestic animal ⟨a cow that ~*s* her calf⟩ **2 :** to move (as one's eyes) in a slinking manner **syn** see LURK
2slink \"\ *n* -s **1 a :** the young of an animal brought forth prematurely; *esp* **:** a calf brought forth before its time **b :** the flesh or skin of such a calf **2** *chiefly dial* **a :** an underdeveloped or undernourished creature **:** WEAKLING **b :** a slinking cowardly person **:** SNEAK **3 :** a stealthy slinking movement or pace ⟨a ~ of the eye⟩
3slink \"\ *adj* [2*slink*] **1 a :** born prematurely or abortively ⟨a ~ calf⟩ **b :** derived from a prematurely born animal ⟨~ meat⟩ **2** *chiefly dial* **:** starved looking **:** THIN, SCRAWNY
slink·er \-kə(r)\ *n* -s **:** one that slinks: as **a :** an animal (as a cow) that gives birth prematurely; *esp* **:** one that does so habitually **b :** LOAFER, SHIRKER, SLACKER
slink·i·ly \'sliŋkəlē\ *adv* **:** in a slinky manner
slink·i·ness \-kēnəs\ *n* -ES **:** the quality or state of being slinky
slink·ing·ly *adv* [*slinking* (pres. part. of 1*slink*) + -*ly*] **:** in a slinking manner **:** so as to slink or seem to slink
slink lamb *n* [3*slink*] **:** a skin from a stillborn or a very young lamb
slinkskin \'=ˌ=\ *n* [2*slink* + *skin*] **:** leather made from the skin of a slink
slinkweed \'=ˌ=\ *n* [1*slink* + *weed*; fr. the belief that it causes cows to miscarry] **1 :** CARDINAL FLOWER **2 :** SWAMP LOOSESTRIFE
1slinky \'sliŋkē, -ki\ *adj* -ER/-EST [2*slink* + -*y*] *chiefly dial* **:** SLINK 2
2slinky \"\ *adj* -ER/-EST [1*slink* + -*y*] **1 :** characterized by slinking **:** stealthily quiet ⟨~ movements⟩ **2 :** sleek and sinuous in outline ⟨a ~ figure⟩; *esp* **:** following the lines of the figure in a gracefully flowing manner — used of woman's clothing ⟨a ~ evening gown⟩
1slip \'slip\ *vb* **slipped** *or archaic* **slipt** \'slipt\ **slipped** *or archaic* **slipt; slipping; slips** [ME *slippen*, fr. MD or MLG; akin to OHG *slipfen*, *slīfan* to glide, slip, ON *sleipr* slippery, Gk *olibros* slippery, *leios* smooth — more at LIME] *vi* **1 a :** to move with a sliding motion ⟨he opened the door and she *slipped* under the wheel —Hamilton Basso⟩ ⟨the red rim of the sun ~*s* out of the sea —Richard Thruelsen⟩ **:** go or pass smoothly and easily ⟨let his mind ~ automatically into the trading routine —Walter O'Meara⟩ **b :** to move quietly and cautiously **:** go stealthily so as to escape notice **:** GLIDE, STEAL ⟨peeped out, saw no one, and thinking himself secure, *slipped* out into the road —David Garnett⟩ ⟨*slipped* from a doorway and followed him —T.M.Johnson⟩ **c :** to elapse quickly and smoothly **:** pass imperceptibly ⟨could see millions of years *slipping* by and the earth spinning still more dizzily —Waldemar Kaempffert⟩ **2 a** (1) **:** to escape from one's mind or consciousness ⟨lately, things seem to ~ away from me —Lenard Kaufman⟩ (2) **:** to become uttered through inadvertence or negligence ⟨her name *slipped* from his lips —Agnes S. Turnbull⟩ **b :** to pass quickly or easily away **:** become lost **:** ESCAPE ⟨the power of the upper classes to act as sole arbiters of taste and fashion was *slipping* from them —Jacquetta & Christopher Hawkes⟩ ⟨the money *slipped* through his fingers⟩ **3 :** to fall into error or fault **:** LAPSE ⟨he is most orthodox and rarely ~*s* —G.C.Sellery⟩ ⟨sometimes ~*s* into rather dreadful puns and hackneyed language —C.K.Kluckhohn⟩ **4 a** (1) **:** to slide out of place or away from a support or one's grasp **:** fall or change direction by sliding ⟨the books *slipped* to the floor⟩ ⟨the chisel *slipped* and cut his hand⟩ (2) **:** to undergo a slip ⟨the younger rock ~*s* from time to time, as some earth movement takes place —*Amer. Guide Series: Wash.*⟩ (3) *of a crystal* **:** to undergo internal sliding along a particular plane **b :** to slide on or down a slippery surface so as to fall or endanger one's balance ⟨had hurt his elbow through dropping his stick and *slipping* downstairs —Arnold Bennett⟩ **c :** to flow smoothly ⟨a gentle stream *slipping* down the face of the cliff —John Muir †1914⟩ **5 :** to get speedily or easily into or out of an article of clothing or wear ⟨began *slipping* into a pair of hip boots —*Buick Mag.*⟩ ⟨*slipped* into his coat⟩ **6 :** to let go of an anchor by letting the cable run overboard ⟨the captain gave the order to ~⟩ **7 a :** to suffer a gradual loss of one's health or capacities **:** DETERIORATE ⟨has *slipped* badly since his last illness⟩ **b :** to suffer a falling off in one's power, standing, or reputation ⟨more scared when he was successful than when he began to ~ —Delmore Schwartz⟩ **c :** to fall off from a standard or accustomed level by degrees **:** DECLINE ⟨as costs and prices rise, sales in some lines will ~ —*Time*⟩ **8 a :** to move the head or body quickly to either side to avoid being hit (as by an opponent's fist) **b :** SIDESLIP **~** *vt* **1 :** to cause to move easily and smoothly **:** SLIDE ⟨*slipped* a little mirror from her handbag —Willa Cather⟩ ⟨~*s* an airplane through openings in drifting clouds —William Beebe⟩ **2 a :** to get away from **:** ELUDE, EVADE ⟨*slipped* his pursuers⟩ **b :** to free oneself from **:** get out of ⟨his horse, having *slipped* the bridle —*Amer. Guide Series: Conn.*⟩ ⟨*slipped* the formal bonds that have held his comedy in restraint —Irving Kolodin⟩ **c :** to escape from (one's memory or notice) ⟨the appointment *slipped* his memory⟩ ⟨was so absorbed in his thoughts that the approaching storm *slipped* his attention⟩ **3 :** CAST, SHED ⟨the snake *slipped* its skin⟩ **4 a** *archaic* **:** NEGLECT, OVERLOOK — sometimes used with *over* **b :** to pass over or set aside **:** leave out of account or consideration **:** OMIT ⟨had *slipped* our claim until another age —Shak.⟩ **c** *obs* **:** to let (an appointed time) go by ⟨did command me to call timely on him; I have almost *slipped* the hour —Shak.⟩ **5 :** to put (a garment) hastily or carelessly — usu. used with *on* ⟨~ on a coat⟩ **6 :** to utter inadvertently ⟨never once did he ~ even the name of . . . that town —Will Irwin⟩ **7 a :** to let loose from a restraining leash or grasp ⟨the puppies were *slipped* and off they tore —*Manchester Guardian Weekly*⟩ **b :** to cause to slip open **:** RELEASE, UNDO ⟨*slipped* the knots that bound him⟩ ⟨in the darkness he *slipped* the night lock and went out —James Jones⟩ **c :** to loosen one's grip on or connection with **:** let go of ⟨*slipped* her lines and began the final leg of her homeward journey —*Crowsnest*⟩ ⟨with her tug *slipped*, she moved at gathering speed into the dark, open sea —J.E.Macdonnell⟩ **d :** to disengage from (an anchor) instead of hauling in ⟨ships began *slipping* their anchors, but her skipper . . . wouldn't ~ his —Max Hunn⟩ **:** get free of (an anchor cable) ⟨*slipped* its cable and made a run for the open sea⟩ **e** *Brit* **:** to detach (a slip carriage) en route ⟨knows all the stations where the train stops or where carriages are *slipped* —Bertrand Russell⟩ **8 a :** to insert, place, or pass quietly or secretly ⟨*slipped* the letter into his pocket when no one was looking⟩ ⟨*slipping* a wink to his brother —L.C.Douglas⟩ **b :** to give or pay on the sly ⟨*slipped* some money to the chief of police —Emmett Kelly⟩ **9** *of a domestic animal* **:** to give birth to prematurely **:** ABORT ⟨some cows ~ their calves in the early stages of pregnancy —*New Zealand Jour. of Agric.*⟩ **10 :** DISLOCATE ⟨*slipped* his shoulder⟩ **:** suffer the slipping of (one's foot) ⟨*slipped* his foot on the patch of oil and fell⟩ **11 :** PALM ⟨~ a card⟩ **12 a :** to transfer (a stitch) from one needle to another without working a stitch — compare DECREASE *vt* 2 **b** [*slip stitch*] **:** to sew (something) with slip stitches **13 a :** to avoid (a punch) by moving the body or head quickly to one side ⟨couldn't believe that he relied on speed of eye and head to ~ such punches —A.J.Liebling⟩ **b :** to cause (a descending parachute) to glide in a particular direction by pulling down on suspension lines on the side toward the desired direction so as to spill air out of the opposite side of the canopy — **slip a cog :** to make a mistake — **slip one's trolley** *slang* **:** to lose one's sanity **:** act irrationally — **slip something over :** to foist something on another **:** get the better of another by trickery or taking him unawares
2slip \"\ *n* -s [ME *slippe*, fr. *slippen* to slip] **1 a** (1) **:** a sloping ramp (as of stone) extending out into the water far enough to serve as a landing place for ships (2) **:** an inclined plane on which a ship is built or upon which it is hauled for repair (3) **:** a ship's berth between two piers or wharves **b :** a narrow passageway; *specif* **:** a mountain pass **:** DEFILE **2 :** the act or an instance of slipping out or away **:** secret or hurried departure, escape, or evasion ⟨under cover of night, gave his enemy the ~ and rejoined his convoy —Edward Breck⟩ **3 a :** a mistake in judgment, policy, or procedure **:** BLUNDER ⟨a ~ of presidential timing —*Time*⟩ ⟨one of the ~*s* a wise man sometimes makes —F.L.Mott⟩ **b :** a false step **:** a usu. slight offense or misdeed ⟨make a slight moral ~ — tell a lie, for instance, or smuggle a silk dress through the customhouse —O.W.Holmes †1894⟩ **c :** an unintentional and trivial mistake or fault **:** ERROR, LAPSE ⟨scan the purely mathematical reasoning to make sure that there are no mere ~*s* in it —A.N.Whitehead⟩ ⟨a ~ of the tongue⟩ **4 :** a leash or lead by which a dog is held and which is so made that it can be quickly slipped **5 a :** the act or an instance of slipping down or out of place or control ⟨a ~ on the ice⟩ **:** a sudden mishap ⟨many a ~ between the cup and the lip⟩ **b :** a movement dislocating the parts of a rock mass **:** the result of such a movement or a joint plane on which such a movement has taken place **:** a fault usu. of slight displacement; *specif* **:** one of the components of a fault movement that is confined to the plane of the fault **:** the displacement itself measured in a fault plane — see DIP SLIP, STRIKE SLIP, TOTAL SLIP **c :** displacement of one part of a crystal with respect to another along a particular plane — called also *slippage* **d :** a fall from some level or standard **:** DECLINE ⟨a ~ in stock prices⟩ **6 :** a garment or covering that slips on easily: as **a :** an undergarment made in dress lengths with shoulder straps or in skirt lengths as petticoats **b** *dial Brit* **:** a child's pinafore **c** *chiefly Brit* **:** BATHING SUIT **d :** a cloth covering for a pillow **:** PILLOWCASE **7 a slips** *pl, archaic* **:** the portions of the wings of a theater from which the scenes are slipped into place and where the actors stand just before their entrances **b** *Brit* **:** the sides of the upper gallery of a theater **8 a :** one of several cricket fielders positioned on the off side of the wicketkeeper and behind point **b slips** *n pl but sing in constr* **:** the part of the field in which the slips are placed — see CRICKET illustration **9 a :** the motion of the center of resistance of the float of a paddle wheel or the blade of an oar through the water horizontally; *also* **:** the difference between a ship's actual speed and the speed which it would have if the propeller worked in a solid **b** (1) **:** retrograde movement of a belt on a pulley or vice versa that is in excess of the movement due to expansion and contraction of the belt as its tension varies — compare CREEP 5b (2) **:** the sliding movement of a link relative to a link block that is due to swinging of the link (3) **:** relative motion of parts (as of a clutch or coupling) of a mechanism designed to have none **c :** the difference between the operating and synchronous speed of an induction motor; *also* **:** the ratio of this difference to the synchronous speed of the motor usu. expressed as a percentage **d** (1) **:** a flow of fluid adjacent to a conduit wall that ceases to be laminar and slides along the surface as if it were a solid (2) **:** the amount of leakage past the piston and valves of a pump or the impellers of a blower usu. expressed as a percentage of the nominal flow **e :** the difference between the effective pitch of an airplane propeller and its mean geometrical pitch usu. expressed as a percentage of the latter **f :** a leakage of gas past the rotor of a gas meter **10 :** one of the projecting ends of the cords with which a book is sewed that are used to fasten the book to its covering boards **11 :** noncontagious abortion of a domestic animal ⟨this type of cow would breed itself out because of ~*s* and deaths in early spring —*New Zealand Jour. of Agric.*⟩ **12 a :** a disposition or tendency to slip easily ⟨good ~ is required of a plastic film to facilitate bag making —Walter Egan⟩ **b :** the quality of a paint or enamel that permits easy application with a brush **13 a :** SIDESLIP **b :** the act or an instance of slipping a parachute **14 :** CHASSÉ 1 **syn** see ERROR, WHARF
3slip \"\ *adj* [1*slip*] **1 a :** operating by slipping or sliding ⟨a ~ bar⟩ **b :** DETACHABLE ⟨a ~ compartment⟩ **2 :** having a slipknot **:** operated by means of a slipknot ⟨a ~ cord⟩ **3 :** capable of being released quickly ⟨a ~ bolt⟩
4slip \"\ *n* -s [ME *slippe*, prob. fr. MD or MLG, split, slit, flap of a garment] **1 a :** a small shoot or twig cut for planting or grafting **:** CUTTING, SCION **b :** DESCENDANT, OFFSPRING ⟨a lazy, conceited, whey-faced ~ of gentility —Sir Walter Scott⟩ **c** (1) **:** a pineapple plant developing from a bud at the base of the fruit (2) **:** a rooted sweet potato sprout **2 a :** a long narrow strip of material ⟨~*s* of smooth oakwood, bleached and split —Thomas Wood †1950⟩ ⟨a glass ~⟩ **b** (1) **:** a piece of paper used for a memorandum or record ⟨deposit ~⟩ ⟨sales ~⟩ (2) **:** a usu. small or narrow piece of paper used as an insert in a book or periodical ⟨a cancel ~⟩ ⟨an errata ~⟩ **c** (1) **:** a portion of the columns of a newspaper or other work struck off by itself (2) **:** GALLEY PROOF **3 a** (1) **:** a young and slender person ⟨a ~ of fourteen, just fresh from school —Richard Free⟩ (2) **:** a small and slender or undeveloped specimen — used with *of* ⟨a ~ of a girl⟩ ⟨a ~ of a boy⟩ ⟨an attractive little ~ of a coloratura soprano —Douglas Watt⟩ (3) *Austral* **:** a young pig **b :** a narrow stretch ⟨a thin ~ of gray beach and blue sea —May Sinclair⟩ **c :** a small or unusually narrow instance or example — used with *of* ⟨a ~ of a room which just held a trestle table and a couple of chairs —Edith C. Rivett⟩ ⟨in hard weather he stayed in his snug ~ of a house —Mary Webb⟩ **d :** a long seat or narrow pew in a church ⟨the interior has the old box pews, or ~*s*, each with an individual door —*Amer. Guide Series: Vt.*⟩ **4** *dial chiefly Eng* **:** a hank of yarn **5 :** an imperfectly castrated cockerel that is seldom able to reproduce but lacks the desirable meat-producing characteristics of the capon
5slip \"\ *vt* **slipped; slipped; slipping; slips 1 :** to write or note upon a slip ⟨this use of the word has been *slipped* and filed⟩ **2 :** to replace a book card in (a book) when returned to a library
6slip \"\ *vt* **slipped; slipped; slipping; slips** [ME *slippen* to cut off, prob. fr. MD or MLG, to split, slit] **:** to take cuttings from (a plant) **:** divide into slips ⟨~ a geranium⟩
7slip \"\ *n* -s [ME *slyp* slime, curds, fr. OE *slypa* slime, paste, pulp; akin to OE *slūpan* to slip — more at SLEEVE] **1 a :** a mixture of fine clay and water having the consistency of cream and used in the casting process, for the decoration of ceramic ware, or as a cement for handles and other applied parts **:** SLURRY **b :** enamel or glaze powdered and suspended in water and ready for application **2 :** SKINNING LOAM
8slip \"\ *vt* **slipped; slipped; slipping; slips 1 :** to convert into slip **2 :** to coat with slip
slipband \'=ˌ=\ *n* [2*slip* + *band*] **:** one of the parallel lines on the crystal grains of a material stressed beyond its elastic limit that are visible only under a microscope and are produced by slippages inside the grains
slip bedding *n* **:** the contortion of the earth's stratification planes by slumping or related disturbance during sedimentation
slipboard \'=ˌ=\ *n* [3*slip* + *board*] **:** a board sliding in grooves
slipbody \'=ˌ=\ *n* [2*slip* + *body*] *Scot* **:** a loose bodice
slip carriage *or* **slip coach** *n* [3*slip*] *Brit* **:** a railroad coach or carriage designed to be detached at an intermediate station where the train does not stop
slipcase \'=ˌ=\ *n* [1*slip* + *case*] **:** a protective container with one open end for books or other objects of similar shape and size — called also *slipcover*
slip casting *n* [7*slip*] **:** the process of forming ceramic ware by pouring slip into usu. plaster molds
slip coupling *n* [3*slip*] **1 :** a form of coupling adapted for use on slip carriages **2 :** a coupling designed to slip at heavy loads and thus relieve the duty on the driving unit
1slipcover \'=ˌ==\ *n* [1*slip* + *cover*] **1 :** a cover that may be slipped off and on; *specif* **:** a protective or decorative usu. cloth or plastic covering for furniture (as sofas and chairs) that is usu. designed to fit closely **2 a :** a paper or fabric cover that is readily slipped on or off a book **:** JACKET **b :** SLIPCASE
2slipcover \"\ *vt* **:** to cover with a slipcover ⟨~ a chair in chintz⟩ ⟨an unusual decorative screen that you can ~ . . . to match the other fabric furnishings —*House Beautiful*⟩

slip decision *n* [⁴*slip*] **:** an advance or early and separate printing of a court's decision that is made available at or shortly after the time it is announced and before it is available in the regular court reports

¹slipe \'slīp\ *vt* -ED/-ING/-S [ME *slypen*] **1** *dial Brit* **:** to remove an outer covering from **:** PEEL, PARE, STRIP **2** *dial Brit* **:** to cut off **:** SLICE

²slipe \"\ *or* **slipe wool** *n* -s **:** pulled wool removed from skins by a lime process

³slipe \"\ *n* -s [ME, fr. MLG *slīpe, slēpe;* akin to MLG *slippen* to slip — more at SLIP] *dial Eng* **:** SLEIGH, SLED

⁴slipe \"\ *n* -s [origin unknown] *dial Brit & Midland* **:** a thin narrow strip esp. of land

slip face *n* [²*slip*] **:** the lee side of a dune where the slope approximates the angle of rest of loose sand that is generally about 33 degrees

slip form *n* [¹*slip*] **:** a form that can be moved slowly as concrete placing progresses and that is used extensively in building tall storage bins and occas. in widening existing pavements

slip friction *or* **slip friction clutch** *n* [²*slip*] **:** a friction clutch permitting slip when excessive power is transmitted

slip gage *n* [¹*slip*] **:** GAGE BLOCK

slip glaze *n* [⁷*slip*] **:** a glazing material applied in a liquid state before firing

slip grab *n* [³*slip*] **:** a pear-shaped link attachment for a whiffletree or evener that grips the skidding chain when the narrow end is down but otherwise permits the chain to slip — called also *grab link*

slip gun *n* **:** a single-action revolver having its trigger tied down or so altered that the piece may be fired by retracting the hammer and allowing it to fall

slip hook *n* **:** a hook so arranged as to be automatically or easily unhooked — called also *trip hook;* compare PELICAN HOOK

sliphorn \'=,=\ *n* **:** TROMBONE

sliphouse \'=,=\ *n* [⁷*slip*] **:** a building where slip is made

slip joint *n* [³*slip*] **1 a :** a telescopic joint between two parts (as a piece of tubing and packing material in a stuffing box) that permits the parts to move in a lengthwise direction **b :** a joint formed by slipping one part over another of nearly the same size and uniting the two (as by brazing) **2 :** a channel or groove cut in an existing wall to receive the ends of the brick of a new wall

slip-joint pliers *n pl but sing or pl in constr* **:** pliers having the joint adjustable to two positions so as to obtain either a wide or a narrow opening for the jaws

slip key *n* [⁴*slip*] **:** a cash register key that upon being depressed actuates a mechanism that certifies a sales slip usu. by printing on it pertinent information (as the number or amount of the sale)

slipknot \'=,=\ *n* [³*slip*] **:** a knot that slips along the rope or line around which it is made; *esp* **:** one made by tying an overhand knot around the standing part of a rope

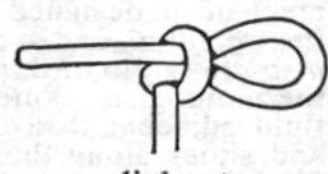

slipknot

slip-lasted \'=,==\ *adj* [¹*slip* + *lasted*, past part. of ⁷*last*] **:** manufactured by the California process — used of shoes

slip law *n* [⁴*slip*] **:** an early and separate print of a statute (as of the U. S. Congress) made available immediately after enactment and before the regular appearance of a permanent edition of collected statutes (as the statutes at large)

slip line *n* [²*slip*] **:** SLIPBAND

slip·man \'slipmən\ *n, pl* **slipmen 1 :** JACKER c(1) **2 :** one who operates a slip or wheeled scoop (as for moving earth or coal)

slip mortise *n* [¹*slip*] **:** a mortise cut through to the end of a piece

slipmouth \'=,=\ *n* **:** any of numerous small compressed slimy bodied percoid fishes (genus *Leiognathus*) with highly protrusible mouths that are widely distributed in the Indian ocean and tropical parts of the Pacific and are often dried for food

slip noose *n* [³*slip*] **:** a noose with a slipknot

slip-off slope \'=,=-\ *n* [¹*slip*] **:** a comparatively gentle slope often produced on the downstream face of a meander spur

slip-on \'=,=\ *n* -s [¹*slip* + *on*] **:** an article of clothing that is easily slipped on or off: as **a :** a glove or shoe without fastenings **b :** a garment (as a girdle) that one steps into and pulls up **c :** PULLOVER

slipover \'=,==\ *n* -s **:** a garment or cover that slips over and off easily; *specif* **:** a sweater that is pulled on over the head

slip·page \'slipij, -pēj\ *n* -s [¹*slip* + *-age*] **1 :** the act or an instance of slipping out of place or failing to hold ⟨permits surgeon to tie with the finest of silk without ~ —*Armamentarium*⟩ ⟨the ~ of the tires on the ice⟩: as **a :** a shifting of threads in fabric when subjected to strain **b :** SLIP 5c **2 :** the act or an instance of falling off from a standard or level or the amount by which something falls off ⟨an indication of the ~ that can take place when training is let go —R.L.Moberly⟩: as **a** (1) **:** a loss in working (as in transmission of power) (2) **:** the difference between theoretical and actual output (as of power) **b** (1) **:** a lag in production of goods (2) **:** the difference between scheduled and actual production

slipped \'slipt\ *adj* [⁴*slip* + *-ed*] *of a heraldic plant* **:** having its stalk attached

slipped coat *n* [*slipped*, past part. of ⁸*slip* + *coat*] **:** FINISHING COAT

slipped disk *n* [*slipped* (past part. of ¹slip) + *disk*] **:** a protrusion of an intervertebral disk and its nucleus pulposus that produces pressure upon spinal nerves resulting in low back pain and often sciatic pain

slipped epiphysis *n* **:** EPIPHYSIOLYSIS

slipped tendon *also* **slipped tendon disease** *n* **:** perosis of poultry

slipped wing *n* **:** a fowl's wing that does not fold closely or that folds with some of the primaries extending below the secondaries

¹slip·per \'slipə(r)\ *adj* [ME *sliper, slipper* — more at SLIPPERY] **1** *chiefly dial* **:** SLIPPERY **2** *chiefly dial* **:** PLIANT, WILLOWY

²slipper \"\ *n* -s [ME, fr. *slippen* to slip + *-er*] **1 a :** a light shoe; *specif* **:** a low-cut shoe that is easily slipped on the foot, is held to the foot by means of the upper usu. without the aid of lacing or other fastening, and is made in various styles for either informal or formal indoor wear **b** *dial* **:** OXFORD 1 **2 a :** one that releases the leash of a hound in a coursing event **b :** ROSSER a **3 a :** SLIPPER BRAKE **b :** GIB 1 **4 :** something that is shaped like a slipper; *specif* **:** the lip of an orchid

³slipper \"\ *vb* -ED/-ING/-S *vt* **1 :** to strike with a slipper ⟨~*ed* him across the fingers⟩ **2 :** to put into slippers ⟨~*ed* her feet in bits of fluff —Truman Capote⟩ ~ *vi* **:** to walk in slippers **:** SHUFFLE ⟨~*ing* across the room from her bed —R.O.Bowen⟩

slipper animalcule *n* [²*slipper*] **:** a ciliated protozoan of the genus *Paramecium* (esp. *P. caudatum*) that is shaped somewhat like a slipper

slipper brake *n* **1 :** a metal plate or skid used under the wheel or pushed against the roadway or track to retard the motion of a vehicle **2 :** a metal plate slipped against a moving part of a machine to retard or stop its motion

slipper chair *n* **:** an often upholstered chair with short legs designed for bedroom use

slip·pered \'slipə(r)d\ *adj* [²*slipper* + *-ed*] **1 :** provided with or wearing slippers ⟨the sixth age shifts into the lean and ~ pantaloon —Shak.⟩ **2 :** suggestive of or suitable to one wearing slippers **:** COMFORTABLE **:** RELAXED ⟨an easy, ~ prose —B.R.Redman⟩ ⟨the ~ ease of a small-town family man —*Time*⟩

slipperflower \'==,=\ *n* [²*slipper*] **1 :** SLIPPERWORT **2 :** SLIPPER PLANT

slipper foot *n* **:** SNAKE FOOT

slipper-foxed \'==;=\ *adj* [²*slipper* + *foxed*, past part. of *fox*] **:** having a vamp extending back over the heel and taking the place of the foxing or counter ⟨a *slipper-foxed* shoe⟩

slipper chair

slip·per·i·ly \'slip(ə)rəlē\ *adv* **:** in a slippery manner

slip·per·i·ness \-rēnəs, -rin-\ *n* -ES **:** the quality or state of being slippery

slipper limpet *or* **slipper shell** *n* [²*slipper*] **:** a mollusk of *Crepidula* or a related genus that is sometimes a serious pest of oyster beds

slipper plant *n* **1 :** a tropical American plant of the genus *Pedilanthus* having slipper-shaped involucres **2** *or* **slipper orchid :** LADY'S SLIPPER

slipper-root \'==,=\ *n* **:** a yellow lady's slipper (*Cypripedium parviflorum*)

slipper satin *n* **:** a strong heavy stiff satin with a high luster that is used chiefly for evening dresses and wraps and women's footwear

slipperweed \'==,=\ *n* **:** JEWELWEED

slipperwort \'==,=\ *n* **:** a plant of the genus *Calceolaria*

slip·pery \'slip(ə)rē, -ri\ *adj, sometimes* -ER/-EST [alter. (perh. influenced by LG *slipperig* slippery) of ME *sliper, slipper* slippery, fr. OE *slipor;* akin to MLG *slipper* slippery, OHG *sleffar*, MLG *slippen* to slip — more at SLIP (slide)] **1 a :** causing one to slide or fall down ⟨a new mountain road ~ with mud —Carleton Beals⟩ ⟨the ~ track made walking difficult —T.E. Lawrence⟩ **b :** tending to slide from the grasp **:** not easily held ⟨a running attack operated by half a dozen fast and ~ runners —Rogers Whitaker⟩ ⟨a ~ fabric⟩ ⟨a ~ fish⟩ **2 a :** not firmly fixed **:** UNCERTAIN, UNSTABLE ⟨to maintain his ~ position he needed more than cash, he needed prestige —G.W.Johnson⟩ **b :** not precise or fixed in meaning **:** AMBIGUOUS, ELUSIVE ⟨his style is so ~ that it is hard to tell what he really believes —J.N. Leonard⟩ ⟨the ~ term romanticism —M.W.Fishwick⟩ **3 a :** not to be trusted **:** SHIFTY, TRICKY ⟨those whom he knew to be ~ and double-faced —C.G.Bowers⟩ ⟨proved to be a ~ witness —Robert Coughlan⟩ **b :** marked by evasion, deceit, or trickery ⟨~ devices⟩ ⟨~ maneuvers⟩ **4 :** IMMORAL, WANTON ⟨~ looks of love —James Thomson †1748⟩

slippery dick *n* **:** a small brightly colored wrasse (*Halichoeres bivittatus*) of the warm western Atlantic

slippery elm *n* **1 a :** a No. American elm (*Ulmus rubra*) with rough leaves, short-pediceled flowers, and hard wood **b :** the wood of slippery elm **c :** the fragrant mucilaginous bark of slippery elm **2 :** FLANNELBUSH

slippery hitch *n* **:** a single hitch with the end doubled back under the standing part in such a way that a pull on the end releases the knot

slipperyroot \'=(=)=,=\ *n* **:** a common comfrey (*Symphytum officinale*)

slippery slide *n* **:** SLIDE 5a(2)

slipping *pres part of* SLIP

slip plane *n* [²*slip*] **:** a plane surface through a crystal along which slip can take place under some conditions without apparently disrupting the crystal

slip proof *n* [⁴*slip*] **:** GALLEY PROOF

slip·py \'slipē, -pi\ *adj* -ER/-EST [¹*slip* + *-y*] **1 :** SLIPPERY ⟨the streets were still ~ and slimy from the rain —Bruce Marshall⟩ **2** *chiefly Brit* **:** ALERT, ALIVE, WIDE-AWAKE ⟨waiter, get this gentleman friend of mine a glass of port, and look ~ —E.F. Benson⟩

sliprail \'=,=\ *n* [³*slip* + *rail*] *Austral* **:** one of a set of movable rails in a fence that can be taken out to form a gateway **:** DRAWBAR ⟨rode down toward the ~s of the scrubbers' paddock —F.D.Davison⟩

slip regulator *n* [²*slip*] **:** a usu. variable rheostat connected across the collector rings of a wound-rotor induction motor for regulating the speed or slip of the motor

slip ring *n* **:** COLLECTOR RING 1 — see MAGNETO illustration

slip rope *n* [³*slip*] **1 :** a rope by which a cable is secured preparatory to clearing hawse **2 :** a rope so fastened that it can easily and quickly be unfastened

slips \'slips\ *n pl but sing in constr* [fr. pl. of ²*slip*] **:** an accidental slipping of a taw from the hand of a marbles player as he is about to shoot

slip scraper *n* [³*slip*] **:** BUCK SCRAPER

slip seat *n* **:** a chair or settee seat either upholstered or made of rushes and built so as to rest in a rabbeted frame from which it can be lifted

slip seed *n* [⁴*slip*] **:** small sweet potatoes produced one year from cuttings for use as seed stock for the next year — compare CROP SEED

slip share *n* **:** a plowshare that is independent of the landside

slip sheet *n* [¹*slip*] **1 :** a sheet of paper placed between newly printed sheets to prevent offsetting **2 :** a protective sheet of paper placed between adjacent surfaces (as of bound books packed together)

slip-sheet \'=,=\ *vt* [*slip sheet*] **1 :** to interleave (as printed sheets) with slip sheets **2 :** to protect (as books) with slip sheets

slip-shelled \'=;=\ *adj* [³*slip*] **:** having a shell that slips off easily — used of nuts

slip·shod \'slip,shäd\ *adj* [¹*slip* + *shod*] **1 a :** wearing shoes or slippers that are loose or worn at the heel **b :** down at the heel **:** SHABBY ⟨~ shoes⟩ ⟨a small ~ girl in a dirty coarse apron —Charles Dickens⟩ **2 a :** careless and informal in style ⟨writes with the fluent ~ ease of a letter writer —*Edinburgh Rev.*⟩ **b :** not caring for or observant of exactness **:** lacking precision **:** INACCURATE ⟨is surprisingly ~ in his own use of words and his own thought —L.S.Woolf⟩ ⟨was at first a ~ observer . . . he had a positive distaste for exactitude —D.C. Peattie⟩ **c :** marked by indifference or carelessness **:** SLOVENLY ⟨these are days of fast, careless, ~ work —E.B.Barrett⟩ ⟨his own research is sketchy and frequently ~ —M.W.Straight⟩

syn SLOVENLY, UNKEMPT, DISHEVELED, SLOPPY: SLIPSHOD may imply an acceptance of the shabby, worn out, imperfect, unsound, or inexact that is careless, indifferent, or apathetic ⟨dressed hastily and roughly, in a *slipshod* way⟩ ⟨though facile, he had the conscientious craftsman's contempt for *slipshod* work —J.D.Spaeth⟩ SLOVENLY is a strong antonym for *neat* or *tidy* implying an extreme disorderly carelessness and lazy negligent indifference ⟨a long column — a *slovenly* column that marched irregularly and out of step —Kenneth Roberts⟩ ⟨she had become *slovenly* at home: she no longer reddened the hearth with pounded brick-dust, she no longer scrubbed the floor boards white and clean. Cobwebs hung in the corners —Lyle Saxon⟩ UNKEMPT implies negligent lack of ordinary care about grooming, smoothing, cleaning, refining, and maintaining ⟨a somewhat dilapidated house, badly in need of a new coat of paint. The garden round it was *unkempt* and weedy and the gate hung askew —Agatha Christie⟩ ⟨abandoned mills, general stores, and *unkempt* houses, an air of crumbling decadence prevailing in the sidehill settlement —*Amer. Guide Series: Vt.*⟩ DISHEVELED may suggest the ruffled disorder or disarray brought on by exertion, strenuous exercise, or coping with a series of exigent demands ⟨the white oxen of Clitumnus are loaded with gaudy flowers, and the dancing maidens are *disheveled* Maenads —J.A.Symonds⟩ SLOPPY may suggest a careless, loose, or messy abandon ⟨couldn't you even take the trouble to notice that you had a spot of soot on your nose tonight . . . why are you so *sloppy?* —Sinclair Lewis⟩

slip·shod·di·ness \-dēnəs\ *n* -ES [irreg. fr. *slipshod* + *-ness*] **:** SLIPSHODNESS

slip·shod·ness *n* -ES **:** the quality or state of being slipshod **:** SLOVENLINESS ⟨a combination of apparent ~ and actual precision —John Gunther⟩

slip sill *n* [³*slip*] **:** a sill that can be slipped into position between the jambs of an opening

slipskin \'=,=\ *n* [¹*slip* + *skin*] **1 :** gray mold rot of grapes caused by a fungus of the genus *Botrytis* **2 :** a grape in which the skin slips readily from the pulp

slip-slop \'slip,släp\ *n* [redupl. of ²*slop*] **1** *archaic* **a :** a watery food **:** a thin weak liquid **:** SLOPS **2** *archaic* **a :** a verbal blunder **:** MALAPROPISM **b :** a person given to making such blunders **3 :** shallow or meaningless talk or writing **:** TWADDLE ⟨the mass of ~ poured forth by the daily and weekly press —Frances Trollope⟩ ⟨the miserable, twaddling ~ that he is obliged to hear from and utter to her —W.M.Thackeray⟩ **4** [imit.] **:** a slip-slopping sound or movement ⟨the scurry of a hare, the ~ of my feet —J.A.Phillimore⟩

¹slip-slop \"\ *adj* [*slipslop*] **1** *archaic* **:** given to or marked by verbal blundering **2 :** lacking in solidity or content **:** INANE, WISHY-WASHY ⟨talked *slip-slop* commonplaces with them; they spoke of the country and the weather, and he of the city —Samuel Lover⟩

²slip-slop \"\ *vi* [imit.] **:** to move about in loose slippers or to make the flapping sound produced by or as if by such movement ⟨laid him in a crib and *slip-slopped* down to serve dinner —Anne Green⟩ ⟨his untidily shod feet *slip-slopping* on the wooden floor —Rafael Sabatini⟩

slipsole \'=,=\ *n* [¹*slip* + *sole*] **1 :** a thin insole **2 :** a half sole inserted between the insole or welt and the outsole of a shoe to give additional height — called also *slip tap*

slipstick \'=,=\ *n* [³*slip*] **:** SLIDE RULE

slip stitch *n* [¹*slip*] **1 :** a concealed stitch for sewing folded edges (as hems, facings, or appliqués) made by alternately running the needle inside the fold and picking up a thread or two from the body of the article **2 :** an unworked stitch; *esp* **:** a knitting stitch that is shifted from one needle to another without knitting in it

slip-stitch \'=,=\ *vt* [*slip stitch*] **:** to sew with slip stitches ⟨*slip-stitch* facing to a garment⟩

slipstone \'=,=\ *n* [¹*slip* + *stone*] **:** a small whetstone having a cross section like that of a wedge and usu. having one or both edges rounded

slip stopper *n* [²*slip*] **:** a cable stopper consisting of a short length of chain with a pelican hook at the end and intended to be used when the cable is let go suddenly

slipstream \'=,=\ *n* [²*slip* + *stream*] **:** the stream of air driven aft by the propeller of an aircraft and having a velocity relative to the engine greater than that of the surrounding body of still air — called also *propeller race, race of the propeller*

slipstring \'=,=\ *n* [¹*slip* + *string*] *archaic* **:** SCAPEGALLOWS

slip switch *n* [¹*slip*] **:** a crossing frog containing either one or two connecting tracks that serve as short turnouts

slipt *archaic past of* SLIP

slip tap *n* [¹*slip*] **:** SLIPSOLE 2

slip tongue *n* **:** a tongue that slips between two steel plates joining the fore hounds of a vehicle and into a stirrup supported under a crossbar with lengthwise movement of the tongue being prevented by a bolt that passes through holes in the tongue and steel plates

slip-tongue wheel *n* **:** a two-wheeled logging truck in which the load is suspended under an axle or arch and whose design is such that on a downgrade the end of the tongue slips out of a stirrup so as to let one end of the logs drop to the road and act as a brake

slip up *vi* [¹*slip* + *up*] **:** to make a mistake **:** BLUNDER ⟨*slipped up* in his calculations⟩

slipup \'=,=\ *n* -s **:** the act or an instance of slipping up **:** MISTAKE ⟨through some ~ — a lost file, a technicality — I was to spend a few mistaken hours here —Andy Logan⟩

slipware \'=,=\ *n* [⁷*slip*] **:** pottery coated with slip to improve the surface or change the color

slipway \'=,=\ *n* [¹*slip*] **:** an inclined way: as **a :** one of the ways on which the cradle of a marine railway travels — usu. used in pl. **b :** BUILDING SLIP **c :** an inclined passageway in the stern of a whaling ship by which whales are hauled in

¹slit \'slit, *usu* -id·+V\ *vt* **slit; slit; slitting; slits** [ME *slitten;* akin to MHG *slitzen* to slit; akin to OE *slītan* to tear apart, OHG *slīzan*, ON *slīta*, Lith *skélti* to split — more at SHELL] **1 a :** to make a slit in **:** cut lengthwise **:** SLASH ⟨~ the huge envelope clumsily with the paper knife —Lawrence Durrell⟩ ⟨his two motorboats ~ the waters of the sound —Scott Fitzgerald⟩ **b :** to cut off or away **:** SEVER ⟨be his tongue ~ for his insolence —P.B.Shelley⟩ **2 :** to cut (as film or paper) into long narrow strips **syn** see CUT

²slit \"\ *n* -s [ME *slitte*, fr. *slitten* to slit] **:** a long narrow cut or opening ⟨a ~ in the jacket⟩ ⟨the window was no more than a ~ in the wall⟩: as **a :** a narrow opening in a dome or in the roof and sidewalls of an observing room through which a telescope is pointed at the celestial bodies **b :** a narrow usu. rectangular opening through which light or other emission is admitted (as to the collimator of a spectroscope) or through which it escapes (as from a black-body cavity) **c :** an aperture in the optical system of photographic sound recorders and reproducers that limits the height of the scanned area to less than a wavelength of the shortest wavelength signal to be recorded or reproduced

³slit \"\ *adj* **1 :** shaped like a slit **:** long and narrow ⟨fat-padded ~ eyes —Weston La Barre⟩ **2 :** having a slit ⟨a ~ skirt⟩ ⟨~ limpet⟩ **3 :** produced through a wide shallow opening formed at the free end of the tongue ⟨a ~ fricative such as \th\⟩ — compare GROOVE

⁴slit \"\ *vt* **slitted; slitted; slitting; slits :** to form into a slit **:** NARROW ⟨morning sunlight flooded in upon him, and he *slitted* his eyes against the glare —J.R.Ullman⟩

slit deal *n* [fr. past part. of ¹*slit*] **:** a deal board ⅝ of an inch thick — compare WHOLE DEAL

slit-drum \'=,=\ *n* **:** a primitive drum orig. consisting of a tree trunk hollowed out like a boat and played by stamping

slite \'slīt\ *n* -s [fr. obs. *slite* to split, wear out, fr. ME *sliten*, fr. OE *slītan* to tear apart — more at SLIT] *dial Eng* **:** WEAR AND TEAR

slit-eyed \'=;=\ *adj* [³*slit* + *eyed*] **:** having narrow eyes

¹slith·er \'slithə(r)\ *vb* **slithered; slithered; slithering** \-th(ə)riŋ\ **slithers** [ME *slideren, slitheren*, fr. OE *sliderian, slidrian*, freq. of *slīdan* to slide] *vi* **1 a :** to slide on or as if on a loose gravelly surface ⟨the sharp stones which were loosened as his toe caps ~*ed* over them —Fred Majdalany⟩ **b :** to move or proceed by slipping or sliding ⟨learnt to skate, ~*ing* over the five miles to and fro along the frozen . . . road —H.W.Nevinson⟩ ⟨horse-drawn sleds ~*ed* across the snowy pavement —Truman Capote⟩ **2 :** to walk or move in a sinuous undulating way **:** GLIDE ⟨a ~*ing* sinister creature who snakes her way out from her table —Leland Miles⟩ ⟨the brown trout ~*ed* among the shallow stones —W.C.Williams⟩ ⟨the traditional ticker tape ~*ed* down on the marching men —*Time*⟩ ~ *vt* **1 :** to cause to slide ⟨the wind had ~*ed* them through that narrow gap —Marguerite Lyon⟩ **2 :** to thin and taper (the hair) with upward strokes of a cutting edge along a small strand

²slither \"\ *n* -s **1 :** loose gravel **:** RUBBLE ⟨cascaded the great talus of ~ and reached the surf-belt of shingle —Christopher Morley⟩ **2 a :** the act or an instance of sliding **:** a gliding or slipping movement ⟨a ~ of his right foot on the wet pavement —Liam O'Flaherty⟩ ⟨was through the door with the smooth ~ of a weasel —J.H.Wheelwright⟩ **b :** a sound produced by or as if by a smooth gliding movement ⟨the soft ~ of the fountain in the sunk garden —Mary Austin⟩ ⟨heard the rush and ~ of breaking waves —William Beebe⟩

slith·ery \-th(ə)rē, -ri\ *adj* [¹*slither* + *-y*] **:** having a slippery surface, texture, or quality ⟨steep footpaths that are coated with ~ mud —Christopher Rand⟩ ⟨the ~ gloss of thick dust —Leslie Charteris⟩

slit lamp *n* [³*slit*] **:** a lamp for projecting a narrow beam of intense light into an eye to facilitate microscopic study (as of the conjunctiva or cornea)

slit·less \'slitləs\ *adj* **:** not having a slit ⟨a ~ spectroscope⟩

slitted *past of* SLIT

¹slit·ter \'slid·ə(r), -itə-\ *vt* -ED/-ING/-S [ME *sliteren, slitteren*, freq. of *slitten* to slit] **:** to cut the edge of (a garment) in ornamental slits

²slitter \"\ *n* -s [¹*slit* + *-er*] **1 :** a slitting machine or device: as **a :** a thin wheel of bronze or soft steel charged with diamond dust or emery for slitting or sawing precious stones **b :** a rapidly revolving sharpened disk for trimming or cutting a web of paper into narrower rolls **c :** a machine for slitting motion-picture film **2 :** an operator of a machine for slitting (as metal, textiles, paper, or plastics)

slitting *pres part of* SLIT

slitting file *n* **:** a blunt file of narrow lozenge section

slitting saw *n* **:** a circular saw or thin milling cutter for cutting metal

slitting shears *n pl* **:** a shearing machine for cutting sheet metal; *esp* **:** ROTARY SHEARS

slit trench *n* [³*slit*] **:** a usu. narrow and relatively shallow trench dug for individual protection during combat esp. against bomb and shell fragments — compare FOXHOLE

slitwork \'=,=\ *n* [*slit* (past part. of ¹*slit*) + *work*] **:** thin boards used as sheathing

¹slive \'slīv\ *vt* -ED/-ING/-S [ME *sliven*, fr. (assumed) OE *slīfan* (whence *tōslīfan* to split); prob. akin to OE *slītan* to tear apart — more at SLIT] *dial chiefly Eng* **:** to slice off or cut through

2slive \"\ *vi* **slove** \'slōv\ **slived; sliving; slives** [obs. *slive* to cause to slip, slip (clothes) on, to slip away, fr. ME *sliven*, alter. of *sleven*, fr. OE *slēfan* to slip (clothes) on — more at SLEEVE] *dial chiefly Eng* : to move furtively : SIDLE

1sliv·er \'slivə(r), *in sense 2 usu* 'slīv-\ *n* -s [ME *slivere*, fr. *sliven* to slive + *-ere* -er] **1 a** : a long slender piece cut or torn off : SPLINTER ⟨a piece of apple pie with a ~ of cheese on top —F.C.Othman⟩ ⟨was building up the fire with split logs and pine ~s —William Faulkner⟩ **b** : something that is small and narrow : FRAGMENT ⟨the initial quarrel over the ~s of land was intense —*Foreign Policy Bull.*⟩ ⟨a ~ of an apartment in an old-fashioned small hotel —Mollie Panter-Downes⟩ **c** : a piece of bait sliced from a small fish **2 a** (1) : a loose soft untwisted strand or rope of textile fiber produced by a carding or combing machine and ready for drawing or roving (2) : a similar strand of wool fiber delivered by a carding machine and ready to be spun into yarn **b** : an untwisted strand of glass fibers produced from molten glass

2sliver \'slivə(r), 'slīv-\ *vb* -ED/-ING/-S *vt* **1** *obs* : to cut off in the form of a sliver ⟨slips of yew, ~*ed* in the moon's eclipse —Shak.⟩ **2** : to cut into slivers : reduce to slivers : SLICE, SPLINTER ⟨chopped the broccoli and ~*ed* the salad —Grace Reiten⟩ **3** : to cut slivers from (a fish) ⟨helped . . . to ~ porgies for the trawls —Sarah O. Jewett⟩ ~ *vi* : to become split into slivers ⟨the war decided that the United States should not ~ into two, three, or four fragments —Allan Nevins⟩

sliver lap *n* : cotton slivers combined into a wide strand and wound into a cylindrical roll

sliver lapper *n* [*sliver lap* + *-er*] : a textile machine for forming sliver laps; *also* : the operator of such a machine

sliv·o·vitz *also* **sliv·o·vic** \'slivə,vits\ *n* -ES [Serbo-Croatian *šljivovica*, fr. *šljiva*, *sliva* plum; akin to Russ *sliva* plum — more at LIVID] : a dry usu. colorless plum brandy made esp. in Hungary and the Balkan countries

sliv·ver \'slivə(r)\ *Scot var of* SLOBBER

sloak *var of* SLOKE

sloa·nea \'slōnēə\ *n, cap* [NL, fr. Sir Hans *Sloane* †1753 Brit. naturalist] : a large genus of tropical timber trees (family Elaeocarpaceae) having alternate leaves, small apetalous flowers with numerous stamens, a spiny or hairy 4-valved capsule, and usu. very hard wood — see BREAKAX; compare IRONWOOD

sloat *var of* SLOTE

slob \'släb\ *n* -s [Ir *slab*, prob. of Scand origin; akin to Sw dial. *slabb* slime, mud — more at SLAB (mud)] **1** *chiefly Irish* **a** : MUD, MIRE, OOZE **b** : a tract of muddy ground; *esp* : 2FLAT 1a (2) **2** : a heavy sludge of sea ice **3** : a slack, ungainly, or common person : someone mean, rude, or undistinguished : BOOR, CLOD, VULGARIAN ⟨a bunch of ~s and stuffed shirts —H.A.Smith⟩ ⟨the translator who ignores or evades this responsibility is a ~ —Rolfe Humphries⟩

1slob·ber \'släbə(r)\ *n* -s [partly fr. ME *slober* mud, slush; partly fr. 2*slobber*; akin to MD *slobbe* slime, mud, mire, *slobberen* to walk through mud or mire, D *slobber* swill, slush and prob. to LG *slubberen* to sip, lap] **1** *chiefly dial* : a sloppy mess (as of rain and sleet or slush and mud) **2** : the slaver or drool of excessive salivation : spittle drooled from the mouth **3** : driveling, sloppy, or incoherent speech or expression : inarticulate utterance ⟨a mere helpless ~ of disconnected vowel noises —Henry James †1916⟩ ⟨some essays . . . I thought were ~, if that is worse than drool —O.W.Holmes †1935⟩ **4 slobbers** \-)z\ *pl but usu sing in constr* : excessive salivation; *specif* : more or less chronic drooling or salivation in rabbits usu. associated with excessive consumption of green feed but sometimes symptomatic of coccidiosis or of dental troubles

2slob·ber \"\ *vb* **slobbered; slobbered; slobbering** \-b(ə)riŋ\ **slobbers** [ME *sloberen*; akin to LG *slubberen* to sip, lap, *sluf* loose, slack, tired, OFris *luf* slack, tired, ON *lūfa* thick hair, MD *lobbe* thick underlip, Lith *lūpa* lip, *slubnas* slack, tired, drooping; basic meaning: slack, loose] *vi* **1 a** : to let saliva fall or dribble from the mouth : DROOL, SLAVER ⟨bit . . . could cause a horse to ~ and bleed at the mouth —Bruce Siberts⟩ **b** : to let liquid spill or dribble from the mouth in eating or drinking **2** : to gush with effusive or unrestrained emotion or sentiment : indulge the feelings unchecked ⟨later writers ~*ed* over the mountains . . . with extensive extracts from the Lake poets —A.S.Pease⟩ ⟨when he reads the works of American historians . . . he can only ~ in abject frustration —C.M.Wilson⟩ ~ *vt* **1 a** : to wet and smear with dribbling saliva or with food or drink spilled from the mouth ⟨the baby ~*ed* his bib⟩ **b** : to spill or let drip so as to smear or soil ⟨~*ed* the medicine on his nightclothes⟩ **2 a** : to kiss very wetly or implant very juicy kisses on **b** : to utter or speak in a slurred, thick, or inarticulate way ⟨~*ed* one song out of his scraggy and ulcerous face —Robert Lynd⟩ **3** : to handle or perform in sloppy or slovenly fashion

slobberchops \'⸗⸗,⸗\ *n pl but sing or pl in constr* [2*slobber* + *chops* (mouth)] : SLOBBERER

slob·ber·er \-bərə(r)\ *n* -s : one that slobbers

slob·ber·han·nes \,s(h)läbər'hänəs\ *n* -ES [G dial. *schlabberhans*, *schlabberhannes* sloppy eater, gossiper, fr. *schlabbern* to eat sloppily, slaver, gossip + *Hans*, *Hannes*, nickname for *Johann*, *Johannes* John — more at SLAVER] : a variation of the game of hearts in which the object is to avoid winning the first and last tricks and any trick containing the queen of clubs

slob·bery \'släb(ə)rē, -ri\ *adj* [ME *slobery*, fr. *slober* slobber + *-y*] **1** : MUDDY, SLUSHY, DIRTY ⟨a ~ and a dirty farm —Shak.⟩ **2 a** : marked by drooling or slobbering **b** : marked by ungoverned or gushy sentimentality **3** : SLACK, SLOVENLY

slob·by \'släbē\ *adj* -ER/-EST [*slob* + *-y*] **1** : MUDDY **2** : SLOBBERY

slob land *n* **1** : muddy soil; *esp* : reclaimed alluvial land **2** : a tract of muddy soil

slob trout *n* : a trout from brackish water (as of an estuary)

1slock \'släk\ *vt* -ED/-ING/-S [ME *sloken*, of Scand origin; akin to ON *slokinn* extinguished, *slokna* to extinguish] *dial Brit* : QUENCH, DRENCH

2slock \"\ *n* -s [prob. fr. 1*slock*] *chiefly Scot* : DRINK, SWALLOW

3slock \"\ *vt* -ED/-ING/-S [ME *slocken*] *dial Eng* : ENTICE, LURE

slock·en \'släkən\ *vt* -ED/-ING/-S [ME *slockenen*, *slokenen*, of Scand origin; akin to ON *slokna* to extinguish, exhaust, *loka* to let hang loosely; akin to LG *slokeren* to hang loosely, MLG *slūren* to drag, trail — more at SLUR] *chiefly Scot* : QUENCH, EXTINGUISH

slod [alter. of earlier *slode*, fr. ME *slood*, fr. OE *slād*] *dial past of* SLIDE

sloe \'slō\ *n* -s [ME *slo*, fr. OE *slāh*, *slā*; akin to OHG *slēha* sloe, Sw *slån* sloe, L *livēre* to be blue — more at LIVID] **1 a** : a small globose and pruinose dark-colored plum with astringent green flesh that is the fruit of the blackthorn and is used esp. for preserves and as a flavoring for liquors **b** : BLACKTHORN 1a **2** : any of various American wild plums **3** : BLACK HAW 1

sloe·ber·ry \'slō- — *see* BERRY\ *n* **1** : the fruit of the common juniper **2** : SLOE 1

sloebush *or* **sloetree** \'⸗,⸗\ *n* [*sloebush* fr. *sloe* + *bush*; *sloetree* fr. ME *slotre*, fr. *slo* sloe + *tre* tree — more at TREE] : BLACKTHORN 1a

sloe–eyed \'⸗'⸗\ *adj* **1** : having soft dark bluish or purplish black eyes **2** : having slanted eyes

sloe gin *n* : a sweet reddish liqueur consisting of grain spirits flavored chiefly with sloeberries from the blackthorn

1slog \'släg *also* -lȯg\ *vb* **slogged; slogged; slogging; slogs** [origin unknown] *vt* **1 a** : to hit hard : BEAT **b** : DRIVE ⟨*slogged* his horse relentlessly on⟩ **c** (1) : to hit hard in cricket (2) : SCORE **2 a** : to make (one's way) by dogged plodding (as in difficult terrain or in mud) **b** : to plod (one's way) perseveringly through a task or career esp. against difficulty, opposition, or adversity ⟨*slogged* his way steadily up through the business ranks⟩ ~ *vi* **1** : to plod heavily (as through mud) : tramp a long or arduous route ⟨*slogged* through the already softening drifts —Farley Mowat⟩ **2** : to work hard and steadily : PLUG ⟨been *slogging* away at this business for 15 years —Laurence Harvey⟩ **syn** see STRIKE

2slog \"\ *n* -s **1 a** : a hard dogged march or tramp : a difficult or plodding advance **b** : a long drudgery of effort : hard plugging application ⟨that long central ~ of the war from Pearl Harbor to the invasion of Normandy —Geoffrey Crowther⟩ **2** : a hard hit at cricket

slo·gan \'slōgən\ *n* -s [alter. of earlier *slogorn*, fr. Gael *sluagh-ghairm* army cry, fr. *sluagh* army + *gairm* call] **1 a** : a war cry or gathering word (as of a Highland clan in Scotland) : a rallying or battle cry **b** : a word or phrase used by a person or group to express a characteristic position or aim, a stand on a contested issue, or a goal of endeavor ⟨the whalemen's ~, "A dead whale or a stove boat" —*Amer. Guide Series: Conn.*⟩ ⟨a widespread decline of cognitive standards, exemplified, for example, in the popular ~ that "it all depends on the point of view" —T.M.Clarke⟩ ⟨years ago we repudiated the ~, "Peace at any price" —Laurence Sears⟩ **2** : a brief striking phrase used in advertising or promotion **3 a** : a word or phrase imprinted on a piece of mail usu. with the cancellation as a commemorative or publicity device **b** : an advertising phrase imprinted on mail together with the postage by a postage meter

1slo·gan·eer \,slōgə'ni(ə)r\ *n* -s [*slogan* + *-eer*] : a coiner or user of slogans esp. for political or commercial purposes ⟨subtle ~s seeking to convert us to their views —H.G. Rickover⟩

2sloganeer \"\ *vi* -ED/-ING/-S : to phrase or disseminate a slogan in order to influence or stimulate thought or action

slo·gan·ize \'⸗⸗,nīz\ *vt* -ED/-ING/-S [*slogan* + *-ize*] : to cast in the form of a slogan : express tersely so as to induce action or instill opinion or belief ⟨scientists, to start a research program, must ~ it, must optimistically forecast great results from it, and report its progress in journalese —*Science*⟩

slog·ger \'slägə(r) *also* -lȯg-\ *n* -s [1*slog* + *-er*] : one that slogs as **a** : PLODDER **b** : a hard-hitting pugilist or cricket batsman : SLUGGER **c** : a hard steady worker

1slogging *n* -s [fr. gerund of 1*slog*] **1** : PLODDING **2** : hard drudging work : PLUGGING ⟨it will require not merely general approval but desperately hard ~ at details in order to frame a practicable plan —*Irish Statesman*⟩

2slogging *adj* [fr. pres part. of 1*slog*] **1** : given to or marked by dogged hard work ⟨it is hard ~ work for the men in the field —K.W.Kuhne⟩ **2** : hard hitting : SLUGGING ⟨a ~ match⟩

slog·wood \'släg,⸗, -lȯg-\ *n* [*slog* (perh. fr. 1*slog*) + *wood*] **1** : a West Indian timber tree (*Beilschmiedia pendula*) of the family Lauraceae **2** : the aromatic durable yellowish brown wood of the slogwood tree

slojd *or* **sloid** *var of* SLOYD

slo·ka \'shlōkə\ *n* -s [Skt *śloka*, lit., sound, fame, hymn, stanza; akin to *śṛnoti* he hears — more at LOUD] : a distich consisting of two lines of 16 syllables each or of four octosyllabic hemistichs that is the chief verse form of the Sanskrit epics

sloke *or* **sloak** \'s(h)lōk\ *n* -s [Ir *sleabhac*] **1** : any of various edible marine algae (as sea lettuce, red laver, and Irish moss) **2** : slime or scum in water

slok·en \'släkən\ *var of* SLOCKEN

1slom·mack \'sləmək, -läm-\ *n* -s [origin unknown] *dial* : an awkward, uncouth, or slovenly person : SLOB

2slommack \"\ *vi* -ED/-ING/-S *dial* : to be messy or ungainly

slom·macky \-kē\ *adj, dial* : repulsively untidy : MESSY

slone \'slōn\ *n* -s [prob. fr. ME *slon*, *sloon*, pl., sloes, fr. OE *slān*, pl. of *slā* sloe — more at SLOE] *dial Eng* : SLOE 1a

1sloom \'slüm\ *n* -s [ME *slume*, *sloumbe* — more at SLUMBER] *dial Brit* : a light sleep : DOZE, SLUMBER

2sloom \"\ *vi* -ED/-ING/-S [ME *slumen*, prob. fr. *slume* slumber] **1** *dial Brit* : DOZE, SLUMBER **2** *dial Brit* : to become weak and flaccid : DECAY, WASTE **3** *dial Brit* : to move or wander slowly or silently : DRIFT

sloomy \-mi\ *adj, dial Brit* : SLEEPY, SLUGGISH

1sloop \'slüp\ *n* -s [D *sloep*, prob. fr. F *chaloupe* — more at CHALOUPE] **1** : a fore-and-aft rigged boat with a single mast that is usu. stepped well forward and a single headsail jib — compare CUTTER **2** : SLOOP OF WAR **3** : LONGBOAT

2sloop \"\ *n* -s [origin unknown] **1** : a single sled or dray for supporting the front end of a log in hauling **2** : a pair of runners with bunks on which short logs may be loaded

3sloop \"\ *vt* -ED/-ING/-S : to haul (logs) down steep slopes on a dray or sloop

sloop·man \-mən\ *n, pl* **sloopmen** [1*sloop* + *man*] : a master or crewman of a sloop

sloop 1

sloop of war **1** : a vessel rigged as a ship or as a brig or as a schooner and mounting from 10 to 32 guns **2** : a warship larger than a gunboat and carrying guns on one deck only **3** *Brit* : a small armed ship

sloosh \'slüsh\ *n* -ES [prob. alter. of 3*slush*] **1** : a lapping or sloshing sound **2** : an act of washing : WASH ⟨gave myself a good ~ with cold water —William Plomer⟩

sloot \'slüt\ *n* -s [D — more at SLUIT] *chiefly Africa* : SLUIT

1slop \'släp\ *n* -s [ME *sloppe*, prob. fr. MD *slop*; akin to OE *oferslop* surplice, stole, slop, ON *sloppr* slop and prob. to OE *slūpan* to slip — more at SLEEVE] **1** : a loose covering garment for workmen (as a smock, smock frock, apron, or overall) **2 a slops** *pl* : the short full breeches worn by men of fashion in the late 16th century **b** *dial* : loose baggy trousers or a trouser leg — usu. used in pl. **3 a slops** *pl* : clothing and other articles sold to sailors : a ship's small stores **b** : cheap ready-made clothing — usu. used in pl.

2slop \"\ *n* -s [ME *sloppe*, prob. fr. OE *sloppe* dung (as in *cū-sloppe* cowslip, lit., cow's dung); akin to OE *slyppe*, *slypa* slime, pulp, paste — more at SLIP] **1** : a mud puddle : soft mud : SLUSH **2** : thin tasteless drink or liquid food — usu. used in pl. ⟨the thin ~s provided on soup lines —*Amer. Guide Series: Oregon*⟩ ⟨had eaten the prison ~ without even suffering the gnawing pain of diarrhea —Douglass Cater⟩ **3** : the spilling or splashing of something liquid or moist or the material spilled or splashed ⟨washing up with ~s of water and bashing of plates —Richard Llewellyn⟩ ⟨shoves her glass in its own ~ over the bar —Brendan Gill⟩ **4 a** (1) : food waste fed to animals : GARBAGE ⟨watching his pig eat ~s —P.E.Green⟩ (2) : a thin gruel for feeding animals ⟨a ~ of skim milk and bran⟩ **b** : excreted body waste — usu. used in pl. ⟨emptying other people's ~s —John Morrison⟩ **5** : STILLAGE **6** : sentimental or undiscerning effusiveness in speech or writing : GUSH

3slop \"\ *vb* **slopped; slopped; slopping; slops** *vt* **1 a** : to spill (something) from a container **b** (1) : to splash (someone or something) with a liquid ⟨passing cars kept *slopping* him as they went through puddles⟩ (2) : to cause (a liquid) to splash ⟨*slopped* water from the pail he carried⟩ **2** : to slobber or spill liquid on ⟨beer drinkers kept *slopping* the bar⟩ **3** : to ladle, serve, or dish out clumsily or messily ⟨his red, swollen hands *slopped* oatmeal into our plates —Ruth Domino⟩ **4** : to eat or drink greedily or noisily : lap up : GOBBLE ⟨*slopped* up great tablespoonfuls of cereal —Hodding Carter⟩ ⟨so long as they could yap and ~ beer —Mickey Spillane⟩ **5** : to feed with slops ⟨*slopped* hogs . . . to get the money to go to college —*Newsweek*⟩ ~ *vi* **1 a** : to plod or tramp in mud or slush ⟨*slopped* along muddy roads⟩ **b** : to slouch or lounge about in slack, slatternly, or slovenly style ⟨continental soldiers *slopped* about in a most unmilitary manner —Bruce Marshall⟩ ⟨for TV, they just ~ around in the living room —*Newsweek*⟩ **2** : to spill or splash over an edge (as of a container) ⟨carried the soup so unsteadily that it *slopped* over⟩ **3** : to go to excess in expression or conduct : be effusive or indiscriminate : GUSH — used with *over* ⟨when an ambitious feature writer ~s over —F.L.Mott⟩ **4** : to exceed, overrun, or overflow boundaries or limits — used with *over* ⟨my personal interests ~ over into related fields —*Amer. Council of Learned Soc. Newsletter*⟩ **5 a** : to move or fit loosely ⟨the plug gage was worn and had begun to ~⟩ ⟨the spindle *slopped* in its bearing⟩ **b** : to make a rhythmic slapping sound (as of a loose-fitting machine part or of plashing waves) ⟨could hear his oars *slopping* in the rowlocks⟩

slop basin *n, Brit* : SLOP BOWL

slop book *n* : a record of clothing and supplies furnished to a British naval crew

slop bowl *n* : a basin or bowl for receiving the leavings of tea or coffee cups at the table

slop chest *n* **1** : a store of clothing and personal requisites (as tobacco) carried on merchant ships for issue to the crew usu. as a charge against their wages

slop chute *n* **1** : a chute toward the rear of a ship for dumping garbage **2** *slang* : a tavern frequented by military men

slop culture *n* : a method of growing plants in which a nutrient solution is regularly poured over the surface of the sand or other medium in which the plants are growing, the surplus running through — compare DRIP CULTURE

1slope \'slōp\ *adv* [ME] *archaic* : in a sloping manner : ASLANT, OBLIQUELY

2slope \"\ *adj* : SLANTING, SLOPING ⟨stagger on the ~ decks —Alfred Tennyson⟩ — often used in combination ⟨*slope*-edged⟩ ⟨*slope*-sided⟩

3slope \"\ *vb* -ED/-ING/-S *vi* **1** : to move in or take an oblique direction : advance in or form a slanting line or course ⟨wide golden fans of light *sloped* down the canyons —Katharine N. Burt⟩ **2** : to incline from the horizontal or vertical : lie or fall in a slanting plane ⟨the bank *sloped* gently down to the water's edge —W.F.Davis⟩ **3** : GO, TRAVEL, WALK ⟨renounces her position and her inheritance, and ~s off into the night —Wolcott Gibbs⟩ ⟨pack and ~ out for cow country —C.T.Jackson⟩ ⟨eight dusty, hungry men *sloped* into the farm kitchen —Ronald Duncan⟩ ~ *vt* **1 a** : to cause to incline or slant : give a slanting position or direction to : BEND ⟨the most obvious method of fitting a pattern to the body is to ~ or curve seam lines along body curves —Evelyn A. Mansfield⟩ **b** : to carry or place (a weapon) in a sloping position **2** : to form or make with a slanting shape or surface ⟨the same man will ~ his margin at one time to the right, at another time to the left —Stephen Paget⟩

4slope \"\ *n* -s **1 a** : ground whose surface forms an angle with the plane of the horizon : a natural or artificial incline (as a hillside or terrace) : ACCLIVITY, DECLIVITY ⟨steep submarine ~s and steep-sided submarine canyons —F.P.Shepard⟩ **b** : a course on an open hillside prepared and graded for skiing — called also *trail* **2** : upward or downward slant or inclination : degree or extent of deviation from the horizontal or perpendicular ⟨the mountains reach 15,000 feet or higher, the average ~ of the flanking ranges being 60 degrees —Francis Kingdon-Ward⟩ **3** : the part of a continent descending toward and draining to a particular ocean ⟨the Pacific ~⟩ **4** : SLANT 2 **5 a** : the trigonometric tangent of the angle made by a straight line with the x-axis **b** : the derivative of a dependent variable y with respect to the independent variable x **6** : an inclined mine shaft; *esp* : the main incline in a colliery

slope angle *n* : the acute angle made by a meridional ray with the axis in a symmetrical optical system

slope arms *n* : a former command and position in the manual of arms with the piece carried as in left shoulder arms except that the muzzle was turned a little to the right or left

sloped *adj* [fr. past part. of 3*slope*] : having a slope : inclined from horizontal or perpendicular : formed or placed with a slant

slope–line approach *n* : a system of lights at an airport so arranged as to form a pair of sharply defined converging lines between which an airplane pilot may make a safe landing

slope·man \'slōpmən\ *n, pl* **slopemen** : a worker who grades slopes of excavations with hand tools

slop·er \-pə(r)\ *n* -s [3*slope* + *-er*] **1** : one that slopes: as **a** : a device for shaping the slopes of a railroad embankment **b** : a basic pattern for garment makers indicating the measurements for each size but having no fullness or design details **2** : SLOPEMAN

slope wash *n* **1** : SHEET EROSION **2** : earth material transported by sheet erosion

slope·ways \'⸗,wāz\ *adv* : in a sloping position or direction : ASLANT

slopewise \'⸗,⸗\ *adv, obs* : SLOPEWAYS

sloping *adj* : having a slanting form, position, or direction : INCLINING, OBLIQUE

slop·ing·ly *adv* : in a sloping manner

slop jar *n* : a large pail often of china used variously in a house without running water to receive waste water from a washbowl, to collect the contents of chamber pots, or to serve as a chamber pot

slop–molding \'⸗,⸗⸗\ *n* : the molding of brick in molds wet with water to prevent sticking in soft-mud process brickmaking — compare SAND-MOLDING

slop–over \'⸗,⸗⸗\ *n* -s **1** : OVERFLOW **2** : EFFUSIVENESS, GUSH, SENTIMENTALITY

slop pail *n* : a pail for toilet or household slops

slopped *adj* [fr. past part. of 3*slop*] **1** : stained or wet with slops **2** : DRUNK, INTOXICATED ⟨~ to the eyes —Mitzi Martin⟩

slop·pi·ly \'släpəlē, -li\ *adv* : in a sloppy manner

slop·pi·ness \-pēnəs, -pin-\ *n* -ES : the quality or state of being sloppy

slopping *pres part of* SLOP

slop·py \'släpē, -pi\ *adj* -ER/-EST [2*slop* + *-y*] **1 a** : muddy or slushy so as to spatter easily : SPLASHY ⟨those bogs can be great, ~ messes of treacle pudding in wet weather —Wynford Vaughan-Thomas⟩ ⟨the race was run over a ~ track —G.F.T. Ryall⟩ **b** : wet or smeared with slopped liquid or moist material : MESSY ⟨the oilcloth was sticky and ~ and smeared⟩ **2** *of a garment* : lacking formality or fastidiousness : ill fitted or worn carelessly **3** : feebly organized or directed : ill concerted or contrived : lacking firmness : CARELESS, LOOSE, SLOVENLY ⟨the misery of all those ~ words will fade as the correct, crisp sentence at last comes to her —L.B.Nicolson⟩ ⟨he was a ~ dresser —W.L.Gresham⟩ ⟨harden ~ thinking —Charlton Laird⟩ **4** : marked by excessive or indiscriminate sentimentality : EFFUSIVE, GUSHING, SOFT ⟨gives much of his time to ~ self-pity —E.F.Meagher⟩ **5** : disturbed with heavy waves : having a rough or choppy surface — used of lakes and seas ⟨hadn't the constitution to handle a heavy steering oar . . . in a ~ sea —R.S.Porteous⟩ **6** : DRUNK, INTOXICATED ⟨he had finished his fourth drink and was getting a little ~ —Edmund Wilson⟩ **syn** see SLIPSHOD

sloppy joe *n* **1** *usu cap J* : a man who is negligent of his clothes or personal appearance **2** : a loose baggy sweater for girls

slops *pl of* SLOP, *pres 3d sing of* SLOP

slopseller \'⸗,⸗⸗\ *n* [1*slop* + *seller*] : a dealer in cheap ready-made clothes

slopshop \'⸗,⸗\ *n* : a slopseller's shop

slop sink *n* : a sink (as in a hospital) in which chamber pots and bedpans are emptied and washed and scrub water is thrown out

slopstone \'⸗,⸗\ *n* [2*slop* + *stone*] : a stone slab or table under a tap

slopwork \'⸗,⸗\ *n* [1*slop* + *work*] **1 a** : the manufacture of cheap ready-made clothing **b** : slop clothing **2** [influenced in meaning by 2*slop*] : hasty slovenly work ⟨no ~ ever dropped from his pen —J.A.Froude⟩

slopworker \'⸗,⸗⸗\ *n* : a worker making cheap ready-made clothing

slopy \'slōpē\ *adj* -ER/-EST [4*slope* + *-y*] : SLOPING

slorp \'slȯ(ə)rp\ *dial Brit var of* SLURP

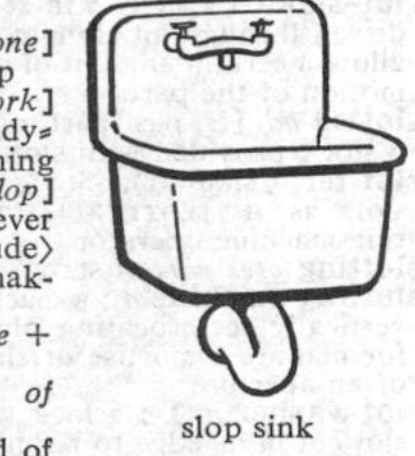

slop sink

1slosh \'släsh\ *n* -ES [prob. blend of 2*slop* and 1*slush*] **1 a** : a wet sloppy condition underfoot : MUD, SLUSH **b** : a tramp through mud, slush, or puddles ⟨a half-mile ~ through a grove of sawed-off trees —Burgess Scott⟩ **2** : a thin poor drink **3** : the slap or splash of liquid (as waves or spilled water) ⟨listened to the ~ of the water against the barge —Willard Robertson⟩ **4** : a small quantity of liquid : DASH ⟨there seemed to be only a ~ of kerosine left⟩ **5** : BLOW, STROKE ⟨caught one chap a ~ on the ear he won't forget —Bruce Marshall⟩

2slosh \"\ *vb* -ED/-ING/-ES *vi* **1** : to slog or splash through water, mud, or slush : FLOUNDER ⟨faster than ~ over a soggy fairway —R.M.Hodesh⟩ **2** : to wander, walk, or loaf about **3** : to move with the lapping motion of a liquid : GURGLE, SPLASH ⟨his stomach ~*ed* with countless cups of coffee —K.M. Dodson⟩ ⟨the water ~*ed* around him, running down his legs —Bill Alcine⟩ ⟨saw about 20 gallons of water ~*ing* around the engine —*Springfield (Mass.) Daily News*⟩ ~ *vt* **1 a** : to splash (something) about in liquid ⟨fills a pan with dry-cleaning fluid and ~*es* the hairpiece around in it —R.F.Wallace⟩ **b** : to splash (a liquid) about on or someone or something ⟨had finished systematically ~*ing* gasoline around —St. Clair

McKelway⟩ **c :** to splash (someone or something) with liquid ⟨workmen are ~*ing* down the open-air-café floors with water —Irwin Shaw⟩ **2 :** to pour hastily or clumsily ⟨was ~*ing* out the drinks behind the counter —Bruce Marshall⟩ **3 :** to gulp down : GUZZLE, SWILL ⟨the beer drinker would have to ~ down more than three quarts in less than three hours —*Newsweek*⟩ **4** *Brit* : BASH, PUNCH, SLAM, STRIKE ⟨you can't very well ~ a child —P.G.Wodehouse⟩

sloshy \-shē,-shi\ *adj* -ER/-EST : SLUSHY

¹slot \'slät, *usu* -äd.+V\ *n* -S [ME, fr. MD; akin to OFris & ON *slot* lock, bolt, OHG *sloz* lock, bolt, *sliozan* to lock, close — more at CLOSE] **1** *dial Eng* : a bolt or bar for fastening a door **2** *dial Eng* : SLAT

²slot \"\ *n* -S [ME, fr. MF *esclot*] **1** *chiefly Scot* : a hollow or depression; *specif* : the hollow running down the middle of the breast **2 a :** a long and narrow opening or groove : SLIT, NOTCH ⟨deliver mail through a ~ in a door⟩ ⟨the musket ~*s* in the fort's hand-hewn walls —J.H.Cutler⟩ ⟨information is coded by cutting ~*s* between adjacent vertical perforations —H.C.Zeisig & P.T.Martin⟩ ⟨spanner wrenches are made with one or two pins to fit into the holes or ~*s* of nuts, collars, sealing rings —T.G.Thompson & R.A.Peterson⟩ ⟨a coin ~ in a vending machine⟩ **b :** a narrow passage, enclosure, or space ⟨a ~ between islands⟩ ⟨they sat close together . . . in their ~ between the stacked, rattling ration boxes —Fred Majdalany⟩ : a small open compartment : PIGEONHOLE **c :** a passage of spanwise extent through an airplane wing located usu. near the leading edge and formed between a main and an auxiliary airfoil for improving the flow conditions over the wing at high angles of attack and thus increasing lift and delaying the stalling of the wing **3 :** a depression in the lift surface of an armature or stator of a dynamo-electric machine into which a portion of the winding is placed **4 a :** a place or a position in an organization, series, sequence, list, or program : NICHE ⟨athletes for athletic ~*s* on college teams —A.E.Lumley⟩ ⟨the chairman's ~⟩ ⟨her name was switched to the "contributing editors" ~ on the masthead —*Time*⟩ ⟨a TV show in the seven-o'clock ~⟩ **b :** the dealer's position in a gambling game **c** (1) **:** the position occupied by the copy editor on the inside of a horseshoe-shaped copydesk — compare RIM (2) **:** the position of copy editor **5** *slang* : SLOT MACHINE

³slot \"\ *vt* **slotted; slotted; slotting; slots 1 :** to cut a slot in : cut or shape by means of a slotting machine ⟨abrasive wheel . . . for cutting off or *slotting* any material —K.B. Lewis⟩ **2 :** to provide with slots ⟨the walls of the convent . . . were *slotted* for machine guns —Laurence Critchell⟩ ⟨a *slotted* collar⟩ **3 :** to pass through a slot ⟨velvet ribbon *slotted* through strands of wool —*Women's Wear Daily*⟩ : put into a slot

⁴slot \"\ *n, pl* **slot** [MF *esclot* horse's hoofprint, track, prob. of Scand origin; akin to ON *slōth* track] **1 :** the track of an animal (as a deer) **2 :** TRAIL

⁵slot \"\ *vt* : to follow the trail of : TRACK

slot bark graft *n* : a modified bark graft in which a wedge-shaped scion is inserted under a loosened tongue of bark on the stock

slot–drill \'=,=\ *vt* : to cut out (as a slot) with a traverse drill

slote *or* **sloat** \'slōt\ *n* -S [ME *sloot*, *slote* bolt, bar, crossbar, fr. MD *sloot*, *slot* bolt — more at SLOT (bolt)] : any of several former devices for moving persons or scenery above or below a theater stage

sloth \'slōth, -ō- *sometimes* -ä-; *sometimes* -ō- *for sense 1*, -ō- *or* -ä- *for sense 4*\ *n, pl* **sloths** \-ths,-thz\ [ME *slouthe*, *slowthe*, fr. *slou*, *slow* slow + -*the* -th — more at SLOW] **1 a :** disinclination to action or labor : SLUGGISHNESS, LAZINESS, IDLENESS, INDOLENCE ⟨the sun . . . is gentle, mellow, and ~ provoking —T.H.Fielding⟩ **b :** spiritual sluggishness and dejection that constitute one of the seven deadly sins : apathy and inactivity in the practice of virtue ⟨war may shake off . . . spiritual ~ —C.D.Lewis⟩ **2** *archaic* : SLOWNESS, TARDINESS **3 :** a pack of bears **4 a :** any of several slow-moving exclusively arboreal edentate mammals that inhabit tropical forests of So. and Central America, have esp. the front pair of limbs very long and provided with long curved claws, have rudimentary tail and external ears, have long coarse and crisp hair grayish or brownish in color but in the native habitat appearing more or less green and harmonizing with the moss and foliage due to a growth of commensal algae, have the habit of hanging from the branches back downward, and feed entirely on leaves, shoots, and fruits **b :** any of various related extinct edentates — see GROUND SLOTH **c :** any of various sluggish arboreal mammals (as the slow loris or the koala)

sloth bear *n* : a common bear (*Melursus labiatus*) of India and Ceylon that has long black hair and very large claws, a brownish muzzle, a white V-shaped mark on the breast, a long snout, and very mobile tongue and lips, that differs from ordinary bears in having very small molars and 4 instead of 6 upper incisors, and that feeds on fruit, insects, and honey

sloth·ful \-thfəl\ *adj* [ME *sloutheful*, fr. *slouthe* sloth + -*ful*] : addicted to sloth : INACTIVE, SLUGGISH, INDOLENT ⟨not ~ anguish, is what you now require, but effort —Nathaniel Hawthorne⟩ ⟨municipal government was corrupt and ~ —H.A.Sinclair⟩ **syn** see LAZY

sloth·ful·ly \-fəlē, -li\ *adv* : in a slothful manner

sloth·ful·ness \-fəlnəs\ *n* -ES : the quality or state of being slothful ⟨that dim ~ of the spirit which a great sorrow . . . will bring —Mary Webb⟩

sloth monkey *n* : LORIS

slot·hound \'=,=\ *n* [⁴*slot* + *hound*] : SLEUTH 1

slot–lip aileron *n* : a combination of an aileron and a slot in which a small hinged flap controls the opening and closing of the slot

slot machine *n* **1 :** a machine (as a vending machine) whose operation is started by dropping a coin into a slot **2 :** a coin-operated gambling machine that pays off according to the matching of symbols on wheels spun by a handle — called also *one-armed bandit*

slot man *n* : a newspaper editor responsible for the layout of news items

slots *pl of* SLOT, *pres 3d sing of* SLOT

slot seam *n* : a seam with a decorative slit formed by bringing two folds together and stitching them onto an underlying piece

slot–spike \'=,=\ *vt* : to secure by a spike driven through an elongated hole so as to allow a certain amount of relative endways motion of the parts

slotted *adj* [fr. past part. of ³*slot*] : having a slot : provided with slots

slot·ter \'släd·ə(r), -ätə-\ *n* -S : one that slots: as **a :** SLOTTING MACHINE **b :** a slotting-machine operator

slotting *pres part of* SLOT

slotting machine *n* : a machine tool with a vertically reciprocating planing tool used for making a mortise or shaping the sides of an aperture

slot seam

slot washer *n* **1 :** a lock washer having a slot cut in its edge to permit the driving of a nail or screw through it after the nut has been tightened to prevent the bolt or nut from turning **2 :** a washer slotted through from the outside to the central hole so that it may be inserted or removed with the bolt in place

slot winding *n* : a winding in which the wires are run in deep grooves (as in armatures of dynamos and motors)

sloubbie *usu cap, var of* SLUBBI

¹slouch \'slau̇ch\ *n* -ES [origin unknown] **1 a :** an awkward clownish fellow : LOUT **b :** one devoid of energy, ambition, or competence : an inefficient person : LOAFER, INCOMPETENT ⟨the ~ whom military drill has transformed into a man —Calvin Coolidge⟩ ⟨if you're only a clerk, you'll have to yield precedence to the ~ who holds the post of manager —M.F.A. Montagu⟩ — often used in negative constructions ⟨no ~ as a comedian⟩ ⟨no ~ at conversation⟩ ⟨a dancer who is no ~ on his feet⟩ **2 :** a gait or posture characterized by ungainly stooping of head and shoulders or undue relaxation of body muscles ⟨walked with shut lips and cold, cruel bearing, that had something of a ~ and a sneer in it —D.H.Lawrence⟩ ⟨all the regular prisoners had the same hollow-gutted ~ —R.O. Bowen⟩ **3 :** SLOUCH HAT **4 :** LAZINESS, SHIFTLESSNESS ⟨saw among them a good deal of ~ — mental, moral, and physical ~ —A.W.Long⟩

²slouch \"\ *adj* **1 :** DROOPING, PENDULOUS ⟨~ ears⟩ **2 :** SLOUCHING, SLOUCHY ⟨he slams ~ scribes —A.L.Hench⟩

³slouch \"\ *vb* -ED/-ING/-ES *vi* **1 :** to move, walk, stand, or sit with a slouch : assume or drop into a slouch : SLUMP ⟨the cur dog ~*ing* across the road —*Amer. Guide Series: Tenn.*⟩ ⟨~*ed* over to the telephone —S.H.Adams⟩ ⟨~*ed* behind the wheel —J.P.Marquand⟩ ⟨some of the others ~*ed* on the table around him —Vincent McHugh⟩ **2 :** to hang down flaccidly : DROOP ⟨a hat with a brim that ~*es*⟩ ~ *vt* **1 :** to cause to hang down or droop ⟨~ the hat over the eyes⟩ **2 :** to make in a slouching manner ⟨~*ed* his way along⟩ **3 :** to cause (the shoulders) to stoop ⟨his head drooped forward, his shoulders were ~*ed* down —O.E.Rölvaag⟩

⁴slouch \'slüch\ *n* -ES [prob. fr. ¹*slouch*] : a pipe by which an engine takes up water

slouch·er \'slau̇chə(r)\ *n* -S : one that slouches : SLOUCH ⟨modern man is an inveterate ~ . . . still rather a simian affair —*Time*⟩

slouch hat *n* : a soft usu. felt hat with a wide flexible brim

slouch·i·ly \'slau̇chəlē, -li\ *adv* : in a slouchy manner ⟨~ dressed⟩

slouch·i·ness \-chēnəs, -chin-\ *n* -ES : the quality or state of being slouchy

slouching *adj* [fr. pres. part. of ³*slouch*] : characterized by a slouch ⟨a tall but ~ figure standing at the bar —Richard Burke⟩ — **slouch·ing·ly** *adv*

slouchy \'slau̇chē, -chi\ *adj* -ER/-EST **1 :** slouching esp. in gait or posture : SLOVENLY ⟨the speaker presents a ~ and indifferent appearance —A.T.Weaver⟩ ⟨there is an indescribably constrained, ~, shabby look to all thus attired —Lafcadio Hearn⟩ **2 :** inefficient because lazy or unenergetic

¹slough \'slü, 'slau̇ *sometimes* 'sləf\ *n* -S [ME *slogh*, fr. OE *slōh*; akin to MHG *slouche* ditch] **1 a :** a place of deep mud or mire : MUDHOLE ⟨walk up steep rises in the road or help rescue horses stalled in a ~ —*Amer. Guide Series: N.J.*⟩ **b** *also* **slew** *or* **slue** \'slü\ (1) **:** a large wet or marshy place : SWAMP ⟨Indians are still living in primitive palm-thatched huts in the ~*s* of the Everglades —Merrill Folsom⟩ (2) **:** a small marshy place lying in a local depression of dry land (as on a prairie); *also* : a depression that becomes marshy or filled with water ⟨thousands of ~*s* and potholes went dry —I.N.Gabrielson⟩ **c** *also* **slew** *or* **slue** (1) **:** a side channel or inlet (as from a river) : a sluggish channel : a small backwater : BAYOU, POND ⟨lakes so close together and so intricately connected by rivers and ~*s* that they may almost be called continuous —Bernard DeVoto⟩ (2) **:** a creek in a marshland, tide flat, or bottomland ⟨a narrow tidal ~, over three miles long —*U. S. Board on Geog. Names Decisions*⟩ **2** *obs* : MUD, MIRE, OOZE **3 :** a state of moral degradation or spiritual dejection into which one sinks or from which one cannot free oneself : an engulfing depth of something (as sin or misery) : MORASS ⟨one of those tireless organizers who come to the rescue of doddering lodges and . . . bring them out of their ~*s* when all hope is gone —C.W. Ferguson⟩ ⟨high hopes ended in such a ~ of frustration, paralysis, and bitterness —W.W.Kaufmann⟩ ⟨music has just kept her nose above the ~ of realism, romance, and melodrama —Clive Bell⟩ ⟨the sooty ~ that submerges so many factory towns —*Amer. Guide Series: Vt.*⟩ ⟨a ~ of self-distrust⟩ ⟨a ~ of mediocrity⟩

²slough \"\ *vb* -ED/-ING/-S *vt* **1 :** to engulf in or as if in a slough **2** *slang* : ARREST, IMPRISON — usu. used with *in* or *up* ~ *vi* : to plod through mud ⟨lumberjacks ~*ing* through swampy lowlands —D.G.Hoffman⟩

³slough \'sləf\ *n* -S [ME *slughe*, *slouh*; akin to MHG *slūch* snake skin, hose, Norw *slo* fleshy part of a horn, D *sluiken* to slip, smuggle, Lith *šliaũžti* to glide, crawl] **1 :** the skin of a snake or other animal that sheds its skin; *esp* : the cast-off skin **2 :** a mass of dead tissue separating from an ulcer : the dead part separating from living tissues in mortification **3 :** something that may be shed or cast off ⟨when shall this ~ of sense be cast —A.E.Housman⟩ ⟨the book is . . . necessarily a study in sociology, concerning itself with the struggles of a new order in casting off the ~ of the old —*Times Lit. Supp.*⟩ **4** *chiefly dial* **a :** an outer skin, covering, or sheath **b :** SHELL, HUSK ⟨the ~ on a fruit⟩ **5 :** a mass of material that has sloughed from the side of a mine working or drill hole **6** [so called fr. the fact that it involves sloughing or discard] **:** a card game that is a variety of frog or solo

⁴slough \"\ *vb* -ED/-ING/-S *vi* **1 a :** to become shed or cast off ⟨a snake skin ~*s*⟩ ⟨the skin of my hand and forearm ~*ed* in patches —J.M.Savidge⟩ ⟨his clothes hung in rags, and some of them had ~*ed* off —Edison Marshall⟩ **b :** to shed or cast off one's skin ⟨the snake ~*s* annually⟩ **c :** to become encrusted with or as if with a slough: as (1) **:** to form a slough : separate in the form of dead tissue from living tissue ⟨a ~*ing* ulcer⟩ ⟨the dead tissue ~*s* slowly⟩ ⟨a ~*ing* of the colon⟩ — often used with *off* (2) **:** to cast off a thin film of scum or mass of bacterial growth or fungus ⟨a filter used in sewage disposal ~*s*⟩ **2 a :** to crumble and fall away : FALL, SLIDE ⟨fragments of rock ~ from the sides of a mine working or drill hole⟩ ⟨the track had disappeared with the ~*ing* of the surface rock —Francis Kingdon-Ward⟩ ⟨a worn stone building with stucco ~*ing* from its face⟩ ⟨stream banks that have a tendency to ~ at high-water level —*Carpentry*⟩ **b :** to drop or fall off : diminish in significance or intensity ⟨trade ~*s* off after Christmas⟩ **3 :** to slip from a bobbin or other package and tangle ⟨yarn ~*s*⟩ — usu. used with *off* ~ *vt* **1 a :** to cast off : throw off : ease off ⟨~ dead tissue⟩ ⟨many of the teeth are supported by soft tissue only; and several of them have been ~*ed* —E.C.Stafne⟩ ⟨a naked tired dark man, ~*ing* water off his thighs —Douglas Newton⟩ **b :** to get rid of, abandon, or discard as irksome, objectionable, deleterious, disadvantageous, outworn, or excrescent ⟨~*ed* their knapsacks —H.M. Robinson⟩ — usu. used with *off* ⟨~*ed* off the unimportant verbiage —P.D.Leedy⟩ ⟨the tendency in furniture . . . to ~ off many of its former crude and ungraceful characteristics —W.R. Storey⟩ ⟨author has ~*ed* off most of her more irritating sentimentalities —*Times Lit. Supp.*⟩ ⟨enlarged his understanding of religion by ~*ing* off most of the cosmological and theological lore associated with it —P.L.Holmer⟩ **2 :** to consume or waste away by forming a slough — usu. used with *away* ⟨the ulcer ~*ed* away the breast⟩ **3 :** to get rid of (a playing card) **syn** see DISCARD

⁵slough \'slü\ *var of* SLUE

⁶slough \'slau̇\ *vt* -ED/-ING/-S [prob. alter. (influenced by ⁴*slough*) of ⁶*slug*] *slang* : to strike heavily

slough bass *see* ¹SLOUGH\ *n* : LARGEMOUTH BLACK BASS

slough grass *see* ¹SLOUGH\ *n* **1 a :** either of two stout annual grasses (genus *Beckmannia*) with broad light green blades and 1-flowered or 2-flowered spikelets in two rows along one side of the rachis **b :** PRAIRIE CORDGRASS **c :** WESTERN WHEATGRASS 1 **2 :** TUSSOCK SEDGE

sloughi *often cap, var of* SALUKI

slough ice *see* ¹SLOUGH\ *n* : slushy ice or snow

slough of despond \,slüəvdə'spänd, ,slau̇əv-, -dē's- *sometimes* -'de,s-\ [fr. The *Slough of Despond*, deep bog into which Christian falls on the way from the City of Destruction and from which Help saves him in the allegory *Pilgrim's Progress* (1678) by John Bunyan †1688 Eng. preacher and writer] **:** a state of extreme depression ⟨the country was in the *slough of despond* —Manfred Nathan⟩ ⟨men climbed out of the *slough of despond* on the ladder of Christian Platonism —Douglas Bush⟩

slough over \;sləf-\ *vt* [⁴*slough*] : SLIGHT, ²GLOSS 1 ⟨dwell on a few of the aspects of group work that are currently being *sloughed over* —W.H.Whyte⟩

¹sloughy *pronunc at* ¹SLOUGH + ē *or* i\ *adj* -ER/-EST [¹*slough* + -*y*] : full of sloughs : MIRY, MUDDY ⟨in a ~, weedy district —Willa Cather⟩ ⟨a ~ creek⟩

²sloughy \'sləfē, -fi\ *adj* [³*slough* + -*y*] : resembling or marked by the presence of the dead matter that separates from living flesh

slounge \'slünj\ *vb* -ED/-ING/-S [alter. (influenced by ¹*slouch*) of ¹*lounge*] *chiefly Scot* : LOUNGE, LOAF

slo·vak \'slō,väk, -vak,-väk\ *also* **slo·vak·ian** \(')=;=ēən\ *or* **slo·vac** *like* SLOVAK\ *n* -S *cap* [*slovak*, *slovac* fr. Slovak *Slovák*, lit., Slav; *slovakian* fr. Slovak *Slovák* + E -*ian*; akin to ORuss *Slovēne*, an East-Slavic people — more at SLAVE] **1 a :** one of a Slavic people of eastern Czechoslovakia **b :** a member of such people **2 :** the Slavic language of the Slovak people

²slovak \"\ *or* **slovakian** \"\ *or* **slovac** \"\ *adj, usu cap* **1 :** of, relating to, or characteristic of the Slovaks **2 :** of, relating to, or characteristic of the Slovak language

slove *past of* SLIVE

¹slov·en \'sləvən *sometimes* -läv-\ *n* -S [ME *sloveyn*, of Flem or LG origin; akin to Flem *sloovin* gossip, woman of low character, LG *sluffen* to walk in a bedraggled manner, *sluf* loose, slack — more at SLOBBER] **1 :** one habitually negligent of neatness or cleanliness esp. in dress or person : one of extremely untidy habits ⟨local ~, who has since washed up, cleaned up —John Ciardi⟩ ⟨no slouchy ~ is he, but a scholar and a gentleman —W.A.White⟩ **2 :** one who is exceedingly lazy and slipshod in any way ⟨the difference between the unpunctual slacker and ~ and the model servant is very perceptible —G.B.Shaw⟩ ⟨a ~ in speech⟩

²sloven \"\ *adj* **1 :** SLOVENLY ⟨jargon . . . often ends as a ~ substitute for freshness and accuracy of statement —Dixon Wecter⟩ **2 :** UNCULTIVATED, UNDEVELOPED ⟨in this great ~ continent —Van Wyck Brooks⟩

¹slo·vene \'slō,vēn *sometimes* =';=\ *or* **slo·ve·nian** \slō'vēnēən, -nyən\ *n* -S *cap* [*slovene* fr. G *Slovene*, *Slowene*, fr. Slovene *Sloven*; *Slovenian* fr. G *Slovene* + E -*ian*; akin to OBulg *Slověne*, a Slavic people — more at SLAVE] **1 a :** a member of a southern Slavic group of people usu. classed with the Serbs and Croats and living in Yugoslavia **b :** a native or inhabitant of Slovenia — called also *Slavonian* **2 :** the language of the Slovenes

²slovene \"\ *or* **slovenian** \"\ *adj, usu cap* [*slovene* fr. ¹*slovene*; *slovenian* fr. G *Slovene*, n. + E -*ian* (adj. suffix)] **1 a :** of, relating to, or characteristic of Slovenia **b :** of, relating to, or characteristic of the Slovenes **2 :** of, relating to, or characteristic of the Slovene language

slov·en·li·ness \'sləvənlēnəs, -lin- *sometimes* -ləl *or* \|vᵊml- *or* \|bᵊml-\ *n* -ES : the quality or state of being slovenly

¹slov·en·ly \|vənlē, -li\ *adj* [¹*sloven* + -*ly* (adj. suffix)] **1 a :** having the habits of a sloven : negligent of neatness and order esp. in dress or person : SLIPSHOD **b :** lazily slipshod ⟨~ in thought⟩ **2 :** characteristic of a sloven : lacking neatness and order ⟨~ dress⟩ ⟨~ thinking⟩ ⟨~ habits⟩ ⟨~ grammar⟩ ⟨~ pronunciation⟩ ⟨~ workmanship⟩ **syn** see SLIPSHOD

²slovenly \"\ *adv* [¹*sloven* + -*ly* (adv. suffix)] : in a slovenly manner

slov·en·ness \|vən(n)əs\ *n* -ES *obs* : SLOVENLINESS

slov·en·ry \|vənrē\ *n* -ES [¹*sloven* + -*ry*] : SLOVENLINESS

slo·vin·cian \slō'vinch(ē)ən\ *n* -S *usu cap* [F *Slovince* (fr. *Slowinze*, fr. Slovincian *Slovenec*) + E -*ian*; akin to Slovene *Sloven* Slovene] : an extinct Slavic language of Pomerania

¹slow \'slō\ *adj* -ER/-EST [ME *slow*, *slaw*, fr. OE *slāw*, *slǣw*; akin to OS *slēu* blunt, dull, weak, slow, OHG *slēo* blunt, dull, ON *sljōr*, *slær* blunt, weak, Skt *srēvayati* he causes to fail] **1 a :** not quick in apprehending or comprehending : mentally dull : STUPID ⟨a ~ student⟩ ⟨a ~ mind⟩ ⟨offers ~ or retarded boys an adjusted program of education —*advt*⟩ ⟨the ~ learner, properly defined, is neither mentally nor emotionally retarded —Agnes Bass⟩ **b :** naturally inert or sluggish ⟨a ~ imagination⟩ **2 a :** lacking in readiness, promptness, or willingness : manifesting dilatoriness or extreme deliberation — often used with *in*, *of*, *to* ⟨they had been far too ~ in giving the colonies their independence —Hugh Gaitskell⟩ ⟨an unimaginative man, ~ of comprehension —*Times Lit. Supp.*⟩ ⟨many industries . . . have been ~ to develop the full value of research —*Defense Against Recession*⟩ **b :** not hasty or precipitate : not quickly aroused or excited ⟨~ to speak ill of a person —F.E.Ross⟩ ⟨a ~ theater audience⟩ **3 a :** moving, flowing, or proceeding without rapidity or at less than the usual speed ⟨a ~ stream⟩ ⟨a ~ train⟩ ⟨the robin has been mentioned as a ~ migrant —F.C.Lincoln⟩ **b :** exhibiting or characterized by retarded motion or speed ⟨a ~ advance⟩ ⟨~ marching⟩ ⟨~ music⟩ ⟨a ~ pace⟩ ⟨~ progress⟩ ⟨a ~ pulse⟩ ⟨a ~ tempo⟩ ⟨a ~ walk⟩ **c :** not acute ⟨a ~ disease⟩ **d** (1) **:** LOW, GENTLE ⟨a ~ fire⟩ (2) **:** heated to a relatively low baking temperature — compare SLOW OVEN **4 :** not happening in a short time : requiring a comparatively great length of time ⟨a ~ convalescence⟩ ⟨a ~ growth⟩ ⟨a ~ process⟩ **5 a :** having qualities that hinder or prohibit rapidity of movement, play, or action ⟨a ~ track is one in which the drying-out process has progressed to the stage where the footing is soft —Dan Parker⟩ ⟨her feet would sop in and out of the ~ mire —Elizabeth M. Roberts⟩ ⟨a ~ putting green⟩ **b** *of a wicket* : in such condition that a bowled cricket ball does not rebound with speed and liveliness — contrasted with *fast* **c :** not operating, taking effect, or responding to treatment immediately or quickly ⟨a ~ filter⟩ ⟨a ~ influence⟩ ⟨a ~ poison⟩ **d :** contributing to a lengthening of exposure time — used of a photographic lens or material **e :** draining slowly : WET — used of paper pulp; compare FREE 20a **6 a :** registering behind or below what is correct ⟨a ~ clock⟩ ⟨a ~ meter⟩ ⟨~ scales⟩ ⟨a ~ taximeter⟩ **b :** that is less than the time indicated by another method of reckoning ⟨standard time is an hour ~*er* than daylight-saving time⟩ **c :** that is behind the time with regard to a specified time or place ⟨local time (6 hrs. 36 min. 46.67 secs. ~ on Greenwich mean time) —G.B. & Charlotte L. Dyer⟩ ⟨Washington is several hours ~ on London⟩ **7 a :** lacking in life, animation, or gaiety : BORING ⟨somebody who's . . . so gay and daring that she'll think I'm ~ —Sinclair Lewis⟩ ⟨things were ~ around Times Square —Herbert Mitgang⟩ **b :** SLOWGOING, UNPROGRESSIVE ⟨a ~ town⟩ **c :** marked by reduced sales or patronage : not brisk : SLACK ⟨business here is a little ~ in summer —W.L.Gresham⟩ ⟨September is always a ~ month —Mary Jane Rolfs⟩ ⟨diamonds were particularly ~ —*Minerals Yrbk.*⟩ ⟨~ sales⟩ **8 :** not steep : GRADUAL ⟨a ~ taper⟩ ⟨a ~ spiral⟩ ⟨party climbed the comparatively ~ ascent —Frank Debenham⟩

syn SLOW, DILATORY, LAGGARD, DELIBERATE, and LEISURELY can apply to persons who take a longer time than is necessary, or sometimes desirable, to perform action or an action. SLOW, wide in its range of application, can apply to anything that is the opposite of quick ⟨a *slow* fuse⟩ ⟨a *slow* walker⟩ sometimes suggesting a more or less discreditable cause ⟨a *slow* careless worker⟩ ⟨*slow* wits⟩ ⟨*slow* in getting results⟩ or extreme care ⟨*slow* craftsmanship, careful and particular⟩ or a natural tempo ⟨*slow* growth⟩ ⟨a *slow* convalescence⟩ or a falling behind because of defect or difficulty ⟨a *slow* watch⟩ ⟨a *slow* train, held up by a storm⟩ DILATORY implies slowness resulting from inertia, procrastination, or indifference ⟨though *dilatory* in undertaking business, he was quick in its execution —Jane Austen⟩ ⟨the trial must not be protracted in duration by anything that is obstructive or *dilatory* —R.H.Jackson⟩ LAGGARD, more censorious than DILATORY, implies failure to do things on time or to observe a demand promptly, implying loitering or a wasting of time ⟨in its coverage of spot news events, radio has been especially *laggard* —R.H.Rovere⟩ ⟨a pupil *laggard* in getting assignments completed⟩ ⟨her body slender and motionless for a moment as though waiting for some *laggard* part to catch up —William Faulkner⟩ DELIBERATE suggests absence of hurry or agitation, or a slowness that is the result of care or calculation ⟨swung his axe steadily, with the *deliberate* measured strokes of a skilled woodsman —C.B.Nordhoff & J.N.Hall⟩ ⟨proceeding in the most *deliberate* and orderly manner —T.S.Eliot⟩ ⟨had been hurrying everyone since the first streak of light, suddenly became *deliberate* —Willa Cather⟩ LEISURELY also implies lack of hurry but suggests rather no pressure of time ⟨moving at a casual, almost *leisurely* pace —*Time*⟩ ⟨the mild wind and the blue skies with the *leisurely* clouds tenting among them —J.H.Wheelwright⟩

²slow \"\ *adv* -ER/-EST : SLOWLY ⟨how ~ time goes —Shak.⟩ ⟨I am going ~ until I am really on my feet again —H.J.Laski⟩ ⟨I would go pretty ~ on that —F.D.Roosevelt⟩ ⟨the engine is idling a trifle ~ —Walt Waron⟩

³slow \"\ *vb* -ED/-ING/-S *vt* **:** to make slow : slacken the speed of : RETARD ⟨investors were ~*ing* the market —*Time*⟩ ⟨the dirt track ~*ed* his pace —*Current Biog.*⟩ — often used with *up* or *down* ⟨a sudden storm will . . . only temporarily ~ down the movement of a freight train —J.N.Efferson⟩ ⟨reader is ~*ed* up by a stream of long words —Milton Hall⟩ ~ *vi* : to go slower : become slower ⟨the river . . . ~*s* on the flat bottom —Alexander Marshack⟩ ⟨the production of such vehicles ~*ed* a bit

—A.F.Harlow〉 — often used with *up* or *down* 〈go all day at high speed, begin to ~ up in the evening —R.S.Rubinow〉 〈his doctor told him to ~ down —*N.Y. Times*〉 **syn** see DELAY

4slow \"\ *n* -s **:** one that is slow

slowbelly \ˈ=,==\ *n, pl* **slowbellies** [1*slow* + *belly*] **1 :** a slothful person **2 :** a heavy indolent glutton **:** HOG

slow board *n* **:** a track-side marker for indicating to railroad engineers the maximum permissible speed in restricted speed zones (as on curves and bridges)

slow-burning \ˈ=ˈ==\ *adj* **:** burning slowly; *esp* **:** made of material treated to resist fire

slow coach *n* **:** one who is slow or is lethargic in temperament **:** one who thinks or moves slowly

slowdown \ˈ=,=\ *n* -s [fr. *slow down,* v.] **:** a slowing down 〈a business ~〉 〈an industrial ~〉 〈a sales ~〉; *specif* **:** a slowing down in the performance of duties by workers as a protest and means toward forcing compliance with demands — compare SIT-DOWN

slower *comparative of* SLOW

slowest *superlative of* SLOW

slow fever *n* **:** a fever that is not acute or a disease characterized by such fever; *esp* **:** INFECTIOUS ANEMIA

slow fire *n* **:** a class of rifle-marksmanship fire in which the time allowed for completing the number of shots is comparatively great (as one minute per round or longer)

slow-foot \ˈ=,=\ *adj* **:** SLOW-FOOTED

slow-footed \ˈ=ˈ==\ *adj* **:** moving at a very slow pace **:** SLOW-GOING, PLODDING 〈a *slow-footed* novel〉 〈a *slow-footed* ship〉 — **slow-foot·ed·ness** \ˈ=ˈ===\ *n* -ES

slowgoing \ˈ=ˈ==\ *adj* **1 :** plodding along in easygoing fashion **2 :** not inclined to be enterprising **:** UNENERGETIC

slow·hound \ˈslō,=\ *n* [alter. (influenced by 1*slow*) of obs. E *sloughhound,* prob. alter. (influenced by E 1*slough*) of E *sleuthhound*] **:** SLEUTH 1

slow·ish \ˈslōish, -ō ēsh\ *adj* **:** somewhat slow 〈a ~ reader〉

slow loris *or* **slow lemur** *n* **:** LORIS 1b

slow·ly *adv* [ME *slowlich, slawly,* fr. OE *slāwlīce,* fr. *slāw* slow + *-līce* -ly — more at SLOW] **:** in a slow manner **:** not quickly, fast, rapidly, early, rashly, or readily **:** TARDILY

slow match *n* **:** a match or fuse made so as to burn slowly and evenly at a known rate and used for firing (as of blasting charges or fireworks)

slow motion *n* **:** the action in a projected motion picture apparently taking place at a speed much slower than that of the photographed action as a result of exposing the film at a rate much faster than that at which it is projected 〈a scene in *slow motion*〉

slow-moving \ˈ=ˈ==\ *adj* **:** SLOW-FOOTED, SLOWGOING; *specif* **:** selling slowly

slow·ness *n* -ES [ME *slawnes,* fr. *slaw* slow + *-nes* -ness] **:** the quality or state of being slow

slow oven *n* **:** a baking oven heated to a temperature between 250° F and 325° F

slow-paced \ˈ=ˈ=\ *adj* **:** moving at a slow rate of speed **:** SLOW-FOOTED

slow pill *n, slang* **:** a depressant illegally administered to a race horse to slow his pace and prevent his winning

slow·poke \ˈslō,pōk\ *n* [1*slow* + *poke*] **:** an annoyingly slow or slowgoing person **:** SLOW COACH 〈journey even inquisitive ~s can make in a dawdling two days and a half —Claudia Cassidy〉

slow-poke \"\ *vi* [*slow poke*] **:** to go like a slowpoke 〈*slow-poked* up and down the river —Louis Armstrong〉

slows \ˈslōz\ *n pl but sing in constr* [fr. pl. of 4*slow*] **:** MILK SICKNESS 1, TREMBLE 3

slow shrimp *n* **:** a small brightly colored Australian anomuran crustacean (*Axius plectorhynchus*)

slow-spoken \ˈ=ˈ==\ *adj* **:** characterized by speaking slowly

slow-up \ˈ=,=\ *n* -s [fr. *slow up,* v.] **:** a slowing up; *specif* **:** a marked decline in activity

slow-witted \ˈ=ˈ==\ *adj* **:** mentally slow **:** DULL

slow·worm \ˈslō,=\ *n* [alter. (influenced by 1*slow*) of ME *slowurm, slaworm,* fr. OE *slāwyrm,* fr. *slā* (akin to Sw *slå* earthworm, Norw *slo* blindworm) + *wyrm* worm — more at WORM] **1 :** BLINDWORM 1 **2** *Austral* **:** a pygopodid lizard

sloyd *also* **slojd** *or* **sloid** \ˈslȯid\ *n* -s [Sw *slöjd* skill, skilled labor; akin to ON *slægth* cunning, sleight — more at SLEIGHT] **:** a system of manual training developed from a Swedish system and designed for training in the use of tools and materials but emphasizing training in wood carving as a means to this end

sloyd knife *n* **:** a single-blade woodworker's knife used in carving, trimming, or slicing

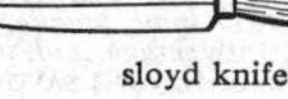

sloyd knife

SLP *abbr, often not cap* [L *sine legitima prole*] without lawful issue

slsmgr *abbr* sales manager

slsmn *abbr* salesman

slt *abbr* **1** searchlight **2** sleet

1slub \ˈsləb, -lu̇b\ *n* -s [obs. D *slubbe,* fr. MD *slubbe, slobbe* slime, mud, mire — more at SLOBBER] *dial Eng* **:** a muddy or slushy mess

2slub \ˈsləb\ *n* -s [origin unknown] **:** a soft thick uneven section in a yarn caused accidentally by knotting during winding or by the inclusion of lint during spinning or intentionally by the twisting of two or more strands at different speeds or by the inclusion of short fibers during spinning

3slub \"\ *vt* **slubbed; slubbed; slubbing; slubs** [back-formation fr. *slubbing*] **:** to draw out and twist slightly (as slivers of wool)

4slub \"\ *n* -s **:** SLUBBING 2

slubbed *adj* [fr. past part. of 3*slub*] **:** made from yarns having decorative slubs

1slub·ber \ˈsləbə(r)\ *vt* -ED/-ING/-S [prob. fr. obs. D *slubberen* to walk through mud or mire, to slubber, fr. MD *slubberen, slobberen* to walk through mud and mire — more at SLOBBER] **1** *dial chiefly Eng* **:** STAIN, SULLY 〈~*ed* with . . . pedantry —John Milton〉 **2 :** to perform in a slipshod fashion **:** run through hastily — usu. used with *over* 〈~ over the business〉

2slubber \"\ *n* -s [3*slub* + *-er*] **1 :** one that produces slubbing **2 :** partly twined or badly twined woolen thread

slub·ber·de·gul·lion \ˈsləbə(r)də,gəlyən, -dē,g-, ,===ˈ==\ *n* [prob. irreg. fr. 1*slubber*] *chiefly dial* **:** a dirty rascal **:** SCOUNDREL, WRETCH

slub·bi \ˈslübē\ *also* **so·lu·bi** \səˈl-\ *or* **sloub·bie** \ˈslü-\ *n, pl* **sleyb** \ˈslāb\ *or* **su·lu·ba** \səˈlübə\ *usu cap* **:** a member of a nomadic Arab people living in an area extending from Damascus to Mosul in the north and in the Tigris-Euphrates region above Baghdad

slub·bing \ˈsləbiŋ\ *n* -s [*slub* of unknown origin + *-ing* (n. suffix)] **1 :** the act or process of drawing out and slightly twisting wool, cotton, or silk **2 :** slightly twisted roving

slubbing billy *n* **:** a machine for slubbing

1slub·by \ˈsləbi, -lu̇bi\ *adj* -ER/-EST [obs. D *slubbe* slub + E *-y* — more at SLUB] *chiefly dial* **:** MUDDY

2slub·by \-bē\ *adj* -ER/-EST [4*slub* + *-y*] *of a textile* **:** having slubs

slubcatcher \ˈ=,==\ *n* [2*slub* + *catcher*] **:** a yarn inspection device on spoolers and winders consisting usu. of a narrow slit that stops slubs and thickenings

slub yarn *n* **:** a yarn with thick and thin sections alternating regularly or irregularly — compare SLUB

slud \ˈsləd, -lu̇d\ *also* **slud·der** \-də(r)\ *n* -s [of Scand origin; akin to Dan *slud* sleet, slush, Icel *slyddā* — more at SLATTERN] *dial Eng* **:** a slippery mass (as of mud or slush)

1sludge \ˈsləj\ *n* -s [prob. alter. of 1*slush*] **1 :** MUD, MIRE; *esp* **:** a muddy deposit (as on tideland or river bed) **:** OOZE **2 :** a muddy or slushy mass, deposit, or sediment: as **a :** the precipitated solid matter produced by water and sewage treatment processes **b :** mud from a drill hole in boring **c :** muddy sediment in a steam boiler **d** (1) **:** SLIME 2d (2) **:** waste from a coal washery **e :** a precipitate or settling from oils; *esp* **:** one (as a mixture of impurities and acid) from mineral oils (as petroleum refined by sulfuric acid or oxidized in automotive engine lubrication or transformer cooling) **3 :** new sea ice forming in thin detached crystals **:** SLOB **4 :** a clump of agglutinated red blood cells; *specif* **:** SLUDGED BLOOD

2sludge \"\ *vb* -ED/-ING/-S *vt* **1 a :** to convert into sludge **b :** to fill in with sludge **c :** to clear of sludge **2 :** to form a sludge of (red blood cells) in small blood vessels **~** *vi* **:** to form sludge

sludge acid *n* **:** waste or spent sulfuric acid; *esp* **:** such acid derived from refining petroleum oils or crude benzenes

sludged blood *n* **:** blood in which the red blood cells become massed along the walls of the blood vessels and reduce the lumen of the vessels and the rate of blood flow

sludg·er \-jə(r)\ *n* -s **:** a device for sludging: as **a :** SAND PUMP **b :** SHELL PUMP **c :** a shovel for sludging out drains

sludgy \-jē,-ji\ *adj* -ER/-EST **:** full of sludge **:** MUDDY, SLUSHY

1slue *var of* SLOUGH

2slue *also* **slew** *or* **slough** \ˈslü\ *vb* -ED/-ING/-S [origin unknown] *vt* **1 :** to turn (as a ship's spar) about a fixed point that is usu. the center or axis **2 :** to turn (something) about **:** TWIST, VEER — usu. used with *around* or *round* 〈*slued* the boat around〉 〈*slued* her head around〉 〈they laughed and *slued* themselves round —Charles Dickens〉 **~** *vi* **1 :** to turn, twist, or swing about **:** PIVOT — usu. used with *around* 〈*slued* around in the saddle —A.B.Guthrie〉 **2 :** to slide and turn or slip out of the course **:** SKID 〈broke her towlines and *slued* across the channel —Marjory S. Douglas〉

3slue *also* **slew** \"\ *n* -s **:** position or inclination after sluing 〈get the mast on the right ~〉

4slue *var of* SLEW

slue-foot \ˈ=,=\ *or* **slue-footed** \ˈ=ˈ==\ *adj* **:** having big, clumsy, or turned-out feet

slue rope *also* **slew rope** *n* **:** a rope used in sluing (as a mast or spar)

1sluff \ˈsləf\ *n* -s [alter. of 3*slough*] **1 :** SLOUGH **2 :** DISCARD 1

2sluff \"\ *vb* -ED/-ING/-S *vt* **:** DISCARD 1 **~** *vi* **:** to discard a playing card

1slug \ˈsləg\ *n* -s [ME *slugge,* of Scand origin; akin to Sw & Norw dial. *slugga* to walk sluggishly, Norw dial. *sluggje* heavy slow person; akin to LG *slokeren* to hang loosely, MLG *slūren* to drag, trail — more at SLUR] **1 :** SLUGGARD **2** *archaic* **:** something (as a vessel, vehicle, or animal) that is slow-moving or sluggish **3 a :** any of numerous chiefly terrestrial pulmonate gastropods that are found in most parts of the world where there is a reasonable supply of moisture, are usu. placed in the family Limacidae though the group is prob. polyphyletic including descendants of shelled snails of several families, are closely related to the land snails but have the shell rudimentary and often buried in the mantle or wanting entirely, have the body when extended long and fusiform with the entire lower surface constituting the foot upon which the animal typically crawls over a film of mucous secreted by the skin, are mostly herbivorous, rasp at herbage with a well-developed radula, and often become serious pests of cultivated plants — see GARDEN SLUG **b :** SEA SLUG 2 **4 :** a smooth soft larva of a sawfly or moth that creeps like a mollusk: as **a :** PEAR SLUG **b :** ROSE SLUG

2slug \"\ *vb* **slugged; slugged; slugging; slugs** [ME *sluggen,* prob. of Scand origin; akin to Sw dial. *slugga* to walk sluggishly] *vi* **1 :** to rest idly **:** remain (as in bed) through laziness 〈~ in sloth and sensual delight —Edmund Spenser〉 **2 :** to move at a sluggish pace **:** LOITER 〈*slugging* on their slow-gaited asses —William Tennant〉 **~** *vt* **1 :** to spend (time) in dawdling or idling 〈the wretch who ~s his life away —James Thomson †1748〉 **2** *obs* **a :** to make sluggish **b :** DELAY, HINDER

3slug \"\ *n* -s [prob. fr. 1*slug*] **1 :** a piece (as a lump, disk, or cylinder) of metal: as **a** (1) **:** a musket ball (2) **:** BULLET; *esp* **:** a revolver bullet **b** (1) **:** a piece of crude metal **:** NUGGET (2) **:** a piece of solid bulk metal roughly shaped for subsequent processing **c** (1) **:** one of the private gold coins issued in California in 1849 (2) **:** a $50 gold piece **d** (1) **:** a thin flat piece of metal formed from a sheet by punching **:** 1BURR 3c (2) **:** a metal disk for insertion in a slot to operate an automatic machine; *esp* **:** one used illegally instead of a coin in such a machine (as a turnstile) **2 a :** a strip of metal similar to a printer's lead but usu. 6 point or larger **b** (1) **:** an identifying line placed by a compositor over matter set by him (2) **:** a line carrying a short title temporarily placed over one portion of matter set in separate takes — called also *galley slug* (3) **:** the short title itself (4) **:** GUIDELINE (5) **:** a line bearing a message or instruction (as a release date or the word *more*) **c :** a solid line either of characters or blank produced by a slugcasting machine **d** (1) **:** a scratch or tear in a negative or plate (2) **:** an anchor on a plate **3 :** a heavy nail or stud driven in a shoe or boot sole in shoe manufacturing **4 a :** a piece of magnetic material used to adjust the inductance of a coil **b :** a hollow metallic or dielectric cylinder used as a transforming element in a wave-guide system **5 :** a large flat-faced disk prepared for the purpose of mixing the ingredients in the manufacture of compressed pharmaceutical tablets **6 :** an irregular freshwater pearl — compare BAROQUE **7 :** a thickened place in a yarn or fabric caused usu. by lint or knots **8 :** a mass of half-roasted ore **9 a :** a small amount of liquor; *esp* **:** the quantity of drink taken in one swallow **:** SHOT, SNIFTER 〈tossed down three stiff ~s of bourbon —Peter DeVries〉 **b :** a detached mass of water or oil that causes impact or water hammer in a circulating system **10 :** the gravitational unit of mass in the fps system to which a pound force can impart an acceleration of one foot per second per second

4slug \"\ *vb* **slugged; slugged; slugging; slugs** *vt* **1 :** to load (as a gun) with slugs **:** insert a slug in 〈~ a rifle〉 〈~ a shoe〉 〈~ a coin machine〉 **2 :** to drive a soft lead bullet through (the bore of a rifle or pistol) in order to determine the exact bore diameter **3 a :** to add a printer's slug to (as a story) **:** insert a slug in (letterpress matter) **b :** to anchor (a printing plate) to a metal base by soldering metal projections into holes in the base **~** *vi* **:** to insert a slug (as in a shoe)

5slug \"\ *n* -s [perh. fr. 3*slug*] **:** a heavy blow; *esp* **:** one given with the fist 〈an epidemic of slaps, ~s, and slights that has threatened to turn . . . bus conductors into public punching bags —*N.Y. Times*〉

6slug \"\ *vb* **slugged; slugged; slugging; slugs** *vt* **1 :** to strike (as a person) heavily (as with the fist or a blunt instrument) 〈~ a man with a length of pipe〉 **2 a :** to drive or propel (a baseball) by batting hard 〈~ the ball over the left field fence〉 **b :** to achieve (as a two-base hit or a home run) by good batting 〈~ four homers in one ball game〉 **~** *vi* **1 :** to fight fiercely with a continuous exchange of heavy blows 〈the two fighters were still *slugging* as the round ended〉 〈the opposed armies *slugged* away in the same area for weeks〉 **2 :** to move forward or push on vigorously against difficulties **:** PLOW 〈a fighting leader who would ~ on through —Fletcher Pratt〉 **syn** see STRIKE

1slug·abed \ˈsləgə,bed\ *n* -s [1*slug* + *abed*] **:** one who stays in bed after his usual or obligated time of getting up **:** SLUGGARD 〈mothers getting their young ~s off to school〉

2slugabed \"\ *adj* **:** of or relating to a slugabed 〈~ habits . . . distressed him —Aldous Huxley〉

slugcast \ˈ=,=\ *adj* [3*slug* + *cast*] **:** produced by slugcasting 〈~ composition〉

slugcasting \ˈ=,==\ *n* [3*slug* + *casting*] **:** the mechanical casting of printer's slugs that are either keyboard assembled or hand assembled **:** LINECASTING

slug caterpillar *n* **:** 1SLUG 4

slug·fest \ˈsləg,fest\ *n* -s [5*slug* + *-fest*] **:** a hard-hitting struggle or contest marked by a sustained and vigorous exchange of heavy blows: as **a :** a boxing match; *esp* **:** one marked by the frequent and sometimes lengthy exchange of hard punches and a minimum of defensive boxing **b :** a baseball game that is marked by heavy hitting and frequent scoring by both teams

1slug·gard \ˈsləgə(r)d\ *n* -s [ME *sluggart, slogard,* prob. fr. *sluggy, sloggy* sluggish, lazy (prob. of Scand origin) + *-art, -ard* -ard; akin to Sw dial. *slugga* to walk sluggishly — more at SLUG] **:** an habitually lazy idle and inactive person 〈go to the ant, thou ~; consider her ways, and be wise —Prov. 6:6 (AV)〉 〈forecast a nation of ~s —Irwin Edman〉

2sluggard \"\ *adj* **:** having the characteristics of a sluggard 〈the people . . . depose the ~ king —J.G.Frazer〉

slug·gard·ly \-lē,-li\ *adj* **:** lazily inactive **:** INDOLENT

slug·gard·ness *n* -ES [ME *slogardnes,* fr. *slogard* sluggard + *-nes* -ness] **:** the quality or state of being a sluggard **:** lazy inactivity **:** INDOLENCE

slugged *past of* SLUG

1slug·ger \ˈsləgə(r)\ *n* -s [4*slug* + *-er*] **1 :** an operator of a slugging machine for nailing top lifts to shoe heels **2 :** a slugging machine used in shoe manufacturing

2slugger \"\ *n* -s [6*slug* + *-er*] **:** one that strikes hard or with heavy blows: as **a :** a prizefighter who punches hard but has usu. little defensive skill 〈a boxer, not a ~ —Chandler Brossard〉 **b :** a hard-hitting batter in baseball **c :** GOON 1 〈employers and labor organizations hiring . . . small armies of ~s —Walter Goodman〉

1slug·ging \ˈsləgiŋ, -gēŋ\ *n* -s [fr. gerund of 6*slug*] **:** illegal use of the fist or forearm on an opponent in football for which a penalty is usu. imposed

2slugging \"\ *n* -s [3*slug* + *-ing*] **:** the act or process of compressing pharmaceutical ingredients into disks — compare 3SLUG 5

slugging match *n* **:** SLUGFEST

slug·gish \ˈsləgish, -gēsh\ *adj* [ME *sluggus, sluggish,* fr. *slugge* sluggard + *-us, -ish* -ish — more at SLUG] **1 :** disinclined (as by nature, habit, or condition) to activity or exertion **:** INDOLENT, TORPID 〈a ~ worker〉 〈a ~ temperament〉 〈some physicians are mentally ~ —*Fortune*〉 〈many freshwater fishes . . . become ~ during cold weather —W.H.Dowdeswell〉 **2 :** slow to respond (as to stimulation or treatment) **:** lacking in vigor, animation, or efficiency 〈a ~ liver〉 〈an old man whose reactions were so ~ he shouldn't have been driving a car —Erle Stanley Gardner〉 〈tonic . . . for a clogged and ~ system —Emily Holt〉 〈turn an otherwise good performance into a ~ one —Warwick Braithwaite〉 **3 a :** markedly slow in movement, flow, or growth 〈a ~ pace〉 〈a ~ stream〉 〈~, wallowing oil tankers —*Amer. Guide Series: Texas*〉 〈his cataract of eloquence suddenly lagged to a ~ trickle —Herman Wouk〉 〈spread over several decades of ~ economic development —*Amer. Guide Series: Va.*〉 **b :** economically inactive or slow-moving **:** DULL, STAGNANT 〈a ~ market〉 〈clothing sales were ~〉 〈stock prices have remained notably ~ —*Fortune*〉 **syn** see LETHARGIC

slug·gish·ly *adv* [ME *sluggusly,* fr. *sluggus* sluggish + *-ly*] **:** in a sluggish manner **:** SLOWLY, INDOLENTLY

slug·gish·ness *n* -ES [ME *sluggusnes,* fr. *sluggus* sluggish + *-nes* -ness] **:** the quality or state of being sluggish: as **a :** disinclination to activity **:** INDOLENCE 〈mental ~〉 **b :** slowness of movement 〈silt adding to the ~ of the creek〉 **c :** economic stagnancy 〈the post-holiday ~ of department store sales〉

slughi *often cap, var of* SALUKI

slug·horn \ˈsləg,hȯrn\ *n* -s [by folk etymology fr. earlier *slogorn* — more at SLOGAN] **1** *obs* **:** SLOGAN 1 **2 :** HORN, TRUMPET

sluglike \ˈ=,=\ *adj* **:** resembling a slug

slugline \ˈ=,=\ *n* **:** 3SLUG 2b, 2c

slugs *pl of* SLUG, *pres 3d sing of* SLUG

slug snail *n* **:** 1SLUG 3

slug·wood \ˈslə,gwu̇d\ *n* [by alter.] **:** SLOGWOOD

slug worm *n* **:** 1SLUG 4

1sluice \ˈslüs\ *n* -s [ME *scluse, escluse,* fr. MF *escluse,* fr. LL *exclusa* dam, sluice, fr. fem. of L *exclusus,* past part. of *excludere* to shut out, exclude — more at EXCLUDE] **1 a :** an artificial passage for water (as in a millstream) fitted with a valve or gate for stopping or regulating the flow **b :** a body of water pent up behind a floodgate or water gate **2 :** a device for letting water in or out or holding it back: as **a :** a dock gate **:** WATER GATE, FLOODGATE **b :** VALVE, PIPE **3 a :** a stream flowing through a floodgate **b :** a conduit (as a channel or stream) that serves to drain or carry off surplus water **4 :** a long inclined trough or flume usu. on the ground (as for washing auriferous earth or floating down logs); *specif* **:** such a contrivance paved usu. with riffles to hold quicksilver for catching gold **5 :** something suggestive of a sluice: as **a :** a rushing or pouring stream **:** SPATE 〈stopped the ~ of free advice —F.B.Gipson〉 〈great ~s of rain —Carleton Beals〉 **b :** a pent-up flood of emotion 〈open the ~s of popular revolt —D.J.Dallin〉

2sluice \"\ *vb* -ED/-ING/-S *vt* **1 :** to cause to flow or pour forth by or as if by floodgates **:** draw off by or through a sluice or sluiceway 〈by this fresh blood that from thy manly breast I cowardly *sluiced* out —John Marston〉 **2 a :** to wash with or in a stream of water running through or from a sluice **b :** to drench, wash, or scour with gushes or floods (as of water) **:** FLUSH, DOUSE 〈~ earth in mining〉 〈~ a pavement with a hose〉 〈hydraulic jets ~ away soil layers bearing tin ore —W.R.Moore〉 〈trying to ~ his face without wetting his cuffs —Richard Llewellyn〉 **3 a :** to transport (as logs) in a sluice or float through a sluiceway **b :** to drive (logs) by releasing a sluice of water **~** *vi* **:** to pour from or as if from a sluice 〈rain *sluicing* down to plaster his ragged shirt to his body —Marcia Davenport〉 **syn** see POUR

sluice box *n* **:** a single section usu. about 12 feet long of a gold-mining sluice

sluice gate *n* **:** the sliding gate of a sluice

sluic·er \-sə(r)\ *n* -s **:** the keeper of a sluice

sluice valve *n* **1 :** SLUICE GATE **2 :** GATE VALVE **3 :** a watertight sliding valve in the watertight floors of a frame in shipbuilding

sluiceway \ˈ=,=\ *n* **1 :** an artificial channel into which water is let by a sluice; *specif* **:** SLUICE 4 **2 :** the opening in a splash dam for passage of logs **3 :** a channel through which a large volume of water has passed (as of meltwater from a glacier)

sluicy \ˈslüsē\ *adj* **:** falling copiously or in streams (as from a sluice) **:** STREAMING 〈~ sheets of rain〉

sluing arch *n* [*sluing* fr. pres. part. of 2*slue*] **:** SPLAYED ARCH

sluit \ˈslüt\ *n* -s [Afrik, fr. D *sloot* ditch, fr. MD; akin to MLG *slōt* ditch, puddle, bog, OFris *slāt,* Sw dial. *slota* to be putrid, ME *sloor* mud — more at SLUR] *chiefly Africa* **:** a deep usu. dry ditch produced by the washing of heavy rains in a large natural fissure **:** GULLY, GULCH

1slum \ˈsləm\ *n* -s *often attrib* [origin unknown] **1 :** a highly congested usu. urban residential area characterized by deteriorated unsanitary buildings, poverty, and social disorganization 〈brought up in an unwholesome ~〉 〈the ~s of the city〉 〈~ clearance〉 〈a ~ district〉 〈creating a rural ~〉 **2 :** cheap articles given as prizes in games of chance (as at carnivals)

2slum \"\ *vi* **slummed; slummed; slumming; slums :** to visit or frequent slums; *esp* **:** to make an excursion into slums out of curiosity or for pleasure — often used in the expression *go slumming* 〈went *slumming* in their evening clothes〉

3slum \"\ *n* -s [perh. fr. G *schlamm* slime, mud, fr. MHG *slam;* prob. akin to obs. E dial. *slemp* to slip away, ON *sleppa* to slide, slip, L *labi* to slide, slip, sink, fall — more at SLEEP] **1 :** SLIME **2 :** a passage at the bottom of a mining pit

4slum \"\ *n* -s [by shortening] **1 :** SLUMGULLION 1b **2 :** SLUMGULLION 3

1slum·ber \ˈsləmbə(r)\ *vb* **slumbered; slumbered; slumbering** \-b(ə)riŋ\ **slumbers** [ME *slumberen, slumeren,* freq. of *slumen* to doze, prob. fr. *slume, sloumbe* slumber, fr. OE *slūma;* akin to MHG *slummern, slumen* to slumber, Norw *slum* sluggish, Norw dial. *sluma* to walk sluggishly, drag one's feet, ME *sloor* mud — more at SLUR] *vi* **1 a :** to sleep lightly **:** DOZE 〈he who keeps Israel will neither ~ nor sleep —Ps 121:4 (RSV)〉 **b :** to lie asleep 〈the girl ~*ed* peacefully —Henry La Cossitt〉 **2 a :** to lie or live as if sunk in sleep or stupor **:** be in a torpid state **:** HIBERNATE 〈the . . . nation ~*ed* through more than two centuries of self-imposed isolation —Louis Wasserman〉 **b :** to remain in a negligent or slothful state **:** IDLE 〈the public conscience ~s〉 〈~*ing* along until shocked into activity〉 〈add to this a report I have been asked to do . . . and you will guess that I have not ~*ed* —H.J.Laski〉 **c :** to lie dormant or latent 〈below the surface ~*ed* deadly memories —*Times Lit. Supp.*〉 **~** *vt* **:** to pass or spend (as time) in or as if in sleep — usu. used with *away* or *out* 〈~*ing* away the best years for productive work〉 **syn** see SLEEP

2slumber \"\ *n* -s [ME *slumbir, slummir,* fr. *slumberen, slumeren* to slumber] **1 a :** a state of sleep or repose **:** SLEEP 〈it was no night for ~〉 〈sank into a deep ~〉 〈fills my ~ with tumultuous dreams —P.B.Shelley〉 **b :** light sleep **:** DOZE 〈at last fell into a ~, and thence into a fast sleep —John Bunyan〉 **2 :** a moral, mental, or physical condition like sleep **:** LETHARGY, TORPOR 〈a great writer arouses us from our dogmatic ~s —Zechariah Chafee〉

3slumber \"\ *adj* **:** of, relating to, or intended for use during slumber 〈a ~ cap〉 〈a ~ robe〉

slum·ber·er \-bərə(r)\ *n* -s [ME *slumbrer, slumerer,* fr. *slumberen, slumeren* to slumber + *-er*] : one that slumbers : SLEEPER

slumberland \ˈ=,=\ *n* : an unreal country that is a realm of sleep

slum·ber·ous *or* **slum·brous** \ˈsləmb(ə)rəs\ *adj* [ME *slumbrous,* fr. *slumbir* slumber + *-ous*] **1 a** : inclined to sleep : heavy with sleep : SLEEPY, SOMNOLENT ⟨~ eyes⟩ ⟨lifting . . . her ~ little boy —Peggy Bennett⟩ ⟨her heavy ~ voice —Meridel Le Sueur⟩ **b** : CALM, PEACEFUL ⟨a ~ town⟩ ⟨a ~ Sunday in June —Maurice Walsh⟩ **2** : inviting or inducing slumber : SOPORIFIC ⟨a ~ sound⟩ ⟨the ~ light is rich and warm —Alfred Tennyson⟩ **3** : marked by, accompanied by, or suggestive of sleep or a condition like sleep : LETHARGIC ⟨a ~ peace pervaded every province —Pearl Buck⟩ ⟨a ~ administration⟩ — **slum·ber·ous·ly** *or* **slum·brous·ly** *adv* — **slum·ber·ous·ness** *n* -ES

slumber party *n* : an overnight gathering of teen-age girls usu. at one of their homes at which they dress in nightclothes but pass the night more in talking than sleeping

slum·bery \ˈsləmb(ə)rē\ *adj* [ME *slumbry,* fr. *slumbir* slumber + *-y*] : SLUMBEROUS

slum·dom \ˈsləmdəm\ *n* -s [¹*slum* + *-dom*] **1** : a district of slums ⟨wandering through ~⟩ **2** : the quality or state of being a slum ⟨a once fashionable district declining slowly into ~ —Osbert Lancaster⟩

slum·gul·lion \,sləmˈgəlyən, ˈ=,==\ *n* [³*slum* + *gullion*] **1 a** : an insipid drink (as weak tea or coffee) **b** : a meat stew **2** : the mixed blood, oil, and salt water that collect on the decks of a ship while the valuable parts of a whale are being handled **3** : a usu. red muddy deposit in mining sluices

slumgum \ˈ=,=\ *n* [³*slum* + *gum*] : the residue consisting chiefly of propolis, cocoons, bits of wax, and honey that remains after removal of the readily extractable honey and wax from honeycombs

slumland \ˈ=,=\ *n* [¹*slum* + *land*] : an area of slums : SLUMDOM ⟨the town is one vast ~⟩

slum·mage \ˈsləmij\ *n* -s [³*slum* + *-age*] *Brit* : impurities that settle out in fermenting vessels and casks

slummed *past of* SLUM

slumming *pres part of* SLUM

slum·mock \ˈsləmək\ *var of* SLOMMACK

slum·my \ˈsləmē, -mi\ *adj* -ER/-EST [¹*slum* + *-y*] : of, relating to, or full of slums ⟨the ~ outskirts of the city⟩

¹**slump** \ˈsləmp\ *vb* -ED/-ING/-S [prob. of Scand origin; akin to Norw *slumpa* to fall, fall upon, Dan *slumpe* to stumble, fall upon, chance upon; akin to LG *slump* marsh, slime, L *labi* to slide, slip, fall — more at SLEEP] *vi* **1 a** : to fall or sink suddenly ⟨ice cracked and he ~*ed* through⟩ **b** : to drop suddenly : fall in a heap : slide down : COLLAPSE ⟨he ~*ed* to the floor with hardly a murmur —*Phoenix Flame*⟩ ⟨slipped on the parquet and ~*ed* headlong —Richard Llewellyn⟩ **2** : to assume an awkwardly drooping posture or carriage ⟨~*ed* onto the leather davenport —J.A.Michener⟩ ⟨she walks slowly . . . ~*ing* at the waist —Constance Walsh⟩ **3** : to fall off : DECLINE, SAG ⟨begins to make a place for himself and then . . . suddenly ~*s* —Edmund Fuller⟩ ⟨sales ~ badly in certain territories —E.H.Shanks⟩ **4 a** : to slip or settle down ⟨rock or earth ~*s* in a landslide or above a rock that is undergoing solution⟩ **b** : to settle slightly and spread out ⟨concrete or mortar will ~ when the form is removed⟩ ~ *vt* : to cause a slump in (a market) **syn** see FALL

²**slump** \"\, ˈslu̇mp\ *n* -s [LG, marsh, slime] *dial Brit* : a marshy or boggy place

³**slump** \ˈsləmp\ *n* -s [LG; akin to Fris *slompe* lump, slump, D *slomp*] *chiefly Scot* : a sizable group or quantity : LUMP, BULK

⁴**slump** \"\ *vt* -ED/-ING/-S *chiefly Scot* : to classify or consider together : LUMP ⟨~*ing* the . . . candidates together —*Scots Mag.*⟩

⁵**slump** \"\ *n* -s [¹*slump*] **1 a** : a marked decline or falling off (as in prices, activity, vigor) : DROP, SAG ⟨a ~ in theater attendance⟩ ⟨fear a ~ in the party vote⟩ ⟨a period of moral ~ —S.H.Adams⟩ ⟨the normal seasonal ~ in tuna deliveries —*Wall Street Jour.*⟩ **b** : a sustained decline in economic activity or in prices : DEPRESSION ⟨a worldwide ~⟩ ⟨a ~ in the wheat market⟩ ⟨the great waste of booms and ~*s* of the business cycle —Will Irwin⟩ ⟨lost all his money in the ~ —Dorothy Sayers⟩ **c** : a period of poor or losing play by a team or individual competitor in a sport : a losing streak ⟨one spring I was in a batting ~ —Ted Williams⟩ ⟨came out of its scoring ~ and won the consolation game —*Ice Hockey Guide*⟩ **2** : the number of inches that a mass of concrete settles after the removal of a cone-shaped metal form into which the fresh concrete has been placed in three layers — see SLUMP TEST **3** : a fall or downward slide (as of earth or rock) : LANDSLIDE **4** *chiefly NewEng* : a dessert made by dropping biscuit dough on cooking fruit ⟨apple ~⟩ ⟨blueberry ~⟩ — compare GRUNT 3

slump bedding *n* : SLIP BEDDING

slump test *n* : a test to determine the consistency of freshly mixed concrete by measuring the slump

slums *pl of* SLUM, *pres 3d sing of* SLUM

¹**slung** *past of* SLING

²**slung** \ˈsləŋ\ *chiefly Scot var of* SLING

slung·shot \ˈsləŋ,=\ *n* [¹*slung* + *shot*] : a weapon consisting of a small mass of metal or stone fixed on a flexible handle or strap

¹**slunk** *past of* SLINK

²**slunk** \ˈsləŋk\ *n* -s [¹*slunk*] : SLINK 1

slunkskin \ˈ=,=\ *n* [²*slunk* + *skin*] : SLINKSKIN

slup \ˈsləp\ *vt* **slupped; slupped; slupping; slups** [perh. alter. of ³*slop*] : to sip or swallow (as soup or beverage) greedily and noisily : SLURP ⟨there wasn't a sound at the table except for Uncle . . . *slupping* his soup —N.R.Nash⟩

¹**slur** *R* ˈslər, + *vowel* -lər·; *-R* -lə̄, + *suffixal vowel* -lər· *also* -lə̄r, + *vowel in a following word* -lər· *or* -lə̄ *also* -lə̄r\ *vb* **slurred; slurred; slurring; slurs** [prob. of LG origin; akin to LG *slurrn* to shuffle, drag the feet, MLG *slūren* to drag, trail — more at SLUR (to soil)] *vt* **1** *obs* : to slide (a die) so as to cheat : TRICK **2 a** : to slide or slip over without due mention, consideration, or emphasis : treat superficially or dissemblingly — often used with *over* ⟨the problem of the illegitimate child . . . is *slurred* over —C.W.Cunnington⟩ ⟨~ over certain facts in one's argument⟩ ⟨*slurring* over the significance of the letter —*Times Lit. Supp.*⟩ **b** : to perform (as a duty) hurriedly : SKIMP ⟨let him not ~ his lesson —R.W.Emerson⟩ ⟨wherefore ~ the . . . ceremony —Alfred Tennyson⟩ **3 a** : to perform (two or more successive musical tones of different pitch) in a smooth or connected manner **b** : to mark (notes) with a slur **4** : to reduce, make a substitution for, or omit (a sound or succession of sounds that occurs or that would occur in speech regarded as exemplary) : make such reduction, substitution, or omission in (one's utterance of (as a word or phrase) ~ *vi* **1** *dial chiefly Eng* : SLIP, SLIDE ⟨~ on ice⟩ **2** : DRAG, SHUFFLE ⟨*slurring* through ankle-deep water —W.E.M.Campbell⟩

²**slur** \"\ *n* -s **1** *obs* **a** : a glide in dancing **b** : a sliding of dice in an attempt to cheat **2 a** : a curved line ⁀ or ‿ connecting musical notes that are to be sung to the same syllable or performed without a break (as with one stroke of a bow) — called also *bind;* compare TIE **b** : the combination of two or more slurred tones **3** : a slurring manner of speech **4** *or* **slur cam** *or* **slur cock** : a device for depressing the sinkers in knitting machines successively by passing over them

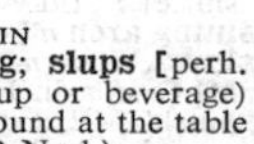

slur 2a

³**slur** \"\ *vb* **slurred; slurred; slurring; slurs** [obs. E dial. *slur* thin watery mud, fr. ME *sloor;* akin to MHG *slier* mud, MLG *slūren* to drag, trail, MD *sluren* to drag, trail, Norw dial. *slura* to hang loose, drag, Lith *sliužti* to diminish, become small and prob. to Goth *slawan* to be silent; basic meaning: to hang loose, be slack] *vt* **1** *dial chiefly Eng* : to soil by smearing : BESMIRCH, SULLY **2** : to cast aspersions upon : run down : DISPARAGE ⟨was always *slurring* her fellow workers⟩ ⟨*slurred* his integrity —Marguerite A. Brown⟩ **3** : to make indistinct : OBSCURE, MASK ⟨with periods, points, and tropes he ~*s* his crimes —John Dryden⟩ **4** : BLUR **1** ~ *vi* : to slip so as to blur or make slurs — used of a sheet being printed

⁴**slur** \"\ *n* -s **1 a** : an insulting or disparaging remark or innuendo : ASPERSION, CALUMNY ⟨his election was due to . . . last minute racial ~*s* on his opponent —William Cox⟩ ⟨the cowardly ~*s* of scandalmongers⟩ **b** : STAIN, BLOT, STIGMA ⟨his actions cast a ~ on his profession⟩ **2** : a blurred or doubled spot or area in printed matter caused by the sliding of the paper on the printing surface at the moment of impression : MACKLE, SMUDGE

¹**slurp** \ˈslərp, -lə̄p, -ləip\ *vb* -ED/-ING/-S [D *slurpen* to lap, sip, slurp, fr. MD *slorpen;* akin to MLG *slorpen* to slurp, Norw *slurpe* to sip — more at ABSORB] *vi* : to make a sucking noise in the process of drinking or eating ~ *vt* : to eat or drink (soft food or liquid) noisily ⟨~*ing* porridge from a wooden spoon —Ogden Nash⟩

²**slurp** \"\ *n* -s : a noisy swallow or ingestion ⟨the puppy gobbled at the food in great ~*s* —Walter Karig⟩

¹**slur·ry** \ˈslər·|ē, -lə·r|, |i\ *n* -ES [ME *slory;* prob. akin to ME *sloor* mud — more at SLUR] **1 a** : a watery mixture or suspension of insoluble matter (as mud, lime, plaster of paris, or wood pulp) ⟨a thin ~ of magnesia⟩ **b** : a mixture of raw materials with water in the manufacture of portland cement by the wet process **c** : a watery suspension of a fungicide or insecticide used esp. in seed treatment **d** : SLIP **2** : REGULUS, MATTE

²**slurry** \"\ *vt* -ED/-ING/-S : to convert (as a powder or concentrate) into a slurry

³**slurry** \"\ *adj* : of, relating to, or involving the use of a slurry ⟨~ methods of seed treatment⟩

⁴**slurry** \"\ *vt* -ED/-ING/-S [ME *slorien,* prob. fr. *slory* slurry] *archaic* : SMEAR, SMIRCH

slurs *pres 3d sing of* SLUR, *pl of* SLUR

¹**slush** \ˈsləsh\ *n* -ES [perh. of Scand origin; akin to Norw *slusk* slop, slush, Sw *slask* wet, slushy weather] **1 a** : partly melted snow : watery snow **b** : a substance resembling melted snow (as a mixture of solid carbon dioxide and acetone) **c** : incoherent ice crystals formed during the early stages of freezing of salt water (as in the Arctic ocean) **2 a** : soft mud : MIRE ⟨the water was dirty with the ~ brought to the surface by the trampling —F.D.Davison⟩ **b** : liquid mud used in well drilling **c** : grout made of portland cement, sand, and water **3** : refuse grease and fat from cooking esp. on shipboard **4 a** : a soft mixture of grease or oil and other materials for protecting the surface of metal parts against corrosion; *esp* : a mixture of white lead and lime for painting the bright parts of machines (as the connecting rods of steamboats) to preserve them from oxidation **b** : liquid enamel applied as a ground coat on metalware **5** : SLUSH PULP **6** : trashy and usu. cheaply sentimental material (as in a book, newspaper, or film) : RUBBISH, DRIVEL, MUSH ⟨syndicated ~⟩ ⟨the dramatic ~ known as soap operas —G.S.Perry⟩ **7** *dial Eng* : a sloppy person : SLOVEN

²**slush** \"\ *vb* -ED/-ING/-ES *vt* **1** : to wet, splash, or soil with slush ⟨we were quite ~*ed* in the mire —R.T.Wilson⟩ **2 a** : to cover with a protective coating of paint or lubricating slush ⟨masts ~*ed* with linseed —W.P.Moore⟩ ⟨bearings . . . ~*ed* with two coatings of pure petrolatum —*Packing & Shipping*⟩ **b** : to apply a finishing material to roughly (as by dipping, spraying, or brushing) **3** : to wash (as a deck) roughly or noisily : SLUICE ⟨waiting . . . for the bo'sun to come aloft to ~ the deck —Herman Smith⟩ **4** : to fill in (as the joints of a wall or of a block pavement) with slush or grout — often used with *in or up* ⟨~ in well all the joints between the tile and brickwork —J.E.Ray⟩ **5 a** : to fill (old mine workings) hydraulically with fine waste material **b** : to transport (as ore or rock) in a scraper that is usu. drawn by a hoist and cable **6 a** : to pump (wet pulp) in paper manufacturing **b** : to extract surplus liquid from (pulp) ~ *vi* **1** : to make one's way through slush : SLOSH, WADE ⟨~*ed* through the mire doggedly —*Century Mag.*⟩ ⟨~*ed* through waist-deep water —L.M.Uris⟩ **2** : to make a splashing sound ⟨shoes ~*ing* in the mud —Shirley A. Grau⟩ ⟨the filthy gutter ~*es* —R.L.Stevenson⟩

³**slush** \"\ *n* -ES : a sound of or as if of slushing through soft mud or snow

slush-cast \ˈ=,=\ *vt* : to cast (as a hollow metal shape) by a process in which metal is poured into a metallic mold and immediately poured out leaving a thin solidified layer of the metal on the walls of the mold

slush casting *n* -s : a hollow casting made by the process of slush-casting

slush·er \-shə(r)\ *n* -s [²*slush* + *-er*] **1** : one that slushes: as **a** : a worker who sprays filler over castings (as sinks or bathtubs) to make a smooth surface for the enamel coating **b** : a device for slushing **2** : SCRAPER 1j

slush fund *n* **1** : a fund raised from the sale of slush and other refuse (as formerly of warships) to obtain small luxuries or pleasures (as for the crew) **2** : a fund for bribing public officials or carrying on corruptive propaganda on behalf of special interests ⟨a *slush fund* to corrupt legislatures, to purchase favors from public officers —W.O.Douglas⟩ ⟨had the support of the trucking interests with the richest *slush fund* in the state —*New Republic*⟩

slush ice *n* **1** : ¹SLUSH 1c **2** : FRAZIL

slush·i·ly \-shəlē, -li\ *adv* : in a slushy manner

slush·i·ness \-shēnəs, -shin-\ *n* -ES : the quality or state of being slushy : SENTIMENTALITY ⟨the ~ of young girls over a crooner⟩

slush·ing oil *n* : a semisolid oil or grease (as a mixture of petrolatum and rosin) used as a protective coating for bright metal surfaces

slush lamp *n* : a crude lamp burning slush, tallow, or grease

slushpit \ˈ=,=\ *n* : an excavation or diked area to receive sludge, mud, and discharged matter from an oil well

slush pulp *n* : paper pulp in water suspension

¹**slushy** \ˈsləshē, -shi\ *adj* -ER/-EST [¹*slush* + *-y* (adj. suffix)] : of, full of, or characterized by slush ⟨~ snow⟩ ⟨a ~ road⟩; *esp* : TRASHY ⟨pander to everything that's shoddy and ~ and third-rate in human nature —John Buchan⟩ ⟨~ songs —MacKinlay Kantor⟩ **syn** see SENTIMENTAL

²**slushy** \"\ *n* -ES [¹*slush* + *-y* (n. suffix)] **1** *slang* : a ship's cook **2** *Austral* : a cook's helper

slut \ˈslət, *usu* -əd·+V\ *n* -s [ME *slutte;* prob. akin to G dial. *schlote* slut, Sw dial. *slåta* slattern, D *slodder* slovenly person, slut — more at SLATTERN] **1** : a lazy, careless, or slovenly woman : SLATTERN ⟨that ~ of a housekeeper —Margaret Kennedy⟩ **2 a** : a lewd or dissolute woman; *esp* : PROSTITUTE ⟨outrageously made up, her cheeks rouged to the eyes . . . she looked more of a ~ than any woman there —W.S.Maugham⟩ **b** : a saucy or brazen girl : HUSSY, MINX ⟨never knew any of these forward ~*s* come to good —Henry Fielding⟩ ⟨a whimsical ~ . . . who is off in peals of wanton laughter —D.B.Dodson⟩ **c** : a servant girl : MAID ⟨a most admirable ~ —Samuel Pepys⟩ **3** : a female dog : BITCH **4** *dial* : a rude lamp or candle; *esp* : one made from a grease-soaked rag

¹**sluth·er** \ˈsləthə(r), -lu̇th-\ *vi* -ED/-ING/-S [alter. of ¹*slither*] *dial Eng* : to slip along : SHUFFLE, SLITHER

²**sluther** \"\ *n* -s *chiefly dial* : the act of shuffling or sliding

slut·tery \ˈslədərē, -lətə-, -ri\ *n* -ES [*slut* + *-ery*] : SLUTTISHNESS

slut·tish \-d·|ish, -t|, |ēsh\ *adj* [ME, fr. *slutte* slut + *-ish*] : having the characteristics of a slut : SLOVENLY, DISORDERLY ⟨the servants awkward, ~, and slothful —Tobias Smollett⟩ ⟨his wife's careless tresses had ~ charm —Vera Caspary⟩ — **slut·tish·ly** *adv* — **slut·tish·ness** *n* -ES

slut·ty \|ē, |i\ *adj* -ER/-EST [ME, fr. *slutte* slut + *-y*] : SLUTTISH

slv *abbr* **1** sleeve **2** solvent

SLW *abbr, often not cap* straight-line wavelength

¹**sly** \ˈslī\ *adj* **slier** *also* **slyer** \-ī(ə)r, -īə\ **sliest** *also* **slyest** \-ī̇əst\ [ME *sli, sleih, slegh,* fr. ON *slœgr* sly, crafty; akin to ON *slā* to strike, beat — more at SLAY] **1** *chiefly dial* **a** : wise in practical affairs : CANNY, SHREWD ⟨has a deal to say in his ~, dry, sententious, proverb way —Robert Burns⟩ **b** : displaying cleverness : INGENIOUS ⟨with ~ skill —Edmund Spenser⟩ **2 a** : artfully cunning : subtle in deceit : CRAFTY, GUILEFUL, WILY ⟨a ~ fox⟩ ⟨a ~ action⟩ ⟨a ~ scheme⟩ ⟨by ~ enticement gives his baneful cup —John Milton⟩ ⟨had played . . . many a ~ trick —Lyle Saxon⟩ ⟨a ~ way of prodding sales —*Business Week*⟩ **b** : trickily secret : SECRETIVE, FURTIVE ⟨he's a ~ one — had it up his sleeve all the time⟩ ⟨a ~ answer⟩ ⟨a ~ glance⟩ ⟨you have been very ~, very reserved with me —Jane Austen⟩ **3** : lightly artful or mischievous : ARCH, ROGUISH ⟨~ jests⟩ ⟨a ~ wit⟩ ⟨churchmen, when off duty, were not averse to ~ irreverences —G.F.Whicher⟩ **4** *chiefly Austral* : carried on or sold clandestinely or illegally : ILLICIT, BOOTLEG ⟨a ~ trade⟩ ⟨selling ~ grog to the convicts —Colin Simpson⟩

syn CUNNING, CRAFTY, TRICKY, FOXY, INSIDIOUS, GUILEFUL, WILY, ARTFUL: SLY suggests devious, furtive, or secretive lack of candor or underhandedness ⟨the *sly* attack which undermines faith in our allies and among ourselves —Dean Acheson⟩ ⟨*sly* fellows to be watched —A.C.Whitehead⟩ CUNNING may apply to an overreaching, circumventing, or evading often by one of low intelligence and usu. by secret or devious means ⟨he's always slipping out at night. They're *cunning* as the devil, these naturals —Dorothy Sayers⟩ ⟨looked up with a *cunning* smile. "A servant can always know his master's secrets if he likes" —Charles Kingsley⟩ CRAFTY may describe adroitness at deceptive scheme and stratagem along with chary caution ⟨the Nazi insanity turned this mild man of conscience into a *crafty* plotter, collector of illegal funds, traffic manager of nocturnal convoys, distributor of forged passports —Hal Lehrman⟩ ⟨as truculent, as relentless in the fight, as *crafty* in legal subterfuge as the Erie men themselves —Matthew Josephson⟩ TRICKY may indicate shifty chicanery ⟨beneath all this glitter of chivalry lay the subtle, busy diplomatist . . . to all who dealt with him he was equally false and *tricky* —J.R. Green⟩ ⟨he avoided the mean and *tricky:* he was always an honorable foe —W.C.Ford⟩ FOXY may suggest practised, wary shrewdness ⟨concealment of his partnership in the Ballantyne firm and the publishing of many of his works either anonymously or under varied pseudonyms reveal a strain of *foxy* secretiveness —Edgar Johnson⟩ INSIDIOUS may apply to carefully masked underhandedness ⟨with the *insidious* undermining of respect for law and government, the vicious conception of republicanism made its appearance —V.L.Parrington⟩ GUILEFUL and WILY describe what is habitually marked by treacherous cunning or astute stratagem unctuously concealed ⟨nor trust in the *guileful* heart and the murder-loving hand —William Morris⟩ ⟨mistaking the light for a beacon, ships were lured to the treacherous reefs, there to be boarded and looted by the *wily* shoremen —*Amer. Guide Series: N.C.*⟩ ARTFUL may apply to calculating crafty deception employing the indirect or factitious ⟨if you can keep her from drink, but you can't keep her; she's that *artful* she'll get it under your very eyes, without you knowing it —Samuel Butler †1902⟩ ⟨as workingmen, under *artful* urging, began to blame the Chinese for all their wrongs —*Amer. Guide Series: Calif.*⟩ — **on the sly** *adv* : SURREPTITIOUSLY, SECRETLY ⟨read it, if at all, *on the sly,* to look for their names —A.C.Spectorsky⟩ ⟨got married *on the sly* —Helen Rich⟩

²**sly** \"\ *vi* **slied; slied; slying; slies** : to move slyly; *esp* : SLIP, SLINK — usu. used with *out* ⟨ready to ~ out the alley door, bent double —*Everybody's Mag.*⟩

sly *abbr* sloppy

slyboots \ˈ=,=\ *n pl but sing in constr* [¹*sly* + *boots*] : a sly, tricky person; *esp* : one who is cunning or mischievous in an engaging, diverting way : SCAMP, WAG ⟨the ~, how she wheedled him —W.S.Gilbert⟩ ⟨an adorable ~ of a child who was often naughty but always forgiven and indulged —Gore Vidal⟩

sly goose *n* : SHELDRAKE

sly·ly *also* **sli·ly** *adv* [ME *slily,* fr. *sli* sly + *-ly*] : in a sly manner: as **a** : SHREWDLY ⟨pointed his remarks by ~ wagging his forefinger —G.B.Shaw⟩ **b** : with covert cunning : SUBTLY ⟨offered her ~ insolent condolences on being married to a barbarian —Charles Kingsley⟩ **c** : in a surreptitious way : FURTIVELY ⟨glanced ~⟩ ⟨~ in love with their colleagues —H.T.Moore⟩ ⟨~ injected commercials —*New Yorker*⟩ **d** : ARTFULLY, ROGUISHLY

sly·ness *n* -ES [ME *sleghness, slinesse,* fr. *slegh, sli* sly + *-ness, -nesse* -ness] : the quality or state of being sly: as **a** : SHREWDNESS, CRAFTINESS ⟨a very weak position of which the bishop with praiseworthy ~ took full advantage —T.S.Eliot⟩ **b** : SECRETIVENESS ⟨led him to escape . . . the next morning with admirable ~ —Jane Austen⟩

¹**slype** *dial Eng var of* ³SLIPE

²**slype** \ˈslīp\ *n* -s [prob. fr. Flem *slijpe* place for slipping in and out, fr. MFlem *slijpen* to slip, slip out; akin to MD *slippen* to slip — more at SLIP] : a narrow passage; *specif* : one between the transept and chapter house or deanery in an English cathedral

sm *abbr* small

SM *abbr or n* -s [NL *scientiae magister*] Master of Science

SM *abbr* **1** senior magistrate **2** sergeant major **3** short meter **4** signalman **5** silver medalist **6** single deck **7** [L *sinistra mano*] left hand; mano sinistra **8** standard matched **9** state militia **10** stipendiary magistrate **11** surface measure **12** surgeon major

Sm *symbol* samarium

sma \ˈsmȯ, ˈsmä\ *Scot var of* SMALL

¹**smack** \ˈsmak\ *n* -s [ME, fr. OE *smæc;* akin to OFris *smek, smaka* taste, MD *smac, smake,* MLG *smak,* OHG *smoc,* ON *smekkr* taste, Lith *smaguriauti* to nibble, eat dainties] **1** : characteristic taste or flavor : SAVOR; *also* : a slight or perceptible taste or tincture ⟨an orange with a bitter ~⟩ ⟨a ~ of the wood in cider⟩ **2** *obs* : LIKING, DELIGHT **3** : a small quantity: as **a** : a trifling portion : little serving : TASTE ⟨a ~ of wine to each child⟩ **b** : a smattering of knowledge or information **syn** see TASTE

²**smack** \"\ *vb* -ED/-ING/-S [ME *smacken,* alter. (influenced by *smack,* n.) of *smachen,* fr. OE *smæccan;* akin to OFris *smekka* to taste, MD *smaken,* OHG *smecken,* ON *smakka* to taste, *smekkr,* n., taste — more at ¹SMACK] *vt, archaic* : to perceive by taste or scent ~ *vi* **1** : to have a taste or flavor ⟨wine that ~*s* of resin⟩ **2** : to have a trace, vestige, or suggestion : reveal or retain a share, hint, or reminder — usu. used with *of* ⟨his talk ~*ed* of the sea⟩ ⟨the plan ~*s* of radicalism⟩

³**smack** \"\ *vb* -ED/-ING/-S [akin to MD & MLG *smacken* to strike, slap, throw] *vt* **1 a** : to close and open (lips) noisily and in rapid succession esp. in eating ⟨~*ing* his lips over the soup⟩ **b** : to consume (food or drink) with evident and sometimes noisy satisfaction **2 a** : to kiss vigorously with or as if with a smack ⟨~*ed* his cousin on the cheek⟩ **b** : to strike (as a person) in such a manner as to produce a smacking sound; *esp* : to strike with the palm of the open hand ⟨~ his ugly face⟩ **3** : to move, place, or bring into contact with a smack ⟨~*ed* down the paper⟩ ⟨~*ing* her hands together⟩ ~ *vi* : to make or give a smack : do something with a smack

⁴**smack** \"\ *n* -s [akin to MD *smac* slap, throw, MLG *smak*] **1** : a quick sharp noise made by rapidly compressing and opening the lips (as in gusto or kissing) **2** : a loud kiss : BUSS ⟨a ~ on the cheek⟩ **3** : a sharp slap with the palm of the open hand or sometimes with another flat surface; *broadly* : any quick sharp resounding blow ⟨hit the ball a powerful ~ with his bat⟩

⁵**smack** \"\ *adv* [⁴*smack*] **1** : with the sudden violence of a smack : squarely and sharply : PLUMP ⟨ran ~ into the wall⟩ **2** : as direct or as evident as a smack : COMPLETELY, UNDEVIATINGLY

⁶**smack** \"\ *n* -s [D *smak* or LG *smack;* prob. fr. MD & MLG *smacken* to strike, slap; fr. the slapping of the sail] : a sailing vessel (as a sloop or cutter) used chiefly in coasting and fishing: as **a** *Brit* : a large fishing vessel strictly fore-and-aft rigged — compare LUGGER **b** *also* **smack boat** : a fore-and-aft-rigged fishing boat having a well in which fish are kept alive — called also *well smack*

smack-dab \ˈ=ˈ=\ *adv* [⁵*smack* + *dab*] *dial* : SQUARELY, EXACTLY ⟨stood *smack-dab* in the middle of the parlor —Helen Eustis⟩

smacked *adj* [fr. past part. of ³*smack*] *chiefly Midland* : GROUND ⟨~ peanut hulls⟩

smack·er \ˈsmakə(r)\ *n* -s [³*smack* + *-er*] **1** : one that smacks **2** *slang* : DOLLAR

smack·er·oo \,smakəˈrü\ *n* -s [alter. of *smacker*] *slang* : DOLLAR

¹**smacking** *adj* [fr. pres. part. of ³*smack*] **1** : BRISK, LIVELY, SPANKING ⟨a ~ breeze⟩ **2** : outstanding in some respect (as size or excellence) — **smack·ing·ly** *adv*

²**smacking** *n* -s [fr. gerund of ³*smack*] : the act of or sound made by one who smacks ⟨gave the child a good ~⟩ ⟨the ~ of the sail against the mast⟩

smacks·man \ˈsmaksmən\ *n, pl* **smacksmen** [*smacks* (gen. of ⁶*smack*) + *man*] : one of the crew of a fishing smack; *also* : the owner of a smack

smack-smooth \ˈ=ˈ=\ *adv (or adj)* [⁵*smack* + *smooth*] : so as to leave or involve no projection, irregularity, or imperfection

smaik \ˈsmāk\ *n* -s [ME] *Scot* : SCOUNDREL, RASCAL

smairt \ˈsmārt\ *Scot var of* SMART

¹small \ˈsmȯl\ *adj* -ER/-EST [ME *smal,* fr. OE *smæl;* akin to OHG *smal* small, ON *smali* small cattle, Icel *smalr* small, Goth *smalista* smallest, L *malus* bad, Gk *mēlon* sheep, goat, Arm *mal* sheep, ram] **1 a :** slight in circumference esp. as compared with length or with another similar thing ⟨a ~ waist⟩ ⟨sausage casings made from the ~ bowel⟩ **b** *archaic* **:** narrow in width esp. as compared with length **2 a :** having little size esp. as compared with other similar things **:** not large or extended in dimensions, girth, or mass ⟨a ~ house⟩ ⟨~ lumps of coal⟩ ⟨the child is ~ for his age⟩ **b :** small in size by reason of incomplete growth **:** IMMATURE, YOUNG ⟨toys for ~ children⟩ ⟨~ plants for bedding⟩ **c** (1) **:** consisting of small pieces or units ⟨the branches yield ~ wood for burning⟩ (2) **:** LITTLE 1a(5) **d** *of a letter* **:** comparatively small in size, usu. less angular than the corresponding capital letter, and in print usu. having a body that does not extend above lower-case x height but in several letters having the overall height increased upward by an ascender or downward by a descender **3** *dial Eng* **:** fine in texture or in the size of constituent particles **:** not coarse or heavy ⟨a ~ misty rain⟩ **4 a :** of little influence, power, or authority **:** of low rank **:** lacking high position or status ⟨the ~ people who are the backbone of the nation⟩ **b :** lacking prominence in a particular sphere **:** minor in rank or ability **:** not noteworthy or great ⟨~ poets⟩: as (1) **:** being such to a limited degree **:** PETTY ⟨~ criminals⟩ (2) **:** having little capital or resources **:** operating on a limited scale in respect to assets, employees, and volume of business ⟨a ~ farmer⟩ ⟨~ manufactories⟩; *also* **:** having or serving a small clientele ⟨~ shops⟩ ⟨a ~ tradesman⟩ **5 :** lacking in strength: as **a** *of the voice* **:** GENTLE, SOFT **b :** very dilute; *esp* **:** deficient in or free from alcohol ⟨the wine was very thin and ~⟩ **6 a :** little in a way that is objectively measurable (as in quantity, amount, value, duration, extent) ⟨a ~ number⟩ ⟨a ~ salary⟩ ⟨a ~ distance away⟩ ⟨waited a ~ space of time⟩ **b :** made up of units that are few in number, little in size, low in value, or otherwise objectively small ⟨a ~ standing army⟩ ⟨~ change⟩ **7 a :** of little consequence, weight, or importance **:** INSIGNIFICANT ⟨a ~ fault⟩ ⟨played a ~ role in the show⟩ **b :** lacking in prominence **:** HUMBLE, MODEST ⟨living in a ~ way⟩ ⟨from such ~ beginnings⟩ **c** *of language* **:** PLAIN, SIMPLE **8 :** limited or slight in degree, intensity, scope, or similar quality **:** less and often markedly less than is usual, expected, or fitting **:** TRIFLING ⟨had ~ interest in public affairs⟩ ⟨paying ~ heed to his mother's warning⟩ ⟨suffered a ~ mishap⟩ **9 a :** lacking in largeness of spirit **:** not large-minded or generous **:** MEAN ⟨a ~ and cruel revenge⟩ ⟨a harsh ~ man⟩ **b :** HUMILIATED, HUMBLED ⟨never felt so ~ in his life⟩

syn SMALL, LITTLE, DIMINUTIVE, WEE, TINY, TEENY, WEENY, MINUTE, MICROSCOPIC, MINIATURE, and PETITE agree in meaning noticeably below the average in magnitude, esp. physical. SMALL and LITTLE are often interchangeable, but SMALL more frequently applies to things whose magnitude is formulated in terms of number, size, capacity, value, or significance ⟨a *small* audience⟩ ⟨a *small* child⟩ ⟨a *small* car⟩ ⟨*small* bills⟩ ⟨a *small* effect upon one's life⟩ ⟨a *small* reputation⟩ or modifies words like *quantity, amount, size,* or *capacity* ⟨a *small* quantity of flour⟩ ⟨rooms of a *small* size⟩ or limits intangible or generally immeasurable things ⟨a *small* mind⟩ ⟨a *small* personality⟩ ⟨a *small* prospect of succeeding⟩ LITTLE is usu. more absolute in implication, often carrying the idea of petiteness, pettiness, or insignificance in literal or figurative size, amount, quantity, or extent ⟨a *little* woman⟩ ⟨our *little* ambitions⟩ ⟨a *little* mind⟩ ⟨a *little* man in all qualities of character⟩ ⟨*little* hope of a cure⟩ LITTLE also often signifies a small amount, a small quantity, or a small extent of (something) ⟨a *little* meat⟩ ⟨a small house and a *little* land⟩ or carries a note of pathos, tenderness, or affection ⟨a *little* heart-rending smile⟩ ⟨a *little* adorable child⟩ DIMINUTIVE can stress not only smallness but often extreme, sometimes abnormal, smallness in comparison ⟨peasants who have wine for their ordinary drink, are of a *diminutive* size —Tobias Smollett⟩ ⟨a little black mustache and *diminutive* chin-beard —George Santayana⟩ ⟨*diminutive* houses and furniture fit only for dolls —W.H.Mallock⟩ ⟨these *diminutive* crabs are scavengers and live in holes in the mud at tide line —*Amer. Guide Series: Fla.*⟩ PETITE applies to a proportionally small but usu. pleasingly trim woman or girl ⟨*petite* in stature: her height is about five feet, her weight, 112 pounds —*Current Biog.*⟩ ⟨a *petite* actress with strong box-office appeal⟩ WEE is homely or dialect for DIMINUTIVE ⟨though my own interest quickened, my *wee* son, then aged one-and-a-half years, grew distinctly bored —O.S.Nock⟩ ⟨a *wee* drop of whiskey⟩ TINY goes farther than DIMINUTIVE in suggesting extreme littleness or smallness by comparison ⟨in my lapel was a *tiny* gold lizard —Victor Canning⟩ ⟨the poisonous ingredient which magnified will kill, but in *tiny* quantities will cure —B.N.Cardozo⟩ ⟨children who squat patiently over those *tiny* little holes in the ground where doodlebugs are thought to live —Carson McCullers⟩ ⟨a wee *tiny* voice⟩ TEENY and WEENY, occurring chiefly in children's or playful or humorous use, denote the same thing as DIMINUTIVE or WEE; the variant forms *teeny-weeny, teeny-tiny, teensy-weensy,* and similar reduplications, merely emphasize diminutiveness more or are more childish or playful ⟨a little *teeny* dog can make enough racket to attract neighbors' attention —*English Digest*⟩ ⟨two veteran progressive-school teachers who have grown a *weeny* bit tired of their energetic, articulate, expressive little charges —Dwight MacDonald⟩ ⟨a *teeny-weeny* little dwarf⟩ ⟨when I was a *teensy-weensy* little girl⟩ MICROSCOPIC applies to or suggests what is small or insignificant enough to be observed usu. only by the use of a microscope ⟨*microscopic* germs⟩ ⟨*microscopic* particles of dust⟩ ⟨the mill workers who labored twelve or thirteen or fourteen hours a day for a *microscopic* wage —F.L.Allen⟩ ⟨traverses rolling farm country, spans creeks, passes through *microscopic* settlements, and penetrates scrubby woodland —*Amer. Guide Series: Pa.*⟩ MINUTE means extremely small in an absolute sense, usu. on a microscopic or near-microscopic scale ⟨mollusks drill *minute* holes in the shells through which they suck the oyster —*Amer. Guide Series: Fla.*⟩ ⟨the *minute* and steady click of Mrs. Millington's needle —Walter de la Mare⟩ MINIATURE applies to what is complete but built, drawn, or made on a very small scale ⟨a *miniature* shower of pink petals —Harriet La Barre⟩ ⟨the park has a swimming pool for children, a *miniature* waterfall, and a small powerhouse and water-wheel —*Amer. Guide Series: Mich.*⟩ ⟨the child was a *miniature* version of the father⟩

²small \"\ *adv* -ER/-EST [ME *smale,* fr. OE *smale,* fr. *smæl,* adj.] **1 :** in or into small-sized pieces **:** FINE ⟨grate ~⟩ ⟨the meat served ~ on toast⟩ **2** *obs* **:** to a slight extent or degree **:** very little **3 :** without force or loudness **:** FAINTLY, TIMIDLY ⟨you may speak as ~ as you will —Shak.⟩ **4 :** in a small way, manner, or size **:** in miniature **5 :** CONTEMPTUOUSLY, DISDAINFULLY ⟨think ~ of one's neighbors⟩

³small \"\ *n* -S [ME *smal,* fr. *smal,* adj.] **1 :** a part that is smaller and esp. narrower than the remainder or than adjacent parts ⟨the ~ of the back⟩; *esp* **:** the posterior part of a whale between the vent and the flukes of the tail **2 a smalls** *pl* **:** small-sized products (as notions, bread, rolls, screws) ⟨kept a good stock of ~*s*⟩ **b smalls** *pl, chiefly Scot* **:** small portions **:** DRIBLETS **c smalls** *pl, chiefly Brit* (1) **:** small articles of clothing (as underclothing) or household linen (2) **:** SMALLCLOTHES 1 **d :** coal, ore, or ore-bearing rock that passes through small meshes of a specified size — usu. used in pl. **e smalls** *pl, Brit* **:** articles of freight under a specified weight (as 200 pounds) for carriage of which an extra charge or surtax is made **3 smalls** *pl, slang* **:** RESPONSIONS — **by small and small :** by slow degrees **:** bit by bit

⁴small \"\ *vb* -ED/-ING/-S [ME *smalen,* fr. *smal,* adj.] *vt, obs* **:** to make small or less **:** LESSEN ~ *vi* **:** to become small or less **:** DIMINISH ⟨the road ~*s* in the distance⟩

small·age \-lij\ *n* -S [ME *smalege,* alter. of *smalache,* fr. *smal* small + *ache* wild celery, parsley — more at ACHE] **:** a strongly scented erect biennial herb (*Apium graveolens*) that is the wild form of the culinary celery and is widely distributed in moist situations in temperate regions

small ale *n* **:** a weak ale brewed with little malt and little or no hops as a mild and cheap drink

small and early *n* **:** an evening party (as an informal reception or dance) attended by comparatively few guests and breaking up early

small arm *n* **:** a firearm capable of being fired while held with one or both hands — usu. used in pl.

¹small beer *n* **1 :** weak or inferior beer **2 :** something of small importance **:** insignificant matters **:** TRIVIA

²small beer *adv* **:** with contempt **:** SCORNFULLY — usu. used with a negative ⟨thought no *small beer* of themselves for having been out of their depths —Thomas Hughes⟩

small-beer \ˈ=ˌ=\ *adj* [¹*small beer*] **:** marked by little importance, significance, or worth **:** TRIVIAL ⟨finding a pleasure in these ~ chronicles —W.M.Thackeray⟩

small-billed water thrush \ˈ=ˌ=-\ *n* **:** NORTHERN WATER THRUSH

small bluet *n* **:** a star violet (*Houstonia patens*)

small bond *n* **:** BABY BOND

small-bore \ˈ=ˌ=\ *adj* **1 a** *of a firearm* **:** having a small or relatively small bore; *esp* **:** having a caliber of .22 inches — distinguished from *big-bore* **b :** of, relating to, or involving the use of small-bore firearms ⟨*small-bore* competition⟩ **2 :** narrow in outlook ⟨*small-bore* politicians⟩

small bower *n* **:** an anchor carried in the bow of a ship

small broomrape *n* **:** a broomrape (*Orobanche minor*) having a loose spike of flowers with two basal bracts and a corolla with rounded lobes — called also *hellroot*

small bugloss *n* **:** a Eurasian annual weed (*Lycopsis arvensis*) naturalized in No. America and having rough hairy leaves and small bluish flowers in one-sided racemes

small calorie *n* **:** CALORIE a

small cane *n* **:** a grass (*Arundinaria tecta*) having large sheaths enfolding the flowering shoots

small capital *n* **:** a letter having the form of and about two thirds the size of a capital letter (as in THESE WORDS) that is typically used for cross reference and in abbreviations (as A.D., B.C.) — abbr. *s. c., sm. cap.*

small chair *n* **:** a chair (as a side chair) that has no arms

small change *n* **1 :** money consisting of small coins — contrasted with *folding money* **2 :** something as trifling, petty, or as quickly circulated as small change

small circle *n* **:** a circle formed on the surface of a sphere by the intersection of a plane that does not pass through the center of the sphere; *specif* **:** such a circle on the surface of the earth — compare GREAT CIRCLE

small claim *n* **:** a debt or claim of small amount and esp. of an amount sufficiently small (as 50 dollars) to bring it within the jurisdiction of a special court of more or less expeditious or summary procedure

small-claims court *n* **:** a special court intended to simplify and expedite the handling of small debts or claims

smallclothes \ˈ=ˌ=\ *n pl* **1 :** knee breeches esp. of the close-fitting type worn in the 18th and early 19th centuries **2 :** small articles of clothing (as underclothing, handkerchiefs, children's garments)

small coal *n* **1** *obs* **:** CHARCOAL **2 :** small-sized coal

small crabgrass *n* **:** a rather small somewhat glabrous and often purplish Eurasian grass (*Digitaria ischaemum*) that is widely naturalized and often a pest in lawns — called also *smooth crabgrass*

small cranberry *n* **:** EUROPEAN CRANBERRY

small debt *n, Brit* **:** SMALL CLAIM

small-debts court *n, Brit* **:** SMALL-CLAIMS COURT

small·en \ˈsmȯlən\ *vt* [¹*small* + *-en*] *dial* **:** to make smaller

smaller *adj* [fr. *smaller,* comparative of ¹*small*] **:** LESSER

smaller pine sawyer *n* **:** a pine sawyer (*Monochamus scutellatus*)

smallest *superlative of* SMALL

small fruit *n* **:** a low-growing plant (as a shrub, bramble, or herb) that produces table fruit; *also* **:** a fruit (as the strawberry, raspberry, or currant) produced on such a plant — compare BUSH FRUIT, CANE FRUIT, TREE FRUIT

small-fruited hickory \ˈ=ˌ==-\ *n* **:** SMALL PIGNUT

small-fry \ˈ=ˌ=\ *adj* [fr. the phrase *small fry*] **1 :** MINOR, UNIMPORTANT ⟨a *small-fry* politician⟩ **2 :** of, relating to, or made up of children **:** intended for children **:** CHILDISH ⟨*small-fry* sports⟩

small game *n* **:** game birds and mammals not classed as big game

small goods *n pl* **1 :** SMALL 2a **2** *Austral* **:** edible meat by-products

small grain *n* **:** a cereal (as wheat, oats, barley, rye, rice) having relatively small kernels or sometimes a relatively small plant as distinguished from a plant (as corn) with large kernels or sometimes from a cereal (as sorghum) with a large plant but small kernels or from a similarly cultured and used seed (as soybean) with a relatively small plant and large seeds

small-headed fly \ˈ=ˌ==-\ *n* **:** a fly of the family Cyrtidae

small helm *n* **:** a helm at only a small angle to the keel of a ship

small henbit *n* **:** IVY-LEAVED SPEEDWELL

smallholder \ˈ=ˌ==\ *n, chiefly Brit* **:** an owner or operator of a small holding

small holding *n, chiefly Brit* **:** a piece of land detached from a cottage, hired or owned by a laboring man, and cultivated to supplement his main income — compare ALLOTMENT

small honeysuckle *n* **:** a yellow honeysuckle (*Lonicera dioica*)

small horde *n, usu cap S&H* [trans. of Kirghiz *kitchi-juz*] **:** a division of the Great Horde

small hours *n pl* **:** hours of the early morning immediately following midnight — used with *the*

smalling *pres part of* SMALL

small intestine *n* **:** the anterior portion of the intestine that is lined with a complex glandular mucous membrane which secretes digestive enzymes and through which digested nutrients pass to enter the blood and lymph — see VILLUS; compare LARGE INTESTINE; see DIGESTION illustration

small·ish \ˈsmȯlish, -lēsh\ *adj* [ME *smalish,* fr. *smal* small + *-ish*] **:** somewhat small **:** slightly below normal size

small laurel *n* **:** MOUNTAIN LAUREL 1

small-leaved linden *also* **small-leaved lime** \ˈ=ˌ=-\ *n* **:** a large spreading European linden (*Tilia cordata*) that has small somewhat cordate dark green leaves and is often cultivated as a shade tree

small line *n* **:** a fishing line for use in shallow water ⟨a *small line* boat⟩

small magnolia *n* **1 :** EVERGREEN MAGNOLIA **2 :** SWEET BAY 2

small mean *n* **:** the second string of a viol — compare GREAT MEAN

small-minded \ˈ=ˈ==\ *adj* **1 :** having few and petty interests, narrow sympathies, or rigid outlook **:** lacking breadth of mind ⟨a *small-minded* man⟩ **2 :** typical of a small-minded person **:** marked esp. by pettiness, narrowness, meanness ⟨*small-minded* conduct⟩ — **small-minded·ly** *adv* — **small-minded·ness** *n* -ES

small money *n* **:** SMALL CHANGE

smallmouth black bass *also* **smallmouthed black bass** *or* **smallmouth bass** *or* **smallmouthed bass** \ˈ=ˌ=-\ *or* **smallmouth** \ˈ=ˌ=\ *n* **:** a black bass (*Micropterus dolomieu*) that lives chiefly in cool clear rivers and lakes, is bronzy green above and lighter below, and has the angle of the jaw falling below the eye — compare LARGEMOUTH BLACK BASS

smallmouth buffalo *n* **:** a common buffalo fish (*Ictiobus bubalus*) that is usu. smaller and slenderer than the bigmouth and black buffalos and is a superior food fish

small·ness *n* -ES [ME *smalnesse,* fr. *smal* small + *-nesse* -ness] **1 :** the quality or state of being small **2 :** something that is small

small nettle *n* **:** an annual European weed (*Urtica urens*) naturalized throughout No. America and having stinging foliage and green flowers in lax elongating clusters that exceed the leaf petioles in length

small octave *n* **:** a musical octave that begins on the first C below middle C — see PITCH illustration

small part *n* **:** a minor role in a theatrical performance

small pastern bone *n* **:** the second phalanx of the functional digit of the foot of an equine

small people *n, chiefly dial* **:** FAIRIES

small pica *n* **:** an old size of type between long primer and pica and approximately 11 point

small pignut *n* **:** a smooth-barked hickory (*Carya ovalis*) with 5 to 7 leaflets; *also* **:** its nearly round small white nut

small potato *n* **:** someone or something of trivial importance or worth and usu. meanly petty ⟨you are a *small potato* in the world —*Times Lit. Supp.*⟩ — usu. used in pl. but sing. or pl. in constr. ⟨he was *small potatoes* in my book⟩

¹smallpox \ˈ=ˌ=\ *n* [¹*small* + *pox*] **1 :** an acute contagious febrile virus disease characterized by constitutional symptoms and successive stages of skin eruptions of which the last is marked by pustules, sloughing, and scar formation **2 :** BITTER PIT

²smallpox \"\ *vt* **:** to infect or scar with smallpox

smallpox plant *n* **:** a pitcher plant (*Sarracenia purpurea*)

small print *n* **:** FINE PRINT ⟨always read the *small print* —D.G. Gerahty⟩

small purple fringed orchis *n* **:** a rather small orchid (*Habenaria psychodes*) of moist parts of northeastern No. America with pink to rosy purple or occasionally white flowers distinguished by a broad lip deeply cleft into three lacerate segments

small reed *n* **:** REED BENT 1

smalls *pl of* SMALL, *pres 3d sing of* SMALL

small sagebrush *n* **:** a very low-growing sagebrush (*Artemisia nova*) of dry uplands of western No. America that is an important browse plant

small-scale \ˈ=ˌ=\ *adj* **1 a :** small in scope; *esp* **:** having a small output or product ⟨a *small-scale* pilot plant⟩ ⟨*small-scale* farms⟩ **b :** occupied with or engaged in a small-scale operation ⟨a *small-scale* retailer⟩ **2** *of a map* **:** having a scale (as one inch to 25 miles) that permits plotting of comparatively little detail — compare LARGE-SCALE

small-seeded false flax \ˈ=ˌ==-\ *n* **:** a weedy annual European false flax (*Camelina microcarpa*) that is a widely naturalized No. American weed, is similar to but generally smaller than gold of pleasure, and has been implicated in livestock poisoning when excessive amounts of the seed are present in feed

smallshot \ˈ=ˌ=\ *n, slang* **:** a person of no importance or prominence

small slam *n* **:** LITTLE SLAM

small soapweed *n* **:** a short-stemmed or acaulescent yucca (*Yucca glauca*) of the central U. S. with usu. white-margined leaves and greenish white pendulous flowers

small solomon's seal *n, usu cap 2d S* **:** a low-growing Solomon's seal (*Polygonatum biflorum*) that is widely distributed in eastern No. America

small spelt *n* **:** EINKORN

small spikenard *n* **1 :** an American spikenard (*Aralia racemosa*) **2 :** WILD SARSAPARILLA 1

small stores *n pl* **:** articles of regulation issue clothing sold for cash by the supply officer of a naval ship or station to naval personnel

small strongyle *n* **:** CYLICOSTOME

small stuff *n* **:** spun yarn, marline, and other small rope that is used aboard ship and is usu. identified by the number of threads or yarns which it contains

smallsword \ˈ=ˌ=\ *n* **:** a light tapering sword designed for thrusting and used esp. in the 18th century for dueling and fencing

small talk *n* **:** light or casual conversation **:** CHITCHAT

small-talk \ˈ=ˌ=\ *vi* [*small talk*] **:** to engage in or be given to small talk

small tiger lily *n* **:** a tall-growing lily (*Lilium parvum*) of moist spots in the coastal mountains of the western U. S. that usu. produces large numbers of small funnelform purple-spotted yellowish orange flowers

small time *n* **:** theatrical and esp. vaudeville circuits where the pay is small and acts are shown three or more times a day

small-time \ˈsmȯlˈtīm\ *adj* [*small time*] **:** belonging to a minor, small-scale, or local organization or to a petty gang obtaining only small returns **:** insignificant in performance and standing

small-tim·er \"+ə(r)\ *n* [*small time* + *-er*] **:** one that is small-time or belongs to a small-time group

small-toothed palm civet \ˈ=ˌ=-\ *n* **:** any of several eastern Asian palm civets (genus *Arctogalidea*)

small-town \ˈ=ˈ=\ *adj* [fr. *small town,* n] **:** of, belonging to, or characteristic of a small city or a large village, its life, or its inhabitants — usu. distinguished from *urban* and *metropolitan* ⟨*small-town* girls⟩ ⟨*small-town* customs⟩ ⟨a *small-town* outlook⟩

small-town·er \"+ə(r)\ *n* -S [*small town* + *-er*] **1 :** a resident of a small town **2 :** a person with small-town characteristics (as of thought or behavior)

small vehicle *n* **:** HINAYANA

smallware \ˈ=ˌ=\ *n* **1** *Brit* **:** small articles of merchandise; *esp* **:** NOTIONS — usu. used in pl. **2** *Brit* **:** narrow fabrics

small white *n* **1 :** CABBAGE BUTTERFLY a **2 a** *usu cap S&W* **:** a British breed of small white hogs that tend to be somewhat chuffy and deficient in lean meat — compare LARGE WHITE **b :** an animal of the Small White breed

small woodbine *n* **:** YELLOW HONEYSUCKLE 1a

¹smal·ly \ˈsmȯlē\ *adv* [ME, fr. *smal* small + *-ly*] **1** *obs* **:** MINUTELY, SCANTILY **2** *obs* **:** in a small quantity, degree, or manner; *also* **:** not numerously or largely **3 :** on a small scale **:** DELICATELY, FINELY, SLENDERLY ⟨~ built⟩

²smally \ˈsmȯlē, ˈsmälē, -li\ *adj* [¹*small* + *-y*] *chiefly dial* **:** rather small

smalt \ˈsmȯlt\ *n* -S [MF, fr. OIt *smalto,* of Gmc origin; akin to OHG *smelzan* to melt — more at SMELT] **1 :** a blue glass made by fusing potassium carbonate, silica, and cobalt oxide and used in powdered form chiefly as a colorant for glass and vitreous enamels — often used in pl. but sing. or pl. in constr. **2 :** a moderate blue that is redder and duller than average copen, redder and deeper than azurite blue, Dresden blue, or pompadour, and greener and deeper than luster blue — called also *cobalt glass, Dumont's blue, king's blue, powder blue, starch blue* **3 :** sand colored for use in producing a rough decorative long-wearing surface with paint

smalt green *n* **:** COBALT GREEN 2

smalt·ite \ˈsmȯlˌtīt\ *also* **smalt·ine** \-ltən, -lˌtēn\ *n* -S [alter. of *smaltine;* *smaltine* fr. F, fr. *smalt* + *-ine*] **:** a tin-white or gray isometric mineral (Co,Ni)As_{3-x} of metallic luster that is an arsenide of cobalt and nickel and is isomorphous with skutterudite and chloanthite (hardness 5.5–6, sp. gr. 6.4–6.6)

smal·to \ˈsmäl(ˌ)tō\ *n, pl* **smaltos** \-ōz\ *also* **smal·ti** \-ltē\ [It, smalt, smalto] **:** colored glass or enamel for use in mosaic work; *also* **:** a piece of such material

smaltz \ˈsmȯlts\ *n* -ES [prob. alter. of *smalts,* pl. of *smalt*] **:** SMALT 1

smar·agd \ˈsmaˌragd\ *n* -S [ME *smaragde,* fr. OF *smaragde, esmeragde, esmeraude, esmeralde* — more at EMERALD] **:** EMERALD

sma·rag·dine \sməˈragdən\ *adj* [L *smaragdinus,* fr. *smaragdus* emerald + *-inus* -ine — more at EMERALD] **:** of or relating to emerald **:** yellowish green in color like an emerald

sma·rag·dite \sməˈragˌdīt\ *n* -S [F, fr. L *smaragdus* + F *-ite*] **:** a mineral consisting of a green foliated amphibole often derived from common diallage

smarm \ˈsmärm\ *or* **smalm** \-älm\ *vb* [origin unknown] *vt, dial* **:** SMEAR ⟨more color in her cheeks, natural, than what they could ~ on out of a box —Richard Llewellyn⟩ ~ *vi* **:** GUSH, SLOBBER ⟨would ~ over me just the way they do over you —Robertson Davies⟩

smarmy \ˈsmärmē\ *adj* -ER/-EST **1 :** SLEEK ⟨*smarmy*-headed —David Walker⟩ **2 :** unctuously or fulsomely flattering **:** SLOBBERY, GUSHING, OILY, INSINUATING ⟨young man with the ~ voice —Noel Coward⟩ ⟨coy and ~ —Bernard Holloway⟩ ⟨~ insincerity —Eric Partridge⟩ ⟨a ~ little melody —*Time*⟩

¹smart \ˈsmär|t, -mä|, *usu* |d·+V\ *vb* -ED/-ING/-S [ME *smerten,* fr. OE *smeortan;* akin to MD *smerten,* *smarten* to pain, hurt, MLG *smerten,* OHG *smerzan* to pain, hurt, L *mordēre* to bite, Gk *smerdnos* terrible, fearful, *marainein* to waste away, Skt *mṛdnāti, mardati* he pulverizes, crushes, destroys, and perh. to L *mort-, mors* death — more at MURDER] *vi* **1 a :** to be the source or seat of a sharp stinging or cutting usu. local and superficial pain ⟨a cut that ~*ed* badly but was not serious⟩ ⟨face ~*ed* where his razor had scraped the skin⟩ ⟨rapid fatigue with burning and ~*ing* of the conjunctiva —G.H.Armstrong⟩ ⟨the ~*ing* of his wounded vanity —G.B.Shaw⟩ **b :** to cause or produce such a pain ⟨this liniment will ~⟩ ⟨a slap that was hard enough to ~⟩ **c :** to feel or have such a pain ⟨was still ~*ing* wherever the acrid fumes had come into contact with his skin⟩ ⟨had ~*ed* more than once under the lash of the cruel overseer⟩ ⟨this liniment will make you ~ but it will do you good⟩ **2 a :** to feel sharp mental pain or distress (as in remorse or in consequence of a real or fancied grievance) : suffer keenly in mind or feelings — usu. used with *under* ⟨~*ing* under the prickings of his own conscience⟩ ⟨~*ing*, evidently, under a sense of wrong —Susan Ertz⟩ ⟨had ~*ed* for years under his father's low opinion of him —Herman Wouk⟩ or with *from* ⟨~*ing* from his dismissal —R.A.Billington⟩ ⟨~*ing* from their defeats —*Wall Street Jour.*⟩ or sometimes with *over* ⟨~*ing* over the civil rights issue —R.E.Lee⟩ or *at* ⟨still ~*ing* at his too candid criticism —W.H.Hudson †1922⟩ ⟨then suddenly ~*ed* at her own pettishness —Sheila Kaye-Smith⟩ **b** : to suffer severely as a penalty — usu. used with *for* ⟨feared that someday he would ~ for this foolishness⟩ ⟨you will be made to ~ for this offense⟩ **~ vt** : to cause to smart : act on as an irritant

²smart \"\ *adj* -ER/-EST [ME *smert, smart*, fr. OE *smeart;* akin to OE *smeortan* to smart — more at ¹SMART] **1 a** *archaic* : causing smarting : attended by smarting : arousing or marked by a sharp stinging or cutting pain ⟨their softest touch as ~ as lizard's stings —Shak.⟩ ⟨a ~ sensation⟩ **b** : so severe as to cause smarting ⟨a ~ thrashing⟩ ⟨winced under the ~ cut of the whip⟩ ⟨administered a ~ reproof⟩ **2 a** : marked by often sudden sharp intensity : showing sharp forceful activity ⟨brought the kettle to a ~ boil⟩ ⟨a ~ rally in oil stocks⟩ ⟨a ~ shock of surprise —Ambrose Bierce⟩ ⟨a ~ shower from the sinking sun —George Meredith⟩ **b** : marked by strength or pungency — used of liquors ⟨a ~ full-bodied wine⟩ ⟨I'm after bringing down a ~ drop —J.M.Synge⟩ **3 a** : marked by or suggesting brisk vigor, speedy effective activity, or spirited liveliness ⟨walking at a ~ pace⟩ ⟨~ trot⟩ ⟨a ~ gust of wind⟩ ⟨a brief but ~ skirmish⟩ **b** : seeming well suited to quick vigorous activity : not weak, flaccid, enervated, or obese ⟨a ~ physique⟩ **4 a** : having or showing mental alertness and quickness of perception, shrewd informed calculation, or contriving resourcefulness : BRIGHT, CLEVER, QUICK-WITTED ⟨wish I was ~ enough to invent something and maybe get rich —Sherwood Anderson⟩ ⟨~ children talk earlier and dull children talk later than the average —Morris Fishbein⟩ ⟨the race is no longer to the strong but to the ~ —F.V.Drake⟩ ⟨when are you going to get ~ and shut up for a while —Harvey Granite⟩ ⟨~ politics⟩ ⟨a ~ move⟩ ⟨a ~ investment⟩ ⟨~ management⟩ **b** : shrewd, sharp, and of questionable honesty esp. in the furthering of self-interest ⟨loaded with prizes for the ~ guys . . . full of booby traps for the unwary —W.H.Upson⟩ ⟨which a few ~ men at the top manipulated in their own interest —Elmer Davis⟩ ⟨making a fast buck . . . ~, a smooth operator —Marc Brandel⟩ **5 a** : marked by keen ready wit and repartee, amusing cleverness, or facetious pertness ⟨the essence of English ~ comedy is its combination of verbal distinction with intellectual impertinence —H.E.Clurman⟩ ⟨had been supposed to be clever and had said ~ things to him —Samuel Butler †1902⟩ **b** : impertinently witty or facetious : FLIP, FRESH, SAUCY ⟨gave his mother a ~ answer⟩ ⟨was punished for being ~⟩ ⟨an unpleasantly ~ attitude toward things that were not funny⟩ **6 a** : dashing in appearance : well turned out : NEAT, TRIM, SPRUCE, TIDY: (1) : showing the trimness of efficient design and careful maintenance : promising speed and reliable performance ⟨a ~ new yacht⟩ ⟨the ~*est* ship of the fleet⟩ ⟨drove his blooded horses to his ~ carriages —John Reed⟩ (2) : stylish in dress : showing careful attention to details of appearance : NATTY ⟨uniform of green faced with orange, *smart*-looking in spite of being patched —Kenneth Roberts⟩ ⟨trim and ~, from her bronze hair so well done to the end of her neat silver-slippered toe —Louis Bromfield⟩ **b** : showing fashion, elegance, richness, dash, modernity, or striking quality : appealing to sophisticated wealthier tastes ⟨the ~ suburban air —*Amer. Guide Series: N.Y. City*⟩ ⟨the hotel . . . is not at all ~ but very comfortable —Willa Cather⟩ **7** : characteristic of or patronized by exclusive ultrafashionable society ⟨the restaurant is small, exclusive, terribly ~ —T.H.Fielding⟩ ⟨locations which are considered ~ or chic because they are the property of privileged circles —Edward Sapir⟩ **8** *chiefly dial* : fairly large : CONSIDERABLE ⟨a ~ price for a broken-down car⟩ **syn** see INTELLIGENT

³smart \"\ *adv* -ER/-EST [ME *smerte, smarte*, fr. *smert, smart*, adj.] : in a smart manner : SMARTLY ⟨will make all his characters talk ~ or epigrammatically —Arnold Bennett⟩ ⟨frankly a good deal of a mug, indifferent to those who cannot play it ~ —Alfred Kazin⟩

⁴smart \"\ *n* -S [ME *smerte;* akin to MLG *smerte* pain, MD *smerte, smarte*, OHG *smerzo* pain, *smerzan* to pain, hurt — more at ¹SMART] **1** : a smarting pain; *esp* : a stinging local pain (as from an injury, blow, or irritant) ⟨a ~ in the eyes⟩ ⟨whimpering over the ~ from the liniment⟩ **2 a** : keen mental pain (as from grief, remorse, affliction, wounded feelings) : poignant distress ⟨only time would cure the ~ of their bereavement⟩ ⟨the ~ of being the underdog —Abram Kardiner⟩ ⟨was not the sort to get over ~*s* —Sir Winston Churchill⟩ **b** *archaic* : pain or distress inflicted or felt as punishment or retribution ⟨stand betwixt us and our deserved ~ —John Milton⟩; *also* : a cause of such pain ⟨a sword that thine enemy's ~ —John Keats⟩ **3** : one that affects smartness (as in dress, speech, manners, attitudes) ⟨the wits and the ~*s* —Sir Walter Scott⟩ ⟨a young Broadway ~ —Joel Sayre⟩ **4** *dial* : a sizable amount

smar·ta \ˈsmärd·ə\ *n* -S *usu cap* [Skt, fr. *smṛti* what is remembered] : a member of a large Hindu sect of Brahmans founded in the eighth century, guided chiefly by the traditions of the smriti, holding the doctrine of Advaita, worshiping all the principal deities equally, and thriving most in south India

smart al·eck *also* **smart-al·ec** *n, pl* **smart alecks** *also* **smart-alecs** \ˈsmär\|d·ˌalək, -mäl, \|t\|-, -lēk, *dial* -ˌel-\ [*Aleck, Alec*, nickname fr. the name *Alexander*] : one that is offensively conceited and bumptious : a self-satisfied self-assertive cocky person with pretensions to cleverness : one combining in himself the characteristic traits of show-off and know-it-all

smart-al·eck·ism \-ˌkizəm\ *or* **smart-al·eck·ry** \-krē\ *n, pl* **smart-aleckisms** *or* **smart-aleckries** : the speech or behavior of a smart aleck : smart-alecky quality or characteristics

smart-al·ecky \-kē, -ki\ *or* **smart-aleck** *also* **smart-alec** *adj* : like, typical of, or being a smart aleck : marked by cockiness and conceit : concerned with or striving for smartness and cleverness for their own sake or at the expense of seriousness and responsibility ⟨had never talked that way to the *smart-aleck* kid before —J.H.Reese⟩ ⟨the *smart-aleck* way you were talking —Alexander Saxton⟩ ⟨dismayingly intelligent and a shade *smart-alecky* —Jean Stafford⟩ ⟨five *smart-alecky* collegians who conspired to rob the till —Bennett Cerf⟩

smarted *past of* SMART

smarted up *adj* : made smart; *esp* : dressed up : spruced up ⟨a woman hates to go on a safari for a cab when she's all *smarted up* —Christopher Morley⟩

smart·en \ˈsmärtᵊn, ˈsmät-\ *vb* **smartened; smartened; smartening** \-t(ᵊ)niŋ\ **smartens** [²*smart* + *-en*] *vt* : to make smart or smarter: **a** : to improve in appearance (as by making neat, trim, spruce, or stylish) ⟨a tightened and ~*ed* version of the modern sports coat —James Lauer⟩ — usu. used with *up* ⟨sent the kids along to ~ themselves up —John Christopher⟩ ⟨newly shaved and ~*ed* up —Thor Heyerdahl⟩ ⟨~ themselves up for the evening meal —Rebecca West⟩ ⟨~*ed* up with a new figurehead —Mollie Panter-Downes⟩ **b** : to make more brisk or vigorous ⟨~ the pace⟩ : brighten up : ENLIVEN — used with *up* ⟨old theme . . . has been ~*ed* up into a refreshing piece of whimsy —*New Yorker*⟩ **c** : to make more alert : sharpen the wits of — used with *up* ⟨could learn a lot . . . ~ you up no end —A.M.Shairp⟩ **~ vi 1** : to smarten oneself : become smart or smarter — used with *up* ⟨everybody tried to ~ up for the festival —Christopher Morley⟩ ⟨~ up boy . . . leave the dumbbells settle the war —Richard Bissell⟩ **2** : to become sharper or more vigorous or intense ⟨a ~*ing* wind⟩ ⟨~ into color as the sun rises —Amy Lowell⟩

smarter *comparative of* SMART

smartest *superlative of* SMART

smart grass *n* [⁴*smart*] : SMARTWEED

smarting *adj* [fr. pres. part. of ¹*smart*] : that smarts: **a** : causing or marked by an acute stinging or cutting sensation ⟨~ pain⟩ ⟨a ~ wound⟩ **b** : feeling or affected by sharp stinging pain ⟨~ eyes⟩ or acute mental distress ⟨~ vanity⟩ — **smarting·ly** *adv*

smart·ish \ˈsmärd·ish\ *adj* [²*smart* + *-ish*] **1** : somewhat smart : fairly smart ⟨a ~ little bar —William Sansom⟩ **2** : of considerable importance or significance (as in amount, number, degree, quality) ⟨a ~ distance⟩ ⟨some ~ lambs . . . fat as snails —A.E.Coppard⟩

smart·less \ˈsmärtləs\ *adj* [⁴*smart* + *-less*] : free from smart

smart·ly *adv* [ME *smertly*, fr. *smert* smart + *-ly*] : in a smart manner : so as to be or seem smart: as **a** : VIGOROUSLY, SHARPLY ⟨paced ~ up and down —Thomas Hardy⟩ ⟨scratched his bare legs ~ —Willa Cather⟩ ⟨was spotted and ~ attacked by two English brigs —Parry Miller⟩ **b** : CURTLY ⟨was returned with the offending lines ~ pencilled out —Mollie Panter-Downes⟩ ⟨severely ⟨reprimanded him ~⟩ **c** : to a notable degree : CONSIDERABLY ⟨~ improved buying —D.C. Morrill⟩ ⟨temperature rose ~⟩ **d** : NEATLY, TRIMLY, PRECISELY ⟨beds ~ turned down —C.W.Morton⟩ ⟨had executed all commands ~ and briskly⟩ ⟨with a plastic disk ~ balanced on his snout —R.N.Hill⟩ ⟨drilled and handled their weapons ~⟩ **e** : CLEVERLY, EFFICIENTLY, CAPABLY ⟨skillfully drawn and ~ administered city plans —Hal Burton⟩ ⟨Department of Agriculture was ~ on the job —*Sydney (Australia) Bull.*⟩ ⟨a ~ directed play⟩ **f** : PERTLY, WITTILY ⟨~ said⟩ ⟨~ turned phrases⟩ ⟨put it so ~ that it seemed to mean more than it did⟩ **g** : FASHIONABLY, STYLISHLY ⟨always dressed ~⟩ ⟨~ tailored black and white linen —Virginia Pope⟩ ⟨~ furnished⟩

¹smart money \ˈ=,=\ *n* [⁴*smart*] **1 a** : money allowed to British soldiers or sailors for wounds and injuries received **b** : a sum paid by an employer to an injured employee **2** : money paid to procure the release of a recruit for the British army **3** : PUNITIVE DAMAGES

²smart money \ˈ=ˈ=\ *n* [²*smart*] **1** : money ventured by a bettor or speculator likely to have inside information; *sometimes* : investments made by alert experienced investors **2** : well-informed bettors or speculators

smart·ness *n* -ES [ME *smartnes*, fr. *smart* + *-nes* -ness] **1** *obs* : something causing smarting pain or distress **2** : the quality or state of being smart in expression, appearance, or movement : liveliness of wit or manner : BRISKNESS, SNAPPINESS ⟨~ of an epigram⟩ ⟨~ of a ship⟩ ⟨~ of a uniform⟩ ⟨~ of a salute⟩ ⟨~ of pace⟩ **3** : the quality or state of being ultrafashionable, elegant, or sophisticated ⟨~ of their address⟩ ⟨crowd . . . had a strong coloring of worldly ~ —Thomas Wolfe⟩ ⟨the ~ which is a characteristic achievement of most French girls —Frank Brookhouser⟩ **4** : ADROITNESS, CLEVERNESS, SHREWDNESS ⟨~ in business⟩ ⟨~ of a scheme⟩; *esp* : questionable shrewdness where self-interest is affected ⟨a certain degree of unscrupulous ~ —A.L.Guérard⟩

smarts *pres 3d sing of* SMART, *pl of* SMART

smart set *n* : ultrafashionable society

smartweed \ˈ=,=\ *n* [⁴*smart* + *weed*] **1** : any of various knotweeds (genus *Polygonum*) with strong acrid juice: as **a** : WATER PEPPER **b** : LADY'S THUMB **2** : a plant (as a nettle) that causes a burning sensation in contact with the skin

¹smarty *or* **smartie** \ˈsmär\|d·\|ē, -mä\|, \|t\|, \|i\ *n* -ES [²*smart* + *-y, -ie*] : one that tries in a callow fashion to be witty or clever : SMART ALECK

²smarty \"\ *adj* -ER/-EST : having the characteristics of a smarty : SMART-ALECKY ⟨attempt to satirize . . . seems thin and even ~ —F.O.Matthiessen⟩ ⟨was full of ~ ideas and had no manners —Margery Allingham⟩

smarty-pants \ˈ==,=\ *n pl but sing in constr* : SMARTY

¹smash \ˈsmash, -aa(ə)sh, -aish\ *vb* -ED/-ING/-ES [perh. blend of ³*smack* and *mash*] *vt* **1 a** : to break in pieces by violence : dash or crush to pieces : SHATTER ⟨~ a teacup⟩ ⟨~ a chair⟩ ⟨lifts his stick and ~*es* the chandelier —Edmund Wilson⟩ ⟨percussion wave that ~*ed* anything it hit at fifty yards —Wirt Williams⟩ ⟨bridge of his nose ~*ed* level with his face —G.B. Shaw⟩ ⟨typhoon ~*ed* all installations —*Americana Annual*⟩ ⟨X rays which ~ the genes and break up the chromosomes —Lee Hancock⟩ **b** : SPLIT 2a (3) ⟨a method of ~*ing* the atom —C.S.Kilby⟩ ⟨the cyclotron that ~*ed* the atom —J.W.Noble⟩ **2 a** (1) : to drive or throw violently esp. with a shattering or battering effect ⟨~ a stone through a window⟩ ⟨~*ed* a fist in his face⟩ ⟨~*ing* bombs into . . . enemy positions —*N.Y. Times*⟩ ⟨the shot ~*ing* an echo back from the gorge —Ernest Hemingway⟩ ⟨~ themselves against stone walls⟩; *also* : to bring about or effect in this way ⟨~*ed* a gap in the hedge —Adrian Bell⟩ ⟨had ~*ed* their way into Singapore two years before —Dave Richardson⟩ (2) : to handle (baggage) in a rough noisy manner **b** (1) : to hit violently : BATTER ⟨~ him in the face⟩ ⟨~ a door in⟩ ⟨~ down a fence⟩ (2) : to hit (as a tennis ball, a shuttlecock) with a very hard overhand stroke — compare DRIVE, KILL **3** : to destroy utterly as if by crushing to pieces or shattering : break up completely : cause to collapse : WRECK — often used with *up* ⟨~ a theory⟩ ⟨~ a tradition⟩ ⟨~ up an organization⟩ ⟨~ all resistance⟩ ⟨~ up a monopoly⟩ ⟨~ a revolt⟩ ⟨found his health ~*ed*⟩ ⟨~*ed* all production records⟩ **4 a** : to force (as into a new form, a more compact form) by pressure : MASH, PRESS ⟨caps to be worn ~*ed* sideways —Lois Long⟩ **b** : to compress (as folded book sections or assembled books) in order to give firmness and uniform bulk and eliminate a tendency to a wedge-shaped back from threads used in sewing — compare NIP 6a, SMASHING MACHINE **~ vi 1** : to move or become propelled with violence or crashing effect ⟨~*ed* into a tree⟩ ⟨~ through a thicket⟩ ⟨~*ed* over from the five-yard line for a touchdown⟩ ⟨raw wind ~*ing* against them —Irwin Shaw⟩ ⟨sea surges and ~*es* —Russell Lord⟩ **2** : to become utterly disrupted or wrecked; *esp* : to go bankrupt — often used with *up* ⟨~*ed* up during the slump⟩ **3** : to break up or go to pieces suddenly as a result of collision or pressure ⟨dish dropped from his grasp and ~*ed*⟩ ⟨had a horrible moment when things seemed to ~ inside me —Mary Deasy⟩ **4** : to execute a smash (as in tennis or badminton)

²smash \"\ *n* -ES **1 a** : a smashing blow ⟨a ~ on the jaw⟩ or attack ⟨two line ~*es* gained seven yards⟩ or the sound of a smashing blow ⟨~ of bat on ball⟩ ⟨the eternal ~ of a handball against the wall —Alfred Kazin⟩ **b** : an attacking shot in tennis or badminton in which the ball or shuttlecock is hit overhead with a powerful downward stroke and travels with great speed and usu. at a sharp angle to the floor or court **2 a** : the condition of being broken to pieces : a state of disaster ⟨the grand ~ that is inherent in every arms race —D.F.Fleming⟩ — often used in the phrases *go to smash, come to smash* ⟨had watched his plans go to ~⟩ ⟨felt his health going to ~⟩ **b** : a fabric defect caused by the breaking of warp or filling yarns **3 a** : a breaking or dashing to pieces or the sound of such breaking ⟨a ~ of crockery in the kitchen⟩; *esp* : a wreck due to collision : CRASH, SMASHUP ⟨a grade-crossing ~⟩ ⟨a bad ~ at the corner⟩ ⟨got in a ~ and a cyclist was killed —Margaret Kennedy⟩ **b** : utter collapse : FAILURE, RUIN, WRECK ⟨the ~ of all his hopes⟩; *esp* : business failure : BANKRUPTCY ⟨the bank ~*es* of 1893 —E.H.Collis⟩ **4 a** : a tall drink served with ice and garnished with fruit or mint and consisting of sprigs of mint, sugar, and soda water muddled in a glass to which is added an alcoholic liquor ⟨brandy ~⟩ ⟨whiskey ~⟩ **b** : a fruit beverage made with crushed or squeezed fruit ⟨cherry ~⟩ **5** : a striking success : HIT ⟨a box-office ~⟩ ⟨musical ~⟩ ⟨sang it for a ~ —R.G.Hubler⟩

³smash \"\ *adv* [²*smash*] : with a resounding crash : SMASHINGLY ⟨the stone went ~ through the window⟩

⁴smash \"\ *adj* [²*smash*] : being a smash : EXTRAORDINARY, OUTSTANDING, SMASHING ⟨~ hit⟩ ⟨the ~ best seller of the year —Orville Prescott⟩ ⟨~ musical show⟩ ⟨a ~ success⟩ ⟨two ~ record hits —Bill Simon⟩

⁵smash \"\ *n* -ES [origin unknown] **1** : counterfeit coin **2** : COIN ⟨twenty-nine dollars in bills and the rest in ~ —Croswell Bowen⟩ **3** *slang* : MONEY

⁶smash \"\ *vt* -ED/-ING/-ES : to pass (counterfeit coin)

smash·able \-shəbəl\ *adj* : capable of being smashed

smash-and-grab \ˈ==ˈ=\ *adj, chiefly Brit* : committed by smashing a shop window and snatching articles displayed within ⟨a *smash-and-grab* robbery⟩

smashboard signal \ˈ=,= -\ *n* : a railroad signal the arm of which is designed to be broken when passed in the stop position

¹smash·er \ˈsmashə(r), -aa(ə)sh-, -aish-\ *n* -S [¹*smash* + *-er*] **1** : something very large or fine or extraordinary of its kind ⟨hotel is a ~ with 1216 rooms —Hedda Hopper⟩ ⟨a ~ of a moustache —Bruce Marshall⟩ ⟨~ of a bride —Richard Llewellyn⟩ **2** : one that smashes or crushes ⟨a ~ of a blow⟩ ⟨heavy freight vehicles which are road ~*s* —John Kemp⟩: as **a** : a laborer who smashes slate or stone with a sledgehammer **b** : SMASHING MACHINE; *also* : an operator of such a machine **3** : a tennis or badminton player who is skilled in executing a smash ⟨can play the baseline but is also a volleyer, a ~ —Alice Marble⟩ **4** : a repairer of smashes in textiles — called also *smash fixer, smash hand, smash piecer* **5** *or* **smasher hat** *Africa* : a soft felt hat with a wide brim

²smasher \"\ *n* -S [⁵*smash* + *-er*] **1** : a receiver of stolen goods **2** : one that puts into circulation counterfeit coin or forged notes

smash·ery \-shərē\ *n* -ES [¹*smash* + *-ery*] : a state of smash : a smashed mass : DESTRUCTION

smashes *pres 3d sing of* SMASH, *pl of* SMASH

smash fixer *or* **smash hand** *or* **smash piecer** *n* : ¹SMASHER 4

smashing *adj* [fr. pres. part. of ¹*smash*] **1 a** : that smashes : CRUSHING ⟨a ~ blow⟩ ⟨~ defeat⟩ **b** : CRASHING ⟨~ chords⟩ **2** : that is a smash or a smasher : extraordinarily impressive or effective ⟨~ success⟩ ⟨a ~ victory⟩ ⟨~ display of power⟩ ⟨~ vote of confidence⟩ ⟨was ~ in that role⟩ ⟨an absolutely ~ costume⟩ ⟨a ~ blonde⟩ — **smash·ing·ly** *adv*

smashing machine *n* : a machine used by bookbinders to smash books or book sections

smashup \ˈ=,=\ *n* -S [fr. *smash up*, v.] **1** : a complete collapse ⟨the ~ of many an ancient civilization —Russell Lord⟩ ⟨warning signals of an economic ~ —*Time*⟩ ⟨an unexpected ~ in health⟩ ⟨trying to prevent a ~ of the family business⟩ **2** : a collision or crash esp. of one or more motor vehicles ⟨a head-on ~⟩ ⟨died in an early morning ~⟩

smatch \ˈsmach\ *n* -ES [ME *smech, smach*, alter. (influenced by *smachen* to taste) of *smack* — more at SMACK] **1** : a slight touch or trace : HINT, SUGGESTION **2** : SMATTERING

smatch·et \ˈsmachət\ *n* -S [prob. fr. *smatch* + *-et*] *Scot* : a contemptible unmannerly person

¹smat·ter \ˈsmad·ə(r), -atə-\ *vb* -ED/-ING/-S [ME *smateren*, prob. of imit. origin like MHG *smetern* to chatter, gossip, Sw *smattra* to clatter, crackle] *vt* **1** *obs* : SPOT, SPATTER, DEFILE **2** : to speak or utter so as to reveal a spotty or superficial knowledge ⟨to ~ French⟩ **3** : to dabble in : study bits of ⟨I have ~*ed* law . . . letters . . . geography —R.L.Stevenson⟩ **4** [influenced in meaning by *shatter*] *Scot* : to break in pieces : SHATTER **~ vi 1** : to talk superficially and disconnectedly : BABBLE, CHATTER **2** : to have a slight, superficial, and spotty knowledge : DABBLE

²smatter \"\ *n* -S **1** : slight piecemeal knowledge : SMATTERING ⟨a ~ of French⟩ **2** *Scot* : small bits : insignificant things : FRAGMENTS **3** : a heterogeneous collection : SMATTERING ⟨a weary ~ of applause —M.W.Straight⟩

smat·ter·er \-ərə(r)\ *n* -S : one that smatters or has a smattering knowledge

¹smattering *n* -S [fr. gerund of ¹*smatter*] **1** : an act of one that smatters ⟨learn a few languages then, and learn them well: a ~ is a frittering —A.L.Guérard⟩ ⟨a unified discipline instead of an elegant ~ —H.J.Muller⟩ **2** : superficial or piecemeal knowledge ⟨picked up a ~ of these languages when they were children —Demaree Bess⟩ ⟨a ~ of carpentry, house painting, bricklaying —Alva Johnston⟩ **3** : an inconsiderable number or amount esp. of similar but distinct individuals or parts : piecemeal collection : SMATTER ⟨weeks passed with only a ~ of lookers —Peter DeVries⟩ ⟨the ~ of Negroes in the balcony —Shelby Foote⟩ ⟨only a ~ of early writing had been printed —Charlton Laird⟩

²smattering \"\ *adj* [fr. pres. part. of ¹*smatter*] : that smatters or is a smattering ⟨~ knowledge of French⟩ ⟨~ dilettantes⟩ — **smat·ter·ing·ly** *adv*

smattery \-rē\ *adj* [²*smatter* + *-y*] : SMATTERING, SUPERFICIAL ⟨a ~ knowledge is equated to education —Eric Partridge⟩

smaze \ˈsmāz\ *n* -S [*smoke* + *haze*] : a combination of haze and smoke similar to smog in appearance but less damp in consistency

sm cap *abbr* small capital

¹smear \ˈsmi(ə)r, -iə\ *n* -S *often attrib* [ME *smere*, fr. OE *smeoru;* akin to OS & OHG *smero* fat, grease, lard, ON *smǫr, smjǫr* fat, butter, Goth *smairthr* fat, *smarna* dung, OIr *smir, smiur* marrow, Gk *smyrid-, smyris* powdered emery, *myron* unguent, perfume] **1 a** (1) *obs* : a fat oily substance : OINTMENT, GREASE (2) : a viscous or sticky substance **b** : a spot made by or as if by an unctuous or adhesive substance : BLOTCH, STAIN, SMUDGE **2** : material smeared on a surface (as of a microscopic slide or of a culture medium); *also* : a preparation made by spreading material on a surface ⟨a fecal ~⟩ ⟨vaginal ~⟩ **3** : a partial glaze on pottery produced by vapor or by brushing off the greater part of an applied glaze **4** : a play of a counting card on one's partner's trick **5** : a glissando esp. when produced on a trombone **6 a** : a deliberate and usu. unsubstantiated charge or accusation intended to foment distrust or hatred against the person or organization so charged ⟨pleaded calmly that those who expound unpopular doctrine be answered factually instead of by ~*s* —Saul Carson⟩ ⟨attack and personal ~ in the familiar manner of rumor and innuendo —Harry Conn⟩ **b** : SMEAR WORD

²smear \"\ *vt* -ED/-ING/-S [ME *smeren, smiren*, fr. OE *smierwan, smerwan, smirwan;* akin to MD & MLG *smeren* to grease, salve, anoint, OHG *smirwen*, ON *smyrva, smyrja* to anoint, *smǫr, smjǫr* fat, butter — more at ¹SMEAR] **1 a** (1) : to overspread with something unctuous, viscous, or adhesive : DAUB ⟨the wood looked new, so he ~*ed* it with oil and ashes —Lyle Saxon⟩ ⟨lived on bread ~*ed* with lard —C.J.Rolo⟩ (2) : to spread (a substance) over a surface ⟨~*ed* 10 minims of machine oil on a condenser lens —J.A.Knight⟩ **b** : to treat (as a wound) by overspreading with a thick or greasy medication **c** : to treat (as young sheep) with a salve to destroy vermin and mat the fleece **2 a** : to stain, smudge, or make dirty by or as if by smearing or rubbing : BESMIRCH, SULLY ⟨the hat . . . had been ~*ed* with grease and dirt in a minor airplane accident —Henry LaCossitt⟩ **b** : to give a quality or appearance to; *specif* : to vilify or blacken the reputation of by applying a debasing or odious epithet or by secretly and maliciously spreading gross charges and imputations ⟨people . . . whose opinions disagree with his; and whom he has ~*ed* by all sorts of distortions and misrepresentations —Elmer Davis⟩ **c** : to obliterate, obscure, blur, blend, or wipe out by or as if by smearing ⟨~*ed* the end of his cigarette on the tray —Hamilton Basso⟩ ⟨~ notes on a trombone⟩ **3 a** : to rush hard (the opposing ball carrier, passer, or kicker of a defensive football team) and throw for a loss **b** : to rout, repulse, or frustrate completely : SMOTHER **4** : FATTEN 1b(2) **5** : to prepare as a smear for microscopic examination : to make a smear of

smear·case *or* **smier·case** \ˈsmir,kās\ *n* [modif. of G *schmierkäse*, fr. *schmieren* to smear, spread (fr. OHG *smirwen*) + *käse* cheese, fr. OHG *kāsi* — more at SMEAR, CHEESE] *chiefly Midland* : COTTAGE CHEESE

smear dab *n* : a brown mottled flatfish (*Microstomus microcephalus*) of the coasts of northern Europe and Iceland that has a slimy skin and is highly esteemed as food; *also* : any of various other flatfishes

smear dock *n* : GOOD-KING-HENRY

smeared *adj* [fr. past part. of *smear*] : having color markings that are ill defined as if rubbed ⟨~ deerskin⟩

smear·er \ˈsmirə(r)\ *n* -S : one that smears

smear·i·ness \-rēnəs\ *n* -ES : the quality or state of being smeary ⟨was conscious of the ~ of the tiled floor —Marjorie Brace⟩

smear·less \-rləs\ *adj* : having no smears : UNSMEARED

smear-sheet \ˈ=,=\ *n* : a newspaper or periodical containing a high proportion of unfounded personal charges or vilification

smear word *n* : an epithet applied to a person or group in order to degrade, blacken, or make unjust or unfounded accusations ⟨time was . . . when independents in politics were rare and *mugwump* was a *smear word* —W.E.Binkley⟩ ⟨strained relations may be expressed in clique formation, subtle whispers and shrugs, *smear words*, discrimination in clubs and dances —F.J. Brown & J.S.Roucek⟩

smeary \ˈsmirē, -ri\ *adj* -ER/-EST **1** : marked by or covered with smears ⟨the ~ marble-topped table —Nicholas Monsarrat⟩ ⟨every page . . . was a mess of ~ erasures —Robert Rice⟩ **2** : liable to cause smears : GREASY, ADHESIVE, VISCOUS ⟨~ white library paste —Pearl Kazin⟩

smec·tic \'smektik\ *adj* [L *smecticus* cleansing, fr. Gk *smēktikos*, fr. *smēktos* (verbal of *smēchein* to wash off, clean) + *-ikos* -ic — more at SMITE] **1 :** PURIFYING, DETERGENT **2 :** of, relating to, or being the phase of a liquid crystal characterized by arrangement of molecules in layers with the long molecular axes in a given layer being parallel to one another and those of other layers and perpendicular or slightly inclined to the plane of the layer — compare CHOLESTERIC 2, NEMATIC

1**smec·tym·nu·an** \smek'timnəwən\ *n* -s *usu cap* [*Smectymnuus*, pseudonym formed fr. the initials of *S*tephan *M*arshall †1635, *E*dmund *C*alamy †1666, *T*homas *Y*oung †1655, *M*atthew *N*ewcomen †1669, and *W*illiam *S*purstowe †1666 Brit. Presbyterian clergymen + E *-an*] **1 :** one of a group of five 17th century English Presbyterian clergymen collaborating in a pamphlet attacking the episcopacy **2 :** an adherent of the Smectymnuans

2**smectymnuan** \"\ *adj, usu cap* **:** of or relating to the Smectymnuans

smed·dum \'smedəm\ *n* -s [fr. (assumed) ME, fr. OE *smedma, smeoduma*] **1** *chiefly Scot* **:** POWDER, DUST; *specif* **:** the flour or powder of ground malt **2** *Scot* **:** spirited vigor **:** SPUNK

1**smeech** \'smēch\ *n* -ES [ME *smech*, fr. OE *smēc, smȳc, smīc*; akin to OE *smoca* smoke — more at SMOKE] *dial Brit* **:** dense smoke

2**smeech** \"\ *vi* -ED/-ING/-ES *Brit* **:** to emit smoke or vapor

1**smeek** \'smēk\ *vt* -ED/-ING/-S [ME *smeken*, fr. OE *smēocan* to emit smoke, fumigate; akin to OE *smoca* smoke — more at SMOKE] *Scot* **:** to clean, cure, dry, drive out, or fumigate by means of smoke or fumes

2**smeek** \"\ *n* -s [ME *smek*, alter. (influenced by *smeken*) of *smech*] *chiefly Scot* **:** dense or black smoke — **smeeky** \-ki\ *adj* -ER/-EST

smeeth \'smēth\ *vt* -ED/-ING/-S [ME *smethen*, fr. OE *smēthan, smēthian*, fr. *smēthe*, adj., smooth — more at SMOOTH] *dial chiefly Brit* **:** SMOOTH

smeg·ma \'smegmə\ *n* -s [NL, fr. L, detergent, soap, fr. Gk *smēgma*, fr. *smēchein* to wash off, clean — more at SMITE] **:** the secretion of a sebaceous gland; *specif* **:** the cheesy sebaceous matter that collects between the glans penis and the foreskin or around the clitoris and labia minora

smegma bacillus *n* **:** an acid-fast bacterium (*Mycobacterium smegmatis*) found in smegma

1**smell** \'smel\ *vb* **smelled** \-ld\ *or* **smelt** \-lt\ **smelled** *or* **smelt; smelling; smells** [ME *smellen, smullen*; akin to MD *smōlen* to smolder, scorch, LG *smelen, smölen* to smolder, scorch, MIr *smāl, smōl, smūal* fire, glow, Russ *smalit'* to scorch, singe; basic meaning: to smolder] *vt* **1 a :** to perceive by the excitation of the olfactory nerves **:** get the odor or scent of through stimuli affecting the sensory nerves of the nasal passages ⟨*smelt* growing things in the park —Ellen Glasgow⟩ **b :** to inhale the odor of (as for enjoyment or testing) **:** SNIFF ⟨~ stew cooking⟩ ⟨~ each perfume offered for sale⟩ **2 :** to detect or become aware of as if by the sense of smell or natural instinct ⟨the censors ~*ed* sex in every realistic literary creation —O.S.J.Gogarty⟩ ⟨very few fail to ~ the tension and the fear in the air of its cities —Patrick O'Donovan⟩ **3 :** to emit the odor of ⟨you ~ sherry, sir —W.M.Thackeray⟩ ~ *vi* **1 :** to exercise the sense of smell: as **a :** to be on the scent for something ⟨the dogs ran ~*ing* through the fields⟩ **b :** to inhale an odor ⟨~ at her salts⟩ **2 a** (1) **:** to have an odor or scent **:** give forth an aroma ⟨the air ~*s* of the sea —Gladys Taber⟩ ⟨lorries rolled by ~*ing* of rubber and oil —Paul Roche⟩ ⟨it ~*s* like violets⟩ (2) **:** to have or exhibit a characteristic aura or atmosphere **:** be suggestive ⟨the accounts . . . seemed to me to ~ of truth —R.S.Bourne⟩ ⟨elimination of anything ~*ing* of policy was necessary in order to secure unanimous agreement —R.C.Tolman⟩ **b** (1) **:** to have an offensive odor **:** STINK ⟨the canals are sewers and, in tactless truth, they ~ —Claudia Cassidy⟩ (2) **:** to appear evil, dishonest, ugly, or disreputable ⟨all this from the moral point of view ~*s* —A.F.Wills⟩ — **smell a rat :** to have a suspicion of something wrong — **smell of the lamp :** to bear marks of study and labor rather than of genius or inspiration **:** seem artificial ⟨to them a discussion of sovereignty in the abstract would have *smelt of the lamp* —C.A.Beard⟩ — usu. used of a literary composition — **smell one's oats :** to pluck up spirit and move with new energy when near one's goal — **smell the bottom** *or* **smell the ground** *of a ship* **:** to lose speed in shallow water and often to veer off course or become heavy on the helm

2**smell** \"\ *n* -s [ME *smel, smul*; akin to *smellen, smullen*, v. — more at 1SMELL] **1 a :** the act or power of perceiving odor **:** olfactory sensation or the capacity for it **:** OLFACTION ⟨canine behavior is largely oriented in terms of ~⟩ **b :** the one of the special senses that is concerned with the perception of the quality of a substance which is classified as odor, is mediated by the olfactory organ, is normally sensitive to volatile or dissolved material in extremely low concentration (as 0.00000001 mg. per liter), is conducted centrally by the olfactory nerve, and is coordinated esp. by centers in the hippocampal convolution **2 :** the property of a thing that affects the olfactory organs **:** a pleasant, unpleasant, or neutral odor ⟨the ~ of fat meat cooking in beans —Jean Stafford⟩ ⟨the sweet, intense ~ of overripe fruit —William Beebe⟩ **3 a :** a very small amount or indication **:** TRACE, HINT ⟨add only a ~ of garlic or the dish will offend most palates⟩ ⟨taking care to avoid any ~ of impropriety in the proceedings⟩ **b :** the quality by which an influence or presence is detected ⟨quite soon danger loses the ~ it had for you — you know it's there, but only because you know it must be there —Elizabeth Bowen⟩ **c :** a pervasive quality **:** AURA, ATMOSPHERE ⟨the ~ of mortality that exudes from the old records —V.L.Parrington⟩ **4 :** an act or instance of smelling

syn SMELL, SCENT, ODOR, AROMA mean, in common, the quality of a thing that makes it perceptible to the olfactory sense, or something perceptible only to that sense. SMELL usu. indicates solely the sensation, usu. devoid of connotation, sometimes but rarely, however, as opposed to AROMA, carrying the suggestion of something unpleasant ⟨the *smell* of oranges and wooden boxes —Kay Fuller⟩ ⟨the spicy *smell* of tobacco —*Amer. Guide Series: Tenn.*⟩ ⟨like all houses . . . had its peculiar *smell* —Samuel Butler †1902⟩ ⟨about the town's political activity there was a *smell* to high heaven⟩ SCENT is associated, in one direction, with the natural odor of living things, esp. animals, and so carries rather vivid connotations; in being associated with the trail an animal leaves, it suggests a finer perception than SMELL; in being the word in Britain equivalent to the American *perfume*, it frequently suggests something pleasant ⟨the *scent* of rabbits roused the dog to alertness⟩ ⟨the *scents* of the countryside —Roy Lewis & Angus Maude⟩ ⟨the rich, vital *scents* of the ploughed ground —Ellen Glasgow⟩ ⟨vibrating among the pale petals of the lilies and setting free their *scent* in short waves of perfume —John Galsworthy⟩ ODOR is sometimes interchangeable with SMELL, often implying unpleasantness ⟨innumerable articles of manufacture carry with them characteristic *odors* —A.C.Morrison⟩ ⟨redolent with the *odor* of West Indian molasses, rum, spices, and China tea —*Amer. Guide Series: Maine*⟩ ⟨the fetid *odor* of a bog, the stench of a carcass in the woods, the delectable reek of ferment in the hay-crammed barn —D.C.Peattie⟩ AROMA suggests an odor that is penetrating or pungent and usu. pleasant as from something savory ⟨the *aroma* of cooking coffee⟩ ⟨African ginger lacks the fine *aroma* of Jamaica ginger but it has an intensely pungent odor —J.W.Parry⟩ ⟨the sweet, burned *aroma* of roasted meat and the penetrating, acid odor of hardwood smoke —Rufus Jarman⟩ ⟨the pervading *aroma* of decay and hopelessness —Harrison Smith⟩

— **smell of the lamp :** the appearance of having been produced by pedantry and plodding scholarship rather than vital inspiration ⟨when he speaks about economic or social issues the *smell of the lamp* hangs about every cliché-cluttered sentence —H.G.Nicholas⟩

smell·able \-ləbəl\ *adj* **:** capable of being smelled

smell·age \-lij\ *n* -s [2*smell* + *-age* (as in *lovage*)] **:** fragrant vegetation; *specif* **:** LOVAGE

smelled *past of* SMELL

smell·er \-lə(r)\ *n* -s **1 :** one that smells; *specif* **:** one that perceives, traces, or tests by the sense of smell **2 :** a tactile bristle **:** VIBRISSA **3 a :** NOSE **b :** a blow on the nose

smell–feast \'⸗,⸗\ *n* [1*smell* + *feast*] **:** one given to finding out and getting invited to good feasts **:** PARASITE, SPONGER

smell·ful \'smelfəl\ *adj, Austral* **:** SMELLY

smell·fun·gus \'smel,fəŋgəs\ *n* [after *Smelfungus*, a hypercritical traveler in *A Sentimental Journey through France and Italy* (1768) by Laurence Sterne †1768 Brit. novelist, who intended this character to satirize Tobias Smollett †1771 Brit. novelist for his descriptions in *Travels through France and Italy* (1766)] **:** a captious critic **:** FAULTFINDER

smell·ie \'smelē, -li\ *n* -s [2*smell* + *-ie*] **:** a motion picture having smells synchronized with the action

smell·i·ness \-lēnəs\ *n* -ES **:** the quality or state of being smelly

smelling *n* -s [ME, fr. gerund of *smellen* to smell — more at SMELL] **:** SMELL 1a

smelling bottle *n* **:** a bottle filled with smelling salts or a scent

smelling salts *n pl* **:** an aromatic preparation of ammonium carbonate (sense c) and ammonia water and often some scent used as a stimulant and restorative (as to avoid or relieve faintness or headache)

smelling–stick \'⸗⸗,⸗\ *n* **:** a common No. American sassafras (*Sassafras albidum molle*) with pubescent twigs and young leaves

smell–less \'smelləs\ *adj* **:** having no smell

smell out *vt* **1 :** to seek or find as if by smelling **:** ferret out ⟨its task remained unchanged: to *smell out* and sweep away ruthlessly all opposition to the dictator —W.C.Bullitt⟩ **2 :** to detect (as a witch) by divination

smells *pres 3d sing of* SMELL, *pl of* SMELL

smell up *vt* **:** to fill with an esp. disagreeable odor ⟨the baggage man reported to the district supervisor that two trunks had *smelled up* his car —E.D.Radin⟩

smelly \'smelē, -li\ *adj* -ER/-EST **:** having a smell; *esp* **:** MALODOROUS

1**smelt** \'smelt\ *n, pl* **smelts** *or* **smelt** [ME, fr. OE; akin to Norw *smelte* whiting] **1 a :** any of various small fishes of the family Osmeridae and esp. of the genus *Osmerus* that closely resemble the trouts in general structure, are translucent greenish above, silvery on the sides, and silvery or white beneath, live along the coasts and ascend the rivers to spawn or are landlocked in lakes, and have delicate tender oily flesh with a distinctive odor and taste: as (1) **:** a common and commercially important food fish (*O. mordax*) of eastern No. America from Virginia northward (2) **:** SPARLING (3) **:** WHITEBAIT 2c **b :** any of various other salmonoid fishes: as (1) **:** any of several fishes of the family Argentinidae (as the capelin) (2) *Brit* **:** SMOLT (3) **:** a small freshwater fish (*Retropinna semoni*) of Australia and New Zealand that has a strong odor of cucumbers **2 :** any of various small fishes of groups other than Salmonoidea resembling the smelt: as **a :** any of several silversides (as a jack smelt, a top smelt, or a grunion) **b :** TOMCOD 1b **c :** SAND LAUNCE **d :** any of various freshwater cyprinid fishes **e :** SAND BORER **3** *obs* **:** an easy mark **:** SIMPLETON

2**smelt** *past of* SMELL

3**smelt** \'smelt\ *vt* -ED/-ING/-S [D or LG *smelten* (fr. MD & MLG, respectively); akin to OHG *smelzan* to melt, OSw *smælta*, OE *meltan* — more at MELT] **1 :** to melt or fuse (as ore) often with an accompanying chemical change usu. to separate the metal **2 :** FLUX, SCORIFY, REFINE, REDUCE

4**smelt** \"\ *n* -s **:** a product of smelting or fusing **:** MELT

5**smelt** \"\ *n* -s [origin unknown] **:** a half guinea

1**smelt·er** \-tə(r)\ *n* -s [3*smelt* + *-er*] **1 a :** one that smelts; *specif* **:** a furnaceman who smelts ore **b :** an owner or operator of a smeltery **2** *or* **smelt·ery** \-tərē\ **:** an establishment for smelting

2**smelter** \"\ *n* -s [1*smelt* + *-er*] **:** a smelt fisherman

smelt·er·man \'⸗⸗mən\ *n, pl* **smeltermen** [1*smelter* + *man*] **:** 1SMELTER 1a

smeuse \'smyüz, -üs\ *n* -s [prob. blend of 1*smoot* and *meuse*] *dial Eng* **:** a hole in a hedge or wall

smew \'smyü\ *n* -s [akin to Fris *smjunt* smew, D *smient*, MHG *smiehe*] **1 :** a merganser (*Mergus albellus*) of northern Europe and Asia that is the smallest of mergansers and one of the most expert divers of all ducks and is in the male white and black with a large white crest **2 :** HOODED MERGANSER

SMG *abbr* submachine gun

smick·er \'smikə(r)\ *vi* [prob. of Scand origin; akin to OSw *smikra, smikkra* to flatter, Dan *smigre*; akin to OE *smicer* handsome, elegant, *smācian* to flatter, OHG *smehhar* slender, *bismītan* to defile, stain — more at SMITE] *archaic* **:** to ogle and smile amorously — used with *at* or *after*

smick·et \'smikət\ *n* [prob. dim. of *smock*] *dial Eng* **:** a woman's smock

smid·dy \'smidi\ *dial Brit var of* SMITHY

smid·gen *or* **smid·geon** *or* **smid·gin** \'smijən\ *also* **smidge** \'smij\ *n* -s [prob. alter. of *smitch*] **:** a small amount **:** BIT

smiercase *var of* SMEARCASE

smi·la·ca·ce·ae \,smīlə'kāsē,ē\ *n pl, cap* [NL, fr. *Smilac-, Smilax*, type genus + *-aceae*] *in some classifications* **:** a family of herbs or somewhat woody vines (order Liliales) having leaves with one to five prominent parallel veins and dioecious flowers with six perianth segments succeeded by globose berries and being commonly included in the family Liliaceae — **smi·la·ca·ceous** \¦⸗⸗¦kāshəs\ *adj*

smi·la·ce·ae \smī'lāsē,ē\ [NL, fr. *Smilac-, Smilax* + *-eae*] *syn of* SMILACACEAE

smi·la·ci·na \,smīlə'sīnə\ *n, cap* [NL, fr. *Smilac-, Smilax* + *-ina*] **:** a genus of American and Asiatic plants (family Liliaceae) with alternate leaves and racemes or panicles of small white flowers succeeded by red, green, or black berries — see FALSE SOLOMON'S SEAL

smi·la·gen·in \,smīlə'jenən, smī'lajənən\ *n* -s [NL *Smilax* (genus name of *Smilax ornata*) + E *-genin*] **:** a steroid sapogenin $C_{27}H_{44}O_3$ that is obtained esp. from a sarsaparilla (*Smilax ornata*) and is stereoisomeric with sarsapogenin

smi·lax \'smī,laks\ *n* [NL, fr. L, a kind of oak, yew, bindweed, fr. Gk; perh. akin to Gk *smilē* wood-carving knife; fr. the use of oak in carving — more at SMITH] **1** *cap* **:** a large widely distributed genus of plants (family Liliaceae) having small greenish flowers in axillary umbels and erect often prickly stems that climb by means of petiolar tendrils — see CATBRIER, SARSAPARILLA **2** *pl* **smilaxes :** a delicate greenhouse twining plant (*Asparagus asparagoides*) of southern Africa having ovate, bright-green cladophylls and being used esp. by florists in bouquet work and as a pot plant

1**smile** \'smīl, *esp before pause or consonant* -īəl\ *vb* -ED/-ING/-S [ME *smilen*; akin to OE *smerian* to laugh at, LG *smilen* to smile, obs. D *smuilen*, OHG *smierōn*, MHG *smielen*, Sw & Norw *smila* to smile, L *mirus* wonderful, *mirari* to wonder, wonder at, Gk *meidian* to smile, Toch A *smi-*, Skt *smayate* he smiles] *vi* **1 :** to have, produce, or exhibit a smile ⟨by this time the infant . . . may even laugh or ~ at his mother —H.R. Litchfield & L.H.Dembo⟩ **2 a :** to look or regard with amusement, ridicule, contempt, or indulgence ⟨~ indulgently at his quiddities⟩ ⟨*smiled* at his own folly for engaging in such a business —Martin Gardner⟩ **b :** to look or seem to look with favor **:** bestow approval **:** be propitious ⟨could hardly be blamed for feeling that Heaven *smiled* on his labors —Sheila Rowlands⟩ ⟨circumstances happen to ~ around him —Glenway Westcott⟩ **c :** to look or appear pleasant or agreeable **:** present a gay, sparkling, thriving, or benignant aspect ⟨a lake, warm and *smiling* and margined with green trees and grass —*Amer. Guide Series: Oregon*⟩ ~ *vt* **1 a :** to affect in some way with a smile or by a smile ⟨*smiling* away her embarrassment —C.S.Forester⟩ **b :** to effect or accomplish by smiling ⟨you thanked them and *smiled* your way out of it before you started crying yourself —Fred Majdalany⟩ **2** *obs* **:** to regard with disdain **:** hold in contempt ⟨~ you my speeches, as I were a fool —Shak.⟩ **3 :** to express by a smile ⟨*smiling* his pleasure at the happy outcome —E.B.George⟩ ⟨*smiled* a doubt as to their capacity —Irving Howe⟩ **4 :** to form one's face into (a smile) ⟨*smiled* a filial smile —Charles Dickens⟩

2**smile** \"\ *n* -s **1 :** a change of facial expression involving a brightening of the eyes and an upward curving of the corners of the mouth with no sound and less muscular distortion of the features than in a laugh that may express amusement, pleasure, tender affection, approval, restrained mirth, irony, derision, or any of various other emotions ⟨an infectious public ~ —*Time*⟩ ⟨the slight superior ~ of the man who is sure that he has the future —O.W.Holmes †1935⟩ ⟨wears a fixed ~ on her made-up face —C.W.Mills⟩ **2 :** a bright, pleasant, gratifying, or encouraging appearance or aspect ⟨the ~ of sunlit sea half a mile or so away —Blanche E. Baughan⟩

smile·ful \-lfəl\ *adj* **:** SMILING

smile·less \'smī(ə)lləs\ *adj* **:** exhibiting no smile **:** SOLEMN — **smile·less·ly** *adv* — **smile·less·ness** *n* -ES

smil·er \'smīlə(r)\ *n* -s [ME, fr. *smilen* to smile + *-er*] **:** one that smiles

smil·et \'smīlət\ *n* -s [2*smile* + *-et*] **:** a little smile

smiley *also* **smily** \'smīlē\ *adj* [2*smile* + *-y*] **:** exhibiting a smile

smil·ing·ly *adv* **:** in a smiling manner

smil·ing·ness *n* -ES **:** the quality or state of exhibiting a smile

smi·lo \'smī(,)lō\ *or* **smilo grass** *n* -s [origin unknown] **:** a perennial mountain rice (*Oryzopsis mileacea*) native to the Mediterranean region and introduced into No. America

smi·lo·don \'smīlə,dän\ *n, cap* [NL, fr. Gk *smilē* woodcarving knife + NL *-odon* — more at SMITH] **:** a New World genus of Pleistocene saber-toothed tigers attaining the size of tigers and having upper canines that extend 7 inches or more below the lower jaw and a gape of fully 90 degrees

1**smin·thu·rid** \smin'thürəd\ *adj* [NL *Sminthuridae*] **:** of or relating to the Sminthuridae

2**sminthurid** \"\ *n* -s **:** a collembolan of the family Sminthuridae

smin·thu·ri·dae \-rə,dē\ *n pl, cap* [NL, fr. *Sminthurus*, type genus (fr. Gk *sminthos* mouse of non-IE origin; akin to Etruscan *isminthians* mouse — + *-urus*) + *-idae*] **:** a family of small jumping collembolans having a short rounded body — compare LUCERNE FLEA

1**smirch** \'smərch, 'sməch, 'smәich\ *vt* -ED/-ING/-ES [ME *smorchen*] **1 a :** to make dirty, stained, or discolored **:** SULLY, SOIL, TARNISH **b :** to smear with something that stains or dirties **:** apply a discoloring agent to ⟨with a kind of umber ~ my face —Shak.⟩ **2 :** to bring into disrepute **:** bring discredit or disgrace upon ⟨the kind of mentalities that delight in ~*ing* the names of public men —A.D.H.Smith⟩

2**smirch** \"\ *n* -ES **1 :** a dirty blurred mark or blot **:** SMEAR, STAIN **2 :** something that tarnishes a reputation **:** a moral flaw

smirchy \-chē\ *adj* -ER/-EST **:** marked with spots or stains **:** SMIRCHED, BEGRIMED

smi·ris \'smīrəs\ *n* -ES [Gk *smyris, smiris* — more at SMEAR] **:** EMERY

1**smirk** \'smərk, 'smək, 'smәik\ *vi* -ED/-ING/-S [ME *smirken*, fr. OE *smearcian* to smile; akin to OE *smerian* to laugh at — more at SMILE] **:** to smile in an affected or conceited manner **:** smile with affected complaisance **:** SIMPER

2**smirk** \'smərk\ *adj, dial chiefly Brit* **:** pleasantly neat and trim **:** AGREEABLE

3**smirk** \'smərk, 'smək, 'smәik\ *n* -s **:** an affected smile **:** SIMPER ⟨the solemnity of the ceremony was broken by ~*s*, whispered jokes, and repressed titters —Robert Graves⟩

smirk·er \-kə(r)\ *n* -s **:** one that smirks

smirk·ing·ly *adv* **:** in a smirking manner

smir·kle \'smərkəl\ *vi* -ED/-ING/-S [freq. of 1*smirk*] *chiefly Scot* **:** SMIRK, SMILE

smirky \'smərkē\ *adj* -ER/-EST **:** SMIRKING

smirr \'smər\ *var of* SMUR

smit \'smit\ *vt* [ME *smitten*, fr. OE *smittian*; akin to OFris *smitta* to dirty, defile, MLG *smitten*, OHG *bismizzan*, *bismīzan* — more at SMITE] **1** *chiefly Scot* **:** STAIN, TARNISH **2** *chiefly Scot* **:** CONTAMINATE, SULLY — often used of persons **3** *chiefly Scot* **:** INFECT

1**smitch** \'smich\ *dial Brit var of* SMUTCH

2**smitch** \"\ *n* -ES [perh. fr. 1*smitch*] **:** SMIDGEN

1**smite** \'smī|t, *usu* |d·+V\ *vb* **smote** \'smōl\ *or archaic* **smit** \'smi|\ **smit·ten** \'smit°n\ *or* **smit** *or* **smote; smiting; smites** [ME *smiten*, fr. OE *smītan*; akin to MD *smiten* to strike, throw, OHG *bismīzan* to defile, stain, OSw *smēta* to daub, smear, spread, Goth *bismeitan* to anoint, Gk *smēn* to wipe off, cleanse, *smēchein* to wash off, clean, Arm *mic* dirt, and perh. to L *mittere* to let go, send, Av *hamista* cast down, suppressed; basic meaning: to rub, throw] *vt* **1 a :** to strike usu. hard esp. with the hand or something held in the hand ⟨blacksmiths *smiting* the anvil —Havelock Ellis⟩ ⟨*smote* the side of his head with his palm —Pearl Buck⟩ **b :** to knock down ⟨to ~ an enemy to the ground⟩ **c** *archaic* **:** to strike or pluck (as the strings of a harp) to produce musical sound ⟨the minstrel *smote* his harp and sang⟩ **d :** to shine upon suddenly ⟨morning sunlight *smote* for the first time mankind's very first space craft —W.F.Jenkins⟩ **2 a :** to kill or severely injure by or as if by smiting **:** afflict with sudden calamity, destruction, or injury **b :** to inflict punishment (as destruction, death, or severe injury) upon as if by a stroke **c :** to attack or afflict suddenly and injuriously ⟨the herd was *smitten* by foot-and-mouth disease —*Irish Digest*⟩ **3 :** to cause to strike ⟨*smote* his hand against his thigh⟩ ⟨~ cymbals together⟩ **4 :** to affect as if by striking forcefully or abruptly **:** impress suddenly ⟨little children *smitten* with the fear of hell —V.L. Parrington⟩ ⟨*smitten* by the view from a crossing ferry —*Newsweek*⟩ ⟨her conscience *smote* her that she should have so much and they should have so little —Rebecca West⟩ ~ *vi* **:** to deliver or deal a usu. heavy blow with or as if with the hand or something held in the hand ⟨the child over 16 who cursed or *smote* at parents might incur the death penalty —*Amer. Guide Series: N.J.*⟩ **syn** see STRIKE

2**smite** \"\ *n* -s **:** a heavy blow **:** a smiting with a hand, weapon, or implement

smit·er \'smīd·ə(r)\ *n* -s [ME, fr. *smiten* + *-er*] **:** one that smites

1**smith** \'smith\ *n* -s [ME, fr. OE; akin to OHG *smid* smith, ON *smithr* smith, craftsman, Goth *aizasmitha* coppersmith, Gk *smilē* wood-carving knife, and perh. to Lith *smailus* pointed, greedy; basic meaning to carve] **1 a :** a worker in metals — often used in combination ⟨*goldsmith*⟩ ⟨*ironsmith*⟩ ⟨*platinumsmith*⟩ **b :** BLACKSMITH 1c **2 :** one who constructs, builds, or produces something **:** MAKER ⟨the ~ of his own fortune —Van Wyck Brooks⟩ — often used in combination ⟨*skismith*⟩ ⟨*tunesmith*⟩

2**smith** \"\ *vt* -ED/-ING/-S [ME *smithen*, fr. OE *smithian*; akin to OHG *smithōn* to forge, fashion, Goth *gasmithon* to produce; denominative fr. the root of E 1*smith*] **:** to make or fashion by beating metal into shape **:** forge on an anvil after heating ⟨~ a sword⟩ ⟨~ a blade⟩

smith·am \'smithəm\ *n* -s [alter. of *smeddum*] **:** ore in fine particles obtained usu. by sifting

smithcraft \'⸗,⸗\ *n* **:** the occupation or technique of a smith

smith·er·eens \,smithə'rēnz\ *also* **smith·ers** \'smithə(r)z\ *n pl* [*smithereens* fr. IrGael *smidirīn*, dim. of *smiodar* fragment; *smithers* fr. IrGael *smiodar*] **:** BITS, FRAGMENTS ⟨blown to ~ in the dynamite pit —Mrs. Patrick Campbell⟩

smith·ery \'smithərē, -ri\ *n* -ES [1*smith* + *-ery*] **1 :** the work, art, or trade of a smith **:** SMITHCRAFT **2 :** SMITHY 1

smith·field \'smith,fēld\ *adj, usu cap* [fr. *Smithfield*, town in the Union of So. Africa] **:** of or belonging to a southern African culture in the Würm glacial period characterized by hunting, rock painting, ground stone tools, and in the later stages by the introduction of pottery of the Bantu type

smithfield bargain *also* **smithfield match** *n, usu cap S* [fr. *Smithfield*, area in London, England where fairs were formerly held] **:** a marriage of convenience in which the size of the marriage settlement is the determining factor

smithfield ham *n, usu cap S* [fr. *Smithfield*, town in southeastern Va.] **:** a smoked ham esp. from a peanut-fed hog that is drier than a Virginia ham

smith·ian \'smithēən\ *adj, usu cap* [Adam *Smith* †1790 Scotch economist + E *-ian*] **:** of, relating to, or having the characteristics of Adam Smith or of his economic theories

smithing coal *n* **:** a grade of caking coal low in sulfur and ash used esp. by blacksmiths

smith·ite \'smi,thīt\ *n* -s [G. F. Herbert *Smith* †1953 Eng. mineralogist + E *-ite*] **:** a mineral $AgAsS_2$ consisting of a silver arsenic sulfide occurring in small red monoclinic crystals (hardness 1.5–2, sp. gr. 4.9)

smith-pe·ter·son nail \'smith'pēd·ə(r)sən-\ *n, usu cap S&P* [after Marius *Smith-Peterson* †1953 American orthopedic surgeon who designed it] **:** a flanged metal nail used to fix the femoral head in fractures of the femoral neck

smith's longspur \'smiths-\ *n, usu cap S* [after Gideon B. *Smith*, 19th cent. Am. physician] **:** a longspur (*Calcarius pictus*) of northwestern No. America

smith·son·ite \ˈsmithsəˌnīt\ *n* -s [James *Smithson* †1829 Brit. chemist and mineralogist + E *-ite*] **1 :** a usu. white or nearly white native zinc carbonate $ZnCO_3$ commonly reniform, botryoidal, stalactitic, or granular and distinguished from hemimorphite by its effervescence with acids (hardness 5, sp. gr. 4.30–4.45) **2 :** HEMIMORPHITE 1

smithwork \ˈ=,=\ *n* **:** SMITHCRAFT

¹smithy \ˈsmithē, |i, *esp Brit* -ith|\ *n* -ES [ME, fr. ON *smithja;* akin to OE *smiththe* smithy, OHG *smitta* smithy, *smid* smith — more at SMITH] **1 :** the workshop of a smith; *esp* **:** BLACKSMITH SHOP — called also *smithery, stithy* **2 :** BLACKSMITH ⟨working with the village ~ —Judith Crist⟩

²smithy \"\ *vt* -ED/-ING/-ES **:** SMITH

smithy coal *n, Brit* **:** SMITHING COAL

smiting *pres part of* SMITE

smit·ing line \ˈsmīd·iŋ-\ *n* **:** a line by which a sail stoppered with yarns is broken out from the deck

smitten *past part of* SMITE

smit·ting \ˈsmitiŋ\ *adj* [fr. pres. part. of *smit*] *dial Brit* **:** INFECTIOUS

smit·tle \ˈsmitᵊl\ *vt* [freq. of *²smit*] **1** *dial Brit* **:** to infect esp. with a contagious disease **2** *dial Brit* **:** GRASP, SEIZE

smkd *abbr* smoked

smkls *abbr* smokeless

sml *abbr* small

smls *abbr* seamless

SMO *abbr* **1** senior medical officer **2** squadron medical officer

smoak \ˈsmōk\ *archaic var of* SMOKE

¹smock \ˈsmäk\ *n* -s *often attrib* [ME *smok,* fr. OE *smoc;* akin to OHG *smocco* adornment, ON *smokkr* woman's stomacher, OE *smūgan* to creep, MHG *smiegen* to press in tightly, ON *smjūga* to creep through, and prob. to ON *mjūkr* soft, gentle — more at MUCUS] **1 a** *archaic* **:** a woman's undergarment; *esp* **:** CHEMISE **b :** SMOCK FROCK **c :** a lightweight loose garment made usu. with smocking or gathering at the shoulders, short or long sleeves, and a front opening and worn esp. for protection of clothing while working **2** *obs* **:** WOMAN

²smock \"\ *vb* -ED/-ING/-S *vt* **1 :** to provide with or clothe in a smock **2 :** to embroider or shirr with smocking ~ *vi* **:** to do smocking

smock 1c

smock–face \ˈ=,=\ *n, archaic* **:** a pale effeminate face; *also* **:** a person having such a face

smock frock *n* **:** a loose shirtlike outer garment of coarse linen or cotton worn by workmen esp. in Europe

smocking *n* -s [fr. gerund of *²smock*] **:** a decorative embroidery or shirring designed esp. to control fullness in garments and made by gathering cloth in regularly spaced round tucks held in place with fancy stitching

smock mill *or* **smock windmill** *n* [so called fr. the fancied resemblance of its shape to a person dressed in a smock] **:** a windmill whose cap alone turns round to meet the wind

smog \ˈsmäg *also* ˈsmȯg\ *n* -s [blend of *¹smoke* and *fog*] **1 :** a fog made heavier and darker by smoke and chemical fumes ⟨one of the worst ~s in London's history was . . . blamed for the deaths of 4000 people —Leonard Parkin⟩ **2 :** something resembling atmospheric smog **:** HAZE 2 ⟨behind the ~ of sophistry . . . lie two real issues —Robert Wuliger⟩

smog·gy \-gē\ *adj* -ER/-EST **:** characterized by or abounding in smog

smok·able *or* **smoke·able** \ˈsmōkəbəl\ *adj* **:** fit for smoking

¹smoke \ˈsmōk\ *n* -s *often attrib* [ME, fr. OE *smoca;* akin to OE *smēocan* to emit smoke, MD *smieken* to emit smoke, MHG *smouch* smoke, Gk *smychein* to smolder, Lith *smáugti* to suffocate, choke] **1 a** (1) **:** the gaseous products of burning carbonaceous materials made visible by the presence of small particles of carbon (2) **:** a similar incompletely burned volatilized product resulting from incomplete combustion and finally settling as soot — compare FLAME 1 **b :** a suspension of solid or liquid particles in a gas **:** FUME 1. **2 a** (1) **:** a mass or column of smoke ⟨the fifty ~s . . . curling from the valley —J.F.Cooper⟩ (2) **:** a smudge used esp. to drive away insects **b** *archaic* **:** FIRESIDE, HEARTH **3 a :** fume or vapor often resulting from the action of heat on moisture ⟨steeds . . . whose breaths dimmed the sun with ~ —John Lyly⟩ **b smokes** *pl* **:** dense white mists occurring in the dry season along the Guinea coast of Africa **4 :** visible or tangible evidence (as of secret activity) ⟨such a hell of a lot of ~ . . . that there must be enough flame to justify refusing a divorce —F.M.Ford⟩ **5 :** something of little substance, permanence, or value ⟨these aspirations and visions were only ~ —Van Wyck Brooks⟩ **6 :** something tending to cloud or obscure ⟨most of the ~ generated by the alleged conflict between poetry and science —C.I.Glicksberg⟩ **7 a** (1) **:** something to smoke **:** TOBACCO — often used in pl. ⟨what they spend each year on ~s is . . . less than what they spend on liquor —Dwight Macdonald⟩ (2) **:** CIGARETTE ⟨a reduction to seven cents a pack on ~s —G.E.Cruikshank⟩ **b** [*²smoke*] **:** an act or spell of smoking tobacco ⟨let's light our pipes and take a short ~ —A.B.Longstreet⟩ **8 a :** a pale blue that is redder and paler than average powder blue or Sistine and redder and duller than average cadet gray **b :** any of the colors of smoke viewed against various usual backgrounds (as smoke blue, smoke brown, smoke gray, smoke yellow) **c :** a neutral slightly reddish dark gray that is darker than grebe or lead **9 a :** cheap liquor **b :** any of various drinks used as a substitute for liquor; *specif* **:** a drink consisting of wood alcohol and water **10 :** SPEED ⟨a pitcher with plenty of ~ on his fast ball⟩ **11 :** NEGRO — often taken to be offensive **12 :** SMOKE CAT

²smoke \"\ *vb* -ED/-ING/-S [ME *smoken,* fr. OE *smocian,* fr. *smoca,* n.] *vi* **1 a** (1) **:** to emit or exhale smoke ⟨hard by a cottage chimney ~s —John Milton⟩ (2) **:** to emit smoke as the result of faulty burning or inadequate draft ⟨the wick . . . flared and *smoked* —D.R.Murphy⟩ **b :** to give off something resembling smoke ⟨the marsh ~s in the sun⟩; *esp* **:** STEAM ⟨the horse's flanks *smoked*⟩ **2** *archaic* **:** to undergo severe pain or punishment **:** SUFFER ⟨some of you shall ~ for it in Rome —Shak.⟩ **3 a :** to spread like smoke ⟨a yellow mist far *smoking* o'er the interminable plain —James Thomson †1748⟩ **b :** to rise like or as if like smoke ⟨the anger of the Lord and his jealousy would ~ against that man —Deut 29: 20 (RSV)⟩ **4 a :** to inhale and exhale the fumes of tobacco or something resembling tobacco from a pipe, cigar, or cigarette ⟨has been *smoking* for six years⟩ **b :** to serve in a specified way for smoking ⟨the larger sizes *smoked* the best —Ben Riker⟩ **5** *archaic* **:** to have a notion or understanding of something **:** COMPREHEND **6 :** to go at a rapid rate **:** SPEED ⟨*smoked* along over the levels as fast as a pack in full cry —Rudyard Kipling⟩ **7** *Austral* **:** to run away **:** ABSCOND **8** *of a clay pigeon* **:** to break into small pieces **:** SHATTER ~ *vt* **1 :** to subject to the action of smoke: as **a :** FUMIGATE ⟨a good day for *smoking* ship —R.H.Dana⟩ **b :** to drive away (as mosquitoes) by smoke **c :** to blacken or discolor with smoke ⟨looked at the sun through *smoked* glasses —Ellen Glasgow⟩ **d :** to cure (as meat) by exposure to smoke ⟨*smoked* ham⟩ ⟨*smoked* salmon⟩ **e :** to stupefy (as bees) by smoke **2** *archaic* **:** to have an inkling or suspicion of **:** SUSPECT ⟨it's a capital notion . . . if he doesn't ~ the trick —Samuel Lover⟩ **3 a :** to inhale and exhale the smoke of **:** use in smoking ⟨*smoked* one cigarette after another⟩ ⟨*smoked* a pipe for many years⟩ **b :** to bring to a specified state by smoking ⟨if a man ~ himself to death —James I⟩ **4** *archaic* **:** to make fun of **:** RIDICULE ⟨*smoked* her and baited her and . . . drove her away —John Keats⟩ **5** *archaic* **:** to take notice of **:** OBSERVE ⟨~ his eyes, how they glare —John Wilson †1854⟩ **6 :** to cover with smoke so as to prevent enemy observation ⟨the wind and terrain were adaptable to *smoking* another mountainside on our right forward flank —G.E.Lynch⟩ **7 :** to cause (a clay pigeon) to break into small pieces

smokeable *var of* SMOKABLE

smoke ball *n* **1 :** a ball or case containing a composition that when ignited emits thick smoke **2 :** PUFFBALL **3 :** a pitch (as in baseball) having great speed

smoke beetle *n* **:** any of several buprestid beetles (genus *Melanophila*) that are attracted to smoke

smoke black *n* **:** a carbon black used as a pigment

smoke blue *n* **:** a dark bluish gray that is redder and darker than teal gray

smoke bomb *n* **:** a chemical bomb containing a smoke-producing substance; *esp* **:** any of various smoke flares that trail a streamer of smoke and are dropped from airplanes to mark targets for air attack, to screen targets from air attack, or to show wind direction over water

smokebox \ˈ=,=\ *n* **:** a chamber in a steam boiler between the flues or flue tubes and the chimney or smokestack

smoke brown *n* **:** a nearly neutral very slightly olive dark gray — called also *asphalt, Vienna smoke*

smoke bush *n* **:** SMOKE TREE

smoke cat *n* **:** a domestic long-haired cat with a light silvery undercoat, ruff, and ear tufts and black topcoat and points; *also* **:** a similarly marked domestic short-haired cat

smoke chamber *n* **:** a part of a fireplace extending from the top of the throat to the bottom of the flue

smokechaser \ˈ=,==\ *n* **:** a forest fire fighter; *esp* **:** one with light equipment that enables him to get to fires quickly — called also *fire chaser*

smoked *past of* SMOKE

smoke door *n* **:** a door in the roof above the gridiron of a theater opened in case of fire to draw the flames up and so prevent their spread to the auditorium

smoked pearl *n* **:** a purplish gray that is bluer than crane or granite and bluer and darker than cinder gray or zinc — called also *mitraille*

smoke–dry \ˈ=,=\ *vt* **:** to dry or cure by means of smoke ~ *vi* **:** to become dried by means of smoke

smoked sheet *n* **:** sheet rubber dried by smoking

smoke eater *n* **1 :** FIRE FIGHTER **2 :** a device used with a smokejack in an enginehouse to draw smoke from a locomotive into a tank or pit for separating the solids in the smoke from the gas

smoke ejector *n* **:** a piece of fire apparatus used for ejecting smoke from a burning building by means of a blower

smoke explosion *n* **:** BACK DRAFT

smokefarthing \ˈ=,==\ *n* [ME *smoke ffardyng,* fr. *¹smoke* + *ffardyng, ferthing* farthing] **:** HEARTH MONEY — usu. used in pl.

smoke feeler *n* **:** EXHAUST-GAS ANALYZER

smoke–filled room \ˈ=,=-\ *n* **:** a hotel room in which a small group of politicians carry on negotiations ⟨meet in a *smoke-filled room* to decide on . . . men and measures —D.D. McKean⟩

smoke fly *n* **:** any of several flies of a genus (*Microsania*) of the family Platypezidae that are attracted to smoke

smoke generator *n* **:** a mechanical device employing a special petroleum product that produces a smokelike screen to protect large areas from enemy observation

smoke gray *n* **:** a pale yellow green that is greener and slightly duller than oyster gray and yellower and less strong than average Nile

smoke helmet *n* **:** a gas mask used in fighting fire; *specif* **:** a gas mask connected by air hose to a pump or air line

smoke hole *n* [ME, fr. *¹smoke* + *hole*] **:** a vent (as in a flue or roof) for smoke

smokehouse \ˈ=,=\ *n* **1 :** a building where meat or fish is cured by means of dense smoke **2 :** a room where hides are softened in the manufacture of leather by means of smoke from a smoldering fire of spent tan

smokejack \ˈ=,=\ *n* **1 :** a contrivance for turning a spit by a fly or wheel moved by the rising gases in a chimney **2 :** a flue built into the roof of an enginehouse to carry away the smoke and gases from the locomotive

smoke jumper *n* **:** a forest fire fighter who parachutes to locations otherwise difficult to reach

smoke·less \ˈsmōkləs\ *adj* **1 :** producing little or no smoke ⟨~ fuel⟩ ⟨~ combustion⟩ **2 :** having little or no smoke ⟨the ~ air⟩ ⟨a ~ city⟩ — **smoke·less·ly** *adv* — **smoke·less·ness** *n* -ES

smokeless powder *n* **:** any of a class of propellants that produce less smoke on explosion than black powder, that typically consist of gelatinized cellulose nitrates either alone or mixed with nitroglycerin or other ingredients, and that are produced in various forms (as solid and perforated cylindrical grains for military use or as flakes and pellets for sporting use) but not in powder form — compare GUNPOWDER

smokelike \ˈ=,=\ *adj* **:** resembling smoke

smoke mask *n* **:** SMOKE HELMET

smoke–oh \ˈ=,=\ *n* -s [*¹smoke* + *oh,* interj.; fr. the practice of smoking during rest periods] *chiefly Austral* **:** a short rest period (as in the midmorning or midafternoon) for workers engaged esp. in manual labor **:** BREAK

smoke out *vt* **1 :** to drive out of a place of hiding or concealment by or as if by the use of smoke ⟨*smoked out* small game by ramming smoldering grass into a hole —*N.Y. Herald Tribune Bk. Rev.*⟩ ⟨came and *smoked* him *out* with tommy guns —Jean Stafford⟩ **2 :** to bring into the open **:** bring to public view or knowledge ⟨would *smoke out* the real intentions of the Syrian government —A.T.Steele⟩

smoke pipe *n* **:** a usu. thin metal pipe connecting a possible source of smoke to a chimney or smokestack

smoke plant *n* **:** SMOKE TREE

smoke pocket *n* **:** a steel angle enclosing the edge of the asbestos curtain in a theater for keeping smoke and flames from getting into the theater in case of fire

smoke pot *n* **:** a can containing a mixture that produces a smoke or smokelike screen

smoke proof *n* [*¹smoke* + *proof,* n.] **:** a test impression of a typefounder's punch obtained by blackening it in a flame and stamping it on paper

smokeproof \ˈ=;=\ *adj* [*¹smoke* + *proof,* adj.] **:** impermeable to smoke; *specif* **:** designed to restrict the spread of smoke through a building — used esp. of a door or partition

smok·er \ˈsmōkə(r)\ *n* -s **1 :** one that smokes: as **a :** a person who dries or preserves by smoke **b :** a person who smokes tobacco **c :** a ship or airplane discharging a smoke screen **d :** an apparatus for producing and directing a stream of smoke at bees so as to quiet them **e** *slang* (1) **:** STEAM LOCOMOTIVE (2) **:** HOTBOX **2 :** a railroad car or compartment in which smoking is allowed **3 :** an informal social gathering for men **4 :** SMOKING STAND

smoke room *n, chiefly Brit* **:** SMOKING ROOM

smoker's heart *n* **:** TOBACCO HEART

smok·ery \ˈsmōkərē\ *n* -ES **:** a place where smoking is done

smokes *pl of* SMOKE, *pres 3d sing of* SMOKE

smoke sail *n* **:** a small sail hoisted close to the galley stovepipe in a head wind for carrying the smoke from the deck

smoke screen *n* **1 :** a screen or cloud of smoke: as **a :** a screen of smoke designed to hinder enemy observation of a military force, area, or activity **b :** a heavy smoke supplied by smudge pots and designed to protect orchards and other plantings from injury by frost **2 :** something designed to obscure, confuse, or mislead ⟨seek immunity from criticism behind a rhetorical *smoke screen* about academic freedom —Sidney Hook⟩

smoke shelf *n* **:** a shelf or baffle in a smoke flue designed to prevent downdraft

smoke shell *n* **:** a projectile that releases smoke on impact

smokestack \ˈ=,=\ *n* **:** a chimney or funnel through which smoke and gases of combustion are discharged from a locomotive, ship, or building

smokestand \ˈ=,=\ *n* **:** SMOKING STAND

smoke talk *n* **:** a talk given at a smoker

smoketight \ˈ=;=\ *adj* **:** impervious to smoke

smoke train *n* **:** a trail of dust and gas left by an exploding meteorite in its passage through the atmosphere

smoke tree *n* **1 :** either of two small shrubby plants of the genus *Cotinus* having large panicles of flowers on plumose pedicels that resemble a cloud of smoke: **a :** an Old World shrub (*C. coggygria*) — called also *Venetian sumac* **b :** an American shrub or shrubby tree (*C. obovatus*) — called also *chittamwood* **2 :** a spiny grayish green leguminous shrub (*Dalea spinosa*) of desert areas of the southwestern U.S. and Mexico that has very sparse foliage and terminal spikes of bluish violet flowers and that is a locally important honey plant yielding a light-colored honey of excellent flavor

smoke tunnel *n* **:** an experimental wind tunnel in which air movements are observed by means of smoke filaments released at suitable points

smoke up *vt* **:** to fill with smoke

smoke washer *n* **:** a device in which smoke is forced upward against a downward spray of water in order to remove the solid particles in the smoke

smoke yellow *n* **:** BEACH 3

smok·i·ly \ˈsmōkəlē, -lī\ *adv* **:** in a smoky manner

smok·i·ness \-kēnəs, -kin-\ *n* -ES **:** the quality or state of being smoky

smoking *adv* [fr. pres. part. of *²smoke*] **:** to a smoking degree ⟨~ hot food⟩

smoking bean *n* [so called fr. the occasional use of the pods for smoking by boys] **1 :** CATALPA **2 :** the long pod of the catalpa

smoking car *n* **:** SMOKER 2

smoking concert *n, Brit* **:** FREE AND EASY 1a

smoking jacket *n* [so called fr. its orig. having been worn for after-dinner smoking] **:** a man's soft dressy jacket for wear at home — compare HOUSECOAT

smoking lamp *n* **:** a lamp on a ship kept lighted during the hours when smoking is allowed

smoking opium *n* **:** PREPARED OPIUM

smoking room *n* **:** a room (as in a hotel or club) set apart for smokers

smoking–room \ˈ==,=\ *adj* [*smoking room*] **:** marked by indecency or obscenity **:** DIRTY, SMUTTY ⟨it is possible even in the *smoking-room* story to perceive some of the characteristics common to all storytelling —W.H.Auden⟩

smoking stand *n* **:** a wood or metal stand for holding an ashtray

smoking tobacco *n* **:** tobacco suitable for the manufacture of cigarettes and pipe tobacco — compare BURLEY, MARYLAND

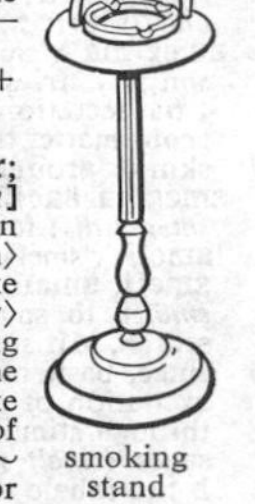

smoking stand

smok·ish \ˈsmōkish\ *adj* [ME, fr. *¹smoke* + *-ish*] **:** somewhat smoky

smo·ko \ˈsmō(,)kō\ *var of* SMOKE-OH

smoky *also* **smokey** \ˈsmōkē, -ki\ *adj* **smokier; smokiest** [ME *smoky,* fr. *¹smoke* + *-y*] **1 a :** emitting smoke esp. in large quantities or in an offensive manner ⟨~ fireplaces⟩ ⟨a ~ torch⟩ **b :** emitting something that resembles smoke ⟨part the ~ flesh, enjoy the feast —Joel Barlow⟩ **2 a :** having the characteristics of or resembling smoke ⟨a ~ mist⟩: as (1) *obs* **:** having the obscuring or unsubstantial quality of smoke (2) **:** having a flavor or odor suggestive of smoke **:** tasting or smelling like smoke ⟨the ~ taste of Scotch whisky⟩ **b :** having a foggy or misty quality **:** HAZY ⟨the ~ outline of the farther shore —Valentine Williams⟩ ⟨the Great *Smoky* Mountains⟩ **3 a :** filled with or marked by the presence of smoke ⟨a ~ kitchen⟩ ⟨autumn is the *smokiest* season —Berton Roueché⟩ **b :** made dark or black by smoke ⟨~ rafters⟩ **4 :** of the color smoke **5 :** having the habit of smoking ⟨*smokey* young men . . . watching football matches —*London Daily News*⟩ **6** *archaic* **:** quick to detect or suspect **7** *of a voice* **:** marked by a low guttural quality suggestive of a torch singer

smoky fungus *n* **:** a parasitic fungus producing dark mycelium on the surface of fruit or twigs of its host

smoky quartz *n* **:** CAIRNGORM

smoky topaz *n* **:** a smoky quartz used for jewelry

¹smol·der *or* **smoul·der** \ˈsmōldə(r)\ *n* -s [ME *smolder;* akin to MD *smölen* to smolder, scorch — more at SMELL] **1 :** SMOKE, SMOTHER, SMUDGE **2 :** a smoldering fire — compare BLAZE **3 :** a disease of narcissus bulbs caused by a fungus (*Botrytis narcissicola*)

²smolder *or* **smoulder** \"\ *vb* **smoldered** *or* **smouldered; smoldered** *or* **smouldered; smoldering** *or* **smouldering** \-d(ə)riŋ\ **smolders** *or* **smoulders** [ME *smolderen,* fr. *smolder,* n.] *vt* **1** *obs* **:** SMOTHER, SUPPRESS, SUFFOCATE **2 :** to blacken with fire or ashes ~ *vi* **1 :** to burn and smoke without flame ⟨the fuse ~*ed* and sputtered⟩ **:** waste away by slow combustion ⟨fire was ~*ing* in the grate⟩ — often used with *out* ⟨it took hours for the ruins to ~ out⟩ **2 :** to exist in a state of suppressed activity **:** be or continue liable to violent outbreak at any moment ⟨the feud ~*ed* for months with no actual shooting⟩ **3 :** to show scarcely suppressed or contained anger, hate, jealousy ⟨her tone was . . . conversational, although . . . her eyes were ~*ing* —James Hensel⟩

smol·der·ing·ly *adv* **:** in a smoldering manner

smo·lensk \smōˈlen(t)sk\ *adj, usu cap* [fr. *Smolensk,* city in western U.S.S.R.] **:** of or from the city of Smolensk, U.S.S.R. **:** of the kind or style prevalent in Smolensk

¹smolt \ˈsmōlt\ *adj* [ME, affable, fr. OE, fair (of the weather); akin to MD *smout, smolt* fair (of the weather), calm, OSw *smultna* to become calm, OHG *smelzan* to melt — more at SMELT] *dial chiefly Eng* **:** SMOOTH, CALM

²smolt \"\ *n* -s [ME (Sc); prob. akin to OE *¹smelt* — more at SMELT] **:** a salmon or sea trout between the parr and grilse stages when it is about two years old and silvery and first descends to the sea

¹smooch \ˈsmüch\ *vt* -ED/-ING/-ES [prob. alter. of *²smutch*] **:** SMUDGE, SMEAR, SOIL ⟨don't want you ~*ing* up these cards —W.L.Gresham⟩

²smooch \"\ *n* -ES **:** SMUDGE, SMEAR ⟨~ of lipstick on his collar⟩

³smooch \"\ *vi* -ED/-ING/-ES [alter. of *²smouch*] **:** KISS, PET ⟨~*ing* in dark corners⟩

⁴smooch \"\ *n* -ES **:** KISS ⟨comes over and plants a big ~ on me —Richard Bissell⟩

smoochy \-chē\ *adj* **:** SMUDGY

smoodge *or* **smooge** \ˈsmüj\ *vi* [perh. alter. of *²smouch*] *chiefly Austral* **1 :** to curry favor in a fawning manner **2 :** ³SMOOCH

¹smoor \ˈsmō(ə)r\ *var of* SMORE

²smoor \ˈsmō(ə)r\ *chiefly Scot var of* SMUR

smoor·ich \ˈsmōrə̇k\ *n* [prob. imit.] *Scot* **:** a stolen kiss

smoot \ˈsmüt\ *n* -s [of Scand origin; akin to ON *smātta* narrow lane; perh. akin to OE *smūgan* to creep — more at SMOCK] *dial Eng* **:** a narrow passageway; *esp* **:** one through which small animals may creep

¹smooth \ˈsmüth\ *adj* -ER/-EST [ME *smothe,* fr. OE *smōth;* akin to OE *smēthe* smooth, OS *smōthi*] **1 a :** having a continuously even surface **:** being without roughness, points, bumps, or ridges esp. to the touch ⟨~ tabletop⟩ ⟨~ fabric⟩ ⟨~ skin⟩ ⟨~ lawn⟩ ⟨~ road⟩ **b :** being without bristles or hair ⟨my brother is a hairy man and I am a ~ man —Gen 27:11 (AV)⟩ **c :** not rough or scabrous **:** not pubescent **:** GLABROUS ⟨a ~ leaf⟩ **d** (1) **:** causing no resistance to a body sliding along its surface **:** FRICTIONLESS (2) *of a reflecting surface* **:** having surface irregularities small compared with the wave length of the reflected radiation **e :** less rough or harsh than is characteristic of the class ⟨~ file⟩; *sometimes* **:** having its points or ridges leveled by wear ⟨~ tire⟩ **2 :** free from all that would obstruct or impede progress **:** easily or comfortably traveled **:** presenting no obstacles or difficulties ⟨broad ~ highways⟩ ⟨trying to make his path ~*er* for him⟩ **3 a :** even and uninterrupted in flow or flight **:** continuously flowing or gliding **:** moving or proceeding without breaks, abrupt changes or transitions **:** not jerky, jolting, or jarring ⟨~ stream⟩ ⟨~ flow of words⟩ ⟨car came to a ~ stop⟩ **b :** capable of easy dexterity and effortlessly controlled movement ⟨~ dancer⟩ **c :** avoiding or minimizing what is harsh or unpleasant or objectionable **:** plausibly flattering **:** INGRATIATING ⟨deceived by the ~ talk of the salesman⟩ ⟨~ villain⟩ ⟨~ handling of an embarrassing situation⟩ ⟨~ explanations of suspicious conduct⟩ **4 a :** calm and unruffled in words, manner or behavior **:** SERENE, EQUABLE ⟨~ disposition⟩ **b :** AMIABLE, COURTEOUS, FRIENDLY **5 :** accompanied by calm weather **:** free from discomfort or difficulty ⟨~ channel crossing⟩ ⟨~ sailing from here on⟩ **6 a :** performed so that each tone within the musical phrase glides or flows into the next **:** LEGATO **b :** moving by small intervals — used of the progression of voice parts in harmonized music **7** *Greek grammar* **a** *of a vowel* **:** sounded without the aspirate ⟨~ vowel⟩ **b** *of a stop consonant* **:** being voiceless, unaspirated, and lenis **8 a :** agreeable or soothing to one's ear, palate, feelings **:** BLAND, MILD ⟨~ tone of voice⟩ ⟨~ syrup⟩ ⟨~ wine⟩ **b :** free from lumps **:** having perfect blending of the elements ⟨~ batter⟩ ⟨~ salad dressing⟩ **c :** having the pungency (as of alcohol) moderated by blending of other ingredients ⟨a ~ cocktail⟩ **9 :** relatively good — used esp. of a poker hand in lowball; compare ROUGH **10 :** forming smooth colonies usu. made up of organisms that form no chains or filaments, show characteristic internal changes, and tend to marked increase in capsule formation and virulence — used of dissociated strains of bacteria; compare MUCOID **syn** see EASY, LEVEL, SUAVE

²smooth \"\ *vb* -ED/-ING/-S [ME *smothen,* fr. *smothe,* adj., smooth] *vt* **1 :** to make smooth, level, or even on the surface **:** remove the surface inequalities and irregularities of ⟨~ soil in a flower bed⟩ ⟨~ the edge of a board⟩ ⟨~ cloth with an iron⟩ ⟨~ a rumpled bedsheet⟩ **2 a :** to free from what is harsh, crude, offending, or disagreeable **:** REFINE, POLISH ⟨~ verses⟩ ⟨sent to a school to ~ and polish his manners⟩ **b :** to make calm **:** SOOTHE **3 :** to minimize (as a fault, a difference) in order to allay anger or ill-will **:** PALLIATE — often used with *over* ⟨~*ing* things over is practically a profession to mothers of families —Margaret Deland⟩ **4 :** to free from obstruction or difficulty **:** make easy ⟨~*ed* his way with bribes⟩ **5 a :** to remove (as wrinkles, creases) from a surface ⟨~*ed* the lines of worry away with her cool fingertips⟩ **b :** to press or rub into a flat form ⟨nervously crumpling and ~*ing* out her handkerchief⟩ **c :** to remove expression from (one's face) **:** COMPOSE **6 :** cause to lie evenly and in order **:** PREEN ⟨took off her hat and ~*ed* down her hair⟩ ⟨hen ~*ing* her ruffled feathers⟩ **7 :** to change a broken line made up of sections of straight lines into (a curve); *specif* **:** to free (a graph) from irregularities by ignoring random deviations **8 :** MONOPHTHONGIZE — used esp. of the change of a vowel before a back consonant in the Anglian dialects of Old English ⟨Anglian ~*ing* of *ēa* to *ē*⟩ ~ *vi* **1** *obs* **:** BLANDISH, FLATTER **2 :** to become smooth ⟨the wind dropped and the waves ~*ed* down⟩

³smooth \"\ *adv* [ME *smothe,* fr. *smothe,* adj., smooth] **:** SMOOTHLY ⟨~ runs the water where the brook is deep —Shak.⟩

⁴smooth \"\ *n* -S [ME *smothe,* fr. *smothe,* adj., smooth] **1 a :** a smooth stretch (as of land); *specif* **:** MEADOW **b :** an intermittent space of smooth water **2 :** the smooth part of anything **:** something that is smooth ⟨learn to take the rough with the ~⟩ **3** [²*smooth*] **:** act of smoothing or state of being smooth **:** a stroke which smooths ⟨give a ~ to his hair⟩ **4** [²*smooth*] **:** a smoothing implement **5 :** the side of a tennis racket on which the binding strings form a continuous line ⟨calling rough or ~ to decide court and service⟩

smooth alder *n* **:** a common alder (*Alnus rugosa*) of the eastern U.S. with smooth bark and leaves green on both sides — called also *hazel alder*

smooth azalea *n* **:** TREE AZALEA

smoothbark \ˈ=,=\ *n* **:** any of several eucalypts having the bark smooth except at or near the base of the trunk — compare STRINGYBARK

smooth beardtongue *n* **:** a commonly cultivated perennial herb (*Pentstemon laevigatus*) with showy slightly irregular tubular purple flowers

smooth-billed ani \ˈ=,=-\ *n* **:** a common ani (*Crotophaga ani*)

¹smoothbore \ˈ=,=\ *adj* [¹*smooth* + *bore,* n.] *of a firearm* **:** having a bore with a smooth surface — compare ⁴RIFLE

²smoothbore \"\ *n* **:** a smoothbore firearm

smooth breathing *n* [trans. of LL *spiritus lenis*] **1 :** a mark ʼ placed over some initial vowels in Greek to show that they are not aspirated (as in ἄγειν pronounced \ˈägān\) **2 :** the absence of aspiration as indicated by the mark ʼ — called also *spiritus lenis;* compare BREATHING 2, ROUGH BREATHING

smooth brome *or* **smooth bromegrass** *n* **:** AWNLESS BROMEGRASS

smooth buckeye *n* **:** a common buckeye (*Aesculus glabra*)

smooth-chinned \ˈ=ˈ=\ *adj* **:** BEARDLESS

smooth crabgrass *n* **:** a weedy European grass (*Digitaria ischaemum*) naturalized in No. America often becoming a troublesome pest

smooth curve *n* **:** a curve with a continuously turning tangent

smooth dogfish *also* **smooth dog** *n* **:** any of various dogfishes that lack spines in front of the dorsal fins — see SMOOTH HOUND; compare SPINY DOGFISH

smoothed *past of* SMOOTH

smoothen \ˈsmüthən\ *vb* **smoothened; smoothened; smoothening** \-th(ə)niŋ\ **smoothens** *vt* **:** to make smooth ~ *vi* **:** to become smooth

¹smoother *comparative of* SMOOTH

²smooth·er \ˈsmüthə(r)\ *n* -S **1 :** one that smooths ⟨a ~ of the way for those who came after him⟩ **2 :** one whose work is to make something smooth: as **a :** one who smooths sheet metal on a hammering machine **b :** one that bevels the edges of optical glass with an abrasive wheel **c :** one that removes blemishes from glassware by means of a gas flame **d :** one that smooths finished fountain pen points with emery paper **3 :** a device or tool for smoothing **:** SLEEKER, SLICKER

smoothest *superlative of* SMOOTH

smooth-faced \ˈ=ˈ=\ *adj* **1 :** BEARDLESS **2 :** having a smooth surface — usu. used of cloth **3 :** bland in countenance or expression

smooth green snake *n* **:** a green snake (*Ophiodrys vernalis*) occupying a somewhat more northerly range than the rough green snake and having dark bluish green or almost blue perfectly smooth scales above and smooth ivory ventral plates

smooth hound *n* **:** a smooth dogfish (*Mustelus mustelus*) common in southern European waters; *broadly* **:** SMOOTH DOGFISH

smoothie *var of* SMOOTHY

smoothing *pres part of* SMOOTH

smoothing box *n* **:** BOX IRON

smoothing iron *n* **1 :** FLATIRON **2 :** an iron slicker used in leather manufacture

smoothing mill *n* **:** a revolvable sandstone wheel used with a stream of water for cutting and beveling glass or stone

smoothing plane *or* **smooth plane** *n* **:** a short finely set plane used for smoothing and finishing

smooth·ish \ˈsmüthish\ *adj* **:** fairly smooth ⟨~ bark⟩

smooth joint *n* **:** TIGHT JOINT

smooth-leaved elm \ˈ=,=-\ *n* **:** a European elm (*Ulmus carpinifolia*) used as an ornamental and having lustrous smooth leaves

smooth log *n* **:** a clean copy of a ship's log

smooth lungwort *n* **:** any plant of the genus *Mertensia; esp* **:** VIRGINIA COWSLIP

smooth·ly *adv* [ME *smothely,* fr. *smothe,* adj., smooth + *-ly*] **:** in a smooth manner **:** without roughness, abruptness, or interruption ⟨~ flowing speech⟩ **:** without difficulties ⟨not be assumed that rents and dues were all paid ~ —*Times Lit. Supp.*⟩

smooth meadow grass *n* **:** KENTUCKY BLUEGRASS

smooth muscle *n* **:** muscle tissue made up of elongated spindle-shaped cells having central nucleus and lacking cross striations that in vertebrates typically form thin sheets associated with visceral structures (as stomach and bladder) performing functions (as peristalsis) not under direct voluntary control and that constitute in most invertebrates the chief or only type of muscle present

smooth·ness *n* -ES [ME *smothenesse,* fr. *smothe,* adj., smooth + *-nesse* -ness] **:** the quality, state, or fact of being smooth **:** absence of irregularities of surface, movement, or functioning

smooth newt *n* **:** a common European newt (*Triturus vulgaris*) — called also *spotted newt*

smooth-running \ˈ=ˈ==\ *adj* **:** that runs smoothly, frictionlessly, or efficiently ⟨*smooth-running* machinery⟩

smooths *pres 3d sing of* SMOOTH, *pl of* SMOOTH

smooth-shaven \ˈ=ˈ==\ *adj* **:** having the face shaven clean of beard and moustache

smooth shelf fungus *n* **:** a fungus of the family Thelephoraceae

smooth skate *n* **:** BARN-DOOR SKATE

smooth snake *n* **:** a harmless European colubrid snake (*Coronella austriaca*) with smooth glossy scales

smooth-spoken \ˈ=ˈ==\ *adj* **:** speaking smoothly **:** fluent and plausible in speech

smooth storax *n* **:** SPRING ORANGE

smooth sumac *n* **1 :** a common No. American sumac (*Rhus glabra*) with glaucous stems and leaves **2 :** DWARF SUMAC

smooth-taper drift *n* **:** DRIFT 4g

smooth tare *or* **smooth vetch** *n* **:** SLENDER VETCH

smooth tongue *n* **:** a genetic variation in cattle believed due to a recessive gene and marked by faulty differentiation of the lingual structures and anemia

smooth-tongued \ˈ=ˈ=\ *adj* **:** ingratiating in speech **:** PLAUSIBLE, FLATTERING

smooth winterberry *n* **:** an often arborescent shrub (*Ilex laevigata*) that lacks prickles on the leaves

smoothy *or* **smooth·ie** \ˈsmüthē, -thi\ *n, pl* **smoothies** [¹*smooth* + *-ie*] **1 a :** a person with polished manners **b :** one who behaves or performs with deftness, assurance, easy competence; *esp* **:** a man with an ingratiating manner toward women **c :** a smooth-tongued person **2** *slang* **:** SLICK 6

¹smore \ˈsmō(ə)r\ *vb* -ED/-ING/-S [ME *smoren,* fr. OE *smorian* to suffocate, strangle] *dial Brit* **:** SMOTHER, SUPPRESS

²smore \"\ *n* -S *chiefly Scot* **:** dense smoke or stifling air

smor·gas·bord *R* ˈsmȯrgəs,bȯrd, -bōrd; *-R* ˈsmȯgəs,bȯ(ə)d, -bōəd\ *n* -S [Sw *smörgåsbord,* fr. *smörgås* bread and butter, open sandwich (fr. *smör* butter + *gås* goose) + *bord* table; fr. a fancied resemblance of lumps of butter to geese; akin to ON *smör, smjör* fat, butter, to ON *gās* goose, and to ON *borth* table — more at SMEAR, GOOSE, BOARD] **1 :** a luncheon or supper buffet offering a variety of foods and dishes (as hors d'oeuvres, hot and cold meats, smoked and pickled fish, sausages, cheeses, salads, relishes) **2 :** MÉLANGE, HODGEPODGE

smør·re·brød \ˈsmœrə,brœth\ *also* **smor·re·brod** \ˈsmȯrə,brȯd\ *n* -S [Dan *smørrebrød,* fr. *smør* butter + *brød* bread; akin to ON *smör, smjör* fat, butter and to ON *brauth* bread — more at BREAD] **:** an hors d'oeuvre served in Danish style on a slice of buttered bread

smor·zan·do \smȯrtˈsän(,)dō\ *also* **smor·za·to** \-ä(,)dō\ *adj* [*smorzando* fr. It, verbal of *smorzare* to tone down, reduce, alter. (influenced by *s-,* fr. L *ex-*) of *ammorzare* to moderate, weaken, extinguish, fr. (assumed) VL *admortiare* to extinguish, fr. L *ad-* + (assumed) VL *-mortiare* (fr. L *mortuus,* past part. of *mori* to die); *smorzato* fr. It, past part. of *smorzare* — more at MURDER] **:** growing slower and softer **:** dying away — abbr. *smorz.;* used as a direction in music

smote *past of* SMITE

¹smoth·er \ˈsməthə(r)\ *n* -S [ME, alter. of *smorther,* fr. *smoren* to smother, fr. OE *smorian* to suffocate, strangle; akin to MD *smoren* to suffocate, stew, MLG *smōren,* and perh. to MD *smōlen* to smolder, scorch — more at SMELL] **1 a :** thick stifling smoke **:** a suffocating smudge or smoky condition **b :** a state of being stifled or suppressed **:** a smoldering or dampened fire **2 :** a dense cloud of fog, foam, spray, snow, or dust ⟨logs . . . rolled and tossed in a creamy ~ —Kenneth Roberts⟩ ⟨come with her tail up in a ~ of flying sand —Mary H. Vorse⟩ **3 :** a confused multitude or rush of things **:** WELTER ⟨~ of flowering creepers and climbers —Jean Devanny⟩ ⟨in a ~ of shoal-water waves that roll you down to leeward —S.E. Morison⟩

²smother \"\ *vb* **smothered; smothered; smothering** \-th(ə)riŋ\ **smothers** [ME *smotheren,* alter. of *smortheren,* fr. *smorther,* n.] *vt* **1 :** to overcome or kill with smoke or fumes **2 a :** to destroy the life of by depriving of air ⟨~ a child with a pillow⟩ ⟨~ seedlings in a tight cold frame⟩ **b :** to overcome or discomfit through or as if through lack of adequate air ⟨such close quarters tend to ~ one⟩ **c :** to suppress (a fire) by excluding oxygen **3 :** to cover or overlay oppressively: as **a :** to cause to smolder rather than blaze by or as if by covering ⟨~ a fire with too much coal⟩ **b :** to suppress or prevent expression, utterance, notice, or knowledge of as though by thick covering ⟨~ a secret⟩ ⟨he ~*ed* his rage⟩ ⟨the bill was ~*ed* in committee⟩ — often used with *up* **c :** to stop or prevent the growth, development, activity, or vitality of by or as if by thick cover or dense concentration around ⟨moralized, intellectualized, and nearly ~*ed* by Harvard —H.S.Canby⟩ ⟨little flowers ~*ed* by the weeds⟩ ⟨~ weeds in a field by planting sorghum⟩ **d :** to cover thickly, settle over, or blanket completely or restrictingly ⟨a record snow ~*ing* the valley⟩ **e :** to overcome quickly and completely **:** vanquish at once and render utterly helpless ⟨Belgian units ~*ed* by the invading Germans⟩ ⟨state ~*ed* Tech by a score of 52–0⟩ **f :** to hit (a golf ball) low along the ground through faulty execution of a lofting stroke **g :** to play (a bowled cricket ball) from above with a sharp downward defensive stroke **4 a :** to cook (meat, vegetables) in a covered pan or pot with very little liquid over low heat ⟨~*ed* round steak and onions⟩ ⟨~*ed* cabbage⟩ **b :** to serve (food) covered with other food cooked or uncooked ⟨gingerbread ~*ed* with whipped cream⟩ ⟨broiled steak ~*ed* with mushrooms⟩ ~ *vi* **1 :** to suffer or die from lack of air ⟨were ~*ing* in the sultry heat⟩ ⟨the child ~*ed* in the locked chest⟩ **2** *dial Brit* **:** SMOLDER **3 :** to undergo suppression, repression, extreme restraint, or concealment ⟨his anger ~*ed* and died⟩ **syn** see SUFFOCATE

³smother \"\ *n* -S **:** SMOTHERING

smoth·er·able \-ərəbəl\ *adj* **:** that may be smothered

smoth·er·a·tion \,sməthəˈrāshən\ *n* -S **:** a smothering or state of being smothered **:** SUFFOCATION ⟨death by ~ in a mine cave-in⟩

smother crop *n* **:** a crop (as buckwheat, soybeans) sown for the purpose of suppressing persistent weeds

smothered mate *n* **:** a checkmate by a knight in chess when movement of the king is completely obstructed by his own men

smoth·er·er \ˈsməth(ə)rə(r)\ *n* -S **:** one that smothers ⟨after three days of a hundred-and-two-degree ~ —Alma Stone⟩

smother fire *n* **:** a smoldering fire

smother fly *n, Brit* **:** APHID

¹smothering *adj* [ME, fr. pres. part. of *smotheren* to smother] **1 :** SUFFOCATING, STIFLING ⟨~ affection⟩ ⟨~ heat⟩ **2 :** SMOLDERING — **smoth·er·ing·ly** *adv*

²smothering *n* -S [fr. gerund of ²*smother*] **:** a disease of tree seedlings occurring esp. in crowded nurseries and characterized by the growth of the leathery fruiting body of a fungus (*Thelephora terrestris*) about the seedling stem

smother-kiln \ˈ==,=\ *n* **:** a kiln in which pottery is blackened by admitting smoke in firing

smoth·ery \ˈsməth(ə)rē\ *adj* **:** tending to smother **:** STIFLING ⟨~ attic⟩ ⟨climbed up the bank and walked under the trees; it was soft and warm and ~ in there —Richard Bissell⟩

¹smouch \ˈsmüch, ˈsmau̇ch\ *n* -ES [imit.] *dial* **:** a slobbery smacking kiss

²smouch \"\ *vb* -ED/-ING/-ES *chiefly dial* **:** to kiss esp. loudly or slobberingly

³smouch *n* -ES [alter. of *smous*] *obs* **:** JEW

⁴smouch \ˈsmau̇ch\ *vt* -ED/-ING/-ES [prob. fr. ³*smouch*] **:** to get by stealing or trickery **:** FILCH, PILFER

⁵smouch *var of* SMUTCH

smoulder *var of* SMOLDER

smous *or* **smouse** *n, pl* **smouses** [D *smous,* prob. fr. Yiddish *shmues* talk, chat — more at SCHMOOZE] **1** *obs* **:** JEW **2** *So Afr* **:** an itinerant peddler

SMP *abbr, often not cap* [L *sine mascula prole*] without male issue

smri·ti *also* **smrti** \ˈsmrid·ē\ *n* -S *often cap* [Skt *smṛti,* lit., what is remembered, fr. *smarati* he remembers — more at MEMORY] **:** the body of Hindu sacred writings containing traditional teachings (as on religious, domestic, and social practice) based on the Vedas and forming the class of shastras below the sruti

smry *abbr* summary

smstrs *abbr* seamstress

¹smudge \ˈsməj\ *vb* -ED/-ING/-S [ME *smogen*] *vt* **1 a :** to make a blurry splotch or streak (as of dirt) on **:** BEGRIME, SMUTCH, SOIL ⟨wiped his brow with his sooty hand, *smudging* it⟩ **b :** to soil as if by smudging ⟨the bright record for child welfare has been *smudged* occasionally by scandals —*Amer. Guide Series: Oregon*⟩ **2 a :** to rub, daub, or wipe in a smeary manner ⟨*smudging* out instead of erasing neatly his first hesitant strokes —*Time*⟩ **b :** to make indistinct **:** BLUR ⟨~ the clean line of the bridges with unnecessary parapets —*Times Lit. Supp.*⟩ ⟨careful distinctions are *smudged* and coarsened —*New Statesman & Nation*⟩ **3 a :** to smoke by means of a smudge (as in repelling mosquitoes); *specif* **:** to protect (an orchard, garden) against frost by means of a smudge — compare ORCHARD HEATING **b :** to cause (a fire) to smoke heavily ~ *vi* **1 a :** to make a smudge ⟨chalks that mark easily but do not ~⟩ ⟨they were *smudging* in the groves —Wright Morris⟩ **b :** to burn with little flame and much thick smoke **2 :** to become smudged ⟨charcoal drawings ~ easily⟩

²smudge \"\ *n* -S **1 a** (1) **:** a blurry spot or streak **:** SPLOTCH, SMEAR ⟨left a ~ at the erasure⟩ ⟨~*s* made by cheap carbon paper⟩ (2) **:** an immaterial stain ⟨cleanse him of every last ~ of impropriety —Richard Hanser⟩ **b :** a smudged condition **:** SOILAGE **c :** an indistinct mass **:** BLUR ⟨ahead lay a chocolate brown ~ of land, huddled in mist —Gerald Durrell⟩ **2 a :** thick or suffocating smoke **:** SMOTHER **b** *or* **smudge fire :** a smoldering mass placed on the windward side (as of a tent) to repel insects or in an orchard or garden to prevent frost **c :** an apparatus for making a smudge fire **3** *Brit* **:** PLUMBER'S SOIL **4 a :** ONION SMUDGE **b :** a disease of wheat, rye, and barley caused by fungi of the genera *Helminthosporium* and *Alternaria* and characterized by brownish or black discoloration of the grains **5 a :** a bid of 4 by a player in auction pitch who is not in the hole that if made wins the game forthwith **b :** the winning of all four points in auction pitch; *also* **:** the reward for this which may be a doubled score or the winning of the game **c :** the game of auction pitch when either of the foregoing rules is incorporated **6 :** a leukocyte that is degenerating

³smudge \"\ *vi* [origin unknown] *chiefly Scot* **:** to be quietly and slyly amused **:** laugh up one's sleeve

smudg·ed·ly \-jədlē\ *adv* [*smudged* (past part. of ¹*smudge*) + *-ly*] **:** in a smudged manner

smudge pot *n* **:** a container in which oil or other fuel is burned to produce a smudge (as in an orchard)

smudg·er \ˈsməjə(r)\ *n* -S **:** one that smudges; *specif* **:** a worker who smudges orchards or groves

smudg·i·ly \-jəlē\ *adv* **:** in a smudgy manner

smudg·i·ness \-jēnəs\ *n* -ES **:** the quality or state of being smudgy

smudgy \ˈsməjē, -ji\ *adj* -ER/-EST [²*smudge* + *-y*] **1** *dial Eng* **:** thick with smoke **:** SMOKY **2** *dial* **:** OPPRESSIVE, STIFLING — used esp. of weather **3 :** soiled by smudging **:** BEGRIMED, STAINED **4 :** lacking distinctness **:** BLURRED

¹smug \ˈsməg\ *adj* **smugger; smuggest** [prob. modif. of LG *smuck* neat, trim, fr. MLG, fr. *smucken* to dress, adorn; akin to MHG *smiegen* to press in tightly — more at SMOCK] **1 :** presenting a smooth, well-groomed appearance **:** NEAT, SLEEK ⟨at one end of the promenade the clean, ~ town drifted into desultory fields —*Strand Mag.*⟩ **2 :** giving an impression of scrupulous correctness and respectability ⟨you are looking ~, man; the honest innkeeper to the life —W.W.Jacobs⟩ **3 :** marked by or suggestive of belief in one's own superiority, virtue, and respectability usu. accompanied by contented resistance to change, provincial lack of vision, or deprecation of others ⟨a ~ glow of self-congratulation radiated from the editorial pages of some of the most respectable newspapers —Max Ascoli⟩ ⟨people relax with a sense of ~ well-being because a law has been enacted which will take care of everything —D.W. Maurer & V.H.Vogel⟩ **syn** see COMPLACENT

²smug \"\ *vt* **smugged; smugged; smugging; smugs :** to make clean or neat **:** SPRUCE, SMARTEN

³smug \"\ *n* -S **:** a smug person **:** PRIG

⁴smug \"\ *vt* **smugged; smugged; smugging; smugs** [prob. back-formation fr. ¹*smuggle*] **:** to run away with in a sneaking manner **:** FILCH

smug·gle \ˈsməgəl\ *vb* **smuggled; smuggled; smuggling** \-g(ə)liŋ\ **smuggles** [LG *smuggeln, smuckeln* & D *smokkelen;* akin to OE *smūgan* to creep — more at SMOCK] *vt* **1 :** to import or export secretly contrary to the law **:** bring into or take out of a country (merchandise, forbidden articles, or persons) contrary to law and with a fraudulent intent ⟨~ Chinese laborers⟩; *specif* **:** to import or export without paying the duties imposed by law ⟨by various ruses liquors were *smuggled* past the inspecting officers —W.M.Babcock⟩ **2 :** to convey or introduce in a surreptitious manner ⟨escaped with his life by being *smuggled* out in a policeman's uniform —S.P.B.Mais⟩ ⟨~ a normative judgment into what purports to be a statement of fact —A.J.Ayer⟩ ~ *vi* **:** to import or export anything in violation of the customs laws

smug·gle·able \-gələbəl\ *adj* **:** that can be smuggled

smug·gler \ˈsməg(ə)lə(r)\ *n* -S [LG *smuggeler, smuckeler* & D *smokkelaar;* LG *smuggeler, smuckeler* fr. *smuggeln, smuckeln* to smuggle + *-er* (akin to G *-er*); D *smokkelaar* fr. *smokkelen* to smuggle] **1 :** one that smuggles **2 :** a ship employed in smuggling

smug·ly *adv* **:** in a smug manner

smug·ness *n* -ES **:** the quality or state of being smug ⟨the little smile of self-satisfaction that gave his face an aspect of ~ —*Strand Mag.*⟩

smur *or* **smurr** \ˈsmər\ *n* [origin unknown] *dial* **:** a drizzly fog or mist

smur·ry \-rē\ *adj, chiefly dial* **:** MISTY, FOGGY, CLOUDY

¹smut \ˈsmət, *usu* -əd·+V\ *vb* **smutted; smutted; smutting; smuts** [prob. alter. of earlier *smot* to stain, fr. ME *smotten;* akin to ME *-smoteren* to soil, stain, MHG *smutzen,* and prob. to Gk *mydan* to be damp — more at MOSS] *vt* **1 :** to stain or mark with a black or dirty substance (as soot) **2 :** to taint or affect with smut or mildew ⟨*smutted* corn⟩ **3 :** SULLY, TAINT, DEFILE **4 :** to clear of smut ⟨~ grain for the mill⟩ ~ *vi* **1 :** to become affected by smut **:** become smutted ⟨treated grain will not ~⟩ **2** *Brit, of fish* **:** to rise at or feed on very small flies

²smut \"\ *n* -S **1 a** (1) **:** a dirty spot or condition **:** SOIL (2) **:** a patch of black or dark hair on an animal (as on the nose of a Himalayan rabbit) **b :** matter that soils or blackens ⟨her lace curtains . . . would already be darkened by the ~ of soft coal —Lewis Mumford⟩; *specif* **:** a particle of soot ⟨when trains went by the garden was filled with smoke and ~*s* —David Garnett⟩ **2 a** (1) **:** any of various destructive diseases of cereal grasses and some other plants caused by parasitic basidiomycetous fungi of the order Ustilaginales and characterized by the transformation of various plant organs into dark brown or black often dusty masses of spores — see COVERED SMUT, FLAG SMUT, LOOSE SMUT (2) **:** any fungus producing such a disease **b :** a similar disease of figs caused by an ascomycetous fungus (*Aspergillus niger*) **3 :** inferior soft coal containing much earthy matter and found esp. at the outcrop **4 :** material (as jokes, pictures, stories) in which a subject is treated in a manner violating accepted standards of decency **:** verbal or graphic obscenity **:** matter felt to be morally fouling **5** *Brit* **:** any of various small flies (as the midge, gnat) **6 :** a dark slate color appearing in a domesticated bird normally of another color

smut ball *n* **1 :** the spore mass into which the ovary of the host is converted by the stinking smut organism — compare ²BUNT **2 :** PUFFBALL

¹smutch \ˈsməch\ *or* **smouch** \ˈsmüch, ˈsmau̇ch\ *n* -ES [prob. irreg. fr. ¹*smudge*] **1 :** a soiling mark or trace **:** dirty spot **:** SMUDGE **2 :** a corrupting or polluting influence or effect **:** BLOT **3 :** SMUT, SOOT, GRIME

²smutch \"\ *or* **smouch** \"\ *vt* -ED/-ING/-ES **1 :** to make black or dirty (as with soot) **:** SMUDGE **2 :** DEFILE, SULLY, TAINT

smutchy \ˈsməchē\ *adj* -ER/-EST **:** DIRTY, STAINED, SMUDGED

smut fungus *n* **:** any fungus of the order Ustilaginales

smut gall *n* **:** an abnormal growth composed of the tissues of the host and a smut fungus (as in boil smut of corn)

smut grass *n* **:** a grass (*Sporobolus poiretii*) native to the West Indies but common in the southern U.S. that often has its tufted wiry stems and narrow panicles infested with a fungus (*Helminthosporium ravenelii*) — called also *blackseed, carpet grass*

smut mill *n* **:** a machine to rid grain of smut

smut sheet *n* **:** WASTE LEAF 1

smut·ter \ˈsməd·ə(r)\ *n* -S **:** one that smuts; *specif* **:** an operator of machinery for cleaning smut and other impurities from grain

smut·ti·ly \ˈsməd·ᵊlē, -ət|, |ᵊl-, |əl-\ *adv* **:** in a smutty manner

smut·ti·ness \|ēnəs, |in-\ *n* -ES **:** the quality or state of being smutty

smut·ty \|ē, |i\ *adj* -ER/-EST **1 :** soiled or tainted with smut **:** affected with smut fungus **:** SMUTTED **2 :** OBSCENE, INDECENT ⟨a ~ joke⟩ **3 :** like smut in appearance (as in color) **:** SOOTY, DUSKY

smyn·thu·ri·dae \smin'thu̇rə,dē\ *syn of* SMINTHURIDAE

¹smyr·na \ˈsmərnə, ˈsmə̄nə, ˈsməinə\ *adj, usu cap* [fr. *Smyrna* (now *İzmir*), Turkey, fr. L, fr. Gk] **:** IZMIR

²smyrna \"\ *n* -S *usu cap* **1 :** a Turkish rug shipped from Smyrna **2 :** a modern industrial carpet produced in Smyrna **3 :** a domestic reversible chenille rug

[1]**smyr·nae·an** \-nēən\ *n* -s *cap* [L *smyrnae*us, adj. & n., Smyrnaean (fr. Gk *smyrnaios*, fr. *Smyrna*) + E *-an*, n. suffix] **:** a native or inhabitant of the ancient city of Smyrna in Asia Minor

[2]**smyrnaean** \"\ *adj, usu cap* [L *smyrnae*us + E *-an*, adj. suffix] **:** of or belonging to Smyrna

smyrna fig *n, usu cap S* **:** a fig orig. grown near Smyrna that requires caprification in order to set fruit — compare COMMON FIG

smyr·ni·ote \-nē,ōt\ *n* -s *cap* [NGk *smyrniōtēs*, fr. *Smyrna* + Gk *-iōtēs* (as in *Sikeliōtēs* Siceliot)] **:** SMYRNAEAN

smyth sewing *or* **smythe sewing** \'smith-, 'smīth-\ *n, usu cap 1st S* [after David M. *Smyth* †1907 Am. inventor] **:** a mechanical method of attaching together the sections of books by means of thread passed through the folds

smy·trie \'smītri, 'smit-\ *n* -s [origin unknown] *Scot* **:** a miscellaneous collection of small creatures or things **:** BUNCH

sn *abbr* **1** sanitary; sanitation **2** [L *sine*] without

SN *abbr* **1** *often not cap* [L *secundum naturam*] naturally **2** serial number **3** shipping note **4** *often not cap* side note **5** *often not cap* [L *sine nomine*] without name

Sn *symbol* [LL *stannum*] tin

snab \'snab\ *n* -s [fr. or akin to Flem *snabbe* beak, beak of land; prob. akin to OHG *snabul* beak — more at NEB] *Scot* **:** the brow of a steep rise

[1]**snack** \'snak\ *vb* [ME *snaken*, prob. fr. MD *snacken* to snap at, bite, chatter — more at SNATCH] *vi* **1** *dial* **:** to snatch something with the teeth **:** SNAP, BITE **2 :** to lunch esp. between meals ~ *vt* **1** *chiefly dial* **:** to go shares on **:** divide into portions and share **2** *chiefly Scot* **:** to seize by or as if by snatching

[2]**snack** \"\ *n* -s [ME *snake*, fr. *snaken*, v.] **1** *chiefly Scot* **:** a snap or snatch with the teeth (as by a dog) **2 :** SHARE — often used in the phrase *go snacks* ⟨go ~s in the profits —*Temple Bar*⟩ **3 a :** a slight amount (as of liquor) **:** TASTE, BIT **b :** food served or taken informally usu. in small amounts and typically under other circumstances than as a regular meal ⟨had coffee and a ~⟩ ⟨took time for a ~ at noon⟩ ⟨dinner was a mere ~⟩

[3]**snack** \"\ *adj* [perh. fr. [2]*snack*] **1** *chiefly Scot* **:** keenly alert **:** CLEVER, QUICK **2** *chiefly Scot* **:** SNAPPISH, PEEVISH

[4]**snack** \"\ *adv, chiefly Scot* **:** with dispatch **:** QUICKLY, SMARTLY

[5]**snack** \"\ *n* -s [origin unknown] **:** a fives ball

snack bar *n* **1 :** a public eating place where snacks are served usu. at a counter **2 :** a counter or shelf in a home at which a snack may be eaten

snack table *n* **:** a small portable table designed to hold food or drink for one person

snack table

[1]**snaf·fle** \'snafəl\ *n* -s [origin unknown] **1** *also* **snaffle bit :** a bridle bit the mouthpiece of which has one or more joints or links and which consists in its simplest form of two bars tapering to where they are joined by a single ring — see BIT illustration, BRIDLE illustration **2 :** a light or gentle restraint or check — compare CURB

[2]**snaffle** \"\ *vt* **snaffled; snaffled; snaffling** \-f(ə)liŋ\ **snaffles 1 a :** to fit or equip with a snaffle ⟨a *snaffled* bridle⟩ **b :** to restrain or check with or as if with a snaffle **2 a** *dial chiefly Brit* **:** STEAL, ROB **b :** to obtain by devious or irregular means **c :** to obtain without delay **:** snap up **syn** see RESTRAIN

[3]**snaffle** \"\ *vi* [prob. alter. of *snuffle*] *chiefly dial* **:** SNUFFLE, SNIFF

snaf·fles \-fəlz\ *n pl but sing or pl in constr* [fr. pl. of [1]*snaffle;* fr. the shape of the flowers] **:** a lousewort (*Pedicularis canadensis*)

[1]**sna·fu** \(')sna¦fü\ *adj* [*s*ituation *n*ormal *a*ll *f*ouled *u*p] *slang* **:** snarled or stalled in confusion **:** AWRY

[2]**snafu** \"\ *n* -s *slang* **:** CONFUSION, MUDDLE

[3]**snafu** \"\ *vt* -ED/-ING/-S *slang* **:** to cause to be in a state of complete confusion and disorder **:** snarl up

[1]**snag** \'snag, -aa(ə)g, -aig\ *vi* **snagged; snagged; snagging; snags** [perh. of Scand origin; akin to Icel *snagga* to quarrel, wrangle, and perh. to ON *snaga*, a kind of ax — more at [2]SNAG] *dial chiefly Brit* **:** to scold aggravatingly **:** NAG, CARP

[2]**snag** \"\ *n* -s [of Scand origin; akin to Norw dial. *snag* projecting point on a headland, islet or skerry, ON *snagi* clothes peg, *snaga*, a kind of ax, and prob. to Norw *snake* to sniff around, snatch at something with the teeth — more at SNATCH] **1 a** (1) **:** a stub or stump remaining on a tree after a branch has been lopped off (2) **:** the rough stub remaining after a branch has been torn off (as by wind); *also* **:** such a roughly broken branch ⟨stumbling through underbrush and over the ~s that littered the ground⟩ **b :** a tree or a branch, log, or stump embedded in a lake or stream bed in such a manner that projecting parts constitute a hazard to navigation **c :** a standing dead tree from which parts or all of the top have fallen; *esp* **:** one that is more than 20 feet tall — compare STUB **d :** a short stub that is left temporarily to support the new growth from the scion when the stock is cut back after some side graft or more often budding operations **2 :** a rough sharp or jagged projecting part or unit **:** PROTUBERANCE: as **a :** a projecting tooth; *also* **:** a stump of a tooth **b :** one of the secondary branches of an antler **:** a small tine or a branch of a tine **3 :** a concealed or unexpected impediment, difficulty, or obstacle **4 a :** a jagged tear made by or as if by catching on a sharp projection **b :** an irregularity that suggests the result of tearing; *esp* **:** a pulled thread in fabric ⟨a *snag* in her stocking⟩ **5 a :** an irregular piece separated from a larger unit ⟨broke off a ~ of bread⟩ **b :** an indefinite amount ⟨came into quite a ~ of money⟩ **syn** see OBSTACLE

[3]**snag** \"\ *vt* **snagged; snagged; snagging; snags 1 :** to lop off (as branches) so as to leave snags **:** hew, trim, or cut roughly or jaggedly **2 a :** to catch on an underwater tree ⟨the boat was *snagged* near the right bank⟩ **b :** to catch (as wool) on sharp bushes or brush **c :** to catch (a line or hook) on underwater weeds or stones **d :** to catch (as clothes) on wire ⟨*snagged* his pants on the barbed wire fence⟩ **e :** to hook (a fish) in the body rather than in the mouth **f :** to hook (a fish) with a snagline **g :** to interrupt or interfere with as if by catching on a snag ⟨commerce . . . has been *snagged* by . . . lack of foreign exchange —*N.Y.Times*⟩ **3 a :** to clear (a river) of snags **b :** to remove rough protuberances from a foundry casting **4 :** to catch or obtain by quick, decisive, and often more or less irregular action ⟨~ a football pass from the opponent⟩ ⟨*snagged* a taxi —Frances Crane⟩ ⟨*snagged* the cake from the pantry while his mother was out⟩ ⟨worked out ways and means of *snagging* a rich husband —Polly Adler⟩

[4]**snag** \"\ *n* -s [origin unknown] *dial Brit* **:** SLOE, BLACKTHORN

snag boat *n* **:** a steamboat with an apparatus for removing impeding debris (as snags) from inland waters

snag·ged \-gəd\ *adj* **:** full of snags **:** SNAGGY, JAGGED; *also* **:** caught on or damaged by a snag

snag·ger \-gə(r)\ *n* -s [[3]*snag* + *-er*] **:** one that snags: as **a :** a billhook for trimming trees **b :** a foundry worker who chips or grinds excess metal from castings **c** *Austral* **:** an inexperienced shearer

snag·gle \-gəl\ *vt* -ED/-ING/-S [freq. of [3]*snag*] **:** [3]SNAG 4

snag·gled \-gəld\ *adj* [*snaggle*tooth + *-ed*] *of teeth* **:** markedly uneven **:** irregularly projecting; *also* **:** broken or decayed to stumps

snaggletooth \'==,=\ *n* [E dial. *snaggle* irregularly shaped tooth (fr. [2]*snag* + *-le*) + *tooth*] **:** an irregular, broken, or projecting tooth — **snaggletoothed** \¦==¦=\ *adj*

snag·gy \-gē, -gi\ *adj* -ER/-EST **:** full of snags ⟨a ~ pole⟩

snagline \'=,=\ *n* **:** a line to which is attached a large number of unbaited fishhooks and which is anchored across the bottom of a river to entangle fish (as paddlefish) nosing about

snag·rel \'snagrəl\ *n* -s [origin unknown] **:** VIRGINIA SNAKEROOT

snags *pres 3d sing of* SNAG, *pl of* SNAG

snag scow *n* **:** a scow employed in pulling snags from inland waterways

snag tree *n* **:** BLACK GUM 1a

[1]**snail** \'snāl, *esp before pause or consonant* -āəl\ *n* -s *often attrib* [ME, fr. OE *snægl, snægel;* akin to OS *snegil* snail, MHG *snegel*, OHG *snecko* snail, *snahhan* to creep, ON *snigill* snail, OIr *snaighim* I creep, Lith *snãke* snail; basic meaning: to creep] **1 :** a freshwater or marine or terrestrial gastropod mollusk esp. when having an external enclosing spiral shell — see BROWN SNAIL, EDIBLE SNAIL, GARDEN SNAIL, LAND SNAIL, VIOLET SNAIL; compare LIMPET, PTEROPOD, SLUG **2 :** a slow-moving or sluggish person or thing **:** one lacking in energy or activity **3 :** something suggesting a snail shell: as **a :** a snail clover or its pod — often used in pl. **b** *or* **snail wheel :** a spiral or volute-shaped cam (as in a watch)

marine snail **:** *a* proboscis, exserted; *b,b,* tentacles; *c* siphon; *d* foot; *e* shell; *f* operculum; *g* caudal cirri

[2]**snail** \"\ *vb* -ED/-ING/-S *vi* **:** to move, act, or go slowly or lazily ⟨the train ~*ed* up the steep grade⟩ ~ *vt* **1 :** to form in or mark with a spiral — used chiefly in horology **2 :** to spend (time) like a snail or drone

[3]**snail** *n* [prob. by folk etymology] *obs* **:** CHENILLE 1

snail bore *or* **snail borer** *n* **:** a boring gastropod mollusk **:** DRILL

snail cloud *n* **:** CUMULOSTRATUS

snail clover *or* **snail medic** *n* **:** any of several medics having helicoid or spirally coiled pods (as *Medicago scutellata*)

snail countersink *or* **snail-head countersink** *n* **:** a countersink used esp. to bevel the ends of holes — see COUNTERSINK illustration

snaileater \'=,==\ *n* **:** OPENBILL

snail·er \-lə(r)\ *n* -s [[2]*snail* + *-er*] **:** an operator of a machine used for snailing and polishing ratchet wheels for clocks and watches

snail·ery \-lərē, -ri\ *n* -ES **:** a place where edible snails are bred and fattened for market

snail fever *n* **:** SCHISTOSOMIASIS

snailfish \'=,=\ *n* **:** SEA SNAIL 2

snailflower \'=,=\ *n* **1 :** a perennial tropical American vine (*Phaseolus caracalla*) that is sometimes cultivated for its racemes of showy purple and yellow flowers and has the corolla keel coiled like a snail shell **2 :** SNAIL CLOVER

snail hawk *n* **:** EVERGLADE KITE

snail-horned \'=¦=\ *adj* **:** having short crooked horns suggesting a snail shell ⟨a *snail-horned* cow⟩

snail·ish \'snālish\ *adj* **:** suggesting a snail esp. in slowness or sluggishness — **snail·ish·ly** *adv*

snaillike \'=,=\ *adj* **:** resembling a snail **:** SNAILISH

snail-paced \'=¦=\ *adj* **:** moving at or characterized by a snail's pace

snail-seed \'=,=\ *n* **:** CAROLINA MOONSEED

snail-slow \'=¦=\ *adj* **:** SNAIL-PACED

snail's pace *n* [ME *snayles pas*] **:** an excessively slow pace or rate of speed ⟨business is progressing at a *snail's pace*⟩

snaily \'snālē\ *adj* [[1]*snail* + *-y*] **1 a :** SNAILISH **b :** infested with snails **2** *Austral* **:** SNAIL-HORNED

snaith \'snāth, -t͟h\ *dial Eng var of* SNATH

[1]**snake** \'snāk, *dial* 'snek\ *n* -s *often attrib* [ME, fr. OE *snaca;* akin to MLG *snake*, ON *snākr, snōkr* snake, *snigill* snail — more at SNAIL] **1 a :** any of numerous oviparous or ovoviviparous scaly limbless reptiles (suborder Serpentes) with a very elongated body that are first known from the Cretaceous and are presumably derived from lacertilian ancestors, that have the branches of the mandible usu. connected in front by an elastic ligament so that the mouth is very distensible, the tongue forked, the tympanum of the ear lacking, the eye permanently covered by a transparent membrane, and one lung usu. reduced or absent, that in many forms produce venoms in modified salivary glands, that are usu. predaceous in habit killing their prey by constriction or by injection of venom through hollow or grooved fangs and swallowing it whole, and that are often valuable destroyers of rodents and other vermin **b :** an elongated limbless lizard or amphibian — not used technically; see GLASS SNAKE **c :** any of various vigorous voracious elongated fishes (as a pike, a pickerel, or a barracuda) — not used technically **2 a** *obs* **:** a poor, miserable, or cringing person **b :** a worthless contemptible fellow; *esp* **:** a perfidious ingrate **3 :** something felt to resemble a snake: as **a** *obs* **:** a tail, curl, or braid of a wig **b :** SERPENT 6 **c :** the flexible stem of a hookah **d :** an arrow buried flat in the grass **e :** PLUMBER'S SNAKE **f :** FISH TAPE **g :** a crooked surface flaw in rolled metal **h :** a baseball curve **i :** an explosive charge in a very long narrow metal case that can be pushed into a minefield by a tank and then exploded to clear a path sometimes of several hundred feet through the field **4** *usu cap* **a :** any of various Shoshonean peoples esp. of the northern Shoshoni, northern Paiute, and Comanche **b :** a member of such people

[2]**snake** \"\ *vb* -ED/-ING/-S *vt* **1 :** to wind (as one's way, one's body in crawling) so as to suggest a snake or snakelike movement **:** move sinuously ⟨a long wagon train *snaking* its way along the slope⟩ **2 a :** WORM 6 **b :** to bind (as backstays) together with small stuff **3 a :** to move (something) by dragging **:** drag forcibly ⟨*snaking* logs down the hill with a chain hitch⟩ ⟨*snaked* out the timber over an old tote road⟩; *also* **:** to move (logs) by skidding **b** *chiefly dial* **:** STEAL, SWIPE **4 :** to flaw (a log) in sawing into board by making a wavy cut ~ *vi* **1 a :** to crawl or move silently, secretly, or sinuously ⟨*snaking* softly through the brush⟩ **b :** to twist in the manner of a snake **:** progress in a spiral ⟨a narrow trail that ~*s* between the trees⟩ **c** *dial Eng* **:** to move stealthily **:** SNEAK **2** *of an arrow* **:** to bury itself in the grass in falling

snakebark \'=,=\ *n* **:** a medium-sized timber tree (*Colubrina ferruginosa*) of Florida and the West Indies with yellowish brown durable wood

snakeberry \'=- — *see* BERRY\ *n* **1** *Brit* **:** BRYONY; *also* **:** the fruit of bryony **2 a :** RED BANEBERRY **b :** a bittersweet (*Solanum dulcamara*); *also* **:** its berry **c :** PARTRIDGEBERRY

snakebird \'=,=\ *n* [so called fr. its snakelike neck] **1 :** any of various fish-eating birds constituting the genus *Anhinga*, having a very long slender neck, small head, and sharp-pointed bill, being mostly blackish brown varied on the upper parts with silvery gray or metallic greenish, chiefly frequenting inland streams, lakes, and swamps, and being very expert swimmers and divers **2** *dial Eng* **:** WRYNECK

snakebit \'=¦=\ *or* **snakebitten** \'=¦==\ *adj* **:** bitten by a venomous snake

snakebite \'=,=\ *n* **1 :** the bite of a snake; *also* **:** the condition of having been bitten by a venomous snake characterized by stinging pain in the puncture wound, constitutional symptoms, and injury to blood or nerve tissue **2 a :** BLOODROOT 1 **b :** a common No. American wake-robin (*Trillium cernuum*) **3** *also* **snakebite remedy** *dial* **:** LIQUOR; *specif* **:** WHISKEY

snake buzzard *n* **:** SERPENT EAGLE

snake cactus *n* **:** a cactus (*Nyctocereus serpentinus*) having clustered cylindric stems and showy red flowers

snake cane *n* **:** a tropical So. American palm (*Kunthia montana*) having a ringed snakelike stem

snake charmer *n* **:** an entertainer who exhibits his professed power to charm or fascinate venomous snakes

snake crane *n* **:** CARIAMA 2

snake dance *n* **1 :** a ceremonial dance in which snakes or their images are handled, invoked, or symbolically imitated by individual sinuous actions **2 :** a group progression in a single-file serpentine path often in celebration of an athletic victory

snake doctor *n* **1 :** HELLGRAMMITE **2 :** DRAGONFLY

snake-eater \'=,==\ *n* **1 :** MARKHOR **2 :** SECRETARY BIRD

snake eel *n* **:** any of numerous scaleless eels of the family Ophichthyidae having no caudal fin and the end of the tail projecting beyond the dorsal and anal fins, abounding in tropical seas, and being often spotted like some of the venomous sea snakes

snake eggplant *n* **:** an eggplant with long cylindric fruit that is curled at the end

snake eyes *n pl* **:** a throw of two aces in craps

snake feeder *n, Midland* **:** DRAGONFLY

snake fence *n* **:** WORM FENCE

snakefish \'=,=\ *n* **1 :** RIBBONFISH 1b **2 :** LIZARD FISH

snakeflower \'=,=\ *n* **1 :** BLUEWEED 1 **2 :** GREATER STITCHWORT **3 :** WHITE CAMPION a **4 :** STARFLOWER b

snake fly *n* **:** any of several insects of the suborder Raphidiodea having a large head and an elongated prothorax that suggests a neck

snake foot *n* **:** a pointed Dutch foot (as on Queen Anne furniture) — see FOOT illustration

snake gentian *n* **:** a lion's foot (*Prenanthes serpentaria*)

snake gourd *n* **1** *or* **snake cucumber :** SNAKE MELON **2 a :** a gourd (*Trichosanthes anguina*) with long contorted green and white edible fruits that become bright orange when fully ripe **b :** BOTTLE GOURD **c :** DISHCLOTH GOURD

snake-grass \'=,=\ *n* **1 :** GREATER STITCHWORT **2 :** a common forget-me-not (*Myosotis scorpioides*) **3 :** SKUNK GRASS

snake hawk *n* **:** SWALLOW-TAILED KITE

snakehead \'=,=\ *n* **1 :** a loose bent-up end of one of the strap rails or flat rails formerly used on railroads **2 a :** TURTLEHEAD **b :** GUINEA-HEN FLOWER **3** *also* **snakehead mullet** *or* **snake-headed fish** \'=¦==-\ **:** a fish of the family Ophicephalidae

snake-hipped \'=¦=\ *adj* **:** having slender and usu. mobile hips

snakehips \'=,=\ *n pl but sing in constr* **:** a swing dance with sideward foot twisting and resultant hip wriggling

snake hole *n* **1 :** a hole bored beneath a boulder and immediately against the bottom of it for blasting **2 :** any of various drill holes in quarrying or bench blasting

snakeholing \'=,==\ *n* -s **:** blasting (as in mining or quarrying) by means of snake holes

snake in the grass 1 : a lurking or unsuspected danger **2 :** a secretly faithless friend

snake juice *n, dial* **:** strong drink; *esp* **:** bad whiskey

snake killer *n* **1 :** SECRETARY BIRD **2 :** ROADRUNNER

snake·less \'=ləs\ *adj* **:** free from snakes ⟨the ~ isle⟩

snake·let \-lət\ *n* -s **:** a young or small snake

snakelike \'=,=\ *adj* **:** resembling a snake esp. in elongate tapering form

snake lily *n* **1 :** BLUE FLAG **2 :** a climbing and twining herb (*Brodiaea volubilis*) that is native to the southwestern U.S. but cultivated elsewhere for its showy umbels of rose-red or pinkish flowers

snake line *n* **:** a small line passed around or between two ropes in a spiral or zigzag

snake·ling \'=liŋ\ *n* -s **:** SNAKELET

snake mackerel *n* **:** a long silvery deep-sea fish (*Gempylus serpens*) chiefly of tropical and southern seas that is highly esteemed for its rich oily flesh and is related to but slenderer than the typical escolar; *broadly* **:** ESCOLAR

snake melon *n* **:** a long sinuous white-fleshed melon that is technically a variety (*Cucumis melo flexuosus*) of the muskmelon but resembles a cucumber in texture and flavor and that is sometimes cultivated usu. as a curiosity — called also *snake gourd*

snake-milk \'=,=\ *n* **:** FLOWERING SPURGE

snake moss *n* **:** a common club moss (*Lycopodium clavatum*)

snakemouth \'=,=\ *also* **snakemouth pogonia** *n* **:** a showy bog orchid (*Pogonia ophioglossoides*) of eastern No. America and Japan having pink flowers suggestive of the open mouth of a snake

snake muishond *or* **snake weasel** *n* **:** a small slender burrowing African muishond (*Poecilogale albinucha*) with the top of the head white — compare STRIPED MUISHOND

snakeneck \'=,=\ *n* **:** SNAKEBIRD 1

snake-necked \'=¦=\ *adj* **:** SIDE-NECKED

snake oil *n* **:** any of various substances or mixtures sold (as by a traveling medicine show) as medicine usu. without regard to their medical worth or properties

snake palm *n* **:** DEVIL'S-TONGUE 2

snakepiece \'=,=\ *n* **:** a diagonal timber connecting the afterbody and the stern frame of a wooden ship

snake pit *n* **1 :** a hospital for mental diseases **2 :** a place of chaotic disorder and distress ⟨the *snake pit* of her alcoholism —John Barkham⟩

snake plant *n* **:** a plant of the genus *Sansevieria*

snak·er \'snākə(r)\ *n* -s **:** SKIDDER a, b

snakeroot \'=,=\ *n* **1 :** any of numerous plants most of which have had repute as remedies for snake bites: as **a :** VIRGINIA SNAKEROOT **b :** BUGBANE 1 **c :** a plant of the genus *Sanicula* **d :** SENEGA ROOT **e :** BUTTON SNAKEROOT **f :** BLAZING STAR 3a **g :** WHITE SNAKEROOT **h :** a plant of the genus *Asarum; esp* **:** WILD GINGER 2a **i :** BITTERBUSH 2 **2 :** the root of a snakeroot

snakes *pl of* SNAKE, *pres 3d sing of* SNAKE

snakes and ladders *n pl but usu sing in constr* **:** a board game in which pictures of snakes and ladders retard or facilitate the players' progress

snake's-head \'=,=\ *n, pl* **snake's-heads 1 a** *or* **snake's-head lily :** GUINEA-HEN FLOWER **b :** a woody composite herb (*Malacothrix coulteri*) with a spotted involucre that grows in dry areas of the southwestern U.S. **2 :** SNAKEHEAD 1

snake's-head iris *n* **:** a tuberous herb (*Iris tuberosus*) of the Mediterranean region having flowers that resemble a serpent's open mouth

snakeskin \'=,=\ *n* **:** leather prepared from the skins of snakes

snake spit *n* **:** CUCKOO SPIT 1

snakestone \'=,=\ *n* **1** *chiefly dial* **:** AMMONITE **2 :** a stone (as the adder stone) or a stony preparation popularly thought efficacious when applied to a snake bite **3 :** AYR STONE

snake's-tongue \'=,=\ *n, pl* **snake's-tongues :** ADDER'S-TONGUE 1

snake turtle *or* **snake tortoise** *n* **:** LONG-NECKED TURTLE

snake violet *n* **:** BIRD'S-FOOT VIOLET

snakeweed \'=,=\ *n* **:** any of several plants popularly associated with snakes (as in appearance, common habitat, or use in treatment of snake bite): as **a :** BISTORT **b :** SNAKEROOT **c :** any of various plantains **d :** a plant of the genus *Gutierrezia* **e :** POISON HEMLOCK 1

snake wire *n* **:** FISH TAPE

snakewise \'=,=\ *adv* [[1]*snake* + *-wise*] **:** so as to resemble a snake; *esp* **:** with a stealthy slithering snakelike movement

snake woman *n, usu cap S&W* **:** a male Aztec leader functioning as the principal executive officer in tribal affairs and ranking equal with the chief

snakewood \'=,=\ *n* **1 :** NUX VOMICA 2 **2 :** an East Indian climbing shrub (*Rauwolfia serpentina*) whose twisted roots and stems resemble serpents **3 :** TRUMPETWOOD **4 :** FRANGIPANI **5 :** LETTERWOOD **6 :** SNAKEBARK **7 :** NAKEDWOOD 1

snakeworm \'=,=\ *n* **:** a traveling mass of army worms of the genus *Sciara*

snak·i·ly \'snākəlē, -li\ *adv* **:** in a snaky manner

[1]**snaking** *adj* [fr. pres. part. of [2]*snake*] **1 :** WINDING, SINUOUS ⟨a ~ river⟩ **2 :** used in snaking ⟨a ~ chain⟩

[2]**snaking** *n* -s [fr. gerund of [2]*snake*] **1 :** the act of one who snakes **2 a :** something that is snakelike in form or arrangement **:** COIL **b :** a persistent directional oscillation of an airplane

snak·ish \'snākish, -kēsh\ *adj* [[1]*snake* + *-ish*] **:** rather snaky

snaky *also* **snakey** \-kē, -ki\ *adj* **snakier; snakiest** [[1]*snake* + *-y*] **1 :** of, formed of, or covered or entwined with snakes ⟨a writhing ~ mass littered the den⟩ **2 :** resembling a snake **:** SNAKELIKE, SERPENTINE ⟨a ~ eel⟩; *usu* **:** having many convolutions **:** SINUOUS, WAVY, WRIGGLY ⟨~ ridges in the sand⟩ ⟨a ~ river⟩ **3 a :** of or typical of a snake ⟨~ cunning⟩ **b :** felt to share the characteristics of a snake (as in slyness, treachery, perfidiousness, venom, spitefulness) ⟨mean ~ ways⟩ ⟨~ treachery⟩ **4 :** abounding in snakes ⟨a ~ forest⟩ **5** *Austral* **:** ANGRY, EXASPERATED, TOUCHY

snal·ly·gas·ter \'snälē,gästə(r)\ *n* -s [perh. modif. of PaG *schnelle geeschter*, lit., quick spirits] **:** a mythical nocturnal creature that is reported chiefly from rural Maryland, is reputed to be part reptile and part bird, and is said to prey on poultry and children

[1]**snap** \'snap\ *vb* **snapped; snapped; snapping; snaps** [D or LG *snappen*, fr. MD & MLG, respectively; akin to MHG *snappen* to snap, stumble, sway, chatter, ON *snapa* to snuffle, snap, and prob. to OHG *snabul* beak — more at NEB] *vi* **1 a :** to make a snap of the jaws **:** seize something with a snap of the mouth ⟨an ill-conditioned cur that ~*s* and snarls⟩ — usu. used with *at* ⟨fish *snapping* at the bait⟩ **b :** to grasp at something eagerly **:** make a pounce or snatch — usu. used with *at* ⟨*snapped* at the invitation⟩ ⟨ready to ~ at any chance for im-

provement⟩ **2 :** to utter sharp biting words **:** bark out irritable or peevish retorts — often used with *at* **3 a :** to break off or in two often with a short snapping sound **:** break suddenly (as under strain or tension) ⟨the twig *snapped*⟩ ⟨the taut cable finally *snapped*⟩ **b :** to give way under stress **:** suddenly yield usu. to the cumulative effect of some strain ⟨after three days of battle his nerve *snapped*⟩ **4 a :** to make a sound that is a snap **:** give out a sharp or crackling sound or a sudden report or click ⟨the fire *snapped* and crackled on the hearth⟩ ⟨damp clothes *snapping* on the line⟩ **b** *of a firearm* **:** to make a sharp sound by the falling of the hammer on an empty chamber or on a round that does not fire; *also* **:** MISFIRE **5 :** to move esp. abruptly in a particular direction or manner usu. in attaining a position of closure ⟨the lid *snapped* down⟩ ⟨her eyes *snapped* shut⟩ ⟨the bolt ~*s* home with a click⟩ **6 :** to emit sparks or flashes (as of wit or sarcasm) ⟨the conversation *snapped* back and forth⟩; *also* **:** to appear to scintillate **:** SPARKLE ⟨eyes *snapping* with fury⟩ ~ *vt* **1 a :** to seize with or as if with a snap of the jaws **:** grasp or snatch suddenly or unexpectedly ⟨the dog *snapped* the meat from the table⟩ ⟨the wind *snapped* the scarf from her hand⟩ **b :** to capture or take possession of suddenly **:** steal by adroitness ⟨ready to ~ the very shoes from our feet⟩ **2 :** to secure (something) to one's own use or possession by prompt decisive action — usu. used with *up* ⟨quick to ~ up a bargain⟩ ⟨a prize to be *snapped* up cheaply⟩ ⟨~ up his offer⟩ **3 a :** to retort to or interrupt with a snappish, cutting, or crushing remark **:** speak to curtly and usu. irritably ⟨*snapped* him short with a curt acknowledgement⟩ ⟨*snapped* them a sharp reply⟩ **b :** to utter (words) curtly, harshly, or abruptly ⟨*snapping* out an answer without a moment's hesitation⟩ **4 a :** to break by snapping **:** break short or in two **:** break apart or into pieces ⟨the blow *snapped* the bone⟩ ⟨wind ~*s* many branches from the trees⟩ **b :** to harvest (as corn or cotton) by breaking from the stem **5 a :** to cause to make a snapping sound usu. in the course of some action or movement ⟨wind *snapping* the sheets on the line⟩ **:** cause to crack ⟨~ a whip⟩ **b :** to cause (as a handgun) to discharge by pulling the trigger **c :** to put into or remove from a particular position or state by a sudden movement or with a snapping sound ⟨~ the lock shut⟩ ⟨*snapped* the top from the bottle⟩ **d :** to make a snapping sound by moving (fingers) against one another **6 a :** to project with a snap **:** FILLIP ⟨snapped a spitball across the classroom⟩ **b :** to make, present, or do without prolonged preparation or delay ⟨~ into a performance or role⟩; *esp* **:** to fire (a projectile) without chance for careful aim ⟨*snapped* a shot at the fleeing bandit⟩ **c** (1) **:** to catch (a cricket batsman) out sharply (as from a snicked ball) — often used with *up* ⟨*snapped* up at the wicket⟩ (2) **:** to put (a football) in play from a position on the ground with a quick continuous motion of the hands **d** (1) **:** to take (a photograph) with a hand-held camera using an instantaneous exposure (2) **:** take a snapshot of ⟨*snapping* the scenery⟩ — **snap off one's head** *also* **snap off one's nose :** to speak to curtly, harshly, or discourteously by way of reply — **snap one's fingers at :** to give no heed to **:** treat with contempt or unconcern — **snap out of it :** to free oneself from something (as a mood or habit) by an effort of will **syn** see BREAK, JERK

²snap \"\ *n* -S **1 :** an abrupt closing (as of the mouth in biting or of scissors in cutting) **:** the action of one that bites or bites at something **:** a biting or snatching with the teeth or jaws ⟨the dog took a ~ at a flea⟩ ⟨a ~ of the scissors cut the string⟩ **2 a** *obs* **:** something snapped up as one's share of profits or booty **b :** a chance to make money easily or quickly; *specif* **:** an easy remunerative post or position **c :** something (as a task or course of study) that is easy and presents no problems ⟨it will be a ~ to win the game⟩ ⟨the literature course was a ~ for him⟩ **3 a :** a small amount **:** BIT, MORSEL ⟨cared not a ~ for his mother's advice⟩ **b** *dial chiefly Brit* **:** a small or hasty meal **:** SNACK; *esp* **:** a miner's lunch eaten while on shift **4 a :** an act or instance of seizing abruptly **:** a sudden gripping or snatching at something **:** a quick short brisk movement ⟨a ~ of the fingers⟩ **b :** a sudden sharp tearing or breaking ⟨felt the ~ of the bone parting⟩ **5 a :** a sudden sharp sound made by or as if by snapping something (as together, apart, into place, off) ⟨the ~ of a twig⟩ ⟨shut the book with a ~⟩ **b :** a brief sharp and usu. irritable speech or retort ⟨took me up with a ~⟩ **6 :** FELLOW, LAD **7 :** a sudden interval of harsh weather ⟨an unexpected cold ~⟩ — compare SPELL 3b **8 a :** a catch or fastening that closes or locks with a click (as one provided with a spring or with parts that fit tightly into each other) ⟨the ~ of a bracelet⟩ ⟨closed the ~*s* on the suitcase⟩ **b :** a device (as a snap hook or snap fastener) having such a catch **9 :** a thin brittle cookie ⟨a batch of lemon ~*s*⟩ ⟨a new chocolate ~⟩ — compare GINGERSNAP **10 a :** SNAP SHOT **b :** SNAPSHOT **c :** SNAPDRAGON **11 a** *or* **snap tool :** a tool having a usu. cup-shaped depression in one end and used in forming rivetheads in riveting **b :** SNAPHEAD **12 a :** the condition of being vigorous in body, mind, or spirit **:** ALERTNESS, ENERGY, GO ⟨a young man with plenty of ~⟩ **b :** a pungent pleasing quality (as of literary style) **:** SMARTNESS **13 :** a fruit that is snapped (as from the fruiting spur): as **a :** a whole mature cotton boll when harvested by snapping — usu. used in pl. **b :** SNAP BEAN **14 :** SCOTCH SNAP **15 a :** an act or instance of snapping a football **b :** CENTER 5a(1) — used chiefly in Canadian football

³snap \"\ *adv* [¹*snap*] **:** with a snapping movement or sound **:** with suddenness or violence **:** BRISKLY ⟨the sail went ~ in the freshening wind⟩

⁴snap \"\ *adj* [¹*snap*] **1 a** *chiefly Scot* **:** QUICK, SMART, ALERT **b :** snapped up or done in a snap **:** secured, given, done, carried through suddenly or without due process or deliberation ⟨a ~ judgment⟩ ⟨such ~ decisions⟩ **c :** called or taken without prior warning ⟨repeated calling of ~ votes has given the cabinet some severe scares —*Atlantic*⟩ **2 :** shutting, fastening, or otherwise coming together with a click or by means of a device that snaps ⟨a ~ lock⟩ ⟨~ closures⟩ ⟨a ~ action⟩ **3 :** unusually easy or simple ⟨a ~ course⟩

snap back *vi* **:** to make a quick or vigorous recovery

snapback \ˈ=,=\ *n* -S [fr. *snap back*, v.] **1 :** a football snap **2 :** a sudden rebound or recovery ⟨predicted a ~ of the market from the present lows⟩

snap bean *n* **1 :** a bean grown primarily for its whole pods that are usu. broken in pieces and cooked as a vegetable while young and tender and before the seeds have become enlarged — see GREEN BEAN, WAX BEAN; compare SHELL BEAN **2 :** one of the edible pods of a snap bean

snap beetle *or* **snap bug** *n* **:** CLICK BEETLE

snapberry \ˈ=,- — *see* BERRY\ *n* **:** CORALBERRY

snap-brim hat \ˈ=,=-\ *also* **snap-brim** *n* **:** a hat usu. made of felt with the brim turned up in back and down in front and with a dented crown

snap catch *n* **:** SPRING CATCH

snap clutch *n* **:** any of several clutches used on major drive parts of harvesting and threshing machinery and so designed as to disengage when subjected to undue strains

snapdragon \ˈ=,==\ *n* **1 a :** a garden plant of the genus *Antirrhinum* (esp. *A. majus*) having showy white, crimson, or yellow bilabiate flowers fancifully likened to the face of a dragon **b :** TOADFLAX **c :** JEWELWEED **2** *archaic* **:** a mummer's representation of a dragon with snapping jaws **3 :** a game in which the players snatch raisins or other tidbits from burning brandy and quickly eat them; *also* **:** any of the materials used in the game — called also *flapdragon* **4 :** a tongs used by glassmakers **5 :** a light to moderate yellow that is redder than amber yellow and stronger and slightly redder than buff (sense 4b)

¹snape \ˈsnāp\ *dial var of* SNEAP

²snape \"\ *vb* -ED/-ING/-S [origin unknown] *vt* **:** TAPER; *specif* **:** to bevel the end of (a timber) to fit against an inclined surface (as of a ship) ~ *vi* **:** to taper a timber

snap fastener *n* **:** a metal fastener consisting essentially of a ball and a socket attached to opposed parts of an article and used to hold meeting edges (as of a garment) together — see FASTENER illustration

snap flask *n* **:** a molding flask for small work having its sides separable and held together by latches so that the flask may be removed from around the sand mold

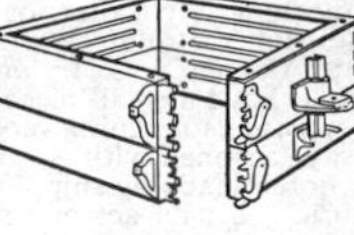

snap flask

snap gage *n* **:** a gage with inside measuring surfaces (as for calipering lengths or diameters)

snap·hance *or* **snap·haunce** \ˈsnap,han(t)s, -hän\ *also* **snap·haan** \|n\ *n* -S [D *snaphaan* highway man, snaphance (influenced in meaning by *snappen* to snap and *haan* hammer of a gun), fr. MD *snaphaen* highwayman, fr. *snappen* to snap, snatch + *haen* cock; akin to OHG *hani* cock — more at SNAP, CHANT] **1 a :** a primitive flintlock **b :** an old-time musket having such a lock **2** *obs* **:** a snap catch or spring catch

snaphead \ˈ=,=\ *n* **1 :** a hemispherical or rounded head on a rivet or bolt **2 :** a riveting snap

snap header *n* **1 :** a half brick appearing like a header in a masonry face but not extending in beyond the facework **2 :** a bond stone not extending through the wall

snaphead rivet *n* **1 :** a rivet with head formed by a snap **2 :** a buttonhead rivet

snapholder \ˈ=,==\ *n* **:** a holder (as a tool holder) actuated by a snap

snap hook *n* **:** SPRING HOOK

snapjack \ˈ=,=\ *n, dial Eng* **:** GREATER STITCHWORT

snap·less \ˈ=ləs\ *adj* **:** having no snap **:** employing or requiring no snaps

snap link *n* **:** a link (as of a chain) with a gap in the side closed by a spring

snap lock *n* **:** a lock shutting with a catch or snap

snap mackerel *n* **:** BLUEFISH 1

snap molding *n* **:** molding with snap flasks

snap-on \ˈ=,=\ *adj* [fr. *snap on*, v.] **1 :** designed to snap into position and fit tightly ⟨dishes with *snap-on* covers⟩ **2 :** attachable by means of snap fasteners ⟨a *snap-on* collar⟩

snap·pable \ˈsnapəbəl\ *adj* **:** capable of being snapped

snapped *past of* SNAP

snapped work *n* **:** masonry laid with considerable use of snap headers

¹snap·per \ˈsnapə(r)\ *vi* [ME *snaperen*; akin to MHG *snappen* to snap, stumble, sway, chatter — more at SNAP] **1** *chiefly Scot* **:** STUMBLE **2** *chiefly Scot* **:** to commit an error **:** make a slip

²snapper \"\ *n* -S *chiefly Scot* **:** a false step **:** SLIP, FAUX PAS

³snapper \"\ *n* -S [¹*snap* + *-er*] **1 :** something that snaps: as **a snappers** *pl* **:** CASTANETS **b :** a small usu. tasseled tip on a buggy whip **c :** CRACKER 2c **d** (1) **:** GREATER STITCHWORT (2) **:** BLADDER CAMPION **a** (3) **:** SNAP BEAN **e** (1) **:** SNAPPING TURTLE (2) **:** GREEN WOODPECKER (3) **:** CLICK BEETLE (4) **:** PHAINOPEPLA **f :** a bit of business, turn of phrase, or other matter that gives new orientation to a situation or utterance **g :** SNAP FASTENER **h :** a small clamshell bucket used esp. for collecting samples of deep-sea mud and ooze **2 :** a person that snaps or that snaps something esp. by way of occupation: as **a :** an irritable snappish individual **:** one who answers or speaks curtly and cuttingly **b :** a glassworker who uses a snapdragon **c :** a taker of snapshots **d :** ²CLIPPER a; *also* **:** a mine car brakeman or coupler **e :** SNAPPER-BACK **3** *pl sometimes* **snapper a :** any of numerous active carnivorous fishes (family Lutjanidae) of warm seas that are important as food and often as sport fishes, commonly resemble bass, attain a length of about two feet, and are usu. red or rose in deep-sea forms but often greenish above in shallow-water forms esp. when young **b :** any of several immature fishes (as the young of the bluefish, rosefish, or red grouper) that somewhat resemble a snapper **c :** an important sparid food fish (*Pagrosomus auratus* or *P. unicolor*) of Australia and New Zealand that is usu. pink or reddish with dark spots when young and becomes bright red when adult — see COCK SNAPPER **4** *slang* **:** WHOPPER

snapper-back \ˈ==,=\ *n* -S [*snap back* + *-er*] **:** a football player who snaps back the ball **:** CENTER

snapper shark *n* **:** MAKO

snapper-up \ˈ==ˈ=\ *n, pl* **snappers-up** [*snap up*, v. + *-er*] **:** one that snaps something up ⟨a *snapper-up* of bargains⟩ ⟨a *snapper-up* of unconsidered trifles —Shak.⟩

snap·pi·ly \ˈsnapəlē, -li\ *adv* **:** in a snappy manner

snap·pi·ness \-pēnəs, -pin-\ *n* -ES **:** the quality or state of being snappy

snapping *adv* [fr. pres. part. of ¹*snap*] **:** NOTABLY, VERY, INTENSELY ⟨a ~ cold day⟩

snapping beetle *also* **snapping bug** *n* **:** CLICK BEETLE

snapping hazel *n* **:** WITCH HAZEL 2a(1)

snap·ping·ly *adv* **:** in a snapping manner **:** with snapping ⟨dogs threatening ~⟩

snapping mackerel *n* **:** BLUEFISH 1

snapping prawn *n, Austral* **:** SNAPPING SHRIMP

snapping shrimp *n* **:** any of numerous small shrimps (family Crangonidae) that make a sharp snapping sound with one of their chelae which is greatly enlarged

snapping tool *n* **:** a stamp for forcing a metal plate into a die to make an impression

snapping turtle *also* **snapping terrapin** *n* **1 :** either of two large edible American aquatic turtles of the family Chelydridae with powerful jaws and a strong musky odor: **a :** a turtle (*Chelydra serpentina*) that has the head covered with smooth skin, has large plates in a double row on the underside of the tail, and is distributed from eastern Canada to Central America and Ecuador **b :** ALLIGATOR SNAPPER 1 **2 :** SOFT-SHELLED TURTLE

snap·pish \ˈsnapish, -pēsh\ *adj* [¹*snap* + *-ish*] **1 a :** given to snapping irritable speech **:** TESTY, IRASCIBLE ⟨a ~ old man⟩ ⟨a ~ disposition⟩ **b :** arising from a harsh irascible nature **:** curt and ungracious **:** CUTTING ⟨a ~ answer⟩ **2 :** inclined or accustomed to bite or snap ⟨a ~ dog⟩ **syn** see IRRITABLE

snap·pish·ly *adv* **:** in a snappish manner **:** with a snap

snap·pish·ness *n* -ES **:** the quality or state of being snappish

snap point *n* **:** SNAPHEAD

snap·py \ˈsnapē, -pi\ *adj* -ER/-EST [¹*snap* + *-y*] **1 :** SNAPPISH **2 :** quickly made or done **:** QUICK, SUDDEN **3 :** full of or characterized by liveliness, briskness, pungency, smartness, or similar quality ⟨~ conversation⟩: as **a** *of weather* **:** CRISP, BRISK **b :** exhibiting a high degree of style or pleasing show ⟨~ clothes⟩ ⟨a ~ dresser⟩ **4 :** emitting or constituting sparks or a series of sharp quick reports **:** CRACKLING ⟨a ~ sound⟩ **5** *of a photographic negative or positive* **:** having a high degree of contrast **syn** see PUNGENT

snappy gum *n, Austral* **:** a eucalyptus (esp. *Eucalyptus haemastoma*) with notably soft or brittle wood

snap ring *n* **1 :** a spring ring that is sprung open and snapped into place in its groove and is used esp. for a piston or other retaining ring function **2 :** an oval or pear-shaped ring used by rock climbers to fasten a rope to a piton

snap-rivet \ˈ=,==\ *vt* **:** to rivet by forming heads with a snap

snap roll *n* **:** a maneuver in which an airplane is made by quick movement of the controls to complete a full revolution about its longitudinal axis while maintaining an approximately level line of flight

¹snaps *pres 3d sing of* SNAP, *pl of* SNAP

²snaps \ˈsnaps, -näps\ *n, pl* **snaps** [Sw & Dan, lit., dram of liquor, fr. LG, dram, mouthful — more at SCHNAPPS] **:** an alcoholic beverage of Scandinavia consisting of ethyl alcohol flavored with various herbs

snapsack \ˈ=,=\ *n* [LG *snappsack*, fr. *snappen* to snap + *sack*, bag, sack — more at SNAP, KNAPSACK] *archaic* **:** KNAPSACK

snapshoot \ˈ=,=\ *vt* [back-formation fr. ¹*snapshot*] **:** to take a snapshot of

snap shooter *n* [⁴*snap* + *shooter*] **:** a gunner that is adept at snap shooting

snapshooter \ˈ=,==\ *n* [*snapshoot* + *-er*] **:** a person that takes snapshots

snap shooting *n* [⁴*snap*] **:** shooting (as a rifle) quickly and without taking deliberate aim with the sights

snap shot *n* [⁴*snap*] **:** a quick shot (as with a rifle) made without deliberately taking aim with the sights

¹snapshot \ˈ=,=\ *n* [⁴*snap* + *shot*] **1 :** a casual photograph made by rapid exposure and usu. with a small hand-held camera **2 :** a brief or transitory view; *also* **:** a mere segment ⟨the letters give us ~*s* of his progress⟩

²snapshot \"\ *adj* **1 :** of, relating to, or having the nature of a snapshot **2 :** produced or executed as hastily as a snapshot

³snapshot \"\ *vt* **snapshotted; snapshotted; snapshotting; snapshots :** SNAPSHOOT

snap·shot·ter \-äd·ə(r), -ätə-\ *n* -S *chiefly Brit* **:** SNAPSHOOTER

snap switch *n* **:** a manually operated electric switch with a blade which makes contact with a snap and in which the speed of making or breaking of the circuit is independent of the speed of operation of the switch

snap table *or* **snap-top table** *n* **:** a tip-top table whose top is held down by a snap catch

snap-the-whip \ˈ=,==ˈ=\ *n* **:** CRACK-THE-WHIP

snap tool *n* **:** SNAP 11a

snap trap *n* **:** a trap that snaps shut when the bait or trigger is disturbed: as **a :** a trap designed to imprison an animal unharmed in a suitable container **b :** a guillotine mouse or rat trap

snap turtle *n* **:** SNAPPING TURTLE

snap up *n, pl* **snap ups** [fr. *snap up*, v.] **:** KIP-UP

snapweed \ˈ=,=\ *n* **:** JEWELWEED

snap willow *n* **:** CRACK WILLOW

snapwood \ˈ=,=\ *n* **:** SPICEBUSH 1

¹snare \ˈsna(a)(ə)r, ˈsne|, |ə\ *n* -S [ME, fr. OE *sneare*, fr. ON *snara*; akin to MD *snaer* cord, string, MLG *snāre* cord, string, OHG *snaraha, snarha* noose, snare, *snuor* cord, Gk *narkē* numbness — more at NARROW] **1 a :** a contrivance typically consisting of a running noose (as of wire or cord) by which a bird or other animal may be caught; *broadly* **:** TRAP, GIN **b :** something by which one is entangled, involved in difficulties, held fast, or impeded in one's progress; *often* **:** something deceptively attractive **:** a misleading lure **2** [prob. fr. D *snaar*, lit., cord, string, fr. MD *snaer*] **a :** one of the gut strings or metal spirals of a snare drum **b :** SNARE DRUM **3 :** a surgical instrument consisting usu. of a wire loop or noose that can be constricted by a mechanism in the handle and used for removing tissue masses (as tonsils, polyps, granulations)

²snare \"\ *vt* -ED/-ING/-S [ME *snaren*, fr. *snare*, n.] **1 a :** to capture or gain possession of by or as if by use of a snare ⟨pigeons *snared* in a trap⟩ ⟨*snaring* the ball out of the air⟩ **b :** to win or attain by artful or skillful maneuvers ⟨~ an important appointment⟩ **2 :** to cause to become enmeshed in unanticipated complexities, difficulties, or distress **:** entangle as if in a snare ⟨urban dissipations that ~ unwary countrymen⟩ **syn** see CATCH

snare drum *n* **:** the smaller common military double-headed drum having a snare or snares stretched across its lower head and sounded by means of two wooden drumsticks — called also *side drum*; see DRUM illustration

snare head *n* **:** the lower head of a snare drum across which the snares are stretched — compare BATTER HEAD

snare·less \ˈ=ləs\ *adj* **:** free from snares

snar·er \ˈsna(a)rə(r), ˈsner-\ *n* -S **1 :** one that snares **2 :** one that uses snares (as in hunting)

snark \ˈsnärk, ˈsnåk\ *vi* [prob. alter. of *snork*] *dial Brit* **:** SNORE, SNORT

¹snarl *R* ˈsnärl, *chiefly before pause or consonant* -rəl, *-R* ˈsnål\ *n* -S [ME *snarle*, prob. fr. *snare* + *-le* (dim. suffix)] **1** *chiefly dial* **:** SNARE, NOOSE, GIN **2 a :** a tangle (as of hairs, thread, lines, plant growths) difficult or impossible to unravel ⟨a ~ of blackberry bushes and a matting underfoot of vine —Edmund Wilson⟩ ⟨a ~ of traffic⟩; *also* **:** a confused or disordered group or mass **:** SWARM ⟨a ~ of people arrived late⟩ **b :** a condition of complication or confusion making orderly procedure or progress difficult or impossible ⟨in the home of the direct primary . . . the system produced an inconclusive ~ —F.L.Paxson⟩ **syn** see CONFUSION

²snarl \"\ *vb* -ED/-ING/-S [ME *snarlen*, fr. *snarle*, n.] *vt* **1 a** *chiefly dial* **:** to catch in a snare or noose; *also* **:** hold fast in a knot or tangle **b** *obs* **:** STRANGLE **c** *obs* **:** to ensnare by arts or wiles as if by a noose; *also* **:** to bring (oneself) into a state of confused disorder **:** enmesh or entangle (oneself) in difficulties **2 :** to get into a tangle **:** cause to become knotted and intertwined ⟨~ one's hair⟩ **3 :** to make excessively or unduly complicated or confused ⟨~ a once simple problem⟩ ~ *vi* **:** to become tangled or snarled **:** be inclined to tangle ⟨this thread ~*s* easily⟩

³snarl \"\ *vb* -ED/-ING/-S [freq. of obs. E *snar* to growl, snarl; akin to MD *snarren* to hum, drone — more at SNORE] *vi* **1 :** to growl with a snapping or gnashing of the teeth (as of an angry dog) **:** utter angry or grumbling sounds with a display of teeth **2 :** to give vent to anger or irritation in rude surly language **:** quarrel, scold, complain, or otherwise show anger or disgust in a growling, snappish, or spiteful manner **3 :** to become expressed by a snarl ⟨their anger ~*s* forth in angry words⟩ ~ *vt* **1 :** to utter or express with a snarl or by snarling **2 :** to bring into a specified situation or condition by snarling ⟨~*ed* himself hoarse⟩

⁴snarl \"\ *n* -S **:** an act or the sound of snarling **:** a surly angry growl ⟨the ~ of the waves changed to a sullen roar⟩

⁵snarl \"\ *vt* -ED/-ING/-S [perh. fr. E dial. *snarl* knot in wood, fr. ¹*snarl*] **:** to form raised work upon the outer surface of (thin metal ware) by the repercussion of a snarling iron

⁶snarl \"\ *n* -S **:** an anvil whose horn has an upturned projecting point over which hollow sheet-metal work in process may be placed when it is to be ornamented with reliefs — compare SNARLING IRON

¹snarl·er \ˈsnärlər, ˈsnålə(r\ *n* -S [³*snarl* + *-er*] **:** one that snarls

²snarler \"\ *n* -S [⁵*snarl* + *-er*] **:** a user of a snarling iron

snarling iron *n* [*snarling* fr. gerund of ⁵*snarl*] **:** a tool with a long beak used in making raised work on metal surfaces by repercussion

snarl·ing·ly *adv* **:** in a snarling manner **:** with a snarl ⟨answered ~⟩

snarl·ish \-lish\ *adj* [³*snarl* + *-ish*] **:** disposed to snarl **:** ugly-tempered

¹snarly \-lē, -li\ *adj* -ER/-EST [¹*snarl* + *-y*] **:** full of tangles and snarls **:** TANGLED ⟨~ yarn⟩

²snarly \"\ *adj* -ER/-EST [³*snarl* + *-y*] **:** marked by snarling ill nature **:** SURLY, PEEVISH

¹snash \ˈsnash\ *n* [origin unknown] *chiefly Scot* **:** INSOLENCE, ABUSE, IMPERTINENCE

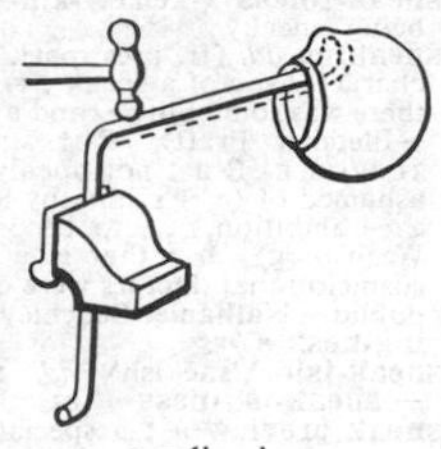

snarling iron

²snash \"\ *vi, chiefly Scot* **:** to speak or act disrespectfully or insolently

snaste *n* [origin unknown] *obs* **:** the wick of a snuffed candle

¹snatch \ˈsnach\ *vb* -ED/-ING/-ES [ME *snacchen, snecchen*; akin to MD *snacken* to snap at, bite, chatter, MLG & MHG *snacken* to chatter, gossip, ON *snaka* to sniff around, Norw *snake* to sniff around, snap at with the teeth] *vi* **1** *obs* **:** to give a sudden snap (as in anger or attack) **:** make a snappish attack **2 :** to attempt to seize something suddenly by or as if by snapping **:** catch at something — often used with *at* ⟨~ at a rope⟩ ~ *vt* **1 :** to take or grasp abruptly or hastily **:** seize (something) hurriedly or in passing ⟨~ a pen⟩ ⟨~*ed* the first opportunity⟩ ⟨~*ing* a glance at his friend⟩; *often* **:** to seize or grab suddenly without permission, ceremony, due process, or legal or moral right **:** steal, win, or otherwise gain irregularly when catching another unawares ⟨~ a kiss⟩ ⟨~*ing* victory from defeat⟩ **2 a :** to remove with suddenness (as by pulling, tearing, concealing, rescuing) — often used with *away* or *off* ⟨~ off his burning clothes⟩ **b :** to remove by death ⟨~*ed* from the bosom of his family⟩ **3 :** to insert (a rope) in a snatch block **4 :** to catch (a fish) by intentionally hooking the body rather than the mouth **syn** see TAKE — **snatch one baldheaded :** to rebuke severely or caustically

²snatch \"\ *n* -ES [ME *snacche*, fr. *snecchen, snacchen*, v.] **1** *obs* **:** TRAP, SNARE **2 :** a snatching at or of something **:** a quick catching or grabbing: as **a :** a lift in which the weight is raised from the floor to the overhead position in one rapid motion — compare CLEAN AND JERK, PRESS **b** *slang* (1) **:** KIDNAPPING (2) **:** a demand for something (as money) — used chiefly in *put the snatch on* ⟨put the ~ on him for a cut of the take⟩ **3 :** a snatched opportunity or period of time **:** an occasional period (as a moment or hour) ⟨sleep only in ~*es*⟩ ⟨work by ~*es*⟩ **4 :** something (as a short period, spell, or stint, an excerpt from a song, a few bars of a melody, a fleeting glimpse, a disconnected portion of a story, a snack) as brief, fragmentary, or hurried as if snatched or done in snatched time ⟨a ~ of spring in January⟩ ⟨sing ~es of old tunes⟩ ⟨you may have heard ~es of the story⟩ **5** *obs* **:** something (as a way of speaking or an argument) with a catch **6 a :** SNATCH BLOCK **b :** SNATCH HOOK **7 a :** VAGINA — usu. considered vulgar **b :** SEXUAL INTERCOURSE — usu. considered vulgar

snatch·able \-chəbəl\ *adj* **:** capable of being snatched

snatch block *n* **:** a block that can be opened on one side to receive the bight of a rope

snatched *adj* **:** that is snatched; *usu* **:** BRIEF, HURRIED ⟨a ~ moment of chat⟩

snatch·er \ˈsnachə(r)\ *n* -s **:** one that snatches: as **a :** THIEF; *esp* **:** one that snatches purses or other articles from his victims **b :** BODY SNATCHER **c :** KIDNAPPER **d :** a slaughterhouse worker who removes viscera

snatch hitch *n* **:** an easily made and broken hook hitch that is used to hook an extra team to a load for pulling it over a difficult spot and then to unhitch quickly while the load is in motion

snatch hook *n* **:** a gang hook designed specif. for foul-hooking fish

snatch·i·ly \-chəlē\ *adv* **:** in snatches **:** so as to be snatchy

snatching *pres part of* SNATCH

snatch·ing·ly *adv* **:** in a snatching manner **:** HURRIEDLY

snatch line *n* **:** a line by which something (as a piece of theatrical scenery) is snatched into position

snatch pickup *n* **:** an action wherein a flying airplane hooks onto a glider or a person or object on the ground and carries or tows it away through the air

snatch team *n* **:** TOW TEAM

snatchy \ˈsnachē, -chi\ *adj, often* -ER/-EST **:** done in or by snatches; *broadly* **:** marked by breaks in continuity **:** INTERRUPTED, SPASMODIC ⟨~ reading⟩ ⟨a ~ conversation⟩

snath \ˈsnath, -neth\ *or* **snathe** \-nāth, -nāth\ *or* **snead** \-nēd,-nād,-ned\ *or* **sneath** \-nēth,-nēth\ *n* -s [ME *snede*, fr. OE *snǣd;* akin to OE *snīthan* to cut, OHG *snīdan*, ON *snītha;* akin to Ukr *snit* block, chunk, Czech *snět* branch, and perh. to MIr *snēid* small, short] **:** the handle of a scythe

snav·vle \ˈsnavəl\ *vt* [alter. of ²*snaffle*] *Austral* **:** to get hold of by fair means or foul **:** rustle up

snaw \ˈsnȯ, ˈsnä\ *chiefly Scot var of* SNOW

snaz·zi·ness \ˈsnazēnə̇s, -zin-\ *n* -ES **:** the quality or state of being snazzy

snaz·zy \-zē, -zi\ *adj* -ER/-EST [origin unknown] **1 :** outstanding in style **:** conspicuously or flashily attractive ⟨his suit was pretty ~ —Wallace Stegner⟩ ⟨a pretty ~ place —Paul Gallico⟩ **2 :** very pleasing ⟨smooth, ~ tunes —E.T.Canby⟩

snd *abbr* sound

SND *abbr* **1** *often not cap* sap no defect **2** static no delivery

¹**sneak** \ˈsnēk\ *vb* **sneaked** \-kt\ *or chiefly dial* **snuck** \ˈsnək\ *or dial* **snook** \ˈsnu̇k\ **sneaked** *or chiefly dial* **snuck; sneaking; sneaks** [akin to OE *snīcan* to creep, sneak along, ON *snīkja* to hanker, Dan *snige* to sneak, OHG *snahhan* to creep — more at SNAIL] *vi* **1 a :** to go stealthily or furtively **:** creep or steal so as to be unobserved ⟨would ~ out over the back fence to avoid boys who were laying for me —John Reed⟩ **:** SLINK ⟨~*ed* away after his ignominious defeat⟩ **b :** to get oneself out or past or through by furtive or artful means ⟨~ out of a difficulty⟩ ⟨his papers always ~ past the examiners⟩ **2 :** to behave in a furtive or servile manner **3 :** to cross a football goal line and score by a quarterback sneak — usu. used with *over* ~ *vt* **1 :** to put, bring, or take in a furtive or artful manner **:** get surreptitiously ⟨~ in a stop at a bar⟩ ⟨~ Christmas gifts into the house⟩ ⟨~ a look at the book during the test⟩ ⟨~ a smoke while the nurse is out⟩; *specif* **:** steal in the manner of a sneak thief ⟨caught him ~*ing* tomatoes when he thought no one was home⟩ **2 a :** to cause (radio or television sound) to come or go with a very gradual change of volume — used with *in* or *out* **b :** to bring in (radio or television sound) at a very low volume ⟨~ bar sounds⟩ **syn** see LURK

²**sneak** \"\ *n* -s **1 :** a person who acts in a stealthy, furtive, or shifty manner **:** a sneaky person; *specif* **:** SNEAK THIEF **2 a :** a stealthy or furtive move **b :** an unobserved departure or escape **3 :** SNEAKER 3 — usu. used in pl. **4 :** the opening lead of a singleton in a card game (as bridge) **5 :** SNEAK PREVIEW **6 :** QUARTERBACK SNEAK — **on the sneak** *adv* **:** in a clandestine manner ⟨speakeasies and clubs . . . operated *on the sneak* —Polly Adler⟩

³**sneak** \"\ *adj* **1 :** carried on secretly **:** CLANDESTINE ⟨handbook operations . . . are now operating on a ~ basis —*New Orleans (La.) Times-Picayune*⟩ **2 :** occurring without warning **:** SURPRISE ⟨a ~ attack⟩ ⟨a ~ flood⟩

sneak boat *n* **:** a boat used in approaching unobserved; *esp* **:** SNEAK BOX

sneak box *n* **:** a boat orig. built for duck shooting having a spoon-shaped bottom and deck with a small cockpit and a dagger board and usu. a boom and gaff mainsail and jib

sneak–cup *n* [¹*sneak* + *cup*] *obs* **:** one who fails to drink his share

sneak current *n* **:** an electric current that though too feeble to blow the usual fuse or to injure at once telegraph or telephone instruments will in time burn them out

sneak·er \ˈsnēkə(r)\ *n* -s **1 :** one that sneaks **2 :** PUNCH BOWL **3 :** a shoe usu. of canvas with a pliable rubber sole worn esp. for sports or hiking — usu. used in pl.; compare TENNIS SHOE

sneak·i·ly \-kəlē, -li\ *adv* **:** in a sneaky manner

sneak·i·ness \-kēnə̇s, -kin-\ *n* -ES **:** the quality or state of being sneaky

sneaking *adj* [fr. pres. part. of ¹*sneak*] **1 :** that sneaks or is characteristic of a sneak **:** FURTIVE, UNDERHAND ⟨felt . . . that there was something ~ and unclean about secret code messages —Fletcher Pratt⟩ **2 :** MEAN, NIGGARDLY, PALTRY, CONTEMPTIBLE **3 a :** not openly expressed as if something to be ashamed of ⟨a ~ sympathy for the rascal⟩ ⟨I have always had a ~ ambition . . . to become a conductor myself —Joseph Wechsberg⟩ **b :** that is a persistent conjecture ⟨had a ~ suspicion that doctors were only one step ahead of the general public —Nathaniel Benchley⟩ — **sneak·ing·ly** *adv* — **sneak·ing·ness** *n* -ES

sneak·ish \ˈsnēkish\ *adj* **:** SNEAKY — **sneak·ish·ly** *adv* — **sneak·ish·ness** *n* -ES

sneak preview *n* **:** a special advanced showing of a motion picture usu. announced but not named

sneaks·by \ˈsnēksbē\ *n* -ES [²*sneak* + *-sby* (as in such proper names as *Grimsby, Ormesby*)] **:** SNEAK

sneak shooting *n* **:** shooting from a sneak boat

sneak thief *n* **:** a thief who steals whatever he can reach without using violence or forcibly breaking into buildings

sneak–up \ˈ=,=\ *n* -s [fr. *sneak up*, v.] **:** SNEAK

sneaky \ˈsnēkē, -ki\ *adj* -ER/-EST **:** marked by stealth, furtiveness, or shiftiness **:** that sneaks or is done in a sneaking manner **:** characteristic of a sneak ⟨a ~ two-faced fellow who breaks all the rules when your back is turned⟩ ⟨called the policeman's hiding behind the billboard a ~ trick⟩

¹**sneap** \ˈsnēp\ *vt* -ED/-ING/-S [ME *snaipen*, prob. of Scand origin; akin to ON *sneypa* to dishonor, disgrace, Icel, to scold, rebuke, OSw *snöpa* to castrate, ON *snubba* to scold — more at SNUB] **1** *dial Eng* **:** CHIDE, REPROVE, CHASTEN ⟨she had a tongue for the ~*ing* of too casual boys —Arnold Bennett⟩ **2** *archaic* **:** to blast or blight with cold **:** NIP ⟨like an envious ~*ing* frost that bites the first born infants of the spring —Shak.⟩

²**sneap** \"\ *n* -s *archaic* **:** REBUKE, SNUB

sneath *var of* SNATH

sneb *var of* SNIB

¹**sneck** \ˈsnek\ *n* -s [ME *snekk, snekke;* prob. akin to ME *snecchen, snacchen* to snatch — more at SNATCH] **1** *dial Brit* **:** the latch or catch of a door **2** *chiefly dial* **:** a clicking sound

²**sneck** \"\ *vb* -ED/-ING/-S [ME *snekken*, fr. *snekk, snekke*, n.] *vt, dial Brit* **:** to fasten (a gate or door) with a latch ~ *vi, dial Brit* **:** LATCH

³**sneck** \"\ *vb* -ED/-ING/-S [origin unknown] *chiefly dial* **:** ¹SNICK

⁴**sneck** \"\ *vt* -ED/-ING/-S [origin unknown] **:** to lay (rubblework) with spalls and fragments to fill the interstices

⁵**sneck** \"\ *n* -s **:** a small roughly squared stone used in snecking

sneckdraw \ˈ=,=\ *or* **sneck drawer** *n* [*sneckdraw* fr. ¹*sneck* + *draw* (v.); *sneck drawer* fr. ME *snek-drawer*, fr. *snek, snekk* sneck + *drawer*] *chiefly Scot* **:** a sly crafty person trying to worm his way in

sneck up *vi* [*sneck* of unknown origin] *chiefly dial* **:** to make oneself scarce — usu. used in the phrase *go sneck up*

sned \ˈsned\ *vt* [ME *sneden*, fr. OE *snǣdan* to cut off, slice — more at SNATH] *chiefly Scot* **:** to lop off (vegetation) **:** PRUNE

¹**sneer** \ˈsni(ə)r, -iə\ *vb* -ED/-ING/-S [prob. akin to MHG *snerren* to chatter, gossip — more at SNORE] *vi* **1** *dial chiefly Brit* **:** to snort in the manner of an animal **2 a :** to smile or laugh with facial contortions that express scorn or contempt **b :** to manifest derision, disdain, or contempt by speaking or writing in a scornfully jeering manner ⟨people are nowadays so cynical — they ~ at everything that makes life worth living —L.P.Smith⟩ **3 :** to make a sound like a sneer ⟨a bullet ~*ing* overhead⟩ ~ *vt* **1 :** to utter with a sneer or sneeringly ⟨~ a reply⟩ **2** *archaic* **:** to treat with sneers **:** sneer at **syn** see SCOFF

²**sneer** \"\ *n* -s **:** the act of sneering **:** a sneering expression, remark, or saying ⟨the lips are pursed in a scornful, supercilious ~ —Harry Luke⟩ ⟨the current ~ that both parties are without cardinal distinctive principles —*No. Amer. Rev.*⟩

sneer·er \-rə(r)\ *n* -s **:** one that sneers

sneer·ful \ˈ=fəl\ *adj* **:** given to sneering

sneer·ing·ly *adv* **:** in a sneering manner

sneer·less \ˈ=lə̇s\ *adj* **:** being without a sneer

sneery \-rē, -ri\ *adj, often* -ER/-EST **:** given to or marked by sneering

sneesh \ˈsnēsh, -nish\ *n* [short for *sneeshing*] *dial Brit* **:** SNUFF

sneesh·ing \ˈsnēshən, -nish-, -shiŋ\ *n* -s [alter. of *sneezing*, fr. gerund of *sneeze*] **1** *dial Brit* **:** SNUFF; *specif* **:** a pinch of snuff **2** *dial Brit* **:** a thing of little value or significance

¹**sneeze** \ˈsnēz\ *vb* -ED/-ING/-S [ME *snesen*, alter. of *fnesen*, fr. OE *fnēosan;* akin to MHG *pfnūsen* to snort, sneeze, ON *fnȳsa* to snort, Gk *pnein* to breathe] *vi* **1 :** to make a sudden violent spasmodic audible expiration of breath through the nose and mouth usu. as a reflex act following irritation of the nasal mucous membrane **2 :** to make a sound like a sneeze ⟨the last wind snarls and ~s —Thomas Hardy⟩ ~ *vt* **1 :** to utter or give forth with a sneeze **2 :** to cause to be or go by sneezing ⟨~ germs over everyone⟩ **3** *slang* **:** to place under arrest — **sneeze at :** to treat lightly **:** DESPISE, CONTEMN — usu. used in the phrase *not to be sneezed at* ⟨there must be many thousands more to whom two dollars is not to be *sneezed at* —*Saturday Rev.*⟩

²**sneeze** \"\ *n* -s **1 :** the act or fact of sneezing **:** a sudden violent audible spasmodic expiration through the nose and mouth **2** *slang* **:** ARREST

sneeze gas *also* **sneezing gas** *n* **:** STERNUTATOR

sneeze·less \ˈ=ləs\ *adj* **:** having no sneeze **:** being unlikely to cause sneezing

sneez·er \ˈsnēzə(r)\ *n* -s **1 :** one that sneezes **2** *slang* **a :** NOSE **b :** a drink of spirits **c :** one that is exceptional or superlative in some respect ⟨a terrible powerful man he was — a real ~ —T.C.Haliburton⟩ **d :** JAIL

sneezeweed \ˈ=,=\ *n* **1 :** any of several plants of the genus *Helenium:* as **a :** a No. American yellow-flowered perennial herb (*H. autumnale*) the odor of which is said to cause sneezing **b :** a stout perennial herb (*H. hoopesii*) of the western U.S. causing spewing sickness in sheep **2 :** a weed (*Centipeda orbicularis*) of the family Compositae of Australia and Tasmania **3 :** SNEEZEWORT 2

sneezewood \ˈ=,=\ *n* **1 :** a South African timber tree (*Ptaeroxylon utile*) of the family Meliaceae **2 :** the hard valuable wood of the sneezewood tree that yields sawdust which causes sneezing

sneezewort \ˈ=,=\ *n* **1** *obs* **:** WHITE HELLEBORE **2 :** a strong-scented Eurasian perennial herb (*Achillea ptarmica*) resembling yarrow but having simple leaves and large flower heads **3 :** SNEEZEWEED 1

sneezy \ˈsnēzē, -zi\ *adj* -ER/-EST **:** given to or causing sneezing

¹**snell** \ˈsnel\ *adj* -ER/-EST [ME *snel, snell*, fr. OE *snell* quick, active, bold; akin to OHG *snel* strong, bold, agile, OS, fresh, active, bold, ON *snjallr* well-spoken, brave] **1** *chiefly dial* **a :** acting or moving swiftly **:** QUICK, EAGER **b :** SHARP-WITTED, ACUTE **2 :** having a keen edge **:** PIERCING, BITING ⟨a ~ wind blew down the street —Christopher Morley⟩

²**snell** \"\ *adv* [ME, fr. OE *snel, snell*, adj.] *dial chiefly Brit* **:** QUICKLY, SWIFTLY, VIGOROUSLY

³**snell** \"\ *n* -s [origin unknown] **:** a short line (as of gut or nylon) by which a fishhook is attached to a longer line

⁴**snell** \"\ *vt* -ED/-ING/-S **:** to attach to or by a snell

snel·len test \ˈsnelən-\ *n, usu cap S* [after Herman *Snellen* †1908 Dutch ophthalmologist] **:** a test for visual acuity presenting letters of graduated sizes to determine the smallest size that can be read at a standard distance

snell's law \ˈsnelz-\ *n, usu cap S* [after Willebrord *Snell* van Royen (Willebrord *Snellius*) †1626 Dutch mathematician] **:** a law in physics: the ratio of the sines of the angles of incidence and refraction is constant for all incidences in any given pair of media for electromagnetic waves of a definite frequency

¹**snel·ly** \ˈsnel(l)i\ *adv* [ME, fr. OE *snellīce*, fr. *snellīc* smart, ready, quick, bold, fr. *snell* + *-līc* -ly] *dial chiefly Brit* **:** SNELL

²**snelly** \-eli\ *adj* [¹*snell* + *-y*] *Scot* **:** CHILL, SHARP

snerp *var of* SNURP

¹**snew** \ˈsn(y)ü\ *vi* [ME *sniwen, snewen*, fr. OE *snīwan;* akin to MD & MLG *snīen* to snow, OHG *snīwan* to snow, ON *snȳr* it is snowing, OE *snāw* snow — more at SNOW] *dial* **:** SNOW

²**snew** \"\ [ME] *dial past of* SNOW

SNF *abbr* solids not fat

¹**snib** \ˈsnib\ *also* **sneb** \ˈsneb\ *vt* **snibbed; snibbed; snibbing; snibs** [ME *snibben*, prob. of Scand origin; akin to obs. Dan *snibbe* to scold, rebuke, obs. Sw *snybba*, ON *snubba* — more at SNUB] **1** *dial Brit* **:** CHECK, RESTRAIN **2** *dial Brit* **:** REBUKE, SNUB **3** *dial Brit* **:** to put an end to **:** cut short

²**snib** \ˈsnib\ *n* -s [ME *snybb*, fr. *snibben*, v.] *chiefly Scot* **:** REBUFF, SNUB

³**snib** \"\ *vt* **snibbed; snibbed; snibbing; snibs** [origin unknown] *Scot* **:** FASTEN, BOLT, BAR ⟨*snibbed* the door —J.M. Barrie⟩

⁴**snib** \"\ *n* -s [origin unknown] *dial Brit* **:** a door fastening **:** BOLT, CATCH

¹**snick** \ˈsnik\ *vb* -ED/-ING/-S [prob. back-formation fr. *snickersnee*] *vt* **1 :** to cut slightly **:** SNIP, NICK ⟨the razor ~*ed* my Adam's-apple —*Sydney (Australia) Bull.*⟩ **2 :** to strike sharply **:** pierce with a thrust **3 :** to hit (a cricket ball) a glancing blow with the edge of the bat usu. inadvertently ~ *vi* **:** to cut, snip, or nick something ⟨~ at the skin until you can get a hold of the splinter with the tweezers —Peter Heaton⟩

²**snick** \"\ *n* -s **1 :** a small cut **:** SNIP, NICK **2 a :** the act or an instance of snicking (as in cricket) **b :** a snicked ball in cricket ⟨with the bat at an angle the most likely result is a ~ —*Calling All Cricketers*⟩

³**snick** \"\ *n* -s [alter. of ²*snack*] *chiefly dial* **:** SHARE — **go snicks** *chiefly dial* **:** SHARE

⁴**snick** \"\ *chiefly dial var of* ¹SNECK

⁵**snick** \"\ *vb* -ED/-ING/-S [imit.] *vt* **:** to put or move so as to make a clicking sound ⟨~*ed* his dagger in and out of the sheath —Donn Byrne⟩ ~ *vi* **:** to make a click ⟨bolts ~*ed* sharply as cartridges snapped into chambers —J.W.Bellah⟩

⁶**snick** \"\ *n* -s **:** a cutting or clicking noise ⟨the plane made a pleasant ~ as it shaved a long wooden curl —Luis Marden⟩ ⟨he clicked on the safety; it made a metallic ~ —Arthur Gordon⟩

⁷**snick** \"\ *n* -s [origin unknown] **:** a knot or irregularity in yarn or wire

¹**snick·er** \ˈsnikə(r)\ *or* **snig·ger** \ˈsnigə(r)\ *vb* **snickered** *or* **sniggered; snickered** *or* **sniggered; snickering** \-k(ə)riŋ\ *or* **sniggering** \-g(ə)riŋ\ **snickers** *or* **sniggers** [imit.] *vi* **1 :** to laugh in a slight, covert, or partly suppressed manner (as in derision or from embarrassment) ⟨they ~ at my graftin', and I laugh in my sleeve . . . at their penetration —T.C.Haliburton⟩ ⟨a fantastic caricature of the Edwardian dandy his grandfather probably ~*ed* at —P.D.Whitney⟩ ⟨like a small boy taking you into a corner to *snigger* at a bawdy story —H.J.Laski⟩ **:** TITTER ⟨chuckled at his readers, ~*ed* at his correspondents, smiled at his own folly —Martin Gardner⟩ **2 :** to make a sound like a snicker ⟨the irreverent red squirrels . . . run and ~ at my approach —John Burroughs⟩ ~ *vt* **:** to utter with or express by a snicker

²**snicker** \"\ *or* **snigger** \"\ *n* -s **:** an act or sound of snickering **:** a slight, covert, or half-stifled laugh ⟨from innuendo, a dropped word here and there, a sly, meaningful ~ —H.A. Sinclair⟩ ⟨raises in you a ~ of derision, a smile of superiority —J.M.Barzun⟩

snick·er·er \ˈsnik(ə)rə(r)\ *n* -s **:** one that snickers

snick·er·ing·ly *adv* **:** in a snickering manner

¹**snick·er·snee** \ˈsnikə(r)ˌsnē, ˌ=ˈ=\ *or* **snick and snee** \-kən|\ *or* **snick–or–snee** \-kə(r)|\ *vi* [alter. of earlier *steake or snye, stick or snee*, fr. D *steken of snijden* to thrust or cut or *steken en snijden* to thrust and cut] *archaic* **:** to engage in cut-and-thrust fighting with knives

²**snickersnee** \"\ *or* **snick–a–snee** \-kə|\ *or* **snick–or–snee** \-kə(r)|\ *n* -s **1** *archaic* **:** the act or practice of engaging in cut-and-thrust fighting with knives **2 :** a large knife or sword

snick·et \ˈsnikə̇t\ *n* -s [³*snick* + *-et*] *dial Eng* **:** something very small or insignificant of its kind

¹**snick·le** \ˈsnikəl\ *vt* -ED/-ING/-S [origin unknown] *dial Brit* **:** SNARE, NOOSE

²**snickle** \"\ *n* -s *dial Brit* **:** SNARE, NOOSE

snick up *var of* SNECK UP

snid·dle \ˈsnidᵊl\ *n* [ME *snyth hill;* prob. akin to OE *snīthan* to cut — more at SNATH] *dial Eng* **:** coarse grass or sedge

¹**snide** \ˈsnīd\ *adj* -ER/-EST [origin unknown] **1 a :** COUNTERFEIT, SPURIOUS ⟨some contractors use ~ oils knowingly, and . . . some have doped linseed oil palmed off on them —Frederick Maire⟩ **b :** practicing deception **:** DISHONEST, CROOKED ⟨taken in by a ~ merchant⟩ **c :** designed to deceive **:** TRICKY ⟨this is a ~ bill, full of tricks and man-traps —H.L.Ickes⟩ **2 :** MEAN, BASE, LOW, CHEAP ⟨tied to a ~ job in a ~ town —Fannie Hurst⟩ ⟨a ~ trick⟩ **3 :** slyly disparaging **:** subtly derisive **:** INSINUATING ⟨she makes many a sharp comparison, but never a mean or ~ one —Bernardine Kielty⟩ ⟨draws a line between legitimate reporting and ~ muckraking —Don Weldon⟩ **4 :** showing malice ⟨nothing very deep or ~, merely good, clean spoofing —*N.Y.World-Telegram*⟩

²**snide** \"\ *n* -s **:** a snide person or thing

sni·der \ˈsnīdə(r)\ *n* -s *usu cap* [after Jacob *Snider* †1866 Amer. inventor] **:** a breech-loading rifle converted from a muzzle-loading rifle and used in the British military service in the late 1860s and early 1870s

snid·ery \-dərē\ *n* -ES [¹*snide* + *-ery*] **:** the practice of sly malicious disparagement

¹**sniff** \ˈsnif\ *vb* -ED/-ING/-S [ME *sniffen;* prob. akin to ME *snivelen* to snivel — more at SNIVEL] *vi* **1 a :** to draw air audibly up the nose **:** smell or snuff with short audible inhalations ⟨lifted the lids of pots and pans, ~*ed* appreciatively —Winifred Bambrick⟩ ⟨~ at several perfumes before choosing one⟩; *also* **:** to clear the nose of mucus by sniffing ⟨got a runny nose and began to ~⟩ **b :** to make a sniffing noise (as to express disdain) ⟨asked what stipend he might expect, and on being enlightened . . . ~*ed* loudly and disdainfully —Elinor Wylie⟩ **2 :** to show or express disdain or scorn **:** be contemptuous — usu. used with *at* ⟨like all who had read through the four volumes she could ~ at those who knew but the abridged versions —J.D.Hart⟩ **3 :** take a curious or suspicious look ⟨turning . . . to politics, he might finance some lunatic group or ~ suspiciously around public libraries —T.D.Parrish⟩ ~ *vt* **1 :** to smell or take by inhalation through the nose ⟨a pack of bloodhounds eagerly ~*ing* the ground⟩ **:** INHALE ⟨threw open the window and ~*ed* the fresh morning air⟩ ⟨addicts who ~ cocaine⟩ **2 :** to utter or express with a sniff or with disdain or scorn ⟨men, she ~*ed*, were poor creatures —Laura Krey⟩ **3 :** to recognize or detect by or as if by smelling ⟨excelled . . . in ~*ing* trouble before it began —*Times Lit. Supp.*⟩ — often used with *out* ⟨German shepherd dogs are parachuted in the Austrian Alps to ~ *out* survivors of avalanches —P.T.White⟩

²**sniff** \"\ *n* -s **1 :** an act or sound of sniffing ⟨the aspirant must school and steel himself to ~s and sneers —H.L. Mencken⟩ ⟨the coughs, sneezes, and ~s of those who had colds⟩ **2 :** a quantity that is sniffed ⟨got a good ~ of sea air⟩ **3 a :** MUGGINS 1b **b :** the first doublet played in the game of muggins

sniff·er \ˈsnifə(r)\ *n* -s **:** one that sniffs

sniff·i·ly \-fəlē, -li\ *adv* **:** in a sniffy manner **:** DISDAINFULLY, SNIFFINGLY ⟨listening to the volume of booing, he said rather ~, "I am not at all impressed" —*Time*⟩

sniff·i·ness \-fēnə̇s, -fin-\ *n* -ES **:** the quality or state of being sniffy

sniff·ing·ly *adv* **:** in a sniffing manner

sniff·ish \ˈsnifish, -fēsh\ *adj* [¹*sniff* + *-ish*] **:** given to sniffing scornfully **:** HAUGHTY, DISDAINFUL, SUPERCILIOUS ⟨an essentially aristocratic movement — superior, ~ and antidemocratic —H.L.Mencken⟩ — **sniff·ish·ly** *adv* — **sniff·ish·ness** *n* -ES

snif·fle \ˈsnifəl\ *vi* **sniffled; sniffled; snif·fling** \-f(ə)liŋ\ **sniffles** [freq. of ¹*sniff*] **1 :** to sniff repeatedly to prevent mucus running from the nose (as in a cold) **2 :** to speak with or as if with sniffling **:** SNIVEL

²**sniffle** \"\ *n* -s **1 :** an act or sound of sniffling **2 sniffles** *pl* **a :** the nasal symptoms (as discharge and congestion) associated with or characteristic of infection of the respiratory tract **b :** a head cold marked by nasal discharge **3 sniffles** *pl but usu sing in constr* **:** bullnose of swine

snif·fler \-f(ə)lə(r)\ *n* -s **:** one that sniffles

sniffle valve *n* **:** SNIFTER VALVE

snif·fly \-f(ə)lē, -li\ *adj* **:** that sniffles

sniffy \ˈsnifē, -fi\ *adj* **:** inclined to sniff haughtily or scornfully **:** DISDAINFUL, SUPERCILIOUS ⟨pay tradesmen . . . in the ~ manner of one whose main purpose in arriving at the shop was to take the dog for a walk —*Punch*⟩

snift \ˈsnift\ *vb* -ED/-ING/-S [short for ¹*snifter*] *chiefly dial* **:** SNIFF

¹**snif·ter** \ˈsniftə(r)\ *vi* [ME *snifteren;* prob. akin to ME *snivelen* to snivel — more at SNIVEL] *dial* **:** SNIFF, SNORT, SNUFFLE

²**snifter** \"\ *n* -s **1** *dial* **a :** SNIFF, SNORT **b snifters** *pl* **:** a cold in the head **2** *dial* **:** a severe wind or storm **3** *Austral* **:** one that is outstanding **:** RIPSNORTER **4 a :** a small drink of distilled liquor **b :** a small amount of a narcotic ⟨takes an occasional ~ of opium —*Time*⟩ **5 :** an addict who takes cocaine by inhaling it **6 :** a large short-stemmed goblet with a bowl narrowing toward the top in which the aroma of brandy can be savored before drinking — called also *inhaler*

snifter 6

snifter valve *or* **snift·ing valve** *n* **1 :** a small valve opening into the atmosphere from a cylinder, from a condenser, or from the air chamber of a steam pump to allow the escape or entrance of air and the release of accumulated water at each stroke of the piston — called also *sniffle valve* **2 :** any of various valves (as in an internal combustion engine) resembling a snifter valve

snif·ty \ˈsniftē\ *adj* **1 :** SNIFFY **2 :** PETTY, MEAN

¹**snig** \ˈsnig\ *n* -s [ME *snygge;* perh. akin to OE *snægl* snail — more at SNAIL] *dial chiefly Eng* **:** a small eel

²**snig** \"\ *vt* **snigged; snigged; snigging; snigs** [origin unknown] **1** *chiefly dial* **:** to chop off **:** LOP **2 a** *chiefly dial* **:** to drag jerkily **b :** to snake or drag (a log) with a rope or chain

¹**snigger** *var of* SNICKER

²**snig·ger** \ˈsnigə(r)\ *n* -s [prob. alter. of ²*sniggle*] *Brit* **:** a fish spear or grapple used esp. by salmon poachers

snig·gers \-gə(r)z\ *interj* [alter. of *God's nigs*, euphemism for *God's nails*] *archaic* — used as a mild oath

¹**snig·gle** \ˈsnigəl\ *vb* **sniggled; sniggled; sniggling** \-g(ə)liŋ\ **sniggles** [¹*snig* + *-le*] *vi* **:** to fish for eels by thrusting the baited hook or needle into their hiding places ~ *vt* **1 :** to catch (an eel) by sniggling **2 :** CREEP, CRAWL, SNEAK **3 :** to catch (as a salmon) by direct snatching with a hook or snare

²**sniggle** \"\ *n* -s **:** a device used in sniggling eels; *esp* **:** a needle to which a line is secured at the middle

³**sniggle** \"\ *vi* [alter. of *snigger*] *chiefly dial* **:** SNICKER

snig·gler \-g(ə)lə(r)\ *n* -s **:** one that sniggles

¹**snip** \ˈsnip\ *n* -s [fr. or akin to D & LG *snip* small piece, snip] **1 a :** a small piece that is snipped off ⟨cut a paper into ~s⟩; *also* **:** something very small **:** FRAGMENT, PARTICLE, BIT ⟨an essay seasoned with ~s from great poets⟩ **b :** a cut, incision, or notch made by snipping ⟨an armhole formed by a ~ in the fabric⟩ **c :** an act or sound of snipping **:** a single stroke of shears or scissors ⟨with a ~ of his shears⟩ ⟨heard the busy ~ of her scissors⟩ **2 :** a small stripe or spot of white on an

animal's face; *esp* **:** a white spot between the nostrils of a horse **3** *archaic* **:** TAILOR **4 :** a presumptuous or impertinent person (as a saucy girl) **:** UPSTART, MINX ⟨the little ~ — the nerve of her —Tom Walters⟩ **5** *archaic* **:** SHARE ⟨let me go ~ with you in this lie —John Dryden⟩ **6** *Brit* **a :** something certain of achievement **:** a sure thing ⟨it is a ~; we will get both of them, and also the guns —Nevil Shute⟩ **b :** a purchase certain not to disappoint **:** a good value for the price **:** BARGAIN, BUY ⟨a real ~⟩ ⟨one small donkey cart . . . a ~ at £15 —*Farmer's Weekly (So. Africa)*⟩

²snip \"\ *vb* **snipped; snipped; snipping; snips** [fr. or akin to D & LG *snippen* to snip; akin to MHG *snipfen* to snap the fingers] *vt* **1** *obs* **:** to snatch quickly **:** snap off; *also* **:** FILCH **2 :** to cut with or as if with shears or scissors ⟨~ off the surplus thread⟩; *specif* **:** to clip suddenly or by bits ⟨~ his budget until it is within his income⟩ **3** *chiefly dial* **a :** to mar by snipping or chipping a piece from **:** CHIP **b :** CURB, CHECK **4 :** to make a snip with (shears or scissors) ~ *vi* **1 :** to make a cut with or as if with shears or scissors; *specif* **:** to make a short quick cut **2 :** to make the characteristic short cutting sound of shears or scissors

¹snipe \'snīp\ *n, pl* **snipes** *also* **snipe** [ME, of Scand origin; akin to ON *snīpa* snipe; akin to MD *snippe* snipe, OHG *snepfa*, and prob. to OHG *snabul* beak — more at NEB] **1 a :** any of several game birds (genus *Capella*) that are widely distributed in the New and Old Worlds esp. in marshy areas, resemble but are slenderer than the related woodcocks and like these have very long slender bills with which they probe in mud after worms and other food, and are usu. variegated above with blackish brown, buff, and chestnut and barred on the tail and sides — see GREAT SNIPE, JACKSNIPE, WHOLE SNIPE, WILSON'S SNIPE **b :** any of various usu. slender-billed birds (as a dowitcher or some of the sandpipers and tattlers) of the suborder Charadrii and esp. of the families Charadriidae or Scolopacidae — usu. used with a qualifying term ⟨the red-breasted ~⟩ **2 a :** a contemptible person **b** *slang* **:** a railway section hand **c** *slang* **:** an enlisted man in the engineering division of a naval vessel **3** *slang* **:** a butt of a smoked cigar or cigarette **4 :** an outdoor advertising poster **5 :** an act of sniping **6** *usu cap* **:** a racing sailboat approximately 15½ feet long and Marconi sloop rigged

²snipe \"\ *vb* -ED/-ING/-S *vi* **1 :** to shoot or hunt snipe **2 a :** to shoot at exposed individuals of an enemy's forces esp. when not in action from a usu. concealed and removed point of vantage ⟨a rifleman missed in mopping up the ridge *sniped* at anyone moving about the camp in an officer's uniform⟩ **b :** to aim a carping or snide attack (as at a competitor) **:** take damagingly critical or sly swipes ⟨other parties of all political shadings have been *sniping* at his regime —Robert Trumbull⟩ **3 :** to post an advertising bill on an available surface (as a post, tree, wall) without permission ~ *vt* **1 :** to shoot at from a usu. concealed and removed point of vantage ⟨~ the enemy column from the treetops⟩ **2 :** to round the end of (a log) for easy skidding

snipe eel *n* **:** any of various very slender deep-sea eels of the family Nemichthyidae having long sometimes recurved beaks — called also *thread eel*

snipefish \'ˌ=ˌ=\ *n* **:** BELLOWS FISH

snipe fly *n* **:** a fly of the family Rhagionidae

snipe hinge *n* **:** an early American Colonial furniture hinge consisting of a pair of half-round iron wires doubled back like cotter pins, linked by the eyes, and clinched into the wood at the sharp outer ends

snipe hinge

snipe hunt *n* **:** a practical joke in which the victim is left in a remote spot holding a bag for fictitious snipe to run into

snipe-nosed \'=ˌ=\ *adj* **:** SNIPY — used esp. of dogs

snip·er \'snīpə(r)\ *n* -S **:** one that snipes: as **a :** one that fires at exposed men of an enemy's force **b :** a worker who snipes logs for skidding **2 :** a prospector or placer miner who works abandoned claims

snip·er·scope \'==ˌskōp\ *n* **1 :** a device based on the principle of the periscope, attached to a rifle near the rear sight and projecting downward into a trench, and used by a soldier to aim and fire his rifle without exposing himself **2 :** a snooperscope for use on a rifle or carbine

snip·i·ness \'snīpēnəs, -pin-\ *n* -ES **:** the quality or state of being snipy

snipped *past of* SNIP

snip·per \'snipə(r)\ *n* -S **:** one that snips: as **a :** a worker who trims off edges (as of hides or sheet metal) **b :** NICKER

snip·per·snap·per \'snipə(r)ˌsnapə(r)\ *n* [origin unknown] **:** WHIPPERSNAPPER

snip·pet \'snipət, *usu* -əd·+V\ *n* -S [¹*snip* + *-et*] **:** a small part, piece, or thing; *specif* **:** a brief literary quotation or quotable passage ⟨on notes ~*s* of information about a few African tribes —*Times Lit. Supp.*⟩

snip·pety \'snipəd·ē, -atē, -i\ *adj* **1 :** that is a snippet **:** ridiculously small **:** PETTY **2 :** made up of snippets ⟨a rather ~ anthology⟩ **3 :** unduly brief or curt **:** SNIPPY ⟨had been ~ to her former friends since she inherited money⟩

snip·pi·ness \-pēnəs, -pin-\ *n* -ES **:** the quality or state of being snippy

snipping *n* -S [fr. gerund of ²*snip*] **:** something snipped off or out **:** CLIPPING

snip·py \'snipē, -pi\ *adj* -ER/-EST [²*snip* + *-y*] **1 :** SHORT-TEMPERED, TART, SNAPPISH **2 :** unduly brief or curt **:** SNIPPETY, FRAGMENTARY **3 :** putting on airs **:** SNIFFY, SUPERCILIOUS

snips \'snips\ *n pl but sing or pl in constr* [²*snip* + *-s*] **:** hand shears used esp. for cutting sheet metal

¹snip-snap \'=ˌ=\ *adv* [¹*snip* + *snap*] **:** in a snip-snap fashion **:** with a snip-snap

²snip-snap \"\ *vi* **1 :** to indulge in snip-snap **2 :** to make a snip-snap sound

³snip-snap \"\ *n* **1 :** a series of snips with shears **2 :** clever quick repartee

⁴snip-snap \'=ˌ=\ *adj* **:** that is or makes a snip-snap **:** given to snip-snapping **:** SNIPPY, SNAPPISH

snip·snap·sno·rum \ˌsnipˌsnap'snōrəm, -nòr-\ *n* -S [LG *snipp-snapp-snurr, snipp-snapp-snorum*, fr. *snipp* + *snapp* + *snurr, snorum*, interjections used during play] **:** a game in which one player lays a card on the table, the others in turn must match its rank if able, the first to do so says *snip*, the second *snap*, and the third *snorum*, and the winner is the one who gets rid of all his cards first — called also *Earl of Coventry*

snip·tious \'snipshəs\ *adj* [¹*snip* + *-tious* (as in *pretentious, captious*)] *chiefly dial* **:** ATTRACTIVE, SMART, FINE

snipy *or* **snipey** \'snīpē, -pi\ *adj* [¹*snipe* + *-y*] **1 a :** resembling a snipe's bill **b** *of an animal* **:** having a long lean narrow head or muzzle **2 :** abounding in snipe

snirl \'snərl\ *vb* [alter. of ²*snarl*] *chiefly Scot* **:** to curl up **:** TWIST, SNARL, WRINKLE

¹snirt \'snərt\ *n* [prob. of imit. origin] *chiefly Scot* **:** an unsuccessfully suppressed snort of laughter

²snirt \"\ *vb, chiefly Scot* **:** to snort esp. with laughter

snir·tle \'snərtᵊl\ *vi* [freq. of *snirt*] *Scot* **:** to laugh with snorts **:** SNIRT

snit \'snit\ *n* -S [origin unknown] **:** a state of agitation or excitement **:** STEW ⟨Wall Street brokers were in a ~ because nobody bought stocks —*Information Please Almanac*⟩

¹snitch \'snich\ *vb* -ED/-ING/-ES [origin unknown] *vi* **:** to give incriminating evidence against someone, esp. an associate **:** INFORM, TATTLE ⟨a Congressional witness doesn't have to ~ on far-past Red acquaintances if . . . his information serves no legislative purpose —*New Republic*⟩ ~ *vt* [prob. influenced in meaning by ¹*snatch*] **:** to take by stealth ⟨~ a ride on the back of a streetcar⟩; *specif* **:** to steal (as something of small value) in a stealthy manner ⟨started out ~*ing* hubcaps and ended up stealing cars⟩ **syn** see STEAL

²snitch \"\ *n* -ES **1** *slang* **:** NOSE **2 :** SNITCHER, INFORMER, STOOL PIGEON

snitch·er \-chə(r)\ *n* -S **:** one that snitches

snitch knot *n* **:** a weaving knot made by passing two free ends through a lark's head knot and tying the free ends in an overhand knot

¹snite \'snīt, *usu* -īd·+V\ *n* -S [ME, fr. OE *snīte*] *dial Eng* **:** SNIPE 1

²snite \"\ *vt* -ED/-ING/-S [ME *sniten*, fr. OE *snȳtan*; akin to MD *snuten* to blow the nose, OHG *snūzen*, ON *snȳta* to blow the nose, OHG *snuzza* nasal mucus — more at SNOT] *dial Brit* **:** to blow (the nose) without benefit of a handkerchief

snithe \'snīth\ *adj* [fr. obs. E *snithe* to cut, fr. ME *snithen*, fr. OE *snīthan* — more at SNATH] *chiefly dial, of wind or weather* **:** SHARP, PIERCING

snits *also* **snitz** *var of* SCHNITZ

¹sniv·el \'snivəl\ *vb* **sniveled** *or* **snivelled; sniveled** *or* **snivelled; sniveling** *or* **snivelling** \-v(ə)liŋ\ **snivels** [ME *snivelen, snevelen*, fr. (assumed) OE *snyflan* (whence *snyflung* sniveling); akin to OE *snofl* phlegm, mucus, D *snuffelen* to nose about, snuffle, MD *snof* head cold, MHG *snupfe* head cold, *snūfen, snūben* to snort, ON *snoppa* snout, Gk *nan* to flow — more at NOURISH] *vi* **1 :** to run at the nose ⟨played with their noses ~*ing* because it was so early in the morning —John Paris⟩ **2 :** to snuff mucus up the nose audibly **:** SNUFFLE **3 :** to cry or whine with snuffling **4 :** to speak or act in a whining, sniffling, tearful, or weakly emotional manner ⟨the actual people ~ every bit as piously as in the gravest legend —Bruce Lancaster⟩ ~ *vt* **1 :** to bring into a specified or implied condition by sniveling **2 :** to utter or express with or by sniveling ⟨don't come ~*ing* you'd like to go back with the pilot —Marguerite Steen⟩

²snivel \"\ *n* -S [ME *snevel*, fr. *snivelen, snevelen*, v.] **1** *archaic* **:** mucus in or from the nose **2 snivels** *pl, dial* **:** HEAD COLD **3 :** an act or instance of sniveling

sniv·el·er \-v(ə)lə(r)\ *n* -S **:** one that snivels; *esp* **:** a whiny or weakly emotional person

sniv·ely *or* **sniv·el·ly** \-v(ə)lē\ *adj* **:** marked by sniveling **:** weakly sentimental **:** TEARFUL, WHINY

SNLR *abbr* services no longer required

SNO *abbr* **1** senior naval officer **2** senior navigation officer

¹snob \'snäb\ *vi* [ME *snobben*, of imit. origin] *archaic* **:** to sob violently

²snob \"\ *n* -S [origin unknown] **1** *dial Brit* **a :** SHOEMAKER, COBBLER **b :** a shoemaker's apprentice **2 a** *archaic* **:** a person not belonging to the upper classes **:** one not an aristocrat **:** COMMONER, PLEBEIAN **b :** one who blatantly imitates, fawningly admires, or vulgarly seeks association with those he regards as his superiors ⟨a ~ . . . would put up with any affront . . . would ignore any rebuff . . . would swallow any rudeness to get asked to a party he wanted to go to —W.S.Maugham⟩ **c** (1) **:** one who tends to rebuff the advances of those he regards as inferior **:** one convinced of his superiority **:** one inclined to social exclusiveness ⟨a wealthy ~ . . . who was anxious to pursue his family tree —Wallace Clare⟩ ⟨incurable old-fashioned ~*s* who regard trade as beneath the dignity of their family —G.B.Shaw⟩ (2) **:** one rightly or esp. wrongly convinced of his superior knowledge or taste within a field or of the intrinsic superiority of his field of interest or hobby ⟨every seat taken by music lovers (not musical ~*s*) —Janet Flanner⟩ ⟨all of us, except a few academic ~*s*, know full well that a Ph.D. is no indication of good teaching —S.H.Horton⟩ **3 :** a game based on cricket and played typically with a stick for a bat and a soft ball

³snob \"\ *vt* **snobbed; snobbed; snobbing; snobs :** to look down upon **:** SNUB

snob appeal *n* **:** qualities in a product (as high price, rarity, foreign origin, or association with an elite) that appeal to the snobbery in a purchaser ⟨whatever advantage the domestic has in price is offset by the imported's *snob appeal* —Barrett McGurn⟩ ⟨the *snob appeal* of articles made in the home of a former court attendant —Virginia A. Oakes⟩

snob·bery \'snäb(ə)rē, -ri\ *n* -ES [²*snob* + *-ery*] **1 :** the quality of being snobbish **:** snobbish conduct or display **:** SNOBBISHNESS **2 :** an instance of snobbish conduct or opinion; *also* **:** a snobbish trait of character ⟨the *snobberies* of empty, albeit high-sounding nomenclatures, from overseas —H.L.Mencken⟩

snob·bish \-bish, -bēsh\ *adj* **:** of, relating to, characteristic of, or befitting a snob ⟨their ~ behavior caused them to lose many of their oldest friends⟩ — **snob·bish·ly** *adv* — **snob·bish·ness** *n* -ES

snob·bism \'snäˌbizəm\ *n* -S **:** SNOBBERY

snob·by \-bē, -bi\ *adj* **:** SNOBBISH

snob·dom \'snäbdəm\ *n* -S **:** SNOBS

snob·ling \-liŋ\ *n* -S **:** a young or petty snob

Sno-Cat \'snōˌkat, *usu* -ad·+V\ *trademark* — used for a tracklaying vehicle designed for travel on snow

¹snod \'snäd\ *adj* [ME (Sc dial.), perh. of Scand origin; akin to ON *snothinn* bald, *snöggr* shorn, bald — more at NOVACULITE] **1** *chiefly Scot* **:** SMOOTH, NEAT, TRIM, SLEEK **2** *chiefly Scot* **:** well-organized **:** ORDERLY

²snod \"\ *vt* **snodded; snodded; snodding; snods** *chiefly Scot* **:** to make smooth, neat, or trim **:** TIDY

snoek \'snük\ *n* -S [Afrik, fr. D, pike, fr. MD *snoec*] *Africa* **:** any of several vigorous active marine fishes: as **a :** BARRACOUTA **b :** BARRACUDA **c :** SNAKE MACKEREL; *also* **:** any of several closely related fishes

snoek·ing \-kiŋ, -kēŋ\ *n* -S **:** fishing for snoek

sno·ho·mish \snō'hōmish, snə'-, -mēsh\ *n, pl* **snohomish** *or* **snohomishes** *usu cap* **1 a :** a Salishan people of the lower Snohomish river valley and Whidbey island, Washington **b :** a member of such people **2 :** a dialect related to Skagit

snoke \'snōk\ *var of* SNOOK

snol·ly·gos·ter \'snälēˌgästə(r)\ *n* -S [prob. alter. of *snallygaster*] **:** an unprincipled but shrewd person

¹snood \'snüd\ *n* -S [fr. (assumed) ME, fr. OE *snōd*; akin to Old Gutnish *snōth* cord, OIr *snáth* thread, OE *nǣdl* needle — more at NEEDLE] **1 a** *Scot* **:** a fillet or band for the hair of a woman and esp. of an unmarried woman **b :** a net or fabric bag for confining a woman's hair pinned or tied on at the back of the head and sometimes attached to the back edge of a hat **2 :** SNELL **3 :** a fleshy protuberance at the base of the bill of a turkey

²snood \"\ *vt* -ED/-ING/-S **1 :** to bind (the hair) with a snood **2 :** to fasten (a hook) with a snell

snood 1b

snood·ing \-diŋ\ *n* -S [¹*snood* + *-ing*] **:** material for a snell

¹snook \'snük\ *vi* -ED/-ING/-S [ME *snoken*, prob. of Scand origin; akin to Norw & Sw *snoka* to sniff around, obs. Dan *snoge*, ON *snaka* — more at SNATCH] **1** *dial* **:** to pry about esp. while sniffing and smelling **2** *dial* **:** SNEAK

²snook \'snük, 'snu̇k\ *n, pl* **snook** *or* **snooks** [D *snoek* pike, snook, fr. MD *snoec* pike] **1 a :** a large vigorous marine percoid sport and food fish (*Centropomus undecimalis*) resembling a pike and widely distributed in warm seas — called also *robalo, sergeant fish* **b :** any of various other fishes of the family Centropomidae **2** [Afrik *snoek*, fr. D, pike] **:** SNOEK **3 :** COBIA **4 :** any of several needlefishes **5** *Austral* **:** a barracuda (*Sphyraena novae-hollandiae*)

³snook *dial past of* SNEAK

⁴snook \'snük, 'snu̇k\ *n* -S [origin unknown] **:** a gesture of derision consisting of a thumbing of the nose — usu. used in the phrase *cock a snook* ⟨small boy . . . consoles himself by cocking a ~ at the policeman's back —Joyce Cary⟩

¹snook·er \'snu̇kə(r)\ *n* -S [origin unknown] **1** *also* **snooker pool :** pool played with fifteen red balls having a value of one each and six variously colored balls having values of from 2 to 7 respectively on which the striker may play only after pocketing a red ball **2 :** a ball that lies in the way of an opponent's direct shot in the game of snooker — often used in the phrase *lay a snooker*

²snooker \"\ *vt* -ED/-ING/-S **1 :** to prevent (an opponent) from making a direct shot in the game of snooker by striking a ball so that it rests between the cue ball and the ball he is to play on **2 :** THWART, DEFEAT

¹snool \'snül\ *n* -S [origin unknown] *Scot* **:** a cringing person

²snool \"\ *vb* -ED/-ING/-S *vt, Scot* **:** to reduce to submission **:** COW, BULLY ~ *vi, Scot* **:** CRINGE, COWER

¹snoop \'snüp\ *vb* -ED/-ING/-S [D *snoepen* to buy or eat something on the sly, eat sweets, fornicate; akin to Fris *snobje* to buy sweets, Norw *snopa* to eat sweets, throw money away on sweets, ON *snoppa* snout, *snapa* to snuffle, snap — more at SNAP] *vi* **:** to look or pry in a sneaking or meddlesome manner **:** search intrusively or pryingly ⟨interception of telephone conversations . . . is an intrusion into the home . . . because its purpose and effect is to ~ into what goes on in the home —Wayne Morse⟩ ~ *vt* **:** to pry into, search for, or doggedly or exhaustively search out and examine the affairs, activities, or contents of ⟨knew he was around, they had ~*ed* him for days —Fletcher Pratt⟩

²snoop \"\ *n* -S **:** SNOOPER

snoop·er \-pə(r)\ *n* -S [¹*snoop* + *-er*] **:** one that snoops: as **a :** a prying meddler **b :** one employed as an inspector, investigator, detective, or spy ⟨a wartime censor — one of the 15,000 ~*s* who . . . opened your mail —Mary Knight⟩ ⟨an increased number of ~*s* dogging him —Joseph Wechsberg⟩ **c :** an airplane working alone to search out, observe, and sometimes attack targets

snoop·er·scope \'==ˌskōp\ *n* **:** a device that enables a person to see an object obscured (as by darkness) by the use of infrared radiation sent out from the device and reflected back to it from the object to produce a visible image on a fluorescent screen

snoop·ery \'snüpərē\ *n* -ES **:** the act or practice of prying or meddling into the affairs of others ⟨reading the published letters of famous men . . . is legitimized and justifiable ~ —J.D. Adams⟩

snoopy \-pē, -pi\ *adj* -ER/-EST **:** given to snooping esp. for personal information about others that is not one's own concern ⟨the aloof but ~ master of thirty thousand employees —Brendan Gill⟩ **syn** see CURIOUS

snoose \'snüs, 'snüz\ *n* -S [Sw, Dan, & Norw *snus*, short for Sw & Dan *snustobak* & Norw *snustobakk* respectively, fr. Sw *snusa* to sniff, snuff & Dan & Norw *snuse* + Sw & Dan *tobak* tobacco & Norw *tobakk*] *dial* **:** SNUFF

¹snoot \'snüt, *usu* -üd·+V\ *n* -S [ME *snute* — more at SNOUT] **1 a :** SNOUT **b** *slang* **:** NOSE ⟨an overpowering compulsion to bust each other on the ~ —H.H.Martin⟩ **2 a :** a grimace expressive of contempt or disgust ⟨made a ~ at us⟩ **b :** SNOOK ⟨little boys making ~*s* across the fence —W.A.White⟩ **3 :** a snooty person **:** SNOB

²snoot \"\ *vt* -ED/-ING/-S **:** to treat with disdain **:** look down one's nose at ⟨the aristocracy snubs the middle class as the middle class ~*s* the workers —*New Republic*⟩

snoot·ful \'=ˌfu̇l\ *n* -S **:** enough alcoholic liquor to cause drunkenness ⟨afraid he'd get a real ~ if he had any more —Syd Bennington⟩

snoot·i·ly \'snü|d·ᵊlē, |t|, |ᵊli, |əl-\ *adv* **:** in a snooty manner

snoot·i·ness \|ēnəs, |in-\ *n* -ES **:** the quality or state of being snooty

snooty \'snüd·ē, -ütē, -i\ *adj* -ER/-EST [¹*snoot* + *-y*] **:** haughtily or arrogantly contemptuous **:** SUPERCILIOUS, SNOBBISH

snoove \'snüv\ *vi* [fr. earlier Sc *snoove* to twirl, turn, of Scand origin; akin to ON *snūa* to turn, twist; akin to OE *snūd* speed, haste, OHG *sniumi* hasty, rapid, Goth *sniumjan* to hurry, L *nēre* to spin — more at NEEDLE] **:** to walk smoothly and steadily **:** make a steady advance

¹snooze \'snüz\ *vi* -ED/-ING/-S [origin unknown] **:** to take a nap **:** DOZE, DROWSE **syn** see SLEEP

²snooze \"\ *n* -S **:** a short sleep **:** NAP ⟨settling himself deliberately for a ~ —Joseph Conrad⟩

snooz·er \-zə(r)\ *n* -S **1 a :** one that snoozes **b :** FELLOW, SCAMP **2 :** ¹DOM PEDRO

snoo·zle \-zəl\ *vb* **snoozled; snoozled; snoozling** \-z(ə)liŋ\ **snoozles** [prob. fr. ¹*snooze* + *-le*] **1** *chiefly dial* **a :** CUDDLE, SNUGGLE **b :** NUZZLE **2** *chiefly dial* **:** DOZE

snoozy \'snüzē, -zi\ *adj* -ER/-EST **:** inclined to snooze **:** DROWSY

sno·qual·mie \snō'kwälmē, snə'-\ *n, pl* **snoqualmie** *or* **snoqualmies** *usu cap* [Snoqualmie *sdokwalbiuqᵘ*] **1 a :** a Salishan people of the Snoqualmie and Skykomish river valleys of west central Washington **b :** a member of the Snoqualmie people **2 :** a dialect related to Skagit

¹snore \'snō(ə)r, -ò(ə)r, -ōə, -ò(ə)\ *vb* -ED/-ING/-S [ME *snoren*; akin to MLG & D *snorren* to drone, hum, MD *snorren* to drone, hum, MLG & MHG, to rattle, gossip, MHG *snerren* to chatter, gossip] *vi* **1** *chiefly Scot* **:** SNORT **2 :** to breathe during sleep with a rough hoarse noise due to vibration of the uvula and the soft palate **3 a :** to make a sound as of snoring **:** ROAR, RUMBLE **b** *of a ship* **:** to cut the waves with a roar ⟨*snoring* along in a good twelve-knot breeze —Vincent McHugh⟩ **4** *dial* **:** DECLARE — used in the expression *I snore* ⟨I ~ I don't think there's much difference —T.C.Haliburton⟩ ~ *vt* **1 :** to spend in snoring — used with *away* or *out* ⟨*snored* away the interval between their own arrival and that of the expected repast —Sir Walter Scott⟩ **2 :** to utter with a snore

²snore \"\ *n* -S [ME, fr. *snoren*, v.] **1 :** an act of snoring **2 :** a noise of or as if of snoring ⟨the deep ~ of distant traffic —Margery Allingham⟩

snor·er \'snōrə(r), 'snòr-\ *n* -S [ME, fr. *snoren* to snore + *-er*] **:** one that snores

snoring disease *n* **:** nasal granuloma of cattle and other ruminants usu. incident to nasal schistosomiasis

snork \'snò(ə)rk, 'snò(ə)k\ *n* -S [fr. E dial. *snork* to snort, snore; akin to MD & MLG *snorken* to snore, MHG *snarchen*, OSw *snarka*, ME *snoren* — more at SNORE] *dial Eng* **:** a snorting sound **:** SNORT

¹snor·kel \'snòrkəl, -ò(ə)k-\ *n* -S [G *schnorchel*, fr. G dial., snout, fr. *schnorchen* to snore; akin to MHG *snarchen* to snore — more at SNORK] **1** *or* **schnor·kel** *also* **schnor·chel** \'shnòrkəl, -ò(ə)k-\ **:** a tube or pair of tubes housing air intake and exhaust pipes that can be extended above the surface of the water for operating submerged submarines **2 :** any of various devices resembling a snorkel in appearance or function: as **a :** a plastic breathing tube fitted at one end with a mouthpiece and at the other with a valve that admits air when projecting above water and closes when submerged and used for swimming near the surface with the head underwater **b :** an air intake tube projecting above water on an automotive vehicle designed to travel submerged

²snorkel \"\ *vi* -ED/-ING/-S **1** *of a submarine* **:** to operate submerged on diesel engines with only a snorkel showing above water **2 :** to swim near the surface of the water with submerged face breathing through a snorkel

¹snort \'snò(ə)rt, -ò(ə)t, *usu* -d·+V\ *vb* -ED/-ING/-S [ME *snorten*; prob. akin to ME *snoren* to snore — more at SNORE] *vi* **1 a :** to force air violently through the nose with a rough harsh sound ⟨a drover's pony . . . sipped the water, ~*ing* at its own shadow —Alice Duncan-Kemp⟩ **b :** to express scorn, anger, indignation, or surprise by a snort ⟨has been known to ~ impatiently at public acknowledgments of his skill —R.L. Taylor⟩ **2** *obs* **:** SNORE **3 a :** to emit explosive sounds like or in the manner of a snort ⟨the bleating and ~*ing* lyricism of the saxophone —F.J.Mather⟩ **b :** to travel with snorting or roaring sounds ⟨an old car was ~*ing* along the road without a muffler —Elizabeth Pollet⟩ ⟨the first iron horse that ever ~*ed* up these mountains —A.W.Long⟩ **4 :** to take in a drug by inhalation ~ *vt* **1 :** to utter with or express by a snort ⟨the horse ~*ed* his relief at the removal of the heavy, burdened saddle and accouterments —Zane Grey⟩ **2 :** to expel or emit with or as if with snorts ⟨a horse ~*ing* grass pollen out of his nostrils —H.L.Davis⟩ **3 :** to inhale (a narcotic drug in powdered form) through the nostrils **syn** see EXCLAIM

²snort \"\ *n* -S **1 :** an act or sound of snorting ⟨gave an astonished ~ of laughter —Kay Boyle⟩ ⟨was mingled with deep, hoarse ~*s*, and we knew that we had disturbed one of the big red deer —William Beebe⟩ **2 :** a drink of usu. straight liquor taken in one draft **3** *Brit* **:** SNORKEL 1

snort·er \'snòr|d·ə(r), -ò(ə)|d·ə(r, |tə-\ *n* -S [¹*snort* + *-er*] **1 :** one that snorts **2** *dial Brit* **:** WHEATEAR **3 :** something that is extraordinary, remarkable, or prominent **:** HUMDINGER ⟨made up his mind to preach the ~ of a sermon —Bruce Marshall⟩ ⟨a real ~ at chess⟩: as **a :** a violent storm or wind ⟨blizzard wasn't long, but she was a ~ —C.T.Jackson⟩ **b :** a bowled ball in cricket that is exceptionally fast or accurate or difficult to play **4 :** SNORT 2 **5 :** an exhaust tube projecting above water on an automotive vehicle designed to travel submerged

snort·ing·ly *adv* **:** in a snorting manner

snorty \|d·ē, |t|, |i\ *adj* -ER/-EST **:** characterized by or given to snorting

¹snot \'snät, *usu* -äd·+V\ *n* -S [ME, fr. OE *gesnot*; akin to OFris *snotta* nasal mucus, MD & MLG *snotte*, OHG *snuzza*,

Norw *snott* nasal mucus, MIr *snūad* river, Gk *nan* to flow — more at NOURISH] **1 :** nasal mucus — usu. considered vulgar **2 :** a snotty person ⟨don't like young ~*s* like you —Irwin Shaw⟩

²**snot** \"\ *vt* -ED/-ING/-S **:** to blow or clear mucus from (the nose) — usu. considered vulgar

snot–rag \ˈ=,=\ *n* **:** HANDKERCHIEF — usu. considered vulgar

¹**snot·ter** \ˈsnäd·ə(r), -ätə-\ *n* -S [akin to ¹*snot*] *dial Brit* **:** nasal mucus

²**snotter** \"\ *vi* **1** *dial Brit* **:** to breathe noisily **:** SNORT, SNORE **2** *dial Brit* **:** SNIVEL, SNIFF ⟨stood blubbering and ~*ing* and twisting his hands —Bruce Marshall⟩

³**snotter** \"\ *or* **snort·er** \ˈsnȯr|d·ər, -ȯ(ə)|d·ə(r, |tə-\ *n* -S [origin unknown] **1 :** a flat rope usu. of sennit secured to a yardarm to which a tripping line is bent and used to strip the lower lift and brace from the yardarm in sending down topgallant and royal yards in a ship of war **2 :** a loop or ring of rope or metal for receiving the lower end of a sprit

¹**snot·ty** \ˈsnäd·ē, -ätē, -i\ *adj* -ER/-EST [¹*snot* + -*y*] **1 :** foul with nasal mucus **:** VISCOUS, SLIMY **2 a :** meanly contemptible ⟨~ little scion of a degenerate family —Laurent Le Sage⟩ **b :** exhibiting unjustified or exaggerated pride **:** SNOOTY, SUPERCILIOUS ⟨you were so ~ when I called you up, I was afraid to talk to you —Dorothy Parker⟩

²**snotty** *or* **snot·tie** \"\ *n, pl* **snotties :** a midshipman, esp. in the British navy

snotty nose *n* **:** nasal myiasis of sheep

snotty–nosed \ˈ==ˈ=\ *also* **snot–nosed** \ˈ=ˈ=\ *adj* **1 :** having a nose running or fouled with nasal mucus **2 :** small and contemptible **:** SNOTTY

snot·ziek·te \ˈsnȯt,zēktə\ *n* -S [Afrik *snotsiekte* (formerly spelled *snotziekte*), fr. *snot* nasal mucus (fr. MD *snotte*) + *siekte* disease, sickness — more at SNOT, LAMSIEKTE] *southern Africa* **:** malignant catarrh of cattle

snouch \ˈsnau̇ch\ *vt* -ED/-ING/-ES [origin unknown] **:** SNUB

¹**snout** \ˈsnau̇t, *usu* -au̇d·+V\ *n* -S [ME *snute, snoute;* akin to MD *snute* snout, G *schnauze*, Norw *snut* snout, and prob. to OHG *snuzza* nasal mucus — more at SNOT] **1 a** *obs* **:** the trunk of an elephant **b :** the long projecting nose of any of various mammals (as a swine); *also* **:** the anterior prolongation of the head of various animals ⟨a weevil with a long ~⟩ **:** ROSTRUM **c :** the human nose esp. when large or grotesque ⟨over the gruesomely fattened ~, her scarlet eyes stared —Jean Stafford⟩ **2 :** something resembling an animal's snout in position, function, or shape: as **a** (1) **:** PROW (2) **:** the projecting front of an automotive chassis **b** (1) **:** NOZZLE (2) **:** MUZZLE **c :** a projecting mass of rock **:** PROMONTORY **d :** the terminal face of a glacier

²**snout** \"\ *vb* -ED/-ING/-S *vt* **:** to furnish with a snout, nozzle, or point ~ *vi* **:** to dig with or as if with a snout **:** GRUB ⟨~*ed* into pails and old crocks in the back yard —Paul de Kruif⟩

snout beetle *n* **:** a beetle of the group Rhynchophora — see WEEVIL

snout butterfly *n* **:** a butterfly of the family Libytheidae having very long palpi carried extended in front of the head

snout·ish \ˈsnau̇d·|ish, -au̇t|, |ēsh\ *adj* **:** SNOUTLIKE ⟨a gross heavy face with a ~ nose⟩

snout·less \ˈsnau̇tləs\ *adj* **:** having no snout

snoutlike \ˈ=,=\ *adj* **:** resembling a snout

snout machine *n* **:** a boring machine or mill in which the cutting tools are carried directly by the spindle without the interposition of a boring bar and the spindle is supported along its entire length by a projecting boss

snout mite *n* **:** any of numerous active slender usu. reddish mites (family Bdellidae) with well-developed and prolonged rostrum

snout moth *n* **:** a moth of the family Pyralididae; *broadly* **:** any of various moths mostly of this or related families having the labial palpi held out forward like a snout

snouty \ˈsnau̇d·ē, -au̇tē, -i\ *adj* -ER/-EST **1 :** SNOUTLIKE **2 :** having a snout and esp. a prominent or remarkable one ⟨the ~ little creatures became a symbol of pamperedness —*New Yorker*⟩

¹**snow** \ˈsnō\ *n* -S *often attrib* [ME *snaw, snow*, fr. OE *snāw;* akin to OHG *snēo* snow, ON *snær, snjōr*, Goth *snaiws*, L *niv-, nix*, Gk *nipha* (acc.), Lith *sniẽgas*] **1 a :** small tabular and columnar white transparent often branched crystals of frozen water that are formed directly from the water vapor of the air at a temperature of less than 32°F and belong to the hexagonal system of crystallization **b** (1) **:** a descent or shower of snow crystals **:** SNOWFALL ⟨another big ~ fell the next day —Bruce Siberts⟩ (2) **:** a usu. consolidated mass of fallen snow crystals ⟨play in the ~⟩ (3) **:** a region or area covered with snow and often with permanent snow — usu. used in pl. ⟨the high ~*s*⟩ **2 :** something resembling snow (as in whiteness, coldness, or transitoriness): as **a :** a dessert made of stiffly beaten whites of eggs, sugar, and fruit pulp ⟨apple ~⟩ **b :** white hair — often used in pl. **c :** any of various congealed or crystallized substances resembling snow in appearance ⟨carbon dioxide ~⟩ ⟨very finely granulated copper sulfate ~⟩ **d** *slang* **:** COCAINE **e :** small transient light or dark spots on a television or radar screen resulting from the same causes as those that produce static in radio **3 :** a period of time consisting of one winter with or without the accompanying seasons — used chiefly in a representation of Amerindian speech ⟨forty ~*s* ago⟩

²**snow** \"\ *vb* **snowed** *or dial* **snew; snowed; snowing; snows** [ME *snawen, snowen*, fr. *snaw, snow*, n.] *vi* **1 :** to fall in or as snow — usu. used with *it* ⟨it had been ~*ing* all day⟩ **2 a :** to fall in the manner of snow ⟨soot ~*s* in my face —Isaac Rosenfeld⟩ **b :** to descend or become distributed in great quantities ⟨telegrams began to ~ on Congress —T.H.White b. 1915⟩ ~ *vt* **1 :** to cause to fall like or as snow ⟨watching the rhododendron ~ its petals on the dark pool —D.C.Peattie⟩ **2 a** (1) **:** to cover with or as if with snow **:** bury in or as if in snow — usu. used with *over* or *under* ⟨cars ~*ed* under by drifts⟩ (2) *slang* **:** to deceive, persuade, or charm glibly (as by the presentation of a large amount of information that is hard to check or the relation of fictitious exploits) ⟨remembered that a Marine should "~" his girl, and started telling her about his campaigns —Dan Levin⟩ **b :** to shut in or imprison with snow — used with *up* or *in* ⟨in the hidden valleys, whole families who, ~*ed* up, never set foot outside their houses from September to May —F.M.Ford⟩ **3 :** to whiten like snow ⟨hair ~*ed* by age⟩

³**snow** \"\ *n* -S [modif. of D *snauw*, prob. fr. LG *snau* beak, snout, snow (vessel); akin to MD *snauwen* to snap at, bite, MLG *snouwen* to snap at, MHG *snöuwen, snouwen* to snort, snap at, and perh. to MHG *snūben, snūfen* to snort — more at SNIVEL] **:** a square-rigged ship that differs from a brig in having a trysail mast close abaft the mainmast

snow apple *n* **:** MUSHROOM

snow azalea *n* **:** an evergreen shrub (*Rhododendron mucronatum*) with white flowers and bristly shoots

¹**snowball** \ˈ=,=\ *n* [ME, fr. *snow* + *ball*] **1 a** (1) **:** a small round mass of snow pressed into shape in the hand for throwing (2) **:** a large round mass of snow formed by rolling in snow until the desired size is attained **b :** shaved ice molded into a ball and flavored with fruit or other syrup **2** *also* **snowball bush :** any of several cultivated white-flowered shrubs of the genus *Viburnum* (as the guelder rose or the Japanese snowball) **3 :** something that snowballs ⟨watching the toll of the steel strike begin to mount in a ~ of statistics —*Christian Science Monitor*⟩

²**snowball** \"\ *vb* -ED/-ING/-S *vt* **1 :** to pelt with snowballs **:** throw snowballs at **2 :** to cause to increase or multiply at a rapidly accelerating rate ⟨helped the newly built organization to ~ its political influence —L.G.Reynolds⟩ ~ *vi* **1 :** to engage in throwing snowballs ⟨little boys, too, were ~*ing* —Virginia Woolf⟩ **2 a :** to increase, accumulate, expand, or multiply at a rapidly accelerating rate ⟨discontent would grow, sabotage increase, passive or overt resistance ~ —F.H.Hartmann⟩ ⟨the differences may ~ into a heated public controversy —*Current History*⟩ **b :** to progress rapidly and with great momentum

snowball cactus *n* **:** any of several cacti that have a covering of long cottony hairs

snowbank \ˈ=,=\ *n* **:** a mound or slope of snow

snow banner *n* **:** a stream of snow blown into the air from a mountain peak that is often pinkish and several miles in horizontal extent

snow bear *n* **:** RED BEAR

snowbell \ˈ=,=\ *n* **:** any of several plants of the genus *Styrax; esp* **:** a shrub or small tree (*S. grandifolia*) of the southeastern U. S. with showy clusters of fragrant white flowers

snowberry \ˈ=- — *see* BERRY\ *n* **1 :** any of various shrubs of the genus *Symphoricarpos* that have white berries; *esp* **:** a low-growing No. American shrub (*S. albus*) with pink flowers in small axillary clusters **2 :** BLOLLY 2 **3 :** CREEPING SNOWBERRY

snowbird \ˈ=,=\ *n* **1 a :** SNOW BUNTING **b :** a finch of the genus *Junco* **c :** FIELDFARE **d :** IVORY GULL **2 a** *slang* **:** a cocaine addict **b :** SKIER **3 :** one of a class of sailing dinghies of about 12 feet in length

snow blanket *n* **:** a surface accumulation of snow that serves to protect and water underlying vegetation

snow blight *n* **:** a disease of conifer seedlings caused by a fungus (*Phacidium infestans*) that attacks the needles under the snow, causes them to turn brown, and covers them with white mycelium

snow–blind \ˈ=ˌ=\ *or* **snow–blinded** \ˈ=ˌ==\ *adj* **:** affected with snow blindness

snow blindness *n* **:** inflammation and photophobia caused by exposure of the unprotected eyes to ultraviolet rays reflected from fields of snow or ice ⟨suffering the excruciating agony of *snow blindness* after two weeks of futile searching in the empty plains —Farley Mowat⟩

snowblink \ˈ=,=\ *n* **:** a white glare in the sky over a snowfield that is brighter than iceblink

snowblower \ˈ=,==\ *n* **:** a machine using blasts of air to remove snow (as from a highway or railroad)

snow boot *n* **:** a boot reaching to the ankle or above for wear in snow

snowbound \ˈ=ˌ=\ *adj* **:** shut in or blockaded by snow

snowbreak \ˈ=,=\ *n* **1 :** a melting of snow **:** THAW **2 a :** a breaking of trees by snow **b :** an area over which there has been such breakage **3 :** a protective barrier (as of planted trees along a highway or railroad) against drifting snow

snowbridge \ˈ=,=\ *n* **:** a bridge of snow across a crevasse in a glacier

snow–broth \ˈ=,=\ *n* **1 :** mixed snow and water **2 :** newly melted snow

snowbrush \ˈ=,=\ *n* **:** any of several white-flowered shrubs of the genus *Ceanothus; esp* **:** a spreading shrub (*C. velutina*) of the mountainous western U.S. with dark green cinnamon-scented leaves and abundant panicles of small white flowers

snow bunny *n* **:** a person and esp. a girl who is a beginner in skiing

snow bunting *n* **:** a finch (*Plectrophenax nivalis*) of northern regions that is related to the longspurs, breeds in the arctic regions, in winter often appears in large flocks both in Europe and the U. S. esp. during snowstorms, and has largely white plumage with upper parts usu. overcast with brown and red during winter and during the summer in the male with black — called also *snowflake*

snowbush \ˈ=,=\ *n* **:** a Polynesian shrub (*Breynia nivosa*) of the family Euphorbiaceae cultivated for the white and green mottled foliage of one of its horticultural varieties

snowcap \ˈ=,=\ *n* **1 :** a covering cap of snow (as on a mountain peak) **2 :** a very small Central American hummingbird (*Microchera albo-coronata*) having a shining white crown — **snow-capped** \ˈ=ˌ=\ *adj*

snow cock *or* **snow chukar** *n* **:** any of several large gallinaceous birds of the genus *Tetraogallus* living almost exclusively above timber line in the mountains of central and western Asia — see HIMALAYAN SNOW COCK

snow crab *n* **:** a specially equipped railroad car that draws snow from the sides of a track onto the track so that it may be thrown further to the side by a rotary plow

snowcraft \ˈ=,=\ *n* **:** skill and experience in judging snow conditions and behavior

snow cup *n* **:** a cup-shaped indentation in snow at high altitudes caused by evaporation

snow devil *n* **:** a column of fine snow blown upward from a surface by the wind

snow·do·nian \(ˈ)snō¦dōnēən, -nyən\ *adj, usu cap* [*Snowdonia*, mountainous area in northwestern Wales + E -*an*] **:** of relating to, or situated in the area of Snowdonia

snowdrift \ˈ=,=\ *n* **1 a :** a bank of drifted snow **b :** drifting snow **2 :** SWEET ALYSSUM

snowdrop \ˈ=,=\ *n* **1 a :** a plant of the genus *Galanthus; esp* **:** a bulbous European herb (*G. nivalis*) bearing nodding white flowers that often appear while the snow is on the ground **2 :** WOOD ANEMONE a

snowdrop anemone *n* **:** a Eurasian herb (*Anemone sylvestris*) having ternately cleft leaves and usu. solitary nodding fragrant white flowers

snowdrop tree *n* **1 :** a plant of the genus *Halesia; esp* **:** SILVER BELL **2 :** FRINGE TREE

snow dust *n* **:** snow borne by the wind in fine particles

snow eater *n* **:** CHINOOK 3b

snowed *past of* SNOW

snowfall \ˈ=,=\ *n* **:** a fall of snow; *specif* **:** the amount of snow that falls in a single storm or in a given period

snow fence *n* **:** a barrier stretched across the path of prevailing winds to deflect drifting snow (as from a building, road, or railroad track)

snowfield \ˈ=,=\ *n* **:** a broad level expanse of snow; *esp* **:** a mass of perennial snow as at the head of a glacier

snow finch *n* **1 :** BRAMBLING **2 :** any of several European and Asian alpine sparrows of the genus *Montifringilla*

snowflake \ˈ=,=\ *n* **1 :** a flake or crystal of snow **2 :** SNOW BUNTING **3 a :** a bulbous plant of the genus *Leucojum* (esp. *L. vernum*) **b :** SWEET WILLIAM

snow flea *n* **:** a small black leaping springtail (*Achorutes nivicolus*) often found in early spring on the snow in vast numbers in the eastern U.S.; *broadly* **:** any of several collembolans with similar habits

snow fly *or* **snow insect** *n* **1 :** any of several minute insects that constitute a genus (*Boreus*) of the order Mecoptera and sometimes appear on the snow in great numbers and in the males have vestigial wings but in the female are wingless **2 :** any of several small American stone flies (esp. *Taeniopteryx nivalis* or *Capnella pygmaea*) often seen on snow **3 :** SNOW GNAT

snow gnat *n* **1 :** a wingless crane fly (genus *Chionea*) found chiefly on snow **2 :** a gnat of the family Chironomidae often seen on snow in spring

snow goggles *n* **:** a piece of wood with two narrow slits used esp. by Eskimos for protection against snow blindness

snow goose *n* **:** a wild goose of the genus *Chen* (*C. caerulescens*) that is usu. white with blackish primaries and a reddish or pinkish bill but exists in a genetic form with dark plumage, breeds chiefly in Arctic America, and migrates south — see BLUE GOOSE, LESSER SNOW GOOSE

snow grass *n* **:** any of several Australian grasses of the genera *Agrostis, Danthonia*, or *Poa*

snow grouse *n* **:** PTARMIGAN

snow guard *n* **:** any of several devices to prevent a slide of snow from a sloping roof

snow gum *n* **:** any of several eucalypts growing at higher elevations in Australia

snowhouse \ˈ=,=\ *n* **:** a house built of snow **:** a snow igloo

snow ice *n* **1 :** ice (as in a glacier) formed by the compacting of snow **2 :** whitish porous ice formed by the freezing of half-melted snow or ice

snowier *comparative of* SNOWY

snowiest *superlative of* SNOWY

snow·i·ly \ˈsnōəlē, -li\ *adv* **:** with or as snow

snow·i·ness \-ōēnəs, -ōin-\ *n* -ES **:** the quality or state of being snowy

snowing *pres part of* SNOW

snow–in–summer \ˌ=='==\ *also* **snow–in–harvest** \ˌ=='==\ *n* **:** any of several plants blossoming at harvesttime: as **a :** a mouse-ear chickweed (*Cerastium tomentosum*) with grayish tomentose foliage and rather large white flowers that is sometimes used as a low border about ornamental plantings **b :** a virgin's bower (*Clematis viorna*) of the eastern U. S. sometimes cultivated for its purplish flowers and showy plumose white achenes

snow job *n, slang* **:** a long involved effort at persuasion or deception with a vast amount of information or fictitious exploits ⟨he didn't talk much — no *snow job* about the money he'd had, the cars he'd owned, the women he'd known —*Prison World*⟩

snow knife *n* **:** a broad-bladed curved knife used by Eskimos for cutting and shaping blocks of snow in building snowhouses

snow lemming *n* **:** PIED LEMMING

snow leopard *or* **snow panther** *n* **:** a showily marked large cat (*Felis uncia*) of the high mountains of central Asia with a long heavy pelt that is grayish white irregularly blotched with brownish black in summer and almost pure white in winter

snow·less \ˈ=,ləs\ *adj* **:** having no snow ⟨along the ~ ridges of the coast —Freya Stark⟩

snow lichen *n* **:** a cream-colored or pale gray lichen (*Cetraria nivalis*) with finely divided crinkled tips found on soil in high mountain areas of northern New England and the northern Rockies

snow light *n* **:** SNOWBLINK

snow lily *n* **:** GLACIER LILY

snow line *n* **1 :** the lower margin of a perennial snowfield **:** the elevation above which some snow remains throughout the year **2 :** the extreme limit from the equator within which no snow falls unmelted and which varies with physical conditions (as elevation and nearness to the sea)

snow·man \ˈsnō,man, -,maa(ə)n, -mən\ *n, pl* **snowmen 1 :** a representation of a man formed from snow and usu. from snowballs **2 a :** a person that works in or with snow **b :** a specialist in the study of snow **3 :** ABOMINABLE SNOWMAN

snowmelt \ˈ=,=\ *n* **:** water from melting of snow

snow·mo·bile \ˈ=mō,bēl\ *n* -S [¹*snow* + auto*mobile*] **:** any of various automotive vehicles for travel on snow

snow mold *or* **snow rot** *n* **1 a :** a disease of cereals caused by a fungus (*Calonectria graminicola*) and characterized by abundant superficial white mycelium when the snow melts **b :** a similar disease esp. of turf grasses caused by a fungus of the genera *Typhula, Sclerotium* or *Fusarium* **2 :** a fungus causing a snow mold

snow mosquito *n* **:** any of several mosquitoes of the far north esp. of the genus *Aedes* with larvae that develop in the water from melting snow

snow mouse *n* **1 :** any of several pale-grayish voles of the Alps and other high mountains of central Europe **2 :** PIED LEMMING

snow–on–the–mountain \ˌ===ˈ==\ *n* **1** *dial Eng* **:** SNOW-IN-SUMMER a **2 :** a spurge (*Euphorbia marginata*) of the western U. S. that has showy white-bracted flower clusters and is used as an ornamental

snow owl *n* **:** SNOWY OWL

snowpack \ˈ=,=\ *n* **:** a field of naturally packed snow that ordinarily melts slowly and yields water for irrigation or power during the early summer months

snow partridge *n* **1 :** a Himalayan gallinaceous bird (*Lerwa lerwa*) having the upper half of the legs feathered, the reddish shanks spurred, the upper parts of the body blackish and narrowly barred with white and rufous, and the under parts of the body chestnut **2 :** SNOW COCK **3 :** PTARMIGAN

snow pear *n* **:** a European pear (*Pyrus nivalis*) used esp. for making pear cider

snow pheasant *n* **1 :** SNOW COCK **2 :** EARED PHEASANT

snow pigeon *n* **:** a pigeon (*Columba leuconota*) of Tibet and the Himalayas having the back, neck, and rump white and the top of the head, ear coverts, and tail blackish

snowplane \ˈ=,=\ *n* **:** a snowmobile propelled by an airplane-type engine and pusher propeller

snow plant *n* **1 :** a fleshy bright red saprophytic herb (*Sarcodes sanguinea*) of the family Pyrolaceae growing in coniferous woods at high altitudes on the sierras of California often appearing and blossoming in early spring while snow is on the ground **2 :** a red-snow flagellate (*Chlamydomonas nivalis*)

¹**snowplow** \ˈ=,=\ *n* [¹*snow* + *plow*] **1 :** any of various devices used for clearing away snow (as from a road or railroad) **2 :** a skiing maneuver consisting of stemming with both skis that is used for coming to a stop, slowing down, or descending slowly

²**snowplow** \"\ *vi, of a skier* **:** to slow down or stop by executing a snowplow

snowplow turn *n* **:** an elementary skiing turn executed by shifting the weight to the ski opposite to the desired direction of the turn while keeping both skis in snowplow position

snow pudding *n* **:** a pudding made very fluffy and light by the addition of whipped egg whites and gelatin

snow pusher *n* **:** a concave scoop similar to a shovel used to remove snow by pushing on a long handle

snow quail *n* **:** WHITE-TAILED PTARMIGAN

snow roller *n* **:** a mass of snow rolled up by the wind that is usu. cylindrical with concave ends

snow rose *n* **:** a low shrub (*Rhododendron chrysanthum*) of cool regions in northeastern Asia sometimes cultivated for its pale yellow flowers

snows *pl of* SNOW, *pres 3d sing of* SNOW

snow scald *n* **:** a disease of cereals and turf grasses caused by fungi of the genus *Typhula* (esp. *T. gramum*) and characterized by white to gray or black mycelium and by reddish brown sclerotia in the roots, stem bases, and leaf sheaths

snowshed \ˈ=,=\ *n* **1 :** a shelter (as a long structure over an exposed part of a railroad) to protect from snow; *esp* **:** a shelter on a mountain or other slope to afford protection against snowslides **2 :** a watershed supplied largely by snowfalls

snow sheen *n* **:** SNOWBLINK

¹**snowshoe** \ˈ=,=\ *n* [¹*snow* + *shoe*] **1 :** any of various devices worn in pairs under the shoes to enable a person to walk on soft snow without sinking; *specif* **:** a light oval wooden frame strengthened by two crosspieces, strung with thongs, and attached to the foot **2 :** INDIAN YELLOW **2 3 :** SNOWSHOE RABBIT

²**snowshoe** \"\ *vi* -ED/-ING/-S **:** to travel on snowshoes — **snowshoeing** \ˈ=,==\ *n* -S — **snowshoer** \ˈ=,==\ *n* -S

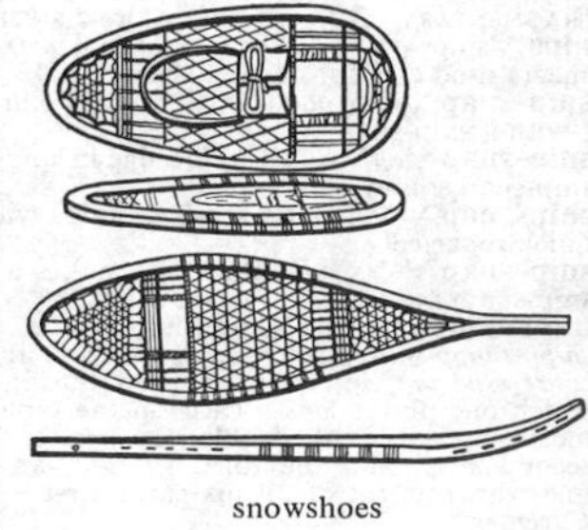

snowshoes

snowshoe rabbit *n* [so called fr. the large, heavily furred feet in winter pelage] **:** a rather large chiefly northern No. American rabbit (*Lepus americanus*) with large heavily furred hind feet and a coat that is brown in summer but usu. white in winter

snowslide \ˈ=,=\ *n* **:** an avalanche of snow

snow snake *n* **:** an implement in the form of a staff several feet long hurled along ice or snowy ground in a No. American Indian game

snow static *n* **:** static resulting from the passage of a vehicle and esp. an airplane through snow or particles of ice

snowstorm \ˈ=,=\ *n* **1 :** a storm of falling snow ⟨alighted at the station in a raging ~ —Willa Cather⟩ **2 :** something resembling a snowstorm ⟨~*s* of white birds lighted on sandbars —J.M.Brinnin⟩

snowsuit \ˈ=,=\ *n* **:** an outfit for winter wear; *esp* **:** a one-piece or two-piece lined garment similar to a ski suit worn by children

snow sweeper *n* **:** a vehicle or car with revolving brushes for sweeping away snow (as from a road or railroad track)

snowthrown \ˈ=ˌ=\ *adj, of a tree* **:** bent or broken by the weight of snow

snow tire *n* **:** an automotive tire with a tread designed to give added traction on snow or ice

snow train *n* **:** a special train to a ski resort or other place suitable for winter sports

snow trillium *n* **:** EARLY WAKE-ROBIN

snow under *vt* **1 :** to overwhelm beyond the capacity for absorbing or dealing with something ⟨*snowed under* by corre-

spondence and paper work —Raymond Chandler⟩ **2 :** to defeat by a large margin ⟨*snowed* him *under* with some 4000 write-in votes for another candidate —H.H.Martin⟩
snow vine *n* **:** PEPPER VINE 2
snow vole *n* **:** SNOW MOUSE 1
snow water *n* **:** water from melted snow
snow–white \ˈ=¦=\ *adj* [ME *snawwhit, snowwhit,* fr. OE *snāwhwīt,* fr. *snāw* snow + *hwīt* white — more at SNOW, WHITE] **:** white as snow — **snow–white·ness** *n*
snowworm \ˈ=,=\ *n* **:** any of several oligochaete worms of the family Enchytraeidae found living in or on snow
snow wreath *n* **1** *dial Brit* **:** SNOWDRIFT **2 :** a deciduous shrub (*Neviusia alabamensis*) of the family Rosaceae native to Alabama that is cultivated for its white feathery flowers
snowy \ˈsnōē, -ōi\ *adj* -ER/-EST [ME, fr. OE *snāwig,* fr. *snāw* snow + *-ig* -y] **1 a :** composed of snow or melted snow **b :** marked by, abounding in, or covered with snow ⟨the *snowiest* night of the year —Beverly Fields⟩ ⟨~ pastures —H.D.Thoreau⟩ **2 :** whitened by or as if by snow ⟨the ground was still ~ with fallen petals —Ellen Glasgow⟩ **:** SNOW-WHITE ⟨its beaches were of ~ coral sand —C.B. Nordhoff & J.N.Hall⟩
snowy campion *n* **:** a perennial smooth herb (*Silene nivea*) of the eastern U.S. with a much-inflated calyx and white notched petals
snowy egret *or* **snowy heron** *n* **:** a small white egret or heron (*Leucophoyx thula* or *Egretta thula*) that is about two feet long, ranges from the southern U.S. southward to Chile, and was formerly extensively hunted for its aigrettes
snowy lemming *n* **:** PIED LEMMING
snowy orchid *n* **:** a slender fringed orchid (*Habenaria nivea*) of eastern No. America with linear firm keeled leaves and white flowers
snowy owl *n* **:** a large diurnal arctic owl (*Nyctea nyctea*) that enters the northern parts of the U.S. and Europe in winter and has no ear tufts and plumage that is sometimes nearly pure white but usu. with dark brownish spots
snowy plover *n* **:** a small plover (*Charadrius alexandrinus nivosus*) of the Gulf coast and the western parts of the U.S. and Mexico that is light gray above with a dark patch on the crown, sides of the head, and each side of the breast and has the underparts and portions of the head white
snowy tree cricket *n* **:** a pale greenish or whitish yellow tree cricket (*Oecanthus fultoni*) widely distributed in No. America
snoz·zle \ˈsnäzəl\ *var of* SCHNOZZLE
SNP *abbr* soluble nucleoprotein
snr *abbr* senior
1**snub** \ˈsnəb\ *vb* **snubbed; snubbed; snubbing; snubs** [ME *snubben,* of Scand origin; akin to ON *snubba* to scold, rebuke, Sw dial., to reproach, cut off; akin to MLG *snubbelen* to chide, and perh. to OHG *snabul* beak — more at NEB] *vt* **1 a :** to check or stop with a cutting retort or remark **:** restrain by reprimanding **:** REBUKE ⟨was quickly *snubbed* when he tried to intercede⟩ **b** *archaic* **:** UPBRAID, SCOLD **c :** to treat with contempt or neglect so as to humiliate or repress **:** ignore with or as if with disdain **:** slight designedly ⟨the ambassador was obviously *snubbed*⟩ ⟨his suggestions were *snubbed*⟩ ⟨whose only concerns were to make history and to ~ the history that had already been made —Jean Stafford⟩; *also* **:** to affect in a specified way by such treatment ⟨*snubbed* into silence⟩ **2 a** *obs* **:** to check or curb the growth or development of **b** *chiefly dial* **:** to break off the end of **:** NIP ⟨~ branches of a tree⟩ **c** *West* **:** DEHORN ⟨~ cattle⟩ **3 a :** to check suddenly (as a rope or chain that is running out) ⟨*snubbed* short, like a downstream trout when fairly hooked —*Century Mag.*⟩ **b :** to increase the tension of (as a rope or belt) by turning around a post, pin, or pulley **:** TAUTEN **c :** to check or restrain the motion of (an animal or thing) by turning an attached line around a post or other available anchoring point ⟨~ a horse to a tree⟩ ⟨as the lariat jerked tight, the rider instantly *snubbed* it tight around the saddle horn —D.A.Brown⟩ **d :** INHIBIT, SUPPRESS, RESTRAIN ⟨air springs *snubbed* out all the undulating motion —*Motor Life*⟩ **e :** to extinguish (a cigarette) by stubbing — usu. used with *out* ⟨*snubbed* the butt out in my saucer —Mickey Spillane⟩ **4 :** to turn the end of (a line) around a post or other available anchoring point **:** tie up short ⟨let the wagons down the steep slope by means of rope *snubbed* around trees —G.R.Stewart⟩ ⟨had *snubbed* the bronc's rein to his saddle horn —Colin Lofting⟩ **5 :** to enlarge (an undercut in a coal mine) by blasting or other means so that the coal rolls forward when it is broken down ~ *vi* **1 :** to snub someone or something **:** give snubs ⟨the ability to ~ and to tell useful fibs —R.H.Rovere⟩ **2 :** to tie up short against a bank or wharf ⟨one by one, the flatboats *snubbed* in at the bank —F.G.Slaughter⟩ ⟨a raft well piloted would outrun a flood and have to ~ up to the bank and wait for the floodwater to catch up —R.G.Lillard⟩ **3 :** to pull a restraining line up taut ⟨when a wind came up, the boat began to ~⟩ ⟨the horse *snubbed* back from the hitchrack⟩ **4 :** to enlarge an undercut in coal mining by blasting or other means so that the coal rolls forward when it is broken down
2**snub** \"\ *n* -S **1 :** an act or an instance of snubbing; *esp* **:** a rebuff or slight intended to check a person or his activity ⟨accepted every unjust rebuke and ~ as part of the day's routine —R.S.Porteous⟩ **2 a :** something that snubs **b :** SNUBBING POST ⟨no ~ in that corral —A.B.Guthrie⟩ **3** [3*snub*] **:** SNUB NOSE
3**snub** \"\ *adj* **1 :** used in snubbing ⟨~ rope⟩ ⟨~ line⟩ **2** *or* **snubbed :** BLUNT, STUBBY, STUMPY ⟨allowed a flicker of indulgent amusement to show itself upon his ~ features —Guy McCrone⟩ ⟨a small pyramid . . . a ~ figure, rather flat and inelegant —Isaac Rosenfeld⟩ — **snub·ness** *n* -ES
4**snub** \"\ *vi* **snubbed; snubbing; snubs** [alter. of 1*snob*] *chiefly Midland* **:** SOB
5**snub** \"\ *n* -S *chiefly Midland* **:** SOB
snub·ber \ˈsnəbə(r)\ *n* -S **:** one that snubs: as **a :** a miner who breaks down the working face of a coal seam with a pick so that it will drop freely when blasted **b :** a device with a drum and a brake used with a cable for lowering logs or vehicles down a steep grade **c :** a device for snubbing a cable **d :** SHOCK ABSORBER
snub·bi·ness \-bēnəs, -bin-\ *n* -ES **:** the quality or state of being snubby
snubbing *n* -S **:** the act of one who snubs **:** SNUB, REBUKE, REBUFF
snub·bing·ly *adv* **:** in a snubbing manner
snubbing post *n* **:** a post around which a line is thrown to snub something
snub·bish \ˈsnəbish\ *adj, of the nose* **:** somewhat snub— **snub·bish·ness** *n* -ES
snub·by \-bē, -bi\ *adj* -ER/-EST **1 a :** SNUB ⟨a ~ nose⟩ **b :** SNUB-NOSED ⟨an impudent, vulgar, ~ little face —Aldous Huxley⟩ **2 :** giving snubs **:** inclined to snub ⟨a ~ manner⟩
snub nose *or* **snubbed nose** *n* **:** a short blunt nose; *esp* **:** one slightly turned up at the tip
snub–nosed \ˈ=¦=\ *adj* **:** having a snub nose **:** SNUB ⟨a *snub-nosed* revolver —Erle Stanley Gardner⟩
snub–nosed auklet *n* **:** CRESTED AUKLET
snub–nosed cachalot *n* **:** PYGMY SPERM WHALE
snub–nosed langur *or* **snub–nosed monkey** *n* **:** any of several rather large langurs (genus *Rhinopithecus*) of western China and Tibet that are distinguished by a large fleshy upturned nose
snub pulley *n* **:** a pulley placed to support an empty conveyor belt in its return
snubs *pres 3d sing of* SNUB, *pl of* SNUB
1**snuck** \ˈsnək\ *chiefly dial past of* SNEAK
2**snuck** \"\ *n* -S [alter. of 2*snack*] *chiefly dial* **:** SHARE — **go snucks** *chiefly dial* **:** SHARE
1**snudge** \ˈsnəj\ *vi* -ED/-ING/-S [origin unknown] **1** *chiefly dial* **:** to be stingy and niggardly **2** *chiefly dial* **:** to cheat esp. in competition **:** FUDGE **3 :** to go about hunched over or as if in deep thought
2**snudge** \"\ *n* -S *archaic* **:** a niggardly miserly fellow
3**snudge** \"\ *vi* -ED/-ING/-S [prob. alter. of 2*snug*] *chiefly dial* **:** SNUGGLE, NESTLE
1**snuff** \ˈsnəf\ *n* -S [ME *snoffe*] **1 :** the charred part of a candlewick **2** *obs* **:** the leavings of a cup or glass of liquor **3 a** *obs* **:** UMBRAGE, PIQUE, OFFENSE — usu. used with *take* **b** *chiefly Scot* **:** a fit of resentment or indignation **:** HUFF
2**snuff** \"\ *vb* -ED/-ING/-S [ME *snoffen,* fr. *snoffe,* n.] *vt* **1 a :** to crop the snuff of (a candle) by pinching or by the use of snuffers so as to brighten the light **b :** to extinguish by or as if by the use of snuffers **:** make extinct **:** put an end to **:** KILL — usu. used with *out* ⟨just in case automation ~s out their jobs —A.H.Raskin⟩ **2** *obs* **:** CLEANSE, PURIFY ~ *vi* **1 :** to become extinguished — usu. used with *out* ⟨the lighted wick gutters, ~s out —Ernest Beaglehole⟩ **2** *slang* **:** DIE ⟨I'll love 'er till I ~ it —C.J.Dennis⟩ — often used with *out* ⟨what a place to ~ out in —Elizabeth Bowen⟩
3**snuff** \"\ *vb* -ED/-ING/-S [akin to D *snoffen, snuffen* to sniff, snuff, MD *snuven* to sniff, snuff, *snof* head cold — more at SNIVEL] *vt* **1 :** to draw in forcibly through the nostrils **:** sniff audibly ⟨~ up a solution of salt and water⟩ ⟨~ the fragrance of the clover⟩ ⟨among the irises and roses . . . ~*ing* in . . . the delicious scent —Virginia Woolf⟩ **2 :** to perceive or detect by smelling **:** SCENT, SMELL **3 :** to sniff at in order to examine — used of an animal ~ *vi* **1 :** to inhale through the nose noisily and forcibly **:** sniff or smell inquiringly **2** *archaic* **:** to sniff loudly in or as if in disgust ⟨the enemies of the church rage and ~ —Joseph Hall⟩ **3 :** to chew or inhale snuff **:** take snuff ⟨smoked and ~*ed* almost to the hour of her death —*Irish Digest*⟩
4**snuff** \"\ *n* -S **:** the act of snuffing **:** SNIFF, INHALATION
5**snuff** \"\ *n* -S [D *snuf* (short for *snuftabak,* fr. *snuffen* to sniff + *tabak* tobacco) & *snuif,* short for *snuiftabak,* fr. *snuiven* to sniff (fr. MD *snuven*) + *tabak*] **1 a :** a preparation of pulverized tobacco to be chewed, placed against the gums, or inhaled through the nostrils **b :** the amount of snuff taken at one time **:** PINCH **2 :** SCENT, SMELL, AROMA, ODOR **3** *or* **snuff brown :** MUMMY BROWN 2b — **up to snuff 1** *chiefly Brit* **a :** not easily deceived **b :** SOPHISTICATED, WORLDLY-WISE **2 :** in good shape or normal condition **:** up to an accepted standard ⟨looked more *up to snuff* than he had at any time since he won —G.F.T.Ryall⟩ ⟨one child mentally not *up to snuff* —Andy Logan⟩ ⟨if his judgment of red and green lights isn't *up to snuff* —Frederick Way⟩ ⟨if your work wasn't *up to snuff* . . . you'd hear about it quick enough —W.H.Whyte⟩
6**snuff** \"\ *vt* -ED/-ING/-S [origin unknown] **:** to lightly buff (the grain side of leather) so as to remove grain imperfections
snuff bottle *n* [5*snuff*] **:** an often elaborately decorated bottle for holding snuff
snuffbox \ˈ=,=\ *n* **1 :** a small box for holding snuff usu. carried about the person **2** *dial Eng* **:** PUFFBALL
snuffbox bean *n* **1 :** a sea bean that is the large seed of a tropical liana **2 :** a plant (*Entada phaseoloides* or *E. scandens*) bearing the snuffbox bean and having tough ropy stems, pinnate leaves ending in a tendril, small spicate flowers, and gigantic sword-shaped woody pods divided into boxlike compartments
snuffbox fern *n* **:** MARSH FERN 1
snuff brush *n, chiefly Midland* **:** a stick or brush used in rubbing snuff on teeth or gums
snuff dipper *n* **:** one that dips snuff
1**snuff·er** \ˈsnəfə(r)\ *n* -S [ME *snoffer,* fr. *snoffen* to snuff +

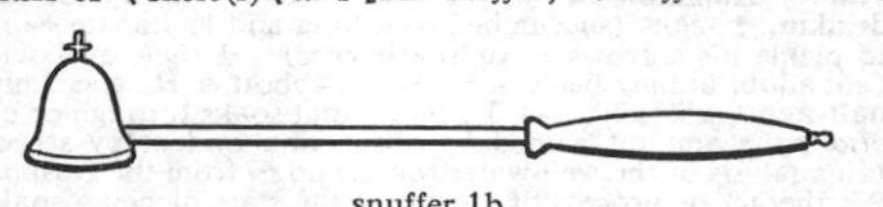

snuffer 1b

-er] **1 a :** a device somewhat like a pair of scissors for cropping and holding the snuff of a candle when its light grows dim or is extinguished — usu. used in pl. but sing. or pl. in constr. **b :** a device for extinguishing candles consisting of a small hollow cone with a handle attached **2** *archaic* **:** one that snuffs cut candles **3 :** a wire used to adjust the wick in a safety lamp — called also *pricker* **4 :** a means for extinguishing an electric arc or preventing ignition by it of combustible material **5 :** a cup-shaped device used for handling incendiary bombs
2**snuffer** \"\ *n* -S [3*snuff* + *-er*] **1 :** one that inhales esp. audibly through the nostrils **2 :** a user of snuff **3 :** PORPOISE
snuff·i·ness \-fēnəs, -fin-\ *n* -ES **:** the quality or state of being snuffy
1**snuffing** *adj* [fr. pres. part. of 3*snuff*] **:** that snuffs disagreeably or disdainfully **:** ARROGANT
2**snuffing** *n* -S [fr. gerund of 2*snuff*] *archaic* **:** the snuff of a wick as removed by snuffers — usu. used in pl.
snuff·ing·ly *adv* **:** in a snuffing manner
snuff·ish \ˈsnəfish\ *adj* [3*snuff* + *-ish*] **:** SNIFFISH, TOUCHY
1**snuf·fle** \ˈsnəfəl\ *vb* **snuffled; snuffled; snuffling** \-f(ə)liŋ\ **snuffles** [akin to D & LG *snuffelen* to nose about, snuffle — more at SNIVEL] *vi* **1 :** to snuff esp. audibly and repeatedly ⟨the tiny dog *snuffled* hungrily over the meat —T.B.Costain⟩ ⟨took her handkerchief . . . and *snuffled* into it —Jean Stafford⟩ **2 :** to breathe through an obstructed nose with a broken sound ⟨a herd of buffalo stomping and *snuffling* around —Jackson Burgess⟩ **3 a :** to speak in a nasal tone ⟨the old man *snuffled* indistinctly in reply⟩ **b** *archaic* **:** to speak in a canting sanctimonious manner **4 :** to make a sound like a snuffle ⟨the wind *snuffling* at the window⟩ ⟨a teletype ~s intermittently —*Lamp*⟩ **5 :** SNIVEL, WHIMPER ⟨the child merely *snuffled* a little⟩ ~ *vt* **1 :** to snuff up ⟨the wind is warm and the horse ~s it —Millen Brand⟩ **2 :** to snuff out ⟨dogs *snuffling* rabbits⟩ **3 :** to snuff at ⟨old hound that used to ~ your door and moan —R.P.Warren⟩ ⟨a snooping dog *snuffled* the thickets —George Heinold⟩
2**snuffle** \"\ *n* -S **1 a :** the act or fact of snuffling **b :** the sound made in snuffling ⟨the snort and ~ of the straining oxen —Victor Canning⟩ **2 :** a nasal twang ⟨talked with an adenoidal ~ —Earle Birney⟩ **3 snuffles** *pl* **:** SNIFFLES **4 snuffles** *pl but usu sing in constr* **:** a respiratory disorder in animals marked esp. by catarrhal inflammation and sniffling: as **a :** a contagious disease of rabbits characterized by nasal discharge, sneezing, rubbing of the nose, and gradual emaciation and caused by a bacterium (*Brucella bronchiseptica*) **b :** BULLNOSE 3
snuf·fler \-f(ə)lə(r)\ *n* -S **1 :** one that snuffles **2 :** one that uses cant
snuff·less \ˈsnəfləs\ *adj* [2*snuff* + *-less*] **:** not requiring snuffing ⟨~ candle⟩
snuf·fli·ness \-f(ə)lēnəs, -lin-\ *n* -ES **:** the quality or state of being snuffly
1**snuffling** *n* -S [fr. gerund of 1*snuffle*] **1 :** the act of snuffling **2 :** SNUFFLE ⟨the ~s of obtuse furry animals grunting and nosing —Virginia Woolf⟩
2**snuffling** *adj* [fr. pres. part. of 1*snuffle*] **:** that snuffles; *specif* **:** SANCTIMONIOUS — **snuf·fling·ly** *adv*
snuf·fly \ˈsnəf(ə)lē, -li\ *adj* -ER/-EST [1*snuffle* + *-y*] **:** SNUFFLING
snuff mill *or* **snuff mull** *n, Scot* **:** SNUFFBOX
snuffs *pl of* SNUFF, *pres 3d sing of* SNUFF
snuff stick *n, chiefly Midland* [5*snuff*] **:** SNUFF BRUSH
1**snuffy** \ˈsnəfē, -fi\ *adj* -ER/-EST [3*snuff* + *-y*] **1 a :** SULKY, PEEVISH **b :** SHORT-TEMPERED **2 :** inclined to haughtiness **:** SUPERCILIOUS, DISDAINFUL ⟨among his mother's ~ colleagues —W.J.Locke⟩ ⟨a ~ seminary for young ladies —Sylvia T. Warner⟩
2**snuffy** \"\ *adj* -ER/-EST [5*snuff* + *-y*] **1 :** resembling snuff (as in color, consistency, or pungency) ⟨~ brown clothing⟩ ⟨~ soil⟩ **2 a :** addicted to the use of snuff ⟨a ~ old man —Henry Watterson⟩ **b :** having unpleasant habits **:** HORRID, DISAGREEABLE ⟨a singularly unattractive, ~ old man —Dorothy C. Fisher⟩ **3 :** soiled with snuff ⟨~ clothes⟩
snuffy ears *n pl but sing in constr* [2*snuffy*] *Austral* **:** LOOSE SMUT
1**snug** \ˈsnəg\ *adj* **snugger; snuggest** [perh. of Scand origin; akin to Sw *snygg* tidy, neat, clean, ON *snöggr* shorn, bald — more at NOVACULITE] **1 a** *of a ship* **:** manifesting seaworthiness (as in design, compactness, or arrangements) **:** adequately prepared for a voyage or esp. for riding a storm **:** TAUT ⟨soon all was ~ aloft, and we were allowed to go below —R. H.Dana⟩ ⟨a comparatively ~ rigged vessel that could leave her three lower sails set in most weather —*Rudder*⟩ **b :** TRIM, NEAT, TIDY — used esp. of a person ⟨a ~ gentleman⟩ **c :** fitting closely but not tightly or uncomfortably **:** not loose or baggy ⟨a ~ coat⟩ ⟨a ~ fit⟩ ⟨stitch bearing retainer by pressing it on until it is ~ —H.F.Blanchard & Ralph Ritchen⟩ **2 a :** enjoying or affording warm secure shelter, safety from intrusion, and opportunity for placid ease and quiet contentment often in unpretentious quarters or quiet ways ⟨his home . . . the ~ haven to which his adventurous forebears retired at the end of their voyages —*Amer. Guide Series: Maine*⟩ ⟨a town that seems especially ~ in winter —Richard Joseph⟩ ⟨sit in the ~ little parlor —*Irish Digest*⟩ **b :** at rest, warmly covered, and safe from cold ⟨~ and warm under blankets and comforters —Willa Cather⟩ ⟨the fisherfolk were all ~ under thatch —G. W.Russell⟩ **c :** affording safe or protected anchorage ⟨the sailboat enthusiast's paradise of ~ harbors —R.W.Hatch⟩ **d :** compact, neat, orderly, and affording or suggesting comfortable sheltered ease or safe smoothness ⟨~ little shops that once offered Cornhill the best soups and jellies —Rebecca West⟩ ⟨a ~ little commune intent on its own affairs —John Buchan⟩ ⟨the street level was broken by three ~ doorways —Harriet LaBarre⟩ **e :** marked by pleasant ease, conviviality, friendly intimacy or cordiality, and secure privacy ⟨~ little dinners with old friends⟩ **3 a :** assuring or affording a degree of comfort and ease ranging from modest adequacy to gratifying ampleness ⟨a ~ little benefice, worth a hundred gold florins a year —Alan Moorehead⟩ ⟨family influence had installed him in a ~ ecclesiastical berth —H.O.Taylor⟩ ⟨his brother made a ~ fortune —Julian Dana⟩ **b** *chiefly Irish* **:** in comfortable financial circumstances **:** fairly well-to-do **4 a :** resorting to or offering safe concealment or a safe retreat ⟨lie ~ until the chase stops⟩ ⟨a ~ hideout⟩ **b** *dial* **:** marked by or given to secretiveness or taciturn reticence ⟨staying ~ about the arrangement⟩ **syn** see COMFORTABLE, NEAT
2**snug** \"\ *vb* **snugged; snugged; snugging; snugs** *vi* **1 a** *archaic* **:** to lie close **:** SNUGGLE — often used with *up* or *together* **b :** to move along close to a confining line or surface ⟨a horse *snugging* along the inner rail of the track⟩ **2 a :** to settle or lie down **:** NESTLE; *specif* **:** to go to bed ⟨dragged the old buffalo hide out to the covered wagon again, *snugged* in the hay and pulled all the horse blankets over us —C.T.Jackson⟩ **b :** to put something in a condition to resist a storm or other onslaught (as by lashing down movables) — often used with *down* ⟨with a good motor, one can ~ down while approaching a harbor —H.A.Calahan⟩ ~ *vt* **1 :** to place in a snug or snuggled-up position **:** cause to fit closely ⟨a belt that ~s the waist⟩ ⟨~ the sole of a shoe to the upper⟩ ⟨overcoat collars turned up and *snugged* close to our necks —S.H. Adams⟩ ⟨she curled up . . . her head *snugged* between her shoulders —D.H.Lawrence⟩ — often used with *down* ⟨found his sons, *snugged* down in a lifeboat, pretending to be castaways —Archie Binns⟩ **2 :** to make snug ⟨push-up sleeves *snugged* by tiny buttons —*Californian*⟩ ⟨tidy up the fields and garden and ~ the place for winter —Hal Borland⟩ — often used with *down, in,* or *up* ⟨*snugged* the farm down for the winter —H.E.Giles⟩ ⟨farmers . . . *snugging* themselves in for the winter —L.C.Douglas⟩ ⟨children were *snugged* up in overcoats, mufflers, and mittens⟩ **3 :** to put away snugly **:** HIDE ⟨pick a pocket and ~ it in a featherbed —W.B.Yeats⟩ **4 a :** to prepare (a ship) for a gale esp. by reducing sail, lowering topmasts, or lashing down movables — usu. used with *down* **b :** to put in a condition to resist a storm or other onslaught — usu. used with *down* ⟨*snugging* down her hatches for the long voyage —W.J.Granbert⟩ ⟨move the aircraft to the parking place and *snug* it down for the night —Nevil Shute⟩ **5 :** to rub (as twine or rope) so as to make smooth and improve the finish
3**snug** \"\ *adv* **:** SNUGLY, NEATLY ⟨a coat that fits ~ across the shoulders⟩ ⟨in harbor, at night berthed ~ —Thomas Wood †1950⟩
4**snug** \"\ *n* -S *Brit* **:** a small private room or a back room in a public house
5**snug** \"\ *n* -S [prob. alter. of 2*snag*] **1** *obs* **:** a jagged projection **2 :** a projecting piece **:** LUG; *esp* **:** one forged under the head of a bolt in order to prevent rotation in screwing up the nut
snug fit *n* **:** a fit (as of mechanical parts) with no allowance **:** the closest fit that can be assembled by hand for parts that are not to move against each other
snug·ger \ˈsnəgə(r)\ *n* -S [2*snug* + *-er*] **:** a device for snugging or making snug
snug·gery \-g(ə)rē, -ri\ *n* -ES [1*snug* + *-ery*] **1** *chiefly Brit* **:** a snug cozy place ⟨underground *snuggeries* for foxes —W.W. Smith⟩; *esp* **:** a small warm comfortable room ⟨little smoking ~ at the end of the passage —W.F.De Morgan⟩ ⟨the inner room . . . was a perfect ~, with walls two feet thick and outside shutters to close at night and . . . rag rugs, red curtains, and feather cushions within —Flora Thompson⟩ **2** *Brit* **:** a parlor or alcove in a public house **:** SNUG
snug·gies \ˈsnəgēz, -giz\ *n pl* [1*snug* + *-ies* (pl. of *-ie*)] **:** women's warm knitted undergarments; *esp* **:** pants of this type
snug·gish \-gish\ *adj* [1*snug* + *-ish*] **:** somewhat snug
1**snug·gle** \ˈsnəgəl\ *vb* **snuggled; snuggled; snuggling** \-g(ə)liŋ\ **snuggles** [freq. of 2*snug*] *vi* **:** to move so as to come near to a person, animal, or thing for warmth or protection or in affection **:** get into or lie in a warm or comfortable position **:** CUDDLE, NESTLE ⟨a baby *snuggling* close to its mother⟩ ⟨~ up in a blanket⟩ ⟨allow aircrews to ~ cozily inside their leaden fuselage —Joseph Wechsberg⟩ ⟨a few houses *snuggling* against a hill⟩ ⟨before he *snuggled* down into the warm domesticity of winter —John Buchan⟩ ~ *vt* **1 a :** to draw (as oneself, one's head, or another) close esp. for comfort or protection or in affection ⟨the dog *snuggled* his muzzle under his master's arm⟩ ⟨kittens *snuggling* a mother cat⟩ **b :** to be or place in a position close to (someone or something) ⟨trapshots used to ~ their cheeks against the combs of their stocks —*Amer. Guide Series: Conn.*⟩ **2 :** to place in a snug position **:** make snug ⟨the ship experiment center is *snuggled* in an out-of-the-way spot —*All Hands*⟩ ⟨*snuggled* the bottle into a lower drawer —David Wagoner⟩
2**snuggle** \"\ *n* -S **:** the action of snuggling
snug harbor *n* **:** a cozy comfortable retreat; *esp* **:** a home for retired seamen
snug·ly *adv* **:** in a snug manner ⟨pipers, with their beribboned bagpipes ~ tucked —W.B.Ready⟩ ⟨while old tenants have sat ~ in their apartments paying a comparatively small rent —Gerda Luft⟩ ⟨extended series of small incidents that must fit ~ together —Arthur Knight⟩ ⟨music is no longer fitted so ~ to the word as before —Alfred Einstein⟩
snug·ness *n* -ES **:** the quality or state of being snug ⟨a fitted shirt . . . with . . . elastic sides and back for ~ —*Car Life*⟩
snum \ˈsnəm\ *vi* [origin unknown] *chiefly dial* **:** VOW, DECLARE — used in the phrase *I snum*
snurl *var of* SNIRL
snurp \ˈsnərp, -nə̄p\ *vi* [of Scand origin; akin to Sw *snäipa* to shrivel up, contract, Norw *snerpa,* Dan *snerpe;* akin to OHG *snerfan* to contract, shrivel up, ON *snarpr* rough, sharp, Goth *atsnarpjan* to touch, and perh. to OE *nearu* narrow — more at NARROW] *dial Eng* **:** to contract into a shriveled form **:** go to pieces
snuz·zle \ˈsnəzəl\ *vi* -ED/-ING/-S [blend of 2*snug* and *nuzzle*] *dial Eng* **:** NESTLE, SNUGGLE
snw *abbr* snow
1**sny** \ˈsnī\ *vi* -ED/-ING/-ES [origin unknown] *dial Eng* **:** ABOUND, TEEM
2**sny** \"\ *vi* -ED/-ING/-ES [origin unknown] **:** to bend upward — used esp. of the edge of a plank near the bow or stern of a ship
3**sny** \"\ *n* -ES **:** the upward curve of the edge of a plank esp. toward the bow or stern of a ship
1**so** \(ˈ)sō, *when followed without pause by a stressed syllable sometimes* sə\ *adv* [ME *so, sa, swa,* fr. OE *swā;* akin to OHG *sō* so, ON *svā,* Goth *swa* so, *swe* as, OL *suad* thus, L *si* if, Gk *hōs* thus, so, Skt *sva* one's own — more at SUICIDE] **1 a :** in a manner or way that is indicated or suggested ⟨many farmers operated a tannery and ~ provided a convenient market for hides —W.M.Kollmorgen⟩ ⟨imposing a pattern which, ~ the author contends, the facts do not warrant —*Brit. Bk. News*⟩ ⟨~ it goes throughout the nation —F.L.Mott⟩ ⟨gave up the life of a missionary in the field to become an administrator . . . it was better ~ —Kemp Malone⟩ ⟨hold the shears right . . . incline the edge ~ —Thomas Hardy⟩ — often used to indicate an exact or close parallel (as between two actions or

situations) ⟨just as in his absence during the war he required weekly reports from the manager . . . ~ now he kept up the same practice —H.E.Scudder⟩; often used with a following clause introduced by *that* or with an infinitive phrase introduced by *as* that shows the logical result or purpose of an action done in a specific manner with the following clause or phrase serving to indicate the desired manner as well as the outcome of the action ⟨the educated people of our country would have to be ~ trained that they could see the dialectical possibility of the opposites of the beliefs they possess —R.M. Weaver⟩ ⟨it ~ happened that . . . the first work bearing this title by a sociologist was published in the same year —L.A. White⟩ ⟨nothing in this constitution shall be ~ construed as to prejudice any claims of the United States —*U. S. Constitution*⟩ ⟨try to hit the snake on the head ~ as to stun it⟩; often used as a substitute in various expressions (1) to express the idea of an entire preceding clause or longer passage ⟨perhaps they take life seriously too, but if ~, that is only because there are things in life . . . worth taking seriously —Clive Bell⟩ ⟨this fly is the most common species of the horseflies, but even ~ it is not abundant —H.L. Van Volkenberg⟩ or (2) to express the idea of a preceding phrase ⟨there seems no logical necessity for local . . . organizations to fall into the hands of reactionaries even though the major national organizations have done ~ —Elmer Davis⟩ or (3) to express approval (as of an action performed in a particular way) sometimes interjectionally ⟨here, just let me turn that curl — there, ~ —T.E.Hook⟩ ⟨if it please you, ~; if not, why, ~ —Shak.⟩ **b :** in the same manner or way **:** ALSO, TOO ⟨always worked on a farm and ~ did his father⟩ ⟨if a metropolis had its hard decorum, ~ had a village —Carl Van Doren⟩ **c :** in the following manner **:** THUS ⟨for ~ the Lord said unto me, I will take my rest —Isa 18:4 (AV)⟩ **d :** forward or as if forward in a manner that is indicated or suggested **:** SUBSEQUENTLY, THEN ⟨~ home and to bed —Samuel Pepys⟩ **2 a** (1) **:** to an indicated or suggested extent or degree ⟨there is usu. some spirit of the age which historians can define, but the shape of things is seldom ~ clear to those who live them —J.W.Krutch⟩ — often used with a following clause that indicates the extent or degree ⟨the difficulties they encountered getting home ~ weakened him that he never recovered his strength —H.E.Starr⟩ ⟨was ~ eloquent he could sell refrigerators to the Eskimos —D.L. Graham⟩ ⟨the nest was . . . in ~ good a state of preservation that it might have been occupied the previous year —*Manchester Guardian Weekly*⟩ ⟨~ gradual was the growth . . . that 90 years after its founding it had but 107 students —*Amer. Guide Series: N.Y. City*⟩; often used with a following infinitive phrase usu. introduced by *as* that indicates the extent or degree by specifying a result or consequence ⟨gossip ~ persistent as to be impossible to ignore —T.H.White b.1915⟩ ⟨had been ~ kind to procure the child a new wardrobe —Mary Charlton⟩ (2) **:** to the same extent or degree **:** to such a degree **:** AS 1 — used chiefly in negative constructions with a following correlative element introduced by *as* ⟨see a bullfight . . . it won't be half ~ gory as you think —T.H.Fielding⟩ ⟨thought that his share wasn't ~ big as his brother's⟩ ⟨never . . . had the condition of the Puritans been ~ deplorable as at that time —T.B.Macaulay⟩ but also in positive constructions ⟨the river was . . . deep enough for a pleasure boat ~ small as theirs —G.K.Chesterton⟩ ⟨if my aunt thought I was defeated ~ easily as that, she . . . was mistaken —R.H.Sampson⟩ ⟨many of our best citizens intend starting to California ~ soon as they can —Pamela Clemens⟩; often used in adjurative phrases ⟨I did see him there, ~ help me⟩ **b :** to a great extent or degree **:** VERY, QUITE, EXTREMELY ⟨had . . . a life of their own, but it was all ~ patterned and convention-ridden —H.S.Bennett⟩ ⟨~ many of the subjects had been photographed ~ often —Norris Harkness⟩ ⟨said that he left her because he loved her ~⟩ — often used in mild negative understatements ⟨isn't ~ slow as a lawyer himself —G.A.Nichols⟩ **c :** to a definite but unspecified extent or degree ⟨I can only move ~ fast —Dave Beck⟩ **d :** most certainly **:** INDEED ⟨said, like a stolid little girl, "I am ~ pregnant" —Maude Hutchins⟩ ⟨"I didn't do it." "You did ~"⟩ **3** — used in place of an adjective to avoid repetition of the adjective ⟨susceptible, but not excessively ~, to the attractions of other women —Anthony Quinton⟩ ⟨is paralyzed but was not born ~⟩ **4 :** for a reason that has just been stated **:** THEREFORE ⟨the records deal mostly with business and ~ are not as valuable . . . as records of a more personal kind —*Notes & Queries*⟩ — **so far from** *prep* **:** rather than **:** instead of — used chiefly to give emphasis by pointing out a marked difference ⟨*so far from* abating, the pestilence grew in virulence —A.M.Young⟩ — **so fashion** *dial* **:** in an indicated way **:** so ⟨I'll knock *so fashion* and peep round the door —Robert Frost⟩

²so \"\ *conj* [ME *so, sa, swa,* fr. OE *swā*] **1 a :** with the result that ⟨the choral work was clean, ~ every word was distinguishable —Douglas Watt⟩ **b :** with the purpose that **:** in order that ⟨separate the marginal items by slashes ~ they won't run together —H.M.Silver⟩ **2 :** provided that — usu. used with *just* ⟨some people don't care who goes hungry just ~ they themselves get enough to eat⟩ **3 a** (1) **:** for that reason **:** THEREFORE ⟨when I speak of these matters I am always accused of being a snob, ~, to illustrate my point, I propose to quote —Nancy Mitford⟩ (2) **:** AND ⟨was getting rather tired by this time, ~ that is why he sang a complaining song —A.A.Milne⟩ **b** (1) — used as an introductory particle ⟨~ here we are at last⟩ occas. reduplicated ⟨~ ~, quoth he, lets attend the time —Shak.⟩ and often to belittle a point under discussion esp. in the phrase *so what* ⟨he took a drink now and then . . . ~ what? He was a man —E.D.Radin⟩ ⟨I may be a numskull scholastically, but what I remember of my family — it was so wonderful. *So* I misspell a word —Helen Traubel⟩ (2) — used interjectionally to indicate awareness of a discovery (as of guilt) ⟨~, that's who did it⟩ or surprised dissent

³so \ˈsō\ *adj* [ME *so, sa, swa,* fr. OE *swā*] **1 :** conforming with actual facts **:** TRUE ⟨cocksure of many things that were not ~ —O.W.Holmes †1935⟩ **2 :** marked by a definite order ⟨insists on having his books just ~⟩

⁴so *pron* [ME, fr. *so, sa, swa,* adv.] **1 :** such as has been specified or suggested **:** the same ⟨became chairman . . . and remained ~ until his death —Marie A. Kasten⟩ ⟨"has she gone?" "I believe ~"⟩ — often used for emphasis at the beginning of a statement ⟨the last day? Why, ~ it is⟩ **2 :** something that approximates what has just been indicated ⟨I've known him 20 years or ~⟩ ⟨back in 1940 or ~ —C.D.Lane⟩ ⟨my joints are somewhat stiff or ~ —Alfred Tennyson⟩ **3 :** THIS ⟨then fold the paper like ~⟩

⁵so *var of* SOL

so *abbr* south; southern

SO *abbr* **1** seller's option **2** senior officer **3** sex offender **4** shipping order **5** ship's option **6** shop order **7** special order **8** staff officer **9** standing order **10** strikeout **11** suboffice **12** supply officer

¹soak \ˈsōk\ *vb* **soaked; soaked** \-kt\ *also* **soak·en** \-kən\ **soaking; soaks** [ME *soken,* fr. OE *socian;* akin to OE *sūcan* to suck — more at SUCK] *vi* **1 :** to remain steeping in water or other liquid **:** to become saturated or softened by immersion ⟨let the beans ~ overnight⟩ ⟨put the clothes to ~⟩ ⟨likes to get in the tub and ~⟩ **2 a :** to enter or pass through something by or as if by pores or interstices **:** PERCOLATE, PERMEATE — often used with *into* ⟨rain ~s into the ground⟩ ⟨blood ~*ing* through the bandage⟩ ⟨the porous quality of the brick into which the light seemed to ~ as if absorbed —Herbert Read⟩ ⟨the warmth ~*ed* into his legs —Oliver La Farge⟩ ⟨dawn was ~*ing* into the sky over the tops of the trees —R.H.Newman⟩ **b :** to penetrate or affect the mind or feelings — usu. used with *in* or *into* ⟨waited for the remark to ~ in —O.S.J. Gogarty⟩ ⟨will let it ~ into my subconscious —W.H.Upson⟩ ⟨the idea of web defense ~*ing* into troops —Tom Wintringham⟩ **3 :** to drink alcoholic beverages intemperately or gluttonously ⟨~*ing* all night at the bar⟩ **4 :** to remain for a considerable time under heat treatment — used esp. of a metal in annealing ~ *vt* **1 :** to permeate so as to wet, soften, or fill thoroughly **:** SATURATE ⟨the meteorologist watched the solid drenching sheets ~ the ground —Hilbert Schenck⟩ ⟨unable to fire a shot because of ~*ed* cartridges and drowned powder horns —F.V.W.Mason⟩ ⟨two entire annual layers had been ~*ed* by the summer meltwater —Walter Schytt⟩ ⟨the house . . . made of sun-*soaked* red brick —Edith Sitwell⟩ ⟨an atmosphere ~*ed* with insatiable interest in international law —G.F.Renier⟩ **2 a :** to place (something) in a liquid or other surrounding element to wet or as if to wet thoroughly **:** SUBMERGE, STEEP ⟨~ the clothes before washing⟩ ⟨~ the negatives in an acid solution⟩ ⟨bread ~*ed* in milk —Agnes Repplier⟩ ⟨~*ed* overnight in vinegar and olive oil —*Amer. Guide Series: La.*⟩ ⟨~*ed* himself in the sunshine —Archibald Marshall⟩ ⟨his irony . . . was ~*ed* in vitriol —Max Lerner⟩ ⟨a drama ~*ed* . . . in blood and rape —Leslie Rees⟩ ⟨books ~*ed* in sentiment —Hubert Herring⟩ ⟨~*ed* himself in booze —V.P.Hass⟩ **b :** to engross the full attention of (a person) in deep and extensive study **:** imbue fully **:** IMMERSE ⟨~ yourself in art⟩ ⟨start right oft not only to expose yourself to, but to ~ yourself in, those fields of knowledge —Bennett Cerf⟩ ⟨~ himself in American history —*Nieman Reports*⟩ ⟨until recently nearly all writers have been ~*ed* in classical and renaissance literature —A.N.Whitehead⟩ **3 a :** to drain or cleanse by washing or absorbing — usu. used with *out* ⟨~ the dirt out of the clothes⟩ ⟨apply a poultice to ~ out the poison⟩ **b** (1) *obs* **:** to exhaust or make poor by emptying or removing ⟨all plants that do draw much nourishment from the earth, and so ~ the earth, and exhaust it —Francis Bacon⟩ (2) **:** to levy an exorbitant or unreasonable charge against (a person or business concern) ⟨neither the newspaper nor its millionaire executives were ever ~*ed* very hard by the tax collectors —D.D.McKean⟩ ⟨~ the rich⟩ ⟨~*ing* the tourist is a popular . . . sport —A.T.Steele⟩ **4 a :** to draw in by or as if by suction or absorption ⟨down the coast bathers cavorted and ~*ed* sun —*Springfield (Mass.) Republican*⟩ — usu. used with *up* ⟨plaster walls ~*ed* up the rain —Virginia D. Dawson & Betty D. Wilson⟩ ⟨partitions ~ up sound —*advt*⟩ ⟨inserting the bar to a length that ~*s* up enough neutrons —Leon Svirsky⟩ ⟨~*ed* up the sunshine —Nelson Glueck⟩ ⟨electronics is ~*ing* up much of the surplus labor and plant space —R.B.Cole⟩ ⟨traveled . . . to ~ up the atmosphere there —Walter Sullivan⟩ ⟨philosophizing about the law does not amount to much until one has ~*ed* in the details —O.W.Holmes †1935⟩ **b :** to intoxicate (oneself) by drinking alcoholic beverages ⟨coming home half ~*ed*, he can hardly climb the stairs⟩ **5 :** to bake (bread) thoroughly **6 :** to beat or punish severely ⟨the jury comes in loaded to ~ an anarchist and a foreigner —Maxwell Anderson⟩ **7 :** to subject (as a metal) to prolonged heat treatment **8 :** to charge (a storage battery) at a low rate

²soak \"\ *n* -S **1 a :** the act or process of soaking **:** the state of being soaked ⟨might as well put them in ~ tonight —Ellen Glasgow⟩ **b :** the liquid in which something is soaked **:** STEEP 2: as (1) **:** a bath for softening dry hides (2) **:** an often hot medicated solution with or in which a body part is soaked usu. long or repeatedly esp. to promote healing, relieve pain, or stimulate local circulation **2** *Austral* **a :** wet land lying esp. at the foot of a local hill **b :** a temporary swamp caused by overflowing surface water **c :** SPRING **3 a :** one who is under the influence of alcohol during most of his waking hours **:** DRUNKARD ⟨a real ~ . . . he hasn't drawn a sober breath in years —Hamilton Basso⟩ **b :** an extended period of hard drinking **:** SPREE ⟨succumbed to a long and legitimate ~ . . . to pickle his sorrows —Audrey Barker⟩ **4** *slang* **:** ¹PAWN 2 ⟨got a job, but my bed's in ~ —E.C.Abbott & Helena Smith⟩

soak·age \-kij, -kēj\ *n* -S **1 :** liquid that soaks through or out; *also* **:** the amount gained by absorption or lost by seepage ⟨an analysis of the well water reveals no ~ from the cesspool⟩ **2 :** the act or process of soaking **:** the state of being soaked ⟨increase the ~ of rain into the geological layers which store water —*Sydney (Australia) Bull.*⟩ ⟨white oak . . . is impervious to ~ through the pores —F.P.Hankerson⟩

soakaway \ˈ⸗⸗ˌ⸗\ *n* -S [fr. *soak away,* v.] *Brit* **:** a depression in the earth's surface into which waters flow and naturally drain away **:** SINK

soak·er \ˈsōkə(r)\ *n* -S *obs* **1 :** one that drains or exhausts **2 a** [short for *old soaker*] *obs* **:** an experienced or elderly person **b :** SOAK 3a **3 :** a worker who carries out a soaking process: as **a :** one who preshrinks woolen cloth with steam **b :** one who soaks hides to clean and soften them **4 :** a long soaking rain ⟨a real good ~ ought to do it . . . a real good all-day rain —C.O.Gorham⟩ **5 :** an absorbent cover of knitted wool for a baby's diaper — often used in pl.

soaking *adv* [fr. pres. part. of ¹*soak*] **:** to a high degree **:** THOROUGHLY — usu. used in phrase *soaking wet*

soak·ing·ly *adv* [ME *sokingly,* fr. *soking* (pres. part. of *soken* to soak) + *-ly*] **1 :** in a slow and steady manner **:** GRADUALLY **2 :** in such manner as to wet thoroughly **:** DRENCHINGLY

soaking pit *n* **:** a deep furnace in which a steel ingot is allowed to stand until its temperature is equalized throughout in preparation for forging or rolling

soaks *pres 3d sing of* SOAK, *pl of* SOAK

so·an \ˈsōˌän\ *also* **so·han** \ˈsōˌhän\ *adj, usu cap* [fr. *Soan, Sohan,* tributary of the upper Indus river in the northwestern part of the Indian subcontinent] **:** of or relating to a Paleolithic culture of West Pakistan characterized by chopping tools

¹so-and-so \ˈsōənˌsō\ *n* -S **1 :** an unnamed or unspecified person or thing ⟨would argue as to whether *so-and-so's* badger could lick such-and-such a dog —*Amer. Guide Series: Nev.*⟩ ⟨the reason he didn't was *so-and-so* —Ring Lardner⟩ ⟨word meaning *so-and-so* —Alexander d'Agapeyeff⟩ **2 :** BASTARD 7 ⟨has often been called an unregenerate *so-and-so* by the opposition —Bill Hatch⟩ ⟨should have given the poor *so-and-so* another chance —Jean Stafford⟩ ⟨you old *so-and-so* . . . how are you, anyway —J.G.Cozzens⟩

²so-and-so \"\ *adv* **:** in an unspecified manner or fashion ⟨instructions were to feed them *so-and-so* and treat them *so-and-so* —H.G.Wells⟩

³so-and-so \"\ *adj* **:** BLANKETY-BLANK ⟨expurgate that profane gentleman's scathing narration of what he terms a *so-and-so* wild-goose chase —G.F.T.Ryall⟩ ⟨you can keep the *so-and-so* car —Harry Bennett⟩

¹soap \ˈsōp\ *n* -S *often attrib* [ME *sope,* fr. OE *sāpe;* akin to MD *sepe* soap, OHG *seifa* soap, OE *sāp* amber, salve, L *sebum* tallow, grease, Toch A *sepal* salve] **1 a :** a cleansing and emulsifying agent that is made usu. either from fats and oils (as a mixture of tallow and coconut oil) by saponification with alkali in the boiling process or the cold process or from fatty acids by neutralization with alkali, that consists essentially of a mixture of water-soluble sodium or potassium salts of fatty acids, and that may contain other ingredients (as sodium carbonate or other builders, perfume, coloring agents, fluorescent dyes, disinfectants, or abrasive material) — sometimes distinguished from *detergent;* compare HARD SOAP, RESIN SOAP, SOFT SOAP, SURFACE-ACTIVE AGENT, TOILET SOAP **b :** a water-soluble salt of a single fatty acid or similar acid **c :** a usu. water-insoluble metal salt other than an alkali-metal salt of a fatty acid or similar acid (as a resin acid or a naphthenic acid) that may be a nuisance (as the calcium and magnesium soaps formed as a curd when ordinary soap is used in hard water) or that may be useful as a paint drier and for other purposes **:** METALLIC SOAP **2 :** soap as prepared esp. for the trade ⟨a full stock of ~*s*⟩ — **no soap :** to no purpose **:** with no results **:** no go ⟨tried to talk the buyer into redrawing the contract . . . but it was *no soap* —F.B.Gipson⟩ ⟨I was asked, I was cajoled . . . I was threatened — but *no soap* —F.H. La Guardia⟩

²soap \"\ *vt* -ED/-ING/-S **1 a :** to rub soap over or into esp. so as to make a lather or coating ⟨~ one's hands⟩ ⟨~*ing* the clothes⟩ ⟨~*ed* crosses on windows and automobiles —*Holiday*⟩ **b :** to treat or scour (as cloth) with a soap solution **2 :** to address in smooth or complimentary speech **:** FLATTER ⟨as I ~*ed* the dean I was sure of having one hearer in my favor —O.W.Holmes †1935⟩ — compare SOFT-SOAP

soap apple *n* **:** the bulb of a soap plant (*Chlorogalum pomeridianum*); *also* **:** the plant itself

soapbark \ˈ⸗ˌ⸗\ *n* **1 a** *also* **soapbark tree :** a Chilean tree (*Quillaja saponaria*) with shining leaves and terminal white flowers **b :** the bark of the soapbark tree that because of its saponin content yields a soapy lather and is used in cleaning and in emulsifying oils — compare QUILLAIC ACID **2** *also* **soapbark tree :** any of several tropical American trees or shrubs of the genus *Pithecolobium* (as *P. bigeminum*) having saponaceous bark

soap·berry \ˈsōp- — *see* BERRY\ *n* **1 a** *also* **soapberry tree :** a tree of the genus *Sapindus* (esp. *S. saponaria*) **b :** the fruit of the soapberry tree that in the common form contains as much as 37 percent saponin **2 :** BUFFALO BERRY

soapberry family *n* **:** SAPINDACEAE

soap-boiler \ˈ⸗ˌ⸗⸗\ *n* **:** one that makes soap by boiling

¹soapbox \ˈ⸗ˌ⸗\ *n* **1 a :** a small box or receptacle designed to hold a bar of soap **b :** a packing box used for shipping soap **2 :** an improvised platform used by a self-appointed, spontaneous, or informal orator ⟨~*es* were carried openly into the classroom and mounted by the orators —Heywood Broun⟩ ⟨need no encouragement to leap on your ~ to tell it to the world —Norris Harkness⟩ ⟨novels are novels and rarely handy ~*es* —Robert Carson⟩

²soapbox \"\ *adj* **1 :** shaped like a soapbox ⟨architects of skyscrapers who found their ~ forms imposed by zoning laws —W.E.Cox⟩ **2 :** of, relating to, or delivered from a soapbox ⟨~ oratory⟩ ⟨distrustful of the whole pattern of ~ politics —Leslie Rees⟩ ⟨the park is the orating ground of the city's ~ evangels —*Amer. Guide Series: Oregon*⟩

³soapbox \"\ *vi* -ED/-ING/-ES **:** to indulge in soapbox oratory ⟨girls who ~*ed* for equal rights —Marybeth Weinstein⟩ ⟨joined picket lines and ~*ed* at breadlines —*Time*⟩ — **soap·box·er** *n*

Soap Box Derby *service mark* — used for a competition in which children usu. 11 to 15 years of age race homemade motorless single-seated vehicles down an inclined raceway

soap brick *n* **:** a small brick used in filling out a course

soap bubble *n* **:** a hollow iridescent globe formed by blowing a film of soapsuds from a pipe

soapbush \ˈ⸗ˌ⸗\ *n* [*soap* + *bush*] **1 :** a deer brush (*Ceanothus integerrimus*) of the western U. S. that is an important browse and honey plant **2 :** SWEET PEPPERBUSH

soap dish *n* **:** a dish for holding soap; *esp* **:** a bathroom or kitchen fixture designed for holding soap

soap dishes

soap earth *n* **:** STEATITE

soaped *past of* SOAP

soap·er \ˈsōpə(r)\ *n* -S [ME *soper,* fr. *sope* soap + *-er* — more at SOAP] **1 :** one that makes or deals in soap **2 a :** a series of tanks in which printed cloth is made colorfast as it is run through a hot solution of water, soap, and a fixing agent **b :** an operator of a soaper **3 :** SOAP OPERA ⟨in radio . . . there were some 40 separate ~*s* a day —Gilbert Seldes⟩

soap·ery \ˈsōpərē\ *n* -ES [¹*soap* + *-ery*] **:** a soap factory

soapfish \ˈ⸗ˌ⸗\ *n* [*soap* + *fish*] **:** any of several fishes constituting the genus *Rypticus* (family Serranidae) of the warmer coasts of America and having scales that are smooth and soapy to the touch

soap flakes *n pl* **:** finely flaked soap prepared for marketing

soapier *comparative of* SOAPY

soapiest *superlative of* SOAPY

soap·i·ly \ˈsōpəlē\ *adv* **:** in a smooth or slippery manner

soap·i·ness \-pēnəs\ *n* -ES **:** the quality or state of being soapy

soaping *pres part of* SOAP

soaplees \ˈ⸗ˌ⸗\ *n pl* [*soap* + *lees* (dregs)] **:** SPENT LYE

soap·less \ˈsōpləs\ *adj* **1 :** being without soap **2 :** UNWASHED, DIRTY

soapless soap *n* **:** DETERGENT c

soap lock *n* [*soap* + *lock*] **1 :** a lock of hair plastered down with soap — usu. used in pl. **2 :** a person wearing a soap lock

soapmaking \ˈ⸗ˌ⸗⸗\ *n* **:** the act, process, or occupation of manufacturing soap

soap nut *n* **1 :** the seed of a soapberry (*Sapindus saponaria*) used for making beads and buttons **2 :** the flat saponaceous pod of an East Indian woody vine (*Acacia concinna*); *also* **:** the plant itself

soap opera *n* [prob. so called fr. the fact that it was formerly often sponsored by soap manufacturers] **:** a radio or television serial drama performed usu. on a daytime commercial program and chiefly characterized by stock domestic situations and often melodramatic or sentimental treatment ⟨unadulterated *soap opera* — a banal story, dripping with sentiment — *Sat. Rev.*⟩

soap orange *n* **:** a wild orange (*Citrus aurantium saponacea*) of Guam and other Pacific islands that has an inedible fruit with saponaceous pulp

soap plant *n* **:** a plant having a part that may be used in place of soap: as **a :** a California plant (*Chlorogalum pomeridianum*) of the family Liliaceae **b :** SOAPWORT 1 **c :** any of several plants of the genera *Agave, Yucca,* and *Zigadenus* found in southwestern U.S. and adjacent Mexico **d :** a soapberry (*Shepherdia canadensis*) having leaves that are silvery on the lower surface

soap powder *n* **:** soap in powdered form made by grinding dried soap chips or by spray-drying crutched soap; *esp* **:** a mixture of soap with large amounts of one or more alkaline builders — compare WASHING POWDER

soaprock \ˈ⸗ˌ⸗\ *n* [*soap* + *rock;* fr. its soapy feel] **:** STEATITE

soaproot \ˈ⸗ˌ⸗\ *n* **1 :** any of several southern European herbs of the genus *Gypsophila* whose roots are used as a substitute for soap **2 :** SAND LILY **3 :** SOAPWORT 1 **4 :** SOAP PLANT a

soaps *pl of* SOAP, *pres 3d sing of* SOAP

soap stock *n* **:** the fatty material from which soap is made; *esp* **:** the foots obtained in refining or hardening oils that contain chiefly fatty acids or their salts and oil

soapstone \ˈ⸗ˌ⸗\ *n* **:** a soft stone having a soapy feel and composed essentially of talc, chlorite, and often some magnetite — compare STEATITE

soapston·er \"+ə(r)\ *n* -S **:** a worker who uses powdered soapstone to clean molds and other equipment used in the rubber industry — called also *talcer*

soapsuds \ˈ⸗ˌ⸗\ *n pl* **:** SUDS 2a, 2b

soap test *n* **:** a test for determining the hardness of water by adding just enough standard soap solution to produce a lasting lather

soap tree *n* **:** any tree that yields saponin; *specif* **:** SOAPBERRY

soapweed \ˈ⸗ˌ⸗\ *n* **:** SOAP PLANT

soapwood \ˈ⸗ˌ⸗\ *n* **1 :** WILD PEAR **2 :** any of several Australian trees with smooth pale yellowish wood **3 :** SOAPBARK 2

soapwort \ˈ⸗ˌ⸗\ *n* **1 :** a European perennial herb (*Saponaria officinalis*) that is widely naturalized or escaped in the U.S. and has coarse pink or white flowers and leaves that yield a detergent when bruised — called also *bouncing Bet* **2 :** COWHERB **3 :** a plant of the family Sapindaceae

soapwort gentian *n* **:** an eastern No. American gentian (*Gentiana saponaria*) whose leaves and unexpanded flower buds resemble those of soapwort

soapy \ˈsōpē, -pi\ *adj* -ER/-EST **1 :** smeared with soap **:** covered with soap **:** LATHERED **2 :** containing or combined with soap or saponin ⟨a ~ water⟩ ⟨a ~ solution⟩ **3 :** resembling or having the qualities of soap **:** SLIPPERY, SMOOTH, SOFT ⟨talc and soapstone have a ~ feel⟩ **4 :** ingratiating or flattering in word or act **:** UNCTUOUS, SUAVE ⟨writes to me requesting in ~ terms what he calls an autographed photograph —O.W. Holmes †1935⟩ ⟨~ supplications for unity — *New Republic*⟩ **5 :** of, relating to, or having the characteristics of soap opera ⟨much of the nighttime drama was equally ~ —*Time*⟩ ⟨the midmorning stimulant that the radio now dishes out in ~ drama —Louise Baker⟩

¹soar \ˈsō(ə)r, ˈsȯ(ə)r, -ōə, -ō(ə)\ *vb* -ED/-ING/-S [ME *soren,* fr. MF *essorer* to expose to the air for drying, throw up in the air, soar, fr. (assumed) VL *exaurare* to expose to the air, fr. L *ex-* ¹ex- + *aura* air — more at AURA] *vi* **1 a :** to mount on wings **:** fly aloft or about ⟨larks ~*ing* into the sky⟩ ⟨birds ~*ed* lower and settled on rooftops —Joseph Hitrec⟩ — often used with *away* ⟨an early gull rose from the water . . . and ~*ed* away into the murk —Nevil Shute⟩ **b** (1) **:** to sail or hover in the air often at a great height **:** GLIDE ⟨vultures ~*ing* above the plain⟩ ⟨a few lilac-colored clouds ~*ed* overhead —G.A.Wagner⟩ (2) *of a glider* **:** to fly without engine power and by means of ascending air currents without loss of altitude **2 :** to go or move upward in position or status **:** RISE ⟨the final rocket . . . ~*ed* twice as high —Jan Struther⟩ ⟨~*ed* in his sophomore year to an eastern record —Eddie Beachler⟩ ⟨his reputation ~*ing* to its zenith —O.S.Nock⟩ ⟨the thermometer ~*ed* up past the century mark —*Sydney (Australia) Bull.*⟩ ⟨up from the eastern sea ~*s* the delightful day —A.E.Housman⟩ **3 :** to ascend to a higher or more exalted level **:** to go beyond earthly or mean things or considerations : TRANSCEND ⟨young ~ing imaginations —John Reed⟩ ⟨his ~ing idealism —H.S.Commager⟩ ⟨his spirit ~ed —Stephen Crane⟩ ⟨a man whose desires ~ed beyond one room —Robertson Davies⟩ — often used with *above* ⟨~ed above the troubles of ordinary people —Marchette Chute⟩ ⟨~ above the facts —A.L.Guérard⟩ **4 a :** to rise to an imposing or majestic stature or height : TOWER ⟨mountainsides . . . ~ 3000 feet from the floor of the narrow valleys —M.J. Herskovits⟩ ⟨half-grown oaks and ~ing poplars —J.A.G. Hungerford⟩ ⟨soldiers filling the impressive square before the ~ing pillars and broad steps —Irwin Shaw⟩ **b :** to go or move to such a height : CLIMB ⟨~ing chairs and tramways of all sorts —William Gilman⟩ ⟨the motorist can be ~ing 284 feet above the ground at one point and boring through a tunnel . . . 30 seconds later —Richard Thruelsen⟩ **5 :** to increase to an uncommon or unprecedented level or amount ⟨unemployment was ~ing —N.M.Clark⟩ ⟨food prices continued to ~ —*Current History*⟩ ⟨~ing hospital costs —Clarence Axman⟩ **6 a :** to sing or play usu. in the higher ranges in an impressive or moving fashion ⟨a soprano voice ~ing ecstatically above the orchestra —Dyneley Hussey⟩ ⟨the welling up of that climactic ~ing of symbolic song —Claudia Cassidy⟩ ⟨~ed effortlessly through two choruses —H.A.Sinclair⟩ **b :** to rise to a high and usu. moving pitch and cadence ⟨no matter what ~ing of verbal eloquence —Leslie Rees⟩ ⟨terse and rich in dialogue . . . the prose ~s in those amazing apostrophes —Douglas Stewart⟩ **7 :** to move or go at a high rate of speed ⟨~ed down that road leaving a trail of dust behind —Frederick Way⟩ ⟨any skier who has ~ed down a slope —*Ford Times*⟩ **~** *vt* **1** *archaic* **:** to lift oneself high in (flight) ⟨whether thy soul ~s fancy's flights beyond the pole —Robert Burns⟩ **2** *archaic* **:** to ascend to or hover through (a height) ⟨~ing the air —John Milton⟩ **syn** see RISE

²soar \"\ *n* -s **1 :** the range, distance, or height attained in soaring ⟨such ~s of fancy⟩ **2 :** the act of soaring : upward flight ⟨the ~ of a lark⟩ ⟨the ~ of song and verse⟩

soar·able \ˈsōrəbəl, ˈsȯr-\ *adj* **:** able to support soaring : permitting soaring ⟨~ winds⟩

soar falcon *or* **soar hawk** *n* [*soar* alter. (influenced by ¹*soar*) of *sore* (as in *sorefalcon*)] **:** SOREFALCON

soaring *n* -s [fr. gerund of ¹*soar*] **:** the act or process of soaring; *specif* **:** the art of operating a heavier-than-air craft without power and without loss of altitude by utilizing ascending air currents

so as *conj* **1 a** *obs* **:** so 1a ⟨I hope you shall receive honorable requital of his amicable ambassade *so as* you shall have no cause to regret his arrival —Elizabeth I⟩ **b :** so 1b ⟨repeated aloud *so as* there'd be no chance of a mistake —G.W.Brace⟩ **2 :** provided that ⟨could play 'em a tune on any sort of pot you please, *so as* it was iron or block tin —Charles Dickens⟩

so·ave \sōˈävā\ *adj* (*or adv*) [It, fr. L *suavis* sweet — more at SWEET] **:** with sweetness or smoothness : in a gentle manner — used as a direction in music

so·a·ve·men·te \sō,ävāˈmentā\ *adv* **:** SOAVE

so·ay \ˈsō(,)ā\ *n* [fr. *Soay*, island of the Hebrides, where the breed originated] **1** *usu cap* **:** an old breed of small dark-brown or blackish sheep that are horned in both sexes **2** -s *often cap* **:** an animal of the Soay breed

¹sob \ˈsäb\ *vb* **sobbed; sobbed; sobbing; sobs** [ME *sobben*] *vi* **1 a :** to catch the breath audibly in a spasmodic contraction of the throat resulting from an intense emotional excitement **b :** to cry or weep with such convulsive catching of the breath ⟨began to ~ a little, like a hurt child —F. Tennyson Jesse⟩ **2 :** to make a sound like that of a sob or sobbing ⟨the loud, rapid, painful, regular intake of *sobbing* breath —Arnold Bennett⟩ ⟨the doves ~ quietly in their cote —Edmund Blunden⟩ ⟨gives . . . the theme to the basses while the horns play a *sobbing* figure —Martin Cooper⟩ **~** *vt* **1 :** to bring (as oneself) to a specified state or condition by sobbing ⟨*sobbed* himself to sleep⟩ **2 :** to utter or pour forth with sobs ⟨had cried enough already, *sobbing* her loneliness into her pillow —Stuart Cloete⟩

²sob \"\ *n* -s [ME *sobbe*, fr. *sobben* to sob] **1 a :** an act of sobbing ⟨~s shook their bodies —George Meredith⟩ ⟨stood for a moment . . . a joyous ~ catching his throat —Wallace Markfield⟩ **b** *archaic* **:** an utterance or sound (as of effort or pain) similar to a sob **2** *obs* **a :** the act of a horse in getting its wind **b :** an interval for a horse to rest **c :** REST, RELIEF **3 :** a sound like that of a sob ⟨~s of the wind in the trees⟩

³sob \ˌe,sōˈbē\ *abbr or n* -s *often cap S&O&B* **:** SON OF A BITCH : BASTARD 7a ⟨what the administration needs most . . . is a ruthless ~ to run its politics —*Time*⟩

sobbed \ˈsäbd\ *adj* [perh. alter. (influenced by ¹*sob*) of *sopped*, past. part. of *sop*, v.] *chiefly dial* **:** thoroughly wet : SOAKED ⟨water-*sobbed* potatoes⟩

sob·ber \ˈsäbə(r)\ *n* -s **:** one that sobs

¹sob·bing \ˈsäbiŋ\ *adj* [perh. alter. (influenced by ¹*sob*) of *sopping*, pres. part. of *sop*, v.] *chiefly dial* **:** thoroughly wet : SOBBED, SOAKED ⟨his shoes are ~⟩

²sobbing \"\ *adv*, *chiefly dial* **:** to a high degree : THOROUGHLY — usu. used in the phrase *sobbing wet*

sob·bing·ly *adv* **:** in a sobbing manner : with sobs

sob·by \ˈsäbē, -bi\ *adj* -ER/-EST [in sense 1, perh. alter. (influenced by ¹*sob*) of *sop*, v., to soak, saturate + -*y*; in sense 2, fr. ²*sob* + -*y*] **1** *chiefly dial* **:** saturated with moisture : WET, SOGGY **2 :** of or relating to sobs or weeping : SENTIMENTAL ⟨sad, ~ little stories in the magazines —*Metropolitan Mag.*⟩ ⟨endeavor to simulate the Italian style . . . results in too much that is strenuous, manifestly ~, and tortured —*Saturday Rev.*⟩

so being *conj* **:** provided that

so·be·it \sōˈbēət\ *conj* [fr. the phrase *so be it*] *archaic* **:** provided that : as long as : IF ⟨the heart of his friend cared little whither he went ~ he were not too much alone —H.W. Longfellow⟩

¹so·ber \ˈsōbə(r)\ *adj*, *usu* -ER/-EST [ME *sobre*, fr. MF, fr. L *sobrius* sober; akin to L *ebrius* drunk] **1 a** (1) **:** sparing in the use of food and drink : restrained in appetite : ABSTEMIOUS ⟨blank as to morals but comparatively ~ in his habits —Dorothy Sayers⟩ ⟨for him the ~ path of moderation appears to be infeasible —J.V.L.Casserley⟩ (2) *archaic* **:** moderate in amount or quantity — used esp. of food or drink⟩ **b :** not given or addicted to the use of intoxicating beverages : ABSTINENT ⟨meet all sorts of men, from ~ traveling missionaries . . . to drunken loafers —Rudyard Kipling⟩ **c :** free from the influence of intoxicating beverages : not drunk ⟨authorities state that a person whose blood contains less than 0.05 percent of alcohol is ~ —*Quarterly Jour. of Studies on Alcohol*⟩ ⟨smelt of port wine, and did not appear to be quite ~ —Charles Dickens⟩ ⟨said he was cold ~⟩ **2 a :** indicating or expressing a thoughtful or grave character or intent ⟨if our pupils are to devote ~ attention to our instruction, we must set a high standard for ourselves —C.H.Grandgent⟩ ⟨had gone into battle . . . with the ~ insouciance, the lighthearted seriousness, so characteristic of the age —Walter Millis⟩ **b** (1) **:** marked by staid or sedate attitude or demeanor : GRAVE, SOLEMN ⟨a group of ~ merchants who detested the leveling tendencies —V.L.Parrington⟩ ⟨pensive nun, devout and pure, ~, steadfast, and demure —John Milton⟩ ⟨the ~ office of sexton —*Countryman*⟩ (2) **:** marked by an earnest or thoughtful demeanor or frame of mind : SERIOUS ⟨was unwontedly ~; his customary levity had . . . deserted him —W.H.Wright⟩ ⟨a ~ and experienced generation, grown old on the battlefields —Sigmund Neumann⟩ **3 a** *archaic* **:** patient or unruffled in bearing or movement : UNHURRIED ⟨pacing back his ~ way, slowly he gained his own array —Sir Walter Scott⟩ **b :** marked by quiet or calmness : PEACEFUL ⟨the sun sinking into a ~ sea⟩ **4** *archaic* **:** of indifferent value : SLIGHT, MEAGER **5** *chiefly Scot* **a :** in poor health : not well : FEEBLE, AILING **b :** UNPRETENTIOUS, HUMBLE **6 a :** indicating or expressing a temperate or moderate character or demeanor ⟨the Puritans . . . with their ~, thrifty, industrious life —Lewis Mumford⟩ ⟨soothes with ~ words their angry mood —John Dryden⟩ **b :** marked by temperance, moderation, or seriousness of character or demeanor ⟨the ~*est* and best man in that countryside, only a little hot and hasty now and then —George Eliot⟩ ⟨the people were quiet, ~, and friendly —Upton Sinclair⟩ **c** *archaic* **:** moderate in ambition or desire ⟨their ~ wishes never learned to stray —Thomas Gray⟩ **7 :** quiet or neutral in color or decoration : SUBDUED ⟨wore no scarlet raiment, but clothed himself in ~ garments —H.O.Taylor⟩ ⟨skies that were ashen and ~ —George du Maurier⟩ ⟨a ~ Georgian colonial with simple details —*Amer. Guide Series: Mich.*⟩ **8 a :** showing no excessive or extreme qualities : RESTRAINED, REASONABLE, TEMPERED ⟨the writing is at once vivid and ~ —*Geog. Jour.*⟩ ⟨the cleanliness, order and ~ luxury of all the dwellings —Arnold Bennett⟩ ⟨the more ~ and less ecstatic types of church —W.L.Sperry⟩ **b :** carefully reasoned or considered : free from fancy or exaggeration : REALISTIC ⟨tried to subdue his riotous senses to the ~ dictates of reason —Ellen Glasgow⟩ ⟨was not a pose of youthful cynicism, but a ~ judgment confirmed by observation and experience —V.L.Parrington⟩ ⟨~ fact⟩ ⟨~ truth⟩ ⟨hope is followed by ~ and critical second thought —John Dewey⟩ **9 :** dictated or guided by sane and sound reason : RATIONAL ⟨being sometimes mad, sometimes ~⟩

syn TEMPERATE, CONTINENT, UNIMPASSIONED: SOBER implies cool composure, dispassionate unprejudiced reason and analysis, or freedom from unreasonable excess ⟨a *sober* book, written without hysteria or excitement —A.T.Steele⟩ ⟨*sober* speech, thoughtfully reasoned and carefully prepared —Jack Gould⟩ ⟨no young giddy thoughtless maiden, full of graces, airs, and jeers — but a *sober* widow —W.S.Gilbert⟩ TEMPERATE implies moderation, self-control, and restraint operating against the excessive, extreme, extravagant, or violent ⟨his *temperate* advice at the early provincial congresses aroused some opposition among the more radical leaders —W.A. Robinson⟩ ⟨the delegates adopted a resolution threatening to rise in armed opposition if any attempt was made to coerce East Tennesseans into the Confederacy. Maynard urged the delegates to be more *temperate* —*Amer. Guide Series: Tenn.*⟩ CONTINENT indicates deliberate accustomed restraint on desires, esp. sexual desires ⟨had the circumstances of their lives given them opportunity they would have been sheer sensualists. Their strength was the strength of men geographically beyond temptation: the poverty of Arabia made them simple, *continent*, enduring —T.E.Lawrence⟩ UNIMPASSIONED indicates lack of ardor and fervor; it may imply accustomed rationality, stoicism, or coldness ⟨in weighed and measured *unimpassioned* words —Robert Browning⟩ ⟨Stephen spoke irritably. He was tired, excited, on fire, and Deborah seemed so *unimpassioned* —Mary Webb⟩ **syn** see in addition SERIOUS

²sober \"\ *vb* **sobered; sobered; sobering** \-b(ə)riŋ\ **sobers** [ME *sobren*, fr. *sobre* sober] *vt* **1 :** to make (a person) serious, grave, or thoughtful ⟨an atmosphere of tense expectancy . . . that ~*ed* everyone —J.R.Perkins⟩ ⟨both had been ~*ed* and sharpened by wide experience —Willa Cather⟩ ⟨the buffet of Providence failed utterly to ~ her frivolous spirit —Robert Grant †1940⟩ ⟨a verdict for libel damages would have a tremendously ~*ing* effect on the guilty party —Norman Cousins⟩ **2 :** to make (a drunken person) sober — usu. used with *up* ⟨trying to ~ him up before taking him home⟩ **3 :** to make (something) neutral or dull in color ⟨the lacy green of trees . . . is ~*ed* by vast fields of brown earth —*Amer. Guide Series: Ark.*⟩ **~** *vi* **1 :** to become sober: as **a :** to become serious or thoughtful ⟨had ~*ed* from youthful cavaliers into . . . astute businessmen —Francis Hackett⟩ **b :** to become neutral or dull in color or tone ⟨the sunset ~*ed* into twilight⟩ **c :** to become sober after being drunk ⟨came home drunk and then ate . . . when they ~*ed* —C.T. Jackson⟩ — usu. used with *up* ⟨the offender apologizes when he ~*s* up —Abram Kardiner⟩ **2 :** to become settled or quiet — usu. used with *down* ⟨~*ed* down and married somebody else and was as sensible as anybody —Ellen Glasgow⟩ ⟨are so high from tension that they need half a dozen drinks to ~ down —Alfred Bester⟩

soberer *comparative of* SOBER

soberest *superlative of* SOBER

so·ber·ing·ly *adv* **:** with a sobering effect ⟨embarrassed by the memory of experiences which once seemed ~ private —Neil Martin⟩

so·ber·ize \ˈsōbə,rīz\ *vb* -ED/-ING/-S [¹*sober* + -*ize*] *vt* **:** to make sober ⟨the honor you have done me has its *soberizing* qualifications —*Times Lit. Supp.*⟩ **~** *vi*, *archaic* **:** to become sober

so·ber·ly *adv* [ME *sobrely*, fr. *sobre* sober + -*ly*] **:** in a sober manner

so·ber·ness *n* -ES [ME *sobrenes*, fr. *sobre* sober + -*nes* -ness] **:** the quality or state of being sober

sobersided \ˈ⸗⸗,⸗⸗\ *adj* [¹*sober* + *sided*] **1 :** of a grave or serious nature : not given to levity : EARNEST, SEDATE ⟨the lean, ~, goateed, frock-coated types the cartoonists love —C.B.Palmer b. 1910⟩ ⟨~ historians of the 17th century —Lindesay Parrott⟩ **2 :** wholly serious in viewpoint or treatment : unrelieved by humor or light touches : SOLEMN ⟨book is no piece of ~ pontificating —*Time*⟩ ⟨a ~ treatise on Congressional organization —R.H.Rovere⟩ ⟨the choreography . . . is ~ and sententious —*Musical America*⟩ — **sobersidedness** *n* -ES

sobersides \ˈ⸗⸗,⸗\ *n pl but sing or pl in constr* [¹*sober* + *sides*] **:** one who is sobersided ⟨is sure to give all but the ~ in the audience some pleasant moments —*Newsweek*⟩ ⟨drew a humorless ~ for his teacher⟩

sob·ful \ˈsäbfəl\ *adj* **:** full of sobs : given to sobbing : drawing forth sobs ⟨in a ~ state⟩ ⟨a ~ story⟩

sobnd *abbr* southbound

sob·o·le \ˈsäbə,lē\ *also* **so·bol** \ˈsō,bäl\ *or* **sob·o·les** \ˈsäbə,lēz\ *n*, *pl* **sobo·les** \-ēz\ *also* **sobols** [L *soboles*, *suboles* sprout, shoot, offspring, fr. *sub-* + root of -*olescere* to grow — more at ADULT] **:** SUCKER, STOLON, SHOOT

sob·o·lif·er·ous \ˌsäbəˈlif(ə)rəs\ *adj* [L *soboles* sprout + E -*iferous*] **:** producing shoots or suckers

so·bor \səˈbȯ(ə)r\ *n* -s *often cap* [Russ, fr. ORuss *sŭborŭ*] **:** an ecclesiastical synod, council, or assembly of the Eastern Orthodox Church

so·bor·nost \-r,nȯst\ *n* -s [Russ, lit., conciliarity, fr. *sobornyĭ* conciliar, fr. *sobor* council] **:** spiritual harmony based on freedom and unity in love : ECUMENICITY; *specif* **:** the principle of spiritual unity and religious community based on free commitment to a tradition of catholicity interpreted through ecumenical councils of the Eastern Orthodox Church — compare CONCILIARITY

so·bra·lia \sōˈbrālēə\ *n*, *cap* [NL, fr. Francisco M. *Sobral*, 18th cent. Span. physician and botanist + NL -*ia*] **:** a genus of tropical American terrestrial orchids having leafy stems and usu. brightly colored solitary or racemose flowers

so·brer·ol \səˈbre,rōl, -rōl\ *n* -s [ISV, fr. Ascanio *Sobrero* †1888 Ital. chemist + ISV -*ol*] **:** a crystalline alcohol $C_{10}H_{16}(OH)_2$ formed by oxidation of alpha-pinene

so·bri·e·ty \səˈbrīəd·ē, sō-, -īət|, |i\ *n* -ES [ME *sobrietie*, fr. MF *sobrieté*, fr. L *sobrietat-*, *sobrietas*, fr. *sobrie-* (fr. *sobrius* sober) + -*tat-*, -*tas* -ty — more at SOBER] **:** the quality or state of being sober ⟨tried to establish rules of ~ in costume . . . to restrain the sartorial excesses —Rosaleen Mills⟩ ⟨able to force himself into ~ despite his alcoholic consumption —Wayne Hughes⟩ ⟨the ~, the earnestness, and the soul-searching . . . come out clearly —T.G.Bergin⟩ ⟨applied himself with scientific ~ to observation of his own life —R.L. Rusk⟩

so·bri·quet \ˈsōbrə,kā, -ket (*usu* -ked·+V), ⸗⸗ˈ⸗\ *or* **sou·bri·quet** \"\ ˈsüb-\ *n* -s [F *sobriquet*, fr. MF *soubriquet* tap under the chin, nickname] **:** an assumed name : a fanciful epithet or appellation : NICKNAME ⟨also had its purely local celebrities . . . with such picturesque ~*s* as "Rowdy Joe" and "Monte Joe" —*Amer. Guide Series: Texas*⟩ ⟨earned the lasting ~ of "Honest John" —G.A.Woods⟩ ⟨referred to it as "that hotbed of radicalism," a trite ~ —G.R.Stewart⟩

sobs *pres 3d sing of* SOB, *pl of* SOB

sob sister *n* **1 :** a journalist who specializes in writing or editing sob stories or other material of a sentimental type ⟨the *sob sisters*, male and female, have filled the magazines and newspapers with sentimental homilies —A.Q.Maisel⟩ ⟨nothing of their marriage would be too intimate for the *sob sisters* to search out and serve to the public in syrupy prose —Vera Caspary⟩ ⟨for fear some . . . *sob sister* would track him down for one of those rags-to-riches human interest yarns —Budd Schulberg⟩ **2 :** a sentimental and often impractical person usu. engaged in good works ⟨the impression that psychiatrists are *sob sisters* who are actuated alone by sympathy for the offender —*Medico-Legal Jour.*⟩ ⟨describes the pacifists as paid agitators, sentimental *sob sisters* —*New Republic*⟩

sob story *n* **1 :** a sentimental story or account designed chiefly to evoke sympathy or sadness ⟨the old *sob story* of youngsters sweltering in the blow rooms of the glass factories and spinning out their lives in cotton mills —*New Republic*⟩ **2 :** a story or account designed to gain sympathy and used as an excuse or rationalization ⟨won't listen to your *sob stories* about absences —Evan Hunter⟩ ⟨your publisher's *sob stories* about how little he can afford —Julian Maclaren-Ross⟩

sob stuff *n* **:** a sob story or other material designed to make a sentimental or strongly emotional appeal ⟨the fineness and restraint of feeling that differentiate it from the coarsely and slushily sentimental child literature, the vulgar *sob stuff* —*Nation*⟩

soc *var of* SOKE

soc *abbr* **1** social; socialist **2** society **3** sociology **4** [L *socius*] companion **5** socket

soc·age *or* **soc·cage** \ˈsäkij, -kēj\ *n* -s [ME *socage*, *sokage*, fr. *soc*, *sok*, *soke* soke + -*age* — more at SOKE] **:** a tenure of land by agricultural service fixed in amount and kind or by payment of money rent only and not burdened with any military service — see FREE SOCAGE, VILLEIN SOCAGE; compare BURGAGE

soc·ag·er \-jə(r)\ *n* -s **:** a tenant by socage : SOKEMAN

so–called \ˈ⸗;⸗\ *adj* **1 :** commonly named : popularly so termed ⟨the privilege of the *so-called* pocket veto —*School & Society*⟩ ⟨his heavy working schedule did not keep the student out of *so-called* campus politics —*Current Biog.*⟩ ⟨closer cooperation with our traditional rivals in the *so-called* Ivy Group —J.B.Conant⟩ **2 :** falsely or improperly so named or designated ⟨deceived by his *so-called* friend⟩ ⟨his *so-called* explanation further confuses the issue⟩

so–called dollar *n* **:** a dollar-size token or medal issued for commemorative purposes or for political propaganda (as an exposition medal or a token issued to propagandize bimetallism or free silver)

soc·cer \ˈsäkə(r)\ *n* -s *often attrib* [by shortening & alter. (influence of -*er*) fr. *association* (in *association football*)] **:** a football game with 11 players on a side in which the ball is advanced by kicking or by propelling it with any part of the body except the hands and arms — called also *association football*

socdolager *var of* SOCKDOLAGER

soce \ˈsōs, ˈsäs\ *n pl* [prob. short for *associates*] *archaic* **:** COMRADES, FRIENDS — used as a term of address

so·cia·bil·i·ty \ˌsōshəˈbiləd·|ē, -lət|, |i\ *n* -ES [ME *socibbilite*, fr. L *sociabilis* sociable + ME -*ite* -ity] **1 a :** the quality or state of being sociable : AFFABILITY ⟨smoke to relieve tension, to express ~ —Vance Packard⟩ **b :** the act or an instance of being sociable ⟨the midmorning coffee break and the other *sociabilities* —David Riesman⟩ **2 :** relative tendency of individuals of one kind (as pine trees) to group themselves together or scatter among individuals of other kinds usu. expressed in terms of gregariousness or dispersion

¹so·cia·ble \ˈsōshəbəl\ *adj* [MF or L; MF *sociable*, fr. L *sociabilis*, fr. *sociare* to join, share (fr. *socius* companion) + -*abilis* -able] **1 :** inclined by nature to community life : inherently disposed to companionship or association with others of the same species : SOCIAL ⟨man is said to be a ~ animal —Joseph Addison⟩ ⟨all large ~ birds make noticeable preparations when about to take wing —E.A.Armstrong⟩ **2 :** inclined to seek or enjoy companionship or social intercourse : AFFABLE, COMPANIONABLE, FRIENDLY ⟨I had been intensely ~, but now I had grown shy —Osbert Sitwell⟩ **b :** marked by or conducive to friendliness or pleasant social relations ⟨ask him to have a dinner and play some ~ pinochle —Mary Barrett⟩ ⟨no more ~ form of traveling to town has been devised than those old river steamers —E.H.Collis⟩ **syn** see GRACIOUS

²sociable \"\ *n* -s **1 a** [short for *sociable coach*] **:** an open four-wheeled carriage having two double seats facing each other and a box for the driver **b :** an S-shaped sofa designed to seat two persons partially facing each other **c :** a vehicle (as a tricycle or airplane) having a seat accommodating two persons side by side **2 :** an informal party or group gathering for general entertainment and encouragement of sociability and frequently having a central activity or interest — called also *social* ⟨giving an ice cream ~ in the grove about the new courthouse —Willa Cather⟩ ⟨enjoying a strawberry ~ on a . . . church lawn —Irving Dilliard⟩

sociable 1b

so·cia·ble·ness *n* -ES **:** SOCIABILITY

sociable weaverbird *n* **:** a southern African weaverbird (*Philetairus socius*) that breeds in colonies having a compound nest in one great umbrella-shaped structure of grass placed in a tree

so·cia·bly \-blē, -li\ *adv* **:** in a sociable manner

¹so·cial \ˈsōshəl\ *adj* [L *socialis*, fr. *socius* companion, ally, associate + -*alis* -al; akin to OE *secg* man, follower, companion, OS *segg*, ON *seggr* man, messenger, companion, Gk *aossein* to help, stand by, Skt *sakha* companion, friend, L *sequi* to follow — more at SUE] **1 :** involving allies or confederates ⟨the *Social* War between the Athenians and their allies⟩ **2 a :** marked by or passed in pleasant companionship with one's friends or associates ⟨leads a very full ~ life⟩ ⟨spent a relaxed ~ evening⟩ : taken, enjoyed, or engaged in with friends or for the sake of companionship ⟨~ drinking⟩ ⟨a ~ game of bridge⟩ **b :** SOCIABLE ⟨difficult for him, although fundamentally a ~ character, to take any great pleasure in the company —Osbert Lancaster⟩ ⟨having to drive home, and not feeling very ~, I drank very little —Nigel Balchin⟩ **c :** composed of sociable persons or formed for the purpose of sociability ⟨a purely ~ club⟩ **d :** of, relating to, or designed for sociability or sociable gatherings ⟨the ~ director of the hotel⟩ ⟨the church has a large ~ hall⟩ **3 a :** forming or having a tendency to form cooperative and interdependent relationships with one's fellows : GREGARIOUS ⟨man is a ~ creature . . . one of the aims of education, therefore, is to teach man how to adjust himself to community living —M.B.Smith⟩ **b :** living together and breeding in more or less organized communities ⟨~ insects are less individuals than standardized, interchangeable units —Ralph Linton⟩ **c** *of a plant* **:** tending to grow in groups or masses so as to form a more or less pure stand — used esp. of forest trees **4 a :** of or relating to human society ⟨~ institutions⟩ ⟨the ~ implications of scientific progress⟩ : of or relating to the interaction of the individual and the group ⟨immature ~ behavior⟩ **b :** of, relating to, or concerned with the welfare of human beings as members of society ⟨~ legislation⟩ ⟨the ~ question⟩ **c** *Roman, civil, & Scots law* **:** of or relating to an association, partnership, or corporation **5 a :** of, relating to, or based on rank or status in a particular society or community ⟨move in different ~ circles⟩ ⟨did not accept him as their ~ equal⟩ ⟨a member of his ~ set⟩ **b :** of, belonging to, or characteristic of the upper classes ⟨a reactionary, solid, stuffy, and ~ —Rosemary Benét⟩ ⟨made fun of her being so ~ and high-tone —Lillian Hellman⟩ ⟨writes a column of ~ gossip⟩ **c :** FORMAL ⟨asked in a ~ voice, very deliberately, if she'd wakened me last night when she came in —Crary Moore⟩

syn GREGARIOUS, COOPERATIVE, CONVIVIAL, COMPANIONABLE, HOSPITABLE: SOCIAL now often indicates having to do with society in general as an interdependent group or as a phenomenon for study ⟨the desire for removing human error, clearing human confusion, and diminishing human misery . . . — motives eminently such as are called *social* —Matthew Arnold⟩ ⟨the *social* order⟩ ⟨plans for *social* reorganization⟩ In its older senses, still quite current, it describes easy pleasant conversational companionship with others conducted on the basis of friendship and equality and enjoyed for its own sake, without ulterior motive ⟨if at times everyone is talking at once it is evidently because of the *social* desire to contribute to the conversation, rather than because of the unsocial disposition to neglect one's neighbor's appreciation —W.C.

Brownell⟩ ⟨of a jovial, *social* disposition, with a host of friends —Allan Westcott⟩ GREGARIOUS indicates tending to flock together with others of one's kind and disliking a solitary existence: it may or may not connote enjoyable sociability ⟨renounced a life of solitude, and became a *gregarious* creature —William Cowper⟩ ⟨without intelligence, man is not social, he is only *gregarious* —Samuel Johnson⟩ ⟨as popular with the seeker after solitude as with the noisily *gregarious* —S.P.B. Mais⟩ ⟨the true Nevadan is *gregarious*, as his passion for clubs and other social circles indicates —*Amer. Guide Series: Nev.*⟩ COOPERATIVE indicates a willingness to work with others for a common end, subordinating immediate personal interests and wishes, and may suggest an attitude conducive to good morale throughout a group ⟨the *cooperative* efforts of all the allies⟩ ⟨while the development of armor called forth the skill of the smith, the multiplication of cannon demanded *cooperative* manufacture on a much larger scale —Lewis Mumford⟩ ⟨the cohesive, *cooperative* nature of American life as opposed to selfish individualism —Bradford Smith⟩ CONVIVIAL suggests jovial or merry enjoyment of others' company, particularly in situations in which eating or drinking is involved ⟨all the social and *convivial* joy and festivity that become youth —Earl of Chesterfield⟩ ⟨at the insistence of a *convivial* uncle and against her better inclination she permits herself to drink three glasses of champagne —Edmund Wilson⟩ COMPANIONABLE suggests a ready affability and warm sympathy that make association easy and pleasant ⟨blessed with a *companionable* roommate⟩ ⟨the trip was the more pleasant because our associates were *companionable*⟩ HOSPITABLE indicates a disposition to greet guests and visitors openly, generously, and warmly ⟨with a few rare exceptions which may arise from sheer lack of time to welcome all newcomers, Arizonans are warmhearted and *hospitable* —*Amer. Guide Series: Ariz.*⟩

²social \"\ *n* -s : SOCIABLE 2

social action *n* : an organized program of socioeconomic reform; *specif* : activity on the part of an interested group directed toward some particular institutional change ⟨a committee for the prevention of juvenile delinquency through *social action*⟩

social anthropology *n* **1** : the study of the social structure of nonliterate societies **2** : CULTURAL ANTHROPOLOGY

social ascidian *n* : any of various ascidians that reproduce by budding like the ordinary compound ascidians but that produce zooids each surrounded by a separate test though remaining connected by stolons

social bee *n* : any of numerous bees (as the bumblebees, honeybees, and stingless bees) of the superfamily Apoidea that live together in colonies

social brethren *n pl, cap S&B* : members of a small religious body organized in 1867 in Illinois on the basis of orthodox evangelical doctrines and a polity formed principally from Baptist and Methodist features

social casework *n* : CASEWORK

social climber *n* : one who attempts to gain a higher social position; *esp* : one ambitious to gain acceptance as a member of fashionable society ⟨the misery of the *social climber* to whose sumptuous party nobody will come —F.L.Allen⟩

social compact *n* : SOCIAL CONTRACT

social contract *n* [trans. of F *contrat social*] **1** : an agreement among individuals by which organized society is brought into being and which serves to regulate the relations of the members of a society with each other and with the government — compare CONTRACT THEORY, POPULAR SOVEREIGNTY, ROUSSEAUISM **2** : an agreement between the community and the ruler that defines and limits the rights and duties of each

social control *n* : the rules and standards of society that circumscribe individual action through the inculcation of conventional sanctions and the imposition of formalized mechanisms

social credit *n, usu cap S&C* : a doctrine that the capitalist system does not distribute sufficient income to keep itself in operation and that national dividends should be declared for consumers to assure a high level of consumption

social dance *n* **1** : a group dance or couple dance done for social and usu. recreational purposes — see BALLROOM DANCE **2** : a gathering held in a ballroom, in a home, or outdoors where people may participate in social dances

social darwinism *n, usu cap D* : an extension of Darwinism to social phenomena; *specif* : a theory in sociology: sociocultural advance is the product of intergroup conflict and competition and the socially elect classes (as those possessing wealth and power) possess biological superiority in the struggle for existence

social democracy *n* [trans. of G *sozialdemokratie*] : the principles and policies of social democrats or of a Social Democratic party

social democrat *n* [trans. of G *sozialdemokrat*] **1** *usu cap S&D* : a member of a Social Democratic party **2** : one who believes in and advocates a gradual and peaceful transition from capitalism to socialism by democratic means

social democratic *adj, usu cap S&D* [trans. of G *sozialdemokratisch*] : of or constituting a political party or group advocating social democracy

social disease *n* **1** : VENEREAL DISEASE **2** : a disease (as tuberculosis) whose incidence is directly related to social and economic factors

social disorganization *n* : a state of society characterized by the breakdown of effective social control resulting in a lack of functional integration between groups, conflicting social attitudes, and personal maladjustment

social distance *n* : the degree of acceptance or rejection of social intercourse between individuals belonging to diverse racial, ethnic, or class groups

social dividend theory of taxation : BENEFIT THEORY OF TAXATION

social dynamics *n pl but often sing in constr* : a branch of social physics that deals with the laws, forces, and phenomena of change in society

social engineering *n* : management of human beings with respect to their place and function in society : applied social science

social evil *n* : PROSTITUTION — used with *the*

social gospel *n* **1** : the application of biblical principles and esp. the teachings of Jesus to social problems **2** *usu cap S&G* : a movement in American Protestant Christianity initiated at the end of the 19th century and reaching its zenith in the first part of the 20th century and dedicated to the purpose of bringing the social order into conformity with the teachings of Jesus Christ

social group work *n* : GROUP WORK

social hedonism *n* : UNIVERSALISTIC HEDONISM

social history *n* **1** : history that concentrates upon the social, economic, and cultural institutions of a people — compare CULTURAL HISTORY **2** : the environmental history of an individual; *specif* : CASE HISTORY

social hygiene *n* : the practice of measures designed to protect and improve the family as a social institution; *specif* : the practice of measures aiming at the elimination of venereal disease and prostitution

social insect *n* : an insect that lives in a colony or community with other individuals of the same species

social insurance *n* : insurance against economic hazards (as loss of income due to unemployment, old age, disability, or death) affecting the individual and his family in which the government participates or secures the participation of the employer and the wage earner or self-employed individual — compare PRIVATE INSURANCE

so·cial·ism \ˈsōshəˌlizəm\ *n* -s **1** : any of various theories or social and political movements advocating or aiming at collective or governmental ownership and administration of the means of production and control of the distribution of goods: as **a** : FOURIERISM **b** : GUILD SOCIALISM **c** : MARXISM **d** : OWENISM **2 a** : a system or condition of society or group living in which there is no private property ⟨trace the remains of pure ~ that marked the first phase of the Christian community —W.E.H.Lecky⟩ — compare INDIVIDUALISM **b** : a system or condition of society in which the means of production are owned and controlled by the state — compare CAPITALISM, LIBERALISM **c** : a stage of society that in Marxist theory is transitional between capitalism and communism and distinguished by unequal distribution of goods and payments to individuals according to their work

¹so·cial·ist \-shələst, *in rapid speech* -shl-\ *n* -s [*socialism* + *-ist*] **1** : one who advocates or practices socialism **2** *usu cap* : a member of a socialist party or political group **syn** see COLLECTIVIST

²socialist \"\ *adj* **1 a** : of or relating to socialism ⟨~ theory⟩ ⟨~ ideas⟩ : adhering to or favoring socialism ⟨a ~ state⟩ ⟨a ~ thinker⟩ **b** : advocating, furthering, or constituting political, economic, or social measures or actions tending toward or regarded as tending toward socialism **2** *usu cap* : of, belonging to, or constituting a political party advocating or associated with the doctrines of socialism ⟨the major ~ parties prior to 1914 were all professedly Marxian —G.E.Hoover⟩; *specif* : of or constituting a minor political party in the U.S. formed by fusion after 1899 of the Social Democratic party and seceders from the Socialist Labor party and having its greatest influence and activity in the early 20th century — compare LABOR 2b

so·cial·is·tic \ˌsōshəˈlistik, -tēk\ *adj* [*socialism* + *-istic*] : of, relating to, or tending toward socialism ⟨government ~ development of peacetime atomic power —*New Republic*⟩

socialist labor *adj, usu cap* : of or constituting a minor U.S. political party formed in 1874 and advocating the attainment of socialism by economic rather than political action

so·cial·ite \ˈsōshəˌlīt, *usu* -īd.+V\ *n* -s *often attrib* [¹*social* + *-ite*] : a socially prominent person

so·ci·al·i·ty \ˌsōshēˈaləd·ē, -lət|, |i\ *n* -ES [L *socialitas*, fr. *socialis* social + *-itas* -ity — more at SOCIAL] **1 a** : the quality or state of being social : SOCIABILITY ⟨though capable of friendship, he is not always much disposed to general ~ —Adam Smith⟩ **b** : an instance of social intercourse : an act of sociability — usu. used in pl. ⟨reminded the other of their early *socialities* —J.G.Lockhart⟩ **2** : the tendency to associate with one's fellows or to form social groups ⟨mammals as a class are not naturally strong on ~ —*Harper's*⟩ : the fact or condition of being associated with others : FELLOWSHIP ⟨the moral sense demands that men should be bound together by ties of ~ —J.W.Beach⟩

so·cial·iza·tion \ˌsōshələˈzāshən, ˌsōshəˌlīˈ-\ *n* -s [in sense 1, fr. *socialism* + *-ization;* in other senses, fr. *socialize* (sense 1) + *-ation*] **1** : the action or process of making socialist or putting on a socialist basis : the state of being socialized ⟨made public ownership of land the first step in ~ —Irving Brant⟩ ⟨the country was quite prepared for ~ of the banking structure —*Accent*⟩ **2** : the process by which a human being beginning at infancy acquires the habits, beliefs, and accumulated knowledge of his society through his education and training for adult status — compare ENCULTURATION **3** : adoption (as by a juvenile court) of a sociological approach to legal procedure

so·cial·ize \ˈsōshəˌlīz\ *vb* -ED/-ING/-s *see -ize in Explan Notes* [in sense 1, fr. ¹*social* + *-ize;* in other senses, back-formation fr. *socialization*] *vt* **1** : to render social; *esp* : to fit or train for society or a social environment ⟨children are *socialized* according to a given cultural pattern —H.A.Murray & C.K. Kluckhohn⟩ **2 a** : to constitute on a socialistic basis ⟨~ the country⟩ : subject to collective or governmental ownership and control ⟨~ the land⟩ ⟨~ industry⟩ — compare NATIONALIZE **b** : to use for social purposes : adapt to social needs or uses ⟨*socializing* science in such a way as to make it more widely available for public use —Kimball Young⟩ **3** : to organize group participation in ⟨teaching that employs the *socialized* recitation instead of the question-and-answer method⟩ **~** *vi* : to participate actively in a social group : enter into or maintain personal relationships with others ⟨*socializing* at backyard barbecues —*Newsweek*⟩ ⟨let the students themselves decide with whom they want to ~ —Vannevar Bush⟩

socialized medicine *n* : administration by an organized group, a state, or a nation of medical and hospital services to suit the needs of all members of a class or all members of the population by means of funds derived from assessments, philanthropy, taxation, or other sources — compare STATE MEDICINE

so·cial·iz·er \-zə(r)\ *n* -s : one that socializes

social justice *n* : a state or doctrine of egalitarianism ⟨the causes of human freedom and of *social justice* —Sir Winston Churchill⟩ ⟨promote the common good and *social justice* —G.J.Schnepp⟩

so·cial·ly \ˈsōshəl|ē, |i, *in rapid speech* -shl|\ *adv* **1** : in a social manner ⟨~ popular⟩ ⟨~ active⟩ **2** : with respect to society ⟨intellectually his superior but ~ his inferior⟩ **3** : by society ⟨~ prescribed values⟩

social medicine *n* : organized investigation of social, genetic, and environmental factors influencing human disease and disability and promotion of methods of prevention of disease and health measures protective of individual and community

social-minded \ˈ==ˈ==\ *adj* : having an interest in society; *specif* : actively interested in social welfare or the well-being of society as a whole

so·cial·ness *n* -ES : SOCIALITY

social order *n* : the totality of structured human interrelationships in a society or a part of it

social organism *n* : society considered as an organic unit analogous to a physiological organism

social organization *n* **1** : the kinship structure of a culture or society esp. as constituted in a stabilized network of rules of descent and residence **2 a** : the system of relationships between persons and among groups with regard to the division of activity and the functional arrangement of mutual obligations within society **b** : the broad institutional interrelationships in a society

social parasitism *n* : a mixobiotic and dependent relation; *specif* : the relation of various ants that lack a worker caste to other kinds of ants within whose nests they dwell and upon whom they depend for all the services normally performed by a species' own workers

social pathology *n* : a study of social problems (as crime or alcoholism) that views them as diseased conditions of the social organism

social philosophy *n* : the study and interpretation of society and social institutions in terms of ethical values rather than empirical relations

social physics *n pl but usu sing in constr* **1** : the science of social phenomena subject to invariable natural laws — compare SOCIAL DYNAMICS, SOCIAL STATICS **2** : the quantitative study of human society : social statistics

social process *n* **1** : a consistent historical change within a society or social institution **2** : a characteristic mode of social interaction

social psychiatry *n* **1** : a branch of psychiatry that deals in collaboration with related specialties (as sociology and anthropology) with the influence of social and cultural factors on the causation, course, and outcome of mental illness **2** : the application of psychodynamic principles to the solution of social problems

social psychology *n* : the study of the manner in which the personality, attitudes, and motivations of the individual esp. as manifested in his behavior reciprocally influence and are influenced by the structure, dynamics, and behavior of the social groups with which he interacts

social realism *n* : a theory or practice (as in painting) of using appropriate representation and symbol to express a social or political attitude

social recovery *n* : an improvement in a psychiatric patient's clinical status without the implication of cure but sufficient to permit his return to his former social milieu

social reg·is·ter·ite \-ˈrejəstəˌrīt\ *n* -s [fr. *Social Register*, a trademark + E *-ite*] : one whose name is listed in a register of persons socially prominent

socials *pl of* SOCIAL

social science *n* **1** : the branches of science that deal with the institutions and functioning of human sooiety and with the interpersonal relationships of individuals as members of society **2** : a science (as economics or political science) dealing with a particular phase or aspect of human society — compare BEHAVIORAL SCIENCE

social scientist *n* : a specialist in the social sciences

social secretary *n* : a personal secretary employed to handle social correspondence and appointments

social security *n* **1** : the principle or practice of public provision for the economic security and social welfare of the individual and his family (as through social insurance or assistance) **2 a** *sometimes cap* : a U.S. government program established in 1935, gradually extended since, and including provisions for old age and survivors insurance, contributions to state unemployment insurance, and old age assistance **b** : a deduction or payment made under the U.S. social security program ⟨deducted three dollars from his check for *social security*⟩ ⟨hasn't received his *social security* for this month⟩

social selection *n* : the differential action of social conditions or agencies on the longevity and reproductive rates of individuals and strains in the population ⟨war is a factor in *social selection*⟩

social service *n* : an activity designed to promote social welfare; *specif* : organized philanthropic assistance of the sick, destitute, or unfortunate (as by a hospital, church or charitable agency) : WELFARE WORK

social statics *n pl but usu sing in constr* : a branch of social physics that deals with the fundamental laws of the social order and the equilibrium of forces in a stable society

social structure *n* **1** : the internal institutionalized relationships built up by persons living within a group (as a family or community) esp. with regard to the hierarchical organization of status and to the rules and principles regulating behavior **2** : the social organization of a society constituting an integrated whole

social studies *n pl* : the part of a school or college curriculum concerned with the study of social relationships and the functioning of society and usu. including courses in history, government, economics, civics, sociology, geography, and anthropology

social system *n* **1** : the patterned series of interrelationships existing between individuals, groups, and institutions and forming a coherent whole : SOCIAL STRUCTURE **2** : the formal organization of status and role that may develop among the members of a relatively small stable group (as a family or club)

social telesis *n* : TELESIS

social unit *n* : a unit (as an individual, a family, or a group) of a society

social wasp *n* : a wasp that lives in a communal nest

social weaverbird *n* : SOCIABLE WEAVERBIRD

social welfare *n* : organized public or private social services for the assistance of disadvantaged classes or groups; *specif* : SOCIAL WORK

social whale *n* : BLACKFISH 2

social work *n* : any of various professional services, activities, or methods concretely concerned with the investigation, treatment, and material aid of the economically underprivileged and socially maladjusted — compare CASEWORK, COMMUNITY ORGANIZATION, GROUP WORK

social worker *n* : one engaged in social work; *specif* : a professionally trained specialist in social work

¹so·ci·ate \ˈsōs(h)ēət\ *n* -s [ME *sociat*, fr. L *sociatus*, past part. of *sociare* to join, share, fr. *socius* companion — more at SOCIAL] *archaic* : COMPANION

²so·ci·ate \-ēˌāt\ *vi* -ED/-ING/-S [L *sociatus*, past part. of *sociare* to join, share] *archaic* : ASSOCIATE ⟨desire to ~ with and to be in their company —Wallace Stevens⟩

so·ci·a·tion \ˌsōs(h)ēˈāshən\ *n* -s [LL *sociation-*, *sociatio* union, association, fr. L *sociatus* (past part.) + *-ion-*, *-io* -ion] **1** : a mode or process of social interaction whether associative or dissociative — compare FORMAL SOCIOLOGY **2 a** : an ecological association that is usu. rather stable and of essentially uniform composition **b** : a community that is subject to seasonal variation

so·ci·a·tive \ˈsōs(h)ēˌād·iv, -ōshəd·iv, -ōs(h)ēəd·iv\ *adj* [L *sociatus* (past part.) + E *-ive*] **1** : expressive of association ⟨the ~ case⟩ **2** : tending to produce social interaction : ASSOCIATIVE

so·ci·a·trist \sōˈsīə·trəst\ *n* -s [*sociatry* + *-ist*] : one who practices sociatry

so·ci·a·try \-rē\ *n* -ES [*socio-* + *-iatry*] : group psychotherapy through the use of sociometric techniques (as psychodrama or sociodrama)

so·cies \ˈsō(ˌ)shēz\ *n, pl* **socies** [NL, fr. E sociation + *-ies* (as in *species*)] : a transitory ecological society of a developmental community : a seral community comparable to a society

so·cié·taire \ˌsōˌsyāˈta(a)(ə)r\ *n* -s [F, lit., member of a group or society, fr. *société* society (fr. MF *societé*) + *-aire* -ary] : a full member of the acting company of the Comédie Française having a voice in the management and sharing in the profits — compare PENSIONNAIRE

so·ci·e·tal \səˈsīəd·ᵊl, sō'-, -ītᵊl\ *adj* [*society* + *-al*] : of or relating to society : SOCIAL ⟨~ evolution⟩ ⟨~ forces⟩ — **so·ci·e·tal·ly** \-ᵊlē\ *adv*

so·ci·e·tary \səˈsīəˌterē\ *adj* [*society* + *-ary*] : SOCIETAL

so·ci·e·tas \sōˈkēəˌtäs, sōˈsīəˌtas\ *n, pl* **societa·tes** \sōˌkēəˈtäˌtās, sōˌsīəˈtād·(ˌ)ēz\ [L] *Roman & civil law* : SOCIETY 3c

societas le·o·ni·na \-ˌlāəˈnēnə, -ˌlēəˈnīnə\ *n* [LL] : LEONINE PARTNERSHIP

societas uni·ver·so·rum bo·no·rum \-ˌünəvərˈsōrəmbəˈnōrəm, -ˌyünə(ˌ)vərˈs-\ *n* [LL] : a partnership including all the property of the partners however acquired : UNIVERSAL PARTNERSHIP

so·cié·té ano·nyme \sōsyātāänōnēm\ *n, pl* **sociétés anonymes** \"\ [F, lit., anonymous society; fr. the fact that it consists of silent partners] *in civil law systems* : a society or corporation in which liability is limited to the capital invested — compare COMMANDITE

société en com·man·dite \-äⁿkōⁿmäⁿdēt\ *n, pl* **sociétés en commandite** \"\ [F, lit., society in commandite] : COMMANDITE

so·ci·e·ties \səˈsīəd·ēz\ *n pl, usu cap* [fr. pl. of ¹*society;* fr. the fact that they were orig. organized into a number of separate societies] : CAMERONIANS

¹so·ci·e·ty \səˈsīəd·ē, sō'-, -ət|, |i\ *n* -ES [MF *societé*, fr. L *societat-*, *societas*, fr. *socie-* (fr. *socius* companion) + *-tat-*, *-tas* -ty — more at SOCIAL] **1 a** : companionship or association with one's fellows : friendly or intimate intercourse : COMPANY ⟨what are lobster and claret compared with the ~ of those we love —W.S.Gilbert⟩ **b** : one's friends or companions : ACQUAINTANCES ⟨widen his range of feminine ~, hitherto restricted —Richard Sullivan⟩ **2** *archaic* : the quality or state of being connected : RELATIONSHIP **3 a** : a voluntary association of individuals for common ends; *esp* : an organized group living or working together or periodically meeting or worshiping together because of a community of interests or beliefs or a common profession : a corporate or cooperative body ⟨a ~ of lawyers⟩ ⟨an agricultural ~⟩ ⟨the Royal *Society*⟩ **b** (1) : an ecclesiastical division of a town in colonial New England — called also *precinct* (2) : a Congregationalist corporation connected with a local church in the U.S. and having control of the ownership of the church buildings as well as the determination and payment of the minister's salary — called also *parish* **c** *Roman, civil, & Scots law* : an association organized under law for some recognized civil or business purpose and having various forms (as of a corporation, a general partnership, a limited partnership, or a community property entity) — compare COMMANDITE, SOCIÉTÉ ANONYME **d** : an association or fraternity among nonliterate peoples; *esp* : one functioning as an esoteric or ritualistic organization ⟨the medicine *societies* of the No. American Indians⟩ ⟨the leopard ~ of West Africa⟩ **4 a** : an enduring and cooperating social group whose members have developed organized patterns of relationships through interaction with one another; *also* : the complex structure of social institutions of such a group **b** : a community, nation, or broad grouping of people having common traditions, institutions, and collective activities and interests **c** : an international social order or community of societies and institutions ⟨a ~ of nations⟩ ⟨the ideal of a Christian world ~⟩ **d** : an autonomous nonliterate or peasant group possessing a distinct cultural heritage ⟨a primitive ~ in New Guinea⟩ **5 a** : a community made up of an aggregate of persons : those who are responsible for the prevailing social order ⟨when I say ~ I mean more than people; I mean people bound together for an end —V.S.Pritchett⟩ **b** : a part of a community that is a unit distinguishable by particular aims or standards of living or conduct : a social circle or a group of social circles having a clearly marked identity ⟨move in polite ~⟩ ⟨in the judgment of good ~⟩ ⟨literary ~⟩ ⟨musical ~⟩ **c** : a part of the community that sets itself apart as a leisure class and that regards itself as the arbiter of fashion and manners ⟨in most towns and smaller cities there is an easily discernible social pattern with a local ~ on top —F.L.Allen⟩ ⟨introduced to ~ at a formal reception⟩ ⟨snubbed by ~⟩ **6 a** (1) **:** a unit assemblage of plants within an association or consociation characterized by a single species or a common habit ⟨the alder ~ within the sugar maple consociation⟩ ⟨an herbaceous ~ in open woodland⟩ (2) **:** ASSOCIATION 8 **b :** the progeny of a pair of insect parents when constituting a social unit (as a hive of bees) **7 :** an interdependent system of organisms or biological units ⟨the skin — the protector, conservator, and inquirer of the ~ of organs —Margaret Gilbert⟩ ⟨the biological organism, a ~ of cells —T.C.Schneirla & Gerard Piel⟩

²society \"\ *adj* **:** of, relating to, or characteristic of fashionable society ⟨with her outdated ~ face highly rouged —G.A. Wagner⟩ **:** dealing with the activities of fashionable society ⟨~ page⟩ ⟨~ reporter⟩

society finch *n* **:** a small white weaverbird that is prob. an artificial variety and possibly derived from an Asiatic bird (*Lonchura acuticauda*)

society islander *n, usu cap S&I* [*Society island* + E *-er*] **:** a native or inhabitant of the Society islands in French Oceania

society men *or* **society people** *n pl, usu cap S* [so called fr. their being orig. organized into separate societies] **:** CAMERONIANS

society screw *n* [fr. its adoption by the Royal Microscopical Society] **:** a standard screw thread for objectives and nosepieces on microscopes used throughout the world

socii *pl of* SOCIUS

¹so·cin·i·an \sō'sinēən\ *n* -s *usu cap* [NL *socinianus*, fr. Faustus *Socinus* (latinized form of Fausto Sozzini) †1604 Ital. theologian who developed Socinianism and his uncle Laelius *Socinus* (latinized form of Lelio Sozzini) †1562 Ital. theologian whose writings influenced the founding of the movement + L *-ianus* -ian] **:** an adherent of Socinus or Socinianism

²socinian \"\ *adj, usu cap* [NL *socinianus*] **:** of or relating to Socinus, the Socinians, or Socinianism

so·cin·i·an·ism \-ə,nizəm\ *n* -s *usu cap* [NL *socinianismus*, fr. *socinianus* socinian + L *-ismus* -ism] **:** the rationalistic doctrines and anti-Trinitarian theological movement originating in the middle of the 16th century in Italy and developed in Poland under the leadership of Socinus who denied the tenets of the Trinity, the divinity of Christ, the personality of the Devil, the native and total depravity of man, substitutionary atonement, the efficacy of the sacraments, and the eternity of future punishment and affirmed instead the tenets that Christ was a man miraculously conceived by the Virgin Mary, that the Holy Spirit is a power or influence exerted by God, that human sin is the imitation of Adam's sin, that salvation is something to be achieved by the imitation of Christ's virtue, and that the Bible is to be interpreted by and as being in accord with human reason

so·cin·i·an·is·tic \sō¦sinēə¦nistik\ *adj, usu cap* [*socinian* + *-istic*] **:** Socinian in character or tendency

so·cin·i·an·ize \sō'sinēə,nīz\ *vt* -ED/-ING/-s *usu cap* [*socinian* + *-ize*] **:** to cause to conform to Socinianism **:** imbue with Socinianism

socio- *comb form* [F, fr. L *socius* associate, companion — more at SOCIAL] **1 :** society ⟨*socio*graphy⟩ **:** social ⟨*socio*gram⟩ **2 :** social and ⟨*socio*educational⟩ ⟨*socio*political⟩ ⟨*socio*religious⟩ **3 :** sociological and ⟨*socio*legal⟩ ⟨*socio*psychiatric⟩

so·cio·biological \¦sōs(h)ē(,)ō+\ *adj* [*socio-* + *biological*] **1 :** relating to the interrelation of social science and biological science or joining their techniques **2 :** having both a social and biological factor

so·cio·biology \"+\ *n* [*socio-* + *biology*] **:** the study of society in terms of the methods and concepts of biological science

so·ci·o·cen·tric \¦sōs(h)ēō¦sen·trik\ *adj* [*socio-* + *-centric*] **:** concerned with or centered on one's own social group — compare EGOCENTRIC, ETHNOCENTRIC — **so·ci·o·cen·tric·i·ty** \,sōs(h)ēōsen·'trisəd·ē\ *n* -ES

so·ci·o·cen·trism \¦=ˌ=¦sen,trizəm\ *n* -s [ISV *sociocentric* + *-ism*] **:** a tendency to assume the superiority or rightness of one's own social group

so·ci·oc·ra·cy \,sōs(h)ē'äkrəsē\ *n* -ES [F *sociocratie*, fr. *socio-* + *-cratie* -cracy] **1 :** a theoretical form of government in which society as a whole has sovereign rights **2 :** the application of scientifically determined principles promoting the interests of society as a whole

so·ci·o·crat \'sōs(h)ēə,krat\ *n* -s [*socio-* + *-crat*] **:** one who advocates sociocracy

so·ci·o·crat·ic \¦=ˌ=¦krad·ik\ *adj* [*socio-* + *-cratic*] **:** of or relating to sociocracy

so·cio·cultural \¦sōs(h)ē(,)ō+\ *adj* [*socio-* + *cultural*] **:** of, relating to, or involving a combination of social and cultural factors

so·cio·drama \"+\ *n* [*socio-* + *drama*] **1 :** a dramatic play in which several individuals act out assigned roles for the purpose of studying and remedying group or collective relationships — compare PSYCHODRAMA **2 :** the application of the principles of psychodrama to the study of intergroup tensions and conflict — **so·cio·dramatic** \"+\ *adj*

so·cio·dynamic \"+\ *adj* [*socio-* + *dynamic*] **:** causing or producing change in a society or social group ⟨morale is a ~ factor in a ship's company⟩

so·cio·economic \"+\ *adj* [*socio-* + *economic*] **1 :** of, relating to, or involving a combination of social and economic factors; *specif* **:** of or relating to income and social position considered as a single factor ⟨a scale to measure family ~ status⟩ **2 :** of or relating to social economics

so·cio·genesis \"+\ *n* [NL, fr. *socio-* + L *genesis*] **:** the evolution of societies or of a particular society, community, or social unit

so·ci·o·ge·net·ic \¦sōs(h)ēōjə¦ned·ik\ *adj* [*socio-* + *-genetic*] **:** of, relating to, or contributing to sociogenesis ⟨~ factors⟩

so·ci·o·gen·ic \-ēō¦jenik\ *adj* [*socio-* + *-genic*] **:** produced or determined by society or social forces ⟨~ factors in mental health⟩

so·ci·o·gram \'sōs(h)ēə,gram\ *n* [*socio-* + *-gram*] **:** a sociometric chart plotting the structure of interpersonal relations in a group situation

so·ci·o·graph·ic \¦sōs(h)ēə¦grafik\ *adj* [*sociography* + *-ic*] **:** of or relating to sociography ⟨a ~ survey⟩

so·ci·og·ra·phy \,sōs(h)ē'ägrəfē\ *n* -ES [*socio-* + *-graphy*] **:** a branch of sociology that concentrates on the descriptive analysis of social groups

so·ci·o·log·ic \¦sōsēə¦läjik, -jēk *also* ¦sōsh(ē)ə¦-\ *or* **so·ci·o·log·i·cal** \-jəkəl, -jēk-\ *adj* [*sociologic* fr. F *sociologique*, fr. *sociologie* sociology + *-ique* -ic; *sociological* fr. *sociology* + *-ical*] **1 a :** of or relating to sociology or to the methodological approach of sociology **b :** involving one or more of the social sciences generally **2 a :** oriented or directed toward social needs and problems ⟨~ jurisprudence⟩ ⟨~ novels⟩ ⟨~ criticism⟩ **b :** social in nature ⟨only human society is truly ~⟩ **3 :** of or relating to interpersonal and collective relationships rather than to individual psychology — **so·ci·o·log·i·cal·ly** \-jək(ə)lē, -jēk-, -li\ *adv*

so·ci·ol·o·gism \,sōsē'älə,jizəm *also* ,sōshē-\ *n* -s [*sociology* + *-ism*] **:** a sociologistic explanation or theory

so·ci·ol·o·gist \-jəst\ *n* -s [ISV *sociology* + *-ist*] **:** a specialist in sociology

so·ci·ol·o·gis·tic \¦sōsē,älə¦jistik, -tēk *also* ¦sōshē-\ *adj* [*sociology* + *-istic*] **:** SOCIOLOGIC; *specif* **:** explaining social phenomena by sociologic principles alone ⟨a ~ interpretation admitting of no biologic or psychologic factors⟩

so·ci·ol·o·gize \,sōsē'älə,jīz *also* ,sōshē-\ *vt* -ED/-ING/-s [*sociology* + *-ize*] **:** to give a sociological character or interpretation to

so·ci·ol·o·gy \-ləjē, -ji\ *n* -ES [F *sociologie*, fr. *socio-* (fr. L *socius* associate, companion) + *-logie* -logy — more at SOCIAL] **1 :** the science of society, social institutions, and social relationships; *specif* **:** the systematic study of the development, structure, and function of human groups conceived as processes of interaction or as organized patterns of collective behavior **2 a :** the scientific analysis of a social institution as a functioning whole and as it relates to the rest of society ⟨the ~ of education⟩ ⟨the ~ of law⟩ ⟨the ~ of business⟩ **b :** an analysis or exposition of the socially significant traits of a specific group, class, or social milieu ⟨a ~ of the blind⟩ ⟨write a ~ of Victorian England⟩ **3** *Brit* **:** SOCIAL ANTHROPOLOGY **4 :** the study of social and behavioral interaction among lower animals (as in a flock of hens) **:** SYNECOLOGY

so·cio·medical \¦sōsē(,)ō+\ *adj* [*socio-* + *medical*] **:** of or relating to the interrelations of medicine and social welfare

so·cio·met·ric \¦sōsēə¦me·trik, -rēk *also* ¦sōsh(ē)ə¦-\ *adj* [*socio-* + *-metric*] **1 :** adapted for or used in the measurement of social phenomena ⟨a ~ scale⟩ **2 :** relating to or constituting a test in which the members of a group are invited to express their feelings with regard to one another

so·ci·om·e·trist \,sōsē'ämə·trəst *also* ,sōshē-\ *n* -s [*sociometry* + *-ist*] **1 :** a specialist in sociometry **2 :** one who administers sociometric tests

so·ci·om·e·try \-rē, -ri\ *n* -ES [ISV *socio-* + *-metry*] **:** the study (as by sociometric test, psychodrama, or sociodrama) of the patterns of interrelation existing in a group of people

so·ci·o·path \'sōs(h)ēə,path\ *n* -s [*socio-* + *-path*] **:** a sociopathic person

so·ci·o·path·ic \¦=ˌ=¦pathik\ *adj* [*socio-* + *-pathic*] **:** of, relating to, or characterized by asocial or antisocial behavior ⟨a ~ personality⟩ — compare PSYCHOPATHIC PERSONALITY

so·ci·op·a·thy \,sōs(h)ē'äpəthē\ *n* -ES [*socio-* + *-pathy*] **:** the condition of being sociopathic

so·cio·political \¦sōs(h)ē(,)ō+\ *adj* [*socio-* + *political*] **:** of, relating to, or involving a combination of social and political factors

so·cio·psychological \"+\ *adj* [*socio-* + *psychological*] **1 :** of, relating to, or involving a combination of social and psychological factors **2 :** of or relating to social psychology

so·cio·sexual \"+\ *adj* [*socio-* + *sexual*] **:** of or relating to the interpersonal aspects of sexuality — **so·cio·sexuality** \"+\ *n*

so·ci·us \'sōshēəs\ *n, pl* **socii** \-ē,ī\ [L — more at SOCIAL] **1 :** ASSOCIATE, COLLEAGUE ⟨was procurator and ~ to the vice-provincial —R.J.Purcell⟩; *specif, cap* **:** the divine friend and companion of man **2 :** a unit in social relationships consisting of an individual

socius cri·mi·nis \-'krimənəs\ *n* [LL] **:** an associate or accomplice in crime **:** ACCESSORY

¹sock \'säk\ *n* -s *see sense 2a* [ME *socke*, *sokke*, fr. OE *socc*, fr. L *soccus*, a low-heeled light shoe, slipper, sock; akin to Gk *sykchos*, a shoe, sock, Av *haxa* sole of the foot] **1** *archaic* **:** a low shoe or slipper **2 a** *or pl* **sox** \-ks\ **:** a knitted or woven covering for the foot usu. extending above the ankle and sometimes to the knee and worn inside the shoe or other footwear **b :** a soft protective covering (as for the head of a golf club) resembling a sock **c :** SOCK LINING **d** [by shortening] **:** WIND SOCK **3 a :** a shoe worn by actors in Greek and Roman comedy **b :** comedy as a literary or theatrical form **:** the comic stage — compare BUSKIN 2b **4 :** a receptacle for savings ⟨in France, the money tends to disappear into the ~; here it goes into circulation —Frank Gorrell⟩ **5 :** a usu. white band of foot color extending to the fetlock ⟨a horse with three white ~s⟩ **6 :** STOCKING 2c

socks 2b

²sock \"\ *vt* -ED/-ING/-s **:** to furnish socks to **:** put socks on

³sock \"\ *n* -s [ME *sok*, *sokk*, fr. MF *soc*, fr. OF — more at SOCKET] *chiefly Scot* **:** PLOWSHARE

⁴sock \"\ *vb* -ED/-ING/-s [prob. of Scand origin; akin to ON *sökkva* to cause to sink, *sökkva* to sink — more at SINK] *vt* **:** to hit, strike, or apply forcefully ⟨hailstones as big as pullet eggs were ~*ing* me on the head —*Springfield (Mass.) Union*⟩ ⟨I pick a good one and ~ it —Babe Ruth⟩ ⟨~*ed* the hot iron to the calf's side —Lewis Nordyke⟩ **~** *vi* **:** to deliver a blow **:** HIT ⟨a miracle that a person as old . . . could ~ as hard or holler as loud as she could —J.T.Farrell⟩ ⟨the bull lunged forward and ~*ed* against the mattress shield that protected the horse —Barnaby Conrad⟩ — **sock it to** *slang* **:** to act, speak, or express oneself forcefully or violently to ⟨they may let you off the first time . . . but the second time they'll *sock it to* you —James Jones⟩ ⟨he really *socked it to* her . . . he had a great talent for obscenity and filth —Albert Morgan⟩

⁵sock \"\ *n* -s **1 :** a vigorous or violent blow ⟨got a ~ in the belly from somebody that made him plenty sick —H.A.Sinclair⟩ **2 :** FORCE, PUNCH ⟨surface-to-surface missiles will add new ~ to the Army's firepower —*Time*⟩

⁶sock \"\ *adj* [⁴*sock*] **1** *slang* **:** having a loud or forceful quality ⟨dazzling chorus work and ~ arrangements —Douglas Watt⟩ **2** *slang* **:** highly successful ⟨wrote a ~ first play and can't get on with a second —*Time*⟩

⁷sock \"\ *vi* [prob. imit.] *dial Eng* **:** SIGH

sock away *vt* [¹*sock*] *slang* **:** to put away (money) as savings or investment ⟨has *socked away* very little of his earnings with which to buy a ranch —*Life*⟩ ⟨had been *socking* money *away* at a faster rate —*Newsweek*⟩

sock·dol·a·ger *or* **sock·dol·o·ger** *also* **soc·dol·a·ger** \säk'däləjə(r)\ *n* -s [perh. alter. (influenced by ⁵*sock*) of *doxology*] **1 :** something that ends or settles a matter **:** a decisive blow or answer **:** FINISHER **2 :** something or someone outstanding or exceptional ⟨a blizzard — a real ~ —Lorna Slocombe⟩

¹sock·er \'säkə(r)\ *chiefly Brit var of* SOCCER

²socker \"\ *n* -s [⁴*sock* + *-er*] *slang* **:** one that socks; *specif* **:** a hard puncher

sock·er·oo \,säkə'rü\ *n* -s [alter. of ²*socker*] *slang* **:** a smash hit

¹sock·et \'säkət, *usu* -əd·+V\ *n* -s [ME *soket* spearhead shaped like a plowshare, support of a spear or pole, socket, fr. AF, dim. of OF *soc* plowshare, of Celt origin; akin to Corn *soch* plowshare, MIr *soc* plowshare, snout of a hog, OIr *socc* hog — more at SOW (hog)] **1 a :** an opening or hollow that forms a holder for something **:** a hollow piece that serves as a standard or support for a pole, rod, shaft, or similarly shaped object ⟨the whip was in its ~ beside him —Kathleen Freeman⟩ ⟨put the flagpole in its ~⟩ ⟨a candle ~⟩ **b :** any of various hollows in body structures in which some other part normally lodges ⟨the bony ~ of the eye⟩ ⟨an inflamed tooth ~⟩; *esp* **:** the depression in a bone with which the rounded head of another bone fits in a ball-and-socket joint ⟨the acetabulum or ~ of the hip joint⟩ **c :** a cavity terminating an artificial limb into which the bodily stump fits ⟨suction ~⟩ **d :** BELL 5i **2 a :** a device to receive and grip the end of a thing (as a rope, tool, incandescent lamp, or shaft of a golf club) ⟨screwed the light bulb into the ~⟩ **b :** any of several fishing tools for catching the outside of pipe or tools lost in an oil well

²socket \"\ *vt* -ED/-ING/-s **1 :** to provide with or support in or by a socket **2 :** to insert, screw, or secure in a socket

socket-and-spigot joint \¦=ˌ=¦=ˌ=-\ *n* **:** BELL-AND-SPIGOT JOINT

socket chisel *n* **:** a chisel that has a tapering hollow tang to receive a handle — see CHISEL illustration

socket head screw *n* **:** a screw having a recess or socket to fit a wrench for turning rather than a slot or external hexagonal or square shape

sock·et·less \'säkətləs\ *adj* **:** not provided or made with a socket

socket punch *n* **:** a hollow punch (as a belt punch) with a cutting edge forming a closed curve

socket washer *n* **:** a washer countersunk to receive a bolt head or nut

socket wood *n* **:** an Australian sassafras (*Daphnandra micrantha*) that has swellings resembling sockets at the branch bases

socket wrench *n* **:** a wrench in the form of a socket or a rod having a hollow end to fit a bolt or nut — compare BOX WRENCH

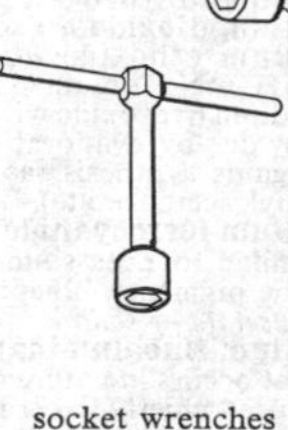

socket wrenches

sock·eye \'säk,ī\ *or* **sockeye salmon** *n* [by folk etymology fr. Salish dial. *suk-kegh* sockeye] **:** a small but very important Pacific salmon (*Oncorhynchus nerka*) attaining an average weight of about 5 pounds and ascending rivers chiefly from the Columbia northward to spawn in late summer or fall — called also *red salmon;* compare KOKANEE

sock in *vt* [¹*sock;* fr. the fact that indications by the wind sock may cause flights to be canceled] **1 :** to close in **:** CONCEAL ⟨bases . . . *socked in* with monsoon clouds squatting on the runways —Wesley Price⟩ **2 :** to restrict from flying ⟨planes *socked in* by fog⟩

socking *pres part of* SOCK

sock·less \'säkləs\ *adj* **:** being without socks

socklike \'=ˌ=\ *adj* **:** resembling a sock

sock lining *n* **:** a thin piece of leather or other material inserted in a shoe over the insole

sock·man \'säkmən\ *archaic var of* SOCMAN

socko \'sä(,)kō\ *adj* [prob. fr. ⁵*sock* + ¹*oh*] **1** *slang* **:** SMASH ⟨some ~ successes in TV —Ethel Merman⟩ **2** *slang* **:** packing a wallop ⟨the ~ lines, the one-two punch lines —*Vogue*⟩

socks *pl of* SOCK, *pres 3d sing of* SOCK

sock suspenders *n pl, Brit* **:** men's garters

so·cle \'säkəl, 'sōkəl\ *n* -s [F, fr. It *zoccolo* sock, wooden shoe, socle, fr. L *socculus*, dim. of *soccus* sock — more at SOCK] **:** a projecting usu. molded member at the foot of a wall or pier or beneath the base of a column, pedestal, or superstructure — compare PLINTH

soc·man \'säkmən, 'sōk-\ *n, pl* **socmen** [ML *sochemannus, sokemannus* — more at SOKEMAN] **:** SOKEMAN

soc·man·ry \-nrē\ *n* -ES [by alter.] **:** SOKEMANRY

so·co \'sō(,)kō\ *n* -s [Pg *socó*, fr. Tupi *soco*, *çoco*] **:** any of several Brazilian herons; *esp* **:** any of certain night herons and bitterns

¹so·co·tran \sə'kō·trən\ *or* **so·co·trine** \-rən\ *or* **so·ko·tron** \-rən\ *adj, usu cap* [*Socotra*, *Sokotra*, island in the Indian ocean + E *-an* or *-ine*] **:** of, relating to, or characteristic of Socotra, an island in the Indian ocean off Cape Guardafui, Africa

²socotran *or* **sokotran** \"\ *n* -s *cap* [*Socotra*, *Sokotra* + E *-an* (n. suffix)] **:** a native or inhabitant of Socotra

so·cra·te·an \¦säkrə¦tēən\ *adj, usu cap* [*Socrates* †399 B.C. Greek philosopher + E *-an*] **:** SOCRATIC

¹so·crat·ic \sə'krad·|ik, sō'-, -at|, |ēk\ *adj, usu cap* [L *socraticus*, fr. Gk *sōkratikos*, fr. *Sōkratēs* Socrates †399 B.C. Greek philosopher + *-ikos* -ic] **:** of or relating to the philosopher Socrates, Socratism, or the Socratics

²socratic \"\ *n* -s *usu cap* **1 :** a follower of Socrates **2 :** a member of one of the minor schools of Greek philosophy (as the Cynic, Cyrenaic, or Megarian) influenced by Socrates — called also *lesser Socratic, minor Socratic*

so·crat·i·cal \|əkəl\ *adj, usu cap* [L *socraticus* + E *-al*] *archaic* **:** SOCRATIC

so·crat·i·cal·ly \|ək(ə)lē\ *adv, usu cap* **:** in the Socratic method

socratic elenchus *n, usu cap S* **:** the method of questioning and cross examination used by Socrates

socratic induction *n, usu cap S* **:** the process of gradually arriving at generalizations through dialectical questions and answers — compare SOCRATIC METHOD

socratic irony *n, usu cap S* **:** pretended ignorance or willingness to learn from others assumed for the sake of making their errors conspicuous by means of adroit questioning

so·crat·i·cism \sə'krad·ə,sizəm\ *n* -s *usu cap* [¹*socratic* + *-ism*] **1 :** SOCRATISM **2 :** a Socratic trait or principle

socratic method *n, usu cap S* **:** the method of inquiry and instruction employed by Socrates esp. as represented in the dialogues of Plato and consisting of a series of questionings the object of which is to elicit a clear and consistent expression of something supposed to be implicitly known by all rational beings

so·cra·tism \'säkrə,tizəm\ *n* -s *usu cap* [*Socrates* †399 B.C. Greek philosopher (fr. L, fr. Gk *Sōkratēs*) + E *-ism*] **:** the philosophy or the method of Socrates to whom are generally ascribed an intense ethical devotion that influenced all later Greek philosophy, the development of the inductive method, and the conception of knowledge or insight as the foundation of virtue — compare DIALECTIC, SOCRATIC METHOD

socy *abbr* society

¹sod \'säd\ *n* -s *often attrib* [ME *sod*, *sodde*, fr. MD or MLG *sode;* akin to OFris *sātha* sod] **1 a :** the upper stratum of the soil that is filled with the roots of grass or other herbs **:** TURF, SWARD **b :** a piece or section of such sod (as for grassing a lawn) **2 a :** the grass-covered surface of the ground ⟨hired nesters to break ~ for 50 cents an acre —F.B.Gipson⟩ ⟨clambered on to the wet-soaked ~ of land —Michael McLaverty⟩ **b :** COUNTRY 2a — usu. used in the phrase *old sod* ⟨would take a trip to the old ~ —J.T.Farrell⟩

²sod \"\ *vt* **sodded; sodded; sodding; sods :** to cover with sod ⟨many gullies on the ridge have been *sodded* with grass —*Amer. Guide Series: Ark.*⟩ ⟨*sodded* earthen bunkers capped three walls —B.A.Roth⟩

³sod \"\ *adj, archaic, of food* **:** boiled or prepared by boiling; *sometimes* **:** SOGGY, UNPALATABLE

⁴sod \"\ [ME *soden* (past pl.), fr. OE *sudon*] *archaic past of* SEETHE

⁵sod \'säd\ *n* -s [short for *sodomite*] *chiefly Brit* **:** BUGGER ⟨you bleary-eyed murderous ~ —Ernest Hemingway⟩ ⟨picture palace for the silly ~s to go and get rid of the rest of their minds in —Richard Llewellyn⟩

sod *abbr* sodium

SOD *abbr* seller's option to double

so·da \'sōdə, *dial* -dē *or* -di\ *n* -s [It, barilla (from which soda is produced), soda, fr. (assumed) ML *soda* barilla (whence ML *sodanum* barilla), perh. fr. Ar *suwwād*] **1 a :** SODIUM CARBONATE; *esp* **:** the decahydrate of the normal salt **b :** SODIUM BICARBONATE **c :** SODIUM HYDROXIDE **2 a :** SODIUM OXIDE **b :** SODIUM — not used systematically ⟨nitrate of ~⟩ **3 a :** SODA WATER 2 **b :** ICE-CREAM SODA **4 :** the faro card that shows face up in the dealing box before play begins

soda alum *n* **:** sodium alum esp. in the isometric crystal form but not isostructural with potash alum — compare MENDOZITE

soda ash *n* **:** commercial anhydrous sodium carbonate Na_2CO_3 obtained as a grayish white powder or as lumps

soda biscuit *n* **1 :** a biscuit leavened with baking soda and sour milk or buttermilk **2 :** SODA CRACKER

soda bread *n* **:** a quick bread leavened with baking soda and sour milk

soda cracker *n* **:** a cracker leavened with bicarbonate of soda and cream of tartar

soda crystals *n pl* **:** SODIUM CARBONATE a(3)

soda fountain *n* **1 :** an apparatus with delivery tube and faucets for drawing soda water **2 :** the equipment necessary for the preparation and serving of sodas, sundaes, and ice cream; *also* **:** the counter at which such items are dispensed

soda-granite \¦=ˌ=¦=ˌ=\ *n* **1 :** a granite containing more soda than potash **2 :** a granite rock differing from normal granite in containing a soda-plagioclase instead of orthoclase

soda jerk \'=ˌ=,jərk, -,jə̄k, -,jəik\ *or* **soda jerker** \'=ˌ=,=ˌ=\ *n* [*soda jerk*, short for *soda jerker*, fr. *soda* + *jerker*] **:** a counterman at a soda fountain

soda lake *n* **:** ALKALI LAKE

soda lime *n* **:** a granular mixture of calcium hydroxide with sodium hydroxide or potassium hydroxide or both and sometimes with other substances (as kieselguhr) used to absorb moisture and acid gases esp. carbon dioxide (as in gas masks, in the rebreathing technique of inhalation anesthesia, and in oxygen therapy)

soda-lime glass *n* [*soda lime*] **:** a lime glass in which soda is used

so·da·list \'sōdᵊləst\ *n* -s *sometimes cap* [*sodality* + *-ist*] **:** a member of a sodality

so·da·lite \-də,līt, -dᵊl,īt\ *n* -s [*soda* + *-lite*] **:** a mineral $Na_4Al_3Si_3O_{12}Cl$ consisting of a sodium aluminum silicate with some chlorine that occurs commonly in dodecahedrons, that is transparent to translucent with a vitreous or greasy luster, that is white, greenish, gray, or blue in color, and that is found in various igneous rocks (hardness 5.5–6, sp. gr. 2.14–2.30)

so·dal·i·ty \sō'daləd·ē, -lətē, -i\ *n* -ES [L *sodalitat-*, *sodalitas* comradeship, association, club, fr. *sodalis* comrade — more at ETHICAL] **1 :** a grouping, association, or joining together based on common purpose or interest **:** BROTHERHOOD, COMMUNITY ⟨whether ape hordes are blood kin or mere territorial *sodalities* —Weston La Barre⟩ ⟨federal ~⟩ ⟨body of ardent and vocal supporters and a formidable ~ of hostile critics —R.J.B. Sellar⟩ **2 :** an organized society or fellowship **:** FRATERNITY, CLUB ⟨endless . . . *sodalities* into which people brigade themselves —John Buchan⟩; *specif* : a lay association of the Roman Catholic Church organized for devotional or charitable purposes **3** *obs* : a chapel used for sodality meetings and devotions

soda lye *n* : a solution (as used in soap-making) of sodium hydroxide

soda mesolite *n* : NATROLITE

soda mica *n* : PARAGONITE

so·da·mide \'sōdə|,mīd, sō'da|, |_məd\ *n* -s [*sodium* + *amide*] : SODIUM AMIDE

soda niter *n* : SODIUM NITRATE

soda pop *n* : a soft drink consisting of water charged with carbon dioxide with added flavoring and a sweet syrup

soda process *n* : a method for making pulp by cooking wood chips at high temperature and pressure in an alkaline solution containing chiefly caustic soda

soda pulp *n* : pulp prepared by the soda process — compare SULFITE PULP, WOOD PULP

so·dar \'sō,där, -dȧ(r\ *n* -s [*sound detecting and ranging*] : an acoustical system operated like radar and initially developed to investigate the atmosphere directly overhead for the prediction of the weather

sodas *pl of* SODA

soda soap *n* : a usu. hard soap made with sodium hydroxide or sodium carbonate

soda–tremolite \¦=+¦==,=\ *n* : a mineral $Na_2CaMg_5Si_8O_{22}(OH)_2$ consisting of an amphibole that differs from tremolite in having sodium in place of half of the calcium

soda water *n* **1** : a weak solution of sodium bicarbonate with some acid added to cause effervescence **2 a** : a beverage consisting of water highly charged with carbon dioxide that is effervescent when not under pressure and is used in the manufacture of soft drinks and with various liquors in highballs and other alcoholic drinks **b** : SODA POP

sod–bound \'=,=\ *adj* [¹*sod*] : impeded in growth or yield by a seemingly crowded condition of the sod usu. resulting from inadequate nitrates in the soil ⟨*sod-bound* grass⟩ ⟨*sod-bound* meadows⟩

sodbuster \'=,==\ *n* : one that breaks the sod: **a** : a breaking or sod plow **b** : a farmer on a homestead **c** : FARMER; *esp* : a farm worker or tiller of the soil

sod cloth *n* : a heavy canvas or duck cloth that extends into the ground at the foot of a tent wall and serves to exclude vermin and rain

sod crop *n* : a crop (as flax or corn) grown on a field of freshly broken sod

sod culture *n* : the culture of fruit trees in sod with or without fertilizing or light tillage

sodded *past of* SOD

¹**sodden** [ME *soden*, fr. OE] *archaic past part. of* SEETHE

²**sod·den** \'säd³n\ *adj* [ME *soden*, fr. *soden*, past part.] **1** *archaic* : BOILED **2 a** : dull or expressionless in cast or appearance from or as if from continued indulgence in alcoholic beverages ⟨a feeble smile crept over his ~ features —Joseph Furphy⟩ ⟨a burly, ~ red-faced man —S.E.White⟩ **b** : dull or mentally inert : TORPID, UNIMAGINATIVE ⟨is emotionally, intellectually, and spiritually . . . too ~ a character to carry the full weight of philosophical understanding —C.I. Glicksberg⟩ ⟨quickens their ~ . . . minds to some sort of glimmering conception of writing as an art —Dorothy C. Fisher⟩ **c** : wearisome or monotonous in delivery or effect : SPIRITLESS ⟨turns in a ~ performance, ranting endlessly about his daughter's conduct —John McCarten⟩ ⟨considering how many ~ and saccharine singers wandered through half a dozen variety shows —Bernard De Voto⟩ **3 a** : heavy with moisture or water : SOAKED, SATURATED ⟨the ~ drumming of the water on the caribou skins of the roof —Farley Mowat⟩ ⟨torrid atmospheric conditions which . . . had reduced the conductor's collar to a ~ wreck —*Sydney (Australia) Bull.*⟩ ⟨the sands were ~ with petroleum that killed fish, destroyed waterfowl —Walter Karig⟩ **b** : settled, unremitting, or oppressively heavy or inert ⟨living in clumsy and ~ ugliness —Galbraith Welch⟩ ⟨depicts ~ hopelessness in the dreary landscape —Curtis Dahl⟩ ⟨the ~ habits of a dead and inferior era —C.G. Burke⟩ ⟨the exhausted, ~ sleep of beasts —F. Tennyson Jesse⟩ ⟨too small a minority to leaven the ~ mass of a people long subject to absolutist rule —V.L.Parrington⟩ **c** : heavy or doughy because of imperfect cooking ⟨~ biscuits⟩ **4** : filled or weighed down with evil : SORDID ⟨exposing the ~ motives behind anti-Semitism —Carl Van Doren⟩ ⟨some very ~, very callous guys operate around these stock joints —Marcus Verner⟩ ⟨drunkenness is a ~ vice —Albert Mowbray⟩

³**sodden** \"\ *vb* **soddened; soddened; soddening** \-d(ᵊ)niŋ\ **soddens** *vt* : to make sodden: **a** : SOAK, SATURATE ⟨bread which has been ~*ed* in water —C.R.A.Martin⟩ **b** : to cause (one's mind) to become dull, stupid, or inert ⟨~*ed* by years of oppression and hardship⟩ **c** : to make (a person) flabby or bloated by alcoholic beverages ⟨a woman ~*ed* and mad with brandy —William Black⟩ ~ *vi* : to become soaked or saturated with moisture or water ⟨the sands ~ as the waves move in⟩

sod·den·ly *adv* : in a sodden condition or manner ⟨tramping ~ homeward through the dust —Booth Tarkington⟩

sod·den·ness \-dᵊn(n)əs\ *n* -ES : the quality or state of being sodden

sodding *n* -s [fr. gerund of ²*sod*] **1** : the action of one that sods **2** : SOD, TURF

sod disease *n* [¹*sod*] : a severe vesicular dermatitis esp. of the feet of young chickens and turkeys ranging on sod that is marked by swelling and frequent sloughing of toes and is thought to be due to a fungus infection

sod·dite \'sä,dīt\ *n* -s [Frederick *Soddy* †1956 Eng. chemist + E *-ite*] : SODDYITE

¹**sod·dy** \'sädē, -di\ *adj* -ER/-EST [¹*sod* + *-y*] : consisting of, covered with, or abounding in sod : TURFY

²**soddy** \"\ *n* -ES [¹*sod* + *-y*] : SOD HOUSE

sod·dy·ite \'sädē,īt\ *n* -s [alter. of *soddite*] : a mineral $(UO_2)_{12}Si_5O_{22}.14H_2O$ consisting of a hydrous uranium silicate occurring in fine-grained pale-yellow aggregates or orthorhombic crystals

sod grass *n* [¹*sod*] : a grass that forms good sod — compare SAINT AUGUSTINE GRASS

sod house *n* : a house with walls built of sod or turf laid in horizontal layers

so·dic \'sōdik\ *adj* [ISV *sod-* (fr. NL *sodium*) + *-ic*] : of, relating to, or containing sodium

so·dio \'sōdē,ō\ *adj* [*sodio-*] : containing sodium in place of hydrogen

sodio- *comb form* [NL *sodium*] **1** : sodium and ⟨*sodio*aluminic⟩ ⟨*sodio*hydric⟩ **2** : containing sodium in place of hydrogen — used in names of organic compounds ⟨*sodio*malonic ester⟩ ⟨*sodio*nitromethane⟩

so·di·um \'sōdēəm\ *n* -s [NL, fr. E *soda* + NL *-ium*] : a silver white soft waxy ductile metallic element of the alkali metal group that has a low melting point and density and high electrical and thermal conductivity, that occurs abundantly in nature in combined form (as rock salt, Chile saltpeter, trona, borax, glauberite, albite), in soils, in the sea and other salt waters, in most plants, and in the animal body esp. in the fluids, that is usu. prepared by electrolysis of a mixture of fused sodium chloride and calcium chloride, that is very active chemically and oxidizes and tarnishes readily in air and burns with a yellow flame, that reacts violently with water to form sodium hydroxide and spontaneously ignitable hydrogen, that is stored under kerosene, other inert hydrocarbon liquid, or in tight containers protected from moisture and air, and that is used sometimes in the form of its amalgam or other alloys or in dispersions in hydrocarbon liquids in making tetraethyl lead and various sodium compounds (as sodium cyanide, sodium hydride, sodium peroxide), in organic synthesis (as in reducing esters to alcohols for making detergents), in metallurgy esp. for removing oxygen or various impurities, in sodium-vapor lamps, and as a heat-transfer agent esp. in cooling valves for internal-combustion engines — symbol *Na;* see ELEMENT table; compare RADIOSODIUM

sodium acetate *n* : either of two sodium salts of acetic acid: **a** : the hygroscopic crystalline normal salt CH_3COONa used chiefly in organic synthesis and photography and as a mordant or as an analytical reagent **b** : the acid salt $CH_3COONa.CH_3COOH$ used chiefly in inhibiting mold and rope in bakery products; sodium hydrogen acetate

sodium acid phosphate *n* : SODIUM PHOSPHATE 1a

sodium acid pyrophosphate *n* : SODIUM PYROPHOSPHATE a

sodium alginate *n* : ALGIN c

sodium alum *n* : a crystalline double salt $NaAl(SO_4)_2.12H_2O$ used similarly to potassium alum; sodium aluminum sulfate dodecahydrate — called also *soda alum*

sodium aluminate *n* : a crystalline compound $NaAlO_2$ used chiefly in water purification, in making synthetic zeolites, and in sizing paper

sodium aluminum fluoride *n* : SODIUM FLUOALUMINATE

sodium aluminum sulfate *n* : a salt $NaAl(SO_4)_2$ occurring either in the anhydrous form as a fine powder used as an acid ingredient of baking powder or in the hydrated forms mendozite and sodium alum

sodium amide *n* : a crystalline compound $NaNH_2$ that decomposes explosively in contact with water, that is usu. made by passing ammonia through molten sodium, and that is used chiefly in making sodium cyanide and in organic synthesis as a strongly basic condensing agent (as in the preparation of indoxyl for making indigo) — called also *sodamide*

sodium antimonate *n* : an antimonate of sodium; *esp* : the meta-antimonate $2NaSbO_3.7H_2O$ obtained as a granular powder and used chiefly as an opacifier for enamels

sodium arsenate *n* : an arsenate of sodium: as **a** : the poisonous secondary orthoarsenate Na_2HAsO_4 or its hydrates that are used chiefly in dyeing and in medicine **b** : the poisonous normal orthoarsenate $Na_3AsO_4.12H_2O$ used chiefly in making other arsenates and insecticides

sodium arsenite *n* : a poisonous substance that is obtained as a concentrated solution or dry powder by treating arsenic trioxide with sodium hydroxide, that consists in some cases of a mixture of sodium ortho-arsenite Na_3AsO_3 and sodium meta-arsenite $NaAsO_2$, and that is used chiefly as an insecticidal bait and weed killer

sodium aurothiosulfate *n* : GOLD SODIUM THIOSULFATE

sodium azide *n* : a poisonous crystalline salt NaN_3 used esp. to make lead azide

sodium benzoate *n* : a crystalline or granular salt C_6H_5COONa used chiefly as a food preservative

sodium biborate *n* : BORAX

sodium bicarbonate *also* **sodium acid carbonate** *n* : a crystalline salt $NaHCO_3$ that is less soluble in water than normal sodium carbonate and gives a weakly alkaline reaction, that evolves carbon dioxide when heated, that is found in nature and is also made by passing carbon dioxide into a solution of the normal carbonate or by purifying the intermediate product of the Solvay process, that is used chiefly in baking powders, in carbonated beverages and effervescent salts, in fire extinguishers, and in medicine as an antacid, and that with carbonic acid constitutes the principal inorganic buffer system of blood and other body fluids; sodium hydrogen carbonate — called also *baking soda, nahcolite, soda*

sodium bichromate *n* : SODIUM DICHROMATE

sodium bifluoride *n* : SODIUM FLUORIDE b

sodium bisulfate *also* **sodium acid sulfate** *n* : a crystalline salt $NaHSO_4$ that gives an acid reaction in solution, that is usu. made by the reaction of sulfuric acid with common salt or sodium sulfate, and that is used chiefly as a flux in pickling metals and as an acid ingredient in dyeing and cleaning compositions; sodium hydrogen sulfate — called also *niter cake*

sodium bisulfite *also* **sodium acid sulfite** *n* : either of two salts usu. obtained by passing sulfur dioxide through a solution of sodium carbonate: **a** : an unstable crystalline salt $NaHSO_3$ that is known esp. in solution and forms sodium metabisulfite on dehydration; sodium hydrogen sulfite **b** : SODIUM METABISULFITE

sodium borate *n* : a sodium salt of a boric acid; *esp* : BORAX — compare SODIUM PERBORATE

sodium borohydride *n* : a hygroscopic crystalline compound $NaBH_4$ that is flammable but remarkably stable in air and decomposes readily in water only above room temperature or in the presence of acid to yield hydrogen and sodium metaborate, that is made in various ways (as from methyl borate and sodium hydride or from diborane and sodium methoxide), and that is used chiefly as a reducing agent for organic compounds — called also *sodium tetrahydroborate*

sodium bromide *n* : a crystalline salt NaBr having a biting saline taste that is used similarly to potassium bromide esp. in medicine and photography

sodium cacodylate *n* : a poisonous deliquescent crystalline or granular salt $(CH_3)_2AsOONa.3H_2O$ used in medicine as an arsenical

sodium carbonate *n* : a sodium salt of carbonic acid: as **a** (1) : the hygroscopic crystalline anhydrous normal salt Na_2CO_3 that is moderately soluble in cold water and gives a strongly alkaline reaction, that was orig. obtained from the ash of sea plants but is now usu. produced by the Solvay process in light and dense forms, and that is used chiefly in making glass, soap powders and soap builders, in water treatment, in the manufacture of pulp and paper, and in the manufacture of sodium hydroxide and other chemicals — called also *soda ash;* compare LEBLANC PROCESS (2) : the crystalline monohydrate $Na_2CO_3.H_2O$ found in nature as thermonatrite and used similarly to the anhydrous salt in photography and medicine (3) : the efflorescent crystalline decahydrate $Na_2CO_3.10H_2O$ found in nature as natron but usu. made artificially by crystallization and used chiefly in washing and bleaching textiles — called also *sal soda, soda, washing soda* **b** : SODIUM BICARBONATE **c** : SODIUM SESQUICARBONATE

sodium carboxymethyl cellulose *n* : a gummy substance that is obtained as a hygroscopic powder or a granular solid by reaction of alkali cellulose and sodium chloroacetate, that is either soluble in water or swells in water, and that is used chiefly as a thickening, emulsifying, and stabilizing agent (as in sizes for textiles and paper and in pharmaceutical ointments) and as a bulk laxative and antacid in medicine : a sodium salt of carboxymethyl cellulose

sodium chlorate *n* : a hygroscopic crystalline salt $NaClO_3$ usu. made by electrolysis of common salt and used as an oxidizing agent (as in dye manufacture) and for the manufacture of perchlorates and perchloric acid, and as a weed killer

sodium chloride *n* : SALT 1a

sodium chlorite *n* : a crystalline salt $NaClO_2$ usu. made by reaction of sodium hydroxide with chlorine dioxide from the reduction of a chlorate and used chiefly as a bleaching and oxidizing agent

sodium chromate *n* : a yellow crystalline salt Na_2CrO_4 made by roasting chrome ore with soda ash and used chiefly in making pigments and other chromium chemicals and in dyeing and processing textiles

sodium citrate *n* : a crystalline salt $Na_3C_6H_5O_7$ used chiefly in foods as a buffering agent, in pharmaceuticals as an alkalizer and cathartic, and in medicine as a blood anticoagulant

sodium cyanide *n* : a highly poisonous deliquescent crystalline salt NaCN usu. made by heating sodium amide with carbon and used chiefly in case-hardening and heat-treating steel, in the cyanide process, in electroplating, and in chemical synthesis

sodium diacetate *n* : SODIUM ACETATE b

sodium dichromate *n* : a poisonous red deliquescent crystalline salt $Na_2Cr_2O_7$ made by oxidizing sodium chromate and used in making pigments, tanning leather, dyeing, cleaning and protecting metals from corrosion, and as an oxidizing agent

sodium dihydrogen phosphate *n* : SODIUM PHOSPHATE 1a

sodium dioxide *n* : SODIUM PEROXIDE

sodium ethoxide *also* **sodium ethylate** *n* : a strong base C_2H_5ONa obtained in solution by reaction of sodium or sodium hydroxide with ethyl alcohol and as a hygroscopic white powder by evaporation of the excess of solvent and used in organic synthesis (as in the condensation of ethyl acetate to ethyl acetoacetate)

sodium ferrocyanide *n* : a yellow crystalline salt $Na_4Fe(CN)_6$ similar to potassium ferrocyanide and used in making iron blue pigments, blueprint paper, and dyes — called also *yellow prussiate of soda*

sodium fluoaluminate *n* : a crystalline complex salt Na_3AlF_6 that occurs in nature as cryolite, is also made synthetically, and is used chiefly in ceramics, in metallurgy esp. as an electrolyte in the production of aluminum from alumina, and as an insecticide — called also *sodium aluminum fluoride*

sodium fluoride *n* : either of two poisonous crystalline salts usu. made by reaction of hydrofluoric acid with soda ash: **a** : the normal salt NaF that is used in trace amounts in the fluoridation of water, in metallurgy, as a flux, as an antiseptic, and as an exterminator **b** *or* **sodium bifluoride** : the corrosive acid fluoride $NaHF_2$ used as a laundry sour, as a preservative esp. for biological specimens, and in tinning steel; sodium hydrogen fluoride

sodium fluoroacetate *n* : a poisonous powdery compound $CH_2FCOONa$ used as a rodenticide — called also *1080*

sodium fluosilicate *n* : a crystalline salt Na_2SiF_6 used chiefly as a laundry sour, as an insecticide, and in ceramics

sodium formate *n* : a deliquescent crystalline salt HCOONa made usu. by passing carbon monoxide (as in the form of producer gas) through heated sodium hydroxide and used chiefly in making formic acid, sodium oxalate, and oxalic acid and in the chrome tanning of leather

sodium hexametaphosphate *n* : a sodium metaphosphate glass formerly regarded as having the composition $(NaPO_3)_6$

sodium hydrate *n* : SODIUM HYDROXIDE — not used systematically

sodium hydride *n* : a flammable gray to white crystalline compound NaH that is made by reaction of hydrogen and sodium, that is decomposed by water to yield hydrogen and sodium hydroxide, and that is used chiefly in organic synthesis and in removing scale from metals

sodium hydrosulfide *n* : a hygroscopic crystalline compound NaSH used chiefly in dehairing hides; sodium hydrogen sulfide

sodium hydrosulfite *n* : a crystalline salt $Na_2S_2O_4$ made by reduction (as of sodium bisulfite or sulfur dioxide with zinc) and used as a reducing agent esp. in dyeing, printing, and stripping textiles and as a bleaching agent; sodium dithionite — not used systematically

sodium hydroxide *n* : a brittle white deliquescent solid NaOH that dissolves readily in water to form a strongly alkaline and caustic solution, that is made usu. by the electrolysis of common salt or by treating soda ash with hydrated lime, and that is used chiefly in making other chemicals, soap and detergents, rayon and cellulose film, and pulp and paper, in petroleum refining, and in bleaching and mercerizing — called also *caustic soda;* compare LYE

sodium hypochlorite *n* : an unstable salt NaOCl made usu. in aqueous solution by passing chlorine into sodium hydroxide solution and used chiefly as a bleaching agent and disinfectant — see JAVELLE WATER b

sodium hyposulfite *n* **1** : SODIUM THIOSULFATE **2** : SODIUM HYDROSULFITE

sodium iodide *n* : a crystalline salt NaI used like potassium iodide

sodium lactate *n* : a hygroscopic syrupy salt $CH_3CHOHCOONa$ used chiefly as an antacid in medicine and as a substitute for glycerol

sodium lamp *or* **sodium–vapor lamp** *n* : a gas discharge lamp using sodium vapor and designed esp. for lighting highways

sodium lauryl sulfate *n* : the crystalline sodium salt $C_{12}H_{25}SO_4Na$ of sulfated lauryl alcohol; *also* : a mixture of sodium alkyl sulfates consisting principally of this salt and used as an anionic detergent, wetting agent, and emulsifying agent

sodium light *n* : the yellow light of glowing sodium vapor consisting chiefly of two monochromatic portions of wavelength 5890 and 5896 angstroms corresponding respectively to the D_2 and D_1 Fraunhofer lines

sodium metabisulfite *n* : a compound $Na_2S_2O_5$ produced as an anhydrous solid or in aqueous solutions and used chiefly as a reducing agent, bleaching agent, and antichlor, in preserving foods and silage, as an antiseptic esp. in the fermentation industries, and in coagulating rubber latex

sodium metaphosphate *n* **1** : any of several crystalline sodium salts $NaPO_3$ or $(NaPO_3)_n$ of a metaphosphoric acid: as **a** : the water-soluble cyclic trimetaphosphate $(NaPO_3)_3$ or $NaPO_3$ I **b** : sodium Kurrol's salt $NaPO_3$ IV **2 a** : a water-soluble sodium phosphate glass having the composition of a sodium metaphosphate — called also *sodium (1:1) phosphate;* compare SODIUM HEXAMETAPHOSPHATE **b** : SODIUM PHOSPHATE GLASS

sodium metasilicate *n* : SODIUM SILICATE b

sodium molybdate *n* : a molybdate of sodium; *esp* : the normal salt Na_2MoO_4 that commonly crystallizes with two molecules of water and is used chiefly in making pigments and in chemical analysis

sodium morrhuate *n* : a pale-yellow granular salt administered in solution intravenously as a sclerosing agent esp. in the treatment of varicose veins

sodium nitrate *n* : a deliquescent crystalline salt $NaNO_3$ esp. occurring in crude form (as caliche) in Chile and also made by reaction of nitric acid and soda ash and used as a fertilizer, as an oxidizing agent (as in explosives), and in curing meat — called also *soda niter;* see CHILE SALTPETER

sodium nitrite *n* : a colorless or yellowish deliquescent salt $NaNO_2$ made usu. by absorption of nitrogen oxide in a solution of soda ash and used chiefly for diazotizing (as in dye manufacture) and in medicine

sodium nitroprusside *n* : a red crystalline salt $Na_2[Fe(CN)_5NO].2H_2O$ made usu. by reaction of a ferrocyanide and nitric acid or of a ferricyanide and nitrous acid and used chiefly in testing for sulfides with which it forms a violet color in alkaline solution; disodium penta-cyano-nitrosyl-ferrate

sodium orthosilicate *n* : SODIUM SILICATE a

sodium oxalate *n* : a poisonous crystalline salt $Na_2C_2O_4$ made by heating sodium formate and used chiefly as a source of oxalic acid and as a reagent in chemical analysis

sodium oxide *n* : an oxide of sodium; *esp* : the hygroscopic amorphous monoxide Na_2O that reacts violently with water to yield sodium hydroxide and that is obtained chiefly as an intermediate in the manufacture of sodium peroxide

sodium pentothal *n* : the sodium salt of thiopental

sodium perborate *n* : either of two crystalline or powdery substances that are compounds of sodium metaborate with hydrogen peroxide and are used chiefly as bleaching agents and oxidizing agents and in mouthwashes and dentifrices: **a** *or* **sodium perborate tetrahydrate** : the compound $NaBO_3.4H_2O$ or $NaBO_2.H_2O_2.3H_2O$ made by reaction of sodium peroxide with a solution of borax or by electrolysis of a solution of borax and sodium carbonate **b** *or* **sodium perborate monohydrate** : the compound $NaBO_3.H_2O$ or $NaBO_2.H_2O_2$ made by dehydration of the tetrahydrate

sodium perchlorate *n* : a crystalline salt $NaClO_4$ made usu. by electrolysis of sodium chlorate and used chiefly in making other perchlorates and perchloric acid

sodium peroxide *n* : a pale-yellow hygroscopic granular compound Na_2O_2 that reacts with water to form sodium hydroxide and hydrogen peroxide, that is made by passing hot dry air over metallic sodium and treating with oxygen the sodium oxide formed, and that is used chiefly as an oxidizing and bleaching agent and in making other peroxy compounds

sodium phosphate *n* **1** : an orthophosphate of sodium known in both anyhydrous and hydrated crystalline forms: **a** : the primary phosphate NaH_2PO_4 that with the secondary phosphate constitutes the principal buffer system of the urine and that is used chiefly in buffer compositions (as in acid cleaning compositions) — called also *monobasic sodium phosphate, monosodium phosphate, sodium acid phosphate, sodium dihydrogen phosphate* **b** : the secondary phosphate Na_2HPO_4 that is used chiefly in water treatment for precipitating polyvalent metals, in cleaning compositions, in process cheeses, in ceramic glazes and enamels, in the textile industry, and in medicine as a laxative and antacid — called also *dibasic sodium phosphate, disodium hydrogen phosphate, disodium phosphate* **c** : the tertiary phosphate Na_3PO_4 that is used chiefly in cleaning compositions and in water treatment — called also *tribasic sodium phosphate, trisodium phosphate* **2** : a phosphate of sodium that is not an orthophosphate — compare SODIUM METAPHOSPHATE, SODIUM PYROPHOSPHATE, SODIUM TRIPOLYPHOSPHATE

sodium phosphate glass *n* : any of various usu. water-soluble glassy substances that in many cases approximate a sodium metaphosphate in composition but are held to be mixtures of sodium polyphosphates and that are used chiefly as sequestering agents in water treatment, as deflocculating agents, and in protecting metals from corrosion; *esp* : SODIUM METAPHOSPHATE 2a

sodium polysulfide *n* : any of several yellow compounds Na_2S_n containing two or more atoms of sulfur in the molecule (as sodium tetrasulfide Na_2S_4) made by dissolving sulfur in an aqueous solution of sodium sulfide or sodium hydroxide and used chiefly in making polysulfide rubbers

sodium potassium tartrate *n* : ROCHELLE SALT

sodium propionate *n* : a deliquescent crystalline salt CH_3CH_2COONa used as a fungicide (as in retarding the growth of mold in the baking and dairy industries)

sodium pyrophosphate *n* : any of four sodium salts of pyrophosphoric acid: as **a** : a crystalline acid salt $Na_2H_2P_2O_7$ used chiefly as a leavening agent, in acid cleaning compositions, and in electroplating; disodium dihydrogen pyrophosphate — called also *sodium acid pyrophosphate* **b** : the crystalline normal salt $Na_4P_2O_7$ used chiefly as a builder in soaps and detergents and as a deflocculant (as in treating drilling muds for oil wells) — called also *tetrasodium pyrophosphate*

sodium pyrosulfite *n* : SODIUM METABISULFITE

sodiums *pl of* SODIUM

sodium salicylate *n* : a crystalline salt HOC_6H_4COONa with a sweetish saline taste used chiefly in medicine as an analgesic, antipyretic, and antirheumatic

sodium sesquicarbonate *n* : a crystalline acid carbonate $Na_2CO_3.NaHCO_3.2H_2O$ or $Na_3H(CO_3)_2.2H_2O$ that occurs in nature as trona or is made synthetically from sodium carbonate and sodium bicarbonate and is used chiefly as a detergent — not used systematically

sodium silicate *n* : any of various water-soluble substances obtained in the form of crystals, glasses, powders, or aqueous solutions usu. by melting silica with a sodium compound (as sodium carbonate or sodium hydroxide): as **a** *or* **sodium orthosilicate** : a corrosive crystalline substance regarded as a salt Na_4SiO_4 or $2Na_2O.SiO_2$ of orthosilicic acid or as a mixture of sodium metasilicate with sodium hydroxide and used chiefly in heavy-duty cleaning compositions **b** *or* **sodium metasilicate** : a crystalline salt Na_2SiO_3 or $Na_2O.SiO_2$ either in the anhydrous or hydrated form used chiefly as a detergent **c** *or* **sodium sesquisilicate** : a corrosive crystalline salt regarded as intermediate in composition between sodium orthosilicate and sodium metasilicate and used in heavy-duty cleaning compositions — not used systematically **d** : WATER GLASS

sodium silicofluoride *n* : SODIUM FLUOSILICATE

sodium sulfate *n* : either of two crystalline sulfates of sodium: **a** : the bitter normal salt Na_2SO_4 occurring in nature as the mineral thenardite and in various salt lakes and brines and used chiefly in detergents, in the manufacture of wood pulp and rayon, and in dyeing and finishing textiles — see GLAUBER'S SALT, SALT CAKE **b** : SODIUM BISULFATE

sodium sulfide *n* : a sulfide of sodium; *esp* : a crystalline compound Na_2S usu. obtained by heating sodium sulfate with coal or hydrogen and used in dehairing hides, in the manufacture of sulfur dyes, as a solvent for these dyes, and as a reducing agent for the nitro group in making amines — compare ²BLACK ASH 2, SODIUM HYDROSULFIDE, SODIUM POLYSULFIDE

sodium sulfite *n* : a sulfite of sodium: as **a** : the crystalline normal salt Na_2SO_3 used chiefly as a reducing agent, bleaching agent, and antichlor, in photographic developing and fixing baths, and in preserving foods **b** : SODIUM BISULFITE **a c** : SODIUM METABISULFITE

sodium sulfydrate *n* : SODIUM HYDROSULFIDE — not used systematically

sodium tetraborate *n* : BORAX

sodium tetrahydroborate *or* **sodium tetrahydridoborate** *n* : SODIUM BOROHYDRIDE

sodium thiocyanate *n* : a hygroscopic crystalline salt NaSCN made usu. by reaction of sodium cyanide with sulfur or sodium polysulfide and used chiefly in dyeing and printing textiles, in processing photographic color film, and as a weed killer

sodium thiosulfate *n* : a hygroscopic crystalline salt $Na_2S_2O_3$ that commonly crystallizes with five molecules of water, that is usu. made by the reaction of sodium sulfite solution with sulfur or of sodium sulfide with sulfur dioxide or in the recovery of sulfur from waste products (as spent oxide), and that is used as a fixing agent in photography, as a reducing agent, bleaching agent, and antichlor, in chemical analysis for the titration of iodine, and in medicine as an antidote in poisoning by cyanides or iodine — called also *hypo, sodium hyposulfite*

sodium tripolyphosphate *n* : a crystalline salt $Na_5P_3O_{10}$ used chiefly as a builder in soaps and detergents, as a sequestering agent, and as a deflocculating agent; penta-sodium triphosphate — not used systematically

sodium tungstate *or* **sodium wolframate** *n* : a tungstate of sodium; *esp* : the normal salt Na_2WO_4 that commonly crystallizes with two molecules of water, is usu. obtained during the extraction of tungsten from its ores, and is used chiefly in making other tungsten compounds and in fireproofing textiles

sodium-vapor lamp *n* : SODIUM LAMP

sod oil *n* [³*sod*] : degras recovered from treated skins by washing with alkali instead of by pressing

so·do·ku \'sōdə,kü\ *n* -s [Jap, fr. Chin (Cant) *shuē* rat + *tūk* poison] : RAT-BITE FEVER b

sod·om \'sädəm\ *n* -s *usu cap* [fr. *Sodom*, city of ancient Palestine destroyed by God for its wickedness (Gen 18:20, 21; 19:24–28)] : a place notorious for vice or corruption

sodom apple *n, usu cap S* : APPLE OF SODOM

sod·om·ite \'sädə,mīt\ *n* -s [ME, fr. MF, fr. LL *Sodomita* inhabitant of Sodom, fr. LGk *Sodomitēs*, fr. *Sodoma* Sodom + Gk -*itēs* -ite] **1** *often cap* : one who practices sodomy — compare BUGGER **2** *usu cap* : a native or inhabitant of Sodom, a city located in ancient times in the region of the Dead Sea which with Gomorrah was destroyed for its wickedness

sod·om·it·ic \,sädə¦mid·ik\ *adj, often cap* [LL *sodomiticus* of the inhabitants of Sodom, fr. *Sodomita* inhabitant of Sodom + L -*icus* -ic] : SODOMITICAL

sod·om·it·i·cal \id·əkəl\ *adj, often cap* [LL *sodomiticus* + E *-al*] **1** *obs* : given to or participating in the practice of sodomy **2** : of, relating to, or involving sodomy — **sod·om·it·i·cal·ly** \-id·ək(ə)lē\ *adv*

sodomitry *n* -ES *often cap* [MF *sodomiterie*, fr. *sodomite* + *-erie* -ry] *obs* : SODOMY

sod·om·ize \'sädə,mīz\ *vt* -ED/-ING/-S [*sodomy* + *-ize*] : to practice sodomy upon ⟨had begun the practice of *sodomizing* younger boys —David Abrahamsen⟩

sod·omy \'sädəmē, -mi\ *n* -ES [ME, fr. OF *sodomie*, fr. LL *Sodoma* Sodom (fr. Gk) + OF *-ie* -y; fr. the homosexual proclivities of the men of the city as narrated in Gen 19:1–11] : carnal copulation with a member of the same sex or with an animal : noncoital carnal copulation with a member of the opposite sex; *specif* : the penetration of the male organ into the mouth or anus of another — compare BESTIALITY, BUGGERY, CUNNILINGUS, FELLATIO, HOMOSEXUALITY, PEDERASTY

sod plow *n* [¹*sod*] **1** : BREAKER 2b **2** : a plow for stirring cultivated meadows

sods *pl of* SOD, *pres 3d sing of* SOD

sod webworm *n* : GRASS WEBWORM

sodwork \'⸗,⸗\ *n* : a construction (as a revetment) made of sods piled up and packed closely together

soe *n* [ME *so, soe*, fr. OE *sā*; akin to ON *sār* large vessel — more at SAY] *obs* : a large wooden tub or pail

soerabaja *usu cap, var of* SURABAJA

soerakarta *usu cap, var of* SURAKARTA

so·ev·er \sə'wevə(r), (,)sō'e-\ *adv* [-*soever* (as in *whosoever*)] **1** : to any possible or known extent : in any conceivable degree or manner — used after an adjective preceded by *how* or a superlative preceded by *the* ⟨how fair ~ she may be⟩ ⟨the most selfish ~ in this world⟩ **2** : of any or every kind that may be specified — used after a noun modified esp. by *any, no*, or *what* ⟨all who are perplexed in any way ~ —J.H. Newman⟩

SOF *abbr* sound on film

so·fa \'sōfə, *dial* -fē *or* -fi\ *n* -s [Ar *suffah* a long bench] **1** : a carpeted and cushioned section of floor raised above the rest in some eastern Mediterranean lands for sitting on : DIVAN **2** : an upholstered couch or settee usu. with arms and a back and often convertible into a bed — compare LOUNGE

sofa bed *n* : an upholstered sofa that can be made to serve as a double bed by lowering its hinged upholstered back to horizontal position — compare SOFA 2, STUDIO COUCH

so·far \'sō,fär, -fä(r\ *n* -s [*sound fixing and ranging*] : a system for locating an underwater explosion at sea by triangulation based on the reception of the sound by three widely separated shore stations that is usable in a search for survivors who drop a special bomb into the sea (as from a lifeboat)

so far as *conj* : as far as

sofa table *n* : a moderate-sized oblong table with small leaves at the ends

sof·fi·o·ne \,säfē'ōnē, ,sōf-, -ō(,)nā\ *n, pl* **soffio·ni** \-ō(,)nē\ [It, fr. aug. of *soffio* puff, blast, fr. *soffiare* to blow, fr. L *sufflare* to inflate, blow upon — more at SUFFLATE] : a jet of steam usu. accompanied by other vapors that issues from the ground in a volcanic region

sof·fit \'säfət\ *also* **sof·fite** \", sä'fēt\ *n* -s [F *soffite*, fr. It *soffitto*, fr. (assumed) VL *suffictus*, past part. of L *suffigere* to fasten underneath — more at SUFFIX] : the underside of a part or member of a building (as of an overhang, ceiling, staircase, cornice, or entablature); *esp* : the intrados of an arch — compare PLANCIER

so·fia \÷sō'fēə, 'sōf- *sometimes* 'sȯf-\ *adj, usu cap* [fr. *Sofia*, capital of Bulgaria] : of or from Sofia, the capital of Bulgaria : of the kind or style prevalent in Sofia

sof·kee \'säfkē\ *n* -s [Muskogee *safki*] *South* : a thin mush or gruel made of cornmeal

¹**soft** \'sȯft *also* 'säft\ *adj* -ER/-EST [ME *softe, soft*, fr. OE *sōfte*, alter. (prob. influenced by *sōfte* softly) of *sēfte*; akin to OS *sāfti* soft, OHG *semfti*, and prob. to Goth *samjan* to please, ON *semja* to arrange, settle, make peace, Skt *samayati* he levels, regulates, *sama* level, same — more at SAME] **1 a** : pleasing or agreeable to the senses : bringing ease, comfort, or quiet ⟨the ~ influences of home⟩ — sometimes used interjectionally to enjoin silence or less haste ⟨~, who comes here —*Shak.*⟩ **b** : having the restfulness of sleep ⟨~ slumbers⟩ **c** (1) : having a bland or mellow rather than a sharp or acid taste or flavor (2) : containing no alcohol — used of beverages ⟨washing down hot dogs with ~ drinks⟩ **d** (1) : having only moderate contrast between light and shadow or between colors or color shades : not bright or glaring : SUBDUED ⟨the ~ shadows of a spring evening⟩ (2) : having or producing little contrast or a relatively short range of tones ⟨~ negative⟩ ⟨~ print⟩ ⟨~ paper⟩ ⟨~ lighting⟩ **e** (1) : free from loudness, harshness, or stridency : quiet in pitch or volume (2) *archaic* : making a low and gentle rather than a loud or harsh sound — used of a musical instrument (3) : MELODIOUS, PLEASING, SENSUOUS ⟨her voice was ~ and thrilling⟩ **f** *of the eyes* : having a liquid or gentle appearance ⟨~ brown eyes —Len Zinberg⟩ **g** : smooth or delicate in texture, grain, or fiber : not rough, coarse, or irritating to the touch ⟨a ~ cashmere⟩ **h** (1) : balmy, mild, or clement in weather or temperature ⟨~ summer nights —Sherwood Anderson⟩ (2) : moving or falling with slight force or impact : not violent ⟨outside there was a ~ rain —Martin Quigley⟩ ⟨~ breezes⟩ **2** : having a surface unbroken by heavy waves : CALM — used of a river or sea **3 a** *obs* : readily endured or supported : involving no severity, harshness, or strain **b** : demanding little work or effort : not toilsome or laborious : EASY, IDLE ⟨given to ~ living and dissolute practices⟩ ⟨young men who married ~ jobs —J.H.Reese⟩ **4 a** : sounding as in *ace* and *gem* respectively — used of *c* and *g* or their sound **b** *of a consonant* : VOICED **c** : constituting a vowel before which there is a \y\ sound or a \y\-like modification of a consonant or constituting a consonant in whose articulation there is a \y\-like modification or which is followed by a \y\ sound (as in Russian) — opposed to *hard*; compare PALATALIZATION **5 a** *archaic* : moving slowly and unhurriedly **b** : slow or moderate in burning — used of a fire **6** : rising gradually : ascending by moderate degrees ⟨a ~ slope⟩ ⟨a ~ crescendo⟩ **7** : having curved or rounded outline : blending easily into the general effect or view : not harsh or jagged ⟨~ hills against the horizon⟩ ⟨a pullover sweater with ~ shoulder lines⟩ **8 a** : evincing mildness of disposition or temper : showing gentleness, kindness, or mercy : COMPASSIONATE **b** (1) : exhibiting sympathetic understanding : tending to ingratiate or disarm : CONCILIATORY, ENGAGING, KIND, SUAVE ⟨a ~ answer turns away wrath —Prov 15:1 (RSV)⟩ ⟨could be great harm in accepting, at face value, whatever ~ words they may utter —*Springfield (Mass.) Republican*⟩ (2) : TENDER, SENTIMENTAL ⟨the ~ utterance of a loving heart⟩ **c** (1) : mild, lenient, or gentle in method or procedure ⟨adopted a policy of slow growth and ~ competition to allow other firms to establish themselves in the industry —A.D.H.Kaplan⟩ ⟨hopes . . . died in the awful gap between tough talk and ~ action —*New Republic*⟩ (2) : based on negotiation and conciliation rather than on a show of power or on threats ⟨had switched to a ~ line as the situation worsened⟩ **d** : emotionally susceptible or responsive : readily affected by sentiment : IMPRESSIONABLE, SUGGESTIBLE **e** : unduly susceptible to influence : readily affected, swayed, or imposed on : COMPLIANT ⟨said their teacher was ~⟩ **f** *obs* : of refined character or gentle breeding **g** : lacking firmness or strength of character : FEEBLE, UNMANLY **h** : amorously intent or emotionally involved or attracted — used with *on* ⟨had always been ~ on the neighbors' daughter⟩ **9 a** : weak or delicate in health or constitution : lacking robust strength, stamina, or endurance : enervated by ease or luxury : not hardened by exercise or effort **b** : weak or deficient mentally : FOOLISH, HALF-WITTED **10** *Scot & Irish* : DAMP, WET, DRIZZLY **11 a** : yielding or giving way to physical pressure : having a surface that does not firmly resist the touch : loose rather than dense in texture or consistency : comfortable or pleasant because not hard **b** : too moist or yielding to support weight : permitting (someone or something) to sink in — used of wet ground **c** : of a consistency that may be shaped or molded : COMPRESSIBLE, MALLEABLE **d** : easily magnetized and demagnetized ⟨magnetically ~ alloys are used for motors, transformers, and other electromagnetic devices⟩ **e** : lacking relatively or comparatively in hardness ⟨~ iron⟩ ⟨~ coal⟩ **12** : characterized by the practical absence of substances (as calcium and magnesium salts) that prevent formation of lather with soap — used of water and water solutions; compare HARD 1c (1) **13** : maturing as a ceramic glaze or object at a relatively low temperature **14** *of glass* **a** : capable of being annealed at a relatively low temperature **b** : readily scratched : having little mechanical hardness **15 a** : having relatively low penetrating power ⟨~ X rays⟩ **b** : *of an electron tube* : containing gas that adversely affects its characteristics **16** : not durable : PERISHABLE **17 a** : tending to decline in price under the influence of selling — used esp. of securities or commodities **b** *of money* : paper as distinct from metallic **c** *of currency* : not convertible into gold nor heavily backed by a gold reserve and typically unstable, low, or depreciating in value; *also* : available to borrowers in ample supply and at low interest rates **d** *of a currency* : not soundly backed nor readily convertible into foreign currencies except under restrictions or at considerable discounts ⟨has attempted, where possible, to shift purchases to ~ currency areas —T.C.Blaisdell⟩ **18** *of brick* : underburned because of its position in the kiln **19** : SOFTWOOD **20 a** *of paper* : being opaque and not brittle or crisp and having under the microscope a slightly fuzzy texture **b** : bound in paperback ⟨*soft*-bound book⟩ ⟨*soft*-back book⟩ ⟨~ bindings⟩ **21** *of news* : unimportant in its economic, political, or larger social bearing ⟨a ~ human-interest story⟩ — compare HARD **22** *of a foundry blast* : weak in force or pressure **23** : containing some of the solids of raw cane sugar that are removed in refining white sugar and being usu. brown and somewhat moist

syn SOFT, BLAND, MILD, GENTLE, LENIENT, and BALMY can mean, in common, pleasantly agreeable because devoid of harshness or roughness in the sensations evoked. SOFT suggests a tranquilizing sensation of mellowness esp. as devoid of pungency, vividness, intensity, stridency, and so on ⟨a *soft* color⟩ ⟨a *soft* voice⟩ ⟨a *soft* answer⟩ ⟨the *soft* glow of the lamp —Louis Bromfield⟩ ⟨a *soft* and smooth climate⟩ BLAND can be often interchanged with SOFT but more generally suggests smoothness and suavity, emphasizing more than SOFT the absence of what might disturb, irritate, stimulate, and so on ⟨it was hot and cold, sweet and sour, fiery and *bland* — all at the same time —Mary Lasswell⟩ ⟨a *bland* diet was prescribed with milk and cream with meals and between meals —*Jour. Amer. Med. Assoc.*⟩ ⟨a *bland* reply to a belligerent accusation⟩ ⟨from the south comes the *bland* air of the gulf —H.T.Kane⟩ ⟨the *bland* influence of encouraging words⟩ MILD and GENTLE both stress moderation and are usu. applied to things that are not, as they might be and often are, harsh, rough, strong, stimulating or violent, often, however, connoting positively pleasurable sensations, a pleasurableness induced by the very moderation of the thing, MILD possibly stressing more an induced mood of serenity, GENTLE possibly implying more an induced placidity and a sense of restrained power or force ⟨a *mild* drink⟩ ⟨a *mild* taste⟩ ⟨a *mild* winter⟩ ⟨a *mild* breeze⟩ ⟨his picture is *mild*, feeble, and contrived, whereas Picasso's is excited, bold, and hardy —J.T.Soby⟩ ⟨a good man, *mild*, charitable, and humane —Tobias Smollett⟩ ⟨a *gentle* hand⟩ ⟨his voice was soft; his manner *gentle* —Robert Tallant⟩ ⟨a tone of *gentle* authority —Martha Bacon⟩ ⟨contrasts of light, shade, and shadow should be *gentle* —A.S.Whiton⟩ LENIENT sometimes applies to something exerting an emollient, relaxing, or assuasive influence, often connoting (from another sense of the word) indulgence or kindliness ⟨a *lenient* hand on his brow⟩ ⟨the weather was *lenient* —H.L.Davis⟩ ⟨poured her a *lenient* rum and water —Christopher Morley⟩ BALMY, applied chiefly to atmospheric conditions, esp. to a breeze or a wind, often adds to the idea of soothing sensation on mind or senses the idea of refreshing influence or even fragrant quality ⟨the *balmy* summer air, the restful quiet —Mark Twain⟩ ⟨it was a lovely soft spring morning at the end of March, and unusually *balmy* for the time of year —Samuel Butler †1902⟩ ⟨the *balmy* trade winds and subtropical sunshine —P.J.C. Friedlander⟩

²**soft** \"\ *n* -s [ME, fr. ¹*soft*] **1 a** : the quality or state of being soft : SOFTNESS **b** : a soft object, material, or part ⟨the ~ of the thumb⟩ **2** : a soft or silly person **3 softs** *pl, Brit* : SHODDY

³**soft** \"\ *adv* [ME *softe, soft*, fr. OE *sōfte*; akin to OS *sāfto* softly, OHG *samfto*; all fr. a prehistoric WGmc adv. fr. the root of OE *sēfte* soft — more at ¹SOFT] : in a soft or gentle manner : SOFTLY

sof·ta \'sȯftə, 'säf-\ *n* -s [Turk, fr. Per *sōkhtah* burnt, kindled (with love of knowledge)] : someone associated with the religious activities of a Turkish mosque; *esp* : a beginner in theological studies

softball \'⸗,⸗\ *n* [¹*soft* + *ball*] **1** : a team game of seven innings closely resembling baseball but played on a smaller diamond with a larger ball under rules requiring an underhand pitch and forbidding a base runner to take a lead until the ball is pitched **2** : a smooth-seamed ball about 12 inches in circumference that is filled with kapok, covered with horsehide or cowhide, and used in the game of softball

soft-bill \'⸗,⸗\ *n* : any of numerous birds with rather fragile weak bills suitable for consuming insects and other small animals as food — compare HARD-BILL

soft black *n* : a vegetable black pigment (as vine black) used esp. in printing inks

soft-boiled \'⸗¦⸗\ *adj* **1** *of an egg* : boiled to a soft consistency **2 a** : SENTIMENTAL **b** : of or relating to literary expression regarded satirically as given to wholesome sentiment and moralism — opposed to *hard-boiled*

soft brome *or* **soft brome grass** *n* : SOFT CHEAT

soft chancre *n* : CHANCROID

soft cheat \'⸗¦chēt\ *or* **soft chess** \'⸗¦ches\ *n* [*soft cheat* fr. ¹*soft* + *cheat*grass; *soft chess* fr. ¹*soft* + *chess*] : a weedy Old World grass (*Bromus mollis*) that is softly pubescent in all parts and is widely naturalized in No. America esp. on the Pacific coast; *also* : a very similar grass (*B. racemosus*)

soft clam *n* : SOFT-SHELL CLAM

soft coal *n* : BITUMINOUS COAL

soft commissure *n* : a commissure of gray matter connecting the optic thalami across the third ventricle of the brain

soft coral *n* : any member of the alcyonarian order Alcyonacea in which the polyp bases fuse into a fleshy mass partially supported by calcareous spicules and which are common in shallow tropical seas (as the Indian ocean)

¹**soft corn** *n* **1** : an Indian corn (*Zea mays amylacea*) having kernels shaped like those of flint corn and composed almost entirely of soft starch — called also *flour corn, squaw corn* **2** : a soft and watery corn whether immature or prematurely frozen as distinguished from hard dry mature corn

²**soft corn** *n* : a usu. moist white corn between two toes

soft-cover \'⸗¦⸗⸗\ *adj or n* : PAPERBACK

soft crab *n* : SOFT-SHELL CRAB

soft-cure \'⸗¦⸗\ *vt* : to cure (tobacco) slowly with limited heat

soft dough *n* : the early part of the dough stage of a cereal grain

soft·en \'sȯfən *also* 'säf- *sometimes* -ftən\ *vb* -ED/-ING/-S [ME *softnen*, fr. ¹*soft* + *-nen* -en] *vt* **1** : to lessen the severity of : make more endurable : ASSUAGE, MITIGATE ⟨have ~*ed* their puritanical code —Paul Blanshard⟩ ⟨pride in his heroism ~*ed* their grief⟩ **2 a** : to render gentle, mild, or compassionate : induce sympathy or mercy in : MELT ⟨the story should ~ the stoniest of hearts —J.D.Adams⟩ **b** : to reduce the harshness or rigor of : make milder or gentler : MOLLIFY ⟨~*ing* him to love by eloquent tenderness —T.L.Peacock⟩ **c** : to make effeminate or weak : leach away the strength or virility of : ENERVATE ⟨ease and luxury had ~*ed* their fiber⟩ **3** : to make less glaring, loud, or sharp : tone down the brightness, contrast, or sound of : round or blend the harsh lines or jagged angles of ⟨dusk and dark clouds were ~*ing* the daylight —Elyne Mitchell⟩ ⟨the contours of the bodies are ~*ed* —Leona Prasse⟩ **4 a** : to make less hard, solid, or compact (as by pounding or annealing) ⟨heat ~*s* iron⟩ **b** : to make less dry or brittle by use of an oil or grease : restore freshness, pliability, or luster to ⟨lotions that ~ dry skin⟩ ⟨used oil to ~ and preserve leather⟩ **c** : to make (hair) more receptive to dye by use of a bleaching solution **5** : to lessen the hardness of (water) esp. by removing or reducing the reactivity of calcium and magnesium ions (as by precipitation, ion exchange, or sequestration) **6** : to remove impurities from (lead) preparatory to desilverizing **7 a** : to weaken the military resistance and morale of esp. by preliminary bombardment or other harassment — often used with *up* **b** : to break the resistance or opposition of (a person) by physical or mental torture ⟨first we'll ~ you up with a little of the pistol-whipping I promised you —Hartley Howard⟩ **8** : to bring down (prices or market demand) ⟨adverse developments . . . have completely demoralized product prices, ~*ed* the price of crude, and are squeezing profits to a minimum —P.C.Spencer⟩ ~ *vi* : to become soft, gentle, pliable, or weak ⟨her expression ~*ed*⟩ ⟨foreign policy ~*ed* as the cold war reached a temporary lull⟩ ⟨thewind was ~*ing* —Vincent McHugh⟩

soft·en·er \-(ə)nə(r)\ *n* -s : one that softens: as **a** : a worker who softens hides, skins, or leather usu. by immersing or tumbling them in water **b** : a textile worker who waxes thread and yarn **c** : a machine or apparatus in which something is softened **d** : a substance added to something (as hard water, molten iron, or rubber in the process of manufacture) to make it soft, malleable, or plastic — compare PLASTICIZER

softening point *n* [*softening* (gerund of *soften*) + *point*] : the temperature or range of temperatures at which a substance softens

softer *comparative of* SOFT

softest *superlative of* SOFT

soft fiber *n* : any of various cordage or textile fibers (as flax, hemp, jute, or ramie) obtained from the stems of plants and typically of softer texture and greater length than hard fibers obtained from leaves : BAST 2

soft-finned \'⸗¦⸗\ *adj* [¹*soft* + *fin* + *-ed*] : having fins in which the membrane is supported entirely or almost entirely by soft or articulated rays — used of the more advanced teleost fishes; opposed to *spiny-finned*

soft flame *n* : a thin shell of flame surrounding a core of unburned gas that is produced by using a small amount of primary air in the mixture and is used as a free flame (as in an oven)

soft focus *n* : unsharpness of a photograph due to intentional diffusion of the lens image

soft-focus \'⸗¦⸗⸗\ *adj* [*soft focus*] **1** *of a photographic image* : having unsharp outlines **2** *of a lens* : producing an image having unsharp outlines

soft fold *n* : the fold that results when paper is lapped

soft fruit *n, chiefly Brit* : SMALL FRUIT

soft goods *n pl* **1** *Brit* **:** DRY GOODS **2 :** goods that are not durable **:** perishable goods — used esp. of textile products
soft grass *n* **:** any of various grasses of the genus *Holcus; esp* **:** VELVET GRASS
soft grit *n* **:** finely ground corncobs, rice hulls, or other siliceous plant wastes used as a mild abrasive in air blasting
soft ground *n* **1 :** a mixture of ordinary etching ground usu. with tallow or grease that is used chiefly to obtain textural lines and effects on the plate by pressing cloth or similar material into the ground or by drawing with a pencil on a piece of paper laid over it **2 :** a process or effect in etching obtained by the use of soft ground
soft hail *n* **:** GRAUPEL
softhead \ˈ=,=\ *n* [¹*soft* + *head*] **1 :** a silly or feebleminded person **:** SIMPLETON **2 :** a fatuous sentimentalist ⟨aren't they the ~*s*, the all too susceptible and sentimental imbeciles? —Aldous Huxley⟩
softheaded \ˈ=ˈ==\ *adj* [¹*soft* + *headed*] **:** having a weak, unrealistic, or uncritical mind **:** lacking judgment **:** IMPRACTICAL ⟨a ~ visionary —*Commonweal*⟩ — **soft·head·ed·ly** *adv* — **soft·head·ed·ness** *n* -ES
softhearted \ˈ=ˈ==\ *adj* [¹*soft* + *hearted*] **:** emotionally responsive **:** MERCIFUL, SYMPATHETIC, TENDER — **soft·heart·ed·ly** *adv* — **soft·heart·ed·ness** *n* -ES
soft hog *n* **:** a hog producing or expected to produce soft pork
softie *var of* SOFTY
softies *pl of* SOFTY
soft·ish \ˈsȯftish, -tēsh *also* ˈsäf-\ *adj* **:** somewhat soft
soft-laid \ˈ=ˈ=\ *adj* **:** having the strands twisted more loosely than those of medium-laid rope
soft lay *n* **:** a rope lay in which the yarns of the strands and the strands of the rope are loosely twisted to secure great strength on a straight pull
soft lead *n* **:** lead containing virtually no impurities other than the precious metals **:** lead that has been put through the process of softening
soft·ling \-ftliŋ\ *n* -S [¹*soft* + *-ling*] **1 :** an effeminate person **:** WEAKLING **2 :** something soft, small, or delicate
¹**soft·ly** *adv* [ME, fr. ¹*soft* + *-ly*] **:** in a soft manner — used interjectionally to enjoin silence or less haste
²**softly** *adj* [¹*soft* + *-ly*] *archaic* **:** SOFT, GENTLE, QUIET
soft maize *n* **:** SOFT CORN 1
soft maple *n* **1 :** any of various maples with soft wood: as **a :** SILVER MAPLE **b :** RED MAPLE **c :** DWARF MAPLE **2 :** the wood of a soft maple tree
soft-mud process *n* **:** a brickmaking process in which water and clay are mixed to a relatively soft consistency and inserted into molds — compare STIFF-MUD PROCESS, SAND-MOLDING, SLOP-MOLDING
soft mute *n* **:** MEDIA 1a
soft·ness \-f(t)nəs\ *n* -ES [ME *softnes*, fr. OE *sōftnes* ease, comfort, fr. *sōfte* soft + *-nes* -ness] **:** the quality or state of being soft
soft-nosed \ˈ=ˈ=\ *adj, of a bullet* **:** having a hard metal jacket that covers all but the nose and encloses a soft core and mushrooming upon striking an object
soft palate *n* **:** the membranous and muscular fold suspended from the posterior margin of the hard palate and partially separating the mouth cavity from the pharynx — called also *velum;* see UVULA
soft paste *n* **1 :** a ceramic body containing refined clay and a glassy frit **2** *or* **soft-paste porcelain :** a soft low-fired translucent ware with a soft-paste body produced in Europe from the 15th through the 18th century — compare HARD PASTE
soft patch *n* **1 :** a patch for a crack in a metallic vessel (as a steam boiler) consisting of a soft material (as putty) covered and held in place by a plate bolted or riveted fast **2 :** a plate and gasket used as a temporary repair to cover a break or hole in a ship's hull
soft pedal *n* **1 :** a foot pedal on a piano that reduces the volume of sound by shortening the stroke of the hammers or by shifting the hammers so that fewer strings are struck for each note **2 :** something that muffles, deadens, or reduces effect **:** DAMPER
soft-pedal \ˈ=ˈ==\ *vb* [*soft pedal*] *vt* **1 :** to use the soft pedal in playing (a musical passage) **2 :** to play down (a fact, an aspect, or a consideration) **:** reduce the effect of **:** CONCEAL, DISGUISE, MUFFLE ⟨time for the club to *soft-pedal* the war heroics —Jack Gould⟩ ⟨this concern is evident, though *soft-pedaled* —*Atlantic*⟩ ~ *vi* **1 :** to play a musical passage with the soft pedal **2 :** to play something down **:** obscure or muffle a fact or consideration
soft phosphate *n* **:** a powdery impure form of tricalcium phosphate of low fertilizer value occurring in natural deposits of phosphate rock and separated from hard rock and pebble phosphates in fertilizer manufacture
soft pine *n* **1 :** a soft-wooded pine; *specif* **:** an American white pine (*Pinus strobus*) **2 :** the wood of a soft pine
soft poplar *n* **:** LARGE-TOOTHED ASPEN
soft porcelain *n* **:** a porcelain made of soft paste
soft pork *n* **:** pork made oily and flabby by feeding hogs on oily feeds (as peanuts or soybeans)
soft ray *n* **:** a fish's fin ray made up of numerous short slightly movable joints giving it some flexibility and usu. dividing into two or more slightly diverging branches — opposed to *spiny ray*
soft-rayed \ˈ=ˈ=\ *adj* **1 :** having soft or articulated rays — used of the fins of some fishes **2 :** having fins with soft or articulated rays — used of fishes; compare SPINY-RAYED
soft roe *n* **:** the testes of a fish **:** MILT
soft rot *n* **:** a mushy watery or slimy decay of plants or their parts caused by bacteria or fungi: as **a :** a disintegration of tissues (as of roots, tubers) caused by a bacterium (*Erwinia carotovora*) **b :** a highly destructive blue mold or storage rot of fruits caused by a mold (*Penicillium expansum*)
soft rush *n* **:** a nearly cosmopolitan rush (*Juncus effusus*) common in marshy areas and having furrowed or striate usu. soft culms — called also *round rush*
softs *pl of* SOFT
soft saw·der \-ˈsädə(r), -ˈsȯd-\ *n* [*soft* + obs. *sawder* solder, fr. ME — more at SOLDER] **:** FLATTERY, BLARNEY
soft-sawder \ˈ=ˈ==\ *vb* [*soft sawder*] *chiefly dial* **:** FLATTER
soft scale *n* **:** a scale insect (esp. family Coccidae) more or less active in all stages; *esp* **:** BROWN SOFT SCALE — compare ARMORED SCALE
soft sell *n* **:** the use of suggestion or persuasion in selling rather than aggressive pressure — compare HARD SELL
¹**soft-shell** \ˈ=ˈ=\ *adj* [¹*soft* + *shell*] **1 :** having a soft or fragile shell esp. as a result of recent shedding **2 :** moderate in policy or doctrine **:** avoiding extreme principles or measures ⟨the sort of *soft-shell* left-of-center man who is for free speech plus the good manners that ensure that nothing offensive will ever be said —Anthony West⟩
²**soft-shell** \ˈ=,=\ *n* [¹*soft-shell*] **1 :** SOFT-SHELLED CRAB **2 :** SOFT-SHELL CLAM **3 :** SOFT-SHELLED TURTLE **4 :** MODERATE, LIBERAL
soft-shell clam *also* **soft-shelled clam** *n* **:** an elongated clam (*Mya arenaria*) of the east coast of No. America having a thin friable shell and long siphons and being considered esp. desirable for steaming
soft-shelled \ˈ=ˈ=\ *adj* **:** SOFT-SHELL
soft-shell crab *or* **soft-shelled crab** *n* **:** a crab that has recently shed its shell and has a very soft new one — distinguished from *hard-shell crab;* see BLUE CRAB
soft-shelled turtle *n* **:** any of numerous fiercely voracious aquatic turtles of the family Trionychidae having a flat, oval, or nearly round shell covered with soft leathery skin instead of with horny plates, a narrow head, nostrils at the end of a fleshy proboscis, and feet broadly webbed with but three claws and living in parts of Africa, Asia, and No. America, including the whole Mississippi valley, the Great lakes, and many southern rivers
soft-shoe \ˈ=ˈ=\ *adj* **:** of or relating to tap dancing done in soft-soled shoes without metal taps
soft silk *n* **:** silk with the natural gum removed
soft-sized \ˈ=ˈ=\ *adj* **:** SLACK-SIZED
soft snap *n* **:** a post, job, or course of study demanding little time or effort
soft soap *n* **1 :** soap of a semifluid consistency made principally with potash or with soda by control of the fluidity by other factors (as the unsaturation of the fat used and the amount of water and glycerol present) and used chiefly in liquid soaps, in blending with hard soaps to increase solubility and lathering properties, and in medicine — see GREEN SOAP **2 :** the art or device of persuasion and flattery **:** BLARNEY ⟨the master of the glad hand and the *soft soap* —H.A.Burton⟩
soft-soap \ˈ=ˈ=\ *vt* [*soft soap*] **:** to soothe or persuade with flattery or blarney ⟨*soft-soaped* him and got him to ride along by giving him an office —*Amer. Mercury*⟩
soft-soaper \ˈ=ˈ=ə(r)\ *n* **:** one that soft-soaps **:** FLATTERER
soft solder *n* **1 :** an alloy of lead and tin that melts below 700° F and is used when melted to join metallic surfaces — compare HARD SOLDER, SILVER SOLDER **2 :** SOFT SAWDER
soft-solder \ˈ=ˈ==\ *vt* [*soft solder*] **:** to repair or join with soft solder
soft sole *n* **:** a soft-soled shoe; *specif* **:** an infant's shoe made with a moccasin seam and soft leather sole

soft sole

soft-spoken \ˈ=ˈ==\ *adj* [³*soft* + *spoken*] **:** speaking softly **:** having a mild or gentle voice **:** SUAVE ⟨as *soft-spoken* as any curate —Heywood Broun⟩
soft spot *n* **1 :** a sentimental weakness **:** an affectionate inclination **:** LEANING ⟨women have a *soft spot* for a man with a broken heart —Rearden Conner⟩ **2 :** a vulnerable point ⟨the major *soft spot* in the West's armor —*World*⟩ **3 :** any business or department of the economy that displays weakness ⟨some *soft spots* have appeared in a number of items, notably in stainless steel and in sheet and strip —*Wall Street Jour.*⟩
soft steel *n* **:** MILD STEEL
soft-stem bulrush *n* **:** GREAT BULRUSH b
soft thing *n* **:** SOFT SNAP
soft tick *n* **:** a tick of the family Argasidae — compare HARD TICK, IXODIDAE
soft toe *n* [¹*soft* + *toe*] **1 :** the toe of a shoe without toe stiffening or toe box **2 :** a shoe having a soft toe
soft touch *n* **1 :** someone who can be easily talked into giving help (as a gift or loan of money) **:** EASY MARK ⟨recognized him early as a *soft touch* for a loan —John Lardner⟩ **2 :** something easily performed or dispatched ⟨it's not a *soft touch;* it's a business⟩ **3 :** an easily defeated opponent **:** someone readily victimized ⟨their traditional football rival promised to be a *soft touch* that year⟩
soft turtle *or* **soft tortoise** *n* **:** SOFT-SHELLED TURTLE
soft waste *n* **:** textile waste from processes prior to spinning that is usu. reworkable — compare HARD WASTE
soft wheat *n* **:** a wheat with soft starchy kernels that are high in starch but typically low in gluten and yield a weak flour esp. suitable for pastry and breakfast foods — compare HARD WHEAT
¹**softwood** \ˈ=,=\ *n* **1 :** the wood of a coniferous tree known orig. from soft European woods but including both soft and hard woods **2** [²*softwood*] **:** a tree that yields softwood **:** an arborescent conifer
²**softwood** \"\ *adj* **1 :** having softwood or made of softwood **2 :** consisting of immature and still soft and pliable tissue ⟨~ cuttings for propagating plants⟩
soft-wooded \ˈ=ˈ==\ *adj* **1 :** having soft wood that is easy to work or finish **2 :** SOFTWOOD 1
softy *or* **soft·ie** \ˈsȯftē, -ti *also* ˈsäf-\ *n, pl* **softies** [¹*soft* + *-y*] **1 :** an excessively sentimental or susceptible person ⟨an old ~ with a weakness for the tingling effect on the spine of massive bands swinging into college songs —John McNulty⟩ **2 :** a weak, effeminate, or foolish person ⟨easy polemic victories, won by browbeating *softies* on the other side —H.L.Varney⟩
¹**sog** \ˈsäg *also* ˈsȯg\ *vb* **sogged; sogged; sogging; sogs** [origin unknown] *chiefly dial* **:** SOAK
²**sog** \"\ *vb* [origin unknown] *dial Eng* **:** DROWSE
so·ga \ˈsōgə\ *n, pl* **soga** *or* **sogas** *usu cap* **1 a :** a Bantu-speaking people of the north shore of Lake Victoria in eastern Africa **b :** a member of the Soga people **2 :** a dialect of Ganda spoken by the Soga people
¹**sog·di·an** *or* **sogh·di·an** \ˈsägdēən *also* ˈsȯg-\ *n* -S *cap* [L *Sogdiani* (pl.), fr. *sogdiani*, pl. of *sogdianus*, adj., Sogdian] **1 :** a native or inhabitant of Sogdiana, a province of the ancient Persian Empire in the region of modern Bukhara **2 :** an Iranian language of the Sogdian people
²**sogdian** *or* **soghdian** \"\ *adj, usu cap* [L *sogdianus*, fr. OPer *Sughuda* Sogdiana, province of the ancient Persian Empire + L *-anus* -an] **1 :** of, relating to, or characteristic of ancient Sogdiana **2 :** of, relating to, or characteristic of the people of ancient Sogdiana
sog·garth \ˈsägərth\ *n* -S [IrGael *sagart*, fr. L *sacerdot-, sacerdos* — more at SACERDOTAL] *Irish* **:** PRIEST
sog·gi·ly \ˈsägəlē, -li *also* ˈsȯg-\ *adv* **:** in a soggy manner
sog·gi·ness \-gēnəs, -gin-\ *n* -ES **:** the quality or state of being soggy: as **a :** WATERINESS, MARSHINESS ⟨the ~ of the land⟩ **b :** DULLNESS, PONDEROUSNESS ⟨the sometimes unbelievable ~ of their prose —T.E.Cooney⟩
¹**sog·ging** \-giŋ\ *adj* [fr. pres. part. of ¹*sog*] **:** SOAKING
²**sogging** \"\ *adv* **:** THOROUGHLY ⟨our clothes were ~ wet⟩
sog·gy \ˈsägē, -gi *also* ˈsȯg-\ *adj* -ER/-EST [¹*sog* + *-y*] **1 :** saturated or heavy with water or moisture: as **a :** WATERLOGGED, SOAKED ⟨slosh over a ~ fairway —R.M.Hodesh⟩ ⟨a thick and ~ mat of fiber —*Monsanto Mag.*⟩ ⟨~ clothes⟩ ⟨~ shoes⟩ **b :** DAMP, HUMID ⟨the air of the lowlands seemed ~ and heavy —Ida Treat⟩ **c :** SODDEN ⟨~ bread⟩ **2 :** heavily dull **:** HEAVY-FOOTED, PONDEROUS, SPIRITLESS ⟨a good deal of . . . ~ conversation about the state of the world —Wolcott Gibbs⟩ ⟨digest large portions of rather ~ educational literature —M.B.Smith⟩ ⟨a ~ prose that makes even sudden death seem tedious —Martin Levin⟩
¹**soh** \ˈsō\ *interj* [origin unknown] *archaic* — used as an expression of surprised annoyance or as a command to calm down
²**soh** *var of* SOL
sohan *usu cap, var of* SOAN
so-ho \sōˈhō\ *n* -ES [ME *so howe, so ho*] — used by hunters on sighting a hare as a call or exclamation; sometimes used interjectionally as an expression of angry surprise or discovery ⟨*so-ho*, caught in the act⟩
soia *var of* SOJA
soi-disant \ˌswädēˈzäⁿ\ *adj* [F, lit., saying oneself] **:** SELF-STYLED, SO-CALLED, PRETENDED — usu. used disparagingly ⟨a *soi-disant* artist⟩ ⟨this *soi-disant* novel —Anthony Boucher⟩ ⟨literary specialists (*soi-disant* or even authentic) —M.A.Pei⟩
soi·gné *or* **soi·gnée** \(ˈ)swänˈyā\ *adj* [F, fr. past part. of *soigner* to take care of, fr. ML *soniare*] **1 :** taken care of painstakingly **:** elegantly maintained **:** MODISH ⟨a *soigné* restaurant⟩ ⟨simple but *soignée* dresses of black crêpe —*New Yorker*⟩ **2 :** dressed with great care and elegance **:** WELL-GROOMED, SLEEK ⟨she was *soignée* in a platinum mink stole —*Time*⟩
¹**soil** \ˈsȯil, *esp before pause or consonant* -ȯiəl\ *vb* -ED/-ING/-S [ME *soilen*, fr. OF *soiller, souiller* to wallow, soil, fr. *soil* pigsty, boar's wallow, prob. fr. L *suile* pigsty, fr. *sus* pig — more at SOW] *vt* **1 :** to stain or defile morally **:** CORRUPT, POLLUTE ⟨why ~ their ears with nasty knowledge —C.W. Cunnington⟩ ⟨~ one's mind with such paltry thoughts —Van Wyck Brooks⟩ **2 :** to make unclean esp. superficially **:** DIRTY 1, SMUDGE, SPOT ⟨~ a rug⟩ ⟨a paste that ~*s* the hands⟩ ⟨his shoes . . . were ~*ed* now from the clay of the airfield —Kay Boyle⟩ ⟨the majestic river . . . ~*ed* with garbage —Herbert Agar⟩ **3 :** to blacken or besmirch (as a person's reputation or honor) by word or deed **:** give a bad name to **:** SULLY, DISGRACE ⟨what hath she done, prince, that can ~ our mothers —Shak.⟩ **4** *chiefly Brit* **:** to paint (as a pipe) with plumber's soil ~ *vi* **1 a :** to wallow in mud — used esp. of a deer or wild boar **b :** to take refuge in water or in a marsh — used of hunted game **2 a :** to become soiled or dirty ⟨this fabric ~*s* easily⟩ **b :** to defecate involuntarily ⟨patients also showed infantile reactions . . . continually wetting and ~*ing* —*Digest of Neurology & Psychiatry*⟩
²**soil** \"\ *n* -S **1 a :** the action of soiling or the condition of being soiled **:** SOILAGE 1, STAIN, SPOT ⟨protect a dress from ~⟩ ⟨hands free from ~⟩ ⟨finger marks or any other kind of ~ —*New Yorker*⟩ **b :** moral defilement **:** CORRUPTION ⟨disburdening herself of the ~ of worldly frailties —Nathaniel Hawthorne⟩ **2 :** something that soils or pollutes: as **a :** foreign matter **:** REFUSE ⟨metal surfaces . . . filled with all types of ~ —R.E.Marce⟩ **b :** SEWAGE ⟨conduits to carry away the ~⟩ **c :** DUNG, EXCREMENT **3 :** PLUMBER'S SOIL
³**soil** \"\ *n* -S [ME, fr. AF, fr. L *solium* seat (influenced in meaning by L *solum* base, floor, ground, soil); prob. akin to L *sedēre* to sit — more at SIT] **1 :** firm land **:** EARTH, GROUND ⟨underfoot the divine ~, overhead the sun —Walt Whitman⟩ ⟨she was as brown as the very ~ itself —Pearl Buck⟩ **2 a :** the upper layer of earth that may be dug or plowed; *specif* **:** the loose surface material of the earth in which plants grow usu. consisting of disintegrated rock with an admixture of organic matter and soluble salts — see HUMUS, NITRIFICATION **b :** the surface earth of a particular place with reference esp. to its composition or its adaptability (as for the farmer, builder, or engineer) ⟨sandy ~⟩ ⟨fertile ~⟩ ⟨a rich ~⟩ ⟨a ~ deficient in alkali⟩ **3 :** COUNTRY, LAND ⟨seek your hero in a distant ~ —Thomas Gray⟩ ⟨left his native ~ never to return⟩ **4 a :** cultivated or tilled ground ⟨works on the ~⟩ **b :** the agricultural life or calling ⟨a son of the ~⟩ ⟨felt a closeness to the ~⟩ **5 :** a medium in which something takes hold and develops ⟨countries where such misery exists are fertile ~ for Communist infiltration —*N.Y. Times Mag.*⟩ ⟨psychiatry flourished in the ~ of curiosity —R.S.Ellery⟩
⁴**soil** \"\ *n* -S [ME *soyle* boar's wallow, small pond, fr. MF *soil, souille* boar's wallow — more at ¹SOIL] **:** a tract of water (as a marsh or pool) in which hunted animals take refuge from their pursuers **:** REFUGE, SANCTUARY — used chiefly in the phrases *run to soil, go to soil, take soil*
⁵**soil** \"\ *vt* -ED/-ING/-S [origin unknown] **1 :** to feed (livestock) in the barn or an enclosure with fresh grass or green food **:** FATTEN **2 :** to purge (livestock) by feeding on green food
⁶**soil** \"\ *n* -S **:** SOILAGE
soil·age \ˈsȯilij, -lēj\ *n* -S [¹*soil* + *-age*] **1 :** the act of soiling or condition of being soiled ⟨a fabric that resists ~⟩ **2** *archaic* **:** REFUSE, SEWAGE **3** [⁵*soil* + *-age*] **:** green crops cut for feeding confined animals
soil air *n* [³*soil*] **:** gases occupying the free pore space in soil
soil auger *n* **:** an auger for taking soil samples
soil binder *n* **:** a plant (as any of various grasses or stoloniferous plants) used to prevent or capable of preventing soil erosion usu. by forming dense mats of roots or of superficial growth
soil cap *n* **:** a layer of mantle rock
¹**soil-cement** \ˈ=ˈ=,= *sometimes* ˈ=ˈ=,=\ *n* **:** an intimate highly compacted mixture of pulverized soil and measured amounts of cement and water used chiefly as a base course for roads and street and airport paving
²**soil-cement** \"\ *adj, of a road* **:** having a hard base or surface composed of earth mixed with portland cement
soil colloid *n* **:** the colloidal complex of soils that consists chiefly of clay and humus and plays an important role in ion exchange and fertility
soil complex *n* **:** a mapping unit consisting of two or more recognized taxonomic units used in detailed soil surveys
soil conditioner *n* **:** a chemical substance (as gypsum) used to improve the structure of the soil and increase its porosity and crumbliness
soil conservation *n* **1 :** the prevention or reduction of soil erosion and soil depletion by protective measures against water and wind damage **2 :** management of soil so as to obtain the largest crop yields feasible and improve the soil at the same time
soil creep *n* **:** slow down-slope movement of earth materials under the influence of gravitation
soiled \ˈsȯi(ə)ld\ *adj* [³*soil* + *-ed*] **:** having soil of a specified character — used chiefly in combination ⟨rich-*soiled*⟩
soil family *n* **:** FAMILY 4g
soil fertility *n* **:** capacity of a soil to provide crops with essential plant nutrients
soil horizon *n* **:** HORIZON 2a
¹**soiling** *n* -S [fr. gerund of ⁵*soil*] **1 :** the act or process of soiling or feeding green food to an animal **2 :** SOILAGE 3
²**soiling** *n* -S [fr. gerund of obs. *soil* to spread with soil, to manure, fr. ³*soil*] **:** the act or process of spreading or filling with soil, dirt, or manure
soiling crop *n* [¹*soiling*] **:** a crop cut green and fed to livestock immediately without further curing or processing
soil·less \ˈsȯi(ə)lləs\ *adj* [³*soil* + *-less*] **:** carried on without soil ⟨the ~ growth of plants⟩ ⟨~ agriculture⟩
soil map *n* **:** a record on a map of an area showing soil types, drains, and other pertinent information
soil mechanics *n pl but sing or pl in constr* **:** the study of the physical properties and utilization of soils esp. in planning foundations for structures and subgrades for highways
soil miller *n* **:** any of several rotary cultivating devices for pulverizing soil
soil-moisture index *n* **:** ability of soil to supply moisture to plants
soil-moisture tension *n* **:** the force per unit area required to remove film water from soil
soil mulch *n* **:** DUST MULCH
soil phase *n* **:** a subdivision of a soil type that deviates from the typical character of the soil type
soil pipe *n* **:** a pipe for liquid wastes carrying human excrement
soil rot *n* **:** a rot caused by organisms in the soil; *specif* **:** pox of sweet potatoes
soils *pres 3d sing of* SOIL, *pl of* SOIL
soil science *n* **:** the study of soil as a natural product **:** PEDOLOGY
soil scientist *n* **:** a specialist in soil science
soil series *n* **:** any of various soils with similar profiles developed from similar parent materials under comparable climatic and vegetational conditions ⟨the Miami *soil series*⟩ — see SOIL TYPE
soil solution *n* **:** the film moisture in the soil together with its dissolved substances
soil stack *n* **:** a vertical soil pipe
soil stripe *n* **:** one of the alternating bands of finer and coarser material comprising a soil structure that are produced in sloping ground by solifluction — usu. used in pl.
soil structure *n* **:** the arrangement of soil particles in various aggregates differing in shape, size, stability, and degree of adhesion to one another
soil survey *n* **:** a systematic study of the soil of an area including classification and mapping of the properties, crop adaptations, and distribution of various soil types
soil type *n* **:** a member of a soil series distinguished primarily by texture ⟨the Miami silt is a distinctive *soil type* of the Miami series⟩
soil·ure \ˈsȯilyə(r)\ *n* -S [ME, fr. OF *soilleure*, fr. *soiller* to soil] **1 :** the act of soiling **:** the condition of being soiled ⟨not making any scruple of her ~ —Shak.⟩ **2 :** STAIN, SMUDGE ⟨a dry, light ~ of dead ashes —William Faulkner⟩
soily \ˈsȯilē\ *adj* -ER/-EST [³*soil* + *-y*] **:** having spots or stains **:** DIRTY ⟨on her ~ neck stealthily hangs her lady's jewels —Gordon Bottomley⟩
soi·ree *or* **soi·rée** \(ˈ)swäˈrā\ *n* -S [F *soirée* evening period, evening party, fr. MF, fr. *soir* evening, fr. L *sero* at a late hour, fr. abl. of *serum* late time, fr. neut. of *serus* late — more at SINCE] **:** an evening party or reception ⟨attending . . . ~*s* in her silk, penthouse parlor —Saul Bellow⟩ ⟨invited to ~*s* where the elite . . . displayed their shoddy splendor —Upton Sinclair⟩
soix·ante-neuf \ˌswä,säntˈnə(r)f, -ˈnəf\ *n* -S [F, lit., sixty-nine] **:** simultaneous cunnilingus and fellatio **:** double fellatio **:** double cunnilingus
¹**soja** \ˈsȯi(y)ə, ˈsōjə, ˈsōyə, ˈsȯyə\ [NL, fr. D, soybean — more at SOYA] *syn of* APIOS
²**soja** \", *dial* ˈsōjē *or* -ōji *or* -ōdə *or* -ōdē *or* -ōdi *or* -ōə\ *also* **soja bean** \ˈ-ˌ- *or* **soia** *like* ²SOJA\ *n* -S [D *soja*] **:** SOYBEAN
¹**so·journ** \ˈsō,jərn, -jōn, -jəin, =ˈ= *sometimes* səˈj-, *chiefly Brit* ˈsäj- *or* ˈsōj- *or* -jən\ *n* -S [ME *soiorn, soiourne*, fr. OF *sojorn*, fr. *sojorner* to sojourn] **1 :** a temporary stay (as of a traveler in a foreign country) ⟨returned . . . after a long ~ in

Europe —Alan McCulloch⟩ ⟨a summer's ~ in the English countryside —Lucien Price⟩ ⟨the Israelite tradition of a prolonged ~ in Egypt —W.F.Albright⟩ **2** *archaic* **:** a temporary dwelling place ⟨long detained in that obscure ~ —John Milton⟩

²**sojourn** \"\ *vi* -ED/-ING/-S [ME *soiornen, soiournen*, fr. OF *sojorner*, fr. (assumed) VL *subdiurnare*, fr. L *sub-* under, during + LL *diurnum* day — more at JOURNEY] **:** to stay as a temporary resident **:** STOP ⟨~*ed* for a month at a mountain resort⟩ ⟨the right . . . to ~ there as long as they pleased —R.B.Taney⟩ **syn** see RESIDE

so·journ·er \-nə(r)\ *n* -S [ME *sojorner*, fr. *soiornen* to sojourn + *-er*] **:** one that sojourns ⟨missionaries and other ~*s* among primitive peoples —*Times Lit. Supp.*⟩: as **a** *obs* **:** GUEST, LODGER ⟨report what a ~ we have —Shak.⟩ **b** *archaic* **:** a student lodging in the house or school where he is taught

so·journ·ment \-nmənt\ *n* -S [²*sojourn* + *-ment*] *archaic* **:** SOJOURN

soke \'sōk\ *also* **soc** \'säk, 'sōk\ *n* -S [ME *soc, sok, soke*, fr. ML *soca*, fr. OE *sōcn* — more at SOKEN] **1 a** *Anglo-Saxon & early Eng law* **:** the right to hold court and do justice with the franchise to receive certain fees or fines arising from it **:** jurisdiction over a territory or over people **b :** any of various other jurisdictions or franchises: as (1) **:** FOLDAGE (2) **:** MILL SOKE **2 :** the district included in a soke jurisdiction or franchise

soke·man \'sōkmən\ *n, pl* **sokemen** [ME, fr. ML *sokemannus, sochemannus*, fr. OE *sōcn* soke + *man*] **:** a man who is under the soke of another **:** a tenant by socage

soke·man·ry \-rē\ *n* -ES [AF *sokemanerie*, fr. ML *sokemannus* sokeman + AF *-erie* -ry] **1 :** tenure of land subject to the soke of another — compare SOCAGE **2 a :** the quality or state of being a sokeman **b :** SOKEMEN

so·ken \'sōkən\ *n* -S [ME *socne, soken* soke, fr. OE *sōcn* act of seeking, inquiry, exercise of judicial power, jurisdiction, district of jurisdiction; akin to ON *sōkn* attack, action at law, parish, Goth *sokns* search, inquiry, OE *sēcan* to search — more at SEEK] **:** a district held by socage **:** SOKE 2

so·khor \(')sō¦kō(ə)r\ *n* -S [origin unknown] **:** any of several sturdily built burrowing cricetid rodents (genus *Myospalax*) of China, Manchuria, and southern Siberia that strongly resemble the American pocket gophers but may be distinguished from them by the greatly reduced eye and by absence of the external ear

so·kol \'sō,kōl\ *n* -S *often cap* [Czech, lit., falcon; akin to Skt *śakuna* bird] **:** a member of any one of various Slavic gymnastic societies of Europe and the U.S.

sokotrine *or* **sokotrine** *usu cap, var of* SOCOTRAN

so·ko·tri \sə'kō·trē\ *n, usu cap* [Ar *Suquṭrī*] **:** a South Arabic dialect very closely related to Mahri and spoken on the island of Socotra

¹**sol** \'sōl, *chiefly Brit* 'säl\ *also* **soh** *or* **so** \'sō\ *n* -S [*sol*, ME, fr. ML, fr. L *solve* purge, a word begun on this note in a medieval hymn to St. John the Baptist; *soh, so*, alterations of *sol* due to simplification of *-l l-* in singing the sequence *sol la* in the ascending scale] **1 :** the fifth tone of the diatonic scale in solmization **2 :** the tone *G* in the fixed-do system

²**sol** \"\ *vt, obs* **:** to sing sol to

³**sol** \'säl, *in sense 3* " *or* 'sōl\ *n* -S [ME, fr. L — more at SOLAR] **1** *usu cap* **:** SUN **2 :** gold as used in alchemy **3** [Mex-Sp, fr. Sp, sun, fr. L] **:** the sunny side or section of a bullfight arena — compare SOMBRA

⁴**sol** \'säl, 'sōl\ *n* -S [ME, fr. MF — more at SOU] **:** an old French coin equal to 12 deniers or ¹⁄₂₀ livre; *also* **:** a corresponding unit of value

⁵**sol** \"\ *n, pl* **so·les** \'sō(,)lās\ [AmerSp, fr. Sp, sun, fr. L; fr. the device on the coin] **1 a :** a Peruvian monetary unit equal to ¹⁄₁₀ libra or pound used before 1930 **b :** the basic monetary unit of Peru since 1930 — see MONEY table **2 :** a coin or note representing one Peruvian sol unit

⁶**sol** \'säl, 'sōl, 'sōl\ *n* -S [*-sol* (as in *hydrosol, alcosol*), fr. *solution*] **1 :** a fluid colloidal system: as **a :** a dispersion of solid particles in a liquid colloidal solution — compare GEL **b :** AEROSOL 1 **2 :** a fraction of a high-molecular-weight compound (as rubber) that dissolves or disperses in a solvent (as ether)

sol *abbr* **1** soldier **2** solenoid **3** solicitor **4** soluble **5** solution

SOL *abbr* **1** shipowner's liability **2** strictly out of luck

¹**so·la** \(')sō¦lä\ *interj* [origin unknown] *obs* **:** HOLLO

²**so·la** *also* **so·lah** \'s(h)ō(,)lä\ *n* -S [Hindi *śolā*] **:** an East Indian shrubby herb (*Aeschynomene aspera*) the pith of which is used for making hats, swimming jackets, and toys — see TOPEE

³**so·la** \'sōlə\ *or* **sola bill** *n* [L *sola*, fem. of *solus* sole, only] **:** an unduplicated bill of exchange

⁴**sola** *pl of* SOLUM

¹**sol·ace** \'säləs *sometimes* 'sōl-\ *n* -S [ME *solas*, fr. OF, fr. L *solacium, solatium* fr. *solari* to console, comfort — more at SILLY] **1 :** comfort in grief **:** alleviation of grief or anxiety ⟨seek ~ in company⟩ ⟨give ~ to a friend⟩ **2 a** *obs* **:** RECREATION **b :** an offsetting diversion **3 :** something that gives solace **:** a source of relief or consolation ⟨books were his only ~⟩ **4** *archaic* **:** a penalty imposed on a member by a printers' chapel for a breach of the rules

²**solace** \"\ *vb* -ED/-ING/-S [ME *solacen*, fr. OF *solacier*, fr. LL *solaciare*, fr. L *solacium* comfort, solace] *vt* **1 :** to give comfort to in grief or misfortune **:** CONSOLE **2 a :** to make (as a place) cheerful **b :** to give (as oneself) diversion **:** ENTERTAIN, AMUSE **3 :** ALLAY, ASSUAGE, SOOTHE ⟨~ grief⟩ **4** *archaic* **:** to impose a solace on (a member of a printers' chapel) ~ *vi, obs* **:** to take or give solace or comfort or diversion **syn** see COMFORT

sol·ace·ful \-fəl\ *adj* **:** full of or tending to bring solace

sol·ace·ment \-mənt\ *n* -S [²*solace* + *-ment*] **1 :** an act of solacing or the condition of being solaced **2 :** something that solaces

sol·ac·er \-ləsə(r)\ *n* -S **:** one that solaces

so·la·cious \sə'lāshəs, sō'l-\ *adj* [ME, fr. MF *solacieus*, fr. OF, fr. *solas* solace + *-eus* -ous] *archaic* **:** affording solace

so·lan \'sōlən\ *n* -S [ME *soland*, fr. ON *sūla* pillar, gannet + *önd* duck — more at SILE, ANAS] **:** SOLAN GOOSE

so·la·na·ce·ae \,sōlə'nāsē,ē\ *n pl, cap* [NL, fr. *Solanum*, type genus + *-aceae*] **:** a large and economically important family of widely distributed, often strongly scented, and sometimes narcotic herbs, shrubs, or trees (order Polemoniales) having alternate leaves and flowers that are often showy and have five stamens and a 2-celled ovary of which each cell contains many ovules — see ATROPA, CAPSICUM, HYOSCYAMUS, LYCOPERSICON, NICOTIANA, PETUNIA, PHYSALIS, SOLANUM — **so·la·na·ceous** \¦sōlə¦nāshəs\ *adj*

so·la·na·les \,sōlə'nā(,)lēz\ *n pl, cap* [NL, fr. *Solanum* + *-ales*] *in former classifications* **:** an order of dicotyledonous plants comprising Solanaceae and related families that are now usu. included among the Polemoniales

so·land \'sōlən(d)\ *n* -S [ME — more at SOLAN] **:** SOLAN GOOSE

so·lan·der case \(')sō¦landə(r)-\ *also* **solander box** *or* **solander** *n* -S *often cap S* [after Daniel C. *Solander* †1782 Swed. botanist in England] **:** a protective often leather-covered and book-shaped case for books and documents usu. with a slide-on top that completely covers the contents

solander case

so·lan·dra \sō'landrə\ *n* [NL, after Daniel C. *Solander* †1782] **1** *cap* **:** a small genus of tall climbing tropical American shrubs (family Solanaceae) having entire shining leathery leaves and large showy solitary white to yellow usu. fragrant flowers — see CHALICE VINE **2** -S **:** any plant of the genus *Solandra*

so·lan goose \¦sōlən-\ *or* **so·lent goose** \-n(t)-\ *n* **:** a very large white gannet (*Sula bassana* syn. *Morus bassanus*) with black wing tips that occurs esp. in Europe and eastern No. America

so·lan·i·dine \sō'lanə,dēn, -dən\ *also* **solanidine-t** *n, sometimes cap T* [*solanidine* ISV *solanine* + *-idine*; *solanidine-t* fr. *solanine* + *-idine* + *-t* (as in *solanine-t*)] **:** a crystalline steroidal alkaloid $C_{27}H_{43}NO$ obtained esp. by hydrolysis of solanine and also occurring with it naturally

so·la·nine \'sōlə,nēn, -,nən\ *also* **so·la·nin** \-,nən\ *n* -S [F *solanine*, fr. L *solanum* nightshade + F *-ine*] **1** *also* **solanine-t** *usu cap T* [*solanine-t* fr. *solanine* + *t*, initial of NL *tuberosum* (specific epithet of *Solanum tuberosum*, a solanaceous plant from which it is produced), fr. L, neut. of *tuberosus* tuberous] **:** a bitter crystalline glycosidal alkaloid $C_{45}H_{73}NO_{15}$ that has the toxic properties of a saponin, that is obtained from several solanaceous plants (as potato sprouts and eyes, tomatoes, and the berries of black nightshade and bittersweet), and that on hydrolysis yields solanidine, glucose, galactose, and rhamnose **2 :** any of several glycosidal alkaloids (as solasonine) related chemically to solanine

so·la·no \sə'lä(,)nō\ *n* -S [Sp, fr. L *solanus*, fr. *sol* sun + *-anus* -an — more at SOLAR] **:** a hot oppressive east wind of the Mediterranean region and esp. of the eastern coast of Spain; *also* **:** a cloudy rain-bringing wind of the same locality and direction

so·la·num \sə'lānəm, -lăn-\ *n* [NL, fr. L, nightshade, prob. fr. *sol* sun + *-anum*, neut. of *-anus* -an] **1** *cap* **:** the type genus of Solanaceae comprising herbs, trees, and shrubs that are widely distributed in tropical and temperate regions, have often prickly-veined leaves, cymose white, purple, or yellow flowers with a rotate corolla and five stamens with long connivent anthers, and a fruit that is a berry, and include several important food and ornamental plants — see EGGPLANT, POTATO; BITTERSWEET, JERUSALEM CHERRY; compare LYCOPERSICON **2** -S **:** any plant of the genus *Solanum*

¹**solar** \'sōlə(r), 'sōl-\ *or* **sol·lar** \'säl-\ *n* -S [ME *soler, solar*, fr. OE *soler, solar*; akin to MD *solre* loft, flat roof, MLG *solder*, OHG *solāri* loft; all fr. a prehistoric WGmc word borrowed fr. L *solarium* part of a house exposed to the sun — more at SOLARIUM] **1 :** an upper room or apartment (as a solarium, a chamber, a rood loft, or a garret); *esp* **:** an apartment for family use in a superior medieval residence ⟨the ladies gathered in the ~ while the lords drank in the great hall of the castle⟩ **2** *usu* **sollar** *or* **sol·ler** \'sälə(r)\ **:** a platform in a Cornish mine shaft and esp. between a series of ladders **:** a longitudinal partition forming an air passage between itself and the roof in a mine working

²**so·lar** \'sōlə(r) *sometimes* -,lär *or* -,lā(r\ *adj* [ME, fr. L *solaris*, fr. *sol* sun + *-aris* -ar; akin to OE & ON *sōl* sun, Goth *sauil*, Gk *hēlios*, Skt *sūra*] **1 :** of, derived from, or relating to the sun and its effects esp. on the earth and other celestial bodies **2 :** born under or subject to the influence of the sun **3 :** produced or operated by the action of the sun's light or heat; *also* **:** utilizing the sun's rays or heat ⟨a ~ engine⟩ — see SOLAR SALT, SOLAR TELEGRAPH **4 :** of, like, or connected with the sun as a deity or symbol of deity **:** descended from or sacred to a sun god **:** devoted to sun worship ⟨~ myths⟩ ⟨a ~ hero⟩

³**solar** \"\ *adj* [alter. (influenced by ²*solar*) of ²*sola*] **1 :** made of sola ⟨a ~ topee⟩ **2 :** intended for use in tropic regions ⟨~ clothing⟩

solar apex *n* **:** a point of the celestial sphere lying in the constellation Hercules toward which the sun and the solar system are moving with respect to the stars in the solar neighborhood at a rate of about 12 miles per second — compare ANTAPEX

solar attachment *n* **:** an attachment to a surveyor's transit or compass for determining the true meridian directly from the sun

solar battery *n* **:** a device consisting of one or more units for converting the energy of sunlight into electrical energy

solar compass *n* **:** SUN COMPASS

solar constant *n* **:** the quantity of radiant solar heat that is received normally at the outer layer of the earth's atmosphere and that has an average value of about 1.94 gram calories per square centimeter per minute

solar corona *n* **:** CORONA 2a(2)

solar cycle *n* **1 :** a cycle of disturbances in the sun and its atmosphere (as the fluctuation in the numbers and areas of sunspots or the form and shape of the corona) of an average length of about 11 years **2 :** CYCLE OF THE SUN

solar day *n* **1 :** the interval between transits of the apparent or mean solar sun across the meridian at any place **2 :** a period of one mean solar day containing 24 hours of solar minutes and seconds

solar diagonal *n* **:** an attachment for a telescope designed to permit direct observing of the sun by means of a prism that discards most of the unwanted heat and light

solar eclipse *n* **:** an eclipse of the sun by the moon — see ECLIPSE illustration

solar ecliptic limit *n* **:** the angular distance from the nodes of the moon's orbit within which an eclipse of the sun may or must occur when the sun and moon are in conjunction there

solar equation *n* **:** the correction of the epacts by —1 required in each century of the Gregorian calendar that begins with a common year instead of a leap year — compare LUNAR EQUATION

solar eyepiece *n* **:** an eyepiece for viewing the sun telescopically with means for diminishing the light and heat (as by partial reflection)

solar flare *n* **:** a sudden and temporary outburst of energy from a small area of the sun's surface that is usu. directly observable only in increased emission of a few spectral wavelengths (as in a hydrogen line and the lines of ionized calcium) but sometimes seen in white light

solar furnace *n* **:** a heating unit utilizing the rays of the sun concentrated by means of a concave mirror

solar heating *n* **:** space heating by capture and conversion of radiant energy from the sun — compare SOLAR FURNACE

solar hour *n* **:** the twenty-fourth part of a mean solar day

solar house *n* **:** a house equipped with glass areas and so planned as to utilize the sun's rays extensively in heating

sol·ar·ism \'sōlə,rizəm\ *n* -S [²*solar* + *-ism*] **:** an interpretation of folk stories and ancient legends as primitive concepts of the nature and action of the sun — compare SOLAR MYTH 2

¹**so·lar·i·um** \sō'la(a)rēəm, sə'l-, -ler-,-lăr-\ *n, pl* **solar·ia** *see sense 2* \-ēə\ [L, sundial, part of a house exposed to the sun, flat house, terrace, fr. *sol* sun + *-arium* — more at SOLAR] **1 :** a Roman sundial or clock (as a water clock) **2** *pl also* **solariums :** an apartment exposed to the sun: as **a :** an apartment on the roof of an ancient dwelling **b :** the solar of a medieval residence **c :** a glass-enclosed porch or living room **:** SUN PARLOR **d :** a room (as in a hospital) for exposure of the body to sunlight (as in sunbathing) or for the treatment of illness by therapeutic light **3 :** a snail of *Architectonica* or a related genus **:** SUNDIAL SHELL

²**solarium** \"\ [NL, fr. L, sundial] *syn of* ARCHITECTONICA

so·lar·iza·tion \,sōlərə'zāshən, -,rī'z-\ *n* -S [²*solar* + *-ization*] **1 :** an act or process of solarizing **2 :** a reversal of gradation sequence in the denser portions of the image obtained on the normal development of photographic films, plates, and papers after giving a very intense or long continued exposure **3 :** the inhibition of starch accumulation in leaves in the presence of intense illumination **4 :** alteration in the light-transmitting capacity of glass that follows prolonged exposure to sunlight or sometimes other radiations

so·lar·ize \'sōlə,rīz\ *vb* -ED/-ING/-S [²*solar* + *-ize*] *vt* **1 :** to expose to sunlight **:** affect or alter in some way by the action of the sun's rays **2 :** to interpret in terms of or color with solarism ⟨~ a myth⟩ **3 :** to subject (photographic materials) to solarization ~ *vi* **1 :** to solarize something **:** engage in solarizing **2** *of a photographic material* **:** to become affected by solarization

solar lamp *n* **:** ARGAND LAMP

solar letter *n* [trans. of Ar *alḥurūf ashshamsīya* — more at SUN LETTER] **:** SUN LETTER

solar mass *n* **:** the mass of the sun amounting to 2×10^{33} grams and being used as a unit for the expression of the masses of other stars, nebulas, and galaxies

solar microscope *n* **:** a projecting microscope using sunlight

solar motion *n* **:** the motion of the sun and solar system with reference to stars in the sun's neighborhood; *also* **:** any of the sun's other motions as a member of the galaxy — compare SOLAR APEX

solar myth *n* **1 :** a myth that concerns a sun god **2 :** a traditional story (as a folk tale or legend) that is interpreted as a primitive explanation of the course, motion, or influence of the sun — compare SOLARISM

solar noise *n* **:** radio noise emitted by the sun and its atmosphere

solar oil *n* **:** any of various mineral oils used esp. as fuel oils or insecticides: as **a :** gas oil from petroleum **b :** an intermediate fraction from crude shale oil

solar parallax *n* **:** the parallax of the sun being the angle subtended at the sun by the semidiameter of the earth, having an adopted value of 8″.80, and constituting the fundamental datum for the dimensions of the solar system

solar physics *n pl but sing or pl in constr* **:** a branch of astrophysics that deals with the constitution of the sun

solar plexus *n* [so called fr. the radiating nerve fibers] **1 :** a nerve plexus situated in the abdomen behind the stomach and in front of the aorta and the crura of the diaphragm, surrounding the coeliac axis and the root of the superior mesenteric artery, containing several ganglia of which the most important are the coeliac ganglia, and distributing nerve fibers to all the abdominal viscera — called also *coeliac plexus* **2 a :** the pit of the stomach **b :** a knockout or nerve-racking blow received in or as if in this spot

solar prominences *n pl* **:** great clouds of luminous hydrogen, calcium, sodium, and other gases floating above the sun's chromosphere, occas. erupting violently outward, and being esp. numerous in regions above sunspots

solar propagation *n* **:** a method of rooting cuttings using a hot-bed in which heat is supplied by radiation of stored sun heat from bricks or stones in the bottom of the frame

solars *pl of* SOLAR

solar salt *n* **:** salt from seawater or other brine evaporated in the sun

solar star *n* **:** a star of spectral type G resembling the sun in spectrum

solar still *n* **:** a small device orig. designed for army and navy fliers forced down in the sea that converts salt water or contaminated water into drinking water by vaporization by the sun's rays and condensation

solar system *n* **:** a star with the group of celestial bodies that are gravitationally bound to it; *esp* **:** the sun with the planets, moons, asteroids, and comets that orbit it

solar telegraph *n* **:** a telegraph for signaling by flashes of reflected sunlight — compare HELIOGRAPH 2

solar telescope *n* **:** a telescope designed for observations of the sun

solar tide *n* **:** the part of a tide due to the tide-producing force of the sun

solar time *n* **:** time either apparent or mean indicated by the sun **:** time expressed in units of mean solar time

solar tower *n* **:** a solar telescope in which light-gathering mirrors are placed at the top of a tall tower to permit the use of long-focus optics without the deterioration of image suffered in horizontal telescopes

solar trap *n* **:** a garden or terrace so oriented as to take advantage of the sun while protected from cold winds

solar type *n* **:** the spectral type of which the sun is the type object — used in designating stars

solary *adj* [L *sol* sun + E *-ary*] *obs* **:** SOLAR 1, 2

solar year *n* **:** the length of a year measured by the sun **:** TROPICAL YEAR

solas *pl of* SOLA

so·las·o·dine \sə'lasə,dēn, -dən; ,sälə'sō,dēn, -dᵊn\ *n* -S [*solasonine* + *solanidine*] **:** a crystalline steroidal alkaloid $C_{27}H_{43}NO_2$ closely related to solanidine and obtained by hydrolysis of solasonine

so·las·o·nine \sə'lasə,nēn, ,sälə'sō,n-, -,nən\ *n* -S [*solaso-* (fr. NL *Solanum sodomaeum*, fr. *Solanum* + *sodomaeum*, neut. of *sodomaeus* of Sodom, fr. LL *Sodoma* Sodom, fr. Gk) + *solanine*] **:** a crystalline glycosidic alkaloid $C_{45}H_{73}NO_{16}$ obtained from several solanaceous plants (as *Solanum sodomaeum*) and closely related to solanine but yielding solasodine on hydrolysis — called also *solanine-S*

sol·as·ter \'sä,lastə(r), ='=\ *n, cap* [NL, fr. L *sol* sun + LL *aster* star — more at SOLAR, ASTER] **:** the type genus of Solasteridae comprising the sun stars — compare ROSE STAR

sol·a·ster·i·dae \,sälə'sterə,dē\ *n pl, cap* [NL, fr. *Solaster*, type genus + *-idae*] **:** a widely distributed family of long-spined starfishes (order Spinulosa) that are typically brightly colored and have numerous arms

sol·ate \'sä,lāt, 'sō,-, 'sō,-\ *vi* -ED/-ING/-S [⁶*sol* + *-ate*] **:** to change to a sol — compare GEL

so·la·ti·um \sō'lāshēəm\ *n, pl* **sola·tia** \-ēə\ [LL *solacium, solatium*, fr. L, solace — more at SOLACE] **:** something that alleviates or compensates for suffering or loss **:** COMPENSATION; *esp* **:** an additional allowance (as for injured feelings)

so·lay \sə'lā\ *vt* [alter. (due to printer's error) of ¹*splay*] **:** to cut (a bream) into serving portions

sold [ME *solde* (past), *sold* (past part.), fr. OE (northern & Midland dial.) *salde* (past), *gesald* (past part.)] *past of* SELL

sol·da·de·ra \,söldə'derə, ,säl-\ *n* -S [AmerSp, fr. Sp, female entertainer, woman of loose morals, lit., woman who works for pay, fr. *soldada* pay, fr. fem. of *soldado*, past part. of *soldar* to pay] **:** a woman that is a camp follower with a Latin-American and esp. a guerrilla military force

sol·da·do \sōl'dä(,)dō\ *n, pl* **soldados** *also* **soldadoes** [Sp, soldier, fr. past part. of *soldar* to pay, fr. *soldo, sueldo* a small coin, pay, salary, fr. LL *solidus, soldus* solidus] **:** a Latin-American soldier

sol·dan \'säldən, 'sōldən, 'sōdᵊn\ *n* -S [ME, fr. MF, fr. Ar *sulṭān*] **1** *usu cap, archaic* **:** the sovereign of a Muslim country **:** SULTAN; *esp* **:** the sultan of Egypt **2 :** a Muslim ruler or prince

sol·da·nel·la \,säldə'nelə, ,sōl-\ *n* [NL, fr. It, soldanella] **1** *cap* **:** a small genus of European low-growing perennial alpine herbs (family Primulaceae) having basal fleshy leaves and nodding scapose blue or pink flowers with the corolla lobes often fringed **2** -S **:** any plant of the genus *Soldanella*

¹**sol·der** \'sädə(r), 'sōd-, *chiefly Brit* 'säld-\ *n* -S [ME *souldour, sowder, sawder*, fr. MF *soldure, soudure, saudure*, fr. *solder, souder, saudar* to solder fr. L *solidare* to make solid, join together, fr. *solidus* solid) + *-ure*] **1 :** a metal or metallic alloy used when melted to join metallic surfaces and usu. applied by means of a soldering iron or a blowpipe with a flux (as rosin, borax, or zinc chloride) to cleanse the surfaces; *esp* **:** an alloy of lead and tin so used **2 :** something (as a shared principle) that serves to unite or cement **:** a common bond

²**solder** \"\ *vb* **soldered; soldered; soldering** \-d(ə)riŋ\ **solders** *vt* **1 :** to unite or make whole by means of solder ⟨~ a joint in piping⟩ ⟨~ a leaky pot⟩ ⟨~ up a hole⟩ ⟨~ sheets of metal together⟩ **2 :** to bring into or restore to firm union as if by the use of solder **:** cause to adhere, knit, close up, or come together as if soldered ⟨a friendship ~*ed* by common interests⟩ — often used with *up* ⟨the union was ~*ed up* by concessions from both sides⟩ ~ *vi* **1 :** to use solder **:** make unions or repairs by means of solder ⟨was ~*ing* away at a free form when I got there⟩ ⟨workmen who like to ~⟩ **2** *obs* **:** to constitute a source of union **3 :** to become united or repaired by or as if by solder ⟨the joint ~*s* easily⟩

sol·der·able \-d(ə)rəbəl\ *adj* **:** capable of being soldered ⟨a ~ leak⟩ or of promoting union with solder ⟨a ~ coating⟩

sol·der·er \-dərə(r)\ *n* -S **:** one that solders; *esp* **:** a worker who joins or repairs metal parts with solder

¹**soldering** *n* -S [fr. gerund of ²*solder*] **1 :** an act or instance of using solder ⟨his ~ was very neat⟩ **2 :** SOLDER 1 **3 :** a joint, repair, or distinctive mark made by soldering **:** a soldered place ⟨the ~*s* should be polished clean⟩

²**soldering** *adj* **:** used in the process of uniting by solder ⟨~ tools⟩ ⟨a ~ flux⟩

soldering bolt *n* **1 :** SOLDERING IRON **2 :** ¹BIT 3a

soldering gun *n* **:** an electric soldering iron with a gun-type grip

soldering iron *also* **soldering copper** *n* **1 a :** a bit or bolt of

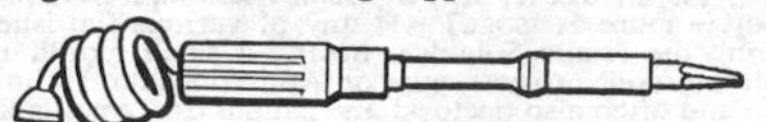

electric soldering iron

copper made with a pointed or wedge-shaped end, furnished

with a handle, and used for soldering **b :** a plumber's grozing iron **2 :** any of various usu. somewhat pointed or wedge-shaped electrically heated devices used for soldering

soldering nipple *or* **solder nipple** *n* **:** a plumbing nipple with a pipe thread on one end and the other end plain for soldering into the end of a pipe

soldering pot *n* **:** a small plumber's furnace (as one used by linemen)

sol·der·less \-də(r)ləs\ *adj* **:** lacking solder **:** containing no solder

soldi *pl of* SOLDO

¹sol·dier \'sōljə(r), *substand & dial* -ōj-, *chiefly Brit sometimes* -ōldyə(r\ *n* -s *often attrib* [ME *souldiour, sodiour, soudier,* fr. OF *souldiour, soudier,* fr. *soulde, soude* pay, fr. LL *solidus, soldus* solidus] **1 a :** a person engaged in military service: as (1) **:** an officer or enlisted man serving in an army **:** a member of an organized body of combatants (2) **:** an enlisted man or woman in military service as distinguished from a commissioned or warrant officer (3) **:** PRIVATE 4a **b :** a skilled, experienced, or valorous warrior **c :** a member of the Salvation Army **2 :** one that fights for a cause, endures hardships, or otherwise conducts himself gallantly **:** a militant leader, follower, or worker ⟨~*s* in the cause of peace⟩ **3 :** any of various animals in some way (as habits, appearance) associated with soldiers: as **a** (1) **:** HERMIT CRAB (2) **:** FIDDLER CRAB **b** (1) **:** one of a caste of wingless sterile individuals that in most termites differ more or less from the workers in their larger size, very large head, and long jaws and that often perform a share in the work of the colonies (2) **:** one of a type of workers among some ants distinguished by exceptionally large head and jaws **c** (1) *dial Eng* **:** RED GURNARD (2) *southern Africa* **:** a silvery pink sparid food fish (*Cheimerius nufar*) widespread in the Indo-Pacific seas (3) **:** SQUIRRELFISH 1 **d :** SOLDIER BEETLE **e :** RED SPIDER **4 :** RED HERRING 1 **5 soldiers** *pl* **:** VIRGINIA STICKSEED **6 :** a person who shirks his work **:** LOAFER, DRONE **7 :** a brick that is placed on end in a wall with its narrow side exposed

²soldier \"\ *vi* **soldiered; soldiered; soldiering** \-(ə)riŋ\ **soldiers 1 a :** to serve or function as a soldier ⟨~*ed* in three wars⟩ **b :** to serve satisfactorily as a soldier **:** behave in a soldierly manner ⟨have to really ~ in such a crack outfit⟩ **2 :** to make a pretense of working while doing only enough to escape punishment or discharge **:** affect a pretense of busyness or working **:** loaf surreptitiously ⟨workers ~*ing* on the job⟩ **3** *chiefly dial* **:** BULLY

soldier ant *n* **1 :** SOLDIER 3b(2) **2 a :** BULLDOG ANT **b :** ARMY ANT

soldier beetle *n* **:** any of various usu. brightly colored and soft-bodied beetles of the family Cantharidae (as *Chauliognathus pennsylvanicus*) that frequent fruit and flowers and include several valuable predators on other insects

soldier bug *n* **:** any of numerous predatory bugs (family Pentatomidae) that suck the blood of other insects

soldier course *n* **:** a course of soldiers in masonry

soldier crab *n* **1 :** HERMIT CRAB **2 :** FIDDLER CRAB

soldierfish \'==,=\ *n* **1 :** SQUIRRELFISH 1 **2 :** RAINBOW DARTER **3 :** a small Australian cardinal fish (*Apogon fasciatus*) or a related fish (*A. conspersus*)

soldier fly *n* **:** any of numerous two-winged flies (family Stratiomyiidae) that are typically marked with colored stripes and have larvae which develop esp. in water, earth, or decaying wood

soldiering *n* -s [fr. gerund of ²*soldier*] **:** the life, service, or practice of one who soldiers

sol·dier·ize \'sōljə,rīz\ *vb* -ED/-ING/-s *vi* **:** SOLDIER 1a ~ *vt* **:** to convert into a soldier **:** force to soldier

soldierlike \'==,=\ *adj* [¹*soldier* + *like*] **:** SOLDIERLY

sol·dier·li·ness \-jə(r)lēnəs, -lin-\ *n* -ES **:** the quality or state of being soldierly

¹sol·dier·ly \-lē,-li\ *adj* [¹*soldier* + -*ly*] **:** being like or befitting a good soldier **:** BRAVE, MARTIAL, HEROIC

²soldierly \"\ *adv* **:** in a soldierly manner **:** so as to be soldierly

soldier of fortune : one who follows a military career wherever there is promise of profit, adventure, or pleasure; *also* **:** a mettlesome adventurer guided by similar aims

soldier prawn *n* **:** an edible Australian deep-water prawn (*Plesionika martia*)

soldier's buttons *n pl but sing or pl in constr* **:** a marsh marigold (*Caltha palustris*)

soldier's-cap \'==,=\ *n, pl* **soldier's-caps 1 :** DUTCHMAN'S-BREECHES **2 :** a monkshood (*Aconitum napellus*)

soldier's heart *n* **:** CARDIAC NEUROSIS

soldier's herb *n* **:** MATICO 1

sol·dier·ship \'sōljə(r),ship\ *n* **:** the status or condition of a soldier

soldiers' home *n* **:** an institution maintained (as by the federal or a state government) for the care and relief of military veterans

soldier's-plume \'==,=\ *n, pl* **soldier's-plumes :** PURPLE-FRINGED ORCHID a

soldier sprag *n* **:** a long sprag used esp. in New So. Wales to support a seam in a coal mine between the top of the holing and the roof

soldier's wind *n* **:** a beam wind favorable either coming or going

soldier turtle *n* **:** PAINTED TURTLE

soldier wood *n* **:** MABI 1

sol·diery \'sōlj(ə)rē, -ri\ *n* -ES [¹*soldier* + -*y*] **1 :** a body of soldiers **:** SOLDIERS, MILITARY **2 a :** the profession or training of a soldier **b :** the art or technique of soldiering

sol·do \'sōl(,)dō\ *n, pl* **sol·di** \-dē\ [It, fr. LL *solidus, soldus* solidus] **1 :** an Italian coin and corresponding unit of value of the 13th century **2 :** an Italian 5-centesimi piece or 1/20 lira

sold-out \(')=;=\ *adj* **:** sold completely and esp. in advance ⟨had a *sold-out* house for both performances⟩

sold-up \(')=;=\ *adj* **:** having the product for the production period in question sold in full or in advance ⟨many mills are reaching a *sold-up* position⟩

¹sole \'sōl\ *n* -s [ME, fr. MF, fr. L *solea* sandal (consisting of a sole with a strap across the instep); akin to L *solum* base, ground, soil] **1 a** (1) **:** the undersurface of a foot or that part of it which is placed on the ground in walking or standing (2) **:** the somewhat concave plate of moderately dense horn that covers the lower surface of the coffin bone in the horse, partly surrounds the frog, and is bounded externally by the wall **b :** FOOT **2 :** the part of a shoe or other article of footwear on which the sole of the foot rests and upon which the wearer treads; *specif* **:** a shaped piece of leather, rubber, or other material forming the bottom or a layer of the bottom of a shoe and often excluding the heel — compare HALF SOLE, INSOLE, MIDSOLE, OUTSOLE, SLIPSOLE; see SHOE illustration **3 :** the bottom or lower part of something or the base on which something rests: as **a** *obs* **:** the foundation or site of a building or city **b** (1) *chiefly dial* **:** the sill of a window or door (2) **:** the horizontal plate on which the studs of a partition bear (3) **:** SOLEPIECE (4) **:** either of two planks resting one on each side on a sliding ways and forming the foundation of the cradle that supports a ship during building **c :** the hearth or flooring of a furnace, oven, or other heating device **d :** the floor of drift, level, or working in a mine **e** (1) **:** the undersurface of a plane through which the blade projects (2) **:** the bottom of the body of a plow **f :** the floor of a cabin on a ship **g** *chiefly dial* **:** the underframe of a vehicle (as a wagon or cart) **h :** the bottom of the inside of a gas retort **i :** the flattened bottom surface of a golf club head **4 a :** the underlying layers of land and esp. of arable land **:** SUBSOIL **b :** the layer of intertwined roots that forms the base of sod or turf **c :** the bottom of a furrow **d :** the lowest part of a valley

²sole \"\ *vt* -ED/-ING/-s **1 :** to furnish with a sole ⟨~ a shoe⟩ **2 :** to serve as a base for or bottom of **3 :** to place the sole of (a golf club) on the ground (as in addressing a ball)

³sole \"\ *n* -s [ME, fr. MF, fr. L *solea* sandal, a flatfish (fr. its shape) — more at ¹SOLE] **1 :** any of various flatfishes constituting the family Soleidae, having a small mouth beyond which the snout projects more or less, reduced or rudimentary pelvic and often also pectoral and caudal fins, small gill openings, and small eyes placed close together, and including superior food fishes (as *Solea solea* of Europe) and others too small to be of commercial value — compare FLOUNDER **2 :** any of various flatfishes of families other than Soleidae esp. when for table use — usu. used with a qualifying term; see PETRALE SOLE, SAND SOLE

⁴sole \"\ *adj* [ME *soul, sool, sole* alone, celibate, fr. MF *seul, sol* alone, fr. L *solus;* prob. akin to L *sed, se* without — more at IDIOT] **1 :** having no spouse **:** UNMARRIED — used chiefly of women **2 :** having no companion **:** SOLITARY, LONELY ⟨sitting ~ by the hearth⟩ **3 a :** having no sharer (as in a right or status) **:** being the only one ⟨the ~ heir⟩ ⟨the ~ product of all this industry⟩ **b :** of unmatched quality or kind **:** UNIQUE **4 :** functioning (as in acting, working, moving) independently and without assistance or interference ⟨the ~ author of this scheme⟩ ⟨let conscience be the ~ judge⟩ **5** *obs* **a :** that is such and no other **:** MERE **b :** ALONE **6 :** belonging, granted, or attributed to the one person or group specified **:** independently accomplished, held, or developed **:** exclusively exercised **:** UNSHARED ⟨the ~ power of the Congress⟩ ⟨~ rights of publication⟩; *sometimes* **:** ENTIRE ⟨~ jurisdiction⟩ **syn** see SINGLE

⁵sole \"\ *adv* **:** SOLELY

⁶sole \"\ *vt* -ED/-ING/-s [origin unknown] **:** to pull roughly

¹so·lea \'sōlēə\ *n, cap* [NL, fr. L, a kind of flatfish — more at SOLE] **:** the type genus of Soleidae

²so·lea \sō'lēə\ *n* -s [MGk, fr. L, sandal, sill — more at SOLE] **:** a platform or a raised part of the floor in front of the inner sanctuary in an Eastern Orthodox church on which the singers stand and the faithful receive communion

sole·cism \'sälə,sizəm *also* 'sōl- *sometimes* 'sōl-\ *n* -s [L *soloecismus,* fr. Gk *soloikismos,* fr. *soloikos* speaking incorrectly (lit., inhabitant of Soloi, fr. *Soloi,* city in ancient Cilicia where a corrupt form of Attic was spoken by colonists + Gk *-ikos* -ic) + *-ismos* -ism] **1 :** an ungrammatical combination of words in a sentence **:** a deviation from the idiom of a language or from the rules of syntax ⟨"he was independent on any patron" is a typical ~⟩; *also* **:** a minor blunder in speech **2 :** a deviation from the proper, normal, or accepted order **:** something (as a theory, situation, act) not consonant with logic, circumstances, known facts, or other standard **:** an absurd incongruity or incompatibility; *sometimes* **:** ANACHRONISM **3 :** a breach of etiquette or decorum **:** an unmannerly act or practice **:** IMPROPRIETY

sole·cist \-,səst\ *n* -s [LL *soloecista,* fr. Gk *soloikistēs,* fr. *soloikos* speaking incorrectly + *-istēs* -ist] **:** a user of solecisms; *also* **:** one who defies convention

sole·cis·tic \'==;sistik, -tēk\ *also* **sole·cis·ti·cal** \-təkəl, -tēk-\ *adj* [*solecist* + *-ic, -ical*] **:** relating to, constituting, or involving a solecism **:** INCORRECT, INCONGRUOUS, UNSEEMLY — **sole·cis·ti·cal·ly** \-tək(ə)lē, -tēk-, -li\ *adv*

sole·cize \'==,sīz\ *vi* -ED/-ING/-s [Gk *soloikizein,* fr. *soloikos* speaking incorrectly + *-izein* -ize] **:** to use solecisms **:** commit a solecism

sole·ciz·er \-zə(r)\ *n* -s [*solecize* + *-er*] **:** SOLECIST

sole corporation *n* [⁴*sole*] **:** CORPORATION SOLE

soled \'sōld\ *adj* [ME, fr. ¹*sole* + *-ed*] **:** having such or so many soles — usu. used in combination ⟨callous-*soled*⟩ ⟨triple-*soled*⟩ ⟨thin-*soled*⟩

sol·e·dad pine \'säl|ə,dad- *sometimes* 'sōl\ *n, usu cap S* [fr. *Soledad* river, San Diego co., California] **:** TORREY PINE

so·le·idae \sə'lēə,dē\ *n pl, cap* [NL, fr. *Solea,* type genus + *-idae*] **:** a family of flatfishes (order Heterosomata) comprising the typical soles and distinguished from the typical flounders (family Pleuronectidae) by the extension of the dorsal fin high on the head and by the covered margin of the preopercle

so·le·i·form \sə'lēə,fōrm, 'sōl-\ *adj* [L *solea* sandal + E *-iform* — more at SOLE] **:** shaped like a slipper **:** CALCEIFORM

¹so·leil \(')sō¦lā\ *adj* [F, sun, fr. (assumed) VL *soliculus,* dim. of L *sol* sun — more at SOLAR] **1 :** finished with a high luster ⟨*soleil* felt or velour⟩ **2 :** woven with a fancy warp rib

²soleil \"\ *n* -s **:** a fabric with a soleil finish or weave

sole leather *n* [¹*sole*] **1 :** a thick strong leather esp. for shoe soles **2** *also* **sole-leather kelp :** any of the larger kelps of the genus *Laminaria*

sole·less \'sōlləs\ *adj* **:** having no sole

sole·ly \'sōl(l)ē, -)i\ *adv* [⁴*sole* + *-ly*] **1 :** without an associate (as a companion or assistant) **:** SINGLY, ALONE ⟨go ~ on one's way⟩ **2 :** to the exclusion of alternate or competing things (as persons, purposes, duties) ⟨done ~ for money⟩ ⟨a privilege granted ~ to him⟩ ⟨rely ~ on oneself⟩

¹sol·emn \'säləm *sometimes* 'sōl-\ *adj* -ER/-EST [ME *solempne, solemne,* fr. MF, fr. L *sollennis, solennis, sollemnis, solemnis* regularly appointed, festive, solemn, prob. fr. *sollus* whole, entire (fr. Oscan; akin to Gk *holos* entire) + *-ennis* (fr. *annus* year) — more at SAFE, ANNUAL] **1 a :** marked by or performed, made, or uttered under circumstances that indicate a full and sober realization and acceptance of all that is involved and usu. accompanied by a specific religious sanction ⟨took a ~ oath on the Bible⟩ ⟨a ~ dedication to the cause of freedom⟩ **b :** made in due and proper form and so as to be legally binding **:** conforming to all legal requirements ⟨a ~ writ⟩ ⟨~ instruments⟩ ⟨made ~ affidavit⟩ ⟨a ~ declaration⟩ **2 a** *archaic, of a day or season* **:** given over to the performance of special rites or ceremonies usu. of a religious character **b :** carried out in accord with accepted religious forms or rites ⟨a ~ blessing⟩ ⟨a ~ curse⟩ **c :** observed or celebrated with unusual pomp and ceremony and usu. after a pattern established by liturgy or tradition ⟨a ~ festival⟩; *specif* **:** distinguished from other services by being celebrated with full liturgy ⟨a ~ high mass⟩ ⟨~ complines⟩ **3** *obs* **a :** SUMPTUOUS, SPLENDID **b :** NOTABLE, DISTINGUISHED **4 a :** notable for marked ceremony and formality **:** characterized by pomp, dignity, and elaborate attention to form ⟨a ~ state dinner⟩ **b** *obs* **:** being such in full form **:** conforming to what is usual in the thing specified **5 a :** of a kind fitted to excite serious reflections or exalted emotions **:** AWE-INSPIRING, SUBLIME ⟨these ~ scenes⟩ **b :** marked by grave sobriety and earnest serious sedateness **:** free from casualness or lighthearted levity ⟨the audience grew ~⟩ ⟨at this ~ moment⟩ ⟨spoke in a ~ and thoughtful manner⟩ **c :** of a serious nature **:** involving responsibility and strict adherence to duty imposed ⟨staked his life on the fulfilling of this ~ charge⟩ ⟨children are a ~ responsibility to their parents⟩ **6 :** SOMBER, GLOOMY ⟨a suit of ~ black⟩ **syn** see CEREMONIAL, SERIOUS

²solemn \"\ *adv* **:** SOLEMNLY

solemn form *n* **:** the form of probate of a will where the will is decreed in open court to be the last will and testament after notice to all interested persons and after hearing the testimony of the attesting witnesses

so·lem·ni·fy \sə'lemnə,fī\ *vt* -ED/-ING/-ES **:** to make solemn

so·lem·ni·tude \-nə,tüd, -nə,tyüd\ *n* -s [L *solemnis* + E *-tude*] **:** SOLEMNNESS

so·lem·ni·ty \sə'lemnəd·ē, -nətē, -i\ *n* -ES [ME *solempnite, solemnite,* fr. OF *solempnité, solemnité,* fr. LL *solemnitat-, solemnitas,* fr. L *solemnis* solemn + *-itat-, -itas* -ity] **1 :** formal or ceremonious observance of an occasion or event **:** such observance as a due of a particular occasion, person, or event ⟨welcomed the visiting statesman with fitting ~⟩; *esp* **:** solemn liturgical celebration of a sacrament, service, or feast day ⟨the *solemnities* of Easter⟩ **2 a :** a solemn event or occasion (as a season, rite, utterance, or feast day) **b :** an observance or proceeding according to due form **:** the formality necessary to make a thing done valid in law **3 :** a solemn condition or quality (as of mien) **:** the state of being serious, dignified, or awe-inspiring ⟨the ~ of his words⟩ ⟨an occasion of great ~⟩

sol·em·ni·za·tion \,säləmnə'zāshən, -,nī'z- *sometimes* ,sōl-\ *n* -s [ME *solemnyzacyoun,* fr. MF *solemnisation,* fr. ML *solemnization-, solemnizatio,* fr. LL *solemnizatus* (past part. of *solemnizare*) + L *-ion-, -io-* -ion] **:** an act of solemnizing or the condition of being solemnized **:** CELEBRATION ⟨the ~ of a marriage⟩

¹sol·em·nize \'==,nīz\ *vb* -ED/-ING/-s *see -ize in Explan Notes* [ME *solempnisen,* fr. MF *solempniser,* fr. LL *solemnizare,* fr. L *solemnis* solemn + LL *-izare* -ize] *vt* **1 :** to hold, conduct, observe, or honor with due formal ceremony or solemn notice ⟨~ this sorrowing natal day to prove our loyal truth —Robert Burns⟩ **2 :** to perform with pomp or ceremony or according to legal forms; *esp* **:** to unite a couple in (marriage) with religious ceremony **:** celebrate (a marriage) with religious rites **3** *obs* **:** to exalt by praising **:** GLORIFY **4 :** to make solemn, serious, or exalted **:** DIGNIFY ~ *vi* **:** to grow solemn **:** speak or act with solemnity **syn** see KEEP

²solemnize \"\ *n* -s *obs* **:** SOLEMNIZATION

sol·em·niz·er \-zə(r)\ *n* -s **:** one that solemnizes

solemnlike \'==,=\ *adv* [¹*solemn* + *like*] *dial* **:** somewhat solemnly

sol·emn·ly *adv* [ME *solemnely, solemply,* fr. *solemne, solempne* solemn + *-ly*] **:** in a solemn manner **:** with solemnity ⟨~ sworn testimony⟩

solemn mass *n, often cap S&M* **:** a mass celebrated with full ceremony including the use of incense and music by an officiating priest assisted by a deacon and subdeacon

sol·emn·ness \-əmnəs\ *n* -ES **:** the quality or state of being solemn

solemn vow *n* **:** an absolute and irrevocable public vow taken by a religious in the Roman Catholic Church under which ownership of property by the individual is prohibited and marriage is invalid under canon law — compare SIMPLE VOW

so·len \'sōlən, -,len\ *n* [NL, fr. L, razor clam, fr. Gk *sōlēn* channel, pipe, a shellfish — more at SYRINGE] **1** *cap* **:** a genus (the type of the family Solenidae) of razor clams **2** -s **:** RAZOR CLAM

solen- *or* **soleno-** *comb form* [Gk *sōlēn-, sōlēno-,* fr. *sōlēn*] **:** channel **:** pipe **:** tube; *also* **:** tubular ⟨*Solenodon*⟩ ⟨*solenocyte*⟩ ⟨*solenostele*⟩

¹sole·na·cean \¦sälə¦nāsh(ē)ən, ¦sōl-\ *also* **sole·na·ceous** \-shəs\ *adj* [NL *Solēn* + E *-acean, -aceous*] **:** of, relating to, or resembling the Solenidae

²solenacean \"\ *n* -s **:** a solenacean mollusk

sole·ness *n* -ES [⁴*sole* + *-ness*] **:** the quality or state of being sole

sole·nette \(')sōl¦net, ¦sōlə¦n-\ *n* -s [irreg. fr. ³*sole* + *-ette*] **:** a small European sole (*Microchirus luteus*) about five inches long and of no commercial value

Sol·en·ho·fen stone \'s|ōlən,hōfən-, 'z|\ *n, usu cap 1st S* [fr. *Solenhofen,* village of west central Bavaria] **:** a limestone found at Solenhofen, Bavaria and valued for lithographic purposes

so·le·ni·al \sō'lēnēəl\ *adj* [NL *solenium* + E *-al*] **:** of, relating to, or involving a solenium

so·len·ich·thy·es \,sōlə'nikthē,ēz\ *n pl, cap* [NL, fr. *solen-* + Gk *ichthyes,* pl. of *ichthys* fish — more at ICHTHUS] **:** a small order of chiefly tropical marine fishes (as the bellows fishes, shrimpfishes, and cornetfishes) that are of varied and sometimes bizarre form but all have the small mouth at the end of a drawn-out tubular snout — compare THORACOSTEI

so·len·i·dae \sō'lenə,dē\ *n pl, cap* [NL, fr. *Solen,* type genus + *-idae*] **:** a family of marine clams (suborder Myacea) with elongated curved shells comprising the razor clams

so·le·ni·um \sō'lēnēəm\ *n, pl* **sole·nia** \-nēə\ [NL, fr. Gk *sōlēnion,* dim. of *sōlēn* channel, pipe] **:** STOLON

so·len·ne \sō'le(,)nā\ *adj* [It, fr. L *solemnis* — more at SOLEMN] **:** SOLEMN — used as a direction in music regarding mood — **so·len·ne·men·te** \sō,lenə'men·(,)tā\ *adv*

so·leno·concha \sō¦lēnə, -lenə+\ *or* **so·leno·conchae** \"+\ [NL, fr. *solen-* + L *concha* shell — more at CONCH] *syn of* SCAPHOPODA

so·leno·cyte \sō'lēnə,sīt, -len-\ *n* -s [*solen-* + *-cyte*] **:** any of various modified tubular flagellated cells occurring in the nephridia of the larvae of some annelids, mollusks, and rotifers and of a few lancelets — **so·leno·cyt·ic** \=¦==¦sid·ik\ *adj*

so·len·odon \sō'lēnə,dän, -len-\ *n* [NL, fr. *solen-* + *-odon*] **1** *cap* **:** a small genus (coextensive with the family Solenodontidae) of atypical and very rare insectivorous mammals of Cuba and Haiti that are nearly 2 feet long and have a long snout, short round ears, hard fur, a long scaly tail, 40 teeth, and a skull with no zygomatic arch **2** -s **:** any mammal of the genus *Solenodon* — **so·len·odont** \-nt\ *adj or n*

so·leno·gas·ter \=¦==¦gastə(r)\ *n* -s [NL *Solenogastres*] **:** APLACOPHORAN

so·leno·gas·tres \=¦==ga(,)strēz\ [NL, fr. *solen-* + Gk *gastr-, gastēr* belly — more at GASTRIC] *syn of* APLACOPHORA

so·leno·glyph \=¦==,glif\ *n* -s [NL *Solenoglypha*] **:** a venomous snake with tubular erectile fangs

sole·nog·ly·pha \,sōlə'näglәfə, ,säl-\ *n pl, cap* [NL, fr. *solen-* + Gk *glyphein* to carve — more at CLEAVE] *in some classifications* **:** a group of venomous snakes with tubular erectile fangs comprising the families Viperidae and Crotalidae

sole·nog·ly·phous \¦==¦==fəs\ *or* **soleno·glyph·ic** \¦sōlənō-¦glifik, ¦säl-; sō¦lēnə¦glifik, -¦len-\ *adj* [NL *Solenoglypha* + E *-ous* or *-ic*] **:** having tubular erectile fangs **:** belonging to the Solenoglypha

so·le·noid \'sōlə,nȯid *sometimes* 'säl-\ *n* -s [F *solénoïde,* fr. Gk *sōlēnoeidēs* shaped like a pipe, fr. *sōlēn-* + *-oeidēs* -oid] **1 :** a coil of wire commonly in the form of a long cylinder that when carrying a current resembles a bar magnet so that a movable core is drawn into the coil when a current flows **2 :** a section of atmosphere bounded by two isobaric and two isosteric surfaces

so·le·noi·dal \¦==¦nȯidᵊl\ *adj* **1 :** of, relating to, or constituting a solenoid **2 :** TUBULAR — used of a mathematical vector field whose divergence is 0 — **so·le·noi·dal·ly** \-ᵊlē\ *adv*

solenoid brake *n* **:** a brake in which the shoes are operated by the magnetic action of a solenoid

solenoid switch *n* **:** a switch operated by a solenoid

solenoid valve *n* **:** a valve operated by a solenoid

sole·nop·sis \,sōlə'näpsəs, ,säl-\ *n, cap* [NL, fr. *solen-* + *-opsis*] **:** a genus of small stinging ants including several abundant tropical and subtropical forms (as the fire ant and thief ant)

so·leno·stele \sō'lēnə,stēl, -len- *also* =¦==¦stēlē\ *n* [*solen-* + *stele*] **:** a siphonostele (as in some ferns) with phloem both internal and external to the xylem — **so·leno·ste·lic** \=¦==¦stēlik\ *adj* — **so·leno·ste·ly** \='==,stēlē\ *n* -ES

so·leno·stom·i·dae \sō,lēnə'stämə,dē, -len-\ *n pl, cap* [NL, fr. *Solenostomus,* type genus + *-idae*] **:** a family of fishes (order Solenichthyes) that is coextensive with the genus *Solenostomus*

so·le·nos·to·mus \,sōlə'nästəməs\ *n, cap* [NL, fr. *solen-* + Gk *stoma* mouth — more at STOMACH] **:** a genus of small fishes (family Solenostomidae) of the tropical Indo-Pacific having a short compressed body and a long tubular snout and a female that carries her eggs in a pouch formed by the coalescence of the pelvic fins with the body

solens *pl of* SOLEN

solent goose *n* [alter. of *soland goose*] **:** SOLAN GOOSE

sol·en·tine \'sälən,tīn, -tēn\ *n* -s [alter. of *celandine*] **:** a jewelweed (*Impatiens capensis*)

so·le·oi·dei \,sōlē'ȯidē,ī\ *or* **so·le·oi·dea** \-dēə\ *n pl, cap* [NL, fr. *Solea* + *-oidei* or *-oidea*] *in some classifications* **:** a suborder or other division of Heterosomata comprising the families Soleidae and Cynoglossidae

solepiece \'=,=\ *n* [¹*sole* + *piece*] **1 :** a timber or girder laid on the ground to take and distribute the thrust of an upright or strut **:** the floor member of a frame **2 a :** a piece on the bottom of the rudder of a wooden ship designed to bring it down to the false keel **b :** a piece joining rudderpost and sternpost in a steel ship **c :** a projection from a ship's keel designed to support a balanced rudder

soleplate \'=,=\ *n* [¹*sole* + *plate*] **1 :** a flattened nucleated mass of soft granular protoplasm surrounding the end of a motor nerve in a striated muscle fiber **2 :** the lower plate of a stud partition on which the bases of the studs butt **3 a:** BEDPLATE **b :** the plate forming the back of a waterwheel bucket **c :** a plate to which a bearing can be wedged and bolted so as to be slightly adjustable **d :** the under surface of a flatiron **:** the surface contacting the material in pressing

soleprint \'=,=\ *n* [¹*sole* + *print*] **:** a print of the sole of the foot; *esp* **:** one made in the manner of a fingerprint and used particularly for the identification of an infant

soleprint

sol·er \'sōlə(r)\ *n* -s [²*sole* + *-er*] **:** one that soles shoes or boots

so·le·ra \sō'lerə\ *n* -s [Sp, crossbeam, stone base, mother liquor, fr. *suelo* ground, floor, dregs, fr.

L *solum* ground, base] **1 :** a set of Spanish sherry vats arranged in tiers usu. three high in a storage shed **2** *also* **solera system :** a system evolved by the sherry producers of Jeres, Spain, whereby young wine in the vats of the top tier of a solera is successively blended into the more mature wine in the vats on the tier below to insure ultimate uniformity **3** *also* **solera sherry** *or* **solera wine :** a wine aged by the Spanish solera system

soles *pl of* SOL *or of* SOLE, *pres 3d sing of* SOLE

sole tile *n* [¹*sole*] **:** a tile with a concave top used esp. to pave sewers

sole tree *n* [¹*sole*] **:** a solepiece used in a mine (as for timbering headings)

so·le·us \ˈsōlēəs\ *n, pl* **so·lei** \-ēˌī\ *also* **soleuses** [NL, fr. L *solea* sole of the foot] **:** a broad flat muscle of the calf of the leg lying immediately below the gastrocnemius, arising from the back and upper part of the tibia and fibula and from a tendinous arch between them, and inserting by a tendon that unites with that of the gastrocnemius to form the Achilles' tendon

¹sol-fa \(ˈ)sōl¦fä, -fȧ, *chiefly Brit* (ˈ)säl-\ *n* -s [¹*sol* + *fa*] **1 :** SOL-FA SYLLABLES **2 :** GREAT SCALE **3 a :** SOLMIZATION **b :** an exercise sung in sol-fa syllables **4 :** TONIC SOL-FA

²sol-fa \ˈ"\ *vb* -ED/-ING/-s *vi* **1 :** to sing or practice the tones of the gamut or scale **2 :** to sing in sol-fa syllables **~** *vt* **:** to sing (as an air or song) to or in sol-fa syllables

sol-fa·er \-ə(r)\ *n* -s [²*sol-fa* + *-er*] **:** one that sol-fas

sol-fa·ist \-əst\ *n* -s [¹*sol-fa* + *-ist*] **:** a user or an advocate of the tonic sol-fa system

sol-fa syllables *n pl* **:** the eight modified Guidonian syllables *do, re, mi, fa, sol, la, ti, do* applied to reading music for the major scale and further modified for the chromatic scale ascending and descending to *do, di, re, ri, mi, fa, fi, sol, si, la, li, ti, do, ti, te, la, le, sol, se, fa, mi, me, re, ra, do* — compare MOVABLE-DO SYSTEM, SOLMIZATION

sol·fa·ta·ra \ˌsälfəˈtärə, ˌsōl-\ *n* -s [It, sulfur mine, sulphurous vent, fr. *solfo* sulphur, fr. L *sulfur*] **:** a volcanic area or vent that yields only hot vapors and gases in part sulfurous and represents a late stage of volcanic activity

sol·fa·taric \¦=¦tarik, -¦tär-\ *adj* **1 :** of or relating to a solfatara or its action **2 :** relating to, caused by, or denoting the transfer of mineral substances within the earth by sublimation or by the chemical and transporting action of steam

sol·fège \(ˈ)säl¦fezh\ *n* -s [F, fr. It *solfeggio*] **1 :** the application of the sol-fa syllables to the tones of the musical scale or to melodies or other voice parts **2 :** an exercise in scales; *specif* **:** a singing exercise using sol-fa syllables **3 :** practice in sight-singing using the sol-fa syllables

sol·feg·gio \säl'fe(ˌ)jō, -ejēˌō\ *n, pl* **solfeg·gi** \-e(ˌ)jē\ *also* **solfeggios** [It, fr. *solfeggiare* to sol-fa, fr. *solfa* sol-fa, fr. *sol* (fr. ML) + *fa* (fr. ML) — more at SOL, FA] **:** SOLFÈGE

sol·fe·ri·no \ˌsälfəˈrē(ˌ)nō\ *n* -s [fr. *Solferino*, village of northern Italy; fr. its being discovered soon after the battle fought there in 1859] **1 :** FUCHSINE I **2 :** a moderate purplish red that is redder, darker, and slightly stronger than average rose, redder and duller than violine pink, redder and paler than magenta rose, and redder and less strong than average fuchsia rose

solgel \ˈ=¦=\ *adj* [⁶*sol* + *gel*] **:** involving alternation between sol and gel states — used esp. of protoplasmic phenomena ⟨~ transformations in the amoeba⟩

¹soli *pl of* SOLO

²so·li \ˈsō,lē\ *adj* [¹*soli*] **:** constituting a solo part usu. to be performed by a section or part of a section in an orchestra or a chorus ⟨~ parts⟩ ⟨~ strings⟩

soli- *comb form* [L, fr. *solus* — more at SOLE] **:** alone **:** solely ⟨*soli*loquy⟩ ⟨*soli*fidian⟩

so·lic·it \səˈlisət, *usu* -əd.+V\ *vb* -ED/-ING/-S [ME *soliciten*, fr. MF *solliciter*, *soliciter* to disturb, take care of (influenced in meaning by L *sollicitus* anxious), fr. L *sollicitare* to disturb, agitate, move, entreat, fr. *sollicitus* anxious, troubled, fr. *sollus* whole, entire (fr. Oscan; akin to Gk *holos* entire) + *citus*, past part. of *ciēre* to move — more at SAFE, HIGHT] *vt* **1** *archaic* **a :** to take charge or care of (as business) **:** MANAGE, FORWARD **b :** to act as solicitor or legal agent for or with reference to **2** *archaic* **:** to make anxious **:** DISQUIET, CONCERN **3 :** to make petition to **:** ENTREAT, IMPORTUNE ⟨~ the king for relief⟩; *esp* **:** to approach with a request or plea (as in selling or begging) ⟨~ one's neighbors for contributions⟩ **4 :** to move to action **:** serve as an urge or incentive to **:** INCITE **5 :** to strongly urge (as one's cause or point) **:** insist upon **6 a :** to entice or lead astray by or as if by specious arguments **:** lure on and esp. into evil **b** *obs* **:** to seek the favor of (a woman) usu. for the purpose of seduction **:** attempt to seduce **c :** to accost (a man) for immoral purposes and usu. in the character of a prostitute **7 :** to endeavor to obtain by asking or pleading **:** plead for ⟨~ an office⟩ ⟨~ alms⟩; *also* **:** to seek eagerly or actively **8 :** to demand as a requisite **:** call for **:** REQUIRE ⟨the situation ~*s* the closest attention⟩ **9 a** (1) **:** to have an effect on (a person or thing) through some natural influence or property (2) **:** to induce (as a phenomenon) by means of such influence or property ⟨~*ing* sparks by rubbing amber with flannel⟩ **b :** to seek to affect (as by moving, inducing, withdrawing) usu. by mild or gentle means ⟨~ a bowel movement with a laxative⟩ ⟨~ an arrow gently and draw it from a wound⟩ **10 :** to serve as a temptation or lure to **:** ATTRACT ⟨that fruit . . . ~*ed* her longing eye —John Milton⟩ ~ *vi* **1 :** to make solicitation **:** IMPORTUNE, PETITION: as **a :** to beg alms **b** *of a prostitute* **:** to offer illicit intercourse to a man **2 :** to serve as a solicitor **syn** see ASK

so·lic·i·tant \səˈlisəd.ənt, -isətənt\ *n* -s [L *sollicitant-, sollicitans*, pres. part. of *sollicitare* to solicit] **:** one who solicits

so·lic·i·ta·tion \sə,lisəˈtāshən\ *n* -s [L *sollicitation-, sollicitatio*, fr. *sollicitatus* (past part. of *sollicitare*) + *-ion-, -io* -ion] **1 :** the pursuit, practice, act, or an instance of soliciting; *often* **:** ENTREATY, IMPORTUNITY ⟨yield to his ~*s*⟩ **2 :** the operation, influence, pressure, or other inducing effect of something that solicits or attracts or draws **:** a moving or drawing force **:** INCITEMENT, ALLUREMENT ⟨unable to resist the ~*s* of appetite⟩

soliciter *n* -s [ME, fr. *soliciten* to solicit + *-er*] *obs* **:** SOLICITOR

so·lic·i·tor \səˈlisəd.ə(r), -is(ə)tə-, *in rapid speech* ˈsl-\ *n* -s [ME *solicitour*, fr. MF *soliciteur* prompter, agent, advocate, fr. *soliciter* to solicit, take care of] **1 :** one that solicits; *esp* **:** a person that acts as an agent in the soliciting of something (as contributions to charity, subscriptions to periodicals, or business for a firm) **2 a** (1) **:** a person formerly admitted to practice law in an English court of chancery or equity (2) **:** a person currently admitted to practice law and conduct litigation in any English court including the officers formerly called attorney-at-law and proctor but distinguished from the barrister in not having the right to plead in open court except in a few minor courts **b :** a law officer of a city, town, department, or government ⟨the city ~⟩ ⟨the ~ of the Interior Department⟩

solicitor general *n, pl* **solicitors general 1 :** the second law officer in the government of Great Britain appointed to assist the attorney general **2 :** an officer under the U.S. government appointed by the president to assist the attorney general **3 :** the chief law officer in some states of the U.S.

so·lic·i·tor·ship \-,ship\ *n* **:** the position or status of a solicitor

so·lic·i·tous \səˈlisəd.əs, -is(ə)təs\ *adj* [L *sollicitus* — more at SOLICIT] **1 :** full of concern or fears **:** APPREHENSIVE, TROUBLED, CONCERNED — often used with *about, for,* or *of* ⟨~ about the future⟩ ⟨~ for the welfare of one's country⟩ **2 :** full of desire **:** anxiously willing **:** EAGER ⟨~ to gain all the benefits⟩ ⟨not ~ to proceed in this affair⟩ **3 :** meticulously careful or attentive ⟨~ in matters of dress⟩ **4 :** manifesting or expressing solicitude or concern ⟨a ~ inquiry⟩ — **so·lic·i·tous·ly** *adv* — **so·lic·i·tous·ness** *n* -ES

so·lic·i·tress \-isə·trəs\ *n* -ES [*solicitor* + *-ess*] **:** a female solicitor

solicitrix *n* -ES [fr. *solicitor*, after such pairs as E *executor: executrix*] *obs* **:** a female solicitor

so·lic·i·tude \səˈlisə,tüd, -isə-,tyüd\ *n* -s [ME, fr. MF or L; MF *sollicitude*, fr. L *sollicitudin-, sollicitudo*, fr. *sollicitus* solicitous + *-tudin-, -tudo* -tude] **1 :** uneasiness of mind due to fear (as of evil, future developments, material want) **:** ANXIETY, DISQUIETUDE ⟨having few wants he had little cause for ~⟩ ⟨even the more peaceful hours . . . had beneath them a perpetual undercurrent of apprehensive ~ —Havelock Ellis⟩ **2 a :** urgently attentive and sometimes excessive care and protectiveness ⟨caring for the sick child with great ~⟩ **b :** an attitude of solicitous concern or attention ⟨inquired after her welfare with marked ~⟩ **3 :** a cause for or source of solicitude — usu. used in pl. ⟨worn by the ~*s* of daily life⟩ **syn** see CARE

so·lic·i·tu·di·nous \sə¦lisə¦tüd(ᵊ)nəs, -isə-¦tyü-\ *adj* [L *sollicitudin-, sollicitudo* + E *-ous*] **:** marked by solicitude **:** SOLICITOUS

¹sol·id \ˈsäləd\ *adj* -ER/-EST [ME *solide*, fr. MF, fr. L *solidus*; akin to Gk *holos*, entire — more at SAFE] **1 a :** having an interior filled with matter **:** being without an internal cavity ⟨the knob is heavy because it is ~⟩ ⟨the stalks of some plants are not ~⟩ ⟨a ~ tire⟩ — opposed to *hollow* **b** (1) **:** set in type without leads or other spacing material between the lines **:** CLOSE ⟨a forbidding page full of ~ black paragraphs⟩ (2) **:** having no intervening space ⟨the ~ elements of a compound word⟩ **c :** not interrupted by any break or opening ⟨the outer walls ~ and windowless⟩ ⟨the law requires a driver to stay on his own side of the ~ line⟩ **2 a :** having or involving three dimensions **:** CUBIC ⟨a ~ paraboloid⟩ ⟨a ~ foot contains 1728 ~ inches⟩ **b :** of, relating to, or dealing with solid magnitudes ⟨a ~ equation⟩ — see SOLID GEOMETRY **3 a :** marked by density or compactness **:** of uniformly close and coherent texture or consistency **:** not disintegrated, loose, or spongy ⟨a ~ mass of rock⟩ ⟨rain fell in ~ sheets⟩ ⟨the surgeon scraped back to ~ healthy bone⟩ **b :** possessing or characterized by the properties of a solid **:** being neither gaseous nor liquid ⟨the pavement is not yet ~⟩ ⟨physics of the ~ state⟩ **4 :** of good and substantial quality or kind ⟨~ comfort⟩: as **a :** having merit or soundness ⟨based his decision on ~ reasons⟩ **b :** made firmly and well **:** STURDY ⟨a ~ chair⟩ ⟨firm ~ walls⟩ **c** (1) **:** full sounding and having a strong rhythmic drive ⟨~ jazz music⟩ (2) **:** excellent in every respect — used esp. of popular music **d** *of immunity* **:** capable of resisting severe challenge ⟨intradermal inoculation of the virulent agent in guinea pigs resulted in ~ immunity in all trials⟩ **5 :** united or consolidated so as to form an integral whole: as **a** *of time* **:** having no break or interruption ⟨stand for three ~ hours⟩ **b :** UNANIMOUS ⟨a ~ delegation⟩ ⟨the ~ vote of a delegation⟩ ⟨group opinion is ~⟩ **c :** united or joined in intimacy **:** being on good terms — used with *with* ⟨make oneself ~ with the chief⟩ **6 a :** having or marked by sound judgment or knowledge **:** thoroughly grounded ⟨~ thinkers⟩ ⟨~ learning⟩ **b :** SERIOUS-MINDED, RELIABLE, PRUDENT; *often* **:** well-established financially **:** having unimpaired credit ⟨~ New Englanders⟩ ⟨the ~ men of the community⟩ **c :** serious in purpose or character **:** not trivial **:** not vain or frivolous ⟨time for ~ reading⟩ **7 :** entirely of one substance, formation, kind, or character: as **a :** entirely of one metal **:** containing the minimum of alloy necessary to impart hardness ⟨~ gold⟩ **b :** being or consisting of a single uniform color or tone **c :** having decorative details worked on solid material ⟨a ~ frame⟩ **syn** see FIRM

²solid \ˈ"\ *adv* **:** SOLIDLY; *often* **:** UNANIMOUSLY

³solid \ˈ"\ *n* -s [ME, fr. L *solidum*, fr. neut. of *solidus*, adj.] **1 :** a magnitude that has the three dimensions length, breadth, and thickness **:** a part of space (as a cube, a sphere) bounded on all sides **2 a :** a substance that does not flow perceptibly under moderate stress, has a definite capacity for resisting forces (as compression, tension, strain) which tend to deform it, and under ordinary conditions retains a definite size and shape — compare GAS, LIQUID **b :** material in solution or suspension that when freed of solvent or suspending medium has the form and qualities of a solid — usu. used in pl. ⟨the ~*s* of the blood⟩ ⟨milk ~*s* include salts, protein, and sugar⟩ — see SOLIDS-NOT-FAT **3 :** something (as a substantial mass) that is solid: as **a :** a compact mass of masonry or comparable fabrication (as a wall or pier) as distinguished from one containing a void or an opening **b :** coal in place that has not been sheared, undercut, or similarly prepared for blasting **c** (1) **:** a solid color (2) **:** a printing plate having an entirely smooth surface without etching or design of any kind that is used for printing a solid color and esp. a tint (3) **:** one of the darkest or heaviest printing areas of a halftone as distinguished from middletone or highlight areas (4) **:** textile or other material of a solid color — usu. used in pl. **d :** a compound word whose members are joined together without a hyphen

sol·i·da·go \ˌsälə'dā(ˌ)gō\ *n* [NL, fr. ML *soldago* an herb reputed to heal wounds, fr. *soldare* to make whole, make sound, fr. L *solidare*, fr. *solidus* solid] **1** *cap* **:** a very large genus of chiefly No. American herbs (family Compositae) that are distinguished from members of *Aster* by no definite characters but usu. have stems resembling wands, small heads with yellow or occas. white ray florets, and an inflorescence which varies from a thyrsoid panicle to axillary capitate clusters — see DYER'S-WEED, GOLDENROD **2** -ES **:** any plant of the genus *Solidago*

solid alcohol *n* **:** a product consisting of ordinary alcohol converted to a gel (as by means of a soap or calcium acetate) and used on a small scale as a fuel

solid angle *n* **:** the angular spread at the vertex of a cone or similar figure measured by the area intercepted on a unit sphere about the vertex as center by the cone surface

sol·i·dar·ic \¦sälə¦darik\ *adj* [*solidarity* + *-ic*] **:** having solidarity

sol·i·dar·i·ly \-¦derəlē\ *adv* **:** in a solidary manner **:** so as to be solidary

sol·i·da·rism \ˈsälədə,rizəm\ *n* -s [*solidarity* + *-ism*] **1 :** SOLIDARITY **2 :** a theory in sociology: the mutual interdependence of members of society offers a basis for a social organization based upon solidarity of interests

sol·i·da·rist \-¦rəst\ *n* -s [*solidarity* + *-ist*] **:** an advocate of solidarism

sol·i·da·ris·tic \¦=¦=¦ristik\ *adj* [*solidarist* + *-ic*] **:** of or relating to solidarity or solidarism **:** based on solidarism ⟨~ concepts⟩

sol·i·dar·i·ty \ˌsälə'darəd.ē, -rətē, -i *also* -der-\ *n* -ES [F *solidarité*, fr. *solidaire* solidary + *-ité* -ity] **1 :** an entire union of interests and responsibilities in a group **:** community of interests, objectives, or standards ⟨~ that knits together innumerable hearts —Joseph Conrad⟩ **2** *Roman, civil, & Scots law* **:** the quality or state of being solidary

sol·i·da·rize \ˈsälədə,rīz\ *vi* -ED/-ING/-S [F *solidariser*, fr. *solidaire* + *-iser* -ize] **:** to come together **:** attain a state of solidarity ⟨the parties of the right failed to ~ in time⟩

sol·i·dary \-,derē\ *adj* [F *solidaire*, fr. MF, fr. L (*in*) *solidum* for the whole, involving all (fr. *in* + *solidum* whole sum, fr. neut. of *solidus* solid) + MF *-aire* -ary — more at IN, SAFE] **1 :** characterized by or manifesting community of interests and responsibilities **2 :** constituting or relating to an obligation in solido under Roman, civil, or Scots law wherein the parties thereto are bound jointly and severally for the entire debt or damages or for the full performance or object of the obligation, or wherein any one party entitled to such an obligation may receive the full debt, damages, performance, or object of the obligation and give a receipt or release binding all others entitled thereto — compare CORREAL

solid board *n* **:** a paperboard made of the same type of material throughout — distinguished from *combination board*

solid box *n* **:** a solid ring bearing for a shaft that is lined with babbitt metal, is not adjustable, and is used esp. on light machinery

solid bulb *n* **:** CORM

solid casting *n* **:** slip casting of ceramic material without pour= off of residue esp. for forming solid pieces or for hollow ware if the mold has a core

solid compound *n* **:** a compound whose components are solid in printing or writing — compare OPEN COMPOUND

solid die *n* **:** a hollow internally threaded screw-cutting tool made in one piece

solid–drawn \¦=¦=\ *adj* **:** drawn out from a heated solid bar esp. by a process of spiral rolling that first hollows the bar and then expands the cavity by forcing the bar over a pointed mandrel fixed in front of the rolls — used of a weldless tube

so·li·deo \ˌsōlə'dā(ˌ)ō, -'thā-\ *n* -s [Sp, fr. the ML phrase *soli Deo sit gloria* to God alone be the glory; fr. the fact that it is removed only on approaching the sanctuary] **:** ZUCCHETTO

solider *comparative of* SOLID

solidest *superlative of* SOLID

solid geometry *n* **:** a branch of geometry that deals with the figures of three-dimensional space

solid hoof *n* **:** a hoof (as of a horse) that forms a continuous encasement of the distal part of a foot — compare CLOVEN FOOT

solid–hoofed \¦=¦=¦=\ *adj* [*solid hoof* + *-ed*] **1 :** SOLIDUNGULATE **2 :** MULE-FOOT

solidi *pl of* SOLIDUS

so·lid·i·fi·able \səˈlidə,fīəbəl, =,==ˈ===\ *adj* **:** capable of being solidified

so·lid·i·fi·ca·tion \sə,lidəfəˈkāshən\ *n* -s [fr. *solidify*, after such pairs as E *ratify: ratification*] **1 :** an act or instance of solidifying **2 :** the condition of being solidified

so·lid·i·fi·er \=ˈ==,fī(ə)r, -īə-\ *n* -s **:** one that solidifies

so·lid·i·fy \səˈlidə,fī\ *vb* -ED/-ING/-ES [¹*solid* + *-ify*] *vt* **:** to make solid or compact or hard: as **a :** to alter (a fluid) to a solid state ⟨~ concrete⟩ **b :** to give a feeling of reality to ⟨details that *solidified* the composition⟩ **c :** to cause to take on strength and assurance ⟨~*ing* one's knowledge⟩ **:** make secure, substantial, or firmly fixed ⟨factors that ~ public opinion⟩ ~ *vi* **:** to become solid **:** HARDEN ⟨hot paraffin *solidifies* as it cools⟩

solid injection *n* **:** the injection of atomized fuel oil into the combustion chamber of a diesel engine under the pressure of the liquid fuel itself — compare AIR INJECTION

sol·id·ish \ˈsälədish\ *adj* **:** comparatively solid

so·lid·i·ty \səˈlidəd.ē, -idətē, -i\ *n* -ES [MF *solidité*, fr. L *soliditat-, soliditas*, fr. *solidus* solid + *-itat-, -itas* -ity] **1 :** the quality or state of being solid **:** lack of an interior cavity **:** DENSITY, COMPACTNESS ⟨stone oppressed him with its indestructible ~ —Aldous Huxley⟩ ⟨felt the rubbery ~ as the club came down —Ernest Hemingway⟩ **2 :** the quality or character (as in a human being, act, institution) of being sound in a moral, mental, financial, or other comparable respect **3 :** something solid **:** a solid body **4** *archaic* **:** space within a closed surface **:** VOLUME **5 :** the ratio of the projected area of the blades of a rotor to the area swept by the blades

solid–looking \¦==¦==\ *adj* [¹*solid* + *looking*] **:** giving an impression of solid worth or substance ⟨*solid-looking* well-fed citizens⟩

sol·id·ly *adv* [¹*solid* + *-ly*] **:** so as to have or give an effect of solidity: as **a** (1) **:** STRONGLY, FIRMLY ⟨~ constructed furniture⟩ (2) **:** SECURELY ⟨set ~ on its base⟩ **b :** on soundly logical or reasonable grounds ⟨the result may be ~ inferred⟩ **c** *archaic* **:** SERIOUSLY, INTENSIVELY **d :** without reservation **:** WHOLLY, UNANIMOUSLY ⟨~ behind the move⟩ ⟨voted the precinct ~ for the party candidate⟩

solid–mouth \¦==¦=\ *also* **solid–mouthed** \¦=¦=\ *adj, of a sheep* **:** having a complete set of teeth — compare BROKEN= MOUTHED

sol·id·ness *n* -ES **:** the quality or state of being solid

solid newel *n* **:** a newel into which the ends of winding stairs are built — distinguished from *hollow newel*

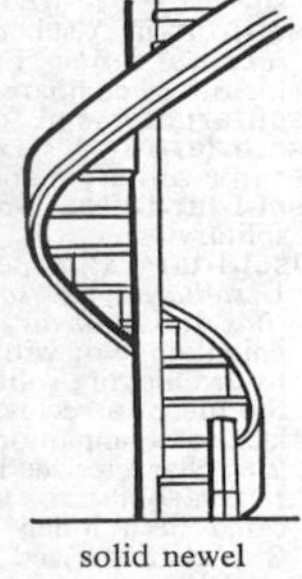
solid newel

solid of revolution [³*solid*] **:** a mathematical solid conceived as formed by the revolution of a plane figure about an axis in its plane

solids *pl of* SOLID

solids–not–fat \¦==¦=¦=\ *n pl but usu sing in constr* **:** the constituents of milk other than butterfat and water ⟨*solids-not-fat* is lowest in summer⟩

solid solution *n* [³*solid*] **:** a homogeneous solid phase (as austenite) capable of existing throughout a range of chemical composition — used chiefly of crystalline materials; often distinguished from *intermetallic compound*; compare MIXTURE

solid system *n* **:** an underground electrical distribution system in which the conductors or cables are buried rather than pulled into ducts

sol·i·dum \ˈsälədəm\ *n* -s [L, neut. of *solidus* solid] **1 :** the dado of a pedestal **2 :** an entire sum **:** WHOLE — used in various phrases (as *in solidum, singuli in solidum*)

sol·id·un·gu·la \ˌsälə'dəŋgyələ\ *n pl, cap* [NL, fr. L *solidus* + *ungula* hoof — more at UNGULA] *in some classifications* **:** a group coextensive with Hippoidea

sol·id·un·gu·lar \¦=¦==lə(r)\ *also* **sol·id·un·gu·lous** \-ləs\ *adj* [L *solidus* solid + *ungula* hoof + E *-ar, -ous*] **:** SOLIDUNGULATE

¹sol·id·un·gu·late \-lət, -,lāt\ *adj* [L *solidus* solid + *ungula* hoof + E *-ate*] **:** having a single hoof on each foot ⟨horses and other ~ mammals⟩

²solidungulate \ˈ"+\ *n* -s **:** a solidungulate animal

sol·i·dus \ˈsälədəs\ *n, pl* **soli·di** \-,dī\ [ME, fr. LL, fr. L *solidus* solid — more at SAFE] **1 :** an ancient Roman gold coin introduced by Constantine as successor to the aureus and used until the fall of the Byzantine Empire **2** [ML *solidus* shilling, fr. LL, a gold coin; fr. its use as a symbol for shillings] **:** DIAGONAL 4 **3 a** *also* **solidus curve** [L, solid, adj.] **:** a curve usu. on a temperature-composition diagram for a binary system that corresponds with a liquidus and that indicates temperatures below which only the solid phase can exist **b** *also* **solidus point :** the point of temperature at which a substance and esp. a metal or alloy is about to melt **:** incipient melting point

so·lier·i·a·ce·ae \sō,lirēˈāsē,ē\ *n pl, cap* [NL, fr. *Solieria* genus of algae + *-aceae*] **:** a family of red algae (order Gigartinales) having multiaxial thalli and inhabiting the warmer seas

soli·fid·i·an \,sōləˈfidēən, ,säl-\ *n* -s [*soli-* + L *fides* faith + E *-ian* — more at FAITH] **:** one who holds that faith alone without achievement or personal merit is sufficient to insure salvation — compare NULLIFIDIAN

soli·fid·i·an·ism \-ēə,nizəm\ *n* -s **:** the doctrine of the solifidians

soli·fluction *also* **soli·fluxion** \¦sōlə, ¦sälə+\ *n* -s [L *solum* ground, soil + *-i-* + *fluction-, fluctio* act of flowing, fr. *fluctus* (past part. of *fluere* to flow) + *-ion-, -io* -ion — more at FLUID] **:** the slow creeping of wet soil and other saturated fragmental material down a slope resulting sometimes in the formation of small terraces **:** the selective movement of soil particles and rock waste in regions of perennially frozen ground by frost action and associated phenomena producing soil structures of various kinds and shapes — compare CONGELITURBATION — **soli·fluctional** \ˈ"+\ *adj*

so·lif·u·gae \səˈlifyə,jē\ [NL, fr. pl. of LL *solifuga*, a venomous ant or spider, alter. of L *salpuga*] *syn of* SOLPUGIDA

soli·fuge \ˈsōlə,fyüj, ˈsäl-\ *n* -s [LL *solifuga*] **:** SOLPUGID

so·lif·u·ge·an \sə¦lifyə¦jēən\ *or* **so·lif·u·gous** \-ˈlifyəgəs\ *adj* [LL *solifuga* + E *-ean* or *-ous*] **:** SOLPUGID

so·lif·u·gid \-ˈlifyəjəd\ *n* -s [NL *Solifugae* + E *-id*] **:** SOLPUGID

so·lig·e·nous \sōˈlijənəs\ *adj* [L *solum* ground + E *-i-* + *-genous*] **:** produced by inflow of surface water or rise of ground water and not by locally precipitated water ⟨a ~ marsh⟩

so·lil·o·quist \səˈliləkwəst\ *n* -s [*soliloquy* + *-ist*] **:** one who soliloquizes

so·lil·o·quize \səˈlilə,kwīz\ *vb* -ED/-ING/-S *see* -IZE *in Explan Notes* [*soliloquy* + *-ize*] *vi* **:** to utter a soliloquy **:** talk to oneself ~ *vt* **:** to say, discuss, or address in a soliloquy — **so·lil·o·quiz·er** \-zə(r)\ *n* -s

so·lil·o·quiz·ing·ly \=ˈ==,===, =,==ˈ===\ *adv* [*soliloquizing* (pres. part. of *soliloquize*) + *-ly*] **:** in the manner of one that soliloquizes

so·lil·o·quy \səˈliləkwē, -wi\ *n* -ES [LL *soliloquium*, fr. L *soli-* + *loqui* to speak] **1 :** the act of talking to oneself **:** a discourse made by one in solitude to oneself **:** MONOLOGUE **2 :** a poem, a discourse, or an utterance of a dramatic character that has the form of a monologue or gives the illusion of being a series of unspoken reflections

so·li·lunar \¦sōlə+\ *adj* [L *sol* sun + E *-i-* + *lunar* — more at SOLAR] **:** LUNISOLAR

soling *pres part of* SOLE

so·ling·en \'zōliŋən, 'sō-\ *adj, usu cap* [fr. *Solingen*, city of northwest Germany] **:** of or from the city of Solingen, Germany **:** of the kind or style prevalent in Solingen

sol·ion \'säl+,-\ *n* -s [*sol*ution + *ion*] **:** an electronic detecting and amplifying device whose operation depends on the movement of ions in a solution

soli·ped \'sälə,ped\ *n* -s [NL *soliped-, solipes*, fr. L *solidus* solid + *ped-, pes* foot — more at SAFE, FOOT] **:** SOLIDUNGULATE

solip·sism \'sōləp,sizəm, 'säləp-, sə'lip-\ *n* -s [L *sol*us alone + *ipse* self + E *-ism* — more at SOLE] **1 :** any of various extreme versions of subjective idealism: as **a** (1) **:** an epistemological theory that the self can know nothing but its own modifications and states (2) *or* **solipsism of the present moment :** an epistemological theory that the self knows or can know only its present modifications and states to the exclusion of future and past states **b** (1) **:** a metaphysical theory that the self is the only existent thing (2) **:** a metaphysical theory that all real entities are modifications and states of the self **:** EGOISM 1a **2 :** the adoption of epistemological solipsism as a premise for a general metaphysical or epistemological theory or as a scientific hypothesis **3 :** extreme indulgence of and concern with the self at the expense of social relationships esp. as expressed in a failure of artistic communication ⟨the poet today must navigate between . . . parochial ~ and commercial success —F.L.Utley⟩

solip·sist \-,səst\ *n* -s [*solipsism* + *-ist*] **:** an adherent or advocate of solipsism ⟨the artist's egoism is outrageous . . . he is by nature a ~ and the world exists only for him to exercise upon it his powers of creation —W.S.Maugham⟩

solip·sis·tic \'sōləp¦sistik, ¦säl-\ *or* **solip·sist** \'==,səst, sə'lip-\ *adj* **:** of or relating to solipsism or solipsists — **solip·sis·ti·cal·ly** \¦sōləp¦sistək(ə)lē, ¦säl-\ *adv*

so·liste \(')sō¦lēst\ *n* -s [F, fr. *solo* (fr. It) + *-iste* -ist — more at SOLO] **:** a minor solo dancer in ballet

sol·i·taire \'sälə,ta(ə)(ə)r, -te|, |ə *sometimes* ,==ˈ=\ *n* -s [F, fr. *solitaire* solitary, adj., fr. L *solitarius*] **1 :** SOLITARY 1 **2 a :** a single diamond or sometimes other gem set alone **b :** a piece of jewelry (as a ring) set with a single diamond ⟨her ear rings were magnificent ~*s*⟩ **3 :** a game designed for one person to play alone: as **a :** any of various card games that typically involve the arranging of cards dealt at random in a prescribed pattern — called also *patience;* see DOUBLE SOLITAIRE **b :** a game played on a board with pegs or balls in which the object is beginning with all the places filled except one to remove all but one of the pieces by jumping **4 :** a large usu. black silk neckcloth worn by men in the 18th century **5 a :** a flightless extinct bird (*Pezophaps solitaria*) related to the dodo but less clumsy and with a smaller bill and formerly inhabiting the island of Rodriguez in the Indian ocean **b :** any of several American fly-catching thrushes (genus *Myadestes*) noted for their sweet song and shyness — see TOWNSEND'S SOLITAIRE

solitaire 4

sol·i·tar·ia \,sälə'terēə, -ta(ə)r-\ *n* -s [NL, fr. fem. of L *solitarius* solitary] **:** a nonmigratory phase occurring in some locusts — compare GREGARIA

solitarian *n* -s [L *solitarius* + E *-an*] *obs* **:** HERMIT, SOLITARY

sol·i·tar·i·ly \¦sälə¦terəlē, -li\ *adv* [ME, fr. [1]*solitary* + *-ly*] **:** in a solitary manner **:** in solitude

sol·i·tar·i·ness \-rēnəs\ *n* -ES **:** the quality or state of being solitary

[1]**sol·i·tary** \'sälə,terē, -ri\ *adj, sometimes* -ER/-EST [ME, fr. L *solitarius*, fr. *solitas* aloneness (fr. *solus* alone + *-itat-, -itas* -ity) + *-arius* -ary — more at SOLE] **1 a :** being, living, or going alone or without companions ⟨a ~ traveler⟩ **b :** given to or enjoying solitude ⟨a person ~ by nature⟩; *also* **:** living the life of a recluse or hermit ⟨~ saint⟩ **c :** suffering from lack of companions **:** LONELY ⟨often alone but never ~⟩ **2 a :** characterized by seclusion, solitude, or lack of inhabitants **:** UNFREQUENTED, DESERTED, DESOLATE ⟨a ~ valley⟩ **b :** located in a lonely place ⟨a ~ mountain camp⟩ ⟨~ ruins⟩ **3 :** characterized by the lack or absence of companions **:** taken, passed, performed, endured, or otherwise dealt with alone ⟨a ~ ramble⟩ ⟨~ tasks⟩ ⟨lead a ~ life⟩ **4 :** SINGLE, INDIVIDUAL, SOLE ⟨a ~ example⟩ **5 a** *of a plant part or organ* **:** not forming part of a group or cluster of parts or organs **:** occurring singly and usu. one to a branch or stem ⟨flowers terminal and ~⟩ **b** *of an organism* **:** living or growing habitually alone **:** not gregarious, colonial, social, or compound ⟨~ tunicates⟩ ⟨some bees are ~ in habit⟩ ⟨some trees are ~ or sporadic in occurrence⟩ **syn** see ALONE, SINGLE

[2]**solitary** \"\ *n* -ES [ME, fr. [1]*solitary*] **1 :** one who lives or seeks to live a solitary life **:** RECLUSE, HERMIT **2 :** SOLITARY CONFINEMENT

solitary ant *n* **:** VELVET ANT

solitary bee *n* **:** any of various bees that do not live in colonies

solitary confinement *n* **:** confinement of a prisoner where he has no intercourse with others

solitary gland *n* **:** any of the small lymph follicles in the submucous tissue and mucous membrane of the intestine

solitary phase *n* **:** SOLITARIA

solitary sandpiper *n* **:** an American sandpiper (*Tringa solitaria*) that is similar in appearance and habit to the Old World green sandpiper and lays its eggs in abandoned nests in trees

solitary snipe *n, dial Eng* **:** GREAT SNIPE

solitary vireo *n* **:** a vireo (*Vireo solitarius*) of eastern No. America having the head bluish gray, the back green, and the wings with two white bars — compare BLUE-HEADED VIREO

solitary wasp *n* **:** any of numerous wasps (as the mud wasps and sand wasps) that do not live in colonies

solitary wave *n* **:** a single wave caused by some special disturbance (as a tidal wave)

soli·terraneous \¦sōlə, ¦sälə-+\ *adj* [L *sol* sun + E *-i-* + *terraneous*] **:** of or relating to the earth and sun; *specif* **:** constituting a period when solar and terrestrial conditions jointly affect weather

sol·i·tude \'sälə,tüd, -ə,tyüd\ *n* -s [ME, fr. MF, fr. L *solitudin-, solitudo*, fr. *solus* alone + *-i-* + *-tudin-, -tudo* -tude — more at SOLE] **1 :** the quality or state of being alone or remote from society **:** SOLITARINESS, ISOLATION, SECLUSION **2 :** a solitary or lonely place (as a desert or wilderness) ⟨living in these ~*s*⟩ **3 a** *obs* **:** SOLENESS, UNIQUENESS **b** *archaic* **:** complete lack **:** DEARTH

sol·i·tu·di·nar·i·an \,==,tüdᵊn'erēən, ,==,tyü-\ *n* -s [L *solitudin-, solitudo* + E *-arian*] **:** RECLUSE

[1]**so·liv·a·gant** \sō'livəgənt\ *n* -s [L *solivagus* wandering alone (fr. *soli-* + *vagus* wandering) + E *-ant* — more at VAGARY] **:** a solitary wanderer

[2]**solivagant** \"\ *adj* [L *solivagus* + E *-ant*] **:** rambling alone **:** marked by solitary wandering

sollar *or* **soller** *var of* SOLAR

sol·ler·et \¦sälə¦ret\ *n* -s [F *soleret, solleret*, fr. MF, dim. of OF *soller* shoe, fr. ML *subtelare*, fr. LL *subtel* hollow of the foot, fr. *sub-* + *talus* ankle] **:** a flexible steel shoe forming part of a medieval suit of armor — see ARMOR illustration

sol·lya \'sälēə, -lyə\ *n, cap* [NL, after Richard H. *Solly* †1858 Eng. botanist] **:** a genus of Australian woody vines (family Pittosporaceae) with evergreen entire leaves, nodding blue flowers in loose cymes, and oblong many-seeded capsules

sol·mi·zate \'sälmə,zāt\ *vb* -ED/-ING/-S [back-formation fr. *solmization*] *vt* **1 :** to sing or represent (music) by the syllables of solmization **2 :** SOL-FA ~ *vi* **:** to sing using solmization

sol·mi·za·tion \,sälmə'zāshən\ *n* -s [F *solmisation*, fr. *solmiser* to sol-fa (fr. *sol* — fr. ML — + *mi* — fr. ML — + *-iser* -ize) + *-ation* — more at SOL, MI] **:** the act, practice, or system of using a set of syllables to denote the tones of a musical scale — compare GREAT SCALE, GUIDONIAN SYLLABLES, SOL-FA SYLLABLES, SOLFÈGE

soln *abbr* solution

[1]**so·lo** \'sō(,)lō\ *n, pl* **solos** \-lōz\ *also* **so·li** \-ō,lē\ [It, lit., alone, fr. L *solus* — more at SOLE] **1 a :** an air, strain, or a whole piece played by a single person or sung by a single voice with or without accompaniment **b :** a musical composition written for performance by one person **2 :** a performance (as a dance or a flight in an airplane) in which the performer has no partner or associate **3 a :** a bid or contract in various card games by which a player chooses to defeat two or more opponents without the benefit of having a partner **b :** a game in skat in which the player undertakes to play without use of the skat **c :** any of several card games in which a bid of solo is permissible **d :** a game derived from ombre

[2]**solo** \"\ *adv (or adj)* **1 :** without a companion **:** in solitude **:** ALONE ⟨experienced enough to fly ~⟩ ⟨left ~ to await the returning hunters⟩ **2 :** of, relating to, or being a solo **:** performed or for performance as a solo **:** UNACCOMPANIED ⟨a ~ air⟩ ⟨excellent ~ voices⟩ ⟨a ~ dance⟩

[3]**solo** \"\ *vb* **soloed; soloed; soloing** \-(,)lōiŋ, -ləwiŋ\ **solos** *vi* **:** to perform by oneself; *esp* **:** to fly solo in an airplane ~ *vt* **:** to fly (an airplane) solo

so·lod *or* **so·loth** \'sōlət\ *n, pl* **solo·di** *or* **solo·ti** \-lədē,-lətē\ *sometimes cap* [Russ *solod* malt; akin to Russ *sol'* salt, L *sal* — more at SALT] **:** any of an intrazonal group of dealkalized compacted clay soils of low productivity formed gradually through drainage and leaching of silty upper layers of solonetz soils

so·lod·iza·tion \,sōlədə'zāshən, -,dī'z-\ *n* -s **:** the process of solodizing or the process of becoming solodized

so·lod·ize \'sōlə,dīz\ *vt* -ED/-ING/-S [Russ *solod* malt + E *-ize*] **:** to develop (a soil and esp. solonetz) through dealkalizing processes including drainage and leaching into solod

so·lod·ous \'sōlədəs\ *adj* [*solod* + *-ous*] **:** made up of or constituting solod

so·lo·ist \'sōləwəst, -(,)lōəst\ *n* -s [[1]*solo* + *-ist*] **:** one (as a singer or aviator) who performs a solo; *esp* **:** a performer of solos at an orchestral or choral concert

so·lo·is·tic \¦sōlə¦wistik, -lō¦is-\ *adj* [*soloist* + *-ic*] **:** of, relating to, or suitable for performance by a soloist ⟨~ writing for wind instruments⟩

so·lo man \'sō(,)lō-\ *n, usu cap S* [fr. *Solo* river, Java] **:** a late Pleistocene Neanderthaloid man known from incomplete skulls and other skeletal remains found near Trinil in Java, usu. considered a distinct species (*Homo soloensis*), and being intermediate in many respects between Java and Peking man on the one hand and typical Neanderthal man on the other

sol·o·mon \'säləmən\ *n* -s *sometimes cap* [after King *Solomon* †ab933B.C. ruler of Israel who was famed for his wisdom as a judge] **:** a very wise man

sol·o·mo·nian \¦sälə¦mōnēən, -ōnyən\ *adj, usu cap* [King *Solomon* + E *-ian*] **:** SOLOMONIC

sol·o·mon·ic \-mänik\ *adj, usu cap* [King *Solomon* + E *-ic*] **1 :** of, relating to, produced by, or characteristic of the Hebrew ruler Solomon ⟨~ literature⟩ **2 :** marked by notable wisdom, reasonableness, or discretion esp. under trying circumstances ⟨a ~ compromise⟩

solomon seal *n, usu cap 1st S* [by alter.] **:** SOLOMON'S SEAL

solomon's lily *n, usu cap S* [after King *Solomon*] **:** BLACK CALLA

solomon's–plume \¦==¦=\ *n, pl* **solomon's–plumes** *usu cap S* **:** FALSE SOLOMON'S SEAL — often used in pl. with sing. or pl. constr.

solomon's seal *n, usu cap 1st S* **1 :** a mystic symbol that consists of two interlaced triangles arranged in a star with six points and often with one triangle dark and one light, is symbolic of the union of soul and body, and has been used as an amulet to guard against fever and other diseases — compare MAGEN DAVID **2** [so called fr. the resemblance of the scars on the rootstock to the symbol] **a :** a plant of the genus *Polygonatum* **b :** any of several plants felt to resemble the Solomon's seal: as (1) **:** TURQUOISEBERRY 1 (2) **:** FALSE SOLOMON'S SEAL

Solomon's seal

so·lon \'sōlən *also* -,län\ *n* -s [after *Solon* †ab559B.C. Athenian lawgiver and one of the Seven Wise Men of Greece] **:** a wise and skillful lawgiver or statesman; *broadly* **:** a member of a legislative body

sol·on·chak \¦sälən¦chak\ *n* -s *sometimes cap* [Russ, salt marsh, fr. *solonyĭ* salty, fr. *sol'* salt; akin to L *sal* salt — more at SALT] **:** any of an intrazonal group of strongly saline soils usu. light colored and without characteristic structural form and typically developed in poorly drained arid or semiarid areas vegetated mostly by halophytes

sol·o·netz *also* **sol·o·nets** \¦sälə¦nets\ *n, pl* **solonetzes** *also* **solonetses** [Russ *solonets* salt not extracted by decoction, fr. *solonyĭ* salty] **:** any of an intrazonal group of dark hard alkaline soils showing columnar structure and containing sulfates, bicarbonates, and other soluble salts which evolve by leaching and alkalizing from solonchak in imperfectly drained semiarid regions — **sol·o·netz·ic** \-tsik\ *adj*

so long \=ˈ=\ *interj* **:** GOOD-BYE

so long as *conj* **1 :** during and up to the end of the time that **:** as long as **:** WHILE ⟨the different key words that we must use are all interconnected, and *so long as* some remain vague, others must . . . share this defect —Bertrand Russell⟩ **2 :** provided that ⟨could . . . do as they pleased *so long as* they attended lectures —John Reed⟩

so·lo·ni·an \sō'lōnēən, sə'l-\ *also* **so·lon·ic** \(')sō¦länik\ *adj* [*Solon* †ab559B.C. Athenian lawgiver + E *-ian, -ic*] **:** of, relating to, or characteristic of Solon, the ancient Athenian lawgiver, or his legislation

solo organ *n* **:** a division of a pipe organ consisting of stops with an individual character suitable for solo effects

solos *pl of* SOLO, *pres 3d sing of* SOLO

solo stop *n* **:** an organ stop of individual tone quality suitable for solo effects

soloth *var of* SOLOD

soloti *pl of* SOLOD

solo whist *n* **:** a card game which is played with the full pack ranking as at whist and in which each player chooses one of seven different declarations he proposes to play

[1]**sol·pu·gid** \säl'pyüjəd\ *adj* [NL *Solpugida*] **:** of or relating to the Solpugida

[2]**solpugid** \"\ *n* -s **:** an arachnid of the order Solpugida

sol·pu·gi·da \-jədə\ *n pl, cap* [NL, fr. *Solpuga*, genus of arachnids (fr. L *salpuga, solpuga, solipuga* a kind of venomous ant or spider) + *-ida*] **:** an order of hairy arachnids having a segmented thorax and abdomen, slender pedipalpi that resemble legs, and strong chelate chelicerae, showing in structure close relationship to the scorpions but breathing by means of tracheae and having no book lungs, and occurring widely in warm regions with the exception of Madagascar and Australia

sol·pu·gid·ea \,sälpyü'jidēə\ *or* **sol·pu·gi·des** \säl'pyüjə,dēz\ [NL, fr. *Solpuga* + *-idea*] *syn of* SOLPUGIDA

solr *abbr* solicitor

sols *pl of* SOL

sol·stice \'sälztəs, 'sōl-, 'sȯl-, -lst-\ *n* -s [ME, fr. OF, fr. L *solstitium*, fr. *sol* sun + *-stitium* (fr. *status*, past part. of *sistere* to come to a stand, cause to stand or stop); akin to L *stare* to stand, be stationary — more at SOLAR, STAND] **1 a :** one of the two points on the ecliptic at which its distance from the celestial equator is greatest and which is reached by the sun each year about June 22d and December 22d **b :** the time of the sun's passing a solstice which occurs on June 22d to begin summer in the northern hemisphere and winter in the southern and on December 22d to begin winter in the northern and summer in the southern hemisphere **c :** the summer solstice or its heat **2 :** a furthest or highest point **:** LIMIT

sol·sti·tial \(')säl¦stishəl, (')sōl-, (')sȯl-, -l¦st-\ *adj* [L *solstitialis*, fr. *solstitium* solstice + *-alis* -al] **:** of, relating to, or characteristic of a solstice and esp. the summer solstice **:** happening or appearing at a solstice or being associated with a solstice

sol·sti·tial·ly \-əlē\ *adv* [*solstitial* + *-ly*] **:** at or toward a solstice

solstitial point *n* **:** SOLSTICE 1a

solubbi *usu cap, var of* SLUBBI

sol·u·bil·i·ty \,sälyə'bilәd·ē, -lətē, -i\ *n* -ES [[1]*soluble* + *-ity*] **1 :** the quality or state of being soluble **2 :** the amount of a substance that will dissolve in a given amount of another substance and is typically expressed as the number of parts by weight dissolved by 100 parts of solvent at a specified temperature and pressure or as percent by weight or by volume

solubility curve *n* **:** a graphic representation of the variation with changing temperature of the solubility of a given substance in a given solvent

solubility product *n* **:** the maximum product of the ionic concentrations or activities of an electrolyte that at one temperature can continue in equilibrium with the undissolved phase

sol·u·bi·li·za·tion \,sälyəbələ'zāshən, -(,)bil-, -,lī'z-\ *n* -s **:** the quality or state of being solubilized

sol·u·bi·lize \'==,bə,līz\ *vt* -ED/-ING/-S *see -ize in Explan Notes* **:** to make soluble or increase the solubility of — compare EMULSIFY

solubilized vat dye *n* [fr. past part. of *solubilize*] **:** a vat dye in the form of a soluble sodium salt of a sulfuric acid monoester of its leuco compound — see DYE table I

sol·u·bi·liz·er \-zə(r)\ *n* -s [*solubilize* + *-er*] **:** an agent that increases the solubility of a substance

[1]**sol·u·ble** \'sälyəbəl\ *adj* [ME, fr. MF, susceptible of being loosened or relaxed or dissolved, fr. LL *solubilis*, fr. L *solvere* to loosen, relax, dissolve + *-bilis* -able — more at SOLVE] **1 a** *archaic* **:** not constipated **:** evacuating normally **b** *obs* **:** having a laxative effect **:** inducing evacuation of the bowels **2 a :** susceptible of being dissolved in or as if in a fluid **:** capable of solution ⟨salt and sugar are ~ in water⟩ ⟨copper and zinc are completely ~ in the liquid state, but are only partially ~ in the solid state —G.E.Claussen⟩ — see FAT-SOLUBLE **b :** EMULSIFIABLE, DISPERSIBLE — used esp. of oils **3 :** subject to being solved **:** susceptible of being disentangled or explained **:** SOLVABLE ⟨a ~ puzzle⟩ ⟨such problems are perfectly ~⟩ — **sol·u·ble·ness** \-bəlnəs\ *n* -ES — **sol·u·bly** \-blē, -bli\ *adv*

[2]**soluble** \"\ *n* -s **:** something (as a substance or problem) that is soluble ⟨leaching of soil ~*s*⟩ — see DISTILLERS' SOLUBLES

soluble blue *n* **1** *often cap S&B* **:** any of several water-soluble acid dyes made by sulfonating the Spirit Blues and used in the form of salts chiefly in writing inks, in laundry blues, and as biological stains — see DYE table I (under *Acid Blue 22*) **2 :** a pigment dispersible in water that is made by treating an iron blue with sodium ferrocyanide or oxalic acid and is used chiefly in permanent writing inks and oxalic blues

soluble coffee *n* **:** a fine powder or a mass of tiny crystal balls produced by dehydration from strong concentrates of brewed coffee and used for the quick preparation of beverage coffee without brewing

soluble dried blood *n* **:** a reddish brown powder made from defibrinated uncoagulated blood and used esp. in making water-resistant glues for plywood, as a clarifying agent, and as a stabilizer and spreader in emulsions (as insecticidal and fungicidal sprays)

soluble glass *n* **:** WATER GLASS 4a

soluble guncotton *or* **soluble cotton** *n* **:** PYROXYLIN 1

soluble nitrocellulose *or* **soluble nitrocotton** *n* **:** PYROXYLIN

soluble oil *n* **1 :** SULFONATED OIL **2 :** an emulsifiable oil (as a mineral oil containing a sulfonated oil or a soap as emulsifier) for use in the form of an aqueous emulsion as a cutting fluid, textile lubricant, or carrier for insecticides; *also* **:** the emulsion formed from such an oil

soluble starch *n* **:** a modified starch that is capable of dissolving in hot water to give a limpid solution and is formed from raw starch esp. by relatively mild treatment with acids, by oxidation, or by heating with glycerol — compare AMYLODEXTRIN

so·lum \'sōləm\ *n, pl* **so·la** *see sense 2* \-lə\ [NL, fr. L, base, ground, earth, soil] **1 :** SOIL, LAND; *esp* **:** a parcel of ground — used esp. in law **2** *or pl* **solums :** the layer of soil which lies above the parent material, in which the natural processes of soil formation take place, and which in well-developed soils is greatly altered from the parent material and includes the A- and B-horizons — called also *true soil;* distinguished from *topsoil*

so–lun *n, pl* **so–lun** \'sō¦lən\ *or* **so–luns** *usu cap* **:** a member of a Mongol people of Chinese Turkestan

So–lunar Tables \sə, (')sō+. . .-\ *trademark* — used for tables containing forecasts of the daily feeding times of fish and game based on tidal conditions

so·lus \'sōləs\ *adv (or adj)* [L — more at SOLE] **:** without companions **:** in solitude **:** ALONE ⟨meditating ~ on the problems of life⟩ — often used in stage directions

solut *abbr* [L *solutus*] dissolved

solute \'säl,yüt *also* 'sō,lüt *sometimes* 'sōl,yüt\ *n* -s [L *solutus*, past part. of *solvere* to dissolve — more at SOLVE] **:** a dissolved substance; *esp* **:** a component of a solution present in smaller amount than the solvent

so·lu·tio \sō'lüd·ē,ō\ *n* [L, lit., loosening] *Roman & civil law* **:** performance of an obligation **:** PAYMENT, DISCHARGE, RELEASE

[1]**so·lu·tion** \sə'lüshən *also* səl'yü-\ *n* -s [ME, fr. MF, fr. L *solution-, solutio* act of loosening, solving, fr. *solutus* (past part. of *solvere* to loosen, solve, dissolve) + *-ion-, -io* -ion — more at SOLVE] **1 a :** an action or process of solving a problem ⟨do your ~*s* quickly and without checking⟩ ⟨you may use tables in the ~ of the examples⟩; *also* **:** the fact or state of a problem's being solved ⟨a difficulty that admits of no ~⟩ **b :** an answer to or means of answering a problem **:** a clearing up **:** EXPLANATION, DENOUEMENT ⟨your ~ of the problem⟩ **c** (1) **:** a set of values of the variables of an equation that satisfies the equation (2) **:** any relation between the variables of a differential equation free from derivatives that upon differentiation yields the given differential equation **2 a** (1) **:** an act or the process by which a solid, liquid, or gaseous substance is homogeneously mixed with a liquid or less commonly a gas or solid that may consist of simple physical mixing of components or may involve chemical change ⟨when silver is dissolved in nitric acid the solute of the resulting ~ is not silver but silver nitrate formed by chemical interaction⟩ (2) *obs* **:** the process of altering material (as by dissolving, fusing, or distilling) through the agency of heat **b :** a mixture formed by a process of solution and having the same chemical composition and physical properties throughout although the concentration can undergo continuous variation within definite limits depending upon the conditions: as (1) **:** a single-phase liquid system in which the particles of dissolved solid, liquid, or gas are held to be molecules or ions — called also *true solution;* often distinguished from *emulsion, sol, suspension* (2) **:** a mixture of gases (3) **:** SOLID SOLUTION (4) **:** SOL **c :** the condition of being dissolved or of constituting the solute of a solution ⟨put the salt in ~ in as little water as possible⟩; *broadly* **:** a state of fluidity (as of material held in an emulsion or suspension) **d** (1) **:** a liquid containing a dissolved substance ⟨a watery ~ of unknown composition⟩ (2) **:** a liquid and usu. aqueous medicinal preparation with the solid ingredients soluble ⟨~*s* are easier to administer than powders⟩ **3 :** a bringing or coming to an end or into a state of discontinuity: as **a :** discharge of a contract by performance (as payment or release) **:** performance of an obligation **b** *obs* **:** a setting free **:** DELIVERANCE, DISCHARGE **c :** a separating from continuity of normally continuous parts **:** SEVERANCE ⟨a violent ~ of the continuity of a joint⟩ **d :** an interruption of continuity **:** DISRUPTION, BREACH, BREAK, DISPERSION ⟨watched the gradual ~ of the clouds as the storm moved on⟩

[2]**solution** \"\ *vt* -ED/-ING/-S **:** to apply a solution to; *esp* **:** to cement with a solution (as of rubber)

so·lu·tion·al \-shənᵊl,-shnəl\ *adj* **:** of, relating to, or constituting a solution

solution heat treatment *n* **:** heating of an alloy to a temperature at which a particular constituent will enter into solid solution followed by cooling at a rate fast enough to prevent the dissolved constituent from precipitating

so·lu·tion·ist \-sh(ə)nəst\ *n* -s [[1]*solution* + *-ist*] **:** a solver of problems; *esp* **:** one who makes a practice or occupation of solving puzzles

solution plane *n* **:** a direction in a crystal of relatively easy solubility (as when the substance is under great pressure) ⟨chemical action along *solution planes* in minerals in rocks has often resulted in schillerization⟩

solution pressure *n* **:** the pressure by which the particles of a dissolved substance are driven into solution and which when equal to the osmotic pressure establishes equilibrium so that the concentration of the solution becomes constant

solutive *adj* [ML *solutivus*, fr. L *solutus* (past part. of *solvere* to loosen) + *-ivus* -ive] *obs* **:** tending to produce relaxation (as of the bowels) **:** LAXATIVE

sol·u·tiz·er \-zə(r)\ *n* -s [*solutize* to treat with organic salts or solvents to impart certain solvent properties (fr. *solute* + *-ize*)

+ *-er*] : an agent (as an organic salt or an organic solvent) for promoting solubility; *esp* : such an agent (as potassium isobutyrate) for use with a caustic solution in removing mercaptans from gasoline

so·lu·tre·an *or* **so·lu·tri·an** \sə'lü·trēən\ *adj, usu cap* [*Solutré*, village of east central France where remains of the period were found + E *-an* or *-ian*] : of or relating to an epoch of the Upper Paleolithic period following the Aurignacian, preceding the Magdalenian, and characterized by stone implements that are typically leaf-shaped and finely flaked on both sides and by the hunting of wild horses for food

solv *abbr* [L *solve*] dissolve

solv·abil·i·ty \ˌ⸗⸗'bilədē, -lətē, -i — *see* SOLVE\ *n* : the quality or state of being solvable

solv·able \'⸗⸗əbəl — *see* SOLVE\ *adj* [*solve* + *-able*] **1** *obs* : able to pay one's debts : SOLVENT **2** *archaic* : SOLUBLE **3** : susceptible of solution or of being solved, resolved, or explained

¹solv·ate \'⸗ˌāt — *see* SOLVE\ *n* -S [*solvent* + *-ate*] : a chemical or physical combination of a solute with a solvent or of a dispersed phase with a dispersion medium — compare HYDRATE

²solvate \"\ *vb* -ED/-ING/-S *vt* : to convert into a solvate ⟨ions are *solvated* to a greater or lesser extent in polar solvents⟩ ⟨molecules are *solvated* by the plasticizer —Donald Druesedow & C.F.Gibbs⟩ ~ *vi* : to become or behave as a solvate

solvated *adj* [fr. past part. of ²*solvate*] : containing combined solvent ⟨a ~ hydrate⟩

solv·a·tion \⸗'āshən — *see* SOLVE\ *n* -S [²*solvate* + *-ion*] : the formation of a solvate; *also* : the state or degree of being solvated — compare HYDRATION, SOLVOLYSIS

sol·vay process \'säl|ˌvā- *also* 'sȯl|\ *n, usu cap S* [after Ernest *Solvay* †1922 Belg. chemist, its inventor] : a process for making sodium carbonate from common salt and limestone that is based on the sparing solubility of sodium bicarbonate and involves burning the limestone to lime and carbon dioxide, passing the carbon dioxide into a strong brine saturated with ammonia to precipitate sodium bicarbonate and leave ammonium chloride in solution, and converting the bicarbonate to soda ash by calcining — called also *ammonia soda process*

solve \'sälv, 'sȯlv *also* 'sä(ů)v *or* 'sȯv\ *vb* -ED/-ING/-S [ME *solven*, fr. L *solvere, soluere* to loosen, free, pay, solve, dissolve, fr. *sed-, se-* apart (fr. *sed, se* without) + *luere* to release, atone for — more at LOSE] *vt* **1** *obs* : to set loose or free **2 a** : to find an answer, solution, explanation, or remedy for : arrive at a clear, definite, and satisfying answer to (the difficult, obscure, or urgent) ⟨the members of these commissions . . . ~ administrative difficulties, and save the state money —*Amer. Guide Series: Del.*⟩ **b** : to perform the operations required to solve (a mathematical problem) : work out **3 a** : to make payment of (as a debt or money) **b** : to free oneself of (an obligation) **4** : to cause to go into solution : DISSOLVE ~ *vi* : to solve something

syn RESOLVE, UNFOLD, UNRAVEL, DECIPHER: SOLVE is the most general in meaning and suggestion in this group; it applies to finding a satisfactory answer or solution, usu. to something of at least moderate difficulty ⟨the mystery and disquieting meaninglessness of existence . . . were *solved* for me now —L.P. Smith⟩ ⟨create a difficulty rather than *solve* one —A.M.Young⟩ RESOLVE, as contrasted with SOLVE, is likely to indicate analytic arrangement and consideration of the various phases or items of a problem or situation rather than finding a final solution or answer and is likely to suggest dispelling of confusion or perplexity by a clear formulation of questions or issues ⟨you may find it of some interest to be told that the law has had to struggle with these problems and to know how it has *resolved* them —B.N.Cardozo⟩ In some situations this process may achieve an answer, esp. a ready or summary one ⟨he was at the same time *resolving* successive tangles of intrigue against himself and his policy —Hilaire Belloc⟩ ⟨it was realized that the method of *resolving* apparent contradictions by liquidating one of the contradictories is not the way to arrive at true solutions —*Times Lit. Supp.*⟩ UNFOLD indicates continuous opening up, clarifying, making more and more clear and patent until a full solution or resolution is apparent ⟨went around and through and behind a situation, *unfolding* it . . . to include possibilities he hadn't known were upon its horizon —Mary Austin⟩ ⟨saw the great truth of evolution *unfolded* —Waldemar Kaempffert⟩ ⟨the method of *unfolding* the course of a plot must in some ways be different in a play meant for acting and in a book meant for reading —C.E.Montague⟩ UNRAVEL stresses the notion of making a clear and orderly rearrangement of something entangled or a simple ordering of something complicated, esp. by patient endeavor ⟨the details are difficult to *unravel* at this distance of time —H.O.Taylor⟩ ⟨a whole elaborate plot may be *unravelled* by discovering the one relevant detail —W. O.Aydelotte⟩ DECIPHER stresses the notion of finding the meaning or significance of something very obscure, clouded, cryptic, or enigmatic ⟨placing of a writer or other artist in his proper rank or in *deciphering* the less obvious intentions of his work —C.E.Montague⟩ ⟨the results, so far as they could be *deciphered* from the puzzling procedure and twisted combinations, confirmed what had gone before —*Atlantic*⟩

sol·ven·cy \'sälvənsē, 'sȯl-\ *n* -ES [¹*solvent* + *-cy*] : the quality or state of being solvent

sol·vend \'⸗ˌvend, ⸗'⸗\ *n* -S [L *solvendus*, gerundive of *solvere* to dissolve] : a dissolved substance in a solution : SOLUTE

¹sol·vent \'sälvənt, 'sȯl-\ *adj* [L *solvent-, solvens*, pres. part. of *solvere* to pay, dissolve] **1** : able or sufficient to pay all legal debts ⟨a ~ merchant⟩ ⟨the estate is ~⟩ **2** : that dissolves or can dissolve : producing a solution or homogeneous mixture ⟨~ fluids⟩ ⟨the ~ action of water⟩ ⟨~ social influences⟩ — **sol·vent·ly** *adv*

²solvent \"\ *n* -S **1** : a substance capable of or used in dissolving or dispersing one or more other substances; *esp* : a liquid component of a solution present in greater amount than the solute : MENSTRUUM 1 ⟨water is a good ~ for many salts, alcohol for many resins, and ether for fats⟩ ⟨the best ~ for a material is usu. related to it in chemical structure —P.O.Powers⟩ — compare PLASTICIZER, THINNER **2** : something that provides a solution (as for a problem) ⟨no ~ has been found for the industrial stagnation⟩ **3** : something that dissipates, disintegrates, or otherwise eliminates or attenuates something and esp. something unwanted ⟨ridicule is a ~ of prejudice⟩

solvent dye *n* : any of a class of dyes that are soluble in varying degree in organic solvents and are usu. insoluble in water — see DYE table I

solvent naphtha *n* : a flammable liquid distillate containing principally xylenes and higher aromatic hydrocarbons and usu. boiling higher than ligroin, obtained esp. from coal-tar light oils or coke-oven-gas light oils or from petroleum cracking, and used chiefly as a solvent and as a raw material for coumarone-indene resins

solv·er \'sälvə(r), 'sȯlv- *also* 'sä(ů)v- *or* 'sȯv-\ *n* -S : one that solves

solves *pres 3d sing of* SOLVE

solving *pres part of* SOLVE

sol·vol·y·sis \säl'väləsəs, sȯl-\ *n* [*solvent* + *-o-* + *-lysis*] : a chemical reaction of a solvent and a dissolved substance with the formation typically of one or two or more new compounds : either hydrolysis or an analogous reaction (as alcoholysis or ammonolysis) in which a solvent other than water plays a role similar to that of water in hydrolysis — compare SOLVATION

sol·vo·lyt·ic \¦⸗ˌvə¦lid·ik\ *adj* [*solvent* + *-o-* + *-lytic*] : of, relating to, or involving solvolysis

sol·vo·lyze \'⸗ˌvəˌlīz\ *vt* -ED/-ING/-S [*solvent* + *-o-* + *-lyze*] : to subject to solvolysis

sol·vus \'sälvəs, 'sȯl-\ *n, pl* **sol·vi** \-ˌvī, -ˌvē\ *also* **solvuses** [NL, fr. L *solvere* to dissolve] : a curve on a temperature-composition diagram indicating the limits of solubility of one solid phase in another — compare LIQUIDUS, SOLID SOLUTION, SOLIDUS

soly *obs var of* SOLELY

soly *abbr* solubility

¹so·ma \'sōmə\ *n* -S [Skt; akin to Av *haoma* haoma, Gk *hyei* it is raining — more at SUCK] **1** : an East Indian leafless vine (*Sarcostemma acidum*) of the family Asclepiadaceae that yields a somewhat acidulous milky juice **2** : an intoxicating plant juice of ancient India used as an offering to the gods and as a drink of immortality by worshipers in Vedic ritual and worshiped in personified form as a Vedic god — compare HAOMA

²soma \"\ *n, pl* **soma·ta** \-məd·ə, -ətə\ *also* **somas** *often attrib* [NL *somat-, soma*, fr. Gk *sōmat-, sōma* body] **1** : the whole of any organism except its germ cells **2** [Gk *sōmat-, sōma*] : BODY 1a — opposed to *psyche* **3** : CELL BODY

-so·ma \'sōmə\ *n comb form* [NL *-somat-, -soma*, fr. Gk *sōmat-, sōma* body; akin to L *tumēre* to swell — more at THUMB] **1** : one having (such) a body — in generic names in zoology ⟨Dolicho*soma*⟩ ⟨Loxo*soma*⟩ and botany ⟨Crosso*soma*⟩ **2** *pl* **-somas** *or* **-soma·ta** \-məd·ə, -ətə\ : body ⟨actino*soma*⟩ ⟨hydro*soma*⟩ : region or portion of a body ⟨meso*soma*⟩ ⟨pro*soma*⟩

somaesthesia *or* **somaesthesis** *var of* SOMESTHESIA

so·mal \'sōməl\ *adj* [²*soma* + *-al*] : SOMATIC

so·ma·li \sō'mälē, sə'-\ *also* **so·mal** \-'mäl\ *n, pl* **somali** *or* **somalis** *also* **somal** *or* **somals** *usu cap* **1 a** : a very tall and dark Cushitic-speaking people of Somaliland apparently of mixed Mediterranean and negroid stock and almost universally Muslim **b** : a member of the Somali people **2** : the Cushitic language of the Somali people

so·ma·lia \sō'mälēə, sə'-, -lyə\ *adj, usu cap* [fr. *Somalia*, former Italian colony in East Africa] : of or from Somalia : of the kind or style prevalent in Somalia : SOMALIAN

¹so·ma·lian \-lēən, -lyən\ *adj, usu cap* [*Somalia* + E *-an*] **1** : of, relating to, or characteristic of Somalia **2** : of, relating to, or characteristic of the people of Somalia

²somalian \"\ *n* -S *cap* : a native or inhabitant of Somalia

somali shilling *also* **so·ma·lo** \-'mä(ˌ)lō\ *n, pl* **somali shillings** *also* **soma·li** \-(ˌ)lē\ *usu cap 1st S* **1** : the basic monetary unit of Somalia — see MONEY table **2** : a coin or note representing one Somali shilling

so many *adj* **1** : constituting an unspecified number ⟨reading . . . *so many* verses before bedtime because it was the Bible —Amy Lowell⟩ **2** : constituting a group or pack ⟨the noblesse stretched in pairs upon logs of wood like *so many* seals upon the rocks —Tobias Smollett⟩

so·ma·plasm \'sōməˌplazəm\ *n* [²*soma* + *-plasm*] : SOMATOPLASM

somat- *or* **somato-** *comb form* [NL, fr. Gk *sōmat-, sōmato-*, fr. *sōmat-, sōma* body] **1 a** : body ⟨*somato*logy⟩ **b** : somatic ⟨*somat*ize⟩ : somatic and ⟨*somato*psychic⟩ **2** : soma ⟨*somato*plasm⟩

-so·ma·ta \'sōməd·ə, -mətə\ *n pl comb form* [NL, fr. Gk *sōmata*, pl. of *sōmat-, sōma* body] : ones having (such) a body — in names of zoological taxa larger than a genus ⟨Hetero*somata*⟩

so·ma·te·ria \ˌsōmə'tirēə\ *n, cap* [NL, prob. irreg. fr. *somat-* + Gk *erion* wool] : the principal genus of eider ducks

so·mat·ic \sō'mad·ik, sə'-, -atik, -ēk\ *adj* [Gk *sōmatikos*, fr. *sōmat-, sōma* body + *-ikos* -ic] **1 a** : of, relating to, or affecting the body or esp. the soma : PHYSICAL, CORPOREAL ⟨~ posture⟩ ⟨~ attitudes⟩ **b** : of, relating to, or affecting the soma as contrasted with reproductive or germ cells ⟨~ tissue⟩ **2 a** : of or relating to the wall of the body : SOMATOPLEURIC, PARIETAL — distinguished from *visceral* **b** : of or relating to the trunk — distinguished from *appendicular* **3** : MESOMORPHIC 2 **syn** see BODILY

so·mat·i·cal·ly \-ək(ə)lē, -ēk-, -li\ *adv* : in a somatic manner : in the soma : in terms of the body

somatic antigen *n* : an antigen of the body of the bacterial cell — distinguished from *flagellar antigen*

somatic cavity *n* : BODY CAVITY; *esp* : COELOM

somatic cell *n* : one of the cells of the body of an individual that become differentiated and compose the tissues, organs, and parts of that individual — distinguished from *germ cell*

somatic crossing-over *n* : crossing-over occurring during mitosis whether in germinal or somatic tissue

somatic mutation *n* : change originating in a somatic cell due to chance loss of genes or to genic change and constituting the cause of chimera formation

so·ma·tist \'sōməd·əst\ *n* -S [ISV *somat-* + *-ist*] **1** : an advocate of medical organicism **2** : one who seeks the causes of mental disorders in brain lesions and other physical conditions

so·ma·ti·za·tion \ˌsōməd·ə'zāshən, -əˌdī'z-, -ətə'z-, -əˌtī'z-\ *n* -S [ISV *somat-* + *-ization*] **1** : the production of physiological dysfunction often resulting in irreversible structural changes by the exaggeration and persistence of an emotional state **2** : the expression of psychological conflict through somatic symptoms including conversion hysteria

so·ma·tize \'sōməˌtīz\ *vb* -ED/-ING/-S [*somat-* + *-ize*] *vt* : to express (as psychological conflicts) through somatic symptoms ~ *vi* : to express psychological conflicts through somatic symptoms

somato- — see SOMAT-

so·ma·to·blast \'sōməd·əˌblast\ *n* [*somat-* + *-blast*] **1 a** : a cleavage cell of an annelid worm that is the precursor of most of the trunk ectoderm, the nervous system, and the nephridia **b** : cleavage cells descended from the primary somatoblast cell of an annelid **2** : the outer layer of cells of the nematogen of a dicyemic mesozoan

so·ma·to·chrome \-ˌkrōm\ *n* [*somat-* + *-chrome*] : a nerve cell having a distinct cytoplasm around its nucleus and taking a deep stain with basic aniline dyes

so·ma·to·cyst \-ˌsist\ *n* -S [*somat-* + *-cyst*] : an air cavity in the float of a siphonophoran — **so·ma·to·cys·tic** \¦⸗⸗⸗¦sistik\ *adj*

so·ma·to·derm \-ˌdərm\ *n* -S [*somat-* + *-derm*] : the mesodermal part of the somatopleure

so·ma·to·gen·ic \¦⸗⸗⸗¦jenik\ *or* **so·ma·to·ge·net·ic** \-jə¦ned·ik\ *adj* [*somat-* + *-genic* or *-genetic*] : originating in, affecting, or acting through the somatic cells — distinguished from *psychogenic*; compare BLASTOGENIC

somatogenic variation *n* : a nonheritable character imposed on the soma by environmental conditions

so·ma·to·log·i·cal \¦⸗⸗⸗+\ *adj* : of or relating to somatology ⟨~ observations⟩

so·ma·tol·o·gy \ˌ⸗⸗'täləjē\ *n* -ES [NL *somatologia* study of the body, fr. *somat-* + L *-logia* -logy] : PHYSICAL ANTHROPOLOGY

so·ma·tome \'sōməˌtōm\ *n* -S [Gk *sōma* body + E *-tome* — more at -SOMA] : SOMITE — **so·ma·tom·ic** \¦⸗⸗¦tämik\ *adj*

so·ma·to·metric \¦sōməd·ə+\ *adj* [ISV *somat-* + *-metric*] : of or relating to somatometry

so·ma·tom·e·try \ˌ⸗⸗'tämə·trē\ *n* -ES : a branch of anthropometry that is concerned with measurement of the body

so·ma·to·phyte \'⸗⸗d·əˌfīt\ *n* -S [ISV *somat-* + *-phyte*] : a plant composed of somatic cells that develop chiefly into adult tissue ⟨all higher plants are ~*s*⟩ — compare ASOMATOPHYTE

so·ma·to·phyt·ic \¦⸗⸗⸗¦fid|ik, -it|, |ēk\ *adj* : of, relating to, or being a somatophyte

so·ma·to·plasm \'⸗⸗⸗d·əˌplazəm\ *n* [*somat-* + *-plasm*] **1** : protoplasm of somatic cells **2** : somatic cells as opposed to germ cells — compare GERM PLASM

so·ma·to·plas·tic \¦⸗⸗⸗¦plastik\ *adj* [fr. *somatoplasm*, after E *plasm: plastic*] : of, relating to, or constituting somatoplasm

so·ma·to·pleure \'⸗⸗⸗ˌplů(ə)r, -ůə\ *n* -S [NL *somatopleura*, fr. *somat-* + Gk *pleura* side — more at PLEURISY] **1** : a complex layer of tissue in the embryo of a craniate vertebrate consisting of the outer of the two layers into which the lateral plate of the mesoderm splits together with the ectoderm that sheathes it externally and giving rise to the body wall and in amniote vertebrates to the amnion and chorion — compare SPLANCHNOPLEURE **2** : a part of an invertebrate embryo that corresponds to but is not necessarily homologous with the vertebrate somatopleure — **so·ma·to·pleu·ric** \¦⸗⸗⸗¦plůrik\ *adj*

so·ma·to·psychic \¦⸗⸗⸗+\ *adj* [*somat-* + *psychic*] **1** : relating to an individual's notions regarding his own body ⟨a ~ delusion⟩ — compare PSYCHOSOMATIC **2** : of or relating to primary somatic diseases (as syphilis or chorea) which produce secondary mental symptoms

so·ma·to·psychological \¦⸗⸗⸗+\ *adj* [*somat-* + *psychological*] : SOMATOPSYCHIC 2

so·ma·to·splanchnic \"+\ *adj* [*somat-* + *splanchnic*] **1** : of, relating to, or made up of the somatic and splanchnic layers of the mesoderm **2** : of or relating to the body and the viscera

so·ma·to·to·nia \¦⸗⸗⸗'tōnēə\ *n* -S [NL, fr. *somat-* + *-tonia*] : a pattern of temperament typical of the mesomorphic individual and marked by predominance of physical over social or intellectual factors and exhibiting aggressiveness, love of physical activity, vigor, and alertness

¹so·ma·to·ton·ic \¦⸗⸗⸗¦tänik\ *adj* [NL *somatotonia* + E *-ic*] : exhibiting somatotonia

²somatotonic \"\ *n* -S : a somatotonic individual : MESOMORPH

so·ma·to·top·ic \¦⸗⸗⸗¦täpik\ *also* **so·ma·to·top·i·cal** \-pəkəl\ *adj* [*somat-* + *top-* + *-ic* or *-ical*] : of, relating to, or mediating the orderly and specific relation between particular body regions (as a hand or the tongue) and corresponding motor areas of the brain ⟨the ~ arrangement within the thalamus⟩

so·ma·to·trop·ic \¦⸗⸗⸗¦träpik\ *or* **so·ma·to·tro·phic** \¦⸗⸗⸗¦trōfik\ *adj* [ISV *somat-* + *-tropic* or *-trophic*] : promoting growth ⟨~ activity⟩

so·ma·to·tro·pin \ˌsōməd·ə'trōpən\ *also* **so·ma·to·tro·phin** \-rəfən\ *n* -S [*somatotropin* ISV *somatotropic* + *-in*; *somatotrophin* alter. (influenced by *troph-*) of *somatotropin*] : GROWTH HORMONE 1

¹so·ma·to·type \'sōməd·əˌtīp, sə'mad·ə,-\ *n* [*somat-* + *type*] **1** : body type : PHYSIQUE **2** : one of the types of body-build differentiated by a classificatory system : a classification of human body-build in terms of the relative development of ectomorphic, endomorphic, and mesomorphic components

²somatotype \"\ *vt* : to determine the somatotype of (as a human body) : classify according to physique

so·ma·to·ty·pol·o·gy \ˌ⸗⸗⸗tī'päləjē\ *n* -ES [*somatotype* + *-o-* + *-logy*] : the study of somatotypes

-soma·tous \¦sāməd·əs, ¦sōm-, -mətəs\ *adj comb form* [LL *-somatus*, fr. Gk *-sōmatos*, fr. *sōmat-, sōma* body — more at -SOMA] : having (such) a body ⟨macro*somatous*⟩

¹som·ber *or* **som·bre** \'sämbə(r) *sometimes* 'sōm-\ *adj* [F *sombre*] **1** : so shaded or full of shadows as to be dark and gloomy : lacking light or brightness : characterized by gloom or shadow : depressingly dark, dusky, or obscure ⟨narrow, ~ streets —*Amer. Guide Series: Va.*⟩ ⟨the bell-chamber was ~ and almost menacing —Dorothy Sayers⟩ **2 a** (1) : gloomy, sullen, melancholy, or dejected in appearance or mood ⟨the city made him ~ and restless —John Cheever⟩ (2) : of a serious mien : GRAVE ⟨~ . . . merchant dignitaries —J.H. Randall⟩ **b** : of a melancholy, dismal, or depressing character ⟨~ thoughts⟩ ⟨a ~ mood⟩ **3** : conveying gloomy suggestions or ideas : DEPRESSING, GRAVE, MELANCHOLY ⟨took on a more ~ and threatening aspect —*Emporia (Kans.) Gazette*⟩ ⟨know the truth, ~ though it may be —Sir Winston Churchill⟩ **4 a** *of color or a color* : of a dull or heavy cast or shade ⟨~ tone⟩ ⟨a more ~ hue⟩ ⟨house . . . painted a ~ Puritan color —A.W.Long⟩ **b** : having or characterized by such a color : dark colored ⟨the ~ leaves of the copper beech —*Amer. Guide Series: N.J.*⟩ **syn** see SERIOUS

²somber *or* **sombre** \"\ *vb* **sombered** *or* **sombred**; **sombered** *or* **sombred**; **sombering** *or* **sombring** \-b(ə)riŋ\ **sombers** *or* **sombres** *vt* : to make somber ~ *vi* : to become or grow somber

³somber *or* **sombre** \"\ *n* -S : GLOOM

som·ber·ly *or* **som·bre·ly** *adv* : in a somber manner ⟨answered him flatly and ~ —Pearl Buck⟩ ⟨stared ~ at the . . . person —Booth Tarkington⟩

som·ber·ness *or* **som·bre·ness** *n* -ES : the quality or state of being somber

som·bra \'sämbrə\ *n* -S [MexSp, fr. Sp, shade, prob. modif. (influenced by Sp *sol* sun, fr. L) of L *umbra* — more at UMBRAGE, SOLAR] : the shady side or section of a bullfight arena — compare SOL

som·bre·ro \səm'bre(ˌ)rō, säm-\ *n* -S [Sp, hat, canopy, fr. *sombra* shade] **1** *obs* : an Oriental sunshade **2** : a high-crowned hat made of felt or straw with a very wide brim usu. rolled at the edges and worn esp. in the Southwest and Mexico

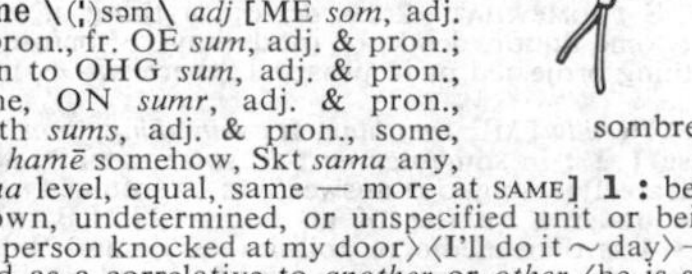

sombrero 2

som·brous \'sämbrəs\ *adj* [F *sombre* somber + E *-ous*] *archaic* : characterized by or manifesting somberness : SOMBER ⟨an avenue of tall and ~ pines —H.W.Longfellow⟩ ⟨the ~ and heavy sound of the billows —Sir Walter Scott⟩

¹some \(ˈ)səm\ *adj* [ME *som*, adj. & pron., fr. OE *sum*, adj. & pron.; akin to OHG *sum*, adj. & pron., some, ON *sumr*, adj. & pron., Goth *sums*, adj. & pron., some, Gk *hamē* somehow, Skt *sama* any, *sama* level, equal, same — more at SAME] **1** : being one unknown, undetermined, or unspecified unit or being or thing ⟨~ person knocked at my door⟩ ⟨I'll do it ~ day⟩ — sometimes used as a correlative to *another* or *other* ⟨he is spending the summer at ~ beach or another⟩ ⟨~ day or other make us a visit⟩ **2** : being one, a part, or an unspecified number of something (as a class, group, species, collection, or range of possibilities) named or contextually implied : being an unspecified or ill-defined individual, kind, or example of something ⟨this criticism applies to ~ students only⟩ ⟨~ gems are hard but the majority are soft⟩ ⟨protective coloring occurs in ~ birds⟩ ⟨the hartebeest is ~ African animal⟩ ⟨requested help from ~ man in the audience⟩ **3** : worthy of notice or consideration : far from negligible : more or less important or striking ⟨that was ~ race⟩ ⟨that was ~ party⟩ **4** : being one of, one kind of, or an undetermined proportion of : being always at least one but often a few and sometimes all of — used as a sign of particularity to indicate that the logical proposition in which it occurs is asserted only of a subclass or certain existent members of the class denoted by the term which it modifies

²some \ˈsəm\ *pron, sing or pl in constr* [ME *som*, adj. & pron., fr. OE *sum*, adj. & pron.] **1** : some one : one person or thing among a number ⟨~ of these days⟩ **2** : one indeterminate quantity, portion, or number as distinguished from the rest : a part of something (as a number or group of persons) ⟨~ had webbed feet, ~ had talons⟩ **3** : some more : an indefinite additional amount or degree ⟨he ran a mile and then ~⟩

³some \(ˈ)səm\ *indefinite article* [¹*some*] : being of an unspecified but appreciable or not inconsiderable quantity, amount, extent, or degree : more than a little : being in number at least or often more than a few ⟨we have ~ good honey⟩ ⟨there is ~ heat in this radiator⟩ ⟨they have ~ land by the river⟩

⁴some \ˈsəm\ *adv* [¹*some*] **1** : ABOUT — usu. used before a numeral ⟨a village of ~ eighty houses⟩ ⟨~ two or three persons⟩ **2** : in some degree or extent : SOMEWHAT ⟨felt ~ better after just one mouthful⟩

¹-some \ˌsəm; *when n immediately precedes, as in "winsome",* (t)səm\ *adj suffix* [ME *-som*, fr. OE *-sum*; akin to OFris *-sum* -some, OHG *-sam*, ON *-samr*, Goth *-sama* -some, *sama* same — more at SAME] : characterized by a (specified) thing, quality, state, or action ⟨awe*some*⟩ ⟨burden*some*⟩ ⟨cuddle*some*⟩ ⟨lone*some*⟩

²-some \"\ *n suffix* -S [ME (northern dial.) *-sum*, fr. ME *sum*, *som*, pron., one, a certain one, some, fr. OE *sum*, pron., one, a certain one, some, one of a group of (so many) members (in such expressions as *syxa sum* one of a group of six members) — more at SOME] : group of (so many) members and esp. persons ⟨four*some*⟩ ⟨two*some*⟩

³-some \ˌsōm\ *n comb form* -S [NL *-somat-, -soma* -soma — more at -SOMA] **1** : -SOMA 2 ⟨chromo*some*⟩ ⟨tropho*some*⟩ ⟨ecto*some*⟩ **2** : chromosome ⟨mono*some*⟩

⁴-some \"\ *adj comb form* [ISV, fr. NL *soma* body, fr. Gk *sōma* — more at -SOMA] : having (such) a body ⟨eury*some*⟩

¹some·body \'səmˌbǝdē, -(ˌ)bədē, -di\ *pron* [ME *sum body*, fr. *sum, som* some + *body*] : one or some person of no certain or known identity : a person indeterminate ⟨if you leave the door open ~ will be sure to come in⟩ ⟨there should be ~ at the office at this hour⟩

²somebody \"\ *n* : a person of position or importance ⟨think oneself a ~⟩ — often used without article ⟨the desire to be ~ is one of the strongest of human motives —*Amer. Quarterly*⟩

some·day \'səmˌdā\ *adv* [ME *sum day*, fr. *sum, som* some + *day*] : at some time in the future ⟨~ a beginning must be made —Lewis Mumford⟩ ⟨may ~ choose to reassert themselves —John Gunther⟩

somedeal \'⸗ˌ⸗\ *adv* [ME *somdele*, fr. OE *sume dǣle*, dat. of *sum dǣl* some part, fairly large amount, fr. *sum* some + *dǣl* part — more at DEAL] *archaic* : in some degree or measure : SOMEWHAT

somegate \'⸗ˌ⸗\ *adv* [¹*some* + *gate* (way)] *Scot* : SOMEHOW, SOMEWHERE

somehow \'⸗ˌ⸗\ *adv* : in one way or another : in some way not yet known or designated : by some means ⟨the thing must be done ~⟩ ⟨he lives ~⟩ ⟨the evidence needed was ~ obtained

—G.G.Coulton⟩ ⟨he has ~ or other got the entire management —Sir Walter Scott⟩
some·one \'səm(,)wən\ *pron* [ME *sum oon*, fr. *sum, som* some + *oon* one] **:** some person **:** SOMEBODY ⟨hoping that ~ will suddenly find out —*Contemporary Rev.*⟩ ⟨then you meet ~ . . . you like —John Van Druten⟩
someplace \'⸗,⸗\ *adv* **:** SOMEWHERE ⟨topples overboard ~ in the middle of the sea —Robert Evett⟩ ⟨really had ~ to go that day —*New Yorker*⟩ ⟨~ in this mess of masonry . . . was a girl —Richard Bissell⟩
somer *obs var of* SUMMER
som·ers \'səmə(r)z\ *adv* [alter. of *somewheres*] *chiefly dial* **:** SOMEWHERE
1**som·er·sault** *also* **sum·mer·sault** \'səmə(r),sȯlt\ *n* -s [MF *sombresaut* leap, alter. of *soubresaut, soubresault*, prob. fr. (assumed) OProv *sobresaut*, fr. OProv *sobre* over (fr. L *super*) + *saut* leap, jump, fr. L *saltus* — more at OVER, SALT] **1 :** an act of turning end over end: as **a :** a stunt or maneuver in which a person stoops down and while remaining in a tuck position rolls end over end on the floor either forward or backward **b :** a leap or jump in which a person turns his heels over his head forward or backward before landing on the floor **c :** a front or back dive executed in tuck, pike, or layout position in which the diver rotates end over end one or more times before entering the water **2 :** an action held to resemble a somersault **:** a reversal of policy, tactics, or position **:** a complete overturn ⟨saying that our present Far Eastern policy represents a complete ~ —*New Republic*⟩ ⟨led Bulgaria in its complete ~ from the camp of the Axis into the fold of the Allies —E.P.Snow⟩
2**somersault** *also* **summersault** \"\ *vi* -ED/-ING/-S **:** to turn or execute a somersault
1**som·er·set** *also* **sum·mer·set** -,set, *usu* -ed·+V\ *n* -s [by alter. (influence of *Somerset*, county in southwest England)] **:** SOMERSAULT
2**somerset** *also* **summerset** \"\ *vb* -ED/-ING/-S *vt* **:** to fling in a somersault **:** cause to turn a somersault ~ *vi* **:** SOMERSAULT
som·er·set·shire \'səmərsət,shi(ə)r; -məsət,shiə, -i(ə)r; -,set-, -,shə(r)\ *or* **som·er·set** \-,sə|t, -,se|, *usu* |d·+V\ *adj, usu cap* [fr. *Somersetshire, Somerset*, county in southwest England] **:** of or from the county of Somerset, England **:** of the kind or style prevalent in Somerset
som·er·ville \'səmə(r),vil, -,vəl\ *adj, usu cap* [fr. *Somerville*, city in northeast Massachusetts] **:** of or from the city of Somerville, Mass. ⟨a *Somerville* street⟩ **:** of the kind or style prevalent in Somerville
-somes *pl of* -SOME
som·esthesia \,sōm+\ *also* **som·esthesis** \(')sōm+\ *or* **som·aesthesia** \,sōm+\ *or* **som·aesthesis** \(')sōm+\ *n, pl* **somesthesias** *also* **somesthesises** [NL, fr. 2*soma* + *esthesia* or *esthesis*] **:** body sensibility including the cutaneous and kinesthetic senses
som·esthetic \,sōm+\ *adj* [fr. *somesthesia*, after such pairs as E *anesthesia*: *anesthetic*] **:** of, relating to, or concerned with bodily sensations
somesthetic area *n* **:** a sensory area of either parietal lobe of the brain
somesthetic receptor *n* **:** a sensory end organ concerned with the reception of stimuli producing one of the generalized sensations (as temperature, pressure, position, or movement)
1**some·thing** \'səm(p)thiŋ, -thēŋ, *in rapid, informal, or dial speech* -mpᵊm\ *pron* [ME *sum thing, som thing* (noun phrase), fr. OE *sum thing*, fr. *sum* some + *thing*] **1 a :** some undetermined or unspecified thing **:** some thing not definitely understood or remembered ⟨~ must be done about it⟩ ⟨he muttered ~ or other⟩ **b :** some thing (as a name or part of a name) not remembered or immaterial ⟨the twelve ~ train⟩ **2 :** some definite but not specified thing **:** an unnamed but positive, concrete, or significant thing — opposed to *nothing* ⟨he has ~ to live for⟩ **3 :** SOMEWHAT **4 :** a person or thing of consequence **5 :** some liquor, drink, or food ⟨have ~ before you go⟩ **6 :** a thing projected or in prospect ⟨there was ~ in the wind⟩
2**something** \"\ *adv* [ME *sumthing*, fr. *sum thing, som thing* (noun phrase)] **1 :** in some degree **:** to some extent **:** SOMEWHAT ⟨the scarcely ambiguous answer was ~ softened —J.A. Froude⟩ ⟨~ under a quarter of an hour —G.N.Boothby⟩ ⟨a man of ~ less than mediocre abilities —Edmund Wilson⟩ **2 :** to a high degree **:** EXTREMELY, VERY ⟨raved ~ fierce⟩ ⟨swears ~ awful⟩
3**something** \"\ *n* [1*something*] **:** a thing of an unspecified or indeterminate nature ⟨felt the presence of an unknown ~⟩
4**something** \"\ *vt* -ED/-ING/-S [1*something*] **:** DAMN, CURSE
some·thing·ness *n* -ES **:** the quality or state of being something **:** real or material existence
1**some·time** \'səm,tīm\ *adv* [ME *sum tim, sum time*, fr. *sum* some + *tim, time* time] **1 a** *obs* **:** at some past time **:** at a certain time or on a particular occasion in the past **:** ONCE ⟨there was ~ . . . founded a certain house —Friar Rush⟩ **b** *archaic* **:** in the past **:** at one time **:** in former times **:** FORMERLY ⟨a large marble stone ~ inlaid with brass —Edward Ledwich⟩ **2** *archaic* **:** once in a while **:** OCCASIONALLY, SOMETIMES ⟨but ~ fear is the beginning of wisdom —Timothy Puller⟩ **3 :** at one time or other hereafter **:** at some time in the future **:** on a future occasion ⟨I'll do it ~⟩ **4 :** at some indefinite or indeterminate time **:** at some not specified or definitely known point of time **:** at some time or other ⟨~ in 1710 or 1711 he was taken to a neighboring town —J.W.Krutch⟩ ⟨~ years ago a . . . sea had filled the valley —R.O.Easton⟩
2**sometime** \"\ *adj* **1 :** having been formerly **:** FORMER, LATE ⟨former military officer, ~ newspaper editor —Dixon Wecter⟩ ⟨~ professor of history at a nearby university⟩ **2** *South & Midland* **:** erratic in loyalties and dependability ⟨a ~ friend⟩
1**some·times** \'səm,tīmz *also* (,)səm't-\ *adv* [1*some* + *times*, pl. of *time*, n.] **1 :** on some occasions **:** at times **:** now and then **:** OCCASIONALLY ⟨writes . . . ~ in captious criticism of some policy or other —Ernestine Evans⟩ ⟨illustrated by excellent and ~ beautiful photographs —*Geog. Jour.*⟩ **2** *obs* **a :** ONCE **b :** FORMERLY
2**sometimes** \"\ *adj, archaic* **:** FORMER, SOMETIME ⟨excelled only by her ~ tutoress —Charlotte Smith⟩
some·way \'səm,wā\ *also* **some·ways** \-āz\ *adv* [*someway* fr. ME *sum way*, fr. *sum, som* some + *way*; *someways* fr. ME *som wayes*, fr. *sumes weis*, gen. of *sum wei* (noun phrase) some way, fr. *sum, som* some + *wei, way* way] **:** in some way or manner **:** by some means **:** SOMEHOW ⟨tried to make him ~ decent —James Joyce⟩ ⟨~ . . . finding money to buy things —W.A. White⟩
1**some·what** \'səm,(h)wä|t, -,(h)wə|, *usu* |d·+V; *sometimes* ,⸗'⸗\ *pron* [ME *somewhat*, fr. *som* some + *what*] **1 :** something (as an amount or degree) that is indefinite or unspecified **:** a part, more or less ⟨he told them ~ of his adventures⟩ ⟨neglect ~ of his duty⟩ **2 :** some unspecified, undetermined, or indeterminate thing **:** SOMETHING **3 :** one (as a previously specified person, thing, or action) having to a greater or lesser extent the character, qualities, or nature of something else ⟨he is ~ of a connoisseur⟩ **4 :** one (as a person or thing) that is important or noteworthy
2**somewhat** \"\ *adv* [ME *somwhat*, fr. *somwhat*, pron.] **:** in some degree or measure **:** to a certain slight or small extent **:** a little **:** SLIGHTLY ⟨the terrain roughens ~ as the watershed . . . is approached —*Amer. Guide Series: Texas*⟩ ⟨the total was ~ above earlier estimates⟩ ⟨speech in ~ different words —Edward Sapir⟩ ⟨the ~ ornately styled . . . church —*Amer. Guide Series: N. H.*⟩ ⟨~ at a loss for words⟩
3**somewhat** \"\ *n* -S [1*somewhat*] **1 :** an undetermined or unspecified quality, character, or amount ⟨matter is an unknown ~ —George Berkeley⟩ **2** [trans. of G *etwas*] *Hegelianism* **:** a reality to which belongs negation as a limit **:** a limited reality
somewhen \'⸗,⸗\ *adv* **:** at some time or other **:** at some indefinite or unknown time **:** SOMETIME ⟨born somewhere and ~ —Marvin Farber⟩ ⟨imposed upon somebody, somehow, somewhere, and ~ —William James⟩
1**somewhere** \'⸗(,)⸗\ *adv* [ME *somwher*, fr. *som* some + *wher* where] **1 a :** in or at some place unknown, unspecified, or undetermined **:** in one place or another ⟨a bleak farmhouse ~ in rural America —Harrison Smith⟩ **b :** in a book or other writing **:** in some part of a literary work ⟨makes a reference to it ~⟩ **2 a :** to some unknown or unspecified place ⟨he's ~ gone to dinner —Shak.⟩ ⟨go ~ out of town⟩ **b :** to a place unspecified or unknown but symbolizing positive accomplishment or progress ⟨getting ~ with his program —Michael James⟩ ⟨seemed to feel that the nine days of talks . . . had led ~ —*N. Y. Times*⟩ **3 :** APPROXIMATELY ⟨~ between five million and twenty million more Democrats —R.H.Rovere⟩ ⟨~ about nine o'clock⟩
2**somewhere** \"\ *n* -S **:** an undetermined or unnamed place ⟨to ~ in France⟩
somewheres \'⸗(,)⸗\ *adv* [1*somewhere* + *-s*] *chiefly dial* **:** SOMEWHERE
somewhile \'⸗,⸗\ *adv* [ME *som while*, fr. *som* some + *while*] *archaic* **:** at some unspecified time **:** at one time or another **:** at times **:** SOMETIMES ⟨with which all lives worth living have been ~ brightened —John Nichol⟩
somewhiles \'⸗,⸗\ *adv* [1*some* + *whiles*, pl. of *while*, n.] *archaic* **:** SOMEWHILE
somewhither \'⸗,⸗⸗\ *adv* **:** to some place **:** SOMEWHERE 2a ⟨the poor young king . . . must go ~ —Thomas Carlyle⟩
somewise \'⸗,⸗\ *adv* [ME *somwise*, fr. *som* some + *wise*, n.] **:** SOMEWAY — used chiefly in the phrase *in somewise* ⟨the father's, brother's love — was changed . . . in ~ —D.G. Rossetti⟩
-somi *pl of* -SOMUS
-so·mia \'sōmēə\ *n comb form* -S [NL, fr. 2*soma* + *-ia*] **:** condition of having (such) a body ⟨*nanosomia*⟩
-so·mic \'sōmik, -mēk\ *adj comb form* [ISV 3*-some* + *-ic*] **:** having or being a body of chromosomes of which one or more but not all members exhibit (such) a degree of ploidy ⟨*hexasomic*⟩ ⟨*monosomic*⟩
som·ite \'sō,mīt\ *n* -S [ISV *som-* (fr. Gk *sōma* body) + *-ite* — more at -SOMA] **:** one of the longitudinal series of segments into which the body of many animals (as articulates and vertebrates) is more or less distinctly divided **:** METAMERE — **so·mit·ic** \sō'mid·ik\ *adj*
som·ma \'sämə\ *n* -S [It, summit, sum, fr. L *summa* — more at SUM] **:** the rim of a volcanic crater or caldera
som·me·lier \,səməl'yā\ *n* -S [F, wine steward, butler, fr. MF, court official charged with transportation of supplies, pack animal driver, fr. OProv *saumalier* pack animal driver, fr. *sauma* pack animal, load of a pack animal, fr. (assumed) VL *sauma* packsaddle (whence ML *sauma*), fr. LL *sagma* — more at SUMPTER] **:** a waiter in a restaurant who has charge of wines and their service **:** a wine steward
somnambul- *comb form* [NL, fr. *somnambulus* somnambulist, fr. L *somnus* sleep + *-ambulus* (as in *funambulus* funambulist) — more at SOMNOLENT, FUNAMBULIST] **:** somnambulism **:** somnambulist ⟨*somnambular*⟩
som·nam·bu·lant \säm'nambyələnt\ *adj* [*somnambul-* + *-ant*] **:** walking or addicted to walking while asleep
som·nam·bu·lar \-lə(r)\ *adj* [*somnambul-* + *-ar*] **:** of, relating to, or characterized by somnambulism
som·nam·bu·late \-,lāt, *usu* -ād·+V\ *vi* [*somnambul-* + *-ate*] **:** to walk when asleep
som·nam·bu·la·tion \⸗,⸗⸗'lāshən\ *n* [NL *somnambulation-, somnambulatio*, fr. *somnambul-* + L *-ation-, -atio* -ation] **:** the action of walking in sleep
som·nam·bule \⸗'⸗,byül\ *n* -S [F, fr. NL *somnambulus*] **:** SOMNAMBULIST
som·nam·bu·lic \(')säm'nambyəlik\ *adj* [ISV *somnambul-* + *-ic*] **:** SOMNAMBULISTIC
som·nam·bu·lism \⸗'⸗⸗,lizəm\ *n* -S [NL *somnambulismus*, fr. *somnambul-* + L *-ismus* -ism] **1 :** the action of walking or the performance of other motor acts while asleep and specif. when the actions are not recalled after waking **2 :** an action performed while asleep
som·nam·bu·list \-ləst\ *n* -S [*somnambul-* + *-ist*] **:** one who is subject to somnambulism **:** one who walks in his sleep **:** SLEEPWALKER
som·nam·bu·lis·tic \(')⸗;⸗⸗;listik, -tēk\ *adj* **1 :** of, relating to, or affected by somnambulism ⟨a ~ state⟩ **2 :** of, relating to, or having the characteristics of a somnambulist
som·nam·bu·lis·ti·cal·ly \-tək(ə)lē\ *adv* **:** in the manner of a somnambulist ⟨moves about the stage ~ —Francis Fergusson⟩
somni- *comb form* [L, fr. *somnus*] **:** sleep ⟨*somnifacient*⟩
som·ni·al \'sämnēəl\ *adj* [F, fr. LL *somnialis*, fr. L *somnium* dream + *-alis* -al; akin to L *somnus* sleep] **:** of or relating to sleep or dreams ⟨vivid recollections of . . . bizarre ~ experiences —H.W.Cushing⟩
1**som·ni·fa·cient** \,sämnə'fāshənt\ *adj* [*somni-* + *-facient*] **:** HYPNOTIC 1
2**somnifacient** \"\ *n* **:** HYPNOTIC 1
som·nif·er·ous \(')säm'nif(ə)rəs\ *adj* [L *somnifer* somniferous (fr. *somni-* + *-fer*) + E *-ous* — more at -FER] **:** tending to induce sleep **:** SOPORIFIC ⟨a ~ potion⟩ ⟨~ prose⟩ — **som·nif·er·ous·ly** *adv*
som·nif·ic \(')säm'nifik\ *adj* [L *somnificus*, fr. *somni-* + *-ficus* -fic] **:** SOMNIFEROUS
som·nil·o·quist \säm'niləkwəst\ *n* -S [*somni-* + *-loquist* (as in *ventriloquist*)] **:** one who talks in his sleep
som·nil·o·quy \-kwē\ *n* -ES [ISV *somni-* + *-loquy* (as in E *ventriloquy*)] **:** the action or practice of talking in sleep
som·ni·o·sus \,sämnē'ōsəs\ *n, cap* [NL, fr. LL, sleepy, fr. L *somnium* dream + *-osus* -ose] **:** a genus of sharks (suborder Squaloidea) to which the Greenland shark belongs
som·nip·a·thy \säm'nipəthē\ *n* -ES [ISV *somni-* + *-pathy*] **:** abnormal or disordered sleep (as in a hypnotic state)
som·niv·o·len·cy \⸗'nivələnsē\ *n* -ES [*somni-* + *-volency* (fr. L *volentia* will, inclination, fr. *volent-, volens* — pres. part. of *velle* to will, wish — + *-ia* -y) — more at WILL] **:** SOPORIFIC
som·no·lence \'sämnələn(t)s\ *also* **som·no·len·cy** \-lənsē, -si\ *n, pl* **somnolences** *also* **somnolencies** [*somnolence* fr. ME *sompnolence*, fr. MF, fr. LL *somnolentia*, fr. L *somnolentus* somnolent + *-ia* -y; *somnolency* fr. LL *somnolentia*] **:** inclination to sleep **:** DROWSINESS, SLEEPINESS — compare HYPERSOMNIA
som·no·lent \-lənt\ *adj* [ME *sompnolent*, fr. MF fr. L *somnolentus*, fr. *somnus* sleep; akin to OE *swefn* dream, sleep, OHG *intswebben* to put to sleep, ON *svefn* dream, sleep, Gk *hypnos* sleep, Skt *svapna*] **1 :** tending to induce drowsiness or sleepiness ⟨the sound had a ~ effect⟩ **2 a :** inclined to sleep **:** heavy with sleep **:** DROWSY, SLEEPY ⟨fasting and watching had made him more than usually ~ —R.H.Barham⟩ **b :** marked by sleepiness, drowsiness, or slowness ⟨the ~ river scene⟩ ⟨a ~ country village⟩
som·no·lent·ly *adv* **:** in a somnolent manner **:** DROWSILY
som·no·rif·ic \,sämnə'rifik, -fēk\ *adj* [blend of *somnific* and *soporific*] **:** SOMNIFEROUS
1**so much** *adv* [ME *so muche* (adverb phrase), fr. 1*so* + *muche*, adv., much] **:** by the amount indicated or suggested ⟨if they lose their way, *so much* the better for us⟩
2**so much** *adj* [ME *so muche* (adjective phrase) such a quantity of, fr. 1*so* + *muche*, adj., much] **1 :** of an equal amount — often used as an intensive ⟨the house burned like *so much* paper⟩ **2 :** of an unspecified amount — often used as an intensive ⟨the common notion of a classic or romantic literature is *so much* nonsense —Irving Kolodin⟩
3**so much** *pron* [ME *so muche*, fr. *so muche* (adjective phrase)] **1 :** something (as an amount or price) unspecified or undetermined ⟨charge *so much* a mile⟩ **2 :** that is all that can be or is to be said or done now ⟨*so much* for the history of the case⟩
so much as *adv* [ME *so muche as*, fr. *so muche* (adverb phrase) + *as*] **:** EVEN ⟨cannot recall that . . . their descendants were *so much as* mentioned in all that time —R.H.Shryock⟩
-so·mus \'sōməs\ *n comb form, pl* **-so·mi** \-,mī\ *or* **-somuses** [NL, fr. Gk *sōma* body — more at -SOMA] **:** one having (such) a body or (so many) bodies ⟨*disomus*⟩ ⟨*nanosomus*⟩
1**son** \'sən\ *n* -S [ME *sone*, fr. OE *sunu*; akin to OHG *sun* son, ON *sonr*, Goth *sunus*, Gk *hyios*, Skt *sūnu* son, *sūte* he begets] **1 a :** the male offspring of human beings ⟨a family consisting of two ~*s*⟩ **b :** a male child ⟨a playground for the ~*s* and daughters of the community⟩ **c :** a male who assumes the role or status of the offspring of human parents (as an adopted child or son-in-law) **d :** a male descendant — usu. used in pl. ⟨the modern-day ~*s* of early pioneers⟩ **2** *cap* **:** the second person of the Trinity **3 :** the male offspring of an animal (as a horse or dog) **4 :** a person closely associated with or deriving from a nation, school, race, belief, or any other formative agent ⟨a nation robbed by war of most of her ~*s*⟩ — often used with *of* ⟨the ~*s* of modern technology⟩
2**son** \'sōn\ *n, pl* **so·nes** \'sō(,)nās\ [AmerSp, fr. Sp, sound, prob. fr. OProv, fr. L *sonus*] **1 :** a folk song of Cuba, Mexico, and Central America **2 a :** a Latin American ballroom dance popular in Cuba and coastal Mexico **b :** the musical accompaniment of such a dance
son- *or* **soni-** *or* **sono-** *comb form* [L *son-, soni-*, fr. *sonus* — more at SOUND] **:** sound ⟨*sonal*⟩ ⟨*sonification*⟩ ⟨*sonobuoy*⟩
son *abbr* **1** sonata **2** southern
so·na·ble \'sōnəbəl\ *adj* [L *sonabilis* noisy, fr. *sonare* to sound + *-bilis* -able] **:** that may be sounded
so·nal \'sōnᵊl\ *adj* [*son-* + *-al*] **:** SONIC — **so·nal·ly** \-nᵊlē\ *adv*
so·nance \'sōnən(t)s\ *n* -S [L *sonare* + E *-ance*] **:** SOUND, SONANCY ⟨the far-off mellow ~ of a cowbell —Edna Ferber⟩
so·nan·cy \-nənsē, -si\ *n* -ES [1*sonant* + *-cy*] **:** the quality or state of being sonant
1**so·nant** \-nənt\ *adj* [L *sonant-, sonans*, pres. part. of *sonare* to sound — more at SOUND] **1** *of a speech sound* **:** VOICED — opposed to *surd* **2** *of a consonant* **:** SYLLABIC
2**sonant** \"\ *n* -S **1 :** a voiced sound **2 :** a syllabic consonant
so·nan·tic \sō'nantik\ *adj, of a consonant* **:** SYLLABIC
so·nant·ize \'sōnən,tīz\ *vt* -ED/-ING/-S **:** VOICE
1**sonant–surd** \'⸗⸗;⸗\ *adj, of a sound* **:** beginning voiced and ending voiceless
2**sonant–surd** \"\ *n* **:** a sonant-surd sound
1**so·nar** \sō'när\ *n* -S [Hindi *sonār*, fr. Skt *suvarṇakāra*, fr. *suvarṇa* gold (fr. *su-* good + *varṇa* color) + *-kāra* worker (fr. *kr̥noti* he makes); prob. akin to Skt *vr̥noti* he covers, holds back — more at WEIR, KARMA] **:** a member of a Hindu artisan caste of goldsmiths and silversmiths
2**so·nar** \'sō,när, -nȧ(r\ *n* -S [*so*und *n*avigation *r*anging] **:** an apparatus that detects the presence and location of a submerged object (as a submarine or underwater mine) by means of sonic and ultrasonic waves which are reflected back to it from the object — compare ECHO RANGING, SOUND RANGING
sonar·man \'⸗,⸗mən\ *n, pl* **sonarmen :** an enlisted man in the navy who operates sonar equipment
so·na·ta \sə'näd·ə, -ätə\ *n* -S [It, fr. *sonare* to sound, fr. L] **:** an instrumental musical composition: as **a :** an early instrumental composition in movements without characteristic structure — see SONATA DA CHIESA, SONATA DA CAMERA **b :** an extended composition for one or two instruments usu. in three or four movements which are contrasted in rhythm and mood but related in tonality and which usu. have an organic unity of sentiment and style — compare SONATA FORM
sonata da cam·era \-də'kam(ə)rə\ *n* [It, lit., chamber sonata] **:** a 17th and 18th century instrumental composition for two or more instruments with continuo consisting chiefly of dance movements
sonata da chie·sa \-dākē'āzə\ *n* [It, lit., church sonata] **:** a 17th and 18th century instrumental composition for two or more instruments with continuo usu. in four movements of which one or more are in fugato style
sonata form *n* **1 :** the musical form of a sonata used not only in the sonata proper but also in the concerto, symphony, and string quartet and other chamber music **2 :** a type of musical structure distinctive of the first movement of the sonata usu. based on two themes or subjects presented in different keys often with transitional episodes and consisting of an exposition giving the principal subject in the tonic key and the secondary subject usu. in the dominant key if the tonic key is major but otherwise in the relative key, a development giving a full thematic working out of one or both subjects, and a recapitulation repeating both subjects in the original key and ending with a coda
son·a·ti·na \,sänə'tēnə\ *also* **son·a·tine** \,sänə'tēn\ *n, pl* **sonatinas** \-'tēnəz\ *or* **sonati·ne** \,⸗⸗'tē(,)nā\ *also* **sonatines** \⸗⸗'tēnz\ [*sonatina* fr. It, dim. of *sonata*; *sonatine* fr. F, fr. It *sonatina*] **:** a short condensed sonata usu. with little or no development section
so·na·tion \sō'nāshən\ *n* -S [ML *sonation-, sonatio*, fr. L *sonatus* (past part. of *sonare* to sound) + *-ion-, -io* -ion] **:** a giving forth of sound **:** SOUNDING
son·chus \'säŋkəs\ *n, cap* [NL, fr. L, sow thistle, fr. Gk *sonchos*] **:** a genus of Old World herbs (family Compositae) comprising the sow thistles and having coarse often spiny-tipped foliage, heads of yellow flowers, and ribbed achenes crowned with soft white pappus
son·dage \(')sän;däzh\ *n, pl* **son·dages** \-zh(əz)\ [F, lit., sounding, fr. *sonder* to sound + *-age* — more at SOUND] **:** a sounding of the earth (as by boring or digging) preliminary to archaeological excavation **:** a trial excavation
sonde \'sänd\ *n* -S [F, lit., sounding line — more at SOUND] **:** any of various devices for testing physical and meteorological conditions at high altitudes above the earth's surface
son·de·li \sän'dälē\ *n* -S [Kannada *sonḍili*, fr. *sunḍa* muskshrew + *ili* rat] **:** MUSKSHREW 1
sone \'sōn\ *n* -S [ISV, fr. L *sonus* sound — more at SOUND] **:** a subjective unit of loudness for a given listener equal to the loudness of a 1000-cycle sound that has an intensity 40 decibels above the listener's own threshold
sones *pl of* SON
song \'sȯŋ *also* 'säŋ\ *n* -S [ME *song, sang*, fr. OE; akin to OHG *sang* song, ON *söngr*, Goth *sangws* song, OE *singan* to sing — more at SING] **1 a :** the act of singing ⟨rejoice in ~⟩ **b :** the art of making or singing vocal compositions ⟨a people famous for their ~⟩ **2 :** poetical composition ⟨a hero honored in ~ and story⟩ **3 a :** a short musical composition made up of mutually dependent words and music which together produce a unique aesthetic response — compare LIED **b :** a group or collection of such compositions ⟨gather and preserve popular ~ —Louise Pound⟩ **4 :** a distinctive sound **:** characteristic noise ⟨the ~ of the wind⟩ ⟨the ~ of birds⟩ **5 a :** a melody or musical setting for a lyric poem or ballad ⟨whistle a ~⟩ **b :** an instrumental composition displaying or suggesting the technique or quality of vocal music **6 a :** the words that are sung with or belong to a particular musical composition **:** LYRICS **b :** a poem of limited length often stanzaic and easily set to music ⟨Shakespeare's ~*s*⟩ **7 a :** a habitual, temperamental, or characteristic manner (as of speaking, reacting, or arguing) ⟨the same old ~ of the party politician⟩ **b :** a violent, abusive, or noisy reaction ⟨put up quite a ~⟩ **8 :** a small amount — used with *for* ⟨a house that sold for a ~⟩
song and dance *n* **1 :** a theatrical performance (as a vaudeville act) combining singing and dancing **2 :** a statement or explanation interesting in itself but not necessarily true or pertinent ⟨gave me a *song and dance* about how busy he was⟩
songbird \'⸗,⸗\ *n* **1 :** a bird that utters a succession of musical tones; *esp* **:** a bird of the suborder Passeres **2 :** a female singer
songbook \'⸗,⸗\ *n* **:** a collection of songs; *specif* **:** a book of hymns or other vocal music
song box *n* **:** SYRINX 3
songcraft \'⸗,⸗\ *n* **:** the art of making songs or verses
song cycle *n* **:** a group of songs based on the same general subject or having some other unifying feature
songfest \'⸗,⸗\ *n* **:** an informal session of group singing of popular or folk songs
song form *n* **:** the form of a song, dance, or similar short musical composition in binary or ternary measure
song·ful \'⸗fəl\ *adj* **:** of or relating to singing **:** MELODIOUS — **song·ful·ly** \-fəlē, -li\ *adv* — **song·ful·ness** \-lnəs\ *n* -ES
son·ghai \säŋ'gī\ *also* **son·ghoi** *or* **son·goi** \-'gȯi\ *or* **songhay** \-'gī\ *n, pl* **songhai** *or* **songhais** *usu cap* **1 a :** a Sudanese people living below Timbuktu in the bend of the Niger that are mostly Muslim **b :** a member of such people **2 :** the language of the Songhai people used widely as a language of commerce throughout the middle Niger valley **3 :** a language family consisting only of Songhai and a few closely related languages or dialects (as perhaps Dyerma)
son·gish *also* **son·geesh** \säŋ'gēsh\ *n, pl* **songish** *or* **songishes** *also* **songeesh** *or* **songeeshes** *usu cap* **1 a :** a Salishan people of Vancouver Island and San Juan Island, Wash. **b :** a member of such people **2 :** the language of the Songish people
son·gle \'säŋgəl\ *n* -S [perh. alter. of E dial. (northern) *single* handful of gleaned grain, fr. E 2*single*] **1** *dial Eng* **:** a handful of gleaned grain **2** *dial Eng* **:** a small quantity
song·less \'⸗ləs\ *adj* **:** lacking in, incapable of, or not given to song — **song·less·ly** *adv*
song·let \'⸗lət\ *n* -S **:** a little song
songlike \'⸗,⸗\ *adj* **:** resembling or suggestive of song

song·man \ˈ≈,mən\ *n, pl* **songmen** : a male choir singer
song of ascents *also* **song of degrees** *usu cap S&A&D* : any one of 15 psalms in the series Ps 120 to 134 sung by Hebrew pilgrims on their way to Jerusalem or possibly while ascending Mount Zion or the steps of the Temple — called also *Gradual Psalm, Pilgrim Psalm, Psalm of Ascents*
son·go fever \ˈsȯŋ(,)gō-, ˈsäŋ\ *n* [*Songo* river, Manchuria, where it was observed among Japanese soldiers in 1939] : epidemic hemorrhagic fever
songs *pl of* SONG
songsmith \ˈ≈,≈\ *n* : a composer of songs
song sparrow *n* **1** : a common sparrow (*Melospiza melodia*) of eastern No. America about six inches long that is brownish above and white below with brownish streaks on the breast forming a blotch in the center and that is noted for its melodious song **2** : any of several western No. American birds that are varieties of the song sparrow and range from Alaska to Mexico
song·ster \ˈsȯŋztə(r), -ŋ(k)st- *also* ˈsäŋ-\ *n* -s [ME, singer, fr. OE *sangestre* woman singer, fr. *sang* song + *-estre* female agent — more at -STER] **1** : one that is skilled in song; *specif* : POET **2** : SONGBOOK; *esp* : a songbook containing popular songs
song·stress \-trəs\ *n* -ES [*songster* + *-ess*] : a female singer esp. of jazz
song thrush *n* **1** : an Old World thrush (*Turdus ericetorum*) that is olivaceous brown above and white below, tinged with buff on the breast, and spotted with blackish brown on the breast and sides — called also *mavis, throstle* **2** : WOOD THRUSH 1
songwriter \ˈ≈,≈≈\ *n* : a person who composes words or music or both esp. for popular songs
soni- — see SON-
son·ic \ˈsänik, -nēk\ *adj* [*son-* + *-ic*] **1** : having a frequency within the audibility range of the human ear — used of waves and vibrations; compare INFRASONIC, SUPERSONIC **2** : utilizing, produced by, or relating to sound waves ⟨~ altimeter⟩ **3** : of, indicating, or relating to the speed of sound in air : having a speed in air of about 1087 feet per second or about 741 miles per hour at sea level — compare HYPERSONIC, SUBSONIC, SUPERSONIC, TRANSONIC **4** : capable of uttering sounds — **son·i·cal·ly** \-nək(ə)lē, -nēk-, -li\ *adv*
sonic barrier *n* : a sudden large increase in aerodynamic drag that occurs as the speed of an aircraft approaches the speed of sound and that is no longer an insurmountable obstacle to traveling faster than sound
sonic boom *n* : a sound resembling an explosion produced when a shock wave formed at the nose of an aircraft traveling at supersonic speed reaches the ground
sonic depth finder *n* : an instrument for determining the depth of a body of water or of an object below the surface by measuring the interval of time between the emission of a sound signal and the return of its echo from the bottom or the object
sonic mine *n* : a naval mine actuated by the sound of a ship's propeller or by the noise of water streaming along the hull
son·ics \ˈsäniks, -nēks\ *n pl but usu sing in constr* : acoustics esp. in its technological and supersonic aspects
so·nif·er·ous \səˈnif(ə)rəs, sōˈ-\ *adj* [*son-* + *-ferous*] : producing or conducting sound ⟨~ marine animals⟩
son·i·fi·ca·tion \,sänəfəˈkāshən\ *n* -s [*son-* + *-fication*] : the act or process of producing sound (as the stridulation of insects)
son–in–law \ˈ≈≈,≈\ *n, pl* **sons–in–law** [ME *sone in lawe*] : the husband of one's daughter
son·less \ˈ≈ləs\ *adj* : not possessing, bereft of, or never having had a son
son·ly *adj* : FILIAL
son·ne camera \ˈsänə-\ *n* [after Fred J. *Sonne* †1965 Am. engineer] : STRIP CAMERA
son·ne·ra·tia \,sänəˈrāsh(ē)ə\ *n, cap* [NL, fr. Pierre *Sonnerat* †1814 Fr. naturalist + NL *-ia*] : a genus (the type of the family Sonneratiaceae) of trees and shrubs having large flowers shaped like bells and succeeded by pulpy berries which in some members (as *S. acida*) are used as a condiment in India — see KAMBALA, PAGATPAT
son·ne·ra·ti·a·ce·ae \,≈≈,≈shēˈāsē,ē\ *n pl, cap* [NL, fr. *Sonneratia*, type genus + *-aceae*] : a small family of tropical trees and shrubs (order Myrtales) having opposite leaves, large flowers with indefinite stamens, and pulpy often edible fruit
¹**son·net** \ˈsänət, *usu* -əd·+V\ *n* -s [It *sonetto*, fr. OProv *sonet* little song, fr. *son* song, sound (fr. L *sonus* sound) + *-et* — more at SOUND] **1** : a fixed verse form of Italian origin consisting of fourteen lines that are typically five-foot iambics rhyming according to a prescribed scheme; *also* : a poem in this pattern or more or less conforming to it — compare CURTAL SONNET, ENGLISH SONNET, PETRARCHAN SONNET, SPENSERIAN SONNET, TAILED SONNET **2** *obs* : a short usu. amatory poem
²**sonnet** \ˈ"\ *vb* **sonneted** *or* **sonnetted**; **sonneted** *or* **sonnetted**; **sonneting** *or* **sonnetting**; **sonnets** : SONNETIZE
¹**son·ne·teer** \,sänəˈti(ə)r, -iə\ *n* -s [alter. (influenced by *-eer*) of earlier *sonnettier*, modif. (influenced by E ¹*sonnet*) of It *sonettiere*, fr. *sonetto* sonnet] **1** : a composer of sonnets **2** : a minor or insignificant poet
²**sonneteer** \ˈ"\ *vb* -ED/-ING/-S : SONNETIZE
son·net·ist \ˈsänəd·əst\ *n* -s : SONNETEER
son·net·ize \-ə,tīz\ *vb* -ED/-ING/-S *vi* : to compose a sonnet ~ *vt* : to compose a sonnet on or to
son·net·ry \ˈsänə·trē\ *n* -ES *archaic* **1** : poetry in sonnet form **2** : the writing of sonnets
sonnet sequence *n* : a series of sonnets often having a unifying theme
son·ny \ˈsənē, -ni\ *n* -ES [¹*son* + *-y*] : a young boy — used chiefly as a term of address
sono- — see SON-
son·o·buoy \ˈsänə+,-\ *n* [*son-* + *buoy*] : a buoy equipped with a hydrophone for detecting underwater sounds and an automatic radio transmitter for transmitting the sounds and developed as a submarine detector to be dropped by parachute from aircraft for transmitting the coded sounds of submerged submarines to air and surface craft
son of a bitch *n, pl* **sons of bitches** : BASTARD 7 — sometimes considered vulgar; sometimes used interjectionally to express surprise or keen disappointment
son of a gun *n, pl* **sons of guns** **1** : SON OF A BITCH — sometimes used interjectionally **2** : a small firework in the form of a tablet that emits a loud crackling sound when scraped on a rough surface
son of god [ME *sone of God*] **1** *often cap S & cap G* : a superhuman or divine being; *specif* : an angel **2** *cap S&G* : God's Messiah — often used as a messianic title ⟨Jesus Christ, the *Son of God*⟩ **3** *cap G* : a person established in the love of God through acceptance of the divine will and guidance ⟨for all who are led by the Spirit of God are *sons of God* —Rom 8:14 (RSV)⟩ **4** *cap G* : an individual viewed in relation to God the Father
son of heaven *usu cap S&H* [trans. of Chin (Pek) *tien*¹ *tzu*³] : one of the former emperors of China
son of man [ME *sone of man*] **1** : a human being : MORTAL **2** *often cap S & sometimes cap M* : God's Messiah; *esp* : God's divine representative destined to preside over the final judgment of the world ⟨the coming of the Messiah, the *son of man*⟩
sono·graph \ˈsänə,graf\ *n* [ISV *son-* + *-graph*] : an apparatus by which sounds or seismic vibrations are recorded or translated into arbitrary phonetic symbols
son·o·luminescence \,≈≈+\ *n* [*son-* + *luminescence*] : the emission of light by various liquids when traversed by high-frequency sound or ultrasonic waves of suitable intensity
so·no·ma oak \səˈnōmə-\ *n, usu cap S* [*Sonoma* County, Calif.] : CALIFORNIA BLACK OAK
so·nom·e·ter \səˈnäməd·ə(r), -ətə-\ *n* [ISV *son-* + *-meter*] **1** : MONOCHORD **2** : AUDIOMETER
son·o–radio buoy \ˈsä(,)nō-\ *n* [*son-* + *radio* + *buoy*] : SONOBUOY
so·no·ra gum \səˈnōrə, -nȯrə-\ *n, usu cap S* [*Sonora*, state in northwest Mexico] : the acidulous gum resin of the creosote bush
sonora ironwood *n, usu cap S* : DESERT IRONWOOD
sonora lac *n, usu cap S* : a substance that resembles lac, is secreted by a scale (*Tachardiella mexicana*) living on the twigs of several Mexican leguminous shrubs, and is used locally for medicine
¹**so·no·ran** \səˈnōrən, -nȯr-\ *adj, usu cap* [*Sonora* + E *-an*] **1** : relating to, situated in, inhabiting, or coming from Sonora **2** : PIMAN 1 **3** : of, relating to, or being the arid division of the Austral biogeographic zone that includes the warmer parts of the western U. S. and central Mexico — see LOWER SONORAN, UPPER SONORAN
²**sonoran** \ˈ"\ *n* -s *cap* : a native or inhabitant of Sonora
sonoran coral snake *n, usu cap 1st S* : a coral snake (*Micrurus euryxanthus* or *Micruroides euryxanthus*) of western Mexico and the U. S. north to Colorado and Utah
so·no·rant \səˈnōrənt, -nȯr-\ *n* -s [*sonorous* + *-ant* (as in ²*sonant*)] **1** : RESONANT **2** : a nonvocalic resonant sometimes with the exclusion of \r\, \y\, and \w\
son·o·rif·er·ous \,sänəˈrif(ə)rəs\ *adj* [L *sonor* sound + E *-iferous*; akin to L *sonus* sound] : SONIFEROUS; *also* : RESOUNDING — **son·o·rif·er·ous·ly** *adv*
so·nor·i·ty \səˈnȯrəd·ē, -när-, -rətē, -i *sometimes* -nōr-\ *n* -ES [ML *sonoritat-, sonoritas*, fr. LL, melody, fr. L *sonorus* + *-itat-, -itas* -ity] **1 a** : the quality or state of being sonorous : SONOROUSNESS, RESONANCE **b** : a sonorous tone or speech **2** : the perceptibility or distinctness of speech sounds when spoken in a context in which stress, pitch, and sound duration are constant ⟨vowels possessing greater ~ than consonants⟩
son·o·riza·tion \,sänərəˈzāshən, -,rīˈz-\ *n* -s [It *sonorizzazione*, fr. *sonorizzare* to sonorize + *-azione* -ation] : VOICING ⟨~ of intervocalic consonants⟩
son·o·rize \ˈ≈≈,rīz\ *vb* -ED/-ING/-S [It *sonorizzare*, fr. *sonoro* sonorous, voiced (fr. L *sonorus* sonorous) + *-izzare* -ize] : VOICE — used esp. of intervocalic consonants in Italian
sono·rous \səˈnōrəs, -ˈnȯr-, ˈsänər-\ *adj* [L *sonorus*; akin to L *sonus* sound — more at SOUND] **1 a** : producing sound (as when struck) ⟨~ metals⟩ **b** : marked by or productive of loud sounds : NOISY ⟨a ~ water fall⟩ **2** : characterized by full or loud sound often with clear or rich tone, marked volume, or easy audibility ⟨a herald chosen for his ~ voice —J.G.Frazer⟩ **3 a** : marked by imposing or impressive effect or style ⟨the ~ sureness of pure philosophy —J.P.Marquand⟩ **b** : marked by excessively heavy high-flown grandiloquent or self-assured effect or style ⟨the cosmic poet, who indulges in vague generalities, magnificent and ~, about his universe —J.L.Lowes⟩ **4** : having a high or an indicated degree of sonority or number of sounds evaluated for sonority ⟨~ sounds like \ä\ and \ȯ\⟩ ⟨one of the least ~ of languages⟩ **syn** see RESONANT
sonorous figures *n pl* : figures (as the geometrical figures of sand on a plate of glass or metal when the bow of a violin is drawn along the edge) formed by the vibrations of a substance emitting a musical tone — called also *Chladni figures*
sono·rous·ly *adv* : in a sonorous manner ⟨a politician who spoke ~⟩
sono·rous·ness *n* -ES : the quality or state of being sonorous ⟨scores of phrases of splendid and empty ~ —S.H.Adams⟩
so·no·vox \ˈsōnə,väks\ *n* -ES [*son-* + L *vox* voice — more at VOICE] : a device that transmits to the larynx recorded human or nonhuman sound whose vibrations substitute prosthetically or for unusual effect for those of the vocal cords
¹**sons** *pl of* SON
²**sons** *also* **sonse** \ˈsän(t)s\ *n* [partly fr. ME (Sc) *sons*, of Celt origin; akin to ScGael & IrGael *sonas* good fortune; partly fr. IrGael *sonas*] **1** *chiefly Scot* : health and happiness, good fortune, luck **2** *chiefly Scot* : ABUNDANCE, PLENTY
³**sons** \ˈsōnz\ *Scot var of* SOWENS
son·ship \ˈ≈,ship\ *n* : the relationship of son to father ⟨it at least brought a deepened realization of the significance of his ~ to God —K.S.Latourette⟩
son·stadt solution \ˈsän,stat-\ *n, usu cap S* [after E. *Sonstadt*, 19th cent. Eng. chemist] : a heavy solution of mercuric iodide in potassium iodide having a maximum specific gravity of 3.2 — called also *Thoulet solution*
sonsy *or* **son·sie** \ˈsän(t)sē\ *adj* [²*sons* + *-y*] **1** *chiefly dial* : bringing or having good fortune : LUCKY **2** *chiefly dial* : attractively buxom : COMELY **3** *chiefly dial* : cheerfully genial **4** *chiefly dial* : comfortably relaxed
son·tag \ˈsän,tag\ *n* -s [after Henriette *Sontag* †1854 Ger. vocalist] : a crocheted or knitted cape with long ends crossed in front and fastened at the back
soo·chow *or* **su·chow** \ˈsü;chaü, -ü;jō\ *adj, usu cap* [fr. *Soochow* (*Suchow*), China] : of or from the city of Soochow in Kiangsu province, China : of the kind or style prevalent in Soochow
soodra *var of* SUDRA
soo·ey \ˈsüē, -üi\ *v imper* [prob. alter. of ¹*sow*] — used as a call to pigs
soogan *var of* SUGAN
¹**soo·gee** \ˈsüjē\ *vb* -ED/-ING/-S [perh. fr. Jap *sōji* cleaning] : to wash down (as the deck and paintwork of a ship) ⟨have his boys ~ the galley —Richard Bissell⟩
²**soogee** \ˈ"\ *n* -s : clean rope yarns used to wash with
soojee *var of* SUJI
sook \ˈsük\ *or* **sook·ie** \-kē,-ki\ *v imper* [alter. of ¹*suck*] *dial* — used as a call to cows
sool \ˈsül\ *vt* -ED/-ING/-S [fr. dial. Brit *sowl, sole, sool* to pull by the ears, of unknown origin] **1** *Austral* : to incite (as a dog) to attack : SIC **2** *Austral* : to urge on
soo·la clover \ˈsülə\ *n* [*soola* modif. of Sp *sulla* — more at SULLA] : SULLA
soo markee *var of* SOU MARKEE
¹**soon** \ˈsün, ˈsün\ *adv* -ER/-EST [ME *sone, soone*, fr. OE *sōna*; akin to OFris *sōn* immediately, OS & OHG *sān, sāno*] **1 a** : at once : without delay : IMMEDIATELY ⟨no ~*er* said than done⟩ **b** : before long : without undue time lapse ⟨smoke ~ disappears⟩ ⟨~ after sunrise⟩ ⟨results were ~ evident⟩ **2** : PROMPTLY, SPEEDILY, QUICKLY ⟨as ~ as possible⟩ ⟨the more help, the ~*er* done⟩ **3** : before the usual, expected, appointed, or actual time ⟨spring came ~ this year⟩ **4** : READILY, WILLINGLY ⟨as ~ walk as ride⟩ ⟨~*er* stay than go⟩ **5** : REASONABLY, ASSUREDLY, CERTAINLY ⟨as ~ expect a call from him as from anyone else⟩
²**soon** \ˈ"\ *adj* -ER/-EST [ME *sone, soone*, fr. *sone, soone*, adj.] **1** *chiefly dial* : EARLY **2** *archaic* : FAST, QUICK
soon·er \ˈsü·nə(r)\ *n* -s [fr. *sooner*, compar. of ¹*soon*] **1** : a person settling on land in the early West before the official date of its being opened to settlement with a view to gaining the prior claim allowed by law to the first settler after the official opening **2** *usu cap* : OKLAHOMAN — used as a nickname
sooner or later *adv* : at some uncertain future time : SOMETIME
soop \ˈsüp\ *vb* [of Scand origin; akin to ON *sōpa* to sweep; akin to OE *swāpan* to sweep — more at SWOOP] *chiefly Scot* : SWEEP
¹**soor** \ˈsü(ə)r\ *chiefly Scot var of* SOUR
²**soor** \ˈsü(ə)r\ *n* -s [origin unknown] : ²THRUSH
soor·kee *or* **soor·ki** *or* **soor·ky** \ˈsürkē\ *n, pl* **soorkees** *or* **soorkis** *or* **soorkies** [Hindi *surkhī*, fr. Per *surkhī*, lit., redness, fr. *surkh* red, fr. MPer *sukhr*; akin to Av *suxra-* bright, Skt *śukra*] *India* : brick pulverized and mixed with lime to form a mortar
soorma *var of* SURMA
¹**soot** \ˈsu̇t *also* ÷ˈsəl *or* ˈsül; *usu* |d·+V\ *n* -s [ME *sot, soot*, fr. OE *sōt*; akin to MLG & ON *sōt* soot, MD *soet*, OIr *sūide*, Lith *suodžiai* (pl.) soot, OE *sittan* to sit — more at SIT] **1** : a black substance formed by combustion or separated from fuel during combustion, rising in fine particles, and adhering to the sides of the chimney or pipe conveying the smoke; *esp* : the fine powder consisting chiefly of carbon that colors smoke and is the result of incomplete combustion — compare FLY ASH **2** : SOOTY BLACK
²**soot** \ˈ"\ *vt* -ED/-ING/-S : to coat, cover, or spread with soot : smudge or soil with soot
soot blowing *n* : removal of soot deposits on the tubes of a steam generator by a blast of air or steam
soot brown *n* : a grayish brown to yellowish brown that is stronger and slightly darker than mummy brown (sense 2b) and very slightly paler than gold bronze — called also *bister, pinecone, teakwood*
soot·er \|d·ə(r), ˈtə-\ *n* -s [¹*soot* + *-er*] : one that removes soot (as from the outside of a boiler)
soot·er·kin \ˈsüd·ə(r)kən, ˈsüd·-\ *n* -s [prob. fr. (assumed) D dial. *zoetkijn*, dim. of D dial. *zoet* soot, fr. MD *soet* — more at SOOT] **1** : an afterbirth formerly held to be produced by Dutch women ⟨delivered of a ~ not unlike to a rat —John Cleveland⟩ **2** : something that is imperfect or unsuccessful; *esp* : an imperfect literary composition ⟨fruits of dull heat and ~s of wit —Alexander Pope⟩ **3** *archaic* : DUTCHMAN
sootfall \ˈ≈,≈\ *n* : the descent of soot from an atmosphere contaminated with smokestack gases and dusts
¹**sooth** \ˈsüth\ *adj* -ER/-EST [ME *soth, sooth*, fr. OE *sōth*; akin to OHG *sand* true, ON *sannr* true, Goth *sunja* truth, Gk *eteos* true, Skt *sant, sat* being, existing, true, good, *satya* true, right, L *esse* to be — more at IS] **1** *archaic* : agreeing with or telling the truth **2** *archaic* : SOFT, SWEET
²**sooth** \ˈ"\ *n* -s [ME *soth, sooth*, fr. OE *sōth*, fr. neut. of *sōth*, adj.] **1** *archaic* **a** : TRUTH, REALITY **b** : FACT; *also* : TRUISM — used interjectionally **2** *obs* : CAJOLERY, BLANDISHMENT
soothe \ˈsüth\ *vb* -ED/-ING/-S [ME *sothen*, fr. OE *sōthian*, fr. *sōth*, adj.] *vt* **1** *obs* : to show, assert, or confirm the truth of : demonstrate or maintain as true **2** *obs* **a** : to uphold or back up; *also* : to humor by complying **b** : to gloss over : PALLIATE, EXTENUATE **3 a** : to please (a person) by or as if by attention or concern : PLACATE, MOLLIFY ⟨~ an angry crowd with promises⟩ **b** : to assuage or relieve as if by softening : ALLEVIATE ⟨~ an inflamed throat⟩ **4 a** : to bring comfort, solace, or reassurance to ⟨~ a troubled mind⟩ **b** : to lead to tranquility or equanimity : dispel the inner agitation of ⟨music's *soothing* of the mind⟩ ⟨~ a frightened child⟩ ~ *vi* : to bring peace, composure, or quietude **syn** see CALM
¹**sooth·er** \-thə(r)\ *n* -s [*soothe* + *-er* (n. suffix)] : one (as a flatterer) that soothes
²**sooth·er** \ˈsüthə(r), ˈsüth-\ *vt* [*soothe* + *-er* (freq. suffix)] **1** *dial* : SOOTHE **2** *dial* : COAX, FLATTER
soothfast \ˈ≈,≈\ *adj* [ME *sothfast, soothfast*, fr. OE *sōthfæst*, fr. *sōth* true + *fæst* fast — more at SOOTH, FAST] **1** *archaic* : firmly fixed in or founded on the truth : REAL, TRUE **2** *archaic* : TRUTHFUL
sooth·ful \ˈsüthfəl\ *adj* [ME *sothfol*, fr. *soth, sooth* truth + *-fol, -ful* -ful — more at SOOTH] *archaic* : TRUE, RELIABLE
soothing *adj* [fr. pres. part. of *soothe*] : having a quieting or sedative effect : CALMING, TRANQUILIZING ⟨~ syrup⟩ — **sooth·ing·ly** *adv* — **sooth·ing·ness** *n* -ES
sooth·less \ˈsüthləs\ *adj* [²*sooth* + *-less*] *archaic* : lacking in faith or fidelity : TREACHEROUS, FALSE
sooth·ly \-thlē\ *adv* [ME *sothly, soothly*, fr. OE *sōthlīce*, fr. *sōthlīc*, adj., true, truthful, fr. *sōth* true + *-līc* -ly — more at SOOTH] *archaic* : in truth : TRULY
¹**sooth·say** \ˈsüth,sā *sometimes* -th-\ *n* -s [back-formation fr. *soothsayer*] **1** : PROVERB **2** : PROPHECY, SOOTHSAYING **3** : OMEN, PORTENT
²**soothsay** \ˈ"\ *vi* **sooth·said** \-,sed\ **soothsaid**; **sooth·say·ing** \-,sāiŋ\ **sooth·says** \-,sez\ [back-formation fr. *soothsayer*] : to practice soothsaying : PREDICT, FORETELL
sooth·say·er \-,sāə(r), -,se(ə)r, -,seə\ *n* [ME *sothseyer*, fr. *soth, sooth* truth + *seyer, sayer* sayer — more at SOOTH, SAYER] **1** : a speaker of truth or wisdom; *esp* : PROGNOSTICATOR **2** : MANTIS
sooth·say·ing \-,sāiŋ\ *n* [²*sooth* + *saying*] **1** : the act of foretelling events **2** : PREDICTION, PROPHECY
soot·i·ly *pronunc at* ¹SOOT +ᵊlē, əl|, |i\ *adv* : in a sooty manner
soot·i·ness *pronunc at* ¹SOOT +ēnəs, in-\ *n* -ES : the quality or state of being sooty
sooting *pres part of* SOOT
soot·less *pronunc at* ¹SOOT +ləs\ *adj* : lacking or not producing soot
sootlike \ˈ≈,≈\ *adj* : resembling soot ⟨a black ~ material⟩
soots *pl of* SOOT, *pres 3d sing of* SOOT
¹**sooty** *pronunc at* ¹SOOT +ē,i\ *adj* -ER/-EST [ME *soty, sooty*, fr. *sot, soot* soot + *-y*] **1 a** : of or relating to soot : producing soot ⟨~ fires⟩ **b** : soiled or smutted with soot ⟨~ buildings⟩ **2** : of a dark color varying from soot brown to sooty black
²**sooty** \ˈ"\ *vt* -ED/-ING/-ES : to cover or soil with soot ⟨*sootied* clothing⟩
sooty albatross *n* : either of two dark-colored albatrosses (genus *Phoebetria*) common in far southern seas
sooty black *also* **soot** *n* : a nearly neutral slightly purplish black that is very slightly redder and lighter than slate black
sooty blotch *n* : a disease of apples and pears caused by an imperfect fungus (*Gloeodes pomigena*) and characterized by sooty blotches on the fruit
sooty kangaroo *n* : a large dark kangaroo (*Macropus fuliginosus*) found only on the Australian Kangaroo Island preserve
sooty mangabey *n* : a dark gray monkey (*Cercocebus fuliginosus*) of West Africa
sooty mold *n* **1** : a dark or black velvety coating of mycelium of various fungi growing in insect honeydew on the leaves, fruit, or other exposed parts of plants, when heavy often interfering with the normal metabolism of the plant, and being esp. common on plants of the genus *Citrus* **2** : a fungus (as members of the family Capnodiaceae and Meliolaceae) that causes or develops as a sooty mold on plants
sooty ore *n* : a black copper ore that is an impure form of chalcocite
sooty shearwater *or* **sooty petrel** *n* : a brownish black shearwater (*Puffinus griseus*) of the south Pacific that migrates in the nonbreeding season to the north Atlantic and north Pacific
sooty stripe *n* : a disease of sorghums caused by a fungus (*Ramulispora sorghi*) and characterized by elongate elliptic lesions which become sooty black as the sclerotia of the fungus develop
sooty tern *n* : a tern (*Sterna fuscata*) that is widely distributed on tropical coasts and is blackish above and white below
sooty wing *n* : a skipper of the genus *Pholisora*
¹**sop** \ˈsäp\ *n* -s [ME *soppe*, fr. OE *sopp*; akin to MLG *soppe* soup, broth, MD *sop* pot liquor, broth, sauce, OHG *sopfa* piece of bread soaked in milk, ON *soppa* soup, OE *sūpan* to swallow, sip, taste — more at SUP] **1** *chiefly dial* : a piece of food (as bread) dipped or steeped in a liquid before being eaten **2** *chiefly dial* : the liquid into which food is dipped before being eaten; *esp* : GRAVY **3** : a wet soppy mess **4** : a foolish spineless individual : MILKSOP **5** *dial Eng* : a tuft of damp green grass mixed in with hay **6** : a conciliatory or propitiatory bribe, gift, or advance ⟨as a ~ to the low-paid teachers . . . the board approved $400-a-year raises —*Time*⟩
²**sop** \ˈ"\ *vb* **sopped**; **sopped**; **sopping**; **sops** *vt* **1** : to steep or dip in or as if in a liquid ⟨~ bread in gravy⟩ **2** : to mop (as water) so as to leave a dry or semidry surface **3** : to give a bribe or conciliatory gift to ~ *vi* **1** : to become completely soaked **2** : to soak in : ooze through
sop *abbr* soprano
SOP *abbr* **1** senior officer present **2** standard operating procedure; standing operating procedure
sope \ˈsōp\ *n* -s [ME, fr. OE *sopa*; akin to OE *sūpan* to swallow, sip, taste — more at SUP] *dial chiefly Brit* : DRINK 3
soph \ˈsäf, ˈsȯf\ *abbr or n* -s sophomore
so·pha *archaic var of* SOFA
so·pher \ˈsōfər\ *n, pl* **so·pher·im** \-rəm, -,rēm\ *often cap* [Heb *sōphēr*] : SCRIBE 1
so·pher·ic \(ˈ)sō;ferik\ *adj, often cap* : of or relating to the sopherim or the literature associated with them
so·phia \sōˈfēə, ˈsäf-,ˈsōf-\ *n* -s *usu cap* [L, fr. Gk, fr. *sophos* skilled, clever, wise + *-ia* -y] : WISDOM; *specif* : divine wisdom — **so·phi·an** \-ən\ *adj, usu cap*
so·phi·an·ism \-ə,nizəm\ *n* -s *usu cap* : a theology or system of thought based on divine wisdom ⟨the *Sophianism* . . . represented by some of the outstanding Orthodox Thinkers of our time —Endre Ivanka⟩ — **so·phi·an·ist** \-ənəst\ *n* -s *usu cap*
soph·ic \ˈsäfik\ *or* **soph·i·cal** \-fəkəl\ *adj* [LL *sophicus*, fr. Gk *sophos* skilled, clever, wise + L *-icus* -ic, -ical] : of, relating to, or full of wisdom : INTELLECTUAL — **sophically** *adv*
sophies *pl of* SOPHY
-sophies *pl of* -SOPHY
sophi·ol·o·gy \,säfēˈäləjē, ,sōf-\ *n* -ES [*sophio-* (fr. *sophia*) + *-logy*] : SOPHIANISM
soph·ism \ˈsä,fizəm\ *n* -s [alter. (influenced by MF *sophisme* & L *sophisma*) of earlier *sophim*, fr. ME, fr. MF *sophime*,

sophisme, fr. L *sophisma,* fr. Gk, clever device, artifice, sophism, fr. *sophizesthai* to become wise, act craftily, deceive, deal in sophisms, fr. *sophos* skilled, clever, wise] **1 :** an argument that is correct in form or appearance but is actually invalid; *esp* **:** an argument used for deception, disputation, or the display of intellectual brilliance ⟨employ a ~⟩ — compare SKEPTICISM **2 :** specious reasoning **:** SOPHISTRY 1 **3 :** SOPHISTRY 4

soph·ist \-fəst\ *n* -s [L *sophista,* fr. Gk *sophistēs,* lit., master craftsman, expert, wise man, fr. *sophizesthai*] **1** *usu cap* **:** one of a class of teachers of philosophy and rhetoric in ancient Greece who became prominent about the middle of the 5th century B.C. and impressed by the conflicting opinions of the early nature philosophers developed subjectivistic, relativistic, and skeptical arguments, were the first to offer anything approaching systematic education beyond the elementary branches, and argued for the natural equality of men, but taught also the art of successful living and partly by virtue of their unorthodox opinions and their acceptance of pay for instruction gradually fell into disrepute **2** *sometimes cap* **:** a learned man, thinker, or sage **3 :** a person employing sophistry **:** a fallacious reasoner

soph·is·ter \-tə(r)\ *n* -s [ME, fr. MF *sophistre,* fr. L *sophista*] **1** *obs* **:** SOPHIST 1 **2 :** SOPHIST 3 **3** *obs* **:** a student in his third or fourth year esp. at an English university

¹so·phis·tic \(ˈ)sə¦fistik, səˈf-,sōˈf-, -tēk\ *adj* [L *sophisticus,* fr. Gk *sophistikos,* fr. *sophistēs* + *-ikos* -ic] **1 a :** tending to or employing sophistry ⟨~ tyrants⟩ **b :** using sophisms ⟨~ rhetoricians⟩ **2 :** of, relating to, or typical of sophists, sophistry, or the ancient Sophists ⟨a ~ age⟩ ⟨~ subtleties⟩ ⟨the ~ movement⟩

²sophistic \ˈ"\ *n* -s **:** the doctrines or procedures of the Sophists or a sophist; *also* **:** SOPHISTRY

so·phis·ti·cal \-tə̇kəl, -tēk-\ *adj* [L *sophisticus* + E *-al*] **1 :** SOPHISTIC **2 :** resembling a sophism; *specif* **:** that appears to be plausible but is actually fallacious ⟨a ~ argument⟩ ⟨a ~ method⟩ — **so·phis·ti·cal·ly** \-k(ə)lē, -li\ *adv* — **so·phis·ti·cal·ness** \-kəlnə̇s\ *n* -ES

¹so·phis·ti·cate \səˈfistə̇kə̇t, -tēk-, -stə,kāt, *usu* |d.+V\ *adj* [ME *sophisticat,* fr. ML *sophisticatus,* past part.] **:** SOPHISTICATED

²so·phis·ti·cate \-stə,kāt, *usu* -ād.+V\ *vb* -ED/-ING/-S [ME *sophisticaten,* fr. ML *sophisticatus,* past part. of *sophisticare,* fr. L *sophisticus* sophistic] *vt* **1 :** to alter deceptively: as **a :** ADULTERATE ⟨rose oil is *sophisticated* with geraniol —R.N. Shreve⟩ **b :** to falsify (as a text, passage, or author) by interpolations, unwarranted changes, or misinterpretation **2 :** to make artificial **:** deprive of genuineness, naturalness, or simplicity: as **a** *archaic* **:** DEBASE, SPOIL, CORRUPT **b :** to deprive of naïveté **:** DISILLUSION **3 a :** to make complicated or complex ⟨~ the mechanism of a watch⟩ **b :** to make aware of complexities and subtleties **:** REFINE **~** *vi* **:** ADULTERATE, CORRUPT, COMPLICATE

³sophisticate *like* ¹SOPHISTICATE\ *n* -s [¹*sophisticate*] **:** a sophisticated person

sophisticated \⸗ˈ⸗⸗,⸗⸗\ *adj* [ML *sophisticatus* + E *-ed*] **1 :** not in a natural, pure, or original state **:** ADULTERATED ⟨a ~ oil⟩ **:** amended unwarrantedly ⟨a ~ text⟩ **2 :** deprived of native or original simplicity: as **a :** highly complicated **:** many sided **:** COMPLEX ⟨~ specifications⟩ ⟨~ search techniques would be needed to locate faint objects —*Space Handbk.*⟩ **b :** WORLDLY-WISE, KNOWING ⟨a ~ adolescent⟩ **3 :** devoid of grossness **:** SUBTLE: as **a :** supremely cultured **:** finely experienced and aware ⟨a ~ columnist⟩ **b :** intellectually appealing **:** devoid of the obvious traditional or popular appeal ⟨a ~ novel⟩ — **so·phis·ti·cat·ed·ly** \⸗ˈ⸗⸗,⸗⸗⸗, ⸗,⸗⸗ˈ⸗⸗⸗\ *adv*

so·phis·ti·ca·tion \sə,fistəˈkāshən\ *n* -s [ME *sophisticacioun,* fr. ML *sophistication-, sophisticatio,* fr. *sophisticatus* + *-ion-, -io* -ion] **1 a :** the use or employment of sophistry **:** sophistical reasoning **:** misrepresentation or falsification in argument **b :** SOPHISM, QUIBBLE **2 :** an act of sophisticating **:** the quality or state of being sophisticated: as **a :** ADULTERATION, ADULTERANT; *also* **:** something adulterated **b :** the quality or the character of being intellectually sophisticated (as through cultivation, experience, or disillusionment) ⟨the text is simple and requires no scientific ~ to be understood —D.L.Wolfle⟩

so·phis·ti·ca·tive \⸗ˈ⸗⸗,kād·iv\ *adj* **:** promoting sophistication **:** tending to sophisticate

so·phis·ti·ca·tor \-ād·ə(r)\ *n* -s **:** one that sophisticates; *esp* **:** one that adulterates

soph·is·try \ˈsäfə̇strē, -ri\ *n* -ES [ME *sophistrie,* fr. MF, fr. *sophistre* sophist + *-ie* -y — more at SOPHISTER] **1 :** reasoning that is superficially plausible but actually fallacious ⟨his masterful but irresponsible ~⟩ **2 :** the employment of sophisms **:** disputation in the actual or supposed manner of the Sophists ⟨rhetorical ~⟩ **3 :** a sophistical argument; *specif* **:** SOPHISM ⟨a maze of *sophistries*⟩ **4 :** the doctrines, principles, or practices of the ancient Sophists ⟨the history of ~⟩

sophists *pl of* SOPHIST

soph·o·cle·an \¦säfə¦klēən\ *adj, usu cap* [*Sophocles* †406 B.C. Greek tragic dramatist + E *-an*] **:** of, relating to, or characteristic of the Athenian tragic poet Sophocles or his dramas

soph·o·more \ˈsäf(ə),m|ō(ə)r, -fˈm,|, |ó(ə)r, |ōə, |ó(ə), *esp in 2-syllable pronunc* ˈsóf-\ *n* -s [prob. fr. Gk *sophos* wise + *mōros* dull, foolish, stupid — more at MORON] **1 :** a student in his second year or with second-year standing at a college; *also* **:** a student in his second year at a secondary school **2 :** a person in the second year of experience ⟨a ~ in organized baseball⟩

soph·o·mor·ic \¦⸗⸗¦⸗⸗, (ˈ)⸗¦⸗⸗, *with last part* -ōrik, -ȯr-, -rēk\ *adj* **1 :** of, relating to, resembling, or characteristic of a sophomore **2 a :** exhibiting a firm and often aggressive conviction of knowledge and wisdom and unaware of limitations and lack of maturity **:** inclined to oversimplify **:** SUPERFICIAL **b :** falsely skeptical **:** given to shallow quibbling

so·pho·ra \səˈfōrə\ *n* [NL, fr. Ar *ṣufayrāʼ,* a tree of the genus *Sophora*] **1** *cap* **:** a genus of trees and shrubs (family Leguminosae) that are natives of the warmer parts of both hemispheres and have odd-pinnate leaves and rather showy flowers with a broad or rounded standard and oblong keel — see JAPANESE PAGODA TREE, KOWHAI, MESCAL BEAN 2 **2** -s **:** any plant of the genus *Sophora*

soph·o·rine \ˈsäfə,rēn, -rə̇n; səˈfōrə̇n\ *n* -s [ISV *sophor-* (fr. NL *Sophora*) + *-ine*] **:** CYTISINE

so·phros·y·ne \səˈfräsᵊn(,)ē\ *n* -s [Gk *sōphrosynē,* fr. *sōphrōn* being of sound mind, prudent, reasonable (fr. *saos, sōs* whole, safe, sound + *-phrōn;* akin to Gk *phrēn* mind) + *-synē,* suffix used to form abstract nouns — more at THUMB, FRENETIC] **1 :** TEMPERANCE 2 **2 a :** SELF-CONTROL **b :** PRUDENCE — contrasted with *hubris*

sophy *n* -ES [L *sophi,* pl. of *sophus,* fr. Gk *sophos,* fr. *sophos* skilled, clever, wise] *obs* **:** a wise man **:** SAGE

-so·phy \,səfē\ *n comb form* -ES [ME *-sophie,* fr. OF, fr. L *-sophia,* fr. Gk *sophia* wisdom, fr. *sophos* skilled, clever, wise + *-ia* -y] **:** knowledge or wisdom concerning (something specified) **:** science or study of (something specified) ⟨anthro*posophy*⟩ ⟨chiro*sophy*⟩ ⟨physio*sophy*⟩

sopite \ˈsō,pīt, ˈsä,p-\ *vt* -ED/-ING/-S [L *sopitus,* past part. of *sopire* to put to sleep, fr. *sopor*] **1 :** to put to sleep **:** LULL **2 :** to put an end to (as a claim) **:** SETTLE

so·por \ˈsōpər, -,pȯ(ə)r\ *n* -s [L; akin to L *somnus* sleep — more at SOMNOLENT] **:** profound or lethargic sleep **:** STUPOR

sopo·rif·er·ous \¦säpə¦rif(ə)rəs, ¦sōp-\ *adj* [L *soporifer* (fr. *sopor* + *-ifer* -iferous) + E *-ous*] **:** characterized by or inducing sleep or stupor **:** SOPORIFIC — **sopo·rif·er·ous·ly** *adv* — **sopo·rif·er·ous·ness** *n* -ES

¹sopo·rif·ic \-fik,-fēk\ *adj* [prob. fr. F *soporifique,* fr. L *sopor* + F *-ifique* -ific] **1 :** causing or tending to cause sleep ⟨a ~ drug⟩ ⟨a ~ speech⟩ **2 :** of, relating to, or characterized by sleepiness or lethargy ⟨~ old men⟩ ⟨~ symptoms⟩ **3 :** tending to dull or deaden awareness or alertness

²soporific \ˈ"\ *n* -s **:** something that is soporific ⟨the ~ of peace and prosperity —Peter Eckstein⟩; *specif* **:** a sleep-inducing drug or medicament

sopo·rif·i·cal \-fə̇kəl, -fēk-\ *adj* **:** SOPORIFIC — **sopo·rif·i·cal·ly** \-k(ə)lē, -li\ *adv*

sopo·rose \ˈ⸗⸗,rōs\ *adj* [*sopor* + *-ose*] **:** full of sleep **:** characterized by or manifesting morbid sleep or sleepiness

sopped *past of* SOP

sop·per \ˈsäpə(r)\ *n* -s **:** one that sops

sop·pi·ness \ˈsäpēnə̇s, -pin-\ *n* -ES **:** the quality or state of being soppy **:** WETNESS

sop·ping \ˈsäpiŋ, -pēŋ\ *adv* [fr. pres. part. of ²*sop*] **:** EXTREMELY, VERY ⟨~ wet⟩

sop·py \-pē,-pi\ *adj* -ER/-EST **1 :** soaked through **:** SATURATED **:** very wet or sloppy **2** *Brit* **:** MUSHY 2 **syn** see SENTIMENTAL

so·pra·ni·no \,sōprəˈnē(,)nō\ *n* -s [It, dim. of *soprano*] **:** a musical instrument (as a recorder or saxophone) higher in pitch than the soprano

so·pran·ist \səˈpranə̇st *also* -rän- *or* -rȧn-\ *n* -s [¹*soprano* + *-ist*] **:** a treble singer

¹so·pra·no \-(,)nō, -_nə, *often* -naw+V\ *n* -s [It, adj. & n., fr. *sopra* above + *-ano* -an] **1 :** the highest voice part in 4-part mixed harmony **2 :** the highest singing voice of women, boys, or castrati — compare ALTO **3 :** a singer (as a woman) with a soprano voice

²soprano \ˈ"\ *adj* [It] **1 :** relating to the soprano voice or part ⟨a ~ clef⟩ **2 :** having a high or treble range ⟨a ~ saxophone⟩ ⟨~ solo⟩

soprano clef *n* **:** the C clef when it is on the first or lower line of the staff — see CLEF illustration

soprano recorder *n* **:** the highest of the four standard members of the recorder family — called also *descant recorder*

sops *pl of* SOP, *pres 3d sing of* SOP

sops in wine 1 : the clove pink once used to flavor wine **2** *also* **sops of wine** *usu cap S&W* **:** a red late summer apple of highly aromatic flavor

sop to cer·be·rus \-ˈsərb(ə)rəs\ *usu cap C* [after *Cerberus,* 3-headed dog guarding the entrance to Hades; fr. the sop given him by Aeneas in Vergil's *Aeneid* (6,417) to engage his attention while Aeneas slipped by — more at CERBERUS] **:** a concession or bribe to conciliate a person otherwise liable to be troublesome

so·ra \ˈsōrə\ *or* **sora rail** *n* -s [origin unknown] **:** a small short-billed No. American rail (*Porzana carolina*) numerous in marshes in the Atlantic states during its migrations

so·ral \ˈsōrəl\ *adj* [NL *sorus* + E *-al*] **:** of or relating to a sorus

sorance *n* -s [¹*sore* + *-ance*] *obs* **:** SORE, INJURY, DISEASE

¹sorb \ˈsȯ(ə)rb\ *n* -s *cap* [G *Sorbe,* fr. Sorbian *serb*] **1 :** WEND **2 :** WENDISH

²sorb \ˈ"\ *n* -s [F *sorbe* fruit of the service tree, fr. L *sorbum*] **1 :** any of several Old World trees related to the apples and pears (as a wild service tree or rowan tree) **2** *or* **sorb apple :** the fruit of a sorb

³sorb \ˈ"\ *vt* -ED/-ING/-S [back-formation fr. *absorb* & *adsorb*] **:** to take up and hold either by adsorption or absorption **:** OCCLUDE

sor·bar·ia \sȯ(r)ˈba(a)rēə\ *n, cap* [NL, fr. *Sorbus* + *-aria*] **:** a small genus of Asiatic shrubs (family Rosaceae) with some compound leaves (as at the base) and panicles of white flowers with 5 to 8 pistils

sor·bate \ˈsȯr,bāt, -,bə̇t\ *n* -s [*sorbic* (*acid*) + *-ate*] **1 :** a salt or ester of sorbic acid **2 :** a sorbed substance

¹sor·be·fa·cient \¦sȯ(r)bə¦fāshənt\ *adj* [L *sorbēre* to suck up, swallow + *facient-, faciens,* pres. part. of *facere* to make, do — more at ABSORB, DO] **:** producing or promoting absorption

²sorbefacient \ˈ"\ *n* **:** a sorbefacient substance

sor·bent \ˈsȯrbənt\ *n* -s [³*sorb* + *-ent*] **:** a substance that sorbs

sor·bet \ˈsȯrbə̇t\ *n* -s [MF, a fruit drink, fr. OIt *sorbetto,* fr. Turk *serbet* — more at SHERBET] **1** *archaic* **:** SHERBET 3 **2 :** a sherbet made with a mixture of fruits

¹sorb·ian \ˈsȯrbēən\ *adj, usu cap* [¹*Sorb* + *-ian*] **:** WENDISH

²sorbian \ˈ"\ *n* -s *cap* **1 :** WEND **2 :** WENDISH

sorb·ic acid \ˈsȯrbik-\ *n* [²*sorb* + *-ic*] **:** a crystalline diolefinic acid $CH_3(CH{=}CH)_2COOH$ obtained from the unripe fruits of the mountain ash or made synthetically and used chiefly as a fungicide and food preservative and in the form of esters in improving drying oils

sor·bi·tan \ˈsȯ(r)bə,tan\ *n* -s [*sorbitol* + *-an*] **:** an inner anhydride $C_6H_{12}O_5$ of sorbitol: as **a :** a synthetic compound made by chemical dehydration of sorbitol and used in making fatty acid esters (as the mono-oleate) and then ethers (as with a polyethylene glycol) for use as emulsifiers and wetting agents; 1,4-anhydro-D-glucitol — called also *1,4-sorbitan* **b :** POLYGALITOL

sor·bite \ˈsȯr,bīt\ *n* -s [Henry C. *Sorby* †1908 Eng. geologist + E *-ite*] **:** tempered martensite having a granular appearance under the microscope — **sor·bit·ic** \(ˈ)⸗¦bid·ik\ *adj*

sor·bi·tol \ˈ⸗bə,tȯl, -tōl\ *n* -s [²*sorb* + *-itol*] **:** a crystalline faintly sweet hexahydroxy alcohol $CH_2OH(CHOH)_4CH_2OH$ that occurs esp. in mountain ash fruits, may be obtained by reduction of L-sorbose but is made industrially by reduction of D-glucose, and is used chiefly as a humectant and softener and in making sorbitan derivatives and ascorbic acid — called also D-glucitol; compare DULCITOL, MANNITOL

sor·bon·ist *also* **sor·bonn·ist** \(ˈ)sȯ(r)¦bänə̇st, -¦bən-\ *n* -s *usu cap* [MF *sorboniste,* fr. *Sorbonne,* a house for impoverished theological students at the University of Paris, now the site of the faculties of arts and letters of the University of Paris (after Robert de *Sorbon* †1274 Fr. theologian, its founder) + *-iste* -ist] **1 :** a member of the faculty of theology or a theological student at the University of Paris **2 :** a graduate of or student at the Sorbonne

sor·bose \ˈsȯr,bōs *also* -ōz\ *n* -s [ISV *sorbitol* + *-ose*] **:** a sweet crystalline unfermentable sugar $C_6H_{12}O_6$ of the ketohexose class existing as two optical isomers: *esp* **:** the levorotatory L-form obtained from sorbitol by fermentation with an acetobacter (*Acetobacter xylinum*) and used chiefly in making ascorbic acid

sor·bo·side \-bə,sīd, -səd *also* -,zīd *or* -zəd\ *n* -s [*sorbose* + *-ide*] **:** a glycoside that yields sorbose on hydrolysis

sorbs *pl of* SORB, *pres 3d sing of* SORB

sor·bus \ˈsȯrbəs\ *n* [NL, fr. L, service tree] **1** *cap* **:** a genus of trees and shrubs (family Rosaceae) distinguished from *Pyrus* and *Malus* by the pinnate leaves, three styles, and carpels that are not cartilaginous — see MOUNTAIN ASH **2** -ES **:** any tree of the genus *Sorbus*

sor·cer·er \ˈsȯ(r)|s(ə)rə(r)\ *n* -s [modif. of MF *sorcier,* fr. (assumed) VL *sortiarius,* fr. L *sort-, sors* lot, chance, decision by lot + *-i-* + *-arius* -ary — more at SORT] **:** a person who practices sorcery **:** MAGICIAN, WIZARD

sor·cer·ess \|s(ə)rə̇s\ *n* -ES [ME *sorceresse,* fr. AF, fr. OF *sorcier* + *-esse* -ess] **:** a female sorcerer

sor·cer·ize \|sə,rīz\ *vt* -ED/-ING/-S [*sorcery* + *-ize*] **:** to transform by sorcery

sor·cer·ous \|s(ə)rəs\ *adj* [*sorcery* + *-ous*] **:** of or relating to sorcery **:** using sorcery **:** MAGICAL

sor·cery \|s(ə)rē\ *n* -ES [ME *sorcerie,* fr. OF, fr. *sorcier* sorcerer + *-ie* -y — more at SORCERER] **:** the use of power gained from the assistance or control of evil spirits esp. for divining **:** divination by black magic **:** NECROMANCY, WITCHCRAFT **syn** see MAGIC

sor·dar·ia \sȯ(r)ˈda(a)rēə\ *n, cap* [NL, fr. L *sordes* dirt, filth + NL *-aria* — more at SWART] **:** a genus of chiefly dung-inhabiting ascomycetous fungi (order Sphaeriales) having scattered hairy-necked perithecia with dark continuous ascospores

sor·des \ˈsȯr(,)dēz\ *n, pl* **sordes** [L] **:** foul matter **:** useless matter **:** REFUSE; *specif* **:** the crusts that collect on the teeth and lips in debilitating diseases with protracted low fever

sor·did \-dəd\ *adj* [L *sordidus,* fr. *sordes* dirt, filth — more at SWART] **1 a :** characterized by filth **:** FILTHY ⟨~ surroundings⟩ **b :** slatternly or foul in appearance **:** SLUTTISH ⟨a ~ mob⟩ **c :** covered with filth **:** DIRTY ⟨~ animals⟩ **2 :** marked by baseness or grossness **:** VILE ⟨~ motives⟩ **3 :** meanly avaricious **:** COVETOUS, NIGGARDLY **4 :** of a dull or muddy color — used in the names of fishes or birds — **sor·did·ly** *adv*

sor·did·ness *n* -ES **:** the quality or state of being sordid

sor·dine \ˈsȯ(ə)r,dēn, ⸗ˈ⸗\ *n* -s [MF *sourdine* — more at SOURDINE] **1 :** a cone-shaped pipe inserted in the mouth of a trumpet to muffle its tone **:** MUTE **2 :** SOURDINE 1a

sor·di·no \sȯrˈdē(,)nō\ *n, pl* **sordi·ni** \-nē\ [It — more at SOURDINE] **1 :** SORDINE 1 **2 :** MUTE

sor·dor \ˈsȯrdər, -,dȯ(ə)r\ *n* -s [NL, fr. L *sordes* dirt, filth + *-or* — more at SWART] **:** REFUSE, DREGS; *also* **:** SORDIDNESS

¹sore \ˈsō(ə)r, -ȯ(ə)r, -ōə, -ȯ(ə)\ *adj* -ER/-EST [ME *sar, sor, soor,* fr. OE *sār;* akin to OS & OHG *sēr* painful, sore, ON *sārr* sore, wounded, L *saevus* fierce, savage, cruel, OIr *sāeth* pain, Lith *šaižus* rough, sharp] **1** PAINFUL, DISTRESSING: as **a :** causing or involving physical suffering or risk ⟨a ~ wound⟩ **b :** painful from overuse, injury, or inflammation **:** SENSITIVE ⟨~ muscles⟩ ⟨a ~ eye⟩; *also* **:** affected by such pain ⟨~ from riding⟩ **c :** causing or likely to cause mental distress ⟨~ news⟩ ⟨a ~ subject⟩ **2 :** attended by strenuous difficulties, hardship, or exertion ⟨in ~ straits⟩ ⟨~ struggles⟩ **3 :** not readily placated or mollified **:** ANGERED, NETTLED, VEXED ⟨~ over a remark⟩ **syn** see BITTER

²sore \ˈ"\ *n* -s [ME *sar, sor, soor,* fr. OE *sār;* akin to OHG *sēr* pain, wound, ON *sār* sore, wound, Goth *sair* pain, OE *sār,* adj.] **1 a :** a place (as an ulcer or boil) in an animal body where the skin and flesh are ruptured or bruised and tender or painful **b :** a wound, bruise, or abrasion that has become infected **:** a suppurating ulcer or boil **c :** LESION **2 :** DISEASE, SICKNESS, HARM **3 :** a source or cause of pain or vexation **:** AFFLICTION, TROUBLE ⟨the ~s of official duties⟩

³sore \ˈ"\ *adv* [ME *sare, sore,* fr. OE *sāre* (akin to OS & OHG *sēro* sorely), fr. *sār,* adj.] **:** SORELY — often used in combination ⟨*sore*-afraid⟩

soredi- *comb form* [NL *soredium*] **:** soredium ⟨*soredi*ferous⟩ ⟨*soredi*form⟩ ⟨*soredi*oid⟩

so·re·di·al \səˈrēdēəl\ *adj* [*soredi-* + *-al*] **:** relating to or derived from a soredium ⟨~ branches⟩

so·re·di·oid \səˈrēdē,ȯid\ *or* **so·re·di·ose** \-,ōs\ *adj* [*soredi-* + *-oid* or *-ose*] **:** having the form or nature of a soredium **:** resembling or functioning as a soredium

so·re·di·um \səˈrēdēəm\ *n, pl* **sore·dia** \-dēə\ [NL, irreg. fr. Gk *sōros* heap + NL *-idium;* akin to L *tumēre* to swell — more at THUMB] **:** one of the vegetative gemmae on the surface of the thallus of a lichen consisting of a tuft of hyphae investing a few algal cells or gonidia — called also *brood bud, hologonidium*

sore-eyed pigeon \ˈ⸗,⸗-\ *n* **:** SHEATHBILL

sorefalcon \ˈ⸗,⸗\ *n* [*sore* (as in *sorehawk*) + *falcon*] **:** a peregrine falcon in the reddish plumage of the first year

sorehawk \ˈ⸗,⸗\ *n* [ME *sor hawke,* fr. *sor* sorrel (fr. MF) + *hawke, hauk* hawk — more at SORREL, HAWK] **:** SOREFALCON

¹sorehead \ˈ⸗,⸗\ *n* [prob. fr. the phrase *as mad as a bear with a sore head*] **1 :** a person easily angered or disgruntled **:** one obdurately contentious and eager to find grievances or faults **2** [¹*sore* + *head*] **:** FOWL POX

²sorehead \ˈ"\ *adj* **:** irritated and disappointed esp. by having one's hopes frustrated ⟨~ politicians⟩

soreheaded \ˈ⸗¦⸗⸗\ *adj* **:** SOREHEAD — **sore·head·ed·ly** *adv* — **sore·head·ed·ness** *n* -ES

sore heels *n pl* **:** HORSEPOX

sore hocks *n pl* **:** an ulcerated condition of the undersurface of the forefeet or hind feet of a domestic rabbit

sor·el \ˈsȯrəl, ˈsär-\ *n* -s [ME *sorelle, sorrel* (also, sorrel horse) — more at SORREL] *Brit* **:** a male fallow deer in the third year

sorel cement \ˈ"-\ *n* [fr. the name *Sorel*] **:** magnesium oxychloride cement consisting of magnesium chloride and calcined magnesia

sore·ly *adv* [ME *sarly, sorly, soorly,* fr. OE *sārlīce,* fr. *sārlic,* adj., grievous, sad, painful, fr. *sār* sore + *-lic* -ly — more at SORE] **:** in a sore manner: as **a :** PAINFULLY, GRIEVOUSLY ⟨~ vexed⟩ **b :** SEVERELY, VIOLENTLY ⟨~ exerted⟩ **c :** EXTREMELY ⟨~ tired⟩

sore mouth *n* **1 :** a highly contagious virus disease of sheep and goats that occurs esp. in young animals, is characterized by extensive vesiculation and subsequent ulceration about the lips, gums, and tongue, and rarely ends fatally but interferes with nutrition and may be complicated by secondary bacterial infection — called also *contagious ecthyma, scabby mouth* **2 :** necrobacillosis affecting the mouth; *esp* **:** CALF DIPHTHERIA

soremuzzle \ˈ⸗¦⸗⸗\ *n* **:** SORE MOUTH 1

sore·ness *n* -ES [ME *sarnes, sornes,* fr. OE *sārnes,* fr. *sār* sore + *-nes* -ness] **1 :** the quality or state of being sore: as **a :** PAINFULNESS ⟨the ~ of a sprain⟩ **b :** mental grief **:** DISTRESS ⟨the ~ of defeat⟩ **c :** SEVERITY, VIOLENCE ⟨the ~ of battle⟩ **2 :** something sore or painful

sorer *comparative of* SORE

sores *pl of* SORE

sore shank *n* **:** rhizoctonia disease (as of tobacco)

sore shin *n* **:** a disease of tobacco, cotton, and other plants beyond the seedling stage caused by any of several soil fungi (as members of the genera *Corticium* and *Pythium*) that girdle the plant near the groundline

sorest *superlative of* SORE

sore throat *n* **:** painful throat due to inflammation of the fauces and pharynx

so·rex \ˈsōr,eks\ *n* [NL, fr. L, shrew; akin to L *susurrus* murmur, hum — more at SWARM] **1** *cap* **:** a large and widely distributed genus (the type of the family Soricidae) of shrews with 32 reddish-brown-tipped teeth **2** -ES **:** any shrew of the genus *Sorex*

sor·ge \ˈzȯrgə\ *n* -s [G, fr. OHG *sorga* — more at SORROW] **:** CONCERN, CARE; *esp* **:** a feeling bordering on anxiety

sor·ghum \ˈsȯrgəm, -ȯ(ə)g-\ *n* [NL, fr. It *sorgo,* perh. fr. (assumed) VL *Syricum* (*granum*), fr. L *Syricum* (neut. of *Syricus* Syrian) + *granum* grain] **1 a** *cap* **:** an economically important genus of Old World tropical grasses that are sometimes naturalized in the New World, are widely grown for grain and herbage even in temperate regions, and are characterized by growth habit and stem form similar to that of Indian corn but have the leaves saw-toothed on their edges and the spikelets in pairs on a hairy rachis — see BROOMCORN, GRAIN SORGHUM, SORGO **b** -s **:** any plant of the genus *Sorghum; esp* **:** any cultivated plant (as a grain sorghum or a sorgo) derived from a common species (*S. vulgare*) **c** -s **:** the seeds of grain sorghum used as cereals and stock feed **d** -s **:** the stalks and leaves of sorghum used for fodder, hay, or silage **2** -s **:** syrup produced by evaporating from stems of any sorgo the juice which resembles cane sugar but contains a high proportion of invert sugars as well as starch and dextrin **3** -s **:** something cloyingly sweet or overly sentimental

sorghum brown *n* **:** WOOD ROSE 2

sorghum midge *n* **:** a minute gall midge (*Contarinia sorghicola*) whose larvae develop in the seed heads of sorghum, broomcorn, and wild grasses

sorghum smut *n* **1 :** a smut attacking sorghum; *esp* **:** HEAD SMUT **2 :** an organism causing a sorghum smut

sor·go *also* **sor·gho** \-(,)gō\ *n* -s [It *sorgo*] **:** any of various sorghums that are cultivated primarily for the sweet juice in their stems from which sugar and syrup are made and are also widely used for fodder and silage — called also *sweet sorghum;* compare GRAIN SORGHUM

sorgo syrup *n* **:** syrup made of sorghum

sori *pl of* SORUS

so·ric·i·dae \səˈrisə,dē\ *n pl, cap* [NL, fr. *Soric-, Sorex,* type genus + *-idae*] **:** a family of small chiefly terrestrial long-snouted mammals (order Insectivora) that comprise the true shrews — compare ELEPHANT SHREW, TALPIDAE

so·ric·i·dent \səˈrisə,dent, -_dənt\ *adj* [NL *soric-, sorex* shrew + *-i-* + *dent-, dens* tooth — more at SOREX, TOOTH] **:** having or characterized by teeth like those of shrews in which the middle pair of incisors are very large and the canines small and unspecialized

¹sor·i·cine \ˈsȯrə,sīn\ *adj* [L *soricinus,* fr. *soric-, sorex* shrew + *-inus* -ine] **:** of, like, or relating to a shrew or the Soricidae

²soricine \ˈ"\ *n* -s **:** SHREW

soricine bat *n* **:** a leaf-nosed bat (*Glossophaga soricina*) of Central and So. America

so·ri·coi·dea \,sȯrəˈkȯidēə\ *n pl, cap* [NL, fr. *Soric-, Sorex* + *-oidea*] **:** a superfamily of insectivores consisting of the shrews, moles, and extinct related forms

sories *pl of* SORY

so·rite \ˈsōr,īt\ *n* -s [Gk *sōros* heap + E *-ite*] **:** ARCHAEOCYTE

so·ri·tes \səˈrīd·(,)ēz\ *n, pl* **sorites** \ˈ"\ [L, fr. Gk *sōritēs, sōreitēs,* fr. *sōros* heap — more at SORUS] **1 :** an abridged form of stating a series of syllogisms in a series of propositions so arranged that the predicate of each one that precedes forms the subject of each one that follows and the conclusion unites the subject of the first proposition with the predicate of the last proposition — compare GOCLENIAN SORITES **2 :** an aggregation of more or less related things, facts, or items

so·rit·i·cal \səˈrid·ə̇kəl\ *also* **so·rit·ic** \-d·ik\ *adj* [*soritical,* fr. Gk *sōritikos* (fr. *sōritēs* + *-ikos* -ic) + *-al;* soritic, fr. Gk *sōritikos*] **:** of or relating to a sorites

sorn \'sȯ(ə)rn\ *vi* -ED/-ING/-S [origin unknown] *chiefly Scot* **:** to impose in order to obtain hospitality **:** SPONGE — **sorn·er** \-nə(r)\ *n* -S *chiefly Scot*

sor·o·ban \'sȯrə,bän\ *n* -S [Jap, fr. Chin (Pek) *suan*[4] *p'an*[2], lit., reckoning board] **:** an abacus used by the Japanese that is a modification of the Chinese suan pan

so·ro·che \sə'rōchē\ *n* -S [AmerSp, fr. Quechua *surúchi*, lit., antimony; fr. the belief that the sickness is due to the presence of the metal in the Andes mountains] **:** mountain sickness esp. in the Andes

so·rop·ti·mist \sə'räptəməst\ *n* -S [blend of *sorority* and *optimist*] **:** a member of a club composed of professional women and women business executives associated primarily for service

so·ro·ral \sə'rōrəl\ *adj* [L *soror* sister + E *-al* — more at SISTER] **:** of, relating to, or in the relationship of a sister **:** SISTERLY

sororal polygyny *n* **:** a polygyny in which the wives are sisters — contrasted with *fraternal polyandry;* compare LEVIRATE, SORORATE

soro·rate \sə'rōrət, -ōr,āt; 'sȯrə,rāt\ *n* -S [L *soror* sister + E *-ate*] **:** the marriage of one man with two or more sisters usu. successively and after the first wife has been found to be barren or after her death — compare LEVIRATE, SORORAL POLYGYNY

so·ro·ri·al \sə'rōrēəl\ *adj* [L *sororius* sororal (fr. *soror* sister) + E *-al*] **:** SORORAL — **so·ro·ri·al·ly** \-ēəlē\ *adv*

so·ror·i·cide \sə'rȯrə,sīd\ *n* -S [in sense 1, fr. ML *sororicidium*, fr. L *soror* sister + *-i-* + *-cidium* -cide (killing); in sense 2, fr. L *sororicida*, fr. *soror* + *-i-* + *-cida* -cide (killer)] **1 :** the act of killing one's sister **2 :** a person who kills his sister

so·ror·i·ty \sə'rȯrəd·ē, -rär-, -ətē, -i\ *n* -ES [ML *sororitas*, fr. L *soror* sister + *-itas* -ity — more at SISTER] **1 :** SISTERHOOD **2 :** a society or club of girls or women (as in a college) — compare FRATERNITY

sor·o·rize \'sȯrə,rīz\ *vi* -ED/-ING/-S [L *soror* + E *-ize*] **:** to associate or hold fellowship as sisters — compare FRATERNIZE

so·rose \'sōr,ōs\ *adj* [NL *sorus* + E *-ose*] **:** bearing sori

so·ro·silicate \,sōr(,)ō+\ *n* [Gk *sōros* heap + E *silicate*] **:** a class of polymeric silicates or a member thereof in which the silicon-oxygen groups are linked into limited clusters by sharing oxygen atoms (as in hemimorphite or in melilite or zunyite) and in some cases a portion of the silicon is replaced by aluminum — compare CYCLOSILICATE, INOSILICATE, NESOSILICATE, PHYLLOSILICATE, TECTOSILICATE

so·ro·sis \sə'rōsəs\ *n, pl* **soroses** \-ō,sēz\ *or* **sorosises** [fr. *Sorosis*, a woman's club incorporated in 1869] **:** an association of women (as for social purposes) **:** a women's club

so·ro·spo·rel·la \,sōrəspə'relə\ *n, cap* [NL, fr. Gk *sōros* heap + *spora* seed + NL *-ella* — more at SPORE] **:** a genus of imperfect fungi (family Moniliaceae) parasitic on various insect larvae and characterized by abundant chlamydospore production and verticillate conidiophores forming nonseptate hyaline spores

so·ro·spo·ri·um \,sōrə'spōrēəm\ *n, cap* [NL, fr. Gk *sōros* heap + NL *-sporium*] **:** a genus of smut fungi having teliospores united in more or less firm ball-like masses with the sori dusty at maturity and including several that cause head smuts in grasses

sorp·tion \'sȯrpshən\ *n* -S [back-formation fr. *absorption* & *adsorption*] **:** the process of sorbing by physical or chemical forces or both **:** ADSORPTION, ABSORPTION ⟨~ of gases and vapors by solids⟩ ⟨~ occurs wherever there is a surface or an interface —J.W.McBain⟩ — compare CHEMISORPTION, IMBIBITION 2a, OCCLUSION 3

sorp·tive \-ptiv\ *adj* **:** relating to sorption

sor·ra \'särə\ *also* **sor·roa** \-rwə\ *Irish & Scot var of* SORROW

[1]sor·rel \'sȯrəl, 'sär-\ *n* -S [ME *sorelle*, fr. MF *sorel*, fr. *sorel*, adj., having the color sorrel, fr. *sor* reddish brown, prob. of Gmc origin; akin to MD *soor* dry, dried out, MLG *sōr* — more at SERE] **1 :** an animal of a sorrel color: as **a :** a light bright chestnut horse often with white mane and tail **b :** a dark red roan horse **2** [fr. *sorrel*, adj., of the color sorrel, fr. ME *sorelle*, fr. MF *sorel*] **:** a brownish orange to light brown that is darker than caramel, slightly yellower than tawny, and redder than raw sienna

[2]sorrel \"\ *n* -S [ME *sorel*, fr. MF *surele*, fr. OF, fr. *sur* sour, of Gmc origin; akin to OHG *sūr* sour — more at SOUR] **:** any of various plants with sour juice: as **a :** [1]DOCK 1 **b :** a plant of the genus *Oxalis* — called also *wood sorrel* **c :** ROSELLE

sorrel dock *n* **:** GARDEN SORREL

sorrel family *n* **:** OXALIDACEAE

sorrel tree *n* **1 :** SOURWOOD **2 :** an Australian hibiscus (*Hibiscus heterophyllus*) with acid foliage **3 :** STAGGERBUSH

sorrel vine *n* **:** a fleshy tropical American vine (*Cissus trifoliata*) with acid compound leaves

sor·ren·tine \'sȯrən,tēn, sə'ren-\ *adj, usu cap* [It *sorrentino*, fr. *Sorrento*, seaport in southern Italy + It *-ino* -ine (fr. L *-inus*)] **:** relating to, situated in, inhabiting, or coming from Sorrento ⟨the *Sorrentine* peninsula⟩

sor·ren·to green \sə'rent·(,)ō-\ *n, often cap S* [fr. *Sorrento*, seaport in southern Italy] **:** a moderate bluish green that is bluer and deeper than porcelain green or sea blue

sorrento work *n, usu cap S* **:** inlaid fretwork (as in wood) esp. when made at or near Sorrento, Italy

sorrier *comparative of* SORRY

sorriest *superlative of* SORRY

sor·ri·ly \'särəlē, -li *also* 'sȯr-\ *adv* [ME *sarily, sorily*, fr. *sary, sory* sorry + *-ly* — more at SORRY] **:** in a sorry manner

sor·ri·ness \-rēnəs, -rin-\ *n* -ES [ME *sarines, sorines*, fr. OE *sārignes*, fr. *sārig* sorry + *-nes* -ness — more at SORRY] **:** the quality or state of being sorry

[1]sor·row \'sä(,)rō, -rə *also* 'sȯ-; -rəw, -rō+V\ *n* -S [ME *sorge, sorwe, sorow*, fr. OE *sorg*; akin to OHG *sorga* care, sorrow, ON *sorg*, Goth *saurga* care, sorrow, OIr *serg* sickness, OSlav *sraga* sickness, Skt *sūrkṣati* he is concerned about something] **1 a :** uneasiness or anguish due to loss (as of something loved or familiar) **:** UNHAPPINESS, SADNESS ⟨~ at the loss of a friend⟩ **b :** a cause of grief or sadness **:** HARM, DAMAGE ⟨the great ~ of a conflagration⟩ ⟨transgressions that were ultimately a permanent ~⟩ **2 :** contrition at having done or caused evil **:** PENITENCE **3 :** a display of grief or sadness **:** LAMENTATION ⟨uneasy in the presence of family ~⟩ **4 a** *chiefly Irish & Scot* (1) **:** MISCHIEF, MISFORTUNE (2) — used as an emphatic negative; often preceded by *the* ⟨the ~ a word or sign out of them —Seumas O'Kelly⟩ **b** *chiefly Scot* **:** PEST, RASCAL

syn GRIEF, HEARTACHE, ANGUISH, WOE, DOLE, REGRET: SORROW is the most general of these terms, implying a sense of loss or of guilt ⟨the widespread *sorrow* that his death aroused —Douglas Cleverdon⟩ ⟨anguish that wept aloud; misery that could find no voice; *sorrow* that was dumb —Oscar Wilde⟩ GRIEF is poignant or extended sorrow ⟨immune to *grief*, even at the death of a loved one⟩ HEARTACHE is usu. an all-embracing hidden sorrow springing from disappointment or loss, as of hope or love ⟨the *heartache* of war, signalized in defeat and death⟩ ⟨reach fame and success after many years of poverty and *heartache*⟩ ⟨the *heartache* of unrequited love⟩ ANGUISH is usu. excruciating or torturing grief or dread ⟨nothing but despair and *anguish* written in every line of Susanna's slim figure —Gerald Beaumont⟩ ⟨the *anguish* of intense fear⟩ WOE is deep or inconsolable misery induced by grief or anguish ⟨the suffering people whose *woes* he has not alleviated —W.P. Webb⟩ ⟨one builds a tight fence around the misfortune, and within that minute enclosure, one sits intent upon one's *woe* —H.A.Overstreet⟩ ⟨bowed now in his *woe* —Agnes S. Turnbull⟩ DOLE is woe given vent to in weeping, moaning, or wailing ⟨giving way to inconsolable, tearful *dole*⟩ REGRET implies a sorrow usu. not outwardly manifest and may designate pain of mind or spiritual anguish induced by disappointment, lost opportunity, or heartache, and ranging in intensity from the mildest of momentary unhappiness at an invitation declined to intense pangs of remorse for a wrong done, though usu. signifying only the lighter, less intense feelings ⟨intense *regret* for lost opportunities⟩ ⟨his bitter *regrets* for past happiness —T.S. Eliot⟩ ⟨in moments of *regret* we recognize that some of our judgments have been mistaken —M.R.Cohen⟩

[2]sorrow \"\ *vb* -ED/-ING/-S [ME *sorgen, sorwen, sorowen*, fr. OE *sorgian*; akin to OS *sorgon* to care, grieve, sorrow, OHG *sorgēn*, Goth *saurgan* to care, grieve, *saurga*, n.] *vi* **1 :** to feel sorrow **:** GRIEVE ⟨~ over the death of a relative⟩ **2 :** to express grief **:** LAMENT ⟨stung to the soul he ~*ed*, and he raged —Alexander Pope⟩ ~ *vt* **:** MOURN, LAMENT **syn** see GRIEVE

sor·row·er \-rəwə(r), -rōə-\ *n* -S **:** one that sorrows

sor·row·ful \-rōfəl, -rəf-\ *adj* [ME *sorowful*, fr. OE *sorgful*, fr. *sorg* sorrow + *-ful*] **1 :** full of or characterized by sorrow ⟨~ widows⟩ **2 :** expressive of or inducing sorrow **:** SAD ⟨~ tale⟩ **3 :** given to melancholy **:** PLAINTIVE ⟨a ~ disposition⟩

sor·row·ful·ly \-f(ə)lē, -li\ *adv* [ME *sorowfully*, fr. *sorowful* + *-ly*] **:** in a sorrowful manner

sor·row·ful·ness \-fəlnəs\ *n* -ES [ME *sorowfulnesse*, fr. *sorowful* + *-nesse* -ness] **:** the quality or state of being sorrowful **:** MISERABLENESS, SADNESS

sorrowing *adj* **:** given to grief, anguish, or lamentation — **sorrow·ing·ly** *adv*

sor·row·less \-rōləs, -rəl-\ *adj* **:** being without sorrow **:** free of grief or trouble

sor·ry \'särē, 'sȯr-, -ri\ *adj* -ER/-EST [ME *sary, sory*, fr. OE *sārig*, fr. *sār* sore + *-ig* -y — more at SORE] **1 :** grieved or grieving over the loss of some good ⟨was ~ to see it moved but I would be *sorrier* to see it destroyed —W.T.Scott⟩ **:** feeling sorrow, regret, or penitence ⟨she began to cry, poor thing, and I felt very ~ for her —W.S.Maugham⟩ ⟨was momentarily ~ that she had not read it —Arnold Bennett⟩ ⟨~ for past transgressions⟩ — often used interjectionally to express polite regret ⟨~, but I disagree⟩ ⟨~; I decline to yield —F.H.Case⟩ **2 :** of melancholy, dismal, or gloomy mien **:** MOURNFUL, SAD ⟨through the ~ routine that follows on the heels of death —B.A.Williams⟩ ⟨the ~ truth is, this book ought not to have been accepted for publication —Kemp Malone⟩ **3 :** inspiring blended sorrow, pity, scorn, and ridicule **:** worthlessly or wretchedly worn-out, unfit, or futile ⟨a ~ underpaid official⟩ ⟨fed us on such ~ chuck —*American Songbag*⟩ ⟨for every good fur-catching dog, there are a hundred ~ ones —F.B.Gipson⟩ ⟨making a ~ spectacle of himself —Joseph Wechsberg⟩ **syn** see CONTEMPTIBLE

[1]sort \'sȯ(ə)r|t, -ȯ(ə)|, *usu* |d· +V\ *n* -S [ME, fr. MF *sorte*, prob. fr. ML & LL; ML *sort-, sors* sort, kind, fr. LL, way, manner, fr. L, lot, decision by lot, chance, fortune; perh. akin to L *serere* to bind together, join — more at SERIES] **1 :** a group or kind established or set up permanently or temporarily on the basis of any characteristic in common ⟨a strange ~ of people⟩ — sometimes used as a zero plural with a preceding *these* or *those* and a following *of* ⟨those ~ of men⟩ **2 a :** a number of things used or adapted to be used together **:** SET, SUIT **b** *archaic* **:** GROUP, CROWD, FLOCK **3 a :** a method or manner of acting **:** WAY, FASHION, MANNER **b :** CHARACTER, QUALITY, DISPOSITION, NATURE ⟨people of an evil ~⟩; *also* **:** INDIVIDUAL, THING ⟨he is really not a bad ~ at all⟩ **4 a :** letter or character that is one element of a font **b :** a character or piece of type (as a symbol, piece fraction, or space) that is not part of a regular font **c :** a matrix that is not stored in a keyboard-controlled channel of a slugcasting machine and must be hand-inserted when used; *also* **:** a character cast or made from such a matrix **5 sorts** *pl* **a :** a grade of a natural resin (as a copal) characterized by largish pieces sorted usu. by color **b :** ungraded gum (as gum arabic) of various sizes **syn** see TYPE — **after a sort :** in a rough, unfinished, or haphazard way **:** after a fashion — **of sorts** *or* **of a sort :** of an inconsequential or mediocre quality ⟨a poet *of sorts*⟩ — **out of sorts :** out of temper **:** VEXED, ILL, DISTURBED

[2]sort \"\ *vb* -ED/-ING/-S [ME *sorten*, fr. *sort*, n.] *vt* **1** *obs* **:** to select as of a certain sort **:** CHOOSE; *also* **:** to distinguish between **2** *obs* **:** to assign by or as if by lot **:** ALLOT **3 a :** to put in a given place or rank according to kind, class, or nature ⟨~ mail⟩ **:** arrange according to characteristics **:** CLASSIFY — often used with *out* ⟨~ out colors⟩ **b :** to separate (a particular thing) from a mass ⟨~ out a defective tool⟩ ⟨quickly ~ out some of the riddles resulting from repressed guilt —R.L. Jenkins⟩ **4** *chiefly Scot* **:** to furnish provision for; *esp* **:** to feed and bed down (an animal) **5** *chiefly Scot* **a :** to put to rights **:** put in order **b :** to set right morally by punishing or scolding ~ *vi* **1 :** to join or associate with others esp. of the same kind — used with *with* ⟨~ with thieves⟩ **2** *obs* **:** to divine by or as if by lot **:** SOOTHSAY; *also* **:** turn out **3** *archaic* **:** SUIT, HARMONIZE, AGREE — used with *with*

sort·able \'sȯ(r)d·əbəl\ *adj* **1 :** capable of being sorted **2** *archaic* **:** SUITABLE, PROPER — **sort·ably** \-blē\ *adv*

sor·ta·tion \sȯ(r)'tāshən\ *n* -S **:** the act or process of sorting ⟨the ~ of mail⟩

sort·er \'sȯr|d·ər, -ȯ(ə)|d·ə(r, |tə-\ *n* -S **:** one that sorts: as **a :** one that sorts hides, skins, and leather according to grade, weight, thickness, and color **b :** one that sorts burned brick or tile according to color and hardness **c :** one that sorts fruit or other food products according to size or condition **d :** a clerical worker who sorts such items as bills, checks, correspondence, or statements (as for mailing or filing) **e :** a machine or device for selecting punch cards or arranging them in groups or in a predetermined order

[1]sor·tie \'sȯr|d·|ē, -ȯ(ə)|d·ə(r), |t|, |i *also* 's,tē *sometimes* ='tē\ *n* -S [F, fr. MF, fr. fem. of *sorti*, past part. of *sortir* to escape, sally, go out] **:** a sudden or rapid emerging or issuing out: as **a :** the sudden issuing of troops from a defensive position to attack or harass the enemy **:** SALLY **b :** one mission or attack by a single plane **c :** the departure of a ship or group of ships from a harbor or anchorage

[2]sortie \"\ *vi* -ED/-ING/-S **:** to issue forth in a sortie **:** sally forth or go out; *specif* **:** to depart from a harbor or anchorage

sor·ti·lege \'sȯ(r)d·lij, -)t°l-, -°l,ej\ *n* -S [ME, fr. ML *sortilegium*, fr. L *sortilegus* foretelling, fr. *sort-, sors* lot + *-i-* + *-legus* (fr. *legere* to gather, select, read) — more at SORT, LEGEND] **1 a :** the act of divination by lots — compare AUGURY **b :** the art or practice of divination by lots **2 :** SORCERY, WITCHERY, ENCHANTMENT ⟨the ~ of suddenly acquired wealth⟩ — **sor·ti·leg·ic** \¦=;=¦ejik\ *or* **sor·ti·le·gious** \¦=;=¦ējəs\ *adj*

sor·ti·leg·er \-¦ijə(r), -,ej-\ *n* -S **:** FORTUNE-TELLER

sorting boom *n* **:** a stout boom used to guide floating logs into the sorting jack

sorting jack *n* **:** a moored raft having a gap through which logs are floated to be sorted by their marks; *also* **:** the space where the sorting is done

sorting tracks *n pl* **:** yard tracks for sorting and classifying railroad cars in detail after they have passed through the classification tracks

sor·ti·ta \sȯ(r)'tēd·ə\ *n* -S [It, fr. fem. of *sortito*, past part. of *sortire* to come out, emerge, fr. F *sortir*] **:** an entrance aria in an opera

sor·ti·tion \sȯ(r)'tishən\ *n* -S [L *sortition-, sortitio*, fr. *sortitus* (past part. of *sortiri* to cast or draw lots, fr. *sort-, sors* lot) + *-ion-, -io* -ion — more at SORT] **:** the act of casting lots **:** determination or appointment by or as if by lot

sortment *n* -S [[2]*sort* + *-ment*] *obs* **:** ASSORTMENT

sort of \-ə(v), -ər\ *adv* **:** kind of ⟨acting *sort of* crazy —Scott Fitzgerald⟩ ⟨I *sort of* thought —Kenneth Roberts⟩ ⟨*sort of* squatly romanesque —James Dugan⟩

sorts *pl of* SORT, *pres 3d sing of* SORT

so·rus \'sōrəs, 'sȯr-\ *n, pl* **so·ri** \-ō,rī, -ȯ,rī\ [NL, fr. Gk *sōros* heap; akin to L *tumēre* to swell — more at THUMB] **:** a cluster of reproductive bodies or spores on a lower plant: as **a :** a clump of sporangia on a fertile frond of a fern **b :** a mass of spores bursting through the epidermis of the host plant of a parasitic fungus **c :** a cluster of gemmae on the thallus of a lichen

-so·rus \'\ *n comb form* [NL, fr. *sorus*] **:** one having sori of a (specified) kind — in generic names of plants ⟨Camptosorus⟩

sor·va \'sȯrvə\ *n* -S [Pg *sôrva* (also, serviceberry), fr. L *sorba*, pl. of *sorbum* serviceberry] **1 :** COUMA **2 :** the edible fruit of the couma **3 :** the latex of the couma which yields a rubber — see BORRACHA

so·ry \'sōrē\ *n* -ES [L, fr. Gk *sōry*] **:** a black earth impregnated with vitriol; *also* **:** VITRIOLS

sos *abbr* sostenuto

SOS \¦e,sō'es\ *n* -S **1 :** an internationally recognized signal of distress in radio code made of three dots, three dashes, three dots and used esp. by ships calling for help **2 :** a call or request for help or rescue ⟨sent an ~ home for more cash⟩

SOS *abbr* **1** services of supply **2** [L *si opus sit*] if occasion require

soshed \'säsht\ *adj* [prob. alter. of E dial. *sossed* soaked, saturated, fr. past part. of E [2]*soss*] **:** DRUNK, INTOXICATED

so·sie \sō'zē\ *n* -S [F, fr. *Sosie*, slave whose form Mercury assumes in the play *Amphitryon* (1667) by Molière †1673 Fr. playwright, fr. L *Sosia*, servant of the Greco-Roman mythological hero Amphitryon in the play *Amphitruo* by Titus Maccius Plautus †184 B.C. Roman playwright] **1 :** a person having an exact likeness with another **:** DOUBLE **2 :** TWIN; *esp* **:** an identical twin

[1]so-so \'=;=\ *adv* [redupl. of [1]*so*] **:** TOLERABLY, PASSABLY ⟨played golf only so-so⟩

[2]so-so \"\ *adj* **:** neither very good nor very bad **:** MIDDLING, PASSABLE, TOLERABLE, INDIFFERENT ⟨business has been only *so-so* lately⟩ ⟨tired of seeing *so-so* movies⟩

[1]soss \'säs\ *n* -ES [ME *sos*, of imit. origin] *dial Brit* **:** MESS, SLOP

[2]soss \"\ *vb* -ED/-ING/-ES *vi* **1** *dial Brit* **:** MESS, SLOP **2** *dial Brit* **:** LAP ~ *vt, dial Brit* **:** LAP

[3]soss \"\ *n* -ES [prob. alter. of obs. E *sosh* thud, thump, of imit. origin] **:** THUMP

[4]soss \"\ *adv, dial Brit* **:** HEAVILY, PLUMP

[5]soss \"\ *vi* -ED/-ING/-ES *dial Brit* **:** to fall heavily

[1]so·ste·nen·te *also* **so·sti·nen·te** \,sōstə¦nentē, -en·(,)tā\ *adj* [It *sostenente*, fr. pres. part. of *sostenere* to sustain, fr. L *sustinēre* — more at SUSTAIN] **:** SUSTAINING; *sometimes* **:** SOSTENUTO

[2]sostenente *or* **sostinente** \"\ *n* -S [*sostenente* alter. of *sostinente; sostinente* short for *sostinente pianoforte*] **:** a device on a piano for attaining a sostenuto effect — compare SOSTINENTE PIANOFORTE

[1]so·ste·nu·to \,sōstə¦nüd·(,)ō\ *adj* [It, fr. past part. of *sostenere* to sustain] **:** SUSTAINED, PROLONGED — used as a direction in music to sustain the notes of a movement or passage to or beyond their full nominal value; abbr. *sost*

[2]sostenuto \"\ *n* -S **:** a movement or passage whose notes are markedly sustained or prolonged

sostenuto pedal *n* **:** a selective damper pedal on a piano that enables the performer to sustain selected tones or chords

sostinente pianoforte *n* [*sostinente* alter. of [1]*sostenente*] **:** one of several musical instruments (as melopiano, piano-violin) combining the ordinary piano with a mechanism for prolonging the tone produced by the strings — compare HARMONICHORD

[1]sot \'sät, -äd·+V\ *n* -S [ME *sot, sott*, fr. OE] **1** *archaic* **:** FOOL, IDIOT **2 :** a person dulled by excessive and continual drinking **:** a habitual drunkard

[2]sot \"\ *vb* **sotted; sotted; sotting; sots** [ME *sotten*, fr. *sott*, *sot* fool] *vt* **1** *archaic* **:** to make a fool or simpleton of **:** BEFOOL, STULTIFY, BEMUSE **2 :** to waste in drunkenness **:** squander sottishly — usu. used with *away* ⟨~ away his time in taverns⟩ ~ *vi* **:** TIPPLE, GUZZLE

[3]sot \"\ *chiefly dial past of* SIT

[4]sot \"\ *adj* [fr. E dial. past part. of E *set*] **1** *dial* **:** SET, FIXED **2** *dial* **:** STUBBORN, OBSTINATE

so·ta·de·an \,sōd·ə¦dēən\ *adj, usu cap* [L *sotadeus* sotadean (fr. Gk *sōtadeios*, fr. *Sōtadēs* Sotades, 3d cent. B.C. Greek satirist) + E *-an*] **:** of, relating to, or characteristic of the ancient Greek poet Sotades or his notoriously scurrilous and licentious verse

sotadean verse *n* **:** a catalectic tetrameter of major ionics having the normal form – –◡◡ | – –◡◡ | – –◡◡ | – –

[1]so·tad·ic \sō'tadik\ *adj, usu cap* [L *sotadicus*, fr. *Sotades* + L *-icus* -ic] **:** SOTADEAN

[2]sotadic \"\ *n* -S *usu cap* [L *sotadicus*, fr. *sotadicus*, adj., sotadic] **:** a Sotadean verse or poem **:** a scurrilous satire

sotadic verse *n, usu cap S* **:** palindromic verse

so·te·ri·al \sō'tirēəl\ *adj* [Gk *sōtēria* deliverance (fr. *sōtēr* savior + *-ia* -y) + E *-al*] **:** of or relating to salvation ⟨~ significance of biblical incidents⟩

so·te·ri·o·log·i·cal \sō¦tirēə¦läjəkəl\ *adj* **:** of or pertaining to soteriology

so·te·ri·ol·o·gy \sō,tirē'äləjē\ *n* -ES [Gk *sōtērion* deliverance, salvation (fr. *sōtēr* savior, fr. *sōzein* to save) + E *-logy*; akin to Gk *sōma* body — more at -SOMA] **:** a branch of theology that deals with salvation as the effect of divine agency

so that *conj* [ME, fr. OE *swā thæt*] **1 :** so 1 ⟨the turf roof of it had fallen entirely in *so that* the hut was of no use to me —R.L.Stevenson⟩ ⟨bombed out all the bridges *so that* the enemy could not retreat⟩ **2** *archaic* **:** provided that ⟨*so that* ye do not serve me sparrow hawks for supper, I will enter —Alfred Tennyson⟩

so·thi·ac \'sōthē,ak\ *also* **so·thi·a·cal** \sō'thīəkəl\ *adj, usu cap* [Gk *Sōthēs* the star Sirius + E *-iac, -iacal* (as in *zodiac, zodiacal*)] **:** SOTHIC

so·thic \'sōthik, 'säth-\ *adj, usu cap* [Gk *Sōthēs* the star Sirius + E *-ic*; fr. the fact that the year began when Sirius first appeared on the eastern horizon at sunrise] **:** relating to the ancient Egyptian year of 365¼ days or to the Sothic cycle

sothic cycle *n, usu cap S* **:** a period of 1460 Sothic years in the ancient Egyptian calendar being the time required for the beginning of the vague year of 365 days to return to its original place in relation to the sun after retrogressing through all the seasons

so·tho \'sō(,)tō\ *n, pl* **sotho** *or* **sothos** *usu cap* **1 :** BASUTO 1 **2 :** a group of closely related Bantu languages comprising Tswana, Northern Sotho, and Southern Sotho **3 :** any of the Sotho languages; *esp* **:** Southern Sotho

so·tie \sō'tē\ *n* -S [F, fr. MF, lit., foolishness, farce, fr. *sot* fool + *-ie* -y] **:** a short topical and farcical play of medieval France performed in costumes combining contemporary dress and fantastic elements (as donkey's ears and cockscombs)

so·tol \'sō,tōl, =¦=\ *n* -S [AmerSp, fr. Nahuatl *tzotolli*] **1 :** a plant of the genus *Dasylirion* (esp. *D. texanum* and *D. wheeleri*) of the southwestern U. S. and adjacent Mexico **2** [MexSp *sotol, sotole*, fr. *sotole* maguey leaf] **:** a distilled liquor made in northern Mexico esp. from the maguey — compare MESCAL, TEQUILA

sots \'säts\ *n pl* [PaG *satz* yeast, leaven, coffee grounds, fr. MHG *saz* settlement, sediment, seat (gen. *satzes*), fr. *sitzen* to sit, fr. OHG *sizzen* — more at SIT] *dial chiefly Midland* **:** YEAST

sot·ted \'säd·əd\ *adj* [ME, short for *assotted*, past part. of *assotten* to be a fool, make a fool of, become infatuated, fr. OF *assoter, asoter* to treat as a fool, fr. *a-* (fr. L *ad-*) + *sot* fool] **:** BESOTTED

sot·ter \'säd·ə(r)\ *vi* -ED/-ING/-S [prob. fr. G dial. *sottern*; prob. akin to OHG *siodan* to seethe — more at SEETHE] *chiefly Scot* **:** SIMMER, BUBBLE, SPUTTER

sot·tish \'säd·|ish, -ät|, |ēsh\ *adj* [[1]*sot* + *-ish*] **:** resembling a sot **:** very foolish **:** DOLTISH, STUPID; *also* **:** INTEMPERATE a — **sot·tish·ly** *adv* — **sot·tish·ness** *n* -ES

sot·to vo·ce \¦säd·(,)ō'vōchē, ¦sä(,)tō-, -'vō(,)chā\ *also* **sotto** *adv (or adj)* [*sotto voce* fr. It *sottovoce*, adv., lit., under the voice; *sotto* short for *sotto voce*] **1 :** under the breath **:** in an undertone; *also* **:** ASIDE, PRIVATELY **2 :** very softly ⟨play the finale *sotto voce*⟩

sou \'sü\ *n, pl* **sous** \'sü(z)\ [F, fr. MF, fr. OF *sol, solt*, fr. LL *solidus, soldus* solidus — more at SOLIDUS] **1 :** [4]SOL **2 :** a 5-centime piece **3 :** a smallest piece of money **:** PENNY, TRIFLE ⟨not a ~ lost⟩

sou *abbr* south; southern

sou·a·ri \sü'ärē\ *n* -S [F *saouari*, fr. Galibi *sawarra*] **:** a tree of the genus *Caryocar*

souari nut *n* **:** the large edible nutlike seed of any of various So. American trees of the genus *Caryocar* (as *C. nuciferum*) that yield a bland oil used in cookery

souari-nut family *n* **:** CARYOCARACEAE

sou·bise \(')sü¦bēz\ *or* **soubise sauce** *n* -S [F *soubise*, after Charles de Rohan, Prince de *Soubise* †1787 Fr. nobleman and military leader, fr. *Soubise*, village in western France that was an ancient seigneury of the Rohan family] **:** a white or brown sauce containing onions or onion purée

sou·bre·saut \,sübrə'sō\ *n* -S [F, leap, fr. MF *soubresault* — more at SOMERSAULT] **:** a ballet jump from the front and a landing on both feet in closed position

sou·brette \sü'bret\ *n* -S [F, fr. Prov *soubreto*, fem. of *soubret* affected, coy, fr. *soubra* to set aside, exceed, surmount, fr. L *superare* to go over, surmount — more at SUPERABLE] **1 a :** a lady's maid in comedies who acts the part of an intrigante **:** a coquettish maidservant or frivolous young woman — compare INGENUE **b :** an actress who plays such a part **2 :** a soprano who sings supporting roles in comic opera

soubriquet *var of* SOBRIQUET

sou·chong \(')sü¦ch|ȯŋ, -¦sh|, -¦j|, |äŋ\ *n* -S [Chin (Pek) *hsiao*[3] *chung*[3], lit., small sort] **1 :** any of several Chinese black teas made from large leaves **2 :** the coarser leaves obtained by screening fired tea

soudanese *usu cap, var of* SUDANESE

¹souf·flé \(')sü¦flā\ *n* -s [F, fr. *soufflé,* adj., puffed, fr. past part. of *souffler* to blow, blow up, puff up, fr. L *sufflare* — more at SUFFLATE] **1 :** an entrée or a dessert made with a white sauce, egg yolks and stiffly whipped egg whites, seasonings, and added ingredients (as tuna, cheese, chocolate) baked until puffed ⟨cheese ~⟩ — compare MOUSSE **2 :** something (as an artistic creation) having a light delicate mixture ⟨happy endings and her ~ of fairies and folklore —*Time*⟩ **3 :** a thin or sheer fabric made with large puffed designs and used for women's dresses

²soufflé \"\ *vt* **souffléed; souffléed; souffléing; soufflés :** to cause (food) to puff up in cooking

³soufflé \"\ *adj* [F, fr. past part. of *souffler* to blow] **1** *of pottery* **:** decorated with very small drops or sprinkles of color as if blown from a bellows **2** *or* **souf·fléed** \-ād\ [*souffléed* fr. ¹*soufflé* + *-ed*] **:** puffed by or in cooking ⟨~ omelette⟩ ⟨~ crackers⟩ ⟨~ mashed potato⟩

⁴souf·fle \'süfəl\ *n* -s [F, fr. *souffler* to blow, blow up] **:** a blowing sound heard on auscultation ⟨the uterine ~ heard in pregnancy⟩

soufflé potatoes *n pl but sing or pl in constr* [trans. of F *pommes de terre soufflées*] **1 :** mashed potatoes with egg yolks, stiffly whipped egg whites, butter, and seasonings baked until puffed **2 :** thinly sliced potatoes fried in deep fat of moderate temperature and then in fat of high temperature until puffed

sou·fri·ère \¦süfrē¦a(a)ə(r)\ *n* -s [F, fr. *soufre* sulfur (fr. L *sulphur*) + *-ière* -ier] **:** SOLFATARA

soufrière bird *n* **:** a solitaire (*Myadestes genibarbis sibilano*) of St. Vincent Island, West Indies, known only from the forested summit of the volcano La Soufrière

sougan *var of* SUGAN

¹sough \'saů, 'səf\ *vb* -ED/-ING/-S [ME *swoghen, swoughen,* fr. OE *swōgan* to sound, rustle, moan; akin to OS *swōgan* to rustle, ON *sægr* tumult, noise, Goth *gaswogjan* to groan, Lith *svagėti* to sound and perh. to Gk *ēchē, ēchos* sound — more at ECHO] *vi* **1 a :** to make a moaning or sighing sound ⟨wind ~*ing* in the branches⟩ **b :** to breathe or sigh noisily ⟨~*ing* in her sleep⟩ **c** *Scot* **:** to breathe one's last **:** DIE — used with *away* **2** *Scot* **:** to preach or pray in a whining tone ~ *vt* **1** *Scot* **:** to hum or whistle (a tune) softly **2** *Scot* **:** to utter or deliver (as a sermon) in a monotonous chanting tone

²sough \"\ *n* -s [ME *swogh, swough,* fr. *swoghen, swoughen* to sough] **1 a :** a moaning, murmuring, or sighing sound (as of the wind) **b :** a deep or noisy sigh **2** *Scot* **:** a flying report **:** RUMOR **3** *Scot* **:** the whiz of a missile or the hiss of a swung sword or club **4** *Scot* **:** a singsong manner of speaking esp. in preaching or praying — **a calm sough** *chiefly Scot* **:** SILENCE

³sough \'səf, 'saů\ *n* -s [ME *sough, swoughe, sogh*] **1** *Brit* **:** a wet place **2** *Brit* **:** DRAIN; *specif* **:** an adit for draining a mine

⁴sough \"\ *vt* -ED/-ING/-S *Brit* **:** to ditch for drainage **:** DRAIN

sought [ME *soughte* (past), *sought* (past part.), fr. OE *sōhte* (past), *gesōhte* (past part.)] *past of* SEEK

¹souk \'sük, 'sůk\ *chiefly Scot var of* SUCK

²souk *var of* SUQ

¹soul \'sōl\ *n* -s [ME *soule,* fr. OE *sāwol, sāwl;* akin to OHG *sēla, sēula* soul, ON *sāla,* Goth *saiwala*] **1 :** the immaterial essence or substance, animating principle, or actuating cause of life or of the individual life **2 a :** the psychical or spiritual principle in general shared by or embodied in individual human beings or all beings having a rational and spiritual nature **b :** the psychical or spiritual nature of the universe related to the physical world as the human soul to the human body — compare LOGOS **c** *cap, Christian Science* **:** ²GOD b(6) **3 a :** the immortal part of man having permanent individual existence ⟨~*s* in paradise⟩ ⟨~*s* consigned to damnation⟩ — contrasted with *body* **b :** a person's total self in its living unity and wholeness — sometimes distinguished from *spirit* ⟨I pray God your whole spirit and ~ and body be preserved blameless —1 Thess 5:23 (AV)⟩ **4 a :** a seat of real life, vitality, or action **:** PERSONALITY, PSYCHE **b :** an animating or essential part **:** a vital principle actuating something ⟨the hidden ~ of harmony —John Milton⟩ ⟨the true French horn, the ~ of orchestral poetry —Ralph Vaughan Williams⟩ ⟨courageous minorities are the very ~ of a democracy —*New Republic*⟩ **c :** moving spirit **:** INSPIRER, LEADER ⟨~ of the rebellion⟩ ⟨~ of an enterprise⟩ **5 a :** man's moral and emotional nature as distinguished from his mind or intellect ⟨an indomitable ~ confronting a whole world, a whole culture —Lionel Trilling⟩ **b :** the quality of expression that effectively presents or arouses emotion and sentiment ⟨what is lacking most in these young dancers . . . is a feeling of ~ —Paul Tassovin⟩ **c :** a manifestation (as affection, generosity, charity, sympathy) of the moral nature ⟨a clever man lacking in ~⟩ ⟨with so much intelligence she needs less ~ than other people —Anne D. Sedgwick⟩ **d :** spiritual or moral force **:** FERVOR ⟨that America has no ~ and will not deserve to have one until she consents to plunge into the abyss of human suffering and sin —Wallace Fowlie⟩ **6 :** human being **:** PERSON — used with a qualifying epithet ⟨a kindly ~⟩ ⟨dear ~⟩ ⟨poor ~⟩ or a number ⟨a village of barely a hundred ~*s*⟩ **7 :** one having a good or noble quality in the highest degree **:** EXEMPLIFICATION, PERSONIFICATION ⟨he is the ~ of honor⟩ ⟨she is the ~ of generosity⟩ **8** *obs* **:** the base of a cannon **syn** see MIND

²soul \'sōl, 'sōl\ *vi* -ED/-ING/-S [fr. All Souls' Day] *dial Eng* **:** to go about on All Souls' Day singing and begging for soul cakes — **soul·er** \-lə(r)\ *n* -s

sou·lard crab *or* **soulard crab apple** \(')sü¦lärd-\ *n, usu cap S* [after James G. Soulard, 19th cent. Am. horticulturist] **:** a hybrid tree (*Malus soulardii*) resembling the parent Iowa crab but having yellowish red fruit

soul bell *n* **:** PASSING BELL

soul cake *n* **:** a round or oval sweet bun traditionally eaten on All Souls' Day in England

souled \¦sōld\ *adj* **:** having a soul **:** possessing soul and feeling — usu. used in combination ⟨whole-*souled* repentance⟩ ⟨brave-*souled* pioneers⟩

soule·tin \sül'taⁿ\ *n* -s *cap* [F, fr. *Soule,* region in southwestern France] **:** a Basque dialect spoken in a district in the department of Basses-Pyrénées in France

soul–force \'≐,≐\ *n* **:** SATYAGRAHA

soul·ful \'sōlfəl\ *adj* **:** full of or expressing feeling, emotion, or sentiment ⟨~ eyes⟩ ⟨~ pose⟩ — **soul·ful·ly** \-fəlē, -li\ *adv* — **soul·ful·ness** *n* -ES

soul house *n* **:** a pottery model of a house set over a grave by the ancient Egyptians as a dwelling for the soul

soul·ish \'sōlish\ *adj* **:** relating to, involving, or suggesting the soul ⟨the ~ situations he discovers are real enough to be compulsory —Walter Lowrie⟩

soul kiss *n* **:** DEEP KISS

soul·less \'sōlləs\ *adj* **:** having no soul ⟨~ corporation⟩ **:** lacking greatness or nobleness of mind or feeling ⟨~ grubbing for profits⟩ — **soul·less·ly** *adv* — **soul·less·ness** *n* -ES

soul·mass \'sōməs\ *n* [ME *soulemasse,* fr. *soule* soul + *masse* mass — more at MASS] **1** *archaic* **:** a mass for the dead **2** *dial Eng* **:** ALL SOULS' DAY

soul mate *n* **:** one of two persons esp. of opposite sex temperamentally suited to each other **:** AFFINITY; *often* **:** a partner in an illicit relationship **:** LOVER, MISTRESS

soul priest *n* **:** a priest who offers prayers for the souls of the dead

soul scot *also* **soul shot** *or* **soul scat** *n* [*soul shot* fr. *soul* + *shot* (alter. of ME *scot* amount of money); *soul scat* alter. of *soul scot* — more at SCOT (amount of money)] **:** a mortuary fee or present paid to the clergy from a deceased's estate

soul–searching \'≐,≐≐\ *n* **:** anxious or conscientious deliberation **:** examination of one's conscience esp. with regard to deeper motives and values **:** SELF-ANALYSIS ⟨could never dismiss any suggestion however fantastic without hours of *soul-searching* —Christopher Isherwood⟩

soul–sick \'≐,≐\ *adj* **:** spiritually ill **:** very dejected or depressed — **soul–sick·ness** *n*

soul sleep *n* **:** PSYCHOPANNYCHY

soul–stuff \'≐,≐\ *n* **:** an impersonal essence vitalizing the body and believed by some peoples of Indonesia and Melanesia to permeate an individual's body and things in contact with his body and to be separable from the body either temporarily (as in dreams) or permanently (as in death)

soulth \'saůlth\ *var of* SOWLTH

¹soum \'süm\ *n* -s [prob. alter. of ¹*sum*] **1** *Irish & Scot* **:** the area of pastureland that will maintain one cow or a fixed number of other stock **2** *Scot* **:** the number of cattle or other stock that can be pastured on a determined amount of land

²soum \"\ *vt* -ED/-ING/-S *Scot* **:** to examine (land held in common) in order to determine the number of cattle or other stock that can be pastured

sou mar·kee *also* **soo markee** \¦sümär'kē\ *n* [F *sou marqué,* lit., marked sou] **1 :** a small 18th century French coin issued for the colonies and formerly circulating in the West Indies and on the No. American mainland **2 :** something of little or no value **:** CONTINENTAL ⟨not worth a *sou markee*⟩

soun *obs var of* SOUND

¹sound \'saůnd\ *adj* -ER/-EST [ME *sound, sund,* fr. OE *gesund;* akin to OS *gisund* sound, OFris *sund* fresh, unharmed, healthy, OHG *gisunt* healthy, Goth *swinths* strong, healthy and prob. to Lith *sumdyti, siumdyti* to rouse, incite] **1 a :** free from injury or disease **:** ROBUST, WHOLESOME ⟨a young man . . . of good parentage, ~ in wind and limb —Henry Miller⟩ ⟨every tooth in her head was ~ —W.M.Thackeray⟩ ⟨a ~ mind in a ~ body⟩ **b :** free from disease, abnormality, or defect impairing or likely to impair usefulness — used of a domestic animal and esp. of a horse; compare UNSOUND **c :** free from flaw, defect, or decay **:** UNIMPAIRED, UNBLEMISHED ⟨~ timber⟩ ⟨a ~ wine⟩ ⟨a ~ wall⟩ ⟨~ fruit⟩ ⟨the masonry . . . is still ~ —*Amer. Guide Series: N.C.*⟩ **2 a :** marked by solidity, firmness, or stability ⟨a building of ~ construction⟩ ⟨established a ~ foundation for future progress⟩ **b :** stable and resistant to volume change when used in construction work — used of hydraulic cements including portland, hydrated lime, quicklime, and aggregates for concrete **c :** solidly or securely based **:** RELIABLE ⟨a ~ economy⟩ ⟨a ~ society⟩ ⟨~ relationships⟩ **d :** financially secure **:** SAFE ⟨a ~ investment⟩ **3 a :** based on truth or right **:** free from error or fallacy ⟨~ advice⟩ ⟨a ~ argument⟩ ⟨~ reasoning⟩ ⟨~ criticism⟩ **b :** based on adequate knowledge or experience **:** CORRECT ⟨~ estimate of the military situation —Carl Bridenbaugh⟩ **c :** showing a high level of accuracy or polish **:** PRECISE ⟨~ scholarship⟩ ⟨paved the way for . . . ~ and fruitful knowledge of antiquity —G.C. Sellery⟩ ⟨a ~ paragraph —L.B.Nicolson⟩ **d** *chess* **:** admitting of no variation advantageous to the opponent — used of a problem or combination **e :** founded in law **:** not defective **:** LEGAL, VALID ⟨a ~ title to land⟩ **f :** agreeing with accepted views **:** ORTHODOX ⟨~ in the faith⟩ ⟨preached ~ doctrine⟩ **4 a :** COMPLETE, THOROUGH ⟨a ~ revenge⟩ ⟨a ~ recovery⟩ **b :** deep and undisturbed — used of sleep ⟨a ~ sleep⟩ **c :** HARD, SEVERE ⟨a ~ whipping⟩ **5 a :** marked by loyalty and dependability **:** TRUSTWORTHY ⟨a ~ friend⟩ ⟨his shipmates pronounced him ~ to the kelson —Herman Melville⟩ **b :** showing high morale **:** not disaffected ⟨a robust and ~ people —Matthew Arnold⟩ **c :** showing good judgment **:** LEVEL-HEADED ⟨a ~ man to have on a governing board⟩ **syn** see HEALTHY, VALID

²sound \"\ *adv* [ME, fr. ¹*sound*] **:** SOUNDLY — used with *asleep* and *sleep* and in combination ⟨~ asleep⟩ ⟨slept ~⟩ ⟨*sound*-thinking citizens⟩

³sound \"\ *n* -s *often attrib* [ME *soun,* fr. OF *son,* fr. L *sonus;* akin to OE *swinn* melody, OIr *senim* sounds, playing, OL *sonere* to sound, Skt *svanati* it sounds, resounds] **1 a :** the sensation perceived by the sense of hearing ⟨the pattern of nerve impulses arriving in the brain is associated with and subjectively experienced as ~ —Otto Stuhlman⟩ **b :** an auditory impression **:** NOISE, TONE ⟨the ~ of thunder⟩ ⟨~*s* of laughter⟩ ⟨the ~ of girls' voices —Pearl Buck⟩ ⟨from the passageway . . . the ~ of footsteps —Kenneth Roberts⟩ **c :** mechanical radiant energy that is transmitted by longitudinal pressure waves in air or other material medium and is the objective cause of the sensation of hearing ⟨the velocity of ~ in air at 32° F is about 1087 feet per second⟩ **2 a :** a speech sound ⟨a peculiar *r-sound*⟩ ⟨an \ō\-*sound*⟩ **b :** value in terms of a single speech sound or a succession of speech sounds ⟨Polish *prz* has pretty much the ~ of *bsch* in German *hübsch* — \psh\⟩ **3** *archaic* **:** RUMOR, TIDINGS ⟨the preachers . . . spread the glorious ~ —William Cowper⟩ **4 a :** noise without meaning **:** mere noise ⟨full of ~ and fury, signifying nothing —Shak.⟩ ⟨systems which . . . deal in ~*s* instead of sense —Jeremy Bentham⟩ **b** *obs* **:** underlying meaning **:** SIGNIFICANCE ⟨the word has no ~, as I may say, to me —Daniel Defoe⟩ **c :** the mental impression conveyed by a particular sound or expression **:** an accompanying implication **:** IMPORT, PORTENT ⟨that confession has a suspicious ~ to me⟩ **5 :** distance within which a particular noise may be heard **:** EARSHOT, HEARING ⟨within ~ of his voice⟩ ⟨the lad was out of sight and out of ~ —S.H.Holbrook⟩ **6 :** recorded auditory material (as on phonograph discs or motion-picture film) ⟨stereophonic ~⟩ ⟨with ~ there came . . . the need of good writing —Irving Pichel⟩ **7 :** a particular musical style characteristic of an individual, a group, or an area ⟨the Nashville ~⟩

⁴sound \"\ *vb* -ED/-ING/-S [ME *sounen,* fr. MF *soner, suner,* fr. L *sonare;* akin to L *sonus* sound] *vi* **1 a :** to make a noise or sound (as with the voice or with an instrument) **:** produce an audible effect ⟨first taught speaking trumpets how to ~ —John Dryden⟩ ⟨a buzzing noise kept ~*ing* in his ears⟩ **b :** RESOUND ⟨~*ing* to strains of soft music⟩ ⟨the echoes of his clever talk were still ~*ing* —V.L.Parrington⟩ **c :** to give a signal by sound **:** SUMMON — used with *to* ⟨the bugle ~*s* to battle⟩ **d** *archaic* **:** to become known by word of mouth ⟨from you ~*ed* out the word of the Lord —1 Thess 1:8 (AV)⟩ **2 a :** to make or convey a certain impression **:** have a certain import when heard **:** SEEM, APPEAR ⟨~*s* good to me⟩ ⟨the whole thing ~*ed* incredible —Burtt Evans⟩ **b** *obs* **:** TEND, LEAN, INCLINE ⟨~ neither to matters of state nor of war —George Puttenham⟩ **c :** to become based or founded — used with *in* ⟨those remedies for rent which ~*ed* in contract —O.W. Holmes †1935⟩ ⟨~ in tort⟩ ⟨~ in damages⟩ ⟨motives ~*ing* in the need of divine salvation —H.O.Taylor⟩ **d :** to have or tend to have the character of a specified thing — usu. used with *in* ⟨~ in folly⟩ ~ *vt* **1 a :** to cause to sound (as a musical instrument) **:** PLAY, STRIKE ⟨~*ing* the gong for breakfast⟩ ⟨hear each instrumentalist ~ his *A* —Warwick Braithwaite⟩ **b :** to produce the sound of **:** PRONOUNCE ⟨~ each syllable carefully⟩ ⟨~ the keynote⟩ **2 :** to put into words **:** VOICE ⟨how dares thy . . . tongue ~ this unpleasing news —Shak.⟩ ⟨encomiums are being ~*ed* —A.H.MacCormick⟩ **3 a :** to make known **:** PROCLAIM ⟨~ his praises far and wide⟩ ⟨~*ed* its purpose of enforcing its new regulations —Fred Russell⟩ **b :** to order, signal, or indicate by a sound ⟨~ retreat⟩ ⟨~ a parley⟩ ⟨the clock ~*s* noon⟩ **4 :** to examine the condition of (something) by causing it to emit sounds and noting their character ⟨~ a piece of timber⟩ ⟨~ the lungs⟩

⁵sound \"\ *n* -s [ME, fr. OE *sund* swimming, capacity for swimming, strait, sea & ON *sund* swimming, strait, sound; akin to MLG *sunt* narrow sea, strait, OHG *swimman* to swim — more at SWIM] **1 a :** a long and rather broad inlet of the ocean generally with its larger part extending roughly parallel to the coast **b :** a long passage of water connecting two larger bodies but too wide and extensive to be termed a strait (as a passage connecting a sea or lake with the ocean or with another sea or a channel passing between a mainland and an island) **2 :** the air bladder of a fish

⁶sound \"\ *vb* -ED/-ING/-S [ME *sounden,* fr. MF *sonder,* fr. *sonde* sounding line, act of sounding, prob. of Gmc origin; akin to OE *sundgyrd* sounding rod, *sundline* sounding line, *sundrāp* sounding lead, ON *sund* strait, sound] *vt* **1 :** to measure the depth of (as by a line and plummet) **:** FATHOM ⟨the crew must often ~ the bottom to be sure of enough water —Lyn Harrington⟩ ⟨~*ing* the distance to the bottom and to the ice overhead —W.R.Anderson & Clay Blair⟩ — see ECHO SOUNDING **2 :** to try to find out (as by discreet questioning) the views or intentions of **:** feel out **:** PROBE ⟨~*ing* various senators as to their willingness to support him —Robert Graves⟩ — often used with *out* ⟨~ him out on the idea⟩ ⟨~*ed* out the old folks about marrying her —Seumas O'Kelly⟩ **3 :** to explore or examine (a body cavity, as the bladder or urethra) with a sound **4 :** to remove the sound and other organs from (fish) **5 :** to carry down (the towline of a boat) when sounding — used of a whale ~ *vi* **1 a :** to ascertain the depth of water esp. with a sounding line ⟨there was fog . . . they crept in, ~*ing* —*Christian Science Monitor*⟩ **b :** to look into or investigate the possibility **:** put out feelers ⟨sent commissioners . . . to ~ for peace —Thomas Jefferson⟩ **c** *of a lead* **:** to go down ⟨deeper than did ever plummet ~ I'll drown my book —Shak.⟩ **2 :** to dive suddenly straight toward the bottom — used of a fish and of a whale, esp. when hooked or harpooned ⟨get to the spot before the whale gathered its wits sufficiently to ~ —R.B.Robertson⟩ — **sound the well :** to measure the depth of water accumulated in the hold of a ship ⟨*sounded the well* . . . in Nos. 1 and 2 holds —F.W.Crofts⟩

⁷sound \"\ *n* -s [obs. *sound* sounding line, act of sounding, fr. MF *sonde*] **:** an elongated instrument or probe by which cavities of the body are sounded or explored for foreign bodies, constriction, or other abnormal conditions (as in the esophagus, urethra, uterus)

⁸sound \'sün(d)\ *dial Brit var of* SWOON

sound·able \'saůndəbəl\ *adj* [⁶*sound* + *-able*] **:** capable of being sounded ⟨one piano left ~ —Thomas Carlyle⟩

sound analyzer *n* **:** a harmonic analyzer for sound waves

sound barrier *n* **:** SONIC BARRIER

soundboard \'≐,≐\ *n* [³*sound* + *board*] **1 a :** a thin resonant board (as the belly of a violin) so placed in an instrument as to reinforce its tones by sympathetic vibration — see VIOLIN illustration **b :** the top board of a wind-chest in an organ **2 :** SOUNDING BOARD 1a

sound boarding *n* **:** boards that hold deafening in partitions or under floors to deaden sounds

sound boat *n* [fr. the *Sound* (Öresund), strait between Denmark and Sweden where these boats are common] **:** a double-ended deep-keel cutter-rigged Danish fishing boat

sound bone *n* [⁵*sound*] **:** a part of the backbone of a fish lying next to the sound

sound bow *n* [³*sound*] **:** the thick part of a bell against which the clapper strikes — see BELL illustration

sound box *n* **1 :** a device in an acoustic phonograph using vibrating needle and thin diaphragm to convert phonograph record groove undulations into sound which is then amplified in a horn **2 :** a hollow chamber in a musical instrument for increasing its sonority

sound cage *n* **:** SOUND PERIMETER

sound camera *n* **:** a motion-picture camera equipped to record a sound track simultaneously with the picture on a single film and in the form of either a photographic or a magnetic record

sound change *n* **:** phonetic or phonemic change

sound–condition \'≐≐¦≐≐\ *vt* **:** to improve the acoustic properties of (as by absorption, damping, selective control, or reflection) ⟨*sound-condition* an auditorium⟩ — **sound–conditioned** \'≐≐¦≐≐\ *adj* — **sound–conditioning** \'≐≐¦≐(≐)≐\ *n*

sound–dead \'≐,≐\ *adj* **:** DEAD 10

sound effects *n pl* **:** effects that are imitative of sounds called for in the script of a play, radio or television program, or motion picture and are produced by various means (as phonograph records, musical instruments, or mechanical devices) ⟨before radio began to grow up in the 1920s, the technique of *sound effects* was extremely limited —Richard Hubbell⟩ ⟨a *sound-effects* girl . . . making radio noises like fire trucks, kisses, waterfalls, telephones —*Harper's*⟩

sound–effects man *n* **:** a technician (as in a radio or television studio) who produces sound effects

¹soun·der \'saůndə(r)\ *n* -s [ME, fr. MF *sondre, sonre,* of Gmc origin; akin to OE *sunor* herd of swine, ON *sonar-* herd of swine, MHG *swaner* herd] **:** a herd of wild swine

²sound·er \"\ *n* -s [⁶*sound* + *-er*] **:** one that sounds: as **a :** a man who measures depths of water with a lead **:** LEADSMAN **b :** a device for making soundings — see DEPTH-SOUNDER

³sounder \"\ *n* -s [⁴*sound* + *-er*] **:** an electromagnetic instrument used in telegraphy that emits clicking sounds from which a message is interpreted

soundest *superlative of* SOUND

sound field *n* **:** a region in a material medium in which sound waves are being propagated

sound figures *n pl* **:** SONOROUS FIGURES

sound film *n* **1 :** a motion-picture film carrying one or more sound records **2 a :** film intended for use in sound recording **b :** a strip of film carrying sound records in addition to the pictures

sound filmstrip *n* **:** SOUND SLIDEFILM

sound·ful \'saůndfəl\ *adj* **:** full of sound **:** MELODIOUS ⟨a ~ crowd⟩ ⟨a ~ harp⟩

sound gear *n* **:** acoustic and sonic underwater submarine detection equipment

soundhead \'≐,≐\ *n* [³*sound* + *head*] **1 :** an attachment for a motion picture projector containing apparatus for smoothing the motion of the film and for converting the sound record information into electrical signals **2 :** the part of a motion-picture printer in which the sound track negative is printed onto the positive film

sound hole *n* **:** an opening in the belly or soundboard in stringed musical instruments serving to increase its elasticity for sympathetic vibration — see VIOLIN illustration

¹sound·ing \'saůndiŋ, -dēŋ\ *n* -s [ME, fr. gerund of *sounden* to sound (measure depths) — more at SOUND] **1 a :** measurement by sounding **b :** the depth so ascertained — see ECHO SOUNDING **c soundings** *pl* **:** a place or part of a body of water where a hand sounding line will reach the bottom **2 :** measurement of the condition of the atmosphere at various heights **3 :** a probe, test, or sampling of opinion or intention **:** INQUIRY, INVESTIGATION ⟨has started ~*s* of farmer sentiment on future farm policy —*N.Y. Times*⟩ — **in soundings** *or* **on soundings :** in water not too deep to be fathomed by a hand sounding line **:** near the coast — **out of soundings** *or* **off soundings :** in water too deep to be fathomed by a hand sounding line

²sounding \"\ *adj* [ME *souning,* fr. pres. part. of *sounen* to sound — more at SOUND] **1 :** EMITTING, REVERBERATING, RESONANT, RESOUNDING, SONOROUS ⟨~ brass and a tinkling cymbal —1 Cor 13:1 (AV)⟩ ⟨a ~ kiss —Osbert Sitwell⟩ ⟨the ~ cataract haunted me like a passion —William Wordsworth⟩ — often used in combination with a preceding adjective or adverb ⟨clear ~⟩ ⟨loud ~⟩ ⟨fine-*sounding* phrases⟩ **2 :** HIGH-SOUNDING ⟨~ commonplaces⟩ ⟨apt to be taken in by ~ phrases —W.F.DeMorgan⟩

sounding arrow *n* **:** WHISTLING ARROW

sounding balloon *n* [¹*sounding*] **:** a balloon sent aloft with self-registering instruments to record and often radio reports of meteorological data

sounding board *n* [*sounding* fr. gerund of ⁴*sound*] **1 a :** a board or structure placed behind or over a pulpit, rostrum, or platform to give distinctness and sonority to the sound (as voice or music) coming from it — see BAND SHELL **b :** a device or agency that gives greater effect (as force, volume, or scope) to or helps propagate opinions or utterances ⟨Congressional hearings provide a *sounding board* comparable to question time in the House of Commons —*Economist*⟩ ⟨uses the newspapermen merely as a *sounding board* —*Atlantic*⟩ **2 :** SOUNDBOARD 1 **3 :** SOUND BOARDING

sounding lead *n* [ME] **:** a mass of lead at the end of a sounding line

sounding line *n* [ME] **:** a line, wire, or cord for sounding that is weighted at one end and is divided for sounding by hand into marks and deeps — called also *lead line*

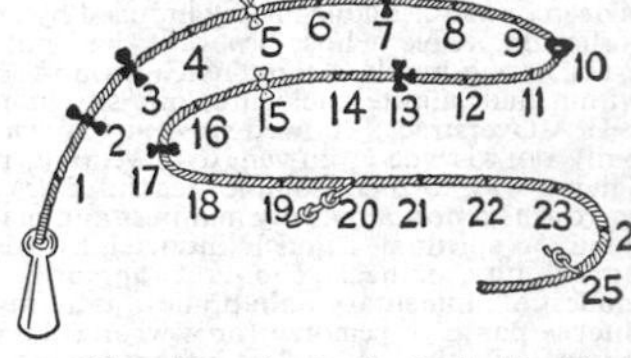

sounding line: 1, 4, 6, 8, 9, 11, 12, 14, 16, 18, 19, 21, 22, 23, 24, deeps; 2, 3, 5, 7, 10, 13, 15, 17, 20, 25, marks

sound·ing·ly *adv* **:** in a sounding manner: as **a :** RESOUNDINGLY ⟨struck his chest ~ —George Meredith⟩ **b :** IMPOSINGLY, IMPRESSIVELY ⟨pronounced the name ~⟩

sound·ing·ness *n* -ES **:** the quality or state of being sounding **:** SONOROUSNESS

sounding pipe *n* **:** a pipe in a water or oil tank on a ship for measuring depth of liquid

sounding rocket *n* **:** a rocket used to obtain information concerning the condition of the earth's atmosphere at various altitudes
sounding stop *n* **:** SPEAKING STOP
sounding tube *n* **:** a glass tube open at the bottom that is lowered to record water pressure and therefore depth as shown by the point reached within it by the water
sound intensity *n* **:** the intensity of a sound in a specified direction measured by the average rate at which sound energy passes through a unit area normal to that direction and commonly expressed in ergs per second per square centimeter
sound-intensity level *n* **:** the relative sound intensity at any point in a sound field as compared with a specified standard intensity that is usu. expressed in decibels above or below the standard
sound knot *n* [[1]*sound*] **:** a knot in lumber that is as hard as the surrounding wood and is so solid and free from decay that it will retain its place in the piece
sound law *n* **:** PHONETIC LAW
sound lens *n* **:** a lens that brings sound waves to a focus (as by having walls of collodion film and being filled with a heavy gas which retards and consequently refracts sound waves)
[1]**sound·less** \'saůndləs, *in rapid speech* -nl-\ *adj* [obs. E *sound* act of sounding + E *-less* — more at SOUND (probing instrument)] **:** incapable of being sounded or plumbed **:** UNFATHOMABLE ⟨~ seas⟩ ⟨the ~ deep⟩
[2]**soundless** \"\ *adj* [[3]*sound* + *-less*] **:** making no sound **:** QUIET, SILENT ⟨tread sure and ~ —Lew Wallace⟩ ⟨his mouth moving in a brief, ~ prayer —Josephine Johnson⟩
sound·less·ly *adv* **:** in a soundless manner **:** without a sound **:** NOISELESSLY, SILENTLY ⟨a lion pacing ~ in his cage⟩ ⟨shot twice, he crumpled ~ to the ground⟩
sound·less·ness *n* -ES **:** the quality or state of being soundless **:** NOISELESSNESS, QUIETNESS ⟨the unnatural ~ was vaguely disturbing⟩
sound-level meter *n* **:** an apparatus for comparing sound-intensity levels usu. in decibels
sound line *n* [*sound* fr. obs. *sound* act of sounding] **:** the line fastened to a harpoon and carried down by a whale when sounding
sound·ly \-lē, -li\ *adv* [ME, fr. [1]*sound* + *-ly*] **:** in a sound manner: as **a :** on a solid basis **:** SECURELY ⟨has established himself ~ in his work —*Bull. of Bates Coll.*⟩ **b :** DEEPLY, PROFOUNDLY ⟨slept ~ through the storm⟩ **c** *obs* **:** in an orthodox manner **:** CORRECTLY **d :** THOROUGHLY ⟨the wound healed ~⟩ **e :** with good sense or judgment **:** in accordance with sound principles ⟨an organization administered ~⟩ ⟨teachers . . . ~ trained —Eric Ashby⟩ **f :** VIOLENTLY, SEVERELY ⟨shook her ~ —Pearl Buck⟩
sound man *n* **1 :** SOUND MIXER **2 :** SOUND-EFFECTS MAN
sound mixer *n* **:** one that controls the volume and tone of sound picked up by microphones (as on a motion-picture set) in order to obtain the desired effects for recording
sound money *n* [[1]*sound*] **:** money not liable to sudden appreciation or depreciation in value **:** stable money; *specif* **:** a currency based on or redeemable in gold — compare PAPER MONEY, SOFT 17
sound motion picture *n* **:** a motion picture accompanied by synchronized recorded sound
sound·ness \'saůnnəs *also* -ndnəs\ *n* -ES [ME, fr. [1]*sound* + *-ness*] **:** the quality or state of being sound: as **a :** healthiness of body or mind ⟨the ~ of his constitution⟩ **b :** financial security **:** SOLVENCY ⟨appraising the ~ of the enterprise⟩ **c :** resistance to damage or disintegration **:** FIRMNESS, SOLIDITY ⟨assure . . . uniformity and structural ~ —*Steel*⟩ **d :** rightness of judgment or conception **:** LEVELHEADEDNESS ⟨the ~ of his educational theories —H.E.Starr⟩ **e :** ORTHODOXY ⟨convinced he had always doubted the ~ of my principles —Joseph Conrad⟩
[1]**sound off** *vi* **1 a :** to play three chords before and after marching from right to left of the line of troops and back during a ceremonial parade or formal guard mount — used of the band or field music **b :** to play the sound off, march as indicated, and play the sound off again **2 :** to count cadence while marching **3 a :** to speak up in a loud voice **b :** to voice one's opinions freely, vigorously, and often somewhat belligerently ⟨*sounded off* on how publishers should run their papers —*Newsweek*⟩
[2]**sound off** *n* **:** the three chords sounded by the band or field music in a military ceremony — often used as a command
sound-on-film \ˌ==ˈ=\ *n* **:** SOUND FILM 1
sound perimeter *n* **:** an apparatus for testing the ability (as of a subject in a psychological experiment) to detect the location of sounds — called also *sound cage*
sound post *n* **:** a small post in an instrument of the viol or violin family set nearly under the bridge as a support and as a transmitter of vibrations to the back
sound-powered telephone \'=,==-\ *n* **:** a light telephone operated by current generated by the speaker's voice
sound pressure *n* **1 :** the difference between the actual pressure at any point in a sound field at any instant and the average pressure at that point — compare ACOUSTIC RADIATION PRESSURE **2 :** the amplitude of the sound pressure
sound printer *n* **:** an operator of a machine for transferring the sound image from the negative to the positive motion-picture film
sound projector *n* **:** a motion-picture projector equipped to reproduce photographically and magnetically recorded sound from one or more sound tracks in synchronism with picture projection from the same film
[1]**soundproof** \'=,=\ *adj* [[3]*sound* + *proof*] **:** impervious to sound ⟨a ~ room⟩ ⟨a ~ studio⟩
[2]**soundproof** \"\ *vt* [back-formation fr. *soundproofing*] **:** to make soundproof **:** insulate so as to obstruct the passage of sound ⟨called for ~*ing* all floors, ceilings, and partitions⟩
soundproof·er \"+ə(r)\ *n* **:** a worker who installs material for soundproofing (as in automobile bodies)
soundproof·ing \"+iŋ\ *n* [[1]*soundproof* + *-ing*] **:** the act or process of soundproofing ⟨the ~ of library cubicles⟩
sound ranging *n* **:** the location of enemy weapons and the adjusting of friendly fire by timing (as with microphones) sounds from accurately surveyed points — compare FLASH RANGING, SONAR
sound recorder *n* **1 :** a mechanism that records sound tracks for sound motion pictures on a separate film from the picture film **2 :** a device for recording sound on disc, tape, or film usu. by electronic means
sound recording *n* **1 :** the act or process of making a record of sound ⟨*sound recording* for 16-millimeter films⟩ **2 :** a film, disc, or tape recording of sound ⟨*sound recordings* for news broadcasts⟩
sounds *pl of* SOUND, *pres 3d sing of* SOUND
sound screen *n* **:** a motion-picture screen made of a porous material to facilitate the transmission of sound from a loud speaker placed behind it
sound shadow *n* **:** a region of relative silence behind a screen opaque to sound waves
sound shift *or* **sound shifting** *n* [trans. of G *lautverschiebung*] **:** PHONETIC CHANGE; *specif* **:** GRIMM'S LAW
sound slidefilm *n* **:** a filmstrip having accompanying sound on a separate disc or magnetic tape that is synchronized manually or automatically with each picture on the filmstrip — called also *sound filmstrip*
sound spectrogram *n* **:** a record produced by a sound spectrograph with time shown along the horizontal axis, frequency shown along the vertical axis, and intensity indicated by varying shades of darkness of the pattern
sound spectrograph *n* **1 :** an instrument that obtains a sound spectrum by analyzing a complex sound into its component elements **2 :** an electronic instrument that produces a time-frequency-intensity analysis of sound recorded on a magnetic tape loop by repeatedly playing the sound into a variable filter and recording the output by means of a stylus on electrically sensitive paper and by synchronizing the movement of the tape loop and the paper so that successive lines drawn by the stylus along the horizontal axis of the paper correspond to the shifting frequency range of the filter
sound stage *n* **:** a room or studio made acoustically suitable (as by soundproofing) for producing sound motion pictures
soundstripe \'=,=\ *n* **:** a longitudinal stripe of magnetic material on a photographic film on which a magnetic sound record is made
sound track *n* **:** the area on a motion-picture film that carries the photographic or magnetic sound record — compare SOUND STRIPE
sound truck *n* **:** a truck equipped with a loudspeaker for broadcasting speeches or music (as for an advertising purpose or in a political campaign) ⟨*sound trucks* drive slowly through the streets blaring forth the candidate's appeal⟩
sound-type \'=,=\ *n* **:** a speech sound whose articulation and acoustic effects are unlike those of any other speech sound **:** a member of the entire stock of allophones in one or more languages
sound wave *n* **1 :** [3]SOUND 1b **2 sound waves** *pl* **:** longitudinal pressure waves in any material medium regardless of whether they constitute audible sound ⟨earthquake waves and ultrasonic waves are sometimes called *sound waves*⟩
sound wormy *n* [short for *sound wormy grade*] **:** a grade of lumber and esp. of chestnut and oak that contains many small wormholes
[1]**soup** \'süp\ *n* -S [F *soupe*, fr. OF, of Gmc origin; akin to ON *soppa* soup — more at SOP] **1** *often attrib* **:** a liquid food having as a base a meat, fish, or vegetable stock, being clear or thickened to the consistency of a thin puree or having milk or cream added, and often containing pieces of solid food (as meat, shellfish, pasta, or vegetables) **2 :** something having the consistency of soup: as **a :** a plastic mixture of solid material with liquid ⟨could not culture it in . . . any of the ~*s* used to grow bacteria —G.W.Gray b.1886⟩ ⟨manufacture . . . bookpaper from a ~ of shredded woodpulp —*Saturday Rev.*⟩; *specif* **:** a very wet concrete or mortar mix **b :** thick wet clouds or fog ⟨talk airplanes down through the ~ by . . . radar —*Boeing Mag.*⟩ **c :** nitroglycerin esp. as used by safecrackers ⟨drove to the powder house . . . to get some ~ for a safecracking job —*N.Y. Times*⟩ **d :** photographic developer ⟨while the prints were in the ~ —Florence Haas⟩ **e :** a thin solution of pyroxylin containing pigments used in coating fabrics (as for artificial leather) **3 :** an unfortunate predicament **:** HOT WATER — used in the phrase *in the soup* ⟨caught him red-handed and now he's in the ~⟩ — **from soup to nuts :** from beginning to end **:** in comprehensive detail ⟨complete equipment for the fisherman — rod, creel, waders, fancy flies, everything *from soup to nuts*⟩
[2]**soup** \"\ *vt* -ED/-ING/-S [fr. earlier *soup* substance injected into a racehorse to speed it up, fr. [1]*soup*] **:** to increase the power or efficiency of ⟨~*ing* the stock engine —*Hot Rod Mag.*⟩ — usu. used with *up* ⟨engineers had ~*ed* up the planes and some could climb as high as 20,000 feet —*All Hands*⟩ ⟨boys . . . buy old cars and ~ them up —Gregor Felsen⟩ ⟨suspended mikes — ~*ed* up to pick up a wider range of sounds —*Newsweek*⟩
[3]**soup** \"\ *n* -S **1** *slang* **:** HORSEPOWER **2** *slang* **:** added power of any kind ⟨using a rifle powder in a pistol cartridge can give a load with too much ~⟩
soup and fish *n* [so called fr. the kind of dishes served at formal dinners] **:** formal evening dress for men
soupbone \'=,=\ *n* **:** a shin, knuckle, or other bone suitable for making soup stock
soup·çon \(')süp¦sōⁿ\ *n* -S [F, suspicion, conjecture, hint, trace, fr. MF *sospeçon* suspicion — more at SUSPICION] **:** a little bit **:** TRACE, TOUCH ⟨a ~ of army rank had slipped . . . insidiously into his voice —J.D.Salinger⟩ ⟨great learning flavored with . . . a ~ of raillery —J.S.Schapiro⟩
souped-up \'=¦=\ *adj* [fr. past part. of *soup up*, v.] **1 :** augmented in power or efficiency ⟨*souped-up* outboards have given new zoom to the water-ski business —*Newsweek*⟩ ⟨racing . . . at 100 miles per hour in *souped-up* jalopies —*Information Please Almanac*⟩ ⟨a *souped-up* fission bomb . . . may release more than ten times the explosive force —*Economist*⟩ **2 a :** heightened in impact **:** made more stimulating or sensational **:** DRAMATIZED ⟨extra billions . . . for a *souped-up* worldwide arms aid program —*Wall Street Jour.*⟩ ⟨sang a *souped-up* version of the national anthem —M.W.Straight⟩ **b :** made physically more attractive **:** GLAMORIZED ⟨a *souped-up* truck boasting luxury items that would make any trucker's mouth water —*Motor Transportation in the West*⟩ **c :** keyed up **:** OVERSTIMULATED ⟨to some *souped-up* American tastes this may seem . . . slightly old-fashioned —Anthony Boucher⟩
soupfin shark \'=,=-\ *also* **soupfin** *n* **:** any of various sharks whose fins when boiled form gelatin used by the Chinese in making soup: as **a :** a common shark (*Galeorhinus zyopterus*) of the California coast **b :** [2]TOPE
soup kitchen *n* **:** an establishment dispensing soup, bread, and other minimum dietary essentials to the needy
[1]**sou·ple** \'süpəl\ *dial var of* SUPPLE
[2]**souple** \"\ *dial Brit var of* SWIPPLE
[3]**souple** \"\ *or* **souple silk** *n* -S [*souple* short for F *soie souple* supple silk; *souple silk* part trans. of F *soie souple*] **:** partially degummed silk
soup-meagre \'=,==\ *n* [F *soupe-maigre*, lit., maigre soup] *archaic* **:** a broth made chiefly from vegetables or fish
soup plate *n* **:** a deep plate usu. having a wide rim and used for serving soup
soup spoon *n* **:** a spoon with a large or rounded bowl for eating soup

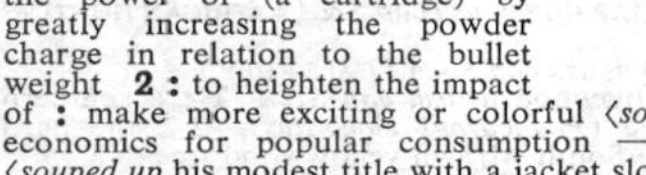

soup plate

soup up *vt* [[2]*soup*] **1 :** to increase the power of (a cartridge) by greatly increasing the powder charge in relation to the bullet weight **2 :** to heighten the impact of **:** make more exciting or colorful ⟨*souping up* textbook economics for popular consumption —Siegfried Mandel⟩ ⟨*souped up* his modest title with a jacket slogan —John Woodburn⟩
soupy \'süpē, -pi\ *adj* -ER/-EST [[1]*soup* + *-y*] **1 a :** having the consistency of soup ⟨a concrete mix should be *mushy* but not ~ —*Building, Estimating & Contracting*⟩ **b :** characterized by emotionalism **:** SENTIMENTAL, MAWKISH ⟨~ operetta melodies . . . made her cry —Mavis Gallant⟩ **2 :** densely foggy or cloudy ⟨~ weather⟩
[1]**sour** \'saů(ə)r, 'saůə, *esp in the South* 'saůwə(r\ *adj* -ER/-EST [ME, fr. OE *sūr*; akin to OHG *sūr* sour, ON *sūrr* sour, Lith *suras* salty, OSlav *syrŭ* moist, raw] **1 :** causing or characterized by the one of the four basic taste sensations produced chiefly by acids ⟨~ pickles⟩ ⟨~ green apples for pies⟩ — compare BITTER, SALT, SWEET **2 a** (1) **:** having the acid taste or smell of or as if of fermentation **:** RANCID, TURNED ⟨~ beer⟩ ⟨~ milk⟩ ⟨the smell of wet clothing is ~ —Norman Mailer⟩ (2) **:** of or relating to fermentation ⟨the ~ process for manufacturing starch⟩ **b :** smelling or tasting of decay **:** PUTRID, ROTTEN ⟨~ breath⟩ ⟨a dense drift of dead nettles — their ~ odor haunting the air —Walter de la Mare⟩ **c** (1) **:** proving unsound or unpopular **:** BAD, WRONG ⟨private lending institutions unloaded their ~ investments on the Treasury —Harrison Smith⟩ — usu. used with *go* or *turn* ⟨not enough people rented them and the project went ~ —*Reporter*⟩ ⟨a proposal which quickly turned ~ even in the Republican camp —*Economist*⟩ (2) **:** robbed of illusion **:** DISENCHANTED ⟨halfway through the book . . . went ~ on Marxism —Alfred Kazin⟩ **3 a :** of a disagreeable kind **:** UNPLEASANT, DISTASTEFUL ⟨find it easier if they . . . do not have to hear too often too much of the ~ truth —Walter Lippmann⟩ ⟨a ~ job, like washing up the dishes after a party —George Weller⟩ ⟨that's a ~ harbor in a sou'east gale —Mary H. Vorse⟩ **b :** of a cross or sullen nature **:** DOUR, MOROSE ⟨a ~ disgruntled man of small position —Margaret Mead⟩ ⟨take a ~ view of recent contributions of nuclear physics to human progress —J.B.Priestley⟩ **c :** expressive of ill humor or dissatisfaction **:** PEEVISH ⟨made a ~ grimace —L.C.Douglas⟩ **d :** taking a hostile attitude **:** DOWN — used with *on* ⟨unions are ~ on the new merger, and may . . . form a new group —*Kiplinger Washington Letter*⟩ **4 a :** acid in reaction and usu. needing drainage as well as liming — used of soil **b** *dial Brit* **:** disagreeable in texture or taste **:** HARSH, RANK — used of grass **5** *archaic* **:** INCLEMENT, MISERABLE — used of weather ⟨~ gusts of wind and rain —Archibald Lovell⟩ **6 a :** containing malodorous sulfur compounds (as hydrogen sulfide and mercaptans) — used esp. of natural gas, petroleum, and petroleum distillates; compare DOCTOR TEST **b :** inaccurate or inferior in quality **:** JARRING, POOR ⟨must hear the ~ note and correct it —C.W.Pearce⟩ ⟨his . . . drives were often wild, his putting ~ —*Time*⟩
syn ACID, ACIDULOUS, TART, DRY: SOUR is often interchangeable with ACID but in addition is applied to that which through fermentation has lost its sweet or neutral taste; it may or may not suggest rancidness ⟨*sour* wine⟩ ⟨*sour* bread⟩ ACID applies to that which has a biting taste in its natural or normal state ⟨*acid* fruits⟩ ACIDULOUS implies a degree of acidity ⟨mineral waters pleasantly *acidulous*⟩ while TART indicates a sharp but often an agreeable acidity ⟨cooks prefer *tart* apples for pies⟩ DRY applies to wines that are bland without being sweet. In more figurative senses, SOUR applies to the peevish or morose; ACIDULOUS and TART to asperity, pungency, or sharpness; ACID to the biting or caustic ⟨a *sour* man was Andrew Bogue that day, and *sourer* was he now. Nor word nor syllable would he utter —William Black⟩ ⟨she's none too well pleased about it. A discarded woman never is; she always turns *sour* on you —Max Peacock⟩ ⟨the *acidulous* tongue . . . had impaired working relationships with his British, Chinese, and American colleagues —John Fischer⟩ ⟨*tart* temper never mellows with age —Washington Irving⟩ ⟨his wit became *acid;* his letters are filled with caustic comment to sharpen the temper of those on the fighting line —V.L.Parrington⟩ DRY may suggest matter-of-fact impersonal presentation of the humorous, sarcastic, or ironic ⟨into these tiny paragraphs he packed his *dry* wit and his easy, good-natured satire on the follies of the day —Eleanor M. Sickles⟩ ⟨a story by Maupassant, *dry* and ironical in its beginning —V.S.Pritchett⟩
[2]**sour** \"\ *n* -S [ME, fr. [1]*sour*] **1 a** (1) **:** something acidulous ⟨film yeasts may develop on . . . pickles, including ~*s* and dills —*Crops in Peace & War*⟩ (2) **:** the primary taste sensation produced by acid stimuli **b :** something unpleasant or distasteful ⟨take the good with the bad, the sweet with the ~⟩ **2 :** an acid or acidic compound (as sodium fluosilicate) used in dilute water solution esp. in bleaching or laundering to neutralize alkali and decompose any remaining bleach or soap — compare GRAY SOUR 2, WHITE SOUR **3 :** a cocktail made with spirituous liquor, lemon or lime juice, sugar, and sometimes also soda water, shaken in ice and strained, and often served garnished with a maraschino cherry and slice of orange ⟨whiskey ~⟩ ⟨gin ~⟩
[3]**sour** \"\ *adv* -ER/-EST [ME, fr. [1]*sour*] **:** SOURLY
[4]**sour** \"\ *vb* -ED/-ING/-S [ME *souren*, fr. [1]*sour*] *vi* **1 a :** to become sour **:** FERMENT, ROT ⟨made a start of yeast in that keg . . . by letting some dough ~ in it —W.F.Harris⟩ ⟨there is no need for carpets to ~ from cleaning —*Boxoffice*⟩ **b :** to become acid or unproductive — used of soil **2 a :** to become peevish or morose ⟨a laughing girl, but she ~*ed* early and took to other ways —A.E.Coppard⟩ **b :** to lose interest **:** become disillusioned or fed up ⟨prospective investors ~*ed* when they found the company would pocket most of the proceeds⟩ — usu. used with *on* ⟨voters can ~ on a man who runs too many times for the same office —J.A. Morris b.1904⟩ **c :** to become impaired **:** go bad **:** DETERIORATE ⟨could . . . feel his grief ~*ing* into jealousy and resentment —Elizabeth Enright⟩ ⟨relations with his neighbors suddenly ~*ed* over the situation⟩ ~ *vt* **1 a :** to cause to ferment ⟨yeast is used to ~ the wort for beer⟩ **b :** to cause to spoil or become acidulous ⟨tainted vessels ~ what they contain —Philip Francis⟩ **c :** to make sour ⟨some grasses ~ land⟩ **2 a :** to cause to deteriorate **:** make distasteful **:** IMPAIR ⟨career was ~*ed* by inability to get along with . . . his colleagues —Lynn Montross⟩ ⟨a taste of Africa during two hunting trips . . . ~*ed* him for city life —*Newsweek*⟩ **b** (1) **:** to make cross or gloomy **:** DISGRUNTLE, IRRITATE ⟨everything in the galley had gone adrift and ~*ed* the cook —Llewellyn Howland⟩ (2) **:** to destroy the faith or enthusiasm of **:** DISAPPOINT, DISILLUSION ⟨refused to intervene . . . this ~*ed* many European idealists —Janet Flanner⟩ — usu. used with *on* ⟨~*ed* me on wealth, made me suspicious of the whole system —W.A.White⟩ **c** *obs* **:** to give a sour expression to ⟨~*ing* his cheeks —Shak.⟩ **3 :** to treat with a dilute acid solution esp. in bleaching, dyeing, and laundering **4 :** to macerate (lime) for plaster or mortar **syn** see EXACERBATE
sour ball *n* **:** a spherical piece of hard candy having a tart flavor — compare ACID DROP
sourball \'=,=\ *n* [*sour ball*] **:** a peevish person **:** GROUCH
sour·berry \'=- —*see* BERRY\ *n* **1 :** EUROPEAN CRANBERRY **2 :** LEMONADE BERRY
sourbush \'=,=\ *n* **1 :** FRENCH MULBERRY 1 **2 :** INDIAN TOBACCO 3
sour-cake \'=,=\ *n* **:** a sour leavened cake of oatmeal or rye
[1]**source** \'sō(ə)rs, 'sȯ(ə)rs, 'sōəs, 'sȯ(ə)s\ *n* -S [ME *sours*, fr. MF *sors*, fr. OF, past part. of *sordre, sourdre* to spring forth, rise, fr. L *surgere* to raise, rise — more at SURGE] **1 a :** the point of origin of a stream of water **:** FOUNTAINHEAD ⟨followed it from its ~ high in the mountains to its calmer reaches —*London Calling*⟩ **b** *archaic* **:** a natural spring or reservoir **:** FOUNT ⟨seven aqueducts brought water from distant ~*s* to Rome —Charles Merivale⟩ **2 a** (1) **:** a generative force or stimulus **:** CAUSE, INSTIGATOR ⟨reliance on local initiative . . . has always been a ~ of strength to American educational institutions —R.H.Wittcoff⟩ ⟨in almost all cases, the psychological ~ of cruel doctrines is fear —Bertrand Russell⟩ ⟨hills . . . are a ~ of scenic and recreational attraction —*Amer. Guide Series: Texas*⟩ (2) *usu cap* **:** ultimate reality **:** GOD ⟨felt close to the *Source* of all that is beautiful and true —Anna Kunz⟩ **b** (1) **:** a point of origin or procurement **:** FOUNTAIN, SUPPLIER ⟨brings us back to . . . the ~ of all significant artistic and intellectual effort — the struggles, aspirations, joys and sorrows of human beings —*Irish Digest*⟩ ⟨the principal ~ of the state's road funds was motor-vehicle fees —*Amer. Guide Series: Mich.*⟩ ⟨dried skim milk is a good ~ of protein for hogs —*Deerfield (Wis.) Independent*⟩ (2) **:** one that initiates or serves as a prototype **:** AUTHOR, MODEL ⟨the ~ of this fresh modern outlook is the prime minister —William Clark⟩ ⟨documenting . . . heavily the writer's ~*s* and his rational intentions —A.J.Guérard⟩ (3) **:** one that supplies information ⟨~*s* close to the chief executive report he is planning to request the Legislature to approve state purchase —E.M.Mills⟩ **c** *archaic* **:** genealogical lineage **:** ANCESTRY ⟨traced his ~ through the most Gothic gentlemen of Spain —Lord Byron⟩ **d :** a point of emanation ⟨it is desirable to have the light ~ accurately located —Terrell Croft⟩ **3 :** a firsthand document or primary reference work ⟨extensive work in the ~*s* — official records, manuscripts, letters, diaries, old books, newspapers —W.G.Carleton⟩ **syn** see ORIGIN
[2]**source** \"\ *vb* -ED/-ING/-S **:** ORIGINATE
source book *n* **:** a fundamental document or record (as of history, literature, art, or religion) upon which subsequent writings, compositions, opinions, beliefs, or practices are based; *also* **:** a collection of such documents ⟨these memoirs are . . . a *source book* for historians —Crane Brinton⟩
source material *n* **1 :** basic raw material ⟨requires . . . actual *source materials* in original languages on cultures, customs, economy —D.H.Clift⟩ ⟨ship nuclear *source materials* to allied nations —*Time*⟩ **2 :** PARENT MATERIAL
source region *n* **:** an extensive region of the earth's surface where large masses of air having uniform temperature and humidity conditions characteristic of the region originate
source rock *n* **:** a rock in which petroleum has originated ⟨oil passes from the *source rock* . . . into the more open spaces of a reservoir rock, where it can accumulate —W.G.Fearnsides & O.M.B.Bulman⟩
sour cherry *n* **1 a :** a rather small round-headed Eurasian tree (*Prunus cerasus*) with grayish bark, white to pinkish flowers, and bright red to almost black soft-fleshed acid edible fruits for which it is widely cultivated — compare SWEET CHERRY; see AMARELLE, MORELLO **b :** the fruit of this tree **2 :** an Australian tree (*Eugenia corynantha*) with sour-tasting red fruits
sour clover *n* **:** any of several plants of the genera *Melilotus* and *Trifolium*; *esp* **:** BITTER CLOVER
sour cream *n* **:** cream soured by the addition of a culture of lactic acid bacteria that produce lactic fermentation
sour crop *n* **:** moniliasis of poultry **:** THRUSH
sourcrout *or* **sourkrout** *var of* SAUERKRAUT

sour·dine \ˈsu̇(ə)rˌdēn, ⸗ˈ⸗\ *n* -s [F, fr. It *sordina, sordino,* fr. *sordo* silent, dull-sounding, deaf (fr. L *surdus*) + *-ina, -ino* (dim. suffixes) — more at SURD] **1 :** any of several obsolete musical instruments distinguished by their low or soft tone: as **a :** a trumpet used in giving soldiers the signal to march **b :** SPINET **2 :** ²MUTE 3

sour dip *n* **:** an acidic solution containing fermenting corn sugar and Epsom salts in which sole leather is dipped in tanning to improve color and feel

sour dock *n* [ME *sour docke,* fr. ¹*sour* + *docke* dock — more at DOCK] **:** any of several docks with sour juice: as **a :** SHEEP SORREL 1 **b :** GARDEN SORREL **c :** CURLED DOCK **d :** CANAIGRE

sour dook \ˈsü(ə)rˌdük\ *n* [¹*sour* + *dook,* of unknown origin] *Scot* **:** BUTTERMILK

sourdough \ˈ⸗ˌ⸗\ *n* [ME *sour dogh,* fr. ¹*sour* + *dogh* dough — more at DOUGH] **1 :** a leaven consisting of dough in which both alcoholic and lactic fermentation is active **2** [so called fr. the use of sourdough in making bread while camping] **:** a veteran inhabitant (as an old-time prospector) of Alaska or northwestern Canada — contrasted with *cheechako*

soured *past of* SOUR

¹**sourer** *comparative of* SOUR

²**sour·er** \ˈsau̇rə(r)\ *n* -s **:** one that sours; *specif* **:** a worker who sours yarn in a solution

sourest *superlative of* SOUR

sour gnat *n, chiefly Midland* **:** any of various minute irritating insects (as an eye gnat or drosophila)

sour gourd *n* **1 a :** CREAM-OF-TARTAR TREE **b :** the acid fruit of the cream-of-tartar tree **2 :** BAOBAB

sour grapes *n pl* [so called fr. the fable ascribed to Aesop, legendary 6th cent. B.C. Greek author of fables, about the fox that tried to get at some grapes but finding that they were beyond his reach disparaged them by saying that they appeared to be sour] **:** disparagement of something that has proven unattainable ⟨his snide remarks about people who make the honor roll are nothing but *sour grapes*⟩

sour grass *n* **1 :** ¹DOCK 1 **2 :** an American plant (*Xerophyllum tenax*) having stiff grasslike foliage **3 :** either of two tropical grasses (*Paspalum conjugatum* or *Tricholaena insularis*) the leaves of which are too sour for cattle to eat

sour greens *n pl* **:** a dock (*Rumex venosus*) of No. America having rose-colored veiny capsules

sour gum *n* **1 :** BLACK GUM — see TREE illustration **2 :** SOURWOOD

sour humus *n* **:** humus harmful to plant growth because of the presence of humic or similar acids

souring *n* -s [fr. gerund of ⁴*sour*] **1 :** an act or instance of turning sour **2** *archaic* **:** a substance (as lemon juice or vinegar) that causes souring

sour·i·quois \ˈsu̇rəˌkwȯi\ *n, pl* **souriquois** *usu cap* [F, of AmerInd origin] **:** MICMAC

sour·ish \ˈsau̇rish\ *adj* [ME, fr. ¹*sour* + *-ish*] **:** somewhat sour **:** ACIDULOUS

sourjack \ˈ⸗ˌ⸗\ *n* [¹*sour* + *jack*] **:** JACKFRUIT 2

sour lime *n* **:** ⁶LIME

sour·ly *adv* **:** in a sour manner ⟨complained ~ that it benefited only the bosses, as usual —Mollie Panter-Downes⟩

sour mash *n* **:** grain mash for brewing or distilling whose initial acidity has been adjusted to optimum condition for yeast fermentation by mash from a previous run

sour milk *n* **1 :** soured milk **2** *dial* **:** BUTTERMILK

sour milk cheese *n, North* **:** COTTAGE CHEESE

sour·ness *n* -ES [ME *sournes,* fr. OE *sūrness,* fr. *sūr* + *-ness* — more at SOUR] **1 :** the quality, state, or degree of being sour **:** ACIDITY **2 :** DISCONTENT, PEEVISHNESS

sour orange *n* **1 :** a tree (*Citrus aurantium*) much used as an understock in grafting **2 :** the fruit of the sour orange tree having somewhat bitter pulp and used esp. in making marmalade — called also *bitter orange, Seville orange*

sour plum *n* **1 :** EMU APPLE **2 :** any of several trees or shrubs of the genus *Ximenia; esp* **:** a tall much-branched often spiny shrub (*X. caffra*) of the northern Transvaal with greenish flowers in axillary clusters followed by orange-red to scarlet fruits

sourpuss \ˈ⸗ˌ⸗\ *n* [¹*sour* + *puss* (face)] **:** GROUCH, KILLJOY

sour rot *n* **:** a soft slimy watery decay of citrus fruits caused by a fungus (*Oospora citri-aurantii*)

sours *pl of* SOUR, *pres 3d sing of* SOUR

sour salt *n* **:** CITRIC ACID

sour sap *n* **:** a winter injury of fruit trees in which there is a stagnation and fermentation of sap at the time uninjured trees are starting growth and which usu. results in death

sour scab *n* **:** CITRUS SCAB

sour·sob \ˈ⸗ˌsäb\ *n* [prob. alter. (influenced by ²*sob*) of *soursop*] **:** any of several plants of the genus *Oxalis*

soursop \ˈ⸗ˌ⸗\ *n* [¹*sour* + *sop* (food)] **1 :** a small tropical American tree (*Annona muricata*) **2 :** the large succulent irregularly ovoid fruit of the soursop tree having short fleshy spines and a slightly acid fibrous pulp — called also *guanabana;* compare SWEETSOP

¹**sour-sweet** \ˈ⸗¦⸗\ *adj* [trans. of MF *aigre-doux*] **:** sweet and sour at the same time ⟨*sour-sweet* molasses⟩; *esp* **:** pleasant but with an acid overtone ⟨a *sour-sweet* smile⟩

²**sour-sweet** \"\ *n* **:** something that is sour-sweet

sourtop \ˈ⸗ˌ⸗\ *also* **sourtop blueberry** *n* **:** CANADA BLUEBERRY

sour trefoil *also* **sour trifoly** *n* **:** a wood sorrel (*Oxalis acetosella*)

sour tupelo *n* **:** OGEECHEE LIME

sourveld \ˈ⸗ˌ⸗\ *n* [¹*sour* + *veld*] **:** African veld that is largely covered with coarse seasonal perennial grasses and affords inferior grazing

sourweed \ˈ⸗ˌ⸗\ *n* **:** SHEEP SORREL

sourwood \ˈ⸗ˌ⸗\ *n* **:** a small tree (*Oxydendrum arboreum*) of the family Ericaceae common along the Alleghenies and having one-sided racemes of white flowers clustered in terminal panicles and sour-tasting leaves that turn brilliant red in the fall — called also *sorrel tree*

¹**sous** \ˈsü\ *adj* [F, prep., under, fr. L *subtus,* adv., below, under; akin to L *sub* under — more at SUB-] **:** of subordinate rank **:** ASSISTANT — used chiefly in titles ⟨~ chef⟩

²**sous** *or* **souse** \ˈsau̇s\ *n, pl* **sous** *or* **souses** [MF *sous,* pl. of *sou* — more at SOU] **1** *archaic* **:** SOU ⟨grapes are a ~ a pound —J.A.Heraud⟩ **2** [so called fr. the fact that a hit in the ring entitled the archer to a sou] **a** *archaic* **:** the outermost ring of an archery target **b :** ¹PETTICOAT 4a

³**sous** *pl of* SOU

sou·sa·phone \ˈsüzəˌfōn ˈsüsə,-\ *n* -s [John P. *Sousa* †1932 Am. bandmaster and composer + E *-phone*] **:** a large circular tuba similar to the helicon but having a flaring adjustable bell

sousaphone

¹**souse** \ˈsau̇s\ *vb* -ED/-ING/-S [ME *sousen,* prob. fr. MF *sous, souce,* n., souse, preservative] *vt* **1 :** to steep in a preservative **:** PICKLE ⟨counter loaded with *soused* herrings —A.J. Cronin⟩ **2 a :** to dip in or as if in water **:** IMMERSE, PLUNGE ⟨*soused* the squealing youngster up and down until . . . it was clean —A.W. O'Neil⟩ ⟨*soused* himself in the literature of the period before writing his term paper⟩ **b :** to wet thoroughly **:** DRENCH, SATURATE ⟨the engines arrived and *soused* the burning houses —George Meredith⟩ **3 a :** to shower or engulf completely **:** SOAK, SUBMERGE ⟨guns . . . *soused* the kopjes with shells —*London Daily News*⟩ **b :** to douse a person with **:** SLOSH, POUR ⟨*soused* one of the buckets in the drunk's face —W.A.White⟩ **4 :** to make drunk **:** INEBRIATE ⟨he was *soused,* but the look in his eyes, the rapt expression . . . weren't due only to drink —W.S.Maugham⟩ ~ *vi* **1 :** to become immersed or drenched; *esp* **:** BATHE **2 :** to get drunk **syn** see DIP

²**souse** \"\ *n* -s [ME *souse,* fr. MF *sous, souz, souce,* of Gmc origin; akin to OHG *sulza* salt water, pickled sausage, OS *sultia* salt water, MD *sulte* pickled pork, OE *sealt* salt — more at SALT] **1 a :** something that is pickled; *esp* **:** pork trimmings, fish, or shellfish chopped, seasoned, cooked, and molded for slicing **b :** a pickling solution **2** *chiefly dial* **:** EAR **3 :** an act or instance of drenching or immersion **:** DIP, WETTING ⟨the storm gets down his neck in an icy ~ —Robert Frost⟩ **4 a :** a habitual drunkard **:** TIPPLER ⟨a ~ on a bar stool —Raymond Chandler⟩ **b :** a drinking spree **:** BINGE ⟨a Sunday morning headache from a Saturday night ~⟩

³**souse** \"\ *n* -s [ME *sowce,* prob. of imit. origin] *chiefly dial* **:** a heavy blow

⁴**souse** *n* -s [ME *souce,* alter. of *sours* start of flight, source — more at SOURCE] *obs* **:** the start of a bird's flight or the stoop of a hawk intercepting it at this point

⁵**souse** \ˈsau̇s\ *vb* -ED/-ING/-S *vi, archaic* **:** to swoop down **:** PLUNGE ~ *vt, archaic* **:** to knock down by swooping upon

⁶**souse** \"\ *adv* **:** with a sudden swoop or splash ⟨~ went the sheep into a murky, muddy pool —Zane Grey⟩

⁷**souse** \"\ *vb* -ED/-ING/-S [prob. fr. ³*souse*] *vt, archaic* **:** to hit hard **:** beat severely ~ *vi, archaic* **:** to come down heavily

⁸**souse** \"\ *adv, chiefly dial* **:** with a strong impact **:** HEAVILY, DIRECTLY

souslik *var of* SUSLIK

sous-sous \ˈsü(ˌ)sü\ *n* [modif. of F *sous-sus,* short for *dessous-dessus,* lit., "underover"] **:** SOUBRESAUT

sou·tache \(ˈ)sü¦tash\ *n* -s [F, fr. Hung *sujtás*] **:** a narrow rounded or flat braid with a characteristic herringbone pattern used as a decorative trimming (as on suits, dresses, uniforms)

sou·tane \(ˈ)sü¦tän\ *n* -s [F, alter. (influenced by ¹*sous*) of MF *sottane,* fr. OIt *sottana,* fem. of *sottano,* fr. ML *subtanus,* adj., lower, under, fr. L *subtus* below, under + *-anus* -an; fr. its being worn under the vestments at religious services — more at SOUS] **:** a cassock worn by secular clergy of the Roman Catholic Church

sou·te·neur \ˌsütəˈnər, +V -ˈnər·; *-R* -ˈnə̄, + *vowel in a word following without pause* -ˈnər· *or* -ˈnə̄ *also* -ˈnə̄r\ *n* -s [F, lit., supporter, provider, fr. OF *susteneur,* fr. *sustenir* to support, provide, sustain + *-eur* -or — more at SUSTAIN] **:** PIMP 1b

sou·te·nu \ˌsütə¦nü\ *adj* [F, fr. past part. of *soutenir* to sustain, fr. OF *sustenir*] *of a ballet movement* **:** executed in a drawn-out manner **:** SUSTAINED

sou·ter *also* **sou·tar** \ˈsütə(r)\ *n* -s [ME *souter, sutor,* fr. OE *sūtere,* fr. L *sutor;* akin to L *suere* to sew — more at SEW] *chiefly Scot* **:** SHOEMAKER

sou·ter·lie·de·ken \ˈsau̇d·ə(r)ˌlēdəkən\ *n* -s [D, fr. MD *souterliedekijn,* fr. *souter* psalter (prob. fr. OF *psautier, sautier*) + *liedekijn* little song, fr. *liet* song (akin to OHG *liod* song) + *-kijn* -kin — more at PSALTER, LAUD, -KIN] **:** one of a 16th century Netherlands collection of monophonic psalm tunes taken from current popular folk melodies and containing rhymed versions of the Psalms

sou·ter·rain \ˌsüdˌəˈrān\ *n* [F, fr. *sous* under + *terrain* ground — more at SOUS, TERRAIN] **:** an underground passage or chamber

souter's clod *n, Scot* **:** a roll of coarse bread

¹**south** \ˈsau̇th\ *adv* [ME *south, suth,* fr. OE *sūth;* akin to OFris *sūth* southward, ON *suthr,* OHG *sund-;* akin to OHG *sunna* sun — more at SUN] **:** to, toward, or in the south **:** SOUTHWARD

²**south** \"\ *adj* [ME, fr. OE *sūthan-,* fr. *sūthan,* adv.; akin to OHG *sundan* from the south; derivative fr. the root of E ¹*south*] **1 a :** coming from the south ⟨a ~ wind⟩ **b** [ME, fr. OE *sūth-,* fr. *sūth,* adv.] **:** situated toward or at the south ⟨the ~ entrance⟩ ⟨the ~ country⟩ **2 :** situated in the direction of the right side of a church looking from the nave toward the altar or chancel

³**south** \"\ *n* -s [ME, fr. ¹*south*] **1 a :** the direction of the south terrestrial pole **:** the direction to the right of one facing east **:** the direction to the right of one facing the sunrise when the sun is near one of the equinoxes **b :** the part of the sky lying to the right of an observer facing east **c :** the cardinal point directly opposite to north — abbr. *S;* see COMPASS CARD **d :** the direction along any meridian toward that pole of the earth viewed from which the earth's rotation is clockwise **e :** the direction on the celestial sphere to the right when one faces the direction of its apparent rotation **:** the direction to the right when one faces the direction of revolution around the sun of the earth and the principal planets **2** *usu cap* **a :** regions or countries lying to the south of a specified or implied point of orientation (as in the U. S. the states lying in general south of Mason and Dixon's Line and the Ohio river) **b :** something (as people, culture, or institutions) characteristic of the South ⟨for years the *South* could be depended upon to vote the straight Democratic ticket⟩ **3 :** the south wind **4** *often cap* **a :** the one of four positions at 90-degree intervals that lies toward the south **b :** a person (as a bridge player) occupying such a position in the course of a specific activity

⁴**south** \ˈsau̇th, ˈsau̇t͟h\ *vi* -ED/-ING/-S **1 :** to move or veer toward the south **2 :** to come to the meridian **:** cross the north-and-south line — used chiefly of the sun and moon

southabout \ˈ⸗⸗ˌ⸗\ *adv* (*or adj*) **:** about in tacking so as to head south; *broadly* **:** toward the south **:** SOUTHWARD

south africa *adj, usu cap S&A* [fr. *South Africa,* republic in southern Africa] **:** of or from South Africa **:** of the kind or style prevalent in South Africa **:** SOUTH AFRICAN

¹**south african** *adj, usu cap S&A* [*South Africa* + E *-an,* adj. suffix] **1 :** of, relating to, or characteristic of southern Africa; *esp* **:** of, relating to, or characteristic of the Republic of South Africa **2 :** of, relating to, or characteristic of South Africans

²**south african** *n, cap S&A* [*South Africa* + E *-an,* n. suffix] **:** a native or inhabitant of the Republic of South Africa; *esp* **:** AFRIKANER

south african hunting dog *n, usu cap S&A* **:** AFRICAN HUNTING DOG

south african ruby *n, usu cap S&A* **:** CAPE RUBY

south african yellowwood *n, usu cap S&A* **1 :** a southern African timber tree (*Podocarpus elongatus*) **2 :** the hard yellow wood of the South African yellowwood tree

south america *adj, usu cap S&A* [fr. *South America,* continent of the western hemisphere] **:** of or from the continent of South America **:** of the kind or style prevalent in South America **:** SOUTH AMERICAN

¹**south american** *adj, usu cap S&A* [*South America* + E *-an,* adj. suffix] **:** of, relating to, or characteristic of South America or its people

²**south american** *n, cap S&A* [*South America* + E *-an,* n. suffix] **:** a native or inhabitant of South America

south american blastomycosis *n, usu cap S&A* [so called fr. its being limited chiefly to South America and distinct from North American blastomycosis] **:** blastomycosis characterized by formation of ulcers on the mucosal surfaces of the mouth that spread to lips, nose, and cheeks, by great enlargement of lymph nodes esp. of the throat and chest, and by involvement of the gastrointestinal tract and caused by a fungus (*Blastomyces brasiliensis*)

south american bullfrog *n, usu cap S&A* **:** a large So. American toothed frog of the genus *Leptodactylus*

south american kino *n, usu cap S&A* **:** kino taken from a So. American tree (*Coccolobis uvifera*)

south american tulipwood *n, usu cap S&A* **:** TULIPWOOD 2a(1)

south american walnut *n, usu cap S&A* **:** CONACASTE

south·amp·ton \(ˈ)sau̇¦tham(p)tən, -au̇th¦ha-\ *adj, usu cap* [fr. *Southampton,* England] **:** of or from the county borough of Southampton, England **:** of the kind or style prevalent in Southampton

south arabic *n, usu cap S&A* **:** a group of Semitic dialects spoken in southern Arabia from at least the third century B.C.

south australia *adj, usu cap S&A* [fr. *South Australia,* Australia] **:** of or from the state of South Australia **:** of the kind or style prevalent in South Australia **:** SOUTH AUSTRALIAN

¹**south australian** *adj, usu cap S&A* [*South Australia* + E *-an,* adj. suffix] **1 :** of, relating to, or characteristic of South Australia **2 :** of, relating to, or characteristic of the South Australians

²**south australian** *n, cap S&A* [*South Australia* + E *-an,* n. suffix] **:** a native or inhabitant of South Australia

south bend \(ˈ)sau̇th¦bend\ *adj, usu cap S&B* [fr. *South Bend,* Ind.] **:** of or from the city of South Bend, Ind. ⟨*South Bend* factories⟩ **:** of the kind or style prevalent in South Bend

southbound \ˈ⸗ˌ⸗\ *adj* **:** traveling or headed in a southerly direction ⟨~ traffic⟩

¹**south by east :** a compass point that is one point east of due south **:** S 11° 15′ E — abbr. *S b E, S by E;* see COMPASS CARD

²**south by east** *adv* (*or adj*) **1 :** toward south by east **2 :** from south by east

¹**south by west :** a compass point that is one point west of due south **:** S 11° 15′ W — abbr. *S b W, S by W;* see COMPASS CARD

²**south by west** *adv* (*or adj*) **1 :** toward south by west **2 :** from south by west

south carolina *adj, usu cap S&C* [fr. *South Carolina,* south Atlantic state of the U. S., fr. ²*south* + *Carolina,* Eng. colony from which No. & So. Carolina were formed — more at CAROLINIAN] **:** of or from the state of South Carolina ⟨a *South Carolina* crop⟩ **:** of the kind or style prevalent in South Carolina **:** SOUTH CAROLINIAN

¹**south carolinian** *adj, usu cap S&C* [*South Carolina* + E *-ian,* adj. suffix] **1 :** of, relating to, or characteristic of South Carolina **2 :** of, relating to, or characteristic of South Carolinians

²**south carolinian** *n, cap S&C* [*South Carolina* + E *-ian,* n. suffix] **:** a native or resident of the state of South Carolina

south celestial pole *n* **:** SOUTH POLE 1a

south central *adj, usu cap S&C* **:** of, relating to, or characteristic of the states of the lower Mississippi valley and east of the Rio Grande

south·cot·ti·an \sau̇thˈkäd·ēən\ *n* -s *usu cap* [Joanna *Southcott* †1814 Eng. woman + E *-ian*] **:** a follower of Joanna Southcott who claimed to be the bride of Christ and in the last year of her life prophesied that she would give birth to another Messiah

south dakota *adj, usu cap S&D* [fr. *South Dakota,* northwestern state of the U. S., fr. ²*south* + *Dakota* (*territory*), former region of the U. S. including No. & So. Dakota — more at DAKOTA] **:** of or from the state of South Dakota ⟨the *South Dakota* badlands⟩ **:** of the kind or style prevalent in South Dakota **:** SOUTH DAKOTAN

¹**south dakotan** *adj, usu cap S&D* [*South Dakota* + E *-an,* adj. suffix] **1 :** of, relating to, or characteristic of South Dakota **2 :** of, relating to, or characteristic of South Dakotans

²**south dakotan** *n, cap S&D* [*South Dakota* + E *-an,* n. suffix] **:** a native or resident of the state of South Dakota

¹**south·down** \ˈsau̇thˌdau̇n\ *n* -s *usu cap* [fr. *South Downs,* England, where it was orig. bred] **:** an important English breed of small medium-wooled hornless mutton-type sheep — compare DOWN

²**southdown** \"\ *adj, usu cap* [fr. *South Downs,* England] **:** of, relating to, or characteristic of a range of pasture hills south of the Thames, England

¹**south·east** \(ˈ)sau̇¦thēst, *in nautical pronunciation also* (ˈ)sau̇-¦ēst\ *adv* [ME *southest,* fr. OE *sūthēast,* fr. *sūth* south + *ēast* east — more at SOUTH, EAST] **:** to, toward, or in the southeast **:** SOUTHEASTWARD

²**southeast** \"\ *n* -s [ME, fr. ¹*southeast*] **1 a :** the general direction between south and east **b :** the part of the southern sky lying east of the observer's meridian **c :** the point of the compass midway between the cardinal points south and east **:** the point directly opposite to northwest — abbr. *SE;* see COMPASS CARD **2** *usu cap* **a :** regions or countries lying to the southeast of a specified or implied point of orientation **b :** something (as people or institutions) characteristic of the southeast ⟨the *Southeast* has benefited greatly from TVA⟩ **3 :** the southeast wind

³**southeast** \"\ *adj* [ME, fr. ¹*southeast*] **1 :** coming from the southeast ⟨a ~ wind⟩ **2 :** situated toward or at the southeast ⟨the ~ corner of his ranch⟩

¹**southeast by east :** a compass point that is one point east of due southeast **:** S 56° 15′ E — abbr. *SE b E, SE by E;* see COMPASS CARD

²**southeast by east** *adv* (*or adj*) **1 :** toward southeast by east **2 :** from southeast by east

¹**southeast by south :** a compass point that is one point south of due southeast **:** S 33° 45′ E — abbr. *SE b S, SE by S;* see COMPASS CARD

²**southeast by south** *adv* (*or adj*) **1 :** toward southeast by south **2 :** from southeast by south

south·east·er \-tə(r)\ *n* **1 :** a strong southeast wind **2 :** a storm with southeast winds ⟨a good, solid ~ . . . smacks the windows with pelting rain —Wyman Richardson⟩

¹**south·east·er·ly** \-tərlē, -li, *-R* -təl- *sometimes* -tᵊl-\ *adv* (*or adj*) [²*south* + *easterly,* adv. or adj.] **1 :** from the southeast ⟨~ gale⟩ **2 :** toward the southeast ⟨held a ~ course⟩

²**southeasterly** \"\ *n* [²*south* + *easterly,* n.] **:** a wind from the southeast ⟨it doesn't take one of those *southeasterlies* long to come up —Norman Lewis⟩

south·east·ern \-tə(r)n, *-R also* -tᵊn\ *adj* [²*southeast* + *-ern* (as in *eastern*)] **1** *often cap* **:** of, relating to, originating or dwelling in, or characteristic of a region (as of the U. S.) conventionally designated Southeast ⟨~ schools⟩ **2 :** situated toward or coming from the southeast ⟨the train comes in at the ~ station⟩

south·east·ern·er *R* -tə(r)nər, *-R* -tənə(r *also* -tᵊnə(r\ *n, usu cap* **:** a native or inhabitant of a southeastern region (as of the U. S.) ⟨the *Southeasterner* has his magnolias⟩

south·east·ern·most \-tə(r)nˌmōst, *esp Brit also* -nməst\ *adj* **:** farthest to the southeast **:** most southeastern

¹**south·east·ward** \-ēstwə(r)d\ *adv* (*or adj*) **:** toward the southeast **:** in a southeast direction ⟨rises in the mountains and flows ~⟩

²**southeastward** \"\ *n* **:** SOUTHEAST ⟨to the ~⟩

south·east·ward·ly *adv* (*or adj*) **:** toward or from the southeastward **:** SOUTHEASTERLY

south·east·wards \-dz\ *adv* **:** SOUTHEASTWARD

southed *past of* SOUTH

south·end \(ˈ)sau̇¦thend\ *or* **southend-on-sea** \(ˈ)⸗¦⸗⸗ˈ⸗\ *adj, usu cap both Ss* [fr. *Southend on Sea,* England] **:** of or from the city of Southend on Sea, England **:** of the kind or style prevalent in Southend on Sea

¹**south·er** \ˈsau̇t͟hə(r)\ *vi* -ED/-ING/-S [¹*south* + *-er* (as in ¹*batter*)] **:** to turn, veer, or shift to the south — used chiefly of the wind

²**souther** \"\ *n* -s [¹*south* + *-er,* n. suffix] **:** a southerly wind ⟨the anchorage offers pretty fair protection from anything except a ~⟩

south·er·li·ness \ˈsət͟hə(r)lēnə̇s\ *n* -ES **:** the situation of being southerly

¹**south·er·ly** \-lē, -li\ *adj* [fr. ²*south,* after E ²*east:* ¹*easterly*] **1 :** situated or directed toward the south ⟨ordered a ~ course —C.S.Forester⟩ **:** SOUTHERN ⟨there was a crack in its ~ wall —Earl Hamner⟩ **2 :** blowing from the south ⟨a ~ wind⟩

²**southerly** \"\ *adv* **1 :** from the south ⟨the wind blew ~⟩ **2 :** toward the south ⟨turned ~⟩

³**southerly** \"\ *n* -ES **:** a wind from the south ⟨the ~ came in with flood tide —G.W.Brace⟩

southerly buster *n* **:** BUSTER 3

south·er·most \-(r)ˌmōst, *esp Brit also* -ˌməst\ *adj* [fr. ²*south,* after such pairs as E ²*east: eastermost*] **:** SOUTHERNMOST

¹**south·ern** \ˈsət͟hə(r)n\ *adj* [ME *southren,* fr. OE *sūtherne;* akin to OHG *sundrōni,* ON *suthrœnn;* derivative fr. the root of E ¹*south*] **1** *often cap* **a :** of, relating to, originating or dwelling in, or characteristic of a region conventionally designated South ⟨~ mansion⟩ ⟨~ belle⟩ **b :** being or characterizing the native speech of the r-dropping population of the southeastern U. S. — compare EASTERN 4, SOUTHERN MOUNTAIN **2 a :** lying toward the south ⟨patients on the ~ side of a hospital recover faster —Herbert Spencer⟩ **b :** coming from the south ⟨~ breezes⟩ **3** *of a sign of the zodiac* **:** situated south of the equator **:** AUSTRAL

²**southern** \"\ *n* -s [ME, fr. ¹*southern*] **1** *usu cap* **:** an inhabitant of the South **:** SOUTHERNER 1 **2** *or* **southern dialect** *usu cap S* **:** the dialect of English spoken in the part of the U. S. that lies south of the southern boundary of Midland and includes most of the Chesapeake Bay area, the coastal plain and the greater part of the upland plateau in Virginia, North Carolina, South Carolina, and Georgia, and the Gulf states at least as far west as the valley of the Brazos in Texas

southern armyworm *n* **:** a climbing cutworm (*Prodenia eridania*) that is destructive to many vegetable crops in southern U. S.

southern bacterial wilt *n* **:** GRANVILLE WILT

southern balsam fir *n* **:** FRASER FIR

southern baptist *n, usu cap S&B* **:** a member of a body of Baptist churches organized in 1845 in the southern U. S. as the Southern Baptist Convention

southern black haw *n* **:** a coarse shrub or small tree (*Viburnum rufidulum*) chiefly of the southeastern U. S. having densely scurfy covering over all or parts of the leaves, petioles and branchlets

southern blight *n* **:** a disease of many vegetable and ornamental plants caused by a fungus (*Sclerotium rolfsii*) and characterized by girdling of the stem near the soil line and the production of round whitish to brown sclerotia on the stems — called also *southern stem rot*

southern blue gum *n* **:** a blue gum (*Eucalyptus globulus*)

southern bright *n* -s *usu cap S* **:** heat-cured tobacco grown in southeastern U. S., harvested by priming, and usu. used in cigarettes

southern buckthorn *n* **:** a shrub or small tree (*Bumelia lycioides*) of the southeastern U. S. with milky sap, smooth or silky oblong to narrowly obovate leaves, dense clusters of small white flowers followed by dark ovoid fruits, and very tough hard wood

southern buddhism *n, usu cap S&B* **:** HINAYANA

southern cabbage butterfly *n* **:** CABBAGE BUTTERFLY c

southern canary grass *n* **:** an annual grass (*Phalaris caroliniana*) with dense oblong panicles found in the southern U. S.

southern cattle fever *or* **southern fever** *n* **:** TEXAS FEVER

southern colonial *n, usu cap S&C* **:** the architectural style culminating in the fine Georgian mansions of the antebellum period

southern corn rootworm *n* **:** a corn rootworm that is the larva of the spotted cucumber beetle

southern cornstalk borer *n* **:** a brown-spotted grayish white caterpillar that is the larva of a straw-colored moth (*Diatraea crambidoides*) and is a destructive pest esp. of corn in the southern U. S.

southern crabapple *n* **:** a partially evergreen small tree (*Malus angustifolia*) native to southeastern U. S. but used as an ornamental having lance-oblong leaves and rose-colored flowers

southern cult *n, usu cap S&C* **:** a religious movement among the Indians of the southern U. S. in the 16th and 17th centuries assumed from certain naturalistic art styles in embossed copper plates, cut and engraved shell gorgets, pottery, and batons or maces found in archaeological sites

southern cypress *n* **:** a bald cypress (*Taxodium distichum*)

southern dewberry *n* **:** any of several brambles of the southern U. S.; *esp* **:** a dewberry (*Rubus trivialis*) with somewhat persistent foliage and oblong black fruit

southern english *n, usu cap S&E* **1 :** the English spoken in the South of England esp. by cultivated people native to or educated there and by many educated people in other parts of the British Empire **2 :** SOUTHERN 2

south·ern·er \R 'sət͟hə(r)nər, -R -t͟hənə(r\ *n* -s **1** *usu cap* **:** a native or inhabitant of the South; *esp* **:** a native or inhabitant of the southern states of the U. S. **2 :** a small light workhorse used chiefly in the southern U. S. for field labor, driving, and riding

southern flounder *n* **:** a dusky olive flounder (*Paralichthys lethostigmus*) of the south Atlantic and Gulf coasts of the U. S.

southern fox grape *n* **:** MUSCADINE 2

southern green stink bug *n* **:** a pentatomid bug (*Nezara viridula*) that is an important pest on citrus in Florida

southern hemisphere *n* **:** the half of the earth that lies south of the equator

south·ern·ism \'sət͟hə(r),nizəm\ *n* -s *usu cap* **1 :** a locution or pronunciation characteristic of the southern U.S. ⟨can detect a phony ~ quicker than most theater men —Joshua Logan⟩ **2 :** an attitude or trait characteristic of the South or Southerners esp. in the U.S. ⟨his *Southernisms* had been thoroughly rubbed away —Robert Lowell⟩

south·ern·ize \-,nīz\ *vt* -ED/-ING/-S *sometimes cap* [¹*southern* + *-ize*] **:** to imbue with qualities native to or associated with a southern region and esp. the southern states of the U. S.

southern leopard frog *n* **:** LEOPARD FROG 2

southern lights *n pl* **:** AURORA AUSTRALIS

south·ern·ly *adj* **:** SOUTHERLY

southern magnolia *n* **:** EVERGREEN MAGNOLIA

southern mongol *n, usu cap S&M* **:** PAREOEAN

southern moss *n* **:** SPANISH MOSS

south·ern·most \'sət͟hə(r)n,mōst, *esp Brit also* -nməst\ *adj* **:** farthest to the south **:** most southern

southern mountain *adj, often cap S&M* **:** being or characterizing the native speech of many mountain-dwellers of the southeastern U. S. who do not drop their r's — compare SOUTHERN 1b

southern paiute *n, usu cap S&P* **1 :** PAIUTE 1 **2 :** the language of the Southern Paiute people

southern pine *n* **1** *or* **southern pitch pine :** LONGLEAF PINE **2 :** a pitch pine (*Pinus rigida*)

southern pine beetle *n* **:** a bark beetle (*Dendroctonus frontalis*) which attacks pines in southern and eastern parts of the U. S.

southern porgy *n* **:** SCUP b

southern prickly ash *n* **:** HERCULES'-CLUB 1a

southern red cedar *n* **:** a red cedar (*Juniperus silicicola*) of the southeastern U. S. differing from the eastern red cedar in having shorter thicker leaves with blunt apexes

southern red lily *n* **:** a bulbous herb (*Lilium catesbaei*) of the southeastern U. S. with showy scarlet purple-spotted flowers

southern red oak *n* **:** RED OAK 1b

southern right whale *n* **:** a right whale (*Eubalaena glacialis*) that is somewhat smaller than the Greenland whale and is widely distributed in temperate seas though nearly extinct in the North Atlantic through overfishing

southerns *pl of* SOUTHERN

southern senega *n* **:** SENEGA 2b

southern spatterdock *n* **:** a spatterdock (*Nuphar sagittifolium*) of flowing waters of the southeastern U. S. that has filmy submersed leaves and narrow oblong to lanceolate floating leaves, sometimes forms obstructive mats in larger streams, and is often planted in aquariums

southern stem rot *or* **southern root rot** *or* **southern wilt** *n* **:** SOUTHERN BLIGHT

southern sugar maple *n* **:** a tree (*Acer barbatum*) chiefly of the southeastern U. S. having whitish gray bark and flowers with a conspicuous long white beard projecting from the throat

southern white cedar *n* **:** a strong-scented evergreen tree (*Chamaecyparis thyoides*) somewhat resembling the American arborvitae but having smaller leaves and globose cones with peltate scales

southernwood \'⸗⸗,⸗\ *n* [ME *southernwode*, fr. OE *sūtherne wudu*, fr. *sūtherne* southern + *wudu* wood — more at SOUTHERN, WOOD] **:** a shrubby European wormwood (*Artemisia abrotanum*) naturalized in America and sometimes used in brewing beer — called also *old man*

southern yellow pine *n* **:** any of several pines; *esp* **:** LONGLEAF PINE

south ethiopic *n, usu cap S&E* **:** a subgroup of Afro-Asiatic languages including Amharic, Argobba, Harari, Gafat, Gurage

south geographical pole *n* **:** SOUTH POLE 1b

south·ing \'sau̇thiŋ\ *n* -s [¹*south* + *-ing*] **1 a :** difference in latitude to the south from the last preceding point of reckoning **b :** southerly progress **:** a going southward **2 a :** crossing of the meridian to the south of the zenith **b :** the distance of any celestial body south of the equator **:** south declination

south·land \'sau̇th,land, -,laa(ə)nd, -,lənd\ *n, often cap* [ME, fr. OE *sūthland*, fr. *sūth* south + *land* — more at SOUTH, LAND] **:** land in the south **:** the south of a country ⟨most of Chile's hundred thousand Germans live in . . . her ~ —Hubert Herring⟩; *specif* **:** DEEP SOUTH ⟨bands from the ~ begin to jazz up their dance numbers —A.C.E.Schonemann⟩

south·land·er \-də(r)\ *n* **:** SOUTHERNER 1

southmost \'⸗,⸗\ *adj* [alter. (influenced by ¹*most*) of ME *southmaist*, fr. OE *sūthmest*, superl. of *sūth* south] **:** SOUTHERNMOST

south·ness *n* -ES **:** the quality or state of being south

¹southpaw \'⸗,⸗\ *n* [²*south* + *paw*] **1 :** LEFT-HANDER; *specif* **:** a left-handed baseball pitcher **2 :** a boxer who leads with the right hand and foot forward while guarding with the left hand

²southpaw \"\ *adj* **1 :** habitually using the left hand **:** LEFT-HANDED ⟨a ~ pitcher⟩ **2 :** done with the left hand ⟨a laboriously printed ~ note —John Mason Brown⟩

south polar distance *n* **:** the angular distance of a celestial body measured along its hour circle from the south celestial pole

south pole *n* **1 a :** the zenith of the heavens as viewed from the south terrestrial pole **b** *often cap S&P* **:** the southernmost point of the earth **:** the southern extremity of the earth's axis — see ZONE illustration **2** *of a magnet* **:** the pole that points toward the south when the magnet is freely suspended

¹south·ron \'sət͟hrən\ *adj, usu cap* [ME (Sc), alter. (influenced by *-on* as in *Briton*) of *southren* southern — more at SOUTHERN] *chiefly Scot* **:** SOUTHERN; *specif* **:** ENGLISH

²southron \"\ *n* -s *usu cap* **:** SOUTHERNER: as **a** *chiefly Scot* **:** ENGLISHMAN **b** *chiefly South* **:** a native or inhabitant of the southern states of the U. S.

souths *pl of* SOUTH, *pres 3d sing of* SOUTH

south sea *adj, usu cap both Ss* [fr. *South Seas*, the waters of the southern hemisphere] **:** of or relating to the seas of the southern hemisphere and esp. the south Pacific ⟨thatched huts and coconut palms of the *South Sea* islands⟩ ⟨*South Sea* pirate schooners with tall, raking masts, loaded to the gunwale with rum and gold bars —Peter Heaton⟩

south sea islander *n, usu cap both Ss&I* [*South Sea islands* + E *-er*] **:** a native or inhabitant of the tropical islands of the South Pacific **:** POLYNESIAN

south-sea·man \(')⸗'⸗mən\ *n, usu cap 1st S* [*South Sea* + *man*] **:** a sailing ship formerly running to or trading in the region of the South Seas

south sea rose *n, usu cap both Ss* **:** OLEANDER

south-seeking pole *n* **:** SOUTH POLE 2

south semitic *n, cap both Ss* **:** SOUTHWEST SEMITIC

south shields \-'shēldz\ *adj, usu cap both Ss* [fr. *South Shields*, England] **:** of or from the county borough of South Shields, England **:** of the kind or style prevalent in South Shields

south slav *n, cap both Ss* **:** a member of the Slovene, Croat, Serb, or Bulgarian peoples of the Balkans including the Serbo-Croatian speaking natives of Macedonia, Dalmatia, Bosnia and Herzegovina; *specif* **:** YUGOSLAV

¹south-southeast \(ˌ)⸗ˌ⸗ˈ⸗\ *adv (or adj)* [ME *south south est*] **1 :** toward south-southeast **2 :** from south-southeast

²south-southeast \"\ *n* **:** a compass point that is two points east of due south **:** S22°30′E — abbr. *SSE*; see COMPASS CARD

south-southerly \(')⸗'⸗⸗⸗\ *n* [so called fr. an imitation of its cry] **:** OLD-SQUAW

¹south-southwest \(ˌ)⸗ˌ⸗ˈ⸗\ *adv (or adj)* **1 :** toward south-southwest **2 :** from south-southwest

²south-southwest \"\ *n* **:** a compass point that is two points west of due south **:** S22°30′W — abbr. *SSW*; see COMPASS CARD

south temperate *adj, often cap S&T* **:** of or relating to the south temperate zone of the earth lying between the tropic of Capricorn and the antarctic circle ⟨*south temperate* seas⟩ — see ZONE illustration

south terrestrial pole *n* **:** SOUTH POLE 1b

¹south·um·bri·an \(')sau̇ˈthəmbrēən\ *n* -s *cap* [²*south* + *-umbrian* (as in *northumbrian*)] **:** a native or inhabitant of Northern Mercia

²southumbrian \"\ *adj, usu cap* **:** of or relating to the northern part of the Anglo-Saxon kingdom of Mercia, south of Northumbria

¹south·ward \'sau̇thwə(r)d\ *adv (or adj)* [ME, fr. OE *sūthweard*, fr. *sūth* south + *-weard* -ward] **:** toward the south

²southward \"\ *n* **:** southward direction or part

south·ward·ly *adv (or adj)* **:** in a southern direction ⟨proceed ~ . . . through the great region of slaves —Hastings Lyon⟩

south·wards \-dz\ *adv* [ME *southwardis*, fr. OE *sūthweardes*, fr. *sūth* south + *-weardes* -wards] **:** SOUTHWARD

¹south·west \(')sau̇ˈthwest, *usual nautical pronunciation* -au̇ˈw-\ *adv* [ME, fr. OE *sūthwest*, fr. *sūth* south + *west*] **:** to, toward, or in the southwest **:** SOUTHWESTWARD

²southwest \"\ *n* [ME, fr. OE *sūthwest*, fr. *sūthwest*, adv.] **1 a :** the general direction between the south and west **b :** the part of the southern sky lying west of the observer's meridian **c :** the point of the compass midway between the cardinal points south and west **:** the point directly opposite to northeast — abbr. *SW*; see COMPASS CARD **2** *usu cap* **a :** regions or countries lying to the southwest of a specified or implied point of orientation **b :** something (as people or institutions) characteristic of the Southwest ⟨the *Southwest* is concerned over the problem of wetbacks⟩ **3 :** the southwest wind

³southwest \"\ *adj* [ME, fr. ¹*southwest*] **1 :** coming from the southwest ⟨a ~ wind⟩ **2 :** situated toward or at the southwest

¹southwest by south : a compass point that is one point south of due southwest **:** S 33° 45′ W — abbr. *SW b S*, *SW by S*; see COMPASS CARD

²southwest by south *adv (or adj)* **1 :** toward southwest by south **2 :** from southwest by south

¹southwest by west : a compass point that is one point west of due southwest **:** S 56° 15′ W — abbr. *SW b W*, *SW by W*; see COMPASS CARD

²southwest by west *adv (or adj)* **1 :** toward southwest by west **2 :** from southwest by west

south·west·er \-tə(r)\ *n* **1 :** a strong southwest wind ⟨for the ~ freshened, and blew three parts of a gale dead into the bay —Charles Kingsley⟩ **2 :** a storm with southwest winds **3 :** SOU'WESTER 2b

¹south·west·er·ly \-tərlē, -li, -R -təl- *sometimes* -tᵊl-\ *adv (or adj)* [fr. ²*southwest*, after E *west: westerly*] **1 :** from the southwest ⟨a ~ weather pattern⟩ **2 :** toward the southwest ⟨this part of US 277 extends ~, then south —*Amer. Guide Series: Texas*⟩

²southwesterly \"\ *n* **:** a wind from the southwest

south·west·ern \-tə(r)n, -R *also* -tᵊn\ *adj* [ME, fr. OE *sūthwesterne*, fr. *sūth* south + *westerne* western — more at SOUTH, WESTERN] **1** *often cap* **:** of, relating to, originating or dwelling in, or characteristic of a region conventionally designated Southwest ⟨~ ranchers⟩ ⟨~ pueblo towns⟩ **2 :** situated toward or coming from the southwest

south·west·ern·er \R -tə(r)nər, -R -tənə(r *also* -tᵊnə(r\ *n, usu cap* **:** a native or inhabitant of a southwestern region (as of the U.S.)

southwest semitic *n, cap both Ss* **:** a division of the Semitic languages consisting of Arabic, South Arabic, and the Semitic languages of Ethiopia

¹south·west·ward \-twə(r)d\ *adv (or adj)* [²*southwest* + *-ward*] **:** toward the southwest **:** in a southwest direction

²southwestward \"\ *n* **:** SOUTHWEST ⟨to the ~⟩

south·west·ward·ly *adv (or adj)* **:** toward or from the southwest **:** SOUTHWESTERLY

south·west·wards \-dz\ *adv* [²*southwest* + *-wards*] **:** SOUTHWESTWARD

southwide \'⸗,⸗\ *adj* **:** including or affecting all the southern states of the U.S. ⟨a ~ conference⟩ ⟨a ~ strike⟩

south ye·men \-'yemən, -'yām-\ *adj, usu cap S&Y* [fr. *South Yemen*, country in southern Arabian peninsula] **:** of or from the country of South Yemen **:** of the kind or style prevalent in South Yemen

¹sou·ve·nir \ˌsüvəˈni(ə)r, -niə\ *n* -s [F, fr. MF, fr. (*se*) *souvenir* to remember, fr. L *subvenire* to come to mind, to come up — more at SUBVENTION] **1 :** an act of remembering **:** RECOLLECTION ⟨eking out her life of ~ in her palace —Eleanor Clark⟩ ⟨flitting ~ . . . of a regal gesture of her mother —Arnold Bennett⟩ **2 :** something that serves as a reminder **:** MEMENTO, REMEMBRANCE ⟨the pressed flower is a ~ from her wedding bouquet⟩ ⟨brought him a pictorial ashtray as a ~ of the trip⟩ ⟨pockmarks in the masonry . . . are ~s of the bomb that exploded there —John Brooks⟩ **syn** see MEMORY

²souvenir \"\ *vt* -ED/-ING/-S **:** to take as a souvenir ⟨guests ~*ed* the green tulle and the pink tiger lilies which had adorned the Royal table —*Sydney (Australia) Bull.*⟩

souvenir sheet *n* **1 :** a block or set of postage stamps or a single stamp printed on a single sheet of paper without gum or perforations and with margins containing lettering or design that identifies some notable event being commemorated **2 :** MINIATURE SHEET 1

sou·ve·rain \ˈsüvəˌrān\ *n* -s [F, modif. (influenced by *souverain* sovereign, fr. OF *soverain*) of E ¹*sovereign*] **:** a gold coin of Brabant and the Low Countries issued from the early 17th century until supplanted by the Belgian coinage of 1832

¹sou·ward \'sau̇wə(r)d\ *adv (or adj)* [by contr.] **:** SOUTHWARD

²souward \"\ *n* -s **:** SOUTHWARD

sou'west·er \(')sau̇ˈwestə(r)\ *n* -s [by contr.] **1 :** SOUTHWESTER ⟨exposure to . . . strong rain-bearing ~s —Katharine S. Woods⟩ **2 a :** a long oilskin coat with buckle fastenings worn esp. by sailors during stormy weather **:** SLICKER **b :** a hat with a wide slanting brim longer in back than in front and often having ear flaps that tie under the chin — called also *southwester*

sou'wester 2b

sou·za·lite \'sōzəˌlīt\ *n* -s [Antonio J. A. de *Souza*, 20th cent. Brazilian mineralogist + E *-lite*] **:** a mineral $(Mg,Fe)_3(Al,Fe)_4(PO_4)_4(OH)_6 \cdot 2H_2O$ consisting of a hydrous basic phosphate of magnesium, iron, and aluminum found with scorzalite in Minas Gerais, Brazil

sov \'säv\ *n* -s [short for ¹*sovereign*] *Brit* **:** SOVEREIGN, POUND

sov *abbr* **1** sovereign **2** soviet

SOV *abbr* shut-off valve

sovenance *n* -s [ME *sovenaunce*, fr. MF *sovenance*, *souvenance*, fr. (*se*) *sovenir*, (*se*) *souvenir* to remember + *-ance*] *obs* **:** REMEMBRANCE

¹sov·er·eign \'säv(ə)rən, -vərn *sometimes* 'səv-\ *also* **sov·ran** \'sävrən\ *n* -s [*sovereign* alter. (influenced by ¹*reign*) of ME *soverein*, *soverain*, fr. OF *soverain*, fr. (assumed) VL *superanus*, fr. L *super* over, above + *-anus* -an; *sovran* alter. (influenced by It *sovrano* sovereign, fr. OIt, fr. OF *soverain*) of *sovereign* — more at SUPER-] **1 a** (1) **:** the supreme repository of power in a political state ⟨the ~ . . . is not himself bound by the law since the law is what he declares it to be —J.H.Hallowell⟩ (2) **:** the person wielding or exercising supreme political power in a political state — compare DICTATOR, MONARCH, RULER (3) **:** a political unit possessing or held to possess sovereignty ⟨a controversy between two ~s . . . the United States on the one hand and the state of California on the other —*U.S.Code*⟩ **b :** one that exercises supreme authority within a limited sphere **:** CHIEF, MASTER **c :** an acknowledged leader **:** ARBITER, SUPERIOR ⟨cupid . . . the anointed ~ of sighs and groans —Shak.⟩ ⟨the true ~s of a country are those who determine . . . its modes of thinking —Van Wyck Brooks⟩ ⟨the rose, ~ among flowers⟩ **2 a :** a gold coin of Great Britain worth 1 pound sterling or 20 shillings, issued from Henry VII to James I and as a coin having 123.274 grains of gold .9166 fine from George III **b :** a gold coin of Saudi Arabia equivalent to 40 riyals

²sovereign \"\ *also* **sovran** \"\ *adj* [*sovereign* alter. (influenced by ¹*reign*) of ME *soverein*, *soverain*, fr. MF *sovrain*, fr. OF, fr. *sovrain*, n., sovereign; *sovran* alter. (influenced by It *sovrano*) of *sovereign*] **1 a :** possessed of controlling power **:** RULING, PREDOMINANT ⟨the king could not be ~ if there were any immunities . . . outside his jurisdiction —Christopher Morris⟩ ⟨in the case of Palestine, the United Nations, for a brief period of history, was able to act as a ~ agent —A.S.Eban⟩ **b :** unlimited in extent **:** ABSOLUTE ⟨the ~ power of the pope over all forms of secular authority —G.H.Sabine⟩ **c :** enjoying autonomy **:** INDEPENDENT, SELF-GOVERNING ⟨a ~ state⟩ ⟨a move to unify command of the separate and ~ armed services⟩ ⟨the right of each individual to be a ~ personality —Geoffrey Bruun⟩ **2 a :** of the most exalted kind **:** SUPREME ⟨in . . . literary style the ~ virtue for the judge is clearness —B.N. Cardozo⟩ ⟨promote . . . the ~ good of the community —George Grote⟩ **b :** superlative in quality **:** EXCELLENT, UNSURPASSED ⟨their ~ sense of humor, never minding the joke that is turned against themselves —Sir Winston Churchill⟩ ⟨the veneration and respect due a ~ creative genius —Roland Gelatt⟩ **c** (1) **:** having generalized curative powers **:** POTENT ⟨diphtheria antitoxin is a specific and ~ remedy when given in sufficient amounts during the first 24 hours —K.F.Maxcy⟩ (2) **:** having universally beneficial application **:** EFFECTIVE ⟨special facets of past human culture remain potentially ~ for our current ills —H.H.Watts⟩ **d :** of an unqualified nature **:** UNMITIGATED, UTTER ⟨kissed the feet of their conquerors, but in ~ contempt —Vincent Sheean⟩ **e :** having undisputed ascendancy **:** LEADING, PARAMOUNT ⟨in recasting the . . . old theology, Calvin accepted as a ~ conception the idea of God as arbitrary and absolute will —V.L.Parrington⟩ **3 :** of, relating to, characteristic of, or befitting a sovereign **:** ROYAL, UNRESTRICTED ⟨a ~ right⟩ ⟨~ equality⟩ **syn** see DOMINANT, FREE

sov·er·eign·ly *adv* [ME *sovrainly*, fr. *soverain*, adj., sovereign + *-ly*] **:** in a sovereign manner **:** AUTONOMOUSLY, SUPREMELY

sov·er·eign·ty *also* **sov·ran·ty** \-ntē, -ti\ *n* -ES [*sovereignty* fr. ME *soveraintе*, *sovereinte*, fr. MF *sovraineté*, fr. *sovraine* (fem. of *sovrain* sovereign) + *-té* -ty; *sovranty* alter. (influenced by *sovran*) of *sovereignty*] **1** *obs* **:** supreme excellence or an example of it ⟨of all complexions the cull'd ~ do meet . . . in her fair cheek —Shak.⟩ **2 a** (1) **:** supreme power esp. over a body politic **:** DOMINION, SWAY ⟨the treaty provided for the cession . . . by Spain of its ~ over the territory of Puerto Rico —Antonio Fernós-Isern⟩ ⟨the gates of Hell shall not prevail against His Church — to believe otherwise is to deny the ~ of God —*Time*⟩ ⟨deprived the railroads of ultimate ~ in . . . rate-making —A.S.Link⟩ (2) **:** freedom from external control **:** AUTONOMY, INDEPENDENCE ⟨the chief cause of modern war has been the fallacy of absolute ~ of the national state —J.T. Shotwell⟩ ⟨~ is not an indivisible whole, since it can be partially ceded to a joint authority —*European Federation Now*⟩ ⟨his mind asserted itself with . . . a strong sense of its own ~ —Leon Edel⟩ **b :** royal position or authority ⟨let the emperor turn his nominal ~ into a real central and autocratic power —Hilaire Belloc⟩ **c :** controlling influence ⟨the ~ of a superior class which gains dominion through social, economic or religious prestige —J.S.Roucek⟩ **3 :** one that is sovereign; *esp* **:** an autonomous state ⟨affirming . . . that Formosa and China are part of the same ~ —*New Republic*⟩

¹so·vi·et \'sōvē,et, -ēət *also* 'säv- *sometimes* ,⸗⸗'et *or* sōv'yet *or* 'sōv,yet *or* 'sōvyət, *usu* -d·+V\ *n* -s [Russ *sovet* council, soviet, fr. ORuss *sŭvětŭ* council] **1 :** an elected organizational unit in Communist countries **:** COMMITTEE, COUNCIL ⟨local ~s concern themselves with matters of public health, education, trade, urban improvement, and new construction —J.N.Hazard⟩ ⟨the system of ~s . . . provides an upward stream of political intelligence, suggestion and accounting from the lower organs and a downward stream of laws, decrees, and instructions from the apex —J.A.Corry⟩ — compare POLITBURO, PRESIDIUM **2 :** a state organized on Communist lines ⟨peasants were willing to seize the land and proclaim a ~ —Clare & Harris Wofford⟩; *esp* **:** one of the associated republics of the U.S.S.R. ⟨incorporate — not in the Union as a ~ but as a member of her hierarchy —*Pleasures of Publishing*⟩ **3 soviets** *pl, usu cap* **:** the people, leaders, or armed forces of the U.S.S.R. ⟨the *Soviets* say they want an increase in East-West trade —*Wall Street Jour.*⟩

²soviet \"\ *adj, usu cap* **:** of, relating to, or associated with the U.S.S.R. or its inhabitants

so·vi·et·ism \-,izəm\ *n* -s *often cap* **1 :** the principles or practices of a Soviet regime; *esp* **:** COMMUNISM ⟨fascism, socialism, and ~ have appeared as new and anticapitalist forms in the contemporary world —A.M.Sievers⟩ ⟨compelled to listen to Russian radio music, and lectures about ~ —Alfred Bilmanis⟩ **2 :** a characteristic expression or embodiment of Soviet ideology ⟨this operetta has a number of standard *Sovietisms* in it —Manny Farber⟩

so·vi·et·iza·tion \,sōvēəd·ə'zāshən, -ət, ,ī'z-\ *n* -s *often cap* **:** conversion to the Soviet system ⟨Russian leadership still seeks security for the Soviet fatherland . . . through undermining of the capitalistic and socialistic democracies and their ultimate ~ —*Foreign Policy Bull.*⟩

so·vi·et·ize *pronunciation at* SOVIET + ,īz\ *vt* -ED/-ING/-S *often cap* [¹*soviet* + *-ize*] **1 :** to bring within the Soviet orbit ⟨quotes their own words to prove that they won't be content until the world has been not only *Sovietized* but Russified —*New Yorker*⟩ **2 :** to imbue with Soviet ideals or bring into line with Soviet policy ⟨tries to *Sovietize* the youth through Marxist-trained teachers and professors —*Education Digest*⟩ ⟨on the heels of the Communist armies march the Communist commissars, who . . . ~ the conquered territory —*N.Y.Times*⟩

so·vi·et·ol·o·gist \,sōvēəd-'äləjəst, -vēə'tä- *also* ,säv-\ *n* -s *often cap* [¹*soviet* + *-ologist* (as in *geologist*)] **:** a specialist in sovietism

soviet style *n, usu cap 1st S* **:** the U.S.S.R. version of the international style of architecture characterized by a heavier reliance on a traditional vocabulary of forms

sö·vite \'sœ̄,vīt\ *n* -s [*Söve*, area in Telemark, mountain region of southern Norway + E *-ite*] **:** a dike rock composed of magmatic calcite and accessory apatite, biotite, and manganophyllite

sov·khoz *also* **sov·khos** \(,)səf'kȯz, sȯv'-, säv'-, -ȯs\ *or* **sov·hoz** \-'hȯ-\ *n, pl* **sovkho·zy** \-ȯzē\ *or* **sovkhozes** [Russ, short for *sovetskoe khozyaĭstvo* soviet farm, fr. *sovetskoe*, adj., soviet (fr. *sovet* soviet) + *khozyaĭstvo* household, economy, farm, fr. *khozyain* head of the house, proprietor] **:** a state-owned farm of the U.S.S.R. paying wages to the workers — compare KOLKHOZ

sov·prene \'säv,prēn\ *n* -s [*sov*iet + *-prene* (as in *neoprene*)] **:** a U.S.S.R. synthetic rubber of the neoprene type

sovran *var of* SOVEREIGN

sovs *pl of* SOV

[1]**sow** \'sau̇\ *n* -s [ME *sowe, suwe*, fr. OE *sugu;* akin to OE *sū* sow, OS *sū, suga*, OHG *sū*, ON *sȳr* sow, L *sus* hog, swine, Gk *hys*, Corn *hoch*, OIr *socc* hog, swine, Skt *sūkara* boar, hog, swine, Toch B *suwo* swine] **1 a :** the adult female of swine; *specif* **:** a female hog of any age that has farrowed — compare GILT **b :** the adult female of various mammals (as the cavy) **c** *archaic* **:** a fat slovenly woman **2 :** a movable protective shed; *specif* **:** CAT 3 **3 :** WOOD LOUSE 1 **4 a** (1) **:** a channel or runner that conducts molten metal to rows of molds in a pig bed (2) **:** mold of larger size than a pig **b :** a mass of metal solidified in such a mold **:** INGOT — compare [1]PIG 5a **c :** SALAMANDER **5** *chiefly Scot* **:** STACK, HEAP

[2]**sow** \'sō\ *vb* **sowed; sown** \'sōn\ *or* **sowed; sowing; sows** [ME *sowen, sawen*, fr. OE *sāwan;* akin to OHG *sāwen, sājen* to sow, ON *sā*, Goth *saian*, L *serere*, Lith *sėti* to sow, Skt *sīra* plow used for seeding, *sāyaka* one suitable for throwing; basic meaning: to drop, throw, scatter] *vi* **1 :** to plant or scatter seed ⟨farmers wait to plough and ~ until after the frost is out of the ground⟩ **2 :** to set something in motion **:** begin an enterprise ⟨may those who ~ in tears reap with shouts of joy —Ps 126:5(RSV)⟩ ~ *vt* **1 a :** to impregnate with or as if with seed ⟨surrounding fields have been *sown* . . . with squash, pumpkin and maize —*Science*⟩ ⟨insects are . . . ~*ing* the lake surface with their eggs —D.C.Peattie⟩ **b :** to put into a growing medium **:** PLANT ⟨~ seeds in vermiculite⟩; *specif* **:** to broadcast (seed) over a wide area ⟨~ clover⟩ **c :** to spread thickly **:** introduce into a selected environment **:** DISTRIBUTE, IMPLANT ⟨half a million anchovy fingerlings were *sown* in the waters of the Gulf —Jack Raymond⟩ ⟨burying a drum of metallic sodium at sea . . . would be tantamount to ~*ing* a mine —John Kobler⟩ **2 :** to set in motion **:** AROUSE, FOMENT ⟨moving . . . from town to village, ~*ing* a suspicion here and a doubt there —Christine Weston⟩ ⟨~ timidity where there should be boldness —G.F. Kennan⟩ ⟨whatever a man ~*s*, that he will also reap —Gal 6:7(RSV)⟩ **syn** see STREW

sow·able \'sōəbəl\ *adj* **:** fit for sowing

so·war \sō'(w)är\ *n* -s [Per *suwār* rider, fr. MPer *asbār, aspwār*, fr. OPer *asabāra-* horseman, fr. *asa-* horse + *-bāra-* carried by, rider] **1 :** a member of an Indian cavalry regiment **:** LANCER **2 :** a mounted orderly

sowback \'=,=\ *n* [[1]*sow* + *back*] **:** a long low hill **:** RIDGE — **sowbacked** \'=,=\ *adj*

sowbane \'=,=\ *n* [[1]*sow* + *bane*] **:** RED GOOSEFOOT; *also* **:** a related herb (*Chenopodium hybridum*) considered fatal to swine

sowbelly \'=,==\ *n* **:** fat salt pork or bacon **:** SIDE MEAT

sowbread \'=,=\ *n* [[1]*sow* + *bread;* fr. the fact that its rootstocks are eaten by swine] **:** a common wild cyclamen (*Cyclamen europaeum*) of central Europe having leaves that are dark green spotted with white above and carmine or white flowers **:** a related European herb (*Cyclamen neapolitanum*) often cultivated for its showy rose or white flowers

sow bug *n* [so called fr. its round shape] **:** WOOD LOUSE 1

sow·der \'sōdər\ *Scot var of* SOLDER

sow·ens \'sōənz, 'süə-\ *n pl but sing or pl in constr* [ScGael *sūghan* liquid of which sowens are made (fr. *sūgh* juice) + E *-s* (pl. suffix); akin to OHG *sūgan* to suck — more at SUCK] **:** a slightly fermented porridge made from the husks and siftings of oatmeal — compare FLUMMERY

sow·er \'sō(ə)r, -ōə\ *n* -s [ME *sower, sawere*, fr. OE *sāwere*, fr. *sāwan* to sow + *-ere* -er — more at SOW] **:** one that sows: as **a :** a planter of seed ⟨the simplest of mechanical ~*s* —Walter Bally⟩ **b :** a distributor of various other objects ⟨a ~ of mines⟩ **c :** a fomenter of discord ⟨a ~ of sedition —*Times Lit. Supp.*⟩

sowf *or* **sowff** \'sau̇f\ *or* **sowth** \-au̇th\ *vt* [prob. alter. of [1]*sough*] *Scot* **:** to sing softly **:** HUM

sow-gelder \'=,==\ *n, archaic* **:** one that spays sows

sow·ing \'sōiŋ\ *n* -s *often attrib* [ME *sowing, sawing*, fr. gerund of *sowen, sawen* to sow] **:** an act or instance of scattering

sowl \'sōl\ *dial var of* SOUL

sowlth \'sau̇lth\ *n* [Ir *samhailt*, lit., likeness] *Irish* **:** GHOST

sowp \'sau̇p\ *chiefly dial var of* SUP

sowre \'sau̇(ə)r\ *archaic var of* SOUR

sows *pl of* SOW, *pres 3d sing of* SOW

sow thistle *n* [ME *sowethistel*, fr. earlier *sugethistel*, fr. OE *sugu* sow + *thistel* thistle — more at SOW, THISTLE] **:** any of several coarse often somewhat spiny annual or perennial weedy herbs constituting the genus *Sonchus*, being native to Europe but naturalized throughout most of the world, and growing esp. in cultivated soils where they are noxious weeds

sow-tit \'=,=\ *n* **:** a wood strawberry (*Fragaria vesca*)

sox *pl of* SOCK

soxh·let apparatus \'säkslət-\ *n, usu cap S* [after Franz von *Soxhlet* †1926 Ger. agricultural chemist, its inventor] **:** an apparatus for use in extracting fatty or other material with a volatile solvent (as ether, alcohol, or benzene) consisting of a vertical glass cylindrical extraction tube that has both a siphon tube and a vapor tube, that is fitted at its upper end to a reflux condenser and at its lower end to a flask so that the solvent may be distilled from the flask into the condenser whence it flows back into the cylindrical tube and siphons over into the flask to be distilled again

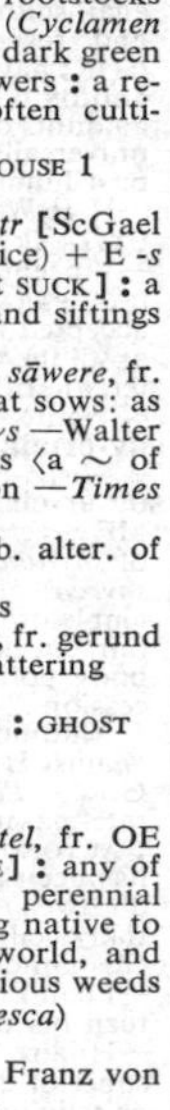

soxhlet extraction *n, usu cap S* **:** extraction in a Soxhlet apparatus

soxhlet extractor *also* **soxhlet** *n, usu cap S* [after Franz von *Soxhlet* †1926] **:** SOXHLET APPARATUS; *esp* **:** the cylindrical extraction tube

soy \'sȯi, *dial* 'sōē *or* -ōi *or* -ōə\ *n* -s [Jap *shōyū*, fr. Chin (Pek) *chiang*[4] *-yu*[2], lit., soybean oil] **1** *or* **soy sauce :** an oriental condiment consisting of a brown liquid sauce made by subjecting boiled beans (as soybeans) or beans and roasted wheat flour to long fermentation and then to long digestion in brine **2** *or* **soy pea :** SOYBEAN

soya *like* [2]SOJA\ *also* **soya bean** *n* -s [D *soja*, fr. Jap *shōyū* soy] **:** SOYBEAN

soyate \'sȯi,(y)āt, 'sō,yāt\ *n* -s [*soy* + *-ate*] **:** a mixture of salts of fatty acids from soybean oil ⟨cobalt ~⟩

soybean \'=¦=, *dial* ¦==¦=\ *n* [*soy* + *bean*] **:** an erect bushy hairy annual legume (*Glycine max*) native to Asia and extensively cultivated in China, Japan, and elsewhere whose seeds yield valuable products (as oil, flour, and meal) and whose plant is used for forage and soil improvement — called also *soja, soya*

Soxhlet apparatus or extractor

soybean lecithin *n* **:** LECITHIN 2b

soybean milk *or* **soya milk** *n* **:** soybean flour or finely ground meal suspended in water and used as a substitute for milk

soybean oil *or* **soya-bean oil** *also* **soy oil** *n* **:** a pale-yellow drying or semidrying oil obtained from soybeans by expression or solvent extraction, containing principally glycerides of linoleic, oleic, linolenic, and palmitic acids and used chiefly as a food, in paints, varnishes, linoleum, printing ink, and soap, and as a source of phosphatides, fatty acids, and sterols — called also *Chinese bean oil*

soybean oil meal *or* **soybean meal** *n* **:** the ground protein-rich residue from the production of soybean oil used chiefly in animal feeds, in adhesives and plastics, in making synthetic protein fibers, and in fermentation media (as for the production of antibiotics)

soy flour *or* **soybean flour** *n* **:** a fine sifted hull-free soybean meal used esp. as human food

so·yot \sō'yōt\ *n, pl* **soyot** *or* **soyots** *usu cap* **1 a :** a Tatar people near the headwaters of the Yenisei in Siberia and Mongolia **b :** a member of such people **2 :** the Turkic language of the Soyot people

so·zol·ic acid \sō'zälik-, -'zōlik-\ *n* [*sozolic* ISV *soz-* (fr. Gk *sōzein* to save) + *-ol* + *-ic;* fr. its antiseptic character — more at SOTERIOLOGY] **:** a mixture of the ortho and para isomers of phenolsulfonic acid $C_6H_4(OH)SO_3H$ obtained as a syrupy liquid or crystalline solid by the action of sulfuric acid on phenol and used as an antiseptic

soz·zle \'säzəl\ *vb* -ED/-ING/-S [alter. of earlier *sossle*, prob. freq. of [2]*soss*] *vt* **1 :** to wash by splashing **:** SPLASH, SOUSE **2 :** to make drunk **:** INTOXICATE ⟨we will sit here and ~ ourselves into a nice coma —Noel Coward⟩ ~ *vi* **:** LOLL, LOUNGE

sozzled *adj* **:** DRUNK ⟨a ~ nightclub customer —Douglas Watt⟩ ⟨gets ~ on the smell of the cork —*Sydney* (*Australia*) *Bull.*⟩

sp *abbr* **1** space **2** spare **3** special; specialist **4** species **5** specific **6** specimen **7** speck **8** speech **9** speed **10** spell; spelled; spelling **11** spine **12** spirit **13** sponge **14** spoon **15** sport

SP *abbr or n* -s a shore patrolman

SP *abbr* **1** self-propelled **2** semipostal **3** shore patrol **4** short page **5** *often not cap* [L *sine prole*] without issue **6** *often not cap* single phase **7** *often not cap* single pole **8** small packet **9** small paper **10** small pica **11** smokeless powder **12** soil pipe **13** standpipe **14** starting point **15** starting price **16** static pressure **17** stern post **18** stirrup pump **19** stop payment **20** stretcher party **21** submarine patrol **22** subprofessional **23** supraprotest

spa \'spä, 'spȯ, 'spȧ\ *n* -s [fr. *Spa*, watering place in eastern Belgium] **1 a :** a mineral spring resorted to for cures **b :** a locality containing a mineral spring resorted to for cures ⟨the town used to be quite the fashionable ~ —Richard Joseph⟩ **c :** a resort hotel situated at a mineral spring **d :** any esp. fashionable resort locality or hotel ⟨ski instructor at a snow-*spa* —John Woodburn⟩ **2** *NewEng* **:** SODA FOUNTAIN

SPA *abbr* **1** special public assistance **2** subject to particular average

[1]**space** \'spās\ *n* -s *often attrib* [ME, fr. OF *espace*, fr. L *spatium* — more at SPEED] **1 a :** lapse of time between two points in time ⟨the brief intermission allowed little ~ to relax⟩ **b :** a period of time **:** SPELL ⟨now there was peace for a ~⟩; *esp* **:** a relatively short interval of time ⟨during the contemplative ~ after breakfast and before work —Rebecca West⟩ ⟨a brief resting ~⟩ — often used in the phrase *space of time* ⟨this ~ of time wrought many changes —I.M.Price⟩ **c :** a specified quantity of time **:** DURATION ⟨this continued by the ~ of two years —Acts 19:10 (AV)⟩ ⟨nine times the ~ that measures day and night —John Milton⟩ ⟨we stood for the ~ of a second or two —Francis Shean⟩ **2 a :** a limited extension in one, two, or three dimensions **:** a part marked off or bounded in some way **:** DISTANCE, AREA, VOLUME ⟨written communication across the intervening ~ was more quickly accomplished —R.H.Brown⟩ ⟨from the ~*s* under the trees about the house one looked toward the south —Elizabeth M. Roberts⟩ ⟨~ left in a petroleum product container to allow for expansion during temperature changes —*Proving Ground*⟩ ⟨inner cells of land plants in contact with the outside air through the interconnecting intercellular ~*s* —*Botanical Rev.*⟩ **b :** an extent or area set apart or available for a particular purpose ⟨the open-air lot would contain 945 parking ~*s* —*Springfield* (*Mass.*) *Union*⟩ ⟨1800 square feet of floor ~⟩ ⟨the seating ~ of an auditorium⟩ ⟨down in the gasoline ~ deep in number five hold —K.M. Dodson⟩ **c :** an unobstructed area (as of land) ⟨an inner zone of parks, public gardens, and open ~*s* —H.W.H.King⟩ ⟨between the clumps of nutmeg and azalea, wide open ~*s* baked in the hot sunshine —R.L.Stevenson⟩ ⟨a land of wide open ~*s* with a sparsely scattered population —*London Calling*⟩ ⟨men whom the free ~*s* of thought frightened —V.L.Parrington⟩ ⟨the social area between built-up conventions and the wide open ~*s* where riotous instincts roam at will —C.W.Cunnington⟩ **d** (1) **:** the shaped volume defined by architectural forms (as walls, roofs, courts, and wings) ⟨translations of architectural ~ into two dimensions —J.P.Coolidge⟩ ⟨the appropriate use of ~ in small rooms has not been fully solved —Gladys Miller⟩ (2) **:** the representation or effect of three-dimensional forms and volumes in painting; *also* **:** an instance of this ⟨the actual lines and colors and ~*s* in a work of art —Clive Bell⟩ **3 :** one of the degrees between or above or below the lines of a musical staff **4 a** (1) **:** a three-dimensional entity that extends without bounds in all directions and is the field of physical objects and events and their order and relationships (2) **:** a part of space unaltered by removal of a material object **b** (1) **:** a mathematical model that pictures physical space as three-dimensional, as partly filled with material bodies, as capable of existence if all physical bodies were destroyed, and as determining but not determined by the relative positions of bodies **:** ABSOLUTE SPACE (2) **:** a mathematical model that pictures physical space as dependent on and solely determined by the relative position and direction of material bodies (3) **:** any of various mathematical models devised to explain observed or postulated phenomena inexplicable upon the assumption of a three-dimensional space unaltered by changes in the relations and state of material bodies — see SPACE-TIME **c :** the a priori form of one's experience of external phenomena **5 a :** the region beyond the earth's atmosphere — see OUTER SPACE **b :** all of the universe beyond the solar system **:** the sidereal universe ⟨interstellar ~⟩ **6 a :** a blank interval between words or lines in written or printed matter **b** (1) **:** a piece of type that is cast less than type high so as not to print and is used to separate words or characters in a line; *specif* **:** such type when narrower than an en quad — compare QUAD (2) **:** a blank area in printing caused by the use of such type; *also* **:** a comparable unexposed area in photocomposition **c :** the measure of room that a typewritten character occupies on the paper or that is left blank by one movement of the space bar ⟨indent the first line several ~*s* —*Modern Language Assoc. Style Sheet*⟩ **d :** the measure of room that a line of typewriting occupies on the paper ⟨drop three ~*s* and indent⟩ **7 a :** a mathematical aggregate of *n* elements and *n* dimensions **b :** a three-dimensional region **8 :** an expanse of empty air extending outward and downward from a particular point ⟨cornices which hung out over ~ on both sides —N. B. Clinch⟩ **9 :** a vague conception of distance and expansiveness induced by a listless or dreamy mental state ⟨was reminded of those dreamy spells of hers, the way she used to go drifting off into ~ —Hamilton Basso⟩ **10 :** a place left open in the pattern of a game of solitaire by the play of a card and made available for occupancy by another card **11 :** an interval in operation during which a telegraph key is not in contact **12 a :** LINAGE 1, 3 ⟨sell ~ for a newspaper⟩ ⟨~ in the newspaper is always restricted —F.L.Mott⟩ ⟨reproduced his delicate drawings badly, paid him by ~ —F.J.Mather⟩ **b :** time available on radio or television esp. to advertisers ⟨air ~ is even more valuable than paper ~ —Joanna Jonsson⟩ **13 :** accommodations obtained or available on a public transportation vehicle ⟨the passenger agent was pretty sure there wouldn't be ~ on the incoming flight —J.S.Redding⟩; *esp* **:** such accommodations when reserved in advance ⟨reserved his ~ two weeks ago⟩ — **in the mean space** *obs* **:** MEANWHILE

[2]**space** \"\ *vb* -ED/-ING/-S *vt* **1 :** to bound in space **:** determine the spatial limits of **2 :** to place at intervals **:** separate by periods of time **:** arrange with spaces between **:** INTERSPACE ⟨houses *spaced* as irregularly as pins on a map —*Amer. Guide Series: N.Y. City*⟩ ⟨~ the children born in a family⟩ — often used with *out* ⟨the farms were small, and *spaced* out from four to five miles apart —H.L.Davis⟩; see SPACE OUT ~ *vi* **:** to leave one or more blank spaces (as in a line of typing)

space absorption *n* **:** the attenuation of the light of stars and galaxies when it encounters interstellar matter within a galaxy or material in the relatively empty regions between galaxies **:** the reddening of starlight by interstellar matter

spaceband \'=,=\ *n* **:** a device consisting typically of a joined pair of thin reciprocally tapered steel wedges that is used as a variable-width space in keyboard slugcasting machines to expand and force the line of assembled matrices out to full measure so that a justified line is cast

space bar *n* **1 :** a bar (as on a typewriter) that on each depression causes the carriage to move one space to the left **2 :** a bar on a monotype keyboard each depression of which causes the setting of one justification space

space cadet *n* **1 :** a youthful astronaut in a space opera **2 :** a usu. juvenile enthusiast for space travel **3** *slang* **:** a pilot who shows off

space charge *n* **:** an electric charge (as the electrons in the region near the filament of a vacuum tube) distributed throughout a three-dimensional region as distinguished from the electrostatic surface charge on a conductor

space-charge effect *n* **:** the limitation of flow of plate current in an electron tube produced by repulsion exerted on electrons leaving the filament by the other electrons in the region between filament and plate

spacecraft \'=,=\ *n* **:** SPACESHIP

space curve *n* **:** a curve in three-dimensional space

space divider *n* **:** DIVIDER 9

spaced payment *n* **:** the payment of parts of a purchase price at stated intervals **:** payment by installments

space error *n* **:** a constant error in the comparison of magnitudes resulting from the differing locations of the magnitudes compared

space flight *n* **:** flight beyond the earth's atmosphere

space formula *n* **:** PERSPECTIVE FORMULA

space group *n* **:** a group or array of symmetry elements on the points of a space lattice

space heater *n* **:** a self-contained unit that warms a room or space by converting to heat in that space the fuel or electric energy supplied to it

space heating *n* **:** heating of spaces esp. for human comfort by any means (as by fuel, electricity, or solar radiation) with the heater either within the space or external to it

space isomerism *n* **:** STEREOISOMERISM

space key *n* **1 :** SPACE BAR 1 **2 :** a key on a monotype keyboard each depression of which causes the setting of a space of fixed width (as one em) **3 :** the key on a key punch that controls the spacing of holes in punched cards

space lattice *n* **:** a three-dimensional pattern of points so arranged as to determine by indefinite repetition sets of equally spaced parallel planes in various directions forming polyhedral cells (as in a honeycomb); *specif* **:** a set of such points occupied by the atoms of a crystal — compare BRAVAIS LATTICE, LATTICE CONSTANT

space·less \'spāsləs\ *adj* **1 :** having no limits **:** BOUNDLESS ⟨a timeless and almost ~ world of the imagination —R.A. Hall b.1911⟩ **2 :** occupying no space ⟨pure meanings, values, and norms are geometrically ~ —P.A.Sorokin⟩

space man \'=,man, -,maa(ə)n\ *n* **:** SPACE WRITER

space·man \-,man, -mən, -,maa(ə)n\ *n, pl* **spacemen 1 :** one who travels or is in training for travel outside the earth's atmosphere **2 :** a visitor to the earth from outer space

space mark *n* **:** the symbol #

space medicine *n* **:** a branch of medicine that deals with the physiologic and biologic effects on the human body of rocket or jet flight beyond the earth's atmosphere — see AVIATION MEDICINE

space motion *n* **1 :** the motion of the earth and other solar system members as they travel through space with the sun **2 :** SPACE VELOCITY

space of fon·tana \-,fän·'tänə, -fən·-, -tanə\ *usu cap F* [after Felice *Fontana* †1805 It. physiologist] **:** any of the spaces between trabeculae of the posterior elastic lamina of the cornea through which the anterior chamber of the eye communicates with Schlemm's canal

space of ret·zi·us \-'retsēəs\ *usu cap R* [after Anders A. *Retzius* †1860 Swed. anatomist] **:** a space between the bladder and the symphysis pubis occupied by fatty tissue

space opera *n* **1 :** a novel, motion picture, radio or television play, or comic strip usu. of a stock type featuring interplanetary travel, beings of outer space often in conflict with the people of earth, and other similar science-fiction themes **2 :** the category of fiction or drama comprising space operas

space out *vt* **1 :** to fill out (a line) by increasing the interword spacing **2 :** to extend the vertical dimension of (a page or form) as by interlinear insertion of leads or furniture **:** BLANK 6

space perception *n* **:** the perception of direction, distance, size, and other spatial facts

spaceport \'=,=\ *n* **:** an installation for testing and launching rockets, missiles, and satellites

space quantization *n* **:** quantization in respect to direction in space ⟨the *space quantization* of an atom in a magnetic field whose quantum states correspond to a limited number of possible angles between the directions of the angular momentum and the magnetic intensity⟩

spac·er \'spāsə(r)\ *n* -s **:** one that spaces: as **a :** a device or piece for holding two members at a given distance from each other ⟨trucks which have ~*s* between dual tires —*Motor Transportation in the West*⟩ ⟨wood ~*s* holding the sides of a concrete form the proper distance apart⟩ ⟨when more than one layer of bars lies at the bottom of a beam or girder the layers are separated by ~*s* —Theodore Crane⟩ **b :** a person or machine that spaces ties at proper intervals in railroad track **c :** a current-reversing device used esp. in cable telegraphy to increase speed of transmission **d :** SPACE BAR

spacer bar *n* **:** a bar used as a spacer (as in sling handling of crates)

space reddening *n, pl* **space reddenings :** an effect of selective space absorption in which the shorter wavelengths of the radiation of a star's or galaxy's light are reduced in intensity more than the longer wavelengths and cause the object to appear redder than it really is

space rule *n* **:** single rule in short regular lengths that is used chiefly in the printing of tables

spaces *pl of* SPACE, *pres 3d sing of* SPACE

space·ship \'spās(h),ship\ *n* **:** a man-carrying vehicle designed to operate in free space outside the earth's atmosphere

space stage *n* **:** an abstract stage setting consisting of a broad arrangement of platforms, flights of steps, and occas. other simple architectural elements backed by a usu. black cyclorama, the actors and properties being spotlighted to appear as if in a black void

space station *or* **space platform** *n* **:** a manned artificial satellite that is designed to revolve in a fixed orbit and serve as a base for scientific observation and experiment, the refueling of spaceships, or the launching of satellites or missiles

space suit *n* **1 :** a suit equipped with air supply and other elaborate provisions intended to make life in free space possible for its wearer **2 :** G SUIT

space-time \'=¦=\ *n* **1 :** the four-dimensional order within which every physical existent may be determined by specifying its three spatial coordinates and one temporal coordinate; *also* **:** the characteristic quality or set of properties of such an order **2 :** the whole or any circumscribed portion of physical reality that is a four-dimensional array of perduring extended things or of events or event particles **3 :** the primordial reality which has no qualities beyond the spatial and temporal and from which further qualities and higher levels of existence evolutionally emerge — compare EMERGENT EVOLUTION

space-time continuum *n* **:** a space of four dimensions which if described would have three space axes and one axis indicating variations in time

space velocity *n* **1 :** the velocity of a star's motion relative to the sun as determined from its proper motion, distance, and radial velocity — called also *space motion* **2 :** the number of volumes of gas or liquid usu. calculated to standard conditions that pass over or through one unit volume (as of a catalyst in a reaction tube) in unit time

space·ward \'spāswə(r)d\ *adv* **:** toward space

space washer *n* **:** a washer used for a distance piece (as on a mandrel)

space writer *n* **:** a writer (as a newspaper reporter or a copywriter) paid according to the space his matter fills in print

spacht·ling compound \'späk(t)liŋ-\ *n* [*spachtling* fr. G *spachteln* to spread with a spatula + E *-ing* — more at SPACKLE] **:** SPACKLE

spacial *var of* SPATIAL

spac·i·ness \'spāsēnəs, -āsin-\ *n* -ES **:** the quality or state of being spacy **:** ROOMINESS

spacing *n* -s **1 :** the act of providing with spaces or of placing at intervals ⟨the ~ of words in a line of type⟩ ⟨the ~ of children born in a family⟩ **2 :** a spatial arrangement **:** an arrangement with intervening spaces ⟨the ~ of the planets at their present distances from the sun —F.L.Whipple⟩ **3 a :** SPACE ⟨the long end of roping at the tack provides a ~ when several flags are hoisted together —*Manual of Seamanship*⟩ ⟨neat ~s of white enamelled wood —Donn Byrne⟩ **b :** the distance between any two objects in a usu. regularly arranged series often measured from the center point of one object to that of the next **c** *of a lock* **:** the distance from the center of the keyhole to the center of the knob hub

spacing strip *n* **:** POLE STRIP

spa·cious \ˈspāshəs\ *adj* [ME, fr. MF *spacieux*, fr. L *spatiosus*, fr. *spatium* space, room + *-osus* -ous — more at SPEED] **1 :** marked by large or ample space: **a :** vast in area; *esp* **:** having broad open expanses ⟨contains within its ~ borders . . . many geographical, climatic, and economic divisions —H.S.Commager⟩ ⟨white villas . . . were scattered upon this ~ map —Nathaniel Hawthorne⟩ **b :** affording much room or space **:** not narrow or constricted **:** ROOMY ⟨a land of villages and ~ countrysides —C.J.Brosnan⟩ ⟨moved to a more ~, rambling residence on a hilltop —E.A.Weeks⟩ ⟨seemed so ~ and beautiful to stand high above the prairie and look around —O.E.Rölvaag⟩ **2 :** marked by largeness, magnitude, or scope: **a :** COMPREHENSIVE, WIDE, EXPANSIVE ⟨the ~ mountain air —R.M.Coates⟩ ⟨one great ~ golden morning followed another —J.C.Powys⟩ ⟨the topic is a ~ one, opening into many other fields —P.A.Wadsworth⟩ **b :** rich, varied, luxuriant or halcyon rather than circumscribed, inhibited, petty, or mean ⟨~ ease and generous enjoyment of life —*Times Lit. Supp.*⟩ ⟨a more ~ and stimulating existence than the farm could offer —H.L.Mencken⟩ ⟨the ~ life of the wealthy in that time before the great wars —H.W.Baehr⟩ **syn** see AMPLE

spa·cious·ly *adv* **:** in a spacious manner **:** on spacious lines **:** EXPANSIVELY ⟨in Cambridge the colleges are prominent and ~ spread out —S.P.B.Mais⟩ ⟨planned my life from the outset largely and ~ —Havelock Ellis⟩

spa·cious·ness *n* -ES **:** the quality or state of being spacious **:** BREADTH, AMPLITUDE, EXPANSIVENESS ⟨strong enough to walk out over the fields, at whose ~ she was amazed —Marcia Davenport⟩ ⟨out of this leisure they created a dignity, ease, and ~ in their lives —William Barrett⟩

spa·cis·tor \ˈspāˌsistə(r)\ *n* -S [¹*space* + *-istor* (as in *transistor*)] **:** a high-frequency semiconductor amplifying device

spack *dial Brit past of* SPEAK

spack·le \ˈspakəl\ *vt* **spackled; spackled; spackling** \-k(ə)liŋ\ **spackles** [*Spackle*] **:** to apply a Spackle paste to **:** fill with Spackle paste

Spackle \"\ *trademark* — used for a dry powder usu. of gypsum plaster, glue, and silica flour that when mixed with water to form a paste is used as a filler or putty to fill in cracks or holes in a surface before painting

spackling compound *n* **:** a Spackle powder

spacy \ˈspāsē, -āsi\ *adj* -ER/-EST **:** characterized by space **:** ROOMY, LARGE ⟨contributed at rather ~ intervals to slightly known magazines —*Amer. Mercury*⟩

spad \ˈspad\ *n* -S [alter. of earlier *spud*, fr. ¹*spud*] **:** a nail one or two inches long made of iron, brass, tin, or tinned iron with a hook or eye at the head and used to mark stations in underground surveying (as of mines)

spad·able \ˈspādəbəl\ *adj* **:** capable of being spaded or shoveled ⟨~ sludge⟩

spa·da·ite \ˈspädəˌīt\ *n* -S [G *spadait*, fr. L. di Medici-*Spada* + G *-it* -ite] **:** a mineral $MgSiO_2(OH)_2.H_2O$(?) consisting of hydrous magnesium silicate

¹**spade** \ˈspād\ *n* -S [ME, fr. OE *spadu, spædu;* akin to OFris *spada* spade, OS *spado*, MHG *spat, spate*, Icel *spathi* spade, Gk *spathē* blade, Hitt *išpatar* spit, OHG *spān* chip of wood — more at SPOON] **1 a :** an implement for turning soil resembling a shovel, adapted for being pushed into the ground with the foot and having a heavy, usu. flat and oblong blade **b** (1) **:** the depth a spade reaches in digging ⟨ditches two ~s deep⟩ (2) **:** the total length of a spade **2 :** any of several spade-shaped instruments: as **a :** a cutting instrument used in flensing a whale **b :** a spade-shaped prong on the underside of the trail of a gun carriage that is embedded in the ground to check recoil of the carriage **c :** a long-handled tool similar in appearance to a garden spade used for compacting and smoothing vertical surfaces of freshly-placed concrete in forms **3 :** the horny formation on the heel of the spadefoot toad

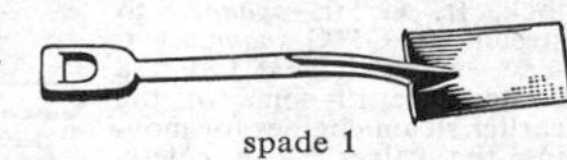
spade 1

²**spade** \"\ *vb* -ED/-ING/-S *vt* **1 a :** to dig up or out with a spade **:** pare off with a spade ⟨~ a garden⟩ ⟨~ a trench⟩ **b :** to place or cover with a spade ⟨~ plants in⟩ ⟨~ fertilizer under⟩ **2 :** to compact and smooth (a vertical surface of freshly placed concrete) by operating a spade up and down between the form and the concrete **~** *vi* **:** to use a spade **syn** see DIG

³**spade** \"\ *n* -S [origin unknown] **:** a three-year-old stag

⁴**spade** \"\ *n* -S [It *spada* or Sp *espada* sword (used as a mark on playing cards), both fr. L *spatha* spatula, broad sword, fr. Gk *spathē* blade — more at ¹SPADE] **1 a :** a usu. black figure ♠ impressed on each card of one of the four suits of a pack of playing cards **b :** a card marked with this figure **c spades** *pl* **:** the suit of cards marked with this figure ⟨he was strong in ~s⟩ **d :** an odd trick in bridge won or contracted for with spades as trumps ⟨I bid one ~⟩ ⟨four ~s bid and made⟩ **e spades** *pl* **:** the winning of the majority of the spades in casino; *also* **:** the score of one point for this **2** *slang* **:** NEGRO; *esp* **:** a dark-skinned Negro — usu. taken to be offensive — **in spades** *adv* [so called fr. the fact that spades are the highest suit in some card games (as bridge)] **1** *slang* **:** EMPHATICALLY, DECIDEDLY, DISTINCTLY, INTENSELY ⟨whether you realize it or not, you've got trouble — *in spades* —Jerry Bradley⟩ ⟨they thought him a stinker, *in spades*, for many years —Inez Robb⟩ ⟨it was a whirlwind romance, *in spades* —Larry Phelps⟩ **2** *slang* **:** without hesitation or glossing over **:** PLAINLY, FRANKLY, RELENTLESSLY ⟨he gave it to me *in spades* and there was nothing I could deny⟩ ⟨I was going to tell him off — *in spades* —Frank Bridges⟩

⁵**spade** \"\ *vt* -ED/-ING/-S [by folk etymology fr. *spay*] *chiefly dial* **:** SPAY

spade beard *n* [¹*spade* & ⁴*spade*] **1 :** an oblong beard with square ends **2 :** a beard rounded off at the top and pointed at the bottom

spade bit *n* **:** a bit having a piece of metal attached to the center of the bar in such a way that when the reins are pulled, the metal piece presses against the roof of the horse's mouth

spadebone \ˈ=ˌ=\ *n, dial chiefly Eng* **:** SCAPULA 1a

spade casino *n* [⁴*spade*] **:** a variation of casino in which spades are worth one point each and the spade jack counts 2 making 24 points in all

spade edge *n* [¹*spade*] *of a shoe* **:** SCOTCH EDGE

spade face *n* **:** the exposed face or surface of a concrete structure that has been finished with the back of the spade

spadefish \ˈ=ˌ=\ *n* **1 :** any of numerous short compressed deep-bodied fishes constituting the family Ephippidae and being widely distributed in warm seas; *esp* **:** a common bluish or dark gray food and sport fish (*Chaetodipterus faber*) of the tropical western Atlantic — called also *angelfish* **2 :** PADDLEFISH

spade foot \ˈ=ˌ=\ *n* **:** a terminal enlargement of the straight square furniture leg esp. of the late 18th century that sweeps outward in an abrupt curve on each side and then gradually tapers downward — see FOOT illustration

spadefoot \ˈ=ˌ=\ *or* **spadefoot toad** *n, pl* **spadefoots** *or* **spadefoot toads :** any of several burrowing toads of the family Pelobatidae in which the inner bone of the tarsus has a strong sharp-edged horny sheath with which they dig

spade·ful \ˈspādˌfu̇l\ *n* -S **:** as much as can be dug out with or carried on a spade ⟨~ of earth⟩

spade graft *n, chiefly dial* **:** ¹SPADE 1b (1)

spade guinea *n* **:** a guinea of George III with a spade-shaped shield on the reverse

spade hand *n* **:** a timepiece hand in form of a spade

spade handle *n* **:** a forked end of a shaft or rod (as a connecting rod) in which a pin is held at both ends

spa·del·la \spəˈdelə\ *n, cap* [NL, prob. fr. LL *spada* sword (alter. of L *spatha* broad sword) + NL *-ella*] **:** a genus of marine worms (group Chaetognatha) resembling those of *Sagitta* but having a broader body and only one pair of lateral fins

spade lug *n* **1 :** a steel spade-shaped attachment to the rim of a tractor drive wheel to prevent slip during traction **2 :** a forked prong to be slipped under a screw or nut for making an electrical connection

spade·man \ˈspādmən\ *also* **spades·man** \-dzm-\ *n, pl* **spademen** *also* **spadesmen :** one who works with a spade **:** SPADER

spade money *n* **:** ancient Chinese money in the form of spade-shaped pieces of bronze

spad·er \ˈspādə(r)\ *n* -S **:** one that spades; *specif* **:** SPADING HARROW

spades *pl of* SPADE, *pres 3d sing of* SPADE

spadework \ˈ=ˌ=\ *n* **1 :** work done with the spade **2 :** the hard plain preliminary drudgery in any undertaking ⟨between the periods of actual negotiations much ~ may be done by both sides in the form of collecting data and preparing for negotiations —D.C.Miller & W.H.Form⟩ — **spadeworker** \ˈ=ˌ==\ *n*

spad·ger \ˈspajə(r)\ *n* -S [prob. alter. of *sparrow*] **1** *Brit* **:** HOUSE SPARROW ⟨always very quick on his feet, like a ~ —Margery Allingham⟩ **2** *slang* **:** a small boy

spa·di·ceous \spāˈdishəs, spəˈd-\ *adj* [L *spadix, spadix* frond torn off a palm tree, brownish color of palm fronds + E *-eous* — more at SPADIX] **1 :** of a bright clear brown or chestnut color **2** [NL *spadic-, spadix* + E *-eous*] **:** bearing flowers on or constituting a spadix

spa·dici·flo·rae \ˌ=ˌdisəˈflōrˌē\ *n pl, cap* [NL, fr. *spadic-, spadix* + *-i-* + *-florae* (fr. LL, fem. pl. of *-florus* -florous)] *in some classifications* **:** an order of monocotyledonous plants comprising the Palmales and Cyclanthales of other classifications

spa·dic·i·form \=ˈdisəˌfȯrm\ *adj* [NL *spadic-, spadix* + E *-iform*] **:** resembling a spadix

spa·di·cose \ˈspādəˌkōs\ *adj* [NL *spadic-, spadix* + E *-ose*] **:** SPADICEOUS 2

spa·dille \spəˈdil\ *n* -S [F, fr. Sp *espadilla*, dim. of *espada* sword (used as a mark on playing cards) — more at SPADE] **:** the highest trump (as the ace of spades in ombre or the queen of clubs in solo)

spading *pres part of* SPADE

spading fork *n* **:** a hand tool with flat tines for turning soil

spading harrow *n* **:** a disc harrow having rotating blades curved at the ends and assembled in the form of a sprocket wheel with the cutting edges out

spad·ish \ˈspādish\ *adj* [¹*spade* + *-ish* (after the phrase *call a spade a spade*)] **:** direct and blunt in manner of expression ⟨~ language⟩ — **spad·ish·ness** *n* -ES

spa·dix \ˈspādiks\ *n, pl* **spadi·ces** \spāˈdīˌsēz, spəˈd-; ˈspādəˌs-\ [NL, fr. L, frond torn off a palm tree, fr. Gk, fr. *span* to draw, pull, tear — more at SPAN] **1 :** a fleshy or succulent spike that is usu. subtended by or enclosed in a leaflike spathe and is the inflorescence characteristic of the arums and palms **2 :** a compressed cone-shaped organ of the male nautilus formed of four modified tentacles and their sheaths and supposed to represent a hectocotylus

spading fork

spa·do \ˈspā(ˌ)dō\ *n, pl* **spado·nes** \spāˈdō(ˌ)nēz, spəˈd-\ [ME, fr. L *spadon-, spado*, fr. Gk *spadōn*, fr. *span* to draw, pull, tear — more at SPAN] **1 :** a castrated man or lower animal **2 :** an impotent person

spa·droon \spəˈdrün\ *n* -S [F dial. (Switzerland) *espadron*, alter. of *espadon* — more at ESPADON] *archaic* **:** a sword lighter than the broadsword and suitable for both cutting and thrusting

spads *pl of* SPAD

spae \ˈspā\ *vt* [ME *span*, fr. ON *spā* — more at SPY] *chiefly Scot* **:** FORETELL, PROPHESY

spaeman *n, pl* **spaemen** *Scot* **:** FORTUNE-TELLER, PROPHET, WIZARD

spaetz·le *or* **spätz·le** \ˈshpetslə, -lē\ *n, pl* **spaetzle** *or* **spaetzles** *or* **spätzle** *or* **spätzles** [G dial. (Alemannic) *spätzle*, dim. of *spatz* sparrow, dumpling, fr. MHG, sparrow, fr. *spar, spare* sparrow (fr. OHG *sparo*) + *-tz*, hypocoristic suffix (fr. OHG *-izo*) — more at SPARROW] **:** the strings and lumps that result when a batter made of eggs, milk, flour, and salt is run through a coarse colander into boiling liquid and that when cooked are used as additions to gravy, goulash, or other stews

spaewife *n, chiefly Scot* **:** a female fortune-teller **:** PROPHETESS, WITCH

spa·ghet·ti \spəˈged·|ē, -et|, |i\ *n* -S [It, fr. pl. of *spaghetto* string, dim. of *spago* cord, string; akin to Sardinian *ispau* cord, string] **1 :** an alimentary paste made in solid strings of small diameter but larger than vermicelli — distinguished from *macaroni* **2** *or* **spaghetti tubing :** SLEEVING **3 :** a trimming with many cords resembling spaghetti for women's dresses

spa·gnuo·lo \ˌspänyəˈwō(ˌ)lō\ *n* -S *cap* [It, lit., Spaniard, fr. *spagnuolo*, adj., Spanish, fr. (assumed) VL *Hispaniolus* — more at HISPANIOLIZE] **:** one of a group of Spanish and Portuguese Jews expelled from Spain in 1492 whose descendants scattered among the Balkan states speak Judeo-Spanish — compare LADINO 4, SEPHARDIM

spagyric \spəˈjirik\ *adj* [NL *spagiricus*] **:** ALCHEMIC, IATROCHEMICAL

spa·hi *also* **spa·hee** \ˈspäˌhē\ *n* -S [MF *spahi*, fr. Turk *sipahi*, fr. Per *sipāhī* horseman, mounted soldier — more at SEPOY] **1 :** one of a corps of largely irregular Turkish cavalry disbanded after the suppression of the Janissaries in 1826 **2 :** one of a corps of Algerian native cavalry in the French army normally serving in Africa

spaik *or* **spake** \ˈspāk\ *Scot var of* ²SPOKE

¹**spain** \ˈspān\ *vt* -ED/-ING/-S [ME *spanen*, fr. OF *espanir*, of Gmc origin; akin to MD *spenen, spennen* to wean — more at SPEAN] *chiefly Scot* **:** WEAN

²**spain** \"\ *adj, usu cap* [fr. *Spain*, country in southwestern Europe] **:** of or from Spain **:** of the kind or style prevalent in Spain **:** SPANISH

spairge \ˈspärj, -perj\ *chiefly Scot var of* SPARGE

spait \ˈspāt\ *chiefly Scot var of* SPATE

spak \ˈspak\ [ME, fr. OE *spæc*] *dial Brit past of* SPEAK

spake [ME *spak*, fr. OE *spæc*] *archaic past of* SPEAK

¹**spa·lac·id** \spəˈlasəd\ *adj* [NL *Spalacidae*] **:** of or relating to the Spalacidae

²**spalacid** \"\ *n* -S **:** a rodent of the family Spalacidae

spa·lac·i·dae \-asəˌdē\ *n pl, cap* [NL, fr. *Spalac-, Spalax*, type genus + *-idae*] **:** a family of Old World muroid rodents comprising the mole rats and extinct related forms — **spal·a·cine** \ˈspaləˌsīn\ *adj*

spa·lax \ˈspāˌlaks\ *n, cap* [NL, fr. Gk, mole; akin to OHG *spaltan* to split — more at SPILL] **:** a genus (the type of the family Spalacidae) of mole rats

spald *var of* SPAULD

spale *also* **spail** \ˈspā(ə)l\ *n* -S [ME *spale, spalle*, perh. of Scand origin; akin to ON *spal-, spölr* rail, bar, *spjald* square tablet — more at SPILL] **1** *dial Brit* **:** LATH, SPLINTER, CHIP **2 :** CROSS-SPALE

¹**spall** *also* **spawl** \ˈspȯl\ *n* -S [ME *spalle* — more at SPALE] **1 :** CHIP, FLAKE; *esp* **:** a small fragment broken from the face or edge of a material (as stone, metal, concrete, glass, or a ceramic product) and having at least one featheredge ⟨~s from marble-dressing operations —H.P.Chandler & Nan Jensen⟩ **2 :** a fragment removed from a rock surface by weathering ⟨few exfoliation ~s detach themselves from the parent mass in the form of lenses —*Jour. of Geol.*⟩ **3 :** CROSS-SPALE

²**spall** *also* **spawl** \"\ *vb* -ED/-ING/-S *vt* **1 :** to break up (ore) with a hammer usu. preparatory to crushing **2 :** to reduce (as irregular stone blocks) approximately to size by chipping with a hammer **3 :** to cause to break off in spalls ⟨avoid ~ing the concrete in drilling⟩ **~** *vi* **1 :** to break off chips, scales, or slabs from the surface or edge often as the result of a rapid change of temperature **:** EXFOLIATE ⟨the dead-burned magnesia produced does not ~ —R.N.Shreve⟩ — often used with *off* or *away* ⟨the ~*ing* off of the outer layers of a rock⟩ ⟨frost action . . . and other unavoidable influences tend to cause the mortar to ~ away from the joints —*Railway Engineering & Maintenance Cycl.*⟩ **2 :** to split off particles as the result of bombardment in such a manner that a large part remains — used of a surface, target, or nucleus

³**spall** \"\ *n* -S [alter. of *spauld*] *archaic* **:** SHOULDER

spall·ation \spȯˈlāshən\ *n* -S [²*spall* + *-ation*] **:** a nuclear reaction in which light particles are ejected as the result of bombardment (as by high-energy protons); *esp* **:** a reaction resulting in numerous products — distinguished from *fission*

spall·er \ˈspȯlə(r)\ *n* -S **:** one that spalls: as **a :** a machine for spalling ore **b :** a laborer who spalls ore

spalling *n* -S **:** loss of spalls from a face or edge (as of brick, stone, or concrete) due to any cause

spalling hammer *n* **:** a large hammer usu. with a flat face and straight peen for breaking and rough-dressing stone

spal·peen \(ˈ)spalˈpēn\ *n* -S [IrGael *spailpín* common laborer, migratory workman, worthless person] **1** *chiefly Irish* **:** a common laborer **2** *chiefly Irish* **:** RASCAL 3 **3** *chiefly Irish* **:** a young boy

¹**spalt** \ˈspȯlt, -palt\ *vb* [prob. fr. G *spalten* to split, fr. OHG *spaltan* — more at SPILL] *dial* **:** SPLIT, SPLINTER

²**spalt** \"\ *n* -S **:** the residue left after cutting shingles from a bolt of wood

Spam \ˈspam, -paa(ə)m\ *trademark* — used for a canned meat consisting primarily of pork products

¹**span** [ME, fr. OE *spann*] *archaic past of* SPIN

²**span** \ˈspan, -paa(ə)n\ *n* -S [ME *spanne*, fr. OE *spann;* akin to OHG *spanna* span, ON *spönn* span, *spenna* to span — more at ³SPAN] **1 a :** the distance from the end of the thumb to the end of the little finger of a spread hand; *also* **:** an English unit of length based on this distance equal to 9 inches **b :** the distance between the tips of the middle fingers when the arms are stretched to the side as far as possible from the body **2 :** something conceived of as an extent, stretch, reach, or spread between two definite limits: as **a :** a limited often small space **b :** a portion of time; *esp* **:** the period of one's life on earth **3 a :** the distance between the supports of a transverse structural member or between the abutments of an arch **b :** a transverse member or the part of one which is between structural supports **:** ARCH, BRIDGE, TRUSS — see BRIDGE illustration **4 :** the amount of material that is grasped and dealt with in a single mental performance ⟨the ~ of attention⟩ ⟨memory ~⟩ **5 :** the maximum distance laterally from tip to tip of an airplane inclusive of ailerons or the lateral dimension of an airfoil — called also *spread*

³**span** \"\ *vb* **spanned; spanned; spanning; spans** [ME *spannen*, fr. OE *spannan;* akin to MD & MLG *spannen* to stretch, span, hitch up, fasten, OHG *spannan* to stretch, span, ON *spenna* to span, L *pendere* to weigh, Gk *span* to draw, pull, tear] *vt* **1 :** to grasp firmly **:** SEIZE **2 a :** to measure by or as if by the hand with fingers and thumb extended; *broadly* **:** to measure in any way ⟨watch the stars and your eye consciously ~s that distance —James Jones⟩ **b :** to encompass with or as if with the fingers **3** *obs* **:** to set a limit to **4 a :** to cross or reach over in space **:** TRAVERSE ⟨took us just three minutes to ~ the bay —Horace Sutton⟩ **b :** to extend across in time ⟨his active career . . . *spanned* the two decades —Vincent Starrett⟩ **5 a :** to form an arch over **:** spread, stretch, or extend across from one limit to another ⟨a rainbow *spanned* the lake —P.B.Shelley⟩ **b :** to cover (as a given space between supports) with a transverse member **6 :** to spread out **:** STRETCH ⟨little paths . . . with tree roots *spanned* across them —Katherine Mansfield⟩ **7 :** to bridge over ⟨a small stream, *spanned* by several rustic bridges —*Amer. Guide Series: Mich.*⟩ **~** *vi* **1 :** to swim along rising to the surface to breathe at more or less regular intervals — used of a whale **2 :** to move in the manner of a looper

⁴**span** \"\ *n* -S [of Scand origin; akin to ON *spann* pail, a measure of butter; akin to ON *spenna* to span — more at ³SPAN] **:** a unit of measure for butter formerly used in northern Scotland

⁵**span** \"\ *vt* **spanned; spanned; spanning; spans** [D *spannen* to stretch, span, hitch up, fr. MD — more at ³SPAN] **1 :** to stretch or pull tight **:** draw firmly ⟨he was on his knees . . . the seat of his trousers perilously *spanned* —Gladys Schmitt⟩ **2** *obs* **:** to cock with a spanner (as a firearm) **3 :** to confine by ropes or other lashings **:** to attach or fasten — often used with *in* **4** [Afrik, fr. MD *spannen*] *chiefly Africa* **:** to attach (a draft animal) to a vehicle

⁶**span** \"\ *n* -S [D, fr. MD, something stretched, team of animals, fr. *spannen* to stretch, span, hitch up — more at ³SPAN] **1 a :** a rope having its ends made fast so that a purchase can be hooked to the bight **b :** a rope made fast in the center so that both ends can be used (as with thimbles) as fairleads **c :** a rope made fast or secured between two uprights (as a jumper stay or the rope between davit heads) **2 a :** a pair of horses, mules, or other animals usu. matched in looks and action and driven together **b** [Afrik, fr. D] **:** a team of two or more pairs of oxen or other animals worked or driven together

⁷**span** \"\ *adv* [fr. *span-* (as in *span-new*)] **:** COMPLETELY ⟨~ white gloves⟩

span blocks *n* [⁶*span*] **:** two blocks each at one end of a span of rope at a masthead for studding-sail halyards

¹**span·cel** \ˈspan(t)səl\ *vt* **spanceled** *or* **spancelled; spanceled** *or* **spancelled; spanceling** *or* **spancelling; spancels** [LG *spanseln*, fr. *spansel*, n.] **:** to tie or hobble with or as if with a spancel **:** FETTER

²**spancel** \"\ *n* -S [LG *spansel*, fr. *spannen* to stretch, fasten, fr. MLG — more at SPAN] **:** a rope hobble or clog esp. for a horse or cow

span-clean \ˈspan¦=, -paan-\ *adj* [⁷*span*] **:** extremely clean

span–counter \ˈ=ˌ==\ *n* [³*span*] **:** an old English game in which a player tries to toss his counter within a span's distance of his opponent's — see SPAN-FARTHING

span·dex \ˈspanˌdeks\ *n* -ES [anagram of *expand*] **:** any of various synthetic textile elastic fibers that are long-chain polymers composed of at least 85 percent of a segmented polyurethane

span dog *n* [⁶*span*] **1 span dogs** *pl* **:** a pair of grappling dogs for hoisting logs and timber **2 :** an iron dog for holding a wooden stave to shape after bending while it cools

span·drel *or* **span·dril** \ˈspandrəl, -paan-\ *n* -S [ME *spaundrell*, dim. of AF *spaundre* spandrel, fr. OF *espandre*, *spandre* to spread, disperse — more at SPAWN] **1 a :** the wall or panel between the extrados of an arch and the next adjacent molding; *specif* **:** an ornamentally treated space between the right or left extrados curve and an enclosing right angle **b :** an area of the shape and nature of a spandrel **2 :** the triangular space beneath the string of a stair **3 :** an exterior wall panel which fills the space beneath a windowsill usu. extending to the top of the window in the story below **4 :** a corner space with scrollwork or other decorative filling between a rounded corner of a design and a squared corner of a rectangular frame line on a stamp

spandrels 1a

spandrel beam *n* **:** the exterior beam in steel or concrete construction that marks the floor level between stories

spandrel frame *n* **:** a triangular framing (as under a stair)

spandrel wall *n* **:** a wall on an extrados to fill the spandrels

¹**span·dy** \ˈspandē, -paan-, -di\ *adv* [alter. of ⁷*span*] **:** COMPLETELY ⟨a ~ new apartment house —*Time*⟩

²**spandy** \"\ *adj* **:** NEAT ⟨two pairs of ~ gloves —Louisa Alcott⟩

spane \ˈspān\ *var of* SPAIN

span–farthing \ˈ=ˌ==\ *n* [³*span*] **:** a game played like span-counter but with farthings

¹**spang** \ˈspaŋ, -aiŋ\ *vb* -ED/-ING/-S [origin unknown] *vt, chiefly Scot* **:** THROW, BANG **~** *vi, chiefly Scot* **:** JUMP, LEAP

²**spang** \"\ *n* -S *chiefly Scot* **:** a sudden violent movement **:** JERK, LEAP, KICK

³**spang** \"\ *adv* **1 :** COMPLETELY ⟨the brooks were . . . all running ~ full to the very edge with snow-water —Dorothy C. Fisher⟩ **2 :** EXACTLY, SQUARELY, DIRECTLY ⟨this roomy place

is ~ in the middle of the theater district —Roger Angell⟩ ⟨jumped ~ onto my seat —G.W.Bagby⟩

⁴spang \"\ *n* -s [prob. of imit. origin] **:** a sharp loud often whining sound ⟨the canyon wall echoes to the ~ of the miner's hammer —*Nature Mag.*⟩ ⟨the ~ of a ricocheting bullet⟩

⁵spang \"\ *vi* -ED/-ING/-S **:** to make a spang **:** CRACK ⟨bullets buzzed in the air and ~*ed* into tree trunks —Stephen Crane⟩

spang·hew \'ˌ=ˌ(h)yü\ *vt* -ED/-ING/-S [alter. of ¹*spang*] *dial Brit* **:** to throw violently into the air; *esp* **:** to throw (a frog) into the air from the end of a stick

¹span·gle \'spaŋgəl, -paiŋ-\ *n* -s [ME *spangel*, dim. of *spang* shiny ornament, spangle, prob. of Scand origin; akin to ON *spang-, spöng* spangle; akin to OE *spang* clasp, buckle, OHG *spanga* clasp, buckle, *spannan* to stretch, span — more at SPAN] **1 :** a small disk or other geometric shape of shining metal or plastic used for sparkling ornamentation esp. on dresses and costumes **2 :** something resembling or suggesting a spangle in sparkle and brilliance: as **a :** a small object that brightly reflects light ⟨a fox . . . wet with gold ~*s* of the dew —Edith Sitwell⟩ **b :** a glittering point of light **3 :** a sparkle or glitter from or as if from spangles **4 :** a glossy or shining mark on the end of a feather

²spangle \"\ *vb* **spangled; spangled; spangling** \-g(ə)liŋ\ **spangles** *vt* **:** to set or sprinkle with or as if with spangles **:** adorn with small brilliant objects **:** give a sparkling appearance or impression to ⟨the sky is . . . *spangled* with stars —Marjorie K. Rawlings⟩ ⟨yellow jasmine *spangled* the forest with gold —B.A.Williams⟩ ⟨an evening sheath . . . *spangled* with black sequins —Lois Long⟩ ~ *vi* **:** to glitter as if covered with spangles **:** GLISTEN, SPARKLE ⟨it *spangled* like a cold star —Eudora Welty⟩ ⟨its countless mirror lakes . . . glow and ~ —John Muir †1914⟩

³spangle \"\ *n, pl* **spangle** *or* **spangles** [origin unknown] **:** a measure of yarn formerly in use in Ireland and Scotland

spangled glass *n* **:** a late nineteenth century American clear glassware having crystalline fleckings usu. of mica suspended in the glass fabric

spanglegrass \'==ˌ=\ *n* **:** SPIKE-GRASS a

span·gler \'spaŋg(ə)lə(r), -paiŋ-\ *n* -s **:** one that spangles

span·glet \-glət\ *n* -s **:** a tiny spangle

span·gly \-g(ə)lē, -li\ *adj* -ER/-EST [¹*spangle* + -*y*] **:** covered with or resembling spangles **:** GLITTERING

spang-new \'spaŋ'=, -paiŋ-\ *adj* [alter. of *span-new*] **:** BRAND-NEW

spango·lite \'spaŋ(g)əˌlīt\ *n* -s [Norman *Spang*, 19th cent. Am. mineralogist + E -*o-* + -*lite*] **:** a mineral $Cu_6Al(SO_4)(OH)_{12}Cl.3H_2O$ consisting of a hydrous basic sulfate and chloride of aluminum and copper in dark-green hexagonal crystals

span·iard \'spanyə(r)d\ *n* -s *cap* [ME *Spaignard, Spaynard, Spanyeart*, fr. MF *Espaignart, Espaniard*, fr. *Espaigne* Spain (fr. L *Hispania*) + -*art*, -*ard* -ard] **1 :** a native or inhabitant of Spain **2 :** a spear grass (*Aciphylla colensoi*) of New Zealand that grows in tufted clumps and has stiff but slender grassy leaf divisions

¹span·iel \'spanyəl, *chiefly archaic or dial* -nᵊl\ *n* [ME *spaynel, spaniell*, fr. MF *espaignol*, lit., Spaniard, fr. OProv *espanhol*, fr. OIt *spagnuolo* — more at SPAGNUOLO] **1 a** *usu cap* **:** any of numerous breeds of small or medium-sized mostly short-legged dogs usu. having long wavy hair, feathered legs and tail, and large drooping ears — see ENGLISH TOY SPANIEL, FIELD SPANIEL, WATER SPANIEL **b** -s *sometimes cap* **:** a dog of one of these breeds **2** -s **:** a cringing servile fawning person ⟨office seekers, . . . ~*s* well-trained to carry and fetch —Walt Whitman⟩

²spaniel \"\ *vb* -ED/-ING/-S *vi* **:** to play about like a spaniel **:** FROLIC, SPORT ~ *vt* **:** to follow esp. fawningly after ⟨the hearts that ~*ed* me at heels —Shak.⟩

spaning *pres part of* SPANE

spani·pelagic \ˌspanə+\ *adj* [ISV *spani-* (fr. Gk *spanios* rare, scarce) + *pelagic*; orig. formed as G *spanipelagisch*; perh. akin to Gk *span* to draw, pull, tear — more at SPAN] *of plankton* **:** living in deep water and coming to the surface rarely — compare AUTOPELAGIC

span iron *n* [⁶*span*] **:** a harpoon usu. secured just below the gunwale of a whaleboat

¹span·ish \'spanish, -nēsh\ *adj, usu cap* [ME *Spainish, Spanish*, fr. *Spain*, country in southwestern Europe + ME -*ish*] **1 a :** of, relating to, or characteristic of Spain **b :** of, relating to, or characteristic of the Spanish people **2 :** dominated by Spain or the Spanish ⟨sailed the *Spanish* Main⟩ **3 a :** of, relating to, or in the Spanish language **b :** of or associated with the literature of Spain **4 :** SPANISH-AMERICAN

²spanish \"\ *n* -ES *see sense 2* **1** *cap* **:** the Romance language of the largest part of Spain and of the countries colonized by Spaniards **2** *pl in constr, cap* **:** the people of Spain **3** *also* **spanish colonial** *usu cap S & sometimes cap C* **:** a style of architecture deriving from the missions and ranch houses of the Spanish settlers in the Southwest and Florida

spanish-american \ˌ===ˌ===\ *adj, usu cap S&A* **1 :** of, relating to, or characteristic of the countries of America in which Spanish is the national language **2 :** of, relating to, or characteristic of communities or sections of communities in the U. S. where Spanish Americans live

spanish american *n, cap S&A* **1 :** a native or inhabitant of a Spanish-American country esp. of Spanish descent — compare LATIN AMERICAN **2 :** a resident of the U. S. whose native language is Spanish and whose culture is of Spanish origin — compare ANGLO-AMERICAN

spanish bayonet *n, usu cap S* **:** any of several plants of the genus *Yucca*; *esp* **:** a stiff short-trunked plant (*Yucca aloifolia*) of the southern U. S. and tropical America with rigid spine-tipped leaves

spanish beard *n, usu cap S* **:** SPANISH MOSS 1

spanish billiards *n, usu cap S* **:** a game closely resembling pin pool except that winning and losing hazards and caroms are scored and that two points are counted for each pin knocked down by the cue ball after contact with an object ball

spanish bluebell *n, usu cap S* **:** SPANISH JACINTH

spanish bowline *n, usu cap S* **:** a knot that is similar to a bowline but has two separate loops and is used esp. as a sling for hoisting or lowering a man

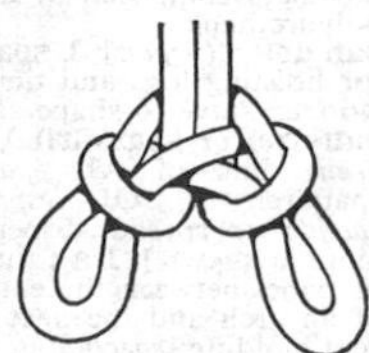
Spanish bowline

spanish broom *n, usu cap S* **1 :** a nearly leafless shrub (*Spartium junceum*) of the family Leguminosae of southern Europe and the Canary Islands that has green flexible twigs which are similar to rushes, are used in basketry, and yield a fiber and that has hand-some fragrant flowers which yield a yellow dye **2 :** a broom (*Genista hispanica*) of southwestern Europe having golden yellow flowers in heads

spanish brown *n* **1** *usu cap S* **:** earth having a dark reddish brown color because of the presence of iron oxide and used as a pigment — compare SPANISH OXIDE **2** *often cap S* **:** INDIAN RED 2b

spanish buckeye *n, usu cap S* **:** BUCKEYE 1c

spanish bugloss *n, usu cap S* **:** ALKANET 1a

spanish burton *n, usu cap S* **:** a tackle with two single blocks — see DOUBLE SPANISH BURTON, SINGLE SPANISH BURTON; BURTON illustration

spanish buttons *n pl but sing or pl in constr, usu cap S* **:** a perennial branching knapweed (*Centaurea nigra*) with hairy leaves and reddish purple to dark purple flowers

spanish carnation *n, usu cap S* **:** PRIDE OF BARBADOS

spanish cedar *n, usu cap S* **1 :** any of several trees of the genus *Cedrela*; *esp* **:** a tropical American tree (*C. odorata*) **2 :** the fragrant wood of Spanish cedar much used for cigar boxes — called also *cigar-box cedar*

spanish chalk *n, usu cap S* **:** a steatite from the Aragon region of Spain

spanish chestnut *n, usu cap S* **1 :** a large tree (*Castanea sativa*) chiefly of the Mediterranean region with large nutritious nuts — called also *sweet chestnut, Italian chestnut* **2 :** the nut borne by the Spanish chestnut

spanish clover *n, usu cap S* **1 :** ALFALFA **2 :** MEXICAN CLOVER **3 :** PRAIRIE BIRD'S-FOOT TREFOIL

spanish cream *n, usu cap S* **:** a molded dessert made of eggs, sugar, milk, and gelatin

spanish curlew *n, usu cap S* **1 :** HEN CURLEW **2 :** WHITE IBIS 1

spanish dagger *n, usu cap S* **1 :** a plant (*Yucca gloriosa*) of the southeastern U. S. resembling the Spanish bayonet but with shorter trunk and smoother leaves **2 :** SPANISH BAYONET

spanish elm *n, usu cap S* **1 :** a large tropical American tree (*Cordia alliodora*) **2 :** the hard grayish wood of the Spanish elm used for building and for many other purposes

span·ish·er \'spanishə(r), -nēsh-\ *n* -s [*Spanish* (*leather*) + -*er*] **1 :** one who treats embossed leather with a special solution and bakes it to obtain a two-tone effect **2 :** a worker engaged in the production of Spanish leather

spanish fir *n, usu cap S* **:** an evergreen tree (*Abies pinsapo*) of the Pyrenees with stiff bright green foliage

spanish flag *n, usu cap S* **1 :** a California rockfish (*Sebastodes rubrivinctus*) having conspicuous bands of red and creamy pink **2 :** a West Indian fish (*Gonioplectrus hispanus*) of the family Serranidae with a bright-red body and yellow stripes along the head and back

spanish flesh *n, often cap S* **:** SEED PEARL 2

spanish fly *n, usu cap S* **1 :** a brilliant green blister beetle (*Lytta vesicatoria*) common in the south of Europe **2 :** CANTHARIS 2

spanish foot *n, usu cap S* **:** a foot on a piece of furniture curved outward with ridges resembling claws

spanish fox *n, usu cap S* **:** FOX 7b

spanish grain *n, usu cap S* **:** grain texture produced on fancy or upholstery leather by embossing

spanish grape *n, usu cap S* **1 :** a wild grape (*Vitis berlandieri*) of Texas and Mexico **2 :** the small purple tangy fruit of the Spanish grape

spanish green *n, often cap S* **:** VERDIGRIS 4

spanish grunt *n, usu cap S* **:** GRAY GRUNT

spanish guitar *n, usu cap S* **:** GUITAR

spanish heath *n, usu cap S* **:** an erect dense shrub (*Erica lusitanica*) native to western Europe but widely grown as an ornamental and having white or pink flowers produced profusely along the entire length of the branches

spanish heel *n, usu cap S* **:** a high leather-covered wooden heel having a straight breast — compare CUBAN HEEL, FRENCH HEEL, SPIKE HEEL

Spanish heel

spanish hogfish *n, usu cap S* **:** LADYFISH b

spanish influenza *n, usu cap S* **:** pandemic influenza

spanish iris *n, usu cap S* **:** a bulbous iris (*Iris xiphium*) of the western Mediterranean region having usu. violet-purple flowers with a short perianth tube — called also *xiphium iris*; compare ENGLISH IRIS, PERSIAN IRIS

spanish jacinth *n, usu cap S* **:** a squill (*Scilla hispanica*) of Spain and Portugal with blue or white flowers resembling those of the hyacinth

spanish jasmine *n, usu cap S* **1** *also* **spanish jessamine :** a large-flowered East Indian jasmine (*Jasminum grandiflorum*) often cultivated for ornament and perfume **2 :** a frangipani (*Plumeria rubra*)

spanish lady *or* **spanish ladyfish** *n, usu cap S* **:** LADYFISH b

spanish leather *n, usu cap S* **:** CORDOVAN 2

spanish lettuce *n, usu cap S* **:** INDIAN LETTUCE 3

spanish licorice *n, usu cap S* **:** LICORICE 1b

spanish lime *n, usu cap S* **:** GENIP 2

spanish lobster *n, usu cap S* **:** any of several large sluggish scyllarian crustaceans (genus *Scyllarides*) used as bait and sometimes for food in the West Indies

spanish mackerel *n, usu cap S* **1 :** any of several mackerels of the genus *Scomberomorus:* as **a :** a mackerel (*S. maculatus*) that is bluish above with oval brown spots on the sides, is found during the warmer months off the American Atlantic coast from Cape Ann to Brazil, and often weighs six to ten pounds **b :** a related but unspotted mackerel (*S. concolor*) occurring on the Mexican and Southern California coast **c :** a large mackerel (*S. commersoni*) that is widespread in the tropical Indo-Pacific, attains a length of six feet, and weighs over 100 pounds **2** *West* **:** JACK MACKEREL a **3 :** CHUB MACKEREL

spanish mahogany *n, usu cap S* **:** a mahogany obtained only from the West Indies and esp. from Santo Domingo and sometimes considered a distinct species (*Swietenia macrophylla*)

spanish measles *n pl but sing or pl in constr, usu cap S* **:** BLACK MEASLES 2

spanish moss *n, usu cap S* **1 :** an epiphytic plant (*Tillandsia usneoides*) that forms pendent tufts of hairlike grayish green strands upon the trunks and branches of many trees in the southern U. S. and the West Indies — called also *black moss, long moss, old-man's-beard* **2 :** a lichen (*Ramalina reticulata*) that forms lacelike masses on many trees in the Pacific coastal U. S.

spanish n *n, usu cap S* **:** the character ñ — compare TILDE

spanish needles *n pl but sing or pl in constr, usu cap S* **1 :** the barbed achenes of any of several plants of the genus *Bidens* **2 :** a common beggar-ticks (*Bidens bipinnata*) of the eastern U. S.

spanish oak *n, usu cap S* **:** any of several oaks of the southern U. S.; *esp* **:** RED OAK 1b

spanish ocher *n, often cap S* **:** OCHER ORANGE

spanish omelet *n, usu cap S* **:** an omelet served with a sauce containing chopped green pepper, onion, and tomato

spanish onion *n, usu cap S* **:** any of several large-bulbed mild-flavored onions

spanish oxide *n, usu cap S* **:** a dull red natural iron oxide pigment — compare INDIAN RED 1a, SPANISH BROWN

spanish oyster *n, usu cap S, Bermuda* **:** PEN SHELL

spanish oyster plant *n, usu cap S* **:** a tall biennial golden thistle (*Scolymus hispanicus*) of southwestern Europe that is sometimes cultivated for its edible roots which resemble but are larger and milder than those of salsify, for its foliage which is eaten like that of the cardoon, and for its flowers which are used as a substitute for saffron

spanish pack *n, usu cap S* **:** a pack of 40 playing cards resembling a 52-card pack but without eights, nines, and tens

spanish paprika *n, usu cap S* **1 :** PIMIENTO 1 **2 :** a paprika produced from pimientos usu. in Spain

spanish peanut *n, usu cap S* **:** a peanut that has small pods and short rounded seeds and is sometimes grown as a forage plant

spanish pear *n, usu cap S* **:** AVOCADO

spanish pepper *n, usu cap S* **1 :** PEPPER TREE 1 **2 :** PEPPER 3

spanish plum *n, usu cap S* **1 a :** the red edible fruit of a tropical American hog plum (*Spondias purpurea*) — called also *red mombin* **b :** the tree that bears the Spanish plum **2 :** FALSE SANDALWOOD 1

spanish potato *n, usu cap S* **:** SWEET POTATO

spanish red *n, often cap S* **1 :** CARTHAMUS RED **2 :** IRON-OXIDE RED

spanish rice *n, usu cap S* **:** rice cooked with onions, green pepper, and tomatoes

spanish rococo *n, usu cap S* **:** the more highly decorated and elaborate period of Spanish Renaissance architecture

spanish sage *n, usu cap 1st S* **:** a sage (*Salvia lavandulaefolia*) of western Europe that has small dark green leaves and is sometimes used as an adulterant of official sage

spanish salsify *n, usu cap 1st S* **:** SPANISH OYSTER PLANT

spanish sauce *n, usu cap 1st S* **:** BROWN SAUCE

spanish scroll *n, usu cap 1st S* **:** an ornamental scroll usu. for the foot of a chair or table consisting of a series of parallel flutes terminating in a sweeping spiral — see FOOT illustration

spanish sheep *n, usu cap 1st S* **:** MERINO 1b

spanish soldier *n, usu cap 1st S* **:** a spear grass (*Aciphylla squarrosa*) of New Zealand

spanish spoon *n, usu cap 1st S* **:** a long-handled shallow dipper or shovel used for digging postholes

spanish stopper *n, usu cap 1st S* **:** GURGEON STOPPER

spanish tea *n, usu cap S* **1 :** MEXICAN TEA **2 :** a West Indian shrub (*Gesneria longiflora*)

spanish thistle *n, usu cap S* **:** BUFFALO BUR

spanish toothpick *n, usu cap S* **:** a bishop's-weed (*Ammi viznaga*)

spanish topaz *n, usu cap S* **:** a yellow variety of rock crystal

spanish trefoil *n, usu cap S* **:** ALFALFA

spanish white *n, usu cap S* **1 :** whiting used as a pigment **2 :** bismuth subnitrate used as a pigment

spanish windlass *n, usu cap S* **:** a device for bringing together two taut lines (as for seizing) in which a small line is passed around the two, its ends are passed around a wooden roller, and a turn of each end is taken around a marlinespike by which the roller may be revolved and the lines hove together

spanish wine *n, often cap S* **:** PIGEON BLOOD

spanish yellow *n, often cap S* **:** a strong orange yellow that is slightly duller than bright maize or nasturtium yellow (sense 2)

¹spank \'spaŋk, -paiŋk\ *vb* -ED/-ING/-S [imit.] *vt* **1 :** to strike with or as if with the open hand; *esp* **:** to slap smartly on the buttocks ⟨in the olden days children were ~*ed* plenty —Benjamin Spock⟩ **2 :** to thrust or propel with a spank ⟨"I like balloons," she said, ~*ing* it into the air with . . . her hand —Joseph Mitchell⟩ **3 :** to reprimand severely ⟨we watch new American novelists being ~*ed* in the public prints —J.H. Burns⟩ ~ *vi* **:** to strike or fall with a spank ⟨the ball . . . would ~ into the round mitt —Richard Wilbur⟩

²spank \"\ *n* -s **1 a :** a blow usu. with the palm of the hand **:** SLAP **b :** a blow resembling a spank ⟨raised his oar and brought it down flat on the water with a tremendous ~ —*Saturday Rev.*⟩ **2 :** the sound produced by a spank

³spank \"\ *vb* -ED/-ING/-S [back-formation fr. ¹*spanking*] *vi* **1 :** to move quickly, dashingly, or spiritedly; *esp* **:** to drive or ride in a smart or stylish manner ⟨used to ~ around . . . in a smart rig that had yellow wheels trimmed in red —James Thurber⟩ **2 :** to sail briskly ⟨sailing craft would come down ~*ing* before the breeze —Richard Jefferies⟩ ~ *vt* **:** to drive (as a horse, vehicle) smartly

¹spank·er \-kə(r)\ *n* -s [origin unknown] **1** *dial* **:** one remarkable of its kind (as for size, speed, quality, appearance) **2 a :** the fore-and-aft sail carried on the aftermast of a square-rigged ship — see SAIL illustration **b :** the aftermast and sail in a schooner of four or more masts **c :** the fifth mast of a six-masted or seven-masted schooner **3 :** a horse capable of good speed **:** a fast trotter or pacer

²spanker \"\ *n* -s [¹*spank* + -*er*] **1 a :** one that spanks **b :** something used as an instrument for spanking ⟨some . . . shovel dirt in the path of the fire; others beat the flames with ~*s* —Philip Pollack⟩ **2 :** a drop-hammer operator who straightens metal parts that become warped during forging

spanker boom *n* **:** the boom for a spanker — see SHIP illustration

¹spank·ing \'spaŋkiŋ, -paiŋ-, -kēn\ *adj* [origin unknown] **1 :** remarkable of its kind **:** unusual or distinctive in some manner ⟨rode the noble animal over the ~ leap —Samuel Lover⟩ ⟨her smocked . . . cotton brought up behind with a ~ bow —*Mademoiselle*⟩ **2 a :** moving or capable of moving with a quick lively pace ⟨drove . . . by buckboard behind a ~ pair of the little mules —J.H.Allen⟩ **b :** DASHING, MERRY ⟨passed our house . . . at a ~ three miles an hour —Ben Riker⟩ ⟨like to be towed astern, riding surfboard . . . at a ~ clip —Jerome Ellison⟩ **c :** being fresh and strong **:** BRISK — usu. used of a breeze ⟨small boats dance on the clear blue waters in the ~ breeze —Bentz Plagemann⟩

²spanking \"\ *adv* **:** EXCEPTIONALLY, VERY ⟨put that away ~ clean last fall —Charles Boswell⟩ ⟨~ new modernistic structures, all concrete and colored glass —Ridgely Cummings⟩

spank·ing·ly *adv* **:** in a spanking manner **:** SPANKING

span-long \'=¦=\ *adj* [²*span* + *long*] **:** having the length of a span

spanned *past of* SPAN

span·ner \'spanə(r), -paan-\ *n* -s [fr. obs. E, instrument for winding the spring of a wheel lock, fr. G, fr. *spannen* to stretch (fr. OHG *spannan*) + -*er* — more at SPAN] **1 :** a contrivance in some of the earlier steam engines for moving the valves **2 a** *chiefly Brit* **:** WRENCH **b :** a wrench that has a jaw or socket to fit a nut or head of a bolt, a pipe, or hose coupling; *esp* **:** one having a tooth or one or more pins in its jaw to fit a hole or slot in an object **3 :** a horizontal cross brace or collar beam **4 :** a pendulum attachment for an ordinary sextant providing an artificial horizon for use when the sea horizon is obscured **5 :** an embroidery-machine worker who adjusts fabric and frames

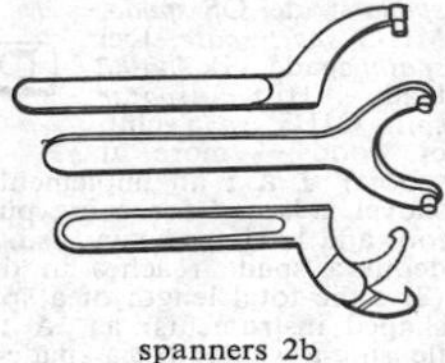
spanners 2b

span·ner·man \-mən\ *n, pl* **spannermen 1 :** a workman who tightens nuts or bolts with a spanner **2 :** a worker who adjusts the rolls of a roughing mill to assure that iron and steel will be of the desired thickness

span-new \'span¦=, -paan-\ *adj* [ME, part trans. of ON *spānnȳr*, fr. *spānn* chip of wood + *nȳr* new — more at SPOON] **:** BRAND-NEW

spanning *pres part of* SPAN

span of apprehension [²*span*] **:** the number of discrete stimulus objects to which a subject can simultaneously attend

span of attention [²*span*] **1 :** SPAN OF APPREHENSION **2 :** the duration of a subject's attention to a given task or set of stimuli

span roof *n* [³*span*] **:** a common roof having two slopes and one ridge with eaves on both sides

spans *pl of* SPAN, *pres 3d sing of* SPAN

spans and snops \-¦snäps\ *n pl but sing in constr* [*spans* fr. pl. of ²*span*; *snops* prob. alter. of *snaps*, pl. of *snap*] **:** an old game in which one player tries to shoot a marble against or to within a span of that of an opponent

span shackle *n* [⁶*span*] **:** a triangular or square shackle in the head of a large bolt driven through the forecastle deck to receive the heel of the fish davit

span-spek \'spänzˌpek, -nˌsp-\ *n* -s [Afrik, alter. of *spaanspek*, fr. *spaans* Spanisch (fr. D *spaansch*) + *spek* bacon, pork fat, fr. MD *spec* — more at SPECK] **:** a usu. somewhat pale-fleshed and moderately sweet muskmelon that is widely cultivated in southern Africa

spanwise \'=ˌ=\ *adj* [²*span* + -*wise*] **:** directed, moving, or placed along the span of an airfoil — compare CHORDWISE

spanworm \'=ˌ=\ *n* [³*span* + *worm*] **:** LOOPER 1

¹spar \'spär, -pȧ(r\ *vt* **sparred; sparred; sparring; spars** [partly fr. ME *sperren*, fr. MD; partly fr. ME *sparren*, fr. OE *gesparrian*; akin to MD & OHG *sperren* to bolt, lock, hamper, ON *sperra* to bolt, bar, *sparri* beam, rafter — more at ²SPAR] **1** *archaic* **:** BOLT, BAR, FASTEN **2 a** *obs* **:** SHUT, CLOSE **b** *obs* **:** to shut up **:** ENCLOSE

²spar \"\ *n* -s [ME *sparre*; akin to MD *sparre* beam, rafter, OHG *sparro*, ON *sparri* beam, rafter, OE *spere* spear — more at SPEAR] **1** *archaic* **:** RAFTER **2 a :** a pole or moderately thick piece of timber **b :** a stout rounded typically solid piece of wood or metal (as a mast, boom, gaff, yard) used to support rigging — see SHIP illustration **c** (1) **:** one of the main longitudinal members of the wing of an airplane that carry the ribs (2) **:** LONGERON **3 :** a thin doubled stick used in fastening thatch on roofs

³spar \"\ *vt* **sparred; sparred; sparring; spars :** to move or assist (a stranded ship) with a spar or with spar and tackle

⁴spar \"\ *vb* **sparred; sparred; sparring; spars** [prob. alter. of ²*spur*] *vi* **1 :** to strike or fight with the feet or spurs like a gamecock **2 :** to contest in words **:** WRANGLE ⟨the gabble of the vegetable men as they *sparred* with women at the open stalls outside their stores —Hortense Calisher⟩ **3 a :** BOX; *esp* **:** to make offensive and defensive gestures without landing a blow in order to draw one's opponent and find or create an opening **b :** to engage in a practice or exhibition bout esp. of scientific boxing with a sparring partner **4 :** to engage in a skirmish ⟨along the ground front . . . troops *sparred* in scattered fights —*N.Y.Times*⟩ **5 :** to move or act slowly or inconclusively **:** STALL ⟨seems to ~ for time by asking that questions be repeated —Jerome Frank⟩ ~ *vt* **:** to teach (a gamecock) to fight **:** train for fighting

⁵spar \"\ *n* -s **1 a :** a movement of offense or defense in boxing **b :** a sparring match or session **2 :** a wrangle or dispute esp. between well-matched opponents **:** a contest of thrust and counter

⁶spar \"\ *n* -s [LG, fr. MLG; akin to OE *spærstān* gypsum, chalk, *spæren* of plaster] **:** any of various nonmetallic usu. cleavable and somewhat lustrous minerals; *esp* **:** such a mineral occurring as gangue in a metalliferous vein — compare CALCSPAR, FELDSPAR, FLUORITE

7spar \"\ *n* -s *usu cap* [fr. *Semper Paratus*, motto of the U.S. Coast Guard fr. NL, always ready] **:** a member of the Women's Reserve of the U.S. Coast Guard formed during World War II

spar·a·ble \'sparəbəl\ *n* -s [alter. of *sparrowbill*] **:** a small headless nail used by cobblers to reduce wear on shoe soles

sparable tin *n* **:** tin ore in grains like sparables

spara·grass \'sparə,gras, -,grəs\ *n* [by folk etymology fr. *sparagus*] *chiefly dial* **:** ASPARAGUS

spar·a·gus \-,gəs\ *n* [modif. of L *asparagus*] *archaic* **:** ASPARAGUS

spa·ras·sis \spə'rasəs\ *n, cap* [NL, fr. Gk *sparassein* to tear, rend; akin to ON *spjörr* rag, Arm *p'ert'* piece ripped off of something, and perh. to OSlav *prožiti, prožati* to tear apart] **:** a genus of fungi (family Clavariaceae) having fleshy, much-branched, leafy sporophores — see YELLOW ROOT ROT

spa·rax·is \spə'raksəs\ *n* [NL, fr. Gk, act of retching; akin to Gk *sparassein* to tear, rend] **1** *cap* **:** a small genus of bulbous plants (family Iridaceae) that are native to the Cape of Good Hope and include several which are cultivated for their brilliantly colored flowers borne in fringed spathes — see WANDFLOWER **2** *pl* **sparaxis :** any plant, flower, or bulb of the genus *Sparaxis*

spar bridge *n* **:** a temporary bridge consisting of round timbers (as tree trunks) lashed together and usu. used for military purposes

spar buoy *n* **:** a buoy consisting of a spar anchored at one end usu. marking the port side of a channel — see BUOY illustration

sparce *var of* SPARSE

spar ceiling *n* **:** SPARRING

sparcity *var of* SPARSITY

spar deck *n* **:** an upper deck of light construction above the main deck

spar-decked \'≈,≈\ *adj* **:** having a spar deck

spar-deck·er \'≈'dekə(r)\ *n* **:** a ship having a spar deck

spar-deck vessel *n* **:** a ship for both cargo and passengers that has two or more decks of lighter construction above the strength deck

1spare \'spa(ə)|(ə)r, -pe|, |ə\ *vb* -ED/-ING/-S [ME *sparen*, fr. OE *sparian*; akin to OFris *sparia* to spare, OHG *sparōn*, *sparēn*, ON *spara*; derivatives fr. the root of E *2spare*] *vt* **1 :** to forbear to destroy, punish, or harm **:** preserve from punishment, injury, or evil **:** show mercy to ⟨~, O Lord, this miserable sinner⟩ ⟨many ships were sunk but a few were *spared*⟩ ⟨woodman, ~ that tree —G.P.Morris⟩ **2 :** to refrain from attacking, scolding, reprimanding, or speaking with necessary or salutary severity to ⟨his sermons *spared* neither high nor low, rich nor poor⟩ ⟨does not *spare* the U.N. and he recommends that it set its house in order —Chester Bowles⟩ **3 :** to relieve (someone) of the necessity of doing or undergoing something **:** EXEMPT ⟨~ him the trouble of answering⟩ ⟨wanted to ~ his parents the expense of sending him to college⟩ ⟨~ yourself quite a bit of . . . weeding —*New Yorker*⟩ **4 :** to refrain from **:** AVOID ⟨nothing is *spared* to . . . make you comfortable —T.H.Fielding⟩ **5 a :** to use stintingly or frugally **:** refrain from the free use or consumption of ⟨~ the rod and spoil the child⟩ — chiefly in negative use ⟨more pancakes, please, and don't ~ the syrup⟩ ⟨come at once and don't ~ the horses⟩ ⟨substantial homes with no *sparing* of paint —R.W. Hatch⟩ **b** *dial chiefly Brit* **:** SAVE 2a ⟨rob a poor man of all he had *spared* —Augusta Gregory⟩ **6 a :** to give up or part with as being not strictly needed **:** dispense with as surplus or extra ⟨could have better *spared* a better man —Shak.⟩ ⟨giving employment . . . to villagers who can be *spared* from the farms —*Geog. School Bull.*⟩ **b :** to have left over or as margin ⟨caught the train with a few minutes to ~⟩ ⟨that rug will cover the floor with a foot to ~⟩ **~** *vi* **1** *obs* **:** DESIST, STOP **2 :** to be frugal **:** live in a saving and stinting manner ⟨some will spend and some will ~ —Robert Burns⟩ **3 :** to refrain from executing judgment or punishment or taking vengeance **:** use mercy or kindness **:** be lenient — **and to spare :** in plenty **:** in superabundance **:** too much ⟨we have enough *and to spare* of bad novels⟩

2spare \"\ *adj* -ER/-EST [ME, fr. OE *spær*; akin to OHG *spar* spare, ON *sparr* spare, OSlav *sporŭ* abundant, OE *spēd* success, speed — more at SPEED] **1 :** not being used **:** held for future or emergency use ⟨~ bedroom⟩ ⟨~ tire⟩ ⟨~ anchor⟩ **2 :** being over and above what is necessary **:** not wanted **:** not presently needed **:** FREE, SUPERFLUOUS ⟨a hobby to occupy his ~ time⟩ ⟨have you any ~ cash you could lend me⟩ **3 :** not liberal or profuse **:** SPARING, CHARY ⟨habitually ~ of speech⟩ ⟨build up the truth of his characters through ~, pungent dialogue —Arthur Knight⟩ ⟨tale proceeds with a ~ and lucid simplicity —*Times Lit. Supp.*⟩ **4 :** lacking fat **:** somewhat thin **:** LEAN ⟨~, alert, and jaunty figure —Thomas Wolfe⟩ ⟨some like their beauty to be luxurious; others see beauty in the gaunt and the ~ —Richard Joseph⟩ **5 :** not abundant or plentiful **:** MEAGER, SCANTY ⟨~ diet⟩ ⟨~ vegetation⟩ **syn** see LEAN, MEAGER

3spare \"\ *n* -s [ME, fr. *sparen*, v.] **1** *obs* **:** an act of showing restraint or mercy — used esp. in the phrase *without spare* **2** *archaic* **:** PLACKET **3** *archaic* **:** frugal use **:** ECONOMY, FRUGALITY — used with *make* **4 a :** a spare tire **b :** a duplicate (as a battery, a pair of eyeglasses) kept in reserve **c** *chiefly Brit* **:** SPARE PART **d :** an extra member of a sports team **5 :** the knocking down of all 10 pins with the first 2 bowls of a frame in bowling — compare STRIKE **6 :** surplus clay trimmed off the mold in the slip-casting process

spare·able \'spa(a)rəbəl, -per-\ *adj* **:** that can be spared

spare hand *n* **:** an additional workman kept for incidental odd jobs or relieving a regular

spare·less \'≈ləs\ *adj* [*2spare* + *-less*] *archaic* **:** UNSPARING

spare·ly *adv* [*2spare* + *-ly*] **1 :** SPARINGLY ⟨drinking gravely and ~ of the . . . punch —Irwin Shaw⟩ **2 :** SPARSELY, MEAGERLY ⟨rooms were ~ furnished —Elizabeth M. Roberts⟩ **3 :** LEANLY ⟨~ built, active little man⟩

spare·ness *n* -ES **:** LEANNESS, THINNESS, MEAGERNESS

spare part *n* **:** an extra part of a vehicle or machine kept for use in emergency or replacement

spar·er \'spa(a)rə(r), -per-\ *n* -s [ME *sparare*, fr. *sparen* to spare + *-are*, *-er* -er — more at SPARE] **:** one that spares; *esp* **:** one that reduces destruction of something (as a bodily substance) ⟨sugar in the diet may act as a ~ of protein⟩

spare·ribs \'spa(a)(r),ribz, -pe(r),ri-, -pa(a)ə,ri-, -peə,ri-\ *n pl* [by folk etymology fr. LG *ribbesper* smoked or pickled pork ribs roasted on a spit, fr. MLG, fr. *ribbe* rib + *sper* spit, spear; akin to OHG *rippi* rib and to OHG *sper* spear — more at RIB, SPEAR] **:** a cut of pork ribs and breastbone separated from the bacon strip

spares *pres 3d sing of* SPARE, *pl of* SPARE

spare-set \'≈'≈\ *adj* [*2spare* + *set*, past part. of *set*] **:** spare in form **:** somewhat thin **:** GAUNT ⟨accosted by a graying, *spare-set* guest —S.H.Adams⟩

spar·ga·ni·a·ce·ae \(,)spär,ganē'āsē,ē\ *n pl, cap* [NL, fr. *Sparganium*, type genus + *-aceae*] **:** a monotypic family of monocotyledonous plants (order Pandanales) — see SPARGANIUM

spar·ga·ni·a·sis \,spärgə'nīəsəs\ *n, pl* **spargania·ses** \-īə,sēz\ [NL, fr. *sparganum* + *-iasis*] **:** SPARGANOSIS

spar·ga·nid \'spärgənəd\ *adj* [NL *sparganum* + E *-id*] **:** of or relating to a sparganum ⟨~ infestation⟩

spar·ga·ni·um \spär'gānēəm\ *n* [NL, fr. L *sparganion* bur reed, fr. Gk, dim. of *sparganon* swaddling band] **1** *cap* **:** a genus (coextensive with the family Sparganiaceae) of marsh or aquatic herbs of temperate regions with simple or branching stems, linear leaves, and monoecious flowers in globose heads — see BUR REED **2** -s **:** any plant of the genus *Sparganium*

spar·ga·no·sis \,spärgə'nōsəs\ *n, pl* **sparganoses** [NL, fr. *sparganum* + *-osis*] **:** the condition of being infected with Sparganum

spar·ga·num \'spärgənəm\ *n, pl* **sparga·na** \-nə\ *also* **sparganums** [NL, fr. Gk *sparganon* swaddling band; akin to Gk *speira* twist — more at SPIRE] **:** an intramuscular or subcutaneous vermiform parasite of various vertebrates including man that is the plerocercoid larva of a tapeworm — often used as though a generic name when referring to such a larva esp. when the adult is unknown ⟨*Sparganum proliferum* is a rare parasite of man⟩; compare LIGULA

1sparge \'spärj\ *vb* -ED/-ING/-S [prob. fr. MF *espargier* to sprinkle, fr. L *spargere* to scatter, strew, sprinkle — more at SPARK] *vt* **1 :** ROUGHCAST, PLASTER **2 a :** to moisten by sprinkling **:** SPRINKLE, BESPATTER; *esp* **:** to spray (mash) with hot water to extract the wort in brewing **b** (1) **:** to heat (a liquid) by means of live steam entering through a sparger (2) **:** to agitate (a liquid) by means of compressed air or gas entering through a sparger **~** *vi* **:** to scatter water about **:** SPRAY

2sparge \"\ *n* -s **:** a sprinkling or spraying; *also* **:** SPRAY

sparge pipe *n* **:** a horizontal perforated water pipe for flushing a urinal — called also *weeper*

sparg·er \-jə(r)\ *n* -s **:** one that sparges **:** SPRINKLER: as **a :** a vessel with a perforated cover for sprinkling clothes **b :** a device with perforated arms for sprinkling the grains in a mash tun **c :** a pipe having either perforations or nozzles through which steam, compressed air, or gas is forced into a liquid in a fermentation process

spar·hawk \'spär,≈\ *n* [ME *sparhauk*, fr. OE *spearhafoc*, fr. *spearwa* sparrow + *hafoc* hawk — more at SPARROW, HAWK] *archaic* **:** SPARROW HAWK

1spar·id \'sparəd\ *adj* [NL *Sparidae*] **:** of or relating to the Sparidae

2sparid *n* -s **:** a fish of the family Sparidae

spar·i·dae \-rə,dē\ *n pl, cap* [NL, fr. *Sparus*, type genus + *-idae*] **:** a large and widely distributed family of deep-bodied marine percoid fishes including the porgies, scups, and sheepsheads that are related to the grunts and snappers but have some of the teeth along the sides of the jaw transformed into large blunt molars — see SEA BREAM

sparing *adj* [ME, fr. pres. part. of *sparen* to spare] **1 a :** economical in the use or expenditure of resources ⟨a ~ father and a spending son —John Clarke⟩ **b :** RETICENT ⟨~ in speech⟩ ⟨~ prose⟩ **2 :** MEAGER, SCANTY ⟨the map is ~ of information⟩ **3 :** capable of preventing or characterized by prevention of waste of a vital substance in metabolism ⟨carbohydrates are ~ agents of body proteins⟩ ⟨aureomycin may exert a ~ action on some vitamins⟩

syn SPARING, FRUGAL, THRIFTY, and ECONOMICAL can mean, in common, tending to save or make unwasteful use of one's money, goods, or resources. SPARING suggests abstention and restraint and can apply to the use of anything, although commonly applying to the use of money or goods ⟨the *sparing* use of words⟩ ⟨*sparing* in all matters of household expense⟩ FRUGAL suggests the absence of all luxury and implies simplicity and temperance ⟨Roman life was a *frugal* thing, sparing in food, temperate in drink, modest in clothing, cleanly in habit —John Buchan⟩ ⟨was *frugal* and he did not, like many of the villagers, spend his money freely at gambling or on foods too delicate for them —Pearl Buck⟩ THRIFTY implies a minimum wastefulness and often a maximum of saving, and usu. suggests industry and frugality ⟨a miserly man who hoards money out of avarice and a *thrifty* man who saves money out of prudence —William Empson⟩ ⟨a *thrifty* people — *thrifty* of property, of speech, of their emotions above all —H.S.Commager⟩ ECONOMICAL, often interchangeable with *thrifty* when the sparing use of money or resources is involved, more distinctly emphasizes prudent management or use of things to their best advantage ⟨an *economical* housewife⟩ ⟨*economical* methods of using building materials⟩ ⟨the *economical* use of words⟩

spar·ing·ly *adv* [ME, fr. *sparing* + *-ly*] **1 :** in a sparing manner **:** MEAGERLY, SCANTILY ⟨~ seasoned food⟩ ⟨~ soluble in water⟩ **2 :** with restraint **:** INFREQUENTLY

spar·ing·ness *n* -ES **:** the quality or state of being sparing

1spark \'spärk, -pȧk\ *n* -s [ME *sperke*, *sparke*, fr. OE *spearca*, *spærca*; akin to MD & MLG *sparke* spark, L *spargere* to scatter, strew, Gk *spargan* to swell, Skt *sphūrjati* it bursts forth, appears] **1 a :** a small particle of a burning substance thrown out by a body in combustion or remaining when combustion is nearly completed ⟨~s from a fire⟩ **b :** a hot glowing particle heated by friction and struck out at the impact of two hard objects (as flint and steel) **2 a :** a luminous disruptive electrical discharge of very short duration between two conductors separated by air or other gas **b :** a small arc of short duration (as often at dynamo brushes) **c :** the discharge in a spark plug **d :** the mechanism (as a button or lever) controlling the discharge in a spark plug **3 a :** a very small glittering body or surface or a transient flash of reflected light **:** SPARKLE **b :** a very small gem **:** SPARKLER; *specif* **:** DIAMOND **4 :** something that ignites or sets off an explosion, conflagration, or other manifestation of suddenly released force ⟨~ that set off the rebellion⟩ **5 :** a latent particle or vestige of some quality or capability having possibilities of growth or development **:** GERM ⟨discern the ~ of promise . . . the barb of fruitful controversy —August Fruge⟩ ⟨a ~ of decency still remained in him⟩ ⟨lacking the least ~ of wit or grace⟩ ⟨vital ~ in a man that makes him an artist —Philip Mason⟩ **6 sparks** *pl but sing in constr* **:** a radio operator on a ship **7 :** SPARK TRANSMITTER **8 :** a person interested in fires and fire fighting **:** BUFF 7a **9 :** GERANIUM LAKE 2

2spark \"\ *vb* -ED/-ING/-S [ME *sparken*; akin to MD & MLG *sparken* to spark, sparkle, OE *spearca* spark — more at 1SPARK] *vi* **1 a :** to throw out sparks **:** SPARKLE ⟨the damp wood crackled and ~*ed*⟩ ⟨her eyes ~*ing* with fury⟩ **b :** to flash out or fall like sparks ⟨fireflies ~*ing* in the gathering darkness⟩ **2 :** to produce sparks **:** convert electrical energy into light and heat by ionization of the air or gas that separates the electrodes (as of a dynamo or a spark plug) **3 :** to respond with enthusiasm or ready acceptance ⟨~*ed* to the idea of an early wedding date⟩ **~** *vt* **1 :** to set off in a burst of activity **:** ACTIVATE ⟨these kindred spirits, articulate men with hair-trigger minds, ~ the president's thinking —Raymond Clapper⟩ **2 :** to stir into intense or sustained activity **:** inspire with zeal and energy **:** INCITE, STIMULATE ⟨a player ~s his team to victory⟩ ⟨his hit ~*ed* a rally that brought in four runs⟩ ⟨the discovery ~*ed* the police to fresh activity⟩ **3** *chiefly Scot* **:** SPATTER, SOIL

3spark \"\ *adj* [*1spark*] **:** of or relating to radio communication carried on with a spark transmitter ⟨~ set⟩ ⟨~ station⟩

4spark \"\ *n* -s [perh. of Scand origin; akin to ON *sparkr* lively, sprightly; perh. akin to OE *spearca* spark — more at 1SPARK] **1 :** a young, beautiful, witty woman **2 a :** a brisk showy gay man **:** BLADE, GALLANT **b :** a hot-tempered person **3 :** LOVER, BEAU

5spark \"\ *vb* -ED/-ING/-S *vt* **1** *obs* **:** show off — used with *it* **2 :** WOO, COURT ⟨the railroad didn't pay him to ~ a girl on its time —T.W.Duncan⟩ **~** *vi* **:** to engage in courting **:** go together as sweethearts

spark advance *n* **:** *2*LEAD 3d(2)

spark arrester *n* **1 :** a device for preventing the escape of sparks from a smokestack; *esp* **:** a framework of wire in the smokebox of a steam locomotive to arrest the escape of cinders **2 :** a device to minimize or prevent electric sparking at a place where a circuit is made and broken

sparkback *or* **sparked-back** \'≈,≈\ *n* **:** TURNSTONE

spark coil *n* **:** an induction coil for producing the spark for an internal-combustion engine

spark discharge *n* **:** an electric discharge accompanied by a spark **:** a disruptive discharge

sparked \'spärkəd, -pȧk-\ *adj* [obs. *spark* speck (fr. *1spark*) + *-ed*] *dial* **:** SPOTTED, STREAKED, VARIEGATED

spark·er \-kə(r)\ *n* -s **1 :** a small firework that gives out sparks **2 :** BEAU, LOVER **3** *Brit* **:** a ship's radio operator **4 :** IGNITER b

spark frequency *n* **:** the number of spark discharges per second in a radio transmitter

spark gap *n* **1 :** a space between two high-potential terminals (as of an induction coil) through which pass disruptive discharges of electricity in the form of sparks — see LIGHTNING ARRESTER illustration, SPARK PLUG illustration **2 :** a device consisting of two electrodes arranged to permit passage between them of disruptive discharges in the form of sparks

spark generator *n* **:** a generator of electric oscillations that utilizes the discharge of a condenser through a spark gap as the source of its alternating-current power

sparkier *comparative of* SPARKY

sparkiest *superlative of* SPARKY

spark·i·ness \-kēnəs, -kin-\ *n* -ES **1 :** the quality or condition of sparkling or of sending out sparks **:** LIVELINESS, VIVACIOUSNESS **2 :** the quality of being mottled or variegated

sparking lamp *n* **:** a small open oil lamp with floating wick

sparking plug *n, Brit* **:** SPARK PLUG

spark·ish \-kish\ *adj* [*4spark* + *-ish*] **1 :** like a gallant or beau **:** GAY **2 :** gaily dressed **:** SHOWY, DAPPER — **spark·ish·ly** *adv* — **spark·ish·ness** *n* -ES

spark knock *n* **:** the sound produced in an internal-combustion engine by operation with the spark too far advanced

1spar·kle \'spärkəl, -pȧk-\ *vb* **sparkled; sparkled; sparkling** \-k(ə)liŋ\ **sparkles** [ME *sparklen*, freq. of *sparken* to spark — more at SPARK] *vi* **1 a :** to throw out sparks **b :** to shine as if throwing out sparks **:** emit small flashes of light **:** SCINTILLATE, FLASH, GLISTEN ⟨dewdrops ~ in the morning sun⟩ **c :** to perform brilliantly ⟨the team hit well and *sparkled* in the field⟩ **2 :** to effervesce with bubbles of released carbon dioxide ⟨wine that ~s⟩ **3 :** to become lively or animated **:** show spirit and fire ⟨her eyes *sparkled* with anger⟩ ⟨the dialogue ~s with wit⟩ **~** *vt* **1 :** to cause to glitter or shine ⟨the sun *sparkled* wet grass⟩ **2 :** to show by or as if by flashes of light ⟨her eyes *sparkled* her pleasure at the compliment⟩

2sparkle \"\ *n* -s [ME, dim. of *sparke* spark — more at SPARK] **1 :** a little spark **:** SCINTILLATION **2 :** the quality of sending out or reflecting flashes of brilliant light ⟨~ of a diamond⟩ ⟨~ of the dancing waves⟩ **3 :** a slight trace **:** SHOWING ⟨now showed only an occasional ~ of his former high spirits⟩ **4 a :** ANIMATION, LIVELINESS, VIVACITY ⟨natural ~ animates her dialogue —*Current Biog.*⟩ **b :** EFFERVESCENCE **5 :** a small brilliant gem

3sparkle \"\ *vb* -ED/-ING/-S [ME *sparklen*, prob. alter. of *sparplen* — more at SPARPLE] *archaic* **:** DISPERSE, SCATTER

spark lead \'≈,lēd\ *n* **:** the amount of advance by which the production of the spark in the cylinders of an internal-combustion engine precedes the arrival of the piston at the top dead center position

spar·kle·ber·ry \'spärkəl, -pȧk- —*see* BERRY\ *n* [prob. by alter.] **:** FARKLEBERRY

sparkle metal *n* **:** matte containing 74 percent copper

spar·kler \-k(ə)lə(r)\ *n* -s **:** one that sparkles: as **a :** DIAMOND **b :** a bright witty vivacious person **c :** a brilliant performer **d :** a firework that throws off brilliant sparks on burning **e :** a toy gun or pistol that produces sparks when the trigger is pulled

spark·less \'spärklə̇s, -pȧk-\ *adj* **:** producing no sparks ⟨~ electric switch⟩ — **spark·less·ly** *adv*

spark·let \-lət\ *n* -s **1 :** a small spark **:** a tiny point of light **2 :** a small sparkling or glittering object ⟨gown adorned with glass ~s⟩ **:** a small spot that is relatively bright against a dark background

spark lever *n* **:** a lever formerly mounted usu. on the steering post of a motor vehicle for controlling the timing of the ignition

sparkling *adj* [ME, fr. pres. part. of *sparklen* to sparkle — more at SPARKLE] **1 a :** having luster or sparkle **:** SHINING, GLISTENING **b :** reflecting brilliant flashes or points of light ⟨~ ice⟩ **2 a :** BRILLIANT, DAZZLING ⟨~ performance of a piano piece⟩ **b :** ANIMATED, LIVELY ⟨~ conversation⟩ **3 :** EFFERVESCENT; *specif* **:** bubbling due to escaping carbon dioxide gas — opposed to *still* ⟨~ Burgundy⟩ — **spar·kling·ly** *adv* — **spar·kling·ness** *n* -ES

sparkling water *n* **:** SODA WATER 2a

sparkling wine *n* **:** an effervescent table wine usu. white but occas. red containing on the average 12 percent alcohol by volume and carbonated by secondary fermentation — compare CHAMPAGNE, DESSERT WINE, TABLE WINE

spar·kly \-k(ə)lē, -li\ *adj* [*1sparkle* + *-y*] **:** tending to sparkle ⟨~ white teeth⟩

sparkover \'≈,≈≈\ *n* -s [fr. *spark over*, v.] **:** a disruptive electric discharge; *esp* **:** an undesired sparking (as in charging a Leyden jar) between two conductors ⟨high-voltage generator operating in a pressure chamber to prevent electrical ~ —*Science*⟩ ⟨~ potential⟩

spark photography *n* **:** photography in which an electric spark discharge provides the only illumination and which is used esp. for photographing rapidly moving objects

spark plug *n* **1 :** a part that fits into the cylinder head of an internal-combustion engine and carries two electrodes separated by an air gap across which the current from the ignition system discharges to form the spark for combustion **2 :** one that initiates, affords the impetus to, or is the most effective or dynamic force in an undertaking or work **:** PRIME MOVER, MAINSPRING ⟨supervisors are the *spark plugs* in any program of vocational education —E.A.Lee⟩ ⟨his responsibility to act as *spark plug* when his team is in the field —C.F.Stubblefield⟩ ⟨the profit motive as a *spark plug* of progress —S.T.Williamson⟩

spark plug: *1* spark gap, *2* ground electrode, *3* center electrode, *4* steel shell, *5* copper gaskets, *6* steel bushing, *7* porcelain insulator, *8* brass cap, *9* center electrode terminal

sparkplug \'≈,≈\ *vt* [*spark plug*] **:** to initiate, give the impetus to, or play the chief role in (an undertaking) ⟨*spark-plugged* the new industrial and economic revolution —F.G.Slaughter⟩ ⟨*spark-plugging* their activities has been a group of dedicated physicians —Milton Silverman⟩

sparkproof \'≈;≈\ *adj* **:** SPARKLESS

sparks *pl of* SPARK, *pres 3d sing of* SPARK

spark spectrum *n* **:** the spectrum of a substance (as a metal) produced by using light from sparks passing between electrodes composed of that substance — compare ARC SPECTRUM

spark transmitter *n* **:** a radio transmitting set using a spark generator

1sparky \'spärkē, -pȧk-, -ki\ *adj* -ER/-EST [*1spark* + *-y*] **1 :** showing or throwing out sparks **2 :** ANIMATED, LIVELY

2sparky \"\ *adj* -ER/-EST [*5spark* + *-y*] **:** inclined toward lovemaking or courting

spar·ling \'spärliŋ\ *n, pl* **sparling** *or* **sparlings** [ME *sperling*, fr. MF *esperling*, *esperlan*, fr. MD *spierlinc*, fr. *spier* shoot, blade of grass + *-linc* -ling — more at SPIRE] **:** a European smelt (*Osmerus eperlanus*)

sparling fowl *n* [*sparling*] *dial Eng* **:** MERGANSER

sparmaker \'≈,≈≈\ *n* **:** a carpenter who finishes and installs spars, masts, and cargo booms

spar·man·nia \spär'manēə\ *n, cap* [NL, fr. Andreas *Sparmann* †1820 Swed. naturalist + NL *-ia*] **:** a small genus of African shrubs or trees (family Tiliaceae) having cordate more or less lobed leaves and silky white flowers with imperfect outer stamens succeeded by echinate capsules — see AFRICAN HEMP

sparmate \'≈,≈\ *n* [*5spar* + *mate*] **:** SPARRING PARTNER

1spar·oid \'spa(a),rȯid\ *adj* [NL *Sparus* + E *-oid*] **:** resembling or related to the Sparidae

2sparoid \"\ *n* -s **:** a sparoid fish

spar·ple \'spärpəl\ *vb* -ED/-ING/-S [ME *sparplen*, *sparpillen*, fr. MF *esparpeillier*, *esparpillier*, fr. (assumed) VL *sparpiliare*, perh. blend of L *spargere* to scatter, strew, sprinkle and *papilio* butterfly — more at SPARK, PAVILION] *archaic* **:** SCATTER, DISPERSE, ROUT, DISSEMINATE

sparred *adj* **:** made of or equipped with spars set at intervals

1spar·ring \'späriŋ, -pȧr-, -rēŋ\ *n* -s [ME, fr. *sparre* spar + *-ing*] **:** fore-and-aft battens secured to the reverse frames of a ship for cargo to rest against

2sparring \"\ *n* -s [fr. gerund of *4spar*] **1 :** scientific boxing **2 :** a skirmishing for advantage; *esp* **:** ARGUMENT, DISPUTE

sparring partner *n* **1 :** a boxer's companion for practice in sparring during training **2 :** one's mate in amicable wrangling or debating **:** a protagonist with whom to sharpen one's wits in argument

spar·row \'spa|(,)rō, |,rə; |,rəw, |,rō+V; *also* 'spe|\ *n* -s [ME *sparwe*, *sparowe*, *sparow*, fr. OE *spearwa*; akin to OHG *sparo* sparrow, ON *spörr*, Goth *sparwa* sparrow, Corn *frau* crow, Gk *sparasion*, a bird resembling a sparrow, *psar* starling, OPruss *spurglis* sparrow] **1 :** HOUSE SPARROW; *broadly* **:** any of various related birds of the genus *Passer* **2 :** any of numerous finches resembling the house sparrow in size and shape and in having plumage streaked with brown or gray — see CHIPPING SPARROW, FIELD SPARROW, HEDGE SPARROW, SAGE SPARROW, SAVANNAH SPARROW, SONG SPARROW, TREE SPARROW **3 :** MOUSE GRAY **4 a :** an undersized person **b :** one who is of aggressively active and markedly self-reliant temperament

sparrowbill \'ˌ,ˌ\ *n* **:** SPARABLE

spar·row·grass \'ˌ,gras, -grəs\ *n* [by folk etymology fr. *sparagus*] *chiefly dial* **:** ASPARAGUS

sparrow hawk *n* [ME *sparowhauk*, fr. *sparwe, sparowe, sparow* sparrow + *hauk* hawk] **1 :** a small Old World hawk (*Accipiter nisus*) similar in habits, size, and general coloration to the American sharp-shinned hawk **2 :** a small No. American falcon (*Falco sparverius*) that is closely related to the European kestrel, is chiefly rufous and slaty blue above and buffy white with dark markings below, and feeds mostly on large insects (as grasshoppers) **3 :** any of various hawks or falcons of small size: as **a :** PIGEON HAWK **b :** BUSH HAWK **4 :** a small anvil used by silversmiths

spar·row·ish \'sparəwish, -rōi- *also* -per-\ *adj* **:** resembling or suggesting a sparrow — **spar·row·ish·ness** *n* -ES

sparrowlike \'ˌ,ˌ\ *adj* **:** resembling a sparrow

sparrow owl *n* **1 :** PYGMY OWL **2 :** LITTLE OWL

sparrow–tail *also* **sparrow–tailed** \'ˌ,ˌ\ *adj* **:** SWALLOW-TAILED

spar·rowy \-rəw|ē, -rō|, |i\ *adj* **1 :** frequented by sparrows **:** infested with sparrows **2 :** SPARROWLIKE

spar·ry \'spärē, -pár-, -ri\ *adj* [*⁶spar* + *-y*] **:** resembling, consisting of, or abounding with spar **:** SPATHIC ⟨~ lode⟩ ⟨~ luster⟩

sparry iron *n* **:** SIDERITE

sparry limestone *n* **:** a coarsely crystalline marble

spars *pl of* SPAR, *pres 3d sing of* SPAR

¹sparse *vt* [L *sparsus*, past part. of *spargere* — more at SPARK] *obs* **:** SCATTER, DISPERSE, DISTRIBUTE

²sparse \'spärs, -pás\ *adv* [L *sparsus*, past part.] **:** SPARSELY, THINLY

³sparse *also* **sparce** \"\ *adj* -ER/-EST [L *sparsus*, past part.] **:** of few and scattered elements **:** having spaces between the component units **:** not thickly grown or settled **:** thinly scattered **:** SCANTY ⟨~ beard⟩ ⟨~ population⟩ ⟨~ shade of one willow tree —Eudora Welty⟩ **syn** see MEAGER

sparse·ly *adv* **:** in a sparse manner **:** SCANTILY, THINLY ⟨~ inhabited country⟩

sparse·ness *n* -ES **:** the quality or state of being sparse

spar·si·ty *also* **spar·ci·ty** \'spärsəd·ē, -pás-, -ətē, -i\ *n* -ES **:** the state of being sparse **:** SCANTINESS ⟨~ of vegetation⟩

¹spar·tan \'spärtᵊn, -pát-\ *n* -S [ME, fr. L *Spartanus*, adj. & n., fr. *Sparta*, city in ancient Greece (fr. Gk *Sparta, Spartē*) + L *-anus* -an] **1** *cap* **:** a native or inhabitant of ancient Sparta **2** *usu cap* **:** a person of great courage and fortitude

²spartan \"\ *adj*, *usu cap* [L *Spartanus*] **1 :** of or relating to Sparta in ancient Greece **2 :** marked by simplicity, frugality, avoidance of comfort and luxury, strict self-discipline, severity of manner, brevity in speech, hardihood in the face of pain or danger ⟨love their homes and often derive a kind of *Spartan* satisfaction from running them —A.C.Spectorsky⟩ ⟨lived with *Spartan* simplicity . . . eating frugal meals of farm produce and sleeping in a camp bed —*N.Y.Times*⟩ ⟨neat and *Spartan* look of military posts all over the world —Henriette Roosenburg⟩

spar·tan·ic \(')spär¦tanik\ *adj*, *usu cap* [L *Spartanus* + E *-ic*] **:** SPARTAN — **spar·tan·i·cal·ly** \-nək(ə)lē\ *adv*, *usu cap*

spar·tan·ism \'spärtᵊn,izəm, -pát-\ *n* -S *usu cap* **:** the moral quality or traits ascribed to the ancient Spartans **:** austerity in mode of living or in self-discipline **:** indomitableness or endurance esp. under great stress; *also* **:** conduct characteristic of such moral quality or traits

spar·tan·ize \-ᵊn,īz\ *vb* -ED/-ING/-S *often cap* [*²Spartan* + *-ize*] *vt* **:** to make Spartan in character **:** imbue with Spartan ideals ⟨tried to ~ his whole household⟩ ~ *vi* **:** to become Spartan in character **:** live in a Spartan manner

spar·tan·ly *adv*, *usu cap* **:** in a Spartan manner **:** with unflinching courage **:** with uncomplaining endurance of pain

spar·te·ine \'spärd·ē,ēn, -d·ēən\ *n* -S [ISV *spart-* (fr. NL *Spartium* genus of shrubs, fr. L *spartum* broom + NL *-ium*) + *-eine*] **:** a liquid tetracyclic alkaloid $C_{15}H_{26}N_2$ obtained esp. from the tops of the common broom and used in the form of its crystalline sulfate esp. formerly in the treatment of tachycardia and other irregularities of the heart

spar·te·rie \'spärd·ərē\ *n* -S [F, fr. *sparte* esparto (fr. L *spartum*) + *-erie* -ery — more at ESPARTO] **:** a fabric or articles made of esparto

spart grass \'spärt-\ *n* [L *spartum* — more at ESPARTO] **1 :** ESPARTO **2 :** a tall rather broad-leaved cordgrass (*Spartina alterniflora*) common in salt marshes of the eastern U.S. and introduced along the European coast and in the Pacific northwest

sparth \'spärth\ *n* -S [ME *sparthe*, fr. ON *spartha*] **:** a battle-ax used by the Irish in the middle ages

spar·ti·ate \'spärd·ē,āt, -rshē-\ *n* -S *cap* [L *Spartiates*, fr. Gk *Spartiatēs*, fr. *Sparta, Spartē* Sparta] **:** a member of the dominant race of ancient Laconia **:** SPARTAN

spar·ti·na \'spärtᵊnə\ *n* [NL, fr. Gk *spartinē* rope, cord; akin to Gk *speira* spiral — more at SPIRE] **1** *cap* **:** a small but widely distributed genus of grasses occurring chiefly in salt marshes along the coastal regions of Europe and No. and So. America and having stiff culms, panicled spikelets, and flowers with three glumes **2** *also* **spartina grass** -S **:** any grass of the genus *Spartina* — called also *cord grass;* see MARSH GRASS, SALT GRASS

spar·tle \'spärtᵊl\ *vi* -ED/-ING/-S [D *spartelen*, fr. MD *spartelen, spertelen, sportelen;* akin to MLG *spartelen, sportelen, spertelen* to sprawl, thrash about, OHG *sprazzalōn*, Norw *spratla* to sprawl, thrash about, OHG *sprinzan* to jump up — more at SPRINT] *Scot* **:** to kick about **:** SPRAWL

spar torpedo *n* **:** an explosive charge mounted on the end of a long spar and designed to be carried to a target by an attacking ship

spar tree *n* **:** a tall tree trimmed and well-guyed and used for supporting the lead blocks for high-line logging

spar·us \'spa(a)rəs\ *n*, *cap* [NL, fr. L, gilthead, fr. Gk *sparos* — more at SPEAR] **:** the type genus of the family Sparidae

spar varnish *n* **:** an exterior waterproof varnish suitable for use on the spars of ships

spar·ver \'spärvər\ *n* -S [ME *sperver, sparver*, fr. MF *esprevier, espervier* sparrow hawk, canopy bed, of Gmc origin; akin to MD *sperware* sparrow hawk, MLG *sparwer, sperwer*, OHG *sparwāri;* all fr. a prehistoric OHG-MD-MLG compound whose first element is represented by OHG *sparo* sparrow, and whose second element is represented by OHG *aro* eagle, altered under the influence of the suffix represented by OHG *-āri* -er — more at SPARROW, ERNE] *obs* **:** the canopy of a bed

spas *pl of* SPA

spasm \'spazəm\ *n* -S [ME *spasme*, fr. MF, fr. L *spasmus*, fr. Gk *spasmos*, fr. *span* to draw, pull, tear — more at SPAN] **1 a :** an involuntary and abnormal contraction of muscle or muscle fibers or of a hollow organ (as an artery, the colon, the esophagus) that consists largely of involuntary muscle fibers — compare CLONUS, TONUS **b :** the state or condition of a muscle or organ affected with spasms ⟨the renal artery went into ~⟩ **2 :** a sudden violent and temporary activity, effort, or emotion **:** BURST, FIT ⟨a ~ of antagonism⟩ ⟨a ~ of economy⟩ ⟨a ~ of fear⟩ ⟨a ~ of nervousness⟩ ⟨a ~ of pain⟩

spas·mat·ic \(')spaz¦mad·ik\ *or* **spas·mat·i·cal** \-d·əkəl\ *adj* [Gk *spasmat-, spasma* spasm (fr. *span* to draw, pull, tear) + E *-ic, -ical*] **:** SPASMODIC

spasm band *n* **:** a jazz band originating during the ragtime period, using chiefly improvised instruments (as cowbells, jug, kazoo), and later being composed primarily of youths performing in the street

spasmed \'spazəmd\ *adj* **:** afflicted with spasms **:** marked by spasms

spas·mic \'spazmik\ *adj* **:** marked by spasms **:** SPASMODIC

spas·mod·ic \(')spaz¦mädik, -dēk\ *or* **spas·mod·i·cal** \-dəkəl, -dēk-\ *adj* [NL *spasmodicus*, fr. Gk *spasmōdēs* spasmodic (fr. *spasmos* spasm) + L *-icus* -ic, -ical] **1 a :** of, relating to, affected or characterized by a spasm **b :** resembling a spasm in being sudden and violent ⟨his body gave a ~ jerk forward —Anthony Trollope⟩ ⟨clutched at the doctor's hand with a ~ movement of despair —W.H.Wright⟩ **2 :** acting or proceeding fitfully or intermittently **:** lacking continuity of effort, production, or activity **:** INTERMITTENT ⟨a continuous discussion of international affairs, not a ~ action at times of crisis —Clement Attlee⟩ ⟨growth of the towns was ~ —*Amer. Guide Series: Mass.*⟩ ⟨streamlining . . . may prove chronic or ~ —C.C.Furnas⟩ **3 :** subject to outbursts of emotional excitement — **spas·mod·i·cal·ly** \-dək(ə)lē, -dēk-, -li\ *adv*

spas·mo·dism \'spazmə,dizəm\ *n* -S [*spasmodic* + *-ism*] **:** spasmodic emotion

spas·mo·dist \-ˌdəst\ *n* -S [*spasmodic* + *-ist*] **:** one that is spasmodic in work or manner

spas·mo·gen·ic \¦spazmə¦jenik\ *adj* [ISV *spasm* + *-o-* + *-genic*] **:** inducing spasm ⟨a ~ drug⟩

spas·mol·y·sis \spaz'mäləsəs\ *n*, *pl* **spasmoly·ses** \-lə,sēz\ [NL, fr. L *spasmus* spasm + NL *-o-* + *-lysis*] **:** the relaxation of muscle spasm

¹spas·mo·lyt·ic \¦spazmə¦lid·ik\ *adj* [ISV, fr. NL *spasmolysis*, after such pairs as NL *hypnosis:* E *hypnotic*] **:** tending or having the power to relieve spasms or convulsions — **spas·mo·lyt·i·cal·ly** \-d·ək(ə)lē\ *adv*

²spasmolytic \"\ *n* -S **:** a spasmolytic agent

spas·mo·neme \'spazmə,nēm\ *n* -S [*spasm* + *-o-* + *-neme*] **:** a contractile filament (as in various stalked protozoans)

spas·mo·phil·ia \,spazmə'filēə\ *n* -S [NL, fr. L *spasmus* spasm + NL *-o-* + *-philia*] **:** an abnormal tendency to convulsions, tetany, or spasms from even slight mechanical or electrical stimulation

spas·mo·phil·ic \¦ˌˌ¦filik\ *or* **spas·mo·phile** \'ˌˌ,fīl\ *adj* [*spasm* + *-o-* + *-philic* or *-phile*] **:** of, relating to, or affected by spasmophilia

¹spas·tic \'spastik, -paas-,-pais-, -tēk\ *adj* [L *spasticus*, fr. Gk *spastikos* drawing, fr. (assumed) *spastos*, verbal of *span* to draw + *-ikos* -ic — more at SPAN] **1 a :** of, relating to, or characterized by spasm ⟨~ colon⟩ **b :** suffering from spastic paralysis ⟨a ~ child⟩ **2 :** characterized by spasms esp. of movement or activity **:** SPASMODIC ⟨a ~ motion of alternate digging and ducking —Van Van Praag⟩

²spastic \"\ *n* -S **:** one suffering from spastic paralysis

spas·ti·cal·ly \-tək(ə)lē, -tēk-, -li\ *adv* **:** in a spastic manner ⟨the ~ gyrating performers —*Time*⟩

spas·tic·i·ty \'stisəd·ē, -ətē, -i\ *n* -ES **:** the state of being spastic

spastic paralysis *n* **:** paralysis marked by tonic spasm of the muscles affected and by increased tendon reflexes — compare CEREBRAL PALSY

¹spat [ME *spatte* (past of *speten* to spit), fr. OE *spǣte*, past of *spǣtan* to spit; akin to OE (northern dial.) *spittan* to spit] *past of* SPIT

²spat \'spat, *usu* -ad·+V\ *n*, *pl* **spat** *or* **spats** [origin unknown] **1 :** a young oyster or other bivalve mollusk either before or after it first becomes adherent **2 :** young oysters ⟨~ is abundant this year⟩

³spat \"\ *vi* **spatted; spatted; spatting; spats 1 :** to emit spawn ⟨oysters ~⟩ **2 :** to become permanently attached to some solid object — used of a mollusk and esp. of an oyster

⁴spat \"\ *n* -S [short for *spatterdash*] **1 :** a covering for the instep and ankle usu. made of cloth or leather with a side closing and a strap under the instep and worn for protection or appearance — usu. used in pl. ⟨dressed in ~s, cutaway, and silk hat⟩ **2 :** a fairing around the wheel of a fixed airplane landing gear

spats 1

⁵spat \"\ *n* -S [prob. of imit. origin] **1 :** a usu. petty quarrel that flares up quickly and is of short duration **2** *chiefly dial* **:** a quick sharp blow **:** SLAP **3 a :** something that spatters **:** a light splash ⟨a ~ of rain⟩ ⟨~s of mud⟩ **b :** a sound like that of rain falling in large drops ⟨the ~ of bullets against a stone wall⟩ **syn** see QUARREL

⁶spat \"\ *vb* **spatted; spatted; spatting; spats** [prob. of imit. origin] *vt* **1** *chiefly dial* **a :** SLAP **b :** to clap together (as the hands) **2 :** to strike with a sound like that of rain falling in large drops ⟨bullets . . . *spatting* the leaves —J.H.Stuart⟩ ~ *vi* **1 :** to quarrel usu. pettily or briefly and repeatedly ⟨a teenager *spatting* with her mother⟩ **2 :** to strike or fall and strike with a sound like that of rain falling in large drops ⟨bullets were *spatting* down —R.H.Newman⟩

¹spa·tan·gid \spə'tanjəd\ *or* **spat·an·goid** \'spatᵊn,gȯid, spə'tan,gȯid\ *or* **spat·an·goi·de·an** \¦spatᵊn¦gȯidēən\ *adj* [*spatangid* fr. NL *Spatangida; spatangoid* fr. NL *Spatangoida; spatangoidean* fr. NL *Spatangoida* + E *-ean*] **:** of or relating to the Spatangina

²spatangid \"\ *or* **spatangoid** \"\ *or* **spatangoidean** \"\ *n* -S **:** a sea urchin of the suborder Spatangina **:** HEART URCHIN

spa·tan·gi·da \spə'tanjədə\ *or* **spat·an·goi·da** \,spatᵊn'gȯidə\ *or* **spat·an·goi·dea** \-dēə\ [NL, fr. *Spatangus* + *-ida* or *-oida* or *-oidea*] *syn of* SPATANGINA

spat·an·gi·na \,spatᵊn'jīnə, -jēnə\ *n pl*, *cap* [NL, fr. *Spatangus* + *-ina*] **:** a suborder of sea urchins (order Exocycloida) comprising numerous more or less flattened approximately heart-shaped sea urchins that exhibit considerable secondary bilateral symmetry — compare CLYPEASTRINA

spa·tan·gus \spə'taŋgəs\ *n*, *cap* [NL, fr. Gk *spatangēs*, a kind of sea urchin] **:** an ill-defined genus (the type of the family Spantangidae) of sea urchins including many of the commonest and best-known heart urchins

¹spatch·cock \'spach,käk\ *n* -S [prob. alter. of *spitchcock*] **:** a fowl split and grilled usu. immediately after being killed and dressed

²spatchcock \"\ *vt* -ED/-ING/-S **1 :** to prepare (as a fowl) for eating as or as if a spatchcock **2 :** to introduce by or as if by interpolation or insertion ⟨task of attempting to ~ the new evidence into an existing framework —*Times Lit. Supp.*⟩ ⟨all the random majesty of the place appeared ~*ed*, rectified, and jumbled —John Cheever⟩

¹spate \'spat, *usu* -ād·+V\ *n* -S [ME] **1 :** FRESHET, FLOOD ⟨every waterfall roars in ~ —E.J.Moran⟩ ⟨an Arkansas River ~ —S.H.Adams⟩ ⟨a migration into the valley that continued in full ~ beyond the middle of the century —*Amer. Guide Series: Va.*⟩ **2** *chiefly Scot* **:** a sudden heavy rainstorm **3 a :** a large number or amount ⟨a ~ of books on gardening⟩ ⟨a ~ of cowboy movies⟩ ⟨a ~ of publicity⟩ **b :** a sudden or strong outburst **:** RUSH ⟨a ~ of anger⟩ ⟨a ~ of words⟩

²spate \"\ *vt* -ED/-ING/-S *chiefly Scot* **:** FLOOD

spatfall \'ˌ,ˌ\ *n* [*²spat* + *fall*] **:** the settling and attachment of young bivalves (as oysters or mussels) to the substrate

spath \'spath, 's(h)pät\ *n* -S [G *spat* (formerly spelled *spath*), fr. MHG *spat, spāt;* akin to OHG *spān* chip, thin slab of wood — more at SPOON] *archaic* **:** ⁶SPAR

spatha \'spathə, -päthə\ *n*, *pl* **spathae** \-,thē, -,thī\ [L, fr. Gk *spathē* blade — more at SPADE] **1 :** a broadsword with blunt point used by the ancient Greeks and Romans **2 :** a long heavy sword used by Britons, Saxons, and Normans

spa·tha·ceous \(')spa¦thāshəs, (')spā¦th-, spə'th-, (')spa¦th-\ *adj* [*spathe* + *-aceous*] **:** having a spathe **:** resembling a spathe

spath·al \'spāthəl, -th-\ *adj* [*spathe* + *-al*] **:** SPATHACEOUS

spathe \'spāth, -th\ *n* -S [NL *spatha*, fr. L, broadsword, fr. Gk *spathē* blade — more at SPADE] **:** a sheathing bract or pair of bracts subtending or enclosing an inflorescence, exhibiting much variation in form and coloring, and occurring typically in plants whose inflorescence is a spadix or in modified form in many monocotyledonous plants (as the irises)

spathed \-āthd, -atht\ *adj* **:** having a spathe

spath·ic \'spathik\ *adj* [*spath* + *-ic*] **:** resembling spar **:** FOLIATED, LAMELLAR, SPATHOSE

spathic iron *or* **spathic iron ore** *n* **:** SIDERITE

spathi·flo·rae \,spatha'flōr,ē, -päth-,-path-\ [NL, fr. *spatha* + *-i-* + *-florae* (fr. LL, fem. pl. of *-florus* -florous)] *syn of* ARALES

spa·tho·dea \spa'thōdēə, spa'th-,spa'th-\ *n* [NL, fr. *spatha* + *-odea*, alter. of *-odes*] **1** *cap* **:** a genus of tropical African evergreen trees (family Bignoniaceae) used as ornamentals in tropical and subtropical regions and having large odd-pinnate or ternate leaves and showy orange or scarlet flowers in terminal panicles or racemes **2** *also* **spa·tho·dia** \"\ -S **:** any plant of the genus *Spathodea*

¹spath·ose \'spa,thōs\ *adj* [*spath* + *-ose*] **:** SPATHIC

²spath·ose \'spā,thōs, -thōs\ *also* **spath·ous** \-thəs, -thəs\ *adj* [*spathe* + *-ose* or *-ous*] **:** SPATHACEOUS

spath·u·late \'spathyələt, -,lāt\ *adj* [LL *spathula, spatula* + E *-ate* — more at EPAULET] **:** SPATULATE ⟨~ petals of a flower⟩

spa·tial *or* **spa·cial** \'spāshəl\ *adj* [*spatial* fr. L *spatium* space + E *-al; spacial* alter. of *spatial* — more at SPEED] **1 a :** of or relating to space ⟨~ pioneers will face such problems as . . . cosmic radiation —*Time*⟩ ⟨elimination of ~ barriers by speedy transportation and communication —John Dewey⟩ ⟨the changing ~ distribution of our population —Sidney Goldstein⟩ **b :** subject to the conditions of space **:** limited by space ⟨it is one of the facts of our being that we are temporal and ~ —Norman Kelman⟩ **2 :** occupying space **:** involving relations in space ⟨this ~ theme fulfills an ancient requirement of the art of architecture — namely, to balance artfully the building masses and open spaces —Walter Gropius⟩ — **spa·tial·ly** \-əlē, -əli\ *adv*

spatial isomerism *n* **:** STEREOISOMERISM

spa·ti·al·i·ty \,spāshē'aləd·ē\ *n* -ES **:** the quality or state of being spatial — distinguished from *temporality*

spa·tial·iza·tion \,spāshələ'zāshən, -,lī'z-\ *n* -S **:** the act of spatializing

spa·tial·ize \'ˌˌ,līz\ *vt* -ED/-ING/-S [*spatial* + *-ize*] **:** to give spatial form to **:** think of as spatial or in space relations **:** localize in space ⟨man . . . invented writing to ~, i.e. preserve, language —Susanne K. Langer⟩ ⟨our inveterate cognitive disposition to ~ everything —H.A.Murray⟩

spa·ti·ate \'spāshē,āt\ *vi* -ED/-ING/-S [L *spatiatus*, past part. of *spatiari*, fr. *spatium* space] **:** ROVE, RAMBLE, STROLL

spatio- *comb form* [L *spatium* — more at SPEED] **1 :** space ⟨*spatio*graphy⟩ **2 :** spatial and ⟨*spatio*temporal⟩

spa·ti·og·ra·phy \,spāshē'ägrəfē\ *n* -ES [*spatio-* + *-graphy*] **:** a science that deals with space beyond the earth's atmosphere; *esp* **:** the description of the physical characteristics of the moon and the planets

spa·tio·temporal \¦spāshē(,)ō+\ *adj* [*spatio-* + *temporal*] **:** having the quality of something that is at once extended and enduring **:** of or relating to the spatial and temporal together **:** of space-time ⟨the important elements of experience are ~ relations —M.M.Deems⟩ ⟨the ~ limits within which our reason functions —*Times Lit. Supp.*⟩ — **spa·tio·temporally** \"+\ *adv*

spats *pl of* SPAT, *pres 3d sing of* SPAT

spat·ted \'spad·əd, -atəd\ *adj* [*⁴spat* + *-ed*] **:** furnished with or wearing spats ⟨he was in Paris . . . still ~, still wearing his cutaway —Djuna Barnes⟩

¹spat·ter \'spad·ə(r), -atə-\ *vb* -ED/-ING/-S [akin to Fris *spatte, spatterje* to spatter, splash, MD *spatten*, Flem *spetteren*] *vt* **1 :** to splash with a liquid or with any wet substance **:** soil by splashing with drops or small portions ⟨~ the floor with grease⟩ **2 :** to scatter by splashing **:** sprinkle around ⟨~ blood⟩ ⟨~ mud on one's clothes⟩ **3 :** to cover with or as if with splashes or spots **:** SPOT ⟨the bare floor ~*ed* with moonlight —Amy Lowell⟩ ⟨green tweed ~*ed* with white silk flecks —*New Yorker*⟩ ⟨mistakes and misrepresentations ~*ed* throughout the whole article —*Times Lit. Supp.*⟩ **4 :** to injure by aspersion **:** DEFAME ⟨as an advocate, he must praise the man whom, a year before, he had ~*ed* with ignominy —J.A. Froude⟩ ⟨satire . . . has an awkward way of ~*ing* its author —*Listener*⟩ ~ *vi* **1 :** to sputter as if ejecting something distasteful **:** SPLUTTER **2 a :** to jet or spurt forth in scattered drops ⟨by hitting the ferrule of the brush against the opposite wrist and causing dots of color to ~ upon the setting —H.F. Helvenston⟩ ⟨spray from one of the hoses ~*ed* over the longshoremen —Vernon Pizer⟩ **b :** to drop or fall with or as if with the sound of heavy drops of rain ⟨earth damp and fragrant from the dew which ~*s* from the overhanging trees —Tom Marvel⟩ ⟨water-stream blows . . . and ~*s* into the basin with a light tinkling —Amy Lowell⟩

²spatter \"\ *n* -S **1 a :** the act or process of spattering or the state of being spattered **:** SPLASHING **b :** SPATTER DASH 2 **c :** the noise of spattering **2 a :** a drop or splash spattered on something **:** a spot or stain due to spattering ⟨clean mud ~*s* off clothing⟩ ⟨wipe grease ~*s* off the wall⟩ **b :** a small number or quantity **:** SPRINKLE ⟨a ~ of rain⟩ ⟨a ~ of applause⟩ ⟨heavy artillery fire and a ~ of infantry raids —*Current History*⟩ ⟨a continual ~ of musketry fire —Kenneth Roberts⟩ **3** *West* **:** RUDDY DUCK

spatter cone *n* **:** a miniature volcanic cone on a crater floor or lava flow from which lava is ejected in drops or gobs

spatterdash \'ˌˌ,ˌ\ *n* [*¹spatter* + *dash*] **:** a usu. knee-high legging worn as a protection from water and mud — usu. used in pl.

spatter dash \"\ *n* [*¹spatter* + *dash*] **1 :** a finish produced on stucco by dashing a very thin mixture of cement and coarse sand against a surface of fresh mortar — called also *roughcast* **2** *usu* **spatter–dash** \"\ **:** a finish produced by spattering paint of a different color on a ground coat

spat·ter·dock \'spad·ə(r),däk, -atə-\ *n* **1 :** the common yellow water lily (*Nuphar advena*) of eastern and central No. America that grows freely in sluggish fresh or sometimes slightly brackish water (as in swamps or about the margin of ponds) **2 :** a plant of the genus *Nuphar* — see SOUTHERN SPATTERDOCK

spatterdash, 18th century

¹spattering *adj* [fr. pres. part. of *¹spatter*] **:** that spatters — **spat·ter·ing·ly** *adv*

²spattering *n* -S [fr. gerund of *¹spatter*] **1 :** SPATTER, SPRINKLING ⟨a ~ of . . . freckles across the bridge of her nose —Irwin Shaw⟩ ⟨only a ~ of irregular lights burned in the palace tenements —D.C.Peattie⟩ ⟨a ~ of applause —J.M. Flagler⟩ **2 :** a method of painting stage scenery in which paint is spattered onto a surface

spatterware \'ˌˌ,ˌ\ *n* **:** earthenware that has spatterwork designs

spatterwork \'ˌˌ,ˌ\ *n* **1 :** a process of reproducing designs by laying them on a surface and spattering the exposed parts with a tinting fluid **2 :** a design made by spatterwork

spatting *pres part of* SPAT

spat·tle \'spad·ᵊl\ *n* -S [ME *spatyl*, fr. MF *spatule* — more at SPATULE] **1 :** SPATULA **2 :** an implement for mottling a molded article with a pigment

spat·u·la \'spachələ\ *n* [LL — more at EPAULET] **1** -S **:** a flat thin flexible dull-edged usu. metal implement used esp. for spreading or mixing soft substances (as paint, plaster, ointment, frosting), scooping, or lifting (as in removing cookies from a pan) **2** *cap* [NL, fr. LL] **:** a genus of ducks consisting of the shovelers and often included in *Anas* **3** -S **:** a spatulate process on the body of an insect

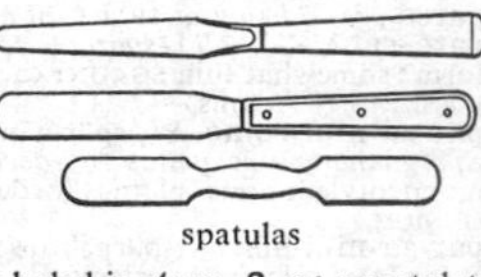
spatulas

spat·u·la·man·cy \-,man(t)sē\ *n* -ES [LL *spatula* spatula, shoulder blade + E *-mancy*] **:** divination by means of an animal's shoulder blade

¹spat·u·late \-chələt, -,lāt\ *adj* [*spatula* + *-ate* (adj. suffix)] **1 :** shaped like a spatula **:** spoon-shaped ⟨spreading her butter on her bread with her broad ~ hand —Jessie Roy⟩ ⟨a ~ leaf⟩ — see LEAF illustration **2** *of a hand* **:** having fingers shaped like spatulas and a palm either broad at the wrist and narrow at the base of the fingers or narrow at the wrist and broad at the base of the fingers usu. held by palmists to indicate energy, love of action, and independence of spirit

²spat·u·late \-,lāt\ *vt* -ED/-ING/-S [*spatula* + *-ate* (v. suffix)] **:** to work or treat with a spatula ⟨after the powder has been incorporated in the water, the mass is *spatulated* thoroughly —M.G.Swenson⟩

spat·u·lat·ed \-,lād·əd\ *adj* [*spatula* + *-ate* + *-ed*] **:** SPATULATE

spat·u·la·tion \ˌ⸗⸗ˈlāshən\ *n* -s **:** the act or process of spatulating or the condition of being spatulate

spat·ule \ˈspa(ˌ)chül\ *n* -s [ME, fr. MF, fr. LL *spatula* — more at SPATULA] **1 :** SPATULA **2 :** a spatulate organ or part

spat·u·li·form \ˈspachələ,fȯrm\ *adj* [*spatula* + *-iform*] **:** SPATULATE

spat·u·lose \-ˈspachə,lōs\ *or* **spat·u·lous** \-ˌləs\ *adj* [*spatula* + *-ose* or *-ous*] **:** SPATULATE

spätzle *var of* SPAETZLE

spaul *obs var of* ¹SPAWL

spauld *also* **spaul** \ˈspȯl(d), -pal-\ *n* -s [ME *spalde, spaulde, spald*, fr. (assumed) OF *espalde*, var. of *espaule* — more at EPAULET] **1** *chiefly Scot* **:** SHOULDER **2** *chiefly Scot* **:** ¹LIMB 2

spa·vie \ˈspāvi\ *n* [by alter.] *chiefly Scot* **:** SPAVIN

spa·vied \-vid\ *also* **spa·viet** \-vit\ *adj, chiefly Scot* **:** SPAVINED

spav·in *also* **spav·ine** \ˈspavən\ *n* -s [ME *spavayne, spaveyne*, fr. MF *esparvain, espavain*] **:** SWELLING; *esp* **:** a bony enlargement of the hock of a horse immediately due to strain but associated with a hereditary predisposition

spav·in·dy \-vəndi\ *adj* [*spavined* + *-y*] *Irish* **:** SPAVINED

spav·ined \-nd\ *adj* [ME *spaveyned*, fr. *spavayne, spaveyne* + *-ed*] **1 :** affected with spavin **2 :** LAME, MAIMED ⟨broken-winded novels, or ~ verses —O.W.Holmes †1894⟩ ⟨an ancient coach and a string of ~ baggage cars —*Time*⟩ ⟨lawyers pictured him as a sad and ~ man, plagued with a bad heart —*Time*⟩

spaw *archaic var of* SPA

¹**spawl** \ˈspȯl\ *vb* -ED/-ING/-S [origin unknown] *archaic* **:** SPIT

²**spawl** *var of* SPALL

¹**spawn** \ˈspȯn *also* -pän\ *vb* -ED/-ING/-S [ME *spawnen*, fr. AF *espaundre*, fr. OF *espandre, spandre* to spread, disperse, fr. L *expandere* to spread out, expand — more at EXPAND] *vt* **1 a :** to produce or deposit (eggs or spawn) — used of an aquatic animal **b :** to induce (fish) to spawn — used esp. of an aquarium fish **c :** to strip spawn from (a ripe fish) esp. for hatchery rearing of fish **d :** to plant with mycelia of the common edible mushroom mostly in the form of spawn bricks ⟨~ beds for growing mushrooms⟩ **2 :** to bring forth **:** GENERATE, PRODUCE ⟨a universe that ~*s* forth only ghouls and ogres —M.D.Geismar⟩ ⟨a blizzard ~*ed* in the Rocky mountains —*N. Y. Herald Tribune*⟩ ⟨impatience and irritation are often ~*ed* by ignorance or misunderstanding —A.E.Stevenson b. 1900⟩ ⟨slums which ~ the criminal elements —John Barkham⟩ ⟨this ideology is ~*ed* out of Communism —A.W. Barkley⟩; *esp* **:** to produce in great quantity ⟨no fewer than 500 private home-study schools . . . had been ~*ed* —J.M.Flagler⟩ ⟨hypotheses might be ~*ed* by the dozens —S.C.Pepper⟩ ⟨last year . . . ~*ed* books by the millions —Harrison Smith⟩ ⟨abundant rains, ~*ing* a profusion of desert wild flowers —*Los Angeles (Calif.) Examiner*⟩ ~ *vi* **1 :** to deposit spawn ⟨silver fish that . . . madly push their way upstream to ~ —*Amer. Guide Series: Mich.*⟩ **2 a :** to give forth young esp. in large numbers or like spawn **:** REPRODUCE **b :** to develop in multitudes or masses

²**spawn** \ˈ"\ *n* -s [ME *spawne*, fr. *spawnen*, v.] **1 a :** the eggs of fishes, oysters, and other aquatic animals that lay many small eggs **b :** the fertilized eggs produced by one pair of fish at one time **2 a :** any product or offspring ⟨Spanish moss, that peculiar ~ of the South —Henry Miller⟩ ⟨our likes and dislikes are often blind, the ~ of instinct or habit —Harry Bear⟩ ⟨shooing away young ~*s* . . . who wanted the glory of having touched the wonderful red machine —Marcia Davenport⟩ **b :** offspring in great numbers or masses **:** numerous issue ⟨mules are ~ of Satan —Francis Yeats-Brown⟩ ⟨the ~ of careless dicta —B.N.Cardozo⟩ **3 :** the seed, germ, or source of something ⟨democracy was . . . the very ~ of anarchy —V.L.Parrington⟩ ⟨the loom and shuttles made the old lady's garage apartment a ~ of noise —*Western Rev.*⟩ **4 :** the mycelium of fungi esp. prepared usu. in the form of bricks for propagating mushrooms **5 :** gelatinous matter **:** BREAK 6d ⟨the ~ of an oil⟩

spawneater \ˈ⸗,⸗⸗\ *n* **:** SPOTTAIL SHINER

spawn·er \-ˌə(r)\ *n* -s **1 :** a mature female fish **2 :** something that produces spawn

¹**spawning** *n* -s [ME *spawnynge*, fr. gerund of *spawnen* to spawn] **1 :** the process of emitting spawn **2 :** the collecting of spawn from ripe fishes

²**spawning** *adj* [fr. pres. part. of ¹*spawn*] **1 :** emitting spawn **2 :** FERTILE, PROLIFIC ⟨the ~ slums of our cities⟩

spawny \-ē\ *adj* **:** resembling spawn; *also* **:** SPAWNING

¹**spay** \ˈspā\ *vt* -ED/-ING/-S [ME *spayen*, fr. MF *espeer* to cut with a sword, pierce, fr. OF, fr. *espee* sword, fr. L *spatha* broadsword — more at SPATHE] **:** to remove or extirpate the ovaries of (as a sow or a bitch) **:** CASTRATE

²**spay** \ˈ"\ *n* -s **1 :** a spayed animal **2 :** SPAYING

³**spay** \ˈ"\ *or* **spay·ad** \-āəd\ *or* **spay·ard** \-āə(r)d\ *n* -s [ME *spayer, spayad*] **:** a male red deer in his third year

spaying *n* -s [fr. gerund of ¹*spay*] **:** the act of castrating a female animal

spd *abbr* **1** ous] **2** sprayed

SPD *abbr, often not cap* steamer pays dues

spdl *abbr* spindle

¹**speak** \ˈspēk\ *vb* **spoke** \ˈspōk\ *or archaic* **spake** \ˈspāk\ *or dial Brit* **spak** \ˈspak\ **spo·ken** \ˈspōkən *sometimes* -kᵊŋ\ *or archaic* **spoke** *or dial Brit* **spak; speaking; speaks** [ME *speken*, fr. OE *sprecan, specan*; akin to OHG *sprehhan* to speak, Gk *spharageisthai* to crackle, Skt *sphūrjati* it roars, crackles] *vi* **1 a :** to utter words or articulate sounds with the ordinary modulation of the voice **:** TALK ⟨swallowed once or twice before she was able to ~ —Mary Austin⟩ ⟨does not find it necessary to ~ . . . at the top of his lungs —B.R. Redman⟩ **b (1) :** to give oral expression to thoughts, opinions, or feelings **:** engage in talk or conversation ⟨not for three years to ~ with any men —Alfred Tennyson⟩ ⟨why don't you ~ for yourself —H.W.Longfellow⟩ **(2) :** to extend a greeting ⟨are embarrassed . . . and they often blush when *spoken* to on the street —Carl Withers⟩ **(3) :** to be on speaking terms ⟨still are ~*ing* after a quarter century of collaboration —Lewis Nichols⟩ **(4) :** to give a rebuke or reprimand ⟨promised to ~ to the boy about his laziness⟩ **c (1) :** to express one's views before a group **:** make a talk or address ⟨*spoke* from one end of the state to the other during the campaign⟩ ⟨*spoke* to the club on gardening⟩ **(2) :** to address one's remarks — usu. used with *to* ⟨I should like to ~ to the nominations —*Report: Standard Oil Co. of N.J.*⟩ **2 a :** to give written expression to thoughts, opinions, or feelings **:** make a written statement ⟨as a writer of great talent he ~*s* with clarity and eloquence —R.K.Carr⟩ ⟨these lines . . . ~ of the saddest thing we know —H.A.Overstreet⟩ **b :** to express oneself ⟨science ~*s* in the conventionalized precision of mathematical language —T.H.Littlefield⟩ — often used in the phrase *so to speak* ⟨here he was at the enemy's gates, so to ~ —C.S.Forester⟩ **c :** to serve as spokesman ⟨associations presuming to ~ for higher education —J.K. Little⟩ ⟨the dominant interests of the electorate for whom they ~ —Cabell Phillips⟩ ⟨writers . . . ~ for their age —Caroline Gordon⟩ **3 a :** to give expression to thoughts, opinions, or feelings by other than verbal means ⟨eyes that ~ too plainly —W.S.Gilbert⟩ ⟨she said nothing at all but her strong fingers *spoke* for her —Louis Bromfield⟩ ⟨actions ~ louder than words⟩ **b :** to communicate by signals **:** SIGNAL ⟨our steamer *spoke* in a short, sharp blast —William Beebe⟩ **c :** to communicate by being interesting or attractive **:** APPEAL ⟨great music . . . is intelligible to children since it ~*s* directly to the emotions —A.N.Whitehead⟩ ⟨nature ~*s* to us . . . through our senses —Susanne K. Langer⟩ **4 a :** to make a request **:** ASK ⟨suppose you ~ for tea —Jane Austen⟩ **b :** to place an order ⟨among the companies which have *spoken* for these later models —Horace Sutton⟩ **5 a :** to make a characteristic or natural sound or noise ⟨and let the kettle to the trumpet ~ —Shak.⟩ ⟨all at once the thunder *spoke* —George Meredith⟩ **b :** to produce a musical sound readily and clearly ⟨discovered that the saxophone ~*s* easily —Deems Taylor⟩ **c :** to emit a sound on being fired ⟨the big guns that *spoke* so thunderously that wild night —H.L.Merillat⟩ **d** *of a hound* **:** to give tongue **:** BARK, BAY **6 a :** to bear witness **:** TESTIFY ⟨if his trial is held in absentia his dossier will ~ in his defense —Kay Boyle⟩ ⟨how the old tub took those tossing seas . . . *spoke* well for her builders —H.A.Chippendale⟩ **b :** to give proof or evidence **:** be indicative or suggestive ⟨his gold . . . *spoke* of riches in the land —Julian Dana⟩ ⟨schools and museums all ~ of the past —D.W.Brogan⟩ **c :** to serve as a symbol ⟨the acres of white marble . . . ~ for the purity of justice —John Mason Brown⟩ **d :** AUGUR ⟨his thrift and industry ~ well for his future⟩ ~ *vt* **1 a (1) :** to utter articulately and with ordinary modulation of the voice **:** PRONOUNCE ⟨once the words were *spoken* she was sorry —Carson McCullers⟩ ⟨~ the speech I pray you . . . trippingly on the tongue —Shak.⟩ **(2) :** to give a recitation of **:** DECLAIM ⟨little girls who were going to ~ pieces, fluttering about in white dresses —Della Lutes⟩ **b :** to make known by speech **:** express orally **:** DECLARE ⟨the English clergy *spoke* their mind very freely on the subject —L.F. Salzman⟩ **c (1)** *archaic* **:** to engage in talk or conversation with ⟨~*ing* him in that . . . tongue —P.J.Bailey⟩ **(2) :** ADDRESS, ACCOST — usu. used with *fair* ⟨a stranger came to the door at eve and . . . *spoke* the bridegroom fair —Robert Frost⟩ **d :** to make communication with **:** HAIL ⟨when you pass other yachts ~ them —H.A.Calahan⟩ **2 a :** to make known in writing **:** STATE ⟨letting the Bible ~ its message to them —J.C.Swaim⟩ ⟨in this passage the man himself is ~*ing* . . . his innermost convictions —H.O.Taylor⟩ **b** *obs* **:** to make reference to **:** MENTION ⟨~ me to her in the best language of affection —Robert Loveday⟩ **c :** to serve as spokesman for **:** REPRESENT ⟨the municipal council . . . had ceased to ~ the sense of the citizens —T.B.Macaulay⟩ **3 :** to use or have the ability to use in talk or conversation ⟨has lived there and ~*s* both Spanish and Portuguese —H.G.Doyle⟩ **4 a :** to make known by other than verbal means **:** REVEAL ⟨his eager smile . . . *spoke* devotion —Hugh Walpole⟩ ⟨what color means, color alone can ~ —Louise Nicholl⟩ **b :** to give proof or evidence of **:** INDICATE, SUGGEST ⟨his various addictions . . . ~ the amateur —F.R. Leavis⟩ **c** *archaic* **:** to demonstrate clearly or undeniably **:** PROCLAIM ⟨his whole person . . . ~*s* him a man of quality —Richard Steele⟩ **d :** to announce by making a characteristic or natural sound ⟨these trumpets ~ his presence —Nicholas Rowe⟩ ⟨the tower-clock *spoke* night —Henry Treece⟩ **5 :** to make a request of **:** ASK ⟨we'd like to ~ some friendly wraith to tell us news —*Bookman*⟩ **6** *archaic* **a :** DESIGNATE, CALL ⟨may'st thou live ever *spoken* our protector —John Fletcher⟩ **b :** to give a description of **:** DEPICT ⟨to ~ him true . . . no keener hunter after glory breathes —Alfred Tennyson⟩ **7 :** to have the significance of **:** SIGNIFY ⟨another long passage that ~*s* volumes for the formalist viewpoint —Hunter Mead⟩ **8 :** to bring into a specified state or position by or as if by speech ⟨*spoke* himself into the common council —*New Monthly Mag.*⟩

syn TALK, CONVERSE: SPEAK is a general term of wide application. It may on occasion differ from TALK in suggesting a weighty formality ⟨*speak* at a university commencement⟩ ⟨*speaking* as a guest of honor⟩ TALK in general may suggest less formality and is likely to implicate auditors or interlocutors ⟨we *talk* in the bosom of our family in a way different from that in which we discourse on state occasions —J.L.Lowes⟩ CONVERSE may imply interchange of opinions and ideas ⟨don't ever remember hearing my parents *converse*, and they never even chatted. My father would expound on law and ritual, my mother would listen —S.N.Behrman⟩

— to speak of : worthy of mention or notice ⟨the islanders had no trees *to speak of* —Harry Luke⟩

²**speak** \ˈ"\ *n* -s [ME *speke*, fr. *speken* to speak] *chiefly Scot* **:** SPEECH, TALK

³**speak** \ˈ"\ *n* -s [by shortening] **:** SPEAKEASY ⟨there would be token raids now and then but the ~ usually opened the next day —C.B.Davis⟩

speak·able \-kəbəl\ *adj* [ME *spekable*, fr. *speken* to speak + *-able*] **1 :** capable of being spoken **:** fit to be spoken **2** *obs* **:** able to speak — **speak·able·ness** *n* -ES — **speak·ably** \-blē, -li\ *adv*

speak down *vi* **:** to speak in a condescending manner ⟨without once *speaking down* to the audience or without once sacrificing artistic quality —R.W.Sarnoff⟩

speakeasy \ˈ⸗,⸗⸗\ *n* -ES **:** a place where alcoholic drinks are illegally sold ⟨asserts that his men are entitled to go into *speakeasies* without warrants and smash everything —*Nation*⟩

speak·er \ˈspēkə(r)\ *n* -s [ME *speker*, fr. *speken* to speak + *-er*] **1 a :** one that speaks ⟨an excellent ~ of French⟩ **b :** a person who addresses an audience **:** one who makes a public speech ⟨the ~ of the evening⟩ ⟨a forceful and logical ~⟩ **c :** one who acts as a spokesman for others; *specif* **:** a spokesman for an Indian nation or people in a council **2 :** the presiding officer of a deliberative assembly; *esp* **:** the presiding officer of a popularly elected legislative body ⟨the *Speaker* of the House of Representatives is the leader of the majority party in that body —W.S.Sayre⟩ ⟨the ~ of the English House of Commons . . . long ago became a wholly disinterested and impartial moderator —F.A.Ogg & P.O.Ray⟩ **3 :** a book of selections for declamation ⟨the readers and ~*s* used in the academies and colleges —E.C.Shoemaker⟩ **4 :** LOUDSPEAKER ⟨from the ~ came a crackling static —Wirt Williams⟩

speak·er·ess \-kərəs\ *n* -ES [*speaker* + *-ess*] **:** a female speaker; *esp* **:** a woman serving as a presiding officer

speaker key *or* **speaker hole** *n* **:** a key or hole on a woodwind instrument to facilitate the production of the upper harmonics

speak·er·ship \ˈ⸗⸗,ship\ *n* [*speaker* + *-ship*] **:** the office of speaker in a legislative body

speakhouse \ˈ⸗,⸗\ *n* **1** *obs* **:** a room for conversation in a convent or monastery **2 :** a large structure used for conferences or councils in some of the islands of the south Pacific

¹**speak·ing** \ˈspēkiŋ, -kēŋ\ *adj* [ME *speking*, fr. pres. part. of *speken* to speak] **1 :** that speaks **:** capable of speech **2 a :** highly significant **:** ELOQUENT ⟨a ~ witness to their permanence —E.A.Freeman⟩ **b :** highly expressive ⟨a face profound and ~ in spite of its silence —Mary Lindsay⟩ **3 :** resembling a living being or a real object **:** STRIKING, FAITHFUL ⟨the ~ portrait of the eldest daughter —Anita Marburg⟩ — **speak·ing·ly** *adv* — **speak·ing·ness** *n* -ES

²**speaking** \ˈ"\ *n* -s [ME *speking*, fr. gerund of *speken* to speak] **1 a :** the act or an instance of uttering words ⟨there has been fine ~ of noble language —*Scots Mag.*⟩ **b :** SPEECH, DISCOURSE ⟨so sweet his ~ sounded —William Morris⟩ **c :** STATEMENT, SAYING ⟨laying aside all malice . . . and all evil ~*s* —1 Pet 2:1 (AV)⟩ **2 :** a political rally ⟨the farmers . . . had come in to attend the ~ —J.S.Buckingham⟩

speaking arc *n* **:** an arc lamp which is used as a telephone receiver and in which the telephonic current is superposed upon the normal current of the lamp

speaking choir *n* **:** a group organized for choral speaking

speaking part *n* **:** a dramatic role containing lines to be spoken

speaking pipe *n* **:** an organ pipe that sounds as contrasted with one that is only for display

speaking rod *n* **:** SELF-READING ROD

speaking stop *n* **:** a stop knob controlling a rank of pipes in a pipe organ

speaking terms *n pl* **1 :** a mutual relationship limited to casual greeting or conversation — used in the phrase *on speaking terms* **2 :** a mutual relationship of intimacy and trust — used with a negative and in the phrase *on speaking terms* ⟨the two brothers weren't on *speaking terms* for years⟩

speaking trumpet *n* **:** a trumpet-shaped instrument for intensifying and directing the sound of the human voice

speaking tube *n* **:** a pipe through which conversation may be carried on (as between persons in different parts of a building)

speak out *vb* [ME *speken out*, fr. *speken* to speak + *out*] *vi* **1 :** to speak loud enough to be heard ⟨asked him to *speak out* or sit down⟩ **2 :** to speak boldly or unreservedly ⟨stand up and *speak out* for the president's whole program —Sinclair Weeks⟩ ⟨*spoke out* . . . forthrightly against the carpetbag militia —*Amer. Guide Series: Ark.*⟩ **3 :** to express an opinion freely and frankly ⟨everyone of us has the obligation to *speak out*, to exchange ideas —Wendell Willkie⟩ ~ *vt* **:** to make known verbally **:** DECLARE ⟨*spoke out* his mind and showed that he was not too well pleased —Augustus Jessopp⟩

speaks *pres 3d sing of* SPEAK, *pl of* SPEAK

speak up *vi* **1 :** to speak strongly or vigorously — usu. used with *for* ⟨*speak up* for truth and justice —Clive Bell⟩ **2 :** to speak loudly and distinctly ⟨was told to *speak up* as the people . . . could not hear him —B.L.K.Henderson⟩ **3 :** to express an opinion freely and fearlessly ⟨we'll never find out how we feel about one another if we don't *speak up* —D.B.Chidsey⟩

speal *var of* SPEEL

speal·bone \ˈspēl,bōn\ *n* [Sc *spealbane*, alter. of *spulebane*, fr. *spule* shoulder (of unknown origin) + *bane* bone, fr. OE *bān* — more at BONE] **:** the shoulder blade used by magicians or medicine men in divination

¹**spean** \ˈspēn\ *vt* [MD *spenen*, fr. *spene* teat; akin to OE *spane* teat, MHG *spenen* to entice, wean, ON *speni* teat, OIr *sine*] *chiefly Scot* **:** WEAN

²**spean** \ˈ"\ *n* -s [origin unknown] *dial Eng* **:** ¹PRONG 2

¹**spear** \ˈspi(ə)r, -iə\ *n* -s [ME *spere*, fr. OE; akin to OHG *sper* spear, ON *spjör* spears, L *sparus* hunting spear, Gk *sparos* gilthead] **1 :** a thrusting or throwing weapon with a long shaft and sharp head or blade used in war or hunting **2 :** something resembling a spear: as **a :** a transverse spike or pole in a cheval-de-frise **b :** a sharp-pointed instrument with barbs used in spearing fish **c :** the tip end of a fishhook with barb and point **d :** LANCE 2c **e :** a body part (as a stylet or barb) that resembles a spear **3 :** SPEARMAN; *esp* **:** a soldier armed with a spear **4 :** a light ray **:** BEAM ⟨the ~*s* of an aurora were stabbing upward to the zenith —S.H.Adams⟩ **5 :** a tool used in recovering equipment lost in a drilled oil well — **under the spear** [fr. the ancient Roman practice of hanging up a spear as a sign that an auction was being held] *obs* **:** for sale at auction

spear 1

²**spear** \ˈ"\ *adj* [ME *spere*, fr. *spere*, n.] **1 :** of, relating to, or resembling a spear **2 :** of or relating to the father **:** MALE ⟨the ~ side of the family⟩ — compare DISTAFF

³**spear** \ˈ"\ *vb* -ED/-ING/-S [¹*spear*] *vt* **1 :** to pierce or strike with or as if with a spear ⟨learning how to ~ salmon⟩ ⟨~*ing* a cake . . . she put it on her plate —Clarissa F. Cushman⟩ **2 :** to impale (cut stalks or plants) on a lath in harvesting tobacco **3 :** to clean out (a hole) with a reamer **4 :** to catch (as a baseball) with a sudden thrust of the arm ~ *vi* **1 :** to thrust with or as if with a spear ⟨hundreds of sharks ~*ing* at the whale —H.A.Chippendale⟩ **2 :** to make a way into or through something in the manner of a spear ⟨the headlight is a white shaft ~*ing* into a misty night —R.M.Neal⟩ ⟨the great cathedral ~*s* into the sky —Amy Lowell⟩

⁴**spear** \ˈ"\ *n* -s [alter. (influenced by ¹*spear*) of ¹*spire*] **1** *obs* **:** STEEPLE **2 a :** a usu. young blade, shoot, or sprout (as of grass) **b (1) :** a stalk of reed grass **(2)** *dial Eng* **:** REEDS; *esp* **:** reeds used for thatching

⁵**spear** \ˈ"\ *vi* -ED/-ING/-S **:** to thrust upward in a shoot, blade, or spear-shaped leaf ⟨how beautiful are oats when the first wavering ranks of green come ~*ing* bravely in the light —D.C. Peattie⟩

⁶**spear** \ˈ"\ *n* -s [alter. of ³*spire*] *Brit* **:** a rod to which the bucket of a mine pump is attached

spear·er \-rə(r)\ *n* -s **:** one that spears

speareye \ˈ⸗,⸗\ *or* **speareye shark** *n* [modif. (influenced by E *spear, eye*) of Afrik *spierhaai*, fr. *spier* muscle, blade (fr. MD; akin to OE *spīr* blade) + *haai* shark, fr. MD *haey* — more at SPIRE, HAYE] **:** a small coastal shark (*Mustelus punctulatus*) of the south Atlantic and Indian oceans that is grayish brown dotted with black

¹**spearfish** \ˈ⸗,⸗\ *n* [¹*spear* + *fish*, n.] **1 :** any of several large powerful pelagic fishes of the genus *Tetrapturus* that are closely related to the marlins and sailfishes but have the first dorsal fin low in front and moderately elevated behind and are widely distributed but rare in all seas **2 :** any of various fishes related to the spearfish

²**spearfish** \ˈ"\ *vi* [¹*spear* + *fish*, v.] **:** to fish with a spear: **a :** to catch fish by means of a barbed spear thrown by hand or propelled by a mechanical device and retrieved by an attached line **b :** to fish underwater with a spear

spearflower \ˈ⸗,⸗\ *n* [¹*spear* + *flower*] **:** a plant or flower of the genus *Ardisia*

spear grass *n* **1 :** any of numerous grasses having spear-shaped inflorescences or stiff pointed leaves: as **a :** COUCH GRASS **b :** BENT 2d **c :** MEADOW GRASS **d :** DITCH REED **e :** SLENDER FOXTAIL **f :** PORCUPINE GRASS 1 **2 a :** a spearwort (*Ranunculus flammula*) **b :** a plant of the genus *Aciphylla* (family Umbelliferae) with prickly leaves; *esp* **:** a New Zealand perennial (*A. colensoi*)

spear gun *n* **:** a gun that propels a spear and is used in underwater spearfishing

spear hand *n, archaic* **:** the right hand

¹**spearhead** \ˈ⸗,⸗\ *n* [ME *spere-hed*, fr. *spere* spear + *hed* head] **1 a :** the sharp-pointed head of a spear **b :** something having a sharp-pointed end; *specif* **:** a sharp device on the end of a lath for piercing tobacco stalks that are to be hung on the lath during curing **2 a :** a military force that precedes others in a thrust or attack **:** the leading element in a military thrust or attack ⟨smashed the American ~ in savage fighting —F.V.W. Mason⟩ **b :** a leading element, force, or influence in an undertaking or development ⟨trained to act as the ~ of miners' demands against the management —Leo Wolman⟩ ⟨the ~ of propaganda is the slogan —S.H.Flowerman⟩ ⟨plastics might be said to be the ~ of the advance in synthetic materials —Howard Marshall⟩

²**spearhead** \ˈ"\ *vt* **1 a :** to take the lead in launching and pressing forward (a military thrust or attack) ⟨airborne troops ~*ed* a massed crossing of the river —Allan Taylor⟩ **b :** to precede in a military thrust or attack ⟨the dive bombers ~*ed* the panzer forces —C.C.Caldwell⟩ **2 a :** to take a leading role in (an undertaking or development) ⟨~*ed* the medical profession's efforts to improve physician-patient relationships —Milton Silverman⟩ ⟨~*ed* the romantic revolution —Florence Bullock⟩ **b :** to serve as leader of in an undertaking or development ⟨~*ed* a group of liberal Democrats who are supporting . . . the censure movement —Anthony Leviero⟩

spear hook *n* **:** SPRING HOOK 2

spear·ing \ˈspiriŋ, -rēŋ\ *n, pl* **spearing** [D *spiering* smelt, fr. MD *spierinc*, fr. *spier* spear; akin to OE *spere* spear — more at SPEAR] **:** a small lizard fish (*Trachinocephalus myops*) widespread in warm seas

spear javelin *n* [¹*spear*] **:** FRAMEA

spear lily *n* **:** a tall perennial herbaceous plant (*Doryanthes excelsa*) that is cultivated in warm regions for its showy globose heads of scarlet flowers with spreading perianths

spear·man \ˈ⸗mən\ *n, pl* **spearmen** [ME *spereman*, fr. *spere* spear + *man*] **:** one armed or equipped with a spear; *esp* **:** a soldier having a spear as a weapon

spearmint \ˈ⸗,⸗\ *n* [¹*spear* + *mint*] **1 :** a common garden mint (*Mentha spicata*) that is widely cultivated for use in flavoring and esp. for its aromatic oil and that resembles peppermint but has slender interrupted spikes **2 :** a moderate to strong green that is bluer and stronger than Hooker's green

spearmint oil *n* **:** an aromatic essential oil obtained from spearmint and used in flavoring

spearnose bat \ˈ⸗,⸗-\ *n* **:** any of several bats of the family Phyllostomatidae and esp. of the genera *Phyllostomus* and *Vampyrum* with a prominently pointed nose leaf

spear penny *n* [trans. of Welsh *ceiniog baladr*] **:** an exaction paid under ancient Welsh law to an injured person by a wrongdoer

spear plate *n* [¹*spear*] **:** STRAPPING PLATE

¹**spearpoint** \ˈ⸗,⸗\ *n* [ME *sperepoint*, fr. *spere* spear + *point*] **1 :** the point of a spear **2 :** SPEARHEAD ⟨the ~ of a general intellectual awakening —Mary Scrutton⟩

²**spearpoint** \ˈ"\ *vt* **:** SPEARHEAD

spear-point chisel *n* **:** a chisel with a triangular point for lathe-turning operations

spear pyrites *n* **:** a marcasite in twin crystals resembling the head of a spear

spear rod *n* [⁶*spear*] *Brit* **:** the main rod of a mine pump

spears *pl of* SPEAR, *pres 3d sing of* SPEAR

spear thistle *n* [¹*spear*] **:** BULL THISTLE 1

spear-thrower \ˈ⸗,⸗⸗\ *n* **:** THROWING-STICK

spearwood \ˈ⸗,⸗\ *n* **1 :** any of several Australian acacias with very hard heavy durable wood; *esp* **:** a widely distributed small or medium-sized tree (*Acacia doratoxylon*) with elongated slightly curved phyllodes and racemes of small flowers **2 :** the wood of a spearwood used chiefly for cabinet work and small articles and by the aborigines for spears

spearwort \ˈ⸗,⸗\ *n* [ME *sperewort*, fr. OE *sperewyrt*, fr. *spere* spear + *wyrt* wort] **:** any of several crowfoots having spear-shaped leaves; *esp* **:** a Eurasian crowfoot (*Ranunculus flammula*) naturalized in Newfoundland

speary \ˈspirē, -ri\ *adj, usu* -ER/-EST **:** resembling a spear; *esp* **:** having a sharp point ⟨evergreens . . . point their ~ tops above the crest of bluffs —W.D.Howells⟩

speat \ˈspāt, spēt\ *chiefly Scot var of* SPATE

spec *abbr or n* **1** special; specialist; specialty **2** species **3** specific; specifically **4** specification **5** specimen **6** spectacle; spectacular **7** spectrum **8** speculation

speci- *or* **specie-** *or* **specio-** *comb form* [*species*] **:** species ⟨*speci*ogenesis⟩ ⟨*speci*ation⟩

¹spe·cial \ˈspeshəl\ *adj, sometimes* -ER/-EST [ME, fr. OF or L; OF *especial,* fr. L *specialis* individual, particular, fr. *species* appearance, kind + *-alis* -al — more at SPY] **1 :** distinguished by some unusual quality **:** UNCOMMON, NOTEWORTHY, EXTRAORDINARY ⟨a ~ occasion⟩; *esp* **:** distinguished by superiority **2 :** regarded with particular favor and affection **:** DEAR, INTIMATE ⟨not a ~ friend of mine⟩ **3 a :** relating to a single thing or class of things **:** having an individual character or trait **:** PECULIAR, UNIQUE ⟨to this ~ evil an improvement of style would apply a ~ redress —Thomas De Quincey⟩ **b :** of or belonging to a particular species **:** constituting a species or kind ⟨a ~ concept⟩ **4 a :** supplemental to the regular **:** EXTRA ⟨a ~ edition of a newspaper⟩ **b :** assigned or provided to meet a particular need not covered under established procedures ⟨a ~ correspondent⟩ ⟨went west on a ~ train⟩ **5 :** confined to a definite field of action **:** designed or selected for a particular purpose, occasion, or other end **:** limited in range ⟨a ~ act of Congress⟩ ⟨a ~ branch of study⟩ ⟨a ~ student in college is not enrolled for the usual degree⟩ **6 :** containing particulars **:** DETAILED, SPECIFIC — opposed to *general* ⟨a ~ confession⟩

syn ESPECIAL, SPECIFIC, PARTICULAR, INDIVIDUAL: SPECIAL indicates the possessing of a quality, character, or identity of one's own, perhaps one out of the ordinary or conspicuously unusual ⟨a *special* diet for these cases⟩ ⟨*special* fatigue duty⟩ ⟨the women never drink in this manner, which is absolutely *special* to men —J.G.Frazer⟩ ⟨land that has *special* charm or outstanding beauty —S.P.B.Mais⟩ ⟨it's not like ordinary photographs. There's something *special* about it —Arnold Bennett⟩ ESPECIAL may add implications of preeminence or preference ⟨Gettysburg is of *especial* interest because of the famous battle —*Amer. Guide Series: Pa.*⟩ ⟨not one of his *especial* chums —Samuel Butler †1902⟩ SPECIFIC is applicable to special traits and characteristics in proportion as the group they characterize is limited; it often describes traits of an individual ⟨get down to *specific* cases⟩ ⟨the pressure on the universities, therefore, to educate men and women for *specific* vocations both increased and diversified —J.B.Conant⟩ ⟨some years ago we read with singular pleasure a new guidebook . . . its *specific* charm was simply that it left out all the gush —C.E.Montague⟩ PARTICULAR, often interchangeable with SPECIFIC, may differ from it in increasing suggestions of individual distinctness and decreasing those of membership in a group ⟨more than three years in the South were a happy experience and a liberalizing education for this *particular* northern boy —E.J.Benton⟩ ⟨any *particular* remark of a psychologist, if true, is unlikely to be startling —I.A.Richards⟩ ⟨a sense for *particular* beauties of nature, rather than a sense for Nature herself —Laurence Binyon⟩ INDIVIDUAL applies to what is clearly isolated or individualized from all else ⟨the *individual* idiosyncrasies of each member of the great family —Sherwood Anderson⟩ ⟨more faith in the collective opinion of all Americans than in the *individual* opinion of any one American —F.D.Roosevelt⟩ ⟨while the political influence of the baronage as a leading element in the whole nation thus steadily mounted, the personal and purely feudal power of each *individual* baron on his own estates as steadily fell —J.R. Green⟩

²special \"\ *adv* [ME, fr. ¹*special*] **:** SPECIALLY, ESPECIALLY

³special \"\ *n* -S [ME, fr. ¹*special*] **1 a** *obs* **:** a favorite or intimate friend or companion; *esp* **:** PARAMOUR **b :** a special thing **:** PARTICULAR — usu. used with *the* ⟨from the general to the ~⟩ **c** *obs* **:** SPECIES, KIND **d :** one outside of or in addition to the regular or normal number, quantity, series, range, or similar category ⟨not a regular, but a ~⟩ ⟨newsboys hawking the afternoon ~*s*⟩ ⟨a store featuring ~*s* on meats⟩ **2 :** one appointed or used for a special service or occasion ⟨the train was a ~ for the football game⟩ **3 a :** a special-delivery letter **b :** SPECIAL-DELIVERY STAMP

special ability *n* **:** an individual's ability in a particular subject (as music or mathematics) or in a particular function (as memorizing) as opposed to his general intelligence

special act *n* **:** an act of a legislature that is not of general application in all territory subject to the legislative power but affects private persons or only part of a class of persons in the same situation or only part of a more general subject matter or is intended to apply only in a particular subdivision of the entire territory subject to the legislative power

special administrator *n* **1 :** an administrator appointed to administer only a designated part of a decedent's assets **2 :** an administrator appointed ex parte without notice to all interested parties to conserve the assets of an estate usu. in some emergency (as in a will contest)

special agent *n* **1 :** an agent authorized by his principal to act in one undertaking or to act in a number of transactions not involving continuous service to the principal **:** an agent following particular instructions in a particular matter whose authority is limited to doing what is reasonable to fulfill those instructions — compare GENERAL AGENT **2 :** a representative of a property insurance company within a specified territory who supervises and assists local agents, recommends the appointment of new agents, and in some cases adjusts losses — called also *fieldman*

special appearance *n* **:** an appearance by a party in court for the sole purpose of attacking the jurisdiction of the court (as for lack of effective service or lack of power to adjudge the cause)

special area *n, Brit* **:** an area forming the subject of special legislation because of disproportionately severe depression and destitution

special assessment *n* **:** a specific tax levied on private property to meet the cost of public improvements that enhance the value of the property

special assumpsit *n* **:** EXPRESS ASSUMPSIT

special bail *n* **1 a :** BAIL ABOVE **b :** BAIL BELOW **2 :** bail given by responsible persons rather than that given solely as a matter of form

special bastard *n* **:** a bastard legitimated by marriage of its parents

special carrier *n* **:** PRIVATE CARRIER

special case *n* **:** a case the proceedings under which are different from those of the regular common law or equity actions: as **a :** an action or proceeding established by statute to provide new rights or remedies **b :** a case reserved for the decision of the court on a question of law, on a case stated, or on a finding of facts by the jury; *also* **:** a case prepared to be so submitted

special collection *n* **1 :** a memorial collection of printed works or manuscripts in a library **2 :** an aggregation of printed or other material of an author or on a special subject

special contract *n* **:** SPECIALTY CONTRACT

special court *n* **:** a court created for an exceptional and temporary purpose (as a commission to try alleged war criminals or a tribunal to hear claims for war damages against a state by nationals of the victorious state)

special court-martial *n* **:** a court-martial consisting of at least three officers, a trial judge advocate, and a defense counsel and having authority to impose no sentence in excess of six months' confinement or forfeiture of two thirds of six months' pay — compare GENERAL COURT-MARTIAL, SUMMARY COURT-MARTIAL

special creation *n* **:** the theoretical independent origin of each biological species through a special act of creation — opposed to *doctrine of descent*

special damage *n* **1 :** damage for which a defendant is responsible but which must be pleaded and proved by plaintiff to be recoverable **2 :** damage not ordinarily expected to be caused by defendant's wrong or breach of duty but in fact caused thereby under circumstances making defendant responsible **3 :** damage peculiar to a plaintiff because of his particular condition or the particular circumstances in which he finds himself, but not ordinarily implied from defendant's wrong or breach of duty **4 :** damage capable of being exactly measured in money or its equivalent as distinguished from damage which must be estimated and concerning which reasonable men might differ **5 :** CONSEQUENTIAL DAMAGE **6 special damages** *pl* **:** compensatory damages awarded for a particular harm or pecuniary loss for which special proof must be made

special delivery *n* **1 :** the delivery of a piece of mail of any class by postal messenger ahead of the regular carrier delivery on prepayment of a fee represented by a special-delivery stamp **2 a** *or* **special-delivery stamp :** a stamp affixed to a piece of mail to obtain special delivery service **b :** a piece of mail sent by special delivery

special demurrer *n* **:** a demurrer for some specified defect of form in a pleading

special deposit *n* **1 :** a deposit (as of valuables or securities) which is usu. primarily for security and in which the identical property deposited is to be returned to its owner — compare GENERAL DEPOSIT, IRREGULAR DEPOSIT **2 :** a deposit of money (as a savings or time deposit) in a bank that bears interest and is not subject to checking

special deputy *n* **:** a deputy authorized to exercise some special function on behalf of another official

special dividend *n* **:** a dividend that typically results from some windfall profit to a company and is not ordinarily expected to be repeated

special duty *n* **:** duty performed by an individual in military service with a unit or activity other than that to which he is assigned but at the same station — compare DETACHED SERVICE

special effect *n* **:** an often illusory effect introduced into a motion picture during processing of the film

special endorsement *n* **1 :** an endorsement on negotiable paper that limits the transfer to a particular person — compare RESTRICTIVE ENDORSEMENT **2 :** a statement on a writ of the nature of the claim or the scope of the relief sought

special finding *n* **:** a finding of a jury or judge sitting to try facts or some particular fact as established by the evidence in an action not including a rendering of a verdict or finding upon the entire matter in issue

special grace *n* **:** grace that relates to eternal salvation — distinguished from *common grace*

special handling *n* **:** the handling of a piece of parcel-post or fourth-class mail as first-class but not as special-delivery matter by the U.S. Post Office on prepayment of a fee represented by a special-handling stamp

special-handling stamp *n* **:** a stamp indicating payment of a fee for postal special handling

special hazard *n* **:** a potential cause of fire peculiar to a particular building or to a process of manufacturing — compare COMMON HAZARD

special injunction *n* **:** an injunction on motion granted to prevent threatened and irreparable injury **:** a temporary or preliminary injunction **:** a prohibitory injunction against specified acts or conduct

special interest *n* **1 :** a particular concern in something usu. by which one is directly affected **2 :** an individual, group, or corporation having a special interest in usu. a particular part of the economy and receiving or seeking through political pressure special advantages from the government often to the detriment of the general welfare — usu. used in pl.

spe·cial·ism \ˈspeshəˌlizəm\ *n* -S [¹*special* + *-ism*] **1 :** specialization in or confinement of interest to a particular field of study, activity, or interest **:** restriction of concern to one branch or aspect of a wider field (as of knowledge); *often* **:** excessive confinement to a specialty ⟨humanists decry the tendency to ~ in modern society⟩ **2 :** a field of specialization **:** a branch or aspect of something in which specialization exists ⟨the several medical ~*s*⟩ ⟨geomorphology and other ~*s* inside the fold of geography —J.K.Wright⟩

special issue *n* **1 :** an issue denying or traversing one or more material points of law or fact but not the whole declaration, complaint, or indictment — compare GENERAL ISSUE **2 :** an issue raised by pleadings that may be determinative of the entire case (as a plea of release or of infancy)

spe·cial·ist \ˈspesh(ə)ləst\ *n* -S *often attrib* [¹*special* + *-ist*] **1 :** a person who devotes or limits his interest to some special branch (as of an activity, business, art, or science): as **a :** a medical practitioner who limits his practice to a particular class of patients (as children) or of diseases (as skin diseases) or of technique (as surgery); *usu* **:** a physician who is qualified by advanced training and certification by a specialty examining board to so limit his practice **b :** a member of a stock exchange who concentrates his activity on a single stock or group of stocks traded at the same trading post and by executing orders for other brokers in such stocks as well as trading for his own account helps maintain a continuous market in the issues in question **c :** an enlisted man (as in the U. S. army) qualified for specialized duties and having a grade ranging from that of a corporal to that of a master sergeant but lacking the rank or command responsibilities of a noncommissioned officer **2 :** one that is extremely specialized in some physiologic respect (as in food habits)

spe·cial·is·tic \ˌ⸗shəˈlistik\ *adj* [*specialist* + *-ic*] **1 :** concerned with or tending toward specialism **2 :** of, relating to, or typical of specialists

spe·ci·al·i·ty \ˌspeshēˈalədē, -lətē, -i\ *n* -ES [ME *specialite, specialitie,* fr. MF or LL; MF *specialité,* fr. LL *specialitat-, specialitas* — more at SPECIALTY] **1 a :** a special or peculiar mark or characteristic **:** a distinctive or distinguishing and sometimes limiting or restrictive quality **:** PARTICULARITY **b specialities** *pl* **:** DETAILS, PARTICULARS **2 :** an object or class of objects marked by some special or peculiar characteristic **:** SPECIALTY 2a **3 a :** an aptitude or special skill in a particular endeavor (as a line of handicraft) **b :** SPECIALTY 3 **4 :** SPECIALTY 2a (1)

spe·cial·iza·tion \ˌspeshələˈzāshən, -ˌlīˈz-\ *n* -S [*specialize* + *-ation*] **1 :** a making or becoming specialized **:** the quality or state of being specialized ⟨the ~ of industry⟩ **2 a :** adaptation in the structure of a body part to the performance of some particular function **:** differentiation that usu. tends toward greatly increased efficiency in one function at the expense of most other functions **b :** adaptation in the structure of an entire organism for life in particular surroundings or for particular habits **c :** a body part or organization adapted to a particular function, situation, or course of life

spe·cial·ize \ˈ⸗shəˌlīz\ *vb* -ED/-ING/-S *see -ize in Explan Notes* [¹*special* + *-ize*] *vt* **1 :** to consider separately **:** ITEMIZE ⟨*specialized* each item —Vicki Baum⟩ **2 :** to limit in scope or interest **:** focus on a special area of knowledge or activity ⟨*specialized* his studies⟩ **~** *vi* **1 :** to go into detail **:** PARTICULARIZE ⟨first give a general outline, then ~⟩ **2 :** to concentrate one's efforts **:** develop or pursue a specialty ⟨~ in copyright law⟩ ⟨their restaurants ~ in Swedish cuisine —*Amer. Guide Series: N. Y.*⟩ ⟨the company ~*s* in jet engines⟩ **3 :** to undergo specialization; *esp* **:** to change adaptively ⟨many organisms ~ for a predacious existence⟩

specialized *adj* [fr. past part. of *specialize*] **1 :** designed or fitted for use or employment in one special line (as of occupation) so that change to another involves a loss in utility **2 :** characterized by or exhibiting biological specialization; *often* **:** highly developed **:** extremely differentiated esp. in a particular direction or for a particular end — compare GENERALIZED

spe·cial·iz·er \ˈ⸗⸗ˌlīzə(r)\ *n* -S [*specialize* + *-er*] **:** SPECIALIST

special jury *n* **1 :** a jury formerly selected by the parties each striking a number of names (as 12 each) from the general list before the jury is impaneled — called also *struck jury* **2 :** a specially selected panel of jurors chosen by the court upon request of a party from a list of better educated or presumably more intelligent prospective jurors for a case involving complicated issues of fact or serious felonies — called also *blue-ribbon jury*

special law *n* **1 :** PRIVATE LAW **2 :** a local law applicable to a particular territory in a state or to a particular political subdivision thereof **3 :** a law unconstitutional because applying without justifiable reason to a particular member or members of but not to an entire class of persons or things in the same situation **:** a law that applies without reasonable basis to or in a particular territory rather than throughout the entire state

special library *n* **:** a privately owned library that forms a unit of a business firm or other organization, specializes in books and other material of special interest to the organization of which it is a part, and usu. serves only the staff or members of this organization

special license *n, Brit* **:** a license granting exceptional privileges; *specif* **:** a license from the Archbishop of Canterbury permitting a marriage to take place at any time or place and without usual preliminary formalities

special lien *n* **:** an attorney's charging lien against a judgment recovered by his efforts **:** PARTICULAR LIEN

spe·cial·ly \ˈspesh(ə)lē, -li\ *adv* [ME, fr. ¹*special* + *-ly*] **:** in a special manner **:** so as to be special **:** ESPECIALLY, PARTICULARLY

special master *n* **:** a master appointed by a court to hear the testimony and make findings of fact in a particular case, make a sale of property under court order, or carry out some other order of a court

spe·cial·ness *n* -ES **:** the quality or state of being special

special order *n* **:** a routine order issued by an authorized military headquarters that includes matter concerning individuals but is not of general interest — compare GENERAL ORDER

special partner *n* **:** a partner who may share in the profits of a general partnership registered under law, who contributes property to the capital thereof but must not exercise control over or be active in partnership affairs, and whose liability for partnership debts providing certain rules of law are observed is limited to his capital and interest in the firm assets — called also *limited partner;* distinguished from *general partner*

special partnership *n* **1 :** PARTICULAR PARTNERSHIP **2 :** LIMITED PARTNERSHIP

special plea *n* **:** a plea (as of infancy, statute of limitations or of frauds, discharge in bankruptcy or release) alleging new and affirmative matter as a defense without denying any allegations of the opponent **:** a plea in bar or in avoidance of what opponent alleges

special pleader *n* **1 :** a counsel who formerly devoted himself to drawing special counts and pleas **2 a :** a lawyer whose occupation is to draw pleadings, give opinions on matters submitted to him, and prepare the papers in various proceedings out of the usual course **b** *Brit* **:** a public officer, notary, barrister or solicitor occupied by such activities **3 :** one advocating a specific proposal (as a law) because of self-interest or on other bases than independent disinterested impartial judgment

special pleading *n* **1 :** the allegation of special or new matter to avoid the effect of matter pleaded by the opposite side and admitted, as distinguished from a direct denial of the matter pleaded **2 :** sophistical or misleading argumentation; *esp* **:** argument that presents one point or phase as if it covered the entire question at issue

special plea in bar *n* **:** a plea in bar admitting the facts alleged but avoiding the action by setting forth particular and new matter — distinguished from *general issue;* compare ISSUE 6a

special power *n* **1 :** a power of appointment (as to testator's widow to appoint testator's estate to such of their issue as she should by her will appoint) created or reserved not for the benefit of the donee but for the benefit of persons or a class of persons that can be reasonably ascertained and not including the donee **2 :** a power described as such in a state statute where the persons or class of persons to whom the disposition of property under the power is to be made are expressly designated or where the power is to transfer, charge, or incumber any estate less than a fee simple

special privilege *n* **:** a privilege granted (as by a law or constitution) to an individual or group to the exclusion of others and in derogation of common right ⟨introduced a bill that would provide for *special privileges* such as tariff and other subsidies to domestic corporations⟩ ⟨the board . . . considered perhaps that scientists felt they were a group apart, entitled to *special privilege* or gentle treatment —Vannevar Bush⟩

special proceeding *n* **:** a judicial proceeding other than an action — used chiefly of such procedure under a code

special property *n* **:** a property right or qualified interest in property (as the interest of a bailee, pledgee, lawful possessor, a conditional vendee prior to full payment, or a lienholder) subordinate to the absolute, unconditional or general property or ownership

special retainer *n* **:** a retainer for a particular law service, case, or matter — distinguished from *general retainer*

special revelation *n* **:** religious revelation accessible only to a particular people or group of people ⟨the *special revelation* available to Christians through faith⟩ ⟨the *special revelation* of God's purposes in the history of Israel⟩ — compare GENERAL REVELATION

special rule *n* **:** a rule obtained from a court upon motion of counsel and not issuing as a matter of course **:** an interlocutory order made in a particular case — compare GENERAL RULE

specials *pl of* SPECIAL

special school *n* **:** a school for pupils who differ from the average so noticeably that they are not suited to ordinary schools; *esp* **:** a school for children of retarded development

special service school *n* **:** a unit in a system of military education (as in the U. S. Army) at which officers and enlisted men of the interested branch receive instruction in the subjects relating to their particular branch — compare GENERAL SERVICE SCHOOL

special service tariff *n* **:** a railroad or other shipping tariff containing regulations and charges for special services (as storage, demurrage, reconsignment, refrigeration)

special session *n* **1 :** an extraordinary session (as of a legislative body) **2 special sessions** *pl* **:** sittings held by two or more British magistrates or justices for the exercise of some special jurisdiction (as the licensing of alehouses) that can be exercised out of quarter sessions — compare GENERAL SESSIONS, PETTY SESSIONS

special settlement *n* **:** a settling of bargains usu. for new issues at a time other than the regular fortnightly settlement on the London stock exchange

special staff *n* **:** a part of the staff of a division or higher unit of an army including representatives of the artillery, engineers, ordnance, quartermaster, signal, and other branches — compare GENERAL STAFF, PERSONAL STAFF

special statute *n* **:** SPECIAL ACT

special term *n* **1 :** a term of court held by a single judge or for a special purpose — used of courts composed of several judges to describe the term at which one alone presides whose judgment may thereafter be reviewed by all or others sitting together **2 :** an extraordinary sitting of a court at a time other than that regularly fixed

special traverse *n* **:** a traverse not in absolute terms but with qualifications — compare COMMON TRAVERSE

special trust *n* **:** an active trust for the accomplishment of a specified purpose

spe·cial·ty \ˈspeshəltē, -ti\ *n* -ES *often attrib* [ME *specialte,* fr. MF *especialté,* fr. LL *specialitat-, specialitas,* fr. L *specialis* special + *-itat-, -itas* -ity] **1 :** a particular, peculiar, or individual circumstance, detail, or characteristic **:** a distinctive or sometimes a restrictive mark or quality ⟨the *specialties* of one's lot in life⟩ **2 a :** an object or class of objects distinguished by some special characteristic, individual quality, or peculiarity: as (1) **:** a legal agreement (as a contract or deed) embodied in a sealed instrument — compare SPECIALTY CONTRACT (2) **:** a product of a special kind, made under a special patent, serving one special purpose or otherwise distinctive (as in excellence) ⟨apple pie was mother's ~⟩ ⟨the ~ of the house was seafood⟩ (3) **:** a security having some unusual character that makes it comparatively free from the influence of general market conditions (4) *or* **specialty good :** an item (as an automobile, novelty, piece of jewelry, or an art object) that has an attraction for the consumer other than price that tends to induce him to put forth special effort to obtain it, is usu. of relatively high unit value, is purchased infrequently in comparison with staple goods, and whose purchase is postponable ⟨a ~ dealer⟩ ⟨luxurious ~ shops⟩ **b :** the state of being special **:** possession of distinctive or peculiar or particular characteristics **3 :** something in which one specializes or of which one has special knowledge: as **a :** a branch of knowledge, science, art, or business to which one devotes oneself whether as an avocation or a profession and usu. to the partial or total exclusion of related matters ⟨a chemist whose ~ is tropical alkaloids⟩ ⟨the major medical *specialties*⟩ **b :** a culture trait characteristic of or restricted to a limited group in a society

specialty contract *n* **:** a contract (as a deed or mortgage) depending for its validity upon the formality of its execution (as in being signed, sealed, and delivered) — called also *formal contract, special contract*

specialty mark *n* **:** insignia worn on an enlisted man's uniform that reveals his specialty or rating — compare RATING BADGE

special verdict *n* **:** a verdict setting forth the specific findings of fact made by the jury on the material issues and leaving the court to make general finding for either party as the law requires on the facts so found

special vert *n* **:** trees in an English crown forest that provide food for deer

special warranty *n* **:** a limited warranty in a transfer or conveyance by which the grantor warrants the property transferred to be free of all liens and encumbrances made by, through, or under him

spe·ci·ate \'spēs(h)ē,āt\ *vi* -ED/-ING/-S [back-formation fr. *speciation*] **:** to form species **:** differentiate into new species

spe·ci·a·tion \,==¦āshən\ *n* -S [*speci-* + *-ation*] **:** formation of biological species or the processes leading to this end whether constituting gradual divergence from related groups (as by an extension of raciation) or occurring abruptly by combination or transformation of genomes (as in the formation of polyploid species) — compare MACROEVOLUTION, SALTATION — **spe·ci·a·tion·al** \¦==¦āshən°l, -shnəl\ *adj*

1**spe·cie** \'spē(,)shē, -,shi *also* -(,)sē *or* -,si\ *n* -S [fr. the phrase *in specie*, fr. L, in kind] **:** money in coin ⟨required ~ payments⟩ — **in spe·cie** \ənz'pē(,)shē, -n'sp-, -,shi *also* -(,)sē *or* -,si; *in senses other than c* " *or* -pēs(h)ē,ē *or* -pekē,ā\ *adv* **:** in or with the same or like form or kind: as **a :** in kind **:** SPECIFICALLY ⟨his duties are *in specie* identical with your own⟩ **b :** in the identical form and without alteration or substitution — used chiefly in law ⟨an agreement to be carried out *in specie*⟩ **c :** in coin or coined money ⟨payment *in specie*⟩ **d :** in a like manner or with similar treatment ⟨ready to return insult *in specie*⟩

2**specie** \"\ *n* -S [back-formation fr. *species*] *nonstand* **:** SPECIES

specie- — see SPECI-

specie jar *n* [2*specie*] **:** a blown glass jar with sheet metal top formerly used for storage (as of herbs or stick candies)

specie payment *n* [1*specie*] **:** payment in coin or bullion as distinguished from payment in paper money

1**spe·cies** \'spē(,)shēz, -,shiz *also* -(,)sēz *or* -,siz\ *n, pl* **species** [L, appearance, form, kind, species, beauty — more at SPY] **1 a :** a class of individuals having common attributes and designated by a common name **:** a logical division of a genus or more comprehensive class **:** a subclass designated by adding to the name or connotation of a genus some specific difference that limits its application to a restricted group ⟨the triangle is a ~ of plane figure⟩ **b :** a limited kind or group having a distinguishing characteristic; *esp* **:** one capable of including variant individuals and of being subsumed in a more inclusive category ⟨mineral ~ are made up of varieties having common basic properties⟩ ⟨one ~ of tramp who wanders from workhouse to workhouse —Osbert Sitwell⟩ **c :** the race of man **:** human beings **:** HUMANITY ⟨progress of the ~ in science⟩ **d** (1) **:** a category of biological classification ranking immediately below a genus or subgenus and being denominated in taxonomic usage by a binomial that consists of the name of its genus followed by a Latin or latinized noun or adjective which is usu. not capitalized and agrees grammatically with the genus name **:** a group of intimately related and physically similar organisms that actually or potentially interbreed and are less commonly capable of fertile interbreeding with members of other groups, that ordinarily comprise differentiated populations limited geographically (as subspecies) or ecologically (as ecotypes) which tend to intergrade at points of contact, and that as a group represent the stage of evolution at which variations become fixed through loss of ability to exchange genes with members of other groups although formerly conceived to be the total progeny of a single distinctive specially created pair — compare NOMENCLATURE 4c; see SPECIFIC EPITHET (2) **:** an individual plant or animal or a kind of plant or animal belonging to a particular species — not used technically **e :** a particular kind of atomic nucleus, atom, molecule, or ion ⟨a great number of new nuclear ~ have been prepared within the last few years in the region of the natural radioactivities —*Science*⟩ ⟨all atoms of a particular radioactive ~ have the same probability of disintegrating —H.D.Smyth⟩ — compare ISOTOPE, NUCLIDE **2 a :** the consecrated eucharistic elements; *specif* **:** the accidents of the eucharistic bread and wine as distinguished in Roman Catholicism from their substance **b** (1) **:** a mental image, phantasm, or sensuous presentation (2) **:** an idea or object of thought that is the similitude of an object in nature whether in the guise of a modification of sense or of a purely intellectual correlative of the natural object; *broadly* **:** FORM, ASPECT, APPEARANCE **c** *obs* **:** a reflected image **:** REFLECTION **d** *obs* **:** an illusory image **:** PHANTOM **3** *obs* **:** the essential quality or distinguishing characteristic of something **4 a :** a component part of a compound medicine **:** SIMPLE **b :** a mixture of chopped or coarsely powdered vegetable drugs; *esp* **:** one used to prepare an aromatic tea or tisane ⟨a pectoral ~⟩ ⟨an emollient ~⟩ **5** *obs* **:** money of gold, silver, or other metal **:** COIN, SPECIE **syn** see CLASS

2**species** \"\ *adj* **:** constituting, being a member of, or selected from a biological species and not belonging to a horticultural variety of hybrid origin ⟨the China rose is a ~ rose⟩ ⟨native American ~ irises⟩

species-group \'=(,)=,=\ *n* **:** ARTENKREIS

species-specific \¦=(,)==¦==\ *adj* **:** exhibiting or characterized by species specificity ⟨a *species-specific* reaction⟩

species specificity *n* **:** the phenomenon involved in the interaction of an agent (as a pathogen, drug, or antigen) and members of a given species that results in a reaction characteristic for that species — compare SUSCEPTIBILITY

spe·ci·es·ta·ler \'shpātsē,e,stälər, -ē,es,dä-\ *n* -S [G *speziestaler*, fr. *spezies* specie (fr. L *species* species) + *taler* — more at TALER] **:** REICHSTALER

specif *abbr* **1** specific; specifically **2** specification

spec·i·fi·able \'spesə,fīəbəl, ,=='===\ *adj* **:** capable of being specified ⟨~ standards⟩ ⟨a ~ logical form⟩

1**spe·cif·ic** \spə'sifik, -fēk\ *adj* [LL *specificus*, fr. L *species* + *-ficus* -fic] **1 :** constituting or falling into the category specified ⟨~ fertilizing agents such as nitrogen or phosphate⟩ **2 :** having a real and fixed relationship to and usu. constituting a characteristic of **:** being peculiar to the thing or relation in question ⟨the ~ qualities of a drug⟩ ⟨a ~ distinction between vice and virtue⟩ ⟨~ symptoms of a disease⟩ **3 :** restricted by nature to a particular individual, situation, relation, or effect **:** PECULIAR ⟨faults ~ to past centuries⟩: as **a** *of a therapeutic agent* **:** exerting a definitive and distinctive influence on a particular part of the body or on the course of a particular disease ⟨quinine is highly ~ for malaria⟩ **b** *of a parasite* (1) **:** capable of living and reproducing in only one kind of host (2) **:** producing a particular disease **c** *of a disease* **:** caused by a particular pathogen (as a microorganism) **d** *of an antigen or antibody* **:** capable of reacting with but one antibody or antigen or with an antibody or antigen in but one way ⟨in complement fixation both antigen and antibody may be either ~ or nonspecific⟩ **4 a :** characterized by precise formulation or accurate restriction (as in stating, describing, defining, reserving) **:** free from such ambiguity as results from careless lack of precision or from omission of pertinent matter ⟨a ~ statement of faith⟩ ⟨~ analysis of the problem⟩ ⟨a ~ agreement⟩ **b :** intended for or restricted to a particular end or object ⟨a ~ deposit in a bank⟩ **5 :** of, relating to, or constituting a species and esp. a taxonomic species ⟨groups of ~ rank⟩ ⟨distinctive ~ characters⟩ **6 :** being any of various arbitrary physical constants and esp. one relating a quantitative attribute to unit mass, volume, or area ⟨~ luminous intensity is the luminous intensity per unit area of source⟩ — see SPECIFIC ENTROPY, SPECIFIC GRAVITY, SPECIFIC HEAT, SPECIFIC HUMIDITY **syn** see EXPLICIT, SPECIAL

2**specific** \"\ *n* -S **1 a :** something peculiarly adapted to its purpose, use, or situation **b :** a drug that has a specific mitigating influence on a disease ⟨quinine is a ~ for malaria⟩ **2 a :** a specific or characteristic quality, trait, mark, or other feature **b :** precise details or distinctions **:** PARTICULARS ⟨music frees us from the ~ and stirs the unconscious depths of our being⟩ **c specifics** *pl* **:** SPECIFICATION 4 ⟨work out the ~s required for putting his program into effect —*New Republic*⟩ **syn** see REMEDY

specific absorptive index *n* **:** absorbance of radiation per unit thickness of layer and concentration of solution

spe·cif·i·cal \-fəkəl\ *adj* [ME, fr. LL *specificus* + ME *-al*] *archaic* **:** SPECIFIC

spe·cif·i·cal·i·ty \=,=fə'kaləd·ē, -lətē, -i\ *n* -ES [*specifical* + *-ity*] **:** the quality or state of being specific

spe·cif·i·cal·ly \spə'sifək(ə)lē, -fēk-, -li\ *adv* [*specifical* + *-ly*] **1 :** in regard to the matter in question **:** with reference to a quality or condition that is specified or inherent ⟨water is ~ heavier than ice⟩ ⟨a product of ~ architectural imagination —R.W.Kennedy⟩ **2 :** with exactness and precision **:** in a definite manner ⟨~ denounced the new tax⟩

spe·cif·i·cate \-fə,kāt\ *vt* -ED/-ING/-S [LL *specificatus*, past part. of *specificare* to specify — more at SPECIFY] **:** to give specificity to **:** SPECIFY

spec·i·fi·ca·tion \,spesəfə'kāshən\ *n* -S [ML *specification-*, *specificatio*, fr. LL *specificatus* + L *-ion*, *-io* -ion] **1 a** *obs* **:** the giving of a definitive or specific quality **b :** conversion of property and esp. of property belonging to another into a new kind of property by labor (as in manufacture); *also* **:** the acquisition of title in property so produced that results under Roman, Scots, or civil law when the article cannot be reduced to its original form **2** *obs* **:** natural or specific character **:** characteristic quality **3 :** the act or process of identifying or making specific through the supplying of particularizing detail **:** a decreasing of generality or vagueness (as of a concept) by determining or supplying characteristics that delimit a more precise applicability; *esp* **:** the replacement of a variable in a propositional function in symbolic logic by a specific value ⟨"the sky is blue" is obtained by ~ from "*x* is blue"⟩ **4 :** a detailed, precise, explicit presentation (as by enumeration, description, or working drawing) of something or a plan or proposal for something: as **a :** a written statement containing a minute description or enumeration of particulars (as of charges against a public officer or of the terms of a contract); *also* **:** a single article, item, or particular or an allegation of a specific act **b :** a written description of an invention or discovery for which a patent is sought that embodies the manner and process of making, constructing, compounding, and using and concludes with a specific and distinct claim of the part, improvement, or combination which the applicant regards as his discovery or invention — compare CLAIM **c :** a written or printed description of constructional work to be done (as in repairing a house or installing machinery in a factory) forming part of the contract, describing qualities of material and mode of construction, and giving dimension and other information not shown in the drawings — usu. used in pl.

spec·i·fi·ca·tive \'spesəfə,kād·iv, spə'sifə,-\ *adj* [LL *specificatus* + E *-ive*] **:** tending or serving to specify — **spec·i·fi·ca·tive·ly** \-d·əvlē\ *adv*

specific capacity *n* **:** the amount of water furnished under a standard unit head **:** the amount of water that is furnished under unit lowering of the surface of the water in a well by pumping

specific character *n* **:** a character distinguishing one species from another or from every other species of the same genus

specific charge *n* **1 :** a charge against specific identifiable property that is essentially the same in effect as a mortgage **2 :** the ratio of the electric charge on a particle to its mass

specific color *n* **:** a color having hue and saturation **:** a chromatic color

specific conductance *n* **:** CONDUCTIVITY

specific cost *n* **:** DIRECT COST

specific duty *n* **:** a duty assessed on an article of a given kind at a flat rate per unit of quantity (as a ton, bushel, or yard) without individual appraisal

specific dynamic action *n* **:** the effect of ingestion and assimilation of food and esp. of protein in increasing the production of heat in the body

specific energy *n* **:** the supposed specific quality of a sensory nerve that has been held to cause it to transmit a particular kind of sensation whatever the nature of the stimulus and that is usu. attributed to interpretive and correlative processes in the central nervous system

specific entropy *n* **:** entropy of a substance per unit mass (as per gram or per mole)

specific epithet *n* **:** the Latin or latinized noun or adjective that follows and agrees grammatically with the genus name in the name of a taxonomic species — called also *trivial name*

specific gravity *n* **:** the ratio of the density of a substance to the density of some substance (as pure water at its temperature of maximum density at 4° C) taken as a standard when both densities are obtained by weighing in air ⟨if one cubic inch of gold weighs in air 19.3 times as much as one cubic inch of water, the *specific gravity* of gold is 19.3⟩

specific-gravity balance *n* **:** a balance used for determining the specific gravity of a liquid or solid by means of the Archimedes' principle

specific-gravity bottle *or* **specific-gravity flask** *n* **:** a pycnometer having the form of a stoppered bottle

specific-gravity bulb *n* **:** a hollow glass bulb so weighted that it will float on a liquid of greater and sink in a liquid of less specific gravity than that marked on the bulb

specific heat *n* **1 :** the ratio of the quantity of heat required to raise the temperature of a body one degree to that required to raise the temperature of an equal mass of water one degree **2 :** the heat in calories required to raise the temperature of one gram of a substance one degree centigrade

specific humidity *n* **:** the mass of water vapor per unit mass of moist air

specific impulse *n* **:** the thrust produced per unit rate of consumption of the propellant usu. specified in pounds of thrust per pound of propellant used per second and forming a measure of the efficiency of performance of a rocket engine

specific ionization *n* **:** the number of ion pairs formed in a gas by an ionizing particle per unit length of its path

spec·i·fic·i·ty \,spesə'fisəd·ē, -sətē, -i\ *n* -ES **:** the quality or state of being specific ⟨contribute a desirable note of ~ to the discussion —H.D.Gideonse⟩; *esp* **:** the condition of being peculiar to a particular individual or group of organisms ⟨host ~ of a parasite⟩

spe·cif·i·cize \spə'sifə,sīz\ *vt* -ED/-ING/-S **:** to make specific **:** give a specific quality to

specific key *n* **:** a key for a single cryptographic message or a small group of messages — compare PERIOD KEY

specific legacy *n* **:** a bequest of a particular identifiable and existing thing or part (as a specified animal) out of a testator's estate — compare GENERAL LEGACY

specific lien *n* **:** PARTICULAR LIEN

specific magnetization *n* **:** the ratio of the magnetization of a substance to the density obtained by dividing the magnetic moment of a specimen by its mass

specific modifier *n* **:** a gene that modifies the effect of one or more other genes

specific name *n* **:** the binomial name of a taxonomic species consisting of the name of its genus followed by a specific epithet

spe·cif·ic·ness *n* -ES **:** the quality or state of being specific

specific performance *n* **:** the performance of a legal contract exactly or substantially according to its terms — used chiefly with reference to such performance as decreed by a court of equity in a case where the common-law remedy of damages would be substantially inadequate and the specific performance not unjust to the defendant

specific rate *n* **:** an insurance rate specif. computed for a particular risk **:** SCHEDULE RATE

specific refractivity *n* **:** the refractivity of a medium divided by its density

specific resistance *n* **:** RESISTIVITY 2b

specific rotation *n* **:** the angle of rotation in degrees of the plane of polarization of a ray of monochromatic light that passes through a tube 1 decimeter long containing the substance in solution at a concentration of 1 gram per milliliter in a polarimeter

specifics *pl of* SPECIFIC

specific stain *n* **:** a dye used in histology and microchemistry that has a specific affinity for particular structural elements or chemical compounds

specific surface *n* **:** the ratio of the total surface of a substance (as an adsorbent) to its volume **:** surface area (as of a finely divided powder) per unit mass

specific volume *n* **:** the volume per unit mass of a substance **:** the reciprocal of the density

specific weight *n* **:** the weight of a substance per unit volume in absolute units equal to the density multiplied by the acceleration of gravity

spec·i·fi·er \'spesə,fī(ə)r, -īə\ *n* -S **:** one that specifies (as by giving details or particulars); *esp* **:** a person who draws up specifications (as for obtaining a patent)

spec·i·fy \-,fī\ *vb* -ED/-ING/-ES [ME *specifien*, fr. OF *specifier*, fr. LL *specificare*, fr. *specificus* specific] *vt* **1 a :** to mention or name in a specific or explicit manner **:** tell or state precisely or in detail ⟨~ the uses of a plant⟩ ⟨clearly *specified* the one he meant⟩ ⟨the bequest *specifies* that the recipient must care for the cat⟩ **b :** to include as an item in a specification ⟨~*ing* oak flooring throughout⟩; *also* **:** to draw specifications of **2 :** to make specific **:** give a specific character or application to ⟨tensions that ~ personal conflicts⟩ ~ *vi* **:** to speak precisely or in detail **:** give full particulars **syn** see MENTION

spec·i·men \'spesəmən *sometimes* -esm-\ *n* -S [L, fr. *specere* to look, look at — more at SPY] **1 a :** a particular single item, part, aspect, or incident that is typical and indicative of the nature, character, or quality of others in the same class or group ⟨a ~ of the melodramatic fiction of the era —T.S. Eliot⟩ ⟨compared ~*s* of their handwriting⟩ ⟨repeated a ~ from which the tenor of the conversation could be readily inferred⟩ **b :** a sample or unit (as of merchandise, a mineral, or a plant) that is deliberately selected for examination, display, or study and is usu. chosen as typical of its kind ⟨a ~ cabinet⟩ ⟨~*s* of a new line of textiles⟩: as (1) **:** a printed sheet showing different styles and sizes of type (2) **:** a sample copy of a printed work; *specif* **:** a condensed sample containing enough of the typography, illustrations, maps, binding, and other features to give an adequate idea of the complete work (3) **:** a postage stamp printed as a sample and bearing the word *specimen* (4) **:** a portion of material for use in testing ⟨a fecal ~⟩ ⟨wool ~*s* for staple testing⟩ **2 a :** something that obviously belongs to a particular category but shows or is noticed by reason of some individual distinguishing character or peculiarity ⟨the scavenging pigs, the dirtiest, leanest, and hungriest ~*s* I have met with —V.G.Heiser⟩ **b :** INDIVIDUAL, PERSON ⟨turned out to be a queer ~⟩ ⟨~*s* like these fellows that hang around the docks⟩ **syn** see INSTANCE

specimen plant *n* **:** a plant grown for exhibition or in the open to display its full development as distinguished from one in a border or other planting

specio- — see SPECI-

spe·ci·os·i·ty \,spēshē'äsəd·ē, -sətē, -i\ *n* -ES [ME *specioustee* beauty, fr. LL *speciositat-*, *speciositas*, fr. L *speciosus* beautiful + *-itat*, *-itas* -ity] **1 :** the quality or state of being specious **2 :** a specious appearance or thing

spe·cious \'spēshəs\ *adj* [ME, fr. L *speciosus* beautiful, showy, plausible, fr. *species* appearance, beauty + *-osus* -ous — more at SPY] **1** *obs* **:** presenting a pleasing appearance **:** pleasing in form or look **:** SHOWY **2 :** superficially beautiful or attractive but not so in reality **:** deceptively beautiful **3 :** apparently right or proper **:** superficially fair, just, or correct but not so in reality **:** appearing well at first view **:** PLAUSIBLE ⟨~ reasoning⟩ ⟨a ~ claim⟩ **4 :** existing to our senses **:** actually known or experienced — see SPECIOUS PRESENT — **spe·cious·ly** *adv* — **spe·cious·ness** *n* -ES

specious present *n* **:** the time span of immediate consciousness **:** interval within which what is earlier may be distinguished from what is later though both are directly present to consciousness

1**speck** \'spek\ *n* -S [ME *specke*, fr. OE *specca*] **1 a :** a small discoloration in or on something **:** SPOT, STAIN ⟨a ~ on paper or cloth⟩ ⟨covered with dark ~*s*⟩ **b :** a small discoloration revealing decay (as in fruit); *broadly* **:** FLAW, BLEMISH ⟨a reputation without a ~⟩ **2 :** a tiny bit of something **:** a small piece, particle, or amount **:** MITE ⟨put just a ~ of milk in the tea⟩ ⟨ore sparkling with ~*s* of gold⟩ ⟨the announcement failed to arouse a ~ of interest⟩ **3 a :** a bacterial or fungous disease of rice characterized by shriveled or specked grains **b :** a disease of plants characterized by small usu. circumscribed lesions — see BACTERIAL SPECK **4 :** something marked or marred with specks: as **a :** imperfect but usable fruit ⟨bought a basket of ~*s* for jelly⟩ **b :** a spotted or speckled fish ⟨when the big ~*s* begin biting⟩ **5 :** a small sand darter (*Ulocentra stigmaea*) common in the southeastern U. S.

2**speck** \"\ *vt* -ED/-ING/-S **1 :** to produce specks and esp. blemishes on or in **:** SPOT, SPECKLE **2 :** to remove specks from (as cloth)

3**speck** \"\ *n* -S [ME *spekke*] *dial Eng* **:** PATCH

4**speck** \"\ *n* [D *spek* (fr. MD *spec*) & G *speck*, fr. OHG *spek*; both akin to OE *spec*, *spic* bacon, blubber, ON *spik*, Skt *sphigī* buttock, *sphāyati* he increases, grows fat — more at speed] *chiefly dial* **:** fat meat: as **a :** BACON, SALT PORK **b :** the blubber of a whale or other marine mammal **c** *Africa* **:** the fat of the hippopotamus esp. when cured for use as bacon

5**speck** \"\ *vi* -ED/-ING/-S [by shortening and alter.] *Austral* **:** PROSPECT 1a

specked \'spekt\ *adj* [ME, fr. *specke* speck + *-ed*] **:** marked or marred with or as if with specks **:** SPOTTED, SPECKLED — **speck·ed·ness** \'spekədnəs\ *n* -ES

speckeldy *var of* SPECKLEDY

speck·er \'spekə(r)\ *n* -S **:** one that specks; *esp* **:** a worker that removes specks from something

speckfall \'=,=\ *n* [4*speck* + *fall*] **:** a fall rove through a block for hoisting blubber and bone aboard a whaler

speck finger *n* [2*speck* + *finger*] **:** ERYSIPELOID

speckier *comparative of* SPECKY

speckiest *superlative of* SPECKY

speck·i·ness \'spekēnəs, -kin-\ *n* -ES **:** the quality or state of being specky

1**speck·le** \'spekəl\ *n* -S *often attrib* [ME *spakle*, *speckle*; akin to MD *speckel* speckle, OE *specca* speck] **:** a small mark, splotch, or speck; *esp* **:** an irregular natural speck (as of color) ⟨white eggs covered with purplish ~*s*⟩ ⟨a *speckle*-bellied goose⟩

2**speckle** \"\ *vt* **speckled**; **speckled**; **speckling** \-k(ə)liŋ\ **speckles 1 :** to mark with small spots or specks **:** SPECK, SPOT ⟨sunlight *speckling* the lawn⟩ ⟨decided to ~ the finish of the floor⟩ **2 :** to dot in the manner of speckles ⟨little lakes *speckled* the land⟩ ⟨a slope *speckled* with houses⟩

specklebelly \'==,==\ *n* [1*speckle* + *belly*] **1 :** WHITE-FRONTED GOOSE **2 :** GADWALL

specklebreast \'==,=\ *also* **speckle-breasted brant** \¦==¦==-\ *or* **speckle-breasted goose** *n* **:** WHITE-FRONTED GOOSE

speckle-cheek \'==,=\ *n* **:** CACTUS WOODPECKER

speck·led \'spekəld\ *adj* [ME *spacled*, fr. *spakle* speckle + -ed] **:** covered or marked with speckles **:** SPOTTED

speckled alder *n* **:** a common shrub (*Alnus rugosa*) of the north temperate zone with oval leaves and catkins that flower much before the leaves expand

speckled bass *n* **:** BLACK CRAPPIE

speckledbill \'==,=\ *n* **:** SURF SCOTER

speckled blotch *or* **speckled leaf blotch** *n* **:** a disease of wheat caused by fungi of the genus *Septoria* and characterized by pinhead-sized light-colored leaf spots that later develop into blackish spore pustules

speckled brant *n* **:** WHITE-FRONTED GOOSE

speckled bullhead *n* **:** BROWN BULLHEAD

speckled crab *n* **:** an active shallow-water crab (*Araneus cribrarius*) that is found from Massachusetts to Brazil and is light brown thickly dotted with white or yellow

speckled hind *n* **:** a large grouper (*Epinephelus drummondhayi*) that is umber brown densely covered with small pearly-white or bluish dots and is a common food fish of the Florida coast

speckled moray *n* **:** HAMLET 2

speck·led·ness \'spekəldnəs\ *n* -ES **:** the quality or state of being speckled

speckled perch *n* **:** BLACK CRAPPIE

speckled trout *n* **1** *or* **speckle trout a :** BROOK TROUT **b :** RAINBOW TROUT; *broadly* **:** any of several trouts of the western U.S. **2 :** SPOTTED WEAKFISH

speckled turtle *or* **speckled tortoise** *n* **:** SPOTTED TURTLE

speckled wood *n* **1 :** LETTERWOOD **2 :** palmyra wood cut transversely so as to give a mottled effect

speck·ledy *also* **speck·eldy** \ˈspekəldē, -di\ *adj* [*speckled* + *-y*] **:** marked with spots or speckles

speckled yellows *n pl but usu sing in constr* **:** a manganese deficiency disease of table beets, sugar beets, and mangels marked by development of yellowish interveinal areas on the leaf that often turn brown and fall out

specklehead \ˈ==,=\ *n* **:** BALDPATE 2

speckles *pl of* SPECKLE, *pres 3d sing of* SPECKLE

speck·less \ˈ=ləs\ *adj* **:** free from specks **:** UNMARKED, SPOTLESS; *esp* **:** perfectly clean — **speck·less·ly** *adv* — **speck·less·ness** *n* -ES

speckling *n* -s [fr. gerund of ²*speckle*] **:** speckled marking

speck·ly \ˈspek(ə)lē, -li\ *adj* -ER/-EST [¹*speckle* + *-y*] **:** marked with speckles **:** SPECKLED

¹**specks** *pl of* SPECK, *pres 3d sing of* SPECK

²**specks** \ˈspeks\ *n pl* [alter. of *specs*] **:** GLASS 2b(2)

specky \-kē, -ki\ *adj* -ER/-EST [¹*speck* + *-y*] **:** marked or marred with specks or spots

specl *abbr* specialist

speclst *abbr* specialist

specs \ˈspeks\ *n pl* **1** [contr. of *spectacles*] **:** GLASS 2b(2) **2** [pl. of *spec*] **:** SPECIFICATIONS

spectable *adj* [ME, fr. L *spectabilis*, fr. *spectare* to look, observe + *-abilis* -able] *obs* **:** VISIBLE; *also* **:** SIGHTLY

spec·ta·cle \ˈspektəkəl, -tēk- *also* -,tik-\ *n* -s [ME, fr. MF, fr. L *spectaculum*, fr. *spectare* to look at, watch, view, freq. of *specere* to look at, catch sight of — more at SPY] **1 a :** something exhibited to view; *usu* **:** something exhibited as unusual and notable **:** a remarkable or noteworthy sight **:** an impressive display esp. for entertainment **b :** an object of curiosity or contempt esp. by reason of silly or inappropriate behavior ⟨made a ~ of herself at the party⟩ **c** (1) **:** a public display appealing or intended to appeal to the eye by its mass, proportions, color, or other dramatic qualities ⟨a great dramatic ~⟩ ⟨a naval ~⟩ ⟨the opening ~ of a circus⟩ (2) **:** a motion picture employing massively impressive scenery and much crowd action, usu. set in past time, and commonly dealing with a historical or religious theme **2 :** a means of viewing or observing: as **a** *obs* **:** an object of glass (as a window or mirror) **b** (1) *obs* **:** an aid to vision (as a spyglass) (2) **:** GLASS 2b(2); *esp* **:** glasses that are supported by the ears as distinguished from goggles or pince-nez — usu. used in pl. and often with *pair* ⟨a new pair of ~*s*⟩ **3 :** any of various things felt to resemble a pair of glasses: as **a spectacles** *pl* **:** a colored marking on an animal either in the form of a double loop (as on the spectacled cobra) or of rings about the eyes (as on some birds) **b :** a frame containing the red and green lights of a railroad semaphore **c :** a device with two handles used to move well-boring tools **d spectacles** *pl, Brit* **:** a cricketer's score of nothing in each of his two innings in a single match **:** PAIR OF SPECTACLES

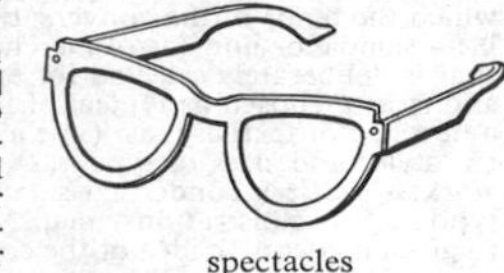

spectacles

spectacle clew *or* **spectacle iron** *n* **:** a steel device consisting of three rings at the clews of square sails into which three ropes or blocks can be hooked

spectacle coot *n* [short for *spectacled coot*] **:** SURF SCOTER

spec·ta·cled \-kəld\ *adj* [*spectacle, spectacles* + *-ed*] **1 :** having or wearing spectacles **2 :** having color markings or patches of naked skin suggesting a pair of spectacles ⟨~ alligator⟩

spectacled bear *n* **:** a bear (*Tremarctos ornatus*) of the Andes mountains

spectacled caiman *n* **:** a caiman with bony ridges about the eyes; *esp* **:** a common caiman (*Caiman sclerops*) that occurs from southern Mexico to the Argentine

spectacled cobra *n* **:** INDIAN COBRA

spectacled coot *or* **spectacled duck** *n* **:** SURF SCOTER

spectacled dolphin *n* **:** any of several dolphins (genus *Lagenorhynchus*) that are distinctively striped in black and white — called also *skunk porpoise*

spectacled eider *n* **:** a chiefly Siberian eider duck (*Somateria fischeri*) that has large white black-margined patches about the eyes

spectacled goose *n, Brit* **:** the common gannet (*Sula bassana*)

spectacled pelican *n* **:** a large predominantly white pelican (*Pelecanus conspicillatus*) of Australia and New Guinea that has the wings and hinder parts somewhat dusky to blackish

spectacled warbler *n* **:** a small Old World warbler (*Sylvia conspicillata*) with a dark slaty gray head and white eye rings

spectacle frame *n* **:** a frame at or near the sternposts through which both shafts pass in a twin-screw ship having the stern bossed out to surround both shafts

spectacle furnace *n* **:** a German shaft furnace with two tapholes

spec·ta·cle·less \-kəl(l)əs\ *adj* **:** having or wearing no spectacles

spectacle pod *n* **:** an annual cruciferous herb (*Dithyrea californica*) of the southwestern U.S. having thin fruits that resemble miniature spectacles

spectacle stone *n* **:** any of the ancient monumental stones of Scotland ornamented with connected or overlapping disks or rude spirals and probably of Celtic origin

¹**spec·tac·u·lar** \(ˈ)spek¦takyələ(r) *sometimes* spək't-\ *adj* [L *spectaculum* spectacle + E *-ar*] **1 :** of, relating to, or constituting a spectacle **:** adapted or intended to excite wonder and admiration by unusual display (as of pomp or scenic effects) ⟨a ~ play⟩ ⟨a ~ display of northern lights⟩ **2 :** of a kind to attract notice distinctly unusual or unexpected ⟨a ~ rise in prices⟩ ⟨a ~ scheme⟩ — **spec·tac·u·lar·i·ty** \(,)spek,takyəˈlarəd·ē *also* spək-\ *n* -ES

²**spectacular** \"\ *n* -s **:** something that is spectacular and esp. is designed to appeal to the eye as a spectacle **:** an unusual display (as of pomp or scenery): as **a :** an action or a sight of a sensational nature ⟨ever a lover of the ~⟩ **b :** a large custom-built advertising display usu. of electric or neon lights and designed to produce a special effect or unusual animation **c :** a long elaborately produced television show featuring noted entertainers

spec·tac·u·lar·ism \spek'takyələ,rizəm *also* spək-\ *n* -s **:** the quality or state of being spectacular

spec·tac·u·lar·ly *adv* **:** in a spectacular manner

spec·tate \ˈspek,tāt\ *vi* -ED/-ING/-S [L *spectatus*, past part. of *spectare*] **:** OBSERVE, WATCH; *esp* **:** to be present as a spectator (as at a sports event)

¹**spec·ta·tor** \ˈspek,tād·ə(r), -atə-, =ˈ==\ *n* -s [L, fr. *spectatus* (past part. of *spectare* to look at, watch, view) + *-or* — more at SPECTACLE] **1 :** one that looks on or beholds; *esp* **:** one witnessing an exhibition (as a sports event) **2** *or* **spectator pump :** a woman's pump designed for casual wear with a medium to high heel and a leather upper often with contrasting color at the toe and heel

spectator 2

²**spectator** \"\ *adj* **1 :** having its main attraction for spectators **:** tending to attract spectators ⟨such ~ sports as racing⟩ **2 :** styled in an informal or casual manner and suitable for use by a spectator at a sports event ⟨a ~ frock⟩

spec·ta·to·ri·al \,spektə¦tōrēəl, -tȯr-\ *adj* [¹*spectator* + *-ial*] **1 a :** of or relating to a spectator **b** *sometimes cap* [after *The Spectator* published in London 1711–12 by Joseph Addison †1719 and Richard Steele †1729] **:** suggesting the critical observations of a periodical essay

spec·ta·tor·itis \(,)spek,tād·əˈrīd·əs\ *n* -ES [¹*spectator* + *-itis*] **:** excessive indulgence in forms of amusement in which one is a passive spectator rather than an active participant

spec·ta·tor·ship \ˈ=,==,ship, =ˈ==,=\ *n* [¹*spectator* + *-ship*] **1 :** the condition of being viewed or submitted for viewing **2 :** the condition of being a spectator esp. as distinguished from a participant

spec·ta·to·ry \(ˈ)spek¦tād·ərē\ *n* -ES [¹*spectator* + *-ory*] **:** a part of a building set apart for spectators; *also* **:** a body of spectators

spec·ta·tress \spek'tā·trəs, ˈ=,==\ *also* **spec·ta·trix** \-triks\ *n* -ES [*spectatress* fr. *spectator* + *-ess*; *spectatrix* fr. L, fem. of *spectator*] **:** a female spectator

spec·ter *or* **spec·tre** \ˈspektə(r)\ *n* -s [F *spectre*, fr. L *spectrum* appearance, specter, fr. *specere* to look — more at SPY] **1 :** a visible disembodied spirit **:** APPARITION, GHOST, PHANTOM **2 :** a ghostly and usu. fear-inspiring vision of the imagination **:** something that haunts or persistently perturbs the mind **:** PHANTASM ⟨the ~ of want⟩ **3 a :** STICK INSECT **b** *or* **specter crab :** GLASS CRAB **c :** SPECTER SHRIMP

specter bat *n* **:** a phyllostome bat; *esp* **:** a large tropical American leaf-nosed bat (*Vampyrum spectrum*)

specter candle *n* **:** BELEMNITE

spec·tered *or* **spec·tred** \-tə(r)d\ *adj* [*specter* + *-ed*] **:** peopled with specters

specter lemur *n* **:** TARSIER

specter of the brocken *usu cap B* **:** BROCKEN SPECTER

specter shrimp *n* **1 :** SKELETON SHRIMP **2 :** GHOST SHRIMP

spectra *pl of* SPECTRUM

spec·tral \ˈspektrəl\ *adj* [L & NL *spectrum* + E *-al*] **1 a :** of, like, or relating to a specter **:** GHOSTLY **b :** lacking in solid substance **:** FALSE, ILLUSORY **2 :** of or relating to a spectrum **:** made by the spectrum ⟨~ analysis⟩ — **spec·tral·i·ty** \spek'tralәd·ē\ *or* **spec·tral·ness** \ˈspektrəlnəs\ *n* -ES — **spec·tral·ly** \-rəlē, -li\ *adv*

spectral bat *n* **:** SPECTER BAT

spectral distribution *n* **:** a function expressing analytically or graphically the relation between radiant or luminous flux per wavelength or frequency interval and wavelength or frequency

spectral lemur *n* **:** TARSIER

spectral line *n* **:** one of a series of linear images of the narrow slit of a spectrograph or similar instrument corresponding to a component of the spectrum of the radiation emitted by a particular source

spectral owl *n* **:** GREAT GRAY OWL

spectral type *n* **:** the type of a star according to a description of its spectrum by means of 10 principal spectral classes, decimal subdivisions of the classes, and symbols indicating special characteristics (as *e* for stars with bright lines, *d* for dwarfs, and *g* for giants)

PRINCIPAL SPECTRAL TYPES

TYPE	SURFACE TEMPERATURE (° KELVIN)	COLOR	MOST PROMINENT SPECTRAL LINES AND BANDS
O	50,000	blue	hydrogen, ionized helium, ionized oxygen, ionized nitrogen
B	20,000	bluish	hydrogen, helium
A	10,000	white	hydrogen
F	7,000	yellowish	hydrogen, ionized calcium
G	5,500	yellow	hydrogen, ionized calcium, metals
K	4,500	orange	ionized calcium, metals, cyanogen
M	3,000	red	titanium oxide, vanadium oxide
R	2,500	red	carbon, carbon compounds
S	2,400	red	zirconium oxide, lanthanum oxide
N	2,000	very red	carbon, carbon compounds

spectro- *comb form* [NL *spectrum*] **1 :** spectral and ⟨*spectro*chemical⟩ **2 :** of or relating to spectra ⟨*spectro*photography⟩ **3** [*spectroscope*] **:** combined with a spectroscope ⟨*spectro*polarimeter⟩

spec·tro·bolometer \¦spek(,)trō+\ *n* [*spectro-* + *bolometer*] **:** a combination of spectroscope and bolometer for determining the distribution of energy in a spectrum **:** SPECTRORADIOMETER

spec·tro·chemical \"+\ *adj* [*spectro-* + *chemical*] **:** of, relating to, or applying the methods of spectrochemistry

spectrochemical analysis *n* **:** the chemical analysis of a mixture of substances or of a complex substance by a study of spectra

spec·tro·chemistry \¦spek(,)trō+\ *n* [*spectro-* + *chemistry*] **:** a branch of chemistry based on a study of the spectra of substances

spec·tro·colorimetry \"+\ *n* [*spectro-* + *colorimetry*] **:** quantitative study of color by means of the spectrophotometer usu. for purposes of chemical analysis

spec·tro·gram \ˈspekt(r)ə,gram, -graa(ə)m\ *n* [ISV *spectro-* + *-gram*] **1 :** a photograph, map, or diagram of a spectrum **2 :** SOUND SPECTROGRAM

spec·tro·graph \-graf, -gaa(ə)f, -graif, -gráf\ *n* [ISV *spectro-* + *-graph*] **1 :** an apparatus for dispersing radiation into a spectrum and for photographing or mapping the spectrum — see CRYSTAL SPECTROGRAPH, MASS SPECTROGRAPH; compare SPECTROGRAM, SPECTROSCOPE **2 :** SOUND SPECTROGRAPH — **spec·tro·graph·ic** \¦==¦grafik\ *adj* — **spec·tro·graph·i·cal·ly** \-fək(ə)lē\ *adv*

spec·trog·ra·pher \spek'trägrəfə(r)\ *n* -s [*spectrography* + *-er*] **:** SPECTROSCOPIST

spec·trog·ra·phy \-fē, -fi\ *n* -ES [ISV *spectro-* + *-graphy*] **:** the art or technique of using the spectrograph

spec·tro·heliogram \¦spek(,)trō+\ *n* [*spectro-* + *heli-* + *-gram*] **:** a photograph of the sun made by monochromatic light usu. of the hydrogen-alpha line in the red or the calcium K line in the violet and showing the sun's faculae and prominences

spec·tro·heliograph \"+\ *n* [ISV *spectro-* + *heli-* + *-graph*] **:** an apparatus for making spectroheliograms consisting of a spectroscopic camera used in combination with a telescope and provided with clockwork for moving the sun's image across the slit — **spec·tro·heliographic** \"+\ *adj*

spec·tro·he·lio·kinematograph \¦spek(,)trō¦hēlēō+\ *n* [*spectro-* + *heli-* + *kinematograph*] **:** a spectroheliograph equipped with a motion-picture camera

spec·tro·he·li·o·scope \,=(,)=ˈhēlēə,skōp\ *n* [ISV *spectro-* + *heli-* + *-scope*] **1 :** SPECTROHELIOGRAPH **2 :** an instrument similar to a spectroheliograph used for visual as distinguished from photographic observations — **spec·tro·he·li·o·scop·ic** \¦=(,)=¦===¦skäpik\ *adj*

spec·trol·o·gy \spek'träləjē\ *n* -ES [L *spectrum* specter + E *-o-* + *-logy*] **:** the study of specters

spec·trom·e·ter \=ˈträməd·ə(r), -mətə-\ *n* [ISV *spectro-* + *-meter*] **1 :** an instrument used in determining the index of refraction by measuring the external angle of a prism of a substance and also its angle of minimum deviation for light of a given kind **2 :** a spectroscope fitted for measurements of the spectra observed with it — compare MASS SPECTROMETER

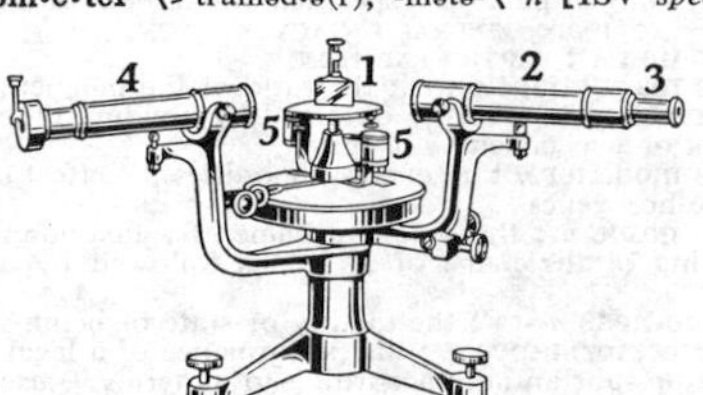

spectrometer: *1* prism, *2* telescope, *3* eyepiece, *4* collimator, *5, 5* magnifying glasses

spec·tro·met·ric \¦spektrə¦me·trik\ *adj* [ISV *spectro-* + *-metric*] **:** of, relating to, or involving spectrometry or the spectrometer

spec·trom·e·try \spek'trämə·trē, -ri\ *n* -ES [ISV *spectro-* + *-metry*] **:** the art or process of using the spectrometer or of measuring wavelengths of rays of a spectrum

spec·tro·microscope \¦spek(,)trō+\ *n* [*spectro-* + *microscope*] **:** a microscope with a spectroscopic attachment — compare MICROSPECTROSCOPE — **spec·tro·microscopical** \"+\ *adj*

spec·tro·photoelectric \"+\ *adj* [*spectro-* + *photoelectric*] **:** varying in photoelectric sensitiveness according to the wavelength of the exciting light

spec·tro·photometer \"+\ *n* [ISV *spectro-* + *photometer*] **:** a photometer for measuring the relative intensities of the light in different parts of a spectrum

spec·tro·photometric \"+\ *adj* [ISV *spectrophotometer* + *-ic*] **:** of, relating to, or involving spectrophotometry or the spectrophotometer — **spec·tro·photometrically** \"+\ *adv*

spec·tro·photometry \"+\ *n* [ISV *spectrophotometer* + *-y*] **:** the art or process of comparing photometrically the relative intensities of the light in different parts of a spectrum **:** the use of the spectrophotometer

spec·tro·polarimeter \"+\ *n* [*spectro-* + *polarimeter*] **:** a combined spectroscope and polarimeter that is used for the determination of the rotatory power of solutions at different wavelengths

spec·tro·polariscope \"+\ *n* [*spectro-* + *polariscope*] **:** a combined spectroscope and polariscope **:** SPECTROPOLARIMETER

spec·tro·pyrheliometer \"+\ *n* [*spectro-* + *pyrheliometer*] **:** an instrument for measuring the energy distribution in the visible and ultraviolet spectrum of emitted radiation from the sun

spec·tro·pyrometer \"+\ *n* [*spectro-* + *pyrometer*] **:** an instrument for optical or spectrophotometric estimation of the temperature of an incandescent substance

spec·tro·radiometer \"+\ *n* [*spectro-* + *radiometer*] **:** an instrument for measuring the energy distribution of emitted radiation that is a combination of spectroscope and radiometer

spec·tro·radiometric \"+\ *adj* [*spectroradiometer* + *-ic*] **:** of, relating to, or involving spectroradiometry or the spectroradiometer

spec·tro·radiometry \"+\ *n* [*spectroradiometer* + *-y*] **:** the art or process of using the spectroradiometer in the study of radiant energy

spec·tro·scope \ˈspektrə,skōp\ *n* [ISV *spectro-* + *-scope*] **:** any of various instruments designed for forming and examining optical spectra and being so constructed that observations are made visually — compare SPECTROGRAPH, SPECTROMETER

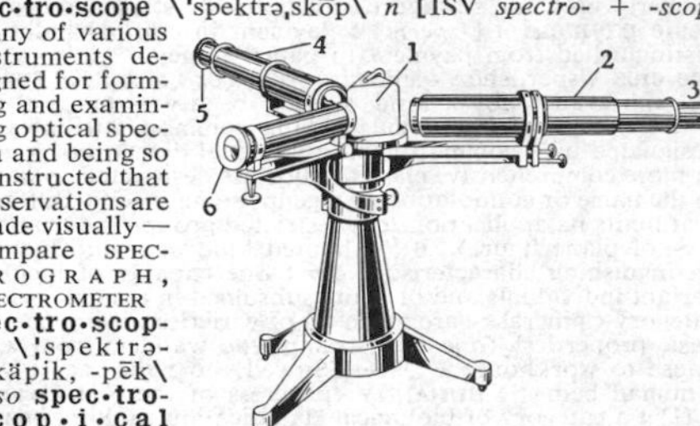

simple form of spectroscope: *1* prism, *2* telescope, *3* eyepiece, *4* collimator, *5* end with slit, *6* tube with micrometer

spec·tro·scop·ic \¦spektrə¦skäpik, -pēk\ *also* **spec·tro·scop·i·cal** \-pəkəl, -pēk-\ *adj* [*spectroscope* + *-ic*, *-ical*] **1 :** of, relating to, or involving spectroscopy or the spectroscope or sometimes spectrograph **2 :** dealing or concerned with spectroscopy — **spec·tro·scop·i·cal·ly** \-pək(ə)lē, -pēk-, -li\ *adv*

spectroscopic binary *n* **:** a binary star in which shifting of lines in the system's spectrum indicates orbital revolution

spectroscopic parallax *n* **:** the parallax of a star indicated by its absolute magnitude as deduced from the relative intensities of selected lines in its spectrum

spec·tros·co·pist \spek'träskəpəst\ *n* -s [ISV *spectroscope* + *-ist*] **:** one who uses the spectroscope **:** an expert in spectroscopy

spec·tros·co·py \-pē, -pi\ *n* -ES [ISV *spectro-* + *-scopy*] **1 a :** the production and investigation of spectra **b :** the art or process of using the spectroscope **2 :** the science of spectroscopic phenomena

spec·trous \ˈspektrəs\ *adj* [*specter* + *-ous*] **:** SPECTRAL

spec·trum \-trəm\ *n, pl* **spec·tra** \-rə\ *or* **spectrums** [NL, fr. L, appearance, image, specter — more at SPECTER] **1 a :** APPARITION, SPECTER **b :** AFTERIMAGE **2 :** an array of the components of an emission or wave separated and arranged in the order of some varying characteristic (as wavelength, mass, or energy): as **a :** a series of images formed when a beam of radiant energy is subjected to dispersion and brought to focus so that the component waves are arranged in the order of their wavelengths (as when a beam of sunlight that is refracted and dispersed by a prism forms a display of colors) — called also *color spectrum* **b :** ELECTROMAGNETIC SPECTRUM **c :** RADIO SPECTRUM **d** (1) **:** the range of frequencies of sound waves to which the human ear is sensitive — called also *acoustic spectrum, acoustical spectrum, sound spectrum* (2) **:** the range of frequencies of a particular sound (as a noise or a speech sound) **3 a :** an intergrading array in which the constituent elements are usu. not sharply isolable **:** a continuous sequence or range ⟨a wide ~ of opinions —Eugene Rabinowitch⟩ ⟨the total ~ of valid inference —J.T.Clark⟩ ⟨considerable deposits of a ~ of minerals ranging from platinum to mica —Smith Hempstone⟩ **b :** kinds of life forms associated with a particular situation (as an environmental region or sensitivity to an antibiotic); *also* **:** a conspectus of such forms

spectrum analysis *n* **:** the investigation of substances or bodies by means of their spectra; *specif* **:** SPECTROCHEMICAL ANALYSIS

spectrum-luminosity diagram *n* **:** a graph with the spectral type of each star plotted as the abscissa and the absolute magnitude as the ordinate

specula *pl of* SPECULUM

spec·u·lar \ˈspekyələ(r)\ *adj* [L *specularis* of a mirror, fr. *speculum* mirror + *-aris* -ar; in senses 3 & 4 influenced in meaning by L *speculari* to observe, examine — more at SPECULUM, SPECULATE] **1** *obs* **:** seen as if through a glass or in a mirror **:** REFLECTED **2 :** of, relating to, or having the qualities of a mirror **:** having a smooth reflecting surface or a metallic luster ⟨a ~ metal⟩ ⟨a ~ surface⟩ **3** *archaic* **:** concerned with, employed in, or assisting sight **4 :** offering an extensive prospect **:** providing a good view **5 :** of, relating to, or conducted with the aid of a medical speculum ⟨a ~ examination⟩ — **spec·u·lar·ly** *adv*

specular angle *n* **:** ANGLE OF REFLECTION

spec·u·lar·ia \,spekyəˈla(a)rēə\ *n* [NL, fr. ML *speculum Veneris* campanula, lit., mirror of Venus + NL *-aria*] **1** *cap* **:** a small genus of annual herbs (family Campanulaceae) distinguished from *Campanula* by the rotate corolla and narrowly oblong ovary — see CORN VIOLET, VENUS'S LOOKING-GLASS **2** -s **:** any plant of the genus *Specularia*

specular iron *or* **specular iron ore** *n* **:** hematite with a metallic luster — called also *specularite*

specular reflection *n* **:** reflection (as of light by a mirror) at a surface having irregularities small as compared with the wavelength of the incident radiation

spec·u·late \ˈspekyə,lāt *sometimes* ÷ -kə-; *usu* -ād·+V\ *vb* -ED/-ING/-S [L *speculatus*, past part. of *speculari* to spy out, observe, examine, fr. *specula* watchtower, fr. *specere* to look, catch sight of — more at SPY] *vt, archaic* **:** to mull over in the mind **:** consider attentively or as an object of study **:** reflect upon ~ *vi* **1 a :** to ponder a subject in its different aspects, relations, and implications **:** indulge in contemplation **:** evolve ideas or theories by mental reexamination of a subject or matter and usu. without experimentation or introduction of new data **b :** to reason a priori **c :** to review something mentally or orally in an idle or casual manner and usu. with an element of doubt or without sufficient evidence to reach a sound or meaningful conclusion ⟨*speculating* about the chances of rain⟩ ⟨we may ~ about strangers⟩ **2 :** to enter into a business transaction or other venture from which the profits, return of invested capital, or other good are conjectural because of the risks involved and knowingly assumed: as **a :** to purchase or sell with the expectation of profiting by anticipated but conjectural fluctuations in price **b :** to engage in hazardous business transactions for the chance of an unusually large profit; *esp* **:** to gamble on a stock or commodity market ⟨~ in coffee⟩ **syn** see THINK

spec·u·la·tion \ˌ==ˈlāshən\ *n* -s [ME, fr. LL *speculation-, speculatio* act of spying out, exploration, contemplation, fr. L *speculatus,* past part. of *speculari* to spy out, examine] **1 a** *archaic* **:** studious or profound consideration of some object or topic **b :** the faculty, act, or process of intellectual examination or investigation: as (1) **:** reasoning taking the form of prolonged and systematic analysis (2) **:** reasoning or theorizing about a matter that transcends experience and does not admit of demonstration **:** reasoning a priori (3) *Hegelianism* **:** reasoning that apprehends the unity of opposing categories, synthesizes them in a broader comprehension, and constitutes the thinking which explains objects of experience by their relation to the absolute personal reason **c :** contemplation or the theoretical as opposed to action or the practical **d :** light, casual, or superficial mental examination or study **:** mere guesswork or surmise ⟨his answer was obviously a product of ~ and not of serious thought⟩ **2** *archaic* **:** capacity for or exercise of the power of seeing: as **a :** comprehending or mental vision ⟨thou hast no ~ in those eyes —Shak.⟩ **b :** physical vision **:** the act of viewing **:** OBSERVATION **3 :** a product of speculation: as **a :** a view, conclusion, opinion, or decision based on thought or attained by reasoning **b :** GUESS, CONJECTURE **4** *obs* **:** OBSERVER **5 a :** an act of speculating (as by engaging in business out of the ordinary, by dealing with a view to making a profit from conjectural fluctuations in the price rather than from earnings of the ordinary profit of trade, or by entering into a business venture involving unusual risks for a chance of an unusually large gain or profit) or the condition of being speculated in ⟨uncontrolled ~ is a danger to the national economy⟩ ⟨land ~ in the 19th century was as common as stock ~ today⟩ — contrasted with *investment* **b :** an individual transaction so entered into ⟨had a successful ~ in cotton futures⟩ **6 :** a card game in which the players buy trumps from one another on a chance of getting the highest trump dealt and winning the pool

spec·u·la·tist \ˈ==ˌlād·əst\ *n* -s [*speculate* + *-ist*] **:** SPECULATOR

spec·u·la·tive \ˈspekyəˌlād·|iv, -ˌləd·|, |t|, |ēv *also* |əv\ *adj* [ME *speculatif,* fr. MF, fr. LL *speculativus,* fr. L *speculatus* + *-ivus* -ive] **1 a :** involving, based on, or constituting speculation **:** not established by demonstration **:** THEORETICAL ⟨a ~ approach to a problem⟩ ⟨~ knowledge⟩ ⟨~ aspects of religion⟩ **b :** given to speculation **:** inclined to make or accept conclusions based on theory rather than demonstration **:** interested in abstractions ⟨the ~ intelligence⟩ ⟨a ~ writer⟩ **c :** forming an object of speculation **:** not subject to clear-cut demonstration or analysis ⟨~ matters⟩ ⟨a ~ concept⟩ **d :** marked by questioning curiosity **:** seeming to speculate ⟨gave him a ~ glance⟩ **2 a** *obs* **:** relating to or concerned with vision **:** VISUAL **b :** giving a wide prospect or view **:** constituting a vantage point for seeing ⟨a ~ height⟩ **3 a :** engaging in or making a practice of taking risks esp. in commercial matters ⟨a ~ trader⟩ **b :** involving relatively high risk and usu. an unusual potentiality for gain ⟨a ~ enterprise⟩ ⟨a ~ crop⟩; *also* **:** appealing primarily to speculators ⟨a ~ stock⟩ ⟨a ~ situation on an exchange⟩ **c :** concerned with economic speculation ⟨a ~ cycle⟩ — **spec·u·la·tive·ly** \|əvlē, -li\ *adv* — **spec·u·la·tive·ness** \|ivnəs, |ēv- *also* |əv-\ *n* -ES

speculative damages *n pl* **:** possible damages (as loss of anticipated profits depending on contingencies) not recoverable at law for lack of reasonable proof thereof **:** conjectural or contingent damages

speculative issue *n* **:** an issue of postage stamps unnecessary for postal requirements prepared chiefly for sale to collectors

speculative philosophy *n* **1 :** a philosophy professing to be founded upon intuitive or a priori insight and esp. insight into the nature of the Absolute or Divine; *broadly* **:** a philosophy of the transcendent or one lacking empirical bases **2 :** theoretical as opposed to demonstrative philosophy

speculative reason *n* **:** reason concerned with the supersensible — used esp. in Kantianism

speculative theology *n* **:** theology founded on or fundamentally influenced by speculative or metaphysical philosophy

spec·u·la·tor \-ˌlād·ə(r), -ātə-\ *n* -s [L, spy, lookout, examiner, fr. *speculatus* (past part. of *speculari* to spy out, examine) + *-or* — more at SPECULATE] **:** one that speculates: as **a :** a person who devotes himself to mental speculation or abstract reasoning **:** CONTEMPLATOR, THEORIST **b** *obs* **:** OBSERVER, LOOKOUT; *also* **:** SPY **c :** a person who speculates in business **:** one that engages in speculation (as in stocks, bonds, real estate) — contrasted with *investor*

spec·u·la·to·ry \ˈ==ˌlaˌtōrē, -tȯrē, -ri\ *adj* [L *speculatus* + E *-ory*] **1** *obs* **:** concerned with or constituting occult speculation **2** *archaic* **:** SPECULATIVE 2b

spec·u·list \ˈspekyələst\ *n* -s [*speculate* + *-ist*] **:** one who observes or considers

spec·u·lum \-ləm\ *n, pl* **specu·la** \-lə\ *also* **speculums** [L, mirror, fr. *specere* to look, look at — more at SPY] **1 :** a tubular instrument for insertion into the opening of a passage of the body esp. to facilitate visual inspection or medication ⟨vaginal ~⟩ **2 a :** an ancient mirror usu. of bronze or silver **b :** a reflector of polished metal or of glass with a film of metal used in optical instruments **3 :** a medieval treatise constituting a survey of life or of philosophy, history, and theology **:** a comprehensive, encyclopedic presentation of a subject aiming to be a compendium of all knowledge and usu. beginning with the Biblical account of creation, giving an outline of history, and thence passing chiefly to theology and scholastic philosophy **4 :** a drawing or table showing the relative positions of all the planets (as in an astrological nativity) **5 :** a patch of color covering the distal portion of the secondaries of most ducks and some other birds (as domestic fowls), exposed in the closed wing, variously colored and often with bluish or greenish iridescence or a frame of a different color, and usu. most brilliant in the adult male

speculum metal *n* **:** an alloy capable of taking a brilliant polish, used for making reflectors, and being commonly a hard brittle alloy of copper and tin in various ratios (as tin 33 to copper 67) with often a little arsenic, antimony, or zinc added to improve the whiteness

spe·cus \ˈspēkəs\ *n, pl* **specuses** *or* **specus** [L, cave, cavity, drain, channel; prob. akin to L *specere* to look — more at SPY] **:** the roofed channel in which the water of an ancient Roman aqueduct flows whether underground or raised on embankments or arches

sped *past of* SPEED

¹speech \ˈspēch\ *n* -ES [ME *speche,* fr. OE *spǣc, spēc, sprǣc, sprēc;* akin to OHG *sprāhha* speech, OE *sprecan, specan* to speak — more at SPEAK] **1 a :** the act of speaking **:** communication or expression of thoughts in spoken words ⟨~ is a means of producing in our hearers the images which are in us —Bertrand Russell⟩ **b :** interchange of spoken words **:** CONVERSATION, TALK ⟨wayfarers, after a first greeting, frequently plod on for miles without ~ —Thomas Hardy⟩ ⟨wanted to have ~ with him and could not —Arnold Bennett⟩ **c :** the sounding or speaking of a musical instrument **d :** a form or method of expression or communication ⟨so profound and poignant is his musical ~ that there is no other eloquence like it —A.T.Davison⟩ ⟨if another ship ever broke into ~ with flags or lamp, most ships' officers of that time panicked —Gavin Douglas⟩ **2 a :** something that is spoken **:** an uttered word **:** STATEMENT ⟨this was nearer a complaint than any ~ she had ever heard from him —Ellen Glasgow⟩ **b :** a usu. formal discourse delivered before or to an audience ⟨will make a ~ to the nation on television⟩ ⟨the queen read her ~ from the throne⟩ ⟨an impromptu ~⟩ **c :** a line or group of lines spoken at one time by a character in a play ⟨one of the most moving ~*es* in the play⟩ ⟨a dramatist with a fondness for writing long ~*es*⟩ **3 a :** a form of spoken communication or expression developed by a particular group of people (as of a nation, region, or class) **:** a language, dialect, or idiom ⟨had to begin by studying their ~ and creating a written language —*Amer. Guide Series: Minn.*⟩ ⟨wrote several treatises in his native ~ —William Grant⟩ ⟨Midland ~⟩ **b :** a manner, style, or pattern of speaking characteristic of a particular individual **:** a distinctive phonetic quality ⟨his ~ is slipshod and unclear⟩ ⟨his ~ is a peculiar blend of New England and the South⟩ **4 a :** the faculty of uttering articulate sounds or words **:** the faculty of expressing thoughts by words or articulate sounds **:** the power of speaking ⟨we stood for some moments, silent and trembling . . . at length I found my ~ —W.H.Hudson †1922⟩ **b :** the art or technique of clear and effective speaking **:** ELOCUTION, PUBLIC SPEAKING ⟨~ is one of the oldest subjects of study in organized instruction —F.H.Knower⟩ **5** *archaic* **:** common report **:** MENTION, TALK ⟨what was the ~ among the Londoners concerning the French journey —Shak.⟩ **syn** see LANGUAGE

²speech \"\ *vb* -ED/-ING/-ES *vi* **:** to make a speech **~** *vt* **:** to speak or make a speech to

speech center *n* **:** a brain center exerting control over the power of speech and being commonly situated in the cortex at the third left frontal convolution

speech community *n* **:** a group of people sharing characteristic vocabulary and grammatical and pronunciation patterns for use in their normal intercommunication ⟨the global English-speaking *speech community*⟩ ⟨the little *speech community* in the body-repair shop⟩

speechcraft \ˈ=ˌ=\ *n* **:** skill in speech **:** RHETORIC

speech day *n* **:** the last day of the school year devoted to prize-giving and oral exercises at some British public schools

speech defect *n* **:** a defect in oral speech (as lisping or stuttering)

speech form *n* **:** LINGUISTIC FORM

speech·ful \ˈspēchfəl\ *adj* **:** full of speech **:** EXPRESSIVE, VOLUBLE — **speech·ful·ness** *n* -ES

speech house *or* **speech room** *n* **:** a room or hall used for audiences or conferences

speech·i·fi·ca·tion \ˌspēchəfəˈkāshən\ *n* -s [fr. *speechify,* after such pairs as E *specify: specification*] **:** the act or an instance of making speeches

speech·i·fi·er \ˈ==ˌfī(ə)r, -īə\ *n* -s [*speechify* + *-er*] **:** one that spouts speeches **:** DECLAIMER

speech·i·fy \-ˌfī\ *vi* -ED/-ING/-ES [¹*speech* + *-ify*] **:** to make a speech **:** DECLAIM, ORATE ⟨makes trips to ~ at industry conventions —F.C.Othman⟩ ⟨a good deal of pompous ~*ing* by the stay-at-homes —H.A.Overstreet⟩

speech island *n* [trans. of G *sprachinsel*] **:** a speech community within a different speech community ⟨Mexican Spanish *speech islands* in the southwestern U. S.⟩ — called also *linguistic island*

speech·less \ˈspēchləs\ *adj* [ME *specheles,* fr. OE *spǣclēas,* fr. *spǣc* speech + *-lēas* -less — more at SPEECH] **1 a :** unendowed with or deprived of the power of speech ⟨~ animals⟩ **b :** marked by lack of speech ⟨~ slumber⟩ ⟨~ death⟩ **2 a :** temporarily deprived of the ability to speak (as through injury, shock, or strong emotion) **:** struck dumb ⟨~ with exhaustion⟩ ⟨~ with grief⟩ **b :** refraining from speech **:** SILENT, RETICENT ⟨a shy and ~ person⟩ **c :** so as to deprive of speech **:** causing speechlessness ⟨the ~ fright of the captain —Herman Melville⟩ **3 a** *obs* **:** expressed or communicated without speech ⟨sometimes from her eyes I did receive fair ~ messages —Shak.⟩ **b :** done or experienced without speech **:** unattended by speech ⟨swaying back and forth in ~ content —Hamlin Garland⟩ **c :** not capable of being expressed in speech **:** beyond the power of speech ⟨a shape of ~ beauty did appear —P.B. Shelley⟩ **syn** see DUMB

speech·less·ly *adv* **:** in a speechless manner

speech·less·ness *n* -ES **:** the quality or state of being speechless

speechlike \ˈ=ˌ=\ *adj* **:** resembling speech

speechmaker \ˈ=ˌ==\ *n* **:** one who makes speeches

speechmaking \ˈ=ˌ==\ *n* **:** the act or practice of making speeches

speech melody *or* **speech tune** *n* **:** the intonation of connected speech **:** the continual rise and fall in pitch of the voice in speech

speech organ *n* **:** any of the organs (as the larynx, tongue, or lips) playing a part in the production of articulate speech

speech-prefix \ˈ=ˌ=ˌ=\ *n* **:** the usu. abbreviated name of a character in a play written or printed before each of his speeches in the play

speechreading \ˈ=ˌ==\ *n* **:** LIPREADING

speech situation *n* **:** an instance of communication having as prerequisites a speaker, an utterance, and a hearer who interprets the utterance

speech sound *n* **1 :** any one of the smallest recurrent recognizably same constituents of spoken language produced by movement or movement and configuration of a varying number of the organs of speech in an act of ear-directed communication **2 :** PHONE **3 :** PHONEME

speech stretcher *n* **:** an electronic instrument for speech analysis that halves the speed of recorded speech and avoids the reduced or lost intelligibility of reduced pitch by doubling the halved pitch

speechway \ˈ=ˌ=\ *n* **:** a mode of speech common to a particular people, group, or region ⟨in the home, the family, the school, and the neighborhood we learn the ~*s* of our community —D.J.Lloyd⟩

¹speed \ˈspēd\ *n* -s [ME *spede,* fr. OE *spēd;* akin to OHG *spuot* prosperity, success, speed, *spāti* late, Goth *spediza* latecomer, L *spes* hope, *spatium* space, Lith *spėtas* leisure, Skt *sphāra* extensive, *sphāyati* it increases, grows fat; basic meaning: to increase, expand] **1 a** *archaic* **:** good fortune **:** favorable issue **:** SUCCESS **b** *archaic* **:** something that falls to one's lot **:** FORTUNE ⟨send me good ~ this day, and show kindness unto my master —Gen 24:12 (AV)⟩ **c** *obs* **:** one that furthers success or provides favorable conditions ⟨now Hercules be thy ~, young man —Shak.⟩ **2 a :** the act, action, or state of moving swiftly **:** CELERITY, DISPATCH, SWIFTNESS ⟨this is the day of ~, of the atom, of wanting to get to places before you start —W.J.MacQueen-Pope⟩ ⟨the animal escaped pursuit by ~ rather than cunning⟩ **b :** rate of motion ⟨a heavy person who moved at a glacial ~⟩ ⟨drove at a reckless ~⟩; *specif* **:** rate of motion irrespective of direction **:** the magnitude of velocity expressed as a particular relationship ⟨the car maintained a ~ of 150 miles per hour⟩ ⟨a record made to be played at a ~ of 33⅓ revolutions per minute⟩ **c :** capacity or power of motion ⟨put all his ~ into the attempt to reach the ball before it hit the ground⟩ **d :** MOMENTUM ⟨set in motion an economic revival that gathered ~ with the hastening sense of crisis —Oscar Handlin⟩ **3 a :** swiftness of performance or execution **:** QUICKNESS ⟨as the minuteness of the parts formed a great hindrance to my ~, I resolved . . . to make the being of a gigantic stature —Mary W. Shelley⟩ ⟨a pastel sketch of flowers, full of life and ~ —Adrian Bell⟩ **b :** rate of performance or action ⟨trying to increase his reading ~⟩ **4 a :** the sensitivity of a photographic film, plate, or paper that is often expressed numerically according to one of several systems **b :** the light gathering power of a lens or optical system expressed as relative aperture **c :** the time during which a camera shutter is open **5 :** a transmission gear in automotive vehicles ⟨shift to low ~⟩ **6 a :** character or level of performance or activity ⟨they need a new night watchman at the dam; that's about your ~ —Elmer Davis⟩ **b :** a person or thing suited to one's tastes **:** CUP OF TEA ⟨bottled beer and a cigar are about their ~ —A.J. Liebling⟩ **7** *of a baseball pitcher* **:** ability to throw a fast ball ⟨has a good curve, but no ~⟩ **syn** see HASTE — **at speed** *adv* **:** RAPIDLY ⟨the motorboat swung in a half circle, bore down upon them *at speed* —Erle Stanley Gardner⟩ ⟨sailed *at speed* across the wind —Eileen Robertson⟩

²speed \"\ *vb* **sped** \ˈsped\ *or* **speeded; sped** *or* **speeded; speeding; speeds** [ME *speden,* fr. OE *spēdan;* akin to MD *spoeden* to speed, OS *spōdian* to prosper, OHG *spuoten* to prosper, succeed; derivative fr. the root of E ¹*speed*] *vi* **1 a :** to experience good fortune **:** fare well **:** PROSPER ⟨regarding the quality of the sheep the shepherds led, asking if the rams ~*ed* —George Moore⟩ **b :** to get along **:** FARE, SUCCEED ⟨a forlorn hope at the best . . . I should like to know how you ~ —Charles Dickens⟩ **2 a :** to go or pass quickly ⟨the work *sped* on at a commendable rate until completed —I.M.Price⟩ ⟨his college years *sped* by —Alexander MacDonald⟩ **b :** to move with speed **:** make haste ⟨ordered an automobile and *sped* directly to the village —H.F.Wilkins⟩ ⟨fighter planes which ~ to intercept and identify —*Lamp*⟩ **c :** to go or drive at an excessive speed ⟨was ~*ing* on the icy highway and the car skidded⟩; *specif* **:** to drive at an illegal speed **:** exceed the speed limit ⟨~*ed* for a while but slowed down when he saw a police car⟩ **3 :** to move, work, or take place at a faster rate — usu. used with *up* ⟨the heart ~*s* up and the blood pressure rises —H.G. Armstrong⟩ ⟨her embezzlements were ~*ing* up —R.T.Moriarty⟩ **~** *vt* **1 a** *archaic* **:** to cause or help to prosper **:** AID ⟨the Saxon bade God ~ him —Sir Walter Scott⟩ **b :** to promote the development or success of **:** ADVANCE, FURTHER ⟨two other things happened that *sped* the process —J.S.Martin⟩ ⟨increasing the supply of banknotes and ~*ing* the inflationary trend —R.A.Billington⟩ **c** *archaic* **:** to bring to a state of satisfaction or sufficiency **:** SATISFY **2 a :** to cause to move quickly **:** HASTEN ⟨*sped* our craft forward —Nora Waln⟩ ⟨he *sped* his pen to complete his treatises on government —U.B.Phillips⟩ ⟨a camaraderie which *sped* the evening hours away all too quickly —Gwen Allmon⟩ **b** (1) **:** to expedite the departure of **:** aid in going or traveling ⟨some villager's departing soul was being ritually *sped* on its difficult road from earth to paradise —Arthur Grimble⟩ ⟨cops obligingly scattering traffic to ~ us on our way —Bennett Cerf⟩ (2) **:** to say good-bye to ⟨~ the parting guest⟩ **c :** to increase the rate of motion or operation of **:** ACCELERATE — usu. used with *up* ⟨~*ed* up the engine⟩ ⟨~*ed* up production⟩ **3 :** to send out (as to a target) **:** DIRECT, DISCHARGE ⟨*sped* arrows from their heavy war bows —F.V.W. Mason⟩ ⟨these short essays . . . *sped* with so intense a seriousness —Edmund Wilson⟩ **4 a** *archaic* **:** to bring to completion **:** FINISH **b** *archaic* **:** DESTROY, KILL **5 :** to set, adjust, or design to or for a definite speed

syn ACCELERATE, QUICKEN, HASTEN, HURRY, PRECIPITATE: SPEED, although usu. throwing stress upon the rapidity of motion or progress ⟨bullets *sped* only a few feet over the Americans' heads —Dave Richardson⟩ ⟨poised to *speed* down the runway —Richard Thruelsen⟩ is also generally used to emphasize the becoming rapid or the achievement of such rapidity as by acceleration or increasing efficiency ⟨his heart *speeded* a little as he neared the cluster of tents —L.C.Douglas⟩ ⟨linked with fourteen miles of highway connections, it *speeds* traffic by shunting through-vehicles away from congested areas and carrying them swiftly across the boroughs —*Amer. Guide Series: N. Y. City*⟩ ACCELERATE emphasizes an increase in rate of motion or progress, not necessarily implying rapidity ⟨*accelerate* your pace⟩ ⟨efforts to *accelerate* our technological progress —H.M.Curtice⟩ ⟨the development of the steamboat *accelerated* the stream of farm products flowing toward the South —*Amer. Guide Series: Ind.*⟩ QUICKEN often adds to the idea of an increase in rapidity the notion of an increase in animation in the action, often also throwing stress upon the shortening of time consumed ⟨how our steps *quickened* when we heard the exhilarating notes of the trumpets and drums —G.E.Fox⟩ ⟨the pace of discovery in geology has been *quickened* by applying the principles and techniques of modern physics —*Scientific American Reader*⟩ HASTEN may add the notion of urgency or of an earlier or sometimes premature outcome ⟨assembled a force of volunteers and . . . *hastened* to the relief of the village —*Amer. Guide Series: Minn.*⟩ ⟨as rapidly as physics and electronics are *hastening* the future —*Time*⟩ HURRY sometimes suggests the notion of a disturbing acceleration of pace and a consequent disorder in the activity or progress ⟨*hurry* home after dark⟩ ⟨events which were *hurrying* the war to the close —H.E.Scudder⟩ ⟨the need for responsive action *hurries* us along and prevents us from ever realising fully what the emotion is that we feel —Roger Fry⟩ PRECIPITATE implies usu. an unexpectedly sudden or abrupt motion or progress ⟨at that instant two animals *precipitated* against his calves, thereby nearly unbalancing him —John Buchan⟩ ⟨one of the bitter disputes was *precipitated* by the question of women's suffrage —*Amer. Guide Series: Tenn.*⟩ ⟨the false charges that the radicals had maliciously *precipitated* the strike —Oscar Handlin⟩

³speed \"\ *adj* [¹*speed*] **:** of or relating to speed **:** regulating, indicating, or attaining speed

¹speedball \ˈ=ˌ=\ *n* **:** a game resembling soccer but permitting a ball caught in the air to be passed with the hands

²speedball \"\ *n, slang* **:** cocaine mixed with heroin or morphine

speedboat \ˈ=ˌ=\ *n* **:** a launch or powerboat designed for high speed

speed·boat·ing \ˈ=ˌ=ˌ=iŋ\ *n* **:** the act, art, or sport of managing a speedboat

speed box *n* **:** a box containing a speed-changing device for the main drive of a lathe or similar machine

speed change lane *also* **speed change area** *n* **:** an acceleration or deceleration lane

speed cone *n* **1 :** STEPPED PULLEY **2 :** one of a pair of conical pulleys connected by a short belt that can be adjusted to permit fine variations of speed

speed control *n* **:** equipment designed to operate automatically under certain conditions to keep the speed of a railroad train within a predetermined rate

speed counter *n* **:** a device for automatically counting the revolutions of an engine or other machine — called also *counter*

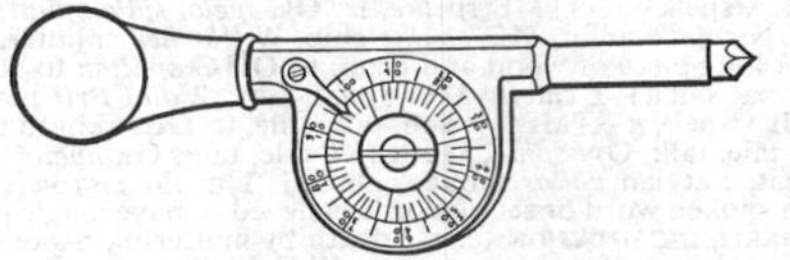

speed counter

speeded *past of* SPEED

speed·er \ˈspēdə(r)\ *n* -s [ME *speder,* fr. *spede* speed + *-er* — more at SPEED] **:** one that speeds: as **a :** any of various devices (as an attachment to a governor) for regulating the speed of a machine or part **b** *also* **speed frame :** a machine for drawing and twisting slivers to form rovings **c :** a small light usu. gasoline-operated vehicle with flanged wheels or solid rubber tires for operation on railroad tracks ⟨spent the next four days riding freight trains and gas ~*s* up and down the main line —H.L.Davis⟩ **d :** one who drives too fast or who exceeds the legal speed limit

speedflash \ˈ=ˌ=\ *n* **:** SPEEDLIGHT

speed·ful \ˈspēdfəl\ *adj* [ME *spedeful,* fr. *spede* speed + *-ful*] *archaic* **:** full of speed **:** RAPID, SPEEDY

speed gear *n* **:** CHANGE GEAR

speedgun \ˈ=ˌ=\ *n* **:** SYNCHRONIZER b

speed·i·ly \ˈspēdᵊl|ē, -dəl|, |i\ *adv* [ME *spedily,* fr. *spedy* speedy + *-ly*] **1 :** in a speedy manner **:** QUICKLY, RAPIDLY ⟨an object traveling ~ through the air⟩ **2 :** PROMPTLY, SOON ⟨you will ~ receive from me a letter of thanks for this —Jane Austen⟩

speed indicator *n* **1** *or* **speed gage a :** SPEED COUNTER **b :** TACHOMETER **2 :** a device (as a display of canvas cones, a flashing or steady display of lights, or a display of flags) for showing the speed of a ship to other vessels in a formation

speed·i·ness \ˈspēdēnəs, -din-\ *n* -ES **:** the quality or state of being speedy

¹speeding *adj* [fr. pres. part. of ²*speed*] **:** moving with speed ⟨a ~ car⟩ ⟨the ~ earth⟩ — **speed·ing·ly** *adv*

²speeding *n* -s [fr. gerund of ²*speed*] **:** the act or action of going fast; *specif* **:** the act of operating a motor vehicle at an excessive or illegal speed ⟨was arrested for ~⟩

speedlamp \ˈ=ˌ=\ *n* **:** SPEEDLIGHT

speed-length ratio *n* **:** the ratio of a ship's speed in knots divided by the square root of her length in feet

speed·less \ˈspēdləs\ *adj* [ME *spedeles,* fr. *spede* success, speed + *-les* -less] *archaic* **:** being without success

speedlight \ˈ=ˌ=\ *n* **:** an electronic flash lamp **:** FLASHTUBE, STROBE

speed limit *n* **:** the maximum speed permitted by law in a given area under specified circumstances

speed·om·e·ter \spəˈdäməd·ə(r), -mətə- *sometimes* spiˈd-\ *n* [¹*speed* + *-o-* + *-meter*] **1 :** an instrument for indicating speed or velocity **:** TACHOMETER **2 :** a device (as on an automobile) that measures distance as well as speed **:** ODOMETER

speed pulley *n* **:** SPEED CONE

speed reducer *n* **:** an apparatus for reducing speed

speeds *pl of* SPEED, *pres 3d sing of* SPEED

speed sprayer *n* : CONCENTRATE SPRAYER
speed·ster \'spēdztə(r), -dst-\ *n* -s [1*speed* + *-ster*] **1** : one that goes or moves at high speed : a person, animal, or vehicle that excels in speed **2** : SPEEDER d
speed test *n* : a psychological test for the maximum speed of performing a task that lies well within the subject's power — compare POWER TEST
speed trap *n* : a stretch of road watched by concealed officers or devices (as radar) to catch motorists who exceed a speed limit
speedup \'=,=\ *n* -s [fr. *speed up*, v.] **1** : the act or action of speeding up : ACCELERATION ⟨a ~ in research and industrial technology is an integral part of the defense program —*U.S. Code*⟩ **2** : an acceleration of the rate of output required of a worker by an employer without increase in pay
speedway \'=,=\ *n* **1** : a public road on which fast driving is allowed; *specif* : EXPRESSWAY **2** : a racecourse for automobiles or motorcycles
speed·well \'spē,dwel\ *n* -s [1*speed* + *well*] : an herb of the genus *Veronica; esp* : a common hairy perennial European herb (*V. officinalis*) with pale blue or lilac flowers in axillary racemes
speedy \'spēdē, -di\ *adj* -ER/-EST [ME *spedy*, fr. *spede* speed + *-y* — more at SPEED] **1** : rapid in motion : going or able to go quickly : SWIFT ⟨forced in time of war to use the heavier= type ~ vehicles —John Kemp⟩ ⟨a ~ runner⟩ **2** : marked by swiftness of motion or action : occurring, accomplished, or arrived at quickly ⟨a ~ journey⟩ ⟨a ~ recovery⟩ ⟨the ~ exhaustion of the soils that were being recklessly cropped —Lewis Mumford⟩ **3** : prompt in action or performance : QUICK ⟨the medication is ~ and effective⟩ **syn** see FAST
speedy cut *or* **speedy cutting** *n* : an injury to a horse's foreleg below the knee that is caused by the shoe of the opposite foot in running
1speel \'spē(ə)l\ *n* -s [ME, of Scand origin; akin to Norw *spel* flat stick, splinter, Sw *spjäla;* akin to ON *spjald* square tablet, OHG *spaltan* to split — more at SPILL] *dial chiefly Brit* : SPLINTER, STRIP
2speel \"\ *vb* -ED/-ING/-S [origin unknown] : CLIMB
speen·ham·land system \(')spēn¦hamlənd-\ *n, usu cap 1st S* [fr. *Speenhamland*, England, where it was first used] : a system of supplementing rural wage payments from local taxes first used in England in the latter part of the 18th century
1speer *or* **speir** \'spēr\ *vb* -ED/-ING/-S [ME (Sc) *speren, spiren*, fr. OE *spyrian* to seek after, follow a track; akin to ON *spyrja* to follow a track, *spor* spoor — more at SPOOR] *chiefly Scot* : ASK, INQUIRE
2speer \'spi(ə)r\ *n* -s [ME *spere*] *dial Eng* : SCREEN, PARTITION
speer·ings \'spērənz, -riŋz\ *n pl* [ME (Sc) *speringes, spiringes*, pl. of *spering, spiring* inquiry, information obtained by inquiry, fr. gerund of *speren, spiren* to inquire] : NEWS, TIDINGS
speis·ko·balt *also* **speiss·co·balt** \'s(h)pī,skō,bȯlt *also* -bält\ *n* -s [G *speiskobalt*, fr. *speise* speiss + *kobalt* cobalt] : SMALTITE
speiss \'s(h)pīs\ *n* -ES [G *speise*, lit., food, fr. OHG *spīsa*, fr. (assumed) VL *spesa*, fr. LL *expensa* expense — more at EXPENSE] : a mixture of impure metallic arsenides produced as a regulus in smelting certain ores — compare MATTE
spek·boom \'spek,büm, -bōm\ *n* -s [Afrik, lit., fat tree, blubber tree, fr. D *spek* fat, blubber, bacon (fr. MD *spec*) + *boom* tree, fr. MD; akin to OHG *boum* tree — more at SPECK, BEAM] : PURSLANE TREE
speke's antelope \'spēks-\ *n, usu cap S* [after John H. *Speke* †1864 Eng. African explorer] : SITATUNGA
spe·lae·an *also* **spe·le·an** \spə'lēən, (')spē¦l-\ *adj* [L *spelaeum*, *speleum* cave (fr. Gk *spēlaion*) + E *-an*] : dwelling or occurring in a cave
spel·der \'speldər\ *vb* -ED/-ING/-S [obs. E *speld* to split open, spread open (fr. ME *spelden*, prob. alter. — influenced by *spelde* splinter — of *spalden* to split, spread open, fr. MLG, fr. OHG *spaltan* to split) + E *-er* (as in *batter*) — more at SPILL] *vt, chiefly Scot* : SPLIT ~ *vi, chiefly Scot* : STRETCH, SPRAWL
speld·ing \'spel(d)ən\ *n* -s [prob. fr. obs. E *speld* to split open + E *-ing*] *Scot* : STOCKFISH 1a
spel·dring *also* **spel·dron** \'speldrən\ *n* -s [*speldring* prob. fr. *spelder* + *-ing; speldron* alter. of *speldring*] *Scot* : STOCKFISH 1a
spele·o·log·i·cal *also* **spelae·o·log·i·cal** \¦spēlēə¦läjəkəl, -pel-\ *adj* [*speleological* fr. *speleology* + *-ical; spelaeological* alter. (influenced by *spelaean*) of *speleological*] : of or relating to speleology
spele·ol·o·gist \,==ˈäləjəst\ *n* -s [ISV *speleology* + *-ist*] : a specialist in speleology
spele·ol·o·gy \-jē\ *n* -ES [ISV *speleo-* (fr. L *speleum* cave, fr. Gk *spēlaion*) + *-logy*; akin to Gk *spēlunx* cave, *speos* cave, grotto] : the scientific study or systematic exploration of caves
speleo·them \'=ə,them\ *n* -s [*speleo-* (fr. L *speleum* cave) + *-them* (fr. Gk *thema* something laid down, deposit) — more at THEME] : a cave deposit or formation
spelican *var of* SPILLIKIN
spelk \'spelk\ *n* -s [ME *spelke*, fr. OE *spelc, spilc* splint; akin to ON *spjalk* splint, MD *spalke* chip, W *fflochen* splinter, Arm *p'elk* long piece of wood and prob. to OHG *spaltan* to split — more at SPILL] **1** *chiefly Scot* : SPLINTER **2** *dial Brit* : SPAR 3
1spell \'spel\ *n* -s [ME, speech, talk, tale, fr. OE; akin to OHG *spel* tale, talk, ON *spjall*, Goth *spill* tale, talk, Gk *apeilē* boast, threat, Latvian *pal'as* rebuke, abuse] **1 a** *obs* : STORY, TALE **b** : a spoken word or set of words believed to have magic power : CHARM, INCANTATION ⟨cause death by muttering ~s over the young shoots of a certain tree —W.D.Wallis⟩ **c** : a state of enchantment ⟨it was the voice that cracked the ~ — that pleasant, homely, wheedling voice which brought with it daylight and common sense —John Buchan⟩ **2** : a strong compelling influence or attraction ⟨even . . . enemies were unable to resist the ~ of his presence —Alvin Redman⟩ ⟨writing under the ~ of the slavery controversy —R.A.Billington⟩
2spell \"\ *vt* **spelled** \-ld\ **spelled; spelling; spells** : to put under or as if under a spell : BEWITCH, CHARM ⟨used witchcraft all these years to ~ the ladies —Ray Bradbury⟩
3spell \"\ *vb* **spelled** \-ld,-lt\ *or chiefly Brit* **spelt** \-lt\ **spelled** *or chiefly Brit* **spelt; spelling; spells** [ME *spellen*, fr. OF *espeller*, of Gmc origin; akin to OE *spellian* to relate, talk, MHG *spellen*, ON *spialla* to talk, mention, Goth *spillon* to relate; denominative fr. the root of E 1*spell*] *vt* **1** : to read slowly and with difficulty ⟨yourselves may ~ it yet in chronicles —Robert Browning⟩ — often used with *out* ⟨laboriously ~ out a newspaper —*Time*⟩ **2 a** : to find out by study or investigation : DISCOVER — often used with *out* ⟨~ out a God in the works of creation —Robert Southey⟩ **b** : COMPREHEND, UNDERSTAND — often used with *out* ⟨found it hard to ~ out his meaning⟩ **c** : to give thought to : CONSIDER — often used with *over* ⟨she *spelt* over the names of the guests at the houses —George Meredith⟩ **3 a** : to name in order the letters of ⟨~*ed* the word correctly⟩ ⟨~*ed* the word incorrectly with two *e's*⟩ : write or print in order the letters of ⟨the two writers ~ the word in two different ways⟩ **b** : to make up (a word) : FORM, COMPOSE ⟨what word do these letters ~⟩ ⟨put the cards through a decoding machine to find out that the holes ~*ed* "order now" —F.W.Boardman⟩ **4** : to add up to : amount to : MEAN, SIGNIFY ⟨sensitiveness without impulse ~*s* decadence —A.N.Whitehead⟩ ⟨crop failure was likely to ~ stark famine —Stringfellow Barr⟩ ~ *vi* **1** : to form words with letters, symbols, or signs ⟨writes well, but ~*s* badly⟩ ⟨~*ed* with difficulty on his fingers —Helen Keller⟩ **2** : to make a suggestion : ASK, HINT ⟨never saw anybody in my life ~ harder for an invitation —Jane Austen⟩
4spell \"\ *n* -s [prob. alter. of ME *speld, spelde* spark, flake, splinter, fr. OE *speld* torch, ember; akin to Goth *spilda* tablet, Gk *sphallein* to cause to fall, OHG *spaltan* to split; basic meaning: split piece of wood — more at SPILL] **1** *dial chiefly Brit* : SPLINTER, FRAGMENT **2** *dial chiefly Eng* : BAR, RUNG **3** : the trap in the game of knur and spell **4** : a splinter raised from the back of an archery bow
5spell \"\ *vb* -ED/-ING/-S [ME *spelen* to spare, leave over, substitute, represent, fr. OE *spelian* to stand in the place of, represent; akin to OE *spala* substitute] *vt* **1** : to supply the place of for a time : take the turn of : RELIEVE ⟨four-carrier teams ~ each other every 15 minutes —*Nat'l Geographic*⟩ ⟨he and the other assistant stage managers ~*ed* each other —Mary McCarthy⟩ **2** : to allow an interval of rest to : REST ⟨it was midday, and we squatted there, ~*ing* the camels —I.L.Idriess⟩ **3** *Austral* : to interrupt grazing of (pasture) esp. in order to prevent transmission of disease among grazing animals ~ *vi* **1** : to work in turns ⟨she had learned to ~ at the oars and help in the camp work —Arthur Mayse⟩ **2** : to rest from work or activity for a time
6spell \"\ *n* -s [prob. alter. (influenced by ME *spelen* to substitute) of ME *spale* substitute, fr. OE *spala*] **1 a** *archaic* : a shift of workers **b** : a period of work taken by an individual or group in rotation with others : TURN ⟨as this work has to be done standing, it is generally shared between the assistants in ~*s* lasting perhaps three hours —*Choice of Careers: Librarianship*⟩ **2 a** : an unbroken period spent in a specified job, occupation, or situation : HITCH ⟨a ~ of clerking . . . during his teens —Jerome Ellison⟩ ⟨a ~ of service in the tropics —D.W.Brogan⟩ ⟨became involved in a gambling scandal and did a ~ in prison —*Times Lit. Supp.*⟩ **b** *chiefly Austral* : a period of rest from work, activity, or use ⟨the tired musterers sitting down . . . and having a ten minutes' ~ and half a pipe —Mary S. Broome⟩ ⟨the motor bike was getting a ~ —F.S. Anthony⟩ **3 a** : an indeterminate period of time ⟨mark time for a ~ —*English Digest*⟩ ⟨a long ~ when he appeared to be petering out —A.M.Mizener⟩ **b** : a stretch of a specified type of weather ⟨a ~ of rain⟩ ⟨a long cold ~⟩ **4** : a period marked by illness, depression, or other abnormal physical or mental state ⟨take me some time to get her to her room if she has one of her weak ~*s* —Robertson Davies⟩ ⟨you mustn't excite yourself . . . you've had a bad ~ —Berton Roueché⟩ : a seizure of some specified sickness or symptom : ATTACK ⟨a ~ of dizziness, like a cough, is then a danger sign —Morris Fishbein⟩ ⟨prolonged coughing ~*s* —H.G.Armstrong⟩ — **by spells** *adv* : INTERMITTENTLY ⟨*by spells* she wept —Winston Churchill⟩
spell·able \'speləbəl\ *adj* : capable of being spelled
spell·bind \'spel¦bīnd\ *vt* [fr. *spellbound*, after E 4*bound*: 1*bind*] : to bind or hold by or as if by a spell or charm : CHARM, FASCINATE ⟨~*ing* her little brother with tales of the wondrous anemones she had seen —P.A.Zahl⟩
spell·bind·er \-,bīndə(r)\ *n* : one that spellbinds ⟨because he is a poet he is a ~ —Gerald Bullett⟩; *specif* : a speaker (as a political orator, actor, or lecturer) able to seize and hold the attention of an audience by force of personality or eloquence ⟨a local ~ swayed the meeting into voting a resolution —John Bird⟩ ⟨the flashy ~ who popularizes himself instead of his subject —J.R.Adams⟩
spellbound \'=¦=\ *adj* [1*spell* + *bound*] : held by or as if by a spell : FASCINATED ⟨can hold a reader almost ~ through every chapter —J.W.Lippincott⟩
spell down *vt* : to defeat in a spelling match
spelldown \'=,=\ *n* -s : a spelling match that begins with all the contestants standing and ends when all but one have been forced by the rules to sit down after misspelling a word
spelled *past of* SPELL
1spell·er \'spelə(r)\ *n* -s [ME, fr. *spellen* to spell + *-er*] **1** : one that spells words ⟨the best ~ in the class⟩ **2** : SPELLING BOOK
2spell·er \"\ *n* -s [perh. fr. 4*spell* + *-er*] : a small branch from the crown of a deer's antler
spell·ful \'spelfəl\ *adj* : full of spells : ENCHANTING
spellican *var of* SPILLIKIN
spelling *n* -s [ME, fr. gerund of *spellen* to spell — more at SPELL] **1 a** : the act of one who spells : the formation of words by letters ⟨his ~ has improved⟩ **b** : the art or technique of forming words by letters according to accepted usage : ORTHOGRAPHY ⟨~ as a subject of instruction is in need of reexamination —*Education Digest*⟩ **2** : a sequence of letters composing a word ⟨where the dictionaries differed, either ~ would do —*Time*⟩
spelling bee *n* : a spelling match : SPELLDOWN
spelling book *n* : a book with exercises for teaching how to spell
spelling-bound \'==,=\ *adj* : deaf to or intolerant of a pronunciation because of its discrepancy with its orthographic representation ⟨too *spelling-bound* to realize that the best= educated speakers often say \'sebᵊm\ for *seven*⟩
spelling pronunciation *n* : pronunciation of a word in which letters or syllables are given their usual sounds in analogous situations rather than the sounds heard among speakers who make greatest use of the word ⟨\'wō(r),sestə(r)\ instead of \'wu̇stə(r)\ for *Worcester*, or \'bōt,swān\ instead of \'bōsᵊn\ for *boatswain* are *spelling pronunciations*⟩
spelling reform *n* : a movement to modify conventional spellings so as to lessen or remove the differences between the orthography and the pronunciation of words — compare REFORMED SPELLING
spelling school *n* : a spelling match in rural schools esp. of the 19th century often serving as the occasion for a social event
spell out *vt* : to explain or state explicitly in unmistakable terms ⟨these views will be further *spelled out* in future speeches —*Newsweek*⟩ ⟨in a brief, seemingly unambitious book, without *spelling* anything *out* . . . gets a great deal said —*Time*⟩
spells *pl of* SPELL, *pres 3d sing of* SPELL
1spelt \'spelt\ *n* -s [ME, fr. OE, fr. LL *spelta*, of Gmc origin; akin to MHG & MD *spelte* split piece of wood, OHG *spaltan* to split; prob. fr. the splitting of the husk during threshing — more at SPILL] : a wheat (*Triticum spelta*) that is of no commercial importance in America but is grown to some extent in Germany and Switzerland and that has lax spikes with spikelets containing two light red kernels — called also *speltz;* compare EMMER
2spelt *chiefly Brit past of* SPELL
1spel·ter \'speltə(r)\ *n* -s [prob. modif. (influenced by It *peltro* pewter) of MD *speauter* spelter — more at PEWTER] **1** : ZINC; *esp* : zinc cast in slabs for commercial use **2** : SPELTER SOLDER
2spelter \"\ *vt* -ED/-ING/-S : to solder with an alloy high in zinc
spelter solder *n* : a zinc solder (as one of three parts of zinc to four of copper) used in soldering copper, iron, and brass
spelt·oid \'spel,tȯid\ *n* -s [1*spelt* + *-oid*] : a variant in wheat having certain characteristics of spelt
speltz \'s(h)pelts\ *n* -ES [G *spelz* spelt, fr. OHG *spelza, spelta*, fr. LL *spelta* — more at SPELT] **1** : SPELT **2** : any of several varieties of emmer
spe·lun·car \spə'ləŋkə(r), (')spē¦l-\ *adj* [L *spelunca* cave + E *-ar*] : of or relating to a cave
spe·lunk·er \-ŋkə(r)\ *n* -s [obs. E *spelunk* cave (fr. ME, fr. MF or L) + E *-er;* MF *spelunque*, fr. L *spelunca*, fr. Gk *spēlunx* — more at SPELEOLOGY] : one who makes a hobby of exploring and studying caves : CAVER — compare SPELEOLOGIST
spe·lunk·ing \-kiŋ\ *n* -s [obs. E *spelunk* cave + E *-ing*] : the hobby or practice of exploring caves
spence \'spen(t)s\ *n* -s [ME *spence, spense*, fr. MF *despense* place for storing supplies, supplies — more at DISPENSE] **1** *dial Brit* **a** : PANTRY **b** : CUPBOARD **2** *Scot* : an inner room usu. near the kitchen
1spen·cer \'spen(t)sə(r)\ *n* -s [after George John, 2d earl *Spencer* †1834 Eng. politician] **1** : a short double-breasted overcoat or jacket worn by men esp. in the 19th century **2** : a woman's fitted jacket of waist length or shorter
2spencer \"\ *n* -s [prob. fr. the name *Spencer*] **1** : a fore-and-aft sail formerly used abaft the foremast or the mainmast, hoisted upon a small supplementary mast, and set with a gaff and no boom **2** : a trysail abaft the foremast or mainmast

spencer 2

1spen·ce·ri·an \(')spen¦sirēən, -¦sēr-\ *adj, usu cap* [Herbert *Spencer* †1903 Eng. philosopher + E *-ian* (adj. suffix)] : of or relating to the philosopher Spencer or Spencerianism
2spencerian \"\ *n* -s *usu cap* [Herbert *Spencer* †1903 + E *-ian* (n. suffix)] : a follower of Spencer
3spencerian \"\ *adj, usu cap* [Platt Rogers *Spencer* †1864 Am. calligrapher the originator of the handwriting + E *-ian*] : of, relating to, or characteristic of a form of slanting handwriting
spen·ce·ri·an·ism \=ˈ==ə,nizəm\ *n* -s *usu cap* : the synthetic philosophy of Spencer that has as its central idea the evolution of the cosmos from relative simplicity to relative complexity through the operation of mechanical forces with the acme of evolution being the equilibration of these forces after which dissolution begins and the cosmos goes back to the ultimate state from which evolution started
spen·cer·ism \'spen(t)sə,rizəm\ *n* -s *usu cap* [Herbert *Spencer* †1903 Eng. philosopher + E *-ism*] : SPENCERIANISM
spen·cer·ite \-rīt\ *n* -s [Leonard J. *Spencer* †1959 Eng. mineralogist + E *-ite*] : a mineral $Zn_4(PO_4)_2(OH)_2.3H_2O$ consisting of a hydrous basic zinc phosphate occurring in pearly white scaly masses and small monoclinic crystals (hardness 2.7, sp. gr. 3.1)
spencer mast *n* : a small mast just abaft the foremast or mainmast and used to hoist the spencer
spen·cer roll \'spen(t)sə(r)-\ *n, usu cap S* [prob. after the name *Spencer*] : beef trimmed from the ribs, rolled, and used for short steaks or for a roast
1spend \'spend\ *vb* **spent** \-nt\ **spent; spending; spends** [ME *spenden*, fr. OE & OF; OE *spendan*, fr. L *expendere* to weigh out, expend; OF *despendre*, fr. L *dispendere* to weigh out — more at EXPEND, DISPENSE] *vt* **1** : to distribute or consume in payment or expenditure : pay out : EXPEND, DISBURSE ⟨~*s* money freely⟩ ⟨*spent* his inheritance within a few years⟩ **2 a** : to exhaust or wear out by use or activity ⟨the silver agitation had by this time *spent* its force —Marian Silveus⟩ ⟨gradually the hurricane *spent* itself —Francis Robinson⟩ ⟨*spent* himself in the service of humanity —D.S. & Jessie Jordan⟩ **b** : to make use of : EMPLOY ⟨prehistorians have *spent* their learning and ingenuity on reconstructing continental invasions —Jacquetta & Christopher Hawkes⟩ ⟨determined to ~ these new bullets . . . more profitably —H.H. Arnold & I.C.Eaker⟩ **c** : to consume wastefully : SQUANDER ⟨~ your rich opinion for the name of a night-brawler —Shak.⟩ **d** *archaic* : DESTROY **3** : to cause or permit to elapse : use the interval of : PASS ⟨have *spent* the greater part of the last year going up and down the countryside —S.P.B.Mais⟩ ⟨~*s* three hours a day on his studies⟩ ⟨*spent* his life in a quiet village⟩ ⟨~ the evening with his friends⟩ **4** : to give up : endure the loss of ⟨to royalize his blood, I *spent* my own —Shak.⟩ ⟨the ship *spent* its mast⟩ ~ *vi* **1** : to expend money or other possession ⟨~*s* without any thought for the next day⟩ **2** *chiefly dial* : to turn out or produce in a specified manner **3** : to become expended ⟨I have no skill to make money ~ well —R.W.Emerson⟩
syn EXPEND, DISBURSE: SPEND is the general term indicating a paying out of money or, sometimes, incurring obligations calling for its being paid ⟨*spend* a hundred dollars for a coat⟩ ⟨*spending* billions on wars⟩ It may apply to using, consuming, or exhausting without tangible or specific return ⟨*spend* time on the project⟩ ⟨*spend* one's life in government service⟩ EXPEND is often but not always applied to larger sums or more important materials and attributes ⟨more than twenty million dollars has been *expended* in the construction —*Amer. Guide Series: N.Y.City*⟩ ⟨during the war years we have *expended* our resources — both human and natural — without stint —H.S. Truman⟩ ⟨this eloquence was always *expended* in expounding the duties of the citizen —H.L.Mencken⟩ DISBURSE is sometimes interchangeable with EXPEND; it indicates a paying out or distributing, often from a public or corporation fund, sometimes by a person or agency other than the one doing the spending or expending ⟨state and federal funds *disbursed* for roads aggregated $34,514,584 —James Brewster⟩ ⟨waiting for the teller to *disburse* those complex payroll accounts —Christopher Morley⟩
— **spend one's mouth** *obs* : give tongue : BARK ⟨coward dogs most *spend their mouths* when what they seem to threaten runs far before them —Shak.⟩
2spend \"\ *n* -s : the act or process of spending money — used in the phrase *on the spend*
spend·able \'spendəbəl\ *adj* : capable of being spent : available for spending ⟨~ income⟩
spend-all \'=,=\ *n* : SPENDTHRIFT
spend·er \'spendə(r)\ *n* -s [ME, fr. *spenden* to spend + *-er*] **1** : one that spends money; *esp* : one that spends lavishly : SPENDTHRIFT ⟨had become a ~ in his middle age —John Lardner⟩ **2** : one that uses up ⟨the most colossal ~*s* of resources in our history —Julian Dana⟩
spending *n* -s [ME, partly fr. gerund of *spenden* to spend & partly fr. OE *spendung*, fr. *spendan* to spend + *-ung* -ing — more at SPEND] **1** : the act of spending : EXPENDITURE ⟨the level of government ~⟩ **2** : the act of consuming : CONSUMPTION
spending money *n* : POCKET MONEY
spending unit *n* : an individual living alone or a family living together and pooling incomes to meet expenses
1spend·thrift \'spen(d),thrift\ *n* [1*spend* + *thrift* (savings)] **1** : one that spends or uses improvidently or wastefully ⟨mobilizing the populace against ~*s* at the public trough —J.R.Aswell & E.J.Michelson⟩ **2** : one who spends his estate (as by drinking or gambling) so as to expose himself or his family to want or suffering or to becoming a charge upon the public
2spendthrift \"\ *adj* : given to or marked by improvident expenditure or use : WASTEFUL ⟨~ property owners who have lived beyond their incomes —G.B.Shaw⟩ ⟨~ duplication of work —H.N.Southern⟩
spendthrift clause *n* : a provision sometimes included in a life insurance policy prohibiting the beneficiary from assigning or anticipating payments coming due and exempting such payments from the claims of creditors of the beneficiary
spend·thrift·i·ness \-ftēnəs, -ftin-\ *n* : the quality or state of being spendthrift : IMPROVIDENCE, WASTEFULNESS ⟨an almost incredible ~ of energy and talent —Carlos Baker⟩
spendthrift trust *n* : a trust created to provide a fund for the maintenance of another and to secure it (as by withholding from him the power to alienate his interest or put a charge upon it or to anticipate or assign the income) against his improvidence or incapacity
spend·thrifty \-ftē, -fti\ *adj* : SPENDTHRIFT
spe·ner·ism \'s(h)pānə,rizəm\ *n* -s *usu cap* [Philipp Jacob *Spener* †1705 Ger. Protestant theologian + E *-ism*] : the pietistic teaching of Spener
1spen·gle·ri·an \(')s(h)peŋ¦(g)lirēən\ *adj, usu cap* [Oswald *Spengler* †1936 Ger. writer on philosophy of history who developed the theory + E *-ian* (adj. suffix)] : of or relating to a theory of world history that holds that major cultures (as the Egyptian, Chinese, or Mayan) undergo similar cyclical developments from birth to maturity to decay, that modern western civilization also is undergoing such a development, and that its decline is consequently predictable
2spenglerian \"\ *n* -s *usu cap* [Oswald *Spengler* †1936 + E *-ian* (n. suffix)] : a follower of the historian Spengler or an advocate of a Spenglerian philosophy of history
spen·se·ri·an \(')spen¦sirēən, -¦sēr-\ *adj, usu cap* [Edmund *Spenser* †1599 Eng. poet + E *-ian*] : of or relating to the poet Spenser or his works
spenserian sonnet *n, usu cap 1st S* : a sonnet in which the lines are grouped into three interlocked quatrains and a couplet and the rhyme scheme is *abab, bcbc, cdcd, ee*
spenserian stanza *n, usu cap 1st S* : a stanza consisting of eight iambic pentameter lines and an alexandrine and having the rhyme scheme *ababbcbcc*
spent \'spent\ *adj* [ME, fr. past part. of *spenden* to spend — more at SPEND] **1 a** : used up : CONSUMED, EXPENDED ⟨the smell of ~ powder —R.H.Newman⟩ ⟨the air, breathed many times and ~ —Edna S. V. Millay⟩ **b** : exhausted of active or effective quality or components ⟨~ fuller's earth⟩ ⟨~ tanbark⟩ ⟨~ grain⟩ **2** : drained of energy or vitality : worn out : EXHAUSTED ⟨saw him come creeping home at dawn, panting and ~ —Pearl Buck⟩ ⟨two ~ old women —Edith Wharton⟩ **3** : exhausted of spawn or sperm — used esp. of fishes or of insects that have laid all their eggs; compare RIPE **4** *of an artificial fly* : tied to imitate the drooping wings of a natural insect that has dropped its eggs or is exhausted
spent acid *n* : acid weakened by use: as **a** : mixed acid that has been used in nitration **b** : acid that has been used in pickling metal articles
spent lye *n* : the alkaline glycerol-containing liquor that results on saponification of fat with boiling lye solution in soapmaking and that is drawn off after cooling from the floating curd
spent oxide *n* : iron oxide that has been used in gas manufacture to purify coal gas by removing chiefly hydrogen sulfide and sometimes cyanogen, that generally has formed a coating on shavings and sawdust, and that may be used as a source of sulfur and of cyanogen compounds

spe·os \'spē,äs\ *n* -ES [Gk, cave — more at SPELEOLOGY] **:** an ancient Egyptian cave temple or tomb

speo·ty·to \,spēə'tīd·(,)ō\ *n, cap* [NL, fr. Gk *speos* cave + *tytō* night owl] **:** a genus of owls (family Strigidae) consisting of the burrowing owls

spe·rate \'spi,rāt\ *adj* [L *speratus*, past part. of *sperare* to hope; akin to L *spes* hope — more at SPEED] *archaic* **:** hoped for **:** to be hoped for; *esp* **:** giving some hope of being paid

spere *obs var of* ¹SPEER

sper·gu·la \'spərgyələ\ *n, cap* [NL, fr. ML, spurry, prob. fr. *spergere* to scatter, strew (alter. of L *spargere*) + L *-ula*, dim. suffix — more at SPARK] **:** a small genus of Old World annual herbs (family Caryophyllaceae) having subulate fascicled leaves, terminal cymes of pentamerous small white flowers, and 5-valved capsules — see CORN SPURRY

sper·gu·lar·ia \,=='la(a)rēə\ *n, cap* [NL, fr. *Spergula* + *-aria*] **:** a genus of chiefly maritime herbs (family Caryophyllaceae) with linear or setaceous and often fleshy leaves and pink or white flowers — see SAND SPURRY

sper·ling \'spərliŋ, -lən\ *n, pl* **sperling** *or* **sperlings** [ME — more at SPARLING] **1** *dial Brit* **:** SMELT; *esp* **:** SPARLING **2 :** a young herring

sperm \'spərm, -pəm,-pəim\ *n, pl* **sperm** *or* **sperms** [ME *sperme*, fr. MF *esperme*, fr. LL *spermat-, sperma*, fr. Gk; akin to Gk *speirein* to sow — more at SPROUT] **1 a :** the male fecundating fluid **:** SEMEN **b :** a male gamete: (1) **:** SPERMATOZOON (2) **:** SPERMATOZOID (3) **:** a sperm nucleus of an angiosperm **2** *archaic* **:** the seed, germ, or originative matter from which something develops **3 a :** SPERM WHALE **b :** a product of the sperm whale (as spermaceti or sperm oil)

sperm- *or* **spermo-** *or* **sperma-** *or* **spermi-** *comb form* [Gk *sperm-, spermo-*, fr. *spermat-, sperma* seed, sperm] **:** seed **:** germ **:** sperm **:** semen ⟨*spermophile*⟩ ⟨*sperm*angium⟩ ⟨*sperma*theca⟩ ⟨*sperm*idine⟩ ⟨*spermi*duct⟩

-sper·ma \"\ *n comb form* [NL, fr. fem. sing. of *-spermus* -spermous] **:** one having (such) a seed or germ — in generic names of plants ⟨Lepido*sperma*⟩

sper·ma·ceti \,==‘sēd·ē, -'sel, |tl, |ī\ *n* -S [ME *sperma cete*, fr. ML *sperma ceti* whale sperm, fr. LL *sperma* sperm + L *ceti*, gen. of *cetus* whale; fr. the belief that it was the coagulated semen of the whale — more at CETE] **1** *also* **spermaceti wax :** a white crystalline waxy solid that separates from sperm oil esp. from the head cavities and from the oils of related cetaceans, consists principally of cetyl palmitate and other esters of fatty acids, and is used chiefly in ointments, cosmetic creams, and candles **2 :** sperm oil containing spermaceti

sper·ma·duct *or* **sper·mi·duct** *or* **sper·mo·duct** \'==mə,dəkt\ *n* [*sperm-* + *duct*] **:** SPERMATIC DUCT

-sper·mae \'spər(,)mē, -pə(-, -pəi(-, -,mī\ *or* **-sper·me·ae** \-,mē,ē, -mē,ī\ *n pl comb form* [NL, fr. *-spermae*, fem. pl. of *-spermus* -spermous] **:** ones having (such) a seed or germ — in higher taxa in botany ⟨Angio*spermae*⟩ ⟨Gymno*spermae*⟩ ⟨Rhodo*spermeae*⟩

sper·ma·gone \'spərmə,gōn\ *n* -S [NL *spermagonium*] **:** SPERMOGONIUM

sper·ma·go·ni·al \,==‘gōnēəl\ *adj* [NL *spermagonium* + E *-al*] **:** of, relating to, or being a spermagonium

sper·ma·go·ni·um *or* **sper·mo·go·ni·um** \,=='gōnēəm\ *n, pl* **spermago·nia** *or* **spermogo·nia** \-ēə\ [NL, fr. *sperm-* + *gonium*] **:** a flask-shaped or depressed receptacle in which spermatia are produced in various ascocarpous fungi and lichens — compare CONCEPTACLE, PYCNIUM

-sper·mal \,spərməl, -pəm-,-pəim-\ *or* **-sper·mous** \-məs\ *adj comb form* [*-spermal* fr. NL *-spermum* + E *-al*; *-spermous* fr. NL *-spermus*, fr. Gk *-spermos*, fr. *spermat-, sperma* seed, sperm — more at SPERM] **:** having (such or so many) seeds **:** seeded ⟨peri*spermal*⟩ ⟨poly*spermous*⟩ ⟨angio*spermal*⟩

sper·mal·ist \'spərməlist\ *n* -S [obs. E *spermal* relating to sperm (fr. E *sperm* + *-al*) + E *-ist*] **:** SPERMIST

sper·maph·y·ta \(,)spər'mafəd·ə\ [NL, fr. *sperm-* + *-phyta*] *syn of* SPERMATOPHYTA

sper·ma·phyte \'spərmə,fīt\ *n* -S [NL *Spermaphyta*] **:** SPERMATOPHYTE

sper·ma·phyt·ic \,=='fid·ik\ *adj* [*spermaphyte* + *-ic*] **:** SPERMATOPHYTIC

sper·mar·i·um \(,)spər'ma(a)rēəm\ *n, pl* **spermar·ia** \-ēə\ [NL, fr. *sperm-* + *-arium*] **:** SPERMARY

sper·ma·ry \'spərmərē\ *n* -ES [NL *spermarium*] **1 :** an organ in which spermatozoa are developed: **a :** TESTIS **b :** a sac dependent from a segmental septum of an oligochaete worm in which the later stages of sperm maturation take place **2 a :** ANTHERIDIUM **b :** POLLEN TUBE

sperm–aster \'=,==\ *n* **:** the centrosome and aster associated with the male pronucleus in the stage of fertilization preceding fusion of pronuclei and usu. giving rise to the first cleavage spindle of the zygote

spermat- *or* **spermato-** *comb form* [MF, fr. LL, fr. Gk, fr. *spermat-, sperma* seed, sperm — more at SPERM] **:** seed **:** spermatozoan ⟨*spermat*angium⟩ ⟨*spermato*phore⟩ ⟨*spermato*cyte⟩ ⟨*Spermato*phyta⟩

sper·ma·ta \'spərməd·ə\ *n pl* [NL, fr. *sperm-* + L *-ata*, neut pl. of *-atus* -ate] **:** HOMOEOMERIES

sper·ma·tan·gi·um \,spərmə'tanjēəm\ *n, pl* **spermatan·gia** \-ēə\ [NL, fr. *spermat-* + *-angium*] **:** a multicellular antheridium characteristic of some algae — compare SPERMATOCYST

sper·ma·teli·o·sis \,==,telē'ōsəs, -,tel-\ *n* -ES [NL, fr. *sperm-* + Gk *teleiōsis* development] **1 :** SPERMIOGENESIS a **2 :** SPERMATOGENESIS

sper·ma·theca \,spərmə+\ *n* [NL, fr. *sperm-* + *theca*] **:** a sac connected with the female reproductive organs of most insects, many other invertebrates, and a few vertebrates (as some amphibians) that receives and retains the spermatozoa often for a long period and until the time for fertilizing the eggs — **sper·ma·thecal** \"+\ *adj*

spermathecal gland *n* **:** a gland in some insects connected with the spermatheca

spermatia *pl of* SPERMATIUM

sper·ma·tial \(')spər'māshəl, spər'm-\ *adj* [NL *spermatium* + E *-al*] **:** of, relating to, or being a spermatium

¹**sper·mat·ic** \,spər'mad·ik, (')spə'm-, (')spəi'm-, ,spə(r)'m-, -at|, |ēk\ *adj* [MF *spermatique*, fr. LL *spermaticus*, fr. Gk *spermatikos*, fr. *spermat-, sperma* seed, sperm + *-ikos* -ic] **1 :** relating to sperm or a spermary **:** carrying or full of sperm **:** resembling sperm **:** SEMINAL, TESTICULAR **2 :** REPRODUCTIVE, ORIGINATIVE, GENERATIVE

²**spermatic** \"\ *n* -S **:** a spermatic part (as an artery, canal, or vein)

spermatical *adj* [ME, fr. LL *spermaticus* + E *-al*] *obs* **:** SPERMATIC

sper·mat·i·cal·ly \|ək(ə)lē, |ēk-, -li\ *adv* **:** in a spermatic manner or relation

spermatic animalcule *n, archaic* **:** SPERMATOZOON

spermatic artery *n* **:** an artery that supplies blood to a testis and that in man is one of a pair which arises from the front of the aorta a little below the renal arteries and passes downward to the spermatic cord of the same side and along it to the testis

spermatic canal *n* **:** INGUINAL CANAL

spermatic capsule *n* **:** a transparent globular sac produced by the male of some mites, containing the spermatozoa, and serving to convey them to the female genital tract

spermatic cord *also* **spermatic funiculus** *n* **:** a cord that suspends the testis within the scrotum, contains the vas deferens and vessels and nerves of the testis, and extends from the internal abdominal ring through the inguinal canal and external abdominal ring downward into the scrotum

spermatic duct *n* **:** an efferent duct of a testis **:** a duct conveying sperm

spermatic fluid *n* **:** SEMEN

spermatic plexus *n* **:** the pampiniform plexus of the spermatic cord

spermatic vein *n* **:** any of the veins leading from the testes, being numerous in man, forming with tributaries from the epididymis the pampiniform plexus in the spermatic cord, and thence accompanying the spermatic artery and eventually uniting to form a single trunk which on the right side opens into the vena cava and on the left into the renal vein

sper·ma·tid \'spərməd·əd\ *n* -S [ISV *spermat-* + *-id*] **:** one of the cells formed by division of the secondary spermatocytes and differentiating into spermatozoa — compare OOTID

sper·ma·tif·er·ous \,spərmə'tif(ə)rəs\ *adj* [NL *spermatium* + E *-ferous*] **:** bearing spermatia

sper·ma·tin \'spərməd·ən\ *n* -S [ISV *spermat-* + *-in*; prob. orig. formed as F *spermatine*] **:** an albuminoid substance from semen

sper·ma·tio·phore \(,)spər'māshēə,fō(ə)r\ *n* -S [NL *spermatium* + E *-o-* + *-phore*] **:** a hypha that gives rise to spermatia

sper·ma·tism \'spərmə,tizəm\ *n* -S [*spermat-* + *-ism*] **1 :** emission of semen **2** [ISV *spermat-* + *-ism*] **:** SPERMISM

sper·ma·tist \-məd·əst\ *n* -S [ISV *spermat-* + *-ist*] **:** SPERMIST

sper·ma·ti·um \(,)spər'māshēəm\ *n, pl* **sperma·tia** \-ēə\ [NL, fr. Gk *spermation*, dim. of *spermat-, sperma* sperm — more at SPERM] **1 :** a nonmotile male gamete of a red alga that conjugates with the egg in the carpogonium **2 :** a nonmotile cell developed in various fungi and lichens by abstriction from a sterigma within a spermagonium and apparently functioning as a male gamete though sometimes considered a conidium (as a pycnospore)

sper·ma·ti·za·tion \,spərməd·ə'zāshən, -mə,tī'z-\ *n* -S [*spermatize* + *-ation*] **:** the quality or state of being spermatized

sper·ma·tize \'==,tīz\ *vb* -ED/-ING/-S [Gk *spermatizein* to sow, fr. *spermat-* + *-izein* -ize] *vi, obs* **:** to produce or shed sperm ~ *vt* **:** to mingle spermatia or rarely sperm with **:** fertilize or diploidize (as rust fungi) by means of spermatia

spermato- — see SPERMAT-

sper·mato·blast \(,)spər'mad·ə,blast, 'spərməd·ə-\ *n* [ISV *spermat-* + *-blast*] **:** a cell or structure producing sperm **:** SPERMATID — **sper·mato·blas·tic** \(,)=;==;'blastik, |===-\ *adj*

sper·mato·cele \(,)spər'mad·ə,sēl, 'spərməd·-\ *n* -S [NL, fr. *spermat-* + *-cele*] **:** a cystic swelling of the ducts in the epididymis or in the rete testis usu. containing spermatozoa

sper·mato·ci·dal \(,)spər'mad·ə'sīd·ᵊl, 'spərməd·-\ *or* **sper·mi·ci·dal** \'spərmə'sīd·ᵊl\ *adj* [*spermat-, sperm-* + *-cidal*] **:** capable of killing or used to kill spermatozoa

sper·mato·cide \-,sīd\ *or* **sper·mi·cide** \'spərmə,-\ *n* -S [*spermat-, sperm-* + *-cide*] **:** an agent that kills spermatozoa

sper·mato·cyst \(,)spər'mad·ə,sist, 'spərməd·-\ *n* [*spermat-* + *-cyst*] **1 :** SEMINAL VESICLE **2 :** a unicellular antheridium in an alga and fungus — compare SPERMATANGIUM — **sper·mato·cys·tic** \(,)spər'mad·ə'sistik, 'spərməd·-\ *adj*

sper·mato·cy·tal \(,)spər'mad·ə'sīd·ᵊl, 'spərməd·-\ *adj* [*spermatocyte* + *-al*] **:** of, relating to, or being spermatocytes

sper·mato·cyte \(,)spər'mad·ə,sīt, 'spərməd·-\ *n* -S [*spermat-* + *-cyte*] **:** a cell giving rise to spermatozoa or spermatozooids — see PRIMARY SPERMATOCYTE, SECONDARY SPERMATOCYTE; compare ANDROCYTE, SPERMATID, SPERMATOGONIUM

sper·mato·genesis \,spərməd·ə, (,)spər,mad·ə+\ *n* [NL, fr. *spermat-* + *genesis*] **:** the whole process of male gamete formation including meiosis of a primary spermatocyte and transformation of the four resulting spermatids into spermatozoa — compare SPERMIOGENESIS

sper·mato·ge·net·ic \(,)spər,mad·əjə'ned·ik, 'spərməd·-\ *or* **sper·mato·gen·ic** \'spərməd·ə'jenik, (,)spər'mad·-\ *adj* [*spermat-* + *-genetic* or *-genic*] **:** of, relating to, or constituting spermatogenesis

sper·ma·tog·e·nous \,spərmə'täjənəs\ *adj* [*spermat-* + *-genous*] **:** producing sperm

sper·ma·tog·e·ny \-nē\ *n* -ES [*spermat-* + *-geny*] **:** SPERMATOGENESIS

sper·mato·go·ni·al \,spərməd·ə'gōnēəl, (,)spər'mad·-\ *also* **sper·mato·gon·ic** \-'gänik\ *adj* [NL *spermatogonium* + E *-al* or *-ic*] **:** of, relating to, or producing spermatogonia

sper·mato·go·ni·um \,===‘gōnēəm, (,)=,==-\ *n, pl* **spermato·go·nia** \-ēə\ [NL, fr. *spermat-* + *gonium*] **:** a primitive male germ cell **:** a testicular cell from which gametes are ultimately produced by meiosis and metamorphosis

sper·ma·toid \'spərmə,tòid\ *adj* [*spermat-* + *-oid*] **:** resembling sperm or a sperm cell **:** SEMINAL 1

sper·ma·tol·y·sis \,spərmə'täləsəs\ *n* [NL, fr. *spermat-* + *-lysis*] **:** dissolution of spermatozoa

sper·mato·lyt·ic \,spərməd·ə'lid·ik, (,)spər'mad·-\ *adj* [ISV *spermat-* + *-lytic*] **:** of, relating to, or promoting spermatolysis

sper·mato·pho·ral \(,)spər'mad·ə'fōrəl, 'spərməd·-; 'spərmə'täfərəl\ *or* **sper·ma·toph·o·rous** \'spərmə'täfərəs\ *adj* [*spermatophore* + *-al* or *-ous*] **:** of, relating to, or being a spermatophore

sper·mato·phore \(,)spər'mad·ə,fō(ə)r, 'spərməd·-\ *n* -S [ISV *spermat-* + *-phore*] **1 :** a capsule, packet, or mass enclosing spermatozoa extruded by the male of various animals and functioning in the insemination of the female (as annelids, mollusks, arthropods, and some vertebrates) **2 :** SPERMATIOPHORE

spermatophore sac *n* **:** a terminal sac in a cephalopod that retains the spermatophores until ready for fertilization

sper·ma·toph·y·ta \,spərmə'täfəd·ə\ *n pl, cap* [NL, fr. *spermat-* + *-phyta*] *in some classifications* **:** a division of higher plants that is coordinate with Bryophyta and Pteridophyta and coextensive with the classes Gymnospermae and Angiospermae

sper·mato·phyte \(,)spər'mad·ə,fīt, 'spərməd·-\ *n* -S [NL *Spermatophyta*] **:** a plant of the division Spermatophyta **:** SEED PLANT — **sper·mato·phyt·ic** \(,)=;==;'fid·ik, |===-\ *adj*

sper·mato·plasm \(,)spər'mad·ə,plazəm, 'spərməd·-\ *n* -S [*spermat-* + *-plasm*] **:** protoplasm of a sperm cell — **sper·mato·plas·mic** \(,)=;==;'plazmik, |===-\ *adj*

sper·mato·rhea *or* **sper·mator·rhoea** \,spərməd·ə'rēə, (,)spər,mad·-\ *n* -S [NL, fr. *spermat-* + *-rrhea, -rrhoea*] **:** abnormally frequent or excessive involuntary emission of semen without orgasm

sper·mato·theca \,spərməd·ə, (,)spər,mad·ə+\ *n* [NL, fr. *spermat-* + *theca*] **:** SPERMATHECA

-sper·ma·tous \'spərməd·əs, -pəm-,-pəim-, -mətəs\ *adj comb form* [Gk *-spermatos*, fr. *spermat-, sperma* seed, sperm — more at SPERM] **:** having (such or so many) seeds **:** seeded ⟨macro*spermatous*⟩ ⟨angio*spermatous*⟩

sper·ma·toxic \'spərmə+\ *adj* [*sperm-* + *toxic*] **:** poisonous to spermatozoa

sper·ma·toxin \"+\ *n* [alter. of *spermotoxin*] **:** a substance (as an antibody) poisonous to spermatozoa or derived from spermatozoa and tending to prevent conception

sper·mato·zo·al \'spərməd·ə'zōəl, (,)spər'mad·-\ *also* **sper·mato·zo·an** \-ōən\ *or* **sper·mato·zo·ic** \-ōik\ *adj* [NL *spermatozoa* + E *-al* or *-an* or *-ic*] **:** of or relating to spermatozoa

spermatozoan \"\ *n* -S [NL *spermatozoa* + E *-an* (n. suffix)] **:** SPERMATOZOON

sper·mato·zo·id \,==='zōəd, (,)=,==-\ *n* -S [NL *spermatozoon* + ISV *-id*] **:** a motile male gamete of a plant (as an alga or a moss, a liverwort, a fern, or a gymnosperm) that is usu. produced in an antheridium and that swims freely by means of two or more anterior cilia prior to fusion with the egg or oosphere — compare SPERMATOZOON, SPERM NUCLEUS **2 :** SPERMATOZOON 1

sper·mato·zo·on \,==='zō,än, (,)=,==-, -ōən\ *n, pl* **spermato·zoa** \-ōə\ [NL, fr. *spermat-* + *-zoon*] **1 :** a motile male gamete of an animal produced in the male reproductive gland usu. in great numbers, varying greatly in form in different animals but usu. consisting of a rounded or elongate head made up chiefly of the greatly condensed nucleus, a thickened middle piece, and a long posterior flagellum that provides motility, discharged in a fluid semen or a gelatinous spermatophore, and under suitable conditions (as of moisture and temperature) capable of actively seeking the typically much larger passive ovum — compare FERTILIZATION, SPERMATOGENESIS **2 :** SPERMATOZOID 1

sper·ma·tu·ria \,spərmə'tùrēə, -mə·'tyù-\ *n* -S [NL, fr. *spermat-* + *-uria*] **:** discharge of semen in the urine

sperm candle *n* **:** a candle made of spermaceti

sperm cell *n* **:** a male gamete **:** a male germ cell — contrasted with *egg cell*

sperm center *or* **sperm centrosome** *n* **:** a sperm-aster presumably derived from the middlepiece of the fertilizing sperm **:** the aster of the first zygotic division

-spermeae — see -SPERMAE

spermi- — see SPERM-

-sper·mia \'spərmēə, -pəm-,-pəim-\ *n comb form* -S [NL, fr. *-spermus* -spermous + *-ia*] **:** condition of having or producing (such) sperm ⟨azoo*spermia*⟩

sper·mi·a·tion \,spərmē'āshən\ *n* -S [*sperm-* + *-ation*] **:** the discharge of spermatozoa from the testis

-sper·mic \'spərmik, -pəm-,-pəim-, -mēk\ *adj comb form* [NL *-spermicus*, fr. LL *sperma* sperm + L *-icus* -ic — more at SPERM] **1 :** -SPERMAL **2 :** being the product of (such) a number of spermatozoa **:** resulting from (such) a multiple fertilization ⟨a tri*spermic* egg⟩ ⟨poly*spermic* fertilization⟩

sper·mi·cide \'spərmə,sīd\ *var of* SPERMATOCIDE

sper·mi·dine \'spərmə,dēn, -,dən\ *n* -S [*sperm-* + *-idine*] **:** a crystalline aliphatic triamine $H_2N(CH_2)_3NH(CH_2)_4NH_2$, found esp. in semen in association with spermine and structurally related to it and to putrescine

sper·mi·du·cal \'spərmə'd(y)ükəl\ *adj* [*spermiduct* + *-al*] **:** of, relating to, or being the sperm ducts — used esp. of glandular structures in oligochaetes

sper·mi·duct *or* **sper·mo·duct** \'spərmə,dəkt\ *var of* SPERMADUCT

-spermies *pl of* -SPERMY

sper·mig·er·ous \(')spər'mijərəs\ *adj* [*sperm-* + *-gerous*] **:** carrying sperm

sperm·ine \'spər,mēn, -,mən\ *n* -S [*sperm-* + *-ine*] **:** a deliquescent crystalline aliphatic tetramine $[-CH_2CH_2NH(CH_2)_3NH_2]_2$ found in semen in combination with phosphoric acid, in blood serum and body tissues, and in yeast and also prepared synthetically

sper·mio·genesis \,spərmēō+\ *n* [NL, fr. *spermio-* (fr. *spermium*) + *genesis*] **1 :** transformation of a spermatid into a spermatozoon **2 :** SPERMATOGENESIS

sper·mio·teliosis \,spərmē(,)ō,telē'ōsəs, -tel-\ *n* -ES [NL, fr. *spermio-* (fr. *spermium*) + Gk *teleiōsis* development] **:** SPERMIOGENESIS 1

sperm·ism \'spər,mizəm\ *n* -S [ISV *sperm-* + *-ism*] **:** a theory formerly widely held in biology: the sperm contains the preformed germ of the embryo — compare OVISM

sperm·ist \-məst\ *n* -S [ISV *sperm-* + *-ist*] **:** an adherent of the theory of spermism

sper·mi·um \'spərmēəm\ *n, pl* **sper·mia** \-ēə\ [NL, prob. fr. Gk *spermeion* sperm, seed, fr. *sperma* — more at SPERM] **:** SPERMATOZOON — used usu. in pl.

sperm nucleus *n* **:** the nucleus of a male gamete; *esp* **:** either of the two nuclei that arise from the generative nucleus of a pollen grain and function in the double fertilization characteristic of seed plants

spermo- — see SPERM-

sper·mo·blast \'spərmə,blast\ *n* [*sperm-* + *-blast*] **:** SPERMATOBLAST — **sper·mo·blas·tic** \'==;'blastik\ *adj*

sper·mo·carp \'==,kärp\ *n* -S [*sperm-* + *-carp*] **:** the oogonium together with the ensheathing cells that develop from underlying cells of the parent thallus after fertilization in various algae (as those of the genera *Chara* and *Coleochaete*)

sper·mo·center \'==+\ *n* [*sperm-* + *center*] **:** SPERM CENTER

sper·mo·derm \-,dərm\ *n* [*sperm-* + *-derm*] **:** TESTA

sper·mog·e·nous \(')spər'mäjənəs\ *adj* [*sperm-* + *-genous*] **:** giving rise to sperms

sper·mo·gone \'spərmə,gōn\ *n* -S [NL *spermogonium*] **:** SPERMAGONIUM

spermogonium *var of* SPERMAGONIUM

sperm oil *n* [so called fr. its being found in the sperm whale] **:** a pale yellow oil that is found with spermaceti in the head cavities and blubber of the sperm whale, is classed chemically as a liquid wax, and is used chiefly as a lubricant (as for light machinery)

sper·mol·y·sis \(,)spər'mäləsəs\ *n* [NL, fr. *sperm-* + *-lysis*] **:** SPERMATOLYSIS

sper·mo·phile \'spərmə,fīl\ *n* -S [NL *Spermophilus*] **:** GROUND SQUIRREL 1c

sper·moph·i·lus \(,)spər'mäfələs\ [NL, fr. *sperm-* + *-philus*] *syn of* CITELLUS

sper·moph·y·ta \-mäfəd·ə\ [NL, fr. *sperm-* + *-phyta*] *syn of* SPERMATOPHYTA

sper·mo·phyte \'spərmə,fīt\ *n* -S [NL *Spermophyta*] **:** SPERMATOPHYTE — **sper·mo·phyt·ic** \'==;'fid·ik\ *adj*

sper·mo·toxin \'spərmə+\ *n* [*sperm-* + *toxin*] **:** SPERMATOXIN

sper·mo·type \'spərmə,tīp\ *n* [*sperm-* + *type*] **:** a botanical type (as a neotype) obtained from a plant grown from the seed of a primary type (as a holotype)

sper·mous \'spərməs, -pəm-,-pəim-\ *adj* [*sperm-* + *-ous*] **:** resembling or made up of sperm

-spermous — see -SPERMAL

sperm·oviduct \'spərm+\ *n* [*sperm-* + *oviduct*] **:** HERMAPHRODITE DUCT

sperm receptor *n* **:** a hypothetical substance in the male gamete that is held to interact with fertilizin and egg receptor in the process of fertilization

sperm sac *n* **:** SPERMATHECA

-sper·mum \'spərməm, -pəm-,-pəim-\ *n comb form* [NL, fr. neut. of *-spermus* -spermous] **:** plant having (such) seeds or (such) a seed characteristic — in generic names ⟨Antho*spermum*⟩

sperm whale *n* [short for *spermaceti whale*] **:** a large toothed whale (*Physeter catodon* syn. *P. macrocephalus*) that has large conical teeth in the lower jaw only and no whalebone, attains a length of about 60 feet, has a large closed cavity in the head containing a fluid mixture of spermaceti and oil and a blubber yielding oil of superior quality, and produces ambergris as a pathological secretion of its intestines — called also *black whale;* see PYGMY SPERM WHALE

sperm-whale porpoise *n* **:** a beaked whale (*Hyperoodon ampullatum* syn. *H. rostratum*)

sperm whaling *n* **:** the search for and capture of sperm whales

-sper·my \,spərmē, -pəm-,-pəim-, -mi\ *n comb form* -ES [Gk *-spermia*, fr. *-spermos* -spermous + *-ia* -y] **1 :** state of having (such or so many) seeds ⟨gymno*spermy*⟩ **2 :** state of exhibiting or resulting from (such) a multiple fertilization ⟨poly*spermy*⟩

sper·o·na·ro \,sperə'nä(,)rō\ *also* **sper·o·na·ra** \-ärə\ *n, pl* **speronaros** *or* **speronaroes** [It *speronara*] **:** a large open boat rowed with oars but also having a lateen sail and used in southern Italian waters

sper·ry·lite \'sperē,līt, -rə,l-\ *n* -S [Francis L. *Sperry*, 19th cent. Canadian chemist + E *-lite*] **:** a platinum arsenide $PtAs_2$ occurring as a mineral near Sudbury, Ontario in grains and minute isometric crystals of a tin-white color and being the only compound of platinum known to occur in nature (hardness 6–7, sp. gr. 10.60)

sperse \'spərs\ *vb* -ED/-ING/-S [by shortening] *archaic* **:** DISPERSE

spes phthis·i·ca \'spā'stizəkə\ *n* [NL, phthisic hope] **:** a state of euphoria believed to occur in patients with pulmonary tuberculosis

spes re·cu·pe·ran·di \'spāsrə,küpə'rän(,)dē\ *n* [LL] **:** hope of recovery of captured goods

spes·sart·ite \'spesə(r),tīt\ *also* **spes·sart·ine** \-,tēn, -,tən\ *n* -S [F, fr. *Spessart*, mountain range in southern Germany + F *-ite, -ine*] **:** a manganese aluminum garnet ideally $Mn_3Al_2(SiO_4)_3$ usu. containing iron, magnesium, or other elements in minor amounts — see GARNET 1

spet \'spe\ *n* -S [F, of Gmc origin; akin to OE *spitu* spit; fr. its long slender shape — more at SPIT (rod)] **:** a small barracuda (*Sphyraena sphyraena*) of southern Europe

¹**spetch** \'spech\ *n* -ES [alter. of *speck* (patch)] **1 spetches** *pl* **:** parings and refuse of leather, hides, or skins used as a byproduct (as for making glue) **2** *dial Brit* **:** a scrap (as of leather) for patching **:** PATCH

²**spetch** \"\ *vt* [prob. fr. ¹*spetch*] *dial Eng* **:** MEND, PATCH

¹**spew** *also* **spue** \'spyü\ *vb* -ED/-ING/-S [ME *spewen*, fr. OE *spīwan*; akin to OHG *spīwan* to spit, ON *spȳja* to spew, Goth *speiwan* to spit, L *spuere*, Gk *ptyein* to spit, Skt *ṣṭhīvati* he spits] *vi* **1 :** VOMIT **2 :** to come in a flood or gush ⟨sewage ~*ed* over the yard⟩ ⟨a violently ~*ing* flood⟩ **3 a :** to ooze forth **:** EXUDE ⟨oil ~*ing* out of the wood⟩ ⟨water ~*ed* slowly from the saturated soil⟩ **b** *of soil* **:** to break away and slip (as when swollen with frost) ~ *vt* **1 :** to eject from the stomach **:** VOMIT ⟨~*ed* out a mass of undigested food⟩ **2 :** to cast forth with or as if with disgust **:** emit or eject with vigor or violence ⟨a volcano ~*ing* out lava⟩ ⟨~*ed* forth his contempt⟩ **3 :** to force out by or as if by pressure **:** EXTRUDE

²**spew** *also* **spue** \"\ *n* -S **1 a :** matter that is vomited **:** VOMITUS **b :** material that exudes or is extruded: as (1) **:** an oily or gummy exudate (as on the surface of leather or a recording disc) (2) **:** an overflow (as of rubber or metal) from a mold

2 *dial Brit* : an afterswarm of bees that is usu. the third or fourth of a season 3 *dial Brit* : a soggy piece of ground : an oozy patch esp. in a field

spew·er \-üə(r), -ủ(ə)r, -üə\ *n* -s : one that spews

spewing sickness *n* : a disease of sheep and cattle caused by eating the sneezeweed (*Helenium hoopesii*) and characterized by weakness, rapid irregular pulse, nausea, and vomiting

spewy \-üi\ *adj* -ER/-EST [1*spew* + *-y*] *of land* : excessively moist or marshy : tending to ooze out water ⟨fields too ~ to cultivate⟩

spey \'spā\ *Austral var of* SPAY

spey·e·ria \spī'(y)irēə\ *n, cap* [NL, fr. A. *Speyer*, 19th cent. Ger. lepidopterist + NL *-ia*] : a large genus of butterflies (family Nymphalidae) that contains the silverspots

spezia *adj, usu cap* [fr. La *Spezia*, seaport in northwest Italy] : LA SPEZIA

spg *abbr* 1 sponge 2 spring

sp gr *abbr* specific gravity

sph *abbr* sphere; spherical

sphac·e·lar·ia \,sfasə'la(a)rēə\ *n, cap* [NL, fr. *sphacelus* gangrene + *-aria*] : a genus of small feathery brown algae (order Sphacelariales) similar to *Ectocarpus* but having the area of growth restricted to large dark brown apical cells

sphac·e·lar·i·a·les \,==,=='ā(,)lēz\ *n pl, cap* [NL, fr. *Sphacelaria* + *-ales*] : an order of small or medium-sized much branched parenchymatous brown algae (class Isogeneratae) that are found chiefly in the lower part of the intertidal zone and grow from apical cells on the branches

sphac·e·late \'sfasə,lāt\ *vb* -ED/-ING/-S [prob. fr. (assumed) NL *sphacelatus*, past part. of *sphacelare* to become gangrenous, fr. NL *sphacelus* gangrene] *vi* : to become gangrenous : MORTIFY ~ *vt* : to cause to become gangrenous — **sphac·e·la·tion** \,=='lāshən\ *n* -s

sphac·e·lat·ed \'==,lād·əd\ *adj* [prob. fr. (assumed) NL *sphacelatus* + E *-ed*] 1 : GANGRENOUS, SLOUGHED ⟨a ~ ulcer⟩ 2 : WITHERED, DECAYED ⟨a ~ root⟩

spha·ce·lia \sfa'sēlēə, sfə's-\ *n* -s [NL, fr. *sphacelus* gangrene + *-ia*] : the conidial stage of ergot (*Claviceps purpurea*) — called also *sphacelial stage* — **spha·ce·li·al** \-lēəl\ *adj*

sphac·e·lo·ma \,sfasə'lōmə\ *n, cap* [NL, fr. *sphacelus* + *-oma*] : a form genus of imperfect fungi that is sometimes included in *Gloeosporium* but is usu. considered as distinct because of the firm acervulus suggestive of a cushion

sphac·e·lo·the·ca \,sfasəlō'thēkə\ *n, cap* [NL, fr. *sphacelus* + *theca*] : a genus of smut fungi bearing teliospores in globose masses that are surrounded by a pseudoparenchymatous layer of tissue

sphac·e·lus \'sfasələs\ *n* -ES [NL, fr. Gk *sphakelos* gangrene] : GANGRENE, NECROSIS; *also* : a gangrenous or necrosed part or mass : SLOUGH

sphaer- *or* **sphaero-** *also* **spher-** *or* **sphero-** *comb form* [LL *sphaer-*, *sphaero-*, fr. L, fr. Gk *sphair-*, *sphairo-*, fr. *sphaira* — more at SPHERE] 1 : ball : sphere ⟨*Sphaero*phorus⟩ ⟨calco*spher*ite⟩ 2 : spherical : consisting of spherical elements ⟨*sphaer*aphides⟩ ⟨*sphero*meter⟩

-sphae·ra \'sfirə, -fērə\ *n comb form* -s [NL, fr. L *sphaera* sphere — more at SPHERE] : ball : sphere — chiefly in taxonomic names ⟨Micro*sphaera*⟩

sphaer·al·cea \,sfi,ral'sēə, -fe,r-\ *n, cap* [NL, fr. *sphaer-* + L *alcea*, a mallow, fr. Gk *alkaia* vervain mallow] : a large genus of chiefly tropical herbs (family Malvaceae) with showy pink or scarlet flowers and mostly globose fruit — see GLOBE MALLOW

sphaer·a·phis \'sfirəfəs, 'sfer-\ *n, pl* **sphae·raph·i·des** \sfə'rafə,dēz\ [NL, fr. *sphaer-* + Gk *rhaphis* needle — more at RAPHIDE] : a spherical aggregation of raphides in a plant ce

sphae·rel·la \sfə'relə\ [NL, fr. *sphaer-* + *-ella*] *syn of* MYCOSPHAERELLA

sphaer·i·a·ce·ae \,sfirē'āsē,ē\ *n pl, cap* [NL, fr. *Sphaeria*, type genus (fr. *sphaer-* + *-ia*) + *-aceae*] : a family of parasitic fungi (order Sphaeriales) having globose and sometimes necked or beaked perithecia usu. with ostioles — **sphaer·i·a·ceous** \¦==¦āshəs\ *adj*

sphaer·i·a·les \,=='ā(,)lēz\ *n pl, cap* [NL, fr. *Sphaeria* + *-ales*] : a large order of ascomycetous fungi (subclass Euascomycetes) that usu. have hard dark perithecia with definite ostioles, that include many economically important plant parasites as well as large numbers of saprophytes, and that in recent classifications are often divided among several orders

sphae·rid·i·al \sfə'ridēəl\ *adj* [NL *sphaeridi*um + E *-al*] : of, relating to, or being a sphaeridium

sphae·rid·i·um \-ēəm\ *n, pl* **sphaerid·ia** \-ēə\ [NL, fr. *sphaer-* + *-idium*] : one of the small organs found on or buried in the test of all recent sea urchins except the Cidaroida suggesting statoliths in structure and possibly subserving a similar function

1**sphae·ri·id** \'sfirēəd\ *adj* [NL *Sphaeriidae*] : of or relating to the Sphaeriidae

2**sphaeriid** \"\ *n* -s : a mollusk of the family Sphaeriidae

sphae·ri·idae \sfə'rīə,dē\ *n pl, cap* [NL, fr. *Sphaerium*, type genus + *-idae*] : a cosmopolitan family of minute freshwater bivalve mollusks (suborder Submytilacea) including some that are intermediate hosts of trematode worms — see SPHAERIUM

sphae·ri·oi·da·ce·ae \,sfirē,ȯi'dasē,ē\ [NL, prob. fr. *Sphaeria*, genus of fungi + *-oides* -oid + *-aceae*] *syn of* SPHAEROPSIDACEAE

sphae·ri·ta \sfə'rīd·ə, -rēd·ə\ *n, cap* [NL, fr. *sphaer-* + L *-ita* -ite] : a genus of amoeboid parasites of the cytoplasm of various algae and protozoans that are usu. considered lower fungi and placed in the order Chytridiales

sphae·rite \'sfi,rīt\ *n* -s [G *sphärit*, fr. *sphär-* sphaer- + *-it* -ite] : a mineral consisting of a light gray or bluish hydrous aluminum phosphate in globular concretions

sphae·ri·um \'sfirēəm\ *n, cap* [NL, fr. Gk *sphairion*, dim. of *sphaira* ball, sphere — more at SPHERE] : a widely distributed genus (the type of the family Sphaeriidae) of small viviparous freshwater bivalve mollusks that have a thin light-colored shell and the siphons separate — see FINGERNAIL CLAM

sphaero- — see SPHAER-

sphaero·bo·la·ce·ae \,sfirōbə'lāsē,ē, -fer-\ *n pl, cap* [NL, fr. *Sphaerobolus*, type genus (fr. *sphaer-* + Gk *bolos* throw) + NL *-aceae*; akin to Gk *ballein* to throw — more at DEVIL] : a monotypic family of fungi (order Nidulariales) in which the more or less spherical gleba is forcibly ejected at maturity

sphaero·car·pa·ce·ae \-ō,kär'pāsē,ē\ *n pl, cap* [NL, fr. *Sphaerocarpus*, type genus + *-aceae*] : a family of liverworts with bilaterally symmetrical gametophytes that is placed in the order Sphaerocarpales or sometimes included in Jungermanniales among the Anacrogynae — see SPHAEROCARPUS

sphaero·car·pa·les \-ā(,)lēz\ *n pl, cap* [NL, fr. *Sphaerocarpus* + *-ales*] : a small order of Hepaticae comprising liverworts with an involucre around each archegonium — see SPHAEROCARPACEAE

sphaero·car·pos \-ō'kärpəs, -,päs\ [NL] *syn of* SPHAEROCARPUS

sphaero·car·pus \-,pəs\ *n, cap* [NL, fr. *sphaer-* + *-carpus*] : the type genus of Sphaerocarpaceae comprising liverworts with a small many-lobed usu. orbicular thallus and with the spores nearly always remaining in tetrads at maturity

sphaero·cobaltite \¦sfi(,)rō, -fe(-+\ *n* [G *sphärokobaltit*, fr. *sphär-* sphaer- + *kobaltit* cobaltite] : COBALTOCALCITE

sphaero·coc·ca·ce·ae \¦=(,)=,kä'kāsē,ē\ *n pl, cap* [NL, fr. *Sphaerococcus*, type genus (fr. *sphaer-* + *-coccus*) + *-aceae*] : a family of red algae (order Rhodymeniales) having a much branched thallus with the cystocarps enclosed in semiglobular swellings of the peripheral tissues — see GRACILARIA — **sphaero·coc·ca·ceous** \¦=(,)=¦=¦kāshəs\ *adj*

sphaero·crystal \'=(,)=+,-\ *n* [*sphaer-* + *crystal*] : SPHAERAPHIS

sphaeroid *var of* SPHEROID

sphaer·o·lite \'sfirə,līt, -fer-\ *n* -s [by alter.] : SPHERULITE

sphaer·o·lit·ic \¦==¦lid·ik\ *adj* [by alter.] : SPHERULITIC

sphae·ro·ma \sfə'rōmə\ *n* [NL, fr. Gk *sphairōma* something made round, fr. *sphairoun* to make round, fr. *sphaira* ball, sphere — more at SPHERE] 1 *cap* : a genus (the type of the family Sphaeromidae) of marine isopod crustaceans having broad oval bodies that can sometimes be rolled into a ball, an abdomen of two segments, and well developed antennae and including destructive borers of pilings and other timbers — see ROCK-BORING ISOPOD 2 -s : any isopod of the genus *Sphaeroma*

sphaero·ne·ma \,sfirə'nēmə, -fer-\ *n, cap* [NL, fr. *sphaer-* + *-nema*] : a genus of imperfect fungi (family Sphaeropsidaceae) having pycnidia with elongated necks and occurring chiefly on dead plant tissue

sphae·roph·o·rus \sfə'räfərəs\ *n, cap* [NL, fr. *sphaer-* + *-phorus*] : a genus (the type of the family Sphaerophoraceae) of gymnocarpous lichens characterized by a foliaceous or fruticose thallus with terminal globose apothecia bearing continuous dark-colored ascospores

sphae·rop·lea \sfə'räplēə\ *n, cap* [NL, fr. *sphaer-* + *-plea* (fr. Gk *pleos* full); akin to L *plenus* full — more at FULL] : a genus of unbranched filamentous green algae (order Cladophorales) having many chloroplasts in each cell arranged in transverse bands and producing more than one egg in each oogonium

sphae·rop·si·da·ce·ae \sfə,räpsə'dāsē,ē\ *n pl, cap* [NL, fr. *Sphaeropsid-*, *Sphaeropsis*, type genus + *-aceae*] : a very large family of imperfect fungi (order Sphaeropsidales) that include various important plant pathogens and are characterized by globose to spheroidal pycnidia with dark leathery or carbonaceous walls — **sphae·rop·si·da·ceous** \=¦==¦dāshəs\ *adj*

sphae·rop·si·da·les \=,=='dā(,)lēz\ *n pl, cap* [NL, fr. *Sphaeropsid-*, *Sphaeropsis* + *-ales*] : an order of imperfect fungi in which the conidia are produced in pycnidia or similar chambered cavities and which include both saprophytes and parasites

sphae·rop·sis \sfə'räpsəs\ *n, cap* [NL, fr. *sphaer-* + *-opsis*] : a form genus of imperfect fungi (family Sphaeropsidaceae) having large unicellular dark pycnospores and including many forms that have been found to be imperfect stages of various other fungi (as members of the genus *Physalospora*)

sphaero·stil·be \,sfirō'stil(,)bē, -fer-\ *n, cap* [NL, fr. *sphaer-* + *-stilbe* (fr. Gk *stilbos* glistening) — more at STILBUM] : a genus of ascomycetous fungi (family Nectriaceae) characterized by red perithecia borne on slender stromatic stalks and 2-celled ascospores and including destructive root parasites esp. of tropical plants

sphaero·the·ca \-'thēkə\ *n, cap* [NL, fr. *sphaer-* + *theca*] : a genus of powdery mildews (family Erysiphaceae) having perithecia with one ascus and unbranched appendages that resemble hyphae — see HOP MILDEW

sphae·rot·i·lus \sfə'räd·ᵊləs\ *n, cap* [NL, fr. *sphaer-* + Gk *tilos* fiber, fr. *tillein* to pluck] : a genus of bacteria (family Chlamydobacteriaceae) having filaments that exhibit false branching and reproducing by both conidia and swarmers

sphag·na·ceous \(')sfag¦nāshəs\ *adj* [NL *Sphagnum* + E *-aceous*] : of or relating to the genus *Sphagnum* or order Sphagnales

sphag·na·les \sfag'nā(,)lēz\ *n pl, cap* [NL, fr. *Sphagnum* + *-ales*] : an order of Musci that is coextensive with the genus *Sphagnum* and is often isolated in a separate subclass

sphag·ni·cole \'sfagnə,kōl\ *n* -s [back-formation fr. *sphagnicolous*] : a sphagnicolous organism

sphag·nic·o·lous \(')sfag¦nikələs\ *adj* [*sphagn*um + *-i-* + *-colous*] : inhabiting or growing in sphagnum ⟨~ rotifers⟩

sphag·nob·rya \sfag'näbrēə\ *n pl, cap* [NL, fr. *Sphagnum* + *-brya* (fr. Gk *bryon* moss) — more at BRY-] *in some classifications* : a subclass of Musci coextensive with the order Sphagnales

sphag·no·phil·ic \¦sfagnə¦filik\ *adj* [*sphagn*um + *-o-* + *-philic*] : living or thriving in sphagnum

sphag·nous \'sfagnəs\ *adj* [NL *Sphagnum* + E *-ous*] 1 : being or made up of mosses of the genus *Sphagnum* ⟨a heavy ~ growth⟩ ⟨~ plants⟩ 2 : abounding in peat sphagnum ⟨a ~ bog⟩

sphag·num \'sfagnəm, -faig-\ *n* [NL, fr. L *sphagnos*, a moss, fr. Gk] 1 *cap* : a large genus (coextensive with the order Sphagnales) of atypical mosses that have a protonema which is not filamentous but resembles the prothallium of a fern, a pseudopodium which is derived from the gametophyte rather than the sporophyte as in other mosses, and leaves which contain abundant colorless aqueous tissue interspersed with chlorophyll-bearing cells and that grow only in very wet acid areas where their accumulated remains become compacted with other plant debris to form peat 2 *or* **sphagnum moss** -s **a** : any plant of the genus *Sphagnum* **b** : a mass of sphagnum plants ⟨damping off can often be prevented by covering the seeds with a thin layer of pulverized ~⟩ ⟨dehydrated ~ was used for surgical dressings during World War I⟩

sphagnum bog *n* : a bog containing sphagnum and usu. other characteristic and acid-tolerant plants (as pitcher plants of the genus *Sarracenia*, sundews, or heaths) and tending to form deposits of peat

sphagnum frog *n* [so called fr. the fact that it was orig. found in a sphagnum bog] : CARPENTER FROG

sphal·er·ite \'sfalə,rīt\ *n* -s [G *sphalerit*, fr. Gk *sphaleros* deceitful, tripping, slippery (fr. *sphallein* to cause to fall) + G *-it* -ite; fr. its being often mistaken for galena — more at SPILL] : a widely distributed ore of zinc composed essentially of zinc sulfide ZnS but often containing iron, manganese, or other elements, occurring in isometric crystals or cleavable masses of resinous to adamantine luster and commonly yellow, brown, or black color, and having highly perfect dodecahedral cleavage (hardness 3.5–4, sp. gr. 3.9–4.1) — called also *blackjack*, *blende*, *false galena*

sphar·gis \'sfärjəs\ [NL] *syn of* DERMOCHELYS

1**sphe·cid** \'sfēsəd\ *adj* [NL *Sphecidae*] : of or relating to the Sphecidae

2**sphecid** \"\ *n* -s : a wasp of the family Sphecidae

spheci·dae \'sfēsə,dē, -fes-\ *n pl, cap* [NL, fr. *Sphec-*, *Sphex*, type genus + *-idae*] : a family of solitary wasps (superfamily Sphecoidea) having the first segment of the abdomen generally prolonged into a long smooth cylindrical petiole and including the mud daubers and some digger wasps

sphe·cius \'sfēsh(ē)əs\ *n, cap* [NL, fr. *Sphec-*, *Sphex* — more at SPHEX] : a cosmopolitan genus of large solitary wasps (family Stizidae) including the cicada killer

1**sphe·coid** \'sfē,kȯid\ *adj* [NL *Sphecoidea*] : of or relating to the Sphecoidea

2**sphecoid** \"\ *n* -s : an insect of the superfamily Sphecoidea

sphe·coi·dea \sfə'kȯidēə\ *n pl, cap* [NL, fr. *Sphec-*, *Sphex* + *-oidea*] : a superfamily of Hymenoptera comprising Sphecidae and related families and in some classifications the true bees — compare APOIDEA

spheges *pl of* SPHEX

sphegi·dae \'sfejə,dē, -fēj-\ [NL, irreg. fr. *Sphec-*, *Sphex* + *-idae*] *syn of* SPHECIDAE

sphen- *or* **spheno-** *comb form* [NL, fr. Gk *sphēn-*, *sphēno-*, fr. *sphēn* — more at SPOON] 1 : wedge : wedge-shaped ⟨*spheno*gram⟩ ⟨*Sphen*odon⟩ 2 **a** : of or relating to the sphenoid ⟨*spheno*tribe⟩ **b** : sphenoidal and ⟨*spheno*mastoid⟩ ⟨*sphen*ethmoidal⟩

sphen·acanthocephala \¦sfēn+\ *n pl, cap* [NL, fr. *sphen-* + *Acanthocephala*] : a small order of Acanthocephala comprising a few parasites of birds that lack a true cephalic extrovert or proboscis

1**sphe·nac·odont** \sfə'nakə,dänt\ *adj* [NL *Sphenacodontia*] : of or relating to the Sphenacodontia

2**sphenacodont** \"\ *n* -s : a sphenacodont reptile or fossil

sphe·nac·odon·tia \=,=='dänchēə, -ntēə\ *n pl, cap* [NL, fr. *Sphenacodont-*, *Sphenacodon*, genus of reptiles (irreg. fr. *sphen-* + *-odont-*, *-odon*) + *-ia*] : a suborder of Pelycosauria comprising primitive Permian reptiles that resemble mammals

sphen·do·ne \'sfendə,nē\ *n* -s [Gk *sphendonē* sling, sphendone — more at SPONDYL] 1 : a headband worn by ancient Greek women 2 : a semicircular part or place (as at the end of an ancient Greek stadium)

sphene \'sfēn\ *n* -s [F *sphène*, fr. Gk *sphēn* wedge; fr. a form of its crystals] : a mineral $CaTiSiO_5$ that is a silicate of calcium and titanium, and often contains columbium, chromium, fluorine, and other elements — called also *titanite*

sphen·ethmoid \(')sfēn+\ *adj* [*sphen-* + *ethmoid*] : of, relating to, or being a bone of the skull that surrounds the anterior end of the brain in many amphibians

sphe·ni·on \'sfēnē,än\ *n* -s [NL, fr. *sphen-* + Gk *-ion*, dim. suffix] : the lower frontal apex of the parietal bone used as a reference point in craniometry

sphe·nis·ci·dae \sfə'nisə,dē\ *n pl, cap* [NL, fr. *Spheniscus*, type genus + *-idae*] : a family of birds (order Sphenisciformes) containing all the existing penguins

sphe·nis·ci·for·mes \=,=='fȯr(,)mēz\ *n pl, cap* [NL, fr. *Spheniscus* + *-iformes*] : an order of flightless aquatic birds comprising the penguins

sphe·nis·co·mor·phae \sfə,niskə'mȯr,fē\ [NL, fr. *Spheniscus* + *-o-* + *-morphae*] *syn of* SPHENISCIFORMES

sphe·nis·cus \-'niskəs\ *n, cap* [NL, fr. Gk *sphēniskos* small wedge, dim. of *sphēn* wedge; fr. the shortness of the wings — more at SPOON] : a genus of penguins that is type of the family Spheniscidae and includes the jackass penguin

sphe·no·basilar *also* **sphe·no·basilic** \¦sfē(,)nō+\ *adj* [*sphenobasilar*, fr. NL *sphenobasilaris*, fr. *sphen-* + *basilaris* basilar, irreg. fr. L *basis* base + *-aris* -ar; *sphenobasilic*, prob. fr. NL *sphenobasil*aris + E *-ic* — more at BASE] : of, relating to, lying between, or distributed to the sphenoid and the basilar part of the occipital bone

sphe·no·ce·pha·lia \,sfēnəsə'fālyə\ *n* -s [NL, fr. Gk *sphēnokephalos* having a wedge-shaped head (fr. *sphēn-* sphen- + *-kephalos* -headed, -cephalous) + NL *-ia*] : SPHENOCEPHALY

sphe·no·ce·phal·ic \¦==sə¦falik\ *or* **sphe·no·ceph·a·lous** \¦==¦sefələs\ *adj* [NL *sphenocephalia* + E *-ic* or *-ous*] : having a wedge-shaped head

sphe·no·ceph·a·ly \,=='sefəlē\ *n* -ES [NL *sphenocephalia*] : the condition of being sphenocephalic

sphen·odon \'sfēnə,dän, -fen-\ *n* [NL, fr. *sphen-* + *-odon*] 1 *cap* : a genus of reptiles comprising the tuatara, being distinguished from all other recent reptiles by the presence of a pineal eye, and usu. placed with the Rhynchocephalia but sometimes segregated in a distinct suborder 2 *or* **sphen·odont** \-änt\ -s [*sphenodont*, fr. NL *Sphenodont-*, *Sphenodon*] : an animal of the genus *Sphenodon* : TUATARA

sphen·odont \-änt\ *adj* [NL *Sphenodont-*, *Sphenodon*] : of or relating to the genus *Sphenodon*

sphe·no·frontal \¦sfē(,)nō+\ *adj* [*sphen-* + *frontal*] : of, relating to, lying between, or distributed to the sphenoid and frontal bones of the skull

spheno·gram \'sfēnə,gram, -fen-\ *n* [*sphen-* + *-gram*] : a cuneiform character (as in an inscription)

sphe·nog·ra·phy \sfə'nägrəfē\ *n* -ES [*sphen-* + *-graphy*] : the art of writing in or deciphering cuneiform characters

1**sphe·noid** \'sfē,nȯid\ *also* **sphe·noi·dal** \(')sfē¦nȯidᵊl\ *adj* [*sphenoid*, fr. NL *sphenoides*, fr. Gk *sphēnoeidēs* wedge-shaped, fr. *sphēn* wedge + *-oeidēs* -oid; *sphenoidal*, fr. NL *sphenoidalis*, fr. Gk *sphēnoeidēs* + L *-alis* -al — more at SPOON] 1 : of, relating to, or situated in the region of a compound bone of the base of the cranium of various vertebrates formed by the fusion of several bony elements with the basisphenoid and in man consisting of a median body from whose sides extend a pair of broad curved winglike expansions in front of which is another pair of much smaller triangular lateral processes while ventrally two large deeply cleft processes extend downward ⟨a ~ sinus⟩ 2 *usu sphenoidal* **a** : relating to or resembling a sphenoid : wedge-shaped **b** : having such symmetry that the general form is a sphenoid — used of a monoclinic crystal with a diad axis of symmetry

2**sphenoid** \"\ *n* -s 1 : a sphenoid bone 2 **a** : a wedge-shaped open form in the monoclinic system of crystallization consisting of two faces related by a diad axis of symmetry — compare DOME **b** : DISPHENOID

sphenoid 2

sphenoidal fissure *n* : a fissure between the greater and lesser wing of the sphenoid bone

sphenoidal group *n* : a group of the tetragonal system of crystalline symmetries of which the sphenoid is the typical form

sphenoidal process *n* 1 : a process on the superior border of the vertical plate of the palatine bone articulating with the sphenoid 2 : a backward prolongation of the cartilage of the nasal septum between the vomer and the perpendicular plate of the ethmoid

sphenoidal sinus *n* : either of two irregular cavities in the body of the sphenoid bone that communicate with the nasal cavities

sphe·noid·itis \,sfē,nȯi'dīd·əs\ *n* -ES [NL, fr. *sphenoides* sphenoid + *-itis*] : inflammation of the sphenoidal sinuses

spheno·lith \'sfēnᵊl,ith, -fen-\ *n* -s [*sphen-* + *-lith*] : a wedge-shaped intrusive mass of igneous rock

sphe·no·mandibular \¦sfē(,)nō+\ *adj* [*sphen-* + *mandibular*] : of, relating to, or joining the sphenoid bone and the lower jaw

sphe·no·maxillary \"+\ *adj* [*sphen-* + *maxillary*] : of, relating to, or joining the sphenoid bone and the upper jaw

sphenomaxillary fissure *n* : the inferior orbital fissure

sphenomaxillary fossa *n* : PTERYGOPALATINE FOSSA

spheno–occipital suture \"+ . . . -\ *also* **spheno–occipital** *n* : the junction between the basisphenoid and basioccipital bones of the mammalian skull that in man is usu. closed by the age of 25

1**sphe·no·palatine** \"+\ *adj* [ISV *sphen-* + *palatine*] : of, relating to, lying in, or distributed to the vicinity of the sphenoid and palatine bones

2**sphenopalatine** \"\ *n* : a sphenopalatine part; *specif* : SPHENOPALATINE GANGLION

sphenopalatine foramen *n* : a foramen between the sphenoidal and orbital parts of the vertical plate of the palatine bone; *often* : a deep notch between these parts that by articulation with the sphenoid bone is converted into a foramen

sphenopalatine ganglion *n* : an autonomic ganglion on the maxillary nerve in the pterygopalatine fossa receiving preganglionic fibers from the facial nerve by way of the greater superficial petrosal nerve, sending postganglionic fibers to the nasal mucosa, palate, pharynx, and orbit, and giving passage to sympathetic fibers from the carotid plexus — called also *Meckel's ganglion*

sphe·no·parietal \¦sfē(,)nō+\ *adj* [*sphen-* + *parietal*] : of, relating to, lying between, or distributed to the region of the sphenoid and parietal bones ⟨~ fissure⟩

sphenoparietal index *n* : the ratio of the breadth of the skull from stenion to stenion to its greatest breadth multiplied by 100

sphe·noph·o·rus \sfē'näfərəs\ *n, cap* [NL, fr. *sphen-* + *-phorus*] : a genus of weevils whose larvae bore in the roots and stems of cereal and other grasses

sphe·no·phyl·la·les \,sfē(,)nōfə'lā(,)lēz\ *n pl, cap* [NL, fr. *Sphenophyllum* + *-ales*] : an order of fossil plants (subdivision Sphenopsida) coextensive with the genus *Sphenophyllum*

sphe·no·phyl·lum \,sfēnə'filəm\ *n, cap* [NL, fr. *sphen-* + *-phyllum*] : a genus of Paleozoic fossil plants that are related to the club mosses and horsetails but are usu. placed in the separate order Sphenophyllales, that have jointed stems, cuneate leaves in whorls of three or multiples of three, and terminal cones or sporophylls, and that occur from the Devonian to the Permian

sphe·nop·sid \sfē'näpsəd\ *n* -s [NL *Sphenopsida*] : a plant or fossil of the subdivision Sphenopsida

sphe·nop·si·da \-psədə\ *n pl, cap* [NL, fr. *sphen-* + *-opsis* + *-ida*] : a subdivision of Tracheophyta comprising vascular plants (as the horsetails and extinct related forms) with jointed stems, small leaves usu. in whorls at distinct stem nodes, and sporangia in sporangiophores and including the orders Hyeniales, Sphenophyllales, and Equisetales — compare LYCOPSIDA, PSILOPSIDA, PTEROPSIDA

sphe·nop·ter·is \-ptərəs\ *n, cap* [NL, fr. *sphen-* + *-pteris*] : a form genus of Paleozoic fossil plants (order Cycadofilicales) based primarily on leaf blades with cuneate pinnules

sphe·no·squamosal \¦sfē(,)nō+\ *adj* [*sphen-* + *squamosal*] : of, relating to, lying between, or distributed to the sphenoid and temporal bones of the skull ⟨~ suture⟩

1**sphen·otic** \(')sfē¦nōd·ik, -näd·-\ *adj* [*sphen-* + *-otic*] : of, relating to, or being an element of the skull of many fishes situated above the prootic and often forming part of the posterior boundary of the orbit

2**sphenotic** \"\ *n* -s : a sphenotic bone or cartilage

1**sphe·no·turbinal** \¦sfē(,)nō+\ *adj* [*sphen-* + *turbinal*] : of, relating to, constituting, or situated near a pair of small curved plates of bone at the anterior and inferior part of the body of the sphenoid bone that in man remain attached to the sphenoid until the age of puberty

2**sphenoturbinal** \"\ *n* -s : a sphenoturbinal bone

spher- — see SPHAER-

spher·al \'sfirəl\ *adj* [LL *sphaeralis*, fr. *sphaer-* + L *-alis* -al] 1 **a** : of, relating to, or having the form of a sphere **b** : resembling a sphere esp. in perfection of symmetry or well-rounded excellence **2 a :** of or relating to the spheres of ancient astronomy **b :** suggesting the music of the spheres **:** HARMONIOUS

sphe·ral·i·ty \sfiˈraləd·ē\ *n* -ES **:** the quality or state of being spheral or spherical

spher·aster \(ˈ)sfi¦rastə(r)\ *n* -S [NL, fr. *sphaer-* + *-aster*] **:** a many-rayed sponge spicule with a spherical central body

sphe·ra·tion \sfiˈrāshən\ *n* -S [¹*sphere* + *-ation*] **:** the act or process of taking the form of a sphere

¹**sphere** \ˈsfi(ə)r, -iə, *chiefly South sometimes* ˈspi-\ *n* -S *often attrib* [ME *spere*, fr. MF *espere*, fr. L *sphaera*, fr. Gk *sphaira* ball, sphere; perh. akin to Gk *spairein* to quiver — more at SPURN] **1 a** (1) **:** the apparent surface of the heavens of which half forms the dome of the visible sky, which is assumed to be spherical and everywhere infinitely distant from the earth, on which the celestial bodies seem to have their places, and on which the various astronomical circles (as of right ascension and declination, the equator, ecliptic) are conceived to be drawn **:** an ideal globe with the astronomical circles in their proper positions on it (2) **:** one of the concentric and eccentric revolving spherical transparent shells in which according to ancient astronomy stars, sun, planets, and moon are set and by which they are carried in such manner as to produce their apparent motions — compare MUSIC OF THE SPHERES **b :** a globe depicting such a sphere; *broadly* **:** GLOBE 1a **2 a :** a globular body **:** one whose major circumferences approximate to circles **:** BALL ⟨ruddy ~*s* burdening the apple boughs⟩: as (1) **:** a celestial body **:** PLANET, STAR (2) **:** a rounded differentiated structure (as a centrosome or idiosome) in protoplasm **b** (1) **:** a body or space bounded by one surface all points of which are equally distant from a point within that constitutes its center — see VOLUME table (2) **:** the bounding surface of such a body or space **3 a :** one of the concentric layers anciently believed to be formed by each of the elements earth, water, air, and fire **b :** natural, normal, or proper place ⟨fish in their underwater ~⟩ **c :** an order of society **:** social position or class **d :** a happier or heavenly region ⟨a future ~, where the injustices of life shall be rectified —W.E.H.Lecky⟩ **4 a** *obs* **:** a course or path encompassing a center **:** the orbit of a heavenly body **:** CIRCUIT **b** (1) **:** the area over which something acts, exerts influence, has its being or significance, or radiates **:** a domain or range of something (as action, knowledge, or influence) **:** field of action or existence **:** COMPASS, PROVINCE ⟨within her narrow ~ of action⟩ ⟨in the ~ of mundane affairs⟩ ⟨the case falls into the ~ of this act⟩ — compare CIRCLE 5b (2) **:** DENOTATION 4 **syn** see FIELD

²**sphere** \"\ *vt* -ED/-ING/-S **1 :** to place in or as if in a sphere or among the spheres **:** raise aloft **:** ENSPHERE **2 a :** to form into a sphere **:** make round or spherical **b :** to make complete **:** PERFECT **3 :** to enclose in or as if in a sphere **:** SURROUND **4** *archaic* **:** to send in a circuit **:** cause to turn in all directions **:** CIRCULATE

sphere crystal *n* **:** SPHAERAPHIS

sphere fungus *n* **:** a fungus of the order Sphaeriales

sphere gap *n* **:** a spark gap (sense 2) in which the electrode terminals are metal spheres

sphere·less \-ləs\ *adj* **:** lacking a sphere and esp. an orbit **:** WANDERING

sphere of influence 1 : a territorial area within which the political influence or the interests of one nation are held to be more or less paramount **2 :** a region more or less under the control of a nation but not constituting a formally recognized protectorate

spheric \ˈsfirik, -fer-, -rēk\ *adj* [MF *spherique*, fr. LL *sphaericus*] **:** of or relating to a sphere or the spheres **:** resembling a sphere **:** SPHERICAL, ORBITAL ⟨~ shape⟩ ⟨~ geometry⟩

spheri·cal \-rəkəl, -rēk-\ *adj* [LL *sphaericus* (fr. Gk *sphairikos*, fr. *sphaira* sphere + *-ikos* -ic) + E *-al*] **1 :** having the form of a sphere or of one of its segments **:** like a sphere **:** GLOBULAR, ORBICULAR ⟨a ~ body⟩ **2 :** of or relating to a sphere **:** having to do with a sphere or with the properties of a sphere ⟨a ~ coordinate⟩ ⟨~ deviation⟩ **3 :** of or relating to the celestial bodies or their spheres ⟨thieves . . . by ~ predominance —Shak.⟩ — **spheri·cal·ly** \-rək(ə)lē, -rēk-, -li\ *adv*

spherical aberration *n* **:** aberration caused by the spherical form of a lens or mirror that gives different foci for central and marginal rays

spherical angle *n* **:** the angle between two intersecting arcs of great circles of a sphere measured by the plane angle formed by the tangents to the arcs at the point of intersection

spherical astronomy *n* **:** a branch of astronomy that deals chiefly with problems relating to the celestial sphere

spherical coordinate *n* **:** any of three coordinates in space two being obtained by constructing in a plane a polar coordinate system and the third being the angle between this plane and a fixed plane containing the polar axis

spherical excess *n* **:** the amount by which the sum of the three angles of a spherical triangle exceeds two right angles

spherical geometry *n* **:** the geometry of figures on a sphere

spheri·cal·i·ty \ˌsfirəˈkaləd·ē, -fer-\ *n* -ES **:** ROUNDNESS, SPHERICITY

spherical lens *n* **:** a lens whose surfaces form portions of perfect spheres

spherical mirror *n* **:** a mirror with a surface that is either concave or convex and forms a portion of a true sphere

spheri·cal·ness *n* -ES **:** the quality or state of being spherical **:** spherical form

spherical perspective *n* **:** curvilinear perspective in which a picture is made upon a spherical surface

spherical polygon *n* **:** a figure analogous to a plane polygon that is formed on a sphere by arcs of great circles

spherical sailing *n* **:** sailing in which the earth is regarded as a spherical or spheroidal figure and allowance is made for the curvature of its surface in directing the course of a ship

spherical sector *n* **:** SECTOR OF A SPHERE

spherical triangle *n* **:** a spherical polygon of three sides

spherical trigonometry *n* **:** trigonometry applied to spherical triangles and polygons

spherical vault *n* **:** a vault having approximately the form of part of a sphere **:** a cupola of circular plan

spherical wedge *n* **:** the portion of a sphere included between two half planes that intersect in a diameter

sphe·ric·i·ty \sfəˈrisəd·ē\ *n* -ES [NL *sphaericitas*, fr. LL *sphaericus* spherical + L *-itas* -ity] **:** the quality or state of being spherical **:** ROUNDNESS; *esp* **:** the degree of perfection of the surface of a sphere

¹**spherics** \ˈsfiriks, -fer-, -rēks\ *n pl but sing in constr* [modif. (influenced by E *-s*, pl. suffix) of NL *sphaerica*, fr. fem. of LL *sphaericus* spherical] **1 :** SPHERICAL GEOMETRY **2 :** SPHERICAL TRIGONOMETRY

²**spherics** \"\ *var of* SFERICS

spherier *comparative of* SPHERY

spheriest *superlative of* SPHERY

spheri·form \ˈsfirəˌfȯrm, -fer-\ *adj* [*sphaer-* + *-iform*] **:** SPHERICAL

sphering *pres part of* SPHERE

sphero- — see SPHAER-

sphero·crystal \ˈsfi(ˌ)rō, -fe(-+,-\ *n* [ISV *sphaer-* + *crystal*] **:** a spherical crystal aggregate

sphero·cyte \ˈsfirəˌsīt, -fer-\ *n* -S [ISV *sphaer-* + *-cyte*] **:** a more or less globular red blood cell that is characteristic of some hemolytic anemias — compare SPHEROCYTOSIS — **sphero·cyt·ic** \¦=ˈsid·ik\ *adj*

sphero·cy·to·sis \ˌ=ˌsīˈtōsəs\ *n* -ES [NL, fr. ISV *spherocyte* + NL *-osis*] **:** a familial anemia in which the red blood cells are smaller than normal and spherical in form and which commonly accompanies congenital hemolytic jaundice

sphero·graph \ˈsfirəˌgraf, -fer-, -ˌgräf\ *n* [*sphaer-* + *-graph*] **1 :** two cardboards used esp. in navigation and astronomy, containing various circles, and turning upon each other in such a manner that any possible spherical triangle may be readily found and the measure of the parts read off by inspection **2 :** a disk ruled with meridians and parallels in stereographic projection for the solution of problems in spherics

spheroid *or* **sphaeroid** \ˈsfiˌrȯid, -fe,r-\ *n* -S [LL *sphaeroides* spherical, fr. Gk *sphairoeidēs*, fr. *sphaira* sphere + *-oeidēs* -oid — more at SPHERE] **:** a figure resembling but not identical to a sphere; *esp* **:** ELLIPSOID OF REVOLUTION

sphe·roi·dal \(ˈ)sfi¦rȯidᵊl, sfəˈr-\ *also* **spheroid** \ˈsfiˌrȯid, -fe,r-\ *adj* **:** having the form of a spheroid **:** consisting of or characterized by spheroids — **sphe·roi·dal·ly** \(ˈ)sfi¦rȯidᵊlē, sfə¦r-, -ᵊli\ *adv*

spheroidal galaxy *n* **:** ELLIPTICAL GALAXY

spheroidal recovery *n* **:** a hypothetical more or less complete resumption by the earth of spheroidal form after distortion (as is sometimes held to follow periods of collapse to tetrahedral shape)

spheroidal state *n* **:** the state of a liquid (as water) when on being thrown on a surface of highly heated metal it gathers in flattened drops or round-edged masses that are at a temperature several degrees below ebullition and are without actual contact with the heated surface owing to a cushion of nonconducting vapor

sphe·roi·di·cal \sfəˈrȯidəkəl, sfeˈr-\ *adj* [*spheroid* + *-ical*] *archaic* **:** SPHEROIDAL — **sphe·roi·di·cal·ly** \-k(ə)lē\ *adv, archaic*

spheroid·ic·i·ty \ˌsfiˌrȯiˈdisəd·ē, -fe,r-\ *n* -ES [*spheroidical* + *-ity*] **:** the quality or state of being spheroidal

spheroid·ism \ˈ=ˌ=ˌdizəm\ *n* -S **1 :** the quality or state of being a spheroid **2 :** spheroidal condition

spheroid·iza·tion \ˌ=ˌ=ˌdəˈzāshən, -ˌdīˈz-\ *n* -S **1 :** the act of spheroidizing steel **2 :** the condition of steel that has been spheroidized

spheroid·ize \ˈ=ˌ=ˌdīz\ *vt* -ED/-ING/-S [*spheroid* + *-ize*] **:** to subject (an iron-base alloy) to prolonged heating near the critical temperature and then to slow cooling so that the iron carbide assumes a globular form — compare ANNEAL, HEAT-TREAT

spherome \ˈsfiˌrōm, -fe,r-\ *n* -S [ISV *sphaer-* + *-ome*; orig. formed as F *sphérome*] **:** CYTOME

sphe·rom·e·ter \sfəˈräməd·ə(r)\ *n* [ISV *sphaer-* + *-meter*; orig. formed as F *sphéromètre*] **:** an instrument for measuring the curvature of a spherical surface

spherometer

sphe·roph·o·rus \sfəˈräfərəs\ *n, cap* [NL, fr. *spher-* + *-phorus*] **:** a genus comprising markedly pleomorphic gram-negative rod-shaped bacteria of uncertain systematic position and including various organisms associated with suppurative and necrotic processes in man and various lower animals — compare BULLNOSE

spheru·la \ˈsfir(y)ələ, -fer-\ *n, pl* **spheru·lae** \-ˌlē, -ˌlī\ *also* **spherulas** [NL, fr. LL *sphaerula* spherule] **:** a small spherical sponge spicule

spheru·lar \-lə(r)\ *adj* [*spherule* + *-ar*] **:** taking the form of or resembling a spherule

spheru·late \-lət, -ˌlāt\ *adj* [*spherule* + *-ate*] **:** covered or set with spherules or tubercles

spherule \ˈsfi(ˌ)rül, -fel, |r(ˌ)yül\ *n* -S [LL *sphaerula*, dim. of L *sphaera* sphere — more at SPHERE] **1 :** a little sphere or spherical body **2** [NL *spherula*] **:** SPHERULA

spheru·lite \ˈsfir(y)əˌlīt, -fer-\ *n* -S [*spherule* + *-ite*] **:** a usu. spherical crystalline body made up of radiating crystal fibers, often found in vitreous volcanic rocks (as obsidian and perlite), and commonly constituting an intergrowth of quartz and feldspar

spheru·lit·ic \¦==ˈlid·ik\ *adj* **:** of, relating to, made up of, or being spherulites

spheru·lit·ize \ˈ==ˌlīd·ˌīz\ *vt* -ED/-ING/-S **:** to convert into spherulites

sphery \ˈsfi(ə)rē\ *adj* -ER/-EST [*sphere* + *-y*] **1 :** of, relating to, or suggestive of the heavenly spheres or the music of the spheres **2 :** STARLIKE

sphet·er·ize \ˈsfed·əˌrīz\ *vt* -ED/-ING/-S [Gk *spheterizein*, fr. *spheteros* their own, their (fr. *spheis* they) + *-izein* -ize; akin to L *se* oneself — more at SUICIDE] **:** to take for one's own **:** APPROPRIATE

¹**sphex** \ˈsfeks\ *n* [NL, fr. Gk *sphēk-*, *sphēx* wasp] **1** *cap* **:** a genus of wasps that is the type of the family Sphecidae **2** *pl* **sphe·ges** \ˈsfē(ˌ)jēz\ *also* **sphexes :** any wasp of the genus *Sphex*

²**sphex** \"\ [NL] *syn of* CHLORION

sphinc·ter \ˈsfiŋ(k)tə(r)\ *n* -S [LL, fr. Gk *sphinktēr* band, sphincter; akin to Gk *sphingein* to bind fast, L *spatium* space — more at SPEED] **:** an annular muscle surrounding and able to contract or close a bodily opening or channel ⟨the anal ~⟩ ⟨a ~ muscle⟩ ⟨suffering from sphincteralgia⟩

sphinc·ter·al \-tərəl\ *adj* **:** of, relating to, or functioning as a sphincter

sphincter ani \-ˈāˌnī, -ˈä(ˌ)nē\ *n* [NL] **:** ANAL SPHINCTER

sphinc·ter·ate \-tərət, -təˌrāt\ *or* **sphinc·trate** \-ŋ(k)trət, -ˌtrāt\ *adj* [*sphincter* + *-ate*] **1 :** provided with or contracted by a sphincter **2 :** constricted in the middle as if by a sphincter

sphinc·ter·ic \(ˈ)sfiŋ(k)¦terik\ *adj* **:** of, relating to, or being a sphincter

sphincter of od·di \-ˈädē\ *usu cap 2d O* [after Ruggero *Oddi*, 19th cent. Ital. physician] **:** a complex sphincter closing the duodenal orifice of the common bile duct

sphinc·ter·ot·o·my \ˌsfiŋ(k)təˈräd·əmē\ *n* -ES [ISV *sphincter* + *-o-* + *-tomy*] **:** surgical incision of a sphincter

sphincter pu·pil·lae \-pyüˈpi(ˌ)lē, -pyüˈpi,lī\ *n* [NL, pupillar sphincter] **:** a broad flat band of smooth muscle in the iris and surrounding the pupil of the eye

sphincter va·gi·nae \-vəˈjī(ˌ)nē\ *n* [NL, vaginal sphincter] **:** the female bulbocavernosus

¹**sphin·did** \ˈsfindəd\ *adj* [NL *Sphindidae*] **:** of or relating to the Sphindidae

²**sphindid** \"\ *n* -S **:** a beetle of the family Sphindidae

sphin·di·dae \-ndəˌdē\ *n pl, cap* [NL, fr. *Sphindus*, type genus + *-idae*] **:** a family of small clavicorn tenebrionid beetles living in dry fungi on trees

sphinges *pl of* SPHINX

¹**sphin·gid** \ˈsfinjəd\ *adj* [NL *Sphingidae*] **:** of or relating to the Sphingidae

²**sphingid** \"\ *n* -S **:** a moth of the family Sphingidae **:** HAWKMOTH

sphin·gi·dae \-jəˌdē\ *n pl, cap* [NL, fr. *Sphing-*, *Sphinx*, type genus + *-idae*] **:** a family of typically large heavy-bodied strong-flying moths with narrow elongated wings that comprise the hawkmoths

sphin·gine \ˈsfinˌjīn, -ˌjən\ *adj* [L *sphing-*, *sphinx* + E *-ine*] **:** resembling a sphinx ⟨my most ~ smile —Aldous Huxley⟩

sphingo- *comb form* [ISV, fr. Gk *sphingein* to bind fast — more at SPHINCTER] **1 :** deflection **:** bending ⟨*sphingo*meter⟩ **2 :** sphingomyelin ⟨*sphingo*sine⟩

sphin·go·lipid *also* **sphin·go·lipide** \¦sfiŋ(ˌ)gō+\ *n* [*sphingo-* + *lipid, lipide*] **:** any of a group of lipids (as sphingomyelins and cerebrosides) that yield sphingosine or one of its derivatives as one product of hydrolysis — compare GLYCOLIPID

sphin·gom·e·ter \sfiŋˈgäməd·ə(r), -inˈg-\ *n* [*sphingo-* + *-meter*] **:** an instrument for measuring the bending of a strut (as by deflection of beams of light)

sphin·go·myelin \¦sfiŋ(ˌ)gō+\ *n* [ISV *sphingo-* (fr. Gk *sphingein* to bind fast) + *myelin*] **:** any of a group of crystalline phosphatides that are obtained esp. from nerve tissue and that on hydrolysis yield a fatty acid (as lignoceric acid), sphingosine or its saturated dihydro derivative, choline, and phosphoric acid

sphin·go·sine \ˈsfiŋgəˌsēn, -ˌsən\ *n* -S [ISV, irreg. fr. *sphingo-* + *-ine*] **:** an unsaturated amino glycol $C_{18}H_{33}(OH)_2NH_2$ obtained by hydrolysis of various sphingomyelins, cerebrosides, and gangliosides

sphinx \ˈsfiŋ(k)s\ *n* [ME *Spynx* the sphinx of Thebes who according to Greek legend destroyed all passers who could not solve the riddle she proposed until Oedipus guessed it and caused the sphinx to kill herself, fr. L *Sphinx*, fr. Gk, the sphinx of Thebes, person resembling the sphinx; akin to Gk *sphingein* to bind fast; prob. fr. the spell she cast — more at SPHINCTER] **1** *pl* **sphinx·es** \-iŋ(k)səz\ *or* **sphin·ges** \-inˌjēz\ **a :** an enigmatic monster in ancient Greek mythology having typically a lion's body, wings, and the head and bust of a woman; *also* **:** a monster resembling a Grecian sphinx in appearance or character **b :** a person who resembles the sphinx of ancient Greece esp. in enigmatic or inscrutable character or in speaking enigmatically **2** *pl* **sphinxes** *or* **sphinges :** an ancient Egyptian image in the form of a recumbent lion having a man's head, a ram's head, or a hawk's head **3** [NL, fr. L *Sphinx*] **a** *cap* **:** the type genus of Sphingidae formerly coextensive with the family but now including only a few hawkmoths with larvae that often assume a position suggestive of the Egyptian sphinx **b** *pl* **sphinges** *also* **sphinxes :** any moth of the genus *Sphinx* or family Sphingidae **:** HAWKMOTH **4** *pl* **sphinxes** *or* **sphinges :** a grayish yellowish brown that is darker than deer and slightly darker than acorn — called also *mustang* **5** *pl* **sphinxes** *or* **sphinges** [L, an ape, perh. chimpanzee, fr. Gk, an ape, fr. *Sphinx*] **:** SPHINX BABOON

sphinx baboon *n* **:** a large West African baboon (*Papio sphinx*) often kept in menageries

sphinx caterpillar *n* **:** the larva of a hawk moth

sphinx·ian \ˈsfiŋ(k)sēən\ *adj* **:** of, relating to, or resembling a sphinx

sphinxlike \ˈ=ˌ=\ *adj* **:** resembling a sphinx esp. in enigmatic inscrutable quality

sphinx moth *n* **:** HAWKMOTH

sphoe·roi·des \sfəˈrȯi(ˌ)dēz\ *n, cap* [NL, fr. *sphoer-* (alter. of *sphaer-*) + L *-oides* -oid] **:** a common genus of globefishes

sphrag·ide \ˈsfraˌjīd, -ˌjəd\ *n* -S [L *sphragid-*, *sphragis*, fr. Gk, seal, signet; fr. the fact that it was sold in sealed packets] **:** LEMNIAN BOLE

sphra·gis·tic \sfrəˈjistik\ *adj* [LGk *sphragistikos*, fr. Gk *sphragistos* sealed (fr. *sphragizein* to close with a seal, fr. *sphragis* seal + *-izein* -ize) + *-ikos* -ic] **:** of or relating to a seal or signet **:** dealing with seals ⟨~ studies⟩

sphra·gis·tics \-ks\ *n pl but usu sing in constr* [LGk *sphragistikē* (fem. of *sphragistikos* sphragistic) + E *-s* (pl. suffix)] **:** the science of seals and signets dealing esp. with their history, age, distinctions of types, manner of use, and legal function **:** SIGILLOGRAPHY

sp ht *abbr* specific heat

sphyg·mic \ˈsfigmik\ *adj* [Gk *sphygmikos*, fr. *sphygmos* pulse + *-ikos* -ic] **:** of or relating to the circulatory pulse

sphygmo- *comb form* [Gk, fr. *sphygmos*; akin to Gk *asphyxia* stopping of the pulse — more at ASPHYXIA] **:** pulse ⟨*sphygmo*gram⟩

sphyg·mo·chronograph \¦sfig(ˌ)mō+\ *n* [*sphygmo-* + *chronograph*] **:** an instrument for recording the movements of the pulse

sphyg·mo·gram \ˈsfigməˌgram\ *n* [ISV *sphygmo-* + *-gram*] **:** a tracing made by a sphygmograph and consisting of a series of curves that correspond to the beats of the heart

sphyg·mo·graph \-ˌraf, -ˌräf\ *n* [ISV *sphygmo-* + *-graph*] **:** an instrument that when applied over an artery records graphically the movements or character of the pulse — **sphyg·mo·graph·ic** \¦==¦==\ *adj* — **sphyg·mog·ra·phy** \sfigˈmägrəfē\ *n* -ES

sphyg·mo·manometer \¦sfig(ˌ)mō+\ *n* [ISV *sphygmo-* + *manometer*; orig. formed as F *sphygmomanomètre*] **:** an instrument for measuring blood pressure and esp. arterial blood pressure

sphyg·mo·manometric \"+\ *adj* [ISV *sphygmomanometry* + *-ic*] **1 :** obtained with a sphygmomanometer ⟨~ readings⟩ **2 :** of or relating to sphygmomanometry — **sphyg·mo·man·ometrically** \"+\ *adv*

sphyg·mo·manometry \"+\ *n* -ES [*sphygmomanometer* + *-y*] **:** determination of blood pressure by use of the sphygmomanometer

sphyg·mom·e·ter \sfigˈmäməd·ə(r)\ *n* [ISV *sphygmo-* + *-meter*] **:** an instrument for measuring the strength of the pulse beat

sphy·rae·ni·dae \-nəˌdē\ *n pl, cap* [NL, fr. *Sphyraena*, type genus + *-idae*] **:** a monotypic family of large active elongated cylindrical small-scaled fishes (suborder Mugiloidea) having a large mouth with a projecting lower jaw and long strong teeth in jaws and palate — see BARRACUDA

sphy·ra·pi·cus \ˌsfīrəˈpīkəs\ *n, cap* [NL, fr. Gk *sphyra* hammer + L *picus* woodpecker — more at PIE] **:** a genus of American woodpeckers consisting of the sapsuckers

sphyr·i·on \ˈsfirēˌän, -ēən\ *n, pl* **sphyrions** \-nz\ *or* **sphyr·ia** \-ēə\ [Gk, small mallet, small hammer, dim. of *sphyra* mallet, hammer] **:** MALLEOLAR POINT

sphyr·na \ˈsfərnə\ *n, cap* [NL, modif. of Gk *sphyra* hammer] **:** a genus (the type of the family Sphyrnidae) of large voracious chiefly tropical sharks including the hammerhead shark

sphyr·ni·dae \ˈsfərnəˌdē\ *n pl, cap* [NL, fr. *Sphyrna*, type genus + *-idae*] **:** a family of sharks that have the head highly modified and that include the hammerheads and bonnetheads

spi·al \ˈspīəl\ *n* -S [ME (Sc) *spyale*, fr. ME *spyen*, *spien* to spy + *-ale*, *-aille* -al] **1** *obs* **:** ESPIAL, WATCH **2** *archaic* **:** SPY, SCOUT

spic *sometimes cap, var of* SPIK

spi·ca \ˈspīkə\ *n, pl* **spi·cae** \-ˌīˌsē, -ˌsī\ *or* **spicas** [L, head (of grain); fr. the resemblance of the successive V-shaped crossings of the bandage to the rows on a head of grain — more at SPIKE] **:** a spiral reverse plain or plaster bandage used to immobilize a limb esp. at a joint ⟨hip ~⟩

spic-and-span *var of* SPICK-AND-SPAN

spi·car·ia \spīˈka(a)rēə\ *n, cap* [NL, fr. L *spica* + NL *-aria*] **:** a form genus of imperfect fungi (family Moniliaceae) characterized by nonseptate hyaline conidia borne in chains on verticillate conidiophores

spi·cate \ˈspīˌkāt, *usu* -ād·+V\ *adj* [L *spicatus*, past part. of *spicare* to furnish with heads of grain, arrange in the shape of heads of grain, fr. *spica*] **:** POINTED, SPIKED; *specif* **:** arranged in the form of a spike **:** resembling a spike ⟨a ~ inflorescence⟩

spi·cat·ed \-ˌkād·əd\ *adj* [L *spicatus* + E *-ed*] **:** SPICATE

¹**spic·ca·to** \spəˈkäd·(ˌ)ō\ *adj* [It, past part. of *spiccare* to detach, make distinct] **:** performed with springing bow **:** ARCO SALTANDO — used as a direction in music for stringed instruments

²**spiccato** \"\ *n* -S **:** something (as technique, a performance, or a passage) that is spiccato

¹**spice** \ˈspīs\ *n* -S *often attrib* [ME, fr. OF *espice*, fr. LL *species* spices, fr. L, sight, outward appearance, sort, fr. *specere* to look — more at SPY] **1 a :** any of various aromatic vegetable products (as pepper, cinnamon, nutmeg, mace, allspice, ginger, cloves) used in cookery to season food and to flavor foods (as sauces, pickles, cakes) **b :** a substance or collection of substances used as a spice ⟨add ~ to a cake⟩ **2 a** *archaic* **:** a small portion, quantity, or admixture **:** DASH, TOUCH, TASTE **b :** something that enriches or alters the quality of a thing esp. in a small degree **:** something that gives zest or pungency **:** a piquant or pleasing flavor **:** RELISH ⟨our friends have all . . . a ~ of mischief in their constitutions —F.A. Swinnerton⟩ ⟨scandals a hundred years old usually lack ~ for anyone save the antiquary —Katharine F. Gerould⟩ **3 :** a pungent or fragrant odor **:** PERFUME **4 :** a brownish orange that is redder and duller than leather, stronger, slightly redder, and darker than gold pheasant, and slightly redder and darker than prairie brown, Windsor tan, Titian, or amber brown

²**spice** \"\ *vt* -ED/-ING/-S [ME *spicen*, fr. *spice*, n.] **1 :** to season with spices **:** mix aromatic or pungent substances with **:** FLAVOR, SEASON ⟨~ a sauce⟩ **2 :** to season as if with spices **:** make spicy, piquant, or pleasing ⟨his chapters are *spiced* with a wealth of curious and amusing detail —*Brit. Bk. News*⟩ ⟨these anecdotes, if *spiced* with derision, remained unflavored by malice —J.B.Cabell⟩ ⟨days of adventure, all the pleasanter for being *spiced* with danger —W.H. Hudson †1922⟩ — often used with *up* ⟨never misses a trick to ~ things up for the ordinary customer —Hal Lehrman⟩

spice·able \-səbəl\ *adj* **:** capable of being spiced

spice·berry \ˈspīs- — *see* BERRY\ *n* **1 :** WINTERGREEN 2a **2 :** RED STOPPER **3 :** SPICEBUSH

spice birch *n* **:** SWEET BIRCH

spice box *n* **:** a box holding or designed to hold spices; *esp* **:** a box fitted with smaller boxes for holding spices

spice brown *n* **:** a variable color averaging a moderate brown that is darker and very slightly yellower and stronger than auburn, redder, darker, and slightly stronger than chestnut brown, yellower and slightly duller than bay, and yellower and duller than toast brown

spice box

spicebush \'ˌ=ˌ=\ *n* **1 :** an aromatic shrub (*Lindera benzoin*) bearing dense clusters of small yellow flowers followed by scarlet or yellow berries — called also *American spicebush* **2 :** any of several shrubs of the genus *Calycanthus; esp* **:** a tall upright shrub (*C. occidentalis*) with slightly fragrant brown flowers — compare CAROLINA ALLSPICE

spicebush swallowtail *n* **:** a rather dark swallowtail butterfly (*Papilio troilus*) of eastern No. America

spice currant *n* **:** GOLDEN CURRANT

spiced \'spīst\ *adj* [ME, fr. past part. of *spicen* to spice] **1 :** flavored with or as if with spice **:** SPICY **2** *obs* **:** NICE, DAINTY, SCRUPULOUS, SQUEAMISH **3 :** filled or impregnated with the odor of spices **:** FRAGRANT

spice·less \'=ləs\ *adj* **:** lacking spice **:** not spiced

spice nut *n* **:** a small crisp highly spiced cookie

spic·ery \'spīs(ə)rē\ *n* -ES [ME *spicerie*, fr. OF *espicerie*, fr. *espice* spice + *-erie* -ery] **1 :** SPICES **2 a** *archaic* **:** a storage place (as a pantry or warehouse) for spices **b** *obs* **:** a spice shop **c** *obs* **:** the department of the royal household connected with the keeping of spices **3 :** a spicy or aromatic quality **:** SPICINESS

spice tree *n* **:** CALIFORNIA LAUREL

spicewood \'=ˌ=\ *n* **:** any of several trees or shrubs having spicy aromatic wood; *esp* **:** SPICEBUSH 1

spicey *var of* SPICY

spicier *comparative of* SPICY

spiciest *superlative of* SPICY

spi·ci·form \'spīsə,fȯrm\ *adj* [prob. fr. (assumed) NL *spiciformis*, fr. L *spici-* (fr. *spica* head of grain) + *-formis* -form — more at SPIKE] **:** shaped like a spike ⟨~ panicle⟩

spi·cig·er·ous \(')spī¦sij(ə)rəs\ *adj* [prob. fr. (assumed) NL *spiciger* spicate (fr. L *spici-* — fr. *spica* head of grain — + *-ger* -gerous) + E *-ous*] **:** SPICATE

spic·i·ly \'spīsəlē, -li\ *adv* **:** in a spicy manner **:** with seasoning (as of spices) **:** PUNGENTLY

spic·i·ness \-sēnəs, -sin-\ *n* -ES **:** the quality of being spicy **:** PUNGENCY

spicing *n* -S **:** SEASONING ⟨its liberal ~ of humor —Hywel Evans⟩

¹spick \'spik\ *n* -S [ME *spyk*, fr. OE *spic* — more at SPECK] *obs* **:** FAT, GREASE, BLUBBER

²spick \"\ *n* -S [MF *espic, spic*, fr. OProv *espic* head (of grain), fr. L *spica* — more at SPIKE] *dial Eng* **:** LAVENDER

³spick \"\ *adj* -ER/-EST [by shortening] **:** SPICK-AND-SPAN

⁴spick *sometimes cap, var of* SPIK

¹spick-and-span *or* **spic-and-span** \¦spikən¦span, -k°ŋ¦-, -paa(ə)n\ *also* **spick-and-span-new** \¦==¦=¦=\ *adj* [*spic-and-span* alter. of *spick-and-span*, short for *spick-and-span-new*, fr. obs. E *spick* spike, nail (alter. of E ¹*spike*) + E *and* + *span-new*] **1 :** quite new **:** FRESH, BRAND-NEW ⟨a *spick-and-span* novelty⟩ **2 :** like new **:** spotlessly clean **:** SPRUCE ⟨his cottage was *spick-and-span* —J.B.Clayton⟩ ⟨a *spick-and-span* figure in his Panama hat and neat clothes —G.K.Chesterton⟩ ⟨automobile owner who likes to keep his car *spick-and-span* —*New Yorker*⟩ **syn** see NEAT

²spick-and-span *or* **spic-and-span** \"\ *adv* **:** in a spick-and-span manner ⟨clean the kitchen *spick-and-span*⟩

spick-and-spandy \-¦spandē, -aan-, -di\ *adj (or adv)* [by alter.] **:** SPICK-AND-SPAN

spick-and-span·ness \-nəs\ *n* -ES **:** the quality or state of being spick-and-span

spick·et \'spikət, *usu* -əd·+V\ *n* -S [ME *spyket*, alter. of ¹*spigot*] *chiefly South & Midland* **:** SPIGOT

spick·le \'spikəl\ *n* -S [by alter.] **:** SPICULE

spick·nel \'spiknəl\ *also* **spig·nel** \-ign-\ *n* -S [origin unknown] **:** a European perennial herb (*Meum athamanticum*) having finely divided strongly aromatic leaves and minute white flowers

spi·cose \'spī,kōs\ *adj* [L *spica* head (of grain) + E *-ose*] **:** having spikes ⟨~ flowers⟩ — **spi·cos·i·ty** \spī'käsəd·ē\ *n* -ES

spi·cous \'spīkəs\ *adj* [L *spica* head (of grain) + E *-ous*] **:** SPICOSE — **spi·cous·ness** *n* -ES

spic·u·la \'spikyələ\ *n, pl* **spicu·lae** \-,lē, -,lī\ [NL, fr. ML, arrowhead, alter. of L *spiculum* arrowhead, arrow] **:** SPICULE, PRICKLE

spic·u·lar \-lə(r)\ *adj* [prob. fr. (assumed) NL *spicularis*, fr. NL *spicula* & L *spiculum* + L *-aris* -ar] **:** of, relating to, or like a spicule **:** SPICULATE ⟨~ ice⟩

spicular cell *n* **:** IDIOBLAST 1a

spic·u·late \-lət, -,lāt, *usu* -d·+V\ *adj* [prob. fr. (assumed) NL *spiculatus*, fr. NL *spicula* & L *spiculum* + L *-atus* -ate] **1 :** covered with or having spicules **:** SPICULAR, PRICKLY **2 :** divided into small spikelets

spic·u·lat·ed \-,lād·əd\ *adj* [prob. fr. (assumed) NL *spiculatus* + E *-ed*] **:** SPICULATE

spic·u·la·tion \,=='lāshən\ *n* -S [*spicule* + *-ation*] **1 :** the formation of spicules **2 a :** the form and arrangement of spicules **b :** the spicular component of a sponge

spic·ule \'spi,kyül\ *n* -S [NL *spicula* & L *spiculum* small sharp organ or part, sting, arrowhead, arrow; L *spiculum* fr. *spica* head of grain) + *-ulum* — more at SPIKE] **1 a :** a small fleshy point or appendage (as the sterigma in basidiomycetous fungi) **b :** SPIKELET **c :** the empty siliceous shell of a diatom **2 a :** one of the numerous small often very minute calcareous or siliceous bodies occurring in and serving to stiffen and support the tissues of various invertebrates (as the majority of sponges and alcyonarians and many radiolarians, holothurians, and compound ascidians) and having forms that are very varied and often characteristic of a species or other group **b :** a spikelike organ ⟨a copulatory ~⟩ **:** SPICULUM 1 **3 :** any minute slender pointed body **:** a needlelike body esp. of bony or other hard material ⟨~s of ice⟩ **4 :** a very small spikelike short-lived prominence appearing close to the chromosphere of the solar atmosphere and occurring in greatest numbers at the sun's poles

spic·u·lif·er·ous \¦spikyə¦lif(ə)rəs\ *adj* [prob. fr. (assumed) NL *spiculifer* spiculiferous (fr. L *spiculi-* — fr. NL *spicula* & L *spiculum* — + *-fer* -ferous) + E *-ous*] **:** bearing spicules

spic·u·lose \'==,lōs\ *adj* [*spicule* + *-ose*] **:** having or full of spicules **:** SPICULIFEROUS

spic·u·lum \-,ləm\ *n, pl* **spicu·la** \-lə\ [L, small sharp organ or part, sting, arrowhead, arrow] **1 :** any of various small spicular organs (as the spines of an echinoderm, the dart of various snails, or a copulatory bristle on a nematode) **2 :** SPICULE

spicy *also* **spicey** \'spīsē, -si\ *adj* **spicier; spiciest** [¹*spice* + *-y*] **1 :** having the quality of spice ⟨a ~ flavor⟩ ⟨clams had steamed in ~ seaweed —Marcia Davenport⟩ **2 :** flavored with spice **:** SPICED ⟨~ foods⟩ **3 :** producing or abounding in spices ⟨~ islands⟩ **4 :** having a fragrance suggestive of spices **:** AROMATIC ⟨blossoms of fervid hue and ~ fragrance —Nathaniel Hawthorne⟩ ⟨the sky is clear and clean, the air ~ —A.E.Coppard⟩ ⟨swampland, ~ with the odor of pine and cedar —*Amer. Guide Series: N.C.*⟩ **5 :** SPIRITED, PEPPERY, ZESTFUL ⟨the ~ and brisk quality of this adorable autocrat is indicated by well-chosen quotations —Agnes de Mille⟩ ⟨a ~ temper⟩ **6 :** PIQUANT, RACY ⟨uttering his famous shrill whistle and a variety of ~ language —*Current Biog.*⟩; *esp* **:** somewhat scandalous or salacious ⟨resisted every temptation to say ~ things in the footnotes —C.R.Sanders⟩ ⟨a ~ gossip⟩ ⟨~ magazines⟩ **syn** see PUNGENT

spicy fleabane *n* **:** a marsh fleabane (*Pluchea camphorata*) with petioled sharply serrate leaves and a round-topped flower cluster

¹spi·der \'spīdə(r)\ *n* -S *often attrib* [ME *spyder*, alter. of *spithre*; akin to OE *spinnan* to spin — more at SPIN] **1 a :** an animal of the order Araneida **b :** any of various other arthropods (as a pycnogonid) esp. of the class Arachnida that resemble the true spiders — usu. used with a qualifying term; see RED SPIDER **2 :** one felt to resemble a spider (as in appearance or in scheming) **3 :** a cast-iron frying pan orig. made with short feet to stand among coals on the hearth **4 :** a metal outrigger to keep a block clear (as of the mast) **5 :** a contrivance consisting of a frame or skeleton having radiating arms or members: as **a :** a frame for strengthening a core or mold in founding **b :** a casting forming the hub and spokes to which the rim of a wheel or pulley is secured **c :** the body or solid hub of a built-up piston **d :** a machine element consisting of a ring with projections outward **e :** a hub with radiating arms interposed between the shaft and the core of a dynamo or motor armature **6 a :** SPIDER CART **b :** SPIDER PHAETON **7 :** SPIDER NEVUS **8 :** SET GAGE **9 :** an obstruction in the teat of a cow; *esp* **:** a small irregular horny growth following bruises or other irritation **10** *often cap* **:** a solitaire or patience game played with two packs of cards dealt in a row of ten piles among which the cards are shifted to assemble them in complete suits **11 :** the part of a dynamic loudspeaker that properly positions the voice coil relative to the magnet and that usu. consists of a flexible fiber ring **12 :** a frame on an explosive mine that when pressed detonates the mine

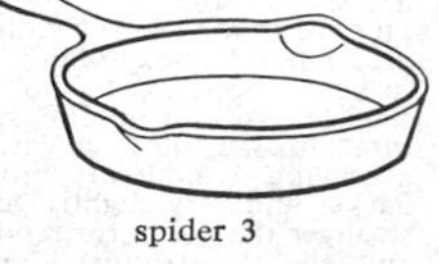

spider 3

²spider \"\ *vb* -ED/-ING/-S **:** to crack or shatter in a radiating pattern of thin lines ⟨the wall was . . . ~*ed* with cracks —A.R. Foff⟩

spider angioma *n* **:** SPIDER NEVUS

spider ant *n* **:** VELVET ANT

spider band *also* **spider hoop** *n* **1 :** a metal band around a ship's mast having sockets for belaying pins **2 :** a metal band around a ship's mast having eyebolts to which the lower ends of the futtock shrouds are secured

spider beetle *n* **:** any of various small destructive beetles of the genus *Ptinus* (as *P. fur* and *P. brunneus*) that resemble spiders and have larvae which feed on woolen goods, fur, feathers, flour, and seeds; *broadly* **:** a ptinid beetle

spider bug *n* **:** a bug of the genus *Ploiaria*

spider cart *or* **spider wagon** *n* **:** a light cart having a high body and large slenderly constructed wheels

spider cell *n* **:** one of the astrocytes typical of the white matter and distinguished from the mossy cells by very long unbranched processes

spider crab *n* **:** any of numerous oxyrhynchan crabs esp. of the large family Majidae having more or less triangular bodies which they often cover with kelp or other plants, a well-developed spiny rostrum, and extremely long legs and including some that are among the largest of crustaceans — see GIANT CRAB

spider diver *n, Brit* **:** LITTLE GREBE

spider fern *n* **:** RIBBON FERN 2

spiderflower \'===,=\ *n* [so called fr. the long stamens] **1 :** a plant of the genus *Cleome* **2 :** any of several shrubs of the genus *Tibouchina* whose flowers have long stamens — see BRAZILIAN SPIDERFLOWER **3 :** GREVILLEA 2

spider fly *n* **1 :** a sheep ked, bat fly, or similar usu. wingless parasitic dipterous insect **2 :** an artificial fly tied to imitate a spider or a spiderlike insect

spider hunter *n* **:** any of various relatively large long-billed East Indian sunbirds of the genus *Arachnothera*

spidering *pres part of* SPIDER

spider·less \'==,ləs\ *adj* **:** lacking spiders **:** free of spiders

spiderlike \'==,=\ *adj* **:** resembling a spider (as in form or manner)

spider lily *n* **1 :** SPIDERWORT 1a **2 :** SAINT-BERNARD'S-LILY **3 :** any of several plants of the genus *Nerine* (as the Guernsey lily) **4 :** a plant of the genus *Hymenocallis*

spider line *n* **:** one of the bits of spider's web or fine platinum wires forming the reticle of an optical instrument **:** CROSS HAIR

spi·der·ling \'==,liŋ, -lēŋ\ *n* -S **1 :** a very young spider esp. where the brood remains on the back of the mother or in the egg sac for a time after hatching **2 :** a plant of the genus *Boerhavia*

spi·der·ly *adj* **:** resembling a spider **:** SPIDERY

spider milkweed *n* **:** a plant of the genus *Asclepiodora*

spider mite *n* **:** RED SPIDER

spider monkey *n* **:** any of numerous monkeys of *Ateles* or a related genus that range from southern Mexico to Paraguay, have long slender limbs, a thumb absent or rudimentary, and a very long and prehensile tail, and are preeminently fitted for arboreal life — see WOOLLY SPIDER MONKEY

spider nevus *n* **:** a nevus formed of dilated capillaries radiating like the legs of a spider

spider orchid *also* **spider orchis** *n* **:** any of various orchids (as members of the genus *Brassia*) having flowers with slender sepals or petals

spider phaeton *n* **:** a very high carriage of light construction with a covered seat in front and a footman's seat behind

spider plant *n* **1 :** SPIDERFLOWER 1 **2 :** SPIDERWORT 1a

spiders *pl of* SPIDER, *pres 3d sing of* SPIDER

spider shell *n* **:** SCORPION SHELL

spider wasp *n* **:** any of various solitary wasps that fill their brood cells with spiders which they kill or paralyze by stinging as food for their young

spider phaeton

spider web *also* **spider's web** *n* **1 :** a silk web constructed by a spider esp. to entrap prey of threads composed of a viscid fluid that is secreted by glands in the abdomen, is discharged through minute orifices in the spinnerets, and hardens on exposure to the air in a form often characteristic of its family or genus — compare COBWEB, ORB WEB **2 :** something that resembles or suggests a spider web in form, arrangement, or function ⟨a *spider web* of railroads⟩ ⟨a *spider web* of airlines⟩ ⟨a *spider's web* of intrigue⟩

spider-web \'==,=\ *vt* [*spider web*] **:** to cover with a web of fine lines suggestive of a spider web ⟨plains in progressive countries are . . . *spider-webbed* with transportation lines —C.L.White & G.T.Renner⟩

spiderwebby \'==,==\ *adj* [*spider web* + *-y*] **1 :** hung with spider webs **:** COBWEBBY **2 :** resembling or suggesting a spider web ⟨~ cracks in ice⟩ ⟨~ trees⟩

spider wheel *n* **:** SPIDER 5b

spiderwort \'==,=\ *n* **1 a :** a plant of the genus *Tradescantia* the ephemeral usu. blue or violet flowers of which have slender hairy stamens **b :** any plant of the family Commelinaceae — called also *dayflower* **2 :** any of several plants (as the Saint-Bernard's-lily and Saint-Bruno's-lily) of genera other than *Tradescantia*

spiderwort family *n* **:** COMMELINACEAE

spi·dery \'spīdərē, -ri\ *adj, sometimes* -ER/-EST **1 a :** resembling or suggesting a spider (as in appearance, nature, or actions) **:** SPIDERLIKE ⟨eyes of horrid dark and ~ things —C.B. Fernald⟩ ⟨a ~ hand clad in a black kid glove —John Galsworthy⟩ ⟨a ~ disposition⟩; *specif* **:** long, thin, and sharply angular like the legs of a spider ⟨~ lines of scaffolding on the monument —Leslie Charteris⟩ or composed of elements having this appearance ⟨a ~ antenna reaching high in the sky —Horace Sutton⟩ ⟨~ bamboo bridges —Alan Moorehead⟩ ⟨write a ~ hand⟩ **b :** resembling or suggesting a spider web; *esp* **:** composed of fine threads or lines in a weblike arrangement ⟨~ lace⟩ **2 :** full of spiders **:** infested with spiders ⟨a ~ thicket⟩

spie *obs var of* SPY

spied *past of* SPY

spie·gel·ei·sen \'spēgə,līz°n\ *also* **spie·gel** *or* **spiegel iron** *n* -S [*spiegeleisen* fr. G, fr. *spiegel* mirror (fr. OHG *spiagal*, fr. L *speculum*) + *eisen* iron, fr. OHG *īsan*; *spiegel* short for *spiegeleisen*; *spiegel iron* part trans. of G *spiegeleisen* — more at SPECULUM, IRON] **:** a variety of pig iron containing 15 to 30 percent manganese and 4.5 to 6.5 percent carbon and used in steelmaking to recarburize and deoxidize the molten metal of the Bessemer converter or the open-hearth furnace — called also *mirror iron*; compare FERROMANGANESE

¹spiel *var of* SPEEL

²spiel \'spēl, *esp before pause or consonant* -ēəl\ *n* -S [short for *bonspiel*] *Scot* **:** a curling match

³spiel \"\ *vb* -ED/-ING/-S [G *spielen* to play, play music, gamble, fr. OHG *spilōn* to hop, dance, play; akin to OE *spilian* to revel, OFris *spilia* to play, *spil, spel* play, MD *spelen* to play, *spel* play, game, OHG *spil* play] *vi* **1 :** to play music ⟨with three or four you just ~ but with the whole band you got to work —Benny Goodman⟩ **2 :** to talk in a voluble often extravagant manner ⟨always ~*ing* about how scientists ought to rule the world, instead of . . . politicians —Sinclair Lewis⟩ ~ *vt* **:** to utter, express, or describe in a voluble often extravagant manner ⟨can quickly memorize answers to 250 questions and ~ them off long afterward —*Science News Letter*⟩

⁴spiel \"\ *n* -S **:** a voluble line of often extravagant talk usu. intended to persuade **:** PITCH

spiel·er \'spēlə(r)\ *n* -S [G, player, gambler, fr. OHG *spilāri* professional entertainer, fr. *spil* play + *-āri* -er] **1** *chiefly Austral* **a :** a person who earns a living by dishonest gambling **:** CARDSHARPER **b :** SHARPER, SWINDLER **2 a :** a person who attracts customers (as to a sideshow) by a voluble line of extravagant claims and skillful persuasion **:** BARKER **b :** one that spiels **:** the giver of a spiel; *specif* **:** a person with a voluble often exaggerated line of talk **c :** BARKER b **d :** a radio announcer (as for a commercial)

¹spi·er \'spīə(r), -īə\ *n* -S [ME *spiere*, fr. *spyen, spien* to spy + *-ere* -er] **:** one that spies

²spier \'spi(ə)r, -iə\ *n* -S [ME *spere*] **:** a fixed and often architecturally treated screen (as in the hall of an English manor house)

³spier \"\ *chiefly Scot var of* ¹SPEER

spies *pl of* SPY, *pres 3d sing of* SPY

¹spiff \'spif\ *n* -S [perh. fr. E dial. *spiff*, adj., smartly dressed, dandified] **:** PUSH MONEY

²spiff \"\ *vb* -ED/-ING/-S [E dial. *spiff*, adj.] **:** SPRUCE ⟨time to ~ up a bit before the company arrived⟩

spiffed *adj* [fr. past part. of ²*spiff*] **1 :** decked out **:** well attired **2** [prob. by shortening & alter. fr. *spifflicated*] **:** INTOXICATED

spiff·i·ly \'spifəlē, -li\ *adv* **:** in a spiffy manner

spiff·i·ness \-fēnəs, -fin-\ *n* -ES **:** the quality or state of being spiffy

spiff·ing \'spifiŋ, -fēŋ\ *adj* [E dial. *spiff*, adj. + E *-ing*] *slang* **:** SPIFFY ⟨a ~ cook and a top-notch dresser —Gertrude Atherton⟩

spiffy \-fē, -fi\ *adj* -ER/-EST [E dial. *spiff*, adj. + E *-y*] **1 :** fine looking **:** SMART ⟨you were sure ~ in your major's uniform —Lillian Ross⟩ **2 :** SPLENDID, EXCELLENT, CLEVER ⟨the ~ thing is to pull off the elections when they won't get balled up with national issues —*New Republic*⟩

spif·li·cate *or* **spif·fli·cate** \'spiflə,kāt, *usu* -ād·+V\ *vt* -ED/-ING/-S [origin unknown] **1 :** to overcome or dispose of by violence **2 :** BEAT

spiflicated *adj* **:** INTOXICATED

spif·li·ca·tion \,=='kāshən\ *n* -S **:** the act of spiflicating or state of being spiflicated

spig \'spig\ *n* -S *sometimes cap* [short for *spigotty*] **:** SPIK — usu. taken to be offensive

spi·ge·lia \spī'jēlyə, -lēə\ *n, cap* [NL, fr. *Spigelius* (latinized form of the name of Adriaan van den *Spieghel* †1625 Flem. botanist and anatomist) + NL *-ia*] **:** a large genus of American herbs (family Loganiaceae) with showy spicate flowers having valvate corolla lobes, and a 2-celled ovary — see PINKROOT

spi·ge·li·a·ce·ae \=,jēlē'āsē,ē\ [NL, fr. *Spigelia* + *-aceae*] *syn of* LOGANIACEAE

spi·ge·lian \=ˈjēlyən, -lēən\ *adj, sometimes cap* [*Spigelius* + E *-an*] **:** relating to or discovered by the Flemish anatomist Adriaan van den Spieghel

spight \'spīt\ *n* -S [by alter.] *archaic* **:** SPITE

spignel *var of* SPICKNEL

spig·net *also* **spig·nut** \'spignət\ *n* -S [by alter.] **:** SPIKENARD 2a

¹spig·ot *also* **spig·got** \'spigət, -ikət, *usu* -əd·+V\ *n* -S [ME *spigot*, perh. fr. (assumed) OProv *espigot*, dim. of OProv *espiga* head (of grain), fr. L *spica* — more at SPIKE] **1 a :** a pin or peg used to stop the vent in a cask **b :** the plug of a faucet or cock **c :** FAUCET, COCK **2 :** the male end of a section of pipe that enters the hub end of the next section **3 :** a large usu. conical spinning tube associated with silk glands of a spider

²spigot \"\ *vt* **spigoted** *or* **spigotted; spigoted** *or* **spigotted; spigoting** *or* **spigotting; spigots :** to provide, plug, or pierce with or as if with a spigot

spigot-and-faucet joint \¦==¦==¦=-\ *n* **:** BELL-AND-SPIGOT JOINT

spigot joint *n* **:** BELL-AND-SPIGOT JOINT

spig·ot·ty *or* **spig·go·ty** \-əd·ē, -ətē, -i\ *n* -ES *sometimes cap* [prob. fr. the broken English utterance *no speaka de English* (meaning "I don't speak English") supposed to be much used by Spanish Americans] **:** SPIK — usu. taken to be offensive

spik *or* **spick** *or* **spic** \'spik\ *n* -S *sometimes cap* [alter. of *spig*] **:** SPANISH AMERICAN; *esp* **:** MEXICAN — usu. taken to be offensive

¹spike \'spīk\ *n* -S *often attrib* [ME *spike, spik*, prob. fr. MD *spike*; akin to MLG *spiker* spike, ON *spīk* splinter, Lith *speigliai* thorns, L *spina* thorn — more at SPINE] **1 a :** a very large nail; *specif* **:** one three or more inches long and often of square section (as a barge spike) **b :** a similar fastener used on railroads for securing rails to ties **2 :** a pointed piece of metal set with the point upward or outward **:** a pointed metal projection: as **a :** one of a row of pointed irons placed (as on the top of a wall) to prevent passage **b :** one of several metal projections set in the sole and heel of a shoe to improve traction (as in logging, baseball, track and field, golf) and made in varying size, shape, and number for different activities — compare CALK, CLEAT, CLIMBING IRON **c :** a needlelike steel spindle set upright in a base and used for temporary filing of papers (as restaurant bills, rejected newspaper copy) **3 :** something suggesting a spike (as in tapering to a point): as **a :** a young mackerel not over six inches long **b :** an unbranched antler of a young deer **c :** a backward projection on the rose comb of a fowl **4** *Brit* **:** a rigid adherent of high church dogma or ritual **5 :** SPIKE DISEASE **6 a :** SPIKE HEEL **b :** a spike-heeled shoe **7 spikes** *pl* **:** a pair of shoes having spikes attached **8** [²*spike*] **:** the act or an instance of spiking a volleyball — see SETUP **9 a :** the pointed element in a graph or tracing: as (1) **:** the sharp up-and-down deflections on a fever chart indicating high and low temperature levels ⟨had a fever with ~s to 102° F⟩ (2) **:** the pointed element in an electroencephalogram wave ⟨the ~ and dome pattern representing the discharges characteristic of petit mal epilepsy⟩ **b :** an unusually high and sharply defined maximum (as of amplitude in a wave train) **10** *slang* **:** HYPODERMIC NEEDLE

spikes 2b (baseball)

²spike \"\ *vb* -ED/-ING/-S *vt* **1 :** to fasten or fix with spikes ⟨all the track he owned had been laid and *spiked* —Bill Collins⟩ **2 a** (1) **:** to disable (a muzzle-loading cannon) temporarily by driving a spike into the vent (2) **:** to disable (a modern breech-loading cannon) by breaking or carrying away part of the breech mechanism **b :** to put an end to **:** suppress or cut off completely **:** QUASH ⟨~ the minority proposal and present one of their own⟩ ⟨~ the rumor by publishing a full account of the affair⟩ **3 a :** to pierce or impale with or on a spike ⟨~ an enemy with a bayonet⟩; *specif* **:** injure with the spikes on one's shoes ⟨in sliding the runner *spiked* the second baseman⟩ **b :** to reject (newspaper copy) by or as if by impalement on a spike ⟨the correspondent may wonder why his piece was *spiked* in favor of an item about the weather —Anthony Wigan⟩ **4 :** to set or furnish with spikes ⟨~ the bottoms of his climbing shoes⟩ **5 a :** to add alcohol or strong spirituous liquor to (beer or a nonalcoholic beverage) ⟨Frenchmen, accustomed to *spiking* coffee with cognac —*Newsweek*⟩ **b :** to increase the effect, interest, or attractiveness of **:** add strength or pungency to ⟨lighten the discussion by *spiking* it with dry humor⟩ ⟨geranium-pink ~s this kitchen and matches the flowers —Kay Hardy⟩ **6 :** to drive (a volleyball) into the opponents' court at a sharp angle with a hard downward blow delivered from a front line position — compare KILL *vt* 8 ~ *vi* **1 :** to form a spike **:** project like a spike ⟨docks which ~ outward from the eastern fringe of the city —E.K.Gann⟩ **2 :** to alternate sharply high points and low points in temperature as shown on a fever chart — **spike one's guns** *or* **spike the guns :** to nullify one's power of hostile action **:** frustrate one's hostile intentions

⟨*spiked the guns* of the opposition by exposing their equal involvement in the scandal⟩

³spike \"\ *n* -s [ME *spik* head (of grain), fr. L *spica* head (of grain), tuft (of a plant); akin to D *spie* peg, pin, L *spina* thorn — more at SPINE] **1 :** an ear of grain **2 :** an elongated indeterminate inflorescence similar to a raceme but having the flowers sessile on the main axis (as in common plantain) — see INFLORESCENCE illustration

⁴spike \"\ *dial Eng var of* ²SPICK

spikebill \ˈ=,=\ *n* **1 :** HOODED MERGANSER **2 :** MARBLED GODWIT

spike buck *n* **:** a male deer typically in its second year with unbranched antlers on both sides

spike bull *n* **1 :** a young male elk with unbranched antlers **2 :** a young bison with short sharp horns

spike camp *n* **:** a temporary or secondary camp site for a forestry crew accessible from the main camp

¹spiked \ˈspīkt\ *adj* [³*spike* + *-ed*] **1 :** bearing ears **2 :** having a spiky inflorescence ⟨~ flowers⟩

²spiked \"\ *adj* [¹*spike* + *-ed*] **:** having sharp points

spiked alder *n* **:** SWEET PEPPERBUSH

spike disease *n* [¹*spike*] **:** a virus disease of the sandalwood tree in the Orient characterized by dwarfed growth of the shoots and narrow stiff crowded leaves

spiked loosestrife *n* **:** PURPLE LOOSESTRIFE

spiked willow herb *n* **1 :** PURPLE LOOSESTRIFE **2 :** SWAMP WILLOW HERB

spikefish \ˈ=,=\ *n* **:** SPEARFISH; *esp* **:** MARLIN

spike-grass \ˈ=,=\ *n* **:** any of several American maritime grasses having large or conspicuous spikelets: as **a :** SEA OAT; *also* **:** any of several related grasses of the genus *Uniola* **b :** SALT GRASS **c :** an annual grass (*Leptochloa fascicularis*) found in ditches and brackish meadows from New England to Florida

spike gun *n* **:** a machine for driving spikes in railroad ties

spike heath *n* **:** an erect but spreading shrubby evergreen heath (*Bruckenthalia spiculifolia*) of southern Europe and Asia Minor that has small bell-shaped pink flowers and is sometimes cultivated as an ornamental

spike heel *n* **:** a very high tapering heel used on women's shoes — compare FRENCH HEEL, SPANISH HEEL

spike heel

spikehorn \ˈ=,=\ *n* **1 :** SPIKE 3b **2 :** a deer having spikes

spike-kill \ˈ=,=\ *vt* **:** to make (a railroad tie) useless by repeated spiking

spike knot *n* **:** a knot in lumber sawed through lengthwise

spike lavender *n* [⁴*spike*] **:** a European mint (*Lavandula latifolia*) that is closely related to the true lavender and yields spike lavender oil — called also *French lavender*

spike lavender oil *or* **spike oil** *n* **:** a pale yellow fragrant essential oil obtained from spike lavender and used chiefly in making soap and in cosmetics

spike·let \ˈ=lət\ *n* -s [³*spike* + *-let*] **:** a small or secondary spike; *specif* **:** one of the small few-flowered bracteate spikes that make up the compound inflorescence of a grass or sedge — see WILD OAT illustration

spikelike \ˈ=,=\ *adj* [¹*spike* & ³*spike* + *like*] **:** resembling a spike

spike·man \ˈ=,mən\ *n, pl* **spikemen :** a spiker of railroad tracks

spike nail *n* [ME *spiknail*, fr. *spike, spik* spike + *nail*] *chiefly dial* **:** SPIKE 1a

spike·nard \ˈspīk,närd, -,nȧd, -,nə(r)d\ *n* -s [ME, fr. MF or ML; MF *spicanarde*, fr. ML *spica nardi* (trans. of Gk *nardou stachys*), fr. L *spica* head (of grain), tuft (of a plant) + *nardi*, gen. of *nardus* nard — more at SPIKE, NARD] **1 a :** a costly ointment with a musky odor valued as a perfume in ancient times — called also *nard* **b :** an East Indian aromatic plant (*Nardostachys jatamansi*) of the family Valerianaceae from the dried roots and young stems of which the ointment spikenard is believed to have been derived **2 a :** an American herb (*Aralia racemosa*) distinguished from wild sarsaparilla by its more aromatic root and its panicled umbels — called also *American spikenard* **b :** any of various other fragrant plants — usu. used in combination ⟨plowman's-*spikenard*⟩

spikenard tree *n* **:** HERCULES'-CLUB 3

spike-pitch \ˈ=,=\ *vi* [prob. back-formation fr. *spike-pitcher*] **:** to work as a spike-pitcher

spike-pitcher \ˈ=,==\ *n* [¹*spike* + *pitcher*; fr. the use of a pitchfork] **:** a member of a threshing or baling crew who pitches bundles, headings, hay, or straw from a stack or derrick to the machine or who helps the hauler unload his wagon at the machine

spike potential *n* **:** the sharp wave of electric negativity that accompanies the passage of an impulse along a nerve and coincides in time of occurrence with the refractory period of the nerve

spik·er \ˈspīkə(r)\ *n* -s **1 :** one that spikes **2 :** a railroad trackman who drives spikes **3 :** a volleyball player who spikes the ball **:** an attack player

spike rush *n* [³*spike*] **:** a sedge of the genus *Eleocharis* — see HAIR GRASS

spikes *pl of* SPIKE, *pres 3d sing of* SPIKE

spiketail \ˈ=,=\ *n* **1** *or* **spiketail coat** \ˈ=,=-\ *or* **spiketailed coat** \ˈ=,=-\ **:** TAILCOAT **2 a :** PINTAIL 1a **b :** SHARP-TAILED GROUSE

spike team *n* **:** a team of three draft animals harnessed two abreast and one leading

spike-tooth harrow \ˈ=,=-\ *n* **:** a pulverizing and smoothing harrow equipped with straight steel teeth set in horizontal bars

spike-tooth harrow

spiketop \ˈ=,=\ *n* **:** STAGHEAD

spike tub *n* [*spike* (alter. of ⁴*speck*) + *tub*] **:** a tub for blubber on a whaling ship

spikeweed \ˈ=,=\ *n* [¹*spike*] **:** any of several annual Californian herbs of the genus *Centromadia* (family Compositae) with spiny involucral bracts; *esp* **:** a common summer annual (*C. pungens*) valued by beekeepers

spik·i·ly \ˈspīkəlē, -li\ *adv* **:** in a spiky manner

spik·i·ness \-kēnəs, -kin-\ *n* -ES **:** the quality or state of being spiky

spiking *pres part of* SPIKE

¹spiky \ˈspīkē, -ki\ *adj* -ER/-EST [³*spike* + *-y*] **1 :** resembling the spike of a flower **2 :** bearing ears

²spiky \"\ *adj* -ER/-EST [¹*spike* + *-y*] **1 :** having a sharp projecting point ⟨~ thorns⟩ **2 :** characterized by acerbity; *specif* **:** rigidly adhering to high church dogma or ritual

spiky jack *n, usu cap J, southern Africa* **:** SPINY DOGFISH

spi·lan·thes \spīˈlan(,)thēz\ *n, cap* [NL, fr. Gk *spilos* spot + NL *-anthes*] **:** a genus of widely distributed herbs (family Compositae) with opposite serrate leaves and yellow or whitish flowers in dense heads

¹spile \ˈspīl, *esp before pause or consonant* -īəl\ *n* -s [prob. fr. D *spijl* stake, peg, fr. MD *spile*; akin to MHG *spīl* point, Icel *spīla* skewer, Gk *spilas* reef, Latvian *spile* wooden peg, L *spina* thorn — more at SPINE] **1** *chiefly dial* **a :** a small splinter of wood **:** SPILL **b :** a stake or post esp. when used for making a fence **2 a :** a large stake driven into the ground as a support for some superstructure **:** PILE **b :** FOREPOLE **3 a :** a small plug used to stop the vent of a cask **:** BUNG **b :** a tapering wooden pin used to stop the hole left in a ship's sheathing by a withdrawn spike or bolt **4 :** a small tube or spout inserted in a sugar maple tree for conducting sap

²spile \"\ *vt* -ED/-ING/-S **1 a :** to plug (as the hole in a cask) with a spile **b :** to draw off (liquor) through a spile **2 :** to supply (as a cask) with a spile **3 :** to make a small vent in (as a cask)

spilehole \ˈ=,=\ *n* **:** a small air hole in a cask or a maple tree **:** VENT

spileworm \ˈ=,=\ *n* [¹*spile*] **:** SHIPWORM

spilikin *var of* SPILLIKIN

¹spil·ing \ˈspīliŋ, -lēŋ\ *n* -s [origin unknown] **1 :** figures showing the distances from the edge of a template or straightedge to points along a curved part of a ship (as a bow plank or plate) — often used in pl. **2 :** the process of laying off the curvature of a structural part (as a beam or plate) on the material before cutting by taking the spiling **3 :** the curvature of a strake

²spiling \"\ *n* -s [¹*spile* + *-ing*] **1 :** a set of piles **:** PILING **2 :** FOREPOLE

spi·lite \ˈspī,līt\ *n* -s [F, fr. Gk *spilos* spot, stain + F *-ite*] **:** a very fine-grained to dense and greenish to gray-green extrusive rock of the gabbro family often vesicular or amygdaloid and generally free from phenocrysts that is composed essentially of the same minerals as diabase and shows an ophitic texture with augite grains between laths of basic plagioclase — **spi·lit·ic** \=ˈlid·ik\ *adj*

¹spill \ˈspil\ *vb* **spilled** \-ld,-lt\ *also* **spilt** \-lt\; **spilled** *also* **spilt; spilling; spills** [ME *spillen*, fr. OE *spillan*; akin to MD *spillen* to waste, squander, *spouden*, *spalden* to split, MLG *spalden*, OHG *spaltan* to split, ON *spjald*, *speld* square tablet, Goth *spilda* tablet, L *spolium* arms or armor stripped from an enemy, Gk *sphallein* to cause to fall, Skt *sphaṭati* it bursts; basic meaning: to split] *vt* **1** *archaic* **a :** KILL, DESTROY ⟨bade her command my life to save or ~ —Edmund Spenser⟩ **b :** to use or spend wastefully **:** WASTE, SQUANDER **c :** to make useless **:** RUIN, SPOIL **2 :** to cause (blood) to be lost by wounding ⟨rushed into battle eager to ~ their enemies' blood⟩ **3 :** to cause or allow to pour, splash, or fall out (as over the edge of a container) and be wasted, lost, or scattered ⟨fill your wine cup exactly full with a single toss of the bottle and without ~*ing* a drop —Lafcadio Hearn⟩ ⟨dropped the bag and ~*ed* sugar all over the floor⟩ ⟨felt of it and ~*ed* the cool tea on the brick floor and filled the bowl again —Pearl Buck⟩ ⟨2,000 plastic balloons ~*ed* out 2,000,000 leaflets —*Time*⟩ **4 a :** to relieve (a sail) from the pressure of the wind so that it can be more easily reefed or furled or to avoid capsizing or carrying away something **b :** to relieve the pressure of (wind) on a sail by coming about or by adjusting it with lines **5 :** to cause to fall from one's place (as on a horse or in a vehicle) **:** throw off, out, or down ⟨a bucking horse that ~*ed* everyone who tried to ride it⟩ **6 :** to give forth in an overflowing manner **:** pour freely ⟨a mockingbird . . . was ~*ing* his wild song over the moonlit woods —Rebecca Caudill⟩ **7 :** to let out (secret information) **:** DIVULGE ⟨would double-cross me and ~ some of the things I had told him —Polly Adler⟩ ~ *vi* **1** *obs* **a** (1) **:** to cause death or destruction (2) **:** PERISH, DIE **b :** DETERIORATE, SPOIL **2 a :** to flow, run, or fall out, over, or off with waste, loss, or scattering as the result ⟨don't shake the table or the coffee will ~⟩ ⟨light ~*ed* out through the windows —Frances & Richard Lockridge⟩ **b :** to cause or allow something to spill **:** waste a substance by letting it pour or fall out ⟨ate his ice cream, careful not to ~ on his new clothes⟩ **3 a :** to spread beyond bounds ⟨more than 1000 persons had filled the main ballroom and ~*ed* over into adjacent parlors —*Newsweek*⟩ ⟨they allow their private thoughts to ~ over into public statements —Norman Cousins⟩ **b :** to come, go, or pass with a turbulent rush **:** pour in an unrestrained, profuse, or disorderly manner **:** TUMBLE ⟨wave after wave of shouting crowds ~*ed* into . . . streets —*Time*⟩ ⟨the shelves of plays, pamphlets, prefaces, novels, and critical works which . . . ~*ed* from his pen —John Mason Brown⟩ **c :** to extend downward in precipitous or profuse disorder **:** descend as if overflowing ⟨the town ~*s* down a hillside and spreads into a valley —W.R.Moore⟩ ⟨great swags of lilac and laburnum ~ over ancient, weathered walls —*advt*⟩ **d :** to be full to overflowing ⟨the sidewalks . . . were soon ~*ing* over with workers —*Facts about Trailer Coaches*⟩ **4 :** to tell secrets **:** betray confidences ⟨would ~ in spite of the gang's threats⟩ **5 :** to fall from one's place (as on a horse or in a vehicle) **:** fall off, out, or down ⟨saw the motorcycle skid and the driver ~ in the dust⟩ — **spill the beans 1 :** to cause embarrassment by indiscreetly divulging information **2 :** to upset a plan or arrangement

²spill \"\ *n* -s **1 a :** an act or instance of spilling ⟨an undirected ~ of population into the suburban areas —Lewis Mumford⟩; *specif* **:** a fall from a place (as on a horse or in a vehicle) or an erect position (as in skiing) ⟨failing to clear the jump, horse and rider took a nasty ~⟩ ⟨broke his leg skiing when he took a ~ at a turn⟩ **b :** an abrupt decline in price ⟨stocks spurted most of the day then took a sharp ~ in the late trading —*New Orleans (La.) Times-Picayune*⟩ **2 a :** a quantity spilled ⟨fetch a cloth to mop up the ~ —Agnes M. Miall⟩ **b** *or* **spill light :** light that escapes from a concentration of theatrical or photographic light (as a spotlight cone) and produces illumination where it is not wanted **3 :** SPILLWAY

³spill \"\ *n* -s [ME *spille, spyll*; prob. akin to MD *spile* stake, peg — more at SPILE] **1 :** a bit of wood split off **:** SPLINTER **2 :** a slender piece of anything: as **a :** a metallic rod or pin on which something turns **b** (1) **:** a small roll or twist of paper or slip of wood used for lighting lamps, pipes, fires (2) **:** a paper sheath into which the tobacco is pushed in making a cigarette (3) **:** a roll or cone of paper serving as a container (as for a bunch of flowers) **c :** a peg or pin for plugging a hole (as in a cask) **:** SPILE **3 :** a scale-filled crack or seam in an ingot; *esp* **:** a lap due to careless rolling **4 :** a metal disk on a wooden rod used to remove matzoth from the oven

⁴spill \"\ *n* -s [perh. fr. ¹*spill*] *archaic* **:** a small sum of money **:** GRATUITY

spill·able \-ləbəl\ *adj* **:** that can be spilled

spill·age \ˈspilij, -lēj\ *n* -s **1 :** the act or process of spilling ⟨replace antifreeze lost by ~⟩ **2 :** the quantity that spills or is spilled over ⟨a trough to divert any ~⟩

spill box *n* **:** a device for maintaining a constant head or pressure on a measuring weir or orifice; *specif* **:** a short flume with long wells at each end and a spillway over which the excess water flows

¹spill·er \ˈspilə(r)\ *n* -s [¹*spill* + *-er*] **1 :** one that spills **2 :** a bowl that results in a strike despite an inaccurate hit

²spiller \"\ *n* -s [alter. of ²*speller*] *archaic* **:** a branchlet on a deer's palm

³spil·ler \ˈspilə(r)\ *n* -s [IrGael *spilēar*] **1 :** a fishing line with many hooks **2 :** the final enclosure of a fish trap from which fishes are bailed into the fishing boat

spil·let \-lət, *usu* -əd·+V\ *n* -s [IrGael *spilēad*] *dial* **:** ³SPILLER

spill·flö·te \ˈspil,flād·ə, -lōd·ə, *G* ˈshpil,flœtə\ *n* -s [G, fr. *spille* spindle (fr. OHG *spilla*) + *flöte* flute, fr. MHG *vloite*, fr. OF *flaute, fleute*; akin to OHG *spinnan* to spin — more at SPIN, FLUTE] **:** a half-covered pipe-organ flue stop of 8-, 4-, or 2-foot pitch that is shaped like a spindle

spil·li·kin \ˈspiləkən, -lēk-\ *also* **spel·i·can** *or* **spel·li·can** \ˈspel-\ *or* **spil·i·kin** *or* **spil·li·ken** *n* -s [prob. alter. of obs. D *spelleken, spelleke* small peg, small pin, fr. MD *spellekijn* small pin, fr. *spelle, spelde* pin + *-kijn* -kin; akin to OE *speld* torch — more at SPELL] **:** JACKSTRAW 2

spill·ing \ˈspiliŋ, -lēŋ\ *n* -s **:** the loss of air from beneath the canopy of a parachute at the outer edges caused by deliberate manipulation of the parachute or by instability

spilling line *n* **:** a rope used for spilling a sail (as by hauling up the foot, brailing in an edge)

spillover \ˈ=,==\ *n* -s [fr. *spill over*, v.] **1 :** the act or process of spilling over; *also* **:** an instance of spilling over **2 :** a quantity that spills over **3 :** an extension of demand from one product to a related one because of insufficient supply

spillpipe \ˈ=,=\ *n* **:** CHAIN PIPE

spills *pres 3d sing of* SPILL, *pl of* SPILL

spill stream *n* **:** an overflow stream (as from a river)

spillway \ˈ=,=\ *n* **1 :** a passage (as a paved apron or channel) for surplus water over or around a dam or similar obstruction **2 :** a channel through which lake water or meltwater from a glacier flows or has flowed over a barrier (as of glacial drift)

spilly \ˈspilē, -li\ *adj* -ER/-EST [³*spill* + *-y*] *of wrought iron or steel* **:** defective from spills

spi·log·a·le \spīˈlägə(,)lē\ *n, cap* [NL, fr. Gk *spilos* spot + *galē, galeē* weasel, ferret — more at GALEA] **:** a genus of mammals (family Mustelidae) comprising the little spotted skunks

spi·lor·nis \spīˈlȯrnəs\ *n, cap* [NL, fr. Gk *spilos* spot + NL *-ornis*] **:** a genus of Asiatic and East Indian high-soaring diurnal birds of prey (family Accipitridae) that have long slender legs and short toes tipped by powerful claws and feed chiefly on reptiles

spi·lo·site \ˈspīlə,sīt\ *n* -s [G *spilosit*, fr. Gk *spilos* spot + G *-it* -ite] **:** a spotted schistose rock produced by contact metamorphism of clay slate usu. by diabase

spilt \ˈspilt\ *past of* SPILL

spilth \ˈspilth *also* -lth\ *n* -s [¹*spill* + *-th*] **1 :** an act or instance of spilling **2 a :** something spilled or freely poured out **b :** REFUSE, RUBBISH

¹spin \ˈspin\ *vb* **spun** \ˈspən\ *or archaic* **span** \ˈspan, -paa(ə)n\ **spun; spinning; spins** [ME *spinnen*, fr. OE *spinnan*; akin to OHG *spinnan* to spin, ON *spinna*, Goth *spinnan* to spin, L *sponte* of one's free will, voluntarily, Gk *span* to draw, pull, tear — more at SPAN] *vi* **1 :** to draw and twist thread **:** make yarn or thread from fiber ⟨watched the jennies ~⟩ ⟨sat by the fireside *spinning*⟩ **2 :** to form a thread, web, or cocoon by extruding a viscous rapidly hardening fluid — used of a spider or silkworm **3 a :** to revolve or whirl rapidly **:** GYRATE, ROTATE ⟨little boys' tops were *spinning* in the spring afternoon⟩ ⟨round about him *spun* the landscape —H.W.Longfellow⟩ **b :** to turn quickly on one's heel **:** face about in place ⟨as one man we *spun* round —Rex Keating⟩ **c :** to rotate or whirl rapidly in dancing **d :** to feel as if revolving **:** be in a whirl **:** REEL ⟨her head was *spinning* at the finality and emptiness of the prospect⟩ **4 :** to stream or spurt (as blood or juice) in a thread or jet **5 :** to last out **:** EXTEND **6 a :** to move swiftly on wheels or in a vehicle ⟨Sunday trippers were *spinning* over the highway in flashing cars⟩ ⟨bicycles *spun* about an indoor track⟩ ⟨~*s* up the river in a little powerboat⟩ **b :** to pass quickly ⟨time ~*s* away when we are occupied⟩ **7** *Brit* **:** to fail in an examination **:** FLUNK **8 a :** to fish with spinning bait (as a spoon) **:** TROLL **b :** to fish with a fixed spool reel and light line **9 a** *of an airplane* **:** to fall in a spin **b :** to spiral rapidly downward **:** fall dizzily and out of control **:** be caught in a vortex ⟨watch a normal-seeming man ~ downward to madness and abnormality —James Kelly⟩ ~ *vt* **1 a :** to draw out and twist (fibers) into yarns or threads by hand or by machine ⟨mills that ~ cotton, flax, or wool⟩ **b :** to produce (yarn or thread) by drawing out and twisting a fibrous material **c :** to convert (pulp or chemical solutions) into rayon or other man-made filaments by extruding, solidifying, and winding **d :** to pass (an appropriate solution or melt) through a spinneret in the production of synthetic fibers (as rayon or nylon) **e :** to form (filaments) by extruding pulp or chemical solutions through spinnerets, solidifying, and winding **f :** to form (wire strands) into cable or wire rope **2 :** to form (a thread, web, or cocoon) by the extrusion of a viscous rapidly hardening fluid — used of a spider or a silkworm **3 a :** to form or produce in a manner resembling a spinning process **:** draw out slowly, by degrees, or at length **:** EXTEND, PROLONG, PROTRACT — usu. used with *out* ⟨possessed the ability to ~ a saga out of their escapades —Benjamin De Casseres⟩ ⟨~*s* a short-story plot into over 90,000 words of torpid action —Anthony Boucher⟩ ⟨~*s* out the small talk of a chance meeting —*Current Biog.*⟩ **b :** to evolve, express, or fabricate by processes of mind or imagination ⟨the most persistent risk that has always attended all *spinning* of yarns —C.E.Montague⟩ ⟨no more can the imagination ~ its fantastic tales of adventure —W.P.Webb⟩ ⟨*spun* a ritual full of cryptic references —C.W.Ferguson⟩ ⟨the theorists *spun* their theories —*Time*⟩ **c :** to make last **:** stretch out the duration of **:** extend in time or space — used with *out* ⟨*spinning* out his glass of port as long as possible —Elizabeth Goudge⟩ **4** *archaic* **:** to spend (time) to no effect — used with *out* **5 :** to cause to turn round rapidly **:** TWIRL, WHIRL ⟨boys *spun* their tops on the sidewalks⟩ **6 a :** to shape (a material) into threadlike form in manufacture ⟨*spun* gold⟩ **b :** to manufacture by a whirling process ⟨began to ~ glass flat by the crown method —Freda Diamond⟩ ⟨the bearings are centrifugally cast by *spinning* the rod with the center of its lower end . . . as the axis of rotation —H.F.Blanchard & Ralph Ritchen⟩ **c :** to form (metal hollow ware) on a mold on a lathe face plate with a roller or other hand tool ⟨a *spun* aluminum canister⟩ ⟨bowls of *spun* copper⟩ **7** *Brit* **:** to fail (a student) in an examination **:** FLUNK **8 :** to put together or construct (something likened to a spider's web) ⟨as the arctic radar net is *spun* —*Time*⟩ **9 :** to throw off (a fragment) by or as if by centrifugal force from a whirling object ⟨*spun* off a couple of independent companies from its corporate structure to satisfy the justice department⟩ **10 a :** to fish (a body of water) with a spinner or spinning bait **b :** to fish (a body of water) with a fixed spool reel and light line **11 :** to set (a phonograph disc record) rotating on a turntable **:** PLAY ⟨was *spinning* records on an all-night radio show⟩ **syn** see TURN

²spin \"\ *n* -s **1 a :** the act of spinning or twirling something ⟨the decision rested on the ~ of a coin⟩ **b :** the revolving or whirling motion imparted by spinning ⟨the ~ of a top⟩ ⟨the ~ given to a cricket ball by a bowler⟩ — compare ²ENGLISH 5, HOOK 6b, ³SLICE **c :** an excursion in a vehicle esp. on wheels ⟨an evening ~ in the car⟩ ⟨out for a ~ in a powerboat⟩ **2 a :** an aerial maneuver or flight condition consisting of a combination of roll and yaw with the longitudinal axis of the airplane inclined steeply downward so that it descends in a helix of large pitch and very small radius with its upper side on the inside of the helix while the angle of attack on the inner wing is maintained at an extremely large value **b :** a plunging descent or downward spiral ⟨when . . . the world enters upon the downward ~, it is desirable that each country should . . . stimulate revival —R.F.Harrod⟩ **c :** a mental whirl **:** a state of confusion or depression ⟨been in a ~ ever since the bankruptcy⟩ **3 a :** a system of velocities of any number of points all due to one and the same definite angular velocity about one and the same axis **b** (1) **:** the rapid rotation of an elementary particle (as an electron) on its own axis or of a system of such particles in orbital motion that is responsible for measurable angular momentum and magnetic moment (2) **:** the angular momentum associated with such rotation **4 :** a quick dance turn on the narrowest possible base **5** *Austral* **:** LUCK ⟨had a good ~ —Ruth Park⟩ ⟨had a tough ~ —Frank Sargeson⟩

spin- *or* **spini-** *or* **spino-** *comb form* [L *spin-, spini-* thorn, spine, fr. *spina* thorn, spine, spinal column — more at SPINE] **1 a :** spinal column **:** spinal cord ⟨*spino*gram⟩ **b :** of, relating to, or involving the spinal cord and ⟨*spino*thalamic⟩ **2 :** spine ⟨*spin*ate⟩ ⟨*spini*form⟩

spi·na \ˈspīnə\ *n, pl* **spi·nae** \-ī,nē\ [L, thorn, spine] **:** an anatomical spine or spinelike process

spina bi·fi·da \-ˈbīfədə, -ˈbif-\ *n* [NL, bifid spinal column] **:** a congenital cleft of the vertebral column with hernial protrusion of the meninges

spi·na·cea \spīˈnāshēə\ *syn of* SPINACIA

spina·cene \ˈspīnə,sēn, -pīn-\ *n* -s [ISV *spinac-* (fr. NL *Spinac-, Spinax* genus of sharks, prob. fr. Gk *spina*, a fish) + *-ene*] **:** SQUALENE

spi·na·ceous \spəˈnāshəs, (ˈ)spī¦n-\ *adj* [irreg. fr. NL *Spinacia* + E *-aceous*] **:** resembling or related to spinach ⟨~ herbs⟩

spin·ach *or* **spin·age** \ˈspinich, -nēch *sometimes* -nij *or* -nēj\ *n, pl* **spinaches** *or* **spinages** [MF *espinache, espinage*, fr. OSp *espinaca*, fr. Ar *isbānakh, isfānākh*, fr. Per *isfānākh*] **1 :** an annual potherb (*Spinacia oleracea*) native to southwestern Asia and cultivated widely for its edible leaves which are used as greens — called also *prickly-seeded spinach* **2 a :** something repellent, obnoxious, or nonexistent **:** something spurious or unwanted ⟨the bankers' pet . . . was just so much ~ as far as the plain people were concerned —Jay Franklin⟩ ⟨the ~ of controlled, cooperative effort —H.A. Moe⟩ **b :** an untidy overgrowth (as an untrimmed lawn or beard) **c :** an inessential, irrelevant, or inharmonious excrescence, addition, or decoration **:** FRILL ⟨a child . . . has no interest in literary and artistic ~ —Rochelle Girson⟩ ⟨might look at the externals of an airplane and see only struts, wires, and other such ~ —*Air World*⟩

spinach aphid *n, chiefly Brit* **:** GREEN PEACH APHID

spinach beet *n* **:** a beet that constitutes a variety (*Beta vulgaris cicla*) of the common beet, is used as an ornamental and potherb, has much-developed leaves, and lacks a fleshy root — called also *leaf beet*

spinach blight *n* **:** a mosaic disease of spinach caused by the cucumber mosaic virus
spinach carrion beetle *n* **:** a black carrion beetle (*Silpha bituberosa*) with a nocturnal black-and-white larva that feeds on spinach and other crop plants in the western U.S.
spinach dock *or* **spinage dock** *n* **:** PATIENCE 3
spinach flea beetle *n* **:** a small glossy bluish black beetle (*Disonycha xanthomelas*) that has a reddish or yellowish abdomen and feeds on spinach and beet leaves
spinach green *n* **:** a moderate yellow green that is greener and deeper than average moss green, duller and very slightly yellower than average pea green, duller than apple green (sense 1), and greener and duller than mosstone — called also *autumn green, gaudy green*
spinach leaf miner *n* **:** a maggot that is the larva of an anthomyiid fly (*Pegomya hyoscyami*) and mines the leaves of beets, spinach, chard, and other crop plants
spinach mustard *n* **:** TENDERGREEN
spinach yellows *n pl but usu sing in constr* **:** SPINACH BLIGHT
spi·na·cia \spə'nāshēə\ *n, cap* [NL, fr. It *spinace* spinach (fr. Sp *espinaca*) + NL *-ia*] **:** a small genus of Asiatic annual herbs (family Chenopodiaceae) having dioecious flowers without bracts and a pistillate calyx that becomes indurated over the one-seeded perianth — see SPINACH
spina ex·ter·na \-,ek'stərnə\ *n, pl* **spinae exter·nae** \-r,nē\ [NL, external spine] **:** a median bony point projecting from the anterior and ventral margin of the sternum of a bird
spina in·ter·na \-in'tərnə\ *n, pl* **spinae inter·nae** \-r,nē\ [NL, internal spine] **:** a median bony point projecting from the anterior and dorsal edge of the sternum of a bird and sometimes uniting with the spina externa
¹spi·nal \'spīnᵊl\ *adj* [LL *spinalis*, fr. L *spina* thorn, spine, spinal column + *-alis* -al — more at SPINE] **1 a :** of, relating to, or situated near the vertebral column, spinal canal, or spinal cord **b :** located in or affecting the vertebral column or spinal cord ⟨~ twinges⟩ ⟨degenerative ~ disease⟩ **2 a :** dependent upon the spinal cord **:** involving in its central nervous path only the spinal cord ⟨a ~ reflex⟩ **b :** having the spinal cord isolated in its functioning from the brain (as by surgical section) ⟨experiments with ~ animals⟩ **3 :** of or relating to a spine **4 :** resembling a spine **:** suggesting a backbone ⟨the two great ~ mountain-systems of the U.S. —Lewis Mumford⟩ **5 :** made for or fitted to the spine ⟨a ~ brace⟩
²spinal \"\ *n* -s **:** SPINAL ANESTHESIA
spinal accessory nerve *n* **:** ACCESSORY NERVE
spinal anesthesia *n* **:** anesthesia produced by injection of an anesthetic into the spinal subarachnoid space
spinal artery *n* **:** any of the arteries that supply the spinal cord and its membranes and adjacent structures, all arising as branches of the vertebral artery but anastomosing and being reinforced or continued by branches of intercostal and lumbar arteries which enter the intervertebral foramina
spinal canal *n* **:** the canal that is formed by the series of neural arches of the vertebrae and that forms a protective bony case about the spinal cord
spinal column *n* **:** the articulated series of vertebrae connected by ligaments and separated by more or less elastic intervertebral fibrocartilages that in nearly all vertebrates forms the supporting axis of the body and a protection for the spinal cord extending from the hind end of the skull through the median dorsal part of the body and to the end of the tail **:** BACKBONE, SPINE; *broadly* **:** the axial skeleton of the trunk and tail of a vertebrate which in the lowest vertebrates and in the embryos of all higher forms is represented by an elastic rod of cellular tissue enclosed in a fibrous sheath in which in higher forms cartilaginous or bony pieces develop and usu. unite in various ways in the different groups to form a longitudinal series of vertebrae — compare NOTOCHORD
spinal cord *n* **:** the thick longitudinal cord of nervous tissue that in vertebrates extends along the back dorsal to the bodies of the vertebrae and is enclosed in the spinal canal formed by their neural arches, is continuous anteriorly with the medulla oblongata, gives off at intervals pairs of spinal nerves to the various parts of the trunk and limbs, serves not only as a pathway for nervous impulses to and from the brain but as a center for carrying out and coordinating many reflex actions independently of the brain, and is composed largely of white matter arranged in columns and tracts of longitudinal fibers about a large central core of gray matter somewhat H-shaped in cross section and pierced centrally by a small longitudinal canal continuous with the ventricles of the brain
spinal fluid *n* **:** CEREBROSPINAL FLUID
spinal foramen *n* **:** an opening under the neural arch of a vertebra that forms a part of the spinal canal when the vertebrae are articulated
spinal fusion *n* **:** surgical fusion of two or more vertebrae for remedial immobilizing of the spine
spinal ganglion *n* **:** a ganglion on the dorsal root of each spinal nerve that is one of a series of ganglia lodging cell bodies of sensory neurons
spi·nalis \spī'nāləs, -nal-; spə'näl-\ *n, pl* **spina·les** \-a(,)lēz, -ā(,)lēz, -ä(,)lās\ [NL, fr. LL, spinal] **:** any of three muscles of the spinal column
spi·nal·ly \'spīnᵊlē, -ᵊli\ *adv* **:** with respect to the spine **:** along the spine
spinal marrow *n* **:** MARROW 1b
spinal nerve *n* **:** any of the paired nerves that leave the spinal cord of a craniate vertebrate by way of the intervertebral foramina, supply muscles of the trunk and limbs, and connect with the nerves of the sympathetic system, that arise by a short motor ventral root and a short sensory dorsal root which bears a spinal ganglion close to the cord and unites with the ventral root just beyond the ganglion forming a nerve of mixed function which passes through the foramen and divides into two mixed nerves of which one supplies dorsal and the other ventral bodily structures, and that normally aggregate 31 pairs in man and are divided according to the part of the cord from which they arise into 8 cervical pairs, 12 thoracic pairs, 5 lumbar pairs, 5 sacral pairs, and one coccygeal pair
spinal puncture *n* **:** puncture of the subarachnoid space in the lumbar region of the spinal cord to withdraw cerebrospinal fluid or inject anesthetic drugs
spinals *pl of* SPINAL
spinal segment *n* **:** a segment of the spinal cord including a single pair of spinal nerves and representing the spinal nervation of a single primitive metamere
spi·na·sterol \'spīnə+\ *n* -s [NL *Spinacia* (genus name of the spinach plant *Spinacia oleracea*) + E *sterol* — more at SPINACIA] **:** any of several unsaturated isomeric phytosterols $C_{29}H_{47}OH$ obtained esp. from spinach leaves or the oil from alfalfa seeds and distinguished by Greek letters ⟨*α-spinasterol*⟩
spi·nate \'spī,nāt\ *adj* [*spin-* + *-ate*] **:** bearing a spine **:** SPINIFORM
spi·na·tion \spī'nāshən\ *n* -s [*spin-* + *-ation*] **:** the distribution and arrangement of spines (as on an insect)
spin casting *n* **:** casting with a light lure or light natural bait and a very light line
spin chute *n* **:** a small parachute attached usu. at the tail to an airplane undergoing flight tests to retard descent and help the pilot regain control if a spin develops
¹spin·dle \'spindᵊl, *chiefly dial* -nᵊl — *compare* SPINDLY\ *n* -s [ME *spindel*, fr. OE *spinel*; akin to OFris *spindel* spindle, OHG *spinila* spindle, OE *spinnan* to spin — more at SPIN] **1 :** a long tapered pin or rod serving as an axis in spinning: **a :** a round stick with tapered ends that is twirled around to form and twist the yarn in hand spinning **b :** the long slender pin by which the thread is twisted in a spinning wheel and on which it is then wound **c :** any of the various rods or pins holding a bobbin in a spinning frame or other textile machine **d :** the pin in a loom shuttle **2 :** something shaped like a spindle **:** a fusiform piece or figure: as **a** *obs* **:** a long stalk or stem of a plant **b :** a spindle-shaped sensory nerve ending — see MUSCLE SPINDLE **c :** the spindle-shaped portion of the achromatic figure along which the mitotic chromosomes are distributed to the daughter nuclei and which is apparently a dynamic product of gelation of the nuclear sap actively concerned in the separation of the chromosomes in mitosis and is no longer regarded as a structural unit of elongated spindle fibers **d :** RACHIS **e :** SPINDLE SHELL **f :** SPINDLE TREE **3 :** any of various more or less slender pins or rods that are suggestive of a spinning-machine spindle which turns or on which something turns: as **a :** the bar or shaft usu. of square section that carries the knobs and actuates the latch or bolt of a lock **b** (1) **:** a turned often decorative piece (as in a baluster) (2) **:** NEWEL **c :** an upright rod or pipe on which the sweep arm revolves in sweeping up a foundry mold or which is used in making a core **d** (1) **:** a revolving piece esp. if less in size than a shaft (2) **:** a horizontal or vertical axle revolving on pin or pivot ends ⟨the live ~ of a lathe⟩ ⟨the ~ of a vane⟩ ⟨the ~ of a capstan⟩ (3) **:** a rod attached to a valve to move or guide it **e :** the part of an axle on which a vehicle wheel turns **4 :** a unit of length used in counting yarns (as flax or jute) ⟨a ~ of flax or jute equals 14,400 yards⟩ **5 a :** the upper main piece of a made mast **b :** a round usu. iron pile or pipe placed on a rock or shoal as an aid to navigation **6 :** the pin of a turntable over which a phonograph record fits
²spin·dle \'spindᵊl, *chiefly dial* -nᵊl — *compare pres part*\ *vb* **spindled; spindled; spindling** \-nd(ᵊ)liŋ, -nliŋ, -nlēŋ, -nlən\ **spindles** *vi* **1 a :** to shoot or grow into a long slender stalk **:** form a stem **b :** to become disproportionately or unwholesomely tall and slender **2 a :** to grow to stalk or stem rather than to flower or fruit **b :** to become thin and useless ~ *vt* **:** to impale, thrust, or perforate on the spike of a spindle file ⟨~ an order slip⟩
spin·dle·age *also* **spin·dlage** \'spind(ᵊ)lij\ *n* -s [¹*spindle* + *-age*] **1 :** textile spindle equipment **:** the total number of spindles in a mill or region **2 :** the active or potential textile production represented by a stated spindleage
spindle attachment *n* **:** CENTROMERE
spindleberry \'spindᵊl- — *see* BERRY\ *n* **:** any of several shrubby spindle trees with showy usu. reddish fruits
spindle body *or* **spindle organ** *n* **:** a spindle-shaped enlargement on the mycelium of a fungus of the family Cladochytreaceae
spindle cell *n* **:** a fusiform cell; *esp* **:** a slender nucleated element that is the thrombocyte of a lower vertebrate and is equivalent in function to the blood platelet of higher forms
spindle-cell sarcoma *n* **:** FIBROSARCOMA
spindled *adj* [fr. past part. of ²*spindle*] **1 :** long and slender like the stalk of a plant **2 :** equipped or made with spindles ⟨a chair with ~ back⟩ **3 :** spiked on a spindle file
spindle fiber *also* **spindle element** *n* **:** one of the apparent filaments constituting the mitotic spindle esp. when construed as an actual physical structure capable of exerting traction
spindle file *n* **:** a device with a projecting spike, nail, or hook on which to stick papers
spin·dle·ful \'spindᵊl,fu̇l\ *n* -s **:** as much as a spindle will hold
spindlehead \'⸗⸗,⸗\ *n* **:** a headstock or tailstock for a spindle or boring bar
spindle-legged *US usu* ¦⸗⸗¦legəd, *Brit usu* -gd\ *adj* **:** having long slender legs
spindle oil *n* **:** a light fluid lubricating oil from petroleum suitable for oiling the spindles of spinning machinery and also for other light high-speed machinery
spin·dler \'spind(ᵊ)lə(r)\ *n* -s [¹*spindle* + *-er*] **:** one that places reels of paper on the spindle of a rotary printing press
spindles *pl of* SPINDLE, *pres 3d sing of* SPINDLE

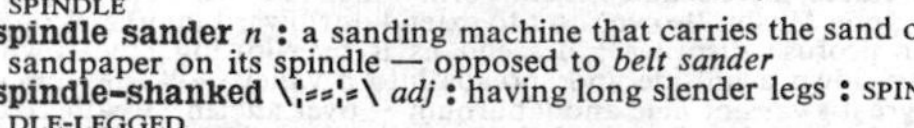
spindle files: *1* desk, *2* wall

spindle sander *n* **:** a sanding machine that carries the sand or sandpaper on its spindle — opposed to *belt sander*
spindle-shanked \'⸗⸗¦⸗\ *adj* **:** having long slender legs **:** SPINDLE-LEGGED
spindleshanks \'⸗⸗,⸗\ *n pl* **1 :** long slender legs **2** *sing or pl in constr* **:** a person having long slender legs
spindle shell *n* **1** *also* **spindle stromb :** any gastropod mollusk of the genus *Tibia* (family Strombidae) having a shell with a long conical many-whorled spire and a long slender anterior canal **2 :** a band shell of the genus *Fusinus* having a shell with a many-whorled spire and a very long straight canal
spindle sprout *or* **spinding sprout** *n* **:** the production of slender sickly shoots by potato tubers that accompanies some diseases (as leaf roll)
spindle stone *n* **:** TEMALACATL
spindletail \'⸗⸗,⸗\ *n* **:** PINTAIL 1a
spindle temper *n* **:** a temper of steel characterized by the presence of about 1.125 percent carbon
spindle tree *n* **:** a shrub or tree of the genus *Euonymus*; *esp* **:** a small erect shrubby tree (*E. europaeus*) of Europe and western Asia with a pink capsule enclosing the orange fruit, tough white wood used esp. for spindles and skewers, and a powerfully cathartic principle in bark and fruit
spindle tuber *n* **1 :** a virus disease of the potato characterized by spindliness and uprightness of tops and by the formation of spindle-shaped tubers **2 :** POTATO MOSAIC
spindle-wood \'⸗⸗,⸗\ *n* **:** the wood of a spindle tree
spin·dli·ness \'spin(d)lēnəs, -lin-\ *n* -ES **:** the quality or state of being spindly
¹spin·dling \-ind(ᵊ)liŋ, -inliŋ, -inlēŋ, -inlən\ *n* -s [fr. gerund of ²*spindle*] **1 :** the act or process of growing in a spindling manner **:** the growth of a plant to stalk rather than to flowers or fruit **2 :** a spindling person, plant, or object
²spindling \"\ *adj* [fr. pres. part. of ²*spindle*] **1 :** conspicuously or disproportionately long and slender or thin ⟨a tall, ~ ghost of a man —Van Wyck Brooks⟩ **2 :** lacking vitality, development, or strength **:** THIN, WEAK, INEFFECTUAL
spin·dly \-in(d)lē, -li\ *adj* -ER/-EST [¹*spindle* + *-y*] **:** exhibiting a tallness and thinness suggesting lack of strength or vitality **:** SPINDLING ⟨guards keep watch from a high, ~ lookout tower —Mollie Panter-Downes⟩ ⟨a sickly ~ child —*Times Lit. Supp.*⟩
spin·drift \'spin,drift\ *n* [alter. of Sc *speendrift*, fr. *speen* to drive before a strong wind (alter. of E ⁴*spoon*) + E *drift*] **1 :** sea spray **:** SPOONDRIFT **2 :** sand, dust, or snow driven before the wind like sea spray
spine \'spīn\ *n* -s [ME, thorn, spinal column, fr. L *spina* thorn, spine, spinal column; akin to Toch A *spin-* hook, Latvian *spina* twig, switch, Skt *sphya* flat sword-shaped piece of wood used in sacrifices] **1 a :** SPINAL COLUMN **b :** something resembling a spinal column in appearance, place, or function **:** something constituting a main strength, central axis, or chief support ⟨the land is flat and marshy before rising to a ~ of low hills —Robert Turley⟩ ⟨he has . . . ~ and starch, in a country sometimes lacking both —John Gunther⟩ ⟨give a ~ of significance to his butterfly existence —Tennessee Williams⟩ **c :** the backbone of a book **d :** the stiff springy quality desired in arrows **2 :** a stiff sharp-pointed plant process (as a modified leaf, leaf part, petiole, or stipule) — compare PRICKLE, THORN **3 :** a stiff sharp process of an animal body: **a :** a sharp-pointed protective outgrowth consisting of an enlarged and modified hair of a mammal (as a porcupine or a hedgehog) **b :** one of the processes that cover most parts of the body of a sea urchin, that serve for defense or for locomotion, and that are borne on rounded tubercles to which they are movably articulated **c :** a radiolarian spicule **d :** a spiny fin ray of a fish **e :** any of various processes esp. of bones **:** a spinous process (as of a vertebra or of the ilium); *specif* **:** a prominent ridge on the back of the scapula **4** *dial Eng* **:** SWARD, TURF **5** *dial Eng* **:** the surface layer or rind of meat **6 :** a pointed mass of viscous or solidified lava that occas. protrudes from the throat of a volcano

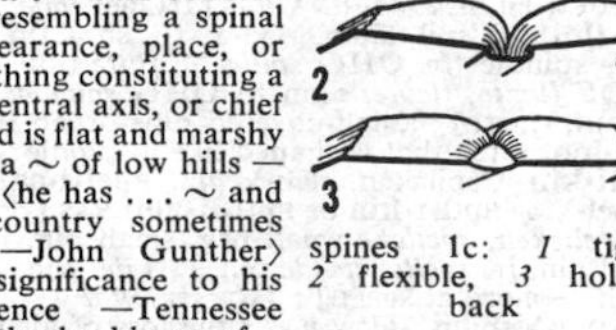
spines 1c: *1* tight, *2* flexible, *3* hollow back

spinebill \'⸗,⸗\ *n* **:** any of various honey eaters of the genus *Acanthorhynchus* having a slender curved and very sharp bill
spinebone \'⸗,⸗\ *n* [ME *spinboon*, fr. *spin, spine* spinal column + *boon* bone] **:** SPINAL COLUMN, BACKBONE
spine cell *n* **:** PRICKLE CELL
spined \'spīnd\ *adj* **:** furnished with a spine **:** SPINY
spine-finned \'⸗¦⸗\ *adj* **:** SPINY-FINNED
spinefoot \'⸗,⸗\ *n, pl* **spinefeet :** any of several rabbitfishes (genus *Siganus*) of the tropical Indo-Pacific capable of inflicting painful wounds with venomous fin spines
spi·nel \spə'nel *sometimes* 'spinᵊl\ *or* **spi·nelle** \spə'nel\ *n* -s [It *spinella, spinello*, dim. of *spina* thorn, fr. L; fr. the pointed crystals — more at SPINE] **1 a :** a mineral $MgAl_2O_4$ consisting of an oxide of magnesium and aluminum that is noted for its great hardness, that usu. forms octahedral crystals varying in color (as from colorless to ruby-red to black), and that is used as a gemstone — see ALMANDINE, BALAS, CEYLONITE, RUBICELLE, SPINEL RUBY **b :** a synthetic substance similar to the mineral spinel that is used as a gemstone, as bearings for watches and various instruments, and as a refractory **2 a :** a member of the spinel series **b :** a member of the spinel group **3 :** a substance (as a sulfide) that has a similar formula and the same crystal structure as a spinel
spine·less \'spīnləs\ *adj* **1 :** having no spines, thorns, or prickles **2 a :** having no spinal column **:** INVERTEBRATE **b :** lacking moral resolution, firmness, or strength of character ⟨a ~, craven fellow —John Lodge⟩
spine·less·ly *adv* **:** in a spineless manner **:** FEEBLY, IRRESOLUTELY
spine·less·ness *n* -ES **:** the quality or state of being spineless
spine·let \'spīnlət\ *n* -s **:** a small spine
spinel group *n* **:** a group of mineral oxides including the spinel series and having the general composition AB_2O_4 in which A represents magnesium, ferrous iron, zinc, or manganese or any combination of them and B represents aluminum, ferric iron, or chromium — see CHROMITE SERIES, MAGNETITE SERIES
spine-like \'⸗,⸗\ *adj* **:** resembling a spine
spi·nel·lid \spə'neləd\ *n* -s [ISV *spinel* + *-id*] **:** a member of the spinel group
spinel pink *n* **:** a moderate purplish red that is bluer and deeper than average rose, redder and deeper than violine pink, and redder and lighter than magenta rose
spinel red *n* **:** a strong red to purplish red that is duller than rose Neyron
spinel ruby *n* **:** a ruby spinel of a deep red color that is used as a gem — not used technically
spinel series *n* **:** a series of isomorphous mineral oxides $(Mg,Fe,Zn,Mn)Al_2O_4$ in the spinel group consisting of spinel, hercynite, gahnite, and galaxite
spine-rayed \'⸗¦⸗\ *adj* **:** SPINY-RAYED
spines *pl of* SPINE
spi·nes·cence \spī'nesᵊn(t)s\ *n* -s [NL *spinescentia*, fr. *spinescent-, spinescens* + L *-ia* -y] **1 :** SPININESS **2 :** SPINATION
spi·nes·cent \(')spī¦nesᵊnt\ *adj* [NL *spinescent-, spinescens*, fr. LL, pres. part. of *spinescere* to be thorny, incho. fr. L *spina* thorn] **:** becoming spiny **:** tapering to a sharp rigid point **:** tending toward spininess **:** SPINOSE, SPINULOSE
spin·et \'spinət\ *n* -s [It *spinetta*, prob. dim. of *spina* thorn, fr. L; fr. the use of quills to pluck the strings — more at SPINE] **1 :** a small harpsichord having a single keyboard **2 a :** a compactly built upright piano of reduced height and usu. reduced keyboard suitable for limited space **b :** a small electronic organ
spinetail \'⸗,⸗\ *n* **1 :** SPINE-TAILED SWIFT **2 :** any of several So. and Central American birds of *Synallaxis, Siptornis*, or related genera of the families Dendrocolaptidae and Furnariidae **3 :** RUDDY DUCK

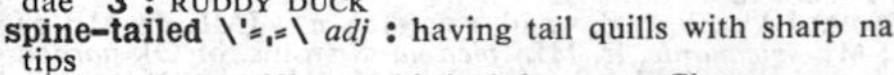
spinet 2

spine-tailed \'⸗,⸗\ *adj* **:** having tail quills with sharp naked tips
spine-tailed swift *n* **:** a bird of the genus *Chaetura*
spinet desk *n* **:** a desk made from or in imitation of a spinet
spiney *var of* SPINY
spin fishing *n* **:** SPINNING 2
spin house *n* [trans. of D *spinhuis*] **:** SPINNING HOUSE
spini- — see SPIN-
spinier *comparative of* SPINY
spinies *pl of* SPINY
spiniest *superlative of* SPINY
spi·ni·fex \'spīnə,feks\ *n* [NL, fr. *spin-* + L *-fex* (fr. *facere* to do, make) — more at SPIN-, DO] **1 a** *cap* **:** a genus of chiefly Australian grasses the seeds of which bear an elastic spine — see SPINY ROLLING GRASS **b** -ES **:** any plant of the genus *Spinifex* **2** -ES **:** any of several Australian grasses of the genus *Triodia* that often form dense almost impassable growths and have stiff and sharp-pointed leaves
spi·ni·form \'spīnə,fȯrm\ *adj* [NL *spiniformis*, fr. *spin-* + L *-formis* -form] **:** like or being a spine
spin in *vi* **:** to crash in an aircraft **:** be out of control in any way
spin·i·ness \'spīnēnəs, -īnin-\ *n* -ES **:** the quality or state of being spiny
spink \'spiŋk\ *n* -s [ME *spynke*, perh. of Scand origin; akin to Sw *spink* small bird, sparrow — more at FINCH] *dial Brit* **:** CHAFFINCH
spin·na·bil·i·ty \,spinə'biləd·ē\ *n* **:** fitness for spinning **:** capability of being spun — used of textile fibers
spin·na·ble \'spinəbəl\ *adj* **:** suitable for spinning **:** capable of being spun
spin·na·ker \'spinəkə(r)\ *n* -s [origin unknown] **:** a large triangular sail set on a long light pole on the side opposite the mainsail on fore-and-aft rigged yachts and used when running before the wind
spin·ner \'spinə(r)\ *n* -s [ME *spinnere*, fr. *spinnen* to spin + *-ere* -er] **1 a** *archaic* **:** a spider that spins a web **b :** MAYFLY **c :** a nightjar (*Caprimulgus europaeus*) **2 :** one that spins: as **a :** a manufacturer engaged in spinning **b** (1) **:** a worker who spins textile fibers (2) **:** a spinning machine **c :** one that tins metal articles by dipping a basket of them in molten tin and then whirling off the excess in a spinning machine **d :** a lathe operator who shapes rings and other round jewelry forms **e :** an operator of a lathe for spinning shaped articles from sheet-metal stock **f :** one that rolls candy strips and cuts them into sticks, drops, or other shapes **3 :** the teller of a yarn **:** one that spins a tale ⟨an extraordinary ~ of yarns —I.L.Salomon⟩ **4 a :** an artificial fly tied to represent one of the Ephemeridae in the imago stage — see LURE illustration **b :** a spoon, blade, or set of wings that revolves when drawn through the water **c :** an angler who uses spinning tackle **5 :** SPINNERET 1 **6 a :** a bowled cricket ball to which spin has been imparted **b :** a bowler of such balls **7 :** SPINNER PLAY **8 :** a padded iron disk revolving for use in polishing stone **9 spinners** *pl* **:** fine wool of high spinning count **10 :** a streamline fairing usu. of sheet metal and roughly conical or paraboloid in form which is attached to a propeller boss and revolves with it **11 :** a movable arrow that is spun on its dial to indicate the number or kind of moves a player may make in a board game
spin·ner·et \,spinə¦ret\ *n* -s [*spinner* + *-et*] **1 :** an organ for producing threads of silk from the secretion of the silk glands **:** a spinning organ: **a :** one of the often distinctly jointed processes usu. numbering six and resembling nipples near the end of a spider's abdomen each bearing minute orifices by which the ducts of the silk glands open to emit streams of secretion that usu. join together to form a single thread **b :** an organ of some insect larvae having a function analogous to that of a spider's spinneret; *esp* **:** a tubule on the labium of many caterpillars by which a double thread made up of separate filaments from paired glands is extruded **2** *or* **spin·ner·ette** \"\ [*spinnerette* fr. *spinner* + *-ette*] **:** a small metal plate, thimble, or cap with fine holes through which a cellulose or chemical solution is forced in the spinning of rayon, nylon, and other man-made filaments
spinner play *n* **:** a football play in which the ball carrier spins around as he either fakes or makes a handoff to another back in an attempt to deceive the opponents about the direction in which the play will go
spin·ner·ular \spə'ner(y)ələ(r); 'spinər,yül-, -nə,rül-\ *adj* **:** of or relating to spinnerets
spin·ner·ule \'spinə(r),yül, -nə,rül\ *n* -s [*spinner* + *-ule*] **:** one of many small tubes on the spinnerets of spiders for discharging the secretion of the silk glands
spin·nery \'spinərē\ *n* -ES [¹*spin* + *-ery*] **:** a spinning mill

spin·ney *also* **spin·ny** \'spinī\ *n, pl* **spinneys** *also* **spinnies** [MF *espinaye* thorny thicket, fr. *espine* thorn, fr. L *spina* — more at SPINE] *Brit* **:** a small wood with undergrowth **:** COPSE, THICKET

spinning *n* -s [ME *spinninge*, gerund of *spinnen* to spin] **1 a :** the operation or business of making fibers or filaments into yarn or thread **b :** the yarn or thread spun **2 :** a method of fishing with a light lure, a fixed spool reel, and light line **3 :** the drawing out of something (as a narration) to excessive length **4 :** rapid rotation ⟨the ~ of the planets⟩ **5 :** the shaping of hollow ware in a lathe by pressing a flat sheet of metal against a revolving form with a hand tool

spinning band *n* **:** [1]BAND 3c

spinning count *n* **:** the number of hanks of yarn that can be spun from one pound of washed combed wool of a given fineness ⟨wool with a *spinning count* of 80 is very fine while one of 40 is chiefly suitable for carpets⟩

spinning dial *n* **:** SPINNER 11

spinning frame *n* **:** a machine that draws, twists, and winds yarn — compare MULE, RING SPINNER

spinning gland *n* **:** SILK GLAND

spinning house *n* [ME *spynnyng hous* building used for spinning, fr. *spynnyng, spinninge* spinning + *hous* house] **:** a former house of correction for prostitutes esp. in England in which inmates were often made to work at spinning

spinning jen·ny \'⸗⸗,jenē, -ni\ *n* [*spinning* + *Jenny*, nickname fr. the name *Jane*] **:** an early machine for spinning wool or cotton by means of many spindles

spinning lathe *n* **:** a lathe used for the shaping of metal hollow ware by pressing flat stock over a revolving form with a hand tool

spinning line *n* **:** a durable rope used to couple or uncouple lengths of pipe in oil well drilling

spinning machine *n* **1 :** a machine for spinning staple fiber or continuous filament into yarn **2 :** a machine for winding insulated covering on electric wires **3 :** a machine for shaping metal hollow ware

spinning mammilla *n* **:** SPINNERET 1

spinning mite *n* **:** RED SPIDER

spinning reel *n* **:** a fishing reel having a fixed spool on which the line is wound by means of an arm or bail actuated by turning the reel handle

spinning ring *n* **:** the circular track on which the traveler of a ring spinner slides

spinning rod *n* **:** a fishing rod designed for casting a spinning lure

spinning tube *n* **:** SPINNERULE

spinning wheel *n* [ME *spynnyngwhele*, fr. *spynnyng, spinninge* spinning + *whele, wheel* wheel] **:** a small domestic machine for spinning yarn or thread in which a wheel drives a single spindle and is itself driven by hand or by foot

spinning wheel

spino- — see SPIN-

spi·no·blast \'spīnə-,blast\ *n* [*spin-* + *-blast*] **:** a free-floating statoblast provided with external barbs or hooks

spi·no·cerebellar \¦spī(,)nō+\ *adj* [*spin-* + *cerebellar*] **:** of or relating to the spinal cord and cerebellum

spinocerebellar tract *n* **:** any of four nerve tracts from the spinal cord to the cerebellum that arise two on each side from a group of large cells in the medial part of the base of the posterior columns of the spinal cord and pass to the cerebellum as both crossed and uncrossed fibers

spin–off \'⸗,⸗\ *n* -s [fr. *spin off*, v.] **:** a transfer of a distinctive business constituting one of two or more businesses owned by a corporation to a corporation controlled by it in return for a distribution to the stockholders of the distributing corporation of all the stock and securities in the transferee corporation without surrender of any stock or securities by the stockholders in the distributing corporation — compare SPLIT-OFF, SPLIT-UP

spi·no·gram \'spīnə,gram\ *n* [*spin-* + *-gram*] **:** MYELOGRAM 2

spi·noid \'spī,nȯid\ *adj* [*spin-* + *-oid*] **:** SPINELIKE

spino–olivary \¦spī(,)nō+\ *adj* [*spin-* + *olivary*] **:** connecting the spinal cord with the olivary body

spin·or \'spinər, -,nȯ(ə)r\ *n* -s [[1]*spin* + *-or*] **:** a quantity that resembles a vector with complex components in two- or four-dimensional space with complex coordinates and that is used esp. in the mathematics of the theory of relativity ⟨the geometrical picture of a two-component ~ requires two plane vectors . . . and these may be of arbitrary lengths and inclined to each other at any angle —*Scientific Monthly*⟩

spi·nose \'spī,nōs\ *adj* [L *spinosus*, fr. *spina* thorn, spine + *-osus* -ose — more at SPINE] **:** full of spines **:** armed with spines **:** SPINELIKE — **spi·nose·ly** *adv* — **spi·nose·ness** *n* -ES

spinose ear tick *n* **:** an ear tick (*Otobius megnini*) of the southwestern U.S. and Mexico that is a serious pest of cattle, horses, sheep, and goats

spi·nos·i·ty \spī'näsəd·ē\ *n* -ES [LL *spinositat-, spinositas*, fr. L *spinosus* spinose + *-itat-, -itas* -ity] **1 a :** the state of having spines **b :** a thorny or prickly quality **:** something nettlesome or difficult (as in a problem or argument) **2 :** a rude or cutting remark or one likely to give pain

spinoso- *comb form* [*spinose* + *-o-*] **:** spinose and ⟨*spinoso*dentate⟩

spi·no·tectal \¦spī(,)nō+\ *adj* [*spin-* + *tectum* + *-al*] **:** TECTOSPINAL

spi·no·thalamic \"+\ *adj* [*spin-* + *thalamic*] **:** connecting the spinal cord and thalamus; *also* **:** involving or affecting nerve fiber tracts connecting these parts

spi·nous \'spīnəs\ *adj* [*spine* + *-ous*] **1 :** difficult or unpleasant to handle or meet **:** BRISTLING, SHARP, THORNY ⟨a ~ humor⟩ **2 a :** having spines, thorns, or prickles ⟨a ~ plant⟩ **b :** having sharp processes (as of bone) ⟨the ~ appendage of a fish⟩ **c :** having the shape of a spine or thorn

spinous process *n* **:** SPINE 3e: as **a :** the median spinelike or platelike dorsal process of the neural arch of a vertebra **:** NEURAL SPINE **b :** a sharp posterior prolongation on each greater wing of the sphenoid bone **c :** a process on the head of the tibia between the articular surfaces for the condyles of the femur

spi·no·zism \spə'nō,zizəm\ *n* -s *usu cap* [ISV *spinoz-* (fr. Baruch *Spinoza* †1677 Du. philosopher) + *-ism*] **:** the philosophy of Spinoza whose fundamental ideas were that all reality is One Substance which has an infinite number of attributes of which only thought and extension are capable of being apprehended by the human mind, that all particular things and particular ideas or states of mind are modes or determinations of these two attributes and all such temporal existences are rigidly connected together in the One Substance in such a manner that all occurrences happen of necessity, and that human bondage to the passions and particular desires is due to an ignorance which fails to apprehend this inevitability so that freedom is to be won through understanding and acquiescing in this necessity and contemplative peace is to be found through the intellectual love of God — compare MONISTIC IDEALISM

spi·no·zist \-,zəst\ *n* -s *usu cap* [ISV *spinoz-* (fr. Baruch *Spinoza*) + *-ist*] **:** an adherent of Spinozism or a specialist in Spinoza's philosophy

spino·zis·tic \spə,nō'zistik, ¦spī(,)nō¦z-\ *adj, usu cap* **:** of, relating to, or typical of Spinoza or Spinozism

spinproof \'⸗,⸗\ *adj* **:** devised so as not to spin **:** incapable of spinning — used esp. of an airplane

spins *pres 3d sing of* SPIN, *pl of* SPIN

spin·ster \'spinztə(r), -n(t)stə-\ *n* -s [ME *spinnestere*, fr. *spinnen* to spin + *-estere* -ster] **1 a :** a woman whose occupation is to spin **b** *obs* **:** a man whose trade is spinning **2 a** *archaic* **:** an unmarried woman of gentle family **b :** an unmarried woman — often used as a legal term **3 :** a woman past the common age for marrying or one who seems unlikely to marry — called also *old maid*

spin·ster·hood \-,hu̇d\ *n* **:** the state or condition of being a spinster **:** OLD MAIDHOOD

spin·ster·ish \-ərish\ *adj* **:** having the habits, appearance, or traits of a spinster **:** OLD-MAIDISH

spin·ster·ly \-ə(r)lē, -li\ *adj* **:** of, relating to, or characteristic of a spinster **:** OLD-MAIDISH

spin·stress \-nzt(ə)rəs, -n(t)st(-\ *n* -ES [*spinster* + *-ess*] **1 :** a woman who spins **2 :** SPINSTER

spin·stry \-rē\ *n* -ES [*spinster* + *-y*] **:** the occupation or product of spinning

spin·thar·i·scope \spin'tharə,skōp\ *n* [Gk *spintharis* spark + E *-scope*; akin to Gk *spinthēr* spark] **:** an instrument consisting of a fluorescent screen and a magnifying lens system for visual detection of alpha rays

spin the bottle *n* **1 :** the game spin the plate when played with a bottle **2 :** a method of choosing a performer (as a partner in a kissing game) according to whom the mouth of a bottle points to when it stops spinning

spin the plate *or* **spin the platter** *n* **:** a game in which something round (as a plate or platter) is spun on edge and the name of a player is called upon which the named player must catch the spinning object before it falls or pay a forfeit

spin·ther·ism \'spin(t)thə,rizəm\ *n* -s [NL *spintherismus*, fr. Gk *spinthēr* spark + L *-ismus* -ism] **:** a subjective sensation as of sparks before the eyes

spin tunnel *n* **:** a vertical wind tunnel in which accurate scale models of aircraft are tested to determine their spinning characteristics

spi·nu·late \'spīnyə,lāt\ *or* **spi·nu·lat·ed** \-ād·əd\ *adj* [*spinulate* fr. *spinule* + *-ate*; *spinulated* fr. *spinulate* + *-ed*] **:** SPINULOSE

spi·nu·la·tion \,spīnyə'lāshən\ *n* -s [*spinule* + *-ation*] **:** an armature of spines or spinules

spi·nule \'spī(,)nyül\ *n* -s [L *spinula*, fr. *spina* thorn, spine + *-ula* — more at SPINE] **:** a small or minute spine

spi·nu·les·cent \¦spīnyə¦lesᵊnt\ *adj* [*spinule* + *-escent*] **:** having small spines **:** somewhat spiny

spi·nu·lo·sa \,spīnyə'lōsə\ *n pl, cap* [NL, fr. L *spinulosa*, neut. pl. of *spinulosus* spinulose] **:** a cosmopolitan order of starfishes lacking conspicuous marginal plates and stalked pedicellariae and often occurring at great depths in the sea

spi·nu·lose \'spīnyə,lōs\ *adj* [NL *spinulosus*, fr. L *spinula* spinule + *-osus* -ose] **:** covered with or having the form of small spines — **spi·nu·lose·ly** *adv*

spi·nu·lous \'spīnyələs\ *adj* [F or NL; F *spinuleux*, fr. NL *spinulosus*] **:** SPINULOSE

spin–up \'⸗,⸗\ *n* -s [fr. *spin up*, v.] **:** the acceleration of the wheels of an airplane by contact with the ground when touching down to land to a peripheral speed equal to the ground speed

spi·nus \'spīnəs, -pēn-\ *n, cap* [NL, fr. Gk *spinos* chaffinch — more at FINCH] **:** a genus of small active often brightly colored finches that commonly includes the siskins and the New World goldfinches and is sometimes considered to constitute a subgenus of *Carduelis*

[1]**spiny** *also* **spin·ey** \'spīnē, -ni\ *adj* **spinier; spiniest** [*spine* + *-y*] **1 :** covered with spines **:** bearing several or many spines, prickles, or sharp processes **2 :** abounding with difficulties, obstacles, or annoyances **:** NETTLESOME, THORNY ⟨a ~ problem —A.C.Fisher⟩ **3 :** slender and pointed like a spine

[2]**spiny** \"\ *n* -ES *Africa* **:** any of several rabbitfishes of the genus *Siganus*

spiny amaranth *or* **spiny pigweed** *n* **:** THORNY AMARANTH

spiny anteater *n* **:** ECHIDNA

spiny catfish *n* **:** a small brown So. American freshwater naked catfish (*Doras cataphractus*) having the pectoral fins armed with hooked spines and a row of spinose bony plates along each side of the body and being sometimes kept in the tropical aquarium where it is an excellent scavenger

spiny clotbur *or* **spiny cocklebur** *n* **:** a European cocklebur (*Xanthium spinosum*) naturalized widely as a weed in waste grounds and having 3-branched spines at the axils of the leaves

spiny crawfish *n* **:** a large Australian crawfish (*Astacopsis senatus*) with a spiny carapace

spiny dogfish *n* **:** any of various dogfishes constituting the family Squalidae and distinguished by the presence of a spine in or immediately anterior to each dorsal fin: as **a :** a common very destructive dogfish (*Squalus acanthias*) of both coasts of the No. Atlantic that becomes about four feet long and has the fin spines stout and prominent **b :** a similar dogfish (*Squalus suckleyi*) of the Pacific coast of No. America

spiny dormouse *n* **:** a small Indian rodent (*Platacanthomys lasiurus*) with long bushy tail, pointed ears, and a pelage of mingled hairs and spines

spiny eel *n* **:** any of several strikingly colored eel-shaped freshwater fishes (order Opisthomi) of Africa and the East Indies having a long slender snout and an anterior dorsal fin consisting of free spines

spiny elm caterpillar *n* **:** the larva of the mourning cloak butterfly

spiny–finned \¦⸗⸗¦⸗\ *adj* **:** having fins with some spiny rays — opposed to *soft-finned*; used of members of the Acanthopterygii

spiny–haired rat \'⸗⸗,⸗-\ *n* **:** a small reddish southeastern Asiatic rat (*Rattus fulvescens* syn. *R. jerdoni*) having flat spines mingled with the hair

spiny–herb \'⸗⸗,⸗\ *n* **:** an annual desert plant of the genus *Chorizanthe* (family Polygonaceae) lacking sheathing stipules and having flowers borne in an involucre which is usu. one-flowered with bracts ending in bristles

spiny lobster *n* **:** an edible crustacean (family Palinuridae) that is distinguished from the true lobster by the simple unenlarged first pair of legs and by the spiny carapace — called also *lobster, rock lobster, sea crawfish;* compare CAPE CRAWFISH, LANGOUSTE

spiny mouse *n* **1 :** any of various mice of the genus *Acomys* that are closely related to the house mouse but distinguished by an almost entirely spiny coat, are native to the Mediterranean area, and are sometimes kept as pets in Europe **2 :** any of several New World fossorial pocket mice (as of the genus *Heteromys*) with spiny pelage

spiny oyster *n* **:** a bivalve mollusk of the family Spondylidae

spiny pocket mouse *n* **:** SPINY MOUSE 2

spiny rat *n* **1 :** any of various So. or Central American rats of *Echimys* and closely related genera having more or less bristly fur — called also *hedgehog rat, porcupine rat* **2 :** SPINY MOUSE 2

spiny ray *n* **:** a fin ray that is stiff, unbranched, pointed at the end, and lacking transverse segmentation, that occurs singly or grouped in the anterior part of the dorsal fin in many fishes or in the first dorsal when there are two as well as in the anal and ventral fins, and that was in former classifications the principal character of the group Acanthopterygii — opposed to *soft ray*

spiny–rayed \¦⸗⸗¦⸗\ *adj* **1 :** having spiny rays — used of a fin **2 :** having fins with one or more spiny rays **:** SPINY-FINNED — used of a fish, esp. of the Acanthopterygii; compare SOFT-RAYED

spiny rolling grass *n* **:** an Australian grass (*Spinifex hirsutus*) with long creeping stems that root freely at the joints and thus of value as a sand binder

spiny–skinned \¦⸗⸗¦⸗\ *adj* **:** having a skin covered with knobs, tubercles, or spines ⟨*spiny-skinned* fishes⟩

spio \'spī(,)ō\ *n, cap* [NL *Spion-, Spio*, perh. fr. L *Spio*, one of the Nereids, fr. Gk *Speiō*] **:** a widely distributed genus (the type of the family Spionidae) of small burrowing marine polychaete worms without tentacles or palps but with enlarged dorsal cirri acting as gills

[1]**spi·o·nid** \'spīənəd\ *adj* [NL *Spionidae*] **:** of or relating to the genus *Spio* or family Spionidae

[2]**spionid** \"\ *n* -s [NL *Spionidae*, family of marine polychaete worms, fr. *Spion-, Spio*, type genus + *-idae*] **:** a spionid worm

spir- *or* **spiri-** *or* **spiro-** *comb form* [LL *spir-*, fr. L *spira* — more at SPIRE] **1 :** coil **:** twist ⟨*Spir*anthes⟩ ⟨*spiri*valve⟩ ⟨*Spiro*chaeta⟩ **2 :** a chemical compound that contains one or more systems of two rings having a single atom in common with a resulting figure-eight arrangement of atoms ⟨*spiro*pentane⟩

spirable *adj* [L *spirabilis*, fr. *spirare* to breathe + *-bilis* -able] *obs* **:** capable of being breathed **:** RESPIRABLE

spi·ra·cle \'spirəkəl, -pīr-\ *n* -s [in sense 1, fr. ME, fr. LL *spiraculum*, fr. L, air hole, spiracle, fr. *spirare* to breathe; in other senses, fr. L *spiraculum* — more at SPIRIT] **1** *obs* **:** BREATH, SPIRIT **2 a :** a usu. small aperture giving a confined space communication with the outer air **:** a breathing hole **:** AIR HOLE, VENT **b :** a steam or gas vent on the surface of a lava flow **3 :** a breathing orifice: **a :** the blowhole of a cetacean **b :** an external tracheal aperture of a terrestrial arthropod that in an insect is usu. one of a series of small more or less elliptical apertures often having a valve and a protective sievelike structure or fringe of hairs and being located along each side of the thorax and abdomen usu. in 10 pairs but sometimes 11 or occas. fewer — see INSECT illustration **c :** one of the orifices or passages that open on the upper back part of the head of many elasmobranchs and some higher fishes (as a sturgeon or the bichir), communicate with the mouth cavity, represent the first postoral visceral clefts of the embryo, in rays serve instead of the mouth as the chief incurrent respiratory openings, and may contain a rudimentary gill **d :** the excurrent aperture of the gill chamber of a tadpole developing from two apertures that unite in a canal which opens on the left side of the body or rarely on the middle of the undersurface

spi·rac·u·lar \(')spī¦rakyələ(r), spə'r-\ *adj* [*spiraculum* + *-ar*] **:** of, relating to, or serving as a spiracle

spi·rac·u·lum \⸗'⸗ləm\ *n, pl* **spiracu·la** \-lə\ [L] **:** SPIRACLE

[1]**spiraea** *var of* SPIREA

[2]**spi·raea** \spī'rēə\ *n, cap* [NL, fr. L, a plant, perh. privet, fr. Gk *speiraia*, perh. fr. *speira* coil — more at SPIRE] **:** a large genus of shrubs (family Rosaceae) that are natives of temperate regions and have small perfect white or pink flowers in dense racemes, corymbs, cymes, or panicles each with five pistils which are alternate with the persistent calyx lobes and which ripen into follicles — see HARDHACK, MEADOWSWEET

[1]**spi·ral** \'spīrəl\ *adj* [ML *spiralis*, fr. L *spira* coil + *-alis* -al — more at SPIRE] **1 a :** winding around a center or pole and gradually receding from or approaching it ⟨a ~ curve⟩ **b (1) :** HELICAL **(2) :** of, relating to, or resembling a spiral **2 :** having one or more strands twisted around a core yarn ⟨a ~ ply yarn⟩ **3 :** advancing to succeeding higher levels through a series of cyclical movements ⟨developed a ~ theory of social evolution⟩

[2]**spiral** \"\ *n* -s **1 a :** the path of a point in a plane moving around a centered point while continuously receding from or approaching it **b :** a three-dimensional curve (as a helix) with one or more turns about an axis **2 :** a single turn or coil in a spiral object **3 a :** something (as a piece of coiled wire or a winding staircase) having a spiral form ⟨a long blue ~ from his cigar ascended —John Galsworthy⟩ **b :** SPIRAL GALAXY **c :** a flight in a spiral path **:** a spiral flight **d :** a kick or pass in which a football rotates on its long axis while moving through the air **e :** a dance movement consisting of concentric circling with steadily diminishing or increasing diameter on a ground level or with rising and falling **f :** a free skating figure consisting of gliding on one foot with speed in a large circle with the body in arabesque position **g :** a synchronized swimming stunt consisting of at least four complete body revolutions executed with the body in a head downward vertical position with the ankles above water followed by complete submergence of the body **h (1) :** an easement curve (as in a railroad track) in which the change of degree of curve is uniform throughout its length **(2) :** a loop built where a railroad line ascends a steep slope for the purpose of gaining distance in order not to exceed the ruling grade **4 :** a continuously spreading and accelerating increase or decrease (as in costs, prices, or wages) ⟨a continuance of the upward ~ of prices —F.D.Roosevelt⟩ ⟨the vicious ~ of deflation —F.L.Allen⟩ ⟨the vicious ~ of arming and counterarming —B.N.Rau⟩ — see INFLATIONARY SPIRAL

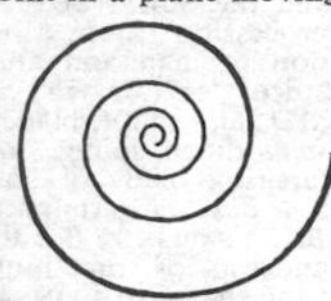

spiral 1a

[3]**spiral** \"\ *vb* **spiraled** *or* **spiralled; spiraled** *or* **spiralled; spiraling** *or* **spiralling; spirals** *vi* **1 a :** to go or move and esp. to rise or fall in a spiral course **:** wind in a spiral manner ⟨the path . . . ~*ed* up the hillside —Harlan Hatcher⟩ ⟨saw a column of cloud slowly ~ from nothingness —Victor Canning⟩ **b :** to follow a spiral path in ascending or descending ⟨our plane ~*s* down toward the . . . airdrome —W.L.White⟩ ⟨the birds ~*ed* high —Adria Langley⟩ ⟨we ~*ed* through the . . . cloud rift and landed —Lowell Thomas⟩ **2 :** to rise or fall in a continuously spreading and accelerating manner ⟨production ~*ed* upward⟩ ⟨the cost of living ~*ed* upward⟩ ⟨profits ~*ed* during the business boom⟩ **3 :** to revolve with a spiral pattern in dancing ~ *vt* **1 :** to form into a spiral **:** turn or twist spirally ⟨section foremen . . . ~*ed* the ends of their curves —*Engineering News*⟩ **2 :** to cause to rise or fall in a continuously spreading and accelerating manner ⟨inflation ~*ed* prices —Henry Coates⟩

[4]**spir·al** \"\ *adj* [[1]*spire* + *-al*] **:** rising to a sharp point **:** tall and tapering or pointed like the spire of a building

spiral axis *n* **:** the axis of a twisted column drawn spirally in order to trace the circumvolutions without

spiral bandage *n* **:** a bandage wound in oblique turns around an extremity — see BANDAGE illustration

spiral bevel gear *n* **:** a bevel gear in which the tooth elements are curved lines (as helical lines)

spiral binding *n* **:** mechanical binding in which a continuous spiral wire or plastic strip is passed through holes at the gutter margin

spiral–bound \¦⸗⸗¦⸗\ *adj* **:** having or bound with a spiral binding ⟨a *spiral-bound* notebook⟩

spiral chute *n* **:** a continuous curved trough spiraled about a column for use in transporting materials to a lower level

spiral conveyor *n* **:** CONVEYER 2a (8)

spiral duct *n* **:** SPIRAL VESSEL

spi·rale \spī'ra(,)lē, -rā(-, spə'ra(,)lā\ *n* -s [NL, fr. ML, neut. of *spiralis* spiral] **:** SPIRALIUM

spiral galaxy *n* **:** a galaxy exhibiting a central nucleus or barred structure from which extend concentrations of matter forming curved arms giving the overall appearance of a gigantic pinwheel — compare SPIRAL NEBULA

spiral ganglion *n* **:** a mass of bipolar nerve cells occupying the spiral canal of the organ of Corti and from their axons forming the cochlear branch of the eighth cranial nerve

spiral gear *or* **spiral gearing** *n* **:** a helical gear used to transmit power between nonparallel shafts

spiral grain *n* **:** a spiral or winding instead of the usual vertical arrangement in the vessels and other elements in the wood from a twisted tree

spiral head *n* **:** an index head whose spindle may be connected by gearing to the feed screw of a milling machine table for the purpose of cutting spirals

spi·ral·i·form \spī'ralə,fȯrm\ *adj* **:** having or based upon the form of a spiral ⟨the ~ system in art⟩

spi·ral·ism \'spīrə,lizəm\ *n* -s **:** the growth of a normally straight stem to form a spiral

spi·ral·i·ty \spī'raləd·ē\ *n* -ES [ISV [1]*spiral* + *-ity*] **:** the quality or state of being spiral **:** the amount or degree of spiral curve

spi·ra·li·um \spī'rālēəm\ *n, pl* **spira·lia** \-ēə\ [NL, fr. ML *spiralis* spiral + NL *-ium*] **:** one of the spirally twisted ribbonlike calcareous supports on the interior of the valve of various extinct brachiopods — see BRACHIOPOD illustration

spi·ral·iza·tion \,spīrələ'zāshən, -,lī'z-\ *n* -s **:** the action or process of spiralizing ⟨~ of chromosomes⟩

spi·ral·ize \'⸗⸗,līz\ *vb* -ED/-ING/-S *vt* **:** to make spiral **:** wind, coil, twist, or cut in a spiral ~ *vi* **:** to gather into a spiral ⟨the chromosomes of the two nuclei begin to ~ —Esko Suomalainen⟩

spi·ral·ly \-rəlē, -li\ *adv* **:** in a spiral manner or course **:** in spiral lines or curves

spiral milling *n* **:** HELICAL MILLING

spiral nebula *n* **:** SPIRAL GALAXY — not used technically

spiral of archimedes *usu cap A* **:** ARCHIMEDEAN SPIRAL

spiral organ *n* **:** ORGAN OF CORTI

spiral reverse bandage *n* **:** a spiral bandage in which the oblique turns are reversed at each turn in order better to adapt to the part — see BANDAGE illustration
spirals *pl of* SPIRAL, *pres 3d sing of* SPIRAL
spiral spring *n* **:** a spring consisting of a wire coiled usu. in a flat spiral or in a helix
spiral stairs *n pl* **:** stairs that are circular in plan and consist entirely of winders
spiral valve *n* **:** a continuous spiral ridge of mucous membrane in the large intestine of fishes of the more primitive groups (as elasmobranchs, ganoids, dipnoans) that makes a number of complete turns increasing the surface for absorption and retarding the passage of food
spiral vessel *n* **:** a trachea or vessel having the walls spirally thickened — called also *spiral duct*
spiral wheel *n* **:** SCREW WHEEL
spi·ran \ˈspī,ran\ *or* **spi·rane** \-rān\ *n* -s [*spir-* + *-an* or *-ane*] **:** a spiro compound
spi·rant \ˈspīrənt\ *n* -s [ISV, fr. L *spirant-, spirans,* pres. part. of *spirare* to breathe — more at SPIRIT] **1 :** a consonant that is not a stop, affricate, nasal, voiced lateral, flap, trill, or semivowel (as in English \f\, \v\, \th\, \t͟h\, \s\, \z\, \sh\, \zh\, or \h\) **2 :** a consonant that is not a stop or affricate **3 :** a member of any classification intermediate between spirant (sense 1) and spirant (sense 2)
spi·ran·tal \(ˈ)spī¦rantᵊl\ *or* **spi·rant** \ˈspīrənt\ *adj* [*spirantal* fr. *spirant,* n. + *-al; spirant* ISV, fr. L *spirant-, spirans,* pres. part. of *spirare*] **:** of, relating to, or of the nature of a spirant
spi·ran·thes \spīˈran(t)(,)thēz\ *n, cap* [NL, fr. *spir-* + *-anthes*] **:** a large widely distributed genus of terrestrial orchids with slender often twisted spikes of white irregular flowers — see SCREW AUGER
spi·ran·tic \(ˈ)spī¦rantik\ *adj* **:** SPIRANTAL
spi·rant·ism \ˈspīrənt·,izəm\ *n* -s **:** spirantal nature ⟨in these sounds ~ is retained —R.F.Spencer⟩
spi·rant·iza·tion \,spīrəntəˈzāshən, -rənt·,īˈz-\ *n* -s **:** the action or process of spirantizing
spi·rant·ize \ˈspīrənt·,īz\ *vt* ED/-ING/-S **:** to make spirantal
spi·ras·ter \(ˈ)spī¦rastə(r)\ *n* -s [NL, fr. *spir-* + *-aster*] **:** a spiral sponge spicule of one or more turns produced on the outside into several spines
spiration *n* -s [L *spiration-, spiratio* action of breathing, fr. *spiratus* (past part. of *spirare* to breathe) + *-ion-, -io* -ion] **1 a** *obs* **:** the action of breathing as a creative or life-giving function of the Deity **b** (1) **:** the act by or manner in which the Holy Spirit proceeds from the Father or from the Father and the Son (2) **:** the relation subsisting by virtue of this procession **2** *obs* **:** the action of breathing as a physical function of man and animals
¹spire \ˈspī(ə)r, -īə\ *n* -s [ME *spir, spire,* fr. OE *spīr;* akin to MD *spier* shoot, blade of grass, ON *spíra* stalk, L *spina* thorn, spine — more at SPINE] **1 :** a slender tapering blade or stalk (as of grass or grain) **2 a** *obs* **:** a germinating plant **:** SPROUT **b** *dial Brit* **:** SAPLING **3 :** the top or end of something and esp. of something held to taper to a point **:** the sharp tip **:** PINNACLE ⟨the ~ of a tree⟩ ⟨a ~ of flame⟩ **4 :** a conical heap or pile **:** a mass of pyramidal form ⟨~s of rock⟩ **5 a :** a steeply tapering roof or analogous pyramidal construction surmounting a tower or towerlike structure **b :** STEEPLE

spire 5a

²spire \"\ *vi* -ED/-ING/-S [ME *spiren,* fr. *spir, spire,* n.] **1 :** to send forth or develop shoots **:** GERMINATE, SPROUT ⟨seeds ~ under suitable conditions⟩ **2** *of a plant* **:** to run to stalk or stem **:** become spindly **3 :** to shoot up into a spire **:** run up taperingly like a spire **:** mount or soar aloft ⟨a towering crag . . . *spired* up —Thomas Gray⟩
³spire \"\ *n* -s [L *spira* coil, twist, fr. Gk *speira;* akin to Gk *sparton* rope, esparto, Lith *spìngti* to choke on something] **1 :** SPIRAL **:** a sinuous winding (as of a serpent) **:** COIL, CURL, TWIST, WHORL **2 :** a series of curls or coils **3 :** the upper part of a spiral shell including the whole series of whorls except the last or body whorl **4 :** SPIRALIUM
⁴spire \"\ *vi* -ED/-ING/-S **:** to rise, fall, or otherwise move in or as if in a spiral **:** mount or soar spirally ⟨up, up ~s the song —Amy Lowell⟩
spi·rea *or* **spi·raea** \spīˈrēə\ *n* -s [NL *Spiraea*] **1 :** a shrub of the genus *Spiraea* **2 :** any of several commonly cultivated plants that resemble members of the genus *Spiraea; esp* **:** a shrub (*Astilbe japonica*) often forced by florists for Easter blooming
spirea aphid *n* **:** GREEN CITRUS APHID
spire-bearer \ˈ=,==\ *n* [*³spire* + *bearer;* trans. of NL *Spirifer*] **:** SPIRIFER 2
¹spired \ˈspī(ə)rd, -īəd\ *adj* [*¹spire* + *-ed*] **1 :** having a spire ⟨a ~ steeple⟩ ⟨a ~ church⟩ **:** characterized by spires ⟨a ~ English village —Mary Ross⟩ **2 :** tapering usu. to a sharp point **:** SLENDER, POINTED ⟨a ~ Engelmann's spruce —R.L. Neuberger⟩
²spired \"\ *adj* [*³spire* + *-ed*] **:** having a spire **:** SPIRAL ⟨a ~ shell⟩
spire·let \ˈspī(ə)rlət\ *n* -s **:** a small spire **:** FLÈCHE
spire lily *n* **:** SUMMER HYACINTH
spi·reme \ˈspī,rēm\ *also* **spi·rem** \-rem\ *n* -s [G *spirem,* fr. Gk *speirēma, speirama* coil, fr. *speira* coil, twist — more at SPIRE] **:** a continuous thread observed in fixed preparations of cells in the prophase of mitosis that gives the appearance of being a strand of chromatin but is generally held to be an observational or technical artifact — compare CHROMOSOME
spire-steeple \ˈ=,==\ *n, archaic* **:** a steeple surmounted by a spire **:** a church spire
spiri- — see SPIR-
spi·ri·cle \ˈspīrəkəl\ *n* -s [*spir-* + *-cle*] **:** one of the minute coiled threads in the coating of some seeds that uncoil when moistened
spi·ri·fer \ˈspīrəfə(r)\ *n* [NL, fr. *spir-* + *-fer*] **1** *cap* **:** a large genus (the type of the family Spiriferidae) of articulate brachiopods that have the arms supported within the shell by long spirally coiled spiralia which form a pair of cones with their apexes directed more or less laterally toward the ends of the long hinge line and that abound in Silurian, Devonian, and Carboniferous formations **2** *or* **spi·rif·er·id** \spīˈrifərəd\ -s [*spiriferid* fr. NL *Spiriferidae* family of brachiopods, fr. *Spirifer,* type genus + *-idae*] **:** any brachiopod of *Spirifer* or a related genus — called also *spire-bearer*
spi·rif·era \spīˈrif(ə)rə\ *syn of* SPIRIFER
spi·rif·er·a·cea \(,)spī,rifəˈrāshēə\ *n* -s [NL, fr. *Spirifer* + *-acea*] **:** a suborder or superfamily of Brachiopoda comprising all the Telotremata with calcareous spiral supports for the arms
spi·rif·er·oid \(ˈ)spī¦rifə,rȯid\ *adj* [NL *Spirifer* + E *-oid*] **:** belonging to or characteristic of the genus *Spirifer* — see BRACHIOPOD illustration
spi·rif·er·ous \(ˈ)spī¦rif(ə)rəs\ *adj* [prob. fr. NL *spirifer* spiriferous (fr. *spir-* + *-fer* -ferous) + E *-ous*] **1 a :** having a spiral part or organ **b :** SPIRED **2** [*spirifer* + *-ous*] **:** containing or characterized by brachiopods of the suborder Spiriferacea — used esp. of rock
spi·ri·form \ˈspīrə,fȯrm\ *adj* [NL *spiriformis,* fr. *spir-* + L *-formis* -form] **:** resembling a spire or a spiral in form
spi·ril·la·ce·ae \,spīrəˈlāsē,ē\ *n pl, cap* [NL, fr. *Spirillum* + *-aceae*] **:** a family comprising rigid more or less spirally curved elongate bacteria that lack endospores and always divide transversely and are sometimes included as a tribe in Pseudomonadaceae — **spi·ril·la·ceous** \¦==¦lāshəs\ *adj*
spi·ril·lar \(ˈ)spī¦rilə(r)\ *adj* [*spirillum* + *-ar*] **:** belonging to the genus *Spirillum* **:** resembling a spirillum
spi·ril·lary \ˈspīrə,lerē, (ˈ)spī¦rilərē\ *adj* [*spirillum* + *-ary*] **:** caused by spirilla
spi·ril·li·ci·dal \(,)spī,riləˈsīdᵊl, =¦==,==\ *adj* [*spirillum* + *-i-* + *-cidal*] **:** destroying spirilla ⟨~ action⟩
spi·ril·lum \spīˈriləm\ *n* [NL, dim. of L *spira* coil, twist — more at SPIRE] **1** *cap* **:** a genus of bacteria formerly coextensive with the family Spirillaceae but now restricted to elongated forms having tufts of flagella at one or both poles and usu. living in stagnant water rich in organic matter — compare RAT-BITE FEVER, VIBRIO **2** *pl* **spiril·la** \-lə\ **a :** any bacterium of the genus Spirillum or of the group to which it belongs — compare SPIRILLACEAE **b :** SPIROCHETE
¹spiring *adj* [fr. gerund of *²spire*] **:** rising taperingly to or as if to a point **:** soaring aloft **:** reaching to a great height ⟨~ summits of vast mountains —Thomas Pennant⟩ ⟨~ grass⟩
²spiring *adj* [fr. gerund of *⁴spire*] **:** rising spirally ⟨a ~ stairway⟩
¹spir·it \ˈspirət, *chiefly dial* ˈsper-; *usu* -əd.+V\ *n* -s *often attrib* [ME, fr. OF or L; OF *spirit, espirit, esperit,* fr. L *spiritus* spirit, breath; akin to ON *fīsa* to break wind, L *spirare* to breathe, and perh. to OSlav *piskati* to play a reed instrument] **1 :** the breath of life **:** the animating or vital principle giving life to physical organisms **2 a :** a supernatural being (as an apparition, specter, sprite, or elf) **b :** a supernatural, incorporeal, rational being or personality usu. invisible to human beings but having the power to become visible at will; *esp* **:** one held to be troublesome, terrifying, or hostile to mankind **c :** a supernatural being held to be able to enter into and possess a person ⟨possessed by a malign ~⟩ **d :** a being having an incorporeal or immaterial nature ⟨God is a ~ —Jn 4:24 (AV)⟩ **3** *usu cap* **a :** the active essence of the Deity serving as an invisible and life-giving or inspiring power in motion ⟨the *Spirit* of God was a silent partner in the production of many of these first Christian . . . sermons —H. H.Meyer⟩ **b :** one manifestation of the divine nature **:** one of the persons of the Trinity **:** HOLY SPIRIT ⟨at Pentecost the *Spirit* came down from heaven as cloven tongues of fire —D. C.Simpson⟩ **4 a :** SOUL ⟨into thy hands I commit my ~ —Lk 23:46 (RSV)⟩ **b :** a disembodied soul existing as an independent entity **:** the soul departed from the body of a deceased person **5 a :** temper or disposition of mind **:** DISPOSITION, MOOD — usu. used in pl. ⟨in good ~s⟩ ⟨in bad ~s⟩ **b :** mental vigor or animation **:** CHEERFULNESS, LIVELINESS, VIVACITY ⟨full of ~s⟩ **6 :** the immaterial intelligent or sentient part of a person **:** the vital principle in man coming as a gift from God and providing one's personality with its inward structure, dynamic drive, and creative response to the demands it encounters in the process of becoming **7 a :** the activating or essential principle of something (as an emotion or frame of mind) influencing a person **b :** an inclination, impulse, or tendency of a specified kind **8** *archaic* **:** the emotional source of hostile or angry feeling in a person **9** *often cap* **:** life or consciousness having an independent type of existence ⟨idealists maintain that the essential nature of the universe is ~⟩ ⟨pantheists assert that ~ pervades the universe⟩ **10** *archaic* **:** a movement of the air **:** a breath of wind **:** BREEZE, WIND ⟨the balmy ~ of the western gale —Alexander Pope⟩ **11 spirits** *pl* **:** bodily constitution that is the source of energy and strength **:** vital power **:** physical energy **:** the normal operation of the vital functions **12 :** a subtle substance (as a kind of breath or vapor) formerly held to permeate the blood and the principal body organs and to animate the body as a physical organism — usu. used in pl.; see ANIMAL SPIRITS, NATURAL SPIRITS, VITAL SPIRITS **13 spirits** *pl, obs* **:** mental constitution that is the source of perception and active thought **:** mental powers **:** INTELLECT ⟨his ~ should hunt after new fancies —Shak.⟩ **14 a :** a special attitude or frame of mind characterizing an individual or group **:** a character, disposition, or temper peculiar to and often animating a particular individual or group **b :** the frame of mind, feeling, or disposition characterizing something (as an action, consideration, or view) **15 a :** a lively or brisk quality in something **b :** stimulated or high characteristics (as liveliness, energy, vivacity, ardor, enthusiasm, or courage) in a person or his actions **16 :** an individual person considered with reference to characteristics of mind or temper **:** one having a character or disposition of a specified nature **17 :** a mental disposition characterized by firmness or assertiveness **:** ARDOR, COURAGE, METTLE **18 a** *archaic* **:** a liquid produced by distillation **b :** the flammable liquid containing ordinary alcohol and water as its main ingredients that is separated by distillation from any alcoholic liquid or mash and that is colorless and flavorless if highly rectified but that in the case of whiskey, brandy, or similar liquors derives its qualities from the nature of the source (as grain or fruit) from which it is made ⟨taxable distilled ~s —*U. S. Code*⟩ — often used in pl.; compare DISTILLED LIQUOR, METHYLATED SPIRIT, PROOF SPIRIT **c :** any of various volatile liquids obtained by distillation and sometimes by cracking (as of petroleum, shale, or wood) and used chiefly as fuels and solvents ⟨shale ~⟩ — often used in pl.; see MOTOR SPIRIT, PETROLEUM SPIRIT, WOOD SPIRIT **d :** ALCOHOL 3, RECTIFIED SPIRIT **e :** any of various usu. volatile organic solvents (as other alcohols, esters, ketones, or hydrocarbons) used similarly to alcohol — compare SPIRIT-SOLUBLE **19** *obs* **:** a volatile agent or essence that is a constituent and usu. life-giving element of a natural body ⟨the ~s . . . that are in all tangible bodies are scarce known —Francis Bacon⟩ **20 a :** the essential character of something **:** characteristic quality esp. as derived from individual genius or personal character **:** the pervading principle of something **b :** the prevailing tone or tendency ⟨the ~ of the age⟩ ⟨the ~ of the enterprise⟩ **c :** the general intent or real meaning of something (as a statement or law) — opposed to *letter* **21 :** an alcoholic solution of a volatile substance (as an essential oil) ⟨~ of peppermint⟩ **:** ALCOHOLATE 2 — called also *essence;* compare ELIXIR 2, TINCTURE **22 :** any of various solutions esp. of tin salts used as mordants in dyeing ⟨aniline ~⟩ ⟨scarlet ~⟩ **23 :** enthusiastic loyalty ⟨school ~⟩ ⟨class ~⟩ ⟨college ~⟩ **24** *Hegelianism* **:** the complex of human institutions (as family, society, state, and church) and productions in art, poetry, science, and culture **25** *cap, Christian Science* **:** ²GOD b(6) **syn** see COURAGE, VIGOR — **in spirits :** in a cheerful or joyful frame of mind **:** ANIMATED, ELATED, HAPPY — **out of spirits :** in a depressed frame of mind **:** LOW-SPIRITED
²spirit \"\ *vt* -ED/-ING/-S **1** *archaic* **:** to make (as the blood or a liquor) more lively or active ⟨our quick blood, ~*ed* with wine —Shak.⟩ **2 :** to infuse with energy, ardor, or life **:** ANIMATE, ENCOURAGE, INSPIRIT, STIMULATE ⟨some rum . . . to ~ me for what was before me —Daniel Defoe⟩ — sometimes used with *up* ⟨~ up our captives —Robert Browning⟩ ⟨inspire some . . . maid to ~ up her countrymen —Thomas Paine⟩ **3** *obs* **a :** to invest with a spirit or animating principle ⟨thy high commands must ~ all our wars —Alexander Pope⟩ **b :** to endow with a special spirit or character **4 a :** to carry off, make away with, or remove rapidly and secretly or mysteriously as if by the agency of a spirit ⟨seemed to ~ the things off the table without sound or effort —R.S.Surtees⟩ ⟨he ~*ed* from the files . . . canceled checks and other records —H.H.Martin⟩ — sometimes used with *away* ⟨residents . . . ~*ed* away the records —*Amer. Guide Series: La.*⟩ **b :** to convey to a destination in a secret or mysterious way ⟨managed to ~ the proprietor out of town —*Amer. Guide Series: Nev.*⟩ ⟨~*ed* his ensemble aboard a westbound liner —Ann M. Lingg⟩ — sometimes used with *away* ⟨was ~*ed* away to a secret hideaway —*Associated Press*⟩ **c :** to abduct or cause to disappear mysteriously **:** KIDNAP — usu. used with *away* ⟨women and children . . . ~*ed* away to America to be sold into bondage —*Amer. Guide Series: N.C.*⟩ ⟨the man was ~*ed* away, badly beaten, and sent back —J.A.Michener⟩ **5** *archaic* **:** to bring about **:** INSTIGATE — usu. used with *up* ⟨determined to ~ up a cruel war —John & William Langhorne⟩
spirit baptism *n, usu cap S* **:** baptismal purification by the Holy Spirit's entry into one's life as an indwelling force
spirit blue *n, often cap S&B* **:** any of several alcohol-soluble triphenylmethane dyes that are phenyl derivatives of pararosaniline or fuchsine — see SOLUBLE BLUE 1; DYE table I (under *Solvent Blue 3*)
spirit butterfly *n* **:** any of numerous delicate butterflies (genus *Ithomia*) of tropical America having gauzy wings nearly destitute of scales
spirit compass *n* **:** a liquid compass using a mixture of alcohol and water
spirit duck *n* **1 :** BUFFLEHEAD **2 :** GOLDENEYE
spirit duplicating *n* [*duplicating* fr. gerund of *³duplicate*] **:** a duplicating-printing process utilizing master sheets that release color through type indentations when a colorless chemical fluid is applied
spir·it·ed \ˈspirəd·əd, -rətəd\ *adj* [*¹spirit* + *-ed*] **1** *obs* **:** impregnated with elements that activate or make more lively **2 :** full of life or vigor **:** characterized by or displaying animation **:** full of spirit or fire **:** showing energy or enterprise **:** having or suggesting vigor ⟨the ~ yet tractable bride —Henry Cavendish⟩ ⟨~ drawings of hunters and racehorses —Harrison Smith⟩ ⟨a ~ debate⟩ ⟨a ~ answer⟩ — often used in combination; see also HIGH-SPIRITED, MEANSPIRITED, PUBLIC-SPIRITED
spir·it·ed·ly *adv* **:** in a spirited manner **:** with animation, liveliness, or vivacity ⟨writes directly and ~ —G.R.Crone⟩
spiritedness *n* -ES **:** the quality or state of being spirited **:** ANIMATION, LIVELINESS, VIVACITY ⟨her natural ~ detested the monotony —George Meredith⟩ — often used in combination ⟨mean-*spiritedness*⟩ ⟨public-*spiritedness*⟩
spir·it·ful \ˈspirətfəl\ *adj* **1** *archaic* **:** full of spirit or vigor **:** ANIMATED, SPIRITED, VIGOROUS ⟨a charming creature . . . but confoundedly smart and ~ —Samuel Richardson⟩ **2** *obs* **:** SPIRITUOUS 3
spirit ground *n* **:** an aquatint ground made by dissolving resin in spirits of wine, evaporating the spirits, and leaving a dry grain on the plate
spirit gum *n* **:** a solution of a gum (as of gum arabic in ether) used esp. for attaching a wig or other false hair to exposed parts of the skin
spir·it·ism \ˈspirəd·,izəm, -rə,ti-\ *n* -s **1 a :** a theory that mediumistic phenomena are caused by spirits of the dead **b :** the action or agency of such spirits **2 :** a belief that natural objects possess indwelling spirits — compare ANIMISM 2 **3 :** SPIRITUALISM 2
spir·it·ist \-əd·əst, -ətə-\ *n* -s **:** one who believes in or attempts to put in practice spiritism; *specif* **:** SPIRITUALIST
spir·it·is·tic \¦spirəd·¦istik, -rə¦tis-\ *adj* **:** of, relating to, or believing in spirits or phenomena connected with spirits
spir·it·ize \ˈspirəd·,īz, -rə,tīz\ *vt* -ED/-ING/-S **:** to implant a spirit in **:** imbue with spirits
spirit lamp *n* **:** a lamp in which a volatile liquid fuel (as alcohol) is burned ⟨made some coffee over a *spirit lamp* —Joseph Conrad⟩

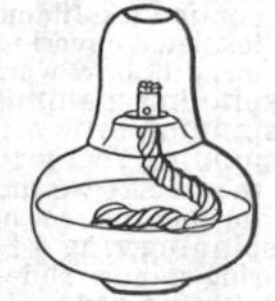
spirit lamp

spir·it·less \ˈspirətləs\ *adj* **1 :** destitute of spirit or vital principle **:** DEAD, LIFELESS ⟨the ~ body should be restored to the earth —Thomas Greenhill⟩ **2 :** wanting animation or cheerfulness **:** lacking lively or cheerful spirits **:** DEJECTED, DEPRESSED, DISPIRITED **3 :** destitute of vigor or energy **:** wanting life, courage, or fire **:** lacking ardor or boldness **syn** see LANGUID
spir·it·less·ly *adv* **:** in a spiritless manner
spir·it·less·ness *n* -ES **:** the quality or state of being spiritless
spirit level *n* **:** LEVEL 1a
spirit of ether : an anodyne mixture of approximately two parts alcohol and one part ether — called also *Hoffmann's drops;* compare COMPOUND SPIRIT OF ETHER
spirit off *vt* **:** to finish (as varnish or lacquer) with a coat of solvent
spirit of hartshorn *or* **spirits of hartshorn :** AMMONIA WATER
spirit of niter 1 : a liquid containing 68 or 70 percent by weight of absolute nitric acid with the remainder water **2 :** ETHYL NITRITE SPIRIT
spirit of nitrous ether : ETHYL NITRITE SPIRIT
spirit of salt *or* **spirits of salt** *archaic* **:** HYDROCHLORIC ACID
spirit of vitriol *archaic* **:** SULFURIC ACID
spir·i·to·so \,spirəˈtō(,)sō, -)zō\ *adj* [It, fr. *spirito* spirit (fr. L *spiritus*) + *-oso* -ose (fr. L *-osus*) — more at SPIRIT] **:** ANIMATED — used as a direction in music
spir·it·ous \ˈspirəd·əs\ *adj* [*¹spirit* + *-ous*] **1** *archaic* **:** resembling or of the nature of spirit **:** PURE, REFINED **2** *obs* **:** characterized by high spirits **:** ARDENT, ANIMATED **3 :** SPIRITUOUS 3
spirit rapping *n* **:** an alleged form of communication with the spirits of the dead by raps — compare SPIRITUALISM 2
spirits *pl of* SPIRIT, *pres 3d sing of* SPIRIT
spirits of turpentine *or* **spirit of turpentine :** TURPENTINE 2a
spirits of wine *or* **spirit of wine :** RECTIFIED SPIRIT, ALCOHOL 3
spirit-soluble \¦==¦===\ *adj* **:** soluble in alcohol or other organic solvent used similarly — often distinguished from *oil-soluble* and *water-soluble* ⟨*spirit-soluble* dyes⟩ ⟨the *spirit-soluble* natural resins⟩
¹spir·i·tu·al \ˈspirəch(ə)wəl, -chəl *sometimes* -rēch-\ *adj* [ME *spirituel, spiritual,* fr. MF & ML; MF *spirituel,* fr. ML *spiritualis,* alter. (influenced by L *spiritus* spirit) of LL *spiritalis,* fr. L, of breathing, of wind, fr. *spiritus* spirit, breath + *-alis* -al — more at SPIRIT] **1 :** of, relating to, or consisting of spirit **:** of the nature of spirit rather than material **:** INCORPOREAL — contrasted with *earthy* **2 a :** of or relating to religious or sacred matters ⟨~ leaders⟩ **b :** SACRED ⟨~ songs⟩ **c :** ecclesiastical rather than lay or temporal ⟨lords ~ and temporal⟩ ⟨eight members, four ~ and four lay⟩ **3 :** of or relating to the moral feelings or states of the soul as distinguished from the external actions **:** reaching and affecting the spirit **4 a :** influenced or controlled by the divine Spirit **:** having a nature in which a concern for the Spirit of God predominates ⟨~ man⟩ **b :** proceeding from or under the influence of the Holy Spirit **:** concerned with religious values **:** seeking earnestly to live in a right relation to God ⟨a ~ Christian⟩ **c :** HOLY, DIVINE ⟨to become ~ and perfected⟩ **d :** RELIGIOUS ⟨Islam's ~ foundations⟩ **5 :** related or joined in spirit **:** spiritually akin **:** having a relationship one to another based on matters of the spirit ⟨her ~ home⟩ ⟨regarded her pastor as her ~ father⟩ ⟨came to believe himself the ~ heir of the French poet —Allen Tate⟩ **6** *archaic* **:** consisting of spirit **:** ALCOHOLIC, SPIRITUOUS **7 :** of, relating to, or coming from the intellectual and higher endowments of the mind **:** INTELLECTUAL, MENTAL — contrasted with *animal* **8 :** highly refined in thought or feeling **9 :** SPIRITED, CLEVER, WITTY **10 :** having to do with spirits, ghosts, or similar supernatural beings or with the world which they are held to people **11 :** SPIRITUALISTIC
²spiritual \"\ *n* -s **1 spirituals** *pl* **:** things (as functions, offices, affairs, matters, or possessions) of a spiritual, ecclesiastical, or religious nature ⟨assigns supremacy to the pope in ~s and to the emperor in temporals —J.R.Lowell⟩ **2 :** a Negro religious song esp. of the southern U. S. distinguished by the graphic narrative method characteristic of the folk ballad and by strongly marked rhythm that is frequently emphasized in singing by swaying or other motions
spiritual bouquet *n* **:** an offering by a Roman Catholic of a number of promised or performed devotional acts undertaken on behalf of a person on special occasions (as name days or anniversaries) or of someone recently deceased esp. as an expression of sympathy
spiritual court *n* [ME *spirituall court,* fr. *spirituel, spiritual, spirituall* spiritual + *court*] **:** ECCLESIASTICAL COURT
spiritual director *n* **:** a confessor in the Roman Catholic Church whose advice and direction are regularly and frequently sought by one seeking spiritual advancement
spir·i·tu·al·ism \-ə,lizəm\ *n* -s [prob. fr. (assumed) NL *spiritualismus,* fr. ML *spiritualis* spiritual + L *-ismus* -ism] **1 :** a doctrine that all that exists is spirit **:** IDEALISM; *esp* **:** metaphysical idealism — compare MATERIALISM **2 a :** a belief that departed spirits hold intercourse with mortals usu. through a medium by means of rapping and other physical phenomena or during abnormal mental states (as trances) **b :** the doctrines and practices of spiritualists **3 :** the quality or state of being spiritual **:** spiritual nature or essence **:** SPIRITUALITY
spir·i·tu·al·ist \-ələst\ *n* -s [prob. fr. (assumed) NL *spiritualista,* fr. ML *spiritualis* spiritual + L *-ista* -ist] **1 :** one whose chief interest is in spiritual things and who tends to interpret things in a spiritual sense **:** a spiritually minded person **:** one whose ideas have a spiritual basis **2 :** one who maintains the doctrine of philosophical spiritualism **3 a :** one who believes in spiritualism **:** one who seeks intercourse with departed spirits **b** *usu cap* **:** a member of a religious organization practicing or believing in spiritualism
spir·i·tu·al·is·tic \¦spirəch(ə)wə¦listik, -chə¦l-, -tēk *sometimes* -rēch-\ *or* **spir·i·tu·al·ist** \ˈ====ləst, ˈ===¦ləst\ *adj* **:** of, relating to, or connected with spiritualism — **spir·i·tu·al·is·ti·cal·ly** \-¦listək(ə)lē, -tēk-, -)li\ *adv*
spir·i·tu·al·i·ty \,spirəch(ə)ˈwaləd·ē, -lətē, -i *sometimes* -rēch-\ *n* -ES [ME *spiritualite,* fr. MF or ML; MF *spiritualité, espiritualité,* fr. ML *spiritualitat-, spiritualitas,* fr. *spiritualis* spiritual + L *-tat-, -tas* -ty] **1 :** something that in ecclesiastical law belongs to the church or to a person as an ecclesiastic or to

religion: as **a spiritualities** *pl* **:** spiritual or ecclesiastical things **:** ecclesiastical possessions or rights of a purely spiritual character **:** fees, dues, or tithes receivable by an ecclesiastic as such **b :** something having a spiritual character; *esp* **:** ecclesiastical property or revenue held or received in return for spiritual services — compare TEMPORALITY **2 :** the whole body of clergy (as in a nation or country) **:** the body of spiritual or ecclesiastical persons **:** CHURCH, CLERGY ⟨subsidies . . . granted to the king by the ~ —Thomas Fuller⟩ — distinguished from *temporalty* **3 :** sensitivity or attachment to religious values and things of the spirit rather than material or worldly interests ⟨a man of deep ~ —R.L.Patterson⟩ **4** *archaic* **:** something incorporeal; *specif* **:** SPIRIT **5** *obs* **:** the quality or state of being spirituous **:** VOLATILITY **6 a :** the quality or state of being spiritual **b :** something having a spiritual as distinguished from a worldly or material character **c :** existence purely in a spiritual state **:** the quality or state of being incorporeal

spir·i·tu·al·iza·tion \ˌspirəch(ə)wələ'zāshən, -chələ-, -ˌlīˈz-*sometimes* -rēch-\ *n* -s [prob. fr. (assumed) NL *spiritualization-, spiritualizatio*, fr. (assumed) NL *spiritualizatus* (past part. of *spiritualizare*) + L -ion-, -io -ion] **:** the action of spiritualizing or the state of being spiritualized

spir·i·tu·al·ize \'⸗⸗⸗⸗ˌlīz, '⸗⸗⸗ˌlīz\ *vt* -ED/-ING/-S [prob. fr. (assumed) NL *spiritualizare*, fr. ML *spiritualis* spiritual + LL *-izare* -ize] **1 :** to make spiritual **:** refine intellectually or morally **:** purify from the corrupting influences of the world **:** give a spiritual character or tendency to **2** *obs* **:** to convert into or impregnate with spirit **:** make volatile or spirituous **3 :** to give a spiritual meaning to **:** take in a spiritual sense — opposed to *literalize* **4 :** to endow with the nature and attributes of a spirit

spir·i·tu·al·iz·er \-zə(r)\ *n* -s **:** one that spiritualizes

spiritual living *n, Brit* **:** BENEFICE

spir·i·tu·al·ly \'spirəch(ə)lē, -ch(ə)wəlē, -li *sometimes* -rēch-\ *adv* [ME *spirituelly, spiritually*, fr. *spirituel, spiritual* spiritual + *-ly*] **1 :** in a spiritual way **:** in connection with things of the spirit — distinguished from *materially* **2 :** in an ethereal or supernatural manner **:** SUPERNATURALLY — distinguished from *naturally*

spiritually-mind·ed \¦⸗⸗(⸗)⸗⸗¦⸗⸗\ *adj* **:** having the mind set on spiritual things **:** filled with holy desires and purposes **:** SPIRITUAL

spiritual-minded·ness *n* -ES **:** the quality or state of being spiritually-minded

spir·i·tu·al·ness *n* -ES **:** the quality or state of being spiritual **:** SPIRITUALITY

spir·i·tu·al·ty *pronunc at* ¹SPIRITUAL + tē\ *n* -ES [ME *spiritualte*, fr. MF *spiritualté*, fr. ML *spiritualitat-, spiritualitas* — more at SPIRITUALITY] **1 spiritualties** *pl* **:** SPIRITUALITY 1a ⟨a complete list of the . . . temporalties and *spiritualties* belonging to a parish church —*English Historical Rev.*⟩ **2 :** SPIRITUALITY 2 ⟨may regard the ~ of England . . . as a body completely organized —William Stubbs⟩

spir·i·tu·el *or* **spir·i·tu·elle** \¦spirə¦chə¦wel, -rē|, |tə¦wel, |·¦twel\ *adj* [*spirituel* fr. F, lit., spiritual; *spirituelle* fr. F, fem. of *spirituel* — more at SPIRITUAL] **:** having or characterized by a highly refined and esp. sprightly, bright, or witty nature ⟨writes with a tenderness which is ~ rather than spiritual —Malcolm Muggeridge⟩ ⟨a personality as *spirituelle* and knowing as any practicing sophisticate's —Jean Stafford⟩

spir·i·tu·os·i·ty \ˌspirəch(ə)'wäsəd·ē\ *n* -ES [fr. *spirituous*, after such pairs as E *generous: generosity*] **:** the quality or state of being spirituous ⟨~ of wines and liquors⟩

spir·i·tu·ous \'spirəch(ə)wəs, -chəs, ÷ -rəd·əs, ÷ -rətəs *sometimes* -rēch-\ *adj* [prob. modif. (influenced by E ¹*spirit* and *-ous*) of Sp *espirituoso*, fr. *espiritu* spirit (fr. L *spiritus*) + *-oso* -ose (fr. L *-osus*) — more at SPIRIT] **1** *archaic* **:** spirited in character or behavior **:** ANIMATED ⟨her once gay and ~ behavior —Eliza Haywood⟩ **2** *archaic* **:** SPIRITUAL **3 :** containing or of the nature of spirit **:** impregnated with alcohol obtained by distillation **:** ALCOHOLIC, ARDENT ⟨~ liquors⟩ ⟨~ beverages⟩

spir·i·tu·ous·ness *n* -ES *obs* **:** SPIRITUOSITY

spir·i·tus \'spirəd·əs, *in ecclesiastical use often* -pirē,tüs *or* -pērē,tüs\ *n* [NL, fr. L, spirit, breath] **1 :** SPIRIT 21 **2** [LL, fr. L, spirit, breath] **:** BREATHING 2

spiritus as·per \-'aspə(r)\ *n* [LL] **:** ROUGH BREATHING

spiritus fru·men·ti \-frü'mentē, -n·,tī\ *n* [NL, lit., spirit of grain] **:** WHISKEY

spiritus le·nis \-'lānəs, -'len-,-'lēn-\ *n* [LL] **:** SMOOTH BREATHING

spirit varnish *n* **:** an artificial varnish composed of a solution of natural or artificial resin, asphalt, or a cellulose ester (as pyroxylin) in a volatile solvent (as alcohol, spirits of turpentine, or amyl acetate) ⟨a common *spirit varnish* is a solution of shellac in alcohol⟩

spirit vinegar *n* **:** VINEGAR 1

spirit wrestler *n, usu cap S&W* [trans. of Russ *dukhoborets* Doukhobor] **:** DOUKHOBOR

spirit writing *n* **:** automatic writing held to be produced under the influence of spirits — compare PNEUMATOGRAPHY

spir·ity \'spirəd·ē\ *adj, dial* **:** SPIRITED, LIVELY

spirit yellow *n, usu cap S&Y* **:** either of two solvent dyes — see DYE table I (under *Solvent Yellow 1* and *3*)

spi·ri·valve \'spīrə+,-\ *adj* [ISV *spir-* + *valve*, n.; prob. orig. formed in F] **:** having a spiral shell — used esp. of a gastropod mollusk

spir·ket·ing \'spərkəd·iŋ\ *n* -s [obs. E *spirket, spurket* space between floor timbers of a ship forward or aft + E *-ing*] **:** planking consisting of timbers that are heavier than the ceiling and are worked above the waterways in a wooden ship — see SHIP illustration

spirketing plate *n* **:** the spirketing in a steel ship

spir·ling \'spərlən\ *n* [ME *spyrlyng*, fr. MD *spierlinc* — more at SPARLING] *chiefly Scot* **:** SPARLING

spi·ro \'spī(ˌ)rō\ *adj* [*spir-*] **:** of or relating to a compound or system that contains two rings having a single atom in common — compare SPIR- 2

¹spiro- *comb form* [ISV *spir-* (fr. L *spirare* to breathe) + *-o-* — more at SPIRIT] **:** respiration ⟨*spirometer*⟩

²spiro- — see SPIR-

spiro atom *n* **:** an atom (as a carbon atom) that is common to two rings in the molecule of a compound

spi·ro·cer·ca \ˌspīrō'sərkə\ *n, cap* [NL, fr. *spir-* + *-cerca* (fr. Gk *kerkos* tail)] **:** a genus of red filarial worms (family Thelaziidae) forming nodules in the walls of the digestive tract and sometimes the aorta of dogs and other canines esp. in warm regions

spi·ro·chae·ta \ˌspīrə'kēd·ə\ *n* [NL, fr. *spir-* + *-chaeta*] **1** *cap* **:** a genus (the type of the family Spirochaetaceae) of spirochetes distinguished by a flexible undulating body with the protoplasm wound spirally around an elastic axis filament and comprising as now restricted various chiefly aquatic forms or formerly these together with important pathogens now placed in the genera *Treponema, Borrelia*, and *Leptospira* **2** *or* **spi·ro·che·ta** \"\ *pl* **spirochae·tae** *or* **spiroche·tae** \-ēd·(ˌ)ē\ **:** any member of the genus *Spirochaeta* **:** SPIROCHETE

spi·ro·chae·ta·ce·ae \ˌspīrə¦kē'tāsē,ē\ *n pl, cap* [NL, fr. *Spirochaeta*, type genus + *-aceae*] **:** a family comprising large coarsely spiral bacteria (order Spirochaetales) that are free-living in fresh or salt water or commensal in the body of oysters — compare TREPONEMATACEAE

spi·ro·chae·ta·les \-ā(ˌ)lēz\ *n pl, cap* [NL, fr. *Spirochaeta* + *-ales*] **:** an order of higher bacteria comprising slender elongated flexuous spiral forms in which the body makes up at least one complete turn of the spiral — compare SPIROCHAETACEAE, TREPONEMATACEAE

spi·ro·chet·al *or* **spi·ro·chaet·al** \¦⸗⸗¦kēd·ᵊl\ *adj* **:** caused by spirochetes ⟨~ jaundice⟩

spi·ro·chete *or* **spi·ro·chaete** \'spīrə,kēt, *usu* -ēd·+V\ *n* -s [NL *Spirochaeta*] **:** a bacterium of the order Spirochaetales many of which cause severe diseases (as syphilis and relapsing fever)

spi·ro·chet·emia \ˌspīrə,kēd·'ēmēə\ *n* -s [NL, fr. *Spirochaeta* + *-emia*] **:** the abnormal presence of spirochetes in the circulating blood

spi·ro·che·tic *or* **spi·ro·chae·tic** \¦⸗⸗¦kēd·ik\ *adj* **:** of, relating to, or caused by spirochetes

spi·ro·che·ti·ci·dal \¦⸗⸗ˌkēd·ə¦sīd·ᵊl\ *adj* [*spirochete* + *-i-* + *-cidal*] **:** destructive to spirochetes esp. within the body of an animal host ⟨a ~ drug⟩

spi·ro·che·ti·cide *or* **spi·ro·chae·ti·cide** \⸗⸗'⸗⸗,sīd\ *n* -s [*spirochete* + *-i-* + *-cide*] **:** an agent (as a drug) capable of killing spirochetes esp. within the human or animal body

spi·ro·chet·osis *or* **spi·ro·chaet·osis** \⸗⸗ˌkēd·'ōsəs\ *n* -ES [NL, fr. *Spirochaeta* + *-osis*] **:** infection with or a disease (as leptospirosis) caused by spirochetes

spi·ro·cyclic \¦spīrō +\ *adj* [*spir-* + *cyclic*] **:** having flower parts in a spiral arrangement that changes phyletically to a cyclic arrangement

spi·ro·de·la \ˌspīrə'dēlə\ *n, cap* [NL, fr. *spir-* + *-dela* (fr. Gk *dēlos* visible, evident); fr. the fact that the spiral vessels are visible through the transparent tissues — more at ADEL-] **:** a genus of aquatic plants (family Lemnaceae) having a membranous spathe and a thallus with a cluster of several rootlets — see GREAT DUCKWEED

spi·ro·gram \'spīrə,gram\ *n* [¹*spiro-* + *-gram*] **:** a graphic record of respiratory movements traced on a moving drum

spi·ro·graph \-raf,-räf\ *n* [ISV ¹*spiro-* + *-graph*] **:** an instrument for recording respiratory movements commonly consisting of a spirometer together with a suitable recording device — **spi·ro·graph·ic** \¦spīrə¦grafik\ *adj*

spi·rog·ra·phis \spī'rägrəfəs\ *n, cap* [NL, fr. *spir-* + LGk *graphis* embroidery, fr. Gk, stylus, fr. *graphein* to write — more at CARVE] **:** a genus of sabelloid annelids with bright-colored gill plumes arranged spirally

spi·ro·gy·ra \ˌspīrə'jīrə\ *n* [NL, fr. *spir-* + *-gyra* (fr. Gk *gyros* ring); akin to Gk *gyros* round — more at COWER] **1** *cap* **:** a genus of freshwater green algae (family Zygnemataceae) having spiral chlorophyll bands and forming slimy masses in still waters and slow streams **2** -s **:** any plant of the genus *Spirogyra*

spi·roid \'spī,rȯid *also* **spi·roi·dal** \(')spī¦rȯid·ᵊl\ *adj* [*spiroid* fr. NL *spiroïdes*, fr. Gk *speiroeidēs*, fr. *speira* coil, twist + *-oeidēs* -oid; *spiroidal* ISV *spiroid* + *-al* — more at SPIRE] **:** resembling a screw **:** spiral in form

spi·ro·loc·u·line \¦spī(ˌ)rō¦lakyə,līn, -ˌlən\ *adj* [*spir-* + *loculus* + *-ine*] **:** having chambers arranged spirally — used of a foraminiferan shell

spi·rom·e·ter \spī'rämәd·ə(r)\ *n* [ISV ¹*spiro-* + *-meter*] **1 :** an instrument for measuring the air entering and leaving the lungs (as in determining the vital capacity of the lungs) **2 :** an instrument used in calibrating gas meters to measure and record the volume of gas

spi·ro·met·ric \¦spīrə¦me·trik\ *adj* [ISV ¹*spiro-* + *-metric*] **:** of, relating to, or using a spirometer ⟨~ studies⟩ **:** of or relating to spirometry

spi·rom·e·try \spī'rämə·trē\ *n* -ES [ISV ¹*spiro-* + *-metry*] **:** measurement of air or gas by use of a spirometer

spi·ro·pentane \¦spī(ˌ)rō+\ *n* [ISV *spir-* + *pentane*] **:** an unstable liquid hydrocarbon C_5H_8 made synthetically — compare STRUCTURAL FORMULA

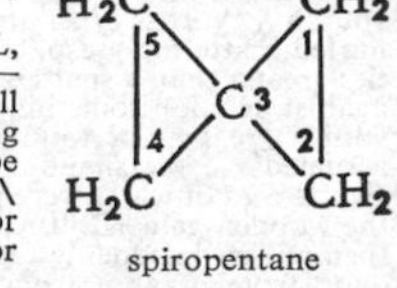

spiropentane

spir·orbis \spī'rȯrbəs\ *n, cap* [NL, fr. *spir-* + L *orbis* circle, disk — more at ORB] **:** a genus of small annelids (family Serpulidae) forming a spirally coiled calcareous tube

¹spi·ros·to·mid \(')spī¦rästəməd\ *adj* [NL *Spirostomidae*] **:** of or relating to the genus *Spirostomum* or family Spirostomidae

²spirostomid \"\ *n* -s [NL *Spirostomidae* family of ciliates, fr. *Spirostomum*, type genus + *-idae*] **:** a spirostomid ciliate

spi·ros·to·mum \spī'rästəməm\ *n, cap* [NL, fr. *spir-* + *-stomum*] **:** a genus (the type of the family Spirostomidae) of large cylindrical elongated heterotrichous ciliates widely distributed in fresh and salt water

spi·ro·trich \'spīrə·,trik\ *n* -s [NL *Spirotricha*] **:** a spirotrichous protozoan

spi·rot·ri·cha \spī'rä·trəkə\ *n pl, cap* [NL, fr. *spir-* + *-tricha*] **:** a large order consisting of euciliate protozoans with well-developed peristome and adoral zone of membranelles and general body cilia that are uniform or variously reduced and fused into cirri and including the suborders Heterotricha, Oligotricha, and Hypotricha

spi·ro·trich·i·da \ˌspīrō·'trikədə\ [NL, fr. *spir-* + *trich-* + *-ida*] *syn of* SPIROTRICHA

spi·rot·ri·chous \(')spī¦rä·trəkəs\ *adj* [NL *Spirotricha* + E *-ous*] **:** of or relating to the Spirotricha

spirt *var of* SPURT

spirtle *vt* [freq. of *spirt*] *obs* **:** SPATTER, SPLASH

spir·u·la \'spir(y)ələ\ *n* [NL, fr. LL, twisted cracknel, fr. L *spira* coil, twist + *-ula* — more at SPIRE] **1** *cap* **:** a genus (coextensive with a family Spirulidae of the order Decapoda) of small cephalopods related to the extinct belemnites, having a many-chambered shell coiled freely in a flat spiral that is comparable to the phragmocone of the belemnite shell and almost enveloped in the soft parts, and occurring in most tropic seas usu. at great depths from which the shells float to the surface and are cast on beaches, although complete specimens of the animal are rare **2** -s **:** a cephalopod of the genus *Spirula*

spir·u·late \'spir(y)ə,lāt, 'spir-\ *adj* [prob. fr. (assumed) NL *spirulatus*, fr. (assumed) NL *spirula* small coil (fr. LL, twisted cracknel) + L *-atus* -ate] **:** spiral in form or arrangement

spi·ru·ra \spī'rùrə\ *n, cap* [NL, fr. *spir-* + *-ura*] **:** the type genus of Spiruridae including various parasites of rodents

¹spi·ru·rid \(')spī¦rùrəd\ *adj* [NL *Spiruridae, Spirurida*] **:** of or relating to the family Spiruridae or the order Spirurida

²spirurid \"\ *n* -s [NL *Spiruridae, Spirurida*] **:** a spirurid worm

spi·ru·ri·da \spī'rùrədə\ *n pl, cap* [NL, fr. *Spirura* + *-ida*] **:** an order of Aphasmidia comprising parasitic nematode worms with the esophagus cylindroid and not divided into three regions, six lips, no buccal stylet, and the musculature polymyarian and including the guinea worm, the filarial worms, and other parasites of vertebrates that all have complex life cycles requiring an invertebrate intermediate host

spi·ru·ri·dae \-ˌdē\ *n pl, cap* [NL, fr. *Spirura*, type genus + *-idae*] **:** a family of nematode worms having the adults parasitic in vertebrates and larval stages in insects and with related forms constituting a distinct superfamily of the order Spirurida — see ASCAROPS

¹spi·ru·roid \-ù,rȯid\ *adj* [NL *Spirura* + E *-oid*] **:** resembling or related to the Spiruridae

²spiruroid \"\ *n* -s **:** a spiruroid worm

¹spiry \'spī(ə)rē, -ri\ *adj* [¹*spire* + *-y*] **1 :** resembling a spire **:** tall, slender, and tapering to a point **:** rising in a slender, tapering form ⟨~ grass⟩ ⟨~ trees⟩ ⟨~ turrets⟩ **2 :** abounding in spires ⟨~ towns⟩

²spiry \"\ *adj* [³*spire* + *-y*] *archaic* **:** of a spiral form **:** curving or coiling in spirals **:** CURLED, SERPENTINE, WREATHED ⟨hid in the ~ volumes of the snake —John Dryden⟩

spis·si·tude \'spisə,tüd, -ə·,tyüd\ *n* -s [ME, fr. L *spissitudo*, fr. *spissi-* (fr. *spissus*) + *-tudo* -tude] *archaic* **:** the quality or state of being thick, dense, or compact **:** DENSITY, VISCOSITY

spis·u·la \'spisələ, -izə-\ *n, cap* [NL, perh. irreg. fr. J. B. von *Spix* †1826 Ger. zoologist] **:** a genus of surf clams that includes a large yellowish white thick-shelled clam (*S. solidissima*) that is the common edible surf clam of the eastern coast of No. America

¹spit \'spi|t, *usu* |d·+V\ *n* -s [ME *spite*, fr. OE *spitu*; akin to MD *spit, spet* spit, OHG *spiz* spit, *spizzi* pointed, Icel *spīta* peg, L *spina* thorn — more at SPINE] **1 a :** a usu. metal stationary or revolving slender pointed rod for holding meat and other foods while cooking before or over a fire **b** *archaic* **:** SWORD **c** *dial Brit* **:** a skewer on which fish (as herring) are hung to dry **d :** SPINDLE 1d **e :** a steel rod on which drawn wire is wound as it leaves drawplates **2 a :** a small point of land commonly consisting of sand or gravel deposited by waves and currents and running into a body of water — compare BAR 2d **b :** a long narrow shoal extending from the shore

²spit \"\ *vt* **spitted; spitted; spitting; spits** [ME *spiten*, fr. *spite*, n.] **1 :** to thrust a spit through **:** fix upon a spit ⟨over the floor were spread the glowing embers of a fire; and across it . . . were *spitted* four whole sheep —Oscar Handlin⟩ **2 :** to fix as if with a spit **:** IMPALE ⟨*spitted* him on a bayonet —Mack Morriss⟩

³spit \", *dial* 'spe|\ *vb* **spit** \"\ *or* **spat** \-pa|\ **spit** *or* **spat** *also dial* **spitted** \-pid·əd, -itəd\ *or* **spit·ten** \-pitᵊn\ **spitting; spits** [ME *spitten*, fr. OE (northern dial.) *spittan*, of imit. origin] *vt* **1 a :** to eject from the mouth (as saliva) **:** EXPECTORATE ⟨got a cigar, bit off the end and ~ it out —Wallace Stegner⟩ **b** (1) **:** to express (scorn, hatred, or malicious feelings) by or as if by spitting ⟨the old man simply *spat* his contempt and stumped away —Roderick Finkayson⟩ (2) **:** to utter with a spitting sound or scornful expression **:** utter in a scornful, malicious, venomous, rapid, or authoritative manner ⟨his father's face, *spitting* the one furious word —John Fountain⟩ ⟨*spat* out the words with unmistakable passion —Helen Howe⟩ **c :** to emit or eject as if by spitting **:** throw forth or out ⟨guns . . . capable of *spitting* heavy flak at guided missiles —*Science*⟩ ⟨a machine . . . cuts the hay as it goes along, places it, ties it with wire, then ~*s* it out the other side —Ralph Gustafson⟩; *specif* **:** to emit (precipitation) in driving particles or short scattered flurries ⟨the sky *spat* rain tentatively —*Springfield (Mass.) Republican*⟩ **2 :** to set fire to **:** start burning ⟨~ a fuse⟩ **~** *vi* **1 a** (1) **:** to eject saliva as a gross insult or as a means of showing aversion or contempt — usu. used with such prepositions as *at, on*, or *upon* ⟨*spat* in their own black, ugly eyes —T.B.Costain⟩ ⟨*spat* contemptuously at the stove —R.H.Newman⟩ (2) **:** to possess or exhibit contempt — usu. used with the phrase *in the eye of* ⟨~*s* in the eye of commercialism with these words —*Ebony*⟩ **b :** to eject saliva **:** EXPECTORATE ⟨~ in the water and watched it bob away —R.O.Bowen⟩ ⟨*spat* into the swept-up heap of rubbish —Herbert Gold⟩ **2 :** to rain or snow slightly or with scattered drops or flakes **:** fall in flurries ⟨the rain ~*s* icily down —Kenneth Tynan⟩ **3 a :** to make a noise like that of expectoration **:** make a sudden short crackling or popping sound **:** SPUTTER ⟨the eggs ~ in the pan —A.R.Foff⟩ ⟨the motor coughed and ~ —R.S.Hillyer⟩ **b :** to emit something or become emitted with a spitting sound ⟨the bullets ~ into the sand below —H.H.Arnold & I.C.Eaker⟩ — **spit cotton 1 :** to spit white cottony saliva esp. from thirst ⟨hadn't had a drink all morning and were *spitting cotton*, they were that thirsty —F.B.Gipson⟩ **2 :** to be angry ⟨better look out; the sheriff's *spitting cotton* —R.B.House⟩ — **spit it out :** to say what is in the mind without further delay — **spit sixpences** *Brit* **:** to spit cotton

⁴spit \"\ *n* -s [ME, fr. *spitten*, v. — more at ³SPIT] **1 a** (1) **:** the secretion normally occurring in the mouth **:** SPITTLE, SALIVA, SPUTUM (2) **:** the act or an instance of spitting **b** (1) **:** a frothing secretion resembling saliva exuded by spittlebugs (2) **:** SPITTLEBUG **2 :** a short distance ⟨followed him into the woods about one good ~ from the door —William Faulkner⟩ **3** [so called fr. a former popular saying that a child with a great resemblance to its father looks as much like him as if it had been spit out of his mouth] **:** perfect likeness **:** COUNTERPART, IMAGE — usu. used in the phrase *spit and image* ⟨the *spit* and image of his father⟩ **4 :** a falling of rain or snow in scattered particles **:** a sprinkle of rain or flurry of snow

⁵spit \'spit\ *n* -s [D, fr. MD; akin to MD *spitten* to dig, spade and prob. to OE *spitu* spit — more at ¹SPIT] **1** *chiefly Brit* **:** the depth of the blade of a spade **2** *chiefly Brit* **a :** a layer of earth as deep as the blade of a spade **b :** a spadeful of earth

spit·al *or* **spit·tle** \'spid·ᵊl, -itᵊl\ *n* -s [*spital* alter. (influenced by *hospital*) of *spittle*, fr. ME *spitel*, modif. of ML *hospitale*, fr. LL, hospice — more at HOSPITAL] **:** LAZARETTO, HOSPITAL; *esp* **:** a charitable institution of a lower class than a hospital for the needy, aged, or infirm

spit and polish *n* [so called fr. the practice of polishing objects such as shoes by spitting on them and then rubbing them with a cloth] **1 :** the action of or materials for a thorough cleaning, polishing, and refurbishing ⟨presented himself for a *spit and polish* —Jessie Wall⟩ ⟨habituated to courtly rhetoric, which is emotion after *spit and polish* have been applied to it —Francis Hackett⟩ **2 :** extreme attention to cleanliness, orderliness, smartness of appearance, and ceremonial esp. at the expense of operational efficiency ⟨reviews, parades, athletics, *spit and polish*, long-standing traditions, and automatic discipline are played up —R.A.Preston⟩

spit-and-polish \¦⸗⸗¦⸗⸗\ *adj* **:** marked by spit and polish ⟨embassies abroad could not do without their *spit-and-polish* doormen —*N.Y.Times*⟩ ⟨a full-time professional soldier, of the old *spit-and-polish* school —Evelyn Eaton⟩

spitball \'⸗,⸗\ *n* **1 :** paper chewed and rolled into a ball to be thrown as a missile **2 :** a baseball pitch delivered after the ball has been moistened with saliva or sweat ⟨sounded the doom of the ~ and other . . . freak pitching deliveries —*Springfield (Mass.) Republican*⟩ — called also *spitter*

spit·ball·er \'⸗,⸗ə(r)\ *n* -s **:** one that throws spitballs

spitbox \'⸗,⸗\ *n* **:** SPITTOON

spit bug *n* **:** SPITTLEBUG

¹spitch·cock \'spich,käk\ *n* [origin unknown] **:** an eel split and grilled

²spitchcock \"\ *vt* **:** to prepare as a spitchcock or in the manner of a spitchcock ⟨~ an eel⟩

spit curl *n* [prob. so called fr. its being sometimes plastered down with saliva] **:** a spiral curl that is usu. plastered on the forehead, temple, or cheek

¹spite \'spīt, *usu* -īd·+V\ *n* -s [ME, short for ¹*despite*] **1 a** *obs* **:** an injury, hurt, or disgrace incurred or inflicted ⟨it is a great ~ to be praised in the wrong place —Ben Jonson⟩ **b** *obs* **:** something that vexes **:** a petty annoyance **2 a :** often petty ill will or hatred toward another accompanied with the disposition to irritate, annoy, or thwart **:** envious or rancorous malice ⟨a little insignificant: not really hate at all, but ~ —C.D.Lewis⟩ **b :** an instance of spite **:** an individual malicious feeling **:** GRUDGE ⟨a normal child has no ~ against work until you have drilled one into him —C.E.Montague⟩ **syn** see MALICE — **in spite of** *prep* **:** in defiance or contempt of ⟨charged *in spite of* superior enemy forces⟩ **:** despite adverse effects of **:** in opposition to all efforts of ⟨*in spite of* careful preparation⟩

²spite \"\ *vt* -ED/-ING/-S [ME *spiten*, fr. *spite*, n.] **1** *obs* **:** to regard with spite **:** DISLIKE, HATE **2 :** to treat maliciously (as by shaming or thwarting) ⟨children are still ready to ~ the older generation —E.H.Erikson⟩ **3 a :** to fill with spite **b :** ANNOY, OFFEND

spite fence *n* **:** an unsightly fence or wall that serves no useful purpose, is so constructed as to be an injury to adjoining property, and is erected and maintained maliciously for the purpose of injuring a neighbor (as by obstructing unreasonably his air, light, or view)

spite·ful \'spītfəl\ *adj, sometimes* **spitefuller**; *sometimes* **spitefullest** [ME, fr. ¹*spite* + *-ful*] **:** filled with or showing spite **:** having or exhibiting a desire to vex, annoy, or injure **:** MALIGNANT, MALICIOUS ⟨growing to hate the very sight of one another, becoming bitter, ~, jealous —W.H.Wright⟩ ⟨because the present law is ~ —A.E.Stevenson †1965⟩ — **spite·ful·ly** \-fəlē, -li\ *adv* — **spite·ful·ness** *n* -ES

spite·less \'spītləs\ *adj* **:** lacking spite **:** not motivated by spite

spite marriage *n* **:** a marriage entered into by one person to vex a third person with whom he is in love

spite of *prep* **:** in spite of ⟨exert your freedom, *spite of* the world —C.W.Hendel⟩

spite-work \'⸗,⸗\ *n* **:** trouble or injury inflicted as revenge for a real or fancied grievance

spitfire \'⸗,⸗\ *n* [³*spit* + *fire*, n.] **1 :** one that emits fire (as a volcano or a cannon) **2 :** a quick-tempered, fiery, or violently emotional person

spit in the ocean : poker in which each player is dealt a hand of cards facedown and combines them with cards faceup on the table to make a poker hand; *specif* **:** a game in which each player is dealt four cards, a fifth card is faced on the take, and the faced card and all others of the same rank are wild

spit·ish \'spīd·ish\ *adj* **:** SPITEFUL

spit·kit *also* **spit·kid** \'spit,kit, -kid\ *n* **1 :** ASHTRAY **2 :** a small ship (as a patrol boat)

spits *pl of* SPIT, *pres 3d sing of* SPIT

¹spit shine *n* **:** a very high gloss on a boot or shoe esp. when partially obtained by the application of saliva

²spit shine *vt* **:** to apply a spit shine to (a boot or shoe)

spit·stick \'spit,stik\ *or* **spit·stick·er** \-kə(r)\ *n* [*spitstick* alter. (influenced by *stick*) of *spitsticker*, fr. D *spitssteker*, fr *spits* pointed (fr. MD, fr. MHG *spiz, spitze*, fr. OHG *spizzi*) + *steker* graver, one that pricks or thrusts, fr. MD, jouster, fr. *steken* to sting, prick, thrust + *-er*; akin to OHG *stehhan* to sting, prick — more at SPIT, STICK] **1 :** a graver that is used esp. to outline designs **2 :** a small pointed chisel (as for making very small sloping cuts between the stones of a setting)

spitted *past of* ²SPIT *or dial past part of* ³SPIT

spitten *dial past part of* SPIT

¹**spit·ter** \ˈspid·ə(r), -itə-\ *n* -S [ME *spittere*, fr. *spitten* to spit + *-ere* -er] **1 :** one that ejects saliva from the mouth **2 :** a short length of fuse nicked to the powder core at about two-inch intervals so that when the fuse is ignited the nicks successively spit fire and are used to light the fuses of a round of loaded holes **3 :** SPITTING SNAKE

²**spitter** \"\ *n* -S [¹*spit* + *-er*] **:** a young deer whose antlers are beginning to shoot or become sharp **:** BROCKET, PRICKET

³**spitter** \"\ *n* -S [E dial. *spit* to spade (fr. ME *spitten* to dig, spade, fr. OE *spittan*) + E *-er*] *dial Brit* **:** SPADE

⁴**spitter** \"\ *n* -S [⁴*spit* + *-er*] **:** SPITBALL

spitting *n* -S [ME, fr. gerund of *spitten* to spit] **:** SPIT

spitting cobra *n* [*spitting* fr. pres. part. of ³*spit*] **:** a venomous elapid snake of the genus *Naja* that ejects its venom toward the victim without striking: as **a :** BLACK-NECKED COBRA **b :** RINGHALS

spit·ting image \ˈspitᵊn- *sometimes* -id·|iŋ- *or* -it| *or* |ēŋ-\ *n* [alter. (influenced by *spitting*, pres. part. of ³*spit*) of the phrase *spit and image*, fr. ⁴*spit*] **:** spit and image **:** SPIT 3

spitting snake *n* **:** a venomous snake (as a ringhals) that discharges its venom at an objective through the air without actually striking with the fangs

¹**spit·tle** \ˈspid·ᵊl, -itᵊl\ *n* -S [ME *spitel*, fr. OE *spitel*; akin to OE *spittan* to dig, spade, MD *spitten* to dig, spade, and prob. to OE *spitu* spit — more at SPIT] *dial Brit* **:** a spadelike implement **:** PEEL

²**spittle** \"\ *n* -S [alter. (influenced by ⁴*spit*) of ME *spetil*, fr. OE *spǣtl*, *spātl*; akin to OE *spittan* to spit — more at SPIT] **1 :** the fluid secreted by the salivary glands **:** SALIVA, SPIT **2 :** the frothy secretion of a spittle insect

³**spittle** *var of* SPITAL

spittlebug \ˈ==,=\ *n* **:** SPITTLE INSECT — usu. used in combination; see MEADOW SPITTLEBUG, PINE SPITTLEBUG, SARATOGA SPITTLEBUG

spittle insect *n* **:** any of numerous small leaping insects of the family Cercopidae with nymphs that live on plants and envelop themselves in a mass of white froth consisting of a fluid secreted from the anus in which bubbles of air are trapped

spit·toon \(ˈ)spi¦tün\ *n* -S [⁴*spit* + *-oon* (as in *balloon* or *doubloon*)] **:** a receptacle for spit; *esp* **:** a low cylindrical or round vessel (as of metal or earthenware) with a funnel-shaped top into which tobacco chewers spit periodically in the course of a chew — called also *cuspidor*

spittoon

spit up *vb* **:** REGURGITATE, VOMIT

spitz \ˈspits *sometimes* ˈshp-\ *n* -ES *sometimes cap* [G, fr. *spitz* pointed, fr. OHG *spizzi*; fr. the shape of the ears and muzzle — more at SPIT] **:** any of several dogs native to northern areas and distinguished by a broad strong stocky body with heavy double coat, a broad somewhat flat head with rather short muzzle and erect prick ears, and a heavily feathered tail tightly recurved over the back: as **a :** a dog regarded as ancestral to a modern breed exhibiting these qualities **b :** a dog of such a modern breed (as a chow chow, samoyed, or pomeranian) **c :** a medium-sized white dog descended from Pomeranian ancestors and often regarded as constituting a separate breed

spit·zer \-tsə(r)\ *n* -S [G, fr. *spitz* pointed (in *spitzgeschoss* pointed bullet) + *-er*] **:** a metal-jacketed pointed bullet

spitz·flö·te \ˈshpits,flād·ə, -lǣd·ə, G -lœtə\ *or* **spitz·flute** \ˈs(h)pits,flüt\ *n* -S [*spitzflöte* fr. G, fr. *spitz* pointed + *flöte* flute, fr. MHG *vloite*, fr. OF *flaute*, *fleute*; *spitzflute* part. trans. of G *spitzflöte* — more at FLUTE] **:** a labial pipe-organ stop with conical metal pipes of 8-foot, 4-foot, or 2-foot pitch and of flute quality

spiv \ˈspiv\ *n* -S [alter. of E dial. *spiff*, n., flashy dresser, fr. E dial. *spiff*, adj., smartly dressed, dandified] **1** *Brit* **:** one who gets his living by his wits without regular employment **:** PARASITE: as **a :** a hanger-on at a racetrack **b :** one engaged in petty black-marketeering and thievery **2** *Brit* **:** one who does not do his full share in an effort **:** SLACKER

spiv·ery *or* **spiv·very** \ˈspivəri\ *n* -ES *Brit* **:** the practice of a spiv **:** obtaining one's living without effort at the expense of others

spi·zel·la \spəˈzelə, spīˈz-\ *n, cap* [NL, fr. Gk *spiza* chaffinch + L *-ella* — more at FINCH] **:** a genus of small American finches including the chipping sparrow, the field sparrow, the tree sparrow, and related birds

spiz·zer·inc·tum \,spizəˈriŋ(k)təm\ *n* -S [E dial. (U.S.) *spizarinctum* cash, specie, prob. irreg. fr. E ¹*specie*] **:** the will to succeed **:** VIM, ENERGY, AMBITION

spk *abbr* speckled

spkl *abbr* sprinkle

spkr *abbr* **1** speaker **2** sprinkler

spl *abbr* special

SPL *abbr, often not cap* [L *sine prole legitima*] without legitimate issue

splach·na·ce·ae \splakˈnāsē,ē\ *n pl, cap* [NL, fr. *Splachnum*, type genus + *-aceae*] **:** a family of mosses (order Funariales) characterized by the swollen neck of the capsule and their growth upon dung or decaying animal tissues — **splach·na·ceous** \(ˈ)=¦nāshəs\ *adj*

splach·noid \ˈsplak,nȯid\ *adj* [NL *Splachnum* + E *-oid*] **:** resembling or related to a moss of the genus *Splachnum*

splach·num \-.nəm\ *n, cap* [NL, fr. Gk *splanchnon* tree moss] **:** a genus (the type of the family Splachnaceae) of rather rare mosses distinguished by a capsule that bears spores only in the upper portion and by its colored lower half being much swollen and composed of loose tissue containing chlorophyll

splack·nuck \ˈsplak,nək\ *n* -S [coined by Jonathan Swift †1745 Eng. satirist as the name of an imaginary animal of approximately human size mentioned in his satire *Gulliver's Travels* (1726)] **:** an odd or peculiar person or animal

splake \ˈsplāk\ *n, pl* **splake** *or* **splakes** [blend of *speckled* (*trout*) and *lake* (*trout*)] **:** a hatchery-produced supposedly fertile hybrid between the American lake trout and the brook trout

splanch·nic \ˈsplaŋknik\ *adj* [NL *splanchnicus*, fr. Gk *splanchnikos*, fr. *splanchnon* entrail + *-ikos* -ic] **1 :** of or relating to the viscera **:** VISCERAL **2 :** of, relating to, affecting, involving, or being the splanchnic nerves

splanch·ni·cec·to·my \,=nəˈsektəmē\ *n* -ES [*splanchnic* + *-ectomy*] **:** excision of a segment of one or more splanchnic nerves to relieve hypertension

splanchnic nerve *n* **:** any of three important nerves situated on each side of the body, formed by the union of branches from the six or seven lower ganglia of the sympathetic system, and being a superior ending in the coeliac ganglion, a middle ending in the solar plexus, and an inferior ending in the renal plexus and lower part of the solar plexus

splanch·ni·cot·o·my \,splaŋknəˈkäd·əmē\ *n* -ES [*splanchnic* + *-o-* + *-tomy*] **:** surgical division of one or more splanchnic nerves

splanchno- *comb form* [NL, fr. Gk, fr. *splanchnon* entrail; akin to Gk *splēn* spleen — more at SPLEEN] **:** viscera ⟨*splanchnomegaly*⟩ ⟨*splanchnoptosis*⟩

splanch·no·coele *or* **splanch·no·coel** \ˈsplaŋknə,sēl\ *n* -S [ISV *splanchno-* + *-coele*, *-coel*] **1 :** the embryonic body cavity when formed by splitting of the mesoderm into somatopleuric and splanchnopleuric layers **2 :** a visceral cavity esp. of a brachiopod

splanch·no·cranium \¦splaŋknə+\ *n* [NL, fr. *splanchno-* + *cranium*] **:** the portion of the skull that arises from the first three visceral arches and forms the supporting structure of the jaws — called also *viscerocranium*; compare NEUROCRANIUM

splanch·nol·o·gy \splaŋkˈnäləjē\ *n* -ES [NL *splanchnologia*, fr. *splanchno-* + *-logia* -logy] **:** a branch of anatomy concerned with the viscera

splanch·no·pleure \ˈsplaŋknə,plu̇(ə)r\ *n* -S [NL *splanchnopleura*, fr. *splanchno-* + *-pleura*] **:** a layer of tissue consisting of the inner of the two layers into which the lateral plate of the mesoderm splits in the embryo of a craniate vertebrate together with the endoderm internal to it and forming most of the walls and substance of the visceral organs — compare SOMATOPLEURE — **splanch·no·pleu·ric** \¦==¦plu̇rik\ *adj*

¹**splash** \ˈsplash, -aa(ə)sh, -aish\ *vb* -ED/-ING/-ES [alter. of ⁴*plash*] *vi* **1 a :** to strike and dash about a liquid or semiliquid substance **:** cause the spattering of a liquid or thinly viscous substance ⟨the children ~⟩ ⟨~*ed* about in the bath —Elizabeth Goudge⟩ **b :** to move through or into a liquid or semiliquid substance and cause splashing ⟨~*ed* across the rich black loam of . . . fields sodden with irrigation water —Rex Keating⟩ ⟨~*ed* overboard and swam ashore —Harriot B. Barbour⟩ **2 a** (1) **:** to become splashed or spattered about or upon **:** spray around or on in drops, columns, sheets, or masses of liquid or semiliquid matter ⟨saw a drop of water ~ down upon the violet script and spread —Willa Cather⟩ ⟨the water ~*ing* out of the tubs upon the stones —Pearl Buck⟩ ⟨the road ~*ed* muddily —Christopher Bloom⟩ (2) **:** to become spread or scattered in the manner of a splashed liquid ⟨the sunlight ~*ed* over her deck and gear —Thomas Wood †1950⟩ **b :** to fall, strike, or move with a splashing sound ⟨kept awake by the ~*ing* of water from the faucet⟩ ⟨a brook ~*ing* over rocks⟩ ~ *vt* **1 a** (1) **:** to dash a liquid or thinly viscous substance upon or against **:** scatter liquid upon in large quantities ⟨poured water into the basin and began to ~ her face —Rumer Godden⟩ — compare SPATTER (2) **:** to soil or stain by a splashed liquid ⟨don't ~ your dress —Margaret Kennedy⟩ **b :** to cause to appear splashed or spattered **:** mark or overlay with patches of a different usu. contrasting color or of a different texture ⟨innumerable peaks, black and sharp, rose grandly into the dark blue sky . . . their sides streaked and ~*ed* with snow —John Muir †1914⟩ ⟨the white tulle is ~*ed* with segments of Alençon-type lace —*New Yorker*⟩ **c :** to cover (a plumbing joint) with melted solder **d :** to outline hastily or carelessly **:** draw, paint, write, or relate sketchily **:** SKETCH ⟨the verbal farce . . . ~*ed* out for us —*Listener*⟩ **e :** to place in a prominent position ⟨insurrectionary proclamations were ~*ed* on the walls of the capital —Bernard Frizell⟩ **f :** to give very conspicuous display to ⟨the papers ~*ed* stories about the dapper little general —*Newsweek*⟩ **2 a :** to strike and dash about (as water or mud) **:** cause (a liquid or thinly viscous substance) to spatter or toss about esp. with force ⟨she puffed and chugged, ~*ing* the brown waters behind her —Tom Marvel⟩ ⟨the pure bright colors which he confidently ~*ed* onto his canvases without even bothering to mix on his palette —*Time*⟩ **b :** to scatter in the manner of a splashed liquid ⟨the sunset colors were ~*ed* brilliantly across the skies —P.E.James⟩ **3 :** to move along (one's way) with splashing ⟨a man, wearing a rubber raincoat which glistened in the headlights . . . ~*ed* his way over toward the car —Erle Stanley Gardner⟩ **4 :** to cause to splash a liquid or other substance ⟨enjoy ~*ing* waterproof boots into deep puddles —Arnold Bennett⟩ **5 a :** to drive (logs) by releasing a head of water confined by a flood dam **b :** to flood (as a shallow river) with a flush of water (as for driving logs) **6 :** to shoot down (as an enemy airplane)

²**splash** \"\ *n* -ES *often attrib* **1 a** (1) **:** liquid hurled or being hurled scatteringly esp. with considerable force or in quantities greater than a spattering, as a result of a surface blow, and against or upon something ⟨the unskilled diver hit the surface with a great ~ of water⟩ ⟨a ~ of paint on his palette had assumed . . . the shape of a distorted skull —Herbert Read⟩ ⟨white ~*es* of water were plunging through the six-inch gap in the wooden gate —Bill Alcine⟩; *specif* **:** water impounded and then released suddenly (as for splashing logs) (2) **:** a spot or daub from or as if from splashed liquid ⟨a mud ~ on the fender⟩ **b** (1) *Brit* **:** a small shallow puddle or pond ⟨an irregular ~ of water to give away its foreignness —Elizabeth Bowen⟩ (2) *Brit* **:** a small amount of soda water ⟨Scotch and a ~ —J.A.Phillips⟩ **c :** a large or irregular conspicuous colored patch upon a background or surface **:** BLOTCH ⟨the blossoming trees dot the countryside with ~*es* of pastel color —*Amer. Guide Series: Texas*⟩ **2 a** (1) **:** the action of striking the surface of a liquid **:** the causing of a liquid to splash ⟨whose placid surface is broken by the swirl and ~ of pickerel and salmon —*Amer. Guide Series: Maine*⟩ (2) **:** the act or process of splashing logs (3) **:** a plunge of short duration and esp. accompanied by vigorous movements into water ⟨will find a warm shower relaxing and a short cold ~ immediately afterward stimulating —Morris Fishbein⟩ **b :** the action of a liquid striking or falling upon something ⟨the steady ~ of a light swell upon the shore⟩ **3 a :** a sound produced by or as if by a body striking upon or in a liquid ⟨tumbled with a sort of ~ upon the keys of a ghostly piano —Scott Fitzgerald⟩ **b :** a sound produced by or as if by a liquid falling, moving forward, being hurled against something, or oscillating back and forth ⟨heard the rain coming down in a ~ —Edmund Wilson⟩; *specif* **:** a splashing sound heard in succession **4 a :** a vivid impression esp. resulting from conspicuous or ostentatious activity or appearance ⟨the son who has made the biggest ~ in the world —Green Peyton⟩ **b** (1) **:** the practice or an instance of ostentatious display ⟨his love of luxury and of ~ —M.D. Geismar⟩ ⟨hard to believe that the magnificence could increase after the first brilliant ~ —C.E.Abernethy⟩ (2) **:** a conspicuous featuring of an item in a newspaper or magazine ⟨the story got a robust front-page ~ —*Newsweek*⟩ ⟨~ headline⟩

splash back *n* **:** SPLASHBOARD

splash block *n* **:** a masonry block placed on the ground below a downspout to divert the water away from the building and to prevent ground washing

splashboard \ˈ=,=\ *n* **1 a :** DASHBOARD 1 **b :** a board or panel (as behind a kitchen sink) to protect against splashes **2 a :** a plank used to close a sluice or spillway of a dam **b :** FLASHBOARD

splash dam *n* **:** a flood dam used to retain a head of water for driving logs

splash·er \ˈsplashə(r), -aash-, -aish-\ *n* -S **1 :** one that splashes **2 :** a guard (as a splashboard) to keep off splashes

splash erosion *n* **:** erosion caused by the splash of falling raindrops

splashes *pres 3d sing of* SPLASH, *pl of* SPLASH

splash guard *n* **:** a flap suspended behind a rear wheel to prevent tire splash from muddying windshields of following vehicles

splash guard

splash·i·ly \-shəlē, -li\ *adv* **:** in a splashy manner ⟨~ printed cotton kimonos —*New Yorker*⟩

splash·i·ness \-shēnəs, -shin-\ *n* -ES **:** the quality or state of being splashy

splash·ing·ly *adv* **:** in a splashing manner

splashings *n pl* [fr. gerund of ¹*splash*] **:** boiled liquor passed over the cooler and refrigerator in brewing and added in the fermentation vessel to reduce the wort to the required gravity

splash-lubricate \ˈ=¦==,=\ *vt* [back-formation fr. *splash lubrication*] **:** to lubricate by splash lubrication

splash lubrication *or* **splash feed** *or* **splash system** *n* **:** lubrication of the parts in a crankcase and cylinder from the splashing about of oil by the crankpin and other moving parts

splash party *n* **:** a party at a swimming pool or beach featuring swimming and other water sports

splash plate *n* **:** a plate (as in the tender of a locomotive) to obstruct and weaken the surge of a surrounding mass of water in motion ⟨water is discharged through tubes located in the troughs, upon *splash plates* which break up the water and distribute it evenly —*Sweet's Catalog Service*⟩

splashy \ˈsplashē, -aash-, -aish-, -shi\ *adj* -ER/-EST [*splash* + *-y*] **1 :** full of dirty water **:** wet and muddy so as to be easily splashed about ⟨a youngster who could resist the temptation of a ~ rain puddle —Ellen L. Buell⟩ **2 :** moving or being moved with a splash or splashing sounds **3 :** tending to or exhibiting ostentatious display **:** SHOWY, SENSATIONAL ⟨a ~ half-page ad —E.J.Kahn⟩ **4 :** consisting of, being, or covered with colored splashes ⟨a short-sleeved dress of . . . black shantung has ~ yellow or white oblongs scattered over it —Lois Long⟩

¹**splat** \ˈsplat, *usu* -ad·+V\ *vb* **splatted; splatted; splatting; splats** [ME *splatten*] *vt* **:** to split open and spread out (a pike) for cooking ~ *vi* **1 :** to flatten on impact ⟨shooting snowballs that *splatted* on the black trunks —Saul Bellow⟩ **2 :** to make a sound characteristic of a bullet flattening on impact

²**splat** \"\ *n* -S **:** a single flat thin often ornamental member of a chairback rising from the seat-rail or one just above it to the top rail used on chairs of the Queen Anne and later styles; *also* **:** a similar horizontal member

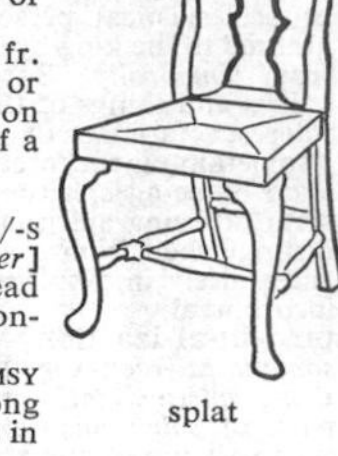
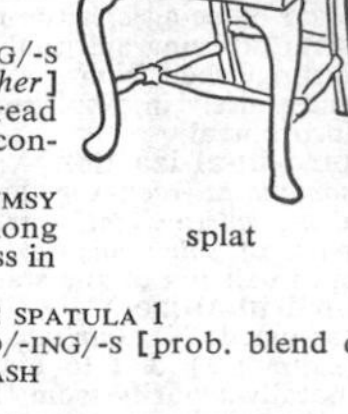
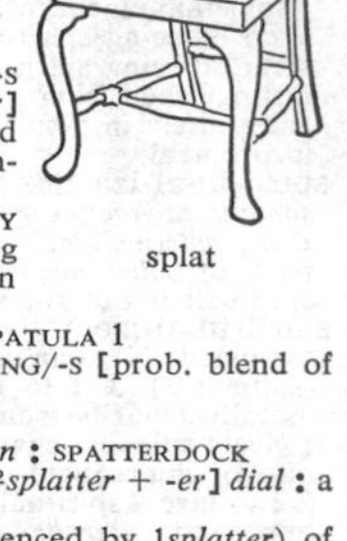
splat

³**splat** \"\ *n* -S [prob. alter. (influenced by ¹*splat*) of ⁸*plat*] *dial Eng* **:** a plot of ground; *also* **:** PATCH, SPOT, BLOTCH

⁴**splat** \"\ *n* -S [back-formation fr. ³*splatter*] **:** any of various splattering or slapping sounds ⟨~ of naked feet on concrete —Wallace Stegner⟩ ⟨the ~ of a bullet⟩

splatch *var of* SPLOTCH

splath·er \ˈspla*th*ə(r)\ *vb* -ED/-ING/-S [prob. blend of ¹*splash* and ¹*blather*] **1** *dial Brit* **a :** SPLASH **b :** to spread about **2** *dial Brit* **:** to speak or tell confusedly

splathering *adj* **1 :** UNGAINLY, CLUMSY **2 :** CONFUSED, RAMBLING ⟨sends a long ~ telegram and never puts her address in it —J.B.Priestley⟩

¹**splatter** *n* -S [alter. of *spatule*] *obs* **:** SPATULA 1

²**splat·ter** \ˈsplad·ə(r), -atə-\ *vb* -ED/-ING/-S [prob. blend of ²*splash* and ¹*spatter*] **:** SPATTER, SPLASH

³**splatter** \"\ *n* -S **:** SPATTER, SPLASH

splat·ter·dock \ˈsplad·ə(r),däk, -atə-\ *n* **:** SPATTERDOCK

splat·ter·er \ˈsplad·ərə(r), -atə-\ *n* -S [²*splatter* + *-er*] *dial* **:** a coot (*Fulica americana*)

splatterfaced \¦==¦=\ *adj* [alter. (influenced by ¹*splatter*) of *platter-faced*] **:** PLATTER-FACED

splatterwork \ˈ==,=\ *n* [¹*splatter* + *work*] **:** art work produced with or as if with a spatula

¹**splay** \ˈsplā\ *vb* -ED/-ING/-S [ME *splayen*, short for *displayen* to spread out, unfold — more at DISPLAY] *vt* **1 :** to cause to spread apart or open outward **:** EXPAND ⟨~*ing* large, meaty hands over the table —Nigel Dennis⟩ — usu. used with *out* ⟨~*ing* out their movable toes, they can move easily over marshy ground —C.D.Forde⟩ **2 :** to turn on one side **:** make oblique (as the side of a door or window) **3 :** to draw together (the ends of staves) in forming a barrel, tub, or bucket ~ *vi* **1 :** to become splayed **:** extend apart or outwards esp. in an awkward or clumsy manner ⟨the front wheels were ~*ing* like a llama's hoofs —A.W.Baum⟩ — usu. used with *out* ⟨four delicate legs that unite in a central shaft near the base and ~ out to support the top —Sheila Hibben⟩ **2 :** to lie at a slant **:** SLOPE, SLANT

²**splay** \"\ *n* -S **1 :** an outward or expanding slope or bevel esp. of the sides of a door or window by which an opening is made larger at one face of the wall than at the other or larger at each of the faces than it is between them **2 :** the degree of outward slope **:** SPREAD, EXPANSION ⟨the ~ of sheers is one-third of their effective length —*Manual of Seamanship*⟩

³**splay** \"\ *adj* **1 :** turned outward esp. in an awkward or ungainly manner ⟨~ knees⟩; *also* **:** broad and flat as from splaying **2 :** CLUMSY, UNGAINLY ⟨something ~, something blunt-edged, unhandy, and infelicitous —Matthew Arnold⟩

⁴**splay** \"\ *vt* [by alter.] *dial* **:** SPAY

splayed arch *n* **:** an arch with its opening at one side larger than at the other so that its intrados face is conical

¹**splayfoot** \ˈ=,=\ *n, pl* **splayfeet** [¹*splay* + *foot*] **:** a foot that is abnormally flattened and spread out; *specif* **:** FLATFOOT

²**splayfoot** \ˈ=¦=\ *or* **splayfooted** \ˈ=¦==\ *adj* [*splayfoot* fr. ¹*splayfoot*; *splayfooted* fr. ¹*splay* + *footed*] **1 :** having a splayfoot **2 :** UNGAINLY, CLUMSY

splaymouthed \ˈ=¦=\ *adj* **:** having a mouth stretched into an awkward gape or grin

¹**spleen** \ˈsplēn\ *n* -S [ME *splen*, fr. MF or L; MF *esplen*, fr. L *splen*, fr. Gk *splēn*; akin to L *lien* spleen, OIr *selg*, OSlav *slězena*, Skt *plīhan*] **1 a :** a highly vascular ductless abdominal organ of vertebrates that resembles a gland in organization but is closely associated with the circulatory system playing a role in the maintenance of blood volume, production of some types of blood cells, recovery of material from worn-out red blood cells, and probably in the production of antibodies and that in man is a dark purplish flattened oblong object of a soft fragile consistency lying near the cardiac end of the stomach and consisting largely of reticuloendothelial and lymphoid tissue enclosed in a fibroelastic capsule from which trabeculae ramify through the tissue of the organ which is divisible into a loose friable red pulp in intimate connection with the blood supply and with red blood cells free in its interstices and a denser white pulp chiefly of lymphoid tissue condensed in masses about the small arteries **b** *archaic* **:** the seat of emotions and passions **:** the source of laughter **2 :** any of various passions or emotions or their manifestations: **a** *obs* **:** violent mirth or merriment; *also* **:** LAUGHTER ⟨haply my presence may well abate thy overmerry ~ —Shak.⟩ **b** *archaic* **:** a fit of anger, malice, or bad temper **c** (1) *obs* **:** a sudden impulse **:** WHIM, CAPRICE ⟨a thousand ~*s* bear her a thousand ways —Shak.⟩ (2) *obs* **:** a capricious temper **d** *obs* **:** a proud courageous impetuous temper **:** manly spirit ⟨leaden age, quicken'd with youthful ~ and warlike rage —Shak.⟩; *also* **:** IMPETUOSITY, HIGH-SPIRITEDNESS **e** (1) **:** latent malevolence or spite **:** violent feelings of anger or spite esp. when suddenly and explosively released ⟨his countrymen vented their ~ at his failure . . . by sending the unfortunate naval commander into exile —A.J. Toynbee⟩ (2) *obs* **:** a feeling of ill will **:** GRUDGE ⟨I have no ~ against you —Shak.⟩ **f :** extreme lowness of spirits **:** MELANCHOLY, DEPRESSION **syn** see MALICE

²**spleen** \"\ *vt* -ED/-ING/-S **:** to arouse the wrath of **:** ANGER

spleen amaranth *n* **:** a tropical American annual weed (*Amaranthus hybridus*) that has dark green or purple foliage and is widely naturalized in the U.S.

spleen·ful \ˈ=fəl\ *adj* **:** full of, displaying, or affected with spleen **:** SPLENETIC

spleen·ic \ˈsplēnik\ *adj* [¹*spleen* + *-ic*] **:** SPLENIC

spleen·less \-ləs\ *adj* **:** having no spleen; *specif* **:** SPLENECTOMIZED

spleen stone *n* **:** a green stone (as jade) formerly used for disorders of the spleen

spleenwort \ˈ=,=\ *n* [¹*spleen* + *wort*; fr. the belief that it has curative powers for disorders of the spleen] **1 :** a fern of the genus *Asplenium* **2 :** a fern of the genus *Athyrium*

spleenwort bush *n* **:** SWEET FERN 2

spleeny \ˈsplēnē, -ni\ *adj* -ER/-EST **1 :** full of or displaying spleen **2** *NewEng* **:** peevish and irritable with hypochondriac inclinations ⟨so ~ when they have the least little thing wrong with them⟩

splen- *or* **spleno-** *comb form* [LL, fr. L, fr. Gk *splēn-*, *splēno-*, fr. *splēn* spleen — more at SPLEEN] **1 :** spleen ⟨*splenectomy*⟩ ⟨*splenoma*⟩ ⟨*splenolysis*⟩ ⟨*splenorrhagia*⟩ **2 :** spleen and ⟨*splenocolic*⟩ ⟨*splenolymphatic*⟩

sple·nal·gia \splēˈnalj(ē)ə, spleˈ-, spləˈ-\ *n* [NL, fr. *splen-* + *-algia*] **:** pain (as neuralgic) in the region of the spleen — **sple·nal·gic** \(ˈ)splē¦naljik, (ˈ)sple¦-, splə¦-\ *adj*

sple·nat·ic \spləˈnad·ik\ *adj* [NL *splenaticus*, alter. of LL *spleneticus* splenetic — more at SPLENETIC] *obs* **:** arising from, due to, or affected by spleen **:** SPLEENFUL

splenative *adj* [*splen-* + *-ative*] *obs* **:** SPLEENFUL

splen·cu·lus \ˈspleŋkyələs\ *n, pl* **splencu·li** \-ə,lī\ [NL, dim. of L *splen* spleen] **:** a small accessory spleen

splen·da·cious *or* **splen·da·ceous** *or* **splen·da·tious** \(ˈ)splen¦dāshəs\ *adj* [*splendid* + *-acious* (as in *loquacious*), *-aceous* (as in *pomaceous*), *-atious* (as in *ostentatious*)] **:** very splendid **:** GORGEOUS

splen·dent \ˈsplendənt\ *adj* [ME, fr. L *splendent-*, *splendens*, pres. part. of *splendēre* to shine] **1 :** shining glossily with light or reflected light ⟨~ planets⟩ ⟨~ luster⟩ **2 :** conspicuously eminent or illustrious

splen·did \-dəd\ *adj, often* -ER/-EST [L *splendidus*, fr. *splendēre* to shine; akin to Gk *splēdos* ashes, Skt *sphuliṅga* spark] **1 a :** marked by, manifestive of, adorned with, or maintained in showy magnificence **:** SUMPTUOUS ⟨a very long, narrow chamber — ~ with chandeliers, Oriental rugs, and gilt furniture —Christopher Rand⟩ ⟨the decoration of the public stage, so far from being merely passable, was strikingly ~ —Leslie Hotson⟩ **b :** brilliantly shining **:** RADIANT, LUSTROUS, BRILLIANT **c :** embellished as if with sumptuous ornaments : FLORID, ORNATE ⟨his creed is set forth . . . in scores of phrases of ~ and empty sonorousness —S.H.Adams⟩ **2 a :** superior or preeminent in accomplishment or distinction : ILLUSTRIOUS, DISTINGUISHED ⟨a great man, a ~ figure in history —H.E.Scudder⟩ **b :** very good, fine, pleasant, or enjoyable : EXCELLENT, PRAISEWORTHY ⟨the ~ cement road —Adria Langley⟩ ⟨prompted by motives which are so ~ —Norman Angell⟩ ⟨the slavery issue offers a ~ illustration of this feature —C.A.M.Ewing⟩ **c :** remarkably pure, complete, or extreme as an embodiment of its type ⟨a miracle of ~ ugliness —Arnold Bennett⟩ ⟨its often ~ lack of intelligibility —C.W. Mills⟩ ⟨~ isolation⟩

syn SPLENDID, RESPLENDENT, GORGEOUS, GLORIOUS, SUBLIME, and SUPERB can all mean having or displaying extraordinarily impressive qualities. All of these terms, like most terms designating superlative qualities, are commonly used interchangeably in hyperbole or as mere indications of great satisfaction in or admiration of something ⟨a *splendid* dish of ice cream —Walt Whitman⟩ ⟨a *splendid* hiker⟩ ⟨a young ROTC student *resplendent* in Air Force blue —Land Kaderli⟩ ⟨a *gorgeous* fat bass voice —*Irish Digest*⟩ ⟨get yourself a *gorgeous* tan —*Read Mag.*⟩ ⟨the deserted boat deck to be a *gorgeous* place to kiss —I.V.Morris⟩ ⟨the *glorious* opportunity of intoxicating themselves at the public expense —J.G.Frazer⟩ ⟨*glorious* onion soup —Ernest Beaglehole⟩ ⟨*sublime* vacation areas —Laurence Lowry⟩ ⟨a *sublime* cocktail⟩ ⟨*superb* hunting and scenic attractions —Tom Marvel⟩ ⟨a *superb* toy⟩ but can be distinguished in more strict use. SPLENDID can apply to what outshines the usual in brilliancy, magnificence, or the like ⟨the courthouse with its portico and spire loomed *splendid* in the distance —Elinor Wylie⟩ ⟨draw the whole opera together in this one *splendid* moment —Robert Craft⟩ RESPLENDENT can apply to what seems to glow or blaze in beauty or splendor ⟨the stars of early evening were *resplendent* —Erle Stanley Gardner⟩ ⟨a *resplendent* butterfly —George Meredith⟩ ⟨she had shown how great and *resplendent* a thing love could be —J.W. Krutch⟩ GORGEOUS can stress a splendor of color or display, sometimes implying a showiness or undue but colorful elaborateness ⟨this *gorgeous* combination of all the hues of Paradise —Henry Adams⟩ ⟨a flair for the exotic and the *gorgeous* —F.O.Matthiessen⟩ ⟨a mass of *gorgeous* upholstery and a labyrinth of luxurious architecture —G.K.Chesterton⟩ GLORIOUS can suggest a radiant beauty or similar extraordinarily admirable quality ⟨all the *glorious* colors of this beautiful range, deep blue and purple in the shadows of the peaks, green and brown where grass and rock mingled —Bram Stoker⟩ ⟨a *glorious* display of fireworks⟩ SUBLIME can imply an elevation or exaltation in contemplation or an impossibility of fully grasping a thing's beauty, power, extent, nobility, or the like ⟨the *sublime* mountain scenery of the West Highlands —O.S.Nock⟩ ⟨the *sublime* but also terrible and sombre experiences and emotions of the battlefield —Sir Winston Churchill⟩ ⟨had been born into that world of stylized drama, of vanity, vulgar pomp and *sublime* grace —*Time*⟩ SUPERB can apply to what has reached or is at a peak of development, competence, grandeur, or magnificence ⟨*superb* political insight —A.M. Schlesinger b. 1917⟩ ⟨*superb* horsemanship⟩ ⟨a *superb* physique⟩ ⟨*superb* cunning⟩ ⟨a *superb* sunset⟩

splen·did·ly *adv* : in a splendid manner

splen·did·ness *n* -ES : the quality or state of being splendid : SPLENDOR, MAGNIFICENCE

splen·dif·er·ous \(ˈ)splenˈdif(ə)rəs\ *adj* [ME, fr. L *splendidus* + E *-ferous*] **1 :** SPLENDID, EXCELLENT, MAGNIFICENT ⟨the oil-rich who worked to live up to the ~ black fountains erupting on their lands —Le Roy Leatherman⟩ **2 :** deceptively splendid ⟨recalls to memory the splendid, or at least ~ days prior to 1929 —G.W.Johnson⟩ — **splen·dif·er·ous·ly** *adv* — **splen·dif·er·ous·ness** *n* -ES

¹splen·dor \ˈsplendə(r) *sometimes* -ˌdȯ(ə)r *or* -ȯ(ə)\ *n* -S *see* *-or in Explan Notes* [ME *splendure*, fr. MF *esplendour*, fr. L *splendor*, fr. *splendēre* to shine — more at SPLENDID] **1 a :** great brightness : brilliant luster : BRILLIANCY ⟨ahead shone the ~ of a showcase full of gold objects —Angélica Mendoza⟩ ⟨the color and delicacy and ~ of soap bubbles —Dorothy Barclay⟩ **b :** sumptuous display, ornament, or ceremonial : gorgeous show : MAGNIFICENCE, POMP, GLORY ⟨entertained at balls noted for their ~ and exclusiveness —*Amer. Guide Series: La.*⟩ **c :** BEAUTY ⟨the harsh ~ of barren mountains —Marion Wilhelm⟩ **d :** EXCELLENCE, VALUE, WORTH ⟨this eloquent and confident look should . . . open the eyes of many . . . to the ~ of their moral heritage —L.P.Curtis⟩ **2 a :** something that exhibits splendor ⟨the east was a ~ of forest fires —William Beebe⟩ **b :** something that contributes to splendor ⟨the vocabulary of poetry increased enormously its store . . . of vague ~*s* —J.L.Lowes⟩ — **in splendor** *of the sun* : represented heraldically with rays

²splendor \"\ *vb* -ED/-ING/-S *see -or in Explan Notes* *vi* : to proceed gloriously, radiantly, or resplendently ~ *vt* : to endow with splendor : ADORN ⟨the winter night is ~*ed* by the stars —Madeline Mason⟩

splen·dor·ous \-d(ə)rəs\ *also* **splen·drous** \-drəs\ *adj* : full of splendor : very bright : SPLENDID

sple·nec·to·mize \spləˈnektəˌmīz\ *vt* -ED/-ING/-S [*splenectomy* + *-ize*] : to excise the spleen of

sple·nec·to·my \-mē, -mi\ *n* -ES [ISV *splen-* + *-ectomy*] : removal of the spleen by surgery

sple·ne·o·lus \spləˈnēələs\ *n, pl* **spleneo·li** \-əˌlī\ [NL, dim. of L *splen* spleen] : an accessory spleen

¹sple·net·ic \spləˈned·ik, -netik, -ēk\ *adj* [LL *spleneticus*, fr. L *splen* spleen + *-eticus* -etic — more at SPLEEN] **1 :** of, relating to, or acting upon the spleen : SPLENIC **2 a** *obs* : having an improperly functioning spleen : afflicted with excessive spleen secretion **b** *archaic* : characterized by or liable to produce melancholy, depression, or moodiness ⟨I could be as *splenetic* as you . . . but my resolution is . . . never to be melancholy —William Cowper⟩ **3 :** marked by morose bad temper, sullen malevolence, or spiteful, peevish anger ⟨heavily biased . . . his book is also ~ in tone —*Times Lit. Supp.*⟩ ⟨~ and railing misanthropy —T.L.Peacock⟩ **syn** see IRASCIBLE

²splenetic \"\ *n* -S : a peevish irritable person

splenetical *obs var of* ¹SPLENETIC

sple·net·i·cal·ly \-ək(ə)lē, -ēk-, -li\ *adv* : in a splenetic manner

splenetic fever *n* : TEXAS FEVER

splen·e·tive \ˈsplenəd·iv\ *adj* [alter. of *splenative*] : SPLENETIC

¹sple·ni·al \ˈsplēnēəl\ *adj* [in senses 1 & 2, fr. NL *splenius* + E *-al*; in sense 3, fr. NL *splenium* + E *-al*] **1 :** of, relating to, or being a thin membrane bone on the inner side of the mandible of many vertebrates below mammals that resembles a splint and is usu. in close relation with the dentary **2 :** relating to a splenius muscle **3 :** of or relating to the splenium

²splenial \"\ *n* -S : a splenial bone

splen·ic \ˈsplēnik, -len-, -nēk\ *also* **sple·ni·cal** \-nəkəl, -nēk-\ *adj* [*splenic* fr. L *splenicus*, fr. Gk *splēnikos*, fr. *splēn* spleen + *-ikos* -ic; *splenical* fr. L *splenicus* + E *-al* — more at SPLEEN] : of, relating to, or located in the spleen

splenic artery *n* : the branch of the coeliac artery that carries blood to the spleen and sends branches also to the pancreas and the cardiac end of the stomach

splenic fever *n* **1** *or* **splenic apoplexy** : ANTHRAX 2 **2 :** TEXAS FEVER

splenic flexure *n* : the sharp bend of the colon under the spleen where the transverse colon joins the descending colon

splenic pulp *n* : the characteristic tissue of the spleen

splenic vein *n* : the vein that carries blood away from the spleen, that in man is formed by five or six large branches which unite a short distance from the spleen, and that joins the superior mesenteric vein to form the portal vein

spleni·fi·ca·tion \ˌsplenəfəˈkāshən, -len-\ *n* -S [F *splénification*, fr. *spléni-* splen- + *-fication*] : SPLENIZATION

sple·ni·tis \spləˈnīd·əs\ *n* -ES [NL, fr. Gk *splēnitis*, fr. *splēn* spleen + *-itis*] : inflammation of the spleen

sple·ni·um \ˈsplēnēəm\ *n, pl* **sple·nia** \-nēə\ [NL, fr. L, plaster, patch, fr. Gk *splēnion* bandage, spleenless person, spleenwort, dim. of *splēn* spleen — more at SPLEEN] : the thick rounded fold forming the posterior border of the corpus callosum and being continuous by its undersurface with the fornix

sple·ni·us \-nēəs\ *n, pl* **sple·nii** \-nēˌī\ [NL, fr. L *splenium* plaster, patch] : a flat muscle of each side of the back of the neck and upper thoracic region in man arising as a single muscle from the ligamentum nuchae, the spinous processes of the last cervical and six upper thoracic vertebrae, and the supraspinous ligament but dividing into a part that inserts into the mastoid process of the temporal bone and the occipital bone and a part that inserts into the transverse processes of the upper two or three cervical vertebrae — called also respectively *splenius capitis, splenius cervicis*

spleni·za·tion \ˌsplēnəˈzāshən, -len-, -ˌnīˈz-\ *n* -S [F *splénisation*, fr. *spléni-* splen- + *-isation* -ization] : the condition of being or process of becoming like a spleen ⟨the ~ of the tissue of a congested lung⟩

spleno- — see SPLEN-

spleno·cyte \ˈsplēnəˌsīt, -len-\ *n* -S [ISV *splen-* + *-cyte*] : a macrophage of the spleen

spleno·gen·ic \ˌ==ˈjenik\ *adj* [*spleno-* + *-genic*] : of splenic origin

sple·noid \ˈspleˌnȯid\ *adj* [ISV *splen-* + *-oid*] : resembling a spleen

spleno·meg·a·ly \ˌsplēnəˈmegəlē, ˌsplen-\ *n* -ES [ISV *splen-* + *-megaly*] : enlargement of the spleen

splent *var of* SPLINT

splen·u·lus \ˈsplenyələs\ *or* **sple·nun·cu·lus** \spləˈnəŋkyələs\ *n, pl* **splenu·li** \-nyəˌlī\ *or* **splenuncu·li** \-kyəˌlī\ [NL, dim. of L *splen* spleen] : a rudimentary or accessory spleen

spleu·chan \ˈsplükən\ *n* -S [ScGael *spliùcan* & IrGael *spliùchan*] *Scot & Irish* : a pouch esp. for holding tobacco or money

¹splice \ˈsplīs\ *vt* -ED/-ING/-S [obs. D *splissen* to split ends into separate strands, splice, fr. MD; akin to MD *splitten* to split — more at SPLIT] **1 :** to fasten together esp. end to end and esp. in order to form a continuous length: as **a :** to unite (two ropes or two parts of a rope) esp. by sticking or tucking the strands of one rope or part between or around each other **b :** to unite (as spars, timbers, or rails) into a single length by lapping together two ends or by applying a piece that laps upon the two ends and binding or making fast; *specif* : to connect (railroad rails) end to end with joint bars **c :** to join (as two lengths of photographic film or paper or recording tape) by or as if by cementing or fusing the ends together; *also* : to transfer (as a sound or picture) to a recording or film by splicing in a piece of recorded tape or film ⟨an audience's laughs have been recorded and are *spliced* into the thirty-minute comedy film —Goodman Ace⟩ **2 :** to attach to, fix in, or join onto something ⟨~ a rope to a chain⟩ ⟨proposing to ~ upon the tariff bill an income tax —N.W.Stephenson⟩; *specif* : to graft (a slip or shoot) into stock by lapping or by applying a piece that laps and binding or making fast **3 :** to make, form, or repair by splicing ⟨bone and ivory knitting needles were often *spliced* in order to obtain the required length —Mary Thomas⟩ ⟨the broken girder can be *spliced* —*New Yorker*⟩ **4 :** to unite in marriage : MARRY ⟨asked the preacher to ~ them⟩ — **splice the main brace** : to give out or drink spirits on a special occasion or after great hardship or effort

²splice \"\ *n* -S **1 :** the act or result of joining or fusing esp. end to end: as **a :** a joining of two cords or ropes or two parts of the same cord or rope made by interweaving or intertwining the strands in such a way that the circumference of the joint is no greater or not much greater than the circumference of the rope — see CHAIN SPLICE, EYE SPLICE, LONG SPLICE, SHORT SPLICE **b :** a joining of the ends of long rigid objects (as spars, timbers, or rails) by lapping the ends or applying a piece lapping both ends and by making fast (as by binding or bolting) **c :** a fused or cemented joint in a length of photographic film or paper or recording tape **2 :** MARRIAGE, WEDDING **3 :** the part of the handle of a cricket bat that is inserted in the blade **4 :** SPLICING 2

splice bar *n* : JOINT BAR

spliced *adj* [fr. past part. of ¹*splice*] : reinforced with an extra thread at heel, foot, and toe — used of knitted hose

splice graft *n* : a plant graft made by cutting both stock and scion across obliquely, fitting the cut surfaces so that the cambiums are in contact, and tying — called also *whip graft*; see GRAFT illustration

splic·er \ˈsplīsə(r)\ *n* -S : one that splices; *specif* : a device for making splices in lengths of photographic film or paper

splicing *n* -S [fr. gerund of ¹*splice*] **1 :** a spliced section or part : SPLICE **2 :** a reinforcement of knitted hose with an extra thread at heel, foot, and toe

splicing chamber *n* : CABLE VAULT

¹spline \ˈsplīn\ *n* -S [origin unknown] **1 :** a thin wood, metal, or plastic strip : SLAT: as **a :** a loose tongue between two pieces of heavy subflooring used in place of a tongue-and-groove joint **b :** a flexible strip used as a guide in drawing curved lines **2 :** FEATHER KEY; *also* : a keyway for a feather key

²spline \"\ *vt* -ED/-ING/-S **1 :** to cut a keyway in for a feather key : SLOT ⟨a *splined* shaft⟩ **2 :** to attach or couple by means of a spline ⟨an exterior of cedar logs *splined* together —*Amer. Builder*⟩ ⟨shell and sleeve assembly *splined* to the armature shaft —Joseph Heitner⟩

spline shaft *n* : a splined shaft; *specif* : one having a number of equally spaced grooves cut in the shaft so as to form a series of projecting keys and fitting into an internally grooved cylindrical member

spline weight *n* : a usu. lead metal weight used for confining a spline to the desired curve — called also *dolphin*

¹splint \ˈsplint\ *or* **splent** \ˈsplent\ *n* -S *often attrib* [ME *splint, splent*, fr. MLG *splinte, splente*; akin to MD *splinte* splint, Norw *splint* wooden nail, wedge, OHG *spaltan* to split — more at SPILL] **1 :** a small plate or strip of metal — see SPLINT ARMOR **2 a (1)** *dial Brit* : LATH **(2) :** a thin strip of wood interwoven with others in caning **(3) :** a piece split off : SPLINTER **(4) :** a rigid or flexible material (as wood, metal, plaster, fabric, or adhesive tape) used to protect, immobilize, or restrict motion in a part ⟨an adhesive ~ on the chest⟩ ⟨a plaster ~ for a fractured leg⟩ ⟨a nasal ~ after rhinoplasty⟩ **b :** SAPWOOD **3 a :** an exostosis on the upper part of the cannon bone of a horse usu. on the inside of the leg — compare PEGGED SPLINT **b :** SPLINT BONE **4 :** SPLINT COAL

²splint \"\ *vt* -ED/-ING/-S **1 a :** to immobilize (as a broken bone) with a splint **b :** to support or brace with or as if with a splint **2 :** to protect against pain by reducing motion ⟨the patient ~*ed* his chest by a fixed position and shallow breathing⟩

splint·age \-tij, -tēj\ *n* -S : the application of splints

splint armor *n* : armor of usu. overlapping thin metal plates allowing the limbs to move freely

splint basket *n* : a usu. rectangular container having the sides and bottom formed from woven or braided splints crossed at right angles, and having some type of handle : MARKET BASKET 1a

splint basket

splint bone *n* **1 :** one of the rudimentary metacarpal or metatarsal bones resembling a splint on either side of the cannon bone in the limbs of a horse and related animals **2 :** FIBULA

splint-bottom \ˈ=ˌ==\ *or* **splint-bottomed** \ˈ=ˌ==\ *adj, of a chair* : having a seat woven of splints

splint coal *n* [so called fr. its splintery fracture] : a very hard bituminous steam coal of dull appearance and laminated structure that gives out intense heat when burning — compare BRIGHT COAL

¹splin·ter \ˈsplintə(r)\ *n* -S [ME, fr. MD *splinter, splenter*; akin to MLG *splinte, splente* splint — more at SPLINT] **1 a (1) :** a thin often jagged or needlelike piece split or rent off lengthwise : SLIVER, CHIP, FRAGMENT ⟨gloves . . . protect a worker from sharp steel ~*s* —Michael Cawley⟩ ⟨the steering wheel . . . was knocked into ~*s* by an enemy shot —Edward Breck⟩ **(2) :** a small jagged or needlelike particle or flash ⟨flying ~*s* of ice —William Beebe⟩ ⟨irradiated for a moment now and then by ~*s* shooting through the darkness —E.K.Brown⟩ **b :** a usu. small group or faction broken away from an organization or body : a dissident faction ⟨this process does seem to split up the whole religious group into many ~*s* —J.O.Nelson⟩ **2 :** SPLINT **3 :** a minute, worthless, or insignificant piece or object ⟨carped at lesser breeds who failed in some ~ of the religious law —*Interpreter's Bible*⟩ ⟨contributed various ~*s* of hackwork —Clifton Fadiman⟩ ⟨no mere ~ of a peak, but a majestic mountain —Claudia Cassidy⟩

²splinter \"\ *vb* **splintered; splintered; splintering** \-nt(ə)riŋ, -n·triŋ\ **splinters** *vt* **1 a :** to split, rend, or break into long thin pieces : SHIVER, SHATTER ⟨the walls were ~*ed* by the explosion⟩ **b :** to split into fragments, parts, or factions ⟨liberal opinion . . . was marshaled, integrated, and effective; it is ~*ed* now —G.W.Johnson⟩ ⟨ownership has been ~*ed* into so many tiny and inadequate parcels —J.D.McGoldrick⟩ **2** *obs* : SPLINT ~ *vi* **1 a :** to become split into long pieces : be shivered ⟨heard the thud of hooves lashing out and timbers ~*ing* —Robinson Jeffers⟩ **b (1) :** to become split into factions ⟨the politicians hope the veterans ~ and never wield their strength together —J.B.Martin⟩ **(2) :** to break away from an organization or entity : SECEDE ⟨will ~ off to form a third party —*Newsweek*⟩ **2 :** to fall or proceed in splinters ⟨the rain was ~*ing*, half frozen, against the kitchen window —Marjorie Housepian⟩

³splinter \"\ *adj* : of, relating to, belonging to, cast for, endorsed by, or being a faction or body broken away or independent from an original, larger, or primary organization or entity : FACTIONAL ⟨~ party⟩ ⟨~ group⟩ ⟨plagued by ~ politics —*Economist*⟩ ⟨the ~ votes . . . are considerably dispersed —Irving Kolodin⟩

splinter bar *n* **1** *Brit* : WHIFFLETREE **2 :** a crossbar in a coach or other vehicle to support the springs **3 :** a bar or other part in a wood-planing machine to decrease splintering of the fibers

splinter deck *n* : a less heavily armored deck usu. just below a ship's protective deck

splin·ter·ize \-təˌrīz\ *vb* -ED/-ING/-S [¹*splinter* + *-ize*] : SPLINTER

splin·ter·less \ˈsplintə(r)ləs\ *adj* : not liable to splinter

splinterproof \ˈ==ˌ=\ *n* : a structure to protect against the splinters of bursting shells or bombs

splin·tery \ˈsplintərē, -n·trē, -ri\ *adj* **1 :** consisting of, resembling, or being embedded with splinters **2 a :** FRAGMENTARY **b :** NEEDLELIKE, ACICULAR, FIBROUS ⟨the ~ fracture of a mineral⟩

splints *pl of* SPLINT, *pres 3d sing of* SPLINT

splintwood \ˈ=ˌ=\ *n* : SAPWOOD

splinty \ˈsplintē, -ti\ *adj* [¹*splint* + *-y*] : SPLINTERY

¹splish-splash \ˈsplish,splash, -aa(ə)sh\ *vi* [redupl. of ¹*splash*] : to make a repeated splashing sound

²splish-splash \"\ *n* : a repeated splashing sound

¹split \ˈsplit, *usu* -id·+V\ *vb* **split** *or archaic* **splitted; split** *or archaic* **splitted; splitting; splits** [D *splitten*, fr. MD; akin to MLG *splīten* to split, slit, MHG *slīzen*, OFris *splīta* to slit, OHG *spaltan* to split — more at SPILL] *vt* **1 a :** to divide or separate from end to end or in a lengthwise direction esp. sharply or suddenly or with force by cleaving or forcing apart usu. along a grain or a seam or by separating layers ⟨~ a board⟩ ⟨~ leather⟩ ⟨~ logs for firewood⟩ ⟨shock ~ the wall along a stud⟩ ⟨his trousers had been ~ down one leg⟩ ⟨girls come down to ~, clean, and pack the fish in barrels —Richard Joseph⟩ ⟨how to ~ clams on rocks —J.H.Wheelock⟩ ⟨~ open a roll and butter it⟩ ⟨~ a few sticks of kindling⟩: as **(1) :** to cause (a sail) to tear or rip ⟨a mainsail ~ by a gale⟩ : have (a sail) torn ⟨~ our mainsail in the storm⟩ **(2) :** to plough (a ridge) so as to cast the earth outward ⟨the ridges were ~ over the potatoes —Adrian Bell⟩ **(3) :** to divide (a pillar or post in a coal mine) by one or more roads **(4) :** to take (a rope) apart by separating the strands **(5) :** to cut (corrugated glass) to a desired width **b :** to affect as if by cleaving or forcing apart ⟨the whole plain . . . is gashed and torn and mauled and ~ —Thomas Wood †1950⟩ ⟨first bass of the season ~ the surface —Gertrude Schweitzer⟩ ⟨his face ~ by a huge yawn —John Wain⟩ ⟨the river ~*s* the town in two⟩ ⟨gorges which ~ the divide —R.L.Neuberger⟩ ⟨cloud was ~ with a flash of flame —R.H.Davis⟩ **2 a (1) :** to break up ⟨the wreck of a ship ~ upon a reef⟩ **(2) :** to tear or rend apart : BURST, RUPTURE ⟨warehouses *splitting* their sides with plunder —F.G.Slaughter⟩ **(3) :** to subject (an atom or atomic nucleus) to artificial disintegration esp. by fission **b :** to affect as if by breaking up or tearing apart : REND, SHATTER ⟨a roar that ~ the air⟩ ⟨series of explosives ~ our ears —J.B.Shaw⟩ : DISORDER, DISINTEGRATE ⟨mind is finally ~ asunder by her abnormal sexual jealousy —*Saturday Rev.*⟩ **3 :** to divide or separate into distinct parts or portions ⟨*splitting* the county into twenty-nine . . . rationing districts —Hal Burton⟩ ⟨scouts had been ~ into small detachments —Georg Meyers⟩ ⟨ornithologists have ~ these again into four more subspecies —Douglas Carruthers⟩ — often used with *up* ⟨*splitting* up the main colors into variants —C.W.H.Johnson⟩: as **a :** to divide between two or more persons : SHARE ⟨~ the loot⟩ ⟨~ up the cost⟩ ⟨~ the physics prize three ways⟩ ⟨~ a bottle of wine at dinner⟩ ⟨this pernicious practice of *splitting* fees —*Time*⟩ ⟨a man has a right to ~ his inheritance —Edward Sapir⟩ ⟨~ the pot at poker⟩ **b :** to divide into opposing factions, parties, or groups ⟨the solid South was ~ by internal revolt⟩ ⟨the issue ~ the village down the middle⟩ ⟨his candidacy ~ the labor vote⟩ **c :** to mark (a ballot) or otherwise cast or register (a vote) so as to vote for candidates of different parties ⟨usually ~ his ticket in national elections⟩ **d :** to divide (an air current) into separate currents (as in mine ventilation) **e :** to separate or break down (a chemical compound) into constituents : effect the cleavage of (as by hydrolysis : ¹CRACK **8** ⟨~ a fat into glycerol and fatty acids⟩ — sometimes used with *up* **f :** to remove by such separation — usu. used with *off* or *out* ⟨~ off carbon dioxide⟩ **g :** to divide (the stock of a corporation) by issuing a larger number of shares to existing shareholders usu. without increase in aggregate par value of capitalization for corporations with par value stock **h :** to win and lose an equal number of (as games or contests) ⟨~ a doubleheader⟩ ⟨~ the first four games⟩ **i :** to discard (one pair from a two-pair hand or one card of a pair) in draw poker to increase one's chance of improving the hand in the draw **j :** to bisect (a stamp) esp. into more than two pieces **4 :** to separate (the parts of a whole) by interposing something ⟨~ an infinitive⟩ ⟨~ the defense in hockey⟩ **5** *slang* : to reveal (as information, secrets) intentionally or unintentionally : BETRAY **6 :** to dilute (liquor) by adding water or a nonalcoholic liquid : CUT ~ *vi* **1 a :** to become divided or separated (as by cleaving, tearing) part from part or from end to end or in a lengthwise direction usu. along a grain or a seam or by the separating of layers ⟨the board ~ while he was driving the nail⟩ ⟨his coat had ~ at the seams⟩ ⟨fingernails showed a tendency to ~⟩ ⟨this wood ~*s* easily⟩ ⟨sails ~ in the storm⟩ **b :** to break apart or into pieces : break up ⟨ship ~*s* on the rock —Shak.⟩ : BURST, RUPTURE ⟨the jar ~ when the water froze⟩ ⟨fruit falls to the ground and ~*s* open⟩ **c (1) :** to part or open as if forced or torn apart by splitting ⟨the sky suddenly ~ open in a flash of lightning⟩ ⟨his face ~ into a wide grin⟩ **(2) :** to burst with laughter ⟨thought he would ~⟩ **2 a (1) :** to become divided up or separated off (as into parts, groups, parties, factions) ⟨stream ~*s* into numerous channels —G.R.Stewart⟩ — often used with *up* ⟨*splitting* up of a language into a number of dialects —Edward Sapir⟩ ⟨the group ~ up into two teams⟩ **(2) :** to break up into divergent or opposing groups ⟨began to ~ into left and right wings and then into smaller groupings —William Petersen⟩ ⟨court ~ four and four⟩ ⟨criticism, like religion, inevitably ~*s* into sects and schisms —C.I.Glicksberg⟩ ⟨~ into dissident groups —H.J. Laski⟩ **(3) :** *of a suit of cards* : to become divided evenly or as nearly so as possible **b :** to sever relations or connections esp. because of disagreement : SEPARATE ⟨~ after six years of marriage⟩ — often used with *with* ⟨had ~ with most of his former friends⟩ or with *from* ⟨caused such a furore by taking in a Negro and *splitting* from the national body —Cleveland Amory⟩ **3 :** to go very fast esp. at a run **4** *slang* : to betray confidence : let out a secret : act as an informer ⟨promised not to ~⟩ — often used with *on* ⟨on the point of *splitting* on the gang —Dorothy Sayers⟩ **5 :** to split one's vote **6 :** to apportion shares ⟨we all ~ equal and that was that —W.L. Gresham⟩ — often used with *with* ⟨said he would ~ with the others⟩ ⟨unwilling to ~ with anyone else⟩ **7 :** to turn up in a split — used of two cards of the same denomination dealt in faro **syn** see TEAR — **split hairs** : to make oversubtle or trivial distinctions : engage in hairsplitting — **split one's sides** : to laugh heartily or immoderately — **split openers** : to discard an essential part of the strength on which one has opened in jackpot — **split straws** : to argue or quarrel over trifling differences — **split tacks** : to tack while an accompanying boat keeps on her course — used of one of two boats or skippers that have been on the same tack — **split the difference** : to reach agreement by compromise involving equal concessions esp. in a disagreement as to a price or to the conclusion of a contract

[2]**split** \"\ *n* -s **1** : a narrow esp. lengthwise break or fissure made by or as if by splitting ⟨a small wedge driven into ~s in either end —Peter Heaton⟩ ⟨a spectacular flight through the deep ~ in the Andes —R.U. & Mary Light⟩ : CLEFT, CRACK, RENT: as **a** (1) : an acute-angled cut made in glassware with a grinding wheel (2) : a check in an article made of glass usu. extending from surface to surface **b** : a lengthwise separation of wood caused by the tearing apart of the wood cells **c** : an earmark on an animal made by slitting the ear — see EARMARK illustration **d** : a position of bowling pins left standing with space for one or more intermediate pins between them — compare RAILROAD **2** : a piece of material that is split off or is made thin by splitting ⟨pegged or nailed the ~s together to get a big enough piece for the door —W.F.Harris⟩: as **a** : a splinter or fragment of wood **b** : a dent in the reed of a loom **c** : any of the underlying sections of a skin made by dividing it into two or more thicknesses **d** : any of the three or four strips into which osiers are cut for some kinds of basketwork — usu. used in pl. **e** : one of two or more narrow fabrics woven as one full-width cloth with selvage strips and then cut apart or split at these strips **3 a** : a breach or separation in an organized or normally cohesive group (as a political party or sect) or between partners or friends : DIVISION; *also* : a faction formed by such separation ⟨another ~ would just about end the party —S.H.Adams⟩ ⟨the ~ in the ranks of the Communist critics —C.I.Glicksberg⟩ ⟨exploiting ~s in the enemy camp —K.T.Chang⟩ ⟨a major ~ between the United States and most of the rest of the free world —McGeorge Bundy⟩ ⟨a rumored ~ between a famous acting couple⟩ **b** : any separation or division into or between esp. divergent or antagonistic elements or forces ⟨the ~ between the integrating and disintegrating tendencies —Lewis Mumford⟩ ⟨the fatal ~ between intellect and emotions —Hans Meyerhoff⟩ ⟨moral and religious ~s that are found in our very makeup as persons —John Dewey⟩ ⟨a very substantial ~ between the anxious egghead and the . . . lowbrow —Rosanna Shamray⟩ ⟨a ~ in his personality⟩ **4** : the act or process of splitting: as **a** : a feat or the movement of lowering oneself to the floor (as by a dancer) or of leaping into the air (as by a gymnast or a figure skater) with the legs extended one to each side or one forward and one backward at right angles to the trunk **b** : the dealing of two cards of the same denomination in the same turn in faro with the result that the dealer takes half the bets on the card of that denomination **c** : SPLIT SHOT **d** : the act or process of splitting the stock of a corporation ⟨recent stock ~s —*Investor's Reader*⟩ ⟨approved a five-for-one ~ of the common stock —Richard Butter⟩ **5** *Brit* **a** : INFORMER **b** : PLAINCLOTHESMAN **6** : a product of division by or as if by splitting: as **a** : any of the air currents in a mine formed by dividing a larger current; *also* : the workings ventilated by such a current **b** : a coal seam separated from another seam by a thick parting **c** *Brit* : a split roll or bun ⟨tea and cider passed around with cakes and ~s —A.T.Quiller-Couch⟩ **7 a** : a small bottle (of some drink) containing about half the quantity of the customary smaller commercial bottle used for that drink; *also* : a drink of half the usual quantity : half glass **b** : a brick of full length and width but half the usual thickness **c** : a share (as of booty, winnings, profits) claimed or promised **d** : an offset on a bulb (as in the narcissus) **e** (1) : the manner in which a suit is divided among the players in a card game (2) : an as nearly as possible even division of cards (as when four are divided 2-2 or five are divided 3-2) **f** : a piece of a bisected stamp **8** : a mixed sweet composed of sliced fruit (as a banana divided lengthwise), ice cream, nuts, and syrups **syn** see BREACH

[3]**split** \"\ *adj* **1** : CLEFT, DIVIDED, FRACTURED, ⟨~ collarbone⟩ ⟨~ lip⟩ ⟨came from a ~ home⟩ ⟨took a ~ vacation⟩ ⟨a badly ~ people⟩ ⟨was ~ between love and hatred —Carson McCullers⟩ ⟨were ~ on the question of women's rights⟩ ⟨executives betray a curiously ~ feeling —W.H.Whyte⟩ **2** : that has been split or split off for use either singly or in combination ⟨fishing rod of ~ bamboo⟩ ⟨~ bandage⟩ ⟨~ hides⟩ **3 a** *of a stock* : that has been split ⟨~ shares⟩ ⟨a ~ issue⟩ **b** *of an order to buy or sell stock* : divided for execution part at one time and price and part at another **c** *of a stock quotation* : given in sixteenths rather than eighths **d** : divided on the London stock exchange into preferred ordinary stock and deferred ordinary stock **4** *of color printing* : using or done by means of a roller or ink fountain divided or adjusted to print two or more separate colors simultaneously ⟨~ fountain work⟩ ⟨~ roller method⟩ **5** *of a network or channel* : broken up to handle more than one program simultaneously **6** : HETEROZYGOUS — used esp. by breeders of cage birds sometimes with *for* ⟨~ for both Cinnamon and Opaline —*All-Pets Mag.*⟩

splitbeak \'⸗,⸗\ *n* : a touraco of the genus *Crinifer*

split bearing *or* **split box** *n* : a shaft bearing made in two pieces that are bolted together

split-board \'⸗;⸗\ *adj* : of or constituting a form of book construction in which the sewing tapes are anchored between laminated cover boards

split bond *n* : a bond in masonry that is formed by using face stretchers that are split lengthwise

split-bottom \'⸗;⸗⸗\ *also* **split-bottomed** \'⸗;⸗⸗\ *adj* : having a seat made of splits ⟨*split-bottom* chair⟩

split brilliant *n* : DOUBLE BRILLIANT

split buck *n* : an offensive play in football in which the quarterback fakes the ball to a back making a cross buck and then hands it to the fullback who goes through the opposite side of the line

split call *n* : a telephone call on a party line that sounds on only half the telephones on the line

split chuck *n* : a hollow spring collet divided through the front into three equally spaced parts

split decision *n* : a decision in a boxing match reflecting a division of opinion among the referee and judges ⟨won a 10-round *split decision*⟩

split die *n* **1** : a cutting or shaping die made in halves for convenience in making and economy in maintenance **2** : a screw-thread die made in one piece with a slit from the outside to the central hole that makes it adjustable as to size

split-down \'⸗,⸗\ *n* -s : the conversion of the outstanding shares of corporation stock into fewer shares

split fence *n* : a strong weighted V-shaped cribwork built on a hillside to deflect an avalanche

splitfinger \'⸗,⸗⸗\ *n* : a West Indian stomatopod crustacean (*Gonodactylus oerstedii*) that often cuts the fingers of its captor with its claws

split flag *n* : a swallow-tailed flag

split flap *n* : a hinged flap attached to the upper surface of a wing of an airplane usu. at the trailing edge to be raised for lateral control or to the lower surface of a wing to be deflected downward for giving increased lift and drag

split-foot \'⸗;⸗\ *adj, of hosiery* : having the sole and instep knitted of different yarns

split fraction *n, chiefly Brit* : PIECE FRACTION

split-hair \'⸗;⸗\ *adj* : minutely exact or precise ⟨this was *split-hair* stuff, this was walking tightrope on a split hair —Ira Wolfert⟩ ⟨a real model railroad runs to a *split-hair* schedule —J.C.Furnas⟩

split-half \'⸗;⸗\ *adj* : relating to, employing, or constituting a method of determining the reliability of a test by dividing the whole test into two halves presumably equivalent in difficulty and scoring the two halves separately ⟨*split-half* techniques⟩ ⟨*split-half* reliability⟩ ⟨*split-half* coefficients⟩

split hand *n* : a hand at bridge with no short suit : hand whose four suits are divided 4-3-3-3

split infinitive *n* : an infinitive with *to* having a modifier between the *to* and the verbal (as in "he hopes to really start")

split joint *n* : TONGUE JOINT

split jump *n* : a jump executed (as by a dancer) with legs extended horizontally and separated by 180 degrees

split key *n* : a key split at one end like a split pin and having similar uses

split kick *n* : a kick executed (as by a dancer) by raising a leg vertically upward

split-knob insulator \'⸗;⸗-\ *n* : a knob-shaped insulator split into two parts with either or both of the opposing surfaces notched for wires — see INSULATOR illustration

[1]**split-level** \'⸗;⸗⸗\ *adj* : divided vertically so that the floor level of rooms in one part is approximately midway between the levels of two successive stories in an adjoining part — used esp. of a dwelling with a one-story portion adjoining a two-story wing ⟨*split-level* design⟩ ⟨*split-level* architecture⟩ ⟨*split-level* house trailers⟩

[2]**split-level** \"\ *n* : a split-level house

split-level in cross section

split-lift \'⸗,⸗\ *n* : the piece of leather in a heel that attaches directly to the sole and is farthest from the top lift

split link *n* : a metal link consisting of two complete turns of a helix pressed flat together

split lug *n* : a lugsail divided below the yard along the line of the mast so that the forward part is practically a jib or foresail with its tack made fast in the bows and its clew shifted by sheets — see LUGSAIL illustration

split moss *n* : a moss of the order Andreaeales

split nut *n* : a screw nut split lengthwise so that it may be opened for quick adjustment

split off *vt* : to separate or remove by or as if by splitting ⟨*split* some kindling *off* from a log⟩ ⟨where only part of the assets of the corporation are *split off* into a new corporation —*U. S. Code*⟩ ⟨*split* the carbon dioxide *off*⟩ ~ *vi* : to separate oneself or become separated or removed by or as if by splitting ⟨pink-tinted granite existing in clean-cleaved layers that *split off* true and fine —Charles Rawlings⟩ ⟨ready to *split off* on the slavery question —S.H.Adams⟩ — often used with *from* ⟨blondness *splits off* from long-headedness —Ruth Benedict⟩ ⟨Miami are supposed to have *split off* from the Chippewa —*Amer. Guide Series: Mich.*⟩

split-off \'⸗,⸗\ *n* -s [*split off*] : an act of splitting off or something that is split off from something else ⟨a succession of left-wing *split-offs*⟩; *specif* : a transfer of a distinctive business constituting one of two or more businesses owned by a corporation to another corporation controlled by the former accompanied by a surrender of part of the stock owned by the stockholders in the distributing corporation for stock in the controlled corporation — compare SPIN-OFF, SPLIT-UP

split page *n* : the first page of the second section of a newspaper

split pattern *n* : a pattern for a casting made in two or more pieces and doweled together to permit separate removal

split pea *n* : a dried hulled pea in which the cotyledons usu. split apart

split personality *n* **1** : SCHIZOPHRENIA; *also* : MULTIPLE PERSONALITY **2** : individual or group behavioral characteristics suggestive of the psychic compartmentalization in multiple personality or of the dissociation from reality in schizophrenia ⟨whole nation has had a *split personality* with respect to civil defense — F.P.Zeidler⟩

split phase *n* : the phase difference of two or more currents into which a single-phase alternating current has been divided

split-phase \'⸗;⸗\ *adj* [*split phase*] : relating to or constituting an alternating single-phase current in a divided circuit when there is a difference of phase between the currents in the two branches

split-phase motor *n* : a motor run by a single-phase alternating current by the use of a phase splitter

split pin *n* : a pin or small cotter with one end split so that it may be spread open to prevent slacking back; *also* : SPRING COTTER

split pit *n* : a breakdown of various peaches caused by inherent weakness and marked by cracking and irregular breakup of the pit and degeneration of the embryo into a gummy mass often accompanied by gummosis of the fruit

split platen *n* : a business-machine platen divided so as to hold a form (as a ledger card) in one section and in the other a continuous listing tape on which is automatically typed or printed information (as credit posted) entered on the form

split pulley *or* **split rigger** *n* : a pulley made in semicircular halves for ease in applying to a shaft — called also *parting pulley*

split rail *n* : a fence rail split from a log

split ring *n* **1** : a metal ring which consists of two complete turns of a helix pressed flat together and upon which objects (as keys) may be strung **2** : a primitive form of commutator for a dynamo or motor consisting of a simple ring or cylindrical shell split axially with the parts insulated from each other **3** : a metal ring used often along with bolts as a timber connector in heavy construction

split rivet *n* : a rivet with a bifurcated shank

split roof *n* : a roof made from strips split from straight-grained timber

split run *n* : a run (as of a newspaper or magazine) in which something (as an illustration or the wording of an advertisement) is changed part way through the run while remaining in the same position in the issue (as for testing the relative effectiveness of the two pieces of copy)

split S *n, often cap 2d S* : a flight maneuver consisting of a half snap roll followed by a pullout to normal flight and accomplishing a 180 degree change in direction accompanied by a loss in altitude

split rivet

splits *pres 3d sing of* SPLIT, *pl of* SPLIT

splitsaw \'⸗,⸗\ *n* : RIPSAW

split scene *n* : a scene on the Elizabethan stage begun in the alcove but extending to the whole stage

split-scion graft \'⸗;⸗⸗-\ *n* : a modified veneer graft in which the scion is split to form two scions

split screen *n* : a technique for projecting onto a television screen images from two cameras side by side or composed into a single picture

split second *n* : a fractional part of a second : any almost imperceptible period of time : FLASH, INSTANT ⟨happened in a *split second*⟩ ⟨one *split second* of surprise —Margery Sharp⟩

split-second *adj* : requiring a split second; *also* : requiring instantaneous precision ⟨*split-second* timing⟩

split-second watch *n* : a stopwatch with two independently controlled sweep-second hands

split session *n* : a regular session of a legislature divided into a preliminary session for organization and introduction of bills, a period of adjournment (as for discussion of proposed legislation with constituents), and a final session for enactment of legislation

split shift *n* : a shift of working hours divided into two or more working periods at times (as morning and evening) separated by more than normal periods of time off (as for lunch or rest)

split shot *or* **split stroke** *n* : a shot or stroke in croquet in which a player drives in different directions his own ball and another ball placed in contact

split shovel *n* : a device for sampling ground ore consisting of a series of parallel troughs separated by gaps of the same width as the troughs and provided with a handle for lifting

split skin *n* **1** : a skin cut open along the belly and legs and spread out flat for drying **2** : leather made from hides of large mammals whose skins are too thick in the natural state and are split into thinner layers for tanning

split stitch *n* : a fine chain stitch for outlining that is formed by bringing the needle through a soft thread

splitstone \'⸗,⸗\ *adj* : made of stones split along the bedding planes into units from one to six feet long and about four inches thick and having a height of one, two or three courses of brick ⟨~ hearth⟩ ⟨~ finish⟩

split switch *n* : a track structure used to divert rolling stock from one railroad track to another and consisting essentially of two movable point rails with necessary fixtures

split T *or* **split T formation** *n* : a variation of the football T formation in which the quarterback either moves along the line of scrimmage with the ball or keeps or pitches the ball depending on the play of the on side end

splittail \'⸗,⸗\ *n* **1** : a California market fish (*Pogonichthys macrolepidotus*) of the family Cyprinidae **2** : PINTAIL **3** : a tail in which some of the feathers are out of line

split-tail perch *n* : either of two surf fishes (*Phanerodon furcatus* or *Damalichthys vacca*) of the Pacific coast of No. America that have deeply forked tails and are common market fishes in California

splitted *archaic past of* SPLIT

[1]**split·ter** \'splid·ə(r), -itə-\ *n or vb* [LG *splittere*, fr. MLG; akin to MLG *spliten* to split — more at SPLIT] : SPLINTER

[2]**splitter** \"\ *n* -s [[1]*split* + *-er*] **1** : one that splits: **a** : a person (as a workman) who splits something: as (1) : a textile worker who splits warps according to the pattern for each beam (2) : an operator of a hide-splitting machine (3) : one that uses a resaw or a ripsaw (4) : one that splits plant shoots into strips for use in basketry (5) : a slaughterhouse worker who by sawing and cleaving lengthwise splits the backbone and neckbone of a cattle or hog carcass **b** : a device or an implement used in splitting something: as (1) : a tool used in splitting the edge of a plate in caulking before finally closing up the part so split (2) : a machine for splitting a hide or skin into two or more thicknesses (3) : a small narrow chisel used by stonemasons (as in carving, lettering) (4) : a butcher's implement for splitting a carcass (5) : any of various devices (as a riffle, a split shovel) for dividing a stream (as of water, ore, earth) into two or more parts **2 a** : one that makes overnice distinctions : HAIRSPLITTER; *also* : one that diffuses his efforts among many interests and accomplishes little : INCOMPETENT **b** : a taxonomist that regards every identifiable variant of living matter as a significant nameable natural unit — compare LUMPER

splitter·man \'⸗⸗mən\ *n, pl* **splittermen 1** : an operator of a machine for cutting defects from wood and splitting it to size for pulp-making machines **2** : BOLTER

split thumb *n* : SPLITFINGER

split ticket *n* : a ticket or ballot cast by a voter who splits his vote : ballot on which the voter has voted for candidates of more than one party — compare STRAIGHT TICKET

[1]**splitting** *adj* [fr. pres. part. of [1]*split*] : that splits or causes to split: as **a** : causing a sensation of rending or piercing : very severe ⟨a ~ headache⟩ **b** : very fast or quick **c** : causing one's sides to split : very funny or comical ⟨~ farce⟩ ⟨~ laugh⟩

[2]**splitting** *n* -s [fr. gerund of [1]*split*] : something split off — usu. used in pl. ⟨~s of mica⟩

splitting chisel *n* : a steel chisel used by a stonecutter

splitting gun *n* : a pointed steel cylinder that is hollow for half its length and is used for splitting very large logs by means of an explosive charge of black powder that is loaded into the pointed end which is then driven into the center end of a log and the powder ignited

splitting plate *n* : a plate used for dividing a mold into halves (as in casting split pulleys)

split turning *n* : a turning (as of a baluster) split vertically and applied decoratively (as to the surface of a chest or cupboard) or used as a spindle in a chairback

[1]**split-up** \'⸗,⸗\ *n* -s [fr. *split up*, v.] **1** : an act or result of splitting up : SEPARATION ⟨*split-up* of the Roman Empire —Sebastian De Grazia⟩ ⟨trying desperately to avoid a domestic *split-up*⟩ **2 a** : the act or process of splitting the stock of a corporation : SPLIT ⟨stock *split-ups* and stock dividends⟩ ⟨a tax-free *split-up*⟩ **b** : the breaking up of a corporation or interrelated group of corporations by legal compulsion or otherwise ⟨*split-up* of utility holding companies⟩ **c** : a transfer of a distinctive business constituting one of two or more businesses owned by a corporation to another corporation controlled by the former accompanied by the surrender of all stock owned by stockholders in the distributing corporation for new stock in both that and in the controlled corporations — compare SPIN-OFF, SPLIT-OFF

[2]**split-up** \'⸗;⸗\ *adj, of the hindquarters of a horse* : lacking substance : SHORT, NARROW; *esp* : lacking sound muscular development between the thighs

split vision *n* : an apparent ability to see out of the opposite corners of the two eyes at the same time : extraordinarily acute peripheral vision

split wheel *n* : SPLIT PULLEY

split wing *n* : a severely slipped wing

splitworm \'⸗,⸗\ *n* : POTATO TUBERWORM

[1]**splodge** \'spläj\ *n* -s [prob. alter. of [1]*splotch*] *chiefly Brit* : SPLOTCH ⟨rook dropped a ~ —Enid Bagnold⟩ ⟨thin green ~ of slime —Stephen Spender⟩

[2]**splodge** \"\ *vb* -ED/-ING/-S *vt, chiefly Brit* : SPLOTCH ⟨newsboys . . . trying to sell a few fresh-*splodged* violet words . . . that told us nothing at all —H.E.Bates⟩ ~ *vi, chiefly Brit* : SPLASH, SLOSH ⟨*splodged* about the streets —A.L.Rowse⟩

splodgy \-jē, -ji\ *adj* -ER/-EST *chiefly Brit* : SPLOTCHY ⟨big ~ brown hands —R.A.W.Hughes⟩

[1]**splore** \'splō(ə)r, -ȯ(ə)r\ *n* -s [origin unknown] **1** *Scot* **a** : FROLIC, MERRYMAKING, FESTIVITY **b** : a drinking bout : CAROUSAL **2** *Scot* : COMMOTION, BROIL

[2]**splore** \"\ *vi* **1** *Scot* **a** : FROLIC, REVEL **b** : RIOT **2** *Scot* : to make an ostentatious display : BRAG, BOAST

[1]**splosh** \'spläsh\ *vb* -ED/-ING/-ES [by alter.] : SPLASH ⟨~*ed* awkwardly through the black Pacific —E.K.Gann⟩ ⟨~*ed* along the rucked road —Adrian Bell⟩ ⟨~*ed* his feet about in the puddle⟩

[2]**splosh** \"\ *n* -ES **1** : SPLASH ⟨plunge with a great ~ into the great social and political agonies of our time —V.S.Pritchett⟩ **2** *slang* : MONEY

[3]**splosh** \"\ *adv* : with a splash or a splashing sound — often used interjectionally

sploshy \-shē, -shi\ *adj* -ER/-EST : SLOPPY ⟨~ slush⟩

[1]**splotch** \'spläch\ *or* **splatch** \'splach\ *n* -ES [*splotch* perh. blend of *spot* and *blotch*; *splatch* alter. (prob. influenced by *splash*) of *splotch*] : a contrasting patch : BLOT, BLOTCH : DAUB, SMEAR : SPOT, STAIN ⟨~*es* of rust⟩ ⟨a ~ of red paint⟩ ⟨his napkin a white ~ on the rug —Josephine Johnson⟩

[2]**splotch** \"\ *or* **splatch** \"\ *vt* -ED/-ING/-ES : to mark with a splotch : cover with splotches ⟨~*ed* face⟩ ⟨dark mass ~*ed* with white —Erskine Caldwell⟩ ⟨his record is ~*ed* and muddy —R.S.Allen⟩ ⟨paintings . . . ~*ed* with conventionally sharp colors —F.J.Mather⟩

splotch·i·ly \'splächəlē, -li\ *adv* : in a splotchy manner : so as to be splotchy

splotch·i·ness \-chēnəs, -chin-\ *n* -ES : the quality or state of being splotchy

splotchy \-chē, -chi\ *adj* -ER/-EST : covered or marked with splotches

splty *abbr* specialty

splunge \'splənj\ *vb* [blend of [1]*splash* and [1]*plunge*] *dial* : PLUNGE

[1]**splurge** \'splərj, -lə̄j, -ləij\ *n* -s [perh. blend of [1]*splash* and [1]*surge*] **1** : an ostentatious or conspicuous demonstration or effort : burst of activity : great display ⟨without ~ or ostentation —*Fortune*⟩ ⟨last carefree ~s of pre-Depression film production —Arthur Knight⟩ ⟨frontier spirit was having its ~ —V.L.Parrington⟩ ⟨orgy of ~ characteristic of an easy-money period —S.H.Adams⟩ **2 a** : SPLASH ⟨dashing away in a ~ of foam —Rose Macaulay⟩ **b** : SPLOTCH ⟨imperfections . . . such as the ~ of the ink in a print —J.C.Tarr⟩

[2]**splurge** \"\ *vb* -ED/-ING/-S *vi* **1** : to make a showy display ⟨of a grave and orderly demeanor . . . never *splurged* —G.D. Brown⟩ ⟨wild flowers ~ —*Time*⟩ **2** : to indulge oneself in some unusual activity, expense, pleasure, luxury ⟨liked to ~ a bit on weekends⟩ — often used with *on* ⟨*splurged* on a steak and strawberries for dessert —Nancy Wilbur⟩ **3** : to splash heavily : SLOSH ~ *vt* : to spend extravagantly, ostentatiously, or as a self-indulgence ⟨swarming into New Orleans to ~ millions during a five-day sports program —*Newsweek*⟩

splurgy \-jē, -ji\ *adj* -ER/-EST : given to or characterized by ostentatious display or extravagance

splurt \'splərt, 'splə̄t, 'spləit, *usu* \|d.+V\ *vb* -ED/-ING/-S [by alter.] : SPURT

[1]**splut·ter** \'splәd·ə(r), -ətə-\ *n* -s [prob. alter. of [2]*sputter*] **1** : a confused noise (as of hasty speaking) ⟨a few ~s from the other end, then laughter —*N.Y. Herald Tribune*⟩ ⟨an occasional ~ of birds among the leaves —Gerald Durrell⟩ **2** : a loud or violent splashing or sputtering ⟨dumped them overside with a sizzle and a ~ —C.S.Forester⟩ ⟨~ of rain came hissing down the chimney —J.C.Powys⟩ ⟨the flaming ~ of the volcano and the rending crash of the earthquake —W.E.Swinton⟩

²splutter \"\ *vb* -ED/-ING/-S *vi* **1 :** to speak hastily and indistinctly ⟨hardly a man in authority today who does not . . . ~ at some of the restrictions —F.L.Allen⟩ **2 :** to make a series of sudden short crackling or popping sounds **:** SPUTTER ⟨bacon ~*ing* in the kitchen —Jan de Hartog⟩ ⟨steam hammer thudding . . . and the electric arcs ~*ing* —Gavin Casey⟩ **3 :** to hurry noisily **:** BUSTLE ⟨the last bus ~*ed* down the highway —D.C.Peattie⟩ ~ *vt* **1 :** to utter hastily and indistinctly **:** STAMMER ⟨he ~*s* a series of observations and analyses which are individually coherent —Robert Halsband⟩ — often used with *out* or *forth* **2 :** to scatter by or as if by splashing ⟨a plane . . . ~*ing* cannon fire —H.E.Bates⟩

splut·ter·er \-d·ərə(r), -tə-\ *n* -S **:** one that splutters

splut·tery \-rē, -ri\ *adj* **:** marked by spluttering **:** suggestive of spluttering ⟨voice was thin and ~ —Leslie Charteris⟩

SPM *abbr* **1** self-propelled mount **2** short particular meter **3** *often not cap* [L *sine prole mascula*] without male issue **4** smaller profit margin **5** *often not cap* strokes per minute

spn *abbr* specimen

SPO *abbr* sea post office

spode \'spōd\ *n* -S *usu cap* [after Josiah *Spode* †1827 Eng. potter] **:** ceramic ware (as bone china, stone china, or Parian ware) made at the works established by Josiah Spode in 1770 at Stoke on Trent, England

spo·di·um \'spōdēəm\ *n* -S [ME, fr. L, fr. Gk *spodion*, dim. of *spodos* wood ash] **1** *obs* **:** a powder obtained as a product or residue of combustion (as soot from melting metals or vegetable ash) **2 :** bone or animal charcoal; *esp* **:** spent bone black from sugar factories used as fertilizer

spod·o·gram \'spädə,gram\ *n* [Gk *spodos* wood ash + E *-gram*] **:** a preparation of ash esp. of a woody portion of a plant that is used in investigating structure and the location of minerals in the plant

spo·dop·tera \spə'däptərə\ *n, cap* [NL, fr. Gk *spodos* wood ash + NL *-ptera*] **:** a genus of noctuid moths whose larvae are armyworms (as the fall armyworm) that include numerous economically important pests

spod·u·mene \'späjə,mēn\ *n* -S [prob. fr. F *spodumène*, fr. G *spodumen*, fr. Gk *spodoumenos*, pres. part. of *spodousthai* to be burnt to ashes, fr. *spodos* wood ash; fr. its becoming ash-colored when exposed to the blowpipe] **:** a monoclinic mineral $LiAlSi_2O_6$ of the pyroxene group that is a lithium aluminum silicate of white to yellowish, purplish, or emerald-green color and that occurs in prismatic crystals often of great size (hardness 6.5–7, sp. gr. 3.13–3.20) — see HIDDENITE, KUNZITE

spof·fish \'späfish\ *adj* [prob. fr. E dial. *spoffle* (alter. of *spuffle*) + E *-ish*] **:** FUSSBUDGETY

¹spoil \'spȯil, *esp before pause or consonant* -ȯiəl; *dial* 'spī(ə)l\ *n* -S [ME *spoile*, fr. MF *espoille*, *espuille*, fr. L *spolium* hide stripped from an animal, armor stripped from an enemy, booty— more at SPILL] **1 a** (1) **:** the plunder taken in war **:** material, land, or property seized or confiscated by the victor of an armed aggression ⟨claim . . . colonies in Africa as its share of the ~*s* of war —Vera M. Dean⟩ ⟨courts his future wife knowing he has already won her as a ~ of war —Richard Corliss⟩ (2) **:** arms or armor stripped from a defeated enemy **b :** something taken unlawfully usu. by stealth ⟨steal from the rich and give the ~*s* to the poor —E.V.Lucas⟩ **2 a :** the act or practice of plundering **:** SPOLIATION ⟨would have given their town up to ~ —Sir Walter Scott⟩ **b** *obs* **:** an act of plunder ⟨the man that hath no music in himself . . . is fit for treason, stratagems, and ~*s* —Shak.⟩ **c :** an object of plunder ⟨fire the palace, the fort . . . leave to the foeman no ~ at all —Rudyard Kipling⟩ **3 a** *obs* **:** an injurious or destructive act **b :** the act of damaging **:** HARM, IMPAIRMENT, RUIN ⟨villainous company hath been the ~ of me —Shak.⟩ **4 a** *obs* **:** the cast skin of a snake **:** SLOUGH **b :** the cast skin of an animal; *also* **:** a treated animal hide ⟨moccasins of the ~ of deer⟩ **c spoils** *pl* **:** animal remains **5 a :** something that is gained by strength or special effort ⟨the ~*s* of a conservative industrial life —Van Wyck Brooks⟩ **b :** a collector's item (as an antique, rare book, or natural specimen) acquired by special and knowledgeable skill or search **6 :** public offices and their emoluments that are the peculiar property of a successful political party or faction to be bestowed for its own advantage — usu. used in pl. ⟨patronage and ~*s* . . . have helped to finance complete party machinery —D.D.McKean⟩ ⟨to the victors belong the ~*s* —W.L.Marcy⟩ **7 :** material (as refuse earth or rock) excavated usu. in mining, dredging, or excavating **8** [²*spoil*] **:** something imperfectly made **:** an object having flaws produced in the process of manufacture **9** [²*spoil*] **a :** a deal in spoil five in which no player wins the pool **b :** the act of winning a trick that causes this result

²spoil \"\ *vb* **spoiled** \-ld, -lt\ *or* **spoilt** \-lt\ **spoiled** *or* **spoilt; spoiling; spoils** [ME *spoilen*, fr. MF *espoillier*, fr. L *spoliare*, fr. *spolium* spoil] *vt* **1 a** *archaic* **:** to despoil (an enemy) esp. of armor and weapons on the field of battle **b** *archaic* **:** DIVEST, STRIP — often used with *of* ⟨made to ~ themselves of soiled arms —Edmund Spenser⟩ **2** *archaic* **:** to seize or take possession of by force or violence **:** PLUNDER ⟨enter into a man's house and ~ his goods —Mt 12:29 (AV)⟩ **3 :** to strip by violent means **:** ROB ⟨deliver him that is ~*ed* out of the hand of the oppressor —Jer 21:12 (AV)⟩ ⟨recovery of property of which it has been ~*ed* —W.E.Channing⟩ **4 :** to sack of valuable possessions **:** PILLAGE ⟨bind the strong man and then he will ~ his house —Mt 12:29 (AV)⟩ **5 :** DEPRIVE ⟨I may ~ the Egyptians of a proverb —J.L.Lowes⟩ **6 :** to cut up (a hen) **:** CARVE ⟨think of the pleasure of calling on the hostess for a ruling as to whether one was . . . ~*ing* a hen —Basil Davenport⟩ **7 :** to cause to decay or perish **:** cause to become of little or no use or value **:** seriously impair **:** MAR, RUIN ⟨the whole island . . . was inundated, and much valuable land ~*ed* —J.A.Steers⟩ ⟨more rain had fallen, the hay crop was *spoilt* —George Moore⟩ ⟨these thoughts . . . *spoilt* my sleep —Nevil Shute⟩ **8 a** *archaic* **:** DESTROY, KILL ⟨go down . . . and ~ them until the morning light, and let us not leave a man of them —1 Sam 14:36 (AV)⟩ **b** *obs* **:** to injure seriously **9 :** RAVISH ⟨am quite sure he would not ~ a virgin —Raymond Chandler⟩ **10 a :** to impair or injure the disposition or character of (a person) usu. by overindulgence, excessive adulation, or praise ⟨~*ed* by the high status accorded to them in their communities —Will Durant⟩ ⟨our only little girl, and . . . we ~ her —Margaret Deland⟩ **b :** to pamper excessively **:** CODDLE ~ *vi* **1 :** to practice plunder and robbery **2 :** to lose the best or valuable properties or qualities **:** become corrupted or tainted ⟨fruit will soon ~ in warm weather⟩ **3 :** to have an excessive desire esp. as a result of long deprivation **:** be extremely eager — usu. used with *for* ⟨was ~*ing* for a fight —Earle Birney⟩ **4 :** to play a defensive game often with marked emphasis on the thwarting of the opponents' efforts to start offensive movements ⟨~*ing* in soccer by constantly kicking the ball out of play⟩ **syn** see DECAY, INDULGE, INJURE

spoil·able \-ləbəl\ *adj* **:** capable of spoiling or of being spoiled

spoil·age \-lij, -lēj\ *n* -S **1 a :** the act of spoiling **b :** something that is spoiled or wasted (as sheets of paper in printing) **2 :** the process of decaying in foods esp. when caused by bacterial or fungal infection

spoil·a·tion \spȯi'lāshən\ *n* -S [alter. (influenced by ²*spoil*) of *spoliation*] **:** SPOLIATION

spoil bank *n* **:** a bank composed of excavated earth

spoil·er \'spȯilə(r)\ *n* -S [²*spoil* + *-er*] **1 :** one that spoils: as **a :** one that plunders **:** PILLAGER, ROBBER ⟨estates soon became very great, tempting the ~ —G.G.Coulton⟩ **b :** one that corrupts, impairs, injures, or makes useless **2 :** a long narrow hinged or retractable plate that extends along the upper surface of an airplane wing and that may be raised above the surface for reducing the lift of the wing and increasing its drag

spoil five *n* [²*spoil* + *five;* fr. the rule that the game is spoiled if no one wins three of the five tricks] **:** a card game in which a pool is won by a player who wins three of the five tricks with a bonus for winning all five

spoil ground *n* **:** an area where excavated material is deposited

spoil heap *n* **:** a pile of refuse material from an excavation

spoil·ing \'spȯiliŋ\ *n* -S [ME, fr. gerund of *spoilen* to spoil] **:** an act of plundering or pillaging **:** a marauding raid

spoiling attack *n* [fr. *spoiling*, pres. part. of ²*spoil*] **:** a limited objective attack launched to disrupt enemy plans or operations

spoil-mold \'=,=\ *n* **:** WASTE MOLD

spoilsman \'=mən\ *n, pl* **spoilsmen** [*spoils* (pl. of ¹*spoil*) + *man*] **:** one who serves a cause or a party for a share of the spoils **:** one who makes or recognizes a demand for public office on the ground of partisan service

spoilsport \'=,=\ *n* [²*spoil* + *sport*] **:** one who spoils or mars sport or diversion ⟨was ~ enough to ask where the money was to come from —*Time*⟩

spoils system *n* **:** a practice of regarding public offices and their emoluments as so much plunder to be taken from the defeated party and distributed to members of the victorious party — opposed to *merit system*

spo·kan *or* **spo·kane** \spō'kan\ *n, pl* **spokan** *or* **spokans** *or* **spokane** *or* **spokanes** *usu cap* **1 a :** a Salishan people of northeastern Washington **b :** a member of such people **2 :** a dialect of Kalispel

spo·kane \(')spō¦kan, -aa(ə)n, *by outsiders also* -kān\ *adj, usu cap* [fr. *Spokane*, city of eastern Wash.] **:** of or from the city of Spokane, Wash. ⟨*Spokane* churches⟩ **:** of the kind or style prevalent in Spokane

spo·kan·ite \-,nīt\ *n* -S *cap* [*Spokane*, city of Wash. + E *-ite*] **:** a native or resident of Spokane, Wash.

¹spoke [ME *spoken* (past pl. & past part.), alter. of *speken* (past pl. & past part.), fr. OE *spǣcon* (past pl.), *gespecen* (past part.)] *past & archaic past part of* SPEAK

²spoke \'spōk\ *n* -S [ME *spake, spoke*, fr. OE *spāca;* akin to OS *spēca* spoke, MD *speke, speec*, OHG *speicha*, MD *spike* spike — more at SPIKE] **1 a :** the radius of a wheel **:** one of the small bars inserted in the hub of a wheel that serve to support the rim **:** a radiating bar or rod on a wheel — see WHEEL illustration **b :** something resembling a wheel spoke **2 :** a bar or rod designed to serve a specific purpose: as **a :** a rung of a ladder **b :** one of the poles used for bearing a coffin to the grave **c :** BALUSTER 1 ⟨the entrance hall was visible through the bannisters' ~*s* —Kay Boyle⟩ **3 :** one of the projecting handles of a steering wheel of a boat **4 a :** a bar of wood or metal to prevent the wheel of a vehicle from turning esp. in going downhill **:** CHOCK **b :** something that impedes **:** an obstacle to a course of action **:** OBSTRUCTION ⟨careless mistakes may be the ~ in the wheel of his advancement⟩ **5 :** STAKE 11 **6 :** a bar in drawnwork consisting of a solid row of buttonholing or overcasting across several threads **7 :** the length of rope that passes through the honda to the hand when spinning the rope

³spoke \"\ *vb* -ED/-ING/-S *vt* **1 :** to furnish with or as if with spokes **2 :** to block or impede with or as if with a spoke ⟨the scheme was my scheme and you might easily have *spoked* my wheel —F.W.Crofts⟩ ~ *vi* **:** to jut out like a spoke ⟨another road that *spoked* into their own —Thomas Wolfe⟩

⁴spoke *n* -S [prob. fr. ¹*spoke*, past part. of *speak*] **1** *dial Eng* **:** TALE, SPEECH **2** *dial Eng* **:** ENCHANTMENT

spoke auger *n* [²*spoke*] **:** a hollow cutter for forming a round tenon on the end of a spoke

spoke·less \-kləs\ *adj* [²*spoke* + *-less*] **:** having no spokes ⟨wagons with ~ wooden wheels —Alan Moore⟩

spo·ken \'spōkən\ *adj* [fr. past part. of ¹*speak*] **1 a :** expressed, told, or delivered by word of mouth **:** ORAL ⟨a ~ message⟩ **b :** used in speaking or conversation **:** UTTERED ⟨the ~ language⟩ **2 :** characterized by speaking in a specified manner — used in combination ⟨the Welsh-*spoken* schoolmaster —Gilbert Highet⟩ ⟨soft-*spoken*⟩ ⟨plain*spoken*⟩

spokeshave \'=,=\ *n* [²*spoke* + *shave*] **1 :** a drawknife or small transverse plane with end handles for planing convex or concave surfaces **2 :** a notched concave scraper prob. used to shape curved or rounded artifacts

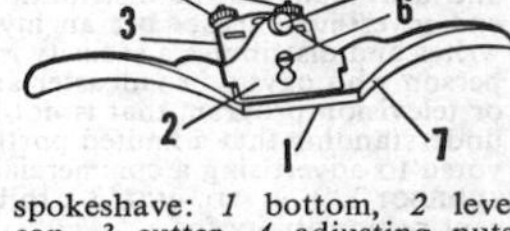

spokeshave: *1* bottom, *2* lever cap, *3* cutter, *4* adjusting nuts, *5* lever cap thumbscrew, *6* lever cap screw, *7* frame and handles

spokes·man \'spōksmən\ *n, pl* **spokesmen** [prob. fr. *spokes* (poss. sing. of ¹*spoke*, past part. of *speak* used as a noun) + *man*] **1 a :** one who speaks as the representative of another; *esp* **:** one delegated by others to express or present their views or opinions publicly ⟨acted as the industry ~ on current problems —*Current Biog.*⟩ ⟨a recognized ~ for the wage earners —William Green⟩ **b :** one that is or becomes an interpreter (as of an era) or an outstanding advocate (as of a cause) ⟨had the chance to become the ~ of the war generation —J.P.Bishop⟩ ⟨great statesmen . . . emerge as personalities and *spokesmen* for ideologies —F.L.Mott⟩ **2 :** one who makes a public address **:** ORATOR, SPEAKER

spokes·man·ship \-n,ship\ *n* **:** the position or status of a spokesman

spokes·woman \'spōks+,-\ *n, pl* **spokeswomen** [*spokes*man + *woman*] **:** a female spokesman

spokewise \'=,=\ *adv* [²*spoke* + *-wise*] **:** in a manner resembling the spokes of a wheel ⟨white dusty trails converge . . . ~ at the small Arab village —George Biddle⟩

spoky *adj* [²*spoke* + *-y*] *obs* **:** having or equipped with parts arranged like the spokes of a wheel

spo·li·ate \'spōlē,āt, *usu* -ād.+V\ *vb* -ED/-ING/-S [L *spoliatus*, past part. of *spoliare* to spoil] *vt* **:** to thoroughly despoil ~ *vi* **:** SPOIL 1 **syn** see RAVAGE

spo·li·a·tion \,==ˈāshən\ *n* -S [ME, fr. L *spoliation-, spoliatio*, fr. *spoliatus* (past part. of *spoliare* to plunder) + *-ion-, -io* -ion — more at SPOIL] **1 a :** the act of plundering **:** pillage or robbery in war **:** DESPOLIATION **b :** the state of having been despoiled or pillaged **2** *eccl & canon law* **a :** the appropriation of the fruits of a benefice whose incumbent has not yet resigned by one duly presented and instituted **b :** a process or writ for possession of a church or its fruits **3 :** injury done to or change made in a document by a stranger to the document — distinguished from *alteration* **4 :** the act of damaging or injuring esp. beyond reclaim or recovery ⟨the ~ of a magnificent piece of scenery —*Scots Mag.*⟩ **5 :** the destruction of a ship's papers or other documents showing its character and the nature of its business usu. when it is suspected of smuggling, carrying contraband of war, or being an enemy's ship

spo·li·a·tor \'==,ād·ə(r)\ *n* -S [L, fr. *spoliatus* + *-or*] **:** one that spoliates **:** SPOILER

spo·li·a·to·ry \'spōlēə,tōrē\ *adj* [L *spoliatus* + E *-ory*] **:** of, relating to, or characterized by spoliation

¹spon·da·ic \(')spän¦dāik, -āek\ *also* **spon·da·i·cal** \-ākəl, -āekəl\ *adj* [*spondaic* fr. F or LL; F *spondaïque* fr. LL *spondaicus*, alter. of *spondiacus*, fr. Gk *spondeiakos*, fr. *spondeios* spondee; *spondaical* fr. LL *spondaicus* + E *-al*] **:** of, relating to, or constituting a spondee **:** consisting of spondees **:** characterized by spondees

²spondaic \"\ *n* -S **:** SPONDEE

spondaic hexameter *n* **:** a hexameter having a spondee instead of a dactyl in the fifth foot

spon·da·ize \'spändā,īz\ *vt* -ED/-ING/-S [*spondaic* + *-ize*] **:** to make spondaic

spon·de·an \spän'dēən, '===\ *adj* [L *spondeum* spondee + E *-an*] **:** having, consisting of, or characterized by spondees

spon·dee \'spän¦dē\ *n* -S [ME *sponde*, fr. MF or L; MF *spondée*, fr. L *spondeum*, fr. Gk *spondeios*, fr. *spondeios* of a libation, fr. *spondē* libation; fr. its use in the solemn music accompanying a libation — more at SPOUSE] **:** a foot consisting of two long or stressed syllables — symbol – – or óó

spon·di·a·ce·ae \,spändē'āsē,ē\ [NL, fr. *Spondias* + *-aceae*] *syn of* ANACARDIACEAE

spon·di·as \'spändē,as\ *n, cap* [NL, fr. Gk *spondias, spodias* bullace] **:** a small genus of tropical trees (family Anacardiaceae) having pinnate leaves and small flowers in terminal panicles, a free ovary that becomes in fruit a fleshy drupe, and astringent leaves and bark — see CIRUELA, HOG PLUM, MOMBIN, OTAHEITE APPLE

spon·du·licks *or* **spon·du·lix** \spän'düliks\ *n pl* [origin unknown] **1** *archaic* **:** FRACTIONAL CURRENCY **2 :** MONEY, FUNDS ⟨you certainly made the ~ fly —Joyce Cary⟩

spon·dyl \'spänd°l\ *or* **spon·dyle** \-n,dīl\ *n* -S [ME *spondyle*, fr. MF, fr. L *spondylus*, fr. Gk *sphondylos, spondylos* vertebra, whorl of a spindle, muscle of a bivalve, a kind of mussel; akin to Gk *sphendonē* sling, *sphadazein* to jerk, be restless, Skt *spandate* he quivers, MHG *spat* spavin] **1** *obs* **:** VERTEBRA **2 :** SPINY OYSTER

spondyl- *or* **spondylo-** *comb form* [Gk *spondylos* spondyl, whorl] **1 :** vertebra ⟨*spondyl*algia⟩ ⟨*spondylo*tomy⟩ **2 :** whorl ⟨*Spondylo*morum⟩

-spon·dy·li \'spändə,lī\ *n pl comb form* [NL, fr. L *spondylus* vertebra] **:** animals having (such) vertebrae — in names of higher taxa ⟨Diplo*spondyli*⟩ ⟨Lepo*spondyli*⟩

spon·dyl·ic \(')spän¦dilik\ *adj* [L *spondyl*us vertebra + E *-ic*] **:** VERTEBRAL

¹spon·dy·lid \'spändələd\ *adj* [NL *Spondylidae*] **:** of or belonging to the Spondylidae

²spondylid \"\ *n* -S **:** a mollusk of the family Spondylidae

spon·dyl·i·dae \spän'dilə,dē\ *n pl, cap* [NL, fr. *Spondylus*, type genus + *-idae*] **:** a family of marine bivalve mollusks (order Filibranchia) comprising the spiny oysters

¹spon·dyl·it·ic \,spändə¦lid·ik\ *adj* [NL *spondyliti*s + E *-ic*] **1 :** of or relating to spondylitis **2 :** affected with spondylitis ⟨~ soldiers⟩

²spondylitic \"\ *n* -S **:** a person affected with spondylitis

spon·dy·li·tis \,spändə'līd·əs\ *n* -ES [NL, fr. *spondyl-* + *-itis*] **:** inflammation of the vertebrae ⟨tuberculous ~⟩ — see RHEUMATOID SPONDYLITIS

spon·dyl·i·um \spän'dilēəm\ *n, pl* **spondyl·ia** \-ēə\ [NL, fr. Gk *spondylion*, fr. *spondylos* muscle of a bivalve — more at SPONDYL] **:** a curved median plate for muscle attachment in the posterior part of one or both valves of a brachiopod

spon·dy·lo·cla·di·um \,spändəlō'klādēəm\ *n, cap* [NL, fr. *spondyl-* + Gk *kladion* twig, dim. of *klados* branch — more at GLADIATOR] **:** a genus of imperfect fungi (family Dematiaceae) characterized by brown septate conidia borne in successive whorls on the conidiophores — see SILVER SCURF

spon·dy·loid \'spändə,lȯid\ *adj* [NL *Spondylus* + E *-oid*] **:** resembling or related to the Spondylidae

spon·dy·lo·lis·the·sis \,spändəlō,lis'thēsəs\ *n* -ES [NL, fr. *spondyl-* + Gk *olisthēsis* dislocation, fr. *olisthanein* to slip, fall — more at SLIDE] **:** forward displacement of a lumbar vertebra and esp. of the fifth lumbar vertebra on the sacrum producing pain by compression of nerve roots

spon·dy·lo·mo·rum \,spändəlō'mōrəm\ *n, cap* [NL, fr. *spondyl-* + L *morum* mulberry — more at MULBERRY] **:** a genus of colonial flagellates related to *Volvox*, having cells with four flagella, two contractile vacuoles, and a cup-shaped chromoplast, forming a 16-celled colony, and sometimes causing a contamination of water supplies

spon·dyl·ous \'spändələs\ *adj* [L *spondyl*us spondyl + E *-ous*] *archaic* **:** VERTEBRAL

spon·dy·lus \"\ *n* [NL, fr. L, a kind of mussel, fr. Gk *spondylos* — more at SPONDYL] **1** *cap* **:** a genus of large, thick, inequivalve, usu. spinose and attached, bivalve mollusks (family Spondylidae) that are remarkable for perfection of the hinge **2** -ES **:** any mollusk of the family Spondylidae **:** SPINY OYSTER

-spon·dy·lus \"\ *n comb form* [NL, fr. L *spondylus* vertebra — more at SPONDYL] **:** animal having (such) vertebrae — in generic names ⟨Palaeo*spondylus*⟩

¹sponge *also* **spunge** \'spənj\ *n* -S *often attrib* [ME *sponge, spounge*, fr. OE *sponge*, fr. L *spongia, spongea*, fr. Gk *spongia;* akin to Gk *spongos* sponge — more at FUNGUS] **1 a :** the elastic porous mass of interlacing horny fibers that forms the internal skeleton of marine animals of low organization belonging to the phylum Porifera (as members of the genera *Hippiospongia* and *Spongia*) and that has great power of absorbing water and becomes soft when wet without losing strength — see GRASS SPONGE, TURKEY SPONGE, VELVET SPONGE, WOOL SPONGE **b :** any one of a large group of chiefly marine animals constituting the phylum Porifera that consist fundamentally of two layers of cells surrounding a central cavity, are permanently attached either solitary or in masses varying greatly in size, shape, color, and consistency, have skeletons composed variously of spongin (as in the commercial sponges) or a siliceous or a calcareous substance the interstices of which are filled with cells and pierced with a system of canals and small cavities opening on the surface through which a current of food-bearing water is maintained by collared flagellated cells lining the canal walls, and reproduce either asexually by budding or sexually by means of egg and sperm cells that form a free-swimming larva — see LEUCON, RHAGON, SYCON **2 a :** a piece of the skeleton of various marine sponges that is used for washing, cleaning, or erasing marks (as of chalk) from blackboards or slates; *also* **:** porous rubber or cellulose material used for washing or swabbing **b** *archaic* **:** something that effaces or blots out existing impressions, memories, or emotions **c** *obs* **:** a process or method of canceling or wiping off indebtedness without making payment **3 a :** a small pad made of multiple folds of gauze or of cotton and gauze used to mop blood from a surgical incision, to carry inhalant medicaments to the nose, or to cover a superficial wound as a dressing **b :** a porous dressing (as of fibrin or gelatin) applied to promote wound healing **c :** a plastic prosthesis used in chest cavities following lung surgery **4 :** a long-handled cylindrical swab for cleaning the bore of a cannon after discharge **5 :** SPONGE BATH **6 a :** a hard drinker **:** DRUNKARD **b :** one who lives upon others **:** a persistently idle or lazy dependent **:** SPONGER **c :** one from whom money may be extorted or information extracted **7 a :** porous elastic soil or a patch of such soil **b :** bread dough after it has been raised or converted into a light porous mass by yeast or leaven **c :** a dessert made light by the incorporation of air usu. through addition of whipped whites of eggs or of gelatin that is whipped after it has jelled ⟨pineapple ~⟩ **d :** LUFFA 3 **e** *obs* **:** pasty iron from a puddling furnace **f :** a metal (as lead, platinum) obtained in porous form usu. by reduction without fusion ⟨titanium ~⟩ — see PLATINUM SPONGE **g :** the egg mass of a crab borne by the female until the larvae hatch **8 :** a light olive brown that is slightly stronger than drab, less strong and slightly redder than average mustard tan, and deeper than the color dust **syn** see PARASITE

²sponge *also* **spunge** \"\ *vb* -ED/-ING/-S [ME *spongen*, fr. ¹*sponge*] *vt* **1 a :** to cleanse or wipe with or as if with a sponge ⟨~ a slate⟩ ⟨~ off his face⟩ ⟨~ the bore of a cannon⟩ **b :** to dampen with a sponge or cloth before ironing ⟨~ trousers⟩ **c :** to spruce up **:** make neat, fresh, and tidy **d :** to apply liquid to with a sponge ⟨~ a patient's back with alcohol⟩ **2 a :** to wipe out (as letters, numbers) with a sponge **:** ERASE, OBLITERATE — used often with *out* ⟨whole paragraphs had been *sponged* out⟩ **b :** to destroy all trace of **:** EFFACE ⟨every stain of his infected and corroding fingers will be *sponged* and . . . blasted from the surface of the earth —Sir Winston Churchill⟩ **3 a :** to stipple (a painted surface) by removing some of the wet paint with a sponge **b :** to decorate (a ceramic surface) by applying mucilaginous pigment with a sponge **c :** to smooth the edges of (ceramic ware) with a damp sponge before firing **4** *obs* **:** to squeeze money or information from **:** extort from **:** DRAIN **5 :** to get (as money, meals, comforts) without cost or return by imposing on generosity or hospitality ⟨nightclub entertainer . . . that ~*s* drinks from the guests —Anthony West⟩ **6 :** to take up or absorb with or as if with a sponge or as a sponge does **:** SOAK, SOP, SWAB — used usu. with *up* ⟨~ up spilled ink⟩ ⟨the state loan . . . managed to ~ up most of the available savings —D.C.McKay⟩ **7 :** to insert a piece of sponge in (a horse's nostril) to impair the breathing and so effect the loss of a race ~ *vi* **1 a :** to absorb, soak up, imbibe like a sponge **b :** to swell out like a sponge **2 a :** to get something at another's cost by imposing on hospitality or good nature ⟨beggar *sponging* for rum —R.L.Stevenson⟩ **b :** to live like a parasite on the generosity of another — usu. used with *on* or *off* ⟨do you expect to go on *sponging* on me the rest of your days —Marcia Davenport⟩ **3 :** to dive or dredge for sponges **4** *of a tobacco leaf* **:** to mottle in curing because of rapid beating or insufficient ventilation

sponge bag *n, Brit* **:** a waterproof case for holding a bath sponge and toilet articles

sponge-bag \'=,=\ *adj, Brit* [*sponge bag;* prob. fr. the frequent use of such fabrics for the outside of sponge bags] **:** CHECKED ⟨*sponge-bag* trousers⟩

sponge bath *n* **:** a bath in which water is applied to the body without actual immersion

sponge biopsy *n* **:** biopsy performed on matter collected with a sponge from a lesion

sponge boat *n* **:** a strongly built sailboat with a high bow used for obtaining sponges

sponge cake *n* **:** a cake made without shortening — distinguished from *butter cake*

sponge cloth *n* **1 :** RATINÉ 2 **2 :** any of various soft porous fabrics loosely woven esp. in honeycomb weave from coarse or nubby yarns and used for clothing, curtains, and cloths for cleaning machinery

sponge crab *n* **1 :** a female crab bearing an egg mass **2 :** any of several crabs commonly found in association with sponges: as **a** (1) **:** GRASS CRAB (2) **:** a crab of the group Dromiacea that decorates its back with sponges or ascidians **b :** any of several hermit crabs of the Pacific coast of No. America that excavate their homes in a living sponge (*Suberites latus*)

sponge finger *n, chiefly Brit* **:** LADYFINGER 2

sponge fly *or* **spongilla fly** *n* [so called fr. its being parasitic in its larva stage on sponges, including those of the genus *Spongilla*] **:** an insect of the family Sisyridae

¹sponge glass *n* **:** a glass-bottomed box or bucket for viewing the sea bottom from the surface in sponge fishing

²sponge glass *n* **:** CELLULAR GLASS

sponge gourd *n* **:** DISHCLOTH GOURD

sponge hook *n* **:** a 3-pronged curved hook attached to a long handle for detaching growing sponges from the bottom

sponge iron *n* **:** iron in porous form or containing many voids; *specif* **:** crude iron made by subjecting the oxide ore to a reducing gas without melting

spongelike \ˈ⸗,⸗\ *adj* **:** resembling a sponge **:** SPONGY, POROUS

sponge mushroom *n* **:** MOREL

spon·geous \ˈspənjəs\ *adj* [ME, fr. L *spongeosus*, fr. *spongea* sponge + *-osus* -ous] *archaic* **:** SPONGY

spong·er \ˈspənjə(r)\ *n* -s **1 :** a man or boat engaged in gathering sponges **2 :** one that sponges something: as **a :** one that smooths greenware with a sponge **b :** an operator of a machine for sponging and shrinking cloth **c :** an operator of a dough-mixing machine **3 :** a parasitical person **:** CADGER ⟨the feckless ~ is held in contempt —*Time*⟩ ⟨easy tolerance of ~*s* looking for a cinch rather than an education —Dixon Wecter⟩ **syn** see PARASITE

sponge rubber *n* **:** porous or cellular rubber resembling a natural sponge in structure that is made usu. by blowing with a gas (as carbon dioxide) liberated during vulcanization by a chemical (as sodium bicarbonate) incorporated in the rubber compound and that is used chiefly in making cushions, vibration dampeners, weather stripping, gaskets, insulation, and other molded products — compare FOAM RUBBER

sponge hooks

sponges *pl of* SPONGE, *pres 3d sing of* SPONGE

sponge tree *n* **:** HUISACHE

spongework \ˈ⸗,⸗\ *n* **:** an irregular pattern of very small interconnecting cavities sometimes produced by solution in cave walls

spongi- *or* **spongio-** *comb form* [L *spongia*] **1 :** sponge ⟨*spongi*colous⟩ ⟨*spongio*logy⟩ **2 :** spongy ⟨*spongio*blast⟩

Spon·gia \ˈspənjēə, ˈspän-\ *n, cap* [NL, fr. L, sponge] **:** a genus of tropical and subtropical sponges that includes various commercially important sponges and is the type of the family Spongiidae

¹-spongia \"\ *n comb form* [NL, fr. L *spongia*] **:** sponge — in generic names of sponges ⟨Astylo*spongia*⟩

²-spongia *pl of* -SPONGIUM

spon·gi·ae \-ē,ē\ [NL, fr. L, pl. of *spongia* sponge] *syn of* PORIFERA

-spongiae \"\ *n pl comb form* [NL, fr. L *spongiae*] **:** sponges — in names of orders and other higher groups of sponges ⟨Silici*spongiae*⟩

spon·gic·o·lous \spənˈjikələs, spän-\ *adj* [*spongi-* + *-colous*] **:** inhabiting sponges

spon·gi·da \ˈspənjədə, ˈspän-\ [NL, irreg. fr. *Spongia* + *-ida*] *syn of* PORIFERA

spon·gi·dae \-jə,dē\ [NL, irreg. fr. *Spongia*, type genus + *-idae*] *syn of* SPONGIIDAE

spongier *comparative of* SPONGY

spongiest *superlative of* SPONGY

spon·gi·idae \spənˈjīə,dē, spän-\ *n pl, cap* [NL, fr. *Spongia*, type genus + *-idae*] **:** a family of horny sponges (order Keratosa) that have solid spongin fibers enclosing an axial core — see SPONGIA

spon·gil·la \spənˈjilə, spän-\ *n, cap* [NL, fr. L *spongia* sponge + NL *-illa*] **:** a genus (the type of the family Spongillidae) of siliceous freshwater sponges that are usu. green in color and form incrustations on submerged objects — **spon·gil·lid** \-ləd\ *n* -s — **spon·gil·line** \-i,lin, -ilən\ *adj*

spongilla fly *var of* SPONGE FLY

spon·gi·ly \ˈspənjəlē\ *adv* **:** in a spongy manner **:** SPRINGILY, POROUSLY

spon·gin \ˈspənjən\ *n* -s [G, fr. L *spongia* sponge + G *-in*] **:** a scleroprotein constituting the chief constituent of the flexible fibers in the skeleton of commercial sponges and in part that of many other sponges

spon·gi·ness \ˈspənjēnəs, -jin-\ *n* -ES **:** the quality or state of being spongy

sponging *n* -s [fr. gerund of ²*sponge*] **1 :** DECATING **2 :** a cold-water or steam treatment for shrinking new woolen goods before cutting out garments

sponging house *n* [*sponging* (gerund of ²*sponge*) + *house*; fr. the extortionate charges made there for food and lodging] **:** a house usu. maintained by a bailiff for keeping debtors for a day to afford opportunity to come to terms with their creditors

spon·ging·ly *adv* [*sponging* (pres. part. of ²*sponge*) + *-ly*] **:** in a sponging manner

spon·gi·o·blast \ˈspənjēō,blast, ˈspän-\ *n* -s [ISV *spongi-* + *-blast*] **1 :** one of the ectodermal cells of the embryonic spinal cord or other nerve center that are at first columnar but become branched at one end and that give rise to the neuroglia cells **2 :** SPONGOBLAST

spon·gi·o·blas·to·ma \,⸗⸗⸗,blaˈstōmə\ *n, pl* **spongioblastomas** *or* **spongioblastoma·ta** \-məd·ə\ [NL, fr. ISV *spongioblast* + *-oma*] **:** a malignant tumor of the central nervous system or the brain composed of spongioblasts

spon·gi·o·cyte \ˈspənjēō,sīt, ˈspän-\ *n* -s [*spongi-* + *-cyte*] **:** a cell of the neuroglia

spon·gi·ol·o·gy \,spənjēˈäləjē, ,spän-\ *or* **spon·gol·o·gy** \späŋˈgä-\ *n* -ES [*spongiology* ISV *spongi-* + *-logy*; *spongology* fr. *spongo-* + *-logy*] **:** the study of sponges

spon·gi·o·plasm \ˈspənjēō,plazəm, ˈspän-\ *n* [ISV *spongi-* + *-plasm*; orig. formed in G] **:** CYTORETICULUM — **spon·gi·o·plas·mic** \,⸗⸗⸗ˈplazmik\ *adj*

spon·gi·o·sa \,spənjēˈōsə, ,spän-\ *n* -s [NL, fr. *substantia spongiosa* spongy substance, fr. L *substantia* substance + *spongiosa*, fem. of *spongiosus* spongious] **:** the part of a bone (as much of the epiphyseal area of long bones) made up of spongy cancellous bone — compare COMPACTA

spon·gi·o·sis \-ˈōsəs\ *n* -ES [NL, fr. *spongi-* + *-osis*] **:** swelling localized in the epidermis and often occurring in eczema

spon·gi·ous \ˈspənjēəs\ *adj* [ME, fr. MF *spongieux*, fr. L *spongiosus*, fr. *spongia* sponge + *-osus* -ous] *archaic* **:** full of small cavities like sponge **:** SPONGY

spon·gi·o·zoa \,spənjēəˈzōə, ,spän-\ [NL, fr. *spongi-* + *-zoa*] *syn of* PORIFERA

-spon·gi·um \ˈspənjēəm, ˈspän-\ *n comb form, pl* **-spon·gia** \-ēə\ [NL, fr. L *spongia* sponge] **:** network of cells or fibrils ⟨neuro*spongium*⟩

spongo- *comb form* [Gk *spong-*, *spongo-*, fr. *spongos* — more at FUNGUS] **:** sponge ⟨*spongo*logy⟩

spon·go·blast \ˈspäŋgō,blast\ *n* [*spongo-* + *-blast*] **:** a cell that produces spongin — **spon·go·blas·tic** \;⸗⸗ˈblastik\ *adj*

spon·go·coel \ˈspäŋgō,sēl\ *n* -s [*spongo-* + *-coel*] **:** the internal cavity of a sponge discharging by way of the osculum

¹spon·goid \ˈspäŋ,gȯid, ˈspəŋ-\ *adj* [Gk *spongoeidēs*, fr. *spongo-* spongo- + *-oeidēs* -oid] **:** resembling sponge **:** SPONGELIKE

²spongoid \"\ *n* -s **:** a spongelike animal or fossil

spon·gos·po·ra \späŋˈgäspərə\ *n, cap* [NL, fr. *spongo-* + *-spora*] **:** a genus of organisms (family Plasmodiophoraceae) resembling the slime molds and characterized by spongelike spore balls each cell of which germinates — see POWDERY SCAB; compare PLASMODIOPHORA

spongy \ˈspənjē, -ji\ *adj* -ER/-EST [¹*sponge* + *-y*] **1 :** having the consistency of a sponge **:** being soft and full of cavities ⟨~ ice⟩ ⟨~ lava⟩ **:** being elastic, porous, and absorbent ⟨~ earth⟩ ⟨~ cheese⟩ ⟨~ roots⟩ **2 :** lacking in strength and solidity **:** not firm or solid ⟨~ area in an iron casting⟩ ⟨~ wood⟩ ⟨~ action of a steering gear⟩ ⟨cities suggest jittery nerves and ~ flesh —A.W.Long⟩ **3 :** moist and soft like a sponge full of water **:** SATURATED, SOGGY ⟨~ clouds⟩ ⟨~ moor⟩

spongy dry rot *n* **:** a dry rot (as of apples) caused by a fungus (*Colletrichum fructus*)

spongy parenchyma *n* **:** loosely and irregularly arranged parenchyma having numerous intercellular spaces found toward the lower surface within many leaves and consisting of irregular, lobed, or stellate cells — compare PALISADE PARENCHYMA

spon·sal \ˈspän(t)səl\ *adj* [L *sponsalis* of a betrothal, spousal — more at ESPOUSAL] **:** SPOUSAL

spon·sa·lia \spänˈsālēə\ *n pl* [L, betrothal — more at ESPOUSAL] **:** a formal promise or contract for a future marriage between persons competent to make such a contract

spon·si·ble \ˈspän(t)səbəl\ *adj* [short for *responsible*] *dial* **:** RESPONSIBLE, RESPECTABLE

spon·sion \ˈspänchən\ *n* -s [L *sponsion-*, *sponsio*, lit., solemn promise, pledge, fr. *sponsus* (past part. of *spondēre* to promise solemnly) + *-ion-*, *-io* -ion — more at SPOUSE] **1** *Roman law* **:** suretyship accessory to oral contracts and available only to Roman citizens **2 :** the act of becoming surety; *esp* **:** a formal pledge made on behalf of another **3 :** an act or engagement on behalf of a state undertaken by an agent not specially authorized or by one who exceeds the limits of his authority and requiring for validity ratification by the state

¹spon·son \ˈspän(t)sən\ *n* -s [prob. by shortening & alter. fr. *expansion*] **:** a projection from the side of a ship or a tank to act as a bearing or protection for some part: as **a :** a structure outside the normal hull of a vessel to give added deck room or stability or protection for paddle wheels or to afford a gun platform **b :** a gun platform projecting from the side of a warship or a tank to give a greater arc of fire **c :** an air chamber along the side of a canoe to increase its stability and buoyancy **d :** a light air-filled structure protruding from the hull of a seaplane to give it steadiness as it rests on water

²sponson \"\ *vt* -ED/-ING/-S **:** to equip with or install on sponsons

¹spon·sor \ˈspän(t)sə(r)\ *n* -s [L, fr. *sponsus* (past part. of *spondēre*) + *-or* — more at SPOUSE] **1** *Roman law* **:** one who binds himself to answer for another's default **:** SURETY **2 :** one who without request intervenes in behalf of another **3** [LL, fr. L, surety] **:** one who at the baptism of an infant or child professes the Christian faith in its name, and guarantees its religious education; *also* **:** one who presents a candidate for confirmation to the bishop **:** GODPARENT **4 :** one who assumes responsibility for some other person or thing: as **a :** one who presents and supports a legislative proposal **b :** an experienced salesclerk or salesperson who instructs and supervises new selling employees **c :** a teacher acting as adviser to a specified student activity ⟨~ to a student council⟩ ⟨homeroom ~⟩ ⟨~ for a class dance⟩ **d :** one who assumes responsibility for a paroled delinquent **5 a :** a corporation that organizes and usu. manages the distribution of the shares of an open-end investment trust **b :** an investment banker who underwrites and distributes a security issue **6 :** a business firm or a person who pays a broadcaster and the performer for a radio or television program that is not in itself commercial with the understanding that a limited portion of the time allotted is devoted to advertising a commercial product

²sponsor \"\ *vt* -ED/-ING/-S **:** to be or stand sponsor for **:** accept responsibility for

spon·so·ri·al \spänˈsōrēəl\ *adj* [¹*sponsor* + *-ial*] **:** of or relating to a sponsor

spon·sor·ship \ˈspän(t)sə(r),ship\ *n* **:** the state of being a sponsor **:** act of sponsoring **:** official or financial support

spon·ta·ne·i·ty \,späntəˈnēəd·ē, |āə-, -ətē, -i *sometimes* -tᵊnˈ|\ *n* -ES [LL *spontaneus* + E *-ity*] **1 :** the quality or state of being spontaneous ⟨the apparent ~ with which a new . . . type of art arose —Herbert Read⟩ ⟨~ of his laughter⟩ **2 :** the source of spontaneous action or expression **:** the quality, innate power, or influence that determines the character ⟨the free play of passion and thought, the graces and arts of life, all that springs from the ~ of nature —G.L.Dickinson⟩

¹spon·ta·ne·ous \spänˈtānēəs\ *adj* [LL *spontaneus*, fr. L *sponte* of one's free will, voluntarily — more at SPIN] **1 :** proceeding from natural feeling or native tendency without external constraint **:** VOLUNTARY ⟨~ expression of affection and gratitude⟩ ⟨a ~ modernist in theology and philosophy —George Santayana⟩ ⟨~ boycott⟩ ⟨~ obedience⟩ **2 :** arising from immediate natural impulse **:** UNPREMEDITATED, IMPULSIVE ⟨~ offer of assistance⟩ ⟨this diary has the ~ quality of a child's observations made for her own pleasure —Ellen L. Buell⟩ ⟨~ improvising on a melody⟩ **3 :** caused by internal energy controlled and directed internally **:** SELF-ACTING ⟨~ movement is characteristic of all living things⟩ ⟨proves that there must be ~ activity as well as derivative activity in the universe —C.H.Whiteley⟩ **4 :** produced without being planted or without human labor **:** NATIVE, INDIGENOUS ⟨~ growth of wood⟩ **5 a :** developing without apparent external influence or force or from some undiscoverable cause ⟨~ nosebleed⟩ ⟨~ fracture⟩ ⟨~ abortion⟩ **b :** not resulting from externally planned or intended modification or treatment ⟨~ remission of nervous symptoms⟩ ⟨~ recovery from a disease⟩ **6 :** occurring or seeming to occur in the natural course of things **:** not apparently contrived or manipulated ⟨the fact that the experiences are ~ and not laboratory products make these cases of the highest importance —W.H.Salter⟩

syn SPONTANEOUS, IMPULSIVE, INSTINCTIVE, AUTOMATIC, and MECHANICAL as applied to human acts (and, with appropriate adjustments, to the person performing the act, excepting possibly the word *automatic*) can mean activated (or acting) without apparent thought or deliberation. SPONTANEOUS applies to acts that come about so naturally, are so unselfconscious and so unaffected or unprompted by ulterior motive or purpose that they seem totally unpremeditated ⟨find ourselves making an immediate and *spontaneous* answer —W.T. Hastings⟩ ⟨his sentiment was *spontaneous* rather than introspective —H.S.Commager⟩ ⟨*spontaneous* laughter⟩ ⟨at ease with us . . . generally gay, always *spontaneous* and natural —Dorothy Bussy⟩ IMPULSIVE applies to apparently involuntary acts actuated suddenly and impetuously on the spur of the momentary feeling or spirit ⟨her childlikeness, her headlong sympathies, the *impulsive* traits that endeared —W.R. Benét⟩ ⟨*impulsive*, reckless and unreliable —A.E.Stevenson b. 1900⟩ INSTINCTIVE stresses the involuntary, often unconscious, character of an instantaneous, spontaneous act, suggesting the compulsion of native predisposition or long conditioning rather than of the will ⟨the *instinctive* movement of his agile frame —Nathaniel Hawthorne⟩ ⟨he did what he did *instinctively* and for no other reason than because it was most natural to him —Samuel Butler †1902⟩ ⟨long and laborious planning to carry out elaborately conceived intellectual effort was not her way. Everything was inborn, *instinctive*, spontaneous —Gamaliel Bradford⟩ AUTOMATIC and MECHANICAL both apply to acts which do not seem to engage the mind. AUTOMATIC usually stresses promptness and invariableness in a response to a given set of stimuli, as from long habit or repetition, often implying a training or discipline and sometimes a precision of response ⟨he said the right thing, performed the appropriate action, so unceasingly, day after day, night after night, that it had become simply *automatic* —Elizabeth Goudge⟩ ⟨his easy, *automatic* smile —Luke Short⟩ ⟨the artist's movements with the pencil were swift and *automatic* — in a few minutes the sketch was complete⟩ MECHANICAL, though it can apply to any act, usu. repeated, performed with little or no conscious ordering of movements, usu. connotes a lifelessness and perfunctoriness of response ⟨shorthand and typewriting, both of which are purely *mechanical* activities —George Sampson⟩ ⟨many of the situations which previously elicited emotional response come to be met in a *mechanical* or routine fashion —J.E.Anderson⟩ ⟨not with any interest or curiosity, but with a dull *mechanical* perception —Charles Dickens⟩

²spontaneous \"\ *adv, archaic* **:** SPONTANEOUSLY ⟨to her lips . . . the minstrel verse ~ came —Sir Walter Scott⟩

spontaneous amputation *n* **:** the spontaneous separation (as in some forms of gangrene) of a necrotic body part

spontaneous combustion *also* **spontaneous ignition** *n* **:** the outbreak of fire in combustible material (as oily rags or damp hay) that occurs without application of direct flame or spark and is usu. caused by slow oxidation processes (as atmospheric oxidation or bacterial fermentation) under conditions not permitting dissipation of heat

spontaneous generation *n* **:** ABIOGENESIS

spon·ta·ne·ous·ly *adv* **:** in a spontaneous manner **:** without external constraint ⟨children . . . will memorize favorite selections ~ —Dorothy Barclay⟩ ⟨woke up ~ at seven-fifteen⟩ **:** without premeditation ⟨acts so ~ that the consequences of his offense do not have time to sink in —R.S.Banay⟩

spontaneous magnetization *n* **:** the magnetization within each magnetic domain of a ferromagnetic substance in the absence of a magnetizing field

spon·ta·ne·ous·ness *n* -ES [¹*spontaneous* + *-ness*] **:** SPONTANEITY

spontaneous recovery *n* **:** reappearance of an extinguished conditioned response without further positive reinforcement

spon·toon \spänˈtün\ *also* **spon·ton** \ˈspäntᵊn\ *or* **es·pon·toon** \,espänˈtün\ *n* -s [F *sponton*, *esponton*, fr. It *spuntone*, *spontone*, fr. *punta* sharp point, fr. (assumed) VL *puncta* — more at POINT] **1 :** a half-pike formerly borne by subordinate officers of infantry **2 :** a policeman's club **:** TRUNCHEON

¹spoof \ˈspüf\ *vb* -ED/-ING/-S [fr. *Spoof*, a hoaxing game invented by Arthur Roberts †1933 Eng. comedian] *vt* **1 :** to deceive by a hoax **:** DELUDE ⟨managed to ~ and terrorize the local officials by impersonating a government inspector —Edmund Stevens⟩ ⟨my old friend had often been ~*ed* but who was still anxious to get at the truth —*Saturday Rev.*⟩ **2 :** to make good-natured fun of often by means of a misrepresentation ⟨the witty screenplay . . . ~*s* this very quality —*Los Angeles (Calif.) Examiner*⟩ ⟨a deft satire . . . it . . . ~*s* traveling salesmen —Amy Loveman⟩ ⟨~ social customs —John McCarten⟩; *also* **:** KID, GUY ⟨they're kidding you . . . don't let them ~ you —Agnes N. Keith⟩ ~ *vi* **1 :** to use or practice deceit ⟨honesty pays . . . if I ~ I shall get found out —Thomas Wood †1950⟩ **2 :** to make fun of a person or thing often by means of a misrepresentation ⟨their type of gently ~*ing* satirical fantasy —*Time*⟩; *also* **:** KID, JOKE ⟨hear a minstrel show man ~ about one oyster in the stew —*Springfield (Mass.) Union*⟩

²spoof \"\ *n* -s **1 a :** HOAX, FEINT ⟨one sees that the whole thing is a clumsy ~ —J.F.Runciman⟩ ⟨one day a supposed ~ might be the real thing —W.R.Frye⟩ **b :** HUMBUG, NONSENSE ⟨only don't try any more ~ about me —Joyce Cary⟩ **2 a :** a light, amiable, humorous, but usu. telling takeoff (as on human nature, customs, or manners) **:** PARODY ⟨a pleasant ~ of all the moonstruck nonsense the movies have been dishing up —John McCarten⟩ ⟨those quiet, unpretentious, but deliciously funny ~*s* of national types and customs —Arthur Knight⟩

spoof·er \-fə(r)\ *n* -s **:** one that spoofs: as **a :** DECEIVER ⟨a ~ is inordinately insincere —*Dalhart (Texas) Texan*⟩ **b :** PARODIST ⟨the ~, the transient bubble-pricker lies in the theatrical deathbed —*Amer. Mercury*⟩

spoof·ery \-fərē\ *n* -ES [²*spoof* + *-ery*] **1 :** DECEIT **2 a :** good-natured ridicule **:** KIDDING, RIBBING ⟨British ~ that is sometimes so gentle that the humor is almost inaudible —*New Yorker*⟩ ⟨a compendium of ~ including cartoons, verse, and prose⟩ **b :** an instance of good-natured ridicule **:** SPOOF 2 ⟨the ballet . . . bringing this ~ of a house party to a realization less anachronistic than a literal reproduction —Irving Kolodin⟩

¹spook \ˈspük *sometimes* ˈspu̇k\ *n* -s [D, fr. MD *spooc*; akin to MLG *spōk* ghost] **1 :** GHOST, SPECTER, APPARITION, HOBGOBLIN ⟨the strange ~ . . . crept out of heaven on a windless night —S.V.Benét⟩; *specif* **:** an apparition in a spiritualistic séance ⟨became a spiritualist, believing in the power of ~*s* —*Amer. Mercury*⟩ **2** *slang* **:** a queer or strange person **:** ODDBALL ⟨a blind date? What is she, a real ~ —Oakley Hall⟩ **3** *slang* **:** GHOST-WRITER ⟨a writer signed to do the movie script as the ~ —Louis Messolonghites⟩ ⟨professional ~ . . . to ghostwrite a novel —David Dempsey⟩ **4** *slang* **:** NEGRO ⟨what's a ~? A Negro — like me —Robert Lowry⟩ ⟨stop talking like a ~ . . . I mean stop talking like most colored folks —Langston Hughes⟩

²spook \"\ *vb* -ED/-ING/-S *vt* **1 :** to inhabit or visit as a spook **:** HAUNT ⟨forces that ~ the old world —W.M.Meredith⟩ **2 a :** to stir up or excite (as a horse or steer) esp. by frightening ⟨if you come up too fast and ~ a deer it takes off —R.E.Maw⟩ ⟨the entire herd got ~*ed* and stampeded into the mountains —H.W.Anderson⟩ **b** *slang* **:** to frighten (a person) often so as to make run, freeze, or tremble **:** SCARE ⟨too shrewd a detective to ~ the pair with direct questions —Chris Edwards⟩ ⟨those kids had me ~*ed* all right . . . they wanted to kill somebody —Ernest Hemingway⟩ **3** *slang* **:** GHOSTWRITE ⟨~*ed* the reminiscences of the actor⟩ ~ *vi* **:** to flee, scramble, tremble, stampede, or balk as a result of fright ⟨wolves would ~ as the plane flew over —*Alaska Sportsman*⟩

spook·ery \-kərē\ *n* -ES [¹*spook* + *-ery*] **:** something that is concerned with or characteristic of spooks **:** something that is spooky ⟨exchange of *spookeries* between disembodied voices —Edmond Taylor⟩ ⟨with this ~ she mingles fragments of mysticism —*Nation*⟩

spookfish \ˈ⸗,⸗\ *n* **:** CHIMAERA

spook·i·ly \-kəlē\ *adv* **:** in a spooky manner ⟨trees rustled ~⟩

spook·i·ness \-kēnəs\ *n* -ES **:** the quality or state of being spooky ⟨skillful lighting gave . . . the right touch of ~ —*Carnegie Mag.*⟩

spook·ish \-kish, -kēsh\ *adj* [¹*spook* + *-ish*] **:** somewhat spooky ⟨big black-raftered kitchen looked ~ and weird —Lucy M. Montgomery⟩

spook·ism \-,kizəm\ *n* -s **:** belief in or the practice of communicating with spooks or spirits; *esp* **:** SPIRITUALISM ⟨dabbler in wireless and ~ has a specially equipped set which collects the voices of the dead —*Sydney (Australia) Bull.*⟩

spook·ist \-kəst\ *n* -s **:** one who believes in or practices spookism

spooky \-kē, -ki\ *adj* -ER/-EST **1 :** resembling spooks or their appurtenances **:** SPECTRAL ⟨did your ~ friend walk last night —*Lippincott's Mag.*⟩ ⟨a ~ outfit of men who drove their stock by night —Will James⟩ ⟨saw a tall ~ staircase —Jean Stafford⟩ **2 :** of, belonging to, or concerning spooks **3 :** suggesting the presence or influence of ghosts **:** EERIE, UNCANNY, HAUNTING ⟨a very ~ place after dark —A.T.Walden⟩ ⟨the silence felt a bit ~ —W.H.Wright⟩ ⟨prescient to the point of being downright ~ —Milton Crane⟩ **4 :** NERVOUS, SKITTISH, JITTERY ⟨~ animals . . . who will buck from nothing more than high spirits —Alice Hager⟩ ⟨the gang was ~ after being questioned —J.K.Harris⟩

spook yeast *n* **:** EMPTINS

¹spool \ˈspül\ *n* -s *often attrib* [ME *spole*, *spule*, fr. MF or MD; MF *espole*, fr. OF, fr. MD *spoele*; akin to OHG *spuola* spool, bobbin, and prob. to OE *speld* thin piece of wood used as a torch — more at SPELL] **1 a :** any of several cylindrical devices which have a rim, ridge, or head at each end and commonly an axial hole for a pin or spindle and on which filamentary or ribbonlike material (as thread, yarn, ribbon, wire, cord, tape) is wound: as (1) **:** a small usu. wooden cylinder for holding sewing thread (2) **:** BOBBIN (3) **:** a holder for a field coil (4) **:** a holder on which sensitized photographic film or paper is wound esp. for use in a camera (5) **:** a holder for the ribbon of a typewriter or similar machine (6) **:** the part of a fishing reel upon which the line is wound **b :** something (as a capstan barrel) resembling or likened to such a spool **2 :** the material or the amount of material wound on a spool ⟨an hour-long ~ and . . . all the missing speeches . . . were recorded on it —Clemence Dane⟩ ⟨two ~*s* were needed to do the stitching⟩

spool 1a(1)

²spool \"\ *vb* -ED/-ING/-S *vt* **1 :** to wind on a spool ⟨film is ~*ed* for use —R.N.Shreve⟩ ⟨skein yarns are ~*ed* —*Leavers*

Lace⟩ **2 :** WIND ⟨~ the rope on the drum⟩ ⟨~ the thread off the bobbin⟩ **~** *vi* **1 :** to wind itself on a spool ⟨cause the cable to ~ properly —*advt*⟩ **2 :** WIND ⟨permitting the drilling line to ~ off the drum —*Primer of Oil Well Drilling*⟩

spool bed *n* **:** a wooden bed with spool-shaped turnings in the spindles and usu. in the rails and posts of the headboard and footboard

spool·er \-lə(r)\ *n* -s [²*spool* + *-er*] **1 :** a worker or machine that winds material (as thread, yarn, wire, cord, tape, film) on spools **:** WINDER **2 :** waste thrown off in spooling cotton yarn

spool heel *n* **:** a heel that has horizontal corrugations and is used on women's shoes

spool pin *n* **:** a spool-shaped pin tumbler used in some cylinder locks to foil picking attempts

spool turning *n* **:** a continuous turning in furniture that resembles rows of spools

spoolwood \ˈ=,=\ *n* [so called fr. its suitability for the making of spools] **1 :** PAPER BIRCH **2 :** the wood of paper birch

spoolwright \ˈ=,=\ *n* **:** a logger who chops out places in stumps or logs along a skid road for the insertion of spools to guide the skidding line

¹**spoon** \ˈspün *sometimes* ˈspu̇n\ *n* -s [ME *spone, spoon,* fr. OE *spōn;* akin to OHG *spān* splinter, chip of wood, ON *spānn, spōnn* chip, spoon, Gk *sphēn* wedge] **1** *obs* **:** a thin piece of wood **:** SPLINTER, CHIP **2 :** a usu. metal, plastic, or wooden eating or cooking implement consisting of a small oval or round shallow bowl with a handle — often used in combination ⟨~ maker⟩ ⟨baby ~⟩ ⟨jelly ~⟩ ⟨teaspoon⟩ **3 :** something that resembles a spoon in shape: as **a** *or* **spoon shovel :** a long bar with a small oval inclined blade at the end used in excavating deep narrow holes **b :** a lever that forms part of the stop motion on a drawing frame **4 :** SPOONFUL ⟨two ~s of sugar⟩ **5 :** WOODEN SPOON 1 **6** *slang* **:** SIMPLETON **7 :** a usu. metal or shell fishing lure shaped like the bowl of a spoon — see LURE illustration **8 :** a wooden golf club made with a slightly shorter and stiffer shaft and more loft than a driver or brassie and used through the green for long high shots — see WOOD illustration **9 a :** HORN SPOON 2 **b :** SCRAPER 1j **10 :** a smudged and crushed loop left in the ice by a figure skater who makes a faulty turn **11 :** a chrysanthemum with long tubular ray florets and a spoon-shaped tip

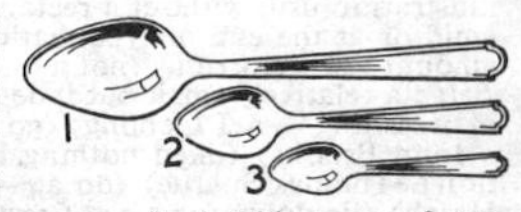

spoons 2: *1* tablespoon, *2* teaspoon, *3* coffee spoon

²**spoon** \"\ *adj* **1 :** used to hold spoons ⟨~ box⟩ ⟨~ rack⟩ **2 :** shaped like a spoon ⟨~ strainer⟩ or the bowl of a spoon ⟨~ shell⟩ **3 :** eaten with or suitable for eating with a spoon usu. because liquid or semisolid ⟨~ food⟩

³**spoon** \"\ *vb* -ED/-ING/-S *vt* **1 :** to take up and usu. transfer in a spoon ⟨they ~ their consommé —Mollie Panter-Downes⟩ ⟨~*ed* the tomatoes into the glass jars —H.D.Skidmore⟩ ⟨mother ~*ed* out bowls of porridge —Margaret Kennedy⟩ ⟨sat placidly ~*ing* up yogurt —*Time*⟩ ⟨the dredge ~*ed* up mud⟩ **2 :** to nestle close to and facing the back of (a person) while lying down **3** [prob. fr. the Welsh custom of an engaged man's presenting his fiancée with a love spoon] **:** to make love to by caressing, kissing, and talking amorously **:** PET, NECK ⟨have ~*ed* other women —Margaret W. Hungerford⟩; *sometimes* **:** WOO, COURT ⟨~*ing* his sister —Kenneth Grahame⟩ **4 :** to propel (a ball) by a stroke having a weak lifting motion **~** *vi* **1 :** to immerse a spoon (as into a liquid) ⟨~*ing* into a bowl of milk toast —William DuBois⟩ **2 :** to nestle close to and facing the back of a person while lying down ⟨sleepers ~*ing* together —Lee Meriwether⟩ — often used with *up* ⟨she tucked the bedclothes around him and then ~*ing* up she fell asleep —Willard Robertson⟩ **3 :** to make love by caressing, kissing, and talking amorously **:** NECK ⟨~*ed* out on the decks—Louis Armstrong⟩ **4 :** to spoon a ball (as a golfball)

⁴**spoon** \"\ *vi* -ED/-ING/-S [origin unknown] *of a boat* **:** to drive steadily and swiftly before or as if before a strong wind

spoon-back \ˈ=,=\ *adj* [²*spoon*] **:** having a back curved slightly to fit the sitter's form — used esp. of chairs of the Queen Anne period

spoonbill \ˈ=,=\ *n* **1 :** any of several wading birds that constitute the family Plataleidae, are closely related to the ibises, and have the bill greatly expanded and flattened at the tip: as **a :** ROSEATE SPOONBILL — see BILL illustration **b :** a common wading bird (*Platalea leucorodia*) of southern Europe, Asia, and northeastern Africa that is pure white and crested **2 a :** SHOVELER **b** *dial Eng* **:** SCAUP DUCK **c :** RUDDY DUCK **d :** PADDLEFISH **3 :** SPOON-BILLED SANDPIPER

spoonbill cat *also* **spoon-billed catfish** *or* **spoonbill** *n* **:** PADDLEFISH

spoon-billed \ˈ=,=\ *adj* **:** having the bill or snout expanded and spatulate at the end

spoon-billed duck *or* **spoon-billed teal** *or* **spoon-billed widgeon** *n* **:** SHOVELER

spoon-billed sandpiper *n* **:** a sandpiper (*Eurynorhynchus pygmeus*) that is characterized by a spatulate bill and inhabits northeastern Asia

spoon bit *n* **:** a wood-boring bit consisting of a grooved shank with a point shaped somewhat like the bowl of a spoon

spoon bow *n* **:** an overhanging bow of a ship whose underside is somewhat spoon-shaped

spoon bread *n, chiefly South & Midland* **:** bread made of cornmeal with or without added rice and hominy and mixed with milk, eggs, shortening, and leavening to a consistency that it must be served from the baking dish with a spoon — called also *batter bread*

spoon chisel *n* **:** a sculptor's bent chisel with the bezel on both sides

spoon·drift \ˈspün,drift\ *n* -s [alter. (influenced by ⁴*spoon*) of earlier *spenedrift,* fr. Sc *speendrift* — more at SPINDRIFT] **:** spray blown from waves during a gale at sea **:** SPINDRIFT

spoon end *n* [²*spoon*] **:** a concave end on a leaf spring to carry a swiveling member

spoon·er \ˈspünə(r)\ *n* -s [³*spoon* + *-er*] **1 :** one that uses a spoon implement ⟨~*s* being rapid professional handlers of the shovel —*Saturday Rev.*⟩ **2 :** one that makes love by spooning

spoon·er·ism \ˈspünə,rizəm\ *n* -s [William A. *Spooner* †1930 Eng. clergyman and educator noted for such lapses + E *-ism*] **:** a transposition of usu. initial sounds of two or more words that generally creates a comic effect (as in *votey heart* for *hearty vote, occupewing a pie* for *occupying a pew*); *esp* **:** such transposition done intentionally and so that the consequent formations are attested words (as in *tons of soil* for *sons of toil, ears and sparrows* for *spears and arrows*)

spoon·er·ize \-,rīz\ *vb* -ED/-ING/-S [Rev. William A. *Spooner* †1930 + E *-ize*] *vt* **:** to make a spoonerism of or in ⟨*spoonerized* recipes and words of advice to householders —*Current Biog.*⟩ **~** *vi* **:** to make spoonerisms

spooney *var of* SPOONY

spoon-fashion \ˈ=,==\ *adv* [¹*spoon*] **:** like spoons placed with the face of one fitting into the back of another ⟨sleep *spoon-fashion*⟩

spoon-feed \ˈ=ˈ=\ *vt* **1 :** to feed (another) by means of a spoon **2 a :** to present (a thing) or to present a thing to (a person or group) so thoroughly or wholeheartedly as to preclude the need of independent thought, initiative, or self-reliance on the part of the recipient ⟨*spoon-feed* material to students⟩ ⟨poet should do all the work and *spoon-feed* his reader —*Fortnightly Rev.*⟩ ⟨claiming that you can prepare Indians for freedom by . . . *spoon-feeding* them —*Senior Scholastic*⟩ **b :** to present (information) or to present information to (a person or group) in a slanted version and with the intention of precluding questioning or revision on the part of the recipient ⟨*spoon-feeding* propaganda through the public schools —*Newsweek*⟩ ⟨fought . . . for free thought against *spoon-fed* thought —*Punch*⟩ ⟨the general public is being *spoon-fed* . . . more and more propaganda —Richard LaCoste⟩ ⟨a *spoon-fed* press⟩ **~** *vi* **1 :** to feed oneself or another by means of a spoon **2 a :** to present a thing so thoroughly or wholeheartedly as to preclude the need of independent thinking, initiative, or self-reliance on the part of the recipient ⟨our *spoon-feeding* pedagogy —H.G.Rickover⟩ **b :** to present information in a slanted version and with the intention of precluding questioning or revision on the part of the recipient ⟨altogether too much bureaucratic *spoon-feeding* about these proposals —*Contemporary Rev.*⟩ **c :** to accept passively that which has been spoon-fed ⟨has self-reliance superseded *spoon-feeding* —*Irish Statesman*⟩

spoonflower \ˈ=,==\ *n* [²*spoon* + *flower;* fr. the spoonlike end of the petiole] **:** YAUTIA a

spoon foot *n* **:** a foot (as on a table or chair) that projects out slightly from the leg and curves up to form a shape similar to that of the bowl of a spoon

spoon·ful \ˈ=,fu̇l\ *n, pl* **spoonfuls** \-lz\ *also* **spoons·ful** \-nz,-\ [ME *sponeful,* fr. *spone* spoon + *-ful*] **:** the amount of material a spoon contains or can contain; *specif* **:** TEASPOONFUL

spoonhunt \ˈ=,=\ *n* [*spoon*wood + *hunt* (of unknown origin)] *NewEng* **:** MOUNTAIN LAUREL 1

spoonhutch \ˈ=,=\ *n* [*spoon*wood + *hutch* (of unknown origin)] **:** BIG LAUREL

spoon·i·ly \ˈspünᵊlē\ *adv* **:** in a spoony manner ⟨how ~ I had managed my good fortune —G.J.Whyte-Melville⟩

spoon·i·ness *also* **spoon·ey·ness** \-nēnəs\ *n* -ES **:** the quality or state of being spoony ⟨restrained . . . from reciprocating my increasing ~ —T.A.Guthrie⟩

spooning *pres part of* SPOON

spoonlike \ˈ=,=\ *adj* **:** resembling a spoon (as in shape or function)

spoon meat *n* [²*spoon*] **:** food (as liquids or semisolids) eaten with or suitable for eating with a spoon ⟨live on *spoon meat* —Thomas Carlyle⟩

spoon nail *n* **:** KOILONYCHIA

spoon oar *n* **:** an oar having the blade so curved as to afford a better hold upon the water in rowing

spoons *pl of* SPOON, *pres 3d sing of* SPOON

spoon shovel *n* **:** SPOON 3a

spoon tool *n* **:** any of various more or less spoon-shaped molder's tools used for smoothing and finishing molds

spoonwood \ˈ=,=\ *n* [¹*spoon* + *wood;* fr. the use of its wood for making spoons] **:** MOUNTAIN LAUREL 1

spoonwood ivy *n* **:** SHEEP LAUREL

spoonwort \ˈ=,=\ *n* [trans. of D *lepelblad* or *lepelkruid*] **:** SCURVY GRASS 1

¹**spoony** *or* **spoon·ey** \ˈspünē\ *n, pl* **spoonies** *or* **spooneys** [¹*spoon* (simpleton) + *-y;* influenced in meaning by ³*spoon*] **:** one who is spoony ⟨a lackadaisical young ~ —Charles Dickens⟩ ⟨playing the lover . . . in the role of a ~ —H.E. Scudder⟩

²**spoony** *or* **spooney** \"\ *adj* **spoonier; spooniest** [¹*spoon* + *-y;* influenced in meaning by ³*spoon*] **1 :** SILLY, FOOLISH; *esp* **:** unduly emotional, sentimental, credulous, or indulgent **:** SOFT ⟨~ enough to let him get off —G.P.R.James⟩ ⟨even my jazz is like a ~ high-school kid's —H.L.Cliburn⟩; *esp* **:** enamored of or in love with to the point of being spoony — usu. used with *over* or *on* ⟨~ over Miss . . . to the point of idolatry —S.J.Perelman⟩ ⟨~ on a gypsy girl —Thomas Hughes⟩ **2 :** expressive or suggestive of spooniness ⟨not a ~ lovelorn effusion, but a good, rational, amusing letter —Bithia Croker⟩ ⟨~ ways and looks⟩

³**spoony** \"\ *n* -ES [*spoon*bill + *-y*] **:** SPOONBILL

spoony·ism *also* **spoon·ey·ism** \-nē,izəm\ *n* -S **:** SPOONINESS

¹**spoor** \ˈspu̇(ə)r, -u̇ə *sometimes* ˈspō(ə)r *or* ˈspōə *or* ˈspȯ(ə)r *or* ˈspȯ(ə)\ *n, pl* **spoor** *or* **spoors** [Afrik, fr. MD *spor, spoor;* akin to OE, OHG, & ON *spor* footprint, track, OE *spurnan* to kick — more at SPURN] **:** a mark (as a footprint), a trail, a scent, a sound, or droppings left by one (as a wild animal) that has passed **:** TRACK, SIGN ⟨~ of three large bulls . . . the tracks unusual in size —*Police Gazette*⟩ ⟨a ~ of blood from a slug in his right thigh —*Time*⟩ ⟨tell roughly how old a ~ is by the color and heat of the droppings —B.D.Nicholson⟩

²**spoor** \"\ *vb* -ED/-ING/-S [prob. fr. Afrik, fr. MD *sporen,* fr. *spor* spoor] *vt* **:** to track by a spoor ⟨~*ing* animals and interpreting every mark on the sand —Frank Debenham⟩ **~** *vi* **:** to track something by a spoor

spoor·er \-u̇rə(r), -ōrə-,-ȯrə-\ *n* -s **:** one that spoors

spor- *or* **spori-** *or* **sporo-** *comb form* [NL *spora* — more at SPORE] **:** seed **:** spore ⟨*spor*ocyst⟩ ⟨*spor*angium⟩ ⟨*spori*cide⟩

-spo·ra \spərə\ *n comb form* [NL, fr. *spora* seed, spore] **:** organism having (such) a sporal characteristic — in generic names (Perono*spora*) ⟨Iso*spora*⟩

spo·rad·ic \spəˈrad·|ik, spō'-, spȯ'-, -at|, |ēk\ *adj* [ML *sporadicus,* fr. Gk *sporadikos* scattered, fr. *sporad-, sporas* scattered; akin to Gk *speirein* to strew, sow — more at SPROUT] **:** occurring occasionally, singly, apart from other things of the same kind, or in scattered instances **:** SEPARATE, SINGLE, ISOLATED ⟨a ~ case of disease⟩ ⟨~ occurrence of a plant⟩ ⟨~ fighting⟩ — **spo·rad·i·cal·ly** \|ək(ə)lē, |ēk-, -li\ *adv*

sporadic e layer *n, usu cap E* **:** a layer of ionization occurring irregularly within the E region of the ionosphere at heights of approximately 60 miles above the surface of the earth and occasionally being capable of reflecting radio waves of very high frequency back to earth at great distances

spo·ra·dic·i·ty \,spōrəˈdisəd·ē\ *n* -ES **:** the quality or state of being sporadic

spo·ra·din \ˈspōrədᵊn\ *n* -s [NL *Sporadina,* genus of gregarines, fr. Gk *sporad-, sporas* scattered + NL *-ina*] **:** a vermiform extracellular fully grown gregarine trophozoite that usu. lacks an epimerite — compare CEPHALIN

spor·al \ˈspōrəl, -ȯr-\ *adj* **:** of, relating to, or having the special characteristics of a spore **:** being a spore

spo·range \spəˈranj, ˈspōr,anj\ *n* -s [NL *sporangium*] **:** SPORANGIUM

sporangi- *or* **sporangio-** *comb form* [NL *sporangium*] **:** sporangium ⟨*sporangi*oid⟩ ⟨*sporangio*spore⟩

sporangia *pl of* SPORANGIUM

spo·ran·gi·al \spəˈranjēəl\ *adj* [NL *sporangium* + E *-al*] **:** of or relating to a sporangium **:** made up of sporangia

spo·ran·gif·er·ous \,spōranˈjif(ə)rəs\ *adj* [*sporangi-* + *-ferous*] **:** bearing sporangia

spo·ran·gi·form \spəˈranjə,fȯrm\ *adj* [*sporangi-* + *-form*] **:** having the form of a sporangium

spo·ran·gi·o·gen·ic \spəˌranjēōˈjenik\ *adj* [*sporangi-* + *-genic*] **:** producing sporangia

spo·ran·gi·oid \spəˈranjē,ȯid\ *adj* [*sporangi-* + *-oid*] **:** resembling a sporangium **:** SPORANGIFORM

spo·ran·gi·ole \-,ōl\ *n* -s [NL *sporangiolum*] **:** a small deciduous few-spored sporangium occurring along with larger sporangia that contain numerous spores in fungi of the family Mucoraceae

spo·ran·gi·o·lum \=,==ˈōləm\ *n, pl* **sporangio·la** \-lə\ [NL, dim. of *sporangium*] **:** SPORANGIOLE

spo·ran·gi·o·phore \spəˈranjēə,fō(ə)r\ *n* -s [*sporangi-* + *-phore*] **:** a stalk or receptacle bearing sporangia

spo·ran·gi·o·spore \-,spō(ə)r\ *n* [*sporangi-* + *spore*] **:** a spore that develops in a sporangium

spo·ran·gite \spəˈran,jīt\ *n* -s [NL *sporangium* + E *-ite*] **:** a fossilized spore case of a plant

spo·ran·gi·tes \,spōranˈjīd·(,)ēz\ *n, cap* [NL, fr. *sporangium* + *-ites*] **:** a form genus of Paleozoic fossil organisms based on spores or spore cases apparently of plants of *Lepidodendron* and *Calamites* or related genera

spo·ran·gi·um \spəˈranjēəm, spō'-, spȯ'-\ *n, pl* **sporan·gia** \-ēə\ [NL, fr. *spor-* + Gk *angeion* vessel, receptacle — more at ANGI-] **:** a case within which spores that are usu. asexual are produced or borne: as **a :** a mother cell that in various bacteria, algae, and fungi produces one or a few cells endogenously **b :** the spore sac of a moss; *broadly* **:** CAPSULE 2b **c :** a complex structure in most ferns and related plants that contains numerous spores nourished by a tapetum and is usu. equipped with an annulus which aids in spore discharge **d :** MICROSPORANGIUM, MEGASPORANGIUM — compare GAMETANGIUM, GONIDANGIUM

¹**spore** \ˈspō(ə)r, ˈspȯ(ə)r, -ōə, -ȯ(ə)\ *n* -s [NL *spora,* fr. Gk, act of sowing, seed; akin to Gk *sporos* act of sowing, seed, *speirein* to sow, strew — more at SPROUT] **1 :** a minute unicellular reproductive or resistant resting body that is often adapted to survive unfavorable environmental conditions and to produce a new vegetative individual when these conditions alter, is morphologically a mass of protoplasm usu. with a single definite nucleus and often with a cell wall and flagella, is capable of producing a new individual directly if asexual or only after union with another similar or dissimilar spore if sexual, and that occurs in many varieties differing in size, form, origin, and other characteristics — see ASCOSPORE, BASIDIOSPORE, CARPOSPORE, CHLAMYDOSPORE, CONIDIUM, ENDOSPORE, EXOSPORE, MEGASPORE, MICROSPORE, OOSPORE, TELIOSPORE, ZOOSPORE, ZYGOSPORE; compare SEED **2 :** any of various small multicellular resistant bodies (as a statoblast or gemmule) that are capable of reproducing a new individual

²**spore** \"\ *vb* -ED/-ING/-S *vi* **:** to produce or have spores **:** reproduce by or as if by spores **~** *vt* **:** to produce or multiply by or as if by sporing **:** SPAWN

-spore \,spō(ə)r, ,spȯ(ə)r, -ōə, -ȯ(ə)\ *n comb form* -s [NL *spora*] **1 :** spore having (such) a characteristic or origin ⟨pycnidio*spore*⟩ **2 :** spore membrane ⟨a dark epi*spore* enclosing a hyaline spore⟩

spore ball *n* **:** a multilocular body which becomes free like a spore and in which each cell is capable of germination (as in members of the genus *Spongospora*) or only some of the cells germinate (as in members of *Urocystis*)

sporebearer \ˈ=,==\ *n* **:** an organism that bears spores; *esp* **:** a bacterium that is difficult to destroy by sterilization because it produces heat-resistant spores

spore case *n* **:** a case containing spores **:** SPORANGIUM

spored \ˌspō(ə)rd\ *adj* [¹*spore* + *-ed*] **:** having spores — often used in combination

sporeformer \ˈ=,==\ *n* **:** an organism that forms spores **:** SPOREBEARER

spore fruit *n* **:** a specialized structure (as an ascocarp) that produces spores **:** FRUITING BODY

spore·ling \ˈspōrliŋ\ *n* -s [¹*spore* + *-ling*] **:** a young new individual developed from a spore; *usu* **:** a young sporophyte **:** PROTHALLIUM

spore mother cell *n* **:** one of the cells of the archespore of a spore-bearing plant whose final divisions result in the production of a spore and usu. of a tetrad of spores

spore print *n* **:** a deposit of spores of a fungus made by allowing the discharged spores to collect on paper or glass and form a print that gives a picture of the arrangement of the gills and of spore color

spore sac *n* **:** SPORE CASE: as **a :** a cavity of the theca of a moss **b :** ASCUS

spori- — see SPOR-

-spor·ic \ˌspōrik, -pȯr-, -pär-, -rēk\ *or* **-spor·ous** \ˌspōrəs, -pȯr-, ˌspərəs\ *adj comb form* [NL *spora* spore + E *-ic* or *-ous*] **:** having (such or so many) spores ⟨carpo*sporic*⟩ ⟨homo*sporous*⟩

spo·ri·ci·dal \ˌspōrəˈsīdᵊl\ *adj* [*spor-* + *-cidal*] **:** tending to kill spores

spo·rid \ˈspōrəd\ *n* -s [NL *sporidium*] **:** SPORIDIUM

spo·ri·desm \ˈspōrə,dezəm\ *n* -s [*spor-* + Gk *desmē* bundle, fr. *dein* to bind, tie — more at DIADEM] **:** a multicellular spore body or chain of independent spores

-spo·rid·ia \spəˈridēə, spō'-, spȯ'-\ *n pl comb form* [NL, fr. pl. of *sporidium*] **:** creatures bearing (such) small spores — in higher taxa in protozoology ⟨Micro*sporidia*⟩ ⟨Cnido*sporidia*⟩

spo·rid·i·al \-ēəl\ *adj* [NL *sporidium* + E *-al*] **:** of, relating to, or producing sporidia **:** developing from a sporidium

spo·ri·dif·er·ous \ˌspōrəˈdif(ə)rəs\ *adj* [NL *sporidium* + E *-ferous*] **:** bearing sporidia

spo·rid·i·um \spəˈridēəm, spō'-, spȯ'-\ *n, pl* **sporid·ia** \-ēə\ [NL, fr. *spor-* + *-idium*] **:** a small spore; *esp* **:** one abjointed from a promycelium (as in various smuts and rusts) — compare BASIDIOSPORE

-spories *pl of* -SPORY

spo·rif·er·ous \-if(ə)rəs\ *adj* [*spor-* + *-iferous*] **:** bearing or producing spores

-spo·ri·um \ˈspōrēəm, -pȯr-\ *n comb form* [NL, fr. *spora* spore + *-ium*] **1** *pl* **-spo·ria** \-ēə\ *also* **-sporiums :** (such) a coat or layer of a spore wall ⟨endo*sporium*⟩ **2 :** plant having (such) a spore — in generic names ⟨Helmintho*sporium*⟩

sporo- — see SPOR-

spo·ro·blast \ˈspōrə,blast\ *n* [ISV *spor-* + *-blast*] **:** a cell of a sporozoan resulting from sexual reproduction and producing spores and sporozoites

spo·rob·o·lo·my·ce·ta·ce·ae \spə,räbəlō,mīsəˈtāsē,ē\ *n pl, cap* [NL, fr. *Sporobolomycet-, Sporobolomyces,* type genus (fr. *spor-* + Gk *-bolos* + NL *-mycet-, -myces*) + *-aceae*] **:** a family of imperfect fungi (order Moniliales) characterized by scanty mycelium and propagation by both budding and repetition

spo·rob·o·lus \spəˈräbələs\ *n, cap* [NL, fr. Gk *spora, sporos* seed + *-bolos* (fr. *ballein* to throw) — more at SPORE, DEVIL] **:** a widely distributed genus of grasses having ample panicles with small one-flowered spikelets each with three glumes and grain that separates easily — see DROPSEED

spo·ro·carp \ˈspōrə,kärp, -ȯr-, -pȯr-\ *n* -s [ISV *spor-* + Gk *karpos* fruit — more at HARVEST] **:** any structure in or on which spores are produced: as **a :** a multicellular body that develops from a fertilized archicarp or procarp of a red alga and produces asexual carpospores **:** CYSTOCARP **b :** a many-celled body (as an ascocarp) producing spores in a fungus **c :** the sporogonium of a moss **d :** an organized mass of sporangia in a fern ally of the families Salviniaceae and Marsileaceae

spo·roch·nus \spəˈräknəs\ *n, cap* [NL, fr. *spor-* + Gk *chnoos, chnous* dust, fine down — more at HYPOCHNUS] **:** a small genus (the type of the family Sporochnaceae) of brown algae characterized by tufts of fine elongated filaments terminating some of the branches of the thallus

spo·ro·cyst \ˈspōrə, ˈspȯrə+,-\ *n* [ISV *spor-* + *cyst*] **1 :** a unicellular resting cell that may give rise to asexual spores (as in various myxomycetes and algae) — compare SPORANGIUM **2 a :** a case or cyst secreted by some sporozoans preliminary to sporogony; *also* **:** a sporozoan encysted in such a case **b :** a saccular body that is the first reproductive form of a digenetic trematode in the molluscan host and buds off cells from its inner surface which develop into rediae within the cavity of the sporocyst — **spo·ro·cys·tic** \ˌ==+ˈ=\ *adj* — **spo·ro·cys·tid** \"+\ *n* -s

spo·ro·cyte \ˈspōrə,sīt\ *n* -s [*spor-* + *-cyte*] **:** SPORE MOTHER CELL

spo·ro·do·chi·um \,spōrəˈdōkēəm\ *n, pl* **sporodo·chia** \-ēə\ [NL, fr. *spor-* + Gk *docheion* holder, receptacle, fr. *dechesthai, dekesthai* to receive, accept; akin to Gk *dokein* to seem good — more at DECENT] **:** an erumpent crowded cluster of conidiophores arising from a stroma in the form of a cushion (as in the Tuberculariaceae)

spo·ro·duct \ˈspōrə, ˈspȯrə+,-\ *n* [ISV *spor-* + *duct*] **:** minute tubes in the wall of the cyst formed by some gregarines for the exit of spores

spo·ro·genesis \ˌ==+\ *n* [NL, fr. *spor-* + L *genesis*] **1 :** reproduction by spores **2 :** spore formation

spo·ro·gen·ic \ˌspōrəˈjenik\ *adj* [*spor-* + *-genic*] **1 :** SPOROGENOUS **2 :** of, relating to, or involving sporogenesis ⟨a ~ cycle⟩

spo·rog·e·nous \spəˈräjənəs, spō'-, spȯ'-\ *adj* [*spor-* + *-genous*] **1 :** producing or adapted to the production of spores ⟨~ hyphae⟩ **2 :** reproducing by spores

spo·rog·e·ny \-nē\ *n* -ES [*spor-* + *-geny*] **:** SPOROGENESIS

spo·ro·gone \ˈspōrə,gōn, -pȯr-\ *n* -s [NL *sporogonium*] **:** SPOROGONIUM

spo·ro·go·ni·al \ˌ==ˈgōnēəl\ *adj* [NL *sporogonium* + E *-al*] **1 :** of, relating to, or producing sporogonia **2 :** SPOROGONIC

spo·ro·gon·ic \-ˈgänik\ *also* **spo·rog·o·nous** \spəˈrägənəs, spō'-, spȯ'-\ *adj* [*sporogony* + *-ic* or *-ous*] **:** of, relating to, involving, or produced by sporogony ⟨~ parasites⟩ ⟨a ~ cycle⟩

spo·ro·go·ni·um \,spōrəˈgōnēəm, -pȯr-\ *n, pl* **sporogo·nia** \-ēə\ [NL, fr. *spor-* + *-gonium* (as in *archegonium*)] **:** the sporophyte of a moss or liverwort consisting typically of a stalk bearing a capsule in which spores are produced, developing from a fertilized egg in the venter of the archegonium, and remaining permanently attached to the gametophyte by the base of the stalk which acts as an absorbing organ

spo·rog·o·ny \spəˈrägənē, spō'-, spȯ'-, -ni\ *n* -ES [ISV *spor-* + *-gony*] **:** reproduction by spores; *specif* **:** spore formation in a sporozoan by encystment and subsequent division of a zygote — distinguished from *schizogony*

spor·oid \ˈspōr,ȯid\ *adj* [*spor-* + *-oid*] **:** resembling a spore

spo·ro·morph \ˈspōrə,mȯrf\ *n* -s [*spor-* + *-morph*] **:** a fossil pollen grain or spore

spo·ront \ˈspōr,änt\ *n* -s [ISV *spor-* + *-ont*] **:** a sporozoan (as a zygote or pansporoblast) that engages in sporogony

spo·ro·phore \'spōrə,fō(ə)r, -pȯr-, -fȯ(ə)r, -fōə, -fȯ(ə)\ *n* -s [ISV *spor-* + *-phore*] **:** a spore-bearing branch or organ **:** the part of the thallus of a sporophyte that develops spores, in fungi is often a conspicuous spore fruit (as in the mushrooms and other basidiomycetes) though sometimes a simple hyphal filament or a mass of hyphae, in ferns, mosses, and liverworts is practically equivalent to the sporophyte, and in seed plants constitutes the placenta — compare GAMETOPHORE — **spo·ro·phor·ic** \¦⸗⸗¦fȯrik\ *adj*

spo·roph·o·rous \spə'räf(ə)rəs, spō'-, spȯ'-\ *adj* [NL *sporophorus*, fr. *spor-* + *-phorus* -phorous] **1 :** SPORIFEROUS **2** [*sporophore* + *-ous*] **:** of or relating to a sporophore

spo·ro·phyll *also* **spo·ro·phyl** \'spōrə,fil, -pȯr-\ *n* -s [ISV *spor-* + *-phyll*] **1 :** a spore-bearing leaf **:** a leaf more or less modified in form and structure that develops sporangia and may resemble and perform the functions of a foliage leaf (as in many ferns) or may be completely altered (as the spike of the adder's-tongue) — see MEGASPOROPHYLL, MICROSPOROPHYLL **2 :** a small foliaceous structure bearing the sporangia in a brown alga of the genus *Alaria* — **spo·roph·yl·lary** \spə'räfə,lerē\ *adj*

spo·ro·phyte \'spōrə,fīt, -pȯr-\ *n* -s [ISV *spor-* + *-phyte*] **:** an individual or generation of a plant exhibiting alternation of generations that bears asexual spores, is usu. not clearly differentiated in algae and fungi, is represented by the sporogonium in bryophytes, and in vascular plants is the conspicuous form ordinarily known — distinguished from *gametophyte* — **spo·ro·phyt·ic** \¦⸗⸗¦fid·ik\ *adj*

spo·ro·plasm \'⸗⸗,plazəm\ *n* -s [*spor-* + *-plasm*] **:** a mass of protoplasm that gives rise to or forms a spore; *esp* **:** the protoplasmic body that is released as an infective amoebula from a cnidosporidian cyst

spo·ro·sac \-,sak\ *n* [*spor-* + *sac*] **1 :** a simple degenerate gonophore of some hydroids that is often little more than a gonad and never medusoid **2 a :** SPOROCYST **b :** REDIA

spo·ro·thrix \-,thriks\ *n* -ES [NL *sporotrich-*, *sporothrix*, fr. *spor-* + Gk *trich-*, *thrix* hair — more at TRICHINA] **:** a fungus of the genus *Sporotrichum*

spo·ro·tri·cho·sis \,spōrə·,trī'kōsə̇s\ *n, pl* **sporotricho·ses** \-kō,sēz\ [NL, fr. *sporotrich*um + *-osis*] **:** infection with or disease caused by fungi of the genus *Sporotrichum*, characterized by nodules and abscesses in the superficial lymph nodes, skin, and subcutaneous tissues, occurring esp. in man and horses, and usu. transmitted through entry of the fungus by way of a skin abrasion or wound (as from prick of a thorn)

spo·ro·tri·chot·ic \¦⸗⸗,⸗¦käd·ik\ *adj* **:** of or relating to sporotrichosis ⟨~ lesions⟩

spo·rot·ri·chum \spə'rä·trə̇kəm\ *n* [NL, fr. *spor-* + Gk *trich-*, *thrix* hair — more at TRICHINA] **1** *cap* **:** a genus of saprophytic or parasitic imperfect fungi (family Moniliaceae) forming hyaline conidia either solitary or in groups and on short conidiophores — see SPOROTRICHOSIS **2** *pl* **sporotri·cha** \-kə\ **:** any fungus of the genus *Sporotrichum*

spor·ous \'spōrəs\ *adj* [*spore* + *-ous*] **:** SPORAL

-sporous — see -SPORIC

spo·ro·zoa \,spōrə'zōə, -pȯr-\ *n pl, cap* [NL, fr. *spor-* + *-zoa*] **:** a large class of strictly parasitic protozoans that pass through a complicated life cycle usu. involving alternation of a sexual with an asexual generation, often require two or more dissimilar hosts to complete their life cycle, are typically immobile and usu. intracellular parasites, and include many serious pathogens (as the malaria parasites, coccidia, and piroplasms) as well as numerous apparently innocuous forms — see ACNIDOSPORIDIA, CNIDOSPORIDIA, TELOSPORIDIA — **spo·ro·zo·al** \¦⸗⸗¦zōəl\ *adj* — **spo·ro·zo·an** \-zōən\ *adj or n*

spo·ro·zo·ite \,⸗⸗'zō,īt\ *n* -s [NL *sporozo*on + ISV *-ite*] **:** a small usu. motile and elongate infective stage of some sporozoans that is introduced into a definitive host by an intermediate host or by escape from a spore, is a product of sexual reproduction, and initiates an asexual cycle in the new host

spo·ro·zo·it·i·cide \,⸗⸗zō'id·ə,sīd\ *n* -s [*sporozoite* + *-i-* + *-cide*] **:** an agent selectively destructive of the sporozoite form of a sporozoan parasite

spo·ro·zo·on \,⸗⸗'zō,än\ *n, pl* **sporo·zoa** \-zōə\ [NL, sing. of *Sporozoa*] **:** SPOROZOAN

spor·ran \'spärən\ *n* -s [ScGael *sporan* purse] **:** a large pouch of skin with the hair or fur on that is worn in front of the kilt by Highlanders in full dress and used as a purse

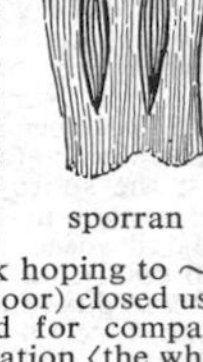

sporran

[1]sport \'spō(ə)r|t, -pȯ(ə)r|, -ōə|, -ȯ(ə)|, *usu* |d·+V\ *vb* -ED/-ING/-S [ME *sporten*, short for *disporten* to disport] *vt* **1** *archaic* **:** to make (as oneself) merry **:** DIVERT, AMUSE, CHEER **2 a** *archaic* **:** to expend (money) in gambling **:** WAGER, BET **b :** to expend wastefully or carelessly (as in riotous living); *also* **:** to spend lavishly and ostentatiously **3 a :** to make public and usu. ostentatious display or use of **:** show off ⟨delighted to ~ his learning in company⟩ ⟨~*ing* the new sedan in the park⟩ **b :** to wear contentedly or with satisfaction ⟨~*ed* a trim little hat at church⟩ **c :** to keep or use as a possession ⟨every clerk hoping to ~ a horse some day⟩ **4** *Brit* **:** to close or keep (a door) closed usu. as an indication that one is too occupied for company **5** [[2]*sport*] **:** to put forth as a sport or bud variation ⟨the white rose ~*ed* a single red-flowered branch⟩ ~ *vi* **1 a :** to amuse oneself by light or playful activity (as by participation in a game or outdoor exercise) **:** FROLIC, ROMP ⟨lambs ~*ing* in the meadow⟩ **b :** to engage or participate in a sport and esp. an active field sport **2 a :** to treat sportively or lightly **:** deal in a sportive or light manner **:** MOCK **b :** to speak or act jestingly or slightingly or without due or serious consideration — used with *with* ⟨~*ing* with things he scarcely hoped to understand⟩ **3** *archaic* **:** to bet habitually **4** [[2]*sport*] **:** to deviate or vary abruptly from type **:** give rise to a sport (as by bud variation) **:** MUTATE **syn** see PLAY — **sport one's oak** *Brit* **:** close one's door against interruption

[2]sport \"\ *n* -s [ME, short for *disport*] **1 a :** something that is a source of pleasant diversion **:** a pleasing or amusing pastime or activity **:** RECREATION ⟨spent the afternoon in ~ and play⟩ **b** *obs* **:** sexual dalliance **:** amorous play **c** *obs* **:** a theatrical performance **d :** a particular play, game, or mode of amusement: as (1) **:** a diversion of the field (as fowling, hunting, fishing, racing, or athletic games); *also* **:** any of various games (as bowling, rackets, basketball) or comparable diversions usu. played under cover (2) **:** a game or contest esp. when involving individual skill or physical prowess on which money is staked **2 a :** something light, playful, or frivolous and lacking in serious intent or spirit **:** PLEASANTRY, JEST **b :** superior or contemptuous mirth **:** MOCKING, MOCKERY, DERISION ⟨then make ~ at me, then let me be your jest —Shak.⟩ **3 :** an occupation that constitutes a diversion ⟨the same old domestic ~ of arguing at table and making up in bed⟩ **4 a :** something tossed or driven about in or as if in play **:** the helpless object of a force ⟨the prey and ~ of wintry winds⟩ ⟨seemed no more than the ~ of misfortune⟩ **b :** a subject of or butt for mirth, mockery, or derision **:** LAUGHING STOCK **5 :** a person interested in sports **:** SPORTSMAN: as **a :** a person with sporting instincts **:** one interested in sports chiefly for the gambling opportunities presented; *broadly* **:** GAMBLER **b :** a person enjoying a gay luxurious life **:** BON VIVANT **c :** a person living up to the high ideals of good sportsmanship esp. as a loser in any contest or situation **d :** a companionable or likable person; *often* **:** FELLOW, COMPANION, CHAP **6 :** an individual exhibiting in whole or in part a sudden spontaneous deviation from type beyond the normal limits of individual variation usu. as a result of mutation esp. of somatic tissue — compare BUD VARIATION **syn** see FUN, [2]PLAY — **in sport** *adv* **:** in a light or jesting manner **:** without serious intent ⟨told him *in sport* that we would all go to Florida⟩

[3]sport \"\ *or* **sports** \|ts\ *adj* **:** of, relating to, or suitable for sports and esp. outdoor sports **:** adapted to use in connection with sports ⟨a ~ roadster⟩ ⟨*sports* equipment⟩; *esp* **:** styled in a manner suitable for casual or informal wear ⟨*sports* coats⟩ ⟨a trim ~ shoe⟩

sport·abil·i·ty \,spōrd·ə'biləd·ē\ *n, archaic* **:** SPORTIVENESS

sport·er \'spōrd·ər\ *n* -s **1 :** one that sports (as a sportsman or a lavish spender) **2 :** one (as a dog or rifle) that is used in sport and esp. in the sport of hunting

sport finder *n* **:** ALBADA FINDER

sport fish *n* **:** a fish primarily of importance for the sport it affords anglers — compare COARSE FISH, GAME FISH, ROUGH FISH

sport·ful \'spōrtfəl, -pȯr-, -ōət-, -ȯ(ə)t-\ *adj* [ME, fr. [2]*sport* + *-ful*] **1 a :** productive of sport or amusement **:** ENTERTAINING, DIVERTING **b :** having an inclination to lighthearted merriment **:** PLAYFUL, FROLICSOME; *usu* **:** inclined to jest or tease playfully **2 :** done in jest or for mere play **:** lacking serious intent **:** SPORTIVE — **sport·ful·ly** \-fəlē, -li\ *adv* — **sport·ful·ness** *n* -ES

sportier *comparative of* SPORTY

sportiest *superlative of* SPORTY

sport·i·ly \'spōrd·ᵊlē\ *adv* **:** in a sporty manner **:** so as to be or appear sporty

sport·i·ness \-d·ēnə̇s\ *n* -ES **:** the quality or state of being sporty

sporting *adj* [fr. gerund & pres. part. of [1]*sport*] **1 a :** SPORT **b :** suitable for or characteristic of a sportsman **:** marked by or calling for sportsmanship ⟨a ~ solution of the problem⟩ **c :** involving such risk as a sports contender may reasonably take or expect to encounter ⟨a ~ chance of success⟩ **2 a :** of, relating to, or preoccupied with dissipation and esp. gambling; *often* **:** FAST, FLASHY ⟨~ gents and their ladies⟩ **b :** engaged or used in prostitution **3 :** tending to produce sports usu. with exceptional frequency ⟨a ~ strain of evening primrose⟩

sporting blood *n* **1 :** instinctive love of sports **2 :** readiness to accept a challenge (as to a contest); *broadly* **:** DARING, COURAGE

sporting editor *n* **:** SPORTS EDITOR

sporting girl *or* **sporting woman** *n* **:** PROSTITUTE

sporting house *n* **1** *archaic* **:** a public place frequented by sportsmen or gamblers **2 :** BROTHEL

sport·ing·ly *adv* **:** in a sporting manner **:** so as to be sporting

sporting page *n* **:** SPORTS PAGE

sporting powder *n* **:** black powder or smokeless powder for use in sporting ammunition

spor·tive \'spōr|d·|iv, -pȯr|, -ōə|, -ȯ(ə)|, |t|, |ēv *also* |əv\ *adj* [[2]*sport* + *-ive*] **1 a :** tending to, engaged in, or productive or provocative of sport **:** GAY, FROLICSOME, PLAYFUL, MERRY **b :** not undertaken or done seriously **:** carried on or out in sport **c :** having an inclination for sexual encounter **:** ARDENT, LUSTY **2 :** relating to or connected with sports and esp. field sports **3 a :** produced as a sport **b :** tending to the production of sports **:** SPORTING 3 — **spor·tive·ly** \|ə̇vlē, -li\ *adv* — **spor·tive·ness** \|ivnə̇s, |ēv- *also* |əv-\ *n* -ES

sportive lemur *n* **:** any of several small slender Madagascan lemurs constituting the genus *Lepilemur* — compare WEASEL LEMUR

sport·less \'⸗lə̇s\ *adj* **:** affording no sport **:** producing no sports

sport of kings 1 : horse racing **2 a :** FALCONRY **b :** HUNTING

[1]sports *pres 3d sing of* SPORT, *pl of* SPORT

[2]sports *var of* SPORT

sports car *also* **sport car** *n* **:** a low-slung open or convertible automobile designed for high-speed transportation on regular roads and having rapid acceleration, more or less smooth horizontal lines, and usu. seats for two people

sports·cast \'spōrt,skast, -pȯr-, -ōət-, -ȯ(ə)t-, -aa(ə)st\ *also* **sport·cast** \-t,k-\ *n* -s [[3]*sport* + broad*cast*] **:** a radio or television broadcast of a sports event or of information about sports — **sports·cast·er** *also* **sport·cast·er** \-tə(r)\ *n* -s

sports·dom \-tsdəm, -tstəm\ *n* -s **:** the realm of sports; *esp* **:** the whole field of organized competitive sport

sports editor *also* **sport editor** *n* **:** a newspaper editor in charge of news about sports

sport shirt *n* **:** a soft shirt styled for casual wear with or without a tie or open at the neck and having long or short sleeves and usu. a square bottom for wear inside or outside the trousers

sports·man \'⸗mən\ *n, pl* **sportsmen :** a person who is active in sports: as **a :** one who engages in the sports of the field and esp. in hunting or fishing **b** *archaic* **:** one who gambles at cards or on sports and esp. on horse racing **:** a sporting man **c :** one who in sports is fair and generous **:** one who in any connection has recourse to nothing illegitimate **:** a person who is a good loser and a graceful winner

sports·man·like \'⸗⸗,⸗\ *adj* **:** characteristic of a sportsman **:** consistent with the ideals of good sportsmanship

sports·man·ly *adj* **:** SPORTSMANLIKE

sports·man·ship \'⸗⸗,ship\ *n* **1** *archaic* **:** skill or an instance of skillful performance in some sport **2 :** conduct becoming to a sportsman and involving fair honest rivalry, courteous relations, and graceful acceptance of results

sports page *n* **:** a page of a newspaper given over to sports news

sports section *n* **:** a section of a newspaper given over to sports news

sportswear \'⸗,⸗\ *n* -s **:** clothing suitable for wearing while engaged in an active sport (as tennis, golf, skiing) ⟨a store specializing in ~⟩; *also* **:** the wearing of such clothing or an occasion on which such clothing might suitably be worn ⟨sell clothing for ~⟩

sportswoman \'⸗,⸗⸗\ *n, pl* **sportswomen :** a female sportsman

sportswriter \'⸗,⸗⸗\ *n* **:** one who writes about sports esp. for a newspaper

sportsy \'spōrtsē\ *adj, sometimes* -ER/-EST [[1]*sports* + *-y*] **1 :** suitable for sportswear **2 :** suggesting sportswear in design, motif, or cut **:** suitable for sport clothes

spor·tu·la \'spȯ(r)chələ\ *n, pl* **sportu·lae** \-chə,lē\ *also* **sportulas** [L, lit., little basket, dim. of *sporta* basket, fr. (assumed) Etruscan *spurta*, fr. Gk *spurid-*, *spuris;* akin to Gk *sparton* plaited rope, esparto — more at SPIRE (spiral)] **:** a gift (as of food or money) usu. from an ancient Roman to one of his clients and often at regular intervals or on prescribed occasions

sporty \'spōr|d·|ē, -pȯr|, -pōə|, -pȯ(ə)|, |t|, |i\ *adj* -ER/-EST **1 :** characteristic of a sport or a sportsman **:** SPORTSMANLIKE **2 a :** notably gay or dissipated **:** FAST, LOOSE ⟨ran around with a very ~ crowd⟩ **b :** FLASHY, SHOWY ⟨~ clothes⟩ **3 :** capable of giving or designed to give good sport **:** suitable for sport or for a particular sport ⟨a ~ little boat⟩ ⟨a ~ golf course⟩

spor·u·lar \'spȯryələ(r), -pär-\ *adj* [NL *sporula* sporule + E *-ar*] **1 :** of, relating to, or having the nature of a sporule **2 :** SPOROID

spor·u·late \-yə,lāt\ *vb* -ED/-ING/-S [back-formation fr. *sporulation*] *vi* **:** to undergo sporulation ~ *vt* **:** to transform into spores

spor·u·la·tion \,⸗⸗'lāshən\ *n* -s [NL *sporula* + ISV *-ation*] **:** the formation of spores; *esp* **:** division into many small spores (as after encystment) — **spor·u·la·tive** \'⸗⸗,lād·iv\ *adj*

spor·ule \'spȯr,yül, -pär-\ *n* -s [F or NL; F *sporule*, fr. NL *sporula*, dim. of *spora* spore] **:** a small spore

-spory \,spōrē, ˌspərē, -ri\ *n comb form* -ES [*-sporic* + *-y*] **:** the quality or state of having (such or such a number of) spores ⟨apo*spory*⟩ ⟨homo*spory*⟩

sposh \'späsh\ *n* [prob. blend of *slush* and [1]*posh*] *dial* **:** soft slushy mud or snow — **sposhy** \-shē\ *adj*

[1]spot \'spät, *usu* -äd·+V\ *n* -s [ME *spotte*, *spot;* akin to MD *spotte* stain, speck, ON *spotti* small piece, bit] **1 :** a taint on character or reputation **:** blemish upon moral purity **:** DISGRACE, STIGMA, FAULT, REPROACH ⟨keep this commandment without ~ —1 Tim 6:14 (AV)⟩ ⟨the only ~ upon the family name⟩ **2 a :** a usu. disfiguring mark on a substance or body made by a deposit of foreign matter **:** discolored place **:** BLOT, SPECK, STAIN ⟨out, damned ~ —Shak.⟩ ⟨a dark ~ that might have been blood⟩ ⟨conscious of a grease ~ on his necktie⟩ ⟨tablecloth had many ~*s*⟩ ⟨one coat is guaranteed to cover all ~*s* and blemishes⟩ ⟨remove all common household ~*s* such as ink, oil, tar, paint, gum —*Sears, Roebuck Cat.*⟩ **b :** such a disfiguring mark or discolored place resulting from natural causes (as injury, disease) ⟨bruised ~ on an apple⟩ ⟨cut out several ~*s* of rot⟩: as (1) **:** a circumscribed area (as of different density, rarefaction) in an organ seen by means of X rays or an instrument (as an ophthalmoscope) ⟨a ~ on the retina⟩ ⟨left him with a ~ on his lungs —Green Peyton⟩ (2) **:** PIMPLE (3) **:** SUNSPOT (4) **:** NEVUS (5) **:** one of the circumscribed discolored areas produced on a plant (as upon leaves, fruits) by various fungi or by nonparasitic agencies — compare RUST **3 :** a small part or area differing to the eye (as in color, finish, composition) from the main ground or surface ⟨a leopard's ~*s*⟩ ⟨black silk with white ~*s*⟩ ⟨orchards made ~*s* of pink among the green meadows⟩ ⟨patterns of transparent ~*s* on photographic film —*Machine Literature Searching*⟩ ⟨added up the ~*s* on the dice⟩ ⟨set of dominoes with badly worn ~*s*⟩ ⟨combed his hair over a bald ~⟩ ⟨saw ~*s* before his eyes⟩: as **a** *obs* **:** BEAUTY SPOT, PATCH **b :** a blaze on a tree **c** (1) **:** a conventionalized design used on playing cards to distinguish suits and indicate values — called also *pip* (2) **:** any similar distinguishing device (as a numeral) used on objects (as billiard balls, paper money) in a set or series (3) **:** an object having a specified number of such designs or devices on its surface or bearing a specified distinguishing numeral ⟨played the six⸗*spot*⟩ ⟨sank the three-*spot* in the corner pocket⟩ ⟨handed the waiter a ten-*spot*⟩ **d** (1) **:** any of the small marks on the bed of a billiard or pool table indicating where balls are to be placed (2) **:** SPOT BALL (3) **:** SPOT STROKE **e** (1) **:** any of the circular marks painted on or embedded in the floor of a bowling alley to indicate the positions of the pins in tenpins and similar games (2) **:** the calculated spot part way down the alley at which a spot bowler aims when attempting to make a strike **f** (1) **:** a small character (as a star or diamond) used in printing as an ornament or eye-arresting device (2) **:** a small simple illustration usu. without a rectangular border or frame placed amid or at the end of type matter **4 a :** a small quantity or amount **:** BIT, PARTICLE ⟨not a ~ of room anywhere⟩ **b** *chiefly Brit* **:** a relatively small but indeterminate amount ⟨doing a ~ of wrestling —A.J.Liebling⟩ ⟨go over . . . for a ~ of lunch —John Brooks⟩ ⟨liked nothing better than a ~ of conversation —Thomas Sugrue⟩ ⟨do a ~ of big-game fishing —Alden Hatch⟩ ⟨lie down for a ~ of rest⟩ ⟨stopped for a ~ of beer⟩; *specif* **:** a smallish amount of liquor **:** DROP, DRINK ⟨could do with a few ~*s* —A.P.Gaskell⟩ ⟨how about having a ~⟩ **5 a :** a particular locality esp. of somewhat limited extent ⟨one of the most beautiful ~*s* in the world⟩ ⟨prepared to move the capital to a safer ~⟩ ⟨selected a ~ for the next annual meeting⟩ ⟨words from all the ~*s* on the earth —Charlton Laird⟩ ⟨any ~ . . . was more endurable than the place she was in —Ellen Glasgow⟩ ⟨hottest ~*s* . . . were Parliament itself, Spain, and Ireland —G.W.Johnson⟩ ⟨two foremost danger ~*s* in the East-West struggle —Carlyle Morgan⟩ **b :** a small extent of space ⟨the exact ~ where the crash occurred⟩ ⟨trying to find a dry ~ for a picnic⟩ ⟨found the right ~ behind the books, and the click of a sliding panel was heard —T.B.Costain⟩ ⟨X marks the ~⟩ ⟨looking for a quiet ~ to fish⟩ **c :** a locality or a building used or suitable for a particular purpose ⟨favorite vacation ~ for New Yorkers⟩ ⟨excellent picnic ~*s*⟩ ⟨his favorite fishing ~⟩ ⟨well-known gambling ~⟩ ⟨cleaning up the vice ~*s*⟩ ⟨famous dining ~*s* —*Ford Times*⟩; *esp* **:** NIGHTCLUB ⟨had a late dinner and then took in a few ~*s*⟩ ⟨tried another ~, where there was dancing —Molly L. Bar-David⟩ ⟨a Chicago jazz ~ —Martin Gardner⟩ **6 :** a small part or area differing from the whole to which it belongs ⟨represented on the tape by invisible magnetic ~*s* —*Univac*⟩ ⟨sensory ~*s* on the skin —R.S.Woodworth⟩ ⟨complained of a sore ~ in his throat⟩ ⟨finger detected a rough ~⟩ ⟨high ~*s* of each publishing season —William Peden⟩ ⟨another dark ~ appeared to be brightening as farm prices steadied —*Dun's Rev.*⟩ ⟨do not have excessively bright ~*s* in their pattern of mental abilities —R.J.Williams⟩ ⟨has ~*s* of very fine acting —Henry Huses⟩ **7 :** a small croaker (*Leiostomus xanthurus*) of the Atlantic coast of the U. S. that is highly esteemed as a panfish and that has a black spot behind the shoulders and 15 oblique dark bars **8 :** a particular position or situation esp. in order of priority (as in a place of employment, an organization, a program or schedule or on a slate or ticket) ⟨the top ~*s* in industry and finance —W.G. Hardy⟩ **:** BERTH, BILLET, POST ⟨finally found a ~ as a receptionist⟩ ⟨a Cabinet ~ here, an undersecretaryship there —E.J. Kahn⟩ ⟨been tried at every ~ except pitcher and catcher —W. B.Furlong⟩ ⟨if he ended up in my ~ one day —Louis Auchincloss⟩; *esp* **:** a place on a program of entertainment ⟨deserve a better ~ on the program —T.W.Duncan⟩ ⟨had a solo ~⟩ ⟨shifted him to a daytime ~⟩ ⟨engaged him for a 15 minute dramatic ~⟩ ⟨has several guest ~*s* lined up⟩ **9 spots** *pl* [[3]*spot*] **:** commodities (as merchandise and cotton) sold for immediate delivery **10 a** [by shortening] **:** SPOTLIGHT ⟨gallery ~*s*⟩ ⟨proscenium ~*s*⟩ ⟨an amber ~⟩ ⟨a battery of baby ~*s* —Christopher Morley⟩ ⟨individually lighted by a ~ in the ceiling —*Lamp*⟩ **b :** the spot of light that results from an electron beam hitting the phosphor in a picture tube and that traces out the television picture **11 a :** a situation with respect to conditions and circumstances **:** POSITION ⟨a tough ~⟩ ⟨in a fine ~ for rapid promotion⟩ **b :** a position of difficulty or embarrassment **:** FIX, PREDICAMENT ⟨was indeed in a dilemma — in a ~ —R.M.Lovett⟩ ⟨one of those ~*s* you get in —J.M.Cain⟩ **12 :** a brief interval between scheduled radio or television programs during which an announcement or advertisement is broadcast; *also* **:** the announcement or advertisement broadcast — **in spots :** at intervals **:** in some respects ⟨not unhappy — except *in spots* —Ellen Glasgow⟩ — **on the spot** *or* **upon the spot** *adv* (*or adj*) **1 :** before moving or without further consideration **:** at once **:** IMMEDIATELY ⟨decided *on the spot*⟩ **2 :** at the place where action is required ⟨sent to investigate *on the spot*⟩ ⟨found everything he needed right *on the spot*⟩ **3 a :** in a position of being held responsible or accountable or of being required to furnish a satisfactory explanation or reply **:** in trouble or difficulty **:** in a spot **b :** in a position of danger esp. of murder or assassination (as by way of reprisal) — often used in the phrase *put on the spot*

[2]spot \"\ *vb* **spotted; spotted; spotting; spots** [ME *spotten*, fr. *spotte*, *spot* spot] *vt* **1 a :** to taint or stain the character or reputation of **:** DISGRACE ⟨may I live *spotted* for my perjury —Francis Beaumont & John Fletcher⟩ **b** (1) *obs* **:** BLAME, ASPERSE (2) **:** give information against **2 :** to mark with a disfiguring or discoloring spot ⟨*spotted* his necktie⟩ **:** stain in spots **:** cover with spots ⟨trail of blood *spotted* the snow⟩ ⟨was *spotted* with mud from top to bottom⟩ ⟨fungus that ~*s* the leaves⟩ **3 :** to mark with a distinctive spot (as for ornament, identification) ⟨a book with edges *spotted* by hand⟩: as **a** *obs* **:** to affix a beauty spot to (the face) **b :** to put a blaze on (a tree) **:** mark (as a line or trail) with blazes **c** (1) **:** to mark (as watch or clock plates, flat surfaces of fine tools) with equally spaced whirls produced by a light abrasive (2) **:** to make a mark on (a surface) as a locating mark for laying out or other operations in machining **d :** to mark (as a railroad tie) by a spot of paint or other means as requiring particular attention **4 :** to single out **:** pick out **:** IDENTIFY: as **a :** to mark or note as a known criminal or as a suspicious person **b :** to pick out or choose in advance (one of a number of contestants) as the winner **c :** to pick out with the eye **:** catch sight of **:** DETECT, NOTICE, RECOGNIZE, SEE ⟨~ a mistake⟩ ⟨*spotted* the fire and turned in an alarm⟩ ⟨among the first to ~ the danger⟩ ⟨how to ~ a subversive⟩ ⟨*spotted* a friend in the distance⟩ ⟨*spotted* him at once for an American⟩ ⟨*spotting* airplanes⟩ **d** (1) **:** to locate (a position) accurately (as on the ground or on a map) ⟨~ the fall of a shell⟩ ⟨gunners were unable to ~ their shots⟩ ⟨*spotted* the position of the battery⟩ ⟨in *spotting* these crime locations . . . use one map with different colored tacks —V.A.Leonard⟩ (2) **:** to observe (a shot) on a target with s spotting scope **5 a :** to form or appear as spots on **:** DOT, STUD ⟨here and there figures *spotted* the twilight —Scott Fitzgerald⟩ ⟨aviation landing-fields with which California is *spotted* —Aubrey Drury⟩ ⟨small boats *spotting* a harbor⟩ **b :** to place in various spots **:** locate at intervals ⟨~ field telephones and observers strategically —*Motor Trend*⟩ ⟨men who represent the firm are *spotted* throughout the country —Victor Boesen⟩ **6 :** to place on an appointed or desired spot **:** put in position ⟨~ a billiard ball⟩ ⟨cameras were *spotted* about twenty feet from the judges' bench —S.J.Perelman⟩ ⟨*spotted* high in the top gallery, the voices floated easily through the hall —Irving Kolodin⟩ ⟨table is small enough to be *spotted* in tight quarters —*Flow Quarterly*⟩: as **a :** to place (as a freight car, truck, trailer, crane) in a desired position for loading or unloading **b :** to prick out or transplant (as young vegetable or flowering plants) **c** (1) **:** to fix in the beam of a spotlight ⟨mass spectacles in which individual acts were *spotted* —Winifred Bambrick⟩ ⟨door is sometimes *spotted* in this manner, with a special mat shaping the light beam —Herbert Philippi⟩ (2) **:** to direct or focus on like a spotlight ⟨his genial smile was *spotted* on everyone in turn —Osbert Sitwell⟩ **d :** to schedule (as a performer, an act, a program) in a particular position or at a particular time : assign a spot to ⟨*spotted* the main bout at ten o'clock⟩ ⟨is *spotted* on a daily pop show —*Down Beat*⟩ ⟨if you have a good program, ~ it opposite another fine show —Gilbert Seldes⟩ **7 :** to rid of a spot or other small defect: as **a :** to touch out (as with India ink, opaque, pencil) defects consisting of clear spots in (a photographic negative) **:** remove similar spots on (a print) with transparent pigment — often used with *out* **b :** to remove a spot or mark from (a fabric) **8 :** to allow as a handicap ⟨*spotted* his opponent five points and still won easily⟩ ⟨~ him two strokes a hole⟩ **:** concede as an advantage ⟨will ~ his rival ten years but nevertheless expected to be the favorite —*N.Y. Times*⟩ ⟨an old timer . . . could have *spotted* the big elephant all his blubber and laid him low in a round —J.T.Farrell⟩ **~ vi 1 :** to become stained or discolored in spots ⟨fungus caused the leaves to ~⟩ ⟨cloth that tends to ~ in the rain⟩ **2 :** to make a spot **:** cause staining ⟨always said gin didn't ~ —Victoria Lincoln⟩ **3 :** to act as a spotter esp. in locating enemy targets ⟨was *spotting* for mortar fire —Mack Morriss⟩; *specif* **:** to locate targets for land batteries or warships from the air ⟨planes had spent the morning *spotting*⟩

³spot \"\ *adj* [¹*spot*] **1 :** being, originating, or done on the spot or on or in or for a particular spot ⟨favored ~ control rather than general restrictions⟩ ⟨~ regulation of traffic —E. G.Mogren & W.S.Smith⟩ ⟨treatment of ~ unemployment —*New Republic*⟩: as **a** (1) **:** on hand for immediate delivery after sale — used of commodities ⟨~ wheat⟩ ⟨~ cocoa⟩ or of services ⟨~ cargo offering⟩ (2) **:** making a specialty of transactions in spot commodities ⟨~ broker⟩ **b** (1) **:** paid or ready for payment at once upon delivery of property purchased ⟨~ cash⟩ (2) **:** involving immediate cash payment ⟨a ~ transaction⟩ (3) **:** engaged in or making a specialty of cash transactions ⟨the ~ market⟩ ⟨a ~ firm⟩ **c :** designed to replace precisely a defective spot ⟨~ insert in a page of standing type⟩ ⟨~ patch for an electrotype⟩ **d :** originating at the scene of a newsworthy event ⟨~ coverage of a foreign election⟩ **e** (1) **:** broadcast between two scheduled radio or television programs or between parts of a scheduled program (as during a station break) ⟨20-second ~ announcements throughout the day —*New Republic*⟩ ⟨well placed ~ commercial campaign —S.H.Britt⟩ (2) **:** originating in or sent out from a local radio or television station for a national advertiser ⟨~ broadcasts⟩ ⟨use of electrical transcriptions in ~ broadcasting⟩ ⟨~ broadcasting . . . represents more than a third of all investment in television time —H.W.McMahan⟩ **2 :** made at random or restricted to a few key or sample places or instances ⟨an adequate job of ~ research, using only the principal references —W.N.Fenton⟩ ⟨a ~ test⟩ ⟨cross-country ~ check on current business —*Banking*⟩ ⟨a small ~ survey of where they go and what they like to eat —Jane Nickerson⟩; *also* **:** selected at random or as a sample ⟨~ questions⟩ ⟨a dozen ~ cities west of the Mississippi⟩

⁴spot \"\ *adv* [¹*spot*] **:** for cash

spot anthracnose *n* **:** any of several plant diseases characterized by light-colored spots with tissue overgrowth forming a raised border; *specif* **:** such a disease caused by fungi of the genus *Sphaceloma* or its perfect stage *Elsinoë*

spot ball *n* **:** the cue ball in billiards marked with a black spot

spot–barred \ˈ=,=\ *adj* **:** constituting or relating to a game (as English billiards) in which the red ball is placed upon the center spot after two spot strokes

spot blight *n* **:** GREASE SPOT

spot blotch *n* **:** a disease of barley characterized by dark-colored elongated spots on the leaves caused by a fungus (*Helminthosporium sativum*) — compare NET BLOTCH

spot board *n* **:** a sighting board laid across the rails in advance of a railroad track-raising gang to indicate the required amount of lift

spot bowling *n* **:** bowling in which a bowler aims at a calculated spot part way down the alley rather than directly at the pins — compare HEADPIN BOWLING

spot card *n* **1 :** a playing card of rank two to nine inclusive **2 :** a playing card except an ace or face card but including the ten

spot–check \ˈ=,=\ *vt* **:** to cause to undergo a spot check **:** sample quickly or roughly **:** test or investigate in a random manner ⟨*spot-checks* income tax returns —J.H.Lavely⟩ ⟨*spot-checked* for accuracy⟩ **~** *vi* **:** to make a spot check ⟨*spot-check* on . . . program reactions for advertisers —*Advertising Age*⟩

spot drawing *n* **:** a small decorative drawing usu. in black and white

spot–drill \ˈ=,=\ *vt* **:** to drill a shallow hole or one just deep enough to locate a spot (as for use as a guide in further drilling)

spot–face \ˈ=,=\ *vt* **:** to machine or face a spot of surface as the seat for a bolt head or nut

spot·fac·er \" + ə(r)\ *n* [*spot-face* + *-er*] **:** a counterbore for use in spot-facing

spot film *n* **:** a roentgenogram of a restricted area in the body taken by means of a radiolucent pressure cone that is pressed upon the spot to be radiographed

spotfin croaker \ˈ=,=-\ *n* [so called fr. the large black spot on the pectoral fin] **:** a large croaker (*Roncador stearnsii*) of the California coast that is metallic steel-blue above and silvery below and is a popular sport fish

spot fire *n* **:** a fire started by flying sparks or embers at a distance from the main fire

spot–grind \ˈ=,=\ *vt* **:** to grind a spot of a surface or any small area

spot lamp *n* **:** SPOTLIGHT

spot lens *n* **:** a condensing lens in which the light is confined to an annular pencil by a small round diaphragm and which is used in dark-field illumination

spot·less \ˈspätləs\ *adj* **:** having no spot; *esp* **:** free from impurity or reproach **:** IMMACULATE, UNSPOTTED ⟨~ white linen⟩ ⟨~ kitchens⟩ ⟨shining ~ silver⟩ **:** BLAMELESS, IRREPROACHABLE, PURE, UNBLEMISHED ⟨his ~ youth⟩ ⟨had kept herself ~⟩ ⟨~ hero⟩ ⟨~ reputation⟩ — **spot·less·ly** *adv* — **spot·less·ness** *n* -ES

¹spotlight \ˈ=,=\ *n* [¹*spot* + *light*] **1 a :** a projected spot or circle of light used to illuminate brilliantly a single person or object or group on a stage while leaving the rest of the stage more or less unilluminated **b :** conspicuous public notice or attention or a place, occasion, or set of circumstances receiving such notice or attention ⟨held the political ~⟩ ⟨hated the ~⟩ ⟨their momentary place in the ~ —J.D.Hart⟩ ⟨wants to get out of the ~ —*Reporter*⟩ ⟨~ shifted westward last week —W.A. Howe⟩ **2 a** (1) **:** a device resembling a small searchlight with an adjustable reflector and consisting typically of an incandescent or arc light in a housing designed to direct a narrow intense beam of light upon a chosen small area (as of a stage or a photographic subject) (2) **:** such a device mounted on an adjustable bracket (as at the side of the windshield of an automobile) so that it can be adjusted to light up objects ahead or to the side **b :** something that illuminates as brilliantly and clearly as a spotlight ⟨series of talks . . . throwing a ~ round the world, illuminating continent after continent —*London Calling*⟩ ⟨throwing a ~ into certain hitherto dark corners of union policy —*Ethyl News*⟩ ⟨succinct penetrating ~*s* on the characters —Fanny Butcher⟩

²spotlight \"\ *vt* **1 :** to illuminate with or as if with a spotlight **:** direct a spotlight upon ⟨dreading the moment when . . . she would be *spotlighted*, pinpointed, impaled, focused upon —A.R.Marcus⟩ ⟨have the whole ghastly process of disintegration *spotlit* —Gwyn Thomas⟩ ⟨a program which ~*s* student musicians —D.R.Meltzer⟩ ⟨discoveries which have recently *spotlighted* this subject —R.W.Murray⟩ **2 :** JACK 1

spotlight·er \" + ə(r)\ *n* **:** one that uses a spotlight; *esp* **:** JACKLIGHTER

spot lighting *n* [¹*spot* + *lighting*] **:** illumination of a part or the whole of an object to a brightness much greater than that of its surroundings by a beam or several beams of light from a distance

spotlike \ˈ=,=\ *adj* **:** resembling a spot

spot line *n* **:** a single line specially rigged to fly a piece of theatrical scenery that cannot be handled by the regular lines

spot–mill \ˈ=,=\ *vt* **:** to mill a spot of a surface or any small area

spot news *n* **:** up-to-date immediately reported news ⟨*spot-news* pictures from the war fronts —John Larkin⟩

spot pass *n* **:** a pass (as in football, basketball, ice hockey) made to a predetermined spot usu. well down the field or court rather than directly to a player

spot plate *n* **:** a porcelain or glass plate usu. with several small depressions for use in spot tests

spot price *n* **:** the price of spot goods — contrasted with *future price*

spot rot *n* **1 :** JONATHAN SPOT **2 :** a general decay of apples in cold storage caused by a fungus (*Botrytis cinerea*) and characterized by brown spots each centering at a lenticel

spotrump \ˈ=,=\ *n* [¹*spot* + *rump*; fr. the white spot on its tail] **:** HUDSONIAN GODWIT

spots *pl of* SPOT, *pres 3d sing of* SPOT

spot sheet *n* **:** a makeready sheet that has been spotted up

spots·man \ˈspätsmən\ *n, pl* **spotsmen :** one that spots, watches, or points out; *esp* **:** SMUGGLER

spot snapper *n* [so called fr. the red blotch below the soft dorsal fin] **:** any of several snappers; *esp* **:** LANE SNAPPER

spot stroke *n* **:** the pocketing of the red ball in English billiards in a top corner pocket from off its own spot so as to leave the cue ball in position for another winning hazard — see SPOT-BARRED

spot·ta·ble \ˈspäd·əbəl, -ätəb-\ *adj* **:** capable of being spotted; *esp* **:** that easily becomes spotted or stained ⟨~ fabrics⟩

spottail \ˈ=,=\ *n* **:** CHANNEL BASS

spottail shiner *n* **:** a common shiner (*Notropis hudsonius*) of lakes and larger streams of the central and northeastern U.S. that is distinguished by a black blotch at the base of the caudal fin

spot·ted \ˈspäd·əd, -ätəd\ *adj* [ME, fr. ¹*spot* + *-ed*] **1 :** marked with spots ⟨the ~ coat of a leopard⟩ ⟨no ~ pony is ever pure Shetland —Ben Riker⟩ ⟨checked, ~, colored and printed petticoats —*Fashions & Fabrics*⟩ **2 a :** marked with disfiguring spots ⟨320 pages; front cover ~⟩ ⟨a ~ youth who lounged against the lorry —I.A.N.Henderson⟩ **b :** SULLIED, TARNISHED ⟨inherited a ~ name⟩ **3 :** characterized or attended by the appearance of spots **4** [fr. past part. of ²*spot*] **:** noticed by others **:** MARKED; *esp* **:** being under watch or suspicion **:** SUSPECTED **5** [fr. past part. of ²*spot*] **:** having an irregular distribution **:** scattered in spots **:** SPOTTY

spotted adder *n* **1 :** MILK SNAKE **2 :** HOGNOSE SNAKE

spotted alder *n* **:** WITCH HAZEL 2a(1)

spotted arum *n* **:** CUCKOOPINT

spotted asparagus beetle *n* **:** a chrysomelid beetle (*Crioceris duodecimpunctata*) that feeds on asparagus in Europe and the northeastern U.S.

spotted bass *n* **1 :** CHANNEL BASS **2 :** SPOTTED BLACK BASS

spotted bat *n* **:** JACKASS BAT

spotted black bass *n* **:** a black bass (*Micropterus pseudoplites*) intermediate in several respects between the largemouth and smallmouth black basses and wide-ranging in the central U.S.

spotted blenny *n* **:** OCELLATED BLENNY

spotted blister beetle *n* **:** a black-spotted gray beetle (*Epicauta maculata*) of the family Meloidae that is destructive in the adult stage to potatoes and other crops

spotted bowerbird *n* **:** a semigregarious bowerbird (*Chlamydera maculata*) of inland scrublands of Australia that builds a very large bower decorated with bright objects (as bleached bone or bits of glass)

spotted bur clover *n* **:** SPOTTED MEDIC

¹spotted cat *or* **spotted catfish** *n* **:** a widely distributed black-spotted catfish (*Ictalurus lacustris*) of the Mississippi drainage and the southeastern U.S. that commonly attains a weight of five pounds and is regarded as superior to most catfishes as food

²spotted cat *n* **:** a wildcat with a blotched or spotted coat; *also* **:** the pelt of such a wildcat

spotted cavy *n* **:** PACA

spotted clover *n* **:** any of several plants of the genus *Medicago* that resemble clover; *esp* **:** SPOTTED MEDIC

spotted cowbane *or* **spotted hemlock** *n* **:** a tall biennial water hemlock (*Cicuta maculata*) of northeastern No. America with purple-mottled stems and clusters of tuberous roots that resemble small sweet potatoes and are extremely poisonous

spotted crake *n* **:** a small European rail (*Porzana porzana*) similar to the American sora — called also *spotted rail*

spotted cranesbill *n* **:** a common wild geranium (*Geranium maculatum*) of eastern No. America with deeply parted leaves and rose-purple flowers

spotted cucumber beetle *n* **:** a rather slender greenish yellow beetle (*Diabrotica undecimpunctata howardi*) that feeds as an adult on the foliage and flowers of various ornamental and crop plants and is a vector of wilt disease of cucurbit plants (as cucumbers and melons) — see SOUTHERN CORN ROOTWORM

spotted cuscus *n* **:** an Australian phalanger (*Phalanger maculatus*)

spotted cutworm *n* **:** a cutworm that is the larva of a noctuid moth (*Amathes c-nigrum*) and that feeds on various crop plants

spotted dead nettle *n* **:** a perennial dead nettle (*Lamium maculatum*) having usu. a pale blotch bordering the leaf midrib

spotted deer *n* **:** AXIS 1

spotted dick *n, often cap S&D* **1** *Brit* **:** SPOTTED DOG 1 **2 :** DALMATIAN 2

spotted dog *n* [prob. alter. of *spotted dick*] **1** *Brit* **:** a suet pudding containing raisins or currants **2 a :** a light-colored dog with dark spots **b** *often cap S&D* **:** DALMATIAN 2

spotted dogfish *n* **:** any of various dogfishes with a blotched or spotted skin; *esp* **:** a common European dogfish (*Scylliorhinus canicula*) sometimes used for food

spotted eagle *n* **:** a small eagle (*Aquila clanga*) ranging from southern Europe to China

spotted eagle ray *n* **:** an eagle ray (*Aetobatus narinari* or *Stoasodon narinari*) widely distributed in warm seas and having the upper surface more or less thickly covered with white or yellow spots — called also *spotted ray*

spotted fever *n* **:** any of various eruptive fevers: as **a :** TYPHUS **b :** ROCKY MOUNTAIN SPOTTED FEVER

spotted fever tick *n* **:** a tick that transmits the rickettsia of Rocky Mountain spotted fever; *esp* **:** a common tick (*Dermacentor venustus*) of western No. America

spotted–finned sunfish \ˈ==,=-\ *n* **:** a spotted sunfish (*Enneacanthus gloriosus*)

spotted flycatcher *n* **:** a flycatcher (*Muscicapa striata*) of Europe

spotted gar *n* **:** a widely distributed gar (*Lepisosteus productus*) of the eastern half of the U.S.

spotted goby *n* **:** a small European goby (*Gobius minutus*) that is gray with numerous dark spots and lives on sandy shores

spotted ground squirrel *n* **:** a brightly patterned ground squirrel (*Citellus spilosoma*) of the western U.S.

spotted grunter *n* **:** a large grunter (*Pomadasys operculare*) widely distributed in coastal waters and tidal estuaries of the Indian ocean and highly esteemed as a food and sport fish in southern Africa

spotted gum *n* **:** either of two Australian eucalypts (*Eucalyptus maculata* and *E. goniocalyx*) with dotted pale leaves

spotted hound *n* **:** a grayish brown black-spotted smooth dogfish (*Mustelus punctulatus*) that is common in warm seas of the Old World

spotted hyena *n* **:** a hyena (*Hyena crocuta* or *Crocuta crocuta*) of Africa south of the Sahara with the coat blotched with black

spotted jewelweed *n* **:** a common American jewelweed (*Impatiens biflora*) with mottled petals

spotted jewfish *n* **:** a grouper (*Promicrops itaiara*) of the West Indies and the west coast of Mexico that is one of the largest of all fishes

spotted knotweed *n* **:** LADY'S THUMB

spotted liver *n* **:** coccidiosis of the liver of the rabbit

spotted loco *or* **spotted locoweed** *n* **:** a perennial locoweed (*Astragalus lentiginosus*) of western No. America that has racemose flowers and often purplish mottled sparsely pubescent pods and is poisonous to livestock

spotted locust *n* **:** LOCUST 3a(2)

spot·ted·ly *adv* **:** SPOTTILY

spotted lynx *n* **:** a southern European lynx (*Lynx pardina*) now chiefly limited to the Spanish Pyrenees that is of a rufous color obscurely spotted with black

spotted medic *n* **:** a spreading annual medic (*Medicago arabica*) having yellow flowers, spotted leaflets, and coiled furrowed pods

spotted moray *n* **:** ²HAMLET 2

spotted–necked otter \ˈ==,=-\ *n* **:** a rather small brown nocturnal southern African otter (*Lutra maculicollis*) with pale markings on the throat and inguinal region

spotted nemophila *n* **:** FIVE-SPOT

spot·ted·ness *n* -ES **:** the quality or state of being spotted

spotted newt *n* **:** SMOOTH NEWT

spotted oak *n* **1 :** a water oak (*Quercus nigra*) **2 :** a black oak (*Quercus velutina*) **3 :** TEXAS RED OAK

spotted orchis *also* **spotted orchid** *n* **1 :** a Eurasian orchid (*Orchis maculata*) with purplish or whitish flowers spotted with purplish brown and palmate tubers **2 :** a leafless orchid (*Dipodium punctatum*) of Tasmania with rose-colored flowers

spotted parsley *n* **1 :** POISON HEMLOCK 1 **2 :** SPOTTED COWBANE

spotted pelidnota *n* **:** a large brownish orange beetle (*Pelidnota punctata*) with black dots on the thorax and elytra that feeds as an adult on grape foliage and as a larva in decaying wood

spotted rail *or* **spotted skitty** *or* **spotted water hen** *n* **:** SPOTTED CRAKE

spotted ray *or* **spotted sting ray** *or* **spotted whip ray** *n* **:** SPOTTED EAGLE RAY

spotted redshank *n* **:** a redshank (*Tringa erythropus*) that is larger than the common redshank and has orange-red legs

spotted rockfish *n* **:** STARRY ROCKFISH

spotted salamander *n* **:** any of various tailed amphibians having dark skin with usu. yellow spots or blotches: **a :** a European salamander (*Salamandra maculosa*) that is black with large yellow or orange blotches — called also *fire salamander* **b :** a common No. American amphibian (*Ambystoma maculatum* syn. *A. punctatum*) with glossy black skin spotted with yellow on the back

spotted sandpiper *n* **:** a common sandpiper (*Actitis macularia*) that breeds throughout No. America and frequents both fresh and salt water, that in summer has the underparts of the adult heavily spotted with black, and that has a plaintive whistling note and when walking or standing bobs its head and tail continually

spotted schaapsteker *n* **:** SCHAAPSTEKER a

spotted skate *n* **:** WINTER SKATE

spotted skunk *n* **:** LITTLE SPOTTED SKUNK

spotted spurge *n* **:** a common milky-juiced weed (*Euphorbia maculata*) of eastern No. America having spotted leaves

spotted sucker *n* **1 :** a sucker (*Minytrema melanops*) chiefly of small rivers of the central and southeastern U.S. that is marked by rows of small black dots occurring one on each scale **2 :** HOG SUCKER

spotted sunfish *n* **1 :** either of two small sunfishes (*Enneacanthus obesus* and *E. gloriosus*) of coastal streams of the eastern U.S. **2 :** STUMPKNOCKER

spotted tree *n* **:** LEOPARD TREE

spotted turtle *also* **spotted terrapin** *or* **spotted tortoise** *n* **:** a small American freshwater tortoise (*Clemmys guttata*) having a blackish carapace on which are scattered round yellow spots

spotted water hemlock *n* **:** SPOTTED COWBANE

spotted weakfish *or* **spotted sea trout** *or* **spotted squeateague** *n* **:** a weakfish (*Cynoscion nebulosus*) of the south Atlantic and Gulf coasts of the U.S.

spotted wilt *n* **:** TOMATO STREAK

spotted wintergreen *n* **:** a No. American evergreen herb (*Chimaphila maculata*) having white-mottled leaves and corymbose or umbellate white or pinkish flowers

spotted woodpecker *n* **:** any of several European and Asiatic woodpeckers having the plumage of variegated black and white: as **a :** GREAT SPOTTED WOODPECKER **b :** a bird (*Dendrocopos minor*) resembling but smaller than the great spotted woodpecker — called also *lesser spotted woodpecker*

spot·ter \ˈspäd·ə(r), -ätə-\ *n* -S **1 :** one that makes a spot; *esp* **:** one that makes or applies a distinctive spot (as for identification or guidance or to mark a defect): as **a :** a device for producing by abrasion frosted or mottled spots on a flat finished metal surface (as for decorative effect or on the ways of machine tools for better holding of lubricants) **b :** DOTTER 2 **c :** one that by means of a microscope locates the correct place for drilling a diamond to be used as a die and drills a tiny starting hole **d :** a device on a railroad car for marking irregularities in the track **e :** a logger who notches trees **f :** a small disk of black metal having a spindle through the center by which it is attached to the target in target practice to indicate the exact position of a hit — called also *spotting disk* **2 :** one that looks out for, keeps watch on, or singles out something ⟨a moralizer and a ~ of universal calamities —R.H. Rovere⟩ ⟨traveled all over the state . . . as a ~ on the trail of oil —Myron Brinig⟩: as **a** (1) **:** DETECTIVE, SPY; *esp* **:** a person privately employed (as by a railroad, a business establishment) to detect dishonesty and irregularities of a particular kind ⟨worked as a ~ for a bus company⟩ ⟨~*s* follow every move of player and dealer —Oscar Lewis⟩ (2) **:** one that checks attendance of workers by locating them on their jobs at various times of the day according to a daily record sheet (3) **:** INVESTIGATOR c **b** (1) **:** one that locates the position of an enemy target and that reports deviations of gunfire from the target; *specif* **:** a naval officer whose duty in battle is to observe the fall of shot and to estimate the corrections necessary to bring the shots on the target (2) **:** an airplane employed in spotting enemy positions or targets; *also* **:** an airman engaged in such spotting (3) **:** a civilian watcher whose duty is to report all approaching airplanes (as by type, direction, speed) **c** (1) **:** a member of a gang of thieves who locates buildings to be robbed (2) **:** one of a gang of hijackers who follows a stolen truck and signals the approach of police **d** (1) **:** an auctioneer's assistant who watches the buyers for bids (2) **:** one that sits with a sportscaster at an athletic event (as a football game) to help identify players **3 :** one that removes spots: as **a :** one that covers imperfections in a photograph by touching them up with a brush or pencil **b** (1) **:** a dry cleaner who removes stains from fabrics by local treatment (2) **:** a solvent used in removing such stains **4 :** one that places something on or in an appointed or desired spot ⟨automatic bowling-pin ~*s* —*Newsweek*⟩: as **a :** one that determines and designates where a load (as from a truck or crane) is to be deposited or a vehicle (as a railroad car, truck, trailer) is to be placed (as for loading, unloading, parking) **b :** CAR PINCHER **c :** CRANE FOLLOWER **d :** a device for moving a freight car into position for loading or unloading **5 :** one that places himself in position to give support or assistance to a tumbler or gymnast if needed to prevent injury

spot test *n* **1 a :** a test conducted on the spot to yield immediate results **b :** a test limited to a few key or sample points or a relatively small percentage of random spots **2 :** a chemical test carried out with one to several drops of solution of the sample and the reagent in which spots (as on filter paper or a spot plate) indicate results usu. by a change in color of the solution or formation of a precipitate

spot·ti·ly \ˈspäd·ᵊl|ē, -ät|, |əl|, |i\ *adv* **:** in a spotty manner **:** so as to be spotty **:** without uniformity ⟨tackled on a major scale, and not just ~ —John Brooks⟩ ⟨account . . . is only ~ absorbing —Hollis Alpert⟩ ⟨rationality as well as unselfishness have existed ~ in the world —Priscilla Robertson⟩

spot·ti·ness \-ād·|ēnəs, -ät|, |in-\ *n* -ES **:** the quality or state of being spotty ⟨economical, clean heat without ~ or drafts —*Better Homes & Gardens*⟩ ⟨the ~ of American labor history is due largely to . . . the business cycles —Roger Burlingame⟩

spotting *pres part of* SPOT

spotting disk *n* [*spotting* (gerund of ²*spot*) + *disk*] **:** SPOTTER 1f

spotting scope *n* **:** a telescope for locating the strike of a bullet on a target

spot·tle \ˈspäd·ᵊl\ *vt* -ED/-ING/-S [²*spot* + *-le*] **:** SPOT, DOT

spot·ty \ˈspäd·ē, -ät|, |i\ *adj* -ER/-EST [ME, fr. ¹*spot* + *-y*] **1 a :** having many spots **:** marked with spots **:** SPOTTED **b** *obs* **:** DEFILED **2 :** occurring in spots **:** lacking uniformity (as in development, effect, quality) **:** IRREGULAR, PATCHY, UNEVEN ⟨~ attendance⟩ ⟨illumination was ~⟩ ⟨~ progress⟩ ⟨book is ~ . . . the whole work is not well integrated —A.L.Guérard⟩ ⟨a weak, ~ piece of music —Alfred Frankenstein⟩ ⟨program . . . was a rather ~ affair —Winthrop Sargeant⟩ ⟨a ~ public-school education, ending in his eleventh year —John Kobler⟩ ⟨medical care is ~ throughout the country —*Fortune*⟩ ⟨a poor musical director presiding over a ~ outfit —H.W.Wind⟩:

a *of a crop* **:** not evenly developed throughout the field **b :** active only in separated places or among a few isolated factors ⟨~ business⟩ ⟨a ~ market⟩ ⟨~ unemployment⟩

spot up *vt* **:** to paste patches of thin paper on (a makeready sheet) so as to give more impression to certain printing areas in a form

1spot-weld \'=,=\ *n* **:** a joint made by spot welding

2spot-weld *vt* **:** to weld two pieces at isolated spots rather than in a continuous seam

spot welding *n* **:** resistance welding in which the current and pressure are restricted to portions of the metal surfaces in contact

spot white *n* **:** SPOT BALL

spot zone *n* **:** SUNSPOT ZONE

spot zoning *n* **:** the illegal singling out of a small parcel of land within the limits of an area zoned for particular uses and permitting other uses for that parcel for the special benefit of its owners and to the detriment of the other owners in the area and not as a part of a scheme to benefit the entire area

1spous·al \'spaůsəl, -aůzəl\ *n* -s [ME *sposail, spousaille*, fr. MF *espousailles* espousal — more at ESPOUSAL] **1** *obs* **:** the married state **:** WEDLOCK **2 a :** the action of espousing esp. in marriage **b :** NUPTIALS — usu. used in pl.

2spousal \"\ *adj* **:** of, relating to, or celebrating marriage **:** CONJUGAL, MATRIMONIAL, NUPTIAL ⟨~ rites⟩ ⟨a fitting symbol of ~ love —W.H.Gardner⟩ ⟨thy ~ bower —Louise Guiney⟩ — **spous·al·ly** \-əlē\ *adv*

1spouse \'spaůs *also* -aůz\ *n* -s [ME *spuse, spouse*, fr. OF *spus, spous, espus* (masc.), *spuse, espouse* (fem.), fr. L *sponsus* (masc.) betrothed man, groom, *sponsa* (fem.) betrothed woman, bride, fr. *sponsus*, past part. of *spondēre* to promise solemnly, betroth; akin to Gk *spendein* to make a libation, promise, *spendesthai* to make a treaty, *spondē* libation, pl. treaty, Skt *spanti* he makes a libation] **1 :** a man or woman joined in wedlock **:** married person **:** HUSBAND, WIFE ⟨I that lady to my ~ had won —Edmund Spenser⟩ ⟨the accompanying ~ and children . . . travel at greatly reduced rates —P.J.C.Friedlander⟩ ⟨a responsible relative such as ~, father, mother, or child —*U.S.Code*⟩ ⟨free and full consent of the intending ~s —*U.N.Declaration of Human Rights*⟩ **2** *obs* **a :** BRIDE, BRIDEGROOM **b :** either one of a betrothed couple **:** FIANCÉ, FIANCÉE **3 a :** the church united in sacred bonds to God or to Christ **b :** a woman who by vow becomes an affianced of Christ **c :** God or Christ united in sacred bonds to the church

2spouse \'spaůz, 'spaůs\ *vt* [ME *spousen*, fr. 1*spouse*] **1** *obs* **:** to unite in marriage **:** give in marriage **2** *archaic* **:** ESPOUSE, WED **3** *obs* **:** AFFIANCE, BETROTH

spouse·hood \'spaůs,hůd *also* -aůz,-\ *n* [ME *spushod*, fr. *spuse* spouse + *-hod* -hood] *archaic* **:** the married state **:** MARRIAGE, WEDLOCK

spouse·less \'=ləs\ *adj* [ME, fr. 1*spouse* + *-less*] **:** having no spouse

1spout \'spaůt, *usu* -aůd·+V\ *vb* -ED/-ING/-S [ME *spouten*; akin to MD *spoiten* to spout, MHG *spiuzen* to spit, ON *spȳta* to spit, *spȳja* to spew — more at SPEW] *vt* **1 :** to throw out (as liquid, vapor, granulated material, tiny objects) in a stream **:** eject in a jet ⟨gleaming metal faucet that ~*ed* clear water —Julian Dana⟩ ⟨farmhouse windows ~*ed* flame and smoke —F.V.W.Mason⟩ ⟨wells ~*ed* 200 barrels an hour —*Amer. Guide Series: Pa.*⟩ ⟨chewing snuff or ~*ing* the brown residue into a tin pail —Earle Birney⟩ — often used with *out* ⟨machines of steel which ~ out pins by the hundred million —G.B.Shaw⟩ ⟨causing the clams . . . to ~ out tiny streams of water —*Amer. Guide Series: Maine*⟩ **2 :** to speak or utter readily, volubly, and at length ⟨fairly ~*ed* technicalities —C.S.Forester⟩ ⟨~*ed* French like a Frenchman⟩ ⟨every cabdriver in town can ~ facts and gossip —John Durant⟩; *often* **:** to speak or utter in a pompous, oratorical, or grandiloquent manner **:** DECLAIM ⟨custom of these judges to ~ extravagant . . . harangues from the bench —C.G.Bowers⟩ ⟨~*ing* Latin invective —F.L. Windolph⟩ ⟨always goes around ~*ing* Shakespeare⟩ ⟨~*s* tag ends of wisdom —Leslie Rees⟩ **3** [2*spout*] *archaic* **:** PAWN **4** [2*spout*] **:** to fit or furnish with a spout ⟨had the roof repaired and the eaves ~*ed*⟩ ⟨teapot poured badly, had not been properly ~*ed*⟩ ~ *vi* **1 :** to issue with force in a strong stream or jet (as of liquid or other material discharged violently through a narrow opening) **:** SPURT ⟨oil was ~*ing* from Western lands —Van Wyck Brooks⟩ ⟨foamy bloody mucus ~*ed* from her mouth and nose —Grace Reiten⟩ ⟨illuminated by flaming jets which seemed to ~ from the trees —John Reed⟩ ⟨pure like a bubbling spring, a fountain ~*ing* out —F.N.Souza⟩ **2 :** to eject liquid or other material in a jet ⟨geyser was ~*ing* freely⟩ ⟨waves were ~*ing* high on the granite cliffs —C.L.Barrett⟩ ⟨he'd shy each time a clam ~*ed* —G.W.Brace⟩; *specif* **:** BLOW 5b **3 :** to talk or speak volubly or at length esp. in a pompous or grandiloquent manner **:** DECLAIM ⟨gave radio concerts, and politicians ~*ed* into the strange instruments —F.L.Allen⟩ ⟨~ about science and rationalism —Harold Strauss⟩

2spout \"\ *n* -s [ME *spoute*; akin to MD *spoite* spout, ME *spouten* to spout] **1 :** a tube, pipe, or conductor through which a liquid is discharged or by which it is conveyed in a stream from one place to another: as **a** (1) **:** a pipe (as in a gargoyle) for carrying off water from the roof of a building (2) **:** DOWNSPOUT (3) **:** GUTTER 2a — usu. used in pl. **b :** the part of a fountain or pump from which water issues **c** (1) **:** a projecting tube or lip for guiding the flow of a liquid poured from a receptacle ⟨broke the ~ off the teapot⟩ ⟨soldered a new ~ on the watering can⟩ (2) **:** a hollow metal device inserted in a hole bored in a maple tree to conduct the sap into a detachable pail **d :** BLOWHOLE 2 **e :** NOZZLE **2 a :** a discharge or jet of water or other fluid matter from or as if from a pipe esp. when ejected with some violence or when rising in a column ⟨surging uprush of invisible ~*s* of warm air —William Beebe⟩: as (1) **:** WATERSPOUT; *also* **:** a downpour of rain (2) **:** a spray of water (3) **:** the blowing of a whale **b :** something appearing as if spouted out ⟨a solitary dark ~ of smoke —Eric Linklater⟩ ⟨violent ~*s* and gusts of burning oil —Nevil Shute⟩ ⟨a rising ~ of debate on guns versus butter —*Fortune*⟩ ⟨a ~ of blasphemies —G.K.Chesterton⟩ **3** *also* **spout fish :** RAZOR CLAM **4 a :** a usu. enclosed trough or chute for conducting bulk materials (as flour, grain) to or from a receptacle **b :** a trough for conducting molten metal from a furnace to a ladle **c** (1) **:** a shoot or lift formerly used in a pawnbroker's shop for transferring pawned articles (2) *archaic* **:** PAWNSHOP **5 :** something resembling or suggestive of a spout on a roof or the spout of a vessel (as in discharging a liquid or in being in the shape of a pipe or a lip) ⟨eyes became two ~*s* —Shak.⟩ ⟨nest high up in the hollow ~ of the big fire-blackened gum —*Sydney (Australia) Bull.*⟩ **6 :** a rush of water to a lower level **:** CASCADE, WATERFALL — **up the spout** *adv* **1** *archaic* **:** in pawn **2 :** in a hopeless condition **:** in a bad way **:** beyond remedy

spout·ed \-aůd·əd, -aůtəd\ *adj* [2*spout* + *-ed*] **1 :** having a spout ⟨~ ceremonial vessels⟩ **2 :** hollowed out in the form of a spout ⟨~ limb of a tree⟩

spout·er \-aůd·ə(r), -aůtə-\ *n* -s [1*spout* + *-er*] **1 :** one that spouts: as **a :** an oil or gas well the flow of which has not been controlled by the engineers **b :** an oratorical or voluble speaker **:** SPEECHIFIER ⟨a ~ who thought he was an orator —W.A.White⟩ **c :** a whale that spouts **2 a :** a whaling vessel **b :** the master of a whaler **3** [2*spout* + *-er*] **:** a worker who controls the flow of grain through the machines and spouts of the milling process

spout hole *n* **1 :** a blowhole of a cetacean **2 :** a nostril of a walrus or seal

spout·ing \-aůd·iŋ, -aůt|, |ēŋ\ *n* -s [2*spout* + *-ing*] **1 :** the system of spouts used to convey rainwater from the roof of a building to the ground **2 :** material from which pieces for making spouts may be cut

spouting horn *n* [*spouting* (pres. part. of 1*spout*) + *horn*] **:** a sea cave with an opening rearward or upward through which water spurts as waves enter the cave

spout·less \'spaůtləs\ *adj* **:** having no spout

spoutlike \'=,=\ *adj* **:** resembling a spout

spout·man \'=mən\ *n*, *pl* **spoutmen 1 :** one who keeps a load (as of grain) level by moving the spout through which the load is being delivered **2 :** one who sets up the chutes and spouts through which concrete is transferred into molding forms

spouty \'spaůd·ē\ *adj* -ER/-EST [1*spout* + *-y*] **:** so wet as to spout water when walked on ⟨~ marshland⟩

spp *abbr* species

SPQR *abbr* **1** [L *senatus populusque Romanus*] the senate and the people of Rome **2** small profits, quick returns

spr *abbr* **1** sapper **2** sprinkled; sprinkler

sprach·ge·fühl \'shpräkgə,fœl\ *n* -s [G, fr. *sprache* language + *gefühl* feeling] **1 :** sensibility to conformance with or divergence from the established usage (as in form or idiom) of a language ⟨the dependable ~ of a skilled linguist⟩ **2 :** a feeling for what is linguistically effective or appropriate ⟨the ~ of the accomplished translator⟩

sprack \'sprak\ *adj* [prob. of Scand origin; akin to ON *sprækr* lively; akin to OE *spearca* spark — more at SPARK] *dial Brit* **:** ALERT, ACTIVE, LIVELY, NIMBLE

sprad·dle \'sprad°l\ *vb* **spraddled; spraddled; spraddling** \-d(°)liŋ\ **spraddles** [prob. of Scand origin; akin to Norw dial. *spradla* to thrash about, ON *sprathka* to kick, thrash about; akin to OHG *spratalōn* to thrash about, *sprinzan* to jump up — more at SPRINT] *vt* **1 :** to spread (the legs) in walking **:** STRADDLE **2 :** SPRAWL ~ *vi* **1 :** to go or walk with a straddling gait **:** STRADDLE **2 :** SPRAWL

spraddle leg *n* **:** perosis of young poultry

spraddle-legged *usu* '=,=¦legəd, *Brit usu* -gd\ *adv* (*or adj*) **:** with the legs wide apart **:** STRADDLE-LEGGED

1sprag \'sprag, -aa(ə)g, -aig\ *adj* [by alter.] *archaic* **:** SPRACK

2sprag \"\ *n* -s [perh. of Scand origin; akin to Sw dial. *spragg, sprägge* branch — more at SPRIG] **:** a piece of timber or metal serving as a prop or brake: as **a :** a post for propping the ore or roof in a mine **b** (1) **:** a rod or shaft applied between the spokes of a wheel of a vehicle to prevent rotation (2) **:** a pointed stake or steel bar let down from a wagon or early automobile body at an angle to the ground to prevent the halted vehicle from rolling downhill

3sprag \"\ *vt* **spragged; spragged; spragging; sprags 1 :** to prop or sustain (as a mine roof) with a sprag **2 :** to check the motion of (a vehicle) by means of a sprag

4sprag \"\ *n* -s [origin unknown] **:** a young codfish

sprag·ger \-gə(r)\ *n* -s [2*sprag* + *-er*] **1 :** a worker who props coal beds with sprags for protection during mining or blasting **2 :** a worker who checks wheels (as of mine cars on inclines) with sprags

sprag road *n* [2*sprag*] **:** a gangway so steep that the wheels of ore cars have to be spragged when going down

sprague's grass \'sprägz-\ *n*, *usu cap S* [after Isaac *Sprague* †1895 Am. illustrator of botanical works] **:** COUCH GRASS

sprague's pipit *n*, *usu cap S* [after Isaac *Sprague*] **:** a pipit (*Anthus spraguei*) found chiefly on the Great Plains — called also *Missouri skylark, sky pipit*

1sprain \'sprān\ *n* -s [origin unknown] **1 :** a sudden or violent twist or wrench of a joint causing the stretching or tearing of ligaments and often rupture of blood vessels with hemorrhage into the tissues **2 :** the condition resulting from a sprain that is usu. marked by swelling, inflammation, hemorrhage, and discoloration — compare STRAIN **3** *also* **spraing** \-āŋ\ **:** internal brown spot of potatoes

2sprain \"\ *vt* -ED/-ING/-S **:** to weaken (a joint or ligament) by sudden and violent twisting or wrenching **:** stretch (ligaments) injuriously without dislocation of the joint — compare STRAIN

3sprain \"\ *vt* -ED/-ING/-S [back-formation fr. *spreined, sprent*, past part. of obs. *sprenge* to sprinkle — more at SPRENT] *archaic* **:** to sprinkle (seed) in sowing

sprain fracture *n* **:** the rupture of a tendon or ligament from its point of insertion at a joint with detachment of a splinter of bone

1spraing \'sprāŋ\ *n* -s [of Scand origin; akin to ON *sprang* lace, Norw *sprang*, a kind of embroidery; prob. akin to Norw *sprang* jump, OE *springan* to jump, spring — more at SPRING] *Scot* **:** a bright streak or stripe

2spraing \"\ *vt* -ED/-ING/-S *Scot* **:** to furnish or adorn with bright streaks or stripes

spraints \'sprānts\ *n pl* [ME *sprayntes*, fr. MF *espraintes*, pl. of *espreinte* piece of otter's dung, fr. fem. of *espraint*, past part. of *espraindre, espreindre* to express, squeeze out — more at EXPRESS] **:** otter's dung

sprang [ME, fr. OE] *past of* SPRING

span·gle \'spraŋgəl, -aiŋ-\ *vb* **sprangled; sprangled; sprangling** \-g(ə)liŋ\ **sprangles** [ME *spranglen*] *vi* **:** to spread out in different directions **:** branch out **:** RAMIFY, STRAGGLE ⟨streams ~ over the countryside⟩ ~ *vt* **1 :** to cause to sprangle **:** DIFFUSE **2 :** to rough up the feathers of (an arrow) as by injury or carelessness

sprangletop \'=,=,=\ *n* **1 :** a tall perennial rhizomatous grass (*Scolochloa festucacea*) that is widely distributed in wet lands and shallow water of northerly parts of the northern hemisphere and is a minor forage grass **2 :** a grass of the genus *Leptochloa*; *esp* **:** an erect wiry perennial grass (*L. dubia*) of the southern U.S. and southward to Argentina that is locally important for forage and hay

spran·gly \-g(ə)lē\ *adj*, *often* -ER/-EST [*sprangle* + *-y*] **:** SPREADING, SPRAWLING

1sprat \'sprat, *usu* -ad·+V\ *or* **spret** \'spret, *usu* -ed·+V\ *n* -s [alter. of (assumed) ME *sprot*, fr. OE *sprott*; prob. akin to OE *sprūtan* to sprout — more at SPROUT] *dial Brit* **:** any of various rushes of the genus *Juncus*

2sprat \"\ *n* -s [alter. of earlier *sprot*, fr. ME, fr. OE *sprott*; prob. akin to OE *sprūtan* to sprout] **1 a :** a small European herring (*Clupea sprattus*) closely related to the common herring and the pilchard **b :** any of various other small or young herrings **2 :** any of numerous small fishes (as anchovy or bleak) not clearly distinguished in popular usage from members of the herring family (*Clupeidae*) **3 :** a small or insignificant person ⟨whip these young ~*s* —Jay Dugan⟩ ⟨a surly . . . ~ of a man —T.B.Costain⟩

3sprat \"\ *vi* **spratted; spratted; spratting; sprats :** to fish for sprats

sprat loon *n* [2*sprat*] **:** RED-THROATED LOON

sprat·ter \-ad·ə(r), -atə-\ *n* -s **:** one that fishes for sprats

sprau·chle \'spräk̇əl\ *vi* [prob. of Scand origin; akin to ON *sprökla* to thrash about, *sparka* to kick; akin to OE *spearca* spark — more at SPARK] *dial Brit* **:** CLAMBER, SCRAMBLE, SPRAWL

1sprawl \'sprȯl\ *vb* -ED/-ING/-S [ME *sprewlen, sprawlen*, fr. OE *sprēawlian*; prob. akin to OE *sprūtan* to sprout — more at SPROUT] *vi* **1 a** *archaic* **:** to lie (as on the ground) thrashing or tossing about **:** struggle convulsively **b :** to creep or clamber with awkward movements of the arms and legs **:** SCRAMBLE ⟨the car slowly fell on its side and two figures ~*ed* out —Irwin Shaw⟩ **2 :** to lie or sit with arms and legs stretched out carelessly or awkwardly **:** spread out ⟨could ~ on her back in the little patch of grass —Elizabeth Janeway⟩ ⟨a child . . . ~*s* across her knees —Laurence Binyon⟩ ⟨the headmaster . . . was ~*ed* out in an easy chair —Grace Metalious⟩ **3 :** to spread or develop irregularly or ungracefully **:** STRAGGLE ⟨bushes are . . . allowed to ~ as they will —Fletcher Steele⟩ ⟨the city ~*s* without apparent logic or plan to the west, north, and south —*Amer. Guide Series: R. I.*⟩ ⟨this novel undeniably ~*s* —Sean O'Faolain⟩ ~ *vt* **1 :** to stretch out (the arms or legs) carelessly or awkwardly ⟨took a chair, ~*ed* out his legs —Erle Stanley Gardner⟩ **2 :** to cause to spread or develop irregularly or stragglingly **:** cause to move erratically **:** SCRAWL ⟨~*s* its . . . winding river across the state line —*Amer. Guide Series: Texas*⟩ ⟨languidly ~*ed* his signature over the document at her urging⟩

2sprawl \"\ *n* -s **1 :** the act, posture, or condition of sprawling ⟨sent him down in a long ~ —Vincent McHugh⟩ ⟨toppled backward to a ~ on the pavement —Scott Fitzgerald⟩ **2 :** an irregularly spread or scattered group or mass **:** a straggling array ⟨a bare and shadeless ~ of adobe barracks —Harvey Fergusson⟩ ⟨the increasing ~ of the curriculum —E.L.Vance⟩ ⟨the rich ~ of her hair —William Faulkner⟩ **3** *dial* **:** resolute spirit **:** SPUNK, GUMPTION ⟨chaps as hadn't the ~ to go a-soldiering —Flora Thompson⟩

sprawl·er \-lə(r)\ *n* -s **1 :** any of various European noctuid moths (esp. *Brachionycha sphinx*) or their larvae **2 :** HELLGRAMMITE

sprawling *adj* **1 :** characterized by clumsy spreading or stretching (as of the arms or legs) **:** UNGAINLY ⟨this ~ gait is characteristic of the crocodiles —W.E.Swinton⟩ **2 :** spreading or developing irregularly or erratically **:** STRAGGLING ⟨a listless, ~ town with sandy streets —*Amer. Guide Series: Texas*⟩ ⟨a ~ book, discursive and prolix —Brendan Gill⟩ **3 :** carelessly irregular **:** SCRAWLY ⟨a letter written in a ~ hand⟩

sprawl·ing·ly *adv* **:** in a sprawling manner

sprawly \'sprȯlē, -li\ *adj* -ER/-EST **1 :** stretching or spreading out in an ungainly or irregular way **:** STRAGGLY, DIFFUSE ⟨an otter cub . . . a tiny, ~, furry handful —F.G.Turnbull⟩ ⟨a big, ~ city —G.S.Kaufman⟩ **2 :** laid on or drawn in an apparently careless fashion **:** SPLASHY ⟨an allover, ~ design of white rickrack —Lois Long⟩

1spray \'sprā\ *n* -s [ME — more at SPRIG] **1 a :** a cluster or mass of small twiggy branches **:** small brushwood ⟨birch ~⟩ **b sprays** *pl*, *dial Eng* **:** twisted willow or hazel for thatching **2 a :** a usu. slim branch or shoot **:** SPRIG ⟨a ~ of apple blossoms⟩ **b :** a bunch or cluster of cut flowers arranged for decorative effect (as on a dress, dinner table, or coffin) ⟨shoulder ~⟩ **c :** something (as a decorative design, ornament, or brooch) resembling a spray ⟨a ~ of brilliants⟩ ⟨rhinestone-set shoulder ~ —*Fashion Digest*⟩ **3 :** a very light bluish green that is duller and slightly greener than average ice green **4 a :** an auxiliary gate, runner, or side channel in a founder's mold **b :** a group of castings made together and connected by sprues and not yet separated and trimmed

2spray \"\ *vi* -ED/-ING/-S **:** to spread out in the form of a spray **:** branch out ⟨orchids . . . ~*ed* from the bowl —Kathryn Grondahl⟩ ⟨branches of climbing vines ~*ed* up its sides —Frederick Faust⟩

3spray \"\ *n* -s [fr. obs. E *spray* to sprinkle, fr. MD *sprayen, spraeyen*; akin to MHG *spræjen, spræwen* to squirt, spray, Sw dial. *språ, språs* to sprout, Gk *speirein* to scatter, sow, sprinkle — more at SPROUT] **1 :** water flying in small drops or particles as blown from waves or thrown up by a waterfall ⟨~ cast up when the heavy rain pounded the flat porch rail —John Updike⟩ **2 a** (1) **:** a jet of fine medicated vapor used either as an application to a diseased part or to charge the air of a room with a disinfectant or deodorizer (2) **:** an instrument for applying such a spray **:** ATOMIZER — compare AEROSOL **b :** a jet of liquid (as water) dispersed by a sprayer **3 a** (1) **:** an application in suspension or solution of a pesticide (2) **:** the material so applied **b :** FOG 3a **c :** a device for applying a vaporized coating (as of paint)

4spray \"\ *vb* -ED/-ING/-S *vt* **1 :** to scatter or let fall (as a solution) in the form of spray ⟨~ a 1 percent solution from an atomizer onto the incision⟩ ⟨antibiotics and body powders that can be ~*ed* instead of dusted on —*Time*⟩ **2 a :** to throw spray upon ⟨the waves ~*ed* us with salt water⟩; *esp* **:** to cover entirely or partially with a liquid, a foam, or sometimes a dust by means of a sprayer or aerosol bomb (as for destroying bacteria or plant pests) **b :** to throw a liquid upon in the form of a spray ⟨stove exploded, ~*ing* them with flaming kerosine —*Pasadena (Calif.) Independent*⟩ **c :** to apply something to by atomizing and allowing to strike the surface in a uniform manner ⟨~*ed* the furniture with paint⟩ **d :** to fire upon scatteringly **:** strew with bullets ⟨opened fire ~*ing* them with buckshot —Meridel LeSueur⟩ ~ *vi* **1 :** to take the form of spray **:** scatter in fine particles ⟨the device causes the water to ~⟩ **2 :** to discharge a liquid as spray

5spray *var of* SPREE

spray boom *n* **:** a pipe with attached nozzles for distributing spray from a tank

spray calendar *or* **spray schedule** *n* **:** a table or chart indicating at what time or stage of development of a plant various pesticidal sprays should be applied

spray crab *n* **:** a small spiny grapsoid crab (*Percnow givvesi*) living on spray-washed rocks

spray drain *n* **:** a drain made by laying tree branches under earth **:** a covered brush drain

spray-dry \'=¦=\ *vt* **:** to dry (as milk, eggs, or soap) by bringing in the form of a spray into contact with hot air or other gases and often recovering in the form of a powder

spray·er \'sprā(ə)r\ *n* -s **1 :** one that sprays: as **a :** one that sprays trees or crops with insecticides **b :** one that sprays surfaces with a coating substance (as paint, enamel, or waterproofing) **c :** one that sprays a finish on cloth **2 :** a device or machine for spraying: as **a :** a vehicle or an attachment to a vehicle for spraying liquids (as insecticides or fungicides) on plants and trees — compare TRACTION SPRAYER **b :** a device or instrument for spraying liquid drugs — compare ATOMIZER **c :** a device for spraying paint on a surface **:** 3SPRAY 3c, SPRAY GUN **d :** an apparatus for spraying liquids on a foundry mold or core

1spray·ey \-āē\ *adj* [3*spray* + *-y*] **:** resembling water spray **:** carrying or throwing spray ⟨a ~ wind from the sea⟩

2sprayey \"\ *adj* [1*spray* + *-y*] **:** consisting of, resembling, or branching out like the sprays of a tree or plant **:** TWIGGY

spray form *n* **:** the form of a tree or shrub as influenced by ocean spray

spray green *n* **:** a pale green that is bluer, lighter, and stronger than celadon gray, yellower, lighter, and stronger than bayberry gray, and bluer and lighter than aloes green

spray gun *n* **1 :** an apparatus resembling a gun for applying substances (as paints or insecticides) in the form of a spray **2 :** GUN 5b

spray nozzle *also* **spray head** *n* **:** an attachment to the end of a spray rod or hose that causes the liquid to be delivered finely and evenly as a spray

spray pond *also* **spray pool** *n* **:** a reservoir in which warmed water is cooled for reuse by evaporation of water discharged from nozzles in spray or mist form over the pond

sprays *pl of* SPRAY, *pres 3d sing of* SPRAY

spray strip *n* **:** a strip that projects from the forepart of a seaplane hull and deflects the spray thrown up when the hull is moving through the water

spray therapy *n* **:** roentgen irradiation of the entire body for therapeutic purposes

1spread \'spred\ *vb* **spread; spread; spreading; spreads** [ME *spreden*, fr. OE *sprǣdan*; akin to OHG *spreiten* to spread, MLG & MD *spreiden, spreden*, OSw *spreda*; causative fr. the root of an intransitive v. represented by OHG *sprītan* to spread, Sw *sprida*; akin to OE *sprūtan* to sprout — more at SPROUT] *vt* **1 a :** to cause to open out or extend over a larger area (as by unfurling, flattening out, or pulling taut) **:** EXPAND ⟨~ a carpet⟩ ⟨a ship with all sails ~⟩ ⟨hammered the metal to ~ it⟩ — often used with *out* ⟨~ out the newspaper⟩ ⟨~ out the roots carefully —Emily Holt⟩ ⟨city ~ out on a level terrain —*Amer. Guide Series: N. H.*⟩ **b :** to cause to reach or thrust out **:** stretch out **:** EXTEND ⟨~*ing* her arms wide to embrace him⟩ ⟨~*s* its wings for flight⟩ ⟨a tree ~*ing* its branches⟩ ⟨~ his hands, palms down on the table —Gilbert Millstein⟩ **c** (1) **:** to expose (one's hand or remaining cards) for the purpose of claiming all or some of the tricks yet to be played (2) **:** to lay down (a combination of cards having value under the rules of the game) **:** SHOW, MELD **2 a :** to distribute over an area **:** SCATTER, STREW ⟨~ fertilizer over the soil⟩ ⟨buildings . . . are ~ around this central point —*Amer. Guide Series: Texas*⟩ ⟨has its armed forces ~ thinly all over the globe —*Wall Street Jour.*⟩ **b :** to distribute over a period of time **:** PROLONG, PROTRACT ⟨~ the cost of medical care⟩ ⟨the work had to be ~ over several weekends⟩; *specif* **:** to distribute (a limited amount of work) among as many workers and for as long as possible by shortening the work hours in a day or reducing the work days in a week **c :** to apply on a surface as an overlayer or cover ⟨~ butter on bread⟩ ⟨the varnish was ~ on every exposed part —Ben Riker⟩ **d** (1) **:** to cover or overlay with ⟨~ the floor with carpet⟩ (2) *archaic* **:** to cover or extend over completely **:** OVERRUN ⟨the velvet down that ~*s* his cheek —Thomas Moore⟩ **e** (1) **:** to prepare or furnish (as a table) for dining **:** SET ⟨~ the board⟩ ⟨~ the tables with the favorite dishes of their absent husbands —J.G.Frazer⟩ (2) **:** to lay out or set down (as a meal) **:** SERVE ⟨~ afternoon tea for us —Eve Langley⟩ ⟨supper was ~ —Thomas Hardy⟩ **f :** RECORD, ENTER ⟨moved . . . that the foregoing resolution be ~ upon the minutes —*Science*⟩ **3 a :** to make more widely known **:** PUBLISH, DISSEMINATE ⟨~ the news⟩ ⟨~ a man's fame⟩ ⟨~ the most glowing reports —T.B.Costain⟩ **b :** to cause to affect an increasing number **:** extend the range or incidence of ⟨~ a disease⟩ ⟨the habit of smoking —Olive Haseltine⟩ ⟨puerperal infection could be ~ in this way —Justina Hill⟩ **c :** DIFFUSE ⟨~ an effluvium⟩ **:** EMIT ⟨the hyacinth ~*ing* its fragrance⟩ **4 a :** to push apart by weight or force **:** make wider and flatter ⟨the locomotive ~*s* the rails⟩ ⟨~ a plate . . . and had to be shod in the paddock —Richard Lane⟩ **b :** to separate (the lips) laterally and bring (them) close together vertically (as in the pronunciation of *ee* in *see*) — compare 6ROUND 1c ~ *vi* **1 a :** to become dispersed, distributed, or scattered **:** flow out readily ⟨the rioters ~ throughout the city⟩ ⟨the odor ~*s* through the room⟩ ⟨a thin paint that ~*s* well⟩ **b :** to become known more widely **:** CIRCULATE ⟨the news ~⟩ ⟨the new ideas were ~*ing* —Tom Wintringham⟩ **c :** to increase in range, incidence, or influence ⟨the disease ~ through the island⟩ ⟨the panic ~ rapidly⟩ ⟨the academy idea had begun to ~ —J.P.Marquand⟩ **2 a :** to extend, grow, or stretch out in length or breadth **:** cover a greater area **:** EXPAND ⟨the city ~*s* over five square miles —*Amer. Guide Series: Mich.*⟩ ⟨the consequences of any big war ~ in circles to infinity —Dixon Wecter⟩ ⟨the shadow ~ across her face —Maude Hutchins⟩ **b :** to extend tendrils, shoots, or new growth **:** UNFOLD ⟨a vine remarkable for its tendency not to ~ and ramble —Willa Cather⟩ **c :** to become extended by heating, drawing, or compressing **d :** to project oneself into new activities ⟨he ~ out into other fields⟩ **3 :** to move apart (as from pressure or weight) **:** SEPARATE ⟨rails ~*ing* under the great weight⟩ ⟨the servant's mouth ~ in a placating grin —T.B.Costain⟩

syn DISSEMINATE, PROPAGATE, CIRCULATE, RADIATE, DIFFUSE: SPREAD, in the sense of broadcasting, publicizing, or making or becoming known widely, is without strong connotation, although it may suggest a scattered strewing ⟨scattered broadcast over the country at government expense, the report did much to *spread* knowledge of the northwest coast —R.A. Billington⟩ ⟨the taste for reading . . . slowly *spread* out toward the lonely clearings to the west —J.D.Hart⟩ DISSEMINATE means and suggests about the same things as SPREAD; it may connote the notion of a hoped-for useful fruition as of seed sown ⟨the need for a cooperative agency in the iron and steel industry for collecting and *disseminating* statistics and information —J.W.Hill⟩ PROPAGATE, applicable to complexes of notions rather than to specific facts or bits of information, may suggest fostering growth by making widespread and increasing the number of possible adherents ⟨mechanical societies sprang into existence, to *propagate* the creed with greater zeal —Lewis Mumford⟩ ⟨the outlandish philosophies that later sectaries were to *propagate* so diligently —V.L.Parrington⟩ CIRCULATE may suggest a passing from person to person as though in a circle and thus to become widely known ⟨this silly story that people are *circulating* —Thomas Hardy⟩ ⟨the satire, *circulating* in manuscript copies, had a great local vogue —E.V. Lucas⟩ RADIATE suggests sending out along radii from a nucleus; it is more likely to apply to matters affective than intellectual ⟨a unity of inspiration that *radiates* into plot and personages alike —T.S.Eliot⟩ ⟨the comments of Arthur Brisbane . . . *radiated* no warmth —A.W.Long⟩ DIFFUSE suggests to make known widely with permeation into small areas or crannies and an overall tingeing effect ⟨the drive behind the American ideal of a universally *diffused* education —Perry Miller⟩ ⟨once literacy has been generally *diffused* among the masses of a society, it tends to become indispensable —Helen Sullivan⟩

— **spread oneself :** to be lavish (as in effort, generosity, hospitality) ⟨*spread themselves* to entertain visiting delegates⟩

2**spread** \"\ *n* -s **1 a :** the act or process of spreading **:** EXPANSION, EXTENSION, DIFFUSION ⟨the ~ of wax under a seal⟩ ⟨the ~ of the great metropolis —*London Calling*⟩ ⟨the ~ of the plague through the city⟩ ⟨a gradual ~ of parliamentary democracy —Bertrand Russell⟩ **b :** the extent or capability of spreading ⟨the ~ of a sail⟩ ⟨elm . . . with a ~ of 146 feet —*Amer. Guide Series: Conn.*⟩ **c** (1) **:** DISPERSION 2a (2) **:** a continuous assemblage usu. of points in mathematics ⟨curves that are one-way ~*s*⟩ **2 :** something spread out: as **a :** a surface area **:** EXPANSE ⟨this giant ~ of land —A.B.Guthrie⟩ **b** *West* (1) **:** a ranch with all its appurtenances ⟨a cattle ~⟩ (2) **:** an expanse of range ⟨a ~ of 100,000 acres⟩ (3) **:** a herd of animals ⟨winter a ~ of 10,000 sheep⟩ **c :** the surface of a cut stone (as a diamond) in relation to its depth **d** (1) **:** a prominent display usu. occupying more than one column and esp. having pictorial illustration in a newspaper or periodical (2) **:** two facing pages (as of a magazine or newspaper) printed with matter that usu. runs across the fold (as a single advertisement or picture or part of an article to be read as a single page); *also* **:** the matter occupying these two facing pages **e :** SPREADHEAD **f** (1) **:** LAYDOWN (2) **:** an intentional exposure (as for the purpose of claiming tricks) of a player's entire hand (3) **:** a combination of cards in rummy that can be or is melded **:** SET (4) **:** the act of melding such a combination **3 :** something spread on or over a surface: as **a :** a food (as butter, jam, jelly, fruit or peanut butter, or deviled meat) used or made for use to spread on bread or crackers ⟨cheese ~⟩ **b :** a usu. sumptuous meal **:** FEAST, BANQUET ⟨a gigantic ~ in honor of the visiting prince —Robert Shaplen⟩ **c :** a plain or decorative cloth used as a cover for a table or a bed **4 :** the distance between two points **:** GAP, DIVERGENCE ⟨the wide ~ between theory and fact⟩: as **a :** the distance between the forelegs of certain quadrupeds (as dogs) **b :** distance from center to center (as of the cylinders of a duplex pump) in machinery **c :** the distance between gage lines at the heel or toe of a railroad frog **d :** SPAN **e** (1) **:** the difference between what the producer is paid for a product and what the consumer pays for it (2) **:** the difference between the highest and lowest price of a product for a given period (3) **:** STRADDLE **f** (1) **:** an option in a put and call in which the put price is different from the call price so that no profit is made unless the price falls or rises below or above the put or call price respectively by more than enough to cover the cost of the option (2) **:** an arbitrage transaction operated by buying and selling simultaneously in two separate markets (as Chicago and New York) when there is an abnormal difference in price between the two markets — see BACKSPREAD (3) **:** the difference between bid and asked prices (4) **:** the difference between any two prices for similar articles ⟨the ~ between the list price and the market price of an article⟩ **g :** DEVIATION f **5 :** something that spreads or fans out: as **a :** a salvo of torpedoes fired just ahead, at, and just abaft the target to ensure a hit **b :** SPREAD FORMATION **c :** a shot in billiards in which the cue ball is made to rebound from the object ball at a considerable angle to its original course

3**spread** \"\ *adj* [fr. past part. of 1*spread*] **1 :** widely extended **:** EXPANDED **2 :** extending across two or more columns of a newspaper or periodical ⟨a two-page ~ advertisement⟩ **3 :** having insufficient depth so that its luster is below standard — used of a gem

spread·abil·i·ty \ˌ⸗⸗ˈbiləd·ē, -lətē, -i\ *n* **:** ease or facility in spreading ⟨the ~ of butter⟩ ⟨the ~ of a paint⟩

spread·able \ˈ⸗⸗bəl\ *adj* [1*spread* + *-able*] **:** capable of being spread ⟨a ~ plastic substance⟩

spreadboard \ˈ⸗,⸗\ *n* **:** a machine that spreads flax and hemp in ropemaking

spread eagle *n* [3*spread*; trans. of MF *aigle esployee*] **1 :** a representation of an eagle with wings raised and legs extended (as in an heraldic device or the silver insigne of the rank of colonel) **2 :** something resembling or suggestive of a spread eagle: as **a :** a man tied (as to a wheel) with arms and legs extended ⟨make a *spread eagle* of you —R.H.Dana⟩ **b :** a glide in figure skating executed with the skates heel to heel in a straight line **c :** a design used esp. in chair and bed backs (as designed by Duncan Phyfe) **3** [so called fr. the spread eagle on the Great Seal of the U. S.] **:** bombastic or high-flown expression esp. of U. S. chauvinistic sentiments ⟨a speech full of *spread eagle*⟩

1**spread-eagle** \ˈ⸗ˈ⸗⸗\ *vb* -ED/-ING/-S [*spread eagle*] *vi* **1 :** to execute a spread eagle (as in skating) **2 :** to stand or move with the arms and legs stretched out **:** SPRAWL ⟨the boys *spread-eagled* across the cinders —J.A.Michener⟩ ~ *vt* **1 a :** to put into the position of a spread eagle **:** stretch out ⟨*spread-eagled* him on a log —R.P.Warren⟩ **b :** to spread over **:** stretch across **:** STRADDLE ⟨the company's plants *spread-eagled* the state⟩ **2 a :** to defeat completely **:** ROUT ⟨threatened to *spread-eagle* the field —Clifford Bloodgood⟩ **b :** to scatter (an opposing team) in football **c :** to break and spread (a wicket) with a bowled ball in cricket

2**spread-eagle** \"\ *adj* [*spread eagle*] **1 :** resembling or suggestive of a spread eagle ⟨sprawled in a *spread-eagle* position⟩ **2 :** marked by bombast and boastful exaggeration esp. of the greatness of the U. S. **:** VAINGLORIOUS ⟨to paint the biggest picture in the world was no inappropriate ambition for that *spread-eagle* era —Dixon Wecter⟩ ⟨a *spread-eagle* orator⟩ ⟨a *spread-eagle* speech⟩

spread-ea·gle·ism \-ə,lizəm\ *n* -s [*spread eagle* + *-ism*] **:** bombastic and vainglorious boasting of the greatness of the U. S. **:** SUPERPATRIOTISM, FLAG-WAVING ⟨resorted to some old-fashioned *spread-eagleism* and even demagoguery —W.G. Carleton⟩

spread-eagle orchid *n* **:** a showy tropical American orchid (*Oncidium carthaginense*) having spreading petals

spreader \ˈspred·ə(r)\ *n* -s [ME *spreder*, fr. *spreden* to spread + *-er*] **1 :** one that spreads, scatters, or diffuses: as **a :** an implement for spreading material (as fertilizer, hay, sand, lime) over an area ⟨heavy trucks with sand ~*s*⟩ **b :** a small knife-shaped implement for use at the table esp. in spreading butter **c :** a worker in a bakery who spreads icing or filling (as on cookies) **d :** PLASTERER **e** (1) *also* **spreading machine :** a machine for coating fabrics esp. with rubber (2) **:** a tender of a spreading machine **f :** a wetting agent (as soap, oil emulsion, or casein) added to fungicides and insecticides to increase their spreading on foliage by lowering the surface tension **g** *or* **spreader dam :** a dike or trench forcing runoff water to disperse over a wide area instead of following a channel **2 :** one that spreads, stretches, or draws out something being processed: as **a :** one that layers cloth on a table for pattern cutting **b** (1) **:** a textile machine for combining and drawing flax fiber into a sliver (2) **:** a similar machine for straightening and evening fibers (as hemp) for rope making (3) **:** any of various textile machines for spreading out the warp threads during winding, fibers for drying, and loops on a knitting machine **c** (1) **:** TACKER a (2) **:** GAMBREL 2 **3 :** one that spreads, holds, or keeps apart: as **a :** a bar holding apart two stays or guys to stretch them and so stiffen a spar (as a topmast or jibboom) — compare CROSSTREE **b :** any of a series of crossbearers that supports a line of rails (as in an adit or heading) **c :** a bar that holds two whiffletrees apart **:** DOUBLETREE **d :** a stick or bar for holding apart the wires of a radio aerial **e :** a small bar or roll so placed as to ensure even tension across a web of paper entering a calender, winder, or printing press

spreader car *n* **:** a car with adjustable wings on each side for pushing earth away from a railroad track to widen the roadbed and for spreading ballast and ditching

spreader-sticker \ˈ⸗⸗ˈ⸗⸗\ *n* **:** a material or combination of materials added to sprays that causes the spray to spread and to stick to the sprayed foliage

spread footing *n* [3*spread*] **:** a footing in building construction that is shallow in proportion to its width and is usu. made of reinforced concrete

spread formation *n* [3*spread*] **:** a double or triple wing offensive formation in football in which the ends are spread three to five yards outside the tackles, the tailback plays seven to eight yards behind the line, and the other three backs are in flanking position close to the line so that they may move quickly downfield to receive a pass

spread glass *n* [3*spread*] **:** CYLINDER GLASS

spreadhead \ˈ⸗,⸗\ *n* [3*spread* + *head*] **:** a newspaper heading in large type usu. extending across two or more columns

spreading *pres part of* SPREAD

spreading adder *n* **:** HOGNOSE SNAKE

spreading board *n* **:** SETTING BLOCK

spreading cotoneaster *n* **:** a Chinese shrub (*Cotoneaster divaricata*) that has pink flowers, spreading branches, and red ellipsoid fruit and is used as an ornamental

spreading decline *n* **:** a disease of citrus trees caused by the citrus nematode and characterized by loss of feeder roots and subsequent progressive decline in vigor

spreading dogbane *n* **:** a milky-juiced No. American perennial herb (*Apocynum androsaemifolium*) having opposite entire leaves and loose spreading cymes of pinkish flowers in early summer — compare RHEUMATISM WEED

spreading factor *n* **:** HYALURONIDASE

spread·ing·ly *adv* **:** EXPANSIVELY, MANIFESTLY ⟨his deeper impression of something beautiful and ~ clear —Henry James †1916⟩

spreading yew *n* **:** any of several cultivated yews that are usu. derived from Japanese species and are characterized by low growth and much horizontal branching

spread misère *n* [3*spread*] **:** a misère game that the bidder plays with all his cards exposed

spread of risk : the extent to which an insurance company by selecting diversified and independent risks that are fairly uniform in size and sufficiently large in number can predict the losses thereon with reasonable accuracy by the law of averages

spreads *pres 3d sing of* SPREAD, *pl of* SPREAD

spread-set \ˈ⸗,⸗\ *vt* **:** to cause the metal of (saw teeth) to flow sidewise (as by swaging)

spready \ˈspredē\ *adj* -ER/-EST **:** having or constituting a hide 60 pounds or more in weight and 6½ feet or more in length — used of a steer or a hide ⟨~ native steers⟩ ⟨a ~ hide⟩

spreagh \ˈsprēk\ *n* -s [alter. of *spreath*] *Scot* **:** a cattle raid **:** FORAY

sprea·ghery *or* **spre·chery** \ˈsprēkərī\ *n* -ES [*spreagh* + *-ery*] **1** *Scot* **:** cattle lifting **:** PLUNDERING **2** *Scot* **:** BOOTY, PLUNDER

spreath \ˈsprēk\ *n* -s [ScGael *sprèidh* cattle, fr. L *praeda* booty — more at PREY] **1** *Scot* **:** PREY, BOOTY; *esp* **:** cattle carried off in a raid **2** *Scot* **:** a cattle raid **:** FORAY

spreck·led \ˈsprekəld\ *adj* [of Scand origin; akin to ON *spreklōttr* speckled, *sprekla* spot; akin to MHG *spreckel* speckle, OE *spearca* spark — more at SPARK] *dial Brit* **:** SPECKLED

1**spree** \ˈsprē\ *or* **spray** \ˈsprā\ *n* -s [perh. alter. of *spreath*] **:** an unrestrained and usu. excessive indulgence in or outburst of any activity **:** SPLURGE, RAMPAGE ⟨a buying ~⟩ ⟨a speculative ~ —*Kiplinger Washington Letter*⟩ ⟨a fishing ~⟩; *esp* **:** an occasion, period, or bout of reckless merrymaking and usu. heavy drinking **:** BINGE, CAROUSAL ⟨inebriated after a ~ in town —*Amer. Guide Series: La.*⟩ — often used in the expressions *on a spree* and *go on a spree* ⟨a pair of undergraduates on a ~ —Lucien Price⟩ ⟨had gone on spending ~*s* —Truman Capote⟩

2**spree** \ˈsprē\ *vi* **spreed; spreed; spreeing; sprees :** to indulge in or go on a spree ⟨~*ing* around —Walt Whitman⟩

3**spree** \"\ *Scot & dial Eng var of* SPRY

spree drinker *n* **:** a chronic alcoholic who suffers from the compulsion to heavy periodic drinking **:** DIPSOMANIAC

spreeuw \ˈspriū\ *n* -s [Afrik *spreeu* starling (formerly spelled *spreeuw*), fr. MD *spreeuwe*, *sprewe*] **:** any of several African starlings of glossy plumage

sprengel explosive \ˈspreŋgəl-, ˈshpreŋəl-\ *n, usu cap S* [after Herman J. P. *Sprengel* †1906 Brit. chemist born in Germany] **:** any of numerous high explosives formed by mixing just before use an oxidizing agent (as nitric acid or potassium chlorate) and a combustible ingredient (as nitrobenzene) neither of which by itself is explosive

sprengel pump *n, usu cap S* [after Herman J. P. *Sprengel*] **:** an air pump in which exhaustion is produced by drops of mercury running down a narrow tube and trapping bubbles of gas between them

sprengel tube *n, usu cap S* [after H. J. P. *Sprengel*] **:** a glass U tube with two capillary ends bent at right angles for use in determining specific gravity esp. of oils and fats by weighing it first filled with the substance to be tested and then filled with water — compare PYCNOMETER

1**sprent** \ˈsprent\ *vb* [ME *sprenten* to jump, spurt, of Scand origin; akin to Sw dial. *sprinta* to jump, hop — more at SPRINT] *vi, dial chiefly Brit* **:** RUN, LEAP, SPRINT ~ *vt, dial chiefly Brit* **:** SPRINKLE, SPLASH, SQUIRT

2**sprent** \"\ *n* -s **1** *dial chiefly Brit* **:** SPRINT, SPRING, LEAP **2** *dial chiefly Brit* **:** HASP, CATCH

3**sprent** \"\ *adj* [fr. past part. of obs. *sprenge* to sprinkle, scatter, fr. ME *sprengen*, fr. OE *sprengan*; akin to MD, MLG, & OHG *sprengen* to make jump, sprinkle, ON *sprengja* to cause to burst; causative fr. the root of E 1*spring*] *archaic* **:** SPRINKLED ⟨the brown hair ~ with gray —Matthew Arnold⟩

spret *var of* SPRAT

sprier *comparative of* SPRY

spriest *superlative of* SPRY

1**sprig** \ˈsprig\ *n* -s [ME *sprigge*; prob. akin to OE *spræc* shoot of a plant, ME *spray*, MD *sprocke* twig, sprig, MLG *sprik*, *sprok* dry twig, OHG *sprahhula* splinter, chaff, ON *sprek* stick, Sw dial. *spragg*, *spragge* branch, and perh. to OE *spearca* spark — more at SPARK] **1 a :** a small shoot **:** TWIG ⟨a ~ of laurel⟩ ⟨a ~ of parsley⟩ ⟨the yard . . . completely bare, no weed no ~ of anything —William Faulkner⟩ **b :** a small division of grass used for propagation **2 a :** a small offshoot or side growth (as of a nerve or vein) **b** (1) **:** HEIR, SCION ⟨a young ~ of nobility —Peter Forster⟩ (2) **:** a young person ⟨a young ~ of a book reviewer —Clifton Fadiman⟩ **c :** a small specimen ⟨a ~ of vivid, unaffected idiom —John Woodburn⟩ **3 a :** an ornament (as a jeweled brooch or a decorative design) resembling a spray, stemmed flower, or leaf **b :** a separate piece of lace (as a flower or foliage motif) usu. appliquéd to the ground **4 :** any of various pointed objects: as **a :** a small headless nail **:** BRAD **b :** GLAZIER'S POINT **c :** DOWEL **5 a :** PINTAIL 1a **b** RUDDY DUCK **c** *Scot* **:** HOUSE SPARROW

2**sprig** \"\ *vt* **sprigged; sprigged; sprigging; sprigs 1 a :** to drive sprigs or brads into **:** secure with sprigs ⟨boots, *sprigged* and screwed soles —*Queensland (Australia) Times*⟩ **b :** to attach (a part) to a piece of raw pottery ⟨~ a handle on the pitcher⟩ **2 :** to mark or adorn with the representation of small branches or plants **:** FIGURE 2a ⟨~ muslin⟩ ⟨white dimity *sprigged* with yellow rosebuds —*New Yorker*⟩ **3 a :** to propagate (a grass) by means of stolons or small divisions **b :** to strip (a shrub or plant) of sprigs ⟨~ a tobacco plant⟩

sprig budding *n* **:** BARK GRAFTING

sprig·ger \ˈsprigə(r)\ *n* -s **:** one that sprigs: as **a :** a machine for driving sprigs into shoes **b :** STRIPPER 1a

sprig·gy \-gē, -gi\ *adj* -ER/-EST **:** having sprigs or small branches ⟨~ branches⟩ ⟨a ~ pattern⟩

spright \ˈsprīt, *usu* -īd·+V\ *archaic var of* SPRITE

spright·ful \-tfəl\ *adj* [*spright* + *-ful*] **:** full of life or spirit **:** SPRIGHTLY — **spright·ful·ly** \-fəlē\ *adv* — **sprightful·ness** \-fəlnəs\ *n* -ES

spright·li·ly \-lə̇lē, -li\ *adv* **:** in a sprightly manner **:** BRISKLY, ANIMATEDLY ⟨setting out on the ascent ~ —Louis Golding⟩

spright·li·ness \-lēnə̇s, -lin-\ *n* -ES **:** the quality or state of being sprightly: as **a :** gay liveliness **:** VIVACITY ⟨beneath her ~ . . . she was seriously inclined —Virginia Woolf⟩ **b :** PIQUANCY ⟨a ~ of flavor, a suggestion of the pineapple, the apricot, the orange —David Fairchild⟩

1**spright·ly** \ˈsprītlē, -li\ *adj* -ER/-EST [*spright* + *-ly*] **1 :** marked by a gay lightness and vivacity (as of movement or manner) **:** SPIRITED ⟨a short ~ dance⟩ ⟨a ~ young girl⟩ ⟨a ~ air⟩ ⟨a ~ style⟩ ⟨gradually through the afternoon her step had become less ~ —Douglass Wallop⟩ ⟨readers prefer ~ trash to dull excellence —H.S.Canby⟩ **2 :** having a distinctively piquant taste ⟨citrus fruits with a ~ blending of tartness and sweetness⟩ **syn** see LIVELY

2**sprightly** \"\ *adv* **:** in a sprightly manner **:** SPRIGHTLILY

sprigtail \ˈ⸗,⸗\ *n* **1 :** PINTAIL 1a **2 :** SHARP-TAILED GROUSE **3 :** RUDDY DUCK

sprigtailed \ˈ⸗,⸗\ *adj* **:** having a sharp-pointed tail ⟨a ~ mare⟩ ⟨a ~ duck⟩

1**spring** \ˈspriŋ\ *vb* **sprang** \ˈspraŋ, -aiŋ\ *or* **sprung** \ˈsprəŋ\ **sprung; springing; springs** [ME *springen*, fr. OE *springan*; akin to OHG *springan* to jump, spring, OFris & ON *springa* to jump, spring, Gk *sperchesthai* to hasten, Skt *sprhayati* he desires; basic meaning: to move fast, jump] *vi* **1 a** (1) **:** to undergo a sudden or violent change in place or position **:** DART, SHOOT ⟨the sparks *sprang* upward as he stirred the fire⟩ (2) **:** to have or display resiliency **:** move or be capable of moving by elastic force ⟨the two halves *sprang* back together again —C.L.Carmer⟩ **b :** to become shattered or cracked **:** BREAK, SPLIT ⟨the veneer ~*s* along the fracture —Andrew Wood & Thomas Linn⟩ **c :** to bend from a straight direction or plane surface **:** become warped **2 :** to issue with speed and force **:** break out ⟨the blood ~*s* from the wound⟩ ⟨the tears ~ from her eyes⟩ **:** issue as a stream ⟨out of these curiously shaped mounds ~*s* an unflagging supply of water —George Farwell⟩ ⟨turned on the first shining water tap, and watched the water ~, steaming, from it —Kay Boyle⟩ **3 a :** to grow as a plant ⟨white heather ~*s* on the mountainsides —Isabel Lawrence⟩ **b :** to issue by birth or descent ⟨both parents *sprang* from wealthy landowners —Cecil Sprigge⟩ ⟨*sprang* from a comfortable corner of the English middle class —J.M. Cameron⟩ **c :** to come into being **:** APPEAR, ARISE, EMERGE ⟨hope ~*s* eternal in the human breast —Alexander Pope⟩ ⟨the horror ~*ing* up in his eyes as it came to him —J.B. Benefield⟩ ⟨towns *sprang* into being where cattle trails and stage lines met —*Amer. Guide Series: Texas*⟩ **:** PROCEED, RESULT ⟨her anxiety had *sprung* from a definite cause —Ellen Glasgow⟩ **d** *archaic* **:** to become visible **:** DAWN ⟨at five the golden light began to ~ —John Keats⟩ **e :** to develop force **:** begin to blow — used with *up* ⟨a breeze suddenly *sprang up*⟩ **4 a :** to make a bound **:** move by means of a leap or leaps ⟨*sprang* toward the door, but was intercepted in her intended flight —T.L.Peacock⟩ ⟨*sprang* across the stream, inviting those who shared his views to follow him —*Amer. Guide Series: Maine*⟩ **b :** to start up suddenly (as from a covert) **c :** to leap or jump up **:** rise suddenly from a resting position ⟨I *sprang* to my feet, for anger had overtaken me —Edita Morris⟩ **5 a :** to stretch out in height or length **:** EXTEND ⟨from its corners ~ four slender minarets —Douglas Carruthers⟩ **b** *of a vault or arch* **:** to start rounding upward from the impost ⟨from rich entablatures ~ graceful arches supporting the vaulted ceilings —*Amer. Guide Series: Pa.*⟩ **6 a** *of a female domestic animal* **:** to show signs of approaching parturition (as by dropping of the enlarged abdomen and swelling of the udder) **b** *of an udder* **:** SWELL ~ *vt* **1 :** to cause to grow, arise, or develop ⟨hoped it would rain very soon, to ~ some new grass —Doris Lessing⟩ ⟨is *sprung* compellingly into life from a powerfully creative, romantic mind —*Times Lit. Supp.*⟩ **2 a :** to start (as game) from cover **:** cause to rise from the earth or from a covert **:** FLUSH ⟨~ a pheasant⟩ **b :** to put to a gallop ⟨*sprang* his horse in front of the ranks —C.L.Carmer⟩ **3 a** (1) **:** to undergo the splitting or cracking of ⟨the ship *sprang* a mast⟩ (2) **:** to bring about the splitting or cracking of ⟨the wind *sprang* the foremast of the ship⟩ **b :** to undergo the opening of (a leak) ⟨having grounded at the mouth of the river as a result of which it *sprung* a leak —*Hispanic Amer. Hist. Rev.*⟩ ⟨the radiator *sprung* a leak —John Steinbeck⟩ **4 a :** to cause to explode ⟨the disturbance of the steamer's approach ~*ing* a myriad of these floating mines —William Beebe⟩ **b :** CHAMBER 4 ⟨a borehole is *sprung* . . . by exploding in the bottom several charges of dynamite —*Blasters' Handbk.*⟩ **5 a :** to cause to shift place or position suddenly **:** make leap up or start forward or out ⟨the wind *sprang* some tiles from the roof⟩ **b** (1) **:** to operate or cause to operate by sudden pressure or movement ⟨*sprang* the watchcase open⟩ (2) **:** to cause to close or operate ⟨~ a trap⟩ (3) **:** to cause (a rattle) to sound by movement of a part **c :** to apply or insert by bending ⟨needed all his strength to ~ in the bar⟩ **d :** to bend by force ⟨~ the steel band⟩ **e :** to move, haul, or swing (a ship) by means of a spring line ⟨to get under way ~ the boat ahead —*Manual of Seamanship*⟩ **f :** to raise (the toe of a shoe last) above the ground line **6 a :** to start (a vault or arch) upward from the impost **b :** to put up (an arch) **c :** ARCH, CURVE ⟨the dog's ribs are well *sprung*⟩ **7 :** to pass over by leaping ⟨the horse *sprang* the narrow fence⟩ **8 :** to give, spend, offer, or pay out (money) ⟨there's nothing really immoral about ~*ing* ten cents for a ball of twine —R.P.Smith⟩ **9 :** to produce or disclose suddenly or unexpectedly ⟨the last page ~*s* a surprise bit of fireworks no reviewer should mention beforehand —*N.Y. Herald Tribune Bk. Rev.*⟩ ⟨my wife *sprung* a dinner party with nearly all my old secretaries on me —O.W.Holmes †1935⟩ **10 :** to make lame **:** STRAIN ⟨its near leg was *sprung* a little, maybe from being worked too hard too young —William Faulkner⟩ ⟨*sprang* every blessed muscle in my . . . leg —John Buchan⟩ **11** *slang* **:** to release or cause to be released from confinement, custody, or military service ⟨there'd be a lawyer down there to ~ him before I got the cell door shut —Leslie Ford⟩

syn SPRING, ARISE, RISE, ORIGINATE, DERIVE, FLOW, ISSUE, EMANATE, PROCEED, STEM can mean, in common, to come up or out of something into existence. SPRING stresses sudden or surprising emergence, esp. after a period of concealed existence or preparation ⟨plants *spring* from seed⟩ ⟨the images that *spring* up in one's consciousness⟩ ⟨it is from the middle class that writers *spring* —Virginia Woolf⟩ ARISE emphasizes chiefly the mere fact of coming into existence or notice, conveying the idea of a vagueness of prior state; when used with *from* it implies a causal connection between subject and object ⟨an argument *arose* during the meal —Zechariah Chafee⟩ ⟨present uncertainties *arise* partly out of far-reaching changes in the American environment —J.D.Millett⟩ ⟨differences in English may *arise* from several causes —*English Language Arts*⟩ RISE and ARISE in this sense of to come into existence are often interchangeable, although RISE may possibly carry some connotation of literal or figurative ascent ⟨empires *rise* and fall within a single man's lifetime —Elspeth Huxley⟩ ⟨a church *rose* in the wilderness —*Amer. Guide Series: Conn.*⟩ ⟨from the South, at last, *rose* that bitter opposition which flowered in a bloody civil war —Carol L. Thompson⟩ ORIGINATE suggests a source or starting point, carrying the idea of inception at that source ⟨at one time it was believed that man *originated* in America —R.W.Murray⟩ ⟨within its area of 84,682 square miles *originate* three great river systems —*Amer. Guide Series: Minn.*⟩ ⟨adult fears *originating* in childhood insecurity⟩ DERIVE also suggests a source, though it usu. does not imply inception, usu. presupposing a prior existence in another form, person, or thing, and connoting descent as by endowment, transference, deduction, imitation, or reproduction ⟨the new playwrights *derive* from him —E.R.Bentley⟩ ⟨the principal income *derives* from coal mining —*Amer. Guide Series: Pa.*⟩ ⟨its criticism *derives* directly from English inspiration —Bernard Smith⟩ FLOW emphasizes often the abundance of the supply, often the ease of provision or production ⟨from the town's shaded public square *flows* justice —*Amer. Guide Series: Va.*⟩ ⟨masterpiece upon masterpiece *flowed* from his brush —*advt*⟩ ⟨a great generosity from which *flowed* gift after gift⟩ ISSUE suggests emergence into existence as from a womb, stressing somewhat a causal force ⟨three conclusions at least *issue* from the perusal —T.S.Eliot⟩ EMANATE applies chiefly to immaterial things, as law, principles, power, or thoughts, connoting the emergence or passage of something impalpable or invisible, suggesting less causal force than ISSUE ⟨the earlier reports which *emanated* from Dumbarton Oaks —Sir Winston Churchill⟩ ⟨the rain-drenched geranium bed, from which *emanated* an odor musky and sweet —J.C.Powys⟩ ⟨the impalpable aura of power that *emanated* from him —Osbert Sitwell⟩ ⟨the criminal organization . . . is extremely powerful, and part of its power *emanates* from the close-knit structure —D.W.Maurer & V.H. Vogel⟩ PROCEED stresses place of origin, or, sometimes, parentage, derivation, or cause ⟨*proceeding* from the premise that half the world does not know how the other half lives —*Dun's Rev.*⟩ ⟨the philosophic movement *proceeded* from little known thinkers and writers⟩ STEM suggests a growing out, as of a stem from a plant, and applies chiefly to things that come into existence through the influence of a predecessor, as a natural outgrowth or subordinate development ⟨one of twenty-five in the class, all but four *stemming* from Maine —M.L.Ernst⟩ ⟨these influences . . . *stem* from warfare, from medicine, from the arts, from religion —D.J.Struik⟩ **syn** see in addition JUMP

²**spring** \"\ *n* -s *often attrib* [ME, fr. OE; akin to OFris *spring*, OS & OHG *gispring* spring, OE *springan* to spring — more at ¹SPRING] **1 a :** a source of a body or reservoir of water (as of a river or well) ⟨a flowing bubble that begins in a hundred trickles and runnels and ∼*s* high up in the mountains —Lewis Mumford⟩ **b** (1) **:** an issue of water from the earth **:** a natural fountain ⟨everybody lived in dugouts or small log houses on ∼*s* or creeks —Bruce Siberts⟩ ⟨had to drill a well when their ∼ ran dry⟩ (2) **:** a natural fountain having specified properties — usu. used in pl. ⟨mineral ∼*s*⟩ ⟨sulfur ∼*s*⟩ ⟨hot ∼*s*⟩ (3) **:** something that resembles a fountain ⟨a ∼ of pity, of affection . . . suddenly welled up within her —Winston Churchill⟩ **c :** a flow or seepage (as of a mineral) from the earth ⟨accumulations of oil which seeped to the surface in ∼*s* —Bliss Isely⟩ ⟨tar ∼*s*⟩ **2 a :** a source of something; *esp* **:** a hidden or ultimate source ⟨this habit of retirement to the inner ∼*s* of being —H.S.Canby⟩ ⟨a custom, a belief, and art, however deep down its ∼*s*, sooner or later rises into social consciousness —A.L.Kroeber⟩ **b** *archaic* **:** the beginning or first appearance of something ⟨never since the middle summer's ∼, met we —Shak.⟩; *specif* **:** DAWN, DAYSPRING ⟨they arose early: and it came to pass about the ∼ of the day —1 Sam 9:26 (AV)⟩ **c :** a first stage **:** a time or state of growth and development ⟨this thirteen-year-old girl, in whose flat childish body the ∼ was beginning to stir —Edith Sitwell⟩ **d :** something that produces action or motion **:** CAUSE, MOTIVE ⟨laying open to his view the ∼*s* of action in both parties —T.L.Peacock⟩ ⟨the ∼*s* of human conduct —A. T.Weaver⟩ **3 :** an exceptionally high or low tide **:** SPRING TIDE **4 a** *chiefly dial* **:** a grove of young trees **:** PLANTATION **b** *chiefly dial* **:** a young undergrowth (as of trees or shrubs) **5 a** (1) **:** an elastic body or device that recovers its original shape when released after being distorted; *specif* **:** one designed for some specific use (as to check recoil, to diminish concussion and jar, to store up energy) — see BREGUET HAIRSPRING, MAINSPRING (2) **:** BEDSPRING **b :** a person likened to a spring (as in tension or contained energy) ⟨a steel ∼ of a man —Claudia Cassidy⟩ **6 a :** the act or an instance of leaping up or forward **:** BOUND ⟨the cat made a ∼ at the mouse⟩ ⟨took the steps at one ∼⟩ ⟨that sudden and inexplicable ∼ forward took place independently . . . in three different regions and cultures —T.I. Cook⟩ **b :** a low leap in which a dancer moves forward, backward, or sideward as weight is transferred from one foot to the other **c** *chiefly Scot* **:** a lively tune or dance ⟨took the pipes, and played a little ∼ —R.L.Stevenson⟩ **7** *of teal* **:** a small flock **8 a :** the season between winter and summer reckoned astronomically as extending from the March equinox to the June solstice **b :** the season comprising the months of March, April, and May **c** *Brit* **:** the season comprising the months of February, March, and April **d :** the season reckoned astronomically in the southern hemisphere as extending from the September equinox to the December solstice **9 a :** capacity for springing **:** elastic power or force **:** ELASTICITY, RESILIENCE ⟨the ironing-out effect of passing trains on track which has a certain amount of ∼ in it —O.S.Nock⟩ **:** BOUNCE, BUOYANCY, ENERGY ⟨there was a new ∼ in their step —Bennett Cerf⟩ **b :** the action of flying back to a normal state or position from a sprung state or position ⟨the ∼ of a bow⟩ **10 :** the point or plane at which an arch or vault curve springs from its impost **11 a :** a crack, fissure, or permanent deformation in a mast or yard **b** (1) **:** a line led from a ship's quarter to its cable so that by hauling in or slacking the line the ship can be made to lie in any desired position (2) **:** a line led diagonally from the bow or stern of a ship to some point upon a wharf and made fast to aid in springing the ship in to the wharf **12** *of a dog* **:** roundness of ribs **:** the state of having the ribs well arched **13 :** the furcula of a springtail **14 :** a more or less flexible pipe bend or elbow designed to accommodate slight changes in length **15 a :** the variation of a shoe at the toe and arch from a horizontal line **b :** a tension at the counter of a shoe caused by cutting the upper shorter at that place **16 a :** KING SALMON **b :** a pelt or fur taken in the spring and usu. no longer prime **syn** see JUMP, MOTIVE

³**spring** \"\ *vt* **sprinqed** \-riŋd\ *or* **sprung** \-rəŋ\ **springed** *or* **sprung; springing; springs :** to fit with springs ⟨the ambulance . . . was the old kind, like a furniture van, but it was well *sprung* —Fred Majdalany⟩ ⟨there were ∼*ed* bunks which folded into the wall —Bill Mauldin⟩

⁴**spring** \"\ *n* -s [alter. of *springe*] *chiefly dial* **:** NOOSE, SNARE

spring·ald \ˈspriŋəld\ *also* **spring·al** \-ŋəl\ *n* -s [prob. fr. ME, a kind of catapult, fr. MF *espringale*, fr. OF, fr. *espringuier* to jump, dance, of Gmc origin; akin to OHG *springan* to jump, spring — more at SPRING] **:** a young man **:** STRIPLING ⟨have any penniless young ∼ defy his parents to marry a green girl —J.H.Wheelwright⟩

spring azure *n* **:** a small blue American butterfly (*Lycaenopsis argiolus*) of the family Lycaenidae

spring back *n* [²*spring*] **:** HOLLOW BACK

springback \ˈ=,=\ *n* [fr. *spring back*, v.] **:** the capacity or tendency of a bent or shaped elastic material (as a metal) to revert to its original form ⟨the forming of magnesium . . . must be done at high temperatures to eliminate ∼ —*Scientific American*⟩

spring base *n* **:** the distance between centers of suspension of an arched spring

spring beam *n* **:** a beam uniting the outboard ends of the paddle beams of a ship and assisting to support the side of a paddle box

spring beauty *n* **1 :** a plant of the genus *Claytonia* (esp. *C. virginica*) sending up in early spring a 2-leaved stem bearing several delicate pink flowers **2 :** a strong to vivid purplish red that is redder and slightly lighter than Tyrian pink

spring bed *n* **1 :** a spring mattress or a bed having a spring mattress **2 :** a long elastic steel plate that serves to press the fibers up to the cutters in a cloth-shearing machine

spring beetle *n* **:** CLICK BEETLE

spring binder *n* **:** a loose-leaf binder having a shaped spring-metal back that opens to receive or release the contents when the covers are opened wide and pressed back

spring binder

springblade knife \ˈ=-,=-\ *n* **:** SWITCHBLADE KNIFE

spring block *n* **:** a block to which a spring is attached; *specif* **:** either of the distance pieces secured one above and the other below an elliptic car spring

springboard \ˈ=,=\ *n* **1 a :** a strong but flexible board of wood, metal, or glass resting on a fulcrum with one end secured and the other projecting over water and used for diving; *specif* **:** one usu. placed at a height of one or three meters above the water and used by fancy divers as a means of getting height for a dive **b :** a flexible board that is usu. secured at one end and is used as a takeoff device for certain gymnastic stunts **c :** a short iron-shod board that is inserted into a notched tree trunk and upon which the axman stands **2 :** a point of departure **:** JUMPING-OFF PLACE ⟨the idea is to use the convention as a ∼ for the campaign —*New Republic*⟩ ⟨sees an opportunity ahead of making the chairmanship a ∼ to higher things —*Atlantic*⟩

spring·bok \ˈ=,bäk, -,bək\ *n, pl* **springbok** *or* **springboks** [Afrik, fr. *spring* to jump (fr. MD *springen*) + *bok* male goat, male deer or antelope, fr. MD *boc*; akin to OHG *springan* to jump and to OHG *boc* male goat — more at SPRING, BUCK] **:** a swift and graceful southern African gazelle (*Antidorcas euchore*) noted for its habit of springing lightly and suddenly into the air and being dark buffy-brown with dark markings and white underparts and a white dorsal stripe that expands into a broad patch of white on the rump

spring bolt *n* **:** a bolt retracted by pressure and shot by a spring when the pressure is released — compare BULLET BOLT

spring brass *n* **:** common brass stiffened by cold working or heat treatment

springbuck \ˈ=,=\ *n, pl* **springbuck** *or* **springbucks** [part trans. of Afrik *springbok*] **:** SPRINGBOK

spring caliper *n* **:** a caliper having legs fastened together with a spring and pivot

spring cankerworm *n* **:** the variably colored looper larva of a widespread No. American geometrid moth (*Paleacrita vernata*) that largely resembles the fall cankerworm but has spines on the abdomen and emerges in spring

spring catch *n* **:** a catch having a spring bolt

spring chair *n* **:** PERCH 3e

spring chicken *n* **1 :** a young table fowl of about three pounds in weight formerly available only from spring hatchings **2 :** a young person ⟨she looks youthful, but she's no *spring chicken*⟩

¹**spring-clean** \ˈ=¦=\ *vt* [back-formation fr. *spring-cleaning*] **:** to give a thorough cleaning to (a place) ⟨*spring-cleaned* the cabin even blacking the stovepipes and stoves —John Onslow⟩ ⟨starlings have started to *spring-clean* their nest box —*Manchester Guardian Weekly*⟩

²**spring-clean** \ˈ=,=\ *n, Brit* **:** SPRING-CLEANING

spring-cleaning \ˈ=¦==\ *n* [²*spring* + *cleaning*] **:** the act or process of doing a thorough cleaning of a place

spring cleavers *n pl but usu sing in constr* **:** a cleavers (*Galium aparine*)

spring clip *n* **1 :** a U-shaped piece of metal used to fasten a leaf spring to the axle of a vehicle **2 :** a small clip working with a spring (as for electrical terminal connections)

spring collet *n* **:** a tempered bushing slotted at the front end and tapered externally to fit another bushing so that when the collet is drawn backward axially (as by a screw action) it closes in and grips the work

spring corn *n* **:** CORN SNOW

spring cotter *n* **:** a cotter formed of elastic metal bent double and used as a split pin — called also *spring key*

spring cowslip *n* **:** a marsh marigold (*Caltha palustris*)

spring cress *n* **:** a small white-flowered cress (*Cardamine bulbosa*) common in wet places in eastern No. America

spring·dans \ˈspriŋ,dän(t)s\ *n* -ES [Norw, fr. *springe* to jump, spring (fr. ON *springa*) + *dans* dance, fr. ON, fr. OF *dance* — more at SPRING, DANCE] **:** a Norwegian leaping dance for men

spring die *n* **:** an adjustable screw-thread die that is made of a hollow cylinder cut away at one end and leaving prongs that are provided with cutting teeth on the inside and are tapered threaded on the outside

spring dwarf *n* **:** a disease of strawberry plants caused by an eelworm (*Aphelenchoides fragariae*) and characterized by twisting, stiffness, and glossiness of the leaves and shortening of the petioles esp. of the central leaves during the early part of the growing season

¹**springe** \ˈsprinj\ *n* -s [ME *springe, sprenge*; akin to OE *springan* to spring — more at SPRING] **1 :** a noose fastened to an elastic body and drawn close with a sudden spring to catch a bird or other animal **2 :** SNARE, TRAP ⟨the herd mind was always laying ∼*s* to catch the unwary —V.L.Parrington⟩

²**springe** \"\ *vb* **springed; springed; springeing; springes** *vt* **:** to catch in a springe **:** ENSNARE ∼ *vi* **:** to set a springe

³**springe** \", ˈsprinzh\ *adj, dial Eng* **:** SUPPLE, AGILE

springed *past of* SPRING

¹**spring·er** \ˈspriŋə(r)\ *n* -s [¹*spring* + *-er*] **1 a :** a stone or other solid laid at the impost of an arch **b :** the lowest voussoir in an arch — see ARCH illustration **c :** SKEWBACK **2 :** one that springs: as **a :** SPRINGBOK **b** (1) **:** SPRINGER SPANIEL (2) **:** a spaniel that flushes game by springing **c** *Africa* (1) **:** any active leaping mullet (2) **:** TENPOUNDER **d :** FLIPPER 2d **e :** WEDGER **3 :** a cow that is nearly ready to calve **4 :** NACHSCHLAG

²**springer** \"\ *n* -s [²*spring* + *-er*] **1 :** an Atlantic salmon that returns to fresh water in the spring **2 :** a young chicken that is larger than a broiler and smaller than a roaster **:** FRYER

³**springer** \"\ *n* -s [³*spring* + *-er*] **:** one that fits with springs; *specif* **:** a worker who fixes springs in places in seats that are to be upholstered

spring·er·le \ˈs(h)priŋərlə\ *n* -s [G dial. (Alemannic), lit., hare, dim. of *springer* jumper, fr. MHG, fr. *springen* to jump (fr. OHG *springan*) + *-er* — more at SPRING] **:** a thick hard cookie that is usu. flavored with anise and has a design impressed in relief upon the dough by means of a carved board or rolling pin and that is traditionally eaten at Christmas in German-speaking countries

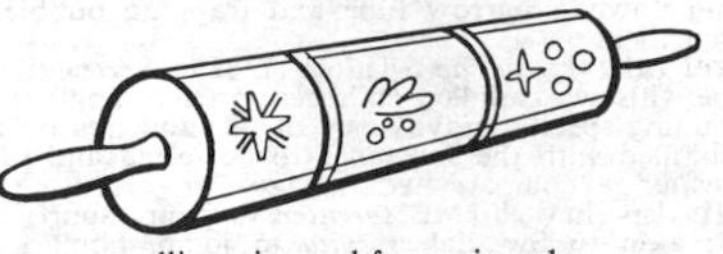
rolling pin used for springerle

springer spaniel *n* [¹*springer*] **:** a medium-sized sporting dog of either of two breeds used chiefly for finding and flushing small game and having a flat or slightly waved coat usu. of white and another color, rather long legs, and a well-feathered tail carried low — see ENGLISH SPRINGER, WELSH SPRINGER SPANIEL

spring faucet *n* **:** a faucet that has to be kept open against the force of a spring that ordinarily keeps it closed

spring fever *n* **:** a lazy or restless feeling often associated with the onset of spring

¹**spring·field** \ˈspriŋ,fēld\ *adj, usu cap* [fr. *Springfield*, Mass., & *Springfield*, Ill.] **1 :** of or from the city of Springfield, Mass. ⟨a *Springfield* park⟩ **:** of the kind or style prevalent in Springfield **2 :** of or from Springfield, the capital of Illinois **:** of the kind or style prevalent in Springfield

²**springfield** \"\ *or* **springfield rifle** *n* -s *usu cap S* [fr. *Springfield*, Mass., where a United States Armory is located] **1 :** a breech-loading .45 caliber rifle used in the U. S. Army from about 1868 to 1893 and by U. S. volunteer troops in the Spanish-American War **2 :** a .30 caliber bolt-operated rifle adopted by the U. S. army in 1903 and used by U. S. troops in World War I — see RIFLE illustration

spring·field·er \-də(r)\ *n* -s *cap* [*Springfield*, Mass. & *Springfield*, Ill. + E *-er*] **:** SPRINGFIELDIAN

spring·field·ian \(ˈ)=¦fēldēən, -dyən\ *n* -s *cap* [*Springfield*, Mass. & *Springfield*, Ill. + E *-ian*] **:** a native or resident of Springfield, esp. Springfield, Illinois or Springfield, Mass.

springfish \ˈ=,=\ *n* [²*spring* + *fish*] **1 :** MILLER'S-THUMB **2 :** SPRINGER 1

spring flood *n* [ME, fr. *spring* + *flood*] **1 :** SPRING TIDE **2 :** a flood (as from a river) occurring in the spring season

spring fly *n* **:** CADDIS FLY

springform \ˈ=,=\ *n* **:** a mold or pan having the upright rim fastened to the bottom by means of a clamp or spring that is released to detach the rim and facilitate removal of the molded or baked food

springform

spring frog *n* **1 :** GREEN FROG **2 :** LEOPARD FROG

spring grain aphis *n* **:** GREENBUG

spring green *n* **:** a variable color averaging a moderate yellow-green that is greener, lighter, and stronger than average moss green, mosstone, average pea green, or spinach green

spring gun *n* **:** SET GUN

spring·haas \ˈspriŋ,häs\ *n, pl* **springhase** \-äsə\ [Afrik, fr. *spring* to jump + *haas* hare, fr. MD *hase*; akin to OHG *haso* hare — more at SPRINGBOK, HARE] **:** JUMPING HARE

spring-hab·it·ed \ˈ=¦habəd·əd\ *adj, of wheat* **:** having growth of such a character as to mature and produce seed in one growing season from spring sowing — compare WINTER-HABITED

spring·halt \ˈspriŋ,=\ *n* [by alter.] **:** STRINGHALT

spring hammer *n* **:** a machine-driven hammer whose blow is caused or increased by the extension of a compressed spring or the expansion of a body of compressed air

springhare \ˈ=,=\ *n* [part trans. of Afrik *springhaas* — more at SPRINGHAAS] **:** JUMPING HARE

spring harrow *n* **:** SPRING-TOOTH HARROW

springhead \ˈ=,=\ *n* **:** FOUNTAINHEAD

spring heath *n* **:** a low European shrub (*Erica carnea*) with very early-blooming bell-shaped red flowers

spring heel *n* **1 :** a heel formed by bending the outsole over a thickness of leather between the sole and the upper at the heel **2 :** a low broad heel with wedge-shaped line at the breast that continues from the bottom of the heel to the surface of the sole at the shank

spring herring *n* **:** ALEWIFE 1a

spring hinge *n* **:** a hinge fitted with a spring to close an opened door automatically

spring hoe *n* **:** a hinged blade for a wheel hoe that is held by a spring so as to yield to obstructions

spring hook *n* **1 :** a hook with a spring snap in its end to prevent accidental unhooking — called also *snap hook* **2 :** a supplementary fishhook that springs down and secures a fish that takes the baited barbed hook — called also *snap hook, spear hook*

springhouse \ˈ=,=\ *n* **:** a small structure built over a spring and used as a cooling place (as for dairy products or meat)

springier *comparative of* SPRINGY

springiest *superlative of* SPRINGY

spring·i·ly \ˈspriŋəlē, -li\ *adv* **:** in a springy manner

spring·i·ness \-ŋēnəs, -ŋin-\ *n* -ES **:** the quality or state of being springy

springing *n* -s [ME, gerund of *springen* to spring — more at SPRING] **1 :** the act, action, or process of one that springs **2 :** the architectural member that constitutes the first upward curvature of an arch or vault; *also* **:** the initial point of such curvature **3 :** the springs with which an automotive vehicle is equipped ⟨allow much softer ∼ to be used at the front than the rear —*Country Life*⟩

springing bow *n* **:** a method of bowing stringed instruments so that the bow rebounds from the string — compare ARCO SALTANDO, SPICCATO

spring·ing·ly *adv* **:** in a springing manner

springing use *n* **:** a use that is limited to arise on the happening of a future event and is not dependent on any preceding use or estate and that is not in derogation of any prior estate or limited on a particular estate

spring iris *n* **:** a dwarf iris (*Iris verna*) with yellow spotted flowers resembling violets

spring key *n* **:** SPRING COTTER

spring lamb *n* **:** a market lamb born in late winter or early spring and sold fat off the dam usu. before July 1st; *also* **:** the meat of such a lamb

spring latch *n* **:** a latch that operates with a spring bolt

spring lay rope *n* **:** a composite rope having three wire and three fiber strands laid alternately around a fiber core

¹**sprin·gle** \ˈspriŋgəl\ *vt* -ED/-ING/-S [prob. by alter.] *archaic* **:** SPRINKLE

²**springle** \"\ *n* -s [prob. fr. ⁴*spring* + *-le*] **:** SPRINGE

spring leaf *n* **:** LEAF 2f (3)

spring·less \ˈ=ləs\ *adj* **1 :** being without a spring **:** lacking springs ⟨equipped with measuring rods and ∼ scales —*Time*⟩ **2 :** lacking in elasticity or vitality ⟨looked at each other with wet eyes, and went off with ∼ steps —Hall Caine⟩

spring·let \-lət\ *n* -s **:** a little spring **:** STREAMLET

spring ligament *n* **:** an elastic ligament of the sole of the foot that connects the calcaneus and navicular bone and supports the head of the astragalus

springlike \ˈ=,=\ *adj* **1 :** having the quality, characteristics, or effect of spring **:** VERNAL **2 :** resembling a spring or the action of a spring

spring lily *n* **:** a white-flowered dogtooth violet (*Erythronium albidum*)

spring line *n* **1 :** SPRING 11b **2 :** an imaginary line connecting the two opposite points at which the curve of an arch or vault begins

spring-load \ˈ=¦=\ *vt* **:** to apply force to or load by means of spring tension or compression

spring lock *n* **:** a lock that fastens with a spring bolt — distinguished from *deadlock*

spring needle *n* **:** a fine steel needle for machine knitting that has a butt at one end and a long flexible hook at the other that curves back to the shank of the needle

spring onion *n* **:** WELSH ONION

spring orange *n* **:** a white-flowered shrub (*Styrax americana*) of the southeastern U. S. having obovoid fruit

spring orchid *or* **spring orchis** *n* **:** SHOWY ORCHIS

spring peeper *n* **:** a small brown tree toad (*Hyla crucifer*) of the eastern U. S. and Canada that has an oblique dark-colored cross on the back, an angular mark between the eyes, and bars on the legs, that breeds in ponds and swamps in the spring, and that has a shrill piping call

spring pin *n* **:** an iron rod fitted between the springs and the axle boxes in locomotives to sustain and regulate the pressure on the axles

spring pole *n* **1 :** a flexible elastic pole used to act as a spring **2 :** an elastic wooden pole from which hand-operated percussion-drilling or other tools are suspended

spring-rail frog \ˈ=,=-\ *n* **:** a frog having a movable wing rail held against the point rail by springs and normally presenting an unbroken running surface to wheels using the main track but operating also to permit the passage of trailing wheels from a diverging track

spring ring *n* : PISTON RING

[1]**springs** *pres 3d sing of* SPRING, *pl of* SPRING

[2]**springs** \'spriŋz\ *adj, usu cap* [fr. *Springs*, Union of South Africa] : of or from the city of Springs, Union of So. Africa : of the kind or style prevalent in Springs

spring salmon *n* : KING SALMON

spring saxifrage *n* : EARLY SAXIFRAGE

spring scale *n* : a scale in which the weight indications depend upon the change of shape or of dimensions of an elastic body or system of such bodies

spring scorpion grass *n* : EARLY SCORPION GRASS

spring set *n* : an arrangement of saw teeth in which alternate teeth are sprung to the right and left to make a saw kerf wider than the thickness of the blade

spring snow *n* : CORN SNOW

spring snowflake *n* : a snowflake (*Leucojum vernum*) with solitary very fragrant green-tipped white flowers borne in spring

spring starflower *n* : a spring-blooming onion-scented Argentine herb (*Spheion uniflora*) of the family Amaryllidaceae that is often cultivated for its bluish white flowers

spring stay *n* **1** : a heavy wire rope running horizontally between the mastheads of a schooner **2** : an auxiliary stay

spring steel *n* : a steel that is processed (as by cold drawing, cold rolling, or heat treating) to give it the elastic properties and yield strength useful in springs

spring switch *n* : a switch consisting of a pair of split switch points held in running position by a stiff coil spring and designed to return to that position after being thrown over by trailing wheels from the diverging route

springtail \'⸗,⸗\ *n* **1** : an arthropod of the order Collembola : COLLEMBOLAN **2** : the furcula of a collembolan

spring temper *n* : a temper induced in steel to increase its upper limit of elasticity by hardening and tempering in the ordinary way and then reheating until the steel assumes a bright blue color; *also* : a similar temper produced in brass by an extreme amount of cold rolling — **spring-tempered** \'⸗¦⸗⸗\ *adj*

springtide \'⸗,⸗\ *n* : SPRINGTIME ⟨in the ~ of his career⟩

spring tide *n* **1** : a tide of greater-than-average range between high and low tide that occurs twice each synodic month around the times of new and full moon when the tidal actions of the sun and moon are nearly in the same direction — compare FLOOD TIDE, NEAP TIDE **2** : a strong or heavy flow ⟨a *spring tide* of prosperity⟩

springtime \'⸗,⸗\ *n* [ME, fr. *spring* + *time*] **1 a** : the season of spring ⟨help him keep his business straighter when it grew more active in ~ —*New Yorker*⟩ **b** : YOUTH ⟨a man still in his prime but past his ~⟩ **c** : an early or flourishing stage of development ⟨the ~ of the national spirit, when the genius of the people formed customs and institutions —W.K.Ferguson⟩ **2** : a deep pink that is bluer, lighter, and stronger than average coral (sense 3b), bluer and deeper than fiesta, and yellower and deeper than begonia

spring tool *n* : a tool having a spring as an essential part of its construction: as **a** : a glassblower's tongs resembling sugar tongs without the spoon ends **b** : a lathe tool with a bend near the point to give a slight spring that makes possible a light finishing cut

spring tooth *n* : a flat coiled steel tooth (as on a cultivating or weeding machine) that digs deeply but springs backward on striking an obstruction

springtooth \'⸗,⸗\ *vt* [*spring tooth*] : to cultivate with a spring-tooth implement

spring-tooth harrow \'⸗,⸗-\ *or* **spring-tooth drag** *also* **spring-tooth** *n* : a harrow with spring teeth

spring training *n* : a period usu. beginning on March 1st and extending until opening day that is used by professional esp. major league baseball teams for conditioning, practice, and exhibition games

spring-trip hoe \'⸗,⸗-\ *n* : a grain-drill furrow opener equipped with a spring hoe

spring-tooth harrow

spring vetch *n* : a vetch (*Vicia sativa*)

spring vetchling *n* : a European perennial herb (*Lathyrus vernus*) with nodding, racemose, violet-blue flowers

spring vise *n* **1** : a spring-actuated vise **2** : a vise for compressing springs

spring wagon *n* : a light wagon equipped with springs and formerly common on farms and ranches ⟨the *spring wagon* the boys used for hauling salt to the cattle —F.B.Gipson⟩

spring washer *n* : an elastic washer; *esp* : a strong flat spiral spring of one or two turns that is sharp-edged at the ends and used as a nut-locking device — compare LOCK WASHER

springwater \'⸗,⸗⸗\ *n* [ME, fr. *spring* + *water*] : water from a natural spring — compare RAINWATER, SURFACE WATER

spring-well \'⸗,⸗\ *n* [[2]*spring* + *well*] : SPRING ⟨go down now to the *spring-well* and give him this —J.M.Synge⟩

spring wheat *n* : wheat that is sown in the spring and harvested in late summer or fall

springwood \'⸗,⸗\ *n* **1** : the portion of each annual ring of wood that develops largely early in the growing season and is softer, more porous, and lighter in weight than the adjoining summerwood because of its higher proportion of larger and thinner-walled cells — called also *earlywood*; compare SUMMERWOOD **2** : a thicket of young trees

springwort \'⸗,⸗\ *n* : a root held in European folklore to have magical properties

springy \'spriŋē, -iŋi\ *adj* -ER/-EST [[2]*spring* + *-y*] **1** : abounding with springs of water : SPONGY ⟨picking his way across the treacherous ~ country —Jeannie Gunn⟩ **2 a** : having an elastic quality : capable of springing back to its original shape after deformation ⟨made crossbows from the ~ horn of the musk ox —Farley Mowat⟩ **b** : having or marked by lightness and vigor of movement ⟨a ~ fellow, well set up —Amy Lowell⟩ ⟨a fine figure of a man tall, lithe, and agile, with a ~ step —A. Conan Doyle⟩ **c** : lively and resilient underfoot ⟨thickly covered with heath and ling and moor plants ~ to the tread —A.L.Rowse⟩ ⟨a ballroom with floor made ~ for dancing —*Amer. Guide Series: Md.*⟩ **syn** see FLEXIBLE

sprink *vt* [ME *sprinken*; akin to ME *sprenklen, sprinclen* to sprinkle — more at SPRINKLE] *obs* : SPRINKLE

[1]**sprin·kle** \'spriŋkəl\ *vb* **sprinkled; sprinkled; sprinkling** \-k(ə)liŋ\ **sprinkles** [ME *sprenklen, sprinclen*; akin to MD, MLG, & MHG *sprenkel, sprinkel* spot, Icel *sprekla* spot, OE *spearca* spark — more at SPARK] *vt* **1 a** : to scatter in drops or particles ⟨it *sprinkled* rain late in the afternoon, just enough to remove some of the dust from the infield —*Nashville Tennessean*⟩ ⟨~ a little bird sand on the feeding board —William Powell-Owen⟩ **b** : to scatter widely : distribute sparsely ⟨a series of model houses *sprinkled* about the grounds —Betty Pepis⟩ **2 a** : to scatter over : BESPRINKLE, SPOT — usu. used with *with* ⟨*sprinkled* that roof with lightning rods —Eudora Welty⟩ ⟨his ill-fitting clothes were usually *sprinkled* with cigarette ashes —Samuel Lubell⟩ **b** : to scatter at intervals in or among : DIVERSIFY, DOT, INTERSPERSE — usu. used with *with* ⟨~s his programs generously with such light works — Green Peyton⟩ ⟨a propaganda tract *sprinkled* with glib half-truths —Theodore Brameld⟩ ⟨a heavily wooded section *sprinkled* with small lakes —*Amer. Guide Series: Pa.*⟩ **c** : to wet lightly ⟨*sprinkled* the flowers⟩ ⟨the rain *sprinkled* the grass⟩ **d** : to spatter small drops of color on the smoothly cut edges of (books) or acid on the surface of (smooth leather) ⟨*sprinkled* edges⟩ ⟨*sprinkled* calf binding⟩ **3 a** : to cleanse with or as if with a few drops of water : PURIFY ⟨our hearts *sprinkled* clean from an evil conscience —Heb 10:22 (RSV)⟩ **b** : to baptize by aspersion or by the application of a few drops of water ~ *vi* **1** : to scatter a liquid in fine drops ⟨shall ~ of the oil with his finger seven times —Lev 14:16 (AV)⟩ **2** : to rain lightly in scattered drops ⟨it began to ~⟩

[2]**sprinkle** \"\ *n* -s **1 a** : the act or an instance of sprinkling ⟨the ~ and trickle filter treatment of sewage —*Building, Estimating & Contracting*⟩; *specif* : a light rain ⟨a brief ~ that hardly wet the ground⟩ **b** : something scattered about or sparsely distributed ⟨they came out of the tunnel into a ~ of lights and houses —Katherine Mansfield⟩ ⟨gathering field peas or the last ~ of late cotton —Frances Gaither⟩ **c** : a small particle intended or suitable for sprinkling — usu. used in pl. ⟨covered it with chocolate ~s —Evan Hunter⟩ **2** : a mottled color effect

[1]**sprin·kler** \'spriŋk(ə)lə(r)\ *n* -s [[1]*sprinkle* + *-er*] **1** : a machine or device for sprinkling: as **a** : a vehicle or an attachment to a vehicle for sprinkling streets or roads **b** (1) : SPRINKLER HEAD (2) : SPRINKLER SYSTEM **c** : a device for spraying plants or lawns **d** : a device for distributing sewage on a filter bed **2** : one that sprinkles: as **a** : one that sprinkles timbers in mines with chemicals to make them proof against fire and rot **b** : one that sprinkles dry coal or dust in a mine with water to prevent explosions **c** : a laundry worker who uses a sprinkler to dampen clothes for ironing **3** : one that believes in baptism by aspersion rather than by immersion

[2]**sprinkler** \"\ *vt* -ED/-ING/-S : to provide with an automatic sprinkler system ⟨stressing the importance of having all schools ~*ed* — *Springfield (Mass.) Daily News*⟩

sprinkler head *n* : the outlet of a sprinkler system that is usu. a valve held closed by a strut having separable parts joined with solder of a predetermined melting point (as 160° F.) that fuses when exposed to fire temperatures and allows the head to open or by a quartz bulb containing a liquid that expands when heated and bursts the bulb

sprinkler leakage insurance *n* : insurance against loss resulting from damage to property caused by the accidental discharge of water from an automatic sprinkler system

sprinkler system *n* **1** : a system for protection against fire in which pipes are distributed for conveying water or other extinguishing fluid to outlets and that is usu. designed to function automatically with the action of heat on the automatic sprinkler head or on a controlling thermostatic system — see DRY-PIPE SYSTEM, WET-PIPE SYSTEM **2** : a system for sprinkling water to lay dust (as in coal mines)

sprinkling *n* -s [ME *sprenkling*, fr. gerund of *sprenklen, sprinklen* to sprinkle — more at SPRINKLE] **1** : the act or process of one that sprinkles **2 a** : a limited quantity or amount : a slight portion : MODICUM ⟨has a ~ of learning⟩ ⟨hasn't even a ~ of common sense⟩ **b** : a small quantity falling or made to fall in scattered drops or particles ⟨a ~ of snow⟩ ⟨a ~ of pepper⟩ **c** : a relatively small number distributed at random : SCATTERING ⟨the sandy soil of the plain had a light ~ of junipers —Willa Cather⟩ ⟨among them were thousands of artisans, a ~ of intellectuals, and political refugees —S.E. Morison & H.S.Commager⟩

sprinkling can *n* : a can used for sprinkling usu. in a flower bed — see CAN illustration

[1]**sprint** \'sprint\ *vb* -ED/-ING/-S [of Scand origin; akin to Sw dial. *sprinta* to jump, hop, ON *spretta* to spurt, start up, jump up; akin to OE *gesprintan* to emit, utter, OHG *sprinzan* to jump up, Gk *spyrthizein* to jump up, OSlav *prędati* to jump, tremble, Skt *spardhate* he contends, fights] *vi* : to run or go at top speed esp. for a relatively short distance ⟨a rabbit ~*ing* back to cover from far out in the field —T.H.White b. 1906⟩ ~ *vt* : to traverse by sprinting

[2]**sprint** \"\ *n* -s **1** : the act or an instance of sprinting : a short run or burst of activity at top speed **2 a** : DASH 7b(1) **b** : a burst of speed in longer races ⟨a ~ at the finish⟩ **c** : a horse race of not more than a mile in distance

sprint·er \-tə(r)\ *n* -s : one that sprints; *esp* : one that competes in sprint races ⟨a champion ~⟩

sprint medley *n* : a medley relay run by a team of four men who run distances of 440 yards, 220 yards, 220 yards, and 880 yards respectively

sprint race *n* : a short footrace of usu. less than a quarter of a mile in distance that is run at top speed

[1]**sprit** \'sprit, *usu* -id·+V\ *n* -s [ME *spret, sprit*, fr. OE *sprēot* pole, spear; akin to OE *sprūtan* to sprout — more at SPROUT] **1** *archaic* : a boat pole **2** : a spar that crosses a fore-and-aft sail diagonally from the mast near the tack of the sail to the upper aftmost corner that it extends and elevates

[2]**sprit** \"\ *vi* **spritted; spritted; spritting; sprits** [ME *sprutten*, fr. OE *sprytan*; akin to MHG *sprützen* to sprout, squirt, Norw *spruta* to spurt, squirt, OE *sprūtan* to sprout — more at SPROUT] : SPROUT, BUD, GERMINATE

[3]**sprit** \"\ *n* -s **1** : SHOOT, SPROUT **2** *chiefly Scot* : a reedy plant : RUSH **3** : a fine speck in unbleached linen — usu. used in pl.

sprite \'sprīt, *usu* -īd·+V\ *n* -s [ME *sprit*, fr. OF *esprit*, fr. L *spiritus* — more at SPIRIT] **1 a** *archaic* : inner being : SOUL ⟨his clear ~ yet reigns o'er earth —P.B.Shelley⟩ **b** : a disembodied spirit : GHOST, SHADE ⟨little ghost ~s of dust sprang up and danced across the shimmering plain —Francis Birtles⟩ **2 a** : ELF, FAIRY ⟨the witch, the ~, the goblin — where are they —E.A.Poe⟩ **b** : an elfish person ⟨he was a tricksy ~ for whom stone walls did not a prison make —Douglas Bush⟩ **3** *or* **sprite crab** : SAND CRAB 1b

sprite·li·ness \-lēnəs, -lin-\ *archaic var of* SPRIGHTLINESS

sprite·ly \-lē, -li\ *archaic var of* SPRIGHTLY

sprit·sail \'spritsəl (*usual nautical pronunc*), -,sāl\ *n* [ME *spretseil, spritseil*, fr. *spret, sprit* sprit + *seil* sail — more at SPRIT, SAIL] **1** : a sail extended by a sprit **2** : a sail formerly hung under the bowsprit from a yard

spritsail yard *n* : a yard across a bowsprit to support a spritsail

sprittail \'⸗,⸗\ *n* [[1]*sprit* + *tail*] : PINTAIL 1a

sprit·ty *or* **sprit·tie** \'sprid·ē, -itē, -i\ *adj* [[3]*sprit* + *-y*] *Scot* : full of rushes

spritz \'s(h)prits\ *vt* -ED/-ING/-ES [PaG *schpritze*, fr. MHG *sprützen* to sprout, squirt — more at SPRIT] *dial* : SPRAY, SQUIRT

spritz·er \-sə(r)\ *n* -s [G, fr. *spritzen* to squirt, spray (fr. MHG *sprützen* to sprout, squirt) + *-er*] : a drink of white wine and soda water

sproat \'sprōt, *usu* -ōd·+V\ *or* **sproat hook** *n* -s [after W. H. *Sproat*, 19th cent. Englishman who invented it] : a light fishhook with a gradual or flattened bend — see FISHHOOK illustration

sprock·et \'spräkət, *usu* -əd·+V\ *n* -s [origin unknown] **1** : a piece of wood fastened to the upper surface of a rafter to effect a change in the angle of the roof where it overhangs the wall of the building **2 a** : a tooth or projection (as on the periphery of a wheel) shaped so as to engage with a chain **b** : SPROCKET WHEEL **c** : a toothed cylinder or wheel that engages the perforations of a motion-picture film to carry it through a mechanism (as a projector)

sprocket wheel *n* : a wheel with cogs or sprockets to engage with the links of a chain or accurately pitched blocks on a cable — see CHAIN GEAR; BICYCLE illustration

sprod \'spräd\ *n* -s [origin unknown] : a sea trout smolt

sprot \'sprät, *usu* -äd·+V\ *archaic var of* SPRAT

[1]**sprout** \'sprau̇t, *usu* -au̇d·+V\ *vb* -ED/-ING/-S [ME *spruten, sprouten*, fr. OE *sprūtan*; akin to OFris *sprūta* to sprout, MD & MLG *sprūten*, OHG *spriozan* to sprout, Goth *sprauto* rapidly, W *ffrwst* haste, Gk *speirein* to scatter, sow, sprinkle, Arm *p'aratem* I disperse, take away; basic meaning: to scatter, sow] *vi* **1 a** : to grow, spring up, or come forth as a sprout ⟨vegetation that ~*ed* in a dried-up watercourse — Francis King⟩ ⟨feathers do not ~ uniformly, but grow in patches —J.M.Downs⟩ ⟨bowler hats banished by the war have been seen ~*ing* like mushrooms —*Britain Today*⟩ ⟨parodies ~*ed* like weeds —J.D.Hart⟩ — often used with *from, out*, or *up* ⟨a long, lean individual with whitish stubble ~*ing* from his lantern jaw —F.V.W.Mason⟩ ⟨limbs ~*ing* out two hundred feet from the ground —Norman Mailer⟩ ⟨giant shopping centers that have ~*ed* up across the country —*Newsweek*⟩ **b** : to send new shoots forth or up : to develop new growth : BUD, GERMINATE ⟨in that area the young grass ~s at least a month earlier —James Stevenson-Hamilton⟩ ⟨the bright green of the ~*ing* bracken —Algernon Blackwood⟩ ⟨potatoes kept too warm will ~ prematurely⟩ **2** : to expand enormously in bulk when heated — used esp. of some forms of graphite mica and esp. vermiculite ~ *vt* **1 a** : to send (as a sprout) forth or up : to cause (a new growth) to develop : GROW ⟨trees ~*ing* their new green leaves⟩ ⟨jurors who ~ beards during overnight deliberations —*N.Y.Times Mag.*⟩ **b** : to cause (a plant or seed) to burgeon or germinate ⟨the big rainy season . . . is as necessary for ~*ing* the seeds of the saguaro —D.C.Peattie⟩ **2** : to support or give rise to (something) in the manner of sprouting ⟨rooftops began to ~ antennae —*Amer. Guide Series: Wash.*⟩ ⟨the same soil can seemingly ~ suburban homes of rare beauty —E.H.Pickering⟩ ⟨may be ~*ing* neuroses like dandelions —G.W.Johnson⟩

[2]**sprout** \"\ *n* -s [ME, fr. *spruten, sprouten*, v.] **1** : the shoot of a plant: **a** : a shoot from the seed **b** : the young growth from a root or tuber **c** : a shoot or sucker from the root or trunk of a tree **2** : something similar or likened to a sprout in appearance or development: as **a** : a person in his early years : OFFSHOOT, SCION ⟨a ~ who wants to go to school but isn't old enough —*New Yorker*⟩ ⟨hanging around to listen were young ~s, 16, 18, seldom 20 —Mari Sandoz⟩ ⟨was now the turn of these young ~s to get their ears beaten back —*Key Reporter*⟩ **b** : a new growth or development ⟨small ~s of liberal thought and practice make their appearance —L.S.Fever⟩ ⟨new ~s included the only large aviation gas refinery —E.O.Hauser⟩ **3 sprouts** *pl* **a** : BRUSSELS SPROUTS **b** : BEAN SPROUTS **c** : KALE **4** : COPPICE 3

[3]**sprout** *vb* [prob. of Scand origin; akin to Norw *spruta* to spurt, squirt — more at SPRIT] *obs* : SPOUT, SPURT

sprout cell *n* : a cell developed by budding from a similar mother cell

sprout·er \'sprau̇d·ə(r), -au̇tə-\ *n* -s : a device for germinating grains (as oats) for feeding livestock

sprout forest *n* : a forest consisting of trees grown from root or stump suckers

sprouting *n* -s **1** : the act or process of one that sprouts **2** : a new growth or shoot : SPROUT

sprouting broccoli *n* : BROCCOLI 2

sprouting crab grass *n* : an annual grass (*Panicum dichotomiflorum*) found chiefly in the southern U.S. that roots much at the lower nodes

sproutland \'⸗,⸗\ *n* : an area covered by a sprout forest

sprout·ling \'sprau̇tliŋ, -lēŋ\ *n* -s : a small sprout or offshoot ⟨a ~ of the giant tree —William Beebe⟩ ⟨his little ~ of a poem —Amy Lowell⟩

[1]**spruce** \'sprüs\ *n* -s *often attrib* [fr. obs. *Spruce* Prussia, fr. ME, alter. of *Pruce*, fr. OF] **1 a** : an evergreen tree of the genus *Picea* marked by dense foliage forming a conical head and widely cultivated for ornament **b** : the light soft moderately strong wood of the spruce tree that is less resinous than pine and is used esp. for timbers, millwork, and musical instruments — compare FIR **c** : any of several other coniferous trees (as the Douglas fir) **2** : a variable color averaging a dark grayish green that is bluer and stronger than average ivy, bluer and darker than Persian green, and bluer, lighter, and slightly stronger than hemlock green **3** : SPRUCE BEER

[2]**spruce** \"\ *adj, often* -ER/-EST [perh. fr. obs. E *Spruce* (*leather*), a kind of smart leather imported from Prussia and used to make jerkins] **1** : SMART, ACTIVE, SPIRITED ⟨a ~, lively air, fashionable dress —Earl of Chesterfield⟩ ⟨the thick orchestral texture is well recorded and some of the chording is admirably ~ —Edward Sackville-West & Desmond Shawe-Taylor⟩ ⟨even pedestrian old stuff is pretty ~ under his editing, and the really good jokes take wing —D.T.W.McCord⟩ **2** : neat, clean-lined, or smart in appearance : TRIM ⟨how ~ he looks in his finery —W.E.M.Campbell⟩ ⟨had great neatness of person, and he continued to wear his ~ black coat and his bowler hat . . . in a dapper, jaunty manner —W.S.Maugham⟩ ⟨the store looked cheerful and ~ and spanking clean —Arthur Cavanaugh⟩

[3]**spruce** \"\ *vb* -ED/-ING/-S *vt* : to make (a person or thing) trim, smart, or spruce ⟨the interior . . . was so *spruced*, so glistening with white paint —Sylvia T. Warner⟩ ⟨*sprucing* himself for the party⟩ — often used with *up* ⟨bought a buggy and came to town *spruced* up in store clothes —W.A.White⟩ ⟨amusement arcades have *spruced* themselves up for the summer season —D.K.Keay⟩ ⟨a short collection of notions . . . some of them *spruced* up as epigrams, others running as long as a page —*New Yorker*⟩ ~ *vi* : to make oneself spruce — usu. used with *up* ⟨makes a mad dash for the comfortable waiting rooms . . . to ~ up a bit —Lynn Grok⟩ ⟨~ up, child, shoulders back, smile, look pleasant —*N.Y.Times*⟩

[4]**spruce** \"\ *adv, often* -ER/-EST : SPRUCELY

spruce aphid *n* : a small deep green aphid (*Elatobium abietinum*) that attacks the needles of spruces

spruce beer *n* : a beverage flavored with spruce: **a** : one made from spruce twigs and leaves boiled with molasses or sugar and fermented with yeast **b** : a fermented beverage made with an extract of spruce twigs and leaves

spruce beetle *n* : a beetle that attacks the spruce; *esp* : any of several bark beetles of the genus *Dendroctonus* whose larvae feed beneath the bark and often cause severe damage

spruce borer *n* : the larva of any of several beetles of the families Cerambycidae and Buprestidae or of various bark beetles that develops in the wood or beneath the bark of spruce trees

spruce bud midge *n* : a cecidomyiid fly (*Rhabdophaga swainei*) that causes bud gall on white spruce in eastern Canada

spruce bud moth *n* **1** : the adult of the spruce budworm **2** : an olethreutid moth (*Zeiraphera ratzeburgiana*) the larva of which feeds on spruce buds in northern U.S. and in Canada

spruce budworm *n* : a caterpillar that is the larva of a tortricid moth (*Choristoneura fumiferana*) and feeds on the needles of the terminal shoots of spruce, balsam fir, and other evergreen trees in the northern U.S. and in Canada

spruce coneworm *n* : the larva of a phycitid moth (*Dioryctria reniculella*) that feeds on young cones of spruce in the northeastern U.S. and eastern Canada

spruce extract *n* : waste sulfite liquor containing salts of ligninsulfonic acids and purified for use chiefly in tanning leather

spruce fir *n* [*spruce* fr. obs. E *Spruce* Prussia] *n* : any of several spruces; *esp* : NORWAY SPRUCE

spruce foliage worm *n* : SPRUCE CONEWORM

spruce gall aphid *n* : any of several aphids of the genus *Adelges* that cause galls on the leaf shoots of spruce trees

spruce green *n* : SEA GREEN 1a

spruce grouse *or* **spruce partridge** *n* : a grouse (*Canachites canadensis*) of the forests of northern No. America chiefly north of the U.S. whose plumage is extensively barred with black with the adult male being nearly black below

spruce gum *n* : an oleoresinous exudation esp. from the red spruce or the black spruce used as a chewing gum or expectorant

spruce·ly *adv* [[2]*spruce* + *-ly*] : in a spruce manner : NEATLY, TRIMLY ⟨he dressed ~ —Robert Graves⟩ ⟨the buildings are ~ painted —*Amer. Guide Series: Wash.*⟩

spruce spider mite *or* **spruce mite** *n* : a dark green spiny mite (*Oligonychus ununguis*) that attacks spruce and other coniferous or deciduous trees in several parts of the U.S.

spruce·ness *n* -ES : the quality or state of being spruce ⟨the army leaves its marks of physical ~ —Dixon Wecter⟩ ⟨the curious confusion of ~ and squalor —W.C.Brownell⟩

spruce oil *n* : a colorless to light yellow pleasant-smelling essential oil obtained from the needles and twigs of various spruces and hemlocks and used chiefly in scenting soap and cosmetics and in medicinal preparations

spruce pine *n* **1** : any of various American pines with light soft wood: **a** : a pine (*Pinus glabra*) of the southern U.S. **b** : YELLOW PINE 1a **c** : WHITE PINE 1a **d** : LODGEPOLE PINE **2** : EASTERN HEMLOCK **3** : any of several spruces; *esp* : BLACK SPRUCE 1

sprucer *comparative of* SPRUCE

spruces *pl of* SPRUCE, *pres 3d sing of* SPRUCE

spruce sawfly *n* : any of several sawflies (family Diprionidae) whose larvae feed on spruce; *esp* : EUROPEAN SPRUCE SAWFLY

sprucest *superlative of* SPRUCE

spruce yellow *n* : a dark orange yellow to light yellowish brown that is very slightly yellower than cotrine

sprucing *pres part of* SPRUCE

sprucy \'sprüsē, -si\ *adj* -ER/-EST [[2]*spruce* + *-y*] : SPRUCE ⟨little tufts of white in her hair . . . looked real ~ —Alma Stone⟩ ⟨you don't look ~ like you did —J.C.Harris⟩

1sprue \ˈsprü\ *n* -s [D *spruw*, fr. MD *sprouwe*; akin to MLG *sprūwe*, a kind of tumor] **:** a chronic deficiency disease characterized by a frothy fatty diarrhea and other digestive disturbances, a sore mouth and tongue, and macrocytic anemia that occurs in a tropical form which attacks chiefly adults and a nontropical form which begins usu. in childhood

2sprue \"\ *n* -s [origin unknown] **1 a :** the hole through which metal or plastics is poured into the gate and thence into a mold **b :** the waste piece cast in this hole **:** DROSS **2 a :** the part of each impression of a drop-forging die that receives the rough bar from which the forging is made and connects the edge of the die block with the gate or flash **b :** the waste portion of a drop forging that fills the sprue in the dies

3sprue \"\ *n* -s [origin unknown] **:** spindling asparagus

spru·er \ˈsprüə(r); -üə(r), -üə\ *n* -s [*2sprue* + *-er*] **:** one that attends to the sprue occupying the gate in the process of casting iron

sprug \ˈsprəg\ *n* -s [origin unknown] *chiefly Scot* **:** HOUSE SPARROW

sprui·ker \ˈsprükə(r)\ *n* -s [Austral. slang *spruik* to give a speech, make a barker's spiel (of unknown origin) + *-er*] *Austral* **:** BARKER

spruit \ˈsprüt, -rāt\ *n* -s [Afrik, shoot, small stream, fr. MD *sprute*, fr. *spruten* to sprout — more at SPROUT] **:** a small often dry tributary stream in southern Africa

sprung [ME *sprungen* (past pl. & past part.), fr. OE *sprungon* (past pl.), *sprungen* (past part.)] *past of* SPRING

sprung hock *n* **:** a horse's hock swollen from strain; *also* **:** the condition or the swelling **:** CURB

sprung rhythm *n* **:** a poetic rhythm designed to approximate the natural rhythm of speech and characterized by the frequent juxtaposition of single accented syllables and the occurrence of mixed types of feet (as the accentual trochee, dactyl, and first paeon) whose sequence is broken or interrupted by outrides

sprung weight *n* **:** weight supported by springs

1sprunt \ˈsprənt, -ȯnt\ *vi* -ED/-ING/-S [prob. of Scand origin; akin to Sw dial. *sprunta* to jump, *sprinta* to jump, hop — more at SPRINT] *dial Eng* **:** to make a quick convulsive movement **:** JUMP, RUN

2sprunt \"\ *n* -s *dial Eng* **:** a spasmodic movement **:** SPRING

3sprunt \"\ *adj* [of Scand origin; akin to Sw dial. *sprant* lively, brisk, *sprinta* to jump, hop] *obs* **:** ACTIVE, BRISK, SPRUCE

spry \ˈsprī\ *adj, usu* -ER/-EST [perh. of Scand origin; akin to Sw dial *sprygg* very lively; perh. akin to Sw dial. *spragg, spragge* branch — more at SPRIG] **:** vigorously active **:** CHIPPER, NIMBLE, BRISK ⟨75 years old and ~ as a kitten —Winifred Bambrick⟩ ⟨his ~, youthful vigor and unimpaired energy —Hervey Allen⟩ ⟨their ~ cockney or colonial idiom —Leslie Rees⟩ **syn** see AGILE

spry·ly *adv* **:** in a spry manner **:** with spryness

spry·ness *n* -ES **:** the quality or state of being spry

SPS *abbr, often not cap* [L *sine prole superstite*] without surviving issue

spt *abbr* **1** seaport **2** spirit **3** support

1spud \ˈspəd\ *n* -s [ME *spudde*; perh. akin to OE *spadu, spædu* spade — more at SPADE] **1** *obs* **:** a short knife **:** DAGGER **2 :** any of various tools or mechanical devices like a spade or a chisel and with a short, thick or widened, and often curved blade: as **a** (1) **:** a sharp narrow spade sometimes with prongs instead of a smooth blade commonly having a long handle and used esp. for digging up large-rooted weeds (2) **:** a similarly shaped implement used for removing the bark from timber **b :** a small shovel with a crowbar point on one end used for digging holes under stumps — called also *stump spud* **c** (1) **:** a broad-bladed socketed stone or metal tool typical of midwestern and eastern No. America (2) **:** a socketed spearhead that is slipped on the end of a lath for spearing tobacco **d :** a long-handled chisel used for cutting holes through the ice **e** (1) **:** a small instrument shaped like a spade for removing foreign bodies esp. from the eye (2) **:** such an instrument for removing wax from the ear **f :** a reamer for enlarging a well around lost tools so that fishing tools can go over the lost article **g :** SPADE LUG **3 :** POTATO **4 a :** one of usu. four sharp-pointed vertical posts or piles that can be forced by a tackle or by power through a socket in a floating or a land dredge or scow to anchor it **b :** one of the two foot pieces of the legs of the A-frame of a floating dipper dredge that are set in the banks of the ditch to steady the dredge and give it support **5 a :** a short connecting piece (as a piece of pipe between a cock and a supply pipe) **b :** a short thick insert or projection (as from a valve or ceramic piece) to which some other part is screwed **6 :** percussion drilling used in starting a well in which a line is used to impart an up-and-down motion to the cable holding the tools to cause them to rise and fall

2spud \"\ *vb* **spudded; spudded; spudding; spuds** *vt* **1 :** to dig, remove, or otherwise treat with a spud ⟨*spudding* up weeds⟩ **2 :** to begin to drill (an oil well) by alternately raising and releasing a spudding bit with the drilling rig ⟨honor those who helped ~ America's first great gusher —*Christian Science Monitor*⟩ — often used with *in* ⟨expected that the well will be *spudded* in before the end of July —*Wall Street Jour.*⟩ ⟨an agreement to ~ in the first well within 30 days —Upton Sinclair⟩ **3 :** to scrape off (as burrs caused by punching or reaming) around holes **4 :** to anchor or hold steady (as a derrick or dredge) by means of spuds ⟨placed in position on the bay bottom and *spudded* in place by H-piles driven within the pipes —P.A.Hakman⟩ ~ *vi* **1 :** to dig with a spud **2 :** to begin to drill an oil well with a spudding bit ⟨company has *spudded* and yesterday was drilling at 582 feet —*Los Angeles (Calif.) Examiner*⟩ — often used with *in* ⟨the driller got busy . . . *spudding* in through the soft, wet earth —*Lamp*⟩

spud casing *n* **:** a well in the hull of a dredge through which a spud can be raised or lowered

spud·der \ˈspədə(r)\ *n* -s **1 a :** one that sets up and operates a well-drilling machine **b :** a light duty drilling rig used primarily to start a new well **2 a :** PEELER 1b **b :** a tool that removes bark from timber **:** BARKER, BARK SPUD

spudding bar *n* **:** a bar having a cutting end for spudding holes

spudding bit *n* **:** a broad dull drilling tool used for the preliminary boring of wells through earth down to rock or other solid substrata

spud·dle \ˈspədᵊl\ *vi* [blend of *1spud* and *puddle*] *archaic* **:** PUDDLE

spud·dy \ˈspədē *also* ˈspu̇dē *or* -di\ *adj* -ER/-EST [*1spud* + *-y*] **:** PUDGY

spue *var of* SPEW

spuf·fle \ˈspəfəl\ *vi* [prob. of imit. origin] *dial Eng* **:** FUSS, BUSTLE

1spule \ˈspül\ *Scot var of* SPOOL

2spule \"\ *n* -s [prob. alter. of *spauld*] *Scot* **:** SHOULDER

spule-bane \ˈ=,=\ *n* [*2spule* + *bane* (bone)] *Scot* **:** SHOULDER BLADE

1spul·zie \ˈspēl(y)i\ *vb* -ED/-ING/-S [alter. (ʒ being taken as *z*) of earlier *spulʒie*, fr. ME (Sc) *spulʒien, spolyen*, fr. MF *espoillier* — more at SPOIL] *chiefly Scot* **:** PLUNDER

2spulzie \"\ *n* -s [alter. (ʒ being taken as *z*) of earlier *spulʒie*, fr. ME (Sc) *spolʒei*, fr. MF *espoille, espuille* — more at SPOIL] **1** *chiefly Scot* **:** an act or instance of unlawfully and violently dispossessing a person of his movables **2** *chiefly Scot* **:** SPOIL, BOOTY

1spume \ˈspyüm\ *n* -s [ME, fr. MF *espume, spume*, fr. L *spuma* — more at FOAM] **:** frothy matter raised on liquids by boiling, effervescence, or agitation **:** FROTH, FOAM, SCUM ⟨shore encumbered by rain-washed boulders and ruffed with sea ~ —Han Suyin⟩ ⟨swung down the gleaming incline while long feathers of ~ streamed out behind his boots —J.R.Ullman⟩ ⟨spat forth among men a ~ of things impure —H.O.Taylor⟩

2spume \"\ *vb* -ED/-ING/-S *vi* **:** FROTH, FOAM ⟨a waterfall . . . steaming and *spuming* among the pebbles —Frederic Prokosch⟩ ⟨the yellow bench of reef *spuming* with surf — John Dos Passos⟩ ~ *vt* **:** to discharge or spout (something) like froth or foam — often used with *forth* ⟨volcanoes ~ forth fire and lava⟩

spu·mes·cence \spyüˈmesᵊn(t)s\ *n* -s [*1spume* + *-escence*] **:** the quality or state of being foamy or frothy

spu·mes·cent \(ˈ)=ˈ=ᵊnt\ *adj* [*1spume* + *-escent*] **:** FROTHY, FOAMY

spu·moid \ˈspyü,mȯid\ *adj* [*1spume* + *-oid*] **:** ALVEOLAR

spu·mo·ni \spüˈmōnē, spəˈm-\ *or* **spumo·ne** \-(,)nā\ *n* -s [It *spumone*, aug. of *spuma* foam, froth, fr. L — more at FOAM] **:** ice cream molded in layers of different colors, flavors, and textures often with candied fruits and nuts and served in sections

spu·mose \ˈspyü,mōs, =ˈ=\ *adj* [L *spumosus*] **:** SPUMY

spu·mous \-məs\ *adj* [ME, fr. L *spumosus*, fr. *spuma* foam + *-osus* -ous, -ose — more at FOAM] **:** SPUMY

spumy \-mē, -mi\ *adj, usu* -ER/-EST [*1spume* + *-y*] **:** marked by or covered with spume **:** of frothy or foamy consistency or appearance

spun [ME *spunnen* (past pl. & past part.), fr. OE *spunnon* (past pl.), *gespunnen* (past part.)] *past of* SPIN

spun-dyed \ˈ=ˈ=\ *adj* **:** dyed during the spinning process — used of a synthetic filament, staple, or yarn

1spung \ˈspəŋ\ *n* -s [prob. alter. of ME *punge*, fr. OE *pung*; akin to MLG *punge* purse, OHG *scazfung*, ON *pungr*, Goth *pungs* purse, and perh. to OE *pocca, pohha* bag, pocket — more at POKE] *chiefly Scot* **:** PURSE

2spung \"\ *vt, Scot* **:** ROB

spunge *var of* SPONGE

spun glass *n* **1 :** FIBER GLASS **2 :** blown glass that has slender threads of glass incorporated in it often in the form of a spiral or network

spun hay *n* **:** hay twisted into ropes for convenient carriage

1spunk \ˈspəŋk\ *n* -s [ScGael *spong* tinder, sponge, fr. L *spongia* sponge — more at SPONGE] **1** *dial Brit* **a :** a small portion or bit **:** SPARK, GLEAM **b :** a small fire **c :** 3MATCH 2a **2 a :** a wood or woody substance prepared for use as tinder **:** TOUCHWOOD, PUNK **b :** any of various fungi used to make tinder **3 :** METTLE, PLUCK, COURAGE ⟨assigned themes on the ~ of great persons who had overcome physical handicaps —Robert Lowell⟩ ⟨enough ~ in the department to resent such an arrogant blow at its prestige —H.L.Ickes⟩ **4 :** SPIRIT, LIVELINESS ⟨as for his musical efforts . . . who could play with such tremendous ~ —William Black⟩ ⟨a story told with rare ~, with the repetition and the surprise action small listeners love —*N.Y. Herald Tribune Bk. Rev.*⟩

2spunk \"\ *vb* -ED/-ING/-S *vi* **1** *Scot* **:** to come to light **:** become known — usu. used with *out* **2** *dial* **:** to assert oneself in a spirited or courageous manner **:** show spirit — usu. used with *up* ~ *vt* **:** to work up **:** muster — usu. used with *up* ⟨has ~*ed* up courage to tell the awful truth about the fallout —*New Republic*⟩

spunk·ie \ˈspəŋki\ *n* -s [*1spunk* + *-ie*] **1** *Scot* **:** IGNIS FATUUS **2** *Scot* **:** LIQUOR **3** *Scot* **:** a spirited or quick-tempered person

spunk·i·ly \ˈspəŋkəlē, -li\ *adv* **:** in a spunky manner

spunk·i·ness \-kēnəs, -kin-\ *n* -ES **:** the quality or state of being spunky

spunky \-kē, -ki\ *adj, usu* -ER/-EST **1 :** full of spunk **:** COURAGEOUS, PLUCKY ⟨the children are ~ and determined —*N.Y. Times Bk. Rev.*⟩ **2** *dial Brit* **:** shining brightly **:** SPARKLING **3 :** IRRITABLE, IRASCIBLE, TESTY ⟨that ~, crotchety, illiterate and wonderfully gifted maker of things —Brendan Gill⟩ ⟨cross and ~, and both too proud to speak —W.M.Carleton⟩ **4 :** full of life **:** ANIMATED, SPIRITED ⟨was . . . an armful of ~ vitality —James Thurber⟩ ⟨were there for ~ debate —*Newsweek*⟩

spun rayon *n* **:** a yarn or fabric made wholly or chiefly of rayon staple ⟨butcher linen made of *spun rayon*⟩

spun silk *n* **:** a yarn or fabric made from short unreelable silk fibers that have been degummed — compare REELED SILK

spun sugar *n* **:** a garnish resembling floss made from sugar boiled to the long thread stage when the threads are gathered up and shaped into the desired forms or heaped upon a stick as a candy

spun yarn *n* **1 :** a textile yarn spun from staple-length fiber **2 :** a small rope or stuff formed of two or more rope yarns loosely twisted and used for seizings esp. on board ship

1spur *R* ˈspər, + *vowel* ˈspər·; *-R* ˈspə̄, + *suffixal vowel* ˈspər· *also* ˈspər, + *vowel in a following word* ˈspər· *or* ˈspə̄ *also* ˈspə̄r\ *n* -s *often attrib* [ME *spore, spure*, fr. OE *spora, spura*; akin to OHG *sporo* spur, ON *spori* spur, OE *spurnan* to kick — more at SPURN] **1 a :** a U-shaped implement with a pointed or rowel-tipped projection that is secured to the heel of a horseman for pricking, managing, or urging on the horse **b spurs** *pl* [ME *spores* knighthood (as in *winnen ones spores* to earn knighthood by a deed of valor)] **:** recognition and reward for achievement ⟨would have won his ~*s* had not a knee injury . . . put him out of the game —*Rugger*⟩ ⟨these guys have earned their battle ~*s* —L.M.Uris⟩ **2 :** an inciting force or stimulus to action **:** GOAD, INCENTIVE ⟨he shot up fast, his ~ the determination to make money and a name —E.A.Weeks⟩ ⟨two professors were immediate ~*s* to trying her hand at writing —*Current Biog.*⟩ ⟨the book is a ~ to both the intellect and the imagination —Ellen L. Buell⟩ **3 :** any of various diagonally set props, braces, or members usu. used in construction: as **a :** a brace (as a rafter or crossbeam) strengthening a post and some connected part **:** STRUT **b :** a reinforcing buttress of masonry **c** (1) **:** a piece of timber fixed on the bilge ways before launching with the upper ends bolted to the vessel's side (2) **:** a curved piece of timber serving as a half-beam to support the deck where a whole beam cannot be placed (3) **:** SPUR SHORE **4 :** a growth, formation, or projection suggestive of a spur in shape or relative size: as **a :** a stiff sharp spine (as on the wings or legs of a bird or insect); *esp* **:** a horny modification of the skin surrounding a bony core attached to the metatarsus of a cock's leg and used in fighting — see COCK illustration **b :** a bony outgrowth (as at a joint margin) **:** OSTEOPHYTE **c :** a projecting root or short branch of a tree: as (1) **:** a short branch bearing fruit buds (2) **:** a branch kept short by annual pruning ⟨a vine cut to 4 ~*s*⟩ **d :** a hollow projecting appendage of a corolla or calyx (as in larkspur or columbine) **5 :** a sharp or pointed usu. metallic object similar to a spur: as **a :** a gaff for a gamecock **b :** a climbing iron **:** GAFF **c :** the bow ram of a warship **d :** a projection or prong on the arm of an anchor **e :** an article like a stilt resting on three points and having one pointing upward to support ceramic ware during firing **f :** the central point on an auger bit or lathe center **g :** 2GRIFFE 1 **h :** the metallic point on either end of a weaving shuttle **i :** the projection of the external hammer of a gun on which the thumb presses in cocking the weapon **j :** one of two or more adjustable buttons or spikes affixed to the back of a wall clock in order to allow the pendulum to swing clear of the walls **k :** one of several clamps with points attached to the hoop of a bass drum to prevent it from rolling and to hold it off the floor **l :** a bundle of several sheets of paper hung to dry in a loft **6 :** an angular projection, offshoot, or branch extending out beyond or away from a main body or formation: **a** *obs* **:** an outer work or salient of a fortification **b :** a ridge or lesser elevation that projects from a mountain, a range of mountains, or a higher land surface to some distance at right angles or in a lateral direction ⟨the western edge is notched . . . by coves and valleys which are separated by fingerlike ~*s* pointing towards the northwest —*Amer. Guide Series: Tenn.*⟩ **c :** a wing dam built out to deflect a river current **d** (1) **:** SPUR TRACK (2) **:** SIDING 3 (3) **:** a side or connecting road running from a main highway or turnpike ⟨problems . . . in the construction of thruway ~*s* —*N.Y. Times*⟩ **e :** a branch of a vein of a mine **7 :** SPUR GEAR **syn** see MOTIVE — **on the spur of the moment :** on impulse **:** prompted by the occasion **:** QUICKLY, SUDDENLY ⟨asked him how he could think up such language *on the spur of the moment* —Max Eastman⟩

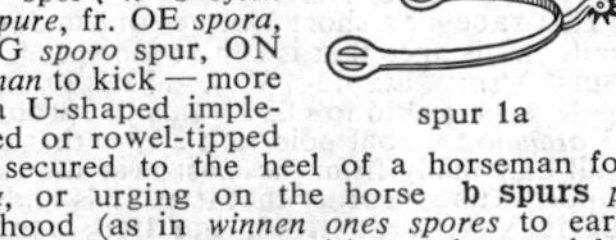

spur 1a

2spur \"\ *vb* **spurred; spurred; spurring; spurs** [ME *sporen, spuren*, fr. *spore, spure*, n.] *vt* **1 :** to prick (a horse) with spurs to go at a faster pace ⟨*spurred* his horse along the crest of the ridge —Zane Grey⟩ **2 :** to incite (a person or thing) to action or accelerated growth or development **:** URGE, STIMULATE ⟨general manager who is *spurred* by idealism —*Times Lit. Supp.*⟩ ⟨*spurred* his players to finish second —*Current Biog.*⟩ ⟨the war has *spurred* interest in the defense programs —*America*⟩ ⟨the rather pallid prose . . . inhibits rather than ~*s* the imagination —J.F.Muehl⟩ — often used with *on* ⟨his own needs ~ him on to invention —Ralph Linton⟩ ⟨*spurred* on by attractive commissions —G.M.Stephenson⟩ **3 :** to furnish with spurs ⟨arriving all booted and *spurred*⟩ **4** *dial Eng* **:** to support or brace with a spur **:** PROP **5 :** to cut back **:** PRUNE, TRIM ⟨number of main branches are *spurred* . . . to within about two inches of their base —F.D.Smith & Barbara Wilcox⟩ ~ *vi* **1 a :** to hurry one's horse with spurs ⟨wheeling the white mustang, he *spurred* away —Zane Grey⟩ ⟨a wounded soldier *spurring* from the field with news of victory —A.B. Osborne⟩ **b :** to proceed in hurried fashion **:** RUSH ⟨*spurred* into the fray —S.H.Adams⟩ **2 :** to strike out or fight with the foot or spur **syn** see URGE

3spur \"\ *n* -s [alter. of *spoor*] **:** the track of an animal (as an otter) **:** SPOOR

spur bit *n* **:** a boring bit having one or more spurs which scribe the periphery of the hole in advance of the cutting lips to guide the bit in the proper direction — compare TWIST BIT

spur blight *n* **:** a disease of raspberries caused by a fungus (*Didymella applanata*) that kills the fruit spurs and causes dark reddish or purple spots on the canes where the leaves arise and eventually browning and graying of the canes

spur·blind \ˈspər, ˈspə̄+,-\ *adj* [alter. (influenced by *1spur*) of *purblind*] *obs* **:** quite or totally blind

spur budding *n* **:** a modified type of shield budding in which the scion consists of a twig or spur having more than one bud

spurdog \ˈ=,=\ *also* **spur dogfish** *n* **:** DOGFISH 1

spur fowl *n* **:** any of several Indian gallinaceous birds of the genus *Galloperdix* related to the bamboo partridges and having two or more spurs on each leg

spurgall \ˈ=,=\ *vt, archaic* **:** to gall with or as if with a spur **:** INJURE, HARASS

spurge \ˈspərj, ˈspə̄j, ˈspəij\ *n* -s [ME, fr. MF *espurge, spurge* purge, spurge, fr. *espurgier* to purge, fr. L *expurgare* — more at EXPURGE] **1 :** any of several plants of the family Euphorbiaceae, esp. of the genus *Euphorbia* **2 :** JAPANESE SPURGE **3 :** ALLEGHENY SPURGE

spur gear *also* **spur gear wheel** *n* **:** the simplest form of toothed wheel used in machinery with radial teeth parallel to the axis of the wheel

spur gear

spurge family *n* **:** EUPHORBIACEAE

spurge flax *n* **1 :** an acrid evergreen European shrub (*Daphne gnidium*) with crowded narrow leaves and fibrous bark **2 :** SPURGE LAUREL 1

spurge laurel *n* **1 :** a low bushy Eurasian shrub (*Daphne laureola*) with oblong evergreen leaves and nearly scentless yellowish flowers **2 :** MEZEREON 1

spurge moth *n* **:** a moth that feeds on euphorbias; *esp* **:** a European hawk moth (*Deilephila euphorbiae*) whose larva feeds on the leaves of devil's milk (*Euphorbia peplus*)

spurge nettle *n* **:** a stinging American herb (*Jatropha stimulosus*)

spurge olive *n* **1 :** MEZEREON **2 :** a daphne (*Daphne oleoides*) of southern Europe related to the mezereon

spur-heeled \ˈ=ˈ=\ *adj* **1 :** having a spur on the heel **2 :** having the claw of the hind toe elongated and straight ⟨the larks are *spur-heeled*⟩

spu·ri·ae \ˈspyu̇rē,ē, -pu̇rē,ī\ *n pl* [NL, fr. LL, fem. pl. of *spurius* false] **:** the feathers of the bastard wing of a bird

spu·ri·ous \ˈspyu̇rēəs, -pyür- *sometimes* ÷ -pər·ē- *or* -pə·rē-\ *adj* [L & LL; LL *spurius* false, fr. L, of illegitimate birth, fr. *spurius*, n., bastard (often used as a praenomen)] **1 :** of illegitimate birth **:** BASTARD ⟨her ~ firstborn —John Milton⟩ ⟨the dominions of both rulers passed away to their ~ or doubtful offspring —E.A.Freeman⟩ **2 a :** outwardly similar or corresponding to something without having its genuine qualities **:** FALSE, COUNTERFEIT ⟨the true ring by which . . . a fossilized survival may be known from a ~ reproduction —Thomas Hardy⟩ ⟨the ~ mechanical substitutes for knowledge and experience now provided through . . . the motion picture —Lewis Mumford⟩ ⟨prone to attach a ~ novelty to the things of the moment simply because they pretend to be new —J.A.R.Pimlott⟩ ⟨first of the . . . dictators to sweep to ~ glory on the upthrust of human arms —Milton Bracker⟩ **b :** simulative in symptoms or development without being pathologically or morphologically genuine ⟨~ labor pains⟩ ⟨~ species⟩ ⟨~ fruit⟩ ⟨the effusion of lymph which gradually degenerates into his ~ bony deposit —Robert Chawner⟩ **3 a :** of falsified or erroneously attributed origin or authorship **:** FORGED, INAUTHENTIC ⟨the ~ lines and passages which scholars used to reject as contradicting the genuine parts of the story —T.A.Jones⟩ ⟨the only known picture . . . albeit a ~ one had been printed some years earlier —James Monaghan⟩ ⟨the regalia became the symbols of sovereignty over all the tribes . . . though their ~ nature was obvious —A.M.Young⟩ **b :** of a deceitful or fictitious nature or quality **:** FRAUDULENT ⟨one of the worst features of the religious decadence . . . was the craftiness of such ~ types of men —Edwin Benson⟩ ⟨a completely ~ witness —M.S.Mayer⟩ ⟨the ~ explanations of the astrologers —G.A.L.Sarton⟩ **c :** faulty in reasoning or conclusion **:** ILLOGICAL, SPECIOUS ⟨~ inferences from obsolescent notions of causality and prediction —Ethel Albert⟩ ⟨no ~ argument, no appeal to sentiment . . . can deceive the American people —F.D.Roosevelt⟩ ⟨incomplete statistical evidence leads to ~ correlations⟩ **4 :** marked by spuriousness or falseness ⟨additions which he inserted . . . to give them a ~ authenticity, into the original manuscript —R.D.Altick⟩ **5 :** of an excrescent or superfluous character **:** undesirably intrusive **:** EXTRANEOUS ⟨the power output of a transmitter must be . . . free from ~ radiations —*Radio Amateur's Handbk.*⟩ ⟨designed . . . to operate so that ~ emissions and responses are completely eliminated —W.P.Corderman⟩ **6 :** irrelevantly inapplicable **:** lacking correspondence to reality **:** vaguely ambiguous **:** PSEUDO ⟨if the terms of our discourse are incompatible or confused . . . then our alleged beliefs are not false, but ~ —Susanne K. Langer⟩ ⟨if, when he utters it, he is not talking about anything, then his use is not a genuine one, but a ~ —Morris Weity⟩ **syn** see COUNTERFEIT

spurious claw *n* **:** a sturdy serrated bristle found on the feet of various spiders

spurious disk *n* **:** the small apparently circular disk of a star as seen in a telescope that limits the resolving power of the telescope and varies inversely with the diameter of the objective — called also *diffraction disk*

spurious fruit *n* **:** ACCESSORY FRUIT

spu·ri·ous·ly *adv* **:** in a spurious manner **:** PRETENTIOUSLY, FALSELY

spu·ri·ous·ness *n* -ES **:** the quality or state of being spurious

spurious primary *or* **spurious quill** *n* **:** the first or outer primary quill (as in certain singing birds) when rudimentary or much reduced in size

spurious vein *n* **:** a longitudinal thickening resembling a true vein or nervure and situated in the membrane of the wing of a fly between the radius and media — compare SYRPHUS FLY

spurious wing *n* **:** BASTARD WING

spurl \ˈspərl\ *vi* [origin unknown] *Scot* **:** SCRAMBLE, SPRAWL

spur·less \ˈ=ləs\ *adj* **:** having no spur

spur·ling line \ˈspərliŋ-, -əl-, -əil-, -lēŋ-\ *n* [*spurling*, of unknown origin] **1 :** a line by which the turning of a ship's wheel moves the indicator of a telltale **2 :** a line stretched across the two forward shrouds of a ship with thimbles spliced in it to serve as a fairlead

spurling pipe *n* **:** a pipe or tube through which an anchor chain passes to the chain locker below the deck of a ship

1spurn \ˈspərn, -pən, -pəin\ *vb* -ED/-ING/-S [ME *spurnen*, fr. OE *spurnan*; akin to OFris *spurna* to kick, OS & OHG *spurnan*, ON *sporna* to kick, L *spernere* to despise, spurn, Gk *spairein* to quiver, Skt *sphurati* he kicks] *vi* **1** *obs* **:** to hit something with the foot **:** STUMBLE **2** *obs* **:** to strike something with the foot **:** KICK — often used with *at* ⟨~ not at stone walls⟩ **3 :** to speak out or act against something in disdainful or contemptuous fashion — usu. used with *at* ⟨~*ing* fearlessly at danger and all enemies⟩ ~ *vt* **1 :** to tread heavily upon (something) **:** KICK, TRAMPLE ⟨then the creature was off, silver hoofs ~*ing* the ground —Elizabeth Goudge⟩ ⟨would have ~*ed* him with her foot save that she did not want to rouse him —C.S.Forester⟩ — often used with *away* ⟨~*ing* away those who had helped him to power⟩ **2 :** to reject (something) with disdain or contempt **:** SCORN ⟨used certain resources and ~*ed* others —Lewis Mumford⟩ ⟨~*ed* a suggestion that he carry a gun —*N.Y. Times*⟩ ⟨the ~*ed* love assuaged his grief in violent activity —Saxe Commins⟩ **syn** see DECLINE

²**spurn** \"\ *n* -s [ME, fr. *spurnen*, v.] **1 :** a blow delivered with the foot **:** KICK **2 :** the act of spurning or kicking **3 :** disdainful rejection **:** contemptuous treatment ⟨the insolence of office, and the ~s that patient merit of the unworthy takes —Shak.⟩

³**spurn** \"\ *n* -s [alter. of ¹*spur*] **1** *archaic* **:** the main root of a tree **2** *archaic* **:** a projecting part **:** SPUR **3 :** a small short pillar of coal left within the seam to support the coal above during holing

spurn·er \-nə(r)\ *n* -s **:** one that spurns

spurnwater \'=,==\ *n* [ME *spurnewater*, fr. *spurnen* to spurn + *water*] **:** a low V-shaped barrier on the forward deck of a ship to throw off seas coming aboard

spur-of-the-moment \;===;==\ *adj* [fr. the phrase (*on the*) *spur of the moment*] **:** occurring or developing without premeditation **:** hastily extemporized ⟨cumulative effect accomplished through . . . what had previously seemed merely *spur-of-the-moment* ideas —Irving Kolodin⟩ ⟨a human equation in live TV that gives it *spur-of-the-moment* touches —Dinah Shore⟩

spur pepper *n* **:** CHILI

spur pruning *n* **1 :** a method of pruning grapevines in which the shoot of the previous season is cut back to a spur with one or two buds **2 :** the removal (as from an apple tree) of fruiting spurs

¹**spurred** *past of* SPUR

²**spurred** \'spərd, 'spə̄d\ *adj* [ME *spored, spurret*, fr. *spore, spure* spur] **1 :** wearing spurs **2 :** having one or more spurs ⟨a ~ flower⟩ ⟨~ outgrowths from the gill covers⟩

spurred butterfly pea *n* **:** a butterfly pea of the genus *Centrosema* (esp. *C. virginianum*)

spurred gentian *n* **:** a plant of the genus *Halenia* (esp. *H. deflexa*)

spur·ri·er \'spər·ēə(r *also* 'spə·rē-\ *n* -s [ME *sporier*, fr. *spore, spure* spur + *-ier* — more at SPUR] **:** one that makes spurs

spurring *pres part of* SPUR

spurr·ite \'spər·,īt\ *n* -s [Josiah E. *Spurr* †1950 Am. geologist + E *-ite*] **:** a mineral $Ca_5(SiO_4)_2(CO_3)$ consisting of a calcium silicate and carbonate and occurring in light gray granular masses

spur rowel *n, heraldry* **:** a mullet pierced

spur·ry *or* **spur·rey** \'spərē\ *n, pl* **spurries** *or* **spurreys** [D *spurrie*, fr. MD *sporie*, fr. ML *spergula* — more at SPERGULA] **1 :** a small white-flowered European weed (*Spergula arvensis*) with whorled filiform leaves **2 :** any of several small herbs of the chickweed family

spur ryal *or* **spur rial** *or* **spur royal** *n* **:** the 15-shilling gold ryal of James I with a design on the reverse resembling the rowel of a spur

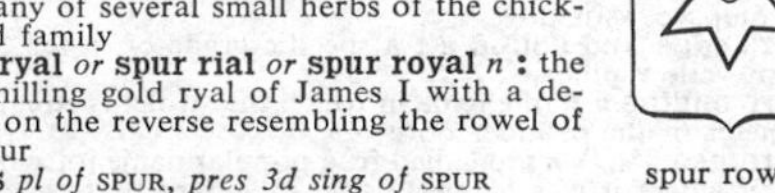
spur rowel

spurs *pl of* SPUR, *pres 3d sing of* SPUR

spur shore *n* **:** a timber or spar designed to hold a boat away from a pier wharf or quay

¹**spurt** *also* **spirt** \'spər|t, 'spə̄|, 'spəi|, *usu* |d·+V\ *n* -s [origin unknown] **1 :** a short period of time **:** MOMENT ⟨leaving for a ~ and returning shortly⟩ **2 a :** a sudden and usu. brief burst or outbreak of effort, activity, or development ⟨the pubertal phase . . . contains the most noticeable growth ~ —G.S.Blum⟩ ⟨the accidental and perhaps temporary ~ in population —S. H.Slichter⟩ ⟨has a little ~ of good fortune —Erle Stanley Gardner⟩ ⟨science and mathematics came in a four-century ~ and then stood still —A.L.Kroeber⟩ **b :** a quick burst or increase in speed of movement or progress ⟨put on an extra ~ and . . . slipped through a hole in the hedge —George Orwell⟩ ⟨his heads-up ball-playing saved many a game . . . in their late season ~ —*Current Biog.*⟩ **c :** a sharp or sudden increase or advance in business activity; *also* **:** the period of such a movement ⟨enjoying a ~ in sales —Vance Packard⟩ ⟨doing a nice business handling the annual ~ in the busy weeks before Christmas —Frederick Way⟩

²**spurt** *also* **spirt** \"\ *vb* -ED/-ING/-S *vi* **:** to make a spurt ⟨has ~*ed* into popularity —Jane Nickerson⟩ ⟨tucked the ball in, ~*ed* at him, driving hard —Irwin Shaw⟩ ⟨possibly its sales will ~ —Lloyd Mangrum⟩ ⟨stocks ~*ed* . . . then took a sharp spill —*New Orleans* (*La.*) *Times-Picayune*⟩ ~ *vt* **:** to cause (something) to make a spurt ⟨we ~ dress sales . . . every time we tie up with a smart society event —*Women's Wear Daily*⟩

³**spurt** *also* **spirt** \"\ *vb* -ED/-ING/-S [perh. akin to MHG *spirzen, spürzen* to spit, *sprützen* to sprout, squirt — more at SPRIT] *vi* **:** to gush suddenly or violently **:** SPOUT ⟨blood was seeping, not ~*ing*, from the head wound —Frances & Richard Lockridge⟩ ⟨hit the ground hard, the dust ~*ing* from beneath his boots —C.J.Clements⟩ ⟨saw smoke billow and flame ~ out —Philip Rooney⟩ ~ *vt* **:** to force out or expel (as a liquid) in a stream or jet **:** SQUIRT ⟨~s water from his mouth⟩

⁴**spurt** *also* **spirt** \"\ *n* -s **1 :** a sudden forceful gushing or shooting forth **:** JET ⟨an intermittent wind with wild ~s of incredibly thin rain —J.C.Powys⟩ ⟨~s of rifle fire stabbed at them —Marjory S. Douglas⟩ ⟨little ~s of low-voiced conversation —H.L.Davis⟩ **2 :** a quick surge of feeling or emotional outburst ⟨in a vicious ~ of temper, flung it into the fire —D. H.Lawrence⟩ ⟨sat there coughing, his sudden ~ of valor . . . knocked out of him —Max Peacock⟩ ⟨inspiration that came and went in ~s —Paul Hume⟩

⁵**spurt** *also* **spirt** \"\ *vi* -ED/-ING/-S [prob. alter. of ¹*sprit*] **:** to shoot up **:** SPROUT ⟨from the grass . . . flame-bright anemones ~*ed* —Elizabeth Bowen⟩ ⟨branches ~ from the trunk⟩

spur·tive \'spərd·iv\ *adj* [¹*spurt* + *-ive*] **:** of the nature of spurts **:** SPASMODIC, SUDDEN

¹**spur·tle** \'spərd·ᵊl\ *n* -s [origin unknown] **1** *chiefly Scot* **:** an implement similar to a spatula used to turn food (as griddle cakes) **2** *chiefly Scot* **:** a wooden stick for stirring porridge **3** *chiefly Scot* **:** SWORD

²**spur·tle** \'spər|dᵊl, 'spə̄|, 'spəi|, |tᵊl\ *vb* **spurtled; spurtled; spurtling** \|dᵊliŋ, |t(ᵊ)liŋ\ **spurtles** [freq. of ³*spurt*] *vt* **:** to cover with spatterings **:** SPRINKLE ~ *vi* **:** to break forth suddenly in a stream or spatter ⟨the white *spurtling* surf —Russell Thacher⟩

spur track *n* **:** a track that diverges from a main line **:** SIDING, BRANCH

spur tree *n* **:** a West Indian tree or shrub (*Petitia domingensis*) of the family Verbenaceae with fragrant white flowers

spur wheel *n* **:** SPUR GEAR

spurwing \'=,=\ *n* **1 :** SPUR-WINGED GOOSE **2 :** SPUR-WINGED PLOVER

spur-winged \'=;=\ *adj* **:** having one or more horny spurs on the bend of the wings

spur-winged goose *n* **:** a long-legged African goose of the genus *Plectropterus* (esp. *P. gambensis*) having a strong spur on the bend of the wing

spur-winged plover *n* **:** any of various plovers; *esp* **:** a plover (*Hoplopterus spinosus*) of northern Africa and neighboring regions with a crested head and underparts chiefly black having a spur on the bend of the wing

spurwort \'=,=\ *n* **:** FIELD MADDER

sput·nik \'spu̇tnik, -pət-,-püt-, -,nēk *also* -,nik; *sometimes* -püt(,)nyik *or* -püt(,)nyik\ *n* -s *sometimes cap* [Russ, traveling companion, satellite, fr. *s*, *so* with + *put'* path + *-nik*, suffix denoting a person engaged in or connected with something specified; akin to OSlav *sŭ* with, *samŭ* same, Skt *sama* equal, same, and to Skt *patha* way, path, course — more at SAME, FIND] **:** SATELLITE 2b ⟨first into space with a ~ —*Newsweek*⟩ ⟨successes in science, ~s, and rocketry —*N.Y. Times*⟩

¹**sput·ter** \'spəd·ə(r), -ətə-\ *vb* -ED/-ING/-S [akin to D *sputteren* to sputter, *spuiten* to spurt, spout — more at SPOUT] *vt* **1 :** to spit or expel (particles of saliva or food) from the mouth with mildly explosive sounds **:** SPLUTTER ⟨cram your mouth so full that if you were to speak you must ~ the contents of it amongst the dishes and the company —Earl of Chesterfield⟩ **2 :** to utter (words or ejaculations) hastily or explosively in confusion or excitement ⟨~*ing* protests he retired from the contest⟩ — often used with *out* ⟨began to laugh, ~*ing* out the story —Dawn Powell⟩ **3 :** to deposit (a metallic film) by electric discharge in which positive gas ions bombarding the cathode cause it to eject atoms of the cathode metal with great speed ~ *vi* **1 :** to spit or expel noisily from the mouth particles of food or saliva ⟨talks while he eats and ~s all over the place⟩ **2 :** to speak, reply, or ejaculate explosively or confusedly from anger or excitement ⟨their response . . . ~*ed* in its indignation —F.L.Paxson⟩ **3 a :** to make explosive or popping sounds in a spasmodic manner often with sparks or bursts of flame ⟨the car ~*ed* down the road —Elizabeth Pollet⟩ ⟨machine guns ~*ed* away hysterically —Erle Stanley Gardner⟩ ⟨candles . . . ~ before the shrines —*Amer. Guide Series: Texas*⟩ **b :** to cease acting or functioning with or as if with such a sputter ⟨the engine ~*ed*, spit, and died⟩ — usu. used with *out* ⟨the excitement . . . appeared to have ~*ed* out —*Newsweek*⟩

²**sputter** \"\ *n* -s **1 :** confused and excited speech or discussion ⟨protesting with a good deal of ~⟩ **2 :** the act or sound of sputtering ⟨can write their names now without a ~ of the pen —Thomas Hardy⟩ ⟨would come the distant cough, ~, choke, then catch, roar, and soon steady droning of the first planes —Benedict Thielen⟩

sput·ter·ing·ly *adv* **:** in a sputtering manner **:** with sputtering

sput·tery \'spəd·ərē, -ətə-, -ri\ *adj* **:** issuing in intermittent bursts **:** SPUTTERING, EJACULATORY

spu·tum \'spyüd·əm, -ütəm\ *n, pl* **spu·ta** \-d·ə, -tə\ *also* **sputums** [L, fr. neut. of *sputus*, past part. of *spuere* to spit — more at SPEW] **1 :** something expectorated and usu. consisting of saliva with or without mucus or other materials from the respiratory passages **2 :** the matter discharged from the air passages in diseases of the lungs, bronchi, or upper respiratory tract that contains mucus and often pus, blood, fibrin, or bacterial products

sputum cup *n* **:** a cup usu. made of paper or thin cardboard to receive and isolate the sputum of a patient with respiratory disease

¹**spy** \'spī\ *vb* **spied; spied; spying; spies** [ME *spien*, fr. OF *espier*, of Gmc origin; akin to OHG *spehōn* to watch, regard, spy, MLG *spēen*, MD *spien*; akin to ON *spā* to prophesy, L *specere* to look, *species* appearance, form, kind, species, Gk *skeptesthai* to view, look, consider, *skopein* to look at, examine, Skt *paśyati* he sees] *vt* **1 a :** to watch (as a person) in a furtive or stealthy manner for the purpose of secretly obtaining information for usu. hostile purposes ⟨*spies* the enemy to determine his direction of march⟩ ⟨take command of the army and . . . sat with his glass, ~*ing* the movements across the water —H.E.Scudder⟩ **b :** to investigate or explore (a country or place) in a secretive or unobtrusive manner — usu. used with *out* ⟨made horseback trips about the vicinity, ~*ing* out the land —Julian Dana⟩ ⟨shareholders started ~*ing* out the landscape in quest of new prospects —*Sydney* (*Australia*) *Bull.*⟩ **2 :** to scrutinize or examine (something) in detail ⟨~*ing* the exhibits at the fair⟩ **3 :** to discover after some search **:** catch sight of **:** DESCRY, NOTICE ⟨the squire in the lead *spied* him . . . and reined in his horse —T.B.Costain⟩ ⟨*spied* the red camellias on the white marble mantel —Olive H. Prouty⟩ **4 :** to search or look for intensively ⟨left at daylight in order to ~ their way . . . through the minefields —Herbert Hoover⟩ — usu. used with *out* ⟨sat at the feet of many European masters . . . ~*ing* out the secrets of their art —Brander Matthews⟩ ~ *vi* **1 :** to observe or search for something **:** LOOK ⟨smoothing her gloves and ~*ing* downward at the folds of her mantle —Arnold Bennett⟩ ⟨you must ~ out for literature as you do for a qualified prescription clerk —Francis Hackett⟩ **2 a :** to watch secretly **:** make furtive or stealthy observations — often used with *into, on,* or *upon* ⟨is usually ~*ing* into other people's business⟩ ⟨is above ~*ing* on his friends⟩ **b :** to seek strategic or related information about a country or people by secret methods of infiltration or investigation ⟨was sent into enemy territory to ~⟩ — usu. used with *on* or *upon* ⟨in order to ~ upon the British —*Amer. Guide Series: Conn.*⟩

²**spy** \"\ *n* -ES [ME *spie*, fr. OF *espie*, of Gmc origin; akin to OHG *speho* watcher, spy, *spehōn* to watch, spy — more at ¹SPY] **1 :** one that spies: **a :** one who keeps secret watch upon a person or thing to obtain information ⟨*spies* who were able to mingle among politicians and gather hot gossip —W.A. Swanberg⟩ ⟨is a sneak, a ~, an informer —Jack London⟩ **b :** one engaged in seeking strategic or related information about a country or people by secret methods of infiltration or investigation **:** secret agent ⟨handicapped by a lack of decent military intelligence . . . had too few scouts and *spies* —F.V.W. Mason⟩; *specif* **:** one who acts in a clandestine manner or on false pretenses (as without regular uniform) to obtain information in the zone of operations of a belligerent with the intention of communicating it to the hostile party **2** [ME *spie*, fr. *spien*, v.] **:** the act or occasion of spying ⟨had the first ~ from a hillock in the glen —John Buchan⟩

spyglass \'=,=\ *n* **:** a small terrestrial telescope

sq *abbr* **1** sequence **2** [L *sequens; sequentes; sequentia*] the following **3** squadron **4** square

sqd *abbr* squad

sqdn *abbr* squadron

SQMS *abbr* staff quartermaster sergeant

sqn *abbr* squadron

sqq *abbr* [L *sequentes; sequentia*] the following

sqr *abbr* square

¹**squab** \'skwäb *also* -wȯb\ *n* -s *see sense 1* [prob. of Scand origin; akin to Sw dial. *skvabb, kvabb* anything soft and thick, Norw dial. *skvabb* paplike mass; prob. akin to OS *quappa* eelpout, OBulg *žaba* toad] **1** *or pl* **squab :** a fledgling bird; *specif* **:** a fledgling pigeon that is about four weeks old and weighs about one pound ⟨the menu featured ~s en casserole⟩ **2 :** one that resembles a squab; *esp* **:** a short fat person **3 a :** COUCH **b :** a removable cushion used esp. in a chair or couch seat **c** *chiefly Brit* **:** the back part of an automobile seat

²**squab** \"\ *adj* **1 :** of, relating to, or having the characteristics of a squab: **a** (1) **:** DUMPY, SQUAT ⟨his ~ white figure stopped growing at fat puppyhood —Haldane Macfall⟩ (2) **:** BROAD, THICK ⟨a ~ nose⟩ **b :** UNFLEDGED **2** *obs* **:** CURT, SHARP

³**squab** \"\ *vb* **squabbed; squabbed; squabbing; squabs** [prob. fr. ¹*squab*] *vt* **1** *dial Brit* **:** CRUSH, SQUASH **2 :** to fill with stuffing (as a cushion) ~ *vi, dial Brit* **:** to squat down

⁴**squab** \"\ *adv* **:** PLUMP

⁵**squab** \"\ *vb* [perh. fr. ³*squab*] **:** SLOP, SPILL

squa·bash \'skwȯ,bash, -wä,b-\ *vt* -ED/-ING/-ES [blend of *squash* and *bash*] **:** to crush esp. with criticism **:** LAMBASTE ⟨his satire . . . ~*ed* on at one blow a set of coxcombs —J.G.Lockhart⟩

squabbed \'skwäbd *also* -wȯbd\ *adj* [fr. past part. of ³*squab*] **:** ²SQUAB 1a(1) ⟨a ~ and thoroughly unattractive figure⟩

squab·ber \-bə(r)\ *n* -s [¹*squab* + *-er*] **:** a pigeon used for commercial breeding purposes

squab·bing \-biŋ\ *adj* [¹*squab* + *-ing*] **:** squab-producing ⟨~ pigeons⟩

squab·bish \-bish\ *adj* [²*squab* + *-ish*] **:** somewhat fat or squat

¹**squab·ble** \'skwäbəl *also* -wȯb-\ *n* -s [prob. of Scand origin; akin to Sw dial. *skvabbel* dispute, Norw *skvabbe* to chatter, babble, rant; prob. of imit. origin] **1 :** a noisy altercation usu. over something insignificant **:** WRANGLE ⟨a mere ~ in the children's schoolroom —Alan Moorehead⟩ ⟨she could better endure a howling brawl . . . a shrill ~ of shrews —Jean Stafford⟩ **2 a :** a futile, aimless, and usu. continuous quarrel **:** BICKERING ⟨because the committee has become the center of a political ~, it seems unlikely that anything will ever come of its activities —Henry LaCossitt⟩ **b :** a minor and often recurrent disagreement (as between groups) **:** DISPUTE ⟨recalled the jurisdictional ~s of the 15th century —Paul Johnson⟩ ⟨an unresolved ~ with the West —William Clark⟩ **syn** see QUARREL

²**squabble** \"\ *vb* **squabbled; squabbled; squabbling** \-b(ə)liŋ\ **squabbles** *vi* **1 :** to quarrel noisily and to no purpose **:** WRANGLE ⟨fight and ~ among themselves in complete and vigorous disregard of any color line —Cabell Phillips⟩ ⟨doctors, nurses, the administrator, and the trustees *squabbled* constantly —*Newsweek*⟩ **2** *of type* **:** to become squabbled ~ *vt* **:** to disarrange (set type) so that the letters or lines stand awry or are mixed and need readjustment — compare ⁴PI

squab·bler \-b(ə)lə(r)\ *n* -s **:** one that squabbles

squab·bly \-b(ə)lē\ *adj, usu* -ER/-EST [¹*squabble* + *-y*] **:** tending toward or characterized by squabbling

squab·by \-bē\ *adj* -ER/-EST [¹*squab* + *-y*] **:** ²SQUAB 1a(1)

squab chicken *n* **:** a young chicken that weighs about 1 to 1¼ pounds and is usu. suitable for an individual serving

squac·co \'skwä(,)kō *also* -wȯ(-\ *or* **squacco heron** *n* -s [It dial. *sguacco*] **:** a small crested heron (*Ardeola ralloides*) that breeds in parts of Asia, Africa, and southern Europe

¹**squad** \'skwäd *also* -wȯd\ *n* -s [MF *esquade, esquadre*, fr. OSp & OIt; OSp *escuadra*, fr. *escuadrar* to square, fr. (assumed) VL *exquadrare;* OIt *squadra*, fr. *squadrare* to square, fr. (assumed) VL *exquadrare;* fr. the men being arranged in square formation — more at SQUARE] **:** a small group of individuals: as **a :** a group of military personnel organized as a team (as for drill or inspection) ⟨on command the ~ moves instantly, smartly, and smoothly —*Drill & Ceremonies*⟩; *esp* **:** a tactical unit that can be easily directed in the field by its leader ⟨using an 11-man rifle ~ for maneuverability and fire power⟩ **b :** a group engaged in a common effort or occupation ⟨a football ~⟩ ⟨a special police ~ of 30 men . . . was on duty —*Springfield* (*Mass.*) *Daily News*⟩ **c :** an auxiliary fire company equipped with special appliances

²**squad** \"\ *vt* **squadded; squadded; squadding; squads :** to arrange in squads

squad *abbr* squadron

squad car *n* **:** an automobile used by police that is equipped with short-wave radiophone connection with headquarters — called also *cruise car, prowl car*

squad·der \-də(r)\ *n* -s [¹*squad* + *-er*] **:** a member of a squad of police

squad leader *n* **:** an enlisted man usu. of noncommissioned officer rank in charge of a squad

squad·rol \(')skwä¦drōl, -wȯ¦d-\ *n* -s [blend of *squad* (car) and *patrol* (wagon)] **:** an automobile that is used by police both as a squad car and as an ambulance

squad·ron \'skwädrən *also* -wȯd-\ *n* -s [It *squadrone* body of soldiers arranged in square formation, squadron, aug. of *squadra* squad, fr. OIt] **1 :** a unit of military organization: **a :** a cavalry unit that is higher than a troop and lower than a regiment — compare BATTALION **b :** a unit of naval administrative and tactical organization that consists of two or more divisions and sometimes additional vessels **c** (1) **:** an aviation unit (as of the U. S. Air Force) higher than a flight and lower than a group and composed of a headquarters and two or more flights (2) **:** a military flight formation **2 :** a relatively large group of individuals ⟨since the war a ~ of younger symphonists has arisen —*Score*⟩ ⟨~s of birds wheel overhead —*Amer. Guide Series: Fla.*⟩ **3** *obs* **:** a division of a town or community or district in New England **4 :** a unit of at least five air explorers of the Boy Scouts

squad·roned \-nd\ *adj* **:** formed into or as if into a squadron

squadron leader *n* **:** a military officer (as in the British Royal Air Force) equivalent in rank to a major in the army

squad room *n* **1 :** a room in a barracks used to billet soldiers **2 :** a room in a police station where members of the force assemble (as for roll call or the assignment of duties)

squad tent *n* **:** a canvas shelter designed to accommodate a military squad

squad wagon *n* **:** a fire truck carrying a squad and its equipment

squad tent

squag·ga \'skwägə\ *n* -s [native name in Australia] **:** a scyllarian crustacean (*Ibacus incisus*) of Australia that is salmon red in color and reaches a length of eight inches

¹**squail** \'skwā(ə)l\ *vb* [origin unknown] *vi, dial chiefly Brit* **:** to throw a weighted stick (as at a bird or fruit on a tree) ⟨~*ed* at the pears with short sticks —Richard Jefferies⟩ ~ *vt, dial chiefly Brit* **:** to strike by throwing a stick

²**squail** \"\ *n* -s [back-formation fr. squails] **:** a disk or counter used in the game of squails

squails \-lz\ *n pl but sing in constr* [prob. alter. (influenced by ¹*squail*) of obs. E *skayles* a form of skittles or ninepins, alter. (prob. influenced by E *skittles*) of ME *kayles* kails — more at KAILS] **:** a game in which disks are driven or snapped from the edge of a table or board at a mark in the center

squa·lene \'skwā,lēn\ *n* -s [ISV *squal-* (fr. NL *Squalus*) + *-ene*] **:** a liquid acyclic triterpene hydrocarbon $[(CH_3)_2C{=}CHCH_2[CH_2C(CH_3){=}CHCH_2]{-}]_2$ that is found esp. in the liver oil of various sharks but also in various plant oils, in yeast, and in human sebum, that is made synthetically from farnesol, that is formed enzymatically from mevalonic acid, and that is a biological precursor of various cyclic triterpenoids and of cholesterol and related steroids

squa·li \'skwā,lī\ [NL, fr. pl. of L *squalus*, a sea fish — more at WHALE] *syn of* PLEUROTREMATA

¹**squal·id** \'skwäləd *also* -wȯl- *sometimes* -wāl-\ *adj, sometimes* -ER/-EST [L *squalidus* — more at SQUALOR] **1 a :** marked by filthiness and degradation usu. from neglect ⟨exchanged . . . ~ and savage dress for a suit of Dutch cloth —Francis Parkman⟩ ⟨ramshackle frame houses . . . notorious firetraps of ~ appearance —*Amer. Guide Series: N. Y. City*⟩ ⟨ministering every year to . . . the poorest, the sickest, the ~*est* human beings —*Saturday Rev.*⟩ ⟨rickety tables . . . surmounted by . . . ~ overflowing ashtrays —John Wain⟩ ⟨rueful ~ poverty that crawled by every wayside —John Morley⟩ **b :** RUN-DOWN, SHABBY ⟨life at a fashionably ~ preparatory school —*New Yorker*⟩ **2** *obs* **a :** DRY **b :** SHAGGY **3 a :** morally debased or repulsive **:** CONTEMPTIBLE, SORDID ⟨a sublime prophet . . . or a ~ quack —La Selle Gilman⟩ ⟨a series of rather ~ little affairs that everybody knew about and nobody mentioned —Ngaio Marsh⟩ **b :** lacking refinement or sophistication **:** CRUDE ⟨finds Voltaire's summary of ancient philosophy ~ —J.H.Seyppel⟩ ⟨such imagination as he can detect is usually commonplace or ~ —Bernard De Voto⟩ **4 :** marked by an unwholesome appearance ⟨his complexion sallow and ~ —E.G.Bulwer-Lytton⟩ **syn** see DIRTY

²**squa·lid** \'skwāləd\ *adj* [NL *Squalidae*] **:** of or relating to the Squalidae

³**squalid** \"\ *n* -s **:** a shark of the family Squalidae

squa·li·da \'skwālədə\ [NL, fr. *Squalus* + *-ida*] *syn of* PLEUROTREMATA

squa·li·dae \-,dē\ *n pl, cap* [NL, fr. *Squalus*, type genus + *-idae*] **:** a family of sharks having a spine in each dorsal fin and comprising the spiny dogfishes and various chiefly small related forms

squa·lid·i·ty \skwä'lidəd·ē, -wȯ'-,-wā'-\ *n* -ES [LL *squaliditas*, fr. L *squalidus* squalid + *-itas* -ity] **:** the quality or state of being squalid

squal·id·ly *adv* **:** in a squalid manner

squal·id·ness *n* -ES **:** SQUALIDITY

squa·li·form \'skwālə,fȯrm\ *adj* [NL *Squalus* + E *-iform*] **:** resembling a shark or dogfish in form

¹**squall** *also* **squawl** \'skwȯl\ *vb* -ED/-ING/-S [of Scand origin; akin to ON *skval* useless chatter, *skvala* to talk noisily, cry out and perh. to ON *skjalla* to clash, clatter — more at SHILL] *vi* **:** to cry or cry out raucously **:** SCREAM ⟨a baby by the fire woke up and began to ~ —Victoria Sackville-West⟩ ⟨~*ed* in terror⟩ ~ *vt* **:** to utter in a strident voice ⟨one of the commonplace psalm tunes, ~*ed* by charity children —*Court Mag.*⟩

²**squall** *also* **squawl** \"\ *n* -s **:** a raucous cry **:** SQUAWK ⟨some clubs, while on the field, keep up a constant ~ of encouragement to their pitchers —R.O.Boyer⟩

³**squall** \"\ *n* -s [prob. of Scand origin; akin to Sw & Norw *skval* splash, ripple, rushing water and prob. to ON *skval* useless chatter] **1 :** a sudden violent wind often accompanied by rain or snow **2 :** a short-lived commotion resembling a squall ⟨his film career . . . has been . . . punctuated with the ~s of scandal —Arthur Knight⟩ **:** SQUABBLE ⟨she could hear another domestic ~ starting next door⟩ **syn** see WIND

⁴**squall** \"\ *vi* -ED/-ING/-S **:** to blow a squall ⟨the raw wind sagged with snow and the storms spat and ~*ed* —Helen Rich⟩

squall cloud *n* **:** a ragged light gray rolling cloud usu. located beneath the dark cloud mass of an advancing thunderstorm

squall·er \'skwȯlə(r)\ *n* -s **:** one that squalls; *esp* **:** a baby that cries excessively

squall line *n* **1 :** an intersection or boundary between the cold and the warm winds of an extratropical cyclone or between the cold air of an advancing anticyclone and the warm air of a cyclone **:** COLD FRONT — called also *wind-shift line* **2 :** a line of squalls often 50 to 200 miles ahead of a cold front

squally \'skwȯlē, -li\ *adj* -ER/-EST [³*squall* + *-y*] **1 a :** marked by squalls ⟨saw the vessel off, on a gray, ~ morning —James Dugan⟩ **b :** GUSTY ⟨the winds . . . are almost always high and ~ —C.D.Forde⟩ **2 :** marked by difficulty or disharmony **:** STORMY ⟨a couple whose home life has been extraordinarily ~ —John McCarten⟩

squa·loid \ˈskwāˌlȯid\ *adj* [NL *Squalus* + *-oid*] **1 :** resembling a shark **2** [NL *Squaloidea*] **:** of or relating to the Squaloidea

squa·loi·dea \skwāˈlȯidēə\ *n pl, cap* [NL, fr. *Squalus* + *-oidea*] **1 :** a suborder of Pleurotremata comprising those sharks (as the spiny dogfishes) that have a compressed or rounded body but in some respects (as in adaptation to bottom-dwelling habits) approach the skates and rays — compare GALEOIDEA, NOTIDANOIDEA **2** *in some classifications* **:** a suborder or other division of elasmobranch fishes comprising the typical sharks — compare SQUATINA

squa·loi·dei \-ēˌī\ [NL, fr. *Squalus* + *-oidei*] *syn of* SQUALOIDEA

squal·or \ˈskwälə(r) *also* -wȯl- *or* -wāl-\ *n* -s [L, roughness, dirt, squalor; akin to L *squalēre* to be dirty, *squalidus* dirty, squalid, *squama* scale] **1 :** the quality or state of being physically squalid ⟨dwellings . . . sinking stage by stage from indigence to ~ —Lewis Mumford⟩ **2 a :** moral baseness **:** CORRUPTION ⟨presenting a picture of political ~ to the country —Russell Baker⟩ **b :** absence of intellectual sensitivity **:** CRASSNESS ⟨depressing ~ of the . . . mind —Dachine Rainer⟩

squa·lus \ˈskwāləs\ *n, cap* [NL, fr. L, a sea fish — more at WHALE] **:** a genus (the type of the family Squalidae) of sharks orig. comprising all the known sharks but now restricted to various typical dogfishes

squam \ˈskwäm *also* -wȯm\ *n* -s [fr. *Squam*, short for *Annisquam*, village in northeastern Mass., where it was orig. worn by fishermen] **:** SOU'WESTER 2b

squam- *or* **squamo-** *comb form* [L, fr. *squama*] **1 :** scale **:** squama ⟨*Squam*ata⟩ ⟨*squam*aceous⟩ **2 :** squamosal and ⟨*squamo*mastoid⟩ **:** squamously ⟨*squamo*cellular⟩

squa·ma \ˈskwāmə\ *n, pl* **squa·mae** \-ˌmē\ [L] **:** a scale or a structure resembling a scale: **a :** an alula, tegula, or calypter at the base of the wing above the halter of a dipterous insect **b :** the exopodite of the antenna (as of certain crustaceans) **c :** SQUAMOSA

squa·ma·ceous \skwəˈmāshəs\ *adj* [*squam-* + *-aceous*] **:** covered with or consisting of scales **:** SCALY, SQUAMOUS

squa·mal \ˈskwāməl\ *adj* [*squam-* + *-al*] **:** SQUAMOSAL

squa·ma·ta \skwəˈmäd·ə, -mād·ə\ *n pl, cap* [NL, fr. *squam-* + *-ata*] **:** an order of reptiles comprising the snakes and lizards and sometimes the extinct Pythonomorpha

squa·mate \ˈskwāˌmāt\ *also* **squa·mat·ed** \-ˌmād·əd\ *adj* [LL *squamatus*, fr. *squama* + *-atus* -ate] **:** SCALY

squa·ma·tion \skwəˈmāshən, -wāˈm-\ *n* -s [*squam-* + *-ation*] **1 :** the state or condition of being scaly or scaled **2 :** the arrangement of scales on an animal **:** SCALATION

squame \ˈskwām\ *n* -s [F, fr. L *squama* scale] **:** SQUAMA

squa·mel·la \skwəˈmelə\ *n, pl* **squamel·lae** \-(ˌ)lē, -ˌlī\ [NL, fr. *squam-* + *-ella*] **:** a diminutive scale or bractlet

squa·mel·late \skwəˈmelət, -wāˈm-; ˈskwāməˌlāt\ *adj* [NL *squamella* + E *-ate*] **:** SQUAMULOSE

squa·mel·lif·er·ous \ˌskwāməˈlif(ə)rəs\ *adj* [ISV *squamell-* (fr. NL *squamella*) + *-iferous*] **:** bearing squamellae

squa·mel·li·form \skwəˈmeləˌfȯrm\ *adj* [ISV *squamell-* (fr. NL *squamella*) + *-iform*; orig. formed as F *squamelliforme*] **:** having the form of a squamella

squa·mi·form \ˈskwāməˌfȯrm\ *adj* [ISV *squam-* + *-iform*] **:** having the shape of a scale

squa·mi·pen·nate \ˌskwāməˈpenˌāt\ *adj* [NL *Squamipennes* + E *-ate*] **:** of or relating to the Squamipennes

squa·mi·pen·nes \ˌ==ˈpe(ˌ)nēz\ *n pl, cap* [NL, fr. *squam-* + *-i-* + *-pennes* (fr. L *penna* feather) — more at PEN] *in some classifications* **:** a suborder of Percomorphi comprising chiefly tropical marine fishes with a narrow deep body and usu. scaly bases on the dorsal and anal fins and including Chaetodontidae, Ephippidae, and various other families

squamish *var of* SQUAWMISH

squa·mo·columnar junction \ˌskwā(ˌ)mō+...-\ *n* [*squam-* + *columnar*] **:** the region in the uterine cervix in which the squamous lining of the vagina is replaced by the columnar epithelium typical of the body of the uterus and which is a common seat of neoplastic change

squa·moid \ˈskwāˌmȯid\ *adj* [*squam-* + *-oid*] **:** SCALY

squa·mo·sa \skwāˈmōsə, -wəˈm-, -ōzə\ *n, pl* **squamosas** \-z\ *or* **squamo·sae** \-ōˌsē, -ōˌzē, ˌī\ [NL, fr. fem. of L *squamosus* squamous] **:** the squamous part of the temporal bone

¹squa·mo·sal \(ˈ)skwāˈmōsəl, skwəˈm-, -ōzəl\ *adj* [L *squamosus* squamous + E *-al*] **:** SCALELIKE: **a :** SQUAMOUS **b** [NL *squamosa* + E *-al*] **:** of, relating to, or constituting a membrane bone of the skull of many vertebrates that is external and more or less dorsal to the auditory capsule and corresponds to the squamous portion of the temporal bone of man

²squamosal \"\ *n* -s **1 :** the squamosal bone **2 :** the pterotic of a teleost fish

squa·mose \ˈskwāˌmōs\ *adj* [L *squamosus*] **:** SQUAMOUS — **squa·mose·ly** *adv* — **squa·mose·ness** *n* -ES

squa·mos·i·ty \skwāˈmäsəd·ē, -wəˈm-\ *n* -ES **1 :** the state or condition of being squamose **2 :** a scaly area (as on the body of an insect)

squa·mous \ˈskwāməs\ *adj* [L *squamosus*, fr. *squama* scale + *-osus* -ose — more at SQUALOR] **1 a :** covered with or consisting of scales **:** resembling a scale **:** SCALY ⟨a ~ stem or bulb⟩ ⟨~ epithelial cells⟩ **b :** of or relating to squamous epithelium **2 :** of, relating to, or constituting the anterior upper portion of the temporal bone of man and various mammals that is a thin flat-edged form bearing the zygomatic process — **squa·mous·ly** *adv*

squamous cell *n* **:** a cell of or derived from squamous epithelium ⟨*squamous-cell* cancers⟩

squamous epithelium *n* **:** stratified epithelium that consists at least in its outer layers of small scalelike cells (as the epidermis of the human skin) — compare COLUMNAR EPITHELIUM

squams *pl of* SQUAM

squamu·la \ˈskwamyələ, -wām-,-wäm-\ *n, pl* **squamu·lae** \-ˌlē, -ˌlī\ [NL, fr. L, small scale, dim. of *squama* scale] **1 :** SQUAMULE **2 :** the tegula of a hymenopteron

squamu·late \-ˌlāt\ *adj* [*squamule* + *-ate*] **:** SQUAMULOSE

squamu·la·tion \ˌ==ˈlāshən\ *n* -s [*squamule* + *-ation*] **:** a squamous arrangement

squamule \ˈ=(ˌ)myül\ *n* -s [NL *squamula*] **:** a small scale: **a :** one of the scalelike lobes of the thallus of a lichen **b :** LODICULE

squamu·li·form \ˈ= myələˌfȯrm\ *adj* [ISV *squamul-* (fr. NL *squamula*) + *-iform*] **:** resembling a squamule

squamu·lose \ˈ=myəˌlōs\ *adj* [*squamule* + *-ose*] **:** squamous with minute scales

¹squan·der \ˈskwändə(r) *also* -wȯn-\ *vb* **squandered; squandered; squandering** \-d(ə)riŋ\ **squanders** [origin unknown] *vt* **1 :** to cause to disperse or spread **:** SCATTER ⟨they drive and ~ the huge Belgian fleet —John Dryden⟩ **2 :** to expend extravagantly or foolishly esp. to the point of depletion **:** throw away **:** DISSIPATE ⟨tied up their fortunes in trust funds so that they could not be ~*ed* by their heirs —Lucien Price⟩ ⟨willing to ~ their lives on the gratuitous work that great art demands —Edmund Wilson⟩ ⟨the most brilliant journalist of my generation . . . often ~*s* his genius for invective —T.S.Eliot⟩ ⟨~*ing* away income by gambling —Bingham Dai⟩ **~** *vi* **1 :** ROAM, WANDER **2 :** to spend in a wasteful manner ⟨they often ~*ed*, but they never gave —Richard Savage⟩ **3 :** to scatter in various directions ⟨many of the enemy . . . ~*ed* like quail from a flushed covey —B.A. Williams⟩ **syn** see WASTE

²squander \"\ *n* -s **:** an act or instance of squandering **:** EXTRAVAGANCE

squan·der·er \-dərə(r)\ *n* -s **:** one that squanders; *esp* **:** WASTREL

squan·der·mania \ˌ=də(r)+\ *n* [¹*squander* + *mania*] **:** the practice of spending money extravagantly esp. by a government ⟨within 6 months he had . . . begun history's most prodigious ~ —D.A.Reed⟩

squanter-squash \ˈskwäntə(r),=\ *n* [alter. of earlier *isquoutersquash* — more at SQUASH] **:** SUMMER SQUASH

squan·tum \ˈskwäntəm *also* -wȯn-\ *n* -s [prob. fr. *Squantum*, former Indian village in eastern Mass.] *NewEng* **:** CLAMBAKE 1a

squar·able \ˈskwa(a)rəbəl, -wer-\ *adj* **:** capable of being squared ⟨only theory ~ with the known facts⟩

¹square \ˈskwa(a)|(ə)r, -we|, |ə\ *n* -s [ME *squyre, square*, fr. MF *esquerre, esquarre*, fr. (assumed) VL *exquadra*, fr. (assumed) VL *exquadrare* to square, fr. L *ex-* ¹ex- + *quadrare* to square — more at QUADRATE] **1 :** an instrument with at least one right angle and two or more straight edges used to lay out or test right angles — see COMBINATION SQUARE, FRAMING SQUARE, TRY SQUARE, T SQUARE **2 a** *obs* **:** the corner or angle of a figure **b** *obs* **:** the side of a rectangle **c :** a rectangle with all four sides equal — see AREA table **3 a :** any of the quadrilateral spaces marked out on a board for playing games **b :** a square piece, surface, or area ⟨a quilt of ~*s* sewn together⟩ ⟨~ of pavement⟩ **c** *obs* **:** the bosom of a woman's dress **d :** a scarf of a square shape **4 :** the product of a number or quantity multiplied by itself ⟨81 is the ~ of 9⟩ **:** the second power of a number **5** *obs* **:** guiding principle **:** PATTERN, RULE, STANDARD **6 a** *obs* **:** justness of workmanship or of conduct **b** *obs* **:** exact proportion **:** REGULARITY **c** *obs* **:** quartile aspect **7 squares** *pl, obs* **:** MATTERS, AFFAIRS, THINGS — used in the phrase *how go the squares* **8 a** *Brit* **:** an open area enclosed by residential buildings and commonly laid out with trees, grass, walks, gardens **b :** an open place or area formed at the meeting of two or more streets ⟨village ~⟩ ⟨market ~⟩ **c :** BLOCK 5e (1), 5e(2) **9 a :** a body of troops formed in solid or hollow rectangle with the ranks that form the sides facing outwards ⟨the brave ~*s* of war —Shak.⟩ **b :** SQUARE DANCE 1 **c :** set 36b **d :** a figure in square dancing performed by moving successively forward, sideward, backward, sideward **10 a :** the upper part of the shank of an anchor to which the stock is attached **b :** the square-ended projection in a clock or watch turned by the key in winding ⟨winding ~⟩ **11 a :** a solid object or piece approximating a cube or having a square as its largest face ⟨~ of cheese⟩ ⟨butter ~*s*⟩ **b :** a molding of square section **c :** a rolled or machined piece (as of steel) with a square section ⟨rounds, bars, and ~*s* are available⟩ **12 :** an unopened cotton flower with its enclosing bracts **13 :** the portion of the board of a book cover that projects beyond the edge of the leaves at the top, fore edge, or bottom ⟨an adequate ~ at the fore edge⟩ **14 :** a builder's unit of floor or roof area equal to 100 square feet ⟨so many shingles per ~⟩; *also* **:** the number of roofing slates or shingles needed per square **15 :** a strong iron frame in a spinning mule to which the carriages are secured **16 :** a person who is an outsider or adversary because of the conventionality, conservatism, or respectability of his taste, behavior, or way of life **:** one who is not in the know **:** FOGY; *also* **:** DUPE, SUCKER — compare BOURGEOIS, PHILISTINE — **at square** *obs* **:** in a state of opposition **:** at variance **:** at odds — **by the square** *obs* **:** PRECISELY, EXACTLY ⟨do you not know my lady's foot *by the square* —Shak.⟩ — **on the square** *adv (or adj)* **1 :** at right angles ⟨plants are set out *on the square* about 30 inches apart —F.D. Smith & Barbara Wilcox⟩ **2 :** in an open, fair manner **:** on the level **:** HONESTLY, HONORABLY ⟨operate a gambling game *on the square*⟩ **3 :** on terms of equality — **out of square 1 :** not at right angles **:** OBLIQUELY **2 :** not in order **:** not regular **:** out of true

²square \"\ *adj* -ER/-EST [ME, modif. (influenced by MF *esquarre* square) of MF *escarré*, past part. of *escarrer* to square, fr. (assumed) VL *exquadrare*] **1 a :** having four equal sides and four right angles **b :** forming a right angle ⟨~ corner⟩ **2 a :** having a width nearly equal to the height and rectangular rather than curving outline ⟨~ cabinet⟩ ⟨~ house⟩ **b :** of a shape suggesting strength and solidity ⟨~ jaw⟩ ⟨~ shoulders⟩ **c** *of a hand* **:** having the palm square at the wrist and at the base of square fingers and usu. held by palmists to indicate qualities of order, practicality, and common sense **d :** rectangular and equilateral in section ⟨~ tower⟩ ⟨~ rod⟩ ⟨pushing ~ pegs into round holes⟩ **3 a** *of a unit of length* **:** converted from a linear unit into a square unit of area having the same length of side **:** SQUARED ⟨~ foot⟩ **b :** being of a specified length in each of two equal dimensions — used after the term of measurement ⟨a room ten feet ~⟩ ⟨a 50 foot ~ courtyard⟩ **4 a :** exactly adjusted or correspondent **:** precisely constructed or aligned **b :** JUST, FAIR, HONEST, STRAIGHTFORWARD ⟨~ in all his dealings⟩ ⟨wanted to do the ~ thing⟩ ⟨a good, ~, explicit fallacy that can be squarely met and . . . refuted —C.S.Peirce⟩ **c :** leaving no balance **:** SETTLED ⟨make an account ~⟩ **d :** EVEN, TIED ⟨the golfers were all ~ on the 17th hole⟩ **e :** SUBSTANTIAL, SATISFYING ⟨~ meal⟩ **f** *of a horse's gait* **:** smooth and regular in movement **g :** having unsophisticated or conservative tastes esp. in entertainment **:** belonging to or characteristic of the respectable law-abiding tradition-bound classes of society ⟨~ audience⟩ ⟨some ~ music⟩; *also* **:** LEGITIMATE, LEGAL ⟨the car has ~ plates on it⟩ ⟨~ name⟩ **5 a :** set at right angles with the mast and keel — used of the yards of a square-rigged ship **b :** at right angles to a line drawn from wicket to wicket and usu. in line with the batting crease — used of cricket fielding positions, fieldsmen, and hits ⟨a ~ cut⟩; compare FINE **6 a :** markedly regular in rhythmic and harmonic structure ⟨~ melody⟩ **b** *of a military group* **:** based primarily on four units ⟨~ army division⟩ — compare TRIANGULAR **7 :** woven with an equal number of warp and weft threads per inch — **get square with :** to get even with **:** get satisfaction for an injury or insult from

³square \"\ *vb* -ED/-ING/-S [ME *squaren*, modif. (influenced by MF *esquarre* square) of MF *escarrer* to square, fr. (assumed) VL *exquadrare* — more at SQUARE (n.)] *vt* **1 a :** to form with right angles and straight edges or flat surfaces **:** make square or rectangular ⟨~ a building stone⟩ ⟨~ a timber⟩ ⟨~ the end of a board⟩ **b :** to measure in order to find or test the deviation from a right angle, straight line, or plane surface **:** apply a try square to **2 :** to bring approximately to a right angle ⟨thrust out his chin and *squared* his shoulders⟩ ⟨stood with feet apart and elbows *squared*⟩ ⟨~ the yards of a ship⟩ **3 a :** to multiply (a number or quantity) by itself **:** raise to the second power **b :** to find a square equal in area to ⟨~ a circle⟩ **c :** to be equal to a square of (a specified size) ⟨*squared* ten feet and ten inches —J.H.Bond⟩ **4 :** to compare with or reduce to a selected standard **:** ADJUST, REGULATE, SHAPE ⟨~ our actions by the opinions of others —John Milton⟩ **5 a :** to make even so as to leave no remainder or difference **:** BALANCE, SETTLE ⟨~ an account⟩ **b :** to even the score of (a contest) ⟨~ a ball game⟩ **6 :** to hold a quartile position respecting ⟨April, when Jupiter ~*s* his Pluto-Mars conjunction in the earthy sign of Taurus —*Time*⟩ **7 :** to mark the surface of (as a paper, a drawing) into squares — often used with *off* **8 a :** to set right **:** straighten out **:** bring into harmonious relation — used with *with* ⟨the corporation must, if it is to survive, ~ itself with the basic beliefs of the American people —E.C. Lindeman⟩ ⟨untamed feudal noble could ~ a good deal of anticlericalism with a conscience that had a . . . horror of . . . heresy —D.W.Brogan⟩ **b** (1) **:** to induce to favorable or satisfactory action or attitude by means of a bribe ⟨~ a watchman⟩ (2) **:** to settle by or as if by a bribe **:** FIX ⟨a friend in city hall can ~ the rap⟩ **~** *vi* **1 :** CONFORM, FIT — used with *with* ⟨making his story ~ with a larger independent body of ideas —Charles Frankel⟩ **2** *obs* **:** to take an opposite position **:** QUARREL — used with *with* **3 :** to settle matters; *esp* **:** to pay the bill — usu. used with *for* or *up* ⟨*squared* for his meal and left the diner⟩ ⟨~ up and go home⟩ **4 :** to take a fighting stance — often used with *up* or *off* ⟨surprised when he suddenly *squared* up to me⟩ ⟨a man *squared* off for his own pride in those days —Gene Tunney⟩ **syn** see AGREE — **square a valve :** to adjust the effective length of a slide-valve rod in a steam engine so that the valve will travel the proper distance past the steam edge of each port — **square by the lifts and braces :** to set the yards at right angles with the keel and with the mast

⁴square \"\ *adv* [²*square*] **1 :** STRAIGHTFORWARDLY, HONESTLY ⟨came ~ out with the truth⟩ ⟨always treated him ~⟩ **2 a :** so as to face or be face to face ⟨the house stood ~ to the road⟩ **b :** at right angles ⟨the path turned ~ to the left⟩ **3 :** with nothing intervening or deflecting **:** head on **:** DIRECTLY ⟨ran ~ into me⟩ ⟨coat buttoned ~ to the chin⟩ ⟨a hole lay ~ in the middle of the road⟩ **4 :** FIRMLY, SOLIDLY ⟨looked him ~ in the eye⟩ ⟨planted his great bulk ~ before his enemy⟩ **5 :** in a square shape **:** so as to form a square ⟨cut a diamond ~⟩ ⟨fold a sheet of paper ~⟩

square alphabet *n* **:** HEBREW ALPHABET 1

square and rabbet *n* **:** ANNULET

square away *vi* **1 :** to square the yards so as to sail before the wind **2 :** to put everything in order or in readiness **:** get ready ⟨is *squaring away* to write the first words of the new chapter —*Atlantic*⟩ **3 :** to take up a fighting stance ⟨a professional fighter he was being compelled to *square away* against —Hamilton Basso⟩ **~** *vt* **:** to put in order or readiness **:** make ready ⟨everything . . . is *squared away*, and satisfaction and contentment reign —W.W.Howells⟩ ⟨helped him *square away* his field scarf and button his blouse —L.M.Uris⟩

square back *n* **:** a flat backbone of a book — compare *round back*

square-backed fiddler \ˈ=ˌ=-\ *n* **:** WOOD CRAB

square body *n* **:** the part of a ship in which the frames run perpendicular to the keel — compare CANT BODY

square bracket *n* **:** ¹BRACKET 4a

square cap *n* **:** MORTARBOARD 2

square capital *n* **:** a simply and elegantly formed erect Roman capital letter used in Roman inscriptions and in the early book hand modeled in the same style without a lowercase letter form — compare CURSIVE, RUSTIC CAPITAL, UNCIAL

SQVARE

square capitals

square center *n* **:** a lathe center with a 4-sided pyramidal point

square centimeter *n* **:** a unit of area equal to a square one centimeter long on each side — see METRIC SYSTEM table

square chain *n* **:** a unit of area equal to a square one chain long on each side or 0.10 acre or 4.047 ares

square check *n* **:** CROSS-CHECK 1b

squared *past of* SQUARE

¹square dance *n* **1 :** a set dance typically danced by four couples arranged to form a hollow square — compare COUNTRY-DANCE, QUADRILLE **2 :** a social gathering for square dancing **:** HOEDOWN 2a

²square dance *vi* **:** to take part in a square dance

square dancer *n* **:** a performer or devotee of square dance

squared circle *n* **:** a boxing ring

square deal *n* **1 :** an honest and fair transaction or trade **2 :** a political program aiming at a fair consideration of the interests of all concerned

squared paper *n* **1 :** paper ruled or printed in squares **:** GRAPH PAPER **2 :** paper that has been trimmed by guillotine so as to be square on at least one corner

square-dress \ˈ=ˌ=\ *vt* **:** SWAGE-SET

square drift *n* **:** DRIFT 4e

square-drill \ˈ=ˌ=\ *vt* **:** to drill a square hole in

squared stone *n* **:** a stone roughly dressed and squared — compare ASHLAR

square edge and sound *n* **:** a specific grade of sawed timbers (as of yellow pine)

square engine *n* **:** an engine in which the stroke is equal to the diameter of the cylinder bore

squareface \ˈ=ˌ=\ *n* [so called fr. a popular name for gin in So. Africa where it was formerly sold in square bottles] **:** cheap hard liquor

squareflipper \ˈ=ˌ==\ *n* [²*square* + *flipper*] **:** BEARDED SEAL

square foot *n* **:** a unit of area equal to a square one foot long on each side — see MEASURE table

square frame *n* **:** a frame in the square body of a ship

square furlong *n* **:** a unit of area equal to a square one furlong on each side or 10 acres or 404.7 ares

square gait *n* **:** OPEN GAIT

squarehead \ˈ=ˌ=\ *n* [²*square* + *head*] **1 :** BLOCKHEAD, DOLT **2 a :** GERMAN — usu. taken to be offensive **b :** SCANDINAVIAN; *esp* **:** SWEDE — usu. taken to be offensive

square-headed \ˈ=ˌ==\ *adj* **:** having a square head ⟨a *square-headed* bolt⟩; *specif* **:** having a straight horizontal lintel or a flat arch ⟨a *square-headed* doorway⟩

square hebrew *n, cap H* **:** HEBREW ALPHABET 2

square inch *n* **:** a unit of area equal to a square one inch long on each side — see MEASURE table

square john \-ˈjän\ *n, sometimes cap J, slang* **:** a law-abiding citizen; *also* **:** one who is not addicted to dope

square joint *n* **:** STRAIGHT JOINT 2

square-jointed \ˈ=ˌ==\ *adj, of a track* **:** having the rail joints opposite

square kilometer *n* **:** a metric unit of area equal to a square that is one kilometer long on each side — see METRIC SYSTEM table

square knot *n* **:** a knot made of two reverse half-knots and used to join the ends of two cords or to tie up and bind bundles and other objects

square knotting *n* **:** knot making for decorative design — compare MACRAME

square-law \ˈ=ˌ=\ *adj* **:** designed so that one variable concerned in the operation is proportional to the square of another ⟨in a *square-law* detector tube the plate-current variations are proportional to the square of grid-voltage variations⟩

square league *n* **:** ¹LEAGUE 2

square leg *n* **:** a fielding position in cricket square with the receiving batsman and on the leg side; *also* **:** a player fielding in this position — see CRICKET illustration

square letter *n* **:** a letter having its horizontal lines at right angles to its up-and-down lines

square-lipped rhinoceros \ˈ=ˌ=-\ *n* **:** WHITE RHINOCEROS

square·ly *adv* **1 :** in a square form or manner **2 a :** in a straightforward manner **:** JUSTLY, HONESTLY ⟨dealt ~ with his customers⟩ **b :** in a straight or direct manner ⟨looked him ~ in the eyes⟩

square·man \-mən\ *n, pl* **squaremen** *Scot* **:** one who uses a square for adjusting or testing his work: as **a :** CARPENTER **b :** STONECUTTER

square mark *n* **:** a mark placed upon running lines (as halyards or braces) to ensure their being secured always at the same point and giving a neat uniform appearance

square-marked toad \ˈ=ˌ=-\ *n* **:** a widespread common toad (*Bufo regularis*) of Africa

square matrix *n, math* **:** a matrix with the number of rows and columns the same

square measure *n* **:** a unit or system of units for measuring area

square meter *n* **:** a unit of area equal to a square one meter on each side **:** CENTARE

square mile *n* **:** a unit of area equal to a square one mile long on each side — see MEASURE table

squaremouthed rhinoceros \ˈ=ˌ=-\ *n* **:** WHITE RHINOCEROS

square-necked grain beetle \ˈ=ˌ=-\ *n* **:** a small reddish beetle (*Cathartus quadricollis*) that feeds on dry cereal products — called also *red grain beetle*

square·ness *n* -ES [ME *squarenesse*, fr. ²*square* + *-nesse* -ness] **:** the quality or state of being square

square notation *n* **:** an early musical notation using square and oblong note heads

square of opposition : a square figure on which may be demonstrated the four logical oppositions by contrariety, subcontrariety, subalternation, and contradiction

square of the circle : QUADRATURE OF THE CIRCLE

square piano *n* **:** a piano having a horizontal frame, an oblong case, and strings parallel with the keyboard

square piano

¹squar·er \ˈskwa(a)rə(r), -werə-\ *n* -s [ME, fr. *squaren* to square + *-er* — more at SQUARE] **1 :** one that squares; *esp* **:** a workman who squares timber or stone **2 :** a square broach **3 :** one who obtains permission (as by offering free passes) to post on private property material advertising a coming entertainment

²squarer *comparative of* SQUARE

square rig *n* **:** a sailing-ship rig in which the sails are bent to the yards carried athwart the mast and trimmed with braces — compare FORE-AND-AFT RIG

square-rigged \ˈ=ˌ=\ *adj* **:** having or equipped with a square rig

square-rig·ger \ˈ=ˌrigə(r)\ *n* **:** a square-rigged craft

square rod *n* **:** a unit of area equal to a square one rod on a side — see MEASURE table

square root *n* **:** a factor of a number that when squared gives the number ⟨either +3 or −3 is the *square root* of 9⟩

squares *pl of* SQUARE, *pres 3d sing of* SQUARE

square sail \ˈ=ˌsəl, -ˌsāl\ *n* **:** a 4-sided sail extended on a yard suspended at the middle from a mast; *specif* **:** a sail set on a yard on the single mast or foremast of a fore-and-aft-rigged ship (as a sloop or schooner) — see SAIL illustration

square-serif \ˈ=ˌ=ˌ=\ *adj* **:** having strokes of equal weight and unbracketed serifs at right angles — used of printed letters

square set *n* **1 :** any of the rectangular sets used in the square-set system of mining **2 :** a group of four couples arranged in a square for a square dance

square set system *n* **:** a method of timbering a mine in which heavy timbers are framed together in rectangular sets 6 or 7 feet high and from 4 to 6 feet long so as to fill in as the ore body is removed by overhand stoping

square shake *n* **:** fair treatment **:** SQUARE DEAL

square shooter *n* **:** an honest person **:** one who plays fairly and justly

square-shouldered \ˈ=ˈ=ˌ=\ *adj* **:** having the shoulders high and well braced back **:** not round-shouldered

squarest *superlative of* SQUARE

square staff *n* **:** STAFF ANGLE

square stake *n* **:** a smith's stake with a square flat top — see STAKE illustration

square stance *n* **:** a golfer's stance in which both feet are parallel to the line of flight used primarily for distance shots — compare CLOSED STANCE, OPEN STANCE

square-stem \ˈ=ˌ=\ *n* **:** any of several plants with prominently angled stems: as **a :** a self-heal (*Prunella vulgaris*) **b :** OSWEGO TEA **c :** an American centaury (*Sabbatia angularis*)

square-stem spike rush \ˈ=ˌ=-\ *n* **:** a spike rush (*Eleocharis quadrangulata*) with square-angled stems

square stern *n* **1 :** a ship's stern having a transom and joining the counter timbers at an angle **2 :** a stern with no overhang

square table *n* **:** VIGENÈRE TABLEAU

squaretail \ˈ=ˌ=\ *n* **1 :** BROOK TROUT **2 :** a small dark long-bodied sluggish pelagic fish (*Tetragonurus cuvieri*) of the Atlantic, Pacific, and Mediterranean that has a compact armor of bony scales, a tail squarish in section, and flesh that is sometimes poisonous

square thread *n* **:** a screw thread so made that the sides, root, and crest of any section formed by a plane that passes through the thread axis are all equal theoretically to one half the pitch

square-thread \ˈ=ˈ=\ *vt* **:** to form a square thread on

square-tipped \ˈ=ˈ=\ *adj* **:** having the tip square

square-toed \ˈ=ˈ=\ *adj* **1 :** having the toe square ⟨*square-toed* boots⟩ **2 :** OLD-FASHIONED, CONSERVATIVE, PRIM — **square-toed·ness** *n* -ES

square up *vi* **:** to arrange one's self along with seven other dancers in a square set ready for square dance figures

square wave *n* **:** the rectangular wave form of a quantity which varies periodically and abruptly from one to the other of two uniform values

square weevil *n* **:** a So. American snout beetle (*Anthonomus vestitus*) closely related to the boll weevil

square wheel *n* **:** a wheel (of a car or locomotive) that has a flat spot on its rim

square yard *n* **:** a unit of area equal to a square one yard long on each side — see MEASURE table

squaring *pres part of* SQUARE

squaring lathe *n* **:** a lathe for shaping square pieces

squaring the circle **:** QUADRATURE OF THE CIRCLE

squar·ish \ˈskwa(a)rish, -wer-, -rēsh\ *adj* **:** somewhat square in form or appearance **:** resembling a square or block ⟨~ windows⟩ ⟨~ house⟩ — **squar·ish·ly** *adv*

[1]**squark** \ˈskwȯ(ə)rk, -ȯ(ə)k\ *n* -S [alter. of [2]*squawk*] **:** SQUAWK, CROAK

[2]**squark** \"\ *vi* -ED/-ING/-S [alter. of [1]*squawk*] **:** SQUAWK, CROAK

squar·rose \ˈskwäˌrōs, -wa,r-\ *also* **squar·rous** \-ˌrəs\ *adj* [L *squarrosus* scurfy, scabby; akin to OSlav *skvrŭna* filth] **:** rough with divergent scales or processes; *esp* **:** having stiff spreading bracts ⟨a ~ involucre⟩ — **squar·rose·ly** *adv*

squar·ru·lose \-ˌr(y)əˌlōs\ *adj* [blend of *squarrose* and *-ule*] **:** somewhat squarrose

squar·son \ˈskwärsᵊn, -wȧs-\ *n* -S [blend of *squire* and *parson*] **:** a landed proprietor who is also a clergyman of the Church of England

[1]**squash** \ˈskwäsh, -wȯ(i)sh, *substand* -wȯ(ə)rsh\ *vb* -ED/-ING/-ES [MF *esquasser*, fr. (assumed) VL *exquassare*, fr. L *ex-* [1]ex- + *quassare* to shake, break into pieces — more at QUASH] *vt* **1 :** to press or beat into a pulp or a flat mass **:** CRUSH ⟨billycock hat ~*ed* low over his forehead —Robert Graves⟩ ⟨~ a fly on the windowpane⟩ **2 a :** to put down **:** SUPPRESS ⟨~ a revolt⟩ ⟨~ a strike⟩ **b :** DISCONCERT, SQUELCH ⟨first overshadowed by . . . his father, then ~*ed* by his contemptuous, ambitious wife —*Time*⟩ ~ *vi* **1 :** to lose shape and flatten out under pressure or impact ⟨guavas . . . fell ~*ing* to the ground —Edwin Granberry⟩ **2 :** to proceed with a splashing or squelching sound ⟨~*ing* through the mud⟩ **3 :** SQUEEZE, PRESS ⟨four of us managed to ~ into the back seat⟩ **4** *of an airplane* **:** to lose altitude in a horizontal position because of loss of airspeed **:** settle vertically

[2]**squash** \"\ *n* -ES **1** *obs* **:** something soft and easily crushed; *specif* **:** an unripe pod of peas **2 :** a sudden fall of a heavy soft body or the sound of such a fall **3 :** a squelching sound made by walking on oozy ground or in water-soaked boots **4 a :** a crushed mass ⟨the crash reduced the car to ~⟩ ⟨the tomatoes have all gone to ~⟩ **b :** a bit of tissue crushed between slide and cover glass and stained in situ, used esp. for cytological study of chromosomes **5** *Brit* **:** a drink of the sweetened juice of a citrus fruit usu. with added soda water **:** ADE ⟨orange ~⟩ ⟨lemon ~⟩ **6 a** *archaic* **:** a soft rubber ball used in the game of squash rackets **b :** SQUASH RACQUETS **7 a :** a crush of people massed together **b :** a crowded social function

[3]**squash** \"\ *adv* **:** with a squash or a squashing sound ⟨you must fall ~ into a bog —Thomas Gray⟩

[4]**squash** \"\ *n, pl* **squashes** *or* **squash** [by shortening & alter. fr. earlier *isquoutersquash*, fr. Natick & Narragansett *askútasquash*, lit., green thing eaten green] **1 :** any of various fruits of plants of the genus *Cucurbita* that are widely cultivated as a vegetable and for livestock feed: as **a :** SUMMER SQUASH **b :** WINTER SQUASH **c :** PUMPKIN 1a (2) **2** *or* **squash vine :** a plant that bears squashes

[5]**squash** \"\ *n* -ES [short for *musquash*] *archaic* **:** MUSKRAT

squash beetle *n* **1 :** a small American black-and-yellow striped beetle (*Acalymma vittata*) often very injurious to the leaves of squash and cucumber **2 :** SQUASH LADYBIRD

squash·ber·ry \ˈ=- — *see* BERRY\ *n* [[4]*squash* + *berry*] **:** the fruit of any of various plants (as the dockmackie) of the genus *Viburnum*; *also* **:** the plant itself

squash bite *n* **:** an impression of the teeth and mouth made by closing the teeth on modeling composition or wax

squash blossom *n* **:** hair dressed in large loops over each ear in a fashion formerly peculiar to Hopi girls

squash borer *also* **squash vine borer** *n* **:** a small clearwing moth (*Melittia satyriniformis*) or its larva that bores in the squash vine

squash bug *n* **:** a brownish black American insect (*Anasa tristis*) of the family Coreidae that is injurious to squash vines

squash flea beetle *n* **:** POTATO FLEA BEETLE

squash blossom

squash·i·ly \-shəlē\ *adv* **:** in a squashy manner ⟨slipped and sat down ~ in the muddy path⟩

squash·i·ness \-shēnəs\ *n* -ES **:** the quality of being squashy ⟨the most repulsive larva of all in its ~ —Compton Mackenzie⟩

squash ladybird *or* **squash ladybug** *n* **:** a ladybird (*Epilachna borealis*) that feeds both as larva and imago on the squash, pumpkin, melon, and cucumber

squash racquets *or* **squash rackets** *n pl but sing in constr* **:** a strenuous singles or doubles game played in a four-wall court with a long handled racket having a small round head and a small black rubber ball with slow bounce which can be played or caromed off any number of walls provided it reaches the front wall above the telltale before hitting the floor — called also *squash;* compare SQUASH TENNIS

squash tennis *n* **:** a racket game resembling squash racquets played by two people only in a four-wall court using a lively inflated ball the size of a tennis ball which bounces very fast and requires great speed in anticipation and turning though less speed of foot and in which points are scored only by the server

squashy \-shē\ *adj* -ER/-EST [[1]*squash* + *-y*] **1 :** easily squashed **:** very soft ⟨~ pillow⟩ **2 :** softly wet **:** BOGGY **3 :** soft because overripe ⟨~ melons⟩

squash yellow *n* **:** a variable color averaging a brilliant yellow that is redder and deeper than butter yellow or average daffodil and redder and stronger than lemon chrome

[1]**squat** \ˈskwä|t *also* -wȯ|; *usu* |d· +V\ *vb* **squatted** *or* **squat; squatted** *or* **squat; squatting; squats** [ME *squatten*, fr. MF *esquater*, *esquatir*, fr. *es-* [1]ex- (fr. L *ex-*) + *quatir*, *catir* to press, fr. (assumed) VL *coactire* to press together — more at DECATING] *vt* **1 a** *obs* **:** to bruise or lay flat with a blow **b** *obs* **:** CRUSH, REPRESS, SILENCE **2 :** to cause to crouch or sit on the ground ⟨*squatted* himself down before the fire⟩ **3 :** to occupy without title or payment of rent ⟨the rest of the mews had long been *squatted* by a low-class colony of private traders —Margery Sharp⟩ ~ *vi* **1 :** to crouch close to the ground to escape observation **:** COWER ⟨*squatting* hare⟩ **2 a :** to sit on one's haunches; *specif* **:** to crouch on the ground with legs fully drawn up before the body **b :** to sit cross-legged **c :** to take or keep a balanced position with knees fully bent and heels raised **d :** to stay persistently or obstinately seated **:** sit still and do nothing ⟨however solidly the officers of the court might ~ on their chairs —Earle Birney⟩ **3 a :** to settle on land without right or title or payment of rent **b :** to settle on public land under government regulation with the purpose of acquiring title **c :** to occupy without permission an abandoned or unguarded empty house **4** *of a ship* **:** to settle by the stern when under way at speed **5** *of clay ware* **:** to soften gradually and slump down

[2]**squat** \"\ *n* -S [ME, fr. *squatten* to crush, squat] **1** *chiefly dial* **:** a heavy fall or blow **2 a :** the act of squatting, crouching, or sitting **b :** the posture of one that squats ⟨horse threw himself into a ~ —F.B.Gipson⟩ **3 a :** a place where one squats; *esp* **:** the lair of a small animal ⟨~ of a hare⟩ **b :** a piece of land claimed by a squatter **4** *dial* **a :** a small mass of ore **b :** a mineral consisting of tin ore and spar **5 :** the amount of squatting of a ship under way ⟨allowance for the well-known ~ of Great Lakes vessels when close to the bottom in narrow channels —*Survey Graphic*⟩

[3]**squat** \"\ *adj* **squat·ter; squat·test** [fr. past part. of [1]*squat*] **1 a :** bent into a sitting position typically resting the weight on the balls of the feet with the haunches close above the heels ⟨the catcher, ~ and ready for the pitch⟩ **b :** sitting on the ground with the body hunched and the legs bent ⟨sitting ~ around the fire⟩ **c :** crouching with the chest and belly close to the ground ⟨a hare ~ on the hillside⟩ **2 :** marked by closeness to the earth, lowness, or disproportionate thickness suggestive of a person squatting **:** gracelessly thick and wanting height or pleasing stature ⟨a ~ red smokestack between two stumpy masts —George Santayana⟩ **syn** see STOCKY

squat·a·ro·la \ˌskwädˌəˈrōlə, -rōlə\ *n, cap* [NL, fr. It dial., black-bellied plover] **:** a genus of birds (family Charadriidae) consisting of the black-bellied plover

squat·a·role *or* **squat·er·ole** \ˈ==ˌrōl\ *n* -S [NL *squatarola*] **:** BLACK-BELLIED PLOVER

squat board *n* **:** a horizontal plane (as a plate or extension of the hull) placed at the level of the water to prevent squatting

squat·i·na \ˈskwätᵊnə\ *n* [NL, fr. L, angelfish] **1** *cap* **:** a genus (coextensive with the family Squatinidae) of sharks having a broadly rounded head with winglike lateral extensions and a broad flattened body that resembles that of a ray and being sometimes placed in a separate suborder but usu. included in Squaloidea **2** -S **:** any shark of the genus *Squatina* **:** MONKFISH — **squat·i·nid** \-ᵊnəd\ *n or adj* — **squat·i·noid** \-ᵊnˌȯid\ *adj*

squat·ly *adv* **:** in a squat manner **:** so as to give a squat appearance ⟨building he envisioned was sort of ~ Romanesque —James Dugan⟩

squat·more \ˈskwätˌmō(ə)r\ *n* -S [[2]*squat* (fall) + *more;* prob. fr. its supposed healing effect on bruises] **:** HORNED POPPY

squat·ness *n* -ES **:** the quality of being squat

squat tag *n* **:** a game of tag in which one may escape being tagged by squatting before being touched — called also *stoop tag*

squat·tage \ˈskwädˌij\ *n* -S [[1]*squat* + *-age*] *Austral* **:** a property (as a sheep run or station) occupied by a squatter

squatted *past of* SQUAT

[1]**squat·ter** \ˈskwä|d·ə(r) |tə- *also* -wȯ|\ *vi* -ED/-ING/-S [prob. of Scand origin; akin to Sw dial. *skvättra* to squander, Dan *skvatte* to sprinkle, Icel *skvetta* to squirt] **1 :** to go along through or as if through water ⟨a school of fish . . . ~*ing* across the bay in an arrowy rush —R.A.W.Hughes⟩ **2 :** to plunge about in or as if in water

[2]**squatter** \"\ *n* -S **:** a loud fluttering noise

[3]**squat·ter** \"\ *n* -S [[1]*squat* + *-er*] **1 :** one that squats: as **a :** one that settles on land without a right or title **b :** one that settles lawfully on government land with the intention of acquiring title **2 a :** PECTORAL SANDPIPER **b :** PARTRIDGE BRONZEWING **3 a :** a person occupying crown land in Australia for sheep raising under a lease or a license; *specif* **:** one holding a sheep run as freehold **b :** the owner or occupant of a sheep run or station in Australia; *specif* **:** one farming on a large scale, coming of a good family, or having a good education

squat·ter·ism \-əˌrizəm\ *n* -S [[3]*squatter* + *-ism*] **:** the practice of acquiring land by squatting

squatter sovereignty *n* **:** POPULAR SOVEREIGNTY 2 — usu. used disparagingly

squatter's right *n* **:** a right to occupancy of or title to land based on adverse possession for the statutory period of time

squatting *pres part of* SQUAT

squat·tish \ˈskwädˌish\ *adj* **:** somewhat squat

squat·tle \ˈskwädᵊl\ *vi* [freq. of [1]*squat*] *archaic* **:** SQUAT, SETTLE

squat·toc·ra·cy \skwädˈäkrəsē\ *n* -ES [[1]*squat* + *-o-* + *-cracy*] **:** the wealthy and influential owners of sheep ranches in Australia ⟨were dependent upon the emerging ~ and the more highly paid government officials —Bernard Smith⟩

squat·ty \ˈskwä|d·ē, |t|, |i *also* -wȯ|\ *adj, sometimes* -ER/-EST [[3]*squat* + *-y*] **:** somewhat squat **:** DUMPY, THICKSET

squat vault *n* **:** a gymnastic vault in which the body is supported on both hands, the knees are flexed and drawn up toward the chest, and the legs pass between the arms as the body passes over the apparatus

squaw \ˈskwȯ\ *n* -S [of Algonquian origin; akin to Natick *squa* female creature, *squàas* woman, Narragansett *squàws*] **1 a :** an American Indian woman — compare SANNUP **b :** FEMALE, WOMAN, WIFE — usu. used disparagingly **2 :** an effeminate person **:** a man of womanish character — usu. used disparagingly **3 :** a form for holding a barrel during the process of crozing and chiming **4 :** a figure target representing a kneeling posture

squaw·ber·ry \ˈ=- — *see* BERRY\ *n* [prob. so called fr. the use of the twigs among the Indians in basketry work] **1 :** DEERBERRY 1 **2 :** PARTRIDGEBERRY 1 **3 :** any of several sumacs; *esp* **:** SQUAWBUSH 2

squawbush \ˈ=ˌ=\ *n* [so called fr. the use of the berries among Indians as a mordant in dyeing] **1 :** CRANBERRY TREE **2 :** a sumac (*Rhus trilobata*) of western No. America with unpleasantly scented trifoliolate or sometimes simple leaves and edible fruit **3 :** any of several shrubs of the genus *Cornus* **4 :** DWARF CORNEL

squaw cabbage *n* **1 :** INDIAN LETTUCE 3 **2 :** any of various plants of the family Cruciferae and esp. of the genera *Caulanthus* and *Streptanthus* believed to have been used as potherbs by the Indians

squaw carpet *n* **1 :** MAHALA MAT **2 :** MOUNTAIN MISERY

squaw corn *n* [so called fr. its extensive cultivation by the American Indians] **:** SOFT CORN 1

squaw currant *n* **:** a spineless shrub (*Ribes cereum*) native to the central and western U. S. having greenish white flowers and a crimson berry

squaw dance *n* **:** a round dance of the Plains Indians and Navaho in which the girls select partners

squaw-drops \ˈ=ˌ=\ *n pl but sing in constr* **1 :** CANCERROOT **2 :** SQUAWROOT 1

squaw duck *n* **:** EIDER

squawfish \ˈ=ˌ=\ *n* **1 :** any of several large cyprinid fishes (genus *Ptychocheilus*) of western No. America: as **a :** a dull-green silver-marked fish (*P. oregonensis*) of the Columbia river **b :** a closely related and nearly indistinguishable fish (*P. grandis*) of central and northern California and parts of the Colorado river system — called also *Sacramento pike* **2 :** a common surf fish (*Taeniotoca lateralis*) of the Pacific coast of No. America

squawflower \ˈ=ˌ=\ *n* **:** PURPLE TRILLIUM

squaw grass *n* **:** a turkey beard (*Xerophyllum tenax*) of the mountains of the Pacific northwest having small white or cream-colored flowers in many-flowered racemes — called also *pine lily*

squaw hitch *n* [prob. so called fr. its use among the Indians] **:** a knot used in tying a pack on an animal

squaw huckleberry *n* **:** DEERBERRY 1

[1]**squawk** \ˈskwȯk\ *vi* -ED/-ING/-S [prob. blend of [1]*squall* and [1]*squeak*] **1 :** to make a loud harsh abrupt raucous outcry ⟨the hens woke up ~*ing* with terror —George Orwell⟩ **2 :** to complain or protest loudly or vehemently or objectionably ⟨his fellow profs . . . ~*ed* about the bonfires the boys built —Christopher Morley⟩ **syn** see COMPLAIN

[2]**squawk** \"\ *n* -S **1 :** the act or noise of squawking **:** a harsh squall ⟨~ of auto horns⟩ ⟨~ of a parrot⟩ **2 :** a noisy, raucous complaint **:** an undignified protest ⟨~*s* of taxpayers⟩ ⟨~*s* from motorists . . . that they have been gypped on speeding charges —*N.Y. Times*⟩ **3 :** BLACK-CROWNED NIGHT HERON

squawk box *n* **:** an intercommunication system speaker **:** LOUDSPEAKER ⟨the *squawk box* announced the kid was circling the ship —*Newsweek*⟩ ⟨interrupted me by buzzing the interoffice *squawk box* —Albert Morgan⟩

squawk duck *n* **:** a duck with brownish spots before and behind the eyes that is a hybrid of the mallard and teal or of the mallard and widgeon

squawk·er \-kə(r)\ *n* -S **:** one that squawks: as **a :** a toy that makes a squawking sound **b :** DUCK CALL **c :** one that complains or protests noisily **d :** INFORMER 3 **e :** SQUAWK BOX

squawking thrush *n* **:** MISTLE THRUSH

squawk sheet *n* **:** a report made out by a pilot listing defects observed in an airplane during the flight

squawky \-kē\ *adj* -ER/-EST [[2]*squawk* + *-y*] **:** HARSH, DISCORDANT, RAUCOUS

squawl *var of* SQUALL

squaw lettuce *n* **:** a waterleaf (*Hydrophyllum occidentale*) of the southwestern U. S. having flowers on stalks that are longer than the leaf stalks and that bear one or two heads of flowers

squaw man *n* **1 :** a white man married to an Indian woman and usu. living as one of her tribe **2 :** BARDASH

squaw mint *n* **:** PENNYROYAL 2

squaw·mish *or* **squa·mish** \ˈskwȯmish\ *n, pl* **squawmish** *or* **squawmishes** *or* **squamish** *or* **squamishes** *usu cap* **1 a :** a Salishan people of the British Columbia coast opposite Vancouver Island **b :** a member of such people **2 :** the language of the Squawmish people

squawroot \ˈ=ˌ=\ *n* [so called fr. its use among Indians as a remedy for female disorders] **1 :** a No. American scaly herb (*Conopholis americana*) that is parasitic on oak and hemlock and has a thick stem with yellow fleshy scales bearing small flowers in their axils **2 :** BLUE COHOSH **3 :** PURPLE TRILLIUM **4 :** YAMP

squaws *pl of* SQUAW

squaw sachem *n* **:** a woman who is a sachem or the wife of a sachem

squaw side *n* [so called fr. the custom among the squaws of some tribes of mounting from the right side of a horse] **:** the right side of a horse

squaw vine *n* **:** PARTRIDGEBERRY 1

squaw-weed \ˈ=ˌ=\ *n* **1 :** RAGWORT **2 :** WHITE SNAKEROOT **3** *also* **squaw waterweed :** PENNYROYAL 2 **4 :** SQUAWBUSH 2 **5 :** HORSEWEED 1

squaw winter *n* [so called fr. the fact that it often precedes Indian summer] **:** a brief early period of wintry weather occurring in the autumn

squaw wood *n* [so called fr. the fact that squaws could gather it since an axe was not needed] **:** the small dead limbs or branches under the live canopy of a tree

squax·on \ˈskwȯksən\ *n, pl* **squaxon** *or* **squaxons** *usu cap* **1 a :** a Salishan people of the southwest Puget sound area, Washington **b :** a member of such people **2 :** a dialect related to Skagit

squdge \ˈskwəj\ *vi* -ED/-ING/-S [prob. imit.] **1 :** OOZE ⟨black mud *squdging* up between their bare toes —M.O.Williams⟩ **2 :** to slosh around (as in ooze or mud)

squdgy \-jē\ *adj, sometimes* -ER/-EST [blend of [3]*squat* and *pudgy*] **:** SQUAT, PUDGY ⟨a ~, ill-shaped body —Carleton Beals⟩

[1]**squeak** \ˈskwēk\ *vb* -ED/-ING/-S [ME *squeken*, prob. of imit. origin] *vi* **1 :** to utter or make a short shrill cry or noise ⟨heard the door . . . ~ upon its wooden hinges —Pearl Buck⟩ ⟨a long lean individual who ~*ed* with a nasal twang —H.A. Chippendale⟩ **2 :** to reveal a secret from or as if from fear of punishment **:** commit an act of betrayal ⟨if somebody ~*ed*, he was quickly smothered and gagged —F.N.Souza⟩ **3 :** to pass, succeed, or win by a narrow margin ⟨his party barely ~*ed* through in congress —G.W.Johnson⟩ ⟨by six months of hard cramming . . . he ~*ed* by the finals —H.H.Martin⟩ **:** barely manage to get by ⟨still ~*ing* by on the manpower available —*Newsweek*⟩ ~ *vt* **:** to utter in a shrill piping tone

[2]**squeak** \"\ *n* -S **1 a :** a sharp shrill usu. short and not very loud cry or sound of the human voice or of an animal ⟨gave a startled ~ as he entered —J.H.Wheelwright⟩ **b :** a sharp shrill piercing noise ⟨the ~ of oars in oarlocks —*New Yorker*⟩ ⟨the ~ and crunch of walking boots on powdery snow —Alan Devoe⟩ **2 a :** CHANCE, OPPORTUNITY ⟨gave him one more ~⟩ **b :** ESCAPE ⟨finally quashed by a 5 to 4 vote . . . a close ~ —H.R.Medina⟩ — usu. used in the phrase *have a narrow squeak* ⟨you've had a narrow ~, but we've pulled you through —O.Henry⟩

squeak·er \-kə(r)\ *n* -S **1 :** one that squeaks: as **a** (1) **:** a young pigeon **:** SQUAB — usu. used of racing pigeons (2) **:** a predominantly gray currawong (*Strepera versicolor*) **b** *Brit* **:** a young pig **c :** any of several African freshwater armored catfishes **d :** a rat kangaroo of the genus *Bettongia* **e :** a noisemaker or a toy instrument that squeaks **f** *Brit* **:** one that betrays **:** INFORMER **2 :** a contest won by a small margin ⟨pitched a 5 to 4 ten-inning ~⟩

squeaky \-kē, -ki\ *adj* -ER/-EST **:** of the nature of, emitting, or tending to emit squeaks ⟨his off-key ~ voice —Lynn Montross⟩ ⟨a ~ door⟩

[1]**squeal** \ˈskwēl, *esp before pause or consonant* -ēəl\ *vb* -ED/-ING/-S [ME *squelen*, prob. of imit. origin] *vi* **1 a :** to cry with a sharp shrill prolonged sound ⟨horses ~*ed* with terror —Kenneth Roberts⟩ ⟨the bird ~*ed* as if in sudden pain —E.A. Armstrong⟩ ⟨~ with delight⟩ **b :** to emit a usu. loud and prolonged shrill piercing noise ⟨chalk ~*ing* on a slate —John Lardner⟩ ⟨heard the brakes ~⟩ **2 a :** to turn informer **:** SQUEAK ⟨he trusted me and I ~*ed* —*Best True Fact Detective*⟩ — usu. used with *on* ⟨marked for death by other prisoners because . . . he ~*ed* on them —*Springfield (Mass.) Union*⟩ **b :** COMPLAIN, PROTEST ⟨individual interests . . . getting hurt . . . are apt to ~ —Bertrum Mycock⟩ ~ *vt* **:** to utter or express with or as if with a squeal ⟨pigs . . . ~ emphatic disapproval of their enforced journey —Leslie Stephen⟩

[2]**squeal** \"\ *n* -S **:** a shrill sharp somewhat prolonged cry or noise; *specif* **:** HOWL 5

squeal·er \-ēlə(r)\ *n* -S **:** one that squeals: as **a :** a European swift (*Apus apus* syn. *Micropus apus*) **b :** HARLEQUIN DUCK **c :** an American golden plover (*Pluvialis dominica*) **d :** a young squab pigeon **e** *dial* **:** WOOD DUCK 1 **f :** a young grouse, partridge, or quail **g :** INFORMER, BETRAYER

squeam \ˈskwēm\ *n* -S [back-formation fr. *squeamish*] **:** QUALM

squea·mish \'skwēmish, -mēsh\ *adj* [ME *squaymisch*, alter. of *squaymous, esquaymous*, fr. AF *escoymous, escoymos*] **1 a :** having or being a stomach easily nauseated ⟨some babies seem to be born more ~ about lumps than others —Benjamin Spock⟩ **b :** inclined to become nauseated : QUEASY, QUALMISH **c :** affected with nausea : NAUSEATED ⟨the violent movement of the ship . . . made me quite ~ —Jack London⟩ **2** *obs* **:** evincing distaste for familiarity : DISTANT, COLD **3 a :** inclined to be easily shocked or offended : PRUDISH **b :** characterized by great or excessive fastidiousness or scrupulousness in conduct or belief ⟨if he were to remain in politics he mustn't be ~ —M.R.Werner⟩ **c :** characterized by extreme fastidiousness about mental or esp. physical surroundings ⟨the mysterious horror of his paintings is heightened by the spellbinding richness of his pigments, and even the ~ do not easily turn away —J.T.Soby⟩ ⟨most psychologists have now abolished the mind and are a little ~ talking about the psyche —A.L. Kroeber⟩ **syn** see NICE

squea·mish·ly *adv* **:** in a squeamish manner

squea·mish·ness *n* -ES **:** the quality or state of being squeamish

squeamy \'skwēmē, -mi\ *adj* -ER/-EST [*squeam* + *-y*] **:** SQUEAMISH

¹squee·gee \'skwē,jē *sometimes* ='= *also* **squil·gee** \" *sometimes* 'skwil,je *or* ='= *or* **squil·la·gee** \'skwilə,je, ,=='= \ *n* -S [prob. imit.] **1 :** a device that consists of a handle and a transverse piece at one end set with a blade of leather or rubber and is used for spreading, pushing, or wiping liquid material on, across, or off a surface (as a pavement, windowpane, or deck) **2 a :** a device constructed like a small squeegee and used (as by a photographer or lithographer) for wiping off excess moisture, transferring material evenly to a surface, or forcing ink, paint, or dye through a stencil or screen **b** *or* **squeegee roller :** a small rubber or plastic roller with a handle used esp. in printing and photography as a squeegee

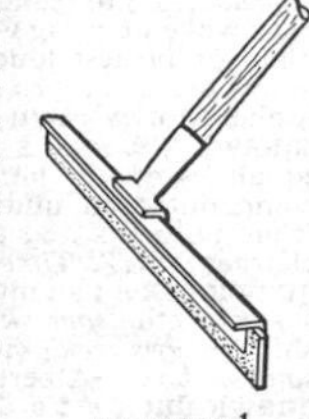
squeegee 1

²squeegee \"\ *vt* **squeegeed; squeegeed; squeegeeing; squeegees :** to smooth, press, or wipe, spread, or remove with or as if with a squeegee (as when removing excess water or solution from the surface of a photographic film or paper)

squeez·abil·i·ty \,skwēzə'bilәd·ē\ *n* **:** the quality of being squeezable

squeez·able \'skwēzәbәl\ *adj* **:** capable of being squeezed; *specif* **:** easily subject to coercion or extortion — **squeez·able·ness** *n* -ES

¹squeeze \'skwēz\ *vb* **squeezed** \-zd\ *or dial* **squoze** \-wōz\ **squeezed** *or dial* **squoze; squeezing; squeezes** [earlier *squease*, alter. of obs. E *quease* to press, squeeze, fr. ME *queysen*, fr. OE *cwȳsan*; akin to Icel *kveisa* stomach cramps] *vt* **1 a** (1) **:** to exert pressure esp. on opposite sides or parts of : press together closely or tightly : COMPRESS ⟨nothing to do . . . but ~ my friends' knees and drink my wine —Kenneth Roberts⟩ ⟨air that had been *squeezed* up so tight that he could not even move his hand through it very easily —J.B.S.Haldane⟩ (2) **:** HUG (3) **:** to pull back on (a trigger) with a steady slow pressure of the finger **b :** to cause to press upon an object ⟨*squeezed* the upper die smoothly down on the blank —John Craig⟩ **c** (1) **:** to extract or emit under pressure ⟨~ the juice from a lemon⟩ ⟨volcanoes formed by lava *squeezed* out of the earth in an exceedingly viscous condition —Howel Williams⟩ (2) **:** to bring into a specified state by or as if by pressure ⟨~ total budgetary outlays two to five billion dollars below the present level —Cabell Phillips⟩ (3) **:** to force, thrust, or cause to pass by pressure ⟨*squeezes* his hand into the hole and grasps the prize —James Stevenson-Hamilton⟩ **2 a** (1) **:** to gain (as valuables, services, or advantages) by extortionary means ⟨come to ~ his land from him in his extremity —Pearl Buck⟩ (2) **:** to force money, goods, or services from by extortionary means : OPPRESS ⟨to ~ the peasants, collectivization has been imposed at great cost —*N. Y. Times*⟩ **b :** to cause economic hardship to ⟨breaks in the supply line from the mainland periodically ~ the islanders —*N. Y. Times*⟩ ⟨not . . . let the farmer be *squeezed* by lowered farm prices and high fixed costs —E.T. Benson⟩ **c :** to reduce the amount of (profits) ⟨climbing cost of cotton *squeezes* mill profits —*Wall Street Jour.*⟩ **3 :** to gain or procure as if by pressure : gain by hard work, adroit maneuvering, close attention to costs, or clever or dubious interpretation of facts ⟨the discount operator can ~ a profit out of a tiny markup —*Advertising Age*⟩ ⟨hard-working farmers ~ the last ounce from their holdings —T.H.Fielding⟩ ⟨thought that no new information can be *squeezed* from the premises of a syllogism —W.F.Doney⟩ **4 a :** to crowd into or within a narrow area : cause to appear squeezed ⟨a single street *squeezed* between the railroad and the canal —*Amer. Guide Series: Md.*⟩ ⟨a small garage, into which, by much maneuvering, he could manage to ~ eight cars —*General Motors Builds Its First 50 Million Cars*⟩ **b :** to provide room, time, or opportunity for within a narrow compass ⟨brought before the courts every single case he could possibly ~ within its provisions —Richard Hayward⟩ — often used with *in* ⟨somewhere in this crowded early life . . . managed to ~ in three years of piano lessons —Gilbert Millstein⟩ **5 :** to gain or win by a narrow margin ⟨just barely *squeezed* out controlling margins in the two houses of Congress —Cabell Phillips⟩ **6 :** to constrain (another player) to discard in bridge so as to unguard a suit **7 a :** to score (a run) by means of a squeeze play **b :** to bring home (a runner) from third base by means of a squeeze play **~** *vi* **1 :** to give way before pressure ⟨the corners of a gray cushion *squeezed* out around his fat back —Earle Birney⟩ **2 a :** to exert physical pressure **b :** to exert economic pressure ⟨would take at least two months for a strike to begin to ~ —*Newsweek*⟩; *specif* **:** to practice extortion or oppression **3 a :** to force a passage : make one's way by pressing ⟨we can all three ~ into my buggy —Ellen Glasgow⟩ ⟨a very stout lady, who could hardly ~ through the door —Fernando Sabino⟩ **b** (1) **:** to ease an automotive vehicle into another traffic lane esp. in preparation for a narrowed pavement ⟨~ to the right⟩ (2) **:** to ease into another traffic lane **4 :** to pass, succeed, gain a victory, or get by narrowly ⟨probably could ~ through the next five months of lean tax collections —*N. Y. Times*⟩ ⟨a measure *squeezed* through both houses —R.A. Billington⟩ **syn** see PRESS — **squeeze the shorts :** to put shorts under pressure to cover their commitments at higher prices (as by making stocks difficult to borrow or by spreading reports of a crop failure in commodities)

²squeeze \"\ *n* -S **1 a :** an act or instance of squeezing : a firm usu. steady and gradually increasing compression of an object esp. between two forces ⟨they give a ~ — not a slap — and exert maximum power only at the end of the stroke⟩ ⟨trigger ~⟩ **b :** a pressing of one person's hand by another's ⟨friendly hands . . . grasping our pencil-cramped fingers, and giving them a firm ~ and a hearty shake —*Phoenix Flame*⟩; *also* **:** HUG **c** (1) **:** the gradual closing of a mine working by the settling of the overlying strata (2) **:** a mine area undergoing a squeeze **d :** pressure or forcing caused by the shoving and crowding of a mass of people ⟨with one final ~, the crowd behind them pushed them along out of the gate —Dorothy C. Fisher⟩ **e :** the pressure with which paper is held against an inked printing surface esp. in a printing press **f :** the shrinkage in bulk of set type when subjected to the pressure of the quoins in locking up ⟨the compositor comes to know just how much allowance he should make for ~ —R.W.Polk⟩ **g :** BAROTRAUMA **2 a :** a quantity squeezed or pressed out from something ⟨a ~ of lemon⟩ **b :** a group crowded together : CROWD ⟨a ~ of people —Emily Hahn⟩; *esp* **:** a crowded social gathering ⟨dinners, card parties, teas, . . . and ~s —C.G. Bowers⟩ **c :** a facsimile impression of an object made in a plastic substance by forcing it into the depressions of the object **3** *Brit* **:** NECK **4** *Brit* **:** an article made of silk : SILK **5 a :** a commission charged by an oriental servant for service ⟨the servant won't let the salesman into the house unless he gets his ~ —*Harper's*⟩ **b** (1) **:** an undercover but usu. recognized and tolerated profit made esp. by an oriental official or middleman on goods or valuables passing through his hands, by an official on government financial transactions, or by anyone in a position that readily lends itself to exploitation (2) **:** GRAFT **c :** the practice of extorting squeeze ⟨resorted to ~ as a means of bringing their income more into proportion to what it cost them to stay alive —Virginia A. Oakes⟩; *also* **:** pressure applied to obtain squeeze ⟨the customary ~ applied to . . . merchants —Darrell Berrigan⟩ **6 a :** an act or instance of squeezing the shorts **b :** financial pressure caused by a narrowing spread between two factors ⟨the ~ between low wages and high prices⟩ ⟨a ~ between high costs and stable selling prices⟩ **c** (1) **:** hardship, inconvenience, or difficulty caused by a shortage ⟨manpower ~⟩ ⟨housing ~⟩ or a tightening of fiscal controls or a withholding of assets ⟨credit ~⟩ or an economic blockade ⟨put a ~ on the city by strict inspection of entering transport⟩ (2) **:** the exploitation of hardship or inconvenience caused by a squeeze to gain an advantage **d** (1) **:** a play or situation in bridge in which one is squeezed — compare END PLAY (2) **:** a situation in canasta or rummy in which one must break up a valuable combination in order to retain a safe discard **e :** SQUEEZE PLAY **7 :** a device for applying pressure or restraint: as **a** *slang* **:** a secret braking device for controlling a wheel of fortune **b :** a device for restraining cattle in a branding chute

squeeze bottle *n* **:** a bottle of flexible plastic that dispenses its contents by being pressed

squeeze–box \'=,=\ *n* **:** ACCORDION

squeeze off *vt* **:** to fire (a round) by squeezing the trigger **~** *vi* **:** to fire a weapon by squeezing the trigger ⟨took a hard aim at the beast's shoulder and *squeezed off* —Edison Marshall⟩

squeeze play *n* **1 :** a prearranged baseball play used when there are less than two outs in which a runner on third base starts for home plate as the ball is being pitched and the batter attempts to bunt to give the runner time to score **2 :** the act or an instance of bringing pressure to bear in order to extort a concession or gain a goal : SQUEEZE ⟨was the victim of a *squeeze play* engineered by his foes . . . and was forced to resign —L.A.Huston⟩

squeez·er \'skwēzә(r)\ *n* -S **1 a :** one that squeezes **b :** a mechanical contrivance that squeezes: as (1) **:** a device for pressing juice from fruit or vegetables ⟨lemon ~⟩ (2) **:** a wire-testing device somewhat like a lemon squeezer in which the wire is subjected to successive bendings until it breaks (3) **:** a pivoted lever device with an eccentric curved end used to curve metal bars or plates (4) **:** a machine for molding bricks (5) **:** a machine for shingling by squeezing — often used in pl.; see CROCODILE SQUEEZER (6) **:** a device for softening and compressing a cork to fit the mouth of a bottle **c :** one that operates a squeezer **2 :** a playing card on which the value and suit are indicated in the upper left-hand corner

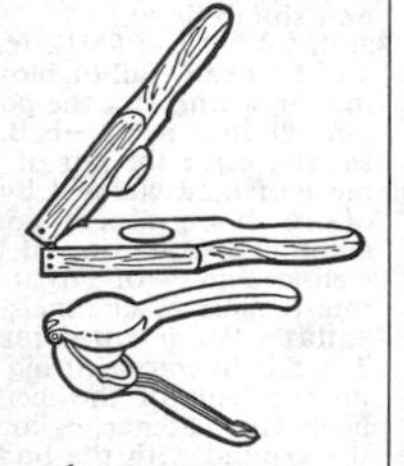
lemon squeezers

squeeze roll *n* **:** one of a pair of rollers designed to exert pressure on material passing between them

squeezes *pres 3d sing of* SQUEEZE, *pl of* SQUEEZE

squeeze track *n* **:** a photographic sound track of the variable density type whose width is manually varied to reduce noise

squeeze–up \'=,=\ *n* -S [fr. *squeeze up*, v.] **:** a rock formation believed to have been squeezed up by volcanic pressure

squeezing *n* -S [fr. gerund of ¹*squeeze*] **1 :** the action of one that squeezes **2 a :** something that is squeezed out or only to be forced out by or as if by squeezing **b :** DREGS — usu. used in pl. **3 :** SQUEEZE 2c

squeezy \'skwēzē\ *adj* -ER/-EST [²*squeeze* + *-y*] **:** accompanied by or suggestive of squeezing; *specif* **:** CRAMPED, CONFINED

squeg \'skweg\ *vi* **squegged; squegged; squegging; squegs** [back-formation fr. *squegger* tube in which the valve oscillates, fr. *squegg-* (blend of *squeeze* and *wedge*) + *-er*; fr. the oscillation's being a form of blocking of the grid] **:** to oscillate in a highly irregular fashion esp. from too much unwanted feedback — used of an electronic system

¹squelch \'skwelch\ *n* -ES [imit.] **1 a :** BLOW, BUFFET **b :** a dull heavy sound of or as if of a blow upon a soft body : THUD ⟨he heard . . . the ~ of turf as she ran toward him —Elizabeth Taylor⟩ **2 :** a sound of or as if of semiliquid matter under suction ⟨the ~ of mud⟩ **3 a :** the act or an instance of suppressing ⟨the producer . . . boldly ignored the ~ and went right ahead . . . in defiance of the industry's rules —Bosley Crowther⟩; *esp* **:** SQUELCHER **b** *or* **squelch circuit :** a circuit in an electronic receiver that cuts off the receiver entirely if the useful signal falls to too low a value and thereby avoids a situation where high noise signals are generated in the absence of wanted signals

²squelch \"\ *vb* -ED/-ING/-ES *vt* **1 a :** to fall or stamp on so as to crush : crush by weight dropped or pressed from above **b** (1) **:** to completely suppress : QUELL ⟨a spirit here which a thousand years of misery had not ~*ed* —Henry Miller⟩ ⟨only three amendments were suggested . . . and each was ~*ed* after a brief word —Dorothy Kahn⟩ (2) **:** SILENCE ⟨presiding at board meetings . . . and ~*ing* shareholders in the middle of sentences —P.G.Wodehouse⟩ **2 :** to cause to emit or move with a sucking sound ⟨their broken shoes ~*ing* water —Marcia Davenport⟩ **~** *vi* **1 :** to emit a sound typical of an object being forcefully withdrawn from mire against the resistance of trapped air : emit a sucking or splashing sound ⟨have manure in my shoes and hear it ~ as I walked —Dylan Thomas⟩ **2 :** to move or proceed splashily in water, slush, or mire or with water or mud in one's shoes and produce a sucking or splashing sound ⟨~ through a miry farm gateway —Adrian Bell⟩ ⟨his feet inside the sodden seaboots ~*ed* icily whenever he moved —Nicholas Monsarrat⟩

squelch·er \-chә(r)\ *n* -S **:** one that squelches; *esp* **:** a retort that eliminates any possible reply

squelchy \-chē\ *adj* -ER/-EST [²*squelch* + *-y*] **:** likely to make a squelching sound : SOFT, PULPY

squench \'skwench\ *vb* [alter. of ¹*quench*] *dial* **:** QUENCH

squet \'skwet\ *n* -S [by shortening] **:** SQUETEAGUE

sque·teague *or* **squi·teague** \skwә'tēg\ *also* **sque·tee** \-ē\ *n, pl* **squeteague** *or* **squiteague** *also* **squetee** [Narraganset *pesukwiteaug*, pl., lit., they make glue; fr. the practice of making glue from swimming bladders of weakfish] **:** GRAY TROUT 1; *also* **:** any of various other weakfishes — usu. used with a qualifying term; see SILVER SQUETEAGUE

¹squib \'skwib\ *n* -S [origin unknown] **1 a :** a small firecracker **b :** a broken firecracker the powder in which burns with a fizz **2 a** (1) **:** a small electric or pyrotechnic device used to ignite a charge (2) **:** a similar device to fire an igniter in a rocket **b :** a small explosive charge used to fire a larger one : DETONATOR **3 a :** a short humorous, satiric, or lampooning writing or speech ⟨the subject of . . . some extremely ribald versified ~s —R.O.Altick⟩ **b :** a short carelessly written piece : SCRIBBLE ⟨continued to send ~s of one sort or another to the newspapers —J.W.Krutch⟩ **c :** FILLER 1d(1) ⟨his deeds and misdeeds hardly would have rated a ~ among the used-car ads —*Newsweek*⟩ **4** *chiefly Brit* **:** an insignificant or cowardly person

²squib \"\ *vb* **squibbed; squibbed; squibbing; squibs** *vi* **1 :** to speak, write, or publish squibs : dispute pettily **2 :** to fire or squirt a squib **~** *vt* **1 a :** to utter in an offhand manner **b :** to make squibs against : LAMPOON **2 :** to shoot off : FIRE

squib·bery \'skwibәrē\ *n* -ES [¹*squib* + *-ery*] **:** the utterance or composition of squibs

squib·bish \-bish\ *adj* **:** somewhat like a squib

¹squid \'skwid\ *n, pl* **squid** *or* **squids** [origin unknown] **1 :** any of numerous 10-armed cephalopods typically having a long tapered body and a caudal fin on each side; *esp* **:** a cephalopod of *Loligo, Ommastrephes*, or a related genus that has the shell reduced to an internal chitinous structure shaped like a pen, often occurs in great schools, and is often used as fish bait and in many areas as food — see ARCHITEUTHIS, DIBRANCHIA; compare CUTTLEFISH **2 a :** bait prepared from a squid **b :** an artificial lure made in imitation of the natural squid used when trolling for tuna **3 :** a usu. metal weighted lure cast when surf fishing **4 :** a many-barreled antisubmarine weapon that fires charges ahead of a ship

²squid \"\ *vi* **squidded; squidded; squidding; squids 1 :** to fish with or for squid **2 :** to cast with a squid lure; *specif* **:** to cast and retrieve a squid lure with rod and reel

squid·der \-d(ә)r\ *n* -S [²*squid* + *-er*] **:** a surf caster who uses artificial lures rather than natural bait

squidge \'skwij\ *n* -S [imit.] **:** SQUELCH 2

squidgy \-jē\ *adj* -ER/-EST [*squidge* + *-y*] **:** unpleasantly damp : CLAMMY ⟨fishermen in ~ rubber boots —Mary H. Vorse⟩ ⟨in the steamy atmosphere my skin had grown ~ as a toad's —Francis Kingdon-Ward⟩

squid hound *n* **:** STRIPED BASS

squid–jigger \'=,==\ *n* -S **:** a group of fishhooks fastened together with radiating points for catching squid

squid–jigging \'=,==\ *n* -S **:** the act or practice of hooking squid with a squid-jigger

squiffed \'skwift\ *or* **squiffy** \-fē, -fi\ *adj* [origin unknown] **:** INTOXICATED, DRUNK

¹squig·gle \'skwigәl\ *vb* **squiggled; squiggled; squiggling** \-g(ә)liŋ\ **squiggles** [blend of ¹*squirm* and ¹*wriggle*] *vi* **1 :** SQUIRM, WRIGGLE **2 :** to write or paint hastily : make scribbles **~** *vt* **1 :** SCRIBBLE ⟨didn't have time to ~ his mark on his correspondence —Bruce Bliven b. 1916⟩ **2 :** to cause to form or form in squiggles

²squiggle \"\ *n* -S **:** a short wavy twist or line : CURL, CURLICUE; *esp* **:** an esp. illegible hastily written bit of handwriting : SCRAWL, SCRIBBLE

squig·gly \-g(ә)lē, -li\ *adj* **:** WRIGGLING, WAVY, TWISTING

squilgee *or* **squillagee** *var of* SQUEEGEE

squill \'skwil\ *n* -S [ME, fr. L *squilla, scilla*, fr. Gk *skilla*] **1 a** (1) **:** a bulbous herb (*Urginea maritima*) of southern Europe and northern Africa that is sometimes grown in gardens for its long racemes of small white flowers — called also *sea onion*; see RED SQUILL (2) **:** any of several other plants of the genus *Urginea* (3) **:** the bulbs of a squill (esp. *U. maritima*) **b :** a plant of the genus *Scilla* **2 a :** the cut and dried fleshy inner scales of the bulb of the white-rooted form of the squill (*Urginea maritima*) or of the younger bulb of a related plant (*U. indica*) of the Orient that contain one or more physiologically active glycosides and are used as an expectorant, cardiac stimulant, and diuretic **b :** RED SQUILL 2 **3** [NL *Squilla*] **:** a crustacean of the genus *Squilla*

squil·la \'skwilә\ *n* [NL, fr. L, a small lobster, squill] **1** *cap* **:** a genus (the type of the family Squillidae) of stomatopod crustaceans that burrow in mud or beneath stones in shallow water along the seashore **2** *pl* **squillas** *or* **squil·lae** \-i,lē, -i,lī\ *also* **squilla :** any crustacean of *Squilla* or a related genus — called also *mantis prawn*

squill blue *n* **:** a light blue that is greener and duller than average forget-me-not (sense 2a) or della Robbia blue — called also *Diana*

squil·lid \'skwilәd\ *n* -S [NL *Squillidae*] **:** a stomatopod crustacean of the genus *Squilla* or family Squillidae

squil·li·dae \'skwilә,dē\ *n pl, cap* [NL, fr. *Squilla*, type genus + *-idae*] **:** a family of stomatopod crustaceans — see SQUILLA

squil·loi·dea \skwә'lȯidēә\ [NL, fr. *Squilla* + *-oidea*] *syn of* STOMATOPODA

squin·a·cy \'skwinәsi, -wēn-\ *n* -ES [ME *swinacie, squinacy* quinsy, modif. of OF *esquinancie, squinancie* quinsy] *dial Brit* **:** PERITONSILLAR ABSCESS

squin·an·cy \-nә(n)si\ *n* -ES [ME, quinsy, fr. MF *esquinancie, squinancie*, fr. OF, alter. (influenced by Gk *synanchē* sore throat, fr. *syn-* + *anchein* to strangle) of *quinancie* quinsy, fr. LL *cynanche* — more at ANGER, QUINSY] **1** *obs* **:** PERITONSILLAR ABSCESS **2 :** a European perennial herb (*Asperula cynanchica*) with narrowly linear whorled leaves formerly thought to cure peritonsillar abscess

¹squinch \'skwinch\ *n* -ES [alter. of obs. E *scunch* sconcheon, short for E *scuncheon*] **1 :** a support (as an arch, lintel, or corbeling) carried across the corner of a room under a superimposed mass (as an octagonal spire or drum resting upon a square tower) — compare PENDENTIVE **2 :** HAGIOSCOPE

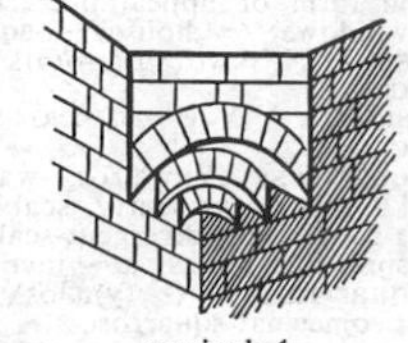
squinch 1

²squinch \"\ *vb* -ED/-ING/-ES [prob. blend of ²*squint* and ¹*pinch*] *vt* **1 a :** to contort (as the face) as a signal or as an involuntary sign (as of pain) **b :** to forcefully but partially screw shut (the eyes) ⟨eyes, permanently ~*ed* against the sun —William Humphrey⟩ **2 :** to compress into a smaller bulk : make more compact **~** *vi* **1 :** FLINCH **2 :** to cause oneself or an object to take up less room ⟨he ~*ed* back in one corner —J.B.Clayton⟩ **3 :** SQUINT ⟨the fire so low she ~*ed* to see —R.P.Warren⟩

³squinch \"\ *adj* **:** characterized or affected by squinching: **a :** SQUINTED ⟨~ eye⟩ **b :** SCREWED, PINCHED ⟨~ face⟩

⁴squinch \'skwinch\ *var of* SQUENCH

squinch owl \'=,=\ *n* [prob. fr. ³*squinch*] *South & Midland* **:** SCREECH OWL

¹squin·ny \'skwinē\ *vb* -ED/-ING/-ES [prob. fr. obs. E *squin* asquint (fr. ME *skuin*) + E *-y* (dim. suffix)] **:** SQUINT

²squinny \"\ *n* -ES **:** SQUINT

³squinny \"\ *adj* -ER/-EST **:** SQUINTY

⁴squinny \"\ *adj* -ER/-EST [prob. alter. (influenced by ¹*squinny*) of *skinny*] **:** long and narrow : SLENDER, THIN

⁵squinny \"\ *vi* -ED/-ING/-ES [origin unknown] **:** WEEP, FRET

¹squint \'skwint\ *adj* -ER/-EST [short for *asquint*] **1 a** *of an eye* **:** looking or tending to look obliquely esp. with envy, disdain, or distrust **b :** characteristic of or likened to the appearance of a squint eye ⟨a ~ look⟩ **c** *of the eyes* **:** not having the visual axes parallel : CROSSED — compare STRABISMUS **2 a** *obs* **:** bearing indirectly **b :** OBLIQUE

²squint \"\ *vb* -ED/-ING/-S *vi* **1 a :** to have an indirect bearing, reference, or aim **b :** to deviate from a true line : run obliquely **2 a** (1) **:** to look obliquely or askance or with a furtive glance (2) **:** to look suspiciously or with envy, malice, or disapproval **b :** to be cross-eyed or strabismic **c :** to look or peer with eyes partly closed (as when blinking from excess light or when sighting a gun) **~** *vt* **1 :** to cause (an eye) to look obliquely or to become crossed **2 :** to cause (an eye) to become partly closed or to peer while partly closed ⟨~*ed* his eyes as he stared up at the number —Erle Stanley Gardner⟩

³squint \"\ *n* -S **1 a :** STRABISMUS **b** (1) **:** the action, habit, or an instance of looking obliquely, furtively, or hastily ⟨detected him taking a hasty ~ at my certificate —Joseph Conrad⟩ (2) **:** an action, habit, or instance of screwing the eyes partly closed **c :** HAGIOSCOPE **2 :** a tendency from the ordinary : an inclination toward some object, course, or procedure : TREND, BENT

squint brick *n* **1 :** a brick cut or molded to an oblique angle **2 :** a brick shaped or molded to a special desired form

squint·er \'skwintә(r)\ *n* -S **:** one that squints

squint–eye \'=,=\ *n* [back-formation fr. *squint-eyed*] **:** a cross-eyed person

squint–eyed \'=;=\ *adj* **1 :** having the character of or having eyes that squint; *specif* **:** CROSS-EYED **2 :** having or exhibiting the character of envy, malice, or disdain : PREJUDICED, MALIGNANT ⟨*squint-eyed* with envy —Catherine D. Bowen⟩

squinting construction *n* **:** a grammatical construction that contains a word or phrase (as *sometimes* in "to die sometimes is noble") interpretable as modifying either what precedes or what follows and if interpreted in one way gives an unintended sense

squint·ing·ly *adv* **:** in a squinting manner

squint quoin *n* **:** a quoin at the corner of a building not forming a right angle

squinty \'skwintē, -ti\ *adj, sometimes* -ER/-EST [³*squint* + *-y*] **:** characterized by or affected with squinting ⟨~ eyes⟩

¹squire \'skwī(ә)r, -īә\ *n* -S [ME *squier*, fr. OF *esquier, escuier*, fr. LL *scutarius* shield bearer — more at ESQUIRE] **1 :** a shield bearer or armor-bearer of a knight — compare PAGE **2 a :** a male attendant esp. on a great personage **b :** a man devotedly attendant on a lady : GALLANT, LOVER **3 a :** a member of the British gentry ranking below a knight and above a gentleman **b :** COUNTRY GENTLEMAN; *esp* **:** the principal landowner in a village or district **c** (1) **:** JUSTICE OF THE PEACE (2) **:** LAWYER (3) **:** JUDGE

²squire \"\ *vb* -ED/-ING/-S [ME *squieren*, fr. *squier* squire]

vt : to attend upon as a squire : serve as an escort to : ACCOMPANY, ESCORT ⟨girlhood, when she had gaily gone to parties, *squired* by boys her own age —Jean Stafford⟩ ~ *vi* : to function as or act the part of a country squire

squire·arch \ˈskwī(ə),rärk\ *n* -S [back-formation fr. *squirearchy*] : a member of the squirearchy

squire·ar·chal \ˌskwīˈrärkəl, (ˈ)skwīˈrä-\ *or* **squire·ar·chi·cal** \-ärkəkəl\ *also* **squir·ar·chal** *like* SQUIREARCHAL\ *adj* [*squirearchal*, *squirearchical* fr. *squirearchy* + *-al* or *-ical*; *squirarchal* fr. *squirarchy* + *-al*] : of, relating to, characteristic of, or belonging to the squirearchy ⟨that image of the right life which has evolved from the aristocratic, ~, and higher official culture —Edward Shils⟩

squire·ar·chy *or* **squir·ar·chy** \ˈskwī(ə),rärkē\ *n* -ES [1*squire* + *-archy*] **1** : the gentry of a country : the landed proprietor class esp. with regard to its political influence ⟨two classes in the community struggling for supremacy: the land-owning ~ allied with the church, and the mercantile classes —C.J. Friedrich⟩ — used esp. of the English government prior to the Reform Bill of 1832 **2** : government by a landed gentry

squire·dom \ˈskwī(ə)rdəm\ *n* -S **1** : the rank, dignity, or estate of a squire **2** : SQUIREARCHY 1

squi·reen \(ˈ)skwīˈrēn\ *n* -S [1*squire* + *-een*] *chiefly Irish* : a petty squire : a gentleman in a small way

squire·hood \ˈskwī(ə)r,hu̇d\ *n* **1** : SQUIREDOM **2** : SQUIREARCHY 1

squire·less \-ī(ə)rləs\ *adj* : lacking a squire; *specif* : UNATTENDED, UNESCORTED

squire·ling \-liŋ\ *n* -S : a young or petty squire

squire·ly \-lē\ *adj* : of, relating to, resembling, or befitting a squire

squire·ship \-ī(ə)r,ship\ *n* : SQUIREDOM

squir·ess \-ī(ə)rəs\ *n* -ES [1*squire* + *-ess*] : the wife of a squire

squir·ish \-rish\ *adj* : characteristic of, resembling, or befitting a squire

squirl \ˈskwər(·ə)l\ *n* -S [prob. blend of 2*squirm* and 2*twirl*] : FLOURISH, TWIST, CURLICUE ⟨signed with a ~ —Elizabeth Bowen⟩

1**squirm** \ˈskwərm, -wəm, -wəim\ *vb* -ED/-ING/-S [perh. imit.] *vi* **1** : to twist about with contortions like an eel or a worm (as from nervousness, embarrassment, or excess of energy) ⟨sleek-haired subalterns who ~*ed* painfully in their chairs when they came to call —Rudyard Kipling⟩ **2 a** : to proceed or move with a writhing motion **b** : to extricate oneself by subtle maneuvering ⟨his reputation for honesty precluded any attempt to ~ out of an obligation —D.G.Hoffman⟩ **3** : to experience acute embarrassment, shame, anguish, remorse, or mental punishment ⟨preparing . . . a grueling cross-examination . . . in which he is going to make me ~ in front of the grand jury —Erle Stanley Gardner⟩ ~ *vt* **1** : to cause to squirm **2** : to execute or accomplish by means of a squirm ⟨~*ed* my way through the crowd —E.M.Benson⟩ **syn** see WRITHE

2**squirm** \ˈ"\ *n* -S : the action or an instance of squirming : WRIGGLE

squirmy \-mē,-mi\ *adj* -ER/-EST [1*squirm* + *-y*] : given to or characterized by squirming ⟨the only other major horror of the barber business . . . is ~ kids —G.S.Perry⟩

squirr \ˈskwər(·)\ *vt* -ED/-ING/-S [prob. alter. of 1*skirr*] *dial Brit* : to throw with a jerk or with the edge foremost

1**squir·rel** \ˈskwər(·ə)l, -wəl,-wəil *also* -wə·rəl *sometimes* -wir(ə)l *or* -wer(ə)l\ *n, pl* **squirrels** *also* **squirrel** [ME *squirel*, *squerel*, fr. MF *esquireul*, *escuriuel*, fr. (assumed) VL *scuriolus*, dim. of (assumed) VL *scurius*, alter. of L *sciurus*, fr. Gk *skiouros*, fr. *skia* shadow + *oura* tail (akin to Gk *orrhos* buttocks) — more at SCENE, ASS] **1 a (1)** : a rodent of the family Sciuridae; *esp* : any of various widely distributed small to medium-sized usu. largely arboreal forms that have a bushy tail and long strong hind limbs which allow them to leap from branch to branch, feed largely on nuts and seeds which they commonly store for winter use, and include numerous small game animals and several economically important fur bearers — see BLACK SQUIRREL, FLYING SQUIRREL, GRAY SQUIRREL, GROUND SQUIRREL, RED SQUIRREL **(2)** : SCALETAIL **(3)** : the fur of a squirrel used in the fur trade; *esp* : the fur of a common Eurasiatic squirrel (*Sciurus vulgaris*) **b** *Austral* : any of various flying phalangers **2** : 4LEAD 5 **3** : one of the small rollers in a carding machine that work with the large cylinder

2**squirrel** \ˈ"\ *vt* -ED/-ING/-S : to store up for future use : HIDE, HOARD ⟨~*ed* away twice as much as he actually expects to use —John Fischer⟩

squirrel cage *n* **1** : a cage for a small animal (as a squirrel) that contains a cylinder revolving upon a horizontal axis when an animal moves within it **2 a** : something resembling a squirrel cage in construction; *specif* : a secondary winding for an induction motor consisting of cylindrically arranged copper bars with ends connected by short-circuiting rings — compare PHASE-WOUND **b** : something resembling a squirrel cage in senselessness or repetitiveness

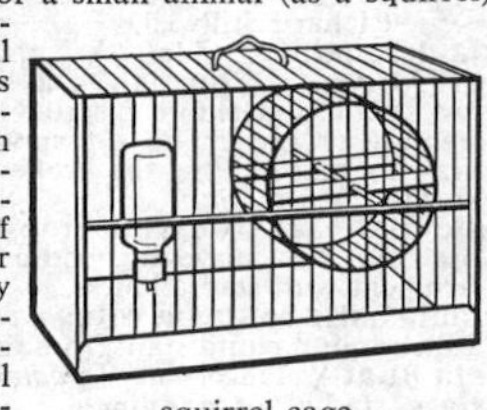

squirrel cage

squirrel–cage \ˈ≈(≈),≈\ *adj* [*squirrel cage*] **1** : consisting of or equipped with an induction motor squirrel cage ⟨*squirrel-cage* rotor⟩ ⟨*squirrel-cage* motor⟩ **2** : endlessly and ploddingly repetitive : constantly returning upon itself in the manner of a treadmill ⟨most of the talk and writing on human nature represents only *squirrel-cage* thinking —C.D.Dam⟩

squirrel corn *n* : a No. American herb (*Dicentra canadensis*) with delicate much-divided leaves and a scapose raceme of cream-colored flowers growing from a cluster of small tubers borne on the rootstock

squirrel cup *n* : a common No. American hepatica (*Hepatica americana*) with bluish to purple or sometimes white or pink flowers — usu. used in pl.

squirrel family *n* : SCIURIDAE

squirrelfish \ˈ≈(≈),≈\ *n* [prob. so called fr. the fact that the sound it makes out of water resembles the bark of a squirrel] **1** : any of numerous small fishes of the family Holocentridae; *esp* : a fish (*Holocentrus ascensionis*) of the West Indies, Bermudas, and adjacent areas that is usu. chiefly bright red with large eyes and large rough scales **2 a** : a pinfish (*Lagodon rhomboides*) **b** : a related grunt of the genus *Haemulon*

squirrel food *n* : any of several plants of the genus *Zigadenus*; *esp* : DEATH CAMAS

squirrel frog *n* : a small tree toad (*Hyla squirella*) of the southern U. S.

squirrel grass *n* : SQUIRRELTAIL 2

squirrel hake *n* : any of several hakes of the genus *Phycis*; *esp* : a common market fish (*P. chuss*) of the Atlantic coast south to Cape Hatteras

squirrel hawk *n* [so called fr. its fondness for ground squirrels] : FERRUGINOUS ROUGHLEG

squir·rel·ly *also* **squir·rely** \-lē,-li\ *adj* [1*squirrel* + *-y*] : extremely odd : crazily peculiar or senseless ⟨just a ~ enough job to appeal to me —Mary McCall⟩

squirrel monkey *n* [so called fr. its being small and arboreal] **1** : any of several small soft-haired So. American monkeys of the genus *Saimiri* (syn. *Chrysothrix*); *esp* : a monkey (*S. sciurea*) having a long nonprehensile tail and being chiefly yellowish gray in color with a white face and black nose **2** : TITI **3** : TAMARIN; *esp* : a Panamanian tamarin (*Leontocebus geoffroyi*)

squirrel mouse *n* : DORMOUSE

squirrel phalanger *or* **squirrel opossum** *n* : FLYING PHALANGER; *esp* : a common Australian flying phalanger (*Petaurus sciureus*)

squirrel rifle *or* **squirrel gun** *n* [so called fr. its being suitable only for small game] : a small-bore rifle introduced into America about 1700 after the adoption of the patched bullet

squirrel's–foot fern *n* : BALL FERN

squirrel shrew *n* : TREE SHREW

squirreltail \ˈ≈(≈),≈\ *n* [1*squirrel* + *tail*] **1** : a tufted perennial grass (*Sitanion hystrix*) that has very bristly spikes disarticulating above each node and resembles lyme grass **2** *also* **squirreltail grass** *or* **squirreltail barley** : any of several grasses of the genus *Hordeum* (as wall barley) with bushy spikes

squirrel tail *n* : a tail arched forward beyond a vertical from its anterior base — used chiefly of fowls

squirring *pres part of* SQUIRR

squirrs *pres 3d sing of* SQUIRR

1**squirt** \ˈskwər|t, -wə|, -wəi|, *usu* |d.+V\ *vb* -ED/-ING/-S [ME *squirten*, *swirten*; akin to LG *swirtjen* to squirt] *vi* **1** : to eject liquid in a thin spurt **2** : to dart suddenly or quickly : move briskly **3** : to come forth in a sudden rapid stream from a narrow orifice : SPURT ~ *vt* **1** : to drive, eject, or inject in a fluid or gaseous stream ⟨~*ed* carbonated water into a glass —Erle Stanley Gardner⟩ **2** : to sprinkle, spatter, splash, or soak by squirting : force a stream of liquid upon ⟨load the hose attachment with soap powder and ~ your dirty car —*New Yorker*⟩ **3** : to cause to squirt a liquid, fluid, or gaseous substance ⟨merrily ~*ing* his seltzer bottle —*Springfield (Mass.) Union*⟩

2**squirt** \ˈ"\ *n* -S [ME, diarrhea, fr. *squirten* to squirt] **1** *dial* : DIARRHEA — usu. used in pl. and with *the* **2 a** : an instrument (as a syringe) for squirting a liquid **b (1)** : a small quick stream : JET, SPURT ⟨took the pipe from his mouth and sent a brown ~ of juice softly into the pebbles —John Hermann⟩ **(2)** : molten metal that is forced through an interstice in an improperly tightened line of matrices at the moment of casting in a slugcasting machine; *also* : an instance of such forcing through of metal **c** : the action or an instance of squirting **3 a** : an esp. young or small upstart or impudent person given to meddling beyond his competence or concern ⟨this young ~ is going too far —S.H.Holbrook⟩ **b** : a young child or youth : KID ⟨giving him nickels to buy lemon ice when he was a ~ —Bernard Malamud⟩

squirt can *n* : an oil can having a flexible bottom that when compressed forces oil out of a tapering spout

squirt·er \-d·ə(r), -tə-\ *n* -S **1** : one that squirts **2** *or* **squirter disease** [so called fr. the fact that the banana squirts when any pressure is applied] : a storage and market disease of bananas marked by dark watery rot of the pulp and caused by a fungus (*Nigrospora sphaerica*)

squirt gun *n* **1** : an often pistol-shaped device having a bulb that squirts out a liquid when pressed and being used for various purposes (as to spray plants or bushes) **2** : WATER PISTOL

squirting cucumber *n* : a Mediterranean plant (*Ecballium elaterium*) of the family Cucurbitaceae having oblong fruit that bursts from the peduncle when ripe and forcibly ejects the seeds

squirty \-d·|ē, -t|, |i\ *adj* -ER/-EST : of the nature of or characteristic of a squirt ⟨three times smarter than these ~ little naval officers —Kenneth Roberts⟩

1**squish** \ˈskwish\ *vb* -ED/-ING/-ES [alter. (influenced by 1*squirt*) of 1*squash*] *vt* **1** : SQUASH ⟨~*ed* her nose against the window pane —R.W.Howard⟩ **2** : to cause to move in or eject a liquid or viscous substance with a splashing or sucking sound ⟨~*ed* his feet . . . deeper into the soft and comfortable mud —K.M.Dodson⟩ ~ *vi* : to move with or emit a sucking, gurgling, or splashing sound : SQUELCH ⟨their wet tennis shoes ~*ed* —Frank Noel⟩

2**squish** \ˈ"\ *n* -ES : a squishing sound

squishy \ˈskwishē\ *adj* -ER/-EST [1*squish* + *-y*] : being soft, yielding, and damp : clammily viscous

1**squit** \ˈskwit\ *n* -S [perh. alter. (influenced by 2*squirt*) of obs. E dial. *skit* skittish person, perh. fr. E 2*skit*] *Brit* : SQUIRT 3a

2**squit** \ˈ"\ *n* -S [by shortening & alter. fr. *squeteague* or *squetee*] : GRAY TROUT 1

squitch \ˈskwich\ *or* **squitch grass** *n* -ES [alter. of *quitch*] : COUCH GRASS 1a

squiteague *var of* SQUETEAGUE

1**squit·ter** \ˈskwid·ə(r)\ *vb* -ED/-ING/-S [alter. (influenced by *-er* as in *blabber*) of obs. E *squit* to squirt, prob. of Scand origin; akin to Icel *skvetta* to squirt — more at SQUATTER] *dial* : SQUIRT

2**squitter** \ˈ"\ *n* -S *dial* : SQUIRT

squiz \ˈskwiz\ *n* [origin unknown] *Austral & NewZeal* : LOOK, GLANCE

squoze *dial past of* SQUEEZE

squush *or* **sqush** \ˈskwəsh, -wu̇sh\ *vb* -ED/-ING/-ES [alter. of 1*squish*] *vt* : SQUASH ~ *vi* : SQUISH

squushy *or* **squshy** \-shē\ *adj* [alter. of *squishy*] : SQUASHY

sr *abbr* **1** seer **2** senior **3** *often cap* senor **4** *often cap* sir **5** *often cap* sister **6** [L *soror*] sister

SR *abbr* **1** saturable reactor **2** seaman recruit **3** sedimentation rate **4** self-rectifying **5** *often not cap* semantic reaction **6** senate resolution **7** sensibility reciprocal **8** service record **9** shipping receipt **10** short rate **11** *often not cap* small ring **12** social-revolutionary **13** sound ranging **14** special regulation **15** star route **16** stateroom **17** stimulus-response **18** storage room **19** subject ratio **20** supplementary regulation

Sr *symbol* strontium

sra *abbr, often cap* senora

SRA *abbr* sulfo-ricinoleic acid

sra·ban \ˈs(h)räbən\ *or* **sra·van** \-ävən\ *n, usu cap* [Skt *śrāvaṇa*] : SAWAN

srad·dha *or* **shrad·dha** \ˈs(h)räd̲ə\ *also* **sradh** \-d\ *n* -S [Skt *śrāddha*, fr. *śraddhā* belief — more at CREED] **1** : a Hindu rite or ceremony performed in behalf of departed ancestors **2** *Hinduism* : religious faith

sra dye \ˌesˌäˈrä-\ *n, usu cap S&R&A* [*sra* fr. sulfo-ricinoleic acid; fr. the use of this acid in treating the dye] : any of a group of disperse dyes — see DYE table I

sra·ma·na \ˈs(h)rəmənə\ *n* -S [Skt *śramana* — more at SHAMAN] *Buddhism* : a religious ascetic

sra·nan ton·go \ˌsrānənˈtäŋ(ˌ)gō\ *n* : TAKI-TAKI

SR and CC *abbr* strikes, riots, and civil commotions

SR and O *abbr* statutory rules and orders

sra·va·ka \ˈs(h)rävəkə\ *n* -S [Skt *śrāvaka*, lit., hearer, listener; akin to Skt *śṛnoti* he hears — more at LOUD] : a direct disciple of the Buddha

SRCC *abbr, often not cap* strikes, riots, and civil commotions

srch *abbr* search

sri *or* **shri** \ˈs(h)rē\ *n* -S [Skt *śrī* majesty, holiness — more at SETH] — used as a conventional title of respect when addressing or speaking of a distinguished Indian

sri·na·gar \srəˈnəgə(r), -näg-\ *adj, usu cap* [fr. *Srinagar*, city in northern India] : of or from the city of Srinagar, India : of the kind or style prevalent in Srinagar

srita *abbr, often cap* senorita

SRM *abbr* speed of relative movement

SRN *abbr* state registered nurse

SRO *abbr* **1** standing room only **2** statutory rules and orders

srta *abbr, often cap* senorita

sru·ti *or* **shru·ti** \ˈs(h)ru̇d·ē\ *n* -S [Skt *śruti* what is heard, fr. *śṛnoti* he hears — more at LOUD] **1** *often cap* : the first class of shastras; *also* : a text of this class **2** : one of the microtones of the musical scale of India

ss *abbr* **1** *often cap both Ss* saints **2** *often cap both Ss* [L *sancti*] saints **3** *often cap both Ss* [L *sanctissimus*] most holy **4** scilicet **5** [L *scriptores*] authors **6** sections **7** [L *semis*] one half

SS *abbr* **1** Sabbath School **2** sacred Scripture **3** same size **4** screw steamer **5** secret service **6** selective service **7** semisteel **8** [It *senza sordini*] without mutes **9** set screw **10** shipside **11** shortstop **12** side seam **13** simplified spelling **14** single-screened **15** single sideband **16** slop sink **17** soap suds **18** social science; social security; social service **19** special session **20** staff surgeon **21** steamship **22** steel sash **23** Sunday school **24** [L *supra scriptum*] written above **25** sworn statement

s's *or* **ss** *pl of* S

SS and C *abbr* supersized and calendered

SSC *abbr* solicitor, supreme court

ss collar *n, cap both Ss* : COLLAR OF SS

SSE *abbr* south-southeast

s–shaped \ˈ≈,≈\ *adj, cap 1st S* : having the shape of a capital S

SSM *abbr* **1** squadron sergeant major **2** staff sergeant major **3** surface to surface missile

ssp *abbr* subspecies

SSR *abbr* Soviet Socialist Republic

SSS *abbr* **1** specific soluble substance **2** strong soap solution

s star *n, usu cap S* : a star of spectral type S — see SPECTRAL TYPE table

SSU *abbr* second, Saybolt universal

SSW *abbr* south-southwest

st *abbr* **1** *often cap* saint **2** stain **3** stamped **4** stand **5** stanza **6** start **7** state **8** statute **9** steam **10** steel **11** stem **12** stere **13** stet **14** stitch **15** stock **16** stone **17** stotinka **18** straight **19** strait **20** street **21** strophe **22** stumped

ST *abbr* **1** *often not cap* [It *senza tempo*] without regard to time **2** shipping ticket **3** *often not cap* short ton **4** single throw **5** sounding tube **6** standard time **7** static thrust **8** *often not cap* steam trawler **9** superintendent of transportation **10** surface tension

-st — see -EST

-st [fr. *-st* (superlative suffix)] *symbol* — used after the figure 1 to indicate the ordinal number first ⟨May 1*st*⟩ ⟨31*st* St.⟩

'st \st\ *vb* [by contr.] *archaic* : HAST ⟨thou'*st*⟩

sta *abbr* **1** *often cap* [It *santa*] saint **2** station; stationary; stationer **3** stator **4** statute

staa·ten·bund \ˈshtätᵊn,bu̇nt\ *n* -S [G, fr. *staaten* (pl. of *staat* state) + *bund* federation, league — more at BUNDESSTAAT, BUND] : a league of states in which each participating state retains full sovereignty : CONFEDERACY 3 — contrasted with *Bundesstaat*

1**stab** \ˈstab, -aa(ə)b\ *n* -S [ME *stabbe*] **1** : a wound produced by or as if by a pointed weapon; *specif* : STAB WOUND **2 a** : a thrust of a pointed weapon **b** : a jerky stroke (as with a bat, mallet, or club) **c** : a billiards shot in which the cue ball is stroked sharply to cause it to remain on the spot occupied by the object ball **d** : a hard jab in boxing **3 a** : a thrust made for a particular purpose ⟨a fish took a ~ at a fly —Richard Bissell⟩ ⟨a quick ~ into unknown country —L. J. Van Der Post⟩ **b** : ATTEMPT, GO, TRIAL ⟨the present reviewer's sections . . . devoted to phrase structure and clause structure represent only a ~ in this direction —R.A.Hall b. 1911⟩ ⟨speaks fluently in French, Italian, Spanish and German and makes a ~ at Hungarian —*Theatre Arts*⟩ ⟨making a ~ at aplomb —Marcia Davenport⟩ ⟨they didn't care to talk to him much even if he did make a ~ at conversation —Will James⟩ **4 a** : a sudden sharp sensation of pain : PANG ⟨a ~ of lumbago⟩ ⟨a sudden strong feeling ⟨a ~ of anxiety⟩ ⟨a ~ of envy⟩ ⟨a ~ of joy⟩ ⟨a ~ of resentment⟩ **b** : a sharply delimited display of vivid color or light ⟨the ~ of the neon sign —*Saturday Rev.*⟩ ⟨a long ~ of lightning —Danforth Ross⟩ ⟨little ~*s* of flame shot from the chimney —O.S.Nock⟩ **5 a** : a culture medium solidified in an upright column in a tube so as to reduce the surface to a minimum — compare SLANT 2d(1) **b** : STAB CULTURE

2**stab** \ˈ"\ *vb* **stabbed; stabbed; stabbing; stabs** *vt* **1 a** : to wound by the thrust of a pointed instrument ⟨~ a man with a dagger⟩ **b** : to pierce with or as if with a pointed weapon ⟨cured me by *stabbing* me in the seat once a fortnight or so with a monstrous hypodermic syringe —G.B.Shaw⟩ ⟨~ an apple with a knife⟩ ⟨a derrick *stabbing* the sky —Ralph Gray⟩: as **(1)** : to puncture (sheets, sections, or cover boards) to facilitate hand stitching or sewing in bookbinding **(2)** : to roughen the surface of (a brick wall) with a point to form a key for plaster **c** : PIERCE 5 ⟨poignant memories *stabbed* him —Marcia Davenport⟩ ⟨children coming home from the factory or the mine ~ the conscience —J.H.Plumb⟩ **2 a** : THRUST, DRIVE ⟨a fork that had been *stabbed* into the navel of a large orange —June W. Brown⟩ ⟨as you arrange the carding, ~ pins through it into the paper —Evelyn A. Mansfield⟩ ⟨man *stabbed* a thumb at a wisp of white ribbon —F.B.Gipson⟩ **b** : to strike (as a golf ball) with a jerky stroke **c** : to hit (a boxing opponent) with a hard jab **3** : to point (a bird) suddenly and without hesitation — used of a hunting dog ~ *vi* : to thrust or give a wound with or as if with a pointed weapon : make a stab : PIERCE ⟨his finger *stabbed* at a blank page —Jan Valtin⟩ ⟨small forces ~ northward looking for a fight —*Current History*⟩ ⟨the thought had *stabbed* through her like a knife —Ellen Glasgow⟩ ⟨misty blue peaks *stabbing* up out of rich forests —Allan Nevins⟩

3**stab** \ˈstab\ *n* -S [prob. alter. of *stob*] *chiefly Scot* : STAKE

4**stab** \ˈ"\ *n* -S [by shortening] *Brit* : ESTABLISHMENT — used of weekly or hourly wages paid by a printing house as distinguished from piecework payments ⟨~ work⟩ ⟨working on ~⟩

stab *abbr* **1** stabilize; stabilizer **2** stable

stab·ber \-bə(r)\ *n* -S **1** : one that stabs **2** : a sailmaker's marlinespike or awl : PRICKER

stabbing *adj* : that stabs : PIERCING ⟨master of the short, ~ phrase —*Times Lit. Supp.*⟩ ⟨~ glare of a fluorescent tube —Lewis Mumford⟩ ⟨knifelike, ~ or sharp pain —*Dental Abstracts*⟩ ⟨the ~ barb with which the stingaree was equipped —Francis Birtles⟩ — **stab·bing·ly** *adv*

stab cell *n* [part trans. of G *stabzelle*, fr. *stab* staff (fr. OHG) + *zelle* cell — more at STAFF] : a young blood granulocyte with densely staining unsegmented nucleus

stab culture *n* : a culture (as of bacteria) made by inoculating deep into a stab

1**sta·bile** \ˈstābəl, -ā,bīl *also* -,bēl *sometimes* ˈstabəl\ *adj* [L *stabilis* — more at STABLE] **1** : not moving : STATIONARY, STABLE **2** : not fluctuating : STEADY — compare LABILE 3 **3** : not decomposing readily : resistant to chemical change ⟨native proteins are never ~ —Otto Rahn⟩

2**sta·bile** \ˈstā,bēl *sometimes* -,bīl *or* -,bil\ *n* -S : an abstract sculpture or construction typically made of sheet metal, wire, and wood — compare MOBILE

sta·bil·i·fy \stəˈbilə,fī\ *vt* -ED/-ING/-ES : to make stable

stab·i·lim·e·ter \ˌstabəˈliməd·ə(r)\ *n* [*stability* + *-meter*] : a device for measuring or indicating stability; *specif* : an apparatus for recording the amplitude and frequency of the motions of an animal or child

sta·bil·i·tate \stəˈbilə,tāt\ *vt* -ED/-ING/-S [ML *stabilitatus*, past part. of *stabilitare*, fr. L *stabilitas*] : to make stable

sta·bil·i·ty \stəˈbiləd·ē, -lətē, -i *sometimes* stāˈ-\ *n* -ES [ME *stabilite*, fr. MF *estabilité*, fr. L *stabilitat-*, *stabilitas*, fr. *stabilis* stable + *-itat-*, *-itas* -ity — more at STABLE] **1** : the quality, state, or degree of being stable: as **a** : the strength to stand or endure without alteration of position or without material change : STEADINESS, FIRMNESS ⟨bridge . . . was frail, with little lateral ~ to withstand the gales —O.S.Nock⟩ ⟨these metals have a structural ~ that should ensure long life —Betty Pepis⟩ ⟨the ~ of a price is the degree to which it stays the same over time —A.P.Lerner⟩ ⟨a recession appeared that showed the lack of ~ in the economy —Oscar Handlin⟩ ⟨cultural ~ — a phenomenon which, in its psychological aspects, is called conservatism —M.J.Herskovits⟩ ⟨political ~, with its accompanying danger of political stagnation —W.C.Brownell⟩ **b** : the state of being in stable equilibrium **c** : the property of a body that causes it when disturbed from a condition of equilibrium or steady motion to develop forces or moments that restore the original condition ⟨the ~ of a projectile⟩ ⟨the ~ of a ship⟩ ⟨the ~ of an airplane⟩ **d** : resistance to decomposition or other chemical change or to physical disintegration ⟨a plastic with a heat ~ of up to 100° C⟩ ⟨salicylamide, an analgesic of wide compatibility and good ~ in pharmaceutical preparations —*Monsanto Mag.*⟩ **e** : PERMANENCE ⟨~ of a color⟩ **2 a** : steadiness or firmness of character, resolution, or purpose : CONSTANCY, STEADFASTNESS ⟨an idea so . . . dishonorable to the ~ of her lover —Jane Austen⟩ ⟨she lacks the ~ and discipline to keep her gift under control —*Time*⟩ ⟨each writer had to find or fashion for himself an artistic credo to serve as a center of ~ — Max Lerner & Edwin Mims⟩ **b** : a vow made by Benedictines and some other monks binding them for life to the monastery in which they make their profession **c** : the state demanded by this vow

sta·bi·li·za·tion \ˌstābələˈzāshən, -bəˌlīˈ- *sometimes* ˌstab-\ *n* -S **1** : the act or process of stabilizing : the state of being stabilized **2 a** : the limitation (as by regulation) of fluctuations of business activity, prices, or employment **b** : the pegging of security prices usu. by an underwriting syndicate **c** : the keeping of the foreign exchange quotation of a currency within a narrow range either by making it convertible or by central bank or stabilization fund action **3** : the state of maximum adjustment between organisms and environment that is characteristic of an ecological climax community

stabilization fund *n* : a fund maintained by a government to control the foreign exchange quotation of its currency — called also *equalization fund*

sta·bi·lize \ˈstābə,līz *sometimes* ˈstab-\ *vb* -ED/-ING/-S [*stabile* + *-ize*] *vt* **1 :** to make stable, steadfast, or firm ⟨sand fences were built and grasses planted to ~ the migratory ridges —*Amer. Guide Series: N.C.*⟩ ⟨advise me where the plant should be *stabilized* —P.A.Zahl⟩ ⟨religious faith . . . ~*s* one's life —Rufus Jones⟩ ⟨the recent arrivals . . . strengthened and *stabilized* the organization they discovered already in existence —Oscar Handlin⟩ **2 :** to make or hold steady : prevent fluctuations of : maintain at a constant level: as **a :** to maintain or to make it possible to maintain the stability of (as an airplane) by means of fixed surfaces or gyroscopic or other devices not manipulated by an operator ⟨a rocket *stabilized* by a gyroscope⟩ **b :** to limit fluctuations of (as business activity, prices, or employment) **c :** to establish a minimum price for (a security) by buying all offerings at that price **3 :** SET 40 ⟨a chemical treatment to ~ a fabric⟩ **~** *vi* **1 :** to become stable, firm, or steadfast ⟨prices received by farmers had *stabilized* —*Dun's Rev.*⟩ ⟨the birthrate has fallen and populations have tended to ~ —Gerard Piel⟩ ⟨when pulse and blood pressure respond and ~ —*Jour. Amer. Med. Assoc.*⟩ **2 :** to prevent regeneration by inserting resistors in the grid circuits of the electron tubes

syn STABILIZE, STEADY, POISE, BALANCE, BALLAST, and TRIM are seldom interchangeable but can mean, in common, to maintain or cause to maintain position or equilibrium. STABILIZE applies to what fluctuates or is unsteady and calls for regulation by an external force ⟨measures to *stabilize* and in the long run to enlarge farm income —*New Republic*⟩ ⟨if the stock rises, the fund can buy fewer shares; if the stock falls, it can buy more, thus tending to *stabilize* the market —*Time*⟩ STEADY applies to what loses, or is subject to loss of, its customary stability, and consequently rocks, shakes, flutters, or tips ⟨*steady* a table by putting a wedge under one leg⟩ ⟨while medics *steadied* trays of instruments against bomb concussions —Bill Alcine⟩ ⟨controlled elections *steadied* authoritarian regimes during the year —M.B.Travis⟩ ⟨a medicine to *steady* the nerves⟩ POISE applies chiefly to what maintains its equilibrium, either by an inherent proper distribution of balancing forces or by a discipline as of muscle or mind, under circumstances which would normally upset it, esp. external forces (as the law of gravity), or in a way that suggests imminent upset ⟨try to see a figure *poised* on a crag or jut of ice over a precipice —Marion Sheridan⟩ ⟨kingfishers *poise* on bare cypress limbs —*Amer. Guide Series: Fla.*⟩ ⟨the world is *poised*, uneasily, dangerously, on a point of decision —*London Calling*⟩ BALANCE also implies an equilibrium resulting from an even distribution of opposing forces but, unlike POISE, carries little suggestion of sustained equilibrium or of forces working to upset ⟨*balance* a pair of scales by putting like weights in both trays⟩ ⟨a military dictatorship of one man who *balances* and plays off the main forces of the country against each other —H.L.Matthews⟩ ⟨her humor . . . *balanced* between dignity and absurdity —*Current Biog.*⟩ BALLAST implies the addition of something heavy or solid to hold down, hold steady, or ensure the stability of something too light or too buoyant; in application to the mind or character it implies something counteracting volatility, frivolity, or uncertainty ⟨*ballast* a canoe in stormy weather with large stones⟩ ⟨the marriage seemed to *ballast* the normally flighty girl⟩ TRIM implies a proper balancing, as of a boat or ship, esp. by moving contents around so that it sits well or fulfills well any of the conditions that make for steadiness ⟨could be *trimmed* on an even keel . . . like scales, in which the weight on one side must be counterposed by a weight in the other —Richard Jefferies⟩ ⟨one man . . . can make quick work of loading and *trimming* a boxcar —*Industrial Equipment News*⟩

sta·bi·liz·er \-zə(r)\ *n* -S **:** one that makes stable: as **a** (1) **:** a substance added to an explosive esp. to make it less liable to spontaneous decomposition (2) **:** a substance added to a plastic or elastomer to maintain its desirable physical and chemical properties (3) **:** a substance added to an emulsion, foam, or other dispersion to prevent change **:** PROTECTIVE COLLOID ⟨~*s* used in the production of chocolate milk⟩ (4) **:** a substance (as gelatin) added to a food mix (as ice cream) to improve and maintain its quality (as of texture or body) **b :** a distilling column for decreasing the evaporative tendency of petroleum products (as gasoline) by removal of gaseous and low-boiling hydrocarbons **c :** a bar-shaped shock absorber for a vehicle (as an automobile) **d :** a gyroscope device to keep ships steady in a heavy sea — compare GYROSTABILIZER **e :** an airfoil providing stability for an airplane; *specif* **:** the fixed horizontal member of the tail assembly of an airplane **f :** a device to hold a tank gun on a target, while the tank is moving over rough ground

¹sta·ble \ˈstābəl\ *n* -S [ME, fr. OF *estable*, fr. L *stabulum*, fr. *stare* to stand — more at STAND] **1 :** a building or part of a building in which domestic animals are lodged and fed; *esp* **:** such a building having stalls or compartments ⟨the horse ~ is in the main barn, the cow ~ is separate⟩ **2 a :** a group of racing horses under one ownership or management; *also* **:** the horses of such a group or the persons concerned with the ownership, operation, or management of such a group **b :** a group or staff of people (as artists, comedians, speakers, writers) engaged to contribute their services or perform when called upon **:** POOL: (1) **:** a group of athletes (as boxers or tennis players) under the direction of a single manager (2) **:** a group of prostitutes working for a pimp **c :** a group of things under a single ownership or management ⟨a ~ of publications⟩ ⟨a ~ of racing cars⟩ ⟨a ~ of five suits —Mel Watkins⟩ **3 stables** *pl* **a :** military duty in the stables **b :** the bugle call to such duty

²stable \"\ *vb* **stabled; stabled; stabling** \-b(ə)liŋ\ **stables** [ME *stablen*, fr. MF *establer*, fr. L *stabulare*, fr. *stabulum*] *vt* **:** to put or keep (as animals) in a stable **:** HOUSE ⟨horses and cows were *stabled* on the lower floor —*Amer. Guide Series: N.C.*⟩ ⟨garage . . . redesigned to ~ neighborhood Cadillacs —*Newsweek*⟩ **~** *vi* **:** to dwell in or as if in a stable

³stable \"\ *adj*, *often* **stabler** \-b(ə)lə(r)\ *often* **stablest** \-b(ə)ləst\ [ME, fr. OF *estable*, fr. L *stabilis*, fr. *stare* to stand + *-abilis* -able — more at STAND] **1 a :** firmly established **:** not easily moved, shaken, or overthrown **:** SOLID, FIXED, STEADFAST ⟨so long upon the moving, rocking sea that the ~ land was a shock to us —Jack London⟩ ⟨the sawmill village with sawdust streets became a ~ community and was incorporated as a city —*Amer. Guide Series: Mich.*⟩ ⟨dictatorship always appears ~ —*Christian Science Monitor*⟩ ⟨~ habits⟩ ⟨a ~ theory⟩ **b :** not subject to sudden change **:** subject to relatively limited fluctuation **:** DURABLE, UNVARYING ⟨~ currency⟩ ⟨a ~ economy⟩ ⟨a general trend toward a ~ population, rather than one that will continue to increase —K.F.Mather⟩ ⟨some industries are quite ~ inasmuch as no basic changes in technique occur for a long period of time —E.B.Alderfer & H.E.Michl⟩ ⟨a relatively ~ society, where class mobility is reasonably low, where the individual remains, both physically and socially, in the place in which he was born —Leslie Cheek⟩ ⟨the personnel of the Supreme Court remained relatively ~ —R.K.Carr⟩ **c :** ABIDING, ENDURING, PERSISTING, PERMANENT ⟨a ~ peace⟩ ⟨your name will travel widely over the world, but will have no ~ habitation —J.A.Froude⟩ **2 a :** steady in purpose **:** firm in resolution **b :** not subject to insecurity or emotional illness **:** SANE, RATIONAL ⟨a ~ personality⟩ ⟨many boys are not emotionally ~ and, as a result, behave in a way that makes some adults believe them to be retarded —H.A.Delp⟩ **3 a :** placed so as to resist forces tending to cause motion or change of motion **:** designed so as to develop forces that restore the original condition when disturbed from a condition of equilibrium or steady motion ⟨an airplane is ~ if, when it is disturbed from a balanced condition of flight (whether level, climbing or gliding), its tendency is to return to that condition —*Skyways*⟩ **b :** of such structure as to resist distortion **c** (1) **:** not readily decomposing or changing otherwise in chemical composition or biological activity (as spontaneously or under the influence of heat, acid, or alkali) ⟨penicillin . . . is ~ at a point about neutrality —*Amer. Scholar*⟩ (2) **:** not readily changing in physical state or properties ⟨a ~ emulsion⟩ ⟨a ~ substance never changes spontaneously into a metastable one —Samuel Glasstone⟩ (3) **:** not spontaneously radioactive or observably so ⟨a ~ isotope⟩ ⟨a ~ nucleus⟩

stableboy \ˈ=,=\ *n* **:** a boy who works around a stable **:** HOSTLER

stable color *n* [³*stable*] **:** a color (as yellow, blue, bluish red, or bluish green) that keeps the same hue though it may lose saturation down to a dead gray as it is viewed in indirect vision

stable entry *n* [¹*stable*] **:** two or more horses owned by the same stable or having the same trainer that are grouped as a single entry in a race and bet on as a unit

stable equilibrium *n* [³*stable*] **:** a state of equilibrium of a body (as a pendulum hanging directly downward from its point of support) such that when the body is slightly displaced it tends to return to its original position — compare UNSTABLE EQUILIBRIUM

stable fly *n* [¹*stable*] **1 :** a two-winged fly (*Stomoxys calcitrans*) that is abundant about stables and often enters dwellings esp. in autumn and that resembles the common housefly but bites severely **2 :** a fly (*Muscina stabulans*) that is related to and similar to the stable fly — called also *false stable fly*

sta·ble·man \ˈ==mən, -,man\ *n*, *pl* **stablemen :** a worker in a stable; *esp* **:** one who takes care of the horses

stablemate \ˈ==,=\ *n* **1 :** a horse stabled with another **:** one of two or more horses having the same owner **2 :** one of two or more boxers having the same manager

stable–meal \ˈ==,=\ *n*, *Scot* **:** the liquor bought to compensate an innkeeper for the accommodation of horses

sta·ble·ness *n* -ES [ME *stablenes*, fr. *stable* + *-nes* -ness] **:** STABILITY

stable oscillation *n* [³*stable*] **:** an oscillation (as of a pendulum, tuning fork, or airplane part) whose amplitude does not increase — compare UNSTABLE OSCILLATION

stable police *n pl* **:** army enlisted men detailed to clean the stables or picket lines and to help in the care of the horses

sta·bler \ˈstāb(ə)lə(r)\ *n* -S [ME *stabyler*, fr. MF *establier*, fr. *estable* stable + *-ier* -er — more at STABLE] **:** one that keeps a stable

stablest *superlative of* STABLE

stabling *n* -S [ME, fr. gerund of *stablen* to stable — more at STABLE] **:** accommodation for animals in a building ⟨~ for 20 horses⟩; *also* **:** the building providing such accommodation ⟨a range of ~ across the court⟩

stab·lish \ˈstablish\ *vb* -ED/-ING/-ES [by shortening] *archaic* **:** ESTABLISH — **stab·lish·ment** \-shmənt\ *n* -S *archaic*

sta·bly \ˈstāblē\ *adv* [ME, fr. *stable* + *-ly*] **:** in a stable manner

stabs *pl of* STAB, *pres 3d sing of* STAB

stab stitch *n* **:** a stitch made with a needle held at right angles to the cloth

stab wound *also* **stab incision** *n* **:** a small surgical opening made into the abdominal cavity for drainage or other purpose

stac *abbr* staccato

stacc *abbr* staccato

stac·ca·tis·si·mo \,stäkəˈtisə,mō\ *adv* (*or adj*) [It, fr. *staccato* + *-issimo*, suffix denoting a high degree (fr. L *-issimus*, superl. suffix)] **:** in a sharper and more detached staccato manner — used as a direction in music

¹stac·ca·to \stəˈkä|d·(,)ō, -ˈká, |(,)tō\ *adj* [It, fr. past part. of *staccare* to detach, short for *distaccare*, fr. OIt, fr. MF *destacher*, fr. OF *destachier* — more at DETACH] **1 a :** cut short or apart in performing **:** DISCONNECTED ⟨~ notes⟩ ⟨~ chords⟩ **b :** marked by short clear-cut playing or singing of tones or chords ⟨a ~ style⟩ — compare LEGATO **2 :** having a sharp abrupt disjointed character or quality ⟨the ~ voice of the telegraph called from settlement to settlement —J.D.Hart⟩ ⟨the book is a series of ~ scenes —Joseph Frank⟩

²staccato \"\ *adv* **:** in a staccato manner — often used as a direction in music; compare TENUTO

³staccato \"\ *n*, *pl* **staccatos** \-ōz\ *or* **stacca·ti** \|d·(,)ē, |(,)tē\ **1 :** an abrupt and disconnected manner of performance (as of a musical instrument); *also* **:** a passage of music so performed **2 :** something (as a manner of expression) that is broken up into brief sharp bursts ⟨in his rapid conversational ~ —Dorothy C. Fisher⟩ ⟨heard the chugging of a tractor, the ~ of its motor coming louder —Kay Boyle⟩

⁴staccato \"\ *vt* -ED/-ING/-S **:** to play, utter, or sound in a staccato manner

staccato mark *n* **:** a pointed vertical stroke or a dot that is put over or under a musical note to be produced staccato

staccato marks

stach·er \ˈstakər\ *Scot var of* STAGGER

stach·y·bot·ryo·toxicosis \,stakə,bä·trēo+\ *n* [NL, fr. *Stachybotrys* + *-o-* + *toxicosis*] **:** a serious and sometimes fatal intoxication of horses fed on moldy hay that is due to a toxic substance elaborated by a mold (*Stachybotrys alternans*)

stach·y·bot·rys \,stakəˈbä·trəs\ *n*, *cap* [NL, fr. Gk *stachys* ear of grain + *botrys* bunch of grapes, grape — more at STING] **:** a genus of imperfect fungi (order Moniliales) characterized by short usu. hyaline conidiophores with whorls of thick hyaline or brown sterigmata each bearing a spore or chain of spores

stach·y·drine \ˈstakə,drēn, -drən\ *n* -S [ISV *stach-* (fr. NL *Stachys*) + *hydr-* + *-ine*] **:** a crystalline alkaloid $C_7H_{13}NO_2$ found in various plants (as alfalfa or Chinese artichoke) **:** the dimethyl betaine of proline

stach·y·ose \ˈstakē,ōs\ *n* -S [ISV *stach-* (fr. NL *Stachys*) + *-ose*] **:** a sweet crystalline sugar $C_{24}H_{42}O_{21}$ of the tetrasaccharide class that is found esp. in the tubers of the Chinese artichoke and yields glucose, fructose, and galactose on hydrolysis

sta·chys \ˈstākəs\ *n* [NL, fr. Gk, ear of grain, base horehound — more at STING] **1** *cap* **:** a large and widely distributed genus of herbs (family Labiatae) having five nearly equal calyx teeth, divergent anther cells, and rounded nutlets — see HEDGE NETTLE **2** -ES **:** any plant of the genus *Stachys*

stach·y·tar·phe·ta \,stakəˈtärˈfēd·ə\ *n*, *cap* [NL, fr. Gk *stachys* + NL *-tarpheta* (prob. irreg. fr. Gk *tarpheia*, fem. of *tarphys* thick; perh. akin to Gk *thrombos* lump — more at THROMB-] **:** a genus of chiefly tropical plants (family Verbenaceae) with solitary axillary flowers — see JAMAICA VERVAIN

stach·y·u·rus \,stakəˈyu̇rəs\ *n*, *cap* [NL, fr. Gk *stachys* + NL *-urus*] **:** a small genus (coextensive with the family Stachyuraceae of the order Parietales) of Asiatic shrubs and trees having regular tetramerous flowers in long drooping racemes and small globose fruits

¹stack \ˈstak\ *n* -S [ME *stak*, fr. ON *stakkr*; akin to OE *staca* stake — more at STAKE] **1 :** a large pile (as of hay, grain in the sheaf, or straw) that is usu. nearly conical but sometimes rectangular, is commonly contracted at the top to a point or ridge, and is often thatched to shed rain **2 a :** a usu. orderly and systematically arranged pile or heap ⟨shuttled back and forth between the sink and the table, building her ~*s* of dried dishes —Lenard Kaufman⟩ ⟨keeps a great ~ of back copies of the magazine —Joseph Mitchell⟩ ⟨a ~ of wood⟩ ⟨a ~ of pancakes⟩ **b :** a large quantity or number ⟨there was a considerable ~ of evidence —G.A.Morran⟩ ⟨often spends his evenings working on ~*s* of papers he has brought home —*Current Biog.*⟩ ⟨has a ~ of money⟩ **3 :** an English unit of measure esp. for wood as fuel that is equal to 108 cubic feet **4 a :** CHIMNEY STACK **b :** a vertical pipe (as to carry off smoke) **:** CHIMNEY, FUNNEL, SMOKESTACK **c :** the part of a blast furnace or cupola above the hearth and melting zone **d :** the exhaust pipe of an internal-combustion engine — compare BAYONET STACK **e :** a fireplace and its chimney for cooking varnish **f :** a set of radiators in a cellar for heating apartments above by hot air conveyed through tin pipes; *also* **:** the tin pipe by which the heat is conveyed to an apartment **5 :** a rocky islet that is commonly steep-sided and near a cliffy shore and that has been isolated by wave erosion — compare CHIMNEY 2c **6 a :** a pyramidal self-supporting pile of arms; *specif* **:** a pile composed of three rifles interlocked by their stacking swivels **7 a** (1) **:** a structure of bookshelves separated by narrow aisles that is one or more stories in height and is used for compact storage of books — usu. used in pl. (2) **:** the portion of a building housing such a structure — usu. used in pl. **b :** a collection of bookcases compactly arranged **8 :** a row of benches containing retorts for use in gas manufacturing **9 :** a number of usu. similar antennas mounted together and operated as part of a single radio system **10 :** an assembled set of calender rolls with the required accessories **11 :** AIR STACK **12 a :** an established quantity of chips sold at one time to a gambler (as in poker) — called also *takeout* **b :** the supply of chips belonging to a cardplayer at any given time

²stack \"\ *vb* -ED/-ING/-S [ME *stakken*, fr. *stak*, n.] *vt* **1 a :** to pile up **:** make into a usu. neat heap or pile ⟨so many millions so tightly packed and ~*ed* into such tall hives —G.S.Perry⟩ ⟨~*ed* the firewood in the cellar⟩ **b :** to place quantities of something on or in **:** LOAD ⟨the floor was ~*ed* high with bales of dry goods —Winston Churchill⟩ ⟨~ the bulkheads with cargoes from every port in the world —*Amer. Guide Series: N. Y. City*⟩ **2 :** to arrange in a stack ⟨~*ed* their arms and lowered their flag —*Amer. Guide Series: La.*⟩ **3 a :** to arrange (cards or a pack of cards) secretly for cheating ⟨the cards were ~*ed* against him⟩ **b :** to weight the composition of dishonestly or unfairly ⟨they ~*ed* juries and stole elections —*Springfield (Mass.) Daily News*⟩ ⟨charged . . . that the conference was ~*ed* against the supporters of federal aid —M.W.Straight⟩ **4 :** to assign (an airplane approaching an airport) by radio to a particular altitude and position within a group circling and waiting a turn to land **5 :** to make the belly of (an archery bow) high and narrow **~** *vi* **1 :** to form a stack **:** HEAP, PILE ⟨the containers are low in cost, set up easily and ~ well —*Appliance Manufacturer*⟩ **2 :** to form a line or group **:** ACCUMULATE — used with *up* ⟨long double lines of cars ~*ed up* on either side of the site —*Springfield (Mass.) Union*⟩

stacked *adj*, *slang*, *of a woman* **:** having a well developed figure **:** BUILT

¹stack·er \ˈstakə(r)\ *n* -S [²*stack* + *-er*] **:** one that stacks: as **a :** one whose work is stacking articles (as for transportation or storage) **b :** an elevator or blast tube attachment to a threshing machine for stacking the straw (as on a wagon) — compare WIND STACKER

²stack·er \ˈstakər\ *Scot var of* STAGGER

stack·freed \ˈstak,frēd\ *n* -S [origin unknown] **:** an eccentric wheel or cam having a spring pressing on it and formerly attached to the barrel of the earliest mainspring-driven timepieces to equalize the force transmitted

stack·garth \ˈstagə(r)th\ *n* -S [ME *stakgarth*, fr. ON *stakkgarthr*, fr. *stakkr* haystack + *garthr* yard — more at STACK, YARD] *dial Eng* **:** STACKYARD

stack gas *n* **:** the gas passing through a smokestack — compare FLUE GAS

stack·hou·sia \stakˈhau̇zēə\ *n*, *cap* [NL, fr. John *Stackhouse* †1819 English botanist + NL *-ia*] **:** a genus of xerophytic mostly Australasian herbs (family Stackhousiaceae) having yellow or white and often gamopetalous flowers

stack·hou·si·a·ce·ae \,stak,hau̇zēˈāsē,ē\ *n pl*, *cap* [NL, fr. *Stackhousia*, type genus + *-aceae*] **:** a family of plants (order Sapindales) having a distinctly lobed ovary that produces a schizocarp

stacking swivel *n* **:** a swivel on a rifle for stacking it

stack process *n* **:** DUTCH PROCESS

stack room *n* **:** a room housing a library stack

stack silage *n* **:** silage made from chopped forage built into a pile above ground

stackstand \ˈ=,=\ *n* **:** a scaffolding for supporting a stack of hay or grain **:** RICKSTAND, STADDLE

stack up *vi* **1 :** to add up **:** TOTAL ⟨this is how things *stack up* today —*Time*⟩ **2 :** to measure up **:** COMPARE, MATCH — usu. used with *against* ⟨how does our product *stack up* against competitive products —Bud Wilson⟩ ⟨how does this ideal secretary *stack up* against the working secretary —Herbert Mitgang⟩

stackyard \ˈ=,=\ *n* **:** a yard or field containing straw or grain in stacks

stac·te \ˈstaktē\ *n* -S [L, myrrh, fr. Gk *staktē*, fr. fem. of *staktos* oozing out in drops, fr. *stazein* to drip — more at STAGNATE] **:** a sweet spice used by the ancient Jews in preparing incense

stac·tom·e·ter \stakˈtäməd·ə(r)\ *n* [Gk *staktos* oozing out in drops + E *-meter*] **:** STALAGMOMETER

stad \ˈstät\ *n* -S [Afrik, town, city, fr. MD *stat*, *stad* place, town, city; akin to OE *stede* place — more at STEAD] *Africa* **:** a native village

stad·dle \ˈstadᵊl\ *n* -S [ME *stathel* base, foundation, support, fr. OE *stathol* (also, heavens, estate, farm); akin to OFris *stathul* base, foundation, OHG *stadal* barn, shed, ON *stöthull* milking shed, OE *stede* place — more at STEAD] **1 :** a small tree or sapling; *esp* **:** a small forest tree **2 a :** the lower part of a stack (as of hay) **b :** the supporting frame or base of a stack

stade \ˈstād\ *n* -S [MF *estade*, fr. L *stadium* — more at STADIUM] **:** STADIUM ⟨the circuit of the course was about six ~*s* —Richard Stillwell⟩

sta·der splint \ˈstādə(r)-\ *n*, *usu cap 1st S* [after Otto *Stader* *b*1894 Am. veterinarian] **:** a splinting device consisting of two stainless steel pins inserted in the bone above and below a fracture or break and a turnbuckle bar joining the pins for drawing and holding the broken ends together

¹stadia *pl of* STADIUM

²sta·dia \ˈstādēə\ *n* -S [It, prob. fr. L, pl. of *stadium*] **1 a :** STADIA ROD **b :** a surveying method using a stadia rod **2 :** an instrument with stadia hairs

stadia hairs *or* **stadia wires** *n pl* **:** horizontal cross hairs (as in a theodolite) equidistant from the central horizontal cross hair

¹sta·di·al \ˈstādēəl\ *adj* [*stadium* + *-al*] **:** of or relating to a stage, stadial, or stadium

²stadial \"\ *n* -S **:** a substage of a glacial stage; *esp* **:** one marked by a readvance of ice

stadia rod *n* **:** a graduated rod used with an instrument having stadia hairs to measure the distance from the observation point to the place where the rod is positioned by observation of the length of rod subtended by the distance between the stadia hairs when these are fixed or of the space between the stadia hairs when they are adjusted to cover a certain definite interval on the rod

sta·dic \ˈstādik\ *adj* [*stadia* + *-ic*] **:** of or relating to a stadia

sta·dim·e·ter \stəˈdiməd·ə(r)\ *n* [*stadium* + *-meter*] **:** an instrument for measuring the distance of an object of known height

sta·di·um \ˈstādēəm\ *n*, *pl* **sta·dia** \-ēə\ *or* **stadiums** [ME, fr. L, fr. Gk *stadion*, alter. (influenced by *stadios* fixed, stable) of *spadion*, fr. *span* to pull, draw, tear — more at SPAN] **1 a** *also* **sta·di·on** \-ē,än\ [*stadion* fr. Gk] **:** any of various ancient Greek units of length equal to 600 Greek feet **b :** an ancient Roman unit of length equal to 625 Roman feet or 606.95 English feet **2 a :** a course for footraces in ancient Greece orig. one stadium in length **b :** a terraced structure with seats for spectators surrounding an ancient Greek running track and typically built in the shape of a long narrow horseshoe **c** *pl usu* *stadiums* **:** a large usu. unroofed structure with tiers of seats for spectators built in various shapes (as circular or elliptic) and enclosing a field usu. used for sports events (as baseball, football, track and field) — compare CIRCUS **3** [NL, fr. L] **:** a phase of development or growth **:** PERIOD; *specif* **:** the interval between any two successive molts in the development of an insect

Stadium Boot *trademark* — used for a usu. ankle-high fleece-lined boot worn by women and children for warmth

stadt·hold·er \ˈstat,hōldə(r)\ *also* **stad·hold·er** \-ad-,\ *n* -S [part trans. of D *stadhouder* (formerly spelled also *stadthouder*), fr. *stad* place, town, city (fr. MD *stat*, *stad*) + *houder* holder — more at STAD] **1 a :** a viceroy in a province of the Netherlands **b :** a chief executive officer of the United Provinces of the Netherlands **2 :** a viceroy or lieutenant governor of a region outside the Netherlands

stadt·hold·er·ate \-ə,rāt\ *n* -S **:** the office or position of a stadtholder

stadt·hold·er·ship \-ə(r),ship\ *n* **:** STADTHOLDERATE

stadt·house \ˈstat+,-\ *n* [part trans. of D *stadhuis* (formerly spelled also *stadthuis*), fr. *stad* town, city + *huis* house] **:** a town hall in a town or colony of the Netherlands

¹staff \ˈstaf, |aa(ə)f, |aif, |af\ *n*, *pl* **staffs** \|fs\ *or* **staves** \|vz, ˈstāvz\ [ME *staf*, fr. OE *stæf*; akin to OHG *stab* staff, ON *stafr* staff, Goth *stabim* (dat. pl.) elemental substances, MIr *sab* shaft, staff, Gk *stemphylon* olive pulp, Skt *stabhnāti*, *stambhate* he supports — more at STAMP] **1 a :** a long stick carried in the hand for support in walking ⟨stumping with his ~ —Robert Browning⟩ ⟨my signs are a rainproof coat, good shoes, and a ~ cut from the woods —Walt Whitman⟩ **b :** a strong usu. rigid rod or bar used to hold or support something

⟨wears a corset with steel *staves* and braces —*Springfield (Mass.) Union*⟩ ⟨a number of hardwood *staves*, fixed crosswise —*Dyestuffs*⟩: as (1) *archaic* : SHAFT 1a(1) (2) : a round bar that is used as a crosspiece (as in a ladder or chair) : RUNG (3) : FLAGSTAFF ⟨twisting the flag around the ~ —*Boy Scout Handbk.*⟩ (4) : a pivoted arbor (as of a wheel or a pinion of a watch) (5) : a vertical bead molding at the angle between walls **c** : CLUB, CUDGEL ⟨a ~ is quickly found to beat a dog —Shak.⟩ **d** : something that upholds or sustains : PROP, SUPPORT ⟨his early successes will be the stout ~ which will support him —H.H.Arnold & I.C.Eaker⟩ **2 a** : a pole with a crook or cross that forms part of the insignia of an ecclesiastic (as a bishop) **b** : a rod carried as a symbol of office or position ⟨*staves* carried by the leading men of the society —L.M. Wulcko⟩ **c** : a rod used by a magician : WAND ⟨over them a gnarled ~ she shook —John Keats⟩ **d** : a small rod or other token handed to a railroad engineer as his authority to proceed over a particular section **3 a** *obs* : STANZA ⟨let me hear a ~ —Shak.⟩ **b** : the horizontal lines with their spaces on which music is written — called also *stave;* compare CLEF, LEDGER LINE **c** : a set of vertical lines for the placement of dance-movement symbols — compare LABAN SYSTEM **4** : any of various graduated sticks or rules used for measuring (as in shipbuilding, surveying) : ROD ⟨setting up gauging *staves*, against which the water level can be read —*Geog. Jour.*⟩ **5** *pl staffs* : the personnel responsible for the functioning of an institution or the establishment or the carrying out of an assigned task under an overall director or head ⟨put together an excellent ~ to assist him in his diplomatic mission⟩ ⟨a small ~ of servants takes care of the house⟩ ⟨is on the editorial ~ of the newspaper⟩: as **a** : the teaching and administrative personnel of an educational institution **b** : the doctors and surgeons regularly attached to a hospital and helping to determine its policies and guide its activities **c** : the personnel of an organization (as an industrial enterprise) that furnishes auxiliary and advisory services and does not participate directly in production — compare ³LINE 6j(2), LINE ORGANIZATION **d** (1) : the officers detailed to serve on the staff of the commander of a fleet or lesser unit (2) : the officers (as in the U.S. Navy) not eligible for command at sea **e** (1) : a group of officers in an army who assist (as by collection and analysis of information, organization of supplies and services, planning of operations) a commanding officer — see GENERAL STAFF, PERSONAL STAFF, SPECIAL STAFF, UNIT STAFF (2) : the noncombatant forces of an army — compare ³LINE 6e(1) **f** : the group of officers and aides appointed to attend upon and serve as escort to a civil executive (as a president or governor) — **at staff's end** *or* **at stave's end** *archaic* : at arm's length

²**staff** \"\ *vt* -ED/-ING/-S : to supply with a staff : provide the necessary personnel for ⟨a large modern plant, finely housed and ~*ed* —*Amer. Guide Series: N.H.*⟩ ⟨we are ~*ing* the faculties of other institutions —McGeorge Bundy⟩

³**staff** \"\ *adj* **1** : of, relating to, or constituting a staff ⟨~ work⟩ ⟨~ officers⟩ ⟨~ personnel⟩ **2** : having an auxiliary or advisory relationship to the stated objective of an organization ⟨the personnel department of a manufacturing concern performs a ~ function⟩

⁴**staff** \"\ *n* -S [prob. fr. G *staffieren* to trim, decorate — more at STAFFAGE] : a building material having a plaster of paris base and used in exterior wall coverings of temporary buildings

staf·fage \stəˈfäzh\ *n* -S [G, fr. *staffieren* to trim, decorate (fr. LG *stafferen*, fr. MLG *stofferen, stafferen*, fr. MD *stofferen*, fr. MF *estoffer* to stuff, trim, decorate) + F *-age* — more at STUFF] : the accessories of an artistic composition; *esp* : human or animal figures added as subordinate elements to the painting of a landscape

staff angle *n* : a corner of metal or wood set into the plaster so as to be flush with the wall surfaces forming an angle in order to secure the corner from injury

staff bead *n* **1** : a bead used to close the joint between a wooden frame and the adjacent masonry **2** : a molded or beaded staff angle

staff cell *n* [trans. of G *stabzelle*] : STAB CELL

staff corps *n* : the personnel of a staff branch of the military service

staff·er *pronunc at* STAFF + ə(r)\ *n* -S : a member of a staff; *specif* : a member of the editorial or reportorial staff of a newspaper, periodical, or press association — compare STRINGER

staf·fette \staˈfet\ *n* -S [MF *estaffette* — more at ESTAFETTE] *archaic* : ESTAFETTE

staff–herd \ˈ=,=\ *vt* : to put (livestock) to graze esp. in charge of a herdsman

staff notation *n* : musical notation in which a staff is used — see PITCH illustration

staff of aesculapius *usu cap A* [after *Aesculapius*, Greco-Roman god of medicine, fr. L, fr. Gk *Asklēpios*] : a conventionalized representation of a staff branched at the top with a single snake twined around it that is used as a symbol of medicine and as the official insignia of the American Medical Association — called also *Aesculapian staff;* compare CADUCEUS

staff of Aesculapius

staff officer *n* **1** : an officer serving on a staff **2** : a member of the Salvation Army attached to a headquarters and responsible for administrative work or for work in a specialized field

staff of life : a staple of diet; *esp* : BREAD ⟨produced a *staff of life* about two feet in length, and cut off a good thick slice for each of them —C.B.Fairbanks⟩

staf·ford \ˈstafə(r)d\ *adj, usu cap* [fr. *Stafford*, England] **1** : of or from the municipal borough of Stafford, England : of the kind or style prevalent in Stafford **2** : STAFFORDSHIRE

¹**staf·ford·shire** \-d,shi(ə)r, -,shiə, -,shə(r)\ *adj, usu cap* [fr. *Staffordshire*, England] : of or from the county of Stafford, England : of the kind or style prevalent in Stafford

²**staffordshire** *or* **staffordshire ware** *n, usu cap S* : glazed ceramic ware produced in Staffordshire during the 18th and 19th centuries

staffordshire terrier *also* **staffordshire bullterrier** *n, usu cap S* : BULLTERRIER

staff ride *or* **staff walk** *n* : a tactical ride or walk for training in staff problems

staff rush *n* : a stiff tufted bog herb (*Juncus conglomeratus*) of the north temperate zone having isolated heads of chaffy flowers — called also *pith rush*

staffs *pl of* STAFF, *pres 3d sing of* STAFF

staff sergeant *n* : a noncommissioned officer rating in the army just below a platoon sergeant and above a sergeant, in the air force just below a technical sergeant and above an airman first class, and in the marine corps just below a gunnery sergeant and above a sergeant — see CHEVRON illustration

staff system *n* : a block system in which a suitably inscribed staff is delivered to the engineer of a train or caught up by the engine while moving as authority giving the right of way to a designated station

staff tree *n* : a tree or shrub of the genus *Celastrus*

staff–tree family *n* : CELASTRACEAE

staff vine *n* : BITTERSWEET 2b

¹**stag** \ˈstag, -aag, -aig\ *n* -S *see sense 1* [ME *stagge*, fr. OE *stagga;* akin to ON *andarsteggi* drake, Icel *steggi* drake, gander, tomcat, male fox, Sw *stagg*, a kind of stiff grass, OE *stingan* to sting — more at STING] **1** *or pl* **stag a** : the adult male of the red deer; *specif* : one five years of age or older — compare HIND **b** : the male of various other deer of the genus *Cervus* **c** : the male of various other large deer (as the caribou) **2** *chiefly Scot* : a young horse; *esp* : a young unbroken stallion **3** : a male animal castrated after the secondary sex characteristics have developed to such a point as to give it the appearance of a mature male **4 a** : a young male domestic fowl: (1) : a market fowl on which the spurs are developing and which is less tender than a fryer but still suitable for roasting (2) : a young gamecock that has not passed through its first full molt **b** *Brit* : TURKEY-COCK **5** *Brit* : INFORMER 3 **6** *Brit* : one who subscribes for shares of an announced issue of stock with the intention of selling at a profit as soon as possible **7 a** : a social gathering of men only ⟨automobile trips and luncheons for the ladies, and banquets and a ~ for the menfolks —*Daily Plumbers Trade Jour.*⟩ **b** : a person who attends a social gathering (as a dance) unaccompanied by someone of the opposite sex ⟨he joined the other ~*s* watching the dancers⟩ ⟨some of them come with their dates . . . but most of the girls are ~*s* —*Accent*⟩

²**stag** \"\ *vb* **stagged; stagged; stagging; stags** *vt* **1** *Brit* : to keep an eye on : spy on **2** : to cut down : SHORTEN; *specif* : to cut off (trousers) at the knees or just above the boot tops ⟨mackinaws and waist overalls, *stagged* at the boot tops —*Amer. Guide Series: Wash.*⟩ ~ *vi* **1** *Brit* : to turn informer **2** *Brit* : to speculate in stocks as a stag **3** : to attend a social function (as a dinner or dance) without a companion of the opposite sex : go stag ⟨had planned to ~ at the class dance —William Du Bois⟩

³**stag** \"\ *adj* **1 a** : restricted to men : for men only ⟨a ~ dinner⟩ ⟨a ~ party⟩ **b** : intended or suitable for a gathering of men only ⟨a ~ movie⟩ **2** : unaccompanied by someone of the opposite sex ⟨three ~ women in beautiful ermine coats —Speed Lamkin⟩

⁴**stag** \"\ *adv* : as a stag ⟨she had a cold, so he went along ~ —Victoria Lincoln⟩ ⟨many girls now prefer to dance ~ at a cotillion —*N.Y.Sun*⟩

stag beetle *n* : any of numerous mostly large lamellicorn beetles (as *Lucanus capreolus* of northeastern U.S. or *L. cervus* of Europe) that constitute the family Lucanidae and have males generally much larger than the females and with long and often branched mandibles suggesting the antlers of a stag and larvae which feed on the rotten wood of dead trees

stagbush *also* **stagbrush** \ˈ=,=\ *n* : BLACK HAW 1

¹**stage** \ˈstāj\ *n* -S [ME, fr. OF *estage* (also, position, place,

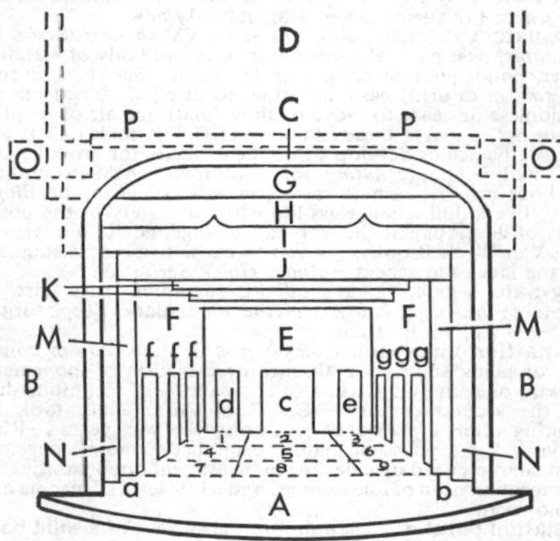

stage 2b(2): proscenium, *A;* wings, *B,B;* proscenium arch, *C;* flies, *D;* back flat, *E;* flats, *F,F;* asbestos curtain, *G;* grand drape, *H;* act drop, *I;* teaser, *J;* borders, *K,K;* returns, *M,M;* tormentors, *N,N;* fly gallery, *O,O;* bridge, *P,P; 1* up right center; *2* up center; *3* up left center; *4* right center; *5* center; *6* left center; *7* down right center; *8* down center; *9* down left center; *a* right first entrance; *b* left first entrance; *c* center entrance; *d* right center entrance; *e* left center entrance; *f,f,f,* right side entrances; *g,g,g,* left side entrances

stay, habitation), fr. (assumed) VL *staticum*, fr. L *stare* to stand + *-aticum* -age — more at STAND] **1 a** : a story of a building : a horizontal division of a structure ⟨a low square tower in four ~*s* —*Amer. Guide Series: Md.*⟩ **b** : one of a series of positions or stations one above the other : GRADE, STEP ⟨the garden that sloped, ~ by ~ precipitously down to the water —F.M.Ford⟩ **c** : a set of shelves : SHELF; *specif* : a tier of shelves (as in a greenhouse) on which potted plants are placed ⟨the height of the glass above the greenhouse ~*s* —*So. African Garden Manual*⟩ **d** : the height of the surface of a river above an arbitrary zero point — see FLOOD STAGE **e** : the distance between two levels (as in hoisting) **2 a** : a raised platform for the better viewing of something by an audience ⟨spoke from a small ~ erected at the edge of the airport⟩ ⟨give order that these bodies high on a ~ be placed to the view —Shak.⟩ **b**(1) : the raised flooring in a theater or auditorium on which plays or other spectacles (as operas or ballets) are enacted (2) : the part of a theater between the proscenium and the rear wall including the acting area, wings, and storage space —called also *stagehouse* (3) : the dramatic art or profession : THEATER — usu. used with *the* ⟨attracted by the ~ ever since she was a child⟩ **c** : a place where something is exhibited or done : a center of attention or a scene of action ⟨all the world's a ~ —Shak.⟩ ⟨those diseases . . . now occupy the center of the medical ~ —R.J.Thomas⟩ ⟨the end of the eighteenth century set the ~ for a new middle-class struggle —Roy Lewis & Angus Maude⟩ **3 a** : a scaffold used to support workmen and their materials ⟨~*s* rigged overside swarmed with . . . shipfitters, busy removing crumpled shell plating —K.M.Dodson⟩ **b** : an elevated structure used for drying fish **c** : LANDING STAGE **d** : a platform used as a base or support; *specif* : the small platform of the stand of a microscope or polariscope on which an object is placed for examination **4 a** : a place of rest formerly provided for those traveling by stagecoach : STATION **b** : the distance between two stopping places on a road : a degree of advance in a journey ⟨proceeded by easy ~*s*, some of them spending the night near my camp —Douglas Carruthers⟩ **c** (1) : STAGECOACH ⟨sat on the slippery leather seat of the old ~ —Margaret Deland⟩ (2) : a motor vehicle that carries mail or passengers (3) : AIR STAGE **5 a** : a period or step in a process, activity, or development ⟨there were three ~*s* in the cutting process —G. S. & Helen McKearin⟩ ⟨came to bat with a teammate on base in the late ~*s* of a close ball game —W.B.Furlong⟩ ⟨aware of the ~*s* in child growth and development —*Current Biog.*⟩ **b** (1) : a period or phase in the course of a disease ⟨the preeruptive ~ of an eruptive fever⟩ ⟨sweating ~ of malaria⟩ (2) : one of two or more operations performed at different times but constituting a single procedure ⟨2-*stage* thoracoplasty⟩ ⟨the operation should be done in two or three ~*s*⟩ (3) : one of the four degrees indicating depth of general anesthesia ⟨~ of excitement⟩ ⟨~ of surgical anesthesia⟩ **c** : one of the steps into which the material development of man or a people is divided : a particular economy ⟨pastoral ~⟩ ⟨hunting ~⟩ ⟨nomadic ~⟩ **d** : a division of a culture or culture period with respect to time, content, or development **e** (1) : a minor subdivision of a stratigraphic series (2) : a part of a cycle of erosion in which the features of the landscape have characteristics that distinguish them from similar features in other parts of the cycle (3) : a subdivision of the Pleistocene epoch ⟨the Illinoian glacial ~⟩; *also* : STADIAL (4) : a particular phase in the historical development of a geologic feature ⟨the Calumet ~ of Lake Chicago⟩ **f** (1) : one of several periods whose beginning and end are usu. marked by some important change of structure in the development and growth of many animals and plants ⟨the larval ~⟩ — see INSTAR (2) : an organism in a specified stage ⟨the tadpole is the larval ~ of a frog⟩ **g** : one complete process or step (as of a fluid passing through one impeller of a multiple-impeller pump) — see PRESSURE STAGE, VELOCITY STAGE **h** : an element or part in a complex electronic contrivance; *specif* : a single tube with its associated components in an amplifier **i** : a propulsion unit of a rocket with its own fuel and container ⟨the first ~ raises all the ~*s* until its fuel is gone⟩ — **on the stage** *adv (or adj)* : in or into the acting profession ⟨has been *on the stage* for many years⟩ ⟨gave up his career to go *on the stage*⟩

²**stage** \"\ *vb* -ED/-ING/-S *vt* **1** *archaic* : to furnish with a scaffold **2** : to put into a play or public show ⟨the quick comedians extemporally will ~ us —Shak.⟩ ⟨his play . . . *staged* only one woman character among airmen —Edmund Fuller⟩ **3 a** : to produce on the stage : put on ⟨*staged* the play in a spectacular fashion⟩ ⟨*staged* a number of new ballets this season⟩ ⟨*staged* the opera with new scenery⟩ **b** : to produce for public view ⟨~ a track meet⟩ ⟨~ a special art exhibition⟩ ⟨~ an elaborate parade⟩ **c** : to bring about or cause to take place esp. in a dramatic or spectacular manner ⟨*staged* a brief hunger strike yesterday —*N.Y.Times*⟩ ⟨*staged* huge protest demonstrations —Anne Bauer⟩ ⟨led his followers to ~ an attempt to release him from custody —L.S.B.Leakey⟩ ⟨the entirely unpredictable . . . weather had decided to ~ a clear sunny day in the middle of December —C.S.Forester⟩ **d** : to arrange or present for public effect : CONTRIVE ⟨*staged* a fake accident⟩ **4** : to place (potted plants) on a layer of sand, gravel, or other medium in a greenhouse **5** : to move (as military personnel, supplies, or equipment) to or establish in a new base in preparation for a further movement or a planned operation ⟨seize bases that would permit *staging* our aircraft forward —F.J.Sackton⟩ **6** : to protect (areas of a printing plate that require no further etching) with a resist of asphalt varnish or other solution ~ *vi* **1** : to travel by stage ⟨after four and a half days of continuous *staging* . . . he arrived —G.R.Stewart⟩ **2** : to establish a military base or position ⟨*staging* there for attacks —*Time*⟩ ⟨ordnance company *staging* for the night nearby —*Yale Rev.*⟩

³**stage** \"\ *adj* **1** : CONVENTIONALIZED, STEREOTYPED ⟨so French as to make him seem almost a ~ Frenchman —Osbert Sitwell⟩ ⟨the face of a ~ curate —Fred Majdalany⟩ **2** : of, relating to, or constituting a manner of pronouncing a language on formal occasions (as in stage acting or public speaking) that is not necessarily identical with any one dialect of the language and that seeks to avoid dialectal features that have the least currency among educated speakers

stage box *n* : a theater box over the proscenium

stage brace *n* : a brace used to support stage scenery (as flats) from behind

stage business *n* : BUSINESS 4

stage carriage *n* : STAGECOACH

stage cloth *n* : a cloth or hanging used about a stage; *specif* : a cloth to cover the floor of a stage

stagecoach \ˈ=,=\ *n* : a heavy usu. four-in-hand closed coach formerly making regular trips between stations and carrying passengers and goods — see ROAD COACH

stagecraft \ˈ=,=\ *n* : the art or practice of effective management of theatrical devices or techniques (as in dramatic composition, acting, directing)

staged *adj* **1 a** : written for or produced on the stage ⟨a ~ version of the novel⟩ **b** : deliberately planned and arranged for effect or deception : CONTRIVED ⟨not going to be taken in by one of those artfully ~ photographs —Philip Guedalla⟩ ⟨~ confessions and railings against sin —Nona B. Brown⟩ **2** : arranged or taking place in stages ⟨called for ~ reduction of both atomic and conventional weapons —*N.Y.Times*⟩

stage direction *n* : a description or direction written or printed in a play (as to describe a character or setting or to indicate a piece of stage business)

stage director *n* **1** : DIRECTOR 1c **2** : STAGE MANAGER

stage door *n* : an entrance to a theater reserved for actors and stage personnel and used also by authorized visitors

stage–door johnny *n, often cap J* : a man who frequents a theater for the purpose of courting an actress or chorus girl ⟨assumed the role of *stage-door Johnny* to serve papers on a burlesque queen —Ralph Ginzburg⟩

stage driver *n* : one that drives a stage

staged tower *n* : a tower in which the stories are strongly marked (as in a Chinese pagoda or a ziggurat)

stage effect *n* : a showy and artificial effect or contrivance ⟨sheer make-believe, *stage effect* and hocus-pocus —Isaac Deutscher⟩

stage fright *n* : nervousness or panic felt by a person appearing or due to appear before an audience — compare BUCK FEVER

stagehand \ˈ=,=\ *n* : a stage worker who handles scenery and properties : SCENESHIFTER

stagehouse \ˈ=,=\ *n* **1** : a house providing facilities for a stage and its passengers **2** : STAGE 2b(2)

stage–keeper \ˈ=,==\ *n* : a stage attendant in the Elizabethan theater

stageland \ˈ=,=\ *n* : the world of the theater ⟨a pure product of ~, and unrelated to any practical experiences of life —Agnes Repplier⟩

stage·man \ˈstājmən\ *n, pl* **stagemen** : one who works on a stage; *specif* : a worker who helps to prepare the stage for the shooting of motion pictures

stage–manage \ˈ=,==\ *vt* [back-formation fr. *stage manager*] **1 a** : to arrange or exhibit with an eye to striking effect ⟨prewar pageantry, pictorially beautiful and brilliantly *stage-managed* —Mollie Panter-Downes⟩ **b** : to arrange or direct from behind the scenes ⟨arrest and trial had been *stage-managed* for a sinister purpose —*Atlantic*⟩ **2** : to act as stage manager for ⟨*stage-managed* a few more productions, but his heart was set on directing —E.J.Kahn⟩

stage management *n* **1** : the act or process of stage-managing **2** : the function of a stage manager

stage manager *n* : one that supervises the physical aspects of a stage production, assists the director during rehearsals, and is in complete charge of the stage during a performance

stage micrometer *n* : a finely divided scale ruled on a microscope slide and used to calibrate the filar micrometer

stage name *n* : an assumed name by which an actor is known professionally

stageplank \ˈ=,=\ *n* **1** : LANDING STAGE ⟨stood on the end of the ~ with the coil of rope in his hand —Mark Twain⟩ **2** : GANGPLANK ⟨the ~ was taken in on schedule —Shelby Foote⟩

stag·er \ˈstājə(r)\ *n* -S [¹*stage* + *-er*] **1** : one that has experience : one that takes part (as in life, a profession, an activity) : HAND ⟨call the roll of the achievements of the new ~*s* —*Va. Quarterly Rev.*⟩ — usu. used in phrases with *old* ⟨a wise old literary ~ —Cyril Connolly⟩; compare OLD HAND 1 **2** *archaic* : ACTOR **3** : STAGE DRIVER **4** : one that applies an acid resistant to the parts of a rotogravure cylinder that are not to be etched

stage right *n* : a right generally protected by copyright to represent a work in a theater with living actors — usu. used in pl.

stag·ery \ˈstājərē\ *n* -ES [¹*stage* + *-ery*] : STAGECRAFT

stages *pl of* STAGE, *pres 3d sing of* STAGE

stage screw *n* : a tapered screw with a handle that resembles a corkscrew and is used to fasten stage braces to the floor

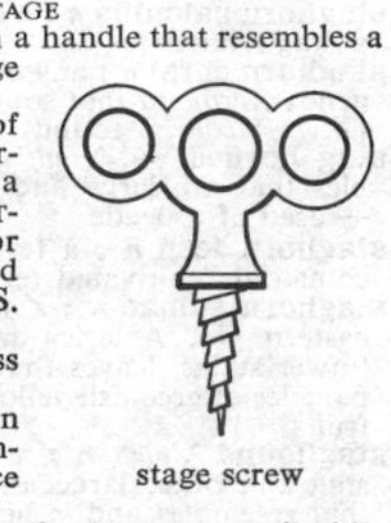

stage screw

stage set *n* **1** : an arrangement of scenery and properties for a particular scene in a play ⟨a house like a *stage set* —Dan Wickenden⟩ **2** : SETTING ⟨wonders if the best *stage set* for learning comes from casual and chance opportunities —Lucy S. Mitchell⟩

stage setting *n* **1** : the act or process of setting the stage **2** : STAGE SET

stage space *n* : the effect esp. in painting of a view limited by a complete block after a very short distance — compare DEEP SPACE

stagestruck \ˈ=,=\ *adj* : fascinated by the stage; *esp* : seized by a passionate desire to become an actor ⟨the youthful who are ~ —John Mason Brown⟩

stage wagon *n* : a wagon used as a stagecoach esp. formerly in thinly settled areas

stage wait *n* : a marked and usu. awkward break in the continuity of the action during a theatrical performance

stage whisper *n* **1** : a loud whisper by an actor that is audible to the spectators but is supposed for dramatic effect not to be heard by one or more of the actors **2** : any distinctly audible whisper

stage–whisper \ˈ=,==\ *vi* [*stage whisper*] : to speak in a stage whisper

¹**stagewise** \ˈ=,=\ *adj* [¹*stage* + *wise*] : theatrically knowledgeable or effective ⟨a ~ director⟩ ⟨less commanding as musical compositions, but bright and ~ —C.M.Smith⟩

²stagewise \"\ *adv* [¹*stage* + *-wise*] **:** with respect to the stage **:** on the stage ⟨known ~ by another name⟩
stagey *var of* STAGY
stag·gard \ˈstagə(r)d\ *or* **stag·gart** \-(r)t\ *n* -s [ME *staggard*, fr. *stagge* stag + *-ard*] **:** a male red deer in its fourth year
stagged *past of* STAG
¹stag·ger \ˈstagə(r), -aig-\ *vb* **staggered**; **staggered**; **staggering** \-g(ə)riŋ\ **staggers** [alter. of earlier *stacker*, fr. ME *stakeren*, fr. ON *stakra* to push, stagger, freq. of *staka* to punt, push, stagger; akin to MLG *staken* to push, OE *staca* stake — more at STAKE] *vi* **1 a :** to have difficulty in remaining erect **:** reel from side to side **:** stand or walk unsteadily **:** SWAY, TOTTER ⟨the man ~*ed*, with his stomach pushed out, under the weight of the demijohn —Jean Stafford⟩ ⟨an intoxicated motorist . . . ~*s* from his car —Wayne Hughes⟩ ⟨the last weary dancers ~*ed* off —Virginia D. Dawson & Betty D. Wilson⟩ **b :** to move on unsteadily **:** make headway or progress with difficulty ⟨the good little ship is ~*ing* along —E.J. Schoettle⟩ ⟨his coach ~*ed* through that wilderness of mud —James Stern⟩ **c** *of an arrow* **:** HOBBLE **d :** to get along or manage despite difficulties — used with *on* or *along* ⟨education, however, has managed to ~ on in spite of these pleasant diversions —F.J.Moffitt⟩ **2 :** to rock violently **:** SHAKE, TREMBLE, VIBRATE ⟨the whole fabric of the ship seemed to ~ —F.W.Crofts⟩ **3 :** to become doubtful and wavering in purpose, thought, or action **:** HESITATE ⟨at whose immensity even soaring fancy ~*s* —P.B.Shelley⟩ ⟨became ~*ed* and perplexed, a skeptic —Charles Lamb⟩ ~ *vt* **1 :** to cause to doubt or hesitate **:** make helpless **:** NONPLUS, PERPLEX ⟨a solution so bizarre as to ~ the imagination —*Newsweek*⟩ ⟨problems so intricate and laborious that they ~ the most patient mathematician —H.M.Davis⟩ **2 :** to cause to sway unsteadily **:** make reel or totter ⟨if a fighter is ~*ed*, watch closely to see how badly he is hurt —Jack Dempsey⟩ ⟨three young girls . . . doing work that would ~ most men —Louise D. Rich⟩ **3 :** to place alternately at equal distances on either side of a middle line: as **a :** to arrange (as spokes or rivets) on each side of a median line alternately **b** (1) **:** to plant alternately on each side of a median line (2) **:** to plant at irregular distances without reference to a definite line **c :** to arrange (a file) so that the tabs on the cards or folders are placed in different positions **4 :** to arrange in a series of overlapping or alternating periods ⟨the move to ~ city business hours to help ameliorate traffic congestion —*Sydney* (*Australia*) *Bull.*⟩ ⟨feeding is ~*ed* in three shifts between 11:45 and 1:30 —*Management Methods*⟩ **5 :** to adjust (as the wings of a biplane) so that the leading edge of one wing projects beyond the leading edge of another wing
²stagger \"\ *n* -s **1 staggers** *pl but usu sing in constr* **a :** an abnormal condition of domestic mammals and birds associated with damage to the central nervous system and marked by incoordination and a reeling unsteady gait **:** MEGRIMS — called also *blind staggers, mad staggers;* compare EQUINE ENCEPHALOMYELITIS, FORAGE POISONING, GID, ⁵KEEL **b :** CAISSON DISEASE **c :** a condition likened to the staggers (as in disorientation) ⟨a bad case of the verbal ~*s* —*Time*⟩ **2 :** a reeling or tottering movement of one trying to walk or stand **:** an unsteady gait or stance ⟨fling saddle and bridle on the horse and ride . . . into the last ~ of exhaustion —William Faulkner⟩ **3** *slang* **:** ATTEMPT, STAB **4 :** the amount of advance of the leading edge of an upper wing of a multiplane (as a biplane) over that of a lower that is expressed as percentage of gap and is measured from the leading edge of the upper wing along its chord to the point of intersection of this chord with a line drawn perpendicular to the chord of the upper wing at the leading edge of the lower wing with all lines being drawn in a plane parallel to the plane of symmetry
³stagger \"\ *adj* **:** marked by an alternating or overlapping arrangement (as of hours of work or study) ⟨a ~ system was set up to relieve overcrowding in the school⟩ ⟨adoption by the theatres of a ~ plan of curtain times —*N.Y.Times*⟩
staggerbush \ˈ==,=\ *n* **:** a shrub (*Lyonia mariana*) of eastern U.S. that is poisonous to stock and has clusters of nodding pinkish white flowers
staggered stance *n* **:** a football stance in which the feet are spread to the width of the hips and the toe of one foot is on a line behind the heel of the other foot
stag·ger·er \-gərə(r)\ *n* -s **:** one that staggers or causes to stagger; *specif* **:** one that shocks or astonishes ⟨the question, nevertheless, was a ~ —J.C.Lincoln⟩
stagger grass *n* **:** either of two plants with slender grassy leaves that are associated with poisoning of cattle or other livestock: **a :** a common atamasco lily (*Zephyranthes atamasco*) of the eastern U. S. which is reputed to cause staggers in horses **b :** FLY POISON 1
staggering *adj* **:** serving to stagger **:** ASTONISHING, OVERWHELMING ⟨in a few years proved an immediate and ~ problem —A.A.Berle⟩ ⟨represents a ~ investment in time, in skilled labor —Charlton Laird⟩ — **stag·ger·ing·ly** *adv*
staggering bob *n* [*bob* fr. E dial., very young calf, prob. fr. *Bob*, nickname for *Robert*] *dial Brit* **:** a very young calf
staggerweed \ˈ==,=\ *n* **1 :** FIELD LARKSPUR **2 :** CORN WOUNDWORT **3 :** SQUIRREL CORN
stagger wire *n* **:** a wire connecting the upper and lower wings of an airplane and lying in a plane substantially parallel to the plane of symmetry
staggerwort \ˈ==,=\ *n* **:** a ragwort (*Senecio aureus*)
stag·gery \ˈstagərē\ *adj* **:** in a reeling condition **:** UNSTEADY ⟨slightly ~ about the legs, and did not disdain his father's hand beneath his elbow —Elizabeth Goudge⟩
stag·gie \ˈstagi\ *n* -s [¹*stag* + *-ie*] *Scot* **:** COLT
stagging *pres part of* STAG
stag·gy \ˈstagē\ *adj* -ER/-EST [¹*stag* + *-y*] **:** having the appearance of a mature male — used of female or castrated domestic animals
staghead \ˈ=,=\ *n* **1 :** a dieback in which the shape of the projecting dead branches suggests a stag's horns **2 :** WITCHES'-BROOM
stag-headed \ˈ=ˈ==\ *adj* **:** having leafless dead limbs at the top ⟨a *stag-headed* oak⟩
stag-head·ed·ness *n* -ES **:** the condition of being stag-headed
staghorn \ˈ=,=\ *n* **1 :** a stag's horn used as a handle for a knife or for ornamental purposes **2 a** *or* **staghorn moss :** a club moss (*Lycopodium clavatum*) **b :** STAGHORN FERN **3 :** STAGHORN CORAL
staghorn calculus *n* **:** a calculus that branches in the shape of a stag's horns
staghorn coral *n* **:** any of several large branching corals of the genus *Acropora* that somewhat resemble antlers; *esp* **:** a coral (*A. cervicornis*) found in waters off Florida
stag-horned \ˈ=ˈ=\ *adj* **1 :** STAG-HEADED **2 :** having mandibles that are large and palmate or branched like an antler — used of a beetle
staghorn fern *n* **:** a fern of the genus *Platycerium; esp* **:** a commonly cultivated fern (*P. bifurcatum*) of Australia
staghorn sumac *n* **:** a small tree or shrub (*Rhus typhina*) of eastern No. America with velvety-pubescent branches and flower stalks, leaves that turn brilliant red in fall, and dense panicles of greenish yellow flowers followed by bright crimson fruits
staghound \ˈ=,=\ *n* **:** a hound formerly used in hunting the stag and other large animals; *specif* **:** a large heavy hound that resembles and is held to be among the ancestors of the modern English foxhound
sta·gi·ary \ˈstājē,erē\ *n* -ES [ML *stagiarius*, fr. *stagium*, *estagium* term of residence (fr. OF *estage* stage) + L *-arius* -ary — more at STAGE] **:** a resident canon
stagier *comparative of* STAGY *or of* STAGEY
stagiest *superlative of* STAGY *or of* STAGEY
sta·gi·ly \ˈstājəlē, -li\ *adv* **:** in a stagy manner **:** THEATRICALLY
sta·gi·ness \-jēnəs, -jin-\ *n* -ES **:** the quality or state of being stagy **:** THEATRICALITY
staging *n* -s [partly fr. ME, fr. ¹*stage* + *-ing;* partly fr. gerund of ²*stage*] **1 :** SCAFFOLDING ⟨a ~ on which he was working —*Springfield* (*Mass.*) *Daily News*⟩ **2 a :** the business of running stagecoaches **b :** the act of journeying in stagecoaches **3 :** the act or art of putting a play on the stage ⟨the steadily evolving character development which is so vital to this kind of ~ —Henry Hewes⟩ **4 :** division of a process (as the expansion of steam in a turbine) into a series of steps or stages **5 :** the moving of troops or materiel forward in several stages or the assembling of troops or materiel in transit in a particular place
staging area *n* **:** an area in which troops are assembled and readied prior to a new operation or mission
stag·i·rite *also* **stag·y·rite** \ˈstajə,rīt\ *n* -s *cap* [L *Stagirites*, fr. Gk *Stagiritēs*, fr. *Stagiros, Stagira*, city in ancient Macedonia + Gk *itēs* -ite] **:** a native or inhabitant of Stagira ⟨Aristotle, the famous *Stagirite*⟩
stag jump *n* **:** a free jump in figure skating in which one leg is bent and drawn up toward the chest and the other extended behind
stag·mom·e·ter \stagˈmämәd·ə(r)\ *n* [Gk *stagma* something that drips (fr. *stazein* to drip) + E *-o-* + *-meter* — more at STAGNATE] **:** an apparatus for the measurement of the number of drops per unit of volume of a liquid
stag·nance \ˈstagnən(t)s, -aig-\ *n* -s **:** STAGNANCY
stag·nan·cy \-gnənsē, -si\ *n* -ES **:** the quality or state of being stagnant
stag·nant \-gnənt\ *adj* [L *stagnant-, stagnans*, pres. part. of *stagnare* to stagnate] **1 :** not running in a current or stream **:** not flowing **:** MOTIONLESS ⟨the ~ water looked uninviting —T.E.Lawrence⟩ **:** STALE ⟨the place was small and close, and the long disuse had made the air ~ and foul —Bram Stoker⟩ **2 a :** not advancing, developing, or growing **:** not active ⟨politically and economically a backward, ~ area —Stringfellow Barr⟩ ⟨something must be done to revive industry so long ~ —V.L.Parrington⟩ **b :** marked by a lack of vitality, activity, or interest **:** DULL ⟨seemed to wish to escape notice, which was easy at this ~ hour of the day —John Buchan⟩ **c** *of a tree* **:** OVERMATURE — **stag·nant·ly** *adv*
¹stag·nate \ˈstag,nāt, -aig-, *usu* -ād·+V\ *vb* -ED/-ING/-S [L *stagnatus*, past part. of *stagnare*, fr. *stagnum* body of standing water, pond, pool, swamp; akin to OBret *staer* river, brook, Gk *stazein* to drip; basic meaning: to drip] *vi* **1 :** to remain motionless or cease to move or flow ⟨maritime air of tropical origin ~*s* . . . over these islands —G.H.T.Kimble⟩ **2 a :** to fail to advance or develop **:** lose the capacity for growth ⟨arts that had been *stagnating* for centuries —A.M.Rosenthal⟩ ⟨without self-criticism a university will ~ —*Current Biog.*⟩ **b :** to live a dull, changeless life without variety or the possibility of development ⟨he wanted a change, he did not wish to ~ —Van Wyck Brooks⟩ ~ *vt* **:** to cause to become stagnant ⟨~ the labor movement —*Amer. Guide Series: N.Y.*⟩
²stag·nate \-gnət, -g,nāt\ *adj* [L *stagnatus*, past part. of *stagnare*] *archaic* **:** STAGNANT ⟨the water dark, deep, turgid, and ~ —William Bartram⟩
stag·na·tion \stagˈnāshən, -aig-\ *n* -s **1 :** the state or condition of being stagnant **:** absence or cessation of movement, growth, or activity **:** TORPOR ⟨a complete ~ of technique during the second century —C.A.Robinson⟩ ⟨again took up painting after a period of ~ during the war years —Rhys Gwyn⟩ **2 :** a phase of mature capitalist economic development characterized by a decline in investment opportunities, an overaccumulation of idle savings, and a low level of income and employment
stagnation point *n* **1 :** a point on the surface of a solid body immersed in a fluid stream which directly faces the stream and at which the stream lines separate **2 :** a point near the leading edge or nose of a body placed in an airstream at which the airflow divides to go on either side of the body
stag·nic·o·la \stagˈnikələ\ *n, cap* [NL, fr. L *stagnum* standing body of water, pond, pool + *-i-* + NL *-cola* — more at STAGNATE] **:** a genus of common freshwater snails (family Lymnaeidae) including intermediate hosts of the sheep liver fluke and of various trematodes of waterfowls that cause schistosome dermatitis in man
stag·nic·o·lous \-ləs\ *adj* [L *stagn*um + E *-i-* + *-colous*] **:** frequenting or living or thriving in stagnant water
stag·num \ˈstagnəm\ *n, pl* **stag·na** \-nə\ [L] **:** a pool of water without an outlet
stag·o·nos·po·ra \,stagəˈnäspərə\ *n, cap* [NL, fr. Gk *stagon-, stagōn* drop (fr. *stazein* to drip) + NL *-o-* + *-spora* — more at STAGNATE] **:** a large cosmopolitan genus of imperfect fungi (family Sphaeropsidaceae) having oblong several-septate hyaline pycniospores and including some forms that cause leaf diseases of economic plants
stags *pl of* STAG, *pres 3d sing of* STAG
stag's horn *or* **stag's horn moss** *n* **:** STAGHORN 2a
stag's-horn sumac *n* **:** STAGHORN SUMAC
stag tick *n* **:** a fly (*Lipoptena cervi*) of the family Hippoboscidae that is parasitic upon the red deer and that has wings on attaining maturity but sheds them soon after settling on its host
stagworm \ˈ=,=\ *n* **:** the larva of a botfly that infests the stag and esp. of a botfly of the genus *Cephenomyia*
stagy *also* **stagey** \ˈstājē, -ji\ *adj* **stagier**; **stagiest** [¹*stage* + *-y*] **:** having characteristics of the stage; *esp* **:** having an artificial and mannered quality **:** THEATRICAL ⟨his father's ~ gesturing for effect —Irwin Shaw⟩
stagyrite *cap, var of* STAGIRITE
¹stahl·ian \ˈstälēən, -lyən\ *adj, usu cap* [Georg Ernst *Stahl* †1734 Ger. physician and chemist + E *-ian*, adj. suffix] **:** of or relating to G. E. Stahl or his doctrine of animism
²stahlian \"\ *n* -s *usu cap* [Georg E. *Stahl* †1734 + E *-ian*, n. suffix] **:** an adherent of G. E. Stahl and his doctrines
¹staid \ˈstād\ *adj* [fr. past part. of ³*stay*] **1 :** SETTLED, FIXED ⟨his ~ opinion⟩ **2 :** SOBER, GRAVE, SEDATE ⟨~ persons⟩ ⟨~ colors⟩ **syn** see SERIOUS
²staid *past of* STAY
staid·ly *adv, archaic* **:** in a staid manner
staid·ness *n* -ES **:** the quality or state of being staid **:** REGULARITY, SEDATENESS, SERIOUSNESS, STEADINESS
staig \ˈstāg\ *chiefly Scot var of* STAG
stail \ˈstāl, *esp before pause or consonant* -āəl\ *n* -s [alter. of ¹*stale*] *Brit* **:** a long straight wooden handle for a tool (as a hoe)
¹stain \ˈstān\ *vb* -ED/-ING/-S [ME *steynen*, partly fr. MF *desteindre* to discolor & partly of Scand origin; akin to ON *steina* to paint — more at DISTAIN] *vt* **1 :** to discolor with foreign matter **:** make foul (as with spots or blemishes) **2 :** to impart to or suffuse with color ⟨like wine that ~*s* a pearly glass —Elinor Wylie⟩ **3 a :** to corrupt or defile morally **:** taint with guilt, vice, or corruption **b :** to inflict a stigma upon **:** bring reproach on **4** *obs* **:** to eclipse by superior beauty or excellence **5** *obs* **:** to obscure the luster of ⟨whether poverty . . . staineth nobility —Henry Peacham⟩ **6 :** to color (as wood, glass, paper, or cloth) by processes affecting chemically or otherwise the material itself **:** tinge with a color combining with or penetrating the substance ⟨~ wood with acids⟩ — compare DYE **7 :** to foil (the scent of the quarry) esp. by the passage of hounds, horses, cattle, or other animals over the track ~ *vi* **:** to receive a stain **:** absorb coloring matter
²stain \"\ *n* -s **1 :** something that stains: as **a :** a discoloration by foreign matter **:** SPOT ⟨a ~ on his shirt⟩ ⟨water ~*s*⟩ ⟨weather ~*s*⟩ ⟨mineral ~*s*⟩ **b :** a discoloration of the skin **:** BLOTCH **c :** a natural spot of color different from the ground ⟨swift trouts, diversified with crimson ~*s* —Alexander Pope⟩ **2** *obs* **:** a cause of reproach or disgrace ⟨~ to thy countrymen, thou hear'st thy doom —Shak.⟩ **3 :** a taint of guilt (as on one's character, conscience, or reputation) **:** a mark of disgrace or infamy **:** a usu. grave blemish **:** STIGMA, TARNISH ⟨on him had fallen . . . the ~ of the massacres —J.A.Froude⟩ ⟨degrades . . . the unhappy issue of the marriage by fixing upon it the ~ of bastardy —R.B.Taney⟩ **4 :** a dye, pigment, or preparation used in staining: **a :** a solution or dispersion of a dye or pigment in a vehicle (as water, alcohols, or oils) that is usu. thinner than a paint or other coating, transparent, and capable of penetrating the pores of wood or other material instead of forming a protective surface **b :** a dye or mixture of dyes used in microscopy to make visible minute and transparent structures, to differentiate tissue elements, or to produce specific microchemical reactions
stain·abil·i·ty \,=nəˈbiləd·ē, -lətē, -i\ *n* **:** the capacity of cells and cell parts to stain specifically and consistently with particular dyes and stains
stain·able \ˈ=nəbəl\ *adj* **:** capable of being stained ⟨a ~ substance⟩
stained \ˈstānd\ *adj* [ME *steyned*, fr. past part. of *steynen* to stain] **1 :** discolored with stains ⟨a ~ and tattered jacket⟩ — often used in combination ⟨her tear-*stained* cheeks⟩ **2 :** colored with stain ⟨a bookcase ~ and waxed⟩ — often used in combination ⟨a brown-*stained* house⟩
stained glass *n* **:** glass colored or stained; *esp* **:** window glass colored throughout by metallic oxides fused into it or remaining white and cased with colored glass or into whose surface the pigments have been burned
stained-glass \ˈ=ˈ=\ *adj* [*stained glass*] **1 a :** of, relating to, or concerned with stained glass **b :** made of or characterized by stained glass ⟨*stained-glass* windows⟩ **2 :** SANCTIMONIOUS ⟨the extirpation of *stained-glass* tones from the preaching of seminary students⟩ ⟨*stained-glass* attitudes⟩
stained paper *n* **:** paper colored on the surface in a calender stack
stain·er \ˈstānə(r)\ *n* -s [alter. (influenced by *-er*) of ME *steynour*, fr. *steynen* to stain + *-our* -or — more at STAIN] **:** one that stains: as **a :** a worker who applies a coloring or finishing stain (as to wood, furniture, or leather goods) **b :** a worker who prepares the dyes for paper-coating mixtures **c :** a pigment used merely to give color to a paint, as distinguished from the base **d :** any of several insects that stain the material on which they feed — see COTTON STAINER
stai·nier·ite \ˈstīnēə,rīt, stīˈni,r-\ *n* -s [D *stainieriet*, fr. Xavier *Stainier*, 20th cent. Belgian geologist + D *-iet* -ite] **:** a rare mineral CoO(OH) consisting of cobalt oxide-hydroxide and occurring in black mammillary masses
stain·less \ˈstānləs\ *adj* **1 :** free from stain, spot, blemish, or stigma **:** IMMACULATE ⟨the ~ purity of her private life —T.B. Macaulay⟩ ⟨a sea captain of ~ reputation —Llewellyn Howland⟩ **2 a :** highly resistant to stain, corrosion, or tarnish ⟨~ iron⟩ ⟨~ silver⟩ **b :** made principally of such a highly resistant material ⟨~ flatware⟩ ⟨~ sills⟩
stain·less·ness *n* -ES **:** the quality or state of being stainless
stainless steel *n* **:** an alloy steel practically immune to rusting and ordinary corrosion having as its essential alloying constituent chromium usu. 12 to 14 percent but sometimes more in content
stair \ˈsta(a)(ə)r, ˈste|, |ə\ *n* -s *often attrib* [ME *steir, steyer*, fr. OE *stǣger;* akin to MD *steger, steiger* ladder, stair, OE *stīg* narrow path, *stīgan* to move, go up or down, OHG *stīgan* to go up, rise, ON *stīga*, Goth *steigan* to go up, rise, OIr *tīagu* I walk, Gk *steichein* to walk, go, Skt *stighnoti* he goes up, rises] **1 :** a series of steps or flights of steps connected by landings for passing from one level to another ⟨a steep ~ . . . provided access to the upper floor attics —G.E. Fussell⟩ ⟨climbing down the steep and tortuous ~ —H.S. Morrison⟩ — often used in pl. but sing. or pl. in constr. ⟨a narrow private ~*s* to connect the upper and lower rooms —Lewis Mumford⟩ ⟨lurked at the foot of one ~*s* —*New Yorker*⟩ ⟨ascended a ~*s* —Scott Fitzgerald⟩ **2 a :** any one step of a series for ascending or descending to a different level (as within a building) **b** *obs* **:** a step by which one progresses or may progress from one stage or elevation to another (as in rank, dignity, preferment, wealth, or power) **3 stairs** *pl* **:** LANDING STAGE
staircase \ˈ=,=\ *n* [*stair* + *case*] **1 a :** the structure containing a stairway **:** an enclosure for stairs (as of walls or railings) **b :** a flight of stairs with the supporting framework, casing, and balusters **2 :** something resembling or held to resemble a staircase ⟨the dead stream was an interminable ~ of ledges —Alan Le May⟩ **3 :** RIVER 4
staircase curve *n* **:** HISTOGRAM
staircase shell *n* **1 :** WENTLETRAP **2 :** SUNDIAL SHELL
stair dance *n* **:** a tap dance performed up and down a small flight of stairs
stair horse *n* **:** one of the inclined members supporting a flight of stairs
stair rod *n* **:** a metal rod or its equivalent for holding a stair carpet in place in the angle between two steps
¹stairstep \ˈ=,=\ *n* [*stair* + *step*] **1 :** a step in a flight of stairs **2 stairsteps** *pl* **:** a flight of stairs
²stairstep \"\ *vi* **:** to move up or down like the steps in a stairway ⟨narrow streets ~ up the slopes —*Geog. School Bull.*⟩
stair-step \ˈ=ˈ=\ *adj* **:** resembling the steps in a stairway ⟨*stair-step* levels of terrain⟩; *esp* **:** moving up or down like steps in a stairway ⟨*stair-step* inflation⟩
stair tower *n* **:** a clearly defined vertical shaft or tower containing stairs
stairway \ˈ=,=\ *n* **:** one or more flights of stairs and usu. connecting landings providing passage from one level (as of a building) to another
stairwell \ˈ=,=\ *n* [*stair* + *well*] **:** a compartment extending vertically through a building in which stairs are located
stair wire *n* **:** a slender stair rod
staithe \ˈstāth\ *n* -s [ME *stathe*, of Scand origin; akin to ON *stōth* landing place, staithe; akin to OE *stæth* bank, shore, OHG *stad, stado* bank, shore, Goth *staths* place, stead — more at STEAD] *dial Eng* **:** a wharf for transshipment esp. of coal (as from railroad cars into ships)
stak·age \ˈstākāj, -kēj\ *n* -s [²*stake* + *-age*] **:** the action of marking channels by stakes
¹stake \ˈstāk\ *n* -s *often attrib* [ME, fr. OE *staca;* akin to MLG *stake* pointed stick, stake, ON *lȳsistaki* candlestick, L *tignum* beam, Lith *stagaras* long dry stalk] **1 :** a pointed piece of wood or other material driven or designed to be driven into the ground usu. for a specific purpose (as a mark of a boundary, site, or claim, support for a plant, part of a framework, or a tethering rod) **2 :** a post or other support to which a person is bound for execution usu. by burning **3 :** execution by burning at a stake **4 a :** something that is staked for gain or loss; *esp* **:** a sum of money or its equivalent risked **b :** the prize set in any contest — often used in pl. **5 :** a small anvil usu. having a tang to enter a hole in a bench top and used by smiths for light work **6 :** something that may be gained or lost (as by the turn of events) **:** something at stake **:** a permanent interest (as in an enterprise or community) ⟨have a ~ in the country⟩ **7 :** a sporting event in which a stake or prize is put up; *specif* **:** STAKE RACE **8 :** a territorial unit of Latter-day Saint Church jurisdiction comprising a group of wards and governed by a stake presidency **9 :** a wooden post formerly used in leather manufacturing to support a blunt semicircular steel blade over which skins are drawn to and fro to be stretched and softened **10 :** a stick inserted upright in a loop, eye, or mortise at the side or end of a vehicle (as a cart, flatcar, or truck) to retain the load **11 :** any of the longest foundation rods of a basket usu. upset from the bottom — see BASKET illustration **12 :** a tool used by a slater **13 :** the part of a riveter frame that carries the stationary die **14 :** a post of stone or wood or both often elaborately ornamented and set up as a rover in archery **15 :** GRUBSTAKE — **at stake :** at issue **:** in jeopardy **:** INVOLVED, IMPLICATED ⟨his honor is *at stake*⟩

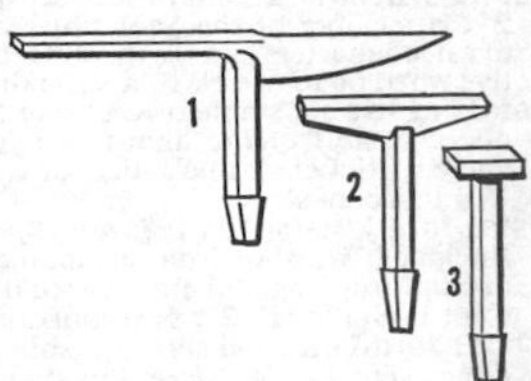

stakes 5: *1* beakhorn, *2* hatchet, *3* square

²stake \"\ *vb* -ED/-ING/-S [ME *staken*, fr. *stake*, n.] *vt* **1 :** to mark the limits of by stakes — usu. used with *out* or *off* **2 :** to tether (an animal) to a stake **3 :** to impale on or transfix with a stake (as formerly in punishment) **4 :** to risk (as one's money or life) upon the issue of competition or upon a future contingency **:** WAGER, VENTURE, BET **5 :** to fasten up or support (as vines or plants) with stakes **6 :** to work (skins) on a stake or in a staking machine in leather manufacturing **:** stretch and flex (leather) to soften it after tanning **7 a :** to back financially **:** support (as a person or enterprise) in order to further chances of success **b :** to advance (as money or supplies) to assist in or in expectation of future success **8 :** GRUBSTAKE ~ *vi* **1 :** to put up a bet **:** WAGER ⟨whether you ~ in pounds or in shillings —*advt*⟩ **2 :** to impale a wheel on the arbor of a clock or watch with the use of hollow punches and with the arbor resting in a die — **stake a claim :** to assert title to something by or as if by placing stakes to satisfy legal requirements ⟨in order to *stake a claim* for a footing in Morocco —Wickham Steed⟩

stake and bound *n* **:** a dead hedge held in place between strong stakes that serves as an obstacle over which horses must jump esp. in fox hunting

stake–and–rider \ˈ⸗⸗ˈ⸗⸗\ *n* **:** a fence having a top bar supported by crossed stakes

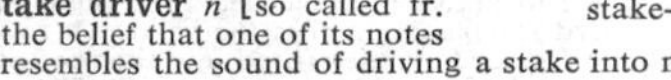

stake-and-rider

stake boat *n* **:** a boat moored to mark the course and esp. the starting point in a race

stake body *n* **:** an open motor-truck body consisting of a platform with stakes inserted along the outside edges to retain a load

stake down *vt* **:** to deposit (as a sum of money) as a wager or stake

stake driver *n* [so called fr. the belief that one of its notes resembles the sound of driving a stake into mud] **:** AMERICAN BITTERN

stakeholder \ˈ⸗,⸗⸗\ *n* **1 :** a person entrusted with the stakes of two or more persons betting against one another and charged with the duty of delivering the stakes to the winner **2 :** a person entrusted with the custody of property or money that is the subject of litigation or of contention between rival claimants in which the holder claims no right or property interest

stake horse *n* **1 :** a horse that runs chiefly in stake races **2 :** a horse of superior quality

stakeman \ˈ⸗,man\ *n, pl* **stakemen :** one who carries and sets stakes for a surveying party

stakemaster \ˈ⸗,⸗⸗\ *n* **:** an official presiding over the stakes of shooting fields in archery

stake net *n* **:** a net held in position by stakes **:** TRAP NET

stake of zion *usu cap Z* [fr. *Zion*, height in the northeastern part of Jerusalem, Palestine that was once the site of Solomon's Temple and the seat of government of the kingdom of Judah] **:** STAKE 8

stake out *vt* **1 :** to assign (as a policeman) to a specified area usu. to conduct a surveillance **2 :** to maintain a police surveillance of (as a suspect or an area)

stakeout \ˈ⸗,⸗\ *n* -S [fr. *stake out*, v.] **:** a surveillance maintained by one or more policemen over an area or a person suspected of criminal activity ⟨a ~ was placed on the home —Courtney McClendon⟩

stake presidency *n* **:** the governing unit of a Latter-day Saint stake consisting of a president and two counselors and a high council of twelve

stak·er \ˈstākə(r)\ *n* -S [ME, fr. *staken* to stake + *-er* — more at STAKE] **1 :** one that stakes: as **a :** PERCHER c **b :** a worker who uses a handpress to fix rivet watch or clock parts together **2** [¹*stake* + *-er*] **:** a plant (as a tomato) of such size that it requires a stake for support when it is planted

stake race *also* **stakes race** *n* **:** a horse race in which the money stake or prize offered is the total contributed by the nominators — compare PURSE RACE

stakerope \ˈ⸗,⸗\ *n* **:** a rope for staking out an animal

stakes *pl of* STAKE, *pres 3d sing of* STAKE

stake truck *n* **:** a truck having a stake body

sta·khanov·ite \stəˈkänə,vīt, -kan-\ *n* -S *usu cap* [Alexei G. *Stakhanov* b1905 Russ. miner who devised a system of higher production + E *-ite*] **:** a worker esp. in the U.S.S.R. whose production is consistently above average and who is therefore awarded recognition and special privileges ⟨said here that *Stakhanovites* . . . make more money than members of the government —Joseph Wechsberg⟩

staking *pres part of* STAKE

stal·ace \ˈstaləs\ *n* -S [irreg. fr. Gk *stalaktos*] **:** a central mass of cells in the root cap of some plants that is evident because its cells are arranged in a distinctly regular radial fashion — called also *columella*

sta·lac·ti·form \stəˈlaktə,fȯrm\ *adj* [¹*stalactite* + *-iform*] **:** resembling a stalactite

¹**stalac·tite** \stəˈlak,tīt *sometimes* ˈstalək-; *usu* -īd.+V\ *n* -S [NL *stalactites*, fr. Gk *stalaktos* dropping, dripping (fr. *stalassein* to let drop, drip) + L *-ites* -ite; fr. the dropping of the waters — more at STALE (urine)] **1 a :** a deposit of crystalline calcium carbonate (as calcite) resembling an icicle, depending from the roof or sides of a cavern, formed by waters that have become saturated with calcium bicarbonate by percolating through and partially dissolving the overlying limestone, and varying from white or colorless to yellow and brown or in some copper mines bright green or blue — compare STALAGMITE **b :** limestone so formed **2 :** a similar formation of some other material ⟨a ~ of lava⟩ **3 :** a small stalactiform projection used in overlapping tiers for ornamentation (as of a vault or capital) in Moorish architecture

²**stalactite** \"\ *or* **stalac·tit·ed** \-īd·əd\ *adj* **:** ornamented with successive rows of stalactites in Moorish architecture ⟨a ~ vault⟩ ⟨~ work⟩

stal·ac·tit·ic \ˌstaləkˈtid·ik\ *also* **stal·ac·tit·i·cal** \-d·əkəl\ *or* **sta·lac·tic** \stəˈlaktik\ *or* **sta·lac·ti·cal** \-təkəl\ *or* **stalac·tit·al** \ˌstaˈlak,tīd·ᵊl, stəˈlak,tī-\ *adj* [*stalactitic, stalactitical* fr. ¹*stalactite* + *-ic* or *-ical*; *stalactic, stalactical* fr. ¹*stalactite* + *-ic* or *-ical*; *stalactital* fr. ¹*stalactite* + *-al*] **1 :** of, relating to, or resembling a stalactite **2 :** covered with stalactites — **stal·ac·tit·i·cal·ly** \ˌstaləkˈtid·ək(ə)lē\ *adv*

sta·lag \ˈs(h)täˌläg\ *n* -S [G, short for *stammlager* base camp, fr. *stamm* base, stem (fr. OHG *stam*) + *lager* camp, place to sleep, bed, fr. OHG *legar* bed — more at STEM, LAIR] **:** a German prison camp for noncommissioned or enlisted prisoners of war

sta·lag·ma \stəˈlagmə, -laig-\ *n* -S [NL, fr. Gk, drop] **:** STALAGMITE 1b

stalag·mite \stəˈlag,mīt, -ˈlaig- *sometimes* ˈstaləg-; *usu* -īd.+V\ *n* -S [NL *stalagmites*, fr. Gk *stalagma* drop, *stalagmos* dropping, dripping + L *-ites* -ite; akin to Gk *stalassein* to let drop, drip — more at STALE (urine)] **1 a :** a deposit of crystalline calcium carbonate more or less like an inverted stalactite formed on the floor of a cave by the drip of water saturated with calcium bicarbonate and often uniting with a stalactite in a complete column **b :** limestone so formed **2 :** a similar formation of some other material

stalagmite marble *n* **:** onyx marble often occurring in a stalagmitic deposit

stal·ag·mit·ic \ˌstaləgˈmid·ik\ *also* **stal·ag·mit·i·cal** \-d·əkəl\ *adj* [*stalagmite* + *-ic* or *-ical*] **:** having the shape or character of or found in stalagmites — **stal·ag·mit·i·cal·ly** \-d·ək(ə)lē\ *adv*

stal·ag·mom·e·ter \ˌstaləgˈmäməd·ə(r), -mətə-\ *n* [Gk *stalagmos* dropping, dripping + E *-meter*] **:** a device characterized by a capillary tube usu. with a flattened tip for determining either the number of drops in a given volume of liquid or the drop weight esp. for use in calculating the surface tension (as of blood or serum) — called also *stactometer* — **sta·lag·mo·met·ric** \stəˌlagməˈme·trik\ *adj* — **sta·lag·mo·met·ri·cal·ly** \-rək(ə)lē\ *adv*

stal·ag·mom·e·try \ˌstaləgˈmämə·trē\ *n* -ES **:** the measurement of surface tension by means of a stalagmometer

¹**stale** \ˈstāl, *esp before pause or consonant* -āəl\ *n* -S [ME, fr. OE *stalu* wood to which harpstrings are fixed; akin to OE *stela* stalk, stem — more at STEAL] **1** *chiefly dial* **:** the stock of an implement (as a rake) **2** *dial Brit* **:** a rung of a ladder **3** *obs* **:** the shaft of an arrow or spear

²**stale** \"\ *adj* -ER/-EST [ME; akin to MD *stel* stale] **1** *obs, of malt liquor* **:** well aged **2 a :** altered in quality through the action of natural processes **:** having undergone physical changes while standing **:** not fresh; *esp* **:** impaired in flavor, odor, or texture by such changes ⟨kept the bread until it was too ~ to eat⟩ ⟨asked the nurse to empty the ~ water and get her a fresh pitcher⟩ **b :** having the unpleasant odor of something that has become stale ⟨a ~ courtyard⟩ **3 :** having lost a former novelty and power of pleasing **:** TRITE, COMMONPLACE ⟨~ and worn phrases —H.D.Gideonse⟩ ⟨news that was ~ by the time it reached him⟩ **4** *archaic* **:** past the age of vigor and attractiveness suitable for marriage **5 a :** impaired in legal force or effect by reason of laches or being allowed to rest without use, action, or demand **:** barred from enforcement by a statute of limitation ⟨a ~ affidavit⟩ ⟨a ~ debt⟩ **b** *of a check* **:** held an unreasonable time after issue before being presented for payment at a bank **6 :** showing a marked loss of vigor, enthusiasm, and effectiveness often due to monotony ⟨many of the old burlesque comics were going ~ for want of fresh material —Henry Hewes⟩ **7 a :** deficient in vitality usu. because of age ⟨a ~ culture of bacteria⟩ **b** *of land* **:** unsuitable as range for the same kind of poultry or livestock because of long use

³**stale** \"\ *vb* -ED/-ING/-S [ME *stalen*, fr. *stale*, n.] *vt* **1 :** to make stale ⟨a smell of previous food *staled* the air —Rose Thurburn⟩ **:** destroy the freshness of ⟨age cannot wither her, nor custom ~ her infinite variety —Shak.⟩ **2** *archaic* **:** to render common **:** CHEAPEN **3 :** to sweat (as sheepskins) at higher temperatures **4** *of an organism* **:** to make (as a culture medium) unsuitable by its metabolic activities for the growth of another kind of organism — used chiefly as a participle or gerund ⟨*staling* products of rhizoctonia⟩ **~** *vi* **:** to become stale: as **a :** to undergo progressive changes in quality of crust, crumb, texture, and flavor ⟨muffins that have *staled*⟩ **b :** to become wearisome, monotonous, or uninteresting ⟨the quickly passing invention of newspaper writers, vaudeville and stage personages . . . will soon ~ —J.P.Bishop⟩

⁴**stale** \"\ *n* -S [ME; akin to MLG *stal* urine of horses, *stallen* to urinate, Gk *stalassein* to let drop, drip and perh. to Lith *įtelžti* to pour in] **:** urine of a domestic animal (as a horse)

⁵**stale** \"\ *vi* -ED/-ING/-S [ME *stalen*; akin to MLG *stallen* to urinate] **:** URINATE — used chiefly of camels and horses

⁶**stale** \"\ *n* -S [ME, bird used as a decoy, fr. AF *estale*, prob. modif. (influenced by OF *estaler* to set, place, fr. *estal* place, stand, stall, of Gmc origin) of OE *stæl*- decoy; akin to OE *stæl* place, stand, OHG *stellen* to set, place, stand — more at STALL] **1** *chiefly dial* **:** a person or thing that lures **:** LURE, DECOY **2** *archaic* **:** a person or thing used as a tool, pretext, or front for illicit or clandestine activity **3** *obs* **:** a butt for ridicule **4** *obs* **:** PROSTITUTE

stale·ly \ˈstā(l)lē, -)i\ *adv* **:** in a stale manner

¹**stalemate** \ˈ⸗,⸗\ *n* [obs. E *stale* stalemate (fr. ME, fr. AF *estale*, lit., fixed position, fr. OF *estal* place, position, stand, stall) + E ³*mate*] **1 :** a drawing position in chess in which only the king can move and although not in check can move only into check **2 :** a position from which neither contestant can derive a winning advantage **:** a drawn contest **:** DEADLOCK

²**stalemate** \"\ *vt* **:** to bring into a stalemate

stale·ness *n* -ES **:** the quality or state of being stale

staling *n* -S [fr. gerund of ³*stale*] **:** gradual decrease and eventual cessation of growth of a fungus in an artificial culture medium believed to be due wholly or in part to progressive increase of the metabolic products of the fungus itself

sta·lin·grad \ˈstälən,grad, -raa(ə)d — *see* DESTALINIZE *for other variants*\ *adj, usu cap* [fr. *Stalingrad*, former name of Volgograd, city in Southeastern U.S.S.R.] **:** of or from the city of Stalingrad, U.S.S.R. **:** of the kind or style prevalent in Stalingrad

sta·lin·ism \-lə,nizəm\ *n* -S *usu cap* [Joseph *Stalin* †1953 Russ. political leader + E *-ism*] **:** the political, economic, and social principles and policies associated with Stalin; *esp* **:** the theory and practice of communism developed by Stalin from Marxism-Leninism — compare BOLSHEVISM, LENINISM, MARXISM, TITOISM, TROTSKYISM

sta·lin·ist \-,nəst\ *n* -S *usu cap* [Joseph *Stalin* †1953 + E *-ist*] **:** a follower of Stalin **:** an adherent of Stalinism

²**stalinist** \"\ *adj, usu cap* [Joseph *Stalin* †1953 + E *-ist*, n. suffix] **:** of, relating to, or having the characteristics of Stalinism or Stalinists ⟨*Stalinist* communists⟩

sta·lin·ize \-,nīz\ *vt* -ED/-ING/-S *usu cap* [Joseph *Stalin* †1953 + E *-ize*] **:** to make Stalinist

sta·li·no \ˈstälə,nō, ˈstal-, -lyənə\ *adj, usu cap* [fr. *Stalino*, former name of Donetsk, city in southwestern U.S.S.R.] **:** of or from the city of Stalino, U.S.S.R. **:** of the kind or style prevalent in Stalino

¹**sta·lin·oid** \ˈstälə,nȯid, ˈstal- — *see* DESTALINIZE *for other variants*\ *adj, usu cap* [Joseph *Stalin* †1953 Russ. political leader + E *-oid*, adj. suffix] **:** favorable to or influenced by Stalinism ⟨*Stalinoid* Marxism⟩ ⟨*Stalinoid* propaganda⟩

²**stalinoid** \"\ *n* -S *usu cap* [Joseph *Stalin* †1953 + E *-oid*, n. suffix] **:** a Stalinoid person

sta·linsk \ˈstäl,linzk, ˈstal, |l,yi-, -n(t)sk\ *adj, usu cap* [fr. *Stalinsk*, former name of Novokuznetsk, city in southern U.S.S.R. in Asia] **:** of or from the city of Stalinsk, U.S.S.R. **:** of the kind or style prevalent in Stalinsk

¹**stalk** \ˈstȯk\ *vb* -ED/-ING/-S [ME *stalken*, fr. OE *bestealcian* to walk stealthily; akin to OE *stealc* steep, lofty, OSw *stjælke* stalk, stem, ON *stjōlr* hinder part, tail — more at STEAL] *vi* **1** *obs* **:** to walk cautiously or furtively **:** STEAL, SLIP **2 :** to pursue quarry or prey stealthily or under cover (as behind a stalking horse) **:** STILL-HUNT ⟨deer are hunted chiefly by *~ing* —*Encyc. Americana*⟩ — compare DRIVE **3 a :** to walk with a stiff ungainly stride ⟨long-legged water birds ~ along the shore⟩ **b :** to walk with long measured steps **:** stride loftily ⟨turned on his heel, and *~ed* stiffly out —Kenneth Roberts⟩ **c :** to move in a silent deliberate manner — used of ghosts and half-personified evils ⟨a specter that *~ed* along the castle walls at midnight⟩ ⟨the terror that *~s* through the city⟩ **~** *vt* **1 a :** to pursue (as game) stealthily and often under cover for the purpose of killing ⟨~ deer⟩ ⟨~ an enemy patrol⟩ ⟨watch a tiger ~ its prey⟩ **b :** to pursue or follow in a stealthy, furtive, or persistent manner ⟨the man was *~ing* him as remorselessly as if he were a criminal —*Time*⟩ **2 :** to move through, recur to, or follow as a specter or evil **:** DOG, HAUNT ⟨a nightmare that *~s* his sleep⟩ ⟨the starvation that *~ed* the winter-devastated land —*N.Y. Times Bk. Rev.*⟩ **3 :** to go through (an area) in search of prey or other quarry ⟨~ the woods for deer⟩

²**stalk** \"\ *n* -S [ME *stalke*, fr. *stalken* to stalk] **1 :** the act or process of stalking prey or other quarry **2 :** a stalking gait

³**stalk** \"\ *n* -S [ME *stalke*; akin to OSw *stjælke* stalk — more at STALK, v.] **1 a :** the main stem of an herbaceous plant often with its dependent parts (as leaves, twigs, fruit) ⟨a ~ of wheat⟩ — often used in combination ⟨corn*stalk*⟩ ⟨bean*stalk*⟩ **b :** a part of a plant by which an organ (as a leaf, fruit) is attached and supported: as (1) **:** the petiole of a leaf (2) **:** the peduncle or pedicel of a flower or fruit (3) **:** the stipe of an ovary (4) **:** the seta of a moss **c :** an organ-bearing stalk with the parts it bears ⟨bought a whole ~ of bananas⟩ **2 :** a slender upright object or supporting or connecting part: as **a :** a long narrow peduncle supporting some part of an animal body ⟨the ~ of the pituitary⟩ or the entire body ⟨the ~ or hydrocaulus that attaches a hydroid to the substrate⟩ ⟨the ~ of some crinoids is many times as long as the body it attaches⟩ **b :** the stack of a chimney **c :** an ornament in the Corinthian capital which resembles the stalk of a plant and from which the volutes and helices spring **3 :** an iron bar with projections that is inserted in a core to strengthen it **:** a core arbor

stalk·able \-kəbəl\ *adj* **:** that can be stalked

stalk borer *n* **:** an insect larva that bores in the stems of plants; *esp* **:** the larva of a noctuid moth (*Papaipema nebris*) that infests the raspberry, strawberry, tomato, aster, and other plants

stalk cell *n* **:** one of the two cells produced by division of the generative cell in the pollen grain of some gymnosperms that bears or supports the body cell

stalk–cutter \ˈ⸗,⸗⸗\ *n* **:** an implement with rotating knives for chopping up cornstalks or cotton stalks in the field in preparation for plowing

stalk disease *n* **:** a stem rot and wilt of the potato caused by a fungus (*Sclerotinia sclerotiorum*)

stalked *adj* **:** having or borne on a stalk

stalked hydatid *n* **:** HYDATID OF MORGAGNI 1

stalked puffball *n* **:** a fungus of the family Tulostomaceae

stalk·er \ˈstȯkə(r)\ *n* -S [ME, fr. *stalken* to stalk + *-er* — more at STALK] **:** one that stalks; *esp* **:** one that stalks game

stalk–eyed \ˈ⸗,⸗\ *adj* **:** having the eyes raised on a stalk — used chiefly of crustaceans

stalk–eyed fly *n* **:** a two-winged fly of *Diopsis* or related genera that has the eyes on the ends of stalks

stalk field *n* **:** a field of cornstalks from which the ears have been harvested

stalk·i·ly \-kəlē\ *adv* **:** in a stalky manner

stalk·i·ness \-kēnəs, -kin-\ *n* -ES **:** the quality or state of being stalky

stalking–horse \ˈ⸗⸗,⸗\ *n* **1 :** a horse or a figure like a horse behind which a hunter stalks game **2 :** something used to cover up a secret project **:** MASK, PRETENSE **3 :** a candidate put forward to divide the opposition in the interest of some faction or to conceal the real candidacy of some other person

stalk·ing·ly *adv* **:** in a stalking manner

stalk·less \ˈ⸗ləs\ *adj* **:** having no stalk

stalk·let \-lət\ *n* -S [³*stalk* + *-let*] **:** a small or secondary stalk

stalklike \ˈ⸗,⸗\ *adj* **:** resembling a stalk

stalks *pres 3d sing of* STALK, *pl of* STALK

stalk shaver *n* **:** an implement on runners with knives cutting cornstalks or stubble at the ground surface for burning (as in the control of the European corn borer)

stalky \ˈstȯkē, -ki\ *adj* -ER/-EST [³*stalk* + *-y*] **1 :** having stalks **2 :** resembling a stalk **:** SLENDER

¹**stall** \ˈstȯl\ *n* -S *often attrib* [ME *stal, stall*, fr. OE *stall, steall*; akin to OHG *stal* stand, place, stall, *stellen* to set, place, ON *stallr* stand, stall, OL *stlocus* place, L *locus* place, *stolidus* dull, *stultus* foolish, Gk *stellein* to set up, make ready, send, Skt *sthalati* he stands] **1 a :** a place where horses or cattle are kept: (1) *obs* **:** STABLE (2) **:** a division of a stable or barn accommodating one animal and often enclosed except at the rear **b :** a compartment in a roundhouse for a locomotive **c :** a space marked off for the parking of a motor vehicle **2** *obs* **a :** a fixed position **:** STAND **b :** a place in or as if in a series **:** STATION, RANK **3 a :** a fixed seat in the chancel of a church usu. forming one of an attached row enclosed or partly enclosed at the back and sides and often having a canopy, separating arms or partitions, a seat that can tip up, a desk for books, and carved ornamentation; *esp* **:** such a seat on either side of the chancel of a cathedral or collegiate church serving as the official seat of a dignitary or residentiary canon ⟨the only minor canon . . . to obtain a prebendal ~ —Leslie Smith⟩ **b :** a long seat with back and arms for worshipers in a church **:** PEW **c :** one of the seats assigned to the knights in a British chapel associated with one of the higher orders of chivalry **d** *Brit* **:** a seat in the forward part of the main level of a theater — usu. used in pl. ⟨people who . . . can't afford the *~s* and are ashamed to be seen in the gallery —G.B.Shaw⟩ **4 :** a booth, stand, or counter at which articles are displayed for sale or a business is conducted ⟨a candy ~ at a fair⟩ ⟨a shooting ~ at a carnival⟩ ⟨coffee ~⟩; *specif* **:** BOOKSTALL ⟨publishers try to get their most handsome volumes into the *~s* just before Christmas —*Time*⟩ ⟨published as ~ ballads —Kenneth Lodewick⟩ **5 :** a protective sheath covering a single finger, thumb, or toe **:** COT **6** *chiefly Brit* **:** a tunnel in which coal is mined by the bord-and-pillar system **:** ROOM, BREAST **7 :** a small partially enclosed compartment ⟨a shower ~⟩: as **a :** CARREL **b :** a usu. roofless enclosure in which ore is roasted **8 stalls** *pl, Brit* **:** the occupants of the stalls in a theater

²**stall** \"\ *vb* -ED/-ING/-S [ME *stallen*, fr. ¹*stall*] *vt* **1 a :** to put into or keep in a stall ⟨the cattle were *~ed* in the house —Gunnar Mickwith⟩ **b** *archaic* **:** to fatten by stall-feeding ⟨better is a dinner of herbs where love is than a *~ed* ox and hatred —Prov 15:17 (AV)⟩ **c** *dial Brit* **:** to cause surfeit in **:** SATIATE **2** *obs* **:** to install in office orig. by formal induction into a stall of office or dignity in a church or chapel **3** *obs* **a :** to assign a place to **b :** to appoint beforehand **:** ARRANGE **c :** to arrange payment of (a debt) by portions due at different times **4 a :** to force to a standstill **:** hinder from going on ⟨help rescue horses *~ed* in a slough —*Amer. Guide Series: N. J.*⟩ ⟨soldiers were *~ed* here for four days by heavy enemy fire —Toni Howard⟩ **b** (1) **:** to cause (an engine) to stop from overload or poor fuel supply **:** KILL (2) **:** to cause (a motor vehicle) to stop by stalling the engine **c :** to cause (an airplane or airfoil) to go into a stall **~** *vi* **1** *obs* **:** to live in the same place **2 a :** to come to a standstill: as (1) **:** to stick fast in mire or snow (2) **:** to stop from engine overload or poor fuel supply **:** DIE **b :** to enter or experience a stall in flying

³**stall** \"\ *n* -S **:** the condition of an airfoil or airplane operating at an angle of attack greater than that corresponding to maximum lift that is characterized by flow breakdown and loss of effectiveness of the controls

⁴**stall** \"\ *n* -S [alter. (influenced by ¹*stall*) of ⁶*stale*] **1** *obs* **:** DECOY **2 :** a pickpocket's confederate who blocks the victim, distracts his attention (as by jostling), and screens the theft **3 :** something used to deceive others about one's intentions **:** DODGE, RUSE, BLIND **4 :** an artifice for delaying or impeding action

⁵**stall** \"\ *vb* -ED/-ING/-S *vi* **1 :** to serve as a pickpocket's stall **2 :** to keep a situation going by some device or trick until relief or change can be effected **:** play for time ⟨charged that he was *~ing* when he did not answer promptly⟩ **3 :** to do less than one's best in a contest in order to deceive one's opponent for some purpose or to husband one's strength **4 :** to maintain possession of the ball (as in basketball) without endeavoring to score to prevent the possibility of a score by the opponents **~** *vt* **:** to divert or delay by evasion or deception ⟨many contractors ~ renegotiation, hoping new renegotiators will be named soon and give them a better break —*Kiplinger Washington Letter*⟩ — often used with *off* ⟨tried to ~ off his creditors till the expected check came⟩

stall·age \-lij, -lēj\ *n* -S [ME, fr. MF *estalage*, fr. OF, fr. *estal* place, stand, stall + *-age* — more at STALE (decoy)] **1** *Eng law* **:** the right of erecting a stall in a fair **2** *Eng law* **:** rent or toll paid for a stall

stall bar *n* **:** a piece of gymnastic apparatus used for corrective and strengthening exercises that consists of uprights about eight feet high and three feet apart secured to a wall and joined by horizontal wooden rungs at about 5-inch intervals

stall bar

stallboard \ˈ⸗,⸗\ *n* **1 a :** a display board formerly attached to the sill of a shop window and often hinging out into the street **b :** a stout sill or rail under the sash in a shop front **2 :** any of a series of successively higher floors on which excavated material is pitched (as in digging sewers)

stalled *adj* [fr. past part. of ²*stall*] *of an animal* **:** suffering from autointoxication usu. due to overfeeding

stall·er \ˈstȯlə(r)\ *n* -S **:** one that stalls

stall–feed \ˈ⸗ˈ⸗\ *vt* **:** to feed in a stall for fattening ⟨*stall-feed* an ox⟩

stalling speed *n* **:** the speed of an airplane in steady flight at its maximum lift coefficient

stal·lion \ˈstalyən\ *n* -S [ME *stalion, stalon*, fr. MF *estalon*, of Gmc origin; akin to OHG *stal* stall — more at STALL] **1 a :** a male horse not castrated **:** a male horse kept for breeding; *also* **:** a mature male of any equine mammal ⟨a zebra ~⟩ **b :** the male of any of various other animals (as dogs, sheep) when kept for or considered in respect to its worth as a stud **2** *obs* **a :** PARAMOUR **b :** COURTESAN **3 :** a man marked by vigorous maleness

stal·lion·er \-nə(r)\ *or* **stal·lion·eer** \ˌ⸗⸗ˈni(ə)r\ *n* -S [*stallion* + *-er* or *-eer*] **:** one supervising or in charge of a stallion (as at public stud)

stallion plague *n* **:** DOURINE

stall·man \ˈ⸗man\ *also* **stallkeeper** \ˈ⸗,⸗⸗\ *n, pl* **stallmen** *also* **stallkeepers :** one who keeps a stall for selling goods (as books)

stall plate *n* **:** a plate with the arms of a knight affixed to his chapel stall

stall reader *n* **:** one that reads books at a bookstall

stallriser \ˈ⸗,⸗⸗\ *n* [¹*stall* + *riser*] *Brit* **:** the part of a store front below a show window

stalls *pl of* STALL, *pres 3d sing of* STALL

stall–warning indicator \ˈ⸗,⸗⸗-\ *n* **:** a flight instrument that warns the pilot that his airplane is approaching a stall

¹**stal·wart** \ˈstȯlwə(r)t *sometimes* -,wȯr|t *or* -,wō(ə)|; *usu* |d.+V\ *adj* [ME, alter. of *stalworth*, fr. OE *stǣlwierthe* serviceable, prob. contr. of *statholwierthe*, fr. *stathol* base, foundation, support + *wierthe* worth — more at STADDLE, WORTH] **1 :** STOUT, STURDY ⟨~ sons . . . well over six feet tall, lean,

long, and resilient —Green Peyton⟩ ⟨the ~ wall of the castle⟩ **2 :** BRAVE, VALIANT, RESOLUTE ⟨a number of ~ men and women who, not counting the cost to themselves, reported on . . . activities to the police —L.S.B.Leakey⟩ **syn** see STRONG

²stalwart \"\ *n* -s [ME, fr. ¹*stalwart*] **1 :** a sturdy or resolute person **2 a :** an unwavering partisan (as in politics) ⟨have ~*s* in both major political parties and have always chipped in heavily to both national campaign coffers —Harry Conn⟩ **b** *usu cap* **:** one of a faction of the Republican party between 1869 and 1877 having a very strong machine and subsequently opposing civil-service reform and conciliation toward the South — compare HALF-BREED 2a

stal·wart·ly *adv* [ME, fr. ¹*stalwart* + *-ly*] **:** in a stalwart manner

stal·wart·ness *n* -ES **:** the quality or state of being stalwart

stal·worth \'stöl(,)wərth\ *archaic var of* STALWART

sta·men \'stāmən\ *n, pl* **stamens** \-nz\ *also* **stami·na** \'stāmənə, 'stam-\ [L, warp, thread, thread spun by the fates at one's birth to determine the length of his life, stamen; akin to Gk *stēmōn* warp, thread, OIr *sessam* act of standing, Skt *sthāman* station, Gk *histanai* to cause to stand; basic meaning: standing upright — more at STAND] **1** *obs* **:** a vital principle or force formerly regarded as the determining factor in longevity **2 :** a microsporophyll of a seed plant **:** the organ of the flower that gives rise to the male gamete, consists of an anther and a filament, is morphologically a spore-bearing leaf though sometimes exhibiting transition to a petal (as in a double flower), occurs usu. in fixed numbers in a given group, and thereby affords an important diagnostic character — see ANDROECIUM; compare PISTIL; see FLOWER illustration

sta·mened \-nd\ *adj* **:** having stamens

stam·in \'stamən\ *n* -s [ME, fr. OF *estamin*, fr. (assumed) VL *staminea*, fr. fem. of L *stamineus* made of threads, fr. *stamin-*, *stamen* thread + *-eus* -eous] **1 a :** a coarse woolen fabric of late medieval use esp. for undershirts of penitents **b :** a rough woolen fabric for clothing similar to linsey-woolsey **2 :** TAMMY

stamin- *or* **stamini-** *comb form* [L *stamin-*, *stamen*] **:** stamen ⟨*stamin*ody⟩ ⟨*stamini*ferous⟩

stam·i·na \'stamənə\ *n* -s [L, pl. of *stamen* warp, thread of life spun by the fates] **1** *pl in constr, archaic* **:** the essential or fundamental parts, elements, or nature of something esp. an organism **2** *pl in constr, archaic* **:** the innate capacities formerly regarded as conditioning or governing the duration of life **3 a :** the strength or vigor of bodily constitution **:** capacity for standing fatigue or resisting disease ⟨the chase, sometimes lasting for miles, calls for unlimited ~ from both dogs and men —*Amer. Guide Series: Tenn.*⟩ ⟨lack of ~ of the population is caused partly by the high rate of infection from parasitic and venereal diseases —Mary Tew⟩ **b :** strength or courage of conviction **:** staying power **:** PERSEVERANCE ⟨displayed little of the moral ~ which characterized the Puritan fathers —R.P.Stearns⟩ ⟨must acquire proficiency in defense and display ~ in purpose —D.D.Eisenhower⟩ ⟨exhibited enough ~ to disagree frequently with the great chief justice —*advt*⟩ ⟨evidence of the ~ of India's indigenous democracy —Vera M. Dean⟩ **c :** the capacity for standing hard or demanding use over an extended period **:** DURABILITY ⟨steelmakers use small amounts of vanadium alloys to give steel ~ —*Hot-Metal Magic*⟩ ⟨enduring ~ built into these trucks —*Newsweek*⟩ ⟨a locker with ~ and correctness of design —*Sweet's Catalog Service*⟩ **4** *archaic* **:** the chief source of support or strength ⟨the infantry is the ~ of a military force⟩ — sometimes pl. in constr.

stam·i·nal \-nᵊl\ *adj* [in sense 1, fr. *stamina* + *-al*; in sense 2, fr. *stamin-* + *-al*] **1 :** of, relating to, or constituting stamina **2 :** of, relating to, or consisting of a stamen

stam·i·nate \-,nə̇t, -,nāt, *usu* |d.+V\ *adj* [*stamin-* + *-ate*] **1 :** having or producing stamens **2** *of a diclinous flower* **:** having stamens but no pistils — compare PISTILLATE; see AMENT illustration

stam·i·nif·er·ous \¦stamə¦nif(ə)rəs\ *adj* [*stamin-* + *-ferous*] **:** bearing or having stamens

stam·i·node \'stamə,nōd\ *n* -s [NL *staminodium*] **:** STAMINODIUM

stam·i·no·di·um \,==ˈnōdēəm\ *n, pl* **stamino·dia** \-dēə\ [NL, fr. *stamin-* + *-odes* -ode + *-ium*] **:** an abortive or sterile stamen (as in the flowers of the genus *Parnassia*)

stam·i·no·dy \'==,nōdē\ *n* -ES [*stamin-* + *-ody*] **:** the metamorphosis of other floral organs into stamens

stam·mel \'staməl\ *n* -s [prob. fr. *stamin* + *-el*] **1** *obs* **:** a coarse woolen clothing fabric usu. dyed red and used sometimes for undershirts of penitents **2** *or* **stammelcolor** \'==,==\ **:** the bright red color of this cloth

¹stam·mer \'stamə(r)\ *vb* **stammered; stammered; stammering** \-m(ə)riŋ\ **stammers** [ME *stameren*, fr. OE *stamerian*; akin to OS *stamarōn* to stammer, MD *stameren*, OHG *stamalōn*, *stamēn*, ON *stamma* to stammer, Goth *stamms* stammering, Lith *stumti* to push] *vi* **1 a :** to make involuntary stops and repetitions in uttering syllables and words **:** hesitate, falter, or block oneself in speaking ⟨is so nervous he ~*s* constantly⟩ ⟨shrank a little at his vehemence, but neither blushed nor ~*ed* —George Meredith⟩ — compare STUTTER **b :** to speak or write haltingly, confusedly, or unclearly ⟨where the pedant theologians mumble and ~, she is articulate —W.L. Sullivan⟩ ⟨living thoughts . . . in the 9th century began to ~ in Latin verses —H.O.Taylor⟩ ⟨appear a much more diffuse, ~*ing*, and incoherent writer than he is —Paul Welsh⟩ **c :** to make a sharp or rattling noise in a spasmodic fashion ⟨my company's light automatics ~*ed* furiously —John Masters⟩ ⟨shutters were ~*ing* and fidgeting at their hooks —Elizabeth Enright⟩ **2** *dial Brit* **:** STAGGER, STUMBLE **~** *vt* **1 :** to utter or speak (something) with involuntary stops or repetitions ⟨"why — why — " ~*ed* the youth struggling with his balking tongue —Stephen Crane⟩ ⟨~*ed* that he was afraid he had not any notes to show — worth seeing —George Meredith⟩ **2 :** to utter or deliver (something) in a confused, halting, or incoherent manner ⟨~*ed* a crude communism in the vernacular —John Buchan⟩ — often used with *out* ⟨contented with a very slight degree of learning, could scarcely ~ out the words of the sacrament —G.G.Coulton⟩

²stammer \"\ *n* -s **1 :** an act or instance of stammering **2 :** defective utterance **:** the involuntary interruption of utterance ⟨when he was at all agitated the ~ became a complete inhibition of speech —F.A.Swinnerton⟩

stam·mer·er \-mərə(r)\ *n* -s **:** one that stammers

stammering *n* -s [ME *stamering*, fr. gerund of *stameren* to stammer] **1 :** the act of one who stammers **2 :** a defective condition of speech characterized by involuntary stops and repetitions or blocking of utterance — compare STUTTERING

stam·mer·ing·ly *adv* **:** in a stammering manner **:** with stammering

stam·nos \'stam,näs\ *n* [Gk; akin to Gk *stēmōn* warp in an upright loom — more at STAMEN] **:** an ancient Greek wine jar with a wide mouth and with handles set horizontally on the shoulders

stamnos

¹stamp \'stamp, -aa(ə)mp, -aimp; *in senses 2a of vt & 2 of vi also* 'stämp *or* -tȯmp\ *vb* -ED/-ING/-S [ME *stampen*; akin to OE *stempan* to stamp, OHG *stampfōn*, ON *stappa* to stamp, L *temnere* to slight, despise, Gk *stembein* to shake up, handle roughly, Skt *stambhate*, *stabhnati* he supports] *vt* **1 :** to pound with a pestle or a heavy instrument; *specif* **:** to crush (ore) by pounding with a stamp **2 a** (1) **:** to strike or beat (something) forcibly with the bottom of the foot or by thrusting the foot downward ⟨the watch officer ~*ing* the deck —R.H. Davis⟩ ⟨~*ing* the mud off his boots⟩ ⟨~*ing* a trail in the deep snow —John Hunt & Edmund Hillary⟩ ⟨~*ed* an incongruous step . . . in a vain effort to dance to the music —Haldane MacFall⟩ (2) **:** to bring down (the foot) forcibly or noisily on the ground or floor ⟨~*s* his feet with rage⟩ ⟨~*ing* her heels with true regimental emphasis —T.B.Costain⟩ ⟨pass unscathed over this burning charcoal although they actually ~ their feet on it —J.G.Frazer⟩ **b :** to extinguish, eradicate, or do away with (something) by or as if by stamping with the foot ⟨are still trying to ~ the spread . . . following the war —T.H.Fielding⟩ — usu. used with *out* ⟨one small fire . . . was easily ~*ed* out —Frank Pemberton⟩ ⟨finally ~*ed* out the cattle thieves —*Amer. Guide Series: La.*⟩ ⟨medical authorities attempted to ~ it out by quarantine measures —*Amer. Guide Series: Fla.*⟩ ⟨strong monarchs are ~*ing* out privy conspiracy and rebellion —S.E.Morison & H.S.Commager⟩ **3 a :** to impress or mark (something) with a special design in intaglio or relief with ink or coloring **b** *obs* **:** to print (a book) with such a process **c :** to impress or mark (something) with a device or design by means of a die and a blow or mechanical pressure **d :** to cut out, bend, or form by a blow or sudden pressure with a stamp or die **e** (1) **:** to impress (lettering or a design) with heated metal type or dies (2) **:** to impress (as a book) with lettering or a design ⟨~*ed* book covers⟩ ⟨~*ed* bindings⟩ ⟨~*ed* cloth⟩ **4 a :** to impress or mark (something) with a device or lettering to authenticate, certify, or register formal or official examination or sanction **b :** to impress (something) with an official mark, stamp, or adhesive label to certify that a government or state tax or duty has been paid **5 a** (1) **:** to adjudge or categorize (a person or thing) as being of good or bad repute or value ⟨little things . . . ~ a girl at her first informal beach party —Alex Atkinson⟩ ⟨long association with agrarian reform ~*ed* him as a radical in the eyes of . . . moderates —R.A. Billington⟩ ⟨~*ed* him as an artist of extraordinary skill and perception —Howard Barnes⟩ ⟨the account of the foundation . . . ~*s* it as fraudulent —G.C.Sellery⟩ (2) **:** to justify or lend approbation or sanction to (a person or thing) ⟨a consummate ability that ~*ed* him the peer of the greatest advocate of the age —W.J.Ghent⟩ ⟨the happy diction and the graceful phrase which literature has ~*ed* with its authority —E.G.Bulwer-Lytton⟩ **b** (1) **:** to mark (a person or thing) with a distinctive or lasting characteristic ⟨an art ~*ed* with great beauty —*Amer. Guide Series: Ind.*⟩ ⟨listlessness rather than vigor ~*s* most of the homeless men —*Amer. Guide Series: Minn.*⟩ ⟨~*ed* the works of Benedictine scholars with a character which they seldom lost —R.W.Southern⟩ (2) **:** to mark or mold one's physical features or appearance with (a distinctive characteristic or cast) **:** TRACE ⟨his paternity was ~*ed* so indelibly on his outer shell —T.B.Costain⟩ **c :** to be a conspicuous characteristic of (something) **:** DISTINGUISH ⟨the chief quality that ~*s* this study of jazz —R.L.Shayon⟩ ⟨corporate ties which had ~*ed* the old monasticism —R.W.Southern⟩ **d** (1) **:** to embed or deeply impress (a fact, idea, or effect) ⟨the Welsh characteristics are indelibly ~*ed* —Wilfrid Goatman⟩ — usu. used with *on* or *upon* ⟨the firm discipline of the Roman Military Academy was ~*ed* on him —L.C.Douglas⟩ ⟨one of the symbolic events that had ~*ed* itself on his mind as a child —Van Wyck Brooks⟩ (2) **:** to impose or firmly mark (an influence, quality, or development) — usu. used with *on* or *upon* ⟨concerned to ~ our civilization upon the world —Bertrand Russell⟩ ⟨developments which were to ~ a new form of papal authority on the church —R.W.Southern⟩ ⟨his genius was ~*ed* on the ecclesiastical architecture —G.M.Trevelyan⟩ **~** *vi* **1 :** to strike, beat, or crush in a manufacturing process **:** POUND ⟨fibers had been fermented, and then separated by . . . ~*ing* —R.K. Johnson⟩ **2 a :** to strike or thrust the foot forcibly or noisily downward ⟨men ~*ing* about with clanking swords —Richard Joseph⟩ ⟨men ~*ed* all over the decks —Anthony Carson⟩ ⟨steps would ~ into the kitchen —Nancy Hale⟩ ⟨~ round in a circle —Wilfred Thesiger⟩ ⟨officers' mounts ~*ed* and steamed before a . . . hitching post —F.V.W.Mason⟩ **b :** to push or beat something down by such stamping with the foot — usu. used with *on* ⟨~ on the accelerator —Green Peyton⟩ ⟨jumping and ~*ing* on the leaves⟩ **c :** to extinguish, extirpate, or do away with something by or as if by such stamping ⟨nearby householders were ~*ing* on the sparks to keep the brush fire from spreading⟩ ⟨decided to ~ on all utterances of a disloyal character —Zechariah Chafee⟩

²stamp \'stamp, -aa(ə)mp, -aimp; *in sense 4 also* 'stämp *or* -tȯmp\ *n* -s *often attrib* [ME *stampe*, fr. *stampen* to stamp] **1 :** a device or instrument for stamping: as **a :** a die or tool for impressing or marking a design or pattern (as of a coin, postage stamp, or plaque) on metal, paper, or other soft or absorbent material **b** (1) **:** a heavy pestle raised by water or steam power for crushing ore (2) **stamps** *pl* **:** STAMP MILL **c :** a bookbinder's embossing tool **d :** a machine for beating and softening hides **2 :** the impression, design, or mark made by stamping or imprinting with a die or tool: as **a :** such an impression or mark used to give authentication, distinctive value, or force to something (as a coin, a document, or goods) **b** (1) **:** an official mark or seal set on something (as a warrant or deed) chargeable with a government or state duty or tax or on papers legally requiring execution under certain conditions to signify that the duty or tax has been paid or the conditions fulfilled (2) **:** POSTMARK **3 a :** a cast, make, or kind marked by distinctive or peculiar qualities or characteristics **:** TYPE ⟨reformers of all ~*s* are prone to regard the existing order as sheer folly —H.J.Muller⟩ ⟨books of a serious ~ —Jane Austen⟩ ⟨does not indicate that the ideal field trial dog is of that ~ —W.F.Brown b. 1903⟩ **b :** a distinguishing or characteristic imprint, sign, or impression **:** MARK ⟨a poet who has left her ~ upon her generation —Sara H. Hay⟩ ⟨these works have the classic ~ upon them —Laurence Binyon⟩ ⟨the very ~ of genius —Alfred Kazin⟩ ⟨in its content and terminology the unmistakable ~ of the backwoods —*Amer. Guide Series: Ind.*⟩ **c :** the lasting imprint or residual impression of something **:** EFFECT ⟨sun and weather . . . and the deeper ~ of his new life have made him physically a stranger —Dixon Wecter⟩ ⟨the ~ of his character upon his style —Arnold Isenberg⟩ **d :** external appearance **:** physical cast or form ⟨the English look gave way to a Celtic ~ on the features of the inhabitants —Richard Joseph⟩ **e :** a sign or certification of worth based on judgment or opinion ⟨implied this to be the very highest ~ of juvenile merit —George Eliot⟩ ⟨carries the ~ of approval⟩ **4 :** an act of stamping; *esp* **:** a forceful downward stroke or step with the foot **5** *obs* **:** something stamped or impressed with a device **:** COIN, MEDAL **6 :** a picture made by an inked impression from an engraved surface **:** ENGRAVING, PLATE **7 a :** a stamped or printed device or slip of paper issued by a government or state at a fixed price and required by law to be affixed to or stamped on various papers or matter as evidence that the government charge or tax is paid — compare POSTAGE STAMP **b :** such a stamp privately printed or issued for any purpose of signification or certification **:** SEAL — compare TRADING STAMP **8 :** a card for gambling marked on the back by the manufacturer — compare READER **9 :** a section of a bloom nicked, partly cut through, or broken off to show the grain

stamp battery *n* **:** BATTERY 9

stamp book *n* **:** a book of or for stamps: as **a :** STAMP BOOKLET **b :** a collector's book for mounting stamps **:** a stamp album **c :** a book in which savings stamps are affixed until they are redeemed or deposited

stamp booklet *n* **:** a book of postage stamps consisting of a few panes of postage stamps separated by sheets of oiled paper stapled together in thin cardboard covers

stamp copper *n* **:** copper-bearing rock that has been or is to be stamped and washed before smelting

stamp duty *n* **:** STAMP TAX

stamped *past of* STAMP

¹stam·pede \(')stam¦pēd, -taam-\ *n* -s [AmerSp *estampida*, fr. Sp, loud noise, crash, fr. *estampar* to pound, stamp, of Gmc origin; akin to OHG *stampfōn* to stamp — more at STAMP] **1 a :** a wild headlong rush or flight of a number of animals usu. due to fright ⟨a ~ of wild animals is no place for a would-be observer —K.K.Darrow⟩ **b :** a sudden retreat or dispersion ⟨this was no disciplined march; it was a ~ —H.G.Wells⟩ **2 :** a sudden often impulsive action or mass movement of a number of persons having a common motive ⟨the migration took on the proportions of a ~ —*Amer. Guide Series: N. Y.*⟩ ⟨discovery of rich silver deposits sets off a ~ of miners —Howard Boston⟩ ⟨a steadily increasing ~ of farm boys escaping . . . farm work for the dullness of city life —M.B. Smith⟩ ⟨delays in delivery would have caused a ~ of postponements —F.A.Swinnerton⟩; *specif* **:** a sudden rush of voters or delegates to support a candidate esp. at a national political convention ⟨the favorite son, never sure that a . . . ~ may not take place at the next moment —H.R.Penniman⟩ ⟨worked desperately to stop the ~, but could not agree on a coalition candidate —I.G.Blake⟩ — compare BREAK 4j **3 :** an extended festival or gathering combining a rodeo, exhibitions, contests, and social events ⟨watched the Calgary ~ grow through the years . . . to a commercialized, supercolossal spectacle —*Time*⟩

²stampede \"\ *vb* -ED/-ING/-S *vt* **1 a :** to cause (as cattle) to run away in a headlong panic ⟨thunderstorms often ~ the cattle⟩ **b :** to cause (a group or army) to retreat or disperse frantically ⟨came the victor *stampeding* armies before him⟩ **2 :** to cause (a group or mass of people) to act or move in an impulsive, unreasoning, or hurried manner ⟨the taverners who would ~ us in to eat and drink —G.G.Coulton⟩ ⟨Indians were *stampeded* into violence —Oliver La Farge⟩ ⟨have refused to allow ourselves to be *stampeded* by fear —Hartley Shawcross⟩ ⟨attempting to ~ government representatives into giving him control over . . . workers —Douglass Cater⟩; *specif* **:** to cause (as voters or delegates) to rush suddenly to the support of a party, ticket, or candidate esp. at a national political convention ⟨observers consider that the . . . electorate was *stampeded* at last year's general election —John Hughes⟩ ⟨gained slowly at first, then shot forward with accretions of a 100 votes at a time, and *stampeded* the convention —H.R. Penniman⟩ **~** *vi* **1 a :** to take to sudden headlong flight in panic ⟨the alarmed herd *stampeding* across the veldt⟩ **b :** to retreat or disperse in a frenzied manner ⟨fired into the roof of the mosque, and the crowd of worshipers *stampeded* —*Time*⟩ **2 :** to move or act usu. in a group or mass in an impulsive, hurried, or unreasoning manner ⟨pulled up stakes and *stampeded* back to China, most of them perishing on the way —A.R.Williams⟩ ⟨prospectors . . . who *stampeded* into the Klondike —Ivor Jones⟩ ⟨companies will now ~ to release . . . their huge backlogs of modern movies —*Wall Street Jour.*⟩ ⟨has . . . *stampeded* out of every war into wholesale demobilization —T.R.Ybarra⟩

stam·pe·do \=ˈpē(,)dō\ *n* -s [AmerSp *estampido* crash, stampede, fr. Sp, loud noise, crash, fr. *estampar* to stamp] *archaic* **:** STAMPEDE

stamped paper *n* **:** postal stationery, postage and revenue stamps, and paper bearing imprinted revenue stamps

stamp·er \'stampə(r), -aam-, -aim-\ *n* -s [ME *stampere*, fr. *stampen* to stamp + *-ere* -er] **:** one that stamps: as **a** (1) **:** one that stamps designs (as on pottery, buttons, fabrics, leather goods) (2) **:** a worker who stamps identifying information on merchandise or its containers (3) **:** STAMPMAN (4) **:** an operator of a machine for stamping bronze or copper to powder **b** (1) **:** an implement for pounding or stamping; *esp* **:** a pestle or heavy metal piece attached to the lower end of a stamp in a stamp battery for crushing ore (2) **:** any of various stamping machines (as for powdering calcined flints or cleansing fabrics in a revolving vessel) **c :** a metal negative from which phonograph records are stamped

stamp hammer *n* **:** a power hammer that moves vertically

stamp·ic \'stampik\ *adj* [²*stamp* + *-ic*] **:** of or relating to stamps or philately ⟨paid ~ tribute to one of her pioneer airmen —L.A.Wolf⟩ ⟨a new issue of stamps is always an event in the ~ world —*Nat'l Stamp News*⟩

stamping *pres part of* STAMP

stamping ground *n* **:** a place much frequented **:** a favorite or habitual resort ⟨accounted for a pretty, tree-lined city on the old buffalo *stamping ground* —Margaret Cousins⟩ ⟨this part of the state was once the *stamping ground* of . . . the outlaw —*Amer. Guide Series: Texas*⟩ ⟨New Orleans is one of his family's *stamping grounds* —Robert Graves⟩

stamp iron *n* **:** a branding iron with the complete brand stamped on it

¹stamp·less \'=lə̇s\ *adj* [²*stamp* + *-less*] **:** being without stamps **:** not bearing any stamp

²stampless \"\ *or* **stampless cover** *n, pl* **stampless** *or* **stampless covers :** a philatelic cover that bears no adhesive stamp; *esp* **:** one transmitted before the beginning of official postal service or before the use of adhesive stamps

stamp·man \'=,mən\ *n, pl* **stampmen :** an operator of a stamp mill — called also *stamper*

stamp mill *or* **stamping mill** *n* **:** a mill in which ore is crushed with stamps; *also* **:** a machine for stamping ore **:** BATTERY 9 — called also *quartz battery*

stamp rock *n* **:** ore or metal-bearing rock requiring stamping before further metallurgical treatment

stamps *pres 3d sing of* STAMP, *pl of* STAMP

stamp seal *n* **:** an ancient stone seal usu. engraved with figures of animals or sometimes (as in China) with characters for stamping identification on personal property — see BUTTON-SEAL

stamp tax *n* **:** a tax or duty collected by means of stamps required to be purchased and affixed to specified articles (as cigarettes, playing cards); *specif* **:** such a tax or duty on specified documents (as deeds, certificates of stock, promissory notes) necessary in legal proceedings — called also *stamp duty*

stan *abbr* **1** stanchion **2** standard

stance \'stan(t)s, -taa(ə)n-, -tain- *also* -tän-\ *n* -s [MF *estance* position, posture, fr. OF — more at STANCHION] **1** *chiefly Scot* **a :** STATION **b :** SITE **2 a :** a place for standing; *esp* **:** a rock platform or ledge on a mountain where a climber can stand at ease or maintain balance without hand support **3 a :** a mode of standing or being placed **:** POSTURE ⟨the threatening ~ of a figure in a picture⟩ **b :** intellectual or emotional attitude **:** general standpoint ⟨moralizing and self-interested ~*s* were compatible —David Riesman⟩ **4 a :** the position of the feet of a golfer or batter preparatory to making a swing — see CLOSED STANCE, OPEN STANCE, SQUARE STANCE **b :** the position of both body and feet from which an athlete starts or operates ⟨crouching ~ of a boxer⟩ ⟨batting ~⟩

¹stanch *also* **staunch** \'stȯnch, -tän-, -tan-, -taa(ə)n-, -tain-, -tȧn-\ *vb* -ED/-ING/-ES [ME *staunchen*, *stanchen*, fr. MF *estancher*, fr. OF, fr. (assumed) VL *stanticare*, fr. L *stant-*, *stans*, pres. part. of *stare* to stand — more at STAND] *vt* **1 :** to check or stop the flowing of ⟨charity . . . ~*ing* the widow's tears —W.E.H.Lecky⟩ **:** stop the flow of blood from (a wound) **2** *archaic* **a :** ALLAY, SATISFY **b :** QUENCH, EXTINGUISH **3 a :** to stop or check in its course **:** put an end to ⟨have somewhat ~*ed* the drain on gold and dollar reserves —*Time*⟩ **b :** to make watertight **:** stop up ⟨~ a leak in a ship⟩ **~** *vi, archaic* **:** to cease flowing or bleeding

²stanch \"\ *also* **staunch** \"\ *n* -ES [ME *staunch*, fr. *staunchen* to stanch] **1** *obs* **:** something that stops or allays **2 :** a floodgate to accumulate water for flashing a boat over a shallow in a stream ⟨we have to have daylight to run the Thames ~*es* —C.S.Forester⟩

³stanch *var of* STAUNCH

stan·chel \'stanchəl\ *n* -s [perh. fr. MF *estanchielle*, dim. of OF *estanche* stay, prop — more at STANCHION] *dial* **:** STANCHION

stanch·er *pronunc at* STANCH + ə(r)\ *n* -s [ME, fr. *stanchen* to stanch + *-er*] **:** one that stanches; *esp* **:** STYPTIC

¹stan·chion \'stanchən, -taan-\ *n* -s [ME *stanchon*, fr. MF *estanchon* prop, supporting post, fr. OF, fr. *estance*, *estanche* position, act of staying, prop, fr. (assumed) VL *stantia* act of standing or staying, fr. L *stant-*, *stans* (pres. part. of *stare* to stand) + *-ia* -y — more at STAND] **1 :** an upright bar, post, prop, brace, or support (as for a roof, a ship's deck, an awning); *specif* **:** an iron mullion in a leaded window **2 :** a device that fits loosely around a cow's neck and limits forward and backward motion while commonly permitting a lateral swinging motion **3 :** a traffic sign mounted on a portable stand

²stanchion \"\ *vt* -ED/-ING/-S **1 :** to provide with stanchions **:** support, prop, or brace with or as if with a stanchion ⟨~*ing* themselves against the wind⟩ ⟨~ a sagging beam⟩ **2 :** to secure (as a cow) by a stanchion ⟨the herd was ~*ed* and fed⟩

stanchion gun *n* **:** a gun mounted on a pivot *esp* **:** a gun fixed to a boat for duck shooting

stanchion 2

stanch·less \'=lə̇s\ *adj* [¹*stanch* + *-less*] **:** that cannot be stanched ⟨~ wound⟩ **:** CEASELESS ⟨the innkeeper's ~ conversational flow —John Kobler⟩ — **stanch·less·ly** *adv*

[1]**stand** \'stand, -aa(ə)nd\ *vb* **stood** \'stu̇d\ **stood; standing; stands** [ME *standen, stonden,* fr. OE *standan, stondan;* akin to OHG *stantan, stān* to stand, ON *standa,* Goth *standan,* L *stare,* Gk *histanai* to cause to stand, set, place, *histasthai* to be standing, *stēnai* to come to a stand, Skt *tiṣṭhati* he stands] *vi* **1 a :** to support oneself on the feet in an essentially erect position — compare LIE, SIT, KNEEL **b :** to be a specified height when fully erect ⟨~*s* six feet two in his socks⟩ ⟨a horse ~*ing* over fifteen hands at the shoulders⟩ **c :** to rise to an erect position **:** stand up **2 a :** to take up or maintain a specified position or posture ⟨~ aloof from an argument⟩ ⟨~ aside and let me pass⟩ ⟨asked the crowd to ~ back⟩ ⟨warned to ~ clear of the swinging boom⟩ ⟨~ at attention⟩ **b :** to hold one's ground **:** maintain one's position ⟨~ firm⟩ ⟨~ fast⟩ ⟨~ still⟩ **:** resist attack ⟨choose whether to run away or ~ and fight it out⟩ ⟨*stood* at bay facing his tormentors⟩ **3 a :** to assume and maintain a particular position or attitude with respect to some question or course of action ⟨how does he ~ on the disarmament question⟩ **:** be firm and steadfast in support or opposition ⟨has always *stood* firmly for states' rights⟩ **b :** to be in a particular state or situation ⟨~*s* revealed as a liar⟩ ⟨~*s* accused of betraying his friend⟩ ⟨his bank account *stood* at low level⟩ ⟨~*s* under heavy obligation to me⟩ **4 :** to hold a course at sea **:** sail in a specified direction ⟨~ out from the shore⟩ ⟨~ for the harbor⟩ **5** *obs* **:** HESITATE, SCRUPLE ⟨~ at murder⟩ **6 a :** to have or maintain a relative position in or as if in a graded scale of value or estimation ⟨~*s* first in his class⟩ ⟨~*s* high with his uncle just now⟩ **b :** to be in a position to gain or lose because of an action taken or commitment made ⟨~*s* to realize a handsome profit on his investment⟩ **7 a :** to choose to play a hand of cards as dealt (as in écarté or twenty-one) **b :** to accept the turnup as trump (as in seven-up) **8** *chiefly Brit* **:** to be a candidate for a position or office **:** RUN ⟨will ~ for reelection in his own district⟩ **9 a :** to rest or remain upright on a base or lower end ⟨a clock *stood* on the mantel⟩ ⟨a ladder ~*ing* against the wall⟩ — opposed to *lie* **b :** to occupy a place or location ⟨an elm ~*s* before the house⟩ ⟨the house ~*s* on a knoll facing the sea⟩ **c :** to be or stay upright in place ⟨trees still ~*ing* after the hurricane⟩ **d :** to stay or remain in the usual position of use ⟨left the dishes ~*ing* on the table⟩ **10 a :** to remain stationary or inactive ⟨the car *stood* in the garage for a week⟩ ⟨~ waiting for the green light⟩; *specif, of a vehicle* **:** to stay briefly (as for loading) in a public or private way **b** *of a liquid* **:** to lie or remain without flowing or circulating or being stirred or shaken up ⟨rainwater ~*ing* in stagnant pools⟩ ⟨let the wine ~ so that the lees will settle⟩ **c :** to gather slowly and remain ⟨sweat *stood* on his brow⟩ ⟨tears ~*ing* in her eyes⟩ **11 :** to be consistent **:** AGREE, ACCORD — used esp. in the expression *it stands to reason* **12 a :** to exist in a definite written or printed form ⟨copy a passage exactly as it ~*s* in the original⟩ ⟨the spelling of a name as it ~*s* in the early charters⟩ ⟨enforce a law just as it ~*s* in the record⟩ **b :** to remain valid or efficacious ⟨the order given last week still ~*s*⟩ **13** *of the wind, archaic* **:** to come from or be in a specified place or condition ⟨the wind ~*s* in the west⟩ **14 a** *of a hunting dog* (1) **:** POINT (2) **:** RANGE ⟨~*s* over more ground than is usual with hounds of other breeds —*Dog World*⟩ **b** *of a male animal* **:** to be available as a sire — used esp. of horses ⟨his sire now ~*s* in France⟩ ⟨the average stallion ~*s* for about seven years⟩ **c** *of a female animal* **:** to accept the male **:** be in heat ~ *vt* **1 a :** to endure or undergo successfully ⟨~ the cold⟩ ⟨~ the test of time⟩ ⟨how his motives would ~ a closer scrutiny⟩ **b :** TOLERATE, BEAR ⟨cannot ~ criticism⟩ ⟨can't ~ the thought of losing all that money⟩ **c :** to endure the presence of ⟨I never could ~ that fellow⟩ **2 :** to resist without yielding or retreating **:** remain firm in the face of ⟨~ gunfire⟩ ⟨~ a siege⟩ **3 :** to submit to **:** agree to abide by **:** accept the result of **:** RISK ⟨~ the judgment of a Roman senate —Joseph Addison⟩ ⟨brought back to ~ trial for forgery⟩ **4 a :** to perform the duty of ⟨as I did ~ my watch upon the hill —Shak.⟩ ⟨*stood* guard over the treasure⟩ **b :** to participate in (a formation) ⟨~ reveille⟩ **5 :** to pay the cost of (as a treat) **:** pay for ⟨I'll ~ you a dinner⟩ ⟨~*ing* drinks for the crowd⟩ **6 :** to set upright **:** cause to stand ⟨picked the child up and *stood* him on his feet⟩ ⟨~ a board on end⟩ **7** *of a hunting dog* **:** POINT, SET ⟨~ game⟩ **8 :** to make available (a stallion) for breeding esp. as a public stud **9 :** to provide standing room for ⟨this bus ~*s* 41 people⟩ **syn** see BEAR — **stand a chance** *or* **stand a show :** to have a likelihood or possibility ⟨he doesn't *stand a chance* with the champion⟩ — **stand and deliver** *archaic* **:** to halt and hand over valuables — **stand by 1 a :** to remain loyal or faithful to **:** SUPPORT, DEFEND ⟨*stand by* the Constitution⟩ ⟨*stood by* her husband through all his troubles⟩ ⟨a strong minority would always *stand by* the king —G.G.Coulton⟩ **b :** to stick to ⟨*stood by* all his promises⟩ **:** MAINTAIN **2 :** to get ready or in position to operate ⟨*stand by* the lifeboats⟩ — **stand by one's guns :** to stick to one's guns — **stand easy** *Brit* **:** to relax in formation **:** stand at ease — often used in commands to troops to give them a rest interval — **stand for 1 :** to be a symbol for **:** REPRESENT, SIGNIFY, DENOTE ⟨white *stands for* purity⟩ ⟨assumed that a consonantal letter *stood for* a consonant and a vowel —A.L.Kroeber⟩ **2 :** to acknowledge or declare as a guiding principle or ideal ⟨*stand for* decency⟩ **3 :** to put up with **:** PERMIT, ENDURE ⟨human sacrifice . . . was more than the Romans . . . could *stand for* —Stuart Piggott⟩ — **stand in hand** *chiefly dial* **:** to be serviceable or advantageous ⟨the architect was possessed of a . . . virtuosity which *stood* him *in hand* in his adopted land —Rexford Newcomb⟩ **:** BEHOOVE — **stand mute** *of a prisoner upon arraignment* **:** to make no answer or to refuse to plead directly or to put himself on trial — **stand on** *or* **stand upon 1 :** to depend upon **:** have a basis in ⟨*stand on* the fifth amendment⟩ **2 :** to insist on **:** regard as important ⟨he will *stand on* his rights⟩ ⟨never *stood on* ceremony with his friends⟩ ⟨*stand* not *upon* the order of your going —Shak.⟩ — **stand one's ground :** to maintain one's position **:** stand firm — **stand on one's own feet** *or* **stand on one's own legs 1 :** to support oneself **:** make a living **:** manage one's own affairs **2 :** to think or act independently — **stand over :** to watch closely and steadily and control the actions of — **stand pat 1 :** to choose to play one's hand as dealt in draw poker without resorting to the draw **2 :** to oppose or resist change; *specif* **:** to oppose any change in the tariff policy of the U.S. — **stand the gaff :** to bear up under trials and difficulties **:** endure stress and strain without weakening or yielding — **stand the racket 1 :** to sustain heavy expense incurred **2 :** to endure consequences — **stand to 1 :** to persevere in using with determination and courage **:** ply with zeal ⟨*stood to* their guns manfully⟩ ⟨now, boys, *stand to* the oars⟩ **2 :** to give support to **:** remain faithful to **:** stand by — **stand together :** to be consistent **:** AGREE — **stand treat :** to pay the cost of food, drinks, or entertainment for others in a group ⟨we all went to a baseball game, myself *standing treat* —Isaac Rosenfeld⟩

[2]**stand** \"\ *n* -s [ME *stand, stond,* fr. *standen, stonden* to stand] **1 a :** an act of stopping or staying in one place **b :** STANDSTILL ⟨the team was finally brought to a ~⟩ **2 a :** a halt (as in a retreat or flight) for defense or resistance **b :** a defensive effort of some duration or degree of success ⟨a gallant ~ at the bridge⟩ ⟨rallied his forces for a final ~⟩ ⟨a record 5th-wicket ~ by a cricket batsman⟩ ⟨desperate goal-line ~⟩ **c** (1) **:** a stop made by a touring theatrical company to give a performance ⟨a one-night ~⟩ (2) **:** a town where such a company stops for a performance **d :** a place for travelers to stop along a road ⟨the old ~ on the stage line —*Amer. Guide Series: Tenn.*⟩ **3 a :** a place or post where one stands **:** STATION, POSITION ⟨a beggar's customary ~ near the gate⟩ ⟨urged to take a definite ~ on the question of civil rights⟩ **b :** a place where the hunter stands awaiting the game that is being driven toward him **4 a :** the place taken by a witness for testifying in court **:** WITNESS-BOX ⟨took the ~ in his own defense⟩ **b :** a section of the tiered seats for spectators of an outdoor sport or spectacle; *also* **:** the occupants of such seats — usu. used in pl. ⟨a roar of applause from the ~*s*⟩ ⟨the ball went into the ~*s* behind third base⟩; compare GRANDSTAND **c :** a raised platform for viewing a race or other spectacle ⟨judges' ~⟩ ⟨the troops saluted as they passed the reviewing ~⟩ **d :** an outdoor platform for speakers or performers **e :** BANDSTAND **f :** a place where a stallion is made available for breeding **5 a :** a small often open-air structure for a small retail business ⟨cigar ~⟩ ⟨roadside fruit ~⟩ ⟨hot-dog ~⟩; *specif* **:** NEWSSTAND ⟨after the latest edition hit the ~*s*⟩ **b :** a site fit for business opportunity ⟨a good ~ for a drugstore⟩ **6 :** a place at which a vehicle regularly stops or is parked when waiting for passengers ⟨bus ~⟩ ⟨taxi ~⟩ **7** *archaic* **:** a large container: as **a :** CASK **b :** TUB ⟨~ of lard⟩ **c :** an open barrel **8** *dial* **:** [1]HIVE 2 **9 a :** a small table **b :** a frame on or in which something may be placed for support ⟨umbrella ~⟩ ⟨music ~⟩ ⟨reading ~⟩ ⟨salt and pepper ~⟩ ⟨~ for firing a rocket⟩ **c :** a base on which something may be placed for exhibit or use **:** STANDARD, PEDESTAL ⟨typewriter ~⟩ **10 a :** the state of the tide at high or low water when there is no sensible change of level **b :** STILLSTAND 2a **11 a** *chiefly Scot* **:** a complete set (as of clothes) **:** SUIT **b** *pl* **stand** *or* **stands** *chiefly Brit* **:** a complete set of arms for one soldier **c :** a set of two or more related rolls in a rolling mill **d :** a unit of drill pipe consisting of two or more lengths coupled together with threaded pipe couplings **e :** a unit of machinery (as for milking, cotton ginning) **12 :** a growth of plants (as trees); *esp* **:** the number or density on a given area ⟨a good ~ of corn⟩ ⟨a mixed ~ of hardwoods and conifers⟩ ⟨timber thinned to a proper ~⟩ — compare CATCH 8 **13** *Africa* **:** LOT 6b **14 :** the erect part of a turned-over collar from the neckline to the crease — compare FALL 1d(3) **15 :** a standing posture ⟨the tumblers ended the stunt in a ~⟩ — **at a stand :** at a standstill **:** in a perplexing situation

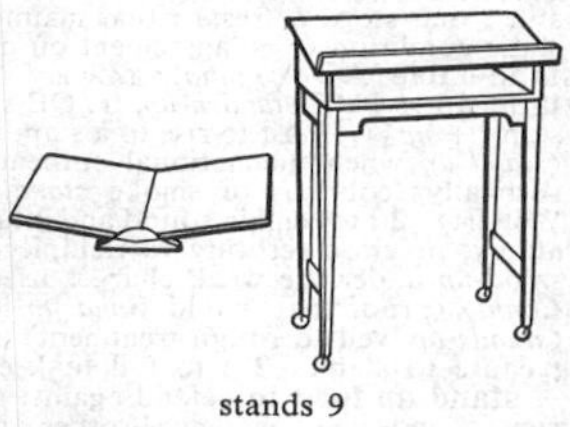

stands 9

stand·age \'standij\ *n* -s [[1]*stand* + *-age*] **1** *Brit* **a :** space or permission for standing ⟨~ for cattle⟩ ⟨~ for bicycles⟩ **b :** a charge for permission to stand **2** *Brit* **:** a reservoir in which water accumulates at the bottom of a mine **:** SUMP

[1]**stan·dard** \'standə(r)d, -aan-\ *n* -s [ME *standart, standard,* fr. MF *estandart, estandard* rallying place, flag to mark a rallying place, fr. OF, prob. of Gmc origin; fr. a compound whose first element is akin to OHG *stantan* to stand and whose second element is akin to OHG *ort* point, corner — more at STAND, ODD] **1 :** a pole or spear bearing some conspicuous object (as a banner) at the top formerly used in an army or fleet to mark a rallying point, to signal, or to serve as an emblem **2 a :** a long narrow tapering flag of considerable size and richness that is personal to an individual or corporation and bears heraldic badges, usu. a motto, and often other devices — distinguished from *banner* **b** (1) **:** the personal flag of the head of a state or of a member of a royal family — compare ROYAL STANDARD (2) **:** a distinctive flag adopted by a government that is not a monarchy for some distinguishing purpose served by the monarch's personal flag under a monarchy **c :** an organization flag carried by a mounted or motorized military unit ⟨regimental ~⟩ **d :** BANNER **e** *obs* **:** STANDARD-BEARER **3 a :** something that is established by authority, custom, or general consent as a model or example to be followed **:** CRITERION, TEST **b :** a definite level or degree of quality that is proper and adequate for a specific purpose **4 :** something that is set up and established by authority as a rule for the measure of quantity, weight, extent, value, or quality; *esp* **:** an original specimen measure or weight (as the international prototype meter and kilogram of the International Bureau of Weights and Measures) or an official copy of such a specimen used as the standard of comparison in testing other weights and measures **5 a :** the fineness of the metal used in coins and the legally fixed weight each coin should have when first minted **b :** STANDARD OF VALUE **6 a** *or* **standard hundred :** any of various units of quantity for timber; *esp* **:** a unit equal to 1980 board feet or 165 cubic feet — called also *Petersburg standard* **b :** STANDARD DEAL **7 a :** a carefully thought-out method of performing a task ⟨auditing ~*s*⟩ **b :** carefully drawn specifications covering manufacturing material or equipment **8** *Brit* **:** a grade in an elementary school ⟨had not gone beyond the fifth ~ of her country school⟩ **9 standards** *pl* **:** the punches (as H M O P h m o p) of a type font that are made first and that serve as a dimensional and design model for the other letters **10** [[2]*standard*] **:** STANDARD ENGLISH **11** *obs* **:** a complete assortment **:** SET, SUIT **12 :** a structure built for or serving as a base or support for something ⟨the ~ for a Sèvres vase⟩ ⟨~ for a set of flags⟩ ⟨power-line ~*s*⟩ ⟨~ for a sewing machine⟩ **13 a :** a tall candlestick in a church; *esp* **:** one of two or more set on a sanctuary or chancel floor **b :** STANDING CUP **c** *obs* **:** a large chest **:** COFFER **14 :** an inverted knee timber placed upon the deck of a ship instead of beneath it **15 :** a plant grown with an erect main stem so that it forms or resembles a tree: as **a :** a fruit tree and esp. an apple grafted on a stock that does not induce dwarfing and grown in an essentially natural form as distinguished from an espalier **b :** an herbaceous plant (as a fuchsia or geranium) pruned and trained to a single stem that is induced to branch when the desired height is attained by pinching out the apical growth **c :** a woody plant (as a rose or wisteria) that is budded on a tall stock and pruned and trained to produce a broad head of scion growth at the top of the stock **16 a :** the large upper posterior petal of some flowers (as the pea) — called also *banner, vexillum* **b :** one of the three inner usu. erect and incurved petals of an iris **17 a :** a tree permitted to remain after coppice felling **b :** a tree from one to two feet in diameter at breastheight **18** [[2]*standard*] **:** a musical composition that has become a part of the standard repertoire

syn STANDARD, CRITERION, GAUGE (*or* GAGE), YARDSTICK, TOUCHSTONE can designate, in common, any measure by which one judges a thing as authentic, good, or adequate or the degree to which it is authentic, good, or adequate. STANDARD applies to any authoritative rule, principle, or measure used to determine the quantity, weight, or extent, or esp. the value, quality, level, or degree of a thing ⟨each generation . . . has its own ideals and its own *standards* of judgment —S.M.Crothers⟩ ⟨the ideal of general cultivation has been one of the *standards* in education —C.W.Eliot⟩ ⟨each breed has a written *standard* of perfection which supposedly describes the ideal specimen —J.W.Cross⟩ CRITERION is the thing, whether formulated into a rule or principle or not, by appeal to which one arrives at or confirms a given judgment, as of value, quality, fitness, or correctness ⟨the sole *criterion* of the truth of illusion is its inner congruity —J.L.Lowes⟩ ⟨the size of sunspots is a meaningless *criterion* in predicting the havoc which may occur to radio transmission —C.L.Dawes⟩ ⟨no exact *criterion* for a just and fruitful apportionment of the surplus wealth —J.A. Hobson⟩ ⟨these laws . . . did establish useful *criteria* of conduct —Oscar Handlin⟩ GAUGE (*or* GAGE), concretely a standard measure or scale or an instrument for measuring something that fluctuates, as in size or height, can in extension apply to any standard measure whether tangible or not ⟨a piece of ⅛ inch thickness fiber or wood makes a convenient *gage* in setting brush holders —*Mill & Factory*⟩ ⟨the *gauges* Hollywood uses to measure a picture's importance —*Time*⟩ ⟨the degree of public acceptance of the opinions of leaders is the ultimate *gauge* of the importance and validity of those opinions —K.A.Rafferty⟩ ⟨the thickness *gage* has leaves of various thickness, and its function is to measure clearances in presswork —*Theory & Practice of Presswork*⟩ YARDSTICK, in this comparison, is a more or less figurative and informal term for any criterion, esp. for something intangible or immaterial ⟨no absolute or universal *yardstick* about what constitutes a frustration —Abram Kardiner⟩ ⟨the consumption of petroleum products, an accurate *yardstick* of economic growth —*Lamp*⟩ TOUCHSTONE, in this comparison, is any simple device by which authenticity or value may be determined, esp. an authentic or superior instance of a class of things by comparison with which another thing may be judged authentic or superior ⟨consistency is a *touchstone* by which the basic doctrine can often be distinguished from the propaganda line —L.C.Stevens⟩ ⟨a Marxist critic using economic determinants, social perspectives, and class consciousness as his *touchstones* —C.I.Glicksberg⟩ ⟨the chief *touchstone* to folklore is the manner in which it is transmitted: one man tells another, one man shows another —D.B.M.Emrich⟩ **syn** see in addition FLAG, MODEL

[2]**standard** \"\ *adj* **1 :** constituting or affording a standard for comparison, measurement, or judgment ⟨~ weight⟩ ⟨~ silver⟩ **2 a :** having qualities or attributes required by law or established by custom ⟨~ insurance policy⟩ ⟨window of ~ width⟩ ⟨~ milk⟩ ⟨~ ginger⟩ **b** *of a fruit or vegetable* **:** of medium-low to inferior quality **:** falling into the third and usu. lowest quality class generally marketed ⟨~ canned tomatoes are often a good buy for cooking⟩ **3 a :** regularly and widely available **:** readily supplied **:** not unusual or special ⟨~ brand of coffee⟩ ⟨~ model of automobile⟩ **b :** well-established and very familiar **:** not novel or experimental ⟨~ automobile transmission⟩ ⟨~ building practice⟩ **4 :** having recognized and permanent value ⟨~ history⟩ ⟨~ authors⟩ ⟨~ reference work⟩ ⟨~ biography⟩ **5 :** substantially uniform and well-established by usage in the speech and writing of the educated and widely recognized as acceptable and authoritative ⟨~ German⟩ ⟨~ pronunciation⟩ ⟨~ spelling⟩ ⟨~ grammar⟩ **6 :** grown in natural form **:** not trained to a wall or support ⟨~ fruit trees⟩ **7** *of a typewriter* **:** heavily constructed for constant service and designed for use on a desk or stand built for the purpose — compare PORTABLE, NOISELESS **8** *cryptography* **:** preserving alphabetic order ⟨DCBAZY . . . GFE is a reversed ~ sequence⟩

[3]**standard** \"\ *vt* -ED/-ING/-S **:** to determine the fineness of (as gold, silver)

standard atmosphere *n* **1 :** an arbitrary ideal set of atmospheric conditions (as used in calculations of aircraft performance); *specif* **:** the international standard specifying a temperature of 15°C and 760 millimeters pressure at sea level with a vertical temperature gradient of −6.5°C per kilometer up to 11 kilometers altitude and uniform temperature of −56.5°C above that level **2 :** ATMOSPHERE 5

standard-bearer \'==,==\ *n* [ME *standart berer,* fr. *standart* standard + *berer* bearer] **1 a :** one that bears a standard or banner **b :** the leader of an organization or movement ⟨the *standard-bearer* of a political party⟩ **2 :** STANDARD-WING

standard-bred \ˌ==ˌ=\ *adj* **:** bred to conform to predetermined standards; *specif* **:** of or relating to the Standardbred breed or an animal of this breed

standardbred \'==,=\ *n* **1** *usu cap* **:** an American breed of light trotting and pacing horses largely of Thoroughbred ancestry bred to attain a standard of speed (as a mile in 2:30 for trotters and in 2:25 for pacers) and noted for their endurance **2** -s *often cap* **:** a horse of the Standardbred breed

standard candle *n* **:** CANDLE 4

standard cell *n* **:** a cell of known electromotive force used in the potentiometer calibration of electrical instruments

standard coin *n* **:** a coin having an intrinsic value equal to its face value — compare TOKEN COIN

standard condition *n* **1 :** a condition specified in a series of scientific tests **2 standard conditions** *pl* **:** a temperature of 0°C and a pressure of 760 millimeters of mercury for use in a comparison of gas volumes

standard cost *n* **:** a predetermined cost based on cost factors assumed to be normal with which a correlated historical cost is compared — compare ACTUAL COST

standard deal *n* **:** a deal board usu. 3 in. x 9 in. x 12 ft. from which other sizes may be sawed

standard deviation *n* **:** the square root of the average of the squares of the deviations from the mean — symbol σ; called also *root-mean-square deviation*

standard distance *n* **:** a distance of 500 yards for capital ships or 250 yards for cruisers in a simple formation — compare DISTANCE 2b(2)

standard dropper *n* **:** DROPPER 4b

standard english *n, usu cap S & cap E* **1 :** the English taught in schools **2 :** English that is current, reputable, and national **3 :** the English that with respect to spelling, grammar, pronunciation, and vocabulary is substantially uniform though not devoid of regional differences, that is well-established by usage in the formal and informal speech and writing of the educated, and that is widely recognized as acceptable wherever English is spoken and understood **4 :** all words entered in a general English language dictionary that are not restricted by a label (as *slang, dial, obs, biol, Scot*)

standard error *n* **1 :** STANDARD DEVIATION **2 :** standard deviation divided by the square root of the number of items in a sample tested **:** the standard deviation of the sample mean

standard fit *n* **:** a fit having standardized allowance and tolerance

standard gage *n* **1 a :** a template, pattern, or other instrument for gauging the dimensions or shape of standardized parts **b :** MASTER GAGE **2 :** a railroad gage of 4 feet 8½ inches

standard gold *n* **:** gold of the legal fineness for coinage **:** COIN GOLD

standard gravity *n* **:** ACCELERATION OF GRAVITY

standard hole *n* **:** a hole machined to a standard of zero allowance plus a specified tolerance, any allowance in the fit being provided for in the size of the shaft intended to fit the hole — compare BILATERAL 5, STANDARD SHAFT

standard hundred *n* **:** STANDARD 6a

stan·dard·iz·able \'standə(r),dīzəbəl, ,=='===\ *adv* **:** capable of being standardized

stan·dard·iza·tion \,standə(r)də'zāshən, -aan-, -(r),dī'-\ *n* -s **:** the act, process, or result of standardizing **:** the condition in which a standard has been achieved or effectively applied

stan·dard·ize \'standə(r),dīz, -aan-\ *vb* -ED/-ING/-S *see -ize in Explan Notes* [[1]*standard* + *-ize*] *vt* **1 :** to reduce to or compare with a standard **:** determine the strength, value, or quality of by comparison with a standard ⟨~ a solution⟩ ⟨~ a voltmeter⟩ **2 :** to bring into conformity with a standard **:** make uniform ⟨*standardized* education⟩ ⟨*standardized* concert repertory⟩ **3 :** to arrange or order the component items of a test (as of intelligence, achievement, or personality) so that the probability of their eliciting a designated class of response varies with some quantifiable psychological or behavioral attribute, function, or characteristic ~ *vi* **:** to adopt a specified product or method as the only one to be produced or utilized ⟨believed the Russians had *standardized* on an A-bomb of considerably greater power —H.W.Baldwin⟩

standard knot *n* **:** a lumber knot that is sound and not over 1½ inches in diameter

standard length *n* **:** the distance on a fish from the tip of the snout or of the lower jaw if projecting forward to the base of the caudal fin

[1]**standard line** *or* **standard route** *n* **:** a railroad line or route upon which the regular or highest rates apply **:** a fast-service route in distinction from slower and perhaps longer routes or from one that is partly by rail and partly by water — compare DIFFERENTIAL ROUTE

[2]**standard line** *n* **:** type casting in which all printed letters and figures regardless of size or style align at the bottom

standard meridian *n* **:** a meridian used for determining standard time

standard money *n* **:** a monetary unit which is designated by a government to serve as the basis of its currency system and into which other types of money in the country are convertible — compare STANDARD OF VALUE

standard of living *or* **standard of life 1 :** the necessities, comforts, and luxuries enjoyed or aspired to by an individual or group **2 :** a minimum of necessities, comforts, or luxuries that is essential to maintaining a person in customary or proper status or circumstances

standard of perfection *or* **standard of excellence :** a compilation of the desired qualities and characteristics of a breed of livestock usu. with indication of the faults to be esp. avoided

standard of value : the commodity that is made the measure of value in any comparison of values; *specif* **:** the basis of value in a monetary system — compare GOLD STANDARD

standard operating procedure *n* **:** STANDING OPERATING PROCEDURE

standard parallel *n* **:** CORRECTION LINE

standard pitch *n* **:** the geometrical pitch of an air propeller measured usu. at a point two-thirds of the radius

standard policy *n* **:** an insurance policy prescribed by statute or otherwise adopted generally by all insurers

standard port *n* **:** a port for which the tides are predicted in tide tables — compare SECONDARY PORT
standard rate *n* **:** a basic or minimum rate established for similar work or occupation within a plant, industry, or community by collective agreement or union rule or by law
standard rose *n* **:** TREE ROSE
standards *pl of* STANDARD, *pres 3d sing of* STANDARD
standard schnauzer *n* **:** a schnauzer of a variety that attains a height of 16¾ to 19¾ inches
standard score *n* **:** an individual test score expressed as the deviation from the mean score of the group in units of standard deviation
standard scottish *or* **standard scotch** *n, often cap 1st S & cap 2d S* **:** English as taught in Scotch schools
standard shaft *n* **:** a shaft machined to a standard of zero allowance minus a specified tolerance — compare STANDARD HOLE
standard silver *n* **:** COIN SILVER
standard solution *n* **:** a solution having a standard or accurately known strength that is used as a reagent in chemical analysis
standard spheroid *n* **:** the ellipsoid of revolution that most nearly coincides with the figure of the earth
standard star *n* **:** a star of known position and proper motion used as a standard in determining time, latitude, and the positions of other celestial bodies
standard test *n* **:** a test (as of intelligence, achievement, or personality) whose reliability has been established by obtaining an average score of a significantly large number of individuals for use as a standard of comparison
standard time *n* **1 :** the time of a region or country that is established by law or general usage as civil time **:** the mean solar time of a meridian that is a multiple of 15 arbitrarily applied to a local area or to one of the 24 time zones and designated as a number of hours earlier or later than Greenwich time **2 :** the amount of time required for a repeated operation by an experienced worker of average skill working at normal pace and with due allowance for relaxation and interruptions
standard unit *n* **:** standard deviation used as a unit of measurement of deviation
standard-wing \'=,=\ *n* **1 :** a bird of paradise (*Semioptera wallacii*) that has two long special feathers standing erect on each wing **2** *or* **standard-winged nightjar :** PENNANT-WINGED NIGHTJAR
standaway \'=,=,=\ *adj* [fr. the phrase *stand away*] **:** standing out from the body ⟨~ neckline⟩ ⟨~ skirt⟩
stand by *vi* [ME *standen by*, fr. *standen* to stand + *by*] **1 a :** to be near at hand **;** be present ⟨made the statement with several witnesses *standing by*⟩ **b :** to remain apart or aloof ⟨how can you *stand by* and let your son ruin himself⟩ **2 a :** to be or to get ready to act ⟨*standing by* to await instructions⟩ ⟨ordered to *stand by* to let go the anchor⟩ **b** *of a transmitting station* **:** to be ready to send signals **c** *of a receiving station* **:** to remain tuned in
¹standby \'=,=\ *n* -s [*stand by*] **1 a :** one to be relied upon esp. in emergencies **b :** a favorite or reliable choice or resource ⟨old ~*s* of the concert repertory⟩ ⟨good old Anglo-Saxon ~*s* of beef, lamb, mutton, ham, and domestic poultry —Thomas Barbour⟩ **2 :** one that is held in reserve ready for use **:** SUBSTITUTE
²standby \"\ *adj* [*stand by*] **1 :** held near at hand and ready for emergency use ⟨~ orchestra in a broadcasting station⟩ ⟨~ equipment⟩ ⟨~ crew for fire fighting⟩ ⟨~ power plant⟩ **2 :** relating to the act or condition of standing by ⟨~ period⟩ ⟨~ time⟩ ⟨~ agreement⟩ ⟨~ pay⟩
stand down *vi* **1 :** to sail with the tide or with the wind **2 :** to leave the witness stand **3** *chiefly Brit* **a :** to go off duty **b :** to retire from taking part (as in a game) or from a position of leadership
stand-down \'=,=\ *n* -s [*stand down*] **:** a period of time off **:** LAYOFF
stand-easy \'=,==\ *n* -ES [*stand easy*] **:** a command to troops to be at ease; *also* **:** the rest interval so authorized
stand·ee \(')stan¦dē, -aan-\ *n* -s [*stand* + *-ee*] **:** one that occupies standing room ⟨~*s* at a play⟩ ⟨~*s* in a ticket queue⟩ ⟨~*s* in a bus⟩
stand·er \'standə(r), -aan-\ *n* -s **1 :** one that stands ⟨~ of a watch⟩; *esp* **:** a member of a hunting party whose duty it is to wait in readiness for game to be driven within shooting range **2 :** BASE, SUPPORT
stander-by \'=='=\ *n, pl* **standers-by :** BYSTANDER
standfast \'=,=\ *n* -s [fr. the phrase *stand fast*] **:** a firm, fixed, or settled position
stand fire *n* [²*stand* + *fire*] **:** a forest fire that ignites the trunks of trees
standholder \'=,==\ *n* [²*stand* + *holder*] **:** an exhibitor in a fair or public exhibition
stand in *vt, chiefly Brit* **:** to be a (specified) expense to **:** COST ~ *vi* **:** to act as a stand-in — **stand in with :** to be in a specially favored position with; *esp* **:** to be in secret and usu. profitable alliance with
stand-in \'=,=\ *n* -s [*stand in*] **1 :** a preferred position **:** a place high in favor **2 a :** someone physically resembling an actor and employed to stand in the actor's place until lights and camera are ready **b :** SUBSTITUTE
¹standing *adj* [ME, fr. pres. part. of *standen* to stand] **1 :** upright on the feet or in place **:** ERECT ⟨~ audience⟩ ⟨~ timber⟩ **2 a :** not being used or operated ⟨~ factory⟩ **b :** not flowing **:** STAGNANT ⟨~ water⟩ **3 a :** remaining at the same level, degree, or amount for an indeterminate period ⟨made me a ~ offer of $10,000 for my house⟩ **b :** kept in use indefinitely **:** remaining valid ⟨one of the ~ problems in physics⟩ ⟨felt her childless state as a ~ reproach to her as a wife⟩ ⟨had a ~ joke with the elevator boy⟩ **c :** kept intact for printing or reprinting or for molding — used of set letterpress matter and sometimes of other printing surfaces (as lithographic stones) ⟨keep the type ~⟩ ⟨~ heads in a newspaper⟩ **4 :** established by law or custom **:** SETTLED, PERMANENT ⟨~ prohibition⟩ **5 a :** not movable **:** fixed in place ⟨~ washtub⟩ **b :** having a supporting base ⟨~ bowl⟩ **6 :** done from a standing position ⟨~ ovation⟩ ⟨~ jump⟩ ⟨race from a ~ start⟩
²standing \"\ *n* -s [ME, fr. gerund of *standen* to stand] **1 a :** a place to stand in **:** SITUATION **:** LOCATION **b :** a position from which one may assert or enforce legal rights and duties **c** *Brit* (1) **:** STABLE (2) **:** a stall (as in a stable) for a domestic animal **2 a :** length of service or experience esp. as determining relative place, rank, pay, or privilege ⟨candidates for the fellowship must be of postgraduate ~⟩ **b :** position or condition in society or in a profession **:** STATUS ⟨lawyer of high ~⟩; *esp* **:** good reputation ⟨among those at the meeting were several men of ~ in the community⟩ **c :** position relative to a standard of achievement ⟨left the college in good ~⟩ ⟨attained a ~ of B in his senior year⟩ or to achievements of competitors ⟨improved their ~ in the baseball league by two places⟩ **3 :** maintenance of position or condition **:** DURATION ⟨custom of long ~⟩ ⟨marriage of many years' ~⟩
standing army *n* [¹*standing*] **:** a permanently organized army of paid soldiers — compare MILITIA
standing barrage *n* **:** a defensive barrage designed to be fired on a particular line
standing bevel *n* **:** a bevel whose angle is obtuse
standing block *or* **standing pulley** *n* **:** a fixed pulley block — distinguished from *running block*
standing committee *n* **:** a committee to consider subjects of a particular class arising during a stated period; *specif* **:** a permanent committee of a legislative body
standing crop *n* **:** a crop not cut or otherwise severed from the soil
standing cup *n* **:** a tall goblet with a foot and a cover
standing cypress *n* **:** a tall erect biennial or perennial leafy-stemmed herb (*Gilia rubra*) having the alternate leaves pinnately divided into slender needlelike leaflets and numerous largely scarlet flowers in a terminal panicle and being native to the southern U.S. but escaped from cultivation and naturalized in areas (as New England) outside its normal range
standing finish *n* **:** the part of the interior fittings esp. of a house that is permanent and fixed
standing height *n* **:** STATURE 1
standing initial *n* **:** a cockup initial
standing lug *n* **:** a lugsail whose yard is not dipped in tacking — compare DIPPING LUG; see LUGSAIL illustration
standing operating procedure *n* **:** established or prescribed tactical or administrative methods to be followed routinely for the performance of designated operations or in designated situations — called also *standard operating procedure;* abbr. *SOP*
standing order *n* **1 :** an instruction or prescribed procedure in force permanently or until specifically changed or canceled: as **a standing orders** *pl* **:** the rules for the guidance and government of parliamentary procedure which endure through successive sessions until vacated or repealed — distinguished from *sessional order* **b standing orders** *pl* **:** routine orders giving authority for the performance of certain prescribed acts for hospitalized patients by the personnel as distinct from specific orders written for a particular patient ⟨blood count and urinalysis on admission are *standing orders*⟩ **2 a :** an order for purchase that holds good until it is filled **b :** an order directing the automatic purchase of succeeding issues of a serial publication
standing part *n* **1 :** the part of a tackle made fast to the block or to any point or object — distinguished from *running part* **2 :** the part of a rope around which turns are taken with the running part in making a knot or bend **3 :** the part of a hook opposite the point
standing press *n* **:** a vertical press in which printed and folded sheets and books are piled and pressed
standing rigging *or* **standing gear** *n* **:** permanent rigging (as stays and shrouds) used primarily to secure the masts and fixed spars of a vessel or to support radio, radar, and other equipment carried aloft — compare RUNNING RIGGING
standing roast *n* **:** a rib roast from which only the heaviest parts of the vertebrae have been removed — compare ROLLED ROAST
standing room *n* [²*standing*] **:** space for standing; *esp* **:** accommodation available for spectators or passengers after all seats are filled
standing rope *n* [¹*standing*] **:** a rope permanently fastened and used as a guy
standing rules *n pl* **:** the rules of a society or organization for details of its government that are created by a majority vote and remain in force until repealed or annulled by a majority vote
standing salt *n* **:** SALTCELLAR
standing valve *n* **:** a foot valve at the bottom of an oil-well pump
standing vise *n* **:** a bench vise at which the operator stands while working
standing vote *n* **:** RISING VOTE
standing wave *n* **:** a single-frequency mode of vibration of a body or physical system in which the amplitude varies from place to place, is constantly zero at fixed points, and has maxima at other points (as at the nodes and antinodes respectively on a violin string or in an organ pipe) — called also *stationary wave*; compare TRAVELING WAVE
standing wave ratio *n* **:** the ratio of the maximum to the minimum signal voltage on a transmission line
standing ways *n pl* **:** GROUND WAYS
stand·ish \'stan(,)dish\ *n* -ES [origin unknown] **:** a stand for writing materials **:** INKSTAND
stand method *n* **:** a practice in forestry of securing reproduction from self-sown seed induced by successive cuttings of trees of different ages in the stand and leading to the development of a stand of trees of the same age
stand of colors : the flags carried by a military unit (as a regiment); *also* **:** a single such flag
stand off *vi* **1 :** to stay at a distance in social intercourse or acquaintance **:** be unapproachable or unobliging **2 :** to sail away from the shore ~ *vt* **1 a :** to hold at a distance **:** keep from advancing **:** REPEL ⟨taking cover they managed to *stand* the Indians *off* until they could make their escape —D.D. Martin⟩ **b :** to put off **:** STALL ⟨able to *stand off* his creditors⟩ **2** *Brit* **:** to remove temporarily from regular employment **:** lay off — **stand off and on** *of a sailing ship* **:** to remain near a coast by sailing toward and then away from the land ⟨*standing off and on* while the captain went ashore⟩
¹standoff \'=,=\ *adj* [*stand off*] **1 :** not cordial **:** not ready to agree or to make friends **:** RESERVED ⟨~ attitude⟩ **2 :** used for holding something (as an electric wire) at a distance from a surface ⟨~ insulator⟩ — see INSULATOR illustration
²standoff \"\ *n* -s [*stand off*] **1 :** the act of standing off **2** *Brit* **:** a rest from work **3 a :** a counterbalancing effect **:** NEUTRALIZATION **b :** TIE, DRAW, DEADLOCK
standoff coat *n* **:** a double coat (as of some dogs) in which thick underhair supports profuse long hair so that it stands out from the body
standoff half *n* **:** a rugby halfback whose position is between the scrum half and the three-quarter backs — called also *fly half*
stand·off·ish \(')stan¦dȯfish, -aan-, -fēsh\ *adj* [¹*standoff* + *-ish*] **:** somewhat cold and reserved **:** lacking cordiality ⟨~ manner⟩ — **stand·off·ish·ly** *adv* — **stand·off·ish·ness** *n* -ES
stand oil *n* **:** a thickened drying oil prepared orig. by exposing to sunlight and air and now usu. by heating **:** BODIED OIL; *esp* **:** linseed oil heated to about 600° F — compare LITHOGRAPHIC VARNISH
stand on *vi* [ME *standen on*, fr. *standen* to stand + *on*] **:** to continue on the same tack or course ⟨whether the approaching ship would *stand on* or give way⟩
stand out *vi* **1 a :** to appear as if in relief **:** PROJECT **b :** to be prominent or conspicuous **:** stick out ⟨success and affluence *stood out* all over him —Hamilton Basso⟩ **2 :** to steer away from shore **3 :** to be stubborn in resolution or resistance **:** not to yield ⟨if you're rich you can afford to *stand out* for a really good contract —Christopher Isherwood⟩ ~ *vt* **:** OUTLAST, ENDURE ⟨*stand out* a storm⟩
¹standout \'=,=\ *n* -s [*stand out*] **:** something outstanding **:** a thing or a person readily distinguishable from others because of excellence or uniqueness ⟨a ~ among the available candidates for the office⟩ ⟨the coat is a ~ in this year's fashions⟩
²standout \"\ *adj* **:** OUTSTANDING ⟨~ performance in an operatic role⟩
stand over *vi* **:** to await consideration or settlement at a later date ⟨resolution will *stand over* until the following session⟩ ~ *vt* **:** to put off **:** POSTPONE
standover \'=,==\ *adj* [fr. the phrase *stand over*] **:** making new growth the next year after harvest ⟨~ crop of sugar cane⟩ ⟨~ cotton⟩ — compare RATOON
¹standpat \'=,=\ *adj* [fr. the phrase *stand pat*] **:** of or relating to or characterized by the policy of standing pat **:** stubbornly conservative
²standpat \"\ *n* -s [fr. the phrase *stand pat*] **:** STANDPATTER
stand·pat·ter \(')stan(d)¦pad·ə(r), -taan-, -patə-\ *n* -s **:** one that stands pat esp. in political matters **:** one that resists or opposes change
stand·pat·tism *also* **stand·pat·ism** \-pad·,izəm\ *n* -s **:** the policy of standing pat **:** resistance to change **:** reluctance to take positive action ⟨~ is timidity —A.L.Guérard⟩
standpipe \'=,=\ *n* **:** a vertical pipe used for holding a liquid: as **a :** a high tank or reservoir that is used to secure a uniform pressure in a water-supply system **b :** a vertical pipe for water that is used to provide fire protection to the upper stories of a high building **c :** a manhole frame

standpipe a

standpoint \'=,=\ *n* [trans. of G *standpunkt*] **:** a fixed point or station **:** a position from which objects or principles are viewed and according to which they are compared and judged ⟨arguing a question from the historical ~⟩ ⟨a good method from the ~ of economy⟩
standpost \'=,=\ *n* **:** a post forming a stand (as for a hydrant)
stands *pl of* STAND, *pres 3d sing of* STAND
¹standstill \'=,=\ *n* -s [fr. the phrase *stand still*] **1 :** cessation of movement forward or backward **:** state of rest **:** STOP ⟨wheels sank in the mud and brought the car to a ~⟩ ⟨death was attributed to cardiac ~ from potassium intoxication —T.R.Harrison⟩ ⟨rate of new building has reached a ~⟩ **2 :** STILLSTAND 3 **3 a :** a state of deadlock ⟨negotiations were at a ~ for the time being⟩ **b :** a state of paralyzing indecision or bafflement **c :** a state of exhaustion or thorough defeat ⟨never met a man she couldn't work to a ~ —Frank Sargeson⟩
²standstill \"\ *adj* [fr. the phrase *stand still*] **:** that stands still **:** that stops or rests **:** that maintains things in a fixed or static condition ⟨a ~ agreement on nuclear testing⟩
stand-table \'=,==\ *n, dial* **:** TABLE
stand up *vb* [ME *standen up*, fr. OE *standan up*, fr. *standan* to stand + *up*] *vi* **1 a :** to rise to a standing position **:** stand erect ⟨*stand up* when the national anthem is played⟩ **b :** to rise vertically ⟨columns of smoke *standing up* to the sky —Ira Wolfert⟩ **2 :** to remain sound and intact under stress, pressure, attack, or close scrutiny ⟨a fieldpiece . . . reported to have *stood up* under the weak charges used —*Amer. Guide Series: Conn.*⟩ ⟨proof that would *stand up* in court —Ross Annett⟩ ⟨*stands up* well to rough treatment⟩ ~ *vt* **1 :** to set on end **:** cause to stand **2 :** to fail to keep an appointment with — **stand up for :** to defend against attack or criticism **:** JUSTIFY, SUPPORT ⟨he was my brother anyway and I'm going to *stand up for* him —Liam O'Flaherty⟩ ⟨has always *stood up for* the rights of the individual —Bradford Smith⟩ — **stand up to :** to meet (as a danger, or obligation) fairly and fully ⟨*stand up to* a promise⟩ ⟨urged by an immense pride to *stand up to* our job —A.W.Long⟩ **:** face boldly **:** defend oneself or one's interests against ⟨had enough nerve to *stand up to* the boss⟩ — **stand up with :** to be best man or bridesmaid for at a wedding ceremony

STANDARD TIME IN 102 PLACES THROUGHOUT THE WORLD WHEN IT IS 12:00 NOON AT NEW YORK

CITY	TIME	CITY	TIME
Adelaide, Australia	2:30 A.M. next day	Los Angeles, California	9:00 A.M.
Alexandria, Egypt	7:00 P.M	¹Madrid, Spain	6:00 P.M.
¹Amsterdam, Netherlands	6:00 P.M.	Manila, Philippines	1:00 A.M. next day
Anchorage, Alaska	7:00 A.M.	Melbourne, Australia	3:00 A.M. next day
Asunción, Paraguay	1:00 P.M.	Mexico City, Mexico	11:00 A.M.
Athens, Greece	7:00 P.M.	Miami, Florida	12:00 NOON
Auckland, New Zealand	5:00 A.M. next day	Montevideo, Uruguay	2:00 P.M.
Baghdad, Iraq	8:00 P.M.	Montreal, Quebec	12:00 NOON
Bangkok, Thailand	12:00 MIDNIGHT	¹Moscow, U.S.S.R.	8:00 P.M.
Belgrade, Yugoslavia	6:00 P.M.	Nairobi, Kenya	8:00 P.M.
Berlin, Germany	6:00 P.M.	Nome, Alaska	6:00 A.M.
Bogotá, Colombia	12:00 NOON	Oslo, Norway	6:00 P.M.
Bombay, India	10:30 P.M.	Ottawa, Ontario	12:00 NOON
Boston, Massachusetts	12:00 NOON	Panama City, Panama	12:00 NOON
¹Brussels, Belgium	6:00 P.M.	¹Paris, France	6:00 P.M.
Bucharest, Romania	7:00 P.M.	Peking, China	1:00 A.M. next day
Budapest, Hungary	6:00 P.M.	Perth, Australia	1:00 A.M. next day
¹Buenos Aires, Argentina	2:00 P.M.	Philadelphia, Pennsylvania	12:00 NOON
Cairo, Egypt	7:00 P.M.	Prague, Czechoslovakia	6:00 P.M.
Calcutta, India	10:30 P.M.	Quito, Ecuador	12:00 NOON
Cape Town, Republic of So. Africa	7:00 P.M.	Rangoon, Burma	11:30 P.M.
Caracas, Venezuela	1:00 P.M.	Regina, Saskatchewan	10:00 A.M.
¹Casablanca, Morocco	6:00 P.M.	Reykjavik, Iceland	4:00 P.M.
Chicago, Illinois	11:00 A.M.	Rio de Janeiro, Brazil	2:00 P.M.
Colombo, Sri Lanka (Ceylon)	10:30 P.M.	Rome, Italy	6:00 P.M.
Copenhagen, Denmark	6:00 P.M.	Saigon, Vietnam	1:00 A.M. next day
Delhi, India	10:30 P.M.	Saint John's, Newfoundland	1:30 P.M.
Denver, Colorado	10:00 A.M.	Saint Louis, Missouri	11:00 A.M.
Detroit, Michigan	12:00 NOON	Salt Lake City, Utah	10:00 A.M.
Djakarta, Indonesia	12:00 MIDNIGHT	San Francisco, California	9:00 A.M.
Dublin, Ireland	5:00 P.M.	San Juan, Puerto Rico	1:00 P.M.
Edmonton, Alberta	10:00 A.M.	Santiago, Chile	1:00 P.M.
Geneva, Switzerland	6:00 P.M.	São Paulo, Brazil	2:00 P.M.
Glasgow, Scotland	5:00 P.M.	Seattle, Washington	9:00 A.M.
Halifax, Nova Scotia	1:00 P.M.	Shanghai, China	1:00 A.M. next day
Havana, Cuba	12:00 NOON	Singapore	12:30 A.M. next day
Helsinki, Finland	7:00 P.M.	Sofia, Bulgaria	7:00 P.M.
Hong Kong	1:00 A.M. next day	Stockholm, Sweden	6:00 P.M.
Honolulu, Hawaii	7:00 A.M.	Sydney, Australia	3:00 A.M. next day
Houston, Texas	11:00 A.M.	Tehran, Iran	8:30 P.M.
Istanbul, Turkey	7:00 P.M.	Tel Aviv, Israel	7:00 P.M.
Jerusalem, Israel	7:00 P.M.	Tokyo, Japan	2:00 A.M. next day
Johannesburg, Republic of So. Africa	7:00 P.M.	Toronto, Ontario	12:00 NOON
Juneau, Alaska	9:00 A.M.	Vancouver, British Columbia	9:00 A.M.
Karachi, Pakistan	10:00 P.M.	Vienna, Austria	6:00 P.M.
Kuala Lumpur, Malaysia	12:30 A.M. next day	¹Vladivostok, U.S.S.R.	3:00 A.M. next day
La Paz, Bolivia	1:00 P.M.	Warsaw, Poland	6:00 P.M.
Leningrad, U.S.S.R.	8:00 P.M.	Washington, D.C.	12:00 NOON
Lima, Peru	12:00 NOON	Wellington, New Zealand	5:00 A.M. next day
¹Lisbon, Portugal	6:00 P.M.	Winnipeg, Manitoba	11:00 A.M.
London, England	5:00 P.M.	Zurich, Switzerland	6:00 P.M.

¹Time is one hour in advance of the standard meridian.

[1]**stand-up** \'ˌ,ˌ\ *adj* [*stand up*] **1 a :** ERECT, UPRIGHT **b** *of a collar* **:** stiffened to stay upright without folding over **2 :** performed in or requiring a standing erect position ⟨*stand-up* lunch⟩ ⟨*stand-up* bar⟩ ⟨*stand-up* comedy act⟩ ⟨*stand-up* boxing stance⟩ **3** *of a fight* **:** characterized by the exchange of blows without maneuvering, dodging, or retreating ⟨a *stand-up*, knockdown brawl⟩ ⟨*stand-up* battle⟩

[2]**stand-up** \"\ *n* -s [*stand up*] **1 :** the quality of standing up to or enduring stress, strain, and wear; *specif* **:** the quality of wearing well when subjected to service **2 :** something that stands erect or is provided with a stand or support to hold it erect ⟨display samples mounted on *stand-ups*⟩ **3 :** the act of failing to keep an appointment

stane \'stān\ *Scot var of* STONE

stan·ford–binet test \'stanfə(r)d \ *or* **stanford revision** *n, usu cap S&B* [fr. *Stanford* University, California] **:** a revision of the Binet-Simon scale prepared at Stanford University **:** an individually administered intelligence test commonly employed with children

[1]**stang** [ME, fr. OE] *archaic past of* STING

[2]**stang** \'staŋ\ *n* -s [ME *stong, stang*, fr. ON *stöng;* akin to OE *steng* pole, *stingan* to thrust, sting, OHG *stanga* pole — more at STING] *dial Brit* **:** POLE, BAR

[3]**stang** \"\ *vb* -ED/-ING/-s [ME *stangen*, fr. ON *stanga* to prick, goad; akin to ON *stinga* to sting — more at STING] *vt, chiefly Scot* **:** STING ~ *vi, chiefly Scot* **:** STING, ACHE, THROB

[4]**stang** \"\ *n* -s [ME, sting, fr. *stangen* to sting] *chiefly Scot* **:** PANG

stan·ge·ria \stan'jirēə\ *n, cap* [NL, fr. William *Stanger* †1854 Eng. surveyor general in Natal + NL *-ia*] **:** a genus of So. African cycads with fernlike foliage and bracted strobiles

stan·hope \'stanəp, -n,hōp\ *n* -s [after Fitzroy *Stanhope* †1864 Brit. clergyman] **:** a gig, buggy, or light phaeton typically having a high seat and closed back

stan·ho·pea \stan'hōpēə\ *n* [NL, after Philip Henry, 4th Earl *Stanhope* †1855 Eng. botanist] **1** *cap* **:** a genus of tropical American epiphytic orchids having a single large leaf, a raceme from each pseudobulb, and large fragrant flowers of various colors and markings with nearly equal sepals and a greatly contorted lip **2** -s **:** any plant of the genus *Stanhopea*

stanhope press *n, usu cap S* [after Charles, 3d Earl *Stanhope* †1816 Eng. scientist, its inventor] **:** a hand-operated printing press that has a system of levers which cause the platen to descend with decreasing rapidity and with increasing force

stanhope process *n, usu cap S* [after Charles, 3d Earl *Stanhope*] **:** a method of stereotyping in which the matrix used is of heat-hardened gypsum and plaster

sta·nine \'stā,nīn\ *n* -s [*standard (score)* + *nine*] **1 :** an aptitude score for aviation students ranging from 1 to 9 based on a battery of tests and weighted for ratings of pilot, bombardier, and navigator **2 :** a score in educational testing on a nine-point scale of normalized standard scores with a standard deviation of 2 and a mean of 5

sta·nit·sa *also* **sta·nit·za** \stə'nitsə\ *n* -s [Russ *stanitsa*, dim. of *stan* station, police district; akin to Skt *sthāna* station, locality, district, *tiṣṭhati* he stands — more at STAND] **:** a village or administrative district in the Cossack regions of Russia

[1]**stank** [ME, fr. OE *stanc*] *past of* STINK

[2]**stank** \'staŋk\ *n* -s [ME, fr. OF *estanc*, prob. fr. *estancher* to check or stop the flowing of — more at STANCH] **1** *dial Brit* **a :** POND, POOL **b :** a ditch containing water **2** *Brit* **:** a small dam **:** WEIR

[3]**stank** \"\ *vt* -ED/-ING/-s *Brit* **:** DAM

stank·ie \'staŋki\ *or* **stank hen** \'staŋk-\ *n* -s [*stankie* fr. *stank (hen)* (fr. [2]*stank*) + *-ie;* fr. its being found near ponds] *Scot* **:** GALLINULE

stann- *or* **stanno-** *comb form* [LL *stannum* tin — more at STANNUM] **:** relating to or containing tin ⟨*stannide*⟩ ⟨*stanniferous*⟩ ⟨*stannotype*⟩ **:** stannic ⟨*stannane*⟩ **:** stannous ⟨*stannite*⟩

stan·nane \'sta,nān\ *n* -s [*stann-* + *methane;* fr. the analogy of its formula to that of methane, CH_4] **1 :** a compound of tin and hydrogen; *esp* **:** the unstable gaseous tetrahydride SnH_4 known chiefly in the form of organic derivatives **2 :** any of various organic derivatives of tin tetrahydride

stan·na·ry \'stanərē\ *n* -ES [ML *stannaria* tin mine, fr. LL *stannum* + L *-aria* -ary] **:** one of the regions in England containing tinworks and formerly placed under jurisdiction of special courts — usu. used in pl.

stan·nate \'sta,nāt\ *n* -s [*stann-* + *-ate*] **:** a salt [as sodium hexa-hydroxo-stannate $Na_2Sn(OH)_6$] of a stannic acid

stan·na·tor \sta'nād·ə(r)\ *n* -s [ML *stannator* tin-miner, irreg. fr. LL *stannum*] **:** a representative from a stannary sent to a stannary assembly

stan·ners \'stanə(r)z\ *n pl* [fr. (assumed) ME (Sc), perh. fr. OE *stǣner* stony ground; akin to OE *stān* stone — more at STONE] *chiefly Scot* **:** the small stones found near or in a body of water

stan·nic \'stanik, -nēk\ *adj* [prob. fr. F *stannique*, fr. LL *stannum, stagnum* tin + F *-ique* -ic —more at STANNUM] **:** of, relating to, or containing tin — used esp. of compounds in which this element is tetravalent; compare STANNOUS

stannic acid *n* [prob. fr. F *acide stannique*] **:** any of various amorphous acid substances that behave like hydrates of stannic oxide and yield stannic oxide when calcined: as **a :** a highly hydrated substance obtainable as a gelatinous precipitate by hydrolysis of stannic chloride by alkali or excess water and forming salts with more alkali — called also *alpha-stannic acid* **b :** a less highly hydrated substance obtainable as a powder by heating or drying alpha-stannic acid — called also *beta-stannic acid*

stannic chloride *n* **:** a mobile liquid compound $SnCl_4$ that fumes in moist air, that is made usu. by the action of chlorine on tin (as in recovering tin from scrap), that when mixed with a little water solidifies to a soft crystalline mass of the pentahydrate and with more water slowly hydrolyzes yielding hydrochloric acid, and that is used chiefly in making other tin compounds but was formerly used in weighting silk and as a mordant and in producing military smoke screens — called also *tin tetrachloride*

stannic oxide *n* **:** the dioxide SnO_2 of tin that occurs in nature as cassiterite, is produced artificially as a crystalline powder when anhydrous, and is used chiefly in ceramic colors, in vitreous enamels and glazes as an opacifier, in glass, and in polishes — see STANNIC ACID

stannic sulfide *n* **:** a yellow compound SnS_2 obtained in amorphous and crystalline forms — see MOSAIC GOLD 1

stan·nide \'sta,nīd\ *n* -s [ISV *stann-* + *-ide*] **:** a compound of tin with a more electropositive element or radical

stan·nif·er·ous \sta'nif(ə)rəs\ *adj* [*stann-* + *-iferous*] **:** containing tin ⟨~ glaze for pottery⟩

stan·nite \'sta,nīt\ *n* -s [G *stannit*, fr. *stann-* + *-it* -ite] **1 :** salt formed in solution when a stannous salt is treated with excess alkali **2** [*stann-* + *-ite*] **:** a mineral Cu_2FeSnS consisting of a steel-gray or iron-black sulfide of copper, iron, and tin, of a metallic luster occurring in granular masses — called also *tin pyrites* (hardness 4, sp. gr. 4.3–4.52)

stan·nous \'stanəs\ *adj* [ISV *stann-* + *-ous*] **:** of, relating to, or containing tin — used esp. of compounds in which this element is bivalent; compare STANNIC

stannous chloride *n* **:** a compound $SnCl_2$ obtained by the action of chlorine, hydrogen chloride or hydrochloric acid on tin either as an anhydrous solid or a crystalline dihydrate and used chiefly in tinning and as a reducing agent and catalyst —called also *tin dichloride;* see TIN CRYSTALS

stannous oxide *n* **:** the monoxide of tin SnO that is obtained as dark lustrous crystals usu. blue-black but sometimes varying in shade (as from brown and red to dark green) and that forms stannic oxide when heated in air

stan·num \'stanəm\ *n* -s [LL *stagnum, stannum*, fr. L, an alloy of silver and lead, prob. of Celt origin; akin to IrGael *stān* tin, Welsh *ystaen*, Corn & Bret *stēn*] **:** TIN — symbol *Sn*

stan·te ma·tri·mo·nio \'stän(,)tā,mä·trə'mōnē,ō\ [NL] **:** while the marriage is in force

stan·za \'stanzə, -aan-\ *n* -s [It, act or place of staying, abode, room, stanza, fr. (assumed) VL *stantia* act of standing or staying — more at STANCHION] **1 :** a division of a poem consisting of a series of lines arranged together in a recurring pattern of metrical lengths and usu. a sequence of rhymes **2** *slang* **a :** a period of performing or showing in one place **:** STAND, ENGAGEMENT; *esp* **:** WEEK ⟨the play is to be held over for another ~⟩ ⟨signed the orchestra for the last ~ in June⟩ **b :** a period (as a half or an inning) into which the duration of a game is divided

stan·zaed \-əd\ *adj* [*stanza* + *-ed*] **:** arranged in, divided into, or composed of stanzas

stan·za·ic \(')stan¦zāik, -aan- -āēk\ *also* **stan·za·i·cal** *adj* [*stanza* + *-ic, -ical*] **:** relating to or consisting of stanzas ⟨~ structure⟩ — **stan·za·i·cal·ly** *adv*

[1]**stap** \'stap\ *Scot var of* STEP

[2]**stap** \"\ *n* -s [origin unknown] *chiefly Scot* **:** a stave of a cask or tub

[3]**stap** \"\ *dial Brit var of* STOP

sta·pe·di·al \stā'pēdēəl, stə'p-\ *adj* [NL *staped-, stapes* + E *-ial*] **:** of, relating to, or located near the stapes

sta·pe·dio·vestibular \stə¦pēdē(,)ō+\ *adj* [*stapedial* + *-o-* + *vestibular*] **:** of or relating to the stapes and the vestibule of the ear

sta·pe·di·us \stə'pēdēəs\ *n, pl* **stape·dii** \-dē,ī\ [NL, fr. *staped-, stapes*] **:** a small muscle of the middle ear of mammals that arises from the wall of the tympanum, is inserted into the neck of the stapes by a tendon that sometimes contains a slender spine of bone, and serves to check and dampen vibration of the stapes

sta·pe·lia \stə'pēlēə\ *n* [NL, fr. J. Bodaeus van *Stapel* †1636 Du. physician and botanist + NL *-ia*] **1** *cap* **:** a large genus of African evil-smelling asclepiads, with succulent leafless toothed stems like the joints of a cactus and oddly colored flowers that are often several inches across and in some a foot or more across **2** -s **:** any plant of the genus *Stapelia* — called also *carrion flower*

sta·pes \'stā(,)pēz\ *n, pl* **stapes** \"\ *or* **stape·des** \stə'pē-,dēz\ [NL *staped-, stapes*, fr. ML, stirrup, alter. (prob. influenced by L *ped-, pes* foot) of LL *stapia*, prob. of Gmc origin; akin to OHG *stapfo* step — more at STEP, FOOT] **1 :** the innermost of the chain of ossicles of the ear of mammals which has the form of a stirrup, a base that occupies the fenestra vestibuli of the tympanum, and a head that is connected with the incus — see EAR illustration **2 :** the inner segment of the columella or sometimes the entire columella of the ear of many nonmammalian vertebrates

staph \'staf\ *n* -s [by shortening] **:** STAPHYLOCOCCUS 2

staph·i·sa·gria \,stafə'sāgrēə\ *n* -s [NL (specific epithet of *Delphinium staphisagria*), fr. L *staphis agria* stavesacre — more at STAVESACRE] **:** the ripe seed of the stavesacre (*Delphinium staphisagria*) used to kill head lice

staphyl- *or* **staphylo-** *comb form* [MF *staphyl-*, fr. L *staphyl-, staphylo-*, fr. Gk, bunch of grapes, uvula, fr. *staphylē* bunch of grapes, swollen uvula, uvula; akin to Gk *stemphylon* olive pulp — more at STAFF] **1 a :** bunch of grapes ⟨*Staphylococcus*⟩ **b :** staphyloma ⟨*staphylotomy*⟩ **2 a :** uvula ⟨*staphylectomy*⟩ **b :** palate ⟨*staphylion*⟩ **3 :** staphylococcic ⟨*staphylocoagulase*⟩ ⟨*staphylodermatitis*⟩

staph·y·lea \,stafə'lēə\ *n, cap* [NL, fr. Gk *staphylē* bunch of grapes; fr. the clustered fruit] **:** a genus of shrubs or small trees (family Staphyleaceae) with opposite leaves and drooping panicles of white or pink flowers succeeded by inflated bladdery capsules — see BLADDERNUT

staph·y·le·a·ce·ae \,stafəlē'āsē,ē\ *n pl, cap* [NL, fr. *Staphylea*, type genus + *-aceae*] **:** a family of plants (order Sapindales) mostly of the north temperate zone that have compound leaves, perfect regular flowers with introrse anthers, and inflated capsular fruit — **staph·y·le·a·ceous** \¦ˌˌˌ¦āshəs\ *adj*

[1]**staph·y·lin·id** \¦stafə¦linəd\ *adj* [NL *Staphylinidae*] **:** of or relating to the Staphylinidae

[2]**staphylinid** \"\ *n* -s [NL *Staphylinidae*] **:** a beetle of the family Staphylinidae

staph·y·lin·i·dae \,ˌˌ'linə,dē\ *n pl, cap* [NL, fr. *Staphylinus*, type genus + *-idae*] **:** a family of beetles consisting of the rove beetles

staph·y·li·noi·dea \,stafələ'nȯidēə\ *n pl, cap* [NL, fr. *Staphylinus* + *-oidea*] **:** a superfamily of beetles including the Staphylinidae and several related families

staph·y·li·nus \,stafə'līnəs\ *n, cap* [NL, fr. Gk *staphylinos*, an insect, prob. fr. *staphylē* bunch of grapes] **:** the type genus of the family Staphylinidae

sta·phyl·i·on \stə'filē,än\ *n* -s [NL, irreg. fr. *staphyl-*] **:** the median point of the posterior edge of the hard palate

staph·y·lo·coagulase \¦stafə(,)lō+\ *n* [*staphyl-* + *coagulase*] **:** a coagulase from pathogenic staphylococci

staph·y·lo·coc·cal \¦stafəlō¦käkəl\ *adj* [NL *Staphylococcus* + E *-al*] **:** of, caused by, produced by, or being a staphylococcus ⟨~ group⟩ ⟨~ infection⟩ ⟨~ organism⟩

staph·y·lo·coc·ce·mia \,stafəlōkäk'sēmēə\ *n* -s [NL, fr. *Staphylococcus* + *-emia*] **:** the presence of staphylococci in the circulating blood — **staph·y·lo·coc·ce·mic** \¦ˌˌˌˌ-¦sēmik\ *adj*

staph·y·lo·coc·cic \¦stafəlō¦käksik, -sēk\ *adj* [ISV *staphylococ-* (fr. NL *Staphylococcus*) + *-ic*] **:** caused by a staphylococcus

staph·y·lo·coc·co·sis \,stafəlōkä'kōsəs\ *n* -ES [NL, fr. *Staphylococcus* + *-osis*] **:** infection with or disease caused by staphylococci; *esp* **:** a disease of poultry and usu. of young turkeys and chickens caused by a staphylococcus (*Staphylococcus aureus*) and characterized by acute septicemia or chronic arthritis

[1]**staph·y·lo·coc·cus** \,stafəlō'käkəs\ *n* [NL, fr. *staphyl-* + *-coccus*] **1** *cap* **:** a genus of nonmotile gram-positive spherical eubacteria (family Micrococcaceae) that occur singly, in pairs or tetrads, or in irregular clusters and as now usu. restricted comprise a few parasites of skin and mucous membranes — compare MICROCOCCUS **2** *pl* **staphylococ·ci** \-äk,sī\ **:** any bacterium of the genus *Staphylococcus; broadly* **:** MICROCOCCUS 2

[2]**staphylococcus** \"\ *n* [NL, fr. *staphyl-* + *-coccus*] *syn of* MICROCOCCUS

staph·y·lo·ma \,stafə'lōmə\ *n* -s [alter. (influenced by LL *staphyloma*) of earlier *staphylome*, fr. MF, fr. LL *staphyloma*, fr. Gk *staphylōma*, fr. *staphylē* bunch of grapes + *-ōma* -oma] **:** a protrusion of the cornea or sclera of the mammalian eye

staph·y·lot·o·my \-'läd·əmē\ *n* -ES [NL *staphylotomia*, fr. Gk, fr. *staphyl-* + *-tomia* -tomy] **1 :** the cutting or removal of the uvula **2** [ISV *staphyl-* + *-tomy*] **:** the surgical removal of a staphyloma

[1]**sta·ple** \'stāpəl\ *n* -s [ME *stapel* staple, post, pillar, fr. OE *stapol* post, pillar; akin to MD *stapel* step, foundation, heap, emporium, OHG *staffal* step, ON *stöpull* pillar, tower, OE *steppan* to step — more at STEP] **1 a :** a U-shaped metal loop both ends of which are driven into a surface to hold the hook, hasp, or bolt of a lock, secure a rope, or fix a wire in place **b :** a small U-shaped wire both ends of which are driven through layers of thin and easily penetrable material (as paper or paperboard) and usu. clinched to hold the layers together **2 :** CHAPLET 4 **3 :** a mine shaft that is smaller and shorter than the principal one and joins different levels **4** *or* **stapling** [*stapling* fr. gerund of [2]*staple*] **:** an angle bar or plate that is fitted closely around the frames and structural members of a ship and passes through decks and bulkheads to secure oil-tightness or watertightness

staples 1

[2]**staple** \"\ *vt* **stapled; stapled; stapling** \-p(ə)liŋ\ **staples** [ME *staplen*, fr. *stapel*, n.] **:** to provide with or secure by staples ⟨~ papers together⟩

[3]**staple** \"\ *n* -s [ME *staple, stapull*, fr. MD *stapel* emporium] **1 :** a town formerly and usu. by royal fiat used as a center for the sale or exportation of commodities (as wool, skin, and leather) in bulk **2 :** a place of supply **:** SOURCE, CENTER ⟨Whitehall naturally became the chief ~ of news —T.B. Macaulay⟩ **3 a :** a commodity that is produced regularly or in large quantities esp. for a wholesale market ⟨where . . . textiles and Welsh coal once led the list of exports, Britain's new ~*s* are . . . —*Time*⟩ **b :** the principal commodity of traffic in a market **:** a chief commodity or production of a place ⟨corn was the great ~ of the Old West —R.A.Billington⟩ **4 a :** a commodity for which the demand is constant and not dependent on variable factors (as season or fashion) ⟨sugar and flour are among a grocer's ~*s*⟩ **b :** something that enjoys widespread and constant use or appeal **:** something that is regular fare ⟨fish is one of the ~*s* of the grizzly's diet —Charles Mulvey⟩ ⟨news and weather reports are ~*s* of television variety shows —Philip Hamburger⟩ ⟨songs from his . . . shows are still . . . ~*s* all over the world —*Newsweek*⟩ **c :** the sustaining or principal element **:** CORE, SUBSTANCE ⟨the Bible . . . as the ~ of their intellectual and spiritual lives —D. R.Meyer⟩ ⟨the ~ of Roman education was always a study of the poets —E.E.Sikes⟩ **5 :** the unworked or natural material from which textiles and other goods are manufactured **:** RAW MATERIAL **6 a** *or* **staple fiber :** natural fiber (as of raw wool, cotton, flax, or hemp) or synthetic fiber (as cut from continuous filaments of rayon or nylon) of relatively short length that when spun and twisted forms a yarn as distinguished from a filament **b :** the length of a piece of such textile fiber ranging from about one inch for some types of cotton to several feet for hemp ⟨tow is flax with short ~⟩

[4]**staple** \"\ *adj* **1** *obs* **:** of, relating to, or being a staple for commodities **2 :** used, needed, or enjoyed constantly usu. by many individuals **:** STANDARD ⟨such ~ items as sugar and flour⟩ ⟨the mesa was our ~ topic of conversation —Willa Cather⟩ ⟨a ~ romantic prop in the construction of historical fiction —E.J.Fitzgerald⟩ **3 :** produced regularly or in large quantities esp. for a wholesale market ⟨such ~ crops as wheat, rice, cotton, flax, sugarcane —V.A.Baker⟩ **4 :** PRINCIPAL, CHIEF ⟨the potato has long been the ~ crop here —*Amer. Guide Series: Va.*⟩ ⟨the ~ diet of all true Mexicans . . . is the tortilla —Green Peyton⟩ **5 :** being or made from textile staple ⟨~ fiber⟩ ⟨~ yarn⟩

[5]**staple** \"\ *vt* -ED/-ING/-s **1 :** to sort or grade (staple) according to its length ⟨~ cotton fiber⟩ **2 :** to convert (material that does not occur naturally as staple) into staple ⟨~ the filament rayon by cutting⟩

staple punch *n* **:** a punch for making two holes simultaneously to receive the points of a staple

[1]**sta·pler** \'stāp(ə)lə(r)\ *n* -s [[3]*staple* + *-er*] **1 :** one that deals in staple goods or in staple fiber **2 :** one that sorts staple according to its length

[2]**stapler** \"\ *n* -s [[2]*staple* + *-er*] **:** one that inserts staples (as in paper or wood): as **a :** a small usu. hand device for inserting the wire staples that bind papers together **b :** STAPLING HAMMER **c :** a workman who inserts staples with a hammer or machine

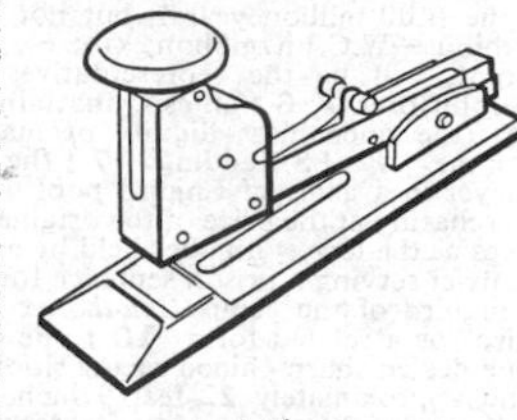

stapler a

staple right *n* [trans. of D *stapelrecht*] **:** a right of forcing any passing vessel either to pay duty or to sell its cargo in the market place orig. possessed by towns in the Netherlands and later introduced into the colony of New Netherland

stapling hammer *n* **:** a tool that resembles a hammer and is used to insert staples esp. in building material

stapp \'stap\ *n* -s [after John P. *Stapp b*1910 Am. biophysicist] **:** a unit of force caused by acceleration and equal to one G acting on a body for one second

stap·ple \'stapəl\ *Scot var of* [1]STAPLE 3

staps *pl of* STAP

[1]**star** \'stär, 'stȧ(r\ *n* -s [ME *sterre*, fr. OE *steorra;* akin to OHG *sterro, sterno* star, ON *stjarna*, Goth *stairno*, L *stella*, Gk *astēr, astron* star, Skt *stṛbhis* (instrumental pl.) by means of stars] **1 a** (1) **:** an object (as a comet, meteor, or planet) in the sky resembling a luminous point and usu. only bright enough to be seen at night; *specif* **:** FIXED STAR (2) **:** a heavenly body (as the sun or moon); *also* **:** EARTH (3) *obs* **:** POLESTAR ⟨there's no more sailing by the ~ —Shak.⟩ **b** (1) **:** a self-luminous gaseous celestial body of great mass whose own gravitation produces high internal pressure and temperature resulting in atomic and nuclear processes that cause the star to emit electromagnetic radiation and to be observable in the visible region of the spectrum if its surface temperature is about 2500° absolute or higher, whose shape is usu. spheroidal, whose size may be as small as the earth or larger than the earth's orbit, and that often is composed of two or more stars in close gravitational association — see BINARY STAR, MULTIPLE STAR, SUPERGIANT, WHITE DWARF (2) **:** one of the self-luminous bodies belonging to a star cluster, globular cluster, star cloud, or galaxy **2 a** (1) **:** a planet or a configuration of the planets influencing one's destiny or fortune — usu. used in pl. (2) **:** fortune or fame esp. with regard to its waxing and waning ⟨during his lifetime he received no such acclaim . . . and . . . after his death his ~ had set apparently not to rise again —A.T.Davison⟩ **b** *obs* **:** DESTINY, FATE ⟨I was not born unto riches, neither is it I think my ~ to be wealthy —Sir Thomas Browne⟩ **3 a :** a conventional figure with five or more points that represents a star ⟨added another

stars 3a

FIFTY IMPORTANT STARS

NAME AND PRONUNCIATION	CONSTELLATION
Achernar \'akər,när, 'ā-\	α Eridani
Albireo \al'birē,ō\	β Cygni
Alcor \'al,kȯr\	80 Ursae Majoris
Alcyone \al'sīə(,)nē\	η Tauri
Aldebaran \al'debərən\	α Tauri
Algenib \al'jenəb, -'ē-\	γ Pegasi
Algol \'al,gäl, -ȯl\	β Persei
Alioth \'alē,äth, -,ȯ-\	ε Ursae Majoris
Alkaid \al'kīd, -ād\	η Ursae Majoris
Almach \'al,mak\	γ Andromedae
Alphard \'al,färd\	α Hydrae
Alphecca \al'fekə\	α Coronae Borealis
Alpheratz \al'ferəts\	α Andromedae *or* δ Pegasi
Altair \al'tī(ə)r, -'ta(a)(ə)r\	α Aquilae
Antares \an'tarēz, aan'taar-\	α Scorpii
Arcturus \ärk't(y)u̇rəs\	α Boötis
Bellatrix \bə'lā·triks\	γ Orionis
Betelgeuse \'bed·ᵊl,jüz, -'ē-\	α Orionis
Canopus \kə'nōpəs\	α Carinae
Capella \kə'pelə\	α Aurigae
Castor \'kastər\	α Geminorum
Deneb \'de,neb, -nəb\	α Cygni
Deneb Kaitos \-'kī¦d·əs, -kā¦, ¦,təs\	β Ceti
Denebola \də'nebələ\	β Leonis
Dubhe \'dübə, 'dəbə\	α Ursae Majoris
Elnath \'el,nath\	β Tauri
Fomalhaut \'fōməl,hȯt, -ə,lȯt, -,ō-\	α Piscis Austrini
Hamal \'haməl\	α Arietis
Markab \'mär,kab\	α Pegasi
Megrez \'mē,grez, -'e-\	δ Ursae Majoris
Menkar \'men,kär\	α Ceti
Merak \'mē,rak\	β Ursae Majoris
Mira \'mīrə\	o Ceti
Mirach \'mī,rak\	β Andromedae
Mirfak \'mi(ə)r,fak\	α Persei
Mizar \'mī,zär\	ζ Ursae Majoris
Phecda \'fekdə\	γ Ursae Majoris
Polaris \pō'la(a)rəs\	α Ursae Minoris
Pollux \'päləks\	β Geminorum
Procyon \'prōsē,än\	α Canis Minoris
Rasalgethi \,rasəl'jed·ē, -ethē\	α Herculis
Rasalhague \,rasəl'hāgwē\	α Ophiuchi
Regulus \'regyələs\	α Leonis
Rigel \'rījəl, -īg-\	β Orionis
Scheat \shē'at, 'shē,at, 'shat\	β Pegasi
Schedar \'shedər\	α Cassiopeiae
Sirius \'sirēəs\	α Canis Majoris
Spica \'spīkə\	α Virginis
Thuban \'th(y)ü,ban\	α Draconis
Vega \'vēgə, -'ā-\	α Lyrae

~ to the flag⟩: as (1) : an unpierced mullet — used esp. in Scottish blazonry (2) : ESTOILE (3) : ASTERISK — compare REFERENCE MARK **b** : an often star-shaped ornament or medal worn as a badge of honor, authority, or rank or as the insignia of an order ⟨awarded the silver ~ for valor⟩ ⟨the single ~ of a brigadier general⟩ ⟨wearing a deputy sheriff's ~⟩ ⟨a campaign ribbon with three battle ~s⟩ **c** : one of a group of usu. four or five conventional stars used to place something in a scale of value ⟨his book could hardly rate three ~s for juvenile reading —*Sydney (Australia) Bull.*⟩ ⟨a five-*star* performance in modern research —J.T.Soby⟩ **4** : something resembling a star or a conventional star: as **a** : a white spot on the forehead of an animal and esp. on a horse **b** : one of the flashing or twinkling lights having no objective existence that are sometimes seen before the eyes esp. as the result of a blow ⟨a body blow that . . . filled his eyes with . . . ~s —F.V.W.Mason⟩ **c** [by shortening] : STARFISH **d** : a small mass of composition used in fireworks (as rockets or mines) that burns with a starlike effect in any of several colors **e** : a bright spot or flaw in the surface of steel that is the end of a pipe which has not been quite cut away **f** : STAR WHEEL **g** : the figure produced by joining the coils or circuits of a polyphase apparatus or system at a common center — see STAR CONNECTION, STAR WINDING **h** (1) : a light figure in a crystal that consists usu. of a bright center and one or more luminous lines radiating from it, is observed best under strong illumination, and is seen esp. in a cabochon-cut gemstone held in the proper orientation (2) : a gemstone showing asterism **i** : STAR FACET **j** : STAR CUT **k** : the multiple forking of a cloud track produced by multiple nuclear disintegration; *also* : a smaller pattern similarly produced in a photographic emulsion **l** : MILL 7c **5 a** (1) : the principal member of a theatrical or operatic company who usu. plays the chief roles (2) : a highly publicized performer whose appearance in a play or motion picture is a major guarantee of its success ⟨the films . . . create ~s out of young actors and actresses —*Britain Today*⟩ (3) : an outstandingly talented performer ⟨a ~ who unquestionably conveyed to the audiences the very essence of the character he was portraying —J.F.Wharton⟩ ⟨track ~⟩ **b** : something that is prominently featured or whose brilliance, distinction, unusualness, or attractiveness attracts attention ⟨a fish long gone (400 million years), but not forgotten, is the ~ of an exhibit —W.C.Fitzgibbon⟩ ⟨the ~s, from a spectator's standpoint, will be the representatives of the military services —John Brehl⟩ **6** : an esp. unattainable goal — often used in pl. ⟨the quenchless dignity of man, the ceaseless questing for the ~s —J.S.Redding⟩ **7** : the privilege open to the first player in a game of English pool who loses his three lives of purchasing at the price of the original stake as many additional lives as the lowest number held by any other player **8** *Brit* : a convict serving a prison sentence for the first time **9** : a hummingbird of the genus *Calothorax* (as the Lucifer hummingbird) or a related form **10** : one of a class of international one-design sharp-chined racing sloops that are Marconi rigged and approximately 22 feet 9 inches in overall length with a sail area of 281 square feet — **stars in one's eyes** : a feeling of elation or optimism ⟨an enamored young girl with *stars in her eyes*⟩

²**star** \"\ *vb* **starred; starred; starring; stars** *vt* **1** : to make (a person) into a star or constellation ⟨a mighty archer *starred* by the gods⟩ **2** : to sprinkle or adorn with or as if with stars : BESPANGLE, DOT ⟨meadows *starred* with buttercups and daisies —Kenneth Roberts⟩ **3 a** : to mark with a star as being superior or preeminent in some way ⟨a monument *starred* in the guidebook⟩ **b** (1) : to mark with or as if with an asterisk (2) : to run or fill out (as an improperly typeset line) with asterisks **4** : to present as a star : advertise or display prominently : FEATURE ⟨the movie ~s a famous stage personality⟩ **5** : to cause (molten antimony) to form starlike patterns on solidifying ~ *vi* **1 a** : to perform as or be a star : play the most prominent or important role ⟨under contract to produce and ~ in two pictures a year —*Current Biog.*⟩ **b** : to perform outstandingly ⟨the third baseman *starred* with a sensational catch⟩ ⟨the author *starred* as journalist, novelist, and playwright⟩ **2** : to become fractured in radiating cracks ⟨the glass *starred* but didn't shatter —*Dupont Mag.*⟩ **3** : to purchase additional lives in English pool **4** : to form starlike patterns on solidifying — used of antimony

³**star** \"\ *adj* **1 a** : of or relating to a star **b** : composed of stars ⟨~ belt⟩ **c** : shaped or arranged like a conventional star ⟨~ punch⟩ **2 a** : marked with a star as a distinguishing mark (as of importance or of excellence) **b** *Brit* : wearing a star that marks the prisoner who wears it as a first offender **3 a** : of, relating to, being, based upon, or concerned with a starred performer or a starring role ⟨~ system⟩ ⟨~ billing⟩ ⟨~ attraction⟩ ⟨~ actors are bad judges of plays —J.B. Priestley⟩ ⟨after his return to film work . . . he played ~ roles in six or more pictures —*Current Biog.*⟩ **b** : of outstanding excellence : PREEMINENT ⟨an athlete⟩ ⟨~ pupil⟩ ⟨a ~ diplomat and intriguer —*Newsweek*⟩ ⟨~ mechanic⟩

⁴**star** \"\ *n* -S [ME, of Scand origin; akin to ON *störr* sedge; akin to OE *starian* to stare — more at STARE] *dial chiefly Brit* : BEACH GRASS, SEDGE

star anise *n* [so called fr. the shape of the fruit] : a tree of the genus *Illicium; esp* : CHINESE ANISE

star aniseed *n* [*star* (in *star anise*) + *aniseed*] : the dried fruit of the Chinese anise used as a spice

star anise oil *or* **star aniseed oil** *n* : a fragrant essential oil obtained from star aniseed and used chiefly as a flavoring agent, expectorant, and carminative — called also *anise oil*

star antimony *n* : refined metallic antimony characterized by crystalline patterns resembling stars or fern leaves on its surface — called also *star metal*

star apple *n* **1** : a tree of the genus *Chrysophyllum; esp* an evergreen tropical American tree (*C. cainito*) that is often cultivated in warm regions for its showy foliage which is dark green above and golden and silky on the undersurface and for its edible purple fruits **2** [so called fr. the starlike figure formed by the carpels in cross section] : the fruit of a star apple

star begonia *n* : a rhizomatous begonia (*Begonia heracleifolia*) having leaves with pointed lobes suggestive of the shape of stars

star-blasting *n, obs* : a baleful influence supposed to be exerted by stars

starbloom \ˈ=,=\ *n* : a pinkroot (*Spigelia marilandica*)

¹**star·board** \ˈstärbərd, ˈstäbəd\ *n* [ME *sterbord* right side of a ship looking forward, fr. OE *stēorbord*, fr. *stēor-* rudder, steering oar + *bord* ship's side; fr. the early practice of steering a ship by means of an oar held in the water over the right side — more at STEER, BOARD] : the right side of a ship or airplane looking forward — opposed to *port*

²**starboard** \"\ *vt* : to turn or put (a helm or rudder) to the right

³**starboard** \"\ *adj* : of, relating to, or situated to starboard — see SHIP illustration

starboard bow *n* : the starboard surface of a ship's hull that curves inward to the stem — distinguished from *port bow*

star boarder *n* : a highly favored and privileged lodger

starboard tack *n* : the tack on which the wind comes from a sailing ship's starboard side

starboard watch *n* : the half of a ship's company that alternates with the port watch in working the ship in successive daily duty periods

star boat *n* : STAR 10

star·bo·lins *also* **star·bow·lines** \ˈstärbələnz\ *n pl* [perh. irreg. fr. ¹*starboard* + -*lings*, pl. of -*ling*, n. suffix] *archaic* : STARBOARD WATCH

starbright \ˈ=,=\ *adj, archaic* : bright as a star; *also* : studded with stars

star cactus *n* : a globular cactus of the genus *Astrophytum* with starlike clusters of spines — called also *bishop's cap, sand dollar*

star capsicum *n* : an ornamental Brazilian shrub (*Solanum capsicastrum*) that resembles the Jerusalem cherry

star carrier *n* : a mail carrier on a star route

star catalog *n* : a list of stars giving their positions for a given epoch, their magnitudes, and usu. other data

¹**starch** \ˈstärch, ˈstäch\ *vt* -ED/-ING/-ES [ME *sterchen*, prob. fr. (assumed) OE *stercan* to stiffen (whence OE *sterced-* firm, resolute); akin to OHG *sterken* to strengthen, OSw *stærkia* to starch, strengthen; causative fr. the root of OE *stearc* stiff, strong — more at STARK] **1 a** : to stiffen with or as if with starch ⟨the sheets were ~*ed* cool and smooth —Anton Vogt⟩ **b** : to make formal, precise or conventional : set into a rigid pattern ⟨derived from times when the English language had not yet been ~*ed* and formalized with definitions and rules of grammar —*Amer. Guide Series: Tenn.*⟩ **2** *obs* : to fasten or attach with starch paste

²**starch** \"\ *n* -ES [ME *sterche*, fr. *sterchen*, v.] **1 a** : a white odorless tasteless granular or powdery complex carbohydrate $(C_6H_{10}O_5)_x$ that is the chief storage form of carbohydrate in plants, is obtained commercially esp. from corn and potatoes, is hydrolyzed by acids to dextrins, hydrol, and finally glucose and by carbohydrases to dextrins or glucose, is insoluble in cold water but swells in hot water and cools to form a paste or gel, gives a characteristic blue color with iodine, is an important foodstuff, and is used otherwise chiefly in adhesives and sizes for paper and textiles, in laundering, and in pharmacy and medicine — compare CELLULOSE, CORNSTARCH, GLYCOGEN, SOLUBLE STARCH **b** : a substance used similarly to starch esp. for stiffening textile fabrics ⟨a permanent ~ for household use is usu. based on an emulsion of polyvinyl acetate or its copolymer with acrylic ester —K.G.Blaikie & M.S.W.Small⟩ **2** : a stiff formal manner : FORMALITY ⟨was there nothing in beautiful manners but foppery, prudery, ~, and affectation —Van Wyck Brooks⟩ **3** : a strengthening vitality : energy and resolution : resolute vigor ⟨he has . . . spine and ~, in a country sometimes lacking both —John Gunther⟩

³**starch** \"\ *adj* -ER/-EST : marked by a stiff formality or preciseness of manner

star-chamber \ˈ=ˈ=,=\ *adj* [*Star Chamber*, a court existing in England from the 15th century until 1641 that exercised wide civil and criminal jurisdiction under rules of procedure well suited to the purposes of absolutist sovereigns] **1** : of, relating to, constituting, or in the manner of a secret oppressive or irresponsible judicial body ⟨it took centuries of bloody struggle to outlaw *star-chamber* sessions, and the principle which requires judicial proceedings to be conducted in public still must be vigorously defended —*San Francisco (Calif.) News*⟩ **2** : of, relating to, constituting, or in the manner of a legislative or executive body that holds closed meetings ⟨*star-chamber* sessions of city councils and school boards —*Fortnight*⟩

star chart *n* : a chart showing the positions of the stars in a region of the sky

starch blue *n* : SMALT 2

starchboard \ˈ=,=\ *n* : a shallow wooden tray used as a container for the powdered starch in which molds or impressions for some candies are made

starch corn *n* : SPELT

star check *n* : STARSHAKE

starch equivalent *n* : the fat-producing capacity of an animal feed or ration expressed as the amount of starch required to produce the same amount of fat

starch·er \ˈstärchər\ *n* -S : one that starches; *specif* : a worker who starches cloth goods by hand or by machine

starch gum *n* : DEXTRIN

star chickweed *n* : GREAT CHICKWEED

starch·i·ly \ˈstärchəlē, ˈstäch-, -li\ *adv* : in a starchy manner

starch·i·ness \-chēnəs, -chin-\ *n* -ES : the quality or state of being starchy ⟨the fresh ~ of her dress —Shirley A. Grau⟩; *esp* : a prim, prudish, or overly dignified formality ⟨deckhands . . . resent the growing ~ of the river cities —Murray Schumach⟩

starch layer *n* : ENDODERMIS

starch·less \-chləs\ *adj* : lacking starch

starch·ly *adv* [³*starch* + -*ly*] *archaic* : STARCHILY, FORMALLY

starch·man \-chmən\ *n, pl* **starchmen** : a worker in the starch room of a candy factory

starch·ness *n* -ES [³*starch* + -*ness*] : starchiness in conduct or manner : stiff formality

starch nitrate *n* : NITROSTARCH

starch room *n* : a room in which starch is applied to candies

starch sheath *n* : ENDODERMIS

starch star *n* : AMYLUM STAR

starch syrup *n* : a syrup made from starch; *esp* : CORN SYRUP

starchy \-chē, -chi\ *adj* -ER/-EST **1 a** : consisting of or containing starch ⟨~ roots⟩ **b** : resembling starch or something starched **2 a** : consisting of or having the characteristics of a stiff aloof and often prudish formality ⟨~ schoolmarms —William Manchester⟩ **b** : marked by a crotchety stiffness of manner or opinion : CRUSTY 2 ⟨a ~ retired colonel⟩

star cloud *n* **1** : a large luminous patch of the Milky Way that can be resolved with optical aid into great numbers of stars appearing to be more densely concentrated than in adjoining areas **2** : an enormous aggregation of stars forming one of the units comprising the nucleus or a spiral arm of a spiral galaxy

star cluster *n* : a relatively compact group of stars forming a gravitating unit and containing either not more than a few hundred stars or tens of thousands of stars

star color *n* : the apparent color of a star measured by its color index

star connection *n* : a method of connecting polyphase circuits in which one end of each phase line is connected to a common neutral point that may be connected to the earth as protection against lightning or to a wire to which all the other neutral points of the system are connected — compare DELTA CONNECTION

star coral *n* : any of numerous stony corals belonging to *Orbicella* and related genera in which the polyp cavities are round or polygonal and contain conspicuous radiating septa

star count *n* : a census of stars in a region of the sky usu. taken on the basis of magnitude, spectral type, or motion

star-crossed \ˈ=,=\ *adj* : not favored by the stars : ILL-FATED

star cucumber *n* : an herbaceous vine (*Sicyos angulatus*) that is native to No. America and that has branched tendrils, greenish white flowers, and prickly fruit

star cut *n* : a cut of a diamond or other gem marked by a hexagonal table bordered by six facets shaped like equilateral triangles — see CUT illustration

star day *n* : a day measured by the stars : SIDEREAL DAY

star density *n* **1** : the number of stars per unit area of a region of the sky **2** : the number of stars in a unit volume of space often expressed as per cubic parsec

star·dom \ˈstärdəm, ˈstäd-\ *n* -S **1** : the status or position of a star ⟨a number . . . reached ~ in the various fields of entertainment —*Current Biog.*⟩ **2** : a body of stars ⟨a select body of guest soloists gathered from the ~ of European music centers —P.V.R.Key⟩

star drag *n* [so called fr. the five spokes on the fixture] : a friction brake on a saltwater fishing reel

star drill *n* : a drill for stone or masonry that has a star-shaped point and that operates by being struck with a hammer and rotated

star drum *n* : a drum (*Stellifer lanceolatus*) of the Atlantic and Gulf coasts of the U. S.

star-duckweed \ˈ=ˈ=,=\ *n* : a duckweed (*Lemna trisulca*) having fronds with very long stalks

stardust \ˈ=,=\ *n* **1** *usu* **star dust a** : a vast multitude of very small stars massed together in the night sky and suggestive of dust particles — not used scientifically **b** : COSMIC DUST — not used scientifically **2 a** : something twinkling in fine particles **b** : something light, fine, and ethereal : GOSSAMER **3** : a feeling or impression of romance, magic, or ethereality

¹**stare** \ˈsta(a)(ə)r, ˈste|, |ə\ *vb* -ED/-ING/-S [ME *staren*, fr. OE *starian*; akin to MD *staren* to stare, OHG *starēn*, ON *stara* to stare, L *strenuus* active, strenuous, Gk *stereos* solid, Lith *starinti* to stiffen; basic meaning: stiff] *vi* **1 a** : to look fixedly often with wide-open eyes (as in fear, wonder, surprise, or impudence) : fasten an earnest and prolonged gaze on an object or look blankly into space ⟨he *stared* into her eyes —Clarissa F. Cushman⟩ ⟨*staring* into the darkness beyond the circle of light —Sherwood Anderson⟩ **b** *archaic* : to glare in anger or madness **2 a** : to have a blank empty appearance ⟨*staring* rows of ghostly blue factory windows —*Amer. Guide Series: Mich.*⟩ **b** : to show oneself conspicuously ⟨loneliness . . . ~s between the lines of this volume —V.S.Pritchett⟩ ⟨*staring* white benches against the green —Fletcher Steele⟩ **3 a** *of hair* : to stand on end : BRISTLE **b** : to appear rough and lusterless — used of the coat of an animal out of condition ~ *vt* **1** : to have an effect upon by staring ⟨uncertain whether to ~ the eye out of its hole —Christopher Isherwood⟩ **2** : to look at with a searching or earnest overall gaze ⟨a fat old lady . . . with the most extraordinary insolence *stared* him up and down —H.J.Kaplan⟩ **syn** see GAZE — **stare one in the face** : to be undeniably and forcefully evident or apparent ⟨the significant difficulties that *stare us in the face* —George Sampson⟩

²**stare** \"\ *n* -S [ME, fr. *staren*, v.] **1** *archaic* : a state of fear or amazement **2** : the act or an instance of staring : a prolonged fixed gaze (as of fear, astonishment, or admiration)

³**stare** \"\ *n, pl* **stares** *also* **stare** [ME, fr. OE *stær* — more at STARLING] *archaic* : STARLING

sta·re de·ci·sis \ˌsta(a)rēdəˈsīsəs\ *n* [L, to stand by decided matters] : the doctrine or policy of following rules or principles laid down in previous judicial decisions unless they contravene the ordinary principles of justice — compare DICTUM

stare down *vt* : to cause to waver or submit by or as if by staring : overcome by calm resolute steadiness of purpose and action : OUTSTARE ⟨though the dog threatened to attack, he was *stared down*⟩ ⟨intending frankly to ~ her down —B.A. Williams⟩

star·er \ˈsta(a)rə(r), ˈster-\ *n* -S : one that stares

sta·rets \ˈstä,rets\ *n, pl* **star·tsy** \ˈstärtsē\ [Russ, lit., venerable old man, fr. *staryĭ* old — more at STOUR] : a spiritual director or religious teacher and counselor in the Eastern Orthodox Church : a spiritual advisor who is not necessarily a priest, who is recognized for his piety, and who is turned to by monks or members of the laity for spiritual guidance

starey *also* **stary** \ˈsta(a)rē\ *adj* **starier; stariest** : staring or given to staring; *specif* : wild, glaring, and fixed esp. as a result of ill health ⟨a dog with ~ eyes⟩

star facet *n* : one of the eight small triangular facets which abut on the table in the bezel of a brilliant — see BRILLIANT illustration

star feed *n* : a feeding device for a machine tool consisting of a star wheel attached to one end of the feed screw and a stop pin clamped so that it contacts with and turns the star wheel at each revolution of the toolhead

star field *n* : a region of the sky containing stars either as seen in a telescope or recorded on a photograph

starfish \ˈ=,=\ *n* : any of numerous echinoderms that constitute the class Asteroidea, that have a body of usu. five radially disposed arms coalescing at the center to form a disk on the lower surface of which is the mouth and containing prolongations of the body cavity and of the digestive tract and other organs, a skeleton composed of small more or less movable ossicles, and ambulacral areas occupying furrows along the under surface of each arm and bearing rows of tube feet by means of which the animal crawls and grasps its prey, and that feed largely on mollusks and esp. oysters

starfish flower *n* : a plant of the genus *Stapelia* (esp. *S. asterias*)

starflower \ˈ=,=\ *n* : any of several plants having star-shaped pentamerous flowers: as **a** : STAR-OF-BETHLEHEM **b** : a plant of the genus *Trientalis* (esp. *T. americana*) **c** : a chickweed of the genus *Alsine* **d** : a plant of the genus *Brodiaea*

starfruit \ˈ=,=\ *n* : a European water plant (*Damasonium stellatum*) of the family Alismataceae having spreading pointed carpels

star·ful \ˈstärfəl\ *adj, archaic* : full of stars : dotted thickly with stars

star gauge *n* **1** : an instrument for measuring bore diameters that consists of a long rod having a micrometer handle and a head fitted to receive adjustable radial steel points **2** : a count of the stars visible in standard areas in different portions of the heavens

star-gauge \ˈ=,=\ *vt* [*star gauge*] : to measure with a star gauge

star·gaze \ˈstär,gāz, -tä,-\ *vi* [back-formation fr. *stargazer*] **1** : to gaze at stars **2** : to gaze raptly or contemplatively

star·gaz·er \-zə(r)\ *n* [¹*star* + *gazer*] **1 a** : one that gazes at the stars: as (1) : ASTROLOGER (2) : ASTRONOMER **b** : one that makes predictions and esp. unjustified predictions **2 a** : any of several marine percoid fishes belonging to the family Uranoscopidae that have the eyes on top of the head looking directly upward and that include several forms (as a common fish (*Astroscopus y-graecum*) of the eastern U. S.) that possess electric organs produced from the modified eye muscles **b** : any of various other fishes having the eyes on the top of the head **3** : a horse that carries its head too high

star·gaz·ing \-ziŋ, -zēŋ\ *n* -S [¹*star* + *gazing*, gerund of *gaze*] **1** : the act or practice of a stargazer **2 a** : absorption in chimerical or impractical ideas **b** : ABSENTMINDEDNESS, DAYDREAMING

star gear *n* : a lobate somewhat star-shaped gear wheel used as a variable gear

star ghost *n* : a faint image often seen accompanying the main image of brighter stars and planets due usu. to reflection from lenses of an eyepiece or of a camera

starglory \ˈ=,==\ *n* : CYPRESS VINE 1

star grass *n* [¹*star* + *grass*] **1** : an herb of the genus *Hypoxis* **2** : COLICROOT 1 **3** : BLUE-EYED GRASS **4** : WATER STARWORT **5** *Austral* : WINDMILL GRASS **6** : any of several grasses of the genus *Cynodon; esp* : GIANT STAR GRASS

star hummingbird *n* : STAR 9

star hyacinth *n* **1** : a spring-blooming European squill (*Scilla amoena*) with pale blue flowers **2** : a star-of-Bethlehem (*Ornithogalum umbellatum*)

starier *comparative of* STAREY *or of* STARY

stariest *superlative of* STAREY *or of* STARY

staring *pres part of* STARE

star·ing·ly *adv* **1** : in a staring manner : with a stare **2** : in an obtrusively obvious manner : GLARINGLY

star ipomoea *n* : a tropical American annual vine (*Quamoclit coccinea*) having red flowers, a long tube with yellow throat, and cupped spreading limb

star jasmine *n* : a Chinese woody vine (*Trachelospermum jasminoides*) with evergreen leaves and white fragrant flowers resembling jasmine flowers — called also *confederate jasmine*

star jelly *n* [so called fr. a popular belief that the gelatinous colonies fall from the stars] : any of several algae that form gelatinous colonies; *esp* : any of various algae of the genus *Nostoc* (esp. *N. commune*) that tend to form irregular or globular firm gelatinous pellets on marshy or frequently inundated ground

¹**stark** \ˈstärk, ˈstäk\ *adj* -ER/-EST [ME, stiff, strong, fr. OE *stearc*; akin to OHG *starc* strong, *gistorchanēn* to coagulate, ON *sterkr* strong, *storkna* to coagulate, Goth *gastaurknan* to become stiff, Lith *strėgti* to freeze, OE *starian* to stare — more at STARE] **1 a** : strongly constructed : STURDY, STOUT **b** : possessing physical strength : ROBUST, VIGOROUS **c** *chiefly Scot, of liquor* : STRONG, INTOXICATING **2 a** : lacking in flexibility or suppleness : rigid in or as if in death ⟨still unburied, lay along the wall, stiff and ~ —R.L.Stevenson⟩ ⟨~ with unbearable wet cold —Helen Rich⟩ **b** : conforming completely to pattern, precept, or doctrine : FIRM, UNBENDING, STRICT ⟨military strength, based of necessity on ~ discipline —H.J. Mackinder⟩ ⟨had a faith in law that was too ~ and literal —Irving Babbitt⟩ **3** : PURE, SHEER, UTTER ⟨~ brutality unredeemed by their tigerish grace —Miriam Allott⟩ ⟨~ denial was his plain course —Arthur Morrison⟩ ⟨~ nonsense⟩ **4** : violently stormy or windy : extremely inclement **5 a** [by shortening] : STARK-NAKED ⟨boys ~ except for breechclouts —Hervey Allen⟩ **b** : BLEAK, BARREN, DESOLATE ⟨the terrain has been rendered even more ~ by deforestation and consequent erosion —*Amer. Guide Series: Minn.*⟩ **c** (1) : having few or no ornaments, attachments, or appurtenances : appearing stripped : BARE, EMPTY ⟨rooms that were as ~ as the rooms of the white cottage had been crowded —D.B.Doner⟩ ⟨winter white offset by ~ branches —Constance Foster⟩ (2) : consisting of or presenting a simple, harsh, or blunt unadorned style or treatment ⟨critics and readers alike have commented on the ~ realism . . . of the torture scenes —Lionel Trilling⟩ ⟨a ~ description of a very graceful movement —Warwick Braithwaite⟩ **6 a** : furnishing or being furnished with an appearance of marked contrast from visual surroundings through outline, color, or texture ⟨crags in ~ outline against the sky⟩ **b** : sharply delineated : glaringly obvious ⟨there is one ~ antithesis which embraces . . . science, politics and philosophy

—Hugh Ross Williamson⟩ ⟨the ~ facts of power politics —John Mason Brown⟩ **syn** see STIFF

²stark \"\ *adv* **1 :** STARKLY **2 :** WHOLLY, ABSOLUTELY, QUITE ⟨~ mad⟩ ⟨rich men who were once ~ poor —Myron Brinig⟩ ⟨eyes shut and mouth ~ open —Douglas Newton⟩

³stark \'shtärk\ *adv (or adj)* [G, lit., strong, fr. OHG *starc*] **:** LOUDLY, FORTE — used as a direction in music

stark effect \'stärk-\ *n, usu cap S* [after Johannes *Stark* †1957 Ger. physicist] **:** the broadening or resolution into components of spectrum lines as the result of subjecting the source of light to an intense electric field — compare ZEEMAN EFFECT

stark·en \'stärkən\ *vb* -ED/-ING/-S [ME *starknen*, fr. ¹*stark* + *-nen* -en] **:** STIFFEN ⟨~*ed* and shrank with decay —Waldo Frank⟩

stark·ly *adv* [ME, fr. OE *stearclīce* strongly, fr. *stearc* stiff, strong + *-līce* -ly] **:** in a stark manner ⟨~ unable to achieve coherence —L.R.Ward⟩: as **a :** in sharp outline or contrast ⟨blackened stone walls rose ~ from the snow—F.V.W.Mason⟩ **b :** in a blunt or spare manner ⟨lit ~ by fluorescent lights —Christopher Rand⟩ ⟨state the problem in ~ realistic terms —*Amer. Guide Series: N. Y.*⟩

stark–naked \'=;==\ *adj* [*stark-naked* alter. (influenced by ²*stark*) of *start-naked*, fr. ME *start naked, stert naked*, fr. *start, stert* tail + *naked* — more at START] **:** wholly naked **:** quite bare

stark·ness *n* -ES [ME *starkenesse* stiffness, fr. *starke, stark* stiff, strong + *-nesse* -ness] **:** the quality or state of being stark

star knot *n* **:** a usu. 5-stranded decorative knot tied in the end of a rope

star–leaved gum \'=,=-\ *n* **:** SWEET GUM 1

star·less \'stärləs, -tȧl-\ *adj* [ME *sterreles*, fr. *sterre* star + *-les* -less] **:** without stars ⟨a ~ night⟩ — **star·less·ly** *adv* — **star·less·ness** *n* -ES

star·let \-lət, *usu* -əd.+V\ *n* -S **1 :** a little star **2 :** a young movie actress who is being coached and publicized for starring roles

starlight \'=,=\ *n* [ME *sterrelight*, fr. *sterre* star + *light*] **:** the light given by the stars

starlight blue *n* **:** a pale purplish blue that is paler and slightly bluer than hydrangea blue, bluer than haze blue, and bluer than moonstone blue

starlighted \'=,==\ *adj* **:** STARLIT

starlights \'=,=\ *n pl* **1 :** DOVE'S-FOOT **2 :** BLUET 1c

¹starlike \'=,=\ *adj* **:** resembling a star: as **a :** shining like a star ⟨a ~ light⟩ **b :** radiated like a star ⟨~ flowers⟩

²starlike \"\ *adv* **:** in the manner of a star

star lily *n* **:** SAND LILY

¹star·ling \'stärliŋ, -tȧl-, -lēŋ\ *n* -S [ME *starling, sterling*, fr. OE *stærlinc*, fr. *stær* starling + *-linc, -ling* -ling; akin to OE *stearn*, a bird, prob. tern, OHG *stara* starling, ON *stari*, L *sturnus* starling, OPruss *starnite* gull] **1 a :** a bird of the family Sturnidae; *esp* **:** a dark brown or in summer plumage greenish black bird (*Sturnus vulgaris*) that has a metallic gloss, is spotted with yellowish white, lives sociably and builds nests around dwellings and structures, and is native to Europe but has been introduced in the U. S., Australia, and New Zealand where it is often a pest — see ROSE-COLORED STARLING **b :** an American bird of the family Icteridae **2 :** BEAVER 6

²starling *obs var of* STERLING

³star·ling \'stärliŋ\ *n* -S [prob. alter. of (assumed) obs. E *staddling*, fr. ME *stadelinge*, fr. (assumed) ME *stadel* foundation, support (alter. of ME *stathel*) + ME *-inge, -ing* -ing — more at STADDLE] **:** a projecting pointed or rounded structure of piles driven close together around a pier of a bridge and often filled with gravel or stone to protect the pier by breaking water, ice, or drift

starling's–egg green \'==,=-\ *n* **:** COURT GRAY

star·ling's law \'stärliŋz-\ *n, usu cap S* [after Ernest H. *Starling* †1927 Eng. physiologist] **:** a statement in physiology: a muscle that is stretched within normal limits at the time of stimulation contracts more strongly than one that is completely relaxed

starling stone *n* **:** the petrified stem of a fossil fern (genus *Psaronius*) that shows in a polished cross section markings resembling those on the feathers of a starling

starlit \'=,=\ *adj* **:** lighted by the stars

star·lite \'stär,līt\ *n* -S [blend of *starlight* and *-lite*] **:** a blue zircon produced by heating a dark brown zircon from Thailand with potassium cyanide

star lot *n* [so called fr. the marking of such a lot with an asterisk in a catalog] **:** a small lot of baled wool (as three bales or less) to be sold at auction

star magnolia *n* **:** an early-blooming Japanese shrubby magnolia (*Magnolia stellata*) that is used as an ornamental and has fragrant often pink-tinged white star-shaped flowers blooming before the leaves unfold

star map *n* **:** a map often made by photography that gives the positions and magnitudes of the stars

star melanose *n* **:** a disease of citrus that results from late spring or summer sprays esp. of copper and is distinguished from melanose by the star-shaped longitudinally split lesions on the leaves

star metal *n* **:** STAR ANTIMONY

star–mop \'=,=\ *n* **:** a tangle for catching starfish

starn \'stärn\ *n* -S [ME *sterne, starne*, of Scand origin; akin to ON *stjarna* star — more at STAR] *Scot* **:** STAR

starn·ie \-ni\ *n* -S [*starn* + *-ie*] *Scot* **:** STARLET 1

star–nosed mole \'=,=-\ *also* **starnose** \'=,=\ *n* **:** a common black long-tailed semiaquatic No. American mole (*Condylura cristata*) distinguished by a series of pink fleshy projections surrounding the nostrils

star nut palm *n* **:** a palm of the genus *Astrocaryum*

starny \'stärni\ *adj* [*starn* + *-y*] *Scot* **:** STARRY

star–of–bethlehem \'==·=(,)=\ *n, pl* **stars–of–bethlehem** *or* **star–of–bethlehem** *usu cap B* [*Bethlehem*, ancient town in Judaea; prob. fr. a supposed resemblance of the flower to the star which according to Mt 2:9 guided the wise men from the East to the place where they were to find the child Jesus in Bethlehem] **1 :** a plant of the genus *Ornithogalum*; *esp* **:** a common Old World herb (*O. umbellatum*) with greenish flowers that is naturalized in the eastern U. S. — called also *sleepy dick* **2 :** AMAZON LILY **3 :** an Australian plant (*Chamaescilla corymbosa*) of the family Liliaceae **4 :** a Tasmanian plant (*Burchardia umbellata*) of the family Liliaceae **5 :** any of several starflowers; *esp* **:** STARWORT **6 :** BLUET 1c

star of david *usu cap S&D* **:** MAGEN DAVID

star of texas *usu cap T* [*Texas*, southwestern state of the U. S.] **:** an annual or biennial composite herb (*Xanthium texanum*) common in the prairie regions of the southern U. S. and also cultivated that has alternate leaves, yellow flower heads solitary or in pairs, and involucral bracts with a whitish margin

star–of–the–earth \'===·'=\ *n* **:** BUCKHORN 3b(1)

star of the veldt **:** DIMORPHOTHECA 2

star pepper *n* **:** BITTER PEPPER

star phlox *n* **:** any of several garden phloxes with narrow sharp-pointed often fringed or cut petals

star pine *n* **:** CLUSTER PINE

star place *or* **star position** *n* **:** the position of a fixed star usu. located by its right ascension and declination — compare MEAN PLACE

star plum *n* **:** STAR APPLE

star primrose *n* **:** a primrose that is a variety (*Primula sinensis stellata*) of the Chinese primrose in which the flowers occur superimposed in umbels

star quartz *n* **:** asteriated quartz

starred \'stärd, 'stȧd\ *adj* [ME *sterred*, fr. *sterre* star + *-ed*] **1 a :** adorned with or as if with stars **b :** marked with or having the shape of a star **2 :** affected in fortune by the stars

starred lizard *n* **:** an agamid lizard (*Agama stellio*) common about the eastern Mediterranean

star·rer \'stärə(r)\ *n* -S **:** a production starring a specified performer

star–ribbed vault *var of* STAR VAULT

star·ri·ly \'stärəlē, -li\ *adv* **:** in starlike fashion, position, character, or manner ⟨the inhabitants of a world of thought ~ remote from theirs —Aldous Huxley⟩

star·ri·ness \-rēnəs\ *n* -ES **:** the quality or state of being starry

starring *pres part of* STAR

star root *n* [so called fr. the fact that the leaves rise directly fr. the root and spread out in star shape] **:** DEVIL'S BIT b

star route *n* [so called fr. the star asterisk used to designate such routes in postal publications] **:** a mail-delivery route in a rural or thinly populated area served by a private carrier under contract who takes mail from one post office to another or from a railroad station to a post office and usu. also delivers mail to private mailboxes along the route — compare RURAL ROUTE

star ruby *n* **:** an asteriated variety of ruby

star·ry \'stärē, -ri\ *adj* -ER/-EST [ME *sterry*, fr. *sterre* star + *-y*] **1 a :** abounding with stars **:** adorned or studded with stars ⟨~ heavens⟩ **b :** of, relating to, consisting of, or proceeding from the stars **:** STELLAR ⟨~ light⟩ **c :** shining like stars **:** SPARKLING ⟨~ with gold and gem —A.E.Housman⟩ **d :** arranged in rays like those of a star **:** STELLATE **2 a :** as high as or seemingly as high as the stars **:** AIRY ⟨~ speculations of what mankind may do —H.G.Wells⟩ **b :** aspiring to stardom ⟨the ~ scrambling of the twain —Osbert Sitwell⟩ **3 :** composed of star performers **:** having an unusual number of stars in the cast ⟨you have to follow up one star program with another even more ~ —I.J.C.Brown⟩

starry campion *n* **:** a catchfly (*Silene stellata*) of the eastern U. S. having white somewhat star-shaped flowers

starry–eyed \'=;=\ *adj* **:** regarding an object or a prospect in an overly favorable light ⟨romantic enough to please the most *starry-eyed* girl —*Times Lit. Supp.*⟩; *specif* **:** VISIONARY ⟨may still think of this conception as radical, crackpot, *starry-eyed* and thoroughly unrealistic —A.L.Guérard⟩ ⟨*starry-eyed* advocates of world government in our time —*Current History*⟩

starry flounder *n* **:** a large dark brown mottled flatfish (*Platichthys stellatus*) of both coasts of the north Pacific that is distinguished by a small mouth with projecting lower jaw and star-shaped tubercles scattered over the head and body and is a commercially important food fish esp. along the California coast

starry grasswort *n* **:** GRASSWORT

starry magnolia *n* **:** STAR MAGNOLIA

starry puffball *n* **:** EARTHSTAR

starry ray *n* **:** a skate (*Raja radiata*) common on the European coasts and occasionally on the Atlantic coast of America having large dorsal spines with stellate bases

starry rockfish *n* **:** a rather small rockfish (*Sebastodes constellatus*) of the southern California and Lower California coast that is chiefly yellow to red above sprinkled with pale dots and fading to yellowish or pinkish white below

stars *pl of* STAR, *pres 3d sing of* STAR

star sapphire *n* **:** a sapphire that when cut with a convex surface and polished exhibits asterism resulting from there being microscopic crystals in various orientations within the gem

star saxifrage *n* **:** a small arctic or alpine saxifrage (*Saxifraga stellaris*) having small starlike white flowers

star scout *n* **:** a boy scout who has been awarded five merit badges — compare EAGLE SCOUT, LIFE SCOUT

starshake \'=,=\ *n* **:** a check in timber beginning near the heart and extending toward the surface in radial cracks or fissures — called also *star check*

star shell *n* [¹*star* + *shell*] **1 :** a shell that on bursting releases a shower of brilliant stars and is used for signaling **2 :** a shell with an illuminating projectile

starshell \'=,=\ *n* [¹*star* + *shell*] **:** a West Indian turban shell (*Astraea longispina*) having the margin of the whorls prolonged by hollow triangular spines; *broadly* **:** any of several other members of the genus *Astraea*

starshine \'=,=\ *n* **:** the glow of the stars **:** STARLIGHT

star·ship \'stär,ship\ *n* **:** a rocket or other ship designed for travel in interstellar space

starshoot *or* **starshot** \'=,=\ *n* -S **:** a star jelly (*Nostoc commune*)

star sight *n* **:** an observation of the altitude of a star made for navigational purposes

star skunk *n* **:** a common skunk of the genus *Mephitis* in which the normal white areas are reduced to one or two small white patches so that the coat is nearly all black

star–spangled \'=;==\ *adj* **1 :** studded with stars **2** [fr. the fact that the flag of the U. S. has frequently been described as star-spangled since the composition of the patriotic song *The Star-Spangled Banner* in 1814 by Francis Scott Key †1843 Am. lawyer] **a :** of, relating to, or characteristic of the U. S. or its citizens ⟨ripsnorting *star-spangled* frontiersmen —R.A.Billington⟩ **b :** extremely patriotic with regard to the U. S.

star spot *n* **:** a bright or dark spot on the surface of a star inferred from photometric or spectroscopic observations and thought to be similar in nature to a sunspot

starstone \'=,=\ *n* **:** an asteriated stone; *esp* **:** STAR SAPPHIRE

star streaming *n* **:** real or apparent systematic drift of the stars

star system *n* **1 :** a group of stars showing common characteristics of location and motion **:** GALAXY **2 :** the dependence upon and extensive advertising of stars in motion pictures and the theater often to the extent of writing or altering a play or screenplay to fit a star's talents

¹start \'stärt, -tȧl, *usu* |d·+V\ *n* -S [ME *start, stert* handle, tail, fr. OE *steort* tail; akin to MD *stert, start* tail, OHG *sterz*, ON *stertr* tail, OE *starian* to stare — more at STARE] **:** a curved or projecting part or section: as **a :** the curved or inclined front and bottom of a waterwheel bucket **b :** the lever of a gin drawn around by a horse

²start \"\ *vb* -ED/-ING/-S [ME *sterten*; akin to MHG *sterzen* to move quickly, stand up stiffly, ON *sterta* to crease, OE *starian* to stare — more at STARE] *vi* **1 a :** to move suddenly and violently from a state of stillness or rest **:** DART, JUMP, SPRING ⟨everywhere men and women ~*ed* from their beds at the shots —Marjory S. Douglas⟩ ⟨~*ed* to his feet angrily —Liam O'Flaherty⟩ — often used with *up* ⟨now falls on her bed, and then ~*s* up —Shak.⟩ **b :** to draw back **:** FLINCH, RECOIL ⟨she skipped forward to the pit . . . but she ~*ed* back in surprise —George Eliot⟩ **c :** to awaken suddenly ⟨~*ed* from my sleep with horror —Mary W. Shelley⟩ ⟨~*ed* from her reverie with a shiver —G.B.Shaw⟩ **d :** to react (as to something that frightens, surprises, or disgusts) with a sudden brief involuntary movement **:** become startled ⟨stepped stealthily, and ~*ed* when a twig snapped underfoot —Margaret Deland⟩ ⟨she never ~*s* or shows surprise —Rose Macaulay⟩ ⟨why do you ~ and seem to fear things that do sound so fair —Shak.⟩ **2 a :** to issue, flow, or enter with sudden force **:** BURST ⟨blood ~*ing* from the wound⟩ ⟨tears ~*ing* from her eyes⟩ **b :** to arise, emerge, or break out suddenly ⟨in a few short paragraphs, the characters ~ into life⟩ — often used with *up* ⟨new settlements ~*ed* up all around them⟩ ⟨a man who ~*ed* up from obscurity⟩ **c :** to come into being, activity, or operation **:** BEGIN, COMMENCE ⟨the blood is all ready and waiting with food, if a baby ~*s* —J.A.O'Brien⟩ ⟨the fever disappears for a few days, only to ~ all over again —Justina Hill⟩ ⟨as soon as the battle ~*ed*, he left his command post —H.L. Merillat⟩ **3 :** to protrude or seem to protrude **:** BULGE ⟨the men of the regiment, with their ~*ing* eyes and sweating faces —Stephen Crane⟩ **4 a :** to work itself open or free **:** become loosened **:** become broken or forced out of place ⟨a nail has ~*ed*⟩ ⟨one of the planks has ~*ed*⟩ **b** *of an arrow* **:** to jump suddenly out of the line of aim when loosed **c** *of book leaves* **:** to extend beyond the regular fore edge because loosened at the backbone **5** *archaic* **:** to deviate from one's course or duty **:** DESERT, REVOLT **6 a :** to begin a forward movement **:** take off on a course or progress **:** set out ⟨the train is ready to ~⟩ ⟨the expedition ~*ed* north⟩ ⟨five cars ~*ed* but only three finished⟩ **b :** to range from a specified initial point ⟨the rates ~ at ten dollars⟩ ⟨the alphabet ~*s* with *A*⟩ ⟨a succession of expressions, ~*ing* with a gentle smile and finishing with a broad grin —Wilfrid Campfield⟩ **7 a :** to begin an activity or undertaking ⟨as soon as you're ready to play, we'll ~⟩ ⟨as a novelist, he ~*s* with a double handicap⟩ ⟨~*ed* in business on a shoestring⟩ **b :** to begin work ⟨when do I ~⟩ — sometimes used with *in* ⟨will ~ in after a brief period of training⟩ **c** (1) **:** to be a contestant or entry in a race or field trial (2) **:** to be in the lineup at the beginning of a game (as baseball or football) ⟨despite his injury, he will ~ in center field⟩ ⟨a left-hander will probably ~ for the home team⟩ ⟨~*ed* at quarterback⟩ **~** *vt* **1 :** to drive from a place of concealment into the open **:** cause to move so as to be discovered **:** FLUSH ⟨~*ed* a deer on the banks of this stream —*Amer. Guide Series: Vt.*⟩ ⟨~ a hare⟩ **2** *archaic* **:** to disturb suddenly **:** STARTLE, ALARM ⟨every feather ~*s* you —Shak.⟩ **3 :** to bring up for consideration or discussion **:** INTRODUCE, PROPOUND ⟨~*ed* a subject in which he expected him to shine —Jane Austen⟩ **4 a :** to bring into being **:** INITIATE, ORIGINATE ⟨~*ed* a story that his opponent was a crook⟩ ⟨~*ed* the modernist movement in art⟩ ⟨~*ed* the custom many years ago⟩ **b :** to set up **:** ESTABLISH, FOUND ⟨~ a college⟩ ⟨~ a newspaper⟩ **5 a :** to cause to become loosened or displaced ⟨the pounding of the waves ~*ed* some of the rivets⟩ **b :** to break out ⟨~ the anchor⟩ **c :** to ease off **:** SLACKEN ⟨~ a rope⟩ **6 a :** DISCHARGE, EMPTY ⟨~ the contents of the barrel into a new cask⟩ **b :** to begin the use of ⟨~ a new keg of beer⟩ ⟨~ a fresh loaf of bread⟩ **7 a :** to set going **:** cause to move, act, or operate ⟨was unable to ~ the car⟩ ⟨wound the clock to ~ it running again⟩ ⟨~*ed* his son in business⟩ **b :** to cause (a motor) to begin running on its own ignition — often used with *up* **c** (1) **:** to enter in a race or contest ⟨plans to ~ the horse in only a few races this year⟩ (2) **:** to put into a game at the beginning ⟨~*ed* the rookie at third but took him out after three innings⟩ **d :** to begin the employment of **:** take on ⟨the company ~*ed* him at the same salary he had been getting on his previous job⟩ ⟨the station ~*ed* him as a news announcer⟩ **e :** to care for during the early stages of growth and development **:** initiate the raising or training of ⟨~*ed* chicks⟩ ⟨a well-*started* coonhound⟩ **8 :** to perform the first stages or actions of **:** enter on ⟨~*ed* studying music at the age of three⟩ ⟨~*ed* to load the truck⟩ ⟨~*ed* what seemed like an impossible job⟩ **syn** see BEGIN — **start something :** to make trouble **:** create a disturbance ⟨a man with a chip on his shoulder who's always trying to *start something*⟩ — **to start with :** at the beginning ⟨standing cans in brine will not stop souring for several hours if the milk is warm *to start with* —*Farmer's Weekly (So. Africa)*⟩

³start \"\ *n* -S [ME *stert*, fr. *sterten*, v.] **1 a :** a sudden involuntary bodily movement or reaction ⟨gave a little ~ of surprise —R.H.Davis⟩ ⟨jerked the reins so hard that her mother came out of her thoughts with a ~ —Margaret Deland⟩ **b :** a brief and sudden action or movement **:** BOUND ⟨nature does nothing by ~*s* and leaps —Roger L'Estrange⟩ ⟨does things by fits and ~*s*⟩ **c** *obs* **:** a sudden excursion or flight ⟨use your legs, take the ~, run away —Shak.⟩ **d :** a sudden capricious impulse or outburst **:** FIT, SALLY ⟨~*s* and aberrations of fancy welling up from springs of suppressed romance —Edith Wharton⟩ **e :** a sudden burst of sound or speech ⟨she did speak in ~*s* distractedly —Shak.⟩ **2 a :** a beginning of movement, activity, or development **:** initial impulse, motion, or action ⟨made a good ~ in life⟩ ⟨the work is off to a promising ~⟩ ⟨the horse made a false ~ and had to be called back⟩ ⟨building ~*s*⟩ ⟨housing ~*s*⟩ **b :** a lead or handicap at the beginning of a race or competition **:** ADVANTAGE, HEAD START ⟨gave them a five minutes' ~ and then went after them⟩ ⟨the early sea trade of the inhabitants of the island world . . . gave them a ~ over their neighbors —Edward Clodd⟩ **c** (1) **:** the act or action of setting into motion **:** the imparting of motion ⟨gave the car a ~ by pushing it⟩ (2) **:** help in beginning or undertaking something (as a career or project) ⟨gave him his ~ in business⟩ ⟨gave him a ~ on the problem⟩ **d :** a place of beginning **:** point of departure ⟨five cars lined up at the ~⟩ ⟨selected the old mill as the ~ of the hike⟩ **3 :** an unusual, interesting, or surprising incident or event **:** a peculiar circumstance ⟨of all the queer ~*s* . . . me, meeting you like this —Richard Dehan⟩ **4 a :** something that has come loose **:** DISPLACEMENT **b starts** *pl* **:** book leaves that have started **5 :** the act or an instance of being a competitor in a race or a member of a starting lineup in a game ⟨finished no worse than second in his last six ~*s*⟩ ⟨pitched an excellent game in his first ~⟩

start·er \|d·ə(r), |tə(r)\ *n* -S **1 :** one who initiates or sets going ⟨one of the ~*s* of the scientific revolution⟩: as **a :** an official who gives the signal to begin a race **b** (1) **:** DISPATCHER a (2) **:** DISPATCHER f **c :** one that does hat sizing **2 a** (1) **:** one that enters a competition or sets out in a race ⟨a late ~ in the contest for the nomination⟩ ⟨an added ~ in the second race⟩ (2) **:** STARTING PITCHER **b :** one that begins to engage in an activity or process ⟨is not a tactful man, nor a slow, easy ~ —John Bird⟩ **3 :** one that causes something (as a mechanism or process) to begin operating: as **a :** a controller that accelerates a motor to normal speed in one direction of rotation but that is not adapted for sustained use in positions intermediate between the off and full-on positions **b :** SELF-STARTER **c :** a strip of foundation placed in a frame or section in a hive to facilitate comb-building by honeybees **d :** material containing microorganisms used to induce a desired fermentation (as in making butter, cheese, or vinegar) and being either a sample of a natural population (as sour cream or vinegar) or a pure culture of a defined microorganism — compare FERMENT 1a **e :** a compound used to start a chemical reaction **f :** a specially prepared food or nutrient used to promote vigorous growth in very young animals or plants ⟨a calf ~⟩ ⟨a chick ~⟩ **g :** a device (as a drill or punch) used for starting a hole **4 a :** something that is the beginning of a process, activity, or series **:** a first step ⟨will sink something over a million dollars into this plant just as a ~ —Green Peyton⟩ ⟨as a ~, the linguists began asking the names of everyday things —*Time*⟩ **b** (1) **:** a card that is cut and turned face up on the top of the stock after cribbage players have discarded for the crib (2) **:** UPCARD **c :** EAVES TILE

starter set *n* **:** a small set of 16 or 20 dishes usu. comprising a service for four persons — compare PLACE SETTING

star thistle *n* **:** any of various plants of the genus *Centaurea*: as **a :** an annual or biennial herb (*Centaurea calcitrapa*) having a basal rosette of deeply toothed leaves, a much branched stem, and axillary or terminal heads of pinkish to purple tubular flowers surrounded by scales tipped with long stout yellow spines and being native to the Mediterranean region but widely distributed by commerce and in many places established as an aggressive weed **b :** BARNABY'S THISTLE **c :** BASKET FLOWER **d :** RUSSIAN KNAPWEED

starthroat \'=,=\ *n* **:** either of two Brazilian hummingbirds of the genus *Heliomaster* whose throat feathers have a metallic luster

star time *n* **:** SIDEREAL TIME

starting *pres part of* START

starting bar *n* **:** GEE-THROW

starting block *n* **:** a device that provides a runner with a rigid surface against which to brace his feet at the start of a race and that consists of two pedals or blocks mounted on either side of a frame usu. anchored in the ground

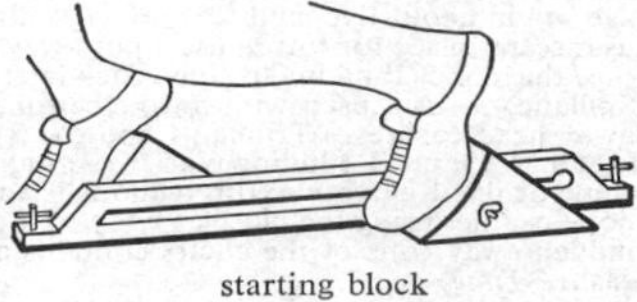
starting block

starting box *n* **:** RHEOSTAT

starting friction *n* **:** STATIC FRICTION

starting gate *n* **:** a mechanically operated barrier used as a starting device for a race

starting grid *n* **1 :** a paved area adjacent to the track on which automobiles line up for the start of a race **2 :** a starting area on the track itself

starting hole *n, archaic* **:** a place of refuge **:** LOOPHOLE ⟨what trick, what device, what *starting hole* canst thou now find out to hide thee —Shak.⟩

start·ing·ly *adv* **:** in a starting manner ⟨why do you speak so ~ and rash —Shak.⟩

starting pitcher *n* **:** a baseball pitcher usu. used in regular rotation (as every fourth day) to start a game and usu. expected to pitch a complete game — compare RELIEF PITCHER

starting punch *n* **:** ³PUNCH 1a(4)

starting sheet *n* **:** a thin sheet of metal which is used as cathode in electrolytic refining and on which the refined metal is electrodeposited

starting torque *n* **:** the torque applied by an electric motor at standstill

¹star·tle \'stär|d·ᵊl, -tȧ|, |tᵊl\ *vb* **startled; startled; startling** \|d·ᵊliŋ, |t(ᵊ)l-\ **startles** [ME *stertlen*, fr. *sterten* to start +

-*len* -le — more at START] *vi* **1** *chiefly Scot* : to run about wildly **2 a** : to move or jump suddenly as in surprise, fear, or alarm ⟨babies who ~ easily —Benjamin Spock⟩ ⟨the nervous creature who ~*s* at every sudden sound —J.H.Newman⟩ **b** : to awake suddenly from sleep or a dormant state ~ *vt* **1** : to excite or rouse by sudden alarm, surprise, fear, or shock : frighten or affect suddenly and usu. not seriously : cause to start ⟨*startled* to see a ghostly silhouette of a submarine —Stewart Beach⟩ **2** *archaic* : to make irresolute : cause to waver ⟨can discover nothing that may ~ a discreet belief —Sir Thomas Browne⟩ **3** : to bring into a specified state by or as if by startling ⟨ferns that the first rain ~*s* to green life —Marjory S. Douglas⟩ ⟨her blank face *startled* the end of his remark out of his mind —Ellen Glasgow⟩ **syn** see FRIGHTEN

2startle \"\ *n* -s **1** : a sudden mild shock as of surprise or alarm : START **2** : a marked tendency to display the startle pattern esp. under conditions of apparently inadequate stimulation

startle pattern *or* **startle reaction** *or* **startle response** *n* : the complex of psychophysiological changes that is elicited in an organism by an unexpected sudden stimulus (as a loud noise) and includes tremor, sweating, palpitation, dry mouth, and a feeling of fear or panic sometimes followed by escape or avoidance reactions

star·tler \|d·ᵊlə(r), |t(ᵊ)l-\ *n* -s : one that startles ⟨the investigation uncovered a ~⟩

startling *adj* **1** : easily frightened : RESTLESS, SKITTISH **2** : causing a momentary shock, fright, surprise, or astonishment by a mild or forcible demand upon the attention : consisting of or exhibiting shocking, bizarre, or extremely or mildly unusual features ⟨~ earthquake shocks —*Amer. Guide Series: Ind.*⟩ ⟨a ~ roadster, all streamlines and cream paint —Sinclair Lewis⟩ ⟨~ economies of expression —Margery Bailey⟩ — **star·tling·ly** *adv* — **star·tling·ness** *n* -ES

star·tlish \|d·ᵊlish, |t(ᵊ)l-\ *also* **star·tly** \|d·ᵊlē |t(ᵊ)lē\ *adj* : SKITTISH — **star·tlish·ness** *n* -ES

start-naked \'stärt¦nākəd\ *dial var of* STARK-NAKED

star tortoise *n* : an Indian tortoise (*Testudo elegans*) with a sculptured carapace, black with yellow markings, and two yellow stars on the black plastron

star trail *n* : a continuous line produced on a photographic plate by the image of a star during an exposure in which the camera or telescope does not follow the diurnal motion of the star or follows the motion of some other celestial body (as a comet) that is being photographed

starts *pl of* START, *pres 3d sing of* START

startsy *pl of* STARETS

star tulip *n* : MARIPOSA LILY

1start-up \'=,=\ *adj* [obs. E *start up*, past part. of E *start up*, v.] *archaic* : UPSTART

2start-up \"\ *n* -s [1*start-up*] **1** *obs* : UPSTART ⟨that young *start-up* hath all the glory of my overthrow —Shak.⟩ **2** [fr. *start up*, v.] : the act or an instance of setting in operation or motion

start-ups \'stärtəps\ *n pl* [fr. *start up*, v.] **1** *obs* : low boots **2** *dial Eng* : LEGGINGS

star turn *n, chiefly Brit* : the featured skit or number in a theatrical production; *broadly* : the most widely publicized person or item in a group

star·va·tion \stär'vāshən, stå'-\ *n* -s : the action or an instance of starving or the state of being starved

starvation wages *n* : wages insufficient to provide the ordinary necessities of life

star vault \'=-\ *or* **star-ribbed vault** \'=,=-\ *n* : a ribbed vault in which the ribs and liernes are arranged in a starlike pattern

starve \'stärv, 'ståv\ *vb* **starved**; **starved**; **starving**; **starves** [ME *sterven*, fr. OE *steorfan;* akin to OFris *sterva* to die, OHG *sterban* to die, OE *starian* to stare — more at STARE] *vi* **1** *obs* : DIE, PERISH **2 a** : to perish from lack of food — often used in the phrase *starve to death* **b** : to suffer extreme hunger ⟨all this time the family had *starved* and gone ragged —Conrad Richter⟩ **3** *archaic* **a** : to die of cold **b** : to suffer greatly from cold ⟨my hands are *starving* while I write in bed —Jonathan Swift⟩ **4** : to suffer or perish from deprivation ⟨pupils are *starving* for means of expression —I.A.Richards⟩ ⟨his horse . . . . almost *starved* for water —J.F.Dobie⟩ ⟨*starving* for lack of intellectual companionship —Robert Grant †1940⟩ ~ *vt* **1** *obs* : KILL, DESTROY **2 a** : to kill with hunger **b** : to deprive of nourishment ⟨seen men *starved*, beaten, herded like cattle —John Fountain⟩ **c** : to cause to capitulate by or as if by depriving of nourishment ⟨~ a person into submission⟩ ⟨*starved* him out by refusing to support his paper —W.E. Smith⟩ **d** : to attempt to cure (a disease) by restricting the diet of the affected person ⟨feed a cold and ~ a fever⟩ **3 a** : to destroy by or cause to suffer from deprivation ⟨*starved* the army of transport —F.M.Ford⟩ ⟨the company avoided bankruptcy by *starving* its depreciation reserves —M.W. Straight⟩ **b** : to suppress or extinguish (a fire) by cutting off fuel **4** *archaic* : to kill with cold

starved brood *n* : a diseased condition of the brood of the honeybee possibly due to an infectious disease

starved·ly \-vədlē, -vd-\ *adv* : in a starved manner : with little nourishment

starve·ling \'stärvliŋ, -tåv-, -lēŋ\ *n* -s : one that starves : one that is thin from or as if from lack of nutriment

starv·er \'stärvər\ *n* -s **1** : one that causes starvation **2** : one that undergoes starvation

star violet *n* **1** : either of two small herbs (*Houstonia patens* and *H. angustifolia*) of the central and southern U. S. **2** : DEWDROP 2

star wheel *n* : a somewhat star-shaped disk used as a ratchet wheel (as in a repeating watch or the feed motion of any of various machines) — compare GENEVA STOP

star winding *n* : a winding used in a polyphase electric machine in which one terminal of each phase coil is connected to a common point and the other terminals are joined to the outside system — compare STAR CONNECTION

starworm \'=,=\ *n* : GEPHYREAN

starwort \'=,=\ *n* [ME *sterrewort*, fr. *sterre* star + *wort*] **1** : any of various chickweeds of the genus *Stellaria* **2** : a plant of the genus *Aster* (as the stiff aster) **3** : any of various plants of the genus *Callitriche* **4** : GRUBROOT **5** : COLICROOT

stary *var of* STAREY

1stash \'stash, -aa(ə)-,-ai- *sometimes* -ā-\ *vt* -ED/-ING/-ES [origin unknown] **1** *chiefly Brit* : to put an end to : break up : STOP, QUIT ⟨~ the business⟩ ⟨~ it⟩ ⟨could ~ up any golden age . . . in about five minutes —H.G.Wells⟩ **2** : to store in a usu. secret place for future use : put away : HIDE, CACHE ⟨had ~*ed* the money thinking to come back later and get it —Mickey Spillane⟩ — usu. used with *away* ⟨began systematically to ~ away her treasures —Truman Capote⟩

2stash \"\ *n* -ES **1** : hiding place : CACHE; *esp* : one for moonshine or illicit narcotics ⟨fifty gallons left in the ~⟩ ⟨caught a dope peddler using the place as a ~⟩ **2** : something stored or hidden away ⟨one of the chairs contains a considerable ~ of cash —*Time*⟩

stash·ie \'stashi\ *n* -s [perh. alter. of *ecstasy*] *Scot* : UPROAR

stasi- *comb form* [Gk *stasis* condition of standing, stoppage, stature, position — more at STASIS] **1** : arrest of development : stoppage ⟨*stasi*morphy⟩ **2** : erect posture ⟨*stasi*phobia⟩ **3** : position ⟨*stasi*metric⟩

-sta·sia \'stāzh(ē)ə, -āsh-\ *n comb form* -s [NL, fr. Gk, fr. *statos* standing (fr. the stem of *histanai* to cause to stand) + -*ia* -y — more at STAND] : condition of standing : stoppage : -STASIS ⟨meno*stasia*⟩ ⟨enhypo*stasia*⟩

stas·i·mon \'stasə,män\ *n, pl* **stasi·ma** \-,mə\ *also* **stasimons** [Gk, fr. neut. of *stasimos* standing, stationary, fr. the stem of *histanai* to cause to stand] : one of the regular choral odes between two episodes in a Greek tragedy possibly sung with the chorus standing in its place in the orchestra — compare PARODOS

stasis \'stāsəs -tas-\ *n, pl* **stases** \-ā,sēz -a,s-\ [NL, fr. Gk, condition of standing, standing still, stoppage, stature, condition, fr. stem of *histanai* to cause to stand + -*sis* — more at STAND] **1** : a slowing or stoppage of the normal flow of fluid or semifluid material in an organ or vessel in the body: as **a** : slowing of the current of circulating blood in arteries or veins ⟨venous ~⟩ **b** : reduced motility of the intestines with retention of feces ⟨colon ~⟩ **2** : an absence of circulatory convection currents in a mass of gas or liquid **3** : a state of static balance or equilibrium among opposing tendencies or forces : QUIESCENCE, STAGNATION ⟨at a point of ~ artistically and spiritually . . . cannot develop any new creative activity —Harrison Smith⟩; *specif* : a state of stable and sometimes sterile equilibrium reached by a society : STAGNANCY ⟨the essential danger of mass media . . . lies in their ability to inflate existing consent to the point of a dull unanimity and so to achieve social and economic ~ —J.T.Klapper⟩

-stasis \'stā|səs, 'sta|, ,stə|\ *n comb form, pl* **-stases** \|,sēz\ [NL, fr. Gk *stasis* condition of standing, standing still, stoppage] **1** : slowing or stoppage of normal flow ⟨hemo*stasis*⟩ **2** : inhibition of the growth without destruction of ⟨bacterio*stasis*⟩ ⟨fungi*stasis*⟩ **3** : tendency toward maintenance of stability ⟨homeo*stasis*⟩ **4** : retention : persistence ⟨tricho*stasis*⟩

stass·furt salt \'sta|sfə(r)t-, 's(h)tä|\ *n, usu cap 1st S* [fr. *Stassfurt*, Germany] : potash salt from large deposits in Germany

stat *abbr* **1** static **2** [L *statim*] immediately **3** stationary **4** statistical; statistician; statistics **5** statuary; statue **6** statute

stat- *comb form* [electro*stat*ic] : electrostatic ⟨*stat*ampere⟩ — in names of electrical units

-stat \,stat, *usu* -ad·+V\ *n comb form* -s [NL -*stata*, fr. Gk -*statēs* one that causes to stand, fr. the stem of *histanai* to cause to stand — more at STAND] **1** : apparatus or agent for keeping (something specified) stable or stationary ⟨gyro*stat*⟩ **2** : device for regulating or for maintaining (something specified) in a constant state ⟨cryo*stat*⟩ ⟨rheo*stat*⟩ ⟨thermo*stat*⟩ **3** : instrument for reflecting (something specified) constantly in one direction ⟨helio*stat*⟩ ⟨sidero*stat*⟩ **4** : device for studying (something specified) in a state of rest ⟨hydro*stat*⟩ **5** : agent causing inhibition of growth without destruction ⟨bacterio*stat*⟩ ⟨fungi*stat*⟩

stat·able *or* **state·able** \'stād·əbəl, -ātə-\ *adj* : capable of being stated ⟨philosophical problems . . . ~ as specific questions —J.E.Smith⟩

stat·al \'stād·ᵊl\ *adj* [1*state* + -*al*] **1** *often cap* : of or relating to a state (as of the U.S. or India) ⟨~ citizenship⟩ ⟨the ~ economy⟩ **2** : of or relating to a national government ⟨the sanctuaries of ~ authority —*Fortnightly Rev.*⟩ **3** *of a passive verb form* : expressing a state or condition (as *was closed* in "the door was closed all day") — contrasted with *actional*

stat·ampere \(')stad·+\ *n* [*stat-* + *ampere*] : the cgs electrostatic unit of current equal to about 3.3×10^{-10} ampere

sta·tant \'stātᵊnt\ *adj* [L *stat*us (past part. of *stare* to stand) + E -*ant*) — more at STAND] *of a heraldic beast* : standing with all feet on the ground and seen in profile ⟨a lion ~⟩

stat·coulomb \(¦)stat+\ *n* [*stat-* + *coulomb*] : the cgs electrostatic unit of charge equal to about 3.3×10^{-10} coulomb

1state \'stāt, *usu* -ād·+V\ *n* -s *often attrib* [ME *stat*, fr. OF & L; OF *estat*, fr. L *status*, fr. *status*, past part. of *stare* to stand — more at STAND] **1 a** : a mode or condition of being : POSITION, NATURE ⟨this mortal ~⟩ ⟨our present ~ of knowledge⟩ ⟨the ~ of his health⟩ ⟨financial ~⟩ ⟨the unsanitary ~ of the building⟩ ⟨a ~ of readiness⟩ ⟨the married ~⟩ **b** (1) : a condition of mind or temperament ⟨a ~ of consciousness⟩ ⟨in a highly nervous ~⟩ (2) : a condition of abnormal tension or excitement (as from anger or fear) ⟨little things piled up on him and he got into a ~⟩ **c** *archaic* : the highest stage of development : ACME, CRISIS — usu. used of a disease **d** : a condition or form of a noun — compare ABSOLUTE STATE, CONSTRUCT STATE, EMPHATIC STATE **2 a** : a condition or stage in the physical constitution of something : STATE OF AGGREGATION ⟨the solid and liquid ~*s*⟩ ⟨water in the vaporous ~⟩ ⟨the best ~ of a metal for the purpose⟩ **b** : one of an indeterminate number of conditions in which an atomic system may exist that is characterized by definite quantities (as of energy, angular momentum, or magnetic moment) and separated from other conditions by finite differences in these quantities **c** : the physical condition of something at one stage in a process: as (1) : a stage of an engraved plate that is distinguished from another stage by a greater or less amount of work on the plate (2) : an impression from the plate in such a stage (3) : a condition of the unfired clay in ceramics ⟨green ~⟩ ⟨raw ~⟩ (4) : a variant (as in type setting or makeup) of an impression or issue of a book (5) : a stage in the growth or development of a plant or animal ⟨buttercups in the green ~⟩ ⟨the larval ~⟩ **3 a** : social position : RANK, STATION ⟨all luxuries befitting the ~ of a marquis —Charles Dickens⟩; *esp* : high rank : EMINENCE ⟨can this imperious lord . . . quit all his ~, descend, and serve again —Alexander Pope⟩ **b** (1) : elaborate or luxurious style or mode of living : MAGNIFICENCE ⟨has a wealthy lover and keeps a considerable ~ —Arnold Bennett⟩ (2) : formal dignity : POMP — usu. used with *in* ⟨rode in ~ to her coronation⟩ ⟨in solemn ~ . . . admitted to the fraternity —R.W. Southern⟩ ⟨lie in ~⟩ **c** : graceful dignity (as in bearing) ⟨keep some ~ in thy exit and vanish —Shak.⟩ ⟨perfect in shapeliness and ~ —A.C.Swinburne⟩ **d** (1) *obs* : a chair with a canopy and often on a dais : THRONE ⟨this chair shall be my ~ —Shak.⟩ (2) *archaic* : CANOPY **4 a** : a body of persons constituting a special class in a society : ESTATE, ORDER ⟨a division of governmental power between the several ~*s* . . . in the community —C.J.Friedrich⟩ **b states** *pl* : the members or representatives of the governing classes assembled in a parliament or diet (as in France before the Revolution, Scotland before the Union, and the United Netherlands) : ESTATE 3b **c** *obs* (1) : a person of high rank (as a noble) ⟨the bold design pleased highly those infernal ~*s* —John Milton⟩ (2) : the ruling persons (as in a country or town) : COUNCIL ⟨consult with the king and ~ —Francis Bacon⟩ **d** : the ruling body or government of a country **5 a** : a body of people permanently occupying a definite territory and politically organized under a sovereign government almost entirely free from external control and possessing coercive power to maintain order within the community : BODY POLITIC, COMMONWEALTH 2, NATION 1b ⟨for Aristotle the ~ was an association of men for the sake of the best moral life⟩ **b** : the political organization that has supreme civil authority and political power and serves as the basis of government ⟨the institutions of Church and ~⟩ **c** : a particular form of government or politically organized society ⟨the secular ~⟩ ⟨the fascist ~⟩ ⟨the welfare ~⟩ **d** : the embodiment of the ethical idea and the moral will of the community in Hegelian philosophy **e** : a colony of social animals (as ants or bees) with organization analogous to that of a human state **6** : the operations, activities, or affairs of the government or ruling power of a country : the sphere of administration and supreme political power of a government ⟨matters of ~⟩ ⟨secrets of ~⟩ ⟨ministers of ~⟩ ⟨Department of ~⟩ **7** *often cap* : one of the bodies politic or component units in a federal system that is more or less independent and sovereign over internal affairs but forms with the other units a sovereign nation ⟨the United *States* of America⟩ ⟨the Indian ~*s*⟩ ⟨the ~*s* of Switzerland are called cantons⟩ **8 a** : a territory governed by a particular nation **b** : a territorial unit in which the general body of law is separate and distinct from the law of any other territorial unit **9** *obs* : PROPERTY, ESTATE 4c **10 a** *archaic* : STATEMENT, ACCOUNT **b** *Brit* : a periodic report of troop numbers and condition ⟨delivered a ~ of the troops⟩

syn CONDITION, MODE, SITUATION, POSTURE, STATUS: STATE, often interchangeable with CONDITION, may but does not always imply genuinely existent characteristics likely to be significant and enduring and discovered or announced after some analysis ⟨shall from time to time give to the Congress information of the *state* of the Union —*U.S.Constitution*⟩ ⟨wharves, piers and docks at the Atlantic ports were brought to what was a high *state* of efficiency for those days —A.F. Harlow⟩ ⟨in a *state* of some excitement, talking eagerly in a rather loud voice —J.D.Beresford⟩ CONDITION may more strongly imply the influence of circumstances on the way of existing, esp. of only temporary circumstances ⟨his mental *condition*⟩ ⟨in a delicate *condition*⟩ ⟨previous *condition* of servitude⟩ ⟨better working *conditions*⟩ ⟨the house is still in good *condition*⟩ ⟨certain weather *conditions*⟩ ⟨by no means relieved of his anxiety and fully aware of the excited *condition* of English opinion he could only await the issue —W.C.Ford⟩ MODE stresses external manifestation and suggests nothing of the concern with underlying reality that may be implicated by *state* ⟨the whole burden of her middle period is the attempt to reach a spiritual equilibrium through a formal *mode* of religious conversion —M.D.Geismar⟩ SITUATION, implying a being placed or located much more than a being formed or composed, may apply to any specific set of circumstances, perhaps individual or interesting ⟨the *situation* in fiction — the desperate girl appealing out of her misery to the Christian priest for help —Rose Macaulay⟩ ⟨he has already won for himself a personal *situation* unparalleled in postwar France, and with it a fighting chance to lead his country —Frank Gorrell⟩ ⟨a play upon a *situation* in which a surgeon is called upon to save the life of the lover of his wife —A.H.Quinn⟩ POSTURE, in this sense often a close synonym for SITUATION, may imply the shaping influence of personal inclination or decision ⟨the type of balance between military and civilian production which will permit us to maintain both a strong economy and a strong military *posture* —H.S.Truman⟩ ⟨showing me in a *posture* of comically servile deference to authority —F.R.Leavis⟩ STATUS may indicate one's state or condition as determined with some definiteness for legal administration or economic or social considerations ⟨new *status* of proprietor — Mary Austin⟩ ⟨the change in the *status* of the Negro, under the Thirteenth Amendment, from three fifths of a person to a whole person in computing state apportionment —Carol L. Thompson⟩ ⟨a married woman's *status* was determined entirely by that of her husband —F.A.Ogg & P.O.Ray⟩ ⟨big business has elevated the function of management to the *status* of the learned professions —*Nation's Business*⟩ ⟨my underprivileged *status* as an ex-convict —Frank O'Leary⟩

— **in a state of nature 1** : naked as when born : NUDE **2** : in a condition of sin : UNREGENERATE **3** : UNCIVILIZED, UNTAMED

2state \"\ *vt* -ED/-ING/-S **1 a** *archaic* : to fix or settle in a position, rank, or condition : PLACE **b** *obs* : to confer possession on : vest a person in **c** : to set by or as if by regulation or authority ⟨meetings are held at *stated* times⟩ **2 a** : to express the particulars of : set forth : RECITE, REPORT ⟨~ the facts of a case⟩ ⟨~ the problem in full⟩ ⟨~ the account in dollars⟩ **b** : to put into words : FRAME, PHRASE ⟨~ the resolution as it is now to be voted upon⟩ **c** (1) : ASSERT, DECLARE ⟨authorities . . . ~ that a young man in good condition can cover up to a hundred miles a day —Richard Joseph⟩ (2) : ANNOUNCE ⟨the opening measures of the first movement where the horns ~ the first theme —Winthrop Sargeant⟩ **3** *obs* : to live in pomp or luxury — used with *it* ⟨began to ~ it . . . as high as ever before —Thomas Fuller⟩ **syn** see RELATE

-state \,=\ *n comb form* -s [Gk *statos* standing, fixed, fr. the stem of *histanai* to cause to stand — more at STAND] : substance produced through a (specified) process ⟨ana*state*⟩ ⟨cata*state*⟩

stateable *var of* STATABLE

state account system *n* : PUBLIC ACCOUNT SYSTEM

state aid *n* : public monies appropriated by a state government for the partial support or improvement of some public local institution (as a library, hospital, or educational institution)

state attorney *or* **state's attorney** *n, usu cap S* : a legal officer appointed to represent a state in the courts : PROSECUTING ATTORNEY, DISTRICT ATTORNEY

state bank *n* **1** : a bank owned, controlled, or operated by a government **2** *usu cap S* : a bank chartered by and operating under the laws of a state of the U.S. — compare NATIONAL BANK 1

state bird *n, usu cap S* : a bird selected (as by the legislature) as an emblem of one of the states of the U.S. ⟨the cardinal is the State bird of North Carolina⟩

state capitalism *n* : a system of capitalism in which capital is largely controlled or owned by the state

state church *n, often cap S&C* : ESTABLISHED CHURCH

state college *n* : a college that is financially supported by a state government, often specializes in a branch of technical or professional education, and often forms part of the state university

statecraft \'=,=\ *n* **1** : the art of conducting state affairs : state management : STATESMANSHIP ⟨one of the greatest problems of ~ now facing our nation —R.K.Carr⟩ — distinguished from *folkcraft* **2** *archaic* : wiliness or chicanery in political dealings ⟨a double treason . . . thought a masterpiece of ~ —T.B. Macaulay⟩

state crown *n, often cap S&C* : IMPERIAL STATE CROWN

stated *adj* [fr. past part. of 2*state*] **1** : set or fixed (as by rule or custom) : ESTABLISHED, REGULAR ⟨the president shall, at ~ times, receive . . . a compensation —*U.S.Constitution*⟩ ⟨~ meetings are held on the first Thursday of every month⟩ **2 a** *obs* : unmistakably known : AVOWED **b** : set down explicitly : DECLARED ⟨allowing certain ~ exceptions⟩ ⟨the ~ value of stock⟩

stated account *n* : ACCOUNT STATED

stated case *n* : CASE STATED

stated clerk *n* : the chief executive officer of an American Presbyterian denomination ranking as the second highest elective officer of the denomination next below the moderator of the General Assembly

stat·ed·ly *adv* : as an established practice : REGULARLY ⟨took a very active part in the academy, visiting the school ~ —H.R. Warfel⟩

stated supply *n* : a clergyman who without formal installation supplies a pulpit for a limited time as a congregation's acting pastor

stated value *n* : the often arbitrary figure rather than the amount received at the time of issuance at which no-par-value stock is carried on the books of a corporation

state flower *n, usu cap S* : a flowering plant selected (as by the legislature or the school children of the state) as the floral emblem of a state of the U.S.

state guard *n* : a military force organized for use within a state in time of war or when the national guard has been called into federal service

state·hood \'stāt,hu̇d\ *n* : the quality, condition, or character of being a state: as **a** : the condition of national independence and sovereignty characterizing a state ⟨modern nationalism has . . . sought full expression in unified and independent ~ — J.S.Roucek⟩ **b** : the condition or status of one of the states of the U.S. ⟨the United States used to administer her territories before they achieved the dignity of ~ —H. W. Van Loon⟩

statehouse \'=,=\ *n* : a building in which governmental affairs (as of a state legislature) are conducted; *specif* : a state capitol ⟨heated discussion of the governor's message in the corridors of the ~⟩

stateism *var of* STATISM

state·less \'stātləs\ *adj* **1** : having no state ⟨looking forward to a ~ society⟩ **2** : having no nationality : owing allegiance to no country ⟨considered himself a citizen of the world, voluntarily ~⟩ **3** : having no citizenship whether from having lost citizenship in a state or from never having acquired effective citizenship in any state ⟨~ persons⟩

state·less·ness *n* -ES : the quality or state of being stateless : the condition of being without citizenship in any country ⟨methods by which ~ may be eliminated —*advt*⟩

state·let \'stātlət\ *n* -s : a small state ⟨the old . . . confederation of Teutonic states and ~*s* —H. W. Van Loon⟩

state·li·ly \'stātləlē, -əli\ *adv* [1*stately* + -*ly*] : in a stately manner : with impressive dignity : DIGNIFIEDLY, FORMALLY ⟨nobody danced more ~ —J.B.Cabell⟩

state·li·ness \-ātlēnəs, -lin-\ *n* -ES : the quality or state of being stately: as **a** : impressiveness in scale or proportion : MAJESTY, GRANDEUR ⟨who can deny to the architecture of nature a certain ~ —W.M.Dixon⟩ **b** (1) : imposing or courtly formality (as in appearance or manner) : ALOOFNESS ⟨his ~ often repelled people⟩ (2) : impressive dignity or loftiness : GRANDNESS ⟨a nobility and ~ of character —Sheldon Cheney⟩ (3) : elevation of style or expression : SUBLIMITY ⟨the ~ of biblical prose⟩

1state·ly \'stātlē, -li\ *adj* -ER/-EST [ME *statly*, fr. *stat* state + -*ly*] **1 a** *obs* : showing consciousness of high birth or rank : HAUGHTY, UNAPPROACHABLE **b** : marked by lofty or imposing dignity : impressively formal : COURTLY, CEREMONIOUS ⟨contrasts of a ~ old order and a somewhat bumptious new — V.L.Parrington⟩ ⟨his wife looks on in ~ aloofness —H.J. Laski⟩ ⟨a ~ pace⟩ ⟨rising in the most ~ manner to open the door —W.M.Thackeray⟩ ⟨the ~ language of old worship — W.L.Sullivan⟩ **2 a** : impressive in size or proportions : MAJESTIC ⟨houses with ~ porticoes —*Amer. Guide Series: Va.*⟩

b : erect and imposing in outline or overall shape ⟨~ old elms⟩ **syn** see GRAND

²stately \"\ *adv* [ME *statly*, fr. *statly*, adj.] **:** in a stately manner: as **a** *obs* **:** in the grand style **:** IMPOSINGLY ⟨men come to build ~ sooner than to garden finely —Francis Bacon⟩ **b :** with a highly dignified or formal carriage or gait **:** CEREMONIOUSLY ⟨a figure . . . with solemn march goes slow and ~ —Shak.⟩

state medicine *n* **:** administration and control by the national government of medical and hospital services provided to the whole population and paid for out of funds raised by taxation — compare SOCIALIZED MEDICINE

state·ment \'stātmənt\ *n* -s [²*state* + *-ment*] **1 :** the act or process of stating, reciting, or presenting orally or on paper ⟨the ~ of a case⟩ ⟨strive . . . for economy of ~ —R.M.Coates⟩ ⟨permits an uninterrupted ~ of the argument —*Brit. Bk. News*⟩ **2 :** something stated: as **a :** a report or narrative (as of facts, events, or opinions) **:** ACCOUNT, RECITAL ⟨take a suspect's ~⟩ **b :** a single declaration or remark **:** ALLEGATION, ASSERTION ⟨his ~s were generally accepted at face value —Edith Diehl⟩ **3 :** PROPOSITION 3a **4 a :** the part of a declaration in a common law action that gives the facts on which the cause of action is based **b :** a formal declaration required by law or made in the course of some official proceeding (as a statement of a witness or of a position of a state in a diplomatic proceeding) **5 a :** a work of art (as in painting, music, or literature) or a part or an aspect of such a work that expresses most clearly and forcefully a theme, basic idea, or intention of the artist ⟨demands that the whole play shall be conceived and composed as ~ —F.R.Leavis⟩ ⟨this was cubism's last influential ~ —Janet Flanner⟩ **b :** the enunciation of a theme in a musical composition ⟨the initial musical ~ and . . . its melodic, rhythmic, and polyphonic deployment —P.H.Lang⟩ **6 :** a financial record or accounting ⟨a ~ of expenses⟩ ⟨a U. S. income tax withholding ~⟩; *specif* **:** a summary of an account showing the balance as of the beginning of, the credits and debts made during, and the balance due as of the end of the accounting period

statement form *or* **statement function** *n* **:** SENTENTIAL FUNCTION

statement of affairs : a statement for a financially embarrassed enterprise showing assets at book and realizable values and claims of creditors classified as preferred, secured, partly secured, and unsecured for the purpose of indicating probable amounts available to creditors in case of liquidation

statement of claim : a plaintiff's first pleading in the English High Court of Justice corresponding to the declaration in common law or the bill in chancery

statement of defense : a defendant's first pleading on an issue of fact in the English High Court of Justice corresponding to the plea in common law and to the answer in equity or under the codes of civil procedure

statemonger \'⸗,⸗⸗\ *n, archaic* **:** a dabbler in political affairs

state of aggregation : one of the three or more fundamental forms, conditions, or states of matter that are commonly considered to include the solid, liquid, and gaseous forms and often others (as the colloidal)

state of war 1 a : a state characterized by the actual existence of open armed hostilities (as between nations) regardless of a formal declaration of war by any party to the conflict **b :** a legal state that comes into being by formal declaration regardless of whether open armed hostilities have taken place, must be officially proclaimed at an end by a similar declaration, and is usu. characterized by such conditions that the rights and duties of belligerents and neutrals to act under the rules of international law applicable to war arise **2 :** the period of time during which a state of war is in effect

state police *n* **:** the police organized and maintained by a state as distinguished from those of a lower subdivision (as a city or county) of the state government

state prison *also* **state's prison** *n* **:** a prison maintained by the state; *esp* **:** the prison or penitentiary for the imprisonment of persons convicted of the more serious crimes (as felonies)

state prisoner *n* **:** POLITICAL PRISONER

sta·ter \'stād·ər, stä'te(ə)r\ *n* -s [ME, fr. LL, fr. Gk *statēr*, a weight, standard coin, fr. the stem of *histanai* to cause to stand, set, place in a balance, weigh — more at STAND] **:** an ancient gold or silver coin of the Greek city-states of any of numerous standards

state religion *n* **:** a religion established by law as the only official religion of a state

stateroom \'⸗,⸗\ *n* **1 :** an apartment of state in a palace or great house **2 a** *usu* **state-room** \"\ *archaic* **:** a commodious room on shipboard usu. for a captain or superior ship's officer **b :** CABIN 2a **3 :** a private room on a railroad car equipped with one or more berths and a toilet

states *pl of* STATE, *pres 3d sing of* STATE

state's attorney *usu cap S, var of* STATE ATTORNEY

state's evidence *n, often cap S* **1 :** one who gives evidence for the prosecution in U.S. state or federal criminal proceedings ⟨turned *state's evidence* against his pals —D.D.Martin⟩ — compare KING'S EVIDENCE **2 :** evidence for the government or prosecution in a criminal proceeding

states general *n pl, often cap S&G* [trans. of D *staten-generaal* & F *états généraux*] **:** a legislative assembly composed of members or representatives of the estates of a nation as distinguished from the states provincial (as the legislative assembly of France before the Revolution or the legislative assembly of the Netherlands from the 15th century to 1796) — compare ESTATE 3b

¹stateside \'⸗,⸗\ *adj, often cap* [(*United*) *States* + *side*] **:** being in, going to, coming from, or characteristic of the U. S. as regarded from outside its continental limits ⟨transferred from Europe to ~ duty⟩ ⟨contrary to ~ custom⟩ ⟨reading a ~ magazine⟩

²stateside \"\ *adv, often cap* **:** in, to, or from the continental U.S. ⟨go ~⟩ ⟨before he could ship ~ —James Jones⟩

state·sid·er \"ə(r)\ *n, usu cap* **:** a native or inhabitant of the continental U.S. as regarded from outside its limits ⟨*Statesiders* employed in government offices on Guam⟩

states·man \'stātsmən\ *n, pl* **statesmen** [*state's* (genitive of ¹*state*) + *man*] **1 a :** one versed in the principles or art of government **:** POLITICIAN; *esp* **:** one actively engaged in conducting the business of a government or in shaping its policies ⟨an assembly of the *statesmen* of many nations⟩ **b :** one who exercises leadership wisely and without narrow partisanship in the general interest ⟨unhappily the republic was subject to men who were mere demagogues and in no sense *statesmen* —T.B.Macaulay⟩ ⟨the ~ differs from the ordinary politician in that he is able to envisage and inspire support for policies that are in the long run, best interests of the most people —J.H. Hallowell⟩ ⟨one of the academic *statesmen* of his era —N.M. Pusey⟩ **2** *dial Eng* **:** a countryman who owns and farms his own land

states·man·like \'⸗⸗,⸗\ *adj* **:** marked by the qualities (as wisdom, breadth of view, or diplomacy) of a statesman **:** befitting a statesman ⟨a man of ~ judgment —Marjory S. Douglas⟩ ⟨a ~ solution of the present perplexities —V.L.Parrington⟩

states·man·ly \-lē,-li\ *adj* **:** STATESMANLIKE

states·man·ship \-,ship\ *n* **1 :** the art or practice of conducting governmental affairs **:** political leadership ⟨those who are fit for the highest duties of ~ such as the final choice of means and ends —G.H.Sabine⟩ ⟨stupid, stubborn ~, without vision or imagination —C.G.Bowers⟩ **2 :** leadership characterized by wisdom, breadth of vision, or regard for the general welfare rather than partisan interest ⟨transforms opportunism into idealism, or politics into ~ —R.B.Perry⟩ ⟨forgot ~ and embraced politics —*N. Y. Herald Tribune Bk. Rev.*⟩ ⟨a task demanding a high level of educational ~ —J.D. Russell & C.H.Judd⟩ ⟨industrial ~⟩ ⟨labor ~⟩

state socialism *n* [trans. of G *staatssozialismus*] **:** socialism that advocates utilizing the power of the state to equalize income and opportunity (as by progressive income and inheritance taxes, by compulsory insurance against old age, unemployment, sickness, and accident, and by state administration of industries, public utilities, common carriers, banking, and housing)

state socialist *n* [trans. of G *staatssozialist*] **:** an advocate of state socialism

state-socialist \'⸗¦⸗(⸗)⸗\ *adj* [*state socialist*] **:** of or relating to state socialism

states' right·er \'stāts'rīd·ə(r), -ītə-\ *n, often cap S&R* [*states' rights* + *-er*] **:** one that advocates strict interpretation of the U. S. constitutional guarantee of states' rights and is opposed to the exercise of federal authority in matters (as education, racial relations, or hours and working conditions) that he regards as the exclusive concern of the individual states

states' rights *n pl, often cap S&R* **:** all rights not vested by the Constitution of the U.S. in the Federal government nor forbidden by it to the separate states

states·wom·an \'stāt,swu̇mən\ *n, pl* **stateswomen** [*state's* (genitive of ¹*state*) + *woman*] **:** a woman who is active in politics or government; *esp* **:** one who holds high public office

state trading *n* **:** international agreements entered into by governments or government agencies for the sale or purchase of commodities

state tree *n, usu cap S* **:** a tree selected (as by the legislature) as an emblem of a state of the U.S.

state trial *n* **1 :** a trial for a political offense (as treason) **2 :** a trial that raises important questions of constitutional or international law

state university *n* **:** a university maintained and administered by one of the states of the U. S. as part of the state public educational system

state use system *n, often cap S* **:** the employment of prison labor in some states of the U. S. in the production of materials exclusively for use in institutions of the state or its subdivisions and not for sale — compare CONVICT LABOR SYSTEM

stateway \'⸗,⸗\ *n* **:** a law or policy of government — contrasted with *folkway*

¹statewide \'⸗¦⸗\ *adj* [¹*state* + *wide* (adj.)] **:** extending throughout a state **:** including all parts of a state ⟨a ~ celebration⟩ ⟨a ~ movement⟩ ⟨~ elective offices⟩

²statewide \"\ *adv* **:** throughout the state ⟨handbills . . . were distributed ~ —*New Republic*⟩

stat·farad \'stat+¦-\ *n* [*stat-* + *farad*] **:** the cgs electrostatic unit of capacitance equal to about 1.113×10^{-12} farads

stat·henry \"+¦-\ *n* [*stat-* + *henry*] **:** the cgs electrostatic unit of inductance equal to about 8.9×10^{11} henries

stath·mo·kinesis \¦stath(,)mō+\ *n* [NL, fr. Gk *stathmos* standing place, post (fr. the stem of *histanai* to stand) + NL *kinesis* — more at STAND] **:** interruption of mitosis (as by colchicine) — compare C-MITOSIS

¹stat·ic \'stad·|ik, -at|, |ēk\ *also* **stat·i·cal** \|əkəl, |ēk-\ *adj* [*static* fr. NL *staticus*, fr. Gk *statikos* causing to stand, skilled at weighing, fr. *statos* (verbal of *histanai* to cause to stand, set, place on a balance, weigh) + *-ikos* -ic; *statical* fr. NL *staticus* + E *-al* — more at STAND] **1 a** *obs* **:** of, relating to, or used in weighing ⟨~ experiments⟩ ⟨~ chair⟩ ⟨~ barometer⟩ **b :** exerting force by reason of weight alone apart from effects of inertia ⟨~ load⟩ **2 :** of or relating to statics **:** of or relating to bodies at rest or forces in equilibrium — compare DYNAMIC **3 a :** showing little change **:** STABLE, STAGNANT ⟨the conception of a ~ universe⟩ ⟨a ~ population⟩ ⟨adjust to the realities of a fairly ~ environment —W.H.Whyte⟩ **b :** rigidly bound by traditional patterns and values **:** UNCHANGING ⟨dynamic modern society contrasted with ~ feudal society⟩ **4 a :** characterized by a lack of movement, animation, or progression ⟨creates ~ characters⟩ ⟨an enormous young woman who is ~ on stage —Roger Dettmer⟩ ⟨the novel is . . . a trifle ~, constructed in episodes —J.H.Jackson⟩ **b :** producing an effect of repose or quiescence ⟨a ~ design⟩ ⟨the Romanesque style is . . . ~ —Nikolaus Pevsner⟩ ⟨perfect fifths . . . sound relatively ~ —Virgil Thomson⟩ **c** *of a verb or verb form* **:** expressing mere existence or state as distinct from action — used esp. in the grammar of American Indian and African languages; compare ACTIVE 3b, NEUTER 1b, STATIVE **5 a :** standing or fixed in one place **:** STATIONARY ⟨a ~ installation⟩ ⟨a ~ dredge⟩ ⟨a ~ antiaircraft gun⟩ **b :** performed in place, on the ground, or in a stationary position ⟨~ firing of a rocket motor⟩ ⟨~ testing of a missile⟩ **c** *of water* **:** stored in a tank and not under pressure for use by pumping in case of fire **6 :** of, relating to, or constituting the labyrinthine sense **7 :** of, relating to, or producing stationary charges of electricity **:** ELECTROSTATIC ⟨~ charges due to friction⟩ ⟨a ~ machine⟩ **8 :** of, relating to, or caused by radio static

²static \"\ *n* -s **1 :** electrical discharges in the atmosphere (as lightning, corona, or electrical storms) **:** ATMOSPHERICS **2 :** atmospheric noise or disturbance resulting from accumulation of electric charges (as from snowflakes, household appliances, or power lines) on or near an antenna and interfering with radio reception

stat·i·cal·ly \|ək(ə)lē, |ēk-, -li\ *adv* **1 :** with static electricity ⟨a wire charged ~⟩ **2 :** in a static manner **:** in stable or unchanging terms ⟨dealt with the problem ~ rather than dynamically⟩ ⟨conceives of life ~⟩

static balancer *n* **:** BALANCER SET 2

stat·i·ce \'stad·ə(,)sē\ *n* [NL, fr. L, a plant of the genus *Armeria* (prob. thrift) that has astringent qualities, fr. Gk *statikē*, fr. fem. of *statikos* causing to stand, astringent — more at STATIC] **1** *cap, in former classifications* **:** a genus of low-growing usu. coastal herbs equivalent to the genera *Armeria* and *Limonium* of modern classification or sometimes synonymous with one or the other of these genera **2 -s :** a plant of *Armeria* or the related genus *Limonium* **:** SEA LAVENDER, THRIFT

static electricity *n* **:** electricity in motionless charges (as on the terminals of an open-circuit battery or on hard rubber after it has been rubbed with cat's fur) or considered without reference to motion

static equilibrium *n* **:** equilibrium of a system whose parts are relatively at rest (as a steel truss resting on piers)

static field *n* **:** ELECTRIC FIELD

static friction *n* **:** the force between two bodies in contact that resists the initiation of sliding motion of one over the other **:** the force required to cause one of the bodies to begin to move when they are at rest — called also *starting friction*

static head *n* **:** the height of a column of water at rest that would produce a given pressure **:** HEAD 14b

static jet thrust *n* **:** the thrust developed by a jet-propulsion engine at rest with respect to the surrounding air

static line *n* **:** a cord or flexible cable attached at one end to a parachute pack and fitted at the other end with means for attachment to some part of an airplane to effect automatic opening of the parachute after the jumper clears the plane without the use of the manual rip cord

static marks *n pl* **:** markings produced by the light from an electrostatic discharge on a light-sensitive material and made visible by development

static metamorphism *n* **:** metamorphism in rock produced by pressure apart from any movement of the rock masses

static oceanography *n* **:** a branch of oceanography dealing with the physical and chemical properties of the ocean waters and the topography and composition of the ocean bottom

static pressure *n* **:** the force per unit area that is exerted by a fluid upon a surface at rest relative to the fluid

static propeller thrust *n* **:** the thrust developed by a propeller when rotating without translation in air that is still except for the effect of the propeller

static refraction *n* **:** the reciprocal of the far point distance of the eye — compare DYNAMIC REFRACTION

stat·ics \'stad·|iks, -at|, |ēks\ *n pl but usu sing in constr* [earlier *static* (fr. NL *statica*, fr. Gk *statikē* art of weighing, fr. fem. of *statikos* skilled in weighing) + *-s* — more at STATIC] **1 :** a branch of mechanics dealing with the relations of forces that produce equilibrium among material bodies — compare DYNAMICS **2 :** SOCIAL STATICS **3 :** the study of an economy that is active but unchanging in its fundamental relationships emphasizing rates of output rather than changes in these rates and dealing with single change and the timeless adjustment of the economy to this change rather than continuous changes and their time sequence

static sensation *n* **:** a sensation of the labyrinthine sense

static stability *n* **:** the degree of stable equilibrium of a body (as a suspended body, a floating ship, or an airplane in flight) capable of rotating out of its equilibrium position measured by the torque necessary to produce a given deflection

static theory *n* **:** STATICS 3

static thrust *n* **:** the thrust developed by an airplane engine that is at rest with respect to the earth and the surrounding air

static tube *n* **:** a usu. closed tube that is used for indicating static as distinct from impact pressure in a stream of fluid (as air), has perforations in its sides, is placed parallel to direction of flow, and has a conical forward end fitted with a branch tube so as to provide for a connection with a manometer

stating *pres part of* STATE

¹sta·tion \'stāshən\ *n* -s *often attrib* [ME *stacioun*, fr. MF *station, estation*, fr. L *station-, statio*, fr. *status* (past part. of *stare* to stand) + *-ion-, -io* -ion — more at STAND] **1 a** *archaic* **:** a state of standing still or of being at rest **:** STILLNESS ⟨her motion and her ~ are as one —Shak.⟩ **b** *archaic* **:** STATIONARY POINT ⟨the planets in their ~s list'ning stood —John Milton⟩ **c** (1) **:** a stop or sojourn at one place **:** HALT ⟨having enjoyed my first ~ here . . . I again commenced my march —John Coulter⟩ (2) **:** tour of duty ⟨left after a short ~ there⟩ **2 :** the place or position in which something or someone stands or is assigned to stand or remain: as **a :** a post of duty ⟨a sentinel's ~⟩ ⟨waiters at their ~s in the dining room⟩ ⟨battle ~s on a ship⟩ **b :** the spot at which an instrument is planted or observations are made in surveying **c** (1) **:** one of the places on a machine tool where the work is subjected to a single operation (2) **:** a position on a conveyor system where materials are loaded or discharged **d :** an enlargement in a mining shaft or gallery used as a landing or passing place or for the accommodation of equipment (as a pump or tank) **e** (1) **:** a position of a ship in a formation or convoy (2) **:** the assigned position of each airplane relative to that of the flight leader in formation flying ⟨hold ~ on the leader⟩ **f** (1) **:** one of the 10 or more divisions on a ship's lines between forward and after perpendicular at which calculations (as of displacement) are made in shipbuilding (2) **:** one of the specified points along the keel or base line marking the places for the ship's frames **3 a :** the act or manner of standing **:** POSTURE ⟨maintain a firm ~⟩ ⟨~ was unsteady with the eyes open or closed —*Diseases of the Nervous System*⟩ **b :** the height and carriage of a gamecock **c :** any of the eight places from which a skeet shooter fires **4 :** a stopping place: as **a** (1) **:** a stopping place in a transportation route (as for taking on passengers or handling freight) (2) **:** the building or buildings connected with such a stopping place **:** DEPOT 3a, 3b (3) **:** an Air Force depot without flying facilities **b :** a place where a missionary stops as regularly as possible to conduct religious services and minister to the needs of the people **c :** one of the stations of the cross **d :** a Christian service held at one of a number of churches on a stated day (as every day in Lent, the ember days, and solemn feasts) **e** *Irish* **:** a priest's stay with a parishioner to confess the neighbors ⟨the night of a ~, when the priest was praising the place she had —Padraic Fallon⟩ **5 :** a sphere of life, duty, or occupation: as **a :** an army post ⟨spent five years at his first ~⟩ **b :** an area of residence (as formerly in India) for British military or civil officers in a district **c :** a place or region to which a government ship or fleet is assigned for duty **d :** a pioneer settlement **:** OUTPOST ⟨tribes were constantly interrupting stage service, attacking ~s —G.R.Stewart⟩ **e** *Austral* **:** RANCH **f :** MISSION STATION **g :** a single church of the Methodist denomination that is a pastor's sole charge as distinguished from a circuit of churches served by one clergyman **6 a :** social standing **:** RANK, POSITION ⟨married above his ~⟩ ⟨a woman of high ~⟩ ⟨the duties of the ~ in which we find ourselves —M.R.Cohen⟩ **b :** the ordinal position in which a number is drawn in lotteries and numbers games **7 a :** a region or situation where a particular kind of plant or animal lives **:** the most characteristic portion of its range **:** HABITAT, BIOTOPE **b :** the exact spot at which a given species or specimen is found or collected **8 a :** a place established and equipped for specialized observation and study of scientific phenomena ⟨a geologic ~⟩ ⟨a seismological ~⟩ ⟨an agricultural experiment ~⟩ **b :** an institution for studying living organisms in their natural surroundings ⟨a marine biological ~⟩ **c :** a place or location for ascertaining or tabulating tidal and current data **9 :** a place established to provide a public service: as **a :** FIRE STATION **b :** POLICE STATION **c :** a post office subsidiary to the headquarters post office of an area **:** a branch post office — see CLASSIFIED STATION, CONTRACT STATION **d** (1) **:** a complete assemblage of radio or television equipment including antenna, transmitting or receiving set, and signal making or reproducing device (2) **:** the place (as a room) in which a radio or television transmitting or receiving station is located **e :** a usu. outdoor place where merchandise is sold **:** STAND **10 :** STATION DAY

²station \"\ *vt* -ED/-ING/-S **:** to assign to or set in a station or position **:** POST ⟨~s his troops on a hill⟩ ⟨~*ed* himself at the only exit⟩ ⟨~*ed* a lady usher to watch a certain drama critic —Gilbert Millstein⟩

station agent *n* **:** a person on duty at a railroad station or depot whose responsibilities vary according to the size of the station — compare STATIONMASTER

sta·tion·al \-shənᵊl,-shnəl\ *adj* **:** of or relating to an ecclesiastical station ⟨a ~ indulgence⟩ ⟨a ~ cross⟩ ⟨a ~ mass⟩

sta·tion·ar·i·ly \¦stāshə¦nerəlē, -li\ *adv* **:** in a stationary manner **:** MOTIONLESSLY ⟨hung ~⟩

sta·tion·ar·i·ness \-rēnəs, -rin-\ *n* -ES **:** the quality or state of being stationary: as **a :** FIXEDNESS, IMMOBILITY ⟨the ~ of the regiment⟩ **b :** STAGNATION ⟨the ~ of an industry⟩

sta·tion·ary \'stāshə,nerē, -ri\ *adj* [ME *stacionarye*, fr. MF & L; MF *stationnaire*, fr. L *stationarius*, fr. *station-, statio* station + *-arius* -ary — more at STATION] **1 a :** fixed in a station, course, or mode **:** standing still **:** IMMOBILE ⟨the shadow remained ~ —Jack London⟩ ⟨a ~ engine⟩ ⟨~ machinery⟩ **b :** not portable ⟨a ~ gun⟩ **c :** having no moving parts ⟨a ~ transformer⟩ **2 :** unchanging in condition **:** STABLE, STATIC ⟨the patient . . . remained relatively ~ —J.D.Teicher⟩ ⟨a ~ population⟩ ⟨a ~ period in philosophy⟩ ⟨no form of living speech can be ~ even though a standard be fixed —George Sampson⟩ **3** *archaic* **:** of or relating to a military post or garrison ⟨the ~ troops retired —Edward Gibbon⟩

stationary air *n* **:** the air that under ordinary circumstances does not leave the lungs in respiration

stationary engine *n* **:** a steam engine permanently placed; *specif* **:** a factory engine

stationary engineer *n* **:** one who operates stationary engines and related equipment

stationary engineering *n* **:** a branch of engineering concerned with the operation of stationary engines and related equipment

stationary flow *n* **:** STEADY FLOW

stationary front *n* **:** the boundary between two air masses neither of which is replacing the other — see FRONT illustration

stationary line *n* **:** INTERSTELLAR LINE

stationary point *n* **:** the point in a planet's apparent path among the stars where for a brief time it seems to be motionless because it is changing from direct to retrograde motion or vice versa

stationary state *n* **1 :** a stable or metastable quantum state **2 :** a condition taken as an operational concept in economic analysis in which economic processes merely reproduce themselves with no changes

stationary wave *n* **1** *or* **stationary vibration :** STANDING WAVE **2 :** a wave in which the water oscillates vertically without progressing

station bill *n* **:** a list of the crew and their duties in case of fire and other emergencies that is posted in the crew's quarters or another conspicuous place on a ship — compare QUARTER BILL

station break *n* **1 :** a pause in a radio or television program or between programs for announcement of the identity of the network or local station **2 :** an announcement or plug given during a station break

station day *n* **:** the fast of Wednesday and Friday in the early Christian church and in the Eastern Orthodox Church

stationed *past of* STATION

sta·tio·ner \'stāsh(ə)nə(r)\ *n* -s [ME *stacioner*, fr. ML *stationarius*, fr. *station-, statio* shop (fr. L, station) + L *-arius* -er — more at STATION] **1** *archaic* **:** a person engaged in the book trade: as **a :** BOOKSELLER **b :** PUBLISHER **2 :** one that sells stationery

station error *n* **:** the difference between the geodetic and the astronomical latitude or longitude of a place caused by a local deviation in the direction of gravity

sta·tio·nery \-shə,nerē, -ri *sometimes* -sh(ə)nər-\ *n* -ES *often attrib* [*stationer* + *-y*] **1 :** materials (as paper, pens, pencils, ink, blankbooks, ledgers, and cards) for writing or typing **2 :** letter paper usu. accompanied with matching envelopes : writing paper ⟨hotel ~⟩ ⟨write him on the company's ~⟩
station hospital *n* : a military hospital usu. located in a communications zone that gives treatment to troops stationed in its immediate area
station house *n* : a house at a post or station: as **a :** POLICE STATION **b :** FIRE STATION **c :** a usu. rural railroad station
stationing *pres part of* STATION
sta·tion·man \'stāshən,man, -,mən\ *n, pl* **stationmen :** one whose work is done from a particular place or station: as **a :** a bottomer in a mine **b :** one that loads and unloads fuel trucks or tank cars **c :** one that operates the controls at a steel rolling mill
stationmaster \'==,==\ *n* : an official in charge of the operation of a railroad station
station point *n* **:** the position of an observer that determines the perspective rendering of the objects or scene being represented in a drawing — compare LINEAR PERSPECTIVE
station pointer *n* **:** an instrument that has three arms of which the two outer are adjustable and the inner is fixed at the zero of a circle and that is used for locating on a chart the position of a place from which the angles subtended by three distant objects whose positions are known have been observed — see THREE-POINT PROBLEM
station pole *or* **station rod** *or* **station staff** *n* **1 :** a rod for marking stations in surveying **2 :** RANGE POLE **3 :** LEVELING ROD
stations *pl of* STATION, *pres 3d sing of* STATION
station selector *n* **:** the element of a radio receiving set that tunes in the signal from any station
stations of the cross *often cap S&C* **1 :** a series of 14 (as in the Roman Catholic and Anglican Churches) or more (as in the Eastern Orthodox Church) images or pictures that symbolize scenes of suffering in the successive stages of Christ's passion and are usu. located in a church or on the road to a church or shrine **2 :** a devotional exercise of a church in which a worshiper pauses before each of the stations of the cross, meditates, and recites appropriate prayers
station track *n* **:** a track at a railroad station on which trains are spotted to receive or discharge passengers and baggage as distinguished from a through track for the passage of trains — called also *house track*
station-type machine tool *n* **:** a machine tool having stations at which various operations are performed on the work
station wagon *n* **:** an automobile that resembles a sedan but has no separate luggage compartment and has a top less rounded in back, a tailgate, and one or more rear seats readily lifted out or folded to facilitate light trucking — called also *beach wagon*
statis *abbr* statistical
stat·i·scope *n* [by alter.] **:** STATOSCOPE
stat·ism *or* **state·ism** \'stād,izəm, -ā,ti-\ *n* -S [[1]*state* + *-ism*; trans. of F *étatisme*] **:** concentration of all economic controls and planning in the hands of a highly centralized government ⟨abandoned her former reliance on ~ in favor of private enterprise —*World*⟩ — compare GOVERNMENTALISM 1
[1]**stat·ist** \-ād·əst, -ātə-\ *n* -S [[1]*state* + *-ist*] **1** *archaic* **:** one versed in state affairs **:** POLITICIAN ⟨hold it, as our ~s do, a baseness to write fair —Shak.⟩ **2** [trans. of F *étatiste*] **:** an advocate of statism ⟨our planners and ~s —Raymond Moley⟩
[2]**statist** \"\ *adj* **:** of, relating to, or advocating statism ⟨a ~ conception⟩ ⟨the partisans of the ~ formula —Gordon Wright⟩ ⟨matter-of-fact acceptance of a ~ and collectivist ideology —Henry Hazlitt⟩
[3]**stat·ist** \'stad·əst, -atə-\ *n* -S [G, back-formation fr. *statistik* statistics — more at STATISTICS] **:** one who collects statistics **:** STATISTICIAN
sta·tis·ti·cal \stə'tistəkəl, -istēk-\ *adj* [*statistics* + *-al*] **:** of, relating to, or dealing with statistics ⟨~ method⟩ ⟨a ~ tabulation⟩ ⟨a ~ study⟩ — **sta·tis·ti·cal·ly** \-istək(ə)lē, -tēk-\ *adv*
statistical engineering *n* **:** the application of statistical inference to engineering experiments
statistical graph *n* **:** a statistical frequency curve
statistical inference *n* **:** the making of estimates concerning a population from information gathered from samples
statistical mechanics *n pl but usu sing in constr* **:** a branch of physics dealing with the application of the principles of statistics to the mechanics of a system consisting of a large number of parts having motions that differ by small steps over a large range
statistical variable *n* **:** a variable having discrete values that differ through random causes and when arranged in order form a statistical distribution or array
stat·is·ti·cian \,stad·ə'stishən, -atə-\ *n* -S [*statistics* + *-ian*] **:** one versed in or engaged in compiling statistics
sta·tis·ti·cism \stə'tistə,sizəm\ *n* -S [*statistics* + *-ism*] **:** proneness to use statistics
sta·tis·tics \stə'tist|iks, |ēks\ *n pl but sing or pl in constr* [G *statistik* (fr. NL *statisticus*, adj., of state affairs, statistical, fr. L *status* state + *-isticus* -istic) + E *-s* — more at STATE] **1 :** a science dealing with the collection, analysis, interpretation, and presentation of masses of numerical data ⟨~ is a branch of mathematics⟩ **2 :** a collection of quantitative data ⟨~ are available on car ownership⟩ **3 statistic** *n sing* [back-formation fr. *statistics*] **a :** a single term or datum in a collection of statistics **b :** a quantity (as the mean of a sample) computed from a statistical sample as an estimate of a population parameter
stat·i·tron \'stad·ə,trän\ *n* -S [electro*static* + *-tron*] **:** ELECTROSTATIC GENERATOR
sta·tive \'stād·iv\ *adj* [NL *stativus*, fr. L *status* (past part. of *stare* to stand) + *-ivus* -ive — more at STAND] **:** expressing existence or state — compare ACTIVE 3b
stato- *comb form* [ISV, fr. Gk *statos*, verbal of *histanai* to cause to stand, set, place on a balance, weigh — more at STAND] **1 :** resting ⟨*stato*blast⟩ ⟨*stato*spore⟩ **2 :** balance **:** equilibrium ⟨*stato*receptor⟩ ⟨*stato*scope⟩
stat·o·blast \'stad·ə,blast\ *n* [ISV *stato-* + *-blast*] **1 :** a bud or germ in many freshwater bryozoans that is enclosed in a chitinous envelope in the parent body, generally serves to preserve the species in winter, and bursts and develops into a new individual in spring **2 :** an internal bud in some sponges that is somewhat analogous to the statoblast of a bryozoan **:** GEMMULE
stato·cyst \-,sist\ *n* [ISV *stato-* + *cyst*] **1 :** a cellular cyst containing one or more statoliths **2 :** an organ of equilibration and orientation that consists of a fluid-filled chamber containing a statolith and is widely distributed among invertebrate animals — compare LABYRINTHINE SENSE, OTOCYST
stat·ohm \'stad·+,-\ *n* [*stat-* + *ohm*] **:** the cgs electrostatic unit of resistance equal to about 8.9×10^{11} ohms
stato·kinetic \¦stad·ō+\ *adj* [*stato-* + *kinetic*] **:** of, relating to, or constituting a kinetic postural reflex that is initiated by stimulation of the semicircular canals through movements of the head and involves compensatory movements of the limbs and eyes — compare STATOTONIC
stat·ol·a·try \stād·'äl·ə·trē\ *n* -ES [[1]*state* + *-o-* + *-latry*] **:** worship of the state **:** advocacy of a highly centralized and all-powerful national government
stat·o·lith \'stad·ᵊl,ith\ *n* -S [ISV *stato-* + *-lith*] **1 a :** the calcareous body in a statocyst **b :** a similar body in the lagena of a fish or amphibian **2 :** any of various starch grains or other solid bodies in the cytoplasm that are thought responsible by their changes in position for changes in orientation of an organ or part — **stat·o·lith·ic** \¦==¦lithik\ *adj*
stator \'stād·ə(r), -tad-\ *n* -S [NL, fr. L, one that stands, fr. *status* + *-or*] **:** a stationary part in a machine in or about which a rotor revolves: as **a** (1) **:** the stationary member of an electrical machine (as an induction motor) (2) **:** the stationary plates of a variable capacitor **b** (1) **:** the case enclosing a turbine wheel (2) **:** the body of stationary blades or nozzles of a turbine — compare ROTOR 1b
stato·receptor \¦stad·ō+\ *n* [*stato-* + *receptor*] **:** a sense organ for the reception of stimuli governing equilibration and orientation in space

stato·scope \'stad·ə,skōp\ *n* [ISV *stato-* + *-scope*] **1 :** a sensitive aneroid barometer for recording small changes in atmospheric pressure **2 :** an instrument for indicating small changes in the altitude of an airplane
stato·spore \-,spō(ə)r\ *n* [*stato-* + *spore*] **:** RESTING SPORE; *esp* **:** a thick-walled resistant spore formed within the frustules of various chiefly marine centric diatoms
stato·tonic \¦stad·ə+\ *adj* [*stato-* + *tonic*] **:** of, relating to, or constituting a tonic postural reflex that is initiated by stimulation of the utricle of the labyrinth through position of the head or movements of the neck muscles and involves alteration of skeletal muscle tone — compare STATOKINETIC
-stats *pl of* -STAT
statua *n* -S [ME, fr. L — more at STATUE] *obs* **:** STATUE ⟨here I will set up her ~ —Christopher Marlowe⟩
stat·u·a·rist \'stachəwərəst\ *n* -S [*statuary* + *-ist*] *archaic* **:** STATUARY 2
[1]**stat·u·ary** \'stachə,werē\ *n* -ES [in sense 1, fr. L *statuaria*, fr. fem. of *statuarius* of a statue; in sense 2, fr. L *statuarius*, fr. *statuarius*, adj.] **1 a :** a branch of sculpture treating of figures in the round ⟨critics of painting and ~ —E.J.Banfield⟩ **b :** STATUES ⟨a group of ~, faintly seen —Matthew Arnold⟩ **2 :** one who practices the art of making statues **:** SCULPTOR ⟨a ~ might have modeled from it —Laurence Sterne⟩
[2]**statuary** \"\ *adj* [L *statuarius*, fr. *statua* statue + *-arius* -ary] **1 :** of or relating to statues ⟨the ~ art⟩ **2 :** consisting of or suitable for statues ⟨a ~ monument⟩ ⟨~ marble⟩
statuary bronze *n* **:** bronze whose surface has been treated with acid to produce the dark brown color frequently given to bronze statues
statuary marble *n* **:** marble of the purest white and of finely crystalline form used in architecture and sculpture
[1]**stat·ue** \'sta(,)chü, -,chə, -,chü, +V *often* -chəw\ *n* -S [ME, fr. MF, fr. L *statua*, fr. *statuere* to set up — more at STATUTE] **1 :** a likeness (as of a person or animal) sculptured, modeled, or cast in a solid substance (as marble, bronze, or wax) **:** IMAGE ⟨a bronze equestrian ~⟩ **2 statues** *pl but sing in constr* **:** a game in which the players dance or whirl around or are taken by the hand in turn and twirled about, freeze in whatever positions they find themselves in when a signal is given or the twirler lets go, and are judged on their poses
[2]**statue** \"\ *vt* **statued; statued; statueing** *or* **statuing; statues 1 :** to adorn (as a walk or park) with statues ⟨a *statued* garden⟩ **2** *archaic* **:** to form a statue of **:** represent in statuary ⟨Herodotus sitteth *statued* —Robert Bridges †1930⟩

statue 1

statue of liberty *usu cap S&L* [fr. the *Statue of Liberty* on Liberty Island in New York harbor; fr. the comparison of the upraised passing arm of the passer to the torch-bearing arm of the statue] **:** an offensive football play in which a back raises an arm as if to throw a pass and the ball is taken from his hand by a teammate who runs behind him
stat·u·esque \¦stachə¦wesk\ *adj* [[1]*statue* + *-esque*] **:** resembling a statue: as **a** (1) **:** having a massive dignity or impressiveness **:** MAJESTIC ⟨a fine, ~ giant —Walter Lippmann⟩ (2) **:** strikingly well-proportioned **:** TALL, SHAPELY ⟨a ~ model⟩ ⟨she measures a ~ 5 feet 8 —Roger Dettmer⟩ **b** (1) **:** immobile or rigid in stance or posture ⟨~ great white heron —J.H.Baker⟩ ⟨~ soldiers⟩ (2) **:** coldly formal **:** INFLEXIBLE ⟨~ piety —W.M.Thackeray⟩ **c :** marked by classic harmony of form but little color, warmth, or feeling **:** MARMOREAL ⟨a composed, ~ little novel —*New Yorker*⟩ — **stat·u·esque·ly** *adv* — **stat·u·esque·ness** *n* -ES
stat·u·ette \¦stachə¦wet, *usu* -ed·+V\ *n* -S [F, dim. of *statue*] **:** a small statue usu. much smaller than life-size — compare FIGURINE
statu-quo-ite \,stā|(,)tü'kwō,īt, ,sta|, |(,)chü-\ *n* -S [(*in*) *statu quo* + *-ite*] **:** an upholder of the existing state of affairs ⟨a perfectibilian and a *statu-quo-ite* were among the guests at this hall —*Times Lit. Supp.*⟩
stat·ure \'stachə(r)\ *n* -S [ME, fr. OF *stature, estature*, fr. L *statura*, fr. *status* (past part. of *stare* to stand) + *-ura* -ure — more at STAND] **1 :** natural height (as of a person or animal) in an upright position **:** standing posture ⟨a man of tall ~⟩ ⟨the fine ~ of the Indian males —*Amer. Guide Series: Oregon*⟩ **2 :** quality or status gained by impressive growth, development, or achievement **:** high caliber **:** PRESTIGE ⟨a playwright of ~ —Henry Hewes⟩ ⟨every piece of work you do adds something to your ~, increases the power and maturity of your experience —Thomas Wolfe⟩ ⟨continues to advance in ~ as a senior institution of learning —N.M.Pusey⟩ **syn** see QUALITY
stat·ured \¦stachə(r)d\ *adj* **:** having a specified stature — usu. used in combination ⟨short-*statured*⟩ ⟨fair-*statured* as the lily and palm —Robert Southey⟩
sta·tus \'stā|d·əs, 'sta|, |təs *sometimes* 'stä| *or* 'stă|\ *n* -ES *often attrib* [L — more at STATE] **1 a :** the condition (as arising out of age, sex, mental incapacity, crime, alienage, or public station) of a person that determines the nature of his legal personality, his legal capacities, and the nature of the legal relations to the state or to other persons into which he may enter **b :** the condition of a political entity (as a state) determining its legal character in relationships with other political entities **2 a :** position or rank in relation to others (as in a social order, community, class, or profession) ⟨the ~ of a father⟩ ⟨the ~ of a doctor⟩ ⟨reduced to the ~ of a guerrilla leader —Woodrow Wyatt⟩ ⟨the city's ~ as a tourist attraction —Winthrop Sargeant⟩ — compare ROLE **b :** relative rank in a hierarchy of prestige ⟨the ~ of a corporation executive in the U.S.⟩ ⟨a rigid ~ system evolved during feudalism⟩ **c :** superior rank **:** high prestige **:** RECOGNITION ⟨academic ~ —Annabel Gray⟩ ⟨her connections gave her ~ in the group⟩ ⟨~ symbol⟩ ⟨~ anxiety⟩ ⟨the ~ seekers ... continually straining to surround themselves with visible evidence of the superior rank they are claiming —Vance Packard⟩ **3 :** state of affairs **:** SITUATION ⟨the ~ of the negotiations between company and union officials⟩ ⟨the inventory ~⟩ **4 :** an abnormal condition of a person or animal **syn** see STATE
status asth·mat·i·cus \-az'mad·əkəs\ *n* [NL, lit., asthmatic state] **:** an attack of asthma of long duration characterized by dyspnea, cyanosis, exhaustion, and sometimes collapse
status ep·i·lep·ti·cus \-,epə'leptəkəs\ *n* [NL, lit., epileptic state] **:** a state in epilepsy in which the attacks occur in rapid succession without recovery of consciousness
status lym·phat·i·cus \-(,)lim'fad·əkəs\ *n* [NL, lit., lymphatic state] **:** a constitutional condition of the body marked by hyperplasia of the lymphatic tissue — called also *lymphatism*
status quo \¦=='kwō\ *n* [L, state in which] **:** the state in which something is **:** the existing state of affairs (as in political or social relationships) at the time in question ⟨seeks to preserve the economic *status quo*⟩ ⟨has a vested interest in the *status quo*⟩
status thy·mi·co·lym·phat·i·cus \-¦thīmə(,)kō(,)lim'fad·əkəs\ *n* [NL, lit., thymicolymphatic state] **:** a condition resembling status lymphaticus with conspicuous enlargement of the thymus
stat·ut·able \'stachəd·əbəl, -chətəb-\ *adj* [[1]*statute* + *-able*] **:** made, introduced, regulated, or imposed by or in conformity to statute **:** STATUTORY, STANDARD ⟨~ provision⟩ ⟨~ age⟩ ⟨~ tonnage⟩
stat·ut·able·ness *n* -ES **:** the quality or state of being statutable
stat·ut·ably \-blē, -bli\ *adv* **:** in a statutable manner **:** conformably to the statutes
[1]**stat·ute** \'sta(,)chü|t *also* -,chə| *sometimes* -,chü| ; *usu* |d·+V\ *n* -S [ME *statut, statute*, fr. OF *statut, estatut, estatu*, fr. LL *statutum*, fr. L, neut. of *statutus*, past part. of *statuere* to stand up, set up, station, fr. *status* position, condition, state — more at STATUS] **1 :** something laid down or declared as fixed or established: as **a :** the edict of a ruler ⟨my acts, decrees, and ~s I deny —Shak.⟩ **b :** a law enacted by or by the authority of the supreme legislative branch of a government and esp. of a representative government **:** the written will of a legislature expressed with all the requisite forms of legislation as distinguished from the common or unwritten law — compare ACT, BILL, COMMON LAW, CONSTITUTION, DECREE, EDICT, ORDINANCE **c :** an act of a corporation or of its founder intended as a permanent rule or law ⟨the ~s of a university⟩ **d :** an international instrument setting up an agency and regulating its scope or authority ⟨the ~ of the Permanent Court of International Justice⟩ **2** *obs* **a :** STATUTE MERCHANT **b :** STATUTE STAPLE **3 :** STATUTE FAIR **4** [ME, influenced in meaning by *statue*] **:** STATUE
[2]**statute** \"\ *vt* -ED/-ING/-S [ME *statuten*, fr. *statut, statute*, n.] **:** to establish (a law) by statute **:** DECREE
[3]**statute** \"\ *adj* [[1]*statute*] **:** fixed by statute **:** STATUTORY ⟨a ~ mile⟩ ⟨a ~ ton⟩
statute-barred \¦=(,)=¦=\ *adj* **:** barred by the statute of limitations
statute book *n* **1 :** an official, semiofficial, or recognized private collection of the statutes of a state or nation as a whole ⟨put a law on the *statute book*⟩ **2 :** the whole body of legislation of a given jurisdiction whether or not published as a whole
statute fair *or* **statutes fair** *n* **:** an annual fair formerly held in English towns and villages for the hiring of servants and farm laborers
statute merchant *n* [ME *statut marchand*, fr. AF *estatu marchaund*, lit., merchant statute] **:** a bond of record formerly in use in England giving the creditor power to seize the property of the debtor for failure to pay at a designated time
statute mile *n* **:** MILE 1a
statute of descent : a statute regulating the descent from ancestor to heir of real and sometimes other property — compare DESCENT 3c
statute of distribution : a statute regulating the distribution of the personal property or estate of a deceased person
statute of frauds : a statute designed to prevent fraudulent practices by requiring that various contracts and causes of action be evidenced by a writing signed by the party to be charged and varying in application to specific contracts according to British and U. S. state laws
statute of limitations *or* **statute of repose :** a statute assigning a certain time after which rights cannot be enforced by legal action — compare LACHES
statute roll *n* **:** a roll containing the engrossed text of a statute
statutes at large : statutes set forth in full in chronological order as enacted as distinguished from abridgments, revisions, codifications, or compilations; *specif* **:** a published compilation containing all the federal laws and resolutions public and private passed and all executive proclamations issued during a session of a congress
statutes of mortmain 1 : any of various English statutes restricting alienation of land in mortmain (as to an ecclesiastical corporation) for the purpose of preserving to the lords the feudal rights of relief, wardship, marriage, and escheat which conveyance in mortmain took away or of preventing undue accumulation of wealth in the hands of corporations **2 :** any of various statutes having purposes similar to those set forth in the English statutes of mortmain
statute staple *n* [ME, contr. of *statute (of the) staple*] **:** a bond of record formerly in use in England giving the creditor powers similar to those given by the statute merchant and acknowledged before the mayor of a staple
stat·u·to·ri·ly \¦stachə¦tōrəlē, -tōr-, -li\ *adv* **:** in a statutory manner **:** by law ⟨~ created privileges —*New Republic*⟩
stat·u·to·ry \'stachə,tōrē, -tōr-, -ri\ *adj* [[1]*statute* + *-ory*] **1 :** of or relating to statutes ⟨~ matters⟩ **2 :** enacted, imposed, created, or regulated by statute ⟨a ~ age limit⟩ ⟨~ duty⟩ ⟨~ restrictions⟩ ⟨a ~ company⟩ ⟨~ attendance at chapel⟩
statutory bond *n* **:** COURT BOND
statutory civilian *n* **:** CIVILIAN 2
statutory crime *n* **:** STATUTORY OFFENSE
statutory declaration *n* **1** *Eng law* **:** a solemn declaration in lieu of an affidavit by a person conscientiously unable to take an oath **2** *Eng law* **:** a voluntary declaration by any person in an affirmation of documents (as written instruments or proofs of debts)
statutory foreclosure *n* **:** a foreclosure that is instituted by a suit in equity and involves the satisfaction of the debt to the extent made possible by a sale of the mortgaged property — distinguished from *strict foreclosure*
statutory guardian *n* **1 :** a guardian appointed by virtue of statutory authority **2** *Eng law* **:** a guardian appointed by deed or will by the father of minor children or by their surviving mother **:** TESTAMENTARY GUARDIAN
statutory instrument *n, Eng law* **:** a rule, order, or administrative regulation having the force of law promulgated by the crown in council, a minister, a local authority, a corporation or other body under power delegated by Parliament
statutory law *n* **:** the law declared by statute in the broadest sense as distinguished from the common or customary law or the law developed in ecclesiastical, equity, admiralty, or other courts without the aid of statute
statutory lien *n* **:** a lien given by statutory provisions and not otherwise existing
statutory next of kin : a blood relative of a person who in case of his death intestate will be entitled by virtue of a statute of distribution to take his personal estate — compare NEXT OF KIN
statutory offense *n* **:** a crime created by statute; *specif* **:** a criminal sexual offense (as rape or attempted rape)
statutory order *or* **statutory rule** *n, Eng law* **:** an administrative regulation promulgated pursuant to authority delegated by Parliament **:** STATUTORY INSTRUMENT
statutory period *n* **:** the period of time prescribed by a relevant statute of limitations
statutory rape *n* **:** sexual intercourse with a female whether willing or unwilling who is below an age fixed by the applicable statute as the age of consent
statutory referendum *n* **:** the submission of ordinary laws to the electorate after they have been passed by a legislative body
statutory rules *n pl, Scots law* **:** the acts of sederunt and acts of adjournal of the Court of Session and subordinate legislation set forth by orders in council and orders and regulations of government agencies and adopted under authority delegated by Parliament **:** STATUTORY INSTRUMENTS
statutory tenant *n* **:** a tenant whose tenancy has expired under the ordinary rules of law but who has rights by statute to pay rent and continue in occupation under rent control or other emergency legislation
statutory trust *n* **:** a trust created or authorized by statute (as for the care of animals or for the beneficiary of an action for wrongfully causing a person's death or for the social security trust funds)
stat·volt \'stat+,-\ *n* [*stat-* + *volt*] **:** the cgs electrostatic unit of potential difference equal to about 300 volts
staty *abbr* stationary
stau·cher \'stakər\ *Scot var of* STAGGER
stau·ding·er equation \'s(h)taudiŋə(r)-\ *n, usu cap S* [after Hermann *Staudinger* †1965 Ger. chemist] **:** an equation for determining the molecular weight of polymeric materials that utilizes the viscosity of solutions of the polymer at definite concentrations
staum·rel \'stamrəl\ *adj* [Sc *staumer* to stagger, stumble (alter. of [1]*stammer*) + *-el*] *Scot* **:** HALF-WITTED
[1]**staunch** *var of* STANCH
[2]**staunch** *or* **stanch** \'stȯnch, -ä-, -á- *sometimes* -a-, -aa(ə)-, -ai-\ *adj* -ER/-EST [ME, fr. MF *estanche*, fem. of *estanc*, fr. OF, fr. *estancher* to stanch] **1 a :** WATERTIGHT, SOUND ⟨a ~ ship⟩ **b :** strongly built **:** SUBSTANTIAL ⟨~ cabin⟩ **2 :** dependable to find, mark, or follow game ⟨~ hound⟩ ⟨drill his dog ... to make him ~ on point —W.F.Brown b.1903⟩ **3 :** constant and steadfast in loyalty **:** firm in principle **:** STEADY, TRUE ⟨the king's ~*est* followers⟩ ⟨~ defender of free speech⟩ ⟨~ friend⟩ ⟨~ ally⟩ **syn** see FAITHFUL
staunch·ly *or* **stanch·ly** *adv* [*staunch* + *-ly*] **:** in a staunch manner ⟨~ conservative⟩ ⟨a ~ defended principle⟩ ⟨he must hold the point ~ until his handler comes up —W.F.Brown b.1903⟩
staunch·ness *or* **stanch·ness** *n* -ES **:** the quality of being staunch **:** LOYALTY, STEADFASTNESS
stau·ri·on \'stȯrē,än, -ēən\ *n* -S [NL, fr. LGk, small cross, dim. of *stauros* pale, stake, cross — more at STEER] **:** the point of intersection of the median and transverse palatine sutures

stauro- *comb form* [LL, fr. LGk, fr. Gk *stauros* pale, stake, cross] **:** cross ⟨*stauro*medusae⟩ ⟨*stauro*scope⟩

stau·rol·a·try \stȯ'räl·ə·trē\ *n* -ES [LL *staurolatria*, fr. LGk *stauro-* + LL *-latria* -latry] **:** worship of the cross or crucifix ⟨Satan's design in advancing ~ to the destruction of thousands of souls —Increase Mather⟩

stau·ro·lite \'stȯrə,līt\ *n* -S [F, fr. *stauro-* + *-lite*] **:** a mineral $(Fe,Mg)_2Al_9Si_4O_{23}(OH)$ consisting of a brown to black basic iron aluminum silicate in prismatic orthorhombic crystals often twinned so as to resemble a cross and generally found embedded in crystalline schists (hardness 7–7.5, sp. gr. 3.65–3.77) — **stau·ro·lit·ic** \¦==¦lid·ik\ *adj*

staurolite

stau·ro·medusae \¦stȯ(,)rō+\ *n pl, cap* [NL, fr. *stauro-* + *medusae*, pl. of *medusa*] **:** an order of Scyphozoa comprising stalked or sessile jellyfish that have an aboral stalk ending in a sucker by which they attach themselves to marine plants and other objects, that both as larvae and adults are creeping or sessile, and that are limited to colder seas of both northern and southern hemispheres — **stauro·medusan** \"+\ *adj or n*

stau·ro·pe·gion \,stäurȯ'pē,yȯn\ *n, pl* **staurope·gia** \-ē(,)yä)\ [MGk or NGk *staurop\=egion*, fr. MGk, act of fastening a cross on the spot where a church is to be built, fr. LGk *stauro-* + MGk *-pēgion* (fr. *pēgnynai* to stick in, fix, fasten together) — more at PACT] *Eastern Church* **:** a church or monastery exempt from the jurisdiction of the local bishop and directly subject to the highest authority of the territorial church

stau·rop·ter·is \stȯ'räptərə̇s\ *n, cap* [NL, fr. *stauro-* + *-pteris*] **:** a genus of fossil plants frequent in the Carboniferous and known only from fronds which have the pinnae disposed in equal pairs

stau·ro·pus \'stȯrəpəs\ *n, cap* [NL, fr. *stauro-* + *-pus*] **:** a genus of chiefly Palaearctic medium-sized dull-colored moths (family Notodontidae) — see LOBSTER MOTH

stau·ro·scope \'stȯrə,skōp\ *n* [ISV *stauro-* + *-scope*] **:** a modified polariscope used to find the position of planes of light vibration in sections of crystals — **stau·ro·scop·ic** \¦==¦skäpik\ *adj* — **stau·ro·scop·i·cal·ly** \-pə̇k(ə)lē\ *adv*

stau·ro·tide \'stȯrə,tīd\ *n* -S [F, fr. *staurot-* (irreg. fr. Gk *stauros* cross) + *-ide* — more at STEER] **:** STAUROLITE

[1]**stave** \'stāv\ *n* -S [back-formation fr. *staves*, pl. of [1]*staff*] **1 :** a wooden stick **:** CUDGEL, STAFF **2 a :** any of the narrow strips of wood or narrow iron plates placed edge to edge to form the sides, covering, or lining of a vessel or structure — see BARREL illustration **b :** a piece shaped like a stave: as (1) **:** a bearing strip for an arch centering (2) **:** a slat of a hayrack **3 a :** any of the bars of a lantern pinion **b :** a bar or round of a rack or ladder **4 a :** a set of verses (as a stanza) ⟨forms that deviate from the common epic measure, such as the Northern lyrical ~*s* —W.P.Ker⟩ **b :** a letter of an alphabet **5 a :** a staff in music notation **b :** a bar or brief passage of music ⟨the quick, eager ~ of the chaffinch —*Scotsman*⟩ **6 :** BOWSTAVE **7 :** the stem of an acanthus leaf in classic architectural ornament

[2]**stave** \"\ *vb* **staved** \-vd\ *or* **stove** \-tōv\ **staved** *or* **stove; staving; staves** *vt* **1 a :** to break in the staves of (a cask) so that the wine or liquor is lost **b :** to lose or destroy (wine or liquor) by smashing the cask **2 a :** to cause a break in (a boat's hull) **:** smash (a hole) in a boat — often used with *in* ⟨whose deckhouse had been *stove* in by the tremendous seas —Homer Bigart⟩ **b :** to crush in **:** break inward ⟨*staved* in several ribs⟩ **3 :** to furnish with or form into staves **4 :** to thrust with great force ~ *vi* **1 a :** to come apart (as a cask or barrel) **:** break up **b :** to become stove in — used of a boat or ship **2 :** to walk or move rapidly **:** HURRY, RUSH — **stave and tail :** to interpose with the staff in bear baiting and hold back the dog by the tail

stave bolt *n* **:** a section of a log to be cut into staves

staved \'stāvd\ *adj* **:** equipped with or made of staves ⟨the ~ wooden tub —Merle Constiner⟩

stave oak *n* **:** WHITE OAK 1b

stave off *vt* **1 :** to beat off (an animal or person) with or as if with a staff or rod **:** drive or fight off **2 :** to ward or fend off (someone) **:** hold back **:** keep away ⟨let's *stave* the greaser *off* till dark —Zane Grey⟩ ⟨often had to *stave off* creditors —W.A. Swanberg⟩ **3 :** to forestall or prevent (something adverse) esp. at the last moment or in extremity **:** DEFLECT, AVERT ⟨the last form of credit that *staved off* foreclosure —*New Republic*⟩

stave pipe *n* **:** a pipe made of wooden staves

[1]**staver** \'stāvər, -tav-\ *vi* [ME *staveren*] *chiefly Scot* **:** to walk restlessly or unsteadily

[2]**stav·er** \'stāvə(r)\ *n* -S [[2]*stave* + *-er*] **:** a bustling energetic person

staverwort \'==,=\ *n* [[1]*staver* + *wort*] **:** TANSY RAGWORT

staves *pl of* STAFF *or of* STAVE, *pres 3d sing of* STAVE

staves·acre \'stāv,zākə(r)\ *n* [ME *staphisagre, staphisagrie*, fr. L *staphis agria*, fr. Gk, fr. *staphis, astaphis* raisin + *agria*, fem. of *agrios* wild, fr. *agros* field — more at ACRE] **1 :** a Eurasian larkspur (*Delphinium staphisagria*) having racemose purple flowers **2 :** the seeds of the stavesacre that contain delphinine, are violently emetic and cathartic, and are used in Eurasia as a fish poison

stavewood \'=,=\ *n* **1 :** PARADISE TREE 1 **2 a :** either of two Australian trees (*Tarrietia argyrodendron* and *T. actinophylla*) that are sometimes grown as ornamentals and yield hard heavy reddish brown lumber **b :** BUNGI-BUNGI

[1]**stav·ing** \'stāviŋ\ *adj* [fr. pres. part. of [2]*stave*] **:** POWERFUL, EXCELLENT

[2]**staving** \"\ *adv* **:** EXTREMELY

[3]**staving** \"\ *n* -S [[1]*stave* + *-ing*] **:** material for forming staves **:** a quantity of staves **:** a casing of staves

[1]**staw** \'stȯ\ [ME (Sc), alter. of ME *stal*, fr. OE *stæl*] *Scot past of* STEAL

[2]**staw** \"\ *chiefly Scot var of* STALL

[3]**staw** \"\ *n* [[2]*staw*] *chiefly Scot* **:** SURFEIT

[1]**stay** \'stā\ *n* -S [ME *stey, stay*, fr. OE *stæg;* akin to MLG *stach* rope, stay, ON *stag* stay, G dial. (Alemannic) *stagen* to get stiff, OE *stēle, stȳle* steel — more at STEEL] **1 :** a large strong rope usu. of wire used to support a mast by being extended forward from the head of one mast down to some other or to some part of the ship **:** a fore-and-aft stay — compare BACKSTAY; see SHIP illustration **2 a :** a guy rope **b :** a tie piece to hold parts together or to contribute stiffness in engineering construction — compare STRUT — **at a long stay :** at such a small angle with the bottom as results when the anchor is not close in — used of an anchor cable — **at a short stay :** at such a large angle with the bottom as results when the anchor is close in — used of an anchor cable — **in stays** *adv* **1 :** in process of going about from one tack to another **2 :** in process of heading into the wind with sails shaking

[2]**stay** \"\ *vb* -ED/-ING/-S *vt* **1 :** to fasten or secure (as a smokestack) with or as if with stays **2 a :** to bring (a ship) about on the other tack **b :** to incline (a mast) forward, aft, or to one side by the stays and backstays ~ *vi* **:** to go about **:** TACK — used of a ship

[3]**stay** \"\ *vb* **stayed** \-ād\ *or* **staid** \"\ *or substand* **stood** \'stu̇d\ **stayed** *or* **staid** *or substand* **stood; staying; stays** [ME *steyen*, fr. MF *estei-, estai-*, stem of *ester* to stand, stop, stay, fr. L *stare* to stand — more at STAND] *vi* **1 :** to halt an advance **:** stop going forward **:** PAUSE ⟨if he paused here at all, he didn't ~ to found a city —Green Peyton⟩ **2 :** to stop doing something **:** CEASE — often used with *from* **3 :** to reach an end **:** become stopped — used of a process or action **4 a :** to remain somewhere or with someone rather than proceed or leave ⟨~ with us until the bridge is repaired —Victor Canning⟩ — often used with *on* ⟨proposed a brief visit but ~*ed* on for months⟩ **b :** to continue in a place or condition **:** remain unmoved or unaltered ⟨the instrument *staid* in tune for a greater period of time —A.E.Wier⟩ **c** (1) **:** to remain in the stomach — often used with *down* ⟨couldn't make spicy foods ~ down⟩ (2) **:** to satisfy appetite substantially — used of food **5 :** to stand firm **:** hold steadfast **6 :** to take up or maintain residence **:** LIVE, LODGE, VISIT ⟨~*ed* overnight at a waterfront hotel⟩ ⟨~*ed* with friends all along his route⟩ **7** *obs* **:** to wait quietly or passively **8** *obs* **:** to become deferred or kept waiting **:** become postponed **9** *obs* **:** HESITATE, DELAY, ABSTAIN **10 :** to keep even in a contest or rivalry — used with *with* ⟨was supremely confident that no rival could ~ with him —Allison Danzig & Joe King⟩ **11 :** to call a poker bet without raising — often used with *in* **12** *obs* **:** to be in waiting or attendance **13 a :** to remain in order to wait ⟨~*ed* neither for time nor tide⟩ ⟨~*ed* for me after the dinner⟩ **b :** to remain in order to share or participate — used with *for* ⟨urged them to ~ for tea⟩ ~ *vt* **1 :** to wait for **:** ABIDE, AWAIT ⟨I will not ~ thy questions —Shak.⟩ **2 :** to last out (a race, contest, or trial of endurance) **:** hold out for the extent or duration of **:** STICK ⟨should not be troubled to ~ the mile and a half —*Sydney* (*Australia*) *Bull.*⟩ ⟨we may not be able to ~ the course against moderately efficient tyranny —*Times Lit. Supp.*⟩ **3 :** to remain during **:** assist at **:** participate in ⟨she ~*ed* the sacrament —Jane Austen⟩ **4 :** to stop the progress or advance of **:** hold from proceeding **:** CHECK, DELAY, DETAIN, RESTRAIN ⟨the huge man in the red shirt ~*ed* his cudgel —Michael Arlen⟩ ⟨do something to ~ bloodshed —Charles Dickens⟩ ⟨might have ~*ed* the ruinous rise in prices —E.H.Youngman⟩ **5** *archaic* **:** to take or hold prisoner **6 :** to stop or keep something from moving **:** hold motionless **:** FIX **7 a :** to prevent, block, or stop from an action or proceeding **:** hold back ⟨there is nothing here . . . to ~ us in our flight —Virginia Woolf⟩ **b :** to stop or suspend the effect or progress of by judicial proceedings or executive mandate ⟨the court of appeals ~*ed* the order⟩ ⟨denied a motion by counsel to ~ the annual meeting⟩ **c** *archaic* **:** to cease from (an action, motion, or process) **8 :** to check the course of (a disease or an evil influence) **:** HALT ⟨that the plague may be ~*ed* from the people —1 Chron 21:22 (AV)⟩ **9 :** ALLAY, CALM, PACIFY ⟨~*ed* the civil war⟩ **10 :** to quiet the hunger of temporarily **:** appease the pangs of appetite of **:** SATISFY ⟨a glass of milk ~*ed* me until meal time⟩ ⟨offered him a snack to ~ his stomach⟩

syn REMAIN, WAIT, ABIDE, LINGER, TARRY: STAY, the most general of these verbs, suggests a continuance in one place for an appreciable time, often as, or in the manner of a visitor or guest ⟨*stay* at a hotel for a week⟩ ⟨*stayed* for the evening meal —Sherwood Anderson⟩ ⟨the itinerant weaver and the household loom *stayed* on in the smaller communities until late in the nineteenth century —*Amer. Guide Series: Mich.*⟩ REMAIN can add the idea of staying after the time of expected departure or a reasonable occasion for departure ⟨the others left but the officer *remained* for an hour more⟩ ⟨went to Europe in the spring of 1806, *remaining* over a year —M.H.Thomas⟩ ⟨no permanent ice *remains*, but snowbanks persist in places —Gladys Wrigley⟩ ⟨in earlier geological periods these were gigantic ranges; today only a few precipitous slopes *remain* —*Amer. Guide Series: Minn.*⟩ ⟨piles of stones *remain* to indicate the site of the mission's gristmill —*Amer. Guide Series: Tenn.*⟩ WAIT implies an event in the future, immediate or distant, for which one stays in anticipation ⟨*wait* for the guests to depart⟩ ⟨if we were to *wait* for the scientists to reach conclusions conducive to certitude, we would have a long wait —L.A.Foley⟩ ⟨when a man disregards current conventions he must *wait* for the future —O.W. Holmes †1935⟩ ABIDE signifies to stay for considerable time, suggesting long residence or a patient waiting or sometimes the staying of one who has found a place of respite or repose and has no immediate intention of leaving ⟨he must get out alone . . . into the wilderness and *abide* there hunting till he had built up his strength and regained his pride —Stuart Cloete⟩ ⟨here she was forced to *abide* —Thomas Hardy⟩ ⟨the foundation of a culture whose influence will *abide* while the world stands —Edward Clodd⟩ LINGER and TARRY both suggest a remaining or staying on in one place by a delaying of departure or of expected procedure in a given direction as from fondness for the place or situation or its concomitants or from uncertainty or recalcitrance ⟨the less casual visitor, with time to *linger*, senses the charm of the old church —*Amer. Guide Series: Texas*⟩ ⟨a young American who is *lingering* in Europe after the First World War —B.R.Redman⟩ ⟨she *lingered* for a few moments to talk with him —Sherwood Anderson⟩ ⟨numerous legends *linger* around this old dwelling —*Amer. Guide Series: Conn.*⟩ ⟨they did not *tarry* in the little settlement but sailed up the Ashley river, and chose a site 18 miles above the town —L.H.Beck⟩ ⟨that night after the guests had *tarried* long over their tea . . . the woman still lingered behind the stove —Pearl Buck⟩ **syn** see in addition DEFER, RESIDE

— **stay put :** to be firmly fixed, attached, or established **:** remain permanently

[4]**stay** \"\ *n* -S **1 a :** a bringing to a stop **:** the action of halting **:** the state of being stopped **:** CHECK **b :** a stopping or suspension of procedure or execution by judicial or executive order ⟨was asked to grant a ~ of execution —*N.Y.Times*⟩ **c :** the cessation of motion, progression, or action **:** a coming to a halt ⟨pressed forward without stop or ~⟩ **d** *obs* **:** something that causes a stop **:** HINDRANCE, OBSTACLE, OBSTRUCTION **2** *obs* **:** MODERATION, SELF-CONTROL **3** *obs* **:** a time of waiting or delay **:** DEFERMENT, POSTPONEMENT **4 :** a temporary residence or sojourn **:** a period of abode ⟨an extended holiday lengthened itself into a ~ of 16 years —J.T.Ellis⟩ **5 :** capacity for endurance **:** STAYING POWER **6 :** a fixed or stationary condition **:** a state without motion forward or back **:** STANDSTILL

[5]**stay** \"\ *n* -S [MF *estaie*, of Gmc origin; akin to MD *staen* to stand, OHG *stān, stēn* — more at STAND] **1 a :** something that serves as a prop **:** BRACE, SUPPORT ⟨special lid ~*s* and pneumatic dampers hold the lid open —*Nat'l Stamp News*⟩ **b :** someone or something that supports or helps **:** an object of reliance ⟨in this kingdom of illusions we grope eagerly for ~*s* and foundations —R.W.Emerson⟩ ⟨this great valiant class, the ~ of domestic England —Bernardine Kielty⟩ **2 a :** a corset stiffened with bones and esp. made in two pieces and laced together — usu. used in pl. **b :** the bones so used — usu. used in pl. **3 :** a series of plain or fancy stitches or a piece of cloth sewn into a garment for reinforcing points of strain, controlling fullness, or preventing stretching **4 :** a corner reinforcement in a rigid paper box

[6]**stay** \"\ *vb* -ED/-ING/-S [partly fr. MF *estaier*, fr. *estaie*, n.; partly fr. [5]*stay*] *vt* **1 a :** to hold up or provide support for **:** PROP, SUSTAIN ⟨a hand on her uncle's chair to ~ herself from falling —George Meredith⟩ **b :** to provide moral support for **:** COMFORT, STRENGTHEN ⟨turned from the man whose friendship had ~*ed* him —Winston Churchill⟩ **2 :** to fix on as a foundation **:** GROUND, REST ⟨all my trust on thee is ~*ed* —Charles Wesley⟩ **3 :** to reinforce or strengthen with stays or supports of various kinds: as **a :** to sew stays into (as a corset) **b :** to reinforce (weak fur pelts) with fabric on the leather side ~ *vi* **1** *obs* **:** to be upheld **:** LEAN, REST — used with *on* or *upon* **2** *obs* **:** to place reliance or confidence **:** show trust **:** DEPEND — used with *on* or *upon* **syn** see BASE

[1]**stay-at-home** \'stāət,hōm, *chiefly Brit* -ə,tōm\ *adj* [fr. the phrase *stay at home*] **:** remaining in one's residence, locality, or country **:** HOMEKEEPING ⟨a *stay-at-home* friend —Jerome Weidman⟩ ⟨while we were still overseas . . . *stay-at-home* doctors had taken over our practices —Milton Silverman⟩

[2]**stay-at-home** \"\ *n* **:** one that remains in his residence, locality, or country **:** one not given to wandering or travel **:** HOMEBODY ⟨travelogues that the *stay-at-homes* must additionally endure from the globe-trotters —Peter De Vries⟩

stay bar *n* [[5]*stay*] **:** a saddle bar passing through the mullions and secured to the jambs in an ornamental window to keep leaded glass in place

stay bolt *n* [[5]*stay*] **:** a bolt or short rod commonly threaded throughout its length and used as a stay to connect opposite plates (as in a steam boiler) that are subjected to a pressure tending to force them apart

stay-bolt tap *n* **:** a long combination cutting tool that successively reams, rough-taps, and finish-taps a stay-bolt hole

stayed *past of* STAY

[1]**stay·er** \'stāə(r)\ *n* -S [[6]*stay* + *-er*] **:** one that stays: as **a :** one that upholds or supports **b :** BONER 1 **c :** an operator of a machine for joining and taping cardboard box parts

[2]**stayer** \"\ *n* -S [[3]*stay* + *-er*] **:** one that stays: as **a :** something that checks or restrains **b :** one having powers of endurance or perseverance ⟨fast horses — sprinters but not ~*s* —G.F.T.Ryall⟩

stay hole *n* [[1]*stay*] **:** an opening in a staysail through which passes one of the hanks joining the sail to the stay

staying *pres part of* STAY

staying power *n* **:** capacity for endurance **:** STAMINA

stay-in strike *or* **stay-in** \'stā,in-\ *n* -S [fr. *stay in*, v.] **:** a slowdown or stoppage of work intended to bring pressure on an employer and concerted by workers who remain in their work place — compare LOCKOUT, SIT-DOWN

staylace \'=,=\ *n* [[5]*stay* + *lace*] **:** a corset lace

stay law *n* [[4]*stay*] **:** a moratory law **:** a law suspending or providing a means of suspending execution of judgments or sale on foreclosure or otherwise suspending legal remedies for a limited time

stay·less \'stālə̇s\ *adj* [[5]*stay* + *-less*] **1** *obs* **:** UNSUPPORTED **2 :** CORSETLESS

stay log *n* [[5]*stay*] **:** an eccentric arm mounted on a lathe as a support for a veneer flitch and permitting alteration of the sweep so as to secure enhanced grain effects in half-round veneer

stay·man convention \¦stāmən-\ *n, usu cap S* [after Samuel M. *Stayman* *b*1909 Amer. bridge expert] **:** a convention in contract bridge of responding to an opening no-trump bid with an artificial bid in clubs to invite a rebid in a four-card major suit by the no-trump bidder if he has one

stay out *vt* [[3]*stay*] **1 :** to remain to or beyond the end of ⟨*stayed out* the whole long performance⟩ **2 :** linger after the departure of **:** OUTSTAY ⟨*stayed* her cousin *out*⟩

staypak \'stā,pak\ *n* -S [[3]*stay* + *pak*, alter. of *packed*] **:** wood densified by pressure and heat and stabilized by its lignin content with no added resin

stay pin *n* [[5]*stay*] **:** a crosspiece or stud in a link of a chain to prevent kinking

stays *pl of* STAY, *pres 3d sing of* STAY

stay·sail \'stāsəl (*usu nautical pronunc*), -ā,sāl\ *n* [[1]*stay* + *sail*] **:** a fore-and-aft sail hoisted on a stay — see SAIL illustration

staysail schooner *n* **:** a schooner without the boom and gaff foresail and with the space between the fore and main masts filled by staysails of various shapes

stay tackle *n* [[1]*stay*] **:** a tackle hooked to a stay and used to lift loads amidships in stowing or discharging holds

stay tap *n* [[5]*stay*] **:** STAY-BOLT TAP

stay tube *n* [[5]*stay*] **:** a fire tube with flared or threaded thickened ends that project through both tube sheets in a steam boiler so as to form stays

stbd *abbr* starboard

STC *abbr* **1** sensitivity-time control **2** short-title catalogue **3** single-trip container **4** state teachers college

std *abbr* **1** seated **2** standard **3** steward

STD \¦e,stē¦dē\ *abbr or n* -S [L *sacrae theologiae doctor*] **:** a doctor of sacred theology

ste *abbr, often cap* [F *sainte*] saint

[1]**stead** \'sted, *dial* 'stid\ *n* -S [ME *stede*, fr. OE; akin to OHG *stat* place, ON *stathr*, Goth *staths*, L *statio* act of standing, station, *statim* on the spot, immediately, Gk *stasis* act of standing, position, Skr *sthiti* act of standing, position, *tiṣṭhati* he stands — more at STAND] **1** *obs* **:** LOCALITY, PLACE **2 :** FARMSTEAD 1 ⟨depicted a Tunisian cattle ~ and its animals —*Nat'l Geographic*⟩ **3 :** ADVANTAGE, AVAIL, SERVICE — used chiefly in the phrase *to stand one in good stead* ⟨took voluminous notes which later stood him in good ~ —W.O.Stevens⟩ ⟨this tradition stands primitive peoples in good ~ —Jane Nickerson⟩ **4 :** a frame on which a bed is laid **:** BEDSTEAD ⟨spool-turned cottage ~*s* —Muriel E. Sheppard⟩ **5 :** the office, place, or function ordinarily occupied or carried out by someone or something else ⟨was again placed in the deputy's ~ at the door —T.S.Stribling⟩ ⟨including rent controls, and the application in their ~ of indirect methods of inflation control —*Current Biog.*⟩ ⟨in the ~ of the traditional view —S.F.Mason⟩ **6** *Scot* **:** IMPRESS, TRACE, TRACK

[2]**stead** \'sted\ *vt* -ED/-ING/-S [ME *steden*, fr. *stede* stead] **1 :** to be of avail to **:** ASSIST, HELP, SUPPORT ⟨the great names cannot ~ him, if he have no life himself —R.W.Emerson⟩ **2 a** *archaic* **:** PLACE, SET **b** *obs* **:** to fill the place of **:** REPLACE ⟨advise this wronged maid to ~ up your appointment, go in your place —Shak.⟩ **3** *archaic* **:** to involve in difficulty or danger **:** BESET

[1]**stead·fast** *also* **sted·fast** \'sted,fast, -aa(ə)st, -aist, -ȧst *also* -fəst\ *adj* [ME *stedefast*, fr. OE *stedefæst*, fr. *stede* place, stead + *fæst* fast, fixed] **1 a :** firmly established **:** fixed in place or position **:** IMMOVABLE ⟨a castle, ~ among storms —Sinclair Lewis⟩ **b :** not subject to change **:** IMMUTABLE ⟨the most ~ of primitive environments, the ocean —Lewis Mumford⟩ ⟨the ~ doctrine of original sin —Ellen Glasgow⟩ **2 :** marked by unwavering steadiness **:** firm in belief, determination, or adherence **:** LOYAL, UNSWERVING ⟨our ~ friend, in peace or war, for many years —H.G.Doyle⟩ ⟨narrow of vision but ~ to principles —Agnes Repplier⟩ **syn** see FAITHFUL

[2]**steadfast** \"\ *adv* [ME *stedefast*, fr. *stedefast*, adj] **:** STEADFASTLY

stead·fast·ly \'=(¦)==\ *adv* [ME *stedefastly*, fr. *stedefast* steadfast + *-ly*] **:** in a steadfast manner

stead·fast·ness \-s(t)nə̇s — *stressed* '=(¦)==\ *n* -ES [ME *stedefastnesse*, fr. *stedefast* steadfast + *-nesse* -ness] **:** the quality or state of being steadfast

steadied *past of* STEADY

steadier *n* -S **:** one that steadies

steadies *pres 3d sing of* STEADY, *pl of* STEADY

stead·i·ly \'stedᵊl|ē, -də̇l|, |i, *dial* 'stid- *also* 'stəd-\ *adv* **:** in a steady manner

stead·i·ment \'stedēmənt\ *n* -S [[2]*steady* + *-ment*] **:** an aid to steadiness **:** the state of being steadied

stead·i·ness \-dēnə̇s, -din-\ *n* -ES **:** the quality or state of being steady

stead·ing \'stediŋ, -dēŋ\ *n* -S [ME *steding*, fr. *stede* stead + *-ing*] **1 a :** FARMHOUSE ⟨for their more permanent homes many of them owned small ~*s* —Jacquetta & Christopher Hawkes⟩ **b :** a small farm or homestead ⟨had left the affairs of the little ~ in a sad muddle —A.J.Cronin⟩ **2** *chiefly Scot* **:** the service buildings or area of a farm

stead·ite \'ste,dīt\ *n* -S [John Edward *Stead* †1923 Eng. metallurgist] **:** a eutectic of iron phosphide Fe_3P and iron that occurs as a microconstituent of high-phosphorus cast iron

stead of *prep, chiefly dial* [by shortening] **:** instead of

[1]**steady** \'stedē, -di, *dial* 'stid- *also* 'stəd-\ *adj* -ER/-EST [[1]*stead* + *-y*] **1 a :** firm in standing or position **:** not tottering or shaking **:** FIXED ⟨holding the box ~ on his shoulder with the other hand —Pearl Buck⟩ **b :** direct or sure in movement or action ⟨with hinged knees and ~ hand to dress wounds —Walt Whitman⟩ **:** UNFALTERING, UNSWERVING ⟨gave him a ~ look —Margaret Deland⟩ ⟨took ~ aim⟩ **c :** keeping nearly upright in a seaway **:** not easily tipped by an external force — used of a ship; compare [9]CRANK, STIFF 7 **d :** serving to hold firm **:** STEADYING ⟨a ~ bearing⟩ **2 a :** marked by an even development, movement, or action **:** not varying in quality, intensity, or direction **:** REGULAR, UNIFORM ⟨a ~ pace⟩ ⟨a ~ breeze⟩ ⟨a ~ light⟩ **:** not changed, replaced, or interrupted **:** CONTINUOUS, UNINTERRUPTED ⟨from then on it was a ~ fight against misfortune —S.H.Adams⟩ ⟨continued to produce a ~ output of books —Evelyn G. Cruickshanks⟩ ⟨a ~ job⟩ ⟨a ~ girl friend⟩ **b :** showing little variation **:** recording little change in the weather ⟨the glass was ~ and the weather good with fair visibility —H.A.Chippendale⟩ **c :** not fluctuating or varying widely (as in price) **:** STABLE ⟨cattle were ~ to off 25 cents per hundredweight —*Wall Street Jour.*⟩ ⟨current quotations show no great improvement but they are *steadier* —*Chem. & Engineering News*⟩ **3 a :** not easily moved or upset **:** CALM, CONTROLLED ⟨~ nerves⟩ ⟨a ~ temper⟩ **:** DISCIPLINED, RESOLUTE ⟨the ~ valor of the warriors whom he had trained —T.B.Macaulay⟩ **b** (1) **:** constant in feeling, principle, purpose, or attachment **:** not fickle or wavering **:** STEADFAST ⟨a conservative and ~ people, are little attracted by tricky trends —*Exhibition of Swiss Bks.*⟩ (2) **:** consistent in performance or behavior **:** DEPENDABLE, RELIABLE ⟨there must be men to tend them, men as ~ as the wheels upon their axles —Aldous Huxley⟩ ⟨a good ~ ballplayer⟩ ⟨a ~ horse⟩ (3) **:** not easily diverted or thrown off ⟨a hound ~ on the scent⟩ **c :** not given to dissipation or excess **:** SOBER ⟨promised to marry another man, a good ~ farmer —Vance Randolph⟩ ⟨grown to be fine women, and good ~ mothers to their children —C.B.Nordhoff & J.N. Hall⟩

syn EVEN, CONSTANT, UNIFORM, EQUABLE: in relation to matters inanimate, STEADY indicates lack of variation, interruption, or change ⟨the light, small, but *steady* and persistent as before —Thomas Hardy⟩ ⟨he first imagined, and then demonstrated, that the geologic agencies are not explosive and cataclysmal, but *steady* and patient —C.W.Eliot⟩ and in relation to persons it may imply a balanced resolution and dependability, a strength of character under stress ⟨intoxicated as he was, he knew enough to charge the steward — a *steady* seaman be it remembered — with the present safety of the ship —Herman Melville⟩ ⟨statesmen, instead of being as they should be, at once mild and *steady*, are at once ferocious and inconsistent —T.B.Macaulay⟩ EVEN may indicate a level, plain quality without rough variation or elevation ⟨had been moving along in an *even* path . . . there was no apparent slope downward, and distinctly none upward —Theodore Dreiser⟩; when used of people it suggests a natural level calmness without the resolution implied by STEADY ⟨support with an *even* temper, and without any violent transports of mind, a sudden gust of prosperity —Henry Fielding⟩ CONSTANT implies a sameness, fixity, consistency, persistence, or regularity more or less measurable and lasting ⟨while there have been several clear and distinct changes in the pattern, the essence of the university tradition has through all these years remained *constant* —J.B.Conant⟩ In reference to persons, it may suggest either loyalty or unchanging fixity ⟨a loyal husband (*constant* if not faithful) —Agnes Repplier⟩ ⟨could never think of him as having been a young man . . . he always thought of him as an unchanging, a measured, deliberate, *constant* quantity, like a Greek letter in a mathematical formula —J.P.Marquand⟩ UNIFORM, less applicable to persons than the preceding words, stresses to a greater degree sameness and lack of variety in salient characteristics as indicated or implied ⟨the various tackle blocks and planks of the wooden ships were cut to *uniform* measure: building became the assemblage of accurately measured elements —Lewis Mumford⟩ ⟨the purpose of this is to afford a requirement of a reasonably *uniform* character for all states cooperating with the federal government —F.D. Roosevelt⟩ EQUABLE stresses lack of extremes and sudden marked changes ⟨a more *equable* winter climate in France —Osbert Sitwell⟩ ⟨in low *equable* tones, curiously in contrast to the strident babble with which natives are accustomed to make day hideous —Rudyard Kipling⟩ and applied to persons and their temperaments it may imply an unruffled complacence ⟨bridge, whist, baccarat, poker, roulette and Monte Carlo — at all these she won and lost, with the same *equable* sangfroid —Rose Macaulay⟩

²**steady** \"\ *vb* -ED/-ING/-ES *vt* **1** : to keep from shaking, reeling, or falling : make or keep firm ⟨she swayed slightly and put a hand out to ~ herself —Nigel Balchin⟩ **2 a** : to bring under control : CALM, COMPOSE, QUIET ⟨drew a deep breath and *steadied* himself with an effort of will —Aldous Huxley⟩ **b** : to make serious or sober : keep from dissipation or irregular habits ⟨as he had no business or profession to ~ him, he traveled rapidly down the primrose path —G.C.Sellery⟩ **c** : to make constant, regular, or resolute ⟨was *steadied* in his determination for a career by his desire to win . . . approbation and love —Lawrason Brown⟩ **3 a** : to keep (a ship) on the course set : keep from veering off course **b** : to cause to proceed at an even pace ⟨~ the horse⟩ ~ *vi* **1** : to settle down : become regular in habits or behavior ⟨led a wild life but *steadied* down after his marriage⟩ **2** : to keep or return to a fixed position or course ⟨the statue tottered but then *steadied* on its base⟩ ⟨they swept round in a long gentle turn and *steadied* on the course —Nevil Shute⟩ **3** : to become more stable ⟨another dark spot appeared to be brightening as farm prices *steadied* —*Dun's Rev.*⟩ **syn** see STABILIZE

³**steady** \"\ *adv* **1** : in a steady manner : STEADILY ⟨the rain was coming down ~ —Richard Bissell⟩ ⟨these poets have seen the city ~ and seen it whole —Thomas Lask⟩ **2** : on the course set : without veering from the direct line of course — used as a direction to the helmsman of a ship

⁴**steady** \"\ *n* -ES **1** : one that is steady; *specif* : a boyfriend or girl friend with whom one goes steady **2** : something that holds firm; *specif* : STEADY REST

steady flow *n* [¹*steady*] : a flow in which the velocity of the fluid at a particular fixed point does not change with time — called also *stationary flow;* compare UNIFORM FLOW

steady-going \ˈ=ˌ==\ *adj* [³*steady*] **1** : CONSTANT, REGULAR ⟨*steady-going* devotion⟩ **2** : of steady habits : SERIOUS, SOBER ⟨a *steady-going* young man⟩

steady load *n* [¹*steady*] : DEAD LOAD 1

steady motion *n* : motion in which the linear and angular velocity or either of them is constant

steady pin *n* [²*steady*] **1** : DOWEL 1 **2** : a device (as a pin or sunk key) used to prevent a pulley from turning on a shaft or spindle **3 a** : a long guide pin attached to a cope or pattern to enable it to be lifted vertically **b** : CORE PRINT

steady rest *n* : a rest in a lathe or grinding machine in which long round pieces of work may rotate but without eccentric movement — called also *center rest;* compare FOLLOW REST

steady state *n* **1** : a state or condition of a system or process (as one of the energy states of an atom) that does not change in time **2** : a condition of stability of a generator or electric system under normal fluctuations of load or voltage **3** : a state of physiological equilibrium esp. in connection with a specified metabolic relation or activity

¹**steak** \ˈstāk\ *n* -S [ME *steyke, steke,* fr. ON *steik;* akin to ON *steikja* to roast on a spit, *stik* stick, stake — more at STICK] **1 a** : a slice of meat cut from a fleshy part of a beef carcass usu. in cross section and usu. cooked or to be cooked by broiling : BEEFSTEAK — see BEEF illustration **b** : a similar slice of a specified meat other than beef ⟨ham ~⟩ ⟨veal ~⟩ **c** : a cross-section slice of a large fish ⟨halibut ~⟩ ⟨swordfish ~⟩ **2** : ground beef prepared for cooking or for serving — see HAMBURGER STEAK, SALISBURY STEAK **3** : FLANK STEAK

²**steak** \"\ *vt* -ED/-ING/-S : to cut (large fish) crosswise into steaks

steak hammer *n* : an implement for pounding meat to make it more tender by breaking down the tissue fibers

steak knife *n* : a table knife having a steel blade often with a serrated edge and a handle of any of various materials (as metal, wood, plastic)

steak set *n* : a small carving set

steak hammers

¹**steal** \ˈstē(ə)l, ˈstā(ə)l\ *n* -S [ME *stele* stalk, stem, handle, fr. OE, stalk, support; akin to ON *stjölr* hinder part, tail, Gk *stelea* handle of an axe, *stellein* to set up, make ready — more at STALL] **1** *dial Brit* : STALK, STEM **2** *dial Brit* : HANDLE, SHAFT

²**steal** \ˈstēl, *esp before pause or consonant* -ēəl\ *vb* **stole** \ˈstōl\ **sto·len** \ˈstōlən *sometimes* -ln\ *or chiefly dial* **stole** \-ōl\ *or dial chiefly Brit* **stoun** *or* **stown** \-ōn\ **stealing; steals** [ME *stelen,* fr. OE *stelan;* akin to OHG *stelan* to steal, ON *stela,* Goth *stilan,* and perh. to Gk *sterein* to deprive, bereave, rob, MIr *serbh* theft] *vi* **1** : to practice theft : take the property of another ⟨thou shall not ~ —Exod 20:15 (RSV)⟩ **2 a** : to leave secretly or unobtrusively ⟨he *stole* quietly out of the picture for ever —Richard Harrison⟩ **b** : to move furtively : attempt to come or go without attracting notice ⟨*stole* over at twilight for an inconspicuous inspection —Margaret Janes⟩ **c** : to move, glide, or elapse gently ⟨a tear *stole* down her cheek⟩ ⟨the months *stole on*⟩ **3 a** : to come upon one gradually or without warning ⟨the white, soft light that ~*s* upon half sleep near morning —Scott Fitzgerald⟩ ⟨shall we ~ upon them . . . at supper —Shak.⟩ **b** : to approach, enter, or take possession by imperceptible degrees ⟨anxiety was ~*ing* over her as if it emanated from her surroundings —Ellen Glasgow⟩ ⟨into her cheeks *stole* a lovely color —Edison Marshall⟩ **4** *of a base runner* : to advance from one base to the next without the aid of a hit or error ⟨are allowed to ~ without a signal —M.F.Mallette⟩ ~ *vt* **1 a** : to take and carry away feloniously and usu. unobserved : take or appropriate without right or leave and with intent to keep or make use of wrongfully ⟨*stole* a car from a parking lot⟩ ⟨*stole* money from the cash register⟩ ⟨who ~*s* my purse ~*s* trash —Shak.⟩ **b** : to appropriate (as another's conception or invention) and use as one's own ⟨*stole* the formula and began to manufacture the product himself⟩ : PLAGIARIZE ⟨his jokes were borrowed and *stolen* all over the country —Eleanor M. Sickels⟩ ⟨*stole* nearly all his plots —Agnes de Mille⟩ **c** : to take away by force or unjust or underhand means : deprive one of ⟨they've *stolen* our liberty from us, and we'll never get it back —Kenneth Roberts⟩ ⟨had *stolen* the nomination from him —A.S.Link⟩ **d** *archaic* : ABDUCT, KIDNAP ⟨such incidents as the child *stolen* by gypsies —E.A.Poe⟩ **e** : to take secretly or without permission ⟨*stole* a kiss from her before she could protest⟩ **f** : to take over : ADOPT, BORROW ⟨the various gyrations have been *stolen* from boxing, basketball, track —*This Week Mag.*⟩ **g** : to appropriate entirely to oneself or beyond one's proper share ⟨has to occupy the center of the stage and ~ the act —Constance Foster⟩ ⟨the young ladies ~ most of the limelight —O.S.Nock⟩ **2 a** : to move, convey, or introduce secretly : SMUGGLE ⟨*stole* a hand into hers —Rumer Godden⟩ ⟨watching for an opportunity to ~ their egg into some nest —John Burroughs⟩ **b** : to aim furtively : direct secretly ⟨*stole* several glances at him with a curiosity very natural under the circumstances —Joseph Conrad⟩ **c** : to accomplish in a concealed or unobserved manner ⟨might even ~ a visit —G.B.Shaw⟩ **3** : to use (an interval of time) for an unscheduled, irregular, or secret purpose ⟨felt he was ~*ing* the time and using it for frivolous thoughts —Virginia D. Dawson & Betty D. Wilson⟩ ⟨~*ing* time off from her other clients to flit in and out of the workrooms —P.E.Deutschman⟩ **4 a** : to win away (as by persuasion or deception) : ENTICE ⟨this savage who *stole* your allegiance from me —T.B.Costain⟩ ⟨the obligation to refrain from deliberately ~*ing* each other's clients —H.S.Drinker⟩ **b** : to take possession of gradually and imperceptibly : withdraw or remove stealthily — often used with *away* ⟨shorter wind, paunches, and hardened arteries had begun to ~ away their lust for life —Dixon Wecter⟩ **5** : to seize, gain, or win by trickery, skill, or daring ⟨a basketball player adept at ~*ing* the ball from his opponents⟩ ⟨show folks know how to ~ that extra bow —Goodman Ace⟩ ⟨a shrewd poker player who ~*s* many pots⟩: as **a** *of a base runner* : to gain (a base) by running without the aid of a hit or an error **b** *baseball* : to intercept and interpret correctly (an opponent's signal) ⟨false moves calculated to keep the enemy from ~*ing* the genuine sign —A.J.Daley⟩ **c** : to make (a run) in cricket by alert opportunism in circumstances where a run would not ordinarily be attempted **6** *of a hen* **a** : to make (a nest) in an out-of-the-way place **b** : to make use of (the nest) of another hen

syn PILFER, FILCH, PURLOIN, LIFT, PINCH, SNITCH, SWIPE, COP: these have in common the sense of to take another's possession without right, without his knowledge or observation. STEAL, the commonest and most general of the group, can refer to any act of taking without right although it suggests strongly a furtiveness or secrecy in the act ⟨*steal* a pocketbook⟩ ⟨*steal* jewels⟩ ⟨*steal* a kiss⟩ ⟨*steal* a glance at someone⟩ PILFER suggests stealing in small amounts ⟨the pantry mouse that *pilfers* our food —*Conservation in the U.S.*⟩ ⟨the ladies of unexceptionable position who are caught *pilfering* furs in shops —L.P. Smith⟩ ⟨*pilfer* the secret files of the foreign office —H.J. Morgenthau⟩ FILCH is close to PILFER but suggests more strongly the use of surreptitious means, esp. quick snatching ⟨the pursuit of a thief who had *filched* an overcoat —McKenzie Porter⟩ ⟨a lot of fellows were too hungry to wait, and so some of the rations were *filched* —Asa Autry⟩ ⟨a bulky, dark youth in spectacles . . . *filching* biscuits from a large tin —Dorothy Sayers⟩ PURLOIN usu. shifts the stress onto the idea of removal or making away with for one's own use, often becoming generalized to include such acts as plundering or plagiarism ⟨had *purloined* $386,920 from the New York realty management firm for which he worked, then absconded —*Time*⟩ ⟨added theft to her other sin, and having found your watch in your bedroom had *purloined* it —Samuel Butler †1902⟩ ⟨I hope to quote him is not to *purloin* —John Dryden⟩ LIFT, when it does not mean specif. to steal by surreptitiously taking from counters or displays in stores, is used frequently in spoken English in the sense of PURLOIN ⟨women shoplifters often work in gangs of three. Two act as shields while the third does the *lifting* —*Irish Digest*⟩ ⟨*lift* money from the cash register⟩ ⟨imitators who *lifted* everything except the shirt off his back —Scott Fitzgerald⟩ PINCH, SWIPE, SNITCH, and COP are virtually interchangeable with FILCH. PINCH and SWIPE are often used in place of STEAL to suggest an act morally less reprehensible ⟨loot having been *pinched* by him from the British ship *Mary Dyer* —*Sydney (Australia) Bull.*⟩ ⟨well-dressed crooks really did steal the Gold Cup at Ascot . . . drove up in a handsome car . . . and *pinched* the cup out of the Royal Enclosure —J.D. Carr⟩ ⟨the bloke who *pinched* my photographs —Richard Llewellyn⟩ ⟨hovering outside the dying butler's bedroom waiting to . . . pop in and *swipe* the old man's private notebooks —*Time*⟩ SNITCH possibly stresses more the removal by quick, furtive snatching ⟨while he was bathing, somebody *snitched* his uniform —P.G.Wodehouse⟩ ⟨*snitched* people's ideas without telling them —Dorothy Sayers⟩ COP usu. lays stress upon quick, often spur-of-the-moment filching or purloining ⟨some woman put on a dinner gown, mingled with guests, *copped* fifty thousand bucks in jewelry —Erle Stanley Gardner⟩ ⟨ran home and *copped* a piece of beefsteak from his old lady —J.T. Farrell⟩

— **steal a march** : to gain an advantage unobserved — **steal one's thunder** : to appropriate or adapt for one's own ends something effective (as an idea or plan) devised or thought out by another

³**steal** \"\ *n* -S **1 a** : the act or an instance of stealing : THEFT ⟨his hand went out and picked up the shears as if he had had that ~ in mind for many years —Wright Morris⟩ **b** : the act or an instance of stealing a base ⟨thrown out on an attempted ~⟩ **2** : a fraudulent or questionable political action or deal ⟨this is the real ~ of the last 10 years —*New Republic*⟩ **3** : BARGAIN ⟨was prepared to let it go, though it was a ~ at the price, for ten dollars —Reed Whittemore⟩

steal·able \-ləbəl\ *adj* [²*steal* + *-able*] : capable of being stolen ⟨though the invasion blueprints weren't stolen, they were ~ —Linnell Jones⟩

steal·age \-lij, -lēj\ *n* -S [²*steal* + *-age*] : STEALING, THEFT ⟨noted any increase in ~ from stores —*Christian Science Monitor*⟩

steal·er \-lə(r)\ *n* -S **1** : one that steals ⟨base ~⟩ ⟨scene ~⟩ **2** *also* **steel·er** \"\ : the endmost plank or plate of a strake that ends short of the stem or stern

¹**stealing** *n* -S [ME *steling,* fr. gerund of *stelen* to steal] : the act of one who steals ⟨accused of ~⟩ ⟨led the league in ~⟩

²**stealing** *adj* [fr. pres. part. of ²*steal*] **1** *archaic* : moving stealthily, softly, or imperceptibly **2** : THIEVING ⟨helpful in the case of a ~ boy or girl —G.E.Gardner⟩ — **steal·ing·ly** *adv*

steals *pl of* STEAL, *pres 3d sing of* STEAL

stealth \ˈstelth *also* -ltth\ *n* -S [ME *stalthe, stelthe;* akin to OE *stelan* to steal] **1 a** *archaic* : the act or an instance of stealing : THEFT ⟨ingratitude makes it worse than ~ —Shak.⟩ **b** *obs* : something that is stolen : BOOTY ⟨pursue the ~ of pilfering wolf —John Milton⟩ **2** : the act or action of going or passing furtively, secretly, or imperceptibly ⟨told him of your ~ unto this wood —Shak.⟩ ⟨the realization of it was creeping through her veins with the deadly ~ of a drug —J.C.Snaith⟩ ⟨with the ~ of years . . . she had lost a little bloom —Francis Hackett⟩ **3** : FURTIVENESS, SLYNESS ⟨equaled this great wood-cat in ~, and far surpassed it in cunning and ferocity —Theodore Roosevelt⟩ — **by stealth** *adv* : in a clandestine manner : SECRETLY ⟨only seven were printed, anonymously, surreptitiously, and *by stealth,* during her lifetime —Louis Untermeyer⟩

stealth·ful \-fəl\ *adj* [*stealth* + *-ful*] *archaic* : STEALTHY

stealth·i·ly \-thəlē, -li\ *adv* : in a stealthy manner ⟨she looked out ~ through the blind of the little window —Charles Kingsley⟩ ⟨the public schools have ~ crept back into the hearts of the intellectuals —Edward Shils⟩

stealth·i·ness \-thēnəs, -thin-\ *n* -ES : the quality or state of being stealthy

stealthy \-thē, -thi\ *adj* -ER/-EST [*stealth* + *-y*] **1** : slow, deliberate, and secret in action or character ⟨the ~ revolution that has produced machine-made society —F.B.Millett⟩ ⟨a ~ owl lived on the roof —E.W.H.Lumsden⟩ **2** : intended to escape observation : FURTIVE ⟨a ~ sound⟩ ⟨a ~ glance⟩ ⟨a ~ movement⟩ **syn** see SECRET

¹**steam** \ˈstēm\ *n* -S *often attrib* [ME *stem, steme,* fr. OE *stēam, stēm, stiem;* akin to D *stoom* steam] **1 a** : a vapor arising from some heated substance : EXHALATION ⟨a ~ of incense⟩ **b** *archaic* : stale air — often used in pl. ⟨every modest flower that needs the pure air and will not grow in ~*s* —James Martineau⟩ **2 a** : the invisible vapor into which water is converted when heated to the boiling point : water in the state of vapor — compare DRY STEAM, WATER VAPOR, WET STEAM **b** : the mist formed by the condensation on cooling of water vapor : visible vapor **3 a** : water vapor kept under pressure so as to supply energy for heating, cooking, or mechanical work; *also* : the power so generated ⟨full ~ ahead⟩ **b** : driving force : ENERGY, POWER ⟨had got here on his own ~, won a lot of scholarships —A.L.Rowse⟩ ⟨hit him a peach of a right . . . but the ~ was gone —A.J.Liebling⟩ **c** : emotional tension ⟨after six months of hard study, he felt the need to let off a little ~⟩ ⟨though not a demonstrative bird, the king penguin occasionally must let off ~ —A.N.T.Rankin⟩ **4 a** : STEAMSHIP ⟨travel by ~⟩ **b** : travel by or a trip in a steamship ⟨the sea voyage — a night and a day's ~ —J.P.O'Donnell⟩ **c** : the occupation of handling ships under steam ⟨a blue-water man who had come into ~ and the home trade to get an easier life —Thomas Wood †1950⟩

²**steam** \"\ *vb* -ED/-ING/-S *vi* **1** : to rise in vapor : issue or pass off as vapor ⟨the heat ~*s* out of the forest —Robert Payne⟩ **2 a** : to give off steam or vapor ⟨the town ~*ed* in a listless heat —Vincent McHugh⟩ ⟨the cows . . . stood in the yards all day, ruminating and ~*ing* —Adrian Bell⟩ **b** : REEK ⟨at that time of year the boardwalk ~*s* with sophistication —*N.Y.Times*⟩ **3 a** : to move or travel by the agency of steam ⟨reaching the little riverside landing . . . after a day and a half of ~*ing* southward —Tom Marvel⟩ ⟨saw the train ~*ing* in —Edith Sitwell⟩ **b** : to move with energy or force as if by the agency of steam ⟨when he ~*s* into second base, say, on a long double —*Time*⟩ ⟨the racket smacked . . . and the white ball came ~*ing* across at me —R.P.Warren⟩ **4** : to generate steam ⟨the boiler ~*s* well⟩ **5** : to be angry : BOIL ⟨was still ~*ing* over the insult he had received⟩ ~ *vt* **1** : to give out as fumes : EXHALE **2** : to apply steam to ⟨women often like to ~ the skin by covering it with hot towels —Morris Fishbein⟩: as **a** : to cook by direct exposure to steam (as in a steamer) or in a vessel surrounded by steam (as in a double boiler) **b** : to expose (cloth) to the action of steam (as in dyeing or shrinking) **3** : to convey by steamship **4** : to move by the action of steam ⟨~*ing* a carrier through the Strait of Gibraltar —Walter Karig⟩ — **steam open** : to unglue by the action of steam ⟨*steam open* the envelope⟩

steam bath *n* **1** : a bath of steam (as for use in a laboratory) — compare WATER BATH **2** : a container for a steam bath

steam beer *n* : a highly effervescent beer brewed in the western U.S.

steam black *n, often cap S&B* : a natural dye — see DYE table I (under *Natural Black 4*)

steamblaster \ˈ=ˌ==\ *n* : one that cleans stone or brick structures with a spray of steam

steam blower *n* : a blower for producing a draft by a jet or jets of steam

¹**steamboat** \ˈ=ˌ=\ *n* : a boat propelled by steam power; *esp* : one designed for river or coastal traffic

²**steamboat** \"\ *vi* : to go or travel by steamboat

steamboat gothic *n, usu cap G* [so called fr. its use in homes of retired steamboat captains in imitation of the style of river steamboats] : an elaborately ornamental architectural style used in homes built in the middle 19th century in the Ohio and Mississippi river valleys

steamboating \ˈ=ˌ==\ *n* [¹*steamboat* + *-ing*] : the business or occupation of operating or working on a steamboat

steamboatman \ˈ=ˌ==\ *n, pl* **steamboatmen** : one engaged in running a steamboat

steamboat ratchet *n* : a sleeve internally threaded at the ends with opposing threads and equipped with a ratchet and handle so that when the sleeve is attached to the ends of two rods the rods may be pulled together by turning it

steam boiler *n* : a boiler for producing steam

steam box *n* **1** : STEAM CHEST **2** : a receptacle in which things are steamed

steam chest *n* : the chamber from which steam is distributed to a cylinder of a steam engine — called also *valve chest*

steam coal *n* : coal suitable for use under steam boilers

steam cock *n* : a cock for passage of steam; *specif* : the upper gauge cock in a steam boiler

steam coil *n* : a coil of pipe through which steam is passed

steam condenser *n* : CONDENSER 2e

steam cure *n* : vulcanization of rubber articles with direct exposure to steam

steam-distill \ˈ=ˌ=ˈ=\ *vb* [back-formation fr. *steam distillation*] *vt* : to subject to steam distillation ~ *vi* : to undergo steam distillation

steam distillation *n* : distillation (as of a substance essentially insoluble in water) assisted by steam that is usu. introduced as a current into the substance to be distilled and carries over with it quantities of the more volatile components to form an aqueous distillate on condensation ⟨by means of *steam distillations,* volatile organic liquids may be separated from relatively nonvolatile impurities —J.H.Perry⟩

steam dome *n* : DOME 4e

steamed *past of* STEAM

steam engine *n* **1** : an engine driven or worked by steam; *specif* : a reciprocating engine consisting essentially of a piston driven in a closed cylinder by steam at a pressure initially much greater than that of the atmosphere and usu. connected rigidly by a piston rod to a crosshead whose reciprocating motion is usu. converted into rotary motion by a connecting rod, crankpin, crank, and crankshaft — compare STEAM TURBINE **2** : LOCOMOTIVE

¹**steam·er** \ˈstēmə(r)\ *n* -S [¹*steam* & ²*steam* + *-er*] **1 a** : a vessel in which articles are subjected to steam **b** : a cooking utensil with a perforated insert to hold food to be steamed **2 a** (1) : STEAMSHIP (2) : a mechanically propelled ship **b** : an engine, machine, or vehicle operated or propelled by steam: as 1) : a fire engine having pumps operated by steam ⟨modern fire trucks ousting the rampaging old horse-drawn ~*s* —*Sat.Eve.Post*⟩ (2) : an automobile driven by steam **3** : one that steams; *specif* : one that cleans or conditions with steam (as in the cleaning of electrolytic refining equipment, the preshrinking of cloth, the blending of tobacco) **4** [so called fr. its suitability for steaming] : SOFT-SHELL CLAM

steamer 1b

²**steamer** \"\ *vi* -ED/-ING/-S : to go or voyage by steamer

steamer chair *n* : DECK CHAIR

steamer duck *n* : any of two flightless and one flying large sea ducks (genus *Tachyeres*) of Patagonia, Tierra del Fuego, and the Falkland islands that swim with a peculiar action suggesting a side-wheel steamboat

steamer rug *n* : RUG 2c

steamer trunk *n* : a trunk suitable for use in a stateroom of a steamer; *esp* : a shallow trunk that may be stowed beneath a berth

steam fit *n* : a steamtight fit

steam fitter *n* : one that installs or repairs steam pipes or other equipment for heating, ventilating, or refrigerating systems

steam fitting *n* : the work or occupation of a steam fitter

steam fog *n* : fog formed by cold air flowing over a warm water surface

steamer trunk

steam gauge *n* : a pressure gauge for steam

steam generator *n* : a large apparatus for converting hot water into steam at high pressure and often with supplementary coils to superheat the steam

steam hammer *n* : a power forging hammer worked directly by steam; *esp* : a hammer guided vertically and operated by a vertical steam cylinder located directly over an anvil

steam harrow *n* **:** a device resembling a spike-tooth harrow that is used for sterilizing soil (as in a greenhouse) with steam escaping from openings in short pipes forced into the soil

steam heat *n* **:** heat given off by steam in condensing

steam–heated \ˈ=ˌ=\ *adj* **:** provided with steam heat

steam heater *n* **1 :** a radiator heated by steam **2 :** a steam-heating apparatus consisting of a boiler, radiators, piping, and the necessary fixtures

steam heating *n* **:** a system of heating (as for a building) in which steam generated in a boiler is piped to radiators in the various parts of the system with the condensed steam being returned to the boiler for recirculation

steamier *comparative of* STEAMY

steamiest *superlative of* STEAMY

steam·i·ly \ˈstēmələ̄, -li\ *adv* **:** in a steamy manner

steam·i·ness \-mēnəs, -min-\ *n* -ES **:** the quality or state of being steamy

1**steaming** *adj* [fr. pres. part. of 2*steam*] **:** giving out or constituting steam or fumes ⟨drove in the big sleigh behind four ~ horses —Louis Bromfield⟩ ⟨there was a ~ mist in all the hollows —Charles Dickens⟩

2**steaming** *adv* **:** to a steaming degree ⟨the night was ~ hot⟩ ⟨the coffee was ~ hot⟩

3**steaming** *n* -S [fr. gerund of 2*steam*] **:** a distance traveled or to be traveled by a steamship in a specified time ⟨these rights did not extend farther than a distance of one hour's ~ from the coast —C.P.Stacey⟩

steam injector *n* **:** a steam-boiler injector

steam iron *n* **:** a pressing iron with a compartment holding water that is converted to steam by the iron's heat and emitted through the sole plate onto the fabric being pressed

steam jacket *n* **:** an outer casing enclosing a hollow space through which steam is circulated to heat the contents of an inner vessel

steam–jacket \ˈ=ˌ=\ *vt* [*steam jacket*] **:** to enclose in a steam jacket

steam joint *n* **:** a steamtight joint

steam knife *n* **:** a hollow-bladed knife heated by steam and used to uncap honeycombs

steam line *n* **:** a graph showing the pressure at which a liquid and its vapor are in equilibrium at any temperature

steam locomotive *n* **:** a locomotive using as motive power steam that is usu. self-generated in the locomotive's own boiler by the combustion of fuel (as coal or oil)

steam loop *n* **:** an arrangement of pipes by which water of condensation can be returned to the boiler without a pump or injector as a result of condensation of boiler steam in a loop of two vertical pipes connected by a horizontal one

steam metal *n* **:** a copper alloy specially designed to endure exposure to steam

steam navvy *n, Brit* **:** STEAM SHOVEL

steam nigger *n* **:** NIGGER 5

steam organ *or* **steam piano** *n* **:** CALLIOPE

steam packing *n* **:** packing made of material (as duck and rubber) resistant to the action of steam

steam point *n* **:** the normal boiling point of pure water that is used as one of the fixed points of the international temperature scale

steam port *n* **:** a port for steam; *esp* **:** one for live steam

steam power plant *n* **:** a plant using steam prime movers to drive electric generating apparatus

steam pump *n* **:** a pump driven by steam or directly by a steam engine; *specif* **:** a combined steam engine and pump with the piston rod and pump plunger directly coupled

steam railroad *n* **1 :** a railroad for steam locomotives **2 :** a railroad required to make reports in accordance with a uniform system of accounts for railroad companies prescribed by the U.S. Interstate Commerce Commission

steam ram *n* **:** a steam pump for deep wells that resembles a pulsometer in action

steam road *n* **:** STEAM RAILROAD

1**steamroller** \ˈ=ˌ==\ *n* **1 :** a steam-driven road roller **2 :** an irresistible or crushing power or force; *esp* **:** one ruthlessly exerted or applied to overcome opposition ⟨the ~ had passed over the insurgents, and the machine had won a new victory —*Rev. of Reviews*⟩

2**steamroller** \"\ *also* **steamroll** \ˈ=ˌ=\ *vb* -ED/-ING/-S [*steamroller* fr. 1*steamroller; steamroll,* back-formation fr. 1*steamroller*] *vt* **1 :** to crush with a steamroller **2 a :** to overwhelm, crush, or coerce by greatly superior force ⟨~ the opposition⟩ ⟨the well-organized majority *~ed* the conference into adopting its proposals without discussion⟩ **b :** to bring by overwhelming force or pressure ⟨*~ed* the bill through the legislature⟩ ⟨*~ed* the bill to defeat⟩ *~ vi* **:** to move or proceed with irresistible force

steam room *n* **:** a room (as in a Turkish bath) that is heated to an extreme temperature by steam

steams *pl of* STEAM, *pres 3d sing of* STEAM

steamship \ˈ=ˌ=\ *n* **:** a ship propelled by the power of steam **:** STEAMER

steam shovel *n* **:** a power shovel operated by steam

steam sizes *n pl* **:** the smallest sorted sizes of anthracite coal — compare PREPARED SIZES

steam still *n* **:** a still heated by steam; *esp* **:** one used in the production of gasoline and naphthas

steam–still \ˈ=ˌ=\ *vb* [1*steam* + *still* (to distill)] **:** STEAM-DISTILL

steam storage locomotive *n* **:** FIRELESS LOCOMOTIVE

steam table *n* **1 a :** a table having openings to hold containers of cooked food over steam or hot water circulating beneath them **b :** a steam-heated table for drying wet matrices in stereotyping **2 :** a tabulation giving data relating to steam saturated at various temperatures and including usu. the pressure, specific volume, density, heat of vaporization, specific enthalpy, and specific entropy

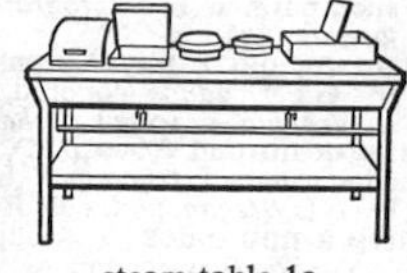
steam table 1a

steamtight \ˈ=ˌ=\ *adj* [1*steam* + *tight*] **:** not permitting the leaking through of steam or of water under pressure of steam

steam trap *n* **:** a device that automatically obstructs the passage of steam (as from a pipe) but permits the escape of condensate or entrained air

steam trawler *n* **:** a small but strongly built steam-driven trawler equipped with an otter trawl

steam turbine *n* **:** a turbine that is driven by the pressure of steam which is discharged at high velocity against the turbine vanes

steam–turbine locomotive *n* **:** a locomotive propelled by a steam turbine

steam up *vb* [2*steam* + *up*, adv.] *vt* **1 :** to cover with steam or vapor ⟨his breath *steamed up* the window pane⟩ **2 :** to supply with energy **:** give impetus to ⟨a drive for bigger government spendings to *steam up* the economy —*Kiplinger Washington Letter*⟩ **3 :** to make angry or excited **:** AROUSE ⟨the injustice of the charges *steamed him up*⟩ ⟨will find the neighbors much more *steamed up* over economic issues —*Time*⟩ **4** *Brit* **:** to feed (a female domestic animal) heavily esp. before parturition in order to induce a heavy milk flow *~ vi* **:** to become covered with steam ⟨his glasses *steamed up* as he came into the warm room⟩

steam valve *n* [1*steam*] **:** a valve for regulating a supply of steam

steam vessel *n* **1 :** a vessel propelled by steam **:** STEAMBOAT, STEAMSHIP, STEAMER **2 :** a mechanically propelled vessel

steam whistle *n* **:** a whistle in which the sound is produced by the action of steam; *esp* **:** one attached to a steam boiler

steamy \ˈstēmē, -mi\ *adj* -ER/-EST **1 :** consisting of or characterized by steam **:** full of steam ⟨from the *steamiest* tropics to the frozen polar regions —C.H.Curran⟩ **2 :** marked by sensual heat **:** HEATED ⟨the object of some ~ yearnings on the part of the comely wife of an older colleague —John McCarten⟩ ⟨summarized the ~ little affairs to be related by the singer —Douglas Watt⟩

stean \ˈstēn\ *n* -S [ME *stene,* fr. OE *stǣne;* akin to OHG *steinna* stone jug, OE *stān* stone] *dial chiefly Eng* **:** an earthenware container for liquids or foods

ste·ap·sin \stēˈapsən\ *n* -S [Gk *stear* fat, suet + E *-psin* (as in *pepsin*) — more at STONE] **:** the lipase in pancreatic juice

stear- *or* **steari-** *comb form* [ISV, fr. *stearic*] **:** related to or derived from stearic acid ⟨*stear*amide⟩ ⟨*steari*-di-oleins⟩

stea·rate \ˈstēəˌrāt, ˈsti,r-, -ˌrət, *usu* -d·+V\ *n* -S [*stear-* + *-ate*] **:** a salt or ester of stearic acid

stear·ic \(ˈ)stēˈarik, ˈstir-\ *adj* [F *stéarique,* fr. Gk *stear* fat, tallow + F *-ique* -ic — more at STONE] **1 :** relating to, obtained from, or resembling stearin or tallow **2 :** of or relating to stearic acid or its derivatives ⟨~ esters⟩

stearic acid *n* **1 :** a waxy crystalline saturated fatty acid $CH_3(CH_2)_{16}COOH$ that occurs esp. as a glyceride in tallow and other animal fats and in cocoa butter and other hard vegetable fats, that is obtained usu. by saponification of these fats or of hydrogenated oils (as soybean oil or cottonseed oil) or by hydrogenation of oleic acid, and that is used chiefly in mixtures with palmitic acid — called also *octadecanoic acid* **2 :** a mixture principally of stearic acid and palmitic acid produced commercially usu. by pressing chilled fatty acid saponification products and used chiefly in rubber compounding, in candles, and in the form of metallic soaps and other derivatives in ointments and cosmetics, lubricants, and coatings

stea·rin \ˈstēərən, ˈstir-\ *n* -S [F *stéarine,* fr. Gk *stear* fat, tallow + F *-ine,* -in, -ine] **1 :** an ester of glycerol and stearic acid; *esp* **:** TRISTEARIN **2** *also* **stea·rine** \", -ˌrēn\ **:** the solid portion of any fat — distinguished from *olein;* compare OLEOSTEARIN **3** *usu* **stearine :** STEARIC ACID 2

stearin pitch *n* **:** 1PITCH 1c

stea·rol·ic acid \ˌstēəˌrōlik-, -rȧl-, (ˈ)sti,r-\ *n* [*stear-* + *-olic*] **:** a crystalline acid $CH_3(CH_2)_7C{\equiv}C(CH_2)_7COOH$ of the acetylene series that is isologous with stearic acid and is obtained indirectly from oleic acid

stea·rone \ˈstēəˌrōn, ˈsti,r-\ *n* -S [*stear-* + *-one*] **:** a crystalline ketone $(C_{17}H_{35})_2CO$ obtainable by heating stearic acid with phosphorus pentoxide

stea·rop·tene \ˌstēəˈräpˌtēn, stiˈr-\ *also* **stea·rop·ten** \-ptən\ *n* -S [ISV *stear-* + Gk *ptēnos* winged; akin to Gk *petesthai* to fly — more at FEATHER] **:** the portion of a natural essential oil that separates as a solid on cooling or long standing — distinguished from *eleoptene*

stear·o·yl \stēˈarəˌwil, ˈstir-, -ˌwēl\ *n* -S [ISV *stear-* + *-yl*] **:** the radical $C_{17}H_{35}CO$— of stearic acid

stea·ryl \ˈstēəˌril, ˈsti,r-, -ēl\ *n* -S [ISV *stear-* + *-yl*] **1 :** STEAROYL **2 :** the univalent radical $C_{17}H_{35}CH_2$— derived from stearyl alcohol

stearyl alcohol *n* **:** an unctuous solid alcohol $CH_3(CH_2)_{16}CH_2OH$ that occurs esp. in whale, porpoise, and dolphin oils but is usu. obtained in a mixture with other solid alcohols by hydrogenation of stearic acid and that has uses similar to those of cetyl alcohol — called also *1-octadecanol*

steat- *or* **steato-** *comb form* [Gk, fr. *steat-, stear* — more at STONE] **:** fat **:** tallow ⟨*steato*lysis⟩ ⟨*steat*osis⟩

ste·a·tin \ˈstēəd·ən, -ətən\ *n* -S [NL *steatinum,* fr. *steat-* + L *-inum,* neut. of *-inus* -ine] **:** 7MULL 2

ste·a·tite \-ˌtīt\ *n* -S [L *steatitis,* a kind of stone, fr. (assumed) Gk *steatitis, steatitēs,* fr. *steat-* + *-itis, -itēs* -ite] **1 :** a massive talc having a grayish green or brown color and forming extensive beds **:** SOAPSTONE **2 :** an insulating porcelain composed largely of steatite and used esp. in radio equipment — **ste·a·tit·ic** \ˌ==ˈtid·ik\ *adj*

ste·a·ti·tis \ˌ==ˈtīd·əs\ *n* -ES [NL, fr. *steat-* + *-itis*] **:** YELLOW FAT

ste·a·tog·e·nous \ˌstēəˈtäjənəs\ *adj* [*steat-* + *-genous*] **:** producing fat **:** causing steatosis

ste·a·tol·y·sis \ˌ==ˈtäləsəs\ *n* [NL, fr. *steat-* + *-lysis*] **:** conversion of neutral fats into glycerol and free fatty acids

ste·a·to·ma \ˌstēəˈtōmə\ *n, pl* **steatomas** \-məz\ *or* **steatoma·ta** \-məd·ə, -ətə\ [NL *steatomat-, steatoma,* fr. L, fr. Gk *steatōmat-, steatōma,* fr. *steat-* + *-ōmat-, -ōma* -oma] **1 :** a sebaceous cyst **2 :** LIPOMA — **ste·a·toma·tous** \ˌ==ˈtämǝd·əs, -tōm-, -ətəs\ *adj*

ste·a·to·pygia \ˌstēəd·əˈpijēə, -pī|, |gēə\ *also* **ste·a·to·py·ga** \-ˈpīgə, ˌstēəˈtäpəgə\ *n* -S [*steatopyga* fr. NL, fr. *steat-* + Gk *pygē* rump, buttocks; *steatopygia* fr. NL, fr. *steat-* + Gk *pygē* + NL *-ia* — more at FOG] **:** an excessive development of fat on the buttocks esp. of females that is common among the Hottentots and some Negro peoples — **ste·a·to·pyg·ic** \ˌstēəd·əˈpijik\ *adj* — **ste·a·to·py·gous** \ˌstēəd·əˈpīgəs, ˌstēəˈtäpəg-\ *adj*

ste·a·to·py·gy \ˈstēəd·əˌpījē, -īgē; ˌstēəˈtäpəjē, -pəgē\ *n* -ES [NL *steatopygia*] **:** STEATOPYGIA

ste·a·tor·nis \ˌstēəˈtȯrnəs\ *n, cap* [NL *Steatornith-, Steatornis,* fr. *steat-* + *-ornith-, -ornis*] **:** a genus (coextensive with the family Steatornithidae) consisting of the oilbird — see STEATORNITHES

ste·a·tor·ni·thes \ˌ==ˈtȯrnəˌthēz, -ˌtȯrˈnī(ˌ)thēz\ *n pl, cap* [NL, fr. pl. of *Steatornis*] **:** a suborder of Caprimulgiformes including the single genus *Steatornis*

ste·a·tor·rhea *or* **ste·a·tor·rhoea** \ˌstēəd·əˈrēə\ *n* -S [NL, fr. *steat-* + *-rrhea*] **:** an excess of fat in the stools resulting from any of several conditions

ste·a·to·sis \-ˈtōsəs\ *n, pl* **steato·ses** \-ōˌsēz\ [NL, fr. *steat-* + *-osis*] **:** FATTY DEGENERATION

stech \ˈstek\ *vb* [origin unknown] *vt, chiefly Scot* **:** CRAM, STUFF *~ vi, chiefly Scot* **:** GORMANDIZE

steck·ling \ˈstekliŋ, -lēŋ\ *n* -S [G, fr. *stecken* to stick, insert (fr. OHG *stecchen*) + *-ling* — more at STICK] **:** a small late-planted plant of a biennial root crop (as beet or carrot) that is usu. dug and stored over winter and replanted the next season for seed production

sted·dle \ˈstedᵊl\ *dial var of* STADDLE

stedfast *var of* STEADFAST

sted·man \ˈstedmən\ *n* -S *usu cap* [after Fabian *Stedman* 17th cent. Eng. printer, its inventor] **:** a system for ringing changes on a set of bells

stee \ˈstē\ *n* -S [alter. of ME *stie,* fr. ON *stigi;* akin to OE *stige* ascent, descent, OHG *stega* flight of stairs, OE *stīgan* to go up — more at STAIR] *dial Eng* **:** LADDER

steed \ˈstēd\ *n* -S [ME *stede,* fr. OE *stēda* studhorse, stallion; akin to OE *stōd* stud — more at STUD] **1 :** HORSE; *esp* **:** a spirited horse for state or war **2 a :** a horse of no mettle or distinction **:** NAG **b :** something (as a bicycle) ridden astride

steed·less \ˈ=ləs\ *adj* **:** lacking a steed

1**steek** \ˈstēk\ *vb* [ME *steken* to pierce, fix, enclose; akin to MLG & MD *steken* to sting, prick, OHG *stehhan* — more at STICK] *chiefly Scot* **:** SHUT, CLOSE

2**steek** \"\ *chiefly Scot var of* STITCH

3**steek** \"\ *n* -S [prob. fr. 2*steek*] *Scot* **:** 4CLIP 5

steek·gras *or* **steek·grass** \ˈstekˌgras\ *n* -ES [Afrik *steekgras,* fr. *steek* prick, sting (fr. MD *steke*) + *gras* grass, fr. MD; akin to OE *stice* stitch and to OE *græs* grass — more at STITCH, GRASS] *southern Africa* **:** a grass of the genus *Aristida*

1**steel** \ˈstēl, *esp before pause or consonant* -ēəl\ *n* -S [ME *stele, stel,* fr. OE *stēle, stȳle;* akin to OHG *stahal* steel, ON *stāl,* Skt *stakati* he resists] **1 :** commercial iron that contains carbon in any amount up to about 1.7 percent as an essential alloying constituent, is malleable when under suitable conditions, is distinguished from cast iron by its malleability and lower carbon content and when of low carbon content from wrought iron by its freedom from slag and by its method of manufacture, and is now usu. produced by refining molten pig iron in a bath that remains completely molten throughout the process — see ALLOY STEEL, BESSEMER STEEL, CARBON STEEL, ELECTRIC STEEL, MILD STEEL, STAINLESS STEEL; BESSEMER PROCESS, OPEN-HEARTH PROCESS **2 a :** steel as a material for manufactured articles **b :** articles characteristically made of steel **c :** the steel part of an article (as the blade of a knife) **3 :** an instrument or implement of or characteristically of steel: as **a** (1) **:** WEAPON; *esp* **:** one for thrusting or cutting — see COLD STEEL (2) **:** weapons or armaments of steel ⟨invaders were driven back by ~⟩ ⟨evils, for which the only remedy is blood and ~ —John Buchan⟩ **b :** an instrument for sharpening knives; *esp* **:** a fluted round rod fitted with a handle and used for this purpose ⟨butcher's ~⟩ **c :** a piece of steel for striking sparks from flint **d :** RAIL 3a,3b(3) ⟨lay ~⟩ ⟨end of ~⟩ **e :** a strip of steel used (as in corsets) for stiffening — compare BONE 5b **4 :** a steellike quality ⟨lacked the ~ a conquistador must have —Bernard De Voto⟩ ⟨the cold ~ of the intellect —Edward Sapir⟩ **5 :** STEEL GRAY **6 a :** the steel manufacturing industry **:** steel manufacturing companies ⟨the growth of ~ since the end of the war —Howard Marshall⟩ ⟨Big *Steel*⟩ **b steels** *pl* **:** stocks or bonds of steel companies

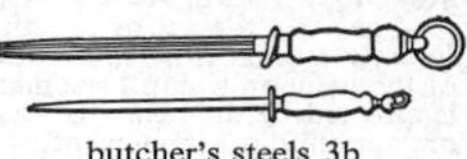
butcher's steels 3b

2**steel** \"\ *vt* -ED/-ING/-S [ME *stelen,* fr. *stele* steel] **1 a :** to overlay, point, or edge with steel ⟨~ a razor⟩ ⟨~ an ax⟩; *specif* **:** to provide (an electrotype) with a nickel or iron-nickel compound face **b :** CASE HARDEN **2 a :** to cause to resemble steel (as in looks or hardness) **b :** to make hard or unbending **:** fill with strong resolution, unyielding determination, or stark insensibility ⟨was sick of the bareness and privation . . . but was *~ing* himself to hold out —Theodore Dreiser⟩ ⟨charge high rates and ~ their hearts against all compassion —G.G.Coulton⟩ ⟨strive rather to ~ them in a new and finer way —E.A.Mowrer⟩ **syn** see ENCOURAGE

3**steel** \"\ *adj* [1*steel*] **1 :** made of steel ⟨~ plate⟩ ⟨~ castings⟩ ⟨~ pen⟩ **2 :** of or relating to the production of steel ⟨the ~ industry⟩ ⟨~ furnace⟩ **3 :** resembling steel in one or more characteristics ⟨~ nerves⟩ ⟨~ courage⟩ — often used in combination ⟨*steel*-jawed⟩ ⟨*steel*-willed⟩

steel band *n* [1*steel*] **:** a band peculiar to the Caribbean islands and esp. Trinidad composed of percussion instruments typically cut out of oil barrels and usu. tuned to a definite pitch — called also *steel orchestra*

steel blue *n* [3*steel*] **1 :** a variable color averaging a grayish blue that is redder and paler than electric, greener and less strong than copenhagen, and redder than Gobelin **2 :** STEEL GRAY **3 :** PRUSSIAN BLUE 2 **4 :** any of the blue colors assumed by steel at various temperatures in tempering — compare TEMPER COLOR **5 :** an iron blue pigment

steel·bow \ˈstēlˌbō, -ˌbau̇\ *n* [ME *stelebow,* fr. *stele* steel + *bow* farm stock; fr. the understanding that the amount must be rigidly preserved and returned — more at BOWER (farm tenant)] **1 :** the farming stock, implements, and other materials formerly supplied to a tenant farmer in Scotland by the landlord under a contract stipulating that these goods must be returned or compensated for at the expiration of the tenancy **2 :** a type of contract formerly in use in Scotland under which a tenant farmer must at the expiration of his tenancy return to his landlord the farming goods supplied by the landlord or compensate him for them

steel bronze *n* [3*steel*] **:** a bronze of about 92 percent copper and 8 percent tin hardened by compression and used as a substitute for steel in making guns — called also *Uchatius bronze*

steel–cage construction \ˈ=ˌ=-\ *n* **:** SKELETON CONSTRUCTION

steel–clad rope \ˈ=ˌ=-\ *n* **:** a hoisting rope whose strands have received an additional external serving of flat strip steel to secure additional wearing surface without a sacrifice of flexibility

steel concrete *n* **:** concrete reinforced with steel

steel–cut \ˈ=ˌ=\ *adj* **1 :** ground or crushed between rolls fitted with cutting teeth into granules of uniform size and freed of powder and chaff ⟨*steel-cut* coffee⟩ ⟨*steel-cut* oats⟩ **2 :** faceted with a steel tool — used esp. of buttons, buckles, and beads having an allover design of facets

steel driver *n* **:** a worker who before the adoption of the power drill drove a steel drill with a heavy hammer into rock or soil to make holes for blasting charges

steeled \ˈstē(ə)ld\ *adj* [ME *steled,* fr. OE *stȳled,* fr. *stȳle* steel + *-ed*] **:** made of steel **:** edged, tipped, or armored with steel ⟨a ~ spear⟩ ⟨a ~ compartment of a battleship⟩

steel electrotype *n* **:** NICKELTYPE

steel emery *n* **:** an abrasive made in the same way as crushed steel but with an intensely hard temper

steel engraving *n* **1 :** the art or process of engraving on steel **2 :** an impression taken from an engraved steel plate

1**steeler** *var of* STEALER

2**steel·er** \ˈstēlə(r)\ *n* -S [2*steel* + *-er*] **1 :** one that steels; *esp* **:** a smith who steels edged tools **2 :** one that inserts steels (as in corsets) **:** BONER

steel eraser *n* [3*steel*] **:** ERASER a

steel–face \ˈ=ˌ=\ *vt* **:** to make (a copper engraving or etching plate) more durable by electroplating with nickel steel

steelfaced electrotype \ˈ=ˌ=-\ *n* **:** NICKELTYPE

steel glass *n* **:** a mirror of steel

steel gray *n* **:** a nearly neutral slightly purplish dark gray that is lighter and slightly bluer than gunmetal — called also *Davy's gray, iron blue*

steel guitar *n* **:** HAWAIIAN GUITAR 1

steel hand *n* **:** a fishing tool used in well drilling to recover objects at the bottom of a well

steelhead \ˈ=ˌ=\ *n* **1** *or* **steelhead trout :** a large-sized silvery anadromous rainbow trout **2** *dial* **:** RUDDY DUCK

steel·ie *also* **steely** \ˈstēlē, -li\ *n, pl* **steelies** [3*steel* + *-ie*] **:** a steel playing marble

steel·i·fi·ca·tion \ˌstēləfəˈkāshən\ *n* -S [fr. *steelify;* after such pairs as E *purify: purification*] **:** the act or process of converting iron into steel

steel·i·fy \ˈ=ˌfī\ *vt* -ED/-ING/-ES [1*steel* + *-ify*] **:** to convert (iron) into steel

steel·i·ness \-lēnəs, -lin-\ *n* -ES **:** the quality or state of being steely

steel jack *n* **:** PUCELLAS

steel–jacketed \ˈ=ˌ===\ *adj, of a bullet* **:** having a steel jacket over a soft metal core

steel·less \ˈstēl(l)əs\ *adj* **:** containing no steel **:** lacking steel

steellike \ˈ=ˌ=\ *adj* **:** resembling steel **:** suggestive of steel (as in strength, severity, or relentlessness)

steelmaker \ˈ=ˌ==\ *n* **:** one that makes steel **:** a steel manufacturer **:** an official of a steel manufacturing company

steelmaking \ˈ=ˌ==\ *n* **:** the process or business of manufacturing steel

steel·man \ˈ=ˌmən\ *n, pl* **steelmen :** STEELMAKER

steel marimba *n* **:** a musical instrument similar to a xylophone but having metal bars

steelmaster \ˈ=ˌ==\ *n* **:** STEELMAKER

steel mill *n* **1 :** a mill (as for coffee or oats) that operates machines with steel grinding surfaces **2 :** a mill where steel is manufactured

steel orchestra *n* **:** STEEL BAND

steels *pl of* STEEL, *pres 3d sing of* STEEL

steel square *n* **:** a carpenter's square made of steel

steel–trap \ˈ=ˌ=\ *adj* [fr. the phrase *as sharp as a steel trap*] **:** extremely quick and penetrating of intellect ⟨a *steel-trap* mind⟩

steel wool *n* **:** an abrasive material composed of long fine steel shavings and used esp. for scouring and burnishing

steelwork \ˈ=ˌ=\ *n* **1 :** work in steel **:** articles or a part or the whole of any structure made of steel **2 steelworks** *pl but sing or pl in constr* **:** a shop or establishment where steel is made

steelworker \ˈ=ˌ==\ *n* **:** one that works in steel and esp. in the manufacturing of it

1**steely** \ˈstēlē, -li\ *adj* -ER/-EST [*steel* + *-y*] **1 :** made of steel **:** consisting of steel **2 :** resembling steel (as in hardness, firmness, color, keenness, or chillness) ⟨night, with the ~ stars above —Aubrey Drury⟩ ⟨a ~ wind⟩ ⟨~ cymbals —Irving Kolodin⟩ ⟨nerves as ~ as those of a steeplejack —*London Daily Telegraph*⟩ ⟨~ fortitude⟩ **3** *of wool* **:** lacking the natural crimp and elasticity

2**steely** *var of* STEELIE

steel·yard \ˈstēlˌyärd, -ˌyȧd, -ˌyə(r)d\ *n* [prob. fr. 1*steel* + *yard* (rod)] **:** a portable balance for weighing designed to be suspended (as from a hook or the free hand of the user) when in operation — called also *lever scales*

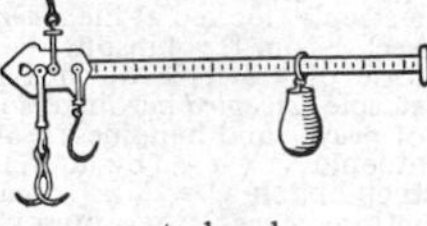
steelyard

1**steen** *or* **stein** *also* **steyn** \ˈstēn, ˈstān\ *vt* -ED/-ING/-S [ME *stenen* to stone, fr. OE *stǣnan;* akin to OHG *steinōn* to stone, Goth *stainjan,* ON *steina* to paint (with mineral colors), OE *stān* stone — more at STONE] **:** to line (an excavation) with stone, brick, cement, or similar material to prevent caving in or washing away of soil ⟨~ a well⟩ ⟨the bottom was but slightly *~ed* and not watertight —G.E.Fussell⟩

²steen *var of* STEAN

³steen \ˈstēn\ *adj* [prob. by shortening & alter. fr. *sixteen*] : UMPTEEN

steen·bok *or* **stein·bok** *also* **stein·bock** \ˈstēn,bäk\ *n, pl* **steenbok** *or* **steenboks** *or* **steinbok** *or* **steinboks** [Afrik *steenbok*, fr. MD *steenboc* ibex — more at STEINBOCK] : any small antelope of the genus *Raphicerus* (as *R. campestris*) of the plains of southern and eastern Africa

steen·bras *also* **steen·brass** \ˈstēn,bras\ *n, pl* **steenbras** *or* **steenbrases** *also* **steenbrass** *or* **steenbrasses** [Afrik *steenbras*, fr. *steen* stone (fr. MD) + *brasem* bream, fr. MD *brasem, bressem* — more at BREAM] : any of several southern African marine sparid food and sport fishes: as **a** : BISKOP **b** : RED STEENBRAS **c** : WHITE STEENBRAS

steening *or* **steining** *also* **steyning** *n* -S [fr. gerund of ¹*steen*] : a lining (as for a well) of stone, brick, or other hard material to prevent caving in or washing away of soil

steenkirk *often cap, var of* STEINKIRK

steen·strup·ine \ˈstēnstrə,pēn, -n,strüpən\ *n* -S [Dan *steenstrupine*, fr. K. J. V. *Steenstrup* †1913 Dan. geologist + Dan *-ine*] : a mineral (La,Ca,Na)(Al,Fe,Mn)(Si,P)(O,OH,F)$_4$(?) consisting of a complex silicate, phosphate, and fluoride of the rare-earth metals, calcium, sodium, aluminum, iron, and manganese, and occurring in dark brown rhombohedral crystals

steenth \ˈstēn(t)th\ *adj* [³*steen* + *-th*] : UMPTEENTH

steen·tjie \ˈstēnchē\ *n* -S [Afrik, dim. of *steenbras*] : a small southern African sea bream (*Spondyliosoma emarginatum*)

¹**steep** \ˈstēp\ *adj* -ER/-EST [ME *stepe*, fr. OE *stēap* high, steep, deep; akin to OE *stēap* cup, OFris *stāp* steep, OHG *stouf* high rock, cup, MHG *stief* steep, ON *staup* lump, knoll, hole in a road, cup] **1** : LOFTY, TALL, ELEVATED, HIGH — used chiefly of a sea ⟨ships steaming into ~ head seas —*Manual of Seamanship*⟩ ⟨the elusive periscope almost impossible to detect in such ~ seas —Stanley Rogers⟩ **2 a** : making a large angle with the plane of the horizon : having a side or slope approaching the perpendicular : PRECIPITOUS ⟨~ hills⟩ ⟨a ~ road⟩ ⟨area of cleared, ~ ground —Evan Williams⟩ **b** *of twill* : having an angle greater than 45 degrees in the twill line **3 a** : mounting or falling precipitously : HEADLONG ⟨a ~ flight of stairs⟩ **b** : characterized by a very rapid decline or increase ⟨the ~ but comparatively brief depression —Clark Warburton⟩ ⟨the persistently ~ fall in immigration —Peter Scott⟩ ⟨a period of ~ decline in our literary standards —Malcolm Cowley⟩ **4** : having precipitous or sharply pitched sides ⟨a ~ roof⟩ ⟨its ~ wooded valleys —R.M.Lockley⟩ **5** : difficult to accept, meet, or perform : ARDUOUS, EXTREME, EXCESSIVE, EXORBITANT, INCREDIBLE ⟨a ~ story⟩ ⟨a ~ tax⟩ ⟨prices are rather ~⟩ ⟨a ~ task⟩

syn ABRUPT, PRECIPITOUS, SHEER: STEEP describes a slope or pitch likely to make ascent difficult or descent or fall sharp, rapid, rushing ⟨the trail . . . then struck up the side of the mountain, growing *steeper* every foot of the way —H.D. Quillin⟩ ⟨a slope of water so *steep* that it made me giddy —R.L.Stevenson⟩ ABRUPT may apply to sudden protuberance or declivity, to sharply broken angles or levels ⟨occasionally the hills slope gently to the waterline, but more often the highlands rise into *abrupt* cliffs —*Amer. Guide Series: Minn.*⟩ ⟨high *abrupt* banks in places become hanging cliffs with a drop of 100 feet or more —*Amer. Guide Series: N.C.*⟩ PRECIPITOUS applies to inclines next to impossible to climb by ordinary procedures, to those approaching the perpendicular ⟨a mountainous region, fronting the Pacific, to which it presents, abruptly, a *precipitous* escarpment —*Amer. Guide Series: Oregon*⟩ ⟨a deep gorge, with *precipitous*, volcanic walls which no man could scale —Jack London⟩ SHEER may suggest an unbroken perpendicular expanse ⟨*sheer* cliffs that fell from the summit to the plain, more than a thousand feet —Willa Cather⟩ ⟨a *sheer* drop of 224 feet into a pool at the base of an overhanging cliff —*Amer. Guide Series: Oregon*⟩

²**steep** \ˈ"\ *adv* : STEEPLY ⟨the cliff rises ~ behind it —Edmund Wilson⟩ ⟨the roof . . . was pitched very ~ to shed water —*Amer. Guide Series: Conn.*⟩ — often used in combination ⟨*steep*-ascending⟩

³**steep** \ˈ"\ *n* -S : a precipitous place : a steep ascent or descent : an object having a steep side or slope ⟨too many thickets and swamps and ~s for practical traveling off the roads —G.W. Brace⟩ ⟨when the toiling cyclists climbed that ~ they had the flat road . . . in front of them —O.S.J.Gogarty⟩

⁴**steep** \ˈ"\ *vi* -ED/-ING/-S : SLOPE; *esp* : to slope abruptly ⟨now the angle of ascent ~*ed* sharply —J.R.Ullman⟩

⁵**steep** \ˈ"\ *vb* -ED/-ING/-S [ME *stepen*; akin to Sw *stöpa* to steep, Dan *stöbe*, and prob. to OE *stēap* cup — more at ¹STEEP] *vt* **1 a** : to soak or let stand in a liquid at a temperature under the boiling point (as for the purpose of cleansing, softening, bleaching, extracting a flavor, or germinating) : INFUSE, MACERATE ⟨rice grains are usually ~*ed* in a solution of sodium hydroxide⟩ ⟨~ coffee⟩ ⟨~ barley⟩ **b** : to soak (corn kernels) in warm water usu. containing a very small amount of sulfur dioxide in the manufacture of starch by the wet milling process **c** : to soak (cellulose pulp) in a dilute solution of sodium hydroxide for the production of alkali cellulose **2** : BATHE, WET, IMMERSE, MOISTEN ⟨~*ed* my wrists and laved my temples —R.L.Stevenson⟩ **3** : to saturate thoroughly : IMBUE ⟨the world was all ~*ed* in sunshine —D.H.Lawrence⟩ ⟨a man ~*ed* in the art of the past —Aline B. Saarinen⟩ ⟨they continued to ~ themselves in the classics —Gilbert Highet⟩ ⟨the annals of those ~*ed* in crime —Ellen Smith⟩ ~ *vi* : to undergo the process of soaking in a liquid (as water) under the boiling point ⟨the tea is ~*ing*⟩ ⟨rosemary . . . ~*ing* in vinegar —J.H. Wheelwright⟩

⁶**steep** \ˈ"\ *n* -S [ME *stepe*, fr. *stepen* to steep] **1** : the state or process of being steeped ⟨put barley in ~ for forty-eight hours⟩ **2** : a bath or solution in which something is steeped (as in dyeing or cleansing) **3** : a tank in which a material (as corn or rice) is steeped ⟨the shelled corn is soaked in a ~ before milling⟩ ⟨the rice starch from the ~ is purified⟩

⁷**steep** \ˈ"\ *adj* [⁵*steep*] : used for steeping ⟨~ tank⟩ ⟨~ tub⟩

steepdown \ˈ=ˌ=\ *adj* [¹*steep* + *down*, adv.] : PRECIPITOUS

steep·en \ˈstēpən, -pᵊm\ *vb* **steepened; steepened; steepening** \-p(ə)niŋ\ **steepens** [¹*steep* + *-en*] *vt* : to make steeper : INCREASE ⟨ice sheets of successive glaciations have ~*ed* the valley sides —Samuel Van Valkenburg & Ellsworth Huntington⟩ ~ *vi* : to become steeper ⟨volcanoes have concave slopes that ~ to the summit —Howel Williams⟩ ⟨the slant of the line ~*ed* to the vertical —Arthur Mayse⟩

steep·er \ˈstēpə(r)\ *n* -S : one that steeps: as **a** : a container (as a tank or vat) in which something is steeped **b** : a worker who steeps barley for the manufacture of malt liquor

steepgrass \ˈ=ˌ=\ *n* [⁶*steep* + *grass*] : a common butterwort (*Pinguicula vulgaris*) used like rennet

steep·i·ness \-pēnəs, -pin-\ *n* -ES [*steepy* + *-ness*] *archaic* : STEEPNESS

steep·ish \-pish, -pēsh\ *adj* : somewhat steep ⟨a very large field with a ~ slope —Roald Dahl⟩

¹**stee·ple** \ˈstēpəl\ *n* -S [ME *stepel*, fr. OE *stīpel, stȳpel, stēpel* tower; akin to OE *stēap* steep — more at STEEP] **1 a** : a tall structure usu. composed of a series of diminishing stories finished at the top with a small spire or cupola surmounting the lower straight-sided story of a church tower **b** : the whole of a church tower **2** : something suggesting or having the shape of a steeple ⟨pressed together their fingertips to form ~s —Scott Fitzgerald⟩

steeple 1a

²**steeple** \ˈ"\ *vb* **steepled; steepled; steepling** \-p(ə)liŋ\ **steeples** *vi* : to rise high in the air like a steeple ⟨looked at the *steepling* mast and loaded keel —Tom Hopkinson⟩ ~ *vt* : to arrange in the form of a steeple or in a form suggestive of a steeple ⟨*steepled* her fingers in the childish gesture of prayer and happiness —Adria Langley⟩

³**steeple** \ˈ"\ *n* -S [by alter.] : ¹STAPLE 1

steeplebush \ˈ=ˌ=\ *n* [so called fr. its steeplelike inflorescences] : HARDHACK 1

¹**steeplechase** \ˈ=ˌ=\ *n* [so called fr. the use of church steeples as landmarks to guide the competitors] **1 a** : a race across country and over barriers (as fences, hedges, and ditches) ridden by a number of horsemen **b** : a similar obstacle race over a circular course typically situated on the inner periphery of a flat-racing track **2** : a usu. 2-mile footrace across country or over a prescribed course obstructed esp. by hurdles, hedges, and water jumps

²**steeplechase** \ˈ"\ *vi* : to run or ride in a steeplechase

steeplechaser \ˈ=ˌ=ˌ=\ *n* **1** : one that rides or runs in a steeplechase **2** : an athlete or a horse trained to run in steeplechases

steeplechasing \ˈ=ˌ=ˌ=\ *n* [fr. gerund of ²*steeplechase*] : the sport of riding in steeplechases

steeple clock *n* : an Early American pointed shelf clock with steeplelike finials bordering each side

steeple–crown \ˈ=ˌ=ˌ=\ *n* **1** : a hat crown that is high and pointed like a steeple **2** : a hat with a steeple-crown — **steeple–crowned** \ˌ=ˌ=ˈ=\ *adj*

steeple cup *n* : a usu. silver standing cup of early 17th century English origin with baluster stem supporting a conical bowl and with a domed cover carrying a steeplelike finial

stee·pled \ˈstēpəld\ *adj* [¹*steeple* + *-ed*] : furnished with or having the form of a steeple : adorned with or as if with steeples ⟨a ~ hill⟩

steeple engine *n* : a vertical back-acting steam engine having the cylinder beneath the crosshead and chiefly used for donkey engines

steeple fork *n* : an earmark on an animal made by a cut removing a rectangular piece from the upper part of the ear — see EARMARK illustration

steeple hat *n* : a steeple-crowned hat

steeple headdress *n* : HENNIN

steeple–head rivet \ˈ=ˌ=ˌ=-\ *n* : a rivet having a head in the form of a cylindrical cone

steeplehouse \ˈ=ˌ=ˌ=\ *n, archaic* : a church building — used esp. by the early Quakers

steeple hunt *n, archaic* : STEEPLECHASE

¹**steeplejack** \ˈ=ˌ=ˌ=\ *n* [¹*steeple* + *jack* (man)] : one whose work is building smokestacks, towers, or steeples or climbing up the outside of such structures to paint and make repairs

²**steeplejack** \ˈ"\ *vi* -ED/-ING/-S : to work as a steeplejack

steeple·less \ˈ=ˌ=ləs\ *adj* : having no steeple ⟨a ~ church⟩

steeplelike \ˈ=ˌ=ˌ=\ *adj* : resembling or suggestive of a steeple

steeples *pl of* STEEPLE, *pres 3d sing of* STEEPLE

steeple skull *or* **steeple head** *n* : OXYCEPHALY

steepletop \ˈ=ˌ=ˌ=\ *n* **1** : a top in the shape of a steeple; *specif* : an octagonal finial (as of an andiron or chair post) tapering to a point **2** [so called fr. its conical blowholes] : GREENLAND WHALE

steepling *pres part of* STEEPLE

steep·ly *adv* [¹*steep* + *-ly*] **1** : at a sharp angle : ABRUPTLY, PRECIPITOUSLY, SHARPLY ⟨the train swept ~ down toward . . . the Swiss border —Joseph Wechsberg⟩ ⟨the ground at once shelves ~ toward the north —James Whyle⟩ ⟨a ~ sloping roof⟩ **2** : at a rapid rate : SWIFTLY ⟨gasoline consumption rose ~ when rationing was ended —*Lamp*⟩ ⟨the ~ declining trend of the population —Alzada Comstock⟩ ⟨dropped ~ into unconsciousness —Irwin Shaw⟩

steep·ness *n* -ES [ME *stepnesse*, fr. *stepe* steep + *-nesse* -ness] : the quality or state of being steep : PRECIPITOUSNESS ⟨the ~ of a gradient⟩

steeps *pres 3d sing of* STEEP, *pl of* STEEP

steep–to \ˈ=ˌ=\ *adj* [¹*steep* + *to*, adv.] : PRECIPITOUS; *esp* : sloping almost perpendicularly downward — used esp. of a shore or shoal ⟨the north side of the cape is *steep-to* —*U. S. Coast Pilot: West Indies*⟩ ⟨found steep-to banks inside against which the ships would have to lie —S.E.Morison⟩

steep–up \ˈ=ˈ=\ *adj* [¹*steep* + *up*, adv.] : STEEP, PRECIPITOUS, STRAIGHT-UP

steepwater \ˈ=ˌ=ˌ=\ *n* [⁶*steep* + *water*] : the solution resulting from steeping (as corn) in water in the manufacture of starch — see INOSITOL a

steepweed \ˈ=ˌ=\ *or* **steepwort** \ˈ=ˌ=\ *n* [⁶*steep*] : STEEPGRASS

steepy \ˈstēpē, -pi\ *adj* [¹*steep* + *-y*] *archaic* : STEEP, PRECIPITOUS ⟨climb the ~ cliffs —John Dryden⟩

¹**steer** \ˈsti(ə)r, -iə\ *n, pl* **steers** *also* **steer** [ME *stere, steer*, fr. OE *stēor* young ox; akin to OHG *stior* young ox, ON *stjōrr*, Goth *stiur*, Skt *sthavira, sthūra* stout, thick, broad, and perh. to L *taurus* bull, Gk *tauros*, MIr *tarb*, ON *thjōrr* — more at ³STEER] **1 a** : a bull castrated before sexual maturity and usu. at an early age — see BEEF **b** : an ox less than four years old ⟨eight thousand head of ~ —Wright Morris⟩ **2** : an entire male bovine : BULL **3** : the hide of a steer

²**steer** \ˈ"\ *vt* -ED/-ING/-S : CASTRATE — used of a bullock

³**steer** \ˈ"\ *vb* -ED/-ING/-S [ME *steren*, fr. OE *stīeran*; akin to OHG *stiuren* to steer, ON *stȳra*, Goth *stiurjan* to establish; all fr. a prehistoric Gmc denominative verb fr. the root of OE *stēor-* rudder, steering oar; akin to ON *stȳri* rudder, *staurr* pale, stake, Gk *stauros* pale, stake, cross, *stylos* pillar, Skt *sthavira, sthūra* stout, thick, *tiṣṭhati* he stands — more at STAND] *vt* **1 a** : to direct the course of : GUIDE, MANAGE, CONTROL ⟨~ a bill through the legislature⟩ ⟨~*ed* the conversation into his favorite channels —T.B.Costain⟩; *specif* : to direct the course of (as a ship) by means of a rudder or similar device or by other mechanical means ⟨~ a bicycle⟩ ⟨~ an automobile⟩ ⟨~ a satellite⟩ **b** : to entice (a prospective customer or victim) to an illicit or disreputable establishment **2** : to set and hold to or pursue (a course) : WEND ⟨see that the boat was ~*ing* her right course for the Narrows —William Black⟩ ⟨an effort to ~ a course between inflation and deflation —*Biddle Survey*⟩ ~ *vi* **1** : to direct the course (as of a ship or automobile) ⟨~ by the stars⟩ ⟨take turns ~*ing*⟩ **2** : to direct one's course : pursue a course of action ⟨~ for home⟩ **3** : to be subject to guidance or direction : obey the helm ⟨an automobile that ~s well⟩ **syn** see GUIDE — **steer large 1** : to steer a ship off the wind **2** : to steer a ship loosely with considerable shifting of the helm — **steer small** : to steer a ship with little shifting of the helm : steer in an almost straight course — **steer clear** : to keep entirely away (as from a danger) : direct one's course so as to avoid any chance of hindrance, contact, harm, or involvement — often used with *of* ⟨tries to *steer clear* of controversial issues —Kathleen Teltsch⟩

⁴**steer** \ˈ"\ *n* -S [ME *stere*, fr. *steren* to steer] : something by which to steer: as **a** *obs* : RUDDER, HELM **b** : directions for steering a course ⟨gave us a ~ toward home⟩ **c** : a hint as to procedure : TIP ⟨give one a friendly ~⟩ ⟨never got a wrong ~ from me yet —H.A.Sinclair⟩ — see BUM STEER **d** : a steering mechanism or arrangement ⟨a truck with a four-wheel ~⟩

⁵**steer** \ˈstēr\ *adj* [ME *stere, steer*; akin to MLG *stūr* stiff, severe, OHG *stiuri, stūri* strong, proud, Skt *sthūra* stout, thick, broad — more at ³STEER] *chiefly Scot* : STRONG, ROUGH

⁶**steer** \ˈsti(ə)r, -iə\ *dial Brit var of* STIR

steer·abil·i·ty \ˌstirəˈbiləd·ē\ *n* : the quality or state of being steerable

steer·able \ˈ=rəbəl\ *adj* [³*steer* + *-able*] : capable of being guided by steering ⟨~ balloon⟩; *also* : capable of being readily shifted ⟨~ antenna⟩

¹**steer·age** \ˈstirij, -rēj\ *n* -S [ME *sterage*, fr. *steren* to steer + *-age*] **1** : the act or practice of steering ⟨the ~ of a ship⟩; *broadly* : DIRECTION, MANAGEMENT, GUIDANCE **2** : the effect of the helm on a ship : the manner in which an individual ship is affected by the helm **3** : a steering apparatus (as of a ship or agricultural implement) **4** *archaic* : a course steered **5 a** (1) *archaic* : a section of the underdeck of the afterpart of a ship situated near the rudder or immediately forward of the main cabin and used for passenger accommodations inferior to those of the cabin (2) : a section in a passenger ship for passengers paying the lowest fares and given inferior accommodations — compare TOURIST CLASS **b** : a compartment in a man-of-war located generally just forward of the wardroom and assigned to midshipmen and other junior officers for quarters

²**steerage** \ˈ"\ *adv* : with steerage accommodations ⟨traveled ~ to Panama —Carl Van Doren⟩

steerage passenger *n* : a passenger in the steerage

steerageway \ˈ=ˌ=ˌ=\ *n* : a rate of motion sufficient to make a boat answer the helm : the slowest forward speed of a ship that will permit steering — compare STERNWAY ⟨the big ships in the van slowed down till they had almost lost ~ —Nicholas Monsarrat⟩

steer·er \ˈstirə(r)\ *n* -S **1** : one that steers: as **a** : STEERSMAN **b** (1) : an accomplice who directs persons to places where they may be swindled : CAPPER ⟨a ~ for a gambling game⟩ (2) : a person employed to entice patrons : TOUT ⟨a ~ for a theater⟩ **2** : something (as a ship) that is steered or responds to steering in some specified way ⟨a quick ~⟩

steerhide \ˈ=ˌ=\ *n* [¹*steer*] **1** : leather made from the hide of a steer **2** : CATTLEHIDE

steering *n* -S [ME *stering*, fr. gerund of *steren* to steer] **1** : the act of one who steers **2 a** : the response (as of a ship) to the action of steering **b** : STEERING GEAR **3** : MANAGEMENT, GOVERNMENT

steering arm *n* : an arm for transmitting the turning force from the steering gear to the drag link esp. of an automotive vehicle

steering bridge *n* : a bridge from which a ship can be steered

steering column *or* **steering post** *n* : the column carrying the steering wheel and enclosing connections to the steering gear of an automobile or other vehicle

steering committee *n* : a managing or directing committee; *specif* : a committee composed of leaders of the majority caucus that determines the order in which business shall be taken up in a U.S. legislative body

steering gear *n* : the mechanism by which something is steered: as **a** : the gear train and linkages between the steering control and road-wheel connections of an automobile **b** : any mechanism giving more powerful control over a boat rudder than that given by the simple tiller

steering head *n* : the assemblages of front-axle end and steering knuckle on which a front wheel of an automobile turns

steering knuckle *n* : a knuckle made to furnish a bearing for an automobile steering wheel, pivoted to the axle, and controlled in its swiveling motion by the steering gear

steering line *n* : the warm front of an extratropical cyclone where the tropical winds rise over the cooler easterly winds

steering lock *n* : the maximum angular range of the steered wheels of an automobile

steering oar *or* **steer oar** *n* : an oar used over the stern or on the quarter in place of a rudder

steering wheel *n* : a hand wheel by means of which one steers: as **a** : a wheel that controls the movements of a ship's rudder **b** : a wheel by which the direction of the road wheels of an automobile is controlled

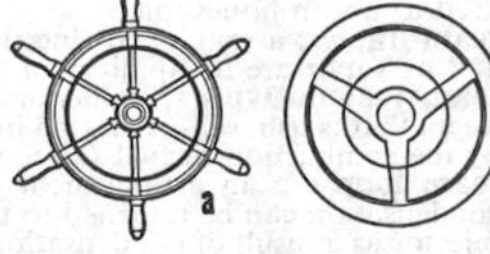

steering wheels

steer joint *n* [³*steer*] : an establishment (as a gambling house) that employs steerers

steer·less \ˈ=ləs\ *adj* : lacking a steer

steers *pl of* STEER, *pres 3d sing of* STEER

steershead \ˈ=ˌ=\ *n* [¹*steer*] : a low tuberous perennial herb (*Dicentra uniflora*) that is native to the mountains of western U.S. and has pink or white flowers few to a stalk and with the narrow outer petals strongly recurved

steers·man \ˈ=mən\ *n, pl* **steersmen** [ME *steresman, stiersman*, fr. OE *stēoresman*, fr. *stēores-* (gen. of *stēor-* rudder, steering oar) + *man* — more at STEER] : one who steers: as **a** : one who steers a ship : HELMSMAN **b** : a worker who steers a raft of logs by means of an oar attached at the back of the raft

steersman·ship \ˈ=ˌ=,ship\ *n* [*steersman* + *-ship*] : the ability a steersman has in steering a ship

steery \ˈstēri\ *n* [⁶*steer* + *-y*] *Scot* : COMMOTION, TUMULT

stees *pl of* STEE

¹**steeve** \ˈstēv\ *adj* [ME *stef* (adv. *steve*)] *chiefly Scot* : STIFF, FIRM, STURDY — **steeve·ly** *adv, chiefly Scot*

²**steeve** \ˈ"\ *vt* -ED/-ING/-S [ME *steven*, prob. fr. Sp *estibar* or Pg *estivar* to pack tightly, fr. L *stipare* to press together, pack tightly — more at STIFF] : to stow esp. in a ship's hold : STUFF, PACK, STOW

³**steeve** \ˈ"\ *vb* -ED/-ING/-S [origin unknown] *vi, of a bowsprit* : to incline upward at an angle with the horizon or the line of the keel ~ *vt* : to set (a bowsprit) at an upward inclination

⁴**steeve** \ˈ"\ *also* **steev·ing** \-viŋ, -vēŋ\ *n* -S : the angle that a bowsprit makes with the horizon or with the keel ⟨was arranged with only slight ~ —E.W.White⟩

steever *var of* STIVER

ste·fan–boltz·mann law \ˈshte,fänˈbōlts,män-\ *n, usu cap S&B* [after Josef *Stefan* †1893 Austrian physicist, its formulator, & Ludwig *Boltzmann* †1906 Austrian physicist who first demonstrated it] : a statement in thermal radiation: the total emissive power of an ideal black body is proportional to the fourth power of its absolute temperature

ste·fan's law \ˈshte,fänz-\ *n, usu cap S* [after Josef *Stefan* †1893] : STEFAN-BOLTZMANN LAW

stef·fen process \ˈstefən-\ *n, usu cap S* [prob. fr. *Steffen*, name of its inventor] : a process for recovering sugar from beet molasses by adding powdered lime to precipitate the sugar as calcium sucrate

steffen's waste *n, usu cap S* : the filtrate obtained from the precipitation of calcium sucrate in the Steffen process and used chiefly as a source of amino acids (as glutamic acid or isoleucine)

¹**steg** \ˈsteg\ *n* -S [ME *stegge*, of Scand origin; akin to Icel *steggi* drake, gander — more at STAG] *dial Brit* : GANDER

²**steg** \ˈ"\ *vi* [prob. fr. ¹*steg*] *chiefly Scot* : STALK

steg- *or* **stego-** *comb form* [Gk *stegē, stegos* roof, fr. *stegein* to cover — more at THATCH] : covering plate or fold ⟨*steg*odon⟩ ⟨*stego*carpous⟩

steg·a·no·gram \ˈstegənə,gram\ *n* [fr. *steganography*, after such pairs as E *cryptography: cryptogram*] *archaic* : a cryptographic writing

steg·a·nog·ra·phy \ˌ==ˈnägrəfē\ *n* -ES [NL *steganographia*, fr. Gk *steganos* covered, reticent (fr. *stegein* to cover) + L *-graphia* -graphy] *archaic* : CRYPTOGRAPHY

steg·a·no·pod \ˈ===,päd\ *also* **steg·a·nop·o·dan** \ˌ==ˈnäpədən\ *n* -S [prob. fr. NL *Steganopodes*; *steganopodan* fr. NL *Steganopodes* + E *-an*] : a steganopodous bird

steg·a·nop·o·des \ˌ==ˈnäpə,dēz\ [NL, fr. Gk, pl. of *teganopod-, steganopous* web-footed, fr. *steganos* covered + *pod-, pous* foot] *syn of* PELECANIFORMES

steg·a·nop·o·dous \ˌ==ˈnäpədəs\ *also* **steg·a·nop·o·dan** \-dən\ *adj* [NL *Steganopodes* + E *-ous, -an*] **1** : having all four toes webbed : TOTIPALMATE **2** : of or relating to the pelicans

-stege \ˌstēj\ *n comb form* -S [Gk *stegē* roof, fr. *stegein* to cover] : covering plate or fold ⟨gastro*stege*⟩ ⟨uro*stege*⟩

stegh \ˈstek\ *var of* STECH

-ste·gite \stə,jīt\ *n comb form* -S [Gk *stegē* roof + E *-ite*] : segment of a carapace ⟨omo*stegite*⟩

ste·go·bi·um \stəˈgōbēəm\ *n, cap* [NL, fr. Gk *stegein* to cover + NL *-o-* + *-bium*] : a cosmopolitan genus of beetles (family Anobiidae) including the drugstore beetle

stego·car·pous \ˌstegəˈkärpəs\ *adj* [*steg-* + *-carpous*] *of a moss* : having a capsule that opens by a deciduous lid

stego·ce·pha·lia \ˌ==səˈfālyə\ *n pl, cap* [NL, fr. *steg-* + Gk *kephalē* head + NL *-ia* — more at CEPHALIC] *in some esp former classifications* : an order or other division of Amphibia comprising all the pre-Jurassic and many later extinct typically tailed and salamandriform amphibians usu. with well-developed limbs and sometimes of large size — compare LABYRINTHODONTIA, LISSAMPHIBIA

¹**stego·ce·pha·lian** \ˌ===ˈfālyən\ *adj* [NL *Stegocephalia* + E *-an*] : of or relating to the Stegocephalia

²**stegocephalian** \ˈ"\ *n* -S : a stegocephalian amphibian

stego·ceph·a·lous \ˌ==ˈsefələs\ *adj* [NL *Stegocephalia* + E *-ous*] : STEGOCEPHALIAN

stego·don \ˈ==,dän\ *n* [NL *Stegodont-, Stegodon*, fr. *steg-* + *-odont-, -odon* -odon] **1** *cap* : a genus of primitive Asiatic Pliocene and Pleistocene mammals that have molar teeth with relatively broad enamel ridges and but little cement and thus are intermediate between elephants and mastodons **2** *or* **stego·dont** \-nt\ -S [*stegodont* fr. NL *Stegodont-, Stegodon*] : an animal or fossil of the genus *Stegodon*

stego·mus \-məs\ *n, cap* [NL, prob. fr. *steg-* + Gk *ōmos* shoulder — more at HUMERUS] : a genus of small short-necked 5-toed reptiles (order Thecodontia) with smooth dermal scutes found in the Triassic of the Connecticut valley

stego·my·ia \ˌ==ˈmī(y)ə\ *n* [NL, fr. *steg-* + *-myia*] **1** *cap, in some classifications* : a genus of mosquitoes including the yellow-fever mosquito (*Aedes aegypti*) and several related mosquitoes **2** -s : any mosquito of the genus *Stegomyia; specif* : YELLOW-FEVER MOSQUITO

stego·saur \'=ˌsȯ(ə)r\ *n* -s [NL *Stegosauria*] : a dinosaur of the suborder Stegosauria

stego·sau·ri \ˌ==ˈsȯˌrī\ [NL, pl. of *Stegosaurus*] *syn of* STEGOSAURIA

stego·sau·ria \ˌ===ˈsȯrēə\ *n pl, cap* [NL, fr. *Stegosaurus* + *-ia*] : a suborder of Ornithischia comprising numerous dinosaurs with strongly developed dorsal bony armor — compare STEGOSAURUS

¹stego·sau·ri·an \ˌ;==ˈsȯrēən\ *adj* [NL *Stegosauria* + E *-an*] : of or relating to the Stegosauria

²stegosaurian \"\ *n* -s : STEGOSAUR

¹stego·sau·roid \ˌ;=ˌ=ˌrȯid\ *adj* [NL *Stegosaurus* + E *-oid*] : resembling or related to the stegosaurs

²stegosauroid \"\ *n* -s : a stegosauroid dinosaur

stego·sau·rus \ˌ=ˈ=ˈsȯrəs\ *n, cap* [NL, fr. *steg-* + *-saurus*] : a genus of large ornithischian dinosaurs of the Upper Jurassic rocks of Colorado and Wyoming being remarkable for their dermal armor and in the best-known species (*S. ungulatus*) having two rows of bony plates along the back

stegs *pl of* STEG

stei·ger·ite \'stīgəˌrīt\ *n* -s [George *Steiger* †1944 Am. chemist + E *-ite*] : a mineral $4AlVO_4.13H_2O$ consisting of hydrous aluminum vanadate and occurring in canary yellow masses in San Miguel valley, Calif.

steigh \'stā\ *var of* STEY

¹stein *var of* STEEN

²stein \'stīn\ *n* -s [prob. fr. G *steingut* stoneware, earthenware, fr. *stein* stone (fr. OHG) + *gut* goods, fr. *gut* good, adj., fr. OHG *guot* — more at STONE, GOOD] **1 a** : an earthenware mug esp. for beer commonly holding about a pint **b** : any large thick mug (as of glass) for beer holding sometimes as much as a quart **2** : the quantity of beer that a stein holds

¹stein·bock \'stīnˌbäk\ *n* -s [G, fr. OHG *steinboc;* akin to OE *stānbucca* ibex, MD *steenboc;* all fr. a prehistoric WGmc compound whose first element is represented by OE *stān* stone and whose second element is represented by OE *bucca* buck — more at STONE, BUCK] : IBEX

²steinbock *var of* STEENBOK

steinbok *or* **steinbuck** *var of* STEENBOK

stein 1a

stein·heim man \'s(h)tīnˌhīm-\ *n, usu cap S* [fr. *Steinheim* am Murr, town of western Germany] : a Lower Paleolithic Neanderthaloid man having some neanthropic characteristics and known from a skull found associated with Acheulean artifacts in western Germany

stein·kern \'s(h)tīnˌkern\ *n* -s [G, fr. *stein* stone + *kern* kernel, grain, fr. OHG *kerno;* akin to OHG *korn* grain — more at CORN] : a fossil consisting of a stony mass that entered a hollow natural object (as a bivalve shell) in the form of mud or sediment, was consolidated, and remained as a cast after dissolution of the mold

stein·kirk *or* **steen·kirk** \'stēnˌkərk\ *n* -s *often cap* [F *steinkerke,* fr. the battle of *Steenkerke,* Belgium, 1692] : a cravat with long hanging ends loosely twisted or looped together and worn esp. in the 18th century by men and women

stein·mann pin \'stīnmən-\ *n, usu cap S* [after Fritz *Steinmann* †1932 Swiss surgeon] : a stainless steel spike used for the internal fixation of fractures of long bones

stein·metz coefficient \'stīnˌmets-\ *n, usu cap S* [after Charles P. *Steinmetz* †1923 Am. electrical engineer] : HYSTERESIS COEFFICIENT

stei·ron·e·ma \ˌstīrəˈnēmə\ *n, cap* [NL, fr. Gk *steiros* barren + NL *-nema*] : a small genus of No. American herbs (family Primulaceae) having yellow flowers with a rotate deeply lobed corolla — see LOOSESTRIFE 3

ste·la \'stēlə\ *or* **stele** \'stēl *also* 'stēlē\ *n, pl* **ste·lae** \-ēˌlē, -lī\ *or* **ste·lai** \-ˌlī\ *or* **steles** [*stela* fr. NL, fr. L, fr. Gk *stēlē; stele* fr. NL, fr. Gk *stēlē;* akin to Gk *stellein* to set up, make ready — more at STALL] **1** : a slab or pillar of stone usu. carved or inscribed and used for commemorative purposes (as to mark a grave) **2** : an inscribed area on a wall **3** : a monument in the form of a pillar

ste·lar \'stēlə(r)\ *adj* [²*stele* + *-ar*] : of, relating to, located in, or resembling a stele ⟨~ tissue⟩

stelar theory *n* : a theory in botany: stem and root are fundamentally alike anatomically since in both the cortex surrounds a central stele

¹stele \'stēl\ *n* -s [ME — more at STEAL] : HANDLE, SHAFT; *esp* : the wooden shaft body of an arrow

²stele \"\ *also* 'stēlē\ *n* -s [NL, fr. Gk *stēlē* stela, boundary post or pillar — more at STELA] : the usu. cylindrical central portion of the axis of a vascular plant that consists of vascular tissue surrounded by a pericycle and often enclosing a central pith and that is in turn enclosed by cortex and in later life by a cork layer and other tissues of which all or part may be sloughed off with age — called also *vascular cylinder;* see ACTINOSTELE, DICTYOSTELE, EUSTELE, MERISTELE, POLYSTELE, PROTOSTELE, SIPHONOSTELE, SOLENOSTELE

-ste·lic \ˌ;stēlik\ *adj comb form* [²*stele* + *-ic*] : having (a specified number or kind of) steles ⟨*astelic*⟩

¹stell \'stel\ *vt* -ED/-ING/-S [ME *stellen,* fr. OE *stellan;* akin to MD & OHG *stellen* to set, place — more at STALL] **1** *Scot* : PUT, PLACE, FIX **2** : DELINEATE ⟨if truly a painter had *stell'd* thee there —Robert Bridges †1930⟩

²stell \"\ *n* -s [prob. fr. ¹*stell*] *chiefly Scot* : a protective enclosure for sheep or cattle

³stell \"\ *n* -s [origin unknown] **1** *dial Eng* : DITCH, DRAIN **2** *dial Eng* : BROOK

stel·lar \'stelə(r)\ *adj* [LL *stellaris,* fr. L *stella* star + *-aris* — more at STAR] **1 a** : of, relating to, or derived from the stars : ASTRAL ⟨an object of ~ size⟩ ⟨~ light⟩ ⟨~ spectrum⟩ **b** : composed of stars ⟨~ ornamentation⟩ **2** : of, relating to, or characteristic of a theatrical, operatic, or film star ⟨building or acquiring ~ names —W.J.Fadiman⟩ **3 a** : CHIEF, LEADING, PRINCIPAL ⟨given a ~ role⟩ **b** : OUTSTANDING, PREEMINENT, FIRST-RATE ⟨a ~ production⟩

stellar eclipse *n* : an eclipse of one star by another in a binary system

stellar energy *n* **1** : the internal energy of a star **2** : the energy radiated by a star **3** : the energy of the stars

stel·lar·ia \steˈla(a)rēə\ *n, cap* [NL, fr. L *stella* star + NL *-aria*] : a genus of herbs (family Caryophyllaceae) having linear to ovate exstipulate leaves and flowers with deeply notched petals and three styles succeeded by ovoid capsular fruits

stellar interferometer *n* : an interferometer attachment to a telescope for measuring objects subtending very small angles (as close double stars)

stellar jay *n* [by alter.] : STELLER'S JAY

stellar nebula *n* [*stellar* + *nebula*] **1** : the nebulosity surrounding a star : a star's shell or envelope of nebulosity **2** : PLANETARY NEBULA

stellar parallax *n* : the heliocentric parallax of a star

stellar vault *n* : STAR VAULT

stel·lary \'steləre\ *adj* [L *stella* + E *-ary*] *archaic* : STELLAR

stel·late \'steˌlāt, *usu* -ād+V\ *adj* [L *stellatus* set with stars, starry, shaped like a star, fr. *stella* star + *-atus* — more at STAR] : resembling a star (as in shape) : pointed, formed, or radiated like a star ⟨a ~ leaf⟩ ⟨a ~ ornament⟩ — **stel·late·ly** *adv*

stellate cell *n* : a cell with radiating cytoplasmic processes; *esp* : KUPFFER CELL

stellate-crystal fungus \ˈ=ˌ=ˈ==-\ *n* [so called fr. the stellate crystals of calcium oxalate formed in connection with the mycelium] *n* : a fungus (*Odontia sacchari*) frequently associated with diseased sugarcane

stel·lat·ed \'=ˌlād·əd\ *adj* [L *stellatus* set with stars, stellate + E *-ed*] **1** : STELLATE **2** : ornamented or dotted with stars ⟨a ~ flag⟩

stellate ganglion *n* **1** : a composite ganglion formed by fusion of the inferior cervical and first thoracic ganglia of the sympathetic chain of a vertebrate animal **2** : a secondary ganglionic center on the course of the pallial nerve near the dorsal border of the internal wall of the mantle of a cephalopod

stellate ligament *n* : a branching ligament uniting the front of the head of a rib with the bodies of two vertebrae and the intervertebral disk between them

stellate reticulum *n* : a loosely-connected mass of stellate epithelial cells that in early stages makes up a large portion of the enamel organ

stel·lec·to·my \stəˈlektəmē\ *n* -ES [*stellate* ganglion + *-ectomy*] : excision of the stellate ganglion

stelled *adj* [L *stella* star + E *-ed* — more at STAR] *obs* : studded with or as if with stars : STARRY

stel·ler·ine \'steləˌrīn, -rən\ *n* -s [Georg W. *Steller* †1746 Ger. naturalist + E *-ine*] : STELLER'S SEA COW

¹stel·ler·oid \-ˌrȯid\ *adj* [NL *Stelleroidea*] : of or relating to the Stelliformia

²stelleroid \"\ *n* -s : an echinoderm of the division Stelliformia

stel·ler·oi·dea \ˌ==ˈrȯidēə\ [NL, fr. F *stelléride* starfish, (irreg. fr. L *stella* star) + NL *-oidea* — more at STAR] *syn of* STELLIFORMIA

stel·ler's eider \'s(h)telə(r)z-\ *also* **steller's duck** *n, usu cap S* [after Georg W. *Steller* †1746 Ger. naturalist] : an eider duck (*Polysticta stelleri*) of Alaska and eastern Asia having a white head and black collar

steller's jay *n, usu cap S* [after Georg W. *Steller*] : a blue jay (*Cyanocitta stelleri*) of western No. America with black to dark-blue fore and upper parts and a conspicuous high crest — see BLUE-FRONTED JAY, LONG-CRESTED JAY

steller's sea cow *n, usu cap 1st S* : an extinct large aquatic mammal (*Hydrodamalis gigas*) formerly common near the Asian coast of the Bering sea and having a relatively small head, no teeth, a laterally lobed tail, and a length of about 25 feet

steller's sea eagle *n, usu cap 1st S* : KAMCHATKAN SEA EAGLE

steller's sea lion *n, usu cap 1st S* : a north Pacific sea lion of the genus *Eumetopias* (*E. jubatus*) that is the largest of sea lions

stel·let·ta \stəˈled·ə\ *n, cap* [NL, dim. of L *stella* star] : a genus of white encrusting sponges (class Demospongiae) with a feltlike covering of slender glassy spicules that is common near the low-tide mark along the Pacific coast of No. America

stel·lif·er·ous \stəˈlif(ə)rəs\ *adj* [L *stellifer* star-bearing, starry (fr. *stella* star + *-ifer* -iferous) + E *-ous*] : having star-shaped markings

stel·li·fi·ca·tion \ˌsteləfəˈkāshən\ *n* -s [fr. *stellify,* after such pairs as E *purify: purification*] : the action of stellifying

stel·li·form \'steləˌfȯrm\ *adj* [NL *stelliformis,* fr. L *stella* star + *-iformis* -iform — more at STAR] : shaped like a star

stel·li·for·mia \ˌ==ˈfȯrmēə\ *n pl, cap* [NL, neut. pl. of *stelliformis*] *in some classifications* : a major division of Echinodermata consisting of the Asteroidea and Ophiuroidea

stel·li·fy \'steləˌfī\ *vt* -ED/-ING/-ES [ME *stellifien,* fr. MF *stellifier,* fr. ML *stellificare,* fr. L *stella* star + *-ificare* -ify] : to turn into or as if into a star : place among the stars : GLORIFY ⟨therefore deserves to be *stellified* by British astronomers —John Ruskin⟩

stelling *pres part of* STELL

stel·lion·ate \'stelyənət, -ˌnāt, *usu* -d·+V\ *n* -s [LL *stellionatus,* fr. L *stellion-, stellio* crafty person (lit., a lizard marked with star-shaped spots, fr. *stella* star) + *-atus* -ate] *Roman, civil, & Scots law* : a fraud not distinguished by a more special name; *esp* : a sale of the same property to different persons or the sale of something as one's own which belongs to another

Stel·lite \'steˌlīt\ *trademark* — used for any of various alloys composed essentially of 75 to 90 percent cobalt and 10 to 25 percent chromium with or without small amounts of other metals added and used esp. for cutting tools, hard wear-resistant surfaces, surgical instruments, and cutlery

stells *pres 3d sing of* STELL, *pl of* STELL

stel·lu·lar \'stelyələ(r)\ *adj* [LL *stellula* (dim. of L *stella* star) + E *-ar*] **1** : having the shape of a small star : STARRY ⟨a ~ light⟩ **2** : radiating like a star ⟨~ markings⟩

¹stem \'stem\ *n* -s *often attrib* [ME, fr. OE *stefn, stemn* stem of a plant or ship; *stefn* akin to MD *steven* stem of a ship, ON *stafn,* OE *stæf* staff; OE *stemn* akin to OHG *stam* stem of a plant, ON *stamn* stem of a ship, Gk *stamnos* wine jar, OE *standan* to stand — more at STAFF, STAND] **1 a** : the main and usu. wholly or predominantly aerial axis, trunk, or body of a tree or other plant; *specif* : the part of the body of a seed plant that originates from the plumule, constitutes the primary axis, produces and supports secondary branches, leaves, flowers, and other appendages, and differs from the root with which it is continuous in having or having a capacity for forming nodes, leaves, and buds, in developing a cuticle and stomata, and in lacking an endodermis and a protective cap over the meristem — see BULB, CORM, TUBER; compare RHIZOME, STOLON **b** : a plant part (as a petiole, peduncle, pedicel, or stalk) that supports one or more leaves, flowers, fruits, or fruiting bodies; *broadly* : any plant part (as the stipe of a kelp) that functions primarily in support **c** : a stalk of bananas including the fruit — compare HAND **2 a** (1) : a piece of timber or cast, forged, or rolled metal to which the sides of a ship are united at the fore end with the lower end scarfed to the keel and the bowsprit resting upon its upper end (2) *chiefly Scot* : a stem or sternpost esp. of a sharp-sterned boat **b** : the forepart of a ship : BOWS, PROW; *also* : a foremost position **3 a** : a line of ancestry : STOCK; *esp* : the main ancestral line from which the branches of a family may be considered to have arisen **b** : a fundamental or primitive line within a natural group of which other members of the group can logically be construed as descendants or offshoots **4 a** : the part of an inflected word that remains unchanged except by phonetic changes or variations throughout a given inflection, is sometimes identical with the root, but is often derived from it with some formative suffix ⟨the root *duc* serves as the ~ of Latin *dux* (ducs), *ducis,* leader, and is developed with suffixes into *ducere,* to lead, *ductor,* leader, *ductus,* act of leading, *ductilis,* ductile⟩ **b** *obs* : an original word that serves as a basis for the formation of derivative words (as by the addition of suffixes) **5** : something felt to resemble a plant stem esp. in being an elongated process projecting from or supporting some structure: as **a** : a main or heavy stroke of a letter; *also* : BODY 10a — see TYPE illustration **b** : the short perpendicular line extending upward on the right or downward on the left from the head of a musical note **c** : the part of a tobacco pipe from the bowl outward; *usu* : the detachable mouthpiece of a tobacco pipe or a cigar or cigarette holder usu. provided with a rimmed mouth end — compare ¹BIT 2c **d** : the cylindrical and usu. solid support of a piece of stemware (as a goblet) **e** : a narrow elongated base or means of attachment by which a sessile animal is made fast ⟨the contractile ~ of a vorticellid⟩ ⟨the horny ~ of a colonial hydroid⟩ **f** : the recording tube of a measuring instrument (as a thermometer) **g** : a shaft of a watch having a threaded top to hold a winding crown and the lower end squared to fit into the winding wheels in the movement and used for winding — see STEM-WINDER **h** : the round portion in some locks about which the ordinary key turns **i** : one of the heavy vertical rods in a stamp battery to which the tappet and boss are attached **j** : a spindle or guide rod on a mechanical part ⟨the rod of a valve is a ~⟩ **k** : AUGER STEM **l** : a thread shank for a button **m** *slang* : a major way (as a street or railroad line) — usu. used in the phrase *main stem* — **from stem to stern** : THROUGHOUT, THOROUGHLY

²stem \"\ *vb* **stemmed; stemmed; stemming; stems** [ME *stemmen,* fr. ¹*stem* (stem of a ship)] *vi* **1** : to head in a particular direction or move forward against or irrespective of an obstacle ⟨a ship *stemming* on against a strong current⟩ **2** : to hold a straight course : STEER ⟨~ toward the sunset⟩ ~ *vt* **1** *archaic* : to oppose or cut with or as if with a ship's stem : RAM **2** *obs* : to hold (a ship) on course : STEER **3 a** : to make headway against (as an adverse tide, current, or wind) ⟨the fish . . . was *stemming* the current at an angle —J.C.Fine⟩ **b** : to go counter to : make progress against

³stem \"\ *vb* **stemmed; stemmed; stemming; stems** [¹*stem* (stem of a plant)] *vi* **1** *archaic* **a** : to grow upward or rise erect like a stem **b** : to produce a stem **2 a** : to grow out or develop like a stem — usu. used with *from* ⟨an illness that ~s from a long-past accident⟩ ⟨our hopes ~ from the one previous success⟩ **b** : to have or trace one's origin or development ~ *vt* **1** : to remove the stem or stem and midrib from ⟨~ cherries⟩ ⟨~ tobacco leaves⟩ **2** : to make stems for or fit with stems (as artificial flowers) **syn** see SPRING

⁴stem \"\ *vb* **stemmed; stemmed; stemming; stems** [ME *stemmen,* fr. ON *stemma;* akin to OE *stam* stammering, ON *stamr* stammering, blocked, *stamma* to stammer — more at STAMMER] *vt* **1 a** : to stop or dam up (as a river) **b** : to check or restrain by or as if by damming ⟨cultivating small plots of land . . . which helps to ~ the erosion of the steep hillside —Pamela Gulliver & P.H.Gulliver⟩ — often used in the phrase *stem the tide* ⟨will not ~ the tide of population that threatens to swamp the developing world —Roger Morris⟩ : STANCH ⟨~ a flow of blood⟩ ⟨~ a wound⟩ **2** : to brace or set firmly (oneself or one's limbs) **3** : to ram or tamp (as a hole) in preparing to blast **4** : to turn (skis) in stemming ~ *vi* **1** : to restrain or check oneself; *also* : to become checked or stanched ⟨after a brief interval the bleeding *stemmed*⟩ **2** : to retard oneself by forcing the heel of one ski or of both skis outward from the line of progress

⁵stem \"\ *n* -s **1** : something that acts in opposition or resistance **2** : an act or instance of stemming on skis

⁶stem \"\ *vt* [alter. of E dial. *steven* to bespeak, fr. ME *stefnen, stevenen* to appoint, specify, fr. OE *stefnan* to appoint, arrange, fr. *stefn* voice, time, occasion — more at STEVEN] *Brit* : to load or contract to load (a ship) with coal within an indicated time

stem anchor *n* [¹*stem*] : the bower anchor carried in the centerline hawsepipe on a clipper-bowed man-of-war

stem back *vb* [⁴*stem*] *vi* : to brace oneself to prevent being driven forward ~ *vt* : to hold in check : brace oneself against

stem blight *n* [¹*stem*] : a fungous blight (as of the peach caused by *Phoma persicae* or of cosmos caused by *Phomopsis stewartii*) primarily attacking the stems of plants

stem body *n* : the portion of a mitotic spindle that lies between the daughter chromosome groups during anaphase and telophase

stem·bok \'stemˌbäk\ *n, pl* **stembok** *or* **stemboks** [by alter.] : STEENBOK

stem borer *n* [¹*stem*] : an insect larva that bores in plant stems; *esp* : a cerambycid larva of the genus *Oberea*

stem break *n* : BROWNING 3a

stem–bud \'=ˌ=\ *n* : PLUMULE

stem canker *n* : a canker disease affecting plant stems; *esp* : RHIZOCTONIA DISEASE

stem cell *n* : an unspecialized and usu. embryonic cell ancestral to one or more specialized cells ⟨one theory regards the hemocytoblast as a *stem cell* from which all the cellular elements of the blood arise⟩; *specif* : an embryonic cell destined to give rise to germ cells and often identifiable in early cleavage

stem christiania *n, often cap C* [⁴*stem*] : a turn in skiing begun by the stemming of one ski and completed by bringing the skis parallel into a christiania during the turn

stem–clasping \'=ˌ==\ *adj* [¹*stem*] : AMPLEXICAUL

stem climber *n* : a plant that climbs by twining

stem correction *n* : a correction applied to the readings of a precise thermometer to allow for the difference in temperature between the liquid in the stem and that in the bulb

stem cutting *n* : a piece of a plant stem or branch including at least one node used in propagation

stem eelworm *also* **stem nematode** *n* : BULB EELWORM

stem–end browning \'=ˌ;=-\ *n* : a storage disease of potatoes of undetermined cause characterized by brownish or black discoloration at the stem end of the tuber

stem–end rot *or* **stem–end decay** *n* : any of various rots (as decay of citrus fruits caused by fungi of the genera *Diplodia, Dothiorella,* and *Phomopsis*) starting at the point of attachment to the plant

stemflow \'=ˌ=\ *n* : rainfall reaching the ground in a forest by draining down the trunks of trees, as distinguished from that dripping from the canopy

stemform \'=ˌ=\ *n* : original or ancestral form

stem ginger *n* : CANTON GINGER

stem girdler *n* : an insect that girdles (as with its jaws or ovipositor) the stems of plants

stemhead \'=ˌ=\ *n* : the top of a ship's stem

stemhead plate *n* : a plate fastened at the bow of a sailboat and used as an attachment for the head stay

stem leaf *n* : a cauline leaf

stem length *n* : the height of the seated human body as measured from the seat of the chair occupied

¹stem·less \'=ləs\ *adj* [¹*stem* + *-less*] : having no stem : ACAULESCENT

²stemless \"\ *adj* **1** [⁴*stem* + *-less*] : not capable of being stemmed **2** [²*stem* + *-less*] : impossible to steer or hold a course against

stemless gentian *n* [¹*stemless*] : a gentianella (*Gentiana acaulis*)

stemless lady's–slipper *n* : a moccasin flower (*Cypripedium acaule*)

stemless thistle *n* : a perennial Eurasian thistle (*Circium acaule*) with a rosette of spiny leaves and one or more usu. sessile crimson to reddish purple flower heads

stem·let \'stemlət\ *n* -s [¹*stem* + *-let*] : a small, slender, or young stem

stemlike \'=ˌ=\ *adj* : resembling or sharing the function of a stem

stem–line \'=ˌ=\ *n* : a long continuous line that is touched by short lines in ogham writing and that is typically the edge of an upright stone

stem·ma \'stemə\ *n, pl* **stem·ma·ta** \-məd·ə\ *also* **stemmas** [NL *stemmat-, stemma,* fr. L, garland, wreath, pedigree (fr. the garlands placed on ancestral images), fr. Gk, garland, wreath, fr. *stephein* to crown, enwreathe] **1 a** (1) : one of the simple eyes of an insect : OCELLUS (2) : a facet of a compound eye of an arthropod **b** : a tubercle on which an antenna is borne **2 a** : a scroll (as among the ancient Romans) containing a list of family names with indication of genealogical or other relations : FAMILY TREE, PEDIGREE **b** : a tree showing the relationships of the manuscripts of a literary work

stem·mat·i·form \steˈmad·əˌfȯrm\ *adj* [NL *stemmat-, stemma* + E *-iform*] : formed like or resembling a stemma

stem·ma·tous \'stemədəs\ *adj* [NL *stemmat-, stemma* + E *-ous*] : of, relating to, or being a stemma : OCELLAR

¹stemmed \ˌstemd\ *adj* [¹*stem* + *-ed*] : having or furnished with a stem — usu. used in combination ⟨long-*stemmed* roses⟩ ⟨a single-*stemmed* plant⟩ ⟨blue-*stemmed* grasses⟩

²stemmed *adj* [fr. past part. of ³*stem*] : having the stem or stems removed ⟨~ berries⟩ ⟨~ tobacco⟩

stem·mer \'stemə(r)\ *n* -s [³*stem* + *-er*] **1** : one that stems: as **a** : a miner's tamping bar for ramming in packing (as clay) over a blasting charge **b** : a machine or device for stemming fruits (as grapes or apples) **c** : STRIPPER 1a **d** : a worker who makes or applies stems of artificial flowers **2** [prob. fr. ¹*stem* (street) + *-er*] *slang* : a beggar seeking money from passersby along the street

stem·mery \-mərē, -ri\ *n* -ES [³*stem* + *-ery*] : a building or place in which tobacco is stemmed

stem·mi·ness \-mēnəs, -min-\ *n* -ES : the condition of being stemmy; *esp* : a tendency of some grasses to produce excessive numbers of stems that reduces their forage or hay value

stemming *pres part of* STEM

stem mother *n* [¹*stem*] : a sexually produced female that produces parthenogenetically a colony of offspring; *esp* : an aphid that develops from an overwintering egg and gives rise to the summer generation — compare FUNDATRIX

stem·my \'stemē, -mi\ *adj* -ER/-EST [¹*stem* + *-y*] : abounding in or mixed with stems; *esp* : consisting largely of stems ⟨a ~ hay from which most of the leaves have been lost in handling⟩ ⟨some grasses become very ~ when mature⟩

ste·mo·na \stəˈmōnə\ *n, cap* [NL, fr. Gk *stēmōn* warp, thread — more at STAMEN] : a small genus of Asian and Australian herbaceous twiners (family Stemonaceae) having alternate leaves and rather large perfect flowers with oddly appendaged somewhat monadelphous stamens

ste·mo·na·ce·ae \ˌstēməˈnāsēˌē\ *n pl, cap* [NL, fr. *Stemona,* type genus + *-aceae*] : a family of herbs (order Liliales) having regular perfect flowers with a 4-parted perianth in two series, four stamens, and a one-celled ovary — **ste·mo·na·ceous** \ˌ;==ˈnāshəs\ *adj*

ste·mo·ni·tis \ˌ==ˈnīd·əs\ *n, cap* [NL, fr. Gk *stēmōn* warp, thread; fr. the threadlike strands of the capillitium] **:** a genus of slime molds (subclass Myxogastres) related to *Physarum* but having an evanescent sporangium and a capillitium formed from branches of the columella

-stemo·nous \ˈstēmənəs, -tem-\ *adj comb form* [fr. (assumed) NL *-stemonus*, fr. Gk *stēmōn* warp, thread — more at STAMEN] **:** having (such or so many) stamens ⟨diplo*stemonous*⟩ ⟨iso*stemonous*⟩

stem·phyl·i·um \stemˈfilēəm\ *n, cap* [NL, fr. Gk *stemphylon* olive pulp + NL *-ium* — more at STAFF] *in some classifications* **:** a genus that comprises imperfect fungi (order Moniliales) with dark greenish brown spores closely resembling those of *Alternaria* but borne singly rather than in chains and is often included in *Alternaria* or sometimes replaced by *Macrosporium*

stempiece \ˈ=,=\ *n* [¹*stem* + *piece*] **:** a piece of timber attached to the stem of a wooden ship beneath the bowsprit for support or ornament

stem·ple *or* **stem·pel** \ˈstempəl\ *n* -s [prob. fr. LG *stempel*; akin to OE *stempan* to stamp — more at STAMP] **:** a crossbar of wood in a mine shaft serving some special purpose (as of a step, supporting timber, or strut)

stempost \ˈ=,=\ *n* [¹*stem* + *post*] **:** the stem of a ship

stem–root \ˈ=,=\ *n* **:** a root (as an adventitious or prop root) arising from a stem above the juncture of stem and basal root

stem–rooting \ˈ=ˈ==\ *adj* **:** tending to form roots on the stem; *esp* **:** forming roots immediately above a basal bulb

stem rust *n* **1 :** a rust attacking the stem of a plant; *esp* **:** a destructive disease of wheat and various other grasses that is caused by a rust fungus (*Puccinia graminis*), is characterized by reddish brown lesions in the uredostage of the parasite and black lesions in the teliospore stage, and involves plants of the genera *Berberis* or *Mahonia* as alternate hosts of the parasite **2 :** the fungus causing stem rust

stems *pl of* STEM, *pres 3d sing of* STEM

stem sickness *n* **:** a disease of clover caused by the bulb eelworm (*Ditylenchus dipsaci*)

stem smut *n* **:** the common smut of rye caused by a fungus (*Urocystis occulta*) in which linear sori occur

stem·son \ˈstem(p)sən\ *n* -s [¹*stem* + *-son* (as in *keelson*)] **:** a piece of curved timber bolted to the stem, keelson, and apron in a ship's frame near the bow

stem stitch *n* **:** an embroidery outlining stitch (as for making stems); *esp* **:** an overlapping stitch that produces a corded appearance

stem turn *n* [⁵*stem*] **:** a skiing turn executed by stemming an outside ski

stem·wards \ˈstemwə(r)dz\ *adv* [¹*stem* + *-wards*] **:** toward a stem (as of a ship)

stemware \ˈ=,=\ *n* **:** hollow ware (as for beverages or desserts) of glass that consists of a rounded hollow body mounted on a usu. solid and basically cylindrical shaft which terminates in a flattened foot

stemware: *1* cordial, *2* cocktail, *3* wine, *4* champagne, *5* goblet, *6* juice, *7* iced tea

stem–winder \ˈ=ˌ==\ *n* **1 :** a stem-winding watch **2 :** one that is first-rate of its kind

stem–winding \ˈ=ˈ==\ *adj* **:** wound by an inside mechanism turned by the knurled knob at the outside end of the stem ⟨a *stem-winding* watch⟩

sten \ˈsten\ *or* **sten gun** *n* -s *usu cap S* [Major *S*heppard, 20th cent. Eng. army officer + Mr. *T*urpin, 20th cent. Eng. civil servant, its designers + *En*gland] **:** a British machine carbine having only 45 parts and weighing from 6 pounds 6 ounces to 8 pounds that uses any rimless 9 millimeter ammunition

sten- *or* **steno-** *comb form* [Gk, fr. *stenos* narrow, close, scanty] **:** close **:** narrow **:** little ⟨*steno*bathic⟩ — opposed to *eury-*

sten *abbr* **1** stencil **2** stenographer; stenography

ste·nan·thi·um \stəˈnan(t)thēəm\ *n, cap* [NL, fr. *sten-* + Gk *anthos* flower + NL *-ium* — more at ANTHOLOGY] **:** a genus of smooth bulbous perennials (family Liliaceae) of No. America and eastern Asia with long grasslike leaves and numerous small flowers in compound racemes — see BRONZE BELLS

¹stench \ˈstench\ *n* -ES [ME, fr. OE *stenc*; akin to OHG *stank* stench, OE *stincan* to emit a smell — more at STINK] **1 a :** an extremely disagreeable smell **:** offensive odor **:** STINK ⟨so many buffaloes were slaughtered . . . that the ~ was fearful —Mari Sandoz⟩ **b :** something resembling or producing the effect of a bad smell ⟨very idea . . . was ~ in his nostrils —C.A.Beard⟩ **c :** a strong heady odor ⟨sweet ~ of magnolia —*Newsweek*⟩ **2 :** something that has an offensive odor **:** ODORANT

²stench \ˈ"\ *vb* -ED/-ING/-ES *vi* **:** STINK ⟨~*ing* fumes issue from . . . crevices and holes —Robert Gibbings⟩ ~ *vt* **:** to cause to stink **:** annoy by stench ⟨the paint ~*es* the whole house⟩

stench bomb *n* **:** STINK BOMB

stench·ful \ˈ=,fəl\ *adj* **:** full of disagreeable smells **:** REEKING

stench trap *n* **:** a trap for permitting outflow of sewage but preventing backflow of foul sewer gases

stenchy \ˈstenchē\ *adj* -ER/-EST [¹*stench* + *-y*] **:** having a stench

¹sten·cil \ˈsten(t)səl\ *n* -s [fr. (assumed) earlier *stansel*, fr. ME *stanselen* to ornament with sparkling colors or pieces of metal, fr. MF *estanceler*, *estenceler*, fr. *estencele* spark, fr. (assumed) VL *stincilla*, alter. of L *scintilla*] **1 a :** material (as a sheet of paper, metal, thin wax, or woven fabric) that is perforated with lettering or a design through which a substance (as ink, paint) is forced onto a surface to be printed **b :** color, ink, or metallic powder used in stenciling **c :** a pattern or design of figures or letters cut into a stencil **d :** an impression left on a surface after stenciling **2 :** a printing process using the stencil principle — compare INTAGLIO, LETTERPRESS, PLANOGRAPHY ⟨silk screen is a form of ~⟩ **3 :** something resembling a stencil **:** an uninspired or insipid repetition usu. of an original idea or plan ⟨the literary ~*s* that represent all cabdrivers as witty —Mark Murphy⟩

A stencil 1a; *B* stencil 1d

²stencil \ˈ"\ *vt* **stenciled** *or* **stencilled; stenciled** *or* **stencilled; stenciling** *or* **stencilling** \-s(ə)liŋ\ **stencils 1 :** to produce by or as if by means of a stencil ⟨~ an address on a packing case⟩ ⟨~ an interoffice memorandum⟩ **2 :** to mark or paint with an inscription or a design by means of a stencil ⟨curtains that you ~*ed* with such pride —Myrtle R. White⟩

stencil brush *n* **:** STIPPLE 3

sten·cil·er *or* **sten·cil·ler** \-s(ə)lə(r)\ *n* -s **:** one that stencils: as **a :** one whose work is decorating or identifying articles by means of stencils **b :** a worker who stencils patterns for the garment cutter

stenciling *or* **stencilling** *n* -s [fr. gerund of ²*stencil*] **:** the art or practice of one that stencils

sten·cil·iza·tion \ˌsten(t)sələˈzāshən, -ˌlīˈz-\ *n* -s [*stencilize* + *-ation*] **:** the act or the product of stenciling esp. by mimeograph

sten·cil·ize \ˈsten(t)sə,līz\ *vt* -ED/-ING/-s [¹*stencil* + *-ize*] **1 :** STENCIL 2 **2 :** to cut into a stencil ⟨the . . . cushion shows through the *stencilized* openings —*Office Equipment Guide*⟩

stencil knife *n* **:** a knife with a wooden handle and a short sharp blade used esp. for cutting stencils and linoleum blocks

stencil paper *n* **:** strong tissue paper impregnated or coated with paraffin or other materials for stencils

¹stend \ˈstend\ *also* **sten** \ˈsten\ *n* -s [ME] *Scot* **:** JUMP, BOUND

²stend \ˈ"\ *also* **sten** \ˈ"\ *vi, Scot* **:** to jump up **:** LEAP, REAR

sten·der dish \ˈstendə(r)-\ *n, sometimes cap S* [after William P. *Stender* 19th cent. Ger. manufacturer] **:** a small circular glass dish with vertical walls and loosely fitting cover used in laboratories usu. to hold stains, culture media, or specimens

sten·dhal·ian \(ˈ)stanˈdälēən, -tanˈd-, -tenˈd-, -dal-, -lyən\ *adj, usu cap* [*Stendhal* (pseudonym of Henri Beyle †1842 Fr. writer) + E *-an*] **:** of, relating to, or having the characteristics of Stendhal or his works ⟨a small but ardent public of *Stendhalian* experts —*Times Lit. Supp.*⟩

ste·ne·cious \stəˈnēshəs\ *or* **ste·noe·cic** \-ēsik\ *adj* [*sten-* + Gk *oikos* house, dwelling + E *-ious* or *-ic* — more at VICINITY] **:** capable of adjusting to or surviving in only a narrow range of environments

steni·on \ˈstenē,än, -ten-\ *n, pl* **stenia** \-nēə\ [NL, fr. *sten-* + *-ion* (as in *rhinion*)] **:** a point on the outer wall of either middle cranial fossa marking the least transverse diameter of the skull in that region

steno \ˈste(,)nō\ *n* -s [by shortening] **1 :** STENOGRAPHER **2 :** STENOGRAPHY

steno- — see STEN-

steno·bath·ic \ˌstenəˈbathik\ *adj* [*sten-* + Gk *bathos* depth + E *-ic* — more at BATHOS] *of a pelagic organism* **:** living within narrow limits of depth — opposed to *eurybathic*

steno·ben·thic \ˌ==ˈben(t)thik\ *adj* [*sten-* + Gk *benthos* depth + E *-ic* — more at BENTHOS] **:** STENOBATHIC

steno·car·dia \ˌ==ˈkärdēə\ *n* -s [NL, fr. *sten-* + *-cardia*] **:** ANGINA PECTORIS — **steno·car·di·ac** \ˌ==ˈ=dē,ak\ *adj*

steno·car·pus \ˌ==ˈkärpəs\ *n, cap* [NL, fr. *sten-* + *-carpus*] **:** a small genus of Australian timber trees (family Proteaceae) with alternate or scattered leaves, umbellate or racemose red or yellow flowers, and leathery follicles with winged seeds — see WHEEL TREE 2

steno·cephalic \ˌ==+\ *adj* [*sten-* + *-cephalic*] **:** having an abnormally narrow head

steno·ceph·a·ly \ˌ==ˈsefəlē\ *also* **steno·ce·phal·ia** \-sə-ˈfālyə\ *n, pl* **stenocephalies** *also* **stenocephalias** [NL *stenocephalia*, fr. *sten-* + *-cephalia* -cephaly] **:** abnormal narrowness of the head

steno·chrome \ˈ==,krōm\ *n* [back-formation fr. *stenochromy*] **:** a print made by stenochromy

steno·chro·my \ˈ==,krōmē\ *n* -ES [ISV *sten-* + *-chromy*] **:** the printing at one impression of a varicolored design

sten·og \stəˈnäg\ *n* -s [by shortening] **:** STENOGRAPHER

ste·nog·a·mous \stəˈnägəməs\ *also* **steno·gam·ic** \ˌstenəˈgamik\ *adj* [*sten-* + *-gamous*, *-gamic*] *of insects* **:** mating in a restricted space **:** requiring no nuptial flight — opposed to *eurygamous*

steno·gastric \ˌstenə+\ *adj* [*sten-* + *gastr-* + *-ic*] **:** having a slender abdomen — used esp. of various insects which later develop large swollen abdomens

steno·gas·try \ˈ==,gastrē\ *n* -ES [*sten-* + *gastr-* + *-y*] **:** a condition in various insects of having a slender abdomen — compare PHYSOGASTRY

steno·glos·sa \ˌ==ˈgläsə, -lȯsə\ *n pl, cap* [NL, fr. *sten-* + *-glossa*] **:** a suborder of Pectinibranchia containing many common marine snails (as the cone shells, olive shells, whelks) which have a concentrated nervous system, a radula, an unpaired esophageal gland, and usu. a well-developed proboscis and including the groups Rachiglossa and Toxoglossa

steno·glos·sate \ˌ==ˈgläsət, -lȯs-\ *adj* [NL *Stenoglossa* + E *-ate*] **:** of or relating to the Stenoglossa

steno·graph \ˈstenə,graf\ *vt* -ED/-ING/-s [back-formation fr. *stenographer*] **:** to write or report in stenographic characters

ste·nog·ra·pher \stəˈnägrəfə(r)\ *n* -s [*stenography* + *-er*] **1 :** a writer of shorthand **2 :** one who is employed (as in an office) chiefly to take and transcribe dictation

steno·graph·ic \ˌstenəˈgrafik, -fēk\ *also* **steno·graph·i·cal** \-fəkəl, -fēk-\ *adj* [*stenography* + *-ic*, *-ical*] **:** of, relating to, or using stenography — **steno·graph·i·cal·ly** \-k(ə)lē, -li\ *adv*

ste·nog·ra·phy \stəˈnägrəfē, -fi\ *n* -ES [Gk *stenos* narrow, close + E *-graphy*] **1 a :** a writing in shorthand esp. by using abbreviations or characters for whole words **b :** shorthand esp. written from dictation or oral discourse **c :** the making of shorthand notes and subsequent transcription of them esp. in typewriting **2 a :** a use of curtailed or reduced forms in representing **b :** a representation using such forms

steno·ha·line \ˌstenəˈhā,līn, -ha,-, -lən\ *adj* [ISV *sten-* + *-haline* (fr. Gk *halinos* of salt, fr. *hals* salt) — more at SALT] *of an aquatic organism* **:** unable to withstand wide variation in salinity of the surrounding water — opposed to *euryhaline*

steno·mer·ic \ˌ==ˈmerik\ *adj* [*sten-* + *mer-* + *-ic*] *of a femur* **:** strongly compressed laterally with a platymeric index of 100 or over

ste·nom·e·ter \stəˈnäməd·ə(r), -mətə-\ *n* [*sten-* + *-meter*] **:** an instrument for measuring distances consisting of a telescope mounted on a tripod and fitted with a micrometer screw so that the distance may be measured to a rod carrying two targets a known distance apart whose images are brought together in the telescope by the micrometer screw

steno·pa·ic \ˌstenəˈpāik\ *also* **steno·pe·ic** *or* **steno·pae·ic** \-pēik\ *adj* [*sten-* + Gk *opaios* having a hole (fr. *opē* hole) + E *-ic*; akin to Gk *osse* (two) eyes — more at EYE] **:** having a small opening for the admission of light ⟨~ spectacles⟩

steno·pel·mat·i·dae \ˌ==(,)pelˈmad·ə,dē\ *n pl, cap* [NL, fr. *Stenopelmatus*, type genus + *-idae*] **:** a family of dull-colored usu. wingless Orthoptera having compressed 3-jointed tarsi and a needle-shaped ovipositor and including the sand crickets and the cave crickets

steno·pel·ma·tus \-ˈmäd·əs\ *n, cap* [NL, fr. *sten-* + Gk *pelmat-*, *pelma* sole of the foot — more at FELL] **:** the type genus of the family Stenopelmatidae

ste·noph·a·gous \stəˈnäfəgəs\ *adj* [ISV *sten-* + *-phagous*] **:** eating few kinds of foods — used esp. of an insect; compare EURYPHAGOUS, MONOPHAGOUS

steno·plastic \ˌstenə+\ *adj* [*sten-* + *plastic*] **:** exhibiting limited capacity for modification or adaptation to new environment **:** not capable of major evolutionary differentiation — opposed to *euryplastic*; compare PSEUDOPLASTIC — **steno·plas·ty** \ˈ==,plastē\ *n* -ES

stenos *pl of* STENO

ste·no's duct \ˈstā(,)nōz-\ *n, usu cap S* [after Nicolaus *Steno* (latinization of *Niels Stensen*) †1687 Dan. anatomist, its discoverer] **:** the duct of the parotid gland opening on the inner surface of the cheek opposite the second upper molar tooth

ste·nose \stəˈnōs, -ōz\ *vt* -ED/-ING/-S [back-formation fr. *stenosis*] **:** to cause stenosis in

stenosed *adj* [fr. past part. of *stenose*] **:** affected with stenosis

ste·no·sis \stəˈnōsəs\ *n, pl* **steno·ses** \-ō,sēz\ [NL, fr. Gk *stenōsis* act of narrowing, fr. *stenoun* to narrow, fr. *stenos* narrow, close] **1 :** a narrowing or constriction of the diameter of any passage, tube, or orifice ⟨mitral ~⟩ **2 :** a virus disease of the cotton plant marked by dwarfing, eroded or perforated leaf margins, and numerous sterile flower buds

steno·sper·mo·car·py \ˌstenəˈspərmə,kärpē\ *n* -ES [*sten-* + *sperm-* + *-carpy*] **:** the production of abortive incompletely developed seeds (as in a seedless grape) with normal development of the berry — compare PARTHENOCARPY

steno·taph·rum \ˌstenəˈtafrəm\ *n, cap* [NL, fr. *sten-* + Gk *taphros* ditch; akin to Gk *thaptein* to bury — more at EPITAPH] **:** a small genus of grasses found in Malaysia and along the seacoast of America and having creeping stems and one-flowered spikelets on one side of a flat corky rachis — see SAINT AUGUSTINE GRASS 1

steno·tele \ˈ==,tēl\ *n* -s [*sten-* + L *tela* warp threads, web — more at TELA] **:** PENETRANT a

steno·therm \ˈstenə,thərm\ *n* [back-formation fr. *stenothermal*] **:** a stenothermal organism

steno·thermal \ˌstenə+\ *also* **steno·thermic** \"+\ *adj* [prob. fr. G *stenotherm* stenothermal (fr. *sten-* + Gk *thermē* heat) + E *-al*, *-ic* — more at THERM] **:** resisting only slight changes of temperature — opposed to *eurythermal*

steno·thermophile \ˌ==+\ *n* [*stenothermy* + *-o-* + *-phile*] **:** a stenothermophilic organism

steno·thermophilic \"+\ *adj* [*stenothermy* + *-o-* + *-philic*] **:** preferring a stenothermal environment

steno·ther·my \ˈstenə,thərmē\ *n* -ES [*stenothermal* + *-y*] **:** the quality or state of being stenothermal

ste·not·ic \stəˈnäd·ik, -ätik\ *adj* [fr. NL *stenosis*, after such pairs as NL *narcosis*: E *narcotic*] **:** relating to or having stenosis

steno·topic \ˌstenəˈtäpik\ *adj* [prob. fr. G *stenotop* stenotopic (fr. *sten-* + *-top*, fr. Gk *topos* place) + E *-ic* — more at TOPIC] **:** having a narrow range of adaptability to changes in environmental conditions — compare EURYTOPIC, STENOTROPIC

steno·trop·ic \ˌ==ˈträpik\ *adj* [alter. (influenced by *-tropic*) of *stenotopic*] **:** having a narrow range of tolerance for variation in environmental conditions — compare STENOTOPIC

¹steno·type \ˈstenə+,-\ *n* [*steno-* (as in *stenography*) + *type*] **1 :** a letter or combination of letters representing a phonogram in stenotypy **2 :** a small machine somewhat resembling a typewriter that records by means of stenotypes

²stenotype \"\ *vt* **:** to record with a stenotype

steno·typ·ist \-pəst\ *n* [¹*stenotype* + *-ist*] **:** an operator of a stenotype

steno·typy \-pē, -pi\ *n* -ES [¹*stenotype* + *-y*] **:** a phonographic writing using ordinary script or printed letters

stens *pl of* STEN

sten·sen's duct *also* **sten·son's duct** \ˈsten(t)sənz-\ *n, usu cap S* [after Niels *Stensen* †1687 Dan. anatomist, its discoverer] **:** STENO'S DUCT

¹stent \ˈstent\ *chiefly dial var of* STINT

²stent \ˈ"\ *vt* -ED/-ING/-S [ME *stenten*, by shortening & alter. fr. *extenten* to stretch out, assess, fr. L *extentus*, past part. of *extendere* to stretch out — more at EXTEND] *chiefly Scot* **:** to stretch out **:** EXTEND

³stent \ˈ"\ *n* -s [ME, by shortening & alter. fr. *extente*] *chiefly Scot* **:** EXTENT 1

⁴stent \ˈ"\ *adj* [prob. contr. of Sc *stentit*, past part. of ²*stent*] *Scot* **:** OUTSTRETCHED, TIGHT

⁵stent \ˈ"\ *also* **stint** \ˈstint\ *n* -s [after Charles R. *Stent* †1901 Eng. dentist, inventor of the compound] **1 :** a compound or a mold made of the compound for holding a surgical graft in place **2 :** something (as a pad of gauze immobilized by sutures) used like a stent

¹stent·er \-ntə(r)\ *n* -s [²*stent* + *-er*] *Brit* **:** ¹TENTER

²stenter \ˈ"\ *vt* -ED/-ING/-S [¹*stenter*] *Brit* **:** ²TENTER

stent net *n* [⁴*stent*] **:** a net used in river fishing that is stretched or extended from the stake by which one end of it is anchored

sten·ton \ˈstentᵊn, -ntən\ *also* **stent·ing** \-tiŋ, -tēŋ\ *n* -s [origin unknown] **:** a short heading driven at right angles to a crosscut in a mining operation

¹sten·tor \ˈstentər\ *n* -s [obs. *stent* to assess (by shortening & alter. fr. obs. *extent*, fr. ME *extenten* to stretch out, assess) + *-or* — more at STENT] *chiefly Scot* **:** a tax assessor

²sten·tor \ˈsten·,tȯ(ə)r, -ō(ə), -ntə(r)\ *n* [after *Stentor*, Greek warrior mentioned in the Iliad famed for his powerful voice, fr. L & Gk; L *Stentor*, fr. Gk *Stentōr*] **1** -s **:** a person having a powerful voice ⟨parliamentary ~*s* —*Time*⟩ **2** [NL, fr. L] **a** *cap* **:** a widely distributed genus of heterotrichous ciliate protozoans that have a trumpet-shaped body attached to the substrate by the smaller end with the mouth at the larger end, are often brightly colored, and are among the largest infusorians **b** -s **:** any protozoan of the genus *Stentor* **3** -s **:** HOWLER MONKEY

sten·to·ri·an \(ˈ)stenˈtōrēən, -tȯr-\ *adj* [²*stentor* + *-ian*] **:** extremely loud **:** capable of powerful utterance or sound ⟨proclaimed the fact in ~ tones —A.A.Berle⟩ ⟨the steamer's ~ foghorn —Nike Anderson⟩ **syn** see LOUD

sten·to·rine \ˈstentə,rīn, -,rən\ *adj* [NL *Stentor* + E *-ine*] **:** of or relating to the genus *Stentor*

sten·to·ri·ous \(ˈ)stenˈtōrēəs, -tȯr-\ *adj* [²*stentor* + *-ious*] **:** STENTORIAN — **sten·to·ri·ous·ly** *adv*

sten·to·ro·phon·ic \ˌstentərəˈfänik\ *adj* [NL *stentorophonicus*, fr. Gk *Stentōr* Stentor + *-o-* + *phōnē* voice + L *-icus* -ic — more at BAN] **:** speaking or sounding very loud **:** STENTORIAN

sten·tor·phone \ˈstentə(r),fōn\ *n* [²*stentor* + *-phone*] **:** a large-scale loud open pipe-organ flue stop of 8-foot pitch

¹step \ˈstep\ *n* -s *often attrib* [ME *step*, *steppe*, fr. OE *stæpe*, *stepe*; akin to OFris *stap*, *stepe* step, footstep, OHG *stapf*, *stapfo* step, footstep, OE *stæppan*, *steppan* to step — more at STEP (v.)] **1 :** something to put the foot on in ascending or descending: **a :** one of a flight of stairs consisting of a riser and a tread **b** (1) **:** a rung of a ladder (2) **:** a flat crosspiece of a stepladder **c :** a flat projecting or projectable footpiece for entering or alighting from a vehicle **d :** a foothold cut in a slope of earth, rock, or ice **2 a :** an advance or movement made by raising the foot and bringing it down in a different position ⟨took two ~*s* toward the door and stopped⟩ **b :** a combination of foot or of foot, leg, and body movements constituting a simple unit or a pattern that is repeated ⟨dancing . . . with such coincidence of ~ and gesture as only years of training could render possible —Lafcadio Hearn⟩ **c :** a pace in military drill — often used in combination ⟨goose ~⟩ **d :** manner of walking **:** STRIDE ⟨came in with his light lithe ~ —Adria Langley⟩ **e :** a mark or impression made by the foot **:** FOOTPRINT ⟨~*s* leading across the beach and disappearing at the water's edge⟩ **f :** the sound of a footstep ⟨heard his ~ on the stairs⟩ **3 a :** the space passed over by the movement of one foot beyond the other in walking ⟨twelve ~*s* or more from my mother's door —William Wordsworth⟩ **b** (1) **:** a short distance ⟨a store located just a ~ from the bank⟩ (2) **:** a distance for walking ⟨lives a good ~ down the road⟩ **c** *obs* **:** a short journey ⟨resolved to take a ~ to Paris for my health —Jonathan Swift⟩ **d :** the vertical distance of one of a set of stairs ⟨built the kitchen two ~*s* lower than the dining room⟩ **4 steps** *pl* **:** progress by or as if by walking **:** COURSE, WAY ⟨vengeance tend upon thy ~*s* —Shak.⟩ ⟨directed his ~*s* toward the river⟩ **5 a :** a degree, grade, or rank in a scale ⟨a ~ higher in the social scale⟩ ⟨rose several ~*s* in my opinion⟩ **b :** a stage in a gradual, regular, or orderly process ⟨achieve the initial ~ in this ambitious plan —Mason Wade⟩ ⟨guided her through every ~ of her career —Jerry Cotter⟩ **c :** promotion to the next higher grade or rank ⟨trusted you would get the ~ within . . . twelve months —Sir Walter Scott⟩ **d :** any one of a graded series of photographic exposures or tones **6 a :** a wood or metal frame on a ship designed to receive an upright shaft; *esp* **:** a block supporting the heel of a mast **b :** the lower bearing block on which a vertical shaft revolves **c :** one of the halves of a split-bearing bushing **7 :** an action, proceeding, or measure often occurring as one in a series ⟨took the unusual ~ of personally remonstrating with the president —W.C.Ford⟩ ⟨took ~*s* toward securing the mouth of the river against Spain —*Amer. Guide Series: La.*⟩ **8 :** pace with or as if with another ⟨two friends kept ~ beside me —A.E.Housman⟩ **9 :** a steplike offset or part usu. occurring in a series; *specif* **:** one of the series of parts of a cone pulley on which the belt runs **10 steps** *pl* **:** STEPLADDER ⟨from the early 18th century, library ~*s* were in use —J.E.Gloag⟩ **11 a :** a musical scale or staff degree **b :** the interval between two contiguous degrees of the staff or scale **c :** WHOLE STEP **12 a :** a steplike shoulder or bench on an otherwise smoothly rising hillside or slope **:** one of a series of terraces rising from a valley floor **b :** a steplike shelf or ledge in the vertical surface of a quarry or mine working **13 :** a change in direction in a line, a surface, or the construction of a solid body; *specif* **:** a break in the form of the bottom of a float or hull of a seaplane that is designed to reduce resistance when under way by rapidly reducing the wetted surfaces as speed increases and that serves to eliminate suction effect and improve longitudinal control in takeoff **14 a :** a change of place due to a motion of translation **b :** the translation that effects such a step — **in step** *adv* (*or adj*) **1 :** with each foot moving to the same time with the corresponding foot of others or in time to music ⟨walking *in step* with the other prisoners —C.K.Ogden⟩ **2 :** in harmony or agreement ⟨keep wages and salaries *in step* with economic conditions —*Report: Electric Auto-Lite Co.*⟩ **3 :** in phase — **on the step** *adv* (*or adj*) **:** in rapid movement over the water with the aft part of the float or hull off the water ⟨trailing a plume of spray . . . she went up *on the step* and was off into space —*Newsweek*⟩ — **out of step** *adv* (*or adj*) **:** not in step ⟨the second platoon was *out of step*⟩ ⟨the right of a man to be *out of step* with society —A.G.Hays⟩

²step \ˈ"\ *vb* **stepped** *or archaic* **stept** \-pt\ **stepped** *or archaic* **stept; stepping; steps** [ME *steppen*, *stepen*, *stapen*, fr. OE *stæppan*, *steppan*; akin to OFris *stapa*, *steppa* to step, MD *stappen*, OHG *stapfōn*, *stepfen* to step, ON *stappa* to pound, stamp — more at STAMP] *vi* **1 a :** to move in any direction by raising the foot and bringing it down in a different position or by moving each foot in succession **:** move the feet (as in walking) ⟨walked . . . to the barn and *stepped* into the saddle —Will Cook⟩ ⟨hunters ~ over the dead animal —J.G. Frazer⟩ ⟨*stepped* ashore at the ferry landing —Louis Bromfield) ⟨*stepped* off the curb and started walking down the hill —Dorothy Baker⟩ ⟨*stepped* out on deck to cool himself —E.K. Gann⟩ ⟨*stepped* down from the ladder⟩ ⟨~ aside to let the doctor pass⟩ ⟨the referee *stepped* between the two boxers⟩ **b :** DANCE ⟨that girl can really ~⟩ **2 a :** to go on foot **:** WALK ⟨what, you are *stepping* westward —Dorothy Wordsworth⟩ ⟨please ~ to the telephone⟩ ⟨*stepped* down to the corner for a newspaper⟩ **b** *obs* **:** to move forward **:** ADVANCE, PROCEED ⟨I am in blood *stepped* in so far —Shak.⟩ **c :** to go or be on one's way **:** DEPART — often used with *along* ⟨well, I must ~ along now⟩ **d :** to move at a brisk or lively pace ⟨they kept us *stepping* all right —W.L.Gresham⟩ **3 a :** to put the foot down **:** TREAD ⟨~ on a rusty nail⟩ **b :** to press down with the foot ⟨~ on the brake⟩ **4 a :** to come as if at a single step ⟨*stepped* into a fortune when his father died⟩ ⟨~ into a good job⟩ **b** *obs* **:** to enter suddenly and in a rash or thoughtless manner ⟨in hot blood hath *stepped* into the law —Shak.⟩ **5 :** to stand erect with the lower end fixed in a step ⟨the foremast ~*s* abaft the forecastle⟩ **~ *vt* 1 :** to take by moving the feet in succession ⟨rose and *stepped* three paces —Rudyard Kipling⟩ **2 a :** to move (the foot) in any direction **:** SET, PLACE ⟨the first man who *stepped* foot on the enemy's soil —S.G.W.Benjamin⟩ **b :** to move over or travel across on foot **:** TRAVERSE ⟨proud too . . . of *stepping* this famous pavement —Virginia Woolf⟩ ⟨deer ~ the highways —Grace H. Flandrau⟩ **3 :** to go through the steps of **:** PERFORM ⟨~ a minuet⟩ **4 :** to make erect by fixing the lower end in a step ⟨a small pole *stepped* in a block of wood served as a mast —Bernard DeVoto⟩ **5 :** to measure by steps ⟨have *stepped* more ground . . . than any man in the country —Samuel Lover⟩ — often used with *off* or *out* ⟨~ off 50 yards⟩ **6 :** to provide or furnish with steps **:** make steps in ⟨~ a key⟩ **7 :** to construct or arrange in or as if in steps **:** build in steps ⟨was . . . *stepped* to ensure that the winter rains did not wash the whole lot into the sea —Brendan Maguire⟩ ⟨the house is *stepped* down the slope —Siegfried Giedion⟩ ⟨craggy peaks with terraces *stepped* up the sides —*Time*⟩ — **step on it 1 :** to increase the speed of a motor vehicle by pressing down on the accelerator **2 :** to increase one's speed **:** hurry up

step- \"\ *comb form* [ME, fr. OE *stēop-*; akin to OFris *stiap-* step-, OHG *stiof-*, ON *stjūp-* step-, OE *āstēpan, āstȳpan* to deprive, bereave, OHG *bistiufen* to deprive of children or parents] **:** related by virtue of a remarriage (as of a parent) and not by blood ⟨*step*aunt⟩ ⟨*step*cousin⟩ ⟨*step*grandchild⟩

step-and-repeat \ˌ═══ˈ═\ *adj* **:** of, relating to, or employing a method in which successive exposures of a single image are made on a printing surface that is being prepared for gang printing

step back *vi* **1 :** to yield ground by moving to the rear ⟨ordered the spectators to *step back*⟩ **2 :** RECEDE ⟨end chimneys which *step back* unattached above the second story —*Amer. Guide Series: N.C.*⟩ **~ *vt* :** to construct (as a building) in an ascending series of steps or stages of diminishing width **:** build so that successive stories or groups of stories recede farther and farther from the front, side, or back ⟨an octagonal tower . . . rising sheer to 13 stories and then *stepped back* three times to a height of 327 feet —*Amer. Guide Series: N.Y.*⟩

step bearing *n* **:** a bearing that supports the lower end of a vertical shaft

step bolt *n* **:** CARRIAGE BOLT

stepbrother \ˈ═ˌ══\ *n* [ME, fr. *step-* + *brother*] **:** a son of one's stepparent by a former marriage

step-by-step \ˌ═(ˌ)═ˈ═\ *adj* **:** marked by successive degrees usu. of limited extent **:** GRADUAL ⟨approach on a *step-by-step* basis a closer association with other nations —Dean Acheson⟩

step-by-step telegraph *n* **:** an electric telegraph in which each letter of the message is indicated by a pointer on a dial

step chair *n* **:** a chair convertible into a stepladder

stepchild \ˈ═ˌ═\ *n, pl* **stepchildren** [ME, fr. OE *stēopcild* orphan, fr. *stēop-* step- + *cild* child — more at CHILD] **1 :** a child of one's wife or husband by a former marriage **2 :** one that fails to receive proper care or attention ⟨music is . . . a ~ in most of our academic institutions —P.H.Lang⟩

step chuck *n* **:** a lathe chuck with recessed shoulders of decreasing diameters for holding flat round work

step-cline \ˈ═ˌ═\ *n* [¹*step*] **:** an irregular or interrupted cline

step-cone pulley \ˈ═ˌ═-\ *n* **:** CONE PULLEY

step cut *n* **:** a cut for diamonds or esp. colored stones forming a series of straight facets that decrease in length as they recede from the girdle and so give the appearance of steps — compare TABLE CUT

stepdame \ˈ═ˌ═\ *n* [ME, fr. *step-* + *dame*] *archaic* **:** STEPMOTHER

step dance *n* **:** a dance in which steps are emphasized rather than gesture or posture; *esp* **:** a solo dance characterized by clogging, tapping, brushing, or kicking

stepdaughter \ˈ═ˌ══\ *n* [ME *stepdoughter*, fr. OE *stēopdohtor* (akin to MHG *stiefiohter*, ON *stjūpdōttir*), fr. *stēop-* step- + *dohtor* daughter — more at STEP-, DAUGHTER] **:** a daughter of one's wife or husband by a former marriage

step down *vt* **1 :** to lower the voltage of (a current) by means of a transformer **2 :** to decrease, retard, or mitigate by or as if by steps ⟨*stepping down* the intensity of the myth into mild contemporary equivalents —Malcolm Cowley⟩ **~ *vi* :** to retire or resign from a position of power or authority ⟨had *stepped down* from active management of the household —Irving Stone⟩

¹step-down \ˈ═ˌ═\ *adj* [*step down*] **:** that decreases, reduces, or retards; *specif* **:** that decreases voltage ⟨*step-down* transformer⟩

²step-down \ˈ═ˌ═\ *n* -s **:** a decrease or reduction in size or amount ⟨a *step-down* in dosage⟩

stepfather \ˈ═ˌ══\ *n* [ME *stepfader*, fr. OE *stēopfæder* (akin to OFris *stiapfeder*, MHG *stiefvater*, ON *stjūpfathir*), fr. *stēop-* step- + *fæder* father — more at FATHER] **:** the husband of one's mother by a subsequent marriage

step fault *n* **:** DISTRIBUTIVE FAULT

step function *n* **:** a function of a single real variable in mathematics that remains constant throughout each of a series of adjacent intervals with the constant value varying from interval to interval

step gauge *n* **1 :** a compound plug gauge consisting of several short cylindrical gauges of graduated diameters on the same axis **2 :** a gauge that consists of a handled body in which a blade slides normally and that is used esp. for measuring shoulders or steps

step grate *n* **:** a fire grate in which the bars rise like steps

stephan- *or* **stephano-** *comb form* [Gk, fr. *stephanos* crown, fr. *stephein* to put round one's head, encircle, crown] **:** crown **:** halo ⟨*Stephan*urus⟩ ⟨*stephano*me⟩ ⟨*Stephano*filaria⟩

steph·a·nan·dra \ˌstefəˈnandrə\ *n, cap* [NL, fr. *stephan-* + *-andra*] **:** a genus of deciduous Japanese and Chinese shrubs (family Rosaceae) with lobed or incised leaves and flowers with four or more petals and a single pistil that produces a follicle

steph·a·ne \ˈstefə(ˌ)nē\ *n* -s [Gk *stephanē*, fr. *stephein* to put round one's head] **:** a headdress that consists of a metal band widest in the middle over the forehead and growing narrower toward the temples and that is often seen in ancient Greek statues of divinities

ste·pha·nian \stəˈfānēən, -nyən\ *adj, usu cap* [F *stéphanien*, fr. (Sanctus) *Stephanus* (Latin form of Saint-Étienne, city in central France where a carboniferous basin representing this division is found) + F *-ien* -ian] **:** of or relating to a division of the Carboniferous — see GEOLOGIC TIME table

ste·phan·i·dae \-ˈfanəˌdē\ *n pl, cap* [NL, fr. *Stephanus*, type genus (fr. Gk *stephanos* crown) + *-idae*; fr. the antennae] **:** a widely distributed family of slender ichneumon flies having many-segmented filamentous antennae and including some that as larvae are parasites on wood-boring insects

ste·pha·ni·on \-ˈfānēən\ *n* -s [NL, fr. Gk, dim. of *stephanos* crown] **:** the point where the coronal suture crosses the superior temporal line — see CRANIOMETRY illustration

steph·an·ite \ˈstefəˌnīt\ *n* -s [G *stephanit*, fr. Archduke *Stephan* of Austria †1867 + G *-it* -ite] **:** a mineral Ag_5SbS_4 consisting of an orthorhombic iron black sulfide of silver and antimony and having metallic luster

steph·a·no·filaria \ˌstefəˌnō+\ *n, cap* [NL, fr. *stephan-* + *filaria*] **:** a genus of filarial worms parasitic in the skin and subcutaneous tissues of ruminants and horses where they may cause dermatitis and extensive degenerative lesions — compare HUMP SORE

steph·a·no·fil·a·ri·a·sis \ˌ══(ˌ)═ˌfiləˈrīəsəs\ *n* [NL, fr. *Stephanofilaria* + *-sis*] **:** infestation with or disease caused by worms of the genus *Stephanofilaria*

steph·a·no·kon·tae \-ˈkän·(ˌ)tē\ *n pl, cap* [NL, fr. *stephan-* + *-kontae* (as in *isokontae*)] *in some classifications* **:** a class or subclass that is approximately equivalent to Oedogoniales and includes green algae having zoospores with a crown or chaplet of cilia — compare HETEROKONTAE, ISOKONTAE

steph·a·nome \ˈstefəˌnōm\ *n* -s [*stephan-* + Gk *-nomos* distributor (fr. *nemein* to distribute) — more at NIMBLE] **:** an instrument for measuring the angular dimensions of fogbows and halos

steph·a·no·tis \ˌ══ˈnōd·əs\ *n* [NL, fr. Gk *stephanōtis* fit for a crown, fr. *stephanos* crown] **1** *cap* **:** a genus of Old World tropical woody vines (family Asclepiadaceae) with fragrant white flowers which corolla has a cylindrical dilated tube and spreading limb — see MADAGASCAR JASMINE **2** -ES **:** any plant of the genus *Stephanotis*

steph·a·nu·rus \-ˈnyürəs\ *n, cap* [NL, fr. *stephan-* + *-urus*] **:** a genus of nematode worms (family Strongylidae) including the kidney worm of swine

step-hop \ˈ═ˌ═\ *n* **:** a dance step consisting of a forward step followed by a hop on the same foot

step in *vi* [ME *stepen in*, fr. *stepen* to step + *in* — more at STEP] **1 :** to make a brief informal visit **:** drop in ⟨*step in* and take your chocolate with her —Elizabeth Inchbald⟩ **2 :** to enter into an affair or dispute often without invitation, permission, or welcome **:** INTERVENE ⟨if the local communities do not meet their responsibilities . . . the federal and state governments will *step in* —C.H.Hood⟩

¹step-in \ˈ═ˌ═\ *adj* [*step in*] **1** *of clothing* **:** put on by being stepped into ⟨*step-in* dress⟩ ⟨*step-in* moccasins⟩ **2 :** of or relating to step-in clothing ⟨*step-in* styles⟩

²step-in \ˈ═ˌ═\ *n* -s **:** an article of step-in clothing: as **a :** a shoe that resembles but usu. has a higher vamp than a pump and that often has concealed goring or elasticized top edging **b step-ins** *pl* **:** a woman's brief panties

step index *n* **:** an index cut into the fore edge of a book in the form of steps with the edge of each set of leaves preceding an indexed leaf being cut away — compare TAB INDEX, THUMB INDEX

step joint *n* **:** a joint used in fastening together the ends of two rails of different height and section

stepladder \ˈ═ˌ══\ *n* **:** a portable set of flat broad steps or treads with a frame hinged to the back for steadying

stepladder

step·less \ˈ═ləs\ *adj* **:** having no steps

steplike \ˈ═ˌ═\ *adj* **:** resembling a series of steps

stepmother \ˈ═ˌ══\ *n* [ME *stepmoder*, fr. OE *stēopmōdor* (akin to MHG *stiefmuoter*, ON *stjūpmōthir*), fr. *stēop-* step- + *mōdor* mother — more at STEP-, MOTHER] **1 :** the wife of one's father by a subsequent marriage **2 :** one that fails to give proper care or attention ⟨the monastery had got the credit of founding a school but had . . . been a ~ to it —*Contemporary Rev.*⟩ **3** *dial* **:** HANGNAIL

step·moth·er·ly *adj* **:** of, relating to, or befitting a stepmother

step·ney \ˈstepnē, -ni\ *or* **stepney wheel** *n* -s *often cap S* [prob. fr. *Stepney* Street, Llanelly, Wales, where it was orig. manufactured] *Brit* **:** a spare spokeless automobile wheel with inflated tire

step-off \ˈ═ˌ═\ *n* -s [fr. *step off*, v.] **1 :** an act or instance of stepping off **2 a :** an abrupt dropping off of a shore line into deep water **b :** a place where such a dropping off occurs

step-on \ˈ═ˌ═\ *adj* [fr. *step on*, v.] **:** opened by means of a pedal ⟨14-quart *step-on* can in chrome-plated steel —*advt*⟩

step out *vi* **1 :** to go away from a place usu. for a short distance and for a short time ⟨just *stepped out* for a while —Erskine Caldwell⟩ **2 :** to go or march at a vigorous or increased pace **3 :** DIE **4 :** to engage in social activities **:** lead an active social life ⟨has really been *stepping out* this past year⟩ **5 :** to be unfaithful — usu. used with *on* ⟨hadn't been married two months before I knew he was *stepping out on* me —James Jones⟩

step-out \ˈ═ˌ═\ *n* -s [*step out*] **:** a well drilled outside but near a proved oil field

stepparent \ˈ═ˌ══\ *n* [*step-* + *parent*] **:** the husband or wife of one's mother or father by a subsequent marriage

steppe \ˈstep\ *n* -s [Russ *step'*, fr. ORuss, lowland] **1 :** one of the vast tracts in southeastern Europe or Asia that are usu. level and without forests **2 :** arid land characterized by xerophilous vegetation and found usu. in large tracts and in regions of extreme temperature range and loess soil — compare GRASSLAND, PAMPA, PLAIN, PRAIRIE, SAVANNA

steppe cat *n* **:** MANUL

stepped \ˈstept\ *adj* [¹*step* + *-ed*] **1 :** having a step or a series of steps **:** arranged or constructed in steps ⟨~ pyramids⟩ ⟨~ gables⟩ **2** *of an arch* **:** consisting of a series of concentric arches of diminishing radius set within one another

stepped footing *n* **:** a footing in which the desired width is secured by a series of steps in about the proportion of one unit of horizontal dimension to two units of vertical dimension

stepped gable *n* **:** a gable that diminishes in width by corbiesteps

stepped gauge *n* **:** STEP GAUGE

stepped gear wheel *n* **:** a gear wheel with two or more complete circular sets of teeth arranged adjacently on the same rim so that the corresponding teeth in the various sets form a series of steps

stepped key *n* **:** BIT KEY

stepped pulley *n* **:** a cone pulley with steps

stepped rack *n* **:** a rack made to mesh with a stepped gear

stepped screw *n* **:** an interrupted screw the divisions of whose surface are stepped

stepped-up \ˈ═ˌ═\ *adj* **:** AUGMENTED, ACCELERATED, INTENSIFIED ⟨a *stepped-up* sales campaign⟩

steppeland \ˈ═ˌ═\ *n* **:** STEPPE 2

step·per \ˈstepə(r)\ *n* -s **:** one that steps: as **a :** a horse with high action **b :** DANCER

stepping *n* -s [ME, fr. gerund of *steppen* to step — more at STEP] **1 :** an act or instance of moving the feet (as in walking) **2 a** (1) **:** lumber suitable for steps (2) **:** wood members esp. formed for use in constructing step treads **b :** an export grade of yellow pine and fir

stepping-off place \ˌ══ˈ═-\ *n* **1 :** the outbound end of a transportation line **2 :** a place from which one departs for unknown territory

stepping-stone \ˈ══ˌ═\ *n* [ME] **1 a :** a stone on which to step in walking (as in crossing a stream) **b :** a raised stone for facilitating an ascent or descent; *specif* **:** HORSE BLOCK **2 :** a means of progress or advancement ⟨the law was a *stepping-stone* to a career in politics —G.S.Bryan⟩ **3 :** a place for a break in or as if in a journey ⟨this *stepping-stone* for airborne supplies on their way to far-flung fronts below the equator —Howell Walker⟩

step rate *n* **:** a rate that changes by regular gradations: as **a :** a life-insurance premium rate that increases or decreases each year **b :** a utilities rate whereby an increase in unit consumption results in a decrease in unit price

step rocket *n* **:** a multistage rocket whose sections are fired successively

steps *pl of* STEP, *pres 3d sing of* STEP

stepsister \ˈ═ˌ══\ *n* [*step-* + *sister*] **:** a daughter of one's stepparent by a former marriage

step socket *n* **:** a socket for a locked-wire rope having a series of gripping blocks of graduated bores to hold the layers

stepson \ˈ═ˌ═\ *n* [ME *stepsone*, fr. OE *stēopsunu* (akin to MHG *stiefsun*, ON *stjūpsonr*), fr. *stēop-* step- + *sunu* son — more at STEP-, SON] **:** a son of one's husband or wife by a former marriage

stepstone \ˈ═ˌ═\ *n* **:** a stone laid before an outside door as a step

step stool *n* **:** a stool with one or two steps that often fold away beneath the seat ⟨use a kitchen *step stool* to reach things on the higher shelves⟩

stept *archaic past of* STEP

step table *n* **:** a small table surmounted by one short shelf or several progressively diminished shelves

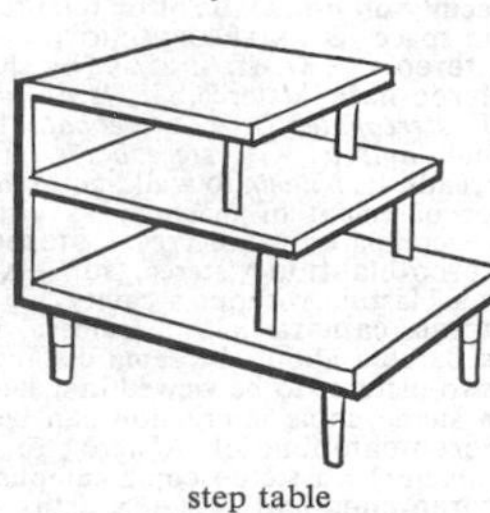

step table

step terrace *n* **:** a stepped terrace on the levels of which farming is done

step trench *n* **:** a trench cut in a series of steps from the base to the top of a mound for determining the cultural levels of an archaeological site

step turn *n* **:** a turn executed in a downhill traverse by lifting the upper ski from the ground, placing it in the desired direction, weighting it, and bringing the other ski parallel

step up *vt* **1 :** to increase the voltage of (a current) by means of a transformer **2 :** to increase, augment, or advance by or as if by steps ⟨the amount of salt mined can be materially *stepped up* —R.E.Crist⟩ ⟨radio and television have *stepped up* . . . the tempo of the news —F.L.Mott⟩ **3 :** to give a promotion to ⟨you're going to be *stepped up* to head clerk —Frederick Way⟩ **~ *vi* 1 :** to come forward often in an interfering, inopportune, or unguarded manner ⟨time for teachers to *step up* and say that there is nothing wrong with teaching something —James Binney⟩ **2 :** to undergo an increase ⟨world trade is *stepping up* —*Kiplinger Washington Letter*⟩ **3 :** to receive a promotion ⟨*stepping up* to the chief executive's chair —*Current Biog.*⟩

¹step-up \ˈ═ˌ═\ *adj* [*step up*] **:** that increases, augments, or advances: as **a** *of a transformer* **:** that increases voltage **b** *of a lease* **:** that provides for increases in rent up to a maximum

²step-up \ˈ═ˌ═\ *n* -s **:** an increase or advance in size or amount ⟨a *step-up* in production⟩

step ward *n* **:** the ward of a lock or key nearest to the pin

stepway \ˈ═ˌ═\ *n* **:** a flight of steps

step wedge *or* **step tablet** *n* **:** an optical wedge in which the change in transmittance with distance along the wedge occurs in discrete adjacent steps

¹stepwise \ˈ═ˌ═\ *adv* **:** in a stepwise manner

²stepwise \"\ *adj* **1 :** marked by or as if by steps **:** GRADUAL ⟨achieved in a ~ struggle for social reform —Fritz Tarnow⟩ ⟨a ~ chemical reaction⟩ **2 :** moving by step to adjacent musical tones ⟨a short melodic line . . . containing mostly ~ progressions —Paul Hindemith⟩

-ster \stə(r), *following a voiced consonant, as in "mobster"*, -ztə- *or* -stə-\ *n suffix* -s [ME *-ster, -stere, -estere*, fr. OE *-estre* female agent; akin to MD *-ster*] **1 :** one that does or handles or operates ⟨*spinster*⟩ ⟨*tapster*⟩ ⟨*teamster*⟩ **2 :** one that makes or uses ⟨*songster*⟩ ⟨*punster*⟩ **3 :** one that is associated with or participates in ⟨*gamester*⟩ ⟨*gangster*⟩

ster *abbr* **1** sterilization; sterilizer **2** sterling

ste·ra·di·an \stəˈrādēən\ *also* **sterad** \ˈsteˌrad, ˈsti,r-\ *n* -s [*steradian* fr. *stere-* + *radian*; *sterad* short for *steradian*] **:** a unit of measure of solid angles that is expressed as the solid angle subtended at the center of the sphere by a portion of the surface whose area is equal to the square of the radius of the sphere

ste·ra·di·an·cy \stəˈrādēənsē\ *n* -ES [*steradian* + *-cy*] **:** the radiant flux from a surface per steradian of solid angle in a specified direction per unit area of cross section of the emission perpendicular to that direction

ster·co·bi·lin \ˌstərkōˈbīlən\ *n* -s [ISV *sterco-* (fr. L *stercus* excrement) + *bil-* (fr. L *bilis* bile) + *-in* — more at BILE] **:** UROBILIN; *esp* **:** a brown levorotatory pigment $C_{33}H_{46}N_4O_6$ found in feces and urine

ster·co·bi·lin·o·gen \-ˌbīˈlinəjən\ *n* -s [ISV *stercobilin* + *-o-* + *-gen*] **:** UROBILINOGEN

ster·co·ra·ceous \ˌstərkəˈrāshəs\ *adj* [L *stercor-, stercus* + E *-aceous*] **:** of or relating to dung **:** being or containing dung

ster·co·ral \ˈstərkərəl\ *adj* [ML *stercoralis*, fr. L *stercor-, stercus* excrement + *-alis* -al — more at DRECK] **1 :** of, relating to, containing, produced by, or being dung **:** FECAL **2 :** living in or feeding on dung

stercoral pocket *n* **:** a pouched diverticulum of the hind intestine of a spider that serves as a reservoir for fecal material

ster·co·ra·nism \ˈstərkərəˌnizəm\ *n* -s *often cap* [ML *stercoranista* Stercoranist + E *-ism*] **:** the body of beliefs peculiar to Stercoranists

ster·co·ra·nist \-ˌnəst\ *also* **ster·co·rar·ian** \ˌstərkəˈra(a)rēən\ *n* -s *often cap* [*stercoranist* fr. ML *stercoranista*, fr. *stercoran-* (irreg. fr. L *stercor-, stercus* excrement) + L *-ista* -ist; *stercorarian* fr. L *stercorarius* stercoral + E *-an*] **:** one who holds that the consecrated elements in the Eucharist are subject to natural processes (as of digestion)

ster·co·ra·rii·dae \ˌstərkərəˈrīəˌdē\ *n pl, cap* [NL, fr. *Stercorarius*, type genus (fr. L *stercorarius* stercoral, fr. *stercor-, stercus* excrement + *-arius* -ary) + NL *-idae*] **:** a family of long-winged sea birds (suborder Lari) comprising the jaegers and skuas and being sometimes ranked as a subfamily of Laridae

ster·co·rary \ˈ══ˌrerē\ *n* -ES [ML *stercorarium* toilet, stercorary, fr. neut. of L *stercorarius* stercoral] *archaic* **:** a place (as a covered pit) for the storage of manure secure from the weather

ster·co·ra·tion \ˌ══ˈrāshən\ *n* -s [L *stercoration-, stercoratio*, fr. *stercoratus* (past part. of *stercorare*) + *-ion-, -io* -ion] **1** *archaic* **:** the act of dressing with manure **2 :** MANURE, DUNG

ster·co·ric·o·lous \ˌ══kəˈrikələs\ *adj* [L *stercor-, stercus* excrement + E *-i-* + *-colous*] **:** living in dung

ster·co·rite \ˈstərkəˌrīt\ *n* -s [L *stercor-, stercus* + E *-ite*] **:** a native microcosmic salt $HNaNH_4PO_4 4H_2O$ occurring in guano

ster·cov·o·rous \(ˈ)stərˈkävərəs\ *adj* [L *stercus* excrement + E *-o-* + *-vorous*] **:** SCATOPHAGOUS — used esp. of an insect

ster·cu·lia \stə(r)ˈkyülēə\ *n* [NL, fr. L *Sterculius* god of cultivation and manuring, fr. *stercus* manure, excrement; fr. the fetid odor of some of the species — more at DRECK] **1** *cap* **:** a genus of tropical trees or shrubs (family Sterculiaceae) having palmate leaves, small paniculate unisexual flowers with 15 anthers, and an ovary with 5 cells that become distinct carpels in the fruit — see BOTTLE TREE, KALUMPANG **2** -s **:** any plant of the genus *Sterculia* — see STERCULIA GUM

ster·cu·li·a·ce·ae \ˌ══ˌlēˈāsēˌē\ *n pl, cap* [NL, fr. *Sterculia*, type genus + *-aceae*] **:** a large family of herbs, shrubs, or trees (order Malvales) distinguished mainly by the numerous monadelphous stamens and 2-celled anthers — see KURRAJONG — **ster·cu·li·a·ceous** \ˌ══ˈāshəs\ *adj*

ster·cu·li·ad \ˈ══lēˌad\ *n* -s [NL *Sterculia* + E *-ad*] **:** a plant of the family Sterculiaceae

sterculia gum *n* **:** any of several vegetable gums that are similar in properties to tragacanth and often used as substitutes for it and that are obtained from tropical Asiatic trees of the genera *Sterculia* and *Cochlospermum* (esp. *S. urens* and *C. gossypium*)

ster·cu·lic acid \(ˈ)stərˈkyülik-\ *n* [NL *Sterculia* + E *-ic*] **:** a crystalline unsaturated fatty acid $C_8H_{17}(C_3H_2)(CH_2)_7$-COOH found as a glyceride in the seeds of a tropical tree (*Sterculia foetida*); 2-octyl-1-cyclo-propene-octanoic acid

stere \ˈsti(ə)r, -te(-\ *n* -s [F *stère*, fr. Gk *stereos* solid] **:** a metric unit of volume equal to one cubic meter — see METRIC SYSTEM table

stere- *or* **stereo-** *comb form* [NL, fr. Gk, fr. *stereos* solid — more at STARE] **1 :** solid **:** solid body ⟨*stereo*spondylous⟩ ⟨*stereo*pticon⟩ **2 a :** stereoscopic ⟨*stereo*camera⟩ **b :** having or dealing with three dimensions of space ⟨*stereo*chemistry⟩ **c :** of, relating to, or considered with respect to stereochemistry ⟨*stereo*specific⟩

stere·id \ˈsterēəd, ˈstir-\ *n* -s [F *stéréide*, fr. Gk *stereoeidēs* of solid nature, fr. *stere-* + *-oeidēs* -oid] **:** a plant cell or cell derivative whose function is primarily mechanical support — compare SCLEREID

¹stereo \ˈsterēˌō, ˈstir-\ *n* -s [by shortening] **1 :** STEREOTYPE **2** [short for *stereoscopy*] **a :** a stereoscopic method, system, or effect; *esp* **:** stereoscopic photography **b :** a stereoscopic photograph **3** [short for *stereophonic*] **a :** stereophonic reproduction **b :** a stereophonic sound system

²stereo \"\ *adj* [*stereo-*] **1 a :** STEREOSCOPIC **b :** STEREOTYPED

2 a : of, relating to, or involving three-dimensional space ⟨~ acuity of vision⟩ **b :** of or relating to the arrangement of atoms in space **3 :** STEREOPHONIC

³stereo \"\ *vt* -ED/-ING/-S [by shortening] **:** STEREOTYPE

stereo·bate \'sterēə,bāt, 'stir-, *usu* -ād.+V\ *n* -s [F or L; F *stéréobate,* fr. L *stereobata* foundation of a column or building, fr. Gk *stereobatēs,* fr. *stere-* + *-batēs* one that treads, fr. *bainein* to walk, go — more at COME] **:** a substructure or basement of masonry as visible above the ground level — compare STYLOBATE — **stereo·bat·ic** \¦≈≈≈¦bad·ik\ *adj*

stereo·blastula \¦sterēə, ¦stir- +\ *n* [NL, fr. *stere-* + *blastula*] **:** a blastula without a cavity

stereo camera *n* **:** a camera having two matched lenses separated about the same distance as a person's eyes so that two pictures to be viewed in a stereoscope or projected to give a stereoscopic impression can be taken simultaneously

stereo·campimeter \¦sterē(,)ō, ¦stir- +\ *n* [*stere-* + *campimeter*] **:** a stereoscopic campimeter

stereo·chemical \¦sterēə, ¦stir- +\ *adj* [*stere-* + *chemical*] **:** of or relating to stereochemistry ⟨~ configurations of steroids⟩ — **stereo·chemically** \"+\ *adv*

stereo·chemistry \"+\ *n* [ISV *stere-* + *chemistry*] **1 :** a branch of chemistry that deals with the spatial arrangement of atoms and groups in molecules **2 :** the spatial relationship of atoms and groups in the molecule of a substance and its effect on the properties of the substance

stereo·chromatic \"+\ *adj* [*stereochromy* + *-atic*] **:** STEREOCHROMIC — **stereo·chromatically** \"+\ *adv*

stereo·chrome \'≈≈≈,krōm\ *n* -s [back-formation fr. *stereochromy*] **:** a stereochromic picture

stereo·chro·mic \¦≈≈≈¦krōmik\ *adj* [ISV *stereochromy* + *-ic*] **:** of, relating to, or done by means of stereochromy — **stereo·chro·mi·cal·ly** \-mək(ə)lē, -li\ *adv*

stereo·chro·my \'≈≈≈,krōmē, -mi\ *n* -ES [ISV *stere-* + *-chromy;* orig. formed as G *stereochromie*] **:** a process of mural painting in which the pigment is fixed by a series of reactions between the lime, fluosilicic acid, and water glass

stereo·cilium \¦≈≈≈+\ *n* [NL, fr. *stere-* + *cilium*] **:** one of the immobile processes that resemble cilia and occur on the free border of various epithelia

stereo·comparagraph \"+\ *n* [*stereocomparator* + *-graph*] **:** a plotting instrument using the stereoscopic principle of parallax for increased accuracy in making small-scale contour maps

stereo·comparator \"+\ *n* [ISV *stere-* + *comparator;* orig. formed as G *stereokomparator*] **:** a stereoscope used in making topographic measurements by the accurate comparison of stereoscopic photographs taken with an instrument having very great distance between the objectives or used in astronomy to detect small motions and brightness changes by stereoscopic examination of two photographs of the same celestial area taken at different times

stereo·fluoroscope \"+\ *n* [*stere-* + *fluoroscope*] **:** an instrument designed to give a three-dimensional image by fluoroscopy — **stereo·fluoroscopic** \"+\ *adj*

stereo·fluoroscopy \"+\ *n* [*stere-* + *fluoroscopy*] **:** stereoscopic fluoroscopy **:** use of the stereofluoroscope

stereo formula *n* **:** PERSPECTIVE FORMULA

stereo·gastrula \¦sterēə, ¦stir- +\ *n* [NL, fr. *stere-* + *gastrula*] **:** a gastrula with no cavity

stere·og·no·sis \,sterēäg'nōsəs, ,stir-\ *n* -ES [NL, fr. *stere-* + *-gnosis*] **:** ability to perceive or the perception of material qualities (as form, weight) of an object by handling or lifting it **:** tactile recognition

stere·og·nos·tic \¦≈≈≈¦nästik\ *adj* [ISV *stere-* + *-gnostic*] **:** of, relating to, or involving stereognosis

stereo·gram \'sterēə,gram, 'stir-, -raa(ə)m\ *n* [ISV *stere-* + *-gram*] **1 :** a diagram or picture representing objects with an impression of solidity or relief **2 :** STEREOGRAPH

¹stereo·graph \-,graf, -aa(ə)f, -aif, -ăf\ *n* [ISV *stere-* + *-graph*] **1 :** a pair of stereoscopic pictures or a picture composed of two superposed stereoscopic images prepared so as to give a three-dimensional effect when viewed with a stereoscope or with special spectacles — compare ANAGLYPH, VECTOGRAPH **2 :** an instrument used in tracing the contours of skulls — compare STEREOGRAPHY **3 :** STEREOTYPER

²stereograph \"\ *vt* **1 :** to prepare (as a picture) for stereoscopic exhibition **2 :** to take a stereoscopic photograph of **3 :** STEREOTYPE 1c

stere·og·ra·pher \,sterē'ägrəfə(r), ,stir-\ *n* -s [*stereograph* + *-er*] **:** one that stereographs: as **a :** one that takes stereoscopic photographs **b :** STEREOTYPER

stereo·graph·ic \¦sterēə¦grafik, ¦stir-, -fēk\ *also* **stereo·graph·i·cal** \-fəkəl, -fēk-\ *adj* [*stereographic* prob. fr. (assumed) NL *stereographicus,* fr. *stereographia* stereography + L *-icus* -ic; *stereographical* fr. (assumed) NL *stereographicus* + E *-al*] **:** made or done according to stereography ⟨a ~ navigation chart⟩ — **stereo·graph·i·cal·ly** \-fək(ə)lē, -fēk-, -li\ *adv*

stereographic projection *n* **:** a map projection of a hemisphere showing the earth's lines of latitude and longitude projected onto a tangent plane by radials from a point on the surface of the sphere opposite to the point of tangency

stere·og·ra·phy \,≈≈'ägrəfē, -fi\ *n* -ES [prob. fr. (assumed) NL *stereographia,* fr. NL *stere-* + *-graphia* -graphy] **1 a :** the art, process, or technique of delineating the forms of solid bodies on a plane **:** a branch of solid geometry showing the construction of all solids that are regularly defined **b :** demonstration of the five regular solids by models cut from flat material and folded **2 :** stereoscopic photography

stereoing *pres part of* STEREO

stereo·isomer \¦sterēō, ¦stir- +\ *n* [ISV *stere-* + *isomer*] **:** any one of the isomers in an example of stereoisomerism ⟨~*s* have the same structure but differ in configuration —C.N. Webb⟩

stereo·isomeric \¦≈≈≈+\ *adj* [*stereoisomerism* + *-ic*] **:** of, relating to, or exhibiting stereoisomerism ⟨the ability of living systems to discriminate between ~ forms of a chemical substance —J.S.Fruton & Sofia Simmonds⟩

stereo·isomeride \"+\ *n* [*stere-* + *isomeride*] **:** STEREOISOMER

stereo·isomerism \"+\ *n* [*stere-* + *isomerism*] **:** isomerism in which atoms are linked in the same order but differ in their arrangement in space — sometimes distinguished from *structural isomerism;* see GEOMETRIC ISOMERISM, OPTICAL ISOMERISM

stereo·kinesis \"+\ *n* [NL, fr. *stere-* + *-kinesis*] **:** a state of immobilization in an insect following strong mechanical stimulation

stere·ome \'sterē,ōm, 'stir-\ *or* **stere·om** \-ē,äm\ *n* -s [G *stereom,* fr. Gk *stereōma* solid body, fr. *stereoun* to make solid, fr. *stereos* solid — more at STARE] **:** mechanical or strengthening tissue: **a :** rigid cellular tissue (as sclerenchyma and collenchyma) of a plant — compare MESTOME **b :** exoskeletal material of an invertebrate

stere·om·e·ter \,≈≈'ämədə(r), -mətə-\ *n* [ISV *stere-* + *-meter;* prob. orig. formed as F *stéréomètre*] **1 :** VOLUMENOMETER **2 :** an instrument used for measuring heights of earth features by means of stereoscopic pairs of aerial photographs

stereo·met·ric \¦≈≈ə¦me·trik, -rēk\ *adj* [NL *stereometricus,* fr. Gk *stereometrikos,* fr. *stereometria* stereometry + *-ikos* -ic] **1 :** relating to stereometry; *usu* **:** having, characterized by, or representing a readily measurable solid form or volume ⟨a house . . . can have variety of interior but the outside is invariably a ~ body —Bruno Zevi⟩ **2 :** made by or relating to a stereometer

stere·om·e·try \,≈≈'ämə·trē\ *n* -ES [NL *stereometria,* fr. Gk, fr. *stereos* solid + *-metria* -metry] **:** the measurement of volumes and other metrical elements of solid figures — distinguished from *planimetry*

stereo·micrograph \¦sterēə, ¦stir- +\ *n* [*stere-* + *micrograph*] **:** a stereoscopic micrograph

stereo·micrography \"+\ *n* [*stereomicrograph* + *-y*] **:** the art of producing stereoscopic micrographs

stereo·micrometer \"+\ *n* [*stere-* + *micrometer*] **:** an apparatus attached to an optical device (as a telescope) for measuring small angles in the field of view by noting the projection on squares seen with the other and naked eye

stereo·microscope \"+\ *n* [*stere-* + *microscope*] **:** a microscope having a set of optics for each eye so arranged that the sets view the object from slightly different directions and make it appear in three dimensions

stereo·pair \'≈≈≈+,-\ *n* [²*stereo* + *pair*] **:** a stereograph consisting of a pair of photographs

stereo·phonic \¦sterēə, ¦stir- +\ *adj* [ISV *stere-* + *phonic*] **:** giving, relating to, or constituting a three-dimensional effect of auditory perspective ⟨sound heard by both ears at once or reproduced through loudspeakers placed in different parts of an auditorium has a ~ quality⟩ ⟨the objective of ~ sound reproduction is to make clear to the listener the spatial aspects of the sound —Charles Fowler⟩ — compare MONOPHONIC — **stere·oph·o·ny** \,≈≈'äfənē, '≈≈ə,fōnē\ *n* -ES

stereo·photogrammetric \¦sterēə, ¦stir- +\ *adj* [ISV *stereophotogrammetry* + *-ic*] **:** of or relating to stereophotogrammetry ⟨~ methods⟩

stereo·photogrammetry \"+\ *n* [ISV *stere-* + *photogrammetry*] **:** photogrammetry involving the use of stereoscopic photographs

stereo·photograph \"+\ *n* [*stere-* + *photograph*] **:** a stereoscopic photograph

stereo·photography \"+\ *n* [ISV *stere-* + *photography*] **:** stereoscopic photography

stereo·photomicrograph \"+\ *n* [*stere-* + *photomicrograph*] **:** a stereophotograph made through a microscope

stereo·photomicrography \"+\ *n* [*stereophotomicrograph* + *-y*] **:** the making of stereophotomicrographs

stereo·planigraph \"+\ *n* [ISV *stere-* + *planigraph*] **:** an instrument for making topographic maps from observations made with a stereocomparator

stereo·plasm \'sterēə,plazəm, 'stir-\ *n* -s [ISV *stere-* + *-plasm*] **:** gelated protoplasm — **stereo·plas·mic** \¦≈≈≈¦plazmik\ *adj*

stereo·plotting \¦≈≈≈+\ *n* [*stere-* + *plotting*] **:** the plotting of a map (as a contour map) from aerial photographs by means of a stereoscopic device

stereo·projection \"+\ *n* [*stere-* + *projection*] **:** the projection of two photographs so as to give a stereoscopic effect

stere·op·sis \,sterē'äpsəs, ,stir-\ *n* -ES [NL, fr. *stere-* + *-opsis*] **:** stereoscopic vision **:** capacity for depth perception

stere·op·ti·can \¦≈≈¦äptəkən, -tēk-\ *adj* [NL *stereopticon* + E *-an*] **:** of, relating to, or like that produced by a stereopticon ⟨a figure with ~ definition⟩

stere·op·ti·cian \¦≈≈,äp¦tishən\ *n* [NL *stereopticon* + E *-ian*] **:** one who tends a stereopticon (as for a lecturer)

stere·op·ti·con \,sterē'äptəkən, ,stir-, -tə,kän\ *n* -s [NL, fr. *stere-* + Gk *optikon,* neut. of *optikos* optic — more at OPTIC] **:** a projector for transparent slides that is often made double so as to produce dissolving views

stereo·radiograph \¦sterēə, ¦stir- +\ *n* [*stere-* + *radiograph*] **:** a stereoscopic radiograph — **stereo·radiographic** \"+\ *adj* — **stereo·radiography** \"+\ *n*

stereo·regular \"+\ *adj* [*stere-* + *regular*] **:** possessing stereochemical regularity in the repeating units of a polymer structure ⟨linear and ~ addition polymers —N.G.Gaylord & H.F.Mark⟩ — **stereo·regularity** \"+\ *n*

stere·or·ni·thes \,sterē'ȯrnə,thēz, ,stir-, -,ȯr'nī(,)thēz\ *n pl, cap* [NL, fr. *stere-* + *-ornithes*] *in former classifications* **:** an artificial or a composite order of very large Miocene Patagonian birds believed to be ratite and mostly included in the order Gruiformes — **stere·or·nith·ic** \¦≈≈,ȯr¦nithik\ *adj*

stereos *pl of* STEREO, *pres 3d sing of* STEREO

stereo·scope \'sterēə,skōp, 'stir-\ *n* [*stere-* + *-scope*] **:** an optical instrument for obtaining from two pictures (as photographs made for the purpose from points of view typically corresponding to the position of the two eyes) a single three-dimensional image by means of two lenses used one with each eye and set sometimes in conjunction with mirrors to deflect rays coming from corresponding points in the two pictures in such a manner as to produce the effect of originating at a single point

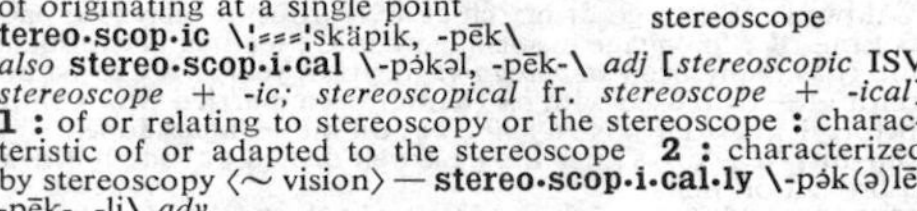

stereoscope

stereo·scop·ic \¦≈≈≈¦skäpik, -pēk\ *also* **stereo·scop·i·cal** \-pəkəl, -pēk-\ *adj* [*stereoscopic* ISV *stereoscope* + *-ic; stereoscopical* fr. *stereoscope* + *-ical*] **1 :** of or relating to stereoscopy or the stereoscope **:** characteristic of or adapted to the stereoscope **2 :** characterized by stereoscopy ⟨~ vision⟩ — **stereo·scop·i·cal·ly** \-pək(ə)lē, -pēk-, -li\ *adv*

stereoscopic camera *n* **:** STEREO CAMERA

stereoscopic microscope *n* **:** STEREOMICROSCOPE

stereoscopic pair *n* **:** STEREOPAIR

stereoscopic radius *n* **:** the limiting distance at which objects are seen in stereoscopic relief amounting with unaided human vision to about 1500 feet

stereoscopic vision *n* **:** STEREOSCOPY 2

stere·os·co·py \,≈≈'äskəpē, '≈≈ə,skōpē, -pi\ *n* -ES [ISV *stere-* + *-scopy*] **1 :** a branch of science that deals with stereoscopic effects and methods by which they are produced **2 :** the seeing of objects in three dimensions

stereo·selective \¦sterēə, ¦stir- +\ *adj* [*stere-* + *selective*] **:** stereochemically selective **:** relating to or being a reaction or process leading to a stereoisomer having one particular configuration regardless of the configuration of the reactant — compare STEREOSPECIFIC — **stereo·selectivity** \"+\ *n*

stereo·sonic \"+\ *adj* [*stere-* + *-sonic*] **:** STEREOPHONIC

stereo·specific \"+\ *adj* [*stere-* + *specific*] **:** stereochemically specific **:** relating to, being, or effecting a reaction or process in which a specific stereoisomer is formed esp. when the product is configurationally related to the reactant either by retention or reversal of the original configuration ⟨~ polymerization⟩ — compare STEREOSELECTIVE — **stereo·specif·ically** \"+\ *adv* — **stereo·specificity** \"+\ *n*

stereo·spon·dyl \,≈≈≈'spänd°l\ *n* -s [NL *Stereospondyli*] **:** an amphibian or fossil of the order Stereospondyli

stereo·spon·dy·li \-də,lī\ *n pl, cap* [NL, fr. *stere-* + *-spondyli*] **:** an order of Labyrinthodontia or formerly a suborder of Stegocephalia including forms with stereospondylous vertebrae

stereo·spondylous \¦≈≈≈+\ *adj* [*stere-* + *spondylous*] **1 :** being or having vertebrae whose component elements are fused into a single piece ⟨most vertebrates are ~⟩ — opposed to *temnospondylous* **2 :** of or relating to the order Stereospondyli

stereo·static \"+\ *adj* [ISV *stere-* + *static;* prob orig. formed as F *stéréostatique*] **:** GEOSTATIC

stereo·tac·tic \-¦taktik\ *adj* [fr. NL *stereotaxis,* after such pairs as NL *hypotaxis:* E *hypotactic*] **:** of, relating to, or involving stereotaxis — **stereo·tac·ti·cal·ly** \-tək(ə)lē\ *adv*

stereo·tax·is \,≈≈≈'taksəs\ *n* [NL, fr. *stere-* + *-taxis*] **:** a taxis in which contact esp. with a solid body is the directive factor

stereo·telescope \¦≈≈≈+\ *n* [*stere-* + *telescope*] **:** TELESTEREOSCOPE

stereo·tom·ic \¦≈≈≈¦tämik\ *or* **stereo·tom·i·cal** \-məkəl\ *adj* [*stereotomic* fr. F *stéréotomique,* fr. *stéréotomie* stereotomy + *-ique* -ic; *stereotomical* fr. *stereotomy* + *-ical*] **:** of or relating to stereotomy

stere·ot·o·mist \,≈≈'äd·əməst\ *n* -s [*stereotomy* + *-ist*] **:** a practitioner of stereotomy

stere·ot·o·my \-mē, -mi\ *n* -ES [F *stéréotomie,* fr. *stéré-* stere- + *-tomie* -tomy] **:** the art or technique of cutting solids (as into arches); *esp* **:** the art of stonecutting

stereo·trop·ic \¦≈≈ə¦träpik\ *adj* [ISV *stereotropism* + *-ic*] **:** of, relating to, or exhibiting stereotropism

stere·ot·ro·pism \,≈≈'ä·trə,pizəm\ *n* [ISV *stere-* + *tropism*] **1 :** a tropism in which contact esp. with a solid body or a rigid surface is the orienting factor — compare HAPTOTROPISM **2 :** STEREOTAXIS

¹stereo·type \'sterēə,tīp, 'stir-\ *n* [F *stéréotype,* fr. *stéré-* stere- + *type*] **1 a** *archaic* **:** STEREOTYPY **b :** a solid metal duplicate of a relief printing surface that is made by pressing a molding material (as wet paper pulp, plaster of paris, clay, or flong) against it to make a matrix and then pouring molten metal into the matrix to make a casting which is sometimes faced with a harder metal (as nickel) to increase durability — compare ALUMINOTYPE, ELECTROTYPE **2 :** something repeated or reproduced without variation **:** something conforming to a fixed or general pattern and lacking individual distinguishing marks or qualities; *esp* **:** a standardized mental picture held in common by members of a group and representing an oversimplified opinion, affective attitude, or uncritical judgment (as of a person, a race, an issue, or an event)

²stereotype \"\ *vt* **1 a :** to make a stereotype from (a relief printing surface) ⟨~ the pages of a newspaper⟩ **b :** to produce by stereotyping ⟨flat and curved *stereotyped* and electrotype plates —*Book Production*⟩ **c :** to emboss in braille characters by use of a stereotyper **2 a :** to fix in a lasting and usu. rigidly precise form **b :** to repeat without variation **:** make standardized or hackneyed **c :** to develop a mental stereotype about ⟨too easy to ~ and dismiss divergent groups⟩

stereotyped *adj* **:** produced by or as if by means of a stereotype **:** repeated by rote or without variation **:** lacking originality or individuality ⟨~ thinking⟩ ⟨~ manners⟩ ⟨~ concepts of other peoples —*Internat'l Social Sci. Bull.*⟩ **syn** see TRITE

stereo·typ·er \-,tīpə(r)\ *n* [ISV ²*stereotype* + *-er*] **:** one that stereotypes: as **a :** a worker who prepares stereotype plates **b :** a machine for embossing thin metal plates with braille characters for use in printing for the blind **c** *or* **stereotypist :** an operator of a stereotyper

stereo·typ·i·cal \¦≈≈≈¦tipəkəl\ *also* **stereo·typ·ic** \-pik\ *adj* [¹*stereotype* + *-ical* or *-ic*] **:** of, relating to, or constituting a stereotype ⟨speaks . . . in terms ~ of the general attitude of the era —David Riesman⟩ — **stereo·typ·i·cal·ly** \-pək(ə)lē\ *adv*

stereotyping *n* [fr. gerund of ²*stereotype*] **:** the process, craft, or business of making stereotypes

stereo·typ·ist \'≈≈≈,tīpəst\ *n* [ISV ²*stereotype* + *-ist*] **:** STEREOTYPER c

stereo·typy \'≈≈≈,tīpē, -pi\ *n* -ES [ISV ¹*stereotype* + *-y*] **1 :** the art or process of making or of printing from stereotype plates **2 a :** frequent and almost mechanical repetition of the same posture, movement, or form of speech (as in the mannerisms of dementia praecox) **b :** formation or a tendency to formation of mental stereotypes

stereo viewer *n* **:** STEREOSCOPE

stereo·vision \¦sterēə, ¦stir- +\ *n* [*stere-* + *vision*] **:** STEREOSCOPY 2

steres *pl of* STERE

ste·re·um \'stirēəm\ *n, cap* [NL, fr. Gk *stereos* solid — more at STARE] **:** a genus of fungi (family Thelephoraceae) having the sporophores resupinate or shelving and the basidial surface smooth — see SILVERLEAF

ster·hydraulic \ster+\ *adj* [prob. fr. F *stérhydraulique,* irreg. fr. *stéré-* stere- + *hydraulique* hydraulic] **:** relating to or being a hydraulic press producing pressure or motion by the introduction of a solid substance (as a screw, a rod, or a rope wound on a roller) into a cylinder previously filled with a liquid **:** resembling such a press in action or principle

steric \'sterik, 'stir-, -rēk\ *adj* [ISV *stere-* + *-ic*] **:** relating to the arrangement of atoms in space **:** SPATIAL — **steri·cal·ly** \-rək(ə)lē, -rēk-, -li\ *adv*

steric hindrance *n* **:** hindrance of chemical action ascribed to the arrangement of atoms in a molecule

sterid \'sterəd, 'stir-\ *also* **steride** \-,rīd, -,rəd\ *n* -s [*sterol* + *-id* or *-ide*] **:** STEROID — used to include sterols

ste·rig·ma \stə'rigmə\ *n, pl* **sterigma·ta** \-məd·ə\ *also* **sterigmas** [NL, fr. Gk *stērigma* support, fr. *stērizein* to prop, support; akin to Gk *stereos* solid — more at STARE] **1 :** one of the slender stalks at the top of the basidium of some fungi from the tips of which the basidiospores are abstricted; *broadly* **:** a stalk or filament from which conidia or spermatia are abjointed — compare PHIALIDE **2 :** one of the persistent peg-shaped projections to which the leaves of some conifers (as spruces) are attached on the twigs — **ster·ig·mat·ic** \¦ste(,)rig¦mad·ik, -,rēg-\ *adj*

ster·i·lant \'sterələnt\ *n* -s [*sterile* + *-ant*] **:** a sterilizing agent; *esp* **:** an herbicide designed to completely eliminate a kind of plant and to have a rather persistent residual effect in the soil

ster·ile \'sterəl, -,rīl\ *adj* [L *sterilis;* akin to Gk *steira* sterile, Goth *stairo* sterile, Skt *starī* sterile cow] **1 a :** failing to produce or incapable of producing offspring ⟨a hybrid that is completely ~⟩ **b :** failing to bear or incapable of bearing fruit or spores ⟨a ~ tree⟩ ⟨~ fungous hyphae⟩ **c :** incapable of germinating ⟨~ spores⟩ **d** *of a flower* **:** lacking a gynecium **:** neither perfect nor pistillate **e :** having or producing no sori ⟨~ fern fronds⟩ **2 :** characterized by deficient fruitfulness **:** BARREN: as **a :** deficient in plant life **:** unproductive of crops or other vegetation ⟨a ~ arid region⟩ ⟨an unusually ~ year⟩ **b :** deficient in ideas or originality of thought ⟨a ~ author⟩ ⟨~ prose⟩ **c :** free from living organisms and esp. microorganisms ⟨a ~ cyst⟩ ⟨dead ~ soil⟩ — compare STERILIZE **3 :** serving no useful purpose **:** withheld from a normal use or function ⟨capital kept ~ through lack of initiative⟩ ⟨excessive and ~ reserves⟩

syn STERILE, BARREN, IMPOTENT, UNFRUITFUL, INFERTILE mean not having or not manifesting the power to produce offspring or bear fruit, literally or figuratively. STERILE implies literal inability, stressing some defect or lack in the reproductive functions; it has a strong figurative use, implying a lack or absence of creative vigor ⟨a *sterile* woman⟩ ⟨a *sterile* ram⟩ ⟨a *sterile* author⟩ ⟨the failure of the three characters to emerge as individuals makes their personal drama seem *sterile* —*Amer. Scholar*⟩ ⟨for him man is always the wanderer in the oppressive and *sterile* world of materialism —Alfred Kazin⟩ ⟨lies at an elevation of from 500 to 1,500 feet, and consists mainly of saline wastes and other *sterile* tracts —*Encyc. Americana*⟩ BARREN applies esp. to a female who has borne no offspring or is incapable of bearing offspring, stressing, literally and figuratively, the lack of issue ⟨a *barren* woman⟩ ⟨a *barren* soil⟩ ⟨nine *barren* years of marriage —Alice Lake⟩ ⟨I am very *barren* of American news —H.J. Laski⟩ IMPOTENT in this sense applies esp. to a male lacking the ability to engage in sexual intercourse and so to produce his kind, carrying more generally the implication of inability to act or suggesting some lack of manliness or natural vigor ⟨an *impotent* man⟩ ⟨nothing is quite so *impotent* in politics as a defeated candidate —W.A.White⟩ ⟨drove the choleric old man into a fit of *impotent* fury —Charles Reade⟩ UNFRUITFUL, interchangeable with BARREN though less forceful and absolute, has a more widespread figurative than literal use ⟨an *unfruitful* orchard⟩ ⟨an *unfruitful* enterprise⟩ ⟨*unfruitful* negotiations between belligerent states⟩ INFERTILE, a factual and neutral word, carries the sense of STERILE, esp. in literal application ⟨an *infertile* marriage⟩ ⟨an *infertile* valley⟩ ⟨an *infertile* line of research⟩

ster·ile·ly \-l(l)ē, -i\ *adv* **:** in a sterile manner **:** so as to be or remain sterile

ste·ril·i·ty \stə'riləd·ē, ste'-, -lətē, -i\ *n* -ES [ME *sterylite,* fr. MF *sterilité,* fr. L *sterilitat-, sterilitas,* fr. *sterilis* sterile + *-itat-, -itas* -ity] **:** the quality or state of being sterile

ster·i·liz·abil·i·ty \,sterə,līzə'biləd·ē, -lətē, -i\ *n* **:** the quality or state of being sterilizable

ster·i·liz·able \¦sterə¦līzəbəl\ *adj* **:** capable of being sterilized

ster·i·liza·tion \,≈≈lə'zāshən, -,lī'z-\ *n* -s **1 :** the act or process of sterilizing: as **a :** the rendering of a body or material free from living cells and esp. microorganisms usu. by killing those present (as by heat) — see FRACTIONAL STERILIZATION; compare PASTEURIZATION **b :** a procedure by which a human or other animal is made incapable of reproduction — compare CASTRATION, SPAYING **c :** a preventing of a monetary factor from exerting its wonted influence ⟨~ of a gold reserve⟩ **2 :** the condition of one that is sterile or sterilized

ster·i·lize \'sterə,līz\ *vt* -ED/-ING/-S *see -ize in Explan Notes* [*sterile* + *-ize*] **:** to cause to become sterile, barren, or unproductive: as **a :** to cause (land) to become unfruitful whether by exhaustion of fertility or deliberately by use of a sterilant **b :** to deprive of the power of reproducing (as by surgical removal or inhibition of function of the reproductive organs) **:** make incapable of germination or fecundation **c** (1) **:** to cause to become void of something desirable (as ideas, emotions, intelligence) ⟨parental pressure that ~*s* an inquiring young mind⟩ (2) **:** to make powerless, ineffective, or useless usu. by restraining from a normal function, relation, or participation ⟨capital *sterilized* by hoarding⟩; *specif* **:** to prevent (gold) from serving as a basis for a monetary expansion **d :** to free from living microorganisms usu. by the use of physical or chemical agents — compare PASTEURIZE

ster·i·liz·er \-zə(r)\ *n* -s **:** one that sterilizes something: as **a :** an apparatus for sterilizing by the agency of boiling water, steam, or dry heat — see AUTOCLAVE **b :** one whose work is sterilizing something (as food, materials, equipment)

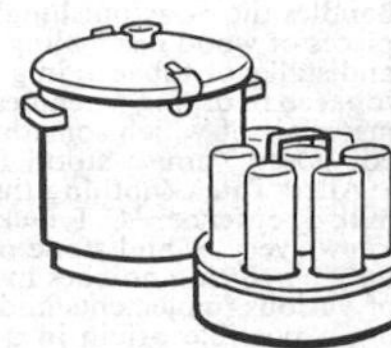

sterilizer for bottles

sterk·fon·tein ape–man \'sterkfən,tān-\ *n, usu cap S* [fr. *Sterkfontein*, farm near Johannesburg, So. Africa, where the specimens were found] **:** an extinct southern African anthropoid (*Australopithecus transvaalensis* or *Plesianthropus transvaalensis*) known from numerous parts of skulls, teeth, and other skeletal fragments recovered from cave bone breccia

ster·let \'stərlət\ *n* -s [Russ *sterlyad'*, of Gmc origin; akin to OHG *sturio* sturgeon — more at STURGEON] **:** a small sturgeon (*Acipenser ruthenus*) found esp. in the Caspian sea and its rivers and highly esteemed for its flavor and its caviar

1ster·ling \'stərliŋ, 'stōl-, 'stəil-, -lēŋ\ *n* -s [ME, prob. fr. (assumed) OE *steorling*, fr. OE *steorra* star + *-ling*; prob. fr. the star engraved on some of the early pennies — more at STAR] **1 a :** the silver penny of medieval England **b :** the legal currency of England and from 1707 of Great Britain **c :** British money **:** British foreign exchange **2 :** sterling silver or articles made of it ⟨a set of ~⟩ — compare PLATE 2, 3a **3 :** an Australian colonist born in England

2sterling \"\ *adj* [ME, fr. *1sterling*] **1 a :** of, relating to, or calculated in terms of British sterling ⟨~ prices⟩ **b :** payable or involving payment in sterling ⟨a ~ bill⟩ ⟨~ exchange⟩ **2 a** *of silver* **:** having a fixed standard of purity from admixture or alloy that is usu. defined legally as represented by an alloy of 925 parts of silver with 75 parts of copper **b :** made of sterling silver **3 :** of full value or first quality **:** conforming to the highest standard **:** GENUINE ⟨~ merit⟩ ⟨a ~ character⟩ — **ster·ling·ly** *adv* — **ster·ling·ness** *n* -ES

sterling area *or* **sterling bloc** *n* **:** the United Kingdom and the countries that tie their currencies to the British pound sterling and pool their foreign exchange resources to a large extent

1stern \'stərn, 'stōn\ *n* -s [fr. (assumed) ME *sterne*, fr. OE *stearn*, a bird, prob. tern — more at STARLING] *dial Brit* **:** TERN

2stern \'stərn, 'stōn, 'stəin\ *adj* -ER/-EST [ME *sterne, stirne, stierne*, fr. OE *styrne, stierne*; akin to OHG *stornēn* to startle, frighten, *storrēn* to project stiffly, Goth *andstaurran* to scold, OE *starian* to stare — more at STARE] **1 a :** having a definite hardness or severity of nature or manner **:** severely strict **:** EXACTING, UNCOMPROMISING, UNBENDING, INFLEXIBLE, RIGOROUS, AUSTERE ⟨equally ~ to himself and others⟩ ⟨a ~ discipline⟩ ⟨~ taskmasters⟩ **b** *obs* **:** lacking pity or mercy **:** CRUEL **c :** proceeding from or characteristic of a severe nature **:** expressive of severe displeasure **:** HARSH ⟨a ~ look⟩ ⟨returned a ~ answer⟩ **2 a :** forbidding or gloomy in appearance **:** lacking in pleasing or attractive aspects **:** INHOSPITABLE, UNINVITING ⟨a ~ coastline⟩ ⟨a ~ land demanding much and returning little⟩ **b :** rigorously severe in style **:** lacking enhancing ornamentation or softening detail ⟨a ~, sturdy, and purely utilitarian hall⟩ **3 :** of a compelling sort **:** INEXORABLE ⟨yielding to ~ necessity⟩ **4 :** of sturdy make or quality **:** having strong power to resist **:** STOUT ⟨made a ~ resolve to win⟩ ⟨only the *~est* spirits can enjoy such a climate⟩ **syn** see SEVERE

3stern \"\ *adv* [ME *sterne, stirne*, fr. *sterne, stirne*, adj.] **:** in a stern manner **:** STERNLY — often used in combination ⟨facing us with *stern*-set face⟩

4stern \'stern\ *var of* STARN

5stern \'stərn, 'stōn, 'stəin, *dial* 'stärn *or* 'stȧn\ *n* -s [ME *sterne*, prob. of Scand origin; akin to ON *stjōrn* act of steering, *stȳra* to steer — more at STEER] **1** *obs* **a :** the helm or tiller of a boat; *also* **:** RUDDER **b :** direction by or as if by a rudder **:** STEERAGE **c :** a post of management or direction ⟨sit at chiefest ~ of public weal —Shak.⟩ **2 :** the after or rear end of a ship; *specif* **:** the portion of the hull abaft the rudderpost or sternpost — see COUNTER illustration **3 :** a hinder or rear part of something **:** the last or a latter part: as **a :** BUTTOCKS, RUMP, BEHIND — not often in formal use **b :** TAIL 1a(1) — used of a hound — **by the stern** *adv* **:** with the stern lower in the water or sinking or settling first ⟨a boat anchored *by the stern*⟩ ⟨sank *by the stern*⟩

6stern \"\ *vb* -ED/-ING/-S [ME *sternen*, fr. *sterne* stern of a ship] *vt* **1** *obs* **:** STEER **2 :** to move (a boat) stern first ~ *vi* **:** to back water **:** row backward

7stern \"\ *adj* [*5stern*] **1 a :** of, relating to, or situated at or near the stern of a ship **b :** fastened or secured to or securing the stern **2 :** following, pursuing, or characterized by pursuit astern

stern- *or* **sterno-** *comb form* [F, fr. Gk, fr. *sternon* — more at STERNUM] **1 :** breast **:** sternum **:** breastbone ⟨*stern*algia⟩ ⟨*stern*ad⟩ **2 :** sternal and ⟨*sterno*cleidomastoid⟩

1sterna *pl of* STERNUM

2ster·na \'stərnə\ *n, cap* [NL, fr. E *stern* tern — more at STERN] **:** a genus of typical terns (family Laridae) including forms that have a slender bill, narrow pointed wings, a forked tail, and mostly white coloration with a black cap and a bluish gray mantle

ster·nad \'stər,nad\ *adv* [*stern-* + *-ad*] **:** toward the sternum

ster·nal \'stərnᵊl, 'stōn-, 'stəin-\ *adj* [NL *sternalis*] **1 :** of, relating to, or involving the sternum **2 a :** situated in the region of the sternum or a sternite **:** VENTRAL **b :** of or relating to a sternite

ster·na·lis \,stər'nāləs\ *n, pl* **sternales** \-(,)lez\ [NL, sternal, sternalis, fr. *stern-* + L *-alis* -al] **:** a muscle nearly parallel to the sternum that is sometimes found on the surface of the pectoralis major

sternal rib *n* **1 :** a rib whose costal cartilage connects with the sternum **:** TRUE RIB **2 :** the ventral segment of a rib of some animals that represents an ossified costal cartilage

stern·berg cell \'stərn,bərg-\ *also* **sternberg–reed cell** \-'rēd-\ *n, usu cap S&R* [after Carl *Sternberg* †1935 Ger. pathologist] **:** a multinucleate acidophil giant cell found in the tissues in Hodgkin's disease

stern·ber·gia \,stərn'bərjēə, ǀjēə\ *n* [NL, fr. Count Kaspar M. von *Sternberg* †1838 + NL *-ia*] **1** *cap* **:** a genus of low bulbous herbs (family Amaryllidaceae) native to the Mediterranean region but widely used as ornamentals and having ribbon-shaped leaves and autumn-blooming yellow flowers that resemble crocuses **2** -s **:** any plant of the genus *Sternbergia*

stern·berg·ite \'stərn,bər,gīt\ *n* -s [Count Kaspar M. von *Sternberg* †1838 Bohemian naturalist + E *-ite*] **:** a dark brown mineral ($AgFe_2S_3$) that is a silver iron sulfide and occurs in tabular crystals or soft flexible laminae

stern board *n* **1 :** a going or falling astern in sailing esp. as caused by missing stays **:** STERNWAY ⟨make a *stern board* into the wind⟩ **2 :** a board forming the flat part of the stern of a small ship

stern boat *n* **:** a ship's boat carried at or near the stern

sterncastle \'ˌ=,=\ *n* [*5stern* + *castle*] **:** AFTERCASTLE

stern chase *n* [*5stern*] **1 :** a chase in which the pursuing vessel follows in the path of the vessel pursued ⟨a *stern chase* is a long chase⟩ **2 :** STERN CHASER

stern chaser *n* **:** a gun so placed (as on a warship) as to be able to fire astern at a vessel that may be in chase

ster·ne·bra \'stərnəbrə\ *n, pl* **sterne·brae** \-,brē, -brī\ [NL, fr. *stern-* + *-ebra* (as in *vertebra*)] **:** a segment of the sternum of a vertebrate — **ster·ne·bral** \-brəl\ *adj*

ster·nel·lum \,stər'neləm\ *n, pl* **sternel·la** \-lə\ [NL, fr. *stern-* + L *-ellum* -el] **:** the posterior plate of a thoracic sternite

sterner *comparative of* STERN

sternest *superlative of* STERN

stern fast *or* **stern line** *n* **:** a line used to secure a boat by the stern

sternforemost \'ˌ='ˌ=(ˌ)=\ *adv* [*5stern* + *foremost*] **:** with the stern in advance **:** BACKWARD; *also* **:** AWKWARDLY

stern frame *n* **1 :** the timbers in a wooden vessel constituting the upper part of stern or counter **2 :** the forging or casting in a steel ship including in one piece the propeller post with boss, the sternpost with gudgeons, and the arch and solepiece

stern gallery *n* **:** a platform around the stern of an old wooden ship

stern hook *n* **:** a horizontal framework for strengthening the attachment of the sides to the sternpost of a ship

sterning *pres part of* STERN

ster·nite \'stər,nīt\ *n* -s [ISV *stern-* + *-ite*] **:** the ventral part or shield of a somite of an arthropod; *esp* **:** the chitinous plate that forms the ventral surface of an abdominal or occas. a thoracic segment of an insect — **ster·nit·ic** \(')stər¦nid·ik\ *adj*

stern knee *n* [so called fr. its shape] **:** STERNSON

stern·less \'ˌ=ləs\ *adj* [ME *sterneles*, fr. *sterne* stern + *-les* -less — more at STERN (rudder)] *obs* **:** RUDDERLESS

stern light *n* **:** a white running light displayed on the stern of a ship

stern·ly *adv* [ME *sternely*, fr. OE *styrnlic, stiernlic*, fr. *styrne, stierne* stern + *-lic* -ly — more at STERN (strict)] **:** in a stern manner **:** with sternness

stern·man \'ˌ=mən\ *n, pl* **sternmen** [*5stern* + *man*] **1** *obs* **:** STEERSMAN **2 :** one (as a rower or paddler) stationed at or occupying the stern of a craft

stern·most \'ˌ=,mōst *also chiefly Brit* -,məst\ *adj* [*5stern* + *-most* (as in *foremost*)] **:** farthest astern

stern·ness \-nnəs\ *n* -ES [ME *sternesse*, fr. *sterne* stern + *-nesse* -ness] **:** the quality or state of being stern

sterno- — see STERN-

1ster·no·clei·do·mas·toid \¦stər(,)nō¦klīdə¦ma,stȯid\ *adj* [NL *sternocleidomastoides*, fr. *stern-* + *cleid-* + *mastoides* mastoid] **:** of, relating to, or constituting a thick superficial muscle on each side arising by one head from the first segment of the sternum and a second from the inner part of the clavicle and inserted into the mastoid and occipital bone

2sternocleidomastoid \"\ *n* **:** a sternocleidomastoid muscle

ster·no·costal \¦stərnə+\ *adj* [*stern-* + *costal*] **:** of, relating to, or situated between the sternum and ribs

ster·no·fa·ci·a·lis \,stər(,)nō,fās(h)ē'aləs, -'āl-, -'al-\ *n, pl* **sternofaciales** [NL, fr. *stern-* + *facialis*, alter. (influenced by *facialis* facial) of *fascialis* fascial] **:** an inconstant slip of muscle arising from the sternum and inserting into the fascia of the neck

1ster·no·hyoid \"+\ *adj* [NL *sternohyoides*, fr. *stern-* + *hyoides* hyoid] **:** of or relating to the sternum and the hyoid bone or cartilage; *specif* **:** constituting a muscle on each side of the midline extending from the medial end of the clavicle and the first segment of the sternum to the body of the hyoid bone

2sternohyoid \"\ *n* **:** a sternohyoid muscle

ster·no·mastoid muscle \¦ˌ=+-\ *n* [*stern-* + *mastoid*] **:** STERNOCLEIDOMASTOID

ster·no·scapular \"+\ *adj* [*stern-* + *scapular*] **:** connecting the sternum and scapula; *specif* **:** constituting a muscle that in many mammals helps to support the anterior part of the body upon the forelimbs

ster·no·the·rus \,ˌ='thirəs\ *n, cap* [NL, fr. *stern-* + Gk *thairos* pivot, axle] **:** a genus of No. American turtles of the family Kinosternidae — see MUSK TURTLE

1ster·no·thyroid \¦ˌ=+\ *adj* [NL *sternothyroides*, fr. *stern-* + *thyroides* thyroid] **:** of, relating to, or situated between the sternum and the thyroid cartilage; *specif* **:** constituting a muscle on each side of the body extending beneath the sternohyoid muscle

2sternothyroid \"\ *n* **:** a sternothyroid muscle

ster·no·tribe \'ˌ=,trīb\ *adj* [*stern-* + *-tribe*] **:** touching the undersurface; *esp* **:** having stamens and pistils so arranged as to touch the sternum of a visiting insect ⟨~ flowers⟩

sternpost \'ˌ=,=\ *n* [*5stern* + *post*] **:** the principal and usu. vertical member at the after end of a ship extending from keel to deck and taking the after ends of the planking in a wooden ship and of the plates in a steel ship

sterns *pl of* STERN, *pres 3d sing of* STERN

stern sheets *n pl* **:** the space in the stern of an open boat not occupied by the thwarts

stern·son \'stərn(t)sᵊn\ *n* -s [*5stern* + *keelson*] **:** the end of a keelson to which the sternpost of a ship is bolted

stern tube *n* **1 :** a long bushing or bearing through the stern of a ship to support the after part of the propeller shaft **2 :** a torpedo tube located at the stern

ster·num \'stərnəm, 'stōn-, 'stəin-\ *n, pl* **sternums** \-mz\ *or* **ster·na** \-nə\ [NL, fr. Gk *sternon* breast, chest, breastbone; akin to OHG *stirna* forehead, Skt *stīrna* spread, strewn, L *sternere* to spread out — more at STREW] **1 :** a bone or cartilage or a series of more or less distinct bony or cartilaginous segments lying in the median ventral part of the body of most vertebrates above fishes, connecting with the ribs or the shoulder girdle or with both, being in man about seven inches long, consisting in the adult of three parts, connecting with the clavicles and the cartilages of the upper seven pairs of ribs, and being in birds modified into a single broad bony plate that usu. bears a high median keel for the attachment of the wing muscles **:** BREASTBONE — see BAT illustration **2 a :** the ventral part of a somite of an arthropod **b :** the whole ventral wall of the arthropod thorax

ster·nu·ta·tion \,stərnyə'tāshən, -yü't-\ *n* -s [L *sternutation-, sternutatio*, fr. *sternutatus* (past part. of *sternutare*, freq. of *sternuere* to sneeze) + *-ion-, -io* -ion; akin to Gk *ptarnysthai* to sneeze, *ptarmos* act of sneezing, OIr *sreod*] **:** the act, fact, or noise of sneezing **:** SNEEZE

ster·nu·ta·tor \'ˌ=,tād·ə(r)\ *n* -s [back-formation fr. *sternutatory*] **:** an agent (as a gas) that induces a flow of nasal secretion or causes sneezing

1ster·nu·ta·to·ry \,stər'nyüd·ə,tōrē\ *or* **ster·nu·ta·tive** \-d·ad·iv, ,stərnyə,tād·iv, -yü,t-\ *adj* [*sternutatory* fr. LL *sternutatorius*, fr. L *sternutatus* (past part. of *sternutare*) + *-orius* -ory; *sternutative* fr. L *sternutatus* + E *-ive*] **:** inducing sneezing; *also* **:** of, relating to, or marked by sneezing

2sternutatory \"\ *n* -ES [LL *sternutatorium*, neut. of *sternutatorius* of sneezing] **:** STERNUTATOR

stern walk *n, chiefly Brit* **:** a gallery around the stern of an old-time man-of-war

stern·ward \'ˌ=wə(r)d\ *or* **stern·wards** \-dz\ *adv (or adj)* [*5stern* + *-ward, -wards*] **1 :** ASTERN 1 **2 :** AFT

stern wave *n* **:** a wave formed at the stern of a boat under way — compare BOW WAVE

sternway \'ˌ=,=\ *n* **:** movement of a ship backward or with her stern foremost — compare STEERAGEWAY

stern·ways \'ˌ=,wāz\ *adv* [*5stern* + *-ways*] **:** toward the stern

stern wheel *n* **:** a paddle wheel at the stern of a boat

stern–wheeler \'ˌ='ˌ=\ *n* **:** a paddle steamer having a stern wheel instead of side wheels

1steroid \'sti(ə),rȯid, -te(-\ *n* -s [ISV *sterol* + *-oid*] **:** any of a class of compounds that are characterized by a polycyclic structure like that of the sterols and that usu. include the sterols and vitamin D as well as many other naturally occurring compounds (as the bile acids and various hormones and glycosides) — compare CHOLESTEROL illustration

2steroid \"\ *or* **ste·roi·dal** \stə'rȯidᵊl, ste'r-\ *adj* [*steroidal* fr. *1steroid* + *-al*] **1 :** resembling a sterol esp. in chemical structure **2 :** of, relating to, or being a steroid

steroid hormone *n* **:** any of numerous hormones (as the sex hormones, cortisone, and adrenocortical hormones) characterized by steroid structure ⟨*steroid hormones* of animal origin —J.S.Fruton & Sofia Simmonds⟩

sterol \'ste,rōl, 'sti,r-, -rōl\ *n* -s [ISV, fr. *-sterol* (as in *cholesterol*)] **:** any of a class of solid complex cyclic alcohols (as cholesterol, ergosterol, and stigmasterol) that are widely distributed in the unsaponifiable portion of lipids in animals and plants and are characterized by a tetracyclic structure involving fusion of a cyclopentane ring to a partially or completely hydrogenated phenanthrene ring system

ster·ras·ter \stə'rastə(r)\ *n* -s [NL, fr. Gk *sterros* firm, solid (akin to Gk *stereos* solid) + NL *-aster* — more at STARE] **:** a spherical sponge spicule with many small rays

ster·rett·ite \'sterə,tīt\ *n* -s [Douglas B. *Sterrett* b1883 Am. geologist + E *-ite*] **:** a mineral $Al_6(PO_4)_4(OH)_6.5H_2O$ consisting of a hydrous basic aluminum phosphate

ster·rinck \'steriŋk\ *n* -s [prob. modif. of NL *Stenorhynchus*, genus of seals, fr. *sten-* + *-rhynchus*] **:** CRABEATER SEAL

ster·ro metal \'ste(,)rō-\ *n* [ISV *sterro* (fr. Gk *sterros* firm, solid) + *metal*] **:** a hard brass containing a little iron

-sters *pl of* -STER

ster·tor \'stərd·ər\ *n* -s [NL, fr. L *stertere* to snore + *-or*; akin to OIr *srennim* I snore, *sreod* act of sneezing — more at STERNUTATION] **:** the act or an instance of producing a snoring or rasping sound in respiration because of obstruction (as in sleep or coma) of air passages of the head

ster·to·rous \-d·ərəs\ *adj* [NL *stertor* + E *-ous*] **1 :** characterized by a harsh snoring or gasping sound **:** exhibiting or marked by stertor ⟨~ breathing⟩ **2 :** marked by snoring ⟨a ~ nap by the hearth⟩ **syn** see LOUD

ster·to·rous·ly *adv* **:** in a stertorous manner

ste·sich·o·re·an \stə¦sikə¦rēən\ *adj, usu cap* [*Stesichorus* †550? B.C. Greek poet + E *-an*] **:** of or relating to Stesichorus the chief early composer of Dorian lyrics and probable establisher of strophe, antistrophe, and epode as the normal structure for choral lyric

1stet \'stet, *usu* -ed·+V\ *vt* **stetted; stetted; stetting; stets** [L, let it stand, 3d pers. sing. pres. subj. of *stare* to stand — more at STAND] **:** to annotate with the word *stet* or otherwise mark (as with a series of subscript dots) to nullify a previous order to delete or omit (a word or passage in a manuscript or printer's proof)

2stet \"\ *n* -s [by shortening] **:** STET PROCESSUS

3stet \"\ *vt* **stetted; stetted; stetting; stets :** to order a stet processus on

stetch \'stech\ *dial chiefly Brit var of* 1STITCH 4

stet·e·feldt furnace \'sted·ə,felt-\ *n, usu cap S* [after Charles A. *Stetefeldt*, 20th cent. Am. mining engineer, its inventor] **:** a shaft furnace in which silver ores are desulfurized and chloridized by dropping them pulverized and mixed with salt through a heated chamber

steth- *or* **stetho-** *comb form* [F *stéth-, stétho-*, fr. Gk *stēth-, stētho-*, fr. *stēthos*] **:** breast **:** chest ⟨*steth*arteritis⟩ ⟨*stetho*meter⟩

stetho·gram \'stethə,gram, -raa(ə)m\ *n* [*steth-* + *-gram*] **:** PHONOCARDIOGRAM

stetho·graph \-,graf, -raa(ə)f, -raif, -rȧf\ *n* [ISV *steth-* + *-graph*] **:** an instrument that records graphically the heart sounds heard through a stethoscope — **stetho·graph·ic** \¦ˌ=¦grafik\ *adj*

ste·thog·ra·phy \stə'thägrəfē, ste'-, -fi\ *n* -ES [ISV *steth-* + *-graphy*; prob. orig. formed as G *stethographie*] **:** PHONOCARDIOGRAPHY

ste·thom·e·ter \ˌ='thäməd·ə(r), -mətə-\ *n* [ISV *steth-* + *-meter*] **:** an apparatus for measuring the expansion of the chest wall during respiration — **stetho·met·ric** \¦stethə¦me·trik\ *adj* — **ste·thom·e·try** \stə'thämətrē, ste'-\ *n* -ES

1stetho·scope \'stethə,skōp *also* 'steth-\ *n* [F *stéthoscope*, fr. *stéth-* + *-scope*] **1 :** an instrument used for the detection and study of sounds within the body (as chest, abdomen) that are conveyed to the ears of the observer through rubber tubing connected with an endpiece placed upon the area to be examined **2 :** an instrument resembling a stethoscope that is used to detect flaws in metal

2stethoscope \"\ *vt* -ED/-ING/-S **:** to examine by means of a stethoscope ⟨*stethoscoped* the patient's chest⟩

stetho·scop·ic \¦ˌ=¦skäpik, -pēk\ *or* **stetho·scop·i·cal** \-pəkəl, -pēk-\ *adj* [*stethoscope* + *-ic* or *-ical*] **:** of, relating to, or obtained or made by means of a stethoscope — **stetho·scop·i·cal·ly** \-pək(ə)lē, -pēk-, li\ *adv*

ste·thos·co·py \stə'thäskəpē, 'stethə,skōpē\ *n* -ES [ISV *stethoscope* + *-y*] **:** examination by means of the stethoscope

stet pro·ces·sus \'stet prō'sesəs\ *n* [L, let the process stop] **:** an entry in law staying all proceedings in an action; *also* **:** an order granting such a stay

stethoscope 1

Stet·son \'stetsən\ *trademark* — used for a broad-brimmed high-crowned felt hat

stet·tin \(')s(h)te¦tēn\ *adj, usu cap* [fr. *Stettin* (now *Szczecin*, Poland), city in the former government district of Stettin in northern Prussia, Germany] **:** of or from the city of Stettin, Germany **:** of the kind or style prevalent in Stettin

Steu·ben \(')st(y)ü¦ben *also* 'ˌ=bən\ *trademark* — used for glassware often of heavy design and decorated with engraved figures

stev *or* **steve** *abbr* stevedore

1steve·dore \'stēvə,dō(ə)r, -dō(ə)r, -ōə, -ō(ə) *also* -v,d-\ *n* -s [Sp *estibador* packer, stower, fr. *estibar* to pack, stow, fr. L *stipare* to press together — more at STIFF] **:** one who works at or is responsible for the loading or unloading of a ship in port

2stevedore \"\ *vb* -ED/-ING/-S *vt* **:** to work at or undertake responsibility for the loading and unloading of (a ship) ~ *vi* **:** to load or unload a ship **:** assume responsibility for loading and unloading cargoes ⟨talked you into coming to this town to ~ —R.F.Mirvish⟩

stevedore knot *or* **stevedore's knot** *n* **:** a stopper knot similar to a figure eight knot but with one or more extra turns

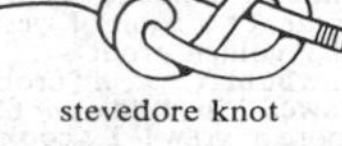

stevedore knot

stev·en \'stevən\ *n* -s [ME, fr. OE *stefn, stemn* voice, sound; akin to OFris *stifne, stemme* voice, OHG *stimna, stimma*, Goth *stibna*] **1** *dial chiefly Brit* **:** VOICE **2** *dial chiefly Brit* **:** NOISE, UPROAR

ste·ven·so·nian \¦stēvən¦sōnēən, -nyən\ *adj, usu cap* [Robert Louis *Stevenson* †1894 Scot. essayist, novelist and poet + E *-an*] **:** of, relating to, or characteristic of Robert Louis Stevenson or his writings **:** having the manner or style of Stevenson ⟨a real essay — *Stevensonian* . . . in its sustained and personal touch —August Heckscher⟩

ste·ven·so·niana \,ˌ=,sōnē'anə, -'änə, -'ānə *also* -'ānə\ *n pl but sing in constr, usu cap* [NL, fr. Robert Louis *Stevenson* †1894 + NL *-ana*] **:** writings by or about Robert Louis Stevenson ⟨a collector and editor of minor *Stevensoniana* —*Yale Rev.*⟩

ste·via \'stēvēə, -vyə\ *n* [NL, irreg. fr. P. J. *Esteve* †1556 Sp. botanist + NL *-ia*] **1 a** *cap* **:** a genus of shrubs and herbs (family Compositae) chiefly of warm regions of the New World having glutinous foliage and white or purplish flowers **b** -s **:** any plant of *Stevia* or the related genus *Piqueria* **2** -s **:** WHITE SNAKEROOT

ste·vi·o·side \'stēvēə,sīd\ *n* -s [NL *Stevia* (genus name of *Stevia rebaudiana*) + E *-oside*] **:** a hygroscopic crystalline intensely sweet glucoside $C_{38}H_{60}O_{18}$ obtained from the leaves of a Paraguayan shrub (*Stevia rebaudiana*)

1stew \'st(y)ü\ *n* -s [ME *stu, stewe*, fr. MF *estuve*, fr. (assumed) VL *extufa*, fr. *extufare* to stew — more at STEW (vb)] **1** *obs* **a :** a utensil used for boiling **b :** something resembling a stew ⟨I have seen corruption boil and bubble till it o'errun the ~ —Shak.⟩ **2 a :** a heated room where hot baths are furnished **b :** a hot bath **3 a :** BROTHEL ⟨squander every penny of their pay in waterfront *~s* —*New Yorker*⟩ **b :** a district characterized by brothels; *typically* **:** a slum area — usu. used in pl. ⟨housed hundreds of free Negroes in the *~s* of those days —*Reporter*⟩ **4 a :** food prepared by stewing in liquid (as water or milk); *esp* **:** a combination of fish or meat usu. with vegetables prepared in this way ⟨beef ~⟩ ⟨oyster ~⟩ **b :** something resembling a cooked stew: as (1) **:** a heterogeneous mixture ⟨a ~ of all the . . . measures ever suggested by anyone —R.H. Rovere⟩ (2) **:** a state of heat and congestion ⟨the tropical ~ of downtown Philadelphia —Alistair Cooke⟩ **5 :** a state of agitating excitement, worry, or confusion ⟨everyone went into a terribly silly ~ about it —Eve Langley⟩

2stew \"\ *n* -s [ME *stewe*, fr. MF *estui* case, tub, tank, fr. *estuier* to enclose, watch, prob. fr. (assumed) VL *studiare* to watch, guard, apply oneself to one thing, fr. L *studium* study — more at STUDY] **1** *Brit* **:** a tank or small pond for keeping fish often until they are wanted for cooking **2 :** an artificial bed of oysters

3stew \"\ *vb* -ED/-ING/-S [ME *stuen, stewen*, fr. MF *estuver*, fr. (assumed) VL *extufare*, prob. fr. L *ex-* 1ex- + (assumed) VL *tufus* hot vapor, fr. Gk *typhos* vapor, smoke; akin to L *fumus* smoke — more at FUME] *vt* **1 :** to boil slowly or with a simmering heat **:** to cook in a little liquid over a gentle fire without boiling ⟨*~ed* the beef for goulash⟩ **2** *archaic* **:** to keep confined in or as if in a hot or stuffy atmosphere — usu. used with *up* **3** *archaic* **:** IMBUE, STEEP ⟨live . . . *~ed* in corruption —Shak.⟩ **4** *obs* **:** to bathe in perspiration ⟨a reeking post, *~ed* in his haste, half breathless, panting —Shak.⟩ **5 :** to bring to an extreme state usu. by worry or excitement — usu. used with *up* ⟨so *~ed* up with anxiety that he couldn't wait —John Morrison⟩ **~** *vi* **1 :** to undergo cooking in or as if in a slow simmering manner **:** become cooked by stewing **2 :** to swelter esp. from confinement in a hot or stuffy atmosphere ⟨a handful of . . . secretaries ~ in the cramped and cluttered Third Room —E.O.Hauser⟩ **3 :** to study hard **:** SWEAT **4 :** to become agitated or worried **:** FRET ⟨been *~ing* over this thing all night —Erle Stanley Gardner⟩ — **stew in one's own juice :** to suffer the discomfort of conditions or circumstances brought about by oneself

[1]**stew·ard** \'st(y)üə(r)d, -)ü(ə)rd, -)üəd\ *n* -s [ME, fr. OE *stīweard, stigweard*, fr. *stī, stig* pen, hall, sty + *weard* ward — more at STY, WARD] **1 :** one called to exercise responsible care over possessions entrusted to him ⟨a ~ of the time, talent, and treasure entrusted to his care⟩ **2 a** *obs* **:** an officer or employee of a household charged with the general administration of its affairs **b :** a head manager of a manor or estate presiding at the manorial courts, auditing accounts, conducting inquests and extents, and controlling the husbandry arrangements **c :** one employed on a large estate usu. to manage its affairs, supervise workmen, collect rents or income, and keep accounts **3 :** SHOP STEWARD **4 a :** a magistrate appointed by the Scottish crown to exercise jurisdiction over lands forfeited to the crown **b :** an English judicial officer joining with the verderers in proceedings under the forest laws **5 a :** an officer in charge of finances (as of a guild or an English municipality) **:** a fiscal agent **b :** one of a body of officers in charge of the finances and some other temporal interests of a local Methodist church **6 a** (1) **:** one employed on board ship to do the catering and superintend culinary affairs (2) **:** an employee on a passenger ship who performs various services for the comfort and needs of the passengers ⟨room ~⟩ ⟨deck ~⟩ **b :** an employee on an airplane, bus, or train who manages the provisioning of food sometimes preparing and serving meals and who may attend to other duties (as seating or the checking of passenger lists, safety belts, and baggage) **7 a :** an officer of a college who has charge of the commons **b :** one appointed to supervise the provision and distribution of food and drink in an institution (as a hotel, club, hospital) **c :** one who operates a commissary **8 a :** one who actively directs affairs **:** MANAGER ⟨the *~s* of a jockey club⟩ **b** *Brit* **:** a person who assists in the supervision of the arrangements of a large gathering of people **:** USHER **c :** an assistant to an animal show judge **9 :** either of two officers of a Masonic lodge whose duties are to collect dues, provide refreshments, and perform other similar services

[2]**steward** \"\ *vb* -ED/-ING/-S *vt* **:** to act as a steward for **:** MANAGE **~** *vi* **:** to perform the duties of a steward

stew·ard·ess \-dəs\ *n* -ES **:** a woman who performs the duties of a steward; *esp* **:** one who attends to the needs of passengers (as on an airplane, ship, or train)

stew·ard·ly *adj* **:** characterized by careful management **:** CAREFUL, FRUGAL, PRUDENT

steward of scotland *cap 2d S* **:** a high officer of the Scottish crown superintending the royal household, administering the crown revenues, and having the privilege of leading the army into battle

stew·ard·ship \-,ship\ *n* [ME *stewardshippe*, fr. *steward* + *-shippe* -ship] **1 a :** the office of steward **b :** the administration of the office of steward and of goods or duties entrusted to one's care **2 a :** the individual's responsibility esp. in certain religious groups for sharing systematically and proportionately his time, talent, and material possessions in the service of God and for the benefit of all mankind **b :** the careful responsible management of something (as an institution) entrusted to one

stew·ards·man \-dzmən\ *n, pl* **stewardsmen** [*stewards* (poss. of [1]*steward*) + *man*] **:** a naval enlisted man who serves food and performs other duties in officers' quarters

stew·ar·tia \s(t)yü'ärsh(ē)ə, -rd·ēə\ *n, cap* [NL, irreg. fr. John *Stuart* †1792 3d Earl of Bute + NL *-ia*] **:** a genus of American and Japanese shrubs or trees (family Theaceae) having large solitary flowers with a 5-celled ovary which becomes a woody capsule — see SILKY CAMELLIA

stew·art·ite \'st(y)üə(r)t,īt\ *n* -s [*Stewart* mine, Pala, Calif., where it was orig. found + E *-ite*] **:** a mineral consisting of a hydrous phosphate of manganese that is brownish yellow in color, is usu. in minute crystals and tufts of fibers, and is found with hureaulite in several pegmatites

stew·art·ry \'st(y)üərtrī\ *also* **stew·ard·ry** \-rdri\ *n* -ES [ME (Sc), fr. [1]*steward* + *-ry*] **1 :** a former administrative district in Scotland under the jurisdiction of a steward **2** *chiefly Scot* **:** the office of a steward

stew·art's disease \'st(y)üə(r)ts-\ *n, usu cap S* [after Fred Carlton *Stewart* †1946 Am. plant pathologist] **:** a disease esp. of sweet corn that is caused by a bacterium of the genus *Erwinia* (*E. stewartii*) transmitted over the winter by the corn flea beetle and that is characterized by wilting, stunting, leaf necrosis, and premature death of affected plants

stew·art white trout \'st(y)üə(r)t-\ *n, often cap S&W* [after *Stewart White* (Stewart Edward White) †1946 Am. fiction writer] **:** a trout of western No. America prob. identical with the golden trout

stewbum \'=,=\ *n* [prob. fr. [1]*stew* + *bum*] **:** DRUNKARD

stewed \'st(y)üd\ *adj* [ME, fr. past part. of *stewen* to stew — more at STEW] **1 :** cooked by stewing ⟨ate a dish of ~ prunes⟩ ⟨a meal of ~ chicken and rice⟩ **2 :** DRUNK ⟨stagger out of the house ~ to the gills —Margaret Long⟩

stewing *pres part of* STEW

stewpan \'=,=\ *n* [[1]*stew* + *pan*] **:** a saucepan with a long handle used for stewing

stewpond \'=,=\ *n* [[2]*stew* + *pond*] *Brit* **:** a pool or tank for keeping fish ⟨*~s* in which fishes were grown and fattened for the table —J.R.Norman⟩

stewpan

stewpot \'=,=\ *n* [[1]*stew* + *pot*] **:** a saucepot with two hand grips used for stewing

stews *pl of* STEW, *pres 3d sing of* STEW

stey \'stā\ *adj* [ME (Sc) *stay*] *chiefly Scot* **:** STEEP

steyn *var of* STEEN

stf *abbr* **1** staff **2** stiff

stg *abbr* **1** staging **2** standing **3** sterling **4** storage

stge *abbr* storage

stgr *abbr* stringer

sth *abbr* south

STH *abbr* somatotropic hormone

stha·nak·va·si \,stänək'väsē\ *or* **stha·na·ka·va·si** \-kə'-\ *n* -s *usu cap* [Skt *sthānakavāsin*, fr. *sthānaka* secular place + *vāsin* living in, inhabiting; akin to Skt *tiṣṭhati* he stands and to Skt *vasati* he lives — more at STAND, WAS] **:** a member of a Jain sect originating in 1473 that rejects the use of all images and idols

sthene \'sthēn\ *n* -s [ISV, fr. Gk *sthenos* strength] **:** an mks absolute unit of force equal to 1000 newtons or 10^8 dynes

sthen·ic \'sthenik, -nēk\ *adj* [NL *sthenicus*, fr. Gk *sthenos* strength, force + L *-icus* -ic; perh. akin to Skt *saghnoti* he takes upon himself, is a match for] **1 :** marked by excessive vitality or nervous energy **:** ACTIVE, STRONG ⟨~ fever⟩ **2 :** indicative of strength and vigor ⟨the ~ personality type⟩ **3 :** PYKNIC

sthn *abbr* southern

stib \'stib\ *n* -s [origin unknown] **:** RED-BACKED SANDPIPER

stib- *or* **stibi-** *or* **stibio-** *also* **stibo-** *comb form* [*stibium*] **:** antimony ⟨*stib*ine⟩ ⟨*stibio*columbite⟩ ⟨*stibo*phen⟩

stib·amine \'stibə,mēn\ *n* [ISV *stib-* + *amine*] **:** a sodium salt of stibanilic acid injected chiefly in the form of a glucoside in the treatment of various tropical diseases

stib·anil·ic acid \¦stibə¦nilik-\ *n* [*stib-* + *anilic*] **:** an unstable acid $NH_2C_6H_4SbO(OH)_2$ containing antimony that is analogous to arsanilic acid and is used in making organic antimonial drugs; *para*-amino-benzene-stibonic acid

stib·ble \'stibəl\ *chiefly Scot var of* STUBBLE

stib·bler \'stiblər\ *n* -s [origin unknown] *Scot* **:** a student of divinity licensed to preach but not called to a ministry

stibble–rig \'==,=\ *n* **1** *Scot* **:** a field of stubble **2** *Scot* **:** the chief reaper

stib·i·al \'stibēəl\ *adj* [NL *stibialis*, fr. L *stibium* + *-alis* -al] **:** ANTIMONIAL

stib·ic \'stibik\ *adj* [*stib-* + *-ic*] **:** ANTIMONIC

stib·i·co·nite \'stibəkə,nīt\ *n* -s [modif. (influenced by *-ite*) of F *stibiconise*, fr. *stib-* + Gk *konis* dust — more at INCINERATE] **:** a mineral $Sb_3O_6(OH)$(?) consisting of a hydrous antimony oxide in yellowish masses or powder

stib·ine \'sti,bēn\ *n* -s [ISV *stib-* + *-ine*] **1 :** a colorless very poisonous gaseous compound SbH_3 of antimony and hydrogen that has a disagreeable odor and burns with a bluish green flame and that is usu. made by decomposing metallic antimonides with acid **2 :** any of a class of organic compounds derived from stibine that are analogous to the arsines

sti·bin·ic acid \stə'binik-\ *n* [ISV *stibine* + *-ic*] **:** any of a series of organic acids of antimony having the general formula $RR'SbOOH$ and analogous to the arsinic acids

stib·io·columbite \¦stibē(,)ō+\ *n* [*stib-* + *columbite*] **:** a mineral $SbCbO_4$ consisting of an oxide of antimony and columbium isomorphous with stibiotantalite

stib·i·o·pal·la·di·nite \,stibēō'palədə,nīt\ *n* [*stib-* + *palladinite* PdO, fr. *palladium* + connective *-n-* + *-ite*] **:** a mineral Pd_3Sb that consists of a native alloy of palladium and antimony

stib·io·tantalite \¦stibē(,)ō+\ *n* [*stib-* + *tantalite*] **:** a mineral $SbTaO_4$ consisting of an oxide of antimony and tantalum isomorphous with stibiocolumbite

stib·i·ous \'stibēəs\ *adj* [*stib-* + *-ous*] **:** ANTIMONIOUS

stib·i·um \'stibēəm\ *n* -s [L *stibium, stibi, stimmi*, fr. Gk *stibi, stimmi*, fr. Egypt *stm*] **1 :** ANTIMONY — symbol *Sb* **2 :** STIBNITE; *esp* **:** stibnite used (as in ancient Egypt) as a cosmetic for painting the eyes

stib·nite \'stib,nīt\ *n* -s [alter. (influenced by E *-ite*) of obs. E *stibine* stibnite, fr. F, fr. *stib-* + *-ine*] **:** a mineral Sb_2S_3 consisting of native antimony trisulfide occurring in prismatic orthorhombic crystals of lead gray color and brilliant metallic luster that show a highly perfect cleavage and are striated vertically and also in massive form and providing the chief source of antimony (hardness 2, sp. gr. 4.62)

sti·bon·ic acid \stə'bänik-\ *n* [NL *stibon*ium + E *-ic*] **:** any of a series of organic acids of antimony having the general formula $RSbO(OH)_2$ and analogous to the arsonic acids — compare STIBANILIC ACID

sti·bo·ni·um \stə'bōnēəm\ *n* -s [NL, fr. *stib-* + ammon*ium*] **:** a univalent ion SbH_4^+ or radical SbH_4 derived from stibine and known only in the form of organic derivatives

stib·o·phen \'stibə,fen\ *n* -s [*stib-* + *phene*] **:** a crystalline antimony derivative $C_{12}H_4Na_5O_{16}S_4Sb.7H_2O$ of pyrocatechol used in the treatment of various tropical diseases

[1]**stich** \'stik\ *n* -s [Gk *stichos*; akin to Gk *steichein* to walk, go — more at STAIR] **:** a measured part of something written esp. in verse **:** LINE, VERSE

[2]**stich** \"\ *n* -s [G, sting, pricking, trick at cards, fr. OHG *stih* sting, pricking — more at STITCH] **:** a trick in various card games (as pinochle) that has scoring value because it is the last one

-stich \,stik\ *n comb form* -s [L *-stichon*, fr. Gk, fr. neut. of *-stichos* having (so many) rows or lines, fr. *stichos* row, line, verse] **:** poem or stanza consisting of (so many) lines ⟨*deca*stich⟩ ⟨*hepta*stich⟩

sti·cha·rion \stə'kär,yȯn\ *n, pl* **sticha·ria** \-(,)yə\ [LGk, dim. of *stichē*, a kind of tunic, fr. Gk *stichos* row, line] **:** an ecclesiastical vestment made in the form of a tunic or long robe similar to an alb and worn by deacons and priests of the Eastern Orthodox Church

sti·che·ron \stə'ki,rän\ *n, pl* **stiche·ra** \-irə\ [MGk *stichēron*, fr. neut. of *stichēros* of verse, fr. Gk *stichos* row, line, verse] **:** a short hymn following usu. a verse from the Psalms in the Eastern Church

stich·ic \'stikik\ *adj* [Gk *stichikos*, fr. *stichos* + *-ikos* -ic] **:** of, relating to, or consisting of lines that are rhythmic units **:** arranged or divided by lines **:** serial in succession or recurrence — **stich·i·cal·ly** \-tikək(ə)lē\ *adv*

stich·id \'stikəd\ *n* -s [NL *stichidium*] **:** STICHIDIUM

sti·chid·i·um \stə'kidēəm\ *n, pl* **stichid·ia** \-ēə\ [NL, fr. Gk *stichidion* small row, small line, dim. of *stichos* row, line] **:** a special branch of the thallus of a red alga bearing tetraspores and often fusiform

sticho·basidial \¦stikō+\ *adj* [Gk *stichos* line + E *basidial*] **:** having the nuclear spindles of the basidia parallel to the longitudinal axis — compare CHIASTOBASIDIAL — **sticho·basidium** \"+\ *n*

stich·o·met·ric \¦stikə¦me·trik\ *or* **stich·o·met·ri·cal** \-rəkəl\ *adj* **:** of, relating to, or characterized by stichometry **:** characterized by lines — **stich·o·met·ri·cal·ly** \-rək(ə)lē\ *adv*

sti·chom·e·try \stə'kämə·trē\ *n* -ES [Gk *stichos* line + E *-metry*] **1 a :** a measurement of books by the number of lines they contain **b :** a list of documents stating how many lines each contains **2 :** division of the text of a book into lines; *esp* **:** division of texts into lines fitted to the sense (as in manuscripts antedating the adoption of punctuation)

stich·o·myth·ia \,stikə'mithēə\ *also* **sti·chom·y·thy** \stə'kämәthē\ *n, pl* **stichomythias** *also* **stichomythies** [Gk *stichomythia*, fr. *stichomythein* to speak dialogue in alternate lines, fr. *stichos* row, line, verse + *mythos* tale, speech, myth — more at MYTH] **:** dialogue esp. of altercation or dispute delivered in alternating lines (as in classical Greek drama)

stich·o·myth·ic \¦stikə¦mithik\ *adj* **:** of, relating to, or constituting stichomythia

sti·chos \'sti,käs\ *n, pl* **sti·choi** \-kȯi\ [Gk — more at STICH] **:** LINE, STICH, VERSE

stich·o·some \'stikə,sōm\ *n* -s [Gk *stichos* row, line + E *-some*] **:** a column of glandular cells associated with the esophagus of various nematodes

-sti·chous \stəkəs\ *adj comb form* [LL *-stichus*, fr. Gk *-stichos*, fr. *stichos* row, line] **:** having (such or so many) rows or sides ⟨*diplo*stichous⟩ ⟨*mono*stichous⟩

sticht·ite \'stik,tīt\ *n* -s [Robert *Sticht* †1922 Australian metallurgist born in U.S. + E *-ite*] **:** a mineral $Mg_6Cr_2(OH)_{16}(CO_3).4H_2O$ consisting of a hydrous carbonate and hydroxide of magnesium and chromium

[1]**stick** \'stik\ *n* -s [ME *stikke*, stik, fr. OE *sticca*; akin to MLG *stikke* stick, OHG *stehho, stecko*, ON *stik, stika* stick, stake, OE *stician* to stick — more at [5]STICK] **1 :** a woody piece or part of a tree or shrub: as **a** (1) **:** a shoot, twig, or slender branch broken or cut off esp. when dry or dead (2) **:** BUD STICK **b :** a cut or broken branch or a piece of chopped wood used as or suitable for fuel — usu. used in pl. ⟨were able to find enough dry *~s* to start a campfire⟩ ⟨cut a few *~s* of kindling⟩ **c :** a stem or branch of any size cut or gathered for use esp. as construction material (as timbers, stakes, staves) or in manufacturing ⟨interwoven willow *~s*⟩ ⟨cane *~s* for oboes —*Time*⟩ ⟨in the postwar world *~s* of timber will be shot full of strengthening plastic —*Science News Letter*⟩; *sometimes* **:** LOG ⟨the big *~s* that housed early Americans and carried the canvas on tall Yankee clipper ships —*Monsanto Mag.*⟩ ⟨started with such a big ~ I couldn't even move one end of it —G.W.Brace⟩ **2 :** a long and relatively slender piece of wood in its natural form or shaped with tools and of a size that can be easily handled **:** ROD, STAFF, WAND ⟨cut himself a hiking ~⟩ ⟨the ~ of a skyrocket⟩ ⟨an apple on a ~⟩ ⟨manicure *~s* of orangewood⟩ ⟨a burnt ~ of a match⟩: as **a** (1) **:** a wooden club or staff used as a weapon ⟨one hand resting on the white ~ in his belt —Kay Boyle⟩ ⟨cop in full kit, his ~ ready in his hand —R.O.Bowen⟩ — compare NIGHTSTICK (2) **:** something suitable for use as a means of compulsion ⟨programs carried on today are nowhere near large enough to be effective either as *~s* or carrots —S.P. Hayes b.1910⟩ ⟨the ~ — the powerful instrumentalities of institutionalized violence —Julian Towster⟩ (3) **:** a beating with or as if with a stick ⟨got a fair share of the ~ —Brian James⟩ **b** (1) **:** DRUMSTICK (2) **sticks** *pl* **:** DRUMMER **c :** WALKING STICK ⟨tossed his hat and ~ on the table —Waldo Frank⟩ ⟨iron-pointed ferrule that distinguishes continental *~s* —Hilton Brown⟩ **d :** any of various implements (as a baseball bat, billiard cue, golf club) used for striking or propelling an object in a game: as (1) **:** HOCKEY STICK ⟨all *~s* shall be made of wood —*Official Ice Hockey Guide*⟩ (2) **:** CROSSE (3) **sticks** *pl* **:** the staves thrown at the target figure in Aunt Sally; *also* **:** the game of Aunt Sally (4) **:** an implement used by a croupier or stickman to retrieve thrown dice **e** (1) **:** a baton symbolizing an office or dignity; *also* **:** a person bearing or entitled to bear such a baton — compare GOLD STICK, SILVER STICK (2) **:** a musical conductor's baton ⟨though no professional conductor, handles the ~ astonishingly well —*N.Y.Times*⟩ **f :** one of the pieces of wood resembling laths that are used to suspend leaves and stalks of tobacco in curing barns and to suspend hands of tobacco in drying machines **3 :** a piece, part, or bit of the total materials of which something (as a building) is constructed or composed ⟨house stood facing her, not a ~ of it changed —Allen Tate⟩ ⟨nothing there . . . not a windbreak tree, windmill, ~ of fence —C.T.Jackson⟩ ⟨had grown up in the town and knew every ~ and stone of it⟩ **4 :** a piece of wood used as a tally by cutting notches in it or as a counter or token **5 :** any of various implements and utensils shaped like a stick or having a possible origin in a stick: as **a :** CANDLESTICK **b :** a violin bow **:** FIDDLESTICK **c** (1) **:** COMPOSING STICK (2) **:** STICKFUL (3) **:** set type occupying two inches of one column esp. of a newspaper; *also* **:** copy for this amount of type (4) **:** the receiving galley of a slugcasting machine **d sticks** *pl* **:** a set of thin narrow rods or slats (as of wood, bone, ivory) on which the folding surface of a fan is mounted **e** *slang* **:** PISTOL **f** (1) **:** CHANTER 3 (2) **:** FIFE (3) **:** FLUTE **g** (1) **:** CONTROL STICK (2) **:** a gearshift lever of an automobile **h :** FOUNTAIN PEN **6 :** something prepared (as by cutting, molding, rolling) in a relatively long and slender often cylindrical form (as for convenience in handling, ease of application or consumption) ⟨cinnamon *~s*⟩ ⟨~ of candy⟩ ⟨~ of sealing wax⟩ ⟨~ of dynamite⟩ ⟨shaving ~ ⟩ ⟨lipsticks and other cosmetic or medicated *~s*⟩ ⟨cucumber *~s*⟩ ⟨pound of butter in *~s*⟩; *specif* **:** a marihuana cigarette **:** REEFER **7 a :** a quantity of eels consisting usu. of 25 eels **b :** a quantity of fish consisting of 25 pounds **8 a :** PERSON — used with a qualifying adjective ⟨queer ~⟩ ⟨a decent old ~ —Robert Graves⟩ ⟨they'd only been kidding you . . . they were good *~s* —David Ballantyne⟩ **b :** a dull, inert, stiff, or spiritless person **:** one that lacks vigor, animation, or geniality ⟨this poor, dim ~ —Jean Stafford⟩ ⟨was also something of a ~ . . . rarely spoke to anyone who was not of her own social station —Aubrey Menen⟩ ⟨such a thing as carrying niceness too far — a girl could end by being a ~ —Hamilton Basso⟩ ⟨is a regular ~ on the stage —Emily Eden⟩ **c :** SHILL; *esp* **:** one working in a carnival **9 a :** a tree trunk or sometimes a tree suitable for timber ⟨next task is to get the big *~s* out of the woods —D.C.Peattie⟩ ⟨a clear ~ of ninety feet was nothing unusual among these giants —G.W. Johnson⟩ **b :** a wood of timber trees **c sticks** *pl* (1) **:** wooded lands **:** rural districts **:** BACKCOUNTRY — used with *the* ⟨bringing in hordes of Indians from the *~s* —*Guatemala News*⟩ ⟨back in the *~s*, far from anything —Bill Wolf⟩ (2) **:** sections of a country remote from or held to be little touched by centers of civilization — used with *the*; compare BACKWOODS, PROVINCES ⟨in case you're from the *~s*, I'll explain it to you —Willard Temple⟩ ⟨a musical comedy during its trial run in the *~s* —J.M.Conly⟩ (3) **:** BUSH LEAGUES — used with *the* ⟨sent him back to the *~s*⟩ **10 a :** an edible plant stem or stalk ⟨celery *~s*⟩ ⟨stewed a few *~s* of rhubarb⟩ **b :** the dry withered stem of a stiffish plant ⟨watering the dry *~s* of hollyhock —Mari Sandoz⟩ **11 a :** MAST ⟨do my sailing with a rag and ~ —H.A.Calahan⟩ ⟨our eyes on the bobbing, varnished ~ of the dinghy —Vincent McHugh⟩ **b :** YARD **12 :** a portion of alcoholic liquor (as brandy, rum) in a nonalcoholic drink ⟨a cup of tea with a ~ in it⟩ **13 :** a single piece or article esp. of furniture ⟨upholstered almost every ~ of furniture herself —E.L.Howe⟩ ⟨some dusty *~s* of Victorian furniture —Margery Allingham⟩ ⟨series of business failures that left him with hardly a ~ to his name⟩ **14 :** LEG — usu. used in pl. ⟨fever left him weak on his *~s*⟩ **15 :** something constructed of sticks: as **a :** a cricket stump — usu. used in pl. **b** (1) **:** a racing or steeplechase hurdle (2) **:** any wooden obstacle (as a fence, gate, stile) to be hurdled (as in hunting) **:** TIMBER 4a **c :** a fireman's ladder **16 sticks** *pl* **:** a violation of the rules of field hockey by raising the stick above the shoulders at either the beginning or end of a stroke **17 a :** a number of bombs arranged for release or released one after another in quick succession from a bombing plane esp. in a spaced series across a target ⟨jettisoning its ~ of bombs —J.W.Bellah⟩ ⟨dropped a few *~s* off target —Jack Alexander⟩ — compare SALVO **b :** a group of parachutists who jump or are assigned to jump one after another in quick succession ⟨our ~ was briefed again on various subjects —T.B.Bruff⟩ ⟨dropping two *~s* of paratroopers simultaneously —J.G.Cozzens⟩ — **hold a stick to** *also* **hold sticks with :** compete with equally **:** survive comparison with — **short end of the stick :** unfair or unfavorable treatment **:** a disadvantageous position — **to sticks** *adv* **1 :** to pieces **:** COMPLETELY, THOROUGHLY ⟨beat being a farmhand all *to sticks*⟩ **2** *also* **to sticks and staves :** into fragments **:** to ruin **:** to the bad — **wrong end of the stick :** a twisted or false version, impression, or account of something ⟨thinks he knows what a teacher means when, in fact, he is getting the *wrong end of the stick* —Alan Road⟩

[2]**stick** \"\ *vt* -ED/-ING/-S **1 :** to arrange (lumber) in stacks esp. with stickers **2 :** to provide a stick as a support for (as a plant, a vine) **3 :** to set (type) in a composing stick **:** COMPOSE ⟨could . . . rustle news, solicit ads, ~ type, make up forms, put the paper to bed —S.H.Adams⟩

[3]**stick** \"\ *adj* **1 :** resembling a stick in shape **:** prepared or made in the form of a stick ⟨~ cinnamon⟩ ⟨a ~ deodorant⟩ **2 :** made of or with sticks ⟨a ~ bridge⟩ ⟨~ chimney⟩

[4]**stick** \"\ *adv* **:** ALTOGETHER, COMPLETELY ⟨~ blind⟩ ⟨~ stark staring mad⟩

[5]**stick** \"\ *vb* **stuck** \'stək\ **stuck; sticking; sticks** [ME *stikken, stiken*, fr. OE *stician*; akin to OS *stekan* to stick fast, OHG *stehhan* to sting, prick, *sticken* to stick, prick, *stecchen* to stick, insert, ON *steikja* to roast, L *instigare* to urge on, incite, instigate, Gk *stizein* to tattoo, Skt *tejate* it is sharp; basic meaning: sharp] *vt* **1 a :** to pierce with something pointed: as (1) **:** to pierce with a pointed weapon **:** wound by a thrust of a pointed instrument **:** STAB (2) *chiefly dial* **:** to pierce with a horn or tusk **:** GORE (3) **:** to make a hole in with a pointed instrument **:** PUNCTURE ⟨man who could ~ a cow for clover bloat —*Time*⟩ **b :** to kill by piercing with a pointed instrument; *esp* **:** to kill (as a pig in butchering) by pressing a knife into the throat **c :** to strike (as fish) or hunt (as wild boar) with a spear ⟨~ salmon⟩ ⟨had *stuck* pigs in India⟩ **2 :** to cause (as a pointed instrument) to penetrate **:** push or thrust so as to pierce or as if to pierce — used with *in* or *into* or with *through* ⟨died from a knife *stuck* in his back⟩ ⟨*stuck* a needle in her finger⟩ ⟨too thick to ~ a pin through it⟩ ⟨accidentally *stuck* his finger in his eye⟩ ⟨*stuck* his umbrella in my ribs⟩ ⟨test by *~ing* a fork into the crust⟩ **3 a :** to fix, fasten, or secure in position by thrusting or pushing in esp. at a pointed or narrow end ⟨~ pins in a pincushion⟩ ⟨~ a marker in the ground⟩ ⟨~ candles in a birthday cake⟩ ⟨*stuck* a flower in his buttonhole⟩ ⟨*stuck* his pipe between his teeth⟩ ⟨a flower *stuck* behind his ear —Judson Philips⟩ ⟨had his pistol *stuck* in his belt⟩ ⟨*stuck* a feather in his hatband⟩ **b** (1) **:** to fix on a point or a pointed implement **:** IMPALE ⟨~ an apple on a fork⟩ ⟨kills a fowl, *~s* it and the banana blossom on a spit —J.G.Frazer⟩ (2) **:** to mount (as an insect specimen) by transfixing with a pin **c :** to push, shove, thrust, or poke (as a part of the body) in a specified direction or into a specified place or position ⟨suddenly *stuck* his arm out⟩ ⟨*stuck* his hands behind him⟩ ⟨sitting with his feet *stuck* out into the aisle⟩ ⟨*stuck* his finger down his collar⟩ ⟨*stuck* his chin out pugnaciously⟩ ⟨an unpleasant way of *~ing* his nose up in the air⟩ ⟨*~s* out his chest and struts away⟩ ⟨~ out your tongue and say "ah"⟩ ⟨prices jump . . . the minute you ~ your head inside the door —T.H.Fielding⟩ ⟨soldier foolish enough to ~ his head over the rock —Burtt Evans⟩ ⟨*stuck* his face into mine⟩ **4 :** to put or set in a specified place or position ⟨~ the letter under the door⟩ ⟨~ a book back on its shelf⟩ ⟨~ a cake in the oven⟩ ⟨~ the washing in the machine⟩ ⟨~ their prepositions in front of the verbs —John Hilton⟩ ⟨*stuck* me in the shore patrol brig —R.O.Bowen⟩ ⟨*stuck* the prettiest girls in the front row⟩ ⟨*stuck* his hat on his head and left⟩ ⟨a cottage *stuck* down among a swarm of other cottages —Morley Callaghan⟩ ⟨*stuck* a few potted plants around the room⟩ **5 a :** to set or furnish with things fixed in or fastened on by or as if by piercing a surface ⟨~ a pincushion full of pins⟩ ⟨an orange *stuck* with cloves⟩ ⟨top of the wall had been *stuck* full of broken glass⟩ ⟨wore a coat *stuck* with badges⟩ **b :** to set or furnish with objects placed about ⟨a brisk trade in pretty things; buildings are *stuck* all over with

them —Clive Bell⟩ ⟨windows *stuck* full of plants and knickknacks on glass shelves⟩ **6 :** to attach by or as if by causing to adhere to a surface (as with pins or an adhesive) ⟨~ a stamp on a letter⟩ ⟨~ down the flap of an envelope⟩ ⟨~ a poster on the wall⟩ ⟨~ up a notice on the bulletin board⟩ ⟨~ a handle on a teapot with glue⟩ **7 a :** to compel to pay (as by beating in a game or gamble or by trickery or imposition) ⟨expert at *~ing* his friends for drinks at liar's dice⟩ ⟨~ his host for the cost of several long-distance calls⟩ **b** (1) **:** CHARGE ⟨what do they ~ you for a meal⟩ (2) **:** OVERCHARGE **:** require to pay or spend exorbitantly ⟨everybody *~s* the dogface —James Jones⟩ ⟨fixed the prices and . . . *stuck* the rich to favor the poor —Marcus Duffield⟩ **8 :** to run or plane (moldings) in a machine in contradistinction to working by hand **9 a :** to bring to a halt **:** prevent the movement or action of **:** keep from proceeding or going back ⟨could not move a yard among people without getting *stuck* —James Cameron⟩ ⟨prevent foreign matter from *~ing* valve —*Air Tools*⟩ ⟨had been *stuck* there for a week by bad weather⟩ ⟨here he was, *stuck* in a shore job —Nevil Shute⟩ ⟨voice is *stuck* somewhere below his larynx —H.A.Overstreet⟩ ⟨got *stuck* halfway up the hill⟩ **b :** to cause to be at a loss **:** BAFFLE, NONPLUS, PUZZLE, STUMP ⟨*stuck* him with the first question they asked⟩ ⟨you can't ~ him about his native land —T.H.Fielding⟩ ⟨getting *stuck* for a word to rhyme with *moon* —R.K.Leavitt⟩ ⟨was *stuck* for a technique that would deal with them adequately —*New Yorker*⟩ **10 a :** to get the better of esp. fraudulently **:** CHEAT, DEFRAUD ⟨had been *stuck* several times in the past year by phony antique dealers⟩ **b :** to saddle with something disadvantageous or disagreeable — usu. used with *with* ⟨it is your car and you are *stuck* with it —Gregor Felsen⟩ ⟨had been *stuck* with the job of washing the dishes⟩ ⟨think you're going to ~ me with a bum rap like that —Courtney McClendon⟩ ⟨went back on the road again, *stuck* with a losing show —F.B.Gipson⟩ ⟨*stuck* with the most complex monetary system left on earth —Richard Joseph⟩ ⟨things like debt and family illness can ~ you —*Time*⟩ **11** *chiefly Brit* **:** BEAR, ENDURE, STAND, TOLERATE **:** put up with ⟨couldn't ~ that pace all day —Adrian Bell⟩ ⟨can't ~ this darned town any longer —Christopher Isherwood⟩ ⟨couldn't ~ life in some stuffy little house —T.H.Raddall⟩ ⟨none of the girls could ~ him —Edith C. Rivett⟩ — often used with *it* ⟨hoped she would try to ~ it a little longer —F.M.Ford⟩ ⟨don't know how I'm going to ~ it till Tuesday —Margaret Kennedy⟩ ⟨were going out to see if we could ~ it —A.R.Williams⟩ **~** *vi* **1 :** to hold to or be held in something tightly or firmly by or as if by being embedded or attached by adhesion: **a :** to become or remain fixed in place by means of a pointed end **:** have the point piercing or held fast in something ⟨was found with a knife *~ing* in his heart⟩ ⟨thorn *stuck* in his finger and broke off⟩ ⟨javelin *stuck* in the ground where it fell⟩ ⟨arrow *stuck* in the target⟩ **b :** to become fixed or fast by or as if by entangling or miring typically after being impelled into a thickly viscous, gluey, or tacky mass ⟨boat *stuck* in the sand⟩ ⟨car *stuck* in the mud⟩ **c :** to become attached by or as if by gluing or plastering ⟨thin silk robe which *stuck* to his sweating barrellike torso —T.B. Costain⟩ ⟨glue had *stuck* to his fingers⟩ ⟨this stamp won't ~⟩ ⟨several pages had *stuck* together⟩ ⟨keep the biscuits from *~ing* to the pan⟩ **2 a :** to remain in a place, situation, or environment **:** continue to stay often as though held firmly, made stationary, or attached ⟨*stuck* on the farm while his brothers traveled⟩ ⟨decided to ~ where he was⟩ **b :** to remain attached or fixed over a period of time as though imbedded in or holding to with tenacious strength or adhesive power ⟨two sentences ~ in my mind —Kenneth Roberts⟩ ⟨boyhood nickname had *stuck*⟩ ⟨anyone so beyond suspicion that no slander can ~ to him —Elmer Davis⟩ ⟨childhood fears that had *stuck* with him⟩ **c :** to remain effective **:** continue or endure esp. in the face of opposition or difficulty **:** have sufficient lasting power and effect to resist efforts to evade, nullify, or make inoperative ⟨many . . . reorganizations in the past have failed to ~ —*New Republic*⟩ — used chiefly in the phrase *make stick* ⟨making the requirements ~ —*New Republic*⟩ ⟨fifteen years before an arrest could be made to ~ —*N.Y.Times*⟩ **d** *chiefly Brit* **:** to put up with existing conditions or circumstances **e :** to refuse to declare in a card game **3 :** to hold to closely, persistently, or steadfastly **:** stay with or near: as **a :** to adhere tenaciously without deviation, digression, interruption, or wavering **:** PERSEVERE — usu. used with *to* ⟨his sermons . . . ~ too closely to the point to be entertaining —T.S.Eliot⟩ ⟨the faculty should ~ to education and abjure finance —R.M.Lovett⟩ ⟨~ to business⟩ ⟨would ~ to his gladiatorial work for the joy and thrill of it —C.E.Montague⟩ or with *at* ⟨~s at his job⟩ ⟨~s persistently at his studies⟩ **b :** to hold or cling (as to a position) with lasting fortitude and resolution despite attack, danger, or the weight of onerous burdens — usu. used with *to* ⟨call upon every American to ~ to his post until the last battle is won —H.S.Truman⟩ ⟨*stuck* to his ship till it sank⟩ ⟨~ to their boards no matter what happens around them —Margaret Biddle⟩ **c :** to remain (as through a series of developments often adverse, trying, or dire) resolute or unshaken in loyalty, friendship, or alliance — usu. used with *by* or *to* ⟨is full of good men . . . they'll help you and ~ by you —Sherwood Anderson⟩ ⟨a man who *stuck* to his friends⟩ **d :** to adhere with strict fidelity, sure reliability, and lack of modification or relaxation induced by temptation, convenience, or opposition — usu. used with *to* ⟨~ to a contract⟩ ⟨translation *stuck* closely to the original⟩ ⟨always *stuck* to his word⟩ sometimes with *by* ⟨*stuck* by his first account⟩ **e :** to keep close to in a quest, chase, vying, or competition matching or countering opposed efforts — usu. used with *with* or *to* ⟨was stronger than his opponent but the latter *stuck* with him and earned a draw⟩ ⟨managed to ~ to the leader's heels for two laps⟩ **4 :** to become fixed in position or hindered in progress or operation by reason of some obstacle or obstruction **:** become blocked or wedged **:** JAM, LODGE ⟨handle had *stuck*⟩ ⟨something had *stuck* in the pipe⟩ ⟨food *stuck* in his throat⟩ ⟨switch had a tendency to ~⟩ ⟨desk drawer always *sticks*⟩ **5 a :** to be reluctant or unwilling **:** be deterred (as by scruples) **:** BALK, HESITATE, SCRUPLE, STOP — usu. used with *at* ⟨was in a hole and would ~ at little to get out of it —John Buchan⟩ ⟨not one who would ~ at calling her at midnight —Aurelia Levi⟩ ⟨with someone else to do the thinking for him he would ~ at nothing —F.W.Crofts⟩ **b :** to be in difficulty **:** become baffled or nonplussed **:** BOGGLE — usu. used with *at* ⟨~ at grammar⟩ ⟨what we ~ at in most religious poetry is not the beliefs but the emotions —J.P. Bishop⟩ **c :** to be unable to proceed (as in a performance, a speech) ⟨memory failed him at the same place he had *stuck* the first time⟩ ⟨*stuck* in the middle of the verse⟩ **6 :** PROJECT, PROTRUDE ⟨had a book *~ing* from his pocket⟩ ⟨spot the house by the air conditioner *~ing* through the window⟩ ⟨aerial *~s* up above the chimney⟩ ⟨nose of the car was *~ing* out of the garage⟩ ⟨wreck of the tiny store *~ing* up in the ruins —C.G.D. Roberts⟩ ⟨tail unit *~ing* high up into the air —*London Calling*⟩ **syn** see ADHERE, DEMUR — **stick in one's craw** *also* **stick in one's crop** *or* **stick in one's gizzard :** to be difficult of digestion **:** be hard to accept **:** be offensive — **stick in one's throat** *of an utterance* **:** to be or become difficult or impossible to speak or repeat **:** remain unexpressed — **stick it on** *chiefly Brit* **:** to charge exorbitantly ⟨those country shops, it's something dreadful the way they *stick it on* —Victoria Sackville-West⟩ — **stick one's neck out :** to lay oneself open (as to attack, criticism, complaint, detection, punishment, reprisal) **:** run the risk of bringing down upon oneself a consequence detrimental to oneself (as by taking another's part, making a decision outside the scope of one's authority, passing judgment on a matter presumed to be beyond one's competence) ⟨when the testing time comes, he isn't afraid to *stick his neck out* —Jack Winocour⟩ ⟨her warmhearted, slaphappy way of *sticking her neck out* —C.J.Rolo⟩ ⟨economists *stuck their necks out* in the capacity of self-appointed forecasters —Fritz Machlup⟩ ⟨avoids *sticking his neck out* politically —*Scotsman*⟩ ⟨*stuck his neck out* many times for liberal causes —R.S.Allen⟩ — **stick together :** to remain united **:** act as a unit **:** stand by and support one another ⟨father seemed to want the family to *stick together* —Isa Glenn⟩ ⟨now or never for the states to find out how to *stick together* and make one nation —Dorothy C. Fisher⟩ ⟨*stick together* against the foreigner —H.L.Matthews⟩ ⟨we *stuck together* in negotiations —Hugh Gaitskell⟩ — **stick to one's fingers :** to be retained wrongfully ⟨as this currency passes from hand to hand, some of it inevitably *sticks to the fingers* that it touches —D.D.McKean⟩ — **stick to one's guns :** to maintain one's position esp. in the face of attack or opposition ⟨France has *stuck to its guns* as far as its principal demands . . . are concerned —Robert Strausz-Hupé⟩ — **stick to one's knitting :** to stick severely to business or to the matter at hand ⟨both airlines *stuck to their knitting* and improved the service on the respective routes —Horace Sutton⟩ — **stick to one's last :** to stick to what one knows best **:** remain within the field of one's special competence ⟨curators . . . shirk any responsibility for exhibits and . . . want to *stick to their lasts* in the research collections —Thomas Barbour⟩ — **stick to one's ribs** *or* **stick to the ribs :** to provide nourishment and protect against hunger ⟨liked a breakfast that would *stick to his ribs*⟩ — **stuck on :** captivated with **:** infatuated with **:** in love with ⟨a girl he had been *stuck on* for a while in high school⟩ ⟨many boys were *stuck on* her⟩ ⟨brought her out to the game with them and she got *stuck on* me —Ring Lardner⟩ ⟨pretty *stuck on* herself, too —S.H.Adams⟩

⁶stick \"\ *n* -s **1 :** a thrust with a pointed instrument **:** STAB **2 a :** a temporary stoppage **:** DELAY, STOP ⟨seemed to be at a ~⟩ **b :** something causing such a stoppage **:** IMPEDIMENT, OBSTACLE ⟨made no ~ at all⟩ **3 :** the quality or power of adhering or causing to adhere **:** adhesive tendency **4 :** a sticky substance; *specif* **:** the thick liquor obtained by evaporation of the liquid from tankage in rendering fats or tankage and mixed with garbage or solid residue from tankage for use as fertilizer or animal feed

stick·abil·i·ty \ˌstikəˈbilədē\ *n* [⁵*stick* + *ability*] **:** ability to endure or persevere

stick·age \ˈstikij\ *n* -s [⁵*stick* + *-age*] **:** an act or the fact of sticking **:** tendency to stick **:** ADHESION ⟨belting conveys the raw dough pieces without ~ —*Bakers Digest*⟩

stick-and-dirt *or* **stick-and-mud** \ˈ==ˌ=\ *adj* **:** made of sticks plastered with clay ⟨*stick-and-dirt* fireplace⟩ ⟨*stick-and-mud* chimneys, the type most often used —*Amer. Guide Series: Texas*⟩

stick and groove *n* **:** a primitive apparatus for kindling fire by friction consisting of a fire-plow and a hearth

stick around *vi* **:** to stay or wait about **:** remain nearby **:** LINGER ⟨was *sticking around* on the chance of being invited to come in⟩ ⟨somebody has to *stick around* and feed it —*New Yorker*⟩ ⟨*stick around* and you'll get your story —Mickey Spillane⟩

stick-at-it-ive \stiˈkad·əd·iv\ *adj* [fr. the phrase *stick at it* + *-ive*] **:** STICK-TO-ITIVE — **stick-at-itive·ness** *n* -ES

stick-at-nothing \ˈ==ˈ==\ *adj* [fr. the phrase *stick at nothing*] **:** that hesitates or scruples at nothing to achieve its purpose **:** DETERMINED, UNSCRUPULOUS ⟨underhand, *stick-at-nothing* brute —Joseph Conrad⟩ ⟨*stick-at-nothing* methods⟩

stick-back \ˈ=ˌ=\ *adj* [¹*stick* + *back*] **:** having a back with spindles driven into the seat and the top rail or bow ⟨Windsor chairs are *stick-back* chairs⟩ ⟨*stick-back* gig —*Amer. Guide Series: N.C.*⟩

stickball \ˈ=ˌ=\ *n* [¹*stick* + *ball*] **:** baseball adapted to playing in streets or small areas and using a broomstick and lightweight ball

stick bean *n* **:** POLE BEAN

stick bowling *n* **:** SKIDDLES

stick bug *n* **1 :** STICK INSECT **2 :** SPIDER BUG **3 :** STILT BUG

stick-button \ˈ=ˌ=\ *n* **:** a common burdock (*Arctium lappa*)

stick candy *n* **:** hard candy molded in the shape of sticks or rods

stick caterpillar *n* **:** any of numerous caterpillars (family Geometridae) that assume the form of a stick or position of a twig when at rest

stick chair *n* **:** SEDAN CHAIR

stick control *n* **:** CONTROL STICK

stick dance *n* **:** any of various dances esp. of western Europe and India in which sticks are beaten against each other by two partners or by the two hands of a dancer

stick-dice \ˈ=ˌ=\ *n* -s **:** a game played by No. American Indians in which variously marked sticks are thrown in the air and scores are settled by the values of the marks that are uppermost when the sticks fall — called also *stick game*

sticked *past of* STICK

¹stick·er \ˈstikə(r)\ *n* -s [⁵*stick* + *-er*] **1 :** one that pierces with a point: as **a** (1) **:** a slaughterhouse worker who sticks a knife into the neck of cattle, sheep, or hogs to sever the jugular vein — called also *bleeder* (2) **:** one that kills poultry by thrusting a knife through the roof of the mouth into the brain **b :** a weapon or implement for piercing as contrasted with slashing **c :** BRAMBLE, BUR, THORN **d :** a sharp projection on a shoe intended to give a racehorse better footing on a muddy track **e :** PINNER 2b **2 :** one that adheres or causes adhesion: as **a** (1) **:** one that sticks faithfully or unswervingly **:** one that remains constant ⟨was a stayer and a ~ —W.A.White⟩ (2) **:** one that persists (as in a task) or that shows powers of endurance ⟨both horse and rider were ~*s*⟩ (3) **:** STONEWALLER **b :** a commodity that does not sell rapidly **c :** an adhesive substance (as glue, casein, resin); *specif* **:** a substance added to a fungicide, insecticide, or other spray or dust to prevent removal of the active ingredients by weathering — compare SPREADER **1f d** (1) **:** a slip of paper with gummed back (as a gummed label, seal, stamp, or philatelist's stamp hinge) that when moistened adheres to a surface against which it is pressed (2) **:** a label bearing the name of an independent candidate in an election sometimes used to stick over a regular name in voting by printed ballot (3) **:** a summons for a parking violation stuck to a motor vehicle **3 :** something or someone puzzling **:** POSER **4 a :** BILLPOSTER **b :** a worker who sticks or pastes one thing into or onto another: as (1) **:** one that inserts extra sheets or sections in newspapers or unbound pamphlets (2) **:** one that repairs marble slabs by sticking them together with shellac (3) **:** one that prepares small pieces of fur for shearing **5 :** a woodworking machine for working rods, moldings, and beadings

²sticker \"\ *n* -s [¹*stick* + *-er*] **1 :** one that gathers sticks (as for fuel) **2 :** a wooden stick or strip placed between boards or plywood sheets stacked in piles to hasten drying and reduce warping — called also *crosser* **3 :** one that uses a stick (as in a game); *esp* **:** an athlete who handles his stick skillfully

sticker-up \ˈ==ˈ=\ *n* -s [*stick up* + *-er*] **1 :** one that finishes ware by sticking parts together **2** *chiefly Austral* **:** one that holds up another (as for robbery) **:** HIGHWAYMAN, BUSHRANGER **3** *Austral* **:** a primitive method of roasting meat on a wooden spit stuck in the ground and leaned over a fire

stick·ery \ˈstikərē\ *adj* [¹*sticker* + *-y*] **:** PRICKLY ⟨hay that he didn't remember as being so ~ —*Southern Lit. Messenger*⟩

stickfast \ˈ=ˌ=\ *n* -s [fr. the phrase *stick fast*] **1 :** one that sticks or causes to stick firmly **2 :** an act of sticking fast

stickfast flea *n, Austral* **:** STICKTIGHT FLEA

stick figure *also* **stick drawing** *n* **:** a drawing representing a human or animal pose by single lines for all parts but the head which is shown usu. as a circle; *esp* **:** such a drawing showing the position of the body members in a dance or sport action

stick figures

stick force *n* **:** the force exerted on the control column by the pilot of an airplane in flight

stick·ful \ˈstikˌful\ *n* -s **:** as much or as many as a stick will hold ⟨makes doughnuts and gives me a whole ~ —Helen Eustis⟩; *specif* **:** as much set type as fills a composing stick

stick game *n* **:** STICK-DICE

stick gig *n* **:** a lightweight two-wheeled carriage for one person

stick grenade *n* **:** a grenade with a handle **:** POTATO MASHER

stickhandle \ˈ=ˌ==\ *vi* [back-formation fr. *stickhandling*, fr. ¹*stick* + *handling*] **:** to maintain control of a puck (as in ice hockey) by clever and deceptive dribbling ⟨*stickhandled* across the ice and cut in from the other wing —H.W.Wind⟩

stick horse *n* **:** HOBBYHORSE 3a

stickied *past of* STICKY

stickier *comparative of* STICKY

stickies *pres 3d sing of* STICKY

stickiest *superlative of* STICKY

stick·i·ly \ˈstikəlē, -li\ *adv* **:** in a sticky manner ⟨~ hot⟩ ⟨squirming heap of maggots came ~ away —Kenneth Roberts⟩

stick-in \ˈ=ˌ=\ *n* -s [fr. *stick in*, v.] **:** STRANDER 2

stick·i·ness \ˈstikēnəs, -kin-\ *n* -ES **:** the quality or state of being sticky

¹stick·ing \ˈstikiŋ, -kēŋ\ *n* -s [ME *stikking*, fr. gerund of *stikken* to stick — more at STICK] **1 :** the action of piercing or stabbing ⟨helpless as calves tied up for ~ —F.V.W.Mason⟩ **2 a :** the action of adhering, holding fast, or holding back; *specif* **:** the action of stonewalling in cricket **b :** material that sticks or has stuck; *specif* **:** GOUGE 4 **c :** an increase in the water resistance at high speed that delays or prevents the take-off of a seaplane **3 :** a molded edge worked on the rails or stiles of a door around the panels or lights

²sticking \"\ *n* -s [¹*stick* + *-ing*] **1 :** sticks for use in supporting plants **2 :** the method or order employed in the use of drumsticks esp. in playing a snare drum

sticking knife *n* **:** a narrow-bladed knife used for killing animals (as poultry) by sticking

sticking-piece \ˈ==ˌ=\ *n, Brit* **:** a piece of beef cut from the lower part of the neck

sticking place *n* **1 :** the place where something stops and sticks fast ⟨screw your courage to the *sticking place* —Shak.⟩ **2 :** the place or point in the neck of an animal where the knife is stuck in slaughtering

sticking plaster *n* **:** an adhesive plaster for closing superficial wounds and similar uses

sticking point *n* **1 :** a place or position at which something sticks **:** STICKING PLACE ⟨go to war only when public opinion is aroused to the *sticking point* —T.K.Finletter⟩ **2 :** a particular (as an item in negotiations) resulting or likely to result in an impasse ⟨*sticking point* is the Soviet refusal to permit inspection of uranium deposits —*World Report*⟩

sticking salve *n* **:** a sticky salve (as for use on wounds)

sticking tommy *n* [*tommy* fr. the name *Tommy*] **:** a candlestick that is equipped with a sharp projecting point for sticking into a floor or wall

stick insect *n* **:** any of various insects of Phasmatidae and related families that are usu. wingless with a long round body sticklike in form and color and long legs often held rigidly in positions resembling twigs of the trees on which they live

stick-in-the-mud \ˈ===ˌ=\ *n* -s **:** one that is slow, dilatory, old-fashioned, or unprogressive; *esp* **:** one that is ultraconservative **:** an old fogy ⟨*stick-in-the-muds* who would live out their days in one town —T.W.Duncan⟩

stick·it \ˈstikət\ *adj* [fr. Sc past part. of ⁵*stick*, fr. ME *stikkyd*] **1** *Scot* **:** IMPERFECT, UNFINISHED ⟨a ~ job⟩ **2** *chiefly Scot* **:** having failed (as in one's intended profession) and given up ⟨a ~ minister⟩

stickjaw \ˈ=ˌ=\ *n* [⁵*stick* + *jaw*] **:** something (as candy or a pudding) that sticks the jaws together and is difficult to chew ⟨sticks of raspberry ~ —Ruth Park⟩

stick lac *n* **:** lac in its natural state that encrusts small twigs and the bodies of lac insects and is scraped off and dried in the shade to become the source of seed lac, lac dye, and shellac wax

¹stick·le \ˈstikəl\ *adj* [ME *stikell*, fr. OE *sticol;* akin to OS *stekul* stony, rough, OHG *stehhal* steep, OE *stician* to stick — more at STICK] **1** *dial Eng* **:** STEEP **2** *dial Eng* **:** moving rapidly ⟨a mile of water . . . bright with ~ runs —R.D.Blackmore⟩

²stickle \"\ *n* -s **1** *dial chiefly Brit* **:** a rapid in a small stream ⟨the little runs and ~*s* —John Buchan⟩ **2** *chiefly Brit* **:** a line of persons placed across a shallow in a stream to prevent passage of an otter into water where it cannot be hunted

³stickle \"\ *vi* **stickled; stickled; stickling** \-k(ə)liŋ\ **stickles** [ME *stightlen, stiglen,* freq. of *stighten* to arrange, place, fr. OE *stihtan, stihtian* to rule, arrange, order; akin to ON *stētta* to support, establish, *stētt* pavement, stepping-stone, degree, rank, *stiga* to climb — more at STAIR] **1** *obs* **:** to separate combatants by intervening **:** act as umpire or mediator **2** *obs* **:** to participate actively **3 :** to contend or hold out esp. pertinaciously and usu. on finical or insufficient grounds **4 :** to feel hesitation or scruples **:** SCRUPLE **syn** see DEMUR

⁴stickle \"\ *n* -s **:** AGITATION, PERTURBATION **:** BEWILDERMENT, PERPLEXITY

stickleaf \ˈ=ˌ=\ *n* [⁵*stick* + *leaf*] **:** any of several rough-leaved herbs of the genus *Mentzelia*

stick·le·back \ˈstikəlˌbak\ *n* [ME *stykylbak*, fr. *stykyl-* (fr. OE *sticel* prick, goad, thorn) + *bak* back; akin to MLG *stekel, stickel* goad, thorn, OHG *stihhil* goad, thorn, ON *stikill* point of a drinking horn, Goth *stikls* drinking vessel (prob. orig. pointed at the bottom), OE *stician* to stick — more at STICK, BACK] **1 :** any of numerous small fishes of the family Gasterosteidae that have two or more free spines in front of the dorsal fin and the ventral fins each reduced to one spine and a small ray, that are scaleless but often have the sides protected by bony plates, that occur in the northern hemisphere in brackish or fresh water or in the sea and are noted for their activity and vigor and for the curious nests which the males construct and guard during the breeding season, and that include the nine-spined stickleback and the two-spined or three-spined stickleback of both Europe and America and the fifteen-spined stickleback of Europe only as well-known forms **2 :** a cleavers (*Galium aparine*)

stick-leg \ˈ=ˌ=\ *adj* **:** having legs like sticks — used of a chair

stick·ler \ˈstik(ə)lə(r)\ *n* -s [³*stickle* + *-er*] **1 :** one that stickles: as **a** (1) *chiefly dial* **:** an umpire in a tournament or other test of strength or skill (2) *obs* **:** one that intervenes in a dispute **:** MEDIATOR **b** *obs* **:** one that participates actively or is an active partisan; *also* **:** MEDDLER **c** (1) *archaic* **:** one that opposes or raises objections — usu. used with *against* (2) **:** one that contends persistently and unyieldingly for something often of trifling importance (as a point of etiquette, a formality) — usu. used with *for* ⟨a ~ for formal clothes at formal functions —E.T.Hellman⟩ ⟨is no ~ for the more rigid military courtesies —Ed Cunningham⟩ ⟨a ~ for dignity —*Newsweek*⟩ **d** *archaic* **:** a backer in a contest **:** SECOND **2 :** something (as a problem, a question) that baffles or puzzles **:** POSER, STICKER ⟨not hard to diagnose. It's the cure that's the ~ —*Los Angeles (Calif.) Examiner*⟩

stick·less \ˈstikləs\ *adj* **:** having no stick

sticklike \ˈ=ˌ=\ *adj* **:** resembling a stick

stick·ling \ˈstikliŋ\ *n* -s [ME *stikeling*; akin to MLG *stekelink*, MD *stekelinc*, OHG *stichelinc;* all fr. a prehistoric WGmc compound whose 1st constituent is represented by OE *sticel* prick, goad, thorn, and whose 2d constituent is represented by E *-ing* — more at STICKLEBACK] **:** STICKLEBACK

stickly *adj* [⁵*stick* + *-ly*] *chiefly Scot* **:** PRICKLY, ROUGH

stick·man \ˈstikˌman, -ˌmaa(ə)n, -ˌmən\ *n, pl* **stickmen** [¹*stick* + *man*] **1 :** one that handles a stick: as **a :** one that supervises the play at a dice table, calls the decisions, and retrieves the dice — called also *dealer* **b :** a player in any of various games played with a stick; *esp* **:** a lacrosse player **c** (1) **:** a worker who moves hogsheads of tobacco by means of a heavy curved stick or an iron bar — called also *hooker-out* (2) **:** a steelworker who moves bars or sheets with hand tongs **d :** CONDUCTOR 6 ⟨the superb ~ — the specialist in baton technique —*Newsweek*⟩ **2 :** STICK FIGURE

stick off *vb, obs* **:** to show to advantage

stick on *vi* **:** to hold fast **:** keep one's place (as on the back of a horse) **:** stay on ⟨was not a good rider but managed to *stick on*⟩

stick out *vi* **1 a :** to jut out **:** PROJECT, PROTRUDE **b :** to be prominent or conspicuous ⟨their writers' prejudices would often *stick out* —Curtis Brown⟩ ⟨antibourgeois notions of the analysts *stick out* all over —C.J.Friedrich⟩ **2 a :** to hold out **:** be persistent (as in a demand or an opinion) **:** refuse to come to agreement or make a settlement ⟨were *sticking out* for a higher price⟩ ⟨*stuck out* for absolute domination —V.S. Pritchett⟩ ⟨a last ditcher, *sticking out* for the rigor of the law —D.B.W.Lewis⟩ **b** *of workmen* **:** STRIKE **~** *vt* **1 :** to endure (as something specified or conditions in general) or see through to the end ⟨*stuck* the first term *out* and then left⟩ ⟨*stuck out* the icy currents —*Newsweek*⟩ ⟨determined to *stick out* a California sojourn —R.G.Hubler⟩ — often used with *it* ⟨*stuck it out*, living on lemonade, glucose tablets and nerves —*Holiday*⟩ ⟨the people *sticking it out* where the dust is thickest and the gulches driest —Russell Lord⟩ ⟨too late now to do anything but *stick it out*⟩ **2 :** to maintain against a person ⟨*stuck* me *out* that . . . it was one of the six best comedies in English —Arnold Bennett⟩ **syn** see BULGE

1stick-out \ˈ⸗,⸗\ *n* -s [*stick out*] **1 :** an act or fact of sticking out; *specif* **:** STRIKE 7a **2 :** one that sticks out

2stick-out \"\ *adj* [*stick out*]**:** sticking out; *esp* **:** PROTUBERANT, PROMINENT

stickpin \ˈ⸗,⸗\ *n* [5*stick* + *pin*] **:** TIEPIN

stick rider *n* **:** a skier who makes excessive use of ski poles

sticks *pl of* STICK, *pres 3d sing of* STICK

stick salve *n* [5*stick*] **:** STICKING SALVE

stickseed \ˈ⸗,⸗\ *n* [5*stick* + *seed*] **:** a plant of the genus *Lappula* characterized by its bristly fruit

sticktail \ˈ⸗,⸗\ *n* [1*stick* + *tail*] **:** RUDDY DUCK

sticktight \ˈ⸗,⸗\ *n* -s [fr. the phrase *stick tight*] **:** one that sticks or adheres closely: as **a :** BUR MARIGOLD **b :** STICKSEED

sticktight flea *n* **:** a tropical flea (*Echidnophaga gallinacea*) that is parasitic esp. on the heads of chickens and is a pest in the southern U.S.

stick-to-it·ive·ness \stikˈtüəd·|ivnəs, ə-t|\ *n* -ES [fr. the phrase *stick to it* + *-ive* + *-ness*] **:** dogged perseverance **:** RESOLUTENESS, TENACITY ⟨has drifted from job to job . . . and lacks *stick-to-itiveness* —Kendall Banning⟩ ⟨not so much a test of marriage as a test of *stick-to-itiveness* —Lewis Nichols⟩

stick·um \ˈstikəm\ *n* -s [5*stick* + *-um* (prob. alter. of *'em*)] **:** something that adheres or causes adhesion **:** a substance that sticks, sticks down, or sticks together ⟨a new ~ for his postage stamps —Bill Hatch⟩

stick up *vi* **:** to stand out from a surface **:** stand upright or on end **:** PROJECT ⟨grain of the wood tends to *stick up*⟩ ⟨a few pilings of an old wharf were still *sticking up* in the water⟩ ~ *vt* **1 a :** to hold up (as at the point of a gun) in order to rob ⟨*stick* a stagecoach *up*⟩; *also* **:** to enter and rob ⟨*stick up* a gas station⟩ ⟨had *stuck* several banks *up*⟩ **b :** to accost for money **:** solicit money from ⟨*stuck* him *up* for the community chest⟩ **2 :** to cook on a spit **3 a :** to finish (as raw clayware) by smoothing — compare FETTLE **b :** to attach (partly formed glass) to a hot iron rod or clamping tool for reheating — **stick up for :** to speak or act in defense of **:** stand up for **:** DEFEND, SUPPORT ⟨afraid to *stick up for* his own beliefs —Virginia Woolf⟩ ⟨haven't got a soul to *stick up for* me —Dorothy Sayers⟩ — **stick up to 1 :** to offer resistance to **:** stand up to ⟨*stick up to* a bully⟩ **2** *dial Brit* **:** 2COURT 2a

1stickup \ˈ⸗,⸗\ *n* -s [*stick up*] **1 :** something that sticks up: as **a :** a stand-up collar **b :** COCKUP 2 **2 :** HOLDUP, ROBBERY ⟨a national wave of ~*s* —*Argosy*⟩ ⟨a grab-and-run ~ in a bank —Alan Hynd⟩ **3 :** graphic material (as lettering) that is pasted on a sheet usu. containing other printed matter; *also* **:** a process using such pasted matter ⟨a map with place-names added by ~⟩

2stickup \ˈ⸗,⸗\ *adj* [*stick up*] **1 :** that projects upward or stands up stiffly ⟨~ collar⟩ ⟨hat with ~ trimming of feathers⟩; *specif* **:** COCKUP 1 **2 :** pasted on or prepared for pasting on ⟨~ lettering⟩

stickup man *also* **stickup** *n* -s **:** HOLDUP MAN

stick vat *n* **:** a tanning vat in which skins are suspended from wooden sticks

stickwater \ˈ⸗,⸗⸗\ *n* [5*stick* + *water*] **:** a viscous quickly decomposing and evil-smelling liquor that is obtained as a by-product in the wet process of manufacturing fish meal and fish oil by cooking the fish with steam and pressing and that is often concentrated by evaporation for use in animal feeds as a source of vitamins and amino acids

stickweed \ˈ⸗,⸗\ *n* [5*stick* + *weed*] **:** any of several plants having seeds that cling to wool or clothing: as **a :** RAGWEED 2a **b :** AGRIMONY **c :** a beggar's-lice (*Lappula virginica*) **d :** GUM SUCCORY

stickwork \ˈ⸗,⸗\ *n* [1*stick* + *work*] **1 :** the use and management of one's stick in offensive and defensive techniques (as in lacrosse, polo, hockey) **2 :** batting ability in baseball

stickwort \ˈ⸗,⸗\ *n* [5*stick* + *wort*] **:** AGRIMONY

1sticky \ˈstikē, -ki\ *adj* -ER/-EST [1*stick* + *-y*] **1 :** resembling a stick **:** WOODY **2 :** *of a person* **:** somewhat wooden **:** lacking animation

2sticky \"\ *adj* -ER/-EST [5*stick* + *-y*] **1 :** having the quality of adhering or of holding or retarding by or as if by adhesion **:** ADHESIVE ⟨stepped in something ~⟩ ⟨road was very ~ after the rain⟩ ⟨quaking and ~ area . . . has been a deathtrap for unwary animals —*Amer. Guide Series: Calif.*⟩: as **a** (1) *of a substance* **:** GLUEY, GLUTINOUS, VISCID, VISCOUS ⟨~ syrup⟩ ⟨paint was still ~⟩ ⟨wad of ~ chewing gum⟩ ⟨black ~ mud⟩ (2) **:** smeared or coated with a sticky substance ⟨table was ~⟩ ⟨wall had been painted and was still ~⟩ ⟨~ cinnamon buns⟩ ⟨how she ever got her face so ~⟩ **b** *of a turf wicket in cricket* **:** having a surface that is temporarily tacky or viscid from drying in the sun after being soaked with rain and that heavily favors spin bowlers **c** *of snow* **:** just beginning to melt **2 :** HUMID, MUGGY ⟨a ~ day⟩ ⟨a hot and ~ hour or two on shore —W.H.Ingrams⟩ **:** moist with perspiration with the clothing sticking to the body **:** CLAMMY, MESSY **3 :** offering or tending to offer resistance: as **a** *of a horse* **:** apt to hesitate at a fence or to jump from a standstill or a trot **b :** apt to impede or be impeded in movement or progress (as by wedging or blocking) ⟨~ windows⟩ ⟨~ valves⟩ ⟨found that control movement . . . was not ~, like many, but free and smooth —*Skyways*⟩ **c** (1) **:** resistant to change **:** not moving **:** RIGID ⟨~ prices⟩ ⟨consumer habits are probably more ~ than variations in the level of income are —H.W.Grayson⟩ ⟨labor supply is ~, perverse, and often unpredictable —L.R.Tripp⟩ (2) **:** hard to sell ⟨reported that television sets had become ~⟩ **:** difficult to secure payment on when due ⟨~ accounts receivable⟩ ⟨~ bank loans⟩ **d** (1) **:** inclined to make difficulties **:** hard to please **:** BALKY, FUSSY, METICULOUS, PARTICULAR ⟨tickets are available if you are not ~ about a special day —*Saturday Rev.*⟩ ⟨ought to be satisfactory to the *stickiest* State Department jurist —V.M.Fry⟩ (2) **:** DIFFICULT, TROUBLESOME ⟨a ~ question⟩ ⟨~ problems⟩ ⟨found the going ~⟩ ⟨the *stickiest* part of the whole operation —*New Yorker*⟩ **4 a :** DISAGREEABLE, PAINFUL, UNPLEASANT ⟨a rather ~ past she wanted to hide —J.B.Priestley⟩ ⟨seemed likely to come to a ~ end⟩ **b :** AWKWARD, STIFF, UNCOMFORTABLE ⟨after a rather ~ beginning became firm friends⟩ ⟨scarcely knew each other, and the talk was decidedly ~ —E.M.Forster⟩ ⟨when royalty is in the audience, things are generally very ~ —*New Yorker*⟩ **5 :** suggestive of a viscid substance or mass (as in lacking strength, solidity, or substance); *esp* **:** characterized by sentimentality **:** SACCHARINE, SLUSHY ⟨a ~ adagio —Wilder Hobson⟩ ⟨a long ~ death scene —*Time*⟩ ⟨a score as ~ as treacle —John McCarten⟩ ⟨invest childhood with a ~ but romantic gloss —Osbert Sitwell⟩

3sticky \"\ *vt* -ED/-ING/-ES **:** to make sticky ⟨children were *stickied* up with popcorn and lollipops and ice cream⟩

stickybeak \ˈ⸗⸗,⸗\ *n* [2*sticky* + *beak*] *Austral* **:** an inquisitive person **:** BUSYBODY

sticky bomb *or* **sticky charge** *or* **sticky grenade** *n* **:** an explosive charge covered with an adhesive that when thrown against an object (as an armored vehicle) sticks until it explodes

sticky cockle *n* **:** NIGHT-FLOWERING CATCHFLY

sticky currant *n* **:** a leafy shrub (*Ribes viscosissimum*) of the western U.S. having black fruit and glandular hispid petioles and branchlets

sticky dog *n, cricket* **:** a wicket that has become sticky

sticky-fingered *also* **sticky-handed** \¦⸗⸗¦⸗⸗\ *adj* **:** given to stealing **:** apt to steal **:** LARCENOUS, THIEVING, THIEVISH

sticky-heads \ˈ⸗⸗,⸗\ *n pl but sing or pl in constr* **:** GUMWEED

sticky laurel *n* **:** a buckbrush (*Ceanothus velutinus*) with gummy twigs and evergreen leaves

stic·ta \ˈstiktə\ *n, cap* [NL, fr. Gk *stiktē*, fem. of *stiktos* tattooed, spotted, fr. *stizein* to tattoo — more at STICK] **:** a large genus (the type of the family Stictaceae) of mainly tropical lichens having a foliaceous lobed thallus that is commonly coriaceous in texture

stic·ta·ce·ae \stikˈtāsē,ē\ *n pl, cap* [NL, fr. *Sticta*, type genus + *-aceae*] **:** a family of common foliaceous lichens comprising the two genera *Lobaria* and *Sticta*

stic·ti·form \ˈstiktə,fȯrm\ *adj* [NL *Sticta* + E *-iform*] **:** resembling in form a lichen of the genus *Sticta*

stic·tis \ˈstiktəs\ *n, cap* [NL, irreg. fr. Gk *stiktos* tattooed, spotted] **:** a genus (the type of the family Stictidaceae) of fungi characterized by sunken pilose perithecia and filiform many-septate hyaline ascospores

stid·dy \ˈstidi\ *dial Brit var of* STITHY

stie *obs var of* STY

stied *past of* STY

stie·gel glass \ˈstēgəl-\ *n, usu cap S* [after Henry William *Stiegel* †1785 Am. glassmaker] **1 :** a late eighteenth century American flint or green glassware made in Pennsylvania; *esp* **:** fine flint glassware with engraved or enameled decoration **2 :** bubbly green glassware resembling some of the eighteenth century Stiegel glasswares

stieng \ˈstēŋ\ *n, pl* **stieng** *or* **stiengs** *usu cap* **1 :** a people related to the Cambodians and inhabiting Thudaumot province of So. Vietnam **2 :** a member of the Stieng people

sties *pres 3d sing of* STY, *pl of* STY

stieve *chiefly Scot var of* 1STEEVE

stife \ˈstīf\ *n* [perh. irreg. fr. 3*stifle*] *dial Brit* **:** a stifling fume or smell

1stiff \ˈstif\ *adj* -ER/-EST [ME *stif*, fr. OE *stīf;* akin to MD *stijf* stiff, MLG *stīf* stiff, ON *stīfla* to dam up, L *stipare* to press together, Gk *steibein* to tread on, Lith *stìpti* to be stiff, Russ *stebel'* stalk] **1 a :** incapable of or resistant to being flexed or bent **:** RIGID ⟨wears a ~ collar⟩ ⟨sitting . . . on the edge of a ~ chair —Scott Fitzgerald⟩ ⟨a palace guardsman, ~ as a poker in his tall busby, stands sentinel⟩ ⟨knots in the gaskets were ~ with frost —C.B.Nordhoff & J.N.Hall⟩ **b :** exhibiting rigor mortis ⟨still unburied, lay . . . ~ and stark —R.L.Stevenson⟩ **c :** lacking in suppleness — used esp. of the muscles and joints ⟨my body was ~ from exertion as well as from cold —Jack London⟩ ⟨tried to smile . . . but her face felt ~ —Margaret Deland⟩ **d** *obs* **:** tightly stretched **:** TAUT ⟨another arrow forth from his ~ string he sent —George Chapman⟩ **e :** impeded in movement (as by friction) — used of a mechanism ⟨clocks whose mannikins went through . . . ~ and elegant movements —Lewis Mumford⟩ **f :** slowed or immobilized by intoxication **:** DRUNK ⟨after drinking . . . in that bar for two hours, I was pretty ~ —W.R.Hecox⟩ **2 a :** characterized by moral courage **:** FIRM, RESOLUTE ⟨has taken a ~ position that it has the power to forbid its contractors to bargain with unions —R.S.Brown⟩ ⟨kept a ~ upper lip for the term of his ordeal —Bruce Dearing⟩ **b :** characterized by obstinacy **:** STUBBORN, UNYIELDING ⟨took a rather ~ . . . stand in defense of his handiwork —Dexter Perkins⟩ **c :** characterized by independence or self-esteem **:** PROUD ⟨passeth by with ~ unbowed knee —Shak.⟩ ⟨too poor to go and too ~ to tell her the reason —*Time*⟩ **d** (1) **:** marked by reserve, decorum, or respect for ceremony **:** FORMAL, PUNCTILIOUS ⟨the easy warmth you knew has given place to a ~ courtesy —H.J.Laski⟩ ⟨brought his hand . . . to the visor of his cap in a ~ salute —Wirt Williams⟩ (2) **:** lacking in ease or grace **:** STILTED, UNBENDING ⟨a style which is lofty but not ~ —C.D.Lewis⟩ ⟨too arid and ~ a melody for song —M.F. Bukofger⟩ **3 :** hard fought **:** PUGNACIOUS, SHARP ⟨salmon give a ~ fight until landed —*Amer. Guide Series: Maine*⟩ ⟨she had driven a ~ bargain —Ann F. Wolfe⟩ ⟨heading into a year of ~ competition —Herbert Koshetz⟩ **4 a** *obs* **:** solidly constructed **:** STURDY, STALWART ⟨make you ready your ~ bats and clubs —Shak.⟩ **b** (1) **:** exerting great force **:** STRONG, VIOLENT ⟨a ~ west wind was whooping in off the prairies —F.B.Gipson⟩ (2) **:** of an energetic or powerful nature **:** FORCEFUL, VIGOROUS ⟨follow . . . on a ~ lope —Bruce Siberts⟩ ⟨landed . . . a ~ left to the head —*Ring*⟩ **c :** containing a relatively large amount of the main ingredient (as alcohol or a medicine) **:** POTENT ⟨a couple of ~ cocktails relaxed him completely⟩ ⟨a ~ dose of cod liver oil⟩ **5 a :** of a dense or glutinous consistency **:** THICK, VISCOUS ⟨the concrete is allowed to stand until it is quite ~ but still workable —*Building Estimating & Contracting*⟩ ⟨a ~ grease that does a good job of protecting metal —*Monsanto Mag.*⟩ ⟨beat the egg whites until ~ —Ruth Hutchison⟩ **b :** consisting of or abounding in clay **:** HEAVY ⟨soils . . . that are wet and ~ —F.D.Smith & Barbara Wilcox⟩ **c :** thickly covered or completely filled **:** CROWDED, PERVADED ⟨an audience ~ with academic dignitaries —Mollie Panter-Downes⟩ ⟨something in the air, intangible, yet ~ with meaning, struck my senses —Edna S. V. Millay⟩ **6 a :** harsh or disagreeable in character **:** SEVERE, TOUGH ⟨get a ~ fine for disorderly conduct —S.H.Holbrook⟩ ⟨Nicaragua objected and ~ notes were exchanged —*Newsweek*⟩ **b :** demanding physical exertion **:** ARDUOUS, RUGGED ⟨~ terrain⟩ ⟨a ~ . . . hike up the trail, among jagged boulders and through crevasses —*Amer. Guide Series: Ark.*⟩ ⟨leading an orchestra is ~ work —Robert Rice⟩ **c :** requiring strenuous mental effort **:** DIFFICULT, EXACTING ⟨the examination was so ~ that none below the highest grades of university honors men . . . could hope to be selected —W.T.Stace⟩ ⟨the casual reader will find certain parts of this book ~ going —Ralph Linton⟩ **7 :** inherently stable **:** not easily heeled over by an external force (as the wind) **:** righting itself quickly when tipped — used of a ship; compare 9CRANK, STEADY 1c **8 a :** excessive in amount **:** EXPENSIVE, STEEP ⟨the rent is a ~ $500 a week —Henry Hewes⟩ ⟨satellite goods paid a ~ duty to enter France —Stringfellow Barr⟩ **b :** maintaining a high level **:** tending to rise **:** BULLISH, UNYIELDING ⟨a ~ market⟩ ⟨buyers . . . find sellers ~ —*London Daily News*⟩ **9 :** UNGUARDED — used in a card game of a high honor that is a singleton

syn STIFF, RIGID, INFLEXIBLE, TENSE, STARK, and WOODEN can mean, in common, so firm or hard as to be difficult or impossible to bend literally or figuratively. STIFF, the most common, can apply to any degree of this condition or to something difficult to work or beat ⟨a *stiff* rod⟩ ⟨a book with *stiff* covers⟩ ⟨hinges that are a bit *stiff*⟩ ⟨a *stiff* pudding⟩ ⟨a *stiff* smile⟩ ⟨to stand straight and *stiff*⟩ RIGID applies to anything so stiff that bending will break it ⟨a *rigid* board⟩ ⟨the *rigid* wings of a plane⟩ INFLEXIBLE is like RIGID but stresses more the lack of suppleness or pliability ⟨an *inflexible* plastic material⟩ ⟨an *inflexible* shaft on a golf club⟩ TENSE, implying tautness, usu. applies to muscles or nerves strained in expectation of activity or by nervous excitement ⟨with muscles *tense* in position to spring⟩ ⟨nerves *tense* with anxiety⟩ STARK implies a stiffness associated with loss of life, warmth, and vitality, often connoting desolation, barrenness, or death ⟨told her once that cut flowers before they actually die . . . stretch themselves out with a palpable jerk, *stark* and rigid —J.C.Powys⟩ ⟨here all the surfaces remained *stark* and unyielding, thin and sharp, like impoverished old maids —George Santayana⟩ ⟨rats . . . danced comically before they died, and lay in the scuppers *stark* and ruffled —Sinclair Lewis⟩ WOODEN, in this application suggesting the hardness and lack of suppleness of wood, implies clumsiness, deadness or heaviness of spirit, or lack of grace or animation ⟨a face that was *wooden* with misery —Rebecca West⟩ ⟨*wooden* humorlessness —*Times Lit. Supp.*⟩ ⟨the *wooden* neatness of routine and failure —Howard Moss⟩

2stiff \"\ *adv, often* -ER/-EST [ME *stif*, fr. *stif*, adj.] **1 :** STIFFLY ⟨stood up straight and ~ —R.L.Stevenson⟩ ⟨wears a uniform that is starched ~⟩ **2 :** to an extreme degree **:** INTENSELY, SEVERELY ⟨bored ~⟩ ⟨scared ~⟩ ⟨advanced into the doctor's consulting room . . . was frightened ~ —Mary McCarthy⟩

3stiff \"\ *vt* -ED/-ING/-S [ME *stiffen*, fr. *stif*, adj.] **1 :** STIFFEN; *esp* **:** to remove the oil in (a French finish) with a rubber **2** *slang* **:** to withhold money from **:** CHEAT, CHISEL; *esp* **:** to refrain from tipping ⟨cabdrivers often get ~*ed*⟩

4stiff \"\ *n* -s [1*stiff*] **1 :** one that is stiff: as **a :** a stiffened article of clothing (as a collar or a petticoat) **b** *slang* (1) **:** negotiable paper **:** MONEY (2) **:** counterfeit bills or a forged check (3) **:** a letter, card, or legal document (as a certificate or license); *esp* **:** a note smuggled between prison inmates (4) **:** something (as a folded newspaper) used by a pickpocket to hide his maneuvers **c** (1) **:** CORPSE, CADAVER (2) **:** a haughty, prim, or boring person (3) **:** DRUNK (4) *slang* **:** CHEAP SKATE, TIGHTWAD; *esp* **:** one who tips poorly or not at all **2 a :** a crude or disreputable fellow **:** BUM, TRAMP ⟨looked like a mission ~ who had wandered uptown from the Bowery —Joel Sayre⟩ ⟨got the breaks, the lucky ~*s* —Jan Peerce⟩ **b :** a blue-collar worker **:** LABORER, HAND ⟨of first importance to every working ~, farmer and businessman in America —E.A.Lahey⟩ ⟨knew enough about the business to hire on as a construction ~ —*Time*⟩; *esp* **:** FLOATER 4 **3 :** a horse not intended to win or certain not to win a race ⟨no way even of knowing if his horse is trying to win or is a ~ just sent out for the exercise —Ernest Havemann⟩ **syn** see VAGABOND

stiff *abbr* stiffener

1stiff-arm \ˈ⸗¦⸗\ *vb* [fr. the noun phrase *stiff arm*, fr. 1*stiff* + *arm*, n.] **:** STRAIGHT-ARM

2stiff-arm \"\ *n* **:** STRAIGHT-ARM

stiff aster *n* **:** a wiry tufted perennial herb (*Aster linariifolia*) of the eastern U. S. with stiff erect rough stems, linear leaves, and large heads of violet flowers terminating the branchlets

stiff-backed \ˈ⸗¦⸗\ *adj* **1 :** rigidly erect ⟨a *stiff-backed* sergeant⟩ **2 :** punctiliously correct **:** HAUGHTY, UNBENDING ⟨a *stiff-backed* aristocrat⟩ ⟨*stiff-backed* Boston⟩

stiff·en \ˈstifən *also* -fᵊm\ *vb* **stiffened; stiffened; stiffening** \-f(ə)niŋ\ **stiffens** [ME *stiffnen*, fr. *stif*, adj., stiff + *-nen* -en] *vt* **1 a** (1) **:** to make stronger or more resolute **:** BOLSTER, SUPPORT ⟨busy . . . reordering his ship, and ~*ing* the morale of his crew —Llewellyn Howland⟩ ⟨felt the honor of the whole army rising within me and ~*ing* my backbone —R.H. Davis⟩ ⟨his papers are ~*ed* with solid facts and a scholar's indignation —E.A.Weeks⟩ (2) **:** to make tougher or more effective ⟨~ the armies . . . with an increasing leaven of mercenaries —J.E.M.White⟩ ⟨recommended ~*ing* the Refugee Relief Act —Dorothy Kahn⟩ (3) **:** to make more obstinate or intransigent ⟨a powerful will ~*ed* by many years of opposition —Helen Macafee⟩ **b** (1) **:** to make tight or hard **:** reduce in resilience **:** TAUTEN, IMMOBILIZE ⟨his sinews ~*ed* themselves in tense readiness —C.G.D.Roberts⟩ ⟨he was ~*ed* straight by back trouble —A.C.Spectorsky⟩; *specif* **:** to knock out (a boxing opponent) ⟨~*ed* the . . . fighter in the first round —*Irish Digest*⟩ (2) **:** BENUMB ⟨spent his evenings ~*ing* himself with gin —V.S.Pritchett⟩ **c :** to make more stilted or inflexible **:** CONSTRICT, FORMALIZE ⟨poetic diction that has ~*ed* into corpses so many orthodox poetic dramas —Leslie Rees⟩ ⟨~*ed* one of the most picturesque of human beings . . . into a stock figure —Carl Van Doren⟩ **2 a :** to make denser or firmer **:** THICKEN, SOLIDIFY ⟨milk well ~*ed* with wheaten flour —G.E.Fussell⟩ ⟨phosphorus ~*s* and strengthens wire —*Monsanto Mag.*⟩; *specif* **:** to reinforce (as an article of clothing) by stitching, sizing, interfacing, interlining, wiring ⟨drapery ~*ed* with stiff starch —F.J.Mather⟩ ⟨hat brims are ~*ed* to hold their shape⟩ **b :** to alter the structure or ballast of (a ship) to prevent excessive heeling **:** STABILIZE **c :** to increase the ratio of inductance to capacity in (an electric circuit) **3 :** to cause to rise or be increased **:** fix at a high level ⟨~ prices⟩ ⟨~ the market⟩ ⟨a definite trend toward ~*ing* of money rates —*Wall Street Jour.*⟩ ~ *vi* **1 a :** THICKEN, HARDEN ⟨mud ~*s* as it dries⟩ **b :** to become physically taut or mentally inflexible ⟨~*ed* in her saddle and tossed her head —T.B.Costain⟩ ⟨my resolve to stick it out ~*ed* —V.G.Heiser⟩ ⟨young feelings ~ in senile works —Malcolm Cowley⟩ **2 :** to increase in strength or difficulty ⟨a ~*ing* breeze⟩ ⟨the climb ~*s* as we near the top⟩ **3 :** to become firmer ⟨stock prices ~*ed* in the final few hours of trading⟩

stiff·en·er \-f(ə)nə(r)\ *n* -s **:** one that stiffens: as **a :** a worker who sizes hats **b :** something (as buckram or a piece of paperboard) used for stiffening a manufactured article; *specif* **:** 5COUNTER 5 **c :** any of a number of vertical angles secured at intervals across the entire width of the web of a large plate girder to prevent buckling **d :** an angle iron, channel, or other structural shape used to increase the rigidity of plating on a ship's bulkhead — called also *stiffening bar* **e :** a structural member other than a flat sheet used to reinforce the frame of an aircraft — compare STRINGER **f :** an alcoholic bracer

1stiffening *n* -s [fr. gerund of *stiffen*] **1 :** the act or process of making or becoming stiff **2 :** STIFFENER

2stiffening *adj* [fr. pres. part. of *stiffen*] **:** making or becoming stiff ⟨a ~ truss for the floor of a suspension bridge⟩ ⟨the days of a ~ cold war —G.E.G.Catlin⟩

stiffening bar *n* **:** STIFFENER d

stiffer *comparative of* STIFF

stiffest *superlative of* STIFF

stiff gentian *n* **:** FIVE-FLOWERED GENTIAN

stiffing *pres part of* STIFF

stiff·ish \ˈstifish\ *adj* **:** moderately stiff: as **a :** fairly rigid or inflexible ⟨the zinnia is a ~ flower⟩ **b :** rather strong ⟨a ~ wind⟩ **c :** tending toward constraint or formality ⟨a ~ diplomatic dinner⟩ ⟨grand old lady, ~, but imposing —O.W. Holmes †1894⟩ **d :** pretty high **:** STEEP ⟨demanded a ~ advance —Burns Mantle⟩

stiff-lamb disease *or* **stiff lamb** *n* **1 :** a deficiency disease of lambs marked by muscular degeneration, difficulty in standing and walking, and general weakness and prostration and thought to be due to inadequate intake of vitamin E **2 :** a condition of young lambs marked by stiffness or lameness

stiffleg derrick \ˈ⸗,⸗-\ *or* **stiffleg** *n* **:** a derrick whose framework rests on a fixed tripod of poles or timbers

stiff·ly *adv* [ME *stifly*, fr. *stif*, adj., stiff + *-ly*] **1 :** in a stiff manner **2 :** to an advanced degree of stiffness

stiff-mud process *n* **:** a brickmaking process in which a stiff mixture of water and clay is extruded in a continuous column through a die and individual bricks are cut by wires from the column as it emerges — compare SOFT-MUD PROCESS

stiff neck *n* **1 a :** fibrositis of the neck muscles **b :** TORTICOLLIS **2 a :** a proud or stubborn person **:** one with a haughty bearing **b :** OBSTINACY ⟨I know thy rebellion and thy *stiff neck* —Deut 31:27 (AV)⟩

stiff-necked \ˈ⸗¦⸗\ *adj* [trans. of Gk *sklērotrachēlos*] **1 :** characterized by arrogance or obstinacy **:** HAUGHTY, STUBBORN ⟨a *stiff-necked* aristocrat⟩ ⟨*stiff-necked* pride⟩ **2 :** STILTED ⟨it is not *stiff-necked* . . . and at its best comes over with simple, unaffected power —*Times Lit. Supp.*⟩ **syn** see OBSTINATE

stiff-necked·ly \ˈ⸗¦nekədlē, -ktlē\ *adv* **:** in a stiff-necked manner

stiff-necked·ness \-kədnəs, -ktn-\ *n* -ES **:** the quality or state of being stiff-necked **:** PRIDE, OBSTINACY

stiff·ness *n* -ES [ME *stifnesse*, fr. *stif*, adj., stiff + *-nesse* -ness] **1 a :** DENSITY, RIGIDITY ⟨14 kinds of varnish each differing in ~ —F.W.Hoch⟩ ⟨toothbrushes vary in the ~ of their bristles⟩ **b :** resistance (as of a structural beam) to bending under stresses within the elastic limit — opposed to *compliance;* compare DEFLECTION 3a **c :** resistance of a ship to rolling **:** STABILITY **2 a :** lack of suppleness **:** INFLEXIBILITY ⟨pains in the limbs and growing ~, finally, paralysis —*Monsanto Mag.*⟩ **b :** firmness of attitude **:** RESOLUTION, OBDURACY ⟨unyielding ~ of will —O.J.Baab⟩ **c :** lack of ease or grace **:** punctilious conduct **:** FORMALITY, CONSTRAINT ⟨the ~ of conventional opera —Arthur Knight⟩ ⟨had given up his ~ and begun to laugh —Vicki Baum⟩

stiffs *pl of* STIFF, *pres 3d sing of* STIFF

stifftail \ˈ⸗,⸗\ *n* **:** RUDDY DUCK

stiff upper lip *n* **:** a determined attitude or effort in the face of trouble — usu. used in the phrase *keep a stiff upper lip*

1sti·fle \ˈstīfəl\ *also* **stifle joint** *n* -s [ME *stifle*] **:** the joint next above the hock and near the flank in the hind leg of various quadrupeds (as horses and dogs) **:** the joint corresponding to the knee in man — see HORSE illustration

2stifle \"\ *vt* -ED/-ING/-S **:** to affect with dislocation of the stifle bone or disease in the stifle — usu. used in passive

3stifle \ˈstīfəl\ *vb* **stifled; stifled; stifling** \-f(ə)liŋ\ **stifles** [alter. of ME *stuflen, stufflen*, prob. modif. of MF *estouffer* to smother, suffocate] *vt* **1** *obs* **:** to kill by submersion **:** DROWN ⟨threw herself into a deep well, in which she was *stifled* —William Bosman⟩ **2 a :** to kill by depriving of oxygen **:** ASPHYXIATE, SUFFOCATE ⟨shall I not then be *stifled* in the vault —Shak.⟩ ⟨every living thing . . . must have perished slowly or suddenly, *stifled* by the mud —Francis Kingdon-Ward⟩ **b** (1) **:** to blanket or envelop to the point of suffocation **:** SMOTHER ⟨the oppressive air *stifled* her, and she felt that her breath . . . was suspended —Ellen Glasgow⟩ (2) *archaic* **:** to extinguish (fire) by covering **:** SNUFF ⟨travelers, armed with felt carpets, were endeavoring to ~ the flame —William Hazlitt †1893⟩ (3) **:** to mute by or as if by enveloping or screening **:** MUFFLE ⟨units can be insulated so they almost entirely ~ noise of operation —Jim Riggs⟩ **3 a :** to cut off (as the voice or breath) **:** SILENCE ⟨engulfing flames soon ~ their cries⟩ **b** *archaic* **:** to withhold from circulation **:** CONCEAL, SUPPRESS ⟨the papers he thought of too much value to be *stifled*, and advised the printing of them —Benjamin Franklin⟩ **c :** to withhold from expression **:** keep in check **:** REPRESS ⟨not the sort of man to ~ anger —J.E.Macdonnell⟩ **d :** to curb or quell by force **:** INHIBIT, RESTRAIN ⟨~ free speech by breaking up meetings . . . and confiscating pamphlets —Zechariah Chafee⟩ ⟨a belligerent right to ~ the trade of an enemy —F.L.Paxson› **e** *archaic* **:** to arrest the flow of **:** ABSORB, OBSTRUCT ‹they stop and ~ . . . the rays which they do not reflect or transmit —Isaac Newton› **f :** to act as a deterrent to **:** deprive of initiative or vitality **:** DISCOURAGE, TRAMMEL ‹the mountain barrier ~s the commerce which might develop —P.E.James› ‹economic controls, which have . . . *stifled* our economy —A.E.Summerfield› ‹vital art is *stifled* by culture, which insists that artists . . . imitate old masters —Clive Bell› **~** *vi* **1 :** to become suffocated by or as if by lack of oxygen **:** SMOTHER ‹no need to ~ in a hot kitchen this summer —*Better Homes & Gardens*› ‹my unsoiled name . . . will so your accusations overweigh, that you shall ~ in your own report —Shak.› **2 :** to undergo repression or restraint ‹why should I ~ in a convent —P.B.Kyne› **syn** see SUFFOCATE

[4]**stifle** \"\ *n* -s **:** a suffocating atmosphere ‹the ~ of the subway —*Everybody's Mag.*›

stifle bone *n* **:** the patella in the stifle of a quadruped

stifled *adj* **:** marked by suffocation or restraint **:** SMOTHERED, REPRESSED ‹almost ~ with resentment —G.B.Shaw› ‹a politely ~ yawn› ‹galvanize the ~ energies of the nation —*Atlantic*› — **sti·fled·ly** *adv*

sti·fler \'stīf(ə)lə(r)\ *n* -s **:** one that stifles

stifling *adj* **:** producing suffocation or restraint **:** OPPRESSIVE, HAMPERING ‹~ heat› ‹stagnation under a ~ orthodoxy —R. A.Lester› — **sti·fling·ly** *adv*

stig·ma \'stigmə\ *n, pl* **stigma·ta** \stig'mäd|ə, 'stigməl, stig'mal, stig'mä|, |tə\ *or* **stigmas** [L *stigmat-, stigma* mark, brand, fr. Gk, mark, tattoo mark, fr. *stizein* to tattoo — more at STICK] **1 a** *archaic* **:** a scar left by a hot iron **:** BRAND ‹when a burning iron is put on the face of an evildoer, it leaveth behind it a . . . ~ —Samuel Rutherford› **b :** a mark of shame or discredit **:** DISGRACE, STAIN ‹the ~ of personal cowardice —William Peden› ‹the pathos and the ~ of slavery —W.L. Sperry› ‹avoid the ~ of being called unprogressive —W.H. Camp› **c :** an identifying mark or characteristic ‹the clothing and characteristic *stigmata* of the profession —R.P.Blackmur› ‹curmudgeonly inability to praise others which has ever been the ~ by which we may recognize the ungenerous —Eric Partridge›; *specif* **:** a symptom of a physical or mental disorder ‹~s of the riboflavin deficiency state include ocular changes —*Therapeutic Notes*› ‹*stigmata* of degeneration, drug addictions, and nervous and mental diseases —H.G.Armstrong› **d :** a mark or label indicating deviation from a norm ‹a further ~ is the tendency for most phrases to end on the tonic —Bruno Nettl› **2 a** *stigmata pl* **:** marks resembling the wounds on the crucified body of Christ and believed to be supernaturally impressed upon the bodies of various persons (as St. Francis of Assisi) **b :** PETECHIA **3** [NL *stigmat-, stigma,* fr. L] **a** (1) **:** a spiracle of an insect or other arthropod or the opening into one of the lung sacs of an arachnid (2) **:** PTEROSTIGMA (3) **:** an androconium forming a conspicuously colored spot on the forewing of the male of various butterflies **b :** a portion of the pistil of a flower usu. apical on the style or ovary and often viscid or rough which receives the pollen grains and upon which they germinate — see FLOWER illustration **c :** the spot or projection on the surface of an ovary at which a Graafian follicle will rupture **d** (1) **:** the eyespot of a protozoan (2) **:** a nephridiopore of an annelid (3) **:** one of the small clefts or perforations in the branchial sac of an ascidian

stig·mal \'stigməl\ *adj* [*stigma* + *-al*] **:** of or relating to a stigma

stigmal plate *n* **:** a chitinized often sculptured or punctate plate covering a respiratory opening in various insect larvae and in ticks

stigmal vein *n* **:** a short vein extending obliquely from the stigma in various hymenopterous insects

stig·mar·ia \stig'ma(a)rēə\ *n* [NL, fr. L *stigma* mark + NL *-aria*] **1** *cap* **:** a form genus of Carboniferous plants based on elongated, cylindrical, and sometimes branched structures that have rounded depressions scattered over the surface and are generally conceded to be underground portions of lepidodendrids (as of the genera *Sigillaria* and *Lepidodendron*) **2** *pl* **stigmariae** *also* **stigmarias :** any plant or fossil of the genus *Stigmaria* — **stig·mar·i·an** \-ēən\ *adj or n*

stig·mar·i·oid \-ē,ȯid\ *adj* [NL *Stigmaria* + E *-oid*] **:** resembling or related to a stigmaria

stig·mas·ter·ol \stig'mastə,rōl, -rōl\ *n* -s [ISV *stigma-* (fr. NL *Physostigma*) + *sterol* — more at PHYSOSTIGMA] **:** a crystalline steroid alcohol $C_{29}H_{47}OH$ obtained esp. from the oil of Calabar beans and from soybean oil usu. in mixtures with sitosterols and used in the synthesis of progesterone

[1]**stig·mat·ic** \(')stig|mad·ik, -at|, |ēk\ *adj* [ML *stigmaticus* branded, fr. L *stigmat-, stigma* mark, brand + *-icus* -ic — more at STIGMA] **1 a** *archaic* **:** having a physical blemish or deformity **b :** having or conveying a social stigma **:** CENSORIOUS, DETESTABLE ‹the ~ status usually accorded an occupying power —R.J.D.Braibanti› **2 :** STIGMAL, STIGMATIFEROUS **3 :** of, relating to, or accompanying supernatural stigmata **4 :** ANASTIGMATIC — used esp. of a bundle of light rays intersecting at a single point ‹~ spectroscope› — **stig·mat·i·cal·ly** \|ək(ə)lē, |ēk-, -li\ *adv*

[2]**stigmatic** \"\ *n* -s **1** *archaic* **:** one marked with a stigma **2 :** one that is believed to bear supernatural stigmata ‹one of the most remarkable ~s in history —*Time*›

stigmatical *adj* [ML *stigmaticus* + E *-al*] **:** STIGMATIC ‹he is deformed, crooked . . . ~ in making, worse in mind —Shak.›

stigmatic cell *n* **:** LID CELL 1

stig·ma·tif·er·ous \,stigmə¦tif(ə)rəs\ *adj* [prob. fr. (assumed) NL *stigmatifer* stigmatiferous (fr. L *stigmat-, stigma* + *-ifer* -iferous) + E *-ous*] **:** bearing a stigma

stig·mat·i·form \stig'mad·ə,fȯrm, 'stigməd-·\ *adj* [prob. fr. (assumed) NL *stigmatiformis,* fr. L *stigmat-, stigma* + *-iformis* -iform] **:** having the form or appearance of a stigma

stig·ma·tism \'stigmə,tizəm\ *n* -s [L *stigmat-, stigma* + E *-ism*] **:** the condition of an optical system (as a lens or mirror) in which rays of light from a single point converge in a single focal point — compare ASTIGMATISM

stig·ma·tist \'stigməd·əst\ *n* -s [L *stigmat-, stigma* + E *-ist*] **:** STIGMATIC 2

stig·ma·ti·za·tion \,stigməd·ə'zāshən, -mətə'z-, -mə,tī'z-\ *n* -s [prob. fr. (assumed) NL *stigmatization-, stigmatizatio,* fr. ML *stigmatizatus* (past part. of *stigmatizare* to stigmatize) + L *-ion-, -io* -ion] **1 :** an act or instance of stigmatizing ‹a government ~ which would deter the public from consideration of the opinions of the party —*Civil Liberty*› **2 :** the production of what are believed to be supernatural stigmata on the body

stig·ma·tize \'stigmə,tīz\ *vt* -ED/-ING/-S *see -ize in Explan Notes* [ML *stigmatizare,* fr. L *stigmat-, stigma* + LL *-izare* -ize] **1 a** *archaic* **:** to brand with a hot iron **b :** to set a stigma upon **:** regard with opprobrium **:** CENSURE, DENOUNCE ‹critics . . . ~ America's technological good fortune as machine-worship —Adrienne Koch› ‹people who so much as whisper during a performance are . . . *stigmatized* as barbarians —Joseph Wechsberg› **2 :** to mark with stigmata ‹a visit to the *stigmatized* seer —*U. S. Daily*› **3 :** DESIGNATE, IDENTIFY ‹I wish . . . that the fates had not *stigmatized* me "writer" —Aldous Huxley›

stig·mo·de·ra \,stigmə'dirə, stig'mädərə\ *n, cap* [NL, prob. fr. *stigmo-* (fr. L *stigmat-, stigma*) + *-dera* (fr. Gk *derē, deirē* neck) — more at DER-] **:** a large chiefly Australian genus of buprestid beetles many of which are brilliant green

stig·mo·nose \'stigmə,nōs *also* -ōz\ *n* -s [*stigmo-* (fr. L *stigmat-, stigma*) + Gk *nosos* disease] **:** a disease characterized by translucent dots in leaves and spotting, dimpling, malformation, and sometimes dwarfing of fruits and caused by punctures made by small insects (as aphids, thrips, or leafhoppers)

sti·kine \stə'kēn\ *n, pl* **stikine** *or* **stikines** *usu cap* **1 a :** a Tlingit people along the Stikine River in Alaska **b :** a member of such people **2 :** the language of the Stikine people

stilb \'stilb\ *n* -s [ISV, fr. Gk *stilbē* lamp] **:** a cgs unit of brightness equal to one candle per square centimeter of cross section perpendicular to the rays

stil·ba·ce·ae \stil'bāsē,ē\ [NL, fr. *Stilbum* + *-aceae*] *syn of* STILBELLACEAE

stil·ba·ceous \(')stil¦bāshəs\ *adj* [NL *Stilbaceae* + E *-ous*] **:** of or relating to the Stilbellaceae

stilb·am·i·dine \(')stil¦bamə,dēn, -,dən\ *n* [*stilb-* (as in *stilbene*) + *amidine*] **:** a diamidine $[NH_2C(=NH)C_6H_4CH=]_2$ derived from stilbene and used chiefly in the form of its crystalline isethionate salt in treating various fungal infections (as systemic blastomycosis)

stil·bel·la \stil'belə\ *n, cap* [NL, fr. Gk *stilbos* glistening + NL *-ella*] **:** a genus (the type of the family Stilbellaceae) of imperfect fungi forming capitate synemata or coremia and bearing continuous hyaline conidia

stil·bel·la·ce·ae \,stilbə'lāsē,ē\ *n pl, cap* [NL, fr. *Stilbella,* type genus + *-aceae*] **:** a family of fungi of the order Moniliales — see STILBELLA

stil·bene \'stil,bēn\ *n* -s [ISV *stilb-* (fr. Gk *stilbos* glistening) + *-ene*] **:** an aromatic hydrocarbon $C_6H_5CH=CHC_6H_5$ occurring in cis and trans forms **:** *sym*-diphenyl-ethylene; *esp* **:** the more stable trans form obtained in large shining crystals (as by heating benzaldehyde with sulfur or by dehydrating benzyl-phenyl-carbinol) useful as phosphors (as in scintillation counters)

stilbene dye *n* **:** any of a class of usu. yellow to orange direct cotton azo dyes derived from stilbene; *also* **:** any of various fluorescent brighteners derived from stilbene

stil·bes·trol \stil'be,strōl, -rōl\ *also* **stil·boes·trol** \" *sometimes* ,stilbō'e,s-\ *n* -s [*stilbene* + *estrus* + *-ol*] **1 :** a crystalline diphenol $(HOC_6H_4CH=)_2$ derived from stilbene and possessing little estrogenic activity; 4,4′-stilbene-diol **2 :** DIETHYLSTILBESTROL

stil·bite \'stil,bīt\ *n* -s [F, fr. Gk *stilbē* lamp + F *-ite;* akin to Gk *stilbos* glistening] **:** a mineral $NaCa_2Al_5Si_{13}O_{36}.14H_2O$ of the zeolite family consisting of a hydrous silicate of aluminum, calcium, and sodium, being white when pure with pearly luster on the cleavage surface, often occurring in sheaflike aggregations of crystals and also in radiated masses, and considered by some to include heulandite (hardness 3.5-4, sp. gr. 2.09-2.21) — called also *desmine*

stil·bum \'stilbəm\ [NL, fr. Gk *stilbon,* neut. of *stilbos* glistening; akin to Gk *stilpnos* glistening and perh. to W *syllu* to gaze] *syn of* STILBELLA

stil-de-grain yellow \'stēldə,graⁿ-\ *n* [*stil-de-grain* fr. F *stil de grain* yellow lake] **:** DUTCH PINK 2

[1]**stile** \'stīl\ *n* -s [ME, fr. OE *stigel;* akin to OHG *stigilla* stile, OE *stīgan* to go up — more at STAIR] **1 a :** steps or rungs to assist a person over a fence while remaining a barrier to livestock **b :** TURNSTILE **2** *archaic* **:** BARRIER, OBSTACLE ‹a lift over the ~ at a crisis of some importance to the party —*Manchester Examiner*›

stile 1a

[2]**stile** *archaic var of* STYLE

[3]**stile** \'stī(ə)l\ *n* -s [prob. fr. D *stijl* post, doorjamb, fr. MD, post, prob. fr. L *stilus* stake, stylus] **1 :** one of the vertical members in a frame or panel (as a door or sash) into which the secondary members are fitted — compare MULLION, RAIL; see DOOR illustration **2 :** a vertical member of a furniture frame (as the vertical continuation of a back leg of a chair to form part of the back)

sti·let *also* **sti·lette** \'stīlət, stə'let\ *n* -s [*stilet* fr. obs. F, stylet, stiletto, fr. MF, stiletto; *stilette* alter. (influenced by *-ette*) of *stilet* — more at STYLET] **:** STYLET 1 — **sti·let·ted** \- əd·əd, -ed·əd\ *adj*

[1]**sti·let·to** *also* **stil·let·to** \stə'led·(,)ō, -e(,)tō\ *n, pl* **stilettos** *or* **stilettoes** [It *stiletto,* dim. of *stilo* dagger, stylus, fr. L *stilus* stake, stylus — more at STYLE] **1 :** a slender dagger with a blade that is thick in proportion to its breadth — compare PONIARD **2 :** something that resembles a dagger; *esp* **:** a pointed instrument for piercing holes for eyelets or embroidery

stiletto 1

[2]**stiletto** \"\ *vt* -ED/-ING/-S *archaic* **:** to stab or kill with or as if with a stiletto

stiletto fly *n* **:** any of numerous small or medium-sized predaceous dipterous flies of the family Therevidae that somewhat resemble the robber flies

[1]**still** \'stil\ *adj* -ER/-EST [ME *stille,* fr. OE; akin to MD *stille* still, OHG *stilli* still, OE *steall* stall — more at STALL] **1 a :** devoid of or abstaining from motion **:** IMMOBILE, STATIONARY ‹each movement has its center, its ~ point —Isaac Rosenfeld› ‹sorrow loomed over her and time was ~ —Ann Ryan› **b** *archaic* **:** tending to remain in one place **:** SEDENTARY ‹in his absence she was a ~ personage —Charlotte Brontë› **c :** having no effervescence **:** not carbonated ‹~ wine› ‹prefer sparkling fruit juices to the ~ products —*Improvements in the Manuf. & Preservation of Grape Juice*› — opposed to *sparkling* **d :** of, relating to, being, or designed for taking a static photograph as contrasted with a motion picture ‹~ camera› ‹~ photography› ‹~ projector› **2 a** (1) **:** uttering no sound **:** disinclined to talk **:** QUIET, TACITURN ‹~ as a mouse› ‹her radio . . . was never ~ —Mavis Gallant› ‹each with each patrols, in ~ society, hand in hand —R.P.Warren› (2) **:** calm in spirit **:** UNPERTURBED ‹my soul was not ~ enough for songs —George Macdonald †1905› **b :** subdued in tone or volume **:** MUTED, SOOTHING ‹a ~ small voice of calm —J.G.Whittier› ‹music by the night wind sent through strings of some ~ instrument —P.B.Shelley› **3 a :** free from agitation **:** TRANQUIL, UNRUFFLED ‹dived so smoothly that she scarcely rippled the ~ water —C.B.Nordhoff & J.N.Hall› **b :** free from noise or turbulence **:** PEACEFUL, SILENT ‹the street was ~, save for the twittering of birds —Winston Churchill› ‹the smack of fist against shoulder was sharp in the ~ barracks —Mack Morriss› ‹~ weather, and dry, powdery snow —O.E.Rölvaag› **c :** caused to revert to a quiescent state **:** SILENCED, STILLED ‹the sound of a voice that is ~ —Alfred Tennyson› **d** *archaic* **:** lacking in incident or excitement **:** DULL, UNEVENTFUL ‹save us . . . from a tedious day, or shine the dullness of ~ life away —William Cowper› **4** *obs* **:** CONTINUED, PERSEVERING ‹by ~ practice, learn to know thy meaning —Shak.›

[2]**still** \"\ *vb* -ED/-ING/-S [ME *stillen,* fr. OE *stillan;* akin to MD & OHG *stillen* to still, ON *stilla;* derivative fr. the root of E [1]*still*] *vt* **1 a :** to cause to subside or die down **:** ALLAY, CHECK ‹as suddenly as it had broken, the gale was ~*ed* —Eric Linklater› **b :** to put an end to **:** restore to order **:** PACIFY, SETTLE ‹the threat of his coming had ~*ed* the . . . revolt —John Buchan› ‹nominal unification . . . had not ~*ed* interservice bitterness —*Time*› **c :** to arrest the motion of ‹before death ~*ed* his hand —G.C.Sellery› **2 a :** to gratify fully **:** APPEASE, ASSUAGE ‹neither beef nor mutton could ~ me —Francis Hackett› **b :** to keep under control **:** OVERCOME, RESTRAIN, SUPPRESS ‹drew a long breath and ~*ed* her shuddering —Laura Krey› ‹unable to ~ his persistent gambling instinct —T.H. White b. 1915› **c :** to calm down **:** LULL, SOOTHE ‹a magic voice that ~*ed* and . . . comforted you —L.C.Douglas› **3 a :** to repress the noise or clamor of **:** HUSH, SILENCE ‹the once-thriving . . . metropolis is ~*ed* by terror —Hal Lehrman› ‹sirens are ~*ed* . . . when they pass hospital or convalescent homes —*Springfield (Mass.) Union*› **b :** to cause to become quiet ‹~*ed* the people before Moses —Num 13:30 (AV)› **~** *vi* **:** to become motionless or silent **:** QUIET ‹the large hand ~*ed* on the heavy knee —Marc Brandel› ‹the river ~*ed* and froze —Hugh MacLennan› ‹music from the dance band ~*ed* —G.A.Wagner› — often used with *down* ‹the wind ~*s* down —*Times Lit. Supp.*› **syn** see CALM

[3]**still** \"\ *adv* [ME *stille,* fr. OE; akin to MD *stille* quietly, OHG *stillo;* adverb fr. the adjective represented by E [1]*still*] **1 :** without noise or motion **:** QUIETLY ‹the girl sat as ~ as an image carved from marble —Louis Bromfield› **2 a :** in a continuous or constant manner **:** ALWAYS, EVER ‹remained for nearly a month . . . ~ widening his acquaintance —W.C. Ford› ‹while we do his goodwill, He abides with us ~ —J.H. Sammis› **b** *archaic* **:** in an uninterrupted manner **:** PROGRESSIVELY ‹~ his courage with his toils increased —Alexander Pope› **c :** in spite of a preceding event or consideration **:** NEVERTHELESS, YET ‹many people who are excessively active in caring for the skin . . . ~ have acne —Morris Fishbein› ‹the old but ~ important truth —M.R.Cohen› **3 a :** to the present time ‹ancient kitchen chimney place with its fireback and crane ~ in position —John Durant› ‹~ . . . revive the customs of their ancestral homelands —*Amer. Guide Series: Minn.*› **b :** at the time in question — used with implication of imminent change ‹drink your coffee while it's ~ hot› ‹~ found themselves a good way from their unit by six o'clock —Earle Birney› ‹teacher noted what words the pupil ~ did not know —Angell Mathewson› **c** *obs* **:** without change in the future ‹discern the coming on of years, and think not to do the same things ~ —Francis Bacon› **d :** to or at a greater distance **:** FARTHER ‹west ~, where the whitish sandy soil is thinly covered with grasses . . . cattle move and graze —Marjory S. Douglas› **e :** in addition **:** beyond this ‹six or seven hundred men . . . and occasionally more ~ —Walt Whitman› ‹~ another example of cultural misunderstanding —A.A.Hill› **4 a** *obs* **:** to a greater extent ‹the guilt being great, the fear doth ~ exceed —Shak.› **b :** EVEN — used as an intensive to stress the comparative degree ‹half a dozen little brigs . . . and eight clumsy gun vessels that were smaller ~ —C.S.Forester› ‹placed him ~ more in the wrong —W.C.Ford›

[4]**still** \"\ *n* -s [ME *stille,* fr. *stille,* adj., still — more at [1]STILL] **1 :** a pervading calm or hush **:** QUIET, SILENCE ‹the ~ of the night› **2 a :** a static photograph ‹the instantaneous ~ which a deer took of himself —*World's Work*›; *specif* **:** a specially posed photograph taken of the actors or scenes of a motion picture production for publicity or documentary purposes **b :** a photograph, map, or chart inserted into a television program **3 :** STILL ALARM

[5]**still** \"\ *conj* [[3]*still*] **:** BUT, NEVERTHELESS ‹~, all men, including dead men, can be wrong —Weston La Barre› ‹~, aside from all other considerations, the relative importance seen in merit . . . may be a real issue —S.L.Payne›

[6]**still** \"\ *vb* -ED/-ING/-S [ME *stillen,* fr. OF *stiller,* fr. L *stillare* to drip, trickle — more at DISTILL] *vi, obs* **:** to trickle down in fine drops **~** *vt, obs* **:** to exude or cause to fall in drops ‹pricks the clouds, ~*s* down the rain —Francis Quarles›

[7]**still** \"\ *vb* -ED/-ING/-S [ME *stillen,* short for *distillen* to distill — more at DISTILL] *vt* **1 :** to subject to distillation ‹~ peaches for brandy› **2 :** to make or extract by distillation ‹~ brandy from peaches› **~** *vi* **:** to perform distillation **:** DISTILL ‹~*ing* was clearly against the law —H.E.Giles›

[8]**still** \"\ *n* -s **1 :** DISTILLERY 2 **2 :** apparatus used in distillation comprising sometimes only the chamber in which the vaporization is carried out or at other times other parts or the entire distillation equipment: as **a :** a vessel or boiler together with a condenser for use in distilling alcoholic liquors or other liquids — compare POT STILL **b :** a fractionating column or tower with or without its condensing equipment and receiver for use in distilling various substances sometimes with decomposition ‹ammonia ~*s*› ‹turpentine ~*s*› ‹petroleum topping ~*s*› ‹cracking ~*s*› — compare RETORT, TAR STILL **c** (1) **:** equipment consisting essentially of an evaporator and a condenser for producing distilled water — called also *water still* (2) **:** a compact device for converting salt water to fresh water ‹floating plastic solar ~*s*› **3 :** a vessel in which manganese dioxide is treated with hydrochloric acid to form chlorine or a bleaching liquor — compare WELDON PROCESS

a simple retort form of still 2: *1* retort, *2* head, *3* tube, *4* condenser

[9]**still** \"\ *adj* -ER/-EST [[8]*still*] **:** of or relating to a still; *esp* **:** remaining as residual matter in a still after distillation ‹~ bottoms› ‹~ coke›

[1]**stil·lage** \'stilij\ *n* -s [modif. of D *stellage* scaffolding, fr. MD, fr. *stellen* to place + *-age* (fr. MF); akin to OHG *stellen* to place — more at STALL] **1 :** a small table or stand (as for casks in a brewery) sometimes equipped with wheels **2 :** a drying stone for ceramic ware shaped but not fired

[2]**stillage** \"\ *vt* -ED/-ING/-S **:** to place on a stillage

[3]**still·age** \"\ *n* -s [[8]*still* + *-age*] **:** the mash from an alcoholic fermentation after removal of the alcohol in a still ‹simple screening of the ~ gives distillers' dried grains —R.S.Aries› — compare DISTILLERS' GRAINS

still alarm *n* **:** a fire alarm transmitted (as by telephone call or by voice communication with the unit directly concerned) without sounding the fire signal apparatus

still and all *adv* **:** after all **:** NEVERTHELESS

still and anon *or* **still an end** *adv* [*still and anon* fr. [3]*still* + *and anon,* fr. *and,* conj. + *anon,* adv.; *still an end* fr. [3]*still* + *an end,* adv.] *obs* **:** from time to time **:** now and then

still and on *adv, chiefly Scot* **:** NEVERTHELESS, YET

stil·la·ti·tious \,stilə¦tishəs\ *adj* [L *stillaticius,* fr. *stillatus,* past part. of *stillare* to drip, trickle] **1 :** falling in drops **2 :** DISTILLED

stil·la·to·ry \'stilə,tōrē\ *n* -ES [ME *stillatorie,* fr. ML *stillatorium,* fr. L *stillatus* (past part. of *stillare* to drip, trickle) + *-orium* -ory] *archaic* **:** STILL, DISTILLERY

still·bay \'stil,bā\ *adj, usu cap* [*Still Bay,* southern coast of Cape Province, South Africa] **:** of or belonging to a Middle Pleistocene culture of East Africa and Cape Province characterized by flake tools and weapons resembling Mousterian and Solutrian types

stillbirth \'⸗,⸗\ *n* **1 :** the birth of a dead fetus — compare LIVE BIRTH **2 :** a viable fetus that is born dead

[1]**stillborn** \'⸗¦⸗\ *adj* **1 :** dead at birth ‹a ~ child› — compare LIVE-BORN **2 :** failing from the start **:** disappointing all expectations **:** ABORTIVE, UNSUCCESSFUL ‹a ~ novel› ‹their first scheme died ~ —J.W.Poling› ‹this ~ treaty marked the failure of Germany to set up a new pattern of alliances —C.E. Black & E.C.Helmreich›

[2]**stillborn** \'⸗,⸗\ *n, pl* **stillborn** *or* **stillborns :** one that is stillborn ‹antigens obtained from infants and ~*s* —*Yr. Bk. of Urology*› ‹the greatest resuscitator of the ~ known to dramatic art —*Everybody's Mag.*›

still box *n* **:** STILLING BASIN

still–burn \'⸗,⸗\ *vt* **:** to burn in the process of distillation

stilled *past of* STILL

[1]**stiller** *comparative of* STILL

[2]**still·er** \'stilə(r)\ *n* -s [[7]*still* + *-er*] **:** DISTILLER

[3]**stiller** \"\ *n* -s [[2]*still* + *-er*] **:** one that calms or quiets

still·ery \'stil(ə)rē\ *n* -ES [[7]*still* + *-ery*] **:** [8]STILL

stillest *superlative of* STILL

still–fish \'⸗,⸗\ *vi* **:** to fish with the line and bait resting still or stationary in the water — **still–fish·er** \'⸗,⸗·⸗\ *n*

still head *n* **:** the top part of a still; *esp* **:** a fractionating column at the top of a still — compare COLUMN 3d

stillhouse \'⸗,⸗\ *n* **:** DISTILLERY 2

still hunt *n* **1 :** a noiseless pursuit or ambushing of game ‹liked the test of holding a small bunch of buffaloes together in the *still hunt* as he picked them off —Mari Sandoz› **2 :** the covert pursuit of an object ‹the typical titled foreigner . . . on a *still hunt* for the American heiress —*N.Y. Sun*›; *esp* **:** a political campaign carried on secretly or underhandedly

still–hunt \'⸗,⸗\ *vb* [*still hunt*] *vi* **:** to ambush or stalk a quarry **:** pursue game noiselessly esp. without a dog ‹if he *still-hunts,* he must be sufficiently versed in woodlore to outwit . . . animals —Don Stillman› **~** *vt* **:** to lie in wait for or approach by stealth **:** AMBUSH, STALK ‹impossible to *still-hunt* mountain lions; they were too alert —H.L.Davis› — **still–hunt·er** \'⸗,⸗·⸗\ *n*

stil·li·cide \'stilə,sīd\ *n* -s [L *stillicidium,* fr. *stilli-* (fr. *stilla* drop) + *-cidium* (fr. *cadere* to fall) — more at DISTILL, CHANCE] **1** *archaic* **:** a continual dripping **2** *Roman, civil, & Scots law* **:** the servitude of eavesdrop binding a servient tenement to receive from the dominant tenement rainwater from the eaves of a building located on the latter

stillier *comparative of* STILLY

stilliest *superlative of* STILLY

[1]**stilling** *pres part of* STILL

[2]**stil·ling** \'stiliŋ\ *n* -s [modif. of D *stelling* scaffolding, fr. MD *stellinge,* fr. *stellen* to place + *-inge* (akin to OE *-ing,* suffix forming nouns from verbs) — more at -ING] **:** STILLION

stilling basin *or* **stilling box** *or* **stilling pool** *or* **stilling well** *n* [*stilling* fr. gerund of [2]*still*] **:** a depression in a channel or reservoir deep enough to reduce the velocity or turbulence of the flow — called also *still box;* compare ORIFICE BOX

stil·lin·gia \stə'linjēə, -inj(ē)ə\ *n* [NL, fr. Benjamin *Stillingfleet* †1771 Eng. botanist + NL *-ia*] **1 a** *cap* **:** a genus of widely distributed herbs or shrubs (family Euphorbiaceae) with alternate leaves, monoecious spicate apetalous flowers, and capsular fruit — see QUEEN'S-DELIGHT **b** -s : any plant of the genus *Stillingia; often* : CHINESE TALLOW TREE **2** -s : the dried root of queen's-delight used as an alterative

stillingia oil *n* : a pale yellow drying oil obtained from the seeds of the Chinese tallow tree

stillingia tallow *n* : CHINESE TALLOW

stil·lion \'stilyən\ *n* -s [alter. of *stilling*] : a cradle for vats in a brewery : STILLAGE

still life *n, pl* **still lifes** *also* **still lives** [trans. of D *stilleven*] **1 a** : a picture consisting predominantly of inanimate objects ⟨so slow in painting *still lifes* that the flowers and fruit in his models would rot before he got them painted —Winthrop Sargeant⟩ **b** : something that resembles such a picture ⟨the novel will remain . . . just an interesting small-town *still life* in which figures are caught in careful needlepoint —James Kelly⟩ **2** : the category of the graphic arts concerned with inanimate objects as subject matter ⟨*still life* . . . is an excellent means of developing a sense of pictorial balance —*Amer. Photography*⟩

still liquor *n* **1** : spent liquid containing manganous chloride from chlorine stills — compare WELDON PROCESS **2** : bleaching liquor made in a still

still·man \'stilmən\ *n, pl* **stillmen 1** : one who owns or operates a still : DISTILLER **2** : a worker who controls the fermentation of beer **3** : one who tends distillation equipment (as in an oil refinery)

still·ness *n* -ES [ME *stilnesse*, fr. OE *stilnes*, fr. *stille*, adj., still + *-nes* -ness] **1 a** : freedom from agitation : CALMNESS, SERENITY ⟨brings with her beauty . . . a capacity for ~ and repose —E.R.Bentley⟩ **b** : absence of movement : IMMOBILITY, LIFELESSNESS ⟨the ~ is so absolute that it seems as if all the winds of the world had . . . dropped out of the air —J.C. Powys⟩ **2 a** : the quality or state of being soundless : QUIET, SILENCE ⟨knew by the ~ and the tenseness that we had reached the outer fringe of the front —Burgess Scott⟩ **b** : a soundless place or environment ⟨polar bears roam the great white ~*es*⟩ **3** *obs* : PATIENCE, FORTITUDE ⟨in peace . . . nothing so becomes a man, as modest ~ —Shak.⟩

still pack *n* : the pack of cards that is not in play when two packs are used (as in bridge) and is shuffled by the next dealer's partner

still return *n* : a fraction of distillate so impure that it must be redistilled

stillroom \'=,=\ *n* [[3]*still*] *Brit* : a room connected with the kitchen where liqueurs, preserves, and cakes are kept and tea, coffee, and other beverages are prepared

stills *pres 3d sing of* STILL, *pl of* STILL

still's disease \'stilz-\ *n, usu cap S* [after Sir George F. *Still* †1941 Eng. pediatrician] : rheumatoid arthritis in children

still·son wrench \'stilsən-\ *n* [fr. *Stillson*, a trademark] : a pipe wrench having an adjustable L-shaped jaw sliding in a sleeve that is pivoted to and loosely encircles the handle so that pressure on the handle increases the grip

[1]**stillstand** \'=,=\ *n* **1** : STANDSTILL **2 a** : an act or instance of stillstanding ⟨represent minor ~*s* locally preserved in the general emergence of the area —W.G.V.Bolchin⟩ **b** : STABILITY ⟨fairly long periods of ~ —C.A.Cotton⟩ **3** : an interval in the light cycle of a variable star when its brightness temporarily stops rising or falling and perhaps forms a secondary maximum or hump in the light curve

[2]**stillstand** \"\ *vi* : to remain stationary with respect to sea level or with reference to the center of the earth — used of a continent, island, or other land area

still water *n* : a part of a stream where the gradient is so gentle that no current is visible

[1]**stil·ly** \'stil(l)ē, |i\ *adv* [ME, fr. OE *stillīce*, fr. *stille*, adj., still + *-līce* -ly] : CALMLY, QUIETLY ⟨~ she glided in —William Allingham⟩

[2]**still·y** \'stil|ē, |i\ *adj* -ER/-EST [perh. fr. [4]*still* + *-y*] : characterized by stillness : CALM, QUIET ⟨the sounds of this most ~ night are almost wholly of the faintly pulsing sea —E.J. Banfield⟩

stilp·no·mel·ane \,stilpnō'me,lān\ *n* -s [G *stilpnomelan*, fr. Gk *stilpnos* glistening + *melan-, melas* black — more at STILBUM, MULLET] : a black or greenish black mineral $K(Fe,Al)_{10}Si_{12}O_{30}(O,OH)_{12}$ (?) occurring in foliated plates, fibrous forms, and velvety bronze-colored incrustations and consisting of a hydrous iron aluminum silicate with a little potassium (sp. gr. 2.77–2.96)

stilp·no·siderite \¦stilp(,)nō+\ *n* -s [G *stilpnosiderit*, fr. Gk *stilpnos* glistening + *sidēros* iron + G *-it* -ite] : LIMONITE

[1]**stilt** \'stilt\ *n* -s *see sense 4b* [ME *stilte* plow handle, crutch, stilt; akin to MD *stelte* wooden leg, crutch, OHG *stelza* stilt, OSw *stylta* crutch, OE *steall* place, position, stall — more at STALL] **1** *dial chiefly Brit* : CRUTCH **2** *dial chiefly Brit* : the handle of a plow **3 a** : one of two poles each with a rest or strap for the foot used to elevate the wearer above the ground in walking and usu. of sufficient length to be steadied at the top by the hand and arm **b** : something that resembles a stilt: as (1) : a pile or post serving to raise a building or other structure above ground or water level (2) : a vertical architectural member that raises the spring of an arch or vault above the apparent or elsewhere established impost (3) : a member placed above or below a column for additional height (4) : any of the piles forming the back of the sheet piling for a bridge starling (5) : a piece of hard-fired clay usu. three-armed with points on each side used to keep articles apart in a pottery kiln **c** : a precarious foundation ⟨rivals . . . can topple governments built on ~*s* as easily as they can hire assassins —Flora Lewis⟩ **4 a** : a long thin leg ⟨white stalky birds on ~*s* —Thomas Wood †1950⟩ **b** *also* **stilt plover,** *pl also* **stilt** : any of various notably long-legged three-toed limicoline birds of the genera *Himantopus* and *Cladorhynchus* related to the avocets, chiefly inhabiting inland ponds and marshes or brackish lagoons, nesting in small colonies, and being mostly white with a black mantle variously extended on the neck and head — called also *longlegs, stiltbird;* see BANDED STILT, BLACK-NECKED STILT, BLACK-WINGED STILT, WHITE-HEADED STILT

stilts 3a

[2]**stilt** \"\ *vb* -ED/-ING/-S *vt* : to raise on or as if on stilts; *specif* : to raise the spring of (an arch or vault) above the apparent or elsewhere established impost ~ *vi, chiefly Scot* : to walk awkwardly and stiffly : LIMP

stiltbird \'=,=\ *n* : STILT 4b

stilt bug *n* : any of various long-legged sluggish bugs (family Neididae) that are closely related to the coreid bugs

stilt·ed \'stiltəd\ *adj* **1 a** : supported on or as if on stilts ⟨a ~ railway trestle⟩ ⟨starting off . . . on her precarious heels with quick ~ steps —Warren Beck⟩ **b** : having the springing higher than the apparent level of the impost ⟨~ arch⟩ **c** : having long thin legs ⟨a ~ crane⟩ **2 a** : artificially elevated : POMPOUS, LOFTY ⟨their conversations are miracles of studied, ~ eloquence —B.R.Redman⟩ **b** : lacking in spontaneity : restricted by convention : FORMAL, STIFF ⟨a ~ letter of acknowledgment⟩ ⟨painting people and tigers . . . in a curiously flat and ~ way —Cyril Ray⟩ ⟨when people try to correct their speech . . . they develop a ~ pronunciation —Charlton Laird⟩ — **stilt·ed·ly** *adv*

stilt·ed·ness *n* -ES : the quality or state of being stilted

stilt·er \-ltə(r)\ *n* -s [[1]*stilt* + *-er*] : one that walks on or as if on stilts — called also *stiltwalker*

stil·ton \'stiltᵊn *also* -lton\ *or* **stilton cheese** *n* -s *usu cap S* [*Stilton*, parish in Huntingdonshire, east central England, where it was originally sold] : a blue-veined cheese with wrinkled rind made of whole cows' milk enriched with cream and usu. aged two years

stilt palm *n* : a palm of the genus *Iriartea*

stilt petrel *n* : a long-legged black-and-white petrel of the genus *Fregetta*

stilt-root \'=,=\ *n* : a prop root of the mangrove

stilt sandpiper *n* : a rather rare American sandpiper (*Micropalama himantopus*) having very long legs and semipalmate feet and a bill somewhat expanded at the tip

stilt wheel *n* : the gauge-wheel attachment to a plow beam for limiting the plowing depth

stilty \'stiltē\ *adj* -ER/-EST **1** : suggestive of stilts **2** : STILTED

stilus *var of* STYLUS

stime \'stīm\ *also* **stim** \-tim\ *n* -s [ME (northern dial.) *stime, styme*] *chiefly Scot & Irish* : the smallest quantity : PARTICLE, GLIMMER

stim·part \'stimpə(r)t\ *n* -s [perh. contr. of *sixteenth part*] : LIPPY

stim·u·la·bil·i·ty \,stimyələ'bilədē, -bilətē, -i *sometimes* ÷-məl-\ *n* : the quality or state of being stimulable

stim·u·la·ble \'==ləbəl\ *adj* [*stimulate* + *-able*] : capable of being stimulated

stim·u·lan·cy \-lənsē\ *n* -ES [[2]*stimulant* + *-cy*] : stimulating quality

[1]**stim·u·lant** \'stimyələnt *sometimes* ÷-məl-\ *n* -s [L *stimulant, stimulans*, pres. part. of *stimulare*] **1** : an agent that produces a temporary increase of the functional activity of a tissue (as the central nervous system) either by direct action (as by excitation) or indirect (as by removal of inhibiting influences) **2** : STIMULUS **3** : an alcoholic beverage — not used technically

[2]**stimulant** \"\ *adj* [L *stimulant-, stimulans*, pres. part. of *stimulare*] : that stimulates

stim·u·late \-,lāt, *usu* -ād.+V\ *vb* -ED/-ING/-S [L *stimulatus*, past part. of *stimulare*, fr. *stimulus* goad] *vt* **1** : to excite to activity or growth or to greater activity or exertion : stir up : GOAD, PRICK, ANIMATE ⟨crop loss might ~ a man to intenser fishing activity —V.W.Turner⟩ : LIVEN ⟨the very controversy his book aroused *stimulated* its sale —Eugene Exman⟩ : AROUSE ⟨establishing the fund . . . to ~ public interest in poetry —*College English*⟩ **2** : to function as a stimulus to; *esp* : to evoke the characteristic physiologic activity of (as a nerve or muscle) **3** : to arouse or affect by a stimulant drug ⟨the caffeine in coffee will ~ the patient⟩ **4** : to administer dope to (a racehorse) to speed running ~ *vi* : to act as a stimulant or stimulus ⟨an academic atmosphere that ~*s* rather than stultifies⟩ **syn** see PROVOKE

stim·u·lat·ing·ly *adv* : in a stimulating manner

stim·u·la·tion \,=='lāshən\ *n* -s [L *stimulation-, stimulatio*, fr. *stimulatus* (past part. of *stimulare*) + *-ion-, -io* -ion] **1 a** : the act or process of stimulating ⟨the ~ of trade by reducing tariffs⟩; *also* : STIMULATIVENESS ⟨enjoy the ~ of the metropolis with its cultural advantages⟩ **b** : the state of being stimulated : altered activity ⟨a test to detect ~ in racehorses⟩ **2** : the stimulating action of various agents on muscles, nerves, or a sensory end organ by which activity is evoked; *esp* : the reaction produced in a sensory end organ by a stimulus that initiates a nerve impulse and results in functional activity of an effector (as a muscle or gland) ⟨gastric secretion induced by ~ of the sense of smell⟩

stim·u·la·tive \'==,lā|d·|iv, -lə|, |t|, |ēv *also* |əv\ *adj* : having power or tending to stimulate — **stim·u·la·tive·ly** \|əvlē, -li\ *adv* — **stim·u·la·tive·ness** \|ivnəs, |ēv- *also* |əv-\ *n* -ES

stim·u·la·tor *also* **stim·u·lat·er** \-,lād·ə(r), -ātə\ *n* -s [*stimulator* fr. LL, fr. L *stimulatus* (past part. of *stimulare*) + *-or; stimulater* fr. *stimulate* + *-er*] : one that stimulates; *specif* : an instrument used to apply a stimulus

stim·u·la·to·ry \-lə,tōrē, -tȯr-, -ri\ *adj* : STIMULATING

stim·u·log·e·nous \¦==¦läjənəs\ *adj* [*stimulus* + *-o-* + *-genous*] : developing as a consequence of stimulation

stim·u·lus \'stimyələs *sometimes* ÷-məl-\ *n, pl* **stim·u·li** \-,lī *also* -,lē\ [L, goad, incentive; akin to L *stilus* stake, stylus — more at STYLE] **1** : something that rouses the mind or spirits or incites to activity : INCENTIVE ⟨the war proved a ~ to agriculture, industry, and commerce —*Amer. Guide Series: N.J.*⟩ **2** : something that produces a temporary increase of physiological activity in an organism or in any of its parts; *esp* : an agent (as an environmental change) capable of directly influencing the activity of living protoplasm (as by inducing a tropism, exciting a sensory end organ, or evoking muscular contraction or glandular secretion) — see HETEROLOGOUS STIMULUS, HOMOLOGOUS STIMULUS

stimulus diffusion *n* : diffusion in which one people receives a culture element from another but gives it a new and unique form

stimulus error *n* : an error in introspective observation of divining the object from which the stimulus comes instead of reporting the impression actually received

stimulus-object \'===,==\ *n* : the physical source of a stimulus : something that produces the energy for stimulation

stimulus-response \¦====¦=\ *adj* : representing the activity of an organism as composed of reactions to stimuli ⟨*stimulus-response* formula⟩ ⟨*stimulus-response* psychology⟩

stimulus threshold *n* : ABSOLUTE THRESHOLD

stimulus word *n* : a word to which the subject reacts (as in an association test)

[1]**sting** \'stiŋ\ *vb* **stung** \'stəŋ\ *or archaic* **stang** \'staŋ, -taiŋ\ **stung; stinging; stings** [ME *stingen*, fr. OE *stingan;* akin to ON *stinga* to sting, stab, Goth *usstangan* to pluck out, Gk *stachys* spike of grain, *stochos* target, aim, guess] *vt* **1 a** : to pierce or wound with a poisonous or irritating process (as a stinger or stinging hair) esp. so as to produce an inflammation or lesion ⟨a great aching welt where a mosquito had *stung* him⟩; *specif* : to wound with an ovipositor (as in laying eggs) ⟨destroy the fruit flies before they begin to ~ the fruit —*Farmer's Weekly (So. Africa)*⟩ **b** : to affect with quick sharp physical pain or smart ⟨driving hail that *stung* their faces⟩ ⟨ginger ~*s* the mouth⟩ ⟨smoke . . . began to ~ his eyes —Frank Cameron⟩ **2 a** : to cause to suffer sharp mental pain : pain keenly ⟨~ him with a sharp reproach⟩ ⟨had been *stung* by remorse⟩ **b** : to stir or incite by a sharp often painful stimulus : GOAD ⟨attacks . . . ~ him to a considerable rage —*English Digest*⟩ ⟨his suffering . . . *stung* their consciences to action —*Times Lit. Supp.*⟩ **3 a** : to get the better of in a financial dealing : OVERCHARGE, CHEAT ⟨never went again to the store that had *stung* him⟩ **b** *slang* : to compel to pay : submit a bill to : STICK, CHARGE ⟨how much did he ~ you for that —J.K. Ewers⟩ ~ *vi* **1** : to wound a person or thing with a sting ⟨scorpions ~ but snakes bite⟩ ⟨an insult that *stung* and rankled⟩ **2** : to feel a keen burning pain or smart ⟨a slap that made his hand ~⟩

[2]**sting** \"\ *n* -s [ME, fr. OE, fr. *stingan*, v.] **1 a** : the act of stinging; *specif* : the thrust of a stinger into the flesh **b** : a wound or pain caused by or as if by stinging ⟨apply wet baking soda to the ~⟩ ⟨crying from the ~ of a cut⟩ ⟨the ~ of sarcasm⟩ ⟨the ~ of tears came to her eyes —Edna Ferber⟩ **2** : STINGER 2 **3** : something that causes a keen pain or stimulation of mind : a stinging element (as the point of an epigram), force, quality, or capacity ⟨a smile that took the ~ out of his rebuke⟩ ⟨practice to put more ~ into his bowling at cricket⟩ **4** : a thin rod used for mounting a model for testing in a wind tunnel

sting and ling \¦stiŋən¦liŋ\ *adv* [Sc *sting* pole (fr. ME, alter. of *steng*, fr. OE) + *and ling*, fr. E *and*, conj. + Sc *ling* (prob. alter. of E *line*, n.); fr. the practice of carrying a load by a rope having both ends attached to a pole resting on the shoulders of the carriers; akin to D *steng* pole, OHG *stengil* stalk, OE *stingan* to sting] *Scot* : WHOLLY, BODILY

sting·a·ree \'stiŋərē, -ri *also* -ŋr-\ *n* -s [by alter.] : STINGRAY; *esp* : ROUND STINGRAY

sting bladder *n* : the larva of the sting moth

stinge \'stinj\ *vi* **stinged; stinged; stingeing; stinges** [back-formation fr. [1]*stingy*] : to act stingily or parsimoniously ⟨not by ~*ing* and paring —Sheila Kaye-Smith⟩

sting·er \'stiŋə(r)\ *n* -s [[1]*sting* + *-er*] **1** : one that stings; *specif* : a sharp blow or remark **2** : any of various sharp organs of offense and defense (as of a bee, scorpion, stingray, wasp) usu. connected with a poison gland or otherwise adapted to wound by piercing and inoculating a poisonous secretion **3** : a cocktail or after-dinner drink of approximately equal parts of white crème de menthe and brandy shaken in ice and strained before serving **4** *slang* : the machine gun or cannon mounted in the tail of an airplane

stingfish \'=,=\ *n* **1** : STONEFISH **2** : SCORPION FISH

stin·gi·ly \'stinjəlē, -li\ *adv* : in a stingy manner

stin·gi·ness \-jēnəs, -jin-\ *n* -ES : the quality or state of being stingy

stinging cell *also* **sting cell** *n* : NEMATOCYST

stinging hair *n* : a glandular hair whose base secretes a stinging fluid (as in nettles)

stinging lizard *n, South* : SCORPION

sting·ing·ly \'stiŋiŋlē, -ŋēŋ-, -li\ *adv* : in a stinging manner

sting·ing·ness *n* : the quality or state of being stinging

stinging nettle *n* : a plant of the family Urticaceae that bears stinging hairs: as **a** : a perennial Eurasian nettle (*Urtica dioica*) established in No. America and having broad coarsely toothed leaves **b** : WOOD NETTLE

stinging tree *n* : an Australian nettle tree (*Laportea gigas*)

sting·less \'stiŋləs\ *adj* : having no sting

stingless bee *n* : any of numerous social bees of *Melipona* and related genera (family Apidae) mainly of tropical America that lack a sting and store honey in waxen cells much like the hive bee to which they are related

sting moth *n* : an Australian moth (*Doratifera vulnerans*) whose larva is armed at each end of the body with four tubercles bearing powerful stinging hairs

stin·go \'stiŋ(,)gō\ *n* -s [irreg. fr. [2]*sting*] **1** *chiefly Brit* : strong ale or beer **2** *slang* : ZEST, ZIP

stingray \'=,=\ *n* : any of numerous rays of Dasyatidae and related families that have one or more large sharp barbed dorsal spines near the base of the whiplike tail capable of inflicting severe wounds, sometimes reach a large size, and in some forms (as on the American Pacific coast) are very destructive to oysters

stings *pres 3d sing of* STING, *pl of* STING

sting winkle *n* : a spinose marine gastropod mollusk (*Tritonalia erinacea*) of the family Muricidae

[1]**stin·gy** \'stinjē, -ji\ *adj* -ER/-EST [prob. fr. (assumed) E dial. *stinge*, n., sting + E *-y;* akin to OE *stingan* to sting — more at STING] **1** *dial chiefly Eng* : BITING, SHARP **2 a** : reluctant to deal out, grant, or part with something : not generous : sparing or scant in giving or spending ⟨too ~ even to get a haircut before his wedding⟩ **b** : meanly scanty or small : MEAGER ⟨complained about his ~ allowance⟩ ⟨a ~ little attic room⟩

syn PARSIMONIOUS, PENURIOUS, CHEESEPARING, PENNY-PINCHING, MISERLY, CURMUDGEONLY, NIGGARDLY, TIGHT, TIGHTFISTED, CLOSEFISTED, CLOSE: STINGY, perhaps the most generally used term in this group, refers to notable want of generosity or liberality in giving, allotting, distributing, a want arising from a certain meanness of spirit ⟨couldn't help being *stingy*, since parsimony ran in their blood —Victoria Sackville-West⟩ ⟨had to request the thirteen states for tax levies, and since the states were jealous, *stingy*, and badly governed, they gave but grudging and inadequate help —Allan Nevins & H.S.Commager⟩ PARSIMONIOUS, PENURIOUS, CHEESEPARING, and PENNY-PINCHING refer to degrees and kinds of frugality. PARSIMONIOUS suggests extreme frugality with stingy wariness about expenditure ⟨a lonely bachelor life in caring for his property and in adding to it by *parsimonious* living —A.W. Long⟩ ⟨had now become strictly *parsimonious* . . . and . . . devoted every energy of his mind to save shillings and pence —Anthony Trollope⟩ PENURIOUS adds a suggestion of meanness to PARSIMONIOUS ⟨*penurious* restrictions upon the payment of legislators designed to discourage them —A.N.Holcombe⟩ CHEESEPARING suggests a parsimoniousness marked by petty mean little economies ⟨an example of *cheeseparing* economy at the dire risk of the national security —Walter Millis⟩ PENNY-PINCHING suggests greedy, wary parsimoniousness in avoiding expense ⟨a *penny-pinching* impresario who overlooked no opportunity to cut down the overhead —Bennett Cerf⟩ MISERLY, CURMUDGEONLY, and NIGGARDLY are derogatory or contemptuous terms for extreme illiberality and aversion to spending or dispensing. MISERLY suggests a morbid pleasure in hoarding, a sordid grasping meanness ⟨expenditure was parsimonious and even *miserly* —J.R.Green⟩ CURMUDGEONLY suggests mean stinginess and crusty irascibility ⟨the *curmudgeonly* old fool cutting off his wife with a bare pittance⟩ NIGGARDLY implies a stinginess in giving, granting, expending whereby one begrudges any contribution to the welfare or happiness of others ⟨we shall not be *niggardly* about this —Hugh Dalton⟩ ⟨*niggardly* monastic prescriptions with regard to gleaning —G.G.Coulton⟩ TIGHT, TIGHTFISTED, CLOSEFISTED, and CLOSE are somewhat informal expressions indicating reluctance and chariness about expending or contributing. TIGHT suggests a general chary stinginess of nature or temperament ⟨what in the name of God's the use of being so *tight* . . . you've got an expense account, haven't you —Dashiell Hammett⟩ TIGHTFISTED and CLOSEFISTED signify an accustomed reluctance to part with money and a careful vigilance against prodigality ⟨you English are a *tightfisted* race —T.B. Costain⟩ CLOSE, not so derogatory as the others, indicates either a certain stinginess or a marked caution about any expenditure ⟨he wasn't as tight as you . . . but he was a little bit *close* so the bargain hung fire —Dashiell Hammett⟩

[2]**stingy** \'stiŋē, -ŋi\ *adj* -ER/-EST [[2]*sting* + *-y*] : able to sting : having a sting or stinging hairs

[1]**stink** \'stiŋk\ *vi* **stank** \'staŋk, -taiŋk\ *or* **stunk** \'stəŋk\ **stunk; stinking; stinks** [ME *stinken*, fr. OE *stincan* to stink, emit a good or bad smell; akin to MD *stinken* to stink, OHG *stinkan* to emit a good or bad smell, and prob. to ON *stökkva* to leap, Goth *stinqan* to make war] **1** : to emit a strong offensive odor ⟨many of the men *stank* of cheap liquor —L.C. Douglas⟩ **2** : to be offensive to morality or good taste ⟨the business ~*s* to high heaven, and you . . . wouldn't dare have it aired before a court-martial —D.J.Greene⟩; *also* : to be in bad repute ⟨a scene of atrocities that will make its name ~ in history⟩ **3** : to possess something to an offensive degree ⟨tourists who are ~*ing* with money⟩ **4** : to be extremely or disgustingly bad in quality or execution ⟨his first performance *stank* and was mercilessly panned by the critics⟩

[2]**stink** \"\ *n* -s [ME, fr. *stinken*, v.] **1** : a strong offensive smell : a disgusting odor : STENCH **2** : an open or public outcry against something offensive : TO-DO ⟨made a big ~ over being accidentally shortchanged⟩ **3 stinks** *pl, Brit* : natural science as a subject of study ⟨science is called ~*s* . . . and neglected —*Spectator*⟩

stink·ard \'stiŋkə(r)d\ *n* -s **1 a** : a mean or contemptible person **b** *usu cap* : one of the common people in the social structure of the Natchez Indians — called also *stinker* **2** : an animal producing a foul odor; *specif* : TELEDU

stink·a·roo *or* **stink·er·oo** \¦stiŋkə¦rü\ *n* -s [irreg. fr. *stinker*] : STINKER ⟨this guy . . . is an insult to the integrity of the industry and a ~ —Otis Ferguson⟩

stink base *n* : PRISONER'S BASE

stink bell *n* : a fetid Californian herb (*Fritillaria agrestis*) common as a weed in grain fields

stinkbird \'=,=\ *n* **1** : HOATZIN **2** : any of various birds (as some wrens and sparrows) that leave a strong scent which may distract or confuse a bird dog

stink bomb *n* : a small bomb charged usu. with chemicals that gives off a foul odor on bursting

stinkbug \'=,=\ *n* : any of various hemipterous insects that emit a disagreeable odor: as **a** : a bug of the family Pentatomidae — called also *shield bug* **b** : SQUASH BUG

stinkbush \'=,=\ *n* **1** : a star anise (*Illicium floridanum*) of the southern U. S. **2** *Austral* : a tree (*Zieria smithii*) of the family Rutaceae

stink cat *n, Africa* : ZORIL

stinkdamp \'=,=\ *n* : sulfureted hydrogen occurring in mine workings

stink·er \'stiŋkə(r)\ *n* -s **1** : one that stinks: as **a** (1) : an offensive or disgustingly contemptible person ⟨a mean little ~ who kills puppy dogs —*Time*⟩ (2) *usu cap* : STINKARD 1b **b** : any of several large petrels (as the giant petrel) that feed on blubber and carrion and have an offensive odor **c** : something (as a play, motion picture) disgustingly poor in quality **d** *slang* : HOTBOX **2** *slang* : something extremely difficult ⟨said the three-hour examination was a real ~ and left him exhausted⟩

stink fly *n* : an insect of the family Chrysopidae

stink gland *n* : a gland that secretes a malodorous substance; *esp* : one of the thoracic or abdominal scent glands of hemipterous insects

stink grass *n* **1** : an ill-scented annual European grass (*Eragrostis megastachya*) that is nearly cosmopolitan as an introduced weed and may under certain circumstances be poisonous to livestock **2** : MOLASSES GRASS

stinkhorn \'=,=\ *n* : an ill-smelling fungus of the order Phallales; *esp* : a common fungus (*Phallus impudicus*) formerly used in preparing a salve for rheumatism — called also *carrion fungus;* compare DICTYOPHORA

[1]**stinking** *adj* [ME *stinkinge*, alter. of *stinkende*, fr. OE *stincende*, pres. part. of *stincan* to stink] **1 :** RANK, OFFENSIVE **2** *slang* **:** offensively drunk — **stink·ing·ly** *adv* — **stink·ing·ness** *n* -ES

[2]**stinking** *adv* **:** to an extreme degree ⟨a ~ drunk bum⟩

stinking ash *n* **1 :** BOX ELDER **2 :** HOP TREE

stinking badger *n* **:** TELEDU

stinking benjamin *n, usu cap B* **:** PURPLE TRILLIUM

stinking cedar *n* **1** *or* **stinking yew :** an evergreen tree (*Torreya taxifolia*) of Florida with fetid leaves resembling those of the yew **2 :** CALIFORNIA NUTMEG

stinking chamomile *n* **:** MAYWEED 1

stinking clover *n* **:** ROCKY MOUNTAIN BEE PLANT

stinking goosefoot *n* **:** a European goosefoot (*Chenopodium vulvaria*) having strong-scented foliage and adventive in eastern No. America

stinking grass *n* **:** STINK GRASS 1

stinking gum *n* **:** an Australian gum tree (*Eucalyptus tereticornis*) whose leaves have a strong sour sickly smell

stinking horehound *n* **:** BLACK HOREHOUND

stinking iris *n* **:** an iris (*Iris foetidissima*) with purple flowers and evil-smelling leaves

stinking mayweed *n* **:** MAYWEED 1

stinking mustard *n* **:** PENNYCRESS

stinking nightshade *n* **:** HENBANE 1a

stinking pea *n* **:** a yellow-flowered shrub (*Cassia bahamensis*) of Florida and the West Indies with flat pods and fetid foliage

stinking pheasant *n* **:** HOATZIN

stinking poke *n* **:** SKUNK CABBAGE 1

stinking rog·er \-'räjə(r)\ *n, usu cap R* [*roger* fr. the name *Roger*] **1 :** any of various evil-smelling plants: as **a :** any of several figworts **b :** HENBANE **c :** BLACK HOREHOUND **2** *Austral* **:** a low-growing marigold (*Tagetes glandulifera*)

stinking smut *n* **:** [2]BUNT

stinking wattle *n* **:** any of various evil-smelling Australian acacias; *esp* **:** GIDGEE 1a

stinking weed *n* **:** COFFEE SENNA

stinking wil·lie \-'wilē\ *n, usu cap W* [*willie* fr. *Willie*, nickname fr. the name *William*] **1** *NewZeal* **:** a ragwort (*Senecio jacobaea*) **2 :** PURPLE TRILLIUM **3 :** SAINT-JOHN'S-WORT

stinking willow *n* **:** MOCK LOCUST

stinko \'stiŋ(,)kō\ *adj* ['*stink* + *-o* (as in *blotto*)] *slang* **:** DRUNK

stink out *vt* **:** to drive out by or as if by subjecting to an offensive or suffocating odor

stinkpot \'=,=\ *n* **1 a :** an earthen jar charged with materials of an offensive and suffocating smell formerly sometimes thrown upon an enemy's deck **b :** POWERBOAT **2 :** MUSK TURTLE **3 :** any of various petrels: as **a :** GIANT PETREL **b :** CAPE HEN **c :** SOOTY ALBATROSS

stinks *pres 3d sing of* STINK, *pl of* STINK

stinkstone \'=,=\ *n* **:** a stone that emits a fetid smell on being struck or rubbed owing to decomposition of organic matter

stink turtle *n* **:** MUSK TURTLE

stink up *vt* **:** to cause to stink ⟨a dead whale washed ashore and *stank up* the countryside —*Time*⟩

stinkweed \'=,=\ *n* **:** any of various strong-scented or ill-smelling plants: as **a :** PENNYCRESS **b :** JIMSONWEED **c :** a wall rocket (as *Diplotaxis tenuifolia* or *D. murinum*) having foliage that is fetid when bruised or crushed **d :** SAND ROCKET **e :** ROCKY MOUNTAIN BEE PLANT **f :** MARSH FLEABANE 1

stinkwood \'=,=\ *n* **1 :** any of several trees with a wood of unpleasant odor: as **a :** either of two trees (*Ocotea bullata* and *Celtis kraussiana*) of southern Africa yielding tough useful timber **b** *Austral* **:** SAND-FLY BUSH **c :** a tree (*Foetidia mauritiana*) of the family Lecythidaceae of the Mascarene islands and Mauritius **d :** YELLOW BUCKTHORN **e :** BLACK GUM **f :** DOGWOOD 2d(1) **2 :** the wood of a stinkwood tree

stinkwort \'=,=\ *n* **1 :** a fetid European herb (*Inula graveolens*) naturalized as a weed in Australia **2 :** JIMSONWEED

stinky \'stiŋkē, -ki\ *adj* -ER/-EST **:** that stinks **:** STINKING

stinky pin·ky \,stiŋkē'piŋkē\ *n* [prob. fr. *pinky* (var. of *pinkie*)] **:** a puzzle that consists in the defining of one phrase with another made up of words that rhyme ⟨*silly filly* is a *stinky pinky* for a foolish horse⟩

[1]**stint** \'stint\ *vb* -ED/-ING/-S [ME *stinten, stenten* to cause to cease, cease, fr. OE *styntan* to blunt, dull; akin to ON *stytta* to shorten; causative fr. the root of the adjective represented by OE *stunt* dull, stupid, MHG *stunz* blunt, short, ON *stuttr* scant; akin to OHG *stōzan* to thrust, push, ON *stauta* to strike, Goth *stautan* to strike, L *tundere* to beat, Skt *tudati* he pushes, strikes, OE *stocc* stock — more at STOCK] *vt* **1** *archaic* **:** to put an end to **:** cause to stop or halt **:** STOP; *specif* **:** to check in growth **:** STUNT **2 a :** to restrain within certain limits **:** BOUND, CONFINE **b :** to limit or restrict with respect to a share or allowance **:** be sparing or frugal with ⟨they will ~ themselves for months to buy a phonograph or bicycle —*New Republic*⟩ **3** *Brit* **a :** to restrict (the use of a common pasture) to a determined number of cattle **b :** to divide (land) into rights of pasturage **c :** to limit (a person) in right of pasturage **4 :** to assign a fixed task to (a person) **:** allot a stint to **5 :** to cause (a mare) to get with foal — usu. used with *to* ⟨~*ed* to a Thoroughbred⟩ ⟨had over a hundred brood mares and began . . . ~*ing* the cream of them to him —J.L.Hervey⟩ ~ *vi* **1** *archaic* **:** STOP, CEASE, DESIST **2 :** to be sparing or frugal ⟨the stingy newspaper will ~ on its editorial costs —*Quill*⟩ ⟨one more mouth to feed, and we'll have to ~ more than we do now —Ellen Glasgow⟩

[2]**stint** \'stint\ *n* -S [ME, fr. *stinten, stenten*, v.] **1** *obs* **:** CESSATION, STOPPAGE, DELAY **2 :** RESTRAINT, RESTRICTION, LIMITATION; *esp* **:** severe or excessive limitations — often used in the phrase *without stint* ⟨during the war years we have expended our resources . . . without ~ —H.S.Truman⟩ **3** *Brit* **a :** the limited number of animals that may be grazed on a piece of common pasture **b :** the right to graze a limited number of animals on a piece of common pasture **4 :** a definite quantity or piece of work or activity assigned by another or set by oneself **:** period of work or activity ⟨did a ~ as a government livestock inspector —*New Yorker*⟩ ⟨started his one-minute ~ in the bell-ringing contest —*N.Y.Times*⟩ **:** TASK ⟨children had no hope of play before their ~*s* were satisfactorily performed —Blanche Sprague⟩ **syn** see TASK

[3]**stint** \"\ *n, pl* **stints** *also* **stint** [ME *stynte*, of unknown origin] **:** any of several small sandpipers: as **a :** RED-BACKED SANDPIPER **b :** LITTLE STINT **c :** TEMMINCK'S STINT **d :** LONG-TOED STINT **e :** LEAST SANDPIPER

[4]**stint** *var of* STENT

stint·ed·ly *adv* **:** in a stinted manner

stint·ed·ness *n* -ES **:** the quality or state of being stinted

stint·er \'stintə(r)\ *n* -S **:** one that stints

stint·ing·ly *adv* **:** in a stinting manner

stint·less \'stintləs\ *adj* **:** having no stint **:** CEASELESS, UNENDING

sti·on \'stīən\ *n* -S ['*stock* + *scion*] **:** a plant consisting of a stock and a scion — **sti·on·ic** \(')stī¦änik\ *adj*

stip *abbr* **1** stipend; stipendiary **2** stipulation

sti·pa \'stīpə\ *n* [NL, fr. L *stupa, stuppa* coarse part of flax, tow — more at STUPE] **1** *cap* **:** a large widely distributed genus of grasses having a one-flowered spikelet and lemma terminating in a long twisted or bent awn — see BUNCHGRASS, FEATHER GRASS, ICHU, NEEDLEGRASS, PORCUPINE GRASS, SLEEPY GRASS **2** *also* **stipa grass** -S **:** any grass of the genus *Stipa*; *specif* **:** ESPARTO

[1]**stipe** \'stīp\ *n* -S [NL *stipes*, fr. L, log, trunk of a tree; akin to L *stipare* to press together — more at STIFF] **1 :** a short stalk or support: as **a :** the stem supporting the cap or pileus of certain fungi **b :** the stemlike part of the thallus of many frondose algae **c :** the petiole of the frond of a fern; *also* **:** the woody caudex of a tree fern **d :** a stalklike prolongation of the receptacle beneath the ovary of a seed plant — compare ANTHOPHORE, CARPOPHORE, GYNOBASE, GYNOPHORE 1 **2 a :** STIPES 1 **b :** a branch of a graptolite colony — **stiped** \-pt\ *adj*

[2]**stipe** \"\ *n* -S [short for [2]*stipendiary*] *chiefly Austral* **:** a stipendiary steward of a jockey club

sti·pel \'stīpəl\ *n* -S [NL *stipella*, dim. of *stipula* stipule] **:** the stipule of a leaflet

sti·pel·late \stī'pelət, stə'p-; 'stīpə,lāt, 'stip-\ *adj* [NL *stipellatus*, fr. *stipella* stipel + L *-atus* -ate] **:** having stipels

sti·pend \'stī,pend, -,pənd\ *n* -S [ME *stipende, stipendy*, fr. L *stipendium*, fr. *stip-, stips* gift, alms + *-pendium* (fr. *pendere* to weigh, pay); perh. akin to L *stipare* to press together — more at STIFF, PENDANT] **1 :** a fixed sum of money typically modest in amount that is paid periodically in compensation for services (as of a clergyman or teacher) **:** SALARY **2 :** a regular allowance paid to defray living expenses; *esp* **:** a sum paid to a student under the terms of a fellowship or scholarship ⟨the scholarship may carry a ~ large enough to take care of the student's entire college expenses —*Harvard College Nat'l Scholarships*⟩ **syn** see WAGE

[1]**sti·pen·di·ary** \stī'pendē,erē\ *adj* [L *stipendiarius*, fr. *stipendium* + *-arius* -ary] **1 :** receiving or compensated by wages or salary **:** performing services for a stated price or compensation ⟨a ~ curate⟩ **2 :** of or relating to a stipend

[2]**stipendiary** \"\ *n* -ES **:** one who receives a stipend: as **a** *Brit* (1) **:** a stipendiary clergyman (2) **:** STIPENDIARY MAGISTRATE **b** *archaic* **:** a mercenary soldier

stipendiary magistrate *n* **:** a salaried British magistrate who is a professional lawyer appointed under statutory provisions to act instead of or in cooperation with unpaid lay justices of the peace

sti·pen·di·um \stī'pendēəm\ *n* -S [L] **:** STIPEND

sti·pend·less \'stī,pendləs, -,pən-\ *adj* **:** having no stipend

sti·pes \'stī,pēz\ *n, pl* **stip·i·tes** \'stipə,tēz\ [NL *stipit-, stipes*, fr. L, log, trunk of a tree; akin to L *stipare* to press together — more at STIFF] **1 :** PEDUNCLE: as **a :** the second basal segment of a maxilla of an insect or crustacean **b :** the second or rarely the first basal segment of the mandible of a millipede — compare MALA 2b **c :** either of the inner and outer platelike pieces that form the major portion of the deutomala of a myriapod **d :** EYESTALK **2 :** STIPE 1

sti·pi·form \'stīpə,fȯrm\ *also* **stip·i·ti·form** \'stipəd·ə,f-, stə'pid-\ *adj* [*stipiform* fr. NL *stipiformis*, fr. *stipes* stipe, stipes + L *-iformis* -iform; *stipitiform* fr. NL *stipitiformis*, fr. *stipit-, stipes* stipe, stipes + L *-iformis* -iform] **:** resembling a stipe or stipes **:** STALKLIKE

stip·i·tal \'stipəd·ᵊl\ *adj* [NL *stipit-, stipes* + E *-al*] **:** of or relating to the stipes

stip·i·tate \'stipə,tāt\ *adj* [NL *stipitatus*, fr. *stipit-, stipes* + L *-atus* -ate] **:** having or borne on a stipe ⟨a ~ pod⟩

stip·i·tat·ic acid \¦stipə¦tad·ik-\ *n* [*stipitatic* fr. NL *stipitatum* (specific epithet of *Penicillium stipitatum*) (neut. of *stipitatus* stipitate) + E *-ic*] **:** a cream-colored solid acid $(HO)_2C_7H_3$-OCOOH related to tropolone and formed from sugar as a metabolic product of a mold (*Penicillium stipitatum*); 3,6-dihydroxy-4-oxo-cyclo-hepta-triene-carboxylic acid

stip·i·ture \'stipə,chu̇(ə)r\ *n* -S [NL *Stipiturus*] **:** a bird of the genus *Stipiturus*

stip·i·tu·rus \,stipə'tu̇rəs, -pə'tyu̇-\ *n, cap* [NL, fr. L *stipit-, stipes* log + NL *-urus*] **:** a genus of small babblers comprising the Australian emu wrens

stip·pen \'stipən\ *n* -S [G, pl. of *stippe* speck, spot, fr. LG, fr. MLG, fr. *stippen* to prick] **:** BITTER PIT

[1]**stip·ple** \'stipəl\ *vt* -ED/-ING/-S [D *stippelen* to spot, dot, fr. *stippel* speck, spot, fr. MD, dim. of *stip* point, dot, fr. *stippen* to prick; akin to MLG *stippen* to prick, MHG *steppen* to stitch, quilt, Russ *stebel'* stalk — more at STIFF] **1 :** to engrave essentially by means of dots and flicks — compare LINE ENGRAVING **2 a :** to make (as in paint, ink) by small short touches that together produce an even or softly graded shadow **b :** to apply (as paint) by repeated small touches **3 :** to produce an effect in as if by stippling **:** dot or spot with shade or color **:** SPECKLE, FLECK, STREAK ⟨sunlight that fell through the trees and *stippled* the sidewalks —Hamilton Basso⟩

[2]**stipple** \"\ *n* -S **1 a :** execution in graphic art by which gradation of light and shade is produced by separate touches of small points, larger dots, or longer strokes **b :** the effect so produced that may show every separate point or touch (as in prints from a stipple plate) or may resemble a mosaic in which the touches tend to run together (as in stippling in strokes from a brush filled with color) **c :** the spattered effect produced on book edges by sprinkling **d :** a finish of paper characterized by small raised dots **2 :** an effect (as in nature) resembling a stipple **3 :** a brush used in stippling

stipple board *n* **:** a drawing board prepared by coating and embossing in such a way that a mark made upon it with crayon or pencil produces the effect of a tone formed by minute dots

stippled *adj* **:** produced or applied by stippling **:** DOTTED, SPOTTED, SPECKLED

stipple engraving *n* **1 :** the act or process of engraving by stippling **2 :** the impression made from a stippled plate

stipple paper *n* **:** a paper similar to stipple board

stip·pler \-p(ə)lə(r)\ *n* -S **:** one that stipples; *specif* **:** an artist or a painter who stipples surfaces

stipple streak *n* **:** a virus disease of the potato characterized by leaf distortion, vein necrosis, and brittleness of stems and petioles

stippling *n* -S **1 :** a stippled effect **2 :** a spotted condition (as in basophilic red blood corpuscles, the retina in diseases of the eye, X rays of the lungs, bones)

stip·ply \-p(ə)lē, -li\ *adj* -ER/-EST **:** resembling stipple **:** somewhat stippled

stip·u·la \'stipyələ\ *n, pl* **stipu·lae** \-,lē, -,lī\ [NL] **:** STIPULE

stip·u·la·ble \'stipyələbəl\ *adj* ['*stipulate* + *-able*] **:** that can be stipulated

stip·u·lar \'stipyələ(r)\ *adj* [NL *stipularis*, fr. *stipula* + L *-aris* -ar] **:** of, resembling, or provided with stipules **:** growing on or like stipules ⟨~ glands⟩ ⟨~ tendrils⟩

[1]**stip·u·late** \'stipyə,lāt, *usu* -ād·+V\ *vb* -ED/-ING/-S [L *stipulatus*, past part. of *stipulari* to make an express demand for some term in an agreement; akin to Umbrian *steplatu* one that makes an express demand for some term in an agreement and perh. to L *stipare* to press together — more at STIFF] *vi* **1 :** to make an agreement or covenant with a person or company to do or forbear something **:** CONTRACT ⟨have *stipulated* for the future disposition and management of those funds —John Marshall⟩ **2 :** to make an express demand for some term in an agreement — used with *for* ⟨fulfilling . . . all the conditions of constraint for which we *stipulated* —Sacheverell Sitwell⟩ **3 :** to agree respecting the conduct of legal proceedings — used with *to* ⟨counsel on both sides will ~ to the receipt of such working papers . . . in evidence —*Jour. of Accountancy*⟩ ~ *vt* **1 :** to specify as a condition or requirement of an agreement or offer (as a contract, treaty, deed, will, law) **:** state as a stipulation ⟨in his will the latter *stipulated* that his sons should all be taught trades —H.E.Starr⟩ ⟨the terms of the Italian peace treaty had *stipulated* the return to Greece of the Dodecanese Islands —R.G.Woolbert⟩ **2 :** to give a guarantee of **:** PROMISE ⟨ceded to the French, who *stipulated* to erect no fortifications on these islands —Jedidiah Morse⟩ **3 :** to agree mutually concerning (conduct or evidence) during legal proceedings ⟨we'll ~ . . . that this man was employed to spy on his wife —Erle Stanley Gardner⟩

[2]**stip·u·late** \-,lət\ *also* **stip·u·lat·ed** \-,lād·əd\ *adj* [*stipulate* fr. NL *stipulatus*, fr. *stipula* + L *-atus* -ate; *stipulated* fr. *stipulate* (fr. NL *stipulatus*) + *-ed*] **:** furnished with stipules

stipulated damages *n pl* **:** damages settled by stipulation **:** liquidated damages

stip·u·la·tion \,stipyə'lāshən\ *n* -S [L *stipulation-, stipulatio*, fr. *stipulatus* (past part. of *stipulari*) + *-ion-, -io* -ion] **1 :** an act of stipulating or something stipulated **:** AGREEMENT, PROVISION: as **a :** an agreement between attorneys respecting the conduct of legal proceedings **b :** a bond or undertaking taken in admiralty courts **c** *Roman law* **:** a formal contract by oral question and answer imposing a duty on the promisor only **d :** a condition, requirement, or item specified in a contract, treaty, deed, will, or law **2 :** a stipulative definition or the process of specifying one **syn** see CONDITION

stip·u·la·tive definition \'stipyə,lād·iv-, -,lət·iv-\ *n* [*stipulative* fr. [1]*stipulate* + *-ive*] **:** a declaration of a meaning that is intended to be attached by the speaker to a word, expression, or symbol and that usu. does not already have an established use in the sense intended — compare DICTIONARY DEFINITION

stip·u·la·tor \-,lād·ə(r)\ *n* -S [L, fr. *stipulatus* (past part. of *stipulari*) + *-or*] **1 :** one that stipulates **2 :** one that proposes a stipulative definition

stip·u·la·to·ry \-,lə,tōrē\ *adj* [[1]*stipulate* + *-ory*] **1 :** of, relating to, or characterized by stipulation **2 :** constituted or contracted by stipulation ⟨~ obligations⟩

stip·ule \'sti(,)pyül\ *n* -S [NL *stipula*, fr. L, stalk, straw; akin to L *stipes* log, trunk of a tree, *stipare* to press together — more at STIFF] **1 a :** one of the pair of leaflike or membranous appendages that arise at the base of the leaf in many plants, vary greatly in size and shape and in degree of adnation to the stem, to the petiole, or to each other, and become modified in some plants to form spines or tendrils and in others to perform all the functions of leaves — see OCREA **b** *also* **stip·u·lode** \'stipyə,lōd\ [*stipulode* fr. *stipule* + *-ode*] **:** one of the leaflike structures arising together with the leaf from the cortex of the basal nodes in some algae of the genus *Chara* **2 :** a newly sprouted feather **:** PINFEATHER

stip·uled \'sti(,)pyüld\ *adj* **:** STIPULATE

stip·u·lif·er·ous \¦stipyə¦lif(ə)rəs\ *adj* [NL *stipulifer* stipuliferous (fr. *stipula* stipule + L *-ifer* -iferous) + E *-ous*] **:** bearing or producing stipules

stip·u·li·form \'stipyələ,fȯrm\ *adj* [*stipule* + *-iform*] **:** having the form of a stipule

[1]**stir** *R* 'stər, + *vowel* -tər·; —*R* -tə̄, + *suffixal vowel* -tər· *also* -tə̄r, + *vowel in a following word* -tər· *or* -tə̄ *also* -tə̄r\ *vb* **stirred; stirred; stirring; stirs** [ME *stiren, steren*, fr. OE *styrian*; akin to MHG *stürn* to poke, incite, ON *styrr* disturbance, and prob. to Skt *tvarate* he hurries — more at TURBID] *vt* **1 a :** to impart movement to; *esp* **:** to cause the slightest movement or change of position of ⟨a faint smile *stirred* her lips —Kathleen Freeman⟩ ⟨tied so tightly he could scarcely ~ a finger⟩ ⟨the great warships easing slowly through the gates of the bay . . . and *stirring* the yachts at anchor —John Durant⟩ **b :** to disturb the quiet of **:** AGITATE ⟨little boats that barely ~ its mysterious black waters —Selby Paul⟩ ⟨coons, coyotes, and owls *stirred* the silence here and there —John Muir †1914⟩ **2 a** (1) **:** to pass a spoon or other implement through (a substance) with a continued circular movement for the purpose of mixing, blending, dissolving, cooling, or preventing sticking of the ingredients ⟨~ the batter until the dry ingredients are blended⟩ ⟨puts sugar in his tea and ~*s* it⟩ ⟨~*s* his pail of paint with a paddle⟩ (2) **:** to mix by or as if by stirring ⟨careful to ~ the ingredients well⟩ ⟨by *stirring* together a mass of . . . facts and superstitions, he arrived at a hierarchy of races —Martin Gardner⟩ — often used with *in* or *into* ⟨~ in the flour gradually to avoid lumping⟩ ⟨~ the beaten eggs into the milk⟩ **b :** to disturb the relative position of the particles or parts of ⟨~ the fire with the poker to make it burn again⟩ ⟨~ the topsoil⟩ — often used with *up* ⟨the cows would wade into the pool and ~ up . . . the mud on the bottom —Vicki Baum⟩ **3 :** BESTIR, EXERT ⟨the wife would . . . ~ herself to sweep the floor —Pearl Buck⟩ **4 :** to bring (a subject or question) into notice or debate **:** RAISE ⟨~ not questions of jurisdiction —Francis Bacon⟩ **5 a :** to excite to activity or strong feeling ⟨an instinct ~*s* her to feed the older grubs —Weston La Barre⟩ **:** INCITE, INFLAME ⟨heroism that ~*s* orators to eloquence⟩ ⟨the increase of illiteracy in children . . . has *stirred* the conscience of the British public —*Britain Today*⟩ ⟨able, as a public speaker, to ~ people . . . to the point of tears —Stewart Cockburn⟩ **:** QUICKEN ⟨peace has no drums and trumpets to ~ the pulse —Amy Loveman⟩ — often used with *up* ⟨she *stirred* up her father to proclaim a campaign against the whites —Negley Farson⟩ **b :** to call forth (as a feeling, memory, or disposition) from a person or group **:** EVOKE ⟨men lacking an arm or leg *stirred* universal pity —Dixon Wecter⟩ ⟨this Vermont watering trough . . . will ~ nostalgic memories —J.H.East⟩ **:** PROVOKE ⟨the inquiry has *stirred* a hot controversy —*N.Y.Times*⟩ — often used with *up* ⟨abolitionists encouraged agitators to come South and ~ up discontent —Helen B. Woodward⟩ ~ *vi* **1 a :** to make a slight movement ⟨a light breeze was *stirring* in the lime trees —T.B.Costain⟩ **:** change one's position slightly ⟨a bed that squeaks if he so much as ~*s*⟩ **:** begin to move (as in rousing) ⟨girl on the floor *stirred*, moaned and sat up —Louis Bromfield⟩ **b :** to make the least movement or excursion **:** move or go at all **:** BUDGE ⟨so intent on this fantastic . . . narrative that she had hardly *stirred* —Walter de la Mare⟩ ⟨it was very wet all day and I didn't ~ out of the house —Lennox Robinson⟩ **2 :** to begin to be active **:** show signs of life ⟨already, although it was still dark, the life of the farm was *stirring* —Ellen Glasgow⟩ ⟨profound forces were *stirring* into a vigorous life that was soon to transform the culture of Europe —I.M.Price⟩ **3 a :** to move in or from a place (as amid prevailing quiet or after inactivity) ⟨in the barn back of the house she could hear the cattle *stirring* about —Sherwood Anderson⟩; *also* **:** to be up and about ⟨up and gone before the others were *stirring*⟩ **b :** to be active or busy **:** move in a brisk or vigorous manner ⟨seemed to be forever busy about something, *stirring* around in the midst of tumult and struggle —W.A.White⟩ **:** exert oneself ⟨the friends of the unfortunate exile . . . were *stirring* anxiously in his behalf —Charles Merivale⟩ **:** be in a state of excitement ⟨the discontents that had been *stirring* in him for at least fifteen years —Carl Van Doren⟩ **4 :** to become an object of notice **:** be current ⟨talk freely on everything that ~*s* —Isaac Watts⟩ **5 :** to pass an implement through a substance with a circular movement (as for the purpose of mixing) ⟨asked to lick the spoon she was *stirring* with⟩ **6 :** to be capable of being stirred ⟨add water till the mixture ~*s* easily⟩

syn STIR and STIR (*up*), ROUSE, AROUSE, AWAKEN, WAKEN, RALLY can mean to inspire or drive someone from inactivity to action of some kind, or (with the exception of RALLY) to inspire or provoke. STIR and STIR (*up*) suggest provocation of a person or his imagination to activity often implying something latent awaiting provocation; or they can apply directly to an emotion or reaction of the person provoked ⟨obstacles only *stirred* the friars to greater efforts —R.A.Billington⟩ ⟨some of them *stir* the imagination and call forth emotions —Douglas Carruthers⟩ ⟨the present Diana had wakened his curiosity, had *stirred* his interest in her —George Meredith⟩ ⟨movements that begin by *stirring up* hostility against a group of people —John Dewey⟩ ⟨matters that *stir* heated controversy —F.A.Ogg & Harold Zink⟩ ROUSE, AROUSE, AWAKEN, and WAKEN all presuppose a state of repose, often sleep or a dormant condition. ROUSE suggests a suddenness in stirring to activity, esp. wakefulness, often applying to incitement by startling, frightening, or upsetting and sometimes suggesting ensuing turbulence ⟨*roused* out of sleep by a heavy pounding on the door —Joseph Wechsberg⟩ ⟨when he was *roused* he spoke with eloquence —R.M.Lovett⟩ ⟨the sight of the brisk flames *roused* the rioters —T.B.Costain⟩ ⟨poetry *roused* in her a clumsy and conventional enthusiasm —Virginia Woolf⟩ ⟨a *rousing* fight⟩ AROUSE is weaker in implication than ROUSE, often suggesting no more than to start into activity ⟨the fact *aroused* no curiosity —John Dewey⟩ ⟨busy *arousing* the public to the danger —W.G. Carleton⟩ ⟨*aroused* sleeping memories —R.L.Cook⟩ ⟨have sought to *arouse* prejudice and fear —F.D.Roosevelt⟩ AWAKEN and WAKEN, implying an ending of sleep, apply chiefly to the stirring to activity of mental or spiritual powers ⟨their assertion that you *awakened* them to think —Irwin Edman⟩ ⟨*awaken* the curiosity of the future scientist —J.B.Conant⟩ ⟨*awaken* the spirit of good will —V.L.Parrington⟩ ⟨employ their talents or *waken* the deepest interest in their lives —Thomas Wolfe⟩ ⟨*wakened* his latent powers of literary expression —C.A.Madison⟩ RALLY implies a gathering together of diffused or disorganized forces that stirs up or rouses, esp. to positive or organized activity ⟨his smiling face *rallied* his friends —Claud Cockburn⟩ ⟨necessary to *rally* all the forces in the country in the name of freedom against a foreign foe —John Dewey⟩ ⟨the prisoner made an effort to *rally* his attention —Charles Dickens⟩

[2]**stir** \"\ *n* -S **1 a :** the state of being stirred **:** a state of disturbance, agitation, or activity **:** COMMOTION ⟨the entrance of the judge and a consequent great ~ . . . stopped the dialogue —Charles Dickens⟩ **:** RESTLESSNESS ⟨an age of ~ and change, a season of new wine and old bottles —John Galsworthy⟩ **:** FLURRY ⟨these visits brought a considerable ~ of . . . business in the provinces —R.W.Southern⟩ **b :** a reaction of widespread notice and discussion ⟨an exposé that created a considerable ~ in the press⟩ **:** IMPRESSION ⟨an obscure family that had till then made little ~ in the world⟩ **2 :** a slight or incipient movement, excitement, or emotion ⟨with every ~ of wind and wheel, the dust blows in choking brown clouds —Marjory S. Douglas⟩ ⟨everywhere there was a faint and genial ~ of spring in the air —Susan Ertz⟩ **3 :** an act of stirring **:** a stirring movement **:** POKE ⟨give the embers a ~⟩

syn STIR, BUSTLE, FLURRY, POTHER, FUSS, ADO: these six nouns all point to a manifest excitement or agitation accompanying an action or event. STIR stresses a restless or brisk movement, usu. of a group or crowd ⟨a great *stir* about the manse that morning, and the boys were dressed in their Sunday clothes —William Black⟩ ⟨the announcement created quite a *stir* in the audience⟩ BUSTLE adds the idea of noisy, obtrusive, often self-important activity ⟨the streets are alive with the hurry and noise of a big city. Then the *bustle* subsides and relative calm is resumed —*Amer. Guide Series: N.C.*⟩ ⟨no such *bustle* of enthusiasm, no such in-and-out of busy workers —S.H.Adams⟩ FLURRY puts stress upon sudden, nervous, usu. short-lived activity, often suggesting undue haste ⟨a *flurry* of excitement⟩ ⟨set off a *flurry* of speculation in the world's oil industry —*Time*⟩ ⟨a *flurry* of ground fire exploded at almost the right altitude to catch the photographic plane —J.A.Michener⟩ POTHER and FUSS both imply unnecessary, often confused, activity or agitation, usu. over trifles. POTHER lays stress upon the agitation or confusion ⟨he was not unused to women, but he was unused to a *pother* of emotion over any one of them —Audrey Barker⟩ ⟨the great hydraulic firms were in a continual *pother* about the water rights —Julian Dana⟩ FUSS usu. stresses more the needlessness of the commotion ⟨those events . . . scarcely warranted the tremendous *fuss* subsequently made about them —Arnold Bennett⟩ ⟨much *fuss* is made of the right of the parent to order the life of his child —*Times Lit. Supp.*⟩ ADO usu. implies fussy activity and waste of energy ⟨everybody seems to know his job and to take over his duties without much *ado* —*Education Digest*⟩ ⟨among . . . speculators there always is considerable *ado* whenever the stock market drops below its preceding lows —*Newsweek*⟩

3**stir** \"\ *n* -s [by alter.] *Scot* : SIR

4**stir** \"\ *n* -s [origin unknown] *slang* : PRISON ⟨an international jewel thief just out of ~ and eager to get back to work —V.P. Hass⟩

stir *abbr* stirrup

stirabout \'=ə,=\ *n* -s [fr. *stir about*, v.] **1** : a porridge of oatmeal or cornmeal boiled in water or milk and stirred during cooking **2 a** : STIR, TUMULT **b** : a bustling person **3** : a combination of pinch shot and push shot used in pool when the cue ball and object ball are too close to a pocket to allow a cut stroke

stir bug *n, slang* : a person mentally unbalanced by prison life

stir crazy *adj, slang* : psychotic as a result of confinement in or as if in prison

stirk \'stərk\ *n* -s [ME, fr. OE *stirc*; akin to MLG *sterke* young cow, Icel *stirtla* sterile cow, L *sterilis* sterile — more at STERILE] **1** *Brit* : a young bull or cow esp. when more than one but less than two years old **2** *Brit* : FOOL

stir·less \'stərləs, -təl-\ *adj* : devoid of stir : MOTIONLESS — **stir·less·ly** *adv* — **stir·less·ness** *n* -ES

stir·ling \'stərliŋ\ *Scot var of* STARLING

stir·ling cycle \'stər|liŋ-, -təl, -təil, |lēŋ-\ *n, usu cap S* [after Robert *Stirling* †1878 Scot. engineer] : a cycle for an air engine using a regenerator and having for its indicator diagram two isothermals and two lines of constant volume

stirling engine *n, usu cap S* : an air engine using the Stirling cycle

stirling's formula *n, usu cap S* [after James *Stirling* †1770 Scot. mathematician] : a formula giving the approximate value of the factorial of any very large number

stir·ling·shire \-ŋ,shi(ə)r, ,shiə, -,shə(r)\ *or* **stirling** *adj, usu cap* [fr. *Stirlingshire*, *Stirling*, county in central Scotland] : of or from the county of Stirling, Scotland : of the kind or style prevalent in Stirling

stir off *vi* **1** : to complete the process of boiling down syrup to a thickness at which the sugar crystallizes and is separated from the molasses **2** : SUGAR OFF

stirp \'stərp\ *n* -s [L *stirp-, stirps*] **1** : a line descending from a common ancestor : STOCK, LINEAGE **2** : the sum of the determinants of whatever nature in a fertilized egg

stir·pi·cul·ture \'stərpə,kəlchər\ *n* [L *stirp-, stirps* + E *-i-* + *culture*] : the breeding of special stocks or races

stirps \'sti(ə)rps, 'stərps\ *n, pl* **stir·pes** \-ir,pās, -ər(,)pēz\ [L *stirp-, stirps* branch of a family, lineage, trunk, root — more at TORPID] **1** : a branch of a family — usu. used in the phrase *per stirpes* **2** : the person from whom a branch of a family is descended **3 a** : a large group of animals comparable to a superfamily **b** : a race or fixed variety of plants

stir·ra *or* **stir·rah** \'stirə\ *n* -s [prob. alter. of *sirrah*] *Scot* : BOY, FELLOW — compare SIRRAH

stir·ra·ble \'stər·əbəl *also* -tərəb-\ *adj* : that can be stirred

stirred *past of* STIR

stir·rer \'stər·ə(r) *also* -tərə(r\ *n* -s [ME *stirer, sterer*, fr. *stiren, steren* to stir + *-er*] : one that stirs: as **a** : a workman who stirs materials (as in baking, sugar refining) **b** : a stirring device in a seed planter **c** : a power-driven apparatus for stirring **d** : a utensil with a long stem and usu. a spoon end for mixing drinks

1**stirring** *n* -s [ME *stiringe, steringe*, fr. OE *styrung, styring*, fr. *styrian* to stir + *-ung, -ing* -ing] : the act of one that stirs : a moving or putting in motion : MOVEMENT, ACTIVITY, AGITATION, INCITEMENT ⟨his grandfather's barn at night with its . . . restless ~ of animals inside —J.P.Marquand⟩ ⟨had already felt little ~s of compunction —Mary Austin⟩

2**stirring** *adj* [ME *stiringe, steringe*, alter. of *stirende, sterende* that stirs, fr. OE *styrende, styriende*, pres. part. of *styrian* to stir] : that stirs; *esp* : EXCITING ⟨~ events such as wars and rescues⟩ ⟨inflamed their patriotism with a ~ oration on their threatened liberties⟩

stir·ring·ly *adv* [ME *steringli*, fr. *stiringe, steringe*, adj. + *-liche, -ly, -li* -ly] : in a stirring manner

stirring plow *n* : a plow with a high abruptly curved moldboard for turning the furrow slice of old land quickly but less completely than a breaker

stirrer d

stir·rup \'stər·əp, 'stə·rəp *also* 'stirəp *sometimes* 'sterəp, *chiefly in dial or substand speech* 'stərp\ *n* -s [ME *stirop*, fr. OE *stigrāp*; akin to OHG *stegareif* stirrup, ON *stigreip*; all fr. a prehistoric NGmc-WGmc compound whose first constituent is akin to OE *stīgan* to go up and whose second constituent is represented by OE *rāp* rope — more at STAIR, ROPE] **1** : a ring or bent piece of metal, wood, or leather made horizontal in one part for receiving the foot of a rider, attached by a strap to a saddle, and used to aid in mounting and as a support while riding — see STOCK SADDLE illustration **2** : a piece resembling a stirrup: as **a** : one used as a support or clamp in carpentry and machinery — compare HANGER 7 **b** : a flat usu. U-shaped steel bar or strap for receiving and supporting one end of a timber joist, beam, or girder **c** : a stirrup-shaped footrest (as used in working bellows) **3** : a rope secured to a yard and having a thimble in its lower end for supporting a footrope — see SAIL illustration, SHIP illustration **4** [trans. of NL *stapes*] : STAPES **5** : the part of a garment or device that passes under the instep

stirrup bar *n* **1** : the horizontal piece of a stirrup **2** : the bar from which a riding stirrup is suspended

stirrup cup *n* **1** : a cup of wine or other drink taken by a rider about to depart **2** : a farewell cup : a parting glass

stirrup iron *n* [ME (Sc) *stirrap irn*, fr. ME *stirrap, strop* stirrup + *irn, iren* iron] : the metal loop of a riding stirrup

stirrup leather *or* **stirrup strap** *n* [*stirrup leather* fr. ME *stirop lethir*, fr. *stirop* stirrup + *lethir, lether* leather; *stirrup strap* fr. *stirrup* + *strap*] : the strap suspending a stirrup — see STOCK SADDLE illustration

stirruplike \'=ə,=\ *adj* : resembling a stirrup

stirrup pump *n* : a portable hand pump held in position by a foot bracket or stirrup and often used (as with a bucket) to supply a short hose for extinguishing small fires

stirrup pump

stirrup-vase \'=ə,=\ *n* : PSEUDAMPHORA

stirs *pres 3d sing of* STIR, *pl of* STIR

stir-up \'=,=\ *n* -s [fr. *stir up*, v.] : an act of stirring up or state of being stirred up : AGITATION, TURMOIL

stir-up sunday \'=,=-\ *n, usu cap both Ss* [so called fr. the first words of the Anglican collect for the day, "Stir up, we beseech thee, O Lord, the wills of thy faithful people"] *Brit* : the Sunday next before Advent

1**stitch** \'stich\ *n* -ES [ME *stiche*, fr. OE *stice* stab, puncture, stitch in the side; akin to OHG *stih* sting, pricking, Goth *stiks* moment, OHG *stehhan* to prick — more at STICK] **1** : a local sharp and sudden pain in the side (as in pleurodynia) **2** : a single complete in-and-out movement of a threaded needle in sewing, embroidering, or suturing **3 a** (1) : a portion of thread left in the material after making one in-and-out movement with a threaded needle in hand sewing (2) : one of the separate lengths of thread, wire, or other material used to hold skin or flesh (as the edges of a wound or incision) during healing (3) : the interlocked section of the threads from needle and shuttle resulting from a single complete motion of the needle through the fabric in machine sewing **b** : the interlacing thread that joins the face and back of a double fabric in weaving **c** : a staple formed by a wire-stitching machine from a coil of wire (as for fastening pamphlets, cartons, novelties) ⟨a wire stitcher that applies ~es as fast as 300 a minute⟩ **4** *dial chiefly Brit* : a narrow ridge of arable land : a ridge between furrows **5** : a least part : least bit ⟨a boat . . . with every ~ of canvas set —Benjamin Disraeli⟩ ⟨refused to do a ~ of work⟩; *specif* : the least bit of clothing ⟨left without a dry ~ on his back⟩ **6** : a single loop of thread or yarn around a knitting needle, crochet hook, or other implement forming one of a series of links in knitted, crocheted, netted, or lace fabric ⟨drop a ~⟩ **7 a** : a stitch or series of stitches formed in a particular manner often for a particular purpose (as basting, buttonholing); *also* : a decorative pattern formed by a stitch (as a French knot) or series of stitches (as satin stitch) worked with a needle or hook through or on cloth or over canvas **b** : a method of fastening leaves (as of pamphlets) with thread or cord drawn by hand or machine through previously pierced holes or with wire staples — usu. used with a qualifier; see DOUBLE STITCH, SADDLE STITCH, SIDE STITCH **syn** see PAIN — **in stitches** *adv* : in a state of uncontrollable laughter ⟨keep cocktail parties *in stitches* with slapstick impersonations —*Time*⟩

2**stitch** \"\ *vb* -ED/-ING/-ES [ME *stichen*, fr. *stiche*, n.] *vt* **1** *obs* : PIERCE, STAB **2 a** (1) : to fasten, join, or close with or as if with stitches ⟨~*ed* his team emblem onto his uniform⟩ ⟨~ the ends of the two strips together⟩ ⟨many literary travelers have . . . ~*ed* their impressions into skillful embroideries —Edward Sapir⟩ — often used with *up* ⟨~ up the rip⟩ (2) : to fasten together (signatures) by passing thread or wire through all the signatures at once — distinguished from *sew* (3) : to unite by means of staples ⟨~ the flaps of a fiber box⟩ **b** : to make, mend, or decorate with or as if with stitches : SEW ⟨~ a seam⟩ : EMBROIDER ⟨~ a sampler⟩ — often used with *up* ⟨~ up torn trousers⟩ **c** : to sew in a hasty manner — usu. used with *up* ⟨~ up a dress to wear this evening⟩ **d** : to sew by first puncturing (as shoe leather) with an awl or needle by hand or by machine **3** *dial* : to form (arable land) into ridges **4** : to form the outline of (a design) on metal by prick-punching through a design on paper fixed to the metal **5** : to strike or pierce at intervals in the manner of stitching ⟨machine guns ~*ed* the sides of buildings —*Springfield (Mass.) Union*⟩ ~ *vi* **1** : to do needlework : SEW **2** : to join something with wire stitches **3** : to move in and out in a stitchlike manner

3**stitch** \"\ *n* -ES [perh. fr. ME *sticche* piece, fr. OE *stycce* — more at STOCK] *dial Eng* : a harvesting shock of about 12 sheaves

4**stitch** \"\ *n* [perh. fr. ME *sticche* piece] **1** *dial Eng* : DISTANCE 2c **2** *dial* : a period of time

stitch aloft *vt* : to stitch (as a shoe or the sole of a shoe) so that the stitches are exposed and not in a covered channel

stitch·bird \'stich,=\ *n* [so called fr. the resemblance of its call to the word *stitch*] : a nearly extinct honey eater (*Notiomystis cincta*) of North Island, New Zealand, of which the male has black, yellow, and white plumage

stitchdown \'=,=\ *n* -s [fr. *stitch down*, v.] **1** : the stitching of the outward-turned lower edge of a shoe upper directly to the sole or sometimes with a welt added over the edge **2** *also* **stitchdown shoe** : a shoe made by the stitchdown process

stitch·er \'stichə(r)\ *n* -s : one that stitches: as **a** : a worker who joins or decorates articles or parts of articles with hand or machine stitching **b** (1) : a machine that joins (as box bottoms) using staples formed from a continuous coil of wire (2) : the operator of such a machine

stitch·ery \-chərē\ *n* -ES : NEEDLEWORK

stitching *n* -s **1 a** : the act of one that stitches **b** : work done by one that stitches **2** : STITCHES; *esp* : a continuous line of stitches **3** : SEWING

stitching horse *n* : a harness maker's clamp for holding work while it is being stitched

stitch in time : a timely action or remedy ⟨a *stitch in time* saves nine⟩

stitchlike \'=,=\ *adj* : resembling a stitch or stitching

stitch rivet *n* : one of several widely spaced rivets used to connect two or more parallel elements of a built-up structural member so that they will act as a unit and will not separate laterally

stitch-rivet \'=|==\ *vt* [*stitch rivet*] : to connect with stitch rivets

stitch watermark *n* : a fortuitous watermark on a stamp caused usu. by the stitches in the wire of the paper machine

1**stitch weld** *n* : a joint made by stitch welding

2**stitch weld** *vt* : to unite by stitch welding

stitch welding *n* : resistance welding in which the weld is made linearly (as between rotating wheels) by a series of spot welds that are spaced rather than overlapping (as in seam welding)

stitch wheel *n* : PRICKER 2c

stitchwork \'=,=\ *n* : NEEDLEWORK; *esp* : TAPESTRY

stitchwort \'=,=\ *n* [ME *stichewort*, fr. OE *sticwyrt* agrimony, fr. *stice* stab, puncture, stitch in the side + *wyrt* herb — more at STITCH, WORT] : any of several plants of the genus *Stellaria*

stith \'stith\ *archaic var of* STITHY

stithy \'stithē, -thē\ *n* -ES [ME *stithy, stethy, stith, stethe*, fr. ON *stethi* (accus. *stethja*); akin to OE *stathr* place — more at STEAD] **1** : ANVIL **2** : SMITHY

1**stive** \'stīv\ *vb* -ED/-ING/-S [ME *stiven*, prob. fr. Sp *estibar* or Pg *estivar* to pack tightly — more at STEEVE] *vt* **1** : to pack tightly : CROWD **2** : to shut up in a warm close place : STIFLE, SUFFOCATE ~ *vi* : SUFFOCATE

2**stive** \"\ *n* -s [obs. D *stuive*, fr. MD *stuve, stuyve* pulverization; akin to MD *stuven, stieven* to raise dust, MLG *stūven* to raise dust, *stübbe* dust, OHG *stoub* dust, *stioban* to raise dust, *stuppi* dust, Goth *stubjus*] : DUST; *esp* : the floating dust in flour mills caused by grinding

3**stive** \"\ *chiefly Scot var of* 1STEEVE

1**sti·ver** *or* **stui·ver** \'stīvə(r)\ *or* **stee·ver** \-tēv-\ *n* -s [D *stuiver*, fr. MD *stuyver, stuver*, a small coin; prob. akin to MLG *stūf* blunt, ON *stubbi* stub — more at STUB] **1** : a unit of value of the Netherlands equal to 1/20 gulden or 5 Dutch cents **2** : a coin representing one stiver **3** : the smallest amount of money ⟨not worth a ~⟩

2**sti·ver** \'stīvə(r)\ *vb* -ED/-ING/-S [prob. irreg. fr. 1*stiff*] *vi* **1** *dial Eng* : to stand up stiff : BRISTLE **2** *dial* : STAGGER, STRUGGLE ~ *vt, dial chiefly Eng* : to cause to stand up stiff : ROUGHEN

stivy \'stīvē\ *adj* [1*stive* + *-y*] : STUFFY

sti·zi·dae \'stizə,dē\ *n pl, cap* [NL, fr. *Stizus*, type genus (fr. Gk *stizein* to tattoo) + *-idae* — more at STICK] : a family of sphecoid wasps that includes the cicada killer

stizo·lo·bi·um \,stīzə'lōbēəm, ,stīz-\ [NL, fr. *stiz-* (fr. Gk *stizein* to tattoo) + *-o-* + *-lobium* (fr. Gk *lobion* small lobe, dim. of *lobos* lobe) — more at SLEEP] *syn of* MUCUNA

stizo·ste·di·on \-'stedēən\ *n, cap* [NL, fr. *stiz-* (fr. Gk *stizein* to tattoo) + *-o-* + *-stedion* (perh. irreg. fr. Gk *stēthion* small breast, dim. of *stēthos* breast)] : a genus of pike perches including the sauger and the walleye

stk *abbr* **1** sticky **2** stock **3** strake

stl *abbr* **1** stall **2** steel **3** stile

STL *abbr or n* -s [L *sacrae theologiae licentiatus*] : a licentiate in sacred theology

stlg *abbr* sterling

stm *abbr* storm

stmfr *abbr* steam fitter

stn *abbr* **1** stainless **2** station

stnd *abbr* stained

sto *abbr* **1** stoker **2** story

STO *abbr* sea transport officer

stoa \'stōə\ *n, pl* **sto·ae** \-ō,ē\ *or* **stoas** [Gk; akin to Gk *stylos* pillar — more at STEER] : an ancient Greek portico that is usu. long and walled at the back with a front colonnade opening on a public place and designed to afford a sheltered promenade or meeting place

stoach \'stōch\ *vb* -ED/-ING/-ES [origin unknown] *dial Eng* : TRAMPLE

stoat \'stōt, *usu* -ōd.+V\ *n, pl* **stoats** *also* **stoat** [ME *stote, stot*] : ERMINE 1a; *broadly* : any of various weasels that have a black-tipped tail — used esp. of the animal when in the brown summer coat

stoa·ting *also* **sto·ting** \'stōd·iŋ\ *n* -s [origin unknown] : invisible stitching used esp. by tailors for joining two edges of fabric

1**stob** \'stäb\ *n* -s [ME, stick, stump; akin to ME *stubb, stubbe* stub — more at STUB] **1** *chiefly dial* : STAKE, POST **2** *chiefly dial* : STUMP; *esp* : the stump of a small tree or a shrub

2**stob** \"\ *dial var of* STAB

stoc·ca·do \stə'käd·(,)ō\ *or* **stoc·ca·ta** \-d·ə\ *n* -s [OIt *stoccata*, fr. *stocco* estoc (fr. MF *estoc*) + *-ata* -ade — more at ESTOC] *archaic* : a thrust with a rapier (as in fencing) : STAB

sto·chas·tic \stə'kastik\ *adj* [Gk *stochastikos* skillful in aiming, proceeding by guesswork, fr. (assumed) *stochastos* (verbal of *stochazesthai* to aim at, guess at, fr. *stochos* target, aim, guess) + *-ikos* -ic — more at STING] : RANDOM ⟨~ processes⟩ ⟨~ variables⟩

sto·chas·ti·cal·ly \-stək(ə)lē\ *adv* : in a stochastic manner

stocks 4

1**stock** \'stäk\ *n* -s [ME *stok*, fr. OE *stocc*; akin to OE *stycce* piece, MD & OHG *stoc* stick, stump, trunk of a tree, OHG *stucki* piece, ON *stokkr* block of wood, trunk of a tree, *stykki* piece, MIr *tūag* ax, bow, *tōcht* part, piece, Skt *tujati, tuñjati* he pushes; basic meaning: to push, strike] **1 a** : a stump of a tree **b** *archaic* : a log or block of wood **c** : something held to resemble a log or stump of wood in having no life or consciousness; *specif* : IDOL — usu. used in the phrase *stocks and stones* ⟨all our fathers worshiped ~s and stones —John Milton⟩ **2** : a supporting framework or structure: as **a** : the support of the block in which an anvil is fixed or of the anvil itself **b stocks** *pl* : the frame or timbers on which a ship rests while under construction ⟨the old-time shipyard in whose ~s were built so many . . . men-o'-war —S.P.B.Mais⟩ ⟨large ships would collapse in the ~s —S.F.Mason⟩ **c** *chiefly Scot* : the outer rail or edge of a bed **d** : the frame bearing the moving parts of a spinning wheel **e** : the casing surrounding and supporting a lock **f** : a frame in which an animal (as a horse or cow) may be slung or otherwise secured esp. for shoeing **3** : a person who is dull, stupid, or lifeless like a block of wood ⟨they stood like ~s, stupidly listening —Dorothy C. Fisher⟩ **4 stocks** *pl* : a frame of timber with holes formerly used to confine the feet or the feet and hands of offenders commonly in a public place by way of punishment — compare PILLORY **5 a** : the main stem of a plant : TRUNK **b** (1) : a living plant or portion of a plant (as a root) designed or prepared for union with a scion in grafting and usu. supplying solely or predominantly underground parts to a graft; *also* : the portion of a grafted plant derived from the stock (2) *or* **stock plant** : a plant maintained primarily for the production of slips or cuttings **6 a** : the crosspiece of an anchor which cants it so that one of the flukes may enter the ground — see ANCHOR illustration **b** : the narrow part of a rudder above the blade **7 a** (1) : the source of a line of descent : the original progenitor : the original (as a man, a race, or a language) from which others have descended or have been derived ⟨one of . . . many sons might well become the ~ of a new dynasty —E.A.Freeman⟩ (2) *obs* : the original source from which something is derived ⟨the sun, the ~ of light —Thomas Fuller⟩ **b** (1) : the progenitor of a family and his direct descendants : the whole group of descendants of one individual : a line of descent : FAMILY, LINEAGE ⟨she comes of good ~⟩ (2) : a compound organism : a colony of individuals (as of interconnected zooids) — compare CLONE **c** : an infraspecific group usu. having unity of descent: (1) : a major anthropological division or primary race of mankind ⟨the main ~s of mankind are usu. held to be the Caucasoids, Mongoloids, and Negroids⟩ (2) : a race, subrace, or group of ethnically closely related people ⟨the Hamite ~ of northern Africa⟩ **d** : the living constituents of a biological group ⟨the ~ of a strain⟩ **e** (1) : a related group of languages (2) : a language family **8** *obs* : TRUNK 1b **9** *chiefly dial* : STOCKING — see NETHERSTOCK, UPPERSTOCK **10 a** *obs* : a sum of money set apart for a specific purpose (as to provide for expenses) **b** *obs* : capital for investment or direct use in a business : principal as distinguished from interest **c** *obs* : something constituting an endowment for a son or a dowry for a daughter **d** *archaic* : BASIS, GROUNDS — usu. used in the phrase *upon the stock of* **11** : the block of wood from which a bell is hung **12 a** : the equipment, materials, or supplies (as of a farm or railroad) ⟨inspectors who report on the sufficiency of the works and ~s of railways —Homersham Cox⟩ — see DEAD STOCK, LIVESTOCK, ROLLING STOCK **b** : LIVESTOCK **13 a** : the wooden part into which the barrel, receiver, and action of a rifle or shotgun are fitted and by which the piece is held for firing **b stocks** *pl* : the often wooden parts fitted to the frame of a handgun to form the grip — compare BUTTSTOCK, TIPSTOCK **c** : the connecting arm between slide and shoulder piece in rapid-fire guns **d** : the long beam of general rectangular shape which forms the basis of the carriage body in field-gun carriages being securely fastened to the axletree, forming the connection with the limber in traveling, and affording the necessary third point of support when the gun is fired **14** *archaic* **a** : property that produces income : ASSETS **b** : the aggregate wealth of a nation **15** : a hive of honeybees **16** : the wooden or iron beam of a plow to which the handles, share, colter, moldboard, and landside are secured **17 a** (1) : the portion of a pack of cards not distributed to the players at the beginning of various games (2) : BONEYARD 3 **b** *obs* : HAND **18** : the hub of a wheel **19** *chiefly Brit* : the capital that a firm employs in the conduct of business (as trading or investing) **20 a** : the part of a tally formerly given to the creditor in a transaction; *specif* : the part given in the English exchequer to the person having lent the monarch money on account **b** (1) : the debt or fund represented by such a stock or a series of such stocks; *specif* : the debt or fund due from a government or a private company or corporation to individuals for money loaned at interest and not divided into shares but instead being divisible and transferable in any amount desired not involving divisions smaller than a specified sum — compare CONSOL, MUNICIPAL SECURITY (2) *chiefly Brit* : a debt, fund, or capital bearing interest at a given rate percent in perpetuity and characterized by the principal not being payable unless at the option of the debtor **c** : a specific debt or fund of such character **d** : a security representing such a debt or fund — usu. used in pl. **21** : a quantity of something accumulated for future use : a store or supply to be drawn upon ⟨lay in a ~ of provisions⟩ ⟨a girl should have . . . ~s of lovely clothes —Robertson Davies⟩ ⟨its members . . . put everything into a common ~ —Norman Goodall⟩ ⟨his own contribution to the general ~ of knowledge —Benjamin Farrington⟩ **22** : a block of wood or metal frame which constitutes the body of a plane and in which the plane iron is fitted : a plane stock **23** *obs* : money invested by a person in a company or partnership **24 a** : any of various pubescent European and Asiatic herbs and subshrubs that constitute the genus *Matthiola*, bear racemes of usu. sweet-scented flowers with 4 long-clawed petals, and include numerous forms chiefly derived from the southern European species (*M. incana*) which are widely cultivated as ornamentals — see BRAMPTON STOCK, TEN-WEEK STOCK **b** : VIRGINIA STOCK **25** : the butt or handle of an implement (as a whip, hunting crop, or fishing rod) **26 a** : the store of goods held by a merchant or manufacturer : the supply on hand : INVENTORY **b** : a quantity (as of completed parts or finished product) held esp. in a storeroom ready for delivery to customers ⟨no publishers' ~s remain of the German edition —*Brit. Bk. News*⟩ **c :** the supply of plants or of seeds of a kind of plant in a nursery, greenhouse, seed house, or other horticultural establishment **27 a :** a wide band or scarf worn about the neck commonly by men during the 18th century and often wrapped twice around and tied in front with a knot ⟨wearing a pearl stickpin in his ~ —Hamilton Basso⟩ **b :** a piece of material worn by some clergymen attached to a clerical collar and covering the chest **28 a :** the proprietorship element in a corporation divided into shares and represented by transferable certificates and giving to the owners a pro rata interest in the assets, the earnings, and except where withheld in the charter the voting power of the business — compare CAPITAL STOCK, COMMON STOCK, CONVERTIBLE, CUMULATIVE, FULLY PAID, GUARANTEED STOCK, NO-PAR, PAR, PARTICIPATING STOCK, PREFERRED STOCK, REDEEMABLE **b :** the proprietorship element of a particular corporation ⟨high quality growth ~s⟩ **c :** a share of such stock **d :** a security representing such a share **29** *Brit* **:** a hard solid brick that has been pressed in a mold — usu. used in pl. **30 :** liquid in which meat, fish, or vegetables are simmered and which is used as a basis for soup, stew, gravy, or sauce **31 a :** a beater in a fulling mill for cloth **b stocks** *pl* **:** a fulling mill for cloth **32 :** the handle or contrivance by which bits are held in boring **:** BITSTOCK, BRACE **33 :** the shorter of the two pieces comprising a square (as a carpenter's square) **34 :** an estimate, evaluation, or appraising survey of something (as of one's position, resources, or prospects) ⟨he took ~ and sought . . . to pick up the threads of his business —Milton Bracker⟩ ⟨the council . . . took ~ of the situation —F.L.Paxson⟩ **35 :** a holder for a threading die and esp. for any of a graduated set of dies for cutting screw threads on bolts and usu. having a pair of relatively long handles **36 :** a small metal container for holy oil used esp. in the Roman Catholic Church **37 a :** raw material from which something is manufactured **:** the basic material used in making or producing something ⟨paper ~⟩ ⟨film ~⟩ — see SOAP STOCK **b :** wood used in the construction of something **:** LUMBER ⟨the saw will cut round ~ to ¾ in. in diameter —*Industrial Equipment News*⟩ **c :** petroleum oil partly or completely refined that is to undergo further processing **38 :** confidence, faith, or value in something ⟨put little ~ in his testimony⟩ ⟨take no ~ in abstract rights —O.W.Holmes †1935⟩ ⟨did not at first take much ~ in it —M.R.Cohen⟩ **39 :** a body of igneous rock that is smaller than a batholith and intruded upward into older formations and that in ground plan is roughly circular or elliptical but in cross section may increase downward **40 stocks** *pl* **:** a machine for softening hides by beating or kneading **41 a :** the stump of a coppice which is expected to furnish new sprouts **b :** growth of a specified kind constituting a forest cover **42 :** material supplied to a break roll or reel in flour milling **43 :** STOCKPILE 2 **44 a :** STOCK COMPANY **b :** the production and presentation of plays by a stock company ⟨the beginning of resident ~ in Seattle —*Amer. Guide Series: Wash.*⟩ ⟨played bit parts in summer ~ —S.T. Williamson⟩ ⟨sold for films or released for ~ —*N.Y.Times*⟩ **45 :** the anterior individual of a chain of asexual annelid worms of *Nais* or related genera **46 a :** STUFF 2c **b :** wet pulp at any point in the manufacturing process **c :** paper on hand or in storage **47 :** a post bearing a holy-water vessel **48 :** the estimation in which someone or something is held ⟨his ~ with the electorate remains high —*Newsweek*⟩ **49 a :** STOCK CAR 2 ⟨racing modified ~s —W.L.Gresham⟩ **b :** a race involving stock cars ⟨winners . . . in the Class B ~s —*Springfield (Mass.) Union*⟩ **syn** see VARIETY — **in stock :** on hand **:** in the store and ready for delivery — **off the stocks 1 :** having been launched — used of a ship **2 :** completed and delivered **:** FINISHED ⟨a book *off the stocks*⟩ ⟨a piece of work *off the stocks*⟩ — **on the stocks** *adv (or adj)* **:** in preparation **:** under construction ⟨the dramatist has a play *on the stocks*⟩ ⟨a frigate is *on the stocks* in a British yard —Anthony Courtney⟩ ⟨through the years that this book has been *on the stocks* —*New Statesman & Nation*⟩ — **out of stock :** having no more on hand **:** sold out

²stock \"\ *vb* -ED/-ING/-S [ME *stokken*, fr. *stok*, n.] *vt* **1 :** to put (as a culprit) in the stocks **:** punish by confinement in the stocks **2** *archaic* **:** to dig or root up **:** EXTIRPATE — often used with *up* **3 :** to make pregnant (a female domestic animal) **:** IMPREGNATE **4 :** to provide (as a rifle, anchor, or bell) with a stock **:** fit to or with a stock **5** *archaic* **:** to make an investment of (funds) **:** put (capital) out at interest **:** INVEST **6 :** to provide with stock **:** equip with a stock of something **:** supply with material requisites **:** furnish with appropriate items ⟨retailers ~*ed* their shelves conservatively —*Dun's Rev.*⟩ ⟨he ~*ed* the farm with . . . Hereford cattle —*Amer. Guide Series: Maine*⟩ ⟨a bar . . . ~*ed* with gins and liquors —Scott Fitzgerald⟩ ⟨~ a stream with trout⟩ ⟨a good sound head . . . well ~*ed* with ideas —Rose Macaulay⟩ — sometimes used with *up* ⟨~ up the place with . . . new specimens —H.L.Davis⟩ **7 :** to let (a cow) retain milk for hours before sale to display the udder to advantage **8 :** to lay up a stock of **:** keep on hand esp. for sale **:** get or have (as merchandise) in stock ⟨stores that ~ everything from plowshares to lamp chimneys —*Amer. Guide Series: Ark.*⟩ ⟨most bookshops do not ~ encyclopedias —Evelyn Kirkland⟩ **9 :** to put (playing cards) into a pack esp. in such a way as to arrange for the purpose of cheating **:** STACK **10 a :** to graze livestock on (as pasture) **b :** to graze (livestock) on land and esp. grassland **11 :** to issue shares in or stocks of (a business enterprise) **12 :** to stamp or knead (as hides) with or as if with stocks in leather manufacturing **13 :** to deliver (logs) from the woods to a railroad or to a mill **14 :** to rough-machine with a stocking cutter ~ *vi* **1 :** to send out new shoots — used esp. of the crown of a plant or a severed trunk or branch **2 :** to put in stock or supplies — usu. used with *up* ⟨~ up for the holiday trade⟩ ⟨~ up on supplies⟩ **3 :** to swell or become swollen — used of a horse's legs and esp. of the part between the pasterns and the hock

³stock \"\ *adv* [ME *stok*, fr. *stok*, n.] **:** COMPLETELY — used in combination ⟨stood *stock*-still⟩ ⟨struck *stock*-dumb⟩

⁴stock \"\ *adj* [¹*stock*] **1 :** used or employed for constant service or application as if constituting a portion of a stock or supply **:** kept regularly in stock or ready for sale or for immediate use ⟨a ~ size of paper⟩ ⟨a ~ model of an automobile⟩ ⟨cars must be clean and ~ —*Illustrated Speedway News*⟩ ⟨a ~ size⟩ **2 a :** suggesting something regularly kept in or as if in stock or ready for use **:** commonly used or brought forward **:** STANDARD ⟨the ~ answer to all these complaints —*Nation*⟩ ⟨humor depending upon ~ situations —*Amer. Guide Series: Tenn.*⟩ ⟨the ~ responses of the slick fictionist —L.O.Coxe⟩ ⟨a ~ jest among English gentlemen —V.L.Parrington⟩ **b :** COMMONPLACE, CONVENTIONAL, TRITE **3 a :** kept for breeding purposes **:** BROOD ⟨a ~ mare⟩ ⟨a ~ bull⟩ **b :** devoted to the breeding and rearing of livestock esp. beef cattle, horses, sheep, and hogs ⟨a ~ farm⟩ **c :** used by or intended for the use of livestock ⟨~ range⟩ ⟨~ train⟩ ⟨~ water⟩ **4 :** of, relating to, or having the characteristics of a stock company ⟨other plays which did not figure as ~ favorites —D.J.Rulfs⟩ ⟨~ actors⟩ **5 a :** employed in handling, checking, or taking care of the stock of merchandise on hand (as in a store or factory) ⟨a ~ girl⟩ ⟨a ~ clerk⟩ **b :** containing the stock **6 :** suitable for fattening ⟨~ cattle⟩

⁵stock \'shtäk, 'stäk\ *n* -S [G, fr. OHG *stoc* stick, stump, trunk of a tree — more at ¹STOCK] **:** STICK; *esp* **:** one used by skiers — sometimes used in combination ⟨alpen*stock*⟩

stock account *n, Brit* **:** a ledger account in bookkeeping with the credit side showing the original capital and additions and the debit side showing withdrawals and losses

¹stock·ade \(')stä'kād\ *n* -S [Sp *estacada*, fr. *estaca* stake, pale (of Gmc origin; akin to OE *staca* stake) + *-ada* -ade (fr. LL *-ata*) — more at STAKE] **1 a :** a line of stout posts or timbers set firmly in the earth in contact with each other, usu. furnished with loopholes, and designed to form a barrier or defensive fortification **b :** a floating barrier of trees chained together to protect a pontoon bridge from floating objects **2 a :** an enclosure or pen made with posts and stakes **b :** an enclosure usu. surrounded by barbed wire in which prisoners are kept **3 :** piling that serves as a breakwater

²stockade \"\ *vt* -ED/-ING/-S **:** to surround, fortify, or protect with a stockade

stock·a·do \stä'kā(,)dō\ *archaic var of* STOCKADE

stock·age \'stäkij\ *n* -S [¹*stock* + *-age*] **:** the amount of military supplies and equipment on hand or scheduled to be on hand in controlled quantities in a given place ⟨build our ammunition reserve ~s to the point where we feel they should be —J.L.Collins⟩

stock-and-bill tackle \'==-'=-\ *n* **:** a small tackle to secure an anchor after it is hove up — called also *stock tackle*

stock·a·teer \,stäkə'ti(ə)r\ *n* -S [¹*stock* + *-ateer* (alter. of *-eteer* —as in *racketeer*—)] **:** a broker dealing in fraudulent securities

stock beer *n* **:** a strong beer that keeps well

stock block *n* **:** a truncated obconical block of wood used as a pattern in making the hole for a stock fire in a forge

stock board *n* **1 :** a loose piece of wood plated with iron around the upper edge and forming the bottom of a brick mold **2 :** STOCK EXCHANGE **3 :** a board of an even width usu. 8, 10, or 12 inches

stock bonus *n* **:** a bonus paid to corporation executives and employees in shares of stock

stock book *n* **1 :** STOCK LEDGER **2 :** STUDBOOK, HERDBOOK **3 :** a book having pages with pockets for holding loose stamps (as stamps in a dealer's stock or the unmounted stamps of a collector)

stock bowler *n, chiefly Austral* **:** a regular bowler on a cricket team — compare CHANGE BOWLER

stockbreeder \'=,==\ *n* **:** one that is engaged in the breeding and care of livestock for the market, for show purposes, or for racing

stock brick *n, Brit* **:** a hard solid brick that is burned in a clamp

stock·bridge \'stäk,brij\ *n* -S *usu cap* [fr. *Stockbridge*, Mass.] **:** a member of the Housatonic band of the Mahican which moved from Massachusetts in 1785 to join the Oneida in northern New York and later united with the Munsee in Wisconsin

stockbroker \'=,==\ *n* **:** one that deals in or executes orders to buy and sell securities

stockbroking \'=,==\ *or* **stockbrokerage** \'=,=(=)=\ *n* **:** the business or work of a stockbroker

stock buckle *n* **:** a buckle for fastening a stock

stockcar \'=,=\ *n* [¹*stock* + *car*] **:** a latticed railroad boxcar for carrying livestock

stockcar

stock car *n* [⁴*stock*] **1 :** an automotive vehicle of a model and type produced commercially and kept in stock for regular sales **2 :** a racing car having the basic chassis of a commercially produced assembly-line model

stock card *n* **:** a brush with bent wire teeth used for carding wool

stock cattle *n pl* **:** all cattle other than beef cattle and steers over three years of age; *esp* **:** cattle for breeding purposes

stock certificate *n* **1 :** a document issued by a joint-stock company to each of its shareholders certifying the amount and character of his holding **2 :** an instrument evidencing ownership of one or more shares of the capital stock of a corporation

stock chute *n* **:** a ramp for loading and unloading livestock

stock clerk *n* **:** one that receives and handles merchandise and supplies in a stock room

stock company *n* **1 a :** a corporation or joint-stock company of which the capital is represented by stock **b :** an insurance company owned and operated for the benefit of stockholders as contrasted with a mutual company **2 :** a theatrical company attached to a repertory theater; *esp* **:** one without outstanding stars

stock dividend *n* **1 :** the payment by a corporation of a dividend in the form of additional shares of its own stock — compare SPLIT-UP **2 :** the stock distributed in a stock dividend

stock dove *n* [ME *stokdouve, stokdove*, fr. *stok* stock + *douve, dove* dove; prob. fr. its living in hollow trees] **1 :** a common European wild pigeon (*Columba oenas*) resembling the rock pigeon but being darker colored and having the rump gray **2 :** an Asiatic dove (*Columba eversmanni*) related to the European stock dove

stock down *vt* **:** to sow (as plowed land) with seed of grass or other permanent forage crop

stock duck *n* **:** MALLARD

stock-dye \'=;=\ *vt* **:** to dye (raw fibers) before processing and esp. spinning in the manufacture of textiles

stock eagle *n, dial Eng* **:** GREEN WOODPECKER

stocked *past of* STOCK

stock·er \'stäkə(r)\ *n* -S **1 :** one that makes or fits stocks esp. of guns **2 a :** a young animal (as a steer or heifer) suitable for being fed and fattened for market **:** a young or light feeder **b :** an animal (as a heifer) suitable for use in a breeding establishment **3 :** one that handles scrap in the stockyard of an iron or steel plant and loads materials for open-hearth melting **4 :** one that prepares stockers for market

stock exchange *n* **1 :** a building or room in which security trading is conducted on an organized system — compare EXCHANGE 5b **2 :** an association or group of people organized to provide an auction market among themselves for the purchase and sale of securities

stock fire *n* **:** a forge fire made in a stock — distinguished from *open fire*

stockfish \'=,=\ *n* [ME *stokfish*, fr. MD *stocvisch*, fr. *stoc* stick, stump, trunk of a tree + *visch* fish; prob. fr. its having been dried on wooden racks; akin to OHG *fisc* fish — more at STOCK, FISH] **1 a :** fish (as cod, haddock, hake, or ling) dried hard in the open air without salt **b :** something held to resemble stockfish in being thoroughly beaten and flattened out ⟨as dead as a ~ —George Meredith⟩ ⟨sat mute as a ~ —Charles Dickens⟩ **2** *also* **stok·vis** \'stäk,fis\ [Afrik *stokvis*, fr. MD *stocvisch*] **:** a hake (*Merluccius capensis*) that is the basis of the leading commercial fishery of southern Africa

stock fly *n* **1 :** STABLE FLY **2 :** HORN FLY

stock guard *n* **:** a barrier for keeping livestock off railroad tracks

stockholder \'=,==\ *n* **1 :** one that holds stock **:** an owner of stocks **:** SHAREHOLDER **2** *archaic* **:** the owner of large herds of cattle or sheep

stockholder of record : the person recorded on the books of the company as the owner of stock although often he is only an agent or trustee for the true owner

stockholding \'=,==\ *n* **1 :** the state or fact of holding stock **:** ownership of stocks ⟨prohibition of unrestricted intercorporate ~ —W.Z.Ripley⟩ **2 :** a holding of stock **:** a specific number of stocks or shares owned — usu. used in pl. ⟨sell ~s he has in corporations —*Springfield (Mass.) Daily News*⟩

stock·holm \'stäk,hō(l)m\ *adj, usu cap* [fr. *Stockholm*, Sweden] **:** of or from Stockholm, the capital of Sweden **:** of the kind or style prevalent in Stockholm

stock·holm·er \-mə(r)\ *n* -S *cap* [Sw, fr. *Stockholm* + *-er*] **:** a native or resident of Stockholm, Sweden

stockholm tar *n, usu cap S* **:** pine tar used in shipbuilding and in the manufacture of cordage

stock·horn \'stäk,hȯrn\ *n* **:** an obsolete Scottish musical instrument similar to the Welsh pibgorn

stock horse *n* **:** a horse used in herding cattle on ranches

stockier *comparative of* STOCKY

stockiest *superlative of* STOCKY

stock·i·ly \'stäkəlē\ *adv* **:** in a stocky manner ⟨a ~ built man⟩

stock·i·nette \,stäkə'net, *usu* -ed·+V\ *n* -S *often attrib* [alter. of earlier *stocking net*] **1** *or* **stockinette stitch :** a knitting pattern that produces a smooth surface on the face and is made on straight needles by alternating rows of knit stitch and purl stitch and on circular needles by knit stitch alone **2 a** *or* **stock·i·net** \"\ **:** a soft circular-knit usu. cotton fabric in stockinette stitch that has considerable natural elasticity, is often napped on the back, and is used esp. for bandages and infants' wear **b :** a garment, bag, or other article made from stockinette

¹stock·ing \'stäkiŋ, -kēŋ\ *n* -S [ME *stokking*, fr. gerund of *stokken* to stock — more at STOCK] **1 :** the action of making or fitting a stock (as to a rifle) **2 :** punishment by detention in the stocks **3** *Scot* **:** livestock and farm implements

²stocking \"\ *n* -S [¹*stock* (stocking) + *-ing*] **1 a :** a close-fitting covering for the foot and leg reaching above the knee and usu. knit of nylon, silk, wool, or cotton **b :** SOCK **2 :** something resembling or held to resemble a stocking: as **a :** a bandage or webbed support for the leg; *esp* **:** one woven or knitted with rubber and used in various disorders of the circulation — called also *elastic stocking* **b (1) :** a broad ring of color on the lower part of the leg of a biped or quadruped differing from the general color; *esp* **:** a white ring between the coronet and the hock or knee of a dark-colored horse **(2) :** the dark feathering of the neck of a Canada goose **c :** a knitted tube of fiber (as rayon) used in making incandescent mantles by impregnation (as with thorium nitrate) — called also *sock* — **in one's stocking feet :** having on stockings but no shoes ⟨went downstairs . . . *in his stocking feet* so as not to wake the others —Hugh MacLennan⟩

³stocking \"\ *vt* -ED/-ING/-S **:** to dress in stockings

stocking cap *n* **:** a knitted cone-shaped cap made usu. long with a tassel or pompon at the point and worn esp. for winter sports or play

stocking cutter *n* **:** a milling gear cutter for removing stock with heavy cuts in preparation for finishing

stock·inged \-ŋd\ *adj* **:** wearing a stocking or stockings ⟨walks about in his ~ feet⟩

stock·ing·er \-ŋə(r)\ *n* -S **:** a stocking knitter or weaver

stocking frame *n* **:** a machine for knitting stockings or other knitted goods

stocking cap

stock insurance company *n* **:** an insurance company with capital contributed by stockholders who control its operations and reap any profits or sustain any losses which may result therefrom and with policies that are ordinarily nonparticipating and always nonassessable

stock-in-trade \'==='=\ *n* **1 :** the equipment necessary to or used in the conduct of a trade or business: as **a :** the goods kept for sale by a shopkeeper **b :** the fittings and appliances of a workman **c :** the aggregate of things necessary to carry on a business **2 :** something held to resemble the standard equipment of a tradesman or business ⟨the light and frivolous charm which was her stage *stock-in-trade* —S.H.Adams⟩ ⟨its civic beauty, its *stock-in-trade*, is being ruined by parked cars —Janet Flanner⟩ ⟨this motive had been a *stock-in-trade* of medieval art —Verena Trudel⟩

stock·ish \'stäkish\ *adj* [¹*stock* + *-ish*] **1 :** resembling a stock **:** STUPID, BLOCKISH ⟨a dull, ~ character —R.L.Stevenson⟩ ⟨fell back into his ~, uncomprehending blankness —Dorothy C. Fisher⟩ **2 :** somewhat stocky ⟨~ of build⟩ — **stock·ish·ly** *adv*

stock·ist \'stäkəst\ *n* -S *Brit* **:** one (as a retailer or distributor) that stocks goods ⟨world's largest ~s of scientific periodicals —*advt*⟩

stock-job *vt* [back-formation fr. *stockjobber* & *stockjobbing*] *obs* **:** to deal with as or in the manner of a stockjobber

stockjobber \'=,==\ *n* [¹*stock* + *jobber*] **:** one that deals in stocks: **a :** a member of the London stock exchange who deals speculatively with brokers or other jobbers and usu. specializes in one class of securities — called also *dealer, jobber* **b :** STOCKBROKER; *esp* **:** one held to be unscrupulous or to deal in stocks of doubtful worth

stockjobbing \'=,==\ *n* -S [¹*stock* + *jobbing*] **:** the business of a stockjobber **:** the buying and selling of stocks **:** dealing in securities often on a speculative basis

stockjudging \'=,==\ *n* -S **:** the appraisal of the quality of livestock in competitions or for educational purposes, either in respect to relative conformity of the animal to breed standards or to performance

stockkeeper \'=,==\ *n* **1 :** one (as a herdsman or shepherd) having the charge or care of livestock **2 :** one that keeps and records stock (as in a warehouse) **:** one that keeps an inventory of goods on hand, shipped, or received

stock ledger *n* **1 :** STORES LEDGER **2 :** a book kept by a corporation in which are entered the names of the stockholders and the amount of the holding of each and sometimes other particulars

stock·less \'stäkləs\ *adj* **:** being without a stock ⟨a ~ anchor⟩

stock list *n* **1 :** a list of the stock issues admitted to dealings on an exchange **2 :** the list of stock issues with prices and volume of turnover published in a newspaper

stock lock *n* **:** a lock enclosed in a wooden case and attached to the face of a door

stockmaker \'=,==\ *n* **:** one that makes stocks; *specif* **:** a workman employed in making the stocks of firearms

stock·man \'stäkmən, -k,man, -,maa(ə)n\ *n, pl* **stockmen 1 :** one occupied in the raising of livestock (as cattle or sheep): as **a** *Austral* **(1) :** COWHAND **(2) :** SHEEPHERDER **b :** a ranch owner **:** one owning herds of cattle or sheep **2 :** one who keeps records or works on stock (as in a store or warehouse)

stock market *n* **1 a :** STOCK EXCHANGE 1 ⟨the New York *stock market*⟩ **b :** a market for particular stocks ⟨the bank *stock market*⟩ **c :** the market for stocks throughout a country ⟨the U.S. *stock market*⟩ **2 :** a market for the sale of livestock

stock melon *n* **:** CITRON

stock option *n* **:** an option giving to the holder the right to purchase a specified number of shares of stock from a corporation at a stated price and by a stated date and constituting a device widely used to provide supplementary compensation to corporation officers and employees

stock pass *n* **:** a culvert or bridge opening under a railroad track primarily for the passage of livestock (as cattle)

stock pea *n* **:** SOYBEAN

stock pigeon *n* **:** STOCK DOVE

¹stockpile \'=,=\ *n* [¹*stock* + *pile*] **1 :** a pile of road metal stored on the roadside and used for road maintenance **2 :** a storage pile or heap of material (as ore or coal) at the surface of a mine **3 a :** a reserve supply of something essential (as processed food or a raw material) accumulated within a country for use during a shortage caused by emergency conditions (as war) ⟨strengthen its civil defense ~ of medical . . . supplies —D.D.Eisenhower⟩ ⟨built up ~s of strategic metals —Richard Rutter⟩ **b :** something held to resemble such a stockpile **:** a gradually accumulated reserve of something and esp. something vital or indispensable ⟨the ~ of basic research information has been seriously depleted —M.H.Trytten⟩ ⟨avert ~s of unsold cars —Bert Pierce⟩ ⟨assets include a ~ of . . . celluloid comedies and dramas —*Wall Street Jour.*⟩

²stockpile \"\ *vt* **1 :** to heap up (as coal or iron ore) **:** accumulate in piles **2 :** to place or store in or on a stockpile **3 :** to accumulate a stockpile of ⟨~ war materials in Europe —A.O.Wolfers⟩ ~ *vi* **:** to accumulate a stockpile

stockpiler \'=,==\ *n* **:** one that stockpiles

stock plant *n* **:** ¹STOCK 5b(2)

stock·port \'stäk,pōrt, -pȯrt\ *adj, usu cap* [fr. *Stockport*, England] **:** of or from the county borough of Stockport, England **:** of the kind or style prevalent in Stockport

stockpot \'=,=\ *n* **1 :** a pot in which stock (as for soup or gravy) is prepared **2 :** something held to resemble a stockpot ⟨the common ~ of melodramatic plots —G.B.Shaw⟩

stock power *n* **:** the irrevocable power of attorney used in making a transfer of a certificate of stock

stockproof \'=;=\ *adj* **:** proof against livestock ⟨an electrified ~ fence⟩

stock purchase warrant *n* **:** a usu. transferable certificate entitling the holder to subscribe to corporate stock at a specified price and often attached to bonds or preferred stock to increase their salability

stock rail *n* **:** the fixed rail in a railroad track against which the switch rail operates

stock raiser *n* **:** one that raises livestock (as beef cattle, horses, sheep, or hogs)

stock raising *n* **:** the act or occupation of raising livestock

stock record *n* **:** STORES LEDGER

stockrider \'=,==\ *n, Austral* **:** COWBOY 3a

stock room *n* **1 :** a storage place for supplies or goods used in a business **2 :** a room (as in a hotel) where commercial travelers may exhibit their goods **:** a sample room

stocks *pl of* STOCK, *pres 3d sing of* STOCK

stock saddle *n* **:** an often ornamented saddle used by cowboys and usu. made with a seat more bowl-shaped than the English saddle, a high pommel with a horn for holding the lariat, a high cantle, and broad skirts and fenders — called also *western saddle*

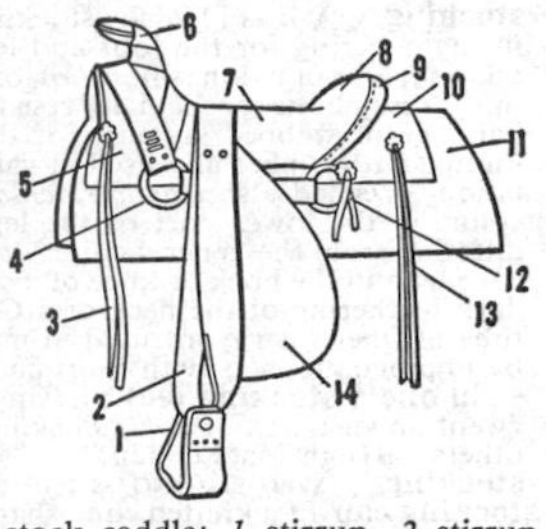

stock saddle: *1* stirrup, *2* stirrup leather, *3* saddle strings, *4* front rigging ring, *5* front jockey, *6* horn, *7* seat, *8* cantle, *9* cantle binding, *10* back jockey, *11* skirt, *12* flank rigging ring, *13* saddle strings, *14* fender

stock-share lease *n* **:** a lease based upon joint ownership of livestock and joint sharing of receipts and expenses by landlord and tenant on a rented farm

stock shot *n* [⁴*stock*] **:** a film clip (as of an historical event or a geographical area) usu. kept in a film library for possible use in future pictures

stock solution *n* [⁴*stock*] **:** a concentrated solution (as of developer) that usu. is diluted with water before use in photography

stock–still \\ˈ=ˈ=\\ *adj* [ME *stok still*, fr. *stok* stock (n.) + *still*] **:** still as a stock or fixed post **:** perfectly still ⟨her wits were *stock-still*, so she did not speak —Owen Wister⟩ ⟨stood *stock-still* and listened⟩

stockstone \\ˈ=ˌ=\\ *n* **:** a stone-bladed tool that is forced over the grain side of leather to stretch it and smooth the grain

stock system \\ˈstäk-\\ *or* **stock's system** *n, usu cap 1st S* [after Alfred *Stock*, 20th cent. German chemist] **:** a system in chemical nomenclature and notation of indicating the oxidation state of the significant element in a compound or ion by means of a Roman numeral that is used in parentheses after the name or part of the name designating this element and ending invariably in *-ate* in the case of an anion and that is placed above and to the right of the symbol for this element ⟨according to the *Stock system* nitrous oxide is named nitrogen(I) oxide, ferrosoferric oxide Fe_3O_4 is iron (II, III) oxide $Fe^{II}Fe^{III}{}_2O_4$, and potassium manganite is potassium manganate (IV) $K_2Mn^{IV}O_3$⟩

stock tackle *n* **:** STOCK-AND-BILL TACKLE

stocktaking \\ˈ=ˌ==\\ *n* -s **1 :** the action of checking or taking an inventory of goods or supplies on hand (as in a store or warehouse) ⟨business is interrupted by ~ February first —*Hosiery & Underwear Rev.*⟩ **2 :** the action of estimating a situation at a given moment (as by considering resources and weaknesses or ground gained and lost) ⟨a sort of summing up and ~ of his career thus far —Kenneth Rexroth⟩

stock tank *n* **:** a tank or artificial pond used for watering livestock

stock ticker *n* **:** TICKER b

stockturn \\ˈ=ˌ=\\ *n* **:** a measure of business volume constituted by the number of times the average inventory of merchandise is sold within a specified period of time usu. a year

stockwhip \\ˈ=ˌ=\\ *n, Brit* **:** a whip with a short handle and a long lash

stock width *n* **:** a piece of lumber cut in an even width from 4 to 12 inches — usu. used in pl.

stockwork \\ˈ=ˌ=\\ *n* [part trans. of G *stockwerk*, fr. *stock* stick, stump, trunk of a tree (fr. OHG *stoc*) + *werk* work — more at STOCK] **1 :** a system of working in ore when it lies not in strata or veins but in solid masses so as to be worked in chambers or stories **2 :** a body or tract of rock so charged with veinlets, nests, or impregnations of ore and esp. tin ore that it can be profitably mined

stocky \\ˈstäkē, -ki\\ *adj* -ER/-EST [¹*stock* + -*y*] **1 :** compact, sturdy, and relatively thick in build **:** short, firm, and solid in shape ⟨*stockier* and better plants are obtained from cuttings —F.W.Card⟩ **2** *dial Eng* **:** HEADSTRONG, BOISTEROUS **3 :** formal in character or manner **:** having a stiff, cold, or severe nature ⟨the ~ virtues of integrity and piety —H.E.Scudder⟩ **syn** THICKSET, THICK, CHUNKY, STUBBY, SQUAT, DUMPY: STOCKY, like other words in this set in indicating a short and wide or thick build, is likely to be complimentary in suggesting compact sturdiness ⟨*stocky* though not chubby —W.A.White⟩ ⟨a *stocky* hard-hitting catcher⟩ THICKSET may describe a thick, solid, burly body ⟨too *thickset* for jockeying —John Masefield⟩ ⟨a *thickset* old policeman⟩ THICK as a synonym for THICKSET in reference to body build or form is dialectal, although it may be used for bodily parts ⟨*thick* lips⟩ ⟨*thick* legs⟩ CHUNKY may indicate a body type ample but robust and solid ⟨short and *chunky*, not quite fat —H.A.Sinclair⟩ ⟨a well-fed, *chunky*, healthy boy⟩ STUBBY, less apt than others in this set to describe human body types, indicates noteworthy lack of height or length and corresponding shortness ⟨outfielders' gloves have longer fingers . . . infielders' gloves have relatively *stubby* fingers —*New Yorker*⟩ SQUAT and DUMPY are usu. uncomplimentary. SQUAT may indicate unshapely lack of height as though suggesting a person squatting ⟨the *squat* misshapen figure that flattened itself into the shadow —Oscar Wilde⟩ ⟨anchored vessels of every sort from *squat* Baltic timber carriers —J.H.Wheelwright⟩ DUMPY may suggest short, lumpish gracelessness of body ⟨stumpy, *dumpy* girls with their rather coarse features, big buttocks and heavy breasts —Arthur Koestler⟩

stockyard \\ˈ=ˌ=\\ *n* **:** a yard for keeping stock; *specif* **:** an enclosure with stables, pens, and sheds which is usu. connected with a railroad and in which cattle, sheep, swine, and horses are kept temporarily for slaughter, market, or shipping

stockyard fever *or* **stockyard pneumonia** *or* **stockyards pneumonia** *n* **:** shipping fever of cattle

stød \\ˈstœd\\ *n* -s [Dan, lit., push, thrust; akin to MLG *stōt* push, thrust, OHG *stōz* push, thrust, *stōzan* to push, thrust — more at STINT] **:** a glottal modification occurring in Danish of the last part of a vowel or consonant sound or a glottal stop following a sound

stod·dard solvent \\ˈstädə(r)d-\\ *also* **stoddard's solvent** *n, usu cap 1st S* [fr. the name *Stoddard*] **:** a straight-run petroleum naphtha fraction of low flammability containing principally aliphatic hydrocarbons and conforming to specifications (as water-white color, distillation range 300° to 400°F, and flash point over 100°F) for use chiefly in dry cleaning — compare PETROLEUM SPIRIT

¹**stodge** \\ˈstäj\\ *vb* -ED/-ING/-S [origin unknown] *vt* **1 a :** to stuff full esp. with food ⟨the young will . . . be *stodged* with tea and buns —Mollie Panter-Downes⟩ **b :** to more than satisfy **:** SATIATE ⟨leaves me to ~ myself with his *Times* —G.B.Shaw⟩ **2 :** to mix or stir up together ⟨all they ever do is ~ some old jello and fruit⟩ ~ *vi* **1 :** to trudge through or as if through muck and mire **:** tramp clumsily and heavily ⟨ought no longer to go *stodging* along in penury —F.M.Ford⟩ **2 :** GORGE ⟨he could eat . . . but he could not ~ —J.M.Barrie⟩

²**stodge** \\"\\ *n* -s **1 :** a thick filling food (as oatmeal or stew) **2 :** something resembling stodge: as **a :** dull stupid ideas **b :** unimaginative tedious literary works ⟨the poor reading public soaked in life-long ~ —*Sydney (Australia) Bull.*⟩ **3 :** a slow plodding person ⟨he's such a ~ —Robertson Davies⟩

stodg·i·ly \\ˈstäjəlē, -li\\ *adv* **:** in a stodgy manner ⟨a ~ respectable real estate man —Anthony Boucher⟩

stodg·i·ness \\-jēnəs, -jin-\\ *n* -ES **:** the quality or state of being stodgy ⟨were it not for a certain ~ . . . this would have been a really fine performance —P.H.Lang⟩

stodgy \\-jē, -ji\\ *adj, sometimes* -ER/-EST [²*stodge* + -*y*] **1 a :** having a thick gluey consistency ⟨good ~ mud —*Canadian Geog. Jour.*⟩ **b :** having a thick texture **:** HEAVY — used esp. of food ⟨gray, ~ war bread stuns the stomach —F.V. & Katharine Drake⟩ **2 :** moving in a slow plodding way esp. as a result of physical bulkiness ⟨the cook's a ~ German woman, a typical hausfrau —W.H.Wright⟩ ⟨an occasional group of ~ sightseers —James Higgins & Gordon Donald⟩ **3 :** characterized by dullness **:** being without lightness or wit **:** BORING, PEDANTIC ⟨these volumes are not ~ . . . they are extremely readable —G.E.Gardner⟩ ⟨many persons . . . become stilted and ~ when they put pen to paper —Raymond Walters b.1912⟩ **4 :** devoid of excitement or interest **:** DULL, PROSAIC ⟨out on a peaceful rather ~ Sunday boat trip —Edna Ferber⟩ ⟨not tied down by . . . the ~ needs of mankind —Harriot B. Barbour⟩ **5 :** extremely old-fashioned in attitude or outlook **:** unwilling to yield to change ⟨received a pompously Victorian letter from his ~ father —E.E.S.Montagu⟩ ⟨who had once been so eager and bright, be so ~ now —Irwin Edman⟩ **6 :** lacking grace or distinction **:** DRAB ⟨~ suburbs whose rows of frame dwellings contrast sharply with . . . opulent mansions —*Amer. Guide Series: N.Y.City*⟩ **7 :** having neither smartness nor style **:** DOWDY ⟨the clothes . . . look ~ after the ones I've been seeing —Dodie Smith⟩ **8 :** adhering too much to tradition **:** stuck in the past **:** being without immediacy or innovation ⟨much better music than the ~ efforts of most . . . composers —H.C.Schonberg⟩

stoep \\ˈstüp\\ *n* -s *chiefly Africa* [Afrik, fr. MD — more at STOOP] **:** PORCH 1

¹**stog** \\ˈstäg\\ *n* -s [prob. alter. of obs. *stock* estoc, thrust with an estoc, fr. MF *estoc* — more at ESTOC] *Scot* **:** STAB

²**stog** \\"\\ *vb* **stogged; stogged; stogging; stogs** [perh. alter. (influenced by *bog*) of ¹*stodge*] *vi, Scot* **:** TRUDGE, PLOD ~ *vt* **:** to cause to be stuck **:** BOG

sto·gie *or* **sto·gy** \\ˈstōgē, -gi\\ *n, pl* **stogies** [fr. *Conestoga*, Pa.] **1** *also* **sto·ga** \\-gə\\ -s **:** a stout coarse shoe **:** BROGAN **2** *also* **sto·gee** \\-gē, -gi\\ -s **:** an inexpensive though not necessarily inferior cigar made in the form of a slender cylindrical roll ⟨still manufactures the . . . ~*s*, which were favored by teamsters and were originally known as Conestogas —G.R. Stewart⟩ ⟨had happily smoked ~*s* rolled by hand —*Time*⟩

¹**sto·ic** \\ˈstōik, -ōēk\\ *n* -s [ME, fr. L *stoicus*, adj. & n., fr. Gk *stōikos*, fr. *Stoa (Poikilē)* Painted Portico, a portico in Athens where Zeno taught (fr. *stoa* portico + *poikilē*, fem. of *poikilos* multicolored, painted) + -*ikos* -ic; akin to Gk *stylos* pillar — more at STEER] **1** *usu cap* **:** a member of a school of philosophy founded by Zeno of Citium about 300 B.C., extensively systematized by Chrysippus of Soli, and later developed and popularized by Seneca, Epictetus, and Marcus Aurelius **2 :** one apparently or professedly indifferent to pleasure or pain **:** one not easily excited or upset ⟨an absolute ~ in the face of mishaps —Thomas Hardy⟩

²**stoic** \\"\\ *or* **sto·i·cal** \\-ōəkəl, -ōēk-\\ *adj* [*stoic* fr. L *stoicus*; *stoical* fr. ME, fr. L *stoicus* + ME -*al*] **1** *usu cap* **:** of, relating to, or resembling the Stoics or their doctrines **2 :** not affected by passion or feeling; *esp* **:** manifesting indifference to pleasure or pain ⟨the ~ courage which enabled him to bear perhaps the most dreadful of human afflictions —W.S.Maugham⟩ ⟨she could only preach ~ patience to herself —Douglas Bush⟩ ⟨a *stoical* person who does not allow a "mere pain" to interfere very much with what he is doing —Harold Shryock⟩ ⟨drenched to the skin but calm and suavely *stoical* —Elinor Wylie⟩ **syn** see IMPASSIVE

sto·i·cal·ly \\-ōək(ə)lē, -ōēk-, -li\\ *adv* **:** in a stoic manner ⟨imagined himself . . . ~ accepting suffering without a word —Aldous Huxley⟩

stoi·chei·om·e·try \\ˌstȯikīˈäməˌtrē\\ *chiefly Brit var of* STOICHIOMETRY

stoi·chi·o·met·ric \\ˌstȯikēəˈme·trik\\ *also* **stoi·chi·o·met·ri·cal** \\-rəkəl\\ *adj* [Gk *stoicheion* element + E -*metric*, -*metrical*] **:** of, relating to, employed in, or obtained by stoichiometry: as **a :** characterized by or being a chemical composition of definite proportions by weight ⟨the zinc oxide is no longer of ~ composition but contains excess zinc atoms —E.E. Hahn⟩ ⟨the coating of lead dioxide obtained on the anode does not correspond to the ~ formula PbO_2 —S.E.Q.Ashley⟩ — compare BERTHOLLIDE, DALTONIDE **b :** characterized by or being a proportion of substances or energy exactly right for a specific chemical reaction with no excess of any reactant or product ⟨combustion is initiated . . . where the fuel and air are close to the chemically correct or ~ proportion —F.P.Durham⟩ ⟨by determining the amount of thrombin formed from known quantities of calcium, one is able to conclude whether the action of the latter is catalytic or ~ —*Science*⟩ ⟨light quanta, like other chemical reactants, enter into the reaction in a ~ manner —J.F.Bonner & A.W.Galston⟩ — **stoi·chi·o·met·ri·cal·ly** \\-rək(ə)lē\\ *adv*

stoi·chi·om·e·try \\ˌstȯikēˈäməˌtrē\\ *n* -ES [Gk *stoicheion* + E -*metry*] **1 :** a branch of science that deals with the application of the laws of definite proportions and of the conservation of matter and also energy to chemical reactions and processes **2 a :** the quantitative relationship of constituents in a chemical entity ⟨aquo-cations of definite ~ characterize crystalline salts —Therald Moeller⟩ **b :** the quantitative relationship between two or more substances esp. in processes involving physical or chemical change ⟨the ~ and reversibility of ion exchange —Robert Kunin⟩

sto·i·cism \\ˈstōəˌsizəm\\ *n* -s **1** *usu cap* **:** the principles or the philosophical system of the Stoics who based an austere ethics on a pantheistic cosmology holding that the world is governed by and is the embodiment of logos, that it is man's duty to conform freely to natural law and his destiny, that virtue is the highest good, and that the wise man should be free from passion equally unperturbed by joy or grief **2 :** the principle or practice of showing indifference to pleasure or pain **:** repression of feeling **:** IMPASSIVENESS ⟨preparing himself with tranquil ~ for the end —P.E.More⟩

stoi·rin \\sthōˈrēn\\ *var of* STOREEN

stoit \\ˈstōt, ˈstȯit\\ *vi* -ED/-ING/-S [perh. fr. D *stuiten* to stop, check, bounce; akin to OHG *stōzan* to push, thrust — more at STINT] **1** *chiefly Scot* **:** STAGGER, LURCH **2** *dial Eng* **:** to jump up

stoit·er \\-tər\\ *vi* -ED/-ING/-S *chiefly Scot* **:** STAGGER, LURCH

¹**stoke** \\ˈstōk\\ *vb* -ED/-ING/-S [D *stoken*, fr. MD, to thrust, poke, stoke; akin to MLG *stōken* to poke, MD *stuken* to push, shove, and prob. to OE *stocc* stock — more at STOCK] *vt* **1 :** to poke or stir up (as a fire) **:** tend the fire of **:** supply with fuel or something resembling fuel ⟨*stoked* the furnace expertly⟩ ⟨*stoked* the fire of his suspicions with lies⟩ **2 :** to feed abundantly or to excess **:** provide more than adequately with food ⟨the scouts *stoked* themselves for the long hike ahead⟩ ~ *vi* **1 :** to poke or stir up a fire **:** tend the fires of furnaces **:** supply a furnace with fuel **2 :** to eat a big meal ⟨the gang fell to and *stoked* in silence —Ronald Duncan⟩

²**stoke** \\"\\ *n* -s [after Sir George G. *Stokes* †1903 Brit. mathematician and physicist] **:** the cgs unit of kinematic viscosity being that of a fluid which has a viscosity of one poise and a density of one gram per cubic centimeter

³**stoke** \\"\\ *or* **stoke–on–trent** \\-ˈtrent\\ *adj, usu cap S&T* [fr. *Stoke on Trent*, England] **:** of or from the city of Stoke on Trent, England **:** of the kind or style prevalent in Stoke on Trent

stokehold \\ˈ=ˌ=\\ *n* **1 :** a space in front of the boilers of a ship from which the furnaces are fed **2 :** a room containing a ship's boilers — called also *fireroom*

stokehole \\ˈ=ˌ=\\ *n* **1 :** the mouth to the grate of a furnace **2 :** the space in front of a furnace where the stokers stand

stok·er \\ˈstōkə(r)\\ *n* -s [D, fr. *stoken* to stoke + -*er*] **1 :** one employed to tend a furnace and supply it with fuel: as **a :** one that tends a marine steam boiler **b** *Brit* **:** a locomotive fireman **2 :** a machine for feeding a fire

stoker's cramp *n* **:** HEAT CRAMPS

stokes' aster \\ˈstōks-\\ *n, usu cap S* [after Jonathan *Stokes* †1831 Eng. botanist] **:** a perennial herb (*Stokesia laevis*) of the southern U.S. that is often cultivated and has large heads of usu. bluish flowers like asters — called also *cornflower aster*

sto·ke·sia \\stōˈkēzh(ē)ə\\ *n* [NL, fr. Jonathan *Stokes* + NL -*ia*] **1** *cap* **:** a monotypic genus of erect perennial herbs (family Compositae) with sometimes yellow or purple flower heads **2** -s **:** any plant of the genus *Stokesia* **:** STOKES' ASTER

stokes·ite \\ˈstōkˌsīt\\ *n* -s [Sir George G. *Stokes* †1903 Brit. mathematician and physicist + E -*ite*] **:** a mineral $CaSnSi_3O_9.2H_2O$ consisting of a hydrous silicate of calcium and tin and occurring in colorless orthorhombic crystals (hardness 6, sp. gr. 3.2)

stokes' law *n, usu cap S* [after Sir George G. *Stokes*] **1 :** a law in physics: the frequency of luminescence excited by radiation does not exceed that of the exciting radiation **2 :** a law in physics: the force required to move a sphere through a given viscous fluid at a low uniform velocity is directly proportional to the velocity and radius of the sphere

stokes litter *also* **stokes stretcher** *n, usu cap S* [after Charles F. *Stokes* †1931 Am. naval medical officer, its inventor] **:** a wire basket conforming in shape to the human body into which an injured, sick, or disabled person can be safely strapped

Stokes litter

stok·roos \\ˈstäˌkrüs\\ *n* -ES [Afrik (*wilde*) *stokroos*, fr. *wild* wild + *stokroos* hollyhock, fr. D, fr. *stok* stick (fr. MD *stoc* stick, stump, trunk of a tree) + *roos* rose, fr. MD *rose*, fr. L *rosa* — more at STOCK, ROSE] *Africa* **:** KENAF

stokvis *var of* STOCKFISH

sto·la \\ˈstōlə\\ *n, pl* **sto·lae** \\-ō,lē\\ *or* **stolas** [L] **:** a long draped robe similar to the Greek chiton worn by women of ancient Rome

¹**stole** [ME *stole* (past), alter. (influenced by *stolen*) of *stal*, fr. OE *stæl*; ME *stole*, *stolen* (past part.), fr. OE *stolen*] *past & chiefly dial past part of* STEAL

²**stole** \\ˈstōl\\ *n* -s [ME, fr. OE, fr. L *stola*, fr. Gk *stolē* equipment, raiment, robe; akin to Gk *stellein* to set up, make ready, send — more at STALL] **1 a :** a long loose garment; *esp* **:** a garment similar to the stola or toga worn in ancient times **b :** STOLA **2 :** an ecclesiastical vestment consisting of a long narrow cloth band worn around the neck and falling from the shoulders of bishops and priests **3 :** a long wide scarf or similar covering worn by women usu. across the shoulders

³**stole** \\"\\ *vt* -ED/-ING/-S **:** to provide a stole for

⁴**stole** \\"\\ *n* -s [ME *stool*, lit., stool — more at STOOL] *archaic* **:** CLOSESTOOL

stoled \\-ld\\ *adj* [²*stole* + -*ed*] **:** having or wearing a stole

stole fee *n* [trans. of G *stolgebühre*] **:** a fee paid by a member of the laity to a priest for the administration of a sacrament or the performance of a rite in the Roman Catholic Church

stole mesh *n* **:** a double mesh in a fishnet

sto·len \\ˈstōlən\\ *adj* [ME, fr. past part. of *stelen* to steal — more at STEAL] **:** obtained or accomplished by theft, stealth, or craft **:** effected in secret ⟨~ hours of pleasure⟩ ⟨managed a ~ base to the delight of the crowd⟩

stol·id \\ˈstäləd\\ *adj, sometimes* -ER/-EST [L *stolidus* unmovable, dull, stolid — more at STALL] **:** having or expressing little or no sensibility **:** not easily aroused or excited ⟨a silent ~ creature who took it all as a matter of course —Virginia Woolf⟩ ⟨spoke in ~ tones —Ellen Glasgow⟩ **syn** see IMPASSIVE

sto·lid·i·ty \\stəˈlidədē, -ətē, -i\\ *n* -ES [L *stoliditas*, fr. *stolidus* + -*itas* -ity] **:** the quality or state of being stolid ⟨all his ~ seemed gone now; he was trembling —W.H.Hudson †1922⟩

stol·id·ly *adv* **:** in a stolid manner ⟨in the winter they had worked . . . enduring ~ the snow and ice —Pearl Buck⟩

¹**stol·kjaer·re** \\ˈstōlˌkyerə\\ *n* -s [Norw *stolkjerre* (formerly spelled *stolkjærre*), fr. *stol* chair, seat (fr. ON *stōll*) + *kjerre* cart, fr. ON *kerra*, prob. fr. MD *carre*, *kerre*, fr. L *carra* — more at STOOL, CAR] **:** a 2-wheeled cart used in Norway with a front seat for two and a rear seat for the driver

²**stolkjaerre** \\"\\ *vi* **stolkjaerred; stolkjaerred; stolkjaerreing; stolkjaerres** **:** to ride in or drive a stolkjaerre

¹**stol·len** \\ˈs(h)tōlən\\ *n, pl* **stollen** [G, fr. MHG *stolle*, lit., post, support, fr. OHG *stollo*; akin to OHG *stellen* to set, place — more at STALL] **:** a repeated section in a meistergesang corresponding to the exposition in classical sonata form — compare ABGESANG

²**stollen** \\"\\ *n, pl* **stollen** *or* **stollens** [G *stolle*, *stollen*, fr. OHG *stollo* post, support] **:** a sweet yeast bread containing fruit and nuts usu. made in a long oval loaf

sto·lon \\ˈstōlən\\ *n* -s [NL, fr. L *stolon-*, *stolo* shoot, branch, sucker of a plant; akin to Arm *steln* branch, stalk, OL *stlocus* place — more at STALL] **1 a :** a horizontal branch from the base of a plant that is either above or below ground and produces new plants from buds at its tip or nodes (as in the strawberry) — called also *runner* **b :** a hypha produced on the surface and connecting a group of conidiophores (as in fungi of the genus *Rhizopus*) **2 :** a more or less prolonged extension of the body wall (as of an anthozoan, hydrozoan, bryozoan, or ascidian) from which buds are developed giving rise to new zooids and thus forming a compound animal in which the zooids usu. remain united by the stolon

sto·lon·ate \\-lənət, -ləˌnāt\\ *adj* [NL *stolon* + E -*ate*] **:** having stolons **:** arising from a stolon

sto·lo·nif·e·ra \\ˌstōləˈnif(ə)rə\\ *n pl, cap* [NL, fr. *stolon* + -*i-* + L -*fera*, neut. pl. of -*fer* -ferous] **:** an order of alcyonarians comprising colonial polyps connected by stolons and supported by a skeleton of calcareous spicules which may be more or less fused into tubes — compare ORGAN-PIPE CORAL

sto·lo·nif·er·ous \\ˌ==ˈnif(ə)rəs\\ *adj* [NL *stolon* + E -*iferous*] **:** bearing or developing stolons — **sto·lo·nif·er·ous·ly** *adv*

sto·lon·iza·tion \\ˌstōlənəˈzāshən\\ *n* -s [ISV *stolon-* (fr. NL *stolon*) + -*ization*] **:** the production of stolons

stolz·ite \\ˈstōlˌzīt\\ *n* -s [G *stolzit*, fr. Dr. *Stolz*, 19th cent. Bohemian scientist + G -*it* -ite] **:** a mineral $PbWO_4$ consisting of a native lead tungstate isomorphous with wulfenite and prob. with scheelite and powellite

stom- *or* **stomo-** *comb form* [NL, fr. Gk, fr. *stoma* — more at STOMACH] **:** mouth **:** stoma ⟨*stomo*daeum⟩ ⟨*stomo*isia⟩

sto·ma \\ˈstōmə\\ *n, pl* **stoma·ta** \\-əd·ə *sometimes* ˈstäm-\\ *also* **stomas** [NL, fr. Gk, mouth — more at STOMACH] **1 :** any of various small and simple openings or inlets (as an insect's spiracle) esp. in a lower animal; *esp* **:** one of the many minute openings among the cells of a serous membrane affording direct communication with the adjacent lymph channels **2 a :** one of the minute openings in the epidermis of leaves, stems, and other plant organs through which gaseous interchange between the atmosphere and the intercellular spaces within the leaf occurs; *usu* **:** the opening together with its associated guard cells and accessory cells **b :** STOMIUM 1 **c :** a fungal ostiole **3 :** an artificial permanent opening in the abdominal wall made in surgical procedures (as colostomy, cecostomy, ileostomy)

¹**-sto·ma** \\stəmə\\ *n comb form, pl* **-stoma·ta** \\ˈstōməd·ə, -mətə *sometimes* ˈstäm-\\ *also* **-stomas** [NL, fr. Gk *stoma*] **1 :** mouth **:** opening **:** stoma ⟨hypo*stoma*⟩ **2** *or* **stomus** **:** creature with (such) a mouth or stoma — in generic names ⟨Bdello*stoma*⟩ ⟨Gnatho*stoma*⟩

²**-stoma** \\"\\ *or* **-stomata** \\"\\ *n pl comb form* [NL, fr. Gk *stomat-*, *stoma* mouth — more at STOMACH] **:** creatures with (such) a mouth or stoma — in higher taxa in zoology ⟨Gnatho*stoma*⟩ ⟨Plagio*stomata*⟩

³**-stoma** *pl of* -STOMUM

¹**stom·ach** \\ˈstəmək, -mēk\\ *n* -s *often attrib* [ME *stomak*, fr. MF *estomac*, fr. L *stomachus* gullet, esophagus, stomach, fr. Gk *stomachos*, fr. *stoma* mouth, opening; akin to MBret *staffu* mouth, W *safn* mouth, Av *staman-* mouth of a dog] **1 a :** a dilatation of the alimentary canal of a vertebrate communicating anteriorly with the esophagus and posteriorly with the duodenum, being typically a simple often curved sac with an outer serous coat, a strong complex muscular wall that contracts rhythmically, and a mucous lining membrane that contains gastric glands, being in some forms (as ruminants) constricted into several chambers that differ in function and structure, providing various digestive enzymes, and grinding and mixing food materials by its muscular action — compare CROP; see GASTRIC JUICE; GREATER CURVATURE, LESSER CURVATURE, PYLORUS; ABOMASUM, OMASUM, RUMEN **b :** a digestive cavity in an invertebrate animal; *esp* **:** a part of the alimentary canal more or less corresponding with the vertebrate stomach **c :** the part of the body that contains the stomach **:** the ventral part of the trunk **:** BELLY, ABDOMEN ⟨she lay on her ~ reading⟩ ⟨a rash on the ~⟩ **2 a :** desire for food caused by hunger **:** APPETITE ⟨had a good ~ for dinner after their climb⟩ **b :** inclination or desire for something other than food — usu. used negatively ⟨no ~ for meeting such a rascal⟩ **3 a :** the seat or source of the feelings **:** emotional power or capacity to meet or withstand a demand on the feelings ⟨needed a strong ~ to meet such challenges⟩ **b :** a particular disposition or mental attitude: as (1) *obs* **:** COMPASSION (2) *obs* **:** TEMPER, SPIRIT, VALOR (3) *obs* **:** PRIDE, ARROGANCE (4) *obs* **:** anger or a display of anger **:** SPLEEN

²**stomach** \\"\\ *vb* -ED/-ING/-S *vt* **1 :** to remember with anger

: take offense at **2** *obs* : ENRAGE, IRRITATE, OFFEND **3 a** : to bear without unfavorable reaction ⟨the prisoner could not ~ his food⟩ **b** : to bear without overt resentment : put up with : BROOK ⟨the legislators should not ~ the proposal⟩ **4** : NAUSEATE, DISGUST ~ *vi, obs* : to be angry : show anger : take offense : feel resentment

stomachache \ˈ⸗,⸗\ *n* : pain occurring in or in the region of the stomach

stom·ach·al \ˈstəməkəl\ *adj* : STOMACHIC

stom·ached \ˈstəməkt\ *adj* [¹*stomach* + *-ed*] : having a stomach — used usu. in combination ⟨large-*stomached*⟩ ⟨weak-*stomached*⟩

stom·ach·er \ˈstəməkə(r), -mek-\ *n* -s [ME *stomaker*, fr. *stomak* stomach + *-er*] **1** : the center front section of a waist or underwaist or a usu. heavily embroidered or jeweled separate piece for the center front of a bodice and worn by men or women in the 15th and 16th centuries and by women later **2** : a usu. large jeweled ornament worn by women on the front of a bodice

¹**stom·ach·ful** \ˈstəməkfəl, -mek-\ *adj* [¹*stomach* + *-ful* (adj. suffix)] **1** *archaic* : OBSTINATE, STUBBORN **2** *archaic* : RESENTFUL, ANGRY **3** *archaic* : COURAGEOUS

²**stom·ach·ful** \-k,fu̇l\ *n* -s [¹*stomach* + *-ful* (n. suffix)] : a quantity sufficient to fill the stomach; *broadly* : all that one can stand or tolerate ⟨had a ~ of his abuse⟩

¹**sto·mach·ic** \stəˈmakik, -akēk\ *also* **sto·mach·i·cal** \-akəkəl, -akēk-\ *adj* [LL *stomachicus*, fr. Gk *stomachikos*, fr. *stomachos* stomach + *-ikos* -ic, -ical] **1** : of or relating to the stomach ⟨~ vessels⟩ **2** : strengthening to the stomach : exciting the action of the stomach ⟨a ~ cordial⟩ — **sto·mach·i·cal·ly** \-akək(ə)lē, -akēk-, -li\ *adv*

²**stomachic** \ˈ"\ *n* -s : a stimulant or tonic for the stomach

stomaching *n* -s [fr. gerund of ²*stomach*] *obs* : a feeling of bitterness, irritation, or anger : RESENTMENT

stom·ach·less \ˈstəməkləs\ *adj* : lacking a stomach

stomach piece *n* : APRON 2c (2)

stomach pump *n* : a suction pump with a flexible tube for removing liquids from the stomach

stomach tooth *n* [so called fr. the gastric disturbance that often attends its appearance] : a lower canine esp. of the first dentition

stomach tube *n* : a flexible rubber tube to be passed through the esophagus into the stomach for introduction of material or removal of gastric contents

stomach worm *n* : any of various nematode worms parasitic in the stomach of mammals or birds; *esp* : a worm (*Haemonchus contortus*) common in domestic ruminants — called also *barber's pole worm, twisted stomach worm*

stom·achy \ˈstəməkē\ *adj* **1** *dial Brit* : IRASCIBLE, IRRITABLE **2** : having a large stomach

sto·mal \ˈstōməl\ *adj* [*stom-* + *-al*] : of, relating to, or situated near a surgical stoma ⟨a ~ ulcer⟩

stomas *pl of* STOMA

-stomas *pl of* -STOMA

stomat- *or* **stomato-** *comb form* [NL, fr. Gk, fr. *stomat-, stoma* — more at STOMACH] : mouth : opening : stoma ⟨*stomat*itis⟩ ⟨*stomato*scope⟩

stomata *pl of* STOMA

¹**-stomata** *pl of* -STOMA

²**-stomata** — see ²-STOMA

stoma·tal \ˈstämədᵊl, ˈstōm-, -ətᵊl\ *adj* [*stomat-* + *-al*] : of, relating to, or constituting plant stomata ⟨~ openings⟩

¹**sto·mate** \ˈstō,māt\ *n* -s [NL *stomat-, stoma*] : STOMA 2

²**stomate** \ˈ"\ *adj* [*stom-* + *-ate* (adj. suffix)] : STOMATOUS

-sto·mate \,stō,māt\ *adj comb form* [*stom-* + *-ate*] : -STOMATOUS

sto·mat·ic \stəˈmad·ik\ *adj* [*stomat-* + *-ic*] : relating to or constituting a stoma

stoma·tit·ic \ˌstōməˈtid·ik, ˌstäm-\ *adj* [NL *stomatitis* + E *-ic*] : of, relating to, or constituting stomatitis ⟨a ~ disorder⟩

stoma·ti·tis \ˌ⸗⸗ˈtīd·əs\ *n, pl* **stomatit·i·des** \-ˈtidə,dēz\ *or* **stomatitises** [NL, fr. *stomat-* + *-itis*] : any of numerous inflammatory diseases of the mouth varying in symptoms with the cause and resulting from various local or systemic causes (as mechanical trauma, irritants, allergy, vitamin deficiency, disease of the blood, or infection) ⟨erosive ~⟩ ⟨vesicular ~⟩

stoma·to·dae·um *or* **stoma·to·de·um** \ˌstōməd·ōˈdēəm, ˌstäm-\ *n, pl* **stomato·daea** *or* **stomato·dea** \-ēə\ *also* **stomatodeums** [NL, fr. *stomat-* + *-odaeum, -odeum* (fr. Gk *hodaion*, neut. of *hodaios* being on the way, fr. *hodos* way) — more at CEDE] : STOMODAEUM

stoma·to·gas·tric \ˌstōmə(ˌ)d·ō, ˌstämə(ˌ)d·ō+\ *adj* [ISV *stomat-* + *gastric*] : of or relating to the mouth and the stomach; *specif* : constituting a system of nerves that ramify over the anterior portion of the alimentary canal in various invertebrates

stoma·to·graph \ˈstōməd·ə,graf, ˈstäm-, -räf\ *n* [*stomat-* + *-graph*] : an instrument for determining and recording variations in size of stomatal apertures (as of a leaf)

stoma·to·log·i·cal \ˌstōməd·ᵊlˈäjəkəl, ˌstäm-\ *also* **stoma·to·log·ic** \-jik\ *adj* : of or relating to stomatology

stoma·tol·o·gist \ˌstōməˈtäləjəst, ˌstäm-\ *n* -s : a specialist in stomatology

stoma·tol·o·gy \-jē, -ji\ *n* -ES [ISV *stomat-* + *-logy*] : a branch of medical science concerned with the mouth and its disorders

¹**stoma·to·pod** \ˈstōməd·ə,päd, ˈstäm-\ *adj* [NL *Stomatopoda*] : of or relating to the Stomatopoda

²**stomatopod** \ˈ"\ *n* -s : a crustacean of the order Stomatopoda : SQUILLA

stoma·top·o·da \ˌstōməˈtäpədə, ˌstäm-\ *n pl, cap* [NL, fr. *stomat-* + *-poda*] : an order of Crustacea coextensive with the division Hoplocarida — **stoma·top·o·dous** \ˌ⸗⸗ˈtäpədəs\ *adj*

stoma·to·po·di·um \ˌstōməd·ōˈpōdēəm, ˌstäm-\ *n, pl* **stoma·topo·dia** \-ēə\ [NL, fr. *stomat-* + *-podium*] : a hypha of a parasitic fungus that passes through a stoma and commonly forms specialized haustoria within a parasitized leaf

stoma·tose \ˈstämə,tōs, ˈstōm-\ *adj* [*stomat-* + *-ose*] : STOMATOUS

stoma·tous \-məd·əs, -mətəs\ *adj* [*stomat-* + *-ous*] : bearing stomata or having a stoma

-stoma·tous \ˌstämədəs, -tōm-, -mətəs\ *adj comb form* [prob. fr. NL *-stomatus*, fr. Gk *stomat-, stoma* mouth — more at STOMACH] : having (such) a mouth or opening : stomatous ⟨cyclo*stomatous*⟩

-stome \ˌstōm\ *n comb form* -s [ISV, fr. NL *-stoma*] : mouth : opening resembling or functioning as a mouth ⟨cyto*stome*⟩

¹**-stomi** *pl of* -STOMUS

²**-sto·mi** \stə,mī\ *n pl comb form* [NL, fr. Gk *stoma* mouth — more at STOMACH] : creatures having (such) a mouth or opening — in names of higher taxa in zoology ⟨Plagio*stomi*⟩ ⟨Aulo*stomi*⟩ ⟨Selacho*stomi*⟩

¹**-sto·mia** \ˈstōmēə\ *n comb form* -s [NL, fr. *stom-* + *-ia* -y] : mouth exhibiting (such) a condition ⟨steno*stomia*⟩

²**-stomia** \ˈ"\ *n pl comb form* [NL, fr. Gk *stomion* mouth — more at STOMION] : creatures sharing (such) a condition of the mouth — in names of higher taxa in zoology ⟨Deutero*stomia*⟩

¹**sto·mi·a·tid** \ˈstōmēəd·əd\ *adj* [NL *Stomiatidae*] : of or relating to the Stomiatidae

²**stomiatid** \ˈ"\ *n* -s : a fish of the family Stomiatidae

sto·mi·at·i·dae \ˌstōmēˈad·ə,dē\ *n pl, cap* [NL, irreg. fr. *Stomias*, type genus (irreg. fr. Gk *stoma* mouth) + *-idae* — more at STOMACH] : a family of small slender usu. scaleless deep-sea fishes having a short head that bears an enormous mouth full of long powerful teeth and a highly distensible stomach and with living and extinct related fishes forming a suborder of the order Isospondyli — compare DRAGONFISH

¹**sto·mi·a·toid** \ˈstōmēə,tȯid\ *adj* [NL *Stomiatidae* + E *-oid*] : resembling or related to the Stomiatidae

²**stomiatoid** \ˈ"\ *n* -s : a stomiatoid fish

-stomies *pl of* -STOMY

sto·mi·on \ˈstōmē,än\ *n, pl* **stomions** \-nz\ *or* **sto·mia** \-ēə\ [NL, fr. Gk, mouth, dim. of *stoma* mouth — more at STOMACH] : the midpoint of the oral fissure determined with the lips closed

sto·mi·um \ˈstōmēəm\ *n, pl* **sto·mia** \-ēə\ *also* **stomiums** [NL, fr. Gk *stomion* mouth] **1** : the thin-walled cells of the annulus marking the line or region of dehiscence of a fern sporangium **2** : the opening in an anther usu. between lip cells through which dehiscence occurs

stomo- — see STOM-

sto·mo·chord \ˈstōmə,kȯrd\ *n* [*stom-* + *-chord* (as in *notochord*)] : a structure in the proboscis of an enteropneust that has been construed as homologous with the chordate notochord — **sto·mo·chord·al** \ˌ⸗⸗ˈkȯrdᵊl\ *adj*

sto·mo·dae·al *or* **sto·mo·de·al** \ˌstōməˈdēəl\ *adj* [NL *stomodaeum, stomode*um + E *-al*] : of, relating to, or derived from a stomodaeum

stomodaeal food *n* : partly digested food regurgitated from the mouth by some social insects (as termites) and used to feed other members of the colony

sto·mo·dae·um *or* **sto·mo·de·um** \ˌ⸗⸗ˈdēəm\ *n, pl* **stomodaea** \-ēə\ *also* **stomodaeums** \-ēəmz\ *or* **stomo·dea** \-ēə\ *also* **stomodeums** [NL, fr. *stom-* + *-odaeum, -odeum* (fr. Gk *hodaion*, neut. of *hodaios* being on the way, fr. *hodos* way) — more at CEDE] : the anterior ectodermal part of the alimentary canal or tract including all formed by invagination of the external body wall — compare PROCTODAEUM; see CTENOPHORE illustration

sto·moi·sia \stəˈmȯisēə\ *n, cap* [NL, perh. fr. *stom-* + Gk *oisos* agnus castus + NL *-ia* — more at WITHY] : a large genus of herbs (family Lentibulariaceae) widely distributed on wet shores and having rootlike bladder-bearing branches, minute or scalelike leaves, and racemose or solitary irregular often spurred mostly yellow flowers — compare BLADDERWORT

-sto·mous \stəməs\ *adj comb form* [NL *-stomus*, fr. Gk *stoma* mouth — more at STOMACH] : -STOMATOUS ⟨gymno*stomous*⟩

sto·mox·ys \stəˈmäksəs\ *n, cap* [NL, fr. *stom-* + Gk *oxys* sharp — more at OXY-] : a genus of blood-sucking flies that includes the stable fly (*S. calcitrans*) and is usu. placed in the family Muscidae but sometimes assigned to a separate family

¹**stomp** \ˈstämp, ˈstȯmp\ *vb* -ED/-ING/-S [alter. of ¹*stamp*] *vt* : STAMP 2 ~ *vi* **1** : STAMP 2 **2** : to dance a stomp — **stomp·er** \-pə(r)\ *n* -s

²**stomp** \ˈ"\ *n* -s **1** : STAMP 4 **2 a** : a jazz dance characterized by heavy stamping **b** : music for a stomp characterized by strong rhythmic drive and a rhythmic repetition pattern **3 a** : a shuffling counterclockwise line dance of Woodland Indians and derivatively of Oklahoma tribes with characteristic antiphonal singing **b** : the running step of this dance

³**stomp** *var of* STUMP

-sto·mum \ˈstōməm, *in sense 2* ˌstəməm\ *n comb form, pl* **-sto·ma** \-mə\ [NL, fr. Gk *stoma* mouth — more at STOMACH] **1** : mouth : opening : stoma ⟨pre*stomum*⟩ **2** : creature with (such) a mouth — in generic names ⟨Amphi*stomum*⟩ ⟨Oesopha*gostomum*⟩

-sto·mus \stəməs\ *n comb form, pl* **sto·mi** \stə,mī\ [NL, fr. Gk *stoma* mouth] **1** : condition of having (such) a mouth ⟨micro*stomus*⟩ **2** : creature with (such) a mouth — in generic names ⟨Agono*stomus*⟩ ⟨Cato*stomus*⟩ ⟨Phyllo*stomus*⟩

¹**-sto·my** \stəmē, -mi\ *n comb form* -ES [ISV, fr. NL ¹*-stomia*] : -STOMIA

²**-stomy** \ˈ"\ *n comb form* -ES [ISV *stom-* + *-y*] : surgical operation establishing a usu. permanent opening into (such) a part ⟨entero*stomy*⟩ or between (such) parts ⟨esophagogastro*stomy*⟩

stond \ˈständ\ *dial Eng var of* STAND

¹**stone** \ˈstōn\ *n* -s *see sense 3* [ME *stan, ston, stoon*, fr. OE *stān*; akin to OHG *stein* stone, ON *steinn*, Goth *stains* stone, L *stiria* icicle, Gk *stia, stion* pebble, *stear* fat, tallow, Skt *styāyate* it congeals, hardens; basic meaning: to harden] **1** : a concretion of earthy or mineral matter of igneous, sedimentary, or metamorphic origin: **a** (1) : such a concretion of indeterminate size or shape : BOULDER, PEBBLE ⟨~*s* rolling down the hill⟩ ⟨gathering ~*s* on the beach⟩ (2) : the substance of this concretion : ROCK ⟨the mountain is solid ~⟩ ⟨trees turned to ~ in the petrified forest⟩ **b** : such a concretion mined, quarried, or shaped in a definite form or size or for a specified function: as (1) : a building block ⟨demolish the structure a ~ at a time⟩ (2) : a paving block : COBBLESTONE ⟨building barricades of the very ~*s* of the streets⟩ (3) : a precious stone : GEM (4) : a mineral matter used for a particular ornamental or commercial purpose ⟨ornaments made of the rarer ~*s* — banded slate, rose quartz, steatite —*Amer. Guide Series: N.J.*⟩ (5) : a pillar or block of stone set as a monument or sign; *esp* : GRAVESTONE ⟨the burying ground, where you can find the ~*s* of veterans of the Revolution —J.P.Marquand⟩ (6) : a rounded missile fired from an arm or a sling ⟨six ~*s* for his sling⟩ (7) : a shaped piece of rock used in a feat of strength (as curling) (8) : MILLSTONE (9) : GRINDSTONE (10) : WHETSTONE (11) : a stand or table with a smooth flat top on which to impose or set type — called also *surface* (12) : a surface upon which a drawing, text, or design to be lithographed is drawn or transferred (13) : a watch jewel **2** : something resembling a small stone or pebble in shape, composition, or hardness: as **a** (1) : CALCULUS 1a (2) : a hard natural growth (as an otolith) found in an animal **b** : TESTIS **c** : HAILSTONE **d** (1) : the hard central portion of a drupaceous fruit (as a peach) (2) : a hard stonelike seed (as of a date) **3** *pl usu* **stone** : any of various units of weight ranging from 4 to 26 pounds: as **a** : an official British unit equal to 14 pounds **b** : a British unit for meat equal to 8 pounds — called also *Smithfield stone* **4** : any of the colors common in stone or weathered rock — see DEEP STONE, HONEY 6, LIGHT STONE, STONE GRAY **5** : CHINA STONE, CORNISH STONE **6** : a small crystalline contamination in glass comprising unmelted batch material or a particle of the melting vessel **7** : a playing piece used in backgammon

²**stone** \ˈ"\ *vb* -ED/-ING/-S [ME *stanen, stonen*, fr. *stan, ston, stoon*, n.] *vt* **1** : to hurl stones or sometimes other missiles at ⟨was *stoned* by abolitionists —Mari Sandoz⟩ ⟨began *stoning* us with empty beer cans —Leslie Waller⟩; *esp* : to kill by hitting with stones ⟨he shall be *stoned* or shot; whether beast or man, he shall not live —Exod 19:13 (RSV)⟩ **2 a** *archaic* : to make (a person) hard or insensitive to feeling ⟨O perjured woman! Thou dost ~ my heart —Shak.⟩ **b** : to make numb or insensible (as from drink or narcotics) ⟨planned to ~ himself with vodka —Truman Capote⟩ **3** : to face, pave, or fortify with stones ⟨has dug a well and is *stoning* it⟩ **4 a** : to free from stones **b** : to remove the stones or seeds of (a fruit) ⟨500 grams of prunes *stoned* in advance —E.V.Knight⟩ **5 a** : to rub, scour, or polish (as leather, dies, machined metal) with a stone **b** : to sharpen with a whetstone ⟨*stoned* and whetted to a razor edge — *Amer. Guide Series: Conn.*⟩ ~ *vi* : to form or develop a stone in the process of growing

³**stone** \ˈ"\ *adj* [¹*stone*] **1** : of, relating to, or made of stone **2** *often cap* : of or relating to the Stone Age ⟨~ culture⟩

stone age *n, usu cap S&A* : the first known period of prehistoric human culture characterized by the use of stone tools — see EOLITHIC, MESOLITHIC, NEOLITHIC, PALEOLITHIC; compare BRONZE AGE, IRON AGE

stone ax *n* [ME *stanax, stonax*, fr. OE *stānæx*, fr. *stān* stone + *æx* ax — more at AX] **1** : a stonecutter's ax : AXHAMMER **2** : a prehistoric stone implement similar to an ax head — compare GROOVED AX, HAND AX, PERFORATED AX

stonebass \ˈ⸗,⸗\ *n* : a large brown grouper (*Polyprion americanus*) of the eastern and southern Atlantic, the Mediterranean, and the seas about Tasmania and New Zealand

stonebird \ˈ⸗,⸗\ *n* **1** : GREATER YELLOWLEGS **2** : FINCH

stonebiter \ˈ⸗,⸗⸗\ *n* : HAWFINCH

stone-blind \ˈ⸗ˈ⸗\ *adj* [ME *stane-blynde*, fr. *stan, ston, stoon* stone + *blynde, blind* blind] : totally blind — **stone-blindness** *n* -ES

stone blue *n* **1** : a variable color averaging a grayish blue that is redder and duller than electric or copenhagen, redder and darker than Gobelin, and duller and slightly redder than old china **2** : AZURITE BLUE

stoneboat \ˈ⸗,⸗\ *n* [ME (northern dial.) *stanboot* fr. *stan* stone + *boot* boat — more at STONE, BOAT] : a flat sledge or drag for transporting stones and other heavy articles or when weighted for smoothing tilled soil or breaking clods — called also *stone drag*

stone boiling *n* : boiling of a liquid by dropping hot stones into it

stone bolt *n* : a bolt grouted into masonry and used to support a member in place

stone borer *n* : an animal that bores stones; *esp* : any of various mollusks of the genus *Lithophaga*

stonebow \ˈ⸗,⸗\ *n* [ME *stonebowe*, fr. *stone, ston* stone + *bowe* bow — more at BOW] : a crossbow or catapult for shooting stones

stone brake *n* **1** : PARSLEY FERN b (2) **2** : a polypody (*Polypodium vulgare*)

stone bramble *n* : a European trailing bramble (*Rubus saxatilis*) with scarlet fruits made up of few drupelets

stonebrash \ˈ⸗,⸗\ *n* : land abounding in stones; *esp* : a subsoil of small stones or finely broken rock

stone brick *n* : a hard brick or firebrick made in Wales

stone-broke \ˈ⸗ˈ⸗\ *adj* : completely broke : lacking funds ⟨could smile at being *stone-broke* till the hundred a week came in —Leonard Merrick⟩

stone bruise *n* **1** : a sore spot on the bottom of the foot without laceration caused by a bruise by a stone or rounded object **2** : an injury to the casing of a pneumatic tire caused by forceful impact with a sharp or hard object

stone canal *n* : a tube in many echinoderms having a wall that contains calcareous deposits and leading from the circumoral ring of the water-vascular system to the madreporite

stone caribou *n* : a large dark caribou (*Rangifer arcticus stonei*) with heavy and well-developed antlers that is widely distributed from central Alaska northward to the arctic slopes

stonecat \ˈ⸗,⸗\ *n* : a catfish (*Noturus flavus*) of the Mississippi valley and Great Lakes area that is related to the smaller madtoms and like them has poisonous pectoral spines

stone cell *n* : BRACHYSCLEREID

stonechat \ˈ⸗,⸗\ *n* **1 a** : a common European singing bird (*Saxicola torquata*) of which the male has a black head, blackish wings and tail, rufous underparts, and white collar, wing spot, and upper tail coverts **b** : any of various other birds of the genus *Saxicola*; *specif* : WHINCHAT **2** : BLUE TIT

stone china *n* : an English chinaware resembling ironstone china; *broadly* : IRONSTONE CHINA

stone circle *n* : a circle of stones constructed by primitive or ancient peoples; *specif* : a circle of upright megaliths usu. enclosing a mound or dolmen — compare CROMLECH

stone clover *n* : RABBIT-FOOT CLOVER

stone coal *n* : ANTHRACITE

stone-cold \ˈ⸗ˈ⸗\ *adj* : completely cold : lacking warmth ⟨by the time he got back to his coffee it was *stone-cold*⟩

stone collar *n* : a large stone ring resembling a horse collar in size and shape and often bearing ancient symbolic decoration that is found in Mexico and the West Indies esp. in Puerto Rico

stone coral *n* : STONY CORAL

stone crab *n* **1** : a large edible crab (*Menippe mercenaria*) found on the southern coast of the U. S. and in the Caribbean area **2** : any of several spiny crabs of the genus *Lithodes*; *esp* : a crab (*L. maia*) of the European coasts

stone crayfish *n* : a freshwater crayfish (*Astacus torrentium*) of central Europe

stonecress \ˈ⸗,⸗\ *n* : a plant of the genus *Aethionema*

stone cricket *n* : a wingless cricket; *esp* : one of the genus *Ceuthophilus* (family Stenopelmatidae) that lives beneath stones and in cellars and caves : CAVE CRICKET

stonecrop \ˈ⸗,⸗\ *n* [ME *stancrop, stooncrop*, fr. OE *stāncrop*, fr. *stān* stone + *crop*] **1** : SEDUM 2; *esp* : a mossy European evergreen creeping sedum (*Sedum acre*) with pungent fleshy leaves and yellow flowers that has been widely introduced as a ground cover and is naturalized in many regions **2** : any of various crassulaceous plants of genera other than *Sedum* — usu. used with a qualifying term; see DITCH STONECROP

stone crusher *n* : a machine for crushing stone

stone curlew *n* **1** : a large-headed and large-eyed bird of the family Burhinidae that is somewhat nocturnal, frequents both open heaths and rocky shores, is widely distributed in the Old World and tropical America, and in some areas is highly regarded as a game bird — called also *thick-knee* **2** *dial Eng* : COMMON CURLEW **3** *South* : WILLET

stonecutter \ˈ⸗,⸗⸗\ *n* **1** : one that cuts, carves, or dresses stone; *specif* : one that sharpens and repairs the buhrstones of a corn-grinding mill or cuts new ones **2** : a machine for dressing stone

stonecutting \ˈ⸗,⸗⸗\ *n* : the art or process of cutting, carving, or dressing stone

stoned *adj* [past part. of *stone*] **1** : DRUNK **2** : being under the influence of a drug taken esp. for pleasure

stone-dead \ˈ⸗ˈ⸗\ *adj* [ME *standed*, fr. *stan* stone + *ded, deed* dead — more at DEAD] : as lifeless as a stone

stone-deaf \ˈ⸗ˈ⸗\ *adj* : totally deaf — **stone-deaf·ness** *n* -ES

stone devil *n* : HELLGRAMMITE

stoned horse *n* [fr. *stoned* having testes, fr. ¹*stone* (testis) + *-ed*] *dial Brit* : STALLION

stone drag *n* : STONEBOAT

stone dresser *n* : STONECUTTER

stone dressing *n* : the act or process of surfacing and shaping blocks of stone

stone dust *n* : ROCK DUST

stoneface \ˈ⸗,⸗\ *n* : LITHOPS 2

stone falcon *or* **stone hawk** *n* : MERLIN

stone fence *n* **1** *chiefly Midland* : STONE WALL **2** : a drink consisting of a mixture of cider and a spirituous liquor

stonefish \ˈ⸗,⸗\ *n* : any of several small dull-colored sluggish spiny scorpion fishes of *Synanceja* or a closely related genus that are widely distributed in shallow seas and about coral reefs of the tropical Indo-Pacific, often simulate seaweeds, and have dorsal spines associated with venom glands and capable of inflicting painful or occas. deadly injuries

stone fly *n* [ME *ston flye*, fr. *ston* stone + *flye* fly — more at STONE, FLY] : any of numerous insects constituting the order Plecoptera, having two pairs of membranous wings with the hinder pair folded in plaits and lying upon the abdomen when at rest, a large free prothorax, and long antennae and cerci, and characterized by an incomplete metamorphosis in which the nymphs are carnivorous, aquatic, and furnished with gills

stone fruit *n* : a fruit with a stony endocarp : DRUPE

stone gray *n* : an olive gray that is greener and lighter than nutria and greener and paler than rat — called also *crystal palace green*

stone-ground \ˈ⸗ˈ⸗\ *adj* : ground in a buhrstone mill ⟨white flour . . . was a great improvement over the gray, coarse *stone-ground* flour —R.M.Wilder⟩

stone hammer *n* [ME *stanehammer*, fr. *stane, stan, ston, stoon* stone + *hammer*] : SPALLING HAMMER

stonehand \ˈ⸗,⸗\ *n* : STONEMAN 1

stonehatch \ˈ⸗,⸗\ *n*, *Brit* : RING PLOVER

stonehearted \ˈ⸗ˈ⸗⸗\ *adj* : STONYHEARTED

stone-horse \ˈ⸗,⸗\ *n* [¹*stone* (testis) + *horse*] *chiefly dial* : STALLION

stone indian *n, usu cap S&I* : ASSINIBOIN

stone·ite \ˈstō,nīt\ *n* -s *usu cap* [Barton W. *Stone* †1844 Am. evangelist + E *-ite*] : CHRISTIAN 1b(3)

stonelaying \ˈ⸗,⸗⸗\ *n* -s : the laying of stones in the process of building; *specif* : the laying of a cornerstone of a building together with the accompanying ceremonies

stone·less \ˈstōnləs\ *adj* : having or containing no stone

stone lichen *n* : a lichen (as *Parmelia saxatilis*) growing on a rock substratum

stone life face *n* : LITHOPS 2

stone lifter *n* **1** : a device, apparatus, or machine for raising large stones **2** : a large-headed slender-bodied stargazer (*Kathetostoma laeve*) of shallow seas about Australia and New Zealand where it burrows through sand and mud and under stones by means of its powerful pectoral fins

stonelike \ˈ⸗,⸗\ *adj* : similar to stone

stone lily *n* : a fossil crinoid

stone·man \ˈstōnmən\ *n, pl* **stonemen** **1** : a compositor who imposes set type on a stone and locks it up in a chase **2 a** : a man working in stone **b** : one who drives stoneheads **3** : STONEMASON

stone marten *n* **1** : a marten (*Martes foina*) of central and southern Europe and Asia having a white patch on the breast and throat — called also *beech marten* **2** : the fur or pelt of the stone marten

stonemason \ˈ⸗,⸗⸗\ *n* : a mason who builds with stone — **stonemasonry** \ˈ⸗,⸗⸗⸗\ *n*

stone mill *n* **1** : BREAKER 2c(4) **2** : a stone-dressing machine **3** : a flour mill with buhrstones instead of steel rollers — **stone-milled** \ˈ⸗ˈ⸗\ *adj*

stone mint *n* : DITTANY 3

ston·en \'stōnən\ *adj* [ME, fr. *ston, stoon* stone + *-en*] *dial chiefly Eng* : made of stone

stone net *or* **stone polygon** *or* **stone ring** *n* : an arrangement of rock fragments and soil particles in a polygonal pattern similar to a net with the finer materials concentrated in the central part of each net or polygon and the coarser materials in the borders as a result of congeliturbation or solifluction — usu. used in pl.

stone oak *n* **1** : a Javanese oak (*Quercus javensis*) having hard ridged acorns **2** : WHITE OAK 1b

stone ocher *n* : ocher found in hard globular masses

stone oil *n* : PETROLEUM

stone parsley *n* **1** : a slender herb (*Sison amomum*) of the family Umbelliferae that is native to Europe and Asia Minor and has aromatic seeds which are used as a condiment **2** : any plant of the genus *Seseli*

stone pine *n* **1** : SWISS PINE **2** : a pine (*Pinus pinea*) of southern Europe that has a wide-spreading flat-topped head and is much cultivated in warm countries for its sweet almondlike seeds — called also *umbrella pine* **3** : NUT PINE a

stone plover *n* : any of various shorebirds: as **a** : STONE CURLEW **b** : BLACK-BELLIED PLOVER **c** : RING PLOVER **d** : DOTTEREL

stone proof *n* : a printer's proof taken from a form on an imposing stone; *specif* : a rough proof made with mallet and planer

ston·er \'stōnə(r)\ *n* -s [ME *staner, stoner,* fr. *stanen, stonen* to stone + *-er* — more at STONE] : one that stones: **a** : one that pelts with stones esp. with intent to kill **b** : one that walls with stones **c** (1) : a device for removing stones from stone fruit (as cherries) (2) : a device for cleaning stones from coffee or wheat **d** : a worker who removes bloom from tanned leather with pumice **e** : a worker who rubs rough edges and burrs from small watch parts or sharpens balance staffs with an oilstone

stone river *or* **stone run** *n* : ROCK STREAM

ston·ern \'stōnərn\ *Scot var of* STONEN

stone roller *n* **1** : HOG SUCKER **2** : a small common cyprinid fish (*Campostoma anomalum*) found chiefly in clear streams of the central U. S.

stoneroot \'≠,≠\ *n* : HORSE BALM 1

stone runner *n* : any of numerous small shorebirds; *esp* : RING PLOVER

stones *pl of* STONE, *pres 3d sing of* STONE

stone sand *n* : finely crushed stone used in place of sand for concrete aggregate

stoneseed \'≠,≠\ *n* : STONEWEED

stone sheep *or* **stone's sheep** *n, usu cap 1st S* : a dark brown northern mountain sheep (*Ovis canadensis stonei*) that is widely but sparsely distributed in the southern Yukon and northern British Columbia and Alberta

stoneshot \'≠,≠\ *n, pl* **stoneshot** : a stone used as a missile

stone snipe *n* : any of several shorebirds; *esp* : GREATER YELLOWLEGS

stone–still \'≠'≠\ *adj* [ME *stanstill, stonstill,* fr. *stan, ston* stone + *still*] : still as a stone : MOTIONLESS ⟨sat *stone-still* for hours —Zane Grey⟩

stone stripe *n* : one of a set of roughly parallel bands of alternately finer and coarser rock debris that result from solifluction or congeliturbation on fairly steep slopes — usu. used in pl.

stone sucker *n* : LAMPREY

stone wall *n* **1** *chiefly North* : a fence made of stones; *esp* : one built of rough stones without mortar to enclose a field — called also *stone fence, rock fence* **2** : an immovable block or obstruction esp. in politics or public affairs ⟨the politicians battered against a *stone wall* of deep-seated popular distrust —*Political Science Quarterly*⟩ **3** : STONE FENCE 2

stone·wall \'stōn,wȯl\ *vb* [*stone wall*] *vi* **1** : to bat in cricket entirely or almost entirely defensively without trying to score runs **2** *chiefly Brit* : to engage in debate or use other parliamentary tactics for the purpose of consuming time and thus obstructing procedure or business : FILIBUSTER ⟨is ~*ing* for time in order to close the missile gap and . . . is actually opposed to negotiations —J.B.Reston⟩ **3** : to build or enclose an area with a stone wall **~** *vt, chiefly Brit* : FILIBUSTER ⟨~ debates . . . to postpone the voting stage —*Sydney (Australia) Sunday Telegraph*⟩ — **stone·wall·er** \-lə(r)\ *n* -s *Brit*

stoneware \'≠,≠\ *n* : an opaque nonporous high-fired clayware that is well vitrified and intermediate in many respects between porcelain and earthenware, is often salt-glazed for utility pieces, and is used esp. for large storage vessels, tile, and ornamental wares — compare STONE CHINA

stoneware clay *n* : a clay suitable for making stoneware because of its plasticity, fusible minerals, and long firing range

stoneweed \'≠,≠\ *n* : any plant of the genus *Lithospermum*

stonewood \'≠,≠\ *n* : the hard close-grained wood of either of two Australian trees (*Callistemon salignus* and *Tarrietia actinophylla*); *also* : either of these trees

stonework \'≠,≠\ *n* [ME *stonwerk, stoonwerk,* fr. OE *stānweorc,* fr. *stān* stone + *weorc* work — more at STONE, WORK] **1 a** : a structure or that part of a structure built of stone esp. with some artistic design or effect : MASONRY ⟨the pier . . . was accounted a most excellent piece of ~ —William Cowper⟩ ⟨a superb example of 14th century ~ with a magnificent timbered roof —S.P.B.Mais⟩ **2** : the process of working in stone : the shaping, preparation, or setting of stone **3** : mining that is done in shale or rock as distinguished from work done in coal

stoneworker \'≠,≠≠\ *n* [¹*stone* + *worker*] : STONECUTTER 1

stonewort \'≠,≠\ *n* **1** : a plant of the family Characeae that is often encrusted with calcareous deposits **2** : SCALE FERN

stone yellow *n* : YELLOW OCHER 1

sto·ney gate \'stōnē-\ *n* [after Bindon B. *Stoney* †1909 Ir. engineer] : a vertical gate moving on rollers and designed for controlling the flow of water from a reservoir or in a canal

ston·i·fy \'stōnə,fī\ *vt* -ED/-ING/-ES [¹*stone* + *-ify*] : PETRIFY

ston·i·ly \'stōnᵊlē, -nᵊli, -nōl-\ *adv* : in a stony manner : without apparent feeling or reaction : DUMBLY ⟨remains ~ indifferent to time and circumstance —Irving Kristol⟩ ⟨in prison sat down ~ to his fate —Marjory S. Douglas⟩ ⟨eyed him ~ —Kenneth Roberts⟩

ston·i·ness \-nēnəs, -nin-\ *n* -ES : the quality or state of being stony ⟨a bigness and a dilapidated dignity and a ~ which carry one back to the Middle Ages —D.H.Lawrence⟩

stoning *pres part of* STONE

stonish *obs var of* ASTONISH

stonishment *obs var of* ASTONISHMENT

stonk \'stäŋk\ *n* -s [perh. of imit. origin] : a heavy concentration of artillery fire ⟨call for a good ~ about five hours before our assault —*Infantry Jour.*⟩ ⟨loosed a ~ on them and wiped them off the face of the earth —Peter Rainier⟩

stonk·er \'stäŋkə(r)\ *vt* -ED/-ING/-S [origin unknown] **1** *Austral* : to hit hard : knock unconscious **2** *Austral* : to baffle completely : OUTWIT, FOIL

¹**stony** *also* **stoney** \'stōnē, -ni\ *adj* **stonier; stoniest** [ME *stany, stony, stoony,* fr. OE *stānig,* fr. *stān* stone + *-ig* -y — more at STONE] **1** : abounding in or having the nature of stone : full of or containing many stones : ROCKY ⟨an infertile ~ ridge —C.B.Hitchcock⟩ ⟨the ground was ~ under heel —David Goldknopf⟩ **2 a** : insensitive to pity or human feeling : HARDHEARTED, OBDURATE ⟨the city wasn't so ~ and inhospitable as she had believed —Ellen Glasgow⟩ ⟨the story should soften the *stoniest* of hearts —J.D.Adams⟩ ⟨presented a ~ front to . . . pleas for herself and the child —S.H.Adams⟩ **b** : manifesting no movement or reaction : DUMB, EXPRESSIONLESS ⟨their faces were ~, their eyes wide open and staring —Jan Valtin⟩ ⟨lighted her own cigarette . . . and smoked in ~, irritating silence —Clive Arden⟩ **c** : fearfully gripping : PETRIFYING ⟨man's . . . ~ knowledge of his own mortality —Maeve Brennan⟩ **3** *archaic* : consisting of or made of stones **4** : similar to stone in substance : HARD ⟨layers are spotted with the ~ remains of ocean forms —*Amer. Guide Series: Minn.*⟩ ⟨the shellfish crawls out of its . . . ~ case —R.W.Emerson⟩ **5** : STONE-BROKE ⟨my father and I were ~ and had a lot of debts —Louis Bromfield⟩

²**stony** *vt* -ED/-ING/-ES [ME *stonien,* fr. MF *estoner* — more at ASTONY] *obs* : to numb the feelings or faculties of (a person) : STUPEFY, STUN

stony-broke \'≠≠'≠\ *adj* : STONE-BROKE

stony coral *n* : a coral with a hard calcareous skeleton

stonyhearted \'≠≠'≠≠\ *adj* : UNFEELING, CRUEL ⟨are used to being called heartless, or at least ~ —*New Yorker*⟩ — **stony-heart·ed·ness** *n* -ES

stony pit *n* : a virus disease of pears characterized by deep pitting and malformation of fruit

stony share *n* : a wingless moldboard plowshare designed for use in stony soils

¹**stood** [ME, fr. OE *stōd*] *past of* STAND

²**stood** *substand past of* STAY

stood·ed \'stüdəd\ *adj* [fr. dial. E past part. of ¹*stand*] *dial Eng* : STALLED, STUCK

¹**stooge** \'stüj\ *n* -s [origin unknown] **1** : a subordinate participant in a comic act or dialogue whose function is to carry on repartee in such manner as to enable a principal comedian to make humorous remarks or appear in a humorous light : STRAIGHT MAN ⟨insults a ~ in the audience —A.J. Liebling⟩ ⟨some boy would play . . . ~ to him in order that this masterstroke of wit should be demonstrated —Robertson Davies⟩ **2 a** : one who plays a subordinate or compliant role to a principal or for some outside force or influence : CHARLIE MCCARTHY ⟨under such conditions directors are likely to be nothing more than paid ~s with far less independence of thought and action —*Corporate Concentration & Public Policy*⟩ ⟨the editor driven into exile . . . and the hoax of a newspaper perpetrated with the help of ~s —B.E.Nelson⟩; *specif* : a subversive agent acting for one government against another ⟨activities of their ~s in the countries of western and southern Europe —J.B.Reston⟩ **b** : PUPPET 4a ⟨a belief that dominion statesmen were . . . mere ~s for astute imperialist rulers —D.W.Brogan⟩ ⟨master strategists have infiltrated . . . ~s into the government —*Atlantic*⟩ **3** : a planted spy : STOOL PIGEON ⟨the company police . . . have ~s watching every move I make —Lawrence Lader⟩ ⟨detectives began contacting informers . . . in hopes that one of these ~s would help put the finger on the elusive bandit —Ray Strinnett⟩

²**stooge** \"\ *vi* -ED/-ING/-S **1** : to act as a stooge ⟨*stooged* for the comedian before starting his own show⟩ ⟨congressmen who ~ for the oil and mineral interests —*New Republic*⟩ **2** : to patrol or cruise in slow or routine flight ⟨two hours of *stooging* it . . . 16,000 feet would find you utterly numb and stiff when you landed —J.R.D.Braham⟩ — usu. used with *around* ⟨*stooging* around over the sea in all weathers —Ralph Michaelis⟩

¹**stook** \'stu̇k, 'stük\ *n* -s [ME *stowke, stouk;* akin to MLG *stūke* tree stump, pile, sleeve, OHG *stūhha* sleeve, ON *stūka,* OE *stocu* sleeve, *stocc* stock — more at STOCK] **1** *chiefly Brit* : ¹SHOCK 1a **2** *Brit* : a pillar of coal left standing as a support for the roof of a mine

²**stook** \"\ *vb* -ED/-ING/-S *vt, chiefly Brit* : to arrange (as grain) in shocks **~** *vi, chiefly Brit* : to work at making shocks (as of grain) — **stook·er** \-kə(r)\ *n* -s *chiefly Brit*

stook·ie \-ki\ *n* -s [prob. fr. ¹*stook* + *-ie*] *chiefly Scot* : FOOL

¹**stool** \'stül\ *n* -s [ME *stol, stool,* seat, chair, stool, fr. OE *stōl;* akin to OHG *stuol* chair, seat, ON *stōll* chair, seat, Goth *stols* chair, throne, OSlav *stolŭ* seat, throne, OE *standan* to stand — more at STAND] **1 a** : a device for sitting usu. consisting of a single wooden or upholstered seat without back or arms supported by three or four props or legs or by a central pedestal on which it may revolve **b** : a low bench or portable support used for stepping, kneeling, or resting the feet : FOOTSTOOL **c** : a base, standard, or small raised platform for supporting something : STAND **2** : a seat used as a symbol of office, authority, or precedence: as **a** : a bishop's seat; *also* : a bishop's see **b** : the seat of a western African chief or head of a lineage that is symbolic of his authority and of the line of continuity between his ancestors and their descendants; *also* : CHIEFTAINCY, KINGSHIP **3 a** : a seat used in evacuating the bowels or in urinating : COMMODE, WATER CLOSET **b** : the act of defecation ⟨violent straining at ~ —H.C.Hopps⟩ **c** : a discharge of fecal matter **4 a** : a tree stump or group of stumps with a common rootstock esp. when associated with suckers or watersprouts **b** : a plant crown from which parts (as shoots, stalks, or layers) grow out or are produced ⟨strong ~s can be layered year after year⟩ **c** : a shoot or growth from a stool : TILLER **d** : a stand of plants with developing stems or shoots ⟨a good ~ of timber⟩ **5 a** : the flat piece corresponding to the sill of a door against which a window shuts **b** : the narrow shelf fitted on the inside against the actual sill **6 a** : a small channel on the side of a ship for the deadeyes of the backstays **b** : a foundation of plates or angles for any auxiliary machinery, piping, or shafting of a ship **7 a** : a real or artificial bird used as a decoy **b** : a group of such decoys ⟨setting out the ~ upwind from the blind⟩ **8** : CULTCH 1a **9** : STOOL PIGEON ⟨among customs informers have been professional ~s —Horace Sutton⟩ — **fall between two stools** : to fail or come to naught because of inability to choose between or reconcile two alternative or conflicting courses of action ⟨a story of *falling between two stools* — the stool of election promises to balance the budget and reduce taxes, and the stool of the hideous cost of new weapons —Stewart Alsop⟩

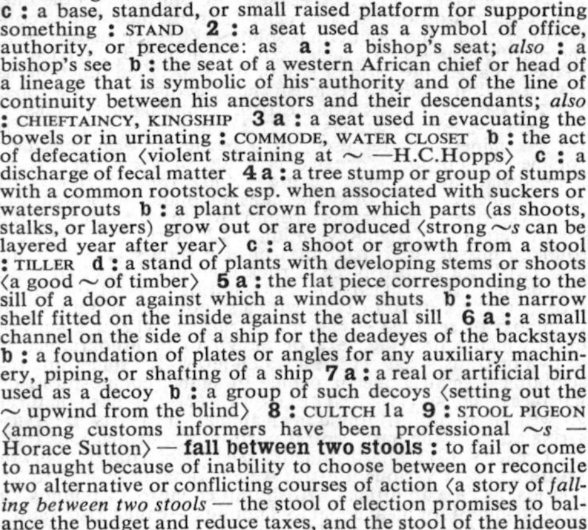

stools 1a

²**stool** \"\ *vb* -ED/-ING/-S *vi* **1** *archaic* : to evacuate the bowels : DEFECATE **2** : to form a stool : throw out shoots after the manner of a stool : TILLER **3** *of wildfowl* : to respond to the lure of a stool ⟨big flights ~*ing* into the decoys —Cameron Hawley⟩ **4** *slang* : to act as a stool pigeon ⟨once you're out of town you're fairly safe unless somebody ~s on you —C.R. Cooper⟩ ⟨~*ed* on a bank job . . . and got me four years —Raymond Chandler⟩ **~** *vt* **1** : to lure (wildfowl) by means of decoys

stoolball \'≠,≠\ *n* : an old English game resembling cricket played chiefly by women

stool bed *n* : a plot of ground in which plants are to be propagated by mound layering

stool end *n* : a supporting pillar of rock in a mine

stool·ie \'stülē, -li\ *n* -s [*stool (pigeon)* + *-ie*] : STOOL PIGEON ⟨~ . . . had turned in an imposing total of 281 counterrevolutionaries and other criminals —*Newsweek*⟩

stool·ing \'stüliŋ\ *n* -s [¹*stool* + *-ing*] : MOUND LAYERING

stool layering *n* : MOUND LAYERING

stool pigeon *n* **1** : a pigeon used as a decoy to draw others within a net **2** : a person acting as a decoy or informer; *esp* : a spy living among or sent into a group to report often to the police on the activities of its members ⟨served . . . as a *stool pigeon,* according to his fellow prisoners, and brought about the execution of a U.S. captain —*Time*⟩

stool shoot *n* : a lateral shoot produced on a woody plant in the absence of a terminal bud

stoon *or* **stoond** \'stün(d)\ *var of* STOUND

¹**stoop** \'stüp\ *vb* -ED/-ING/-S [ME *stupen, stoupen,* fr. OE *stūpian;* akin to MD *stupen* to bow, bend, ON *stūpa* to stand upright, to tower, Norw *stupa* to fall down, plunge, OE *stēap* high, steep, deep — more at STEEP] *vi* **1 a** : to bend the body forward and downward sometimes simultaneously bending the knees : LEAN ⟨the figures ~*ed* and rose with the lifting whips —Mary Austin⟩ ⟨he ~*ed* cowering to the ground —Pearl Buck⟩ ⟨he ~*ed* over his labor —Charles Dickens⟩ —often used with *down* ⟨~*ed* down to take a necklace . . . from the floor —Francis Yeats-Brown⟩ **b** : to stand or walk with a temporary or habitual forward inclination of the head, body, or shoulders ⟨~*ed* through the door of the camp —Lyndall Hadow⟩ ⟨~*ed* along the shore under the headwall of the beach —G.W.Brace⟩ ⟨stood before her, a tall, very thin man, ~*ing* a little —Michael Arlen⟩ **c** *Brit* : to lower the head in following a scent ⟨hounds . . . unlikely to ~ successfully for so weak a scent —E.G.W.W. Harrison⟩ **2** : to assume a position of subservience or subjection : humble oneself : BOW, SUBMIT ⟨~*ing* before the conqueror⟩ **3 a** : to descend from a superior rank, dignity, or status — usu. used with *to* ⟨couldn't believe that God ever ~*ed* to such trivial engagements —L.C.Douglas⟩ ⟨either the audience didn't measure up to his brand of humor, or he wouldn't ~ to theirs —H.J.Higdon⟩ ⟨that masculine dignity which forbids our ~*ing* to conquer . . . the common speech of a foreign people —G.G.Coulton⟩ **b** : to lower oneself morally or in a degrading fashion ⟨did not ~ habitually to falsehood and subterfuge to gain her end —Ellen Glasgow⟩ ⟨will ~ to robbing a bombed store —J.Coughlan⟩ ⟨he ~*ed* to fraud —Hilaire Belloc⟩ **4 a** *archaic* : to move down from a height : ALIGHT ⟨ready now to ~, with wearied wings and willing feet —John Milton⟩ **b** : to fly or dive down swiftly usu. to attack prey ⟨the big eagles were ~*ing* closer —David Walker⟩ ⟨when a falcon ~s for the kill he is traveling more than two miles a minute —H.M.Robinson⟩ **~** *vt* **1 a** : to cause (a person or thing) to move lower or bow down : PROSTRATE, OVERCOME **b** : DEBASE, DEGRADE ⟨~*ing* his talents to an unworthy cause⟩ **2** *obs* : to take or let down (as a sail or flag) **3** : to bend (a part of the body) forward and downward ⟨he ~*ed* his head to hers —Maurice Hewlett⟩ ⟨his shoulders were ~*ed* as if he were bearing a great bundle —Stephen Crane⟩ ⟨the bullocks . . . ~*ed* their heads to the grass —Adrian Bell⟩ **b** *dial Eng* : to cause (as a cask) to incline downward : TILT

²**stoop** \"\ *n* -s **1 a** : an act of bending the body forward : STOOPING **b** : a temporary or habitual forward bend of the back and shoulders ⟨walking bent for 50 yards before he can get the ~ out of his back —F.B.Gipson⟩ ⟨walked with a ~ as if laden with invisible burdens —Maurice Samuel⟩ **2** : the descent of a bird esp. on its prey : SWOOP ⟨the ~ of a hawk —V.C.Heilner⟩ ⟨hover . . . high above their quarry to descend in a terrific, vertical ~ on the unsuspecting larger bird —*Wyo. Wild Life*⟩ **3** : a lowering of oneself (as from a moral or dignified plane) : CONDESCENSION, CONCESSION

³**stoop** \"\ *n* -s [ME *stulpe, stowpe* post, pillar; akin to MLG *stolpe* beam, post, *stülpen* to turn upside down, OLG *stelpōn* to stagnate, ON *stolpi* post, pillar, Latvian *stùlbs* post, and prob. to OHG *stellen* to place, set — more at STALL] **1** *dial Brit* : POST, PILLAR; *specif* : a large pillar (as of coal) left to support the roof of a mine **2** *Scot* : a chief supporter : PROP, MAINSTAY

⁴**stoop** *var of* STOUP

⁵**stoop** \'stüp\ *n* -s [D *stoep,* fr. MD; akin to OHG *stuofa, stuoffa* step of a building, MLG *stōpe* step of a building, OE *stæpe, stepe* step — more at STEP] : a porch, platform, entrance stairway, or small veranda at a house door ⟨mounted a folding stepladder chair on the front ~ and addressed them —Sinclair Lewis⟩ **syn** see BALCONY

stoop

stoop and roop *adv* [origin unknown] *chiefly Scot* : COMPLETELY

stoopball \'≠,≠\ *n* [⁵*stoop* + *ball*] : a game similar to baseball in which a player throws a ball against a stoop or building and runs to base while other players seek to capture the rebound and put him out — compare KICKBALL, PUNCHBALL

stoop crop *n* : a crop (as of a vegetable) that requires extensive hand labor and stooping in cultivating and harvesting

stooped *past of* STOOP

stooping *pres part of* STOOP

stoop·ing·ly *adv* : in a stooping manner : with a stoop

stoop labor *n* **1** : the work required or executed in cultivating or harvesting a stoop crop ⟨supports himself and his family by odd jobs and *stoop labor* in the fields —Dwight Macdonald⟩ **2** : workers employed to cultivate or harvest stoop crops ⟨migrant workers are imported by contract as *stoop labor* in the beet fields —Roscoe Fleming⟩

stoop laborer *n* : one that does stoop labor

stoops *pres 3d sing of* STOOP, *pl of* STOOP

stoop tag *n* : SQUAT TAG

stoor \'stu̇(ə)r\ *var of* STOUR

stoot \'stüt\ *dial Brit var of* STOUT

stoo·ter \'stōd-ə(r)\ *n* -s [D *stoter* (formerly spelled *stooter*), fr. MD, lit., one that pushes or stamps, fr. *stoten* to push, stamp; akin to OHG *stōzan* to push — more at STINT] *archaic* : an old Dutch coin of base silver worth two and a half stivers

¹**stop** \'stäp\ *vb* **stopped** *or archaic* **stopt** \-pt\ **stopped** *or archaic* **stopt; stopping; stops** [ME *stoppen,* fr. OE *-stoppian;* akin to OFris *stoppia* to stop up, stuff, OLF *stuppon,* OHG *stopfōn;* all fr. a prehistoric WGmc word borrowed fr. (assumed) VL *stuppare* to stop with tow, fr. L *stuppa* tow — more at STUPE] *vt* **1 a** *obs* : to keep confined : prevent the escape of ⟨still the envious flood *stopped* in my soul, and would not let it forth —Shak.⟩ **b** : to hinder or prevent the passage of ⟨~ the inlets of fresh experience —Roger Fry⟩ ⟨applied a styptic pencil to ~ the blood⟩ **c** : to keep out : INTERCEPT ⟨weatherstripped the windows to ~ drafts⟩ ⟨most of the rain is *stopped* by the outer hills —Francis Kingdon-Ward⟩ **d** : to get in the way of : suffer the impact of : be wounded or killed by ⟨treats the male natives with bluster and hard knocks, even at the risk of *stopping* a shovel-headed spear —Leslie Rees⟩ ⟨easy to ~ a bullet along a lonely stretch of road —Harvey Fergusson⟩ ⟨*stopped* one in the last battle of the war⟩ **2** *chiefly Scot* : THRUST, PUSH, INSERT **3 a** (1) : to close up or block off access to (an opening) : PLUG ⟨sometimes they refuse to listen, and are seen to ~ their ears —B.N.Cardozo⟩ — often used with *up* ⟨the entrance to the cave was *stopped* up with rocks⟩ (2) : to close off (a burrow) from use esp. by foxes ⟨*stopped* the earths in the neighboring fields before the hunt⟩ **b** (1) : to make impassable : CHOKE, OBSTRUCT ⟨a narrow gangway, which one person could ~ —Anthony Trollope⟩ (2) : to fill or partially fill (a passage) with some obstruction — often used with *up* ⟨if your nose is badly *stopped* up for long, the infection may back up —*X-Rays & You*⟩ **c** (1) : to cover over or fill in (a hole or crevice) ⟨the hole in the window was *stopped* with a piece of cardboard —Christopher Isherwood⟩ ⟨built of hewn logs, the interstices *stopped* with clay —*Amer. Guide Series: N.C.*⟩ (2) : to pack (a horse's feet) with some substance ⟨at nightfall ~ the feet with wet tow —Richard Ford⟩ (3) : to dress over (as with plaster) : POINT 2a(1) (4) *chiefly Brit* : to put a filling in (a tooth) ⟨gnashed his formidable jaws, gleaming with teeth which had been newly *stopped* —S.H.Adams⟩ **4 a** : to cause to give up or change a mode of behavior or course of action ⟨tried to ~ him from continuing to make a fool of himself⟩ ⟨tried to ~ her from spending so much time before the mirror⟩ **b** : to keep from carrying out a proposed action : hold back : RESTRAIN ⟨pleaded with him to ~ him from resigning⟩ ⟨*stopped* him from making a speech that would have ruined him⟩ **5 a** : to interrupt or prevent the continuance or occurrence of : cause to cease ⟨teach people how to ~ burglaries in their homes or business places —Rufus Jarman⟩ ⟨unable to ~ the noise of the children⟩ ⟨*stopped* the epidemic⟩ **b** : DISCONTINUE ⟨*stopped* work at noon⟩ ⟨the phone *stopped* ringing⟩ **c** : to cause to discontinue operating or working ⟨*stopped* the presses to put in a new lead story⟩ **d** : to interrupt in a speech or statement ⟨*stopped* him short as he was trying to explain his mistake⟩ ⟨~ me if you've heard this one before⟩ **6 a** : to deduct or withhold (part or all of a sum due) in order to satisfy a claim or obligation ⟨each worker pays the equivalent of ten cents a week, which is *stopped* from his wages by the employer —D.W. & Jean Orr⟩ **b** : to instruct one's bank not to honor or pay ⟨~ a check⟩ ⟨~ payment on a check⟩ **7 a** : to arrest the progress or motion of : bring to a standstill : cause to halt ⟨*stopped* him with an upraised fat hand —Kenneth Roberts⟩ ⟨was *stopped* in his tracks by a shout from the barn —*Time*⟩ ⟨the violation consists in *stopping* goods in interstate commerce —T.W. Arnold⟩ ⟨*stopped* the car⟩ ⟨~ thief⟩ **b** : to check with a counter blow or movement : PARRY **c** : to check by means of a weapon : bring down ⟨missed his first shot, but *stopped* a bird with his second⟩ **d** (1) : to defeat in a prizefight by a knockout ⟨*stopped* his last opponent in three rounds⟩ (2) : to defeat in a game or contest ⟨*stopped* the opposing team by a wide margin⟩ **e** : to give pause to : BAFFLE, NONPLUS ⟨handles at a fast clip questions that have *stopped* the industrial experts —*N.Y. Times*⟩ **8 a** : to regulate the pitch of (as a violin string) by pressing with the finger **b** : to regulate the pitch of (a wind instrument) by closing one or more finger holes or by thrusting the hand or a mute into the bell **9 a** : to pay out (a cable) gradually in anchoring a ship **b** : to make fast (as a sail) with stops **10** *chiefly Brit* : ¹PINCH 1b (2) **11 a** : to hold an honor card and enough protecting cards to be able to block (a bridge suit) before an opponent can run off many tricks ⟨*stopped* his spades⟩ **b** (1) : to hold both of two honors

that can be melded in (a suit or rank) (2) **:** to prevent (a meld) by such holding ⟨the double ace of spades ~*s* 100 aces and a spade flush⟩ **12** *chiefly Brit* **:** PUNCTUATE **~** *vi* **1 a :** to cease activity or operation ⟨the motor *stopped*⟩ ⟨the rain *stopped*⟩ ⟨his heart *stopped*⟩ **b :** to come to an end **:** CLOSE, FINISH ⟨carried his bow over his shoulder, but the resemblance to the accepted picture *stopped* there —T.B.Costain⟩ ⟨then the din gradually dies down, the music ~*s* —Lafcadio Hearn⟩ **c :** to cease to extend ⟨the blue jacket *stopping* at his waist —Wirt Williams⟩ ⟨the highway ~*s* in the middle of nowhere⟩ **d :** to end abruptly **:** break off ⟨it doesn't end; it ~*s* —Arnold Bennett⟩ **2 a :** to cease to move on **:** stand still **:** HALT ⟨*stopping* for a moment in his walk —Edith Sitwell⟩ ⟨the horse *stopped* short at the fence⟩ ⟨*stopped* dead to listen for a suspicious sound⟩ **b :** to interrupt oneself in an activity or speech ⟨*stopped* for a while to have lunch⟩ ⟨*stopped* short when he discovered his error⟩ ⟨*stopped* to catch his breath⟩ **c :** to take time to consider **:** PAUSE ⟨had she *stopped* to think, she would have recalled . . . the plank there —Laura Krey⟩ **3 a :** to hold back **:** HESITATE ⟨doesn't ~ at the most outrageous lies⟩ ⟨~*s* at nothing to gain his ends⟩ **b :** to cease from a course of action **:** DESIST ⟨his tactics succeeded for a while, but he didn't know where to ~⟩ **4 a** (1) **:** to interrupt a trip (as for rest or a meal) ⟨decided to ~ at the next roadside restaurant for lunch⟩ — sometimes used with *off* ⟨*stopped off* on the way home to pick up some food⟩ (2) **:** to break one's journey ⟨decided to ~ for a few days at the state park⟩ — often used with *over* ⟨*stopped* over to visit his cousins⟩ (3) **:** to make a regularly scheduled halt (as for taking on or dropping passengers) ⟨the express train doesn't ~ at this station⟩ ⟨the bus ~*s* at the next corner⟩ **b :** to spend a short time **:** reside temporarily ⟨arranged to ~ at a hotel —Agnes S. Turnbull⟩ **c** *chiefly Brit* **:** REMAIN, STAY ⟨she'd ~ in bed all morning —Rosamond Lehmann⟩ ⟨his dad fell into that terrible rage with him because he had *stopped* out all night —Edith Sitwell⟩ **d :** to make a brief call **:** drop in — usu. used with *by* ⟨suggested that she ~ by that evening to talk things over —Polly Adler⟩ **5 :** to bring up a narrow wooden strip (as a molding) against a flat or curved surface **6 :** to become choked **:** CLOG ⟨the sink ~*s* up constantly because of the gooey messes the children pour into it⟩

syn QUIT, DESIST, CEASE, DISCONTINUE: STOP is a rather general term indicating suspending or interfering with moving or progressing ⟨the entrance of the judge, and a consequent great stir and settling-down in the court, *stopped* the dialogue —Charles Dickens⟩ ⟨you might as well try and *stop* a young tank —Rose Macaulay⟩ CEASE may differ in applying to conditions, states, or existences rather than to actions or activities ⟨*stopped* (but not *ceased*) the car⟩ ⟨the infielder *stopped* (but not *ceased*) the ball⟩ but often the two are interchangeable ⟨iron works . . . were erected here in 1795 but *ceased* activity in 1838 —*Amer. Guide Series: N.H.*⟩ ⟨these people suddenly *ceased* muttering, but redoubled their gesticulations —E.A. Poe⟩ CEASE may or may not carry with it the idea of gradual slow cessation of activity ⟨the soft woman gradually *ceased* her chirp —George Meredith⟩ ⟨outside in the street all noises suddenly *ceased* —Sherwood Anderson⟩ DESIST, a somewhat more formal word, is likely to indicate holding off, forebearing, refraining from going on, through self-restraint, consideration of others, expediency, or lack of success ⟨had *desisted* in his effort to press love upon her because they were to be married —Sherwood Anderson⟩ ⟨swindler and murderer *desisted* because they felt the latent strength of his personality —Osbert Sitwell⟩ DISCONTINUE is not a very expressive word; it stresses the fact of suspension of some activity, course, accustomed occupation, or habit and may be used more freely than others in this set with tangible objects ⟨*discontinue* the manufacture of motorcycles or motorbikes as part of the company's manufactures⟩ QUIT may suggest either finality or peremptoriness in a person's stopping an activity or employment or acceptance of defeat and futility in continuing an endeavor or struggle ⟨such of the owners as were not wedded to the industry *quit* —P.A.Rollins⟩ ⟨had no thought of *quitting* the struggle —Sir Winston Churchill⟩ **syn** see in addition RESIDE

— **stop one's mouth :** to make silent; *specif* **:** KILL ⟨threatened to *stop his mouth*⟩ — **stop the show :** to draw so much applause that the action on stage must temporarily halt ⟨a song that *stops the show* at every performance⟩ ⟨*stops the show* with her dance in the first act⟩

²stop \"\ *n* -s [ME, fr. *stoppen*, v.] **1 :** CESSATION, END, FINISH ⟨his death put a ~ to the project —J.W.Ellison b. 1891⟩ ⟨time, that takes survey of all the world, must have a ~ —Shak.⟩ **2 a** (1) **:** a graduated set of organ pipes of like kind and tone quality (2) **:** a corresponding set of vibrators or reeds of a reed organ (3) **:** STOP KNOB ⟨pulled out all the ~*s*⟩ **b :** a means of regulating the pitch of a musical instrument: as (1) **:** the closing of an aperture in the air passage of a wind instrument (2) **:** pressure of the finger upon a string of a string instrument **c :** a device in a harpsichord or similar instrument for modifying the power and quality of the tones produced **3 :** something that impedes, obstructs, or brings to a halt **:** IMPEDIMENT, OBSTACLE, OBSTRUCTION ⟨as soon as I had enough men I put out ~*s* on the motor road —*Yale Rev.*⟩ ⟨a groove is made on one side of a length of bone or horn and a raised knob or ~ is left at one end —Agnes Allen⟩: as **a :** DAM, WEIR **b** (1) **:** an opaque barrier for preventing the passage of light through certain portions of an optical system (as at the margin, in the axial zone, or in radial sectors); *specif* **:** the aperture of a camera lens (2) **:** a marking of a series (as of f-numbers) on a camera for indicating settings of the diaphragm **c :** a valve so placed to be used as a shutoff (as in disconnecting water or gas service) **d :** a drain plug **:** STOPPER **4 a** (1) **:** a device or piece (as a pin block, pawl, or strip of wood) for arresting or limiting motion or for determining the position to which a part will be brought (2) **:** a short feather key **b :** STOPWORK **c** (1) **:** a small piece of material (as canvas or line) used to bind or secure something ⟨secure a furled sail with ~*s*⟩ (2) **:** a projection on a mast or spar to support something or keep it from slipping down **d :** a bookbinder's hand tool used to stop a line at its intersection with another and thereby save mitering **e** (1) **:** MARGIN STOP (2) **:** a tabulator stop **5 a :** the act of impeding or bringing to a halt or the state of being impeded or brought to a halt **:** CHECK ⟨the shortstop made a great ~ on a hard grounder⟩ ⟨the train was brought to a sudden ~⟩ **b :** a guard or counter in boxing that prevents an opponent's blow from landing; *esp* **:** a blow delivered as the opponent is in the act of leading **c :** the act of preventing a goal (as in hockey, soccer) by catching or deflecting a shot **:** SAVE **6 a :** the act of coming to a halt **:** a cessation of motion or operation ⟨a brief ~ for mopping-up operations —*Current Biog.*⟩ ⟨within six months she was mastering spirals, sit-down spins and ~*s* —*Time*⟩ **b :** a halt in a journey or trip **:** STAY ⟨made a long ~ to see the famous ruins⟩ ⟨the ship made a brief ~ to refuel⟩ **c :** a point or place for stopping ⟨an old town by the sea is a must ~ —Eleanor Early⟩; *specif* **:** a point at which a public means of conveyance (as a train, bus, or airplane) regularly stops to take on or let off passengers or goods **7 a** *chiefly Brit* **:** any of several punctuation marks ⟨if commas are used rightly the other ~*s* will sort themselves out —Ernest Gowers⟩ **b** — used in telegrams and cables to indicate a period **c :** a pause or break in a verse that marks the end of a grammatical unit **8 a** (1) **:** an order stopping payment (as of a check or note) by a bank (2) **:** the act of making such an order **b :** STOP ORDER **9 :** a consonant in the articulation of which there is a stage (as in the *t* of *apt*, the *p* of *apt*, and the *g* of *tiger*) when the breath passage is completely closed at the nose by raised velum and elsewhere by lips, tongue, or glottis — compare ²NASAL 2a **10 a :** a card in some games (as Michigan or fan-tan) that stops a sequence when played; *also* **:** the termination of a sequence by such a card **b stops** *pl but sing in constr* **:** any of several games having as an essential feature the stopping of play when the card specified to be played next is not available; *specif* **:** MICHIGAN **11 :** a depression in the face of an animal at the junction of forehead and foreface: as **a :** an indentation between muzzle and forehead in a dog (as a bulldog) — see DOG illustration **b :** an angular indentation between bill and forehead in some pigeons **c :** a line where the forehead meets the snout in a dolphin **12** *chiefly Brit* **:** one posted to prevent game animals from breaking away when located

³stop \"\ *adj* **1 :** serving to stop **:** designed to stop ⟨~ line⟩ ⟨~ signal⟩ ⟨~ valve⟩ **2 :** marked by stoppage of sound ⟨~ consonant⟩ ⟨~ articulation⟩

stop-and-go \ˌ==ˈ=\ *adj* **:** of, relating to, or involving frequent stops; *esp* **:** controlled or regulated by traffic lights ⟨*stop-and-go* driving⟩ ⟨*stop-and-go* highways⟩

stopback \ˈ=,=\ *n* [fr. *stop back*, v.] **:** a condition in peach and pear nursery stock caused by the attack of the tarnished plant bug (*Lygus oblineatus*) and characterized by the death of the tender terminal bud of the principal shoot and the forcing of the development of lateral shoots

stopbank \ˈ=,=\ *n, Austral* **:** LEVEE

stop bath *n* **:** an acid rinse bath between a photograph developer and the fixing bath used to check development of a negative or print by neutralizing the alkali in the developer — called also *short-stop*

stop bead *n* **:** a molding fastened to the inner side of a window frame on the face of the pulley stile and completing the groove in which the inner sash is to slide

stopblock \ˈ=,=\ *n* **:** a bumping post or buffer at the end of a railroad track

stopboard \ˈ=,=\ *n* **:** a board to restrain or check motion; *specif* **:** TOEBOARD

stop bud *n, Brit* **:** CROWN BUD

stop card *n* **:** a card (as in canasta) that when played on the discard pile prevents the taking of that pile

stop clock *n* **:** a timing device similar to a stop watch but larger in size usu. electrically operated and often designed for measuring very brief time intervals

stopcock \ˈ=,=\ *n* **1 :** a cock for stopping or regulating flow (as through a pipe) **2 :** the turning plug, stopper, or spigot of a faucet

stopcocks

stop-cylinder press *n* **:** a cylinder press in which the cylinder revolves only when the bed makes its printing stroke and remains stationary on the return stroke — compare TWO-REVOLUTION PRESS

stop down *vt* **:** to reduce the effective aperture of (a lens) by means of a diaphragm **~** *vi* **:** to make a lens opening smaller by means of a diaphragm

stop drill *n* **:** a drill with a collar on its shank to limit the depth of penetration

¹stope \ˈstōp\ *n* -s [prob. fr. LG *stope*, lit., step (of a building), fr. MLG *stōpe* — more at STOOP] **:** a usu. steplike excavation underground for the removal of ore that is formed as the ore is mined in successive layers — see BOTTOM STOPE, OVERHAND STOPE, RILL STOPE, SHRINKAGE STOPE

²stope \"\ *vb* -ED/-ING/-S *vi* **:** to mine by means of a stope **~** *vt* **:** to extract (ore) from a stope

stope drill *n* **:** STOPER

stop·er \ˈstōpə(r)\ *n* -s **1 :** a drillman who works in a stope **2 :** a hammer drill mounted on a pneumatic feed cylinder and used for drilling vertical and inclined holes in stopes — called also *stope drill*

stop-fluted \ˈ=ˌ==\ *adj* **:** having stopped fluting

stop fluting *n* **:** STOPPED FLUTING

stop gage *n* **:** a gage for determining the length of stock for a setup

¹stopgap \ˈ=,=\ *adj* [¹*stop* + *gap*; after the phrase *stop a gap*] **:** serving to fill a gap **:** TEMPORARY ⟨only offered as a convenient ~ way of thinking of the phenomena —A.G.N.Flew⟩ ⟨a ~ measure⟩ ⟨a ~ program⟩

²stopgap \"\ *n* [¹*stop* + *gap*; after the phrase *stop a gap*] **1 :** something that serves as a temporary expedient **:** MAKESHIFT ⟨the export of goods and lending of money alone are only emergency ~*s* —R.P.Russell⟩ **2 :** one who occupies an office or position temporarily **:** SUBSTITUTE ⟨had simply been acting as a ~ for his brother-in-law —*Contemporary Rev.*⟩ **syn** see RESOURCE

stoping *n* -s [fr. gerund of ²*stope*] **:** a process by which ore is stoped; *specif* **:** the process whereby intrusive igneous magmas are thought to make space for themselves by detaching and engulfing fragments of the invaded rocks

stop knob *n* **:** one of the handles by which the player of an organ draws or shuts off a particular stop or controls the mechanical accessories (as a coupler, tremolo)

stop·less \ˈstäpləs\ *adj* **:** having no stop — **stop·less·ness** *n* -ES

stoplight \ˈ=,=\ *n* **1 :** a light on the rear of a motor vehicle that is illuminated when the driver presses the brake pedal to slow down or stop **2 :** TRAFFIC SIGNAL

stop log *n* **:** one of a set of usu. square pieces (as of wood or metal) that serve to form a dam or to check the flow of water

stop-loss \ˈ=,=\ *adj* [¹*stop* + *loss*] **:** designed to prevent further loss

stop-loss order *n* **:** STOP ORDER

stop motion *n* **:** a device for stopping a machine or a part either automatically or at will

stop-motion *adj* **:** TIME-LAPSE

stop net *n* **1 :** a smaller seine auxiliary to a larger one to prevent the escape of fish **2 :** a net used to enclose a portion of shoreline at high tide so as to entrap fish as the tide goes out

stop netting *n* **:** the using of a stop net to catch fish

stop nut *n* **1 :** an adjustable nut used on an adjusting screw to limit motion in a particular direction **2 :** a nut with a fiber or plastic insert that binds it against vibration and eliminates the need for a lock washer or jam nut

stop off *vt* **1 :** to fill in solid (a part of a mold) where a part of the cavity left by a pattern is not wanted for the casting **2 :** to stop out

¹stop-off \ˈ=,=\ *n* -s [fr. *stop off*, v.] **:** the act, privilege, or an instance of making a stopover

²stop-off \"\ *adj* [*stop off*] **:** serving to stop off ⟨various other *stop-off* coatings were tested and found to be unstable —*Chem. Abstracts*⟩

stop order *n* **:** an order to a broker to buy or sell at the market when the price of a security advances or declines to a designated level

stop out *vt* **1 :** to cover part of (a printing surface) with something that does not print or that prevents printing: as **a :** to cover (areas on a negative being prepared for photoengraving) with an opaque substance to prevent light action; *also* **:** to cover (areas on a plate) with a resist to prevent etching **b :** to cover a portion of (a case) with wax so as to prevent electrodeposition in an area that is to be blank in the finished electrotype **2 :** to cover (teeth) with black wax to make invisible

stopover \ˈ=,==\ *n* -s [fr. *stop over*, v.] **1 a :** a stop at an intermediate point in one's journey **:** an interruption in a journey ⟨driving north with leisurely ~*s* to look at the animals —Alan Moorehead⟩ **b :** the act of breaking one's journey (as by train) with the privilege of continuing on a later conveyance of the same carrier **2 :** a stopping place on a journey ⟨the village is a delightful ~ for travelers —*Amer. Guide Series: Mich.*⟩

stop·pa·ble \ˈstäpəbəl\ *adj* [¹*stop* + *-able*] **:** capable of being stopped

stop·page \ˈstäpij, -pēj\ *n* -s [ME, fr. *stoppen* to stop + *-age* — more at STOP] **:** the act of stopping or the state of being stopped ⟨~ of hostile seaborne traffic —Walter Karig⟩ ⟨practically immune from ~*s* due to the weeds which infest so many of our waterways —Dick Gregson⟩: as **a :** deduction from pay as a fine or to reimburse an employer for a sum due from an employee **b :** obstruction of an organ of the body **c :** the stopping, seizure, or detention of a person, public carrier, or goods in transit (as for examination for contraband) **d :** the act or an instance of stopping payment **e :** STRIKE ⟨negotiations have broken down in other industries, and ~*s* are threatened —H.S.Truman⟩ ⟨government seizure of the railroads . . . to forestall a nationwide ~ —C.T.Lucey⟩ **f :** the complete obstruction of the breath passage or of the nonnasal part of it that is one stage in the production of some consonants — compare STOP 9 **g :** a failure of an automatic or semiautomatic firearm to extract or eject a spent case or to load or fire a new round

stoppage at source : the levying of taxes on the thing sought to be taxed (as income) at its source rather than on the person who receives the benefit or substance of it — called also *collection at source*; compare WITHHOLDING TAX

stoppage in transitu : the right of a seller of goods to stop them while on their way to the buyer and resume possession of them (as on discovery of the buyer's insolvency)

stop payment *n* **:** a depositor's order to a bank to refuse to honor a specified check drawn by him

stopped \ˈstäpt\ *adj* [ME, fr. past part. of *stoppen*] **1 a :** closed up or obstructed ⟨a ~ bottle⟩ ⟨a ~ nose⟩ **b** (1) *of an organ pipe* **:** closed at the top and producing thereby a pitch approximately an octave lower than that of an open pipe of the same length (2) *of a note* **:** obtained by stopping a string, pipe, or finger hole of a musical instrument **2 :** brought to a halt **:** CHECKED ⟨hang onto a ~ automobile or streetcar —Anthony Bailey⟩ **3 :** marked by stoppage ⟨~ consonant⟩ ⟨~ release⟩ **4** *of a bridge suit* **:** prevented from being run

stopped couplet *n* **:** CLOSED COUPLET

stopped diapason *n* **:** a foundation stop in a pipe organ consisting of wooden pipes closed at the top and sounding a powerful flute tone

stopped flute *n* **:** a flute filled for part of its length by a convex molding

stopped fluting *n* **:** a stopped flute or series of stopped flutes

¹stop·per \ˈstäpə(r)\ *n* -s [ME, fr. *stoppen* to stop + *-er* — more at STOP] **1 :** one that brings to a halt or causes to stop operating or functioning **:** CHECK ⟨do not appear to have been very effective bullet ~*s*, since the sheet of steel was so thin —J.C.Swaim⟩ ⟨conversation ~⟩ ⟨show ~⟩: as **a** (1) **:** a short piece of rope having a knot and lanyard at one end with a hook at the other (2) **:** a contrivance (as a length of rope or chain) to secure a rope or chain or to check it while running (3) **:** a device to secure a rowlock **b :** a device or appliance to stop machinery **c** (1) **:** a card that will stop the run of a suit (2) **:** both of two high cards whose possession by a pinochle player assures that no other player can make a certain meld **d :** a baseball pitcher depended on to win important games or to stop a losing streak of his team; *also* **:** an effective relief pitcher **e :** something that seizes the attention ⟨good pictures of babies, animals, and pretty girls are the conventional ~*s* because they are so high in human interest and attention value —Daniel Melcher & Nancy Larrick⟩ **2 :** one that closes, shuts, or fills up ⟨the rock was the ~ in the bottleneck —Burtt Evans⟩: as **a :** something (as a bung or cork) used to plug an opening ⟨oval bottles . . . with ground-glass ~*s* —Lois Long⟩ **b :** a composition to stop up holes **c :** one that applies a coating of stopping paste **d :** EARTH STOPPER **3 a :** any of several trees of the genus *Eugenia* (esp. *E. axillaris*) of Florida and the West Indies with hard close-grained wood **b :** WHITE STOPPER

²stopper \"\ *vt* -ED/-ING/-S **1 :** to close or secure with a stopper **:** fit a stopper on ⟨the big problem in wine manufacture was how to ~ the bottles —*Scots Mag.*⟩ **2 :** to close as if with a stopper **:** PLUG ⟨babies — their mouths ~*ed* up with pacifiers —Jean Stafford⟩

stopper knot *n* **:** a knot used to prevent a rope from passing through a hole or opening

stop·per·less \-(r)ləs\ *adj* **:** not having a stopper

stop·per·man \-(r)mən\ *n, pl* **stoppermen :** a foundry worker who makes or repairs fire-clay stoppers for ladles and sets them in place

stop·ping \ˈstäpiŋ, -pēŋ\ *n* -s [ME, fr. gerund of *stoppen*] **1 :** the act of one that stops ⟨a violinist whose ~ is phenomenal⟩ **2 :** material for stopping up or filling in a fissure or cavity **:** FILLING, PACKING ⟨the fleeting glimpse of gold ~ in his side teeth —Margery Allingham⟩ **3 :** a partition or door (as in a mine) to direct or prevent an air current **4 :** the placing of punctuation marks **:** PUNCTUATION **5 :** the solid end of an archery pile

stopping condenser *or* **stopping capacitor** *n* **:** a capacitor used in a circuit to prevent the flow of direct current but permit the flow of alternating current

stopping in transit : a special service by carriers that permits a shipper to unload part of a shipment at intermediate points and then send the remainder to a final destination at a through rate plus stopping charge

stop plank *n* **:** one of a set of planks set in grooves to form a dam — compare FLASHBOARD

stop plate *n* **:** a plate for stopping or limiting the travel of a part (as a rod or valve); *specif* **:** a plate serving as an end bearing for the axle of a railroad car to prevent or limit end play

¹stop·ple \ˈstäpəl\ *n* -s [ME *stoppell*, fr. *stoppen* to stop + *-ell* (suffix denoting an instrument)] **:** something that closes an aperture **:** STOPPER: as **a** (1) **:** a plug for closing a finger hole in a flute or flageolet to change the scale tone (2) **:** the plug in the end of a stopped organ pipe **b :** EARPLUG 2 ⟨a ~ must be fitted into the ear canal so that noise does not leak around the edges —*Nat'l Safety News*⟩

²stopple \"\ *vt* **stoppled; stoppled; stoppling** \-p(ə)liŋ\ **stopples :** to close the mouth of with or as if with a stopple **:** STOPPER

stop press *n* [¹*stop* + *press*] *chiefly Brit* **:** a space or column in a newspaper containing last-minute news items usu. printed from a fudge ⟨hadn't seen anything in the *stop press* or the early papers —Christopher Bush⟩

stop-press \ˈ=,=\ *adj* [¹*stop* + *press*] **1 :** made or inserted while a printing press is stopped in the course of a run ⟨a *stop-press* alteration⟩ ⟨a *stop-press* correction⟩ **2 :** of up-to-the-minute significance or interest **:** TIMELY ⟨many a worthy book of scholarship might be all the better for . . . relating itself to the *stop-press* facts of life —James Cameron⟩

stop rod *n* **:** a stop-motion rod on a loom

stops *pres 3d sing of* STOP, *pl of* STOP

stop screw *n* **:** a screw for mounting or holding a stop

stop seine *n* **:** STOP NET 1

stop sign *n* **:** a usu. octagonal sign requiring vehicles to stop before entering or crossing a thoroughfare

stop street *n* **:** a street on which a vehicle must stop just before entering a through street

stopt *archaic past of* STOP

stop tester *n* **:** an instrument for determining the distance required to stop a vehicle by measuring its deceleration

stop thrust *n* **:** a counteroffensive movement made by a fencer to arrest an opponent's attack — compare TIME THRUST

STOP

stop sign

stop valve *n* **:** a valve closed or opened at will (as by hand) for preventing or regulating flow (as of a liquid in a pipe); *specif* **:** the valve in an engine steam pipe for controlling or checking the passage of steam

stop volley *n* **:** a soft shot in tennis intended to carry just over the net short of the reach of one's opponent

stopwatch \ˈ=,=\ *n* **:** a watch having a hand that can be started or stopped at will (as by pressing a small button on the edge of the watch) to register exact elapsed time (as of a race) — compare FLYBACK

stopwatch

stopwater \ˈ=,==\ *n* [²*stop* + *water*] **:** any of various devices or procedures for securing watertightness: as **a :** a plug of soft wood driven into a hole bored in the seam of a scarf **b :** canvas backed with red lead or other material and fitted between metal parts (as of a ship)

stopwork \ˈ=,=\ *n* [²*stop* + *work*] **1 :** a device to prevent tight winding of the mainspring of a watch or clock — compare MALTESE CROSS **2** [¹*stop* + *work*] *Austral* **:** stoppage of work **:** STRIKE

stor *abbr* storage

¹stor·able \ˈstōrəbəl, ˈstȯr-\ *adj* [¹*store* + *-able*] **:** that may be stored ⟨reserves of ~ commodities —*New Republic*⟩ — contrasted with *perishable*

²storable \"\ *n* -s **:** something that may be stored for an extended period of time without serious loss from spoilage or evaporation and without danger — usu. used in pl. ⟨~s such as wheat and cotton⟩

stor·age \-rij, -rēj\ *n* -s *often attrib* [¹*store* + *-age*] **1 a :** space for storing ⟨~ available at low rates⟩ ⟨~ cabinet⟩ ⟨~ room⟩ **b :** a place for storing ⟨area, which was being used as a ~ for war matériel —*N.Y. Times*⟩ ⟨granaries and other unheated crop ~s —*Nat'l Fire Codes*⟩ ⟨insulation requirements for fruit and vegetable ~s —P.D.Close⟩ ⟨the development of water ~s in arid regions⟩ **c :** an amount stored; *esp* **:** the total amount (as of water in a reservoir) that can be stored in a place ⟨the dam . . . has a total ~ of eight billion cubic feet of water —*Amer. Guide Series: Maine*⟩ **2 a :** the act of storing or state of being stored ⟨off-street ~ of automobiles⟩ ⟨underground ~ of natural gas⟩ ⟨lake, created primarily for upstream ~ —*Amer. Guide Series: Nev.*⟩ ⟨meat packed for ~⟩; *specif* **:** the safekeeping of goods in a warehouse or other depository ⟨place goods in ~⟩ — compare COLD STORAGE **b :** the price charged for keeping goods in a storehouse ⟨to charge ~⟩ **c :** the holding and housing of goods from the time they are produced until their sale **3 :** the production by means of electric energy of chemical reactions that when allowed to reverse themselves generate electricity again without serious loss — see STORAGE CELL **4 :** MEMORY 6

storage bellows *n pl but sing or pl in constr* **:** a chamber in a pipe organ in which the compressed air supplied by the blower is kept at a uniform pressure by means of weights or springs

storage car *n* **:** a railway car for hauling mail and parcels that do not require sorting and distribution en route — compare RAILWAY MAIL CAR

storage cell *or* **storage battery** *n* **1 :** a cell that converts chemical energy into electrical energy by reversible chemical reactions and that may be recharged by passing a current through it in the direction opposite to that of its discharge — called also *accumulator, secondary battery* **2 :** a connected group of two or more storage cells

storage in transit : the storing at an intermediate point of goods that are to be reshipped to their final destination within a prescribed period; *also* **:** the charge for such storage at through rates

storage life *n* **:** SHELF LIFE

storage spot *n* **:** a spotting of fruits and vegetables originating in storage; *specif* **:** a disease of citrus fruits characterized by light-colored or brown sunken spots of varying size and shape — called also *pox*

storage track *n* **:** a railroad yard track for cars awaiting use or other disposition

storage tube *n* **:** MEMORY TUBE

storage wall *n* **:** a built-in combination esp. of cabinets, closets, and open shelves set against or forming a broad wall space (as the side of a room)

storage yard *n* **:** a railroad yard for cars not in use

sto·rax \'stō,raks, 'stȯ,-\ *n* -ES [ME, fr. LL, storax, tree (of the genus *Styrax*) yielding storax, alter. of L *styrax* — more at STYRAX] **1 :** a resin derived from various trees of the genus *Styrax* (as *S. officinalis*) and formerly used for incense **2 a :** a balsam obtained from the bark of an Asiatic tree (*Liquidambar orientalis*) as a grayish brown fragrant liquid containing resin, styrene, and cinnamic acid and used as an expectorant and sometimes in perfumery — called also *Levant storax* **b :** a similar balsam from the sweet gum (*L. styraciflua*) — called also *American storax, sweet gum;* compare LIQUIDAMBAR **3 :** a shrub or tree of the genus *Styrax*

storax family *n* **:** STYRACACEAE

¹**store** \'stō(ə)r, 'stȯ(ə)r, -ōə, -ó(ə)\ *vb* -ED/-ING/-S [ME *storen*, fr. OF *estorer* to construct, restore, store, fr. L *instaurare* to renew, restore, perform, fr. *in-* ²in- + *-staurare* (fr. a base akin to Gk *stauros* pole, stake) — more at STEER] *vt* **1 :** FURNISH, PROVIDE, SUPPLY, FILL ⟨bins *stored* with grain⟩ ⟨his head was *stored* with chaotic but vivid impressions —Frances Gaither⟩; *esp* **:** to stock or furnish against a future time ⟨~ a ship with provisions⟩ **2 :** to collect as a reserved supply **:** lay away **:** ACCUMULATE ⟨~ vegetables for winter use⟩ ⟨energy from the sun may be *stored* in the form of fat as well as carbohydrates . . . and proteins —R.E.Coker⟩ ⟨energy *stored* in a condenser can be computed —W.H.Timbie & Vannevar Bush⟩ — often used with *up* or *away* ⟨build dams to ~ up water —R.W. Murray⟩ ⟨memories *stored away*⟩ **3 a :** to leave or deposit in a store, warehouse, or other place for keeping, preservation, or disposal **:** CACHE, STOW ⟨potatoes *stored* in a basement⟩ ⟨in the early days of the passenger car it was almost unheard of to ~ it on the street —J.C.Ingraham⟩ ⟨the center mall is often used to ~ snow plowed from the pavement in winter months —A.G.Bruce & John Clarkeson⟩ ⟨honey *stored* in hives⟩ **b :** to record (information) in an electronic device (as a computer) from which the data can be obtained as needed **4 :** to have space for **:** provide storage room for **:** HOLD ⟨elevators to ~ surplus wheat⟩ ~ *vi* **1 :** to take on or store away supplies ⟨ships *storing* in the harbor⟩ **2 :** to undergo storing esp. without spoilage ⟨foods should ~ well at room temperatures or in the refrigerator —Callie Coons⟩ ⟨an egg that will ~ 60 percent longer —*Springfield (Mass.) Daily News*⟩

²**store** \"\ *n* -s [ME *stor*, fr. OF *estor*, fr. *estorer*] **1 a :** something that is stored or kept for future use ⟨~ for ten days⟩ ⟨through all his active years he drew heavily on his physical ~ —W.A.Slade⟩ **b stores** *pl* **:** articles (as of food) accumulated for some specific object and issued or drawn upon as needed **:** STOCK, SUPPLIES ⟨issue ~s upon proper written authority⟩ ⟨charged with payment for the coal, oil and other consumable ~s —*Railway Gazette*⟩ ⟨over 700 lb. of ~s — oxygen, tents, food, fuel, cookers, climbing gear — must be lifted —John Hunt & Edmund Hillary⟩ **c :** something accumulated or amassed **:** a source from which things may be drawn as needed **:** a reserve fund ⟨a ~ of provisions⟩ ⟨a ~ of sound advice —R.A.Billington⟩ ⟨their dwindling ~ of undergraduate days —*Dartmouth Alumni Mag.*⟩ — often used in pl. ⟨continued education . . . will provide increasing ~s of information —C.W.Eliot⟩ **2 a** *obs* **:** LIVESTOCK **b** *Brit* **:** a young or unfinished meat animal suitable for growing on and fattening **3** *archaic* **:** POSSESSIONS **4 :** STORAGE — usu. used with *in* or *out of* ⟨fresh fruits and vegetables, whether in transit or in ~ —*Fruit & Vegetable Storage & Pre-packaging*⟩ ⟨when placing eggs in ~ —*Dublin Sunday Independent*⟩ ⟨our furniture, out of ~ last week —Mary Shaw⟩ **5 :** something that is highly valued or greatly relied upon **:** TREASURE — used with *set* or *lay* or *put* ⟨setting a great ~ on precedent —E.M. Coulter⟩ ⟨such schedules did not set light ~ on life and property —H.O.Taylor⟩ ⟨her mother set such ~ by the terrarium —Jean Stafford⟩ ⟨lay great ~ by tradition⟩ ⟨readers, who never put much ~ by the polite, personal essay —*Time*⟩ **6 stores** *pl* **:** the raw or unworked material supplies of a manufacturing concern **7 :** a large quantity, supply, or number **:** ABUNDANCE ⟨intended to bake a ~ of brambles for you to take —G.W.Brace⟩ **8 :** a place of deposit for goods esp. in large quantities **:** STOREHOUSE, WAREHOUSE, MAGAZINE ⟨meat ~⟩ ⟨rope ~⟩ ⟨explosives ~⟩ ⟨quartermaster's ~⟩ — see COLD STORE **9 a :** a business establishment where goods are kept for retail sale ⟨grocery ~⟩ ⟨furniture ~⟩; *esp* **:** a retail establishment having a large diversified stock of goods ⟨thoroughfares lined with modernized ~s and up-to-date shops —*Amer. Guide Series: Pa.*⟩ — see CHAIN STORE, DEPARTMENT STORE, RETAIL STORE; compare SHOP **b stores** *pl but sing or pl in constr, Brit* **:** a retail establishment often consisting of a number of departments **c :** a commercial establishment (as a bank, restaurant, or dry-cleaning shop) ⟨~s and offices will be closed for the holiday⟩ **d :** a building, room, or suite of rooms occupied by or suitable for occupancy by a store ⟨~ for rent⟩ ⟨several ~s under construction⟩ **10** *slang* **a :** an establishment or setup used by swindlers as a front to gain the confidence of victims **b :** an establishment (as a carnival concession) employing shills or barkers to entice customers **11 :** a space or compartment on a gameboard for the keeping of pieces when not in play **12** *chiefly Brit* **:** MEMORY 6 — **in store 1 :** in a state of accumulation **:** in readiness **:** in preparation ⟨a faint promise of the excitement we had been told was *in store* for us —T.C.Roughley⟩ ⟨benefits which the activities of human intelligence may have *in store* for us —H.A.Kramers⟩ **2** *obs* **:** in abundance

³**store** \"\ *adj* **1 a** *or* **stores :** of, relating to, kept in, or used for a store ⟨~ barge⟩ ⟨the *stores* trucks are due on the dock about the same time —Wirt Williams⟩ **b :** used for storing ⟨fill the big red ~ crock with water at night —Flora Thompson⟩ ⟨~ jar⟩ **c :** purchased from a store as opposed to natural or homemade **:** COMMERCIAL, MANUFACTURED, BOUGHT, READY-MADE ⟨~ clothes⟩ ⟨~ bread⟩ ⟨~ teeth⟩ **2** *archaic* **:** ABUNDANT, PLENTIFUL — used postpositively ⟨ships thou hast ~ —Alexander Pope⟩ **3** *Brit* **a :** STOCK 3 **b :** suitable for fattening ⟨strolled past the pens of ~ cattle —Adrian Bell⟩

store–bought \'ₛ,ₛ\ *adj* **:** STORE 1c ⟨*store-bought* clothes⟩ ⟨a *store-bought* haircut⟩

store–boughten \'ₛ,ₛₛ\ *dial var of* STORE-BOUGHT

store card *n* **:** a token issued by a private business concern for relieving a public scarcity of small change or for advertising purposes

store cheese *n* **:** CHEDDAR; *esp* **:** sharp cheddar

stored *past of* STORE

sto·reen \sthō'rēn\ *n* [IrGael *stōirīn*, dim. of *stōr* store, treasure, fr. E ²*store*] *Irish* **:** DARLING

¹**storefront** \'ₛ,ₛ\ *n* [²*store* + *front*] **1 :** the front side of a store or store building facing a street ⟨old-time ~s with cast-iron columns —Richard Bissell⟩ **2 :** a building, room, or suite of rooms having a storefront ⟨churches occupying ~s⟩

²**storefront** \"\ *adj* **1 :** occupying a room or suite of rooms in a store building at street level and immediately behind a storefront ⟨operated from a ~ office —Val Adams⟩ **2 :** of, relating to, or characteristic of a storefront church ⟨~ evangelists⟩

storefront church *n* **:** a city church that utilizes storefront quarters as a meeting place and that usu. holds services of a highly emotional nature

storehouse \'ₛ,ₛ\ *n* [ME *storhous*, fr. *stor* store + *hous* house] **1 :** a building for storing goods (as provisions) **:** MAGAZINE, WAREHOUSE; DEPOT, STORE **2 :** an abundant supply or source **:** REPOSITORY ⟨the sea is the world's greatest ~ of raw materials —J.P.Tully⟩ ⟨an author's memory is a ~ of sensations —R.W. Stallman⟩

storehouse beetle *n* **:** a ptinid beetle (*Gibbium psylloides*) that has a cosmopolitan distribution and is injurious to most animal and vegetable foods

store·keep \'ₛ,kēp\ *vi* [back-formation fr. *storekeeper*] **:** to manage a store ⟨guess I'll buy him out and ~ for a while —Sinclair Lewis⟩

storekeeper *also* **storeskeeper** \'ₛ,ₛₛ\ *n* [²*store* + *keeper*] **1 :** one that has charge of supplies (as military or naval stores) **:** a manager of a warehouse **:** STOCK CLERK; *specif* **:** an enlisted man (as in the U. S. Navy) who performs clerical and manual duty in the supply department of a ship or station **2 :** one who operates a retail store **:** MERCHANT, SHOPKEEPER

storekeeping \'ₛ,ₛₛ\ *n* [²*store* + *keeping*] **:** the occupation of keeping a store **:** the management of a store

store·man *also* **stores·man** \'ₛmən\ *n, pl* **storemen** *also* **storesmen 1 :** STOREKEEPER **2 :** a man who stores goods (as in a storehouse)

store order *n* **:** an order for goods made out for an employee on the general supply store of a company

store pay *n* **:** payment for goods or work in articles from a shop or store

stor·er \'stōrə(r)\ *n* -s **:** one that stores: as **a :** one that maintains in store or places in storage **b :** one that lays aside for emergency **:** HOARDER

sto·re·ria \stə'rirēə\ *n, cap* [NL, fr. David H. *Storer* †1891 Am. obstetrician and naturalist + NL *-ia*] **:** a common genus of harmless No. American gray or brown colubrid snakes

storeroom \'ₛ,ₛ\ *n* **1 :** a room for the storing of goods or supplies **:** LUMBER ROOM **2 :** space for storing in a storehouse or repository **3 :** STOREHOUSE 2 ⟨the prodigious ~ of his mind —F.H.Taylor⟩ ⟨his ~ of anecdotes and illustrations is rich and varied —Ben Bradford⟩ **4 :** a room used or designed for the display of merchandise on sale

¹**stores** *pres 3d sing of* STORE, *pl of* STORE

²**stores** *var of* STORE

storeship \'ₛ,ₛ\ *n* **:** a ship used to carry supplies

stores ledger *n* **:** a perpetual inventory record esp. of raw materials and manufacturing supplies

storewide \'ₛ,ₛ\ *adj* **:** including all or most merchandise throughout a store ⟨a ~ sale⟩ ⟨~ clearance⟩

storey *var of* STORY

storeyard \'ₛ,ₛ\ *n* **:** a yard that is used for storing goods or supplies

sto·ri·at·ed \'stōrē,ād·əd\ *adj* [ML *historiatus* historiated + E *-ed* — more at HISTORIATED] **:** HISTORIATED

sto·ri·a·tion \,ₛₛ'āshən\ *n* -s [ML *historiatus* + E *-ion*] **:** ornamentation with designs representing historical subjects

¹**sto·ried** \'stōrēd, 'stȯr-, -rid\ *adj* [¹*story* + *-ed*] **1 :** decorated with designs representing scenes from story or history ⟨a ~ frieze⟩ ⟨a ~ tapestry⟩ ⟨~ windows richly dight —John Milton⟩ **2 :** having a history **:** celebrated in story or history **:** interesting from the stories that relate to it ⟨a country with a ~ past —V.G.Heiser⟩ ⟨these are ~ mountains —Cornelius Weygandt⟩ ⟨a ~ family⟩

²**storied** *or* **sto·reyed** \'stōrēd, 'stȯr- -rid\ *adj* [³*story, storey* + *-ed*] **1 :** having stories ⟨dwarfing the petty, ~ dwellings —Edwin Benson⟩ — often used in combination ⟨a two-*storied* house⟩ **2** *of wood* **:** characterized by somewhat regular transverse rows when viewed in tangential section **:** having the appearance of ripple marks ⟨~ cambium⟩

sto·ri·er \'stōrēə(r)\ *n* -s [ME, fr. *storie* story + *-er* — more at STORY] **1** *obs* **:** HISTORIAN **2 :** a teller of stories

stories *pres 3d sing of* STORY, *pl of* STORY

sto·ri·ette \,stōrē'et\ *n* -s [¹*story* + *-ette*] **:** a brief story or tale

sto·ri·fy \'stōrə,fī\ *vt* -ED/-ING/-ES [¹*story* + *-fy*] **:** to narrate or describe in story

sto·rin \sthō'rēn\ *var of* STOREEN

storing *pres part of* STORE

sto·ris \'stōrəs\ *n, pl* **storis** [Dan, fr. *stor* large, big (fr. ON *stōrr*) + *is* ice, fr. ON *īss* — more at STOUR, ICE] **:** a floating mass of closely crowded icebergs and floes

¹**stork** \'stȯ(ə)rk, -ó(ə)k\ *n, pl* **storks** *also* **stork** [ME, fr. OE *storc;* akin to MLG & MD *storc* stork, OHG *storah*, ON *storkr* stork, OE *stearc* stiff, strong; fr. its stiff legs — more at STARK] **:** any of various large mostly Old World wading birds having a long stout bill, constituting the family Ciconiidae, and related to the ibises and herons — see ADJUTANT BIRD, BLACK STORK, JABIRU, MARABOU, OPENBILL, SADDLE-BILL, WHITE STORK; compare WOOD IBIS

²**stork** \"\ *adj* [fr. the nursery story that children are brought into the world by storks] **:** relating to the birth of a child ⟨~ cards⟩ ⟨a ~ shower⟩

stork–billed kingfisher \'ₛ,ₛ-\ *n* **:** any of various long-tailed kingfishers (genus *Pelargopsis*) of southeastern Asia and the East Indies having a sharp-pointed bill with the culmen ridged at the base

storksbill \'ₛ,ₛ\ *n* **1 :** a plant of the genus *Pelargonium* **2 :** a plant of the genus *Erodium; esp* **:** ALFILARIA

¹**storm** \'stȯ(ə)rm, -ó(ə)m\ *n* -s *often attrib* [ME, fr. OE; akin to OS & MD *storm*, OHG *sturm*, ON *stormr* storm, OE *styrian* to stir — more at STIR] **1 a :** a violent disturbance of the atmosphere attended by wind and usu. by rain, snow, hail, sleet, or thunder and lightning **:** TEMPEST — see TROPICAL STORM; compare CYCLONE, HURRICANE **b :** a heavy fall of rain, snow, or hail whether accompanied with wind or not **c :** stormy weather ⟨captured their . . . varying moods in sun, ~ and snow, —*Brit. Bk. News*⟩ **d :** wind having a speed of 64 to 72 miles per hour — see BEAUFORT SCALE table **e :** a serious disturbance of any element of nature ⟨ionospheric ~⟩ — see MAGNETIC STORM **2 :** a disturbed or agitated state **:** a sudden or violent commotion ⟨the economic ~s of the 1930s —*Woolworth's First 75 Years*⟩ ⟨the ~s of adolescence⟩ ⟨whose life has been a passage through ~s of emotion —P.E.More⟩ ⟨a ~ of birds in the . . . trees —W.B.Yeats⟩ **3 a :** PAROXYSM, CRISIS **b :** a sudden increase in the symptoms of a disease ⟨thyroid ~⟩ **c :** a sudden heavy influx or onset ⟨the ~ of paperbacks now flooding the country —Harrison Smith⟩ ⟨the ~ of students now entering college⟩ **4 :** a heavy discharge of objects (as missiles) or actions (as blows) ⟨a ~ of arrows⟩ ⟨a ~ of petals⟩ **5 :** a tumultuous outburst ⟨a ~ of protests⟩ ⟨no words could be heard above the ~ of catcalls —E.S.Bates⟩ **6 :** a violent assault on a defended position **7 storms** *pl* **:** STORM WINDOWS ⟨put up the ~s⟩ — **by storm** *adv* **:** by or as if by employing a bold swift frontal movement esp. with the intent of defeating or winning over quickly and completely ⟨attack a fort *by storm*⟩ ⟨take an audience *by storm*⟩

²**storm** \"\ *vb* -ED/-ING/-S [ME *stormen*, fr. *storm*, n.] *vi* **1 a :** to blow with violence ⟨the wind . . . ~*ed* in at nearly 40 miles an hour —J.A.Michener⟩ **b :** to rain, hail, snow, or sleet esp. in a violent manner or with high wind — usu. used with *it* ⟨it was ~*ing* in the mountains⟩ **2 :** to attack by storm ⟨armored divisions ~*ing* toward the city⟩ ⟨the attackers ~*ed* ashore at sunrise⟩ **3 :** to be in or to exhibit a violent passion **:** RAGE ⟨~*ing* at the unusual delay⟩ **4 :** to rush about or move impetuously, violently, or angrily ⟨the mob ~*ed* through the streets⟩ ⟨jumped into his clothes and ~*ed* over to the office —Nathaniel Benchley⟩ ⟨on such occasions the river ~s down in a rush —J.H.Moolman⟩ ~ *vt* **:** to attack, take, or win over by storm ⟨~ a fort⟩ ⟨trying to ~ the public by a mannerism —O.W.Holmes †1935⟩ ⟨they simply ~*ed* their audiences —Philip Carr⟩ **syn** see ATTACK

storm and stress *n, often cap both Ss* [trans. of G *sturm und drang*] **:** STURM UND DRANG

storm beach *n* **:** a low rounded ridge of coarse gravel or shingle constructed by storm waves at the inner margin of a beach beyond the reach of ordinary waves

stormbird \'ₛ,ₛ\ *n* **1 :** PETREL; *esp* **:** STORM PETREL **2 :** a bird (as the man-o'-war bird) thought to presage storms

storm blue *n* **:** a variable color averaging a grayish blue that is redder and less strong than electric, redder and duller than copenhagen, and redder and darker than Gobelin

storm boat *n* **:** a light fast craft used to transport attacking troops across streams

storm boot *n* **:** a woman's high-cut boot made of heavy waterproofed leather

stormbound \'ₛ,ₛ\ *adj* **:** cut off from outside communication by a storm or its effects **:** stopped or delayed by storms ⟨~ ports⟩ ⟨~ travelers⟩

storm breeder *n* **:** a cloud or weather condition regarded as portending storm; *also* **:** WEATHER BREEDER

storm cellar *or* **storm cave** *n* **:** CYCLONE CELLAR

storm center *n* **1 :** the center of the area covered by a storm; *esp* **:** the place of lowest pressure in a cyclonic storm — compare EYE 2h **2 :** a focus of controversy or disturbance **:** a central point around which trouble revolves

storm cloud *n* **1 :** a cloud that portends a storm **2 :** a threat of serious disturbance or trouble

storm coat *n* **:** a heavy lined fabric overcoat usu. waterproofed and with a fur collar

stormcock \'ₛ,ₛ\ *n* **1 :** MISTLE THRUSH **2 :** FIELDFARE **3 :** GREEN WOODPECKER **4 :** STORM PETREL

storm current *n* **:** a current caused by a storm wind

storm door *n* **:** an additional door placed outside an ordinary outside door to prevent entrance of wind, cold, and rain and to reduce heat losses — compare STORM WINDOW

storm drain *n* **1 :** a drain carrying waste water other than sewage from a building to a storm sewer **2 :** STORM SEWER

storm·er \'stȯrmər\ *n* -s **:** one that storms: as **a :** one that rages **b :** one that attacks by storm

storm flag *n* **1 :** a small national flag flown (as at a U. S. Army post) only in stormy weather and measuring usu. 9 feet 6 inches by 5 feet **2 :** a square red flag with a square black center displayed singly, in pairs, or in combination with various pennants to indicate the approach of a storm

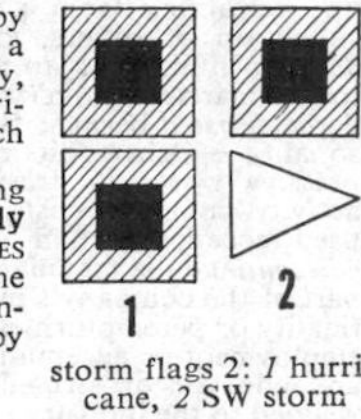

storm flags 2: *1* hurricane, *2* SW storm

storm·ful \'stȯrmfəl\ *adj* **:** abounding with storms **:** STORMY — **storm·ful·ly** \-fəlē\ *adv* — **storm·ful·ness** *n* -ES

storm glass *n* **:** a vertical glass tube the contents of which are supposed to indicate changes in the weather by changes in their appearance

stormier *comparative of* STORMY

stormiest *superlative of* STORMY

storm·i·ly \'stȯ(r)məlē, -li\ *adv* **:** in a stormy manner

storm in a teacup : TEMPEST IN A TEAPOT

storm·i·ness \-mēnəs, -min-\ *n* -ES **:** the quality or state of being stormy ⟨~ increases toward the higher latitudes —P.E. James⟩

storming *adj* [fr. pres. part. of ²*storm*] **:** that storms ⟨equity markets made a ~ start to the week —*Financial Times (London)*⟩

storming party *n* **:** a military party assigned to storm a position

storm jib *n* **:** a small jib used in stormy weather

storm lane *n* **:** a narrow belt over which storm centers pass with a certain degree of regularity and with frequency

storm lantern *or* **storm lamp** *n, chiefly Brit* **:** HURRICANE LAMP 1

storm·less \'stȯrmləs\ *adj* **:** having no storms — **storm·less·ness** *n* -ES

storm level *n* **:** the somewhat indefinite imaginary plane several feet above mean sea level to which storm waves occas. climb

storm mizzen *n* **:** a triangular sail set on a temporary stay abaft the mizzen

storm petrel *n* **:** any of various small petrels; *esp* **:** a small sooty black petrel (*Hydrobates pelagicus*) marked with white on wing and tail coverts and frequenting the north Atlantic and Mediterranean — called also *stormy petrel*

storm porch *n* **:** a small roofed structure designed to protect an outside door of a dwelling in cold weather

stormproof \'ₛ,ₛ\ *adj* **:** impervious to damage by storm **:** so tight as to exclude penetration by wind, rain, or snow in time of storm

storm rack *n* **:** FIDDLE 3

storm rubber *n* **:** a low-cut rubber overshoe having a high front that covers the instep

storms *pl of* STORM, *pres 3d sing of* STORM

storm rubber

storm sail *n* **:** any of numerous small strong heavy sails that are bent and set in stormy weather

storm sewer *n* **1 :** a sewer designed to carry water wastes except sewage **2 :** STORM DRAIN

storm signal *n* **1 :** a signal (as a flag, pennant, or cone) announcing the approach of a storm esp. of marked violence **2 :** STORM WARNING 2

storm stay *n* **:** a temporary stay for a storm sail

storm thrush *n, Brit* **:** MISTLE THRUSH

storm tide *n* **:** a high tide that is significantly higher than normal due to onshore winds reinforcing tidal action

storm track *n* **:** the path of the center of a storm

storm trooper *n* **1 :** a member of the shock troops **2** *sometimes cap S&T* **:** a member of the Sturmabteilung **:** BROWNSHIRT **3 :** a member of a politico-military body similar in aims or function to the Sturmabteilung ⟨the *storm troopers* of some yet undefined totalitarianism —Dixon Wecter⟩

storm troops *n pl* **1 :** SHOCK TROOPS **2** *sometimes cap S&T* **:** troops belonging to the Sturmabteilung of Nazi Germany

storm warning *n* **1 a :** a display of storm signals **b :** a notification (as a radio report) that gives warning of an approaching storm **2 :** a happening that warns of a difficult or involved state of affairs lying ahead ⟨the *storm warnings* he sees for education —*Saturday Rev.*⟩ ⟨the surest *storm warning* that something exciting was about to happen —John Mason Brown⟩

storm welt *n* **:** a welt attached to a shoe between upper and sole around the outside edge of the sole so as to seal out moisture

storm wind *n* **1 :** a heavy wind **:** a wind that brings a storm **:** the blast of a storm **2 :** STORM 1d

storm window *n* **1** *or* **storm sash :** a sash placed outside an ordinary window as a protection against severe weather — compare STORM DOOR **2 :** a dormer window or other protected window raised from a roof

stormy \'stȯrmē, 'stȯ(ə)mē, -mi\ *adj* -ER/-EST [ME, fr. *storm* + *-y*] **1 :** relating to, characterized by, or indicative of a storm **:** subject to storms **:** TEMPESTUOUS ⟨a ~ day⟩ ⟨a ~ autumn⟩ ⟨severed by a wide and ~ sea from the rest of the world —James Bryce⟩ **2 :** marked by turmoil or fury **:** characterized by, subject to, or indicative of heated disagreements or strong emotional outbursts : PASSIONATE, TURBULENT ⟨a ~ conference⟩ ⟨a ~ life⟩ ⟨provoke ~ and uncontrollable emotional responses —Lewis Mumford⟩ ⟨a violent, ~ eloquence —J.L.Motley⟩ ⟨her deep ~ eyes —Thomas Hardy⟩ **3 :** having alternating exacerbations and remissions of symptoms ⟨convalescence ran a ~ course⟩ ⟨the course of the disease is usually extremely ~ —Joseph Stokes⟩

stormy petrel *n* **1 :** STORM PETREL **2 :** one fond of strife **:** a harbinger of trouble ⟨became the *stormy petrel* of his time at home, at school —Floyd Stovall⟩

stor·nel·lo \stȯ(r)ˈne(ˌ)lō\ *n, pl* **stornel·li** \-elē\ [It, prob. fr. *stornare* to turn aside, fr. OIt, fr. OF *destorner, destourner* — more at DETOUR] **:** a short Italian street song often consisting of only three lines rhyming *aba*

¹story \ˈstōrē, ˈstȯrē, -ri\ *n* -ES [ME *storie*, fr. OF *estorie, estoire*, fr. L *historia* — more at HISTORY] **1 a** *obs* **:** a connected narrative of important events esp. of the remote past **b** *archaic* **:** a historical record **:** a work of history **c** *archaic* **:** history as a branch of knowledge **2 a :** an account of some incident or event; *often* **:** a tale written or told esp. for the entertainment of children ⟨used to tell *stories* to his grandchildren at night —Vance Randolph⟩ **b :** a statement regarding the facts pertinent to a situation in question ⟨the man's ~ of the robbery was not convincing⟩ **c :** a detailed account of the career of a particular individual or of the sequential facts in a given case ⟨write the ~ of one's life⟩ ⟨the ~ of the ocean⟩ ⟨the ~ of atomic power⟩ ⟨the ~ of public housing⟩ **d :** ANECDOTE; *esp* **:** an amusing one ⟨his speech contained several good *stories*⟩ **e :** the events in the history of a person or thing that taken together are of sufficient interest and significance to serve as likely subject matter for an account ⟨there's a ~ in every one of your fellow passengers —Richard Joseph⟩ **f :** background information that clarifies a situation or affair ⟨what's the ~ on this deal⟩ ⟨get the whole ~ before commenting⟩ ⟨but figures give only part of the ~ —*New Republic*⟩ **3 a :** a prose or verse narrative of incidents arranged according to their time relationship **:** a fictional work that recounts objective events or a stream of thought or interactions of these **b :** a fiction that is shorter or has a more unified plot than the usual novel ⟨detective *stories*⟩ ⟨Western *stories*⟩; *specif* **:** SHORT STORY **c :** the intrigue or plot of a narrative or dramatic work; *broadly* **:** a narrative thread upon which a composition is based ⟨the ~ of a ballet⟩ **d :** a rewrite or condensation of a literary work in which dramatic values are emphasized and which serves as the basis of the script of a film play **4 :** an historical, legendary, or literary subject depicted in sculptural or pictorial art ⟨~ pictures popular in the 19th century⟩ — compare HISTORY 4a(2) **5 a** *archaic* **:** a groundless rumor **b :** a widely circulated report or rumor ⟨a ~ going round⟩ **6 :** FIB, LIE, FALSEHOOD **7 a :** the composition or telling of stories ⟨a feat long celebrated in song and ~⟩ **b :** TRADITION, LEGEND, ROMANCE ⟨castle walls and snowy summits old in ~ —Alfred Tennyson⟩ **8 a :** an account in a news organ or news broadcast ⟨human-interest ~⟩ ⟨feature ~⟩ **b :** the subject of a news account **:** material for news accounts ⟨the biggest *stories* of the year⟩ **9 :** an arrangement (as of pictures or tableaux) that in sequence and often with the aid of accompanying text tells a connected narrative ⟨the first series of picture *stories* the photographer did —*Current Biog.*⟩

²story \"\ *vb* -ED/-ING/-ES [ME *storien*, fr. *storie*, n.] *vt* **1** *archaic* **:** to tell in historical relation **:** make the subject of a story **:** narrate or describe in story **2 :** to adorn with a story or a scene from history ~ *vi* **:** to tell a story; *specif* **:** to tell a falsehood ⟨*storied* about his age⟩

³story *or* **sto·rey** \"\ *n, pl* **stories** *or* **storeys** [ME *storie*, fr. ML *historia, istoria* picture, story of a building, fr. L *historia* history, story (narrative); prob. fr. pictures adorning the windows of medieval buildings — more at HISTORY] **1 a :** a set of rooms on one floor level of a building excluding the attic level and usu. the cellar or basement level **:** the habitable space between two floors or between a floor and the roof of a building ⟨the first ~ of a house⟩ ⟨the attic ~⟩ ⟨a building ten *stories* high⟩ — often used in combination ⟨a single-*story* house⟩ ⟨a forty-*story* building⟩ — see HALF STORY; compare FIRST FLOOR, FLOOR, MEZZANINE, SECOND STORY **b :** a horizontal division of a building's exterior not necessarily corresponding exactly with the stories within **2 :** one of a series of tiers arranged horizontally one over another ⟨beehives arranged in *stories*⟩ ⟨the three *stories* of the cave —J.H.Bretz⟩

story-and-a-half \ˈ‧‧‧‧ˈ‧\ *adj* **:** consisting basically of one story with additional minor rooms in the attic ⟨a *story-and-a-half* brick house⟩

storyboard \ˈ‧‧ˌ‧\ *n* **:** a panel or series of panels on which is tacked a set of small rough drawings depicting consecutively the important changes of scene and action in a planned film or television show or act ⟨imperative to lay out the story of the film on a ~ —Raymond Spottiswoode⟩

storybook \ˈ‧‧ˌ‧\ *n* **:** a book containing a story **:** a book of stories ⟨~s for children⟩

sto·ry·less \ˈ‧‧ləs\ *adj* **:** being without a story **:** UNSTORIED

story line *n* **:** the plot of a story or play ⟨novels with a strong *story line*, lots of action, and other surefire ingredients —Malcolm Cowley⟩

story pole *or* **story rod** *n* **:** a pole cut to the proposed clear height between finished floor and ceiling and often marked with minor dimensions (as for door trims and dadoes) that is used esp. by carpenters and bricklayers

storyteller \ˈ‧‧ˌ‧‧\ *n* **:** a teller of stories: as **a :** one that relates anecdotes **b :** one that recites tales orally in public **c :** STORYWRITER **d :** FIBBER, LIAR **e :** one employed at a play center or library to tell stories to children ⟨their favorite ~ never objected to interruptions⟩

storytelling \ˈ‧‧ˌ‧‧\ *n* **:** the telling of stories

storywriter \ˈ‧‧ˌ‧‧\ *n* [ME *storiewriter*, fr. *storie* story + *writer*] **:** a writer of stories

stoss \ˈstäs\ *adj* [G *stoss-*, fr. *stossen* to push, thrust, fr. OHG *stōzan* — more at STINT] **:** facing toward the direction from which an overriding glacier impinges ⟨the ~ slope of a hill⟩ ⟨the ~ side of a knob of rock⟩ ⟨drumlins are . . . steeper and broader on the ~ end —O. D. Von Engeln⟩ — opposed to *lee*

¹stot *also* **stott** \ˈstät\ *n* -S [ME *stot, stott*, fr. OE *stot*; akin to MLG *stūt* thigh, buttocks, OHG *stiuz* buttocks, ON *stūtr* horn, stump, ox, OHG *stōzan* to thrust, push — more at STINT] **1** *dial Brit* **:** a young bull **2** *dial Brit* **:** a usu. young steer

²stot \"\ *vb* **stotted; stotted; stotting; stots** [origin unknown] *vi* **1** *chiefly Scot* **:** BOUNCE, REBOUND, JUMP **2** *chiefly Scot* **:** to walk with an irregular step **:** STAGGER, LURCH ~ *vt*, *chiefly Scot* **:** BOUNCE ⟨a series of rebounds . . . comparable to patting or *stotting* an india-rubber ball —Douglas Kennedy⟩

³stot \"\ *n* -S **1** *Scot* **a :** REBOUND **b :** a hard blow **2** *Scot* **a :** JUMP; *esp* **:** a leap in dancing **b :** SWING, RHYTHM

stoter *var of* STOOTER

stoting *var of* STOATING

sto·tin·ka \stəˈtiŋkə\ *n, pl* **stotin·ki** \-kē\ [Bulg] **1 :** a Bulgarian monetary unit equal to ¹⁄₁₀₀ lev — see MONEY table **2 :** a coin representing one stotinka

¹stot·ter \ˈstätə(r)\ *vi* -ED/-ING/-S [freq. of ²*stot*] *dial Brit* **:** STAGGER, STUMBLE

²stot·ter \-tər\ *n* -S *Scot* **:** STUMBLE

stoun *dial chiefly Brit past part of* STEAL

¹stound *also* **stoun** \ˈstaünd, ˈstün(d)\ *n* -S [ME *stund, stond, stound*, fr. OE *stund*; akin to OFris *stunde* time, hour, OHG *stunta* period of time, point in time, time, hour, ON *stund* period of time, hour, OE *standan, stondan* to stand — more at STAND] **1** *archaic* **:** TIME, WHILE, MOMENT **2 a** *chiefly Scot* **:** a throbbing pain **:** PANG, ACHE **b** *chiefly Scot* **:** THRILL **c** *archaic* **:** a loud noise **:** UPROAR

²stound *also* **stoun** \"\ *vi* -ED/-ING/-S *chiefly Scot* **:** to feel a pang **:** ACHE, SMART ⟨my heart it ~s with anguish —Robert Burns⟩

³stound *also* **stoun** \"\ *vt* -ED/-ING/-S [ME *stunden, stonden*, prob. fr. *stund, stouned*, past part. of *stounen*, fr. OF *estoner* — more at ASTONY] *archaic* **:** to stupefy with or as if with a blow **:** STUN, ASTOUND

⁴stound \"\ *n* -S **1** *archaic* **:** STUPOR **2** *archaic* **:** a state of amazement

stoup *also* **stoop** \ˈstüp\ *n* -S [ME *stowp*, prob. of Scand origin; akin to ON *staup* cup — more at STEEP] **1** *chiefly Scot* **:** BUCKET, PAIL **2 a :** a container for beverages: as (1) **:** a large glass (2) **:** TANKARD (3) **:** FLAGON ⟨set me the ~s of wine upon that table —Shak.⟩ **b :** the contents of a stoup ⟨bade him come aboard and drink a ~ —Hope Muntz⟩ **3 :** a basin at the entrance of a Roman Catholic church to contain holy water in which those entering may dip their fingers before blessing themselves

stoup 3

¹stour \ˈstü(ə)r\ *adj* [ME *stor, stur*, fr. OE *stōr*; akin to OFris *stōr* large, big, OS *stōri*, OHG *stuori*, ON *stórr* large, big, Russ *staryĭ* old, Lith *storas* thick, OE *standan, stondan* to stand — more at STAND] **1** *chiefly Scot* **:** STRONG, HARDY **2** *chiefly Scot* **:** SEVERE, STERN, INFLEXIBLE **3** *obs* **:** having a coarse texture **:** ROUGH, STIFF **4** *chiefly Scot* **:** HARSH, RASPING, DEEP

²stour *also* **stoure** \"\ *n* -S [ME *stur, stour*, fr. OF *estor, estour, estur*, of Gmc origin; akin to OHG *sturm* storm, tumult, battle, combat — more at STORM] **1 a** *archaic* **:** BATTLE, FIGHT, CONFLICT **b** (1) *dial Brit* **:** TUMULT, UPROAR (2) *chiefly Scot* **:** STORM **2** *chiefly Scot* **:** DUST, POWDER **3 a** *archaic* **:** a time of tumult **b** *obs* (1) **:** TIME, OCCASION (2) **:** PLACE

³stour \"\ *vi* -ED/-ING/-S [alter. of ¹*stir*] *Scot* **:** to move quickly **:** FLY

stoury *also* **stour·ie** \ˈstüri\ *adj* [²*stour* + -*y*, -*ie*] **1** *dial Brit* **:** DUSTY **2** *dial Brit* **:** marked by driving snow

¹stoush \ˈstaüsh\ *vt* -ED/-ING/-ES [prob. of imit. origin] **1** *Austral* **:** to hit hard **:** STRIKE, THRASH **2** *Austral* **:** DEFEAT

²stoush \"\ *n* -ES *Austral* **:** FIGHT, BRAWL, VIOLENCE

¹stout \ˈsteüt\ *n* -S [ME, fr. OE *stūt*; prob. akin to ON *stūtr* horn, stump, ox — more at STOT] *dial Brit* **:** HORSEFLY

²stout \ˈstaüt, *usu* -aüd·+V\ *adj* -ER/-EST [ME, fr. OF *estout* bold, proud, arrogant, powerful, silly, of Gmc origin; akin to MLG *stolt* proud, arrogant, stately, MHG *stolz* proud, arrogant, stately, MD *stolt, stout* bold, brave, and prob. to OHG *stelza* stilt — more at STILT] **1 a** *obs* **:** FIERCE, MENACING **b** *archaic* **:** displaying insolent conceit **:** ARROGANT, HAUGHTY ⟨as ~ and proud as he were lord of all —Shak.⟩ **2 :** characterized by physical or moral bravery **:** COURAGEOUS, VALIANT ⟨proves himself a ~ fellow in battle⟩ ⟨pioneers with strong backs and ~ hearts⟩ **3 a** *archaic* **:** expressive of opposition **:** DEFIANT, HOSTILE ⟨~ demeanor of the few bishops who refused to take the oaths —John Evelyn⟩ **b** *archaic* **:** unalterably set **:** OBSTINATE, STUBBORN ⟨his old ~ will and hardened heart —J.H.Newman⟩ **c :** perseveringly resolute **:** FIRM, STAUNCH ⟨a ~ pillar of the . . . church —S.H.Holbrook⟩ **d :** relentlessly harsh **:** IMPLACABLE ⟨has now become a ~ foe of backsliders⟩ **4 a :** physically strong **:** LUSTY, POWERFUL ⟨the ~ vigorous frame . . . fitted the peasant-preacher for the hard life he had chosen —J.R.Green⟩ **b :** sturdily constructed **:** DURABLE, SOLID ⟨their feet were protected by ~ boots —F.V.W.Mason⟩ ⟨~ wooden barricades . . . have been built across the streets —Mollie Panter-Downes⟩ **c :** full of energy **:** VIGOROUS, FORCEFUL ⟨a ~ tail wind was giving a friendly boost —W.D. Patterson⟩ ⟨the nation is safer with ~ criticism going on in Washington —*New Republic*⟩ **d :** physically healthy **:** HEARTY, ROBUST ⟨are you ~ enough to be the general nurse —Charles Lamb⟩ **e :** resistant to stress or pressure **:** TOUGH, RIGID ⟨a few yards of ~ rope for towing purposes —*Amer. Guide Series: Ariz.*⟩ ⟨room, within the ~ framework of routine, for more individual whim —Joyce Cary⟩ **5 a :** large in diameter — used of a plant or its parts ⟨a small tree with ~ spreading branches —W.C.L.Muenscher⟩ **b :** having body or substance — used esp. of liquor ⟨~ homemade beer —*Amer. Guide Series: Texas*⟩ **c :** excessively fat **:** CORPULENT, PORTLY ⟨a big ~ woman with . . . an enormous bosom —Arnold Hill⟩ **d :** broad in proportion to length — used of an animal or its parts ⟨the vertebrae were ~ with slightly biconcave ends —W.E.Swinton⟩ **e :** of bulky proportions **:** HEAVY, THICK ⟨this ~ volume of over 400 pages —R.J.Cruikshank⟩ **syn** see FAT, STRONG

³stout \"\ *adv* [ME, fr. *stout*, adj.] *archaic* **:** STOUTLY

⁴stout \"\ *vi* -ED/-ING/-S [ME *stouten*, fr. *stout*, adj.] **:** to maintain a resolute or defiant attitude — usu. used in the phrase *to stout it out* ⟨a fool to resign . . . he should have ~*ed* it out —Margaret Todd⟩

⁵stout \"\ *n* -S [²*stout*] **1 :** a heavy-bodied brew that is darker and sweeter than porter and is made with roasted malt and a relatively high percentage of hops **2 a :** a fat person ⟨the genial ~ who sang —Bennett Cerf⟩ **b :** a clothing size designed for the large figure ⟨men's suits are available in longs, shorts, regulars, and ~s —*Women's Wear Daily*⟩

stout·en \ˈstaüt°n\ *vb* **stoutened; stoutened; stoutening** \-aüt(°)niŋ\ **stoutens** [²*stout* + -*en*] *vt* **:** to make stout ⟨~ a resolve⟩ ~ *vi* **:** to become stout ⟨she's ~*ed* so she couldn't make the dress meet on her —Ellen Glasgow⟩

stouth \ˈstüth\ *n* [ME *stulth, stouth*, of Scand origin; akin to ON *stuldr* theft, *stela* to steal — more at STEAL] *Scot & dial Eng* **:** THEFT, ROBBERY

stouth and routh *n, Scot* **:** PLENTY

stouthearted \ˈ‧ˈ‧‧\ *adj* **:** having a stout heart or spirit: **a :** COURAGEOUS, VALIANT ⟨a ~ fellow who sustained the drag and turmoil of an active career in the deserts —Humphrey Bullock⟩ **b :** RECALCITRANT, STUBBORN ⟨hearken unto me, ye ~, that are far from righteousness —Isa 46:12(AV)⟩ — **stoutheart·ed·ly** *adv*

stouthearted·ness *n* -ES **:** the quality or state of being stouthearted

stouth·rief \ˈstüˌthrēf\ *also* **stouth·rife** \-rīf\ *n* [ME (Sc) *stouthreif*, fr. *stouth* + *reif*] *Scot* **:** robbery with violence

stout·ish \ˈstaüd·ish\ *adj* **:** somewhat stout **:** inclined toward corpulence

stout·ly *adv* [ME, fr. *stout* + -*ly*] **:** in a stout manner: **a :** RESOLUTELY, STUBBORNLY ⟨stood ~ for the interests of the colony —J.T.Adams⟩ **b :** SOLIDLY, STRONGLY ⟨the square ordered to be ~ enclosed as protection in case of . . . attack —*Amer. Guide Series: Del.*⟩ **c :** VIGOROUSLY ⟨applauded him ~ after each number —*New Yorker*⟩

stout·ness *n* -ES [ME *stoutnes*, fr. *stout* + -*nes* -ness] **1 a** *obs* **:** PRIDE, ARROGANCE **b** *archaic* **:** OBDURACY **c :** the quality or state of being strong physically or morally **:** FIRMNESS, FORTITUDE **2 :** bulkiness of structure; *esp* **:** CORPULENCE

stouts *pl of* STOUT, *pres 3d sing of* STOUT

¹stove \ˈstōv\ *n* -S *often attrib* [ME, fr. MD or MLG, heated room, steam room; akin to OE *stofa* steam room, OHG *stuba* heated room, steam room, ON *stofa*; all fr. a prehistoric WGmc-NGmc word derived fr. (assumed) VL *extufa*, fr. *extufare* to heat with steam, fr. L *ex-* ¹ex- + (assumed) VL *tufus* steam, fr. Gk *typhos* smoke, steam — more at TYPHUS] **1** *obs* **a :** a steam room or hot air chamber for inducing sweating **:** STEW ⟨you shall sweat there . . . as well as in all the ~s in Sweden —Ben Jonson⟩ **b :** a room heated by a furnace ⟨found him in his ~ with one hand dandling his child . . . in the other holding a book —Thomas Fuller⟩ **2 a :** a portable or fixed apparatus that burns fuel or uses electricity to produce heat (as for cooking or heating) — compare FRANKLIN STOVE, OIL-STOVE, OVEN, POTBELLY, RANGE **b :** a device that generates heat for special purposes (as for heating tools or heating air for a hot blast) — compare CHECKERWORK 3 **c :** KILN **d :** FOOT STOVE **e** *Brit* **:** GRATE **3** *chiefly Brit* **:** a hothouse usu. having a controlled humid atmosphere and used esp. for the cultivation of tropical exotics ⟨orchids requiring ~ conditions⟩; *broadly* **:** GREENHOUSE

²stove \"\ *vt* -ED/-ING/-S **1 a** *archaic* **:** to keep (a person) in a heated room ⟨mistaken medical opinions . . . induced physicians to ~ their patients —Thomas Beddoes⟩ **b :** to subject to heat **:** dry in or as if in a stove ⟨the bars of soap . . . are *stoved* by being placed on shallow trays in stacks in a long rectangular tunnel —T.P.Hilditch⟩ ⟨dirty clay pipes were *stoved* in a brick oven and restored —F.W.Burgess⟩ **2** *chiefly Brit* **:** to raise (plants) in a stove (sense 3) **3** *chiefly Scot* **:** STEW **4 a :** to expose (as damp yarn or cloth to be bleached or clothing to be disinfected) to sulfur dioxide **b :** to treat (a silk cocoon) with heat to kill the chrysalis

³stove *past of* STAVE

⁴stove \ˈstōv\ *vt* -ED/-ING/-S [fr. *stove*, past part. of ²*stave*] **:** STAVE 2

stove bolt *n* **:** a bolt with a round or flat slotted head and a square nut, resembling a machine screw but usu. having coarser threads and used for joining metal parts — see BOLT illustration

stove coal *n* **:** anthracite coal of a medium size but larger than chestnut — see ANTHRACITE table

stove distillate *n* **:** a distilled petroleum oil suitable for use in stoves

stove-in \ˈ‧ˈ‧\ *adj* [fr. past part. of *stave in*, v.] **1 :** smashed inward ⟨a *stove-in* barrel —Cicely F. Smith⟩ **2 :** STOVE-UP ⟨a *stove-in* horse —S.S.Field⟩

stove length *n* **:** a length of firewood suitable for use in a stove

stove lifter *n* **:** LIFTER 2d

¹sto·ven \ˈstōvən\ *n* -S [ME, fr. OE *stofn*; akin to ON *stofn* stump of a tree, *stūfr* stump — more at STUB] *dial Brit* **:** STUMP

²stoven \"\ *adj* [*stove* (past part. of ²*stave*) + -*en* (as in *gotten*)] **:** broken in **:** STAVED, SMASHED

stovepipe \ˈ‧ˌ‧\ *n* **1 :** pipe of large diameter usu. made of sheet steel in lengths and angular or curved pieces and used as a stove chimney or to connect a stove with a flue **2** *or* **stovepipe hat :** a very tall silk hat

stove plant *n* **:** a plant from a warm climate that has to be grown in a greenhouse to survive in temperate climates

stove polish *n* **:** a blacking (as graphite) used for polishing stoves

¹sto·ver \ˈstōvə(r)\ *n* -S [ME, modif. of AF *estovers* — more at ESTOVERS] **1** *dial chiefly Eng* **:** FODDER; *esp* **:** fodder for use in winter **2 :** HAY, STUBBLE; *esp* **:** the refuse of a field crop (as the stalks and leaves of corn after the ears are harvested) used as feed for cattle ⟨corn ~⟩ ⟨sorghum ~⟩ — compare CORN FODDER

²stov·er \"\ *n* -S [²*stove* + -*er*] *chiefly Brit* **:** one that stoves; *esp* **:** a worker who tends a drying stove

stoves *pl of* STOVE, *pres 3d sing of* STOVE

stove-up \ˈ‧ˈ‧\ *adj* [fr. past part. of *stave up*, v.] **:** suffering physical discomfort caused by injury, illness, exercise, or overwork **:** BATTERED, WORN-OUT ⟨horses . . . too old and *stove-up* for saddle work —F.B.Gipson⟩ ⟨several of the men were *stove-up* . . . and even some of the women showed signs of having been kicked or stepped on —H.L.Davis⟩

stovewood \ˈ‧ˌ‧\ *n* **:** wood sawed into stove lengths

¹stow \ˈstō\ *vb* -ED/-ING/-S [ME *stowen*, fr. *stowe*, n., place, fr. OE *stōw*; akin to OFris *stō* place, OHG *stouwen* to complain, accuse, command, ON *eldstō* hearth, Goth *stojan* to judge, Gk *stylos* pillar — more at STEER] *vt* **1 a** *obs* **:** to put in a particular spot **:** PLACE ⟨his eye had ~*ed* her in his heart —William Warner⟩ **b :** to find at least temporary quarters for **:** HOUSE, LODGE ⟨~*ed* the patient in the hospital emergency room⟩ **2** *obs* **:** to put to use **:** BESTOW, SPEND ⟨there ~s his treasure —Edward Young⟩ **3 a :** to put away **:** keep in reserve **:** STORE ⟨small buildings where fishermen ~*ed* their gear —S.T. Williamson⟩ ⟨grabs the sheep and ~s it in the tucker-bag —William Power⟩ — often used with *away* ⟨taking his hat off, and wiping his head with the handkerchief ~*ed* away in its crown —Mary S. Broome⟩ **b** *obs* **:** to lock up for safekeeping **:** CONFINE ⟨the mariners all under hatches ~*ed* —Shak.⟩ **c :** to roll up (a sail) **:** FURL ⟨~ the jib⟩ **4 a :** to dispose in an orderly fashion **:** ARRANGE, PACK ⟨the cargo was ~*ed* in a thoroughly workmanlike . . . manner —F.W.Crofts⟩ ⟨went on ~ing cigarettes on the shelf —David Ballantyne⟩ **b :** to fill with cargo **:** LOAD ⟨six warships . . . ~*ed* to the hatches with scientific gear —Julian Dana⟩ **5** *slang* **:** to put aside **:** save for another time ⟨those . . . not asking questions told those who were to ~ it, and give the lieutenant a chance —Frances & Richard Lockridge⟩ **6 a** *archaic* **:** to fill with contents **:** CROWD ⟨compared his mind to the magazine of a pawnbroker, ~*ed* with goods of every description —Sir Walter Scott⟩ **b :** to cram in (food) — usu. used with *away* ⟨the more of this heavenly food you can ~ away the more you are admired —Hugh Cave⟩ **c :** to fill up (as a stope) with waste ~ *vi* **:** to fit into a storage space **:** PACK, STORE ⟨a stout rope ladder . . . which ~s neatly in a box on the floor —P.W.Kearney⟩ ⟨the anchor ~s at the hawsepipe —A.M.Knight⟩ **syn** see SET

²stow \ˈstü, ˈstaü\ *vt* [origin unknown] *Scot & dial Eng* **:** CUT, CROP, TRIM

³stow *n* -S [by alter.] *obs* **:** STOVE

⁴stow \ˈstō\ *n* -S [by shortening] **:** STOWBORD

stow *abbr* stowage

stowable \ˈstōəbəl\ *adj* **:** capable of being stowed

stow·age \ˈstōij, -ōēj\ *n* -S [ME, fr. *stowen* to stow + -*age*] **1 a :** an act or process of stowing ⟨facilitate the ~ of wine casks —G.S.L.Clowes⟩ **b :** goods in storage or to be stowed ⟨crates and other ~ piled up on the dock⟩ **c :** the manner of stowing ⟨faulty ~ . . . causes a cargo shift —E.B.Garside⟩ **2 a :** storage capacity ⟨she has excellent ~ for food and water —Peter Heaton⟩ **b :** a place or receptacle for storage ⟨a ~ in a London granary containing 500 tons of . . . wheat —R.W. Owen⟩ ⟨booms situated amidships . . . constituted the ~ for spare spars —*Manual of Seamanship*⟩ **3 :** STORAGE ⟨jewels of rich and exquisite form . . . and I am something curious, being strange, to have them in safe ~ —Shak.⟩

stow away *vi* **:** to secrete oneself aboard a vehicle as a means of obtaining transportation ⟨escaped internment by *stowing away* in an automobile trunk —*Newsweek*⟩

stowaway \ˈ‧‧ˌ‧\ *n* -S [*stow away*] **1 :** an unregistered passenger **:** one who stows away ⟨tickets were inspected and three ~s thrown off —John Masters⟩ **2 :** a hiding place ⟨the window-seat top lifts up, and this makes another good ~ for toys —*London Daily Express*⟩

stow·bord *also* **stow·board** \ˈstōˌbōrd\ *n* -S [*stowbord* alter. of *stowboard*; *stowboard* fr. ²*stow* + *board*] **:** a heading used by miners for stowing rubbish or waste

stowce *or* **stowse** \ˈstōs\ *n* -S [origin unknown] *archaic* **:** a windlass for hoisting ore

¹stow·er \ˈstaüə(r)\ *n* -S [ME *sture, store*, of Scand origin; akin to ON *staurr* pole, stake — more at STEER] *dial Brit* **:** POLE, POST; *specif* **:** a punting pole

²stower \"\ *var of* ¹STOUR

³stow·er \ˈstō(ə)r\ *n* -S [¹*stow* + -*er*] **:** one that stows; *esp* **:** STEVEDORE

stown [ME (Sc) *stowin*, alter. of ME *stolen*, fr. OE] *dial chiefly Brit past part of* STEAL

stownet \ˈ‧ˌ‧\ *n* [¹*stow* + *net*] **:** a funnel-shaped sprat trawl usu. made with several sections of different mesh which diminishes in size toward the small end and usu. anchored in a tideway

stowre \ˈstü(ə)r\ *var of* ¹STOUR

stows *pres 3d sing of* STOW, *pl of* STOW

stp *abbr* **1** stamp; stamped **2** stepping **3** stop; stopping

STP *abbr* standard temperature and pressure

stpd *abbr* stumped

str *abbr* **1** seater **2** steamer **3** straight **4** strainer **5** strait **6** stream **7** strength **8** stretch **9** striking **10** string; stringed **11** stroke **12** strophe **13** structural

STR *abbr* submarine thermal reactor

stra·bis·mal \strəˈbizməl\ *adj* [NL *strabismus* + E -*al*] **:** of, relating to, or typical of strabismus — **stra·bis·mal·ly** \-məlē\ *adv*

stra·bis·mic \-mik\ *adj* [NL *strabismus* + E -*ic*] **1 :** STRABISMAL **2 :** failing to perceive clearly or accurately **:** not based on straight clear observation or analysis ⟨a ~ judgment⟩

stra·bis·mom·e·ter \ˌ‧‧ˈmäməd·ə(r)\ *n* [NL *strabismus* + E -*o-* + -*meter*] **:** an instrument for measuring the degree of strabismus

strabis·mom·e·try \-ə·trē\ *n* -ES [NL *strabismus* + E -*o-* + -*metry*] **:** measurement of the degree of strabismus

stra·bis·mus \strəˈbizməs\ *n* -ES [NL, fr. Gk *strabismos* act or condition of squinting, fr. *strabizein* to squint, fr. *strabos* squint-eyed + -*izein* -ize — more at STROPHE] **:** inability of one eye to attain binocular vision with the other because of imbalance of the extrinsic eye muscles — called also *manifest strabismus, squint*; see LATENT STRABISMUS

strad \ˈstrad, -aa(ə)d\ *n* -S *usu cap* [by shortening] **:** STRADIVARIUS

¹strad·dle \ˈstrad°l\ *vb* **straddled; straddled; straddling** \-d(°)liŋ\ **straddles** [irreg. fr. *stride*] *vi* **1 a :** to part the legs wide **:** stand, sit, or walk, with the legs wide apart; *esp* **:** to sit astride **b** *of the legs* **:** to spread apart **2 :** to spread out irregularly **:** SPRAWL ⟨branches *straddled* in every direction⟩ **3 :** to be noncommittal **:** favor or seem to favor two apparently opposite sides **4 :** to buy in one market and sell short in another ~ *vt* **1 :** to stand, sit, or be astride of **2 :** to be noncommittal in regard to **:** favor or seem to favor both sides of ⟨~ an issue⟩ **3 :** to double (the blind) in playing poker **4 a :** to bracket with artillery fire **b :** to land a straddle on — used esp. of a firing ship with respect to a target

²straddle \"\ *n* -s **1 a :** the act or position of one who straddles **:** the act of standing, sitting, or walking, with the legs wide apart **b :** the distance between the feet or legs of one straddling **2 :** something that straddles or suggests straddling (as in sprawling irregular form or bracketing relation): as **a :** a vertical post (as one of those which support a horizontal set in a mine shaft) **b :** a gunnery salvo landing with part of its shots short of the target and part over the target **3 :** a noncommittal or equivocal position; *also* **:** assumption of such a position (as in politics) **4 a :** an option giving the holder the right to demand of the seller that he deliver at a particular price or compel him to accept at the same price within a specified time specified securities or commodities — compare SPREAD **b :** the state of being long in one market and short in another **5 :** a doubling of the blind in a draw poker game

³straddle \"\ *adv* [²*straddle*] **:** ASTRADDLE

straddleback \'==,=\ *adv* **:** ASTRADDLE

straddlebug \'==,=\ *n* **1 :** a long-legged insect (as a tumblebug) **2 :** a wooden tripod used to mark a boundary (as of a mining claim) **3 :** STRADDLE CARRIER

straddle carrier *n* **:** a vehicle that straddles a pile of lumber or other material, lifts it with adjustable arms, and moves it or loads it onto trucks or other vehicles

straddle–face \'==,=\ *vt* **:** to face with a straddle mill

straddle–fashion \'==,==\ *adv* **:** ASTRADDLE

straddle–legged \'==¦legəd, *esp Brit* -gd\ *adv (or adj)* **:** with the legs wide apart **:** astride of something **:** ASTRADDLE

straddle mill *n* **:** a side milling cutter esp. when used in pairs a fixed distance apart so as to straddle the work

strad·dler \'strad(ᵊ)lə(r)\ *n* -s **:** one that straddles: as **a** *Brit* **:** a tool that straddles a railroad rail to bear upon the projecting ends of a tie plate and is used in driving tie plates into the track **b :** a weeding hoe that straddles a row

straddle trench *n* **:** a trench used as a latrine

straddle truck *n* **:** STRADDLE CARRIER

straddle vault *n* **:** a gymnastic vault in which the body passes over the apparatus in a sitting position with the legs spread wide to each side

straddleways \'==,=\ *adv* **:** in a straddling manner

straddlewise \'==,=\ *adv* **:** STRADDLEWAYS

strad·dling·ly *adv* **:** in a straddling manner **:** so as to straddle

strad·i·ot \'stradēət, *usu* -əd.+V\ *n* -s [MF, fr. It *stradiotto;* fr. Gk *stratiōtēs* soldier, fr. *stratia* army, military campaign, fr. *stratos* army, host — more at STRATUM] **:** a light cavalryman recruited esp. from Albania, Dalmatia, or Greece and employed in the Venetian and other armies in the 15th and 16th centuries

stradi·vari \,stradə'värē, ,sträd-, ,stradə'va(a)rē\ *n* -s *usu cap* [after Antonio *Stradivari* †1737 Ital. violin maker] **:** STRADIVARIUS

stradi·vari·us \,stradə'va(a)rēəs, ,strädə'värēəs\ *n* -ES *usu cap* [after Antonius *Stradivarius* (latinization of *Antonio Stradivari*)] **:** a stringed instrument (as a violin) made by Antonio Stradivari of Cremona whose instruments are famed for beauty of tone and design

¹strafe \'strāf *sometimes* -raf *or* -räf\ *vt* -ED/-ING/-s [fr. the G phrase *Gott strafe England* God punish England, popular as a slogan of the Germans in World War I] **1 :** to rake (as ground troops or an airfield) with fire at close range and esp. with machine-gun fire from low-flying airplanes or formerly with artillery fire **2 :** to censure savagely — **straf·er** \-fə(r)\ *n* -s

²strafe \"\ *n* -s **:** a strafing attack

straf·for·di·an \stra'fōrdēən\ *n* -s *usu cap* [Thomas Wentworth, 1st Earl of *Strafford* †1641 Eng. statesman + E *-ian*] **:** a follower of Thomas Wentworth, Earl of Strafford, esp. in the House of Commons in 1641

¹strag·gle \'stragəl, -raig-\ *vb* **straggled; straggled; straggling** \-g(ə)liŋ\ **straggles** [ME *straglen*, perh. irreg. fr. *straken* to move, proceed; akin to OE *streccan* to stretch — more at STRETCH] *vi* **1 :** to wander from the direct course or way **:** ROVE, STRAY; *specif* **:** to wander from a line of march or desert a line of battle **2 :** to wander off or become separated from others of its kind **:** be, become, or occur as if dispersed ⟨branches that ~ out too far⟩ ⟨hair *straggling* over her collar⟩ ~ *vt* **:** to spread scatteringly ⟨shabby houses were *straggled* along the slope⟩

²straggle \"\ *n* -s **:** a straggling body or arrangement (as of persons or objects) ⟨a man . . . with a ~ of a beard —J.C. Snaith⟩ ⟨a ~ of outbuildings⟩ ⟨a little ~ of mourners —Elizabeth Bowen⟩

strag·gler \-g(ə)lə(r)\ *n* -s [¹*straggle* + *-er*] **:** one that rambles without settled direction: as **a** *obs* **:** VAGABOND, TRAMP **b :** one that is separated by wandering off in some irregular manner from others ⟨crop the ~s in the hedge⟩ **c :** one that departs from the company to which he belongs or from the direct or proper course (as a bird that strays out of its usual range) ⟨sent a crew to round up the ~s from the herd⟩ **d** (1) **:** a soldier who wanders from his unit on the march or from the area assigned his unit (2) **:** a man who has been an unauthorized absentee from naval service for more than 72 hours but who has not been absent long enough to have been declared a deserter

straggling *n* -s [fr. gerund of ¹*straggle*] **:** the condition of one that straggles; *esp* **:** a statistical variation in some property (as in range or angle of travel of particles passing through matter)

strag·gling·ly *adv* [*straggling* (pres. part. of ¹*straggle*) + *-ly*] **:** in a straggling manner **:** so as to straggle

strag·gly \-g(ə)lē, -li\ *adj* -ER/-EST [¹*straggle* + *-y*] **:** spread out or scattered irregularly and without planned order **:** arranged as if by straggling into place ⟨a ~ hamlet⟩ ⟨a ~ beard⟩

strag·u·lum \'stragyələm\ *n, pl* **stragu·la** \-lə\ [NL, fr. L, covering, spread; akin to L *sternere* to spread out, strew — more at STREW] **:** the mantle of a bird

¹straight \'strāt, *usu* -ād.+V\ *adv* -ER/-EST [ME *streght, streit,* fr. past part. of *strecchen* to stretch] **:** without deviation, delay, or other interruption: as **a :** in a manner involving no hesitation or delay **:** STRAIGHTWAY, IMMEDIATELY ⟨come ~ home⟩ **b :** in a direct and uninterrupted course **:** without curving or turning aside **:** DIRECTLY ⟨the arrow flew ~ to the mark⟩ ⟨the road ran ~ for several miles⟩; *also* **:** so as to penetrate usu. without deviation from course ⟨bored a hole ~ through the wall⟩ ⟨the tunnel goes ~ through the mountain⟩ **c :** with the body erect **:** UPRIGHT ⟨sentinel pines stood ~ along the crest⟩ **d :** in an honest or honorable manner ⟨a man willing to run ~ should make a success of this business⟩ ⟨swore to go ~ if he got out of the mess⟩ **e :** without hesitation or equivocation **:** STRAIGHTFORWARDLY, OPENLY ⟨~ denied the charge⟩ ⟨told him ~ we'd stand for no more loafing and neglect⟩

²straight \"\ *adj* -ER/-EST [ME *streght, streit, straight,* fr. past part. of *strecchen* to stretch] **1 a :** free from curves, bends, or angles **:** having no irregularities in course ⟨~ hair⟩ ⟨fine ~ timber⟩ ⟨an unusually ~ stream⟩ **b :** of, relating to, or constituting a one-dimensional continuum that is determined throughout its length by any two points included in it **:** taking a course like that of a taut uninterrupted cord made fast at opposite ends **:** progressing or projected in an unvarying direction **2 :** DIRECT, UNINTERRUPTED: as **a** (1) **:** leading or passing directly from one point to another ⟨sought a ~*er* way from his home to the office⟩ (2) **:** holding to a direct or proper course or method **:** proceeding directly and without disorder or confusion ⟨~ reasoning⟩ ⟨a ~ thinker⟩ **b :** CANDID, FRANK, STRAIGHTFORWARD ⟨a ~ speech⟩ ⟨a ~ answer to the charge⟩ **c :** coming directly from a trustworthy source ⟨a ~ tip on the horses⟩ **d :** composed of elements arranged in some logical order (as of descending values) ⟨following the ~ sequence of events⟩ **e :** having the cylinders of an internal-combustion engine arranged in a single straight line **f** *of type matter* **:** set in ordinary paragraphs of uniform width and without display lines, tabular matter, varied typefaces, or other features that tend to slow production **3** *chiefly Scot, of a mountain* **:** STEEP **4 a :** exhibiting no deviation from the vertical or horizontal **:** not leaning, bending, or inclining ⟨the picture is not quite ~⟩ **b** *of a cricket bat* **:** held with blade at right angles to the ground **5 :** exhibiting no deviation from what is established or accepted as usual, normal, or proper: as **a :** conforming to justice and rectitude **:** exhibiting truth, fairness, and honesty **:** UPRIGHT, FAIR, VIRTUOUS ⟨a ~ man of business⟩ ⟨known for his ~ dealing⟩ **b :** properly ordered or arranged **:** free from irregularity or confusion **:** correctly kept **:** CORRECT, NEAT ⟨in the general confusion, this room alone was ~⟩ ⟨his accounts were found to be ~⟩ ⟨set the kitchen ~⟩ **c :** free from extraneous matter **:** UNMIXED, UNDILUTED, UNMODIFIED ⟨played a ~ old rule game⟩ ⟨writes ~ humor⟩ **d :** making no exceptions or deviations in one's support of something accepted as right (as a principle, policy, party) ⟨a ~ Republican⟩; *also* **:** cast for all the regular candidates of a party ⟨a ~ ballot⟩ **e :** having a fixed price for each regardless of the number sold ⟨cigars 10 cents ~⟩ **f** (1) **:** not deviating from the general norm of human personality — used of dramatic representation or performers ⟨a ~ part⟩ ⟨an excellent ~ actor⟩ (2) *of music* **:** played or to be played as written usu. without improvisation or syncopation **g :** STRAIGHT-TIME **6 :** SEVERE, RIGID, STERN, RIGOROUS **7** *of a credit obligation* **a :** made without special security or endorsement **b :** repayable in full on a specified maturity date

³straight \"\ *vt* -ED/-ING/-s [ME *streghten* (Sc *strauchten*), fr. *streght* straight] **1** *obs* **:** STRETCH **2** *chiefly Scot* **:** STRAIGHTEN

⁴straight \"\ *n* -s [²*straight*] **1 :** something that is straight: as **a :** a straight line or arrangement ⟨the garden was laid out on the ~⟩ **b :** a level place, part, or area **:** PLAIN **c :** a straight extent (as of a road) **:** STRAIGHTAWAY; *esp* **:** the portion of a racetrack between the last turn and the winning post **d :** a true, honest, upright report or way of life **:** one involving no concealment, trickery, or dishonesty ⟨tell us the ~ of it⟩ ⟨had been on the ~ for several years⟩ **e :** a shoe adapted for wear on either foot and made with no deviation in the forepart of the foot in relation to the heel **f :** GRAIN 6d **2 a :** a sequence (as of shots, strokes, or moves) resulting in a perfect score in a game or contest **b :** first place at the finish of a horse race **:** WIN — compare PLACE, SHOW **3 :** a combination in a poker hand that consists of five cards in sequence but not all in the same suit and beats three of a kind but loses to a flush — see POKER illustration — **out of straight :** CROOKED, AWRY

straight a *adj, usu cap A* [²*straight* + *a*] **:** having or constituting a first-class record of achievement ⟨a *straight A* student through high school⟩

straight accent *n* **:** MACRON

straight and narrow *n* [prob. fr. ¹*strait;* fr. the admonition of Mt 7:14(AV), "strait is the gate and narrow is the way which leadeth unto life"] **:** the way of propriety and rectitude — used with *the* ⟨kept to the *straight and narrow* for the rest of his life⟩

straight angle *n* [²*straight*] **:** an angle whose sides lie in the same straight line but extend in opposite directions from the vertex **:** one that is equivalent to one half a complete turn, π radians, 180 degrees, or two right angles — compare ROUND ANGLE; see ANGLE illustration

straight arch *n* **:** a flat arch

¹straight–arm \'=,=\ *n* **:** an act or instance of warding off a football tackler with the arm fully extended from the shoulder, elbow locked, and the palm of the hand placed firmly against any part of his body — called also *stiff-arm*

²straight–arm \"\ *vt* **1 :** to ward off (an opponent) with or as if with a straight-arm **2 :** to clear (a passage) by using a straight-arm ~ *vi* **:** to use a straight-arm in warding off an opponent

¹straightaway \'==,=\ *adj* [fr. the phrase *straight away,* fr. ¹*straight* + *away*] **1 a :** moving or projected away and on a straight or direct course ⟨a ~ shot at a low-flying bird⟩ ⟨a ~ bird⟩ ⟨a plane in ~ flight⟩ **b :** acting in one direction ⟨a ~ napper for textiles⟩ **2 :** constituting a straightaway ⟨the longest ~ bar in the hemisphere —Horace Sutton⟩ ⟨a ~ track⟩ **3 a :** constituting or presented in the form of an orderly progression ⟨a ~ story⟩ **b :** free from confusing disorder **:** CLEAR, STRAIGHTFORWARD ⟨written sometimes in ~ English, sometimes in lyrical double-talk —*Time*⟩ **4 :** IMMEDIATE ⟨a ~ gain in income⟩ ⟨made a ~ reply⟩

²straightaway \"\ *n* -s **:** a straight course: as **a :** the straight part of a closed racecourse; *also* **:** a straight track for racing **b :** a straight and unimpeded stretch on a highway or waterway

³straightaway \"\ *adv* **1 :** without hesitation or delay **:** IMMEDIATELY ⟨found an answer ~⟩ **2 :** from a straight position and without anticipatory shifts ⟨a baseball player who hits ~⟩

straight–backed \'=¦=\ *also* **straight–back** \'=¦=\ *adj* **:** having a straight back ⟨a *straight-backed* chair⟩

straight–billed curlew \'=¦=-\ *n* **:** MARBLED GODWIT

straight bill of lading : a nonnegotiable shipping document prescribed by law and consigning goods to a specific party — compare ORDER BILL OF LADING

straightbred \'=¦=\ *adj* **1 :** carrying blood of a single breed, strain, or type ⟨a ~ Angus heifer⟩ — compare CROSSBRED **2 :** descended in all lines from one specified ancestor — compare LINEBRED

straight chain *n* **:** an open chain of atoms having no side chains (as the sequence of carbon atoms in normal butane $CH_3-CH_2-CH_2-CH_3$) — opposed to *branched chain*

straight–cut \'=¦=\ *adj* **:** having the leaves cut lengthwise — used of smoking tobacco

straight dye *n* **:** a dye containing not more than a small amount (as less than 5 percent) of admixed substances excluding salt

straight dynamite *n* **:** DYNAMITE 1b

¹straightedge \'=,=\ *n* [²*straight* + *edge*] **1 :** a bar or piece of wood, metal, or plastic (as a board or rule) having one or more long edges made straight within a desired degree of accuracy and used esp. for testing straight lines and surfaces or drawing straight lines **2 :** STRAIGHT RAZOR

²straightedge \"\ *vt* **:** to make the edge of (work) straight **:** test with a straightedge

straight·en \'strāt³n\ *vb* **straightened; straightened; straightening** \-t(ᵊ)niŋ\ **straightens** [²*straight* + *-en*] *vt* **:** to make straight: as **a :** to alter from a crooked to a straight form **:** cause to become straight or extended ⟨exercise helped to ~ the injured arm⟩ — sometimes used with *out* ⟨~*ed* himself out on the couch⟩ **b :** to make correct **:** put in order — usu. used with *out* or *up* ⟨~ out your accounts⟩ ⟨had to ~ up the house⟩ ⟨the doctor ~*ed* out her trouble⟩ **c :** to put on the correct road or course (as by reforming or explaining) — usu. used with *out* ⟨discipline without love never ~*ed* out anyone⟩ ⟨he misunderstood but a few words should ~ him out⟩ ~ *vi* **:** to become straight: as **a :** to bring the body to an erect position ⟨the wilting flowers ~*ed* in the rain⟩ — usu. used with *up* ⟨~ up, there's no excuse for slouching⟩ **b :** to alter for the better **:** reach a desirable adjustment — usu. used with *out* and sometimes with *up* ⟨determined to ~ up and make something of himself⟩ ⟨these problems tend to ~ out automatically⟩ — **straighten one's face :** to compose one's features **:** assume an aspect of sober concentration

straight·en·er \-t(ᵊ)nə(r)\ *n* -s **:** one that straightens ⟨a hair ~⟩; *esp* **:** one whose work is straightening or making level by hand or by machine

straighter *comparative of* STRAIGHT

straightest *superlative of* STRAIGHT

straight face *n* **:** a face giving no evidence of emotion and esp. of merriment — **straight–faced** \'=¦=\ *adj*

straight flour *n* **:** flour recovered from bolted wheat meal and containing the whole product of milling except bran and shorts

straight flush *n* **:** a poker hand containing five cards of the same suit in sequence and except when there are wild cards being the highest-ranking hand — see ROYAL FLUSH; POKER illustration

straight–flute \'=¦=\ *or* **straight–fluted** \'=¦=\ *adj, of a drill* **:** having straight flutes

straightforth \'=¦=\ *adv, archaic* **:** STRAIGHTFORWARD, STRAIGHTWAY

¹straightforward \'=¦==\ *also* **straightforwards** \(ˈ)=¦==\ *adv* [¹*straight* + *forward, forwards*] **:** in a straightforward manner

²straightforward \"\ *adj* **1 :** proceeding in a straight course or manner **:** leading directly onward **:** DIRECT, UNDEVIATING **2 a :** free from circumlocution or obscurity **:** OUTSPOKEN, CANDID, FRANK, HONEST ⟨a ~ account of the accident⟩ ⟨their behavior was perfectly ~⟩ **b :** accurately defined or definable **:** CLEARCUT, PRECISE ⟨their responsibility is ~⟩ ⟨a case of ~ automatism⟩ — **straight·for·ward·ly** *adv* — **straight·for·ward·ness** *n* -ES

straight–from–the–shoulder \¦==¦==\ *adj* [*straight from the shoulder,* phrase applied to a blow in boxing] **:** characterized by bold vigor of thought and presentation and by freedom from mincing or quibbling ⟨a *straight-from-the-shoulder* analysis of the problem⟩

straight–front \'=¦=\ *adj* **:** having a straight front, edge, border, or other leading part

straight grain *n* **:** grain in wood characterized by wood fibers that run parallel to the long axis of the piece; *also* **:** a graining (as of leather) in which the distinctive elements run in straight lines — **straight–grained** \'=¦=\ *adj*

straighthead \'=,=\ *n* **:** a disease of the rice plant in which the heads remain sterile and therefore erect when normal heads are drooping and which is caused by disturbed water relations

straightheaded \'=¦==\ *adj* [²*straight* + *headed*] **:** SQUARE-HEADED ⟨a ~ window⟩

straight hit *n, chiefly Austral* **:** a fielding position in cricket between long on and long off and usu. near the boundary; *also* **:** a player fielding in this position

straighting *pres part of* STRAIGHT

straight internship *n* **:** a medical internship in which the intern works under supervision in a single department or service ⟨had his *straight internship* in surgery⟩ — compare ROTATING INTERNSHIP

straight·ish \'strād·|ish, -āt|, |ēsh\ *adj* **:** somewhat straight

straightjacket *var of* STRAITJACKET

straight joint *n* **1 :** a continuous floor joint transverse to the length of the boards **2 :** a joint between pieces of wood without tongues, dowels, or other fittings — called also *square joint*

straight–laced *var of* STRAITLACED

straight life annuity *n* **:** an annuity for life **:** LIFE ANNUITY

straight life insurance *n* **:** ORDINARY LIFE INSURANCE

straight line *n* **:** a curve traced by a point traveling invariably in the same direction **:** a one-dimensional continuum of zero curvature **:** the collection of all points whose coordinates satisfy a linear equation in two-dimensional geometry or two simultaneous linear equations in three-dimensional geometry

straight–line \'=¦=\ *adj* **1 :** being a mechanical linkage or equivalent device designed to produce or copy motion in a straight or approximately straight line **2 a :** having the principal parts arranged in a straight line ⟨a *straight-line* compressor having the steam and air cylinders in a straight line⟩ **b :** relating to or constituting a production system with parts or facilities arranged for performance of consecutive operations without backtracking or deviating from a straightforward course ⟨plant layout on a *straight-line* basis⟩ ⟨savings effected by *straight-line* organization⟩ **3 :** spread uniformly or spreading accumulation or payments uniformly and esp. in equal segments over a course covering a given term ⟨*straight-line* amortization of the discount on bonds⟩ ⟨comparison of results from a *straight-line* and a sinking-fund method⟩

straight–lined \'=¦=\ *adj* **:** having straight lines **:** RECTILINEAR, UNDEVIATING; *also* **:** arranged in straight lines

straight–line depreciation *n* **:** periodic reduction in the book value of an asset by a fixed percentage of its original cost based on its estimated life — compare DEPRECIATION CHARGE

straight–line frequency condenser *n* **:** a variable condenser used in a tuned radio circuit in which a given change of setting of the movable plates corresponds to the same change of frequency for all settings

straight–line gale *n* **1 :** a gale of several days' duration blowing over the same region and from the same quarter **2 :** a long streak of violent wind not related to any deflection of isobars

straight–line method *n* **:** a method of calculating periodic depreciation that involves subtraction of the scrap value from the cost of a depreciable asset and division of the resultant figure by the anticipated number of periods of useful life of the asset — compare COMPOUND-INTEREST METHOD

straight–line rate *n* **:** a rate based on a straight price for each unit

straight·ly *adv* [ME, fr. ²*straight* + *-ly*] **:** in a straight manner **:** so as to be straight

straight man *n* **:** an actor or other entertainer whose main function is to feed lines to a comedian

straightneck \'=,=\ *n* **:** a squash of summer crookneck type but having a straight neck

straight·ness *n* -ES **:** the quality or state of being straight

straight–of–breadth \,==ˈ=\ *n* **:** DEAD FLAT

straight off *adv* [¹*straight* + *off*] **:** immediately and without hesitation **:** at once

straight organ *n* **:** a pipe organ containing no borrowed or unified stops

straight out *adv* **:** without concealment or hesitation **:** DIRECTLY ⟨told the whole story *straight out*⟩

¹straight–out \'=,=\ *n* -s [*straight out*] **:** a person who is uncompromising esp. in adhering to a political party or policy

²straight–out \'=¦=\ *adj* [*straight out*] **1 :** acting without concealment, obliquity, or compromise **2 :** being such and no other **:** UNQUALIFIED, THOROUGHGOING ⟨*straight-out* resentment⟩

straight paper *n* [²*straight*] **:** negotiable paper signed or endorsed by one individual

straight peen *n* **:** a narrow round-edged peen of a hammer that is parallel to the handle — see PEEN illustration

straight poker *n* **:** closed poker in which players bet on the five cards dealt to them and then have a showdown without drawing

straight–pull \'=¦=\ *adj, of a firearm* **:** having the motion of the bolt straight forward and back so that the locking and unlocking is effected without rotation ⟨a *straight-pull* rifle⟩

straight rail *n* **:** a carom billiards game in which points are scored by causing the cue ball with or without cushion contact to strike both object balls simultaneously or alternately

straight razor *n* **:** a razor with a rigid steel cutting blade that is hinged to a case which forms a handle when the razor is open for use — see RAZOR illustration

straight–run \'=¦=\ *adj* **1 :** involving or produced in the course of petroleum refining by fractionation essentially without cracking or other pyrolytic change ⟨*straight-run* distillation⟩ ⟨*straight-run* gasoline⟩ **2** *of chicks* **:** being sold as hatched; *specif* **:** not sexed

straights *pres 3d sing of* STRAIGHT, *pl of* STRAIGHT

straight shooter *n* [¹*straight*] **:** a thoroughly upright straightforward person

straight–side \'=¦=\ *or* **straight–sided** \'=¦==\ *adj* [²*straight*] **:** having straight sides

straight sinus *n* **:** a venous sinus of the brain formed by junction of the great cerebral vein and inferior sagittal sinus and terminating by confluence with the right and left transverse sinuses

straight ticket *n* **:** a ballot cast for all the candidates of one party — compare SPLIT TICKET

straight time *n* **1 :** the regularly established working time of employees during a standard period (as a week) excluding time lost through absence or gained through overtime ⟨in most industries *straight time* still exceeds 35 hours a week⟩ **2 :** the rate of pay applicable for straight-time work ⟨had 40 hours at *straight time* and 12 hours of overtime pay⟩

straight–time \'=¦=\ *adj* [*straight time*] **1 :** constituting or taking place in straight time ⟨*straight-time* work⟩ ⟨40 *straight-time* hours⟩ **2 :** constituting or fixed at a regular base rate per hour, day, week, or month and excluding any overtime pay, merit bonus, shift differential, or commission ⟨a two dollar an hour *straight-time* rate⟩ ⟨*straight-time* pay⟩

straight–up \'=¦=\ *adj* [fr. the phrase *straight up,* fr. ¹*straight* + *up*] **1 :** ERECT, UPRIGHT, PERPENDICULAR ⟨lilies nodding from tall *straight-up* stalks⟩ **2 :** timed exactly **:** being or ending at precisely the time stated or desired ⟨*straight-up* noon⟩

¹straightway \'=¦=\ *adv* [ME *streght way,* fr. *streght* straight + *way*] **1 :** in a direct course **:** DIRECTLY ⟨his ashes invariably fell . . . either ~ or down one of the letter pages —J.D.Salinger⟩ **2 :** without delay or hesitation **:** FORTHWITH ⟨fell ~ to gambling⟩ ⟨~ the clouds began to drift apart⟩

²straightway \"\ *adj* [²*straight* + *way*] **:** having or affording a straight way; *esp* **:** allowing something (as a fluid) to pass directly ⟨~ valve⟩ ⟨~ flues⟩

straightway drill *n* **:** a straight-flute drill

straightway pump *n* **:** a pump with suction valves below and discharge valves above the plunger so arranged as to provide a straightaway flow of the fluid pumped

straightways \'ˌ=ˌ=\ *adv* [²*straight* + *-ways*] *archaic* **:** STRAIGHTWAY

straight whiskey *n* **:** pure unadulterated grain whiskey matured in new charred white oak barrels and being between 80 and 110 proof

straik \'strāk\ *chiefly Scot var of* STROKE

¹**strain** \'strān\ *n* -S [ME *streen, strene,* fr. OE *strēon, strīon* treasure, acquisition, procreation, progeny; akin to OE *strīenan* to gain, OHG *striunan* to gain, *gistriuni* gain, L *strues* heap — more at STRUCTURE] **1 a** *archaic* **:** OFFSPRING, CHILDREN **b :** a line descended or derived from a particular ancestral individual **:** PROGENY, DESCENDANTS ⟨the weakness of this royal ~ increased from generation to generation⟩; *also* **:** LINEAGE, ANCESTRY ⟨came of a sturdy peasant ~⟩ **c :** a selected group of organisms sharing or presumed to share a common ancestry and usu. lacking clear-cut morphological distinctions from related forms but having distinguishing physiological qualities (as high drought resistance in a plant, superior milk production in cattle, or increased virulence in a microorganism) ⟨a high-yielding ~ of winter wheat⟩; *broadly* **:** a specified infraspecific group (as a stock, line, or ecotype) **d :** a class of persons or things **:** KIND, SORT ⟨discussions of the highest ~⟩ **2 a :** inherited or inherent character, quality, or disposition ⟨may this valiant ~ remain a part of our national heritage⟩ **b :** a tendency or quality that is inherent though often incongruous as if inherited intact **:** TRACE, STREAK ⟨a ~ of madness in the family⟩ ⟨his character is marred by a ~ of fanaticism⟩ **3 a :** a period or other well defined short subdivision of a musical composition or movement; *often* **:** TUNE, AIR **b :** a distinct portion of an ode or other poem; *also* **:** a passage of verbal or musical expression **c :** a stream or outburst of forceful, vigorous, or impassioned speech **4 a :** the tenor, pervading note, burden, tone, manner, style, of an utterance (as a song, poem, speech, book) or of a course of action or conduct ⟨he spoke in a noble ~⟩ ⟨there was a ~ of woe in his story⟩ **b :** MOOD, TEMPER ⟨in a philosophizing ~⟩ **syn** see VARIETY

²**strain** \"\ *vb* -ED/-ING/-S [ME *streinen, strainen,* fr. MF *estreindre, estraindre,* fr. L *stringere* to bind tight, press together; akin to Gk *strang-, stranx* drop squeezed out, *strangos* twisted, flowing drop by drop, *strangalē* halter, MIr *srengim* I draw] *vt* **1 a :** to draw tight **:** cause to clasp firmly ⟨the bandage should be ~*ed* tightly over the scalded surface to minimize blistering⟩ **b :** to stretch to maximum extension and tautness ⟨the wire must be ~*ed* into position if the fence is to be firm and erect⟩ ⟨~ a canvas over a frame⟩ **2 a :** to exert (as oneself) to the utmost **:** put to great stress or effort **:** use or cause to function with extreme vigor ⟨~*ing* himself to a final burst of speed⟩ ⟨~*ed* her ear at the keyhole⟩ **b :** to injure (as oneself or a body part) by overuse or misuse ⟨~*ed* his heart by overwork⟩ ⟨~*ed* herself moving the piano⟩ — compare SPRAIN **c :** to injure by making too great a demand on or by exposure to excessive tension or other force ⟨the storm ~*ed* the timbers of the ship⟩ **d :** to cause a change of form or size in (a body) by application of external force **3 :** to squeeze or clasp tightly: as **a :** to press closely in one's arms **:** HUG — usu. used in the phrase *strain to one's breast* **b :** to compress painfully or harmfully **:** CONSTRICT **c** *obs* **:** to exert pressure upon so as to cause distress **:** AFFLICT **d** (1) **:** to take firmly in one's hand or grip ⟨~*ing* his hand in tearful farewell⟩ ⟨~*ed* her tense hands together⟩ (2) *obs* **:** to seize (prey) with the claws (3) *obs* **:** to grasp firmly and wield or brandish (a weapon) **4 a :** to cause to pass through a strainer or other separatory device (as a filter, cloth, or porous body) usu. by pressure, suction, or the force of gravity ⟨~ the gravy free from lumps⟩ **b :** to remove by straining — usu. used with *out* ⟨~ the lumps out of the gravy⟩ **5 a :** to stretch beyond its proper limit **:** do violence to in respect to intent or meaning ⟨a very ~*ed* interpretation of the passage⟩ ⟨the interests of justice are rarely served by ~*ing* the law⟩ **b :** to tax unduly ⟨it would ~ anyone's conscience to agree⟩ **6** *obs* **a :** to urge (as a request) with importunity **:** PRESS **b :** to squeeze out **:** EXTORT **7 :** to raise to a high degree, pitch, or emotional state ~ *vi* **1 a :** to make violent efforts **:** stretch or extend to a maximum in coping with an exerting or difficult task **:** STRIVE ⟨muscles ~*ing* to raise the stone⟩ ⟨his eyes ~ to catch a glimpse of the sea⟩ **b :** to sustain a strain, wrench, or distortion usu. in effecting an effort or resisting a force ⟨ships ~*ing* at their anchors⟩ **c :** to make a vigorous effort to eject something usu. from the body: as (1) **:** to retch in attempting to vomit (2) **:** to contract the muscles forcefully in attempting to defecate — often used in the phrase *strain at stool* **2 a :** to pass through a strainer or other separatory device **:** become filtered ⟨the liquid ~*s* readily⟩ **b :** to pass through something easily as if through a strainer **:** TRICKLE ⟨water ~*ing* through sandy soil⟩ **c :** to pass from something as if being separated with a strainer **:** OOZE, EXUDE ⟨muddy water ~*ed* from her hair⟩ ⟨juice ~*ing* from the overripe fruits⟩ **3 a :** to make great difficulty or resistance **:** BALK ⟨a horse ~*ing* at the lead⟩ ⟨ye blind guides, which ~ at a gnat, and swallow a camel —Mt 23:24 (AV)⟩ **b :** to take exception **:** SCRUPLE — usu. used with *at* ⟨anyone would ~ at such an interpretation⟩ **syn** see DEMUR — **strain a point :** to go beyond a usual, accepted, or proper limit or rule **:** stretch one's conscience or authority usu. because of exceptional circumstances ⟨willing to *strain a point* because of his excellent record⟩ — **strain courtesy** *archaic* **:** to be excessively or unnecessarily punctilious in the minutiae of courtesy **:** use an excess of civility

³**strain** \"\ *n* -S **1 :** an act of straining or the condition of being strained: as **a :** excessive physical or mental tension ⟨subject to severe ~ in action⟩; *also* **:** a force, influence, or factor causing such tension ⟨the wind pressure was a ~ on the ship's rigging⟩ ⟨her responsibilities were a constant ~⟩ **b :** excessive or difficult exertion or labor **:** a violent or overtaxing effort ⟨gave a great ~ and heaved the load aboard⟩ **c :** a hurt or injury of a body part or organ resulting or such as results from excessive tension, effort, or use ⟨suffered from heart ~⟩; *usu* **:** an injury resulting from a wrench or twist and involving overstretching of muscles or ligaments ⟨foot ~⟩ ⟨back ~⟩ — compare SPRAIN **d :** deformation of a material body and esp. of an elastic solid under the action of applied forces **2 :** something reachable only by straining **:** an unusual reach, degree, height, or intensity **:** PITCH ⟨a ~ of excitement quite beyond my reach⟩ **3** *archaic* **:** a misconstruction obtained by stretching a meaning (as of a word or passage) **:** a strained interpretation of something said or written **4** *obs* **:** the track or hoofmarks of a deer **syn** see STRESS

strain·able \'strānəbəl\ *adj* **:** capable of being strained — **strain·able·ness** \-bəlnəs\ *n* -ES — **strain·ably** \-blē\ *adv*

strain band *n* [³*strain*] **:** a reinforcing band of canvas on a sail

strain diagram *or* **strain sheet** *n* **:** STRESS SHEET

strained \'strānd\ *adj* [fr. past part. of ²*strain*] **1 :** subjected to great or excessive tension **:** WRENCHED, WEAKENED ⟨~ relations⟩ **2 :** done or produced with straining or excessive effort **:** FORCED ⟨~ wit⟩ **3 :** made uniform by or as if by passage through a strainer **4 :** distorted in sense **:** forced beyond what is reasonable or equitable — **strained·ly** \-n(ə)dlē, -li\ *adv* — **strained·ness** \-nədnəs, -n(d)nəs\ *n* -ES

strain·er \'strānə(r)\ *n* -S **1 :** one that strains something through or out: as **a :** a utensil or device (as a screen, sieve, or filter) to retain or hold back solid pieces or particles while a liquid passes through — compare COLANDER **b :** a worker that strains paper-coating mixtures to smooth and clean them **c :** an operator of a mill for breaking up devulcanized scrap rubber and removing the cord and fabric **2 :** any of various devices for stretching or tightening something ⟨a fence ~⟩: as **a :** a small rod with ends sharpened and bent at right angles used in basketry to keep a stake in position **b :** a reinforcement (as a strip of wood or a piece of glued canvas) for the back of a carriage panel

strainer 1a

strain gage *n* [³*strain*] **:** EXTENSOMETER

straining *pres part of* STRAIN

straining arch *or* **strainer arch** *n* [*straining arch* fr. *straining* (pres. part. of ²*strain*) + *arch; strainer arch* fr. *strainer* + *arch*] **:** a construction (as a flying buttress) that suggests an arch and is designed to resist end thrust

straining beam *or* **straining piece** *n* **:** a short piece of timber in a truss used to hold in place the ends of struts or rafters

strain·ing·ly *adv* [*straining* + *-ly*] **:** in a straining manner **:** so as to strain or produce a strain

straining sill *n* **:** a straining beam on the tie beam of a truss to resist at each end the foot of a diagonal strut

strain insulator *n* [³*strain*] **:** a strong electrical insulator used to insulate a wire in tension

strain·less \'=ˌləs\ *adj* [³*strain* + *-less*] **1 :** free from strain or straining tension **2** *of a ring in a chemical compound* **:** characterized by bond angles in the structure that are approximately the same as those in comparable acyclic compounds ⟨~ 5- and 6-membered rings in natural organic products⟩ — compare BOAT FORM, CHAIR FORM; BAEYER STRAIN THEORY — **strain·less·ly** *adv*

strain·om·e·ter \strā'nämәd·ә(r)\ *n* [³*strain* + *-o-* + *meter*] **:** EXTENSOMETER

strains *pl of* STRAIN, *pres 3d sing of* STRAIN

strain shadows *n pl* **:** inhomogeneity of interference colors as seen with a polarizing microscope in a crystal that has been deformed

strainslip \'=ˌ=\ *n* **:** fracturing in rock accompanied by slight displacement **:** geologic faulting on a minute scale

strain theory *n* [³*strain*] **:** a theory in chemistry that accounts for strain in the structure of molecules; *esp* **:** BAEYER STRAIN THEORY

¹**strait** \'strāt, *usu* -ād·+V\ *adj* -ER/-EST [ME *streit, strait, straight,* fr. OF *estreit,* fr. L *strictus,* fr. past part. of *stringere* to bind tight, press together — more at STRAIN] **1** *archaic* **a :** giving little room **:** not broad **:** NARROW ⟨~ is the gate, and narrow is the way, which leadeth unto life and few there be that find it —Mt 7:14 (AV)⟩ **b :** limited in space or time **:** RESTRICTED **c :** closely fitting **:** tightly drawn **:** CONSTRICTED, TIGHT, CLOSE **2** *archaic* **:** STRICT, RIGOROUS, EXACTING ⟨the ~*est* sect of our religion —Acts 26:5 (ASV)⟩ **3 a** *obs* **:** DEFINITE, EXACT **b** *chiefly dial* **:** strictly limited as to meaning or application **4 :** INTIMATE, FAMILIAR ⟨a ~ alliance⟩ **5 a :** DISTRESSFUL, DIFFICULT **b :** limited as to means or resources **:** STRAITENED **6** *obs* **a :** PARSIMONIOUS, MEAN, STINGY **b :** inadequate through scantiness of dimensions **syn** see NARROW

²**strait** \"\ *adv* [ME *streit,* fr. *streit,* adj.] **:** STRAITLY: as **a** *obs* **:** TIGHTLY; *also* **:** STINGILY **b** *obs* **:** SECURELY **c :** in a manner likely to cause hardship **:** OPPRESSIVELY **d** *obs* **:** STRICTLY, PRECISELY

³**strait** \"\ *n* -S [ME *streit, strait,* fr. *streit, strait,* adj.] **1 a** *archaic* **:** a narrow space or passage **b :** a comparatively narrow passageway connecting two large bodies of water ⟨the *Strait* of Gibraltar⟩ — often used in pl. **c :** a neck of land **d** *obs* **:** RAVINE, GORGE **2 straits** *pl, obs* **:** cloth of single width **3 :** a condition of distressing narrowness or restriction **:** a situation of perplexity or distress **:** DIFFICULTY, NEED — often used in pl. ⟨reduced to pitiful ~*s*⟩ ⟨in dire ~*s*⟩ **syn** see JUNCTURE

⁴**strait** \"\ *archaic var of* STRAIGHT

strait-bodied \'=ˌ=ˌ=\ *adj* [¹*strait* + *bodied*] *of a fitted garment* **:** made with stays

strait·en \'strāt°n\ *vb* **straitened; straitened; straitening** \-t(°)niŋ\ **straitens** [¹*strait* + *-en*] *vt* **1 a :** to make strait or narrow ⟨~*ed* the bed of the river with high embankments⟩ **b :** to hem in or confine usu. in a narrow space ⟨the arable land was ~*ed* between the mountains and the sea⟩ **2 a** *archaic* **:** to restrict (a person) usu. in respect to freedom or rights **b :** to make narrow in respect to scope, range, or similar property ⟨the decision of the court ~*ed* the range of his authority⟩ ⟨such experiences . . . ~ the mind —Osbert Sitwell⟩ **3 a :** to afflict physically or mentally **:** subject to distress, want, or anguish ⟨a man ~*ed* by misfortune⟩ **b :** to afflict or distress by reason of some deficiency — usu. used with *for* or *in* ⟨I am rather ~*ed* in time —William Cowper⟩ **c :** to cause to suffer or ebb by reason of insufficient funds **:** reduce (as oneself) to poverty ⟨~*ing* himself to keep up appearances⟩ ⟨old people living in ~*ed* circumstances⟩ **4** *obs* **a :** to make tense or tight **:** TIGHTEN **b :** to make more severe **:** increase the rigor of ~ *vi* **:** to become narrow **:** NARROW

¹**straitjacket** *or* **straightjacket** \'=ˌ=ˌ=\ *n* [¹*strait* + *jacket*] **1 :** a cover or overgarment of strong material (as canvas) used to bind the body and esp. the arms closely in restraining violent motion of an irresponsible person (as one that is insane) **2 :** something that restricts or confines like a straitjacket ⟨escape the ~ of a one-crop economy —D.L.Cohn⟩

²**straitjacket** *or* **straightjacket** \"\ *vt* **:** to confine in or as if in a straitjacket ⟨society ~*ed* and enslaved the organic impulses —C.I.Glicksberg⟩

straitlace \'=ˌ=\ *vt* [back-formation fr. *straitlaced*] **:** to bind tightly with or as if with laces **:** CONFINE, RESTRAIN

straitlaced *or* **straightlaced** \'=ˌ=\ *adj* [²*strait* + *laced*] **1 :** wearing or having a bodice or stays tightly laced **2 a** *obs* **:** stubbornly or rigidly self-contained and uncommunicative **:** STIFF, CONSTRAINED **b :** notably and usu. excessively strict in manners, morals, or opinion (as on matters of religion or propriety) **:** intensely or unreasonably scrupulous — **strait·laced·ly** \-stlē, -sədlē\ *adv* — **strait·laced·ness** \-stnəs, -sədn-\ *n* -ES

strait·ly *adv* [ME *streitly,* fr. *streit* strait + *-ly*] **:** in a strait manner **:** STRICTLY, NARROWLY

strait·ness *n* -ES [ME *streitnesse,* fr. *streit* strait + *-nesse* -ness] **:** the quality or state of being strait

straits dollar \'strāts-\ *n, usu cap S* [fr. *Straits* Settlements, former British crown colony on the Strait of Malacca] **:** a dollar formerly issued by British Malaya and used in much of southern and eastern Asia and the East Indies

straits·man \'strātsmən\ *n, pl* **straitsmen** \"\ [fr. the *Straits,* name used formerly to designate the Strait of Malacca, or Bass strait, Australia] **1 :** a ship equipped and suited for service in and about the Strait of Malacca **2** *usu cap* **:** a native or resident of Australia in the vicinity of Bass strait

straits tin *n, usu cap S* [fr. *the Straits*] **:** tin from the Malay peninsula constituting a market standard for high-quality tin

strait-waistcoat \'=ˌ(ˌ)=ˌ=\ *n, chiefly Brit* **:** STRAITJACKET

straitwork \'=ˌ=\ *n* [¹*strait*] *Brit* **:** mining by the bord-and-pillar system

¹**strake** \'strāk\ *n* -S [ME; akin to OE *streccan* to stretch — more at STRETCH] **1 a :** an iron band made up of separate pieces by which the fellies of a wheel are secured to each other; *also* **:** one of the pieces making up such a band **b** (1) **:** a continuous band of hull planking or plates on a ship — see SHIP illustration (2) **:** the width of such a band **c :** one of the rings forming the shell of a steam boiler **d :** a run of clapboarding along the side of a house **2 a :** a striped marking usu. of a distinctive color from that with which it is associated **:** STREAK **b :** a narrow strip or stretch (as of land or mown grass)

²**strake** \"\ *vb* -ED/-ING/-S **:** STREAK

³**strake** \"\ *chiefly dial var of* STROKE

⁴**strake** [ME (northern dial.) *strake* (past), fr. OE *strāc* (past)] *obs var of* STRUCK

straked *adj* [¹*strake* + *-ed*] **:** having or equipped with strakes

stramash \'straməsh, strə'mash\ *n* -ES [prob. imit.] **1** *chiefly Scot* **a :** DISTURBANCE, COMMOTION, RACKET ⟨a terrible ~ to make about a wee lapse —J.D.Scott b. 1917⟩ **b :** BROIL, BRAWL ⟨provoked not a few ~*es* by asking . . . why they did not go back to their banks and braes —Wilson Neill⟩ **2** *chiefly Scot* **:** CRASH, SMASHUP ⟨a wild ~ into the other car —G.B. Shaw⟩

stramazon *n* -S [It *stramazzone,* fr. *stramazzare* to knock down, fr. *stramazzo* mat, mattress, fr. *strame* straw, litter, fr. L *stramin-, stramen*] *obs* **:** a descending cut or slash with the extreme edge of a sword delivered from the wrist

stra·min·eous \strə'minēəs\ *adj* [L *stramineus* of straw, fr. *stramin-, stramen* straw, litter, fr. *sternere* to strew, spread out, lay flat — more at STREW] **1** *archaic* **a :** consisting of straw **b :** of the nature of or resembling straw; *specif* **:** VALUELESS **2 :** STRAW-COLORED

stram·mel \'straməl\ *n* [prob. of F origin; akin to F dial. *étramiller* to scatter straw, fr. MF *estramer,* fr. OF *estraim* straw, fr. L *stramin-, stramen*] *chiefly Scot* **:** STRAW

stra·mo·ni·um \strə'mōnēəm\ *n* -S [NL] **1 :** THORN APPLE 2 **2 :** the dried leaf of the thorn apple that is used in medicine similarly to belladonna esp. in asthma and contains the alkaloids atropine, hyoscyamine, and scopolamine

stramp \'stramp\ *vb* -ED/-ING/-S [prob. blend of *stamp* and *tramp*] **1** *Scot & dial Eng* **:** STAMP **2** *Scot & dial Eng* **:** TRAMPLE

¹**strand** \'strand, -aa(ə)nd\ *n* -S [ME *strand, strond,* fr. OE *strand;* akin to MLG & MD *strant* shore, beach, ON *strönd* border, edge, seashore, L *sternere* to spread out — more at STREW] **1 :** the land bordering a body of water **:** SHORE: as **a** (1) **:** the beach of the ocean, a sea, or an arm of the ocean (2) **:** the land alternately covered and uncovered by the tide **b :** the bank of a stream **2** *obs* **:** WHARF, QUAY **3** *archaic* **:** a faraway region

²**strand** *vb* -ED/-ING/-S *vt* **1 a :** to run, drive, or cause to drift onto a strand **:** run aground **:** BEACH ⟨pearly nautilus shells . . . have been found ~*ed* . . . far south —Joyce Allan⟩ ⟨left our boats ~*ed* —William Beebe⟩ **b :** to leave behind by or as if by the receding of water ⟨the cave suddenly drained off and ~*ed* the fish —*Amer. Guide Series: Tenn.*⟩ ⟨the skull . . . which the hurricane had left ~*ed* in the fork of a big water oak —W.F. Davis⟩ **2 :** to place in an unfavorable position **:** leave without means of coping with the surroundings ⟨when a wild and open land becomes . . . settled, certain men will be ~*ed* in the new, restricting, and alien environment —Francis Ratcliffe⟩; *specif* **:** to leave in an alien town or country without funds or means to depart ⟨he returned . . . almost penniless after paying his railroad fare from the . . . town where the company had been ~*ed* —*Current Biog.*⟩ ~ *vi* **:** to become stranded **:** become propelled onto a shore ⟨the ship ~*ed* at length on the island —Isobel Hutchison⟩

³**strand** \"\ *n* -S [ME *strand, strond, strund,* perh. fr. ¹*strand*] **1** *Scot & dial Eng* **a :** STREAM, CURRENT **b :** SEA **2** *Scot & dial Eng* **:** CHANNEL, GUTTER

⁴**strand** \"\ *n* -S [ME *strond,* of unknown origin] **1 a** (1) **:** fibers or filaments twisted, plaited, or laid parallel to form a unit for further twisting or plaiting into yarn, thread, rope, or cordage **:** one of the components of a plied yarn, thread, or rope ⟨6-*strand* embroidery floss⟩ (2) **:** one of the wires twisted together or laid parallel to form a wire rope or cable or an electrical conductor **b :** a thread, yarn, string, rope, wire, or cable esp. when of suitable length, strength, or construction for a particular purpose ⟨miles of open downland without a ~ of barbed wire —Anthony West⟩ ⟨the tug pulls, tightening the steel ~ —C.G.Bell⟩ **2 :** an element (as a yarn, thread, filament, or reed) of a woven or plaited material **3 :** an elongated or twisted and plaited body resembling a rope ⟨a ~ of pearls⟩ ⟨wet ~*s* of hair were plastered on her cheek —Sheila Kaye-Smith⟩ **4 :** a continuous patterned or structured whole forming a unity within a complex organization or activity ⟨several ~*s* of melody are heard at once —Robert Donington⟩ ⟨the wife comes back . . . to pick up the ~*s* of married life again —C.A.Lejeune⟩ **5** *South* **:** a pile of wood 8 feet by 4 feet by from 12 inches to 24 or 30 inches

⁵**strand** \"\ *vt* -ED/-ING/-S **1 :** to break a strand of (a rope) accidentally **2 a :** to form (as a rope) from strands **b :** to play out, twist, or arrange in a strand ⟨six pairs of copper wires insulated with polyethylene are ~*ed* around a steel core —*Annual Report of Amer. Tel. & Tel. Co.*⟩ ⟨fourteen hundred feet of . . . hose were ~*ed* from the catch basin over the hill to the reservoir —*Fyr-Fyter News*⟩ **3 a :** to lay a thread along an edge of (as a buttonhole) as a foundation for buttonholing **b :** to carry (an attached yarn) along the back in knitting having colored designs

strand·er \-də(r)\ *n* -S [⁵*strand* + *-er*] **1 :** a machine that makes strands into cable or rope **2 :** a steelworker who guides bars by the use of hand tongs from the roughing mill into other rolls for further processing — called also *edger, poke-in, pony rougher, stick-in*

strand fishery *n* [¹*strand*] **:** a fishery pursued from the shore rather than a boat

strandflat \'=ˌ=\ *n* **:** a wave-cut platform **:** an elevated wave-cut terrace

stranding *n* -S [fr. gerund of ²*strand*] **:** the running aground of a ship upon a strand, rock, or bottom so that it is fast for a time esp. when such a running aground is accidental or done to avoid a worse impending danger (as a sinking)

strand·less \'=ˌləs\ *adj* [¹*strand* + *-less*] **:** having no shore ⟨a ~ expanse of water⟩

strandline \'=ˌ=\ *n* **:** SHORELINE, BEACH; *often* **:** a shoreline above the present water level

strand·loop·er \'strand,lüpər\ *n* -S *usu cap* [Afrik, fr. *strand* shore (fr. MD *strant*) + *looper* runner, fr. MD *loper,* fr. *lopen* to run + *-er* — more at STRAND, LEAP] **1 :** one of a late prehistoric coastal race of southern Africa possibly related to both Bushman and Hottentot **2 :** a coast-dwelling Bushman

strand·man \'=ˌmən\ *n, pl* **strandmen** [⁵*strand*] **:** an operator of a machine for bending and cutting wire

strand mole *n* **:** MOLE RAT c

strand plover *n* [¹*strand*] *Brit* **:** BLACK-BELLIED PLOVER

strands *pl of* STRAND, *pres 3d sing of* STRAND

strand wolf *n* **:** BROWN HYENA

¹**strang** \'straŋ\ *dial var of* STRONG

²**strang** *dial past of* STRING

¹**strange** \'strānj\ *adj* -ER/-EST [ME, fr. OF *estrange,* fr. L *extraneus* external, foreign, strange, fr. *extra* outside — more at EXTRA-] **1 a :** of, relating to, coming from, characteristic of, or being a different country, region, or town **:** FOREIGN, ALIEN ⟨the immigrant press came . . . under surveillance . . . because of the ~ tongues in which most were published —Oscar Handlin⟩ **b :** not native to or naturally belonging in a place, body, or person **:** of external origin, kind, or character ⟨something ~ had been inhaled —*X-rays & You*⟩ **c :** belonging to or characteristic of an alien people or group ⟨lacked sympathy for ~ customs —Agnes Repplier⟩ ⟨there shall be no ~ gods among you —Ps 81:9 (RSV)⟩ **2 a :** not before known, heard, or seen **:** NEW, UNFAMILIAR ⟨the name . . . though it was ~ to me, was well known to some there —R.L.Stevenson⟩ ⟨sent to the front . . . to join a ~ outfit under enemy fire —Gordon Harrison⟩ **b** (1) **:** exciting attention, curiosity, surprise, wonder, or awe because of novelty, eccentricity, or exceptional greatness, power, or attributes **:** out of the ordinary **:** strikingly uncommon or unnatural **:** UNUSUAL, EXTRAORDINARY, EXCEPTIONAL ⟨a ~ world indeed, replete with . . . even more weird inhabitants —F.G.Slaughter⟩ ⟨resorts to ~ shapes, odd forms without beauty —E.M.Bridge⟩ ⟨a ~ exaltation that was indefinable —Liam O'Flaherty⟩ (2) **:** difficult to comprehend or believe **:** UNACCOUNTABLE ⟨it's ~, the queer sort of people who win the lotteries —Ruth Park⟩ ⟨a ~ petulance that runs through the writings of the social engineers —W.H. Whyte⟩ **3 :** discouraging familiarities **:** RESERVED, DISTANT, COLD ⟨why did you break off our confidences and become quite ~ to me —G.B.Shaw⟩ **4 :** lacking skill, experience, knowledge, or acquaintance **:** UNACCUSTOMED, UNVERSED ⟨I know thee well; but in thy fortunes am unlearn'd and ~ —Shak.⟩

syn SINGULAR, UNIQUE, PECULIAR, ECCENTRIC, ERRATIC, ODD, QUEER, QUAINT, OUTLANDISH, CURIOUS: STRANGE, a rather general term, applies to the foreign, unnatural, inexplicable, or new or to anything unfamiliar that defies a ready explanation or commands attention by its novelty ⟨the headlands, snow-crowned, take on an icy glaze that sharpens their *strange* silhouettes —*Amer. Guide Series: Maine*⟩ ⟨a *strange* story of a mountain in Numidia which was inhabited by a commonwealth of cats —Agnes Repplier⟩ ⟨a *strange* sort of love, to be entirely free from that quality of selfishness which is frequently the chief constituent of the passion —Thomas Hardy⟩ SINGULAR may suggest individual strangeness of or as if of something unusual or notably different from others of its group; it may be a close synonym of STRANGE ⟨by the *singular* magic of his personality —Osbert Sitwell⟩ ⟨the taxi driver had lugged the parcel into the terminal for the woman, and then — proving himself a *singular* example of his species — had broken a ten-dollar bill for her when it developed that the clerk had insufficient change —E.J.Kahn⟩ ⟨*singular* that a woman of that age should flush so readily —W.S.Maugham⟩ UNIQUE may describe that which is singular (or individual) and unparalleled ⟨a privilege *unique* not only in the British Army but I believe in any army there has ever been —J.S.Bradford⟩ ⟨the *unique* task of setting up an observation post directly at the South Pole —Walter Sullivan⟩ ⟨a glass conservatory full of tropical blossoms of quite *unique* and almost monstrous beauty —G.K. Chesterton⟩ PECULIAR describes anything markedly different, unusual, or puzzling; it is sometimes a close synonym of the terms following ⟨she had put herself in a *peculiar* light, namely, that of agreeing to marry when she was already supposedly married —Theodore Dreiser⟩ ⟨the *peculiar* individuals are those whose behavior is odd and somewhat unpredictable —Carney Landis & Mary Bolles⟩ ECCENTRIC implies a noticeably unusual deviation from the usual, normal, or established ⟨what sort of burglars are they who steal silver, and then throw it into the nearest pond — it was certainly rather *eccentric* behavior —A. Conan Doyle⟩ ⟨this architectural curiosity was erected in 1815 by an *eccentric* Irishman —*Amer. Guide Series: Va.*⟩ ERRATIC may suggest a wandering or deviating, sometimes capricious, from the accustomed or expected so that predictability is impossible ⟨geniuses are such *erratic* people —G.B.Shaw⟩ ⟨his moods were *erratic*, and nobody could be certain how he would behave at any particular moment —Thomas Hardy⟩ ODD may apply to a departure from normal tinged with the fantastic, whimsical, or paradoxical ⟨the *oddest* sense of being herself invisible; unseen; unknown —Virginia Woolf⟩ ⟨it was an *odd* argument that developed. Allnutt was perfectly prepared by now to throw away the life that had seemed so precious to him —C.S. Forester⟩ ⟨it is *odd* that, when we whip her, Madam should love us the more —George Meredith⟩ QUEER may describe the eccentric or odd slightly tinged with the questionable, dubious, reprehensible, or threatening ⟨something *queer* floating by the bank. It was the body of an old woman, gutted, but not gutted enough to sink —Marjory S. Douglas⟩ ⟨a *queer*, wild, half-starved, half-crazy loveliness —Katharine N. Burt⟩ QUAINT may suggest a pleasing or attractive oddness usu. due to some old-fashioned suggestion ⟨one of those *quaint* figures, in the stately ruff, the cloak, tunic, and trunk hose of three centuries ago —Nathaniel Hawthorne⟩ ⟨*quaint* little tank engines, with tall chimneys, cowcatchers and highly polished steam domes —O.S.Nock⟩ OUTLANDISH applies to what is odd as bizarre, foreign, barbaric, or exotic ⟨wholly independent, and withal *outlandish*, they have left me a memory of pigtails and gongs and fluttering red paper —John Reed⟩ CURIOUS, often interchangeable with others in this group, may apply to what merits or invites close scrutiny or examination through its strange or singular nature ⟨*curious* and suspicious circumstances had of late been discovered —Rose Macaulay⟩ ⟨the *curious* expression "pure serene" — Amy Lowell⟩ ⟨the writ of habeas corpus has had a most *curious* history —Edward Jenks⟩

2**strange** \"\ *adv* : STRANGELY

strange·ly *adv* [ME, fr. 1*strange* + *-ly*] : in a strange manner

strange·ness *n* -ES [ME *strangenesse*, fr. 1*strange* + *-nesse* -ness] : the quality or state of being strange

1**stran·ger** \'strānjə(r)\ *n* -S [ME, fr. MF *estrangier* foreign, foreigner, fr. *estrange* strange, foreign] **1** : one who is strange: as **a** (1) : one who comes from a foreign land : FOREIGNER (2) : a resident alien; *specif* : GER **b** : one not in the place where his home is; *specif* : one in the family or house of another as a guest, visitor, or intruder ⟨thy ~ that is within thy gates —Deut 5:14(AV)⟩ **c** : a person or thing that is unknown or with whom one is unacquainted ⟨a total ~⟩ ⟨it's a ~ — and so was the young woman who owns it —Hartley Howard⟩ **d** (1) : one who does not belong to or is not permitted to take part in the activities of a group, organization, or society (2) : someone not a priest : LAYMAN **e** : an acquaintance who has been long absent : an acquaintance who has not been seen for a longer period than usual **f** *or* **stranger in blood** : one who is not a relation; *specif* : one not closely enough related or not so circumstanced as to give rise to the consideration of love and affection ⟨risk giving inheritance rights to offspring begotten by some ~ —H.M.Parshley⟩ **g** : one not privy or party to an act, contract, or title : a mere intruder or intermeddler : one that interferes without right : a third party : VOLUNTEER ⟨actual possession of land gives a good title against a ~ having no title⟩ **h** (1) *obs* : something that is not indigenous : something (as a plant or animal) of exotic origin (2) : something not of the nature of or characteristic of a person, class, thing, or set of concepts **i** : a newborn child **2 a** : one ignorant of or unacquainted with a thing, person, fact, or set of ideas ⟨a man of sociable disposition . . . though a ~ to books —C.H. Grandgent⟩ ⟨no ~ to aesthetic studies —Joseph Frank⟩ **b** : one spiritually alienated from an object or group ⟨a ~ to his religion —Ruth Park⟩ ⟨living as ~*s* to themselves —Marguerite Young⟩ **3** : any of several things (as a tea leaf floating in a cup of tea) or occurrences (as a moth flying toward one) that according to folklore forebode the arrival of an unexpected visitor

2**stranger** \"\ *adj* [ME, fr. 1*stranger*] : of, relating to, or being a stranger : FOREIGN, ALIEN

3**stranger** *vt* -ED/-ING/-S [1*stranger*] *obs* : ESTRANGE, ALIENATE

stran·ger·hood \-ˌhu̇d\ *n* : the quality or state of being a stranger

stranger·ship \-ˌship\ *n* [1*stranger* + *-ship*] : STRANGERHOOD

strangest *superlative of* STRANGE

strange woman *n* [so called fr. the use of the expression in Prov 5:3(AV)] : PROSTITUTE

strang·ite \'straŋˌīt\ *n* -S *usu cap* [James J. *Strang* †1856 Am. religious leader + E *-ite*] : a member of a religious body that was organized by J. J. Strang in Wisconsin in 1844, that regards itself as the original and only true Church of Christ of Latter-day Saints, and that holds its founder to be the only legitimate successor to Joseph Smith

1**stran·gle** \'straŋgəl, -aiŋ-\ *vb* **strangled; strangled; strangling** \-g(ə)liŋ\ **strangles** [ME *stranglen*, fr. MF *estrangler*, fr. L *strangulare*, fr. Gk *strangalan*, fr. *strangalē* halter — more at STRAIN] *vt* **1 a** : to compress the windpipe of until death results from stoppage of respiration : choke to death by compressing the throat with or as if with a hand or rope : THROTTLE **b** : to interfere with or obstruct seriously or fatally the normal breathing of ⟨the bone wedged in his throat and *strangled* him⟩ ⟨the tear gas *strangled* the convicts⟩ **2 a** : to hinder the growth of (an organism) : deny a vital necessity (as air, water, or food) to : choke off or out **b** : to suppress, hinder, or halt the rise, expression, or development of by extreme restrictions or stringency ⟨expression of biological needs is *strangled* by social pressures —Abram Kardiner⟩ ⟨the states ~ local initiative —T.C.Desmond⟩ ⟨*strangling* her trade would neither cause immediate hardship . . . nor stop an army —John Sparkman⟩ **c** : to check free utterance of ⟨a *strangled* gasp of anguish —O.E.Rölvaag⟩ ~ *vi* **1** : to become strangled : undergo an esp. severe interference of breathing ⟨she chokes very easily, and sometimes ~*s* —Grace Reiten⟩ **2** : to die from or as if from interference with breathing ⟨several prisoners in the hold *strangled*⟩ **syn** see SUFFOCATE

2**strangle** \"\ *n* -S [by shortening] : STRANGLEHOLD

stranglehold \'⸗⸗ˌ⸗\ *n* [1*strangle* + *hold*] **1** : an illegal wrestling hold by which one's opponent is choked **2** : a force, influence, or vantage point from which pressure might be brought to bear which chokes or suppresses freedom of movement, development, or expression

stran·gler \'straŋglə(r), -aiŋ-\ *n* -S **1** : one that strangles **2** *Brit* : CHOKE 2a

strangler fig *also* **strangler** *n* -S : any of several epiphytic vines or trees: as **a** : PITCH APPLE **b** : a fig (*Ficus aurea*) of the southeastern U.S. with sessile spheroidal or obovoid fruit — called also *golden fig*

strangler tree *n* : a plant of the genus *Clusia; esp* : PITCH APPLE

stran·gles \-gəlz\ *n pl but sing or pl in constr* [fr. pl. of obs. *strangle* act of strangling, fr. ME, fr. *stranglen* to strangle] : an infectious febrile disease of horses and other equines that is caused by a bacterium (*Streptococcus equi*), is characterized by inflammation and congestion of mucous membranes and a tendency to swelling and suppuration of the intermaxillary and cervical lymph nodes, usu. affects young animals, has a low mortality rate, and confers subsequent immunity after one attack — called also *colt distemper;* compare BASTARD STRANGLES

strangletare \'⸗⸗ˌ⸗\ *n* **1** : a European tare (*Vicia hirsuta*) with hirsute 2-seeded pods naturalized in No. America **2** : a broomrape of the genus *Orobanche*

strangleweed \'⸗⸗ˌ⸗\ *n* : DODDER

strangling fig *n* [*strangling* (pres. part. of 1*strangle*) + *fig*] : STRANGLER FIG

1**stran·gu·late** \'straŋgyəˌlāt, -aiŋ-, *usu* -ād·+V\ *vb* -ED/-ING/-S [L *strangulatus*, past part. of *strangulare* to strangle] *vt* : STRANGLE, CONSTRICT ~ *vi* : to become constricted so as to stop circulation ⟨the hernia will ~ and become painful⟩

2**strangulate** \-ˌlət, -ˌlāt, *usu* -d·+V\ *adj* [L *strangulatus*] : strongly constricted as though compressed by bands ⟨the ~ petiole of an ant or wasp⟩

strangulated blade *n* [*strangulated* (past part. of 1*strangulate*) + *blade*] : a prehistoric flint blade with opposing lateral notches on each margin

strangulated hernia *n* : a hernia in which the blood supply of the herniated viscus is so constricted by swelling and congestion as to arrest its circulation

stran·gu·la·tion \ˌ⸗⸗'lāshən\ *n* -S [L *strangulation-, strangulatio*, fr. *strangulatus* (past part. of *strangulare* to strangle) + *-ion-, -io* -ion] **1** : the action or process of strangling or the state of being strangled ⟨put to death by ~, the instrument of death being the cotton cloth —J.G.Frazer⟩ **2** : inordinate compression or constriction of a tube or part (as the throat or bowel) esp. to a degree that causes a suspension of breathing, circulation, or the passage of contents **3** : the action or process of constricting, choking off, or killing natural, normal, or desirable growth, development, or activity ⟨the gradual ~ of industry and individual initiative by bureaucracy —*Economist*⟩

stran·gu·ry \'straŋgyərē, -aiŋ-, -ri\ *n* -ES [ME, fr. L *stranguria*, fr. Gk *strangouria*, fr. *strang-, stranx* drop squeezed out + *ourein* to urinate (fr. *ouron* urine) + *-ia* -y — more at STRAIN, URINE] : a slow and painful discharge of urine drop by drop produced by spasmodic muscular contraction of the urethra and bladder

stran·ner \'stranə(r)\ *n* -S [origin unknown] : a steelworker who guides bloom through rolling mills until sheets reach the right gauge

strany \'strani\ *n* -ES [origin unknown] *dial Brit* : a murre (*Uria troille*)

1**strap** \'strap\ *n* -S *often attrib* [alter. of *strop* band or loop of leather or rope or metal, fr. ME, band or loop of leather or rope, fr. OE, thong for securing an oar; akin to MLG & MD *strop* strap, MHG *strupfe;* all fr. a prehistoric Gmc word borrowed fr. L *struppus, stroppus* band, thong, strap, fr. Gk *strophos* twisted band, cord — more at STROPHE] **1 a** : a band, plate, or loop of metal for binding objects together or for clamping an object in position; *also* : a flexible thin flat strip of metal fastened around a box, crate, bale, or bundle for security **b** : a projecting metal tang esp. when used for attaching or connecting **c** : metal strips, posts, or rods used for support or reinforcement **d** : a thin flat section of conducting material (as copper) forming part of an electrical connection **e** : a flat piece of lead in a storage battery to which the plates of a group are connected **2 a** : a piece of rope or metal passing around a block or deadeye holding it together and used for fastening it to something — called also *strop* **b** : a rope with its ends spliced together used esp. in slinging weights; *also* : a short cable with an eye at each end **3** : a narrow usu. flat strip or thong of a flexible material and esp. leather used variously (as for securing, holding together, or wrapping): as **a** : a strip of leather, cloth, or webbing fitted with a clasp or buckle for adjustment and used for fastening, securing, or holding together **b** : something made of a strap, a part of one, or of a combination of two or more forming a loop ⟨a carriage ~⟩ ⟨a ~ in a bus⟩ **c** : a band (as of adhesive plaster) used to approximate edges (as of a wound) or to hold a dressing in position **d** : a strip of leather used for flogging; *also* : the use of a strap for inflicting punishment ⟨a little boy who has been out later than he should and who is afraid . . . of getting his father's ~ —Vernon Jarratt⟩ **e** : a piece of leather or strip of wood covered with a suitable material for sharpening a razor : STROP **f** : BELT 2 **g** : SHOULDER STRAP **h** : a flexible strap or belt (as of cloth to which an abrasive is glued and which runs over pulleys or over a pulley and a rod or plate) used for buffing **i** : any of several wide leather strips cut and fitted to blankbook backbones and extending upon the boards between bands **j** : a band or fillet used in strapwork **k** : a flattened strip of cable (as connected to an automobile storage battery) **l** : a strip of paper used to bind a bundle of paper currency **4** *or* **strap shoe** : a shoe fastened with a usu. buckled strap **5** *Brit* : CREDIT **6** *Irish* **a** : a forward impudent girl or woman : HUSSY **b** : HARLOT

2**strap** \"\ *vb* **strapped; strapped; strapping; straps** *vt* **1 a** (1) : to secure with or attach by means of a strap ⟨*strapping* mail in bundles —*U.S.Post Office Manual*⟩ ⟨*strapped* to the pulpit is a curious wooden megaphone —Charles Gordon⟩ ⟨~ on an oxygen tank —Stuart Chase⟩ (2) : to bind (as a sprained joint or painful muscles) with overlapping strips of adhesive plaster (3) : to constrict as if by a strap ⟨his khaki bush shirt *strapped* him as though it were made with stays —Joseph Hitrec⟩ ⟨a decent man *strapped* by dogma —*New Republic*⟩ **b** : to fit, furnish, or equip with a strap ⟨~ a book⟩ ⟨~ the deadeye⟩ **2** : to beat or punish with a strap ⟨would not ~ his pupils —H.S.Canby⟩ **3** : STROP **4** : to cause to suffer from an extreme scarcity ⟨*strapped* its people to keep up the arms race —*Atlantic*⟩ ⟨financially *strapped* due to the depression —Jerome Ellison⟩ **5** : to rub down (a horse) : GROOM ~ *vi, Brit* : to busy oneself : apply oneself actively or energetically : buckle down

s trap *n, cap S* : an S-shaped trap used in plumbing

S trap

strap bolt *n* **1** : LUG BOLT **2** : a bolt with a flat portion in the center so that the whole may be bent into a U shape

strap brake *n* : BAND BRAKE

strap drill *n* : a simple drill operated by means of a thong twisted about the shaft

strap fern *n* : a common tropical American fern (*Campyloneuron phyllitidis*) with long narrow strap-shaped leaves that is found in soil or as an epiphyte

strap game *n* : a swindling game in which a strap or belt is folded in the middle and then rolled up tightly with the victim betting that he can place a pencil in the loop so as to hold the strap when both ends are pulled

strap graft *n* : a graft similar to a bark graft except that the scion is so prepared that a flap of bark will cover the cut end of the stock and can be inserted under the bark of the stock on the side opposite the scion

strap hammer *n* : a heavy hammer (as a helve hammer or drop hammer) in which the head is suspended by a strap

straphang \'⸗ˌ⸗\ *vi* -ED/-ING/-S [back-formation fr. *straphanger*] *chiefly Brit* : to ride in a conveyance as a straphanger

straphanger \'⸗ˌ⸗⸗\ *n* [1*strap* + *hanger*] **1 a** : a passenger in a subway, streetcar, bus, or train who clings for support while standing to one of the short straps or similar devices running along the aisle **b** : a regular passenger on public transportation : COMMUTER **2** : a usu. curved piece of strap fastened at the ends and used to secure a pipe or rod suspended from above or against a vertical surface

strap hinge *n* : a hinge with long flaps by which it is fastened to the surface of a door and the adjacent wall — compare BUTT HINGE

strap hinges

strap joint *n* : a joint formed by butting together the two pieces to be joined and riveting a metal strap to each piece

strap key *n* : TAPPING KEY

strap-laid \'⸗¦⸗\ *adj* : consisting of or being flat rope made by stitching together side-by-side two cable-laid ropes

strap leather *n* : tanned cowhide leather used esp. for luggage straps

strap·less \'⸗ˌləs\ *adj* : having no strap; *specif* : made or worn without shoulder straps ⟨~ bathing suit⟩ ⟨~ evening gown⟩

strap oyster *n, dial* : an uncommonly narrow oyster

1**strap·pa·do** \strə'pā(ˌ)dō, -pä(ˌ)-\ *n* -S [modif. of It *strappata* sharp pull, strappado, fr. *strappare* to pull sharply, prob. of Gmc origin; akin to G dial. *strapfen* to stretch tight, MD *strof* tense, sharp] **1** : a former punishment or torture consisting of hoisting the subject by a rope sometimes fastened to his wrists behind his back and letting him fall to the length of the rope; *also* : a machine or device used in the infliction of this torture **2** *archaic* : a beating with or as if with a strap

2**strappado** \"\ *vt* -ED/-ING/-S *obs* : to punish or torture by or as if by the strappado

strap·pan \'strapən\ *Scot var of* STRAPPING

strapped *past of* STRAP

strap·per \'strapə(r)\ *n* -S [2*strap* + *-er*] **1** : a person unusually large, robust, or formidable **2** : one that uses a strap: as **a** : one that harnesses or grooms horses or takes care of horses in a stable **b** : one that attaches, removes, or attends to straps

1**strapping** *adj* [fr. pres. part. of 2*strap*] : having or being a vigorously sturdy constitution : ROBUST — **strappingly** *adv*

2**strapping** *n* -S [fr. gerund of 2*strap*] **1 a** : the act or process of strapping; *esp* : a beating with or as if with a strap **b** : the application of adhesive plaster in overlapping strips upon or around (as a sprained ankle or the chest in pleurisy) to serve as a splint to reduce motion or to hold surgical dressings in place upon a surgical wound; *also* : material so used **2 a** : straps or material for straps **b** : a trimming for women's clothes made of one or more narrow bands of contrasting material or color and often applied over seams

strapping plate *n* : a long narrow strip of sheet iron or mild steel used as a strap in making a butt joint with two sections of a wooden main rod in a mine shaft

strap rail *n* : a railroad rail consisting of a metal strap placed upon a wooden rail

straps *pl of* STRAP, *pres 3d sing of* STRAP

strap-toothed whale \'⸗¦⸗-\ *n* [so called fr. the shape of the base of its mandibular tooth] : a cowfish (*Mesoplodon layardi*) of southern seas having the front portion of the body gray and the hind portion black with yellow-tipped tail flukes

strapwork \'⸗ˌ⸗\ *n* : decorative design of narrow fillets or bands folded, crossed, and sometimes interlaced

strapwort \'⸗ˌ⸗\ *n* : a European maritime weed (*Corrigiola littoralis*) naturalized in eastern No. America

stras·bourg \'strä|sˌbu̇rg, 'stra|, |zˌb- *sometimes* 'strȯ|; -a|sˌbərg, |zˌb- *sometimes* -ȯ|\ *adj, usu cap* [fr. *Strasbourg*, city of northeast France] : of or from the city of Strasbourg, France : of the kind or style prevalent in Strasbourg

strasbourg goose *n, usu cap S* : a goose fattened so as to enlarge the liver for use in pâté de foie gras

strasbourg turpentine *n, usu cap S* : an oleoresin obtained chiefly from a silver fir (*Abies alba*)

strass \'stras\ *n* -ES [F *stras, strass*, prob. fr. the name of its inventor] : PASTE 4

strata *pl of* STRATUM

strat·a·gem \'strad·|əjəm, -at|, |ējəm *also* |əˌjem\ *n* -S [It *stratagemma*, fr. L *strategema*, fr. Gk *stratēgēma*, fr. *stratēgein* to be a general, maneuver, fr. *stratēgos* general, fr. *stratos* army, host + *-ēgos* (fr. *agein* to lead) — more at STRATUM, AGENT] **1 a** : an artifice or trick in war for deceiving and outwitting the enemy **b** : a cleverly contrived trick or scheme for gaining an end ⟨on our guard against the ~*s* of evil rhetoric —R.M.Weaver⟩ **c** : skillfulness in the employment of stratagems : ability to devise cunning plans to gain an end ⟨without ~, but in plain shock and even play of battle —Shak.⟩ **2** *obs* : a violent or bloody act **syn** see TRICK

strat·a·gem·i·cal \¦⸗⸗¦jeməkəl\ *adj* [*stratagem* + *-ical*] : characterized by stratagem — **strat·a·gem·i·cal·ly** \-mək(ə)lē\ *adv*

stratal \'strā|d·əl, |tᵊl, -ra| *also* -rä| *or* -rå|\ *adj* [NL *strat*um + E *-al*] : of or relating to a stratum or strata

strat·e·get·ic \¦strad·ə¦jed·ik\ *or* **strat·e·get·i·cal** \-d·əkəl\ *adj* [*strategetic* fr. Gk *stratēgētikos*, MS var. (as if fr. *stratēgētos* — assumed verbal of *stratēgein* to be a general — + *-ikos* -ic) of *stratēgikos* strategic; *strategetical* fr. Gk *stratēgētikos* + E *-al* — more at STRATAGEM] : STRATEGIC

stra·te·gian \strə'tēj(ē)ən\ *n* -S [*strategy* + *-an*] : STRATEGIST

stra·te·gic \-jik, -jēk\ *also* **stra·te·gi·cal** \-jəkəl, -jēk-\ *adj* [*strategic* fr. Gk *stratēgikos* of a general, fr. *stratēgos* general + *-ikos* -ic; *strategical* fr. Gk *stratēgikos* + E *-al* — more at STRATAGEM] **1** : of, relating to, or concerned with strategy ⟨~ strength⟩ ⟨~ considerations⟩ ⟨on account of their ~ value to the enemy, I destroyed the bridges —R.H.Davis⟩ **2** : marked by or done in accordance with strategy ⟨this ~ retreat was the promise of victory —C.A. & Mary Beard⟩ **3 a** : necessary to or of great value or importance in the initiation, conduct, or completion of a strategic plan ⟨it is not probable that any enemy would attack . . . across thousands of miles of ocean, until it had acquired ~ bases from which to operate —F.D. Roosevelt⟩ ⟨~ roads⟩ ⟨the retention of a strong ~ reserve⟩; *specif* : required for the conduct of war but obtainable at least in part only from outside the country — compare CRITICAL **b** : of great or vital importance within an integrated whole or to the taking place of a planned or unplanned occurrence ⟨reinforced with belting leather at the corners and other ~ spots —*New Yorker*⟩ ⟨at ~ points where agricultural products were processed . . . towns grew rapidly —*Amer. Guides Series: N.Y.*⟩ ⟨there are four ~ areas of the economy: inventories, durables, business construction, and housing —H.H.Villard⟩ ⟨constriction of arteries in ~ areas of the brain —*Jour. Amer. Med. Assoc.*⟩ **4** : designed or trained to strike an enemy at the sources of his military, economic, or political power and esp. to destroy rear area bases and supply depots, industrial centers, and communications networks ⟨~ bomber⟩ ⟨~ air warfare⟩

stra·te·gi·cal·ly \-jək(ə)lē, -jēk-, -li\ *adv* [*strategical* + *-ly*] **1** : in a strategic manner : for purposes of strategy ⟨deliberately and ~ condescending —L.A.Fiedler⟩ **2** : with regard to strategy : from a strategical view ⟨winning the war ~ and losing it politically —J.R.Newman⟩

stra·te·gics \-jiks, -jēks\ *n pl but sing in constr* [L *strategica*, fr. Gk *stratēgika*, fr. neut. pl. of *stratēgikos* of a general] : STRATEGY

strat·e·gist \'strad·əjəst, -ratə-\ *n* -S [*strategy* + *-ist*] : one skilled in strategy

stra·te·gus \strə'tēgəs\ *or* **stra·te·gos** \", -ˌgäs\ *n, pl* **strate·gi** \-ēˌjī\ *or* **strate·goi** \-ēˌgȯi\ [L *strategus*, fr. Gk *stratēgos* — more at STRATAGEM] **1** : a leader of an ancient and esp. an ancient Greek army **2** : an officer associated with the hipparch as chief executive of the boule in the Achaean and Aetolian Leagues

strat·e·gy \'strad·əjē, -ratə-, -ji\ *n* -ES [Gk *stratēgia* office of a general, generalship, piece of strategy, fr. *stratēgos* general + *-ia* -y] **1 a** (1) : the science and art of employing the political, economic, psychological, and military forces of a nation or group of nations to afford the maximum support to adopted policies in peace or war (2) : the science and art of military command exercised to meet the enemy in combat under advantageous conditions — compare TACTICS **b** : a variety of or instance of the use of strategy ⟨the ~ of the counterattack rather than of the offensive —H.W.Baldwin⟩ ⟨collective security through a world organization is a ~ of defense like any other —J.T.Shotwell⟩ **2 a** : a careful plan or method or a clever stratagem ⟨vulnerable to one of three merchandising *strategies* —Vance Packard⟩ ⟨drafted the ~ it followed in election campaigns —*Current Biog.*⟩ **b** : the art of devising or employing plans or stratagems toward a goal ⟨the clever manager's conception of political ~ —S.H.Adams⟩

strat·for·dian \strat'fōrdēən\ *n* -S *cap* [*Stratford* on Avon, municipal borough of central England and birthplace of William Shakespeare, or *Stratford*, city of southeast Ontario + E *-ian*] **1** : a native or resident of Stratford on Avon, England or of Stratford, Ontario **2** : one who believes that William Shakespeare was the author of the dramatic works usu. attributed to him

strath \'strath\ *n* -S [ScGael *srath;* akin to MIr *srath* wide valley, Welsh *ystrad* — more at STRATUM] **1** : a flat wide river valley or its bottomland **2** : a wide tract of level land embracing parts of several adjacent valleys **3** : a partially developed peneplain

strath·spey \(')strath¦spā\ *n* -S [fr. *Strath Spey*, district of northeast Scotland] **1** : a Scottish dance similar to but slower than the reel **2** : music for the strathspey : music having its duple or quadruple rhythm characterized by the Scotch snap

strath terrace *n* : a remnant of a dissected strath

strati *pl of* STRATUS

strati- *comb form* [NL *stratum*] : stratum ⟨*strati*form⟩ ⟨*strati*graphy⟩

stra·tic·u·late \strəˈtikyələt, -ˌlāt\ *adj* [fr. (assumed) NL *straticulum* (dim. of *stratum*) + E *-ate*] **:** characterized by thin parallel strata

strat·i·fi·ca·tion \ˌstrad·əfəˈkāshən, -ratə-\ *n* -s [NL *stratification-, stratificatio*, fr. *stratificatus* (past part. of *stratificare* to stratify) + L *-ion-, -io* -ion] **:** the act or process of stratifying or state of being stratified **:** a stratified formation **:** disposal or growth in layers: as **a :** the arrangement of sedimentary rocks in layers **b :** the placing of seeds in damp sand, peat moss, or sawdust to facilitate germination that is a necessary procedure for seeds requiring moisture or low temperature or both during their resting period or afterripening period **c :** stratified variation in the richness of the mixture in a cylinder of an internal combustion engine **d** (1) **:** a formation of social classes, castes, strata, or levels into a hierarchy of prestige (2) **:** a graded system of individual statuses within a group, community, or organization **e :** arrangement (as of a forest) in vertical layers of vegetation so as to make maximum use of available light **f :** arrangement of the waters of a lake into hypolimnion and epilimnion separated by a thermocline as a result esp. of differences in specific gravity brought about by natural warming of the waters above the thermocline **g :** the division of a statistical population into groups on any basis esp. in order to select a sample from each group

stratification plane *n* **:** a division between two layers of sedimentary rock that often marks changes in the circumstances of deposition

stratified sample *n* [*stratified* (past part. of *stratify*) + *sample*] **:** a statistical sample obtained by breaking the universe down into smaller parts made up of relatively homogeneous units and taking a sample from each part

strat·i·form \ˈstrad·əˌfȯrm, -ratə-\ *adj* [*strati-* + *-form*] **1 :** having a stratified formation **:** consisting of roughly parallel bands or concentric zones **2** [NL *stratus* + E *-iform*] **:** having the form of a stratus

strat·i·fy \-ˌfī\ *vb* -ED/-ING/-ES [NL *stratificare*, fr. *stratum* + L *-ificare* -ify] *vt* **1 a :** to form, deposit, or arrange in strata ⟨*stratified* alluvium⟩ **b** (1) **:** to divide or arrange into classes, castes, or social strata ⟨important cultural differences often ~ husbands and wives . . . of the very same religious affiliation —M.L.Barron⟩ ⟨society was rather distinctly *stratified* into four classes —*Amer. Guide Series: N.C.*⟩ (2) **:** to divide into a series of graded statuses ⟨a *stratified* religious hierarchy⟩ **c :** to determine the arrangement and order of the strata of ⟨~ an archeological site⟩ **2 a :** to place (seed) in damp sand, peat moss, or sawdust **b :** to preserve (tree seeds) by spreading in layers alternating with sand, earth, or other moisture-holding medium **~** *vi* **:** to become arranged in strata ⟨convected heat . . . has a tendency to cause the air to ~ —P.D.Close⟩ ⟨all society . . . tends to ~ in lines of wealth distribution —V.L. Parrington⟩

stra·tig·ra·pher \strəˈtigrəfə(r)\ *n* -s [*stratigraphy* + *-er*] **:** a geologist who specializes in stratigraphy

strat·i·graph·ic \ˌstrad·əˈgrafik, -ratə-, -fēk\ *also* **strat·i·graph·i·cal** \-fəkəl, -fēk-\ *adj* [*stratigraphic* fr. *stratigraphy* + *-ic; stratigraphical* fr. *strati-* + *-graphical*] **:** of, relating to, or determined by stratigraphy — **strat·i·graph·i·cal·ly** \-fək(ə)lē, -fēk-, -li\ *adv*

stratigraphic geology *n* **:** STRATIGRAPHY 2

stratigraphic separation *or* **stratigraphic throw** *n* **:** PERPENDICULAR SEPARATION

stratigraphic sequence *n* **:** a chronologic succession of sedimentary rocks

stratigraphic trap *n* **:** a natural reservoir in which oil or gas may be confined because of changes in porosity and permeability of the strata rather than as a result of their structural attitudes

stra·tig·ra·phist \strəˈtigrəfəst\ *n* -s [*stratigraphy* + *-ist*] **:** STRATIGRAPHER

stra·tig·ra·phy \-fē, -fi\ *n* -ES [ISV *strati-* + *-graphy*] **1 :** the arrangement of strata esp. as to position and order of sequence **2 :** the branch of geology that deals with the origin, composition, distribution, and succession of strata **3 :** the determination of time sequence in the culture and physical types of peoples by study of the relative locations of the layers of material that are found in archeological excavation — compare SHARD

[1]**strat·io·my·iid** \ˌstrad·ēōˈmī(y)əd\ *or* **strat·io·my·id** \-īəd\ *adj* [NL *Stratiomyiidae*] **:** of or relating to the Stratiomyiidae

[2]**stratiomyiid** \"\ *or* **stratiomyid** \"\ *n* -s **:** a fly of the family Stratiomyiidae **:** SOLDIER FLY

strat·io·my·ii·dae \ˌ⸗⸗⸗ˈmī(y)əˌdē\ *n pl, cap* [NL *Stratiomyia*, type genus (fr. Gk *stratios* of an army, warlike + NL *-myia*) + *-idae*] **:** a family of small often brightly colored two-winged flies comprising the soldier flies and having saprophagous or predacious terrestrial or aquatic larvae

[1]**strato-** *comb form* [NL *stratus*] **:** stratus and ⟨*strato*cirrus⟩ ⟨*strato*cumulus⟩

[2]**strato-** *comb form* [*stratosphere*] **:** stratosphere ⟨*strato*-chamber⟩ ⟨*strato*-flying airplanes —*Science News Letter*⟩

strato·cirrus \ˌstra\|d·ō, -rā\| *also* -rä\| *or* -rȧ\| +\ *n* [NL, fr. [1]*strato-* + *cirrus*] **:** a low dense cirrostratus cloud classed with the altostratus

stra·toc·ra·cy \strəˈtäkrəsē, -si\ *n* -ES [Gk *stratos* army + E *-cracy*] **:** a military government **:** government based on an army

strato·cumulus \ˌstra\|d·ō, -rā\| *also* -rä\| *or* -rȧ\| +\ *n* [NL, fr. [1]*strato-* + *cumulus*] **:** stratified cumulus consisting of large balls or rolls of dark cloud which often cover the whole sky esp. in winter, give at times an undulated appearance, and do not bring rain — see CLOUD illustration

stra·ton·ic \strəˈtänik\ *or* **stra·ton·i·cal** \-nəkəl\ *adj, usu cap* [Gk *Stratōn* Strato, 3d cent. B.C. Greek philosopher + E *-ic* or *-ical*] **:** of, relating to, or typical of Strato of Lampsacus

stratose \ˈstrāˌtōs, -ra-, *also* -rä,- *or* -rȧ,-\ *adj* [NL *stratum* + E *-ose*] **:** arranged in strata

strato·sphere \ˈstrad·əˌsfi(ə)r, -iə\ *n* [F *stratosphère*, fr. NL *stratum* + *-o-* + F *sphère* sphere, fr. L *sphaera* — more at SPHERE] **1 :** an upper portion of the atmosphere above seven miles more or less depending on latitude, season, and weather in which temperature changes but little with altitude, clouds of water are rare, and there is practically no deep convection — called also *isothermal region* **2 a :** a very high or the highest region on a graded scale ⟨meat prices are in the ~ —Joseph & Stewart Alsop⟩ ⟨the ~ of English society —*New Yorker*⟩ **b :** the top part of an object or region ⟨a sooty ~ of struts and girders —Berton Roueché⟩ ⟨the leafy ~ of the forest —Edmond Taylor⟩ **c :** a highly abstract or experimental field of endeavor ⟨pressing their value analyses into a disembodied ~ of transcendental mathematics —A.L.Locke⟩ ⟨~ of modern art —D.C. Rich⟩

strato·spher·ic \ˌ⸗⸗ˈsfirik, -fer-, -ˈrēk\ *also* **strato·spher·i·cal** \-rəkəl, -rēk-\ *adj* [*stratosphere* + *-ic, -ical*] **1 :** of, relating to, or designed for use in the stratosphere **2 :** extremely high ⟨rearmament at ~ costs —Drew Middleton⟩ ⟨a severe critic whose standards are somewhat ~ —Rosalyn Krokover⟩ **3 :** remote from common sense or exact scientific thinking **:** MYSTICAL 3a, METAPHYSICAL 2a ⟨a solid point of reference by which to check . . . ~ philosophies of and about history —Garrett Mattingly⟩

stratous \ˈstrā\|d·əs, \|təs, -ra\| *also* -rä\| *or* -rȧ\|\ *adj* **1** [NL *stratum* + E *-ous*] **:** composed of strata **2** [NL *stratus* + E *-ous*] **:** resembling stratus clouds

strato·volcano \ˌstra\|d·ō, -rā\| *also* -rä\| *or* -rȧ\|+\ *n* [NL *stratum* + E *-o-* + *volcano;* fr. its cone's being built up of successive layers of ash and lava] **:** a volcano composed of explosively erupted cinders and ash with occasional lava flows — contrasted with *shield volcano*

stratum \ˈstrā\|d·əm, \|təm, -ra\| *also* -rä\| *or* -rȧ\|\ *n, pl* **strata** \-d·ə, -tə\ *also* **stratums** [NL, fr. L, spread, bed, fr. neut. of *stratus*, past part. of *sternere* to strew, spread out, lay flat; akin to Gk *stratos* (encamped) army, MIr *srath* wide valley — more at STREW] **1 :** a bed or layer artificially made **:** a coat of some material spread uniformly over a surface or upon another coat **:** LAYER ⟨the chaff, packed into a whole bay of the barn, was in *strata* —Adrian Bell⟩ **2 a :** a tabular mass or thin sheet of sedimentary rock or earth of one kind formed by natural causes and made up usu. of a series of layers lying between beds of other kinds **b :** BED **c :** a region of the sea or atmosphere that is analogous to a stratum of the earth ⟨winds tend to drive the surface water away . . . to be replaced by cold water upwelling from deeper *strata* —R.E.Coker⟩ **d :** a layer of tissue; *esp* **:** one of several superimposed membranes that go to make up an organ **e :** a layer in which archaeological material (as artifacts, skeletons, and dwelling remains) is found on excavation **f :** a vertical layer of vegetation (as of herbs, shrubs, or trees) in a plant community **3 a :** a part of a historical or sociological series representing a period or a stage of development ⟨the technique of skin dressing . . . belongs to an older ~ of Plains culture than the buffalo-skin tipi —Edward Sapir⟩ **b :** a socioeconomic level of society comprised of persons of the same or similar status esp. with regard to education or culture — compare CLASS ⟨wide *strata* of the intellectuals, professionals, and bureaucrats were penetrated ideologically —James Burnham⟩ ⟨the upper administrative *strata* of a typical large factory —E.H.Jacobson & S.E.Seashore⟩ **4 :** one of a series of layers, levels, or gradations in an ordered system ⟨filtered down to him through different *strata* of thought —V.L.Parrington⟩ ⟨the whole subject of colds is overlaid by ~ upon ~ of folklore, superstition, and pseudoscience —C.H. Andrewes⟩ ⟨the more controversial mental *strata* lying between scientific, philosophical, and theological thought —*Times Lit. Supp.*⟩ ⟨the fairy-tale ~ of experience —F.R.Leavis⟩ **5 :** one of the divisions into which a population is divided in statistical stratification ⟨the counties of the United States may be grouped into 30 or more *strata* in terms of their population density —L.W.Doob⟩ **6 :** a group of linguistic phenomena characterized by the possession of common features (as of age or origin)

stratum corneum *n, pl* **strata cornea** [NL, lit., horny layer] **:** the outer more or less horny part of the epidermis including all the layers superficial to the Malpighian layer or only those that are superficial to the stratum granulosum and stratum lucidum

stratum ger·mi·na·ti·vum \-ˌjərmənəˈtīvəm\ *n, pl* **strata germinati·va** \-və\ [NL, lit., germinative layer] **:** the innermost layer of the epidermis consisting of a single row of columnar epithelial cells that continually divide and replace the rest of the epidermis as it wears away; *sometimes* **:** MALPIGHIAN LAYER

stratum gran·u·lo·sum \-ˌgranyəˈlōsəm\ *n, pl* **strata granulo·sa** \-sə\ [NL, lit., granulous layer] **1 :** a layer of granular cells lying immediately above the stratum germinativum in most parts of the epidermis **2 :** the layer of dentin in contact with the cementum of a tooth

stratum lu·ci·dum \-ˈlüsədəm\ *n, pl* **strata luci·da** \-də\ [NL, lit., lucid layer] **:** a thin somewhat translucent layer of cells lying superficial to the stratum granulosum in many parts of the epidermis

stratus \ˈstrā\|d·əs, \|təs, -ra\| *also* -rä\| *or* -rȧ\|\ *n, pl* **strati** \-d·ˌī, -ˌtī\ [NL, fr. L, past part. of *sternere* to spread out — more at STREW] **:** a cloud form characterized by relatively greater horizontal extension and comparatively lower altitude (2000 to 7000 feet) than the cumulostratus or cirrostratus — see CLOUD illustration

stratus cu·mu·li·for·mis \-ˌkyümyələˈfȯrməs\ *n, pl* **strati cumulifor·mes** \-ˌmēz\ [NL] **:** a stratus cloud resembling the cumulus in form

stratus mac·u·lo·sus \-ˌmakyəˈlōsəs\ *n, pl* **strati maculo·si** \-ōˌsī\ [NL, lit., spotted stratus] **:** MACKEREL SKY

straucht *or* **straught** \ˈsträkt\ *Scot var of* STRAIGHT

strauss·ian \ˈs(h)trau̇sēən\ *adj, usu cap* [Richard *Strauss* †1949 Ger. conductor and composer + E *-ian*] **:** of or relating to Richard Strauss or his musical compositions

stra·vage *or* **stra·vaig** \strəˈvāg\ *vi* [prob. by shortening and alter. fr. *extravagate*] *chiefly Scot* **:** SAUNTER, STROLL, WANDER

[1]**straw** \ˈstrȯ\ *n* -s [ME *straw, stree*, fr. OE *strēaw, strē;* akin to OHG *strō* straw, ON *strā*, OE *strēowian, strewian* to strew — more at STREW] **1 a :** stalks of grain after threshing usu. mixed with leaves and chaff, used as bedding for cattle, for packing, for fodder, in papermaking, or woven, plaited, or braided for various uses (as for a hat) **b :** a natural fiber (as buntal) or an artificial fiber (as nylon) woven, plaited, or braided to serve various uses (as for a mat, hat, bag, or box) **c :** any of various dry or stalky residues of plant growth that are put to practical use (as for bedding or packing) — see PINE STRAW **2 :** a stalk or stem of grain (as of wheat, rye, oats, or barley); *also* **:** a stalk of buckwheat, beans, or peas **3 a** (1) **:** something of small worth or significance ⟨grateful for such ~s as the garden and the weather —Will Scott⟩ ⟨another ~ toward helping them carry out their project —Robert Grant †1940⟩ — usu. used in such phrases as *care a straw* ⟨didn't care a ~ about the case —O.W.Holmes †1935⟩ ⟨wasn't worth making a fuss about, because it didn't really matter a ~ —Ellen Glasgow⟩ (2) **:** something too insubstantial to provide support or help in a desperate situation ⟨clutches at the ~ of falsehood —H.M. Parshley⟩ ⟨even active unionists tend to grasp at strange ~s for support —Bob Senser⟩ (3) *or* **straw in the wind :** a slight fact that is an indication of a coming event ⟨some of the *straws in the wind* include an increase in the printing of paper yen —Lindesay Parrott⟩ **b :** CHAFF 3 ⟨the mass of irrelevant trivialities and repetitions in doubtful taste which form the ~ of a considerable part of this book —*Books Abroad*⟩ **c :** MAN OF STRAW **4 :** a thing made of straw: as **a** *obs* **:** PIPE 1a(1) **b :** STRAW HAT **c :** a prepared tube originally cut from a wheat straw for sucking up a beverage ⟨the nurse brought him some clear consommé and a bent glass ~ —Oakley Hall⟩ **5 :** a thing shaped like a straw; *esp* **:** a short narrow strip of pastry ⟨cheese ~s⟩ **6** *or* **straw yellow :** a pale yellow that is deeper than cream, deeper and slightly greener than ivory, and greener and stronger than leghorn — **in the straw** *adv (or adj)* **:** in childbed

[2]**straw** \"\ *vt* -ED/-ING/-S [ME *strawen*, fr. [1]*straw*] **1 :** to cover (a surface) with or as if with straw **2 :** to provide with straw ⟨steers ~ed to weather a blizzard —James Still⟩

[3]**straw** \"\ *adj* [[1]*straw*] **1 :** made of straw ⟨~ basket⟩ ⟨~ seats⟩ ⟨~ broom⟩ **2 :** of, relating to, or used for straw ⟨~ barn⟩ **3 :** of the color of straw ⟨his ~ hair flopped wildly on his forehead —Wirt Williams⟩ **4 :** of little or no value **:** WORTHLESS **5 :** of, relating to, resembling, or being a man of straw ⟨a ~ structure which bore almost no resemblance to the Greek philosopher's manner of thinking —Martin Gardner⟩ ⟨purchase any property . . . either in his own name or by use of a ~ party —W.H.Husband & F.R.Anderson⟩ **6 :** of, relating to, or concerned with the discovery of preferences by means of a straw vote ⟨~ polls that seek to sample public opinion —W.E. Binkley & Malcolm Moos⟩ ⟨the poll . . . is conducted by seven crews of ~ takers —A.J.Liebling⟩

[4]**straw** \"\ *vt* -ED/-ING/-S [ME *strawwen, strawen*, fr. OE *strēawian, strēowian* to strew — more at STREW] **:** STREW **syn** see STREW

straw bail *n* **:** worthless or insufficient bail

straw ballot *n* **:** STRAW VOTE

straw bass *n* **:** LARGEMOUTH BLACK BASS

straw bed *n* **:** a mattress filled with straw

straw·berry \ˈstrȯˌberē, -b(ə)rē, -ri — *see* BERRY\ *n, often attrib* [ME, fr. OE *strēawberige*, fr. *strēaw* straw + *berige, berie* berry; perh. fr. the resemblance of the achenes on the surface to fragments of straw] **1 a :** a juicy edible usu. red fruit produced by a plant of the genus *Fragaria* and being an enlarged pulpy receptacle bearing numerous seedlike achenes rather than a true berry **b :** a plant of the genus *Fragaria* including many that are cultivated for their fruits **2 a :** a variable color averaging a moderate red that is very slightly yellower, lighter, and stronger than cerise, very slightly yellower, darker, and stronger than claret (sense 3a), lighter and very slightly yellower and stronger than Harvard crimson (sense 1), and bluer, slightly lighter, and very slightly stronger than Turkey red **b :** a grayish red that is bluer and deeper than appleblossom and bluer and darker than bois de rose **c** *of textiles* **:** a moderate purplish red that is bluer and deeper than average rose and redder and duller than violine pink **3 :** a small strawberry-colored mark or bruise

strawberry aphid *n* **:** any of several aphids that feed on strawberry plants; *esp* **:** a common and widely distributed aphid (*Chaetosiphon fragaefolii*) that is the chief insect vector of mosaic diseases of strawberries

strawberry bass *n* **:** BLACK CRAPPIE

strawberry blite *n* **:** an annual weedy herb (*Chenopodium capitatum*) of the north temperate zone with succulent stems, small greenish flowers, and red pulpy fruit — called also *strawberry pigweed*

strawberry blonde *n* **:** a woman of blonde complexion and yellowish red hair

strawberry bush *n* **1 a :** a No. American shrub (*Euonymus americanus*) having crimson pods and seeds with a scarlet aril **b :** [2]WAHOO a **2 :** STRAWBERRY SHRUB

strawberry cactus *n* **:** a low caespitose cactus (*Echinocereus enneacanthus*) of southern Texas and Mexico

strawberry clover *n* **:** an Old World clover (*Trifolium fragiferum*) like the white clover but having an inflated pink or reddish calyx

strawberry comb *n* **:** a low rounded comb of a fowl that suggests a half strawberry and is characteristic of Malay and silky fowls — see COMB illustration

strawberry crab *n* **:** a small European spider crab (*Eurynome aspera*) having the back covered with pink tubercles

strawberry crinkle *n* **:** an insect-transmitted virus disease of the strawberry characterized by the development in young leaves of small chlorotic areas which fail to grow so that the leaf becomes crinkled and distorted

strawberry crown borer *or* **strawberry borer** *or* **strawberry root borer** *n* **:** a weevil (*Tyloderma fragariae*) whose larva bores in the crown of the strawberry

strawberry crown miner *n* **:** the caterpillar of a gelechiid moth (*Aristotelia fragariae*) which mines the leaves of strawberry plants

strawberry crown moth *n* **:** a clearwing moth (*Ramosia bibionipennis*) whose larva is destructive to strawberry, blackberry, and raspberry plants; *also* **:** an aegeriid moth with similar habits

strawberry fern *n* **:** a tropical American fern (*Hemionitis palmata*) sometimes cultivated for its roundish 3-parted coarsely lobed fronds

strawberry festival *n* **:** a community festival (as a card party, church supper, or bazaar) held usu. in strawberry season at which strawberry shortcake is served

strawberry finch *n* **:** AVADAVAT

strawberry flea beetle *n* **:** a small metallic blue or greenish American flea beetle (*Altica ignita*) that feeds on the foliage of strawberries

strawberry fly *n* **:** DEERFLY

strawberry gallbladder *n* **:** a gallbladder in which cholesterol is deposited in the lining of the organ in a pattern resembling the surface of a strawberry **:** CHOLESTEROSIS

strawberry geranium *or* **strawberry saxifrage** *n* **:** an eastern Asiatic saxifrage (*Saxifraga sarmentosa*) with numerous creeping stolons, round leaves, and racemes of small red-and-white flowers — called also *mother-of-thousands*

strawberry guava *n* **1 a :** a subtropical shrub or small tree (*Psidium cattleianum*) **b :** the dark-crimson fruit of this plant much used either fresh or preserved **2 :** FEIJOA

straw·ber·ry·ing \-iŋ, -ēŋ\ *n* -s [*strawberry* + *-ing*] **:** the act of gathering or looking for strawberries

strawberry leaf *n* **:** a representation of the leaf of a strawberry plant used as a symbol of the rank or estate of an earl, duke, or marquis

strawberry leaf roller *n* **:** any of several moth larvae that roll up and feed on strawberry leaves; *also* **:** a moth (esp. *Ancylis comptana*) whose larva is a strawberry leaf roller

strawberry leaf spot *or* **strawberry leaf blight** *also* **strawberry rust** *n* **:** a disease of the strawberry plant caused by a parasitic fungus (*Mycosphaerella fragariae*) and characterized esp. by the tan to white more or less circular spots with a usu. clear cut margin — compare LEAF SCORCH b

strawberry mark *n* **:** a birthmark consisting of a hemangioma that is somewhat like a strawberry in appearance

strawberry nettle *n* **:** a Polynesian plant (*Elatostema pedunculatum*) of the family Urticaceae with red fruits that resemble strawberries

strawberry pear *n* **1 :** the red ovoid slightly acid fruit of a West Indian cactus **2 :** a cactus (*Hylocereus undatus*) that bears strawberry pears and has triangular stems and large showy flowers

strawberry perch *n* **:** BLACK CRAPPIE

strawberry pigweed *or* **strawberry spinach** *n* **:** STRAWBERRY BLITE

strawberry pink *n* **:** a deep pink to yellowish pink

strawberry raspberry *n* **:** a low herbaceous or subshrubby Asiatic bramble (*Rubus illecebrosus*) cultivated for its large multi-parted leaves, large white flowers, and showy red edible fruits — called also *balloonberry*

strawberry roan *n* **1 :** roan with a decidedly red ground color **2 :** a horse of a strawberry roan color

strawberry root aphid *n* **:** an aphid (*Aphis forbesi*) that damages strawberries by sucking the sap from the roots

strawberry root weevil *n* **:** a small black beetle (*Brachyrhinus ovatus*) of the family Curculionidae whose larva lives in the soil and feeds on the roots or girdles the crown of strawberry plants

strawberry rootworm *n* **:** a grub that is the larva of a small brownish black-spotted leaf beetle (*Paria fragariae*) and that lives in the soil and feeds on the roots of strawberries

strawberry sawfly *n* **:** a small black sawfly (*Empria maculatus*) whose larva eats the leaves of the strawberry plant

strawberry shrub *n* **:** CAROLINA ALLSPICE

strawberry-shrub family *n* **:** CALYCANTHACEAE

strawberry slug *n* **:** the larva of a strawberry sawfly

strawberry tassel *n* **:** PURPLE MILKWORT

strawberry tomato *n* **:** GROUND-CHERRY 2; *esp* **:** a stout hairy annual herb (*Physalis pruinosa*) of eastern No. America with sweet globular yellow fruits

strawberry tongue *n* **:** a tongue that is red from the swollen congested papillae typical of scarlet fever

strawberry tree *n* **1 :** a European evergreen tree (*Arbutus unedo*) with fruit resembling strawberries and racemose white flowers — called also *Irish strawberry, madrona* **2 :** a strawberry bush (*Euonymus americanus*); *also* **:** [2]WAHOO a

strawberry vine *n* **:** STRAWBERRY 1b

strawberry weevil *n* **1 :** a small weevil (*Anthonomus signatus*) that severs the stems of the strawberry and lays eggs in the buds **2 :** STRAWBERRY CROWN BORER

strawberry wine *n* **:** a dark red that is yellower and duller than cranberry and yellower, lighter, and stronger than average garnet or average wine

strawbill \ˈ⸗ˌ⸗\ *n* **:** HOODED MERGANSER

strawboard \ˈ⸗ˌ⸗\ *n* **:** board made of straw pulp and commonly used for packing and boxmaking

straw bond *n* **:** a bond whose sureties are worthless

straw boss *n* **1 :** an assistant to a foreman in charge of supervising and expediting the work of a small gang of workmen (as in a logging camp or factory or on a road gang) **2 :** a member of a group of workers who supervises the work of the others in addition to doing his own job

straw-boss \ˈ⸗ˈ⸗\ *vt* [*straw boss*] **:** to function as a straw boss at or over ⟨was *straw-bossing* the dam work —*Reader's Digest*⟩

strawbreadth \ˈ⸗ˌ⸗\ *n* **:** a very small distance

straw cat *n* **:** PAMPAS CAT

straw color *n* **:** a light yellow color like that of dry straw

strawed *past of* STRAW

straw·en \ˈstrȯən\ *adj* [ME, fr. [1]*straw* + *-en*] *archaic* **:** made of straw

straw fiddle *n* **:** a xylophone in which wooden bars are supported on rolls of straw

strawflower \ˈ⸗ˌ⸗\ *n* **1 :** any of several everlasting flowers; *specif* **:** an Australian annual herb (*Helichrysum bracteatum*) much grown for its heads of chaffy brightly colored long-keeping flowers **2 :** any of several herbs of the genus *Uvularia*

straw hat *n* **:** a hat of woven or plaited straw

strawhat \ˈ⸗ˌ⸗\ *or* **strawhat theater** *n* [*strawhat* fr. *strawhat theater*, fr. *straw hat* + *theater;* fr. the former fashion of wearing straw hats in summer] **:** a summer theater ⟨prepares packages of his own which he distributes to his playhouses and to a few other ~s —Henry Hewes⟩

strawing *pres part of* STRAW

straw·ish \ˈstrȯish, -ēsh\ *adj* **:** somewhat resembling straw esp. in color

straw itch *n* **:** GRAIN ITCH

straw·less \'=ˌləs\ *adj* **:** containing no straw
straw line *n* **:** a light cable used to haul the heavier cables of a rigging used in skidding logs
straw man *n* **:** MAN OF STRAW
strawmote \'=ˌ=\ *n*, *dial Eng* **:** a single straw
straw-necked ibis \'=ˌ=-\ *n* **:** an Australian ibis (*Threskiornis spinicollis* or *Carphibis spinicollis*) with modified feathers of the lower neck that are yellow and stiff and resemble straw
straw oil *n* **:** a high-boiling petroleum distillate similar to gas oil used chiefly in purifying coke-oven gas and other industrial gases
straw plait *n* **:** braided straw (as for making hats)
straw ride *n* **:** HAYRIDE
straws *pl of* STRAW, *pres 3d sing of* STRAW
straw sedge *n* **:** a common sedge (*Carex straminea*) of eastern No. America
strawsmear \'=ˌ=\ *n* **1** *or* **strawsmall** \'=ˌ=\ *Brit* **:** WHITETHROAT 1 **2** *Brit* **:** GARDEN WARBLER **3** *Brit* **:** WILLOW WREN
strawstack \'=ˌ=\ *n* **:** a pile of grain straw from which the grain has been threshed
strawstacker \'=ˌ==\ *n* [*strawstack* + *-er*] **:** one that piles straw in a stack
straw stem *n* **:** a wineglass stem pulled out of the substance of the bowl; *also* **:** a wineglass having such a stem
straw vote *n* **:** an unofficial vote (as taken at a chance gathering or by letters of inquiry) to indicate the relative strength of opposing candidates or issues — called also *straw ballot*
strawwalker \'=ˌ==\ *n* **:** a device inside a thresher or combine that consists of reciprocating notched bars to push the straw to the rear of the machine
straw wine *n* **:** a sweet dessert wine that resembles liqueur and is produced from grapes partially dried often on straw and in the sun before fermentation
strawworm \'=ˌ=\ *n* **1 :** CADDISWORM **2 :** any of several larval chalcid flies that injure the straw of wheat and other grains (as barley)
strawy \'strȯi, -ōē\ *adj* -ER/-EST [¹*straw* + *-y*] **1 :** of, relating to, resembling, consisting of, or containing straw **2** *obs* **:** WORTHLESS, TRIFLING
strawyard \'=ˌ=\ *n*, *Brit* **:** a yard littered with straw for wintering or fattening livestock
straw yellow *n* **:** STRAW 6
¹**stray** \'strā\ *vb* -ED/-ING/-S [ME *straien*, fr. MF *estraier* fr. (assumed) VL *extragare*, fr. L *extra-* outside + *vagari* to wander — more at EXTRA-, VAGARY] *vi* **1 a :** to wander from company, from confinement or restraint, or from the proper limits **:** rove at large ⟨leaving a gate open so that cattle ~ —Agnes M. Miall⟩ ⟨the two had ~*ed* apart where the woods were deepest —Mary Austin⟩ **b :** to leave a natural or accustomed habitat or environment ⟨fruit trees and ~*ed* garden flowers deep in the woods —Bernard DeVoto⟩ ⟨the most courteous . . . of eighteenth-century grands seigneurs ~*ed* out of his age into ours —Gerald Abraham⟩ ⟨of adults . . . at least one-tenth might never have ~*ed* outside in their lives —G.G. Coulton⟩ **2 a :** to roam about without fixed direction or purpose **:** wander at random ⟨fetid back alleys where we sometimes ~*ed* —Marvin Barret⟩ **b :** to move in a winding course **:** MEANDER **c :** to move without voluntary control or under external compulsion ⟨my hand automatically ~*s* towards my pocket —*Sydney (Australia) Bull.*⟩ ⟨eyes ~*ing* absently around the room⟩ **3 a** (1) **:** to engage temporarily or momentarily in sinful, immoral, or other than praiseworthy actions or thoughts **:** ERR (2) **:** to think or utter ideas contrary to or different from an accepted dogma ⟨those who ~*ed* from the party line —Kurt Glaser⟩ **b :** to become distracted from an argument or chain of thought **:** take up a tangential point ⟨I have ~*ed* from my . . . role of historian . . . to indulge in a bit of prophecy —J.B. Conant⟩ **4 :** to wander accidentally from a direct or chosen route **:** lose one's way **:** DEVIATE ⟨~*ed* off the road . . . in the dark of the moon —Mary Webb⟩ ⟨the unit ~*ed* across the border by mistake —*Springfield (Mass.) Union*⟩ **5 :** to present a haphazard or unkempt appearance ⟨black hair that ~*ed* carelessly about her face —Liam O'Flaherty⟩ ⟨a leading article (which regrettably ~*s* from page to page among the advertisements) —*Times Lit. Supp.*⟩ ~ *vt* **1** *archaic* **:** to cause to stray **2** *archaic* **:** to roam through or over
²**stray** \"\ *n* -S [ME, fr. AF *estray*, fr. OF *estraié*, past part. of *estraier* to stray] **1 a** (1) **:** a domestic animal that has left an enclosure or its proper place and company and wanders at large or is lost subject to impoundment and if unredeemed to forfeiture **:** ESTRAY (2) **:** an animal that has strayed ⟨the shepherd rounded up the flock's ~*s*⟩ (3) **:** an unidentified domestic animal (as a dog or an unbranded steer) wandering at large **b** (1) **:** a person or thing that strays or has strayed **:** a detached, isolated, or vagrant individual **:** STRAGGLER, WAIF ⟨harbored white renegades and ~*s* from hostile tribes —*Amer. Guide Series: Tenn.*⟩ ⟨do not own more than three books other than casual contemporary ~*s* —J.W.Krutch⟩ (2) **:** an animal or plant found outside its natural range or habitat or out of season **c** *obs* **:** a group of strayed animals, people, or things ⟨hast thou seen a ~ of bullocks and of heifers pass this way —Joseph Addison⟩ **2** [ME, fr. *straien* to stray] *archaic* **:** the act or process of going astray or of strolling aimlessly ⟨I would not from your love make such a ~ —Shak.⟩ **3** *Brit* **:** common land or pasturage; *also* **:** the right to allow one's stock to stray and feed thereon **4 a :** an electrical effect that is not produced by a transmitting station and that disturbs the reception of receiving apparatus **b :** an electric wave or current causing a stray — compare ATMOSPHERICS **5 :** an unexpected formation encountered in drilling an oil or gas well
³**stray** \"\ *adj* [²*stray*] **1 a :** escaped from confinement, supervision, or restraint or from a group of its kind ⟨a ~ cow⟩ ⟨~ dog⟩ ⟨~ child⟩ **b :** having been lost, misplaced, or forgotten ⟨the other fellows take handkerchiefs home and ~ coats sometimes —Janet Frame⟩ **2 :** wandering lost, aimless, or isolated from the normal or principal body, habitat, or course ⟨details picked up from ~ survivors —John Mason Brown⟩ ⟨account for every ~ traveller in the mountains —Owen Wister⟩ ⟨a ~ enemy group may at any time swoop down —Ed Cunningham⟩ **3 a :** occurring or appearing sporadically or at random ⟨~ acquaintances met with in hotel rooms and aeroplanes —*Geog. Jour.*⟩ ⟨the white dogwood were ~ handfuls of confetti in the young green —Horace Sutton⟩ **b :** touched upon or met with only in passing or in haste **:** OCCASIONAL, INCIDENTAL ⟨a series of scenes that (except for ~ ones) register honestly —John Kerry⟩ ⟨one or two ~ expressions that have evaded revision —*Times Lit. Supp.*⟩ ⟨a ~ weekly hour of hygiene —Hortense Calisher⟩ **c :** scattered about ⟨on our knees retrieving ~ cigarettes —A. Conan Doyle⟩ ⟨collecting ~ hairs from the farm horses' tails —W.P.Smith⟩ ⟨~ members of the congregation moved by the spirit may be prophesying in unknown tongues —W.L.Sperry⟩ **4 :** not serving any useful purpose **:** UNWANTED ⟨necessarily results in serious errors when ~ light . . . is not absorbed by the optical system —H.A.Stahl⟩ ⟨insulate them . . . so that no ~ current is introduced into the circuit —A.C.Morrison⟩ **5 :** written hastily or thoughtlessly and published in obscure or ephemeral journals ⟨wrote only one complete novel and a few ~ pieces and fragments —Henri Peyre⟩
strayaway \'==ˌ=\ *n* -S [¹*stray* + *away*] **:** one that strays away
strayed *past of* STRAY
stray energy *or* **stray power** *n* **:** electrical losses (as in a dynamo) due to friction, hysteresis, or eddy currents as distinguished from the loss from electric resistance in the conducting apparatus
stray·er \'strāə(r), -re(ə)r, -reə\ *n* -S **:** one that strays **:** STRAY
straying *pres part of* STRAY
stray line *n* **:** the portion of a log line which is run out to allow the chip to get clear of the stern eddies before the reckoning is begun
strays *pres 3d sing of* STRAY, *pl of* STRAY
strd *abbr* strand
¹**streak** \'strēk\ *n* -S [ME *strek*, *streke*, *strik*, *strike*, fr. OE *strica* line, streak; akin to MD *streke* line, stroke, OHG *strich*, Goth *striks* line, stroke, L *striga* row, furrow — more at STRIKE] **1** *obs* **:** a linear mark or cut ⟨in the microscope . . . you may see the very ~*s* —Henry Power⟩ **2 a :** an irregular or indistinct stripe on the coat of an animal or the plumage of a bird ⟨a magnolia warbler . . . his bluish gray back and yellow breast crossed by a black band from which black ~*s* run downward —W.P.Smith⟩ **b** (1) **:** an irregular strip or line of contrasting color or texture causing variation in or on a surface ⟨faded ~*s* in a curtain where the sun hits it⟩ ⟨bacon with a thick ~ of lean⟩ (2) **:** an incision made by chipping a pine tree for obtaining turpentine **c :** the color of the fine powder of a mineral obtained by scratching, pulverizing, or rubbing against a hard white surface, often differing from the color of the mineral in mass, and being important as a distinguishing character esp. for minerals having metallic luster **d :** an imperfection in glass consisting of a wavy or colored line that distorts an image **e** (1) **:** a threadlike striation (2) **:** inoculum implanted (as with a needle drawn across the surface) in a line or stripe upon a solidified culture medium (3) **:** STREAK CULTURE **f** (1) **:** any of several virus diseases of plants (as the potato, tomato, raspberry, or sugarcane) resembling mosaic but usu. producing at least some linear markings — compare BLUESTEM 2, TOMATO STREAK (2) **:** a disease of sweet peas caused by a bacillus (*Erwinia lathyri*) and characterized by brownish spots or streaks on the stem, petioles, and leaves **3 a :** a narrow band of light ⟨the first grey ~*s* of dawn —R.S. Porteous⟩ ⟨a ~ of moonlight came in through the window —Sherwood Anderson⟩ ⟨burning oil flew outwards in a ~ —Nevil Shute⟩ **b :** a dart of lightning **:** BOLT ⟨in dazzling ~*s* the vivid lightnings play —William Cowper⟩ ⟨off like a ~, heading . . . down the homestretch —*N. Y. Times*⟩ **4 a :** a slight admixture (as of an inherent character) **:** STRAIN, TRACE ⟨the ~ of extreme stubbornness . . . was both his strength and his misfortune —J.K.Galbraith⟩ ⟨a ~ of Indian blood in him —A.W.Long⟩ **b :** a brief run (as of luck) ⟨when he hits a ~ . . . everything's dandy —Hamilton Basso⟩ **c :** a consecutive series (as of victories or defeats) ⟨had a long winning ~ and took the . . . lead —A.J.Liebling⟩ **d :** a short interval or transitory phase **:** FIT, SPELL ⟨got started on one of her talking ~*s* —Erskine Caldwell⟩ **5 a :** a long irregular strip (as of land or water) ⟨a ~ of deep green brush marks the course of a creek —*Amer. Guide Series: Ark.*⟩ **b :** a narrow layer (as of ore) **:** SEAM, VEIN ⟨struck a pay ~ at a thousand feet⟩
²**streak** \"\ *vb* -ED/-ING/-S *vt* **1 :** to make streaks on or in **:** STRIATE ⟨the water was ~*ed* with the sunset colors —R.H. Newman⟩ ⟨the sense of living nature seems to ~ some of his more recent pages —Cecil Sprigge⟩ **2 :** to prepare a streak culture of ~ *vi* **1 a :** to make streaks ⟨ribbons of rust ~ down . . . from patches of corrugated iron on the roof —James Reynolds⟩ **b :** to rush swiftly **:** BOLT, ROCKET ⟨lightning ~*s* from cloud to cloud⟩ ⟨reporters . . . ~*ed* through the crowd and out of the doors searching for telephones —Erle Stanley Gardner⟩ ⟨jet planes ~*ed* to three new transcontinental speed records —*Newsweek*⟩ ⟨when the nurse opened the door, the cat ~*ed* in —Henrietta Weigel⟩ **2 :** to become streaked ⟨hair beginning to ~ with gray⟩
³**streak** \"\ *vt* -ED/-ING/-S [ME *streken* to stroke, prob. fr. MD — more at STROKE] *obs* **:** RUB, SMEAR ⟨with the juice of this I'll ~ her eyes —Shak.⟩
⁴**streak** *archaic var of* STRAKE
⁵**streak** \'strek\ *var of* STREEK
streak culture *n* **:** a culture inoculated with a streak
streaked \'strēkt, -kəd\ *adj* [fr. past part. of ²*streak*] **1 :** marked with or as if with stripes or linear discolorations **:** GRIZZLED, STRIATED ⟨~ hair⟩ ⟨~ lumber⟩ **2 :** physically or mentally disturbed **:** stricken with illness or anxiety **:** SICK, UPSET ⟨looked so ~ and so chopfallen, that I felt . . . sorry for him —T.C.Haliburton⟩
streaked-back plover \'=ˌ=-\ *n* **:** TURNSTONE
streaked bass *n* **:** STRIPED BASS
streak·er \'strēkə(r)\ *n* -S [¹*streak* + *-er*; fr. the usu. seven black stripes from gill cover to tail base of the yellow bass] **1 :** YELLOW BASS **2 :** WHITE BASS 1
streak·i·ly \-kəlē, -li\ *adv* **:** in a streaky manner
streak·i·ness \-kēnəs, -kin-\ *n* -ES **:** the quality or state of being streaky
streak lightning *n* **:** CHAIN LIGHTNING
streak plate *n* **:** a piece of white unglazed porcelain on which to test the streak of a mineral
streaky \'strēkē, -ki\ *adj* -ER/-EST [¹*streak* + *-y*] **1 a :** resembling or characterized by streaks ⟨a smoky fleece . . . brushed to give a ~ effect —*Women's Wear Daily*⟩ **b :** marked with streaks ⟨fat legs and dirty, ~ face —Hugh Walpole⟩ **c :** having alternate streaks of fat and lean ⟨~ bacon⟩ **2 :** APPREHENSIVE ⟨as nervous and ~ about it as a cat on a hot rock —H.L.Davis⟩ **3 :** of mixed quality **:** VARIABLE, UNRELIABLE ⟨humans are the most ~ of conceivable things —H.G.Wells⟩
¹**stream** \'strēm\ *n* -S *often attrib* [ME *strem*, *streme*, fr. OE *strēam*; akin to OHG *stroum*, *strōm* stream, ON *straumr* stream, OIr *sruaimm* river, OSlav *struja* flow, Gk *rhysis* flow, *rhein* to flow, Skt *sravati* it flows, *sarati* it runs, flows — more at SERUM] **1 a :** a body of running water flowing in a channel on the surface of the ground, in a cavern below the surface, or beneath or in a glacier ⟨cross the river . . . not far from where General Washington forded the ~ —Gladys Taber⟩ — compare CREEK, RIVER; see CURRENT table **b :** BROOK, RIVULET **2 a :** a steady succession (as of words or events) ⟨let loose a ~ of commentary and discussion —R.W.Southern⟩ ⟨life presents a perpetual ~ of problems —W.J.Reilly⟩ **b :** a constantly renewed supply ⟨the balanced budget . . . injects as much into the income ~ as it takes away —J.G.Gurley⟩ ⟨a steady ~ of material flowed into the Smithsonian from . . . all over the world —D.S. & Jessie Jordan⟩ **c :** a continuous procession moving in one direction ⟨sent a ~ of miners pouring . . . west —R.A.Billington⟩ ⟨a ~ of Sunday traffic⟩ ⟨goats followed him — a long ~ that pattered on small sharp hoofs behind him —Stuart Cloete⟩ **3 a :** an outpouring of a fluid from a source or container ⟨a ~ of water . . . from a fire nozzle —W.Y.Kimball⟩ ⟨pour a sticky ~ of syrup from a pitcher⟩ ⟨a reaction ~ can be switched from one line to the other —*Chem. & Engineering News*⟩ **b :** an effusion of a bodily fluid ⟨~*s* of sweat pour down his back⟩ **c :** an unbroken flow (as of gas or particles of matter) ⟨moisture was kept at a high level by a deep ~ of persistent northerly winds —*Farmer's Weekly (So. Africa)*⟩ ⟨an electric current is a ~ of . . . electrons —Leonard Engel⟩ **d** (1) **:** a valley glacier ⟨ice ~*s* coalesced to form a piedmont glacier —*Jour. of Geol.*⟩ (2) **:** a lava flow esp. long and narrow ⟨dated lava ~*s* —W.J.Miller⟩ (3) **:** sand grains moving or having moved downwind in a fairly continuous mass ⟨the dune advances . . . down the sand ~ —*Geog. Jour.*⟩ — compare ROCK STREAM **4 a :** a streak of light ⟨the ashen ~ of daybreak —Ellen Glasgow⟩ **b** *obs* **:** the tail of a comet ⟨saw another comet . . . but the ~ not so long as the former —John Evelyn⟩ **5 a :** a relatively narrow well-defined and usu. swift oceanic current ⟨the Gulf ~⟩ **b :** the center of a body of running water where the current is swiftest ⟨anchored out in the ~ and came ashore in a launch⟩ **c :** the propulsive current of running water ⟨floating straight, obedient to the ~ —Shak.⟩ ⟨row against the ~⟩ **d :** a prevailing attitude or group ⟨in full accord with the main ~ of British policy —*New Statesman & Nation*⟩ **e :** a dominant influence or line of development ⟨the two ~*s* of heredity . . . that shaped his life —C.A.Dinsmore⟩ ⟨academicians, men out of the main creative ~ of their time —Donald Mintz⟩ ⟨eddies in the great ~ of baroque music —P.H.Lang⟩ **6 streams** *pl*, *archaic* **:** flowing waters ⟨a river . . . pours its ~*s* through a narrow vale —Sir Walter Scott⟩ **syn** see FLOW — **on stream :** in or into production ⟨the refinery could be *on stream* within four or five weeks —Clifton Daniel⟩ ⟨our Baton Rouge plant . . . will go *on stream*, it is expected, in June of this year —*Ethyl News*⟩
²**stream** \"\ *vb* -ED/-ING/-S [ME *stremen*, fr. *strem*, *streme* stream] *vi* **1 a :** to flow in or as if in a stream ⟨a river ~*s* to the sea⟩ ⟨firelight and dance music ~ out from its windows —Douglas Stewart⟩ ⟨a cooler wind was beginning to ~ through the . . . palms —Jean Boley⟩ ⟨capes and headlands . . . ~*ing* away into the west —H.H.Finlayson⟩ ⟨wealth ~*ing* through his fingers —Joseph Conrad⟩ **b :** to emit a beam of light **:** leave a bright trail ⟨a falling star ~*ed* down the blue vault —O.S.J. Gogarty⟩ **2 a :** to exude a bodily fluid in profuse amounts ⟨holding his pocket handkerchief before his ~*ing* eyes —Lewis Carroll⟩ **b :** to become saturated with a discharge of bodily fluid ⟨~*ing* with perspiration under the hot klieg lights⟩ **3 :** to become fully extended by or as if by a current **:** trail out at full length ⟨kelps, anchored to rocks while ~*ing* out in the water —R.E.Coker⟩ ⟨outthrust neck and ~*ing* legs are characteristic of its flight —*Nat'l Geographic*⟩ ⟨the boy, with hair ~*ing* back, was rushing helter-skelter down the hill —John Galsworthy⟩ **4 :** to pour in large numbers in one direction ⟨passengers . . . ~*ed* ashore on seven of the eight gangways —Vernon Pizer⟩ ⟨rooks went ~*ing* across the windy sky —Mary Webb⟩ ⟨innumerable requests and invitations . . . ~ in —Robert Bendiner⟩ ~ *vt* **1 :** to emit or cause to flow **:** EXUDE ⟨his eyes ~*ed* tears⟩ **2 :** to wave or display fully extended ⟨its radiator grille ~*ing* a flag —Kathryn Grondahl⟩ **3 :** to put into the water **:** allow (a tow) to run out to full length ⟨~ an anchor buoy⟩ ⟨~ a paravane⟩ ⟨~ a grass line so that the other ship can grapple it and pick it up —*Manual of Seamanship*⟩ **4 :** to subject to the action of water as a means of exposing ore **:** WASH ⟨slaves were ~*ing* the gravel for tin ore —Charles Kingsley⟩ **syn** see POUR
stream anchor *n* **:** a light anchor for use with a bower in narrow waterways
stream cable *n* **:** the cable of a stream anchor
stream capture *n* **:** CAPTURE 3
¹**stream·er** \'strēmə(r)\ *n* -S [ME *stremer*, fr. *stremen* to stream + *-er* — more at STREAM] **1 a :** a flag that streams in the wind; *esp* **:** PENNANT **b :** a wavy band resembling a fluttering pennon ⟨clouds . . . like ~*s* of snow —O.E.Rölvaag⟩ **c :** a narrow free-floating strip (as of cloth or crepe paper) ⟨a hat with ~*s* down the back⟩ ⟨a hall festooned with ~*s*⟩ **d :** STREAMER FLY **e :** a ribbon poster esp. used in a window or store display and often having a single line of wording **f :** BANNER 4 **g :** a parachute that streams out from the pack but fails to blossom **2 a** *obs* **:** the tail of a comet **b :** a long gauzelike extension of the solar corona brighter at the base and fading to invisibility at the end, sometimes showing filamentous structure, and visible only during a total solar eclipse **c streamers** *pl* **:** AURORA BOREALIS **d :** a visible brush discharge streaming out from some part of an electric circuit or charged body — compare CORONA 2g **3 :** one that washes sand or gravel in search of ore **syn** see FLAG
²**streamer** \"\ *vt* -ED/-ING/-S **:** to provide or decorate with streamers
streamer fly *n* **:** any large wet fisherman's fly with long streamer feathers, hair, or other appendages extending out behind the hook and from the head
stream feeding *n* **:** a method of feeding in which sheets are overlapped as they approach the front guides on the feedboard of a printing press
streamflow \'=ˌ=\ *n* **:** water flowing in a stream channel; *specif* **:** the velocity and volume of such water
¹**stream·ing** \'strēmiŋ, -mēŋ\ *n* -S [ME *streming*, fr. gerund of *stremen* to stream — more at STREAM] **:** an act or instance of flowing; *specif* **:** CYCLOSIS
²**streaming** *adj* [fr. pres. part. of ²*stream*] **:** issuing in or suffused with streams **:** FLOWING, RUNNING ⟨a ~ cold⟩ ⟨a ~ umbrella⟩ ⟨a ~ sunset⟩ — **stream·ing·ly** *adv*
streaming potential *n* **:** a potential difference that arises across a capillary tube or membrane when a liquid is forced through it — compare ZETA POTENTIAL
stream jam *n* **:** a log jam that reaches neither shore — called also *center jam*
stream·less \'=ˌləs\ *adj* **:** having no stream
stream·let \-lət\ *n* -S [¹*stream* + *-let*] **:** a small stream
¹**streamline** \'=ˌ=\ *n*, *often attrib* [¹*stream* + *line*] **1 a :** LINE OF FLOW ⟨~*s* of liquid flowing in a constricted tube —H.B. Lemon & Michael Ference⟩ **b :** the path of a fluid particle relative to a solid body past which the fluid is moving in smooth flow without turbulence ⟨consider the ~*s* . . . around the plane parts —S.A.Moss⟩ **2 a :** a contour offering minimum resistance to a current ⟨probably no animal or plant in the water is without some touch of ~ —R.E.Coker⟩ ⟨the ~ of an airfoil⟩ ⟨the island . . . was formed generally in a ~ —Norman Mailer⟩ **b :** a fluid line ⟨~ may not improve the performance of a typewriter but it makes it look efficient⟩
²**streamline** \'=ˌ=\ *vt* **1 a :** to adapt to a line of flow ⟨even without human assistance the controls of an airplane tend to ~ themselves⟩ **b :** to provide with a contour offering minimum resistance to a current ⟨the fish is the first organism to have its hind appendage . . . ~*ed* into it —A.L.Kroeber⟩ ⟨the nose is well ~*ed* with aluminum cowling giving a bullet-like appearance —*Aero Digest*⟩ **c :** to design with flowing contours ⟨~ apparatus for greater cleanliness and safety —D.E.Pierce⟩ **2 :** to bring up to date **:** renovate in appearance or attitude **:** MODERNIZE ⟨wants to ~ his people by treading on their fondest superstitions —Joseph Hitrec⟩ ⟨the archaic judiciary system has been ~*ed* —T.H.Fielding⟩ ⟨~ the text, to bring it closer to the contemporary stage —John Mason Brown⟩ **3 a :** to impose order or discipline upon **:** INTEGRATE, ORGANIZE ⟨everything is ~*ed* — doctrine, tactics, production, armaments, all integrated, all enshrined in a single dynamic —Lewis Hastings⟩ **b :** to make simpler or more efficient ⟨machines that extrude damp clay . . . ~ the work of clay modelers —*Ford Times*⟩ ⟨enacted legislation combining our armed forces into a single department of defense to ~ our defense machinery —*Think*⟩ **c :** to reduce to a minimum ⟨school terms were ~*ed* . . . to get the graduate sooner for industry —E.C.McVoy⟩
streamlined \'=ˌ=\ *adj* **1 a :** affording minimum resistance to a current **:** contoured to reduce drag ⟨a ~ yacht⟩ ⟨~ engine nacelles⟩ ⟨~ hounds chase a fleeing mechanical rabbit —*Amer. Guide Series: Ark.*⟩ ⟨go easy on ice cream till we get the figure a bit more ~ —*Auckland (New Zealand) Weekly News*⟩ **b :** stripped of nonessentials **:** SIMPLIFIED, COMPACT ⟨a ~ ticket . . . replacing the long tickets previously used for transcontinental travel —*Wall Street Jour.*⟩ ⟨all-steel kitchens, ~ and efficient, with no empty spaces or useless nooks —Harriette Arnow⟩ **c :** effectively integrated **:** ORGANIZED ⟨the shrinking of the world . . . requires ~ and internationally uniform laws of aviation —*Air Transportation*⟩ **2 :** having fluid lines **:** CURVILINEAR ⟨~ watch bracelet⟩ ⟨~ pressure cooker⟩ **3 :** brought up to date **:** MODERNIZED ⟨jumped from the oxcart to the ultra ~ —*Holiday*⟩ ⟨has fashioned . . . a ~ version of the . . . novels —J.T.Winterich⟩ **4 :** of, relating to, or characteristic of streamline flow **:** LAMINAR ⟨the flow of the unagglutinated blood is laminar or ~ —*Science*⟩
streamline flow *n* **:** an uninterrupted flow (as of air) past a solid body in which the direction at every point remains unchanged with the passage of time **:** LAMINAR FLOW — compare TURBULENT FLOW
streamliner \'=ˌ==\ *n* **:** one that is streamlined; *esp* **:** a streamlined train
streamlining *n* [fr. gerund of ²*streamline*] **1 a :** contouring for minimum resistance to a current ⟨the ~ of aircraft⟩ **b :** curvilinear design ⟨the ~ of household appliances is more decorative than functional⟩ **2 :** revision to increase efficiency or eliminate what is obsolete or nonessential **:** MODERNIZATION, SIMPLIFICATION ⟨the ~ of factory operations —*Nat'l Stationer*⟩ ⟨~ certainly reduced the number of opportunities for misunderstanding —*Jour. of Accountancy*⟩
stream of consciousness 1 : individual conscious experience considered as a series of processes, intrapsychic events, or experiences continuously moving forward in time — compare CONSCIOUSNESS 3 **2 :** INTERIOR MONOLOGUE
stream orchid *n* **:** a helleborine (*Epipactis gigantea*) native to western No. America and having greenish or purplish pendulous flowers — called also *giant helleborine*
stream piracy *n* **:** CAPTURE 3
streams *pl of* STREAM, *pres 3d sing of* STREAM
streamside \'=ˌ=\ *n* **:** the land bordering on a stream
stream terrace *n* **:** one of a series of terraces cut usu. out of solid rock by successive changes in the regimen of a stream from alluviation to downcutting — called also *river terrace*; compare ALLUVIAL TERRACE
stream tin *n* **:** cassiterite occurring in the form of rolled fragments or pebbles in alluvial deposits
streamway \'=ˌ=\ *n* **1 :** the current of a stream **2 :** the bed or course of a stream
streamwort \'=ˌ=\ *n* [¹*stream* + *wort*] **:** a plant of the family Haloragaceae
streamy \'strēmē, -mi\ *adj* -ER/-EST [ME *stremy*, fr. *strem*, *streme* stream + *-y* — more at STREAM] **1 :** abounding in streams **2 :** resembling or issuing in a stream
streb·li·dae \'strebləˌdē\ *n pl*, *cap* [NL, fr. *Strebla*, type genus (fr. Gk *streblos* twisted, crooked) + NL *-idae* — more

at STROPHE] **:** a small widely distributed family of dipterous flies the adults of which are external parasites on bats

streek \'strēk\ *vb* -ED/-ING/-S [ME (northern dial.) *streken,* fr. OE *strec-,* stem of *streccan* to stretch] *vt* **1** *chiefly Scot* **:** STRETCH, EXTEND **2** *chiefly Scot* **:** to lay out (a dead body) ~ *vi* **1 :** to fall or lie prostrate **:** stretch out **2** *obs* **:** to extend toward or to something **:** REACH

¹streel \'strē(ə)l\ *vi* [perh. fr. IrGael *straoillim* I trail, *straoilleān* loiterer] **1** *chiefly Irish* **:** to saunter idly and aimlessly **:** trail along **:** STRAGGLE ⟨tinkers ~*ed* into view —Mervyn Wall⟩ **2** *chiefly Irish* **:** to trail or float in the manner of a streamer ⟨the peat smoke ~*ing* off —Naomi Mitchison⟩

²streel \"\ *or* **streel·er** \-lər\ *n* -S *chiefly Irish* **:** an untidy slovenly person **:** SLATTERN

¹streen *obs var of* STRAIN

²streen \'strēn\ *n* [by shortening] *Scot* **:** YESTREEN

¹street \'strēt, *usu* -ēd.+V\ *n* -S [ME *strete,* fr. OE *strǣt;* akin to OFris *strēte* street, OHG *straza, strazza;* all fr. a prehistoric WGmc word borrowed fr. LL *strata* paved road, fr. L, fem. of *stratus,* past part. of *sternere* to spread out, throw down — more at STREW] **1 a** *obs* **:** a paved road **:** HIGHWAY ⟨until recently the Canterbury road was known as the *Street* —*Chicago Daily Tribune*⟩ **b** (1) **:** a public thoroughfare esp. in a city, town, or village including all area within the right of way (as sidewalks and tree belts) and sometimes further distinguished as being wider than an alley or lane but narrower than an avenue or boulevard and as separating blocks rather than penetrating them ⟨another alley that . . . gave on a through ~ —Paul Bowles⟩ — contrasted with *road;* abbr. *st.* (2) **:** the strip of a public thoroughfare reserved for vehicular traffic ⟨a pedestrian killed while crossing the ~⟩ (3) **:** a public thoroughfare including the property abutting it ⟨lives on a fashionable ~⟩ ⟨has an office on Main *Street*⟩ **c :** the roadway in front of or between the barracks or tents of a company or battery ⟨instruction in . . . shelter tent pitching, in the battery ~ —C.P.Smith⟩ **d :** a promising line of development or a channeling of effort ⟨in a crucial election year . . . was shrewdly working both sides of the ~ —*Time*⟩ ⟨this . . . method of furthering economic development can operate at full effectiveness only as a two-way ~ —*Atlantic*⟩ **2 :** the people occupying property along a street ⟨the whole ~ is up in arms over the rezoning proposal⟩ **3** *usu cap* **a :** a district (as Wall Street, Fleet Street) identified with a particular profession ⟨the *Street's* top ten banking houses —*Time*⟩ ⟨coming back as editor to the *Street* —*London Daily Chronicle*⟩ **b :** the people who work there ⟨railroads continued to act well in the opinion of the *Street* —*Wall Street Jour.*⟩ **4 a :** the life or profession of a prostitute ⟨found in opium dens . . . new contingents of women discovered on the ~ —Alfred Buchanan⟩ — usu. used in pl. ⟨a woman of the ~*s*⟩ **b :** the poor or derelict of a city ⟨children of the ~, clad in rags —Heinrich Harrer⟩ **c** *slang* **:** release from confinement **:** FREEDOM, LIBERTY ⟨you won't go right back on it when you make the ~ again —Nelson Algren⟩ **5 :** the common man ⟨in Socrates the ~ conquered the intelligentsia and the aristocracy —C.P.Rodocanachi⟩ — **on the street** *adv (or adj)* **1 :** out of doors in the city ⟨met him *on the street*⟩ **2 a :** idle, homeless, or out of a job ⟨his paper folded; and he's *on the street* —D.M.Mankiewicz⟩ **b :** in the company of the idle, homeless, or derelict in an urban area ⟨boys returning home . . . are amused at the bebops, forgetting their own days *on the street* —C.K.Myers⟩ — **up one's street** *or* **down one's street :** suited to one's abilities or tastes ⟨violence did not dismay them; it was right *down their street* —Raymond Chandler⟩

²street \"\ *adj* [ME *strete,* fr. *strete,* n.] **1 :** of or relating to the thoroughfares of an urban area: as **a :** adjoining or giving access to a street ⟨~ door⟩ **b :** carried on or taking place in the streets ⟨~ fighting⟩ ⟨~ beggary⟩ **c :** living or working on the streets ⟨~ gamin⟩ ⟨~ vendor⟩ **d :** located in, used for, or serving as a guide to the streets ⟨fluorescent ~ lighting⟩ ⟨a ~ directory⟩ **e :** performing in or heard on the streets ⟨~ band⟩ ⟨~ music⟩ ⟨~ cries⟩ **f** (1) **:** suitable for wear on the street ⟨~ clothes⟩ ⟨~ makeup⟩ (2) **:** of a length that does not touch the ground — used of women's dresses in lengths reaching to the knee, calf, or ankle **2 a :** of or relating to the common man ⟨~ humor⟩ **b :** associated with the business of a particular district (as Wall Street) ⟨~ dollar market⟩ **c :** established by trading outside the exchange in a financial center ⟨~ price⟩ ⟨~ rate⟩ **3 :** caused by a street virus ⟨~ distemper⟩

street arab *n, often cap A* **:** a homeless vagabond in the streets of a city and esp. an outcast boy or girl **:** GAMIN

street broker *n* **:** an independent stockbroker who trades elsewhere than on an exchange floor

streetcar \'ˌ=,=\ *n* **:** a vehicle on rails used primarily for transporting passengers and usu. operating within the city limits — compare TROLLEY CAR

street certificate *n* **:** a stock certificate endorsed in blank by the registered owner and guaranteed by a broker that circulates freely from seller to buyer in the market without requiring a transfer on the books of the corporation

street cleaner *or* **street sweeper** *n* **:** one that cleans streets; *esp* **:** an employee of a municipal sanitation department

street edition *n* **:** an edition of a newspaper intended for sale on newsstands or street corners as distinguished from an edition intended primarily for home or office delivery

street elbow *n* **:** a pipe elbow with a female thread on one end and a male thread on the other

street elbow

street·ful \'=,fu̇l\ *n* -S **:** as much or as many as a street will hold

street girl *n* **:** PROSTITUTE

streetlamp \'=,=\ *n* **:** STREETLIGHT

street·let \'=lət\ *n* -S [*street* + *-let*] **:** a very narrow street

streetlight \'=,=\ *n* **:** a light (as an arc lamp) usu. mounted on a pole and constituting one of a series spaced at intervals along a public street or highway

street loan *n* **:** CALL LOAN

street name *n* **:** a recognized broker, dealer, or bank in a financial district in whose name securities may be registered as a convenience for holding certificates and facilitating transfer; *specif* **:** NOMINEE 3

street offense *n, Eng law* **:** an offense (as loitering for purposes of prostitution, ringing doorbells without cause, blowing horns or making noise to cause people to assemble) occurring in the street and classified as such by statute

street orderly *n, chiefly Brit* **:** STREET CLEANER

street organ *n* **:** a crude reed organ played on the streets and operated by turning a crank

street paper *n* **:** commercial paper sold through a dealer rather than to a bank and usu. of lower quality than bank paper

street piano *n* **:** a rudimentary mechanical piano played on the streets and operated by turning a crank or handle — called also *hurdy-gurdy*

street piano

street plate *n* **:** one of several steel plates that can be bolted to the track of a crawler tractor to provide a flat ground contact

street railway *n* **:** a line operating streetcars or buses

streets \'strēts\ *adv* [fr. pl. of *street*] **:** by a wide margin **:** far and away ⟨a nice woman, ~ above these other callers —Katherine Mansfield⟩ ⟨had run the house for thirty shillings a week less, and run it ~ better —F.M.Ford⟩

street virus *n* **:** virulent or natural virus (as of rabies) as distinguished from virus attenuated in the laboratory

streetwalker \'=,==\ *n* **:** PROSTITUTE

streetwalking \'=,==\ *n* **:** PROSTITUTION

street·ward \'=wə(r)d\ *adv (or adj)* **:** toward the street

Stre·ga \'strāgə\ *trademark* — used for a sweet spicy orange-flavored yellow liqueur

streik \'strēk\ *Scot & dial Eng var of* STREEK

stre·litz·ia \strə'litsēə\ *n, cap* [NL, fr. Charlotte Sophia †1818 Princess of Mecklenburg-*Strelitz* and wife of George III of England + NL *-ia*] **:** a small genus of usu. large African herbs (family Musaceae) resembling the banana, rarely having a woody base, and having rigid glaucous distichous leaves and richly colored flowers with three sepals and three very irregular petals — compare BIRD-OF-PARADISE

strem·ma·to·graph \'stremədə,graf\ *n* [Gk *stremmat-, stremma* twist, thread (akin to Gk *strephein* to turn) + E *-graph* — more at STROPHE] **:** an instrument for determining the fiber stresses in rails under moving trains

streng·ite \'streŋ,īt\ *n* -S [G *strengit,* fr. Johann A. *Streng* †1897 Ger. mineralogist + G *-it* -ite] **:** a mineral $FePO_4 \cdot 2H_2O$ consisting of a hydrous iron phosphate, occurring mostly in pale red botryoidal masses, and being isomorphous with variscite (sp. gr. 2.87)

strength \'streŋ(k)th, 'stren(t)th\ *n, pl* **strengths** \-ths, 'streŋks\ [ME *strengthe, strenthe,* fr. OE *strengthu;* akin to OHG *strengida* strength, *strengi* strong — more at STRONG] **1 a :** moral courage ⟨~ to surmount the horrors and humiliations of . . . defeat —Patrick O'Donovan⟩ ⟨the inner ~ of self-restraint —A.E.Stevenson †1965⟩ **b :** physical force or vigor **:** BRAWN, VITALITY ⟨the lion's natural weapons . . . ~ and cunning —James Stevenson-Hamilton⟩ ⟨as the day went on, her ~ lessened —Millen Brand⟩ **c** (1) **:** ability to produce an effect **:** INFLUENCE ⟨the ~ of his personal prestige —A.L. Funk⟩ ⟨a policy based on peace through ~ —R.M.Makins⟩ (2) **:** a quality of flour that determines the volume and texture of the loaf and depends on the amount and kind of protein present (3) **:** energy content ⟨testing the ~ of a new high explosive⟩ **d** *archaic* **:** healthy condition **:** PRODUCTIVENESS — used of soil ⟨westwardly . . . the soil again improves in ~ —Charles Vancouver⟩ **2 a** (1) **:** a source of power or influence ⟨the magnificent sense of history and tradition which is one of the ~*s* of the Roman Catholic Church —*Newsweek*⟩ (2) **:** a strong attribute or inherent asset ⟨make it clear what you consider are the ~*s* and weaknesses of the book —Raymond Walters b. 1912⟩ ⟨children . . . exhibit special gifts and ~*s* relatively early —Gertrude H. Hildreth⟩ ⟨it was Napoleon's ~ neither to admit defeat nor to be trapped by stubborn adherence to a ruinous course —Oscar Handlin⟩ **b** *archaic* **:** a secure retreat **:** FORTRESS, STRONGHOLD ⟨all the forts and ~*s* of the realm —Robert Barret⟩ **c** (1) **:** a strong position ⟨negotiate from ~⟩ (2) *obs* **:** a protective barrier **:** EMBANKMENT, FORTIFICATION **3 a :** military might ⟨made it easier for power-seeking nations to build ~ for the second world war —T.F. Hawkins⟩ **b** *obs* (1) **:** military forces (2) **:** a fighting force **c** *archaic* **:** ability to withstand assault ⟨castle's ~ will laugh a siege to scorn —Shak.⟩ **d :** ability to withstand stress or deformation **:** the quality of bodies by which they endure the application of force without breaking **:** TOUGHNESS, COHESION ⟨the ~ of igneous rocks⟩ ⟨the rubber does not attain full ~ until vulcanization is complete —*Dun's Rev.*⟩ — compare BREAKING STRENGTH, COMPRESSIVE STRENGTH, FATIGUE STRENGTH, TENSILE STRENGTH **e** (1) **:** the number of personnel or units on a military muster roll ⟨the struggle . . . was terrific, costing each side about one third of its ~ —*Amer. Guide Series: Tenn.*⟩ ⟨Commonwealth has a powerful ~ of naval bases around the world —Quentin Reynolds⟩ (2) **:** the authorized complement of a military unit ⟨suggested that we bring the regiment up to ~ with carefully certified officers —Oliver La Farge⟩ ⟨sufficiently valuable assistants to be put on the ~ —*Manchester Guardian Weekly*⟩ (3) **:** large numbers ⟨forces landed in ~ in three places —*Infantry Jour.*⟩ **f :** the number of personnel on a roster of any kind ⟨an employed ~ of 70,000 —*Country Life*⟩ **g** *archaic* **:** a sufficient number ⟨without . . . their crews he had no longer ~ enough to navigate the ship —George Anson⟩ **h :** available means of support **:** reserves that can be mobilized at will **:** RESOURCES ⟨economic and industrial . . . ~*s* of the Communist and anti-Communist blocs —*N. Y. Times*⟩ **4 a** (1) **:** velocity or amount of flow **:** relative quantity or degree **:** INTENSITY, VOLUME ⟨~ of the wind⟩ ⟨the ~ and direction of sea currents vary considerably at different times of the year —W.H.Dowdeswell⟩ ⟨it is not sufficient to know merely the overall ~ of a noise —S.S.Stevens⟩ (2) **:** the phase of a tidal current when its velocity is greatest; *also* **:** the velocity at that time **b :** fervor or predominant inclination **:** PROFOUNDNESS, VEHEMENCE — used of a mental or emotional attitude ⟨~ of conviction⟩ ⟨the overwhelming ~ of British opinion —A.P.Ryan⟩ **c :** degree of coloration or dilution **:** GRADATION, POTENCY ⟨each part of the engraving should print at its exact ~ —John Southward⟩ ⟨~*s* are given as percentages of alcohol by volume —O.A.Mendelsohn⟩ **d :** degree of ionization in solution — used of acids and bases; compare ACIDITY 1a, BASICITY 1 **e :** vigor of demand **:** rising tendency in prices ⟨~ in consumer buying⟩ ⟨stock markets were displaying remarkable drive and ~ —*London Financial Times*⟩ **5 a** *obs* **:** legal backing **:** AUTHORITY ⟨thou hast the ~ of laws —Shak.⟩ **b :** the true facts or general significance **:** GIST, TENOR ⟨intent to have an explanation . . . and I'll get the ~ of matters soon enough —Rex Ingamells⟩ **c :** degree of importance or credibility **:** SOUNDNESS, WEIGHT ⟨~ of an argument⟩ ⟨~ of legal evidence⟩ **d :** BASIS — used in the phrase *on the strength of* ⟨a fussy housewife scalding the entire pantry on the ~ of one ant in the cookie jar —H.L.Davis⟩ ⟨new sawmills were established on the ~ of anticipated canal trade —*Amer. Guide Series: Ind.*⟩ **6 :** force of expression or treatment **:** clarity of definition ⟨it was this titan's spirit which gave such drive and ~ to the mightiest of his plays —John Mason Brown⟩ ⟨the film finds pictorial ~ in its fine blending of bare reality and shattering glitter —Cecile Starr⟩ ⟨the building masses are . . . well related, endowing the structure with a silhouette of great ~ —*Amer. Guide Series: N. Y. City*⟩ **syn** see POWER — **from strength to strength :** vigorously forward **:** from one high point to the next ⟨the Horse of the Year Show goes *from strength to strength* . . . no waiting, no tedium —John Board⟩

strength deck *n* **:** the uppermost continuous deck that resists longitudinal bending

strength·en \-thən\ *vb* **strengthened; strengthened; strengthening** \-th(ə)niŋ\ **strengthens** [ME *strengthnen,* fr. *strengthe* strength + *-nen* -en] *vt* **1 a :** to give moral support to **:** ENCOURAGE, HEARTEN ⟨means of ~*ing* the brethren and converting the pagans —*Episcopal Churchnews*⟩ **b :** to give added weight or incentive to **:** CORROBORATE, ENHANCE ⟨the probability of the ascription of this passage to Democritus is ~*ed* by the latest research —Benjamin Farrington⟩ **2 a :** to give added strength or vigor to ⟨~ a defensive position⟩ ⟨coarse foods ~ the jaws —Morris Fishbein⟩ ⟨although union membership has dropped off in some places, union organization has been . . . ~*ed* in other places —*Amer. Guide Series: N. C.*⟩ **b :** to increase in power or amount **:** improve in effectiveness **:** AUGMENT, INTENSIFY ⟨its offices were regularly employed to ~ the personal machine of the governor —D.W. McConnell⟩ ⟨nothing . . . would so ~ the hand of democracy as the gift of literacy —Jerome Ellison⟩ ⟨our program of aid to scientific education . . . was enlarged and ~*ed* —*Report: Monsanto Chem. Co.*⟩ ⟨working together helps to ~ family life —Mary S. Switzer⟩ ⟨the course might be ~*ed,* further, by . . . more effective integration of movies, visual aids, and other motivational devices —S.B.Zuckerman⟩ **c :** to heighten the artistic effect of **:** make more expressive ⟨the design is ~*ed* by two slightly projecting corner piers —*Amer. Guide Series: Minn.*⟩ ~ *vi* **1 :** to become stronger **:** increase in power or intensity ⟨the light ~*ed* minute by minute, and then the day came —John Connell⟩ ⟨intellectual faculties ~*ed,* and men . . . gained facility in moulding their Latin —H.O.Taylor⟩ **2 :** to go higher **:** RISE ⟨the carrier's shares ~*ed* on the declaration of a 75-cent dividend and the announcement that the stock would go on a . . . quarterly basis —J.G.Forrest⟩

syn INVIGORATE, FORTIFY, ENERGIZE, REINFORCE: STRENGTHEN applies to any increasing of force, vigor, power, intensity, or effectiveness ⟨*strengthening* the shelf with an additional brace⟩ ⟨be silent if you can say nothing to *strengthen* me in my resolution —Israel Zangwill⟩ ⟨*strengthened* his entire staff with specialists wherever they were needed —*Buick Mag.*⟩ ⟨a new science *strengthened* by proof and generalization —H.J.J. Winter⟩ INVIGORATE applies to whatever endows with vigor, vitality, animation, or energy ⟨fresh air and sunshine will help to *invigorate* the body and improve nutrition —Morris Fishbein⟩ ⟨gave their support to *invigorated* nationalist movements —Oscar Handlin⟩ FORTIFY suggests strengthening often against attack of any sort, use calculated to damage, or condition conducive to impairment or enervation ⟨*fortified* by many recruits from the demobilized armies of Europe —C.E.Black & E.C.Helmreich⟩ ⟨*fortified* her argument with quotations —H.O.Taylor⟩ ⟨*fortified* by 68 tables and 75 figures, as well as by the testimony of witnesses —D.D.McKean⟩ ENERGIZE may suggest a rousing into activity along with a strengthening and heartening to sustain that activity ⟨the imagining of beautiful settings can be more sensitizing, *energizing,* and exhilarating than the imagining or reporting of ugly settings —C.A. Smart⟩ ⟨when a man and woman are successfully in love, their whole activity is *energized* and victorious —Walter Lippmann⟩ REINFORCE applies to strengthening by augmenting with new forces or force, power, or effectiveness ⟨fresh troops *reinforcing* the defenders⟩ ⟨concrete *reinforced* with steel⟩ ⟨the simple country fare provided by the home farm was *reinforced* by a regular supply of more exotic dainties —Osbert Lancaster⟩ ⟨when we consider the codes of responsibility that exist in the various professions, we find generally that they do not usually come into being by means of legislation, although they may frequently be confirmed or *reinforced* by statutes —Lister Hill⟩

strength·en·er \-th(ə)nə(r)\ *n* -S **:** one that strengthens

¹strengthening *n* -S [fr. gerund of *strengthen*] **1 :** an act or instance of reinforcing ⟨advised an immediate ~ of the faculty —J.E.Pomfret⟩ **2** *archaic* **:** REINFORCEMENT ⟨piers of brick or stone . . . to be a ~ to the building —B.G.Gerbier⟩

²strengthening *adj* [fr. pres. part. of *strengthen*] **1 :** tending to strengthen ⟨a ~ element in the design —R.E.M.Wheeler⟩ **2 :** increasing in strength or intensity ⟨objects became clearer in the ~ light⟩

strengthening card *n* **:** a queen, jack, ten, or nine led from a short suit in whist in the hope that it will establish a card in one's partner's hand

strength·ful \-thfəl\ *adj* [ME, fr. *strengthe* strength + *-ful* — more at STRENGTH] *archaic* **:** full of strength **:** STRONG

strength·less \-thləs\ *adj* [ME *strentheles,* fr. *strenthe* strength + *-les* -less] **:** having no strength ⟨the ~ dead —A.E.Housman⟩ — **strength·less·ly** *adv* — **strength·less·ness** *n* -ES

strength of field : FIELD INTENSITY

strengths *pl of* STRENGTH

strengthy \'streŋ(k)thi, -en(t)thi\ *adj* [ME *strengthy, strenthy,* fr. *strengthe, strenthe* strength + *-y*] *Scot & dial Eng* **:** STRONG

stren·u·os·i·ty \ˌstrenyə'wäsəd·ē, -sətē, -i\ *also* **stre·nu·i·ty** \strə'nyüə-\ *n* -ES [*strenuosity* fr. *strenuous* + *-ity; strenuity* fr. ME *strenuite,* fr. L *strenuitat-, strenuitas,* fr. *strenuus* strenuous + *-itat-, -itas* -ity] **:** the quality or state of being strenuous

stren·u·ous \'strenyəwəs\ *adj* [L *strenuus* — more at STARE] **1 a :** vigorously active **:** ENERGETIC ⟨to hustle and to be ~ . . . seem to be prominent American virtues —M.R.Cohen⟩ ⟨a tender sort of fancy rather than a ~ imagination —F.J. Mather⟩ ⟨implement the Full Employment Act by ~ measures —*New Republic*⟩ **b :** intensely eager **:** FERVENT, ZEALOUS ⟨a family of intellectual energy and ~ Puritanism —F.A.Christie⟩ **2 :** full of power **:** LUSTY, LOUD ⟨a mud puddle in ~ motion —Nathaniel Hawthorne⟩ ⟨the recorded tone is exemplary, even in the most ~ fortissimo —Edward Sackville-West & Desmond Shawe-Taylor⟩ **3 a :** marked by or calling for physical energy or stamina **:** ARDUOUS, RIGOROUS ⟨relaxing . . . after a ~ day's work —Hervey Allen⟩ ⟨fog, high seas, and strong winds made the crossing a ~ one —M.M.Hunt⟩ **b :** marked by unusual difficulty or tension **:** HARD, EXACTING ⟨a ~ examination⟩ ⟨his occupation is sedentary from a physical standpoint, ~ from a nervous and mental standpoint —H.G.Armstrong⟩ **syn** see VIGOROUS

stren·u·ous·ly *adv* **:** in a strenuous manner **:** STRONGLY, VIGOROUSLY ⟨objected ~ to the stand his party was taking —J.D.Hicks⟩ ⟨campaigned ~ to increase the farm population —*Amer. Guide Series: Minn.*⟩

stren·u·ous·ness *n* -ES **:** STRENUOSITY

¹strep \'strep\ *n* -S [by shortening] **:** STREPTOCOCCUS 2

²strep \"\ *adj* **:** STREPTOCOCCAL

strep·era \'strepərə\ *n* [NL, fr. LL *streperus* noisy] **1** *cap* **:** a genus of bluish black Australian birds (family Cracticidae) often with snowy white undertail coverts **2** -S **:** any bird of the genus *Strepera* **:** CURRAWONG

strepho·sym·bo·lia \ˌstre(ˌ)fō,sim'bōlēə\ *n* -S [NL, fr. Gk *strepho-* (fr. *strephein* to turn) + *symbolon* sign, symbol + NL *-ia* — more at STROPHE, SYMBOL] **:** reversal or transposition of phrases, words, or letters or of any symbols esp. in reading — **strepho·sym·bol·ic** \-¦sim¦bälik\ *adj*

stre·pi·to·so \ˌstrepə¦tō(ˌ)sō\ *adj (or adv)* [It, fr. *strepito* noise (fr. L *strepitus*) + *-oso* (fr. L *-osus* -ose)] **:** NOISY, IMPETUOUS — used as a direction in music

strep·i·tous \'strepəd·əs\ *also* **strep·i·tant** \-əd·ənt\ *adj* [*strepitous* fr. L *strepitus* fr. *strepere* to make noise; *strepitant* fr. L *strepitant-, strepitans,* pres. part. of *strepitare,* freq. of *strepere* — more at OBSTREPEROUS] **:** characterized or accompanied by much noise **:** CLAMOROUS, NOISY, BOISTEROUS ⟨the *strepitant* racket of the streets — Christopher Morley⟩

strepo·gen·in \ˌstrepə'jenən; strə'päjənən, -ˌnen\ *n* -S [ISV *strepo-* (prob. fr. ¹*strep* + *-o-*) + *-genin*] **:** a peptide that is formed by partial hydrolysis of insulin and other proteins, that contains glutamic acid and other amino acid units, and that is essential for the growth of various microorganisms (as *Streptococcus pyogenes* and *Lactobacillus casei*) and of mice

strepsi- *comb form* [NL, fr. Gk, fr. *strepsis* act or instance of turning, fr. *strephein* to turn — more at STROPHE] **:** turned **:** twisted ⟨*strepsi*tene⟩

strep·sic·e·ros \strep'sisərəs, -ˌräs\ *n* [NL, fr. L, addax, fr. Gk *strepsikerōs,* fr. *strepsi-* + *-kerōs* (fr. *keras* horn) — more at HORN] **1** *cap* **:** a large genus of African antelopes comprising the kudus, harnessed antelopes, nyalas, and related forms **2** *pl* **strepsiceros :** any antelope of the genus *Strepsiceros*

strep·si·ne·ma \ˌstrepsə'nēmə\ *n* -S [NL, fr. *strepsi-* + *-nema*] **:** chromatin threads in the strepsitene stage

strep·sip·tera \strep'siptərə\ *n pl, cap* [NL, fr. *strepsi-* (fr. Gk, fr. *strepsis* act or instance of turning) + *-ptera;* fr. the twisted front wings] **:** a group formerly included in the Coleoptera but now regarded as a separate order and comprising minute insects which are parasitic as larvae in other insects, in which the females remain permanently in the host and degenerate into a sac wherein the eggs hatch and the larvae develop, and which undergo a hypermetamorphosis in the course of larval development — compare STYLOPS, XENOS

strep·sip·ter·al \(')=¦==rəl\ *or* **strep·sip·ter·an** \-rən\ *or* **strep·sip·ter·ous** \-rəs\ *adj* [NL *Strepsiptera* + E *-al* or *-an* or *-ous*] **:** of or relating to the Strepsiptera

strep·sip·ter·on \-tə,rän\ *or* **strep·sip·ter·an** \-ˌrən\ *n* -S [*strepsipteron* fr. NL, fr. *Strepsiptera; strepsipteran* fr. NL *Strepsiptera* + E *-an*] **:** an insect of the order Strepsiptera

strep·si·tene \'strepsə,tēn\ *n* -S [ISV *strepsi-* + *-tene;* prob. orig. formed as F *strepsitène*] **:** late diplotene in which the successive loops between chiasmata give the appearance of threads twisted together

strept- *or* **strepto-** *comb form* [NL, fr. Gk, fr. *streptos* twisted, pliant, fr. *strephein* to twist, turn — more at STROPHE] **1 :** twisted **:** twisted chain ⟨*Strepto*coccus⟩ ⟨*strept*aster⟩ ⟨*Strepto*myces⟩ **2 :** streptococcus ⟨*strepto*septicemia⟩ **3 :** streptomycin ⟨*strept*amine⟩

strep·ta·mine \'streptə,mēn, -mən\ *n* [*strept-* + *amine*] **:** a cyclic diamino alcohol $(HO)_4C_6H_6(NH_2)_2$ obtained from streptomycin or streptidine by alkaline hydrolysis

strep·tas·ter \strep'tastə(r)\ *n* -S [NL, fr. *strept-* + *-aster*] **:** a sponge spicule having the form of a modified aster in which the rays do not meet at a common center but radiate from an axis

strep throat *also* **strep sore throat** *n* [²*strep*] **:** SEPTIC SORE THROAT

strep·ti·dine \'streptə,dēn, -dən\ *n* -S [*strept-* + *-idine*] **:** a cyclic basic alcohol $(HO)_4C_6H_6[NHC(=NH)NH_2]_2$ that is obtained from streptomycin by acid hydrolysis and is a guanidine derivative related to scyllitol

strep·to·bacillary \ˌstreptō+\ *adj* [NL *streptobacillus* + E *-ary*] **:** caused by a streptobacillus

¹strep·to·bacillus \"+\ *n* [NL, fr. *strept-* + *Bacillus*] **1** *cap, in some classifications* **:** a genus of bacteria of obscure systematic position that is sometimes placed in *Actinomyces* and that includes a species (*S. moniliformis*) which causes one form of rat-bite fever **2** *pl* **strepto·bacilli** \"+\ **:** any of

various bacilli in which the individual cells are joined in a chain
²streptobacillus \"\ [NL] *syn of* CLOSTRIDIUM
³streptobacillus \"\ [NL] *syn of* LACTOBACILLUS
strep·to·bi·o·sa·mine \,==bīˈōsə,mēn, -,mȯn\ *n* [*strept-* + *biose* + *amine*] **:** a glycosidic compound $C_{13}H_{23}NO_9$ structurally resembling a disaccharide, obtained along with streptidine from streptomycin by hydrolysis, and in turn yielding streptose and *N*-methyl-L-glucosamine on hydrolysis
strep·to·car·pus \,streptəˈkärpəs\ *n* [NL, fr. *strepto-* (fr. Gk, fr. *streptos* twisted) + *-carpus*] **1** *cap* **:** a genus of usu. stemless African herbs (family Gesneriaceae) having showy blue or purple flowers that have two stamens and a funnel-shaped corolla with a 2-lipped limb and are followed by a linear spirally twisted capsule splitting into 2 or 4 valves — see CAPE PRIMROSE **2** -ES **:** any plant of the genus *Streptocarpus*
strep·to·coc·cal \;==ˈkäkəl\ *or* **strep·to·coc·cic** \-äk(s)ik, -)ēk\ *adj* [NL *streptococci* + E *-al* or *-ic*] **:** of, relating to, or caused by streptococci ⟨a ~ sore throat⟩ ⟨~ organisms⟩
streptococcal mastitis *also* **streptococcic mastitis** *n* **:** bovine mastitis caused by infection of the udder with a streptococcus (*Streptococcus agalactiae* or occas. a related form), characterized by chronic progressive fibrotic changes in one or more quarters of the udder, passed readily from cow to cow in milking, and found most prevalent among stabled cattle esp. in winter
strep·to·coc·ci·ci·dal \;==;käk(s)ə;sīdᵊl\ *adj* [NL *streptococci* + E *-cidal*] **:** tending to kill streptococci
strep·to·coc·co·sis \,==,käˈkōsəs\ *n* -ES [NL, fr. *streptococci* + *-osis*] **:** infection with or disease caused by hemolytic streptococci
strep·to·coc·cus \,==ˈkäkəs\ *n* [NL, fr. *strept-* + *-coccus*] **1** *cap* **:** a genus of nonmotile chiefly parasitic gram-positive bacteria (family Lactobacillaceae) that divide in only one plane, occur in pairs or chains but not in packets, do not form zoogleal masses nor ferment inulin, rarely have capsules, and include various important pathogens of man and domestic animals as well as forms important as starters in the manufacture of dairy products **2** *pl* **streptococ·ci** \-ä,kī, -ä(,)kē, -äk,sī, -äk(,)sē\ **a :** any bacterium of *Streptococcus* or a closely related genus **b :** a coccus occurring in chains
strep·to·dor·nase \,streptōˈdȯr,nās\ *n* -S [*strept-* + *deoxyribonuclease*] **:** a deoxyribonuclease from hemolytic streptococci that causes hydrolysis of deoxyribonucleic acid and deoxyribonucleoprotein outside of living cells or in the nuclei of degenerating cells and dissolves pus and that is usu. administered in a mixture with streptokinase
strep·to·kinase \;==+\ *n* [*strept-* + *kinase*] **:** a proteolytic enzyme from hemolytic streptococci that is active in promoting dissolution of blood clots by catalyzing a fibrin-dissolving system present in the euglobulin fraction of blood and that is usu. administered in a mixture with streptodornase to remove clotted blood or fibrinous or purulent accumulations — see PLASMIN
strep·to·lysin \"+\ *n* [*strept-* + *lysin*] **:** an antigenic hemolysin that is produced by various streptococci (as *Streptococcus pyogenes*)
strep·to·my·ces \,==ˈmī,sēz\ *n* [NL, fr. *strept-* + *-myces*] **1** *cap* **:** the type genus of Streptomycetaceae comprising numerous bacteria that produce chains of conidia from aerial hyphae and including some that form antibiotics as by-products of their metabolism — see POTATO SCAB, STREPTOMYCIN **2** *pl* **streptomyces** \"\ *or* **streptomyce·tes** \-,mīˈsēd·ēz, -ētēz\ **:** any bacterium of the genus *Streptomyces*
strep·to·my·ce·ta·ce·ae \,==,mīsəˈtāsē,ē\ *n pl, cap* [NL, fr. *Streptomycet-*, *Streptomyces*, type genus + *-aceae*] **:** a family of higher bacteria (order Actinomycetales) that form vegetative mycelia which rarely break up into bacillary forms, have conidia borne on sporophores, and are typically aerobic soil saprophytes but include a few parasites of plants or animals — see STREPTOMYCES
strep·to·my·cin \,==ˈmīsᵊn\ *n* -S [NL *Streptomyces* + E *-in*] **:** an antibiotic organic base $C_{21}H_{39}N_7O_{12}$ that is produced by a soil actinomycete (*Streptomyces griseus*), that is active against many bacteria, and that is administered chiefly in the form of salts in the treatment of tuberculosis, tularemia, and other infections caused esp. by gram-negative bacteria — compare DIHYDROSTREPTOMYCIN
strep·to·neu·ra \,==ˈn(y)u̇rə\ *n pl, cap* [NL, fr. *strept-* + *-neura*] **:** a large subclass of Gastropoda including the majority of marine, some freshwater, and the operculate land gastropods having the loop of visceral nerves twisted into a figure 8 with the right half crossing in dextral forms above the left, sexes usu. separate, and in most forms an operculum
¹strep·to·neu·ran \;==;nyu̇rən\ *or* **strep·to·neu·ral** \-rəl\ *or* **strep·to·neu·rous** \-rəs\ *adj* [NL *Streptoneura* + E *-an* or *-al* or *-ous*] **:** of or relating to the Streptoneura
²streptoneuran \"\ *n* -S **:** a mollusk of the subclass Streptoneura
strep·tose \ˈstrep,tōs *also* -ōz\ *n* -S [*strept-* + *-ose*] **:** an unstable hydroxy dialdehyde $(HO)_3C_4H_5(CHO)_2$ formed from streptomycin or streptobiosamine by hydrolysis; 3-*C*-formyl-5-deoxy-L-lyxose
strep·to·sty·lic \;streptō;stīlik\ *adj* [*strept-* + *-stylic*] **:** having the quadrate bone movably articulated with the squamosal — used of a reptile
strep·to·thri·cin \,==ˈthrīsᵊn, -risᵊn\ *n* -S [NL *Streptothric-*, *Streptothrix* + E *-in*] **:** an antibiotic basic substance that is produced by a soil actinomycete (*Streptomyces lavendulae*) and is active not only against bacteria but to some degree against fungi
strep·to·thrix \ˈ==,thriks\ *n* [NL, fr. *strept-* + *-thrix*] **1** *cap, in some classifications* **:** a genus of higher bacteria that somewhat resemble molds, have branched filaments which abstrict conidia, and comprise forms now usu. placed in *Actinomyces* or in *Leptothrix* **2** *pl* **strep·to·thri·ces** \,==ˈthrī,sēz\ **:** any bacterium of the genus *Streptothrix*
strep·to·tri·cho·sis \,streptō,trīˈkōsəs\ *also* **strep·to·thri·cho·sis** \-,thrī-\ *n* -ES [NL, fr. *Streptotrich-*, *Streptothric-*, *Streptothrix* + *-osis*] **:** actinomycosis caused by actinomycetes that do not form club-shaped bodies about the granules in lesions and usu. taking the form of a more or less chronic suppurative process that attacks chiefly mucous surfaces and lymph glands — compare FARCY 2
stre·py·an \strāˈpēən, ˈ===\ *adj, usu cap* [*Strepy*, village in eastern Belgium where implements of the culture were found + E *-an*] **:** of or relating to a pre-Chellean culture stage in Belgium characterized by primitive types of worked flints — compare MESVINIAN
¹stress \ˈstres\ *n* -ES *often attrib* [ME *stresse*, short for *distresse* distress — more at DISTRESS] **1** *obs* **:** DISTRESS 3b **2** *chiefly dial* **:** DISTRESS 1 **3 a :** a condition existing within an elastic material because of strain or deformation by external forces or by nonuniform thermal expansion and being expressed quantitatively always in units of force per unit area **b :** a physical, chemical, or emotional factor (as trauma, histamine, or fear) to which an individual fails to make a satisfactory adaptation, and which causes physiologic tensions that may be a contributory cause of disease ⟨continued ~ may result in gastric ulcer⟩ ⟨cramps before a school examination may be a response to the ~ of worry⟩ ⟨~ diseases are hazards of modern life⟩ — see ADAPTATION SYNDROME **4 a :** the state or condition of strain and esp. of intense strain **:** constraining force or influence **:** PRESSURE ⟨~ of circumstances⟩ ⟨~ of weather⟩ **b :** a condition held to be similar to such a state of strain **:** EMPHASIS, IMPORTANCE, SIGNIFICANCE, URGENCY, WEIGHT ⟨lay ~ on a particular argument⟩ **5** *archaic* **:** intense effort **:** strained activity or exertion toward the accomplishment of anything ⟨pursue, with ~ of mental faculties, a train of argument —Richard Polwhele⟩ **6 :** intensity of utterance given to a speech sound, syllable, or word producing relative loudness as its acoustic correlate — compare ACCENT; PRIMARY, SECONDARY, TERTIARY, WEAK **7 a :** relative force or prominence of sound in verse esp. when due to intensity or energy of utterance **:** volume or loudness of sound **b :** a syllable having relative force or prominence **:** a strong syllable **8 :** ACCENT 6a,6c **9 :** the thickening of the stroke of a letter esp. when curved
syn STRESS, STRAIN, PRESSURE, TENSION, SHEAR, THRUST, and TORSION can apply in common to the action or effect of force exerted within or upon a thing. STRESS and STRAIN, the comprehensive terms, can be interchangeable in the basic sense above, but STRESS is technically applied to the force exerted when one body, or a part of one, presses upon, pulls upon, pushes against, or tends to stress, compress, or twist another body or part of one, STRAIN technically denoting the alteration in size or shape resulting from stress. PRESSURE commonly applies to a weighing down upon or a pushing against a surface ⟨the *pressure* of 3000 pounds upon the cement floor caused some cracking⟩ ⟨the *pressure* of air in the tire was about 30 pounds per square inch⟩ TENSION applies to the stress exerted and the strain effected by two forces pulling in opposite directions and causing or tending to cause extension ⟨the *tension* of a violin string⟩ ⟨the *tension* between an outward and a downward force⟩ SHEAR applies to a stress or strain occurring when a force in the plane of one area or section tends to cause it to slide upon a parallel plane or contiguous section ⟨the estimated *shear* in a layer of rock was not enough to cause a landslide⟩ THRUST applies to the pressure exerted by one part or structure against another, esp. when one member exerts a diagonal or horizontal outward thrust against the other ⟨the *thrust* of a rafter against a supporting wall⟩ TORSION applies to the strain or the deformation produced by twisting, esp. as displayed in a nonrigid body ⟨the *torsion* of a wire filament exposed to magnetic force tending to twist it⟩ ⟨the *torsion* strength of a metal column⟩
²stress \"\ *vt* -ED/-ING/-ES [ME *stressen*, partly by shortening fr. ME *distresse* distress & partly fr. MF *estrecier* to constrain, force, fr. (assumed) VL *strictiare*, fr. *strictia* constraint, force, stress, fr. L *strictus*, past part. of *stringere* to draw tight, press together — more at STRAIN] **1** *archaic* **a :** to subject to hardship, affliction, or oppression **b :** DISTRESS 3 **2 :** to subject to phonetic stress **:** ACCENT **3 :** to subject to physical stress **4 :** to lay stress on **:** place emphasis on **:** make emphatic **:** EMPHASIZE
stress accent *n* **1 a :** an accent or variation of prominence dependent on variation of stress **b :** a greater than minimal degree of stress given a vowel or syllable **2 :** a set of phonemes of stress
stress diagram *n* **:** a diagram that results from the graphical analysis of the stresses in a framed structure
stressed skin *n* **:** aircraft construction in which the torsion forces are resisted by shear in the usu. metal skin without aid of struts — compare MONOCOQUE
stresses *pl of* STRESS, *pres 3d sing of* STRESS
stress·ful \ˈstresfəl\ *adj* **:** full of or subject to stress ⟨emotional stability in ~ situation —P.M.Symonds⟩ ⟨living in these ~ times —*Commonweal*⟩ ⟨had been 12 ~ hours in the air —A.C. Fisher⟩
stress·ful·ly \-fəlē\ *adv* **:** in a stressful manner ⟨the plaintiff ~ contends —M.V.Barnhill⟩
stress-group \ˈ=,=\ *n* **:** a unit of speech sound constituted by a single primary stress and usu. marked by relatively open juncture or pause before and after **:** a single syllable with primary stress or a series of syllables united by the fact that among them there is only one with primary stress
stressless *adj* **:** having no stress **:** not accented — **stresslessness** *n* -ES
stress-meter \ˈ=,==\ *n* **:** STRESS-VERSE
stress-rhythm \ˈ=,==\ *n* **:** rhythm based on recurrence of stress
stress sheet *n* **:** a skeleton drawing of a structure (as a roof truss or a bridge) showing the stress to which each member will be subjected
stress-strain curve \ˈ=;=-\ *n* **:** a chart or curve showing the relation between the load or stress on a structural member or specimen of material and the corresponding strain or deformation
stress-verse \ˈ=,=\ *n* **1 :** verse having rhythm produced by recurrence of stresses without regard to number of syllables or any fixed distribution of unstressed elements **2 :** verse having cadence produced by arrangement of stressed and unstressed syllables **:** accentual meter, as distinguished from meter based on temporal quantity
¹stretch \ˈstrech\ *vb* -ED/-ING/-ES [ME *strecchen*, *strechen*, fr. OE *streccan*; akin to OFris *strekka* to stretch, MD *strecken*, OHG *strecchan* to stretch, OE *stræc*, *strec* firm, rigid, MHG & MD *strac* straight, stiff, OHG *starēn* to stare — more at STARE] *vt* **1 :** to extend (as oneself, one's limbs, or one's body) in a reclining position — often used with *out* ⟨~*ed* himself out on the bed⟩ **2 :** to reach out **:** hold out **:** put forth **:** EXTEND ⟨~*ed* his arm to take the book —Cedomilj Mijatovic⟩ ⟨~*ed* forth a lean and quivering hand —Zane Grey⟩ ⟨the tree ~*ed* its branches over the road⟩ **3 a :** to extend in length ⟨~ one's arms⟩ ⟨~*ed* his legs cautiously⟩ **b :** to expand (wings) esp. for flight **4 :** to cause (as a person) to lie at full length **:** **a** *chiefly dial* **:** to lay out for burial **b :** to fell with or as if with a blow ⟨fired again . . . and ~*ed* him dying upon the sand —R.W. Thorp⟩ **5 a :** to cause the limbs of (a person) to be pulled or distended forcibly esp. in torture (as upon a cross or the rack) **b** *archaic* **:** to hang by the neck **:** execute by hanging **:** HANG **6 :** to straighten (oneself) esp. by rising to full height **:** draw up (one's body) from a cramped, stooping, or relaxed position **:** extend (as the arms or the legs) usu. in weariness ⟨awoke and ~*ed* himself⟩ **7 :** to be bring to a rigid state of evenness or straightness by applying force at the ends or edges **:** pull taut ⟨tent . . . made of caribou skin ~*ed* on a framework —Ivor Jones⟩ **8 a** (1) **:** to expand, enlarge, or distend esp. by force **:** extend forcibly in length or width **:** enlarge in girth or capacity by pressure **:** draw or pull out ⟨~ . . . glass threads or fibers to the thinness necessary —Freda Diamond⟩ ⟨~ a hose into a building⟩ (2) **:** to expand as if by physical effort ⟨the understanding must be ~*ed* to take in the image of the universe —Francis Bacon⟩ **b :** to open wide ⟨tales . . . to ~ the wind eye of the oldest salts —Marjory S. Douglas⟩ **c :** STRAIN ⟨~*ed* his already thin patience⟩ **9 :** to cause to reach or continue (as from one point to another or across a space) ⟨~ a wire between two posts⟩ ⟨~ a curtain across the room⟩ **10 a** (1) **:** to amplify or enlarge beyond natural or proper limits **:** extend often unduly the scope, application, or meaning of ⟨~*es* the word . . . by giving it two entirely separate meanings —N.F.Busch⟩ ⟨the general-welfare clause . . . could easily be ~*ed* to give unlimited powers to the central government —Frank Meyer⟩ ⟨the law tacitly permits the rules to be ~*ed* —Norman Birkett⟩ ⟨~*ed* credibility far in reaching the solution —A.C.Ward⟩ (2) **:** to expand (as by improvisation) to fulfill a larger function ⟨~ the . . . appropriation to finance the relief of European children —Will Irwin⟩ ⟨~ one egg for two recipes —Molly L. Bar-David⟩ ⟨~ a budget⟩ **b :** to impair the accuracy of **:** exaggerate in narration ⟨~ the truth⟩ **11 :** to cause (a horse) to stand with the front legs stretched forward and the hind legs stretched backward **12 :** to extend or attempt to extend (a hit) into one involving one or more extra bases usu. by fast or daring running ⟨~ a single into a double⟩ ⟨cut down while trying to ~ the hit⟩ **~** *vi* **1 :** to press onward eagerly **:** proceed rapidly or energetically ⟨~ onward in thy fleet career —Sir Walter Scott⟩ **2** *obs* **:** to possess the capacity, force, or power to stand or endure strain ⟨so far as my coin would ~ —Shak.⟩ **3** *obs* **:** to possess a specified range of action **:** have a specified extent of application ⟨makes himself supreme lord . . . as far as his civil jurisdiction ~*es* —John Milton⟩ **4 a :** to become extended in length or in breadth or both **:** have a specified extent in space **:** be continuous to a certain point or over a certain distance or area **:** EXTEND, REACH, SPREAD ⟨pipeline . . . will ~ some 24.5 miles —*Wall Street Jour.*⟩ ⟨rolling fields ~ westward to the river's edge —*Amer. Guide Series: Conn.*⟩ ⟨attacks on a front that ~*es* from the mountains to the sea⟩ **b :** to extend over a continuous period of time ⟨their authorship ~*ed* . . . over a score of years —Leslie Rees⟩ ⟨this game . . . seems to ~ back to time immemorial —Geoffrey Boumphrey⟩ ⟨in the years which ~ ahead —Harold Wincott⟩ **5 :** to become extended or bear extension without breaking — used esp. of elastic or ductile substances ⟨rubber ~*s* easily⟩ **6 a :** to extend oneself, one's body, or one's limbs ⟨he awoke, yawned, and ~*ed*⟩ **b :** to lie down at full length ⟨~*ed* on the ground and took a nap⟩ ⟨between chores you ~*ed* by the fire —Mary Austin⟩ **7 :** to strain the truth **:** EXAGGERATE **8 :** to sail by the wind usu. under all sail **9 :** to exert oneself vigorously esp. in rowing **10 :** to stall for time (as by slowing the tempo of action) to enable a radio or television program to finish on schedule — **stretch a point :** to go beyond what is strictly warranted in making a claim or concession (as in an argument or bargain) — **stretch one's legs 1 :** to extend the legs; *specif* **:** to straighten the legs from a sitting position ⟨rose from the chair and *stretched his legs*⟩ **2 :** to take a walk in order to relieve the cramped feeling, stiffness, or fatigue caused by prolonged sitting **:** take a walk for exercise
²stretch \"\ *n* -ES **1 a** *archaic* **:** an act held to exceed the scope of authority, a commission, law, justice, propriety, or principle ⟨the unwarrantable ~ . . . which that house made in their last sitting —Thomas Paine⟩ **b :** an exercise (as of power, prerogative, or the law) held to be unwarranted **c** *archaic* **:** an instance of stretching the truth **:** an exaggerated statement **d :** an exercise of something (as the imagination or understanding) beyond ordinary or normal limits ⟨it was a ~ of his patience to hear himself addressed on a family matter —George Meredith⟩ ⟨not even by the longest ~ of the imagination can the sensitive listener be persuaded —Warwick Braithwaite⟩ **e :** an often undue extension of the scope or application of something ⟨a ~ of language⟩ **2 :** the extent to which something may be stretched **:** extreme reach ⟨defy the utmost ~ of your malice —Samuel Richardson⟩ ⟨one end is held at full ~ —Francis Yeats-Brown⟩ **3 :** the act of stretching or the state of being stretched: as **a :** the action of physically extending, expanding, or dilating something ⟨fixation of a muscle in ~ —C.R.Houck⟩ **b** (1) **:** the action of stretching the body or limbs (as in waking up or preparing to rest) ⟨that first comfortable ~ on the sand —*Read Mag.*⟩ (2) **:** the action of a baseball pitcher in fully extending himself (as by raising both arms with hands together over his head) before his windup and pitch **c :** a state of tension **:** the condition of being drawn taut ⟨the string . . . is kept at its ~ by means of a stiff piece of stick —Daniel Johnson⟩ ⟨keeping the thongs still upon the ~ —George Anson⟩ **4 a :** an extent in length **:** a continuous line, length, or distance **:** a continuous portion of something reckoned in length (as a journey, road, or river) ⟨a long ~ of the pipeline —Hardiman Scott⟩ ⟨killed all fish life in a ~ of creek —Bill Wolf⟩ ⟨suspended by . . . nothing except a ~ of stiff wire —P.E.Deutschman⟩ ⟨a particular ~ of speech —Bruce Pattison⟩ ⟨~*es* of narrative⟩ **b :** a continuous surface or expanse (as of land or water) ⟨~*es* of woodland dotted with lakes —*Amer. Guide Series: Maine*⟩ ⟨a tropical ~ of country in the south of India —Aubrey Menen⟩ **5 a :** a single prolonged period of time characterized by an activity or condition without intermission or interruption **:** an unbroken continuance of an activity or condition for a period of time ⟨he believed in regular ~*es* of work —Osbert Sitwell⟩ ⟨go on typing for eighteen hours at a ~ —Aldous Huxley⟩ ⟨pause . . . for unbearably long ~*es* —J.F.Wharton⟩ **b :** a continuous space, expanse, or period ⟨sustain unity of character over a ~ of time —Roger Manvell⟩ ⟨these notes were taken over a ~ of years —A.C.Ballard⟩ **c :** a run on one tack in sailing **d** *archaic* **:** a continuous journey or march **6 a :** an exertion of mental or physical powers **:** a state characterized by a straining of mind or body to the utmost ⟨keep the mind athletic and the spirit on the ~ —R.P.Blackmur⟩ ⟨keep his mental faculties at the ~ —J.N.Hall⟩ **b :** a strain or exhausting effort of mind **7 :** a walk to relieve the fatigue of prolonged sitting **8 a :** a sentence or term of imprisonment ⟨serving a ten-year ~ for counterfeiting —Bennett Cerf⟩ ⟨land a man in prison for quite a ~ —F.J.Warburg⟩ **b :** a period of service (as in the armed forces) ⟨did a short ~ in the infantry —Anthony Leviero⟩ ⟨during his ~ with a southern newspaper⟩ **9 :** the outward run of a mule carriage away from the rollers in spinning **10 a :** either of the straight sides of a racecourse ⟨a half-mile track with its shorter ~*es* —Jeremiah Tax⟩; *esp* **:** HOMESTRETCH 1 ⟨in the ~ the jockey looked back⟩ — see BACKSTRETCH **b :** the final or concluding stage (as in a baseball pennant drive or an election campaign) **11 a :** the capacity for being stretched **:** ELASTICITY ⟨no loss of ~ . . . or adhesive qualities —*Lancet*⟩ ⟨has a three-inch ~ to the yard —*New Yorker*⟩ **b :** liability to increase in size as a result of tension or moisture ⟨knit fabrics have considerable ~⟩
³stretch \"\ *adj* **:** characterized by a capacity to stretch **:** ELASTIC ⟨~ hosiery⟩ ⟨~ nylon⟩
stretch·abil·i·ty \,strechəˈbiləd·ē, -lətē, -i\ *n* **:** the quality or state of being stretchable **:** ELASTICITY, RESILIENCE
stretch·able \ˈ=chəbəl\ *adj* **:** capable of being stretched ⟨~ bandages⟩
stretch·berry \ˈ=- — *see* BERRY\ *n* [³*stretch* + *berry*; fr. the elastic tissue in the pulp of the berries] **1 :** the fruit of a bristly or prickly greenbrier (*Smilax bonanox*) **2 :** the plant producing stretchberries
stretched *past of* STRETCH
stretch·er \ˈstrechə(r)\ *n* -S *often attrib* [ME *strecher*, fr. *strechen* to stretch + *-er* — more at STRETCH] **1 :** one that stretches: as **a :** a workman who stretches textiles or metal **:** a tender of a stretching machine **b :** a device or machine for stretching or expanding something (as a boot, carpet, fence, glove, saw, trousers, or wire) by applied force — often used in combination; see CURTAIN STRETCHER **c :** a stick or one of several sticks used to keep a fishnet expanded **d :** one of the rods pivoted at the ends to the ribs and to the tube that slides upon the handle in opening or closing an umbrella **e :** the frame upon which an artist's canvas is stretched for painting **f :** a piece of wood or metal used to spread the clews of a hammock **g :** one whose work is to straighten something specified ⟨iron ~⟩ ⟨silk ~⟩ ⟨spindle ~⟩ ⟨yarn ~⟩ **h :** a jointed rod or bar that when straightened raises a collapsible top or hood (as of a vehicle) **i :** a textile worker who operates a tenter **j :** an operator of a machine for shaping finger rings **k :** a machine operator who softens skins for hatter's fur **2 a :** a narrow crosspiece in a boat for a rower to brace his feet against — called also *boat stretcher* **b :** a temporary crosspiece to keep the sides of a boat from being crushed together **3 :** an overstretching of the truth **:** an exaggerated story or yarn **:** a tall tale ⟨a true book with some ~*s* —Mark Twain⟩ **4 :** a brick or stone laid with its length parallel to the face of the wall — compare BOND 6, HEADER **5 a :** a timber or rod used esp. when horizontal as a tie in framed work **b :** STRETCHER BAR **6 a :** TAIL FLY **b :** LEADER 1i(2) **7 :** the usu. horizontal bracing member or set of members reaching between and steadying the legs of a piece of furniture (as a chair or table) **:** a part of the underframing serving as a stay or brace between the legs **8 a :** a litter usu. made of canvas stretched on a frame for carrying disabled or dead persons **b** *chiefly Austral & NewZeal* **:** a folding canvas cot **9 :** a display folder simulating a book cover or series of covers (as for explanatory or advertising purposes)

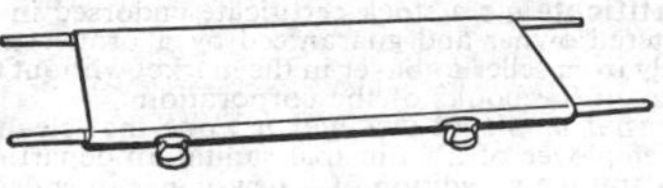

stretcher 8a

stretcher bar *n* **1 :** an extensible pillar attached to a rock drill to secure it in place **2 :** a bar or rod used as a distance piece
stretcher-bearer *n* **:** one who carries one end of a stretcher esp. for conveying sick or wounded from place to place (as from a battlefield to an ambulance)
stretcher bond *n* **:** a bond with all the bricks or ashlars laid as stretchers breaking joint
stretcher course *n* **:** a course in which all the bricks are laid as stretchers
stretcher key *n* **:** a thin wooden wedge pressed into the joints of a stretcher to tighten an artist's canvas
stretcher·man \ˈ==mən\ *n, pl* **stretchermen :** an operator of a machine for stretching and flattening metal sheets
stretcher strip *n* **:** a side member of a stretcher used for oil or water-color painting
stretches *pres 3d sing of* STRETCH, *pl of* STRETCH
stretching *pres part of* STRETCH
stretching bond *n* **:** STRETCHER BOND
stretching course *n* **:** STRETCHER COURSE
stretch-out \ˈ=,=\ *n* -S [fr. *stretch out*, v.] **1 :** a system of industrial operation in which workers are required to do extra work and esp. to operate more machines than formerly

either with slight or with no additional pay **2 :** an economizing measure that spreads a limited quantity over a larger field than orig. intended; *specif* **:** a slackening of production schedules in defense planning so that a previously decided upon quantity of military goods will be produced over a longer period than initially stipulated

stretch runner *n* **:** a racehorse that makes a strong bid in the homestretch

stretch spinning *n* **:** the elongation of man-made textile filaments after they have left the spinneret but before they have finally solidified

stretchy \'strechē, -chi\ *adj* -ER/-EST [¹*stretch* + -*y*] **1 :** having a capacity or tendency to stretch esp. unduly ⟨~ nylon⟩ **2 :** having length of body — used esp. of a pig

stretch yarn *n* **:** synthetic yarn that will stretch under tension and contract when released made from usu. thermoplastic filaments that have been given a permanently-set corkscrew twist and then plied or reverse-twisted and used esp. for hosiery

¹**stret·to** \'stred·(,)ō, -e(,)tō\ *adv* [It, lit., narrowly, closely, fr. *stretto* narrow, close, pressed together, fr. L *strictus*, past part. of *stringere* to draw tight, press together — more at STRAIN] **:** more quickly — used as a direction in music

²**stretto** \"\ *or* **stret·ta** \-ed·ə, -etə\ *n, pl* **stret·ti** \-ed·(,)ē, -e(,)tē\ *or* **strettos** \-ed·(,)ōz, -e(,)tōz\ *or* **stret·te** \-ed·(,)ā, -e(,)tā\ *or* **strettas** [*stretto* fr. It, lit., narrow, close, pressed together; *stretta* fr. It, fr. fem. of *stretto*] **1 a :** the overlapping of answer with subject in a musical fugue **b :** the part of a fugue characterized by the cumulative effect of this overlapping **2 :** a concluding passage performed in a quicker tempo

streu·sel \'strüsəl, ¦zəl, 's(h)trȯil\ *n* -S [G, lit., something strewn, sprinkling, fr. MHG *ströusel* something strewn, sprinkling, fr. *ströun, ströuwen* to scatter, strew, fr. OHG *strewen*] **:** a crumbly mixture of fat, sugar, and flour and sometimes nuts and spices that is used as topping or filling for cake

streuselkuchen \'=,==\ *n* [G, fr. *streusel* + *kuchen* cake — more at KUCHEN] **:** coffee cake that is baked with a topping of streusel

¹**strew** \'strü\ *vb* **strewed; strewed** \-üd\ *or* **strewn** \-ün *sometimes* -üən\ **strewing; strews** [ME *strewen, strowen*, fr. OE *strewian, strēowian*; akin to OHG *strewen* to strew, ON *strá*, Goth *straujan* to strew, L *sternere* to spread out, throw down, Gk *stornynai* to spread, strew, Skt *stṛṇāti* he scatters, strews] *vt* **1 :** to spread by scattering **:** SCATTER — used esp. of solids separated or separable into parts or particles ⟨the ground . . . upon which the poultry grower ~*s* his seed —S.R. Guard & Lloyd Graham⟩ ⟨the growth hormone . . . can be *strewn* freely on lawns —*Harvard Foundation Newsletter*⟩ ⟨obstacles being *strewn* along the water's edge —P.W.Thompson⟩ ⟨little balls of paper were ~*ed* over the bed —Arnold Bennett⟩ **2 :** to cover more or less thickly by or as if by scattering something over or on ⟨with flowers thy bridal bed I ~ —Shak.⟩ ⟨~*ed* the stones . . . with the straw —Padraic Colum⟩ ⟨the forest floor is *strewn* with large granite boulders —G.R.Stewart⟩ **3** *archaic* **:** to raze to the ground **:** cast down **:** lay low **4 :** CALM 1 **5 :** to become dispersed over as if scattered ⟨boulders that ~*ed* the mountainside —D.J.Rankin⟩ **6 :** to spread abroad **:** DISSEMINATE ⟨may ~ dangerous conjectures in ill-breeding minds —Shak.⟩ ~ *vi* **:** to strew seed

syn STREW, STROW, STRAW, SCATTER, SOW, and BROADCAST agree in meaning to throw, scatter, sprinkle, or spread around loosely or at intervals as by casting from the hand. STREW and the rarer STROW and STRAW imply spreading around more or less at random but suggesting a wide coverage ⟨*strew* a floor with rushes⟩ ⟨a sidewalk *strewn* with leaves⟩ ⟨clothes *strewn* around a room⟩ ⟨may *strow* the dust with holy water for her peace —John Bennett⟩ ⟨an ancient usage to *straw* the path that leads from her father's house to the family washing well with handfuls of these flowers —Llewelyn Powys⟩ SCATTER implies a separation of parts or pieces, distinctly suggesting a haphazard throwing about or dispersal of small units ⟨*scatter* toys all over the floor⟩ ⟨no railroad *scatters* its soot over the neat white frame houses —Corey Ford⟩ ⟨many bullets or shot which *scattered* out of the mouth of the gun —Tom Wintringham⟩ ⟨the majority of the dwellings being *scattered* over the town's edge —*Amer. Guide Series: Oregon*⟩ SOW, always implying the strewing of seed, applies to something like seed that can be disseminated throughout a group ⟨*sowed* the area with bombs —Nevil Shute⟩ ⟨*sow* seeds of reason and understanding throughout the world —A.E. Stevenson †1965⟩ ⟨*sowing* dissension in our ranks —Kenneth Roberts⟩ ⟨those problems with which literature is *sown* so thick —Virginia Woolf⟩ BROADCAST in this connection implies a scattering widely or in all directions ⟨*broadcast* very fine seed⟩ ⟨antitoxin should be used only in certain cases of exposed, susceptible individuals, not *broadcast* unnecessarily —Justina Hill⟩ ⟨university presses . . . all have one highly commendable objective — to help *broadcast* scholarship —B.L. Stratton⟩ ⟨used the Senate floor to *broadcast* the obscene objections that had been made against the confirmation —Sidney Hyman⟩

²**strew** \"\ *n* -S **:** a number of things scattered about **:** a disorderly mess ⟨a ~ of oak trunks lay everywhere —A.P. Terhune⟩

strew·er \'strüə(r), -ü(ə)r, -üə\ *n* -S **:** one that strews

strewing herb *n* **:** an herb formerly strewn over the floor in private rooms, banquet halls, churches, and similar places for the fragrance of flower or foliage

strew·ment \-mənt\ *or* **strew·ing** \-iŋ, -ēŋ\ *n* -S [*strewment* fr. ¹*strew* + -*ment*; *strewing* fr. ME *strewing, strowing*, fr. gerund of *strewen, strowen* to strew] *archaic* **:** something (as flowers) strewed or designed for strewing ⟨she is allow'd . . . her maiden ~*s* —Shak.⟩

stria \'strīə\ *n, pl* **stri·ae** \-ī,ē, -ī,ī\ [L, furrow, channel, hollow — more at STRIKE] **1 :** a fillet esp. between flutes of columns or pilasters **2 a :** a minute groove or channel **:** a threadlike line or narrow band (as of color) esp. when one of a series of parallel grooves or lines ⟨the *striae* produced on a rock by rock fragments held in a glacier⟩ ⟨the *striae* on a shell⟩ ⟨the *striae* of the light in a vacuum tube⟩ **b :** a narrow structural band or line ⟨a ~ of nervous matter in the brain⟩ **3 :** an elongated imperfection in glass caused by variation in temperature of the furnace or by unequal density of materials used **4 :** a stripe or line (as on the skin) distinguished from the surrounding tissue by color, texture, or elevation ⟨the *striae* in the skin in pregnancy resulting from stretching and rupture of the elastic fibers⟩ **5 :** STRIÉ

stria lon·gi·tu·di·na·lis \-,lanjə,t(y)üdᵊn'aləs, -äl-, -äl-\ *n, pl* **striae longitudina·les** \-a(,)lēz, -ā(,)lēz, -ä,lās\ [NL, longitudinal stripe] **:** either of a pair of longitudinal elevations near the middle line of the upper surface of the corpus callosum

stri·ar·ia \strē'a(a)rēə\ *n, cap* [NL, fr. L *stria* hollow + NL -*aria*] **:** a genus (the type of the family Striariaceae) of hollow filamentous brown algae of the north Atlantic having the filaments commonly tapering to either extremity

stri·a·tal \(')strī¦ād·ᵊl, -ātᵊl\ *adj* [NL *striatus* striated + E -*al*] **1 :** of or relating to the corpus striatum **2 :** of or relating to the striae longitudinales

¹**stri·ate** \'strī,āt, *usu* -ād·+V\ *adj* [NL *striatus*] **:** STRIATED

²**striate** \"\ *vt* -ED/-ING/-S [NL *striatus* striated] **:** to mark with or as if with striae

stri·at·ed \(')=¦ād·əd, -ātəd\ *adj* [NL *striatus* striated (fr. L, past part. of *striare* to form furrows, fr. *stria* furrow, channel) + E -*ed*] **1 :** marked with striae ⟨a ~ crystal⟩ **2 :** of, relating to, or being striated muscle

striated muscle *n* **:** muscle tissue made up of elongated multinucleate fibers enclosed in a delicate sarcolemma and marked by transverse dark and light bands that presumably indicate differing physical or chemical states of the cytoplasm, the fibers in vertebrates being bound together by a perimysium to form the muscles that clothe the skeleton of a vertebrate and are the organs productive of voluntary activity, and in arthropods forming all or most of the musculature

stri·a·tion \=¦āshən\ *n* -S [²*striate* + -*ion*] **1 a :** the fact or state of being striated **b :** arrangement of striae **2 :** one of a series of parallel stripes or lines **:** STRIA **3 :** one of the alternate light and dark bands occurring in the discharge in the positive column of a vacuum tube between limits of low pressure due to alternate loss and recovery of electron energy through ionization and acceleration

stri·a·tum \,=¦ād·əm\ *n, pl* **stria·ta** \-ād·ə\ [by shortening] **:** CORPUS STRIATUM

stri·a·ture \'strīəchə(r)\ *n* -S [L *striatura* fact of having furrows or channels, arrangement of furrows, fr. *striatus* (past part. of *striare* to form furrows, fr. *stria* furrow, channel) + -*ura* -ure — more at STRIKE] **:** STRIATION

strich *n* -ES [prob. modif. of L *strix* — more at STRIDENT] *obs* **:** SCREECH OWL

strick \'strik\ *n* -S [ME *stric, strik*, prob. of LG or D origin; akin to MLG *strik* rope, MD *stric* knot, rope; akin to OFris *strik* rope, OHG *stric* rope, *stricchan* to rope, twine, OE *strician* to knit] **:** a bunch of heckled flax, jute, or hemp

strick·en \'strikən\ *adj* [fr. past part. of ¹*strike*] **1** *archaic* **:** having reached an advanced stage — usu. used in the phrase *stricken in years* **2 :** having the contents leveled off even with the top ⟨a ~ measure of grain⟩ **3 :** hit or wounded by or as if by a missile ⟨a ~ deer that left the herd long since —William Cowper⟩ **4 a** (1) **:** afflicted with or overwhelmed by or as if by disease, misfortune, or sorrow ⟨was ~ at the height of his career⟩ ⟨wrapped the ~ man in his coat and sat down beside him —Irving Bacheller⟩ ⟨shows how a ~ region . . . can adjust valiantly to harsh conditions —Muna Lee⟩ — often used in combination ⟨grief-*stricken*⟩ ⟨palsy-*stricken*⟩ ⟨panic-*stricken*⟩ ⟨poverty-*stricken*⟩ (2) **:** showing the effect of or as if of disease, misfortune, or sorrow ⟨the whole company had a ~ look —Kenneth Roberts⟩ ⟨the most ~ landscape we had yet seen —George Farwell⟩ **b :** made incapable or unfit **:** INCAPACITATED ⟨destroyers . . . swarmed around the ~ vessel —*Springfield (Mass.) Union*⟩ — **strick·en·ly** *adv*

stricken field *n* **:** a field that has been the scene of a conflict **:** BATTLEGROUND

stricken hour *n* **:** a whole hour as marked by the striking of a clock

¹**strick·le** \'strikəl\ *n* -S [ME *strikell*; akin to MD *strekel* strickle, ME *striche, strek* strickle, OE *strīcan* to pass over lightly, stroke — more at STRIKE] **1 :** an instrument for removing surplus grain from the top of a measure **2 a :** an instrument for whetting scythes **b :** a straightedge fed with an abrasive for sharpening knives arranged helically on a cylinder **3 :** a template consisting of a board or plate with a beveled edge of definite contour used to sweep or strike up a mold, core, or part of a mold in sand or loam

²**strickle** \"\ *vt* **strickled; strickled; strickling** \-k(ə)liŋ\ **strickles :** to smooth or form with a strickle

strict \'strikt\ *adj* -ER/-EST [L *strictus*, past part. of *stringere* to draw tight, press together — more at STRAIN] **1 :** particularly severe in requirement **:** permitting no evasion ⟨had always been under the ~*est* orders not to enter —T.B.Costain⟩ ⟨the only court in equity capable of overruling ~ law —Henry Adams⟩ **2 :** maintained absolutely without deviation **:** COMPLETE, THOROUGH ⟨had been meeting his two friends only in ~ secrecy —Upton Sinclair⟩ ⟨occupy the position of ~ neutrality —E.M.Coulter⟩ **3** *archaic* **:** drawn close **:** TIGHT ⟨she wildly breaketh from their ~ embrace —Shak.⟩ **4 a** *bot* **:** of upright erect habit ⟨a ~ stem or plant⟩ **:** being straight and not lax or drooping ⟨a ~ inflorescence⟩ **b** *biol* **:** OBLIGATE **5 :** rigorous in exercising control **:** severely disciplinary ⟨though ~ in some ways she had shown herself unexpectedly lenient in others —Archibald Marshall⟩ **6 a** *archaic* **:** compressed in extent **:** CONSTRICTED, NARROW **b :** closely restricted ⟨remained in ~ custody⟩ **7** *archaic* **:** CLOSE, INTIMATE ⟨there never was a more ~ friendship —Richard Steele⟩ **8 :** inflexibly adhered to **:** firmly maintained ⟨demanded ~*er* discipline —E.W.Parks⟩ ⟨held his pupils under ~ control —L.M.Crosbie⟩ ⟨congestion . . . makes ~ supervision of speed imperative —*Amer. Guide Series: R.I.*⟩ **9 :** characterized by severity **:** rigorously austere ⟨aren't half so ~ now about mourning as they used to be —Arnold Bennett⟩ **10 :** completely accurate **:** EXACT, PRECISE ⟨in the ~ sense of the word every writer . . . deals with life —M.R.Cohen⟩ ⟨aim at ~ historical accuracy —G.G.Coulton⟩ **11 :** conforming closely to a set pattern **:** adhering rigidly to a conventionally fixed norm ⟨a development of several centuries into a ~ form —T.S. Eliot⟩ ⟨the opera is written in the ~ twelve-tone style —K.H. Wörner⟩ ⟨the verse . . . for all its freedom and variety, is nevertheless very ~ —F.R.Leavis⟩ **12 :** unswerving in conformance to principle ⟨an earnest and a ~ Moslem —W.N.Ewer⟩ ⟨regarded as uncanonical by all ~ churchmen —F.M.Stenton⟩ **syn** see RIGID

strict constructionist *n* **:** one who favors giving a narrow conservative construction of a given document or instrument; *specif* **:** one who favors a strict construction of the Constitution of the United States — compare LOOSE CONSTRUCTIONIST

strict counterpoint *n* **:** counterpoint limited harmonically to musical triads and first inversions in which appogiaturas and chromatic tones are forbidden and usu. divided into five species: (1) note against note of the cantus firmus; (2) two notes to one; (3) four notes to one; (4) syncopated; (5) figurate or florid

strict deposit *n, law* **:** SPECIAL DEPOSIT

strict foreclosure *n* **:** a proceeding in equity that determines by decree the amount due on a mortgage, fixes a time within which the mortgagor debtor must pay it, and vests in case of his default absolute title in the mortgagee forever free of any right of the mortgagor to redeem and that is often used where the value of the mortgaged property does not exceed the mortgage debt — distinguished from *statutory foreclosure*; compare LEGAL FORECLOSURE

stric·ti ju·ris \,strik,tī'jürəs, ,striktē'yü-\ *adv* [L] **:** of or by strict law esp. as distinguished from equity

strict implication *n* **:** IMPLICATION 2b(2)

stric·tis·si·mi ju·ris \strik'tisə,mī'jürəs, -əmē'yü-\ *adv* [L] **:** of or by the strictest law **:** having the law or the instrument or transaction creating the rights in question construed most strictly in favor of one and against the other party

strict law *n* **:** STRICTUM JUS 1

strict·ly \'strik(t)lē\ *adv* [ME, fr. L *strictus* + ME -*ly* — more at STRICT] **:** in a strict manner **:** without latitude **:** CLOSELY, PRECISELY, RIGOROUSLY, STRINGENTLY, POSITIVELY ⟨the reporter was ~ on his own —Bruce Catton⟩ ⟨effectiveness as a novelist is so ~ a function of skill —Bernard DeVoto⟩ ⟨certain rules need to be ~ carried out —Agnes M. Miall⟩

strict·ness \-k(t)nəs\ *n* -ES **:** the quality or state of being strict **:** PRECISION, SEVERITY ⟨the orders of the . . . government had been executed with absolute ~ —W.H.G.Kingston⟩

strict settlement *n, Eng law* **:** a settlement in which in general there is a limitation of lands to a person for life and after his death to the eldest male child in succession with trustees to preserve contingent remainders and with certain rights being given to the younger children

stric·tum jus *or* **strictum ius** \,strikəm'jəs, -m'yüs\ *n* [L, strict law] **1 :** the law by its letter without considering equities **2** *Roman law* **:** the jus civile of the city of Rome — compare PRAETORIAN LAW

stric·ture \'strikchə(r)\ *n* -S [ME, fr. LL *strictura* contraction, stricture, fr. L *strictus* (past part. of *stringere* to draw tight, press together) + -*ura* -ure; in senses 4 & 5, influenced in meaning by L *strictus*, past part. of *stringere* to touch lightly, graze — more at STRAIN, STRIKE] **1 :** an abnormal narrowing of the lumen of a tubular organ from various causes (as inflammation, scar tissue, cancer) **:** CONSTRICTION **2** *obs* **:** a beam of light **:** SPARK **3 :** something that closely restrains or limits **:** RESTRICTION ⟨a ~ against disclosure of classified information —Douglass Cater⟩ ⟨a relaxation of tariffs and of ~*s* upon international currency —*Current Biog.*⟩ **4 :** an adverse criticism **:** critical remark **:** CENSURE ⟨wasn't keen about rousing her suspicions or ~*s* —David Walden⟩ **5** *obs* **:** a slight touch **:** SIGN, TRACE

strid \'strid\ *n* -S [fr. the *Strid*, narrowest part of a channel of the Wharfe river in west central Yorkshire, England] **:** a narrow ravine **:** GORGE

strid·dle \'stridᵊl\ *vb* [back-formation fr. *stridling*] **1** *Scot & dial Eng* **:** STRADDLE **2** *Scot & dial Eng* **:** STRIDE

¹**stride** \'strīd\ *vb* **strode** \-rōd\ **strid·den** \-ridᵊn\ **strid·ing** \-rīdiŋ\ **strides** [ME *striden*, fr. OE *strīdan*; akin to MLG *striden* to straddle, OHG *stritan* to quarrel, fight, ON *stritha* to fight, *strīthr* strong, hard, stiff, OE *starian* to stare — more at STARE] *vi* **1 a** *obs* **:** to stand with the legs wide apart **:** STRADDLE **b :** to give the appearance of standing astride ⟨hills rising from the water and the *striding* bridges —R.L. Shayon⟩ ⟨antennas would ~ north Atlantic ice caps —K.E. Mundt⟩ **2 :** to move or walk with or as if with long steps ⟨*strode* to the door —J.C.Lincoln⟩ ⟨was his custom to ~ up and down the street —*Amer. Guide Series: Oregon*⟩ **3 :** to take a very long step ⟨*strode* over the pail —Arnold Bennett⟩ ~ *vt* **1 :** BESTRIDE, STRADDLE **2 :** to pass over at a step **:** step over **3 :** to move or walk over, along, or about with or as if with long measured steps ⟨found the great man impatiently *striding* the floor —*Time*⟩

²**stride** \"\ *n* -S [ME *stride, stryde, strede*, fr. OE *stride*; akin to MLG *strede* stride, OE *strīdan* to stride] **1 a :** the distance measured by a long step **b :** the distance covered by a runner in one leg cycle **2 a** (1) **:** an act of striding **:** a lengthy walking step ⟨merely marched . . . briskly, stamping hard at every ~ —D.L.Busk⟩ ⟨walked . . . with a kind of finality in the ~, as though she had made up her mind —R.P.Warren⟩ (2) **:** something resembling a stride ⟨gathered many honors in his ~ through a long and useful life —A.W.Long⟩ ⟨a giant crane lifted steel girders with an effortless ~ —Louis Bromfield⟩ **b :** a long dance step **3 :** a standing position in which the legs are spread apart either laterally or forward and back **4 :** a stage of progress **:** a decisive movement toward a future goal **:** ADVANCE ⟨have made extraordinary ~*s* in invention —T.W.Arnold⟩ ⟨the ~*s* made in recent years in keeping the American public informed —Lou Smyth⟩ **5 a :** an act of locomotion consisting of a cycle of movements completed when an animal's feet regain the initial relative positions; *also* **:** the distance traversed in such a movement — used esp. of a horse **b :** the most effective natural pace **:** the full motion or height of activity ⟨he had just got into his ~ when the lady interrupted him with a remark —W.S.Maugham⟩ ⟨the laughter threw the Minister out of his ~, he . . . presently brought his remarks to a close —E.H.Collis⟩ **6 :** a manner of walking with distinctively long steps ⟨watched her lithe ~ . . . as she drew away —Zane Grey⟩ ⟨swinging his arms and stepping higher . . . so that his ~ was one of majesty —Roark Bradford⟩ **7 strides** *pl, Brit* **:** TROUSERS — **in stride** *adv* **:** without changing the normal pace **:** with no loss of equilibrium **:** without interference with regular activities ⟨if a man can't take his bad luck *in stride*, he isn't emotionally mature —P.B.Gilliam⟩

strideleg \'=,=\ *or* **stridelegs** \'=,=\ *adv, chiefly Scot* **:** ASTRIDE

stri·den·cy \'strīdᵊnsē, -si\ *also* **stri·dence** \-dᵊn(t)s\ *n, pl* **stridencies** *also* **stridences :** the quality or state of being strident ⟨argued strongly but without ~ for idealism —Norman Cousins⟩ ⟨and the cities grew in size and in ~ —F.L. Allen⟩

stri·dent \-dᵊnt\ *adj* [L *strident-, stridens*, pres. part. of *stridere, stridēre* to make a harsh noise, to creak, hiss; akin to Gk *trizein* to screech, creak, hiss, *strix* owl, L *strix* screech owl; all of imit. origin] **1 a :** marked by insistent, discordant, harsh, shrill, or grating noise or sound **:** characterized by an annoying often abnormal sibilance ⟨his mouth opens . . . and from it comes a noise, a ~ sigh, a raucous moan —Douglas Newton⟩ ⟨the ~ babble with which natives are accustomed to make the day hideous —Rudyard Kipling⟩ ⟨talks at the top of a very high and ~ voice —Rose Macaulay⟩ **b :** having an unpleasant usu. irritating effect **:** loudly or obtrusively commanding notice or recognition **:** BLATANT ⟨the colors are pure, but they are not ~ —H.D.Walker⟩ ⟨his writing took on a faster tempo and a more ~ tone —Max Lerner⟩ **2 :** characterized by friction that is comparatively turbulent in that there are two friction-producing components in the articulation instead of only one ⟨\sh\, which has both tongue-teeth and tongue-palate friction, is ~, but \th\, which has tongue-teeth friction only, is not⟩ — compare MELLOW **syn** see LOUD, VOCIFEROUS

stri·dent·ly *adv* **:** in a strident manner ⟨the cheap alarm clock ticked ~ —T.O.Heggen⟩

strident stop *n* **:** AFFRICATE

strid·er \'strīdə(r)\ *n* -S [¹*stride* + -*er*] **:** one that strides; *esp* **:** WATER STRIDER

strides *pres 3d sing of* STRIDE, *pl of* STRIDE

stri·dha·na \'strē,dənə\ *also* **stri·dhan** \-dən\ *n* -S [Skt *strīdhana*, fr. *strī* woman + *dhana* property — more at DHAN] *Hindu law* **:** any property belonging to a woman; *esp* **:** property absolutely at her disposal and going to her heirs upon her death intestate

striding *pres part of* STRIDE

striding compass *n* **:** a compass on a theodolite for orientation

striding level *n* **:** a tube-shaped level fastened to a frame having two inverted Y's and mounted on a theodolite

strid·ling \'stridlən, -liŋ\ *or* **stridlings** \-lənz, -liŋz\ *adv* [ME *stridling, stridlinges*, fr. *striden* to stride + -*ling*, -*linges* -ling, -lings] *chiefly Scot* **:** ASTRIDE

stri·dor \'strīdə(r)\ *n* -S [L, fr. *stridere, stridēre* to make a harsh noise] **1 :** a harsh, shrill, or creaking noise ⟨the pine grove, where . . . the boughs made a ~ —R.P.Warren⟩ **2 :** a harsh vibrating sound during expiration in cases of obstruction or spasm of the air passages ⟨laryngeal ~⟩

strids *pl of* STRID

strid·u·lant \'strijələnt\ *adj* [*stridulation* + -*ant*] **:** STRIDULATING, STRIDULOUS

strid·u·late \-,lāt, *usu* -ād·+V\ *vi* -ED/-ING/-S [back-formation fr. *stridulation*] **:** to make a shrill often vibrating noise **:** produce a stridulation

strid·u·la·tion \,=='lāshən\ *n* -S [F, fr. L *stridulus* shrill, squeaky + F -*ation*] **1 :** a usu. high-pitched creaking or musical sound made by the males of many insects (as the katydids or crickets) and sometimes by the females by rubbing together specially modified parts of the body **2 :** the act of stridulating

strid·u·la·tor \'==,lād·ə(r), -ātə-\ *n* -S [*stridulate* + -*or*] **:** one that stridulates

strid·u·la·to·ry \'== lə,tōrē, -tȯr-, -ri\ *adj* [*stridulation* + -*ory*] **:** able to stridulate **:** used in stridulation **:** STRIDULOUS

strid·u·lent \'==lənt\ *adj* [L *stridulus* shrill, squeaky + E -*ent*] **:** STRIDENT, STRIDULOUS

strid·u·lous \-ləs\ *adj* [L *stridulus*, fr. *stridere, stridēre* to creak — more at STRIDENT] **1 a :** making a shrill, creaking sound **:** SQUEAKY ⟨the ~ cries of the gulls —Jean Stafford⟩ **b :** having or producing the effect of a harshly unpleasant grating sound ⟨these harsh and ~ pieces . . . had an instantaneous success with the public —Oscar Cargill⟩ **2 :** characteristic of or affected with stridor — **strid·u·lous·ly** *adv*

strié \'strē¦ā\ *n* -S [F, fr. *strié*, adj., striated, fluted, grooved, fr. L *striatus*, past part. of *striare* to form furrows — more at STRIATED] **:** a striped design used esp. in textiles that consists of faint streaked vertical lines of color close in tone to the background

strife \'strīf\ *n* -S [ME *strif*, fr. OF *estrif*, prob. fr. *estriver* to fight — more at STRIVE] **1 a :** the state or condition of distrust or enmity **:** often bitter sometimes violent conflict or dissension ⟨the grace of universal peace and the folly of human ~ —M.R. Cohen⟩ ⟨a law that . . . comes nearest to eliminating labor ~ —A.G.Larke⟩ **b :** an act of contention **:** FIGHT, QUARREL, STRUGGLE ⟨some twenty of them fought in this black ~ —Shak.⟩ ⟨was nominated for governor as a result of the factional ~ within the . . . party —H.C.Hockett⟩ **2 :** exertion or contention for superiority **:** a contest usu. for a desired goal or result ⟨a strange ~ of wishes, for and against —Thomas Hardy⟩ **3** *archaic* **:** the act of striving **:** earnest endeavor ⟨we will pay with ~ to please you —Shak.⟩ **syn** see DISCORD

strife·less \-ləs\ *adj* **:** free from strife

strif·fen *or* **strif·fin** \'strifən\ *or* **strif·fon** \-fən\ *n* -S [prob. fr. ScGael *streafon* fringe, striffen] *dial* **:** a thin skin **:** MEMBRANE

strift \'strift\ *n* -S [fr. *strive*, after such pairs as E *thrive: thrift*] **1 :** the act of striving **2 :** STRIFE

strig \'strig\ *n* -S [perh. alter. of ¹*string*] **1 a :** the footstalk of a leaf or flower **b** *dial Eng* **:** the rachis of a hop strobile **c :** the fruiting raceme of the common currant **2 :** a thin narrow part or attachment of various tools

¹**stri·ga** \'strīgə\ *n, pl* **stri·gae** \-ī,jē, -,jī\ *or* **strigas** [NL, fr. L, furrow, windrow, swath — more at STRIKE] **1 :** a pointed appressed rigid hairlike scale or bristle **2 :** a flute in a column **3 :** STRIATION — **stri·gal** \-gəl\ *adj*

²**striga** \"\ *n, cap* [NL] **:** a genus of seed plants (family Scrophulariaceae) living as root parasites esp. on corn, sugarcane, and other grasses in the eastern tropics

stri·gate \'strī,gāt\ *adj* [NL *striga* + E -*ate*] **:** having strigae

strig·e·ata \ˌstrijēˈäd·ə, -ˈād·ə\ *n pl, cap* [NL, fr. *Strigea*, genus of trematodes + *-ata*] *in some classifications* **:** a suborder of Prosostomata comprising digenetic trematode worms parasitic as adults in the blood or intestines of vertebrates and including such medically important forms as the schistosomes

¹strig·e·id \ˈ==ˌəd\ *adj* [NL *Strigeidae*] **:** of or relating to the Strigeidae

²strigeid \"\ *n* -s **:** a digenetic trematode of the family Strigeidae

stri·ge·i·dae \strəˈjēəˌdē\ *n pl, cap* [NL, fr. *Strigea*, type genus (prob. fr. *striga* bristle) + *-idae*] **:** a family of digenetic trematodes having the anterior end flattened or cuplike and the posterior end cylindrical and including various parasites of mammals and birds — see ALARIA

stri·ges \ˈstrīˌjēz\ *n pl, cap* [NL, fr. pl. of L *strix* screech owl — more at STRIDENT] *in some classifications* **:** a group of birds equivalent to Strigiformes formerly made a suborder of Coraciiformes or Raptores

strig·i·dae \ˈstrijəˌdē\ *n pl, cap* [NL, fr. *Strig-*, *Strix* type genus + *-idae*] **:** a family of birds (order Strigiformes): **a** *in former classifications* **:** a family coextensive with Strigiformes **b** *in some esp former classifications* **:** a family equivalent to Tytonidae **c :** a family comprising all the owls except the barn owls — compare TYTONIDAE; see BUBONIDAE

strig·i·for·mes \ˌ==ˈfȯrˌmēz\ *n pl, cap* [NL, fr. *Strig-*, *Strix* + *-iformes*] **:** an order of birds of prey that comprises the owls and is usu. divided into the families Tytonidae and Strigidae

strig·il \ˈstrijəl\ *n* -s [L *strigilis;* akin to L *stringere* to touch lightly, graze — more at STRIKE] **1 :** an instrument usu. of metal or ivory used by the ancient Greeks and Romans for scraping the skin esp. after the athletic exercises of the palaestra and at the bath **2 :** a pectinate structure in many insects at the apex of the front tibia formed from the tibial spur and used to clean the antennae and other parts of the body **3 :** one of a group of undulating or slightly curved vertical channels, reedings, or flutings often carved on flat surfaces as ornament and used esp. in Roman architecture

strig·i·late \ˈstrijələt, -ˌlāt, *usu* -d·+V\ *adj* [*strigil* + *-ate*] **:** having a strigil

strig·i·la·tor \ˈ==ˌlād·ə(r)\ *n* -s [*strigilate* + *-or*] **:** any of various myrmecophiles or termitophiles that feed by licking the surface of the bodies of the ants or termites with which they live

strig·i·lis \ˈstrijələs\ *n, pl* **strigi·les** \-əˌlēz\ [L] **:** STRIGIL

strig·il·lose \-əˌlōs\ *adj* [NL *strigilla* (dim. of *striga* bristle) + E *-ose* — more at STRIGA] **:** finely strigose

stri·gine \ˈstrīˌjīn, -ˌjən\ *adj* [NL *Strig-*, *Strix* + E *-ine*] **:** relating to the Strigidae **:** OWLLIKE

stri·gol·nik \strəˈgälnik\ *n, pl* **strigolniks** \-ks\ *also* **strigolni·ki** \-nəkē\ *usu cap* [Russ *Strigol'nik*, lit., cutter, shearer; akin to OSlav *strišti* to cut, shear, L *stringere* to touch lightly, graze; fr. the practice ascribed to the sect's leader of himself cutting the hair of new converts — more at STRIKE] **:** one of a Russian sect that broke away from the Eastern Orthodox Church in the 14th century in protest against the practice of charging fees for the administration of sacraments

stri·gose \ˈstrīˌgōs, =ˈ=\ *adj* [NL *strigosus*, fr. *striga* bristle + L *-osus* -ose — more at STRIGA] **1 :** provided with strigae ⟨a ~ leaf⟩ — compare HISPID **2 :** STRIATED **:** marked with fine closely set grooves

stri·gous \ˈstrīgəs\ *adj* [NL *strigosus*] **:** STRIGOSE 1

strig·o·vite \ˈstrigəˌvīt\ *n* -s [G *strigovit*, fr. *Striegau*, Silesia (now Strzegom, Poland) + G *-it* -ite] **:** a mineral $Fe_3(Al,Fe)_3Si_3O_{11}(OH)_7$ consisting of a basic silicate of iron and aluminum of the chlorite group and occurring in dark green crystalline incrustations

strigs *pl of* STRIG

strig·u·la \ˈstrigyələ\ *n, cap* [NL, dim. of *striga* bristle] **:** a genus (the type of the family Strigulaceae) of pyrenocarpous lichens characterized by minute rosettes growing on the surface of the leaves of tropical evergreens

strik·able \ˈstrīkəbəl\ *adj* **:** capable of being struck

¹strike \ˈstrīk\ *vb* **struck** \ˈstrək\ **struck** \"\ *also* **strick·en** \ˈstrikən\ **striking** \ˈstrīkiŋ\ **strikes** [ME *striken*, fr. OE *strīcan;* akin to OFris *strīka* to pass over lightly, smooth, stroke, go, proceed, MLG *strīken*, OHG *strīhhan*, to pass over lightly, smooth, stroke, go, L *stria* furrow, channel, *striga* row, furrow, swath, *stringere* to touch lightly, graze, OPruss *strigli* thistle, OSlav *strišti* to shear, cut; basic meaning: to stroke] *vi* **1 :** to take a course **:** PROCEED, GO ⟨*struck* into the woods and walked home along the . . . river —Jean Stafford⟩ ⟨you must ~ east from here —T.B.Costain⟩ ⟨*struck* off through the jungle on a trail along the foothills —H.L.Merillat⟩ ⟨the road . . . *struck* down into the sand hills —H.L.Davis⟩ **2 a :** to deliver or aim a stroke, blow, or thrust **:** HIT ⟨~ while the iron is hot⟩ ⟨~ at the dog with a stick⟩ ⟨~ at the nail with a hammer⟩ ⟨a rattlesnake ready to ~⟩ ⟨the hurricane *struck* . . . with the force of a battering ram —H.A. Chippendale⟩ ⟨the lightning *struck* again⟩ ⟨if trouble ~*s*⟩ ⟨a shortage of nurses when the epidemic *struck*⟩ **b :** to cast a stone in curling so as to hit and remove another from play **c :** to make a stroke with an oar **3 a :** to come into contact or collision ⟨*struck* against the stove as she fell⟩ **b** *of a ship* **:** to run aground **:** STRAND **c** *of light* **:** FALL ⟨the sunbeam *struck* full on his face⟩ **d** *of a sound* **:** to become audible ⟨hark! a deep sound ~*s* like a rising knell —Lord Byron⟩ **e** *of oyster spat* **:** to become fixed to something **f** *of a hound* **:** to find the scent of the quarry **4 :** to delete, efface, or cancel something with or as if with a stroke of the pen ⟨a motion to ~ on the ground that there was no corroboration —R.B.Keech⟩ **5 :** to lower a flag usu. as a sign of surrender ⟨pull alongside of the frigate to ascertain if she had *struck* —Frederick Marryat⟩ **6 :** to attempt to bring about destruction, defeat, or overthrow as if by a blow or stroke ⟨had *struck* at the very heart of his faith —Mary Deasy⟩ ⟨ideas that ~ at the foundation of democracy⟩ **7 a :** to come to be indicated by the sounding of a clock, bell, or chime ⟨left the house just after six o'clock *struck*⟩ **b :** to make known the time of day by sounding ⟨the clock *struck* as he entered the room⟩ **8** *obs* **:** to cause suffering or pain ⟨this sorrow's heavenly; it ~*s* where it doth love —Shak.⟩ **9 :** to go through a medium **:** PIERCE, PENETRATE ⟨a chill was *striking* through her flesh to the marrow of her bones —Ellen Glasgow⟩ ⟨an irresistible impulse to ~ nearer the heart of the truth —R.B.West⟩ **10** *obs* **:** STEAL, ROB **11 a :** to engage in battle **:** FIGHT ⟨exhorting the multitude to ~ for freedom —W.C.Taylor⟩ **b :** to make a military attack ⟨fast vessels which could ~ and get away —W.P.Webb⟩ ⟨bombers *struck* at the munitions factories⟩ **12 :** PULSATE, THROB ⟨his heart *struck* heavily when the house was visible —George Meredith⟩ **13 a :** to produce fire with flint and steel ⟨~ on the tinder . . . give me a taper —Shak.⟩ **b :** to become ignited ⟨the match wouldn't ~⟩ **14 :** to come suddenly or unexpectedly **:** LIGHT ⟨*struck* on a new plan to solve the problem⟩ **15 a :** to pull on a fishing rod in order to set the hook in the mouth of a fish **b** *of a fish* **:** to seize the bait **16 :** to move quickly **:** DART, SHOOT ⟨has tossed a sheet of paper into the fire and seen it . . . ~ to flame —George Meredith⟩ **17 a** *of a plant cutting* **:** to take root **b** *of a seed* **:** GERMINATE **18 :** to make an impression ⟨what ~*s* at a first reading —*Times Lit. Supp.*⟩ ⟨would ~ on pure minds with a force like mathematical demonstration —John Keble⟩ **19 :** to engage in a temporary stoppage of work in order to bring about compliance with demands made on an employer ⟨voted to ~ for higher wages⟩ **20 a :** to take effect in the process of curing ⟨the salt has *struck*⟩ **b :** to cause a color to sink in (as in a glass coated with a composition and reheated) **:** become set **21 :** to make a sudden beginning **:** LAUNCH ⟨the orchestra *struck* into another waltz⟩ **22 :** to thrust oneself forward often in a sudden, unexpected, or vigorous manner ⟨sees no brawl but he must ~ into the midst of it —Sir Walter Scott⟩ **23 :** to act or serve as the orderly of a military officer **24 :** to form an arc (as between the two carbons of an electric arc) **25 :** to have a geological strike **26 :** to make a determined effort **:** work diligently **:** STRIVE ⟨as a boy . . . he had decided to ~ for a commission in the Royal Navy —J.A.Michener⟩ ⟨overborne by a sense of futility in *striking* for what seems unattainable —W.P.Webb⟩ ~ *vt* **1 a :** to deliver a stroke, blow, or thrust at **:** HIT ⟨~ the boy with the back of the hand⟩ ⟨~ the dog with a stick⟩ ⟨a deer *struck* by an arrow⟩ ⟨~ the whale with a harpoon⟩ ⟨a hurricane *struck* the town⟩ ⟨a house *struck* by lightning⟩ ⟨their herds are *struck* by an epidemic —Wilfred Thesiger⟩ ⟨this rise in living costs . . . ~*s* especially the poorer people of the country —P.E. James⟩ **b** (1) **:** to drive or remove with or as if with a blow ⟨*struck* the knife from his hand⟩ (2) **:** to remove or separate by or as if by cutting ⟨*struck* a branch from the tree⟩ **c** (1) *of a bird of prey* **:** to attack and sink the talons into (2) *of a snake* **:** to sink the fangs into **d :** to deliver or deal by or as if by some bodily action **:** INFLICT ⟨who would be free, themselves must ~ the blow —Lord Byron⟩ **e :** to produce by or as if by a blow or stroke ⟨waving wide her myrtle wand she ~*s* a universal peace —John Milton⟩ **2 a** (1) **:** to haul down (as a sail) (2) **:** to lower (as a flag) usu. as a sign of surrender ⟨made the ship — maybe with the aid of a ball across her bows — ~ her colors —Eva M. Tappan⟩ (3) **:** to lower (as a cargo) into a ship's hold — usu. used with *down* **b :** to dismantle and take away ⟨~ a stage set⟩ **c** (1) **:** to take down (a tent) ⟨shall be glad to help you ~ the tent —David Walker⟩ (2) **:** to take down the tents of (a camp) ⟨were to ~ camp at sunrise —Irving Stone⟩ **d :** to lower gradually (an arch or vault centering) so as to permit the arch or vault to reach safely its final state of equilibrium **3 a :** to bring suffering or death to as if with a blow ⟨heavily the hand of the Lord had *stricken* him —John Bruce⟩ **b :** to afflict suddenly **:** lay low ⟨was *stricken* with the bends —P.J.Costello⟩ ⟨was *struck* down at the height of his young glory —Richard Pollock⟩ **4 a :** to engage in (a battle) **:** FIGHT **b :** to make a military attack on ⟨the planes returned safely after *striking* their targets⟩ ⟨the first platoon *struck* the retreating enemy⟩ **5 :** to delete, efface, or cancel with or as if with a stroke of the pen ⟨*struck* this appropriation from the defense budget —*Army-Navy-Air Force Jour.*⟩ ⟨have *struck* out a few pages which are merely a newspaper abridgment of an address —O.W.Holmes †1935⟩ ⟨*struck* down a . . . law requiring each state employe to take an oath —*N.Y.Times*⟩ ⟨demanded that the . . . professors be fired and the book *stricken* off the list —Green Peyton⟩ ⟨not only suppress the book but have it *struck* out of the catalog —G.B.Shaw⟩ **6 a :** to penetrate in a sharp or painful manner **:** PIERCE ⟨the news of the loss *struck* him to the heart⟩ **b :** to cause to penetrate ⟨his voice *struck* a chill into the girl's heart —A. Conan Doyle⟩ **c :** to send down or out ⟨trees that ~ deep roots⟩ **7** *obs* **a :** to rub gently ⟨~ his hand over the place and recover the leper —2 Kings 5:11(AV)⟩ **b :** to spread on a surface **:** SMEAR ⟨take of the blood and ~ it on the two side posts —Exod 12:7(AV)⟩ **8 a :** to level (as a measure of grain) by scraping off with a strickle what is above the rim **b :** to smooth or form (as a mold in founding) with a strickle — often used with *out* or *up* **c :** to dress and smooth (a mortar joint between bricks or stones) with a trowel **9 a :** to indicate by sounding ⟨the clock of the church . . . ~*s* the hours —Arnold Bennett⟩ ⟨her ship's bell is now being used . . . for *striking* the end of the day —H. A.Chippendale⟩ **b :** to cause to sound the time ⟨*struck* my repeater again and found that midnight was past —*Nat'l Observer*⟩ **10 a** (1) **:** to bring into forceful contact ⟨*struck* his head on a rafter⟩ ⟨~ the knee against the dashboard⟩ (2) **:** to shake (hands) in confirmation of an agreement ⟨let us ~ hands upon the bargain —Jane Austen⟩ (3) **:** to thrust suddenly ⟨*struck* the spurs in his horse and galloped away —Irving Bacheller⟩ **b :** to come into contact or collision with ⟨the car skidded and *struck* a tree⟩ ⟨a ship ~*s* the reef⟩ ⟨*struck* the table as he fell⟩ ⟨the hissing sound of the rain as it *struck* the river's surface —J.C.Powys⟩ **c** *of light* **:** to fall on ⟨the sun ~*s* him full in the face⟩ **d** *of a sound* **:** to become audible to ⟨nor shout nor whistle ~*s* his ear —William Wordsworth⟩ **e** *of a hound* **:** to find the scent of (the quarry) **11 a :** to cause to fall into a specified mental or emotional state ⟨at this they were all . . . *struck* into their dumps —John Bunyan⟩ **b** (1) **:** to cause to be affected with a strong emotion ⟨a sight that *struck* them with horror⟩ (2) **:** to cause (a strong emotion) to fall suddenly or enter ⟨eyes that ~ terror into junior clerks —Constance Foley⟩ **c** *archaic* **:** DEPRESS, SHOCK ⟨this *struck* . . . the enthusiasts of the King's side as much as it exalted the Scots —Gilbert Burnet⟩ **d :** to cause to become as a result of or as if of a sudden blow ⟨a stray bullet *struck* the man dead —Horace Sutton⟩ ⟨was reportedly *struck* dumb with stage fright —*Current Biog.*⟩ **12 a :** to cast (as candles) in a mold **b :** to convert (metal) into coins **:** MINT **c** (1) **:** to produce by stamping with a die or punch ⟨~ a medal⟩ (2) **:** to hit with a die or punch ⟨wanted coins that were sharply *struck* —*Numismatist*⟩ **d :** to cause (a hot tool or die) to make an impression in bookbinding **e** (1) **:** to produce (as a bank note) by imprinting **:** PRINT (2) **:** STAMP ⟨~ a handstamp⟩ **f** *obs* **:** to imprint on the mind ⟨those beauties which ~ a sort of melancholy —Earl of Shaftesbury †1713⟩ **13 a :** to produce (as fire) by or as if by the percussion of flint and steel ⟨could not be unaware that my remarks did not ~ fire —R.M.Lovett⟩ **b :** to cause to ignite by friction ⟨would have to ~ a match every now and then to read the compass —William Faulkner⟩ **14 :** to make and ratify the terms of ⟨in this informal way the bargain is *struck* —W.T.C.King⟩ **15 a :** to play by strokes on the keys or strings ⟨~*s* the golden lyre —Alexander Pope⟩ **b :** to produce by or as if by playing a musical instrument ⟨~ a few chords on the piano⟩ ⟨he and his companions *struck* a discordant note in this firelit room —John Buchan⟩ **16** *obs* **:** STEAL, ROB **17 a :** to mark (as land) by plowing once up and down the field — often used with *off* **b :** to mark out (as a line) usu. with a compass or chalk line **:** DRAW **18 a :** to hook (a fish) by means of a sharp pull on the line ⟨rely on speed, not strength, when *striking* your trout —*Field & Stream*⟩ **b** *of a fish* **:** to snatch at (the bait) **:** SEIZE **19** *obs* **:** BROACH 3a **20 a** (1) **:** to come into the mind of **:** occur to ⟨it ~*s* me he has moved too far too fast —Irving Kolodin⟩ ⟨the oddity of the premature thanksgiving *struck* them both and they laughed —Israel Zangwill⟩ (2) **:** to appear to the judgment of **:** IMPRESS ⟨always *struck* strangers that way until the novelty wore off —J.P.Marquand⟩ ⟨no wonder they ~ us as silent —Thornton Wilder⟩ ⟨the young always ~ her as infinitely funny —G.W. Brace⟩ **b :** to make a strong impression on **:** appear remarkable to ⟨a spectacle . . . calculated to ~ a highly cultivated, a reflecting, an imaginative mind —T.B.Macaulay⟩ ⟨the name seemed to ~ them all —Jane Austen⟩ ⟨what *struck* me was that he told me very little that I cared to hear —O.W.Holmes †1935⟩ ⟨the first thing that *struck* me was the blue of the sky —Sam Pollock⟩ **c :** to catch and hold ⟨~*s* the attention and focuses the fugitive experience onto itself —Hunter Mead⟩ ⟨has painted the things that have *struck* her eye —*Newsweek*⟩ **21 a :** to transform by or as if by magic **b :** BEWITCH **22 a :** to precipitate (a dye) by a mordant **b :** to cause (a dye) to be adsorbed on an inert carrier in making an organic pigment **23 :** to select the members of (a jury) **:** FORM **24 :** to reach with a sounding line ⟨~ soundings⟩ **25 :** to arrive at by the balancing, counterposing, or canceling out of opposing elements or considerations **:** achieve by or as if by computation or calculation ⟨~ the optimum balance between secrecy and openness —J.G.Palfrey⟩ ⟨for the time being a compromise has been *struck* —C.J.Friedrich⟩ ⟨~ an average⟩ ⟨~ a mean⟩ **26 :** to make a request or demand of ⟨gaze at him and ~ him for his autograph —Mark Twain⟩ **27 :** to smooth and stretch (as skins) while wet in leather manufacturing — often used with *out* **28 :** to cause to become impregnated with salt in the process of curing **29 :** to lade (as a liquor) into a cooler **30 a** (1) **:** to reach in the course of traveling **:** come to ⟨*struck* the main road after a short drive⟩ ⟨an easterly route that eventually ~*s* the river⟩ (2) **:** to succeed in reaching **:** ATTAIN ⟨after an unpromising beginning he finally *struck* his stride as a concert pianist⟩ **b** (1) **:** to come upon in or as if in the course of traveling **:** run across ⟨the most unpractical person I ever *struck* —Sheila Kaye-Smith⟩ ⟨the best sea story I have *struck* in years —H.J.Laski⟩ (2) **:** to come across in the course of prospecting or drilling **:** DISCOVER ⟨this peasant . . . had the luck to ~ water —Norman Douglas⟩ ⟨~ oil⟩ **31 a :** to engage in a temporary stoppage of (work) in order to bring about compliance with demands made on an employer **b** (1) **:** to engage in a strike against (an employer) (2) **:** to suspend or cripple the operation of (as a factory) by engaging in a strike **32 :** to assume temporarily **:** take on ⟨*striking* what appeared to them to be most belligerent attitudes —Thomas Barbour⟩ ⟨~ a pose⟩ **33 a :** to place (a plant cutting) in a medium for growth and the development of roots ⟨less than 10 percent of the cuttings *struck* in sand finally rooted⟩ **b :** to propagate (a plant) esp. by means of cuttings **34 :** to make one's way by taking **:** proceed along ⟨*struck* their path across the fields —Algernon Gissing⟩ **35 :** to cause (an arc) to form (as between the carbon electrodes of an arc lamp) **36 :** to form a thin preliminary deposit on (an article in an electroplating bath) at a rapid rate preliminary to a longer and slower deposition **37** *of an insect* **:** to oviposit on

syn STRIKE, HIT, SMITE, PUNCH, SLUG, SLOG, SWAT, CLOUT, SLAP, CUFF, BOX: of this group, all of which indicate the coming or bringing into contact with or as if with a sharp blow, STRIKE, HIT, and SMITE are the more general terms. STRIKE, the most general of the words, may indicate the motion of aiming or dealing the blow, the motion prior to contact with the hand, fist, instrument, weapon, or missile ⟨*strike* at the enemy and miss⟩ ⟨*strike* out at random⟩ It may indicate various types of contact from a light, often stroking contact ⟨the light breeze *struck* the ship on the north side⟩ to a forcible collision or blasting contact ⟨the car *struck* a post and overturned⟩ ⟨the lightning *struck* the house⟩ ⟨*strike* a man down with a heavy blow⟩ ⟨the enemy *struck* with full force⟩ It may suggest several types of physical or emotional effect or impression ⟨*strike* someone dead⟩ ⟨*strike* a line on paper⟩ ⟨*strike* out a name from a list⟩ ⟨to be *struck* by the beauty of the scenery⟩ ⟨grief-*stricken*⟩ ⟨conscience-*stricken*⟩ or it may be used to indicate any of the types of contact suggested by any of the other words in this group. HIT, although it is used in most of the situations in which STRIKE occurs, emphasizes more than STRIKE the physical or figurative contact with or impact upon an object, usu. something aimed at; it usu., though not necessarily, stresses forcefulness ⟨*hit* a child on the wrist⟩ ⟨the shell *hit* the tank and tore through the side⟩ ⟨the depression *hit* hard all elements of society⟩ ⟨*hit* the right road home⟩ ⟨*hit* the winning number in a lottery⟩ SMITE, largely a rhetorical or book word, usu. stresses the injuriousness or destructiveness of the contact and often suggests a motivation of anger or desire for vengeance ⟨with the hammer she *smote* Sisera, she *smote* off his head —Judg 5:26 (AV)⟩ ⟨conscience-*smitten*⟩ ⟨disease-*smitten*⟩ ⟨*smitten* with grief or love⟩ PUNCH, SLUG, SLOG, SWAT, and CLOUT are generally used to suggest the giving of various kinds of usu. sharp or heavy blows. PUNCH suggests a quick blow with or as if with the fist ⟨would handcuff everybody rather than face the risk of having their noses *punched* by somebody —G.B.Shaw⟩ SLUG emphasizes the heaviness of the impact and usu. suggests a certain viciousness in the delivery of the blow ⟨was attacked by an assault suspect, who *slugged* him with a 5-ft. iron pipe —*Time*⟩ SLOG emphasizes the heavy, usu. haphazard quality of the blows ⟨the two fighters were so tired they merely *slogged* rather than hit each other with clean, precise blows⟩ SWAT suggests a forceful, slapping blow, usu. with such an instrument as a bat, weapon, or flyswatter ⟨in off moments he would *swat* the regiment of cockroaches —Paul de Kruif⟩ ⟨*swat* flies⟩ ⟨*swat* a baseball out of the ball park⟩ CLOUT suggests a heavy careless blow usu. with the hand or fist ⟨a shoe *clouted* his skull and inflicted a fracture —Hugh McCrae⟩ ⟨they *clout* our heads the moment our conclusions differ from theirs —G.B.Shaw⟩ SLAP, CUFF, and BOX all suggest blows of varying force with the open hand. SLAP is the most general and indicates a sharp, usu. stinging blow with or as if with the palm of the hand ⟨*slap* a person in the face⟩ ⟨*slapped* the coverlet angrily —Kenneth Roberts⟩ CUFF suggests a blow often forcible enough to dizzy or throw off balance and often dealt with the back of the hand ⟨it was pointed out . . . that children could be hurried and delayed, *cuffed* and bribed, into becoming adults —Margaret Mead⟩ BOX suggests the delivery of an openhanded blow but is usu. limited to one against the ears ⟨the mother *boxed* her child's ears in a fit of temper⟩ **syn** see in addition AFFECT

— **strike a docket** *Brit* **:** to enter a creditor's affidavit and bond in bankruptcy

²strike \"\ *n* -s [ME *strik*, *strike*, fr. *striken*, v.] **1** *archaic* **:** a bunch of hackled flax, jute, or hemp prepared for drawing into slivers **2** *dial chiefly Eng* **:** a dry measure varying from two pecks to four bushels **3 a :** a strickle for leveling a surface by striking off superfluous material or for striking up a mold in founding **b :** a broad smooth stick for removing superfluous clay in molding bricks **4 :** an act or instance of striking ⟨the ~ of a rattlesnake⟩ ⟨the ~ of the clock⟩ **5 a :** the unit quantity of malt used in making ale or beer **b :** excellence or strength of ale or beer ⟨three hogsheads of ale of the first ~ —Sir Walter Scott⟩ **6 a :** the impression on a coin, token, or medal made by a die or punch **b** (1) **:** the impression on a stamp made by a printing plate (2) **:** the impression on a stamp made by a handstamp **7 a :** a temporary stoppage of work by a body of workers designed to enforce compliance with demands (as changes in wages, hours, or working conditions) made on an employer — compare LOCKOUT, STAY-IN STRIKE **b :** a temporary stoppage of normal operations and activities designed as a protest against an action or condition ⟨a buyers' ~⟩ ⟨hunger ~⟩ **8 a :** the direction of the line of intersection of a horizontal plane with an uptilted bedding plane, vein, fault, slaty cleavage, schistosity, or similar geological structure **b** (1) **:** the trend of a linear geological feature or structure (2) **:** the orientation of a tabular particle in a sediment or rock **9 a :** a pull on a fishing rod designed to set the hook in the mouth of a fish **b :** a pull on a line made by a fish in taking the bait **10 :** the mass of moist sugar crystals left in a pan after a boiling in the manufacture of sugar **11 :** a sudden or unexpected stroke of good luck; *esp* **:** a sudden discovery of oil or of a rich vein of ore ⟨made a lucky ~ and in three months had realized a considerable fortune —H.W.H.Knott⟩ **12 a :** a pitched ball (as in baseball) recorded against a batter ⟨it's one-two-three ~*s*, you're out at the old ball game —Jack Norworth⟩: (1) **:** a pitch at which a batter swings and misses (2) **:** a pitch passing through the strike zone at which a batter does not swing (3) **:** a foul bunt not caught on the fly (4) **:** a foul ball hit with less than two strikes on the batter and not caught on the fly (5) **:** a foul tip caught by the catcher before it hits the ground **b :** a disadvantage that makes achievement difficult **:** HANDICAP ⟨his racial background was a second ~ against him —K.D.Miller⟩ **13 :** an act or instance of knocking down all the bowling pins with the first ball of a frame — compare SPARE **14 :** a piece of copper that carries an impression driven into it by a typefounder's punch and that after hand finishing becomes a matrix for forming the face of type **15 a :** an act of obtaining or attempting to obtain money by importunity, threat, or blackmail **b** *or* **strike bill :** a legislative bill designed to be harmful to a person or corporation if enacted into law and introduced in order to obtain a bribe for its withdrawal **16 :** a striking mechanism (as for a clock) **17 a :** a part of a lock designed to be struck by another part **b :** a part of a lock that prevents a retracted bolt from shooting forward **c :** a metal fastening on a doorframe into which the bolt of a lock is projected in order to secure the door **18 :** establishment of roots and plant growth (as by rooting of cuttings or germination of seeds) ⟨an excellent ~ of oats⟩ ⟨had a 70 percent ~ on his cuttings⟩ **19 a :** a thin initial electrodeposit **b :** an electrolyte used in making such a deposit **20 a :** cutaneous myiasis of sheep **:** FLY-STRIKE ⟨body ~⟩ ⟨tail ~⟩ ⟨blowfly ~⟩ — compare MULES OPERATION **b :** STRUCK 2 **21 a :** a military attack; *esp* **:** an air attack on a single objective ⟨air ~*s* on the more important road junctions —*Infantry Jour.*⟩ **b :** a group of airplanes taking part in such an attack ⟨in the afternoon a second ~ was flown off —Fletcher Pratt⟩ **22 :** the amount of dye absorbed by the fiber but not diffused through it in the first brief period of dyeing **23 :** the act or process of dismantling a stage set **24 :** an individual unit of a design on china or other dinnerware in the decalcomania process

strike–a–light \ˈ==ˌ=\ *n* **:** a device consisting of or including a piece of flint to be struck by steel or pyrites in order to obtain sparks

strike–anywhere match \(ˈ)=ˈ==ˌ=-\ *n* **:** KITCHEN MATCH

strike back *vi* **1 :** to return a blow ⟨*struck back* angrily at his opponent⟩ ⟨decided to *strike back* at the critics⟩ **2 :** BACKFIRE 3

strike–back \ˈ=ˌ=\ *n* -s [*strike back*] **:** burning at the fuel injector of an air-fed burner **:** BACKFIRE 2b

strike below *vt* **:** to lower into or as if into a ship's hold **:** carry below ⟨perishables are stacked on deck under cover, awaiting rigid Navy inspection before they are *struck below* —*All Hands*⟩

strike benefit *or* **strike pay** *n* **:** a payment made by a union to provide subsistence to strikers ⟨well-financed unions always provide *strike benefits* covering the minimum cost of living —H.A.Millis & R.E.Montgomery⟩
strike board *n* **:** ⁵LUTE 2
strikebound \'ˌ=ˌ=\ *adj* **:** subjected to a strike ⟨a ~ factory⟩
strikebreaker \'ˌ=ˌ==\ *n* **:** one engaged in strikebreaking: **a :** one hired to replace a striking worker **b :** one hired to supply replacements for striking workers
strikebreaking \'ˌ=ˌ==\ *n* **:** action designed to break up a strike
strike–dog \'ˌ=ˌ=\ *n* **:** the dog of a pack that customarily first closes with game — called also *striker*
strike fault *n* **:** a geological fault whose trend coincides approximately with the strike of associated strata
strike in *vi* **1** *obs* **:** to enter into competition **:** TRY ⟨advises me to *strike in* for some preferment —Jonathan Swift⟩ **2** *obs* **:** to associate as a confederate or collaborator ⟨*strike in* with him and help him to dupe his father —John Dryden⟩ **3 a** *archaic* **:** to fall into or express agreement ⟨a shifting adversary . . . will *strike in* with any opinion —Richard Bentley †1742⟩ **b** *obs* **:** to prove compatible **:** fit in **4 :** to intervene or interrupt in a sudden or unexpected manner ⟨*strike in* with a foolish suggestion⟩ **5 :** to disappear from the surface with subsequent internal effects ⟨lived only a few days after the disease *struck in*⟩ ~ *vt* **1 :** IMPRINT ⟨presses adequate for *striking in* names and addresses⟩ **2 a :** to draw (a line) from one point on the surface of a sheet to another point with a ruling machine **b :** to make (perforations that do not extend from edge to edge) in a sheet
strike–in \'ˌ=ˌ=\ *n* -S [*strike in*] **:** the relative penetration of ink into paper that is being printed
strike joint *n* **:** a joint whose horizontal direction is the same as that of the strike of the rock
strike·less \'strīkləs\ *adj* **:** marked by the absence of strikes
strike measure *n* **:** LEVEL MEASURE
strike note *or* **strike tone** *n* **:** the apparent pitch produced by a bell when it is first struck — compare HUM NOTE
strike off *vt* **1 :** to compose with facility **:** produce in an effortless manner ⟨*struck off* a sonnet for the occasion⟩ **2 :** to depict clearly and exactly **:** hit off ⟨had too much phlegm to *strike off* the grand passions or reach the sublime parts of painting —Tobias Smollett⟩ **3 :** to remove excess freshly placed concrete, mortar, or plaster from (a surface) by operating a straightedge over the forms or screeds
strike–off \'ˌ=ˌ=\ *n* -S [*strike off*] **:** a straightedge used to remove excess freshly placed concrete, mortar, or plaster from a surface
strike out *vt* **1 :** to create or form with apparent ease **:** produce as if by a stroke ⟨*struck out* the fundamental method . . . now used by all aesthetic historians —Gilbert Highet⟩ **2 :** to enter vigorously and suddenly on ⟨breaking free from the family tradition and *striking out* a line of his own —Sheila Kaye-Smith⟩ **3 :** to retire (a baseball batter) by a strikeout ⟨allowed two walks and *struck out* eight⟩ ~ *vi* **1 :** to enter vigorously and suddenly upon a course of action ⟨had *struck out* for himself and refused to live the tame easy life that he could have lived —Frank Sargeson⟩ **2 :** to set out in a vigorous or sudden manner ⟨*struck out* in the direction . . . the miller had indicated —T.B.Costain⟩ **3 :** to make an out in baseball by a strikeout ⟨had a single, walked, and *struck out* twice⟩
strikeout \'ˌ=ˌ=\ *n* -S [*strike out*] **:** an out in baseball resulting from a batter's being charged with three strikes
strikeover \'ˌ=ˌ==\ *n* -S [fr. the phrase *strike over*] **:** an act or instance of striking a typewriter character on a spot already occupied by another character
strike pan *n* **:** a vacuum pan with steam coils for increasing the rate of evaporation in sugar manufacturing
strike plate *n* **:** STRIKE 17c
strik·er \'strīkə(r)\ *n* -S [¹*strike* + *-er*] **1 :** one that strikes ⟨no blow can be struck but it recoils on the ~ —R.W.Emerson⟩ **2** *obs* **:** a dissolute person **3 :** STRICKLE **4 :** a player in any of several games who strikes: **a :** a batsman in cricket **b :** a billiards player whose turn it is at the table **c :** a player having last struck the ball in court tennis **d :** a player (as in squash) whose turn it is after the ball in play has hit the front wall **5 a :** a clock or watch that strikes **b :** any of various devices designed to strike: as (1) **:** the hammer of the striking mechanism of a clock or watch (2) **:** the part of the action that immediately delivers the blow to the primer of a firearm (3) **:** a small plunger intermediary between the firing pin and the primer that ignites the charge of a torpedo (4) **:** a device on a pen-ruling machine for raising and lowering a pen (5) **:** a device for putting a machine or part in gear with a driving mechanism (6) **:** a reciprocating projecting piece in a loom used to actuate a finger periodically to deliver the pick **6 a :** a worker engaged in any of various occupations that involve striking: as (1) **:** BLACKSMITH 1c (2) **:** one who dresses off the clay bricks with a strike in molding (3) **:** one who stretches and smooths wet hides and skins by hand or machine **b :** an oiler on a ship **c** (1) **:** a fisherman who rows a driveboat (2) **:** a shrimp fisherman who uses a trawl **7 a :** a worker who assists another: as (1) **:** one who assists a truck driver in loading and driving (2) **:** one who helps a furnaceman shape steel plates **b** (1) **:** an enlisted man detailed as an officer's orderly (2) **:** an enlisted man employed by an officer to do odd jobs for extra pay during off-duty hours **8 :** a worker who is on strike **9** *or* **striker plate :** STRIKE 17c **10 :** MORDANT 1 **11 :** STRIKE-DOG **12 :** a navy enlisted man who is working for a petty officer's rate
striker boat *n* **:** DRIVEBOAT
striker–out \'ˌ=ˌ=, ˌ=ˌ='\ *n* -S [*strike out* + *-er*] **1 :** a player who receives the service in a racket game **2 :** SETTER 2h
strikes *pres 3d sing of* STRIKE, *pl of* STRIKE
strike shift *n* **:** the component of the shift parallel with the strike of a fault — compare DIP SHIFT
strike slip *n* **:** the part of a fault displacement that is recorded by the separation of orig. continuous beds or veins measured horizontally in the plane of the fault
strike–through \'ˌ=ˌ=\ *n* -S [fr. *strike through*, v.] **:** the penetration of ink through paper that is being printed
strike up *vi* **1 :** to start singing or playing ⟨then an organ in a gallery *strikes up* —Arnold Bennett⟩ **2 :** to begin to be sung or played ⟨a march *struck up* and the parade began⟩ ~ *vt* **1 a :** to begin to sing or play ⟨the band *struck up* a set of waltzes —W.G.Smith⟩ **b :** to cause to begin singing or playing ⟨*strike up* the band⟩ **2 :** to cause to begin **:** set afoot ⟨easier to *strike up* acquaintanceships with local people —Richard Joseph⟩ ⟨*strike up* a conversation with the neighbors —W.H. Whyte⟩
strike valley *n* **:** a valley parallel to the strike of the underlying rocks of a region — called also *longitudinal valley*
strike zone *n* **:** the area (as between the knees and shoulders of a batter in his natural stance) over home plate through which a pitched baseball must pass to be called a strike
¹**striking** *n* -S [ME, fr. gerund of *striken* to strike — more at STRIKE] **1 :** an act or instance of one that strikes **2 a :** something (as a coin) produced by striking **b :** the things struck at one time ⟨a huge ~ of a token coinage —P.K.Anderson⟩ **3 :** STRIKE 6
²**striking** *adj* [fr. pres. part. of ¹*strike*] **1 :** that strikes; *esp* **:** attracting attention or notice through unusual or conspicuous qualities ⟨one of the most ~ and fearful figures in our early fiction —V.L.Parrington⟩ ⟨~ contradictions between what musical people admire and what they like —Virgil Thomson⟩ ⟨have been few more ~ examples of ingenuity —Edward Clodd⟩ ⟨beautiful tweeds . . . made into ~ suits —Catherine Paul⟩ **2 :** of, relating to, or constituting a device for striking or putting in gear a machine or part of a machine **syn** see NOTICEABLE
striking angle *n* **:** ANGLE OF FALL
striking bag *n* **:** PUNCHING BAG
striking circle *n* **:** a semicircular area in front of each goal in field hockey which extends out from the goal line to a maximum distance of 15 yards and from which the ball must be hit in order to score a goal — see FIELD HOCKEY illustration
striking distance *n* **:** the distance through which it is possible to reach an object by striking **:** the distance at which a force is effective when directed at an object
striking energy *n* **:** the kinetic energy of a bullet at the instant of impact
striking hammer *n* **:** SLEDGEHAMMER
strik·ing·ly *adv* **:** in a striking manner **:** to a striking degree ⟨one of the most ~ picturesque bridges of any English town —S.P.B.Mais⟩
strik·ing·ness *n* -ES **:** the quality or state of being striking
striking–out machine \'ˌ=ˌ='ˌ=-\ *n* **:** a machine used in the finishing of leather for smoothing and stretching — called also *setting-out machine*
striking pin *n* **:** PIN 8
striking plate *n* **:** KEEPER 2b
striking platform *n* **:** a prepared flat surface at right angles to the axis of a stone from which flakes are struck for the production of stone tools
striking reed *n* **:** BEATING REED
striking stile *n* **:** the stile of a door containing the lock — compare HANGING STILE
striking voltage *n* **:** the minimum voltage sufficient to arc across a given gap
¹**string** \'striŋ\ *n* -S [ME *streng, string*, fr. OE *streng*; akin to MD *strenge, stringe, strenc* rope, cord, strap, OHG *strang* rope, cord, ON *strengr* rope, cord, string, L *stringere* to bind tight, press together — more at STRAIN] **1 a :** a small cord (as of vegetable fiber) used to bind, fasten, or tie **:** a cord larger than a thread and smaller than a rope **b :** a gallows rope **c :** a cord for leading or controlling a person or an animal **:** LEASH **2 a** *archaic* **:** a cord (as a tendon or ligament) of an animal body **b :** a plant fiber (as a fine root, the vein of a leaf, or the tough fiber connecting the halves of a string-bean pod) **3 a :** the gut or wire cord of a musical instrument — see VIOLIN illustration **b strings** *pl* (1) **:** the bowed stringed instruments of an orchestra ⟨glanced at the golden forest of 52 ~*s* on my left . . . and gave the downbeat —Joseph Levine⟩ (2) **:** the players of such instruments esp. in an orchestra — compare WIND **4 :** BOWSTRING **5 :** a cord or drawstring used as a closure (as on an article of clothing or a bag) **6 a :** a group of objects threaded on a string esp. if enough to fill it ⟨a ~ of onions⟩ ⟨a ~ of fish⟩ **b :** the cord of a necklace **:** the thread on which beads or gems are strung ⟨a ~ of pearls⟩ **7 :** a cord or leather thong that ties together the leaves and covers of a book bound in the photograph-album style **8 :** a slender vein of ore in a mine **9 :** RIBBON 1c **10 a :** a series of things arranged in or as if in a line ⟨a ~ of cars waiting at a red light⟩ ⟨rapid formation of bars along the shore has produced a ~ of lagoons —P.E.James⟩ **b :** a group of business properties spread out or scattered geographically ⟨still visits the first drugstore of his ~ —*Monsanto Mag.*⟩ ⟨a ~ of filling stations⟩ ⟨a ~ of newspapers⟩ **11 a :** a column of animals, vehicles, or persons moving in single file **:** TRAIN **b :** the horses that belong to one stable or owner **:** STUD **c :** a group or set of horses or draft animals; *esp* **:** the group of saddle horses assigned to a cowhand for his exclusive use ⟨each rider had his ~ of two to six horses, usually belonging to the employer —W.S.Campbell⟩ — compare ³MOUNT 3b **12 a :** a recourse, means, or expedient by which to accomplish an end or purpose ⟨they have a second ~. The husband has farmed as a hobby all his life —Rebecca West⟩ ⟨he has two ~*s* to his bow⟩ **b :** a group of players or contestants ranked according to rated skill or proficiency ⟨the first ~ of the basketball team —Oakley Hall⟩ ⟨a second ~ quarterback⟩ **13 :** a series or succession in time **:** SEQUENCE ⟨his long ~ of single-handed successes made rich fare for . . . crime reporters —Al Spiers⟩ ⟨looking at once into a ~ of stories —Virginia D. Dawson & Betty D. Wilson⟩ **14 a :** one of the inclined sides of a stair supporting the treads and risers — see CLOSE STRING, OPEN STRING **b :** STRINGCOURSE **c :** an inside range of ceiling planks corresponding to the sheer strake of a ship and bolted to it **15 :** a cord used to manipulate a puppet **16 a :** a score or tally of an indoor game sometimes (as in billiards) marked by buttons threaded on a string or wire **b :** a fixed or standard number of turns at play in a game or competition **17** *billiards* **a :** BALKLINE 1 **b :** the action of lagging for break **c :** a wire strung with buttons usu. stretched above a table for the recording of points **18 :** the number of shots prescribed for each shooter in an event of a small arms target match ⟨a ~ of 10 or 20 shots —Townsend Whelen⟩ **19 :** LINE 12a **20 a :** proofs of matter set by one compositor usu. pasted in a strip to facilitate measurement of his work **b :** newspaper clippings of his printed stories pasted on a strip or sheet of paper as a record by a news correspondent paid by the line **21 strings** *pl* **a :** conditions or obligations attached to something ⟨it was his privilege to stay . . . there were no ~*s* attached —Morley Callaghan⟩ **b :** CONTROL, DOMINATION ⟨freed from the occupation's ~*s* —Lindesay Parrott⟩ **22 :** a yellowish gray that is paler and slightly greener than sand and greener and slightly duller than natural **23 :** a transparent line in glass resulting from the slow solution of a large grain of sand or foreign material **24 a :** a set of well-drilling tools and equipment esp. for percussion well drilling **b :** all of the casing or pipe of one size used in a well **25 :** a set of bombs dropped on a target in rapid succession **:** STICK **syn** see CONDITION — **on the string :** subject to one's influence **:** dangling at one's pleasure ⟨kept three suitors *on the string* for months⟩
²**string** \"\ *vb* **strung** \'strəŋ\ *or dial* **strang** \-raŋ, -raiŋ\ **strung** *also* **stringed; stringing; strings** [ME *strengen*, fr. *streng, string*, n.] *vt* **1 :** to fit (a bow) with a string **:** BRACE **2 a :** to equip (a musical instrument) with strings **b :** to bring the strings of (a musical instrument) to the required pitch **:** TUNE **3 :** to make tense **:** key up ⟨the whiskey had *strung* her up to recklessness —Dorothy Sayers⟩ **4 a :** to thread on or as if on a string ⟨*strung* beads by the hour⟩ **b :** to hang or thread (as a rope or wire) with objects ⟨*strung* the rope with the birds taken in our day's bag⟩ **c :** to tie, hang, or fasten with string **d :** to put together (as words or ideas) like objects threaded on a string ⟨words form the thread on which we ~ our experiences —Aldous Huxley⟩ **5 :** to hang (a person) by the neck **:** put to death by hanging ⟨*strung* him up from the nearest tall tree⟩ **6 :** to remove the strings of **:** clean of strings ⟨the beans have been *strung* —*Commonweal*⟩ **7 a :** to extend or stretch like a string ⟨*strung* electric light wires from tree to tree on the lawn⟩ **b :** to set out or stretch in a line, succession, or series ⟨merchants were ~*ing* their prosperous modern houses along this fairly new business thoroughfare —T.D.Clark⟩ **8 a :** to furnish (a book) with strings when binding **b :** to tie (the raised band of a book) with string or cord to preserve shape after covering **9 :** to thread (primed tobacco leaves) on twine or wire and attach to laths for hanging in the barn to dry **10 :** to pull (a wire) through the dies of a drawbench — used with *up* **11 :** to foist off a tall story on **:** pull the leg of **:** FOOL ⟨cowboys ~*ing* tenderfeet with tall tales —Carl Van Doren⟩ ~ *vi* **1 :** to be put to death by hanging **:** be hanged **2 :** to move, progress, or lie in a string or series ⟨the islands ~ along the coast⟩ ⟨the men were ~*ing* over the beach —Norman Mailer⟩ **3 :** to form into strings **:** become stringy (as a viscous fluid) **4 :** LAG 2b
³**string** \"\ *adj* [¹*string*] **1 :** of, containing, or like string **2 a :** STRINGED 1 **b :** relating to stringed musical instruments, the players of stringed instruments, or the music performed on stringed instruments ⟨~ orchestra⟩ **c :** imitating the tone quality of bowed stringed musical instruments ⟨~ stop of a pipe organ⟩
string *abbr* stringendo
string along *vi* **:** to go along ⟨prompts them to *string along* with the people's choice —*Time*⟩ ~ *vt* **1 :** to keep (someone) dangling or waiting ⟨told me to *string* him *along* —Dorothy Sayers⟩ **2 :** DECEIVE, FOOL ⟨let him *string* himself *along* with illusions and false expectations —H.L.Davis⟩
string and ray rot *n* **:** a disintegration of heartwood of the butts of oaks caused by a fungus (*Polyporus berkeleyi*)
string bag *n* **:** a bag made of string; *esp* **:** a mesh bag of heavy string with two handles at the top used for carrying packages

string bag

string bass *n* **:** CONTRABASS
string bean *n* **1 :** SNAP BEAN — used esp. of some older varieties that have stringy fiber on the sutures of the pods **2 :** a tall excessively thin person ⟨that *string bean* of a kid —R.F.Mirvish⟩
stringboard \'ˌ=ˌ=\ *n* **:** a board or built-up facing used in stair building to cover the ends of the steps and hide the true string
string correspondent *n* **:** a news correspondent who is paid space rates
stringcourse \'ˌ=ˌ=\ *n* **:** a horizontal band running around a building usu. on the outside ⟨a brick ~ between the first and second stories —*Amer. Guide Series: Va.*⟩ — compare BLOCKING COURSE
string development *n* **:** RIBBON DEVELOPMENT
stringed \'striŋd\ *adj* **1 :** having strings **2 :** produced by strings ⟨~ noise —John Milton⟩
stringed instrument *n* **:** a musical instrument whose tone is produced on taut strings by drawing a bow across them (as in the violin), by plucking them (as in the harp or guitar), by striking them (as in the piano), or by blowing upon them (as in the aeolian harp); *esp* **:** a member of the violin or viol family
strin·gen·cy \'strinjənsē, -si\ *n* -ES **:** the quality or state of being stringent: as **a :** RIGOR, SEVERITY, STRICTNESS ⟨the best parlor and the awful moral *stringencies* —G.W.Brace⟩ **b :** a pressing want or scarcity **:** tightness of money or credit ⟨financial ~ threatened to complete the ruin —*Amer. Guide Series: Mass.*⟩ **c :** cogency or convincing force of reasoning or argument ⟨theoretical ~⟩
strin·gen·do \strĕn'jen(ˌ)dō\ *adv* [It, verbal of *stringere* to press, squeeze, tie together, fr. L, to bind tight, press together — more at STRAIN] **:** with quickening of tempo (as to a climax) — used as a direction in music
strin·gent \'strinjənt\ *adj* [L *stringent-, stringens*, pres. part. of *stringere* to bind tight, press together — more at STRAIN] **1 :** sharp, astringent, or bitter to the senses esp. of taste ⟨the air was thin and clear, ~ with wood smoke —A.J.Cronin⟩ **2 a :** binding, drawing, or pressing tight ⟨the most ~ confinement that can be laid upon a human being —Lee Rogow⟩ **b :** marked by rigor, strictness, or severity **:** rigidly controlled by rule or standard **:** not loose or lax ⟨a tested touchstone of ~ thinking —Yakov Malkiel⟩ ⟨~ training in pioneer life —John Hersey⟩ ⟨extremely ~ libel laws —*Meet The British*⟩ ⟨colleges with the most ~ admissions requirements —N.O.Frederiksen⟩ **3 :** marked by money scarcity, credit strictness, or market decline ⟨money policies were more ~ —*Dun's Rev.*⟩ **syn** see RIGID
strin·gent·ly *adv* **:** in a stringent manner **:** STRICTLY ⟨game laws are ~ enforced —*Amer. Guide Series: Texas*⟩
string·er \'striŋə(r)\ *n* -S [ME *strynger*, fr. *streng, string* string + *-er*] **1 :** one that strings ⟨wire ~*s* sweated down the road, setting up lines —*Newsweek*⟩ **2 :** a string, rope, or wire often equipped with snaps on which fish are strung by a fisherman **3 a :** a narrow vein or irregular filament of mineral traversing a rock mass of different material **b :** a line or linear zone of specified objects or material ⟨narrow tongues of forest will . . . follow ~*s* of favorable soil —A.A.Nichol⟩ ⟨~*s* of gravel on a tidal flat⟩ ⟨~*s* of pumice⟩ **4 a :** a long horizontal timber used to connect uprights in a frame or to support a floor **b :** a string in stair building **c :** a tie in a truss **5 a :** a longitudinal member in any of various kinds of construction: as **a :** such a member extending from bent to bent of a railroad bridge and carrying the track **b :** a longitudinal sleeper borne on the transverse ties of a railroad track **c :** a longitudinal girder, plank, or plate used in ship construction as a strengthening member — see SHIP illustration **d :** a longitudinal member used (as in a fuselage or wing) to reinforce the skin in a semimonocoque airplane **6 a :** STRING CORRESPONDENT **b :** a newspaper reporter who serves another publication or a news agency part time — distinguished from *staffer* **7 :** one that holds a specified competitive rating or is estimated as of specified excellence or efficiency — usu. used in combination ⟨pulled out his first-*stringers* after piling up a wide scoring margin⟩ ⟨sent their second-*stringer* to review the play⟩ **8 :** a sequence in rummy or panguingue
stringer lode *n* **:** a lode that consists of many small irregular reticulated stringers with the intervening country rock
stringer plate *n* **:** one of the plates forming the outer strake of a ship's deck and being usu. heavier than those used for the rest of the deck — see SHIP illustration
string figure *n* **1 :** a figure representing any of various objects that is made by passing a string around the fingers of both hands sometimes with the help of a second person ⟨anthropologists find the making of *string figures* common in many simple cultures⟩ — compare CAT'S CRADLE **2** *or* **string game :** a game of making string figures
string·ful \'striŋˌfu̇l\ *n, pl* **stringfuls** *also* **stringsful** \-ŋ,fu̇lz, -ŋz,fu̇l\ **:** the quantity or number of objects that can be threaded on a string
string galvanometer *n* **:** a galvanometer for measuring oscillating currents by the lateral motions of a silver-plated quartz fiber traversed by the current and stretched under adjustable tension perpendicular to the field of an electromagnet
string·halt \'striŋˌhȯlt\ *n* **:** a lameness in the hind legs of a horse caused by muscular spasms possibly of nervous origin and causing excessive flexure in locomotion — called also *springhalt*
string·halt·ed \-təd\ *also* **string·halty** \-tē\ *adj* **:** suffering from stringhalt — **string·halt·ed·ness** *n* -ES
string·i·ness \'striŋēnəs, -ŋin-\ *n* -ES **:** the quality or state of being stringy
stringing *n* -S [partly fr. ¹*string* + *-ing*; partly fr. gerund of ²*string*] **1 :** straight lines of inlay in furniture decoration **2 :** the threading of primed tobacco and attaching of it to laths **3 :** the gut, silk, or nylon with which a racket is strung
string insulator *n* **:** a series of two or more suspension insulators flexibly connected
string lead *n* **:** lead in thin strips
string·less \'striŋləs\ *adj* **:** having no strings
stringlike \'ˌ=ˌ=\ *adj* **:** resembling a string (as in shape or tone)
string line *n* **:** BALKLINE 1
string·man \'striŋmən\ *n, pl* **stringmen :** STRING CORRESPONDENT
string organ *n* **:** a reed organ having a set of vibrators or free reeds joined by rods with wires or strings that are thus made to vibrate with them and give musical tones resembling those both of the harmonium and pianoforte
stringpiece \'ˌ=ˌ=\ *n* **:** a long piece of heavy timber usu. used horizontally in a construction: as **a :** the heavy squared timber lying along the top of the piles forming a dock front or timber pier **b :** a temporary horizontal timber used in shoring — compare NEEDLE 4 **c :** STRING 14a
string proof *n* **:** the density at which a boiling syrup threads
string quartet *n* **1 :** a quartet of performers on stringed musical instruments usu. including a first and second violin, a viola, and a cello **2 :** a composition for string quartet
strings *pl of* STRING, *pres 3d sing of* STRING
strings·man \'striŋzmən\ *or* **string·man** \-ŋm-\ *n, pl* **stringsmen** *or* **stringmen :** a player on a stringed musical instrument
string tie *n* **:** a narrow necktie
string tone *n* **:** tone like that of a violin or related instrument
stringways \'ˌ=ˌ=\ *n pl* **:** courses separated by strings for individual contestants (as in swimming, sprinting, and dog races)

string tie

stringy \'striŋē, -ŋi\ *adj* -ER/-EST [¹*string* + *-y*] **1 a :** consisting of strings or small threads **:** FIBROUS, FILAMENTOUS ⟨a ~ root⟩ **b** (1) **:** resembling or suggestive of a string **:** marked by length and thinness ⟨~ hair⟩ (2) **:** lean and muscular in build **:** SINEWY, WIRY ⟨~ old cowboys still rolling their cigarettes —J.B.Priestley⟩ ⟨his tough, ~ body —Georg Meyers⟩ **2 :** capable of being drawn out to form a string (as a glutinous substance) **:** GLUEY, ROPY, VISCID ⟨~ tenacious exudate —A.J.Steigman & C.H.Scott⟩ **3 a** *of cotton* **:** matted in rope form during poor ginning or picking **b** *of wool* (1) **:** slightly matted during scouring (2) **:** lacking normal crimp **4 :** having a tone like that of a violin or related instrument; *esp* **:** thin, edgy, and nasal in quality **5 :** STRINGHALTED
stringybark \'ˌ==ˌ=\ *n* **1 :** any of several Australian eucalypts with fibrous inner bark — compare SMOOTHBARK **2 :** the bark of a stringybark tree
stringybark pine *n* **:** an Australian cypress pine (*Callitris parlatorei*)

stringy kelp *n* **:** a kelp (*Alaria fistulosa*)
stringy sap *n* **:** an inferior sap of the sugar maple milky in color, ropy in texture, and deficient in sugar
¹strinkle *n* [ME *strenkil, strinkil,* prob. alter. (influenced by *strewen* to strew) of *sprenkil, sprinkil;* akin to ME *sprenklen* to sprinkle] *obs* **:** SPRINKLER; *esp* **:** ASPERGILLUM
²strin·kle \ˈstriŋkəl\ *vb* [ME *strenklen, strinklen,* prob. alter. of *sprenklen, sprinklen*] *chiefly dial* **:** SPRINKLE
stri·o·la \ˈstrīələ\ *n, pl* **stri·o·lae** \-ə,lē\ [NL, dim. of *stria*] **:** a faint or minute stria
stri·o·late \-ə,lāt\ *or* **stri·o·lat·ed** \-ād·əd\ *adj* [NL *striola* + E *-ate* or *-ated* (fr. *-ate* + *-ed*)] **:** having striolae
¹strip \ˈstrip\ *vb* **stripped** *also* **stript** \-pt\ **stripped** *also* **stript; stripping; strips** [ME *stripen, strepen, strupen, strippen,* fr. OE *-striepan, -strypan* to plunder, rob; akin to MD *stropen* to plunder, strip, OHG *stroufen*] *vt* **1 a :** to remove the clothing of **:** make naked **:** BARE ⟨~ the child completely for a doctor's examination —H.R.Litchfield & L.H.Dembo⟩ **b :** to divest (one) of outer garments ⟨*stripped* him of his robe⟩ ⟨*stripped* himself to the trunks⟩ **c :** to remove (as clothing) from a person **:** take off ⟨it was a privilege to help the king ~ off his shirt —*Irish Digest*⟩ **2 a :** to deprive (someone) of a uniform, the insignia of rank or office, or a decoration ⟨*stripped* two generals of their stars⟩ **b :** to divest (one) of honors, privileges, or functions ⟨*stripped* the sultan of both his legislative and executive powers —*New Statesman & Nation*⟩ **c :** to remove the externals or trappings of (something) **:** divest of adventitious or superficial matters ⟨*stripped* his proposition to the bare bones —A.H.Vandenberg †1951⟩ **3 :** to remove the accessory equipment of **:** DISMANTLE ⟨was sure the car would be either *stripped* or stolen —Kathryn Grondahl⟩ **4 :** to deprive (one) of possessions **:** PLUNDER, SPOIL **5 a :** to peel the rind, bark, or skin from **b :** to denude (a plant) of fruit or leaves **c :** to make bare or clear (as by cutting, grazing, or removing objects from) **:** empty off or out ⟨the church . . . was sold to a housebreaker who *stripped* it of its valuables —S.P.B.Mais⟩ **d :** to pull, tear, or scrape off (as skin or other covering) **:** wrest away ⟨*stripped* the feathers from fowl⟩ ⟨*stripped* the bark from trees⟩ ⟨*stripped* the film from a photographic plate⟩ ⟨~ the paint from a surface⟩ **6 :** to milk dry at the end of a milking by pressing the last available milk from the teats ⟨~ a cow⟩ **7 :** to remove (a ring or jewel) from finger or arm **8 a** (1) **:** to pick the cured leaves from the stalks of (tobacco) (2) **:** to remove strings of leaves of (primed tobacco) (3) **:** to remove tobacco strings from (laths) (4) **:** to pick, sort, and tie (tobacco leaves) into hands **b :** to remove the midrib from (tobacco leaves) **9 a :** to tear or damage the screw thread of (a bolt or nut) **b :** to cause impairment or distortion of (a screw thread) **10 :** to remove the overburden from (a mineral deposit) in mining **11 :** to bare (an ingot of steel) by removing the mold **12 a :** to remove fiber and embedded waste from (the teeth of a card) **b :** to transfer (carded fiber stock) from the carding cylinder to another **13 :** DEGUM **14 :** to separate (a plating or sheet of electrodeposited metal) from the base metal on which plated **15 a :** to remove the most volatile parts or lightest fractions of (as by distillation or by passage of steam or inert gas) **:** TOP ⟨~ coke-oven gas of benzene⟩ ⟨coke *stripped* by nitrogen purge gas —*Industrial & Engineering Chemistry*⟩ **b :** to separate (one or more components) from a mixture or solution ⟨in a natural-gasoline plant, gasoline fractions are *stripped* from rich oil —*Glossary of Terms Used in Petroleum Refining*⟩ **16 a :** to remove (a dye or part of the color) from yarn or fabric by boiling or treating with a chemical — compare DISCHARGE 6a **b :** to remove dye or part of the color from (yarn or fabric) — compare DISCHARGE 6b **17 :** to gather (as grass seed) with a mechanical beater or a hand comb that removes the seed heads for curing and subsequent threshing **18 a :** to lead from (a bridge hand) a series of winning cards that must be got rid of preparatory to executing an end play **b :** to remove (playing cards usu. of low rank) from a pack in a game requiring a smaller pack **19 :** to press eggs or milt out of (a fish) **20 :** to separate (a weapon) into the component parts **:** DISASSEMBLE ⟨could ~ and reassemble a machine gun in the dark⟩ **21 :** to remove the rigging of (a ship) **:** UNRIG **22 :** to draw all line from (a fishing reel) esp. during the run of a fish **23 :** to remove waste material from (a cut and creased board or sheet) before folding into a carton **24 :** to mount (a photographic negative or positive) in position on copy to be used for making a printing plate esp. by photoengraving — sometimes used with *in* **25 :** to remove (forms) from concrete after the concrete has hardened **26 :** to remove the old hair from (a dog) **:** PLUCK **27 :** to shear off surface metal from (a bullet) under excessive bore velocities ⟨found he was *stripping* bullets and fouling his gun barrel with overloads⟩ ~ *vi* **1 :** to take off clothes **:** undress wholly or partly ⟨ricksha men were enjoined not to ~ to the loincloth when at work —D.C. Buchanan⟩ ⟨we *stripped* in the dressing room —H.D.Schwartz⟩ **2 :** to separate or come off (as skin, bark, or rind) **:** PEEL **3 :** to strip tobacco **4 :** to undergo stripping — used of a bullet **5 :** to become damaged, distorted, or torn — used of a screw thread or a threaded part **6 :** to perform a striptease
syn DIVEST, DENUDE, BARE, DISMANTLE: STRIP may imply a pulling or tearing off or a rapid or thorough depriving of a covering, investment, or furnishing ⟨shot wayfarers from ambush, *stripped* the bodies to the skin —*Amer. Guide Series: Tenn.*⟩ ⟨a reading of the speech today, *stripped* of its emotional trappings —S.H.Adams⟩ ⟨had to sell even the few books that Sylvia had left him when she had *stripped* his house —F.M. Ford⟩ DIVEST may indicate a taking off or away of vesture or of whatever is vested in one as a distinction or mark of special privilege or treatment ⟨*divesting* capitalists of further increments of power —M.R.Cohen⟩ ⟨the king is thus *divested* of his kingship and now becomes merely a corpse —J.G.Frazer⟩ ⟨has begun to *divest* himself of his vast estates —William Clark⟩ DENUDE calls attention to the bareness or barrenness resulting from a stripping or divesting ⟨stripped of its vines and *denuded* of its shrubbery, the house would probably have been ugly enough —Willa Cather⟩ ⟨modern agriculture more and more *denudes* the land of the protective cover and food that wild creatures need —G.S.Perry⟩ BARE is a closer synonym to *uncover* or *reveal* than to STRIP; it seldom implies anything about the nature of the action but may implicate its purpose ⟨*bare* one's head in respect⟩ ⟨not afraid to strip themselves of a goodly portion of their clothes and *bare* their skin to the sun's rays —H.A.Overstreet⟩ ⟨the letter *bares* the motives of her own conduct —H.O.Taylor⟩ DISMANTLE now usu. indicates stripping a building, ship, or machine of furnishings and equipment ⟨his ship being laid up for a month and *dismantled* for repairs —Joseph Conrad⟩ ⟨this mine had been sunk to the tenth level, before the ore crusher, enginehouse, and headframe were *dismantled* —*Amer. Guide Series: Minn.*⟩
²strip \"\ *n* -s **1 :** tobacco leaf from which the midrib has been removed **2 strips** *pl* **:** milk strippings **3 :** STRIPTEASE **4** *also* **strip play :** the stripping of a bridge hand **:** ELIMINATION
³strip \"\ *n* -s [alter. of ME *stripe* — more at STRIPE] **1 a :** a narrow piece of about even width ⟨a ~ of cloth⟩ ⟨a ~ of paper⟩ ⟨a ~ of board⟩ **b :** a long narrow area of land or water ⟨a ~ of wood⟩ **2** *obs* **:** a decorative piece of cloth or lace for the neck and bosom **3 a :** a shallow cast ingot of brass for rolling into sheets **b :** a rolled piece of metal (as iron or steel) of the thickness of sheet metal but relatively long and narrow **4 :** COMIC 3a **5 a :** lumber under eight inches wide and not more than one inch thick **b :** ²STICKER 2 **6** *Brit* **:** a trough for transporting and settling particles of ore suspended in water at a mine **7 :** the draft of a pattern **8 :** three or more postage or other stamps or stickers attached in a row either horizontally or vertically — compare BLOCK 5g **9 :** a narrow piece of wood or metal on which usu. four to six electric-light bulbs are arranged in line and which is used in theatrical stage lighting **10 :** the path or course on which a race is run **11 :** the area usu. of rubber, cork, or linoleum on which a fencing bout takes place **12 :** AIRSTRIP
⁴strip \"\ *vt* **stripped; stripped; stripping; strips 1 :** to affix a strip of paper or cloth to (the edge of a pad) or over (the fold of a lining, section, cover, or insert of a book) either inside or outside usu. by machine **2 :** to split (rolled material) down the roll lengthwise by hand
⁵strip \"\ *n* -s [AF *estrepe,* fr. OF *estreper* to estrepe] **:** ESTREPEMENT
⁶strip \"\ *vt* [ME *strypen* to move fast; prob. akin to MD *stripe* strip, stripe — more at STRIPE] *archaic* **:** OUTSTRIP
⁷strip \"\ *Scot var of* STRIPE
strip bridge *n* [¹*strip*] **:** DRAWBRIDGE
strip building *n* [³*strip*] *Brit* **:** the building of usu. low-cost dwellings in long parallel rows with minimum land use — compare HOUSING DEVELOPMENT, HOUSING PROJECT
strip camera *n* **:** a shutterless camera (as an aerial camera) in which the film moves past an exposing slit at a rate synchronized with that of the ground image
strip census *n* **:** an estimate of the numbers of a wild animal in an area by counting individuals along a typical strip and assuming a uniform population
strip count *n* **:** a piece tally of surfaced lumber based on the width, length, and thickness of the rough sizes used
strip-crop \ˈ=,=\ *vb* [³*strip* + *crop*] *vt* **:** to practice strip-cropping on ~ *vi* **:** to practice strip-cropping
strip-cropping \ˈ=,==\ *n* [fr. gerund of *strip-crop*] **:** the growing of separate crops in successive narrow strips that on sloping land follow an approximate contour and so check wind or water erosion — called also *strip farming*
strip cup *n* [¹*strip*] **:** a metal cup with the opening covered with a fine wire mesh or dark cloth into which foremilk is drawn for examination to detect gross abnormalities (as clots or ropiness) that may indicate the presence of disease in the udder
¹stripe \ˈstrīp\ *n* -s [ME; prob. akin to ⁴*stripe*] *Scot* **:** a small stream **:** RIVULET
²stripe \"\ *n* -s [ME, perh. fr. MLG *strippe* strap, lash; akin to MD *stripe* strip, stripe] **:** a stroke or blow with a rod or lash ⟨was laying on the prescribed number of ~*s* so lustily that the punished man's screams rent the air —F.V.W.Mason⟩
³stripe \"\ *vt* -ED/-ING/-S **:** to beat or lash with a rod or whip
⁴stripe \"\ *n* -s [ME, strip, fr. MD, stripe, strip; akin to OIr *sriab* stripe, OE *strica* line, streak — more at STREAK] **1 a :** a line or long narrow section of something differing in color or texture from the parts adjoining ⟨a white ~ down the center of the highway⟩ **b** (1) **:** a textile design consisting of vertical or horizontal lines or bands against a plain background and created by various weaving, printing, or finishing processes (2) **:** a fabric with a striped design **c :** a long narrow strip (as of land) **2 a :** a piece of gold, silver, silk, cotton, or other braid (as on the sleeve of a coat) used to indicate military rank or length of service — see HALF-STRIPE, SERVICE STRIPE **b :** CHEVRON **3 :** a distinct shade or variety (as of character, opinion, or partisan affiliation) **:** CLASS, KIND, SORT, TYPE ⟨men of a different moral ~ from the God-fearing, stolid farmers —Rex Lardner⟩ ⟨artists of every ~ —Celestine Sibley⟩ ⟨a man of paler ~ would be content to net for herring —J.W.Noble⟩ **4 a :** BARLEY STRIPE **b :** STREAK 2f **5 :** a narrow white mark extending down the face of a horse from between the eyes to the bridge of the nose **6 :** STRIPED BASS **7 stripes** *pl* **:** a prisoner's distinctive horizontally striped uniform **syn** see TYPE
⁵stripe \"\ *vt* -ED/-ING/-S **:** to make stripes on **:** form with lines of different colors or textures **:** variegate with stripes
stripe blight *n* **:** a disease of oats caused by a bacterium (*Pseudomonas striafaciens*) and characterized by water-soaked spots and streaks
stripe canker *n* **:** BLACK THREAD
striped \ˈstrīpt, -pəd\ *adj* [perh. fr. MD *stripet,* fr. *stripe* stripe, strip + *-et* -ed] **:** having stripes or streaks
striped alder *n* **1 :** a black alder (*Ilex verticillata*) **2 :** WITCH HAZEL 2a(1)
striped bass *n* **:** any of several fishes of the family Serranidae: as **a :** an anadromous sea bass (*Roccus saxatilis*) that is native to the Atlantic coast of the U. S. but introduced and common also on the Pacific coast, is olivaceous above and yellowish silvery on the sides and below, is marked with numerous longitudinal black stripes, is highly esteemed as a game fish and as food, and frequently reaches 20 and possibly sometimes 100 pounds in weight **b** (1) **:** WHITE BASS 1 (2) **:** YELLOW BASS
striped blister beetle *n* **:** a common No. American blister beetle (*Epicauta vittata*) that is sometimes a pest on alfalfa and other crops
striped bloodwort *n* **:** RATTLESNAKE WEED 1
striped cucumber beetle *n* **:** a yellowish black-striped beetle (*Acalymma vittata*) that feeds as a larva on the underground parts of cucumbers and other cucurbits and as an adult on foliage and flowers of cucurbits and other crop plants and that is a vector of bacterial wilt and of cucumber mosaic — compare CUCUMBER BEETLE
striped dace *n* **:** BLACKNOSE DACE
striped dogfish *n* **:** LUI-HAAI
striped dolphin *n* **:** SPECTACLED DOLPHIN
striped flea beetle *n* **:** a flea beetle (*Phyllotreta striolata*) having a yellow line on each elytron and being a pest of cabbage and other brassicas
striped gentian *n* **:** a marsh gentian (*Gentiana villosa*)
striped gopher *or* **striped ground squirrel** *n* **:** a ground squirrel that is striped; *esp* **:** THIRTEEN-LINED GROUND SQUIRREL
striped gourami *n* **:** a small labyrinth fish (*Colisa fasciata*) of India marked with alternate diagonal bands of red and blue that is sometimes kept in the tropical aquarium
striped grass *n* **:** RIBBON GRASS
striped grunt *n* **:** GRAY GRUNT
striped head *n* **:** HUDSONIAN CURLEW
striped hyena *n* **:** a strongly marked hyena (*Hyaena hyaena*) of parts of Africa and southern Asia east to India — see HYENA illustration
striped lizard *n* **:** RACE RUNNER
striped maple *or* **striped dogwood** *n* **:** a maple (*Acer pennsylvanicum*) of eastern No. America with striped bark and large thin 3-lobed leaves — called also *moosewood*
striped marlin *n* **:** a sport fish (*Makaira mitsukurii*) of the Pacific ocean that is purplish blue above with the back crossed by 15 light blue bands
striped mouse *n* **1 :** JUMPING MOUSE **2** *or* **striped rat :** any member of an African genus (*Arvicanthus*) of murid rodents having longitudinal dark stripes along the back
striped muishond *n* **:** a muishond (*Ictonyx striata*) that resembles a ferret in size and form and is often tamed — compare SNAKE MUISHOND
striped mullet *n* **:** a gray mullet (*Mugil cephalus*) of the European and American coasts and the Pacific ocean
striped muscle *n* **:** STRIATED MUSCLE
striped opossum *n* **:** any of several brightly marked nocturnal phalangers (genera *Dactylopsila* and *Dactylonax*) of Queensland and New Guinea having the fourth finger more or less strikingly elongated
striped-pants \ˈ=;=\ *adj* [*striped pants;* fr. the wearing of striped trousers as semiformal attire] **:** overattentive to formality, protocol, or partying and social activity ⟨*striped-pants* diplomacy⟩
striped perch *n* **:** any of various more or less striped fishes resembling typical perch: as **a :** YELLOW PERCH **b :** a rainbow perch (*Hypsurus caryi*) **c** *Austral* **:** a small percoid fish (*Helotes sexlineatus*) blue and silver with narrow brown stripes along each side
striped polecat *n* **:** ZORIL
striped schaapsteker *n* **:** SCHAAPSTEKER b
striped shore crab *n* **:** a very common Pacific shore crab (*Pachygrapsus crassipes*) with a squarish carapace transversely striped usu. with purple and the chelae reticulated with purple
striped skunk *n* **:** any of several skunks of the genus *Mephitis*
striped snake *n* **:** a snake with longitudinal stripes on its back; *esp* **:** GARTER SNAKE
striped squirrel *n* **1 :** a squirrel with stripes on the back; *esp* **:** CHIPMUNK **2** *also* **striped spermophile :** THIRTEEN-LINED GROUND SQUIRREL
striped surf fish *or* **striped surf perch** *n* **:** a rainbow perch (*Taeniotoca lateralis*)
striped surmullet *n* **:** a mullet (*Mullus surmulletus*) of southern Europe
striped tree squirrel *n* **:** an Asiatic squirrel of the genus *Tamiops* that resembles the American chipmunk but is arboreal
striped tuna *n* **:** OCEANIC BONITO
stripe·less \ˈstrīpləs\ *adj* **:** having no stripes
strip·er \ˈstrīpə(r)\ *n* -s [in sense 1, fr. ⁵*stripe* + *-er;* in other senses, fr. ⁴*stripe* + *-er*] **1 :** one that stripes: as **a :** one that paints stripes (as on furniture, vehicle parts, or musical instruments) **b :** a worker who cuts and finishes expansion joints in concrete pavement **c :** a brush usu. with a tapering point for drawing stripes **d :** a knitting machine device that automatically changes yarns for patterns (as stripes) **2 :** a navy man who wears stripes on his sleeve to indicate rating or length of service — usu. used in combination; compare FOUR-STRIPER **3 a :** STRIPED BASS a **b :** WHITE BASS 1
stripe rust *n* **:** a rust of wheat, rye, barley, and other grasses caused by a fungus (*Puccinia glumarum*) that produces elongated yellow streaks of sori — called also *yellow rust, yellow stripe rust*
stripes *pl of* STRIPE, *pres 3d sing of* STRIPE
stripe smut *n* **1 :** a smut of grasses caused by a fungus (*Ustilago striaeformis*) and characterized by long narrow nearly black sori on leaves and sheaths **2 :** smut of rye caused by a fungus (*Urocystis occulta*)
strip farming *n* [³*strip*] **1 :** the distribution of farmlands into long strips for allotment to individual farmers formerly practiced in Europe to prevent unfairness caused by differing soils **2 :** STRIP-CROPPING
stripfilm \ˈ=,=\ *n* **:** FILMSTRIP
stripier *comparative of* STRIPY
stripiest *superlative of* STRIPY
strip-in \ˈ=,=\ *n* -s [¹*strip* + *in*] **1 :** a stripped photographic negative or positive **2 :** an instance of stripping in
strip·i·ness \ˈstrīpēnəs\ *n* -ES **:** the quality or state of being stripy
striping *n* -s [fr. gerund of ⁵*stripe*] **1 :** the act or process of marking with stripes ⟨worked for uniformity in the ~ of highways⟩ **2 a :** the stripes marked or painted on something **b :** a design of stripes
striplight \ˈ=,=\ *n* [³*strip*] **:** a row of small floodlights mounted on a trough reflector and used for theater borderlights, footlights, and general stage illumination
strip·ling \ˈstripliŋ, -lēŋ\ *n* -s [ME, prob. fr. *stripe* strip + *-ling*] **:** an adolescent boy or girl **:** one not yet fully matured into manhood or womanhood
strip map *n* [³*strip*] **:** a map (as for an aviator) showing only a narrow band of territory (as 500 miles long and 10 miles wide)
strip method *n* **:** a method of conservative lumbering by which timber is cleared in relatively narrow strips through a forest and reproduction on the cleared strips is obtained by the seed sown from the adjoining woodland
strip mill *n* **:** a rolling mill for producing long continuous strips of flat rolled metal
strip mine *or* **strip pit** *n* [¹*strip*] **:** a mine near the earth's surface that is worked by stripping; *esp* **:** a coal mine situated along the outcrop of a flat dipping bed
strip-mine \ˈ=;=\ *vt* [*strip mine*] **:** to mine (an ore) from a strip mine
strip miner *n* [*strip mine* + *-er*] **:** a strip mine worker
strip·pa·ble \ˈstripəbəl\ *adj* [¹*strip* + *-able*] **:** capable of being stripped or pulled off ⟨~ vinyl coatings⟩ ⟨~ coal⟩
strip·page \-pij\ *n* -s [¹*strip* + *-age*] **:** material stripped from something (as branches from trees)
stripped *adj* [fr. past part. of ¹*strip*] **:** having clothes, a covering, or something accessory or superfluous removed ⟨a ~ automobile⟩ ⟨an athlete ~ to fighting weight⟩
stripped atoms *n pl* **:** atoms from which outer electrons have been removed permitting closer packing of the atoms and great densities — compare ATOMIC THEORY
stripped deck *n* **:** a pack of playing cards from which cards usu. of low rank have been removed (as in hearts and some poker games)
stripped·ness *n* -ES **:** the quality or state of being stripped
stripped plain *n* **:** a plain floored by a resistant flat-lying stratum from above which weaker rocks have been removed by erosion
strip·per \ˈstripə(r)\ *n* -s [¹*strip* + *-er*] **1 :** one that strips: as **a :** a worker who strips stems from moistened tobacco leaves and ties the leaves into books — called also *sprigger, stemmer* **b :** a worker who removes hides or skins from drying frames salvaging the tacks and piling the skins **c :** one of a group of workers who remove sheets of refined copper from the starting plates on which they were deposited by electrolysis **d :** a quarry worker who cleans up dirt left by a power shovel in exposing the rock **e :** one that strips fish of milt or roe **f :** one that strips photographic negatives or positives **2 :** a device that strips or peels (as bark from osier or insulation from wires) **3 a :** a machine that strips the seed heads from the stalks of grass and hay in harvesting **b :** an implement usu. with slots between revolving rolls for stripping cotton **c** *or* **stripper-harvester :** a harvester-thresher that beats the heads and grain from wheat or other crops without cutting the straw **4 a :** a metal plate or one of a pair of plates one on each side of a cutting die punch that strips the work from the punch and prevents it from being dragged up on the upstroke **b :** a machine for smoothing down files for subsequent recutting **c :** a metal point in a capstan for clearing away the cable as it unwinds **5 :** any of the various small card-clothed rollers in textile manufacturing that strip fiber from one cylinder and carry it to another and esp. from a worker to the main cylinder **6 a :** an apparatus in which volatile material is removed **b :** a solvent used to remove deposits (as paint or varnish) from surfaces **7 :** a card trimmed in a wedge shape so that it can be pulled easily from the pack (as by a cardsharper) **8 :** a cow that has nearly stopped giving milk **9 :** an oil well that has fallen off in production to a few barrels or less per day **10 :** STRIPTEASER ⟨a ~ in a honky-tonk —James Jones⟩ **11 :** STRIP MINER
stripper bolt *n* **:** SHOULDER SCREW
stripping *n* -s [ME, fr. gerund of *strippen* to strip] **1 :** the action of one that strips **2 :** something that is stripped: as **a strippings** *pl* **:** the last milk drawn at a milking usu. distinctly richer in fat and freer from bacteria than the foremilk **b :** OVERBURDEN 2a **3 :** DIGGING 2 **4 a :** the removal of cured tobacco leaves from the stalks or from the laths **b :** the removal of the foliage from the stem of a plant or flower **5 :** the shearing off of surface metal from a bullet that is driven at excessive velocity through a gun barrel by an overload of powder and fails to acquire spin from the rifling **6** [³*strip* + *-ing*] **:** material (as leather) that is cut into strips
stripping film *n* **:** photographic film supplied with an emulsion layer coated on the surface of a transparent film support such that all or selected portions of the processed or unprocessed emulsion may be easily removed as a continuous layer for transfer to another surface
stripping knife *or* **stripping comb** *n* **:** a metal blade with a serrated edge used for plucking or stripping the coat of a dog
strip·pit *or* **strip·ped** \ˈstripət\ *Scot & dial Eng var of* STRIPED
strip planking *n* [³*strip*] **:** the planking of a carvel-built boat or ship with narrow slightly tapered strips to make flush joints and a smooth outside hull as distinguished from the lap joints of a clinker-built boat
strip play *n* **:** STRIP 4
strip poker *n* [¹*strip*] **:** a poker game in which players pay their losses with articles of clothing that they take off
strips *pres 3d sing of* STRIP, *pl of* STRIP
strip survey *n* [³*strip*] **:** a valuation survey of a strip of forest land chosen as an average sample from which to estimate the value of a larger area
strip system *n* **:** STRIP FARMING 1
stript *past of* STRIP
¹strip·tease \ˈstrip¦tēz\ *n* [¹*strip* + *tease*] **:** a burlesque act in which a female performer removes her clothing piece by piece in view of the audience
²striptease \"\ *vi* **:** to perform a striptease
strip·teas·er \-zə(r)\ *n* [¹*striptease* + *-er*] **:** an actress who performs a striptease — called also *ecdysiast, peeler, stripper, teaser*
strip template *n* [³*strip*] **:** POLE STRIP
strip·teuse \(ˈ)strip¦tərz, -¦təz, -¦tüz, -¦təz\ *n* -s [¹*strip*tease + *danseuse*] **:** STRIPTEASER
strip windows *n pl* [³*strip*] **:** RIBBON WINDOWS
stripy \ˈstrīpē\ *adj* -ER/-EST [³*stripe* + *y*] **:** having, occurring in, or marked by stripes or streaks
stri·sci·an·do \,strēshēˈän(,)dō\ *adv* (*or adj*) [It, fr. verbal of *strisciare* to drag, trail, fr. *striscia* track, trail, streak, prob. of imit. origin] **1 :** in a slurred or smooth manner — used as a direction in music **2 :** GLISSANDO

strive \'strīv\ *vi* **strove** \'strōv\ *also* **strived; striv·en** \'strivən\ *or* **strived** *or chiefly dial* **strove; striving; strives** [ME *striven*, fr. OF *estriver* to fight, contend, of Gmc origin; akin to obs. D *strijven* to contend, endeavor, MHG *streben* to endeavor, Gk *striphnos* firm, hard, ON *strītha* to fight — more at STRIDE] **1 a :** to struggle in opposition or contention **:** carry on a conflict **:** CONTEND, CONTEST — used with *against* or *with* ⟨we ~ against butchers —Irwin Shaw⟩ ⟨~ not with your superiors in argument —George Washington⟩ **b :** to contend for dominance, mastery, or superiority **:** conduct war **:** FIGHT **c :** to compete as a rival **:** VIE ⟨grief and perplexity . . . ~ within her —Anne D. Sedgwick⟩ **d** *obs* **:** to struggle against physical obstacles **:** buck opposing forces, resistance, or difficulty **e :** to advance laboriously **:** make headway with effort **:** WORK ⟨*strove* not only for the advancement of learning but also for the conversion of the heathen —Kemp Malone⟩ **2 :** to devote effort or energy **:** try hard or earnestly **:** ATTEMPT, ENDEAVOR — often used with an infinitive ⟨*strove* to make the most of every minute —Osbert Sitwell⟩ ⟨a goal toward which he had always perseveringly *striven*⟩ **syn** see TRY

striv·er \-və(r)\ *n* -S [ME, fr. *striven* to strive + *-er*] **:** one that strives ⟨a man of talent and a true ~ after the highest human status —John Dollard⟩

[1]striving *n* -S [ME, fr. gerund of *striven* to strive] **1 :** CONFLICT, CONTEST, RIVALRY ⟨there were strenuous ~*s* for place, profit, promotion, and power —D.C.Mearns⟩ **2 :** a straining effort ⟨these works cost him mighty ~*s* and struggles through long years —Abram Chasins⟩

[2]striving *adj* [ME, fr. pres. part. of *striven* to strive] **:** marked by strenuous effort, rivalry, or conflict — **striv·ing·ly** *adv*

[1]strix \'striks\ *n* -ES [L *strig-, strix* furrow, groove, flute; akin to L *striga* furrow — more at STRIKE] **:** a fluting of a column

[2]strix \"\ *n, cap* [NL *Strig-, Strix*, fr. L, screech owl — more at STRIDENT] **:** a variously restricted genus of owls: **a** *in former classifications* (1) **:** a large genus containing most owls except the barn owls (2) **:** a genus comprising the barn owls **b :** the type genus of the family Strigidae comprising owls that lack ear tufts and including the tawny owl and the barred owl

stroam *var of* STROME

strobe \'strōb\ *n* -S [by shortening & alter. fr. *stroboscope*] **1 :** STROBOSCOPE **2 :** STROBOTRON ⟨~ photography⟩

strob·ic \'sträbik\ *adj* [Gk *strobos* action of whirling + E *-ic* — more at STROPHE] **:** having or appearing to have a spinning motion

strobic disk *n* **:** a disk marked with a set of concentric rings or toothed wheels that is moved in a circular path without causing it to revolve on its own axis causing the figures to appear to revolve on their axes

stro·bi·la \strə'bīlə\ *n, pl* **strobi·lae** \-ˌlē\ [NL, fr. Gk *strobilē* plug of lint twisted so as to resemble a pinecone, fr. *strobilos* pinecone — more at STROBILUS] **:** a linear series of similar structures: as **a :** the chain of segments forming the body of a tapeworm **b :** the chain of individuals produced by repeated transverse fission of a scyphozoan scyphistoma larva — **stro·bi·lar** \-lə(r)\ *adj*

strob·i·la·ceous \ˌsträbə'lāshəs\ *adj* [NL *strobilaceus*, fr. *strobilus* strobile + L *-aceus* -aceous] **1 :** relating to or resembling a strobile **2 :** bearing strobiles

strob·i·late \'sträbəˌlāt\ *vi* -ED/-ING/-S [back-formation fr. *strobilation*] **:** to become a strobila **:** undergo strobilation

strob·i·la·tion \ˌ==='lāshən\ *also* **strob·i·li·za·tion** \ˌsträbələ'zāshən\ *n* -S [NL *strobila* + ISV *-ation, -ization*] **:** asexual reproduction by transverse division of the body into segments which develop into zooids, proglottids, or separate individuals in many coelenterates and worms

strob·ile *also* **strob·il** \'sträbəl\ *n* -S [NL *strobilus*] **:** STROBILUS **2 :** a spike with persistent overlapping bracts that resembles a cone and is the pistillate inflorescence of the hop **3** [NL *strobila*] **:** STROBILA — **strob·i·lif·er·ous** \ˌsträbə'lif(ə)rəs\ *adj*

strob·i·line \'sträbələn\ *adj* [NL *strobila* + E *-ine*] **:** STROBILACEOUS

strob·i·lo·cer·cus \ˌsträbəlō'sərkəs\ *n, pl* **strobilocer·ci** \-'sərˌsī\ [NL, fr. *strobila* + Gk *kerkos* tail] **:** a larval tapeworm that has undergone strobilization and eversion from its bladder while still in the intermediate host

strob·i·loid \'sträbəˌlȯid\ *adj* [NL *strobilus* + E *-oid*] **:** resembling or having to do with a strobilus ⟨a ~ theory of the descent of angiosperms⟩

strob·i·lo·my·ces \ˌsträbəlō'mīˌsēz\ *n, cap* [NL, fr. Gk *strobilos* whirling or twisted object + NL *-myces*] **:** a genus of fungi (family Boletaceae) similar to *Boletus* but with a shaggy scaly cap and the tubes not easily separating from the pileus

strob·i·loph·y·ta \ˌsträbə'läfəd·ə\ [NL, fr. *strobilus* + *-o-* *-phyta*] *syn of* GYMNOSPERMAE

strob·i·lus \'sträbələs\ *n, pl* **strobi·li** \-bəˌlī\ [NL, fr. LL, pinecone, fr. Gk *strobilos* whirling or twisted object, ball, top, pinecone, fr. *strobos* action of whirling — more at STROPHE] **1 a :** a conelike aggregation of sporophylls (as in the club mosses and horsetails) **b :** the cone of a gymnosperm **2 :** STROBILA

strobilus theory *n* **:** a theory in evolutionary botany: the sporophyte of the vascular plant derives from a primitive form resembling or equivalent to a strobilus of sporophylls

stro·bo·scope \'strōbəˌskōp, -räb-\ *n* [Gk *strobos* action of whirling + ISV *-scope*] **:** an instrument that is used for observing motion in such a way that moving objects (as machine parts) appear to be slowed down or stationary, that is used esp. for determining speeds of rotation or frequencies of vibration, and that is made in the form of a revolving disk with holes around the edge through which an object is viewed or a rapidly flashing light that illuminates an object intermittently or a cardboard disk with marks to be viewed under intermittent light

stro·bo·scop·ic \ˌ==='skäpik, -pēk\ *adj* [ISV *stroboscope* + *-ic*] **:** of, by means of, utilizing, or relating to a stroboscope ⟨~ effect⟩ ⟨~ photography⟩ ⟨~ light⟩—**stro·bo·scop·i·cal·ly** \-pək(ə)lē, -pēk-, -li\ *adv*

stro·bo·tron \'===ˌträn\ *n* -S [*stroboscopic* + *-tron*] **:** a gas-filled electron tube with a cold cathode used esp. as a source of stroboscopic light

strock·le \'sträkəl\ *n* -S [origin unknown] **:** a shovel with a turned-up edge used by glassworkers

strode *past of* STRIDE

stro·ga·noff \'strȯgəˌnȯf\ *adj* [after Count Paul *Stroganoff* 19th cent. Russ. diplomat] **:** sliced thin and cooked in a sauce of consommé, sour cream, mustard, onion, and condiments — used postpositively ⟨beef ~⟩ ⟨chicken ~⟩

[1]stroke \'strōk\ *vt* -ED/-ING/-S [ME *stroken*, fr. OE *strācian*; akin to MD *streken* to stroke, OHG *streihhōn* to stroke, *strihhan* to pass over lightly, smooth — more at STRIKE] **1 a :** to rub gently in one direction ⟨*stroking* his beard⟩ ⟨~ a cat's fur⟩ **b :** to pass the hand over gently in kindness or tenderness **:** CARESS, SOOTHE **2 a :** to smooth or arrange by repeatedly drawing the hand or a tool over or through **b :** to draw across a surface repeatedly in order to sharpen **:** WHET, HONE **3 :** to draw milk from (as a cow) esp. by stripping **4 :** to give a finely fluted surface to (a stone) — **stroke the wrong way :** to annoy by offending the tastes or prejudices of **:** RUFFLE

[2]stroke \"\ *n* -S [ME *stroke, strake;* akin to MLG *strek* stroke, MHG *streich*, OE *strīcan* to move, pass over lightly, stroke — more at STRIKE] **1 :** the act of striking with the hand; *esp* **:** a deliberately aimed swinging blow with a weapon or implement ⟨no man could withstand his sword ~⟩ ⟨dealt him several stinging ~*s* with the whip⟩ ⟨ringing ~*s* of the ax⟩ **2 :** a single unbroken movement without pause or reversal of direction ⟨sketched a likeness with a few ~*s* of a pencil⟩; *esp* **:** one of a series of repeated or to-and-fro movements ⟨~*s* of a pendulum⟩ ⟨painting with firm level ~*s*⟩ **3 a :** a blow on a drum; *esp* **:** a full accented beat as distinguished from a tap or a roll **b :** a striking of the ball in a game (as cricket, billiards, tennis) **c :** the act of striking or attempting to strike the ball that constitutes the scoring unit in golf ⟨win a match by two ~*s*⟩ ⟨accepted a penalty ~ for lifting the ball out of an unplayable lie⟩ ⟨a 10-*stroke* handicap⟩ **4 :** a sudden action or process producing an impact ⟨~ of lightning⟩ or a quick or unexpected result ⟨~ of fortune⟩ ⟨~ of luck⟩ **5 a** *obs* **:** the result or effect of a blow **:** INJURY **b** (1) **:** APOPLEXY (2) **:** LITTLE STROKE **6 a :** one of a series of propelling beats or movements against a resisting medium ⟨wing ~ of a bird⟩ ⟨swimming ~⟩ ⟨paddling with quick, stabbing ~*s*⟩ ⟨a rowing pace of 30 ~*s* to the minute⟩ **b :** the member of a rowing crew who sits nearest the stern and sets the tempo for the other rowers **7 a :** a vigorous or energetic effort by which something is done, produced, or accomplished ⟨brilliant diplomatic ~⟩ ⟨without doing a ~ of work⟩ ⟨~ of genius⟩ **b** *Brit* **:** a gratifying quantity of work or business **c :** a delicate or clever touch in a narrative or description or construction **:** a well-turned phrase or a deftly managed bit of plotting **d :** a series of moves and exchanges (in chess and checkers) resulting in a clear advantage for one side **8 a :** a movement of the arm or baton in beating time **b :** the movement of the bow in one direction on a stringed instrument **c :** HEARTBEAT **9 a :** the movement in either direction of a mechanical part (as a piston plunger, piston rod, crosshead) having a reciprocating motion **b :** the entire distance passed through in such a movement ⟨the piston is at half ~⟩ ⟨ratio of piston ~ to bore of a cylinder⟩ **10 :** the sound of a bell being struck ⟨at the ~ of twelve⟩ **11** *obs* **:** method or manner of touching or playing a musical instrument; *also* **:** MELODY **12** [[1]*stroke*] **:** an act of stroking or caressing ⟨the ~ of wind and water on land —Russell Lord⟩ **13 a :** a mark or dash made by a single movement of an implement (as a pen, engraving tool, or brush) ⟨the ~ dividing numerator and denominator in the fraction ¾⟩ **b** *obs* **:** a distinguishing feature **:** CHARACTERISTIC **c :** one of the lines of a letter of the alphabet or other graphic character ⟨a typeface having great contrast between thick and thin ~*s*⟩ ⟨Bodoni has a lively quality caused by the contrast of the heavy ~*s* and the hairlines —W.S.Cowell⟩ **d :** a heavy line connecting the stems of two or more notes in a musical notation **14 :** the truth-functional operator that is the constant element in an alternative denial, that is commonly interpreted as "not both", that is symbolized |, and that can be used alone with only propositional symbols to construct a formally complete propositional calculus ⟨the alternative denial *p|q* is read *p stroke q*⟩ — **at a stroke** *or* **at one stroke** *adv* **:** all at once **:** IMMEDIATELY ⟨his life savings wiped out *at a stroke*⟩

[3]stroke \"\ *vb* -ED/-ING/-S *vt* **1 a :** to mark with a short line ⟨dotted the *i*'s and *stroked* the *t*'s⟩ **b :** to cancel by drawing a line through — used usu. with *out* ⟨*stroked* out the last name on the list⟩ **c :** to join the stems of (musical notes) by a stroke **2 :** to set the stroke for (the crew of a rowing boat) **:** set the stroke for the crew of (a rowing boat) **:** row as stroke of **3 :** HIT ⟨~ a single over second base⟩; *esp* **:** to propel (a ball) with a controlled swinging blow ⟨~ a cue ball in billiards⟩ **4 :** to strike (a key) in typewriting ~ *vi* **1 :** to execute a stroke ⟨polo team showed bold riding and accurate *stroking*⟩ **2 a :** to pull an oar or serve as stroke ⟨*stroked* for the freshman crew —*Current Biog.*⟩ **b :** to row at a certain number of strokes a minute ⟨the crew was *stroking* at 32⟩ **3 :** to strike the keys in typewriting ⟨clean, even *stroking* is desirable for good impressions⟩

stroke function *or* **stroke operation** *n* [[2]*stroke*] **1 :** STROKE 14 **2 :** ALTERNATIVE DENIAL; *sometimes* **:** JOINT DENIAL

stroke hole *n* **:** a golf hole at which a stroke is received by a player in a handicap match

stroke in *vt* [[1]*stroke*] *Brit* **:** to feed (a sheet) into a cylinder press

stroke·let \-klət\ *n* -S [[2]*stroke* + *-let*] **:** LITTLE STROKE

stroke oar *n* **1 :** the oar nearest the stern usu. on the port side **2 :** STROKE 6b

stroke play *n* **:** MEDAL PLAY

strok·er \-kə(r)\ *n* -S [[1]*stroke* + *-er*] **1 :** one that strokes; *specif* **:** one who pretends to heal or cure by stroking **2** *Brit* **a :** a small tool with which sheets are stroked toward the grippers in hand-feeding a cylinder press **b :** a similarly functioning part in an automatic feeder

stroker–in \'=='=\ *n, pl* **strokers–in** *Brit* **:** one who hand-feeds sheets into a cylinder press

strokes *pres 3d sing of* STROKE, *pl of* STROKE

strokes·man \'strōksmən\ *n* [*strokes* (gen. of [2]*stroke*) + *man*] *archaic* **:** STROKE 6b

stroking *pres part of* STROKE

strok·ings \'strōkiŋz\ *n pl* [fr. gerund of [1]*stroke*] **:** STRIPPING 2a

[1]stroll \'strōl\ *vb* -ED/-ING/-S [prob. fr. G dial. *strollen*] *vi* **1 :** to walk in a leisurely or idle manner **:** take a walk **:** SAUNTER, RAMBLE **2 :** to go habitually from place to place in search of occupation or profit **:** ROVE, WANDER ⟨~*ing* players⟩ ⟨~*ing* musician⟩ ~ *vt* **:** to walk at leisure along or about ⟨~ the streets of the village⟩

[2]stroll \"\ *n* -S **:** an idle and leisurely walk **:** RAMBLE ⟨go for a ~ in the country⟩

stroll·er \-lə(r)\ *n* -S [[1]*stroll* + *-er*] **1 :** one that walks along in a leisurely manner **:** one that strolls or saunters ⟨Sunday afternoon ~*s*⟩ **2 a :** a wandering beggar **:** VAGRANT, TRAMP **b :** an itinerant peddler **3 :** a strolling player **:** an itinerant actor **4 :** a four-wheel usu. folding carriage designed as a chair in which a baby may be pushed ⟨the two-year-old prefers a ~ to a carriage⟩ — called also *go-cart*

stroller 4

stroller tan *n* **:** MIKADO BROWN

stro·ma \'strōmə\ *n, pl* **stroma·ta** \-məd·ə\ [NL *stromat-, stroma*, fr. L, bed covering, fr. Gk *strōmat-, strōma* bed covering, spread, bed, fr. *stornynai* to spread, strew — more at STREW] **1 a :** the supporting framework of an animal organ typically consisting of connective tissue **b :** the spongy protoplasmic framework of some cells (as red blood cells, muscle cells, nerve cells) **2 a :** a compact mass of fungous tissue on or in which perithecia or pycnidia are produced often intermingled with tissue of the host or substrate **b :** the proteinaceous matrix throughout which the granules of chlorophyll are dispersed in a chloroplast — **stro·mal** \-məl\ *adj* — **stro·ma·tal** \-məd·ᵊl\ *adj*

stro·ma·te·i·dae \ˌstrōmə'tēəˌdē\ *n pl, cap* [NL, fr. *Stromateus*, type genus (fr. Gk *strōmateus* bed covering, a fish marked with patchwork colors, fr. *strōmat-, strōma* bed covering) + *-idae*] **:** a large family of chiefly small marine fishes (as the harvest fish and the dollarfish) having a short compressed body, smooth scales, feeble spines, and a series of toothlike processes in the esophagus behind the pharyngeal bones that with a few related forms constitutes a distinct suborder of Percomorphi — **stro·mat·e·oid** \strə'madˌēˌȯid\ *adj or n*

stro·mat·ic \strə'mad·ik\ *adj* [NL *stromat-, stroma* + E *-ic*] **:** relating to, resembling, or constituting a stroma **:** STROMAL

stro·ma·tin \'strōməd·ən\ *n* -S [ISV *stromat-* (fr. NL *stromat-, stroma*) + *-in*] **:** a protein in the stroma of some cells (as red blood cells) comparable to keratin that is present in the stroma of some cells (as red blood cells)

stro·ma·top·o·ra \ˌstrōmə'täpərə\ *n, cap* [NL, fr. *stromat-, stroma* + *-o-* + *-pora*] **:** a genus (the type of the family Stromatoporidae) of extinct hydrozoans that form thick concentric laminae of reticulated calcareous tissue with scattered tubules for the zooids and with related hydrozoans constitute extensive beds in various Paleozoic and esp. Devonian rocks — **stro·ma·top·o·roid** \ˌ=='täpəˌrȯid\ *adj or n*

stro·ma·tous \'strōməd·əs\ *adj* [NL *stromat-, stroma* + E *-ous*] **:** having or forming a stroma **:** affecting a stroma

stromb \'sträm(b)\ *n* -S [NL *Strombus*] **:** a mollusk or shell of the genus *Strombus* or family Strombidae

strom·bi·dae \-mbəˌdē\ *n pl, cap* [NL, fr. *Strombus*, type genus + *-idae*] **:** a family of large marine gastropod mollusks (suborder Taenioglossa) comprising numerous chiefly tropical conchs — see STROMBUS

strom·bi·form \-mbəˌfȯrm\ *adj* [NL *Strombus* + ISV *-iform*] **:** resembling a member of the genus *Strombus* in form

strom·bite \'strämˌbīt\ *n* -S [NL *Strombus* + ISV *-ite*] **:** a petrified shell of a gastropod of the genus *Strombus*

[1]strom·boid \-ˌbȯid\ *adj* [NL *Strombus* + ISV *-oid*] **:** resembling or related to the genus *Strombus*

[2]stromboid \"\ *n* -S **:** a stromboid mollusk

strom·bo·li·an \sträm'bōlēən\ *adj, often cap* [*Stromboli*, volcano in the Lipari islands + E *-an*] **:** relating to volcanic eruptions that explode violently and eject incandescent dust, scoria, and bombs with little water vapor

strom·bus \'strämbəs\ *n* [NL, fr. L, a kind of spiral snail, fr. Gk *strombos* a snail — more at STROPHE] **1** *cap* **:** a genus of marine gastropod mollusks (family Strombidae) having a heavy obconical shell with a short conical spire and usu. a much expanded outer lip, a horny operculum, a narrow foot, long snout, and long eye peduncles — see KING CONCH **2** -ES **:** any mollusk of the genus *Strombus*

strome \'strōm\ *vi* [alter. of *stroam*, perh. blend of *stroll* & *roam*] *dial chiefly Eng* **:** STRIDE, STROLL

stro·mey·er·ite \'strōˌmīəˌrīt\ *n* -S [G *stromeyerit*, fr. Friedrich *Strohmeyer* †1835 Ger. chemist + G *-it* -ite] **:** a steel gray mineral CuAgS consisting of silver copper sulfide of metallic luster and usu. occurring in compact masses (hardness 2.5–3, sp. gr. 6.15–6.3)

ström·ming \'strœmiŋ\ *n* -S [Sw, fr. *ström* stream; akin to ON *straumr* stream — more at STREAM] **:** a small Baltic herring

stro·muhr \'strōˌmù(ə)r\ *n* -S [G, lit., stream clock, fr. *strom* stream (fr. OHG *strōm*) + *uhr* hour, clock, fr. MHG *ur* hour, fr. MLG or MD *ure*, fr. OF — more at STREAM, HOUR] **:** a rheometer designed to measure the amount and speed of blood flow through an artery

[1]strong \'strȯŋ *also* 'sträŋ\ *adj* **stron·ger** \-ŋgə(r)\ **stron·gest** \-ŋgəst\ [ME, fr. OE *strang;* akin to OHG *strango* strongly, *strengi* strong, brave, hard, ON *strangr* strong, severe, L *stringere* to bind tight, press together — more at STRAIN] **1 a :** having great muscular power **:** capable of exerting great bodily force ⟨~ as a bull⟩ **b :** accomplished or supported by marked physical power ⟨rows with a ~ stroke⟩ ⟨~ kick⟩ ⟨~ thrust with a spear⟩ **2 a :** able to bear or endure **:** ROBUST, RUGGED ⟨~ runner⟩ ⟨~ health⟩ **b :** able to withstand stress or violence **:** not easily broken or injured ⟨~ furniture⟩ **c :** tending to higher prices — sometimes distinguished from *firm* ⟨a ~ market⟩ **3 :** having or exhibiting moral or intellectual force, endurance, or vigor ⟨mistook an opinionated mind for a ~ one —C.H.Sykes⟩ ⟨~ ruler⟩ ⟨~ president⟩ **4 a :** having great resources of wealth ⟨~ bank⟩ ⟨~ national economy⟩ or of talent ⟨~ cast of actors⟩ ⟨among the ~*er* teams in the baseball league⟩ **b :** being of a specified effective number — used postpositively ⟨army 10 thousand ~⟩ ⟨each choir was over 150 ~ —Warwick Braithwaite⟩ **5 a :** striking or superior of its kind **:** capable of making a clear or deep impression esp. on the mind or imagination ⟨bears a ~ resemblance to his father⟩ ⟨~ picture⟩ **b :** effective or efficient esp. in a particular direction **:** able to accomplish a result ⟨if you are ~ on logic —W.J.Reilly⟩ **c :** MASSIVE, IMPORTANT ⟨~ vein of coal⟩ **d :** FULL 3e(1) **e** *of printing type or a slug* **:** cast slightly over point size **6 a :** having a particular quality in a great degree **:** intense in degree **:** CONCENTRATED ⟨~ salt solution⟩ ⟨~ coffee⟩ ⟨~ dislike⟩ ⟨~ light⟩ ⟨~ feelings of the farmers about foreign competition —Roy Lewis & Angus Maude⟩ **b :** EXTREME, UNCOMPROMISING ⟨~ views on raising children⟩ ⟨denounced in the ~*est* terms⟩ **c** *of a color* **:** high in chroma **d :** containing a large proportion of alcohol ⟨~ beer⟩ **e :** having a high degree of ionization in solution — used of an acid or a base ⟨hydrochloric acid and sulfuric acid are ~ acids⟩; compare WEAK 11 **f** *of tobacco* **:** having a high nicotine content or otherwise strongly flavored ⟨perique is a ~ tobacco⟩ **g :** having great refractive or magnifying power ⟨~ lens⟩ ⟨uses ~ eyeglasses⟩ **7** *obs* **:** GROSS, FLAGRANT, NOTORIOUS ⟨heinous, ~, and bold conspiracy —Shak.⟩ **8 :** URGENT, COMPELLING ⟨~ grounds for believing him guilty⟩ ⟨~ desire for recognition⟩ **9 :** ARDENT, ZEALOUS ⟨the whole family are ~ Republicans⟩ ⟨~ believer in astrology⟩ **10 :** moving with force or rapidity ⟨~ tide⟩ ⟨~ wind⟩ ⟨~ pulse⟩ **11 a** *obs* **:** DIFFICULT, HARD **b :** relatively hard to digest **:** SOLID ⟨~ foods⟩ **12 a :** not easily captured or subdued ⟨~ fortress⟩ ⟨~ military position⟩ **b :** well established **:** firmly fixed **:** not easily altered or eradicated ⟨~ prejudice⟩ ⟨~ belief⟩ ⟨~ custom⟩ **c :** not easily upset or nauseated ⟨~ stomach⟩ ⟨~ head for hard liquor⟩ **13 :** having an offensive or too intense odor or flavor ⟨~ cheese⟩ ⟨~ breath⟩ **14** *of soil* **:** PRODUCTIVE, FERTILE **15** *of flour or wheat* **:** containing a high percentage of gluten **:** cohesive and tenacious and producing bread of good texture and form **16 a** *of a verb* **:** forming its past tense by a change in the root vowel and its past participle usu. by the addition of *-en* with or without change of the root vowel (as *strive, strove, striven; break, broke, broken; drink, drank, drunk*) — opposed to *weak;* compare IRREGULAR **b** *of a noun or adjective declension* **:** retaining the old declensional endings characteristic of the vowel stems in Proto-Germanic — opposed to *weak* **17 a :** bearing a degree of stress greater than the minimal degree occurring in the language ⟨~ stress⟩ ⟨~ syllable⟩ ⟨~ ending of a line of verse⟩ **b :** EMPHATIC — used of forms of chiefly monosyllabic words (as pronouns, auxiliaries) that have minimal stress in some contexts ⟨*am* is a ~ form in "I'm not going today but I am going tomorrow"⟩ ⟨Modern English *off* descends historically from the old ~ form of *of*⟩ **18** *chiefly Austral* **a** *of wool* **:** broad-haired or coarse-fibered **b** *of sheep* **:** having such wool **:** STRONG-WOOLLED

syn STOUT, STURDY, STALWART, TOUGH, TENACIOUS: STRONG is a general term indicating marked physical power, great size or number, soundness for withstanding strain, or marked force, vigor, or intensity ⟨a *strong* constitution⟩ ⟨a *strong* army⟩ ⟨a *strong* brace⟩ ⟨*strong* liquor⟩ ⟨a *strong* color⟩ STOUT suggests power to resist or endure; of things it is applicable to a texture or construction resisting strain, and of persons to an ability to resist with undaunted resolution ⟨mooring the ship with *stout* ropes⟩ ⟨*stout* fences for keeping the cattle in⟩ ⟨the *stout* defenders of the fortress⟩ ⟨and let our hearts be *stout*, to wait out the long travail, to bear sorrows that may come, to impart our courage unto our sons —F.D.Roosevelt⟩ STURDY applies to what is marked by staying power or resistance arising from firm resolution, rugged or vigorous growth, or solid construction ⟨it was easy in this country to idealize the farmers as the *sturdy* yeomanry who embodied all the virtues associated with the original Anglo-Saxon love of liberty —John Dewey⟩ ⟨a kick delivered with all the strength of the blacksmith's *sturdy* leg sent him sprawling on all fours —C.B.Nordhoff & J.N.Hall⟩ STALWART may suggest a firm, strong dependability, often accompanied by notable mental or physical strength ⟨it is a hard life: those that survive are *stalwart*, rugged men, literally mighty men of valour who neither know nor desire comforts —L.D.Stamp⟩ ⟨a *stalwart* Federalist, he was a good hater of all Jacobins —V.L.Parrington⟩ TOUGH may suggest resistant, vigorous hardiness able to withstand hard strain and enervation ⟨a *tough* and durable material⟩ ⟨the *toughest* old salts imaginable — not pretty to look at, but fellows, by their faces, of the most indomitable spirit —R.L.Stevenson⟩ ⟨a *tough* ruthless power bent on dominating the world and suppressing our freedom —Vannevar Bush⟩ TENACIOUS implies a stubborn or resolute holding on, retaining, maintaining, or adhering despite forces that would discourage, weaken, dislodge, or thwart ⟨her power of recuperation was wonderful. There was something *tenacious* about that lily-frail body of hers, a clutch on existence which one could not reconcile with its patent weakness —Jack London⟩ ⟨stubborn, willful, *tenacious*, undiscouraged by adversity —T.H.Fielding⟩

— **strong for :** markedly prejudiced in favor of **:** attaching great importance to ⟨*strong for* hi-fi just now⟩

[2]strong \"\ *adv* [ME *stronge, strong*, fr. OE *strange*, fr. *strang* strong (adj.)] **:** STRONGLY ⟨had the love of adventure ~ in their Irish blood —*Irish Digest*⟩ ⟨still going ~ after 40 years of hard work⟩ ⟨reversible . . . topcoat . . . is coming back ~ —*New Yorker*⟩ ⟨wind blowing ~ from the West⟩

[3]strong \"\ *n* -S [[1]*strong*] **:** FORTE 2

strong arm *n* **1 :** physical strength **:** POWER, FORCE ⟨*strong arm* of the law⟩ **2 :** undue force **:** VIOLENCE **3** *also* **strong–armer** \-ˌŋˌärmə(r)\ -S **:** a person using violence **:** THUG

[1]strong–arm \'=,=\ *adj* [*strong arm*] **:** having or using undue force **:** VIOLENT ⟨*strong-arm* methods of strikebreaking⟩

[2]strong–arm \"\ *vt* **1 :** to use force upon **:** handle roughly

: beat up : ASSAULT ⟨*strong-armed* by a vice squad⟩ **2** : to intimidate by threat of violence ⟨*strong-arming* small business into paying protection money⟩ **3** : to rob by violence
strongback \ˈ≈‚≈\ *n* **1** : a spar lashed from one boat davit to the other to which the boat is secured at sea **2** : a heavy timber or metal beam or bar for taking a strain; *specif* : a post to support a light deck used by passengers
strongbark *also* **strongback** \ˈ≈‚≈\ *n* : a small tree (*Bourreria ovata*) of the family Ehretiaceae of southern Florida and the West Indies with strong hard brown wood streaked with orange and edible berries from which a beverage is made
strongbox \ˈ≈‚≈\ *n* : a chest or case for money or valuables made very strongly : a small safe ⟨papers locked away in his ~⟩
strong breeze *n* : wind having a speed of 25 to 31 miles per hour — see BEAUFORT SCALE table
strong drink *n* [ME *strong drinke*, fr. [1]*strong* + *drinke* drink] : intoxicating liquor
stronger *comparative of* STRONG
strongest *superlative of* STRONG
strong gale *n* : wind having a speed of 47 to 54 miles per hour — see BEAUFORT SCALE table
strong grade *n* : a phase of an ablaut series of vowels that receives more than minimum stress
strongheaded \ˈ≈¦≈≈\ *adj* [[1]*strong* + *headed*] : STUBBORN, HEADSTRONG — **strongheaded·ly** *adv* — **strongheaded·ness** *n* -ES
stronghearted \ˈ≈¦≈≈\ *adj* [ME *strong herted*, fr. [1]*strong* + *herted* hearted] : BRAVE, COURAGEOUS — **stronghearted·ness** *n* -ES
stronghold \ˈ≈‚≈\ *n* [ME *strong holde*, fr. [1]*strong* + *holde* hold] **1** : a fortified place : a place of security or survival : FORTRESS, REFUGE ⟨one of the last ~*s* of the ancient Gaelic language —George Holmes⟩ **2** : a place occupied or dominated by a special group or faction ⟨a Puritan ~⟩
strong·ish \-ŋish, -ŋgish\ *adj* : somewhat strong ⟨~ wind⟩
strong language *n* : markedly or unwarrantedly forcible or vehement manner of expression or choice of words
strong·ly *adv* [ME *strongliche*, fr. OE *stranglīce*, fr. *stranglīc* strong, robust, fr. *strang* strong + *-līc* -ly (adj. suffix)] : in a strong manner : POWERFULLY, FORCIBLY, FIRMLY, BOLDLY, EMPHATICALLY
strong man *n* **1** : a man who exhibits feats of muscular strength ⟨*strong man* in a circus⟩ **2** : a man with the power of planning and executing work : a man capable of taking responsibility ⟨he is the *strong man* in their organization⟩ **3** : one who leads or controls by force of will and character or by military methods; *often* : DICTATOR
strong mayor *n* : a mayor in a mayor-council method of municipal government who is given by charter a large degree of control and responsibility — compare COUNCIL-MANAGER PLAN, WEAK MAYOR
strong-minded \ˈ≈¦≈≈\ *adj* : having a vigorous mind : marked by independence of thought and judgment — **strong-minded·ly** *adv* — **strong-minded·ness** *n* -ES
strong·ness *n* -ES [[1]*strong* + *-ness*] : the quality or state of being strong : STRENGTH, VIGOR
strongpoint \ˈ≈‚≈\ *n* : an organized tactical locality in a defensive position
strong room *n* **1** : a room for money or valuables specially constructed to be fireproof and burglarproof **2** : a special room for violently disturbed mental patients
strong sand *n* : molders' sand with an admixture of loam to increase its adhesiveness
strong side *n* : the side of a football formation having the greatest number of players
strong suit *n* **1** : a long suit that contains high cards **2** : a quality or characteristic in which one excels : one's forte
strong water *n* [trans. of NL *aqua fortis*] **1** *archaic* : ACID; *esp* : NITRIC ACID **2** *archaic* : distilled liquor
strong-weak \ˈ≈ˈ≈\ *adj* : having features of both strong and weak conjugations ⟨*tell, told* is a *strong-weak* verb⟩
strong-woolled \ˈ≈¦≈\ *or* **strong-wool** \ˈ≈‚≈\ *adj, chiefly Austral* : having the relatively coarse-fibered wool characteristic of crossbred or mutton-type sheep; *also* : CROSSBRED
stron·gyle \ˈstränˌjīl\ *also* **stron·gyl** \-njəl\ *n* -S [NL *Strongylus*] **1** : any of various roundworms constituting the family Strongylidae and related to the hookworms; *esp* : a worm of *Strongylus* or closely related genera that is parasitic in the alimentary tract and tissues of the horse and may induce severe diarrhea and debility — compare CYLICOSTOME, PALISADE WORM **2** [NL *strongyla*, fr. Gk *strongylē*, fem. of *strongylos* round, compact — more at STRONGYLUS] : a rod-shaped biradiate sponge spicule with blunt ends
[1]**stron·gy·lid** \-njələd\ *adj* [NL *Strongylidae*] : of or relating to the Strongylidae
[2]**strongylid** \ˈ"\ *n* -S : a nematode worm of the family Strongylidae
stron·gyl·i·dae \strănˈjiləˌdē\ *n pl, cap* [NL, fr. *Strongylus*, type genus + *-idae*] : a large family of nematode worms (suborder Strongylina) that are parasites of vertebrates and have a globular to cylindrical buccal capsule and a circlet of laminar processes about the mouth — see CHABERTIA, OESOPHAGOSTOMUM, STRONGYLUS
stron·gy·li·do·sis \ˌstränjələˈdōsəs\ *n* -ES [NL, fr. *Strongylidae* + *-osis*] : STRONGYLOSIS
stron·gyl·i·form \strănˈjiləˌfȯrm\ *adj* [*strongyle* + *-iform*] **1** : resembling strongyles **2** *of a larval nematode worm* : having the esophagus intermediate in character between the rhabditiform and filariform types
stron·gy·lin *or* **stron·gy·line** \ˈstränjələn, -jəˌlīn\ *n* -S [NL *Strongylina*] : a nematode worm of the suborder Strongylina
stron·gy·li·na \ˌstränjəˈlīnə\ *n pl, cap* [NL, fr. *Strongylus* + *-ina*] : a suborder of Rhabditida that comprises nematode worms parasitic as adults in vertebrates often with a complex life cycle involving an invertebrate larval host and includes important parasites (as the strongyles and the hookworms) of man and domestic animals
stron·gy·lo·cen·trot·i·dae \ˌstränjəlōsenˈträdəˌdē\ *n pl, cap* [NL, fr. *Strongylocentrotus*, type genus + *-idae*] : a large and nearly cosmopolitan family of typical sea urchins (order Centrechinoidea)
stron·gy·lo·cen·tro·tus \-ˈtrōdəs\ *n, cap* [NL, fr. Gk *strongylos* round, compact + *kentrōtos* prickly, fr. *kentroun* to provide with a prick or sting, fr. *kentron* sharp point — more at STRONGYLUS, CENTER] : a widely distributed genus of sea urchins (family Strongylocentrotidae) that includes the common green urchin (*S. drobachiensis*) of the No. American coasts and the small purple urchin (*S. purpuratus*) of the Pacific coast as well as other common forms
[1]**stron·gy·loid** \ˈstränjəˌlȯid\ *adj* [NL *Strongyloidea*] : of or relating to the Strongyloidea
[2]**strongyloid** \ˈ"\ *n* -S [NL *Strongyloidea*] : a worm of the superfamily Strongyloidea
stron·gy·loi·dea \ˌ≈≈ˈlȯidēə\ *n pl, cap* [NL, fr. *Strongylus* + *-oidea*] : a superfamily of parasitic nematode worms (order Rhabditida) comprising the hookworms, strongyles, and related forms
stron·gy·loi·des \ˌstränjəˈlȯiˌdēz\ *n, cap* [NL, fr. *Strongylus* + *-oides* -oid] : a genus (the type of the family Strongyloididae) of rhabditid nematode worms having both free-living males and females and parthenogenetic females parasitic in the intestine of various vertebrates and including some medically and economically important pests (as *S. stercoralis*) of man
stron·gy·loi·di·a·sis \ˌstränjəˌlȯiˈdīəsəs\ *also* **stron·gy·loi·do·sis** \-ˈdōsəs\ *n* -ES [NL, fr. *Strongyloides* + *-iasis*, *-osis*] : infestation with or disease caused by nematodes of the genus *Strongyloides* occas. parasitic in the intestines of many vertebrates including man
stron·gy·lo·plas·ma·ta \ˌstränjəlōˈplazmədə\ *n pl, cap* [NL, fr. Gk *strongylos* round, compact + *plasmata*, pl. of *plasmat-, plasma* form, mold, body — more at STRONGYLUS, PLASMA] : inclusion bodies grouped taxonomically as organisms
stron·gy·lo·sis \ˌstränjəˈlōsəs\ *n* -ES [NL, fr. *Strongylus* + *-osis*] : infestation with or disease caused by strongyles
stron·gy·lote \ˈstränjəˌlōt\ *adj* [Gk *strongylos* round + E *-ote* (as in *tylote*)] : having one end rounded — used chiefly of sponge spicules
stron·gy·lus \ˈstränjələs\ *n, cap* [NL, fr. Gk *strongylos* round, compact; akin to L *stringere* to bind tight, press together — more at STRAIN] : a genus (the type of the family Strongylidae) of parasitic nematode worms comprising worms with a pair of elongated buccal glands and including gastrointestinal parasites of the horse — see PALISADE WORM
stron·tia \ˈstränch(ē)ə, -ntēə\ *n* -S [NL, fr. E *strontian*] **1** : the strontium oxide SrO **2** : STRONTIUM HYDROXIDE — used chiefly commercially
stron·ti·an \-ən\ *n* -S [fr. *Strontian*, village in Argyllshire, Scotland, where it was discovered] : STRONTIUM
stron·ti·an·if·er·ous \ˌstränch(ē)ə¦nif(ə)rəs, -ăntēə¦-\ *adj* [*strontian* + *-iferous*] : containing or yielding strontium
stron·ti·an·ite \ˈstränch(ē)əˌnīt, -ăntēə,-\ *n* -S [*Strontian*, village in Argyllshire, Scotland + E *-ite*] : a mineral $SrCO_3$ consisting of native strontium carbonate and occurring as an orthorhombic, pale-green, white, gray, or yellowish mineral in masses of radiating needle-shaped or spear-shaped crystals or in fibrous massive forms (hardness 3.5–4, sp. gr. 3.68–3.71)
strontian white *n* : STRONTIUM WHITE
strontian yellow *n* **1** : strontium yellow or a pigment of the same color **2** : a brilliant greenish yellow that is greener and deeper than mimosa yellow
stron·tic \ˈsträntik\ *adj* [NL *strontium* + ISV *-ic*] : of or relating to strontium
stron·ti·um \ˈstränch(ē)əm, -ntēəm\ *n* -S [NL, fr. *strontia* + *-ium*] : a silver-white soft malleable and ductile bivalent metallic element of the alkaline-earth group that occurs only in combination esp. as strontianite and celestite, that is usu. obtained by electrolysis of its fused chloride or by thermal reduction of its oxide with aluminum, that turns yellowish in air, and that yields compounds capable of imparting a crimson color to flames and pyrotechnic compositions — symbol *Sr;* see ELEMENT table
strontium carbonate *n* : a crystalline salt $SrCO_3$ occurring naturally as strontianite and used chiefly in fireworks, in iridescent glass, and in making other strontium compounds
strontium hydroxide *n* : a deliquescent solid $Sr(OH)_2$ that forms a crystalline octahydrate, that dissolves in water to form a decidedly alkaline solution, and that is used chiefly in making soaps and greases and in refining beet sugar and recovering sugar from the molasses by the formation of insoluble sucrates
strontium 90 *n* : a heavy radioactive isotope of strontium having the mass number 90 and a half life of 25 years that is present in the fallout from nuclear explosions and is particularly hazardous because like calcium it can be assimilated in biological processes and deposited in the bones of human beings and animals — symbol Sr^{90} or ^{90}Sr; called also *radiostrontium*
strontium nitrate *n* : a salt $Sr(NO_3)_2$ that crystallizes from hot strong solutions in anhydrous form and from cold solutions as the tetrahydrate and that is used chiefly in fireworks, flares, and tracer bullets
strontium oxide *n* : an oxide of strontium; *esp* : the crystalline monoxide SrO resembling lime and barium monoxide
strontium salicylate *n* : a crystalline salt $Sr(C_7H_5O_3)_2.2H_2O$ used esp. formerly in medicine similarly to sodium salicylate
strontium sulfate *n* : a crystalline salt $SrSO_4$ occurring naturally as celestite and used chiefly in making other strontium compounds
strontium titanate *n* : a crystalline compound $SrTiO_3$ used chiefly as an additive to barium titanate ceramic bodies
strontium white *n* : strontium sulfate used as a pigment, extender, or filler
strontium yellow *n* : strontium chromate $SrCrO_4$ used as a yellow pigment although it has little tinting strength
strook *obs var of* STRUCK
stroop *var of* STROUP
stroot *obs var of* STRUT
[1]**strop** \ˈsträp\ *n* -S [ME — more at STRAP] : STRAP: **a** : a short rope with its ends spliced to form a circle **b** : a band usu. of leather backed with liner canvas for sharpening a razor
[2]**strop** \ˈ"\ *vt* **stropped; stropped; stropping; strops** **1** : to furnish (as a pulley block) with a strop **2** : to sharpen (a razor) on a strop
stroph- *or* **stropho-** *comb form* [Gk, fr. *strephein* to twist turn — more at STROPHE] : twisting : turning ⟨*strophosis*⟩ ⟨*stropho*cephaly⟩
stro·phan·thi·din \strəˈfan(t)thədən\ *n* -S [ISV *strophanthin* + *-idin*] : a very toxic crystalline steroidal gamma-lactone $C_{23}H_{32}O_6$ obtained by hydrolysis of strophanthin, cymarin, and various other glycosides
stro·phan·thin \-thən\ *n* -S [NL *Strophanthus* + ISV *-in*] : any of several glycosides or mixtures of glycosides obtained from African apocynaceous plants of the genera *Strophanthus* and *Acocanthera:* as **a** *also* **strophanthin-K** [*strophanthin-K* fr. *Strophanthus kombé*, plant from which it is produced] : a bitter very toxic crystalline steroidal glycoside $C_{36}H_{54}O_{14}$ from the seeds and bark of an east African woody vine (*Strophanthus kombé*) that yields strophanthidin, cymarose, and glucose on hydrolysis and that is used similarly to digitalis and in Africa as an arrow poison — called also *k-strophanthin* **b** *also* **strophanthin-G** [*strophanthin-G* fr. *Strophanthus gratus*, plant from which it is produced] : OUABAIN **c** : CYMARIN

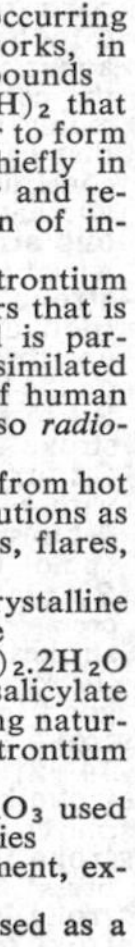

strop b

stro·phan·thus \-thəs\ *n* [NL, fr. Gk *strophos* twisted band + NL *-anthus*; fr. the twisted segments of the corolla — more at STROPHE] **1** *cap* : a genus of tropical Asiatic and African trees, shrubs, or woody vines (family Apocynaceae) that have showy flowers with a glandular calyx and a tubular corolla with five appendaged and twisted lobes and include several African forms with poisonous seeds as well as forms (as *S. kombé*) that furnish strophanthin **2** -ES : the dried cleaned ripe seeds of any of several plants of the genus *Strophanthus* (as *S. kombé* and *S. hispidus*) that are in moderate doses a cardiac stimulant like digitalis but in larger doses a violent poison and that have strophanthin as their most active constituent
stro·pha·ria \strəˈfa(a)rēə\ *n, cap* [NL, fr. Gk *strophos* + NL *-aria*] : a genus of brown spored gill fungi (family Agaricaceae) closely related to *Agaricus* but having gills and stipe united
stro·phe \ˈstrōfē, -fī\ *n* -S [Gk *strophē*, lit., act of turning, fr. *strephein* to twist, turn; akin to Gk *strophos* twisted band, cord, *streblos* twisted, crooked, *strabos* squint-eyed, *strobos* action of whirling, *strombos* whirling or spiral object, top, snail] **1** : the movement of the classical Greek chorus while turning from one side to the other of the orchestra — compare ANTISTROPHE **2 a** : a rhythmic system composed of two or more lines repeated as a unit; *esp* : such a unit recurring in a series of strophic units not all of which have the same internal structure — distinguished from *stanza;* compare ANTISTROPHE **b** : any arrangement of lines together as a unit : STANZA **c** : the part of a Greek choral ode sung during the strophe of the dance : the first of the three divisions of each section of a full Pindaric ode
stroph·ic \ˈsträfik, -rōf-, -fēk\ *also* **stroph·i·cal** \-fəkəl, -fēk-\ *adj* [*strophe* + *-ic*, *-ical*] **1** : relating to, containing, or consisting of strophes **2** : having the same music for successive stanzas of a song — compare THROUGH-COMPOSED — **stroph·i·cal·ly** \-fək(ə)lē\ *adv*
stroph·i·o·late \ˈsträfēəˌlāt, -rōf-\ *adj* [NL *strophiolatus*, fr. *strophiolum* + *-atus* -ate] : furnished with a strophiole
stroph·i·ole \-ēˌōl\ *n* -S [NL *strophiolum*, fr. L, small wreath, dim. of *strophium* breastband, headband, fr. Gk *strophion*, fr. dim. of *strophos* twisted band, cord — more at STROPHE] **1** : an excrescence like a crest about the hilum of some seeds (as of spurge) **2** : CARUNCLE
stropho- — see STROPH-
stroph·o·me·na \ˌsträfəˈmēnə\ *n, cap* [NL, irreg. fr. Gk *strophōma* hinge (akin to Gk *strephein* to turn) + *mēnē* moon; fr. its hinge and concavo-convex shell — more at STROPHE, MOON] : a genus (the type of the family Strophomenidae) of extinct brachiopods having a long hinge, sharply limited muscle scars, and resupinate shell
stroph·o·men·i·dae \-ˈmenəˌdē\ *n pl, cap* [NL, fr. *Strophomena*, type genus + *-idae*] : a family of Ordovician to Permian brachiopods that are usu. isolated in a distinct superfamily or suborder of Telotremata but are sometimes placed in a separate order — see STROPHOMENA
stroph·u·lus \ˈsträfyələs\ *n, pl* **strophu·li** \-yəˌlī\ [NL, fr. Gk *strophos* twisted band — more at STROPHE] : a rash in infants marked by red or sometimes whitish papules surrounded by reddish halos and popularly associated with teething distress — called also *red gum, tooth rash*
stropped *past of* STROP
strop·per \ˈsträpə(r)\ *n* -S : one that strops; *esp* : a device for sharpening double-edged razor blades
stropping *pres part of* STROP
strops *pl of* STROP, *pres 3d sing of* STROP
strossers *n pl* [origin unknown] *obs* : TROUSERS
stroud \ˈstrau̇d\ *n* -S [prob. fr. *Stroud*, urban district of Gloucestershire, England, and woolen manufacturing center] **1** *also* **stroud·ing** \-diŋ\ : a coarse heavy woolen cloth usu. in plain weave formerly used in trade with No. American Indians **2** : a blanket or garment of stroud

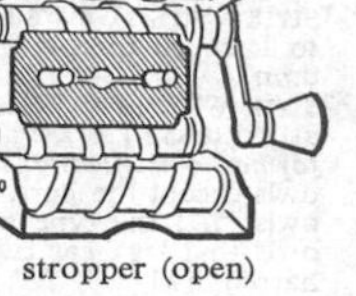

stropper (open)

stroup \ˈstrüp\ *n* -S [ME *stroupe*, fr. ON *strūpi*, *strjūpi*; akin to Norw dial. *strop* narrow opening, and prob. to Gk *stryphnos* astringent — more at STRUBBLY] **1** *dial chiefly Eng* : WINDPIPE **2** *chiefly Scot* : SPOUT
strove [ME *stroof* (past)] *past & chiefly dial past part of* STRIVE
strow \ˈstrō\ *vt* **strowed; strown** \-ōn\ *or* **strowed; strowing; strows** [ME *strowen* — more at STREW] *archaic* : SCATTER **syn** see STREW
stroy *vb* -ED/-ING/-S [ME *struyen, stroyen*, short for *destruyen, destroyen* — more at DESTROY] *obs* : DESTROY
strsph *abbr* stratosphere
strub·bly \ˈstrəb(ə)lē, ˈstrüb-\ *adj* [PaG *schtruwwlich;* akin to OS *strūf* shaggy, OHG *strūben* to stand on end (of hair), MHG *strobel* shaggy, Gk *stryphnos* astringent, sour, harsh, Lith *strubas* lopped off short, OE *starian* to stare — more at STARE] *dial* : UNTIDY, UNKEMPT
struc *abbr* structure
[1]**struck** [ME *strook* (past), fr. OE *strāc* (past)] *past of* STRIKE
[2]**struck** \ˈstrək\ *adj* **1** : affected strongly with love, affection, or fancy for — used with *with* or *on* ⟨~ with a girl⟩ ⟨~ on his dad —*Reader's Digest*⟩ **2 a** : closed or affected by a labor strike ⟨a ~ factory⟩ ⟨a ~ employer⟩ **b** : worked on or produced in a struck establishment ⟨~ work⟩ **3** : figured on the basis of contents being level with the top edge ⟨a sand-hauling truck with a ~ capacity of 15 cubic yards and a heaped capacity of 17 cubic yards⟩ **4** : affected by strike : FLYBLOWN ⟨~ sheep⟩
[3]**struck** \ˈ"\ *n* -S [[2]*struck*] **1** : STRIKE 20a **2** : enterotoxemia esp. of adult sheep
struck joint *n* **1** : a joint in which the mortar is recessed at the bottom with a trowel while the mortar is still green — see JOINT illustration **2** : a joint whose surface has been smoothed with a trowel
struck jury *n* : a special jury of 12 members selected from 48 taken by the sheriff indifferently from those qualified to act as special jurymen, reduced to 24 by the attorney for each side striking out the names of 12, and chosen from these 24 by the ordinary methods
struck measure *n* : LEVEL MEASURE
struct *abbr* structure
struc·tur·al \ˈstrəkchərəl, -ksh(ə)rəl\ *adj* **1 a** : of or relating to structure or a structure : affecting structure : used in building structures : CONSTRUCTIONAL ⟨a ~ error⟩ ⟨~ clay⟩ ⟨these metals have a ~ stability that should insure long life for the furniture in which they are used —Betty Pepis⟩ ⟨stands at the ~ center of the story —Charles Lee⟩ **b** : of or relating to the load-bearing members or scheme of a building as opposed to the screening or ornamental elements ⟨the ~ details of a house consist of floor joists, rafters, wall and partition studs, supporting columns . . . foundations —*Building, Estimating & Contracting*⟩ **c** : involved in or caused by structure esp. of the economy ⟨modern ~ unemployment⟩ **2** : of, relating to, or involving the physical makeup of a plant or animal body and esp. its plan of organization ⟨~ defects in the central nervous system —D.M.Hegsted & F.J.Stare⟩ ⟨the true wing is a ~ peculiarity of birds⟩ **3** : of, relating to, or resulting from the arrangement of rock bodies : resulting from the effects of folding or faulting of the earth's crust : TECTONIC ⟨a ~ plateau⟩ ⟨a ~ ridge⟩ ⟨a ~ valley⟩ **4 a** : of or relating to the social structure; *specif* : involving the arrangement of social status and stratification into a hierarchical class system **b** : stressing social structure and the interdependence of social institutions ⟨the ~ emphasis of social anthropologists⟩ **5** : concerned with or relating to structure rather than history or comparison ⟨~ linguistics⟩ : emphasizing the systematic relations of formal distinctions in a language ⟨~ grammar⟩
structural basin *n* : BASIN 4a
structural color *n* : a color or color component due to interference of light (as in thin films), diffraction (as by a grating), refractive dispersion (as in a rainbow), differential scattering, or differential polarization ⟨colors of most bodies are due largely to selective absorption with some superposed *structural color*⟩
structural engineering *n* : a branch of civil engineering dealing primarily with the design and construction of structures (as bridges, buildings, dams)
structural formula *n* : an expanded molecular formula show-

structural formulas

compound	molecular formula	with bonds	with covalent bonds and unshared electrons	with electrons
water	H_2O	H–O–H	H–Ö–H	H:Ö:H
acetic acid	$C_2H_4O_2$	CH_3-CO-O-H H H-C-C-O-H H O	H H-C-C-Ö-H H :O:	H H:C:C:Ö:H H :O:
methyl formate	$C_2H_4O_2$	H-CO-O-CH_3 H H-C-O-C-H O H		

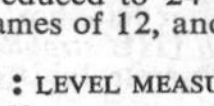

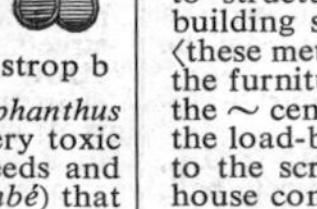

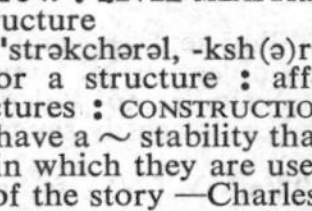

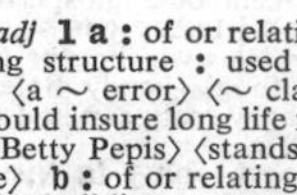

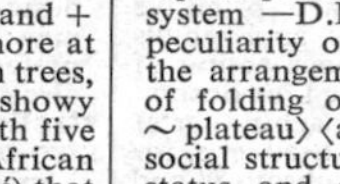

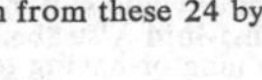

ing the arrangement within the molecule of atoms and of bonds depicted usu. by lines or of valence electrons depicted usu. by dots — see KEKULÉ FORMULA, PERSPECTIVE FORMULA; compare BENZENE RING, OCTET 3; CHOLESTEROL illustration, CIS-TRANS ISOMERISM illustration, INDIGO illustration, MENTHANE illustration

structural-functional \¦=(=)=¦=(=)=\ *adj* **:** combining the approaches of the structuralist and functionalist schools of sociology and social anthropology; *specif* **:** analyzing established institutional relationships and their societal functioning

structural geology *n* **:** a branch of geology that deals with the form, arrangement, and internal structure of rocks — called also *geotectonic geology*

structural iron *n* **:** iron worked or cast in structural shapes

struc·tur·al·ism \'strəkchərə,lizəm, -ksh(ə)r-\ *n* -s **1 :** a theory that emphasizes the importance of structure as contrasted with function in mental life: as **a :** the introspective analysis of consciousness **b :** ORGANICISM b **2 :** the practice of structural methods in linguistics

structural isomerism *n* **:** isomerism in which atoms are linked in a different order — sometimes distinguished from *stereoisomerism;* compare POSITION ISOMERISM

¹struc·tur·al·ist \'strəkchərələst, -ksh(ə)r-\ *n* -s **1 :** an adherent or follower of structuralism **2 :** one stressing the more formal, organizational aspects of social life (as embodied in kinship regulations, marriage forms, clan and moiety systems)

²structuralist \"\ *also* **struc·tur·al·is·tic** \¦=(=)=¦listik\ *adj* **:** of or relating to structuralism

struc·tur·al·iza·tion \,strəkchərələ'zāshən, -ksh(ə)r-, -,lī'z-\ *n* -s **1 :** the process of structuralizing **2 a :** assimilation into a formal social structure ⟨the ~ of clerical duties⟩ **b :** embodiment of social and cultural patterns of thought in the individual personality ⟨the ~ of a person's outlook by his environment⟩

struc·tur·al·ize \'=(=)=,līz\ *vt* -ED/-ING/-S **:** to embody in structural or material form: as **a :** to embody (a function or group of functions) in an organic or other organizational structure **b :** to incorporate into a formal pattern or institution ⟨culture ~s individual behavior⟩

structural lumber *n* **:** lumber that is intended for use where working stresses are required and that is two or more inches thick and four or more inches wide

struc·tur·al·ly \-ˌlē, -li\ *adv* **:** in a structural manner **:** in regard to structure

structural psychology *n* **:** STRUCTURALISM 1

structural steel *also* **structural** *n* -s **1 :** rolled steel in structural shapes **2 :** steel suitable for structural shapes

structural terrace *n* **:** a local flattening in an otherwise uniformly tilted series of strata

struc·tur·a·tion \,strəkchə'rāshən, -kshə'-\ *n* -s **1 :** the interrelation of parts in an organized whole **2 :** STRUCTURALIZATION 2b

¹struc·ture \'strəkchə(r), -ksh-\ *n* -s [ME, fr. L *structura,* fr. *structus* (past part. of *struere* to pile up, arrange, build) + *-ura* -ure; akin to L *strues* heap, *sternere* to spread out, throw down — more at STREW] **1 :** the action of building **:** CONSTRUCTION **2 a :** something constructed or built ⟨a laboratory housed in a temporary wooden ~⟩ ⟨the dam is a massive ~⟩ ⟨demolish any building, highway, road, railroad, excavation, or other ~ —T.W.Arnold⟩ ⟨a ~ of posts or stakes across a stream —F.W. Bradley⟩ ⟨~s experimented with . . .: oxygen-pressure suits, oxygen-pressure balloon gondolas and pressure cabin airplanes —H.G.Armstrong⟩ ⟨all vegetable fibrous ~s felted from a water suspension on a wire screen —*Paper & Paperboard*⟩; *esp* **:** a building of imposing size **:** EDIFICE ⟨the civic auditorium . . . is the city's most important public ~ —*Amer. Guide Series: Mich.*⟩ **b :** something made up of more or less interdependent elements or parts **:** something having a definite or fixed pattern of organization ⟨leaves and other complex plant ~s⟩ ⟨a glandular ~ at the base of the brain⟩ ⟨light provided by a fluorescent ~⟩ ⟨collapse the delicate, incomplete ~ of agreement —Kenneth Love⟩ ⟨the Nazi ~ of falsified facts and perverted history —Alfred Frankfurter⟩ ⟨any object which is in some sense an organized whole is said to have, or to be characterized by, ~ —W.C.Clement⟩ ⟨the political and institutional ~ of the Commonwealth has been built, and continues to develop, round this living core of tradition and culture —H.D.Hall⟩ ⟨events, or material objects, whose mutual spatial relationships are regarded as constant, constitute a ~ —L.A.White⟩ **3 :** the manner of construction **:** the way in which the parts of something are put together or organized **:** FORM, MAKEUP ⟨a rambling country house, basically Gothic in plan, ~, and mass —H.S.Morrison⟩ ⟨~ means the ways in which the stars are organized into clusters and other multiple systems —G.W.Gray b.1886⟩ ⟨primitive societies are . . . pretty rigid and uniform in ~ —J.D.Adams⟩ ⟨the ~ of a novel⟩ **4 :** the arrangement of particles or parts in a substance or body ⟨the ~ of soil⟩ ⟨the ~ of a plant⟩ ⟨the ~ of an animal⟩: as **a :** the arrangement and mode of union of the atoms in a molecule — compare CONSTITUTION 4 **b :** the attitude and relative positions of rock masses consequent upon deformative processes (as folding, faulting, and igneous intrusion) ⟨an anticlinal ~⟩ ⟨a basin-and-range ~⟩ ⟨an alpine ~⟩ **c :** the arrangement of a rock mass with respect to the larger features (as jointing, columnar and platy parting, bedding) — compare TEXTURE **5 :** the interrelation of parts as dominated by the general character of the whole ⟨economic ~⟩ ⟨financial ~⟩ ⟨personality ~⟩ ⟨political ~⟩ ⟨symphonic ~⟩ ⟨tax ~⟩ — see SOCIAL STRUCTURE **6 :** the elements or parts of an entity or the position of such elements or parts in their external relationships to each other: as **a** (1) **:** the components of a language (as phonemes, morphemes) and the way in which they are related — compare PHONEMICS, MORPHOPHONEMICS, MORPHOLOGY, SYNTAX (2) **:** the finite system of such components and their relations **b** (1) **:** the composition of conscious experience with its elements and their combinations (2) **:** GESTALT (3) **:** the anatomical basis of behavior consisting esp. of nerve and muscle tissue **7 :** the element that is common to all true interpretations of a logical or mathematical calculus

²structure \"\ *vb* **structured; structured; structuring** \-kchər, -ksh(ə)r + *-ing*\ **structures** *vt* **1 :** to form into an organized structure **:** BUILD, ORGANIZE ⟨the author has *structured* his book as a simple chronology —E.B.Pettet⟩ ⟨this book succeeds in *structuring* an admirable vantage point —J.G. Brin⟩ ⟨the male in the old-style mammal was largely *structured* for aggressive competition —Weston La Barre⟩ ⟨the way in which our collegiate education is *structured* —E.A.Walker⟩: as **a** (1) **:** STRUCTURALIZE (2) **:** to put into a meaningful frame of reference ⟨a theory to ~ empirical research⟩ ⟨the part of television in *structuring* public events⟩ **b :** to establish the relationship between components of: as (1) **:** to define the psychological relationships in ⟨~ a situation⟩ ⟨~ the perceptual field⟩ (2) **:** to formalize the role of (as a psychotherapist or a patient) (3) **:** to set up the rules or the agenda to be followed in (as an interview or a test) with respect to interpersonal conduct **2 :** to assign (a linguistic element) to a function or a relation within a system ~ *vi* **:** to function or become related — used of a linguistic element

structured *adj* **:** having definite structure **:** exhibiting organized structure or differentiation of parts

struc·ture·less \'==ləs\ *adj* **:** lacking definite structure or organization; *usu* **:** devoid of cells **:** HOMOGENEOUS ⟨a ~ membrane⟩ — **struc·ture·less·ness** *n* -ES

stru·del \'s(h)trüdᵊl\ *n* -s [G, lit., whirlpool, fr. MHG; akin to OHG *stredan* to bubble, Gk *rhothos* roar of the waves, noise, Skt *sarati* it flows — more at SERUM] **:** a sheet of paper-thin dough rolled up with any of various fillings and baked

¹strug·gle \'strəgəl\ *vb* **struggled; struggled; struggling** \-g(ə)liŋ\ **struggles** [ME *struglen*] *vi* **1 :** to make violent, strenuous, labored, or convulsive exertions or efforts against difficult or forceful opposition or impeding or constraining circumstances **:** STRIVE, CONTEND ⟨they *struggled* about the trough as furiously as a litter of pigs —T.B.Costain⟩ ⟨with the driven rationality of church fathers *struggling* to formulate and express the accepted import of the Faith delivered to the saints —H.O.Taylor⟩ ⟨the story of the human spirit *struggling* with sin —R.A.Hall b.1911⟩ ⟨*struggled* bravely against poverty —C.M.Fuess⟩ ⟨the law has had to ~ with these problems —B.N.Cardozo⟩ ⟨the point of view I am *struggling* to attack —T.S.Eliot⟩ **2 :** to proceed with difficulty or with great effort ⟨*struggled* through ancient exits never big enough to handle the crowd —Claudia Cassidy⟩ ⟨the lamplight *struggled* out through the fog —Oscar Wilde⟩ ⟨fell over prostrate trees, sank into deep holes and *struggled* out —Willa Cather⟩ ⟨ancient Egypt was just *struggling* out of barbarism —Geoffrey Boumphrey⟩ ⟨the band *struggled* through the . . . national anthem —*Time*⟩ ⟨the college *struggled* along until 1855 —*Amer. Guide Series: La.*⟩ ~ *vt* **:** to bring to a desired state or condition by or as if by a struggle ⟨*struggled* down the last of his emotions —R.L. Stevenson⟩ **syn** see TRY

²struggle \"\ *n* -s **1 :** an act of earnest striving **:** a violent effort or exertion (as to obtain an object, overcome a difficulty, or avert an evil) ⟨if he makes no effort — shrinking without a ~ from his duty — he himself will not the less certainly perish —Thomas De Quincey⟩ ⟨a ~ for freedom of thought⟩ ⟨a ~ with disease⟩ ⟨the boy had a ~ for a living⟩ ⟨the orchestra's ~ for survival⟩ **2 :** CONTEST, CONTENTION, STRIFE ⟨the ~ between the natural sciences and religion ended in an armistice —Zechariah Chafee⟩ ⟨attempts to express in musical form the ~ between sacred and profane love —Edward Sackville-West & Desmond Shawe-Taylor⟩ ⟨the ~ with communism⟩ ⟨a ~ over a political issue⟩ ⟨a legal ~⟩ ⟨in the course of the ~ he was made prisoner and harshly treated —E.M.Coulter⟩

struggle for existence : the automatic competition of the members of a natural population for a limited supply of vital necessities resulting in elimination of inadequately adapted individuals and hence in selection of the better-adapted as breeding stock — compare NATURAL SELECTION

strug·gler \-g(ə)lə(r)\ *n* -s **:** one that struggles

struggling *adj* **:** engaged in a struggle esp. to overcome poverty or obscurity ⟨a ~ artist⟩ ⟨a ~ school⟩ — **strug·gling·ly** *adv*

struld·brug \'strəl(d),brəg\ *n* -s *usu cap* [*Struldbrug,* one of a class among the inhabitants of the imaginary country Luggnagg, in the book *Gulliver's Travels* (1726) by Jonathan Swift †1745 Eng. satirist, composed of persons who can never die] **:** one of a class of imaginary persons who can never die but who are declared dead in law at the age of 80 and live on wretchedly at state expense

¹strum \'strəm\ *n* -s [ME *strom, strumme*] **:** STRAINER ⟨a wickerwork ~ for straining malt⟩ ⟨a metal ~ for a suction pipe of a pump⟩

²strum \"\ *vb* **strummed; strummed; strumming; strums** [imit.] *vt* **:** to play on or as if on (a stringed musical instrument) esp. in an offhand or careless way **:** THRUM ⟨~ a guitar⟩ ⟨the howling winds *strummed* the rigging —H.A.Chippendale⟩ ~ *vi* **:** to play on or as if on a stringed musical instrument ⟨a rain of missiles that *strummed* against the canvas —Lilian Brown⟩

³strum \"\ *n* -s **:** the act or sound of strumming ⟨the ~ of typewriters —John Summerson⟩

stru·ma \'strümə\ *n, pl* **stru·mae** \-ü,mē, -,mī\ [L, scrofulous enlargement of glands, goiter] **1 :** enlargement of an organ (as a breast or lymph gland); *specif* **:** GOITER **2** [NL, fr. L] **:** a cushion-shaped swelling on any organ; *esp* **:** a swelling at the base of the capsule in many mosses

stru·mel·la \strü'melə\ *n, cap* [NL, fr. L *struma* + NL *-ella*] **:** a form genus of imperfect fungi (family Tuberculariaceae) characterized by ovate nonseptate brown conidia

strum·mer \'strəmə(r)\ *n* -s **:** one that strums (as on a piano or mandolin)

stru·mose \'strü,mōs\ *adj* [L *strumosus* having a scrofulous swelling of glands, fr. *struma* + *-osus* -ose] **:** having a struma

stru·mous \-məs\ *adj* [L *strumosus*] **:** having, relating to, or connected with a struma; *specif* **:** GOITROUS

¹strum·pet \'strəmpət, *usu* -əd·+V\ *n* -s [ME *strumpet, strompet*] **:** PROSTITUTE, HARLOT

²strumpet \"\ *vt* -ED/-ING/-S **1** *obs* **:** DEBAUCH **2 :** to brand as a strumpet **3 :** BELIE, SLANDER

strung *past of* STRING

strung-up \'=¦=\ *adj* [fr. past part. of *string up,* v.] **:** HIGH-STRUNG

¹strunt \'strənt, -rünt\ *n* -s [obs. E *strunt,* adj., stubby, perh. alter. of E ¹*stunt*] **1** *chiefly Scot & dial Eng* **:** the stump of a tail **2** *chiefly Scot & dial Eng* **:** a tail denuded of feathers or hair

²strunt \"\ *vt, dial chiefly Eng* **:** to dock (a tail)

³strunt \"\ *n* -s [origin unknown] *dial Brit* **:** DISPLEASURE, AFFRONT, OFFENSE

⁴strunt \'strənt\ *vi* [by alter.] *Scot* **:** STRUT

⁵strunt \"\ *n* -s [origin unknown] *Scot* **:** LIQUOR

¹strut \'strət, *usu* -əd·+V\ *vb* **strutted; strutted; strutting; struts** [ME *strouten,* fr. OE *strūtian* to exert oneself; akin to MHG *strūzen* to resist, ON *strūtr* conical upper part of a hood, L *struma* scrofulous enlargement of glands, goiter, OE *starian* to stare — more at STARE] *vi* **1 :** to become turgid **:** SWELL ⟨freshly cut unwilted tobacco plants ~ when exposed to rain⟩ **2 :** to walk with a lofty proud gait and an erect head; *esp* **:** to walk with pomposity or affected dignity **:** SWAGGER ⟨pompous little dictator swells with pride and importance as he ~s up and down his study —Martin Turnell⟩ ⟨when he has a little spurt of good fortune, he patronizes all his friends and starts to ~ —Erle Stanley Gardner⟩ ⟨the simple words have been made to ~ and posture and take on an emphasis which makes them ridiculous —Virginia Woolf⟩ ~ *vt* **1 :** to stretch or thrust out **:** PROTRUDE, BULGE, DISTEND ⟨should the udder still remain highly *strutted* —*Dairy Goat*⟩ **2 a :** to walk over with a swaggering gait **:** stride proudly over **b :** to deliver (as a speech or an actor's lines) in a swaggering manner **c :** to parade (as fine clothes or jewelry) with a show of pride ⟨the boys who labor in the music halls and show shops *strutted* their most elaborate accomplishments —*N.Y.Times*⟩ — **strut one's stuff** *slang* **:** to display one's best work **:** show off

²strut \"\ *n* -s **1 a :** a bar (as a member in a frame, structure, or machine) designed to resist pressure in the direction of its length ⟨a basement floor may be used as a ~ between opposite walls —C.W.Dunham⟩ ⟨a ~ supporting a rafter⟩ ⟨an airplane landing-gear ~⟩ ⟨a ~ of thin bone in the cavity of a long bone⟩ — compare BRACKET, STAY, TIE; see ROOF illustration **b :** an outboard support between the stern tube and the propeller on a ship having more than one propeller shaft **2 a :** the act of strutting **:** a pompous step or walk ⟨his walk was a self-important ~ —A.W.Turnbull⟩ **b :** OSTENTATION

³strut \"\ *vt* **strutted; strutted; strutting; struts** [²*strut*] **:** to provide, stiffen, support, or hold apart with or as if with a strut

strutbeam *n* **:** a beam used as a strut; *specif* **:** COLLAR BEAM

struth \'strüth\ *interj* [short for *God's truth*] — used as a mild oath

stru·thi·an \'strüthēən, -ü͟th-\ *adj* [NL *Struthio* + E *-an*] **:** STRUTHIOUS

stru·thi·form \'strüthə,fȯrm, -ü͟th-\ *or* **stru·thii·form** \-thēə-,fȯrm, -t͟hē-\ *adj* [*struthi-* (fr. NL *Struthio*) + *-form* or *-iform*] **:** resembling an ostrich

stru·thio \'strüthē(,)ō, -ü͟th-\ *n, cap* [NL *Struthion-, Struthio,* fr. LL, ostrich, irreg. fr. Gk *strouthos* ostrich, sparrow; perh. akin to OE *thrysce* thrush — more at THRUSH] **:** a genus (the type of the family Struthionidae) of birds comprising the African ostriches — **stru·thi·oid** \'==,ȯid\ *adj or n*

stru·thio·mi·mus \,==(,)=ˈmīməs\ *n, cap* [NL, fr. *Struthio* + *-mimus*] **:** a genus of small light-boned saurischian dinosaurs lacking teeth, resembling ostriches in size and proportions, and found in the Upper Cretaceous of Alberta, Canada

stru·thi·o·nes \,==ˈō,nēz\ *n pl, cap* [NL, fr. LL, pl. of *struthion-, struthio* ostrich] **1** *in former classifications* **:** a major division of Aves equivalent to Ratitae **2** *in some classifications* **:** a suborder or other group equivalent to Struthioniformes

stru·thi·on·i·dae \,==ˈänə,dē\ *n pl, cap* [NL, fr. *Struthion-, Struthio,* type genus + *-idae*] **:** a family of ratite birds (order Struthioniformes) comprising the African ostriches or made coextensive with the order or in former classifications including also the rheas and various other ratite birds

stru·thi·on·iform \¦==¦änə,fȯrm\ *adj* [NL *Struthioniformes*] **:** of or relating to the Struthioniformes **:** resembling an ostrich

¹stru·thi·on·i·for·mes \,==,==ˈfȯr,mēz\ *n pl, cap* [NL, fr. *Struthion-, Struthio* + *-iformes*] **:** an order of tall terrestrial birds (superorder Neognathae) comprising the ostriches and related extinct birds

²struthioniformes \"\ [NL, fr. *Struthion-, Struthio* + *-iformes*] *syn of* TINAMIFORMES

stru·thi·o·nine \'==,ə,nīn, -,nən\ *adj* [NL *Struthion-, Struthio* + E *-ine*] **:** STRUTHIOUS

stru·thi·ous \'==,əs\ *adj* [L *struthio* ostrich + E *-ous*] **:** of or relating to the ostriches and related birds **:** RATITE

strut·ter \'strəd·ə(r), -ətə-\ *n* -s [ME *strouter* one that blusters, fr. *strouten* to swell, bulge, bluster + *-er* — more at STRUT] **:** one that struts

¹strutting *adj* [ME *stroutinge* that swells or bulges, fr. pres. part. of *strouten* to swell, bulge] **:** that struts — **strut·ting·ly** *adv*

²strut·ting \'strəd·iŋ, -ətiŋ, -ēŋ\ *n* -s [²*strut* + *-ing*] **:** STRUTS; *specif* **:** BRIDGING 2

strut·ty \'strəd·ē, -ətē, -i\ *adj* -ER/-EST **1 :** inclined or disposed to strut ⟨he was smallish and ~ —H.L.Davis⟩ **2 :** marked by a strut ⟨his ~, bull-like posture —Adria Langley⟩

stru·vite \'strü,vīt\ *n* -s [Sw *struveit,* fr. H. C. G. von *Struve* †1851 Russ. diplomat + Sw *-it* -ite] **:** a mineral $Mg(NH_4)(PO_4).6H_2O$ consisting of a hydrous ammonium magnesium phosphate and occurring in white orthorhombic-hemimorphic crystals (hardness 2, sp. gr. 1.7)

strych·nia \'striknēə\ *n* -s [NL, fr. *Strychnos*] **:** STRYCHNINE

strych·nic \-nik, -nēk\ *adj* [ISV *strychn-* (fr. NL *Strychnos*) + *-ic*] **:** of, relating to, or produced by strychnine ⟨~ poisoning⟩

¹strych·nine \'strik,nīn, -,nən, -,nēn\ *n* -s [F, fr. NL *Strychnos* + F *-ine*] **1 :** a very poisonous bitter crystalline alkaloid $C_{21}H_{22}N_2O_2$ obtained from various plants of the genus *Strychnos* (as nux vomica and St.-Ignatius's-bean) and used in medicine chiefly in the form of the sulfate or phosphate as a tonic and stimulant for the central nervous system and also as a rodenticide **2 :** NUX VOMICA 2

²strychnine \"\ *vt* -ED/-ING/-S **:** to poison by strychnine

strych·nin·ism \-,nizəm\ *n* -s [ISV ¹*strychnine* + *-ism*] **:** a toxic condition produced by the excessive use of strychnine **:** chronic strychnine poisoning

strych·nin·iza·tion \,=(,)=nə'zāshən, -,nī'z-\ *n* -s [¹*strychnine* + *-ization*] **:** the act of strychninizing

strych·nin·ize \'=(,)=,nīz\ *vt* -ED/-ING/-S [¹*strychnine* + *-ize*] **:** to subject to the action of strychnine

strych·nos \'striknəs, -,näs\ *n, cap* [NL, fr. L, nightshade, fr. Gk] **:** a large genus of tropical trees and woody tendril-climbing vines (family Loganiaceae) having 3- to 5-nerved leaves, cymose flowers with a salver-shaped corolla, and a 2-celled ovary that becomes in fruit a berry with a thick rind — see CURARE, NUX VOMICA, STRYCHNINE; compare BRUCINE

stry·mon \'strī,män\ *n, cap* [NL, prob. fr. Gk *Strymōn* Strymon, river in southwestern Bulgaria and northern Greece] **:** a large and widely distributed genus of hairstreak butterflies including a few (as *S. melinus*) with larvae that are destructive pests of various economic plants

strype *Scot var of* ¹STRIPE

STS *abbr* **1** serologic test for syphilis **2** special treatment steel

stsm *abbr* statesman

¹stu·art \'st(y)üə(r)t, -)u̇(ə)rt, -)üət, *usu* -d·+V\ *n* -s *usu cap* [*Stuart,* Scottish and English royal house] **:** a member or supporter of the British house of Stuart

²stuart \"\ *adj, usu cap* **:** of, relating to, or characteristic of the periods or reigns of the Stuart kings of England — compare JACOBEAN, CAROLINE, RESTORATION

stu·ar·tia \st(y)ü'ärsh(ē)ə, -rd·ēə\ *syn of* STEWARTIA

¹stub \'stəb\ *n* -s *often attrib* [ME *stubb, stubbe,* fr. OE *stubb, stybb;* akin to ON *stubbi* stub, *stūfr* stump, Gk *stypos* stem, stump, *typtein* to beat, strike — more at TYPE] **1 a :** the part of a tree or plant that remains fixed in the earth when the stem is cut down or broken off **:** STUMP, SNAG ⟨solitary woodpeckers were drilling on the dead ~s —Hugh Fosburgh⟩ **b :** a short piece of a broken or trimmed branch remaining on the stem or trunk **2 :** something fashioned or worn to a short or blunt shape: as **a :** an old or worn nail or piece of iron **b :** FENCE 6 **c :** STUB TENON **d :** a short broad file with a handle projecting at an angle suitable for filing broad flat surfaces **e :** a pen with a short blunt nib **f :** a usu. cylindrical and often metallic protuberance used to tune or adjust the impedance of transmission lines at such high frequencies that conventional coils and condensers are impractical **3 :** a short blunt portion (as of a pencil, candle, or cigarette) remaining after the larger part has been broken off or used up **4 :** something that appears cut short or stunted **:** a rudimentary growth (as of a feather or horn) **5 a :** a small portion of each leaf (as of a checkbook or receipt book) permanently attached to the backbone for memoranda of the contents of the part filled out and torn away **b :** the portion of a ticket (as of admission or of a checking service) torn off and returned to the user for verification or identification **6 :** GUARD 9a, 9b **7 :** a vertical column at the extreme left side of a statistical or mathematical table usu. containing items of subject matter that are treated in vertical columns to its right **8 :** STUB TRACK

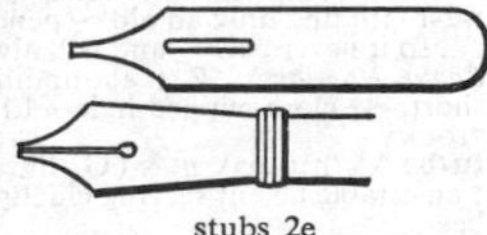

stubs 2e

²stub \"\ *vt* **stubbed; stubbed; stubbing; stubs** [ME *stubben,* fr. *stubb, stubbe,* n.] **1 a :** to grub or dig up by the roots **:** root out — usu. used with *up* ⟨*stubbing* up thornbushes⟩ ⟨the forest was gradually felled and *stubbed* up —A.C.Benson⟩ **b :** to remove trees, stumps, or scrub growth from (land) ⟨~s the heath to make his garden⟩ **c :** to hew or cut down (a tree) close to the ground **2 a** *archaic* **:** to reduce or wear down to a stub **b :** to make (as a knife or pencil) blunt at the point **3 :** to lame (a horse) by allowing to walk over stubs ⟨brought the horse home badly *stubbed*⟩ **4 a :** to crush or drive (as stone) into the ground **:** PULVERIZE **b :** to extinguish (as a cigarette) by crushing ⟨finished his cigarette, *stubbed* it on the floor —Victor Canning⟩ — often used with *out* ⟨smoked her cigarette . . . then she *stubbed* it out —Elizabeth Goudge⟩ **5 :** to strike (one's foot or toe) against a stub or stone ⟨*stubbed* his toe and fell heavily⟩ **6 :** GUARD 6 **7 :** to pluck the pinfeathers from (a fowl) ⟨birds are usually *stubbed* by female labor —W.P.Blount⟩

stub axle *n* **:** an axle supporting only one wheel and carried at the other end on the vehicle frame or some other support

stub·bi·ness \-bēnəs, -bin-\ *n* -ES **:** the quality or state of being stubby

¹stub·ble \'stəbəl\ *n* -s *often attrib* [ME *stuble, stubbel, stouple,* fr. OF *estuble, stuble,* fr. L *stupula* stalk, straw, alter. of *stipula* — more at STIPULE] **1 a stubbles** *pl* **:** a stump of a cultivated plant (as wheat, corn, clover, beans, or grasses) left in the ground after cutting or harvest ⟨the crisp fresh ~s dotted with shocked-up wheat and oats —Anthony West⟩ **b :** such stumps left in a field or area ⟨cattle are seen in the rice ~ during the fall and winter —*Amer. Guide Series: La.*⟩ **2 :** the straw of grain or other stalks remaining after the harvest **3 :** a rough surface or growth resembling stubble; *esp* **:** a short growth of beard ⟨the black unshaven ~ of his jaw —R.P. Warren⟩ **4 :** short wool left on the sheep after shearing ⟨leaves enough ~ to protect sheep from cold —*advt*⟩ **5 :** a blunt bristle (as in some mutant of drosophilas)

²stubble \"\ *vt* **stubbled; stubbled; stubbling** \-b(ə)liŋ\ **stubbles :** to leave in stubble **:** cover with stubble ⟨the *stubbled* prairies spread around her —Ethel Wilson⟩ ⟨black whiskers *stubbled* the small chin —K.M.Dodson⟩

stubbleberry \'== — *see* BERRY\ *n* **:** WONDERBERRY

stubble crop *n* **1 :** a crop (as soybeans, buckwheat, turnips) sown on stubble after the grain is harvested for turning under as green manure **2 :** a ratoon crop esp. of sugarcane

stubble field *also* **stubble** *n* -s **:** a field covered with stubble after harvesting

stubble goose *n* **:** GREYLAG

stubble mulch *n* **:** a lightly tilled mulch of stubble and plant residue left on the surface of the ground to prevent erosion, conserve moisture, and add organic matter to the soil

stubble-mulch farming *n* **:** TRASH FARMING

stubble plow *n* **:** a stirring plow with a steep moldboard for stubble land

stubble quail *n* **:** an Australian quail (*Coturnix pectoralis*)

stubble spurge *n* **:** SPOTTED SPURGE

stub·bly \'stəb(ə)lē, -li\ *adj* -ER/-EST **1 :** covered with stubble **:** STUBBLED ⟨our walk across ~ fields —May Sarton⟩ **2 :** resembling stubble ⟨having ~ hair —G.K.Chesterton⟩

1stub·born \'stəbə(r)n\ *adj* -ER/-EST [ME *stibourne, stuborn, stoburne,* perh. irreg. fr. *stubb, stubbe* stub — more at STUB] **1 a :** unreasonably or perversely unyielding in character or quality **:** PIGHEADED, MULISH ⟨break the ~ will which had been perverted at the source —Henry Miller⟩ ⟨jeopardized . . . by his ~ and tactless maneuvers —A.L.Funk⟩ ⟨~ carelessness⟩ **b :** fixed, resolute, or justifiably unyielding in character or purpose **:** DETERMINED, DOGGED ⟨the resources of the ~ mind, the stout heart —A.E.Stevenson †1965⟩ ⟨~ yeomen who parade their independence —V.L.Parrington⟩ ⟨~ conviction⟩ ⟨~ courage⟩ ⟨~ resistance⟩ **c :** unyielding, defiant, or resolute in cast or appearance ⟨had a ~ profile, like a willful horse —Katherine A. Porter⟩ ⟨under the ~ arch of their brows —Walter O'Meara⟩ **2 a :** difficult to handle, work, or manage **:** RESISTANT, REFRACTORY ⟨was able to start a ~ fire engine —V.G.Heiser⟩ ⟨the lashes standing ~ and thick along the lowered lid —Kay Boyle⟩ ⟨sometimes the soil proved too ~ for even this hardy people —*Amer. Guide Series: N.H.*⟩ ⟨methods for dealing with ~ problems —Theodore Draper⟩ **b :** difficult to treat or cure **:** unresponsive to care **:** CHRONIC, PERSISTENT ⟨methods . . . dermatologists use today in treating ~ cases —Marjorie Vetter⟩ ⟨~ germ plasm's successive ways of surrounding itself with an ever more secure environment —Weston La Barre⟩ ⟨only a pathological condition could account for a depression so ~ and dangerous —L.C.Douglas⟩ **3 :** hard, stiff, or rigid in texture or substance ⟨in a lapidary inscription . . . shapes easy to cut in ~ material would be his chief concern —F.W Goudy⟩ ⟨gathering force . . . to break the ~, granite headlands —*Amer. Guide Series: Maine*⟩ **4 :** performed or carried on in a stubborn manner ⟨a result of long and ~ fighting —*Times Lit. Supp.*⟩ ⟨made a ~ living from repertory troupes for 8 years —*Current Biog.*⟩ **5 :** continually and unremittingly existent **:** ENDURING ⟨the ~ life of small religious bodies transplanted in America from Europe —W.L.Sperry⟩ ⟨the family . . . most ~ of all social units —Edward Sapir⟩ ⟨a ~ tradition of hope—A.M.Schlesinger b.1917⟩ ⟨in the face of ~ facts —Norman Kelman⟩ **syn** see OBSTINATE

2stubborn \"\ *vt* -ED/-ING/-S **:** to make stubborn

stubborn child *n* **:** a minor (as in the state of Massachusetts) who refuses to submit to the lawful commands of parent or guardian and may be punished by six months imprisonment or by a fine — compare WAYWARD CHILD

stubborn disease *n* **:** a persistent virus disease of citrus characterized by shortened internodes resulting in stiff brushy growth, by the appearance of chlorotic leaves early in the season, and by a reduced crop of often acorn-shaped fruit — see ACORN DISEASE

stub·born·ly *adv* [ME *stoberlie,* fr. *stibourne, stuborn, stoburne* stubborn + *-lie, -ly* -ly] **:** in a stubborn manner **:** with stubbornness

stub·born·ness \-n(n)əs\ *n* -ES [ME *styburnesse, stobournesse,* fr. *stibourne, stuborn, stoburne* stubborn + *-nesse* -ness] **:** the quality or state of being stubborn

stub·by \'stəbē, -bi\ *adj* -ER/-EST [1*stub* + *-y*] **1 a :** resembling a stub **:** short and thick or wide in growth or development ⟨~ fingers⟩ ⟨~ arms⟩ **b :** short and thickset in build **:** SQUAT ⟨a ~ little fellow⟩ **c (1) :** short, broad, or blunt in design ⟨an awkward ~ gun in his hand —H.D.Skidmore⟩ ⟨big air-cooled engine and ~ wings —T.W.Lawson⟩ ⟨might cause great chunks of the ice shelf to tumble down upon our ~ vessel —Glen Jacobsen⟩ **(2) :** short, broad, or blunt from use or wear ⟨finding only an old ~ pencil⟩ ⟨filing the flat of the blade . . . so it never gets ~ and will always bite into the wood —*Boy Scout Handbk.*⟩ **2 :** abounding with stubs **:** BRISTLY ⟨his short, ~, close-clipped hair —Elizabeth M. Roberts⟩ **syn** see STOCKY

stu·be \'s(h)tübə\ *n* -S [G, lit., room — more at BIERSTUBE] **:** an establishment serving chiefly alcoholic beverages and esp. beer

stub end *n* **:** either end of a connecting rod containing the bearing for the crankpin or the crosshead pin

stub–end feeder *n* **:** a feeder that connects a load with its only source of power

stub feather *n* **:** PINFEATHER

stub hoe *n* **:** a stout hoe for grubbing up stubs or stumps

stub mortise *n* **:** a mortise passing only part way through the timber

stubrunner \'=,==\ *n* **:** a corn planter or cotton planter furrow opener adapted for use in trashy soil

stubs *pl of* STUB, *pres 3d sing of* STUB

stub station *n* **:** a railroad station at which the tracks terminate — compare THROUGH STATION

stub switch *n* **:** a railroad switch in which the track rails are cut off squarely at the toe and the point rails are thrown to line up with the lead rails

stub tenon *n* **:** a tenon to fit a stub mortise

stub tooth *n* **:** a short gear tooth of great strength with a large angle of obliquity

stub track *n* **:** a track connected with another at one end only

1stuc·co \'stə(,)kō\ *n, pl* **stuccos** *or* **stuccoes** [It, of Gmc origin; akin to OHG *stucki* piece, crust — more at STOCK] **1 a :** a material now usu. made of portland cement, sand, and a small percentage of lime and applied in a plastic state to form a hard covering for the exterior walls or surfaces of a building or structure **b :** a fine plaster of high quality used in the decoration and ornamentation of interior walls **2 :** STUCCOWORK **3 :** DEAUVILLE SAND

2stucco \"\ *vt* **stuccoed; stuccoed; stuccoing; stuccoes** *or* **stuccos 1 :** to overlay or decorate with stucco ⟨the doorcases are generally ~*ed,* with Ionic or Roman Doric shafts supporting . . . pediments —*Country Life*⟩ **2 :** to coat (as a wall) with stucco ⟨streets lined with gray ~*ed* houses —J.M.Brinnin⟩

stuccowork \'=(,)=,=\ *n* **:** decoration, design, or work done in stucco

stuck *past of* STICK

stuck·ling \'stəklən, 'stůk-\ *n* [origin unknown] *dial Eng* **:** an apple turnover

stuck–up \'=;=\ *adj* [fr. past part. of *stick up*] **:** assuming or exhibiting an unwarranted attitude of superiority or self-importance **:** CONCEITED ⟨knew . . . that if she sat out the dance she would at once be damned as *stuck-up* —E.A.McCourt⟩

1stud \'stəd\ *n* -S *often attrib* [ME *stod,* fr. OE *stōd;* akin to OHG *stuot* stud, ON *stōth* stud, OE *standan* to stand — more at STAND] **1 a :** a group of broodmares and stallions kept for breeding ⟨dictated the break-up of this mare's wonderful ~ —*London Calling*⟩ **b :** a group of animals kept or maintained for selective propagation ⟨a ~ of light canaries could very soon be transformed into one of dark selfs —*All-Pets Mag.*⟩ **2 :** an establishment or farm where horses are kept for breeding ⟨one of the most modern and well equipped trotting ~*s* in this state —*Sporting Life*⟩ **3 a :** a group of horses bred or kept by one owner ⟨owner of a ~ of blooded horses —C.G.Bowers⟩ ⟨each omnibus claimed the services of a ~ of ten horses —Hugh McCausland⟩ **b :** a group of animals of a particular kind belonging to one owner ⟨my own ~ built from six generations of red siskin breeding —*All-Pets Mag.*⟩ **4 a** [by shortening] **:** STUDHORSE **b :** a male animal kept for breeding esp. for public use for a fee — compare BROOD 4 **c :** an outstanding plant selected for use in breeding because of inherent desirable qualities — used esp. of orchids **d** *slang* **:** a young male person ⟨an oily ~ in a second-hand sports jacket —Al Hine⟩ **5 :** STUD POKER — **at stud** *or* **in stud** *adv* **:** in the function of a stud **:** for breeding ⟨getting only 16 foals during the 11 years he stood *at stud* —Dennis Craig⟩ ⟨was placed *in stud* after being retired and had three foals —F.G.Menke⟩

2stud \"\ *n* -S *often attrib* [ME *stode,* fr. OE *studu;* akin to MHG *stud* prop, post, ON *stoth* post, OE *stōw* place — more at STOW] **1 a** *obs* **:** an upright prop or support used in a building **:** PILLAR, POST **b :** one of the smaller uprights in the framing of the walls of a building to which sheathing, paneling, or laths are nailed or fastened **:** SCANTLING **c :** the height of a room from floor to ceiling ⟨built a house at least 15 by 15 feet with a seven-foot ~ —*Springfield (Mass.) Republican*⟩ **2 :** something attached to, fixed in, or projecting from a surface: as **a :** a boss, rivet, or nail with a large head used (as on a shield, bridle, bag, or belt) for ornament or protection **b :** a solid button with a shank or eye on the back that is inserted through one or more eyelets usu. in a garment to serve as a fastener or ornament ⟨~*s* for a dress shirt⟩ ⟨~ earrings⟩ **3 :** a short branch of a plant or tree **:** STUB, SPUR **4 :** any of various infixed pieces (as a rod or pin) projecting from a machine and serving chiefly as a support or axis: as **a :** a short live spindle or mandrel (as in the change gear for a screw-cutting lathe) **b :** STUD BOLT **c :** a metal piece in a timepiece to which is attached the outer or upper coil of a hairspring **d :** a projecting pin or dowel on a loose piece used in pattern-making **e :** a chaplet with a baseplate and a disk top **f :** an iron brace across the link of a chain cable **g :** a part that conducts electric current from a terminal to a contact of a switch **h :** CLEAT

3stud \"\ *vt* **studded; studded; studding; studs 1 :** to furnish (a building or wall) with studs ⟨an old house with low-studded rooms⟩ **2 :** to adorn, cover, or protect with studs ⟨likes to ~ her jewelry with semiprecious cabochons —*New Yorker*⟩ ⟨players . . . wearing a pair of *studded* shoes —Don Iddon⟩ ⟨gatehouse with original *studded* door —Nikolaus Pevsner⟩ **3 :** to mark or set (a place or thing) with a number of prominent objects ⟨several small islands ~ the broad sweep of water —*Amer. Guide Series: Maine*⟩ ⟨miles of green tundra . . . *studded* by scattered patches of trees —L.R.Huber⟩ ⟨its pansy-like red blossom *studded* thickly with tiny hairs tipped with . . . dew —Laura Krey⟩ ⟨figures of speech thickly ~ his work —J.G.Southworth⟩ **4 :** to secure with studs

stud *abbr* student

stud block *or* **stud box** *n* **:** a device for screwing home a stud bolt that consists of a rectangular block turned with a wrench — compare STUD DRIVER

stud bolt *n* **:** a bolt with threads on both ends designed to be screwed permanently into a fixed part at one end and to receive a nut on the other

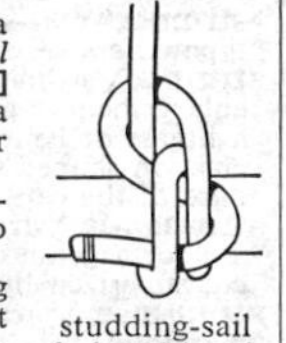
stud bolt

studbook \'=,=\ *n* **:** an official record of the pedigree of purebred animals (as horses and dogs); *also* **:** a book in which such records are published

stud chain *n* **:** a chain having links braced with studs

stud·der \'stədə(r)\ *n* -S **:** a worker who inserts watch hairsprings into studs

stud·die *or* **stud·dy** \'stədi, -tüdi\ *Scot & dial Eng var of* STITHY

studding *n* -S [fr. gerund of 3*stud*] **1 :** the uprights of the wall framing of a building **2 :** wood prepared for use as studding **3 :** the height of a room as determined by its studs

stud·ding sail \'stən(t)səl (*usual nautical pronunc*), 'stədiŋ ,sāl\ *n* [*studding* (of unknown origin) + *sail*] **:** a light sail set at the side of a principal square sail of a vessel in free winds to increase its speed — see SAIL illustration

studding–sail halyard bend *n* **:** a knot similar to a fisherman's bend used to secure a rope to a spar

studding-sail halyard bend

1stud·dle \'stədᵊl\ *n* -S [ME *stodul* sley of a loom, fr. OE *stōdla;* akin to MHG *stuodel* post, OE *standan* to stand — more at STAND] **:** a prop or stud used in timbering; *esp* **:** a piece or post separating the frames, rings, or sets used in timbering a mine shaft

2stud·dle \", 'stůd-\ *vt* [prob. alter. (influenced by 1*stir*) of *muddle,* v.] *dial* **:** to muddy (as water) by stirring up **:** ROIL

stud driver *n* **:** a device for driving or firing home a stud usu. consisting of an impact wrench or a percussion torque tool — compare STUD BLOCK

stu·dent \'st(y)üdᵊnt\ *n* -S *often attrib* [ME, fr. L *student-, studens,* fr. *student-, studens,* pres. part. of *studēre* to be eager, be diligent, study — more at STUDY] **1 :** a person engaged in study **:** one devoted to learning: as **a :** one enrolled in a class or course in a school, college, or university **:** PUPIL **b :** one who independently carries on a systematic study or detailed observation of a subject ⟨a ~ of human nature⟩ ⟨to ~*s* of ships and the sea, the Museum offers a valuable library —Dana Burnet⟩ **2** *often cap* **:** a member of a university foundation (as at Christ Church, Oxford)

student body *n* **:** the students of a school, college, or university

student council *n* **:** a group of students at a school or college elected by their fellow students to represent them in school government and usu. charged with drawing up and enforcing rules and penalties independently or with faculty assistance, coordinating extracurricular activities, and organizing the school's social life

student government *n* **:** the organization and management of student life, activities, or discipline by various student organizations (as the student council) in a school or college

student lamp *n* **:** an adjustable desk reading lamp with a tubular shaft, one or two arms to support a shaded light, and an oil reservoir; *also* **:** a similar electric lamp

student lamp

stu·dent·ship \'==,ship\ *n* **1 :** the state or condition of being a student ⟨would not be a charge on her during the expensive years of ~ —O.S.J.Gogarty⟩ **2** *Brit* **:** a grant for university study — compare SCHOLARSHIP

student teacher *n* **:** one studying to be a teacher; *esp* **:** a student usu. in his last year at a college or teacher-training institution who is engaged in practice teaching at a demonstration school, in a public-school system, or at a cooperating private school

student teaching *n* **:** PRACTICE TEACHING

student volunteer *n* **:** a Protestant Christian student volunteering to devote his life to missionary work overseas

stud fee *n* **:** a fee paid the owner of an animal at public service by the owner of the female to be bred

studfish \'=,=\ *n* [prob. fr. 2*stud* + *fish*] **:** either of two brightly colored American killifishes: **a :** a killifish (*Xenisma catenatum*) of eastern Tennessee and the Ozark region **b :** a killifish (*X. stellifer*) of the Alabama river

studhorse \'=,=\ *n* [prob. fr. (assumed) ME *stodhors,* fr. OE *stōdhors,* fr. *stōd* stud + *hors* horse] **:** a stallion kept esp. for breeding

stud·ied \'stədēd, -did\ *adj* **1 :** well-read or versed in some branch of learning or activity **:** KNOWLEDGEABLE, LEARNED ⟨well ~ in geometry⟩ ⟨an able and ~ man⟩ **2 :** carefully considered or prepared **:** THOUGHTFUL ⟨the legal profession . . . gives its ~ acceptance to the program —*New Republic*⟩ ⟨his upright example . . . and carefully ~ lectures to the boys —Thomas Woody⟩ **3 :** produced or marked by conscious design or premeditation **:** intentionally conceived ⟨appareled for effect and so posed that its very casualness is ~ —John Mason Brown⟩ ⟨there is a note of biting irony and ~ insult —V.L. Parrington⟩ ⟨his attitude was . . . that of watchful waiting and ~ indifference —James Purdy⟩ **syn** see DELIBERATE

stud·ied·ly *adv* **:** in or with a studied manner ⟨the ~ polite disrespect of our chamber-music halls —H.J.Foss⟩ ⟨the proliferation of temporary art galleries among ~ picturesque restaurants —H.R.Lottman⟩

stud·ied·ness *n* -ES **:** the quality or state of being studied

stu·dio \'st(y)üdē,ō, -(,)dyō\ *n* -S *often attrib* [It, lit., study, fr. L *studium* — more at STUDY] **1 a :** the working place of a creative worker (as a painter or sculptor) **b :** a place for the study or practice of various performing or individual arts (as dancing, singing, acting) **2 :** a group of buildings including offices, laboratories, and stages where motion pictures are made **3 :** a room or place maintained and esp. equipped for the transmission of radio or television programs

studio apartment *n* **:** an apartment having a room with high ceiling and large windows similar to or serving as an artist's studio

studio couch *n* **:** an upholstered usu. backless couch that can be made to serve as a double bed by sliding from underneath it the frame of a single cot — compare SOFA BED

stu·dious \'st(y)üdēəs, -dyəs\ *adj* [ME, fr. MF or L; MF *studieux,* fr. L *studiosus,* fr. *studium* study + *-osus* -ose] **1 :** given to study **:** assiduous in the pursuit of learning ⟨a mind which had never found occasion to be ~ or analytical —S.H. Adams⟩ **2 a :** of, relating to, or concerned with study or learning ⟨a man of ~ and methodical habits —Harold Callender⟩ ⟨to read the great books . . . with intelligent appreciation is one of the last achievements of a ~ life —O.W.Holmes †1935⟩ **b :** favorable or suited for study or contemplation ⟨within these ~ walls⟩ **3 a :** diligent in purpose **:** of earnest intent ⟨if we were more ~ to write prose that could be read aloud with pleasure —A.T.Quiller-Couch⟩ **b :** marked by or evincing purposefulness or diligence ⟨a ~ effort was made to avoid representing the human figure realistically —R.W. Murray⟩ **c :** deliberately planned **:** STUDIED ⟨drove into the club with ~ calm . . . for the natives must not suspect that they were agitated —E.M.Forster⟩

stu·dious·ly *adv* [ME *studiousli,* fr. *studious* + *-li* -ly] **:** in a studious or studied manner ⟨followed his finger . . . and ~ copied letter by letter —Edward Bok⟩ ⟨real issues are kept ~ away from public notice —Christopher Hollis⟩

stu·dious·ness *n* -ES **:** the quality or state of being studious

1stu·dite \'st(y)ü,dīt\ *n* -S *usu cap* [*Studius,* 5th cent. A.D. Rom. official + E *-ite*] **:** a Studite monk of the Eastern Orthodox Church

2studite \"\ *adj, usu cap* **:** of or relating to a monastery founded at Constantinople in the 5th century A.D. by a Roman official named Studius and reorganized by St. Theodore; *also* **:** of or relating to the rule codified in this monastery by St. Theodore

stu·di·um gen·er·a·le \'st(y)üdēəm,jenə'ra(,)lē, -rā(,)-; 'stüdēəm,genə'rä,lā\ *n, pl* **stu·dia genera·lia** \-dēə . . . lēə\ [ML, universal studying place] **:** a place or institute of studies where people from all parts of the world may come to study any subject; *esp* **:** a medieval university

stud link *n* **:** a link of a stud chain; *also* **:** the bracing member of such a link

studmaster \'=,==\ *n, Austral* **:** one owning or supervising a stud of sheep

stud–mate \'=,=\ *vt* **:** to breed (poultry) by mating selected pairs — compare FLOCK-MATE, PEN-MATE

stud poker *n* ['*stud* + *poker*] **1 :** poker in which each player is dealt his first card facedown and his other four cards faceup with a round of betting taking place after each of the last four rounds **2 :** a variant (as seven-card stud) of stud poker

stud rivet *n* **:** SCREW RIVET

studs *pl of* STUD, *pres 3d sing of* STUD

stud welding *n* **:** the process of welding a stud to a plate or flat surface by the combined use of heat and pressure

stud wheel *n* **:** a wheel journaled on a stud

studwork \'=,=\ *n* **:** work supported, strengthened, held together, or ornamented by studs ⟨walls . . . of ~ with lath and plaster —Fiske Kimball⟩

1study \'stədē, -di\ *n* -ES [ME *studie,* fr. OF *studie, estudie* state of perplexity or reverie, application of the mind to the acquirement of knowledge, study, fr. L *studium* eagerness, application of the mind to the acquirement of knowledge, study; akin to L *studēre* to be eager, be diligent, study and prob. to L *tundere* to beat — more at STINT] **1 :** a state of absorbed contemplation, perplexity, or reverie **:** ABSTRACTION ⟨paused and appeared to be in a deep ~ —Alexander MacDonald⟩ ⟨the long silences that meant I was lost in ~ —Eve Langley⟩ **2 a :** the application of the mental faculties to the acquisition of knowledge ⟨is in your own power greatly to improve . . . by ~, observation, and reflection —Earl of Chesterfield⟩ ⟨hours of ~ and careful thought —Bruce Payne⟩ ⟨years of ~ in school and college⟩ **b :** such application of the mind in a particular field or to a specific subject matter ⟨scholarship . . . which illuminates the ~ of the family —Lynn White⟩ ⟨taking up the ~ of history⟩ ⟨enter upon the ~ of law⟩ **c (1) :** a careful examination or analysis of a phenomenon, development, or question usu. within a limited area of investigation ⟨plunged into the ~ of latex —Clarence Woodbury⟩ ⟨*studies* have been made of individual cases and of groups of adolescents —H.R. Douglass⟩ — often used with *under* ⟨further reductions are under ~ —D.D.Eisenhower⟩ **(2) :** a paper or monograph in which such a study is published ⟨these two volumes constitute the ablest ~ on the iron and steel industry —*Current Biog.*⟩ ⟨publishes *studies* and reports⟩ **3 a :** a building or room furnished esp. with books and devoted to study or literary pursuits ⟨set out my typewriter in the ~ . . . to write —Worth T. Hedden⟩ **b** *obs* **:** the books contained in such a study or in a collection **c** *obs* **:** a place of learning **:** UNIVERSITY, STUDIUM GENERALE **d :** the lower level of the inner stage of an Elizabethan playhouse often used to represent an indoor scene **4 a** *obs* **:** an expressed inclination **:** DESIRE, INTEREST **b :** a consciously reasoned effort **:** PURPOSE, ENDEAVOR ⟨a continuance of those favors which it will ever be my ~ to deserve —W.S.Gilbert⟩ ⟨it has been the ~ of my life to avoid those weaknesses —Jane Austen⟩ **5 a :** an organized branch or department of learning **:** SUBJECT ⟨what are your favorite *studies* —G.B.Shaw⟩ ⟨was . . . on the faculty of graduate *studies* —Edna Yost⟩ **b :** the activity or work of a student ⟨the curriculum for graduate ~ —E.B.Nyquist⟩ ⟨returning to his *studies* after vacation⟩ **c :** something that is the object of one's study ⟨was pompous and wonderfully conceited, his every word and every gesture a careful ~ —Marcia Davenport⟩ ⟨about the use of making this sugar . . . I said I made it my ~ —H.D.Thoreau⟩ **d :** something attracting close attention or examination usu. by reason of contrast or conflict ⟨it was quite a ~ to watch the faces round the table — in the struggle between good manners and amusement —Rachel Henning⟩ ⟨a ~ in conflicting emotions —T.B.Costain⟩ ⟨the whole show a ~ in tolerant condescension —David Driscoll⟩ **6 :** one who memorizes something (as a part in a play) — usu. used with a qualifying adjective ⟨is not considered a fast ~, but once he has learned a role he has it for good —H.C.Schonberg⟩ **7 a :** an artistic production in any of the fine arts intended as a preliminary outline or esp. as an experimental expression or interpretation of specific features or characteristics ⟨a number of his drawings were *studies* of beggars, clowns, cripples, and street musicians —*Current Biog.*⟩ ⟨a ~ in tunes, all of them beautiful and separate —Leonard Bernstein⟩ ⟨whether dancing in dramatic roles . . . or *studies* in pure dance —*Current Biog.*⟩ **b :** a literary work serving as an experimental or esp. as an exploratory analysis or portrayal of carefully observed features of character or motivation ⟨a particularly successful ~ of the type of grievance-ridden, unhappy . . . misfit —R.P.Fleming⟩ ⟨a topical ~ of life in a wartime services canteen —Leslie Rees⟩ ⟨a brilliantly intuitive ~ of war and the emotions of men in combat —*Time*⟩ **8 :** a musical composition usu. devoted entirely to a special problem of instrumental technique **:** ÉTUDE

2study \"\ *vb* -ED/-ING/-ES [ME *studien,* fr. OF *estudier,* fr. ML *studiare,* fr. L *studium,* n., study] *vi* **1 a :** to apply the mind to the acquirement of knowledge through reading and reflection, observation, or experiment ⟨he might have *studied* through the literature to the mind of that century —T.S.Eliot⟩ **b :** to undertake formal study of a subject or course ⟨*studied* at Manual Arts high school —Lillian de Tagle⟩ ⟨*studied* with the faculty of law at the university —*Current Biog.*⟩ ⟨*studied* under him at the university —*Current Biog.*⟩ **2** *dial* **a :** to consider deeply **:** MEDITATE, REFLECT — usu. used with *about* ⟨looking at the oil in the bottle and smelling it and tasting it, and ~*ing* about what it meant —H.H. Martin⟩ **b :** to deliberate something with oneself **:** DEBATE ⟨stood digging a bare big toe into the dirt and *studied* awhile —F.B.Gipson⟩ — usu. used with *on* or *about* ⟨I'm ~*ing* on whether I ought to sell —Jean Stafford⟩ **3 :** to consider something as one's aim **:** ENDEAVOR ⟨I *studied* to appear calm . . . so as to draw him on to say more —W.H.Hudson †1922⟩ ⟨appears to ~ to repress these things in his poetry —David Daiches⟩ ~ *vt* **1 a :** to read (a book or writing) in close detail often with the intent of learning for recall ⟨was set to ~*ing* the Talmud for 15-hour stretches —*Current Biog.*⟩ ⟨stopped and *studied* a big sign in front of a large store —Irving Bacheller⟩ **b :** to learn (as a part) for playing ⟨you could . . . ~ a speech of some dozen or 16 lines —Shak.⟩ ⟨waiting in the wings ~*ing* his part⟩ **2 a :** to apply the mind to the learning or understanding of (an area of knowledge) ⟨learns a good deal by simply ~*ing* human nature⟩ ⟨*studies* the advances in his profession every free moment⟩ **b :** to occupy oneself with the formal study of (a subject, course, or activity) ⟨planning to ~ medicine⟩ ⟨*studies* the violin at the conservatory⟩ ⟨attends night school to ~ typing⟩ **c :** to do special reading about for a specific purpose — usu. used with *up* ⟨thought I knew something . . . because I'd *studied* it up in a book —Calder Willingham⟩ **3 :** to make a plan for : PLOT, DESIGN ⟨he *studies* our overthrow and generally seeks our destruction —Robert Burton⟩ — usu. used with *out* ⟨works hard ~*ing* out a new system⟩ **4 a** : to observe or analyze in detail (a phenomenon, development, or question) usu. within a restricted area with a view to some action : INVESTIGATE ⟨experts ~ tides and ocean currents —H.M. Parshley⟩ ⟨~*ing* the mood of people in different quarters —Evelyn G. Cruickshanks⟩ ⟨~*ing* and attempting to solve the economic problem —*Current Biog.*⟩ **b** : to examine closely to understand or determine something ⟨each still ~*ing* the other with interest —Agnes S. Turnbull⟩ ⟨the brakeman . . . took advantage of each curve to ~ the train —*Monsanto Mag.*⟩ ⟨*studied* the flames as if seeking the answer . . . in their restive pattern —Walter O'Meara⟩ **5** : to employ thought and careful attention in ⟨the epistle . . . was *studied* and recopied and elaborated —Anthony Trollope⟩ **6** : to pay heed to or be solicitous for (a person's feelings or convenience) ⟨needed a home and a wife who would ~ his comfort —Edith Sitwell⟩ **syn** see CONSIDER

[3]study \ˈstədi, -tüdi\ *Scot & dial Eng var of* STITHY

study group *n* : a group of people joining in the study of a particular topic and usu. meeting at scheduled intervals to discuss individual observations, reading, and research

study hall *n* **1** : a large room or hall in a school set aside for students to study and do homework in usu. under the supervision of a teacher or an older student **2** : a period in a student's day scheduled for study and homework usu. in a study hall

study home *n* : a child-care institution; *esp* : one in which disturbed children undergo psychiatric observation and diagnosis

[1]stuff \ˈstəf\ *n* -s [ME *stuff, stuffe,* fr. MF *estoffe* stuff, material, fr. OF, fr. *estoffer* to equip, stock — more at [2]STUFF] **1** : materials, supplies, or equipment used in various human activities: as **a** *obs* : military baggage : IMPEDIMENTA **b** : bullets or shells fired from a gun : PROJECTILES ⟨were throwing broadsides at him . . . and ~ was going past him from both sides and killing —Ira Wolfert⟩ ⟨our own ~ was pouring back on them, and the power of the weapons was impressive —Fred Majdalany⟩ **c** *obs* : the furnishings and chattels of a place or household **d** : PERSONAL PROPERTY, CLOTHING, POSSESSIONS ⟨my ~ is all unpacked —Joseph Dever⟩ **e** : MONEY ⟨he is out for the ~, and when he gets it he salts it away —P.G.Wodehouse⟩ ⟨is a moneyed writer burdened with even more of the ~ through inheritance —J.S.Sandoe⟩ **2** : material to be manufactured, wrought, or used in construction : raw or partially prepared material: as **a** : building materials ⟨got all the ~ ready for building his house⟩ **b** : wood for use in carpentry ⟨well furred inside with clear half-inch pine ~ —Emily Holt⟩ **c** : fibrous pulp fully beaten and ready for the paper machine — called also *stock;* compare HALF STUFF **d** : a finished textile suitable for clothing; *esp* : wool or worsted material **e** : a composition of tallow, fats, and oil used to fill the pores of leather **f** : a mixture of tallow, tar, and turpentine used as a preservative on wooden ships **3** *chiefly Scot & Irish* : GRAIN, PULSE **4 a** : literary or artistic matter, productions, or compositions ⟨some contemporary . . . material, and some ~ on the early history of toleration —H.J.Laski⟩ ⟨most writers can't cut their own ~ —Claire Callahan⟩ — often used disparagingly ⟨seems to be all the same — the old picaresque ~ —Arnold Bennett⟩ **b** : material written for a newspaper or periodical : COPY ⟨turns in good ~ from his beat⟩ **c** : writing, discourse, or ideas of little value : RUBBISH ⟨novels are so full of nonsense and ~ —Jane Austen⟩ ⟨there is so much vulgar, trivial ~ on the air —D.W.Brogan⟩ ⟨mechanized organs of public opinion . . . are feeding us the same old ~ —Norman Woelfel⟩ **5 a** : an unspecified material substance or aggregate of matter ⟨investigating the age of the universe and the creation of the ~ of which it is made —George Gamow⟩ ⟨decided that hydrogen was the primordial ~ of the universe —Waldemar Kaempffert⟩ ⟨volcanic rock is curious ~⟩ **b** : a solid, liquid, or gaseous matter processed or synthesized for various uses: as (1) : a medical preparation : POTION (2) : an alcoholic beverage ⟨that ~'s too strong on an empty stomach —C.S.Barry⟩ (3) : NARCOTICS ⟨mentioned to me that if I needed any weed or ~ to let her know —J.B.Martin⟩ ⟨you've been pushing the ~ —Wenzell Brown⟩ (4) : COMMODITY, MERCHANDISE ⟨brings the ~ in by freight car⟩ ⟨when the ~ didn't move, advertised the lines widely —Susan Strom⟩ (5) : fissionable material ⟨plutonium . . . was the ~ of the early atom bombs —Bertram Mycock⟩ **6 a** : the fundamental material of which something is made or consists : ESSENCE ⟨tendencies that are part of the very ~ of warfare —Tom Wintringham⟩ ⟨the ~ of greatness⟩ ⟨the ~ of tradition⟩ ⟨the ~ of life⟩ **b** : the basic qualities of a person or character : capacity for accomplishment in an activity or mode of existence ⟨exhibits the ~ of manhood⟩ ⟨was not the ~ of which the revolutionary is made —Liam O'Flaherty⟩ ⟨must not expect to find in ordinary men the ~ of martyrs —Walter Lippmann⟩ ⟨she was of sterner ~ now —C.S.Forester⟩ ⟨proves that heroes are not made of pretty ~ —Frederic Morton⟩ **c** : the substance or material forming the basis of a literary work or artistic production ⟨their adventures are real and make the ~ of a stirring novel —H.U.Ribalow⟩ ⟨contained all the ~ of opera and was dramatically well-pointed —Norman Demuth⟩ ⟨slick work, but . . . he doesn't get down to the real ~ —Arnold Bennett⟩ **d** : a body of knowledge or subject matter ⟨philosophical physics . . . describes the ~ as a mathematical probability —W.L.Sullivan⟩ ⟨the procession of presidents and wars in . . . history is dull ~ indeed if presented in a vacuum —W.R.Steckel⟩ ⟨learning about the heavens from Ptolemy and his Arab commentators — real ~ at last —R.W. Southern⟩ ⟨this is primer ~ today to . . . meteorologists —Carey Longmire⟩ **7 a** : a mode or manner of acting or talking : the actions or talk of a person in specific circumstances ⟨rough ~ isn't tolerated —Bill Wolf⟩ ⟨no funny ~ now —Carl Jonas⟩ ⟨disturbing the peace, ~ like that —R.O.Bowen⟩ ⟨imagine a player getting away with that ~ today —Ted Williams⟩ **b** : an activity or branch of knowledge requiring specialized study, practice, or skill ⟨struck us as a lad who knew his ~ — who could handle affairs of state or breeze through a . . . luncheon with equal aplomb —*New Republic*⟩ ⟨with the plane's crew doing its ~ dodging the fireworks —T.B.Bruff⟩ **c** : an action, attitude, or development eliciting approval or commendation ⟨that's the ~, don't give up⟩ **8** : LIVESTOCK ⟨beds down . . . on the outside edge of the herd away from the horned ~ —R.F.Adams⟩ ⟨box stalls are necessary for . . . young ~ —*Producing Farm Livestock*⟩ **9 a** : the spin or rotation imparted to a thrown, rolled, or hit ball to make it curve or change course ⟨no difference how hard you hit the ball or how much ~ you put on it in the way of spin . . . unless you have accuracy —J.D.Budge⟩ **b** : the speed or esp. the variety of pitches or curves of a baseball pitcher ⟨the greatest pitcher of my time . . . had tremendous ~ —Ted Williams⟩ ⟨has a wide assortment of curves, sliders, and slow ~ —Lou Boudreau⟩

[2]stuff \"\ *vb* -ED/-ING/-S [ME *stuffen,* fr. MF *estoffer* to equip, stock, fr. OF, prob. fr. MHG *stopfen* to stop up, stuff, fr. OHG *stopfōn* — more at STOP] *vt* **1** *obs* **a** : to supply (a fortification or commander) with stores, arms, or men : GARRISON **b** : to endow or equip (a person) with provisions, arms, or money **c** : to furnish (a house or place) with chattels, equipment, or accessories : STOCK **2 a** (1) : to fill (a receptacle) to fullness or distention by packing things in : CRAM ⟨had to . . . ~ the jar —Ida Pruitt⟩ — usu. used with *with* ⟨bags ~*ed* with papers —Van Wyck Brooks⟩ ⟨things you have to ~ your pockets with —Richard Joseph⟩ (2) : to insert a bill or communication in (an envelope) for mailing ⟨their fingers stiff from ~*ing* and addressing envelopes —George Sklar⟩ ⟨~*ed* and addressed the invitations —Carl Jonas⟩ **b** : to fill (as one's stomach) to fullness : SURFEIT ⟨got out the coffeepot . . . and before he could say a number she was ~*ing* him —Arthur Miller⟩ ⟨~*ing* ourselves with cake and sandwiches —Alice F. Webb⟩ ⟨beef calves . . . which he ~*s* for months with corn silage —John Bird⟩ ⟨~ a cold and starve a fever⟩ **c** : to prepare (meat or vegetables) for cooking or eating by filling or lining with a seasoned mixture ⟨used to ~ veal with bread crumbs and butter and sage . . . and onion —Margaret A. Barnes⟩ **d** : to fill (as a cushion or ticking) with a soft material or padding ⟨spent the morning ~*ing* the mattresses⟩ ⟨made of leather and ~*ed* with shoddy and cotton waste —*Amer. Guide Series: Conn.*⟩ **e** : to fill out the skin of (an animal or bird) for mounting **f** : to crowd (an interior or place) with people ⟨hopped aboard . . . the already ~*ed* rear of the bus —Eula Long⟩ ⟨the church was ~*ed* full —R.C.Wood⟩ **g** : to fill (as a hole or opening) by packing in material : stop up : PLUG ⟨~*ed* the keyhole to shut out prying eyes —*Amer. Guide Series: Conn.*⟩ ⟨~*s* woodchuck holes with rocks and dirt⟩ ⟨~*ing* the wound with cotton⟩ **h** : to furnish or fill (a house or room) to excess ⟨lived in attic rooms ~*ed* with fantastic objects and furniture —Virginia D. Dawson & Betty D. Wilson⟩ **3 a** : to clutter or fill (a person's mind) — usu. used with *with* ⟨those whose heads are ~*ed* with facts —A.J.P.Taylor⟩ ⟨has a mind ~*ed* with ideas, hungry for argument —Virginia Woolf⟩; often used disparagingly ⟨~*s* the people with lies that gag an honest man —Kenneth Roberts⟩ ⟨~*ed* right up to the ears with his own slogans —David Driscoll⟩ **b** (1) : to crowd or fill (as a work, book, or discourse) — usu. used with *with* ⟨the book is . . . ~*ed* with delectable stories —Mark Van Doren⟩; often used disparagingly ⟨tracts ~*ed* with a sodden morality —V.L.Parrington⟩ ⟨the appearance of a travelogue ~*ed* with melodrama —*Time*⟩ (2) : to expand or fill (a book or work) chiefly to enlarge the bulk or content : PAD — usu. used with *out* ⟨scanty material, ~*ed* out with appreciation and conjecture —T.S.Eliot⟩ ⟨~*ed* out their pages with platitudes —Virginia Woolf⟩ **4** : to congest or block (as the nasal passages) ⟨sounded ~*ed* up . . . had been crying again —J.H.Reese⟩ ⟨his throat got ~*ed* —Liam O'Flaherty⟩ **5 a** : to insert or fit snugly or tightly : TUCK ⟨secret documents ~*ed* under his shirt —Bernard Kalb⟩ — usu. used with *into* ⟨got her ~*ed* into the closet —Robert Murphy⟩ ⟨~ the greenbacks into my wallet —H.A.Overstreet⟩ **b** : to cause to enter or fill : THRUST, PRESS — usu. used with *in* or *into* ⟨~*ed* it deep down in his mind —Richard Llewellyn⟩ ⟨knowledge . . . can never be knowledge that is ~*ed* in —H.A.Overstreet⟩ ⟨have ~*ed* too many of the facts . . . into my intellectuals —L.P.Smith⟩ ⟨any set mold into which the material has to be ~*ed* —Carlos Lynes⟩ ⟨~*ing* . . . any preoccupation with her concerns out of sight —Helen Howe⟩ **6** : to impregnate (leather) for softening and preserving — usu. used with *with* ⟨the leather goods are ~*ed* with a mixture of hot oil and tallow, or fat liquored —*New Zealand Jour. of Agric.*⟩ **7** : to fill (a ballot box) with fraudulent votes ⟨another type of corrupt practice is ~*ing* the ballot boxes —D.D.McKean⟩ ~ *vi* : to eat gluttonously : GORGE ⟨had finished ~*ing* in the dining room —H.A. Chippendale⟩ **syn** see PACK

[3]stuff *vt* [ME *stuffen,* fr. MF *estouffer*] *obs* : STIFLE, SUFFOCATE

stuff chest *n* : CHEST 1e

stuffed shirt *n* : a smug conceited usu. pompous person with an inflexibly conservative or reactionary attitude ⟨nothing of the *stuffed shirt* in him . . . never put on airs —W.S.Maugham⟩ ⟨at the heart of the legends . . . discovers a *stuffed shirt,* a faker, or a moral monster —DeLancey Ferguson⟩ ⟨a *stuffed shirt* with a starched mind⟩

stuff·er \ˈstəfə(r)\ *n* -s **1** : one that stuffs: as **a** (1) a worker who stuffs hides or skins with grease by hand or by machine (2) : a worker who stuffs articles (as sausage casings, dolls, cushions) **b** (1) : a worker who puts articles (as ads, bills, powder, folded garments) into envelopes or similar containers (2) : a clerk who sorts invoices or statements and inserts them in the proper ledgers for use by bookkeepers and posting clerks **2 a** : an enclosure (as a leaflet or blotter) inserted in an envelope in addition to a bill, statement, or notice usu. for advertising purposes **b** : a piece of cardboard or pieces of paper placed in an envelope that is mailed for a philatelic purpose **3** : a series of extra threads or yarn running lengthwise in a fabric to add weight and bulk and to form a backing esp. for carpets

stuff gown *n* **1** : a gown of stuff; *esp* : one that in England forms the distinctive garb of a junior barrister — compare SILK GOWN **2** : a junior barrister

stuff·i·ly \ˈstəfəlē, -li\ *adv* : in a stuffy manner

stuff·i·ness \-fēnəs, -fin-\ *n* -ES : the quality or state of being stuffy

stuff·ing \ˈstəfiŋ, -fēŋ\ *n* -s **1** : the act or process of one that stuffs **2** : something that stuffs or fills: as **a** : a filling used to stuff upholstered furniture, cushions, bedding, or similar items **b** : a seasoned mixture used to stuff meat, vegetables, or eggs; *esp* : a composition (as for poultry) of bread, onion, celery, and condiments **c** : material of slight value added merely to fill space : PADDING ⟨saw that the author of it would need to . . . reject ~ and divagation —F.A.Swinnerton⟩ **d** : material used as stuffers ⟨printing classes can turn out excellent home-contact material, letter ~ —L.W.Kindred⟩ **3** : INNARDS ⟨would knock the ~ out of an antagonist upon a point of dogma —O.W.Holmes †1935⟩

stuffing box *n* : a device that is designed to prevent leakage along a piston rod, propeller shaft, or other moving part passing through a hole in a cylinder or other vessel containing steam, water, or oil and that consists of a box or chamber made by enlarging the hole and a gland to compress the contained packing

stuffing nut *n* : a nut used to tighten or adjust a stuffing box

stuff·less \ˈ=ləs\ *adj* : lacking stuff or substance ⟨a ~ sound —F. Tennyson Jesse⟩ ⟨a ~ ghost —Edna S. V. Millay⟩

stuff·over \ˈstə,fōvə(r)\ *also* **stuffed-over** \ˈstəf,tō-\ *adj* [*stuffover* alter. of *stuffed-over,* fr. *stuffed* (past part. of [2]*stuff*) + *over,* adv.] *Brit* : OVERSTUFFED

stuffs *pl of* STUFF, *pres 3d sing of* STUFF

stuffy \ˈstəfē, -fi\ *adj* -ER/-EST **1** *obs* : containing stuff or substance : SUBSTANTIAL **2** : SULLEN, ILL-HUMORED ⟨wrong feeding may have much to do with . . . ~, ill-natured, contractive individuals —H.A.Overstreet⟩ **3 a** : lacking oxygen : oppressive to the breathing : STALE, CLOSE ⟨it was hot and ~, and the air was gray with smoke —W.S.Maugham⟩ ⟨popping into the ~ little office —Vicki Baum⟩ **b** : stuffed or choked up ⟨the ~ feeling in the head —H.G.Armstrong⟩ **4** : lacking in vitality or interest : DULL, STODGY ⟨a woodenly earnest, relentlessly ~ sort of fellow . . . not very strong on humor —Alan Devoe⟩ ⟨the press conference . . . was far from solemn and ~ —Stafford Derby⟩ **5** : provincial in outlook : narrowly inflexible in standards of conduct : SELF-RIGHTEOUS ⟨am abiding by the rather involved, ~ code of ethics —R.L. Riggs⟩ ⟨resistance to ~ taboos and pieties —N.E.Nelson⟩ ⟨against the orders of a rather ~ police commissioner —S.H. Adams⟩

stug·gy \ˈstəgi, -tùgi\ *adj* [origin unknown] *dial* : THICKSET, STOCKY, STURDY

stuiver *var of* STIVER

stull \ˈstəl\ *n* -s [perh. modif. of G *stollen* post, support, fr. OHG *stollo* — more at STOLLEN] **1** : a round timber used to support the sides or back of a mine **2 a** : one of a series of props wedged between the walls of a stope to hold up a platform for supporting miners, ore, or waste or to protect miners from falling stones **b** : a platform held up by stulls

stull·er \-lə(r)\ *n* -s : one that places or works at stulls

stulm \ˈstəlm\ *n* -s [perh. modif. of G *stollen* adit, post, support] : an approximately horizontal passageway into a mine : ADIT

stul·ti·fi·ca·tion \,stəltəfəˈkāshən\ *n* -s [fr. *stultify,* after such pairs as E *fortify: fortification*] : the act or process of stultifying : the state of being stultified

stul·ti·fy \ˈ==,fī\ *vt* -ED/-ING/-ES [LL *stultificare* to make foolish, fr. L *stultus* foolish + *-ficare* -fy — more at STALL] **1** : to allege or prove (oneself or another) to be of unsound mind so that the performance of some act may be avoided **2 a** : to cause to appear or be stupid, foolish, or absurdly illogical ⟨the dullards become more *stultified* than ever —C.H.Grandgent⟩ ⟨incidents will have occurred tending to ~ conclusions —James Stevenson-Hamilton⟩ ⟨how like the man to ~ himself, to prove all his own theories wrong —Clemence Dane⟩ ⟨the court did not ~ itself by claiming that its ruling fulfilled any logical, legal progression toward racial equality —C.S.Dowdey⟩ **b** : to impair, invalidate, or reduce to futility or uselessness esp. through debasing or repressive influences : FRUSTRATE, NULLIFY ⟨the psychiatrist *stultifies* his role if he allows such misunderstandings to develop —C.P.Printzlien⟩ ⟨demand for fresh leadership . . . is running smack into the ~*ing* seniority system —T.R.Ybarra⟩ ⟨the slavish traditionalism that *stultifies* most contemporary ecclesiastical art —*Time*⟩ ⟨centralization . . . *stultifies* their local initiative —Hugh McDiarmid⟩ ⟨*stultified* by the oppressive atmosphere of her earlier life —Martin Levin⟩

stul·til·o·quence \,stəlˈtiləkwən(t)s\ *n* -s [L *stultiloquentia,* fr. *stultus* foolish + *loquent-, loquens* (pres. part. of *loqui* to speak) + *-ia* -y] : senseless or silly talk : BABBLE — **stul·til·o·quent** \(ˈ)=ˈ==kwənt\ *or* **stul·til·o·quen·tial** \,=,==ˈkwenchəl\ *adj*

stul·til·o·quy \-kwē\ *n* -ES [L *stultiloquium,* fr. *stultus* foolish + *-loquium* (fr. *loqui* to speak)] : STULTILOQUENCE

[1]stum \ˈstəm\ *vt* **stummed; stummed; stumming; stums** [D *stommen,* fr. *stom,* n.] *archaic* : to renew (wine) by mixing with must and reviving fermentation

[2]stum \"\ *n* -s [D *stom* (approximate trans. of F *muet* in *vin muet* stum), fr. *stom,* adj., mute, fr. MD; akin to OFris *stumm* mute, OHG *stum* mute, OE *stamerian* to stammer] : unfermented or partly fermented grape juice; *esp* : must in which fermentation has been artificially arrested

[1]stum·ble \ˈstəmbəl\ *vb* **stumbled; stumbled; stumbling** \-b(ə)liŋ\ **stumbles** [ME *stumblen, stomblen,* prob. of Scand origin; akin to Norw dial. *stumle* to stumble, Sw dial. *stumla;* akin to OE *stamerian* to stammer — more at STAMMER] *vi* **1 a** : to fall into sin, error, or waywardness : ERR ⟨though we *stumbled* and we strayed, we were led by evil counsellors —Rudyard Kipling⟩ ⟨man is *stumbling* blindly through a spiritual darkness —O.N.Bradley⟩ **b** : to falter through lack of knowledge or experience : BLUNDER ⟨people *stumbling* and learning and going forward to meet the realities of life and death —Marjorie Vetter⟩ ⟨this thought staggers, and reels and ~*s* —Martin Gardner⟩ ⟨how many people in the final survey will ~ over the same obstacle —S.L.Payne⟩ ⟨the problem that . . . other commanders had *stumbled* against —Tom Wintringham⟩ **c** : to come to a block or obstacle to belief ⟨~ at the doctrine of the elect⟩ : SCRUPLE, DEMUR **d** : to make a slip in speaking : MISPRONOUNCE, STAMMER ⟨voices that ~ and trip over proper names —F.L.Mott⟩ ⟨tongue *stumbled* at the start —T.B.Costain⟩ **2** : to lose one's footing in walking or running so as to stagger or fall : TRIP ⟨*stumbled,* laughed, lay there a moment . . . then got up —O.E. Rölvaag⟩ ⟨*stumbled* and then, recovering herself, broke into a trot —Ellen Glasgow⟩ ⟨grumbled whenever we *stumbled* in a shell hole —J.P.O'Neill⟩ **3 a** : to walk or move in an unsteady or clumsy manner : STAGGER ⟨strained and *stumbled* in their exertions like fat sheep —Stephen Crane⟩ ⟨*stumbled* along the broken path —B.L.K.Henderson⟩ ⟨*stumbled* through the dark hall —Erskine Caldwell⟩ **b** : to proceed, speak, or act in a hesitant or faltering manner ⟨*stumbled* haphazardly through the 5th and 6th forms —Margaret A. Barnes⟩ ⟨*stumbled* through the first prayer —Maeve Brennan⟩ ⟨its plot creaks and ~*s* awkwardly —Orville Prescott⟩ ⟨the bassoon ~*s* along precariously —P.H.Lang⟩ **4 a** : to come or happen unexpectedly — usu. used with *on* or *upon* ⟨floundering around in the woods . . . *stumbled on* a blockhouse —P.W. Thompson⟩ ⟨cannot adventure very long with an electron microscope . . . without *stumbling* upon something new —L.A. White⟩ ⟨was so certain he had *stumbled* on the truth —T.B. Costain⟩ ⟨is looking for one thing and ~*s* on something much bigger —W.P.Webb⟩ **b** : to fall or move carelessly or inadvertently — usu. used with *into* ⟨was not long before he *stumbled* into a new folly —H.E.Scudder⟩ ⟨traveler who ~*s* into this world of passionate violence —Mark Schorer⟩ ⟨*stumbled* into a job —Frank O'Leary⟩ ⟨*stumbled* into immortality —David Dempsey⟩ ~ *vt* **1** : to cause (a person or thing) to stumble : TRIP ⟨*stumbled* my shin against a bedpost to give pain to my rage —Herbert Gold⟩ **2** : to cause to hesitate : CONFOUND, PERPLEX ⟨the problem ~*s* him⟩

[2]stumble \"\ *n* -s **1** : a trip in walking or running : TUMBLE ⟨taking a bad ~⟩ **2** : an inadvertent error : SLIP, BLUNDER ⟨conversation . . . is a mass of ~*s,* clumsy returns, and points missed —J.M.Barzun⟩ ⟨a republic . . . must needs make many ~*s* by the way —Katharine L. Bates⟩

stumblebum \ˈ==,=\ *n* **1** : a punch-drunk, clumsy, or inept boxer ⟨was just a strawman built up craftily with knockouts over ~*s* —*Ring*⟩ **2** : a clumsy, inept, or blundering person ⟨has filled most of his . . . staff with third-raters and ~*s* —E.K.Lindley⟩

stumbling block *n* **1** : a bar or hindrance to righteous living **2** : an impediment to belief or understanding : PERPLEXITY ⟨most difficult of statistical measurement and thus . . . the greatest *stumbling block* to the market analyst —S.B.Hunt⟩ **3** : an obstacle in the way of a planned or progressive development or act ⟨*stumbling blocks* that the industry must be prepared to avoid —J.N.Robertson⟩

stum·bling·ly *adv* : in a stumbling manner ⟨as long as he could ~ follow their thoughts —Susan Ertz⟩

stum·bly \ˈstəmb(ə)lē, -li\ *adj* -ER/-EST **1** : given to stumbling **2** : apt to cause one to stumble ⟨weaved along ~ forest paths —*Newsweek*⟩

stu·mer *also* **stu·mour** \ˈst(y)ümə(r)\ *n* -s [origin unknown] **1** *Brit* : FRAUD, SHAM; *esp* : a bad or forged check **2** *Brit* : FAILURE, DUD, WASHOUT; *esp* : a horse that loses a race usu. through fixing **3** *Brit* : MISTAKE, BONER

stum·mel \ˈs(h)tüməl\ *n* -s [G, lit., stump, butt, fr. OHG *stumbal* stump, piece cut off; akin to OE *stæf* staff — more at STAFF] : the bowl and shank of a tobacco pipe

[1]stump \ˈstəmp\ *n* -s [ME *stumpe, stompe;* akin to MD *stompe, stomp* stump, OHG *stumpf* stub, stump, *stomp* blunt, OHG *stumpf* stub, stump, *stumpf* mutilated, OE *stempan* to stamp — more at STAMP] **1 a** : the basal portion of a limb or other part of the body remaining after the rest of it is removed ⟨the ~ of his severed hand —Hamilton Basso⟩ ⟨closure of the duodenal ~ —F.W.Bancroft⟩ **b** : a rudimentary or vestigial growth or part of an organism ⟨the cervical ~⟩ ⟨motor nerve ~⟩ **2 a** : the part of a tree or plant remaining in the earth after the stem or trunk is cut off : STUB — compare SNAG **b** : a walnut stub including the underground portion that is used in making veneers **c** : the base of a tree **d** : the stalk of a plant after the leaves have been removed ⟨cabbage ~*s*⟩ **3 a** : LEG — usu. used in pl. ⟨stir your ~*s,* step lively⟩ **b** : an artificial leg ⟨wore . . . a heavy wooden ~, which made a wooden sound as he walked —Osbert Sitwell⟩ **4 a** : the remaining part of something that has been worn down or used up : STUB ⟨pencil ~⟩ ⟨cigarette ~⟩ **b** : the portion of a worn or broken tooth remaining in the gum ⟨having the ~*s* extracted⟩ **c** : a mountain peak reduced from a former height or size by some natural force ⟨~*s* of much higher mountains of an earlier day —W.W.Atwood †1949⟩ **d** : the stub of a ship's mast ⟨the hulks or prison ships were old vessels reduced to their ~*s*⟩ **5 a stumps** *pl* : hair cut down or growing close to the skin : STUBBLE **b** : PINFEATHER **6 a** : a short pillar used as a barrier or marker : POST **b** : a small pillar at the entrance to a room in a mine **7 a** : one of the three pointed rods used in cricket that are stuck in the ground and topped with two bails to form a wicket **b** [short for *stumper*] : WICKETKEEPER **8 a** *archaic* : a tree stump used as a platform esp. by a political speaker **b** : a place or occasion for political public speaking ⟨supported it actively on the ~ and was elected —J.C.Yonge⟩ **9 a** : a small piece or projection in a lock for the attachment of another part or the reception of a screw or a rivet **b** : FENCE 6 **10** : a miniature anvil in a watchmaker's staking set — **go on the stump** *or* **take the stump** : to go before the public or about the country as a political speaker or supporter of a cause ⟨*went on the stump* in his home state —S.H.Adams⟩ ⟨*took the stump* in a state campaign —*Springfield (Mass.) Republican*⟩ — **up a stump** *slang* : blocked in one's efforts : NONPLUSSED, PERPLEXED ⟨problems that sometimes got me *up a stump* —O.W.Holmes †1935⟩

[2]stump \"\ *adj* : shaped like or suggesting a stump ⟨a ~ arm⟩

[3]stump \"\ *vb* -ED/-ING/-S *vt* **1** : to cut off a part of : reduce to a stump : TRIM ⟨~*ing* the plants⟩ **2** : to dismiss (a cricket batsman who is out of his ground in attempting to play a bowled ball) by breaking the wicket with the ball — sometimes used with *out;* abbr. *st* **3 a** : to challenge to do something difficult or daring **b** : to block the progress or efforts of : PERPLEX, CONFOUND ⟨a mystery that still ~*s* everyone —*New Yorker*⟩ ⟨to become a universal genius and ~ the experts —*Nation's Business*⟩ ⟨a problem that had ~*ed* the mind of man for ages —M.R.Cohen⟩ **4 a** : to dig out by the roots ⟨~*ed* all the trees on the place⟩ **b** : to take or burn stumps out of (land) ⟨land . . . which we hoped to ~ and plow ready for sowing —Alice F. Webb⟩ **5** *chiefly Brit* **a :** to pay out or come across with (money) — usu. used with *up* ⟨have been very decent and ~*ed* up half a quid each —Dorothy Sayers⟩ **b :** to cause (a person) to become penniless ⟨coming home from the races ~*ed*⟩ **6 :** to travel over (a region) making political speeches or supporting a cause ⟨~*ed* the country by air, train, and automobile caravans —T.L.Stokes⟩ ⟨was ~*ing* the country for the league —Dixon Wecter⟩ **7 a :** to walk over heavily or clumsily ⟨~*ing* the deck by the hour⟩ ⟨rising laboriously to the tips of my . . . shoes, I ~*ed* the width of the bed and back again —Agnes deMille⟩ **b :** to strike (as the toe) against something : STUB ⟨those stupid roads . . . where you ~*ed* your toe all the time —Samuel Selvon⟩ ~ *vi* **1 :** to walk heavily or noisily : STUMBLE ⟨spat his contempt and ~*ed* away —Roderick Finlayson⟩ ⟨~*ed* through the puddles —Mollie Panter-Downes⟩ ⟨~*ing* along eagerly on his iron support —T.B.Costain⟩ **2** *chiefly Brit* **:** to pay over money — usu. used with *up* ⟨if this was a bank, they'd have to ~ up —Richard Llewellyn⟩ **3 :** to go about making political speeches or supporting a cause ⟨~*ed* harder than ever, covering every county in the state —*Time*⟩ — often used with *for* ⟨~*ing* for these devices and their morale-building . . . virtues —David Riesman⟩

4stump \"\ *n* -S **:** DARE, CHALLENGE

5stump \" *or* **stomp** \'stämp\ *n* -S [F or Flem; F *estompe*, fr. Flem *stump, stomp*, lit., stub, fr. MD *stompe, stomp* — more at ¹STUMP] **:** a short thick roll of leather or paper cut to a point or any similar implement used to rub down the lines of a crayon or pencil drawing in shading it or for shading drawings by producing tints and gradations from crayon in powder

6stump \'stəmp\ *vt* -ED/-ING/-S **:** to tone or treat (a crayon drawing) with a stump

stump·age \-pij, -pēj\ *n* -S **1 :** the value of or price paid for timber as it stands uncut in the woods **2 :** uncut marketable timber ⟨growing scarcity of accessible cedar ~ —*Jour. of Forestry*⟩

stump·er \'stəmpə(r)\ *n* -S **:** one that stumps: as **a :** one that removes tree stumps **b :** WICKETKEEPER **c :** a perplexing or difficult question **:** POSER ⟨a real question . . . a ~ —Benjamin DeMott⟩ **d :** STUMP SPEAKER ⟨the most indefatigable campaigner and best . . . ~ —Hodding Carter⟩ **e :** one that adjusts the mandrel on a tube-welding machine **f :** an operator of a felting machine

stumping *n* -S **:** a method of cultivating various plants (as blueberry bushes) by cutting mature bushes to the ground and covering the stubs with a mixture (as peat and sand) that is rich in humus

stump·ish \'stəmpish, -pēsh\ *adj* **:** of, relating to, or suggesting a stump ⟨called him a ~ man —H.S.Canby⟩

stump–jumper \'=,==\ *n* **1** *slang* **:** STUMP SPEAKER **2** *slang* **:** a person from a backwoods area

stump–jump plow \'=,=-\ *also* **stump–jumper** \'=,==\ *n* **:** a plow so constructed as to pass over the stumps or roots in newly cleared land

stumpknocker \'=,==\ *n* **:** a small brown-speckled sunfish (*Lepomis punctatus*) of the southeastern U.S. resembling the bluegill and esteemed as a panfish

stumpland \'=,=\ *n* **:** land full of the stumps of trees ⟨the best forests had been reduced to great stretches of ~ —*Amer. Guide Series: Minn.*⟩

stump·less \'=‚ləs\ *adj* **:** cleared of stumps

stump mast *n* **1 :** a lower mast with no topmast rigged **2 :** a broken mast

stumpnose \'=,=\ *n* [trans. of Afrik *stompneus*] *Africa* **:** any of several sea breams: as **a :** SILVER BREAM a; *esp* **:** WHITE STUMPNOSE **b :** RED STUMPNOSE

stump rot *n* **1 :** a disease of the tea bush in which the main central stem is rotted by a tooth fungus (*Irpex destruens*) **2 :** BUTT ROT

stumps *pl of* STUMP, *pres 3d sing of* STUMP

stump sock *n* **:** a special sock worn over an amputation stump with various types of prostheses

stump speaker *n* **:** one that does stump speaking

stump speaking *n* **:** speaking addressed to the general public during a political campaign or in support of a cause ⟨avoided public office and *stump speaking* but . . . engaged actively in party management —L.C.Hatch⟩

stump speech *n* **:** a speech made in the course of stump speaking

stump spud *n* **:** SPUD 2b

stumpsucker \'=,=\ *n* [¹*stump* + *sucker*] **:** CRIBBER b

stump sucker *n* [¹*stump* + *sucker* (shoot)] **:** a shoot growing from a stump

stump–tail \'=,=\ *or* **stump–tailed lizard** \'=¦=-\ *n* **:** an Australian scincoid lizard (*Trachysaurus rugosus*) having a short thick tail resembling its head in form

stump–tailed macaque *or* **stump–tailed monkey** *n* **:** a dark reddish brown pink-faced short-tailed macaque (*Macaca speciosa*) found in eastern Asia from Tibet to Indochina and Malaysia

stump topmast *n* **:** a topmast with no topgallant mast rigged

stump tracery *n* **:** tracery in late German Gothic architecture in which the molded bar seems to pass through itself in its convolutions and is then cut off short so that a section of the molding is seen at the end of each similar stump

stump tree *n* **:** KENTUCKY COFFEE TREE

stumpwood \'=,=\ *n* **1 :** wood from the base of a tree **2 :** STUMP 2b

stump work *n* **:** an elaborate colored embroidery with intricate padded designs and scenes in high relief esp. popular in 17th century England

1stumpy \'stəmpē, -pi\ *adj* -ER/-EST [¹*stump* + *-y*] **1 :** full of short hard stalks or stubble ⟨walking through the ~ grass⟩ **2 a :** short and thick like a stump ⟨his ~ old umbrella —G.K.Chesterton⟩ ⟨bunches of ~ chimneys —Nigel Dennis⟩ ⟨a squat red smokestack between two ~ masts —George Santayana⟩ ⟨a ~ building⟩ **b :** having a short thick build **:** STUBBY ⟨is a block of a woman, thick and ~ and wide —Claudia Cassidy⟩ ⟨~ ungainly figure —R.H.Sampson⟩ **3 :** full of or abounding in stumps ⟨a hand-to-mouth existence on wheat and corn grown in ~ clearings —*Appalachia*⟩

2stumpy \"\ *n* -ES **1 :** one that is stumpy or has a stump **2 :** a pole-masted Thames barge **3** *Brit* **:** MONEY, CASH

stums *pres 3d sing of* STUM, *pl of* STUM

1stun \'stən\ *vt* **stunned; stunned; stunning; stuns** [ME *stonen, stunen*, modif. of OF *estoner* — more at ASTONY] **1 a :** to cause to lose consciousness (as by a blow or concussion) ⟨gone about like a man half *stunned* —Rose Macaulay⟩ ⟨could ~ a rabbit or a squirrel with a stone —Helen Eustis⟩ **b :** to bewilder or daze with noise, clamor, or din **:** BENUMB ⟨a deafening crash *stunning* the ear drums —Fred Majdalany⟩ ⟨*stunned* into speechlessness by the abruptness and violence of the assault —W.A.Swanberg⟩ ⟨had been *stunned* by the terrific . . . bombardment —P.W.Thompson⟩ **2 a :** to shock or paralyze with strong emotional impression **:** STUPEFY ⟨still too *stunned* and dazed by the suddenness with which events had happened —Samuel Butler †1902⟩ ⟨*stunned* and reeling under her invective —D.G.Gerahty⟩ ⟨almost *stunned* by the surprise —A.W.Long⟩ **b** (1) **:** to overcome with astonishment or disbelief **:** CONFOUND, PERPLEX ⟨preparing a statement to ~ the company when we got the floor —Stuart Chase⟩ ⟨*stunned* me the other day by telling me she had attended a bullfight —G.S.Weight⟩ (2) **:** to overcome with pleasure or beauty ⟨the natural beauty of the desert ~*s* the visitor⟩ **3 a :** to bruise (as building stone) so as to cause spalls in the surface **b :** to scratch roughly (as by coarse sand under the saw in the kerf) **syn** see DAZE

2stun \"\ *n* -S **1 :** the effect of something that stuns **:** SHOCK ⟨the ~ of the blow . . . did not even dent his massive skull —James Jones⟩ ⟨bucklings and crashes and then the inside ~ of an explosion —Saul Bellow⟩ **2 :** one of the various strokes of the cue in snooker

stun·dism \'s(h)tün,dizəm\ *n* -S *usu cap* [Russ *shtundizm*, fr. *shtunda* + *-izm* -ism] **:** the religious movement of the Stundists or their principles and practices

stun·dist \-dəst\ *n* -S *usu cap* [Russ *shtundist*, fr. *shtunda* Stundism, body of Stundists (fr. G *stunde* lesson, hour, fr. OHG *stunta* point in time, hour) + *-ist*; fr. their meetings for Bible study or prayer — more at STOUND] **:** one of a Russian denomination of Protestants originating about 1860 under German influence and emphasizing evangelical piety

stun·do–baptist \'s(h)tün(,)dō+\ *n, usu cap S&B* [*stundist* + *-o-* + *baptist*] **:** an adherent of a Russian religious movement originating in the 19th century with the union of various Stundists and Russian Baptists

stung [ME *stungen* (past pl. & past part.), fr. OE *stungon* (past pl.), gestungen (past part.)] *past of* STING

stunk [ME *stunken* (past pl. & past part.), fr. OE *stuncon* (past pl.), *stuncen* (past part.)] *past of* STINK

stun·kard \'stəŋkərd\ *adj* [origin unknown] *Scot* **:** STUBBORN, SULLEN

stunned *adj* **1 :** affected by stunning **2 :** caused by or as if by stunning ⟨the hurt look and the ~ silence —Robert Payne⟩ ⟨a ~ sensation held her emotions imprisoned —Ellen Glasgow⟩ ⟨for a ~ moment she lay, wondering —Dorothy Sayers⟩

stun·ner \'stənə(r)\ *n* -S **:** one that stuns: as **a :** something that amazes or astounds; *esp* **:** an unexpected event or development ⟨the ~ was what happened . . . on Saturday —G.F.T.Ryall⟩ **b :** a person or thing of unusual qualities or attractiveness ⟨the flashiest kind of girls — genuine ~*s* —R.L.Taylor⟩ ⟨would make a ~ of a table decoration —*New Yorker*⟩

stunner hitch *n* **:** a double Blackwall hitch

stun·ning \'stəniŋ, -nēŋ\ *adj* **1 a :** causing or capable of causing a state of bewilderment, shock, or insensibility ⟨its black powder blew forth a ~ detonation and volume of smoke —S.E.White⟩ ⟨with one ~ blow, laid the poor fellow senseless on the floor —R.L.Stevenson⟩ **b :** causing a high degree of surprise, astonishment, or consternation ⟨the sharecroppers' strike . . . came as a ~ protest against landlords —V.P.Hass⟩ ⟨no more ~ tax bills —J.H.Reese⟩ ⟨~ defeat⟩ ⟨~ collapse⟩ ⟨~ announcement⟩ **2 a :** of excellent quality or effect **:** SPLENDID, FIRST-RATE ⟨the book is a ~ piece of workmanship —*Current Biog.*⟩ ⟨the product of one of the most ~ talents today —Ann F. Wolfe⟩ **b :** emotionally impressive **:** ASTOUNDING, SENSATIONAL ⟨a breathtaking and . . . ~ midair extravaganza —*Monsanto Mag.*⟩ ⟨contributed ~ decorations for the adornment of sacred buildings —Edgar Levy⟩ ⟨a ~ performance⟩ ⟨a ~ recording⟩ **c :** extremely attractive **:** HANDSOME, GOOD-LOOKING ⟨was quite ~ . . . had a beautiful high-bosomed figure —Helen B. Woodward⟩ ⟨huge areas of glass, ~ colors, unusual new fabrics —*Newsweek*⟩ ⟨many ~ photographs of Canada's backwoods wilderness —William Murray⟩

stun·ning·ly *adv* **:** in a stunning manner **:** with a stunning effect ⟨sensitively directed and ~ photographed —Arthur Knight⟩ ⟨printed up two ~ handsome brochures —R.H. Rovere⟩

stun·poll \'stən,pōl\ *n* [irreg. fr. ¹*stone* + *poll*] *dial Eng* **:** a stupid person **:** DUNCE

stuns *pres 3d sing of* STUN, *pl of* STUN

stun·sail *or* **stun·s'l** \'stən(t)səl\ *n* [by contr.] **:** STUDDING SAIL

1stunt \'stənt, *dial* " *or* -tùnt\ *adj* [prob. of Scand origin; akin to ON *stuttr* short, scant — more at STINT] **1** *chiefly dial* **:** STUBBORN, ANGRY **2** *chiefly dial* **:** STUNTED, UNDERSIZED, CURTAILED, BLUNT **3** *chiefly dial* **:** ABRUPT

2stunt \"\ *vb* -ED/-ING/-S *vt* **:** to hinder the normal growth, development, or progress of **:** DWARF, CHECK ⟨covered largely with ~*ed* pine woods —*Amer. Guide Series: N.J.*⟩ ⟨heifers will be ~*ed* and ruined, as they will calve at 18 months —*Farmer's Weekly* (*So. Africa*)⟩ ⟨physical and mental development became ~*ed* during . . . childhood —Dorothy Gardner⟩ ⟨superabundance of mechanical diversions ~*ed* men's souls —Bruce Marshall⟩ ~ *vi, archaic* **:** to become arrested in growth or development ⟨undernourished plants will ~⟩

3stunt \"\ *n* -S [²*stunt*] **1 :** a check in growth **2 :** a plant or animal that has been checked in growth; *esp* **:** a dwarfed plant **3 :** a disease of plants in which reduction in size is a marked symptom: as **a :** a virus disease of chrysanthemum characterized by smaller plants and leaves, smaller and often much earlier flowers, and bleaching of flower color esp. of the red and bronze varieties **b :** a similar virus disease of dahlia **c :** a disease of lettuce caused by a fungus of the genus *Pythium*

4stunt *vb* [prob. alter. of ³*stump*] *Scot* **:** STAMP

5stunt \"\ *n* -S [prob. alter. of ⁴*stump*] **1 a :** a feat or performance displaying notable strength or skill **:** TRICK ⟨a moored float with diving board and tower permits aquatic ~*s* —*Amer. Guide Series: Maine*⟩ ⟨standing with one foot on the seat, sitting on the handlebars, and similar ~*s* —W.L. Gresham⟩ ⟨one of his ~*s* . . . was to fly between two trees where the opening was narrower than his wingspread —*Amer. Guide Series: Calif.*⟩ **b :** a book or work marked chiefly by the display or exercise of skill or ingenuity **:** TOUR DE FORCE ⟨in a way this book is a ~, for the portraits are actually medallion heads —*New Yorker*⟩ ⟨the kind of literary ~ one remembers much more respectfully from a youthful reading than from a mature rereading —John Mason Brown⟩ ⟨too trickily written . . . too discontinuous in its drama to be more than a serious ~ —*Time*⟩ **2 :** an unusual feat or act performed or undertaken chiefly to gain attention or publicity ⟨in a money-raising ~ for the sports fund, he was fined a penny for every inch of waistline —Keith Ellis⟩ ⟨won the trip in a radio program advertising ~ —W.H.Davenport⟩ ⟨looked upon filibustering as a political ~ —Lindsay Rogers⟩

6stunt \"\ *vb* -ED/-ING/-S *vi* **1 a :** to perform stunts ⟨~*ed* without nets or any safety devices —Saul Bellow⟩ ⟨lugged a unicycle up the trail and ~*ed* on the summit —Andrew Hamilton & Chandler Harris⟩ **b :** to do stunts with an airplane ⟨its pilot was ~*ing* and . . . took a nose dive —Jean Stafford⟩ **2 :** to do unusual or startling things to attract attention or gain publicity ⟨sentimentalists, political agitators . . . and ~*ing* newspapers —A.A.Calwell⟩ ~ *vt* **:** to do stunts with (an airplane)

stunt·ed·ness *n* -ES **:** the quality or state of being stunted

stunt man *n* **:** one who professionally doubles for an actor in the performance of dangerous stunts

stunty \'stəntē, -ti\ *adj* -ER/-EST **:** characterized by stunts **:** given to performing stunts **:** FLASHY ⟨his advertising was flamboyant, ~, tricky —Don Wharton⟩ ⟨~ flying⟩

stu·pa \'st(y)üpə\ *n* -S [Skt *stūpa*] **:** a hemispherical or cylindrical mound or tower artificially constructed of earth, brick, or stone, surmounted by a spire or umbrella, and containing a relic chamber; *esp* **:** a Buddhist mound forming a memorial shrine of the Buddha — compare CHAITYA, DAGOBA

1stupe \'st(y)üp\ *n* -S [ME *stupe, stuppe*, fr. L *stupa, stuppa* coarse part of flax, tow, fr. Gk *styppē*; perh. akin to Gk *styphein* to contract, be astringent, Skt *stukā* tuft of hair] **:** a cloth wrung out of hot water for external application sometimes with an added medicament as an irritant to stimulate local circulation ⟨a turpentine ~⟩

2stupe \"\ *vt* -ED/-ING/-S **:** to foment (a part of the body) with a stupe

3stupe \"\ *n* -S [short for ²*stupid*] *slang* **:** a stupid person **:** FOOL

1stu·pe·fa·cient \¦st(y)üpə¦fāshənt\ *adj* [L *stupefacient-, stupefaciens*, pres. part. of *stupefacere* to stupefy] **:** bringing about a stupor **:** STUPEFYING

2stupefacient \"\ *n* -S **:** something promoting stupefaction **:** NARCOTIC

stu·pe·fac·tion \,==¦fakshən\ *n* -S [NL *stupefaction-, stupefactio*, fr. L *stupefactus* (past part. of *stupefacere*) + *-ion-, -io* -ion] **:** the quality or state of being stupefied

stu·pe·fac·tive \¦==¦faktiv\ *adj* [ML *stupefactivus*, fr. L *stupefactus* (past part. of *stupefacere*) + *-ivus* -ive] *archaic* **:** STUPEFACIENT

stu·pe·fi·er \'==,fī(ə)r, -īə\ *n* -S **:** one that stupefies

stu·pe·fy \'st(y)üpə,fī\ *vb* -ED/-ING/-ES [MF *stupefier*, modif. (influenced by MF *-fier* -fy) of L *stupefacere*, fr. *stupēre* to be benumbed, be astonished, be stupefied + *facere* to make — more at DO] *vt* **1 a :** to make physically stupid, dull, or insensible **:** BENUMB ⟨concoctions of hemp and mandragora . . . to ~ the sensibilities of individuals who must undergo pain —*Science*⟩ ⟨people warped and *stupefied* by pellagra responded quickly to balanced diet —*Amer. Guide Series: Tenn.*⟩ **b :** to blunt or deaden the faculties of perception and understanding of ⟨such a power . . . enervates, extinguishes, and *stupefies* a people —Alexis de Tocqueville⟩ ⟨has not *stupefied* his countrymen into imitating his own mannerisms —*Times Lit. Supp.*⟩ ⟨the whole ~*ing* theological word game —H.J.Muller⟩ **2 :** to shock with surprise, astonishment, or consternation **:** STUN, ASTOUND ⟨the shape of the monolith . . . and the fanged feline deity left me wondering and *stupefied* —Angélica Mendoza⟩ ⟨was *stupefied* by the impact of this tragedy —B.A. Williams⟩ ⟨the amount of work their painstaking delicacy . . . represented was ~*ing* to think of —H.L.Davis⟩ ~ *vi* **:** to become stupid, dull, or torpid **syn** see DAZE

stu·pe·fy·ing·ly *adv* **:** in a stupefying manner **:** with a stupefying effect

stu·pen·dous \st(y)ü'pendəs, ÷ -njəs\ *adj* [L *stupendus*, gerundive of *stupēre* to be astonished] **1 :** causing astonishment or wonder **:** AWESOME, MARVELOUS ⟨that retribution follows guilt, in ways the most mysterious and ~ —Sheridan Le Fanu⟩ ⟨the still surviving walls and moats which form so ~ a feature of the place —*Country Life*⟩ ⟨a ~ occasion⟩ ⟨a ~ silence⟩ **2 :** of amazing size or greatness **:** PRODIGIOUS ⟨a ~ field of grass on which . . . some 10,000 wild animals were roaming —Alan Moorehead⟩ ⟨a facade ~ in its proportions —O.S.Nock⟩ ⟨~ labors⟩ ⟨~ demand⟩ ⟨~ war production⟩ ⟨~ uproar⟩ **syn** see MONSTROUS

stu·pen·dous·ly *adv* **:** in a stupendous manner **:** to a stupendous degree ⟨her nose ~ aquiline —Charles Dickens⟩ ⟨a group of ~ ignorant men⟩

stu·pen·dous·ness *n* -ES **:** the quality or state of being stupendous

stu·pent \'st(y)üpənt\ *adj* [L *stupent-, stupens*, pres. part. of *stupēre*] *archaic* **:** CONFUSED, BEWILDERED, DUMBFOUNDED

stu·pe·ous \-pēəs\ *adj* [L *stupeus, stuppeus* made of tow, fr. *stupa, stuppa* tow + *-eus* -eous] **:** resembling tow **:** having long loose scales or matted filaments **:** STUPOSE

1stu·pid \'st(y)üpəd\ *adj* -ER/-EST [MF *stupide*, fr. L *stupidus*, fr. *stupēre* to be benumbed, be astonished, be stupefied; akin to Gk *typtein* to beat, strike — more at TYPE] **1 a :** slow of mind **:** UNIMAGINATIVE, OBTUSE, INSENSITIVE ⟨came to regard them as ~, sensual, veritable children of Adam —V.L.Parrington⟩ ⟨will defy the most phlegmatic and ~ spectator to behold it without admiration —Tobias Smollett⟩ ⟨bellowed into his ear as if he were deaf instead of ~ —Anthony Trollope⟩ **b :** given to unintelligent decisions or acts **:** UNTHINKING, IRRATIONAL ⟨while he may be wrong . . . he is never ~ —G.W.Johnson⟩ ⟨consider myself at least ~ for not having profited from many opportunities —Emery Neff⟩ ⟨reality is right under your ~ nose —Lionel Trilling⟩ **c :** lacking intelligence or reasoning power **:** BRUTISH ⟨getting the better of ~*er* beasts —G.A.Morgan⟩ **2 a :** dulled in feeling or sensation **:** being in a state of stupor **:** TORPID ⟨~ with drink —Sherwood Anderson⟩ ⟨~ with the lust of gain and the sloth of slavery —Van Wyck Brooks⟩ ⟨let fall the ~ inanimate limbs of the gone wretch —George Meredith⟩ **b :** incapable of feeling or sensation **:** INANIMATE ⟨nothing is quite so ~ as a fact —A.L.Guérard⟩ ⟨the ~ rain came down in buckets —J.W.Ellison b.1929⟩ **3 :** marked by or resulting from dullness or unintelligent thinking **:** SENSELESS ⟨a ~ refusal to be realistic —W.F.Hambly⟩ ⟨appalling capacity of collective man for ~, blind, self-destructive behavior —H.J. Muller⟩ ⟨takes everything seriously in a ~ and unimaginative fashion —K.T.Bluth⟩ ⟨it is ~ to wait until a probable enemy has gained a foothold from which to attack —F.D.Roosevelt⟩ **4 :** lacking interest or point **:** DREARY, BORING ⟨went to an awfully ~ evening . . . Monday night —Rachel Henning⟩ ⟨would not have minded his going to this ~ lunch —A.J. Cronin⟩ ⟨a really ~ performance⟩ **5** *dial Eng* **:** OBSTINATE, MULISH

syn DULL, DENSE, CRASS, DUMB: STUPID applies to a sluggish, slow-witted want of intelligence or comprehension, often congenital or accustomed; it may apply to a senseless, benumbed, or dazed condition ⟨so *stupid* and so obstinate that it was impossible to get him to do or understand anything —Anthony Trollope⟩ ⟨*stupid* with liquor and unable to understand that the ambulance had already gone —Scott Fitzgerald⟩ ⟨sleepy and *stupid* after a broken night and a hard day's work —Dorothy Sayers⟩ DULL strongly implies sluggish labored slowness of mind, with utter lack of quickness, brightness, or liveliness ⟨a *dull*, ambitionless, vegetating individual —J.A.Brussel⟩ ⟨with its impotent ruling classes and its *dull* and puritanical middle classes —Edward Shils⟩ DENSE applies to a blockheaded thick imperviousness or insensitive obtuseness ⟨she never offered to take me over the house, though I gave her the broadest hints — she's very *dense* —Clive Arden⟩ CRASS suggests a fatheaded grossness precluding delicacy, discrimination, or refinement ⟨in deep disgust at the farrier's *crass* incompetence to apprehend the conditions of ghostly phenomena —George Eliot⟩ ⟨a *crass* bonehead capable of sneering at the progress of the human race —Don Marquis⟩ DUMB may apply to an imperceptive vexatious obtuseness ⟨that the nutmegs were easily sold and eagerly bought is beside the story; the wonder is that we Southerners were so *dumb*, we did not know the difference —Erskine Caldwell⟩ ⟨I guess I was pretty *dumb* that morning, but a fellow in love never sees beyond his own nose —Vicki Baum⟩

2stupid \"\ *n* -S **:** a stupid person ⟨the generals were ~*s* —Stephen Crane⟩ ⟨such a ~ with my hands —John Selby⟩

stu·pid·i·ty \st(y)ü'pidəd·ē, -dətē, -i\ *n* -ES [MF *stupidité*, fr. L *stupiditat-, stupiditas*, fr. *stupidus* + *-itat-, -itas* -ity] **1 :** the quality or state of being stupid ⟨induced more by sudden alarm, coupled with blindness and ~ —James Stevenson-Hamilton⟩ **2 :** a stupid idea or act ⟨was keeping a diary of the captain's *stupidities* —Joanna Spencer⟩ ⟨tensions that lead to the *stupidities* of war —P.S.Henshaw⟩

stu·pid·ly *adv* **:** in a stupid manner

stu·pid·ness *n* -ES **:** the quality or state of being stupid **:** STUPIDITY

stuping *pres part of* STUPE

stu·por \'st(y)üpə(r)\ *n* -S [ME, fr. L, fr. *stupēre* to be benumbed, be astonished, be stupefied] **1 :** a physical or mental condition characterized by great diminution or suspension of sense or feeling **:** NUMBNESS, STUPEFACTION ⟨sleep produced by a bromide is . . . more of a ~ than natural sleep —D.W. Maurer & V.H.Vogel⟩ ⟨in a drunken ~ sold his wife to another —*Brit. Bk. News*⟩; *specif* **:** a chiefly mental condition marked by absence of spontaneous movement, greatly diminished responsiveness to stimulation, and usu. impaired consciousness — compare COMA **2 :** a state of apathy or torpor resulting often from stress or shock ⟨was in a ~ of mental weariness —Sherwood Anderson⟩ ⟨had collapsed for a moment in a ~ of pain —Marguerite Steen⟩ ⟨discomforts were minor, almost unnoticed in the leaden ~ of marching —Norman Mailer⟩ ⟨have recovered from the ~ of defeat —Sigmund Neumann⟩

stu·por·if·ic \¦==¦rifik\ *adj* **:** causing stupor ⟨was all ready to knock myself out with something really ~ —Christopher Morley⟩

stu·por·ose \'==,rōs\ *adj* [ML *stuporosus*, fr. LL, inducing stupor, fr. L *stupor* + *-osus* -ose] **:** STUPOROUS ⟨if so much drug is given that the patient becomes ~ —*Lancet*⟩ ⟨the patient . . . gradually became more anergic, ~, and silent in interviews —W.C.M.Scott⟩

stu·por·ous \-rəs\ *adj* [ML *stuporosus*] **:** attended or affected with stupor ⟨chronic intoxication may be manifested . . . by a dull, ~, almost comatose condition —D.W.Maurer & V.H.Vogel⟩ ⟨in demented children . . . ~ and hallucinatory conditions are rare —*Psychological Abstracts*⟩ ⟨stargazers as well as ~ bookworms —Charles Michelson⟩

stu·pose \'st(y)ü,pōs\ *adj* [ML *stuposus, stupposus*, fr. L *stupa, stuppa* tow + *-osus* -ose — more at STUPE] **:** composed of or having tufted or matted filaments like tow

stupp \'stəp, 'stüp\ *n* -S [G; prob. akin to OHG *stoub* dust — more at STIVE] **:** a black deposit obtained in distilling mercury ores and consisting of a mixture of soot, hydrocarbons, mercury and its compounds, and ore dust

stuprate *vt* -ED/-ING/-S [L *stupratus*, past part. of *stuprare*, fr. *stuprum* defilement — more at TYPE] *obs* **:** to have sexual intercourse with (a woman); *esp* **:** RAPE

stupration *n* -S [prob. fr. (assumed) NL *stupration-, stupratio*, fr. L *stupratus* (past part. of *stuprare*) + *-ion-, -io* -ion] *obs* **:** the act of violating a woman **:** SEDUCTION, RAPE

stu·prum \'st(y)üprəm\ *n* -s [L, defilement, dishonor, stuprum] **1** *Roman & civil law* **:** sexual intercourse between a man and an unmarried woman other than one in slavery or concubinage **2** *Roman & civil law* **:** illicit intercourse contrary to morality **3** *Roman & civil law* **:** unchastity of a woman

stu·pu·lose \'st(y)üpyə,lōs\ *adj* [NL *stupulosus*, fr. L *stupa*, *stuppa* tow + *-ula* + *-osus* -ose] **:** covered with fine short hairs

stur·di·ly \'stərdəlē, 'stə̄d-, 'stəid-, -li\ *adv* [ME, fr. [1]*sturdy* + *-ly*] **:** in a sturdy manner

stur·di·ness \-dēnə̇s, -din-\ *n* -ES [ME *sturdinesse*, fr. [1]*sturdy* + *-nesse* -ness] **:** the quality or state of being sturdy

[1]stur·dy \'stərdē, 'stəd-, 'stəid-, -di\ *adj* -ER/-EST [ME, fr. OF *estourdi*, *estordi* stunned, thoughtless, rash, past part. of *estourdir*, *estordir* to stun, fr. (assumed) VL *exturdire* to be dizzy as a thrush that is drunk from eating grapes, fr. L *ex-* + *turdus* thrush — more at THRUSH] **1** *obs* **:** brave, resolute, or fierce in combat **2** *archaic* **a :** difficult to manage **:** stubbornly rebellious **b :** OPINIONATED, OBSTINATE **3 a :** resistant to destruction **:** firmly built or constituted **:** STOUT ⟨a ~ peasant cottage of stucco and unpainted wood —Ida Treat⟩ ⟨the ~ oaks of the forest⟩ ⟨the *sturdiest* types of airplanes —F.J. Brown & J.S.Roucek⟩ **b :** resistant to disease or unfavorable weather **:** HARDY ⟨the *sturdiest* of creepers, facing the ferocious winds of the hills, the tremendous rains . . . and bitter frost —Richard Jefferies⟩ ⟨sumac and huckleberry hiding the less ~ flowers —*Amer. Guide Series: Minn.*⟩ **c :** sound or enduring in design or execution **:** SOLID, SUBSTANTIAL ⟨his ~, matter-of-fact exegesis with its resolute rejection of forced and fantastic interpretation —H.E.W.Fosbroke⟩ ⟨all delicate veining and spongy texture very unlike the ~ Maine landscapes he used to do —Carlyle Burrows⟩ ⟨conducts a ~ performance of the overture —Irving Kolodin⟩ **4 a :** characterized by or reflecting physical strength or vigor **:** ROBUST ⟨was a ~, handsome, high-colored woman —Carl Van Doren⟩ ⟨compact, broad, and ~ of limb —Joseph Conrad⟩ **b :** characterized by or expressive of mental vigor or vitality **:** UNSWERVING, RESOLUTE ⟨a ~ race, self-reliant and independent in temper —Allan Nevins & H.S.Commager⟩ ⟨developed into the *sturdiest* of fighters for reform —L.G.Vander Velde⟩ ⟨our democratic faith was ~ —F.D.Roosevelt⟩ ⟨~ common sense⟩ **syn** see STRONG

[2]sturdy \"\ *n* -ES **:** GID

sturdy beggar *n* **:** an able-bodied beggar or recipient of charity or relief who is capable of earning his own living

stur·geon \'stərjən, 'stə̄j-, 'stəij-\ *n* -s [ME, fr. OF *estourjon*, *esturgon*, of Gmc origin; akin to OE *styria* sturgeon, OHG *sturio*, ON *styrja*] **1 a :** any of various usu. large ganoid fishes of *Acipenser* and related genera that are widely distributed in the north temperate zone in both fresh and salt water, that have a heterocercal tail, a prolonged head with a toothless protrusile mouth on its undersurface, and an elongate body covered with tough skin protected by five rows of bony plates, and that are valued for their flesh and esp. for their roe which is made into caviar — compare BELUGA, STERLET **b :** fresh or cured sturgeon flesh **2 :** any of several fishes (as a paddlefish) related to and somewhat resembling the true sturgeons

stur·ine *also* **stur·in** \'stər·,ēn, -ər·ə̇n, 'st(y)ů,rēn, -ůrə̇n\ *n* -s [ISV *stur-* (fr. NL *sturio* — specific epithet of the sturgeon *Acipenser sturio* —, fr. ML, sturgeon, of Gmc origin; akin to OHG *sturio* sturgeon) + *-ine* or *-in*] **:** a protamine in the spermatozoa of sturgeon

sturm's theorem \'stůrmz-\ *n, usu cap S* [after Jacques Charles François *Sturm* †1855 Fr. mathematician] **:** a theorem by which the number and position of the real roots between given limits of an algebraic equation are determined

sturm und drang \¦shtůr,můnt'dräŋ\ *n, usu cap S&D* [G, storm and stress, fr. *Sturm und Drang* (1776), drama by Friedrich Maximilian von Klinger †1831 Ger. dramatist and novelist] **1 :** a literary movement of the latter half of the 18th century in Germany characterized by a revolt against the strictures that the Enlightenment and a sterile imitation of French literature imposed, by the exaltation of nature, intuition, and inborn genius as the wellsprings of literature, and by works that typically are loosely constructed, written in realistic language, and marked by rousing action and high emotionalism and that frequently deal with the individual in revolt against the injustices of society **2 :** storm and stress **:** TURMOIL ⟨can no longer endure the buffetings of fate, the *Sturm und Drang* of life —*Times Lit. Supp.*⟩

stur·nel·la \,stər'nelə\ *n, cap* [NL, fr. L *sturnus* starling + *-ella*] **:** a genus of passerine birds (family Icteridae) including the meadowlarks

stur·ni·dae \'stərnə,dē\ *n pl, cap* [NL, fr. *Sturnus*, type genus + *-idae*] **:** a large family of passerine birds consisting of the Old World starlings and related birds and having ten primaries and characters somewhat intermediate between the crows and the American grackles — see STURNUS

stur·nine \'stər,nīn, -ˌnə̇n\ *adj* [LL *sturninus* colored like a starling, fr. L *sturnus* starling + *-inus* -ine] **:** of, relating to, or resembling a starling

stur·noid \-,nȯid\ *adj* [NL *Sturnus* + E *-oid*] **:** resembling or related to the starlings

stur·nus \-ˌnəs\ *n, cap* [NL, fr. L, starling — more at STARLING] **:** the type genus of Sturnidae including the common starling

stur·shum \'stərshəm, 'stə̄sh-, 'stəish-\ *also* **stur·tion** \-shən\ *n* -s [by shortening & alter.] **:** NASTURTIUM

[1]sturt \'stərt\ *n* [ME, contention, wrangling, alter. of *strut*, *strout* contention, combat; akin to MHG *strūz* combat, OE *strūtian* to exert oneself — more at STRUT] *chiefly Scot* **:** DISTURBANCE, TROUBLE ⟨amid the ~ of war —*Edinburgh Rev.*⟩ ⟨memories of early ~ and strife —John Buchan⟩

[2]sturt \"\ *vb* [ME *sturten* to fight, wrangle, fr. *sturt*, n.] *chiefly Scot* **:** STARTLE, STIR, VEX, ANNOY

sturt·ite \'stərd·,īt\ *n* -s [Charles *Sturt* †1869 Eng. explorer + E *-ite*] **:** a mineral $Mn_3FeSi_4O_{11}(OH)_3.10H_2O$(?) consisting of a rare hydrous silicate of iron, manganese, calcium, and magnesium and occurring in black compact masses

sturt's desert pea \'stərts-\ *also* **sturt pea** *n, usu cap S* [prob. fr. the name *Sturt*] **:** a glory pea (*Clianthus speciosus*) that is a sprawling shrubby perennial with long villous stems and pinnate leaves, that is noted for its scarlet black-marked flowers, and that is widely distributed in dry parts of Australia

stuss \'stəsh\ *n* -ES [Yiddish *shtos*, *stos*, fr. G *stoss* push, blow, fr. OHG *stōz* push, thrust — more at STØD] **:** faro in which cards are dealt by hand and the banker takes all bets on splits

stut \'stət, 'stůt\ *vb* [ME *stutten*] *dial* **:** STAMMER, STUTTER

[1]stut·ter \'stəd·ə(r), -ətə-\ *vb* **stuttered; stuttered; stuttering** \-əd·əriŋ, -ətər-, -ə·tr-\ **stutters** [freq. of *stut*, fr. ME *stutten;* akin to D *stotteren* to stutter, MLG *stotern*, *stötern* to stutter, OHG *stōzan* to thrust, push, L *tundere* to beat — more at STINT] *vi* **1 a :** to speak with involuntary disruption or blocking of speech (as by spasmodic repetition or prolongation of vocal sounds) — compare STAMMER **b :** to make sounds similar to or in the manner of a stutter ⟨thunder which ~*ed* far away in the distant ranges —Jean Stafford⟩ ⟨listens to the ~*ing*, muttering rumble of war —*Times Lit. Supp.*⟩ ⟨the one candle ~*ing* like an idiot's tongue —Edith Sitwell⟩ **2 :** to move or act in a halting or spasmodic manner ⟨schools are ~*ing* to an end —*Isis*⟩ ⟨a brilliant idea stands still and ~*ing* —V.S.Pritchett⟩ ~ *vt* **:** to say, speak, or sound with or as if with a stutter ⟨can only ~ his reply⟩ — often used with *out* ⟨the telegraph ticked the gladdest message . . . when it ~*ed* out its first letters —L.D.Lewis⟩ — **stut·ter·er** *n*

[2]stutter \"\ *n* -s **1 :** an act or instance of stuttering ⟨can hardly speak without a ~⟩ ⟨the ~ of the rain along the balconies —Elizabeth Bowen⟩ ⟨the heavy ~ of aerial fire —Walt Sheldon⟩ **2 :** STUTTERING 2 ⟨had a ~ but he was quite understandable —O.S.J.Gogarty⟩

stuttering *n* -s **1 :** the act of one who stutters **2 :** a disorder of vocal communication marked by involuntary disruption or blocking of speech (as by spasmodic repetition or prolongation of vocal sounds), by fear and anxiety, and by a struggle to avoid speech errors — compare STAMMERING

stut·ter·ing·ly *adv* **:** in a stuttering manner

stutt·gart \'s(h)tůt,gär|t, -tüt-, -gȧ| *sometimes* 'stət-; *usu* |d· +V\ *adj, usu cap* [fr. *Stuttgart*, city in southern Germany] **:** of or from the city of Stuttgart, Germany **:** of the kind or style prevalent in Stuttgart

stuttgart disease *also* **stuttgart's disease** *or* **stuttgart dog plague** *or* **stuttgart syndrome** *n, usu cap Stuttgart* **:** canine leptospirosis; *esp* **:** a severe highly contagious form of canicola fever marked by predominantly renal infection with nephritis and uremia, intense calf diphtheria, and bloody vomitus and diarrhea and commonly leading to collapse and death

stuttgart pitch *n, usu cap S* **:** INTERNATIONAL PITCH 2

stwd *abbr* steward

s-twist \'=,=\ *n, cap S* **:** a crossband twist

stwy *abbr* stairway

[1]sty *or* **stye** *vi* **stied; stied; stying; sties** [ME *styen*, fr. OE *stīgan* to go up — more at STAIR] *obs* **:** ASCEND, MOUNT, CLIMB

[2]sty *also* **stye** \'stī\ *n, pl* **sties** *also* **styes** [ME *sty*, fr. OE *sti*, *stig* sty, pen, hall; akin to ON *-stī* sty and perh. to OE *stān* stone — more at STONE] **1 :** a pen or enclosure for swine **:** enclosed housing for swine **2 a :** an unkempt or filthy abode or lodging place ⟨her house was a perfect ~⟩ **b :** a low or vicious place **:** one catering to the viler instincts ⟨a ~ of immorality⟩

[3]sty \"\ *vb* **styed; styed; stying; sties** [fr. (assumed) ME *styen*, fr. OE *stigian*, fr. *stī*, *stig*, n.] *vt* **1 :** to pen up (swine) **2 :** to lodge or keep in or as if in a sty ~ *vi* **:** to live in a sty

[4]sty *or* **stye** \"\ *n, pl* **sties** *or* **styes** [short for obs. E *styan*, fr. (assumed) ME *styan*, alter. of OE *stīgend*, fr. *stīgan* to go up, rise] **:** an inflamed swelling of a sebaceous gland at the margin of an eyelid

sty·ca \'stīkə\ *n* -s [irreg. fr. OE (Northumbrian dial.) *stycas* lepta (in a translation of the Gospels at Mk 12:42); akin to OE *stycce* piece — more at STOCK] **:** a debased copper sceat issued by the kings of Northumbria during the 7th to 9th centuries

styf·siek·te \'stāf,sēktə, 'stīf-\ *or* **styf·ziek·te** \-,zē-\ *n* -s [Afrik *styfsiekte*, fr. *styf* stiff (fr. D *stijf*, fr. MD) + *siekte* disease, sickness, fr. MD, fr. *siek*, *siec* ill, sick — more at STIFF, SICK] *Africa* **:** aphosphorosis of cattle marked by faulty bone structure and lameness — compare LAMSIEKTE

styg·ian \'stij(ē)ən\ *adj, often cap* [L *stygius* stygian (fr. Gk *stygios*, fr. *Styg-*, *Styx* Styx, mythical stream considered to be the chief river of the subterranean world of the dead) + E *-an*] **:** of, relating to, or associated with the river Styx: as **a :** HELLISH, INFERNAL, GLOOMY **b :** characteristic of death **:** DEATHLY ⟨upon those roseate lips a ~ hue —William Wordsworth⟩ **c :** INVIOLABLE ⟨a ~ oath⟩

[1]styl- *or* **stylo-** *comb form* [L *stylo-*, fr. Gk *styl-*, *stylo-*, fr. *stylos* — more at STEER] **:** pillar ⟨*Styl*aster⟩ ⟨*stylo*lite⟩

[2]styl- *or* **styli-** *or* **stylo-** *comb form* [*styl-* fr. earlier *stil-*, fr. L, stalk, fr. *stilus* stake, stalk, stylus; *styli-* fr. earlier *stili-*, fr. ML *styli-* stylus, fr. L *stilus; stylo-* fr. *styl-* + *-o-*] **1 :** style **:** styloid process ⟨*styl*ate⟩ ⟨*styli*ferous⟩ ⟨*stylo*graphic⟩ **2 :** of or relating to a styloid process and ⟨*stylo*mastoid⟩

sty·lar \'stīlə(r)\ *adj* [alter. of earlier *stilar*, fr. L *stil-* + E *-ar*] **1 :** of, relating to, or having the character of a style in writing **2 a :** of, relating to, or constituting an elongated process ⟨a ~ prominence on a shell⟩ **b :** leading to the ovary of a seed plant ⟨a ~ canal⟩

-sty·lar \¦stīlə(r)\ *adj comb form* [Gk *stylos* pillar + E *-ar*] **:** having (such or so many) pillars **:** having (such) columniation ⟨amphi*stylar*⟩ ⟨hepta*stylar*⟩

stylar-end rot \¦==¦=-\ *n* **:** a disorder of limes and sometimes lemons that is of unknown cause and is characterized by a pale firm area of decay about the stylar end of the fruit

sty·las·ter \stī'lastə(r), -laas-\ *n* [NL, fr. [1]*styl-* + *-aster*] **1** *cap* **:** a genus of delicate usu. pink hydrocorals (order Stylasterina) **2** -s **:** any coral of the genus *Stylaster* or sometimes of the order Stylasterina

sty·las·te·ri·na \stī,lastə'rīnə, -rēnə\ *n pl, cap* [NL, fr. *Stylaster* + *-ina*] **:** an order of hydrocorals (class Hydrozoa) that are closely related to the millepores with which they were formerly included in the order Hydrocorallina

sty·late \'stī,lāt\ *adj* [prob. fr. (assumed) NL *stylatus*, fr. NL [2]*styl-* + L *-atus* -ate] **1 :** having a persistent style ⟨~ ovaries⟩ **2 a :** bearing a style or stylet ⟨~ insects⟩ **b :** having the form of a stylet ⟨a ~ ovipositor⟩

[1]style \'stīl, *esp before pause or consonant* -īəl\ *n* -s [ME, alter. (prob. influenced by Gk *stylos* pillar) of *stile*, fr. L *stilus* stake, stylus, manner of writing, style; akin to Av *staēra* mountain peak, OHG *stehhan* to prick — more at STICK] **1 :** an instrument used by the ancients in writing on waxed tablets and made with one of its ends sharp and the other blunt, smooth, and somewhat expanded for the purpose of making erasures by smoothing the wax **2 a :** mode of expressing thought in oral or written language: as (1) **:** a manner of expression characteristic of an individual, a period, a school, or other identifiable group (as a nation) ⟨a classic ~⟩ ⟨a flowery 18th century prose ~⟩ (2) **:** the aspects of literary composition that are concerned with mode and form of expression as distinguished from content or message ⟨his ~ is so graceful that one regrets he has nothing to say⟩ (3) **:** the manner, tone, or orientation assumed in discourse ⟨spoke in the ~ of a master to slaves⟩ ⟨took a very lofty ~ with us⟩ **b :** the custom followed (as in a business, editorial, or printing office) in spelling, capitalization, punctuation, and typographic arrangement and display **3 a :** a proper, generally recognized, or legally acceptable appellation **:** an official, distinctive, or honorific designation **:** mode of address **:** NAME, TITLE ⟨the king did not have the ~, Majesty, until the 16th century⟩ ⟨were in partnership under the ~, Acme Trading Company⟩ **b :** an attributive or qualifying designation ⟨gave himself the ~ of scholar⟩ **4 a :** manner or method of acting or performing esp. as recognized or sanctioned by some standard (as of law or custom) ⟨gave them a hearty welcome in the old-country ~⟩; *often* **:** one that is distinctive or characteristic of or attributed to some group or period ⟨singing in the Italian ~⟩ ⟨Renaissance ~ of painting⟩ ⟨oppressed by the formal ~ of the court⟩ **b :** a way or manner of living or behaving that is deemed elegant or in accord with fashion **:** a fashionable luxurious mode of life **:** fashionable elegance ⟨lived in ~⟩ ⟨a woman of ~⟩ **c** (1) **:** the peculiarly distinctive technique or methods characteristic of or identified with a particular individual usu. in the performance of a particular activity ⟨easy to recognize him by his ~ on the course⟩ (2) **:** an individual's typical way of life **:** his attitudes and their expression in a self-consistent manner as developing from childhood **d :** movement and manner in dancing as evolved in relation to a dance type, sex, tribe, region, or period **5 :** something felt to resemble the ancient style (as in appearance or use): as **a** (1) **:** the gnomon of a dial whose shadow marks the hour on the dial (2) **:** a pen or other writing instrument esp. as a symbol of authorship (3) **:** a blunt pointed surgical instrument (4) **:** a pointed tool used in engraving **:** GRAVER (5) **:** ETCHING NEEDLE (6) **:** a phonograph needle **:** STYLUS **b :** the usu. elongated portion of a pistil that connects the ovary with the stigma of a plant **:** a filiform prolongation of a plant ovary bearing a stigma at its apex — see FLOWER illustration **c** (1) **:** a slender bristle or other elongated process on an animal (as on the anal region or at the tip of the antenna of an insect or crustacean) (2) **:** a uniradiate sponge spicule that is blunt at one end (3) **:** a central calcareous process in the gastropores or sometimes also in the dactylopores of a coral of the order Stylasterina (4) **:** any of several small cusps or elevations of the cingulum of a molar tooth — see HYPOSTYLE, MESOSTYLE, METASTYLE, PARASTYLE (5) **:** EMBOLUS 3 **6 a** (1) **:** a quality that gives distinctive excellence to something (as artistic expression) and that consists esp. in the appropriateness and choiceness of the elements (as subject, medium, form) combined and the individualization imparted by the method of combining (2) **:** distinction of structural quality (as line, color, design, decoration) in dry goods (as for apparel, fabrics, interior decoration) (3) **:** the overall appearance and carriage of an animal esp. as an expression of personality and competence in action **b** (1) **:** a particular type of architecture based on distinctive qualities of design or decoration ⟨churches in the Gothic ~⟩ (2) **:** a combination of shape and ornamentation distinguishing an extensive group of artifacts (as ceramics) **c :** a general category based on somewhat similar characteristics (as of outward appearance) ⟨a modern ~ of furniture⟩ ⟨a Roman ~ of profile⟩ **syn** see FASHION

[2]style \"\ *vb* -ED/-ING/-S *vt* **1 :** to designate (as a person) by an identifying term **:** TERM, NAME, CALL ⟨an old lawyer *styled* judge by his friends⟩ ⟨does not hesitate to ~ himself scientist⟩ **2 :** to impart a particular style to ⟨carefully *styled* prose⟩: as **a :** to cause to conform to a customary style (as for publication) ⟨took hours to ~ the manuscript⟩ **b :** to design and make in accord with the prevailing mode; *esp* **:** to impart a new or distinctive design or quality to ⟨dresses *styled* for summer sports⟩ **c :** to impart a fashionable quality to (as by advertising) in order to stimulate sales **:** make stylish ⟨a campaign to ~ the new model⟩ ~ *vi* **:** to impart a style or stylish quality to something; *esp* **:** to make an article fashionable by advertising

[3]style \"\ *archaic var of* STILE

[1]-style \,stīl\ *n comb form* -s [LL *-stylon*, fr. L, neut. of *-stylos* characterized by the presence of (so many) pillars, fr. Gk, fr. *stylos* pillar — more at STEER] **1 a :** structure characterized by the presence of (so many) pillars ⟨poly*style*⟩ **b :** structure with pillars ⟨cyrto*style*⟩ **2 :** animal part felt to resemble a pillar ⟨blasto*style*⟩ ⟨pygo*style*⟩

[2]-style \"\ *adj comb form* [L *-stylos*, fr. Gk, fr. *stylos* pillar] **:** characterized by the presence of (so many) pillars ⟨di*style*⟩

stylebook \'=,=\ *n* **:** a book explaining, describing, or illustrating the prevailing, accepted, or authorized style ⟨a dressmaker's ~⟩ ⟨a government ~ for printers⟩

styled \¦stī(ə)ld\ *adj* [[1]*style* + *-ed*] **:** having a specified style or number of styles — used in combination ⟨hetero*styled*⟩ ⟨short-*styled*⟩

style·dom \'=ˌdəm\ *n* -s **:** the world of fashion

style·less \'stī(ə)llə̇s\ *adj* **:** lacking in style **:** UNSTYLISH ⟨a ~ costume⟩ — **style·less·ness** *n* -ES

stylelike \'=,=\ *adj* **:** resembling a style esp. in elongated pointed form ⟨a ~ process⟩

style of life : STYLE 4c(2)

style pen *n* **:** a stylographic pen

styl·er \'stīlə(r)\ *n* -s **:** STYLIST 2

style sheet *n* **:** a compilation of style rules often in the form of a card, pamphlet, or booklet

sty·let \'stīlə̇t, *usu* -ə̇d+V\ *n* -s [F, stylet, stiletto, fr. MF *stilet* stiletto, fr. OIt *stiletto* — more at STILETTO] **1 a :** a slender surgical probe **b :** a thin wire inserted in a catheter to maintain rigidity or in a hollow needle to maintain patency **2 a :** a style of a flowering plant **b :** a relatively rigid slender elongated organ or appendage on an animal **:** a small style **3 :** a small poniard **:** STILETTO **4 :** a pointed instrument or tool for making marks (as in graving)

sty·let·ed \-lə̇d·ə̇d\ *adj* **:** having a stylet

sty·let·i·form \stī'led·ə,fȯrm\ *adj* **:** resembling or having the shape of a stylet

style up *vt* **:** to give a stylish or fashionable turn to (as something essentially utilitarian) **:** modify so as to impart style to ⟨*styled up* country denims trim enough for street wear⟩

stylewort \'=,=\ *n* [*style-* (fr. NL *Stylidium*) + *wort*] **:** a plant of the family Stylidiaceae

styli *pl of* STYLUS

styli- — see STYL-

-sty·lic \¦stīlik, -lēk\ *adj comb form* [Gk *stylos* pillar + E *-ic*] **:** being or having (such) a connection of the jaw and skull ⟨hyo*stylic*⟩ ⟨strepto*stylic*⟩

sty·lid·i·a·ce·ae \(,)stī,lidē'āsē,ē\ *n pl, cap* [NL, fr. *Stylidium*, type genus + *-aceae*] **:** a family of herbs or shrubs (order Campanulales) of the southern hemisphere and esp. Australasia that have simple leaves and clustered perfect or unisexual flowers with a slightly irregular corolla followed by capsules bearing seeds with fleshy endosperm — **sty·lid·i·a·ceous** \(¦)=¦==¦āshəs\ *adj*

sty·lid·i·um \stī'lidēəm\ *n* [NL, fr. [1]*styl-* + *-idium*] **1** *cap* **:** the type genus of the family Stylidiaceae comprising mostly Australian herbaceous perennials that have racemes, panicles, or corymbs of showy flowers commonly with elastic stamens and are often cultivated as greenhouse ornamentals **2** -s **:** any plant or flower of the genus *Stylidium*

-stylies *pl of* -STYLY

sty·lif·er·ous \(')stī¦lif(ə)rəs\ *adj* [[2]*styl-* + *-ferous*] **:** bearing one or more styles

sty·li·form \'stīlə,fȯrm\ *adj* [alter. of earlier *stiliforme*, fr. NL *stiliformis*, fr. ML *styli-* stylus + L *-formis* -form — more at STYL-] **:** resembling a style or stylus **:** bristle-shaped; *esp* **:** terminating in a long slender point ⟨a ~ antenna⟩

styling *n* -s [fr. gerund of [2]*style*] **1** [fr. gerund of [2]*style* "to shape or design by means of a stylus"] **:** ornamentation done with a style or stylus **2 :** the act or process of correcting a literary work with the purpose of improving the method or manner of expression **3 a :** the act or process of imparting a stylish quality or a particular style to; *esp* **:** the alteration of the style of something usu. to increase the sales appeal or utility or to improve the appearance **b :** the way in which something is styled

sty·li·on \'stīlēən\ *n, pl* **sty·lia** \-ēə\ *also* **stylions** [NL, irreg. fr. [2]*styl-*] **:** an anthropometric reference point consisting of the end of the styloid process of the radius — called also *styloid point*

styl·ish \'stīlish, -lēsh\ *adj* **:** having style **:** conforming to an accepted standard and esp. to one of current fashion — **styl·ish·ly** \-lə̇shlē, -lēsh-, -li\ *adv* — **styl·ish·ness** *n* -ES

styl·ism \'stī,lizəm\ *n* -s [ISV [1]*style* + *-ism;* prob. orig. formed as F *stylisme*] **:** concern with style (as in art or literature) as an end in itself **:** undue preoccupation with style

styl·ist \-ˌlə̇st\ *n* -s [ISV [1]*style* + *-ist*] **1 :** one who is a master or model of style: as **a** (1) **:** a writer or speaker who is eminent in matters of style (2) **:** a critic of literary style **b :** a sports performer noted for precision and excellence in form **2 :** one who develops, designs, or advises on styles ⟨a fashion ~⟩ ⟨a hair ~⟩ ⟨an industrial ~⟩: as **a :** one who decides points of style or makes or enforces style rules (as in a publishing house or editorial office) **b :** a coordinator of fashions in a store

sty·lis·tic \(')stī¦listik, -tēk\ *also* **sty·lis·ti·cal** \-tə̇kəl, -tēk-\ *adj* [*stylistic* ISV *stylist* + *-ic; stylistical* fr. *stylistic* + *-al*] **:** of or relating to style esp. in the use of language — **sty·lis·ti·cal·ly** \-tə̇k(ə)lē, -tēk-, -li\ *adv*

sty·lis·tics \-tiks, -tēks\ *n pl but sing or pl in constr* [ISV *stylist* + *-ics*] **1 :** an aspect of literary study that emphasizes the analysis of various elements of style (as metaphor and diction) **2 :** the study of the devices in a language (as rhetorical figures and syntactical patterns) that produce expressive value

sty·lite \'stī,līt\ *n* -s [LGk *stylitēs*, fr. Gk *stylos* pillar + *-itēs* -ite — more at STEER] **:** one of a class of ascetics who lived as hermits on the tops of pillars chiefly in Syria and after the time of the famous pillar hermit Simeon Stylites († A.D.459) — called also *pillar saint*

styl·iza·tion \,stīlə̇'zāshən, -,lī'z-\ *n* -s [ISV *stylize* + *-ation*] **1 :** the quality or state of being stylized **2 :** an act or instance of stylizing

styl·ize \'stī(ə),līz\ *vt* -ED/-ING/-S *-see -ize in Explan Notes* [trans. of G *stilisieren*] **:** to cause to conform to a style **:** give a formal quality to by causing to conform to a set plan or style **:** CONVENTIONALIZE: as **a :** to cause (an object represented in sculpture or in pictorial art) to conform to a style of expression often extreme in character rather than to the appearance of nature **b :** to design (theatrical matter) according to a stylistic pattern esp. so that the mise-en-scène, costumes, and other elements are illustrative of the idea of the play **c :** to emphasize inherent rhythmic or pictorial qualities of (a movement in dancing) so as to enhance artistic rather than natural effects; *also* **:** to employ such emphasis as the basis of (one's technique) in designing or staging dances

[1]sty·lo \'stī(,)lō\ *n* -s [by shortening] **:** STYLOGRAPH

[2]stylo \"\ *n* -s [modif. of NL *Stylosanthes*] **:** a leguminous plant (*Stylosanthes gracilis*) grown in warm parts of Australia for pasture

stylo- — see STYL-

sty·lo·bate \'stīlə,bāt\ *n* -s [L *stylobates*, *stylobata*, fr. Gk *stylobatēs*, fr. *stylos* pillar + *-batēs* one that treads, fr. *bainein* to walk, go — more at COME] **:** a continuous flat coping or pavement on which a row of architectural columns is supported; *esp* **:** the uppermost step of a stereobate supporting a peristyle — see SUBBASE

sty·lo·ce·rite \,stīlō'si,rīt\ *n* -s [[1]*styl-* + *cer-* (fr. Gk *keras* horn) + *-ite* — more at HORN] **:** an often spinous process on the outer aspect of the first antennae of a crustacean — see NATANTIA

sty·lo·chus \'stīləkəs\ *n, cap* [NL, fr. [2]*styl-* + Gk *ochos* one that holds, fr. *echein* to have, hold — more at SCHEME] **:** a genus (the type of the family Stylochidae) of large polyclad flatworms with an oval flat body, short tentacles, and pharynx with several accessory lobes

sty·lo·glos·sus \,stī(,)lō'gläsəs, -glȯs-\ *n, pl* **styloglos·si** \-lä,sī, -lȯ,sī\ [NL, fr. [2]*styl-* + *-glossus* (fr. Gk *glōssa* tongue) — more at GLOSS] **:** a muscle arising from the styloid process of the temporal bone and inserted along the side and underpart of the tongue

sty·lo·gonidium \ˌstī(ˌ)lō+\ *n* [NL, fr. ²*styl-* + *gonidium*] : PYCNOSPORE

sty·lo·graph \ˈstīlə,graf, -raa(ə)f, -aif, -äf\ *n* [²*styl-* + *-graph*] : a stylographic pen

sty·lo·graph·ic \ˌ÷÷ˈgrafik, -fēk\ *also* **sty·lo·graph·i·cal** \-fəkəl, -fēk-\ *adj* [*stylographic* fr. ²*styl-* + *-graphic; stylographical* fr. *stylographic* + *-al*] **1** : of, relating to, or used in stylography ⟨~ tablets⟩ **2** : of, relating to, or being a fountain pen that has a fine writing point fitted with a needle which by the pressure of the point on a surface is pushed back to release the flow of ink ⟨a ~ pen⟩ ⟨~ writing⟩ — **sty·lo·graph·i·cal·ly** \-fək(ə)lē, -fēk-, -li\ *adv*

sty·log·ra·phy \stīˈlägrəfē, -fi\ *n* -ES [²*styl-* + *-graphy*] : a mode of writing or tracing lines by means of a style or similar instrument on cards or tablets

sty·lo·hy·al \ˌstī(ˌ)lōˈhīəl\ *n* -S [²*styl-* + *hyoid* + *-al*, adj. suffix] : an element of each side of the hyoid arch between the epihyal and tympanohyal that appears as a distinct element of the anterior cornu of the hyoid bone in many mammals — see STYLOID PROCESS

sty·lo·hy·oid \ˌ÷(ˌ)÷ˈhī,ȯid\ *also* **sty·lo·hy·oi·de·us** \ˌ÷(ˌ)÷,hīˈȯidēəs\ *n, pl* **stylohyoids** \-dz\ *also* **stylohyoi·dei** \-dē,ī\ [NL *stylohyoideus*, fr. ²*styl-* + *hyoides* hyoid bone + L *-eus* -eous] : a slender muscle connecting the back part of the styloid process and the body of the hyoid bone

sty·loid \ˈstī,lȯid\ *adj* [NL *styloides*, fr. Gk *styloeidēs*, fr. *styl-* (irreg. — influenced by Gk *stylos* pillar — fr. L *stilus* stylus) + *-oeidēs* -oid — more at STYLE] : resembling a style : STYLIFORM — used esp. of slender pointed skeletal processes

styloid point *n* : STYLION

styloid process *n* : any of several long slender pointed bony processes; *esp* : one from the lower side of the temporal bone of man corresponding to the tympanohyal and stylohyal of other mammals

sty·lo·lite \ˈstīlə,līt\ *n* -S [ISV ¹*styl-* + *-lite*] : a small longitudinally grooved column of the same material as the rock in which it occurs often resulting from the slipping under vertical pressure of a part capped by a shell through adjacent parts not so capped though one or more layers (as of limestone) may be affected by stylolitic structure throughout where there is no capping object — **sty·lo·lit·ic** \ˌ÷÷ˈlid·ik\ *adj*

sty·lo·mandibular \ˌstī(ˌ)lō+\ *adj* [²*styl-* + *mandibular*] : of, relating to, or being a ligament connecting the styloid process of the temporal bone and the angle of the lower jaw

sty·lo·mastoid \"+\ *adj* [²*styl-* + *mastoid*] **1** : of, relating to, or being a foramen that occurs on the lower surface of the temporal bone between the styloid and mastoid processes and forms the termination of the facial canal **2** : of or associated with the stylomastoid foramen ⟨~ vessels⟩

sty·lo·met·ric \ˌstīləˈme·trik\ *adj* : of, relating to, or involving the methods of stylometry

sty·lom·e·try \stīˈlämə·trē, -tri\ *n* -ES [¹*style* + *-o-* + *-metry*] : the study of the chronology and development of an author's work based esp. on the recurrence of particular turns of expression or trends of thought

sty·lom·ma·toph·o·ra \stī,läməˈtäfərə\ *n pl, cap* [NL, fr. ¹*styl-* + Gk *ommat-, omma* eye + NL *-o-* + *-phora;* akin to Gk *ōps* eye — more at EYE] : a suborder of Pulmonata comprising gastropods with the eyes situated at the tips of retractile tentacles and including the common land snails and slugs — **sty·lom·ma·toph·o·rous** \(ˌ)÷÷÷ˈ÷f(ə)rəs\ *adj*

sty·lo·nych·ia \ˌstīləˈnikēə\ *n, cap* [NL, fr. ¹*styl-* + *onych-* + *-ia*] : a common genus of marine and freshwater, ovoid or reniform, hypotrichous ciliates related to *Oxytricha* and distinguished by long well-developed caudal cirri

sty·lo·pharyn·ge·us \ˌstī(ˌ)lōfəˈrinjēəs, -,farənˈjēəs\ *n, pl* **stylopharyn·gei** \-jē,ī\ [NL, fr. ²*styl-* + *pharyngeus*, adj., pharyngeal — more at PHARYNGEAL] : a slender muscle connecting the base of the styloid process and side of the pharynx

¹**sty·lo·pid** \ˈstīləpəd, -,pid\ *adj* [NL *Stylopidae*] : of or relating to the Stylopidae

²**stylopid** \"\ *n* -S [NL *Stylopidae*] : an insect of the family Stylopidae; *broadly* : STYLOPS 2

sty·lop·i·dae \stīˈläpə,dē\ *n pl, cap* [NL, fr. *Stylop-, Stylops*, type genus + *-idae*] : a family of insects (order Strepsiptera) that have protuberant eyes and are parasites of other insects (as bees)

sty·lo·piza·tion \ˌstīləpəˈzāshən, -,pīˈz-\ *n* -S [NL *Stylop-, Stylops* + E *-ization*] : the condition of being or the process of becoming stylopized

sty·lo·pized \ˈstīlə,pēzd\ *adj* [NL *Stylop-, Stylops* + E *-ize* + *-ed*] : altered by the presence of a parasitic stylops usu. with inhibition of normal sexual development so that an intersexual state results ⟨a ~ female wasp⟩

sty·lo·podium \ˌstīləˈpōdēəm\ *n, pl* **stylopo·dia** \-dēə\ [NL, fr. ²*styl-* + *-podium* (fr. Gk *podion* small foot, base) — more at PEW] : a disk-shaped or conical swelling or expansion at the base of the style in plants of the family Umbelliferae

sty·lops \ˈstī,läps\ *n* [NL *Stylop-, Stylops*, fr. ¹*styl-* + *-op-, -ops* -ops] **1** *cap* : a large genus (the type of the family Stylopidae) comprising many of the better known strepsipterons **2** *pl* **stylops** *also* **stylopses** : any insect of the genus *Stylops; broadly* : an insect of the order Strepsiptera

stylos *pl of* STYLO

sty·lo·san·thes \ˌstīləˈsan(ˌ)thēz\ *n, cap* [NL, fr. Gk *stylos* pillar + NL *-anthes* — more at STEER] : a genus of herbs (family Leguminosae) that are widely distributed in warm regions and have pinnately trifoliolate leaves and yellow flowers in small terminal or axillary clusters — see PENCIL FLOWER, STYLO

sty·lo·spore \ˈstīlə,spō(ə)r\ *n* [ISV ¹*styl-* + *-spore;* prob. orig. formed in F] : PYCNOSPORE

sty·lo·typ·ite \ˈstīlə,tī,pīt\ *n* -S [G *stylotyp* stylotypite (fr. *styl-* ¹styl- + *typ* type, fr. LL *typus*) + E *-ite* — more at TYPE] : a mineral (Cu,Fe,Ag)$_3$SbS$_3$ that is a sulfide of antimony, copper, silver, and iron and occurs in black orthorhombic crystals (hardness 3, sp. gr. 4.7-5.2)

-sty·lous \ˈstīləs\ *adj comb form* [¹*style* + *-ous*] : having (such) a style or (such or so many) styles — in descriptive terms in botany ⟨dolicho*stylous*⟩ ⟨mono*stylous*⟩

sty·lus *also* **sti·lus** \ˈstīləs\ *n, pl* **sty·li** \-ī,lī\ *also* **styluses** [in sense 1, fr. NL, alter. (prob. influenced by Gk *stylos* pillar) of L *stilus* stake, stylus; in other senses, modif. (prob. influenced by Gk *stylos* pillar) of L *stilus* — more at STYLE] **1 a** : STYLE 5b **b** : STYLE 5c, STYLET 2b; *esp* : any of various small pointed processes on the external genitalia of an insect **2** : INDICATOR, POINTER; *esp* : the gnomon of a sundial **3** : an instrument for writing or marking: as **a** (1) : STYLE 1 (2) : an ancient writing instrument for use on papyrus or parchment **b** (1) : a hard-pointed piece (as of glass or other material) used for tracing or writing on carbon paper so as to make impressions on the paper beneath the carbon (2) : a hard-pointed pen-shaped instrument for drawing, tracing, lettering, shading, ruling, or handwriting on stencils used in a reproducing or duplicating machine **c** (1) : NEEDLE 5b (2) : a cutting tool used to produce an original record groove during disc recording — called also *cutting stylus* **d** : a hard-pointed instrument for punching the dots in writing braille with a braille slate **e** : a device that traces a recording (as of a kymograph or an electrocardiograph) on paper

-sty·ly \ˌstīlē, -li\ *n comb form* -ES [ISV ¹*style* + *-y*] : condition of having (such or so many) styles — in botanical terms ⟨hetero*styly*⟩

styme *var of* STIME

¹**sty·mie** \ˈstīmē, -mi\ *n* -S [perh. fr. Sc *stymie* person with poor eyesight, fr. E *styme* + *-ie*] **1** : a condition that exists on a golf putting green when the ball nearer the hole lies in the line of play of another ball **2** : a thoroughly distressing and thwarting situation

²**stymie** \"\ *vt* **stymied; stymied; stymieing; stymies** : BLOCK, CHECK, THWART ⟨~ a plan⟩

stym·pha·lian \(ˈ)stimˈfālēən, -lyən\ *adj, usu cap* [Gk *stymphalios* Stymphalian (fr. *Stymphalos* Stymphalus, mountain in Arcadia near the lake formerly called Stymphalis and now called Zaraka) + E *-an*] : of or relating to Lake Zaraka in Arcadia that according to Greek mythology was haunted by man-eating birds slain by Hercules

sty·phe·lia \stīˈfēlēə, -lyə\ *n, cap* [NL, fr. Gk *styphelos* rough + NL *-ia;* perh. akin to Gk *typtein* to beat, strike — more at TYPE] : a large genus of mostly Australasian heathlike shrubs (family Epacridaceae) having the calyx and corolla usu. colored alike

styph·nate \ˈstif,nāt\ *n* -S [ISV *styphn-* (in *styphnic acid*) + *-ate*] : a salt of styphnic acid

styph·nic acid \ˈstifnik-\ *n* [*styphnic* ISV *styphn-* (fr. G — in G *styphninsäure* styphnic acid —, irreg. fr. Gk *stryphnos* astringent) + *-ic* — more at STRUBBLY] : an explosive yellow crystalline astringent acid $(NO_2)_3C_6H(OH)_2$ obtained usu. by nitration of resorcinol; 2,4,6-trinitro-resorcinol — compare PICRIC ACID

styp·sis \ˈstipsəs\ *n* -ES [NL, fr. LL, astringency, contraction, fr. Gk, fr. *styphein* to contract + *-sis*] : the application or use of styptics

¹**styp·tic** \ˈstiptik, -tēk\ *adj* [ME *stiptik*, fr. L *stypticus*, fr. Gk *styptikos*, fr. (assumed) Gk *styptos* (verbal of Gk *styphein* to contract, be astringent) + Gk *-ikos* -ic — more at STUPE] **1 a** : having an astringent effect : tending to contract or bind **b** : having a harsh, acrid, or acid effect or flavor ⟨the laughter they excite is more ~ than warm —R.A.Cordell⟩ **2** : tending to check bleeding ⟨the ~ effect of cold⟩; *esp* : having the property of arresting oozing of blood (as from a shallow surface injury) when applied to a bleeding part ⟨a ~ agent⟩ — compare HEMOSTATIC

²**styptic** \"\ *n* -S [ME *stiptik*, fr. LL *stypticum*, fr. Gk *styptikon*, fr. neut. of *styptikos*, adj.] : an agent (as a drug) having a styptic effect

styp·ti·cal \-tәkəl\ *adj, archaic* : STYPTIC

styptic collodion *n* : a collodion preparation containing a styptic (as tannin) and used on minor cuts and wounds to stop bleeding

styptic cotton *n* : cotton prepared by impregnating with a styptic agent and drying and applied to minor wounds to stop bleeding

styp·tic·i·ty \stipˈtisəd·ē\ *n* -ES [ME *stipticite*, fr. ML *stypticitat-, stypticitas*, fr. L *stypticus* styptic + *-itat-, -itas* -ity] : styptic quality : ASTRINGENCY

styptic pencil *n* : a cylindrical stick of a paste vehicle medicated with a styptic substance (as alum) and applied to small wounds to stop bleeding

styptic weed *n* : a senna (*Cassia occidentalis*)

styra·ca·ce·ae \ˌstīrəˈkāsē,ē, ˌstir-\ *n pl, cap* [NL, fr. *Styrac-, Styrax*, type genus + *-aceae*] : a widely distributed family of shrubs and trees (order Ebenales) having flowers with a 5-lobed corolla and 10 stamens and a dry or drupaceous fruit — see STYRAX — **styra·ca·ceous** \ˌ÷÷ˈkāshəs\ *adj*

styra·cin \ˈstīrəsən, ˈstir-\ *n* -S [F *styracine*, fr. L *styrac-, styrax* + F *-ine* -in] : a crystalline compound $C_{18}H_{16}O_2$ extracted esp. from storax and balsam of Peru; cinnamyl cinnamate

sty·rac·i·tol \stīˈrasə,tōl, -tōl\ *n* -S [NL *Styrac-, Styrax* + E *-itol*] : a crystalline heterocyclic polyhydric alcohol $C_6H_{12}O_5$ that is obtained from the fruit of a Japanese shrubby tree (*Styrax obassia*) or made synthetically and that is an inner ether of D-mannitol; 1,5-anhydro-D-mannitol

sty·rax \ˈstī,raks\ *n* [L *styrac-, styrax* storax, tree (of the genus *Styrax*) yielding storax, fr. Gk *styrak-, styrax*] **1** -ES : STORAX 1, 2 **2** [NL *Styrac-, Styrax*, fr. L] **a** *cap* : a large genus (the type of the family Styracaceae) of shrubs and trees that have usu. pubescent leaves and pendulous racemes of flowers with the petals distinct or slightly united and that include forms yielding commercially important resins — see BENZOIN 1, STORAX 1 **b** -ES : any plant of the genus *Styrax* : STORAX 3

styre·nate \ˈstīrə,nāt, ˈstir-\ *vt* -ED/-ING/-S [*styrene* + *-ate*] : to combine with styrene, alpha-methyl-styrene, or a similar polymerizable monomer ⟨*styrenated* drying oils, and *styrenated* alkyds as a base for many protective coatings —*Encyc. of Chem. Technol.*⟩ — **styre·na·tion** \ˌ÷÷ˈnāshən\ *n* -S

styrene \ˈstī,rēn *also* ˈsti,r-\ *n* -S [ISV *styr-* (fr. L *styrax*) + *-ene*] **1 a** : a fragrant mobile liquid unsaturated hydrocarbon $C_6H_5CH{=}CH_2$ that is obtained by the distillation of storax or the decomposition of cinnamic acid or more often from ethylbenzene either by catalytic dehydrogenation or by oxidation to acetophenone followed by partial reduction and dehydration, that polymerizes in the presence of air or peroxides to yield polystyrene, and that is used chiefly in making synthetic rubber, resins, and plastics and in improving drying oils — called also *phenylethylene, vinylbenzene;* see GR-S **b** : POLYSTYRENE **c** : STYRENE PLASTIC **2** : a bivalent radical $-CH(C_6H_5)CH_2-$ derived from styrene by breaking of the double bond — called also *phenylethylene*

styrene plastic *n* : any of various synthetic plastics made from styrene by polymerization or copolymerization

¹**styr·i·an** \ˈstirēən\ *n* -S *cap* [*Styria*, province of southeastern Austria + E *-an*, n. suffix] : an inhabitant or native of Styria

²**styrian** \"\ *adj, usu cap* [*Styria* + E *-an*, adj. suffix] : of or relating to Styria

sty·rol \ˈstī,rōl, ˈsti,r-, -rōl\ *n* -S [ISV *styr-* (fr. L *styrax*) + *-ol;* prob. orig. formed as G] : STYRENE 1a

styryl \ˈstīrəl, ˈstir-\ *n* -S [ISV *styr-* (fr. L *styrax*) + *-yl*] : a univalent radical $C_6H_5CH{=}CH-$ derived from styrene by removal of one of the hydrogen atoms attached to the omega carbon atom

styth *or* **stythe** \ˈstīth, -t͟h\ *n* -S [prob. alter. of *stife*] *dial Brit* : BLACKDAMP

SU *abbr* **1** sensation unit **2** service unit **3** set up **4** Siemens's unit

sua·be flute \ˈswäbə-\ *n* [*suabe* prob. modif. of L *suavis* sweet — more at SWEET] : a wood flute organ stop of 4-foot pitch with a bright clear tone

suabian *usu cap, var of* SWABIAN

su·abil·i·ty \ˌsüəˈbiləd·ē, -lətē, -i\ *n* : the quality or state of being suable

su·able \ˈ÷əbəl\ *adj* [*sue* + *-able*] : capable of being sued : subject to be called to answer in court — **su·ably** \-blē, -li\ *adv*

su·ae·da \süˈēdə\ *n, cap* [NL, fr. Ar *suwayd*] : a genus of herbs and shrubs (family Chenopodiaceae) bearing fleshy terete leaves and small flowers with a persistent 5-lobed perianth — see BURROWEED, SEA BLITE, SEEPWEED

suage *var of* SWAGE

sua·kin gum \ˈswäkən-\ *n, usu cap S* [fr. *Suakin*, seaport on Red sea, northeastern Sudan] : TALHA GUM

suan pan *or* **swan pan** \ˈswänˈpän\ *n* [Chin (Pek) *suan*⁴-*p'an*², lit., reckoning board] : an abacus employed by the Chinese and containing balls movable along rods held by a wooden frame

su·ant \ˈsüənt\ *var of* SUENT

sua·rez·ian \(ˈ)swäˈrezēən\ *adj, usu cap* [Francisco *Suárez* †1617 Span. theologian + E *-ian*] : of, relating to, or typical of the Spanish Jesuit Francisco Suárez or his political, philosophical, and theological doctrines

sua·rez·ian·ism \-ə,nizəm\ *n* -S *usu cap* : the theories of Francisco Suárez characterized by criticism of the concept of the divine right of kings, by belief that a ruler derives his authority directly from the people and only indirectly from God, and by a moderate scholasticism differing from Thomism primarily in rejecting a real though accepting a rational distinction between essence and existence and in a tendency to Molinism

sua·si·ble \ˈswāsəbəl, -äzə-\ *adj* [LL *suasibilis*, fr. L *suasus* (past part. of *suadēre* to advise, urge) + *-ibilis* -ible] : capable of being persuaded : easily persuaded

sua·sion \ˈswāzhən\ *n* -S [ME, fr. L *suasion-, suasio*, fr. *suasus* (past part. of *suadēre* to advise, urge) + *-ion-, -io* -ion; akin to L *suavis* sweet — more at SWEET] : the act or an instance of urging, convincing, or persuading : PERSUASION ⟨moral ~⟩

¹**sua·sive** \ˈswāsǀiv, ǀēv *also* -āz *or* ǀəv\ *adj* [L *suasus* (past part.) + E *-ive*] : tending to persuade : having a capacity for persuading : PERSUASIVE ⟨a ~ speaker⟩ ⟨~ eloquence⟩ — **sua·sive·ly** \ǀəvlē, -li\ *adv* — **sua·sive·ness** \ǀivnəs,ǀēv- *also* ǀəv-\ *n* -ES

²**suasive** \"\ *n* -S : something (as a force, speech, or influence) that exerts a suasive effect

sua·so·ria \swəˈsōrēə, -sȯr-\ *n, pl* **suasori·ae** \-rē,ē, -ē,ī\ [L, fr. fem. of *suasorius* persuasive, fr. *suasus* + *-orius* -ory] : an ancient Roman oration dealing with a problem of conscience

suave \ˈswäv, -â-\ *adj, often* -ER/-EST [MF, fr. L *suavis* pleasant, sweet — more at SWEET] **1** : blandly pleasant esp. to the senses ⟨the ~ light of afternoon —Elinor Wylie⟩ ⟨wind laden with the ~ odor . . . of madonna lilies —Norman Douglas⟩ **2 a** : smoothly affable and polite though often without deep interest or sincerity : superficially gracious in manner ⟨a ~ greeting⟩ ⟨affable, ~, moderate men, all of them perfectly and smugly convinced of their respectability —Ezra Pound⟩ **b** : smooth in performance or finish : highly finished ⟨a ~ mastery of technique⟩ ⟨a ~ surface⟩ ⟨one could wish that the book . . . was somewhat *suaver* in style —*Newsweek*⟩

syn URBANE, DIPLOMATIC, BLAND, SMOOTH, POLITIC: SUAVE suggests polished, smooth, well-mannered facilitation of easy and frictionless dealings with others, with affability, politeness, and persuasiveness all markedly checked from offensive excess or obvious fulness ⟨his voice was as smooth and *suave* as his countenance . . . murmuring his regret for having missed us at his first visit —A. Conan Doyle⟩ ⟨they could be as *suave* in advancing their bromides as we could be gauche in establishing our originalities —John Mason Brown⟩ URBANE suggests blended well-mannered and composed cultivation, poise, and wide social experience and an inbred or studied courtesy facilitating pleasant social relationships ⟨so *urbane*, sophisticated, and cultured that a stranger, meeting the Congressman for the first time, would be likely to think he had grown up in the lobby of the Waldorf-Astoria rather than in the backwoods of Missouri —Volta Torrey⟩ ⟨an active, *urbane*, gregarious gentleman . . . who likes to dine out, is fond of travel, is interested in people, and keeps his enthusiasm for life —Rosemary Benét⟩ DIPLOMATIC stresses the tactfulness necessary to ensure lastingly smooth relationships ⟨busy, active, *diplomatic* managing of the party —E.E.Hale⟩ BLAND stresses lack of irritation and implies a placid outlook, mild disposition, general affability, and complaisant benignness ⟨a distinguished-looking old cleric with a sweet smile and a white tie, he's just honorable and *bland* —George Santayana⟩ ⟨polished in his manners, exquisitely neat in his appearance and his *bland* conversation never rose above a calm level —Ruth Garland⟩ SMOOTH suggests an easy suavity making for pleasant, frictionless relationships ⟨they themselves were *smooth* in manner, and they saw to it that in their presence life had no rough edges —Mary Webb⟩ POLITIC suggests expedient, shrewd, and tactful handling of others by diplomacy, manipulation, or ingratiation ⟨the mayors and corporations as a rule guided their cities through difficult times with *politic* shrewdness —Edwin Benson⟩ ⟨the generosity shown by the *politic* conqueror to his prisoners —W.H.Prescott⟩

suave·ly *adv* : in a suave manner : with suavity

suave·ness *n* -ES : the quality or state of being suave : SUAVITY

suav·i·ty \ˈswävəd·ē, ˈswav-, -vətē, -i *sometimes* ˈswāv-\ *n* -ES [ME *suavitee*, fr. MF *suavité*, fr. L *suavitat-, suavitas* pleasantness, sweetness, fr. *suavis* pleasant, sweet + *-itat-, -itas* -ity] **1** : the quality or state of being suave: as **a** (1) : mildness and pleasantness to the sense of smell or taste : FRAGRANCE ⟨eggs and butter and perhaps a bit of onion give both flavor and ~ —Scott Seegers⟩ (2) : pleasing sweetness (as of sound or expression) ⟨music performed with great ~⟩ **b** : the condition of being blandly pleasing to the mind : superficial and urbane agreeableness ⟨replied with ~⟩ ⟨the ~ of their manners⟩ **2** : something that is suave : AMENITY — usu. used in pl. ⟨the *suavities* of polite society⟩

¹**sub** \ˈsəb\ *adj* [short for *subordinate*] : AUXILIARY, SUBORDINATE, SECONDARY ⟨a ~ post office⟩ ⟨a ~ theme in a music⟩

²**sub** \"\ *n* -S [by shortening] : SUBSTITUTE

³**sub** \"\ *vb* **subbed; subbed; subbing; subs** [in sense 1, short for ²*substitute;* in sense 2, short for *subsistence*] *vi* **1** : to act and esp. work as a substitute ⟨*subbing* for the absent men⟩ **2** *chiefly Brit* : to provide or accept a portion of wages in advance as a subsistence allowance ~ *vt* **1** [by shortening] : SUBEDIT **2** [by shortening] : SUBIRRIGATE **3** [short for *substratum*] : to apply a substratum to (a photographic film or plate)

⁴**sub** \"\ *n* -S [by shortening] : SUBMARINE

⁵**sub** \"\ *n* -S [short for *substratum*] : a photographic substratum

sub- *prefix* [ME, fr. L, under, below, from below, up, near, further, after, fr. *sub*, prep. — more at UP] **1** : under : beneath : below ⟨*sub*soil⟩ ⟨*sub*cutaneous⟩ ⟨*sub*pier⟩ ⟨*sub*dominant⟩ ⟨*sub*hymenial⟩ **2 a** : subordinate : secondary : next lower than or inferior to ⟨*sub*center⟩ ⟨*sub*freshman⟩ ⟨*sub*genus⟩ **b** : subordinate portion of : subdivision of : derived from ⟨*sub*committee⟩ ⟨*sub*culture⟩ ⟨*sub*district⟩ ⟨*sub*science⟩; *also* : with repetition (as of a process) so as to form, stress, or deal with subordinate parts or relations ⟨*sub*classify⟩ ⟨*sub*let⟩ ⟨*sub*branch⟩ ⟨*sub*contract⟩ **3 a** : somewhat : slightly : less than completely or perfectly : inadequately : less than normally ⟨*sub*acid⟩ ⟨*sub*dominant⟩ ⟨*sub*ovate⟩ ⟨*sub*arcuate⟩ ⟨*sub*clinical⟩ ⟨*sub*acute⟩ ⟨*sub*convulsive⟩ **b** (1) : containing only a relatively small proportion or less than the normal amount of (such) an element or radical ⟨*sub*oxide⟩ — not used systematically; compare PROT- (2) : basic — in names of salts ⟨*sub*acetate⟩ ⟨*sub*nitrate⟩; not used systematically **4 a** : almost : nearly ⟨*sub*alate⟩ ⟨*sub*caulescent⟩ ⟨*sub*abdominal⟩ ⟨*Sub*akhmimic⟩ **b** : falling nearly in the category of and often adjoining : bordering upon ⟨*sub*adult⟩ ⟨*sub*arid⟩ ⟨*sub*arctic⟩ **c** : immediately following : after ⟨*sub*apostolic⟩ ⟨*Sub*-Mycenaean⟩

sub *abbr* **1** subaltern **2** subcontractor **3** sublieutenant **4** submerge; submerged **5** subordinate **6** subscriber; subscription **7** subsidiary **8** suburb; suburban **9** subway **10** supplementary unemployment benefit

sub·abdominal \ˌsəb+\ *adj* [*sub-* + *abdominal*] *of a ventral fin* : situated nearly far enough back to be considered abdominal

sub·account \"+\ *n* [*sub-* + *account*] : a subordinate or secondary account (as in a business record)

sub·acetate \ˌsəb+\ *n* [*sub-* + *acetate*] : a basic acetate ⟨verdigris is a ~ of copper⟩

sub·acid \"+\ *adj* [L *subacidus*, fr. *sub-* + *acidus* acid — more at ACID] **1 a** : moderately sour to the taste ⟨~ fruit juices⟩ **b** : somewhat biting (as in manner, style, or presentation) : rather tart ⟨~ prose⟩ ⟨a little ~ kind of . . . impatience —Laurence Sterne⟩ **2 a** : containing less than the normal or usual amount of acid ⟨a ~ salt⟩ **b** : having a hydrogen-ion concentration of 5.5 to 6.0 — used esp. of leaf-mold soils — **sub·acidly** \"+\ *adv* — **sub·acidness** \"+\ *n*

sub·acidity \ˌ÷+\ *n* : the quality or state of being subacid; *esp* : HYPOCHLORHYDRIA

sub·acute \ˌsəb+\ *adj* [*sub-* + *acute*] : moderately acute ⟨a ~ angle⟩: as **a** : having a tapering but not sharply pointed form ⟨a ~ flower petal⟩ ⟨large ~ spines on some sea urchins⟩ **b** (1) : falling between acute and chronic in character ⟨~ endocarditis⟩ (2) : less marked in severity or duration than a corresponding acute state ⟨~ pain⟩ ⟨~ inflammation⟩ — **sub·acutely** \"+\ *adv*

sub·adult \ˌsəb+\ *n* [*sub-* + *adult*] : an individual approaching the adult age or the termination of the growing period : one that has passed through the juvenile period but has not yet attained typical adult characteristics

sub·aerial \"+\ *adj* [*sub-* + *aerial*] : taking place in the open air : situated or occurring on or immediately adjacent to the surface of the earth: as **a** : of, relating to, or taking place on a land surface as distinguished from a subaqueous or subterranean ⟨~ erosion⟩ ⟨a ~ valley⟩ **b** : situated or growing at or just above the surface of the ground ⟨~ roots⟩ — **subaerially** \"+\ *adv*

sub·aesthetic \"+\ *adj* [*sub-* + *aesthetic*] : involving or occurring at a level below the developed aesthetic ⟨~ motor functioning out of which art accomplishments can develop —A.L.Kroeber⟩

sub·age \ˈ÷+,-\ *n* [*sub-* + *age*] : a distinguishable subdivision of a geologic age usu. characterized by the occurrence of some specific phenomenon (as a deposition of loess or a glacial recession)

sub·agency \ˌsəb+\ *n* [*sub-* + *agency*] : a subordinate agency commonly originated by the agency to which it belongs rather than by the primary authority from which its parent agency stems ⟨government agencies spawning *subagencies*⟩

sub·agent \"+\ *n* [*sub-* + *agent*] : a subordinate agent : a person to whom an agent delegates with the authorization of his principal the performance of some duty, act, or responsibility owed by him to the principal

su·bah \ˈsübə\ *n* -s [Per *ṣūba* province, fr. Ar] **1 :** a province or division of the Mogul Empire or its government **2 :** SUBAHDAR

su·bah·dar *or* **su·ba·dar** \ˌ==ˈdär\ *n* -s [Per *ṣūbadār*, fr. *ṣūba* province + *-dār* having, holding, fr. OPer *dar-* to hold] **1 :** a governor of a subah **2 :** the chief native officer of a native company in the former British Indian army having a position about equivalent to that of captain

su·bah·dary \-ˈdärē, -ri\ *or* **su·bah·ship** \ˈsübəˌship\ *n, pl* **subahdaries** *or* **subahships** [*subahdary* fr. *subahdar* + *-y; subahship* fr. *subah* + *-ship*] **:** the office or jurisdiction of a subahdar **:** SUBAH 1

sub·akhmimic *also* **sub·achmimic** \ˈsəb+\ *n* -s *usu cap* [*sub-* + *Akhmimic, Achmimic*] **:** a late dialect of Coptic standing between Sahidic and Akhmimic

sub·alary \ˈsəb+\ *adj* [*sub-* + *alary*] **:** situated under the wings

sub·alate \"+\ *adj* [*sub-* + *alate*] **:** having a form suggesting a wing esp. in being thin and somewhat triangular

sub·alimentation \ˈsəb+\ *n* [*sub-* + *alimentation*] **:** insufficient or inadequate nutritional intake

sub·alkaline \ˈsəb+\ *adj* [*sub-* + *alkaline*] **:** having a hydrogen-ion concentration of 8.0 to 8.5 — used esp. of soils of various limestone or salt-marsh regions

sub·allocate \"+\ *vt* [*sub-* + *allocate*] **:** to provide a share of from a source or supply provided or available to one or more subordinate agencies ⟨the provincial treasury will ~ funds to the districts⟩ — **sub·allocation** \"+\ *n*

sub·almoner \ˈsəb+\ *n* [*sub-* + *almoner*] **:** an under almoner **:** an assistant to an almoner

sub·alpine \"+\ *adj* [*sub-* + *alpine*] **1 :** of or relating to the region about the foot and lower slopes of the Alps **2 :** of, relating to, or constituting high upland slopes immediately below the timberline ⟨spruce and fir are characteristic ~ floral elements⟩ — compare MONTANE

subalpine fir *n* **:** ALPINE FIR

¹sub·al·tern \səˈbȯltə(r)n *sometimes* ˈsə,bȯ-, *chiefly Brit* ˈsəbəltən\ *adj* [LL *subalternus*, fr. L *sub-* + *alternus* alternate, fr. *alter* other (of two) — more at ALTER] **1 :** ranked or ranged below **:** inferior in status or quality **:** SUBORDINATE ⟨the congenitally ~ type of man —H.L.Mencken⟩: as **a :** relating to or typical of subordinate status ⟨~ fears⟩ **b :** held or holding from one who is himself a vassal ⟨a ~ manor⟩ ⟨a ~ vassal⟩ **c** *chiefly Brit* **:** holding a rank below that of captain **2** [ML *subalternus*, fr. LL, subordinate] **:** particular with reference to a related universal or general ⟨"some S is P" is a ~ proposition to "all S is P"⟩

²subaltern \"\ *n* -s **1 a :** a person holding a subordinate position or being inferior in respect to some quality or characteristic ⟨natural ~s, ill-trained and uninterested⟩ **b** *chiefly Brit* **:** a commissioned officer below the rank of captain **2** [ML *subalternus*, fr. *subalternus*, adj.] **:** a subaltern proposition **:** a logical subalternate

sub·al·ter·nant \ˌsə,bȯlˈtərnənt, -bal-\ *n* -s [ML *subalternus* + E *-ant*] **:** SUPERALTERN

¹sub·alternate \(ˌ)səb+\ *adj* [ML *subalternatus*, past part. of *subalternare* to subordinate, fr. LL *subalternus* subordinate] **1 :** inferior in quality or status **:** SUBORDINATE ⟨a ~ art⟩ ⟨a study ~ to his earlier work⟩ **2** [*sub-* + *alternate*] **:** nearly alternate but with a tendency to become opposite ⟨the secondary lateral veins of a pinnate leaf are often ~⟩ — **sub·alternately** \"+\ *adv*

²subalternate \"\ *n* **:** a particular logical proposition that follows by immediate inference from a universal one of like quality and identical terms

sub·alternation \"+\ *n* [ML *subalternation-, subalternatio*, fr. *subalternatus* (past part. of *subalternare* to subordinate) + L *-ion-, -io* -ion] **1 :** the quality or state of being subalternate **:** succession by turns **:** SUBORDINATION **2 :** the relation of a logical subalternate to a superaltern — see OPPOSITION 2a(2)

subaltern genus *n* **:** a logical genus that may be a species of a higher genus ⟨the genus *book* is a *subaltern genus* since it is also a species of the genus *printed matter*⟩ — compare TREE OF PORPHYRY

sub·al·ter·ni·ty \ˌsə,bȯlˈtərnəd·ē, -bal-\ *n* -ES [¹*subaltern* + *-ity*] **:** the quality, state, or position of being subaltern

sub·angular \ˈsəb+\ *adj* [*sub-* + *angular*] **:** somewhat angular **:** free from sharp angles though not smoothly rounded ⟨~ quartz particles⟩ — **sub·angularly** \"+\ *adv*

sub·antarctic \"+\ *adj* [ISV *sub-* + *antarctic*] **:** of, relating to, or being a region just outside the antarctic circle

su·ba·nun \süˈbä,nün\ *n, pl* **subanun** *or* **subanuns** *usu cap* [Cebuan, fr. Subanun *Subanen*, from *subā* upstream + *-nen* people, language] **1 a :** any of the pagan peoples on the Zamboanga peninsula of western Mindanao, Philippines **b :** a member of such people **2 :** the Austronesian language of the Subanun peoples

sub·apical \ˈsəb+\ *adj* [*sub-* + *apical*] **:** situated below or near an apex — **sub·apically** \"+\ *adv*

sub·aponeurotic \"+\ *adj* [*sub-* + *aponeurotic*] **:** lying beneath an aponeurosis

sub·apostolic \"+\ *adj* [*sub-* + *apostolic*] **:** of, relating to, or being the age immediately following that of the apostles ⟨the ~ church⟩

sub·apparent \"+\ *adj* [*sub-* + *apparent*] **:** imperfectly apparent **:** perceived with difficulty ⟨a ~ shadowing⟩

sub·appressed \"+\ *adj* [*sub-* + *appressed*] **:** imperfectly or partially appressed ⟨~ pubescence on a leaf⟩

sub·apterous \ˈsəb+\ *adj* [ISV *sub-* + *apterous*] **:** BRACHYPTEROUS

sub·aquatic \"+\ *adj* [ISV *sub-* + *aquatic*] **1 :** SUBAQUEOUS **2 :** somewhat aquatic ⟨a marginal ~ flora⟩

sub·aqueous \"+\ *adj* [*sub-* + *aqueous*] **1 a :** being or found under water or beneath the surface of water ⟨viewing the ~ fauna from a glass-bottomed boat⟩ **b :** adapted for use under water **:** SUBMARINE ⟨a ~ helmet⟩ **c :** suggesting or typical of the underwater world (as in remoteness or dimness) ⟨a soft ~ light⟩ ⟨the ~ world of the underconscious —Vernon Young⟩ **2 :** formed or taking place in or under water ⟨~ canyons⟩

sub·arachnoid \"+\ *adj* [ISV *sub-* + *arachnoid*] **:** of, relating to, or situated under the arachnoid membrane ⟨~ processes⟩: as **a :** constituting the space between the arachnoid membrane and the pia mater **b :** involving the subarachnoid space and the fluid that is contained therein ⟨a ~ meningitis⟩

su·ba·rae·an *or* **su·ba·re·an** \ˌsübəˈrēən\ *n* -s *usu cap* [*subaraean* prob. fr. NL *Subaraeus* Subaraean (fr. *Subartu*, ancient region of northern Mesopotamia inhabited by the Subaraeans) + E *-an; subarean* fr. *Subartu* + E *-ean*] **1 :** a member of an ancient people inhabiting the region stretching westward from the Zagros mountains of Iran **2 :** a language of uncertain relationship used by the Subaraeans and esp. by the Mitannians

sub·arch \ˈsəb+,-\ *n* [*sub-* + *arch*] **:** a subordinate arch esp. when one of two or more grouped in a larger arch

sub·arctic \ˈsəb+\ *adj* [ISV *sub-* + *arctic*] **:** of, relating to, or being regions immediately outside of the arctic circle or regions that for various reasons (as altitude) are similar to these in climate or conditions of life — compare ALPINE

sub·arcuate \"+\ *also* **sub·arcuated** \"+\ *adj* [*sub-* + *arcuate* or *arcuated*] **:** somewhat arched or bowed

sub·arcuation \"+\ *n* [*sub-* + *arcuation*] **:** the construction of subordinate arches under a main arch; *also* **:** arches so constructed

sub·area \"+\ *n* [*sub-* + *area*] **:** a subdivision of an area

sub·arid \"+\ *adj* [*sub-* + *arid*] **:** moderately or slightly arid **:** characterized by or constituting a climate somewhat deficient in moisture — compare SUBHUMID

sub·artesian \ˈsəb+\ *adj* [*sub-* + *artesian*] **:** of, relating to, or being water that rises naturally in a well to a height appreciably above that of the surrounding water table but does not flow out of the well

sub·ascending \"+\ *adj* [*sub-* + *ascending*] **:** rising somewhat obliquely upward from a flattened basal attachment ⟨a ~ keel on a papilionaceous flower⟩

sub·assemble \"+\ *vt* [back-formation fr. *subassembly*] **:** to fabricate (as parts) into a subassembly **:** prepare (a structural unit) as a subassembly

sub·assembler \"+\ *n* [*subassemble* + *-er*] **:** a worker that puts together subassemblies in the process of manufacture

sub·assembly \"+\ *n* [*sub-* + *assembly*] **1 :** a structural unit manufactured or assembled separately but designed to be incorporated with other units in the final assembly of a finished product **2 :** the act or process of preparing subassemblies ⟨a ~ line⟩

sub·astral \ˈsəb+\ *adj* [*sub-* + *astral*] **:** located lower than the stars; *specif* **:** TERRESTRIAL ⟨lowly ~ beings⟩

¹sub·astringent \"+\ *adj* [*sub-* + *astringent*] **:** mildly astringent

²subastringent \"\ *n* **:** a subastringent substance

sub·atlantic \"+\ *adj, usu cap A* [ISV *sub-* + *Atlantic* ocean] **1 :** located beneath the Atlantic ocean ⟨a *sub-Atlantic* cable⟩ **2 :** of, relating to, or being a postglacial climatic period believed to have begun in northwestern Europe about 850–500 B.C. and to be continuing in existence at the present time

sub·atmospheric \"+\ *adj* [*sub-* + *atmospheric*] **:** less or lower than that of the atmosphere ⟨~ temperatures⟩

sub·atomic \"+\ *adj* [*sub-* + *atomic*] **:** of, relating to, or being the phenomena occurring inside of atoms or particles smaller than atoms ⟨the harnessing of ~ energy —Bernard Jaffe⟩

sub·audible \"+\ *adj* [*sub-* + *audible*] **1 :** having a frequency or intensity below the limit of hearing **2 :** scarcely perceptible to the ear ⟨a ~ conversation⟩ ⟨a ~ humming sound⟩

sub·au·di·tion \ˌsə,bȯˈdishən\ *n* [LL *subaudition-, subauditio*, fr. *subauditus* (past part. of *subaudire* to understand, fr. L *sub-* + *audire* to hear) + L *-ion-, -io* -ion — more at AUDIBLE] **1 :** the act of understanding or supplying something not expressed **2 :** something that is understood or supplied in comprehending a text

sub·au·di·tur \ˌsə,bȯˈdīd·ər, -ī,tər\ *n* -s [LL, it is understood, 3d pers. sing. pres. indic. of *subaudire* to understand] **:** something understood or implied in connection with what is expressed

sub·au·rale \ˌsə,bȯˈra(ˌ)lē, -rā-, -rä-\ *n* -s [NL, fr. neut. of *subauralis* of below the ear, fr. L *sub-* + NL *auralis* of the ear, fr. L *auris* ear + *-alis* -al — more at EAR] **:** an anthropometric landmark consisting of the lowest point on the lobe of the ear when the head is held in the eye-ear plane

sub·auricular \ˈsəb+\ *adj* [*sub-* + *auricular*] **:** situated below the ear

sub·average \"+\ *adj* [*sub-* + *average*] **:** of a lower level or quality than some norm ⟨~ minds⟩ ⟨~ education⟩

sub·axillary \"+\ *also* **sub·axillar** \"+\ *adj* [*sub-* + *axillary* or *axillar*] **1 :** situated below the axilla **2 :** situated below or beneath an axil ⟨a ~ bud⟩

sub·basal \"+\ *adj* [*sub-* + *basal*] **1 :** situated near or below a base or basal part ⟨a ~ color band on an insect wing⟩ **2** [*subbase* + *-al*] **:** of, relating to, or constituting a subbase

sub·base \ˈsəb+,-\ *n* [*sub-* + *base*] **1 a :** another base, foundation, or other underlying support placed below that which ordinarily forms the base **b :** the lowermost part of a base; *specif* **:** the lowest member of an architectural base (as when divided horizontally) or of a baseboard or pedestal **c :** material placed under or designed for use under a base **2 :** an alternate or satellite air base subordinate to a main air base commander either directly or administratively or logistically

sub-base \ˈ=,=\ *n* [¹*sub* + *base*] **:** a submarine base

sub·basement \ˈsəb+\ *n* [*sub-* + *basement*] **:** a basement or an underground story or one of several such located below the true basement of a building

sub·bass \ˈsəb+,-\ *n* [*sub-* + *bass*] **:** a 16- or 32-foot pipe organ stop used usu. in a pedal organ

subbed *past of* SUB

sub·bifid \ˈsəb+\ *adj* [*sub-* + *bifid*] **:** somewhat or incompletely forked ⟨a ~ tongue⟩

sub·bing \ˈsəbiŋ, -bēŋ\ *n* -s [fr. gerund of ²*sub*] **1 :** an act of serving as a substitute **2 :** SUBIRRIGATION **3** [¹*sub* + *-ing*] **:** SUBSTRATUM e

sub·bituminous \ˈsəb+\ *adj* [*sub-* + *bituminous*] **:** of, relating to, or being coal of lower rank than bituminous coal but higher than lignite

sub·boreal \"+\ *adj* [ISV *sub-* + *boreal*] **1 :** very cold **:** approaching the frigid ⟨a ~ climate⟩ **2 :** of, relating to, or constituting a postglacial period preceding the boreal and characterized by relatively warm dry climate **3 :** of, relating to, or constituting a biogeographic zone that approaches the boreal in climatic condition

sub·bot·nik \səˈbȯtnik\ *n, pl* **subbotni·ki** \-nəkē\ *also* **subbotniks** *usu cap* [Russ, fr. *subbota* Saturday (fr. L *sabbatum* Sabbath, Saturday) + *-nik* (as in *raskolnik*) — more at SABBATH] **:** SABBATARIAN 3

sub·bourdon \ˈsəb+\ *n* [*sub-* + *bourdon*] **:** a 32-foot covered wood pedal stop in a pipe organ of large scale

sub·brach·i·al \ˈsəbˈbrakēəl\ *also* **sub·brach·i·an** \-ēən\ *adj* [*subbrachial* fr. NL *subbrachialis*, fr. L *sub-* + *brachialis* brachial; *subbrachian* fr. NL *Subbrachiales* + E *-an* — more at BRACHIAL] **:** located beneath or nearly beneath a pectoral fin ⟨ventral fins ~⟩

sub·brach·i·a·les \ˌsəb,brakēˈā(ˌ)lēz\ *n pl, cap* [NL, fr. pl. of *subbrachialis* subbrachial] *in some esp former classifications* **:** a division of soft-finned fishes having the ventral fins beneath or nearly beneath the pectoral fins

sub·brachycephal \ˈsəb+\ *n* [NL *subbrachycephalus*, fr. *sub-* + *brachycephalus* brachycephal] **:** a subbrachycephalic individual

sub·brachycephalic \"+\ *adj* [NL *subbrachycephalus* + E *-ic*] **:** having a cephalic index of 80–83

sub·brachycephaly \"+\ *n* [NL *subbrachycephalus* + E *-y*] **:** the quality or state of being subbrachycephalic

¹sub·branch \ˈ=+,-\ *vi* [*sub-* + *branch* (v.)] **:** to divide into subbranches

²subbranch \"\ *n* [*sub-* + *branch* (n.)] **1 :** a branch of a branch ⟨complex organizations that ramify into branches and ~es⟩ **2 :** a branch (as of a business firm) that is of secondary importance and usu. less complete in function or service than a main branch

sub·breed \"+,-\ *n* [*sub-* + *breed*] **:** a distinguishable race or strain within a breed

sub·cabinet \ˈsəb+\ *n* [*sub-* + *cabinet*] **1 :** a cabinet designed to form a base (as for a piece of apparatus) **2 :** an unofficial advisory group selected by some U.S. presidents esp. from members of the several executive departments

sub·calcarine \"+\ *adj* [*sub-* + *calcarine*] **:** situated below the calcarine fissure

sub·caliber \"+\ *adj* [*sub-* + *caliber*] **1 :** smaller than the caliber of a gun ⟨a ~ projectile⟩ **2 :** of, relating to, used in, or effected by firing a subcaliber projectile

sub·callosal \"+\ *adj* [*sub-* + *callosal*] **:** situated below the corpus callosum ⟨the ~ gyrus⟩

sub·campanulate \"+\ *adj* [ISV *sub-* + *campanulate*] **:** somewhat ventricose at the base and usu slightly recurved at the margin **:** not quite bell-shaped ⟨a mushroom with a ~ pileus⟩

sub·capillary \ˈsəb+\ *adj* [ISV *sub-* + *capillary*] **:** of less than capillary dimensions ⟨~ pores in rock⟩

sub·capsular \"+\ *adj* [*sub-* + *capsular*] **:** situated or occurring beneath or within a capsule ⟨a ~ abscess⟩ ⟨~ cataracts⟩

sub·caption \"+\ *n* [*sub-* + *caption*] **:** a secondary headline (as in an advertisement)

sub·carbide \"+\ *n* [*sub-* + *carbide*] **:** a carbide having less than the ordinary proportion of carbon ⟨~ of iron Fe_4C is reputed to be a constituent of commercial iron⟩

sub·carbonate \"+\ *n* [*sub-* + *carbonate*] **:** a basic carbonate (as bismuth subcarbonate)

sub·carboniferous \ˈsəb+\ *adj or n, usu cap* [*sub-* + *carboniferous*] **:** MISSISSIPPIAN

sub·carcinogenic \"+\ *adj* [*sub-* + *carcinogenic*] **:** inadequate to produce a carcinogenic effect

sub·cardinal \"+\ *adj* [*sub-* + *cardinal* (vein)] **:** of, relating to, situated near, or being either of two veins in the mammalian embryo or the adult of some lower vertebrates that develop one on each side in the abdominal region ventromedial to the mesonephros and in the mammal participate in the formation of the inferior vena cava and the renal veins

sub·carinate \"+\ *adj* [ISV *sub-* + *carinate*] **:** somewhat or incompletely keeled ⟨a ~ scale⟩

sub·carrier \"+\ *n* [*sub-* + *carrier*] **:** a low-frequency carrier in an electronic system (as a telemetering system or a multichannel radio system) used to modulate a main carrier and often being itself modulated to carry information

sub·cartilaginous \"+\ *adj* [MF *subcartilagineux*, fr. *sub-* + *cartilagineux* cartilaginous — more at CARTILAGINOUS] **1 :** partially cartilaginous **2 :** situated under a cartilage

sub·casing \"+\ *n* [*sub-* + *casing*] **:** a rough frame that forms a base over which the finish casing of a door or window opening is applied

sub·cast \"+,-\ *n* [*sub-* + *cast*] **:** a secondary swarm (as of bees)

sub·caste \"+,-\ *n* [*sub-* + *caste*] **:** a subdivision of a caste

¹sub·caudal \ˈsəb+\ *adj* [*sub-* + *caudal*] **:** situated under or on the ventral side of the tail ⟨a ~ pouch⟩

²subcaudal \"\ *n* **:** a subcaudal plate or shield

sub·caudate \"+\ *adj* [*sub-* + *caudate*] **:** having an imperfect or abridged prolongation ⟨a ~ wing of a butterfly⟩

sub·caulescent \"+\ *adj* [ISV *sub-* + *caulescent*] **:** nearly acaulescent

sub·celestial \"+\ *adj* [*sub-* + *celestial*] **:** situated beneath the heavens; *specif* **:** MUNDANE

sub·cellar \"+\ *n* [*sub-* + *cellar*] **:** a cellar beneath a story wholly or partly underground; *usu* **:** a cellar under a cellar **:** SUBBASEMENT

sub·center \"+\ *n* [*sub-* + *center*] **:** a secondary center; *esp* **:** a center (as for business, shopping, amusement) located outside the main business area of a city

sub·central \"+\ *adj* [*sub-* + *central*] **1 :** located under a center: as **a :** situated below the central sulcus **b :** situated below the centrum of a vertebra **2 :** nearly central **:** not quite central — **sub·centrally** \"+\ *adv*

sub·cerebral plane \ˈ=+-ˈ-\ *n* [*sub-* + *cerebral*] **:** an anthropometric landmark consisting of the plane passing through a line crossing the lower angles of the parietal bones and the point where the superciliary ridge joins the cheek bone

sub·chairman \ˈsəb+\ *n* [*sub-* + *chairman*] **:** a substitute or subordinate chairman

sub·chanter \"+\ *n* [*sub-* + *chanter*] **1 :** SUCCENTOR **2 :** VICAR CHORAL

sub·chapter \"+\ *n* [*sub-* + *chapter*] **:** a subdivision of a chapter (as of a code of laws)

subchaser \ˈ=,==\ *n* [¹*sub* + *chaser*] **:** SUBMARINE CHASER

sub·chela \ˈsəb+\ *n, pl* **subchelae** [NL, fr. *sub-* + *chela*] **:** a grasping organ of the limbs of some crustaceans (as of the genus *Squilla*) in which the terminal segment folds back against the next one

sub·chelate \"+\ *adj* [*sub-* + *chelate*] **1 :** imperfectly chelate **2** [NL *subchela* + E *-ate*] **:** ending in a subchela

sub·chief \ˈsəb+,-\ *n* [*sub-* + *chief*] **:** a subordinate chief **:** a chief of secondary rank or authority

sub·chloride \ˈsəb+\ *n* [ISV *sub-* + *chloride*] **1 :** a binary chloride containing a relatively small proportion of chlorine ⟨calomel is the ~ of mercury⟩ **2 :** a basic chloride (as an oxychloride)

sub·chondral \"+\ *adj* [*sub-* + *chondral*] **:** situated below or beneath cartilage

sub·chordal \"+\ *adj* [*sub-* + *chordal*] **:** situated below the notochord

sub·chorionic \"+\ *adj* [*sub-* + *chorionic*] **:** underlying the chorion

sub·choroid \"+\ *adj* [*sub-* + *choroid*] **:** lying or occurring between the choroid coat of the eye and the retina

sub·cinc·to·ri·um \ˌsək,siŋ(k)ˈtōrēəm, ÷ ˌsə,si-\ *or* **suc·cinc·to·ri·um** \ˌsək,siŋ(k)ˈtōrēəm\ *n* -s [LL, fr. L *subcinctus, succinctus* (past part. of *subcingere, succingere* to tuck up, gird about) + *-orium* -ory — more at SUCCINCT] **:** a vestment consisting of an ornamental square of cloth suspended from the girdle and worn by the pope of the Roman Catholic Church when celebrating a solemn mass

sub·cin·gu·lum \ˌsəbˈsiŋgyələm\ *n* -s [LL *subcingulum, succingulum*, fr. L, girdle, fr. *subcingere, succingere* to tuck up, gird about + *-ulum* (neut. of *-ulus* -ule)] **:** a vestment consisting of a girdle or belt circling the waist from which hangs the subcinctorium of the papal vestments when the pope of the Roman Catholic Church is celebrating a solemn mass

sub·circular \ˈsəb+\ *adj* [*sub-* + *circular*] **:** nearly circular **:** not quite circular

sub·civilized \"+\ *adj* [*sub-* + *civilized*] **:** partially civilized

sub·claim \"+,-\ *n* [*sub-* + *claim*] **:** a subordinate claim **:** a claim dependent on or arising out of another

sub·clamatores \ˈsəb+\ *n pl, cap* [NL, fr. *sub-* + *Clamatores*] *in former classifications* **:** a superfamily of passerine birds comprising the broadbills

sub·clan \ˈsəb+,-\ *n* [*sub-* + *clan*] **:** a subdivision of a clan commonly tracing descent from a particular ancestor and forming a single community

sub·class \"+,-\ *n* [*sub-* + *class*] **:** a primary division of a class: as **a :** a biological taxonomic category below a class and above an order **b :** SUBSET

sub·classify \ˈsəb+\ *vt* [*sub-* + *classify*] **:** to form or formulate a detailed classification of **:** divide into subclasses

sub·clause \ˈsəb+,-\ *n* [*sub-* + *clause*] **:** a subordinate clause

sub·clavate \ˈsəb+\ *adj* [*sub-* + *clavate*] **:** somewhat club-shaped

sub·cla·via \ˌsəbˈklāvēə\ *n* -s [NL, fr. fem. of *subclavius* subclavian] **:** SUBCLAVIAN ARTERY

¹sub·cla·vi·an \ˈsəbˈklāvēən\ *adj* [NL *subclavius* (fr. L *sub-* + *clavis* key) + E *-an* — more at CLAVICLE] **:** located under the clavicle **:** of, relating to, or being a subclavian part

²subclavian \"\ *n* -s **:** a subclavian part

subclavian artery *n* [trans. of NL *subclavia arteria*] **:** the proximal part of the main artery of the arm or forelimb extending in man from its point of origin to the outer border of the first rib and arising on the right side from the innominate artery and on the left from the arch of the aorta — see AXILLARY ARTERY

subclavian groove *n* **:** either of two grooves for the passage of the subclavian artery and vein along the first rib

subclavian muscle *n* [trans. of NL *subclavius musculus*] **:** SUBCLAVIUS

subclavian vein *n* **:** the proximal part of the main vein of the arm from the end of the axillary vein at the level of the first rib to its junction with the internal jugular vein to form the innominate vein

sub·cla·vi·us \ˌsəbˈklāvēəs\ *n, pl* **subcla·vii** \-vē,ī\ [NL, fr. *subclavius*, adj., subclavian] **:** a small muscle on each side of the body extending from the first rib and its cartilage to the under surface of the clavicle

sub·climax \ˈsəb+\ *n* [*sub-* + *climax*] **:** a stage or community in an ecological succession immediately preceding a climatic or regional climax; *esp* **:** such a stage or community when held in relative stability for a long time or indefinitely through edaphic or biotic influences or by fire — compare DISCLIMAX

sub·clinical \"+\ *adj* [*sub-* + *clinical*] **:** marked by only slight abnormality and not being such as to give rise to overt symptoms **:** not detectable by the usual clinical tests ⟨a ~ infection⟩ ⟨a ~ vitamin deficiency⟩ — **sub·clinically** \"+\ *adv*

sub·clone \"+,-\ *n* [*sub-* + *clone*] **:** a selected line within a clone

sub-cloud car \ˈ=ˈ=-\ *n* **:** a car which may be lowered from an airship by means of a cable to a position below obscuring clouds to permit observation of the ground

sub·clover \ˈsəb+\ *n* [by shortening] **:** SUBTERRANEAN CLOVER

sub·coastal \"+\ *adj* [*sub-* + *coastal*] **:** situated below a coast — used of a submerged plain of a continental shelf

subcoat \ˈ=,=\ *n* [*sub-* + *coat*] **:** a coat or layer of material underlying another coat; *usu* **:** a coat (as of paint) applied before and intended to form a base for an outer coat

sub·collateral \ˈsəb+\ *adj* [*sub-* + *collateral*] **:** of, relating to, or being a convolution of the tentorial surface of the temporal lobe of the cerebrum lying external to the collateral fissure

sub·collegiate \"+\ *or* **sub·college** \"+\ *adj* [*sub-* + *collegiate* or *college*] **:** offered to or adapted to the needs of students not intending or inadequately prepared to attend college ⟨courses at the ~ level⟩ ⟨studies of ~ grade⟩

sub·columnar \ˈsəb+\ *adj* [*sub-* + *columnar*] **:** partially or imperfectly columnar

sub·coma \ˌsəb+\ *adj* [*sub-* + *coma*] **:** inadequate to produce coma ⟨~ doses of insulin⟩
sub·commission \"+\ *n* [*sub-* + *commission*] **:** a secondary or subordinate commission
sub·commissioner \"+\ *n* [*sub-* + *commissioner*] **1 :** a commissioner subordinate in rank or authority to another **2 :** a member of a subcommission
sub·committee \"+\ *n* [*sub-* + *committee*] **:** a committee forming a subdivision of a primary or standing committee from which its responsibility and authority derive and usu. being charged with a specific or limited function
sub·company \"+\ *n* [*sub-* + *company*] **:** a subsidiary company (as of an industrial corporation)
sub·conchoidal \"+\ *adj* [*sub-* + *conchoidal*] **:** partially or indistinctly conchoidal ⟨a rock with ~ fracture⟩
sub·conical \"+\ *or* **sub·conic** \"+\ *adj* [*sub-* + *conical* or *conic*] **:** nearly or approximately conical
sub·conjunctival \"+\ *adj* [ISV *sub-* + *conjunctival*] **:** situated or occurring beneath the conjunctiva ⟨~ hemorrhage⟩ — **sub·conjunctivally** \"+\ *adv*
[1]**sub·conscious** \ˌsəb+\ *adj* [*sub-* + *conscious*] **1 :** existing in the mind but not immediately available to consciousness **:** affecting thought, feeling, and behavior without entering awareness ⟨~ motive⟩ ⟨~ reflex⟩ — compare UNCONSCIOUS **2 :** imperfectly conscious **:** partially but not fully aware ⟨the persistence of ~ dream activity for several minutes after waking —*Psychological Abstracts*⟩ — **sub·consciously** \"+\ *adv* — **sub·consciousness** \"+\ *n*
[2]**subconscious** \"\ *n* **:** the mental activities just below the threshold of consciousness; *also* **:** the aspect of the mind concerned with such activities that is an entity or a part of the mental apparatus overlapping, equivalent to, or distinct from the unconscious
sub·contiguous \"+\ *adj* [*sub-* + *contiguous*] **:** almost touching
sub·continent \"+\ *n* [*sub-* + *continent*] **1 :** a landmass (as Greenland) of great size but smaller than any of the usu. recognized continents **2 :** a vast and more or less self-contained subdivision of a continent ⟨the Indian ~ stretches northward into the Himalayas and comprises all of the Indian peninsula including Pakistan⟩ — **sub·continental** \"+\ *adj*
[1]**sub·contract** \"+\ *vb* [*sub-* + *contract* (v.)] *vt* **1** *obs* **:** to cause to become betrothed a second time **2 a :** to engage a third party to perform under a subcontract all or part of (work included in an original contract) **b :** to undertake (work) under a subcontract ~ *vi* **:** to let out or undertake work under one or more subcontracts **:** make a subcontract
[2]**sub·contract** \"+\ *n* [*sub-* + *contract* (n.)] **:** a contract subordinate to a previous or prime contract and made between one or more parties to the original contract and a third party; *esp* **:** an agreement to perform all or a specified part of the work or to provide all or certain specified materials required in another contract
sub·contractor \"+\ *n* [*sub-* + *contractor*] **:** an individual or business firm that contracts to perform part or all of another's contract **:** a maker or performer of subcontracts
sub·contraoctave \"+\ *n* [*sub-* + *contraoctave*] **:** the musical octave that begins on the fourth C below middle C — see PITCH illustration
sub·contrariety \"+\ *n* [fr. [1]*subcontrary*, after E *contrary*: *contrariety*] **:** the relation existing between subcontrary propositions in logic **:** the relation of two propositions with identical terms which is such that both may be true but both cannot be false — see OPPOSITION 2a(2)
[1]**sub·contrary** \"+\ *adj* [LL *subcontrarius*, fr. L *sub-* + *contrarius* contrary — more at CONTRARY] **:** contrary in an inferior degree; *specif* **:** having the relation of subcontrariety
[2]**subcontrary** \"\ *n* **:** a subcontrary proposition in logic
sub·convulsive \"+\ *adj* [*sub-* + *convulsive*] **1 :** inadequate to produce convulsion ⟨~ doses of insulin⟩ **2 :** approaching the convulsive in character ⟨a ~ reaction to noise⟩
sub·cool \"+\ *vt* [*sub-* + *cool*] **:** SUPERCOOL
sub·coracoid \"+\ *adj* [*sub-* + *coracoid*] **:** situated or occurring under the coracoid process of the scapula ⟨a ~ dislocation of the humerus⟩
sub·cordate \"+\ *adj* [*sub-* + *cordate*] **:** incompletely cordate **:** nearly heart-shaped ⟨a ~ leaf⟩
sub·coriaceous \"+\ *adj* [*sub-* + *coriaceous*] **:** somewhat coriaceous
sub·corneous \"+\ *adj* [*sub-* + *corneous*] **1 :** situated under a horny part or layer **2 :** partially horny
sub·cortex \"+\ *n* [NL, fr. *sub-* + *cortex*] **:** the parts of the brain (as the corpus striatum and internal capsule) immediately adjoining the cerebral cortex
sub·cortical \"+\ *adj* [*sub-* + *cortical*] **:** situated beneath or below a cortex; *usu* **:** of, relating to, involving, or being nerve centers below the cerebral cortex ⟨~ lesions⟩ ⟨~ sensation⟩ — **sub·cortically** \"+\ *adv*
sub·costa \ˌsəb+\ *n* [NL, fr. L *sub-* + *costa* rib — more at COAST] **:** the subcostal vein of an insect's wing
[1]**sub·costal** \"+\ *adj* [NL *subcostalis*] **1 :** situated below a rib ⟨a ~ muscle⟩ **2 :** of, relating to, or being the primary vein of an insect's wing next behind the costal vein
[2]**subcostal** \"\ *n* -S [NL *subcostalis*] **:** a subcostal part (as a muscle or wing vein)
subcostal artery *n* **:** either of a pair of arteries that are the most posterior branches of the thoracic aorta and course beneath the last pair of ribs
subcostal cell *n* **:** one of the cells between the costal and subcostal veins of an insect's wing
sub·cos·talis \ˌsəb,kä'stāləs, -täl-, -tȧl-\ *n, pl* **subcostales** \-a(ˌ)lēz, -ā(ˌ)lēz, -ȧ,lās\ [NL, fr. *subcostalis* situated below or within the rib, fr. *subcosta* + L *-alis* -al] **:** any of a variable number of small muscles arising on the inner surface of a rib and inserted into the inner surface of the first, second, or third rib below
sub·coxa \ˌsəb+\ *n* [NL, fr. *sub-* + *coxa*] **:** the proximal part of the coxa of an arthropod appendage esp. when forming an element distinct from the coxa — **sub·coxal** \"+\ *adj*
sub·crepitant \"+\ *adj* [*sub-* + *crepitant*] **:** partially crepitant **:** indistinctly crepitant
sub·crescentic \"+\ *adj* [*sub-* + *crescentic*] **:** nearly or irregularly crescentic
sub·critical \"+\ *adj* [*sub-* + *critical*] **1 :** less or lower than critical in respect to a specified factor: as **a** *of temperature* **:** lower than that critical for the hardening of a metal **b** *of a mass of fissionable material* **:** of insufficient size to sustain a chain reaction **2 a :** occurring at or involving the use of subcritical temperatures ⟨~ annealing⟩ **b :** constituting or designed for use with fissionable material of subcritical mass ⟨a ~ reactor⟩ ⟨storing fissionable material in ~ chunks⟩ — **sub·critically** \"+\ *adv*
sub·crossing \"+\ *n* [*sub-* + *crossing*] **:** a minor or secondary crossing (as over a railway line)
sub·crust \'səb+,-\ *n* [*sub-* + *crust*] **:** a layer underlying a crust; *esp* **:** the lower course of a bituminous macadam or concrete roadbed
sub·crustal \ˌsəb+\ *adj* [ISV *sub-* + *crustal*] **:** situated, acting, or occurring below a crust and esp. the crust of the earth
sub·crystalline \"+\ *adj* [*sub-* + *crystalline*] **:** obscurely crystalline **:** partially crystallized
sub·cultural \"+\ *adj* [*sub-* + *cultural*] **1 :** of, relating to, or constituting a subdivision of a social culture ⟨a special ~ framework within the Anglo-American area —John Gillin⟩ **2 :** existing prior to or on a lower level than that of cultural integration ⟨persistence of ~ traits⟩ ⟨~ experiences⟩
[1]**sub·culture** \"+\ *n* [*sub-* + *culture*] **1 a :** a culture (as of bacteria) derived from another culture **b :** an act or instance of subculturing or of producing a subculture **2 :** an ethnic, regional, economic, or social group exhibiting characteristic patterns of behavior sufficient to distinguish it from others within an embracing culture or society ⟨a criminal ~⟩
[2]**subculture** \"\ *vt* **:** to culture (as bacteria) anew on a fresh medium by inoculation from an older culture
sub·curative \ˌsəb+\ *adj* [*sub-* + *curative*] **:** inadequate to produce a cure ⟨~ amounts of one drug may become curative when given with another⟩
sub·current \"+\ *n* [*sub-* + *current*] **:** an obscure or secondary current (as of thought)
sub·cutaneous \"+\ *adj* [LL *subcutaneus*, fr. L *sub-* + *cutis* skin — more at HIDE] **1 :** situated or occurring beneath the skin ⟨~ fat⟩ **2 :** intended for use or made under the skin **:** HYPODERMIC ⟨a ~ injection⟩ ⟨~ needles⟩ **3 :** living beneath the skin ⟨a ~ parasite⟩ — **sub·cutaneously** \"+\ *adv*
subcutaneous mite *n* **:** a widely distributed mite (*Laminosioptes cysticola*) that is an internal parasite of the fowl, turkey, goose, and some other birds
sub·cuticle \ˌsəb+\ *n* [NL *subcuticula*] **:** a layer (as of cells or fibers) lying beneath or forming the inner aspect of a cuticle **:** HYPODERMIS
sub·cuticula \"+\ *n* [NL, fr. *sub-* + *cuticula*] **:** SUBCUTICLE
sub·cuticular \"+\ *adj* [NL *subcuticula* + E *-ar*] **1 :** of, relating to, or being a subcuticle **2** [*sub-* + *cuticular*] **:** situated or occurring beneath a cuticle ⟨~ differentiation⟩ — **sub·cuticular·ly** \"lē, -li\ *adv*
sub·cutis \ˌsəb+\ *n* [NL, fr. LL, beneath the skin, fr. L *sub-* + *cutis* skin] **:** the deeper part of the dermis
sub–cycle \'=,==\ *n* **:** a float propelled like a bicycle and used by a lifeguard at a beach
sub·cylindrical \ˌsəb+\ *also* **sub·cylindric** \"+\ *adj* [*sub-* + *cylindrical*, *cylindric*] **:** nearly cylindrical
subd *abbr* subdivision
sub·deacon \ˌsəb+\ *n* [ME *subdecon*, *subdekene*, fr. LL *subdiaconus*, fr. L *sub-* under, below + LL *diaconus* deacon — more at SUB-, DEACON] **1 :** one in holy orders who ranks below a deacon and whose duties in the Eastern Orthodox and formerly the Roman Catholic Churches include the preparation of holy vessels for the Eucharist or mass **2 :** an ecclesiastic whose duty is to read the epistle in various religious services
sub·deaconate \"+\ *n* [*subdeacon* + *-ate*] **:** SUBDIACONATE
sub·deaconry \"+\ *n* [*subdeacon* + *-ry*] **:** the order or office of subdeacon
sub·dean \"+\ *n* [ME *subdene*, *sudene*, fr. MF *souzdeien*, fr. ML *subdecanus*, fr. L *sub-* + LL *decanus* dean — more at DEAN] **:** an under dean **:** the deputy or substitute of a dean
sub·deanery \"+\ *n* [*subdean* + *-ery*] **:** the office or rank of subdean
sub·deb \ˌsəb+\ *n* [by shortening] **:** SUBDEBUTANTE
sub·debutante \"+\ *n* [*sub-* + *debutante*] **1 :** a young woman on the verge of becoming a social debutante **2 :** a girl in her middle teens ⟨styles for ~*s*⟩
sub·decanal \"+\ *adj* [ML *subdecanus* subdean + E *-al*] **:** of or relating to a subdean or subdeanery
sub·decimal \"+\ *adj* [*sub-* + *decimal*] **:** resulting from division by a multiple of ten
sub·deity \"+\ *n* [*sub-* + *deity*] **:** a minor member of a pantheon **:** a subordinate deity of a polytheistic religious system
[1]**sub·delegate** \"+\ *n* [ML *subdelegatus*, fr. L *sub-* + ML *delegatus* delegate — more at DELEGATE] **:** a deputy for a delegate; *often* **:** one to whom a delegated power or responsibility is transferred usu. for a particular case or situation
[2]**sub·delegate** \"+\ *vt* [ML *subdelegatus*, past part. of *subdelegare* to subdelegate, fr. L *sub-* + *delegare* to delegate] **:** to transfer (as a power or right delegated to oneself) to another ⟨~ legislative powers to an executive branch⟩ — **subdelegation** \ˌsəb+\ *n*
sub·dentate \ˌsəb+\ *also* **sub·dentated** \"+\ *adj* [*sub-* + *dentate*, *dentated*] **:** partially or imperfectly dentate ⟨leaves with margins ~⟩
sub·department \"+\ *n* [*sub-* + *department*] **:** a subdivision of a department
sub·depot \"+\ *n* [*sub-* + *depot*] **:** a military depot that operates under the jurisdiction of another depot and usu. performs only specified depot functions
sub·derivative \"+\ *n* [*sub-* + *derivative*] **:** a word derived from a derivative ⟨*friendliness* is a ~ from *friendly* which is derived from *friend*⟩
sub·dermal \"+\ *adj* [*sub-* + *dermal*] **:** SUBCUTANEOUS
sub·desert \"+\ *n* [*sub-* + *desert*] **:** a stretch of arid land that is less arid than typical desert
sub·diaconal \ˌsəb+\ *adj* [LL *subdiaconalis*, fr. *subdiaconus* subdeacon + L *-alis* -al — more at SUBDEACON] **:** of or relating to a subdeacon or a subdeaconry
sub·diaconate \"+\ *n* [LL *subdiaconatus*, fr. *subdiaconus* subdeacon + L *-atus* -ate] **:** the office or rank of a subdeacon
sub·diapente \"+\ *n* [*sub-* + *diapente*] **:** a fifth below — used as a direction in music
sub·dilution \"+\ *n* [*sub-* + *dilution*] **1 :** a fractional dilution of a solution of known concentration ⟨prepared 0.1, 0.01, and 0.001 molar ~*s* from a molar solution⟩ **2 :** the act of preparing a subdilution ⟨obtained an accurate solution by ~⟩
sub·dimension \"+\ *n* [*sub-* + *dimension*] **:** one of the partial dimensions or dimensions of constituent elements that make up the dimensions of an object
sub·disjunctive \"+\ *n* [NL *subdisjunctivus*, fr. L *sub-* + *disjunctivus*, adj., disjunctive — more at DISJUNCTIVE] **:** a disjunctive conjunction connecting words or word groups that have the same reference ⟨in "report to the chairman or head of the department" *or* is a ~⟩
sub·dividable \ˌsəb+\ *adj* [*subdivide* + *-able*] **:** capable of being further divided **:** suitable for subdividing
sub·divide \"+\ *vb* [ME *subdividen*, fr. LL *subdividere*, fr. L *sub-* further + *dividere* to divide — more at SUB-, DIVIDE] *vt* **1 :** to further divide (that which has already been divided) **:** divide the parts of into more parts ⟨the functional divisions were then *subdivided* into geographic classes⟩ **2 :** to divide into several parts ⟨bulkheads ~ the ship into watertight compartments⟩; *esp* **:** to divide (a tract of land) into building lots **:** lay out a subdivision on (unimproved land) ~ *vi* **:** to separate or become separated into subdivisions — **sub·divider** \"+\ *n*
sub·divisible \ˌsəb+\ *adj* [*subdivision* + *-ible*] **:** susceptible of subdivision
sub·division \"+\ *n* [LL *subdivision-*, *subdivisio*, fr. *subdivisus* (past part. of *subdividere* to subdivide) + L *-ion-*, *-io* -ion] **1 a :** the act or process of subdividing **b :** an instance or example of subdividing **2 :** something produced by subdividing: as **a :** a part made by subdividing ⟨a ~ of a taxonomic division⟩ **b :** a tract of land surveyed and divided into lots for purposes of sale — compare DEVELOPMENT — **sub·divisional** \"+\ *adj*
sub·dolichocephalic \ˌsəb+\ *also* **sub·dolichocephalous** \"+\ *adj* [*subdolichocephalic* fr. NL *subdolichocephalus* subdolichocephalic person (fr. *sub-* + *dolichocephalus* dolichocephal) + E *-ic*; *subdolichocephalous* fr. NL *subdolichocephalus*] **:** having a cephalic index of 77.7–80 — **subdolichocephalism** \"+\ *or* **sub·dolichocephaly** \"+\ *n*
sub·do·lous \'səbdələs\ *adj* [L *subdolus*, fr. *sub-* + *dolus* fraud, deceit — more at TALE] **:** somewhat sly **:** CRAFTY, CUNNING, ARTFUL
sub·dominance \ˌsəb+\ *n* **:** the quality or state of being subdominant
[1]**sub·dominant** \"+\ *adj* [*sub-* + *dominant*] **1 :** incompletely dominant **2 :** being or having the quality of a subdominant ⟨~ chords⟩ ⟨~ life-forms in an ecological community⟩
[2]**subdominant** \"\ *n* [*sub-* + *dominant* n.] **:** something dominant to an inferior or partial degree: as **a :** the fourth musical degree of the major or minor scale (as F in the scale of C) **b :** a species or life-form that is ecologically important but subordinate in influence to the dominants of a community or is characteristic of a structural subunit or partial area of a community ⟨shrubs may be prominent ~*s* in a forest community⟩ ⟨sometimes forbs behave as seasonal ~*s* in grasslands⟩
sub·dorsal \"+\ *adj* [*sub-* + *dorsal*] **:** situated nearly on the dorsal surface — **sub·dorsally** \"+\ *adv*
sub·drain \'səb+,-\ *n* [*sub-* + *drain*] **:** a perforated or plain underground drain
sub·drainage \ˌsəb+\ *n* [*sub-* + *drainage*] **:** natural or artificial drainage from beneath
sub·drill \"+\ *vt* [*sub-* + *drill*] **:** to drill (a hole) to a size that leaves sufficient metal for finishing by reaming
sub·du·able \səb'd(y)üəbəl\ *adj* **:** capable of being subdued
sub·du·al \səb'd(y)üəl\ *n* -S [*subdue* + *-al* (n. suffix)] **:** the act of subduing
sub·duct \səb'dəkt\ *vb* [L *subductus*, past part. of *subducere* to withdraw] **:** WITHDRAW, SUBTRACT, DEDUCT, REMOVE
sub·duc·tion \-kshən\ *n* -S [LL *subduction-*, *subductio*, fr. L *subductus* (past part. of *subducere*) + *-ion-*, *-io* -ion] **1 a :** the act of taking away **:** WITHDRAWAL **b :** arithmetical subtraction; *also* **:** DEDUCTION **2 :** the act or process of subduing
sub·due \səb'd(y)ü\ *vt* -ED/-ING/-S [ME *subduen*, *sodewen* (prob. influenced in meaning by L *subdere* to put under, subdue), fr. MF *soduire* to seduce, deceive (prob. influenced in meaning by L *seducere* to seduce), fr. L *subducere* to withdraw, lit., to lead up, lead away, fr. *sub-* up, further + *ducere* to lead — more at SEDUCE, SUB-, TOW] **1 :** to conquer by force or by superior power and bring into subjection **:** VANQUISH, CRUSH ⟨where Norman forces *subdued* the English⟩ **2 a :** to bring (as a person) into subjection or order by or as if by persuasion, intimidation, or threat of punishment ⟨~ a wilful child⟩ **b :** to bring under control esp. by an exertion of the will **:** CURB ⟨*subduing* her foolish fears⟩ ⟨determined to ~ this unruly desire⟩ **c** *archaic* **:** to bring (a disease) under control by treatment **3 :** to prepare (land) for the growing of crops **:** bring under cultivation **4 :** to reduce the intensity or degree of **:** make less prominent **:** tone down ⟨with an effort *subdued* his angry speech⟩ ⟨voices became *subdued* as the twilight deepened⟩ ⟨a soft hairdo helped to ~ her heavy features⟩ **syn** see CONQUER
subdued *adj* [fr. past part. of *subdue*] **1 :** brought under control by or as if by military conquest **2 :** reduced or lacking in force, intensity, or vividness **:** toned down ⟨~ colors⟩ ⟨a ~ voice⟩ **3 :** characterized by broadly rounded elements as if weathered or eroded ⟨~ landforms⟩ ⟨a ~ topography is typical of old landmasses⟩ **syn** see TAME
sub·dued·ly \-ü(ə)dlē, -li\ *adv* **:** in a subdued manner
sub·dued·ness \-ü(ə)dnəs\ *n* -ES **:** the quality or state of being subdued
sub·du·er \səb'd(y)üə(r), -dů(ə)r, -düə\ *n* -S **:** one that subdues
subduing *adj* **:** tending to produce subdual ⟨~ reflections⟩ — **sub·du·ing·ly** *adv*
sub·dural \ˌsəb+\ *adj* [ISV *sub-* + *dural*] **:** situated or occurring under the dura mater or between the dura mater and the arachnoid membrane ⟨the ~ space⟩ ⟨~ hemorrhage⟩ — **sub·durally** \"+\ *adv*
sub·dwarf \'səb+,-\ *n* [*sub-* + *dwarf*] **:** a star having higher surface temperature for its mass and luminosity than is usual to stars of the main sequence and therefore having relatively high density and lying to the left of the main sequence on the spectrum-luminosity diagram
sub·economic \ˌsəb+\ *adj* [*sub-* + *economic*] **1 :** lacking in economic importance ⟨a pest present in ~ numbers⟩ **2 :** not justifiable on purely economic grounds ⟨~ public housing projects⟩
sub·edit \"+\ *vt* [back-formation fr. *subeditor*] **1 :** to act as subeditor of **2** *chiefly Brit* **:** COPYREAD
sub·edition \"+\ *n* [*sub-* + *edition*] **:** an issue of a printed work bibliographically categorized as of lesser status than an edition because done from plates leased from the original publisher or reproduced by photolithography from an original printing
sub·editor \"+\ *n* [*sub-* + *editor*] **1 :** an assistant editor **2** *chiefly Brit* **:** COPYREADER — **sub·editorial** \"+\ *adj*
sub·editorship \"+\ *n* [*sub-* + *editorship*] **:** the position or status of a subeditor
sub·effective \"+\ *adj* [*sub-* + *effective*] **:** inadequate to produce an effect ⟨a ~ dose of medicine⟩
sub·elliptic \"+\ *or* **sub·elliptical** \"+\ *adj* [*subelliptic* ISV *sub-* + *elliptic*; *subelliptical* fr. *sub-* + *elliptical*] **:** somewhat elliptic
sub·encephalon \ˌsəb+\ *n* [NL, fr. *sub-* + *encephalon*] **:** the midbrain and hindbrain together
sub·endemic \"+\ *adj* [*sub-* + *endemic*] **:** largely localized in one natural area **:** occurring mostly in one environment ⟨a ~ flora⟩
sub·endocardial \"+\ *adj* [*sub-* + *endocardial*] **:** situated or occurring beneath the endocardium or between the endocardium and myocardium ⟨~ blood loss⟩
sub·endorse \"+\ *vt* [*sub-* + *endorse*] **:** to provide with a secondary or additional endorsement — **sub·endorsement** \"+\ *n*
sub·endothelial \ˌsəb+\ *adj* [*sub-* + *endothelial*] **:** situated under an endothelium
sub·enfeoff \"+\ *vt* [*sub-* + *enfeoff*] **:** SUBINFEUDATE
sub·entire \"+\ *adj* [*sub-* + *entire*] **1 :** almost entire **2 :** having few denticulations
sub·entitle \"+\ *vt* [*sub-* + *entitle*] **:** to provide with a subtitle
sub·entry \ˌsəb+\ *n* [*sub-* + *entry*] **:** an entry (as in a catalog or an account) made under a more general entry
sub·epicardial \"+\ *adj* [*sub-* + *epicardial*] **:** situated or occurring beneath the epicardium or between the epicardium and myocardium
sub·epidermal \"+\ *adj* [*sub-* + *epidermal*] **:** lying beneath or constituting the innermost part of the epidermis
sub·epithelial \"+\ *adj* [*sub-* + *epithelial*] **:** situated or occurring beneath an epithelial layer; *sometimes* **:** SUBCUTANEOUS
sub·equal \"+\ *adj* [NL *subaequalis*, fr. L *sub-* + *aequalis* equal — more at EQUAL] **:** approximately but not exactly equal
sub·equatorial \"+\ *adj* [ISV *sub-* + *equatorial*] **:** approximately equatorial; *usu* **:** of, relating to, or constituting a region just outside the equatorial region
sub·equivalve \"+\ *adj* [ISV *sub-* + *equivalve*] **:** having shell valves that are slightly unequal in size ⟨a ~ mollusk⟩
su·ber \'sübə(r)\ *n* -S [L, prob. of non-IE origin; akin to the source of Gk *syphar* wrinkled skin] **:** corky plant tissue **:** PHELLEM; *esp* **:** the outer bark of the cork oak
su·ber·ate \-ə,rāt\ *n* -S [F *subérate*, fr. *subér-* (in *subérique* suberic) + *-ate*] **:** a salt or ester of suberic acid
sub·erect \ˌsəb+\ *adj* [*sub-* + *erect*] **:** standing or growing in a nearly erect position **:** ASCENDING ⟨a ~ shrub⟩
su·be·re·ous \(')sü¦birēəs\ *or* **su·ber·ic** \-berik\ *adj* [*subereous* fr. L *subereus*, fr. *suber* + *-eus* -eous; *suberic* fr. L *suber* + E *-ic*] **:** of, relating to, or derived from cork **:** SUBEROSE
suberic acid *n* [F *subérique*, fr. L *suber* cork oak, cork + F *-ique* -ic] **:** a crystalline dicarboxylic acid $HOOC(CH_2)_6COOH$ obtained usu. by alkaline hydrolysis of suberin or by oxidation of cork, castor oil, or ricinoleic acid with nitric acid; octane-dioic acid
su·ber·i·fi·ca·tion \sü,berəfə'kāshən\ *n* -S [ISV *suberi-* (fr. L *suber*) + *-fication*] **:** production of or conversion into cork or suberin
su·ber·in \'sübərən\ *n* -S [F *subérine*, fr. L *suber* + F *-ine* -in] **:** a complex fatty substance that constitutes an important part of cork cell walls and is found also in or between many other cells and that on alkaline hydrolysis yields suberic acid, phellonic acid, and phloionic acid among other products — compare CUTIN, SUBERIZATION
su·ber·ite \-ə,rīt\ *n* -S [NL *Suberites*] **:** a sponge of the genus *Suberites* or family Suberitidae
su·ber·i·tes \,=='rīd·(ˌ)ēz\ *n, cap* [NL, fr. L *suber* cork oak, cork + NL *-ites*] **:** a genus (the type of the family Suberitidae of the class Demospongiae) of fleshy, erect or encrusting monaxial sponges that have no microscleres or spongin, that have megascleres shaped like needles with heads, and that include forms which often live on shells occupied by hermit crabs
su·ber·iza·tion \,sübərə'zāshən, -ˌrī'z-\ *n* -S [ISV *suberize* + *-ation*] **:** conversion of plant cell walls into water-impervious corky tissue through infiltration with suberin — compare CUTINIZATION, LIGNIFICATION
su·ber·ize \'sübə,rīz\ *also* **su·ber·in·ize** \-ərə,nīz\ *vt* -ED/-ING/-S *see -ize in Explan Notes* [*suberize* fr. L *suber* cork oak, cork + E *-ize*; *suberinize* fr. *suberin* + *-ize*] **:** to cause or effect the suberization of
su·ber·one \-ə,rōn\ *n* -S [F *subérone*, fr. *subér-* (in *subérique* suberic) + *-one*] **:** CYCLOHEPTANONE
su·ber·ose \-ə,rōs\ *also* **su·ber·ous** \-ərəs\ *adj* [NL *suberosus*, fr. L *suber* cork oak, cork + *-osus* -ose — more at SUBER] **:** having a corky texture resulting from or like that resulting from suberization
su·ber·yl·arginine \ˌsübərəl+\ *n* [*suberyl* (fr. F *subéryle*, fr. *subér-* — in *subérique* suberic — + *-yle* -yl) + *arginine*] **:** a monoamide derived from suberic acid and arginine and obtained by hydrolysis of bufotoxins
sub·esophageal \ˌsəb+\ *adj* [*sub-* + *esophageal*] **:** situated or occurring under the esophagus
sub·essential \"+\ *adj* [*sub-* + *essential*] **:** important but not absolutely essential

sub·falcate \ˌsəb+\ *adj* [*sub-* + *falcate*] **:** nearly but not quite falcate **:** irregularly falcate

sub·family \"+\ *n* [ISV *sub-* + *family*] **:** a taxonomic category next below a family ⟨a ~ of languages⟩; *specif* **:** a biological taxonomic category below a family and above a genus — see -INAE

sub·fauna \"+\ *n* [NL, fr. *sub-* + *fauna*] **:** a localized fauna

sub·febrile \"+\ *adj* [ISV *sub-* + *febrile*] **:** of, relating to, or constituting a body temperature very slightly above normal but not febrile

sub·fertile \"+\ *adj* [*sub-* + *fertile*] **:** of less than normal fertility though still capable of producing fertilization ⟨~ semen⟩

¹sub·feu \"+,-\ *n* [*sub-* + *feu*] **:** a feu held of a vassal as such

²sub·feu \ˌsəbˈfyü\ *vb* **:** SUBINFEUDATE

sub·fibrous \ˌsəb+\ *adj* [*sub-* + *fibrous*] **:** somewhat fibrous ⟨a ~ consistency⟩

sub·fief \ˈsəb+,-\ *n* [*sub-* + *fief*] **:** a fief that is granted out of and is part of another fief

sub·fix \ˈsəb,fiks\ *n* [*sub-* + *-fix* (as in *prefix*)] **:** a subscript sign, letter, or character

sub·floor \ˈsəb+,-\ *n* [*sub-* + *floor*] **:** a rough floor laid as a base for a finished floor

sub·flooring \ˌsəb+\ *n* [*sub-* + *flooring*] **1 :** SUBFLOORS ⟨the ~ of a building⟩ **2 :** material for use in a subfloor ⟨the cheapest pine ~⟩

sub·flora \"+\ *n* [NL, fr. *sub-* + *flora*] **:** a localized flora

sub·fluoride \"+\ *n* [*sub-* + *fluoride*] **:** a fluoride containing a relatively small proportion of fluorine ⟨silver ~ Ag_2F⟩

sub·fluvial \"+\ *adj* [*sub-* + *fluvial*] **1 :** situated, taking place, or formed at the bottom of a body of water (as a river) ⟨~ cables⟩ ⟨a ~ deposit of silt⟩ **2 :** passing under a river ⟨a ~ tunnel⟩

sub·focal \"+\ *adj* [*sub-* + *focal*] **:** located or occurring below the focus of attention **:** not clearly conscious

sub·foreman \"+\ *n* [*sub-* + *foreman*] **1 :** a supervisory employee subordinate to a foreman **2 :** a member of a work crew functioning esp. temporarily as a foreman **:** a working foreman

sub·form \ˈsəb+,-\ *n* [*sub-* + *form*] **:** a subordinate or derivative form ⟨~*s* of the Gothic in 19th century writing⟩

sub·fornicate \ˌsəb+\ *adj* [*sub-* + *fornicate*] **:** somewhat arched

¹sub·fossil \"+\ *adj* [ISV *sub-* + *fossil*] **:** of less than typical fossil age though not strictly recent **:** having lost the organic constituents (as fats and proteins) produced in vital activities but not yet having had them replaced (as by mineralization)

²subfossil \"\ *n* **:** a subfossil specimen

sub·fossorial \"+\ *adj* [*sub-* + *fossorial*] **:** showing some modification adaptive to a fossorial way of life ⟨an insect with ~ forelimbs⟩

sub·foundation \"+\ *n* [*sub-* + *foundation*] **:** a secondary foundation **:** SUBGRADE

sub·fraction \"+\ *n* [*sub-* + *fraction*] **1 :** a fraction of a fraction **2 :** a small fraction — **sub·fractional** \"+\ *adj*

sub·frame \ˈsəb+,-\ *n* [*sub-* + *frame*] **:** a secondary frame: as **a :** a frame for the attachment and support of a finish frame (as of a window or door) **b :** a frame for the support of panels used as a wall finish

sub·freezing \ˌsəb+\ *adj* [*sub-* + *freezing*] **:** lower than is required to produce freezing **:** characterized by a temperature lower than 0° C ⟨~ temperatures⟩ ⟨~ conditions⟩

sub·fulgent \"+\ *adj* [*sub-* + *fulgent*] **:** somewhat shining **:** moderately lustrous

sub·functional \"+\ *adj* [*sub-* + *functional*] **:** having little or no apparent function ⟨a ~ appendage on an insect⟩

sub·fusc \ˌsəbˈfəsk\ *adj* [L *subfuscus* brownish, dusky, fr. *sub-* near, almost + *fuscus* dark brown, blackish — more at SUB-, DUSK] **1 :** SUBFUSCOUS **2 :** having little of brightness or appeal **:** DRAB, DINGY ⟨the moment when the word *Austerity* was to take to itself a new ~ and squalid twist of meaning —Osbert Sitwell⟩ ⟨that gray, impoverished, ~ community —Marguerite Steen⟩

sub·fus·cous \-skəs\ *adj* [L *subfuscus*] **:** somewhat fuscous **:** DUSKY

subg *abbr* subgenus

sub·galea \ˌsəb+\ *n* [NL, fr. *sub-* + *galea*] **:** a segment of the maxilla of an insect usu. attached to the stipes and bearing the galea

sub·gallate \"+\ *n* [*sub-* + *gallate*] **:** a basic gallate (as bismuth subgallate)

sub·generic \"+\ *also* **sub·generical** \"+\ *adj* [*subgeneric* ISV *sub-* + *generic*; *subgenerical* fr. *sub-* + *generical*] **:** of, relating to, or constituting a subgenus — **sub·generically** \"+\ *adv*

sub·genital \"+\ *adj* [*sub-* + *genital*] **:** situated below the genital organs

sub·genotype \"+\ *n* [*sub-* + *genotype*] **:** a species that is the type of a subgenus

sub·genus \"+\ *n* [NL, fr. L *sub-* + *genus*] **:** a category in biological taxonomy below a genus and above a species

sub·giant \"+\ *n* [*sub-* + *giant*] **:** a star of such color and luminosity that it falls above the main sequence of the spectrum-luminosity diagram yet is not in the region of ordinary giant stars

sub·gingival \ˌsəb+\ *adj* [*sub-* + *gingival*] **:** situated or occurring beneath the gums and esp. between the gums and the basal part of the crowns of the teeth ⟨~ deposits of tartar⟩

sub·glabrous \"+\ *adj* [ISV *sub-* + *glabrous*] **:** imperfectly glabrous **:** slightly rough or hairy

sub·glacial \"+\ *adj* [*sub-* + *glacial*] **1 :** of, relating to, or formed in or by the bottommost part of a glacier or the area immediately underlying a glacier ⟨~ channels⟩ ⟨the ~ floor⟩ **2 :** POSTGLACIAL ⟨postglacial (or ~) stream-cut canyons —*Jour. of Geol.*⟩ — **sub·glacially** \"+\ *adv*

sub·glenoid \"+\ *adj* [*sub-* + *glenoid*] **:** situated beneath the glenoid fossa of the shoulder

sub·globose \"+\ *adj* [*sub-* + *globose*] **:** imperfectly or nearly globose — **sub·globosely** \"+\ *adv*

sub·glottal \"+\ *adj* [*sub-* + *glottal*] **:** SUBGLOTTIC

sub·glottic \"+\ *adj* [ISV *sub-* + *glottic*] **:** situated or occurring below the glottis

sub·grade \ˈsəb+,-\ *n* [*sub-* + *grade*] **1 :** a subordinate level in a scale (as of rank or quality) ⟨~ is used in some classifications at a supraphylar level⟩ **2 :** a layer (as a stratum or surface) immediately beneath some principal layer; *specif* **:** a surface of earth or rock leveled off to receive the foundation of a structure (as a road, pavement, building, sewer) or the ballast of a railroad

sub·graywacke \ˌsəb+\ *n* [*sub-* + *graywacke*] **:** a graywacke characterized by introduced mineral cement and deposition from normal subaqueous currents

¹sub·group \ˈsəb+,-\ *n* [*sub-* + *group*] **:** a subordinate group usu. of individuals sharing some common quality that makes them distinguishable from other members of a major group to which they belong ⟨the Britannic ~ of the Celtic languages —Isidore Dyen⟩ ⟨the ~ of the professional criminal . . . has basic similarities . . . to the subgroup of the industrialist —R.K.Merton⟩

²sub·group \ˈ;=;=\ *vt* **:** to divide into subgroups

sub·gular \ˌsəb+\ *adj* [*sub-* + *gular*] **:** situated on the lower part of the throat ⟨a ~ scale on a reptile⟩

sub·halide \"+\ *n* [*sub-* + *halide*] **:** a halide (as a subchloride) containing a relatively small proportion of halogen

sub·harmonic \"+\ *n* [ISV *sub-* + *harmonic*] **:** a component of a periodic wave having a frequency that is an integral submultiple of the fundamental frequency ⟨the ~ having half the fundamental frequency is the second ~⟩ — compare HARMONIC

¹sub·head \ˈsəb+,-\ *n* [*sub-* + *head*] **1 :** any of the heads under which each of the main divisions of a subject may be subdivided **2 :** a heading or caption subordinate to a main headline, heading, or title esp. when inserted as a divider between sections (as of a newspaper or periodical article or story or the text of a book)

²sub·head \ˈ;=;=\ *vt* **:** to provide (as a manuscript or discourse) with subheads **:** introduce by a subhead

sub·heading \ˌsəb+\ *n* [*sub-* + *heading*] **:** SUBHEAD

sub·health \ˈsəb+,-\ *n* [*sub-* + *health*] **:** imperfect health **:** a condition of reduced vigor in the absence of overt ailment

sub·he·dral \ˌsəbˈhēdrəl\ *adj* [*sub-* + *-hedral*] **:** incompletely bounded by crystal planes **:** partly faced

sub·hepatic \ˌsəb+\ *adj* [ISV *sub-* + *hepatic*] **:** situated or occurring under the liver

sub·himalayan \"+\ *adj, usu cap H* **:** situated under or at the foot of the Himalaya mountains

sub·holding company \ˌsəb+-\ *n* [*sub-* + *holding company*] **:** a holding company in which a controlling interest is held by another holding company

¹sub·ho·los·te·an \ˌsəbhōˈlästēən\ *adj* [NL *Subholostei* + E *-an* (adj. suffix)] **:** of or relating to the Subholostei

²subholostean \"\ *n* -S [NL *Subholostei* + E *-an* (n. suffix)] **:** a ganoid fish of the order Subholostei

sub·holostei \"+\ *n pl, cap* [NL, fr. *sub-* + *Holostei*] *in some classifications* **:** an order comprising ganoid fishes that are generally more primitive than the Holostei and being more or less equivalent to the order Archistia

sub·horizontal \ˌsəb+\ *adj* [*sub-* + *horizontal*] **:** not quite horizontal in position or orientation

¹sub·human \"+\ *adj* [*sub-* + *human*] **:** less than human: as **a :** failing to attain the level (as of morality or intelligence) associated with normal human beings ⟨a ~ child⟩ ⟨treating the natives as ~⟩ **b :** unsuitable to or unfit for human beings ⟨~ conditions of life⟩ ⟨a ~ spectacle⟩ **c :** approaching that normal to man ⟨a dog with ~ intelligence⟩ **d :** of, relating to, or belonging to an infrahuman group ⟨the ~ primates⟩ ⟨the army ant . . . presents the most complex instance of organized mass behavior . . . in any ~ animal —T.C.Schneirla & Gerard Piel⟩

²subhuman \"\ *n* **:** a subhuman individual; *esp* **:** a person so deficient in ordinary human characteristics as to seem a member of a different species ⟨such moronic ~*s* —*Time*⟩

sub·humanity \ˌsəb+\ *n* **1 :** subhuman behavior **2 :** SUBHUMANS

sub·humid \"+\ *adj* [*sub-* + *humid*] **:** not quite humid **:** slightly to moderately humid and usu. more humid than subarid

sub·hyaline \"+\ *adj* [*sub-* + *hyaline*] **:** somewhat or imperfectly hyaline

sub·hymenium \"+\ *n* [NL, fr. *sub-* + *hymenium*] **:** the hypothecium of a fungus

sub·icteric \"+\ *adj* [ISV *sub-* + *icteric*] **:** very slightly jaundiced **:** indicative of a slight jaundice ⟨a ~ tint in the skin⟩

su·bic·u·lar \səˈbikyələ(r)\ *adj* [NL *subiculum* + E *-ar*] **:** of, relating to, or constituting a subiculum

su·bic·u·lum \-ləm\ *n, pl* **subicu·la** \-lə\ [NL, fr. L *subic-*, *subex* underlayer, support (fr. *subicere*, *subjicere* to throw under) + *-ulum* (neut. of *-ulus* -ule) — more at SUBJECT] **1 a :** a part of the hippocampal convolution that borders the fissure of the hippocampus **b :** the entire hippocampal gyrus **2 :** a felted mass of hyphae forming a basal stratum in which perithecia or pycnidia are situated

sub·imaginal \ˌsəb+\ *adj* [NL *subimagin-*, *subimago* + E *-al*] **:** of, relating to, or being a subimago

sub·imago \"+\ *n* [NL, fr. *sub-* + *imago*] **1 :** a stage in the development of some insects (as the mayflies) between the nymph and imago in which the insect is able to fly but becomes mature only after a further molt **2 :** an insect in the subimaginal stage — see DUN

sub·incandescent \"+\ *adj* [*sub-* + *incandescent*] **:** heated but below the point of incandescence

sub·incise \"+\ *vt* [back-formation fr. *subincision*] **:** to perform subincision upon

sub·incision \"+\ *n* [*sub-* + *incision*] **:** a ritual mutilation performed as a part of puberty rites among some native Australian and Fijian groups that involves slitting the underside of the penis with permanent opening of the urethra

¹sub·index \"+\ *n* [*sub-* + *index*] **1 :** a mathematical subscript **2 :** an index to a division of a main classification

²subindex \"\ *vt* **:** to make a subindex of or for **:** provide with a subindex

sub·indicative \"+\ *adj, archaic* [obs. E *subindicate* to indicate slightly (fr. LL *subindicatus*, past part. of *subindicare* to subindicate, fr. L *sub-* + *indicare* to indicate) + E *-ive* — more at INDICATE] **:** slightly or indirectly indicative

sub·in·feu·date \ˌsəˌbinˈfyüˌdāt, *usu* -ād.+V\ *also* **sub·in·feud** \-ˈfyüd\ *vt* [back-formation fr. *subinfeudation*] **:** to make subinfeudation of

sub·infeudation \ˌsəb+\ *n* [*sub-* + *infeudation*] **:** the granting of feudal lands by a vassal lord to another to hold as vassal of himself rather than of his own superior; *also* **:** the relation or tenure of a vassal so holding land

sub·infeudatory \"+\ *n* -ES [*subinfeudation* + *-ory*] **:** a tenant holding by subinfeudation

sub·influent \ˌsəb+\ *n* [*sub-* + *influent*] **:** an organism functioning like but less effectively than an influent in an ecological community

sub·inguinal \ˌsəb+\ *adj* [*sub-* + *inguinal*] **:** situated below Poupart's ligament

sub·inoculate \"+\ *vt* [*sub-* + *inoculate*] **:** to introduce (infective material) from a laboratory strain into a potential host — used esp. of a virus — **sub·inoculation** \"+\ *n*

sub·integumental \"+\ *adj* [*sub-* + *integumental*] **:** situated or occurring under an integument; *specif* **:** SUBCUTANEOUS

sub·intelligential \"+\ *adj* [*subintelligential* fr. LL *subintelligent-*, *subintelligens* (pres. part. of *subintelligere* to understand implicitly, fr. L *sub-* secretly, under + *intelligere* to understand) + E *-al*] **:** implying something beyond what is obvious to the mind **:** INTIMATING

sub·in·tel·lig·i·tur \ˌsəˌbintᵊlˈijəd·ər\ *n* -S [LL, it is implicitly understood, 3d pers. sing. pres. indic. of *subintelligere*] *archaic* **:** a meaning or understanding (as of a statement) implied but not expressed

sub·intent \ˌsəb+\ *n* [*sub-* + *intent*] **:** a subordinate meaning, purpose, or proposal

sub·interval \"+\ *n* [*sub-* + *interval*] **:** an interval that is a subdivision of a larger or major interval (as in music or mathematics)

sub·intestinal \"+\ *adj* [*sub-* + *intestinal*] **:** situated beneath or on the ventral aspect of an intestine

sub·intimal \"+\ *adj* [*sub-* + *intimal*] **:** situated beneath an intima and esp. between the intima and media of an artery

sub·introduce \"+\ *vt* [LL *subintroducere*, fr. L *sub-* secretly, under + *introducere* to introduce — more at SUB-, INTRODUCE] **:** to bring in secretly or surreptitiously

sub·involution \"+\ *n* [ISV *sub-* + *involution*] **:** partial or incomplete involution ⟨~ of the uterus⟩

sub·irrigate \"+\ *vt* [*sub-* + *irrigate*] **:** to water from beneath (as by the periodic rise of a water table); *esp* **:** to irrigate below the surface (as by a system of underground porous pipes) — **sub·irrigation** \ˌ;=+\ *n*

su·bi·ta·men·te \ˌsüˌbēd·əˈmen·(ˌ)tā\ *adv* [It, fr. *subito*, adj., sudden, fr. L *subitus*] **:** SUBITO — used as a direction in music

sub·i·ta·ne·ous \ˌsəbəˈtānēəs\ *adj* [L *subitaneus* — more at SUDDEN] **:** formed or taking place suddenly or unexpectedly **:** SUDDEN, HASTY; *esp* **:** undergoing or ready for immediate development ⟨~ summer eggs that develop without a period of dormancy⟩

sub·item \ˈsəb+\ *n* [*sub-* + *item*] **:** an item (as a brief note) that forms a subdivision of a larger topic

su·bi·to \ˈsübēd·ˌō\ *adv* [It, fr. L, fr. *subitus* sudden, unexpected — more at SUDDEN] **:** IMMEDIATELY, SUDDENLY — used as a direction in music

su·bi·ya \süˈbē(y)ə\ *n, usu cap* **:** an archaic Bantu language of Northern Rhodesia

subj *abbr* **1** subject; subjective; subjectively **2** subjunctive

sub·ja·cen·cy \(ˌ)səbˈjāsᵊnsē, -si\ *n* -ES **:** the quality or state of being subjacent

sub·ja·cent \-sᵊnt\ *adj* [L *subjacent-*, *subjacens*, pres. part. of *subjacēre* to lie under, fr. *sub-* + *jacēre* to lie — more at ADJACENT] **:** lying under or below: as **a :** lower than though not directly below ⟨hills and ~ valleys⟩ **b :** occurring below the surface ⟨a ~ fire⟩ **c :** antecedent and in some degree causative **:** UNDERLYING ⟨can infer a set of ~ causal events, when only the effects are available for direct scrutiny —A.C.Danto⟩ ⟨~ factors in a crime⟩ — **sub·ja·cent·ly** *adv*

¹sub·ject \ˈsəbjəkt, -jekt *sometimes* -ˌjekt\ *n* -S [ME *suget*, *subget*, fr. MF, fr. L *subjectus* subject, inferior (fr. *subjectus*, past part.) & *subjectum* foundation, subject of a proposition (trans. of Gk *hypokeimenon*), fr. neut. of *subjectus*, past part. of *subjicere*, *subicere* to bring under, throw under, fr. *sub-* + *-jicere*, *-icere* (fr. *jacere* to throw) — more at JET] **1 :** one that is placed under the authority, dominion, control, or influence of someone or something: as **a :** one bound in allegiance or service to a feudal superior **:** VASSAL **b** (1) **:** one subject to a monarch or ruler and governed by his law (2) **:** one who lives in the territory of, enjoys the protection of, and owes allegiance to a sovereign power or state — compare CITIZEN 2 **c** *obs* **:** a person under the spiritual oversight, care, or direction of a religious superior **d** *obs* **:** those who owe allegiance to a particular sovereign or rule **:** CITIZENRY **2 a** *obs* **:** the material from which a thing is formed **:** material substance **b** (1) **:** that of which a quality, attribute, or relation may be affirmed or in which it may inhere **:** the theme of a discourse or predication **:** the identical reference of related thoughts **:** a material either physical or ideal in which differences may appear (2) **:** SUBSTRATUM; *esp* **:** substantive reality that is material or essential being (3) **:** something that sustains or is embodied in thought or consciousness **:** the thinking agent **:** the mind, ego, or reality of whatever sort that supports or assumes the form of mental operations — distinguished from *object* ⟨the individuality of the organism corresponds to, though it is not necessarily identical with, the psychological ~, while to the environment and its changes corresponds the objective continuum —James Ward⟩ **3 :** something that forms a basis (as for action, study, discussion, or use): as **a** (1) **:** the underlying theme or topic of a branch of knowledge or study ⟨the ~ of mathematics is quantities and their manipulations⟩ (2) **:** a branch of knowledge or study esp. when arranged and formulated for teaching as an integrated part in a system of studies ⟨each pupil took courses in five ~*s* including electives⟩ ⟨found the ~ of chemistry difficult⟩ **b :** REASON, MOTIVE, CAUSE ⟨a ~ of dispute⟩ ⟨gave them no ~ for complaint⟩ **c** (1) **:** one that is acted upon (as in an operation or process) ⟨a ~ of debate⟩ ⟨the helpless ~ of his cruelty⟩ (2) **:** an individual whose reactions or responses are studied (as in the testing of a physiological or psychological phenomenon) ⟨the ~*s* of a nutritional experiment⟩ ⟨the ~ was cued to run a maze⟩ (3) **:** a dead body for anatomical study and dissection **d** (1) **:** something concerning which something is said or done **:** a thing or person treated of ⟨let's say no more on that ~⟩ ⟨treated religion as the first and greatest of ~*s*⟩ ⟨the ~ of your essay⟩ ⟨a ~ worthy of a great dramatist⟩ (2) **:** something (as an incident, scene, figure, group) that is represented or indicated in a work of art **e** (1) *or* **subject term :** the term of a logical proposition that denotes what the proposition is about; *also* **:** matter denoted by such a term **:** the topic of an affirmation or denial — contrasted with *predicate* (2) **:** a word or word group denoting that of which something is affirmed or predicated **:** a term that is construed with or without modifiers as the nominative of a verb and is grammatically either a noun or a word, phrase, or clause used as a noun equivalent **f** (1) **:** the principal theme or melodic phrase on which a musical composition or movement is based (2) **:** the antecedent or dux of a contrapuntal work (as a fugue or canon) **g :** a plant having particular horticultural qualities or suitable for a definite site or effect ⟨make good hedge ~*s*⟩ ⟨a difficult ~ only suitable for the expert with fully equipped greenhouse⟩ **syn** see CITIZEN

²subject \"\ *adj* [ME *suget*, *subget*, fr. MF, fr. L *subjectus*, past part.] **1 :** falling under or submitting to the power or dominion of another ⟨children ~ to their parents⟩: as **a :** owing allegiance to or being a subject of a particular sovereign or state ⟨a colony is ~ to the mother country⟩ ⟨a ~ race⟩ **b :** SUBJECTED **c :** OBEDIENT, SUBMISSIVE ⟨be ~ to the laws⟩ **2 a :** suffering a particular liability or exposure ⟨~ to very severe draughts⟩ ⟨~ to temptation⟩ **b :** PRONE, DISPOSED ⟨very ~ to colds⟩ **3** *archaic* **:** situated under or below **:** SUBJACENT **4 :** likely to be conditioned, affected, or modified in some indicated way **:** having a contingent relation to something and usu. dependent on such relation for final form, validity, or significance ⟨democratic representatives whose acts are ~ to discussion and criticism —M.R.Cohen⟩ ⟨a treaty ~ to ratification⟩ **syn** see LIABLE

³sub·ject \səbˈjekt *sometimes* ˌsəbˌjekt\ *vb* -ED/-ING/-S [ME *subjecten*, fr. L *subjectare* to put under, freq. of *subjicere*, *subicere* to bring under — more at SUBJECT (n.)] *vt* **1 a :** to bring under control or dominion **:** SUBJUGATE ⟨~*ing* primitive peoples to colonial rule⟩ **b :** to reduce to subservience or submission **:** make (as oneself) amenable to the discipline and control of a superior ⟨a servant should ~ himself to his master⟩ **2 a :** to make liable **:** PREDISPOSE ⟨his conduct ~*ed* him to needless suffering⟩ **b :** to make accountable **:** SUBMIT ⟨refused to ~ himself to their judgment⟩ **c :** to make (a piece of commercial paper) subject to discount **3** *obs* **:** to cause to lie beneath or below **4 :** to cause to undergo or submit to **:** make submit to a particular action or effect **:** EXPOSE ⟨hated to ~ his wife to such company⟩ ⟨unwilling to ~ himself to any inconvenience⟩ ~ *vi, obs* **:** to be or become subject

sub·ject·able \-təbəl\ *adj* **:** capable of being made subject

subject card *n* **:** a catalog card serving as a subject entry in a library card catalog

subject catalog *n* **:** a catalog in which books or other materials are listed only under the subjects treated and arranged alphabetically or by classes

subject cataloging *n* **:** a form or portion of the library cataloging process that not only describes a title but classifies it and assigns subject headings — contrasted with *descriptive cataloging*

subjected *adj* [fr. past part. of ³*subject*] **1 a :** brought into a state of subjection **:** made subject **:** SUBJUGATED **b :** SUBMISSIVE, OBEDIENT **2** *archaic* **:** situated below **:** LOW-LYING — **sub·ject·ed·ly** *adv* — **sub·ject·ed·ness** *n* -ES

sub·ject·hood \-ˌhu̇d\ *n* **:** the status or position of a subject person

sub·jec·ti·fi·ca·tion \(ˌ)səbˌjektəfəˈkāshən\ *n* -S [fr. *subjectify*, after such pairs as E *fructify*: *fructification*] **:** the act or process of subjectifying

sub·jec·ti·fy \(ˌ)səbˈjektəˌfī\ *vt* -ED/-ING/-ES [¹*subject* + *-ify*] **:** to identify with a subject or interpret in terms of subjective experience

sub·jec·tion \(ˌ)səbˈjekshən\ *n* -S [ME *subjeccioun*, fr. MF *subjection*, fr. LL *subjection-*, *subjectio*, fr. L, act of bringing under, fr. *subjectus* (past part. of *subjicere*, *subicere* to bring under) + *-ion-*, *-io* -ion — more at SUBJECT] **1 a** *obs* **:** the exercise of lordship or control **:** lordly sway or rule **b :** the act of subduing or subjecting **:** SUBJUGATION ⟨planned the ~ of the rebels⟩ ⟨determined on the ~ of his baser nature⟩ **2 :** the quality or state of being subject and esp. under the power, control, or government of another ⟨the general ~ of women prior to the 20th century⟩: as **a** *obs* **:** obedient submissiveness **:** SUBORDINATION **b** *archaic* **:** a legal obligation (as by contract or pledge) to submit to the will of another **:** HOMAGE **c** *archaic* **:** the condition of being under obligation or liability **3 :** attachment of a subject to a predicate in logic — compare PREDICATION

sub·jec·tion·al \-shənᵊl, -shnəl\ *adj* **:** of, relating to, or involving subjection

¹sub·jec·tive \(ˌ)səbˈjektiv, -tēv *also* -təv\ *adj* [ME, relating to submissiveness, fr. ML *subjectivus*, fr. L *subjectus* (past part. of *subjicere*, *subicere* to bring under) + *-ivus* -ive] **1 :** of, relating to, or constituting a subject: as **a** *obs* **:** of, relating to, or characteristic of one that is subject esp. in lack of freedom of action or in submissiveness **b** [LL *subjectivus*, fr. L *subjectum* subject of a proposition + *-ivus* -ive — more at SUBJECT] **:** being or relating to a grammatical subject; *specif* **:** NOMINATIVE **2 a :** of or relating to the real or essential being of that which supports qualities, attributes, or relations **:** SUBSTANTIAL, REAL — compare OBJECTIVE 1b(1) **b** (1) *Kantianism* **:** of, relating to, or determined by the mind, ego, or consciousness as the subject of experience and knowledge ⟨~ reality⟩ (2) **:** characteristic of or belonging to reality as perceived or known as opposed to reality as it is in itself or independent of mind **:** PHENOMENAL — compare OBJECTIVE 1b(2) **c :** of, relating to, or being whatever in experience or knowledge is conditioned by merely personal characteristics of mind or by particular states of mind as opposed to what is determined only by the universal conditions of human experience and knowledge — compare OBJECTIVE 1b(3) **3 :** arising from within or belonging strictly to the individual often as contrasted with something modified by the physical or social environment or by the presence of an interpreter: as **a** : peculiar to a particular individual modified by individual bias and limitations : PERSONAL ⟨a ~ impression⟩ ⟨~ judgments⟩ **b** : arising from conditions within the brain or sense organs and not directly caused by external stimuli ⟨~ sensations⟩ **c** : placing undue stress on one's opinions, fancies, or moods : excessively or moodily introspective **d** : arising out of or identified by means of an individual's attention to or awareness of his own states and processes ⟨a ~ symptom of disease⟩ ⟨a ~ study of fatigue⟩ **e** : lacking in reality or substance : existing in the mind alone : ILLUSORY, FANCIFUL **f** (1) : making prominent the individuality of a writer or an artist (2) : modified or affected by the personal views, mental and emotional background, or other special characteristics of the artist ⟨a ~ painting⟩ ⟨~ writers⟩ — **sub·jec·tive·ly** \-tə̇vlē, -li\ *adv* — **sub·jec·tive·ness** \-tivnə̇s, -tēv- *also* -təv-\ *n* -ES

²**subjective** \"\ *n* -S **1** : something that is subjective ⟨the overemphasis of the individual and the ~ in modern philosophy —John Dewey⟩ **2** : NOMINATIVE

subjective complement *n* : a grammatical complement relating to the subject of an intransitive verb ⟨in "he had fallen sick" *sick* is a *subjective complement*⟩

subjective idealism *n* **1** : the theory that nature does not have any real existence independent of perceiving minds : BERKELEIANISM **2** : the doctrine that an absolute ego dialectically evolves the world : FICHTEANISM — contrasted with *objective idealism*

subjective theory *n* : MORAL THEORY

subjective time *n* : time that is subjectively experienced; *specif* : the subjective feeling of duration with its absolute given present — called also *experiential time, private time;* contrasted with *objective time*

subjective utility *n* : the utility or satisfaction an article gives to an individual based upon his personal judgment and desires rather than upon market judgment

subjective validity *n* : validity relative to the conditions of the thinking subject either to the universal limitations of human experience and knowledge or to personal limitations (as ignorance) or circumstances of individual judgment

subjective verb *n* : an intransitive verb

sub·jec·tiv·ism \(ˌ)səbˈjektə̇ˌvizəm\ *n* -S [ISV ¹*subjective* + *-ism*] **1 a** : any of various epistemological theories that limit knowledge to conscious states and elements; *specif* : SUBJECTIVE IDEALISM **b** : any of various theories, doctrines, or viewpoints that attach great or supreme importance to the subjective elements in experience: as (1) : KANTIANISM (2) : the doctrine that truth is relative to human nature : PROTAGOREANISM **2** : either of two doctrines in ethics: **a** : the supreme good or the end of ethical conduct is the realization of some type of subjective experience or feeling (as pleasure) **b** : individual feeling or apprehension is the ultimate criterion of the good and the right

sub·jec·tiv·ist \-ˌvə̇st\ *n* -S : an adherent or advocate of subjectivism

sub·jec·tiv·is·tic \(ˌ)=ˌ==ˈvistik, -tēk\ *adj* [ISV *subjectivist* + *-ic*] : of or relating to subjectivism

sub·jec·tiv·i·ty \ˌsəbˌjekˈtivədē, -jək-, -vətē, -i\ *n* -ES [NL *subjectivitat-, subjectivitas,* fr. *subjectivus* subjectivistic (fr. LL & ML, subjective) + L *-itat-, -itas* -ity — more at SUBJECTIVE] **1** : subjective character, quality, state, or nature esp. in an artistic or literary work : the individuality of an artist as expressed through his work or performance **2** : SUBJECTIVISM **3** : the quality of an investigator that affects the results of observational investigation (as in scientific observation) by reason of the individual and peculiar characteristics and reaction of or response to the media by the aid of which the investigations are conducted — compare PERSONAL EQUATION **4** : the testing of truth solely by standards which can be applied only by the individual subject making the judgment (as by some subjective impression or feeling or by an arbitrary individual purpose or will to believe) instead of by some objective criterion accessible to others (as logical reasoning, history, verification in generally accessible experience) or even by some traditional external authority frankly recognized as such

sub·jec·tiv·iza·tion \(ˌ)səbˌjektə̇və̇ˈzāshən, -ˌvīˈz-\ *n* -S : an act or instance of subjectivizing

sub·jec·tiv·ize \(ˌ)=ˈ=tə̇ˌvīz\ *vt* -ED/-ING/-S [¹*subjective* + *-ize*] : to make subjective : handle (as data) in a subjective manner

sub·ject·less \ˈsəbjə̇ktlə̇s, -jēk-\ *adj* : having no subject or subjects

subject matter *n* [ME *matere subject,* trans. of LL *materia subjecta,* trans. of Gk *hypokeimenē hylē,* lit., underlying matter] **1** *archaic* : matter acted upon (as in a process or by a skill) : material from which something is formed **2** : matter presented for consideration: as **a** : the essential facts, data, or ideas that constitute the basis of spoken, written, or artistic expression or representation; *often* : the substance as distinguished from the form esp. of an artistic or literary production **b** : a subject of thought or study; *often* : conveyable material (as information, knowledge, skill) actually made available by a branch of knowledge or in a course of study : the available factual content of a branch or course as distinct from technique or method of instruction or factors inherent in the individual learner **c** : the topic of dispute in a legal matter

subject-object \ˈ==ˈ==\ *n* **1** : something that is at once subject and object **2 a** : the ego as object of its own knowledge **b** : a self-conscious being (as man)

subject-objectivity \ˈ==ˌ=ˌ=ˈ===\ *n* : the essential character or status of a subject-object

subject-predicate \ˈ==ˈ===\ *adj* **1** : of, relating to, characterized by, or taking the form of analysis into subjects and predicates analogous to the basic grammatical structure of the Indo-European languages ⟨*subject-predicate* logical structure⟩ **2** : having the form of a predicate attached to a subject ⟨a *subject-predicate* proposition⟩

subjects *pl of* SUBJECT, *pres 3d sing of* SUBJECT

subject·ship \ˈ==ˌship\ *n* : the status or condition of a subject individual

subject substantive *n* : a simple grammatical subject

subject-superject \ˈ==ˈ==\ *n* : a subject that is a superject

subject term *n* : SUBJECT 3e(1)

sub·join \ˌsəbˈjȯin, ˈsəb'-\ *vt* [MF *subjoin-,* stem of *subjoindre* to subjoin, fr. L *subjungere,* lit., to bring under, subjugate, fr. *sub-* + *jungere* to bring together, join — more at YOKE] : to add after something and esp. something said or written : place immediately after or next to something ⟨let me ~ another example⟩; *esp* : to annex (subordinate or supplementary matter) as an appendix ⟨~*ed* a statement of expenses to his report⟩

sub·join·der \-ndə(r)\ *n* -S [*sub-* + *-joinder* (as in *rejoinder*)] : an additional remark

sub·joint \ˈsəb+ˌ-\ *n* [*sub-* + *joint*] : a secondary joint (as of a segment of an arthropod limb)

sub ju·di·ce \ˌsəbˈjüdəˌkā, -ˈjüdəˌsē\ *adv* [L] : before a judge or court : under judicial consideration : not yet decided

sub·ju·ga·ble \ˈsəbjəgəbəl\ *adj* [L *subjugare* to subjugate + E *-able*] : capable of being subjugated

sub·ju·gate \-ˌgāt, *usu* -ād·+V\ *vt* -ED/-ING/-S [ME *subjugaten,* fr. L *subjugatus,* past part. of *subjugare* to bring under the yoke, subjugate, fr. *sub-* + *jugare* to join, yoke, fr. *jugum* yoke — more at YOKE] **1** : to bring under the yoke of power or dominion : conquer by force and compel to submit as a subject to the government of another ⟨colonial powers *subjugating* native peoples⟩ **2 a** : to force to submit to control and governance : make submissive or subject : MASTER ⟨~ a wild horse⟩ ⟨*subjugated* his unruly nephew⟩ **b** : to bring or hold under strict control or into a subordinate position ⟨had to ~ his own feeling⟩ **syn** see CONQUER

sub·ju·ga·tion \ˌ==ˈgāshən\ *n* -S [LL *subjugation-, subjugatio,* fr. L *subjugatus* (past part.) + *-ion-, -io* -ion] : an act of subjugating or the state of being subjugated ⟨the distinction between outright conquest and ~ on the one hand and mere military occupation on the other —E.H.Litchfield⟩ ⟨~ of personal inclination to the good of the group⟩

sub·ju·ga·tor \ˈ==ˌgād·ə(r), -ātə-\ *n* -S [L, fr. *subjugatus* (past part. of *subjugare*) + *-or*] : one that subjugates

sub·jugular \ˌsəb+\ *adj* [*sub-* + *jugular*] : situated nearly far enough forward to be jugular — used of the ventral fins of some fishes

sub·junc·tion \səbˈjəŋ(k)shən\ *n* [LL *subjunction-, subjunctio,* fr. L *subjunctus* (past part.) + *-ion-, -io* -ion] **1** : an act of subjoining or the state of being subjoined **2** : something subjoined ⟨a ~ to a sentence⟩

¹**sub·junc·tive** \-tiv, -tēv *also* -təv\ *adj* [LL *subjunctivus* (trans. of Gk *hypotaktikos*), fr. L *subjunctus* (past part. of *subjungere* to subjoin) + *-ivus* -ive — more at SUBJOIN] : of, relating to, or constituting a verb form or set of verb forms that represents an attitude toward or concern with a denoted act or state not as fact but as something entertained in thought as contingent or possible or viewed emotionally (as with doubt, desire, will) ⟨the ~ mood⟩ ⟨*bless* in "God bless you" and *write* in "I suggest that he write a letter" are ~ verb forms⟩ — compare IMPERATIVE, INDICATIVE

²**subjunctive** \"\ *n* -S **1** : the subjunctive mood; *also* : a verb or verbal form denoting it **2** : SUBJUNCTIVE EQUIVALENT

subjunctive equivalent *n* : a verb phrase formed in English with a modal auxiliary (as *shall, should, may, might*) and functioning in a manner comparable to the subjunctive mood

sub·junc·tive·ly \-tə̇vlē, -li\ *adv* : in a subjunctive manner : with a subjunctive ⟨expressed his doubt ~⟩

subjv *abbr* subjunctive

sub·kingdom \ˌsəb+\ *n* [*sub-* + *kingdom*] **1** : a subordinate kingdom **2** : a primary division of a taxonomic kingdom

¹**sub·labial** \"+\ *adj* [*sub-* + *labial*] : situated below a lip or labium

²**sublabial** \"\ *n* : a sublabial part : INFRALABIAL

sub·laciniate \ˌsəb+\ *adj* [*sub-* + *laciniate*] : partially or imperfectly laciniate

sub·lanceolate \"+\ *adj* [*sub-* + *lanceolate*] : nearly lanceolate

sub·lap·sar·i·an \ˌsəbˌlapˈsa(a)rēən, -ser-\ *adj or n* [NL *sublapsarius* (fr. L *sub-* + *lapsus* lapse, fall + *-arius* -ary) + E *-an* — more at LAPSE] : INFRALAPSARIAN

sub·lap·sar·i·an·ism \-əˌnizəm\ *n* -S [*sublapsarian* + *-ism*] : INFRALAPSARIANISM

sub·late \ˌsəˈblāt\ *vt* -ED/-ING/-S [L *sublatus* (suppletive past part. of *tollere* to take away, lift up), fr. *sub-* up + *latus* carried, suppletive past part. of *ferre* to carry — more at SUB-, TOLERATE, BEAR] **1** *obs* : to take away : REMOVE **2 a** (1) : NEGATE, DENY (2) : CANCEL, ELIMINATE **b** : to cancel but also preserve and elevate (an element in a dialectic process) as a partial element in a synthesis ⟨evil is not evaded, but *sublated* in the higher religious cheer of these persons —William James⟩

¹**sub·lateral** \ˌsəb+\ *adj* [*sub-* + *lateral*] : situated near a side (as of the body)

²**sublateral** \"\ *n* : a channel (as in an irrigation or sewage system) leading to or from a main lateral; *usu* : a channel of least importance

sub·la·tion \ˌsəˈblāshən\ *n* -S [LL *sublation-, sublatio,* fr. L, act of lifting up, fr. *sublatus* (suppletive past part. of *tollere* to lift up, take away) + *-ion-, -io* -ion] **1** : the act of taking or carrying away : REMOVAL **2** : the act or process of sublating

sub·la·tive \ˌsəˈblād·iv\ *adj* [L *sublatus* + E *-ive*] : able or tending to take away : concerned with taking something away ⟨the ~ case of the Magyar language⟩

sub·leader \ˈsəb+\ *n* [*sub-* + *leader*] **1** : a person in a position of authority but subordinate to a leader of greater prominence **2** *chiefly Brit* : an article or paragraph (as in a periodical) in a prominent but not the first position

¹**sub·lease** \ˈ=+ˌ-\ *n* [*sub-* + *lease*] : a lease which is given by a tenant or lessee to another person of part or all of the leased premises for a shorter term than his own term and under which he retains some rights or interest under his original lease : a derivative lease — compare ASSIGNMENT

²**sub·lease** \ˈ=+\ *vt* **1** : to convey (a leased property) to another person under a sublease : grant a sublease of **2** : to take or hold (a leased property) from the original lessee under a sublease : take a sublease of

sub·lenticular \ˌsəb+\ *adj* [*sub-* + *lenticular*] : approaching the lenticular : almost doubly convex in outline

sub·lessee \"+\ *n* [*sub-* + *lessee*] : a tenant under a sublease

sub·lessor \"+\ *n* [*sub-* + *lessor*] : one that grants a sublease

¹**sub·let** \ˌsəb+\ *vt* [*sub-* + *let*] **1 a** : to lease or rent all or part of (a leased or rented property) to another person ⟨they rent a little house . . . and ~ most of the rooms —Edmund Wilson⟩ **b** : to lease or rent all or part of (a leased or rented property) from the original lessee or tenant ⟨move into the apartment they have just ~ —Murray Schumach⟩ **2** : SUBCONTRACT 2a ⟨when a building contractor ~*s* work —*Amer. Builder*⟩

²**sublet** \"\ *n* : property that is or may be sublet

sub·lethal \ˌsəb+\ *adj* [ISV *sub-* + *lethal*] : less but usu. only slightly less than lethal — **sub·lethally** \"+\ *adv*

sub·leukemic \"+\ *adj* [*sub-* + *leukemic*] : not marked by the presence of excessive numbers of white blood cells in the circulating blood ⟨~ leukemia⟩

sub·level \ˈsəb+\ *n* [*sub-* + *level*] : a level that is lower than another express or implied level ⟨a ~ of physiological activity⟩ ⟨the use of ~ caving in mining large bodies of ore⟩

sub·license \"+\ *n* [*sub-* + *license*] : a subordinate license granted to another by one already having a license

sub·licensee \"+\ *n* [*sub-* + *licensee*] : a subordinate licensee : a holder of a sublicense

sub·lieutenancy \"+\ *n* [*sub-* + *lieutenancy*] *chiefly Brit* : the status or position of a sublieutenant

sub·lieutenant \"+\ *n* [*sub-* + *lieutenant*] *chiefly Brit* : an officer ranking next below a lieutenant

sub·lim·able \səˈblīməbəl\ *adj* [¹*sublime* + *-able*] : capable of being sublimed ⟨a ~ chemical⟩

¹**sub·li·mate** \ˈsəbləˌmāt, *usu* -ād·+V\ *vb* -ED/-ING/-S [L *sublimatus,* past part. of *sublimare* to lift up, raise — more at SUBLIME] *vt* **1** *obs* **a** : to elevate to a place of dignity or honor **b** : to give a more elevated character to **2** [ML *sublimatus,* past part. of *sublimare* to refine, sublime, fr. L, to raise, lift up] **a** : to cause to sublime ⟨~ sulfur⟩ **b** *archaic* : to improve or refine as if by subliming **c** *obs* : to get or extract by or as if by subliming **3** : to direct the energy of (an impulse) from a primitive aim to one that is higher in the cultural scale esp. in the course of psychoanalysis ⟨~ sexual curiosity into artistic or scientific production⟩ ~ *vi* : to undergo sublimation

²**sub·li·mate** \-ˌmāt, -ˌmə̇t, *usu* -d·+V\ *n* -S [ML *sublimatum,* fr. neut. of *sublimatus,* past part. of *sublimare* to sublime] **1** : MERCURY CHLORIDE **b** **2** : a chemical product obtained by sublimation

sub·li·ma·tion \ˌ==ˈmāshən\ *n* -S [ME *sublimacion* act or process of subliming, fr. MF & ML; MF *sublimation,* fr. ML *sublimation-, sublimatio,* fr. *sublimatus* (past part. of *sublimare* to sublime) + L *-ion-, -io* -ion] **1** : the act or process of sublimating: as **a** : the act or process or an instance of subliming of a chemical entity — compare DISTILLATION 1, EVAPORATION 1a **b** [LL *sublimation-, sublimatio* act of raising, fr. L *sublimatus* (past part. of *sublimare* to raise, lift up) + *-ion-, -io* -ion; trans. of G *sublimierung*] : discharge of instinctual energy and esp. that associated with pre genital impulses through socially approved activities **2 a** : a product of sublimating **b** : the condition of being sublimated — **sub·li·ma·tion·al** \ˌ==ˈmāshənᵊl, -shnəl\ *adj*

sublimation pressure *n* : the pressure of equilibrium at a definite temperature of a vapor in contact with its solid

sublimation vein *n* : a vein of mineral matter formed by condensation from the vaporous state

sub·li·ma·tive \ˈsəbləˌmād·iv\ *adj* [*sublimation* + *-ive*] : tending to produce or assist in the production of psychic sublimation

sub·li·ma·tor \-ˌmād·ə(r)\ *n* -S [¹*sublimate* + *-or*] : one that sublimates

¹**sub·lime** \səˈblīm\ *vb* -ED/-ING/-S [ME *sublimen,* fr. MF *sublimer,* fr. ML *sublimare* to refine, purify, sublime, fr. L, to lift up, raise, fr. *sublimis* uplifted, high] *vt* **1 a** : to cause to pass from the solid to the vapor state by the action of heat and again condense to solid form ⟨many chemicals (as naphthalene, benzoic acid, and iodine) are *sublimed* to rid them of impurities⟩ **b** : to produce, purify, or release by heating a containing mixture ⟨~ pure sulfur from an unpure mixture⟩ **2** [F *sublimer,* fr. L *sublimare*] **a** : to elevate or exalt esp. in dignity or honor : render finer (as in purity or excellence) **b** : to convert (something inferior) into something of higher esteem or worth ⟨selfishness *sublimed* into care for the public welfare⟩ **3** : to cause to rise upward ⟨the sun's hot rays ~ the morning dew⟩ ~ *vi* **1** *of a chemical entity* : to undergo sublimation : pass directly from the solid to the vapor state ⟨ammonia vapor ~*s* from solid crystals⟩ **2** : to become elevated or exalted (as in dignity or honor) : become finer (as in purity or excellence)

²**sublime** \"\ *adj* -ER/-EST [L *sublimis* uplifted, high, sublime, fr. *sub-* up + *-limis* (fr. *limin-, limen* threshold) — more at SUB-, LIMB] **1 a** : lofty in conception or expression : grand or exalted in thought or manner ⟨the *sublimest* lines in English prose⟩ ⟨a ~ style difficult to maintain⟩ **b** : elevated or exalted in character : of outstanding spiritual, intellectual, or moral worth ⟨in a ~ spirit of sacrifice⟩ ⟨~ devotion⟩ ⟨a ~ Christian leader⟩ **c** : tending to inspire awe or uplifting emotion usu. by reason of elevated beauty, nobility, grandeur, solemnity, or similar character ⟨the ~ beauty of that night⟩ ⟨a ~ peace settled about us⟩ **d** : outstanding as such : very great : NOTABLE ⟨turned out to be a ~ husband⟩ ⟨you ~ idiot⟩ ⟨the ~ stench in a city of evil smells —W.H.Hudson †1922⟩ **2 a** *archaic* : high in place : raised to a great height : lifted up **b** *obs* : lofty of mien : HAUGHTY, PROUD **c** (1) : of exalted rank or high estate (2) *usu cap* : SUPREME — used in a style of address (as to former Turkish sovereigns) **3** *obs* : elevated by joy : ELATED **syn** see SPLENDID

³**sublime** \"\ *n* -S **1** : things that are sublime : the sublime aspect of anything : the quality of sublimity — usu. used with *the* ⟨we see little of the literary ~ in current writing⟩ ⟨from the ~ to the ridiculous⟩ **2** : the supreme degree or utmost point : ACME

sublimed blue lead *n* : BLUE LEAD 2

sublimed sulfur *n* : sulfur that has sublimed; *esp* : FLOWERS OF SULFUR

sublimed white lead *n* : a white pigment composed essentially of basic lead sulfate and formed by fuming lead ore of a particular type

sub·lime·ly *adv* **1** : in a sublime manner : with sublimity **2** : UTTERLY, COMPLETELY ⟨~ content⟩ ⟨~ self-satisfied⟩

sub·lime·ness *n* -ES : the quality or state of being sublime

sub·lim·er \səˈblīmə(r)\ *n* -S : one that sublimes

sub·liminal \ˌsəb+\ *adj* [*sub-* + L *limin-, limen* threshold + E *-al* — more at LIMB] **1** : falling below the threshold of stimulation (as for nerve or muscle) : inadequate to produce a sensation or a perception : too small for discrimination **2 a** : existing or functioning outside the area of conscious awareness : influencing thought, feeling, or behavior in a manner unperceived by personal or subjective consciousness ⟨~ perception⟩ ⟨the ~ mind⟩ — compare SUBCONSCIOUS, SUPRACONSCIOUS, UNCONSCIOUS **b** : designed to influence the mind on levels other than that of conscious awareness and esp. by presentation too brief to be consciously perceived ⟨~ techniques in TV advertising⟩ — **sub·limi·nal·ly** \-nᵊlē, -ᵊli\ *adv*

subliminal self *also* **subliminal** *n* -S : the portion of an individual's personality that lies below or beyond the reach of his personal awareness — compare SUBCONSCIOUS, SUPRACONSCIOUS, UNCONSCIOUS

sub·limi·na·tion \ˌ=ˌ==ˈnāshən\ *n* -S [*subliminal* + *-ation*] : the use of subliminal techniques (as in advertising)

subliming *pres part of* SUBLIME

sub·lim·i·ty \səˈblimədē, -ətē, -i\ *n* -ES [L *sublimitas,* fr. *sublimis* high, sublime + *-itas* -ity — more at SUBLIME] **1** : something that is sublime: as **a** : exalted character, ideals, or conduct : noble quality or elevation (as of thought, feeling, style) **b** : high dignity, honor, or position : exalted office or status — sometimes used as a title or form of address **c** : the highest or supremest level, degree, phase, or development of something : ACME **2** : the quality or state of being sublime and esp. of awakening awe, reverence, or a similar emotion or of producing a sense of vastness, power, or similar quality

sub·limize \ˈsəbləˌmīz, səˈblīˌ-\ *vt* -ED/-ING/-S [²*sublime* + *-ize*] : to give a sublime character to

sub·line \ˈsəb+ˌ-\ *n* [*sub-* + *line*] : a subdivision of a line (sense 6a)

sub·linear \ˌsəb+\ *adj* [*sub-* + *linear*] **1** : almost linear ⟨a ~ arrangement of parts⟩ **2** : placed below a line of written or printed characters

sub·lineation \"+\ *n* [*sub-* + *lineation*] : UNDERLINING

sub·lingua \ˌ=+\ *n, pl* **sublinguae** [NL, fr. L *sub-* + *lingua* tongue — more at TONGUE] : a process or fold covered with modified or hardened mucous membrane and occurring on the floor of the mouth in some animals (as lemurs)

sub·lingual \"+\ *adj* [NL *sublingualis,* fr. L *sub-* + ML *lingualis* lingual — more at LINGUAL] **1** : situated or occurring under the tongue **2** : of, relating to, or situated near the sublingual gland

sublingual gland *n* : a small salivary gland on each side of the mouth lying beneath the mucous membrane in a fossa in the mandible near the symphysis

sub·literary \ˌsəb+\ *adj* : of a quality below that acceptable as standard literature ⟨~ fiction . . . does not bother to blur the distinction between bad and good —G.P.Winship⟩

sub·literate \"+\ *adj* [*sub-* + *literate*] : imperfectly literate ⟨letters from ~ folk —J.G.Randall⟩

sub·literature \"+\ *n* [*sub-* + *literature*] : impermanent literature: as **a** : inferior literature that does not survive the test of time **b** : written material (as reports) duplicated in impermanent form (as by mimeographing or microfilming) usu. primarily for use by the staff of the issuing organization

sub·lithographic \"+\ *adj* [*sub-* + *lithographic*] *of limestone* : approaching in texture the fine grain of lithographic limestone

¹**sub·littoral** \"+\ *adj* [*sub-* + *littoral*] : situated, occurring, or formed on the watery side of a shoreline or littoral zone ⟨~ deposits⟩ : constituting the sublittoral ⟨a distinct ~ zone⟩

²**sublittoral** \"\ *n* : the deeper part of the littoral portion of a body of water: **a** : the region in an ocean between the lowest point exposed by a low-low tide and the margin of the continental shelf **b** : the region in a lake between the deepest growing rooted vegetation and the hypolimnion

sub·lobular \"+\ *adj* [*sub-* + *lobular*] : situated at the bases of the lobules of the liver

sub·luminous \"+\ *adj* [*sub-* + *luminous*] : partially luminous : approaching the state of luminosity

sub·lunar \"+\ *adj* [LL *sublunaris*] : SUBLUNARY

sublunar point *n* : the point on the earth's surface at which the moon is in the zenith

¹**sub·lu·nary** \ˈsəblüˌnerē, ˌsəbˈlünərē\ *adj* [modif. (influenced by ²*lunary*) of LL *sublunaris,* fr. L *sub-* + *lunaris* lunar — more at LUNAR] **1** : situated beneath the moon or within the orbit of the moon — compare SUPERLUNARY **2** : characteristic of or pertinent to this world : TERRESTRIAL, MUNDANE ⟨in a religious epoch those whose main interest is in secular affairs tend . . . to find transcendental motives for ~ action —Aldous Huxley⟩ — compare TRANSLUNARY **syn** see EARTHLY

²**sublunary** *n* -ES *obs* : something sublunary

sub·lunate \ˌsəb+\ *adj* [*sub-* + *lunate*] : nearly crescentic in form

sub·lustrous \"+\ *adj* [*sub-* + *lustrous*] : somewhat or imperfectly lustrous

sub·luxated \"+\ *adj* [*subluxation* + *-ed*] : partially dislocated ⟨a ~ vertebra⟩

sub·luxation \"+\ *n* [NL *subluxation-, subluxatio,* fr. L *sub-* + LL *luxation-, luxatio* dislocation — more at LUXATION] : partial dislocation (as of one of the bones in a joint)

subm *abbr* **1** submarine **2** submerge; submerged

sub·machine gun \ˌsəb+-\ *n* [*sub-* + *machine gun*] : a lightweight automatic or semiautomatic portable firearm designed usu. for firing from the shoulder or hip

sub·main \ˈ=+ˌ-\ *n* [*sub-* + *main*] : a main (as in a sewer, gas, electrical, or drainage system) having a number of lesser mains feeding into or branching from it but being itself subsidiary to a larger main

sub·maintenance \ˈ=+\ *adj* [*sub-* + *maintenance*] : inadequate for the maintenance of bodily health ⟨a ~ ration⟩

sub·man \ˈ=+ˌ-\ *n, pl* **submen** [*sub-* + *man*] : a man or a being who has human characteristics in a very inferior degree : a brutal or stupid man

sub·marginal \ˌsəb+\ *adj* [*sub-* + *marginal*] **1** : situated near a boundary : adjacent to a marginal part or structure ⟨a ~ cell in an insect wing⟩ **2 a** : less than marginal : falling below the minimum necessary for some end (as the obtaining of an economic return or the living of a normal life) ⟨attempting to crop ~ hill farms⟩ ⟨the children in the one fourth of our nation that subsist on ~ levels —Leon Eisenberg⟩ ⟨a ~ diet⟩ **b :** dealing with or dependent upon something (as a way of life) that is submarginal ⟨~ farmers⟩ — **sub·marginally** \"+\ *adv*

sub·marginate \"+\ *also* **sub·margined** \"+\ *adj* [*sub-* + *marginate* or *margined*] : having a border near the edge or margin

1sub·marine \"+\ *adj* [*sub-* + *marine*] **1 :** being, acting, growing, or used under water and esp. in the sea ⟨~ boats⟩ ⟨~ plants⟩ **2 :** suggestive of the undersea world ⟨an illusive ~ glimmer⟩

2submarine \"\ *n* -s **1 :** a submarine organism (as a plant or coral) **2 :** something (as an explosive mine) designed to function underwater; *specif* **:** a submersible ship armed with torpedoes, guns, and guided missiles and propelled by diesel engines, electric motors, or nuclear-powered steam turbines that operates below the surface of the sea — compare TORPEDO BOAT

3submarine \"\ *vb* -ED/-ING/-S [*2submarine*] *vt* **:** to make an attack upon or to sink by means of a submarine and esp. by torpedoing ~ *vi* **1 :** to be, move, or function beneath the sea: as **a :** to handle a submarine **b :** to swim or dive underwater **2** *of a defensive lineman in football* **:** to throw the head and shoulders beneath the knees of two opposing players and then draw the feet up so that the opponents slide over the back

submarine bell *n* **:** an underwater sound transmitting device using the strokes of a bell to send messages or to send at stated intervals a signal as an aid to navigation in a fog

submarine canyon *n* **:** CANYON 1b

submarine chaser *n* **:** a boat fitted to operate offensively against submarines

submarine geology *n* **:** geology of the ocean floor

submarine process *n* **:** a method of color correcting an offset printing plate by rubbing away details of dots under water

sub·ma·rin·er \ˌsəbməˈrēnə(r); ˌsəbˈmarənə(r) *also* -mer-\ *n* -s [*2submarine* + *-er*] **:** a member of a submarine crew

submarine sandwich *also* **submarine** *n* [so called fr. its shape] **:** POOR BOY

submarine sentry *n* **:** KITE 7a

submarine telegraph *n* **1 :** the sending of a message or messages by means of submarine telegraph cable **2 :** a system of communication by means of submarine telegraph cable

submarine telegraph cable *or* **submarine cable** *n* **:** a telegraph cable laid under water to connect stations separated by water

submarine telephone *n* **:** a system of signaling under water (as from a buoy to a ship) by the use of submerged bells and special receivers

sub·master \ˈsəb+\ *n* [ME, fr. *sub-* + *master*] **:** a subordinate or assistant master; *usu* **:** an assistant or deputy principal of a school

sub·mature \"+\ *adj* [*sub-* + *mature*] **:** incompletely matured or differentiated — used esp. of a topographic feature — **sub·maturely** \"+\ *adv*

sub·maxilla \"+\ *n, pl* **submaxillae** *also* **submaxillas** [NL, fr. *sub-* + *maxilla*] **:** the lower jaw or inferior maxillary bone; *specif* **:** the human mandible

1sub·maxillary \"+\ *adj* [*sub-* + *maxillary*] **1 :** of, relating to, or situated below the lower jaw **2 :** of, relating to, or associated with the submaxillary gland

2submaxillary \"\ *n* **:** a submaxillary part (as an artery, bone, ganglion, or gland)

submaxillary ganglion *n* **:** an autonomic ganglion situated on the lingual branch of the mandibular nerve above the deep part of the submaxillary gland, receiving preganglionic fibers from the facial nerve by way of the chorda tympani, sending postganglionic fibers to the submaxillary and sublingual glands, and giving passage to sympathetic fibers from the external maxillary plexus

submaxillary gland *n* **:** a salivary gland inside of and near the lower edge of the mandible on each side and discharging by Wharton's duct into the mouth under the tongue

sub·maximal \ˈsəb+\ *adj* [*sub-* + *maximal*] **:** almost maximal

sub·medial \"+\ *adj* [*sub-* + *medial*] **1 :** SUBMEDIAN **2 :** lying under the middle — **sub·medially** \"+\ *adv*

sub·median \"+\ *adj* [*sub-* + *median*] **:** situated next to a median part or the midline ⟨a ~ tooth on the radula of a mollusk⟩

sub·mediant \"+\ *n* [*sub-* + *mediant*] **:** the sixth musical degree (as A in the scale of C) of the major or minor scale midway between the subdominant and the upper tonic — called also *superdominant*

submen *pl of* SUBMAN

sub·men·tal \ˈsəbˈmentᵊl\ *adj* [in sense 1, fr. *sub-* + *mental;* in sense 2, fr. NL *submentum* + E *-al*] **1 :** situated under the chin **2 :** of or relating to the submentum

submental artery *n* **:** a branch of the external maxillary artery that passes near the submaxillary gland and is distributed to the muscles of the jaw

sub·men·tum \səbˈmentəm\ *n, pl* **submen·ta** \-tə\ [NL, fr. *sub-* + *mentum*] **:** the basal part of the labium of an insect

sub·merge \səbˈmərj, -məj, -məij\ *vb* -ED/-ING/-S [L *submergere*, fr. *sub-* + *mergere* to plunge — more at MERGE] *vt* **1 :** to cause to pass under water **:** put under water ⟨~ your hand to test the heat of the water⟩ **2 :** to cover or overflow with water **:** INUNDATE ⟨the stream overflowed and *submerged* the town⟩ **3 :** to lose sight of, obscure, or cover up as if under a layer of water ⟨personal lives *submerged* by professional responsibilities⟩ ⟨the original argument was *submerged* in irrelevancies⟩ ⟨~ oneself in trivia⟩ ~ *vi* **1 :** to plunge into water or other fluid **2 :** to become submerged, buried, or covered as if by a fluid **syn** see DIP

submerged *adj* [fr. past part. of *submerge*] **1** *of a plant* **:** SUBMERSED **2 :** sunk in poverty and misery ⟨the ~ tenth of society that lacks all that makes life pleasant⟩ **3 :** HIDDEN, CRYPTIC ⟨a ~ gene effect⟩

submerged-tube boiler \ˈ=ˌ=ˈ=-\ *n* **:** a steam boiler in which the tubes emerge below the waterline in the steam drum

sub·merge·ment \-mənt\ *n* -s [ISV *submerge* + *-ment*] **:** SUBMERSION

sub·mer·gence \-jən(t)s\ *n* -s **1 :** the quality or state of being submerged **2 a :** the act of submerging something **b :** the distance or degree to which something is submerged

sub·mer·gent \-nt\ *adj* **:** partly submerged **:** incompletely submerged

sub·mer·gible \-jəbəl\ *adj* **1 :** capable of being submerged ⟨a ~ body⟩ **2 :** capable of functioning under water ⟨a ~ pump⟩

sub·mer·sal \-səl\ *adj* [*1submerse* + *-al*] **:** marked by or occurring during submersion ⟨a ~ period⟩ ⟨~ activities of amphibians⟩

1sub·merse \səbˈmərs, -məs, -məis\ *vt* -ED/-ING/-S [L *submersus*, past part. of *submergere* to plunge under, submerge] **:** SUBMERGE

2submerse \"\ *adj* [L *submersus*, past part.] *of a plant* **:** SUBMERSED

sub·mersed \-st\ *adj* [L *submersus* (past part. of *submergere*) + E *-ed*] **:** SUBMERGED: as **a :** covered with water **b :** growing or adapted to grow under water

1sub·mers·ible \-səbəl\ *adj* [ISV *1submerse* + *-ible*] **:** SUBMERGIBLE

2submersible \"\ *n* -s **:** a boat capable of submerging **:** SUBMARINE

sub·mer·sion \səbˈmərzhən, -məʃ, -məiʃ, ǀsh-\ *n* -s [LL *submersion-, submersio*, fr. L *submersus* (past part. of *submergere* to plunge under, submerge) + *-ion-, -io* -ion] **1 :** the act or process of submerging **2 :** the quality or state of being submerged

sub·metallic \ˈsəb+\ *adj* [*sub-* + *metallic*] **1 :** somewhat or imperfectly metallic ⟨a ~ luster⟩ **2 :** METALLOID ⟨such ~ elements as bismuth⟩

sub·meter \"+\ *n* [*sub-* + *meter*] **:** one of two or more meters for measuring different sections of a supply

sub·metering \"+\ *n* -s [*submeter* + *-ing*] **:** the retail sale through individual meters to tenants in large office or apartment buildings of electric current or gas purchased for the entire building by the owners at wholesale rates

sub·microgram \"+\ *adj* [*sub-* + *microgram*] **:** having a mass less than one microgram

sub·micron \"+\ *n* [NL, fr. *sub-* + *micron*] **:** a very small particle that can be seen only with the ultramicroscope; *specif* **:** one less than 1 × 10^{-4} centimeters in diameter

sub·microscopic \"+\ *adj* [ISV *sub-* + *microscopic*] **1 :** too small to be resolved and made visible by the ordinary light microscope — compare ULTRAMICROSCOPIC **2 :** of, relating to, or dealing with the very minute ⟨the ~ world⟩

sub·miliary \"+\ *adj* [ISV *sub-* + *miliary*] **:** less than miliary **:** smaller than a millet seed ⟨~ lesions⟩

sub·miniature \"+\ *adj* [ISV *sub-* + *miniature*] **:** smaller than miniature **:** very small — used esp. of a very compact assembly of electronic equipment

subminiature camera *n* **:** a miniature camera using film 16 millimeters wide for still photography

sub·miniaturization \ˈsəb+\ *n* -s [*subminiature* + *-ization*] **:** the action or process of making something subminiature ⟨the ~ of electronic components⟩

sub·minimal \"+\ *adj* [*sub-* + *minimal*] **:** smaller than the minimum that is required for a particular result ⟨a ~ stimulus⟩

sub·min·is·ter \səbˈminəstə(r)\ *vt* [L *subministrare*, fr. *sub-* + *ministrare* to serve — more at MINISTER] *archaic* **:** SUPPLY, FURNISH

sub·miss \səbˈmis\ *adj* [L *submissus*, past part. of *submittere* to let down, lower — more at SUBMIT] **1** *archaic* **:** SUBMISSIVE, HUMBLE **2** *archaic* **:** low in tone **:** SUBDUED

sub·mis·si·ble \-səbəl\ *adj* [L *submissus* + *-ible*] **:** capable of being submitted **:** SUBMITTABLE

sub·mis·sion \səbˈmishən\ *n* -s [ME, fr. MF, fr. L, act of letting down, lowering, fr. *submissus* (past part. of *submittere* to let down) + *-ion-, -io* -ion] **1 a :** a legal agreement by which parties engage usu. under the penalties of a bond to submit matters of controversy between them to the decision of arbitrators named or unnamed **b :** an act of submitting something (as for consideration, inspection, or comment) ⟨the ~ of his sketch for the mural⟩ **c** (1) **:** something that is submitted ⟨received more ~s than we could possibly publish⟩ (2) **:** a point of view, theory of a case, or proposal advocated ⟨included the ~ that 300,000 people should move out to new industrial towns —Eric Keown⟩ **2 a :** the condition of being submissive **:** humble or compliant behavior **:** humble or submissive deference in conduct or bearing **b submissions** *pl, archaic* **:** behavior expressive of submission **:** humbly deferent conduct **3 :** an act of submitting; *usu* **:** a yielding of power or authority or a surrendering of person and power to the control of another **4** *obs* **:** CONFESSION

sub·mis·sion·ist \-shənəst\ *n* -s **:** one who advocates submission

sub·mis·sive \səbˈmisiv, -sēv *also* -səv\ *adj* [L *submissus* (past part.) + E *-ive*] **:** inclined or ready to submit **:** expressing submission **:** YIELDING, OBEDIENT, HUMBLE ⟨~ demeanor⟩ ⟨a ~ race⟩ **syn** see TAME

sub·mis·sive·ly \-səvlē, -li\ *adv* **:** in a submissive manner **:** so as to be or appear submissive

sub·mis·sive·ness \-sivnəs, -sēv- *also* -səv-\ *n* -ES **:** the quality or state of being submissive

sub·miss·ly \səbˈmislē\ *adv* [*submiss* + *-ly*] *archaic* **:** HUMBLY, SUBMISSIVELY

sub·mit \səbˈmit, *usu* -id.+V\ *vb* **submitted; submitted; submitting; submits** [ME *submitten*, fr. L *submittere* to let down, lower, set under, fr. *sub-* + *mittere* to send, throw — more at SMITE] *vt* **1 a :** to yield to the will or authority of **:** SURRENDER ⟨~s his will to divine authority⟩ ⟨~ an undertaking . . . to the Senate —Vera M. Dean⟩ **b :** to cause to be subjected ⟨*submitting* himself to a series of literary influences —F.B.Millett⟩ ⟨~ metal to high heat and pressure⟩ **2 a** *obs* **:** to expose to peril or danger ⟨*submitting* me unto the perilous night —Shak.⟩ **b** *archaic* **:** LOWER, BEND ⟨will ye ~ your necks —John Milton⟩ **3 a :** to send or commit for consideration, study, or decision **:** REFER ⟨~ a question to the court⟩ ⟨texts of revised and new conventions, to be *submitted* to the International Red Cross Conference —J.S.Pictet⟩ **b :** to present or make available for use or study **:** OFFER, SUPPLY ⟨~ a report⟩ ⟨~ a manuscript to a publisher⟩ ⟨always ~ your judgment to others with modesty —George Washington⟩ **c :** AFFIRM, SUGGEST ⟨I ~ that it was the wrong decision —E. M.Zacharias⟩ ~ *vi* **1 a :** to bow to the will or authority of another **:** YIELD ⟨~ to an alien law —Frank Altschul⟩ **b :** to allow oneself to become subjected ⟨~ to an interview⟩ ⟨~ to an operation⟩ **2 a :** to grant precedence **:** DEFER ⟨~ to . . . superior intelligence, political wisdom and tough leadership —M.S.Handler⟩ **b :** to become resigned **:** acquiesce uncritically ⟨was obliged to give up the point and ~ —Jane Austen⟩ ⟨the inhabitants . . . will no longer ~ to the evils of the trade —E.V.Buckholder⟩ **syn** see YIELD

sub·mit·tal \-mid·ᵊl, -itᵊl\ *n* -s **:** an act of submitting

sub·mit·tance \-itᵊn(t)s\ *n* -s **:** SUBMISSION

sub·mit·ter \-id·ə(r), -itə-\ *n* -s **:** one that submits

sub·mit·ting·ly *adv* **:** in a submitting or submissive manner

sub mo·do \ˌsəbˈmō(ˌ)dō\ *adv* [LL] **:** under a qualification, condition, or restriction

sub·molecule \ˈsəb+\ *n* [ISV *sub-* + *molecule*] **:** a particle of less than molecular dimensions or state of organization

sub·montane \ˈsəb+\ *adj* [LL *submontanus*, fr. L *sub-* + *montanus* of a mountain — more at MOUNTAIN] **1 :** lying or passing under a mountain or range of mountains ⟨a ~ stream⟩ **2 :** situated at the foot or near the base of a mountain or range of mountains — **sub·mon·tane·ly** *adv*

sub·motive \"+\ *n* [*sub-* + *motive*] **:** a subordinate, secondary, or hidden motive

sub·mountain \"+\ *adj* [*sub-* + *mountain*] **:** lying under a mountain

sub·mucosa \"+\ *n* [NL, fr. *sub-* + *mucosa*] **:** the layer of areolar connective tissue directly under a mucous membrane — **sub·mucosal** \"+\ *adj*

sub·mucous \"+\ *adj* [ISV *sub-* + *mucous*] **:** lying under or involving the tissues under a mucous membrane

submucous coat *n* **:** SUBMUCOSA

sub·multiple \ˈsəb+\ *n* [*sub-* + *multiple*] **:** a number or quantity that divides another exactly ⟨8 is a ~ of 72⟩

sub·mundane \"+\ *adj* [*sub-* + LL *mundanus* of the earth, of the world — more at MUNDANE] **:** UNDERGROUND, SUBTERRANEAN

sub·muscular \"+\ *adj* [*sub-* + *muscular*] **:** situated beneath a muscle or muscular layer

sub–mycenaean \"+\ *adj, usu cap M* **:** belonging to a date and style later than the Mycenaean but before the distinctly Greek

sub·mytilacea \"+\ *n pl, cap* [NL, fr. *sub-* + *Mytilacea*] **:** a suborder of Eulamellibranchia comprising bivalve mollusks with an equivalve shell, an external ligament, a mantle that is only slightly closed, and siphons that if present are short

sub·narcotic \"+\ *adj* [*sub-* + *narcotic*] **:** somewhat narcotic; *esp* **:** insufficient to produce deep sleep ⟨barbiturates in ~ amounts⟩

sub·na·sale \ˌsəbˌnāˈzā(ˌ)lē -ˈs\, ǀāl-, ǀäl-\ *n* -s [NL, fr. *sub-* + *nasale*, neut. sing. of *nasalis* nasal, fr. L *nasus* nose + *-alis* -al — more at NOSE] **:** SUBNASAL POINT 2

subnasal point \ˈsəb+-\ *n* [*sub-* + *nasal*] **1 :** ACANTHION **2 :** a point on the living where the nasal septum and the upper lip meet in the midsagittal plane — called also *subnasale*

sub·nascent \"+\ *adj* [L *subnascent-, subnascens*, pres. part. of *subnasci* to grow beneath, fr. *sub-* + *nasci* to be born — more at NATION] **1** *obs* **:** growing beneath **2 :** growing up or arising from beneath something

sub·nation \"+\ *n* [*sub-* + *nation*] **:** a subdivision of a nation often distinguished by community of culture and interests rather than by administrative dependency ⟨the South is . . . a ~ with its own history, its own patterns of behavior and its own national consciousness —Malcolm Cowley⟩ — **sub·national** \"+\ *adj*

sub·neural \ˈsəb+\ *adj* [*sub-* + *neural*] **:** situated under the central nervous system

sub·nitrate \"+\ *n* [ISV *sub-* + *nitrate*] **:** a basic nitrate (as bismuth subnitrate) — compare OXYNITRATE

sub·niv·e·an \ˌsəbˈnivēən\ *adj* [fr. *sub-* + L *niveus* of snow + E *-an* — more at NIVEOUS] **:** situated or occurring under the snow ⟨~ burrows and runways —W.A.Fuller⟩

sub nom·i·ne \ˌsəbˈnämə,nā, -ˌnē, -ˈnōmə,nā\ *adv* [L] **:** under the name **:** under the caption or title

1sub·normal \ˈsəb+\ *n* [in sense 1, fr. NL *subnormalis*, fr. L *sub-* + *normalis* normal; in sense 2, fr. *2subnormal* — more at NORMAL] **1 :** the projection of the normal of a curve on the x-axis **2 :** one who is below the range of normality; *esp* **:** a person of subnormal intelligence

2subnormal \"\ *adj* [ISV *sub-* + *normal*] **1 :** lower or smaller than normal ⟨a ~ temperature⟩ ⟨repeated ~ harvests⟩ **2 :** having less of something and esp. of intelligence than is normal ⟨~ children⟩ — **sub·normality** \"+\ *n* — **sub·normally** \"+\ *adv*

sub·no·ta·tion \ˌsəbˌnōˈtāshən\ *n* [LL *subnotation-, subnotatio* act of signing underneath, fr. L *subnotatus* (past part. of *subnotare* to mark underneath, fr. *sub-* + *notare* to mark, sign, note) + *-ion-, -io* -ion — more at NOTE] **:** a written answer to an inquiry addressed by a private citizen upon some matter of law or policy to an emperor, sovereign, or pope

sub·nucleus \ˈsəb+\ *n* [NL, fr. *sub-* + *nucleus*] **:** a subdivision of a nucleus esp. of nervous tissue

sub·nutrition \"+\ *n* [*sub-* + *nutrition*] **:** inadequate feeding (as of livestock) whether quantitative or qualitative

sub·oblique \ˈsəb+\ *adj* [*sub-* + *oblique*] **:** not quite oblique

sub·obsolete \"+\ *adj* [*sub-* + *obsolete*] **:** not clearly defined **:** OBSCURE ⟨a ~ marking on an insect wing⟩

sub·occipital \"+\ *adj* [NL *suboccipitalis*, fr. L *sub-* + ML *occipitalis* occipital — more at OCCIPITAL] **1 :** situated below the occipital bone **2 :** situated below the occipital lobe of the brain

suboccipital nerve *n* **:** the first cervical nerve

sub·oceanic \"+\ *also* **sub·ocean** \"+\ *adj* [*sub-* + *oceanic* or *ocean*] **1 :** situated, taking place, or formed beneath the ocean or the bottom of the ocean ⟨~ light⟩ ⟨~ oil resources⟩ **2 :** concerned with the sea bottom ⟨~ physiography⟩

sub·octave \"+\ *n* [*sub-* + *octave*] **1 a :** a range of tones lower than two octaves below middle C **b :** SUBCONTRAOCTAVE **2 :** SUBOCTAVE COUPLER

suboctave coupler *n* **:** an organ coupler for making the tone an octave below sound together with the tone struck

1sub·ocular \"+\ *adj* [LL *subocularis*, fr. L *sub-* + LL *ocularis* of the eyes — more at OCULAR] **:** situated below the eye

2subocular \"\ *n* **:** a subocular part; *esp* **:** one of the small scales between the eye and the upper labials of some reptiles

sub·oesophageal ganglion \ˈsəb+ . . . -\ *n* [*suboesophageal* fr. *sub-* + *oesophageal*] **:** a ganglionic mass formed in an insect by the fusion of the nerve ganglia of the 4th, 5th and 6th body segments

sub·office \"+\ *n* [*sub-* + *office*] **:** a secondary office (as of a post office or bank) that often provides only some of the services of the corresponding main office

sub·officer \"+\ *n* [*sub-* + *officer*] **:** a subordinate officer

sub·opaque \"+\ *adj* [ISV *sub-* + *opaque;* prob. orig. formed in F] **:** partially or imperfectly opaque **:** nearly opaque

sub·operation \"+\ *n* [*sub-* + *operation*] **:** a subordinate operation; *usu* **:** an operation that forms a specific phase of a larger operation or process ⟨dividing the process into ~s⟩

sub·opercle \"+\ *n* [NL *suboperculum*, fr. *sub-* + *operculum*] **:** a bony plate immediately below the opercle in a gill cover of a fish

1sub·opercular \"+\ *adj* [in sense 1, fr. *sub-* + *opercular;* in sense 2, fr. NL *suboperculum* + E *-ar*] **1 :** situated below an opercle **2 :** of, relating to, or being the subopercle

2subopercular \"\ *n* **:** a subopercular part; *esp* **:** SUBOPERCLE

sub·operculum \ˈsəb+\ *n* [NL] **:** SUBOPERCLE

sub·opposite \"+\ *adj* [*sub-* + *opposite*] **:** nearly opposite ⟨leaves ~⟩

sub·optimal \"+\ *adj* [ISV *sub-* + *optimal*] **:** less than optimal ⟨a ~ diet⟩

sub·optimum \"+\ *adj* [NL, fr. *sub-* + *optimum*] **:** SUBOPTIMAL

sub·oral \"+\ *adj* [*sub-* + *oral*] **:** situated or occurring beneath the mouth

sub·orbicular *also* **sub·orbiculate** *or* **sub·orbiculated** \"+\ *adj* [*suborbicular, suborbiculate* ISV *sub-* + *orbicular* or *orbiculate; suborbiculated* fr. *sub-* + obs. E *orbiculated*, fr. L *orbiculatus* orbiculate + E *-ed*] **:** nearly orbicular **:** approximately circular

1sub·orbital \"+\ *adj* [*sub-* + *orbital*] **1 :** situated beneath the orbit of the eye; *also* **:** SUBOCULAR **2 :** being or involving less than one orbit ⟨the first manned ~ flight —Courtney Sheldon⟩

2suborbital \"\ *n* **:** a suborbital part (as a bone)

sub·order \ˈsəb+\ *n* [*sub-* + *order*] **1 :** a subdivision of an order ⟨a soil ~⟩; *esp* **:** a taxonomic category below an order and above a family **2 :** a smaller or subordinate architectural order as distinguished from the principal or main supporting order

sub·or·di·na·cy \səˈbȯ(r)dᵊnəsē, -ᵊnəsi *sometimes* -dən-\ *n* -ES **:** the quality or state of being subordinate **:** SUBORDINATION

sub·ordinal \ˈsəb+\ *adj* [NL *subordin-, subordo* suborder, fr. L *sub-* + *ordo* order] **:** of, relating to, or constituting a suborder

sub·ordinary \"+\ *n* [*sub-* + *ordinary*] **:** any of several common heraldic bearings less important than an ordinary

1sub·or·di·nate \səˈbȯrd(ᵊ)nət -ȯ(ə)d- *sometimes* -dənə̇t *or* -dᵊn,āt *or* -də,nāt; *usu* ǀd.+V\ *adj* [ME *subordinat*, fr. ML *subordinatus*, past part. of *subordinare* to place in a lower order, fr. L *sub-* + *ordinare* to put in order — more at ORDAIN] **1 :** placed in a lower order, class, or rank **:** holding a lower or inferior position ⟨making the executive ~ to the legislative branch of government⟩ ⟨a ~ branch of study⟩ ⟨~ peoples⟩ **2 :** of, relating to, or involving subordination or subordinates: as **a :** submissive to or falling under the control of a higher authority ⟨a ~ kingdom⟩ **b :** of, belonging to, or constituting a clause that functions as a noun, adjective, or adverb in a larger sentence ⟨~ construction⟩ ⟨~ clause⟩ **c :** grammatically subordinating ⟨~ conjunction⟩ — **sub·or·di·nate·ly** *adv* — **sub·or·di·nate·ness** *n* -ES

2subordinate \"\ *n* **:** one that is subordinate: as **a :** one who stands in order or rank below another — distinguished from *principal* **b :** a member of an ecological community other than a dominant

3sub·or·di·nate \-dᵊn,āt *sometimes* -də,nāt, *usu* -ād.+V\ *vt* [ML *subordinatus*, past part. of *subordinare* to subordinate] **1 :** to place in a lower order or class **:** make or consider as of less value or importance ⟨~ one creature to another⟩ **2 :** to make subject or subservient ⟨~ the passions to reason⟩

subordinating *adj* **:** having the capacity to subordinate or the function of subordinating; *usu* **:** introducing a subordinate clause **:** joining a subordinate to a main clause ⟨*if* in "I will come if I can" and *until* in "they fished until it was dark" are ~ conjunctions⟩ — **sub·or·di·nat·ing·ly** \ˈ=ˈ==ˌ==,\ =,==ˈ===\ *adv*

sub·or·di·na·tion \sə,bȯ(r)dᵊnˈāshən *sometimes* -dəˈnā-\ *n* [ML *subordination-, subordinatio*, fr. *subordinatus* (past part. of *subordinare*) + *-ion-, -io* -ion] **1 :** the act of subordinating (as by making secondary or subject): as **a :** arrangement or classification into grades or ranks from highest to lowest **b :** the doctrine or practice under the law of bankruptcy and equity by which particular claims under the equities may not be paid before others or before sufficient assets are available to first meet such others or by which particular claims are allowed conditionally rather than wholly disallowed **c :** expression in the form of a subordinate clause **d :** arrangement of arches in architectural orders **2 a :** the quality or state of being subordinate to another **:** inferiority of rank or dignity **b :** the quality or state of being subordinate to authority **:** obedient submission — opposed to *insubordination* **3 a :** an arrangement produced by an act of subordination **b** *obs* **:** GRADE, RANK; *also* **:** a position of inferior status

sub·or·di·na·tion·ism \-shə,nizəm\ *n* -s **:** a doctrine in theology: the second and third persons of the Trinity are subordinate (as in order or essence) to the first person and the Holy Spirit is subordinate to the Son

sub·or·di·na·tion·ist \-sh(ə)nəst\ *n* -s **:** a person adhering to the doctrine of subordinationism

sub·or·di·na·tive \səˈbȯ(r)dᵊn,ād·iv, -d(ᵊ)nəd-\ *adj* **:** tending to or expressing subordination: as **a :** grammatically subordinating **b** *linguistics* **:** having only one head — used of an endocentric construction (as *my books*); opposed to *coordinative*

sub·orn \səˈbȯ(ə)rn, -ȯ(ə)n\ *vt* -ED/-ING/-S [MF *suborner*, fr. L *subornare*, fr. *sub-* secretly, under + *ornare* to furnish, prepare, embellish — more at ORNATE] **1 a :** to induce (as a person) by secret or underhanded means to do some improper or unlawful thing : incite secretly : INSTIGATE ⟨~*ed* government to the unlawful purposes of business —H.M. Kallen⟩ **b** : to induce or persuade (a person) to commit perjury; *also* : to obtain (testimony) by such action **2** *obs* **a** : to make secret or stealthy provision of **b** : EQUIP, ADORN **3** *obs* : to bring forward in support of an unworthy object

sub·or·na·tion \(,)sə,bȯ(r)'nāshən, ,səbə(r)'n-\ *n* -s [MF, fr. ML *subornation-, subornatio,* fr. L *subornatus* (past part. of *subornare* to suborn) + *-ion-, -io* -ion] : an act or instance of suborning: as **a** : the procuring of some end by secret, underhanded, or improper methods : the inducing (as by bribes or persuasion) of someone to do something improper or unlawful **b** (1) : the crime of procuring a person to commit perjury (2) : testimony procured by subornation : perjured testimony

sub·orn·er \sə'bȯrnər, -ō(ə)nə(r\ *n* -s : one that suborns

sub·oscines \¦səb+\ *n pl, cap* [NL, fr. *sub-* + *Oscines*] *in former classifications* : a superfamily of birds equivalent to the suborder Menurae

su·bo·ti·ca \'sübə,tētsə, ,==ˈ==\ *adj, usu cap* [fr. *Subotica,* Yugoslavia] : of or from the city of Subotica, Yugoslavia : of the kind or style prevalent in Subotica

sub·ovate *or* **sub·ovated** \¦səb+\ *adj* [*sub-* + *ovate* or obs. E *ovated,* fr. L *ovatus* ovate + E *-ed* — more at OVATE] : not quite ovate : approximately ovate

sub·ovoid \"+\ *adj* [ISV *sub-* + *ovoid*] : not quite ovoid : approximately ovoid

sub·oxide \"+\ *n* [ISV *sub-* + *oxide*] : an oxide (as carbon suboxide) containing a relatively small proportion of oxygen — compare PROTOXIDE

sub·pallial \"+\ *adj* [*sub-* + *pallial*] : occurring under a pallium; *usu* : situated beneath or derived from structures beneath the pallium of the brain

subpar \'səb+¦-\ *adv (or adj)* [*sub-* + *par*] : below a standard or normal level : less than par ⟨a reluctance by departments to push out ~ people, for fear of not being allowed to replace them —R.M.Williams⟩

subpar *abbr* subparagraph

sub·paragraph \¦səb+\ *n* [*sub-* + *paragraph*] : a subordinate paragraph esp. of a formally drafted document (as a contract or law)

sub·parallel \"+\ *adj* [*sub-* + *parallel*] : nearly parallel : not quite parallel

sub·passage \"+\ *n* [*sub-* + *passage*] : the passage of a strain of microorganisms obtained from one kind of animal through another (as for increasing its virulence)

sub·pectinate \"+\ *adj* [ISV *sub-* + *pectinate*] : somewhat pectinate : imperfectly pectinate

sub·pectoral \"+\ *adj* [ISV *sub-* + *pectoral*] **1** : situated under the pectoralis muscles **2** : situated or seeming to arise beneath the chest

sub pe·de si·gil·li \,səb'pe,dāsə'gi(,)lē\ *adv* [L, lit., under the foot of the seal] : under seal

sub·peduncular \¦səb+\ *adj* [*sub-* + *peduncular*] : situated beneath a peduncle and esp. beneath one of the peduncles of the brain

sub·periosteal \"+\ *adj* [*sub-* + *periosteal*] : situated or occurring beneath the periosteum ⟨~ bone deposition⟩ — **sub·periosteally** \"+\ *adv*

sub·permanent \"+\ *adj* [*sub-* + *permanent*] : moderately permanent : PERSISTENT — **sub·permanently** \"+\ *adv*

subpermanent magnetism *n* : a metastable state of magnetization that is liable to loss through vibration or mechanical shock

sub·petiolar \¦səb+\ *adj* [*sub-* + *petiolar*] : concealed within the base of the petiole ⟨the leaf buds of the plane tree are ~⟩

sub·phonemic \"+\ *adj* [*sub-* + *phonemic*] : ALLOPHONIC, PHONETIC ⟨in Italian, \ŋ\ is merely a ~ variant of \n\⟩

sub·phrenic \"+\ *adj* [ISV *sub-* + *phrenic*] : situated or occurring below the diaphragm

sub·phylar \"+\ *adj* [NL *subphylum* + E *-ar*] : of, relating to, or constituting a subphylum

sub·phylum \"+\ *n* [NL, fr. *sub-* + *phylum*] : a primary division of a phylum

sub·pial \"+\ *adj* [*sub-* + *pial*] : situated or occurring beneath the pia mater

sub·placenta \"+\ *n* [NL, fr. *sub-* + *placenta*] : DECIDUA

sub·plantigrade \"+\ *adj* [*sub-* + *plantigrade*] : having the heel raised when walking but standing flat-footed ⟨many carnivores are ~⟩

sub·plate \'səb+,-\ *n* [*sub-* + *plate*] : a plate (as of metal) placed beneath something usu. for protection or support

sub·platyhieric \¦səb+\ *adj* [*sub-* + *platyhieric*] : having a sacrum of moderate length and breadth with a length-breadth index of 100 to 106 — compare DOLICHOHIERIC, PLATYHIERIC

sub·pleural \"+\ *adj* [ISV *sub-* + *pleural*] : situated between the pleura and the body wall — **sub·pleurally** \"+\ *adv*

sub·plinth \'səb+,-\ *n* [*sub-* + *plinth*] : a plinth under and projecting slightly beyond a principal plinth

sub·plot \"+,-\ *n* [*sub-* + *plot*] **1** : a subordinate plot in fiction or drama **2** : a subdivision of a plot (as of land)

subplow \"+¦-\ *vb* [*sub-* + *plow*] : SUBTILL

¹sub·poe·na *also* **sub·pe·na** \sə'pēnə, ÷ -ēnē, -ēni *sometimes* (,)səb'p- *or* ÷ -pēnyə\ *n* -s [ME *suppena, sub pena,* fr. L *sub poena* under penalty; fr. the opening words of the writ] **1** : a writ commanding a person designated in it to attend court under a penalty for failure — see SUBPOENA AD TESTIFICANDUM, SUBPOENA DUCES TECUM **2** : the process by which a defendant in an equity action is commanded to appear and answer the plaintiff's bill

²subpoena *also* **subpena** \"\ *vt* -ED/-ING/-S : to serve or summon with a writ of subpoena ⟨had been ~*ed* to appear at the inquest —Kamala Markandaya⟩

sub poe·na \,səb'pēnə\ *adv* [L] : under penalty

subpoena ad tes·ti·fi·can·dum \-,ad,testəfə'kandəm\ *n, pl* **subpoenas ad testificandum** [NL, under penalty to give testimony] : a writ commanding a person to appear in court for testifying as a witness

subpoena du·ces te·cum \-'dü,kās'tākəm, -tā,küm\ *n, pl* **subpoenas duces tecum** [NL, under penalty you shall bring with you] : a writ commanding a person to produce in court certain designated documents or other evidence ⟨the district attorney started serving *subpoenas duces tecum* on witnesses —Erle Stanley Gardner⟩

sub·polar \¦səb+\ *adj* [ISV *sub-* + *polar*] : not quite polar : SUBARCTIC, SUBANTARCTIC

sub·population \"+\ *n* [*sub-* + *population*] **1** : an identifiable fraction or subdivision of a population **2** : a specific biotype within a natural population

sub·port \'səb+¦-\ *n* [*sub-* + *port*] : a subordinate or secondary port (as of entry)

sub·post office \¦səb+\ *n, Brit* : a branch post office : a postal station

sub·potency \"+\ *n* [*sub-* + *potency*] : reduced capacity to transmit hereditary characters

sub·potent \"+\ *adj* [*sub-* + *potent*] : less than usu. or normally potent; *esp* : exhibiting genetic subpotency

sub·prefect \"+\ *n* [*sub-* + *prefect*] : an official subordinate to a prefect; *esp* : a French administrative official in immediate charge of an arrondissement — **sub·prefectorial** \"+\ *adj* — **sub·prefecture** \"+\ *n*

sub·press \'səb+,-\ *n* [*sub-* + *press*] : a small press mounted usu. between the bed and ram of a larger main punch press, used for small and delicate work (as on jewelry), and having its plunger actuated by the slide of the main press

sub·principal \¦səb+\ *n* [*sub-* + *principal*] **1** : an assistant or subordinate principal (as of a school) **2** : a secondary or bracing rafter **3** : an open diapason subbass in a pipe organ

sub·prior \"+\ *n* [ME, fr. ML, fr. *sub-* + *prior* — more at PRIOR] : the vicegerent or assistant of a prior

sub·problem \"+\ *n* [*sub-* + *problem*] : a problem that is contingent on or forms a part of another more inclusive problem

sub·professional \"+\ *adj* [*sub-* + *professional*] **1** : functioning or qualified to function at a level below the professional but distinctly above the clerical or labor level and usu. under the direct supervision of a professionally trained person ⟨~ and clerical assistants⟩ **2** : designed to provide a foundation and background for professional training ⟨the premedical course is basically ~ education⟩

sub·pubescent \"+\ *adj* [*sub-* + *pubescent*] : somewhat hairy

sub·punch \'səb+¦-\ *vt* [*sub-* + *punch*] : to punch to a size smaller than the finished dimension so that sufficient material is left for finishing (as by drilling or reaming)

sub·purlin \¦səb+\ *n* [*sub-* + *purlin*] : a light architectural member resting on purlins and usu. running at right angles to them

sub–pyrenean \"+\ *adj, usu cap P* : situated at the foot of or to the south of the Pyrenees mountains

sub·quadrangular \"+\ *adj* [*sub-* + *quadrangular*] : nearly quadrangular : quadrangular but with the corners rounded

sub·quadrate \"+\ *adj* [*sub-* + *quadrate*] : nearly square : square but with the corners rounded

¹sub·quality \"+\ *n* [*sub-* + *quality*] : an underlying quality ⟨a ~ of beauty running through his serious writing⟩

²subquality \"\ *adj* [*sub-* + *quality* (adj.)] : of an inferior quality ⟨~ products⟩

sub·race \'səb+,-\ *n* [*sub-* + *race*] : a subdivision of a race; *esp* : a division of a primary human race that is developed in a limited area by inbreeding, social selection, and environmental influences — **sub·racial** \¦səb+\ *adj*

sub·radius \¦səb+\ *n* [NL, fr. *sub-* + *radius*] : a radius of the fourth order in some coelenterates that intervenes halfway between an adradius and the adjacent perradius or interradius

sub·ramose *also* **sub·ramous** \"+\ *adj* [NL *subramosus,* fr. L *sub-* + *ramosus* branched — more at RAMOSE] : somewhat branched: as **a** : having blunt short processes or projections that are arranged like branches **b** : having few or sparse branches

sub·range \'səb+,-\ *n* [*sub-* + *range*] : a subordinate range (as of hills)

sub·rational \¦səb+\ *adj* [*sub-* + *rational*] : almost or nearly rational

sub·reader \"+\ *n* [*sub-* + *reader*] : an underreader in the Inns of Court formerly reading the texts discoursed on by the reader

sub·recent \"+\ *adj* [*sub-* + *recent*] : of, relating to, or being a period of indefinite and variable duration extending from the final part of the Pleistocene to the full establishment of the geologically Recent

sub·rectangular \"+\ *adj* [*sub-* + *rectangular*] : approximately rectangular

sub·refraction \"+\ *n* [*sub-* + *refraction*] : a state of refraction (as of the atmosphere) that is less than normal and is usu. associated with a sharp vertical gradient of some physical factor (as temperature)

sub·region \"+\ *n* [ISV *sub-* + *region*] **1** : a subdivision of a region ⟨economic ~*s* of the U. S.⟩ **2** : one of the primary divisions of a biogeographic region — **sub·regional** \"+\ *adj*

sub·regulus \"+\ *n* [LL, fr. L *sub-* + *regulus* prince, petty king, fr. *reg-, rex* king + *-ulus* -ule — more at ROYAL] : a petty prince : a vassal ruler

sub·rep·ta·ry \¦sə'breptərē\ *adj* [L *subreptus* (past part. of *subrepere* to creep under, crawl, fr. *sub-* + *repere* to creep) + E *-ary* — more at REPTILE] : adapted primarily to crawling ⟨a mollusk with a broad ~ foot⟩

sub·rep·tion \(,)sə'brepshən\ *n* -s [LL *subreption-, subreptio,* fr. L, act of stealing, fr. *subreptus* (past part. of *subripere* to snatch away, take away secretly) + *-ion-, -io* -ion — more at SURREPTITIOUS] **1 a** : secret, underhanded, unlawful, or unfair representation through suppression or fraudulent concealment of facts **b** : a deduction drawn from such representation **2** *canon & Scots law* : the obtaining of or attempting to obtain a dispensation from ecclesiastical authority or a gift from the sovereign by concealing the truth — distinguished from *obreption*

sub·rep·ti·tious \,sə,brep¦tishəs\ *adj* [L *subreptitius, subrepticius* secret, clandestine, surreptitious, fr. *subreptus* (past part. of *subripere*) + *-itius, -icius* -itious] **1** : of, relating to, or involving subreption **2** *obs* : SURREPTITIOUS — **subreptitiously** *adv*

sub·reputable \¦səb+\ *adj* [*sub-* + *reputable*] : of slightly questionable reputation

sub·resin \"+\ *n* [ISV *sub-* + *resin*] : the part of a natural resin that dissolves in hot alcohol and is deposited on cooling — **sub·resinous** \"+\ *adj*

sub·ri·dent \¦sə¦brīdᵊnt\ *adj* [L *subrident-, subridens,* pres. part. of *subridēre* to smile, fr. *sub-* + *ridēre* to laugh — more at RIDICULOUS] : wearing or offered with a smile ⟨a ~ answer⟩ — **sub·ri·dent·ly** *adv*

sub·rigid \¦səb+\ *adj* [*sub-* + *rigid*] : not perfectly rigid; *usu* : designed to resist shock by reason of inherent flexibility ⟨a ~ framework⟩

sub·risive \-rīs¦iv, -riz¦, -rīz¦\ *adj* [L *subrisus* (past part. of *subridēre* to smile) + E *-ive*] : SMILING ⟨the sudden ~ humor that lighted his gray eyes —Leslie Ford⟩

sub·ro·gate \'səbrō,gāt\ *vt* -ED/-ING/-S [L *subrogatus,* past part. of *subrogare* to substitute — more at SURROGATE] : to put in the place of another : SUBSTITUTE; *esp* : to apply the legal doctrine of subrogation to

sub·ro·ga·tion \,==ˈgāshən\ *n* [ME *subrogacioun* substitution, fr. MF *subrogation,* fr. ML *subrogation-, subrogatio,* fr. L *subrogatus* (past part.) + *-ion-, -io* -ion] **1** : an act of subrogating: as **a** : the substitution of one for another as a creditor so that the new creditor succeeds to the former's rights in law and equity : a legal operation by which a third person who pays a creditor succeeds to his rights against the debtor as if he were his assignee — compare SUBSTITUTION 1a **b** : succession by an insurance company after payment of a loss to the insured's rights against the party responsible for the loss (as against a person negligently or willfully causing fire damage to insured property) **2** : the legal relation created by an act of subrogation

sub·ro·gee \¦==¦gē, -¦jē\ *n* -s [*subrogate* + *-ee*] : one who acquires by subrogation rights belonging to another

sub·ro·gor \-¦gō(ə)r\ *n* -s [*subrogate* + *-or*] : one who yields rights to another in subrogation

sub ro·sa \,sə¦brōzə\ *adv* [NL, lit., under the rose; fr. the ancient custom of hanging a rose over the council table to indicate that all present were sworn to secrecy and prob. connected with the legend that Cupid gave a rose to the god of silence Harpocrates to keep him from revealing the indiscretions of Venus] : without publicity or notice : COVERTLY, PRIVATELY, CONFIDENTIALLY

sub–rosa \"\ *adj* [*sub rosa*] : designed to be secret or confidential : shunning publicity : SECRETIVE ⟨a *sub-rosa* report⟩ ⟨a *sub-rosa* group⟩ ⟨two very distinct patterns to the summer bachelor scene, *sub-rosa* and glaringly public —Linda Francke⟩

sub·rostral \¦səb+\ *adj* [*sub-* + *rostral*] : situated beneath or below a rostrum

sub·rotund \"+\ *adj* [L *subrotundus,* fr. *sub-* + *rotundus* round — more at ROUND] : nearly but not quite round : ROUNDISH

sub·rounded \"+\ *adj* [*sub-* + *rounded*] : partially rounded; *esp* : exhibiting such wear that some but not all edges are rounded ⟨~ sand⟩

sub·routine \"+\ *n* [ISV *sub-* + *routine*] : a subordinate routine; *esp* : a sequence of computer instructions for performing a specified task that can be used repeatedly in a program or in different programs

subs *pl of* SUB, *pres 3d sing of* SUB

subs *abbr* **1** subscription **2** subsidiary **3** subsistence **4** substantive **5** substitute

sub·salicylate \¦səb+\ *n* [*sub-* + *salicylate*] : a basic salicylate (as bismuth salicylate)

sub·saline \"+\ *adj* [*sub-* + *saline*] : somewhat salty : salty but not excessively so

¹sub·sample \"+\ *vt* [*sub-* + *sample* (v.)] : to draw samples from (a previously screened or selected group or population) : sample a sample of

²subsample \"\ *n* : a sample or specimen obtained by subsampling : a subordinate sample ⟨~*s* are . . . representative to a lesser degree than the total samples —J.C.Davies⟩

sub·saturated \¦səb+\ *adj* [*sub-* + *saturated*] : approximately but not completely saturated — **sub·saturation** \"+\ *n*

sub·scale \'səb+,-\ *n* [*sub-* + *scale* (plate)] : an oxidation product developed within the substance of rather than on the surface of a metal

¹sub·scapular \¦səb+\ *adj* [NL *subscapularis,* fr. *sub-* + *scapularis* scapular] : situated under the scapula : of or relating to the ventral or in man the anterior surface of the scapula; *esp* : being a body part (as an artery or a vein or muscle) that courses in whole or in part beneath the scapula

²subscapular \"\ *n* : a subscapular part

subscapular artery *n* : the largest branch of the axillary artery arising opposite the lower border of the subscapularis muscle and passing back to the inferior angle of the scapula to anastomose with arteries of that region

subscapular fascia *n* : a thin sheet of fascia fixed to the circumference of the subscapular fossa

subscapular fossa *n* : the concave depression of the anterior surface of the scapula

sub·scap·u·lar·is \,səb,skapyə'la(a)rəs\ *n* -ES [NL, fr. *subscapularis,* adj., subscapular] : a large triangular muscle that fills up the subscapular fossa, arises from the surface of the scapula, and is inserted into the lesser tubercle of the humerus

sub·science \¦səb+\ *n* [*sub-* + *science*] : a branch of a science that has developed some degree of specialization and autonomy in its own right ⟨geometry is a ~ of mathematics⟩

sub·scleral \"+\ *adj* [*sub-* + *scleral*] : SUBSCLEROTIC

sub·sclerotic \"+\ *adj* [*sub-* + *sclerotic*] : situated or occurring between the sclerotic and choroid coats of the eyeball

sub·scribe \səbz'krīb, -b'sk-\ *vb* [ME *subscriben,* fr. L *subscribere,* fr. *sub-* + *scribere* to write — more at SCRIBE] *vt* **1** : to write (as one's name) underneath : sign (one's name) to a document **2 a** : to sign with one's own hand : give consent to or bind oneself to the terms of (something written) by appending one's name **b** : to attest by appending one's name ⟨officers ~ their official acts⟩ **c** *obs* : to sign away : RESIGN, YIELD **d** (1) : to promise to give ⟨each man *subscribed* ten dollars⟩ (2) : CONTRIBUTE ⟨each *subscribing* . . . that which it can do best —W.J.Haley⟩ **3** *chiefly Brit* : to give support to or concur in : FAVOR, SANCTION ⟨unable to . . . ~ their beliefs —T.E.Lawrence⟩ **4** *obs* : to declare with or as if with signature : PUBLISH ⟨I will ~ him a coward —Shak.⟩ **~** *vi* **1** : to sign one's name to a letter or other document **2 a** : to give approval to something written by signing — often used with *to* ⟨found him unwilling to ~ to the agreement⟩ **b** : to set one's name to a paper in token of promise to give something (as a sum of money); *also* : to give something in pursuance of a promise so made **c** (1) : to enter one's name for a publication (as a book or newspaper) or service — usu. used with *for* and sometimes with *to* (2) : to agree to take and pay for something (as stock) by signing one's name to a formal agreement; *esp* : to make a signed application for securities of a new offering — usu. used with *for* ⟨*subscribed* for 1000 shares⟩ **3** *obs* : to become surety **4** *obs* : YIELD, SUBMIT **5 a** : to be in accord : ACQUIESCE, AGREE — usu. used with *to* ⟨~ to a doctrine⟩ **b** : ADHERE, BELONG ⟨~ to the masculine gender⟩ **syn** see ASSENT

sub·scrib·er \-bə(r)\ *n* : one that subscribes: as **a** : one that signs something (as a letter, document, agreement) **b** : one that agrees or consents **c** : one that favors, aids, or supports (as by money contribution, moral influence, personal membership) **d** : an individual having commercial telephone equipment installed on his premises

¹sub·script \'səbz,kript, -b,sk-\ *n* [L *subscriptus,* past part. of *subscribere* to write underneath] : something written below (as a subscript sign or letter); *esp* : a subscript character affixed to a symbol to distinguish it in its class

²subscript \"\ *adj* [L *subscriptus,* past part. of *subscribere*] : written below or beneath: as **a** : being a usu. smaller character printed or written immediately below another character ⟨the ~ cedilla of ç⟩ **b** : being a usu. smaller character printed or written lower than but not immediately below another ⟨the ~ 2 of H_2O⟩ — compare ADSCRIPT, SUPERSCRIPT

sub·scrip·tion \səbz'kripshən, -b'sk-\ *n, often attrib* [ME *subscripcioun,* fr. L *subscription-, subscriptio* thing written underneath, subscription, fr. *subscriptus* (past part. of *subscribere* to write underneath) + *-ion-, -io* -ion] **1 a** : a formal approval or acceptance of some outline of principles (as of ecclesiastical articles of faith) attested by the signing of one's name **b** : the act of signing one's name (as in attesting or witnessing a document) **c** : consent, agreement, approval, or support conveyed or such as would be conveyed by signed confirmation **2** : something that is subscribed: **a** : matter appended at the end of a document or writing; *esp* : a signed response by a sovereign written below a written inquiry as to a matter of law or policy — compare RESCRIPT **b** : a written name : SIGNATURE; *also* : a paper to which a signature is attached **c** *obs* : SUBSCRIPT **d** (1) : a sum subscribed ⟨his ~ to a fund⟩ (2) : the whole amount realized from or pledged by subscribers to a particular offering ⟨the ~ amounted to over 3000 dollars⟩ **e** (1) : a method of issuing a published work in which the publisher agrees to a concession in price to those who buy in advance of publication — see SUBSCRIPTION BOOK (2) : a purchase by prepayment of the future issues of a periodical usu. for a fixed period (as a year) ⟨renewed her ~ to the journal⟩ (3) : application to purchase securities of a new issue **f** : a method of offering or supporting a series of public performances (as of plays or concerts) **g** : a part of a prescription that contains directions to the pharmacist **3** *obs* : SUBMISSION, OBEDIENCE

subscription book *n* **1** : a book containing a list of subscribers **2** : a book sold by subscription usu. through personal solicitation by an agent

subscription edition *n* **1** : an edition published after a required number of subscriptions has been guaranteed **2** : an edition usu. in a special format and binding sold only to subscribers

sub·scrip·tion·ist \-sh(ə)nəst\ *n* : one who seeks or canvasses for subscriptions

subscription library *n* : a lending library to which borrowers pay a membership fee either instead of or in addition to a specific charge for books borrowed

subscription list *n* : a list or record of subscriptions and subscribers

subscription warrant *n* : a certificate or other document constituting legal evidence of a subscription right

sub·sea \'səb,sē\ *adj* [*sub-* + *sea*] : SUBMARINE, UNDERSEA

sub·sect \'səb+,-\ *n* [*sub-* + *sect*] **1** : a sect directly derived from another **2** : a minor sect

sub·section \¦səb+\ *n* [*sub-* + *section*] **1** : a subdivision or a subordinate division of a section ⟨~ of a report⟩ **2** : a subordinate part or branch ⟨a ~ of a gene⟩

sub·segment \"+\ *n* [*sub-* + *segment*] : a subordinate segment; *specif* : a distinguishable portion of an arthropod appendage that appears to be but is not morphologically homologous to a true segment ⟨~*s* of the insect tarsus⟩

sub·sel·li·um \(,)səb'selēəm\ *n, pl* **subsellia** \-ēə\ [L, fr. *sub-* + *sella* seat, chair — more at SETTLE] : a low seat or bench; *esp* : MISERICORD

sub·semitone \¦səb+\ *n* [*sub-* + *semitone*] : the leading note of a key in medieval music : SUBTONIC

subsense \'səb+,-\ *n* [*sub-* + *sense*] : a subordinate division of a sense

sub·sensible \¦səb+\ *adj* [*sub-* + *sensible*] : deeper than the reach of the senses : situated beyond sensory perception

sub·septate \"+\ *adj* [*sub-* + *septate*] : imperfectly septate : having a partial septum

sub·se·quence \'səbsəkwən(t)s, -bsēk-, -,kwen- *also* -bz(,)k- *or* -b(,)sk- *sometimes* -bzə(,)k- *or* -bzē(,)k-\ *n* [LL *subsequentia* that which follows, succession, fr. L *subsequent-, subsequens* (pres. part.) + *-ia*] **1** : the quality or state of being subsequent **2** : something that comes subsequently : a later or following event

¹sub·se·quent \-nt\ *adj* [ME, fr. L *subsequent-, subsequens,* pres. part. of *subsequi* to follow closely, fr. *sub-* near, closely + *sequi* to follow — more at SUE] **1** : following in time : coming or being later than something else ⟨~ events⟩ ⟨a period ~ to the war⟩ **2** : following in order of place : SUCCEEDING ⟨a ~ clause in a treaty⟩ **3** [so called fr. its being subsequent in origin to the system of which it is a part] : developed along a belt of underlying weak rock and therefore adjusted to the regional structure ⟨a ~ stream⟩ — **sub·se·quent·ly** *adv* — **sub·se·quent·ness** *n* -ES

²subsequent \"\ *n* **1** : one that follows after in time or in position **2** : a subsequent stream

subsequent condition *n* : CONDITION SUBSEQUENT

subsequent drainage *n* : drainage by means of a subsequent stream

sub·se·quen·tial \¦==¦kwenchəl, ¦=¦kw-, ¦=¦skw-\ *adj* [*subsequent* + *-al*] : SUBSEQUENT — **sub·se·quen·tial·ly** \-ch(ə)lē, -li\ *adv*

subsequent to *prep* : at a time later or more recent than : SINCE ⟨*subsequent to* our discussion⟩

subsequent valley *n* : a valley eroded by a subsequent stream

sub·sere \ˈsəb+,-\ *n* [*sub-* + *sere*] : a secondary succession arising after an ecological climax community has been interrupted (as by fire or human agency)

sub·serosa \¦səb+\ *n* [NL, fr. *sub-* + *serosa*] : subserous tissue

sub·serous \"+\ *adj* [ISV *sub-* + *serous*] : located under a serous membrane ⟨a ~ uterine fibroid⟩

sub·serve \(,)səbˈsərv, -ˈsə̄v,-ˈsəiv\ *vb* [L *subservire*, fr. *sub-* + *servire* to serve — more at SERVE] *vi* : to hold or function in a subordinate position in respect to something ⟨the lesser need must ~ to the greater⟩ ~ *vt* **1 a** : to serve as an instrument or means in carrying on (as an activity) or out (as a plan) or in furthering the ends of (as a person) ⟨if we are going to ~ the purpose for which rent control was adopted —*Congressional Record*⟩ **b** : to function for or serve to promote the betterment, welfare, or effectiveness of ⟨an organism in which every part has its place and ~*s* the whole —Frank Thilly⟩ **c** : to be in accord with : accord honor or respect to ⟨Napoleon's star rose as long as he *subserved* the great ideas of the French revolution —Lucien Price⟩ **2** *archaic* : to avail (oneself) of something

sub·ser·vi·ate \-vē,āt\ *vt* -ED/-ING/-S [¹*subservient* + *-ate*] : to reduce to a subordinate or subservient place or condition

sub·ser·vi·ence \-vēən(t)s\ *also* **sub·ser·vi·en·cy** \-nsē, -nsi\ *n, pl* **subserviences** *also* **subserviencies** [L *subservire* to be subservient, to subserve + E *-ence* or *-ency*] **1** : the quality or state of functioning in serving or promoting : the condition of one that subserves ⟨these proposals are made in ~ to the end in view⟩ **2** : the quality or state of being subordinate or subordinated to something ⟨~ to sensation —Marjorie Grene⟩ ⟨the emancipation of American literature from its ~ to England —*Amer. Guide Series: Mass.*⟩ **3 a** : excessive willingness to submit to the control or demands of another ⟨repudiated the administration's ~ to foreign interests⟩ **b** : servile inferiority : obsequious servility ⟨felt no ~ in working for him —Emery Neff⟩

¹**sub·ser·vi·ent** \-nt\ *adj* [L *subservient-, subserviens*, pres. part. of *subservire* to be subservient, to subserve] : fitted or disposed to subserve: as **a** : useful in an inferior capacity : SUBORDINATE **b** : serving to promote some end **c** : obsequiously submissive : SERVILE, TRUCKLING

syn SERVILE, MENIAL, SLAVISH, OBSEQUIOUS: SUBSERVIENT implies compliance and obedience, perhaps abject and marked by cringing or truckling, of one very conscious of a subordinate, dependent position ⟨the *subservient* smirk which comes only of generations of tip-seeking ancestors —Jack London⟩ ⟨editors and journalists who express opinions in print that are opposed to the interests of the rich are dismissed and replaced by *subservient* ones —G.B.Shaw⟩ SERVILE is likely to suggest the mean submissive cringing or fawning of a slave ⟨*servile* and fawning as he had been before, he was now as domineering and bellicose —Jack London⟩ ⟨the manner of a prince doling out favors to a *servile* group of petitioners —Theodore Dreiser⟩ MENIAL may suggest lower domestic tasks and offices; it may suggest degradation or sordidness ⟨competing against a mass of unemployed, they accepted the most *menial* and worst paid jobs —Oscar Handlin⟩ ⟨the scullery boy peeled the potatoes and did other *menial* tasks out on the open platform —O.S.Nock⟩ SLAVISH, in this sense derived from and suggesting *slave*, may connote abjectness, debasement, or extremely hard drudging toil ⟨which attacks the poor companion bore with meekness, with cowardice, with a resignation that was half generous and half hypocritical — with the *slavish* submission —W.M.Thackeray⟩ OBSEQUIOUS may suggest fawning, unctuous, or sycophantic compliance with and attention to those being served ⟨brutal and arrogant when winning, they are bootlicking and servilely *obsequious* when losing —D.L.Cohn⟩

²**subservient** \"\ *n* -S : one that is subservient

sub·ser·vi·ent·ly *adv* : in a subservient manner : with subservience

sub·ser·vi·ent·ness *n* -ES : SUBSERVIENCE

sub·sessile \¦səb+\ *adj* [NL *subsessilis*, fr. L *sub-* + *sessilis* low, dwarf (of plants) — more at SESSILE] : nearly but not quite sessile

¹**sub·set** \ˈsəb+¦-\ *vb* [*sub-* + *set* (v.)] *Scots law* : SUBLET

²**sub·set** \ˈsəb+,-\ *n* [*sub-* + *set*] : a set (as of data) that is itself an element of a larger set; *esp* : a mathematical set each of whose elements is also an element of a given set

sub·sexual \¦səb+\ *adj* [*sub-* + *sexual*] : approaching but not clearly characterizable as sexual ⟨a ~ parthenogenetic reproduction involving nuclear changes analogous to meiosis but without reduction⟩

sub·shining \"+\ *adj* [*sub-* + *shining*] : somewhat lustrous

sub·shock \ˈsəb+,-\ *adj* [*sub-* + *shock*] **1** : inadequate to produce fully developed insulin shock ⟨~ doses of insulin⟩ **2** : of, relating to, or constituting insulin shock therapy in which the dosage is kept below the level necessary to produce deep coma

sub·shrub \"+,-\ *n* [*sub-* + *shrub*] **1** : a perennial plant having woody stems except for the terminal part of the new growth which is killed back annually **2** : UNDERSHRUB 2

sub·shrubby \"+,-\ *adj* [*sub-* + *shrubby*] : somewhat shrubby : like or being a subshrub

sub·side \səbˈsīd\ *vi* -ED/-ING/-S [L *subsidere*, fr. *sub-* + *sidere* to sit down, sink; akin to L *sedēre* to sit — more at SIT] **1** : to sink or fall to the bottom : SETTLE, PRECIPITATE **2** : to tend downward : become lower : DESCEND; *esp* : to flatten out so as to form a depression ⟨the soil *subsided* over the old dump⟩ **3** : to let oneself settle down : EASE, SINK ⟨*subsided* into a chair⟩ **4** : to fall into a state of quiet : cease to rage : settle down : become tranquil : ABATE ⟨the sea ~*s*⟩ ⟨the tumult will ~⟩ ⟨the fever has *subsided*⟩ **syn** see FALL

sub·sidence \səbˈsīdᵊn(t)s, ˈsəbsədən-\ *n* -S [L *subsidentia*, fr. *subsident-, subsidens* (pres. part. of *subsidere* to subside) + *-ia*] **1** : something (as a sediment in a liquid) that has subsided **2** : the act or process of subsiding : a falling, lowering, or flattening out ⟨the ~ of waves after a storm⟩ ⟨his anger underwent a quick ~⟩

sub·siden·cy \-nsē\ *n* -ES [L *subsidentia*] *archaic* : SUBSIDENCE

sub·sident \-nt\ *adj* [L *subsident-, subsidens*, pres. part. of *subsidere* to subside] : falling to the bottom : SUBSIDING

sub·sid·er \səbˈsīdə(r)\ *n* -S : one (as a settling tank or separator) that subsides or permits of or accelerates the process of subsidence

sub·sid·i·ar·i·ly \(,)səb¦sidē¦erəlē, -li *also* ÷ -ˈsidər-\ *adv* : in a subsidiary manner : so as to be subsidiary

sub·sid·i·ar·i·ty \-,sidēˈarəd-ē\ *n* -ES **1** : the quality or state of being subsidiary **2** : a theory in sociology: functions which subordinate or local organizations perform effectively belong more properly to them than to a dominant central organization

¹**sub·sid·i·ary** \(,)səbˈsidē,erē, -ri *also* ÷-dər-\ *adj* [L *subsidiarius* of or relating to a reserve, fr. *subsidium* army reserve, subsidy + *-arius* -ary] **1 a** : functioning in the provision of aid, support, or other benefit usu. in a subordinate or inferior status or capacity ⟨a ~ subject in a course of study⟩ ⟨~ details that lend finish to the ensemble⟩ **b** (1) : of secondary importance or prominence : SUPPLEMENTARY, MINOR, TRIBUTARY ⟨a ~ stream⟩ ⟨~ crops⟩ (2) : belonging to or controlled by another ⟨a ~ company⟩ **2 a** : of, relating to, or constituting a subsidy ⟨a ~ payment to an ally⟩ **b** : aided or maintained by a subsidy ⟨raised a force of ~ troops⟩

²**subsidiary** \"\ *n* -ES : one that is subsidiary: as **a** : ASSISTANT **b** : a subordinate theme or motive in music; *esp* : one occurring as subject of an episode in an extended work **c** *also* **subsidiary company** : a company wholly controlled by another that owns more than half of its voting stock — compare AFFILIATE 2b(1) **d** : a subsidiary goal in polo

subsidiary cell *n* **1** : ACCESSORY CELL **2** : a cell of an elevated circular group of cells surrounding the base of a multicellular hair in the epidermis of some plants

subsidiary coin *n* : a coin esp. of silver of a denomination smaller than the basic monetary unit (as half-dollar, quarter, dime) — compare MINOR COIN

subsidiary ledger *n* : a ledger which is supplementary to a controlling account in a general ledger and in which detailed accounts of a like class are kept

subsiding reservoir *n* : SETTLING RESERVOIR

sub·si·diz·able \ˈsəbsə,dīzəbəl, ˈsəbzə-, ,==ˈ===\ *adj* : capable of being subsidized

sub·si·di·za·tion \,==dəˈzāshən, -,dīˈz-\ *n* -S **1** : the act or practice of subsidizing **2** : money or other benefits obtained as a subsidy

sub·si·dize \ˈsəbsə,dīz *sometimes* ˈsəbzə-\ *vt* -ED/-ING/-S *see -ize in Explan Notes* [*subsidy* + *-ize*] : to furnish with a subsidy: as **a** : to purchase the assistance of by the payment of a subsidy **b** : to aid or promote (as a private enterprise) with public money ⟨~ a steamship line⟩ — **sub·si·diz·er** \-zə(r)\ *n* -S

sub·si·dy \ˈsəbsədē, -di *also* ˈsəbzə-\ *n* -ES *often attrib* [ME *subsidie*, fr. L *subsidium* army reserve, support, help, fr. *subsidere* to settle down, subside — more at SUBSIDE] **1** *archaic* : something intended to aid, support, or comfort **2** : a grant or gift of money or other property made by way of financial aid: as **a** : a sum of money formerly granted by the British Parliament to the crown and raised by extraordinary or special taxation in distinction from the proceeds of the customs or other taxes levied by royal prerogative **b** : money or other support exacted by a ruler usu. for a special purpose or occasion **c** : money granted by one state to another (as to a friendly power to aid in the prosecution of a war) **d** : a grant of funds or property from a government (as of the state or a municipal corporation) to a private person or company to assist in the establishment or support of an enterprise deemed advantageous to the public either as a simple gift or a payment of an amount in excess of the usual charges for a service (as in carrying the mails) or funds to aid in establishing or maintaining a service or equipment larger or more powerful than the state of trade would warrant (as for the building and keeping in service of ships designed for use as cruisers and auxiliaries in war); *broadly* : an entire payment from a government for services (as for carrying mail) which includes both compensation for actual services and a subsidy proper

sub·sieve \ˈsəb+,-\ *adj* [*sub-* + *sieve*] : of, relating to, made up of, or being particles small enough to pass freely through a 44 micron separatory sieve ⟨the ~ fraction of a clay⟩ ⟨particles in the ~ range⟩

sub si·len·tio \,səbsəˈlenchē,ō, -b,sīˈl-; -bsəˈlentē,ō\ *adv* [L] : under or in silence : without notice being taken or without making a particular point of the matter in question ⟨assumed *sub silentio* that the Supreme Court would have the power to review . . . legislation —J.P.Roche⟩

sub·silicate \¦səb+\ *n* [ISV *sub-* + *silicate*] : a basic silicate

sub·silicic \"+\ *adj* [*sub-* + *silicic*] : containing little silica ⟨a ~ rock⟩ — distinguished from *persilicic*

sub·sill \ˈsəb+,-\ *n* [*sub-* + *sill*] : a secondary sill (as under a shop front or on a mudsill)

sub·sinuous \¦səb+\ *adj* [*sub-* + *sinuous*] : imperfectly sinuous : nearly but not quite sinuous

¹**sub·sist** \səbˈsist\ *vb* -ED/-ING/-S [LL *subsistere* to stay alive, exist, be, fr. L, to remain standing, stand up, fr. *sub-* up + *sistere* to stand, cause to stand; akin to L *stare* to stand — more at SUB-, STAND] *vi* **1 a** : to have existence : be or remain alive : BE ⟨enabling a noble action to ~ as it did in nature —Matthew Arnold⟩ **b** : PERSIST, CONTINUE **2** *archaic* : to exist in a particular way or condition or have a particular form **3** : to be maintained with food and clothing : have the necessities of life ⟨the town ~*s* on what mining activities remain —*Amer. Guide Series: Calif.*⟩ ⟨many adult persons can ~ . . . on less than half the amount of protein recommended —*Science*⟩ **4 a** : HOLD, OBTAIN; *specif* : to hold true or good ⟨relations ~ between terms⟩ **b** : to have existence as a concept rather than in fact; *specif* : to be conceivable as the subject of a true statement ⟨"the round square does not ~" is just as true as "the present King of France does not exist" —Bertrand Russell⟩ ~ *vt* **1** *obs* : to keep up or in existence : keep alive **2** : to support with provisions : FEED, MAINTAIN ⟨~*ing* troops off the country⟩

²**subsist** \"\ *n* -S [short for *subsistence*] *Brit* : payment of wages on account

sub·sist·ence \-tən(t)s\ *n* -S *often attrib* [ME, fr. LL *subsistentia* (trans. of Gk *hypostasis*), fr. *subsistent-, subsistens* (pres. part. of *subsistere* to exist, be) + L *-ia*] **1 a** (1) : existence in reality : the condition of having substance or constituting an independent identifiable entity ⟨an abstraction without real ~⟩ (2) *obs* : condition or manner of existing (3) : HYPOSTASIS **2** (4) *archaic* : something that exists in reality : a material or substantial entity (5) : the condition of remaining in existence : PERSISTENCE (6) : INHERENCY ⟨~ of a quality in a body⟩ **b** *Scholasticism* (1) : the mode by which substance becomes individualized (2) : something in a reality by reason of which it is what it is (3) : a singular rational component of the human personality that is wholly self-contained and endowed with inalienable rights **c** (1) : the metaphysical status of something that subsists (sense 4b) (2) : the character possessed by whatever is logically conceivable **2** : means of subsisting: as **a** : the irreducible minimum (as of food and shelter) necessary to support life ⟨a barren land providing no more than ~⟩ **b** : a mode of obtaining or a source of the necessities of life : LIVELIHOOD ⟨his small patrimony was enough for a ~⟩ ⟨won his ~ dealing in the castoffs of other people⟩ **c** : a source or supply of food ⟨their livestock was their sole ~⟩ **d** *or* **subsistence money** *or* **subsistence allowance** (1) : money given in advance (as to a soldier or workman) to meet the basic needs of life while awaiting a payday (2) : an allowance for expenses incurred in performance of a duty while temporarily away from one's residence (3) : a cash allowance to a member of a military organization given in lieu of food **3** : the providing of the necessities to animal life : the furnishing of support ⟨farming is no easy means of ~⟩ **syn** see LIVING

subsistence economy *n* : an economy which is not based on money, in which buying and selling are absent or rudimentary though barter may occur, and which commonly provides a minimal standard of living — compare SUBSISTENCE FARMING

subsistence farming *or* **subsistence agriculture** *n* **1** : farming or a system of farming designed to provide all or essentially all the goods required by the farm family usu. without any significant surplus for sale ⟨primitive farming is normally *subsistence farming*⟩ — compare GENERAL FARMER, MIXED FARMING, MONOCULTURE **2** : farming or a system of farming that produces a minimum and often inadequate return to the farm operator : economically marginal farming — compare SHARECROPPER

subsistence homestead *n* : a piece of realty comprising a dwelling unit and sufficient land for the raising of supplementary food for a family not primarily dependent on the land for livelihood

subsistence stores *n pl* : military stores consisting principally of articles of the ration but including also other items (as candy, toilet articles) needed by the individual

subsistence theory *n* : a theory in economics: wages tend toward the lowest level that will provide subsistence — compare IRON LAW OF WAGES, WAGE-FUND THEORY

sub·sist·en·cy \-nsē\ *n* -ES [LL *subsistentia*] *archaic* : SUBSISTENCE

¹**sub·sist·ent** \səbˈsistənt\ *adj* [LL *subsistent-, subsistens*, pres. part. of *subsistere* to stay alive, exist, be — more at SUBSIST] **1** : having being : SUBSISTING ⟨a ~ spirit⟩ **2** : INHERENT ⟨qualities ~ in matter⟩

²**subsistent** \"\ *n* -S **1** : something (as an object or substance) having existence **2** : an abstract entity

sub·sis·ten·tial \(¦)səb,si¦stenchəl\ *adj* [LL *subsistentia* existence, substance, reality + E *-al*] : of or relating to subsistence and esp. to the hypostases in the Trinity or to one of them

sub·sist·ing·ly *adv* : so as to subsist : in a subsisting manner

sub·sizar \¦səb+\ *n* [*sub-* + *sizar*] : a subsidized student (as at Cambridge University) ranking below a sizar in achievement and amount of stipend

sub·size \ˈsəb+¦-\ *adj* [*sub-* + *size*] : of less than usual, standard, or normal size

sub·social \¦səb+\ *adj* [*sub-* + *social*] : incompletely social : tending to associate gregariously but lacking fixed or complex social organization ⟨~ insects⟩

sub·society \"+\ *n* : a social subgroup or subculture

¹**sub·soil** \ˈsəb+,-\ *n* [*sub-* + *soil*] : the stratum of weathered material that underlies the surface soil

²**subsoil** \"\ *vt* : to turn, break, or stir the subsoil of

sub·soil·er \-ə(r)\ *n* -S : one that subsoils land: as **a** (1) : SUBSOIL PLOW (2) : an attachment to a lister that prepares a seedbed in the bottom of the furrow (3) : an attachment to a plow frame for breaking up the plow sole **b** : the operator of a subsoiler

subsoil plow *n* : a plow without a moldboard that is used for stirring without turning over the deeper soil usu. beneath previously plowed furrows

sub·solar \¦səb+\ *adj* [*sub-* + *solar*] : situated under the sun : having the sun in the zenith; *specif* : situated between the tropics

subsolar point *n* : the point on the earth's surface at which the sun is in the zenith — compare CIRCLE OF POSITION

sub·sonic \¦səb+\ *adj* [ISV *sub-* + *sonic*] **1** : of, relating to, or being a speed less than that of sound in air — compare SONIC, TRANSONIC **2** : moving, capable of moving, or utilizing air currents moving at a subsonic speed **3** : INFRASONIC 1

subsonic flow *n* : directed motion of a fluid medium in which the velocity is less than that of sound in the medium throughout the region under consideration

sub·space \ˈsəb+,-\ *n* [*sub-* + *space*] : a space each of whose points is contained in a given space but which does not itself contain all the points of the given space

sub·specialty \¦səb+\ *n* [*sub-* + *specialty*] : a subordinate field of specialization (as in medicine) ⟨proctology was formerly considered a ~ of surgery⟩

sub·speciation \"+\ *n* -S [NL *subspecies* + E *-ation*] : formation of or division into subspecies : RACIATION

sub spe·cie ae·ter·ni·ta·tis \,səb¦spekē,ā,ī,ternəˈtäd·əs\ *adv* [NL, lit., under the aspect of eternity] : in its essential or universal form or nature

sub·species \¦səb +\ *n* [NL, fr. L *sub-* + *species*] : a subdivision of a species: as **a** : a taxonomic category that is the lowest generally used taxon, ranks immediately below a species, and designates a morphologically distinguishable group whose members are at least partially isolated geographically but interbreed successfully with members of other subspecies of the same species where their ranges adjoin and overlap **b** : a named subdivision (as a race or variety) of a taxonomic species — not used technically **syn** see VARIETY

sub·specific \"+\ *adj* [*sub-* + *specific*] **1** : of, relating to, or constituting a subspecies ⟨~ rank⟩ ⟨a ~ distinguishing character⟩ **2** : of less than specific rank or significance ⟨a ~ race⟩ — **sub·specifically** \"+\ *adv*

sub·spherical \"+\ *adj* [*sub-* + *spherical*] : imperfectly spherical : nearly but not quite spherical : SPHEROIDAL — **sub·spherically** \"+\ *adv*

sub·spiniform \"+\ *n* [*sub-* + *spiniform*] : a part or process (as on an insect) that suggests a spine

sub·spinous \"+\ *adj* [*sub-* + *spinous*] **1** : somewhat spinous **2 a** : situated beneath the spinal column **b** : INFRASPINOUS

sub·spontaneous \"+\ *adj* [*sub-* + *spontaneous*] : occurring only indirectly under the influence of man ⟨many plants make a ~ establishment in new areas when grazing alters the previous flora⟩

subst *abbr* **1** substantive **2** substitute

sub·stage \ˈsəb+,-\ *n* [*sub-* + *stage*] **1** : a subdivision of a stage and esp. of a geological stage **2** : an attachment to a microscope by means of which accessories (as mirrors, diaphragms, condensers or Nicol prisms) are held in place beneath the stage of the instrument

sub·stalagmite \¦səb+\ *n* [*sub-* + *stalagmite*] : a compact noncrystalline deposit of calcium carbonate — **sub·stalagmitic** \"+\ *adj*

sub·stance \ˈsəbztən(t)s, -bst-\ *n* -S [ME, fr. OF, fr. L *substantia*, fr. *substant-, substans* (pres. part. of *substare* to stand under, stand firm, fr. *sub-* + *stare* to stand) + *-ia* — more at STAND] **1 a** : essential nature : ESSENCE — used esp. of the divine nature and then distinguished from *hypostasis* ⟨being of one ~ with the Father —*Nicene Creed*⟩ **b** : a fundamental part, quality, or aspect : essential quality or import : the characteristic and essential part ⟨the ~ of his address⟩ ⟨distinguish a question of ~ from one which is merely procedural —*Va. Law Rev.*⟩ ⟨considering the plan in its ~ as well as its practical advantages⟩ **c** *Christian Science* : ²GOD b(6) **2 a** [trans. of Gk *ousia*] : something that underlies all outward manifestations whether unique (as in monism), one of two (as in dualism), or one of a large or infinite number (as in pluralism) : ultimate reality whether material or spiritual : the abiding part of existence or an existing thing as distinguished from what is accidental to it : the real essence or nature of a thing: as **a** *Aristotelianism & Scholasticism* (1) : the primary category presupposed by all the others : something that is the real subject of predication and cannot itself be predicated of anything : SUBJECT ⟨~ . . . is that which is neither predicable of a subject nor present in a subject; for instance, the individual man or horse —E.M.Edghill⟩ (2) : the essence of an existing thing : something that makes a thing what it is or gives it its essential nature (3) : something that supports attributes or modes or exists as the material of individuation : SUBSTRATUM (4) : an individual being considered as an existent entity : a subsistent entity compounded of matter and form (5) : GENUS 2 (6) : UNIVERSAL 2a (3) — compare NOMINALISM, REALISM 2 **b** *Cartesianism* (1) : something that depends on no other thing for its existence (2) : something that depends only on God for its existence **c** *Spinozism* : the universal underlying principle that exists and can be conceived independently of any other thing — compare MODE 6 **d** *Leibnizianism* : MONAD 1c **e** : an unknowable imperceivable entity that is the bearer of qualities ⟨if anyone will examine himself concerning his notion of pure ~ . . . he will find he has no other idea of it at all, but only a supposition of he knows not what support of such qualities which are capable of producing simple ideas —John Locke⟩; *also* : a complex of qualities together with its unknowable bearer **f** *Humean philos* : a collection of qualities regarded as constituting a unity ⟨the idea of a ~ . . . is nothing but a collection of simple ideas, that are united by the imagination, and have a particular name assigned them, by which we are able to recall . . . that collection —David Hume †1776⟩ **g** *Kantianism* : a permanent subsisting imperishable substratum necessary for the existence and perception of change in time : that which must be posited in order to assume the duration of a thing rather than a succession of phenomena ⟨we can only give to a phenomenon the name of ~ because we admit its existence at all times —Friedrich Max Müller⟩ **3** *archaic* : an underlying assurance : BASIS, GROUND **4 a** : material from which something is made and to which it owes its characteristic qualities ⟨the special ~*s* of nerve tissue⟩ ⟨a fabric of unknown ~⟩ **b** (1) : a distinguishable kind of physical matter (2) : a piece or mass of such substance ⟨struck by some hard ~⟩ ⟨an oily ~⟩ ⟨cork is a ~ with distinctive properties⟩ **c** : matter of definite or known chemical composition : an identifiable chemical element, compound, or mixture — sometimes restricted to compounds and elements ⟨water is a liquid derived from two gaseous ~*s*⟩ ⟨a chemically pure ~⟩ **5** : material possessions : ESTATE, PROPERTY, RESOURCES ⟨a man of ~⟩ **6 a** *obs* : the whole amount or tally of something : QUANTITY **b** : the greater part : MAJORITY ⟨dissipated the ~ of his fortune in a few short years⟩ **c** *or* **substance number** : BASIS WEIGHT **7** : a material object as distinguished from something shadowy or visionary; *also* : SOLIDITY, SUBSTANTIALITY ⟨an old building but of marked ~⟩ — **in substance** *adv* : in respect to essentials : SUBSTANTIALLY, FUNDAMENTALLY ⟨accurate *in substance*⟩

sub·stance·less \-ləs\ *adj* : lacking in substance : deficient in matter, content, or worth ⟨a ~ charge⟩

substance of schwann *usu cap 2d S* \-ˈshw¦än, -ˈshf¦, -ˈshv¦\ [after Theodor *Schwann* †1882 Ger. anatomist] : MEDULLARY SHEATH

¹**sub·standard** \¦səb +\ *adj* [*sub-* + *standard*] : deviating from or failing to attain to or qualify under some standard or norm: as **a** (1) : of a quality lower than that specified as acceptable under a standard prescribed by law ⟨~ canned goods⟩ (2) *of housing* : deficient in amenities (as sanitary accommodations,

living space, safety facilities, or maintenance) in respect to a substandard set by legal or other authoritative sources **b :** conforming to a pattern of linguistic usage existing within a speech community but not that of the prestige group in that community in choice of word (as *set*, for *sit*), form of word (as *brung*, for *brought*), pronunciation (as *twicet*, for *twice*), grammatical construction (as the boys *is* growing fast), or idiom (as *all to once*, for *all at once*) — compare NONSTANDARD **c :** constituting a greater than normal chance of loss to an insurer due to some inherent and determinable cause (as poor health or unusual fire hazard) ⟨a ~ life⟩ ⟨a ~ risk⟩; *also* **:** covering a substandard risk usu. in return for an extra premium ⟨~ insurance⟩ **d** *of motion-picture film* **:** narrower than 35 millimeters

²substandard \"\ *n* [in sense 1, fr. *sub-* + *standard*, n.; in sense 2, fr. ¹*substandard*] **1 :** a secondary standard used in measurement and esp. to check the accuracy of commercial measuring devices (as scales) **2 :** something (as a way of living) that is substandard

sub·stan·tia \səbz'tanch(ē)ə, -b'st-\ *n, pl* **substanti·ae** \-chē,ē\ [NL, fr. L, substance] **:** anatomical material, substance, or tissue

sub·stan·tia·ble \-ch(ē)əbəl\ *adj* [*substantiate* + *-able*] **:** capable of being substantiated

¹sub·stan·tial \səbz'tanchəl, -b'st-, -taan-\ *adj* [ME *substancial*, fr. LL *substantialis*, fr. L *substantia* substance + *-alis* -al — more at SUBSTANCE] **1 a :** consisting of, relating to, sharing the nature of, or constituting substance **:** existing as or in substance **:** MATERIAL ⟨~ life⟩ ⟨the ~ realities⟩ ⟨most ponderous and ~ things —Shak.⟩ **b :** not seeming or imaginary **:** not illusive **:** REAL, TRUE ⟨the ~ world⟩ ⟨a mere dream neither ~ nor practical⟩ **c :** being of moment **:** IMPORTANT, ESSENTIAL **2 a :** adequately or generously nourishing **:** ABUNDANT, PLENTIFUL ⟨set a ~ table⟩ ⟨after that too ~ dinner⟩ **b :** possessed of goods or an estate **:** moderately wealthy **:** WELL-TO-DO ⟨a ~ man⟩; *often* **:** having a good and well-maintained income-producing property ⟨a ~ farmer⟩ ⟨the more ~ tradesmen⟩ **c :** considerable in amount, value, or worth ⟨made a ~ gain on the transaction⟩ **3 a :** having good substance **:** firmly or stoutly constructed **:** STURDY, SOLID, FIRM ⟨a ~ house⟩ ⟨~ cloth⟩ **b :** having a solid or firm foundation **:** soundly based **:** carrying weight ⟨a ~ argument⟩ ⟨~ evidence⟩ **4 a :** being that specified to a large degree or in the main ⟨a ~ victory⟩ ⟨a ~ lie⟩ **b :** of or relating to the main part of something **syn** see MASSIVE

²substantial \"\ *n* -s [ME *substancial*, fr. *substancial*, adj.] **:** something that is substantial: as **a :** something having substance or actual existence **b :** something having good substance or actual value **c :** something of moment **:** an important or material matter, thing, or part

substantial damages *n pl* **:** damages which bring about actual economic loss or for which compensation in a substantial amount is awarded as distinguished from nominal damages awarded only to vindicate a legal right

substantial form *n* [ME *forme substancial*, trans. of ML *forma substantialis*, trans. of Gk *ousiōdes eidos*] **:** the form or nature that according to the scholastics gives to an individual substance its specific or generic character

sub·stan·ti·a·lia \=,=chē'ālēə\ *n pl* [NL, fr. neut. pl. of LL *substantialis* substantial] *Scots law* **:** the formally essential parts of a deed

sub·stan·tial·ism \='=chə,lizəm\ *n* -s **:** either of two doctrines in philosophy: **a :** one holding that constant realities or substances underlie phenomena **b :** one holding that matter is a real substance rather than an aggregation of centers of force

sub·stan·tial·ist \-ləst\ *n* -s **:** a proponent of a doctrine of substantialism

sub·stan·ti·al·i·ty \=,=chē'aləd·ē, -lətē, -i\ *n* -ES [LL *substantialitas*, fr. *substantialis* substantial + L *-itas* -ity] **:** the quality or state of being substantial **:** CORPOREITY, MATERIALITY

sub·stan·tial·ize \='=chə,līz\ *vt* -ED/-ING/-S **:** to make substantial **:** give substance to

subs·stan·tial·ly \səbz'tanch(ə)lē, -b'st-, -taan-, -li\ *adv* [ME *substancially*, fr. *substancial* + *-ly*] **:** in a substantial manner **:** so as to be substantial

sub·stan·tial·ness \-chəlnəs\ *n* -ES **:** SUBSTANTIALITY

substantial right *n* **:** a legal right affecting or involving a matter of substance as distinguished from matters of form **:** a right materially affecting those interests which a man is entitled to have preserved and protected by law **:** a material right

sub·stan·tia ni·gra \-'nīgrə, -'nig-\ *n, pl* **substantiae ni·grae** \-(,)grē\ [NL, lit., black substance] **:** a layer of deeply pigmented gray matter in the midbrain separating the cerebral peduncles from the tegmentum above

substantia pro·pria \-'prōprēə\ *n, pl* **substantiae propri·ae** \-ē,ē\ [NL, lit., the tissue proper] **:** the layer of lamellated transparent fibrous connective tissue that makes up the bulk of the cornea of the eye

sub·stan·ti·ate \səbz'tanchē,āt, -b'st-, -taan- *sometimes* -n(t)sē-, *chiefly substand* -nchə,wāt; *usu* -ād·+V\ *vt* -ED/-ING/-S [NL *substantiatus*, past part. of *substantiare* to substantiate, fr. L *substantia* substance — more at SUBSTANCE] **1 :** to impart substance or material form or being to **2 a :** to put into concrete form **:** EMBODY **b :** to make solid or firm **3 :** to establish the existence or truth of by proof or competent evidence **:** VERIFY ⟨~ a charge⟩ **syn** see CONFIRM

sub·stan·ti·a·tion \=,==='āshən, *chiefly substand* =,=='wāshən\ *n* -s **1 :** an act of substantiating (as by proving) **2 :** something adduced as proof **:** EVIDENCE — **sub·stan·ti·a·tive** \='==,ād·iv, *chiefly substand* ='==,wā-\ *adj*

sub·stan·ti·a·tor \='==,ād·ə(r), -,ātə-, *chiefly substand* -,wā-\ *n* -s **:** one that substantiates something

sub·stan·ti·fi·ca·tion \səbz,tantəfə'kāshən, -b,st-\ *n* -s [fr. *substantify*, after such pairs as E *magnify*: *magnification*] **:** an act or product of substantifying

sub·stan·ti·fy \='==,fī\ *vt* -ED/-ING/-ES [ML *substantificare*, fr. L *substantia* substance + *-ficare* -fy] **1 :** to give substance or substantive character to **2 :** SUBSTANTIVATE

sub·stan·tious \səbz'tanchəs, -b'st-\ *adj* [MF *substancious*, *substancieus*, fr. OF *substance* + *-ious*, *-ieus* -ious] *chiefly Scot* **:** HEAVY, POWERFUL, SUBSTANTIAL, EFFECTUAL

sub·stan·ti·val \,səbztən·'tīvəl, -bst-\ *adj* **:** of, relating to, or having the nature or function of a substantive — **sub·stan·ti·val·ly** \-vəlē\ *adv*

sub·stan·ti·vate \'səbztəntə,vāt, -bst-; səbz'tantə,v-, -b'st-\ *vt* -ED/-ING/-S **:** to convert into or use as a substantive ⟨the tendency to ~ adjectives⟩ — **sub·stan·ti·va·tion** \,==tə'vāshən, =,=-\ *n* -s

¹sub·stan·tive \'səbztəntiv, -bst-\ *n* -s [ME *substantif*, fr. MF, fr. *substantif*, adj., having or expressing substance, fr. LL *substantivus* self-existent, substantive] **1 a :** a word or part of speech that names or identifies something **:** a noun or noun equivalent (as a pronoun, phrase, or absolute adjective) ⟨in "the good die young" *good* is a ~⟩ **b :** a categorematic term **2 :** an independent thing or person **:** a self-existent entity

²substantive \", *in senses other than 2c & 3 also* səbz'tantiv *or* -b'st- *or* -taan- *or* -'tēv *or* -ntəv\ *adj* [ME, fr. LL *substantivus*, fr. L *substantia* substance + *-ivus* -ive — more at SUBSTANCE] **1 :** having the character of an independent self-subsistent entity or thing **:** existing in its own right **:** not derivative or dependent **:** SELF-CONTAINED **2 a** (1) **:** having the character or status of or referring to something that is real rather than apparent **:** FIRM, SOLID (2) **:** enduring or permanent as distinguished from transitory **b :** belonging to the essence or intrinsic nature of the substance as distinguished from something that is accidental or qualifying **:** ESSENTIAL **c :** betokening or expressing existence ⟨the ~ verb is the verb *to be*⟩ **d** (1) **:** of, relating to, or being a dye that requires no mordant or a dyeing process involving such a dye **:** DIRECT — opposed to *adjective* (2) **:** having a specific affinity for a fiber (as wool or cellulose) **3 a :** having the nature or function of a grammatical substantive ⟨a ~ phrase⟩ **b :** relating to or having the character of a noun or pronominal term in logic **:** CATEGOREMATIC — contrasted with *adjective* **4 :** considerable in amount or numbers **:** SUBSTANTIAL **5 :** definite rather than contingent in status ⟨a ~ appointment to an office⟩

substantive expression *n* **:** a word or combination of words that functions as a substantive

substantive genitive *n* **:** a genitive that includes in its denotation the meaning of a qualified noun to be understood with it ⟨in "I spent the night at my brother's" *brother's* is a *substantive genitive* carrying the implication "residence"⟩

substantive law *n* **:** a branch of law that prescribes the rights, duties, and obligations of persons to one another as to their conduct or property and that determines when a cause of action for damages or other relief has arisen

sub·stan·tive·ly \-ntəvlē, -li\ *adv* **1 :** in a substantive manner **:** in substance **:** ESSENTIALLY **2 :** as a substantive ⟨the phrase is here used ~⟩

sub·stan·tive·ness \-ntivnəs, -ntēv-, -ntəv-\ *n* -ES **:** the quality or state of being substantive

substantive right *n* **:** a right (as of life, liberty, property, or reputation) held to exist for its own sake and to constitute part of the normal legal order of society — compare REMEDIAL RIGHT

sub·stan·tiv·i·ty \,səbztan·'tivəd·ē, -bst-\ *n* -ES **1 :** SUBSTANTIALITY **2 :** the attraction between a substance (as dye) in solution and a fiber — compare AFFINITY 2b

sub·stan·tiva·tion \,==(,)tivə'zāshən, səbz,tantəv-, -b,sta-, -,vī'z-\ *n* -s **:** an act or instance of substantivizing

sub·stan·tivize \'==ti,vīz, ='=tə,v-\ *or* **sub·stan·tize** \'==-,tīz\ *vt* -ED/-ING/-S [*substantivize* fr. ¹*substantive* + *-ize*; *substantize* fr. ¹*substantive* + *-ize*] **:** to convert into or use as a substantive ⟨an adjective can easily be *substantivized*⟩

sub·station \'səb+,-\ *n* [*sub-* + *station*] **:** a station subordinate or subsidiary to another station: as **a :** a station which is subsidiary to a central station and at which high-tension electricity from the central station is transformed to electricity lower in potential and converted if desired to continuous current or to alternating current of a different frequency **b :** a small post-office station (as a contract station in a drug store or a station set up at a convention for handling philatelic mail) **c :** a subordinate station that rebroadcasts messages from a primary station of a communication system

substellar point \¦səb+. . .-\ *n* [*substellar* fr. *sub-* + *stellar*] **:** the point on the earth's surface at which a particular star is in the zenith

sub·sternal \"+\ *adj* [ISV *sub-* + *sternal*] **:** situated or perceived beneath the sternum ⟨~ pain⟩

substile *var of* SUBSTYLE

sub·stit·u·end \səbz'tichə,wend, -b'st-\ *n* -s [NL *substituendum*] **:** something that can be or is substituted in a logical relation

sub·stit·u·en·dum \(,)=,=='wendəm\ *n, pl* **substituen·da** \-də\ [NL, fr. neut. of L *substituendus*, gerundive of *substituere* to substitute] **:** something that is to be substituted in a logical relation

¹sub·stit·u·ent \='==wənt\ *n* -s [L *substituent-*, *substituens*, pres. part. of *substituere* to substitute] **:** something that is or may be substituted; *usu* **:** an atom or group substituted for another or entering a molecule in place of some other part that is removed ⟨aniline derivatives containing an alkyl or halogen ~ —*Veterinary Bull.*⟩

²substituent \"\ *adj* **:** functioning as a substituent

sub·sti·tut·abil·i·ty \,səbztə,tüd·ə'biləd·ē, -bst-, -tə-,tyü-, -ütə-, -lətē, -i\ *n* **:** capacity for being substituted **:** the quality or state of being substitutable

sub·sti·tut·able \'==,==bəl\ *adj* **:** capable of being substituted or sometimes of substituting (as for one another)

¹sub·sti·tute \'səbztə,tüt, -bst-, -tə-,tyüt, *rapid often* -bz,t(y)üt *or* -b,st(y)-; *usu* -üd +V\ *n* -s [ME, fr. L *substitutus*, past part. of *substituere* to put under, put in the place of, substitute, fr. *sub-* + *-stituere* (fr. *statuere* to set, place, stand up) — more at STATUTE] **1 :** a person who takes the place of or acts instead of another: as **a :** an heir instituted under Roman, civil, or Scots law to succeed to property in case another heir named cannot or will not accept the succession **:** a conditionally appointed heir named to take possession in case another heir loses his ownership through default of some condition (as under a will or settlement) **b :** a person who enlists for military service in the place of a conscript or drafted man **2 :** something that is put in place of something else or is available for use instead of something else ⟨honey is an excellent ~ for sugar in many recipes⟩: as **a :** something cheaper or inferior that is used instead of a standard article ⟨margarine is not a ~ but a distinctive article⟩ ⟨use of galvanized iron as a ~ for lead in flashing⟩ **b :** an artificial product used to replace a natural ⟨a valuable milk ~ prepared from soybeans⟩ **c :** a word or grammatical feature that replaces another word, a phrase, or a clause, in a context ⟨a pronoun serves as a ~⟩ **3 a :** any of several connections used for joining oil-well appliances that are of different sizes or that have different joint details — called also *sub* **b :** a special tool or part used in place of a regular tool **syn** see RESOURCE

²substitute \"\ *vb* -ED/-ING/-S [L *substitutus*, past part. of *substituere* to substitute] *vt* **1 a :** to put in the place of another **:** EXCHANGE ⟨~ a new technique for the old one⟩ **b :** to introduce (as an atom or group) by substitution ⟨~ sulfur for oxygen in a molecule⟩ **2** *obs* **:** to invest with delegated authority **:** designate as a delegate **3 :** to replace with another ⟨~ yesterday's steady opinions with the latest fancies⟩ ⟨names like *Jane* are always *substituted* by the pronoun *she* —R.A.Hall b. 1911⟩ **4 :** to nominate (a person) to take a remainder — compare SUBSTITUTION 1a(3) ~ *vi* **:** to function, serve, or act as a substitute

³substitute \"\ *adj* [L *substitutus*, past part. of *substituere*] **1 :** serving as or fitted for use as a substitute ⟨a ~ food⟩ **2 :** involving the use of substitutes ⟨~ feeding of infants⟩

substitute broker *n* **:** a person making a profession of securing military substitutes esp. during the American Civil War

substituted *adj* [fr. past part. of ²*substitute*] **:** put in the place of another: as **a :** appointed by a person to take the place of himself or another or of something else and esp. to act in his own stead or to act on the happening of a particular event in the stead of another **:** appointed by substitution ⟨a ~ executor⟩ ⟨a ~ legacy⟩ **b :** having been subjected to a substitution reaction or having some of its parts replaced ⟨alcohol is a ~ water⟩ ⟨methylamine is a ~ ammonia⟩

substituted service *n* **:** the service of a legal writ, process, or summons otherwise than by personal service (as by leaving it at a defendant's place of business or residence or with his agent, by mail, or by publication)

substitute fiber *n* **:** a living parenchyma cell with the form of a fiber, simple pits, and relatively thick walls that occurs esp. in sapwood

sub·sti·tut·er \-üd·ə(r), -ütə-\ *n* -s **:** one that substitutes

sub·sti·tut·ibil·i·ty *n* -ES [by alter.] **:** SUBSTITUTABILITY

sub·sti·tu·tion \,səbztə'tüshən, -bst-, -tə-'tyü-\ *n* -s *often attrib* [ME *substitucion*, fr. MF *substitution*, fr. LL *substitution-*, *substitutio*, fr. L *substitutus* (past part. of *substituere* to substitute) + *-ion-*, *-io* -ion] **1 :** the substituting of one person or thing for another: as **a** *Roman law* (1) **:** the nomination of someone to be heir upon the failure of an heir previously named to take an inheritance — called also *common substitution*, *vulgar substitution* (2) **:** the similar nomination of a person to take as heir in place of or to succeed a descendant under puberty and in the potestas of the testator in case of the descendant's failure to take the inheritance or on his death before puberty or to succeed a descendant of any age who is a lunatic (3) **:** a designation by a testator that names one to whom property is to be handed over by the person named as heir or by his heir and that gives rise to a fideicommissum; *also* **:** a designation under civil law of a person to succeed to another as beneficiary of an estate used as a means of settling property and involving a fideicommissum **b :** the replacing of a quantity by its equal or of a variable by a value of it or of an algebraic expression or function by one that is equal in value **c** (1) **:** a chord that produces an unexpected or less likely resolution in place of a likelier resolution (2) **:** a change of fingers on a digital of a keyboard instrument **d :** a chemical reaction in which one or more atoms or groups in a molecule are replaced by equivalent atoms or groups to form at least two products; *esp* **:** the replacement of hydrogen in an organic compound by another element or group ⟨the ~ of one chlorine atom for one hydrogen atom of methane gives methyl chloride⟩ — often contrasted with *addition*; compare EXCHANGE 2e **e :** the replacing of a linguistic form by a substitute in a context **f** (1) **:** the replacing in Greek or Latin prosody of a foot required or expected at a given place in a given meter by another which is equivalent in temporal quantity (2) **:** the using in a metrical series in modern prosody of a foot other than the prevailing foot of the series or of a silence that replaces expected sound and occupies the time of a foot or syllable — compare INVERSION, IONIC DISPLACEMENT **g** (1) **:** the deceptive replacing of one material or product by another of less worth (2) **:** the natural economic tendency for the less costly of two or more operations or agencies to replace the more costly **h** (1) **:** the turning from an obstructed desire to another desire whose gratification is socially acceptable (2) **:** the turning from an obstructed form of behavior to a different and often more primitive expression of the same tendency ⟨a ~ neurosis⟩ (3) **:** the reacting to each of a set of stimuli by a response prescribed in a key ⟨a ~ test for speed of learning new responses⟩ **2 :** something that functions as a substitute or exists in a particular relation as a result of an act of substituting: as **a :** material substituted ⟨the ~ was found to be harmless⟩ **b :** a sound change consisting in the replacement or apparent replacement of one vowel or consonant by another **c :** an instance of linguistic substitution **d :** a cipher or method of ciphering that replaces message letters or polygraphs with substitutes

sub·sti·tu·tion·al \¦==(·)¦t(y)üshənᵊl, -shnəl\ *adj* **:** of, relating to, or constituting substitution — **sub·sti·tu·tion·al·ly** \-ᵊl¦ē, -əl|, |i\ *adv*

sub·sti·tu·tion·ary \-shə,nerē, -ri\ *adj* **:** of or relating to substitution **:** serving by way of a substitute **:** SUBSTITUTIONAL

substitution instance *n* **:** a statement in logic derived from a statement form by substitution of constants for variables

substitution rule *n* **:** a principle in logic specifying what expressions may be substituted for one another ⟨a *substitution rule* specifying that the definiendum may replace the definiens⟩

substitution tables *n pl* **:** tables of sentences in which equivalents may be substituted for their elements and which are used esp. in grammar drill

substitution vein *or* **substitution deposit** *n* **:** a metalliferous vein formed by the partial or complete substitution of the vein material for the original rock or mineral — called also *replacement vein*

sub·sti·tu·tive \'səbztə,tüd·|iv, -bst-, -tə-,tyü-, -üt|, |ēv *also* |əv\ *adj* [L *substitutus* (past part.) + E *-ive*] **:** tending to afford or furnish a substitute **:** suitable as a replacement **:** making or capable of substitution ⟨~ behavior⟩ — **sub·sti·tu·tive·ly** \|əvlē, -li\ *adv*

sub·story \¦səb +\ *n* [*sub-* + *story*] **:** a lower story; *specif* **:** a layer of forest growth that does not reach to the canopy ⟨a ~ of shrubby growth and young replacement⟩

sub·stract \səbz'trakt, -b'st-\ *vb* -ED/-ING/-S [LL *substractus*, past part. of *substrahere* to draw from beneath, withdraw, alter. (influenced by L *subs-*, var. of *sub-*) of L *subtrahere* — more at SUBTRACT] **:** SUBTRACT ⟨so far from adding to, it will ~ from, the quantity of labor necessary —Jeremy Bentham⟩

sub·strac·tion \-kshən\ *n* -s [ML *substraction-*, *substractio*, fr. LL *substractus* (past part.) + L *-ion-*, *-io* -ion] **1 :** SUBTRACTION ⟨rendering back to us with additions or ~*s*, the beauty which existing things have of themselves presented to him —Thomas Carlyle⟩ **2 :** secret misappropriation of property and esp. from a decedent's estate **:** EMBEZZLEMENT

sub·stratal \¦səb +\ *adj* [*substratum* + *-al*] **:** of or relating to a substrate or substratum **:** BASIC, UNDERLYING

¹sub·strate \'səbz,trāt, -b,st-\ *n* -s [ML *substratum*] **1 :** SUBSTRATUM **2 a :** ¹BASE 2b(1), CARRIER 9b **b :** the base on which an organism lives ⟨the soil is the ~ of most seed plants while rocks, soil, water, tissues, or other media are ~*s* for various other organisms⟩ **3 a :** a substance acted upon (as by an enzyme) ⟨an enzyme-*substrate* complex⟩ **b :** a source of reactive material (as a nutritive medium) ⟨cultures developing on a nutrient agar ~⟩

²substrate \"\ *adj* **:** of, relating to, forming, or taking place in a substrate; *sometimes* **:** BASIC, FUNDAMENTAL

sub·stra·tist \¦səbz¦trād·əst, -b¦st-\ *n* -s [*substratum* + *-ist*] **:** one that explains some feature of a language by reference to a substratum

sub·stra·tive \-ād·iv\ *adj* [*substratum* + *-ive*] **1 :** of, relating to, or constituting a substrate or substratum **2 :** UNDERLYING, FUNDAMENTAL

sub·stratose \¦səb+\ *adj* [*sub-* + *stratose*] **:** indistinctly or irregularly stratified

sub·stratosphere \"+\ *n* [ISV *sub-* + *stratosphere*] **:** the region of the atmosphere just below the stratosphere — **sub·stratospheric** \"+\ *adj*

sub·stratum \¦səb+\ *n, pl* **substrata** *also* **substratums** [ML, fr. neut. of L *substratus*, past part. of *substernere* to spread under, strew under, fr. *sub-* + *sternere* to strew — more at STREW] **:** something that is laid or spread under or that underlies and supports or forms a base for something else **:** an underlying structure, layer, or part **:** FOUNDATION: as **a** (1) **:** a permanent characterless support of properties of a thing or reality **:** substance as a support of attributes (2) **:** such a support regarded as a cause of a thing or its properties **b :** the material of which something is made and from which it derives its special qualities ⟨protoplasm is the material ~ of life⟩ **c :** a layer of rock or earth beneath the surface soil; *specif* **:** SUBSOIL **d :** SUBSTRATE 2, 3 **e :** a thin coating (as of hardened gelatin) on the support of a photographic film or plate to facilitate the adhesion of the sensitive emulsion **f :** a language that is extinct in a particular region but is believed by some linguists to have left traces of its structure in a current or more recently introduced language of that region as a result of imperfect learning of the introduced language by the native population

sub·striate \"+\ *adj* [*sub-* + *striate*] **:** marked indistinctly with striations

sub·struct \(¦)səbz¦trəkt, -b¦st-\ *vt* -ED/-ING/-S [L *substructus*, past part. of *substruere* to build beneath, fr. *sub-* + *struere* to arrange, build — more at STRUCTURE] **:** to build or lay beneath

sub·struc·tion \-kshən\ *n* -s [L *substruction-*, *substructio*, fr. *substructus* (past part.) + *-ion-*, *-io* -ion] **:** the underlying or supporting part of a fabrication (as a building or dam) — **sub·struc·tion·al** \-kshənᵊl, -shnəl\ *adj*

sub·structural \¦səb +\ *adj* **:** of, relating to, or constituting a substructure

sub·structure \"+\ *n* [*sub-* + *structure*] **:** UNDERSTRUCTURE, GROUNDWORK: as **a :** the foundation of a building or other structure **b :** the earth roadway supporting the ballast and track of a railway line

sub·stylar \"+\ *adj* **:** of or relating to the substyle

sub·style *or* **sub·stile** \'səbz,tīl, -b,st-\ *n* [*sub-* + *style* or obs. E *stile* style, fr. ME — more at STYLE] **:** a straight line on which the gnomon of a dial is erected and which constitutes the common section of the face of the dial and a plane perpendicular to it passing through the gnomon

sub·sulfate \¦səb+\ *n* [*sub-* + *sulfate*] **:** a basic sulfate

sub·sul·tive \səb'səltiv\ *adj* [L *subsultus* (past part. of *subsilire* to leap up) + E *-ive*] **:** SUBSULTORY

sub·sul·to·ry \-tərē\ *adj* [L *subsultus* (past part. of *subsilire* to leap up, fr. *sub-* up + *-silire*, fr. *salire* to leap) + E *-ory* — more at SUB-, SALLY] **:** involving irregularity of movement or advance **:** BOUNDING, LEAPING

sub·sum·able \(,)səb'süməbəl *sometimes* -b'zü-\ *adj* **:** capable of being subsumed

sub·sume \-m\ *vt* -ED/-ING/-S [*sub-* + L *sumere* to take up, take — more at RESUME] **1 :** to view, list, or rate as component in an overall or more comprehensive classification, summation, or synthesis **:** encompass as a part, example, or phase **:** classify as part of a larger schema or judge as a specific instance governed by a general principle ⟨Newtonian physics has not been overthrown so much as *subsumed* into a more embracing scheme —*Times Lit. Supp.*⟩ **2** *obs* **:** ASSUME, DEDUCE; *also* **:** to sum up **:** SUMMARIZE **syn** see INCLUDE

sub·summation *n* [irreg. (influence of *summation*) fr. *subsume* + *-ation*] **:** an act or product of subsuming

sub·summit \¦səb+\ *adj* [*sub-* + *summit*] **:** situated or occurring somewhat below an adjacent summit

sub·sump·tion \səb'səm(p)shən\ *n* -s [NL *subsumption-*, *subsumptio*, fr. *subsumptus* (past part. of *subsumere* to take under, subsume) + L *-ion-*, *-io* -ion] **1 :** the minor premise in the former syllogistic criminal procedure under Scots law containing an affirmation of the accused's guilt, a narrative of the material facts, or comparable matter **2 a :** something that is under the sumption of a presentation in formal logic **:** the minor premise of a syllogism **b :** something that is subsumed

⟨apprehension is a ~ under cognition⟩ **3 a :** the act or process of subsuming : a bringing under a major category **b :** the condition of something that is subsumed

sub·sump·tive \-(p)tiv\ *adj* : of, relating to, assuming the nature of, or containing a subsumption

sub·suretyship \¦səb+\ *n* [*sub-* + *suretyship*] : the relation between two or more sureties who are bound to answer for the same duty where one has the whole duty of performance with respect to the other

1sub·surface \"+\ *n* [*sub-* + *surface*] **1 :** soil situated just above the subsoil; *broadly* : rocks or other earth materials near but not exposed at the surface of the ground **2 :** the portion of a body of water that lies immediately below the surface

2subsurface \"\ *adj* **1 :** being, occurring, or used under a surface ⟨~ printing⟩ ⟨a ~ flow of water⟩ **2 :** of, relating to, or being something located or concealed beneath a surface (as of the ground) ⟨~ riches⟩

subsurface tillage *n* : a method of stirring the soil with underground blades that leave stubble or other vegetation on or near the surface — called also *subtillage*; compare TRASH FARMING

subsurface tiller *n* : an implement designed to loosen soil below the soil surface

sub·system \¦səb +\ *n* [*sub-* + *system*] : a secondary or subordinate system — **sub·systemic** \"+\ *adj*

sub·tack \'səb+,-\ *n* [*sub-* + *tack*] : a sublease under Scots law

sub·tangent \¦səb+\ *n* [*sub-* + *tangent*] : the projection on the x-axis of the portion of the tangent to a curve between the x-axis and the point of tangency

sub·tartarean \"+\ *adj* [*sub-* + *tartarean*] : being or living under Tartarus

sub·tectal \"+\ *adj* [*sub-* + L *tectum* roof (akin to L *tegere* to cover) + E *-al* — more at THATCH] : of, relating to, or being the alisphenoid bone in the skull of a fish

sub·teen \'=¦=\ *n* [*sub-* + *teen*] : a child approaching adolescence; *esp* : a girl under 13 years of age for whom clothing in the size range 8–14 is designed

sub·temperate \¦səb+\ *adj* [*sub-* + *temperate*] **1 :** slightly temperate : somewhat less than typically temperate ⟨a ~ climate⟩ **2 :** of or relating to the colder parts of the temperate zones

sub·tenancy \"+\ *n* : the quality or state of being a subtenant

sub·tenant \"+\ *n* [*sub-* + *tenant*] : one who rents something (as a tenement or land) of one who is himself a tenant in respect to the property in question

sub·tend \¦səb¦tend, ˌsəb't-\ *vt* -ED/-ING/-S [L *subtendere* to stretch beneath, fr. *sub-* + *tendere* to stretch — more at THIN] **1 a :** to be opposite to and extend from one side to the other of ⟨a hypotenuse ~*s* a right angle⟩ **b :** to fix the angular extent of with respect to a fixed point or object taken as the vertex ⟨the angle ~*ed* at the eye by an object of given width and a fixed distance away⟩ ⟨a central angle ~*ed* by an arc⟩ **c :** to determine the measure of by marking off the endpoints or boundary of ⟨a chord ~*s* an arc⟩ ⟨a coral atoll, circular in form, ~*ed* a shallow lagoon —J.A.Michener⟩ **2 a :** to underlie so as to include ⟨lesser loyalties which this supreme loyalty ~*s* —C.C. Morrison⟩ **b :** to occupy an adjacent and usu. lower position to and often so as to embrace or enclose ⟨a bract ~*ing* a flower⟩

subtense \-n(t)s\ *adj* [L *subtensus*, past part. of *subtendere* to stretch beneath] : of, relating to, or constituting an object (as a pole or rod of known length) used to ascertain a distance without actual measurement by observing the subtended angle from a given point ⟨~ method⟩ ⟨~ transit⟩

sub·tentorial \¦səb+\ *adj* [*sub-* + *tentorial*] : situated or occurring under the tentorium ⟨a ~ tumor⟩

sub·tenure \"+\ *n* [*sub-* + *tenure*] : the tenure of a subtenant

sub·terete \"+\ *adj* [*sub-* + *terete*] : not precisely cylindrical : nearly terete

sub·ter·fuge \'səbtə(r),fyüj\ *n* -S [LL *subterfugium*, fr. L *subterfugere* to run away secretly, fr. *subter-* (fr. *subter*, adv. & prep., secretly, under) + *fugere* to run away; akin to L *sub*, prep., under, below, up — more at UP, FUGITIVE] **1 a :** deception by artifice or stratagem to conceal, escape, avoid, or evade ⟨employing ~ to get her own way⟩ **b :** a deceptive device or stratagem ⟨malingering or some other ~ is resorted to in order to save face —H.G.Armstrong⟩ **2** *obs* : a place of retreat or concealment : REFUGE **syn** see DECEPTION

sub·terminal \¦səb+\ *adj* [*sub-* + *terminal*] : situated or occurring near but not precisely at an end ⟨a ~ collapse⟩ ⟨a ~ band of color on the tail feathers⟩

1sub·ter·rane \¦səbtə¦rān\ *adj* [L *subterraneus*] : SUBTERRANEAN

2subterrane \"\ *or* **subterrain** \"\ *n* -S [L *subterraneum* subterranean place, fr. neut. of *subterraneus* subterranean] **1 :** the bedrock or the rocks beneath a particular geological formation **2 :** SUBTERRANEAN

1sub·ter·ra·nean \-nēən, -nyən\ *or* **sub·ter·ra·ne·ous** \-nēəs\ *adj* [*subterranean* fr. L *subterraneus* underground, subterranean + E *-an; subterraneous* fr. L *subterraneus*, fr. *sub-* + *-terraneus* (fr. *terra* ground, earth + *-aneus*, fr. *-anus* -an) — more at TERRACE] **1 :** being or lying under the surface of the earth : situated in the earth or underground ⟨~ springs⟩ — opposed to *surficial* **2 a :** functioning, operating, or suitable for operating beneath the surface of the earth **b :** existing or working in secret : HIDDEN — **sub·ter·ra·nean·ly** *adv*

2subterranean \"\ *n* -S [L *subterraneus* + E *-an* (n. suffix)] **1 :** one who lives, develops, or works underground **2 :** an underground cave or room : CAVERN

subterranean caterpillar *n* : any of various large grayish black caterpillars that are larvae of moths of the genus *Oxycanus*, live in burrows in the ground, and emerge at night to feed on the foliage of pasture plants (as grass) — see PORINA

subterranean clover *n* : a low-growing spreading and branching annual clover (*Trifolium subterraneum*) prob. native to the Mediterranean region, valued for pasturage esp. in Australia and in parts of No. America, and burying the ripening seed heads in the soil like the peanut

sub·ter·rene \¦səbtə¦rēn\ *adj or n* [L *subterrenus*, fr. *sub-* + *terrenus* of earth, earthly, fr. *terra* earth] : SUBTERRANEAN

1sub·terrestrial \¦səb +\ *adj* [*sub-* + *terrestrial*] : SUBTERRANEAN

2subterrestrial \"\ *n* : one (as an animal) that lives underground

sub·tertian malaria \"+. . .-\ *n* [*subtertian* fr. *sub-* + *tertian*] : FALCIPARUM MALARIA

sub·tetanic \¦səb+\ *adj* [*sub-* + *tetanic*] : of less than tetanic force : approaching tetany or tetanus and esp. in form or degree of contraction ⟨a ~ convulsion⟩

sub·thalamic \"+\ *adj* [*sub-* + *thalamic*] **1 :** situated below the thalamus **2** [NL *subthalamus* + E *-ic*] : of or relating to the subthalamus ⟨a ~ nucleus⟩

sub·thalamus \"+\ *n* [NL, fr. *sub-* + *thalamus*] : the ventral part of the thalamus

sub·thoracic \"+\ *adj* [ISV *sub-* + *thoracic*] *of the ventral fins of some fishes* : situated not quite far enough forward to be thoracic

sub·threshold \"+\ *adj* [*sub-* + *threshold*] : inadequate to produce a response ⟨~ dosage with a drug⟩ ⟨a ~ stimulus⟩

sub·ti·a·ba \ˌsübtē'äbə\ *n, pl* **subtiaba** *or* **subtiabas** *usu cap* **1 a :** an Indian people of western Nicaragua **b :** a member of such people **2 :** a Supanecan language of the Subtiaba people

sub·tile \'səd·ᵊl, -ə(b)tᵊl,-əbtəl\ *adj, sometimes* **subtiler** \-əd·ᵊlə(r), -ət(ᵊ)lə-, -btᵊlə-, -btələ-\ *sometimes* **subtilest** \-əd·ᵊləst, -ət(ᵊ)lə-, -əbtᵊlə-, -əbtələ-\ [ME *subtile, subtil*, fr. MF *subtil*, alter. (influenced by L *subtilis* fine, thin, subtle) of OF *soutil, sotil* subtle — more at SUBTLE] **1 :** SUBTLE: as **a :** of a delicate or tenuous nature : ELUSIVE ⟨a ~ aroma⟩ ⟨the ~ threads of life —D.L.Sharp⟩ **b :** marked by craft or cunning : ARTFUL, WILY ⟨fishing . . . is made the ~ excuse for getting away again for a day among the plants —*Amer. Botanist*⟩ **2 a :** keenly perceptive ⟨a ~ sense⟩ **b :** keenly felt or perceived ⟨a ~ joy⟩ — **sub·tile·ly** \-əd·ᵊl¦ē, -ət(ᵊ)l¦, -əbtᵊl¦, -əbtəl¦, ¦i\ *adv*

sub·ti·lin \'səbtələn\ *n* -S [*subtil-* (fr. NL *subtilis*, — specific epithet of *Bacillus subtilis* — fr. L, thin, fine, minute) + *-in*] : a polypeptide antibiotic or mixture of antibiotics that is similar to bacitracin and is produced by a soil bacterium (*Bacillus subtilis*)

sub·til·ist \'səd·ᵊləst, 'sə(b)tᵊl-, 'səbtəl-\ *n* -S [*subtile* + *-ist*] : one given to subtlety

sub·til·i·ty \ˌsəb'tiləd·ē, -lətē, -i\ *n* -ES [ME *subtilite*, fr. MF *subtilité*, alter. (influenced by L *subtilis*) of *sutilté, soutilleté* — more at SUBTLETY] **1 :** SUBTLETY **2 :** something that is subtile or subtle

sub·til·iza·tion \ˌsəd·ᵊlə'zāshən, ˌsə(b)tᵊl-, ˌsəbtəl-, -ᵊlˌī'z-, -əˌlī'z-\ *n* -S : an act or instance or the practice of subtilizing : SUBTLETY

sub·til·ize \'səd·ᵊlˌīz, 'sə(b)tᵊlˌīz, 'səbtəˌlīz\ *vb* -ED/-ING/-S *see -ize in Explan Notes* [ML *subtilizare*, fr. L *subtilis* fine, thin, subtle + LL *-izare* -ize] *vt* : to make subtile: as **a :** RAREFY, REFINE, SUBLIMATE, EXALT **b :** to clarify and sharpen (as the mind or senses) : make keen **c :** to treat with subtlety : introduce fine-drawn or nice distinctions into the use, discussion, or interpretation of ⟨~ words⟩ ⟨*subtilized* his activities⟩ ~ *vi* : to use subtlety : analyze, argue, or deal with materials in a subtle fashion ⟨*subtilized* more than other poets⟩

sub·til·iz·er \-zə(r)\ *n* -S : one that subtilizes

sub·till \'səb¦til\ *vb* [*sub-* + *till*] *vt* : to practice subsurface tillage on ~ *vi* : to practice subsurface tillage

sub·till·age \-lij\ *n* [*sub-* + *tillage*] : SUBSURFACE TILLAGE

sub·til·ty *like* SUBTILETY\ *n* -ES [ME *subtiltee*, alter. (influenced by L *subtilis*) of *sutilte* subtlety — more at SUBTLETY] : subtlety or an instance of it

1sub·title \'səb+¦-\ *n* [*sub-* + *title*] **1 a :** a secondary title ⟨in *Uncle Tom's Cabin, or Life Among the Lowly* the ~ is *Life Among the Lowly*⟩ — called also *alternative title* **b :** an explanatory title ⟨in *The Behavior of Organisms; an Experimental Analysis* the ~ is *an Experimental Analysis*⟩ **2 a :** a printed translation of foreign language dialogue appearing near the bottom of the screen of a motion picture **b :** a printed statement or fragment of dialogue appearing between the scenes of a silent motion picture

2subtitle \"\ *vt* : to give a subtitle to

sub·titular \¦səb+\ *adj* [fr. *subtitle*, after E *title: titular*] : of, relating to, or being a subtitle

sub·tle \'səd·ᵊl, 'sətᵊl\ *adj* **subtler** \-d·ᵊlə(r), -t(ᵊ)lə-\ **subtlest** \-d·ᵊləst, -t(ᵊ)lə-\ [ME *sutil, sotil*, fr. OF *soutil, sotil*, fr. L *subtilis* finely woven, fine, thin, refined, keen, subtle, fr. *sub-* + *-tilis* (fr. *tela* web); akin to L *texere* to weave — more at TECHNICAL] **1 a :** DELICATE, ELUSIVE ⟨~ aroma of sandalwood⟩ ⟨~ lights and shadows⟩ ⟨fawn fled with shy and ~ steps —Elinor Wylie⟩ **b :** difficult to understand : OBSCURE ⟨found the . . . situation ~, not to say opaque —Ruth McKenney⟩ **c :** hard to distinguish or describe : IMPERCEPTIBLE, INTANGIBLE ⟨~ distinctions among consonants⟩ ⟨intuitions . . . too ~ to be formulated —B.N.Cardozo⟩ ⟨~ hints of impending disaster —Leland Miles⟩ **2 a :** PERCEPTIVE, REFINED ⟨a great artist's ~ vision —Herbert Read⟩ ⟨China's complex and ~ language —*Time*⟩ **b :** marked by insight or sensitivity ⟨~ music⟩ ⟨a ~ characterization⟩ ⟨~ proportions of the Parthenon⟩ **3 a** (1) : SKILLFUL, INGENIOUS ⟨a clever and ~ diplomat —Charlton Laird⟩ (2) : demanding skill or ingenuity ⟨as ~ as the delicate incision of a great surgeon —Ezra Pound⟩ **b :** characterized by craft or indirection : DEVIOUS, WILY ⟨a ~ scheme⟩ ⟨~ diplomacy and wary tactics —Arnold Bennett⟩ **c :** having a covert and usu. injurious effect : INSIDIOUS ⟨a ~ insinuation⟩ ⟨a ~ technique of infiltration —C.E.Black & E.C. Helmreich⟩ — **subtleness** \-d·ᵊlnəs, -tᵊl-\ *n* -ES

sub·tle·ty \'səd·ᵊltē, 'sətᵊl-, -ᵊlti\ *n* -ES [ME *sutilte, sotilte*, fr. OF *sutilté, soutilleté, sutilitet*, fr. L *subtilitat-, subtilitas*, fr. *subtilis* fine, subtle + *-itat-, -itas* -ity] **1 :** the quality or state of being subtle: as **a :** the quality of being tenuous, intangible, indefinable, abstruse, or remote **b :** mental acuteness or penetrativeness : the power or practice of drawing delicate distinctions; *also* : the quality in a mental operation or its product that results from such power **2 :** something that emanates from a subtle person or mind: as **a :** a fine-drawn or delicate distinction : a refinement of analysis, perception, or comprehension ⟨avoid *subtleties* in a popular discussion⟩ **b :** an ingenious contrivance; *esp* : a decorative and sometimes edible confection made in an ornamental design **c :** an instance of craft or guile ⟨the *subtleties* of a twisted mind⟩ **3 :** something that is subtle and esp. tenuous, impalpable, or difficult to perceive or trace

sub·tly *also* **sub·tle·ly** \'səd·ᵊl¦ē, 'sət(ᵊ)l¦, ¦i\ *adv* [ME *sutelly, sotily, sotilich*, fr. *sutil, sotil* subtle + *-ly, -lich* -ly] : in a subtle manner : with subtlety : so as to be subtle

1subtone \'səb+,-\ *n* [*sub-* + *tone*] : UNDERTONE

2subtone \"\ *adj* : relating to or constituting clarinet playing esp. of popular music in which the tones are played very softly and usu. in the lower register with little wind pressure from the player

sub·tonic \¦səb+\ *n* [*sub-* + *tonic*] : the seventh degree of the musical scale

sub·torrid \"+\ *adj* [*sub-* + *torrid*] : SUBTROPICAL

1sub·total \"+\ *adj* [*sub-* + *total*] : somewhat less than complete : nearly total ⟨~ removal of the thyroid gland⟩ — **sub·totally** \"+\ *adv*

2subtotal \"\ *n* [*sub-* + *total* (n.)] : the sum of part of a series of figures

3subtotal \"\ *vt* : to determine a subtotal for ⟨~*ing* each column⟩ ~ *vi* : to determine subtotals

sub·tract \səb'trakt\ *vb* -ED/-ING/-S [L *subtractus*, past part. of *subtrahere* to draw from beneath, withdraw, fr. *sub-* + *trahere* to pull, draw — more at TRACE] *vt* **1** *archaic* : to withdraw or take away orig. by stealth : WITHHOLD; *also* : to take away (common land) by enclosing **2** *archaic* : to remove (as oneself) from some specified situation : take elsewhere **3 :** to take away (as a part, a quantity, or a number) by deducting — used with *from* or *out of* ⟨~ 5 from 9⟩; compare SUBTRACTION c ~ *vi* : to perform a subtraction : calculate by subtraction

sub·tract·er \-ktə(r)\ *n* -S : one that subtracts

sub·trac·tion \-kshən\ *n* -S [ME *subtraccion*, fr. LL *subtraction-, subtractio*, fr. L *subtractus* (past part. of *subtrahere*) + *-ion-, -io* -ion] : an act, operation, or instance of subtracting: as **a :** the withdrawing or withholding from one a right (as customary services, fealty, rents, suit and service, conjugal rights, and tithes) to which he is entitled **b :** a process of logical abstraction whereby one class is excepted from another in which it is naturally included or a connotation is withdrawn from another connotation which includes it **c :** a mathematical process in which one number or quantity is deducted from another and which can be generalized by the formula $m-s=r$ in which the remainder r when added to the subtrahend s always reproduces the minuend m : the inverse of addition — **sub·trac·tion·al** \-kshənᵊl, -kshnəl\ *adj*

subtraction sign *or* **subtraction mark** *n* : a mathematical symbol used to indicate that a particular quantity is to be subtracted from another to which it is joined by the symbol : a symbolic representation of the relation of subtrahend and minuend — symbol −

sub·trac·tive \-ktiv, -ktēv *also* -ktəv\ *adj* **1 :** tending to subtract : constituting or involving subtraction ⟨a ~ error in spelling⟩ ⟨a ~ correction⟩ **2 :** formed by absorption of light passing through component colorants in turn — see SUBTRACTIVE PRIMARY **3 a :** being or relating to a process of reducing each of the densities of a photographic image by an approximately constant amount **b :** of or relating to the controlled mixing or superposition of several colored substances (as dyes or pigments) that selectively absorb and transmit or reflect light to form a colored positive photographic image ⟨a ~ process⟩ — compare ADDITIVE 5 — **sub·trac·tive·ly** \-ktəvlē, -li\ *adv*

subtractive primary *n* : one of a set of colorants comprising red, yellow, and blue or more exactly magenta, yellow, and cyan each of which is capable of absorbing from the spectrum of incident daylight some part that the others would reflect and which are therefore combinable to produce a maximum number of object colors — compare ADDITIVE PRIMARY

sub·tra·hend \'səbtrəˌhend\ *n* -S [L *subtrahendum*, neut. of *subtrahendus*, gerundive of *subtrahere* to withdraw] : a quantity that is to be deducted from a minuend in the mathematical operation of subtraction

sub·translucent \¦səb+\ *adj* [*sub-* + *translucent*] : translucent only at the edges ⟨~ minerals⟩

sub·transparent \"+\ *adj* [*sub-* + *transparent*] : imperfectly or partially transparent : SEMITRANSPARENT

sub·treasurer \"+\ *n* [*sub-* + *treasurer*] : a subordinate treasurer; *specif* : an assistant treasurer of the U. S. formerly in charge of a subtreasury

sub·treasury \"+\ *n* [*sub-* + *treasury*] : a subordinate treasury or place of deposit; *specif* : any of nine former branch treasuries of the U. S.

sub·triangular \"+\ *adj* [NL *subtriangularis*, fr. L *sub-* + LL *triangularis* triangular — more at TRIANGULAR] : nearly but not quite triangular ⟨a ~ skull⟩

sub·tribe \'səb+,-\ *n* [*sub-* + *tribe*] **1 :** a subdivision of a tribe **2 :** a small or subordinate tribe

1sub·tropical *also* **sub·tropic** \"+\ *adj* [ISV *sub-* + *tropical* or *tropic*] **1 :** nearly tropical : of, relating to, or being the regions bordering on the tropical zone **2** *of a plant* : requiring climatic conditions typical of subtropical regions to survive ⟨even near the equator vegetation at 5000 feet is ~ rather than tropical⟩

2subtropical \"\ *n* : a plant requiring a subtropical environment to thrive

sub·tropics \¦səb+\ *n pl* [*sub-* + *tropics*] : subtropical regions

sub·truncate \"+\ *adj* [*sub-* + *truncate*] : nearly but not quite truncate ⟨a ~ fin⟩

sub·tu·ber·ant \¦səb¦t(y)üb(ə)rənt\ *adj* [*sub-* + *-tuberant* (as in *protuberant*)] : of, relating to, or being a mountain supposedly formed by the lifting action of underlying intrusive igneous rock

sub·type \'səb+,-\ *n* [*sub-* + *type*] : a type that is subordinate to or included in another type ⟨the blood group ~*s*⟩

sub·typical \¦səb+\ *adj* [*sub-* + *typical*] **1 :** of or relating to a subtype **2 :** deviating somewhat from a type

subu·late \'sübyələt, 'səb-, -əˌlāt\ *adj* [NL *subulatus*, fr. L *subula* awl + *-atus* -ate; akin to OHG *siula* awl, OSlav *šilo* awl, L *suere* to sew — more at SEW] : linear and tapering to a fine point ⟨a ~ leaf⟩

subu·li·corn \-ˌləˌkȯrn\ *adj* [ISV *subuli-* (fr. L *subula* awl) + *-corn*] : having or being subulate antennae

subu·lu·ra \ˌ=='lu̇rə\ *n, cap* [NL, fr. L *subula* awl + NL *-ura*] : a genus of nematode worms (family Heterakidae) including a common parasite (*S. brumpti*) of the ceca of gallinaceous birds

sub·umbonal \¦səb+\ *adj* [*sub-* + *umbonal*] : situated beneath or forward of the umbones of a bivalve shell

sub·umbrella \"+\ *n* [*sub-* + *umbrella*] : the concave undersurface of the bell-shaped or disk-shaped body of a jellyfish — **sub·umbrellar** \"+\ *adj*

sub·ungual \"+\ *also* **sub·un·gui·al** \"+¦əŋgwēəl\ *adj* [*subungual* ISV *sub-* + *ungual; subunguial* alter. (influenced by L *unguis* nail, claw) of ISV *subungual* — more at NAIL] : situated under a nail, hoof, or claw ⟨a ~ abscess⟩

sub·ungulata \¦səb+\ *n pl, cap* [NL, fr. *sub-* + *Ungulata*] *in some classifications* : a major division of Eutheria comprising the mammalian orders Hyracoidea, Proboscidea, and sometimes Sirenia together with a variable group of extinct forms — **sub·ungulate** \"+\ *adj or n*

sub·unit \"+\ *n* [*sub-* + *unit*] : a secondary or subordinate unit : a unit that forms a discrete part of a more comprehensive unit

1sub·urb \'səˌbərb, -ˌbə̄b, -ˌbəib *sometimes* -ˌbə(r)b\ *n* -S [ME, fr. L *suburbium*, fr. *sub-* under, near + *urb-, urbs* city — more at SUB-] **1 a :** an outlying part of a city or town : a smaller place adjacent to or sometimes within commuting distance of a city ⟨the Connecticut shore has become a ~ of New York City⟩ **b suburbs** *pl* : the residential area on the outskirts of any city or large town — used with *the* ⟨live in the ~*s*⟩ **2 suburbs** *pl* : the near vicinity : PERIPHERY, ENVIRONS ⟨carries them to the brink of rebirth and the ~*s* of destruction —R.P. Blackmur⟩

2suburb \"\ *adj* **1 :** SUBURBAN **2** *obs* **a :** of or characteristic of life in the suburbs of the City of London in the 16th and 17th centuries **b :** LOOSE, DISSOLUTE

1sub·ur·ban \sə'bər¦bən, -'bə̄¦, -'bəi¦\ *adj* [L *suburbanus*, fr. *sub-* + *urb-, urbs* city + *-anus* -an] **1 :** of, relating to, inhabiting, or located in the suburbs ⟨a ~ home⟩ **2 :** characteristic of life in the suburbs: as **a** *obs* : SUBURB 2, DISSOLUTE **b :** lacking in finish or elegance : PROVINCIAL **c :** blending or characterized by the blending of the urban and rural ⟨~ recreation⟩

2suburban \"\ *n* -S **1 :** a dweller in the suburbs : SUBURBANITE **2 :** STATION WAGON

sub·ur·ban·ite \¦bəˌnīt, *usu* -īd·+V\ *n* -S : a dweller in the suburbs

sub·ur·ban·iza·tion \səˌbərbənə'zāshən, -ˌbə̄b-, -ˌbəib-, -ˌnī'z-\ *n* -S : the quality or state of being suburbanized

sub·ur·ban·ize \='==ˌnīz\ *vt* -ED/-ING/-S : to make suburban : give a suburban character to ⟨*suburbanizing* the untamed places —Wilfred Thesiger⟩

sub·ur·ban·ly *adv* : so as to be suburban

sub·urbed *pronunc at* 1SUBURB +d\ *adj* : having a suburb

sub·ur·bia \sə'bərbēə, -'bə̄b-,-'bəib-\ *n* -S [1*suburb* + *-ia*] **1 :** the suburbs of a city **2 a :** suburbanites as a distinctive social element **b :** the manners, styles, and customs typical of suburban life

sub·ur·bi·car·i·an \¦səˌbərbə¦ka(a)rēən\ *adj* [LL *suburbicarius* (fr. L *sub-* + LL *urbicarius* of the city, fr. L *urbicus* of the city — fr. *urb-, urbs* city + *-icus* -ic — + *-arius* -ary) + E *-an*] : being in the suburbs or near the city : of or relating to the suburbs ⟨one of the ~ dioceses surrounding the city of Rome⟩

sub·vaginal \¦səb+\ *adj* [*sub-* + *vaginal*] : situated under or inside a sheath

sub·valuation \"+\ *n* [*sub-* + *valuation*] : a secondary or subordinate valuation; *specif* : a valuation under Scots law of the teinds made by the subcommissioners and validated only through confirmation by the High Commission or since 1707 by the Teind Court

sub·varietal \"+\ *adj* [*subvariety* + *-al*] **1 :** of or relating to a subvariety ⟨a ~ character⟩ **2** [*sub-* + *varietal*] : of less than varietal significance ⟨~ variations⟩

sub·variety \"+\ *n* [*sub-* + *variety*] : a minor variety or strain in a more general one : a subdivision (as a strain or line) of a variety

sub·vassal \"+\ *n* -S : a person who is a vassal of a vassal

1sub·ven·tion \səb'venchən\ *n* -S [ME *subvencioun* state subsidy, fr. MF *subvention*, fr. LL *subvention-, subventio* act of giving aid, assistance, fr. L *subventus* (past part. of *subvenire* to come to help), fr. *sub-* up + *venire* to come) + *-ion-, -io* -ion — more at SUB-, COME] **1 :** a providing of assistance or support; *esp* : the granting of financial aid (as to an undertaking) **2 :** aid and esp. pecuniary aid granted either to an individual or an organization: as **a :** ENDOWMENT **b :** a subsidy from a government or foundation

2subvention \"\ *vt* -ED/-ING/-S : to provide with a subvention : support by means of subventions : SUBSIDIZE

sub·ven·tion·ize \-chəˌnīz\ *vt* -ED/-ING/-S : SUBVENTION

sub·verbal \¦səb+\ *adj* [*sub-* + *verbal*] : NONVERBAL

sub·ver·sion \səb'vər¦zhən, -və̄¦, -vəi¦ *also* ¦sh- *sometimes* ˌsəb'v- *or chiefly in rapid speech* ˌsə'v-\ *n* -S [ME *subversioun*, fr. MF *subversion*, fr. LL *subversion-, subversio*, fr. L *subversus* (past part. of *subvertere* to overturn, overthrow) + *-ion-, -io* -ion] **1 :** the act of subverting or state of being subverted : overthrow from the foundation : DESTRUCTION ⟨~ of a government⟩ **2** *obs* : a cause of overthrow or destruction

sub·ver·sion·ary \¦zhəˌnerē, ¦sh-, -ri\ *adj* : SUBVERSIVE

1sub·ver·sive \¦s¦iv, ¦ēv *also* ¦z¦ *or* ¦əv\ *adj* [L *subversus* (past. part. of *subvertere*) + E *-ive*] : tending to subvert : having a tendency to overthrow, upset, or destroy ⟨hypocrisy is a vice ~ of manhood⟩; *esp* : intended to cause the overthrow of a government by unlawful means — **sub·ver·sive·ly** \¦əvlē, -li\ *adv* — **sub·ver·sive·ness** \¦ivnəs, ¦ēv- *also* ¦əv-\ *n* -ES

2subversive \"\ *n* -S : a person engaged in subversive activities or planning or attempting to subvert legally constituted authority esp. by the employment of unconstitutional means

sub·ver·siv·ism \-ˌvizəm\ *n* -S : the quality or state of being subversive

sub·vert \səb'vər¦t, -və̄¦, -vəi¦ *sometimes* ˌsəb'v- *or chiefly in rapid speech* ˌsə'v-; *usu* ¦d·+V\ *vb* [ME *subverten*, fr. MF *subvertir*, fr. OF, fr. L *subvertere* to turn upside down, overturn, overthrow, fr. *sub-* down, under + *vertere* to turn — more at WORTH] *vt* **1 :** to overturn or overthrow from or as if from a foundation : ruin utterly : RAZE, DEMOLISH ⟨who . . . labor to ~ these great pillars of human happiness —George Washington⟩ **2 :** to pervert or corrupt (a person) by an undermining of morals, allegiance, or faith : ALIENATE ⟨propaganda that ~*s* foreign-born citizens⟩ **3 a :** to bring to nothing, destroy, or greatly impair the existence, sovereignty, influence, wholeness of esp. by insidious undermining ⟨tear down our free institutions and ~ our form of government into a tyranny —*New Republic*) **b :** to make invalid or futile **:** CONFUTE, DEFEAT ⟨amorous sweet things, enough to make one fancy the adage ~*ed* that stolen fruits are sweetest —George Meredith⟩ **~ *vi* :** to overthrow something completely **:** DESTROY, OVERTURN **syn** see OVERTURN

sub·vert·er \|d·ə(r), |tə-\ *n* -s **:** one that subverts

sub·vert·ible \|d·əbəl, |təb-\ *adj* **:** capable of being subverted

sub·vertical \ˌsəb+\ *adj* [*sub-* + *vertical*] **:** nearly but not quite vertical

sub·visible \"+\ *adj* [*sub-* + *visible*] **:** invisible unless magnified

sub·vitreous \"+\ *adj* [*sub-* + *vitreous*] **:** not quite vitreous

sub·vocal \"+\ *adj* [*sub-* + *vocal*] **:** characterized by the occurrence in the mind of words in speech order with or without inaudible articulation of the speech organs ⟨thinking is ~ talking⟩ — **sub·vocally** \"+\ *adv*

sub·vo·la \ˈsəbˌvōlə, ˈsəbvələ\ *n* [NL, fr. L *sub-* + *vola* hollow of the hand, palm, sole] **1 :** the interval between the second and fifth fingers **2 :** the hypothenar eminence

sub·water \ˈsəb+\ *vt* [*sub-* + *water*] **:** to furnish water to (plants) below the surface of the ground so that the water rises about the roots by capillary attraction **:** SUBIRRIGATE

¹sub·way \ˈsəbˌwā\ *n* [*sub-* + *way*] **1 :** an underground way or gallery: as **a :** a passage under a street (as for pedestrians, electric cables, water mains) **b :** a usu. electric railway built partly or entirely underground and usu. for local transit in metropolitan areas **c :** UNDERPASS **2 :** a subway train ⟨the ~ pounds along over a steel viaduct —Blake Ehrlich⟩

²subway \"\ *vi* -ED/-ING/-S **:** to travel by subway

sub·weight \ˈsəb+,-\ *n* [*sub-* + *weight*] **:** a section of an assembled weight (as a unit of an elevator counterweight)

sub·xerophilous \ˌsəb+\ *adj* [*sub-* + *xerophilous*] *of a plant* **:** preferring but not confined to a dry habitat

sub–zero \"+\ *adj* **1 :** registering less than zero on some scale, esp. Fahrenheit ⟨*sub-zero* temperatures⟩ **2 :** characterized by or suitable for sub-zero temperature ⟨*sub-zero* weather⟩ ⟨*sub-zero* clothing⟩

sub·zone \ˈsəb+,-\ *n* [*sub-* + *zone*] **:** a subdivision of a zone **:** a secondary or subordinate zone

suc *abbr* **1** succeeded **2** successor **3** suction

succ *abbr* **1** succeeded **2** successor

suc·cade \(ˌ)səˈkād\ *n* -s [ME *socade*, fr. MF *succade*, *sucrade* sweet, candied fruit, succade, fr. OProv *sucrado*, adj., sweet, sugary, sugared, fr. past part. of *sucra* to sugar, fr. *sucre* sugar, fr. OIt *zucchero* — more at SUGAR] **:** a preserve or confection made from fruit **:** preserved or crystallized fruit

succah *var of* SUKKAH

suc·ce·da·ne·ous \ˌsəksəˈdānēəs\ *adj* [L *succedaneus*, fr. *succedere* to succeed] **:** of, relating to, or serving as a succedaneum **:** SUBSTITUTED

suc·ce·da·ne·um \-ˌ==ˈ=nēəm\ *n*, *pl* **succedaneums** \-ēəmz\ *or* **succeda·nea** \-ēə\ [NL, fr. neut. of L *succedaneus*] **1 :** one that succeeds to the place of another **:** SUBSTITUTE **2** *obs* **:** REMEDY, MEDICINE

suc·ce·dent \səkˈsēdᵊnt\ *adj* [L *succedent-*, *succedens*, pres. part. of *succedere* to succeed] **1 :** SUCCEEDING, SUBSEQUENT **2 :** of or relating to the 2d, 5th, 8th, and 11th mundane houses

suc·ceed \səkˈsēd *sometimes* sik-\ *vb* -ED/-ING/-S [ME *succeden*, fr. L *succedere* to go up, follow after, follow, succeed, fr. *sub-* up, after + *cedere* to go, proceed, yield — more at SUB-, CEDE] *vi* **1 a :** to come next after or replace another in an office, position, or role or in possession of an estate **:** fill a vacancy in an inherited, elective, or appointive position ⟨upon the death of his father he ~*ed* to a considerable fortune and to his father's position as rector —J.D.Wade⟩; *specif* **:** to inherit sovereignty, rank, or title ⟨upon the death of the president the vice-president would ~⟩ ⟨an instructor in biology . . . before ~*ing* to the chairmanship of the department of biology —*Current Biog.*⟩ **b :** to follow or take place after another esp. in a natural, prescribed, or necessary order, course of events, or development ⟨one idea would ~ to another with a rush —Osbert Sitwell⟩ ⟨slate has ~*ed* to thatch, and brick to timber —T.B.Macaulay⟩ ⟨the ~*ing* fifteen years . . . were uneventful —J.C.Fitzpatrick⟩ **2 a :** to turn out well **:** result favorably according to plans or desires ⟨the formula and ingredients that finally ~*ed* remain the top company secrets —*Monsanto Mag.*⟩ **b :** to attain a desired object or end **:** accomplish what is attempted or intended **:** be successful ⟨~*ed* in regaining the offensive after a smashing defeat —*Reporter*⟩ ⟨mental abilities high enough to enable them to ~ in college —*Clearing House*⟩ **c :** to attain or be in a thriving, prosperous, or popular state ⟨will produce high quality grapes for wine on gravels where hardly any other crop will ~ —G.G.Weigend⟩ ⟨~*s* with our public —E.R. Bentley⟩ **3** *obs* **:** to turn out **:** RESULT, EVENTUATE ⟨whether the manner of their operation would ~ contrary —Richard Waller⟩ **4** *obs* **:** APPROACH ⟨will you to the cooler cave ~ —John Dryden⟩ **5** *obs* **:** to become the property of a person through inheritance **:** DESCEND ⟨a ring . . . that downward hath ~*ed* in his house from son to son —Shak.⟩ **~ *vt* 1 a :** to be the event or thing immediately following on or one of the events or things following upon in an ordered sequence or chain of events ⟨simplicity of concept ~*s* complexity of calculation —E.T.Bell⟩ ⟨the past is merely a series of messes, ~*ing* one another by discoverable laws —E.M.Forster⟩ ⟨the cathedral ~*ed* a frame building —*Amer. Guide Series: Ark.*⟩ **b :** to come after or follow in an office, position, role, or title **:** fill a vacancy as heir or elected or appointed successor to ⟨~*ed* her father as keeper of the lighthouse —*Amer. Guide Series: R.I.*⟩ **2** *obs* **:** to fall heir to **:** INHERIT **3** *obs* **:** to follow the example of ⟨~ thy father in manners as in shape —Shak.⟩ **4 :** to make successful **:** cause to prosper

syn SUCCEED, PROSPER, THRIVE, and FLOURISH can mean in common to attain the desired end, or increase or enlarge in that attainment. SUCCEED means to gain one's purpose ⟨*succeed* in passing a civil service examination⟩ ⟨*succeed* in business⟩ ⟨*succeed* in becoming president⟩ ⟨this government *succeeded* for seventy years —J.P.Boyd⟩ PROSPER implies continued success ⟨if a genuine democratic revolution should *prosper* —H.N.Brailsford⟩ ⟨education *prospers* by economy —R.W.Livingstone⟩ ⟨the oyster-fishing industry that *prospered* here in the middle-nineteenth century —*Amer. Guide Series: N.Y. City*⟩ THRIVE adds to PROSPER the idea of vigorous growth ⟨dictatorship *thrives* on poverty and war *thrives* on dictatorship —*New Republic*⟩ ⟨the era in which most American firms were born and *thrived* —C.F.Robinson⟩ ⟨the lumber industry *throve* during the boom days by meeting the needs of rush building —*Amer. Guide Series: Texas*⟩ FLOURISH suggests a thriving or prospering, esp. during a period when the thing is at the peak of its development or productivity ⟨if physics and chemistry and biology have *flourished*, morals, religion, and aesthetics have withered —J.W.Krutch⟩ ⟨three expensive but *flourishing* weeklies devoted to absolutely nothing but the life of the rich and the titled —Aldous Huxley⟩ ⟨the demagogue *flourishes* most luxuriantly where negligence is flagrant and the abuse of power is arrogant —A.W.Long⟩ **syn** see in addition FOLLOW

suc·ceed·er \-də(r)\ *n* -s [ME, fr. *succeden* to succeed + *-er*] *archaic* **:** SUCCESSOR

succeeding *n* -s [ME *succeding*, fr. gerund of *succeden* to succeed] *obs* **:** CONSEQUENCE, RESULT

suc·cent \səkˈsent\ *vb* -ED/-ING/-S [back-formation fr. *succentor*] *vt* **:** to sing the close or second part of (a verse) esp. in responsive singing **~ *vi* :** to act as succentor

suc·cen·tor \-tə(r)\ *n* -s [LL, leader, succentor, fr. L *succentus* (past part. of *succinere* to sing to, sing after, fr. *sub-* to, after + *canere* to sing) + *-or* — more at SUB-, CHANT] **1 :** one that succents **2 :** a precentor's deputy or assistant esp. in a monastery or cathedral

suc·cen·tu·ri·ate \ˌsəkˌsenˈt(y)u̇rēət, -ēˌāt\ *adj* [L *succenturiatus*, past part. of *succenturiare* to recruit into a Roman century, fr. *sub-* + *centuriare* to divide into hundreds — more at CENTURIATE] **:** SUPPLEMENTAL, ACCESSORY ⟨a ~ placental lobe⟩

suc·cès de scan·dale \səkˌsādəˌskäⁿˈdäl\ *n* [F, lit., success of scandal] **:** the reception accorded a work of art that wins popularity or notoriety because of the scandalous nature of its contents or of its relation to a scandal ⟨so antireligious and sacrilegious that they . . . achieved a tumultuous *succès de scandale* —H.E.Clurman⟩ ⟨a *succès de scandale* won by its anecdotes about the members of the . . . aristocracy —Anthony West⟩

suc·cès d'es·time \-ādeˈstēm\ *n*, *pl* **succès d'estime** [F, lit., success of esteem] **:** the reception accorded a work of art that wins critical respect but not popular success ⟨the satirical comedies which had brought him a small amount of money and a large *succès d'estime* —*Atlantic*⟩

succès fou \-āˈfü\ *n* [F, lit., mad success] **:** an extraordinary success ⟨the performance . . . according to one of the more ecstatic members of the entertainment committee . . . was a *succès fou* —Cornelia O. Skinner⟩

suc·cess \səkˈses *also* sik-\ *n* -ES [L *successus*, fr. *successus*, past part. of *succedere* to follow, succeed — more at SUCCEED] **1** *obs* **:** something that ensues **:** OUTCOME, CONSEQUENCE, ISSUE ⟨what is the ~ —Shak.⟩ **2** *obs* **a :** COURSE, SEQUENCE, SUCCESSION **b :** a group that proceeds in temporal sequence; *specif* **:** LINEAGE **3 a :** the degree or measure of attaining a desired end **:** kind of fortune ⟨the poor ~ of the book disgusted him —Aldous Huxley⟩ ⟨the ~ of the performance is judged by its volume and enthusiasm —*Amer. Guide Series: Fla.*⟩ **b :** a succeeding fully or in accordance with one's desires **:** favorable termination of a venture ⟨I believe very little in the fortune . . . to which men attribute their ~*es* and reverses —George Meredith⟩ ⟨in pursuing this task she had, at first, cheering hopes of ~ —Matthew Arnold⟩; *specif* **:** the attainment of wealth, position, esteem, favor, or eminence ⟨the first book has been published and had a great ~ —L.L. Day⟩ **4 a :** a person achieving success ⟨as a dance student . . . was . . . an immediate ~ —*Current Biog.*⟩ ⟨a ~ as a rich man's wife —Pearl Buck⟩ **b :** an undertaking that succeeds or confers success ⟨the play was an immediate ~⟩ ⟨a remarkable series of ~*es* in experimentation⟩

suc·cess·ful \-esfəl\ *adj* **1 :** resulting or terminating in success **:** having the desired effect ⟨a ~ experiment⟩ **2 :** gaining or having gained success; *esp* **:** having attained wealth, position, or fame ⟨a ~ writer⟩ ⟨a ~ banker⟩ **3** *of a plant or animal group* **:** represented by diverse forms and occupying a wide variety of ecological niches — **suc·cess·ful·ly** \-fəlē, -li\ *adv* — **suc·cess·ful·ness** *n* -ES

suc·ces·sion \səkˈseshən *also* sik-\ *n* -s [ME, fr. MF or L; MF, fr. L *succession-*, *successio*, fr. *successus* (past part. of *succedere* to follow, succeed) + *-ion-*, *-io* -ion] **1 a :** the order in which or the conditions under which one person after another succeeds to a property, dignity, title, or throne — compare APOSTOLIC SUCCESSION **b :** the right of a person or line to succeed **c :** the line having such a right **2 a :** the act or process of following in order of time or place **:** a repeated following up of one by another **:** SEQUENCE **b** (1) **:** the change in legal relations by which one person comes into the enjoyment of or becomes responsible for one or more of the rights or liabilities of another person ⟨a son's ~ to the estate of his father⟩ ⟨the ~ of one king to another⟩ **:** the act or process of one person's taking the place of another in the enjoyment of or liability for his rights or duties or both; *also* **:** the right or duty to take another's place by succession or the rights and duties succeeded to — see SINGULAR SUCCESSION, UNIVERSAL SUCCESSION (2) **:** the act or process of a person's becoming beneficially entitled to a property or property interest of a deceased person whether by operation of law upon his dying intestate or by testamentary disposition **c :** the whole estate of a deceased including all assets and all liabilities **d :** the action or process of one state taking over or following upon another and becoming entitled to the former's rights and position in international law **e :** the continuance of corporate personality ⟨a corporation which has unlimited ~⟩ **f :** change in the composition of an ecosystem as the available competing organisms and esp. the plants respond to and modify the environment esp. when leading to some relatively stable community structure ⟨the highlights of the ~ were the weed, grass, and forest communities, developed in that order⟩ **g :** the process of change in an inhabited area through invasion by a different human population group or through a different utilization of real estate ⟨the ~ from residence to business in an urban district⟩ **3 a :** a series of descendants, heirs, successors, or members of a dynasty following by right and in order from an initial member ⟨for him and for his ~ granted . . . a tribute —Shak.⟩ ⟨had no antecedent and no fit ~ —Henry Adams⟩ **b** *obs* (1) **:** a group of people of somewhat homogeneous age succeeded to their ancestors **:** GENERATION (2) **:** succeeding generations **:** POSTERITY **c :** a number of persons or things that follow each other in sequence **:** a continuous and uninterrupted series ⟨preserved . . . by a ~ of private owners —C.P.Fitzgerald⟩ ⟨a ~ of rooms, one after the other, extending over a great length —*Amer. Guide Series: La.*⟩ **d :** a group, type, or series that succeeds or displaces another; *specif* **:** an inclusive stratigraphic sequence involving any number of stages, series, or systems, or parts thereof

suc·ces·sion·al \-shənᵊl, -shnəl\ *adj* **1 :** of, relating to, or forming part of a succession ⟨~ forest⟩ **2 :** in a regular order **:** CONSECUTIVE — **suc·ces·sion·al·ly** \-ᵊlē, -əl|, |i\ *adv*

successional speciation *n* **:** gradual evolution from and replacement of one species by another

succession duty *n*, *chiefly Brit* **:** INHERITANCE TAX 1

suc·ces·sion·ist \-sh(ə)nəst\ *n* -s **:** one who upholds the validity and necessity of the apostolic succession

succession of crops 1 : sustained seasonal production of a particular crop either by repeated sowings or by selecting varieties maturing at different times **2 :** the culture of two or more short-life crops planted in turn

succession state *n* **:** one of a number of states that succeed a former state in sovereignty over a certain territory

succession tax *n* **1 :** ESTATE TAX **2 :** INHERITANCE TAX 1

suc·ces·sive \səkˈsesiv, -esēv *also* sik- *or* -esəv\ *adj* [ME, fr. ML *successivus*, fr. L *successus* (past part. of *succedere* to follow, succeed) + *-ivus* -ive] **1** *obs* **a :** inherited or capable of being inherited by succession **:** descending or transmissible to the next in a succession **:** HEREDITARY **b :** inheriting by succession **c :** being the next to inherit **2 a :** following in succession or serial order **:** following one upon another **:** coming in order **:** CONSECUTIVE ⟨their fourth ~ victory⟩ ⟨the product of the ~ labors of innumerable men —Lewis Mumford⟩ **b :** being a successor or one of a group of consecutive successors to a person, thing, or item ⟨the idea of a world order, ~ to both the pagan and the Christian —Paul Rosenfeld⟩ ⟨the book . . . was followed by many ~ editions —J.T.Howard⟩ **c :** characterized by or manifesting succession **:** produced or arranged in succession ⟨the angles between ~ points may be measured —R.E.Davis⟩ — **suc·ces·sive·ly** \-ivlē, -li\ *adv* — **suc·ces·sive·ness** \-esivnəs, -esēv- *also* -esəv-\ *n* -ES

suc·ces·siv·i·ty \(ˌ)səkˌseˈsivəd·ē\ *n* -ES **:** the quality or fact of being successive **:** successive development

suc·cess·less \səkˈsesləs *also* sik-\ *adj* **:** being without success **:** UNSUCCESSFUL — **suc·cess·less·ly** *adv* — **suc·cess·less·ness** *n* -ES

success line *n* **:** LINE OF THE SUN

suc·ces·sor \səkˈsesə(r) *also* sik-, *archaic* ˈsəksəˌsō(ə)r\ *n* -s [ME *successour*, fr. OF, fr. L *successor*, fr. *successus* (past part. of *succedere* to follow, succeed) + *-or* — more at SUCCEED] **:** one that follows; *esp* **:** a person who succeeds to a throne, title, or estate or is elected or appointed to an office, dignity, or other position vacated by another

suc·ces·sor·ship \-ˌship\ *n* **:** the quality or state of being a successor

successor state *n* **:** SUCCESSION STATE

success story *n* **:** a real or fictitious narrative of a poor or unknown person who rises to fortune, acclaim, or brilliant achievement

succi *pl of* SUCCUS

succin- *or* **succino-** *comb form* [L *succin-*, *sucin-*, fr. *succinum*, *sucinum* amber] **1 :** amber ⟨*succinic* (acid)⟩ ⟨*succinite*⟩ ⟨*succiniferous*⟩ **2 :** succinic acid ⟨*succinamide*⟩ ⟨*succinonitrile*⟩

suc·cin·a·mate \(ˌ)səkˈsinəˌmāt; ˌsəksəˈnamət, -aˌmāt\ *n* -s [*succinamic* + *-ate*] **:** a salt or ester of succinamic acid

suc·ci·nam·ic acid \ˌsəksəˈnamik-\ *n* [*succinamide* + *-ic*] **:** a crystalline compound $H_2NCOCH_2CH_2COOH$ that is the half amide of succinic acid

suc·cin·a·mide \(ˌ)səkˈsinəˌmīd; ˌsəksəˈnaməd, -aˌmīd\ *n* [ISV *succin-* + *amide*] **:** a crystalline compound $H_2NCOCH_2CH_2CONH_2$ that is the amide of succinic acid

suc·ci·nate \ˈsəksəˌnāt\ *n* -s [ISV *succin-* + *-ate*] **:** a salt or ester of succinic acid

suc·cin·chlorimide \ˌsəksən+\ *n* [*succin-* + *chlorimide*] **:** a crystalline compound $C_2H_4(CO)_2NCl$ that has an odor like that of chlorine and is used as a disinfectant and chlorinating agent; *N*-chloro-succinimide — not used systematically

suc·cinct \səkˈsiŋ(k)t *also* ˌsəkˈsi- *or* ÷ səˈsi- *or* ÷ ˌsəˈsi-\ *adj*, *often* -ER/-EST [ME, fr. L *succinctus*, past part. of *succingere* to gird from below, tuck up, gird about, fr. *sub-* under, up + *cingere* to gird — more at SUB-, CINCTURE] **1 a** *archaic* **:** encircled with or as with a girdle **b** *archaic* **:** adorned, wrapped, or bound up by a girdle **c :** supported by a band of silk around the middle ⟨the ~ pupa of a butterfly⟩ **2 a :** marked by brief and compact expression or by extreme compression and lack of unnecessary words and details ⟨the displacement of the long-drawn-out epic similes by pithy and ~ comparisons —J.L. Lowes⟩ **b :** brief to the point of curtness ⟨a very ~ refusal⟩ **3 :** lacking fullness in cut **:** CLOSE-FITTING ⟨~ little nipped-in suits —Lois Long⟩ **syn** see CONCISE

suc·cinct·ly \-ŋ(k)tlē, -ŋklē, -li\ *adv* **:** in a succinct manner **:** with concise and precise brevity

suc·cinct·ness \-ŋtnəs, -ŋkn-\ *n* -ES **:** the quality or state of being succinct

succinctorium *var of* SUBCINCTORIUM

suc·cin·ea \(ˌ)səkˈsinēə\ *n*, *cap* [NL, fem. of L *succineus* of amber, fr. *succinum* amber; fr. the color of the shell] **:** a cosmopolitan genus (the type of a family Succineidae) of amphibious or terrestrial pulmonate snails

suc·ci·ne·idae \ˌsəksəˈnēəˌdē\ *n pl*, *cap* [NL, fr. *Succinea*, type genus + *-idae*] **:** a family of small often amber-colored snails (suborder Stylommatophora) that comprises the amber shells — see SUCCINEA

suc·cin·ic acid \(ˌ)səkˈsinik-\ *n* [F *succinique*, fr. *succin-* + *-ique*] **:** a crystalline dicarboxylic acid $HOOCCH_2CH_2COOH$ that occurs widely both free and combined (as in amber, lignite, turpentine oils, and animal fluids), that is formed in the Krebs cycle and in various fermentation processes, that is usu. made by hydrogenation of maleic acid or fumaric acid, and that is used chiefly as an intermediate (as for pharmaceuticals and synthetic resins); butane-dioic acid — compare MALIC ACID

succinic anhydride *n* **:** a crystalline cyclic compound $C_2H_4(CO)_2O$ obtained by dehydration of succinic acid and used similarly as an intermediate

succinic dehydrogenase *n* **:** an iron-containing flavoprotein enzyme that catalyzes often reversibly the dehydrogenation of succinate to fumarate in the presence of a hydrogen acceptor (as a phenazine dye) and that is widely distributed esp. in animal tissues, bacteria, and yeast — see SUCCINOXIDASE

succinic oxidase *n* **:** SUCCINOXIDASE

suc·ci·nif·er·ous \ˌsəksəˈnif(ə)rəs\ *adj* [*succin-* + *-iferous*] **:** yielding amber

suc·cin·i·mide \(ˌ)səkˈsinəˌmīd; ˌsəksəˈniˌmīd, -məd\ *n* [ISV *succin-* + *imide*] **:** a crystalline cyclic imide $C_2H_4(CO)_2NH$ obtainable (as by heating with ammonia) from succinic acid or succinic anhydride

suc·ci·nite \ˈsəksəˌnīt\ *n* -s [in sense 1, fr. F, fr. *succin-* + *-ite*; in sense 2, fr. G *succinit*, fr. *succin-* + *-it* -ite] **1 :** amber-colored grossularite **2 :** AMBER

succino- — see SUCCIN-

suc·cin·oxidase \ˌsəksən+\ *n* [*succin-* + *oxidase*] **:** the entire complex system containing succinic dehydrogenase and cytochromes that catalyzes the reaction between succinate ion and molecular oxygen with the formation of fumarate ion ⟨in rat liver cells, ~ activity is associated with the mitochondria, and in heart muscle it is localized in particles . . . that correspond cytologically to the mitochondria of other tissues —J.S.Fruton & Sofia Simmonds⟩

suc·ci·nyl \ˈsəksənᵊl, -ˌnil\ *n* -s [ISV *succin-* + *-yl*] **1 :** the bivalent radical $-OC(CH_2)_2CO-$ of succinic acid **2 :** the univalent radical $HOOC(CH_2)_2CO-$ of succinic acid — not used systematically

suc·ci·nyl·choline \ˌ==(ˌ)=+\ *n* [*succinyl* + *choline*] **:** a basic compound that has an action like that of curare and that is administered intravenously chiefly in the form of its crystalline dihydrochloride $C_{14}H_{30}Cl_2N_2O_4.2H_2O$ as a skeletal relaxant in surgery

suc·ci·nyl·sulfathiazole \"+\ *n* [*succinyl* + *sulfathiazole*] **:** a crystalline sulfa drug $C_{13}H_{13}N_3O_5S_2$ used esp. for treating gastrointestinal infections

suc·ci·sa \səkˈsīsə, -īzə\ *n*, *cap* [NL, fr. fem. of L *succissus*, past part. of *succidere* to cut from below, fr. *sub-* + *-cidere* (fr. *caedere* to cut) — more at CONCISE] **:** a genus of European herbs (family Dipsacaceae) differing from the closely related *Scabiosa* chiefly in having the scales of the receptacle as long as the flowers — see BLUE SCABIOUS

suc·civ·o·rous \(ˌ)səkˈsivərəs\ *adj* [ISV *succi-* (fr. L *succus*, *sucus* juice, sap) + *-vorous* — more at SUCCULENT] **:** PHYTOSUCCIVOROUS

¹suc·cor \ˈsəkə(r)\ *n* -s *see -or in Explan Notes* [ME *succur*, *sucur*, *socur*, fr. earlier *sucurs*, *socours*, taken as pl., fr. OF *secors*, *sucors*, fr. ML *succursus*, fr. L, past part. of *succurrere* to run up, run to help] **1 a :** relief from difficulty, want, or distress **:** AID, HELP, ASSISTANCE **b :** something that furnishes relief ⟨religion was their chief ~ —*Time*⟩ **c** *or* **succors** *pl* **:** military assistance in supplies and esp. men **:** REINFORCEMENTS ⟨can no longer draw ~ from this ally —Matthew Arnold⟩ ⟨the inconsiderable ~*s* . . . were easily intercepted —Edward Gibbon⟩ **2** *chiefly dial* **:** a sheltered place **:** a building used as a shelter **:** REFUGE

²succor \"\ *vt* -ED/-ING/-S *see -or in Explan Notes* [ME *sucuren*, *soucouren*, fr. OF *secorir*, *sucurir*, fr. L *succurrere* to run up, run to help, help, fr. *sub-* up + *currere* to run — more at SUB-, CURRENT] **1 :** to go to the aid of (one in difficulty, want, or distress) **:** HELP; *specif* **:** to provide with reinforcements or supplies **:** RELIEVE ⟨an escort vessel . . . sent to ~ four vessels . . . under attack by submarine —E.L.Beach⟩ **2 :** to cure, alleviate, or mitigate ⟨attempts to ~ the various distresses of these people —Jerome Stone⟩ **3** *chiefly dial* **:** to provide a shelter for

suc·cor·ance \-rən(t)s\ *n* -s [¹*succor* + *-ance*] **:** DEPENDENCE

suc·cor·er \-rə(r)\ *n* -s [ME *socourer*, fr. MF *secoreor*, *sucureor*, fr. OF, fr. *secorir*, *sucurir* to help + *-eor* -or] **:** one that succors

suc·cor·rhea *or* **suc·cor·rhoea** \ˌsəkəˈrēə\ *n* -s [NL, fr. *succo-* (fr. L *succus*, *sucus* juice, sap) + *-rrhea*, *-rrhoea* — more at SUCCULENT] **:** excessive flow of a juice or secretion

suc·co·ry \ˈsəkərē\ *n* -ES [alter. (prob. influenced by MD *suckereie* succory, modif. — influenced by MD *suker* sugar — of *cichorei*, fr. MF *cichorée*) of ME *cicoree* — more at SUIKERBOS, CHICORY] **1 :** CHICORY 1; *broadly* **:** a plant of the genus *Cichorium* **2 :** any of various composite plants other than the chicory — used in combination; see BLUE SUCCORY, GUM SUCCORY, LAMB SUCCORY

succory blue *n* **:** CHICORY 3

suc·co·tash \ˈsəkəˌtash, -taa(ə)sh, -taish\ *n* -ES [of Algonquian origin; akin to Narraganset *msakwataš* something broken into pieces (as corn from the cob), succotash, Natick *msakutahas*] **1 :** a mixture of lima beans or shell beans and kernels of green corn cooked together **2 :** a mixture of two grain crops (as oats and barley) sown together

¹succoth *or* **succot** *or* **succos** *pl of* SUCCAH

²succoth *or* **succot** *or* **succos** *cap*, *var of* SUKKOTH

suc·cu·ba \ˈsəkyəbə\ *n*, *pl* **succu·bae** \-ˌbē\ [LL, prostitute] **:** SUCCUBUS

suc·cu·bous \ˈsəkyəbəs\ *adj* [L *succubare* to lie under + E *-ous*] **1** *of leaves* **:** being so arranged that the posterior margin of each overlaps the anterior margin of the next older **2 :** having succubous leaves ⟨~ liverworts⟩ — compare INCUBOUS

suc·cu·bus \ˈsəkyəbəs\ *n*, *pl* **succu·bi** \-ˌbī\ [ME, fr. ML, alter. (influenced by LL *incubus*) of LL *succuba* prostitute, lit., one who lies under, fr. L *succubare* to lie under, fr. *sub-* + *cubare* to lie down — more at HIP] **1 :** a demon assuming female form to have sexual intercourse with men in their sleep — compare INCUBUS **2 :** DEMON, FIEND **3 :** STRUMPET, WHORE

suc·cu·lence \ˈsəkyələn(t)s\ *n* -s [F, prob. fr. (assumed) NL *succulentia*, fr. L *succulentus* succulent + *-ia* -y] **1 :** the quality or condition of being succulent **:** JUICINESS **2 :** fresh or juicy food of wild or cultivated plant origin ⟨fodder should contain some ~⟩; *also* **:** SILAGE

suc·cu·len·cy \-nsē,-nsi\ *n* -ES [prob. fr. (assumed) NL *succulentia*] : SUCCULENCE

1suc·cu·lent \-nt\ *adj* [L *succulentus, suculentus*, fr. *succus, sucus* juice, sap; akin to L *sugere* to suck — more at SUCK] **1 a** : full of juice : JUICY ⟨roasted ~ fresh meat —Charles Rawlings⟩ **b** *of a plant* : having fleshy and juicy tissues **2** : full of vitality, freshness, or richness — **suc·cu·lent·ly** *adv*

2succulent \"\ *n* -S **1** : a succulent plant (as a cactus) **2 succulents** *pl* : SUCCULENCE 2

succulent feed *n* : SUCCULENCE 2

suc·cu·lom·e·ter \ˌsəkyəˈlämədˌə(r)\ *n* [*succulence* + *-o-* + *-meter*] : an instrument for measuring the moisture content of a fresh or processed vegetable product (as an ear of corn)

suc·cumb \səˈkəm\ *vi* -ED/-ING/-S [F & L; F *succomber*, fr. L *succumbere* to fall down, yield, fr. *sub-* + *-cumbere* to lie down (akin to L *cubare* to lie down) — more at HIP] **1** : to yield and cease to resist or contend before a superior strength, overpowering appeal or desire, or inexorable force ⟨~*ed* to her drowsiness —Willa Cather⟩ ⟨the free economic system ~*ed* to the strains of war —C.E.Black & E.C.Helmreich⟩ **2** : to cease to exist : DIE ⟨disease ravaged the voyagers, more than half of whom ~*ed* —*Amer. Guide Series: N.C.*⟩ ⟨590 businesses ~*ed* —*Dun's Rev.*⟩ **syn** see YIELD

suc·cum·bence \səˈkəmbən(t)s\ *or* **succumbency** \-nsē\ *n, pl* **succumbences** *or* **succumbencies** [*succumbence* fr. *succumb* + *-ence*; *succumbency* prob. fr. ML *succumbentia* failure in a cause, fr. L *succumbent-, succumbens* (pres. part. of *succumbere*) + *-ia* -y] : the act or process of succumbing

1suc·cur·sal \səˈkərsəl\ *adj* [F *succursale*, fr. ML *succursus* assistance, help + F *-ale* (fem. of *-al*) — more at SUCCOR] : of the nature of a branch or offshoot : SUBSIDIARY, AUXILIARY ⟨a ~ church of a cathedral⟩ ⟨a ~ bank⟩

2succursal \"\ *also* **suc·cur·sale** \"\ *n* -S [F *succursale*, fr. *succursale*, adj., succursal] : a succursal institution (as a dependent monastery or a branch of a business)

suc·cus \ˈsəkəs\ *n, pl* **suc·ci** \ˈsəˌkī, ˈsəkˌsī\ [L — more at SUCCULENT] : JUICE; *specif* : expressed juice (as of a fruit) for medicinal use

succus en·ter·i·cus \-ˌenˈterəkəs\ *n* [NL, intestinal juice] : a fluid that is secreted in small quantity by Lieberkühn's glands of the small intestine, is highly variable in constitution, and typically contains various enzymes (as erepsin, lipase, and lactose), enterokinase, mucus, salts, and water

suc·cus·sa·to·ry \səˈkəsəˌtōrē\ *adj* [obs. E *succussation* shaking, succussion (fr. ML *succussation-, succussatio*, fr. L *succussatus* — past part. of *succussare*, freq. of *succutire* to throw up from below — + *-ion-, -io* -ion) + E *-ory*] : characterized by up-and-down vibrations of short amplitude — used of an earthquake; compare SUSSULTATORY

suc·cus·sion \səˈkəshən\ *n* -S [L *succussion-, succussio*, fr. *succussus* (past part. of *succutere* to throw up from below, fling up, fr. *sub-* up + *quatere* to shake) + *-ion-, -io* -ion — more at SUB-, QUASH] : the action or process of shaking or the condition of being shaken esp. with violence: **a** : a shaking of the body to ascertain if fluid is present in a cavity and esp. in the thorax **b** : the splashing sound made by succussion

suc·cus·sive \-ˈkəsiv\ *adj* [L *succussus* (past part. of *succutere*) + E *-ive*] : SUCCUSSATORY

1such \(ˈ)səch, (ˌ)sich (*i is less frequent when stress is primary*), *chiefly dial* (ˈ)sech\ *adj* [ME *such, swuch, swulch, swilch*, fr. OE *swelc, swilc, swylc*; akin to OHG *sulih, solih* such, ON *slíkr*, Goth *swaleiks*; all fr. a prehistoric Gmc compound whose first and second constituents respectively are represented by OE *swā* so and by OE *gelīc* like — more at SO, LIKE] **1 a** : of a kind or character about to be indicated, suggested, or exemplified ⟨will do ~ things as counsel an immigrant on buying a second-hand car —Robert Crichton⟩ ⟨a bag ~ as a doctor carries⟩ ⟨coarse fish, ~ as carp, catfish, and the like —Alexander MacDonald⟩ **b** : having a quality to a degree to be indicated ⟨his joy at seeing her was ~ that he wept —Henry La Cossitt⟩ ⟨had organized with ~ success that after four years of operation he was able to retire —Frank Monaghan⟩ **2 a** : having a quality already or just specified — used to avoid repetition of a descriptive term ⟨never to accept a thing as true unless it appears to me clearly and evidently to be ~ —R.B.Sewall⟩ **b** : of this or that character, quality, or extent : of the sort or degree previously indicated or implied ⟨had snorted with disdain at ~ vulgarity —C.S.Forester⟩ ⟨were rejoicing over ~ plenty of water —Henry Lapham⟩ ⟨by ~ a rigorous process of natural selection, those that reach maturity are tough —H.L.Hoskins⟩ **c** : previously characterized or specified : AFOREMENTIONED ⟨to take possession . . . of any horse for any of the purposes aforesaid and to detain ~ horse —*Australian Jockey Club*⟩ **3** : of so extreme a degree or quality ⟨this is ~ nonsense⟩ ⟨I never ate ~ food before⟩ ⟨I've never seen ~ a crowd⟩ ⟨~ a day⟩ **4** : not conspicuous of its kind : neither better nor worse : MEDIOCRE ⟨the meal, ~ as it was, was served quickly⟩ ⟨the house, ~ as it is, is at your disposal⟩ **5** : of the same class, type, or sort : in the same category : SIMILAR ⟨established twenty ~ libraries in the colonies —G.H.Doane⟩ ⟨in all ~ matters . . . developed an extraordinary efficiency —F.J. Mather⟩ **6** : such and such ⟨a simple matter to report that these films were shown in ~ a place to so many people —Cecile Starr⟩

2such \"\ *pron* [ME *such, swilch*, fr. OE *swelc, swilc*, fr. *swelc, swilc*, adj.] **1** : such a person or thing or such persons or things ⟨the father of ~ as dwell in tents —Gen 4:20 (AV)⟩ ⟨a general philosophy of life, if it may be called ~ —T.S.Eliot⟩ **2** : someone or something that has been or is being stated, implied, or exemplified ⟨~ was the result of his efforts⟩ ⟨if ~ is the decision, nothing further should be done⟩ ⟨~ is life⟩ **3** : someone or something similar : a person or thing of the same kind ⟨regarded a little water coloring and ~ as a polite accomplishment —Alfred Werner⟩ ⟨ship . . . planes and munitions and ~ in return for raw materials —*New Republic*⟩ — **as such** \ˈaz-ˌsəch, əzˈs-\ *adv* : in itself ⟨*as such* the gift was worth little⟩

3such \"\ *adv* [ME *such, swilch*, fr. OE *swelce, swilce*, fr. *swelc, swilc*, adj.] **1 a** : to such a degree : SO ⟨I have never seen ~ tall buildings⟩ ⟨~ a fine person⟩ **b** : ESPECIALLY, VERY ⟨physically, he was not in ~ good shape —Jay Leyda⟩ ⟨hasn't been in ~ good spirits the last few days⟩ **2** : in such a way ⟨the light is refracted ~ that the point of light appears as a streak —H.G. Armstrong⟩

1such and such *pron* [ME] : something not specified or not requiring to be specified ⟨made him lay himself out to prove that *such and such* is the true view of the facts —*Notes & Queries*⟩ ⟨showed very clearly that *such and such* was often true —K.A.Menninger⟩

2such and such *adj* : not specifically mentioned or designated : not yet specified : not requiring specification now ⟨what we have objectively before us is *such and such* a race or group of people —A.L.Kroeber⟩

such a one *pron* [ME *such an on*] **1** : one of this or that kind : one of a specified or understood kind ⟨he knows who is a likely witch and takes *such a one* in hand by commonsense methods —W.W.Howells⟩ **2 a** : one of a kind to be indicated or specified ⟨*such a one* as may be found in any small town⟩ **b** : one of the same kind ⟨just *such a one* as his father⟩ **3** *archaic* : someone not named ⟨telling you then . . . that *such a one* and *such a one* were past cure —Shak.⟩

1suchlike \ˈ=,=\ *adj* [ME, fr. *1such* + *like*] : of like kind : SIMILAR ⟨a locker which normally held stationery, ink, and ~ equipment for writing —William McFee⟩

2suchlike \"\ *pron* [ME, fr. *1suchlike*] **1** : persons or things of the same kind or of similar character ⟨waiters, kitchen hands and ~ —*Times Lit. Supp.*⟩ ⟨gorgeously colored feminine finery — gowns and ~ —Haldane Macfall⟩ **2** : someone or something of the same sort : a similar person or thing ⟨less often a nobleman than a tramp or ~ —C.W.Cunnington⟩

such·ness *n* -ES **1** : the quality or state of being such : essential or characteristic quality ⟨without any apparent regard to the ~ of her environment, she sat down —J.D.Salinger⟩ **2** *Buddhism* : nameless and characterless reality in its ultimate nature — called also *tathata, thusness*

1suchow *usu cap, var of* SOOCHOW

2su·chow \ˈsüˌchau̇, -üˈjō\ *adj, usu cap* [fr. *Suchow*, China] **1** : of or from the city of Suchow in Shantung province, China : of the kind or style prevalent in Suchow **2** : IPIN

suchwise \ˈ=,=\ *adv* [ME] *archaic* : in such a manner : SO

1suck \ˈsək\ *vb* -ED/-ING/-S [ME *soken, souken*, fr. OE *sūcan*; akin to OHG *sūgan* to suck, ON *sūga*, L *sugere* to suck, MBret *sunaff* juice, Gk *hyei* it is raining, Lith *sunkti* to filter, ooze, Toch B *swese* rain] *vt* **1 a** (1) : to draw (a liquid) into the mouth by a partial vacuum caused by motion of the mouth; *specif* : to draw (milk) from a breast or udder by motion of the mouth or lips (2) : to draw or remove by application of the tongue or lips : LICK, LAP ⟨~ food particles from the tongue⟩ (3) : to draw by or as if by a vacuum created by application of the mouth to a tube ⟨~ the membrane from the throat, using a tube —Morris Fishbein⟩ ⟨the bee that ~*s* from mountain heath her honey —William Wordsworth⟩ (4) : to draw by or as if by suction, absorption, inhalation ⟨a vacuum pump ~*s* the steam out of the cloth —Werner Von Bergen & H.R.Mauersberger⟩ ⟨was nearly ~*ed* under by a bog —*Brit. Bk. News*⟩ ⟨the pull of gravity . . . would ~ the blood away from his head —J.A. Michener⟩ ⟨the sun ~*ed* up the rain . . . —H.L.Merillat⟩ **b** *archaic* : to absorb (a characteristic) in infancy ⟨thy valiantness was mine, thou *suck'st* it from me —Shak.⟩ **c** : to gather or exhaust a supply of ⟨~*ed* away their specie reserves —S.E. Morison & H.S.Commager⟩ ⟨the bemused spinster ~*ing* culture from galleries —H.S.Canby⟩ ⟨~*ing* strength all round for the savage struggle —Liam O'Flaherty⟩ **d** : to affect and esp. involve in an enterprise by compulsion or deceit ⟨all of us . . . have been ~*ed* out of our native soil and scattered in every unlikely corner of the world —Michael Howard⟩ — usu. used with *in* or *into* ⟨inadvertently ~*ed* into the . . . intrigue —Martin Levin⟩ ⟨~*ed* into . . . jury duty —H.J.Laski⟩ ⟨found themselves . . . ~*ed* in as the purveyors of gossip —Alan Barth⟩ **2 a** (1) : to draw liquid or semifluid substance from by a partial vacuum caused by motion of the mouth ⟨~ an orange⟩; *specif* : to suck milk from (a breast or udder) (2) : to draw from or consume by applying the lips or tongue to or across the surface of or by or as if by a vacuum created by applying the mouth to a tube ⟨~ out the trachea —A.R.Koontz⟩ ⟨~ a lollipop⟩ (3) : to apply the mouth or its parts to in the manner of a child sucking the breast ⟨~*s* his thumb⟩ ⟨~*ing* his empty pipe —Ellen Glasgow⟩ **b** : to gather or exhaust the resources, strength, or vitality of ⟨a body ~*ed* and wasted by disease⟩ **3** : SUCKLE, NURSE **4** : to fawn upon ~ *vi* **1 a** : to draw milk from a breast or udder **b** : to draw something in by or as if by producing a vacuum ⟨the thirsty hot winds above ~ constantly at the soil —W.P.Webb⟩ **c** : to draw air — used of a pump that fails to draw fluid because of low water or a defective valve **d** : to draw in the mouth over or around an object in the manner of a child at the breast ⟨pensively . . . and slowly ~*ed* at his pipe —Haldane Macfall⟩ **2** : to flow or splash against a shore somewhat forcefully and in waves esp. so as to undermine or wash away part of its substance ⟨the tide drained and ~*ed* at the mud flats —Nicholas Monsarrat⟩ **3** : to become sucked so as to make a sound or motion ⟨his pipe ~*ed* hollowly —Walter Machen⟩ ⟨flanks ~*ed* in and out, the long nose resting on his paws —Virginia Woolf⟩ **4** : to act in an obsequious manner ⟨when they want votes . . . the candidates come ~*ing* around —W.G.Hardy⟩ — **suck dry** : to draw all the vitality, resources, or strength of : EXHAUST ⟨several centuries of essentialist thought have *sucked dry* reality —*Modern Schoolman*⟩ — **suck the blood of 1** : to exhaust the financial resources of **2** : to exhaust the vitality of — **suck the monkey 1** *Brit* : to drink from the bottle; *also* : to drink liquor from a cask by means of a straw or tube inserted in a small hole **2** *Brit* : to drink rum from a coconut emptied of its milk — **suck up to** *slang* : to truckle to : APPLE-POLISH ⟨*sucked up to* the boss for advancement —*Fortune*⟩

2suck \"\ *n* -S [ME *souke*, fr. *souken* to suck] **1 a** : the act of sucking; *specif* : the act of sucking milk ⟨a child at ~⟩ **b** : a sucking movement or force ⟨the strong ~ of the undertow⟩ **2** *obs* : milk drawn or to be drawn from the breast **3** : a small draft : SIP **4** : WHIRLPOOL **5** *slang* : an obsequious person : TOADY; *also* : the influence an obsequious person has over another

3suck \", ˈsu̇k\ *var of* SOCK

suck-bottle \ˈ=,==\ *n* : NURSING BOTTLE

suck-egg \ˈ=,=\ *n* **1** : a young, foolish, or contemptible person **2** : an animal (as a weasel or cuckoo) that sucks eggs

1suck·en \ˈsəkən\ *n* -S [alter. of *soken*] *Scots law* : the lands subject to the thirlage of a mill

2sucken \"\ *adj* [short for obs. E *bond-sucken*, fr. E *bond* (bound) — *1sucken*] *Scot* : being or belonging to a suckener

suck·en·er \-k(ə)nər\ *n* -S *Scots law* : a tenant bound to grind his grain at the mill of a sucken

1suck·er \ˈsəkə(r)\ *n* -S [ME *soker, souker*, fr. *soken, souken* to suck + *-er* — more at SUCK] **1 a** : one that sucks esp. a breast or udder : SUCKLING; *specif* : an unweaned domestic animal **b** : a device for creating or regulating suction (as a piston or valve in a pump) **c** (1) : a plaything consisting of a soft leather disk suspended from a string that when wet clings to a surface of an object and lifts it (2) : a pipe or tube through which something is drawn by suction (3) : one of several cup-shaped vacuum-operated rubber devices to pick up and carry material in bookbinding; *specif* : one that feeds material in a folding or gathering machine **d** (1) : an organ in various animals for adhering or holding consisting in its simplest form of a soft pad or disk often somewhat concave that when closely applied to an object adheres as a result of atmospheric pressure : a sucking disk — see ECHINOCOCCUS illustration (2) : a mouth (as of a leech) adapted for sucking or adhering or both (3) : a tube foot of an echinoderm ending in a sucking disk **2** : a person who lives by extortion or parasitism **3 a** : a shoot originating from the roots or lower part of the stem of a plant and usu. developing rapidly often at the expense of the plant; *also* : an accessory propagative shoot ⟨a ~ of pineapple⟩ **b** : HAUSTORIUM **4 a** : any of numerous freshwater fishes of the family Catostomidae that are closely related to the carps but are distinguished from them by the structure of the mouth which usu. has thick soft lips and of the lower pharyngeal bones, that live and feed near the bottom, that in the case of larger forms ascend small streams and brooks to spawn, that have inferior flesh frequently eaten in regions where they are abundant, and that except for two Asiatic species are confined to No. America — see BUFFALO FISH, HOG SUCKER, REDHORSE **b** : any of various marine or freshwater true fishes (as the lumpfish, remora, or clingfish) with a sucking organ or mouth like that of a sucker — often used with a qualifying adjective **c** : HAGFISH **d** : LAMPREY **5** : LOLLIPOP b **6 a** (1) : a person easily cheated or deceived; *specif* : a mark for a gambler or confidence man (2) : a person irresistibly attracted by a specific type of object ⟨I've always been a ~ for animal acts —Al Hine⟩ **b** : GREENHORN **c** : a customer or frequenter of a circus, carnival, gambling establishment, or racetrack or a nonprofessional investor in securities **d** : ILLINOISAN — used as a nickname

2sucker \"\ *vb* **suckered; suckered; suckering** \-k(ə)riŋ\ **suckers** *vt* **1** : to remove suckers from ⟨~ tobacco⟩ **2** : to make a sucker of : CHEAT, DECEIVE, SWINDLE ⟨got ~*ed* out of six grand —Gerald Hughes⟩ ~ *vi* : to form or send out suckers ⟨corn ~*s* abundantly⟩

sucker bait *n* : a lure (as the promise of easy money) to attract a person to be swindled

sucker bet *n* : a bet offered at incorrect odds

suck·ered \-kə(r)d\ *adj* : provided with suckers

suck·er·el \ˈsək(ə)rəl\ *n* -S [*1sucker* + *-el*] : a slender somewhat compressed sucker (*Cycleptus elongatus*) of the Mississippi drainage that is dark or bluish gray above and lighter below, has a small head and eyes, and may attain a weight of over five pounds

suckerfish \ˈ==,=\ *n* : SUCKER 4; *esp* : REMORA

sucker foot *n* **1** : one of the terminal prolegs of a caterpillar **2** : one of the tube feet of an echinoderm

sucker-footed bat \ˈ==,==-\ *n* : a small golden-furred Madagascan insectivorous bat (*Myzopoda aurita*) having adhesive suckers on the soles of the feet

sucker list *n* : a list of the names, addresses, and sometimes telephone numbers of persons who are likely to be purchasers or donors, to whom advertising matter might profitably be sent, or to whom personal application might be made ⟨purchased a *sucker list* from another seller of watered stock⟩ ⟨on the *sucker lists* of all the local charities⟩

sucker mouth *n* : the small oval cavity left by the disarticulation of the seed in oats

sucker rod *n* : a jointed rod connecting a pump plunger in a well with a walking beam or pumping jack at the surface

sucker shift *n* : a deceptive shift in football used to lure opposing linemen offside

suckfish \ˈ=,=\ *n* **1** : REMORA **2** : a Pacific coast clingfish (*Caularchus maeandricus*) found in tide pools

suck fly *n* [so called fr. the fact that it sucks the sap from the leaves] : TOBACCO BUG

suckhole \ˈ=,=\ *n* **1** *dial* : WHIRLPOOL **2** *dial* : a spot of quicksand

suck in *vt* **1** : CHEAT, DECEIVE **2** : to contract, flatten, and tighten (the abdomen) by inhaling deeply

suck-in \ˈ=,=\ *n* -S [*suck in*] *Brit* : the process of being cheated : DECEPTION, FRAUD ⟨you never got such a *suck-in* in all your life —Frank O'Connor⟩

sucking *adj* [ME *souking*, fr. pres. part. of *souken* to suck — more at SUCK] **1** : not yet weaned ⟨~ pig⟩ **2** : very young : not full-fledged ⟨~ dove⟩

sucking coil *n* : a coil that draws in an iron core when carrying current

sucking fish *n* **1** : REMORA **2** : LAMPREY

sucking louse *n* : a louse of the order Anoplura characterized by possession of mouthparts adapted to sucking the body fluids of the host — compare BIRD LOUSE

sucking stomach *n* **1** : a food reservoir in some sucking insects connected with the esophagus by a tube **2** : the crop of an insect **3** : a widening of the posterior esophagus in spiders that functions as a pump

sucking wound *n* : a perforating wound of the chest through which air enters and leaves during respiration

1suck·le \ˈsəkəl\ *vt* **suckled; suckled; suckling** \-k(ə)liŋ, -lēŋ\ **suckles** [prob. back-formation fr. *1suckling*] **1 a** : to give suck to **b** : REAR, FOSTER, NOURISH ⟨*suckled* on miracles, religious and astrological —Josephine Pinckney⟩ **2** : to nurse at or from : SUCK **3** : to take in as nourishment ⟨from whose lusty, healthy breast my father had *suckled* the first of that fine strength —Rafael Sabatini⟩

2suckle \"\ *also* **sucklebush** \ˈ==,=\ *n, pl* **suckles** *also* **sucklebushes** [*suckle* fr. ME *sokel* clover, honeysuckle, short for *honysokel, honysoukel* honeysuckle; *sucklebush* fr. *2suckle* + *bush* — more at HONEYSUCKLE] : HONEYSUCKLE

1suck·ler \-k(ə)lə(r)\ *n* -S [*1suckle* + *-er*] **1** : SUCKLING **2** : an animal that suckles its young : MAMMAL

2suckler \"\ *n* -S [*2suckle* + *-er*] *dial Eng* : the flowering head of a clover

1suck·ling \ˈsəkliŋ, -lēŋ\ *n* -S [ME *sokeling*, fr. *soken* to suck + *-ling* — more at SUCK] : a young child or animal before it is weaned

2suckling \"\ *n* -S [ME *sokeling*, fr. *sokel* suckle + *-ing*] **1** *also* **suckling clover** : HOP CLOVER **2** : a tall-growing European honeysuckle (*Lonicera periclymenum*) sometimes cultivated for its richly fragrant flowers

suck-rock \ˈ=,=\ *n* : CHITON 2

sucks *pres 3d sing of* SUCK, *pl of* SUCK

suckstone \ˈ=,=\ *n* : REMORA

SUCL *abbr* set up in carloads

su·clat \səˈklät\ *n* -S [Hindi *suqlāt*, fr. Per *saqalāt* a rich cloth] *India* : any of various woolens; *specif* : European broadcloth

sucr- *or* **sucro-** *comb form* [ISV, fr. F *sucre*, fr. OF — more at SUGAR] : sugar ⟨*sucroacid*⟩

sucr *abbr* successor

su·crase \ˈsüˌkrās, -āz\ *n* -S [ISV *sucr-* + *-ase*] : INVERTASE

su·crate \ˈsüˌkrāt, -ˌkrət\ *n* -S [ISV *sucr-* + *-ate*] : a metallic derivative of sucrose ⟨strontium ~⟩ — compare SACCHARATE 2

1su·cre \ˈsü(ˌ)krā\ *n* -S [Sp, after Antonio José de *Sucre* †1830 So. American liberator] **1** : the basic monetary unit of Ecuador — see MONEY table **2** : a coin representing one sucre

2sucre \"\ *adj, usu cap* [fr. *Sucre*, Bolivia] : of or from Sucre, the constitutional capital of Bolivia : of the kind or style prevalent in Sucre

su·cri·er \ˌsükrēˈā\ *n* -S [F, fr. *sucre* sugar + *-ier* -er] : a sugar bowl usu. with cover

su·crose \ˈsüˌkrōs *also* -ōz\ *n* -S [ISV *sucr-* + *-ose*] : a sweet water-soluble crystalline dextrorotatory nonreducing disaccharide sugar $C_{12}H_{22}O_{11}$ that occurs naturally in most land plants esp. in the juices, fruits, and roots and that is hydrolyzed by mineral acids or by invertase into equal parts of D-glucose and D-fructose — compare SACCHAROSE; GLUCOSE illustration

1suc·tion \ˈsəkshən\ *n* -S *often attrib* [LL *suction-, suctio*, fr. L *suctus* (past part. of *sugere* to suck) + *-ion-, -io* -ion — more at SUCK] **1 a** : the act or process of sucking ⟨suck the membrane from the throat . . . by direct mouth-to-mouth ~ —Morris Fishbein⟩ **b** *Brit* : the imbibing of liquor **2 a** (1) : the act or process of exerting a force upon a solid, liquid, or gaseous body by reason of a reduced air pressure over part of its surface (2) : the force so exerted ⟨~ on the upper surface of an airplane wing⟩ ⟨surfaces that adhere through ~⟩ ⟨pumped up by ~⟩ **b** : the drawing in in an internal-combustion engine of a gaseous mixture during the suction stroke; *also* : the power or capacity to draw in such mixture **c** *or* **suction drainage** : the act or process of removing secretions or fluids from hollow or tubular organs or cavities by means of a tube and a device (as a suction pump) that operates on negative pressure **3** : the capacity for absorbing moisture or wet paint **4** : the amount the share point of a moldboard plow is turned down to cause the share to descend or be drawn into the soil a predetermined distance **5** : a pipe, fitting, or other device used in a machine that operates by suction

2suction \"\ *vt* -ED/-ING/-S : to remove from a body cavity or passage by suction ⟨a small amount of mucus could be ~*ed* through the trachea —Leon Unger⟩

suction anemometer *n* : an anemometer consisting of an inverted siphon half-filled with water that measures a difference in water level due to the wind's force

suction box *n* **1** : a box with a perforated cover over which the wire of a paper machine passes and to which suction is applied in order to remove water from the wet paper web **2** : a box connected with a suction pump and used (as for drying or cleaning) in a manufacturing process

suction cleaner *also* **suction sweeper** *n* : VACUUM CLEANER

suction couch *n* : a rotary suction box that functions also as a couch roll

suction cup *n* : a cup of glass or of a flexible material (as rubber) in which a partial vacuum is produced when applied to a surface and which is used variously (as to bring blood to the surface of the skin, for traction or holding, or as part of a plunger)

suction dredge *n* : a dredging machine using a centrifugal pump to draw up mud, sand, and silt through a suction tube

suction force *or* **suction pressure** *or* **suction tension** *n* : DIFFUSION PRESSURE DEFICIT

suction pump *n* : a common pump in which the liquid to be raised is pushed by atmospheric pressure into the partial vacuum under a retreating valved piston on the upstroke and reflux is prevented by a nonreturn valve in the pipe

suction socket *n* : a socket on an artificial leg that is held to the stump by the suction of negative pressure maintained within the socket

suction stop *also* **suctional stop** *n* : a voice stop in the formation of which the air behind the articulation is rarefied with consequent inrush of air when the articulation is broken — compare PRESSURE STOP

suction stroke *n* : the stroke of the piston in an internal-combustion engine that effects the drawing in of the gaseous mixture to the engine cylinder

1suc·to·ria \ˌsəkˈtōrēə\ *n pl, cap* [NL, fr. neut. pl. of *suctorius* suctorial] : a class of complex protozoans (subphylum Ciliophora) which have cilia only early in development and in which the mature form is fixed to the substrate, lacks locomotor organelles or cytostome, and obtains food through specialized suctorial tentacles — compare ACINETA, PODOPHRYA

2suctoria \"\ [NL] *syn of* HIRUDINEA

3suctoria \"\ [NL] *syn of* SIPHONAPTERA

4suctoria \"\ [NL] *syn of* RHIZOCEPHALA

suc·to·ri·al \ˌsəkˈtōrēəl\ *adj* [NL *suctorius* (fr. L *suctus* — past part. of *sugere* to suck — + *-orius* -ory) + E *-al* — more at SUCK] **1** : adapted for sucking : serving to draw up fluid or to adhere by suction ⟨~ mouths⟩ **2 a :** provided with suctorial organs ⟨a ~ fish⟩ **b :** living by sucking the blood or juices of animals or plants **3** [NL *Suctoria* + E *-al*] **:** of or relating to the Suctoria

suc·to·ri·an \ˌsəkˈtōrēən\ *n* -s [NL *Suctoria* + E *-an*] **1 :** a suctorial animal **2 :** one of the Suctoria

su·cu·pi·ra \ˌsükəˈpirə\ *n* -s [Pg, fr. Tupi *sucupira, sapupira*] **:** any of several tropical So. American timber trees esp. of the genera *Bowdichia* or *Diplotropis* of the family Leguminosae; *also* **:** the hard heavy dark wood of a sucupira that resembles acapu and is used esp. for wagon hubs and in shipbuilding

su·cu·ri \ˌsükəˈrē\ *or* **su·cu·riu** \ˌsükəˈrēˌü\ *or* **su·cu·ru·ju** \ˌsukərəˈzhü\ *or* **su·cu·ry** \ˌsükəˈrē\ *n, pl* **sucuris** *or* **sucurius** *or* **sucurujus** *or* **sucuries** [Pg *sucuri, sucuriu, sucuriju,* fr. Tupi *sucuriuh*] **:** ANACONDA 2

¹sud \ˈsəd, (ˈ)süd\ *Scot & dial Eng var of* SHOULD

²sud \ˈsəd\ *var of* SUDS

su·da·dero \ˌsüdəˈde(ˌ)rō\ *n* -s [Sp, sweat cloth, handkerchief, saddle cloth, fr. *sudar* to sweat, fr. L *sudare* — more at SWEAT] **:** a broad piece (as of leather) attached to a stirrup strap to protect a rider's leg from sweat

su·da·men \süˈdāmən\ *n, pl* **sudam·i·na** \-damənə\ [NL *sudamin-, sudamen,* fr. L *sudare* to sweat — more at SWEAT] **:** a transient eruption of minute translucent vesicles caused by retention of sweat in the sweat glands and in the corneous layer of the skin and occurring after profuse perspiration

su·dam·i·nal \(ˈ)süˈdamənᵊl\ *adj* [NL *sudamin-, sudamen* + E *-al*] **:** of or relating to sudamen ⟨~ eruptions following severe sweating —H.F.Swift⟩

¹su·dan \(ˈ)süˈdan, -daa(ə)n *sometimes* -dᵊn *or* -dȧn\ *adj, usu cap* [fr. *the Sudan,* region of north central Africa] **1 :** of or from the Sudan in northern Africa between the Sahara and the rainy tropics extending from the Atlantic ocean to the mountains of Ethiopia or to the Red sea **:** of the kind or style prevalent in the Sudan **:** SUDANESE **2 :** of or from the Republic of the Sudan in northeastern Africa **:** of the kind or style prevalent in the Republic of the Sudan **:** SUDANESE

²sudan \"\ *n* -s **1** *often cap* **:** a dark grayish yellow to light olive brown **2** *usu cap* **:** any of several azo solvent dyes some of which have a specific affinity for fatty substances and are used as biological stains — see DYE table I

sudan brown *n, often cap S* **:** a moderate to strong brown that is redder than oak and yellower and slightly darker than Vassar tan — called also *brown bread*

¹su·da·nese *also* **sou·da·nese** \ˌsüdᵊnˈēz, -dəˈnēz, -ēs\ *n, pl* **sudanese** *also* **soudanese** *cap* [*sudanese* fr. *the Sudan,* region of north central Africa + E *-ese; soudanese* fr. F *soudanais,* fr. *Soudan* the Sudan + *-ais* -ese] **1 :** a native or inhabitant of the Sudan belonging to one of various racial and linguistic groups including Arab and Arabic-speaking peoples, peoples of Hamitic affiliation (as the Tuaregs), and numerous Negro and negroid peoples **2 :** a native or inhabitant of the former Anglo-Egyptian Sudan or the Republic of the Sudan in northeast Africa

²sudanese *also* **soudanese** \"\ *adj, usu cap* **:** of or relating to the Sudan, to the former Anglo-Egyptian Sudan, or to the Republic of the Sudan **:** SUDAN

sudan IV *also* **sudan** *n* -s *usu cap S* **:** a red disazo solvent dye used chiefly as a biological stain and in ointments for promoting (as in the treatment of burns, wounds, or ulcers) the growth of epithelium — called also *scarlet red;* see DYE table I (under *Solvent Red 24*)

sudan grass *also* **sudan** *n* -s *usu cap S* **:** a vigorous tall-growing annual grass (*Sorghum vulgare sudanensis*) with usu. prominently awned spikelets that is adapted for growth in semiarid regions and is widely cultivated for hay and fodder

sudan gum *n, usu cap S* **:** gum arabic collected in the Sudan chiefly from one species of acacia (*Acacia senegal*) — compare KORDOFAN GUM

¹su·dani \süˈdanē, -ni *sometimes* -dᵊn- *or* -dȧn-\ *adj, usu cap* [Ar *Sūdānīy* of the Sudan, fr. *Sūdān* the Sudan] **:** SUDANESE

²sudani \"\ *n* -s *cap* **1 :** SUDANESE **2 :** an Arabic dialect spoken in the Sudan

¹su·dan·ic \(ˈ)=ˈ=ik, -ēk\ *adj, usu cap* [fr. *the Sudan* + E *-ic*] **:** SUDANESE

²sudanic \"\ *n, cap* **:** the languages neither Bantu nor Hamitic spoken in a belt extending from Senegal to southern Sudan one large part of which has been shown to be related and with Bantu to form the Niger-Congo family and another large part of which forms the Chari-Nile family

su·dan·iza·tion \(ˌ)süˌdanəˈzāshən, ˌsüdᵊn-\ *n* -s *usu cap* **:** the act or process of Sudanizing ⟨the rate at which *Sudanization* of the administration, judiciary and security forces is to take place —*Economist*⟩

su·dan·ize \süˈdaˌnīz, ˈsüdᵊnˌīz\ *vt* -ED/-ING/-S *often cap* [*sudanese* + *-ize*] **:** to make Sudanese; *esp* **:** to staff with Sudanese

sudano- *comb form, usu cap* [ˈ*sudan*] **1 :** Sudanese **:** Sudanese and ⟨*Sudano*-Guinean⟩ **2 :** Sudan dye ⟨*sudanophil*⟩ ⟨*sudanophobic*⟩

su·dan·o·phil \süˈdanəˌfil\ *or* **su·dan·o·phil·ic** \(ˌ)=ˌ==ˈfilik\ *adj* [*sudano-* + *-phil* or *-philic*] *of a tissue or tissue element* **:** staining selectively with Sudan dyes; *also* **:** containing lipoid — **su·dan·o·phil·ia** \(ˌ)=ˌ==ˈfilēə\ *n* -s

su·dar·i·um \süˈda(a)rēəm\ *n, pl* **sudar·ia** \-ēə\ [L, fr. *sudare* to sweat + *-arium* -ary — more at SWEAT] **1 :** a linen square carried by the upper classes in Roman times (as for wiping perspiration from the face) **:** HANDKERCHIEF **2 :** an image of the face of Christ painted on a cloth and used as an aid to devotion **:** VERONICA **3 :** SUDATORIUM

su·da·ry \ˈsüdərē\ *n* -ES [ME, fr. L *sudarium*] **1** *archaic* **:** SUDARIUM **2** *obs* **:** WINDING-SHEET, SHROUD **3 :** HUMERAL VEIL

su·da·tion \süˈdāshən\ *n* -s [L *sudation-, sudatio,* fr. *sudatus* (past part. of *sudare* to sweat) + *-ion-, -io* -ion] **:** SWEATING

su·da·to·ri·um \ˌsüdəˈtōrēəm\ *n, pl* **sudato·ria** \-ēə\ [L, fr. *sudatus* + *-orium*] **:** a sweat room in a bath

¹su·da·to·ry \ˈsüdəˌtōrē\ *adj* [L *sudatorius,* fr. *sudatus* + *-orius* -ory] **:** producing sweating

²sudatory \"\ *n* -ES [L *sudatorium*] **:** SUDATORIUM

sud·bur·ite \ˈsədbəˌrīt\ *n* -s [fr. *Sudbury* district, Ontario, Canada + E *-ite*] **:** a basic hypersthene-bearing basalt composed of bytownite, hypersthene, augite, and magnetite, often vesicular, and sometimes somewhat metamorphosed

sudd \ˈsəd\ *n* -s [Ar, lit., obstruction] **:** floating vegetable matter that is composed chiefly of papyrus stems and an aquatic grass (*Vossia procera*) often intermixed with ambatch and that forms obstructive masses in the upper White Nile

¹sud·den \ˈsədᵊn\ *adj* [ME *sodain, sodein,* fr. MF *sodain, sudain,* fr. L *subitaneus,* fr. *subitus* sudden, unexpected, fr. past part. of *subire* to come up, occur unexpectedly, fr. *sub-* up + *ire* to go — more at SUB-, ISSUE] **1 a :** happening without previous notice or with very brief notice **:** coming or occurring unexpectedly **:** not foreseen or prepared for ⟨caught out walking by a ~ thundershower⟩ ⟨took a ~ almost miraculous turn for the better⟩ **b :** changing angle or character all at once **:** PRECIPITOUS ⟨slopes gradually downwards toward the ~ drop of the icefall —John Hunt and Edmund Hillary⟩ **:** ABRUPT ⟨this ridge forms an important and ~ break between the land of abundant ground water . . . and the dry land —P.E.James⟩ **c :** come upon or met with unexpectedly ⟨watching for ~ turns in the road⟩ **2 a :** characterized by or manifesting hastiness **:** RASH, HEADLONG ⟨a red setter . . . too ~ to be a friend —May Sarton⟩ **b** *obs* **:** characterized by swift action **:** FAST-MOVING, QUICK, ALERT ⟨appearing goodly to the ~ eye —John Milton⟩ **3 a** *archaic* **:** made, provided, brought about, or acting in a short time **:** PROMPT, IMMEDIATE ⟨he acquaints the citizens with the king's peril . . . and requests their ~ assistance —John Cleveland⟩ ⟨hire assassins or put ~ poison in my evening drink —P.B.Shelley⟩ **b** *obs* **:** executed or executing on the spur of the moment **:** IMPROMPTU, EXTEMPORE ⟨do it without invention, suddenly, as I with ~ . . . speech purpose to answer —Shak.⟩ **c** *obs* **:** shortly to come or be **:** EARLY, SOON ⟨tomorrow, in my judgment, is too ~ —Shak.⟩ **syn** see PRECIPITATE

²sudden \"\ *adv* **:** SUDDENLY ⟨~ I heard a voice —Alfred Tennyson⟩

³sudden \"\ *n* -s *obs* **:** an unexpected occurrence **:** EMERGENCY — **of a sudden** *or* **on a sudden** *also* **on the sudden** *adv* **:** sooner than was expected **:** at once **:** SUDDENLY ⟨withdrew his opposition all *of a sudden* —W.M.Thackeray⟩ ⟨the driver had swerved *on a sudden* to avoid a file of geese —Ellen Glasgow⟩ ⟨an effect, *on the sudden,* of real sublimity —Walter Pater⟩

sudden death *n* **1 :** unexpected death that is instantaneous or occurs within minutes from any cause other than violence ⟨*sudden death* following coronary occlusion⟩ ⟨from battle and murder and from *sudden death,* good Lord, deliver us —*Bk. of Com. Prayer*⟩ **2 :** decision by a single throw of dice or toss or spin of a coin in gambling **3 a :** a single full game played to break a tie **b :** competition to break a tie that terminates the moment one side scores or gains the lead in an overtime period or play-off **4 :** a disease of cloves (as in Zanzibar and Madagascar) of unknown cause marked by the extreme rapidity with which death of the tree follows a slight chlorosis and wilting

sud·den·ly *adv* [ME *sodeinliche,* fr. *sodein* sudden + *-liche* -ly] **:** in a sudden manner

sud·den·ness \-dᵊn(n)əs\ *n* -ES **:** the quality or state of being sudden

sud·dent \-dᵊnt\ *dial var of* SUDDEN

suddenty *n* -ES [ME *sodeinte, sodentie,* fr. MF *sodeineté,* fr. *sodein* sudden + *-té* -ty] *obs* **:** SUDDENNESS — **of a suddenty** *or* **on a suddenty** *adv* **1 :** SUDDENLY **2** *Scots law* **:** without premeditation

su·dle \ˈsədᵊl, ˈsu̇d-\ *n or vb* [prob. fr. MHG *sudelen;* akin to G dial. *sudel* swamp, bog, Gk *hyei* it is raining — more at SUCK] *Scot & dial Eng* **:** STAIN, SOIL

sud·dy \ˈsədē, -di\ *adj* -ER/-EST [*sud* + *-y*] **:** SUDSY

¹su·de·ten \süˈdātᵊn\ *also* **su·det·ic** \(ˈ)=ˈdedik\ *adj, usu cap* [fr. *Sudeten,* mountain ranges in northern Czechoslovakia] **1 :** of, relating to, or being a semicircular chain of mountain ranges in the provinces of Bohemia and Silesia extending around the northern and western borders of Czechoslovakia **2 :** of, relating to, or being all the borderlands of Bohemia and Moravia

²sudeten *or* **sudeten german** \"\ *n* -s *cap S&G* **:** a German-speaking native or inhabitant of the Sudeten region

su·do·motor \ˌsüdə+\ *adj* [*sudo-* (fr. L *sudor* sweat) + *motor*] *of nerve fibers* **:** controlling the activity of sweat glands

su·do·rif·er·ous \ˌsüdəˈrif(ə)rəs\ *adj* [LL *sudorifer* sudoriferous (fr. L *sudor* sweat + *-ifer* -iferous) + E *-ous*] **:** producing or conveying sweat ⟨~ glands⟩ ⟨a ~ duct⟩

¹su·do·rif·ic \-fik\ *adj* [NL *sudorificus,* fr. L *sudor* sweat + *-i-* + *-ficus* -fic — more at SWEAT] **:** causing or inducing sweat **:** DIAPHORETIC ⟨~ herbs⟩

²sudorific \"\ *n* -s **:** a sudorific agent or medicine

su·do·rip·a·rous \ˌsüdəˈripərəs\ *adj* [NL *sudoriparus,* fr. L *sudor* + *-i-* + *-parus* -parous] **:** SUDORIFEROUS

su·dra *also* **shu·dra** \ˈs(h)üdrə\ *n* -s *usu cap* [Skt *śūdra*] **1 :** a member of the fourth ancient Hindu varna formed chiefly from conquered non-Aryans and assigned by classical law to menial occupations involving manual labor **2 :** a Hindu belonging to one of a large group of modern lower castes traditionally derived from the ancient Sudra varna — compare BRAHMAN, HARIJAN, KSHATRIYA, VAISYA

¹suds \ˈsədz\ *n pl but sing or pl in constr* [prob. fr. MD *sudde, sudse* (sing.) marsh, bog; akin to OE *sēothan* to seethe — more at SEETHE] **1 a** *obs* **:** FILTH, DREGS **b :** DUMPS — usu. used in the phrase *in the suds* **2 a :** water impregnated with soap and typically containing bubbles and froth **:** a foamy soap solution **b :** the froth or bubbles formed on soapy water ⟨arms white with ~⟩ **c :** a washing in water containing suds ⟨trousers usually require only one ~ —N.J. Berg⟩ **3 a :** FOAM, FROTH ⟨the ~ cast up by the waves⟩ **b** *slang* **:** BEER **4** *also* **sud :** soapy waste liquor formed by the scouring of wool before bleaching and containing grease

²suds \"\ *vb* -ED/-ING/-ES *vt* **:** to wash (as a garment) in suds ~ *vi* **:** to form suds ⟨a soap that ~es easily⟩

sudsy \ˈsədzē, -zi\ *adj* -ER/-EST [¹*suds* + *-y*] **:** full of suds **:** FROTHY, FOAMY

¹sue \ˈsü\ *vb* **sued; sued; su·ing; sues** [ME *suen, suwen, siwen, sewen,* fr. OF *sivre, suivre, suir,* fr. (assumed) VL *sequere,* fr. L *sequi* to follow, come or go after; akin to Gk *hepesthai* to follow, Skt *sacati* he accompanies, follows] *vt* **1** *obs* **a :** to go in pursuit of **:** try to overtake **:** CHASE **b :** to come after (as in time, order, or logical sequence) **:** ensue upon **:** result from **c :** to be a follower or servant or attendant or disciple of **d :** to guide or govern by (as an intention, one's will) **e :** to engage in as a pastime, occupation, or profession **:** PRACTICE **f :** to follow up **:** PROSECUTE, CONTINUE **2 :** to make petition to or for **:** SOLICIT, URGE **3 :** to pay court or suit to **:** WOO **4 a** *early Eng law* (1) **:** to follow or attend upon (a feudal superior) or to resort to (the superior's mill) for the grinding of grain (2) **:** to follow or seek (a court) in order to assist the court in administering justice usu. as a doomster or in order to obtain justice (3) **:** to follow (a person) to a court in order to act as a witness or compurgator in an action in the court **b :** to follow or go to (a court) in order to obtain legal redress ⟨*sued* the court for a writ of recovery⟩ **c :** to seek justice or right from (a person) by legal process **:** bring an action against **:** prosecute judicially **d :** to proceed with (a legal action) and follow up to proper termination **:** gain by legal process ~ *vi* **1 :** to follow someone or something **2 :** to make a request or application **:** PETITION, ENTREAT, PLEAD — usu. used with *for* or *to* **3 :** to pay court or suit **:** WOO ⟨he loved . . . but *sued* in vain —William Wordsworth⟩ **4 a** *early English feudal law* **:** to perform the duties or part of one who sues a superior court or person **b :** to take legal proceedings in court **:** seek in law ⟨~ for damages⟩

²sue *var of* SEW

sue and labor clause *n* [¹*sue*] **:** a clause ordinarily inserted in a marine insurance policy by which the insured contracts to sue, labor, and travel for, in, and about the defense, safeguard, and recovery of the insured property and the insurer agrees to bear his proportion of the expenses voluntarily incurred therefor

¹suede *or* **suède** \ˈswād\ *n* -s *often attrib* [fr. the phrase *suède gloves,* part translation of F *gants de Suède* Swedish gloves] **1 :** leather finished by buffing with an emery wheel usu. on the flesh side to produce a napped surface and used esp. for handbags, shoes, gloves, sports coats **2** *or* **suede cloth :** a woven or knitted fabric of wool, cotton, rayon finished with a very short smooth nap to give the texture and appearance of suede leather and used for sportswear, shirts, gloves **3 :** a light to moderate brown that is slightly yellower than tanbark or mocha bisque — called also *café crème*

²suede *also* **suède** \"\ *vb* -ED/-ING/-S *vt* **:** to give a suede finish or nap to (a fabric or leather) ~ *vi* **:** to give cloth or leather a suede finish

¹su·ent \ˈsüənt\ *adj* [alter. of ME *suaunt, suante* following, agreeable, smooth, fr. MF *suiant, suant,* pres. part. of *suir* to follow — more at SUE] **1** *dial* **:** SMOOTH, EVEN, REGULAR, STEADY **2** *dial* **:** EQUABLE, AGREEABLE **3** *dial* **:** PLACID, QUIET, GRAVE, DEMURE — **su·ent·ly** *adv, dial*

²suent \"\ *adv, dial* **:** in a suent manner

sue out *vt* [ME *suen out,* fr. *suen* to sue + *out*] **:** to obtain by suit **:** petition for and take out or apply for and obtain in judicial proceedings ⟨*sue out* a writ in chancery⟩ ⟨*sue out* a pardon⟩

su·er \ˈsüə(r), ˈsu̇(ə)r, -üə\ *n* -s [ME, fr. *suen* to sue + *-er*] **:** one that sues

suer·te \ˈswer(ˌ)tā\ *n* -s [Sp, lot, chance, luck, suerte, fr. L *sort-, sors* lot, chance — more at SORT] **:** a skilled movement or pass in a bullfight

su·et \ˈsüət, usu -əd·+V\ *n* -s [ME *swet, sewet,* fr. (assumed) AF *suet, sewet,* dim. of AF *sue, seu,* fr. L *sebum* tallow, suet — more at SOAP] **:** the hard fat about the kidneys and loins in beef and mutton that when melted and freed from the membranes forms tallow — compare LEAF FAT

suet pudding *n* **:** a boiled or steamed pudding made with chopped suet, flour, bread crumbs, raisins, and spices

su·ety \-d·ē, -tˌ|, |i\ *adj* [*suet* + *-y*] **:** of, full of, or like suet

sueve \ˈswēv\ *n* -s *cap* [LL *Suevus,* fr. L *suevus* Suevian (adj.), fr. *Suevi*] **:** SUEVIAN

sue·vi \ˈswāˌvē, -wēˌvī\ *or* **sue·bi** \-bē,-bī\ *n pl, cap* [L *Suevi, Suebi,* of Gmc origin; akin to G *Schwaben* Swabians] **:** SUEVIANS

¹sue·vi·an \-ˌvēən\ *n* -s *cap* [L *Suevi* + E *-ian,* n. suffix] **:** one of an ancient Germanic people prob. of many distinct tribes mentioned by Caesar as dwelling east of the Rhine and by Tacitus as extending to the Elbe and the Baltic; *also* **:** one of a Germanic horde from this region that overran France and Spain early in the 5th century A.D.

²suevian \"\ *or* **sue·vic** \-ˌvik\ *adj, usu cap* [L *Suevi* + E *-ian,* adj. suffix, or *-ic*] **:** of or relating to the Suevians

su·ez \süˈez, süˈez, *chiefly Brit* ˈsüiz\ *adj, usu cap* [fr. *Suez,* seaport city of Lower Egypt] **:** of or from the city of Suez, Egypt **:** of the kind or style prevalent in Suez

suf *abbr* suffix

suff *n* -s [origin unknown] *obs* **:** the shoreward surge of the sea

suff *abbr* **1** sufficient **2** suffix **3** suffragan

suf·fect \(ˈ)səˈfekt\ *n* -s [L (*consul*) *suffectus,* fr. *consul* + *suffectus,* past part. of *sufficere* to put in place of — more at SUFFICE] **:** a Roman consul elected to complete the term of one who vacated office before the end of the year

suf·fer \ˈsəfə(r)\ *vb* **suffered; suffered; suffering** \-f(ə)riŋ\ **suffers** [ME *soffren, suffren, sufferen,* fr. OF *soffrir, souffrir,* fr. (assumed) VL *sufferire,* fr. L *sufferre* to bear up, endure, suffer, fr. *sub-* up + *ferre* to bear — more at SUB-, BEAR] *vt* **1 :** to submit to or be forced to endure the infliction, imposition, or penalty of **:** bear as a victim ⟨~ martyrdom⟩ ⟨~ a year's imprisonment⟩ **:** to be subjected to physical or mental pain because of **:** endure with distress ⟨~ thirst⟩ ⟨~ insults⟩ **:** to feel keenly or acutely ⟨~ pain of body⟩ ⟨~ grief of mind⟩ **:** labor under ⟨the greatest handicap which our side ~s in entering the political conference —Willson Woodside⟩ **2 :** to go or pass through (as harm or loss) **:** UNDERGO ⟨most or all genes ~ mutational changes from time to time —Theodosius Dobzhansky⟩ **:** EXPERIENCE ⟨the company ~*ed* a 35% drop in sales the first quarter —*Wall Street Jour.*⟩ **:** SUSTAIN ⟨records that had ~*ed* damage during storage⟩ **3 :** to endure or undergo without sinking **:** have power to resist or sustain **:** to bear up under **:** SUPPORT ⟨~ through half an hour of standing in line for the sake of a five-minute ride⟩ — used chiefly in negative statements ⟨shrubs that cannot ~ a cold winter⟩ ⟨never able to ~ the slightest pain⟩ **4 a :** not to forbid or hinder **:** ALLOW, PERMIT ⟨in later years ~*ed* his beard to grow long —K.W.Colgrove⟩ **b :** to put up with **:** TOLERATE ⟨too proud of its revolutionary tradition to ~ dictatorship gladly —W.L.Burn⟩ **5** *chiefly dial* **:** to cause pain or suffering to ~ *vi* **1 :** to submit to or endure death, affliction, penalty, or pain or distress ⟨contracted rheumatoid arthritis and ~*ed* intensely⟩ ⟨make him ~ for his mistake⟩; *sometimes* **:** to endure such willingly or patiently ⟨martyrs who ~*ed* for Christ's sake⟩ **2 :** to be the one acted upon as distinguished from the one acting ⟨matter cannot act — it can only ~⟩ **3 :** to sustain loss or damage ⟨business ~s greatly from a long-continued depression⟩ **4 a :** to be in a state of disability (as from ill health, anxiety, error) **:** be subject to something disabling ⟨too many of them ~ from nervous or heart disabilities —H.W.Baldwin⟩ ⟨~s from the fallacy of supposing that everyone feels as he does⟩ **b :** to be at a disadvantage **:** labor under a handicap ⟨for years the school had ~*ed* from lack of funds —*Amer. Guide Series: Mich.*⟩ ⟨the story ~s by comparison with the shorter ones —Louise Anderson⟩ ⟨the men . . . ~*ed* from no lack of self-esteem —Van Wyck Brooks⟩ **syn** see BEAR, EXPERIENCE, LET

suf·fer·able \-f(ə)rəbəl\ *adj* [ME *suffrable,* fr. MF *soufrable,* fr. OF, fr. *souffrir* to suffer + *-able*] **1** *obs* **a :** able to suffer or endure **:** PATIENT **b :** ALLOWABLE, PERMISSIBLE **2 :** that can be suffered **:** ENDURABLE, TOLERABLE — **suf·fer·able·ness** \-nəs\ *n* -ES — **suf·fer·ably** \-blē,-bli\ *adv*

suf·fer·ance \ˈsəf(ə)rən(t)s\ *n* -s [ME *suffrance,* fr. OF *soufrance,* fr. *souffrir* to suffer + *-ance*] **1 :** patient endurance **:** forbearance under provocation **:** LONG-SUFFERING ⟨still have I borne it with a patient shrug, for ~ is the badge of all our tribe —Shak.⟩ **2** *archaic* **:** an act, state, or instance of suffering **:** PAIN, MISERY ⟨~s that you had borne —Shak.⟩ **3 :** consent or sanction that is not explicit but is implied by a lack of interference or the failure to enforce a prohibition **:** toleration of something that is usu. disapproved or illegal **:** passive or tacit permission — used usu. with *on, by,* or *through* ⟨he remains here on ~⟩ ⟨by ~ only were they allowed to enter the country⟩; *specif* **:** the legal condition of one continuing in the possession of an estate after his right to it has expired and without express leave from the owner — used with *at* or *by* ⟨a tenant at ~⟩ ⟨estates by ~⟩ **4 :** power or ability to endure or withstand **:** ENDURANCE ⟨it is beyond ~⟩ **5 :** BILL OF SUFFERANCE

sufferance wharf *n* **:** a licensed private wharf where dutiable goods may be kept until the duty is paid

suf·fer·er \-fərə(r)\ *n* -s [ME *suffrer,* fr. *suffren* to suffer + *-er*] **:** one that suffers; *esp* **:** one that endures or undergoes suffering or who sustains inconvenience or loss ⟨a new drug giving relief to hay fever ~s⟩ ⟨emergency aid given to flood ~s⟩

¹suffering *n* -s [ME *suffring,* fr. gerund of *suffren* to suffer] **1 :** the state or experience of one who suffers **:** the endurance of or submission to affliction, pain, loss **2 :** a pain endured or a distress, loss, or injury incurred ⟨rise from a bed of ~⟩ ⟨experience untold ~⟩ ⟨endured many ~s⟩ ⟨no one . . . better prepared by habitual ~ —Jane Austen⟩ **syn** see DISTRESS

²suffering *adj* [ME *suffring,* fr. pres. part. of *suffren* to suffer] **1 a :** that suffers **b :** characterized by or proceeding from suffering **2 :** ILL, SICK ⟨is he very ~ —Owen Wister⟩ — **suf·fer·ing·ly** *adv*

suf·fete \ˈsəˌfēt\ *n, pl* **suf·fetes** \ˈsəˌfēts, ˈsəfəˌtēz\ [L *sufet-, sufes, suffet-, suffes,* of Punic origin; akin to Heb *shōphēṭ* judge] **:** one of the two annually elected chief magistrates of ancient Carthage

suf·fice \səˈfīs *sometimes* -īz\ *vb* -ED/-ING/-S [ME *suffisen, sufficen,* fr. MF *suffis-,* stem of *suffire,* fr. L *sufficere* to put under or in place of, provide, suffice, fr. *sub-* under, in place of + *-ficere* (fr. *facere* to do, make) — more at SUB-, DO] *vi* **1 :** to be enough **:** to meet or satisfy a need **:** to be adequate or sufficient ⟨a hint will ~⟩ ⟨ten bombs *sufficed* to destroy the fort⟩ — often used with an impersonal *it* ⟨~ it that without leisure there is no liberty —G.B.Shaw⟩ **2 :** to measure up to a standard **:** satisfy all requirements **:** be competent, capable, equal to a task ⟨what words or tongue of seraph can ~ —John Milton⟩ **3** *obs* **:** to permit within fixed limits **:** allow or admit of something ~ *vt* **1 :** to be enough for (a person) **:** give a sufficiency to **:** satisfy the needs or appetite of ⟨education that *sufficed* our forefathers⟩ ⟨enough food to ~ an army⟩ **2 :** to serve to satisfy (a want, appetite) **:** APPEASE ⟨this ~s present needs⟩ **3** *obs* **a :** to be capable of **b :** supply adequately **:** REPLENISH, FURNISH ⟨the power appeased, with winds *sufficed* the sail —John Dryden⟩

suf·fic·er \-īsə(r) *sometimes* -īzə-\ *n* -s **:** one that suffices

suf·fi·cience \səˈfishən(t)s\ *n* -s [ME, fr. LL *sufficientia*] *archaic* **:** SUFFICIENCY

suf·fi·cien·cy \-nsē,-nsi\ *n* -ES [LL *sufficientia,* fr. L *sufficient-, sufficiens* sufficient + *-ia* -y] **1 :** sufficient means to meet one's obligations or satisfy one's needs **:** COMPETENCY; *also* **:** a modest but not parsimonious scale or way of living **:** adequate comfort **2 :** the quality or state of being sufficient or adequate to the end proposed **:** ADEQUACY ⟨question the ~ of the equipment⟩ **:** ENOUGH ⟨eat a ~⟩ **3 :** the character or fact of being qualified **:** ABILITY, CAPACITY ⟨the ~ of present laws to meet a severe financial crisis⟩ **4 :** CONCEIT, SELF-CONFIDENCE, SELF-SUFFICIENCY ⟨the master had not flinched . . . nor . . . did he betray the least ~ —R.L.Stevenson⟩

¹suf·fi·cient \-nt\ *adj* [ME, fr. L *sufficient-, sufficiens,* fr. pres. part. of *sufficere* to suffice] **1 :** marked by quantity, scope, power, or quality to meet with the demands, wants, or needs of a situation or of a proposed use or end ⟨an ample sum, one ~ to supply those wants of hers —Thomas Hardy⟩ ⟨have not ~ information to state the exact damage —F.D. Roosevelt⟩ **2** *archaic* **:** adequately qualified or competent **3** *obs* **a :** excessively self-confident **b :** WEALTHY, WELL-TO-DO **4** *archaic* **:** well-made **:** SUBSTANTIAL **5** *of a bid in bridge* **:** higher in rank than the bid over which it is made

syn ENOUGH, ADEQUATE, COMPETENT: SUFFICIENT is likely to refer to a quantity or scope that meets the demands of a specific situation ⟨like ninety-nine percent of those who are taught the classics, I never acquired *sufficient* proficiency to read them with pleasure —Bertrand Russell⟩ ⟨a pinch from his snuffbox was an honor *sufficient* to turn the head of a young enthusiast —T.B.Macaulay〉 ENOUGH, often placed after the noun it modifies, as in *men enough, money enough*, is less exact and more approximate than SUFFICIENT in its suggestion 〈my country! and 'tis joy *enough* and pride for one hour's perfect bliss to tread the grass of England once again —William Wordsworth〉 ADEQUATE may suggest barely meeting a requirement, with nothing excessive or ample remaining 〈vocabulary . . . was perfectly *adequate* to the clear and forceful statement of his ideas —Aldous Huxley〉 ADEQUATE is wider in its sphere of use than SUFFICIENT or ENOUGH 〈you can get along quite comfortably if you're just *adequate*, but it's different with an artist —W.S.Maugham〉 COMPETENT, usu. not used in reference to counting or physical measurement like others in this set, may be entirely complimentary or may imply some of the slighting suggestion of ADEQUATE 〈her *competent* steely mind never rested —Rebecca West〉 〈*competent* narrative or exposition, skilled but not beautiful or artistic writing such as deserves the name of literature —Samuel Alexander〉

²sufficient \"\ *n* -s : SUFFICIENCY, ENOUGH 〈ate till he had ~〉

sufficient condition *n* **1** : a cause, ground, or condition such that if it be given the thing in question is assured **2** : CONDITION 2a(3)

suf·fi·cient·ly *adv* [ME, fr. ¹*sufficient* + -*ly*] : in a sufficient manner or to a sufficient degree

suf·fi·cient·ness *n* -ES [¹*sufficient* + -*ness*] : SUFFICIENCY

sufficient reason *n* **1** : LAW OF SUFFICIENT REASON **2** : SUFFICIENT CONDITION

sufficing *pres part of* SUFFICE

¹suf·fix \'səˌfiks\ *n* -ES [NL *suffixum*, fr. L, neut. of *suffixus*, past part. of *suffigere* to fasten underneath, fasten to, fr. *sub-* + *figere* to fasten — more at DIKE] **1** : an affix occurring at the end of a word, base, or phrase — compare PREFIX **2** : SUBINDEX 1

²suf·fix \", (ˌ)sə'f-\ *vt* -ED/-ING/-ES [partly fr. L *suffixus*, past part. of *suffigere* to fasten to; partly fr. ¹*suffix*] : to add or annex to the end of a word, base, or phrase : attach as a suffix

suf·fix·al \'səˌfiksəl, (ˌ)ₛ'ₛₛ\ *or* **suf·fix·i·al** \(ˌ)sə¦fiksēəl\ *adj* [¹*suffix* + -*al* or -*ial*] : of, relating to, or being a suffix

suf·fix·a·tion \ˌsəˌfik'sāshən\ *n* -s [²*suffix* + -*ation*] : formation or inflection by means of suffixes

suf·flam·i·nate \sə'flamәˌnāt\ *vt* -ED/-ING/-S [L *sufflaminatus*, past part. of *sufflaminare* to check, brake, fr. *sufflamin-, sufflamen* brake, fr. *sub-* + (assumed) L *flagmen, flamen* chock, prop; akin to OE *balca* ridge — more at BALK] : OBSTRUCT, IMPEDE

suf·flate \(ˌ)sə'flāt\ *vt* -ED/-ING/-S [L *sufflatus*, past part. of *sufflare* to blow up, inflate, fr. *sub-* up + *flare* to blow — more at SUB-, BLOW] : to blow up; INFLATE, INSPIRE

suf·fla·tion \(ˌ)sə'flāshən\ *n* -s [L *sufflation-, sufflatio*, fr. *sufflatus* + -*ion-*, -*io* -ion] : an act or instance of sufflating; *specif* : INSPIRATION

suf·fo·cate \'səfəˌkāt, *usu* -ād·+V\ *vb* -ED/-ING/-S [L *suffocatus*, past part. of *suffocare* to choke, stifle, fr. *sub-* + *fauces, foces* (pl.) throat] *vt* **1** : to stop the respiration of (as by strangling or asphyxiation) : deprive of oxygen by any means : make unable to breathe **2** *obs* : to compress so as to impede or prevent breathing 〈let not hemp his windpipe ~ —Shak.〉 **3 a** : to overcome or make extremely uncomfortable by want of cool fresh air **b** : to impede or stop the development, growth, or activity of as though by depriving of air ~ *vi* : to become suffocated: **a** : to die from being unable to breathe 〈the children locked in the chest *suffocated*〉 **b** : to be very uncomfortable through lack of air 〈she was *suffocating* in the hot little kitchen〉 **c** : to become checked, stultified, or enervated in growth or development

syn ASPHYXIATE, STIFLE, SMOTHER, CHOKE, STRANGLE, THROTTLE: SUFFOCATE commonly refers to conditions in which breathing is impossible through lack of available oxygen or through presence of noxious or poisonous gas 〈prisoners *suffocated* in the underground dungeon〉 SUFFOCATE also refers to situations in which breathing is impossible because mouth and nose are covered 〈*suffocating* under the mud and earth which had fallen over his head〉 ASPHYXIATE is likely to refer to situations in which death comes through poisonous gases in the air or through lack of sufficient oxygen 〈*asphyxiated* by the chlorine gas in the cellar〉 STIFLE is likely to refer to situations in which breathing is difficult or impossible through lack of adequate fresh air and, often, presence of heat 〈closing a hatch to stop a fire and the destruction of a cargo was justified even if it was known that doing so would *stifle* a man below —O.W.Holmes †1935〉 SMOTHER is likely to be used in situations in which the supply of oxygen is inadequate for life; it often suggests a deadening pall of smoke, dust, or other impurity in the air 〈*smothered* by the dust after the explosion〉 〈a smell of soot which *smothered* the scent of wistaria and iris —Louis Bromfield〉 SMOTHER also refers to situations in which the mouth and nose are covered so that one cannot breathe 〈was *smothered* with a cushion〉 CHOKE suggests difficulty in breathing through constriction, obstruction, or extreme irritation within the throat 〈*choked* to death by a brutal marauder〉 〈*choking* on a chicken bone lodged in the throat〉 〈*choking* as he breathed the acrid smoke〉 STRANGLE also refers to constriction of the throat, obstruction of the windpipe, or irritation but it is more likely to indicate fatality or quite serious condition 〈fingers itched to *strangle* him —R.W. Buchanan〉 〈*strangling* on a chicken bone〉 THROTTLE may suggest external compression of the throat done forcefully for the purpose of subduing or overcoming resistance 〈heartbeats . . . so violent that they seemed . . . *throttling* hands to her throat —Edith Wharton〉

suf·fo·cat·ing·ly \'ₛₛˌₛₛₛ, ₛₛ'ₛₛₛ\ *adv* [*suffocating* (pres. part. of *suffocate*) + -*ly*] : in a suffocating manner

suf·fo·ca·tion \ˌsəfə'kāshən\ *n* -s [L *suffocation-, suffocatio*, fr. *suffocatus* + -*ion-*, -*io* -ion] : the act of suffocating or state of being suffocated : stoppage of breathing — compare ASPHYXIA

suf·fo·ca·tive \'səfəˌkāt·iv\ *adj* [L *suffocatus* + E -*ive*] : tending or able to choke or stifle 〈~ catarrh〉

¹suf·folk \'səfək *sometimes* -ˌfōk *or* -ˌfōk\ *adj, usu cap* [fr. *Suffolk*, county of eastern England] : of or from the county of Suffolk, England : of the kind or style prevalent in Suffolk

²suffolk \"\ *n* **1** *usu cap* : any of several English breeds of livestock: as **a** : a breed of black-faced hornless sheep derived in part from the Southdown, producing excellent mutton, but having a light fleece and being somewhat rangy **b** : a breed of chestnut-colored draft horses having a deep heavy body, a large head, and short legs — called also *Suffolk punch* **2** -s *often cap* : an animal of any of the Suffolk breeds

suffolk punch *n, usu cap S* : SUFFOLK 1b

suffr *abbr* suffragan

¹suf·fra·gan \'səfrə|gən, -rē|, ÷ |jən\ *n* -s [ME *suffragan*, fr. MF, fr. ML *suffraganeus*, fr. *suffragium* support, assistance, intercessory prayer — more at SUFFRAGE] **1** *or* **suffragan bishop a** : a diocesan bishop (as in the Roman Catholic Church and the Church of England) subordinate to a metropolitan **b** : BISHOP SUFFRAGAN **c** : a Protestant Episcopal bishop elected by a diocese as assistant to the diocesan without right of succession, having no share in the jurisdiction of the diocese, and taking such duties as are assigned to him from time to time — compare BISHOP COADJUTOR **2** *obs* : ASSISTANT, DEPUTY, AGENT

²suffragan \"\ *adj* **1** : of or being a suffragan **2** : subordinate to a metropolitan or archiepiscopal see

suf·fra·gan·ship \-ˌship\ *n* [¹*suffragan* + -*ship*] : the office or rank of a suffragan

¹suf·frage \'səfrij, -rēj, ÷ 'səfər-\ *n* -s [in senses 1 & 2, fr. ME, fr. MF, fr. ML *suffragium* vote, support, assistance, prayer for intercession, fr. L, vote, political support, interest, prob. fr. *sub-* + *fragor* noise (of vote by acclamation); in other senses, fr. L *suffragium* — more at BRAY] **1** : an intercessory prayer or petition (as in a liturgy) — usu. used in pl. **2** *obs* : AID, HELP, ASSISTANCE **3 a** : a vote of assent given by a member of a body to a proposal or nomination — usu. used in pl. **b** : an opinion or decision in favor of a person or thing : APPROVAL, SANCTION **4** : an object (as a pebble or paper ballot) used for voting **5 a** : the vote or opinion of a group of persons : CONSENSUS **b** : a vote given in deciding a controverted question or election : the casting of a vote 〈no state shall be deprived of its equal ~ in the senate —*U.S.Constitution*〉 〈refrain from any word that may . . . influence your ~s in the election —Edward Gibbon〉 **6** : the right or privilege of voting in political matters or the exercise of such right; *esp* : the right or power to participate in electing public officials and adopting or rejecting legislation in a representative form of government : FRANCHISE — see MANHOOD SUFFRAGE, UNIVERSAL SUFFRAGE, WOMAN SUFFRAGE

²suffrage \"\ *vb* -ED/-ING/-S [L *suffragare, suffragari*; akin to L *suffragium* vote, support] *vi, obs* : to give one's vote, approval, or support ~ *vt, archaic* : to elect, sanction, or support by one's suffrage

suf·frag·ette \ˌsəfrə¦jet, -rē¦j-, *usu* -ed·+V\ *n* -s [¹*suffrage* + -*ette*] : a woman who militantly advocates suffrage for her sex

suf·frag·ett·ism \-ed·ˌizəm, -eˌti-\ *n* -s : militant advocacy of the extension of suffrage to women

suf·frag·i·nis \sə'frajənəs\ *n* -ES [NL *os suffraginis*, lit., bone of the suffrago] : the long bone of the pastern that is a common site of fracture in racehorses

suf·frag·ism \'səfrəˌjizəm, -rēˌj-\ *n* -s [¹*suffrage* + -*ism*] : advocacy of the extension of suffrage (as to women)

suf·frag·ist \-jəst\ *n* -s [¹*suffrage* + -*ist*] : one who advocates an extension of suffrage (as to women)

suf·fra·go \sə'frā(ˌ)gō\ *n* -s [NL *suffragin-, suffrago*, fr. L, prob. fr. *sub-* + *frangere* to break — more at BREAK] **1** : the hock of a horse **2** : the tarsal joint of a bird : KNEE

suf·fru·tes·cent \ˌsəˌfrü¦tesᵊnt\ *adj* [NL *suffrutescent-, suffrutescens*, fr. L *sub-* + NL *frutescent-, frutescens* frutescent, fr. L *frutex* shrub + -*escent*, -*escens* -escent — more at FRUTICOSE] *of a plant or stem* : having a base that is somewhat woody and does not die down each year

suf·fru·ti·cose \(ˌ)sə¦früd·əˌkōs\ *also* **suf·fru·ti·cous** \(ˌ)sə'früd·əkəs\ *adj* [NL *suffruticosus*, fr. L *sub-* + *fruticosus* fruticose] : woody and perennial at the base but remaining herbaceous above 〈a low ~ perennial〉

suf·fru·tic·u·lose \ˌsə(ˌ)frü¦tikyəˌlōs\ *adj* [NL *suffruticulosus*, fr. L *sub-* + NL *fruticulosus* fruticulose, fr. *fruticulus* (dim. of L *frutic-, frutex* shrub) + L -*osus* -ose] *of a lichen* : somewhat or imperfectly fruticose

suffs *pl of* SUFF

suf·fumigate \(ˌ)sə+\ *vt* [L *suffumigatus*, past part. of *suffumigare* to fumigate from below, fr. *sub-* + *fumigare* to fumigate] : to fumigate from below : send fumes upward upon

suf·fumigation \(ˌ)sə+\ *n* [LL *suffumigation-, suffumigatio*, fr. L *suffumigatus* + -*ion-*, -*io* -ion] **1** : the act or process of suffumigating (as in magic rites or in treatment) **2** : a fume, smoke, or vapor used in suffumigating

suf·fus·able \sə'fyüzəbəl\ *adj* : that can be suffused

suf·fuse \sə'fyüz\ *vt* -ED/-ING/-S [L *suffusus*, past part. of *suffundere* to pour underneath, suffuse, fr. *sub-* + *fundere* to pour — more at FOUND (melt)] **1** : to spread over or through in the manner of fluid or light : FLUSH, FILL 〈when purple light shall next ~ the skies —Alexander Pope〉 **2** : to pour so as to overspread **syn** see INFUSE

suf·fused·ly \-z(ə)dlē\ *adv* [*suffused* (past part. of *suffuse*) + -*ly*] : in a suffused manner

suf·fu·sion \sə'fyüzhən\ *n* -s [L *suffusion-, suffusio*, fr. *suffusus* + -*ion-*, -*io* -ion] **1** : the act or process of suffusing or state of being suffused with something; *specif* : the spreading of a fluid of the body into the surrounding tissues 〈a ~ of blood〉 **2** : a coloring spread over a surface (as the face)

suf·fu·sive \-üsiv, -üziv\ *adj* [L *suffusus* + E -*ive*] : that suffuses : tending to overspread or to diffuse itself

¹su·fi \'süfē\ *n* -s *usu cap* [Ar *ṣūfīy*, lit., (man) of wool, fr. *ṣūf* wool; prob. fr. the woolen dress worn by the ascetic] : an ascetic Muslim mystic : an adherent of Sufism

²sufi \"\ *adj, usu cap* : of or relating to the Sufis or Sufism

su·fic \-fik\ *adj, usu cap* [¹*sufi* + -*ic*] : SUFISTIC

su·fism \-ˌfizəm\ *also* **su·fi·ism** \-ˌfēˌiz-\ *n* -s *usu cap* [¹*sufi* + -*ism*] : ascetic Islamic mysticism originating in the 8th century and developing esp. in Persia into a system of elaborate symbolism of which the goal is communion with the deity through contemplation and ecstasy

su·fis·tic \(')sü¦fistik\ *adj, usu cap* [¹*sufism* + -*istic*] : of, relating to, or in accordance with Sufism

sug *abbr* suggested; suggestion

su·ga·mo \sü'gä(ˌ)mō\ *n* -s [Jap] : an aquatic plant (*Phyllospadix scouleri*) of the family Potamogetonaceae that occurs along the north Pacific coasts from the northwestern U.S. to Japan and is grown in Japan for fertilizer and fiber

su·gan *or* **soo·gan** *or* **sou·gan** *or* **sug·gan** \'sügən, 'sůg-, 'səg-\ *n* -s [IrGael *sūgān*; akin to ScGael *sūgan* sugan] **1** *chiefly Irish* : a hand-twisted rope of straw or heather **2** : a coarse blanket used by cowboys and ranchmen

¹sug·ar \'shůgə(r)\ *n* -s [ME *sucre, sugre, suger*, fr. MF *çucre, sucre*, fr. ML *zuccarum, succarum*, fr. OIt *zucchero*, fr. Ar *sukkar*, fr. Per *shakar*, fr. Prakrit *sakkara*, fr. Skt *śarkarā* gravel, grit, sugar; akin to Skt *śarkara* pebble] **1 a** : a sweet crystallizable substance that consists entirely or essentially of sucrose, that is colorless or white when pure and usu. yellowish to brown otherwise, that occurs naturally in the most readily available amounts in sugarcane, sugar beet, sugar maple, sorghum, and sugar palms, that is obtained commercially principally by processing the juice expressed from sugarcane or the aqueous extract of sliced sugar beets and refining so that the final product is the same regardless of the source, and that forms an important article of human food and is used also chiefly as a condiment and preservative for other foods and for drugs and in the chemical industry as an intermediate — see BEET SUGAR, BROWN SUGAR 1, CANE SUGAR, INVERT SUGAR, MAPLE SUGAR 1, SACCHAROSE **b** : any of a class of water-soluble compounds (as glucose, fructose, xylose, sucrose, maltose, or raffinose) that vary widely in sweetness, comprise the simpler carbohydrates, include not only the monosaccharides but also the oligosaccharides, may be reducing or nonreducing, and typically are optically active **2** : a unit (as a spoonful, cube, or lump) of sugar 〈how many ~s in your tea〉 **3** : SUGAR BOWL 〈offering ~s, creamers in styles to match —*Edison Electric Appliances Cat.*〉 **4** *slang* : MONEY 〈undergoing an operation that cost heavy ~ —Mickey Spillane〉 〈spend my good ~ on a taxi —*Auckland (New Zealand) Weekly News*〉 **5** — used as an interjection to express annoyance or disappointment

²sugar \"\ *vb* **sugared; sugared; sugaring** \-g(ə)riŋ\ **sugars** [ME *sugren*, fr. *sugre* sugar] *vt* **1** : to make pleasing, palatable, or deceptively attractive : SWEETEN, SUGARCOAT 〈novels heavy with moral teaching and ~*ed* with romance —*Amer. Guide Series: N.Y.*〉 〈~*ing* the reproach with the expression of endearment —Vicki Baum〉 — often used with *over* or *up* 〈with devotion's visage . . . we do ~ o'er the devil himself —Shak.〉 〈his inclination to ~ up reality —David Tilden〉 **2** : to sprinkle sugar on : mix sugar with : put sugar into 〈~ a cake〉 〈~ the mixture to taste〉 〈~ tea〉 ~ *vi* **1** : to form sugar 〈continued stirring will cause a syrup to ~〉 **2** : to become granular in texture : GRANULATE 〈a varnish that ~s〉

³sugar \"\ *adj* [¹*sugar*] **1** : made or derived from sugar **2** : having the sweetness of sugar **3** : attracted to sugar **4** : used with sugar or in the making of sugar

⁴sugar \"\ *usu cap* — a communications code word for the letter *s*

sugar ant *n* : an ant that is attracted to sweet foods: as **a** : PHARAOH ANT **b** : any of several Australian ants of the genus *Camponotus*

sugar apple *n* **1** : SWEETSOP 2 **2** : BIRIBA

sugar ash *n* : BOX ELDER

sugar bag *n* **1** *Austral* : a wild bees' nest **2** *Austral* : honey from a wild bees' nest

sugar basin *n, Brit* : SUGAR BOWL

sugar beet *n* : a white-rooted beet grown for the sugar in its roots

sugar beet eelworm *or* **sugar beet nematode** *n* : a widely distributed destructive nematode worm (*Heterodera schachtii*) native to the Old World but found in several areas of No. America that attacks the roots of sugar beets

sugar beet root aphid *n* : a root aphid (*Pemphigus populivenae*) that causes severe injury to sugar beet, beet, and mangel crops in the western U.S.

sugar beet root maggot *n* : the larva of a fly (*Tetanops myopaeformis*) of the family Otitidae that infests the roots of sugar beets in the western U.S. and parts of Canada

sugarberry \'ₛₛ- — *see* BERRY\ *n* **1** : a hackberry with sweet edible fruits: as **a** : the common eastern hackberry (*Celtis occidentalis*) **b** : a large hackberry (*C. laevigata*) chiefly of the lower Mississippi valley that has orange or yellow fruit **2** : JUNEBERRY

sugarbird \'ₛₛ,ₛ\ *n* [prob. trans. of Afrik *suikervogel*] **1** : any of various honeycreepers, honey eaters, and sunbirds that suck the nectar of flowers **2** : EVENING GROSBEAK

sugar bowl *n* : a bowl-shaped vessel that has usu. two handles and a cover and is used for holding sugar or sugar cubes

sugar bowl

sugar brake *n* : SENSITIVE FERN

sugar bush \'ₛₛ,ₛ\ *n* **1** *or* **sugar grove a** : a grove or collection of sugar maples **b** : a woods in which sugar maples predominate — called also *sugar orchard* **2** *usu* **sugar-bush** [trans. of Afrik *suikerbos*] : any of several plants of the genus *Protea*; *esp* : a southern African shrub (*P. mellifera*) **3** *usu* **sugar-bush** : an evergreen shrub or small tree (*Rhus ovata*) of the southwestern U.S. with reddish yellow flowers in dense spikes and glandular hairy fruits

sugar camp *n, chiefly Midland* : SUGAR BUSH

sugar candy *n* [ME *sugre candy* — more at CANDY] **1** : hard candy made from pure sugar **2** : something sweet or pleasant

sugar-candy \¦ₛₛ¦ₛₛ\ *adj* [*sugar candy*] : deliciously and usu. cloyingly sweet 〈*sugar-candy* novels —*Irish Statesman*〉

sugarcane \'ₛₛ,ₛ\ *n* **1** : a stout tall perennial grass that is usu. considered to constitute a species (*Saccharum officinarum*) but is known only as a cultigen or escape in warm or tropical regions, occurs in distinct forms with characteristic qualities and different chromosome numbers and possibly constitutes a hybrid complex, and has flat 2-ranked leaves, many-jointed stalks, and a large terminal flower cluster — see NOBLE CANE, SUGAR 1 **2** : sugarcane plants 〈a plantation of ~〉

sugarcane beetle *n* : a destructive beetle (*Euetheola rugiceps*) that burrows in the base of the sugarcane

sugarcane borer *n* : the larva of a pyralidid moth (*Diatraea saccharalis*) that bores in sugarcane in the southern U.S. and the West Indies

sugarcane gummosis *n* : COBB'S DISEASE

sugarcane leafhopper *n* : a jassid bug (*Perkinsiella saccharicida*) injurious to sugarcane

sugarcane mosaic *n* : an important virus disease of sugarcane characterized by chlorotic streaking of the leaves, stunting of the plants, and a greatly reduced yield of sugar

sugarcane smut *n* **1** : a disease of sugarcane caused by a smut fungus (*Ustilago scitaminea*) **2** : the fungus causing sugarcane smut

sugarcane wax *n* : a wax that occurs as a thin layer on the outside of the stem of the sugarcane, that is usu. obtained as a by-product in the manufacture of cane sugar as a hard green to brown or tan solid, and that is used chiefly in polishing materials

sugarcoat \'ₛₛ¦ₛ\ *vb* [¹*sugar* + *coat* (v.)] *vt* **1** : to coat (as a food or drug) with sugar or candy 〈~ almonds〉 〈~ pills〉 **2 a** : to make (something difficult, harsh, or unpleasant) superficially easy, attractive, or palatable : SWEETEN 〈~*ing* the classics for children〉 〈~*ed* the punishment with promises of future rewards〉 **b** : to conceal (something ugly or evil) under a deceptively pleasing exterior : gloss over 〈adept at ~*ing* their vicious purpose〉 〈~ the real facts〉 ~ *vi* : to embellish something harsh or unpalatable : conceal a bitter truth by glossing over it 〈makes a practice of ~*ing*〉

sugarcoating *n* [fr. gerund of *sugarcoat*] **1** : the act or process of sugarcoating **2** : something that sugarcoats 〈using fiction as a ~ for their lectures —*Dial*〉

sugar corn *n* : SWEET CORN

sugar crop *n* : a crop (as sugarcane or sugar beets) grown for the extraction of sugar

sugar daddy *n* : a wealthy older man lavishing gifts and luxuries on a young woman whom he squires about or keeps as his mistress 〈the air of a chorus girl who has just been given a bracelet by her *sugar daddy* —Louis Bromfield〉

sugar diabetes *n* : DIABETES MELLITUS

sugar eat *or* **sugar lick** *or* **sugar party** *n* : SUGARING OFF 2

sugared *adj* [ME *sugred, sucred*, fr. *sugre, sucre* sugar + -*ed*] **1** : containing sugar : SWEETENED 〈~ water〉 **2** : deliciously appealing or alluring : HONEYED 〈~ temptation〉 **3** : SUGARCOATED 〈~ almonds〉 〈a ~ speech〉

sug·ar·er \'shůgərə(r)\ *n* -s [¹*sugar* + -*er*] *Brit* : SHIRKER

sugar grape *n* : SAND GRAPE

sugar grass *n* : any saccharine sorghum; *esp* : SORGO

sugar gum *n* : either of two Australian gum trees (*Eucalyptus corynocalyx* and *E. gunnii*) having sweetish leaves that livestock browse upon

sugarhouse \'ₛₛ,ₛ\ *n* : a building where sugar is made or refined; *specif* : a shed where maple sap is boiled and maple syrup and maple sugar are made

sugarhouse molasses *n* : thin molasses remaining after refining of granulated sugar

sug·ar·i·ness \'shůg(ə)rēnəs, -rin-\ *n* -ES : the quality or state of being sugary

sugaring *n* -s [fr. gerund of ²*sugar*] **1** : the act or process of making sugar **2** : granulation found in some marbles and thought to be caused by the differential expansion coefficients of the grains

sugaring off *n, pl* **sugaring offs** **1** : the act or process of converting maple syrup into sugar **2** : a party held at the time of sugaring off at which the refreshments consist of doughnuts, pickles, and boiled-down maple syrup poured on snow — called also *sugar eat*

sugar lerp insect *n* : a psyllid bug (*Spondyliaspis eucalypti*) that secretes large amounts of lerp honey

sug·ar·less \'shůgə(r)ləs\ *adj* : containing no sugar 〈~ tea〉

sugarloaf \'ₛₛ,ₛ\ *n* [ME *sugarlaf*, fr. *suger* sugar + *laf* loaf] **1** : refined sugar molded into a solid cone 〈in my boyhood in eastern Europe a ~ was still a familiar object —E.G.Gudde〉 **2** : a hill or mountain resembling a sugarloaf in its conical or conoidal shape

sugar-loaf \'ₛₛ,ₛ\ *also* **sugar-loafed** \"t\ *adj* : shaped like a sugarloaf : CONOIDAL 〈a *sugar-loaf* mountain〉

sugar maple *n* : any of several maples having a sweet sap; *specif* : a maple (*Acer saccharum*) of eastern No. America having gray bark, 3- to 5-lobed leaves, flowers in nearly sessile corymbs, and hard close-grained wood that is much used for cabinetwork esp. in the curly-grained form and having sap that is the chief source of maple syrup and maple sugar — see BIRD'S-EYE MAPLE; TREE illustration

sugar-maple borer *n* : a maple borer that attacks sugar maple and is the larva of a black and yellow beetle (*Glycobius speciosus*)

sugar mite *n* : any of several mites of the genus *Glycyphagus* that often infest unrefined sugar and dried fruits

sugar mule *n* : a large mule suitable for work on a sugar plantation — distinguished from *cotton mule*

sugar off *vi* : to complete the process of boiling down the syrup in making maple sugar until it is thick enough to crystallize : approach or reach the state of granulation

sugar of lead : LEAD ACETATE a

sugar on snow : maple syrup boiled to the soft-ball stage and poured on snow or ice

sugar orchard *n, chiefly New Eng* : SUGAR BUSH

sugar palm *n* : any of several palms yielding sugar: as **a** : GOMUTI **b** : NIPA 3a **c** : a Philippine palm (*Corypha elata*)

sugar pea *n* : EDIBLE-PODDED PEA

sugar pear *n* **1** : JUNEBERRY **2** : a cultivated pear noted for its sweet flavor

sugar pine *n* : a lofty pine (*Pinus lambertiana*) of California and Oregon having leaves in fives, cones often 18 inches long, a soft reddish brown wood that is used for interior finishings and shingles, and heartwood that yields a sugary exudate

sugarplum \'ₛₛ,ₛ\ *n* **1** : a small candy or confection usu. in the form of a ball or disk : COMFIT, SWEETMEAT 〈ready-made . . . as hand for glove or tongue for ~ —Robert Browning〉 〈visions of ~s danced in their heads —Clement Moore〉 **2** : something that is a sugarplum (as in sweetness or desirability): as **a** : sweet words : FLATTERY 〈pelt with gilt ~s —Anthony Trollope〉 **b** : a gift or bribe offered to conciliate a person : SOP 〈stop his mouth with a ~〉 **c** : something esp. choice of its kind : PLUM 4b, PRIZE **3** : JUNEBERRY

sugar puncture *n* **:** puncture of a definite region in the medulla oblongata resulting in glycosuria
sugars *pl of* SUGAR, *pres 3d sing of* SUGAR
sugar sand *n* **:** granular mineral matter present in boiling maple syrup before filtration
sugar sheath *n* **:** the parenchyma surrounding the xylem in the root of the sugar beet
sugar shell *n* **:** a spoon for serving sugar that often has a bowl molded in the form of a seashell
sugarsop \ˈ==,=\ *n, archaic* **:** a sweetened and spiced sop
sugar sorghum *n* **:** SORGO
sugar squirrel *or* **sugar opossum** *n* **:** a small widely distributed Australian opossum (*Petaurus breviceps*) that is largely silvery gray with a bushy and often white-tipped tail and that in habits and appearance much resembles a flying squirrel
sugar–stick \ˈ=,=\ *n* **:** STICK CANDY ⟨jars of striped *sugar-stick* —*Spectator*⟩
sugar–tit *also* **sugar–teat** \ˈ==,=\ *n* **:** sugar tied up in a nipple-shaped cloth for a child to suck ⟨fighting, while all these legislators were sucking *sugar-tits* —Kenneth Roberts⟩ ⟨*sugar-tit* children . . . coddled and comforted —Lillian Smith⟩—called also *pacifier*
sugar tongs *n pl* **:** a pair of usu. silver tongs with claw-shaped or spoon-shaped ends for serving lump sugar

sugar shell

sugar tree *n* **1 :** SUGAR MAPLE **2 :** an Australian shrub or small tree (*Myoporum platycarpum*) with linear leaves and small white flowers
sugar vinegar *n* **:** vinegar made from refuse sugary or starchy materials by alcoholic and acetic fermentations
sugar wood *n* **1 :** SUGAR MAPLE **2 :** SUGAR TREE 2
sug·ary \ˈshu̇g(ə)rē, -ri\ *adj* [¹*sugar* + *-y*] **1 :** containing, resembling, or tasting of sugar **:** sweet with sugar ⟨~ food⟩ ⟨~ flavor⟩ ⟨~ delicacies⟩ **2 a :** exaggeratedly or ostentatiously sweet (as in manner or expression) **:** SACCHARINE, HONEYED ⟨a ~ smile⟩ ⟨her soft, ~ voice —Katherine Mansfield⟩ ⟨~ amiability coated . . . an inherent weakness in her own psyche —Margaret Hay⟩ **b :** cloyingly sweet **:** SENTIMENTAL ⟨~ verses⟩ ⟨~ melodies⟩ ⟨~ and unconvincing . . . fiction —Katharine F. Gerould⟩ **3 :** having a granular texture ⟨~ marble⟩
sug·bu·ha·non \ˌsəgˈbüə,nän\ *n, usu cap* [Cebuan *Sugbu* Cebu Island + *-hanon* language of] **:** CEBUAN 2
sugg *abbr* suggested; suggestion
suggan *var of* SUGAN
sug·gest \sə(g)ˈjest\ *vb* -ED/-ING/-S [L *suggestus*, past part. of *suggerere* to put under, heap up, furnish, suggest, fr. *sub-* + *gerere* to bear, wage — more at CAST] *vt* **1 :** to put (as an idea, proposition, or impulse) into the mind: as **a** *obs* (1) **:** to seek to influence the mind of **:** URGE ⟨two spirits do ~ me still —Shak.⟩ (2) **:** to insinuate esp. an evil or false thought into the mind of **:** TEMPT, SEDUCE ⟨what serpent hath ~*ed* thee —Shak.⟩ **b :** to call forth (as a desire or mood) **:** AROUSE, EVOKE ⟨indirectly ~ the desired attitude —Dorothy Barclay⟩ ⟨the pleasant voice that enticed and ~*ed* the most improbable falsehoods from witnesses —Rose Macaulay⟩ **c :** to mention (something) as a possibility **:** put forward by implication **:** HINT, INTIMATE ⟨~ that a change of government is necessary⟩ ⟨~ strongly . . . that he bring his wife along for the interview —W.H.Whyte⟩ **d :** to propose (something) as desirable or fitting ⟨~ a stroll after lunch⟩ ⟨~*ed* several thesis subjects⟩ ⟨~*ed* . . . a special committee to work on plans for a possible settlement —*New Republic*⟩ **e :** to offer (as an idea or theory) for consideration **:** present as a hypothesis **:** THEORIZE ⟨this, I ~, is what happened⟩ ⟨~*ed* the conception of poetry as a living whole —T.S.Eliot⟩ ⟨~*s* other reasons why music is powerful in the building . . . of personality —H. A.Overstreet⟩ **2 a :** to call or bring to mind (as an idea, mood, or object) by a process of logical thought or natural association of ideas **:** give rise to the idea of **:** EVOKE ⟨the explosion . . . ~*ed* sabotage —F.L.Paxson⟩ ⟨the scientist ~*s* an ant, putting forth great efforts to lug one . . . apparently unimportant grain of sand —Oliver La Farge⟩ ⟨a setting which is brilliantly ~*ed* —*Times Lit. Supp.*⟩ ⟨the folk customs that ~ themselves for study —Phyllis Greenacre⟩ **b :** to serve as an incentive, motive, or reason for **:** INSPIRE, PROMPT ⟨a short story ~*ed* by an actual incident⟩ ⟨television may ~ new forms and expression —Leslie Rees⟩ ⟨this incident ~*s* significant reflections —M.R.Cohen⟩ ⟨physical comfort . . . ~*s* that students shall occupy alternate seats —*College of William & Mary Cat.*⟩ **3 :** to give an indication or impression of **:** imply the presence of **:** ADUMBRATE, SHADOW ⟨open gambling that ~*ed* collusion with public officials⟩ ⟨his impulsive gestures ~*ed* a passion he had never shown to her —Morley Callaghan⟩ ⟨admirable works, yet they ~*ed* . . . aloofness from the sordid realities —V.L.Parrington⟩ ~ *vi* **1** *obs* **:** to work insidiously upon a person's mind **:** TEMPT ⟨devils . . . do ~ at first with heavenly shows —Shak.⟩ **2 :** to arouse ideas or feelings by a process of association
syn IMPLY, HINT, INTIMATE, INSINUATE: SUGGEST may involve communicating or implanting an idea by calling attention to some notion likely to be associated with it by starting a mental association naturally leading to the notion in question ⟨the business of words in prose is primarily to state; in poetry, not only to state, but also (and sometimes primarily) to *suggest* —J.L.Lowes⟩ ⟨a steamer on the Thames or lines of telegraph inevitably *suggest* the benefits of civilization, man's triumph over Nature —L.P.Smith⟩ IMPLY is close to SUGGEST in denotation and connotation; it differs in seeming to require more analytical or systematic inference to grasp the implied meaning ⟨had always *implied* that there had been something irregular in Dr. Winter's accounts —Edith Wharton⟩ ⟨an era when the scientific point of view no longer *implies* this determinism —Edmund Wilson⟩ HINT refers to communication by slight, indirect, or covert suggestion, with a minimum of straightforward implicit expression ⟨as thou with wary speech . . . hast *hinted* —John Keats⟩ ⟨repeatedly *hinted* at in political thought —Alex Comfort⟩ INTIMATE may stress delicacy as contrasted with blunt forthrightness in expression ⟨*intimated* that there had been danger in his coming just then —Arnold Bennett⟩ ⟨"I never put it so strong as that," said the old lady, looking rather shocked. She had *intimated* as much many times —Archibald Marshall⟩ INSINUATE often indicates covert indirect reference artfully introduced and usu. calculated to depreciate or denigrate ⟨the *insinuated* scoff of coward tongues —William Wordsworth⟩ ⟨the voice that *insinuates* that Jews and Negroes and Catholics are inferior excrescences on our body politic —Max Lerner⟩
sug·gest·ibil·i·ty \=,=ˈbiləd·ē, -lətē, -i\ *n* -ES **:** the quality or state of being suggestible **:** susceptibility to suggestion or influence ⟨the ~ of an actor⟩ ⟨surgically induced malleability and ~ . . . make reeducation possible —*Digest of Neurology & Psychiatry*⟩ ⟨the itching ~ of irresolute and halfhearted men —Ralph Bates⟩
sug·gest·ible \=ˈ=əbəl\ *adj* [*suggest* + *-ible*] **:** easily influenced by suggestion **:** susceptible mentally to external influences esp. to the opinions of others ⟨a bewildered, ~ boy —H.N.Fairchild⟩ ⟨the hypnotic subject is very ~ —G.H. Estabrooks⟩ ⟨whipped up their . . . pathologically ~ population into a frenzy —E.A.Hooton⟩ ⟨too ~ to possess a style of his own —F.O.Matthiessen⟩
sug·ges·tio fal·si \sə(g)ˈjes(h)chē,ōˈfȯl(t),sī\ *n* [NL] *law* **:** suggestion of an untruth **:** false statement as opposed to suppression of the truth — compare SUPPRESSIO VERI
sug·ges·tion \sə(g)ˈjes(h)chən\ *n* -s [ME, act of suggesting, fr. MF, fr. L *suggestion-, suggestio*, fr. *suggestus* (past part. of *suggerere* to suggest) + *-ion-, -io* -ion] **1** *obs* **:** incitement to evil **:** INSTIGATION, TEMPTATION ⟨thy ~, plot, and damned practice —Shak.⟩ **2 a :** the act or process of suggesting ⟨a letter written at a friend's ~⟩ **b :** something suggested: as (1) **:** PROPOSAL ⟨his ~*s* . . . had the force of commands —S.H. Adams⟩ (2) **:** INTIMATION, HINT ⟨his whispered ~ of something significant about to happen —Sherwood Anderson⟩ (3) **:** PROMPTING, INSPIRATION ⟨strange . . . that I should need a ~ from the *Iliad* —Thomas De Quincey⟩ **3 :** information given without oath in a legal action **:** an entry on the record for the action of the court of a material fact or circumstance (as the death or insolvency of a party) **4 a :** the process by which one thought leads to another esp. through association of ideas **:** the power of imaginative or artistic re-creation of experience **:** EVOCATION ⟨fear of the dark . . . seems to be entirely due to ~ —Bertrand Russell⟩ ⟨poetry achieves its finest effects by ~⟩ ⟨stimulates the observer with extraordinary ~ in his paintings —Howard Devree⟩ **b :** the act or process of impressing something (as an idea, attitude, or desired action) upon the mind of another ⟨visual ~ . . . far more powerful than the written word —Roy Lewis & Angus Maude⟩ ⟨situational factors influencing the process of ~ —T.E.Coffin⟩ **c :** a means or process of influencing attitudes and behavior hypnotically ⟨produced a hypnotic state very rapidly and by extremely simple ~ —C.P.Oberndorf⟩ **5 :** a slight indication or touch **:** SOUPÇON, TRACE ⟨a ~ of blue in the gray⟩ ⟨a sprightliness of flavor, a ~ of the pineapple, the apricot, the orange —David Fairchild⟩
sug·ges·tive \-estiv, -tēv *also* -təv\ *adj* [L *suggestus* (past part. of *suggerere* to suggest) + E *-ive*] **1 a :** giving a suggestion or hint **:** INDICATIVE, SIGNIFICANT ⟨the list is ~ rather than comprehensive⟩ ⟨his choice of writers is ~ of his bias —V.L.Parrington⟩ ⟨the peculiar distribution is very ~ —F.A. Geldard⟩ ⟨pediments on the wings, ~ of gable ends —*Amer. Guide Series: R.I.*⟩ **b :** full of suggestions **:** stimulating thought **:** PROVOCATIVE, SEMINAL ⟨provided a ~ running commentary on the era —Lloyd Morris⟩ ⟨a great variety of ~ ideas —M.R.Cohen⟩ **c :** stirring mental associations **:** PREGNANT, EVOCATIVE ⟨hauntingly ~ stories⟩ ⟨the poetry is . . . elusive and ~ —Richard Eberhart⟩ **2 :** suggesting or tending to suggest something considered improper or indecent **:** OFF-COLOR, RISQUÉ ⟨~ song lyrics⟩ ⟨a sly, ~ wink —A.M.Sampley⟩ ⟨a magazine of smutty jokes and ~ pictures —*Sydney (Australia) Bull.*⟩
sug·ges·tive·ly \-tə̇vlē, -li\ *adv* **:** in a suggestive manner **:** MEANINGFULLY, SIGNIFICANTLY ⟨picks up the empty bottle ~ —Erle Stanley Gardner⟩
sug·ges·tive·ness \-tivnəs, -tēv- *also* -təv-\ *n* -ES **:** the quality or state of being suggestive: as **a :** stimulation to thought **:** INSPIRATION ⟨your ~ . . . and affection have enriched life to me —O.W.Holmes †1935⟩ **b :** EVOCATIVENESS ⟨his writing was . . . possessed of an extraordinary power of ~ —J.T. Farrell⟩ **c :** intimation of or allusion to something held improper or obscene ⟨~ tended to take the place of honest bawdry —W.B.Adams⟩
sug·gil·la·tion \,sə(g)jəˈlāshən\ *n* -s [L *sugillation-, sugillatio*, fr. *sugillatus* (past part. of *sugillare, suggillare* to beat black and blue) + *-ion-, -io* -ion] **:** ECCHYMOSIS, BRUISE; *esp* **:** one that develops post-mortem ⟨~*s* of the head are not reliable signs of infanticide —*Ciba Clinical Symposia*⟩
sugh \ˈsü, ˈsüf, ˈsük\ *chiefly Scot var of* SOUGH
sugi \ˈsü(,)gē\ *n, pl* **sugi** *or* **sugis** [Jap] **:** JAPANESE CEDAR
su·i·ci·dal \ˌsüəˈsīdᵊl\ *adj* [¹*suicide* + *-al*] **1 :** of the nature of, relating to, or tending toward suicide **:** SELF-DESTRUCTIVE ⟨medical examiner said that death was ~ —*Springfield (Mass.) Daily News*⟩ ⟨the ~ implications of thermonuclear attack —Denis Healey⟩ ⟨mountain travel at that season was ~ —R. A.Billington⟩ **2 :** characterized by an impulse to commit suicide ⟨~ insanity⟩ ⟨I have had influenza and . . . feel ~ —G.B.Shaw⟩ **3 :** destructive of one's own interests ⟨knew it would be ~ to voice his true opinions in such a group⟩
su·i·ci·dal·ly \-ᵊlē,-ᵊli\ *adv* [*suicidal* + *-ly*] **:** in a manner suggestive of, tending toward, or risking self-destruction or the destruction of one's own interests **:** SELF-DESTRUCTIVELY ⟨the attack was . . . dangerous, almost ~ so —Frank Yerby⟩ ⟨the ouzel . . . flies ~ through a waterfall —Irving Petite⟩ ⟨a country ~ weakening its economy⟩
¹**su·i·cide** \ˈsüə,sīd\ *n* -s [L *sui* (gen.), *sibi* (dat.), *se* (accus. & abl.) oneself + E *-cide*; akin to OE *sīn* his, OHG *sih* (accus.) oneself, *sīn* his, ON *sik* (accus.) oneself, *sīnn* one's own, Goth *sik* oneself, *seins* his, L *suus* one's own, Gk *he* (accus.) oneself, *hos, heos* one's own, Skt *sva* oneself, one's own] **1 a :** the act or an instance of taking one's own life voluntarily and intentionally **:** SELF-DESTRUCTION ⟨the death was adjudged a ~⟩ **b :** the deliberate and intentional destruction of his own life by a person of years of discretion and of sound mind **:** FELO-DE-SE 2 ⟨civilizations . . . in which ~ was considered a completely honorable act —*New Republic*⟩ **c :** ruin of one's own interests ⟨drove into revolt or artistic ~ every student with an ounce of vitality in him —Clive Bell⟩ ⟨the proposal . . . is likely to be an invitation to political ~ —Frank Gorrell⟩ **2 :** one that commits or attempts self-murder **:** FELO-DE-SE 1 ⟨had a ~'*s* temperament, careless of life —J.H.Plumb⟩
²**suicide** \"\ *vb* -ED/-ING/-S *vi* **:** to commit suicide ⟨the unfortunate man had *suicided* —D.D.Martin⟩ ~ *vt* **:** to put (as oneself) to death **:** KILL ⟨after Brutus, aged twelve, had *suicided* himself —E.M.Forster⟩
³**suicide** \"\ *adj* **1** [¹*suicide*] **:** constituting a suicide ⟨his ~ brother —E.A.Mowrer⟩ ⟨the problem of the ~ blonde —J.P. O'Donnell⟩ **2** [¹*suicide*] **a :** resulting in or likely to result in the death of the individual or a high proportion of deaths in a participating group or unit — usu. used of a military or naval operation ⟨one-way ~ bombing missions⟩ ⟨supposed to make any attempt at invasion a ~ attack —*Coast Artillery Jour.*⟩ **b :** engaging in or intended to engage in such an operation ⟨~ pilot⟩ ⟨a ~ squad⟩ ⟨leaving a ~ force . . . to fight a rearguard action —F.B.Gipson⟩
suicide clause *n* **:** a provision limiting the liability of an insurer to a return of net premiums paid if a policyholder whether sane or insane commits suicide within a stipulated period
¹**su·id** \ˈsüəd\ *or* **su·id·i·an** \(ˈ)süˈidēən\ *adj* [*suid* fr. NL *Suidae; suidian* fr. NL *Suidae* + E *-ian*] **:** of or relating to the Suidae
²**suid** \"\ *or* **suidian** \"\ *n* -s **:** a swine of the family Suidae
su·idae \ˈsüə,dē\ *n pl, cap* [NL, fr. *Sus*, type genus + *-idae*] **:** a family of nonruminant artiodactylous mammals consisting of the wild and domestic swine but in modern classifications excluding the peccaries
su·iform \ˈsüə,fȯrm\ *adj* [NL *Suiformes*] **:** of or relating to the Suiformes
su·ifor·mes \ˌsüəˈfȯr,mēz\ *n pl, cap* [NL, fr. L *sus* swine, hog + NL *-iformes* — more at SOW] *in some classifications* **:** a suborder of Artiodactyla that comprises numerous nonruminant mammals including swine, peccaries, hippopotamuses, and extinct related forms
sui·gen·der·ism \ˌsü,īˈjendə,rizəm, ˌsüēˈj-\ *n* -s [L *suus* one's own + E *-i-* + *gender* + *-ism* — more at SUICIDE] **:** the state or the period of development (as in childhood or early adolescence) in which one becomes chiefly interested in or attracted toward persons of the same sex — contrasted with *altrigenderism*
sui ge·ner·is \ˌsü,īˈjenərəs; ˌsüēˈje-, -ēˈge-\ *adj* [L, of its own kind] **:** constituting a class alone **:** UNIQUE, PECULIAR ⟨possesses certain *sui generis* qualities —John Mason Brown⟩ — usu. used predicatively or postpositively ⟨the man is *sui generis* —John McCarten⟩ ⟨a history book *sui generis* —Max Wolff⟩
sui heredes *pl of* SUUS HERES
sui ju·ris \ˌsü,īˈju̇rəs, ˌsüēˈyü-\ *adj* [L, lit., of one's own right or authority] **1 :** having full legal capacity to act on one's own behalf **:** not subject to the authority of another — opposed to *alieni juris* **2 :** qualified to enjoy full civil rights (as of holding public office or serving on a jury)
sui·ker·bos *also* **sui·ker·bosch** \ˈsäkə(r),bäs, ˈsük-, -bȯs\ *or* **sui·ker·bos·sie** \-sē\ *n, pl* **suikerboses** *also* **suikerbosches** *or* **suikerbossies** [*suikerbos, suikerbosch* fr. Afrik, fr. *suiker* sugar (fr. MD *suker*, fr. MF *sucre*) + *bos, bosch* bush, fr. MD *bosch; suikerbossie* fr. Afrik, fr. *suiker* + *bossie*, dim. of *bos* — more at SUGAR, BUSH] **:** SUGAR BUSH 2
sui·mate \ˈsü,ī, ˈsüē+,-\ *n* -s [L *sui* (gen.) of oneself + E *mate* — more at SUICIDE] **1 :** checkmate forced by the side that is checkmated — called also *self-mate* **2 :** a chess problem in which suimate is required
su·ina \süˈīnə, -ˈēnə\ *n pl, cap* [NL, fr. L *sus* swine, hog + NL *-ina*] **:** a division of Artiodactyla (suborder Suiformes) that comprises the swine, peccaries, and closely related extinct forms and is occas. enlarged so that it becomes almost exactly coextensive with Suiformes
su·ine \ˈsü,īn\ *adj* [NL *Suina*] **:** of or relating to the Suina
suing *n* -s [fr. gerund of ¹*sue*] **:** legal prosecution **:** SUIT
su·int \ˈsüənt, ˈswint\ *n* -s [F, fr. MF, fr. *suer* to sweat, fr. L *sudare* — more at SWEAT] **:** the dried perspiration of sheep that is deposited in the wool chiefly in combination with fatty acids and that is rich in potassium salts — compare YOLK
suio·goth \ˈswēə,ˈsüyō+,-\ *n, cap* [NL *Suiogothi* (pl.) Goths of southern Sweden, fr. L *Suiones* + LL *Gothi* Goths] **:** a Scandinavian Goth; *esp* **:** a Goth from southern Sweden
sui·o·nes \ˈswēə,nēz, süˈīə-\ *n pl, usu cap* [L, of Gmc origin; akin to ON *Svīar* Swedes — more at SWEDE] **:** an ancient Teutonic people of what is now Sweden
sui·pes·ti·fer infection \ˌsü,ī,ˌpestəfə(r)-, ˌsüē\ *n* [NL *suipestifer* (specific epithet of *Salmonella suipestifer*, a bacterium causing the disease), fr. L *sus* swine + *-i-* + *pestifer* pestilential — more at SOW, PESTIFEROUS] **:** NECROTIC ENTERITIS
¹**suit** \ˈsüt, *usu* -üd·+V\ *n* -s [ME *siute, sute, suite* act of following, pursuit, petition, retinue, attendance, sequence, set of things, esp. of clothes, fr. OF *sieute, siute* act of following, pursuit, retinue, attendance, fr. fem. of (assumed) OF *sieut* (past part. of OF *suir* to follow), fr. (assumed) VL *sequitus*, past part. of (assumed) VL *sequere* to follow — more at SUE] **1** *archaic* **a :** an act of following (as game or a quest) **:** PURSUIT **b :** SUITE 1 ⟨in his ~ was . . . a young gentleman —Meriwether Lewis⟩ **2 a :** attendance (as at a royal court or a manor) owed according to feudal law by a vassal to his king or lord ⟨~ to some form of court was incumbent upon all landholders —F.M.Stenton⟩ **b :** the required resort of a tenant to a particular mill for his grinding — compare SUCKEN **3 a :** recourse or appeal to a feudal superior for justice or redress of grievances ⟨made ~ to the king in council⟩ **b :** the attempt to gain an end by legal process **:** prosecution of right before any tribunal **:** LITIGATION ⟨an added reason for early institution of ~ —Joseph Schneider⟩ **c :** an action or process in a court for the recovery of a right or claim **:** a legal application to a court for justice ⟨a civil ~⟩ ⟨a criminal ~⟩ ⟨a ~ in chancery⟩ ⟨no ~ . . . having been instituted to recover the debt —*Detroit Law Jour.*⟩ **4 :** an act or instance of suing or seeking by plea or entreaty **:** PETITION, APPEAL ⟨his ~ to the Muse —*Nation*⟩; *specif* **:** solicitation in marriage **:** COURTSHIP, WOOING ⟨mocks all her wooers out of ~ —Shak.⟩ ⟨had her father's consent to his ~⟩ **5 a :** SUITE 2 — used chiefly of armor, sails, clothes, and cards and counters in games ⟨a ~ of medieval armor⟩ ⟨~*s* of sails for . . . racing yachts —*Amer. Guide Series: N.Y. City*⟩ **b** *of hair* **:** HEAD 3a, GROWTH ⟨a beauty with big quick eyes and a heavy ~ of hair —Elizabeth M. Roberts⟩ **6 :** a set of garments **:** OUTFIT, COSTUME: as **a** *obs* **:** LIVERY; *esp* **:** that of the members of a retinue **b** *archaic* **:** HABIT; *esp* **:** one worn by a religious **c :** UNIFORM **d :** an outer costume of two or more parts that harmonize or match in material and color (as a jacket, vest, and trousers for men or a jacket and skirt for women) **e :** BATHING SUIT **f :** a set of underwear **g :** a costume designed to be worn for a special purpose or under particular conditions ⟨gym ~⟩ ⟨space ~⟩ **7 a** (1) **:** all the cards in a pack of playing cards bearing the same spot or symbol (as spades or hearts) — called also *color* (2) **:** all the bones in dominoes bearing the same number ⟨the ~ of sixes⟩ (3) **:** all the counters in a game (as tiles in mah-jongg) having the same name or symbol **b :** all the cards or counters given a special function by the rules of a game though not necessarily similarly marked ⟨a trump ~⟩ **c :** the cards or counters held by a player in a particular suit ⟨a 5-card ~⟩ **d :** the suit led or last played ⟨follow ~⟩ **8 :** AGREEMENT, HARMONY ⟨manual strength . . . in ~ with the ferocity of his manners —Agnes Repplier⟩ **syn** see PRAYER

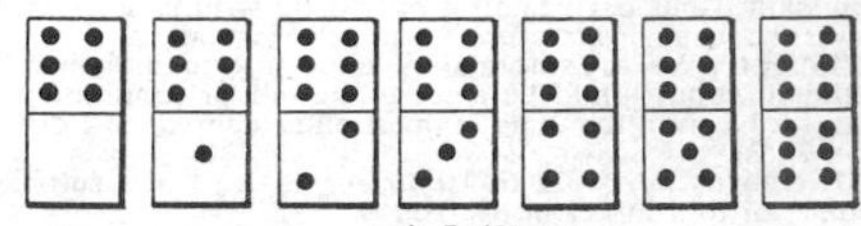
suit 7a(2)

²**suit** \"\ *vb* -ED/-ING/-S *vi* **1** *obs* **:** to make a plea **:** PETITION, SUE **2 :** to be in accordance **:** AGREE, SQUARE — usu. used with *with* ⟨the position ~*s* with his abilities⟩ ⟨steady principles . . . which will ~ with common practice and experience —David Hume †1776⟩ **3 :** to be appropriate, acceptable, or satisfactory ⟨a restaurant . . . that would ~ —F.W.Crofts⟩ ⟨she'll ~, and we'll make her feel at home —Rex Ingamells⟩ ~ *vt* **1** *obs* **:** to arrange (as materials) in a set or order **:** ASSORT **2** *obs* **a :** to appeal for **:** BEG ⟨if we had merit to deserve it, we needed not ~ it of God —William Struther⟩ **b :** to ask the hand of in marriage **:** COURT, WOO **3 :** to outfit with clothes **:** DRESS ⟨did ~ me all points like a man —Shak.⟩ ⟨~*ed* in black⟩ **4 :** to make agree or harmonize with something **:** ACCOMMODATE, ADJUST, FIT, ADAPT — usu. used with *to* ⟨~ the action to the word⟩ ⟨you must ~ your frock to his flowers —Oscar Wilde⟩ ⟨~ their game to their opponents —Robert Collis⟩ **5 a :** to be proper or right for or appropriate to **:** accord with **:** BEFIT ⟨the right word . . . is the one that ~*s* the time and the occasion —E.S.McCartney⟩ ⟨a long handle that did not ~ my grip —O.S.J.Gogarty⟩ **b :** to be becoming to **:** MATCH ⟨a lipstick that ~*ed* her coloring⟩ ⟨the Bible name ~*s* you —Katharine N. Burt⟩ **6 a :** to answer the needs, desires, or requirements of **:** PLEASE ⟨~*s* me fine⟩ ⟨an arrangement that ~*ed* him perfectly⟩ ⟨something to ~ every palate —Peter Forster⟩ ⟨the weather exactly ~*s* us —Martha Kean⟩ **b :** to provide or furnish (as a customer) with something (as merchandise) that proves satisfactory **:** SATISFY ⟨aim to ~ all our patrons⟩
suit·abil·i·ty \ˌsüd·əˈbiləd·ē, -ütə-, -lətē, -i\ *n* **:** the quality or state of being suitable: as **a :** COMPATIBILITY ⟨a marriage of pure inclination and ~ —Charles Dickens⟩ **b :** FITNESS, QUALIFICATION ⟨unfounded accusations reflecting on their loyalty and ~ —Sidney Hook⟩ ⟨the ~ of the land for cultivation⟩ **c :** APPROPRIATENESS ⟨due regard for . . . ~ of style —L.R.McColvin⟩
¹**suit·able** \ˈsüd·əbəl, -ütə-\ *adj* [²*suit* + *-able*] **1** *obs* **:** matching or correspondent (as in character, condition, or kind) **:** LIKE, SIMILAR ⟨in his face youth smiled celestial and to every limb ~ grace diffused —John Milton⟩ **2 a :** adapted to a use or purpose **:** FIT ⟨food ~ for human consumption⟩ ⟨a ~ stream for canoeing⟩ ⟨a style ~ for news announcements —F.L.Mott⟩ **b :** appropriate from the viewpoint of propriety, convenience, or fitness **:** PROPER, RIGHT ⟨a movie ~ for children⟩ ⟨a ~ employment⟩ ⟨clothes ~ for the occasion —James Laver⟩ ⟨pronounced a ~ epitaph —W.R.Inge⟩ **c :** having the necessary qualifications **:** meeting requirements **:** APT, QUALIFIED ⟨find a ~ actor for the role⟩ ⟨looked about for a ~ art school⟩ **syn** see FIT
²**suitable** \"\ *adv, archaic* **:** in a suitable manner **:** CONFORMABLY ⟨clothed and attended ~ to their father's birth —Eliza Parsons⟩
suit·able·ness *n* -ES [¹*suitable* + *-ness*] **:** SUITABILITY
suit·ably \-blē,-bli\ *adv* **:** in a suitable manner: as **a** *obs* **:** CONFORMABLY ⟨brutes . . . act ~ to their whole nature —Joseph Butler⟩ **b :** APPROPRIATELY ⟨trying to look ~ scandalized —H.W.Carter⟩ ⟨a testimonial address, ~ engraved —*Amer. Guide Series: Md.*⟩ **c :** FITLY, RIGHTLY ⟨the only director to stage the play ~⟩ **d :** in accordance with requirements **:** PROPERLY ⟨~ treated metal⟩
suit and service *also* **suit service** *n* [¹*suit*] **1 :** the obligation of being in attendance at a feudal court and of serving one's suzerain **2 :** HOMAGE, FEALTY; *also* **:** one's full duty
suitcase \ˈ=,=\ *n* [¹*suit* + *case*] **:** TRAVELING BAG; *esp* **:** one that is rigid, flat, and rectangular
suitcase farmer *n* **:** a grower of wheat or other crops who lives outside the community except during the plowing, seeding, and harvesting seasons, often has a farm without buildings, and does much of the farming by hired custom operators

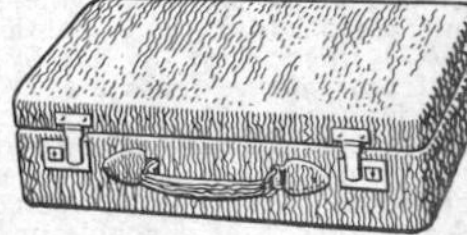
suitcase

suit court *n* **:** the feudal court in which tenants owe attendance

suit-dress \ˈ=,=\ *n* : a woman's two-piece costume that consists usu. of a lightweight jacket and skirt and is worn either as a dress or suit

suite \ˈswēt, *esp in sense 2e* ˈswē| *or* ÷ˈsüt; *usu* |d.+V\ *n* -s [F, alter. of OF *siute* — more at SUIT] **1** : a company of followers or attendants : RETINUE; *esp* : the personal staff (as assistants and secretaries) accompanying a ruler, diplomat, or dignitary on official business ⟨he and his ~, including his wife, secretarial attachés, and servants —H.A.Chippendale⟩ **2** : a series or group of things forming a unit or constituting a complement or collection : SET: as **a** (1) : a group of rooms designed for occupancy as a unit : APARTMENT ⟨a ~ of offices⟩ ⟨executive ~⟩ ⟨bridal ~⟩ ⟨the house . . . contains ninety ~*s* of three to six rooms —*N.Y. Times*⟩ (2) : two adjoining bedrooms in a railroad car having a removable partition for separate or joint occupancy **b** (1) : an instrumental musical form in vogue during the 17th and 18th centuries consisting of a series of usu. 3 to 5 dances (as allemande, gigue) in the same or related keys often with an elaborate prelude — compare SONATA (2) : a modern instrumental composition in several movements having sometimes almost the dimensions of a symphony but wholly free as to the character and number of its movements (3) : a long orchestral concert piece in suite form that is an arrangement by either the original composer or another of material drawn from a longer work (as an opera or ballet) **c** : a collection of rocks having some characteristic in common (as rock type or origin) **d** : SERIES 6a **e** : a set of matched furniture for a room ⟨a bedroom ~⟩ ⟨had a three-piece ~ in the living room⟩ **3** : SEQUEL ⟨the same inevitable ~ of rationalizations —Norman Mailer⟩

¹suit·ed \ˈsüd·əd, -ütəd\ *adj* [¹*suit* + *-ed*] : dressed in a suit — often used in combination ⟨velvet-*suited*⟩

²suited \"\ *adj* [fr. past part. of ²*suit*] **1** : CONFORMABLE, AGREEABLE ⟨the language of every speech community is ~ to the interests of that culture —Stuart Chase⟩ **2** : ADAPTED, APT ⟨farmlands particularly ~ to the growing of sugar beets —*Amer. Guide Series: Mich.*⟩

sui·ter's grass \ˈsüd·ə(r)z-\ *n, usu cap S* [prob. fr. the proper name *Suiter*] : a reed fescue (*Festuca elatior arundinacea*) that resembles orchard grass and is sometimes cultivated esp. in the northeastern U. S. for grazing

suithold \ˈ=,=\ *n* : a feudal tenure of a superior in consideration of suit at his court

suit·ing \ˌsüd·iŋ, -ütˌ, |ēŋ\ *n* -s [¹*suit* + *-ing*] : a fabric for men's and women's suits

¹suit·or \ˈsüd·ə(r), -ütə-\ *n* -s [ME *suter, sutor, suitor*, fr. AF *suter, suitor*, fr. L *secutor* follower, pursuer, fr. *secutus* (past part. of *sequi* to follow) + *-or* — more at SUE] **1** *archaic* : one of a retinue : FOLLOWER **2 a** : one in attendance upon a feudal superior **b** : one that petitions or entreats : PLEADER, PETITIONER ⟨she hath been a ~ to me for her brother —Shak.⟩ ⟨a petition, signed by the parties . . . who are ~*s* for the bill —T.E.May⟩ **c** : one that sues at law or prosecutes an action in a court of justice : a party to a suit : LITIGANT **3** : one that courts a woman or seeks to marry her : WOOER ⟨had difficulty choosing between her two ~*s*⟩ ⟨a ~ for the old king's daughter —A.C.Whitehead⟩

²suitor \"\ *vb* -ED/-ING/-S *vi, archaic* : to behave as a suitor : court a woman ~ *vt, archaic* : to seek (a woman) in marriage : WOO ⟨the miller's son . . . ~*ed* me —Sir Walter Scott⟩

suit-preference signal *n* : the play or discard in contract bridge of an unnecessarily high card to ask one's partner to lead the higher of two available suits and of a low card to ask him to lead the lower

suits *pl of* SUIT, *pres 3d sing of* SUIT

suit service *var of* SUIT AND SERVICE

sui·vez \(ˈ)sw(ʸ)ēˈvā\ *v imper* [F, 2nd pl. imper. of *suivre* to follow, fr. OF — more at SUE] **1** : FOLLOW — used as a direction in music for the accompanist or orchestra to follow the soloist **2** : SEGUE 2

su·ji *or* **su·jee** \ˈsü(ˌ)jē\ *n* -s [Hindi *sūjī*] *India* : wheat granulated but not pulverized

¹suk \ˈsük\ *n, pl* **suk** *or* **suks** *usu cap* **1** : a Nilotic people on the Ethiopian border and in the region of Lake Baringo in Kenya **2** : a member of the Suk people

²suk *var of* SUQ

su·key *also* **su·kie** *or* **su·ky** \ˈsükē\ *or* **suke** \-k\ *n, pl* **sukeys** *also* **sukies** *or* **sukes** [fr. *Sukey*, nickname for *Susanna*] *dial* : TEAKETTLE

su·kha·va·ti \səˈkävəd·ē, -ˈkəv-\ *n* -s *usu cap* [Skt *sukhavatī, sukhāvatī*, fr. fem. of *sukhavat, sukhāvat* blissful, fr. *sukha* bliss, happiness, fr. neut. of *sukha* running smoothly, agreeable, happy, fr. *su* good, well + *kha* cavity, axle hole, fr. *khanati* he digs — more at HYGIENE] : PURE LAND

su·ki·ya·ki \skē(y)ˈäkē, ˌsükē-, ˌsükē-\ *n* -s [Jap, fr. *suki-* (as in *sukimi* slices of fish) + *yaki* roasting] : meat, soybean curd, onions, bamboo shoots, and other vegetables cooked in soy sauce, sake, and sugar usu. at the table

suk·kah *or* **suc·cah** \ˈsükə, -(ˌ)kä\ *n, pl* **suk·koth** *or* **suk·kot** \ˈsüˌkōt(h), -ˌkōs, -kəs\ *or* **suk·kos** \-ˌkōs, -kəs\ *or* **sukkahs** *or* **suc·coth** *or* **suc·cot** *or* **suc·cos** *or* **succahs** [Heb *sukkāh*] : a booth or shelter with a roof of branches and leaves erected near a home or in or near a synagogue and used esp. for meals and for temporary residence during the celebration of the Sukkoth festival

suk·koth *or* **suc·coth** *or* **suk·kot** *or* **suk·kos** *or* **suc·cot** *or* **suc·cos** \ˈsüˌkōt(h), -ˌkōs, -kəs\ *n pl but sing in constr, usu cap* [Heb *sukkōth*, pl. of *sukkāh* thicket, hut, booth, arbor] : a Jewish religious festival of thanksgiving celebrated orig. as an autumn harvest festival that is commemorative of the temporary shelters of the Jews during their wandering in the wilderness and that begins on the 15th day of Tishri and lasts 7 days or 9 days with the annexed holidays of Shemini Atzereth and Simhath Torah — called also *Feast of Booths, Feast of Tabernacles*

suklat *var of* SUCLAT

su·ku·ma \səˈkümə\ *also* **su·ku** \-ü\ *n, pl* **sukuma** *or* **sukumas** *also* **suku** *or* **sukus** *usu cap* **1** : a Bantu-speaking people living south of Lake Victoria in East Africa that is the largest community of Tanganyika **2** : a member of the Sukuma people

sul- *comb form* [*sulfonic*] : sulfonic ⟨*sul*tam⟩ ⟨*sul*tone⟩

su·la \ˈsülə\ *n, cap* [NL, fr. ON *súla* gannet, pillar — more at SILE] : a genus (the type of the family Sulidae) of seabirds comprising the boobies

sul·cal \ˈsəlkəl\ *also* **sul·car** \-kə(r)\ *adj* [NL *sulcus* + E *-al* or *-ar*] **1** : of or relating to a sulcus **2** : GROOVE

sul·cate \ˈsəlˌkāt\ *also* **sul·cat·ed** \-ād·əd\ *adj* [*sulcate* fr. L *sulcatus*, past part. of *sulcare* to furrow, plow, fr. *sulcus* furrow; *sulcated* fr. L *sulcatus* + E *-ed*] : scored with furrows : furrowed or grooved esp. lengthwise

SULCL *abbr* set up in less than carloads

sul·co·marginal \ˌsəl(ˌ)kō+\ *adj* [L *sulcus* + E *-o-* + *marginal*] : situated at the margin of the spinal cord adjacent to the ventral median fissure

sul·cu·lus \ˈsəlkyələs\ *n, pl* **sulcu·li** \-yəˌlī\ [NL, dim. of *sulcus*] : a small sulcus

sul·cus \ˈsəlkəs\ *n, pl* **sul·ci** \-lˌsī\ [NL, fr. L, furrow; akin to Gk *holkos* track, trace, furrow, *helkein* to drag, pull, OE *sulh* plow, measure of land (cultivated by one plow), Arm *helg* slow, sluggish, Toch B *sälk* to pull, drag forward] : FURROW, GROOVE, FISSURE; *esp* : a shallow furrow on the surface of the brain separating adjacent convolutions

sulcus lu·na·tus \-lüˈnād·əs\ *n, pl* **sulci luna·ti** \-āˌtī\ [NL, crescent-shaped groove] : a small inconstant semilunar furrow on the lateral surface of the cerebral hemisphere reputed to occur most often in the brains of primitive peoples

sulcus of ro·lan·do \-rōˈlan(ˌ)dō, -län-\ *usu cap R* [after Luigi *Rolando* †1831 Ital. anatomist] : CENTRAL SULCUS

sulcus ter·mi·na·lis \-ˌtərməˈnāləs\ *n, pl* **sulci termina·les** \-ā(ˌ)lēz\ [NL, lit., terminal groove] **1** : a V-shaped groove separating the anterior two thirds of the tongue from the posterior third and lodging the circumvallate papillae **2** : a shallow groove on the outside of the right atrium of the heart

suld \ˈsəld, ˈsüd\ *archaic var of* SHOULD

sulf- *or* **sulfo-** *or* **sulph-** *or* **sulpho-** *comb form* [*sulf-, sulfo-* fr. F, fr. L *sulfur*; *sulph-, sulpho-* modif. (influenced by *sulphur*) of F *sulf-, sulfo-* — more at SULFUR] : sulfur ⟨*sulf*hydryl⟩ ⟨*sulfo*ne⟩ ⟨*sulf*onium⟩ ⟨*sulfo*cyanic⟩: as **a** : sulfide ⟨*sulf*arsenide⟩ ⟨*sulfo*chloride⟩ **b** : derived from sulfuric acid : sulfuric ⟨*sulf*amide⟩ **c** *usu* **sulfo-** : containing the sulfonic acid group esp. replacing hydrogen : sulfonic ⟨*sulfo*amino⟩ ⟨*sulfo*benzoic⟩ **d** : SULFON- 2 ⟨*sulfo*chlorinate⟩ **e** : THI- ⟨*sulfo*cyanate⟩

¹sul·fa *also* **sul·pha** \ˈsəlfə\ *adj* [short for *sulfanilamide*] **1** : related chemically to sulfanilamide — compare SULFA- **2** : consisting of, containing, or utilizing a sulfa drug

²sulfa *also* **sulpha** \"\ *n* -s : SULFA DRUG

sulfa- *or* **sulf-** *also* **sulpha-** *or* **sulph-** *comb form* [*sulfa-, sulf-* fr. *sulfanilamide*; *sulpha-, sulph-* alter. (influenced by *sulphur*) of *sulfa-, sulf-*] : derived from or otherwise closely related to sulfanilamide: as **a** : SULFANILAMIDO- ⟨*sulfa*diazine⟩ **b** : containing sulfanilyl ⟨*sulf*acetamide⟩

sul·fa·cet·a·mide *also* **sul·fa·cet·i·mide** \ˌsəlfəˈsed·əˌmīd, -ˌməd\ *n* [*sulfacetamide* ISV *sulfa-* + *acetamide*; *sulfacetimide* alter. (influenced by *imide*) of *sulfacetamide*] : a sulfa drug $H_2NC_6H_4SO_2NHCOCH_3$ that has acid properties in solution and that is used chiefly for treating infections of the urinary tract and in the form of its sodium derivative for infections of the eye; *N*-sulfanilyl-acetamide

sul·fa·diazine \ˈsəlfə+\ *n* [*sulfa-* + *diazine*] : a sulfa drug $H_2NC_6H_4SO_2NHC_4H_3N_2$ derived from pyrimidine and sulfanilamide and used in the treatment of meningitis, pneumonia, and intestinal and other infections

sulfa drug *n* : any of a class of synthetic organic antibacterial usu. crystalline drugs (as sulfadiazine or sulfathiazole) that are sulfonamides closely related chemically to sulfanilamide ⟨the *sulfa drugs* are antibacterial agents, bacteriostatic rather than germicidal in action, which are used alone or in various combinations with each other or with antibiotics in the treatment of many types of infection such as those caused by β-hemolytic streptococci or pneumococci —M.E.Hultquist⟩

sul·fa·guanidine \"+\ *n* [*sulfa-* + *guanidine*] : a sulfa drug $H_2NC_6H_4SO_2NHC(=NH)NH_2$ used esp. formerly in treating intestinal infections — called also *sulfanilylguanidine*

sul·fa·mate \ˈsəlfəˌmāt\ *n* -s [*sulfamic* + *-ate*] : a salt or ester of sulfamic acid

sul·fa·mer·a·zine \ˌsəlfəˈmerəˌzēn, -ˌzən\ *n* [*sulfa-* + *-mer* + *azine*] : a sulfa drug $C_{11}H_{12}N_4O_2S$ that is a monomethyl derivative of sulfadiazine and is similarly used and also in veterinary medicine

sul·fa·meth·a·zine \ˌsəlfəˈmethəˌzēn, -ˌzən\ *n* [*sulfa-* + *meth-* + *azine*] : a sulfa drug $C_{12}H_{14}N_4O_2S$ that is a dimethyl derivative of sulfadiazine and is used similarly and also in veterinary medicine

sul·fa·mez·a·thine \-ezəˌthēn, -ˌthən\ *n* -s [by alter.] *chiefly Brit* : SULFAMETHAZINE

sul·fam·ic acid \ˌsəlˈfamik-\ *n* [ISV *sulf-* + *amide* + *-ic*] **1** : a strong crystalline acid H_2NSO_3H made usu. by reaction of sulfuric acid, sulfur trioxide, and urea and used chiefly as a weed killer, in cleaning metals, and in the form of salts as a flameproofing or softening agent for paper and textiles : the half amide of sulfuric acid **2** : any of a group of organic derivatives $RNHSO_3H$ or R_2NSO_3H of sulfamic acid that are stable if the R represents alkyl but unstable if one R is aryl or acyl

sulf·am·ide \ˌsəlˈfaˌmīd, ˈsəlfəˌm-, -ˌməd\ *n* [ISV *sulf-* + *amide*] **1 a** : a crystalline neutral compound $SO_2(NH_2)_2$ obtainable by treating sulfuryl chloride with ammonia : the amide of sulfuric acid **b** : any of several derivatives of this compound **2** : SULFONAMIDE

sulf·a·mid·ic acid \ˌsəlfəˈmidik-\ *n* [*sulfamide* + *-ic*] : SULFAMIC ACID

sul·fam·o·yl \ˌsəlˈfaməwəl\ *or* **sul·fa·myl** \ˈsəlfəˌmil\ *n* -s [*sulfamic* + *-oyl* or *-yl*] : the univalent radical H_2NSO_2- of sulfamic acid

sul·fa·nil·a·mide \ˌsəlfəˈniləˌmīd, -ˌməd\ *n* [*sulfanilic* + *amide*] **1** : a crystalline sulfonamide $H_2NC_6H_4SO_2NH_2$ that is made usu. by the action of ammonia and then alkali on *N*-acetyl-sulfanilyl chloride, that is the parent compound of most of the sulfa drugs, and that is used less than sulfadiazine and other sulfa drugs : the amide of sulfanilic acid **2** : a derivative of sulfanilamide; *esp* : SULFA DRUG

sulfanilamido- *comb form* [*sulfanilamide*] : containing the univalent radical $H_2NC_6H_4SO_2NH$- derived from sulfanilamide ⟨2-*sulfanilamido*pyrimidine⟩

sul·fan·i·late \ˌsəlˈfanəˌlāt\ *n* -s [*sulfanilic* + *-ate*] : a salt or ester of sulfanilic acid

sul·fa·nil·ic acid \ˌsəlfəˈnilik-\ *n* [ISV *sulf-* + *anilic*; prob. orig. formed as F *sulfanilique*] : a crystalline acid $H_2NC_6H_4SO_3H$ made by sulfonating aniline and used chiefly as a dye intermediate; *para*-amino-benzenesulfonic acid — compare METANILIC ACID, ORTHANILIC ACID

sul·fan·i·lyl \ˌsəlˈfanəˌlil\ *n* -s [*sulfanilic* + *-yl*] : the univalent radical $H_2NC_6H_4SO_2$— of sulfanilic acid

sul·fan·i·lyl·guanidine \-ˈ=,=,=+\ *n* [*sulfanilyl* + *guanidine*] : SULFAGUANIDINE

sulf·antimonide \ˈsəlf+\ *n* [*sulf-* + *antimonide*] : a compound that is both a sulfide and an antimonide

sul·fa·pyrazine \ˈsəlfə+\ *n* [*sulfa-* + *pyrazine*] : a sulfa drug $C_{10}H_{10}N_4O_2S$ derived from pyrazine and sulfanilamide and used similarly to sulfadiazine

sul·fa·pyridine \"+\ *n* [*sulfa-* + *pyridine*] : a sulfa drug $C_{11}H_{11}N_3O_2S$ derived from pyridine and sulfanilamide, used in small doses in the treatment of one type of dermatitis and esp. formerly against pneumococcal and gonococcal infections

sul·fa·pyrimidine \"+\ *n* [*sulfa-* + *pyrimidine*] : a sulfa drug derived from pyrimidine; *esp* : SULFADIAZINE

sul·fa·quinoxaline \"+\ *n* [*sulfa-* + *quinoxaline*] : a sulfa drug $C_{14}H_{12}N_4O_2S$ derived from quinoxaline and used esp. in veterinary medicine

sulf·arsenide \ˈsəlf+\ *n* [*sulf-* + *arsenide*] : a compound that is both a sulfide and an arsenide

sulf·arsphenamine \"+\ *n* [*sulf-* + *arsphenamine*] : an orange-yellow powder essentially $C_{12}H_{10}As_2N_2O_2(CH_2SO_3Na)_2$ that is similar to neoarsphenamine and arsphenamine in structure and uses

sulfas *pl of* SULFA

Sul·fa·sux·i·dine \ˌsəlfəˈsəksəˌdēn, -ˌdən\ *trademark* — used for succinylsulfathiazole

sul·fat·ase \ˈsəlfəˌtās\ *n* -s [ISV ¹*sulfate* + *-ase*] : any of various esterases that accelerate the hydrolysis of sulfuric esters and that are found esp. in invertebrate and other animal tissues and in microorganisms

¹sul·fate *or* **sul·phate** \ˈsəlˌfāt, *usu* -ād·+V\ *n* -s [*sulfate* fr. F, fr. L *sulfur* + F *-ate*; *sulphate* modif. (influenced by *sulphur*) of F *sulfate*] : a salt or ester of sulfuric acid of which most of the salts except those of barium, lead, strontium, and calcium are fairly soluble in water

²sulfate *or* **sulphate** \"\ *vb* -ED/-ING/-S *vt* **1** : to treat or combine with sulfuric acid, a sulfate, or a related agent : convert into a sulfate; *esp* : to convert (an organic compound) into a sulfuric monoester containing the acid group —OSO_2OH ⟨*sulfated* alcohols are important anionic detergents⟩ — compare SULFONATE **2** : to form a deposit of a whitish scale of lead sulfate on (the plates of a storage battery) ~ *vi* : to become sulfated

sulfated oil *n* : any of numerous water-soluble oils obtained usu. by treating unsaturated or hydroxylated fatty oils (as various fish oils or castor oil) or their fatty acids with concentrated sulfuric acid so that the essential product is a sulfuric monoester — compare SULFONATED OIL

sulfate group *or* **sulfate ion** *n* : the bivalent group or anion SO_4 or —OSO_2O— characteristic of sulfuric acid and sulfates

sulfate of potash : POTASSIUM SULFATE a — used chiefly of the fertilizer grade

sulfate paper *n* : unbleached or bleached paper made wholly from sulfate pulp

sulfate process *n* : an alkaline process for making pulp from wood chips in which the cooking liquor contains chiefly sodium hydroxide together with considerable amounts of sodium sulfide derived from the reduction of sodium sulfate added during the recovery process

sulfate pulp *n* : wood pulp prepared by the sulfate process

sulfate turpentine *or* **sulfate wood turpentine** *n* : TURPENTINE 2d

Sul·fa·thal·i·dine \ˌsəlfəˈthaləˌdēn, -ˌdən\ *trademark* — used for phthalylsulfathiazole

sul·fa·thiazole \ˈsəlfə+\ *n* [*sulfa-* + *thiazole*] : a sulfa drug $H_2NC_6H_4SO_2NHC_3H_2NS$ derived from thiazole and sulfanilamide, seldom prescribed because of its toxicity, but formerly used esp. in the treatment of pneumococcus and staphylococcus infections

sul·fat·ic \ˌsəlˈfad·ik\ *adj* [ISV ¹*sulfate* + *-ic*] : of, relating to, resembling, or containing a sulfate

sul·fa·tion \ˌsəlˈfāshən\ *n* -s : the process of sulfating or becoming sulfated

sul·fa·tize \ˈsəlfəˌtīz\ *vt* -ED/-ING/-S [ISV ¹*sulfate* + *-ize*] : to convert into sulfate (as sulfide ores by roasting)

sulfato- *also* **sulphato-** *comb form* [¹*sulfate*] : containing the sulfate group — esp. in names of coordination complexes ⟨ammonium tri-*sulfato*-cerate $(NH_4)_2[Ce(SO_4)_3]$⟩

sul·fen·ic acid \ˌsəlˈfenik-\ *n* [*sulf-* + *en-* + *-ic*] : any of a series of monobasic organic acids of sulfur having the general formula RSOH and known almost exclusively in the form of derivatives (as acid halides and amides) — compare SULFINIC ACID, SULFONIC ACID

sul·fen·yl \ˌsəlˈfenᵊl\ *n* [*sulfenic* + *-yl*] : the radical of a sulfenic acid ⟨benzene-*sulfenyl* chloride C_6H_5SCl⟩

sulf·hemoglobin \ˈsəlf+\ *n* [ISV *sulf-* + *hemoglobin*] : a green pigment formed by the reaction of hemoglobin with a sulfide in the presence of oxygen or hydrogen peroxide and found in putrefied organs and cadavers

sulf·he·mo·glo·bi·ne·mia \ˌsəlfˌhēməˌglōbəˈnēmēə, -ˌheməˌ-\ *n* -s [NL, fr. ISV *sulfhemoglobin* + NL *-emia*] : the presence of sulfhemoglobin in the blood

sulf·hydrate \ˈsəlf+\ *also* **sul·phy·drate** \ˌsəlˈfīˌdrāt\ *n* [ISV *sulf-* + *hydrate*] : HYDROSULFIDE — not used systematically

sulf·hy·dryl \ˌsəlfˈhīdrəl\ *also* **sul·phy·dryl** \-lˈfī-\ *n* -s [ISV *sulf-* + *hydr-* + *-yl*] : the mercapto group

sul·fi·da·tion \ˌsəlfəˈdāshən\ *n* -s : the process of sulfiding

¹sul·fide *or* **sul·phide** \ˈsəlˌfīd, -lfəd\ *n* -s [ISV *sulf-* + *-ide*; prob. orig. formed as G *sulfid*] **1** : a compound of sulfur analogous to an oxide with sulfur in place of oxygen: **a** : a binary compound of sulfur usu. with a more electropositive element : a salt of hydrogen sulfide ⟨~*s* of iron⟩ ⟨the metallic ~*s* except those of the alkali metals are usu. insoluble in water and occur in many cases as minerals⟩ — compare DISULFIDE 1, POLYSULFIDE **b** : a compound of sulfur with more than one element ⟨many minerals (as tetrahedrite) are double or multiple ~*s*⟩ — compare SULFOSALT **2** : a compound of sulfur analogous to an ether with sulfur in place of oxygen : an ester of hydrogen sulfide ⟨ethyl ~ $(C_2H_5)_2S$⟩ — called also *organic sulfide, thioether*; compare DISULFIDE 2, MUSTARD GAS

²sulfide *or* **sulphide** \"\ *vt* -ED/-ING/-S : to treat with or convert into a sulfide — compare XANTHATE

sulfide dye *or* **sulfide color** *n* : SULFUR DYE

sulfide toning *n* : SULFUR TONING; *esp* : this process when the final bath is in a solution of sodium sulfide

sul·fid·ic \ˌsəlˈfidik\ *adj* [ISV ¹*sulfide* + *-ic*] : of, relating to, or containing sulfide

sul·fi·dize \ˈsəlfəˌdīz\ *vt* -ED/-ING/-S *see -ize in Explan Notes* : SULFIDE

sul·fil·i·mine \ˌsəlˈfiləˌmēn, -ˌmən\ *n* [*sulf-* + *-il* + *imine*] : any of a class of compounds containing a nitrogen-to-sulfur bond, having the general formula $R'NSR_2$, and formed by reaction of an organic sulfide with a chloramide (as chloramine-T) and alkali

sul·fi·mide \ˈsəlfəˌmīd, -ˌməd\ *n* [ISV *sulf-* + *imide*] : an imide of a carboxylic-sulfonic acid; *esp* : SACCHARIN

sulfin- *or* **sulfino-** *comb form* [*sulfinic*] : containing the group —SO_2H characteristic of the sulfinic acids

sul·fi·nate \ˈsəlfəˌnāt\ *n* -s [*sulfin-* + *-ate*] : a salt or ester of a sulfinic acid

sul·fin·ic acid \ˌsəlˈfinik-\ *n* [ISV *sulf-* + *-in* + *-ic*] : any of a series of monobasic organic acids of sulfur having the general formula RSO_2H and obtained by reducing the chlorides of sulfonic acids and in other ways — compare SULFOXYLIC ACID

sul·fi·nyl \ˈsəlfəˌnil\ *n* -s [*sulfin-* + *-yl*] : the bivalent group or radical >SO occurring in sulfoxides, sulfinic acids, and derivatives of the acids : THIONYL — used esp. of organic compounds

sul·fi·sox·a·zole \ˌsəlfəˈsäksəˌzōl\ *n* [*sulfa-* + *isoxazole*] : a sulfa drug $C_{11}H_{13}N_3O_3S$ derived from sulfanilamide and isoxazole and used similarly to other sulfanilamide derivatives but because of its greater solubility it is less likely to produce renal damage

sul·fi·ta·tion \ˌsəlfəˈtāshən\ *n* -s [ISV *sulfite* + *-ation*] : the process of sulfiting

sulfitation cake *n* : the residue of sugarcane juice from filter presses that has been treated by sulfitation and formed into a cake containing lime and phosphorus and used for fertilizer

¹sul·fite *or* **sul·phite** \ˈsəlˌfīt, *usu* -īd·+V\ *n* -s [*sulfite* fr. F, alter. (influenced by ¹*-ite*) of *sulfate*; *sulphite* modif. (influenced by *sulphur*) of F *sulfite*] : a salt or ester of sulfurous acid — **sul·fit·ic** \ˌsəlˈfid·ik\ *adj*

²sulfite *or* **sulphite** \"\ *vt* -ED/-ING/-S : to treat with sulfur dioxide, sulfurous acid, or a sulfite

sulfite liquor *n* : the bisulfite solution used in making pulp by the sulfite process

sulfite paper *n* : paper made wholly from sulfite pulp

sulfite process *n* : an acid process for making pulp from wood in which chips are cooked at high temperature and pressure in a solution of bisulfite of calcium, magnesium, sodium, or ammonium

sulfite pulp *n* : wood pulp prepared by the sulfite process ⟨*sulfite pulps* are particularly useful for writing papers because of their . . . strength —J.P.Casey⟩

sulfito- *also* **sulphito-** *comb form* [¹*sulfite*] : containing the sulfite group SO_3 — esp. in names of coordination complexes ⟨sodium *sulfito*aurate(III) $Na[Au(SO_3)_2]$⟩

sulfo- — see SULF-

sul·fo acid \ˈsəl(ˌ)fō-\ *n* [*sulfo* short for *sulfonic*] **1** : THIO ACID **2** : SULFONIC ACID

sul·fo·benzoic acid \ˌsəl(ˌ)fō+. . .-\ *n* [ISV *sulf-* + *benzoic*] : any of three isomeric crystalline acids $HO_3SC_6H_4COOH$ that are sulfonic derivatives of benzoic acid, that are made either from benzoic acid by sulfonation in the case of the meta isomer or from the corresponding toluenesulfonic acid by oxidation in the case of the ortho or para isomer, and that are used in organic synthesis

sul·fo·bis·muth·ite \ˌsəlfəˈbizməˌthīt, -ism-, -ˌthīt\ *n* [*sulf-* + *bismuth* + *-ite*] : any of various compounds of metals with sulfur and trivalent bismuth

sul·fo·bo·rite *or* **sul·pho·bo·rite** \ˌsəlfəˈbōrˌīt, -ˈbȯˌrīt\ *n* -s [G *sulfoborit*, fr. *sulf-* + *borat* borate + *-it* -ite] : a mineral $Mg_6H_4(BO_3)_4(SO_4)_2.7H_2O$ consisting of hydrous acid sulfate and borate of magnesium

sul·fo·chloride \ˈsəl(ˌ)fō+\ *n* [ISV *sulf-* + *chloride*] **1** : a compound with sulfur and chlorine that is analogous to an oxychloride ⟨phosphorus ~ $PSCl_3$⟩ **2** : SULFONYL CHLORIDE

sul·fo·chlorinate \"+\ *vt* [*sulf-* + *chlorinate*] : to convert (as a paraffin hydrocarbon) into a sulfonyl chloride by introducing the —SO_2Cl group

sul·fo·chlorination \"+\ *n* : conversion by sulfochlorinating

sul·fo·cyanate \"+\ *n* [ISV *sulf-* + *cyanate*] : THIOCYANATE — not used systematically

sul·fo·cyanide \"+\ *n* [ISV *sulf-* + *cyanide*] : THIOCYANATE — not used systematically

sul·fo·fi·ca·tion \ˌsəlfəfəˈkāshən\ *n* -s [*sulf-* + *-fication*] : a process of oxidation by which sulfur and sulfur compounds (as sulfides) are converted into sulfates esp. in soils by the agency of bacteria

sul·fo·fy \ˈsəlfəˌfī\ *vt* -ED/-ING/-ES [*sulf-* + *-fy*] : to subject to or produce by sulfofication

sulfo group *n* [*sulfo* short for *sulfonic*] : the sulfonic group

sul·fo·halite *or* **sul·pho·halite** \ˈsəl(ˌ)fō+\ *n* [*sulf-* + *halite*] : a mineral $Na_6ClF(SO_4)_2$ consisting of fluoride, chloride, and sulfate of sodium

sulfon- *also* **sulphon-** *comb form* [*sulfon-* ISV *sulfonic*; *sulphon-* fr. obs. E *sulphonic*, fr. *sulphone* sulfone (ISV *sulf-* + *-one*) + E *-ic*] **1** : sulfonic ⟨*sulfon*amido⟩ ⟨*sulfon*methane⟩ ⟨*sulfon*phthalein⟩ **2** : sulfonyl

sul·fo·nal \ˈsəlfəˌnal, ˌ==ˈ=\ *n* -s [fr. *Sulfonal*, a trademark] : SULFONMETHANE

sul·fon·a·mide \ˌsəlˈfänəˌmīd, -ˈfōn-, ˌsəlfəˈnaˌm-, -ˌməd\ *n* [*sulfon-* + *amide*] **:** the amide of a sulfonic acid characterized by the grouping $-SO_2N<$ consisting of nitrogen attached to sulfonyl ⟨benzene-*sulfonamide* $C_6H_5SO_2NH_2$⟩; *esp* **:** SULFA DRUG ⟨the bacteriostatic action of ~*s* is antimetabolite in nature —*U.S. Dispensatory*⟩ — see SULFANILAMIDE

¹sul·fo·nate \ˈsəlfəˌnāt\ *n* -S [ISV *sulfonic* + *-ate*] **:** a salt or ester of a sulfonic acid

²sulfonate *also* **sul·pho·nate** \"\ *vt* -ED/-ING/-S [*sulfonate* fr. ¹*sulfonate; sulphonate* fr. obs. E *sulphonate*, n., salt or ester of a sulfonic acid, fr. E *sulphon-* (fr. obs. E *sulphonic* sulfonic) + E *-ate*] **:** to introduce the sulfonic group into (an organic compound) **:** convert into a sulfonic acid or salt or halide (as by treating with concentrated sulfuric acid, oleum, or chlorosulfonic acid); *broadly* **:** to treat (an organic substance) with sulfuric acid or a related agent regardless of the nature of the products — compare SULFATE 1

sulfonated oil *n* **:** any of numerous water-soluble oils that are obtained usu. by treating various fatty oils or fatty acids with concentrated sulfuric acid or oleum by a process now considered to be essentially sulfation in most cases rather than true sulfonation and that are used chiefly as wetting and emulsifying agents, as dyeing assistants and lubricants in the textile industry, and in fat-liquoring of leather — compare SULFATED OIL, TURKEY-RED OIL

sul·fo·na·tion \ˌ==ˈnāshən\ *n* -S [ISV ²*sulfonate* + *-ion*] **:** the process of sulfonating

sul·fo·na·tor \ˈ==ˌnād·ə(r)\ *n* -S **:** one that sulfonates **:** an acid-resistant vessel used for the sulfonation of organic substances

sul·fon·chloramide \ˌsəlˌfōn+\ *n* [*sulfon-* + *chloramide*] **:** a sulfonamide in which chlorine is attached to the nitrogen atom **:** an *N*-chloro-sulfonamide — not used systematically; compare CHLORAMINE-T, DICHLORAMINE-T

sul·fone \ˈsəlˌfōn\ *n* -S [ISV *sulf-* + *-one*; prob. orig. formed as G *sulfon*] **:** any of a class of organic compounds that are characterized by the sulfonyl group doubly united by means of its sulfur usu. with carbon (as with two hydrocarbon radicals or a single bivalent radical) and that are in general crystalline stable compounds made by oxidation of organic sulfides and in other ways; *esp* **:** diaminodiphenyl sulfone or a derivative or closely related compound used in medicine chiefly in the treatment of leprosy

sul·fone·phthalein *also* **sul·fon·phthalein** \ˌsəlˌfōn, -fän+\ *n* [*sulfone, sulfon-* + *phthalein*] **:** any of a group of organic compounds (as phenolsulfonephthalein or bromocresol purple) that are analogous to the phthaleins and like them are intensely colored in alkaline solution and that are made by condensation of phenols with anhydrides or acid chlorides of *ortho*-sulfobenzoic acid or its derivatives

sul·fon·eth·yl·meth·ane \ˌsəlˌfōˌnethəlˈmeˌthān, -lˌfäˈ-\ *n* [*sulfon-* + *ethyl* + *methane*] **:** a crystalline hypnotic sulfone $CH_3C(C_2H_5)(SO_2C_2H_5)_2$ that is an ethyl analogue of sulfonmethane

sul·fon·ic \ˌsəlˈfänik\ *adj* [ISV *sulfone* + *-ic*] **:** being, containing, or derived from the univalent acid group $-SO_3H$ or $-SO_2OH$

sulfonic acid *n* **:** any of numerous acids that are characterized by the sulfonic group and may be regarded as derived from sulfuric acid by replacement of a hydroxyl group by either an inorganic anion or a univalent organic radical; *esp* **:** any of a class of organic acids (as toluenesulfonic acids or phenolsulfonic acids) that have the general formula RSO_3H when only one sulfonic group is present, that are in general stable, easily water-soluble, strong acids, that are made esp. in the case of the aromatic acids by direct sulfonation, and that are used often in the form of salts chiefly as catalysts, detergents, and intermediates (as for dyes) — compare CHLOROSULFONIC ACID, PETROLEUM SULFONATE, SULFINIC ACID

sul·fo·ni·um \ˌsəlˈfōnēəm\ *n* -S [NL, fr. *sulf-* + *-onium*] **:** a univalent cation H_3S^+ or radical H_3S analogous to oxonium with sulfur in place of oxygen and known esp. in the form of organic derivatives (as triethyl-*sulfonium* iodide) made usu. by reaction of an organic sulfide with an alkyl halide — compare -THIONIUM

sul·fon·methane \ˌsəlˌfōn, -ˌfän+\ *n* [*sulfon-* + *methane*] **:** a crystalline hypnotic sulfone $(CH_3)_2C(SO_2C_2H_5)_2$ made from acetone by reaction with ethyl mercaptan followed by oxidation

sul·fo·nyl \ˈsəlfəˌnil\ *n* -S [ISV *sulfon-* + *-yl*] **:** the bivalent group or radical $>SO_2$ occurring in sulfones, sulfonic acids, and derivatives of the acids **:** SULFURYL — used esp. of organic compounds

sulfonyl chloride *n* **:** the chloride of a sulfonic acid

sul·fo·salt \ˈsəlfəˌsȯlt\ *n* [ISV *sulf-* + *salt*] **:** a compound (as tetrahedrite) that is either a salt of an inorganic thio acid or a double or multiple sulfide

sul·fo·selenide \ˌsəl(ˌ)fō+\ *n* [*sulf-* + *selenide*] **:** a substance (as cadmium red) consisting of or containing both a sulfide and a selenide

sulf·ox·ide \ˌsəlˈfäkˌsīd, -ksəd\ *n* [ISV *sulf-* + *oxide*] **:** any of a class of organic compounds that are characterized by the sulfinyl group doubly united by means of its sulfur with carbon (as with two hydrocarbon radicals or a single bivalent radical), that are usu. made by oxidation of organic sulfides, and that yield sulfones on further oxidation

sulf·ox·one sodium \ˌsəlˈfäkˌsōn-\ *n* [*sulfoxone* alter. (influenced by *ox-*) of *sulfone*] **:** a crystalline salt $SO_2(C_6H_4\text{-}NHCH_2SO_2Na)_2$ made by the condensation of diaminodiphenyl sulfone and sodium formaldehydesulfoxylate and used in the treatment of leprosy

sulf·ox·y·late \ˌsəlˈfäksəˌlāt\ *n* -S [ISV *sulfoxylic* + *-ate*] **:** a salt or ester of sulfoxylic acid or one of its organic derivatives; *esp* **:** FORMALDEHYDESULFOXYLATE

sulf·ox·yl·ic acid \ˌsəlˌfäkˈsilik-\ *n* [ISV *sulf-* + *ox-* + *-yl* + *-ic*] **:** a hypothetical acid $S(OH)_2$ or HSO_2H known in the form of various organic derivatives — compare FORMALDEHYDESULFOXYLIC ACID, SULFINIC ACID

¹sul·fur *or* **sul·phur** \ˈsəlfə(r)\ *n* -S [ME *soufre, sulphre, sulphur* brimstone, fr. OF & L; ME *soufre* fr. OF, fr. L *sulphur, sulfur*; ME *sulphre, sulphur* fr. L *sulphur, sulfur, sulpur*, prob. fr. Oscan] **1 :** a nonmetallic multivalent tasteless odorless water-insoluble element that occurs in large quantities either free esp. in yellow orthorhombic crystals or in masses often associated with limestone, gypsum, and other minerals (as in volcanic regions in Sicily and Japan and in salt domes in Louisiana and Texas) or combined esp. in sulfides (as pyrites and galena) and sulfates (as gypsum and barite), that is also a constituent of proteins and various other compounds found in animals and plants, that exists in several allotropic forms including the ordinary yellow orthorhombic alpha form stable below 95.5°C and changing successively to a pale yellow monoclinic crystalline beta form, a pale yellow mobile liquid, and a dark red to brown very viscous liquid as the temperature is raised to about 200°C, that burns in air with a blue flame forming sulfur dioxide and a trace of sulfur trioxide, that resembles oxygen chemically but is less active and more acidic, and that is used chiefly in making sulfur dioxide, sulfuric acid, carbon disulfide, and other sulfur compounds, in the pulp and paper industry, in rubber vulcanization, in metallurgy, in petroleum refining, in black powder, matches, and fireworks, in agriculture as a fungicide and insecticide, and in medicine in treating skin diseases — called also *brimstone;* symbol *S;* see FLOWERS OF SULFUR, FRASCH PROCESS, HYDROGEN SULFIDE, PLASTIC SULFUR, PRECIPITATED SULFUR, RHOMBIC SULFUR; ELEMENT table **2** *sulphur, archaic* **:** a sulfide or similar compound of sulfur **3** *sulphur* **:** something (as excited, inflamed, or scathing talk or language) that suggests sulfur

²sulfur *or* **sulphur** \"\ *adj* **:** of, relating to, or resembling sulfur **:** containing or impregnated with sulfur

³sulfur *or* **sulphur** \"\ *vt* -ED/-ING/-S **:** to treat with sulfur, with fumes of burning sulfur or sulfur dioxide, or with sulfites (as in fumigating, bleaching, or preserving) **:** SULFURIZE ⟨~*ing* is necessary in the preparation of most kinds of dried fruit —T.H.Jackson & Barbara Roger⟩

sul·fu·rate *or* **sul·phu·rate** \ˈsəlf(y)əˌrāt\ *vt* -ED/-ING/-S [LL *sulfuratus, sulphuratus*, past part. of *sulfurare, sulphurare* to sulfurize, fr. L *sulfur, sulphur*] **:** SULFURIZE, THIONATE — **sul·fu·ra·tion** \ˌ==ˈrāshən\ *n* -S

sulfurated lime solution *n* **:** VLEMINCKX' SOLUTION

sulfurated potash *n* **:** a mixture composed principally of potassium polysulfides and potassium thiosulfate that is obtained by heating sublimed sulfur and potassium carbonate as liver-brown lumps changing to yellowish and decomposing in air and that is used chiefly in treating skin diseases and in producing color effects on brass and other metals — called also *liver of sulfur*

sul·fu·ra·tor \ˈ==ˌrād·ə(r)\ *n* -S **:** an apparatus used in sulfuring or sulfurizing

sulfur bacterium *n* **:** a bacterium (as many members of the Rhodobacteriinae) possessing the power of reducing sulfur compounds

sulfur black *n, often cap S&B* **:** any of several black sulfur dyes; *esp* **:** one made from 2,4-dinitrophenol — see DYE table I (esp. under *Sulfur Black* 1)

sulfur chloride *n* **:** a chloride of sulfur: as **a :** a yellow fuming irritating corrosive toxic liquid S_2Cl_2 that is made usu. by reaction of chlorine with molten sulfur and often contains sulfur or sulfur dichloride and that is used chiefly as a chlorinating or sulfurizing agent or as both simultaneously, in making vulcanized oils, and in the cold cure of rubber; di-sulfur dichloride — called also *sulfur monochloride* **b :** SULFUR DICHLORIDE

sulfur dichloride *n* **:** a dark brown or reddish liquid SCl_2 that resembles the sulfur chloride S_2Cl_2 and is used for similar purposes

sulfur dioxide *n* **:** a compound SO_2 that is toxic esp. to plants, that occurs in the gases from volcanoes, in many volcanic springs, and in variable amounts in the atmosphere, that is produced as a heavy colorless nonflammable gas of pungent suffocating odor usu. by burning sulfur or sulfides (as pyrite) and is present in the waste gases from many smelting and other industrial processes, that is easily condensed to a colorless liquid boiling at −10°C and is usu. sold in liquid form, and that is used chiefly in making sulfuric acid, sulfites, other sulfur compounds, and sulfite pulp, and in petroleum refining as a reducing and bleaching agent, as a preservative, disinfectant, and fumigant, and as a refrigerant — see SULFUROUS ACID

sulfur dye *or* **sulfur color** *n* **:** any of a class of sulfur-containing dyes that are made by heating various organic compounds (as aromatic polyamines or indophenols) with sulfur or alkali polysulfides and are used chiefly in dyeing cotton and other cellulose fibers — called also *sulfide dye;* see DYE table I

sul·fu·re·ous *or* **sul·phu·re·ous** \ˌsəlˈfyu̇rēəs\ *adj* [L *sulfureus, sulphureus*, fr. *sulfur, sulphur, sulpur* sulfur + *-eus* -eous] **:** consisting of sulfur **:** having the qualities of sulfur esp. when burning **:** impregnated with sulfur **:** sulfur-colored **:** SULFUROUS — **sul·fu·re·ous·ly** *adv* — **sul·fu·re·ous·ness** *n* -ES

¹sul·fu·ret \ˈsəlf(y)əˌret\ *n* -S [NL *sulfuretum*, fr. L *sulfur* — more at SULFUR] **:** SULFIDE

²sulfuret \"\ *vt* **sulfureted** *or* **sulfuretted; sulfureted** *or* **sulfuretted; sulfureting** *or* **sulfuretting; sulfurets :** to combine or impregnate with sulfur

sulfureted hydrogen *n* **:** HYDROGEN SULFIDE

sulfur family *n* **:** the three elements sulfur, selenium, and tellurium located in group VIA of the periodic table

sulfur flour *n* **:** crude or refined sulfur ground and usu. sized — called also *flour sulfur;* compare FLOWERS OF SULFUR

sulfur hexafluoride *n* **:** an inert gaseous compound SF_6 that has high dielectric strength and is used as an electric insulator

sul·fu·ric *or* **sul·phu·ric** \ˌsəlˈfyu̇rik, -rēk\ *adj* [*sulfuric* fr. F *sulfurique*, fr. L *sulfur* + F *-ique* -ic; *sulphuric* modif. (influenced by *sulphur*) of F *sulfurique*] **1 :** of, relating to, or containing sulfur **:** derived from or by the use of sulfuric acid — used esp. of compounds in which this element has a higher valence as contrasted with the sulfurous compounds ⟨~ esters⟩ **2** *usu sulphuric* **:** SULFUROUS 2

sulfuric acid *n* **1** *obs* **:** SULFUR TRIOXIDE **2 :** a heavy corrosive high-boiling oily liquid dibasic acid H_2SO_4 that is colorless when pure, that was made in early times by distilling green vitriol and is now made commercially from sulfur dioxide by oxidation either in the chamber process usu. giving an acid of 65 to 78 percent strength or in the contact process involving conversion of the sulfur dioxide to sulfur trioxide on contact with a catalyst (as of platinum or vanadium oxides) followed by absorption of the trioxide in strong sulfuric acid to form acid of 98 to 99 percent strength or oleum, that is a strong acid and oxidizing agent, that combines energetically with water evolving much heat and is consequently a good drying and dehydrating agent, and that is the most widely used acid in industry (as in the manufacture of superphosphate and other fertilizers, chemicals, detergents, pigments and dyes, explosives, rayon, and storage batteries and in petroleum refining and in pickling metals) — called also *oil of vitriol;* compare PYROSULFURIC ACID

sulfuric anhydride *n* **:** SULFUR TRIOXIDE

sulfuric ether *n* **:** ETHER 3a

sul·fu·ri·za·tion \ˌsəlf(y)ərəˈzāshən\ *n* -S **:** the process of sulfurizing

sul·fu·rize *or* **sul·phu·rize** \ˈsəlf(y)əˌrīz\ *vt* -ED/-ING/-S *see -ize in Explan Notes* [*sulfurize* fr. F *sulfuriser*, fr. L *sulfur* + F *-iser* -ize; *sulphurize* modif. (influenced by *sulphur*) of F *sulfuriser*] **:** to combine or impregnate with sulfur or one of its compounds **:** SULFUR ⟨*sulfurized* lubricating and cutting oils⟩

sulfur match *n* **:** ³MATCH 2a

sulfur monochloride *n* **:** SULFUR CHLORIDE a — not used systematically

sulfur mustard *n* **:** MUSTARD GAS

sulfur oil *or* **sulfur olive oil** *n* **:** a green oil of inferior grade obtained from the expressed marc of olives by extraction with carbon disulfide and used in making soap

sul·fu·rous *or* **sul·phu·rous** \ˈsəlf(y)ərəs, *in sense 1 also* ˌsəlˈfyu̇r-\ *adj* [L *sulfurosus, sulphurosus*, fr. *sulfur, sulphur* sulfur + *-osus* -ose] **1 :** of, relating to, or containing sulfur **:** resembling or emanating from sulfur esp. when burning **:** SULFUREOUS ⟨~ gases⟩ — used esp. of compounds in which this element has a lower valence as contrasted with the sulfuric compounds **2** *usu sulphurous* **a :** of, relating to, or characterized by thunder **:** SULTRY ⟨*sulphurous* atmosphere⟩ **b :** of or heavy with the smoke of gunpowder ⟨*sulphurous* fumes⟩ **c :** of, relating to, or dealing with hellfire **:** INFERNAL ⟨the *sulphurous* pit —Shak.⟩ ⟨*sulphurous* sermons⟩ **d :** SCORCHING, SCATHING, VIRULENT, VITRIOLIC ⟨*sulphurous* denunciations⟩ **e :** highly profane **:** BLASPHEMOUS ⟨*sulphurous* language⟩ — **sul·fu·rous·ly** *adv* — **sul·fu·rous·ness** *n* -ES

sulfurous acid *n* **1 :** SULFUR DIOXIDE **2 :** an unstable weak dibasic acid H_2SO_3 that is known esp. in solutions of sulfur dioxide in water and in the form of its salts and that is a good reducing and bleaching agent forming sulfuric acid as it is oxidized

sulfurous anhydride *or* **sulfurous acid anhydride** *n* **:** SULFUR DIOXIDE

sulfur oxide *n* **:** any of several oxides of sulfur: as **a :** SULFUR DIOXIDE **b :** SULFUR TRIOXIDE

sulfur point *n* **:** the boiling point of sulfur — compare INTERNATIONAL TEMPERATURE SCALE

sulfurs *pl of* SULFUR, *pres 3d sing of* SULFUR

sulfur spring *n* **:** a spring whose waters contain compounds of sulfur (as hydrogen sulfide with its characteristic odor)

sulfur subchloride *n* **:** SULFUR CHLORIDE a

sulfur toning *n* **:** any of several processes in which the silver of a printing-out or developed image is caused to combine with sulfur, effecting a change in color and producing a color ranging from a yellowish to a purplish brown — compare SULFIDE TONING

sulfur trioxide *n* **:** a compound SO_3 that is a heavy low-boiling strongly acid corrosive liquid when first produced at ordinary temperatures but that polymerizes readily to three or more solid forms including a stable modification resembling asbestos, that is formed by the union of sulfur dioxide and oxygen (as in the contact process for making sulfuric acid) but is usu. made by distillation of strong oleum, that gives off irritating toxic fumes in air and combines violently with water evolving much heat and forming sulfuric acid, that is a powerful oxidizing agent and sets fire to materials like excelsior and sawdust on contact, and that is used chiefly as a sulfonating and sulfating agent (as in making detergents)

sulfur water *n* **:** a natural water (as in a spring) containing combined sulfur and esp. hydrogen sulfide

sul·fury \ˈsəlfərē\ *adj* [¹*sulfur* + *-y*] **:** of, relating to, or resembling sulfur **:** SULFUREOUS, SULFUROUS

sul·fur·yl \ˈsəlf(y)əˌril\ *n* -S [ISV ¹*sulfur* + *-yl*] **:** the bivalent radical or cation $>SO_2$ of sulfuric acid **:** SULFONYL — used esp. in names of inorganic compounds

sulfuryl chloride *n* [ISV] **:** a pungent corrosive liquid SO_2Cl_2 obtained usu. by direct union of sulfur dioxide and chlorine by means of catalysts and used chiefly as a chlorinating and sulfonating agent since it dissociates when heated or in the presence of catalysts

sul·fy·drate \ˌsəlˈfīˌdrāt\ *n* -S [alter. of *sulfhydrate*] **:** HYDROSULFIDE — not used systematically

su·li·dae \ˈsüləˌdē\ *n pl, cap* [NL, fr. *Sula*, type genus + *-idae*] **:** a small family of sea birds (order Pelecaniformes) comprising the boobies and gannets

¹sulk \ˈsəlk\ *vi* -ED/-ING/-S [back-formation fr. ¹*sulky*] **:** to be sullen or morose in mood **:** be moodily silent **:** refuse advances or intercourse with others for a time **:** nurse a grievance

²sulk \"\ *n* -S **1 :** the state or condition of one sulking — often used in pl. **2 :** a sulky mood or spell — often used in pl.

sul·ka \ˈsəlkə\ *n, pl* **sulka** *or* **sulkas** *usu cap* **1 :** a Papuan people on New Britain Island, Bismarck Archipelago **2 :** a member of the Sulka people

sulk·er \ˈsəlkə(r)\ *n* -S **:** one that sulks

sulk·i·ly \ˈsəlkəlē, ˈsəu̇k-, -əli\ *adv* **:** in a sulky manner

sulk·i·ness \-kēnəs, -kin-\ *n* -ES **:** the state of being sulky

¹sulky \-kē, -ki\ *adj* -ER/-EST [prob. alter. (influenced by *-y*, adj. suffix) of earlier *sulke* hard to sell, slow, sluggish, perh. back-formation fr. past part. of OE *āsolcen* lazy, sluggish, indifferent, fr. past part. of *āseolcan* to be lazy, slow; akin to MHG *selken* to drop, fall, OIr *selg* hunt, Skt *srjati* he releases, shoots, emits] **1 a :** sulking or inclined to sulk **:** given to spells of sulking ⟨a ~ refusal to acknowledge facts —Bertrand Russell⟩ **b :** suggestive of sulkiness **:** MOODY ⟨rather ~ good looks —Dorothy Sayers⟩ **2 a :** slow in movement or response **:** SLUGGISH, INACTIVE ⟨a ~ fire that declines to flame —Edward Sackville-West & Desmond Shawe-Taylor⟩ **b :** DULL, GLOOMY ⟨a ~ day⟩ **3 :** having wheels and usu. a seat for the driver ⟨~ cultivator⟩ ⟨~ plow⟩ **syn** see SULLEN

²sulky \"\ *n* -ES [prob. fr. ¹*sulky*] **1 :** a light 2-wheeled cart (as used for trotting races) having a seat for the driver only and usu. no body **2 :** a sulky vehicle (as a plow, a lister, or a cultivator) **3 :** a light stroller **4 :** an arch mounted on wheels or crawler tracks and used in logging

¹sull \ˈsəl\ *n* [short for *sullow*] *dial* **:** PLOW

²sull \"\ *vi* -ED/-ING/-S [back-formation fr. *sullen*] *South & Midland* **:** to be sullen or balky **:** SULK

³sull \"\ *n* -S [by shortening] **:** SULLAGE 3

sul·la \ˈsələ\ *or* **sulla clover** *n* -S [Sp *sulla*, prob. fr. LL *sylla*, an herb] **:** a European herb (*Hedysarum coronarium*) valued for forage and cultivated for its pink flowers — called also *French honeysuckle*

sul·lage \ˈsəlij\ *n* -S [prob. fr. MF *souiller* to soil + E *-age* — more at SOIL] **1 :** drainage or refuse esp. from a house, farmyard, or street **:** SEWAGE ⟨drains to remove ~ from the inhabited area —*Science & Culture*⟩ **2 :** mud deposited by water **:** SILT **3 :** scoria on molten metal in the ladle

sul·len \ˈsələn\ *adj, often* -ER/-EST [earlier *sollen, sollein*, fr. ME *solein, solain* sullen, solitary, single, prob. fr. MF *solain* (attested only in the sense of "food for a single person"), prob. fr. (assumed) VL *solanus*, fr. L *solus* alone — more at SOLE] **1 a :** ill-humoredly unsociable **:** gloomily or resentfully silent or repressed ⟨a ~ mood⟩ ⟨a ~ crowd⟩ ⟨the population ~ and impoverished —H.W.H.Knott⟩ **b :** relating to or indicative of a gloomy, resentful, or surly mood **:** suggesting a state of repressed anger ⟨began collecting the remaining things with ~ hands —Dorothy M. Richardson⟩ ⟨a ~ voluptuous mouth —Edmund Wilson⟩ **2 :** OBSTINATE, REFRACTORY, INTRACTABLE ⟨~ oxen⟩ **3 a :** of a dull color **:** of somber hue **:** LOWERING ⟨a ~ sky⟩ ⟨a chain of ~ clouds —Ellen Glasgow⟩ ⟨the waves were ~, heavier than usual —K.M.Dodson⟩ **b :** dull or deep of sound **:** of mournful tone ⟨the ~ roar of a vast cataract —William Beckford⟩ ⟨the ~ bawling of steers —Green Peyton⟩ ⟨the ~ murmur of the bees —Oscar Wilde⟩ **4 :** DISMAL, SAD, MELANCHOLY ⟨rain fell with a ~ splash —Marcia Davenport⟩ **5 :** moving sluggishly and resentfully or as if resentfully ⟨just a ~ line of men falling back —R.H. Newman⟩ ⟨~ rivers⟩

syn GLUM, MOROSE, SURLY, SULKY, CRABBED, SATURNINE, DOUR, GLOOMY: SULLEN applies to gloomy ill-humored refusal to be sociable or responsive ⟨her stolid exterior seemed to cloak a *sullen* resentment at the fact that she should be questioned at all —W.H.Wright⟩ ⟨sitting till three in the morning, staring at the dead fire in *sullen* apathy —G.D. Brown⟩ ⟨with *sullen*, defiant hatred still burning in their eyes —Robert Alden⟩ GLUM indicates silent dismal dispiritedness ⟨mutes at funerals could not look more *glum* than the domestics —W.M.Thackeray⟩ ⟨a *glum* guitarist who stared lifelessly into the innards of his guitar —*Time*⟩ MOROSE describes bitter, cynical, or misanthropic uncommunicative ill humor ⟨she has tempted him to drink again because he is so *morose* when he is sober that she cannot endure living with him —G.B. Shaw⟩ ⟨in the keener moments of consciousness of his loneliness, she found him *morose*, until, unable to sing or laugh with the songs and laughter of that house, he came at times to believe he was *morose* himself —E.T.Thurston⟩ SURLY applies to repelling churlish or rude sulkiness ⟨the *surly* expression of an active boy detained within walls while other boys were shouting in the park —Gertrude Atherton⟩ ⟨the family pictures glared at the spectator in the eyes like some *surly* animal, that had lost its good humor when it outlived its playfulness —Nathaniel Hawthorne⟩ SULKY may suggest a childish display of displeasure or resentment marked by sullen peevishness ⟨stared at the newcomer with a *sulky* scowl, as much as to say, Who the devil are you —W.M. Thackeray⟩ ⟨he was silent now, watching her with *sulky*, mistrustful eyes —Christine Weston⟩ CRABBED refers to accustomed, harsh, forbidding, morose crossness ⟨an old crone who knew magic and could be asked for help, but who was apt to be *crabbed* and was best left alone —W.W.Howells⟩ ⟨*crabbed* theologians involved in tenuous subtleties and disputing endlessly —V.L.Parrington⟩ SATURNINE describes heavy forbidding taciturn gloom ⟨the severe, skeptical eyes, the querulous eyebrows, the thin peevish lips, the big pedantic nose . . . display a *saturnine* master bore —D.B.W.Lewis⟩ DOUR may describe uncommunicative grim obstinacy ⟨drank in silence; when deep in his cups he became more and more *dour* and taciturn —C.B.Nordhoff & J.N.Hall⟩ ⟨the pleasure-loving Cavaliers were not sympathetic with the *dour* denials of enjoyment that prevailed in some of the other colonies —*Amer. Guide Series: Va.*⟩ GLOOMY describes a cheerless, sullen, or melancholy depression of spirits ⟨constitutionally *gloomy*, a congenital pessimist who always saw the doleful side of any situation —W.A.White⟩ ⟨a heart full of *gloomy* forebodings, and a brain whirling with wild fancies —Charles Kingsley⟩

sul·len·ly *adv* **:** in a sullen manner

sul·len·ness \-lən(n)əs\ *n* -ES **:** the quality or state of being sullen

sul·lens \-lənz\ *n pl* [*sullen* + *-s* (pl. suffix)] *chiefly dial* **:** a sullen mood **:** SULKS

sul·low \ˈsə(ˌ)lō, -lə\ *n* -S [ME *solow, suluh*, fr. OE *sulh* — more at SULCUS] *chiefly dial* **:** PLOW

¹sul·ly \ˈsəlē, -li\ *vb* -ED/-ING/-ES [prob. fr. MF *souiller* to soil — more at SOIL] *vi, obs* **:** to become soiled, tarnished, or defiled ~ *vt* **:** to make soiled or tarnished **:** BESMIRCH, STAIN, DEFILE ⟨no cruelties *sullied* his name —Brian Fitzgerald⟩ ⟨neologisms with which I will not ~ your ears —R.W.Chapman⟩ ⟨wholesale disruption of war unsettles and *sullies* the minds of millions —R.S.Ellery⟩ ⟨charm of its houses and buildings is somewhat *sullied* by coal smoke deposits —*Amer. Guide Series: N.H.*⟩

²sully \"\ *n* -ES *archaic* **:** SOIL, TARNISH, STAIN ⟨little spots and *sullies* in his reputation —*Spectator, 1711*⟩

sulph- *or* **sulpho-** — see SULF-

sulpha *var of* SULFA

sulpha- *or* **sulph-** — see SULFA-

sulphate *var of* SULFATE

sulphate green *n* **:** a light to moderate bluish green

sulphato- — see SULFATO-

sulphide *var of* SULFIDE

sul·phine yellow \'səl,fēn-\ *n* [*sulphine* fr. obs. E *sulphine* compound containing sulfur, fr. E *sulf-* + *-ine*] **:** a dark grayish to dark yellow that is slightly darker than pyrite yellow and very slightly lighter and stronger than bister green

sulphite *var of* SULFITE

sulphito- — see SULFITO-

sulphoborite *var of* SULFOBORITE

sulphohalite *var of* SULFOHALITE

sulphon- — see SULFON-

sulphonate *var of* SULFONATE

sul·pho rhodamine \'səl(,)fō+\ *n, usu cap S&R* [*sulpho* short for obs. E *sulphonic* — more at SULFON-] **:** an acid dye — see DYE table I (under *Acid Red 52*)

1sulphur *var of* SULFUR

2sul·phur \'səlfə(r)\ *or* **sulphur butterfly** *n* -S **:** any of numerous butterflies of *Colias* and related genera (family Pieridae) usu. having the wings chiefly yellow or orange with a black border — see CLOUDED SULPHUR, CLOUDLESS SULPHUR

sulphur and molasses *n* **:** a preparation sometimes taken as a spring tonic because of the laxative influence of sulfur ⟨looks woebegone . . . as if he needed a good belt of *sulphur and molasses* —John McCarten⟩

1sulphurate *adj* [L *sulphuratus, sulfuratus,* fr. *sulphur, sulfur* + *-atus* -ate] *obs* **:** of or relating to sulfur **:** SULFUROUS

2sulphurate *var of* **sulfurate**

sulphur-bottom \'=₌,=₌\ *also* **sulphur-bottom whale** *n* [so called fr. the yellowish splotches on its belly] **:** BLUE WHALE

sulphur candle *n* **:** a disinfecting candle composed chiefly of sulfur and giving off fumes of sulfur dioxide when burned

sulphur-crested cockatoo \'=₌,=₌-\ *n* **:** a large white Australian cockatoo (*Kakatoe galerita*) that has a showy erectile yellow crest, is often a destructive raider of grain crops, and is often kept as a pet

sulphureous *var of* SULFUREOUS

sulphur granule *n* **:** one of the small yellow bodies found in the pus of actinomycotic abscesses and consisting of clumps of the causative actinomycete

sulphuric *var of* SULFURIC

sulphurize *var of* SULFURIZE

sulphur ore 1 : PYRITE **2 :** native sulfur

sulphurous *var of* SULFUROUS

sulphur plant *also* **sulphur flower** *n* [so called fr. the yellow color of some of the plants] **:** any of several plants of the genus *Eriogonum* of the western U. S.

sulphur shower *or* **sulphur rain** *n* **:** a shower of yellow pollen often seen in spring that is carried by the wind from conifers (as pines)

sulphur sponge *n* **:** a bright yellow sponge; *esp* **:** a boring sponge (*Cliona celata*)

sulphurweed *also* **sulphurwort** \'=₌,=\ *n* **:** either of two European plants (*Peucedanum officinale* and *P. palustre*) the dried roots of which when burned emit a sulfurous odor

sulphur whale *n* **:** BLUE WHALE

sulphur yellow *n* **1 :** a variable color averaging a brilliant greenish yellow that is yellower and paler than average lemon yellow (sense 1a) **2 :** a light greenish yellow that is greener and deeper than Martius yellow — called also *brimstone, citrus*

sulphydrate *var of* SULFHYDRATE

sulphydryl *var of* SULFHYDRYL

sul·pi·cian \,səl'pishən\ *n* -S *usu cap* [F *sulpicien,* fr. Compagnie de Saint-*Sulpice* Society of St. Sulpice (fr. Église *Saint-Sulpice,* church in Paris of which the founder of the Sulpicians Jean Jacques Olier †1657 was a pastor) + F *-ien* -ian] **:** a member of a Roman Catholic society of diocesan priests that was established in France in 1642 with the purpose of contributing teachers for ecclesiastical seminaries

sul pon·ti·cel·lo \,sül,päntə'che(,)lō\ *adv* [It] **:** with the bow kept near the bridge so as to bring out the higher harmonics and thereby produce a nasal tone — used as a direction in music for a stringed instrument

sul·tam \'səl,tam\ *n* -S [*sul-* + lac*tam*] **:** any of a class of inner amides of amino sulfonic acids characterized by the sulfonyl-imido grouping $-SO_2NH-$ in a ring and analogous to lactams

sul·tan \'səlt³n, -tən *sometimes* -l,tan *or* -l,tän *or* -l,tàn *or* sül'tän *or* sül'tán\ *n* [MF, fr. Ar *sulṭān* ruler, dominion, sultan] **1** -S **:** a king or ruling sovereign esp. of a Muhammadan state **2** [so called fr. its being orig. fr. Turkey] **a** *usu cap* **:** an obscure breed of white domestic fowls having the shanks and toes slaty blue and heavily feathered, a V-shaped comb, a crest, muffs, and five toes **b** -S **:** a bird of this breed **3** -S **:** CRIMSON LAKE 2

sul·tana \,səl'tanə\ *n* -S [It, fem. of *sultano* sultan, fr. Ar *sulṭān*] **1 :** a female member of a sultan's family; *esp* **:** a sultan's wife **2** *also* **sultana bird** [so called fr. its rich exotic plumage] **:** a purple gallinule of the genus *Porphyrio* **3 a :** a pale yellow seedless grape grown chiefly in the Mediterranean region as a source of raisins and of a delicate white wine **b :** the raisin of this grape **4 :** a dark red to purplish red that is less strong than plum violet and duller than neutral red

sul·tan·ate \'səlt³nət, -tənət, -t³n,āt, -tə,nāt, *usu* -d·+V\ *n* -S [F *sultanat,* fr. *sultan* (fr. MF) + *-at* -ate] **1 :** the office, dignity, or power of a sultan **2 :** a state or country governed by a sultan

sul·tane \,səl'tān\ *n* -S [F, fr. fem. of *sultan*] **:** an elaborate gown trimmed with buttons and loops and worn around 1700

sul·tan·ess \'səlt³nəs\ *n, archaic* **:** SULTANA

sul·tan·ic \¦səl¦tanik\ *adj* **:** of, relating to, or characteristic of a sultan ⟨~ splendor⟩

sul·ta·nin \'səltənən\ *n* -S [Ar *sulṭānīy* royal, fr. *sulṭān* ruler, sultan] **:** an old Turkish gold coin in value somewhat less than a sequin

sul·tan·ism \'səlt³n,izəm\ *n* -S **:** a characteristic or practice of a sultan **:** DESPOTISM

sul·tan·ship \-,ship\ *n* **:** the office, rank, or dignity of a sultan

sul tasto \,sül'tä(,)stō\ *adv* [It] **:** with the bow kept over the fingerboard so as to produce a soft thin tone — used as a direction in music for a stringed instrument

sul·tone \'səl,tōn\ *n* -S [*sul-* + lac*tone*] **:** any of a class of inner esters of hydroxy sulfonic acids characterized by the sulfonyl-oxy grouping $-OSO_2-$ in a ring and analogous to lactones

sul·tri·ly \'səltrəlē, -əli\ *adv* **:** in a sultry manner

sul·tri·ness \-rēnəs, -rin-\ *n* -ES **:** the quality or state of being sultry

sul·try \-rē, -ri\ *adj* -ER/-EST [obs. E *sulter* to swelter (alter. of E 1*swelter*) + E *-y*] **1 a :** oppressively hot and humid **:** SWELTERING ⟨a ~ day⟩ ⟨~ weather⟩ ⟨~ islands⟩ **b :** burning hot **:** TORRID ⟨~ deserts⟩ ⟨a ~ sun⟩ **2 a :** hot with passion or anger ⟨the meeting disperses with ~ mutterings —J.B. Boothroyd⟩ **:** affected by, exciting, or capable of exciting strong sexual desire **:** PASSIONATE, SENSUAL, VOLUPTUOUS ⟨a ~ actress⟩ ⟨wish I could talk as low and throaty and ~ as she does —Calder Willingham⟩ ⟨the music was ~ —Thurston Scott⟩ **b :** LURID, SCABROUS ⟨~ language⟩ ⟨has a number of ~ comments to make about love —Douglas Watt⟩

1su·lu \'sü(,)lü\ *n, pl* **sulu** *or* **sulus** *usu cap* [Malay *Suluk,* fr. Taw-Sug *sulúg* current] **:** TAW-SUG

2sulu \"\ *n* -S [Fijian] **:** a garment made similar to the lavalava and worn esp. by Fijians and other Melanesians

sulubba *pl of* SLUBBI

su·lung \'sü,lüŋ\ *n* -S [ME *suling,* fr. OE *sulung,* fr. *sul, sulh* plow, measure of land — more at SULCUS] **:** any of various old Kentish units of land area (as one of 120 acres) corresponding to the carucate and the hide

sul·van·ite \'səlvə,nīt\ *n* -S [*sul-* + *van*adium + *-ite*] **:** a mineral Cu_3VS_4 consisting of a sulfide of copper and vanadium that occurs in bronze-yellow masses (hardness 3.5, sp. gr. 4.0)

sul·ze \'zültsə\ *n* -S [G, calf's-foot jelly, brine, fr. OHG *sulza* brine; akin to OHG *salz* salt — more at SALT] **:** CALF'S-FOOT JELLY

1sum \'səm\ *n* -S [ME *summe, somme,* fr. OF, fr. L *summa,* fr. fem. of *summus* highest, topmost; akin to L *super* over — more at OVER] **1 a :** an indefinite or specified amount of money ⟨received occasional ~*s* of money⟩ ⟨a ~ of fifty dollars⟩ ⟨are paid only a nominal ~ for their services —F.A.Ogg & P.O. Ray⟩ ⟨if all ~*s* for armaments were used to build libraries —Alfred Stefferud⟩ **b** *archaic* **:** a quantity of goods having a set value ⟨taxes assessed in ~*s* of tobacco⟩ **2 a :** the whole amount **:** an existent total ⟨duty to maintain and preserve the ~ of human knowledge —H.J.J.Winter⟩ **b :** an aggregate of distinct usu. specified things **:** a discrete whole ⟨history is not merely a ~ of events⟩ ⟨possessed of such various talents in the arts . . . as in their ~ to approach genius —Osbert Sitwell⟩ **3 :** the ultimate end **:** the utmost degree **:** HEIGHT, SUMMIT ⟨reached the ~ of human bliss⟩ ⟨saw the war . . . as the very crown and ~ of human folly —Rose Macaulay⟩ **4 a :** a summary of the chief points or thoughts **:** EPITOME, SUMMATION ⟨the ~ of this criticism follows —C.W.Hendel⟩ **b :** the main or essential point **:** GIST ⟨the ~ of the evidence⟩ ⟨attempting to convey the ~ of the book in a short phrase or sentence —J.E.Miller⟩ **5** *obs* **:** NUMERAL; *esp* **:** INTEGER **6 a** (1) **:** the aggregate of two or more numbers, magnitudes, quantities, or particulars **:** the result of performing an addition ⟨the ~ of 5 and 7 is 12⟩ (2) **:** the limit of the sum of the first *n* terms of an infinite series as *n* increases indefinitely **b :** numbers to be added **:** a column of figures **:** a problem in arithmetic — often used with *do* ⟨a child trying to do a difficult ~ in mental arithmetic —C.D.Lewis⟩ **c sums** *pl* **:** arithmetic esp. as a school subject ⟨singing is quite as important in education as ~*s,* spelling, or writing —George Sampson⟩ **d :** the result of logical addition or alternation

syn AMOUNT, AGGREGATE, TOTAL, WHOLE, NUMBER, QUANTITY: SUM may indicate the result of simple addition ⟨the *sum* of two and three⟩ and usu. applies to simple obvious putting together of things ⟨a personality is never a mere *sum* of traits and cannot be explained by the most complete inventory —H.J.Muller⟩ AMOUNT may be used of more accumulative or combinative processes ⟨the *amount* of snow that we usu. have in the northern United States —Richard Joseph⟩ ⟨a considerable *amount* of business experience —C.W.Mitman⟩ ⟨a considerable *amount* of unhappiness and poverty in his early youth —A.E. Wier⟩ AGGREGATE may stress the notion of separate distinct individuals or discrete particulars grouped together ⟨these larger *aggregates,* the enlarged family, ingroup, the tribe, the clan —Abram Kardiner⟩ ⟨not a logical unity, but an *aggregate* of notions of various origins —J.O.Evjen⟩ TOTAL suggests completeness comprehending inclusiveness and perhaps magnitude of result ⟨a large gold *total,* mostly through small, individual operations —*Amer. Guide Series: Wash.*⟩ ⟨a *total* of one million casualties⟩ WHOLE may refer to a unified or integrated totality ⟨society as a *whole,* acting through its laws, its schools, its publications —R.M.Weaver⟩ ⟨the history as a *whole* is deficient on the economic side —Allen Johnson⟩ NUMBER may suggest an aggregate of countable units, in contrast to AMOUNT, which is usu. used with uncountables ⟨the *number* of corpuscles in this *amount* of blood⟩ ⟨the *number* of accounts involved in this *amount* of trade⟩ QUANTITY is broadly used in reference to anything measurable but usu. applies to what is measured in bulk ⟨if pleasure be the sole good, the only possible criterion of pleasures is *quantity* of pleasure —Clive Bell⟩ ⟨farm country that produces wheat, corn, vegetables and fruit as well as *quantities* of poultry and milk —*Amer. Guide Series: Md.*⟩ ⟨a *quantity* of silvery-yellow hair —Elinor Wylie⟩ ⟨large *quantities* of silt —W.H.Dowdeswell⟩

— in sum *adv* [ME *in summe, in somme,* fr. MF *en summe, en somme,* fr. L *in summa*] **:** in short **:** BRIEFLY

2sum \"\ *vb* **summed; summed; summing; sums** [ME *summen, sommen,* fr. OF *summer, sommer,* fr. ML *summare,* fr. L *summa* sum] *vt* **1 :** to ascertain the sum of **:** count or calculate the number, amount, or total of **:** add together **:** cast up ⟨~ a column of figures⟩ ⟨the costs . . . can rarely be set down in a neat row and *summed* —Harold Koontz & Cyril O'Donnell⟩ ⟨this term is obtained by *summing* the numbers in the bottom left-hand corners of the boxes —Lester Guest⟩ ⟨~ the cards on the tabulator —F.J.Gruenberger⟩ **2 :** to sum up ⟨the body of thought brought to America by the immigrant Puritans . . . may be *summed* in a phrase as Carolinian liberalism —V.L. Parrington⟩ **3** *obs* **:** to bring to consummation or perfection **:** make complete **:** reach the goal or full development of ⟨there was the venture *summed* and satisfied —Christopher Marlowe⟩ **~** *vi* **1 :** to reach a sum **:** AMOUNT — used with *to* or *into* ⟨benefactions that ~ into the thousands⟩ **2 :** to do sums in arithmetic

sum *abbr* **1** [L *sumat*] let him take **2** [L *sume, sumendus*] take; to be taken **3** [L *sumendum*] must be taken

su·ma \'sümə\ *n, pl* **suma** *or* **sumas** *usu cap* [Sp, of AmerInd origin] **1 :** a people or group of peoples of the state of Chihuahua, Mexico **2 :** a member of the Suma people or peoples

su·mac *or* **su·mach** *also* **shu·mac** \'s(h)ü,mak *sometimes* -,mäk *or* -,màk *or* 'shü,māk\ *n* -S [ME *sumac,* fr. MF, fr. Ar *summāq*] **1 a :** a shrub or tree of the genus *Rhus* — often restricted to the innocuous members of the genus; see LAUREL SUMAC, POISON SUMAC, SQUAWBUSH, STAGHORN SUMAC; compare POISON IVY, POISON OAK **b** (1) **:** the wood of a sumac (2) **:** a material used in tanning and dyeing consisting of the dried and powdered leaves and panicles of various sumacs **2 :** any of several shrubs and trees (as of the genera *Ailanthus* and *Myrica*) in some respect resembling though not closely related to members of the genus *Rhus* **3 :** BUCKTHORN BROWN

sumac family *n* **:** ANACARDIACEAE

sumac wax *n* **:** JAPAN WAX

su·man \'sümən\ *adj, usu cap* [*Sumo* + *-an*] **1 :** of, relating to, or characteristic of the Sumo people **2 :** of, relating to, or characteristic of the Sumo language

sum and substance *n* **:** GIST ⟨the *sum and substance* of an argument⟩

1su·ma·tra \sə'mä·trə\ *adj, usu cap* [fr. *Sumatra,* island in Indonesia] **:** of or from the island of Sumatra **:** of the kind or style prevailing in Sumatra **:** SUMATRAN

2sumatra \"\ *n* **1** S *often cap* **:** a violent squall common in the strait between Sumatra and the Malay peninsula **2** *also* **sumatra game a** *usu cap S&G* **:** an Oriental breed of long-tailed greenish black game fowls **b** -S *usu cap S & sometimes cap G* **:** a bird of the Sumatra breed — compare CUBALAYA

sumatra camphor *n, usu cap S* **:** BORNEO CAMPHOR

sumatra leaf *n, usu cap S* **:** a thin elastic uniformly light-colored leaf tobacco raised in Sumatra and extensively used for cigar wrappers

1su·ma·tran \-rən\ *adj, usu cap* [*Sumatra,* island in Indonesia + E *-an*] **1 :** of, relating to, or characteristic of the island of Sumatra **2 :** of, relating to, or characteristic of the people of Sumatra

2sumatran \"\ *n* -S *cap* **:** a native or inhabitant of Sumatra

sumatra seed *n, usu cap 1st S* **:** Sumatra leaf tobacco grown in the U.S.

sumatra wax *n, usu cap S* **:** GONDANG WAX

sum·ba·wa·nese \süm¦bäwə¦nēz, -ēs\ *n, pl* **sumbawanese** *cap* [*Sumbawa* Island, Indonesia + E *-nese* (as in *Chinese*)] **1 :** a native or inhabitant of Sumbawa Island **2 a :** an Indonesian people on Sumbawa Island **b :** a member of such people

sum·bul *or* **sam·bul** \səm'bül\ *also* **sum·bal** \-'bäl\ *n* -S [Ar *sunbul*] **1 :** the root of a muskroot (*Ferula sumbul*) formerly used as a tonic and antispasmodic **2 :** GARDEN HELIOTROPE 1 **3 :** SPIKENARD 1a

sum·dum \,səm'dəm\ *n, pl* **sumdum** *or* **sumdums** *usu cap* [Tlingit *s'aodān*] **1 :** a Tlingit people at Port Houghton, Alaska **2 :** a member of the Sumdum people

su·men \'sümən\ *n* -S [L, fr. *sugere* to suck — more at SUCK] **1** *archaic* **:** a sow's udder esp. regarded as a delicacy **2** *obs* **:** the fat of something **:** RICHNESS

1su·meri·an \sü'merēən, -'mir-\ *adj, usu cap* [F *sumérien,* fr. *Sumer,* ancient region of lower Babylonia + F *-ien* -ian] **1 :** of, relating to, or characteristic of Sumer **2 :** of, relating to, or characteristic of the people of Sumer

2sumerian \"\ *n* -S *cap* **1 :** a native of Sumer **2 :** the language of the Sumerian people surviving as a literary language after the rise of Akkadian ⟨*Sumerian* is very well known today, though archaic . . . texts still offer much difficulty to the interpreter —W.F.Albright⟩

su·mer·ic \-'merik\ *adj, usu cap* [*Sumer,* ancient region of lower Babylon + E *-ic*] **:** SUMERIAN

sumero- *comb form, usu cap* [1*Sumerian*] **1 :** Sumerian ⟨*Sumero*logy⟩ **2 :** Sumerian and ⟨*Sumero*-Assyrian⟩

su·mero-akkadian \sü'me(,)rō, -'mi(,)rō+\ *adj, usu cap S&A* **:** of, relating to, or constituting the Sumerian and Akkadian languages, cultures, or peoples

su·mero-babylonian \"+\ *adj, usu cap S&B* **:** SUMERO-AKKADIAN

su·me·rol·o·gist \,sümə'räləjəst\ *n* -S *usu cap* **:** a specialist in Sumerology

su·me·rol·o·gy \-jē\ *n* -ES *usu cap* [*Sumero-* + *-logy*] **:** the study of the history, language, and archaeology of the Sumerians

su·mi \'sümē\ *n* -S [*Jap*] **:** soot of burned plants and glue made into solid cakes and used esp. by Chinese and Japanese artists for black-and-white paintings

sum·less \'səmləs\ *adj* **:** UNCOUNTABLE, INCALCULABLE, INESTIMABLE ⟨the ~ tale of sorrow —A.E.Housman⟩ — **sum·less·ness** *n* -ES

sum·ma \'sümə, 'sümə; 'səmə\ *n, pl* **sum·mae** *see sense 1* \-,mī; -,mē\ [ME, fr. L — more at SUM] **1** *pl also* **summas** *obs* **:** SUM, SUM TOTAL **2** [ML, fr. L] **a :** a treatise or series of treatises covering a whole field or department of learning; *esp* **:** one of the comprehensive scholastic works (as the Summa Theologica of St. Thomas Aquinas) **b :** a work or series of works that is a synthesis of human knowledge **c :** a synthesis or summary of any subject ⟨a ~ of the principal dogmas of the Church —*America*⟩ ⟨a ~ of a writer's work⟩

sum·ma·bil·i·ty \,səmə'biləd·ē\ *n* **:** capability of being summed

sum·ma·ble \'səməbəl\ *adj* [2*sum* + *-able*] **:** capable of being summed

sum·ma cum lau·de \¦sümə,küm'laüdə, ¦sümə,küm-, -dē, -dā; ¦səmə,kəm'lȯdē\ *adv (or adj)* [L, with highest praise] **:** with highest distinction — used as a mark of meritorious achievement in the academic requirements for graduation from school or college; compare CUM LAUDE, MAGNA CUM LAUDE

summa genera *pl of* SUMMUM GENUS

sum·mand \'sə,mand, =¦=\ *n* -S [ML *summandus,* gerundive of *summare* to sum — more at SUM] **:** a term in a summation **:** ADDEND

sum·mar \'səmər\ *adj* [MF *sommaire,* fr. ML *summarius*] *Scot law* **:** SUMMARY

sum·mar·i·ly \(,)sə'merəlē, -li *also* 'səmərəl-\ *adv* **:** in a summary manner or form ⟨was ~ relieved of his command⟩ ⟨the case was tried ~ without a jury —O.W.Holmes †1935⟩ ⟨not a theory to be dismissed ~ with raised eyebrow and shrugged shoulder —Eric Partridge⟩

sum·mar·i·ness \-rēnəs\ *n* -ES **:** the quality or state of being summary

sum·ma·rist \'səmərəst\ *n* -S [2*summary* + *-ist*] SUMMARIZER, SUMMIST 1

sum·ma·riz·able \'səmə,rīzəbəl, ,==¦===\ *adj* **:** capable of being summarized ⟨a ~ story⟩

sum·ma·ri·za·tion \,səmərə'zāshən, -mə,rī'-\ *n* -S **1 :** the act of summarizing **2 :** SUMMARY

sum·ma·rize \'səmə,rīz\ *vb* -ED/-ING/-S [2*summary* + *-ize*] *vt* **:** to tell in or reduce to a summary **:** present briefly **:** sum up **:** RECAPITULATE **~** *vi* **:** to make or be able to make a summary

1sum·ma·ry \'səmərē, -ri *sometimes* -mr-\ *adj* [ME, fr. ML *summarius,* fr. L *summa* sum, whole + *-arius* -ary (adj. suffix) — more at SUM] **1 a :** constituting or containing a summing up of points **:** covering the main points concisely **:** summarizing very briefly ⟨a ~ formulation of an enormously large situation —A.L.Kroeber⟩ ⟨check the opening and ~ sentences —S.C. Brownstein & Mitchel Weiner⟩ ⟨a ~ chapter⟩ **b :** lacking detailed explanation **:** BRIEF, TERSE ⟨a history of the Philosophic Neurosis, although that's a too ~ name —Irwin Edman⟩ **2** *obs* **:** lacking specific detail **:** GENERAL **3** *obs* **:** SUPREME, MAXIMUM **4 a :** done or occurring without delay or formality **:** quickly executed ⟨violent outbursts of wrath and ~ chastisements —Margaret Mead⟩ ⟨the ~ briskness of the drawing —R.M.Coates⟩ ⟨no resentment at the ~ way in which he has been treated —R.F.Kilvert⟩ **b :** of, relating to, or using a summary proceeding or procedure **:** used in or done by summary proceeding ⟨a ~ order⟩ ⟨special ~ courts⟩ — opposed to *plenary* **c :** accomplished or performed too quickly with inadequate consideration, preparation, or space allotted ⟨the letters to him reproduced here, ~ and unimportant as many of them are —*Times Lit. Supp.*⟩ **syn** see CONCISE

2summary \"\ *n* -ES [L *summarium,* fr. *summa* + *-arium* -ary (n. suffix)] **:** a short restatement of the main points (as of an argument) for easier remembering, for better understanding, or for showing the relation of the points **:** RECAPITULATION, RÉSUMÉ, SUMMATION ⟨proceeded to give a brief ~ of the points he had covered⟩

summary court-martial *n* **:** a court-martial consisting of one commissioned officer and having authority to impose no sentence in excess of one month's confinement or forfeiture of two-thirds of one month's pay — compare GENERAL COURT-MARTIAL, SPECIAL COURT-MARTIAL

summary judgment *n* **:** a judgment granted without a formal trial when it appears on the pleadings and other showing to the court that there is no genuine issue of fact and that the moving party is entitled to judgment as a matter of law

summary jurisdiction *n* **:** the authority or power of a court to use a summary procedure

summary procedure *n* **:** the procedure followed in a summary proceeding

summary proceeding *n* **:** a civil or criminal proceeding in the nature of a trial conducted without the formalities (as indictment, pleadings, and a jury) required by the common law, authorized by statute, and used for the speedy and peremptory disposition of some minor matter

sum·mat \'səmət\ *dial var of* SOMEWHAT

sum·mate \'sə,māt\ *vb* -ED/-ING/-S [back-formation fr. *summation*] **:** to add together **:** sum up

sum·ma·tion \(,)sə'māshən\ *n* -S [ML *summation-, summatio,* fr. *summatus* (past part. of *summare* to sum) + L *-ion-, -io* -ion — more at SUM] **1 :** the act or process of finding or forming a sum or total amount **:** ADDITION — symbol Σ **2 :** an aggregate formed esp. by accumulation or accretion **:** SUM TOTAL, RESULTANT **3 :** cumulative action or effect; *specif* **:** the process by which a sequence of stimuli that are individually inadequate to produce a response are cumulatively able to induce a nerve impulse **4 :** SUMMING-UP ⟨writes with shiny images, spare but eloquent ~*s* of scenes and people —E.A. Davidson⟩; *specif* **:** a speech in court summing up the arguments in a case

sum·ma·tion·al \-shən³l\ *adj* **:** of or relating to a summation **:** produced by summation

summation tone *n* **:** a combination tone whose frequency is equal to the sum of the frequencies of the two tones generating it

sum·ma·tive \'səməd·iv\ *adj* [*summation* + *-ive*] **:** ADDITIVE, CUMULATIVE

sum·ma·tor \'sə,mād·ə(r)\ *n* -S **:** one that summates

sum·ma·to·ry \'səmə,tōrē\ *adj* [ML *summatus* (past part. of *summare* to sum) + E *-ory* — more at SUM] **:** of, relating to, or serving as a summation ⟨his endings have that glowing ~ quality —Clifton Fadiman⟩

summed *adj* [ME *sommed,* fr. past part. of *summen, sommen* to sum; trans. of MF *sommé* — more at SUM] *obs* **:** fully developed or equipped **:** COMPLETED, PERFECTED, FULL-FLEDGED — used esp. of antlers or plumage

1sum·mer \'səmə(r)\ *n* -S *often attrib* [ME *sumer, somer,* fr. OE *sumor;* akin to OS, OHG, & ON *sumar* summer, OIr *sam,* W *haf,* Av *ham-* summer, Skt *samā* year, half year, season] **1 a :** the season between spring and autumn reckoned astronomically as extending from the June solstice to the September equinox **b :** the season comprising the months of June, July, and August **c** *Brit* **:** the season comprising the part of the year extending from mid-May to mid-August **d :** a period of warm weather or sunshine ⟨regions of everlasting ~⟩ ⟨we have had no ~ yet⟩ **e :** the warmer half of the year — contrasted with *winter* **f :** the dry season in the tropics **g :** the season reckoned astronomically in the southern hemisphere as extending from the December solstice to the March equinox **2 a :** one of the years of one's life esp. when young or vigorous ⟨a girl of seventeen ~*s*⟩ **b :** early middle age **:** the period of maturing powers ⟨still in the ~ of one's life⟩ **3 :** a character or condition suggestive of summer (as in warmth, brightness, or lushness)

2**summer** \"\ *vb* **summered; summered; summering** \-m(ə)riŋ\ **summers** [ME *someren*, fr. *sumer, somer*, n.] *vi* **:** to pass the summer ⟨~*ing* or wintering at vacation resorts —Graenum Berger⟩ ~ *vt* **1 :** to keep or carry through the summer **:** provide with pasture during the summer ⟨sheep and cattle are ~*ed* on the surrounding ranges in the mountains —*Amer. Guide Series: Oregon*⟩ **2 :** to infuse with summer heat or brightness **:** make summery — **summer and winter 1 :** to spend the whole year **2 :** to harbor, protect, cherish, or be loyal to always or unceasingly **3** *Scot* **:** to talk endlessly

3**summer** \"\ *n* -s [ME *somer, summer* packhorse, beam, fr. MF *somier*, fr. (assumed) VL *sagmarius*, fr. LL *sagma* packsaddle + L *-arius* -ary — more at SUMPTER] **:** a large horizontal beam or stone variously supported and used esp. in architecture and building: as **a :** the lintel of a door or window **:** BREASTSUMMER **b :** a stone forming the cap of a pier (as to support a lintel or arch) **c :** a principal floor timber (as a girder or lintel supporting other members) — called also *summertree* **d :** a horizontal longitudinal timber in a framing

4**summer** \"\ *n* -s [2*sum* + *-er*] **:** one that sums

summer beam *n* [3*summer*] **:** 3SUMMER a, c, d

summer cohosh *n* **:** a bugbane (*Cimicifuga americana*) of eastern No. American woodlands with chaffy-coated seeds

summer cress *n* **:** WATERCRESS 1

summer crookneck *n* **:** any of several crooknecks that are summer squashes and in the original and many surviving forms have typical crookneck form and bright to deep yellow warty rinds but in many improved forms have a straight neck and pale yellow smooth skins — compare WINTER CROOKNECK

summer cypress *n* **:** a densely branched Eurasian herb (*Kochia scoparia*) cultivated for its foliage which turns red in autumn

summer diarrhea *or* **summer complaint** *n* **:** diarrhea prevalent in hot weather and usu. caused by ingestion of food contaminated by various microorganisms responsible for gastrointestinal infections

summer disease *n* **:** BLUE COMB

summer duck *n* **1** *dial Eng* **:** GARGANEY **2** *dial* **:** WOOD DUCK 1

summer dwarf *n* **:** a dwarfing disease of strawberries caused by an eelworm (*Aphelenchoides besseyi*) and differing from spring dwarf esp. in occurring later in the growing season

summer egg *n* **:** a thin-shelled often parthenogenetic egg that is ready for immediate development when deposited — compare WINTER EGG

summer ermine *n* **:** the tawny brown summer fur of the ermine

summer fallow *n* **1 :** land plowed and frequently tilled during the summer in preparation for a crop the next year **2 :** the practice of summer-fallowing

summer-fallow \'ˌˌ,ˌˌ\ *vt* **:** to plow and work (land) in summer in order to prepare for sowing in the fall or the following spring **:** plow and let lie fallow

summer finch *n* **:** an American sparrow of the genus *Aimophila*; *esp* **:** a finch (*A. aestivalis*) of the southeastern U. S.

summer flounder *n* **:** a mottled greenish brown white-spotted flounder (*Paralichthys dentatus*) of the coast of the U. S. from Cape Cod to the Carolinas having the eyes and color on the left side of the body

summer forest *or* **summergreen forest** *n* **:** a deciduous forest in temperate regions as contrasted with a tropical rain forest or with northern coniferous forests

summer forget-me-not *n* **:** ANCHUSA 2

summer grape *n* **:** a wild grape (*Vitis aestivalis*) native to eastern No. America but widely cultivated in Europe that bears rather small pleasantly flavored berries and has superior powers of resisting the attacks of the phylloxera

summer grass *n* **:** any of several grasses; *esp* **:** CRABGRASS

summer hail *n* **:** hail formed by the freezing of raindrops from cumulonimbus clouds and their alternate catch of rain and snow through their oscillations in height — compare WINTER HAIL

summer haw *n* **:** MAYHAW

summer heat *n* **:** a temperature (as of 76° F) indicated on some thermometers as the approximate average temperature of summer in the temperate zone

summer heliotrope *n* **:** GARDEN HELIOTROPE 1

summer herring *n* **:** GLUT HERRING

summer house *n* [ME *somer hous*] **1 :** a country house for residence in summer **2** *usu* **summerhouse** \'ˌˌ,ˌ\ **:** a rustic covered structure in a garden or park to provide a cool shady retreat in summer

summer hyacinth *n* **:** a southern African herb (*Galtonia candicans* syn. *Hyacinthus candicans*) cultivated for its spicate white bell-shaped flowers — called also *Cape hyacinth*

summerier *comparative of* SUMMERY

summeriest *superlative of* SUMMERY

sum·mer·i·ness \'səmərēnəs\ *n* -ES **:** the quality or state of being summery

1**summering** *n* -s [ME, fr. gerund of *someren* to summer — more at SUMMER] **1 a :** the provision of pasture for livestock during the summer **b :** the pasture provided for the summering of livestock **c :** the summer regimen of livestock (as horses) **2 a :** a spending of the summer (as at a resort) **b** *archaic* **:** a summer pleasure (as an excursion)

2**sum·mer·ing** \'səməriŋ\ *n* -s [3*summer* + *-ing*] **:** the first mass of masonry laid (as on a pier or column) esp. when it begins an arched construction

sum·mer·ish \'səmərish\ *adj* **:** suggestive of or resembling summer **:** rather summerlike ⟨~ weather⟩

sum·mer·ite \-mərīt\ *n* -s **:** one who summers in a place

summer kitchen *n* **:** a small building adjacent to a house and used as a kitchen in warm weather

sum·mer·less \'səmə(r)ləs\ *adj* **:** having no summer

summer lightning *n* **:** HEAT LIGHTNING

summerlike \'ˌˌ,ˌ\ *adj* **:** characteristic of or resembling summer ⟨~ weather⟩

summer lilac *n* **1 :** DAME'S VIOLET **2 :** BUTTERFLY BUSH **3 :** any of several California shrubs of the genus *Ceanothus*

sum·mer·li·ness \'səmə(r)lēnəs\ *n* -ES **:** the quality or state of being summerly

1**sum·mer·ly** \-lē\ *adj* [1*summer* + *-ly*] **:** belonging to or typical of summer **:** SUMMERY ⟨~ solar radiation —*Jour. of Geol.*⟩

2**summerly** \"\ *adv* **:** in a summerly manner

summer mastitis *n* **:** bovine mastitis that occurs sporadically esp. in cattle on summer pasture, is caused by a pus-forming bacterium (*Corynebacterium pyogenes*), and may take an acute fatal course or one which is progressive and chronic

summer mustard *n* **:** CHARLOCK

summer oil *n* **1 :** an oil that solidifies partly or wholly in cold weather: as **a :** cottonseed oil from which the stearin has not been removed **b :** a heavy mineral lubricating oil **2 :** any of several highly refined oils used as foliage sprays to control insects (as the codling moth)

summer pumpkin *n, chiefly Brit* **:** SUMMER SQUASH

summer rape *n* **:** a rough-leaved annual rape (*Brassica napus annua*) widely grown in Europe for its seeds that are used for bird food

summer rash *n* **1 :** PRICKLY HEAT **2 :** an inflammation of the sebaceous glands and hair follicles of the skin of horses in areas rubbed by harness

summerroom \'ˌˌ,ˌ\ *n, archaic* **:** SUMMERHOUSE

1**summers** *pl of* SUMMER, *pres 3d sing of* SUMMER

2**sum·mers** \'səmə(r)z\ *adv* **:** during the summers ⟨has worked ~ as a news reporter —*Atlantic*⟩

summersault *var of* SOMERSAULT

summer sausage *n* **:** a sausage that has been dry-cured, smoked, and hardened and that keeps well without refrigeration ⟨cervelat is a *summer sausage*⟩ — called also *dry sausage*

summer savory *n* **:** an erect annual savory (*Satureia hortensis*) with oval leaves and pink flowers that is used for the flavoring of meats, soups, salads, or other dishes — compare WINTER SAVORY

summer school *n* **:** a school or school session conducted in summer esp. during July and August: **a :** a program of instruction offered during the summer by a school, college, or university enabling students to accelerate their progress toward a degree or make up credits lost through absence or failure **b :** a summer program offered by a college or university for professional workers (as teachers) wishing to round out their professional or general education

summer's darling *n* **:** FAREWELL-TO-SPRING

summerset *var of* SOMERSET

summer sheldrake *n* **:** HOODED MERGANSER

summer snipe *n* **:** the common European sandpiper (*Actitis hypoleucos*)

summer snowflake *n* **:** a plant (*Leucojum aestivum*) with clusters of pure white flowers borne in late spring and early summer — compare SPRING SNOWFLAKE

summer solstice *n* **1 :** the point in the sky occupied by the sun on or about June 22d when summer begins in the northern hemisphere **:** the June solstice **2 :** the time at which the sun reaches the June solstice for dwellers in the northern hemisphere or the December solstice for those in the southern hemisphere

summer sores *n pl but sing or pl in constr* **:** a skin disease of the horse caused by larval roundworms (genus *Habronema*) deposited by flies in skin wounds or abrasions where they cause intense inflammation with exudate and local necrosis followed by destruction of the parasites and gradual healing by granulation of the lesions

summer spore *n* **:** a spore (as the urediospores of the rusts) of brief vitality that germinates without resting and serves to propagate the plant during the summer — compare WINTER SPORE

summer squash *n* **:** any of various fruits of plants that are derived from a squash (*Cucurbita pepo melopepo*) and are used as a vegetable while immature and before hardening of the seeds and rind — see CYMLING, SUMMER CROOKNECK, VEGETABLE MARROW; compare PUMPKIN, SQUASH, WINTER SQUASH, ZUCCHINI

summer stock *n* **:** theatrical productions of repertory companies organized for the summer season and presented esp. in playhouses at summer resorts

summer stone *n* **:** 3SUMMER a,b

summer sweet *n* **:** a sweet pepperbush (*Clethra alnifolia*)

summer tanager *or* **summer redbird** *n* **:** a tanager (*Piranga rubra*) of the middle and southern U.S. the male of which is deep red and the female yellowish olive above and yellow beneath

summer teal *n* **1 :** BLUE-WINGED TEAL **2** *dial Eng* **:** GARGANEY

summertide \'ˌˌ,ˌ\ *n* [ME *sumertid, somertid*, fr. *sumer, somer* summer + *tid* time — more at SUMMER, TIDE] **:** SUMMERTIME

summertime \'ˌˌ,ˌ\ *n* [ME *somertime*, fr. *somer* summer + *time*] **:** the summer season **:** a summerlike period

summer time *n, chiefly Brit* **:** DAYLIGHT SAVING TIME

summertree \'ˌˌ,ˌ\ *n* [ME *somere tree*, fr. *somer, somere* summer (beam) + *tree* — more at SUMMER, TREE] **:** 3SUMMER c

summer trout *n* **:** WEAKFISH; *esp* **:** a common weakfish (*Cynoscion regalis*)

summer truffle *n* **:** a truffle (*Tuber aestivum*)

sum·mer-up \'səmə'rəp\ *n, pl* **summers-up** [*sum up* + *-er*] **:** one who sums up ⟨the *summer-up* of a literary period⟩

summer warbler *or* **summer yellowbird** *n* **:** YELLOW WARBLER 1a

summer-weight \'ˌˌ'ˌ\ *adj* **:** adapted in weight or texture to summer wear ⟨*summer-weight* clothes⟩ ⟨*summer-weight* shoes⟩

summerwood \'ˌˌ,ˌ\ *n* **:** the portion of each annual ring of a woody plant that develops largely during the latter part of the growing season but not necessarily in the summer and that compared with the springwood is less porous, is usu. harder and heavier, consists largely of smaller and thicker-walled cells, and in softwoods is often darker — called also *latewood*

sum·mery \'səmərē, -ri\ *adj, often* -ER/-EST **1 :** of, relating to, or like summer ⟨create an atmosphere of ~ somnolence and repose —R.M.Coates⟩ ⟨the fragrant ~ hay —J.H.Wheelwright⟩ **:** suggestive of summer ⟨a ~ laugh⟩ ⟨six thin, ~ girls —Truman Capote⟩ **2 :** suitable for summer **:** SUMMER-WEIGHT

summer yellowlegs *n pl but sing or pl in constr* **:** LESSER YELLOWLEGS

summing *pres part of* SUM

summing-up \'ˌˌ'ˌ\ *n, pl* **summings-up** [fr. gerund of *sum up*] **:** the act or statement of one who sums up **:** a conclusion in which the points made are reviewed and the conclusions set forth; *specif* **:** a lawyer's summation to a jury

sum·mist \'səməst\ *n* -s [ML *summista*, fr. *summa* + L *-ista* -ist — more at SUMMA] **1 :** a writer of a summa; *specif* **:** one of the medieval philosophers who wrote a philosophical or theological summa **2** *archaic* **:** one who abridges or epitomizes

sum·mit \'səmət, *usu* -əd·+V\ *n* -s *often attrib* [ME *somette*, fr. MF *somete, sommete*, fr. OF, dim. of *sum, som* top, summit, fr. L *summum*, fr. neut. of *summus* highest, topmost — more at SUM] **1 :** TOP, CREST, APEX, VERTEX ⟨the ~ of a wave⟩ ⟨the ~ of a column⟩ ⟨the ~ of a pole⟩: as **a :** the highest point, ridge, or level of a mountain or other feature **:** PEAK ⟨climb to the ~ of the mountain⟩ ⟨a range with ~*s* over 10,000 feet high⟩ ⟨the ~ of a plateau⟩ **b :** the point of highest elevation reached (as by a road or canal) ⟨stopped at the ~ to see the view⟩ **c :** the apex of a pyramid ⟨an octahedron with tetrahedral ~*s*⟩ **d (1) :** the highest level of officials; *esp* **:** the diplomatic level of chiefs of state or heads of government ⟨a meeting at the ~⟩ ⟨~ conference⟩ ⟨~ parley⟩ **(2) :** a conference of highest-level officials (as chiefs of state or heads of government) **2 :** the utmost height **:** the highest degree **:** PINNACLE ⟨the ~ of human fame⟩ ⟨confronting him at the ~ of his wrath —Anthony Quinton⟩

sum·mit·less \-tləs\ *adj* **:** lacking a summit

sum·mit·ry \-trē\ *n* -ES **:** the use of a summit conference for international negotiation

summity *n* -ES [ME *summite*, fr. MF *summité, sommité*, fr. LL *summitat-, summitas*, fr. L *summus* + *-itat-, -itas* -ity] **1** *obs* **:** SUMMIT **2** *obs* **:** one at the summit

summit yard *n* **:** HUMP YARD

sum·mon \'səmən\ *vb* -ED/-ING/-S [ME *sumnen, somenen, somonen, somounen*, fr. OF *somondre, semondre*, fr. (assumed) VL *summonēre*, alter. of L *summonēre* to remind secretly, give a hint to, fr. *sub-* + *monēre* to remind, warn — more at MIND] *vt* **1 :** to issue a call to convene **:** CONVOKE ⟨~ a council of state⟩ ⟨~ a lodge meeting⟩ **2 :** to command by service of a summons or other statutory notice to appear in court **:** CITE ⟨~ a jury⟩ ⟨~ witnesses⟩ ⟨the same defendants were ~*ed* to court again —*Current Biog.*⟩ **3 :** to call upon for specified action ⟨~ one to be in readiness⟩ **4 :** to bid to come or go **:** command or request the presence or service of **:** send for **:** CALL ⟨~ a physician⟩ ⟨bell still ~*s* the parishioners to worship —*Amer. Guide Series: N.H.*⟩ **5 :** to evoke esp. by an act of the will **:** stir or bring to activity **:** call forth **:** call up **:** bring together **:** CONJURE, AROUSE ⟨~*ing* all his strength he arose to speak —S.E.Morison⟩ ⟨each conflict ~*ed* heroic effort from the nation —Dixon Wecter⟩ ⟨when tunes could not be ~*ed* by turning a knob —Nancy Mitford⟩ ⟨poetry of such pure quality cannot be ~*ed* at will —C.D.Lewis⟩ — often used with *up* ⟨endure hardship and ~ up energy for a struggle —John Dewey⟩ ⟨can ~ up arguments from businessmen themselves —H.T.Simmons⟩ ~ *vi* **:** to issue a summons

sum·mon·er \-nə(r)\ *n* -s [ME *somonour*, fr. MF *somoneur, semoneur*, fr. *somon-, semon-* (stem of *somondre, semondre* to summon) + *-eur* -or] **:** one that summons; *specif* **:** one that serves a summons or delegates another to do so

1**sum·mons** \'səmənz\ *n, pl* **summonses** *also* **summons** [ME *somouns*, fr. OF *somonse, semonse*, fr. fem. of *somons, semons*, past part. of *somondre, semondre* to summon] **1 :** the act of summoning; *esp* **:** a call by authority or by the command of a superior to appear at a place named or to attend to some duty **2 :** a warning or citation to appear in court **:** a notice of the beginning of a particular proceeding in court and of the action to be taken therein: as **a :** the original writ by which an action was begun in old common-law practice **b :** a written notification signed by the proper officer to be served on a person warning him to appear in court at a day specified to answer to the plaintiff upon pain of judgment against the defendant for default in so doing **c :** a subpoena to appear as a witness **d :** an order to appear to answer a criminal charge usu. for a minor offense where arrest of the defendant is not regarded as appropriate or necessary **e** *Scots law* **:** a writ in the king's name to cite a defendant to appear and answer **3 :** an imperative call or a calling (as to arms or to death) **:** something (as a signal or knock) that summons ⟨were interrupted at that point by a ~ for tea —Maurice Cranston⟩

2**summons** \"\ *vt* -ED/-ING/-ES **:** SUMMON; *esp* **:** to take out a summons against

summons case *n, Eng law* **:** a case in which the offense is a minor one for which a police officer may without arrest notify a person to appear in court at a fixed time and place

sum·mum bo·num \ˌsüməm'bōnəm, ˌsüməm'-; ˌsəməm'-\ *n* [L] **:** the supreme or highest good usu. in which all other goods are included or from which they are derived

summum ge·nus \-'gānəs; -'jēnəs\ *n, pl* **sum·ma gen·era** \ˌsümə'genərə, ˌsüm-; ˌsəmə'jenərə\ [NL] **:** a genus that can undergo logical division **:** a genus that cannot be classed as a species — compare TREE OF PORPHYRY

summum jus \-'yüs, -'yüs; -'jəs, -'jüs\ *n* [L, highest law] **:** strict legal right **:** exact law **:** STRICTUM JUS — distinguished from *equity*

sum·mut \'səmət\ *dial var of* SOMEWHAT

sum·ner \'səmnə(r)\ *archaic var of* SUMMONER

sum·ner line \'səmnə(r)-\ *n, usu cap S* [after Thomas H. *Sumner*, 19th cent. Am. sea captain] **:** a line of position determined by Sumner's method

sumner's method *n, usu cap S* [after T. H. *Sumner*] **:** a method of determining one's position on the earth in which two approximate latitudes or longitudes are assumed (as from the dead reckoning), the corresponding longitudes or latitudes are calculated from an observation of a heavenly body with the point of observation being somewhere in the line joining the points so determined, and a similar line is determined from another heavenly body or from a later observation of the same body with the intersection of the two lines fixing the point of observation

1**su·mo** \'sü(,)mō\ *also* **su·mu** \-mü\ *n, pl* **sumo** *or* **sumos** *usu cap* [Sp *zuma, zumo, zumu*, of AmerInd origin] **1 a :** a people of Nicaragua **b :** a member of such people **2 :** a language of the Sumo people

2**su·mo** \'sü(,)mō\ *n* -s [Jap *sumō*] **:** a Japanese form of wrestling in which a contestant loses the match if he is forced out of the ring or if any part of his body except his feet touches the ground

1**sump** \'səmp\ *n* -s [ME *sompe*, fr. MD *somp* morass, pool — more at SWAMP] **1** *chiefly dial* **a :** SWAMP, MORASS ⟨~*s* of bottomless mud, bordered by patches of coarse swamp grass and standing puddles —H.L.Davis⟩ **b :** a pool or puddle esp. of dirty water **c :** DIRT, MUD **2 :** a round clay-lined pit of stone used in metallurgy for collecting fused metal **3 :** a pit, depression, reservoir, or tank serving as a drain or a receptacle for liquids to be salvaged or further disposed of: as **a :** CESSPOOL **b :** an open drain for carrying off dripping liquids (as in factories) **c :** a depression made in a water channel to facilitate the emptying of the channel **d** *also* **sump pit :** a pit at the lowest point in a circulating or drainage system (as the oil-circulating system of an internal-combustion engine) **e** *chiefly Brit* **:** OIL PAN **4** *Brit* **:** CRANKCASE **5** [G *sumpf*, lit., marsh, fr. MHG — more at SWAMP] **a :** the portion of a mine shaft which extends below the working levels and into which the water drains **b :** an excavation smaller than and ahead of the regular work in driving a mine tunnel or sinking a mine shaft **c :** SUMPING CUT **6** *or* **sump drain :** a device by means of which deep body cavities (as the pelvis) are drained of accumulated fluids by suction

2**sump** \"\ *vb* -ED/-ING/-S *vt* **:** to make a sump in; *specif* **:** to depress (the bottom of a channel) ~ *vi* **:** to dig or form a sump; *specif* **:** to make a sumping cut

sump·er \-pə(r)\ *n* -s **:** one that sumps; *specif* **:** a worker who oils and greases coal-cutting machines and positions the cutter for the undercutting of the coal face

sump fuse *n* **:** a fuse used in blasting under water

sumph \'səmf, 'sùmf\ *n* -s [origin unknown] *Scot & dial Eng* **:** a stupid or sulky person

sumping cut *n* **:** the preliminary undercut in a face of coal made by a continuous cutter

sumping shot *also* **sump shot** *n* **:** a shot or blast for making a sump or deepening a mine shaft

sum·pit \'səmpət\ *or* **sum·pi·tan** \-pə,tan\ *n* -s [Malay, fr. *sumpit* act of shooting with a blowgun] **:** a Malaysian blowgun

sump·man \'səmpmən\ *n, pl* **sumpmen :** SUMPER: **a :** a pitman's helper **b :** a worker who assists a shaft-sinking crew by putting supporting timbers in place

sump pump *n* **:** a pump to remove accumulations of water or other liquid from a sump pit

sump·si·mus \'səmpsəməs\ *n* -ES [L, we have taken — more at MUMPSIMUS] **:** a strictly correct expression or usage substituted for an old popular error — compare MUMPSIMUS

sump·ter \'səm(p)tə(r)\ *n* -s [ME, fr. MF *sommatier, sommetier*, fr. (assumed) VL *sagmatarius*, fr. LL *sagmat-, sagma* packsaddle (fr. Gk, covering, packsaddle) + L *-arius* -ary; prob. akin to Gk *sattein* to fill, stuff, load] **1 :** PACK, SADDLEBAG **2 :** a pack animal **:** BEAST OF BURDEN

sump·tion \'səm(p)chən\ *n* -s [ME *sumpcion*, fr. ML *sumption-, sumpsio*, alter. of L *sumption-, sumptio* action of taking, fr. *sumptus* (past part. of *sumere* to take) + *-ion-, -io* -ion — more at ASSUME] **1 :** ASSUMPTION 7 **2 :** MAJOR PREMISE

sump·tu·ary \'səm(p)chə,werē, -ri\ *adj* [L *sumptuarius*, fr. *sumptus* expense, cost (fr. *sumptus*, past part. of *sumere* to take, spend) + *-arius* -ary] **1 :** relating to or regulating expenditure esp. on clothes and food **:** controlling extravagance ⟨~ reforms⟩ ⟨~ edicts⟩ **2 :** of or relating to sumptuary laws

sumptuary law *n* **1 :** a law common in the 13th to 15th centuries to prevent extravagance in private life by limiting expenditure for clothing, food, and furniture **2 :** a law designed to regulate habits primarily on moral or religious grounds but regarded as justified under the police power of the state

sump·tu·os·i·ty \,səm(p)chə'wäsəd-ē\ *n* -ES [MF or LL; MF *sumptuosité*, fr. LL *sumptuositat-, sumptuositas*, fr. L *sumptuosus* + *-itat-, -itas* -ity] **1 :** expensive magnificence or elegance **:** lavish display **:** LUXURIOUSNESS ⟨most children like ~ —Sylvia T. Warner⟩

sump·tu·ous \'səm(p)chəwəs, -)chəs, -)sh-\ *adj* [MF *sumptueux*, fr. L *sumptuosus*, fr. *sumptus* expense, cost + *-osus* -ous] **1 a :** involving large outlay or expense **:** COSTLY, LAVISH ⟨the ~ dinner given by a railroad king —Julian Maclaren-Ross⟩ ⟨a ~ piece of bookmaking —Lionel Stevenson⟩ ⟨a ~ education —O.S.J.Gogarty⟩ ⟨general effect is one of an overpowering ~ vulgarity —Arnold Bennett⟩ **b :** OPULENT, MAGNIFICENT ⟨~ furnishings⟩ **2 :** extravagantly or luxuriously dressed, fed, or housed **:** living in luxury **syn** see LUXURIOUS

sump·tu·ous·ly *adv* **:** in a sumptuous manner **:** LAVISHLY, LUXURIOUSLY, OPULENTLY ⟨a ~ furnished house⟩ ⟨a ~ illustrated book⟩

sump·tu·ous·ness *n* -ES **:** the quality or state of being sumptuous

sum·ra \'səmrə\ *n, pl* **sumra** *or* **sumras** *usu cap* **:** one of an early Rajput people inhabiting the lower Sind region of West Pakistan

sums *pl of* SUM, *pres 3d sing of* SUM

sum total *n* [ME *somme total* (trans. of ML *summa totalis*), fr. *somme* sum + *total*, adj.] **1 :** an aggregate of sums **:** a total arrived at through the counting, figuring or casting up of sums ⟨the *sum total* of one's liabilities⟩ **2 a :** the aggregate amount esp. of something not calculable **:** total result **:** TOTALITY ⟨the *sum total* of the day's pleasure⟩ **b :** GIST

sumu *usu cap, var of* SUMO

sum up *vt* **1 :** to be the sum of **:** bring to a total ⟨10 victories *summed up* his record⟩ **2 :** to bring or collect into a small compass **:** state succinctly **:** SUMMARIZE, RECAPITULATE, EPITOMIZE ⟨*sum up* the evidence presented⟩ ⟨values they can *sum up* in a few simple formulas —Herbert Croly⟩ ⟨came at the end of an epoch in culture and *summed* it *up* magnificently —R.A.Hall b.1911⟩ ⟨a phrase which *sums up* the quality of the cathedral schools —R.W.Southern⟩ ~ *vi* **1 :** to present a summary or recapitulation **2 :** to be expressed or summarized ⟨it *sums up* in exactly three words —W.A.Johnston⟩

sum-up \'ˌ,ˌ\ *n* -s [*sum up*] **:** SUMMING-UP, SUMMARY ⟨listeners who might have missed the earlier pickups were able to get a clear-cut *sum-up* —A.N.Williams b.1914⟩

1**sun** \'sən\ *n* -s *often attrib* [ME *sunne, sonne*, fr. OE *sunne*; akin to OFris *sunne* sun, OS, OHG, & ON *sunna*, Goth *sunno*, Av *xvəng* (gen.), L *sol* — more at SOLAR] **1 a (1) :** the luminous celestial body that in the Ptolemaic system is one of the seven planets revolving around the earth ⟨the ~ rises⟩ ⟨the ~ sets⟩ ⟨the ~ came up upon the left —S.T.Coleridge⟩ ⟨was on his way before the ~ was up —John Seago⟩ ⟨the ~ went down behind the hill⟩ **(2) :** the star around which the earth and other planets revolve, by which they are held in their orbits, from which they receive heat and light, and which has a mean distance from earth of 93,000,000 miles, a linear diameter of 864,000 miles, a mass 332,000 times greater than earth, a mean density about one fourth that of earth, and a chemical constitution generally like that of earth but so hot that it remains completely gaseous in spite of the enormous pressure exerted by the mutual attraction of its particles **b :** a celestial body like the sun : a luminary center of a system : another star ⟨a flying rout of ~s and galaxies —E.M.Forster⟩ **2 :** the heat or light radiated from the sun : SUNSHINE ⟨standing in the full ~ in the parking lot —J.G.Cozzens⟩ ⟨so beautifully tanned by the ~⟩ ⟨the photographer has captured their . . . varying moods in ~, storm, and snow —*Brit. Bk. News*⟩ **3 :** one resembling the sun usu. in brilliance or illuminative power : one having a shining or radiant quality ⟨anecdotes about the man . . . , the central ~ he became for a host of surrounding satellites —Irving Kolodin⟩ **4** *usu cap* : SUN-GOD **5 a :** the rising or setting of the sun ⟨between ~ and ~⟩ ⟨a man works from ~ to ~ but woman's work is never done⟩ **b :** a period of daylight : DAY ⟨but one ~'s length off from my happiness —Elizabeth B. Browning⟩ **6 :** temperature produced by the sun; *also* : CLIMATE ⟨thought he would freeze there in the arctic ~⟩ **7 :** a sunlike object: as **a :** a heraldic representation of a sun surrounded with rays **b :** PARHELION **8 :** GLORY, POWER, SPLENDOR ⟨young men fresh from the wars striding . . . luminous with the ~ of conquest —Hassoldt Davis⟩ ⟨problems of the human mind over which the ~ of hope seemed to be rising —Van Wyck Brooks⟩ **9 :** an astrological hot and dry temperate masculine diurnal planet which if well aspected is fortunate, the mansion of which is Leo, the exaltation 19° Aries, the depression 19° Libra, and the orb 15° — **in the sun** *adv (or adj)* **1 :** without worry or care ⟨loves to live *in the sun* —Shak.⟩ **2 :** in the public eye ⟨too much *in the sun* —Shak.⟩ — **under the sun** *adv (or adj)* : in the world : on earth ⟨hope for decent living *under the sun* —R.J.Slavin⟩ ⟨can study almost anything *under the sun* —R.M.Hodesh⟩

[2]**sun** \"\ *vb* **sunned; sunned; sunning; suns** *vt* **1 :** to expose to or as if to the rays of the sun : place in the sunshine ⟨nursemaids *sunning* their charges beside the sea —D.G.Gerahty⟩ ⟨*sunned* himself . . . in the rays of his great friendships —*Amer. Guide Series: N.J.*⟩ **2 :** to shine upon : illumine or irradiate like the sun ⟨dandelions ~ the lawn —Philip Booth⟩ **3 :** to affect by or as if by sunlight or exposure to it ~ *vi* **1 :** to become exposed to sunlight : bask in the sun ⟨patchwork quilts *sunning* on the back fence —*Amer. Guide Series: N.C.*⟩ ⟨they swam and *sunned* and ate —Elizabeth Hardwick⟩ **2 :** to emit radiance : SHINE

sun-and-planet motion \ˈ⸗⸗ˈ⸗⸗-\ *n* : an epicyclic train of two wheels of which the wheel on a central axis is usu. rotated by the other wheel

sun-and-planet wheels: *1* sun gear, *2* planet wheel, *3* connecting rod, *4* flywheel

sun animalcule *n* : a protozoan of the order Heliozoa; *esp* : a large freshwater protozoan (*Actinophrys sol*) with numerous flexible radiating axopodia

sun·a·pee trout \ˈsənə(ˌ)pē-\ *n, usu cap S* [fr. *Sunapee* Lake, N. H.] : a brilliantly colored char (*Salvelinus aureolus*) of Sunapee and other lakes of New Hampshire and Maine closely related to the saibling of Europe

sun arc *n* : a large lamp that is used in making motion pictures and that reflects light by a parabolic mirror — called also *sun lamp, sun spot*

sunback \ˈ⸗,⸗\ *adj* : having a low-cut back for tanning and coolness — used of an article of wearing apparel ⟨sleeveless and ~ housedresses —*Women's Wear Daily*⟩ ⟨boleros make perfect cover-ups for ~ play frocks —*Springfield (Mass.) Republican*⟩

sunbaked \ˈ⸗,⸗\ *adj* **1 :** baked by exposure to sunshine ⟨~ bricks⟩ **2 :** heated, parched, or compacted esp. by excessive sunlight ⟨the city had returned to its ~ quiet —Rudyard Kipling⟩

sunbath \ˈ⸗,⸗\ *n* : exposure to sunlight or to a sunlamp

sun·bathe \ˈsən,bāth\ *vi* [back-formation fr. *sunbather*] : to take a sunbath

sunbather \ˈ⸗,⸗⸗\ *n* [¹*sun* + *bather*] : one that takes sunbaths

sunbeam \ˈ⸗,⸗\ *n* [ME *sunnebem, sonnebem*, fr. OE *sunnebēam, sunbēam*, fr. *sunne* sun + *bēam* beam — more at SUN, BEAM] **1 :** a beam or ray of light of the sun **2 a :** one that radiates happiness; *esp* : a bright merry child **b :** a member of a Salvationist organization for younger girls similar to Brownies **3 :** BANANA 2

sunbeam snake *n* : a harmless snake (*Xenopeltis unicolor*) of the family Xenopeltidae of southeastern Asia and Malaya having smooth black or brown highly iridescent scales

sunbeamy \ˈ⸗,⸗⸗\ *adj* : of or resembling a sunbeam : CHEERFUL, SHINING

sun bear *n* : a small bear (*Helarctos*, or *Ursus, malayanus*) of southern Asia, Java, Sumatra and Borneo that is about four feet long, has a short broad head, fine short glossy mostly black fur but brownish on the nose with a white or orange band on the chest, and is easily tamed

sun·berry \ˈsən- — *see* BERRY\ *n* : WONDERBERRY

sunbird \ˈ⸗,⸗\ *n* **1 :** any of numerous small brilliantly colored birds of the family Nectariniidae that are native to Africa, southern Asia, the East Indies, and Australia, that in external appearance and habits somewhat resemble hummingbirds but have a curved bill and are true singing birds **2 :** SUN-GREBE

sun bittern *n* : SUN-GREBE

sunblasted \ˈ⸗,⸗⸗\ *adj* : scorched by the sun ⟨open ~ country —Marjory S. Douglas⟩

sunblind \ˈ⸗,⸗\ *n, chiefly Brit* : AWNING

sunblink \ˈ⸗,⸗\ *n, Scot* : a glimmer of sunlight

sun blotch *n* : a virus disease of avocados characterized by yellow or brownish red streaks on twigs and fruit, rough corky bark, and decumbent older stems

sunbonnet \ˈ⸗,⸗⸗\ *n* : a woman's bonnet worn for protection from the sun; *esp* : a cloth poke bonnet with or without a ruffle but usu. with a free-hanging extension at the lower edge of the back resembling a small cape

sun·bow \ˈsən,bō\ *n* : an arch resembling a rainbow made by the sun shining through vapor or mist

sunbreak \ˈ⸗,⸗\ *n* **1 :** a breaking forth of the sun at sunrise; *also* : SUNBURST **2** *or* **sunbreaker** \ˈ⸗,⸗⸗\ : BRISE-SOLEIL

sunbright \ˈ⸗,⸗\ *adj* **1 :** having a brightness that rivals the sun ⟨those other . . . ~ minds —John Mason Brown⟩ **2 :** flooded with sunshine ⟨morning is fresh and ~ —H.B. Alexander⟩

sunbonnet

sunbrowned \ˈ⸗,⸗\ *adj* : tanned by exposure to the sun ⟨held her hand . . . and kissed its soft ~ skin —Marcia Davenport⟩

[1]**sun·burn** \ˈsən,bərn, -bə̄n, -bəin\ *vb* [back-formation fr. *sunburned*] *vt* : to burn or discolor by the sun ~ *vi* : to become burned or discolored by the sun

[2]**sunburn** \"\ *n* **1 :** inflammation of the skin of variable degree caused by overexposure to sunlight — compare ERYTHEMA SOLARE **2 a :** development of chlorophyll in potato tubers that have been exposed to light **b :** SUNSCALD **c :** the discoloration of some fruits due to excessive sunlight at ripening time **3 :** FRENCH BEIGE

sunburned *or* **sunburnt** \ˈ⸗,⸗\ *adj* **1 :** affected by sunburn; *specif* : reddened or tanned by sunburn ⟨old wrinkled ~ hands —J.C.Powys⟩ **2 :** seared by the sun ⟨a badly ~ suburban lawn —John Brooks⟩

sun burner *n* : a circle or cluster of gas burners formerly used in lighting large rooms

[1]**sunburst** \ˈ⸗,⸗\ *n* [¹*sun* + *burst*] **1 a :** a sudden flash of sunlight esp. through a break in the clouds ⟨off to the west the sky was pink which meant there would be a ~ —Ysabel Rennie⟩ **b :** something resembling a burst of sunlight ⟨the annual ~ of azaleas . . . that brightens the garden —*Monsanto Mag.*⟩ ⟨that brief, Renaissance ~ of the human intellect —Alan Moorehead⟩ **2 a :** a jeweled brooch representing a sun surrounded by rays ⟨a ~ in his turban —Hamlin Garland⟩ **b :** a design in the form of conventionalized rays diverging from a central point ⟨the gilt-faced clock in the ~ on the restaurant's wall —Elizabeth Bowen⟩ **3 :** the Japanese ensign bearing the device of a rising sun and rays radiating to all points in red on a white field **4 :** a moderate to strong orange that is yellower and lighter than carrot red, lighter than Mars yellow, and slightly yellower and stronger than zinc orange

[2]**sunburst** \"\ *adj* : pleated, tucked, or stitched in lines radiating from a circular edge ⟨blouse with a ~ yoke⟩ ⟨seven slivers of ~ fan pleats set in . . . below the hips —Lois Long⟩

sunck *also* **suncke** \ˈsəŋk\ *n* -s [of Algonquian origin; akin to Natick *sonksq* wife of a sachem, queen, fr. *sonqhuau* he prevails, overcomes + *squa* woman] *archaic* : a female American Indian chief — called also *sunk squaw;* compare SAGAMORE

sun-clock \ˈ⸗,⸗\ *n* : SUNDIAL

sun compass *n* : a navigational compass that uses the sun and its calculated bearing to establish direction esp. in high latitudes

sun crack *n* : a crack due to the sun's heat esp. in dried mud : MUD CRACK — **sun-cracked** \ˈ⸗,⸗\ *adj*

suncup \ˈ⸗,⸗\ *n* : a yellow-flowered evening primrose (*Oenothera ovata*) found along the Pacific coast of the U.S. — called also *golden eggs*

sun-cure \ˈ⸗ˈ⸗\ *vt* [back-formation fr. *sun-cured*, fr. ¹*sun* + *cured*] : to cure (tobacco) by exposing the suspended leaves to the direct rays of the sun

sund *abbr* sundries

sun·dae \ˈsəndē, -di *also* -n(ˌ)dā\ *n* -s [prob. alter. of ¹*sunday*] **1 :** a portion of plain ice cream served with a topping (as crushed fruit, syrups, nuts) **2 :** a footed dish with a shallow bowl used for serving sundaes, sauces, and similar food

sun dance *n* : a solo or group solstice rite of American Indians: as **a :** a rite performed in Peru by a masked impersonator of the sun-god **b :** a rite performed in the area of Lake Michigan in imitation of the sun's course **c :** a rite of the Great Plains region often accompanied by votive self-torture by suspension from a pole

[1]**sun·da·nese** \ˌsəndəˈnēz, -ēs\ *adj, usu cap* [Malay *Sunda* western Java + E *-nese* (as in *Chinese*)] **1 :** of, relating, or belonging to the Sundanese or their language **2** [*Sunda* isles, islands of the Malay archipelago + E *-nese* (as in *Chinese*)] : inhabiting or native to the Sunda isles

[2]**sundanese** \"\ *n, pl* **sundanese** *usu cap* **1 :** one of the people of western Java **2 :** the Austronesian language of the Sundanese people

sun·da·ri \ˈsəndə,rē\ *n* -s [Skt *sundarī*] : SUNDRI

[1]**sun·day** \ˈsəndē, -di *also* -n(ˌ)dā\ *n* -s *usu cap* [ME *sunnenday, sonnenday, sonday, sunday*, fr. OE *sunnandæg;* akin to OFris *sunnandei* Sunday, OS *sunnundag*, OHG *sunnūn tag*, ON *sunnudagr, sunnundagr;* all fr. a prehistoric WGmc-NGmc compound formed fr. components represented by OE *sunne* sun and *dæg* day; trans. of L *dies solis*, trans. of Gk *hēmera hēliou* — more at SUN, DAY] **1 :** the first day of the week regarded by most Christians as a day for rest from secular employments and for public religious worship : the Christian Sabbath kept as a weekly commemoration of the day of Christ's resurrection and as the Christian analogue of the Jewish Sabbath **2 :** a newspaper circulated on Sunday

[2]**sunday** \"\ *adj, usu cap* **1 :** of, relating to, or associated with Sunday **2 :** BEST ⟨*Sunday* manners⟩ ⟨his new white *Sunday* suit —Eudora Welty⟩ **3 :** engaging in a pursuit only on Sundays or in spare time : AMATEUR, DILETTANTE ⟨*Sunday* painters multiply —J.D.Adams⟩ ⟨got behind a *Sunday* driver who was poking along admiring the scenery⟩

[3]**sunday** \"\ *vi* -ED/-ING/-S *usu cap* : to spend Sunday : engage in Sunday activities ⟨the religion . . . is Seventh Day Adventist and you do your *Sundaying* on Saturday —Julien Hyer⟩

sunday best *n, usu cap S* : clothing suitable for churchgoing; *esp* : one's best clothing worn on Sundays and for special occasions ⟨scrubbed behind the ears and with Eton collar and bow tie proclaiming this was *Sunday best* —K.D.Miller⟩

sunday citizen *n, usu cap S, obs* : a citizen in his Sunday clothes

sun·day·fied \-ˌfīd\ *adj, usu cap* [¹*Sunday* + *-fied* (past part. of *-fy*)] : given a character, appearance, or expression appropriate to or typical of Sunday ⟨the solemn silence and *Sundayfied* air . . . seeming to forbid any levity —F.T.Bullen⟩

sunday-go-to-meeting \ˈ⸗(ˌ)⸗,⸗ˈ⸗⸗\ *adj, usu cap S* : appropriate for Sunday churchgoing ⟨a *Sunday-go-to-meeting* expression⟩ ⟨had your *Sunday-go-to-meeting* garments made for you by a tailor —W.F.Harris⟩

sun·day·ish *pronunc at* SUNDAY +ish\ *adj, usu cap* : resembling Sunday ⟨a strange *Sundayish* hush . . . that morning —*Harper's*⟩

sun·day·ism \"+,izəm\ *n* -s *often cap* : SABBATARIANISM

sunday letter *n, usu cap S* : DOMINICAL LETTER

sunday punch *n, usu cap S* **1 :** a hard punishing blow; *esp* : a blow in boxing intended to knock out an opponent ⟨saved his *Sunday punch* for five rounds —*Time*⟩ **2 :** a tactic or maneuver resembling a Sunday punch ⟨their man was saving his *Sunday punch* for the end of the campaign —*Newsweek*⟩

sun·days \ˈsəndēz, -diz *also* -(ˌ)dāz\ *adv, usu cap* : on Sunday repeatedly : on any Sunday ⟨they would go riding *Sundays* in the park⟩

sunday school *n, usu cap 1st S & often cap 2d S* **1 :** a school held on Sunday for purposes of religious education **2 :** the pupils or teachers and pupils of a Sunday school

sunday supplement *n, usu cap 1st S* : the section of a Sunday newspaper consisting of material other than news and usu. including pictures, comic strips, and light often sensational reading matter

sun deck *n* **1 :** the usu. upper deck of a ship that is exposed to the most sun **2 :** a roof or terrace used for sunning

sun·der \ˈsəndə(r)\ *vb* **sundered; sundered; sundering** \-d(ə)riŋ\ **sunders** [ME *sundren, sunderen*, fr. OE *gesundrian, syndrian;* akin to MLG *sunderen* to sunder, OHG *suntarōn*, ON *sundra;* derivative fr. the root of OE *sundor* apart, OHG *suntar* aside, apart, ON *sundr* asunder, Goth *sundro* aside, apart; akin to L *sine* without, Gk *ater* without, apart from, Toch A *sne* without, Skt *sanutar* aside from, far away] *vt* : to break or force apart, in two, or off from a whole : separate usu. by rending, cutting, or breaking, or by intervening time or space : SEVER ⟨the Romans ~*ed* copper-bearing rock by alternately playing fire and water on it —*New Yorker*⟩ ⟨the major races are not always clearly ~*ed* by language —Edward Sapir⟩ ~ *vi* : to become parted, disunited, or severed ⟨pressing hands sharply for pledge of good faith, they ~*ed* —George Meredith⟩ **syn** see SEPARATE

sun·der·land \ˈsəndə(r)lənd\ *adj, usu cap* [fr. *Sunderland*, England] : of or from the county borough of Sunderland, England : of the kind or style prevalent in Sunderland

sundew \ˈ⸗,⸗\ *n* [trans. of ML *ros solis*] : a plant of the genus *Drosera* or of the family Droseraceae — compare ALDROVANDA, DROSOPHYLLUM, RORIDULA

sundew family *n* : DROSERACEAE

sundial \ˈ⸗,⸗⸗\ *n* **1 :** an instrument to show the time of day by the shadow of a gnomon on a usu. horizontal plate or on a cylindrical surface **2** [so called fr. the fact that its leaves incline up to 90 degrees to follow the sun] : a common lupine (*Lupinus perennis*) of the eastern U.S.

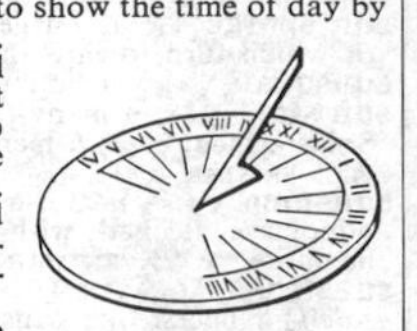

sundial 1

sundial shell *n* : a marine gastropod mollusk of *Architectonica* or a related genus; *also* : the shell of a sundial shell

sun disk *n* : an ancient symbol of the Near East consisting of a disk with conventionalized wings emblematic of the sun-god (as Ra in Egypt, Ashur and later Ahura-Mazda in southwestern Asia)

sun dog *n* **1 :** PARHELION **2 :** a small nearly round halo on the parhelic circle most frequently just outside the halo of 22 degrees — called also *dog, weather gall*

sun·down \ˈsən,dau̇n\ *n* -s [prob. alter. of *sun going down*, fr. ME *sonne goyng downe*] **1 :** the time the sun disappears for the night ⟨visitors are asked to leave at ~ —Frederick Nebel⟩ ⟨they would be back . . . about ~ —Ellen Glasgow⟩ **2 :** a broad-brimmed hat for women **3 :** a light yellowish brown that is redder, lighter, and stronger than khaki or walnut brown and lighter, stronger, and slightly redder than cinnamon

sun·down·er \-nə(r)\ *n* **1** *Austral* : HOBO, TRAMP **2** *chiefly Brit* : a drink taken at sundown ⟨let's have our ~s back on the veranda —Stephen Longstreet⟩ **3 :** a very strict naval officer that formerly compelled midshipmen to return from shore leave at sundown **syn** see VAGABOND

sundress \ˈ⸗,⸗\ *n* : a dress with an abbreviated bodice usu. exposing the shoulders, arms, and back

sun·dri \ˈsəndrē\ *or* **sun·dra** \-rə\ *n* -s [Skt *sundarī*] **1 :** any of several trees of the genus *Heritiera; esp* : an East Indian tree (*H. formes*) with a bark rather rich in tannin and a hard close-grained reddish to dark brown wood that is strong, durable, and resistant to decay and is much used locally for boat-building **2 :** the wood of a sundri

sun·dries \ˈsəndrēz, -riz\ *n pl* [¹*sundry* + *-es*] : miscellaneous articles, details, or items of inconsiderable size or amount individually

sun·dries·man \-zmən\ *n, pl* **sundriesmen** *chiefly Brit* : one that deals in sundries

sundrops \ˈ⸗,⸗\ *n pl but sing or pl in constr* : any of several day-flowering herbs of the genus *Oenothera* (esp. *O. fruticosa*)

[1]**sun·dry** \ˈsəndrē, -ri\ *adj* [ME *sindry, sundry, sondry*, fr. OE *syndrig;* akin to OHG *suntarīg* sundry, OE *sundor* apart — more at SUNDER] **1** *obs* : different or distinct for each : RESPECTIVE ⟨his ministers heaven's palace fill to have their ~ tasks assigned —John Wesley⟩ **2 a** *obs* : variously different : SEPARATE ⟨like to a meadow full of ~ flowers —Shak.⟩ **b :** more than one or two : MISCELLANEOUS, SEVERAL ⟨a guard of ~ horsemen —Charles Dickens⟩ ⟨~ sciences commonly known as social —I.A.Richards⟩ **3** *obs* : DIVERSE ⟨how many and how ~ are the evils wherewith our mortal state is endangered —Angel Day⟩ **4 :** of or relating to sundries ⟨a state's ~ revenue⟩

[2]**sundry** *adv* [ME *sindry, sundry, sondry*, fr. OE *syndrige*, fr. *syndrig*, adj.] *obs* : SEPARATELY, APART, ASUNDER

[3]**sundry** *pron, pl in constr* [ME *sindry, sundry, sondry*, fr. *sindry, sundry, sondry*, adj.] : an indeterminate number : DIVERS ⟨she danced with ~ who asked her —Donn Byrne⟩

sune \ˈsün\ *chiefly dial var of* SOON

sunfall \ˈ⸗,⸗\ *n* : SUNSET

sunfast \ˈ⸗,⸗\ *adj* : resistant to fading by sunlight ⟨~ dyes⟩

[1]**sunfish** \ˈ⸗,⸗\ *n* [¹*sun* + *fish*] **1 a :** OCEAN SUNFISH **b :** any of several rare related forms of the genus *Ranzania* **2 :** any of numerous American freshwater fishes constituting the family Centrarchidae and having a deep compressed body and usu. a brilliant metallic coloration — see PUMPKINSEED 1, LONGEAR SUNFISH **3 :** OPAH **4 :** a moonfish (*Vomer setipennis*) **5 :** THREADFISH 1 **6 :** BASKING SHARK 1 **7 :** a large jellyfish

[2]**sunfish** \"\ *vi, West* : to buck by bringing the shoulders alternately nearly to the ground and raising them ⟨the bronc . . . lunged, broke rhythm and ~*ed* —Dan Cushman⟩

sunfish·er \"+ə(r)\ *n, West* : a bucking horse

sunfish family *n* : CENTRARCHIDAE

sunflower \ˈ⸗,⸗⸗\ *n, often attrib* **1 :** a plant of the genus *Helianthus; esp* : COMMON SUNFLOWER **2 :** HELIOTROPE 1 **3 :** any of various plants that either bear a superficial likeness to the common sunflower or open in the sunshine: as **a :** GUMWEED **b :** POT MARIGOLD **c :** a rockrose of the genus *Helianthemum* **d :** BALSAMROOT **4 a :** a variable color averaging a strong orange yellow that is yellower and stronger than Spanish yellow and stronger and slightly yellower than average marigold **b :** SUNFLOWER YELLOW

sunflower beetle *n* : a chrysomelid beetle (*Zygogramma exclamationis*) that feeds on and sometimes extensively defoliates the sunflower

common sunflower

sunflower chest *n* : CONNECTICUT CHEST

sunflower coral *n* : a discoid fossil of the genus *Receptaculites*

sunflower family *n* : COMPOSITAE

sunflower maggot *n* : the larva of a trypetid fly (*Strauzia longipennis*) that bores in the stems of the common sunflower

sunflower moth *n* : the larva of a moth (*Homoeosoma electellum*) that feeds on the developing head of the common sunflower in many parts of U.S. and Canada

sunflower oil *or* **sunflower-seed oil** *n* : a pale yellow semidrying or drying fatty oil expressed from the seeds of the common sunflower and used chiefly in foods, soaps, varnishes, and paints

sunflower oil cake *n* : the residual cake remaining after the expression of oil from sunflower seed and used chiefly as a cattle feed

sunflower seed weevil *n* : any of several weevils (genus *Desmoris*) with larvae that feed and develop in sunflower seeds

sunflower star *n* : a large 20-rayed starfish (*Pycnopodia helianthoides*) resembling in form a conventionalized representation of a sunflower

sunflower tree *n* : FRINGE TREE

sunflower yellow *n* : a brilliant yellow — called also *balge yellow;* compare SUNFLOWER

[1]**sung** [ME *sungen* (past pl. & past part.), fr. OE *sungon* (past pl.), *gesungen* (past part.)] *past of* SING

[2]**sung** \ˈsu̇ŋ\ *adj, usu cap* [fr. the *Sung* dynasty (960–1280), comprising 18 sovereigns of China] : of, relating to, or having the characteristics of the period of the Sung dynasty and esp. of the art forms developed during that period ⟨*Sung* wares⟩ ⟨*Sung* Chinese collectors⟩

[1]**sungar** *var of* SANGAR

[2]**sun·gar** \ˈsu̇ŋ,gär, ˈsəŋ-\ *n, cap* : DZUNGAR

sun gear *n* : the gear wheel on the central axis in a sun-and-planet motion — see SUN-AND-PLANET MOTION illustration

sun gem *n* : a Brazilian hummingbird (*Heliactin cornuta*) that has in the male two tufts of glittering purple green and golden feathers on the head and a white breast

sun-glade \ˈ⸗,⸗\ *n* : the bright reflection of sunlight on an expanse of water

sunglass \ˈ⸗,⸗\ *adj* [back-formation fr. *sunglasses*] : of or relating to sunglasses ⟨a low-priced ~ lens —*Newsweek*⟩

sunglasses \ˈ⸗,⸗⸗\ *n pl* : glasses used to protect the eyes from the sun

sung·lo \ˈsu̇ŋˈlō\ *n* -s [fr. *Sunglo* Mt., Anhwei prov., China] : a green Chinese tea characterized by large loosely rolled leaves

sunglasses

sunglow \ˈ⸗,⸗\ *n* : a brownish yellow or rosy flush often seen in the sky before sunrise or after sunset that is due to solar rays scattered or diffracted from particles in the lower and upper air

sung mass *n, often cap S&M* : a mass that is chanted or intoned

sun-god \ˈ⸗,⸗\ *n* **1 :** a god that represents or is the personification of the sun in various religions **2 :** a strong reddish orange that is yellower and paler than poppy or paprika and slightly lighter than scarlet vermilion

sun-grebe \ˈ⸗,⸗\ *n* : any of several tropical American and African birds (family Heliornithidae) — called also *finfoot, sun bittern*

sun-grown \ˈ⸗ˈ⸗\ *adj* : grown in the open : exposed to the sun ⟨*sun-grown* tobacco⟩ — compare SHADE-GROWN

sun hat *n* : a broad-brimmed hat often with a high crown worn for protection from the sun

sun-heat \ˈ⸗,⸗\ *n* : heat coming from the sun ⟨in few regions is a more regular and generous outpouring of *sun-heat* available —C.M.Longfield⟩

sun helmet *n* : a hat worn for protection from the sun; *esp* : TOPEE

sun hemp *var of* SUNN

su·ni \ˈsünē\ *n* -s [native name in southeastern Africa] : either of two very small delicately built antelopes (*Nesotragus moschatus* and *N. livingstonei*) of southeastern Africa

[1]**sunk** \ˈsəŋk\ *adj* [fr. past part. of ¹*sink*] **1 :** SUNKEN 2 ⟨a small lean . . . man with ~ cheeks weathered to a tan

—John Masefield⟩ **2 a :** lowered or reduced esp. in status or value **b :** depressed in spirits ⟨when he did not arrive she was rather ~⟩ **3 :** SUNKEN 1 **4 :** recessed rather than projected ⟨a ~ fillet⟩ **5 :** absolutely finished **:** done for ⟨if he couldn't somehow raise the money, he was ~⟩

²sunk \"\ *n* -s [origin unknown] **1** *chiefly Scot* **:** a seat or bank of turf **2** *chiefly Scot* **:** a pad of straw used as a saddle or as a cushion

sunk center *n* **:** the portion of a watch dial that is depressed below the common surface to provide clearance for a hand

sunk cost *n* **:** a cost already incurred that is not subject to variation or revision and that is usu. represented by a fixed asset purchased and in use

sunk·en \ˈsəŋkən\ *adj* [fr. past part. of ¹*sink*] **1 a :** SUBMERGED; *esp* **:** lying at the bottom of a body of water ⟨~ treasure⟩ ⟨a ~ ship⟩ **b :** covered with a watery surface ⟨a ~ marsh⟩ **2 :** fallen in **:** HOLLOW, RECESSED ⟨hunger gave their faces a ~ look⟩ ⟨noticed the slightly ~ cheeks underneath the trimmed beard —Joseph Conrad⟩ **3 :** settled below the normal level ⟨a ~ porch gave a forlorn look to the little house⟩ ⟨that ~ avenue shaded by cypress trees —Marguerite Young⟩ **4 :** SUNK 4 ⟨three bedrooms, a ~ living room —*Springfield (Mass.) Republican*⟩

sunk enamel *n* **:** CHAMPLEVÉ

sunken cord *or* **sunk cord** *n* **:** any of several cords that lie in grooves across the backbone of a hand-sewn book — compare RAISED BAND

sunken garden *also* **sunk garden** *n* **:** a formal garden usu. in a depression or with terraces around it

sun·ket \ˈsəŋkət, ˈsu̇ŋ-\ *n* -s [fr. Sc *sunket* something, alter. of *somewhat*] *Scot & dial Eng* **:** a delicacy in food (as a fancy cake or tart)

sunk fence *n* **:** a ditch with a retaining wall used to divide lands without defacing a landscape — called also *ha-ha*

sunk fly *n* **:** WET FLY

sunk initial *n* **:** an initial placed to align at its top and bottom with two or more text lines

sunk key *n* **:** a key that fits into keyways in both the shaft and the secured member in machinery — compare SADDLE KEY

sunk panel *n* **:** a panel forming a shallow recess below the face of its framing or other surrounding surface

sunk relief *n* **1 :** sculptural relief in which the outlines of modeled forms are incised in a plane surface beyond which the forms do not project **2 :** sculpture or a sculptural form executed in sunk relief

sunk squaw *n* [*sunk* alter. of *sunck*] **:** SUNCK

sunk winding *n* **:** SLOT WINDING

sun lamp *n* **1 :** SUN ARC **2** *usu* **sunlamp** \ˈ=,=\ **:** an electric lamp designed to emit radiation of wavelengths from ultraviolet to infrared and used esp. for therapeutic purposes or for producing tan artificially

sun·less \ˈsənləs\ *adj* **:** lacking the beneficial rays of the sun **:** having no sunshine **:** CHEERLESS, DARK ⟨ran through caverns measureless to man down to a ~ sea —S.T.Coleridge⟩

sun letter *n* [trans. of Ar *alḥurūf ashshamsīya*; fr. the fact that the *l* of the Ar definite article *al* is assimilated to the initial *sh* of *shams* sun, used as a type word] **:** an Arabic consonant to which the *l* of the preceding definite article *al* is assimilated in pronunciation — called also *solar letter;* opposed to *moon letter*

sunlight \ˈ=,=\ *n* [ME *sunneliht, sonneliht*, fr. *sunne, sonne* sun + *liht* light — more at SUN, LIGHT] **1 :** the light of the sun **:** SUNSHINE **2 :** a light source and color filter combination that simulates sunlight in spectral quality and is used in testing photographic film

sunlight burner *n* **:** SUN BURNER

sunlighted \ˈ=,==\ *adj* **:** SUNLIT

sunlight yellow *n* **:** a variable color averaging a light yellow that is greener and lighter than jasmine, greener, lighter, and stronger than popcorn or maize, and greener, stronger, and slightly lighter than chrome lemon

sunlike \ˈ=,=\ *adj* **:** resembling the sun

sun line *n* **:** LINE OF THE SUN

sunlit \ˈ=,=\ *adj* **:** lighted by or as if by the sun ⟨the peaceful and ~ years of the early part of this century —*Current Biog.*⟩

sun moss *n* **:** SUN PLANT 1

sunn \ˈsən\ *or* **sunn hemp** *or* **sun hemp** \ˈsən-\ *n* -s [*sunn*, fr. Hindi *san*, fr. Skt *śaṇa*] **1 :** an East Indian plant (*Crotalaria juncea*) with slender branches, simple leaves, and yellow flowers **2 :** the fiber of the sunn closely resembling that of true hemp, lighter and stronger than jute, and used for ropes and bags, and to some extent for oakum, canvas, and coarse cloth — called also *Bengal hemp, Bombay hemp, Indian hemp*

sun·na *also* **sun·nah** \ˈsu̇nə\ *n* -s [Ar *sunnah*] **1** *often cap* **:** the body of Islamic custom and practice based on Muhammad's words and deeds **2 a :** a personal or communal custom or practice ⟨follow the ~ of his ancestors⟩ **b :** a collection of such practices

sunned *past of* SUN

sun·ni \ˈsu̇nē\ *n* -s *usu cap* [Ar *sunnīy*] **1 :** the Muslims comprising the larger of the two major branches of Islam that adheres to the orthodox tradition of the sunna, acknowledges the first four caliphs as rightful successors of Muhammad, and recognizes as orthodox any of four schools of jurisprudence — compare SHIʿA **2 :** SUNNITE **3 :** the branch of Islam formed by the Sunni

sun·ni·ly \ˈsənᵊlē\ *adv* **:** in a sunny manner ⟨she smiled ~ at him⟩

sun·ni·ness \-nēnəs\ *n* -ES **:** the quality or state of being sunny ⟨a ~ of disposition that delighted us all⟩

sunning *pres part of* SUN

sun·nism \ˈsu̇,nizəm\ *n* -s *usu cap* [*sunna* + *-ism*] **:** the religious system or distinctive tenets of the Sunni

sun·nite \-,nīt\ *n* -s *usu cap* [Ar *sunnīy* + E *-ite*] **:** a Muslim belonging to the Sunni branch of Islam

sunnud *var of* SANAD

¹sun·ny \ˈsənē, -ni\ *adj* -ER/-EST [ME *sunni*, fr. *sunne, sonne* sun + *-i, -y* -y] **1 :** characterized by brilliant sunlight **:** full of sunshine ⟨a ~ springtime weekend —R.S.Monahan⟩ **2 :** exhibiting happiness and gaiety **:** exceptionally cheerful and bright **:** MERRY, OPTIMISTIC ⟨passing suddenly from ~ moods to fits of depression —R.S.Boardman⟩ ⟨a ~ frankness and openness of spirit —J.R.Green⟩ ⟨men and women . . . forever ~ and full of virtue —Sinclair Lewis⟩ **3 :** exposed to, brightened, or warmed by the sun ⟨a ~ room decorated with flowered wallpaper and potted palms —*Amer. Guide Series: N.Y. City*⟩ ⟨small lacquered leaves which . . . glisten like water in a ~ wind —Andrew Young⟩ **4 :** originating with or proceeding from or as if from the sun ⟨a ~ beam danced above her head⟩ **5 :** resembling the sun esp. in color or brilliance ⟨~ bushes of cup of gold —S.M.Spencer⟩

²sunny \"\ *n* -ES **:** a pumpkinseed (*Lepomis gibbosus*) ⟨angling for *sunnies* with flies —*Texas Game & Fish*⟩

sunny side *n* **1 :** the side exposed to the sun's rays ⟨liked to walk down the *sunny side* of the street⟩ **2 :** the favorable optimistic aspect ⟨a child usually sees only the *sunny side*⟩ — **on the sunny side of :** younger than ⟨perhaps she is *on the sunny side of* forty but I doubt it⟩

sunny-side up \ˈ==,=ˈ=\ *adj, of an egg* **:** fried on one side only

sun orange *n* **:** a strong reddish orange that is paler and much yellower than poppy or paprika and yellower, lighter, and slightly stronger than fire red

sun orchid *n* **:** any of several chiefly Australian terrestrial orchids (genus *Thelymitra*) with showy brightly colored and sometimes fragrant flowers that are borne in terminal racemes and typically open only in bright sunlight

sun-pain \ˈ=,=\ *n, South & Midland* **:** intermittent neuralgic headache

sun parlor *n* **1 :** a glass enclosed porch or living room with a sunny exposure **2 :** SUN PORCH 2

sun perch *n* **:** SUNFISH 2

sun pillar *n* **:** a light pillar extending vertically above and below the sun

sun plant *n* **1 :** a cultivated portulaca **2 :** a plant that grows normally in a sunny habitat where it receives light of relatively high intensity — compare SHADE PLANT

sunpocket \ˈ=,==\ *n* **:** SOLAR TRAP

sun porch *n* **1 :** SUN PARLOR 1 **2 :** a wire-floored and usu. wire-enclosed pen raised above the ground adjoining a poultry house and used to provide fresh air and sunlight for birds with a minimum exposure to contaminated soil

sunproof \ˈ=ˈ=\ *adj* **:** impervious to the sun's rays **:** resistant to fading or damage by sunlight

¹sunray \ˈ=,=\ *n* [¹*sun* + *ray*] **1 a :** a ray of sunlight **b :** a representation esp. in art of a sunray **2 :** ANTIMONY YELLOW

²sunray \"\ *adj* **:** SUNBURST

sunrise \ˈ=,=\ *n* [ME *sunne rise*, prob. fr. *sunne rise* (as in such phrases as *tofore the sunne rise* before the sun rises), fr. *sunne* sun + *rise*, 3d pers. pres. subj. of *risen* to rise] **1 a :** the apparent rising of the sun above the horizon **:** atmospheric effects that accompany the sun's appearance **:** the time the sun appears whether in fair or cloudy weather **b :** the time when the upper limb of the sun as affected by refraction appears above the sensible horizon as a result of the diurnal rotation of the earth **2 :** the beginning or start of something ⟨in a dull condition at ~ of that century —G.M. Trevelyan⟩

sunrise clam *or* **sunrise shell** *n* **:** SUNSET SHELL

sunrise service *n, sometimes cap both Ss* **:** an Easter religious service observed at sunrise often in an outdoor setting

sunrise wall *n* **:** the plane of the earth's shadow in the atmosphere at sunrise or the region of changing ionization near this shadow that affects radio fading

sunrising \ˈ=,==\ *n* [ME *sonne rising*, fr. *sonne* sun + *rising*] **1 :** SUNRISE 1 **2 :** the quarter in which the sun rises ⟨the winter ~⟩

sun-room \ˈ=,=\ *n* **:** SUN PARLOR 1

sunrose \ˈ=,=\ *n* **1 :** HELIANTHEMUM 2 **2 :** SUN PLANT 1

suns *pl of* SUN, *pres 3d sing of* SUN

sunscald \ˈ=,=\ *n* **:** an injury of woody plants (as fruit or forest trees) characterized by localized death of the tissues and sometimes by cankers and caused when it occurs in the summer by the combined action of both the heat and light of the sun — see WINTER SUNSCALD

sunscreen \ˈ=,=\ *n* **:** a chemical agent used in suntan preparations for filtering out ultraviolet light

sunset \ˈ=,=\ *n* [ME *sonne set*, prob. fr. *sonne* sun + *set*] **1 a :** the apparent descent of the sun below the horizon **:** the atmospheric effects that accompany the sun's disappearance **:** the time the sun disappears **b :** the time when the upper limb of the sun as affected by refraction disappears below the sensible horizon as a result of the diurnal rotation of the earth **2 :** a period of decline; *esp* **:** the time of old age ⟨the keynote of this ~ of her life was her serene religious faith —Martha T. Stephenson⟩ ⟨the . . . ~ of the secure Victorian world —DeLancey Ferguson⟩ **3 :** a pale orange yellow that is redder and stronger than freestone and slightly yellower and duller than peachblow

sunset clam *n* **:** SUNSET SHELL

sunset gun *n* **:** a cannon fired at sunset or as part of the ceremony of lowering the flag at the end of a day

sunset lily *n* **:** a lily that is a variety (*Lilium pardalinum giganteum*) of the leopard lily and is distinguished by crimson and golden flowers thickly spotted with purple-black

sunset red *n* **:** a strong reddish orange that is yellower and paler than poppy, paler than paprika, and redder, slightly lighter, and stronger than fire red

sunset shell *n* **1 :** any of a family (Tellinidae) of marine equivalve clams having the shell marked with bands of various colors radiating out from the umbones **2 :** a similarly marked bivalve mollusk

sunsetting \ˈ=,==\ *n* [ME *sunne settynge*, fr. *sunne* sun + *settynge, setting*, gerund of *setten* to set] **1 :** SUNSET 1 **2 :** the quarter in which the sun sets

sun·set·ty \ˈsən,sed·ē\ *adj* [¹*sunset* + *-y*] **:** of, resembling, or characteristic of sunset ⟨give the appearance of something ~ and gorgeous —Amy Lowell⟩

sunset wall *n* **:** the plane of the earth's shadow in the atmosphere at sunset or the region of changing ionization near this shadow that affects radio fading

sunset yellow FCF *n, usu cap S&Y* **:** the monoazo dye Food Yellow 3 used esp. in coloring orange drinks — compare DYE table I

sunshade \ˈ=,=\ *n* **:** a shield or baffle, that deflects or redirects the sun's rays: as **a :** PARASOL **b :** AWNING **c :** BRISE-SOLEIL **d :** LENS HOOD

sun shell *n* **:** SUNDIAL SHELL

¹sunshine \ˈ=,=\ *n* [¹*sun* + *shine*] **1 a** (1) **:** the sun's light **:** the sun's direct rays neither scattered nor reflected (2) **:** the sun's light when sufficiently strong to cast a shadow **b** *obs* **:** SUNBURST **c :** the warmth and light given by the sun's rays **d :** a spot or surface on which the sun's light shines as distinguished from surrounding shadow **2 :** something resembling or suggesting the brightness of sunshine **:** a person, thing, condition, or influence that radiates warmth or cheer **:** a source of happiness ⟨last years were spent . . . in the ~ of his home circle —W.L.Worcester⟩ ⟨a good laugh is ~ in a house —W.M.Thackeray⟩

²sunshine \"\ *adj* **1 :** SUNNY 1 **2 :** radiating optimism **:** CHEERFUL, HAPPY ⟨a writer of the ~ type —H.J.Laski⟩ **3 :** FAIR-WEATHER ⟨more than just a ~ friend⟩

sunshining \ˈ=,==\ *adj* [¹*sun* + *shining*] **:** SUNSHINY ⟨that ~ June day —Robert Lowry⟩

sun·shiny \ˈsən,shīnē, -ini\ *adj* [¹*sunshine* + *-y*] **:** bright with or as if with the rays of the sun **:** full of happiness **:** JOYOUS, RESPLENDENT ⟨a ~ day⟩ ⟨looked down at all the ~ faces⟩

sun-shot \ˈ=,=\ *adj* **:** shot or permeated with sunshine ⟨in the limpid *sun-shot* air —Amy Lowell⟩

sun-shower \ˈ=,==\ *n* **:** a light rain while the sun shines

sun side *n* [ME *sonne-syde*, fr. *sonne* sun + *syde, side* side — more at SUN, SIDE] **:** SUNNY SIDE 1

sun sight *n* **:** an observation of the altitude of the sun made for navigational purposes

sun's mean longitude *n* **:** the geocentric celestial longitude which the sun would have if its apparent annual motion in the ecliptic were at a uniform average or mean angular velocity

sun spider *n* **:** WIND SCORPION

sunspot \ˈ=,=\ *n* **1 :** FRECKLE **2 :** a spot on the surface of the sun; *specif* **:** one of the dark spots that appear from time to time consisting commonly of a blue-black umbra with a surrounding penumbra of lighter shade and usu. visible only with the telescope **3** *usu* **sun spot :** SUN ARC

sunspot cycle *or* **sunspot period** *n* **:** the time between maxima in the varying numbers of sunspots averaging about 11 years but sometimes being many years shorter or longer

sunspot number *n* **:** an arbitrary numerical value that is used to describe the sun's spottedness, is the number of individual spots plus 10 times the number of disturbed regions, and depends upon the instrumental equipment and personal equation of the observer

sunspotted \ˈ=,==\ *adj* **:** having sunspots

sunspotted·ness *n* -ES **:** the state of having sunspots

sunspot zone *n* **:** either of two zones within which nearly all sunspots occur: **a :** a zone north of the solar equator between 10 degrees and 30 degrees in solar latitude **b :** a zone correspondingly south of the solar equator

sun spurge *n* **:** a spurge (*Euphorbia helioscopia*) the flowers of which turn toward the sun

sunsquall \ˈ=,=\ *n* **:** a large jellyfish

sun star *n* **1 :** a many-rayed starfish belonging to the family Solasteridae; *esp* **:** a member of the genus *Solaster* **2 :** SUNFLOWER STAR

sunstone \ˈ=,=\ *n* **1 :** a brilliant variety of oligoclase flecked with minute scales of hematite **2 :** AVENTURINE

sunstroke \ˈ=,=\ *n* [trans. of F *coup de soleil*] **:** heatstroke caused by direct exposure to the sun

sunstruck \ˈ=,=\ *adj* **:** affected or touched by the sun ⟨violet valleys and the ~ ridges —Wallace Stegner⟩

sunsuit \ˈ=,=\ *n* **:** an abbreviated playsuit in one-piece or two-piece style worn usu. for sunbathing and play

sunsuit for a child

sun's way *n* **:** the path in interstellar space along which the solar system is traveling

sunt *also* **sant** \ˈsənt\ *n* -s [Ar *sant*, fr. Copt *šonte*, fr. Egypt *šanḏa, šanḏat*] **:** BABUL; *esp* **:** the pod of the babul

suntan \ˈ=,=\ *n, often attrib* **1 :** a browning of the skin from exposure to the rays of the sun **2 a :** a moderate orange color **b :** a light brown to light or moderate yellowish brown

suntans \ˈ=,=\ *n pl* **:** a tan-colored summer uniform

sun temperature *n* **:** the temperature shown by a thermometer exposed fully to sunshine

sun thermometer *n* **:** a black-bulb thermometer used for showing sun temperatures

sun time *n* **:** time by the sun **:** APPARENT TIME

sun-trap \ˈ=,=\ *n* **:** SOLAR TRAP

sun tree *n* **:** a showy Japanese evergreen tree (*Chamaecyparis obtusa*) that is often cultivated as an ornamental and for its fragrant weather-resistant lumber — called also *fire tree, hinoki*

sun trout *n, Midland & South* **:** GRAY TROUT 1

sunup \ˈ=,=\ *n* -s [¹*sun* + *up* (adv.)] **:** SUNRISE

sun valve *n* **:** a device operated by the heat and light of the sun by which beacon lights or other apparatus may be automatically turned off during the daytime

sun visor *n* **:** a sun shield usu. of green mica affixed above the windshield of an automobile

¹sun·ward \ˈsənwə(r)d\ *or* **sun·wards** \-dz\ *adv* [¹*sun* + *-ward, -wards*] **:** toward the sun ⟨hunched his shoulders ~, eager to meet it halfway —Jessamyn West⟩

²sunward \"\ *adj* **:** facing the sun ⟨the ~ side of the earth —H.N.Russell⟩

sun watch *n* **:** a small sundial fitted as a watch

sunweed \ˈ=,=\ *n* **:** SUN SPURGE

sun wheel *n* **:** SUN GEAR

¹sun·wise \ˈsən,wīz\ *adv* [¹*sun* + *-wise*] **:** in the direction of the sun's apparent motion **:** from left to right **:** CLOCKWISE

²sunwise \"\ *adj* **:** moving sunwise **:** CLOCKWISE

su·nya·ta \ˈshünyə,tä\ *n* -s [Skt *śūnyatā*, lit., emptiness, void, fr. *śūnya* empty, void] **1** *Buddhism* **:** the nonexistence of the elements of things and of the self **2 :** ultimate truth or reality interpreted (as in Madhyamika) as absolutely devoid of distinguishing characteristics and beyond even being and nonbeing **:** the transcendental void

sun yat-sen·ism \ˈsün'yät'se,nizəm\ *n* -s *usu cap 1st S&Y* [*Sun Yat-sen* †1925 Chinese statesman and revolutionary leader + E *-ism*] **:** the principles propounded by Sun Yat-sen in his founding of the first Chinese republic

sun yellow *n, usu cap S&Y* **:** the stilbene dye Direct Yellow 11 — compare DYE table I

¹sup \ˈsəp\ *vb* **supped; supped; supping; sups** [ME *soupen, suppen*, fr. OE *sūpan, suppan* to swallow, sip; akin to OHG *sūfan* to drink, sip, MHG *supfen* to sip, ON *sūpa* to drink, swallow, OE *sūcan* to suck — more at SUCK] *vt* **1** *obs* **:** ABSORB, CONSUME **2 a** *chiefly dial* **:** to take into the mouth in sips (as a liquid or liquid food) **b :** to take or drink in swallows or gulps **:** DRINK, SWALLOW — used with *off* or *up* ~ *vi, chiefly dial* **:** to take food and esp. liquid food into the mouth a little at a time either by drinking or with a spoon — **sup sorrow :** to experience sorrow or remorse

²sup \"\ *n* -s **1 a :** a mouthful esp. of liquor or broth **:** SIP **b :** a small quantity (as of a liquid) ⟨a ~ of tea⟩ **2** *dial* **:** QUANTITY, AMOUNT ⟨take a good ~⟩

³sup \"\ *vb* **supped; supped; supping; sups** [ME *soupen, suppen*, fr. OF *soper, super, souper*, fr. *soupe* piece of bread soaked in broth, soup — more at SOUP] *vi* **1 :** to eat the evening meal **:** take supper **2 :** to make one's supper — used with such prepositions as *on, upon,* or *off* ⟨~ on roast beef⟩ ~ *vt* **1** *obs* **:** to provide with supper **:** entertain at supper **2 :** to feed (an animal) at night; — often used with *up*

sup *abbr* **1** superfine **2** superior **3** superlative **4** superseded **5** supine **6** supplement; supplementary **7** supply **8** support **9** [L *supra*] above **10** supreme

su·pa \ˈsüpə\ *n* -s [Tag] **1 :** an Indo-Malayan tree (*Sindora supa*) of the family Leguminosae whose sap yields an oil widely used as an illuminant in the Philippines **2 :** the tough durable wood of the supa

su·pa·necan \,süpəˈnekən, -nāk-\ *n, pl* **supanecan** *or* **supanecans** *usu cap* [*Su*btiaba + Tla*panec*] **:** a language family of the Hokan stock comprising Subtiaba of Nicaragua and Tlapanec of Mexico

su·pa·ri \süˈpärē\ *n* -s [Hindi *supārī*] **:** BETEL NUT

su·pawn *or* **sup·pawn** \səˈpȯn\ *n* -s [D *sappaen*, of Algonquian origin; akin to Massachuset *saupaun* mush, lit., softened by water] *chiefly NewEng* **:** HASTY PUDDING 2

supchgr *abbr* supercharger

¹supe \ˈsüp\ *n* -s [by shortening] **1 :** SUPERNUMERARY **2** *slang* **:** SUPERINTENDENT

²supe \"\ *vi* -ED/-ING/-S **:** to act as a supernumerary

³supe \"\ *vt* -ED/-ING/-S [alter. (influenced by *super*charge) of ²*soup*] **:** to soup up ⟨guided missiles — *suped-*up versions of . . . V-2 rockets —F.V.Drake⟩

¹su·per \ˈsüpə(r)\ *n* -s **1** [short for *supernumerary, superintendent, supervisor*] **a :** SUPERNUMERARY; *esp* **:** a supernumerary actor **b :** one in a position of authority or superiority **:** SUPERINTENDENT, SUPERVISOR **2** [short for obs. *superhive*, fr. *super-* + *hive*] **:** a removable upper story of a beehive containing sections for the storage of honey **3** [E thieves' slang, alter. of *souper*, prob. fr. *white souper* silver watch, fr. *white soup* melted silver from stolen articles + E *-er*] **:** WATCH 7a **4** [³*super*] **a :** a superfine or superior grade or quality **:** an extra large size **b :** an article of merchandise of a superfine grade, quality, or large size **5** [by shortening] **:** SUPERPHOSPHATE **6** [origin unknown] **:** a thin loosely woven open-meshed starched cotton fabric used esp. for reinforcing books **7** [by shortening] **:** SUPERMARKET

²super \"\ *vb* -ED/-ING/-S *vt* **:** to reinforce (as a book backbone) with super ~ *vi* **:** to perform as a super

³super \"\ *adj* **1** [by shortening] **:** SUPERFICIAL 1b **2** [short for *superfine*] **a** (1) **:** of a superfine grade or quality (2) **:** of great worth, value, excellence, or superiority ⟨tiered tables make ~ end tables for a small sofa —*Better Homes & Gardens*⟩ ⟨add mint to chocolate syrup for a ~ sundae sauce —*Parents' Mag.*⟩ **b :** possessing the greatest size, power, complexity, intensity, or development **:** being very great ⟨~ atomic bomb⟩ ⟨~ truck⟩ ⟨~ drugstore⟩ ⟨a plaster casting . . . in bilious ~ gloss colors —I.A.N.Henderson⟩ **c** (1) **:** exhibiting the characteristics of its type to a great or excessive degree ⟨clowns . . . are, in essence, ~ realists —John Grierson⟩; *specif* **:** manifesting excessive loyalty ⟨~ patriot⟩ (2) **:** carried, developed, or made use of to an excessive degree ⟨~ secrecy⟩ ⟨the assumption that safety lies in setting up forbidden signs . . . is what a ~ legalism leads to —W.E.Binkley⟩ **d :** embracing in its structure or authority complexes of its own nature ⟨such a business-labor-agricultural council would develop into a ~ lobby with coercive powers —*New Republic*⟩

⁴super \"\ *adv* **1 :** VERY, EXTREMELY ⟨a brand-new ~ special stove —*Parents' Mag.*⟩ **2 :** EXCESSIVELY ⟨inclined to be ~ critical of the present era hunters —Ed Shearer⟩

super *abbr* **1** superfine **2** superheterodyne **3** superior

super- *prefix* [L, over, above, in addition, fr. *super*, adv. & prep. — more at OVER] **1 a** (1) **:** over and above **:** higher in quantity, quality, or degree **:** more than ⟨*super*standard⟩ ⟨*super*conscious⟩ (2) **:** in addition **:** extra ⟨*super*tax⟩ (3) **:** of a secondary character ⟨*super*parasite⟩ **b** (1) **:** exceeding a norm ⟨*super*alkalinity⟩ ⟨*super*secretion⟩ (2) **:** in excessive degree or intensity ⟨*super*ingenious⟩ ⟨*super*refined⟩ **c :** surpassing all or most others of its kind or class (as in power, size, or complexity) ⟨*super*bomber⟩ ⟨*super*weapon⟩ ⟨*super*state⟩ **2 a :** situated or placed above, on, or at the top of ⟨*super*tower⟩ ⟨*super*glacial⟩; *specif* **:** situated on the dorsal side of **b :** next above or higher ⟨*super*octave⟩ ⟨*super*tonic⟩ **3 :** having the (specified) ingredient present in a large or unusually large proportion ⟨*super*oxide⟩ — compare BI- 4a, PER- 1b(1) **4 :** having an additional dimension ⟨*super*cube⟩ ⟨*super*surface⟩ **5 :** constituting a more inclusive category than that specified ⟨*super*family⟩ ⟨*super*species⟩ **6 :** superior in status, title, or position ⟨*super*sovereign⟩

su·per·a·bil·i·ty \,süp(ə)rəˈbiləd·ē\ *n* [*superable* + *-ity*] **:** SUPERABLENESS

su·per·a·ble \ˈsüp(ə)rəbəl\ *adj* [L *superabilis*, fr. *superare* to go over, surmount, overcome, excel (fr. *super* over) + *-abilis* -able — more at OVER] **:** capable of being overcome or conquered **:** SURMOUNTABLE — **su·per·a·ble·ness** \-nəs\ *n* -ES — **su·per·a·bly** \-blē\ *adv*

su·per·abound \ˌsüpə(r)+\ *vi* [ME *superabounden*, fr. LL *superabundare*, fr. L *super-* + *abundare* to abound] **1 :** to abound or prevail in greater measure **2 :** to be very or too abundant **:** abound to excess or to an unusual extent ⟨~*ing* moisture⟩

su·per·abundance \"+\ *n* [ME, fr. LL *superabundantia*, fr. *superabundant-*, *superabundans* superabundant, overflowing + L *-ia* -y] **1 :** the quality or state of being superabundant **:** great abundance ⟨~ of wealth⟩ **2 :** EXCESS, SURPLUS ⟨get rid of a ~ of grain⟩

su·per·abundancy \"\ *n* -ES [LL *superabundantia*] **:** SUPERABUNDANCE

su·per·abundant \"+\ *adj* [ME, fr. LL *superabundant-*, *superabundans* overflowing, fr. pres. part. of *superabundare* to superabound] **:** abounding to a great, abnormal, or excessive degree **:** being considerably more than is sufficient ⟨~ zeal⟩ ⟨~ crops⟩ ⟨~ grace⟩ — **su·per·abundantly** \"+\ *adv*

su·per·acid \ˌsüpə(r)+\ *adj* [*super-* + *acid*] **1 :** excessively acid ⟨~ solutions of perchloric acid in acetic acid⟩ **2 :** having a pH value of 3.5–4.0 — used of a highly acid soil (as bog peat)

su·per·add \"+\ *vt* [ME *superadden*, fr. L *superaddere*, fr. *super-* + *addere* to add] **1 :** to add over and above **:** add in extra or superfluous amount ⟨the loss of his position was ~*ed* to the loss of his home⟩ ⟨a ~*ed* ornamentation⟩ **2 :** to make an addition; *specif* **:** to say in addition **:** add to what has been mentioned

su·per·addition \"+\ *n* [LL *superaddition-*, *superadditio*, fr. L *superadditus* (past part. of *superaddere* to superadd) + *-ion-*, *-io* -ion] **1 :** the act or process of superadding **2 :** something that has been superadded — **su·per·additional** \"+\ *adj*

su·per·aerodynamics \"+\ *n pl but sing in constr* [*super-* + *aerodynamics*] **:** the study of the mechanical properties of a fluid of such low density that the mean free path of its molecules is large in comparison with the dimensions of a body moving in the fluid

su·per·agency \"+\ *n* [*super-* + *agency*] **:** a large complex governmental agency esp. when set up to supervise and coordinate a group of other agencies

su·per·alimentation \"+\ *n* [*super-* + *alimentation*] **:** the action or process of overfeeding

su·per·alkaline \"+\ *adj* [*super-* + *alkaline*] **1 :** excessively alkaline **2 :** having a pH value of 10.0–10.5 — used of any of the most highly alkaline soils found in deserts

su·per·altar \"+\ *n* [ME *superaltare*, fr. ML, fr. L *super-* + *altare* altar; fr. its being used on top of an unconsecrated altar or table] **:** a portable altar consisting of a small square of precious marble **:** ALTAR STONE 2

su·per·al·tern \ˌsüpəˈrȯltə(r)n\ *n* -S [*super-* + *-altern* (as in *subaltern*)] **:** a universal proposition in traditional logic that is a ground for the immediate inference of a corresponding subalterne

su·per·an·nu·a·ble \ˌsüpəˈranyəwəbəl\ *adj* [*superannua*tion + *-able*] *Brit* **:** that will entitle a person to superannuation pay on completion of a qualifying term ⟨~ position⟩

¹**su·per·an·nu·ate** \ˌsüpəˈranyəwət\ *adj* [ML *superannuatus*] **:** SUPERANNUATED

²**superannuate** \"\ *n* -S **:** one retired or disqualified on account of old age or reaching an age limit

³**su·per·an·nu·ate** \-ˌwāt, *usu* -ād.+V\ *vb* -ED/-ING/-S [back-formation fr. *superannuated*] *vt* **1 :** to make, declare, or prove obsolete or out-of-date ⟨the press ~*s* the town crier —Helen Sullivan⟩ **:** disqualify or reject on account of age or antiquity **2 :** to retire and usu. pension because of old age or infirmity ~ *vi* **1 :** to become retired or ineligible because of age **2 :** to become stale by lapse of time

superannuated *adj* [ML *superannuatus* (past part. of *superannuari* to be too old, fr. L *super-* + *annus* year) + E *-ed* — more at ANNUAL] **:** rated no longer fully or passably efficient in one's job because of age **:** incapacitated or disqualified for active duty by advanced age

su·per·an·nu·a·tion \ˌ==ˌ==ˈwāshən\ *n* [³*superannuate* + *-ion*] **1 :** the action or process of superannuating or the state of being superannuated **2 :** an allowance to one superannuated **:** a retirement allowance

su·per·an·nu·i·tant \-üədˈənt\ *n* [blend of *superannuate* and *annuitant*] **:** a recipient of a superannuation

su·per·an·nu·i·ty \ˌsüpərəˈn(y)üədˌē\ *n* [blend of *superannuate* and *annuity*] **:** SUPERANNUATION 2

su·per·au·rale \ˌsüpəˌrȯˈra(ˌ)lē, -ˌrȯˈrā-, -ˌraủˈrä(-\ *n* -S [NL, prob. fr. neut. of *superauralis* of above the ear, fr. L *super-* + *auris* ear + *-alis* -al — more at EAR] **:** the highest point on the upper edge of the helix of the ear

su·perb \süˈpərb, səˈp-, -pəb, -pəib\ *adj*, *often* -ER/-EST [L *superbus* excellent, proud, haughty, fr. *super* over, above + *-bus* (fr. the root of *fui* I have been) — more at SUPER-, BE] **1 a :** exhibiting a majestic grace or grandeur **:** STATELY, LORDLY ⟨the ~ main shaft . . . rises in an almost unbroken line —*Amer. Guide Series: N. Y. City*⟩ ⟨the ~ masculinity of good Spanish dancing —Claudia Cassidy⟩ **b :** possessing or exhibiting nobility of birth, mien, position, or character **:** NOBLE, MAJESTIC ⟨~ as the ancient doings of the gods of old —Alice D. Estes⟩ **c** (1) **:** magnificently ornate **:** RICH, ELEGANT, SUMPTUOUS ⟨this coronation . . . was probably the most ~ . . . anybody now living has seen —Mollie Panter-Downes⟩ (2) **:** brilliantly colored — used chiefly of a bird **2 :** of supreme excellence, value, goodness, or beauty **:** of the highest quality ⟨our left has provided ~ political leadership —A.M. Schlesinger b.1917⟩ ⟨portfolios of ~ photographs —*Amer. Guide Series: N.H.*⟩ **syn** see SPLENDID

su·per·bi·ty \-bədˌē\ *n* -ES [MF *superbité*, fr. *superbe* haughty (fr. L *superbus*) + *-ité* -ity — more at SUPERB] **:** HAUGHTINESS, ARROGANCE ⟨the vaulting ambition and ~ of youth —T.H. White b.1906⟩

su·per·block \ˈsüpə(r)+ˌ-\ *n* [*super-* + *block*] **:** a very large residential or commercial block barred to through traffic, crossed by pedestrian walks and sometimes access roads, and usu. spotted with open greens or grassed malls

su·perb·ly *adv* **:** in a superb manner

su·perb·ness *n* -ES **:** the quality or state of being superb

su·per·bomb \ˈsüpə(r)+ˌ-\ *n* [*super-* + *bomb*] **:** an extremely powerful bomb; *esp* **:** HYDROGEN BOMB

superb paradise bird *or* **superb bird of paradise** *n* **:** a bird of paradise (*Lophorina superba*) having in the male a large erectile fan-shaped tuft on each shoulder, a gorget of metallic green feathers on the breast, and a deep violet or nearly black color with green reflections

superb warbler *n* **:** BLUECAP 2b

¹**su·per·calender** \ˌsüpə(r)+\ *n* [*super-* + *calender*] **:** a calender stack of highly polished alternating metal and compressed paper or cotton rolls used to give an extra finish to paper — compare FRICTION CALENDER

²**supercalender** \"\ *vt* **:** to process (paper) in a supercalender

su·per·cargo \ˌsüpə(r)+\ *n*, *pl* **supercargos** *or* **supercargoes** [alter. (influenced by *super-*) of *supracargo*, modif. (influenced by *supra-*) of Sp *sobrecargo*, fr. *sobre-* over (fr. L *super-*) + *cargo* — more at CARGO] **1 :** an officer or person in a merchant ship whose duty is to manage the commercial concerns of the voyage **2 :** a foreign factor handling marine cargo

supercede *var of* SUPERSEDE

su·per·celestial \ˌsüpə(r)+\ *adj* [LL *supercaelestis* supercelestial (fr. L *super-* + *caelestis* celestial) + E *-al*] **1 :** above the heavens **2 :** higher than celestial esp. in spirituality or divinity

su·per·central \"+\ *adj* [*super-* + *central*] **:** situated above a center or central structure and esp. the central sulcus of the brain

su·per·centrifuge \"+\ *n* [*super-* + *centrifuge*] **:** a centrifuge designed to operate at higher than normal speeds to perform separations impossible in standard centrifuges — compare ULTRACENTRIFUGE

¹**su·per·charge** \ˈsüpə(r)+ˌ-\ *vt* [*super-* + *charge*] **:** to charge greatly or excessively with vigor, energy, tension, emotion or material supplying one of these ⟨a bitter struggle for power . . . in a *supercharged* political atmosphere —Mary K. Hammond⟩ ⟨he ~*s* his ready flow of speech with slang —*English Digest*⟩ ⟨a supplementary pellet *supercharged* with vitamins and minerals —*Jour. Amer. Med. Assoc.*⟩: as **a :** to supply a charge to the intake of (an internal-combustion engine or other prime mover) at a pressure higher than that of the surrounding atmosphere **b :** PRESSURIZE 1

²**supercharge** \"\ *n* **:** a great or excessive charge ⟨that ~ of zest which generates gaiety in others —John Mason Brown⟩ ⟨the use of ~*s* must be avoided . . . otherwise excessive wear of the guns will result —*U. S. War Dept. Technical Manual*⟩

supercharged engine *n* [*supercharged* (past part. of ¹*supercharge*) + *engine*] **:** an internal-combustion engine equipped with or using a supercharger

su·per·charg·er \-jə(r)\ *n* [¹*supercharge* + *-er*] **:** a device (as a blower, compressor, or pump) to increase the volume air charge of an internal-combustion engine over that which would normally be drawn in through the pumping action of the pistons and to compensate for the lower density of air in altitude operation of aircraft engines or the deficiency of air charge in high-speed automotive operation; *also* **:** a similar device for increasing air pressure — see CABIN SUPERCHARGER

¹**su·per·cil·i·ary** \ˌsüpə(r)ˈsilēˌerē\ *adj* [irreg. (influenced by *-ary*) fr. NL *superciliaris*, fr. L *supercilium* eyebrow + *-aris* -ar] **1 :** of, relating to, or adjoining the eyebrow **:** SUPRAORBITAL ⟨a ~ line of color on a bird⟩ **2 :** SUPRACILIARY

²**superciliary** \"\ *n* -ES **:** a superciliary part or marking

superciliary ridge *or* **superciliary arch** *n* **1 :** a prominence on the frontal bone above the eye caused by the projection of the frontal air sinuses **2 :** the projecting upper part of the orbit of various animals

¹**su·per·cil·ious** \ˌsüpə(r)ˈsilēəs, -lyəs\ *adj* [L *superciliosus*, fr. *supercilium* eyebrow, pride, haughtiness (fr. *super-* + *-cilium* — akin to L *celare* to hide) + *-osus* -ous — more at HELL] **1 :** arrogantly superior **:** HAUGHTY, DISDAINFUL ⟨though elated by his rank, it did not render him ~ —Jane Austen⟩ ⟨translators . . . ~ about the possibility of using Basic English for such international conferences —Mark Starr⟩ ⟨shaggy ~ camels —L.C.Stevens⟩ **2 :** expressive of contempt **:** SCORNFUL, SNEERING ⟨his lip curls in a ~ smile⟩ **syn** see PROUD

²**supercilious** \"\ *adj* [L *supercilium* eyebrow + E *-ous*] *archaic* **:** SUPERCILIARY

su·per·cil·ious·ly *adv* **:** in a supercilious manner

su·per·cil·ious·ness *n* -ES **:** the quality or state of being supercilious

su·per·cil·i·um \ˌsüpə(r)ˈsilēəm\ *n*, *pl* **supercil·ia** \-ēə\ [L, eyebrow, ridge, pride] **1 a :** the region of the eyebrows **:** EYEBROW **b :** the overhanging margin of a bony cavity (as of the acetabulum) **2 a :** a fillet surmounting the cymatium in a Roman cornice **b :** a fillet above or below the scotia of an Attic base **c :** the lintel of a door

su·per·class \ˈsüpə(r)+ˌ-\ *n* [*super-* + *class*] **:** a category in taxonomy ranking between a phylum or division and a class

su·per·colossal \ˌsüpə(r)+\ *adj* [*super-* + *colossal*] **:** extremely colossal

su·per·columnar \"+\ *adj* [*super-* + L *columna* column + E *-ar*] **1 :** built above a column or colonnade **2 :** marked by superposition of columns

su·per·columniation \"+\ *n* [*super-* + *columniation*] **:** the superposition of one order of columns above another

su·per·commentary \"+\ *n* [*super-* + *commentary*] **:** a commentary upon a commentary

su·per·compression \"+\ *n* [*super-* + *compression*] **:** the compression of a portion of a compressed fuel-air mixture during the last stages of the compression stroke in a mixed-cycle internal-combustion engine to a much higher temperature than the remainder

su·per·conduct \"+\ *vi* [back-formation fr. *superconductivity*] **:** to exhibit superconductivity

su·per·conduction \"+\ *n* [*super-* + *conduction*] **:** electrical conduction in a superconductive substance

su·per·conductive \"+\ *adj* [prob. back-formation fr. *superconductivity*] **:** exhibiting superconductivity

su·per·conductivity \"+\ *n* [*super-* + *conductivity*] **:** abnormally high conductivity; *specif* **:** a complete disappearance of electrical resistance in a metal (as lead, mercury, vanadium, or tin) at temperatures near absolute zero — called also *supraconductivity*

su·per·conductor \"+\ *n* [*super-* + *conductor*] **:** a superconductive substance or body

¹**su·per·conscious** \"+\ *adj* [*super-* + *conscious*] **1 :** transcending human consciousness **2 :** of, relating to, or possessing the highest consciousness or a margin of consciousness above that within the ordinary range of attention — compare SUBCONSCIOUS — **su·per·consciousness** \"+\ *n*

²**superconscious** \"\ *n* **:** the superconscious part of the mind or psychic activity

su·per·contract \ˌsüpə(r)+\ *vi* [*super-* + *contract*] **:** to shrink irreversibly — used esp. of keratin fibers and substances (as hair or wool) containing keratin — **su·per·contraction** \"+\ *n*

super contract bridge *n* [³*super*] **:** contract bridge played with a joker added to the regular pack

su·per·cool \ˌsüpə(r)+\ *vt* [*super-* + *cool*] **:** to cool below the freezing point without solidification or crystallization **:** UNDERCOOL

su·per·cres·cence \ˌsüpə(r)ˈkresᵊn(t)s\ *n* -S [fr. *supercrescent*, after such pairs as E *excrescent: excrescence*] **:** a parasitic organism

su·per·cres·cent \-nt\ *adj* [L *supercrescent-*, *supercrescens*, pres. part. of *supercrescere* to grow over, fr. *super-* + *crescere* to grow — more at CRESCENT] **:** growing on a thing **:** PARASITIC

su·per·critical \ˌsüpə(r)+\ *adj* [*super-* + *critical*] **:** capable of carrying on a chain reaction in such a manner that the rate of reaction increases — used esp. of fissionable material

su·per·crust \ˈsüpə(r)+ˌ-\ *n* [*super-* + *crust*] **:** the top course of a concrete or bituminous-macadam pavement

su·per·dainty \ˌsüpə(r)+\ *adj* [*super-* + *dainty*] **:** extremely dainty

su·per·dominant \"+\ *n* [*super-* + *dominant*] **:** SUBMEDIANT

su·per·du·per *also* **su·per·doo·per** \ˌsüpə(r)ˈd(y)üpə(r)\ *adj* [redupl. of ³*super*] **:** extremely super **:** of greatest excellence, size, complexity, intensity, or impressiveness

su·per·duty \ˌsüpə(r)+\ *adj* [*super-* + *duty*] **:** designed to withstand extremely hard use; *esp* **:** designed to withstand use under extreme heat ⟨~ alloys for jet engines⟩

supered *past of* SUPER

su·per·ego \ˌsüpə(r)+\ *n* [*super-* + *ego*] **:** a major sector of the psyche that is mostly unconscious but partly conscious, that develops out of the ego by internalization or introjection in response to advice, threats, warnings, and punishment esp. by parents but also by teachers and other authority, that reflects parental conscience and the rules of society, and that serves as an aid in character formation and as a protector for the ego against overwhelming id impulses

su·per·elevate \"+\ *vt* [prob. back-formation fr. *superelevation*] **:** BANK 1c

su·per·elevation \"+\ *n* [*super-* + *elevation*] **1 :** the vertical distance between the heights of inner and outer edges of highway pavement or railroad rails **2 :** additional elevation

su·per·eminence \"+\ *n* [LL *supereminentia*, fr. *supereminent-*, *supereminens* supereminent + L *-ia* -y] **:** the quality or state of being supereminent **:** distinguished eminence

su·per·eminent \ˌsüpə(r)+\ *adj* [LL *supereminent-*, *supereminens* rising above, prominent, fr. L, pres. part. of *supereminēre* to rise above, fr. *super-* + *eminēre* to stand out, be prominent — more at EMINENT] **1 a :** being extremely high or highest **b :** being the most distinguished in rank or esp. excellence **:** eminent to a conspicuous degree **:** of very remarkable attainments or quality **2 :** extremely conspicuous **:** exhibiting esp. noticeable characteristics — **su·per·eminently** \"+\ *adv*

su·per·empirical \"+\ *adj* [*super-* + *empirical*] **:** experienced or experiencing by more than empirical means **:** TRANSCENDENT, TRANSCENDENTAL

su·per·encipherment \"+\ *n* [*super-* + *encipherment*] **:** an enciphering of what already is a cryptogram esp. in code

su·per·endurance \"+\ *n* [*super-* + *endurance*] **:** extremely great power of endurance

su·per·er·o·gant \ˌsüpəˈrerəgənt\ *adj* [ML *supererogant-*, *supererogans*, pres. part. of *supererogare* to perform beyond the call of duty] **:** SUPEREROGATORY

su·per·er·o·ga·tion \ˌsüpəˌrerəˈgāshən\ *n* -S [ML *supererogation-*, *supererogatio*, fr. *supererogatus* (past part. of *supererogare* to perform beyond the call of duty, fr. LL, to expend in addition, fr. L *super-* + *erogare* to expend money from the public treasury after asking the consent of the people, fr. *e-* + *rogare* to ask) + L *-ion-*, *-io* -ion — more at RIGHT] **1 :** the act or process or an instance of performing more than is required by duty or obligation; *specif* **:** the performance beyond what is considered by the Roman Catholic Church to be necessary for salvation of good deeds of the kind believed to have been done by the saints or to be capable of being done by men **2 :** the act or process or an instance of performing more than necessary to complete an undertaking ⟨repeating the experiment would be an act of ~⟩

su·per·erog·a·tive \ˌsüpərəˈrägəd·iv\ *adj* [ML *supererogatus* + E *-ive*] **:** SUPEREROGATORY

su·per·erog·a·to·ri·ly \ˌ==ˌrägəˌtōrəlē, -tȯr-, -li\ *adv* **:** in a supererogatory manner

su·per·erog·a·to·ry \-ˌtōrē, -ˌtȯr-, -ri\ *adj* [ML *supererogatorius*, fr. *supererogatus* + L *-orius* -ory] **1 a :** of, relating to, or characterized by supererogation **b :** observed or performed to an extent not enjoined or required ⟨~ acts⟩ **2 :** that can be dispensed with **:** SUPERFLUOUS, NONESSENTIAL ⟨metaphors . . . are pleasurable accessories . . . which are ~ when one comes down to the business of understanding what is said —R.M. Weaver⟩

su·per·essential \ˌsüpə(r)+\ *adj* [ML *superessentialis*, fr. L *super-* + *essentia* essence + *-alis* -al] **:** having or being an essence transcending others **:** possessing or consisting of the supreme essence — **su·per·essentially** \"+\ *adv*

¹**su·per·es·sive** \ˌsüpəˈresiv\ *adj* [*super-* + *-essive* (as in *inessive*)] *of a grammatical case* **:** denoting position or location on or upon

²**superessive** \"\ *n* -S **:** the superessive case or a word in it

su·per·ette \ˌsüpəˈret\ *n* -S [¹*super* + *-ette*] **:** a supermarket operating on a scale smaller than usual as measured by space occupied or volume of business

su·per·excellent \"+\ *adj* [LL *superexcellent-*, *superexcellens*, fr. pres. part. of *superexcellere* to excel greatly, fr. *super-* + *excellere* to excel] **:** extremely or supremely excellent **:** excellent in an uncommon degree ⟨the ~ work of professional historians —A.J.Nock⟩

su·per·existent \"+\ *adj* [*super*natural + *existent*] **:** having a supernatural existence

su·per·familial \ˌsüpə(r)+\ *adj* [*superfamily* + *-al*] **:** having the scope of or constituting a superfamily

su·per·family \"+\ *n* [*super-* + *family*] **:** a category of taxonomic classification ranking next above a family and being equivalent to a suborder or falling between the suborder and family

su·per·fat·ted \ˌ==ˈfad·əd\ *adj* [*super-* + *fat* (n.) + *-ed*] **:** containing unsaponified fat ⟨~ toilet soaps⟩

su·per·fecundation \ˌsüpə(r)+\ *n* [*super-* + *fecundation*] **1 :** successive fertilization of two or more ova from the same ovulation esp. by different sires — compare SUPERFETATION **2 :** fertilization at one time of a number of ova excessive for the species

su·per·female \"+\ *n* [*super-* + *female*] **:** a sterile female having three X-chromosomes and two sets of autosomes — compare SUPERMALE

su·per·fetation \"+\ *n* [ML *superfetation-*, *superfetatio*, fr. L *superfetatus* (past part. of *superfetare* to conceive anew while still with young, fr. *super-* + *fetare* to bring forth young, hatch, fr. *fetus*, *foetus* act of bringing forth, young) + *-ion-*, *-io* -ion — more at FETUS] **1 :** successive fertilization of two or more ova of different ovulations resulting in the presence of embryos of unlike ages in the same uterus and occurring normally in various viviparous fishes and sometimes claimed to take place anomalously in mammals including man — compare SUPERFECUNDATION **2 :** fertilization of an ovule by two or more kinds of pollen **3 :** the process or product of the production or accretion of one thing upon another esp. in an uninterrupted superabundant cumulative development ⟨the close, technical style in which they make their discoveries known: the dense syntax and ~ of ideas —A.J.Carr⟩ ⟨a ~ of fantasies —E.M.Forster⟩

su·per·fice \ˈsüpə(r)fəs\ *n* -S [ME, fr. MF, fr. L *superficies* top, surface — more at SUPERFICIES] **:** SUPERFICIES

¹**su·per·fi·cial** \ˌsüpə(r)ˈfishəl\ *adj* [ME, fr. LL *superficialis*, fr. L *superficies* top, surface + *-alis* -al] **1 a :** of or relating to a surface **:** lying on, not penetrating below, occurring in, or affecting only the surface or surface layers ⟨multiple ~ wounds of the left and right thigh —Ernest Hemingway⟩ ⟨the ~ area of the wall —*Code for Dwelling Construction*⟩ ⟨the ~ layers of water through which light penetrates —R.E.Coker⟩ **b** *of a unit of measure* **:** not solid or linear **:** SQUARE ⟨~ foot⟩ **c :** of, relating to, or being the unconsolidated formations (as glacial drift or alluvium) that constitute most of the surface of the land **:** SURFICIAL **2 a** (1) **:** not penetrating beneath or farther than the easily or quickly apprehended features of a thing **:** concerned only with the obvious or apparent **:** CURSORY, HASTY, CASUAL ⟨the newspapers' ~ report . . . never gave the true picture —*Farm Jour.*⟩ ⟨current but mostly ~ explanations —Franz Alexander⟩ (2) **:** lacking in depth or substantial qualities **:** not profound **:** SHALLOW ⟨his thinking was ~ and fuzzy —W.E.Davies⟩ ⟨the religion . . . from which ~ knowledge estranges us —W.R.Inge⟩ ⟨his talents were . . . wasted in the production of ~ trash —R.A.Hall b.1911⟩ (3) **:** lacking in thoroughness of intellect, scholarship, or wisdom **:** not given to soundness ⟨~ research workers . . . often lack the . . . breadth of view to prevent them from giving absurd interpretations to their statistical results —M.R. Cohen⟩ ⟨children who seem to care little about learning and whose minds are definitely ~ in character —Morris Fishbein⟩ **b :** seen on the surface **:** EXTERNAL ⟨their ~ defect . . . cannot blind us to the sterling workmanship —W.B.Adams⟩ ⟨~ changes in costume and creed —Lewis Mumford⟩ **c :** presenting only an appearance or a semblance **:** not far-reaching, significant, or genuine ⟨the ~ differences of accent which are inevitable in such an international language —David Abercrombie⟩ ⟨maintaining the ~ charm of a glib intellectual —Arthur Knight⟩ — **su·per·fi·cial·ly** \-sh(ə)lē, -li\ *adv* — **su·per·fi·cial·ness** \ˌ==ˈfishəlnəs\ *n* -ES

²**superficial** \"\ *n* -S **1 :** a person or thing that is superficial **2 :** a superficial aspect, character, or quality ⟨the American novel of today is only English in ~*s* —*Times Lit. Supp.*⟩

superficial blastula *n* **:** PERIBLASTULA

superficial cleavage *n* **:** meroblastic cleavage in which a layer of cells is produced about a central mass of yolk (as in many arthropod eggs) — compare DISCOIDAL CLEAVAGE

superficial fascia *n* **:** the thin layer of loose fatty connective tissue underlying the skin and binding it to the parts beneath

su·per·fi·cial·ist \ˌsüpə(r)ˈfish(ə)ləst\ *n* -S **:** a person whose knowledge, understanding, or insight is superficial

su·per·fi·ci·al·i·ty \ˌsüpə(r)ˌfishēˈaləd·ē, -lətē, -i\ *n* -ES [¹*superficial* + *-ity*] **1 :** the quality or state of being superficial **2 :** one that is superficial

su·per·fi·cial·ize \-ˈfishəˌlīz\ *vt* -ED/-ING/-S **:** to make superficial

superficial temporal artery *n* **:** the one of the two terminal branches of each external carotid artery that arises behind the parotid gland and passes upward between the mandibular condyle and the auditory meatus to the zygoma

¹**superficiary** *adj* [LL *superficiarius* built on another man's land, fr. L *superficies* surface, building on the surface of the ground + *-arius* -ary] *obs* **:** SUPERFICIAL

²**su·per·fi·ci·ary** \-ˈfishēˌerē\ *n* -ES [LL *superficiarius*, fr. *superficiarius* built on another man's land] *Rom & civil law* **:** one who has built on the soil of another usu. by agreement with him for an annual rental

su·per·fi·cies \-ˈfish(ˌ)ēz, -shēˌēz\ *n*, *pl* **superficies** [L, top, surface, building on the surface of the ground, fr. *super-* + *-ficies* (fr. *facies* form, shape, face) — more at FACE] **1 a :** a depthless surface of a geometric body **:** the boundary or one of the boundaries of a solid or the border between two regions of space ⟨the ~ of a cube⟩ **b :** the outer surface of a body **:** superficial area ⟨the earth, from the ~ to an unknown depth —William Bartram⟩ **2 :** the purely external aspects, features, or characteristics of a thing **:** superficial appearance ⟨the audience is held by the substance of the play rather than by the ~ of the production —R.W.Speaight⟩ **3** *Rom & civil law* **a :** everything on the surface of a piece of ground or of a building so closely connected by art or nature as to constitute a part of it (as houses or other structures, fences, trees, or vines) **b :** a real right or servitude consisting in a right in perpetuity or for a long term to enjoy the superficies of land on payment of an annual or periodic rent — compare EMPHYTEUSIS, GROUND RENT

su·per·fine \ˌsüpə(r)+\ *adj* [*super-* + *fine*] **1 :** very refined or delicate ⟨overly nice ⟨this ~, extraordinary sort of gallantry —Jane Austen⟩ **2 :** of extremely fine size or texture ⟨~ file⟩ **3 :** very fine in quality or grade — used esp. of merchandise ⟨ornate creations, stiff with gold and silver and made of . . . ~ Flemish cloth, or of rich Italian silks —H.S.Bennett⟩

su·per·fines \ˈsüpə(r)ˌfīnz\ *n pl* **:** merchandise graded as superfine

su·per·finish \ˌsüpə(r)+\ *vt* [*super-* + *finish*] **:** to polish (a metal surface) to a mirrorlike finish by the use of hard abrasive stones at low pressure under a flood of lubricant of proper viscosity

su·per·fix \ˈsüpə(r)ˌfiks\ *n* [*super-* + *-fix* (as in *prefix*)] **:** a recurrent predictable pattern of stress that characterizes small stretches of speech whose constituents are parallel in relationship ⟨the ~ for *flattop* and *redhead* is \ˈ=ˌ=\⟩

su·per·flu·ent \süˈpərfləwənt\ *adj* [ME, fr. L *superfluent-, superfluens*, pres. part. of *superfluere* to overflow, be superfluous — more at SUPERFLUOUS] **1 :** characterized by or given to superfluity **:** SUPERFLUOUS **2 :** SUPERABUNDANT **3 :** flowing or floating above or from or on the top

su·per·fluid \ˌsüpə(r)+\ *n* [*super-* + *fluid*] **:** matter (as helium II) in a unique state characterized by extraordinarily large thermal conductivity and capillarity — **su·per·fluidity** \"+\ *n*

su·per·flu·i·ty \ˌsüpə(r)ˈflüəd·ē, -üətē, -i\ *n* -ES [ME *superfluitee*, fr. MF *superfluité*, fr. LL *superfluitat-, superfluitas*, fr. L *superfluus* superfluous + *-itat-, -itas* -ity] **1 a :** a superabundant excess **:** an amount greatly beyond what is sufficient, necessary, or advantageous **:** a copious oversupply ⟨this book has . . . a ~ of introductions and summaries —M.G.Singer⟩ **b :** the quality or state of being extra or superfluous **:** WASTEFULNESS ⟨there is no ~ in the means employed —C.R.Darwin⟩ **c :** a thing that is unnecessary or in excess **:** a superfluous or dispensable thing ⟨do not permit children to indulge in *superfluities* . . . until essentials are met —Mary Ines⟩ **2 :** immoderate and esp. luxurious living, habits, or desires **:** PRODIGALITY, EXTRAVAGANCE **syn** see EXCESS

su·per·flu·ous \süˈpərfləwəs, səˈp-, -pəf-, -pəif- *also* -fləs *or* ÷-fələs\ *adj* [ME, fr. L *superfluus* running over, superfluous, fr. *superfluere* to overflow, be in excess, fr. *super-* + *fluere* to flow — more at FLUID] **1 a :** exceeding what is sufficient, necessary, normal, or desirable **:** SUPERABUNDANT, SURPLUS, NONESSENTIAL, SUPEREROGATORY ⟨eliminating ~ words and replacing loose phrases with single words that express the thought —*N.Y. Times*⟩ ⟨armed ships allow nothing ~ to litter up the deck —Herman Melville⟩ ⟨silver plate . . . was the most suitable outlet for ~ wealth . . . when modern facilities for investment did not exist —Edwin Benson⟩ **b** *obs* (1) **:** unpleasantly excessive (2) **:** ABNORMAL ⟨a blind man, or a lame, or he that hath a flat nose, or any thing ~ —Lev 21:18 (AV)⟩ (3) **:** INORDINATE ⟨purchased at a ~ rate —Shak.⟩ **c :** exceeding the octave compass in an ecclesiastical mode **2 a** *obs* **:** WASTEFUL, EXTRAVAGANT **b :** doing something unnecessary, irrelevant, or frivolous ⟨so ~ as to demand the time of day —Shak.⟩ — **su·per·flu·ous·ly** *adv* — **su·per·flu·ous·ness** *n* -ES

su·per·flux \ˈsüpə(r)ˌfləks\ *n* [ML *superfluxus* action of overflowing, fr. L *superfluxus*, past part. of *superfluere* to overflow] **1 :** SUPERABUNDANCE, SUPERFLUITY **2 :** an excessive flowing

super foot *n* [³*super*] **1** *Austral* **:** a superficial foot **:** SQUARE FOOT **2** *Austral* **:** BOARD FOOT

su·per·frontal \ˌsüpə(r)+\ *n* [ML *superfrontalis*, fr. L *super-* + ML *frontale* altar frontal, fr. L, ornament for the forehead — more at FRONTAL] **:** a cloth which is placed over the top of an altar and hangs down a few inches over the frontal

superfuse *vt* [L *superfusus*, past part. of *superfundere* to pour on or over, fr. *super-* + *fundere* to pour — more at FOUND] **1** *obs* **:** POUR **2 :** SUPERCOOL

su·per·fusibility \ˌsüpə(r)+\ *n* **:** the quality, state, or condition of being superfusible

su·per·fusible \ˌsüpə(r)+\ *adj* [*superfuse* + *-ible*] **:** capable of being supercooled

superfusion \"+\ *n* [LL *superfusion-, superfusio* act of pouring on or over, fr. L *superfusus* + *-ion-, -io* -ion] **:** an act or instance of superfusing

su·per·galaxy \"+\ *n* [*super-* + *galaxy*] **:** an aggregation of great numbers of galaxies **:** a large cluster of galaxies

¹su·per·gene \ˈsüpə(r)ˌjēn\ *adj* [*super-* + *-gene* (as in *hypogene*)] **1 :** deposited or enriched by generally downward-moving solutions — used esp. of an ore deposit; opposed to *hypogene;* compare ENRICHMENT **2 :** of or relating to a process of deposition by generally downward-moving solutions

²supergene \"\ *n* [*super-* + *gene*] **:** a group of linked genes acting as an allelomorphic unit

su·per·generic \ˌsüpə(r)+\ *adj* [*super-* + *generic*] **:** of or relating to groups or characters of higher rank than generic

su·per·giant \"+\ *n* [*super-* + *giant*] **1 :** a very gigantic object **2** *or* **supergiant star :** a star of very great intrinsic luminosity and enormous size characterized by the sharpness of its spectral lines

su·per·glacial \ˌsüpə(r)+\ *adj* [*super-* + *glacier* + *-al*] **:** on, of, or relating to the surface of a glacier ⟨~ rivers⟩

su·per·glottic \"+\ *adj* [*super-* + *glottic*] **:** situated above the glottis

su·per·government \"+\ *n* [*super-* + *government*] **1 :** an international governing body having the power to enforce its decisions upon member nations **2 :** government by a group or body that has no authority to govern but that can force its decisions upon a legitimate government ⟨~ by private enterprise —Catherine Bauer⟩ ⟨a ~ by labor unions which may tax at will —David Lawrence⟩ **3 :** a government with extremely broad or thorough-going powers

¹su·per·heat \" + \ *vt* [*super-* + *heat*, v.] **1 a :** to heat (a liquid) above the boiling point without converting into vapor **b :** to heat (a vapor not in contact with its own liquid) so as to cause to remain free from suspended liquid droplets ⟨~*ed* steam⟩ **2 a :** to heat very much; *esp* **:** OVERHEAT ⟨unbuttoned his coat . . . to cool his ~*ed* blood —Josephine Pinckney⟩ **b :** to excite, intensify, or exaggerate excessively

²su·per·heat \ˈsüpə(r)+,-\ *n* [*super-* + *heat*, n.] **1 :** the extra heat imparted to a vapor in superheating it from a dry and saturated condition; *also* **:** the corresponding rise of temperature **2 :** the difference in temperature between the lifting gas inside a balloon envelope and the outside air

su·per·heater \ˌsüpə(r)+\ *n* **:** one that superheats esp. steam or other gases; *esp* **:** a coil or other device through which steam from a boiler passes to be superheated

su·per·het \ˌsüpə(r)ˌhet, *usu* -ed·+V\ *n* -S [by shortening] **:** SUPERHETERODYNE

¹su·per·heterodyne \ˌsüpə(r)+\ *adj* [*super*sonic + *heterodyne*] **:** of or relating to a form of beat reception in which beats are produced of a frequency above audibility but below that of the received signals and the current of the beat frequency is then rectified, next amplified, and finally rectified again so as to reproduce the sound in a telephone receiver — compare HETERODYNE

²superheterodyne \"\ *n* **1 :** superheterodyne reception **2 :** a radio set which receives superheterodyne reception

³superheterodyne \"\ *vt* **:** to handle (radio signals) by superheterodyne methods

superhigh frequency \ˌsüpər+ . . .-\ *n* [*super-* + *high*] **:** a radio frequency in the next to the highest range of the radio spectrum — see RADIO FREQUENCY table

su·per·highway \ˌsüpə(r)+\ *n* [*super-* + *highway*] **:** a broad arterial highway (as an expressway, freeway, parkway, or turnpike) designed for high-speed traffic

su·per·historical \"+\ *adj* [*super-* + *historical*] **:** taking place or having significance outside the historical process ⟨we are now told that the fall of man is ~ —A.C.Knudson⟩

¹su·per·human \"+\ *adj* [*super-* + *human*] **1 :** being above the human **:** SUPERNATURAL, DIVINE ⟨~ beings⟩ ⟨~ agency⟩ **2 :** being beyond human capacity or strength **:** exceeding normal human power, size, or capability **:** EXTRAORDINARY, HERCULEAN ⟨~ courage⟩ ⟨~ effort⟩ ⟨~ tasks⟩ — **su·per·humanity** \"+\ *n* — **su·per·humanly** \"+\ *adv* — **su·per·humanness** \"+\ *n*

²superhuman \"+\ *n* [trans. of G *übermensch*] **:** SUPERMAN

su·per·humanize \"+\ *vt* [¹*superhuman* + *-ize*] **:** to make superhuman

su·per·humeral \"+\ *n* [LL *superhumerale, superumerale*, fr. L *super-* + *humerus, umerus* shoulder + *-ale*, neut. of *-alis* -al — more at HUMERUS] **:** something (as an ephod, pall, amice, or stole) worn or carried on the shoulders

su·per·implicant \"+\ *n* [*super-* + *implicant*] **:** SUPERALTERN

su·per·implication \"+\ *n* [*super*altern + *implication*] **:** the relation of a superaltern to a subalternate — compare OPPOSITION 2a(2)

su·per·imposable \"+\ *adj* **:** capable of being superimposed

su·per·impose \"+\ *vt* [*super-* + *impose*] **1 :** to place in a covering position **:** OVERLAY ⟨a transparent mask . . . is *superimposed* over the print —*Eastman Kodak Monthly Abstract Bull.*⟩ **2 a :** to cause to become attached, united, coexistent, or interrelated in the manner of a layer, stratum, or accretion ⟨a number of waves of different frequencies *superimposed* upon each other —F.E.Terman⟩ ⟨habits which have been *superimposed* upon other habits —J.W.M.Whiting & O.H.Mowrer⟩ ⟨laws of statutory character *superimposed* on the growing body of common law —F.A.Ogg & Harold Zink⟩ **b :** to add or impose without integrating **:** attach as an unassimilated entity ⟨his symbolism is too often something *superimposed* —E.R.Bentley⟩ ⟨*superimposed* imperatives have validity only to the extent that individuals freely assent to them —Vivian J. McGill⟩

superimposed *adj* [fr. past part. of *superimpose*] **1 :** LAYERED, STRATIFIED ⟨~ rocks⟩ **2 :** of, relating to, or being a river or a drainage system let down by erosion through the formations on which it was developed into underlying formations of different structure unconformable beneath

su·per·imposition \"+\ *n* **:** an act or instance of superimposing

su·per·imposure \ˌsüpə(r)+\ *n* -S [*superimpose* + *-ure*] **:** something that has been superimposed

su·per·impregnate \"+\ *vt* [*super-* + *impregnate*] **:** to subject to the process of superfetation

su·per·impregnation \"\ *n* [*super-* + *impregnation*] **:** SUPERFETATION

su·per·incumbent \"+\ *adj* [L *superincumbent-, superincumbens*, pres. part. of *superincumbere* to lie down on top of, fr. super- + *incumbere* to lie down on — more at INCUMBENT] **1 :** lying or resting on something else esp. so as to exert pressure ⟨~ layers of living and dead plants cut off the air and arrested decomposition —F.D.Smith & Barbara Wilcox⟩ **2 :** pressing heavily **:** BURDENSOME **3 :** *of pressure* **:** coming from above — **superincumbently** *adv*

su·per·individual \ˌsüpə(r)+\ *adj* [*super-* + *individual*] **:** of, relating to, or being an organism, entity, or complex of more than individual complexity or nature ⟨whenever a . . . number of individual agents carry on some relatively lasting organized cooperation . . . a ~ collectivity to which all of them belong will be found to exist —F.W.Znaniecki⟩

su·per·induce \"+\ *vt* [L *superinducere* to bring in on top of, fr. *super-* + *inducere* to lead in — more at INDUCE] **1 a :** to bring into a relationship of wife or heir so as to supplant one already established **b :** to install in a post having an incumbent **2 :** to introduce by way of addition or superimposition **:** bring in over or above that already existing **:** bring about or cause to exist as an addition or accretion ⟨a spiritual meaning *superinduced* upon the literal —*Encyc. Americana*⟩ **3 :** to draw, put, or place so as to cover or conceal — used with *over* or *upon*

su·per·inducement \"+\ *n* [*superinduce* + *-ment*] **:** SUPERINDUCTION

su·per·induction \ˌsüpə(r)+\ *n* [L *superinductus* + E *-ion*] **:** the act or process of superinducing or the state of being superinduced

su·per·infect \"+\ *vt* [back-formation fr. *superinfection*] **:** to cause or produce superinfection

su·per·infection \"+\ *n* [ISV *super-* + *infection*] **:** reinfection or second infection with the same type of bacteria or other parasites ⟨tuberculous ~⟩

supering *pres part of* SUPER

su·per·in·tend \ˌsüp(ə)rənˈtend, -pərn-\ *vb* -ED/-ING/-S [LL *superintendere*, fr. L *super-* + *intendere* to intend, attend, direct attention to — more at INTEND] *vt* **:** to have or exercise the charge and oversight of **:** oversee with the power of direction **:** SUPERVISE ⟨~*ed* publication of a score of good plays —Leslie Rees⟩ ⟨a committee on finance to ~ all appropriations —Allan Nevins⟩ **~** *vi* **:** to exercise supervision **:** have charge or oversight

su·per·in·tend·ence \ˌ=(=)=ˈtendən(t)s\ *n* -S [ML *superintendentia*, fr. LL *superintendent-, superintendens* (pres. part. of *superintendere* to superintend) + L *-ia* -y] **:** the act or function of superintending **:** care and oversight for the purpose of direction **:** SUPERVISION ⟨a part of good ~ to check up constantly —W.C.Voss⟩

su·per·in·tend·en·cy \-dənsē\ *n* -ES [*superintendent* + *-cy*] **1 :** the office, post, or jurisdiction of a superintendent **2 :** SUPERINTENDENCE

¹su·per·in·tend·ent \ˌsüp(ə)rənˈtendənt, -pərn-\ *n* -S [ML *superintendent-, superintendens* overseer, fr. LL, pres. part. of *superintendere* to superintend] **1 a** *obs* **:** BISHOP **b :** a Protestant Christian minister charged with the general supervision of churches within a certain territory or district ⟨a Methodist ~⟩ **2 :** one who has the oversight and charge of a place, institution, department, organization, or operation with the power of direction ⟨~ of schools⟩ ⟨~ of public works⟩ ⟨~ of a railroad division⟩: as **a :** the executive head of a police department **:** a chief of police **b :** BUILDING SUPERINTENDENT

²superintendent \ˌ=(=)=ˈ==\ *adj* [LL *superintendent-, superintendens*] **:** OVERSEEING, SUPERINTENDING

superintendent general *n, pl* **superintendents general** [¹*superintendent* + *general*, adj.] **:** one exercising authority over a number of superintendents

su·per·in·tend·ent·ship \ˌ=(=)=ˈ==ˌship\ *n* [¹*superintendent* + *-ship*] **:** SUPERINTENDENCY

su·per·in·tend·er \-də(r)\ *n* -S **:** one that superintends **:** SUPERINTENDENT

¹su·pe·ri·or \səˈpirēə(r), -pēr- *sometimes* süˈp-\ *adj* [ME, fr. MF *superieur*, fr. L *superior*, comp. of *superus* that is above, upper, fr. *super* over, above — more at OVER] **1 :** situated higher up or farther from a bottom or base **:** HIGHER, UPPER **2 a** (1) **:** of higher degree or rank ⟨insubordinate to his ~ officer⟩ ⟨the eight ~ grades were limited to girls —Robert Lowell⟩ (2) **:** taking precedence ⟨a ~ allegiance to a foreign government —Sidney Hook⟩ ⟨certain rights are ~ to constitutions and to statute laws —Isaac Lippincott⟩ (3) **:** of high degree or rank ⟨~ classes of society⟩ **b** (1) **:** of a higher order, nature, or kind ⟨~ wisdom derived from experience —G.T.Trewartha⟩ (2) **:** not material or natural **:** SPIRITUAL, SUPERNATURAL ⟨the subtle and ~ meaning which underlay the literal meaning of Holy Writ —G.C.Sellery⟩ (3) **:** having or seeming to have a higher level of reality or existence ⟨they are more immediate than the world of friendship, nutrition, and fatigue . . . and they are frequently ~ to it —Bernard DeVoto⟩ **3 :** courageously or serenely indifferent (as to something painful, disheartening, or demoralizing) **:** staunchly unyielding in self-control or morale ⟨he is ~ to that fear —G.B.Shaw⟩ **4 a** (1) **:** of more importance, value, usefulness, or merit **:** of higher quality, accomplishment, or significance ⟨true progress is something ~ to your puffing engines and clicking telegraphs —C.B.Fairbanks⟩ ⟨a class of ~ children⟩ ⟨a smaller proportion . . . of ~ looks and a minuscule number of superlative ones —Katharine T. Kinkead⟩ (2) **:** of greater force, influence, or efficaciousness ⟨the uplifting movements proved to be far ~ to the processes of erosion —W.W.Atwood †1949⟩ ⟨overcome by a ~ opponent⟩ (3) **:** greater in quantity or amount ⟨retreated before ~ numbers⟩ ⟨nor is the tuition greatly ~ to that of the tax-supported schools —B.K.Sandwell⟩ ⟨escaped by ~ speed —Edward Breck⟩ **b** *of a railroad train* **:** having the right of way over another **c :** notably excellent of its kind **:** surpassingly good ⟨men of delicate fancy, urbane instinct and aristocratic manner — in brief, ~ men —H.L. Mencken⟩ ⟨he may have graduated to a more ~ abode —Allan Forbes & R.M.Eastman⟩ ⟨delighted in his ~ ability to memorize —*Current Biog.*⟩ ⟨the paintings on the north wall appear to be by a different and slightly ~ hand —O.Elfrida Saunders⟩ ⟨the ~ durability of parchment —G.G.Coulton⟩ **5 :** SUPERSCRIPT — used usu. postpositionally ⟨"line 57ᵇ" is read "line five seven b ~"⟩; contrasted with *inferior* **6 a** *of a part of the upright body* **:** situated above another and esp. another similar part — distinguished from *inferior* **b** *of a part of the quadrupedal body* (1) **:** situated in a more anterior position (2) **:** situated more dorsad than another and esp. another similar part **:** DORSAL **7** *of a part of a plant* **a :** situated above another organ: (1) *of a calyx* **:** attached to and apparently arising from the ovary (2) *of an ovary* **:** free from the calyx or other floral envelope **b :** ADAXIAL **c :** situated near the top of the stipe — used esp. of the annulus of a mushroom **8 :** more comprehensive ⟨a genus is ~ to a species⟩ ⟨forming a ~ unit out of diversity —Manès Sperber⟩ **9 :** affecting or assuming an air of superiority **:** SUPERCILIOUS, HAUGHTY ⟨moments when the modern audience can feel ~ and amused —Delmore Schwartz⟩

²superior \"\ *n* -S **1 a :** one who is above another in rank, station, or office ⟨went first to his immediate ~⟩: as (1) **:** a head of a religious house or a religious order ⟨~ of the monastery⟩ (2) **:** the lord or his heir in feudal law from whom a vassal receives a fee and to whom he owes allegiance and tribute **b :** one that surpasses another in quality, merit, or excellence **2 :** a superscript character (as in printing)

³superior \"\ *adv* **:** in a superior manner **:** with superiority

superior alveolar canal *n* [¹*superior*] **:** the anterior, middle, or posterior canal in the maxilla that transmits nerves and blood vessels to the teeth

superior colliculus *n* **:** either member of the anterior and higher pair of quadrigeminate bodies that together constitute a primitive center for vision

superior conjunction *n* **:** a conjunction in which a lesser or secondary celestial body passes farther from the observer than the primary body around which it revolves ⟨*superior conjunction* of Venus to the sun⟩

superior court *n* **1 :** a court of general jurisdiction intermediate between the inferior courts (as a magistrate's court, justice of the peace court, or a district court) and the higher appellate courts **2 :** a court with juries having original jurisdiction

su·pe·ri·or·ess \-rērəs\ *n* -ES [²*superior* + *-ess*] **:** a superior of a religious order of women or of a convent

superior ganglion *n* [¹*superior*] **:** the upper of two ganglia on the vagus nerve at its exit through the jugular foramen — called also *jugular ganglion*

superior general *n, pl* **superiors general** [²*superior* + *general*, adj] **:** the superior of an entire religious order or congregation

su·pe·ri·or·i·ty \səˌpirēˈȯrəd·ē, -pēr-, -ˈär-, -ətē, -i *sometimes* (ˌ)süˌp-\ *n* -ES [MF *superiorité*, fr. ML *superioritat-, superioritas*, fr. L *superior* + *-itat-, -itas* -ity — more at SUPERIOR] **1** *obs* **:** the position, office, rank, dignity, authority, or jurisdiction of a superior **2 a :** the quality or state of being superior: as (1) **:** the possession or application of greater or esp. prevailing force ⟨gained the ~ over the enemy army⟩ (2) **:** the possession of superior rank, authority, or dignity ⟨men free and independent . . . amongst whom there was no natural ~ or subjection —John Locke⟩ (3) **:** the quality or state of surpassing in degree or amount ⟨immigration played an important part, in maintaining a numerical ~ of men over women —*President's Commission on Immigration & Naturalization*⟩ (4) **:** the quality or state of surpassing in virtue, merit, excellence, or worth ⟨the ~ of their equipment to the enemy's —*Current Biog.*⟩ (5) **:** the quality or state of exhibiting disdain or conceit **:** HAUGHTINESS, SUPERCILIOUSNESS ⟨had none of the condescension of the foreigner, no white man's ~ —Walter Lippmann⟩ **b :** a superior characteristic or detail ⟨the man of creative imagination pays a ghastly price for all his *superiorities* and immunities —H.L.Mencken⟩ **3 :** DOMINIUM DIRECTUM

superiority complex *n* **1 :** an exaggerated conviction of one's own superiority **2 :** an excessive striving for or pretense of superiority to compensate for supposed inferiority

su·pe·ri·or·ly *adv* [¹*superior* + *-ly*] **1 :** in or to a higher position or direction ⟨those branches of the aorta which are ~ oriented —H.T.Karsner⟩ **2 a :** in a superior manner **:** BETTER ⟨~ equipped troops⟩ **b :** in a condescending or haughty manner **:** SUPERCILIOUSLY ⟨~ puffed away . . . the absurd misgivings of women —Arnold Bennett⟩

superior nasal spine *n* [¹*superior*] **:** FRONTAL NASAL SPINE

superior oblique *n* **:** OBLIQUE 2b(1)

superior olive *n* **:** a small gray nucleus situated dorsal to the inferior olive and made up of cells in the auditory path

superior pharyngeal *n* **:** PHARYNGOBRANCHIAL

superior planet *n* **:** a planet whose orbit lies outside that of the earth

superior servant *n* **:** an employee or agent to whom the principal has delegated such control or management of a business as to make the employee or agent a vice-principal and not a fellow servant of other employees in case of injury due to negligence — compare FELLOW SERVANT

superior slope *n* **:** the slope between the banquette and the exterior crest of a fortification

superior tide *n* **:** the tide of the hemisphere having the moon above the horizon

superior vena cava *n* **:** the portion of the caval system of a vertebrate that brings blood back from the head and anterior part of the body to the heart

superior wing *n* **:** one of the anterior pair of wings of an insect

su·pe·ri·us \səˈpirēəs\ *n* -ES [ML, fr. L, neut. of *superior* higher, upper — more at SUPERIOR] **:** the highest or treble voice part in medieval music

su·per·ja·cent \ˌsüpə(r)ˈjāsᵊnt\ *adj* [L *superjacent-, superjacens*, pres. part. of *superjacēre* to lie over or upon, fr. *super-* + *jacēre* to lie; akin to L *jacere* to throw — more at JET (to spout)] **:** lying above or upon **:** OVERLYING, SUPERINCUMBENT ⟨~ rocks⟩

su·per·ject \ˈsüpə(r)ˌjekt\ *n* -S [*super-* + *-ject* (as in *subject*)] **:** an individual or an actual entity that progressively emerges through feelings and the attainment of satisfactions ⟨for the philosophy of organism, a subject emerges from the world a ~ rather than a subject —A.N.Whitehead⟩ — **su·per·jec·tive** \ˌ==ˈjektiv\ *adj*

su·per·labial \ˌsüpə(r)+\ *adj or n* [*super-* + *labial*] **:** SUPRALABIAL

¹su·per·la·tive \səˈpərləd·iv, süˈp-, -pəl-,-pəil-, -lət|\ *adj* [ME *superlatif*, fr. MF, fr. LL *superlativus*, fr. L *superlatus* — suppletive past part. of *superferre* to carry over, raise high — (fr. *super-* + *latus*, suppletive past part. of *ferre* to bear, carry) + *-ivus* -ive — more at BEAR, TOLERATE] **1 :** belonging to or constituting the degree of comparison that is usu. expressed in English by placing *most* before an adjective (as *most beneficial*) or adverb (as *most fully*) or by suffixing *-est* to it (as *oldest, soonest*) and that typically denotes an unsurpassed or extreme level of the quality, quantity, or relation expressed by the adjective or adverb ⟨the ~ degree⟩ ⟨the irregular ~ forms *farthest* and *worst*⟩ — compare COMPARISON 3, COMPARATIVE 1, POSITIVE 2a **2 :** most eminent of its kind **:** superior to the highest degree **:** having no peers **:** surpassing all others **:** SUPREME ⟨the protection and preservation of ~ scenery —*Chronica Botanica*⟩ ⟨a man of ~ talent and character —C.S. Forester⟩ **3 :** EXAGGERATED, EXCESSIVE — **su·per·la·tive·ly** \|əvlē, -li\ *adv* — **su·per·la·tive·ness** \|ivnəs\ *n* -ES

²superlative \"\ *n* -S **1 a :** the superlative degree of comparison in a language **b :** a superlative form of an adjective or adverb **2 :** the superlative or utmost degree of something **:** PEAK, ACME ⟨so many highest ~*s* achieved by man —Thomas Carlyle⟩ **3 :** a superlative person or thing **:** something that is superlative or of the utmost degree in its kind **4 :** an exaggerated expression esp. of praise ⟨he spoke in ~*s* —C.B. Kelland⟩

su·per·lattice \ˌsüpə(r)+\ *n* [*super-* + *lattice*] **:** a space lattice of an alloy system (as a copper-gold alloy) in which each kind of atom tends to occupy definite geometrical positions instead of having a random distribution

su·per·linear \"+\ *adj* [L *super-* + *linea* line + E *-ar*] **:** SUPRALINEAR

su·per·liner \ˈsüpə(r)+,-\ *n* [*super-* + *liner*] **:** an outstandingly fast, safe, and luxurious passenger liner of great size

su·per·lingua \ˌsüpə(r)+\ *n* [NL, fr. *super-* + *lingua*] **1 :** either of a pair of dorsolateral lobes arising from the hypopharynx of an insect **2 :** MAXILLULA
superlong \"+\ *adj* [*super-* + *long*] **:** OVERLONG
su·per·lunary *also* **su·per·lunar** \ˌsüpə(r)+\ *adj* [L *super-* + *luna* moon + E *-ary, -ar* — more at LUNAR] **:** being above the moon **:** CELESTIAL, HEAVENLY — compare SUBLUNARY
su·per·male \ˈsüpə(r)+,-\ *n* [*super-* + *male*] **:** a sterile male having one X chromosome and three or more sets of autosomes — compare SUPERFEMALE
su·per·man \ˈsüpə(r),man, -maa(ə)n\ *n, pl* **supermen** [trans. of G *übermensch*] **1 :** an ideal superior man: as **a :** one that according to the philosophy of Nietzsche has learned to discipline himself by foregoing fleeting pleasures and sublimating his baser drives to attain happiness and dominance through possessing and exercising creative power and is of a type that has appeared at rare intervals in history **b :** a future man produced in an evolutionary struggle for survival or by selective breeding **c :** one fitted to survive in an egoistic striving for mastery **2 :** a person of extraordinary power or achievements in one field or in general **:** an extraordinarily great or successful person **:** a superhuman individual ⟨social illiterates who are simultaneously scientific *supermen* —Mark Starr⟩ ⟨an omnicompetent administration by *supermen* —Roscoe Pound⟩ **3 :** a fictional hero represented as having extraordinary physical prowess or performing highly improbable feats and depicted with such scant attention to his mental and emotional makeup that he appears rather stupid ⟨when . . . the ~ of this book went down to defeat, it was more in terms of plot than actuality —J.D.Hart⟩
su·per·man·hood \-,hu̇d\ *n* [*superman* + *-hood*] **:** the quality or state of being a superman
su·per·man·ly \-lē\ *adj* [*superman* + *-ly*] **:** of, relating to, or characteristic of a superman
su·per·market \ˈsüpə(r)+,-\ *n* [*super-* + *market*] **:** a departmentized self-service chain or independent retail market that sells foods, convenience goods, and household merchandise arranged in open mass display
su·per·maxilla \ˌsüpə(r)+\ *n* [NL, fr. L *super-* + *maxilla* jaw — more at MAXILLA] **:** the upper jaw — **su·per·maxillary** \"\ *adj*
su·per·microscope \"+\ *n* [*super-* + *microscope*] **:** a microscope having either an unusually great range of magnifying power (as in an electron microscope) or other features (as adaptability to infrared and ultraviolet) that make it superior to the ordinary microscope
su·per·microscopic \"+\ *adj* [*super-* + *microscopic*] **:** SUBMICROSCOPIC
su·per·multiplet \"+\ *n* [*super-* + *multiplet*] **:** a spectral multiplet of exceptional complexity
su·per·mundane \"+\ *adj* [LL *supermundanus*, fr. L *super-* + *mundus* world + *-anus* -an] **:** transcending the earthly **:** DIVINE, CELESTIAL, SUPERNATURAL ⟨~ idealism —A.L.Locke⟩ ⟨some ~ urge . . . for liberty, for happiness, for truth —*Biosophical Rev.*⟩
¹**su·per·nac·u·lum** \ˌsüpə(r)ˈnakyələm\ *adv* [NL, fr. *super nagulum, super naculum* (part. trans. of G *auf den nagel*, lit., on the nail), fr. L *super* over, on + NL *nagulum, naculum* nail, fr. G *nagel* fingernail, fr. OHG *nagal*; fr. the practice of turning the emptied glass upside down on the thumbnail without emitting a drop — more at OVER, NAIL] **:** to the last drop — used chiefly in the phrase *to drink supernaculum*
²**supernaculum** \"\ *n* -s **:** something and specif. an alcoholic beverage of superior quality ⟨the most interesting California sherry, a ~ —S.P.Lucia⟩
su·per·nal \süˈpərnᵊl\ *adj* [ME, fr. MF, fr. L *supernus* supernal (fr. *super* over, above) + MF *-al* — more at OVER] **1 a :** being or coming from above **:** that is or emanates from on high **:** of or from heaven — opposed to *infernal* ⟨could not help but interpret the plague as a visitation from heaven, a ~ punishment for the sins of men —E.S. Le Comte⟩ ⟨some ~ reality that had its being . . . outside the cosmos —John Dewey⟩ **b :** of a heavenly or spiritual character ⟨the beauty and the ~ happiness of a soft and quiet death —Lytton Strachey⟩; *specif* **:** ETHEREAL ⟨a ~ melody⟩ **2 a :** located in or belonging to the sky or celestial regions **:** of or from the firmament ⟨subterranean and ~ deluges —Thomas Carlyle⟩ **b :** situated at or near the top — **su·per·nal·ly** \-ᵊlē\ *adv*
¹**su·per·natant** \ˌsüpə(r)+\ *adj* [L *supernatant-, supernatans*, pres. part. of *supernatare* to float, fr. *super-* + *natare* to swim — more at NOURISH] **:** floating on the surface ⟨the copra was boiled with water and the ~ fat skimmed off —T.P.Hilditch⟩
²**supernatant** \"\ *n* -s **:** a supernatant substance
su·per·nate \ˈsüpə(r),nāt\ *n* -s [by shortening] **:** SUPERNATANT
su·per·national \ˌsüpə(r)+\ *adj* [*super-* + *national*] **:** consisting of, affecting, or having jurisdiction over more than one nation ⟨modern military techniques . . . afford the most persuasive argument for ~ government —C.J.Friedrich⟩
su·per·nationalism \"+\ *n* **1** [*super-* + *nationalism*] **:** excessive pride or attachment to one's country **:** extreme nationalism or patriotism **2** [*supernational* + *-ism*] **:** advocacy of the formation of supernational organizations or governments **:** INTERNATIONALISM
su·per·nationalist \"+\ *n* [*super-* + *nationalist*] **:** an extreme nationalist ⟨the rallying point for extreme reactionary and . . . ~ leaders —E.K.Lindley⟩
¹**su·per·natural** \"+\ *adj* [ML *supernaturalis*, fr. L *super-* + *natura* nature + *-alis* -al] **1 a :** of, belonging to, having reference to, or proceeding from an order of existence beyond the physical universe that is observable, and capable of being experienced by ordinary means **:** transcending nature in degree and in kind or concerned with what transcends nature ⟨a ~ divine order which directs history from outside and keeps man in touch with the eternal world through the Church and the sacraments —*Times Lit. Supp.*⟩ ⟨the ~ character of the soul⟩ **b :** being, having reference to, or proceeding from God or a god, demigod, spirit, or infernal being ⟨among primitive peoples today, the ~ scene is infinitely variegated —J.B.Noss⟩ ⟨inquired . . . whether the strangers were ~ beings, or men of flesh and blood —W.H.Prescott⟩ ⟨attributed to the sun and the moon ~ powers, made gods of them and worshiped them —*College English*⟩ **c :** divine as opposed to human, or spiritual as opposed to material ⟨to make students conscious of the fact that they are not merely natural men but that they have a ~ destiny —*St. John's University Cat.*⟩ ⟨man's ~ life, the life of the soul above the natural life of the body —M.W.Baldwin⟩ **2 a :** differing from the natural only in degree by being much more than is natural or normal **:** SUPERHUMAN, PRETERNATURAL ⟨has come up with almost ~ speed —George Weller⟩ **b :** EXTREME, EXCESSIVE ⟨curs and mongrels . . . endowed with ~ powers of yelping —Rachel Henning⟩ **3 a :** ascribed to agencies or powers above or beyond nature or based upon such an ascription **:** initiated, effected, continued, or supported by means that transcend the laws or observed sequences of nature ⟨the ~ origin of life⟩; *esp* **:** MIRACULOUS ⟨possess the gift of second sight, and the power to wreak ~ vengeance upon those who offend them —Herman Melville⟩ ⟨did not mention the ~ events . . . for fear of encouraging skeptical laughter —Robert Graves⟩ **b :** attributable to or liable to be attributed to the action or presence of a ghost, spirit, or other invisible agent **:** EERIE, OCCULT ⟨something ~, a stirring as it were of the roots of the hair —W.B.Yeats⟩ — **su·per·naturally** \"+\ *adv* — **su·per·naturalness** \"+\ *n* -ES
²**supernatural** \"\ *n* **1 :** something that is supernatural **:** the supernatural order of existence **:** divine operation, influence or intervention — used with *the* ⟨the ~ is in its ultimate essence incomprehensible on our plane of existence —*Register*⟩ **2 :** something of supernatural origin **:** something miraculous or marvelous **3 :** a supernatural being, force, or essence ⟨the object itself (water, tree, or rock) which was worshiped as a ~ —W.A.L.Elmslie⟩
su·per·naturalism \ˌsüpə(r)+\ *n* [¹*supernatural* + *-ism*] **1 :** the quality or state of being supernatural **2 :** belief in the supernatural; *specif* **:** a doctrine or creed that asserts the reality of an existence beyond nature and the control and guidance of nature and of man by an invisible power
su·per·naturalist \"+\ *n* [¹*supernatural* + *-ist*] **:** an advocate or adherent of supernaturalism
su·per·naturalistic \ˌsüpə(r)+\ *adj* [*supernaturalist* + *-ic*] **:** of or relating to supernaturalism
su·per·naturality \ˌsüpə(r)+\ *n* [ML *supernaturalitat-, supernaturalitas*, fr. *supernaturalis* supernatural + *-itat-, -itas* -ity] **1 :** the quality or state of being supernatural **:** SUPERNATURALISM **2 :** a supernatural event or thing
su·per·naturalize \"+\ *vt* [¹*supernatural* + *-ize*] **1 :** to make supernatural **:** endow with supernatural qualities **2 :** to treat as supernatural
supernatural virtue *n* **:** THEOLOGICAL VIRTUE
su·per·nature \ˈsüpə(r)+\ *n* [*super-* + *nature*] **:** a realm or sphere of the supernatural ⟨for Plato, wisdom meant a knowledge not of nature, but of the ~ constituted by the ideas —Benjamin Farrington⟩
su·per·normal \ˌsüpə(r)+\ *adj* [*super-* + *normal*] **1 :** exceeding the normal or average ⟨~ employment, such as may occur in a war situation —Clark Warburton⟩ ⟨a phase of ~ excitability —C.H.Best & N.B.Taylor⟩ **2 :** being beyond natural powers esp. of man **:** not explicable naturally **:** PARANORMAL ⟨~ faculties of the mind —*Bell's Miscellany*⟩ ⟨~ manifestations⟩ ⟨a ~ experience⟩ — **su·per·normality** \"+\ *n* — **su·per·normally** \"+\ *adv*
su·per·nova \"+\ *n* [NL, fr. *super-* + *nova*] **:** one of the rarely observed nova outbursts in which the maximum intrinsic luminosity may reach 100 million times that of the sun
¹**su·per·nu·mer·ary** \ˌsüpə(r)ˈn(y)ümə,rerē, -,reri\ *adj* [LL *supernumerarius*, fr. L *super-* + *numerus* number + *-arius* -ary] **1 :** exceeding the usual, stated, or prescribed number ⟨a ~ tooth⟩ ⟨extra ribs, as well as other ~ internal parts —*Science News Letter*⟩; *specif* **:** not enumerated among the regular components of a group and esp. of a military organization or staff or of the line elements of a military organization ⟨offered the ~ position of inspector general —J.S.Roucek⟩ **2 :** exceeding what is necessary, required, or desired **:** SUPERFLUOUS ⟨the redundant subheading and ~ asterisk —*Punch*⟩ **3 :** being the more numerous ⟨in any population with an unbalanced sex composition . . . a larger number of members of the ~ sex remains in this group —*William & Mary Quarterly*⟩
²**supernumerary** \"\ *n, pl* **supernumeraries 1 :** a supernumerary person or thing: as **a :** a person employed not for regular service but for use in case of need **b :** an individual in excess of the number authorized for a given military or naval unit ⟨carried about two thousand men, including *supernumeraries* on a training course for sea experience —Stanley Rogers⟩ **c :** a person serving no apparent function ⟨reducing them both to the role of irrelevant *supernumeraries* —J.C. Powys⟩ **d :** an inert added member of a chromosome set **2 :** an actor employed to play a walk-on (as in a mob scene or spectacle)
supernumerary bud *n* **:** ACCESSORY BUD
supernumerary rainbow *n* **:** a faintly colored rainbow sometimes seen because of atmospheric interference next to a primary or secondary rainbow
supero- *comb form* [L *superus* upper — more at SUPERIOR] situated above ⟨*superoanterior*⟩ ⟨*superomedial*⟩
su·per·octave \ˌsüpə(r)+\ *n* [*super-* + *octave*] **1 :** the octave above a specific note or tone **2 :** a metal labial pipe-organ stop of 2-foot pitch
su·per·order \"+\ *n* [*super-* + *order*] **:** a taxonomic category ranking between an order and a subclass or a class when no subclass is recognized and in the latter case equivalent to a subclass
su·per·ordinal \"+\ *adj* [fr. *superorder*, after E *order: ordinal*] **:** of or relating to a superorder
su·per·ordinary \"+\ *adj* [*super-* + *ordinary*] **:** superior to or in excess of the ordinary ⟨a man of ~ probity —Jeremy Bentham⟩
¹**su·per·or·di·nate** \ˌsüpə(r)ˈrȯrd(ᵊ)nət\ *adj* [*super-* + *-ordinate* (as in *subordinate*)] **1 :** superior in rank, class, or status ⟨the ~ whole may be represented for a person by a social unit —Andras Angyal⟩ ⟨two racial groups in ~ and subordinate positions —T.C.Cothran⟩ **2 :** bearing the logical relation of superordination
²**superordinate** \"\ *n* -s **:** a person or thing in a superordinate position
³**su·per·or·di·nate** \,==ˈrȯrdᵊn,āt\ *vt* -ED/-ING/-S **:** to make superordinate ⟨the prosodic modifications which subordinate and ~ the heavy stresses in discourse —Stanley Newman⟩
su·per·or·di·na·tion \,===ˈāshən\ *n* **1** [LL *superordination-, superordinatio*, fr. *superordinatus* (past part. of *superordinare* to appoint in addition, fr. L *super-* + *ordinare* to arrange, appoint) + *-ion-, -io* -ion — more at ORDAIN] **:** ordination of a person to fill a station already occupied; *esp* **:** the ordination by an ecclesiastical official of his own successor **2** [*super-* + *-ordination* (as in *subordination*)] **a :** the act or process of superordinating **:** DOMINANCE **b :** the relation of a universal proposition to a particular with the same terms
¹**su·per·organic** \ˌsüpə(r)+\ *adj* [*super-* + *organic*] **:** of or relating to the sociocultural organization of a society including its language, arts, technology, and ethical and religious convictions conceived as a separate class, level, or order possessing independent properties of continuity, transmission, and capacity for change not necessarily derived from, or influenced by, organic or psychological factors ⟨culture is ~ and superindividual —A.L.Kroeber⟩
²**superorganic** \"\ *n* **:** the superorganic order of existence **:** the complex of superorganic phenomena — used with *the* ⟨material culture . . . is changing most rapidly and forcing the other parts of the ~, such as family life and religion, to make adjustments to it —W.F.Ogburn & M.F.Nimkoff⟩
su·per·organicism \ˌsüpə(r)+\ *n* **:** a sociological theory that asserts the reality or emphasizes the importance of superorganic phenomena
su·per·organicist \"+\ *n* **:** an advocate or adherent of superorganicism
su·per·organism \ˌsüpə(r)+\ *n* [*super-* + *organism*] **1 :** a huge or superior organism; *specif* **:** an organism that transcends through mind the organic or physical **2 a :** society or the state that is an integration of human beings into a whole comparable to the human organism in the diversity of its units and their mutual interdependence and in its superiority to yet limited dependence on the physically organic from which it springs **b :** a colony of social organisms (as ants) in which the members and castes are integrated in much the same way as the organs of a multicellular individual
su·per·ovulate \"+\ *vt* [back-formation fr. *superovulation*] **:** to induce excessive ovulation in (as by administration of hormones)
su·per·ovulation \"+\ *n* [*super-* + *ovulation*] **:** response to a superovulating technique; *broadly* **:** production of exceptional numbers of eggs at one time
su·per·oxide \"+\ *n* [*super-* + *oxide*] **:** a compound characterized by the univalent anion O_2^- consisting of two oxygen atoms, by paramagnetism, and by hydrolysis to hydrogen peroxide and oxygen ⟨potassium ~ KO_2⟩ — called also *hyperoxide*, compare PEROXIDE
su·per·ox·ol \ˌsüpəˈräk,sȯl, -k,sōl\ *n* -s [*super-* + *peroxide* + *-ol*] **:** a commercially produced hydrogen peroxide solution of 30 percent concentration
su·per·parasitism \ˌsüpə(r)+\ *n* **1** [*superparasite* + *-ism*] **:** HYPERPARASITISM **2** [*super-* + *parasitism*] **:** parasitization of a host by more than one parasitic individual usu. of one kind — used esp. of parasitic insects
su·per·particular \"+\ *adj* [LL *superparticularis*, fr. L *super* + *particula* small part + *-aris* -ar — more at PARTICLE] **:** of or relating to a ratio in which the greater term exceeds the less by a unit ⟨the ratios of 4 to 3 and of 8 to 7 are ~⟩
su·per·par·ti·ent \ˌsüpə(r)ˈpärd·ēənt\ *adj* [LL *superpartient-, superpartiens*, fr. L *super* + *partient-, partiens*, pres. part. of *partire* to divide — more at PART] **:** of or relating to a ratio in which the greater term exceeds the less by more than a unit ⟨the ratios of 5 to 3 and of 10 to 7 are ~⟩
su·per·patriot \ˌsüpə(r)+\ *n* [*super-* + *patriot*] **:** an excessively patriotic individual — **su·per·patriotic** \"+\ *adj*
su·per·patriotism \"+\ *n* [*superpatriot* + *-ism*] **:** excessive patriotism
su·per·personal \"+\ *adj* [*super-* + *personal*] **:** transcending the personal ⟨God's ~ being takes in and transcends all aspects of personality —Will Herberg⟩ ⟨technology . . . can be viewed as impersonal or ~ —A.L.Kroeber⟩
su·per·personality \"+\ *n* [*super-* + *personality*] **:** a deity or a collection of persons constituting a transcendent personality ⟨the people, once endowed with a will, had to be exalted into a ~ —K.R.Popper⟩
su·per·phosphate \ˌsüpə(r)+\ *n* [*super-* + *phosphate*] **:** any of various commercial phosphate fertilizers obtained as white to gray granules or powders by acidulating ground insoluble phosphate rock: as **a :** a product made by acidulating with sulfuric acid, consisting essentially of soluble primary calcium phosphate, calcium sulfate, and smaller amounts of secondary calcium phosphate, and containing usu. about 20 percent of available phosphoric acid — called also *acid phosphate, ordinary superphosphate* **b :** a product made by acidulating with phosphoric acid, consisting essentially of primary calcium phosphate, and containing usu. 40 to 50 percent of available phosphoric acid — called also *concentrated superphosphate, double superphosphate, treble superphosphate, triple superphosphate*
su·per·physical \ˌsüpə(r)+\ *adj* [*super-* + *physical*] **:** being above or beyond the physical world or explanation on physical principles **:** HYPERPHYSICAL, METAPHYSICAL
su·per·polyamide \ˌsüpə(r)+\ *n* [*super-* + *polyamide*] **:** a polyamide (as nylon) capable of forming fibers
su·per·polymer \"+\ *n* [*super-* + *polymer*] **:** a polymer (as a superpolyamide) composed of very large molecules — compare HIGH POLYMER, MACROMOLECULE
su·per·pos·able \ˌsüpə(r)ˈpōzəbəl\ *adj* **:** capable of being superposed
su·per·pose \-ōz\ *vt* -ED/-ING/-S [prob. fr. F *superposer*, back-formation fr. *superposition*] **1 :** to place or lay over or above so as to rest or to be one of a vertical series or tier **:** superimpose with or without contact ⟨films taken on two successive days can be *superposed* —G.R.Harrison⟩ ⟨*superposed* rock strata⟩ **2 a :** to cause to occupy the same position as and coexist with another ⟨~ an electric wave upon another⟩ ⟨~ two images from different light sources⟩ **b :** to lay (a geometric figure) upon another so as to make all like parts coincide **3 :** SUPERIMPOSE ⟨~ modern industry on a backward agriculture —*Atlantic*⟩
superposed *adj* [fr. past part. of *superpose*] **1 :** growing or situated vertically over another part or organ **2** *of floral parts* **:** OPPOSITE ⟨stamens ~ to petals⟩
su·per·po·si·tion \ˌsüpə(r)pəˈzishən\ *n* [F, fr. LL *superposition-, superpositio* action of laying on, fr. L *superpositus* (past part. of *superponere* to place on top, lay on, fr. *super-* + *ponere* to place) + *-ion-, -io* -ion — more at POSITION] **:** the act or process of superposing or the state of being superposed
superposition eye *n* **:** an insect eye in which all light rays except those entering the central facet of a group of facets are intercepted — compare APPOSITION EYE
superposition principle *n* **:** a statement in physics: if two or more physical causes are vectorially additive and if the effects are proportional to the causes, the effects are vectorially additive
su·per·power \ˈsüpə(r)+,-\ *n* [*super-* + *power*] **1 :** power that is excessive, abnormal, or superior to existing power **2 a :** an extremely powerful nation; *specif* **:** one of a very few dominant states in an era when the world is divided politically into these states and their satellites **b :** an international governing body able to enforce its will upon the most powerful states **3 :** electric power developed by the coordinated utilization of all available power plants in a large area as connected parts of one system — **su·per·powered** \"+,-\ *adj*
su·per·race \ˈsüpə(r)+,-\ *n* [*super-* + *race*] **:** a race or nation of men held to be superior to others
su·per·rational \ˌsüpə(r)+\ *adj* [*super-* + *rational*] **:** transcending the power of reason ⟨~ intuition⟩
su·per·realism \"+\ *n* [trans. of F *surréalisme*] **:** SURREALISM
su·per·realist \"+\ *n* [trans. of F *surréaliste*] **:** SURREALIST
su·per·refractory \"+\ *n* [*super-* + *refractory*] **:** a superior pure oxide refractory
su·per·regeneration \"+\ *n* [*super-* + *regeneration*] **:** regeneration in an electronic circuit that by periodic usu. supersonic changes in the operating conditions (as a reduction of the operating voltage of a tube) prohibits free oscillation and gives the circuit a very high sensitivity to radio signals
su·per·regenerative \"+\ *adj* [*superregeneration* + *-ive*] **:** of or relating to superregeneration
supers *pl of* SUPER, *pres 3d sing of* SUPER
su·per·salesman \ˌsüpə(r)+\ *n* [*super-* + *salesman*] **:** an extremely successful salesman — **su·per·salesmanship** \"+\ *n*
su·per·salt \ˈsüpə(r)+,-\ *n* [*super-* + *salt*; fr. the excess of acid over base] **:** an acid salt
su·per·saturate \ˌsüpə(r)+\ *vt* [*super-* + *saturate*] **:** to add to beyond saturation ⟨a *supersaturated* solution⟩ ⟨*supersaturated* vapor⟩ — **su·per·saturation** \"+\ *n*
su·per·scribe \ˈsüpə(r),skrīb, ,==ˈ=\ *vt* [L *superscribere*, fr. *super-* + *scribere* to write — more at SCRIBE] **1 :** to write or engrave on the top or surface of, outside, or directly above an object ⟨interlinear corrections . . . are often hidden by smudges or by *superscribed* Latin characters —W.H.Bennett⟩ ⟨bars *superscribed* to distinguish the numerals from words —D.E. Smith⟩ **2 :** to write or engrave on the top or surface, outside, or directly above ⟨~ each letter with a number indicating its relative order alphabetically —J.M.Wolfe⟩; *specif* **:** to write a name, title, greeting, description, or esp. an address on the outside, head, or cover of ⟨must be sent by registered post . . . and must be *superscribed* "Tenders for Agricultural Implements" —*Times of India*⟩ ⟨the epistle was *superscribed* "To the Laodicians" —T.W.Manson⟩
¹**su·per·script** \ˈ==,skript\ *n* [L *superscriptus*, past part. of *superscribere* to superscribe] **1** *obs* **:** an address written at the head of a letter **2** [²*superscript*] **:** a superscript character
²**superscript** \"\ *adj* [L *superscriptus*, past part. of *superscribere*] **1 :** of, relating to, or being a usu. smaller character printed or written directly above another character (as the tilde in ñ) **2 :** of, relating to, or being a usu. smaller character printed above and to the side of another character (as the ³ in a^3) — compare ADSCRIPT, SUBSCRIPT
su·per·scrip·tion \,==ˈskripshən\ *n* [ME, fr. MF, fr. LL *superscription-, superscriptio*, fr. L *superscriptus* (past part. of *superscribere* to superscribe) + *-ion-, -io* -ion] **1 :** something that is written or engraved on the surface of, outside, or above something else (as an address on a letter or envelope, an inscription, title, or description) ⟨letters to His Majesty the King bear the ~ —"To the King's Most Excellent Majesty" —Noreen Routledge⟩ ⟨coins worn by abrasion must be accepted so long as the ~ thereon can be distinguished —*U.S. Post Office Manual*⟩ ⟨some that bear the ~ "A Psalm of David" —A.J.Feldman⟩ **2 :** the part of a pharmaceutical prescription which contains the Latin word *recipe* or the sign ℞
su·per·secret \ˌsüpə(r)+\ *adj* [*super-* + *secret*] **:** extremely secret
su·per·sed·able \ˌsüpə(r)ˈsēdəbəl\ *adj* **:** capable of being superseded
su·per·sede *or* **su·per·cede** \ˌsüpə(r)ˈsēd\ *vb* -ED/-ING/-S [MF *superseder* to refrain from, postpone, fr. L *supersedēre* to sit above, be superior to, forbear, refrain from, fr. *super-* + *sedēre* to sit — more at SIT] *vt* **1** *law* **a :** POSTPONE, DEFER **b :** to fail to proceed with **:** DISCONTINUE **c** *obs* **:** to refrain from **:** OMIT, FORBEAR **d :** to suspend the operation (of a judgment or order) by means of a supersedeas **2** *obs* **:** to omit mention of **3 a :** to make obsolete, inferior, or outmoded ⟨the lapse of time has *superseded* his astronomical system —Benjamin Farrington⟩ **b :** to make void **:** ANNUL, OVERRIDE ⟨established the principle that the welfare of a child *superseded* judgments rendered by the courts —*Current Biog.*⟩ **c :** to make superfluous or unnecessary ⟨this brief account . . . is intended to ~ the necessity of a long and minute detail —Jane Austen⟩ **4 :** to take the place of and outmode by superiority **:** supplant and make inferior by better or more efficiently serving a function ⟨the automobile began to ~ the horse —*Amer. Guide Series: Minn.*⟩ ⟨the canal never paid . . . because railroads soon *superseded* it —Samuel Van Valkenburg & Ellsworth Huntington⟩ **5 a :** to cause to be supplanted in a position or function ⟨in course of time this organization would have to be *superseded* by another —Shlomo Katz⟩ **b :** to succeed to the position, office, or function of **:** take the place of ⟨the department . . . *superseded* the geologic and economic survey —*Amer. Guide Series: N.C.*⟩ ⟨~ another as chairman⟩ **6 :** to follow after in the course of time ⟨as truth prevails over error . . . goodness tends to ~ badness —Samuel Alexander⟩ **7 :** to take

precedence over ⟨the movement for adjournment ~s the bill under discussion⟩ ~ *vi* **:** to defer action **:** FORBEAR ⟨~ to name the many other difficulties —F.W.Newman⟩ **syn** see REPLACE

su·per·se·de·as \,==ˈsēdēəs\ *n, pl* **supersedeas** [ME, fr. ML, fr. L, you shall desist, 2d sing. pres. subj. of *supersedēre* to supersede; fr. the occurrence of the word in the writ] **1 a :** a common-law writ commanding a stay of legal proceedings issued under various conditions and esp. to stay an officer from proceeding under another writ **b :** an order staying proceedings esp. of an inferior court that is issued under statutory authority **2** *obs* **:** something that serves as a stay or check

superseded suretyship *n* [fr. past part. of *supersede*] **:** provision for continuity of protection when a new fidelity bond replaces one previously covering the same employees

su·per·sed·ence \,==ˈsēdᵊn(t)s\ *n* -s [*supersede* + *-ence*] **:** SUPERSEDURE

su·per·sed·er \¦==¦sēdə(r)\ *n* -s **:** one that supersedes

su·per·se·de·re \,süpə(r)səˈdārē\ *n* -s [L *supersedēre* to supersede] **:** a judicial order or a private agreement among creditors in Scots law granting a debtor stay of diligence

su·per·se·dure \,süpə(r)ˈsējə(r)\ *n* -s [*supersede* + *-ure*] **:** the act or process of superseding; *specif* **:** the replacement of an old or inferior queen bee by a young or superior queen either naturally by the honeybees or artfully by the beekeeper — compare DEQUEEN

su·per·seniority \¦süpə(r)+\ *n* [*super-* + *seniority*] **:** seniority unrelated to length of actual service; *esp* **:** additional service sometimes credited to a union official or veteran or granted temporarily to insure a union official being employed while holding office — called also *synthetic seniority*

¹su·per·sensible \"+\ *adj* [*super-* + *sensible*] **:** being above or beyond that which is perceivable or apparent to the senses ⟨seeks ~ goals such as eternal life, justice, both social and individual, the progress of human culture and science, the development of moral codes —Peter Dunne⟩ **:** SPIRITUAL, PSYCHICAL

²supersensible \"\ *n* -s **1 :** a supersensible entity **2 :** the sphere of supersensible entities ⟨his teaching that genuine knowledge is knowledge of the ~, the transcendental —G.C. Sellery⟩

su·per·sensitive \¦süpə(r)+\ *adj* [*super-* + *sensitive*] **1 :** HYPERSENSITIVE **2 :** that has been supersensitized ⟨a ~ emulsion⟩ **3 :** that will function on contact with a very light object — used of a fuze in an artillery shell — **su·per·sensi·tiveness** \"+\ *n*

su·per·sensitivity \"+\ *n* [*supersensitive* + *-ity*] **:** HYPERSENSITIVITY

su·per·sensitization \"+\ *n* **:** the act or process of supersensitizing

su·per·sensitize \"+\ *vt* [*supersensitive* + *-ize*] **1 :** HYPERSENSITIZE **2 a :** to increase the sensitizing effect of (a dye) by using with another dye or compound so that their combined effect is greater than the sum of their separate effects **b :** to increase the speed of (an emulsion) by means of a chemical

su·per·sensitizer \"+\ *n* [*supersensitize* + *-er*] **:** a dye or other compound used in photography to increase the sensitizing effect of a dye

su·per·sensory \"+\ *adj* [*super-* + *sensory*] **:** being above or beyond the power of the senses ⟨~ perception⟩

su·per·sensual \"+\ *adj* [*super-* + *sensual*] **:** transcending sense **:** SUPERSENSIBLE, IDEAL

su·per·sensuous \"+\ *adj* [*super-* + *sensuous*] **:** SUPERSENSUAL

su·per·septal \"+\ *adj* [NL *super-* + *septum* + E *-al*] **:** located above a septum

su·per·serviceable \"+\ *adj* [*super-* + *serviceable*] **:** doing or offering superfluous and unwanted services **:** OVEROFFICIOUS

su·per·ses·sion \,süpə(r)ˈseshən\ *n* -s [ML *supersession-, supersessio*, fr. L *supersessus* (past part. of *supersedēre* to supersede) + *-ion-, -io* -ion] **:** the state of being superseded **:** removal and replacement **:** SUPERSEDURE ⟨the ~ of national imperialism by a genuinely international government —J.A. Hobson⟩

su·per·ses·sive \¦==¦sesiv\ *adj* [L *supersessus* + E *-ive*] **:** superseding or tending to supersede

su·per·ses·sor \-esə(r)\ *n* -s [L *supersessus* + *-or*] **:** SUPERSEDER

su·per·size *or* **su·per·sized** \¦süpə(r)+\ *adj* [*super-* + *size* or *sized*] **:** of extremely large size

¹su·per·sonic \¦süpə(r)¦sänik, -nēk\ *adj* [L *super-* + *sonus* sound + E *-ic* — more at SOUND] **1 :** having a frequency above the audibility range of the human ear or greater than about 20,000 cycles per second — used of waves and vibrations; compare INFRASONIC, SONIC **2 :** utilizing, produced by, or relating to supersonic waves or vibrations ⟨~ testing of metal⟩ ⟨~ disintegration of a chemical⟩ **3 :** of, indicating, or relating to speeds from one to five times the speed of sound in air — compare SONIC, TRANSONIC **4 :** moving, capable of moving, or utilizing air currents moving at supersonic speed ⟨~ airplane⟩ ⟨~ wind tunnel⟩ **5 :** relating to supersonic aircraft or missiles ⟨~ age⟩ **6 :** having a quality (as speed, virtue, or intensity) to an extreme degree **:** SUPER ⟨a recording of almost ~ realism — Irving Kolodin⟩ ⟨a ~ version . . . delivered breathlessly in one minute flat —Winston Brebner⟩ — **su·per·son·i·cal·ly** \-nək(ə)lē, -nēk-, -li\ *adv*

²supersonic \"\ *n* -s **:** a supersonic wave or frequency

su·per·son·ics \,==ˈ==niks, -nēks\ *n pl but usu sing in constr* [fr. ¹*supersonic*, after such pairs as E *economic: economics*] **:** the science of supersonic phenomena

supersonic velocity *n* **:** a fluid velocity relative to a body in the fluid that is greater than the local velocity of sound in the fluid

su·per·sound \ˈsüpə(r)+,-\ *n* [*super-* + *sound*] **:** ULTRASOUND

su·per·species \¦süpə(r)+\ *n* [*super-* + *species*] **:** ARTENKREIS

su·per·spectacle \"+\ *n* [*super-* + *spectacle*] **:** something extremely spectacular

su·per·speed \ˈsüpə(r)+,-\ *adj* [*super-* + *speed*] **:** designed to operate at exceedingly high speeds ⟨~ film⟩ ⟨~ airplane⟩

su·per·spinous \¦süpə(r)+\ *adj* [*super-* + *spine* + *-ous*] **:** SUPRASPINOUS

su·per·state \ˈsüpə(r)+,-\ *n* [*super-* + *state*] **1 a :** SUPERGOVERNMENT 1 **b :** a regional group having governmental powers over a group of states **2 :** a totalitarian state **3 :** SUPERPOWER 2a

su·per·sti·tion \,süpə(r)ˈstishən\ *n* -s [ME *superstician*, fr. MF, fr. L *superstition-, superstitio*, fr. *superstit-, superstes* standing over (as witness, victor, or survivor) (fr. *super-* + *-stit-* — akin to *stare* to stand) + *-ion-, -io* -ion — more at STAND] **1 a :** a belief, conception, act, or practice resulting from ignorance, unreasoning fear of the unknown or mysterious, morbid scrupulosity, trust in magic or chance, or a false conception of causation ⟨the ~ that a black cat crossing one's path portends bad luck⟩ ⟨~s such as child-sacrifice, divination, soothsaying, enchantments, sorceries, charms (by magic knots, spells, or incantations), ghosts, spiritualistic mediums, necromancy —D.R.Scott⟩ **b :** an irrational abject attitude of mind toward the supernatural, nature, or God resulting from such beliefs, conceptions, or fears **2 a :** idolatrous religion **b :** IDOLATRY ⟨an alien religion whose ~s and ritual were regarded with abhorrence —J.H.Plumb⟩ **3 :** a fixed irrational idea **:** a notion maintained in spite of evidence to the contrary ⟨the ~ that society can only be built on a foundation of unconditional command and absolute obedience —Karl Renner⟩

su·per·sti·tion·ist \-sh(ə)nəst\ *n* -s **:** a person addicted to superstition

su·per·sti·tion·less \-shənləs\ *adj* **:** not given to superstition

su·per·sti·tious \¦süpə(r)¦stishəs\ *adj* [ME *superstitious*, fr. MF *superstitieux*, fr. L *superstitiosus*, fr. *superstitio* superstition + *-osus* -ous] **1 a :** of, relating to, proceeding from, characterized by, or manifesting superstition ⟨while . . . I used to ascribe the horror he felt . . . to a reasonable cause . . . I came to realize that in origin it, too, was ~ —Osbert Sitwell⟩ **b :** addicted to or swayed by superstition ⟨the darkness and the strange blue streetlights make him . . . ~ —Alexander Forbes⟩ **c :** of, relating to, or used by the adherents of a creed regarded as a superstition **2** *obs* **:** excessively or morbidly scrupulous **:** PUNCTILIOUS **3** *obs* **:** extravagant in loving **:** overly devoted — **su·per·sti·tious·ly** *adv* — **su·per·sti·tious·ness** *n* -ES

superstitious use *n, Eng law* **:** the use of a gift or bequest (as of land) for the maintenance of religious rites not tolerated by the law

superstr *abbr* superstructure

su·per·stratum \¦süpə(r)+\ *n* [*super-* + *-stratum* (as in *substratum*)] **1 :** an overlying stratum or layer **2 :** a language spoken for a limited time in the past in a region usu. by a dominant minority

su·per·strength \"+\ *n* [*super-* + *strength*] **:** extremely great strength

su·per·struct \¦süpə(r)¦strəkt\ *vt* -ED/-ING/-S [L *superstructus*, past part. of *superstruere* to build on or over — more at SUPERSTRUCTURE] **:** to build over or on a structure **:** erect on a foundation

su·per·structural \¦süpə(r)+\ *adj* **:** of, relating to, or resembling a superstructure

su·per·structure \ˈsüpə(r)+,-\ *n* [L *superstructus* (past part. of *superstruere* to build on or over, fr. *super-* + *struere* to build) + E *-ure* — more at STRUCTURE] **1 :** a structure built on or as a vertical extension of something else **:** something that is raised on a foundation: as **a :** all of a building above the basement **b :** the structural part of a ship above the main deck **c :** the ties, rails, and fastenings of a railroad track in distinction from the roadbed **2 :** an entity, concept, or complex naturally or logically arising from or being based or imposed upon another more original or fundamental entity, concept, or complex ⟨this credit ~ rested on commodities, the collateral, rather than on the hard money —W.P.Webb⟩ ⟨a small nubbin of fact . . . used as the foundation for a ~ of inference and suspicion —Elmer Davis⟩; *specif* **:** an organization of ideas (as an ideology) or of persons (as a state bureaucracy) conceived as existing on a higher less functional level in relation to the fundamental operation of society ⟨the principle that the form of economy determines the political ~ —L.S. Feuer⟩ ⟨saying that religion is a mere ~ . . . in the class struggle —David Riesman⟩ **3 :** a regular arrangement of the atoms of a solute in the solvent crystals of an alloy that is characteristic of the solute and not of the solvent

superstructure deck *n* **:** a partial deck above a weather deck and not reaching to the sides of the vessel

su·per·substantial \¦süpə(r)+\ *adj* [LL *supersubstantialis*, fr. L *super-* + *substantia* substance + *-alis* -al] **:** being above material substance **:** of a transcending substance — **su·per·substantiality** \"+\ *n*

su·per·subtle \"+\ *adj* [*super-* + *subtle*] **:** extremely or excessively subtle — **su·per·subtlety** \"+\ *n*

su·per·system \"+\ *n* [*super-* + *system*] **:** a system made up of systems

su·per·tanker \"+\ *n* [*super-* + *tanker*] **:** an exceptionally large and fast tanker

su·per·tax \"+,-\ *n* [*super-* + *tax*] **:** a tax in addition to the usual or normal tax: as **a :** SURTAX **b :** a graduated income tax in addition to the normal income tax imposed in the United Kingdom on the amount by which the total income of a person exceeds a certain sum

su·per·temporal \¦süpə(r)+\ *adj* [*super-* + *temporal*] **:** being beyond time **:** ETERNAL

su·per·ter·ra·nean \¦süpə(r)tə¦rānēən, -ānyən\ *also* **su·per·ter·ra·ne·ous** \-ānēəs\ *adj* [*super-* + *-terranean, -terraneous* (as in *subterranean, subterraneous*)] **:** lying, dwelling, or active above or on the earth's surface

su·per·ter·rene \¦süpə(r)tə¦rēn, -te¦r-\ *adj* [LL *superterrenus*, fr. *super-* + *terra* earth — more at TERRACE] **:** SUPERTERRANEAN

su·per·terrestrial \¦süpə(r)+\ *adj* [*super-* + *terrestrial*] **:** SUPERTERRANEAN

su·per·tonic \"+\ *n* [*super-* + *tonic*] **:** the second tone of the musical scale

su·per·tunic *or* **su·per·tunica** \"+\ *n* [ML *supertunica*, fr. L *super-* + *tunica* tunic] **:** a loose garment worn over a tunic; *specif* **:** a coronation robe

superv *abbr* supervision

su·per·vene \¦süpə(r)¦vēn\ *vb* -ED/-ING/-S [L *supervenire* to come upon, come in addition, fr. *super-* + *venire* to come — more at COME] *vi* **:** to take place after or late in the course of something else as an additional, adventitious, or unlooked-for development with intervening or countering effect ⟨what generally spoils long novels is the untimely *supervening* creative fatigue —Arnold Bennett⟩ ⟨an event *supervened* that brought disaster to my uncle's family —George Santayana⟩ ~ *vt* **:** to supervene upon **:** follow after **:** SUPERSEDE ⟨the new development is further *supervened* the following year —H.M. Muncheryan⟩ **syn** see FOLLOW

su·per·ve·nience \¦süpə(r)ˈvēnyən(t)s\ *n* -s [fr. *supervenient*, after such pairs as E *excellent: excellence*] **:** the character, condition, or fact of being supervenient

su·per·ve·nient \¦==¦vēnyənt\ *adj* [L *supervenient-, superveniens*, pres. part. of *supervenire* to supervene] **:** coming or occurring as something additional, extraneous, or unexpected

su·per·ven·tion \,süpə(r)ˈvenchən\ *n* -s [LL *supervention-, superventio*, fr. L *superventus* (past part. of *supervenire* to supervene) + *-ion-, -io* -ion] **:** the act, process, or an instance of supervening ⟨the ~ of an interest stronger than his practical interests —Susanne K. Langer⟩

su·per·vis·al \¦süpə(r)¦vīzəl\ *n* -s [¹*supervise* + *-al*] **:** SUPERVISION ⟨~ by the central government —Thomas Carlyle⟩

¹su·per·vise \ˈsüpə(r),vīz *also* ,==ˈ=\ *vt* -ED/-ING/-S [ML *supervisus*, past part. of *supervidēre* to look over, inspect, oversee, fr. L *super-* + *vidēre* to see — more at WIT] **1** *obs* **:** to look over in order to read **:** PERUSE, SCAN **2 :** to coordinate, direct, and inspect continuously and at first hand the accomplishment of **:** oversee with the powers of direction and decision the implementation of one's own or another's intentions **:** SUPERINTEND ⟨~ the future disposition of voting shares —*Current Biog.*⟩ ⟨~ the newspaper's own foreign and domestic correspondents —Bruce Westby⟩ ⟨*supervised* the young institution in a paternalistic way —H.E.Starr⟩

²supervise *n* -s *obs* **:** PERUSAL

supervised study *n* [fr. past part. of ¹*supervise*] **:** study or preparation of lessons by a class or group in the presence of a teacher who maintains order and may assist individual pupils in improving methods and habits of study

su·per·vis·ee \,==,vīˈzē\ *n* -s [¹*supervise* + *-ee*] **:** a person being supervised

su·per·vi·sion \,süpə(r)ˈvizhən *also* ˈ==,==\ *n* -s [ML *supervision-, supervisio*, fr. *supervisus* (past part. of *supervidere*) + L *-ion-, -io* -ion] **:** the act, process, or occupation of supervising **:** direction, inspection, and critical evaluation **:** OVERSIGHT, SUPERINTENDENCE ⟨under the ~ of an unbiased international commission —*Current Biog.*⟩

su·per·vi·sor \ˈ==,vīzə(r) *also* ,==ˈ==\ *n* -s [ME, fr. ML, fr. *supervisus* + L *-or*] **1 :** one that supervises a person, group, department, organization, or operation: as **a :** such a person having authority delegated by an employer to hire, transfer, suspend, recall, promote, assign, or discharge another employee or to recommend such action **b :** the popularly elected chief administrative official of a township or other county subdivision in some states of the U.S. **c :** ROADMASTER 1 **d :** an officer of a school system who assists and supervises teachers in curriculum planning and methods of instruction or in the teaching of a special subject ⟨~ of music⟩ ⟨art ~⟩ **2** *obs* **:** ONLOOKER, SPECTATOR **3** *archaic* **:** one who reads over esp. a book for correction **:** REVISER

supervisor district *n* **:** BEAT 9a

su·per·vi·so·ri·al \-,vīˈzōrēəl\ *adj* [*supervisor* + *-ial*] **:** of or relating to a supervisor

su·per·vi·sor·ship \¦süpə(r)¦vīzə(r),ship\ *n* [ME, fr. *supervisor* + *-ship*] **:** the office or function of a supervisor

su·per·vi·so·ry \¦süpə(r)¦vīz(ə)rē, ¦i\ *adj* [ML *supervisus* (past part. of *supervidēre* to supervise) + E *-ory*] **:** of or relating to supervision ⟨~ position⟩

su·per·voltage \¦süpə(r)+\ *adj* [*super-* + *voltage*] **:** of or relating to very high X-ray voltage ⟨~ radiation therapy⟩

su·per·woman \ˈsüpə(r)+,-\ *n, pl* **superwomen** [*super-* + *woman*] **:** a superior woman **:** a strong-minded, efficient, and forceful woman

su·per·zealot \¦süpə(r)+\ *n* [*super-* + *zealot*] **:** an extremely earnest zealot

supes *pl of* SUPE, *pres 3d sing of* SUPE

su·pi·nate \ˈsüpə,nāt\ *vb* -ED/-ING/-S [L *supinatus*, past part. of *supinare* to lay backward or on the back] *vt* **:** to cause to assume a position of supination ~ *vi* **:** to assume a position of supination

su·pi·na·tion \,süpəˈnāshən\ *n* -s [L *supinatus* (past part. of *supinare* to lay backward or on the back, fr. *supinus* supine) + E *-ion*] **1 :** a rotation of the hand and radius around the ulna so that the palm is turned up; *also* **:** the position resulting from this movement — opposed to *pronation* **2 :** a corresponding movement of the foot and leg

su·pi·na·tor \ˈsüpə,nād·ə(r)\ *n* -s [NL, fr. L *supinatus* + *-or*] **:** a muscle that produces the motion of supination; *specif* **:** a deeply situated muscle of the forearm that arises in two layers from the lateral epicondyle of the humerus and adjacent parts of the ligaments and bones of the elbow and passing over the head of the radius is inserted into its neck and the lateral surface of its shaft

¹su·pine \səˈpīn, (ˈ)sü¦p-\ *adj* [L *supinus* lying on the back, moving backward; akin to L *sub* under, up — more at UP] **1 a :** lying on the back or with the face upward — opposed to *prone* **b :** marked by supination **2 :** manifesting mental or moral lethargy **:** indifferent to one's duty or welfare or others' needs **:** lacking stamina **:** ABJECT ⟨condition of static lethargy and ~ incuriousness —Aldous Huxley⟩ ⟨the clergy as a whole were therefore obedient and ~ —G.M.Trevelyan⟩ **3** *archaic* **:** leaning or sloping backward **:** INCLINED **syn** see INACTIVE, PRONE

²su·pine \ˈsü,pīn\ *n* -s [ME *supyn*, fr. LL *supinum*, fr. L, neut. of *supinus* lying on the back] **1 :** a Latin verbal noun either in the accusative case in *-um* used after verbs of motion to denote purpose (as in *abiit piscatum* "he's gone fishing") or in the ablative in *-u* used as an ablative of specification (as in *difficile dictu* "hard to say") **2 :** an English infinitive with *to*

su·pine·ly \səˈpīnlē, (ˈ)sü¦p-, -li\ *adv* **:** in a supine manner ⟨called the tune to me, who ~ took it up —Jean Stafford⟩

su·pine·ness \-īnnəs\ *n* -ES **:** the quality or state of being supine ⟨~ and dogmatism take the place of inquiry —*Harper's*⟩

suping *pres part of* SUPE

su·pin·i·ty \səˈpinəd·ē, süˈp-\ *n* -ES [L *supinitat-, supinitas*, fr. *supinus* supine + *-itat-, -itas* -ity] **:** SUPINENESS ⟨Eastern government rested not so much on consent or force, as on the common ~ —T.E.Lawrence⟩

supls *abbr* supplies

supp *or* **suppl** *abbr* supplement; supplementary

suppawn *var of* SUPAWN

supped *past of* SUP

sup·pe·da·ne·um \,səpəˈdānēəm\ *n, pl* **suppeda·nea** \-ēə\ [LL, footstool, fr. neut. of *suppedaneus* under the feet] **1 :** a support for the feet on a cross used for crucifixions **2 :** PREDELLA 1a

¹sup·per \ˈsəpə(r)\ *n* -s *often attrib* [ME *soper, super, supper*, fr. OF *soper, super, souper*, fr. *soper, super, souper* to eat the evening meal — more at SUP] **1 a :** a meal taken at the close of the day; *esp* **:** the evening meal when dinner is taken at midday **b :** a social affair featuring a supper; *specif* **:** an evening social (as a box social) esp. for raising funds for charitable or other purposes ⟨church ~⟩ ⟨pie ~⟩ **c :** a usu. light evening meal ⟨have ~ after the theater⟩ **2 :** EUCHARIST 1a

²supper \"\ *vb* -ED/-ING/-S *vt* **1 :** to give supper to **:** entertain at supper **2 :** to feed and bed (as a horse) at night ~ *vi* **:** to eat one's supper

³supper \"\ *n* -s [¹*sup* + *-er*] *Scot* **:** one that sups **:** SUCKER

supper club *n* [¹*supper*] **:** NIGHTCLUB

sup·per·less \ˈsəpə(r)ləs\ *adj* [¹*supper* + *-less*] **:** lacking supper

suppertime \ˈ==,=\ *n* [ME *soper tyme*, fr. *soper* supper + *time, tyme* time] **:** the time at which it is customary to eat supper

sup·ping \ˈsəpən, ˈsüp-,ˈsüp-, -piŋ\ *n* -s [ME, fr. gerund of *suppen* to sup, sip] *dial Brit* **:** soft or liquid food **:** BROTH

sup·plant \səˈplant, -laa(ə)nt,-laint,-lánt\ *vt* -ED/-ING/-S [ME *supplanten*, fr. MF *supplanter* fr. L *supplantare* to overthrow by tripping up, throw down, fr. *sub-* + *planta* sole of the foot — more at PLACE] **1** *obs* **:** to cause to fall **:** trip up **2** *archaic* **:** to cause the downfall of **:** bring low in estate, power, potency, or virtue **3 :** to supersede (another) esp. by force, trickery, or treachery **:** usurp the place or possessions of ⟨the pretty young wife finds herself . . . having been ~*ed* by a brisk, unlovely woman —Gerald Bullett⟩ **4 a** (1) *obs* **:** to root out **:** UPROOT (2) **:** to completely remove from a situation and replace **:** eradicate and supply a substitute for ⟨~ hysteria with common sense —Bradford Smith⟩ ⟨the attempt of an alien administration to ~ the vernacular —R.M.Lovett⟩ ⟨attempts to ~ the representational theory by a position which it considers more adequate —Hunter Mead⟩ **b :** to take the place of **:** oust from a position and serve as a substitute for esp. by reason of superior excellence or power ⟨this cheap and useful material rapidly ~*ed* the expensive iron —Tom Marvel⟩ ⟨it supplements rather than ~s the private agencies —*Times Lit. Supp.*⟩ **syn** see REPLACE

sup·plan·ta·tion \(,)sə,plan·ˈtāshən\ *n* -s [ME, fr. MF, fr. LL *supplantation-, supplantatio*, fr. L *supplantatus* (past part. of *supplantare* to overthrow) + *-ion-, -io* -ion] **:** the act or process of supplanting **:** DISPOSSESSION, SUPERSESSION

sup·plant·er *pronunc at* SUPPLANT +ə(r)\ *n* -s [ME, fr. *supplanten* to supplant + *-er*] **:** one that supplants

¹sup·ple \ˈsəpəl, ÷ˈsüp-\ *adj, usu* **suppler** \-p(ə)lə(r\ *usu* **supplest** \-p(ə)ləst\ [ME *souple*, fr. OF, yielding, pliant, fr. L *supplic-, supplex* submissive, suppliant, lit., bending under, fr. *sub-* + *-plic-* (akin to *plicare* to fold) — more at PLY] **1 a :** characterized by suggestibility, yielding compliance, or complaisance often to the point of being artfully or servilely obsequious **b :** characterized by ready adaptability to new situations, flexibility, and responsiveness ⟨the ~ spirit is hidden under an external directness and rough assertion — Hilaire Belloc⟩ **2 a :** characterized by an ability to bend, twist, or fold without creases, cracks, breaks, or other injuries **:** pliant, soft, and yielding in texture ⟨~ leather⟩ **b :** characterized by ease and readiness in bending or other actions and often by grace and agility **:** not stiff and awkward **c :** easy and fluent without stiffness, awkwardness, or turgidity ⟨sang with a lively, ~ voice —Douglas Watt⟩ ⟨his painting . . . is remarkably ~ in line and pattern —R.M.Coates⟩ **3** *Scot* **:** SLY, CUNNING

syn LIMBER, LITHE, LITHESOME, LISSOME: SUPPLE suggests easy flexibility of musculature, excellent coordination, and light, free, unlabored movement; in extended uses it suggests easy, resilient, graceful movement or flow ⟨mere manual labor stiffens the limbs, gymnastic exercises render them *supple* — Richard Jefferies⟩ ⟨in good condition, — not fat, like grass-fed cattle, but trim and *supple*, like deer —John Burroughs⟩ ⟨his use of language is always expert. Serviceable, *supple*, it is capable of a variety of effects —Dayton Kohler⟩ LIMBER may stress the fact of easy flexibility facilitating ready motion ⟨keeping his players *limber* during the off-season⟩ ⟨accustomed to mountain climbing, *limber* and agile⟩ LITHE suggests supple, slender, nimble grace ⟨the jungle and the wilderness lurked in the uplift and downput of his feet. He was cat-footed, and *lithe* —Jack London⟩ ⟨a *lithe* movement of her apparently boneless little figure —F. Tennyson Jesse⟩ LITHESOME may suggest agile vigor ⟨the warlike carriage of the men, and their strong, *lithesome*, resolute step —A.W.Kinglake⟩ LISSOME suggests light feminine graceful bearing or activity ⟨the *lissome* ladies who make their living modeling the latest French fashions —*Time*⟩ ⟨she only wanted wings to fly away, easy and light and *lissome* —J.C.Ransom⟩ **syn** see in addition FLEXIBLE

²supple \"\ *vb* -ED/-ING/-S [ME *souplen*, fr. *souple* supple] *vt* **1 :** to reduce the resoluteness or violence of **:** make pacific or complaisant ⟨mollify the hearts and ~ the tempers of your race —Laurence Sterne⟩ **2** *obs* **:** to soothe or alleviate by application of a salve **3 :** to make supple **:** treat so as to make flexible or pliant ⟨the rawhide was worn and *suppled* into a fair grade of dry tan leather —H.L.Davis⟩ ~ *vi, archaic* **:** to become soft, pliant, or complaisant

¹sup·ple·jack \ˈ==,jak\ *n* [¹*supple* + *Jack*, proper name] **1 :** any of various woody climbers having tough pliant stems: as **a :** a tall-climbing glabrous woody vine (*Berchemia scandens*) of the southern and central U.S. — called also *rattan vine* **b :** any of various tropical American plants of the genera *Paullinia* and *Serjania* from some of which canes are made **c** (1) **:** a small glabrous Australian tree (*Ventilago viminalis*) of the family Rhamnaceae with flexible sometimes twining branches (2) **:** an Australian clematis (*Clematis aristata*) **d :** a lawyer (*Rubus australis*) **2 :** a cane made from the stem of a supplejack

2supplejack \"\ *n* [*supple* + *Jack*, proper name] **:** JUMPING JACK

sup·ple·ly *also* **sup·ply** \p(ə)lē, -li\ *adv* **:** in a supple manner

1sup·ple·ment \'səpləmənt\ *n* -s [ME, fr. L *supplementum*, fr. *supplēre* to fill up, complete, supply + *-mentum* -ment — more at SUPPLY] **1 :** something that supplies a want or makes an addition **:** something that completes, adds a finishing touch, or brings closer to completion or a desired state ⟨one of the real services of the historical novel is not that it can be a substitute for history, but that it can be . . . a ~ —T.C.Chubb⟩ ⟨the policy of apartheid is only a political ~ to an economic policy that depends on cheap native labor —Emory Ross⟩ ⟨prescribe a vitamin ~⟩: as **a :** a part added to or issued as a continuation of a book or periodical to make good its deficiencies, correct its errors, bring it up to date, or provide special features not ordinarily included ⟨issued . . . in fourteen volumes and subsequently kept up to date by nine annual ~*s* —H.W.H. Knott⟩ ⟨Sunday ~⟩ ⟨magazine ~⟩ **b :** a material added to a pesticidal spray or dust to improve a physical or chemical property (as adhesiveness or wettability) — compare SPREADER 1f **c :** a feedstuff rich in protein used to balance a livestock ration **2 :** the quantity by which an arc or an angle falls short of 180 degrees

2sup·ple·ment \-,ment, -mənt — *see* 2-MENT\ *vt* -ED/-ING/-S **:** to fill up or supply by additions **:** add something to **:** fill the deficiencies of: as **a :** to serve as a supplement for ⟨the frontiersman depended for game to ~ his meager larder —R.A. Billington⟩ **b :** to supply a supplement for ⟨he signed mutual defense treaties . . . and ~*ed* many with favorable commercial agreements —R.E.Lee⟩

1sup·ple·men·tal \;səplə;mentᵊl\ *adj* [*1supplement* + *-al*] **1 :** serving to supplement **:** of the character of a supplement **:** SUPPLEMENTARY ⟨~ angle⟩ ⟨~ appropriations⟩ **2 :** of, relating to, or being an answer, bill, or plea filed or served in aid of an original one to supply some defect in the latter or to set forth new facts which cannot be added by amendment — **sup·ple·men·tal·ly** \-ᵊlē, -ᵊli\ *adv*

2supplemental \"\ *n* -s **:** a supplementary thing **:** SUPPLEMENT ⟨~*s* for the civilian agencies totaled more than a billion dollars —*U.S.News & World Report*⟩

supplemental air *n* **:** the air that can still be expelled from the lungs after an ordinary expiration — compare RESIDUAL AIR

supplemental irrigation *n* **:** irrigation that supplements rainfall

sup·ple·men·tar·i·ly \;səplə(,)men·;terəlē, -,mən-·, -rəli; -;men·trəl-, -ntərəl-\ *adv* [*1supplementary* + *-ly*] **:** as a supplement **:** in addition

1sup·ple·men·tary \;səplə;mentərē, -n·trē, -ri\ *adj* [*1supplement* + *-ary*] **:** that is or is added as a supplement **:** ADDITIONAL ⟨~ volume⟩ ⟨~ reading⟩

2supplementary \"\ *n* -ES **:** one that is supplementary

supplementary angles *n pl* **:** two angles or arcs whose sum is 180 degrees

supplementary cost *n* **:** the general cost of an undertaking as a whole including administration, interest, taxes, general maintenance, depreciation, and obsolescence — distinguished from *prime cost*

supplementary factor *n* **:** MODIFIER 3

supplementary proceedings *n pl* **1 :** proceedings under a code or practice act for the examination of a judgment debtor or others to discover property for payment of the judgment **2 :** proceedings ancillary to or in modification of an earlier action or suit (as a petition to modify a decree for alimony or custody of children or one to appoint a receiver)

sup·ple·men·ta·tion \,səplə(,)men·'tāshən, -,mən-·\ *n* -s [*2supplement* + *-ation*] **:** the act or process or an instance of supplementing ⟨dietary ~⟩ ⟨~ of state unemployment benefits —R.A.Lester⟩

sup·ple·ment·er \'səplə,mentə(r)\ *n* -s [*2supplement* + *-er*] **:** one that supplements

sup·ple·ness \'səpəlnə̇s, ÷'sūp-\ *n* -ES [*1supple* + *-ness*] **:** the quality or state of being supple **:** EASE, FLEXIBILITY, ELASTICITY ⟨the ~ of youthful fingers —*Amer. Guide Series: Mich.*⟩

suppler *comparative of* SUPPLE

supples *pres 3d sing of* SUPPLE

supplest *superlative of* SUPPLE

sup·ple·tion \sə'plēshən\ *n* -s [ML *suppletion-, suppletio* act of completing, supplementing, fr. L *suppletus* (past part. of *supplēre* to fill up, complete, supply) + *-ion-, -io* -ion — more at SUPPLY] **:** the occurrence of phonemically unrelated allomorphs of the same morpheme whether that morpheme is a base (as *go*, past tense *went; bad*, comparative *worse*) or an affix (as plural ending *-es* in *boxes, -en* in *oxen*)

sup·ple·tive \sə'plēd·iv, 'səpləd-·\ *adj* [LL *suppletivus* supplementary, fr. L *suppletus* + *-ivus* -ive] **:** characterized by or constituting an instance of suppletion — **sup·ple·tive·ly** \-d·ə̇vlē\ *adv*

sup·ple·to·ry \sə'plēd·ərē, 'səplə,tōrē\ *adj* [L *suppletus* + E *-ory*] **:** supplying deficiencies **:** SUPPLEMENTARY

suppletory oath *n* **:** a restricted oath formerly administered to a party not competent as a general witness but offering documents in evidence and asked to make just and true answers to questions put by the court to prove the authenticity of the documents

suppliable *adj* [*1supply* + *-able*] *obs* **:** capable of being supplied

1sup·pli·ance \-īən(t)s\ *n* -s [*1supply* + *-ance*] **:** the act or process of supplying **:** SUPPLY

2sup·pli·ance \'səplēən(t)s\ *also* **sup·pli·an·cy** \-nsē\ *n, pl* **suppliances** *also* **suppliancies** [*suppliance* fr. *2suppliant*, after such pairs as E *benevolent: benevolence; suppliancy* fr. *2suppliant* + *-cy*] **:** SUPPLICATION, ENTREATY ⟨bow . . . in ~ for wisdom —D.D.Eisenhower⟩

1sup·pli·ant \'səplēənt\ *n* -s [ME, fr. MF, fr. pres. part. of *supplier* to supplicate, fr. L *supplicare* — more at SUPPLICATE] **:** one who supplicates **:** PETITIONER ⟨reducing him to the position of a ~ for her favors —H.M.Parshley⟩

2suppliant \"\ *adj* [MF, pres. part. of *supplier* to supplicate] **:** marked by or expressive of supplication **:** humbly imploring ⟨does not come to the temple as a ~ sinner seeking forgiveness —O.J.Baab⟩ — **sup·pli·ant·ly** *adv*

1sup·pli·cant \'səplə̇kənt, -lēk-\ *adj* [L *supplicant-, supplicans*, pres. part. of *supplicare* to supplicate] **:** asking submissively **:** SUPPLICATING, ENTREATING — **sup·pli·cant·ly** *adv*

2supplicant \"\ *n* -s **:** SUPPLIANT ⟨tapped on the door like a ~, and waited . . . with his hat in his hand —Berton Roueché⟩

sup·pli·cat \-plə̇,kat\ *or* **sup·pli·cate** \-kāt\ *n* -s [*supplicat* fr. L, he makes supplication, 3d sing. pres. indic. of *supplicare;* fr. the wording of the petition; *supplicate* fr. ML *supplicatus*, fr. L *supplicatus*, past part. of *supplicare*] **:** SUPPLICATION; *specif* **:** a formal written petition for a degree or for incorporation at an English university

sup·pli·cate \'səplə,kāt, *usu* -ād·+V\ *vb* -ED/-ING/-S [ME *supplicaten*, fr. L *supplicatus*, past part. of *supplicare* to supplicate, fr. *supplic-, supplex* submissive, suppliant — more at SUPPLE] *vi* **:** to make a humble entreaty **:** pray beseechingly; *specif* **:** to present a supplicat ~ *vt* **1 :** to entreat as a supplicant **:** ask humbly and earnestly of ⟨must fall on his knees and ~ the God of his fathers —S.L.Terrien⟩ **2 :** to ask for earnestly and humbly **:** entreat for in the manner of a supplicant ⟨~ a blessing⟩ **syn** see BEG

sup·pli·cat·ing·ly \'==,===, ,=='===\ *adv* [*supplicating* (pres. part. of *supplicate*) + *-ly*] **:** in a supplicating manner

sup·pli·ca·tion \,səplə'kāshən\ *n* -s [ME, fr. MF, fr. L *supplication-, supplicatio*, fr. *supplicatus* (past part. of *supplicare* to supplicate) + *-ion-, -io* -ion] **1 :** the act or process of supplicating **:** humble and earnest entreaty ⟨pained by such tender, such flattering ~ —Jane Austen⟩ **2 a** (1) *archaic* **:** a formal written petition (2) **:** SUPPLICAT **b :** a humble and earnest petition **:** ENTREATY, SOLICITATION ⟨the last ~ . . . I make of you is, that you will believe this of me —Charles Dickens⟩ **c :** a humble prayer to a deity for mercy, aid, or special blessing ⟨kneeling together on a spit of sand, with their arms raised in ~ —R.L.Stevenson⟩ **3** *obs* **:** a public religious observance of thanksgiving or religious humiliation in ancient Rome **:** a day set apart for such an observance

sup·pli·ca·tor \'==,kād·ə(r), -ātə-\ *n* -s [LL, fr. L *supplicatus* + *-or*] **:** SUPPLICANT

sup·pli·ca·to·ry \'səplə̇kə,tōrē, -lēk-, -tȯr-, -ri\ *adj* [ME, fr. ML *supplicatorius*, fr. L *supplicatus* + *-orius* -ory] **:** of the nature of, containing, or expressive of supplication **:** BESEECHING

sup·pli·ca·vit \,səplə'kāvə̇t\ *n* -s [L, he has made supplication, 3d sing. perf. indic. of *supplicare* to supplicate; fr. the opening word of the writ] **:** a writ formerly issuing out of the Court of Chancery or King's Bench for taking surety to prevent one from injuring the applicant for the writ

sup·pli·er \sə'plī(ə)r, -īə\ *n* -s **:** one that supplies: as **a :** a country or area that supplies a raw material or commodity **b :** a manufacturer that produces a part for use in the product of another part ⟨a ~ to the auto industry⟩

suppling *pres part of* SUPPLE

1sup·ply \sə'plī\ *vb* -ED/-ING/-ES [ME *suppleen, supplien*, fr. MF *souplier, soupleier*, fr. L *supplēre* to fill up, supplement, supply, fr. *sub-* up + *plēre* to fill — more at SUB-, FULL] *vt* **1 a** *obs* **:** to make additions to by way of supplement **b :** to add (something essential or lacking) as a supplement **2 a :** to provide satisfaction or compensation for (as a need or defect) **:** make good by providing a substitute **:** fill adequately ⟨an age which *supplied* the lack of moral habits by a system of moral attitudes and poses —T.S.Eliot⟩ ⟨the laws by which the material wants of men are *supplied* —*Bull. of Bates Coll.*⟩ **b :** to satisfy a need or desire for **:** provide or furnish with **:** bring up or make available a quantity of **:** YIELD ⟨had taken to poaching as a means of ~*ing* fresh meat for the table —H.D.Quillin⟩ ⟨the millrace built to ~ power to the mission's sawmill —*Amer. Guide Series: Tenn.*⟩ ⟨the moral code of each generation . . . *supplies* a norm or standard of behavior —B.N.Cardozo⟩ ⟨a youngster in school *supplied* me the answer —Bryan MacMahon⟩ **c** (1) **:** to provide that which is required or desired by **:** satisfy the needs or wishes of **:** furnish with or as if with supplies, provisions, or equipment ⟨a contract to ~ the railroad with fuel —D.L.Graham⟩ ⟨wells were drilled to ~ the town's water system —*Amer. Guide Series: Ark.*⟩ (2) **:** to furnish (organs, tissues, or cells) with pathways for transmission or a vital element (as a nerve impulse) — used of nerves and blood vessels **3 a** (1) **:** to substitute for another in (a function) (2) **:** to occupy (a position) as a substitute; *specif* **:** to serve as a supply in (a church or pulpit) **b :** to serve instead of **:** take the place of **:** REPLACE ⟨a bold peasantry . . . when once destroyed, can never be *supplied* —Oliver Goldsmith⟩ ~ *vi* **:** to serve as a supply ⟨he *supplied* on Sundays in church pulpits of various denominations —Virginia D. Dawson & Betty D. Wilson⟩ **syn** see PROVIDE

2supply \"\ *n* -ES *often attrib* [ME *supplye*, fr. *supplien* to supply] **1** *obs* **:** ASSISTANCE, SUCCOR, AID **2 :** something that supplies or is supplied to a person or thing: **a** *obs* **:** REINFORCEMENTS — often used in pl. **b :** a clergyman that serves as a substitute for another or as a temporary or incompletely functioning pastor ⟨since the church's organization, the pulpit has been filled by *supplies* —*Presbyterian Life*⟩ **c** *obs* **:** a supplement esp. to a book **d :** the quantity or amount (as of a commodity) needed or available ⟨the state's ~ of antiquities is not alarmingly diminished —*Amer. Guide Series: Md.*⟩ ⟨the need for a ~ of symbols . . . to designate various things —Jack Guendling⟩ ⟨beer was in short ~ in that hot weather —Nevil Shute⟩ **e :** items or a quantity (as provisions, clothing, arms, or raw material) available for use, exploitation, or development or esp. set aside to be dispensed at need **:** STORES, STORE ⟨two crocodiles looking greedily . . . at this ~ of succulent beef —Francis Birtles⟩ — usu. used in pl. ⟨ensuring fresh *supplies* of managerial talent —Roy Lewis & Angus Maude⟩ **f :** an amount of money provided (as by a legislature) to meet the annual national expenditures or those not covered by other revenues — usu. used in pl. ⟨the power of giving or withholding the *supplies* at pleasure is one of absolute supremacy —T.E.May⟩ **3 :** the act, process, or an instance of filling a want or need or of providing someone or something ⟨manufacture, acquisition, provision and ~ of services and goods —*Federal Guide (Australia)*⟩ ⟨the town became a base of ~ for cowboys —*Amer. Guide Series: Texas*⟩ ⟨engaged in the ~ of raw materials to industry⟩ **4 a :** the quantities of goods or services offered for sale at various prices — compare DEMAND **b :** the desire for general purchasing power seeking its end by an offer of specific commodities or services **5 :** something that contains, delivers, maintains, or regulates a supply ⟨~ line⟩ ⟨~ depot⟩ ⟨the traces that supply one leaf constitute the leaf ~ —A.J.Eames & L.H.MacDaniels⟩

3supply *var of* SUPPLELY

supply pastor *or* **supply preacher** *n* [*2supply*] **:** SUPPLY 2b

supply price *n* **:** the lowest price at which a given amount of commodities will be offered under given conditions

1sup·port \sə'pō(ə)r\t, -pȯ(ə)r\, -pōə\, -pȯ(ə)\, *usu* \d.+V\ *vt* -ED/-ING/-S [ME *supporten*, fr. MF *supporter*, fr. LL *supportare* to bear, endure, fr. L, to carry, convey, fr. *sub-* + *portare* to carry — more at FARE] **1 :** to endure esp. in silence or with courage **:** BEAR, SUFFER, TOLERATE ⟨wondered how he could ~ the sun, even with his helmet —Paul Bowles⟩ **2 a** (1) **:** to uphold by aid, countenance, or adherence **:** actively promote the interests or cause of ⟨the art work of the federal agencies has been ~*ed* enthusiastically —*Amer. Guide Series: Minn.*⟩ ⟨an established judicial system ~*ed* by the executive power of the state —John MacNeill⟩ (2) **:** to uphold or defend as valid, right, just, or authoritative **:** ADVOCATE ⟨would ~ the principle of arbitration —C.L.Jones⟩ ⟨the treaties . . . represent public opinion . . . and will be ~*ed* by the people —Vera M. Dean⟩ (3) **:** to argue in favor of **:** vote for ⟨he refused to ~ the . . . party's choice —Gay Talese⟩ ⟨~*ed* increasing the base pay of servicemen —*Current Biog.*⟩; *also* **:** to advocate, endorse, vote for, or implement the policies, principles, or candidacy of ⟨he ~*ed* the administration . . . in practically all its major measures —T.P.Abernethy⟩ ⟨the state delegation . . . ~*ed* him on the first ballot —G.S.Dumke⟩ **b** (1) **:** to provide means, force, or strength that is secondary to **:** back up ⟨scattered eight hits, walked three and fanned two as his mates ~*ed* him brilliantly in the field —Deane McGowen⟩ ⟨body of . . . missionaries and businessmen, ~*ed* rather than led by a handful of politicians —D.W.Brogan⟩ (2) **:** to give assistance to (a primary battle force) by providing supplies, serving as a reserve, or furnishing additional or covering combat strength ⟨a base-building and base-stocking operation to ~ the great air and cross-channel attacks —G.A.Lincoln⟩ ⟨ahead of his main line, where they could not be ~*ed* by the rest of the troops —Tom Wintringham⟩ ⟨mortars and machine guns ~*ed* the attack⟩ (3) **:** to attend upon (a person) esp. as an assistant on a ceremonious occasion ⟨the mayor . . . will attend the old Parish Church, ~*ed* by the Council and civic bodies, in state —Austin Edwards⟩ (4) **:** to act with (a star actor) (5) **:** to provide a musical background for **:** ACCOMPANY ⟨the orchestral sound was always strong enough to ~ the voices —Irving Kolodin⟩ (6) **:** to bid in bridge so as to show support for (one's partner or his suit) **c** (1) **:** to serve as verification, corroboration, or substantiation of ⟨historic evidence ~*s* such guesses —Brewton Berry⟩; *also* **:** to provide with verification, corroboration, or substantiation ⟨his alibi that he had been home all afternoon . . . was ~*ed* by neighbors —Woody Klein⟩ (2) **:** to provide amplification or clarification of ⟨tests, keys, teachers' manuals, and the like, to ~ and supplement their textbooks —*Textbooks in Education*⟩ **3 a :** to pay the costs of **:** MAINTAIN ⟨the association is ~*ed* financially by membership dues —Helen T. Geer⟩ ⟨few graduate students ~ their studies from personal funds —M.H. Trytten⟩; *also* **:** to supply with the means of maintenance (as lodging, food or clothing) or to earn or furnish funds for maintaining ⟨~*s* his own and his brother's family⟩ **b :** to provide a basis for the existence or subsistence of **:** serve as the source of material or immaterial supply, nourishment, provender, fuel, raw material, or sustenance of ⟨the island could probably ~ three, though no more —A.B.C.Whipple⟩ ⟨the flax crop ~*s* an important linen industry —Samuel Van Valkenburg & Ellsworth Huntington⟩ ⟨to ~ study and research . . . these are . . . the outstanding collection of microfilm reproductions —*Univ. of Mich. Bull.*⟩ **c :** to have or put into circulation enough money (as from trade, wages, manufacture, or taxes) to maintain ⟨the town ~*s* a grammar school, a large high school, a movie, and two hotels —*Amer. Guide Series: Nev.*⟩ ⟨one of the large machine shops . . . that ~ the town industrially —*Amer. Guide Series: Vt.*⟩ **4 a :** to hold up or in position **:** serve as a foundation or prop for **:** bear the weight or stress of **:** keep from sinking or falling ⟨octagonal piers ~ Gothic arches along the nave —*Amer. Guide Series: Minn.*⟩ **b :** to serve as a heraldic supporter of ⟨the shield of this monarch is ~*ed* on each side by an angel habited —F.J.Grant⟩ **c :** to give one's arm to **d** *obs* **:** to be the subject or ground of (an attribute) **e :** to assume and give the appearance of having (as a character) ⟨~*ed* a general behavior in the world which could not hurt their credit or their purse —Richard Steele⟩ **f :** to maintain (a price) at a high level by purchases or loans ⟨a wool bill ~*ing* the domestic price for wool at 42 cents —F.A.Barrett⟩; *also* **:** to maintain the price of (as an agricultural commodity) by purchases or loans ⟨mandatory for the secretary to ~ six basic crops — cotton, corn, rice, peanuts, wheat and tobacco — at 90 percent of parity —Jean Begeman⟩ **5 :** to keep from fainting, sinking, yielding, or losing courage **:** COMFORT, STRENGTHEN ⟨beneath the sadness her indomitable pride ~*ed* her —Ellen Glasgow⟩ **6 :** to maintain in condition, action, or existence ⟨the fuel had not been of that substantial sort which can ~ a blaze long —Thomas Hardy⟩ ⟨~ respiration⟩ ⟨~ the fiction that the man had left in the night —*Amer. Guide Series: Tenn.*⟩

syn SUSTAIN, PROP, BOLSTER, BUTTRESS, BRACE: SUPPORT is applicable to a variety of uses with the general meaning or suggestion of carrying or leaning from or as if from below, of maintaining or holding up the weight or pressure of, and of forestalling sinking or falling back ⟨beams *support* the roof⟩ ⟨he *supports* the greater muscular tension involved with less evident fatigue —W.C.Brownell⟩ ⟨*support* the Constitution⟩ SUSTAIN may center attention on the fact of constantly holding up or of maintaining undiminished ⟨*sustain* the weight of office⟩ ⟨for nine years, Napoleon has been *sustained* by the people of France with a unanimity such as the United States never knew —C.B.Fairbanks⟩ ⟨this intellectual interest is great enough to *sustain* the reader through the analytical labyrinths we must search together —Hunter Mead⟩ PROP may imply a weakness, a tendency to fall, sink, or recede, a need for strengthening or reinforcing on the part of the thing being treated ⟨*propping* up the table with a packing case⟩ ⟨trying to *prop* up the decaying structures of last-century imperialism —G.L.Kirk⟩ ⟨the plot, a slim tale of vengeance, is psychologically shallow and *propped* up by unpardonable coincidences —Anthony Boucher⟩ BOLSTER blends the suggestions of SUSTAIN and PROP; it may suggest a supporting comparable to that afforded an invalid by pillows ⟨*bolster* up the falling fortunes of the East India Company —V.L.Parrington⟩ ⟨*bolster* the diminishing lumber trade within the next 75 years —*Amer. Guide Series: N. J.*⟩ ⟨assign some extra instruments to *bolster* the choir's volume of sound —P.H.Lang⟩ BUTTRESS may suggest strengthening, reinforcing, or stabilizing, sometimes massive, at a stress point, in the manner of an architectural buttress ⟨combat business slumps and to *buttress* the economy so that danger of another depression will be reduced to a minimum —*Newsweek*⟩ ⟨a code of laws *buttressed* by divine sanctions which should be unshakable —Benjamin Farrington⟩ ⟨the popular success formula is *buttressed* by evidence from the careers of an impressive minority —R.B.Morris⟩ BRACE may suggest supporting or strengthening so that the thing treated is made firm, unyielding, or rigid against pressure ⟨*brace* the shelf with an angle iron⟩ ⟨then he *braced* himself against a giant oak on his front lawn and experienced a savage kind of exaltation as the elements raged around him —Bennett Cerf⟩ ⟨the shoring up of a tottering political system, which is precisely the problem that we face in trying to *brace* the western democracies —G.W.Johnson⟩

2support \"\ *n* -s *often attrib* [ME, fr. *supporten* to support] **1 :** the act, process, or operation of supporting or the condition of being supported ⟨the ~ by society of increasingly skilled specialists —Jacquetta & Christopher Hawkes⟩ ⟨carried a large club, partly for the ~ of his weak legs —Sherwood Anderson⟩ ⟨appeared . . . to testify in ~ of universal military training —*Current Biog.*⟩: as **a :** the assistance given one military unit by another ⟨methods of ~ by machine-gun fire —*Combat Forces Jour.*⟩ ⟨the transfer of battalions between regiments . . . is done as seldom as possible in order to avoid complicating administrative ~ —M.L.Powell⟩ — see CLOSE SUPPORT **b :** acting by a company or actor that supports a star **2 :** one that supports **:** a supporting means, agency, medium, proof, or reserve **:** PROP ⟨building a steel frame as a structural ~ for the fabric of stone or brick —*Amer. Guide Series: Minn.*⟩ ⟨the first to use canvas as a ~ for painting in oil —C.W.H. Johnson⟩ ⟨one under our special supervision and the other with our cordial ~ —W.F.Brown b.1903⟩: as **a :** a means of livelihood, sustenance, or existence ⟨each son was expected to contribute to his own ~ —Carol L. Thompson⟩ ⟨the only financial ~ which a magazine could expect was from its readers —D.M.Potter⟩; *also* **:** a person or agency that furnishes support ⟨he is his family's sole ~⟩ — compare PRICE SUPPORT **b** (1) **:** one of the two primary subdivisions of an advance or rear guard: (2) **:** a military element in an outpost (3) **:** a body of troops designated to support or reinforce a unit in action (4) **:** a part of a unit held in reserve **c :** a company, actor, or actress playing with a star **d :** a supporting layer of cellulosic material, glass, or plastic on which a photographic light-sensitive layer is coated **e :** sufficient strength (as four cards of the suit or three cards including the queen or jack-ten) in a bridge suit bid by one's partner to justify raising it **f** (1) **:** SUPPORTER d (2) **:** SUSPENSORY **g :** a musical accompaniment or background **h :** corroborating or substantiating evidence, testimony, or documents ⟨the suggested hypothesis led necessarily to searching for ~ in the psychological sciences —S.J. Beck⟩ **3 :** REST 2a(3) **syn** see LIVING

sup·port·able \|d·əbəl, |təb-\ *adj* [*1support* + *-able*] **:** capable of being supported ⟨many debtors had gone into debt up to the maximum limits ~ by boom incomes —*Defense Against Recession*⟩

sup·port·ance \|tᵊn(t)s\ *n* -s [ME, fr. *supporten* to support + *-ance*] **1 :** SUPPORT **2** *Scots law* **:** aid enabling a person otherwise incapable to go to kirk or market so as to validate a conveyance of heritage made within 60 days next before death

supportation *n* -s [ME *supportacion*, fr. MF, fr. ML *supportation-, supportatio*, fr. LL, endurance, bearing, fr. *supportatus* (past part. of *supportare* to endure) + L *-ion-, -io* -ion — more at SUPPORT] **1** *obs* **:** SUPPORT **2** *obs* **:** SUPPORTANCE 2

supported *past of* SUPPORT

supported joint *n* [*supported* (past part. of *1support*) + *joint*] **:** a rail joint in a railroad rail having a tie directly under the rail ends — compare SUSPENDED JOINT

sup·port·er \|d·ə(r), |tə-\ *n* -s [ME, fr. *supporten* to support + *-er*] **:** one that furnishes or acts as a support: as **a :** one that adheres to, advocates, or endorses a person, group, or program ⟨a firm ~ of the imperial claims to temporal domination —R.A. Hall b. 1911⟩ ⟨he was not a leader, he was an effective ~ of leaders —Charles Moore⟩ **b :** one that supports another on a ceremonious occasion ⟨his majesty proceeded to the altar attended by his ~*s* —*Whitaker's Almanack*⟩ **c :** GARTER 1 **d :** a woven or knitted band or elastic device for supporting a part ⟨a wrist ~⟩ **:** SUSPENSORY **e :** a figure (as of a man, animal, or angel) placed one on each side of an escutcheon and exterior to it

supporting *pres part of* SUPPORT

supporting distance *n* [*supporting* (gerund of *support*) + *distance*] **:** the distance beyond which one military unit cannot come to the aid of another before it is defeated

sup·port·ing·ly *adv* [*supporting* (pres. part. of *1support*) + *-ly*] **:** so as to support

sup·port·ive \|d·iv, |tiv\ *adj* [*1support* + *-ive*] **:** furnishing support; *specif* **:** serving to sustain the strength and condition of a patient ⟨administration of fluids, glucose, and proteins is ~ against liver failure⟩

sup·port·less \|tlə̇s\ *adj* **:** lacking support

support mission *n* [*2support*] **:** an air attack in close support of ground forces against enemy ground forces

supports *pres 3d sing of* SUPPORT, *pl of* SUPPORT

suppos *abbr* suppository

sup·pos·able \sə'pōzəbəl\ *adj* [*1suppose* + *-able*] **:** capable of being supposed **:** PRESUMABLE, CONCEIVABLE — **sup·pos·ably** \-blē, -bli\ *adv*

sup·pos·al \-zəl\ *n* -s [ME, fr. ¹*suppose* + *-al*] **1** : the act or process of supposing **2** : something supposed : HYPOTHESIS, CONJECTURE, SUPPOSITION; *specif* : a proposition in logic or the content of a proposition that is neither affirmed nor denied, neither believed nor disbelieved, but merely noted or put forward for remark

¹sup·pose \sə'pōz, *rapid often* 'spōz\ *vb* -ED/-ING/-S [ME *supposen*, fr. MF *supposer*, modif. (influenced by *poser* to put, place) of ML *supponere* to suppose, assume, fr. L, to put under, substitute (perfect stem *suppos-*), fr. *sub-* + *ponere* to put, place — more at POSITION, POSE] *vt* **1** *obs* : ANTICIPATE **2 a** : to lay down as a postulate or use. a hypothesis or assumption : accept tentatively as true or real : assume as true for the sake of argument or exposition ⟨~ an epidemic of typhoid should break out —K.F.Zeisler⟩ ⟨this is the form we have *supposed* them to have in the above discussion —W.S.Sellars⟩ **b** (1) : to hold as belief or opinion : BELIEVE, THINK ⟨the new recruits *supposed* with some reason that they were advancing democratic objectives —M.W.Straight⟩ (2) : to think probable or in keeping with the facts : entertain as likely or probably true ⟨it is *supposed* that the pressure . . . may reach three hundred pounds per square inch —W.J.V.Osterhout⟩ (3) : to believe on slight grounds or without grounds : hold mistakenly or without sufficient proof : PRESUME ⟨the imagination feigns something unknown and invisible which it ~*s* to continue the same despite all variation of quality —Frank Thilly⟩ ⟨numerous pretty things, or things *supposed* to be pretty —Herbert Spencer⟩ **3 a** : to form a conception of : CONCEIVE, IMAGINE ⟨your mother says "Pray send my dear love". There is hardly room to add mine, but you will ~ it —William Cowper⟩ **b** : to have a notion or suspicion of : APPREHEND, SUSPECT **4** *obs* : PRETEND **5** *archaic* : to put in place of another : SUBSTITUTE **6** : to imply as an antecedent : PRESUPPOSE ⟨every sound taxing system ~*s* such a surplus —J.A.Hobson⟩ ~ *vi* : CONJECTURE, THINK, OPINE

²suppose \"\ *n* -s : SUPPOSITION, CONJECTURE ⟨would baffle the wildest ~ —George Woodbury⟩

sup·posed \-zd *sometimes* -zəd\ *adj* [fr. past part. of ¹*suppose*] **1 a** : believed to be or accepted as such usu. on slight grounds or in error : erroneously imputed or ascribed ⟨the ~ necessary laws of economics —M.R.Cohen⟩; *also* : IMAGINED ⟨certain ~ evils which perhaps are not very real evils —A.B.Walkley⟩ **b** : EXPECTED — used in the phrase *be supposed to* ⟨the United States was ~ to present the greatest ratification difficulties —E.P.Chase⟩ **c** : UNDERSTOOD — used in the phrase *be supposed to* ⟨you will be ~ to refer to my grandaunt —G.B.Shaw⟩ **2 a** : PRETENDED — used in the phrase *be supposed to* ⟨twelve hours are ~ to elapse between Acts I and II —A.S.Sullivan⟩ **b** : ALLEGED — used in the phrase *be supposed to* ⟨we are ~ to be stable and weary and lacking new ideas —A.E.Stevenson b. 1900⟩ **3 a** : INTENDED — used in the phrase *be supposed to* ⟨it explains considerable but has to be strained beyond belief to explain all it is ~ to —H.J.Muller⟩ **b** : DESIGNED — used in the phrase *be supposed to* ⟨what's that button ~ to do⟩ **4 a** : under orders : REQUIRED — used in the phrase *be supposed to* ⟨the soldier . . . was ~ to furl the side flaps in the morning —Norman Mailer⟩ **b** : PERMITTED — used in the phrase *be supposed to* ⟨you're not ~ to leave the guardroom at all this morning —Robert Lowry⟩ — **sup·pos·ed·ly** \-zədlē, -li\ *adv*

sup·pos·er \-zə(r)\ *n* -s [¹*suppose* + *-er*] : one that supposes

supposing *conj* [fr. pres. part. of ¹*suppose*] : if by way of hypothesis : on the assumption that ⟨~ a large cube of white material to be placed on sandy ground of an orange hue —C.W.H.Johnson⟩

sup·pos·it \sə'päzət\ *n* -s [NL *suppositum*, fr. L, neuter of *suppositus*, past part. of *supponere* to place under — more at SUPPOSE] : an individual that is philosophically substance or subject — called also *suppositum*

sup·po·si·tion \,səpə'zishən\ *n* -s [ME, fr. LL *supposition-, suppositio* hypothesis, conjecture (influenced in meaning by Gk *hypothesis*, lit., act of placing under), fr. L, act of placing under, fr. *suppositus* (past part. of *supponere* to place under) + *-ion-, -io* -ion — more at HYPOTHESIS, SUPPOSE] **1 a** : something (as a hypothesis, conjecture, theory, or surmise) that is supposed ⟨on the ~ that . . . language so largely contributes to making us men —A.A.Hill⟩ ⟨an entirely gratuitous ~ on my part —W.F.De Morgan⟩ **b** : the act or process of supposing and esp. of assuming something tentatively, hypothetically, or for the sake of argument ⟨not the old psychology of ~, but the new psychology of practical investigation —George Sampson⟩ **c** *obs* : the state of being uncertain and subject to surmise ⟨he is sufficient, yet his means are in ~ —Shak.⟩ **2** : fraudulent substitution or alteration; *specif* : FORGERY **3** : one of the various connotations that a term may have in different passages

sup·po·si·tion·al \¦səpə¦zishən°l, -shnəl\ *adj* [*supposition* + *-al*] : CONJECTURAL, HYPOTHETICAL

sup·po·si·tious \-shəs\ *adj* [contr. of *supposititious*] **1** : SUPPOSITITIOUS ⟨a ~, misguided philosophy, a pseudo science —W.W.Howells⟩ **2** : based on supposition ⟨this . . . ~ contract between ruler and ruled in prehistoric times —V.L.Parrington⟩

sup·pos·i·ti·tious \sə¦päzə¦tishəs\ *adj* [L *suppositicius* substituted, spurious, fr. *suppositus* (past part. of *supponere* to place under, substitute) + *-icius* -itious; in senses 2 & 3 influenced in meaning by E *supposition*] **1 a** (1) : fraudulently substituted for something else (2) : not being what it purports to be : SPURIOUS, COUNTERFEIT ⟨despatched a lawyer . . . to enlarge upon the theme of his father's ~ affluence —John Kobler⟩ **b** *of a child* (1) : presented as a genuine heir (2) : ILLEGITIMATE **2** : IMAGINARY, FABULOUS ⟨the ~ toga in which popular imagination had garbed his impressive form —S.H.Adams⟩ **3** : of the nature of a supposition : HYPOTHETICAL ⟨whether the anticipation be mine or that of a ~ observer —Victor Lowe⟩ — **sup·pos·i·ti·tious·ly** *adv* — **sup·pos·i·ti·tious·ness** *n* -ES

sup·pos·i·tive \sə'päzəd·iv\ *adj* [LL *suppositivus*, fr. L *suppositus* (past part. of *supponere* to place under — influenced in meaning by Gk *hypothetikos* hypothetical) + *-ivus* -ive — more at SUPPOSE] : characterized by, involving, or implying supposition : SUPPOSED

¹sup·pos·i·to·ry \sə'päzə,tōrē, -tȯr-, -ri\ *n* -ES [ML *suppositorium*, fr. LL, neut. of *suppositorius* placed under, fr. L *suppositus* + *-orius* -ory] : a solid preparation made usu. of medicated cocoa butter or glycerinated gelatin in the form usu. of a cone, cylinder, or oval for introduction into a tubular body cavity (as the rectum, vagina, or urethra or the teat of a cow) where it melts at body temperature and releases the medicament it contains

²suppository \"\ *adj* [ML *suppositus* (past part. of *supponere* to suppose) + E *-ory*] : SUPPOSITIOUS 2

sup·pos·i·tum \sə'päzəd·əm\ *n*, *pl* **supposi·ta** \-d·ə\ [NL — more at SUPPOSIT] : SUPPOSIT

sup·press \sə'pres\ *vt* -ED/-ING/-ES [ME *suppressen*, fr. L *suppressus*, past part. of *supprimere* to press under, suppress, fr. *sub-* + *premere* to press — more at PRESS] **1 a** : to put down or out of existence by or as if by authority, force, or pressure : SUBDUE ⟨the incipient uprising had been completely ~*ed* —S.G.Inman⟩ **b** : to force into impotence or obscurity **c** : to extinguish by prohibiting, dissolving, or dispersing ⟨empowered the governments to . . . ~ all opposition parties —C.E. Black & E.C.Helmreich⟩ **2** : to keep from public knowledge: as **a** : to refrain from divulging : leave undisclosed ⟨a famous penal institution the name of which I prefer to ~ —Henry Miller⟩ **b** : to prohibit or interdict the publication or revelation of : cause to be withheld or withdrawn from circulation ⟨foreign correspondent's copy is not censored, but certain news is ~*ed* —R.H.Sollen⟩ ⟨union halls were closed, papers ~*ed* —Meridel Le Sueur⟩ **3 a** : to exclude from consciousness ⟨the satisfaction of a ~*ed* creative wish —T.S.Eliot⟩ ⟨they ought when thus . . . ~*ed* to give some sign in disorder of the conscious life —Havelock Ellis⟩ **b** : to keep from giving vent to : hold back ⟨it has been hard to ~ the question —*Reporter*⟩ ⟨disciplined to ~ his personal impulses —Green Peyton⟩ **4** *obs* : to press down : COMPRESS **5** *obs* : RAPE **6 a** : to stop or check the flow of : arrest the discharge of ⟨~ a cough⟩ ⟨a ~ hemorrhage⟩ **b** : to inhibit the growth or development of : cause to become abortive or vestigial : STUNT ⟨growth of an apical bud usually ~*es* that of adjacent lateral buds⟩ **syn** see CRUSH

sup·press·ant \-°nt\ *adj* [*suppress* + *-ant*] *med* : SUPPRESSIVE

sup·pressed \-st\ *adj* [fr. past part. of *suppress*] **1** : subjected to, marked or affected by, or manifesting suppression ⟨~ emotion⟩ ⟨~ organ⟩ **2** : having the crown below the main forest canopy where it receives little or no direct light and is retarded, stunted, or even killed ⟨a forest with many ~ trees⟩ — **sup·pressed·ly** \-stlē, -sədlē\ *adv*

suppressed inflation *n* : REPRESSED INFLATION

sup·press·ible \-səbəl\ *adj* [*suppress* + *-ible*] : capable of being suppressed ⟨no book . . . is ~ if the publisher and author are unashamed and unapologetic —M.L.Ernst⟩

sup·pres·sion \sə'preshən\ *n* -s [L *suppression-, suppressio*, fr. *suppressus* (past part. of *supprimere* to suppress) + *-ion-, -io* -ion] **1 a** : the action of suppressing or the state of being suppressed ⟨an excuse for slanting the news and for outright ~ of the facts —Liston Pope⟩ ⟨the ~ of rebellion⟩ **b** : an instance of suppressing **2 a** : stoppage of a bodily function or a symptom ⟨~ of urine secretion⟩ ⟨~ of a cough⟩ **b** : the failure of development of a bodily part or organ **c** : retardation or stoppage of growth in a tree or its branches caused by insufficient light or nutrition — compare SUPPRESSED 2 **3** : the conscious intentional exclusion from consciousness of a thought or feeling — contrasted with *repression* **4** : the control of a forest fire after its discovery : the extinction and limitation of the spread of a forest fire

sup·pres·sio ve·ri \sə¦presē,ō've,rī, -vä,rē\ *n* [NL] *Roman, civil, & Scots law* : suppression of the truth — compare DOLUS, SUGGESTIO FALSI

sup·pres·sive \sə'presiv\ *adj* [L *suppressus* + E *-ive*] : tending to suppress : effecting suppression ⟨opposed the ~ measures used by the government —S.G.Inman⟩; *specif* : serving to suppress activity, function, symptoms ⟨treatment of malaria by ~ but not curative drugs⟩ ⟨a ~ agent for cough⟩

sup·pres·sor \sə'presə(r)\ *n* -s [LL, fr. L *suppressus* + *-or*] : one that brings about suppression ⟨a noise ~ for a jet⟩: as **a** : a gene with no detectable effect other than to suppress the normal expression of another nonallelic gene when both are present — compare EPISTATIC **b** : a device (as a spark plug resistor) to suppress interfering radio signals or noise by the use of special circuits or circuit elements

suppressor grid *n* : a grid usu. located between the screen grid and plate of an electron or vacuum tube to prevent the passage of secondary electrons from one to the other

sup·pu·rate \'səpyə,rāt, *usu* -ād.+V\ *vb* -ED/-ING/-S [L *suppuratus*, past part. of *suppurare* to suppurate, fr. *sub-* + *pur-, pus* pus — more at FOUL] *vt* : to cause to generate pus : bring to a head ~ *vi* : to discharge pus ⟨afraid the wound will ~⟩

sup·pu·ra·tion \,==¦rāshən\ *n* -s [L *suppuration-, suppuratio*, fr. *suppuratus* + *-ion-, -io* -ion] : the formation of, conversion into, or act of discharging pus ⟨an abscess is a localized area of ~⟩ ⟨~ in a wound⟩

sup·pu·ra·tive \'səpyə,rād·iv\ *adj* [L *suppuratus* (past part. of *suppurare* to suppurate) + E *-ive*] : attended with suppuration ⟨~ arthritis⟩

sup·pu·ta·tion \,səpyə'tāshən\ *n* -s [ME, fr. L *supputation-, supputatio*, fr. *supputatus* (past part. of *supputare* to count up, reckon, fr. *sub-* + *putare* to consider, think) + *-ion-, -io* -ion — more at PAVE] *archaic* : the act or process or an instance of calculating : COMPUTATION, RECKONING

supr *abbr* **1** superior **2** supreme

su·pra \'süprə, -ü(,)prä, -ü(,)prȧ\ *adv* [L] : ABOVE; *esp* : in the earlier part of this writing ⟨for additional examples see ~⟩

supra- *in pronunciations below*, ¦== = ¦süprə *sometimes* -ü(,)prä *or* -ü(,)prȧ\ *prefix* [L *supra-*, fr. *supra* above, on top, beyond, further back, earlier (adv. & prep.); akin to L *super* over — more at OVER] **1 a** : above : higher than ⟨*supra*-anal⟩ **b** : transcending ⟨*supra*national⟩ **2** : situated on the dorsal or upper side of ⟨*supra*esophageal⟩ ⟨*supra*cranial⟩ **3** : prior to ⟨*supra*lapsarian⟩

supra-angular \¦==+\ *adj* [*supra-* + *angular*] : of, relating to, or being a bone in the lower jaw of some vertebrates (as reptiles and birds) situated above the angular

supra-auricular \"+\ *adj* [*supra-* + *auricular*] **1** : situated above the auricle of the ear **2** *of a feather* : situated above the auriculars

supra-auricular point *n* : a craniometric point at the top of the external auditory meatus vertically above the auricular point — see CRANIOMETRY illustration

su·pra·branchial \¦== *at* SUPRA-+\ *adj* [*supra-* + *branchial*] : situated over the gills — used esp. of the upper part of the pallial chamber of a bivalve mollusk

su·pra·cardinal vein \"+ . . . -\ *n* [*supra-* + *cardinal*] : either of two veins in the mammalian embryo and various adult lower vertebrate forms located in the thoracic and abdominal regions dorsolateral to and on either side of the descending aorta and giving rise to the azygous and hemiazygous veins and a part of the inferior vena cava

su·pra·caudal \"+\ *adj* [*supra-* + *caudal*] : situated above the tail — used esp. of the pygal and suprapygal bones and corresponding horny shields of a turtle's carapace

su·pra·cervical \"+\ *adj* [*supra-* + *cervical*] : situated or occurring above a neck or cervical process ⟨~ hysterectomy⟩

su·pra·choroid *or* **su·pra·choroidal** \"+\ *adj* [*suprachoroid* fr. NL *suprachoroideus*, fr. *supra-* + *choroides* choroid; *suprachoroidal* fr. NL *suprachoroideus* + E *-al*] : of, relating to, or being the layer of loose connective tissue situated between the choroid and sclerotic coats of the eyeball

su·pra·cho·roi·dea \,==kə'rȯidēə\ *n* -s [NL, fr. *lamina suprachoroidea* suprachoroid layer] : the suprachoroid layer of the eyeball

su·pra·ciliary \¦== *at* SUPRA- +\ *adj* [*supra-* + *ciliary*] : of, relating to, or being any of several small shields situated above the orbit but below the supraoculars in various lizards and snakes

su·pra·clavicle \"+\ *n* [*supra-* + *clavicle*] : a bone that usu. connects the clavicle with the posttemporal in the pectoral arch of a fish — called also *scapula*

su·pra·clavicular \"+\ *adj* [*supra-* + *clavicular*] **1** : situated above the clavicle **2** : of or relating to the supraclavicle

su·pra·commissure \"+\ *n* [*supra-* + *commissure*] : a small commissure anterior to the pineal body

su·pra·conductivity \"+\ *n* [*supra-* + *conductivity*] : SUPERCONDUCTIVITY

su·pra·conscious \"+\ *adj* [*supra-* + *conscious*] : existing or functioning above the level of the conscious, rational, and logical

su·pra·cor·a·coi·de·us \¦==,kȯrə'kȯidēəs\ *n* -ES [NL, fr. *supra-* + *coracoides* coracoid] : a muscle that is important to the body support of limbed reptiles, underlies the front part of the pectoral muscle, arises from the coracoid, and passes to the underpart of the humerus

su·pra·dental \¦== *at* SUPRA- +\ *adj* [*supra-* + *dental*] : ALVEOLAR 3, CEREBRAL 3a

su·pra·diaphragmatic \"+\ *adj* [*supra-* + *diaphragmatic*] : situated or performed from above the diaphragm ⟨~ vagotomy⟩ — **su·pra·diaphragmatically** \"+\ *adv*

su·pra·dorsal \"+\ *adj* [*supra-* + *dorsal*] **1** : situated on the back **2** : of, relating to, or being a series of bony or cartilaginous elements present in some vertebrates above the basidorsals and interdorsals in the primitive vertebral column

su·pra·esophageal \"+\ *adj* [*supra-* + *esophageal*] : situated above or over the dorsal aspect of the esophagus

supraesophageal ganglion *n* : the main mass of nervous tissue of the insect and some other invertebrates located in the head and dorsal to the esophagus : BRAIN 1b, CEREBRUM 2

su·pra·foliaceous \¦== *at* SUPRA- +\ *adj* [*supra-* + L *folium* leaf + E *-aceous* — more at BLADE] : inserted on the stem above a leaf

su·pra·foliar \"+\ *adj* [*supra-* + L *folium* leaf + E *-ar*] : growing upon a leaf

su·pra·glacial \"+\ *adj* [*supra-* + *glacier* + *-al*] : of, relating to, or situated or occurring at the surface of a glacier

su·pra·glottal *or* **su·pra·glottic** \"+\ *adj* [*supra-* + *glottal* or *glottic*] **1** : situated above or anterior to the glottis — used of organs functioning in the production of sound and esp. speech **2** *of a phoneme* : produced by the action of supraglottal organs

su·pra·hepatic \"+\ *adj* [*supra-* + *hepatic*] : situated above or on the surface of the liver ⟨a ~ abscess⟩

su·pra·human \"+\ *adj* [*supra-* + *human*] : SUPERHUMAN

su·pra·hyoid muscle \"+ . . . -\ *n* [*supra-* + *hyoid*] : any of several muscles (as the mylohyoid and geniohyoid) passing upward to the jaw and face from the hyoid bone

su·pra·ilium \"+\ *n* [NL, fr. *supra-* + *ilium*] : a cartilaginous epiphysis at the sacral end of the ilium of some animals

¹su·pra·labial \"+\ *adj* [*supra-* + *labial*] : of, relating to, or situated above the upper lip — used esp. of scales bordering the upper jaw on each side of the rostral in snakes and lizards

²supralabial \"\ *n* -s : a supralabial scale or plate

¹su·pra·lap·sar·i·an \,== *at* SUPRA- +,lap'sa(a)rēən, -ser-\ *n* -s [*supra-* + L *lapsus* fall + E *-arian* (as in *Trinitarian*) — more at LAPSE] : one that adheres to the doctrine of supralapsarianism — compare INFRALAPSARIAN

²supralapsarian \¦==,=¦===\ *adj* : of or relating to the doctrine of supralapsarianism

su·pra·lap·sar·i·an·ism \,==,='==ə,nizəm\ *n* -s [¹*supralapsarian* + *-ism*] : the doctrine that God decreed both election and reprobation prior to creation and then allowed the fall of man as a means of carrying out his divine purposes — compare INFRALAPSARIANISM

su·pra·lateral \¦== *at* SUPRA- +\ *adj* [*supra-* + *lateral*] : situated high up on the side of the body

su·pra·liminal \"+\ *adj* [*supra-* + L *limin-, limen* threshold + E *-al* — more at LIMB] : lying above a threshold: as **a** : existing or being above the threshold of consciousness : CONSCIOUS **b** : exceeding the stimulus threshold or the difference threshold — **su·pra·liminally** \"+\ *adv*

su·pra·linear \"+\ *adj* [*supra-* + L *linea* line + E *-ar*] : situated above the regular lines of a text ⟨~ and marginal comments⟩; *usu* : of, relating to, or being a system of Masoretic writing in which the vowels appear immediately above the consonants

su·pra·littoral \"+\ *adj* [*supra-* + *littoral*] : of, relating to, constituting, or living in the marginal zone of a body of water that is above ordinary high tide mark

su·pra·loral \"+\ *adj* [*supra-* + *loral*] : situated above the lores

su·pra·marginal \¦== *at* SUPRA- +\ *adj* [*supra-* + *marginal*] **1** : situated above a margin or marginal part ⟨a ~ scute⟩ **2** : of better than marginal quality : SUPERIOR ⟨~ lands⟩

su·pra·mastoid \"+\ *adj* [*supra-* + *mastoid*] : situated above the mastoid bone — used esp. of inconstant bony ridges of the temporal and parietal bones

su·pra·maxilla \"+\ *n* [NL, fr. *supra-* + *maxilla*] : one of the elements forming the upper jaw of various primitive bony fishes

su·pra·maxillary \"+\ *adj* [*supra-* + *maxillary*] **1** : of or relating to the upper jaw **2** : extending over the lower jaw

supramaxillary nerve *n* **1** : the marginal mandibular branch of the facial nerve extending along the lower jaw and distributed to the muscles of the lower lip and chin **2** : the maxillary division of the trigeminal nerve

su·pra·maximal \¦== *at* SUPRA- +\ *adj* [*supra-* + *maximal*] : higher or greater than a corresponding maximal ⟨a ~ stimulus⟩

su·pra·meatal \"+\ *adj* [*supra-* + LL *meatus* + E *-al*] : situated above a meatus and esp. the external auditory meatus ⟨the ~ triangle⟩

su·pra·mental \"+\ *adj* [*supra-* + *mental* (of the chin)] : situated above the chin

su·pra·molecular \"+\ *adj* [*supra-* + *molecular*] : higher in organization or more complex than a molecule; *often* : composed of many molecules

su·pra·mundane \"+\ *adj* [*supra-* + *mundane*] : transcending the mundane : SPIRITUAL, CELESTIAL

¹su·pra·nasal \"+\ *adj* [*supra-* + *nasal*] : situated above the nose or a nasal part ⟨a ~ scale⟩

²supranasal \"\ *n* : a supranasal scale of a reptile

su·pra·national \¦== *at* SUPRA- +\ *adj* [*supra-* + *national*] : extending beyond or free of the political limitations inhering in the nation-state ⟨~ authority⟩ ⟨~ agencies⟩ ⟨~ languages⟩

su·pra·natural \"+\ *adj* [*supra-* + *natural*] : transcending the natural : SUPERNATURAL

su·pra·normal \"+\ *adj* [*supra-* + *normal*] : transcending the normal : greater than expected or usual

su·pra·nuclear \"+\ *adj* [ISV *supra-* + *nuclear*] : situated above a nucleus; *specif* : situated cortically with respect to a nucleus of the brain

¹su·pra·occipital \"+\ *adj* [*supra-* + *occipital*] **1** : situated over or in the upper part of the occiput **2** : of, relating to, or being a median bone of the cranium lying above the foramen magnum and forming part of the occipital bone in the adult of the higher vertebrates but distinct in the young and in lower forms

²supraoccipital \"\ *n* : a supraoccipital bone

¹su·pra·ocular \¦== *at* SUPRA- +\ *adj* [*supra-* + *ocular*] : situated above the eye : SUPRAORBITAL; *esp* : lying above the orbit and usu. in contact with the frontal of a reptile ⟨~ scales⟩

²supraocular \"\ *n* : a supraocular part (as a scale)

su·pra·optic \¦== *at* SUPRA- +\ *adj* [*supra-* + *optic* (*chiasma*)] : situated above the optic chiasma; *esp* : being a small nucleus of closely packed neurons overlying the optic chiasma and intimately connected with the neurohypophysis

su·pra·optimal \"+\ *adj* [*supra-* + *optimal*] : greater than optimal

su·pra·orbital \"+\ *adj* [NL *supraorbitalis*, fr. *supra-* + ML *orbita* orbit + L *-alis* -al] : situated or occurring above the orbit of the eye ⟨a ~ headache⟩ : SUPRAOCULAR

supraorbital artery *n* : a branch of the ophthalmic artery supplying the orbit and parts of the forehead

supraorbital nerve *n* : a branch of the frontal nerve supplying the forehead, scalp, cranial periosteum, and adjacent parts

supraorbital notch *n* : a notch or foramen in the bony border of the upper inner part of the orbit serving for the passage of the supraorbital nerve, artery, and vein

supraorbital point *n* : OPHRYON

supraorbital ridge *or* **supraorbital torus** *n* : SUPERCILIARY RIDGE

supraorbital vein *n* : a vein draining the supraorbital region and uniting with the frontal to form the angular vein

su·pra·ordinate \¦== *at* SUPRA- +\ *adj* [*supra-* + L *ordin-, ordo* order + E *-ate*] : of or concerned with higher ranks or orders ⟨~ tests in which given species are to be associated with logically proper genera⟩ — **su·pra·ordination** \"+\ *n*

su·pra·organism \"+\ *n* [*supra-* + *organism*] : an organized society (as of a social insect) that functions as an organic whole

su·pra·personal \"+\ *adj* [*supra-* + *personal*] : transcending the merely personal

su·pra·phylar \"+\ *adj* [*supra-* + *phylar*] : being at a level above a phylum

su·pra·position \"+\ *n* [*supra-* + *-position* (as in *superposition*)] : SUPERPOSITION

su·pra·protest \"+\ *n* [modif. of It *sopra protesto* upon protest] : an acceptance or payment of a bill by a third person for the honor of the drawer after protest for nonacceptance or nonpayment by the drawee

su·pra·pubic \"+\ *adj* [*supra-* + *pubic*] : situated or performed from above the pubis ⟨~ prostatectomy⟩ — **su·pra·pubically** \"+\ *or* **su·pra·pubicly** \"+\ *adv*

su·pra·pygal \"+\ *adj* [*supra-* + *pygal*] **1** : situated above the rump **2** : of, relating to, or being one or more median bones between the pygal bone and last neural bones or a shield between the supracaudal and last neural shields in the carapace of some turtles

su·pra·rational \"+\ *adj* [*supra-* + *rational*] : transcending the rational : based on or involving factors not to be comprehended by reason alone ⟨held that God never acts in a ~ manner —K.S.Latourette⟩

¹su·pra·renal \"+\ *adj* [NL *suprarenalis*, fr. L *supra-* + *renes* (pl.) kidneys + *-alis* -al] : situated above or anterior to the kidneys; *specif* : ADRENAL

²suprarenal \"\ *n* -s : a suprarenal part; *esp* : ADRENAL GLAND

su·pra·re·nal·ec·to·my \,süprə,rēn°l'ektəmē\ *n* -ES [ISV ²*suprarenal* + *-ectomy*] : ADRENALECTOMY

suprarenal gland *also* **suprarenal body** *n* : ADRENAL GLAND

su·pra·ren·a·lin \,süprə'renəlǝn\ *n* -s [²*suprarenal* + *-in*] : EPINEPHRINE

su·pra·scapula \¦== *at* SUPRA- +\ *n* [NL, fr. *supra-* + *scapula*] **1** : a cartilaginous or partly ossified plate attached to the superior end of the scapula in various amphibians and reptiles **2** : the posttemporal of a fish

su·pra·scapular \"+\ *adj* [NL *suprascapularis*, fr. *supra-* + *scapula* + L *-aris* -ar] **1 :** situated above the scapula **2** [NL *suprascapula* + E *-ar*] **:** of, relating to, or being a suprascapula

suprascapular artery *n* **:** a branch of the thyrocervical trunk that passes obliquely from within outward across the root of the neck and over the coracoid ligament to the back of the scapula

suprascapular ligament *n* **:** CORACOID LIGAMENT

suprascapular notch *n* **:** a deep notch in the upper border of the scapula at the base of the coracoid process giving passage to a branch of the brachial plexus that supplies the supraspinatus and infraspinatus muscles

su·pra·script \'≈≈ *at* SUPRA- + ,skript\ *adj or n* [L *supra-* + *scriptus*, past part. of *scribere* to write — more at SCRIBE] **:** SUPERSCRIPT

su·pra·segmental \¦≈≈ *at* SUPRA- +\ *adj* [*supra-* + *segment* + *-al*] **1 :** situated above or anterior to segments or segmental parts **2 :** developed in addition to segments or segmental parts: as **a :** of, relating to, or being the parts of the brain that constitute the cerebellum and cerebral cortex together with associated white matter and nuclei, are increasingly developed in higher vertebrates, and cannot be identified with specific parts of the primitive metameric chordate pattern — compare NEOPALLIUM, SEGMENTAL **b :** of or relating to significant features of pitch, stress, and juncture accompanying or superadded to vowels and consonants when the latter are assembled in succession in the construction of a speaker-to-hearer communication ⟨segmental and ~ components⟩

suprasegmental phoneme *n* **:** one of the phonemes (as pitch, stress, juncture, nasalization, voice or voicelessness in clusters) of a language that occur simultaneously with a succession of segmental phonemes — called also *prosodeme*

su·pra·sellar \¦≈≈ *at* SUPRA- +\ *adj* [ISV *supra-* + NL *sella* + ISV *-ar*] **:** situated or rising above the sella turcica — used chiefly of tumors of the hypophysis

su·pra·sensuous \"+\ *adj* [*supra-* + *sensuous*] **:** transcending the merely sensuous or sensory

su·pra·solar \"+\ *adj* [*supra-* + *solar*] **:** exceeding the sun in size or other characteristics

su·pra·species \"+\ *n* [*supra-* + *species*] **:** ARTENKREIS

su·pra·spinal \"+\ *adj* [*supra-* + *spinal*] **:** situated above a spine; *esp* **:** situated over the spinous process of the scapula

su·pra·spi·na·tus \,≈≈,spī'nād·əs\ *n* -ES [NL, fr. *supra-* + L *spina* spine + *-atus* -ate — more at SPINE] **:** a muscle of the back of the shoulder arising from the supraspinous fossa of the scapula and inserted into the top of the greater tubercle of the humerus

su·pra·spinous \¦≈≈ *at* SUPRA- +\ *adj* [*supra-* + *spinous*] **1 :** SUPRASPINAL **2 :** situated above or on the dorsal side of the vertebral spines

supraspinous ligament *n* **:** a fibrous cord joining the tips of the spinous processes of the vertebrae from the seventh cervical to the sacrum and continued forward to the skull as the ligamentum nuchae

su·pra·squamosal \¦≈≈ *at* SUPRA- +\ *n* [*supra-* + *squamosal*] **:** SUPRATEMPORAL

su·pra·stapedial \"+\ *adj* [*supra-* + *stapedial*] **:** situated above the stapedial part of the columella of the ear

su·pra·sternal \"+\ *adj* [*supra-* + NL *sternum* + E *-al*] **:** situated above or measured from the top of the sternum ⟨~ height⟩

su·pra·ster·na·le \¦≈≈(,)stər'na(,)lē, -nā(-, -nä(-\ *n* -S [NL, fr. *supra-* + *sternum* + *-ale*, neut. of L *-alis* -al] **:** the deepest point in the hollow of the suprasternal notch lying at the middle of the anterior-superior border of the sternal manubrium

suprasternal notch *n* **:** a depression of the external surface of the neck above the sternum and between the lower ends of the sternocleidomastoid muscles

suprasternal space *n* **:** a long narrow space in the lower part of the deep cervical fascia containing areolar tissue, the sternal part of the sternocleidomastoid muscles, and the lower part of the anterior jugular veins — called also *space of Burns*

su·pra·stigmal *also* **su·pra·stigmatal** \¦≈≈ *at* SUPRA- +\ *adj* [*supra-* + NL *stigmat-*, *stigma* stigma + E *-al*] **:** placed or developing above a stigma and esp. a spiracle

¹su·pra·temporal \"+\ *adj* [*supra-* + *temporal* (bone)] **:** situated above or relating to the upper part of the temporal bone or region

²supratemporal \"\ *n* **:** SUPRATEMPORAL BONE

³supratemporal \"\ *adj* [*supra-* + *temporal* (secular)] **:** transcending temporal affairs

supratemporal arch *n* [¹*supratemporal*] **:** a bony arch in the skull of many reptiles bounding the supratemporal fossa below and formed typically of the postfrontal, the postorbital, and a process of the squamosal

supratemporal bone *n* **1 :** a bone of the back and side of the skull in close relation with the squamosal in many reptiles **2 :** a small bone at the back of the skull in front of and a little to the outside of the posttemporal in fishes

su·pra·tentorial \¦≈≈ *at* SUPRA- +\ *adj* [*supra-* + *tentorial*] **:** situated above or affecting the structures overlying the tentorium of the brain ⟨progressive ~ disease⟩

su·pra·ter·ra·ne·ous \,≈≈tə¦rānēəs, -te¦r-\ *adj* [*supra-* + *-terraneous* (as in *subterraneous*)] **:** SUPERTERRANEAN

su·pra·threshold \¦≈≈ *at* SUPRA- + *threshold*] **:** supramaximal for threshhold ⟨a ~ stimulus⟩

su·pra·tonsillar \"+\ *adj* [*supra-* + L *tonsillae* tonsils + E *-ar*] **:** situated above the palatine tonsil

su·pra·trochlear nerve \"+ . . . -\ *n* [*supra-* + *trochlear*] **:** a branch of the frontal nerve supplying the skin of the forehead and the upper eyelid

su·pra·ventricular \¦≈≈ *at* SUPRA- +\ *adj* [*supra-* + *ventricular*] **:** situated or occurring above ventricles (as of the heart); *usu* **:** AURICULAR

su·pra·ver·sion \¦süprə¦vərzhən *also* -rsh-\ *n* -S [*supra-* + *-version* (as in *retroversion*)] **:** extension of a tooth beyond the plane of occlusion

su·pra·vital \¦≈≈ *at* SUPRA- +\ *adj* [ISV *supra-* + L *vita* life + ISV *-al* — more at VITAL] **:** constituting or relating to the staining of living tissues or cells surviving after removal from a living body by dyes that penetrate living substance but induce more or less rapid degenerative changes — compare INTRAVITAM — **su·pra·vitally** \"+\ *adv*

su·prem·a·cist \sə'preməsəst, sü'p- *sometimes* -rēm-\ *n* -S [*supremacy* + *-ist*] **:** an advocate or adherent of some concept of group supremacy; *esp* **:** WHITE SUPREMACIST

su·prem·a·cy \sə'preməsē, sü'p-, -məsi *sometimes* -rēm-\ *n* -ES [*supreme* + *-acy* (as in *primacy*)] **1 :** the quality or state of being supreme; *also* **:** supreme authority or power **2 :** the position of being accepted or established as superior to all others in some field or activity ⟨naval ~⟩ ⟨the ~ among dramatists⟩

su·prem·a·tism \-mə,tizəm\ *n* -S [*suprematist* + *-ism*] **:** an art movement and theory originated by Kazimir Malevich in 1913 and concerned with the pictorial arrangement of austere geometric nonobjective form

su·prem·a·tist \-mətəst\ *n* -S [F *suprématie* supremacy (modif. of E *supremacy*) + E *-ist*] **:** an advocate or user of suprematism in art

¹su·preme \sə'prēm, (')sü¦p-, *rapid sometimes* 'sp-\ *adj, sometimes* -ER/-EST [L *supremus*, superlative of *superus* that is above, upper, fr. *super* over, above — more at OVER] **1 :** highest in altitude **:** LOFTIEST **2 a :** highest in rank or authority (as within the state or church) **:** holding or exercising power that cannot be exceeded or overruled **:** DOMINANT **b :** of, relating to, or characteristic of one having such rank or power **3 a :** not exceeded by any other in degree, quality, or intensity **:** greatest possible ⟨~ love⟩ ⟨a ~ folly⟩ **b :** characterized by highest excellence or achievement **:** OUTSTANDING ⟨~ among musicians⟩ **4 a :** ULTIMATE, FINAL ⟨made the ~ sacrifice on the field of battle⟩ **b :** of utmost importance **:** CRUCIAL ⟨the ~ hour in our history⟩

²supreme \"\ *n* -S **:** one that is supreme: as **a** *usu cap* **:** SUPREME BEING **b :** the highest state or degree **:** HEIGHT ⟨this ~ of loveliness⟩

³su·prême \sə'prēm, sü'p-, -rām\ *n* -S [F, fr. *suprême* supreme, fr. MF, fr. L *supremus*] **1 :** a rich white sauce made of chicken stock and cream — called also *sauce suprême* **2** *also* **supreme :** a tall footed sherbet glass with a large bowl **3 a :** a made dish (as an entree) dressed with a sauce suprême ⟨a ~ of sole⟩ **b** *also* **supreme :** a dessert served in a suprême

supreme being *n* **1** *cap S & B* **:** the eternal and infinite Spirit **:** God as the creator and end of man **2 :** a god who dominates all the lesser gods and daemons of a pantheon and who is generally conceived as the creator of all **3 :** a power or being to which all else is subordinate or upon which all else is ultimately dependent

supreme court *n* **1 :** the highest judicial tribunal in a political unit (as a nation or state) ⟨the U. S. *Supreme Court* has both original and appellate jurisdiction⟩ ⟨the *Supreme Court* of Canada . . . renders decisions in disputes between the provinces and the Dominion —*Canadian Citizenship Series*⟩ — compare COURT OF CASSATION, COURT OF SESSION, HIGH COURT OF JUSTICE, SUPREME COURT OF JUDICATURE **2 :** a court of original jurisdiction in New York and formerly in New Jersey that is subordinate to a final court of appeals and constitutes the general trial court of the state

supreme court of judicature *usu cap S&C&J* **:** a consolidated system of superior courts comprising the High Court of Justice together with the Court of Appeal and the Court of Criminal Appeal and having jurisdiction in England and Wales

supreme good *n* [trans. of L *summum bonum*] **:** SUMMUM BONUM

supreme judicial court *n, usu cap S&J&C* **:** a judicial court of last resort (as in Maine or Massachusetts)

su·preme·ly *adv* **:** in a supreme manner **:** so as to be supreme

su·preme·ness *n* -ES **:** the quality or state of being supreme

sups *pres 3d sing of* SUP, *pl of* SUP

supsd *abbr* supersede

supt *abbr* **1** superintendent **2** support

sup·tion \'səpshən\ *n* -S [origin unknown] *dial* **:** BODY, SUBSTANCE, FLAVOR ⟨chewing tobacco until the ~ is out of it —Malcolm Cowley⟩

supv *abbr* supervise

supvr *abbr* supervisor

suq *also* **souk** *or* **suk** \'sük\ *n* -S [Ar *sūq* market] **:** a marketplace in the Muslim East

su·qua·mish \sə'kwämish, 'skw-, -wȯm-\ *n, pl* **suquamish** *or* **suquamishes** *usu cap* **1 a :** a Salishan people of the area directly west of Puget Sound, Washington **b :** a member of such people **2 :** a dialect related to Skagit

sur \'sər\ *prep* [F, fr. L *super* over — more at OVER] **:** ON, UPON — used chiefly in law reports and in the names of proceedings ⟨a writ of entry ~ disseisin —George Booth⟩ ⟨~ motion for a new trial —*U. S. Daily*⟩

sur- *prefix* [ME, fr. OF *sour-*, *sur-*, fr. L *super-* — more at SUPER-] **1 a :** over **:** SUPER- ⟨*sur*print⟩ ⟨*sur*revise⟩ ⟨*sur*fuse⟩ **b :** excessive ⟨*sur*cloy⟩ ⟨*sur*excitation⟩ **2 :** above **:** up ⟨*sur*anal⟩ ⟨*sur*base⟩

sur *abbr* **1** surcharged **2** surface **3** surplus **4** surrendered

¹su·ra \'su̇rə\ *n* -S [Skt *surā*, lit., wine, spirituous liquor] **:** the fermented juice of various East Indian palms (as the palmyra and toddy palm)

²su·ra *also* **su·rah** \'su̇rə\ *n* -S [Ar *sūrah*, lit., row] **:** one of the sections or chapters of the Koran

su·ra·ba·ja *or* **soe·ra·ba·ja** *or* **su·ra·ba·ya** \¦su̇rə¦bīyə, -¦bīə\ *adj, usu cap* [fr. *Surabaja* or *Soerabaja* or *Surabaya*, Java] **:** of or from the city of Surabaja, on the island of Java, Indonesia **:** of the kind or style prevalent in Surabaja

su·rah \'su̇rə\ *n* -S [prob. alter. of ²*surat*] **:** a soft light lustrous fabric usu. made of silk or rayon in twill weave and used for clothing (as dresses or neckties)

su·ra·kar·ta *or* **soe·ra·kar·ta** \¦su̇rə¦kärd·ə\ *adj, usu cap* [fr. *Surakarta* or *Soerakarta*, Java] **:** of or from the city of Surakarta, on the island of Java, Indonesia **:** of the kind or style prevalent in Surakarta

su·ral \'su̇rəl\ *adj* [NL *suralis*, fr. L *sura* calf of the leg + *-alis* -al; perh. akin to L *surus* branch — more at SURCULUS] **:** of or relating to the calf of the leg; *esp* **:** relating to branches of the popliteal artery or vein that ramify in this area

sur·a·min \'su̇rəmən\ *or* **suramin sodium** *n* -S [prob. fr. *surra* + *-am* + *-in*] **:** a trypanocidal drug $C_{51}H_{34}N_6Na_6O_{23}S_6$ obtained as a white powder and administered intravenously in the early stages of African sleeping sickness

sur·anal \'sər+\ *adj* [*sur-* + *anal*] **:** above the anus or an anal part (as an anal fin)

suranal plate *n* **:** PYGIDIUM b

¹su·rat \sů'rat, 'sü(,)rət\ *adj, usu cap* [fr. *Surat*, India] **:** of or from the city of Surat, India **:** of the kind or style prevalent in Surat

²surat \"\ *n* -S [fr. *Surat*, India, where it was produced] **1 :** any of several Indian cottons having coarse dark fibers **2 :** a usu. uncolored cotton cloth made from surat

sur·base \'sər,bās\ *n* [*sur-* + *base*] **1 :** a molding immediately above the base of a wall (as of a wainscoted room) **2 :** a cornice or a series of moldings at the top of the base of a pedestal or podium — see DADO illustration

sur·based \-st\ *adj* [F *surbaissé* depressed, flattened, surbased (fr. past part. of *surbaisser* to lower from above, depress, flatten, fr. *sur-* + *baisser* to lower, fr. *bas* low, fr. MF) + E *-ed* — more at BASE] **1 :** having the curve center below the springing line of imposts ⟨~ arch⟩ ⟨~ vault⟩ **2 :** having a surbase

surbate *vb* -ED/-ING/-S [ME *surbaten*, fr. MF *surbatu*, past part. of *surbatre* to beat up, fr. *sur-* + *battre* to beat, fr. L *battuere* — more at BAT] *vt, obs* **:** to make footsore ~ *vi, obs* **:** to become footsore

¹sur·cease \,sər'sēs, sə̄'-, səi'-\ *vb* -ED/-ING/-S [ME *surcesen*, alter. (influenced by *cesen* to cease) of *sursesen*, fr. MF *sursis*, past part. of *surseoir* to refrain, delay, fr. L *supersedēre* — more at SUPERSEDE] *vi* **1 :** to desist from or leave off some action **:** take a respite **:** discontinue a proceeding **2 :** to come to an end **:** become discontinued **:** CEASE ~ *vt* **1** *obs* **:** to put an end to **:** cause to cease **:** bring to an end **2 :** to desist or refrain from **:** give up **:** ABANDON, DISCONTINUE ⟨the hobbyhorse *surceased* his capering —Sir Walter Scott⟩

²sur·cease \'≈,≈, ,sər'-, sə̄'-, səi'-\ *n* -S **:** CESSATION 1; *esp* **:** a temporary suspension, intermission, or respite ⟨been in the public eye almost without ~ —Angelica Gibbs⟩ ⟨finding . . . ~ from care —*Cosmopolitan*⟩

¹sur·charge \'sər,chärj, 'sə̄,chäj, 'səi,chäj *sometimes* ,sər'- *or* sə̄'- *or* səi'-\ *vt* [ME *surchargen*, fr. MF *surcharger*, fr. *sur-* + *charger*, *chargier* to charge — more at CHARGE] **1 a :** to charge too much **:** subject to an excess or burdensome charge or tax **:** OVERCHARGE **b :** to charge (one) an extra or additional fee usu. for some special service **c :** to show an omission in (an account) for which credit ought to have been given **d** *Brit* **:** to charge (as one of the members) for an expense incurred outside statutory limitations by a local government body **:** charge (a public official) for monies improperly spent **2** *Brit* **:** OVERSTOCK; *esp* **:** to put more cattle into (as a common) than a person has a right to do or more than the herbage will sustain **3 a** *obs* **:** to weigh down in the manner of a physical burden **:** bear heavily upon ⟨the greatest affairs ~ him . . . not —Robert Leighton⟩ **b :** to fill to overflowing **:** OPPRESS, OVERWHELM ⟨the atmosphere . . . was *surcharged* with war hysteria —H.A.Chippendale⟩ ⟨*surcharged* with pent-up feelings, she wrote —Louis Untermeyer⟩ **c :** to fill to excess **:** OVERCROWD — usu. used in passive ⟨the hospital wards are *surcharged*⟩ **4 a :** to place an additional and usu. excessive physical weight or burden upon **:** OVERBURDEN, OVERLOAD **b** *archaic* **:** SURFEIT **c :** to impregnate to repletion **:** give an excessive charge to ⟨winds blowing from the sea are generally *surcharged* with moisture —Charles Lyell⟩ **5 a :** to add a new denomination figure to or to mark a surcharge on (a stamp) ⟨the 1c stamp was *surcharged* 3c⟩ ⟨the 2c stamps were *surcharged* to supply a shortage of another denomination⟩ **b :** OVERPRINT ⟨~ a stamp⟩ ⟨~ a banknote⟩ **6 :** to charge (a bearing) upon another heraldic bearing ⟨on a pointed oval shield . . . is *surcharged* a kite-shaped shield —Allan Marquand⟩

²surcharge \'≈,≈\ *n* **1 :** the action of surcharging a common **2 a :** a charge in excess of the usual or normal amount **:** an additional tax, cost, or impost ⟨the 10 percent ~ on postal cards purchased in quantities of 50 or more —*Publishers' Weekly*⟩ **b :** an additional rate added to the usual charge in transportation ⟨a ~ for jet airplane service⟩ ⟨a sleeping car ~⟩ **c** (1) **:** an instance of surcharging an account (2) **:** a statement of such surcharging **3 :** an additional and usu. excessive charge, load, burden, or supply **4 :** the action of surcharging or the state of being surcharged **5 a** (1) **:** an overprint on a stamp; *specif* **:** one that alters the denomination (2) **:** a stamp bearing such an overprint **b :** an overprint on a currency note **6 :** the earth behind a retaining wall and above a horizontal plane at the elevation of the top of the wall

sur·cin·gle *or* **cir·cin·gle** \'sər,siŋgəl, 'sə̄,-, 'səi,-\ *n* -S [ME *sursengle*, fr. MF *surcengle*, fr. *sur-* + *cengle* belt — more at CINGLE] **1 :** a belt, band, or girth passing around the body of a horse and usu. used to bind something (as a saddle or pack) fast to the horse's back **2 :** the girdle or cincture of a cassock

sur·coat \'sər,kōt, 'sə̄,-, 'səi,-\ *n* [ME *surcote*, fr. MF, fr. *sur-* + *cote* coat — more at COAT] **1 a** *or* **sur·cote** \"\ **:** a fitted coat or robe made in short or long styles with or without sleeves and often with a fur lining and worn by men and women in late medieval times **b** (1) **:** a sleeved or sleeveless tunic of late medieval times worn over armor and often emblazoned with heraldic devices (2) **:** a similar garment worn on formal occasions by members of various orders of knighthood **2 :** an outdoor jacket usu. hip length and belted worn chiefly by men and boys

sur·cu·lose \'sərkyə,lōs\ *or* **sur·cu·lous** \-ləs\ *adj* [L *surculosus*, fr. *surculus* sucker + *-osus* -ose] **:** having numerous branches arising from near the base ⟨a ~ coral⟩ **:** producing suckers

sur·cu·lus \'sərkyələs\ *n, pl* **surcu·li** \-yə,lī\ [L, dim. of *surus* branch, stake; akin to OE *swer*, *swēor* pillar, column, MHG *swir* stake, pole, Gk *herma* prop, support, Skt *svaru* stake] **:** SUCKER 3a

¹surd \'sərd, 'sə̄d, 'səid\ *adj* [L *surdus* dull-sounding, silent, deaf; akin to L *susurrus* hum, murmur — more at SWARM] **1 :** lacking sense **:** lacking reason or rationale **:** INSENSATE, IRRATIONAL ⟨the ~ mystery and the strange forces of existence —D.C.Williams⟩ **2 :** VOICELESS — used of speech sounds; opposed to *sonant*

²surd \"\ *n* -S **:** one that is surd: as **a :** an irrational radical with rational radicand ⟨$\sqrt{3}$ and $\sqrt[3]{\frac{2}{5}}$ are ~s⟩ **b :** a surd speech sound **c :** an unknown or irrational quality ⟨the uncharted ~ at the heart of European politics —William Barrett⟩

¹sure \'shu̇(ə)r, 'shu̇ə *sometimes* 'shər *or* 'shə̄, *esp South, NewEng, & Brit* 'shō(ə)r *or* 'shōə *or* 'shȯ(ə)r *or* 'shȯ(ə), *chiefly substand South* 'shō\ *adj, often* -ER/-EST [ME *sure*, *sur*, fr. MF *sur*, fr. L *securus* safe, secure — more at SECURE] **1** *obs* **a :** free from danger or exposure to risk **:** secure from liability to injury or destruction **b :** safely secured from doing or certain not to do some specified action ⟨make thee ~ enough from adding this lewdness to thine other abominations —Joseph Hall⟩ **c :** safely in one's possession or under one's control **:** unlikely to escape, become lost, do harm, or create disturbance; *esp* **:** DEAD ⟨cut his throat, so making him ~ —Philemon Holland⟩ **2 a :** firmly settled or established **:** unlikely to be overthrown or displaced or to yield **:** FAST, STABLE, STEADFAST, STEADY, STRONG ⟨a ~ foundation⟩ ⟨a ~ hold⟩ **b :** unfailing in character or condition **:** ENDURING, UNFALTERING ⟨a ~ faith⟩ **3 :** marked by complete dependability or reliability (as in fulfilling expectations, hopes, or trust) **:** entirely trustworthy or dependable **:** certain not to fail or disappoint expectation **:** RELIABLE ⟨a ~ messenger⟩ ⟨a ~ remedy⟩ ⟨the *surest* means to this end⟩ ⟨the English had ~ supplies of food —George Bancroft⟩ **4 a :** assured in mind **:** having no doubt or fear **:** marked by or given to feelings of confident certainty and conviction esp. of the rightness of one's judgment or intuition **:** characterized by an unwavering or unreserved certainty ⟨this same suggestion of ~ and calm conviction in some of the judgments —B.N.Cardozo⟩ ⟨did not release his bomb until he was ~ of a direct hit —F.D. Roosevelt⟩ ⟨~ that he would come⟩ ⟨always a very ~ person⟩ **b :** marked by firmness, assurance, and steadiness (as in deportment, bearing, execution, or handling) **:** characterized by a lack of wavering or hesitation ⟨~ brush strokes⟩ ⟨a ~ hand⟩ **5 :** objectively certain **:** admitting of no doubt, condition, or qualification **:** marked by unquestionable fact, verity, or substantiation **:** INDUBITABLE, INDISPUTABLE, POSITIVE ⟨the evidence is ~⟩ ⟨spoke from ~ knowledge⟩ **6** *obs* **a :** contracted or promised in marriage **:** BETROTHED **b :** bound by loyalty or an oath of allegiance (as to a person or party) ⟨made that party ~ unto him —Richard Baker⟩ **7 a :** bound to come about or to happen **:** certain to eventuate **:** ASSURED ⟨moving to ~ disaster⟩ ⟨his success is ~⟩ **b :** destined esp. by fate **:** BOUND ⟨he is ~ to win⟩

syn CERTAIN, POSITIVE, COCKSURE: SURE and CERTAIN are often interchangeable; in the few situations in which they do differ, SURE may be used with judgments or expressions that are subjective or intuitive, CERTAIN with those that rest on indubitable evidence ⟨wonderful how she managed that light note when you were *sure* she couldn't be feeling it —Mary Austin⟩ ⟨of this I am quite *sure*, that there is no inconsistency or natural repugnance between this poetical and religious faith in the same mind —William Hazlitt⟩ ⟨trust me one day more . . . without more *certain* guarantee, than this poor face you deign to praise so much —John Keats⟩ ⟨the only dependable foundation of personal liberty is the personal economic security of private property. The teaching of history is very *certain* on this point —Walter Lippmann⟩ POSITIVE intensifies sureness or certainty; it indicates conviction of one's rightness with no suggestion of doubt; it may but does not necessarily suggest an unduly strong or opinionated conviction forcefully expressed ⟨an assertive *positive* man . . . had his own notion of what a young man should be —Sherwood Anderson⟩ ⟨so much more *positive* than most of his customers, and he impressed his own convictions on them so determinedly, that he had his own way —H.E.Scudder⟩ COCKSURE almost always suggests presumptuous vanity, self-assuredness, or cocky lack of consideration of all details ⟨a people which . . . had been regarded as brash to the point of arrogance, *cocksure* to the verge of folly, and so wholly certain of its future and itself that travelers wrote books about the national assurance —Archibald MacLeish⟩ **syn** see in addition CONFIDENT

— to be sure *adv* **1 :** without doubt **:** CERTAINLY ⟨*to be sure* I am⟩ **2 :** it must be acknowledged **:** ADMITTEDLY — usu. used to introduce an exception or limitation ⟨they were brave, *to be sure*, but ineffectual⟩

²sure \"\ *adv* [ME, fr. *sure*, *sur*, adj.] **:** SURELY ⟨~, I'll be there⟩

³sure \"\ *n* -S **:** CERTAINTY — compare FOR SURE

sure enough *adv* **:** as one might confidently expect **:** CERTAINLY, DEFINITELY, POSITIVELY ⟨in most cases the spontaneity is there, *sure enough* —*Times Lit. Supp.*⟩

sure-enough \'≈≈,≈\ *adj* [*sure enough*] **:** ACTUAL, GENUINE, REAL ⟨the life for a *sure-enough* man —A.B.Guthrie⟩ ⟨upriver to look at a *sure-enough* fish wheel —*Christian Science Monitor*⟩

surefire \'≈¦≈\ *adj* [¹*sure* + *fire*] **:** certain to produce a usu. specified or desired result **:** proved by experience to be reliable **:** DEPENDABLE ⟨a ~ device⟩ ⟨a ~ winner⟩ ⟨a ~ recipe⟩ ⟨made my production . . . once an unpredictable operation — entirely ~ —*New Yorker*⟩

surefooted \'≈¦≈\ *adj* [¹*sure* + *footed*] **1 :** unlikely to make a slip or error (as in judgment or execution of policy) **:** proceeding surely ⟨most ~ of the statesmen who dealt with the depression —Walter Lippmann⟩ ⟨a director as ~ and experienced as this one —Aline B. Saarinen⟩ **2 :** sure of foot **:** unlikely to stumble, fall, slip, or skid **:** moving firmly and confidently on or as if on foot ⟨on ~ donkeys —M.O.Williams⟩ ⟨a ~ tractor⟩

sure·foot·ed·ness *n* -ES **:** the quality or state of being surefooted ⟨the ~ of the mountain goat⟩

sure-handed \'≈¦≈\ *adj* **:** having or held to have hands that are sure in performing some action **:** proficient and confident in performance ⟨promising playwrights . . . *sure-handed* enough to turn out top-drawer scripts with any consistency —Henry Hewes⟩

sure·ly *adv* [ME *surly*, fr. *sur* sure + *-ly* — more at SURE] **1 :** in a sure manner: **a** *archaic* **:** SAFELY, SECURELY ⟨he that walketh uprightly walketh ~ —Prov 10:9 (AV)⟩ **b** (1) **:** with assurance or confidence ⟨people who respond immediately and ~ to works of art —Clive Bell⟩ (2) **:** without doubt **:** CERTAINLY, UNDOUBTEDLY ⟨the tremendous growth that is ~ ahead in this country —C.F.Craig⟩ **c** *obs* **:** in a faithful manner **:** LOYALLY ⟨that I may ~ keep mine oath —Shak.⟩ **2 :** ASSUREDLY,

INDEED, REALLY — often used as an interjection or intensive or to qualify a statement

sure·ness *n* -ES [ME *surnes*, fr. *sur* sure + *-nes* -ness] **:** the quality or state of being sure **:** CERTAINTY, CONFIDENCE ⟨impeccable ~ of hand —Laurence Binyon⟩ ⟨~ of purpose and steadiness of gait —O.E.Rölvaag⟩

surer *comparative of* SURE

su·res \ˈsü,rās\ *n pl* [Sp, pl. of *sur* south, of Gmc origin; akin to OE *sūth* south — more at SOUTH] **:** southerly winds on the coasts of Chile and Peru

sureseater \ˈ⸗,⸗⸗\ *n* [*sure* + *seater;* fr. there usu. being empty seats] **:** ART THEATER

sures par·dos \-ˈpär,dōs\ *n pl* [Sp, lit., drab sures] **:** sures accompanied by fog

surest *superlative of* SURE

[1]**sure thing** *n* **:** something that is or is held to be certain (as to succeed or bring success) **:** something reliable in behavior or development **:** something (as a bet) upon which one allegedly cannot lose ⟨a positively *sure thing* in a race —Joel Sayre⟩ ⟨a *sure thing* does not arouse us emotionally —John Dewey⟩

[2]**sure thing** *adv* **:** CERTAINLY — often used interjectionally

su·rette \sü'ret\ *n* -S [F, sourish, dim. of *sur* sour, of Gmc origin; akin to OHG *sūr* sour — more at SOUR] **:** a tropical American tree (*Byrsonima crassifolia*) having hard dark-colored wood and edible yellow acid berries

sure·ty *R* ˈshu̇r(ə)|d·|ē, |t|, |i *sometimes* ˈshər-; *–R* ˈshu̇ə|, ˈshōə|, ˈshō(ə)|, ˈshu̇rə|, ˈshōrə|, ˈshȯrə| *sometimes* ˈshə̄\ *n* -ES [ME *surte*, fr. MF *surté*, fr. L *securitat-, securitas* safety, security — more at SECURITY] **1 :** the state or condition of being sure: as **a** *obs* **:** safety or security from danger **b :** certainty of knowledge (as of a fact or an event) ⟨there is no ~ he ever reached the river —Julian Dana⟩ ⟨unable to predict a development with ~⟩ **c :** confidence and sureness in action ⟨a bit less ~ of walk —Donald Windham⟩ **2 a :** something that confirms or makes sure **:** a pledge or other formal engagement given for the fulfillment of an undertaking **:** GUARANTEE **b :** ground of confidence or security (as against loss or damage or for payment or the performance of some act) **3 a :** a person formerly given or giving himself as a gage or pledge **:** HOSTAGE **b :** one (as a sponsor at baptism or a bondsman) who makes a pledge in behalf of another and accepts certain accruing responsibilities **:** a person who is bound on an obligation from which another by the discharge of a duty should relieve him **:** one who has become legally liable for the debt, default, or failure in duty (as appearance in court or payment of a debt) of another — compare PRINCIPAL

surety bond *n* **:** a written instrument evidencing a contract of suretyship **:** a bond guaranteeing performance of a contract or obligation — compare FIDELITY BOND

surety company *n* **:** a company whose primary business is acting as a surety for the performance of obligations esp. by the issuing of surety bonds

sure·ty·ship \-,ship\ *n* **:** the state of being surety **:** the obligation of one who is surety **:** the obligation of a person to answer for the debt, default, or failure in duty of another — compare GUARANTY

sur·excitation \¦sər+\ *n* [*sur-* + *excitation*] **:** excessive excitation

[1]**surf** \ˈsərf, ˈsəf, ˈsəif\ *n* -S *often attrib* [origin unknown] **1 a :** the swell of the sea that breaks upon the shore (as upon a sloping beach) **b :** the breaking waves or their foam, splash, and sound **2 :** something that looks like, sounds like, or otherwise is held to resemble surf ⟨a ~ of dust rising back of the carriage —Gilbert Parker⟩ ⟨a constant ~ of yells . . . from hundreds of cell windows —Jan Valtin⟩

[2]**surf** \"\ *vi* -ED/-ING/-S **1 a :** to bathe in the surf **b :** to ride the surf (as on a surfboard) **2 :** to swell, break, or otherwise behave in a manner suggesting surf ⟨the lace frill of her dress ~*ed* white in the sun —William Sansom⟩ ⟨tides of . . . commerce caught up and ~*ed* over me —Christopher Morley⟩

[1]**sur·face** \ˈsərfəs, ˈsəf-, ˈsəif-\ *n* -S [F, fr. *sur-* + *face*, fr. OF — more at FACE] **1 :** the exterior or outside of an object or body **:** the outermost or uppermost boundary **:** one or more of the faces of a three-dimensional thing **:** a plane of a solid ⟨the uneven ~ of the earth⟩ ⟨on the ~ of the water⟩ ⟨planks with a rough ~⟩ ⟨the octagonal ~*s* of a diamond⟩ **2 :** a two-dimensional locus of points **:** the boundary or portion of the boundary of a three-dimensional region ⟨a plane ~⟩ ⟨a spherical ~⟩ **3 :** something held to resemble the surface of an object or body: **a :** the part of something that is presented to a viewer with little or no examination **:** the outward appearance or characteristics of something **:** the external aspect ⟨the ~ of society⟩ ⟨deep beneath the ~ of the legal system —B.N.Cardozo⟩ **b :** someone or something without depth **:** a mere outside **:** one that is superficial in nature **4 :** a complete airfoil used for sustentation or control or to increase stability **5 :** the condition of a railroad track marked by vertical evenness or smoothness over short distances ⟨the track is in ~⟩ **6 a :** PRINTING SURFACE ⟨autographic works printed from ~*s* actually produced by the artist —Barnett Freedman⟩ ⟨printing done from relief ~*s*⟩ **b :** STONE 1b(11) — **on the surface** *adv* **:** to all outward appearances **:** so far as one can see ⟨the entire system was, at least *on the surface*, remarkably efficient —F.A.Ogg & Harold Zink⟩ ⟨*on the surface* there is no apparent relationship between the two books —Harrison Smith⟩

[2]**surface** \"\ *vb* -ED/-ING/-S *vt* **1 :** to give a surface to: as **a :** to plane (as lumber) or make smooth **b :** to apply the surface layer to ⟨the towers are *surfaced* with steel plates —*Amer. Guide Series: N.Y. City*⟩ ⟨~ a highway⟩ **c :** to finish (as furniture or a marble slab) esp. by polishing or varnishing **d :** to give a usu. specified surface to ⟨walls *surfaced* with cream stucco —*Amer. Guide Series: N.C.*⟩ **2 :** to bring to the surface ⟨two wells . . . ~ more than 6,000 gallons of water a minute —Gaston Burridge⟩ ~ *vi* **1 :** to work on or at the surface — used esp. of a gold digger who works the ground superficially or a tracklayer who brings the top of the rail to a true grade line **2 :** to come or rise to the surface (as of the water) ⟨a submarine *surfaced* outside the harbor⟩ ⟨a subway downtown, the line ~*s* after three miles —A.H.Brown⟩ ⟨the truth began to ~ —Robert Jackson⟩

[3]**surface** \"\ *adj* **1 a :** of, located on, or designed for use at the surface of something ⟨designing ~ instruments for the detection of oil deposits —W.J.Reilly⟩ ⟨~ forces⟩ ⟨~ vessels⟩ ⟨~ runoff of water⟩ **b :** situated on the surface of the earth rather than in the air or underground ⟨~ transportation⟩ ⟨~ communications⟩ **c** (1) **:** of or relating to surface mail ⟨~ postage⟩ (2) **:** handled as surface mail ⟨~ parcel post⟩ **2 :** acting upon or against a surface ⟨a ~ grinder⟩ **3 :** working at or near the surface ⟨~ mining⟩ **:** worked at or near the surface ⟨~ mines⟩ **4 a :** appearing on the surface only **:** lacking depth ⟨accurate ~ realism —R.A.Cordell⟩ ⟨improvements in ~ conditions but not in fundamental weaknesses⟩ **b :** SUPERFICIAL ⟨~ friendships⟩

surface-active \¦⸗⸗¦⸗⸗\ *adj* **:** modifying the properties of a liquid medium at a surface or interface usu. by reducing surface tension or interfacial tension ⟨all detergents are *surface-active* but not all surface-active agents are detergents —F.D.Snell⟩

surface-active agent *n* **:** a substance useful for its cleansing, wetting, dispersing, or similar powers ⟨*surface-active agents* . . . in dilute aqueous solution —Donald Price⟩ — called also *surfactant;* see DETERGENT c; compare WETTING AGENT

surface–bent \¦⸗⸗¦⸗\ *adj* **:** bent so as to be not straight in the vertical plane ⟨a *surface-bent* railroad rail⟩

surface car *n* **:** a car (as a streetcar) for transportation on land as opposed to a subway or elevated car

surface carburetor *n* **:** a carburetor in which air is charged by being passed over the surface of gasoline

surface chemistry *n* **:** a branch of chemistry that deals with the properties of surfaces or phase boundaries and with the chemical changes occurring at a surface or interface

surface color *n* **1 a :** the color ascribed to an opaque substance or object **b :** a color extending no farther than the surface **2 :** color determined by selective reflection at the surface (as the yellow color of gold) **3 :** a color localized in the surface of an object and conforming to the orientation, configuration, and texture of that surface — compare BULKY COLOR, FILM COLOR

surface-colored paper \ˈ⸗⸗,⸗⸗-\ *n* **:** a safety paper for postage stamps having color on the side which is to receive the design

surface cooler *n* **:** a tank of cold water or other liquid-cooling medium for cooling milk in cans

surface creep *n* **:** a stage in the wind erosion process in which sand grains are moved along the ground surface by impact of other grains in saltation

surfaced *adj* **:** having or provided with a usu. specified kind of surface ⟨~ roads⟩ — often used in combination ⟨a smooth-*surfaced* stone⟩

surface density *n* **:** a quantity (as mass or electricity) per unit area distributed over a surface

surface dive *n* **:** a dive made from the surface of the water to varying depths and executed headfirst in tuck or pike position or feetfirst

surfaced lumber *n* **:** lumber dressed by a planer

surface energy *n* **:** the energy associated with the intermolecular forces at the interface between two media ⟨the *surface energy* per unit area equals the surface tension⟩ — called also *free surface energy*

surface fire *n* **:** a forest fire that burns only surface litter and undergrowth

surface gauge *n* **1 :** a scriber mounted in an adjustable stand for marking off castings or testing the accuracy of plane surfaces and used with a surface plate **2 :** a gage for measuring ordinates of points on a surface of the work from a reference plane

surface gravity *n* **:** intensity of the force of gravity at the surface of the earth or a celestial body

surface harden *vt* **:** to harden the surface of (as steel) by a case hardening process or other method (as induction or flame)

surface integral *n* **:** the limit of the sum of products formed by multiplying the area of a portion of a surface by the value of a function at any point in this area, the summation covering the entire surface and the area of the largest portion approaching zero

surface layer *n* **:** a layer (as a layer of moisture) having a resistivity different from that of the body on which it is deposited

sur·face·ly *adv* **:** on the surface **:** SUPERFICIALLY ⟨aspects of life as ~ lived —Sheldon Cheney⟩

surface mail *n* **1 :** mail carried by land or sea transportation rather than by air **2 :** the postal system or services handling surface mail

sur·face·man \ˈ⸗⸗mən\ *n, pl* **surfacemen 1 :** a man who works on the surface (as on the roadbed of a railroad or the surface works of a mine) **2 :** a repairer of road surfaces

surface measure *n* **:** the surface area of a board **:** board measure when the board is one inch thick

surface noise *n* **:** a hissing sound in the background of a phonograph record reproduction produced when the needle passes along a groove of less than perfect smoothness of surface — called also *needle scratch*

surface of revolution : a surface held to be formed by the revolution of a plane curve about a line in its plane

surface plate *n* **:** a steel instrument of precision having a dressed flat surface or sometimes two surfaces at right angles and used as a standard of flatness

surface printing *n* **1 :** LETTERPRESS **2 :** PLANOGRAPHY

sur·fac·er \ˈsərfəsər; ˈsəfəsə(r, ˈsəif-\ *n* -S **:** one that surfaces: as **a :** a machine for planing or dressing the surface (as of wood, metal, or stone) — compare BUZZ PLANER, CYLINDER PLANER **b :** a device used in preparing railroad ties for tie plates **c :** one that surfaces furniture **d :** an undercoat of paint used to level up inequalities of a surface **e :** a worker who grinds and polishes optical lenses **f :** SEASONER c **g :** a worker who smooths the faces of watch wheels and reduces them to the proper thickness by rubbing them on a wet emery-paper surface

surface railway *n* **:** a railway whose tracks are mainly on the surface rather than beneath it (as in a subway) or above it on a superstructure (as in an elevated railway)

surface resistance *n* **:** the electrical resistance of a surface layer to a current

surface rib *n* **:** a merely ornamental rib on the surface of a vault **:** LIERNE

surfaces *pl of* SURFACE, *pres 3d sing of* SURFACE

surface-size \ˈ⸗⸗,⸗\ *vt* **:** to treat the surface of (paper) with a sizing agent (as glue or starch) **:** TOP-SIZE — compare BEATER-SIZE, TUB-SIZE

surface soil *n* **:** the upper 5 to 8 inches of the soil layer **:** the portion of the soil usu. tilled

surface switch *n* **:** a snap switch designed for mounting on a plane surface and requiring no enclosing parts (as a box)

surface tension *n* **:** a condition that exists at the free surface of a body (as a liquid) by reason of intermolecular forces unsymmetrically disposed about the individual surface molecules and is manifested by properties resembling those of an elastic skin under tension; *specif* **:** the force per unit length of any straight line on the surface that the surface layers on opposite sides of the line exert upon each other

surface water *n* **:** natural water that has not penetrated much below the surface of the ground **:** drainage water — compare GROUNDWATER, RAINWATER, SPRINGWATER

surface wave *n* **:** an earthquake vibration propagated in the earth's outer shell — contrasted with *body wave*

surfacing *n* -S [fr. gerund of [2]*surface*] **1 :** the action of one that surfaces: **a :** the action or process of digging gold on the surface of the ground **b :** the motion of a tool or part of a tool used in making or finishing a surface **c :** the action of bringing the top of a railroad rail to a true grade line **2 :** material forming or used to form a surface ⟨the ~ for a road⟩ ⟨wash the ~ for gold⟩ ⟨stucco ~ crudely painted to simulate black marble —H.S.Morrison⟩

surfacing machine *n* **:** SURFACER a

sur·fac·tant \,sər'faktənt\ *n* -S [*surface-active agent*] **:** SURFACE-ACTIVE AGENT

sur·facy \ˈsərfəsē\ *adj* [[1]*surface* + *-y*] **:** characterized by surface rather than depth **:** SUPERFICIAL ⟨his music has a ~ brilliance —Irving Lowens⟩

surfbird \ˈ⸗,⸗\ *n* [[1]*surf* + *bird*] **:** a shorebird (*Aphriza virgata*) of the Pacific coasts of No. and So. America related to the turnstones but somewhat like the golden plover in form and habits and readily distinguished in all plumages by its tail which is blackish at the tip and broadly white at the base

[1]**surfboard** \ˈ⸗,⸗\ *n* **:** a long narrow buoyant board used in the sport of riding the surf

[2]**surfboard** \"\ *vi* **:** to ride the surf on a surfboard — **surf·board·er** \"+ə(r)\ *n*

surfboat \ˈ⸗,⸗\ *n* **:** a boat fit for use in heavy surf; *esp* **:** one built strong and buoyant and with a marked sheer to ride the seas better

surf cast *vi* **:** to engage in surf casting

surf caster *n* **:** one that engages in surf casting

surf casting *n* **:** the technique or act of casting artificial or natural bait into the open ocean or in a bay where waves break on a beach

surf clam *n* **:** any of various typically rather large surf-dwelling edible clams constituting the family Mactridae — called also *hen clam, sea clam;* see SPISULA

surf coot *n* **:** SURF SCOTER

surf duck *n* **:** SCOTER; *esp* **:** SURF SCOTER

surfed *past of* SURF

[1]**sur·feit** \ˈsərfət, ˈsəf-, ˈsəif-, *usu* -əd·+V\ *n* -S [ME *surfait, surfet*, fr. MF *sourfait, seurfet*, fr. past part. of *sourfaire* to reach too high, lit., overdo, fr. *sour-, sur-* sur- + *faire* to make, do, fr. L *facere* — more at DO] **1 :** an overabundant supply, yield, or amount of something **:** EXCESS, SUPERFLUITY ⟨a murder with a ~ of clues and motives —*London Calling*⟩ ⟨hard to choose . . . from such a ~ of riches —Martin Levin⟩ **2 a :** an intemperate or immoderate indulgence in something (as food or drink) usu. to a degree that causes physical disorders ⟨died of a ~ of sprats —T.C.Chubb⟩ **b** *obs* **:** the amount (as of food or drink) taken intemperately or in excess ⟨his loathing stomach . . . shall cast the precious ~ up again —Richard Blackmore⟩ **3** *archaic* **:** a sickness arising from excess in eating and drinking **:** sickness caused by intemperance ⟨he died of a ~ caused by intemperance —Oliver Goldsmith⟩ **4 :** disgust caused by excess **:** SATIETY ⟨supplied abundantly and even to ~ —Edmund Burke⟩

[2]**surfeit** \"\ *vb* -ED/-ING/-S [ME *surfeten*, fr. *surfet* surfeit] *vt* **:** to feed, supply, or give to surfeit **:** disgust or sicken by excess **:** fill to satiety or repletion **:** CLOY ⟨a large and corpulent individual ~*ed* . . . with good eating —Theodore Dreiser⟩ ⟨the public was already ~*ed* with . . . histories —Edmund Wilson⟩ ~ *vi* **1** *archaic* **:** to indulge excessively or to satiety in any gratification (as of the appetite or senses) ⟨a merrier set of gourmands . . . never ~*ed* in genial diet —E.K.Kane⟩ **2 a** *obs* **:** to suffer from overindulgence **:** become sick esp. from food or drink taken in excess ⟨they are as sick that ~ with too much as they that starve with nothing —Shak.⟩ **b** *archaic* **:** to become nauseated or disgusted with an excess of something **:** become sick of something overabundant ⟨so early dost thou ~ with the wealth —H.F.Cary⟩ **syn** see SATIATE

sur·feit·er \"+ə(r)\ *n* -S *archaic* **:** one (as a glutton or libertine) that surfeits or cloys

surfeit water *n* **:** a water formerly used to cure surfeit

surf·er \ˈsərfər\ *n* -S **1** *dial* **:** SURF SCOTER **2 :** one that rides a surfboard

surf fish *n* **1 :** any of numerous small or medium-sized fishes that constitute the family Embiotocidae, live chiefly in shallow water along the Pacific coast of No. America, and resemble perches in form but differ from them in their anatomy and in being viviparous **2 :** any of several croakers (family Sciaenidae) of the Pacific coast of No. America **3 :** SURF SMELT

surf–fish *vi* **:** to angle along the ocean shore with tackle esp. designed to cast a natural or artificial bait up to a distance of 200 yards

surfgrass \ˈ⸗,⸗\ *n* [[1]*surf* + *grass*] **:** a grasslike aquatic plant of the genus *Phyllospadix* (family Potamogetonaceae) living on rocky ocean shores and having narrow linear basal leaves and small dioecious flowers borne on the side of a flattened spadix

surf green *n* **1 :** a light to moderate green that is yellower and less strong than Neptune **2 :** a moderate yellowish green that is yellower, lighter, and stronger than tarragon, yellower and paler than malachite green, and yellower and stronger than verdigris

sur·fi·cial \¦sər¦fishəl\ *adj* [*surface* + *-icial* (as in *superficial*)] **1 :** of or relating to a surface and esp. the earth's surface — opposed to *subterranean* **2 :** SUPERFICIAL 1c

surfing *pres part of* SURF

surfle *vt* -ED/-ING/-S [perh. alter. of *sulfur*, n.] *obs* **:** to wash or tint (as the face) with a cosmetic

surf line *n* **:** a line of foam-crested waves breaking on a formation (as a shoal) near the surface

surf·man \ˈ⸗mən\ *n, pl* **surfmen :** one who is skilled in handling a boat in surf; *specif* **:** one employed in the lifesaving branch of the U.S. Coast Guard

surfperch \ˈ⸗,⸗\ *n* **:** SURF FISH 1

surf plant *n* **:** a plant (as a kelp) growing where it is exposed to tidal action **:** CUMATOPHYTE

surf reel *n* **:** a free spool multiplying fishing reel used in surf-fishing

surf–riding \ˈ⸗,⸗⸗\ *n* **:** the sport of riding the surf esp. on a surfboard

surf rod *n* **:** a two-handed fishing rod usu. more than seven feet overall designed specif. for use with a surf reel

surfs *pl of* SURF, *pres 3d sing of* SURF

surf scoter *n* **:** a common American scoter (*Melanitta perspicillata*) of which the adult male has conspicuous white markings on the head and neck with otherwise black plumage and the female and young are grayish brown — called also *surf coot*

surf smelt *n* **:** a pale greenish smelt (*Hypomesus pretiosus*) of the coast of California and northward that spawns in the surf

surf snipe *n* **:** SANDERLING

sur·fuse \,sər'fyüz\ *vb* [*sur-* + *fuse*] **:** SUPERCOOL

sur·fu·sion \-üzhən\ *n* **:** the state of being surfused

surf whiting *n* **:** SILVER WHITING

surfy \ˈsərfē\ *adj* -ER/-EST [[1]*surf* + *-y*] **:** of, abounding in, or resembling surf ⟨a ~ shore⟩

surg *abbr* **1** surgeon **2** surgery **3** surgical

[1]**surge** \ˈsərj, ˈsəj, ˈsəij\ *n* -S *often attrib* [prob. fr. MF *sourge-*, alter. (influenced by L *surgere*) of *sourj-*, stem of *sourdre* to rise, surge, fr. L *surgere* to rise, go straight up, fr. *subs-* (var. of *sub-* up) + *regere* to lead straight, rule — more at SUB-, RIGHT] **1 :** a swelling, rolling, or sweeping forward like that of an oncoming billow or series of billows **:** an onward rush **:** a violent rising and falling ⟨a ~ of interest⟩ ⟨intermittent ~*s* of enthusiasm⟩ ⟨the musketry sounded in long irregular ~*s* —Stephen Crane⟩ ⟨the ~ of the hills⟩ **2 a :** a large wave or billow **:** a great rolling swell of water ⟨the sea was rolling in immense ~*s* —R.H.Dana⟩ **b :** a series of such swells or billows **3 :** the tapered part of a windlass barrel or a capstan on which a cable surges **4 a :** a movement (as a slipping or slackening) of a rope or cable **b :** a sudden jerk or strain caused by such a movement **5 :** a barometric wave apparently independent of and unexplained by existing barometric gradients **6 :** a transient variation of current in an electrical circuit (as when a motor is started) **:** a sudden rise and fall of voltage — compare TRANSIENT CURRENT

[2]**surge** \"\ *vb* -ED/-ING/-S [MF *sourgir*, fr. OSp *surgir*, fr. L *surgere* to rise, go straight up] *vi* **1 :** to rise and fall with much motion **:** toss on the waves **:** ride atop the waves ⟨the vessel at anchor *surged* in the heavy sea⟩ **2** *obs* **:** to rise like a spring from its source or a river from underground **3 a :** to rise and move in surges, high waves, or great billows **:** swell in an agitated manner ⟨the sea . . . ~*s* on its limestone cliffs —Harrison Smith⟩ **b :** to rise in a surge **:** swell or heave with great force ⟨a wave ~*s*⟩ **4 :** to slip around a windlass, capstan, or bitts — used esp. of a rope **5 :** to rise suddenly to an excessive or abnormal value **:** rise to and fall from such a value successively — used esp. of current or voltage **6 :** to rise, heave, blow, sound, or otherwise move with a surge or in surges ⟨a great glow of . . . tenderness *surged* through him —O.E.Rölvaag⟩ ⟨the incessant traffic ~*s* past —Margaret Devlin⟩ ⟨millions of farmers . . . *surged* westward —R.A. Billington⟩ ⟨the music of the organ *surged* through the church⟩ ~ *vt* **1 :** to cause to rise or fall in surges **:** cause to move in a surge **2 :** to let go or slacken gradually (as a rope) ⟨~ a hawser to prevent its parting⟩ **syn** see RISE

surge chamber *n* **:** SURGE TANK

surge gap *n* **:** a spark gap (as in an arrester) for the discharge of surges due to lightning

surge·less \-jləs\ *adj* **:** free from surges ⟨~ seas⟩

sur·gen·cy \-jənsē\ *n* -ES [[2]*surge* + *-ency*] **:** a personality factor characterized by quickness and cleverness

sur·gent \ˈsərjənt\ *adj* [L *surgent-, surgens*, pres. part. of *surgere* to rise] **:** rising in a surge **:** swelling in surges or waves ⟨~ seas⟩

sur·geon \ˈsərjən, ˈsəj-, ˈsəij-\ *n* -S [ME *surgien*, fr. AF, contr. of OF *serurgien, cirurgien*, fr. *serurgie, cirurgie* surgery + *-ien* -ian — more at SURGERY] **1 :** a medical specialist who performs surgery **:** a physician qualified to treat those diseases that are amenable to or require surgery — compare INTERNIST **2 :** the senior medical officer of a military unit **3 :** SURGEONFISH

surgeon apothecary *n, Brit* **:** a surgeon who is also an apothecary **:** a general practitioner

surgeon commander *n* **:** an officer in a medical corps (as of the British Navy) having the rank of commander

sur·geon·cy \-nsē\ *n* -ES [*surgeon* + *-cy*] *Brit* **:** the office or position of a surgeon ⟨a vacant ~⟩

surgeon dentist *n* **:** an oral surgeon

surgeonfish \ˈ⸗⸗,⸗\ *n* [*surgeon* + *fish;* fr. the lancelike spines suggesting a surgeon's instruments] **:** any of numerous spiny-finned fishes of the family Teuthididae that are related to the Moorish idols but are usu. less conspicuously colored and have a more elongate body, bear on each side near the base of the tail one or more movable lancelike spines, and occur in most warm seas esp. in the East Indies — called also *tang*

surgeon general *n, pl* **surgeons general 1 a :** the chief of the medical service of the U. S. Army having the rank of major general **b :** the chief of the Bureau of Medicine and Surgery in the U. S. Navy having the rank of rear admiral **c :** the chief medical officer of the U. S. Air Force **2 :** the chief medical officer in the U. S. Bureau of Public Health or of a state public health bureau **3 :** one of the ten members of the medical staff of the British Army

surgeon major *n, pl* **surgeons major :** the ranking surgeon of a regiment in the British Army

surgeon's agaric *n* **:** a preparation in the form of a powder or thick feltlike sheets of an agaric (*Fomes fomentarius*) formerly used as a hemostatic

surgeon's knot *n* **:** any of several knots used in tying ligatures or stitches; *esp* **:** a reef knot in which the first knot has two turns

surgeon's knot

sur·gery \ˈsərj(ə)rē, ˈsə̄j-, ˈsəij-, -ri\ *n* -ES [ME *surgerie*, fr. OF, contr. of *serurgerie*, *cirurgerie*, fr. *serurgie*, *cirurgie* (fr. L *chirurgia*, fr. Gk *cheirourgia*, fr. *cheirourgos* working with the hand — fr. *cheir* hand + *-ourgos* working, fr. *-o-* + *ergon* work — + *-ia* -y) + *-erie* -ery — more at CHIR-, WORK] **1 :** a branch of medicine that is concerned with diseases and conditions requiring or amenable to operative or manual procedures ⟨orthopedic ~⟩ ⟨new techniques in brain ~⟩ **2 :** the treatment of other than human ills or diseases by methods analogous to or as drastic as those of a surgeon ⟨the agonizing ~ of revolution —John Strachey⟩ ⟨a superb piece of literary ~ —Norman Cousins⟩ — see TREE SURGERY **3 a** *Brit* **:** a room or office (as in a general practitioner's house) where a doctor sees and treats patients **b :** the room (as in a doctor's or dentist's offices) or the quarters (as in a hospital) where surgery is performed ⟨the patient walked into the doctor's ~⟩ ⟨the patient was anesthetized in ~⟩ **4 a :** the work done by a surgeon ⟨the operation was a skillful piece of bloodless ~⟩ **b :** OPERATION ⟨he had a ~ at six o'clock⟩

surges *pl of* SURGE, *pres 3d sing of* SURGE

surge tank *n* **:** a standpipe or storage reservoir at the downstream end of a closed aqueduct or feeder pipe (as for a water wheel) to absorb sudden rises of pressure and to furnish water quickly during a drop in pressure — called also *surge chamber*

sur·gi·cal \ˈsərjəkəl, ˈsə̄j-, ˈsəij-, -jēk-\ *adj* [*surgeon* + *-ical*] **1 :** of, relating to, or concerned with surgeons or surgery **2 :** requiring surgical treatment ⟨~ appendix⟩ — distinguished from *medical* **3 :** resulting from surgery ⟨~ fever⟩ **4 :** done by or used in surgery or surgical conditions ⟨~ gauze⟩ ⟨~ stocking⟩ **5 :** held to resemble medical surgery esp. in precision or incisiveness ⟨a ~ insight into character —F.A. Pottle⟩ ⟨as a tool of analysis it was ~ in its keenness —H.A. Overstreet⟩ ⟨a ~ precision⟩

surgical diathermy *n* **:** surgery by electrocoagulation

surgical knot *n* **:** SURGEON'S KNOT

sur·gi·cal·ly \-jək(ə)lē, -jēk-, -li\ *adv* **:** by or as if by means of surgery **:** in a surgical manner ⟨~ polished corridors —Alan Brien⟩ ⟨almost ~ exact work —Winthrop Sargeant⟩ ⟨~ clean⟩

surgical needle *n* **:** a needle designed to carry sutures when sewing tissues

surging *pres part of* SURGE

surgy \ˈsərjē\ *adj* [¹*surge* + *-y*] *archaic* **:** rising in or like surges or billows **:** abounding in surges ⟨over the ~ main —Alexander Pope⟩

su·ri·a·na \ˌsu̇rēˈänə\ *n, cap* [NL, fr. Joseph D. *Surian*, 18th cent. Fr. botanist] **:** a genus of tropical seashore shrubs or small trees (family Surianaceae) with narrow densely-clustered leaves and small yellow flowers — see BAY CEDAR 2

su·ri·a·na·ce·ae \ˌsu̇rēəˈnāsēˌē\ *n pl, cap* [NL, fr. *Suriana*, type genus + *-aceae*] **:** a monotypic family of dicotyledonous plants (order Geraniales) — see SURIANA

su·ri·ca·ta \ˌsu̇rəˈkädə\ *n, cap* [NL, fr. F *surikate*] **:** a genus of mammals (family Viverridae) consisting of the suricates

su·ri·cate \ˈsu̇rəˌkāt\ *also* **su·ri·cat** \-kat\ *n* -S [F *surikate*, prob. fr. native name in southern Africa] **:** a burrowing mammal (*Suricata tetradactyla*) of southern Africa that is related to the mongooses but has only four toes, is grayish banded with black, is diurnal and social in habits and in some respects behaves like a prairie dog, and is often kept as a pet

su·ri·nam \ˈsu̇rəˌnam\ *adj, usu cap* [fr. *Surinam*, northern So. America] **:** of or from Surinam **:** of the kind or style prevalent in Surinam

surinam cabbage tree *n, usu cap S* **:** a tree (*Andira retusa*) of Guiana having bark that is used as an anthelmintic and cathartic — compare WORM BARK

surinam cherry *n, usu cap S* **1 a :** a Barbados cherry (*Malpighia glabra*) with rose to purple flowers and deep red fruits **b :** the edible aromatic fruit of this tree **2 a :** a Brazilian tree (*Eugenia uniflora*) often cultivated in California and Florida for its spicy red fruit that resembles a cherry **b :** the fruit of this tree

surinam cockroach *n, usu cap S* **:** a widely distributed dark brown tropical cockroach (*Pycnoscelus surinamensis*)

surinam disease *n, usu cap S* **:** PANAMA DISEASE

su·ri·nam·er \ˈsu̇rəˌnamə(r)\ *n, cap* [*Surinam* + E *-er*] **:** SURINAMESE

¹**su·ri·nam·ese** \ˌsu̇rəˌnaˈmēz, -ēs\ *adj, usu cap* [*Surinam* + E *-ese* (adj. suffix)] **1 :** of, relating to, or characteristic of Surinam **2 :** of, relating to, or characteristic of the people of Surinam

²**surinamese** \"\ *n, pl* **surinamese** *cap* [*Surinam* + E *-ese* (n. suffix)] **:** a native or inhabitant of Surinam

surinam quassia *n, usu cap S* **1 :** a tree (*Quassia amara*) growing in tropical America and the West Indies **2 :** the drug obtained from the Surinam quassia

surinam toad *n, usu cap S* **1 :** an aquatic aglossate toad (*Pipa pipa* syn. *P. americana*) of the Guianas and parts of Brazil of which the eggs as they are laid are distributed by the male over the back of the female where they become embedded in the skin each in a separate cavity with a lid formed from the outer capsule of the egg and within which the tadpole lives and metamorphoses **2 :** AGUA

sur les pointes \ˌsərləˈpwaⁿt, -ant\ *adv (or adj)* [F] *ballet* **:** on the tips of the toes

sur·li·ly \ˈsərləlē, ˈsə̄l-, ˈsəil-, -əli\ *adv* **:** in a surly manner **:** with gloomy ill nature **:** RUDELY

sur·li·ness \lēnə̇s, lin-\ *n* -ES **:** the quality or state of being surly **:** gloomy ill nature **:** surly character or manner **:** RUDENESS

¹**sur·ly** \lē, li\ *adj, often* -ER/-EST [alter. of obs. E *sirly*, fr. ME, fr. *sir* + *-ly* — more at SIR] **1** *obs* **:** arrogant in manner or bearing **:** DOMINEERING, HAUGHTY, IMPERIOUS ⟨be opposite with a kinsman, ~ with servants —Shak.⟩ **2 :** ill-natured, abrupt, and rude **:** churlishly cross **:** CRABBED ⟨answered in a ~ voice⟩ ⟨a ~ dog⟩ ⟨a ~ old man⟩ **3 a :** making or accompanied by threatening sounds **:** menacing, gloomy, or dismal in appearance ⟨~ weather⟩ **b :** difficult to manage **:** INTRACTABLE — used chiefly of soil **syn** see SULLEN

²**surly** \"\ *adv* **:** in a haughty or imperious manner ⟨a lion . . . went ~ by —Shak.⟩

sur·ma *or* **soor·ma** \ˈsu̇rmə\ *n* -S [Per *surma*] **:** native antimony sulfide used in India to darken the eyelids

sur·mark *or* **sir·mark** \ˈsərˌmärk\ *n* [*surmark* fr. *sur-* + *mark*; *sirmark* prob. alter. (influenced by ¹*sir*) of *surmark*] **1 :** a mark made on the molds of a ship when building to show where the frames should be beveled **2 :** a cleat temporarily placed on the side of a ship on the ways or in a ship dock to support the ribband against which the shores rest

sur·mis·able \sə(r)ˈmīzəbəl\ *adj* **:** capable of being surmised ⟨regardless of all known or ~ laws —*N. Y. Herald Tribune*⟩

¹**sur·mise** \sə(r)ˈmīz\ *vb* -ED/-ING/-S [ME *surmisen*, fr. MF *surmis*, *surmise*, masc. & fem. past part. of *surmetre* to charge, accuse, prob. fr. L *supermittere* to throw upon, fr. *super-* + *mittere* to throw — more at SMITE] *vt* **:** to imagine without certain knowledge **:** infer on slight grounds **:** form a notion of on slight proof **:** GUESS, SUPPOSE ⟨then she knew that what before she but *surmised* was true —John Dryden⟩ ⟨a delicate matter to ~ the thoughts of men —Emma Hawkridge⟩ ⟨he *surmised* that this was the true situation⟩ **~** *vi* **:** to make a surmise or guess **:** indulge in conjecture **syn** see CONJECTURE

²**sur·mise** \sə(r)ˈmīz; ˈsərˌm-, ˈsə̄,-, ˈsəi,-\ *n* -S [ME, fr. MF, accusation, fr. *surmetre* to charge, accuse] **1** *archaic* **a :** SUSPICION 1 ⟨a very painful ~ arose concerning her character —Ann Radcliffe⟩ **b :** a slight trace or sign **:** SUSPICION 3 ⟨some faintest ineffectual ~ of mercy —Thomas Carlyle⟩ **2** *obs* **:** an unfounded allegation or charge **3** *obs* **:** the action of surmising or imagining **4 :** a thought or idea based on scanty evidence **:** a random conclusion **:** CONJECTURE, GUESS ⟨what he expressed as a mere ~ was transcribed by others as a positive statement —Richard Semon⟩

sur·mis·er \sərˈmīzər\ *n* -S **:** one that surmises

sur·mount \sərˈmau̇nt\ *vt* [ME *surmounten*, fr. MF *surmonter*, fr. *sour-* sur- + *monter* to rise, mount — more at MOUNT] **1 a** *obs* **:** to surpass in quality or attainment **:** EXCEL ⟨kings courts ~ poor shepherds cells —Francis Quarles⟩ **b** *archaic* **:** to exceed in amount or magnitude **:** amount to more than ⟨their increment ~*s* daily their decrease —Matthew Hale⟩ **2 :** to rise above or surpass in height ⟨extinct volcanic centers ~ them near the core of the plateau —*Jour. of Geol.*⟩ **3 :** to rise superior to **:** get the better of **:** prevail over **:** OVERCOME ⟨~ an obstacle⟩ ⟨~ an aversion⟩ ⟨~ a temptation⟩ **4** *obs* **:** SURPASS 3 ⟨thy thoughts of love to me ~ the power of number to recount —John Wesley⟩ **5 :** to climb over **:** get to the top of and over **:** mount and cross to the other side of ⟨~ one crag after another⟩ **6 a :** to stand or lie at the top of **:** remain on the top of **:** CROWN, TOP ⟨a cross ~*s* the steeple⟩ ⟨the house . . . ~*s* a knoll —*Amer. Guide Series: N. Y. City*⟩ **b :** to place above so as to cover partly another heraldic charge ⟨a silver crane on a gules shield, ~*ed* by a crown —M.B. Grosvenor⟩ **syn** see CONQUER

sur·mount·able \-təbəl\ *adj* **:** capable of being surmounted **:** SUPERABLE ⟨situations of measurable and ~ danger —C.P. Romulo⟩

surmounted arch *n* **:** a stilted semicircular arch

sur·mullet \ˌsər+\ *n, pl* **surmullets** *also* **surmullet** [F *surmulet*, fr. MF *sormulet*, prob. fr. *sor* reddish brown + *mulet* mullet — more at SORREL, MULLET] **:** a mullet of the family Mullidae

¹**sur·name** \ˈsərˌnām, ˈsə̄,-, ˈsəi,-\ *n* [ME, fr. *sur-* + *name*] **1 a :** a name added onto an original or baptismal name from some pertinent or accidental circumstance (as occupation, place of residence, or physical appearance) **b** *obs* **:** a second name or an alternative title given to one (as a person, object, or place) **2 a :** the name borne in common by members of a family as distinguished from an individualizing forename **:** the inherited last name taken by children and changed only legally (as by adoption or by a woman's taking her husband's name) **b** *obs* **:** a cognomen of the ancient Romans

²**surname** \"\ *vt* **:** to give a surname to: as **a :** to give a family name to ⟨an earlier family *surnamed* from that parish —Charles Partridge⟩ **b :** to give an additional name, title, or epithet to ⟨his successor Cosmo, *surnamed* the Great —William Robertson †1793⟩ ⟨the Joan of this story is *surnamed* Regan —Ken Smith⟩ **c** *obs* **:** to call by another or additional name **:** DESIGNATE ⟨the great pyramids, *surnamed* the world's wonders —William Lithgow⟩

sur·nape *or* **sur·nap** \ˈsərˌnap\ *n* -S [ME, fr. MF *sournappe*, fr. *sour-* sur- + *nappe* tablecloth — more at NAPKIN] **:** a cloth resembling a napkin used in medieval times for washing at meals

sur·nay *or* **sur·nai** \ˈsu̇rˌnī\ *n* -S [Per *surnāī*] **:** an Oriental oboe

sur·nominal \ˌsər+\ *adj* [*sur-* + *nominal*] **:** of or relating to a surname ⟨~ forms⟩ ⟨~ characteristics⟩

sur·pass \sərˈpas, -paa(ə)s, -pais, -pás\ *vt* [MF *surpasser*, fr. *sur-* + *passer* to pass, fr. OF — more at PASS] **1 :** to become better, greater, or stronger than **:** exceed in quality, degree, or performance **:** become superior to **:** go beyond in action or achievement ⟨the reality ~*ed* all expectations⟩ ⟨he ~*ed* all his contemporaries in skill⟩ **2 :** to pass beyond **:** go over **:** OVERSTEP ⟨nor let the sea ~ his bounds —John Milton⟩ **3 :** to transcend the reach, capacity, or powers of **:** go beyond the bounds or limits of **:** become more than can be attained, achieved, or apprehended by ⟨her beauty ~*es* all description⟩ ⟨the task ~*ed* his skill⟩ **4 :** to extend beyond or above ⟨mountain masses . . . ~*ed* the level of perpetual snow —*Nature*⟩ **syn** see EXCEED

sur·pass·er \-sə(r)\ *n* **:** one that surpasses

¹**surpassing** *adj* **:** eminently excellent **:** greatly exceeding others **:** excelling something of ordinary character **:** of a very high degree ⟨the geometric pattern is of a ~ intricacy —R.H. Rovere⟩ ⟨a ~ performance⟩ ⟨a writer of ~ skill⟩

²**surpassing** *adv* **:** SURPASSINGLY ⟨a large and ~ ugly town —John Foster⟩

sur·pass·ing·ly *adv* **:** in a surpassing degree **:** EXCEEDINGLY ⟨she was a ~ beautiful woman —R.H.Davis⟩ ⟨the movie was a ~ stupid Western —T.O.Heggen⟩

¹**sur·plice** \ˈsərplə̇s, ˈsə̄p-, ˈsəip-\ *n* -S [ME *surplis*, fr. OF *surpliz*, fr. ML *superpellicium*, fr. L *super-* + ML *pellicium* shepherd's coat of skins, fr. L, neut. of *pellicius* made of skins, fr. *pellis* skin; fr. the fact that it was orig. worn over the fur coats customary in the churches of northern countries — more at FELL] **1 :** a loose white ecclesiastical vestment with large open sleeves that generally extends to the knees in length and that usu. is worn as a tunic over other garments by clergymen, acolytes, lay readers, and choristers in the Anglican, Roman Catholic, Moravian, and other churches **2 :** the cotta worn by Roman Catholic clergymen

surplice 1

²**surplice** \"\ *adj* **:** having the neckline extended on each side from the shoulder often to the opposite side seam with the lines crossing in the center ⟨a ~ collar⟩ ⟨a ~ closing of a dress⟩

sur·pliced \-st\ *adj* **1 :** wearing a surplice ⟨~ priests⟩ **2 :** having a surplice collar or neckline

¹**sur·plus** \ˈsər(ˌ)pləs, ˈsə̄(-, ˈsəi(-\ *n* -ES [ME, fr. MF, fr. ML *superplus*, fr. L *super-* + *plus* more — more at PLUS] **1 a :** the amount that remains when use or need is satisfied **b :** an excess of receipts over disbursements ⟨budget ~⟩ ⟨cash ~⟩ — opposed to *deficit* **c :** an excess of the net worth of a corporation over the par or stated value of its capital stock — compare CAPITAL SURPLUS, EARNED SURPLUS, PAID-IN SURPLUS, RESERVE ACCOUNT 3, UNDIVIDED PROFITS **2** *Brit* **:** the amount remaining **:** REST **syn** see EXCESS

²**surplus** \"\ *adj* **1 :** being more than sufficient for use or need **:** constituting a surplus ⟨the steady stream of ~ population from the farms —B.K.Sandwell⟩ ⟨sales of ~ wheat to Asian countries⟩ ⟨the poem . . . heavy with ~ phrasing —William Arrowsmith⟩ **2 :** remaining after the end of a period of specific need or use; *specif* **:** designed for but not used in war usu. as a result of a cessation of hostilities ⟨~ war material⟩ ⟨~ army blankets⟩ ⟨~ jeeps⟩

sur·plus·age \-sij\ *n* -S [ME, fr. ML, fr. ¹*surplus* + *-age*] **1 :** SURPLUS 1a ⟨characterized by literary ~⟩ **2 a :** a quantity of material (as words or matter) that is excessive and nonessential or useless ⟨say what you have to say . . . with no ~ —Walter Pater⟩ **b** (1) **:** matter introduced in legal pleading that is not necessary or relevant to the case and may therefore be rejected **:** matter in a pleading not material to it in form or substance — distinguished from *inducement* (2) **:** a part of a verbal document that is immaterial thereto in both matter and form **syn** see EXCESS

surplus value *n* **:** the difference in Marxist theory between the value of work done or of commodities produced by labor and the usu. subsistence wages paid by the employer — compare LABOR THEORY OF VALUE

¹**sur·print** \ˈsərˌprint\ *vt* [*sur-* + *print*] **1 :** OVERPRINT 1a **2 :** to superimpose (a negative) on a resensitized film already bearing a developed negative in making a printing plate that is to contain both images ⟨a photoengraving made from a line negative with a halftone negative ~*ed* on top of it⟩

²**surprint** \"\ *n* **1 :** OVERPRINT **2 a :** a surprinted image **b :** a plate made from a surprinted negative

sur·pris·able *R* sə(r)ˈprīzəbəl; *-R* səˈ-\ *adj* **:** capable of being surprised **:** liable to surprise

sur·pris·al \-zəl\ *n* -S **:** the action of surprising **:** the state of being surprised **:** SURPRISE ⟨warfare . . . by ambush and ~ —Washington Irving⟩

¹**sur·prise** *also* **sur·prize** \-īz\ *n* -S *often attrib* [*surprise* fr. ME, fr. MF, fr. fem. of OF *surpris*, past part. of *surprendre* to take over, fr. *sur-* + *prendre* to take, fr. L *prehendere* to seize, grasp; *surprize* alter. (influenced by ⁵*prize*) of *surprise* — more at PREHENSILE] **1 a** (1) **:** the action of assailing unexpectedly or attacking without warning **:** the sudden attacking and capture of something (as a fort or body of troops) unprepared ⟨a fortified camp . . . capable of resisting ~*s* —J.A.Froude⟩ (2) **:** the action of coming upon unexpectedly or taking unawares — used esp. in the phrase *take by surprise* **b :** an instance of taking unawares **c** *obs* **:** a sudden attack of illness or emotion **2 a :** something that surprises **:** an occasion for, a cause of, or a quality arousing astonishment **:** something (as an event) unexpected or astonishing ⟨many of the psychologic ~*s* of the first flight are pleasant —H.G.Armstrong⟩ ⟨his development . . . was probably a ~ to himself —A.W.Long⟩ ⟨offering few intellectual ~*s* —Harry Levin⟩ **b :** a pie or other fancy dish with agreeably surprising contents **3 :** the emotion excited by something sudden, unexpected, or contrary to expectation: **a** *archaic* **:** terror, perplexity, or alarm caused by a sudden attack or calamity ⟨gave a ~ and fear made me to quit the house —Shak.⟩ **b :** ASTONISHMENT, WONDER ⟨she never starts or shows ~ —Rose Macaulay⟩ ⟨the ~ which I felt on first learning of the award —E.C.Willatts⟩ ⟨gave a cry of delighted ~ —W.S.Maugham⟩ **4 :** the state of being mentally or emotionally surprised ⟨in his ~ he dropped the book⟩

²**surprise** *also* **surprize** \"\ *vt* -ED/-ING/-S [*surprise* fr. MF, fr. OF, fem. of *surpris*, past part. of *surprendre*; *surprize* alter. (influenced by ⁵*prize*) of *surprise*] **1** *obs* **a :** to take hold of **:** affect strongly and suddenly **:** SEIZE ⟨all on a sudden miserable pain *surpris'd* thee —John Milton⟩ ⟨*surprised* with joy at the motion —Daniel Defoe⟩ **b :** to seize and hold in one's possession **:** CAPTIVATE, OVERCOME, OVERPOWER ⟨power, like new wine, does your weak brain ~ —John Dryden⟩ **2 a :** to attack unexpectedly and without warning **:** assail suddenly **:** make an unexpected assault upon ⟨*surprised* the little garrison . . . and captured the arsenal —*Amer. Guide Series: Md.*⟩ ⟨at dawn the household was *surprised* by a sudden Indian attack —*Amer. Guide Series: N.H.*⟩ **b** (1) **:** to take suddenly by storm **:** seize or capture by a sudden and unexpected attack (2) *archaic* **:** to take possession of by force **:** make captive **:** take prisoner **:** CAPTURE, SEIZE **3 a :** to take unawares (as in an act or by an unexpected visit) **:** come upon abruptly or without warning **:** catch in the act ⟨police *surprised* the burglars leaving the store⟩ **b :** to bring out or to light by a sudden and unexpected action **:** detect, uncover, or elicit by taking (as a person) unawares ⟨*surprised* the secret of his murderous past through a stolen letter —Henri Peyre⟩ ⟨sometimes *surprised* a tragic shadow in her eyes —Willa Cather⟩ **4 a** *obs* **:** to ensnare or implicate by something (as a sudden disclosure or proposal) that takes one unawares **b :** to lead, impel, drive, or cause to do something or bring into some state in a sudden and unexpected way **:** lead on or betray into something not intended ⟨his debate . . . had *surprised* him into attacking the authority of the Pope —Stringfellow Barr⟩ ⟨*surprised* into an indiscretion⟩ **5 :** to strike with wonder or amazement because unexpected or different from what has been anticipated **:** affect with an emotion (as astonishment, awe, shock, or unexpected pleasure, disgust, or delight) ⟨the morning skies . . . *surprised* her daily as if they were uncommon things —Rebecca West⟩ ⟨his conduct *surprised* me⟩

syn ASTONISH, ASTOUND, AMAZE, FLABBERGAST: SURPRISE may indicate coming upon another suddenly and with startling effect; it may apply to any unexpected or unanticipated development bringing a degree of wonder ⟨the enemy was *surprised* —*Infantry Jour.*⟩ ⟨apt not only to be interested but also to be *surprised* by the experience life was holding in store for him —Joseph Conrad⟩ ASTONISH may indicate a surprising with the most unlikely, the unaccountable, or the incredible that virtually dazes one ⟨in the fashion of the magician who *astonishes* twice, once with the trick and again with its secret —L.J.Halle⟩ ⟨a flight that will *astonish* the world —Francis Stuart⟩ ASTOUND applies to the effect of what confounds, shocks, or stuns as unprecedented ⟨the girl was *astounded* and alarmed by the altogether unknown expression in the woman's face —Joseph Conrad⟩ ⟨*astounded* his congregation by putting up for sale a mulatto slave girl —*Amer. Guide Series: N. Y. City*⟩ AMAZE suggests astonished bewilderment or perplexity ⟨it *amazed* her that this soft little creature could be thus firm —George Meredith⟩ ⟨nothing *amazes* these people more than to see a man, apparently sane, meekly submitting to outrageous extortion —Norman Douglas⟩ FLABBERGAST may suggest thorough astonishment and often bewilderment or dismay ⟨his appointment *flabbergasted* those who knew his record⟩

surprised *past of* SURPRISE

sur·prised·ly \-zədlē, -zd-, -li\ *adv* **:** in the manner of one surprised

surprise party *n* **1 :** a party in honor of a person secretly arranged and provided for by friends as a surprise **2 :** an event or other occurrence held to resemble a surprise party in being unexpected although often of an unpleasant nature

sur·pris·er \-zə(r)\ *n* -S **:** one that surprises

surprises *pl of* SURPRISE, *pres 3d sing of* SURPRISE

surprising *adj* **1 :** of a nature to excite surprise **:** causing amazement or wonder esp. by being unexpected **:** AMAZING, ASTONISHING, UNLOOKED-FOR ⟨the commission's report shows a ~ lack of hard, factual data —*Monsanto Mag.*⟩ ⟨with ~ rapidity . . . their economic condition improved —*Amer. Guide Series: Oregon*⟩ **2** *archaic* **:** exciting admiration **:** ADMIRABLE

sur·pris·ing·ly *adv* **:** in a surprising manner or degree ⟨the casualties . . . had been ~ light —Alexander Forbes⟩ ⟨a ~ deft motion —Earle Birney⟩

surprize *var of* SURPRISE

surr *abbr* **1** surrender; surrendered **2** surrogate

sur·ra *also* **sur·rah** \ˈsu̇rə, ˈsərə\ *n* -S [Marathi *sūra* wheezing sound] **:** a severe Old World febrile and hemorrhagic disease marked by edema and anemia, caused by a flagellated protozoan (*Trypanosoma evansi*) transmitted by biting insects (as horseflies of the family Tabanidae), and commonly fatal in horses, mules, and camels although cattle and dogs often recover — compare TRYPANOSOMIASIS

sur·re·al·ism \səˈrēəˌlizəm *also* ¦sərˈ¦r *or* (ˈ)sē¦r\ *or* (ˈ)sü(r)¦r\ *or* (ˈ)su̇(ə)¦r\ *sometimes* ¦āə- *or* ¦sər-\ *or* ˈsəˈr\ *or* ˈsu̇r\ *n* [F *surréalisme*, fr. *sur-* + *réalisme* realism, fr. *réal* real (fr. MF) + *-isme* -ism — more at REAL] **:** the principles, ideals, or practice of producing fantastic or incongruous imagery in art or literature by means of unnatural juxtapositions and combinations

¹**sur·re·al·ist** \-ləst\ *or* **sur·re·al** \ēəl, ¦āəl\ *or* **sur·re·al·is·tic** \sə¦rēə¦listik, ¦sər-, ¦sə-r, -tēk *also* ¦sər-¦r *or* (ˈ)sē¦r *or* (ˈ)sü(r)¦r *or* (ˈ)su̇(ə)¦r *sometimes* ¦āə- *or* ¦su̇r\ *adj* [*surrealist* fr. F *surréaliste* realist; *surreal* back-formation fr. *surrealism*; *surrealistic* fr. ²*surrealist* + *-ic* — more at REALIST] **1 :** of, relating to, or having the characteristics of surrealism ⟨a ~ film⟩ ⟨~ art⟩ ⟨~ literature⟩ ⟨a ~ painter⟩ **2 :** of, relating to, or resembling mental free association

²**surrealist** \"\ *n* **:** one that adheres to, practices, or follows surrealism

sur·re·al·is·ti·cal·ly \-tik(ə)lē\ *adv* **:** in a surrealist manner ⟨the ice runs ~ riot in a phantasma of frozen sculpture —Glen Jacobsen⟩

sur·rebut \ˌsər+\ *vi* [*sur-* + *rebut*] **:** to reply by or in a surrebutter

sur·rebutter *also* **sur·rebuttal** \"+\ *n* [*sur-* + *rebutter*, *rebuttal*] **:** the reply in common law pleading of a plaintiff to a defendant's rebutter

sur·rejoin \"+\ *vi* [*sur-* + *rejoin*] **:** to reply by or in a surrejoinder

sur·rejoinder \"+\ *n* [*sur-* + *rejoinder*] **1 :** the answer in common law pleading of a plaintiff to a defendant's rejoinder **2 :** an answer (as to a rejoinder) held to resemble a surrejoinder in common law pleading

¹**sur·ren·der** \səˈrendə(r)\ *vb* **surrendered; surrendered; surrendering** \-d(ə)riŋ\ **surrenders** [ME *surrenderen*, fr. MF *surrendre*, fr. *sur-* + *rendre* to deliver, yield — more at RENDER] *vt* **1 :** to make a surrender in law of: as **a :** to give up (an estate) to the holder in remainder or reversion **b :** to relinquish (as rights or claims under a patent) to the grantor **c :** to deliver (the principal) into lawful custody **2 a :** to yield to the power, control, authority, or possession of another **:** give or deliver up possession of upon compulsion or demand **:** cease trying to retain or control and agree to yield ⟨~*ed* the fort⟩ ⟨forced to ~ the ship⟩ ⟨the continental firm ~*s* the dollars to its own bank at the official exchange rate —R.F.Mikesell⟩ **b :** to give up completely or agree to forgo esp. in favor of another **:** abandon, resign, or relinquish

possession of usu. for the sake of another **:** assent to loss of possession or exercise of or power or control over ⟨~*ed* his chair to the lady⟩ ⟨benefits bestowed by science which we are not anxious to ~ —J.W.Krutch⟩ **3 a :** to give (oneself) up into the power of another esp. as a prisoner **b :** to give (oneself) over to something (as an influence or course of action) **:** abandon or devote (as oneself) entirely to something without restraint, reservation, or further resistance ⟨the individual . . . has ~*ed* himself to destructive ideologies —F.E.Hill⟩ ⟨~*ed* his mind to more frivolous pursuits —George Meredith⟩ **~** *vi* **:** to give oneself up into the power of another **:** YIELD ⟨ordered the troops to ~⟩ ⟨the enemy must soon ~⟩ **syn** see RELINQUISH

²surrender \"\ *n* -s [ME, fr. AF, fr. MF *surrendre* to deliver, yield (taken as a n.)] **1 a :** the action of yielding one's person or giving up the possession of something into the power of another **:** ABANDONMENT, RESIGNATION ⟨complete ~ of initiative to the adversary —S.L.A.Marshall⟩ ⟨the heroine's . . . ~ to drugs, nymphomania, or catatonic dementia —Malcolm Cowley⟩ **b :** the action of yielding a particular estate to the person who has an immediate estate in remainder or reversion, merging the surrendered estate in the greater one ⟨the ~ of a lease to the landlord before its expiration⟩ ⟨the ~ of a legal tenancy in a copyhold estate to the lord of the manor⟩ — compare RELEASE, RENUNCIATION **c :** the relinquishment by a patentee of his rights or claims under a patent **d** *or* **surrender by bail :** the delivery of a principal into lawful custody by his bail **e :** the assignment of his assets to his creditors by a usu. bankrupt debtor **f :** the voluntary cancellation of the legal liability of an insurance company by the insured and beneficiary for a consideration — see SURRENDER VALUE **g :** the delivering up of a fugitive from justice by one government (as of a foreign country) to another — compare EXTRADITION 1 **2 :** an instance of surrendering

surrender charge *n* **:** a forfeit or penalty generally charged by a life insurance company against the value of a policy surrendered or allowed to lapse

sur·ren·der·ee \sə¦rendə¦rē\ *n* -s [¹*surrender* + *-ee*] **:** one to whom a surrender (as of an estate) is made

sur·ren·der·or \sə'rendərə(r), sə¦rendə¦rȯ(ə)r\ *n* -s [¹*surrender* + *-or*] **:** one that makes a surrender (as of an estate)

surrender value *n* **:** the cash value of an insurance policy that may be taken in cash or applied to the purchase of fractional paid-up or extended term insurance

sur·ren·dry \sə'rendrē\ *n* -ES [¹*surrender* + *-ry*] *archaic* **:** SURRENDER

sur·rep·ti·tious \¦sər·əp¦tishəs, ¦sə·rəp-\ *adj* [ME *surrepticious*, fr. L *surrepticius*, *surreptitius*, fr. *surreptus* (past part. of *surripere*, *subripere* to snatch away, take away secretly, fr. *sub-* secretly, under + *-ripere*, fr. *rapere* to seize) + *-icius*, *-itius* -itious — more at SUB-, RAPID] **1 :** marked or accomplished by fraud or suppression of truth ⟨a ~ ordinance⟩ **2 a :** executed, obtained, used, done, or attended with often clever or deft circumvention of proper standards, sanction, or authority **:** enjoyed by stealth **:** CLANDESTINE ⟨a ~ removal of goods⟩ ⟨~ pleasures⟩ **b :** of fraudulent, spurious, or unauthorized issue **:** made or introduced fraudulently ⟨a ~ copy of a book⟩ **c :** acting in secret or by stealth **:** doing something clandestinely **:** SLY, STEALTHY ⟨glancing at the clock with a ~ eye —H.S. Scott⟩ **syn** see SECRET

sur·rep·ti·tious·ly *adv* **:** in a surreptitious manner ⟨publication was continued ~ during the war —*Amer. Guide Series: Va.*⟩

surreverence *obs var of* SIR-REVERENCE

¹sur·rey \'sər·|ē, 'sə·r|, |i\ *adj*, *usu cap* [fr. *Surrey*, county in southern England] **:** of or from the county of Surrey, England **:** of the kind or style prevalent in Surrey

²surrey \"\ *n* -s [fr. *Surrey (cart)*, English pleasure cart with an open spindle seat introduced into the U.S. in 1872, fr. *Surrey*, county in southern England where it was first built] **1 :** a four-wheel 2-seated pleasure carriage resembling a cabriolet but having a straight or nearly straight bottom and sometimes cut under **2 :** an early motor vehicle resembling a surrey in design

surrey

surrey green *n*, *often cap S* **:** a grayish yellow green to pale green that is darker than the color tea

sur·ro·ga·cy \'sərəgəsē\ *n* -ES **:** the office of surrogate

¹sur·ro·gate \'sərə,gāt, *usu* -ād·+V\ *vt* -ED/-ING/-S [L *surrogatus*, past part. of *surrogare*, *subrogare* to substitute, fr. *sub-* in place of, under + *rogare* to ask — more at RIGHT] **:** to put in the place of another: **a :** to appoint as successor, deputy, or substitute for oneself **b :** SUBSTITUTE

²sur·ro·gate \-,gāt, -,gət, *usu* -d·+V\ *n* -s [L *surrogatus*, past part. of *surrogare*, *subrogare* to substitute] **1 a :** a person appointed to act in place of another **:** DELEGATE, DEPUTY, SUBSTITUTE ⟨the Lord Chief Justice . . . acted as ~ for the Earl Marshal —*Notes & Queries*⟩ ⟨college presidents or their ~*s* appealed for a revival of idealism —M.J.Adler⟩ **b :** the deputy of an ecclesiastical judge (as a bishop or a bishop's chancellor) in the Church of England; *esp* **:** one who grants marriage licenses **c :** a local judicial officer in New York and some other states who has jurisdiction over the probate of wills and testaments and the settlement of estates and often has power to appoint and supervise guardians of infants and other incompetent persons — compare PREROGATIVE COURT **2 a :** something that replaces or serves as a substitute for another ⟨the letter *y* as a ~ for *i* —Arthur Minton⟩ ⟨regard written language as only a ~ of oral communication —J.B. Carroll⟩ **b :** an artificial or synthetic product used as a substitute for a natural product **c :** a representation of a person substituted through symbolizing (as in a dream) for conscious recognition of the person ⟨persons like teachers who represent mother ~*s* —R.R.Sears⟩ **syn** see RESOURCE

³surrogate \"\ *adj* **:** constituting a surrogate **:** serving in place of or standing for something else **:** SUBSTITUTE ⟨a sort of ~ father to him —Brendan Gill⟩ ⟨introduces a native girl to offer the grieving husband a ~ satisfaction —John Barkham⟩

sur·ro·ga·tion \,sərə'gāshən\ *n* -s [ML *surrogation-*, *surrogatio*, fr. L *surrogatus* (past part.) + *-ion-*, *-io* -ion] **1 :** the action of surrogating **:** SUBSTITUTION, SUBROGATION **2 :** an instance of surrogating

¹sur·round \sə'raůnd\ *vb* -ED/-ING/-S [ME *surrounden* to overflow, modif. (influenced by *rounden* to round) of MF *suronder*, *souronder*, fr. LL *superundare*, fr. L *super-* + *undare* to rise in waves, fr. *unda* wave — more at ROUND, WATER] *vt* **1** *obs* **:** to flow over the banks of **:** FLOOD, INUNDATE, OVERFLOW, SUBMERGE **2** [influenced in meaning by ⁶*round*] **:** to be situated or found around, about, or in a ring around: as **a :** to throng, press, or cluster around ⟨the crowd ~*ed* the victor⟩ **b :** to live around on all or most sides ⟨clearly distinct from the more negroid people who ~ them —C.D. Forde⟩ **c :** to form or be in the retinue, entourage, or court of ⟨flatterers who ~ the duke⟩ **d :** to be present around, about, or near in the character of an attribute, characteristic, or natural or accustomed motif ⟨we sit ~*ed* by objects which perpetually express the oddity of our own temperaments —Virginia Woolf⟩ **e :** to constitute part of the determining environment or accustomed condition of **:** ENVIRON ⟨the snow and ice which ~ the earth's polar regions —J.G.Vaeth⟩ **f :** to form a ring around **:** extend around or about the edge of **:** constitute a curving or circular boundary for **:** lie adjacent to all around or in most directions **:** ENCIRCLE ⟨woodland patches ~ the village —*Amer. Guide Series: Vt.*⟩ ⟨house ~*ed* on three sides by a wide veranda —*Amer. Guide Series: N.H.*⟩ **g** (1) **:** to envelop in or as if in a cloud or mist ⟨a fog ~*s* the ship⟩ ⟨complete secrecy ~*ed* the meeting —*Current History*⟩ ⟨the silence that ~*ed* them —Walter O'Meara⟩ (2) **:** to encase or cover like pulp around a core ⟨a hard black shell ~*ed* by a pulpy, fibrous covering —Tom Marvel⟩ **h :** to occur or be next, near, adjacent to, or before and after in a sequence or order ⟨the years that ~*ed* the American Revolution⟩ **3 :** to cause to be encompassed, encircled, or enclosed with something ⟨~*ed* himself with outstanding men —*Phoenix Flame*⟩ ⟨sought to ~ the international liquor traffic with serious restrictions —D.W.McConnell⟩ **4 a** *obs* **:** CIRCUMNAVIGATE **b** *chiefly Midland* **:** to pass or walk around **5 :** to enclose (as a city or a body of troops) so as to cut off communication or retreat **:** INVEST **~** *vi*, *obs* **:** to overflow the banks — used of a body of water

syn ENVIRON, ENCIRCLE, CIRCLE, RING, ENCOMPASS, COMPASS, GIRD, GIRDLE, HEM: SURROUND is a general term not esp. rich in connotation and often interchangeable with the following in situations indicating a being all around rather than a having gone all around, a traversing on a circular course ⟨the noisy, slovenly, argumentative militiamen who had *surrounded* Boston —Kenneth Roberts⟩ ⟨the unseen power which *surrounds* us —W.R.Inge⟩ ENVIRON is likely to suggest lasting situation around, as though enclosing, and forming part of an environment ⟨the passions and motives of the savage world which underlies as well as *environs* civilization —W.D. Howells⟩ ENCIRCLE may stress the idea of a circle, either a circle described by a route, march, or voyage or one enclosing something with or as if with something tangible, material, and lasting ⟨the close which *encircles* the venerable cathedral —T.B. Macaulay⟩ ⟨faster planes now *encircle* the world in a few hours⟩ CIRCLE means and connotes about the same things as ENCIRCLE; the latter may more strongly suggest completeness or perfect roundness of the figure described ⟨his eyes were darkly *circled* —Booth Tarkington⟩ ⟨the Vernon House . . . is *circled* with two rows of windows —*Amer. Guide Series: R.I.*⟩ RING is a close synonym, sometimes more vivid, for CIRCLE; it is not, however, generally used to indicate a traversing or course ⟨a septuagenarian whose few sad last grey hairs, *ringing* an otherwise completely bald head —*Irish Digest*⟩ ENCOMPASS suggests an encircling which includes, discourages entrance or exit, or ensheathes and envelops ⟨the strong fortress-walls which had long *encompassed* him —Charles Dickens⟩ ⟨whenever he moved beyond the walls . . . the drawn swords and cuirasses of his trusty bodyguard *encompassed* him thick —T.B.Macaulay⟩ ⟨nature was a presence which *encompassed* him widely —R.L.Cook⟩ COMPASS often suggests an enclosing which covers and protects or which envelops and weighs down ⟨we must be humble, for we are *compassed* by mysteries —W.R.Inge⟩ GIRD may indicate an encircling of or as if of the waist of a person, esp. with whatever arms, strengthens, or encourages ⟨Christian religious energy *girded* its loins with the cords of Francis and Dominic —H.O.Taylor⟩ GIRDLE may suggest any encirclement like that of a belt, sash, or zone ⟨the great coastal plain which *girdles* the United States —Forrest Morgan⟩ HEM, in this sense, is likely to suggest an encirclement that confines and prevents or makes difficult escape, exit, or activity ⟨the constables were *hemmed* in so closely that they could make no use of their pikes —T.B.Costain⟩ ⟨the rocky walls which, with the deep-flowing river, *hemmed* Matadi in on all sides —Tom Marvel⟩

²surround \"\ *n* -s **1 a :** a method of hunting wild animals (as the buffalo or the vicuña) by surrounding a herd and driving the animals into a circle, a ravine, or other place from which they cannot escape **b :** the action of hunting by this method **c :** the area encompassed by hunters using this method **2 :** something that surrounds: as **a** *chiefly Brit* **:** something (as a border or edging) surrounding or nearly surrounding a central object or area ⟨the brass ~ of the electric bell —Elizabeth Bowen⟩ ⟨took tea out on the paved ~ of the swimming pool —G.A.Wagner⟩ ⟨the ~ of low brown hills —Louis Allen⟩ ⟨a fireplace ~⟩ **b :** the area of illumination surrounding a test object on a motion picture or television screen ⟨the ~ should be about of equal brightness with the test field —R.S. Woodworth⟩

sur·round·er \-də(r)\ *n* -s **:** one that surrounds

surrounding *n* -s [fr. gerund of ¹*surround*] **1 surroundings** *pl* **:** the circumstances, conditions, or objects by which one is surrounded **:** ENVIRONMENT ⟨extraordinarily uninterested in his physical ~*s* —Arnold Bennett⟩ ⟨the village is . . . notable for the great beauty of its ~*s* —*Amer. Guide Series: N.H.*⟩ **2 :** ENTOURAGE — sometimes used in pl.

surrounds *pres 3d sing of* SURROUND

sur·royal \,sər+\ *n* [ME *surryal*, fr. *sur-* + *ryal*, *royal* tres-tine, royal antler — more at ROYAL] **:** one of the terminal tines above the royal antler of a stag or other large deer usu. attained at the age of four years — see ANTLER illustration

sur·sass·ite \,sər'sa,sīt\ *n* -s [*Sursass* (Oberhalbstein), eastern Switzerland, its locality + E *-ite*] **:** a mineral $Mn_5Al_4Si_5O_{21}.3H_2O$ of the epidote group consisting of a hydrous silicate of manganese and aluminum

sursum- *comb form* [L *susum*, *sursum* under, from below, upwards, fr. *subs-* (var. of *sub-*) + *versum*, neut. of *versus*, past part. of *vertere* to turn — more at WORTH] **:** upward ⟨*sursumvergence*⟩

sur·sum cor·da \¦sərsəm'kȯrdə, ¦sůr-\ *n* [LL, lift up the hearts; fr. the words addressed by the celebrant to the congregation before the eucharistic preface] **1** *often cap S&C* **:** a versicle or portion of Christian liturgy inviting the congregation to join in thanksgiving to God **2 :** something held to resemble the sursum corda: **a :** an incitement to fervor or courage **b :** an exaltation of mood or spirits

sur·tax \'sər,taks, 'sə̄,-\ *n* [*sur-* + *tax*] **:** an additional or extra tax: as **a :** a special tax levied against certain classes of persons or goods over and above the general charge upon the whole group **:** an extra charge (as on a railroad for special accommodations) **b :** a graduated income tax in addition to the normal income tax imposed on the amount by which the net income of an individual exceeds a specified sum — called also *additional tax*; compare SUPERTAX **c :** a supplementary tax added at a later date than the normal rates (as in customs duties) **d :** the charge made on a semipostal stamp above the amount required for postage

sur·ti \'sərd·ē\ *n* -s *usu cap* [native name in India] **:** MURRAH

¹sur·tout \,sər'tü, -üt\ *n* -s [F, fr. *sur* over (fr. L *super*) + *tout* all, fr. L *totus* — more at OVER] **1 :** a man's fitted coat or overcoat; *esp* **:** FROCK COAT **2 :** a woman's hood with a mantle

²surtout \"\ *adv* [F] **:** over all; *specif* **:** above other heraldic charges

sur·tur·brand \'sərd·ər,brand\ *n* -s [Icel *surtarbrandr* jet, surturbrand, fr. *Surtr*, giant fire demon in Scandinavian legend (akin to ON *svartr* black) + Icel *brandr* firebrand, fr. ON — more at SWART, BRAND] **:** a variety of lignite in Iceland and the Faeroes occurring in seams between beds of volcanic rock

su·ru·cu·cu \¦surəkə¦kü, -rəkü¦kü\ *n* -s [Tupi *surucucú*] **:** BUSHMASTER

surv *abbr* **1** survey; surveying; surveyor **2** surviving

sur·veil·lance \sə(r)'vālən(t)s *also* -lyən-\ *n* -s [F, fr. *surveiller* to watch over (fr. *sur-* + *veiller* to watch, fr. L *vigilare* to watch, wake, fr. *vigil* awake, watchful) + *-ance* — more at VIGIL] **1 :** close watch kept over one or more persons **:** continuous observation of a person or area (as to detect developments, movements, or activities) ⟨place a suspected person under police ~⟩ ⟨~ of air traffic by radar⟩ **2 :** close and continuous observation for the purpose of direction, supervision, or control ⟨club facilities . . . are conducted under close ~ of the U. S. Forest Service —Jean Lunzer⟩ ⟨place the disputed territory under UN ~⟩

sur·veil·lant \-nt\ *n* -s [F, fr. pres. part. of *surveiller* to watch over] **:** one that exercises surveillance over another

¹sur·vey \sə(r)'vā, ,sər'-, sə̄'-, səi'-, '=,=\ *vb* **surveyed; surveyed; surveying; surveys** [ME *surveyen*, fr. MF *surveer*, *surveeir*, *surveoir* to look over, survey, fr. *sur-* + *veer*, *veeir*, *veoir* to look, see — more at VIEW] *vt* **1 a :** to look over or examine with reference to condition, situation, or value **:** examine and ascertain the state of **:** APPRAISE, ESTIMATE, EVALUATE ⟨hired to ~ a manor for its extent, value, ownership, and liabilities⟩ **b :** to have oversight of **:** SUPERVISE **c :** to make a usu. statistical survey of ⟨~ population growth in the southern counties⟩ **d** (1) **:** to make an investigation and fix responsibility for destruction, loss, or damage of (as military equipment) (2) **:** to inspect (as equipment or supplies) to determine whether retention as serviceable or condemnation as unserviceable is advisable (3) **:** to retire (as men or equipment) from active duty after inspection **2 :** to determine and delineate the form, extent, and position of (as a tract of land, a coast, or a harbor) by taking linear and angular measurements and by applying the principles of geometry and trigonometry **3 a :** to view from or as if from a high place or a commanding position **:** take an inclusive or overall view of **:** consider or study comprehensively **:** examine to the whole extent ⟨silently ~*ed* the beautiful panorama below them —L.C.Douglas⟩ ⟨~ almost the whole mass of contemporary literature —S.E.Hyman⟩ **b :** make, write, or present a survey of **:** outline or describe in or as if in an overall inclusive generalized study ⟨a series of lectures which ~ the entire field of cardiology —*Bull. of Meharry Med. Coll.*⟩ **c** *obs* **:** OBSERVE, PERCEIVE, SEE **4 :** to view with a scrutinizing eye **:** examine carefully and closely the salient features or details of **:** look carefully into or through **:** inspect closely, searchingly, or in detail **:** SCRUTINIZE ⟨she . . . ~*ed* herself in the pier glass —James Joyce⟩ ⟨he ~*ed* us in a lordly way —Alan Harrington⟩ **5 :** to grade and measure (lumber) **~** *vi* **:** to make a survey **syn** see SEE

²sur·vey \'sər,vā, 'sə̄,-, 'səi,- *sometimes* sə(r)'vā *or* ,sər'- *or* sə̄'- *or* səi'-\ *n* -s *often attrib* **1 a** (1) **:** a critical examination or inspection often of an official character for an implied or specified purpose **:** the action of ascertaining facts regarding conditions or the condition of something to provide exact information esp. to persons responsible or interested ⟨~ of a state's roads⟩ ⟨a ~ of the schools in the area⟩ ⟨unemployment ~*s*⟩ (2) **:** an examination of a ship or a part of its cargo or equipment to determine its condition, responsibility for damage, and disposition to be made (3) **:** a study of a specified area or aggregate of units (as human beings) usu. with respect to a special condition or its prevalence or with the objective of drawing conclusions about a larger area or aggregate **:** a systematic collection and analysis of data and esp. statistical data on some aspect of an area or group ⟨a telephone ~ of major U.S. companies . . . in the atom business —Ray Cromley⟩ ⟨made a ~ . . . of farm production in the Midwest —*Current Biog.*⟩ **b :** a report, study, or document presenting the results of such an examination **2 a :** the action of looking at something from a high or commanding position **:** a general or comprehensive view ⟨resumed her ~ of the landscape —Anne D. Sedgwick⟩ **b :** a broad undetailed consideration or treatment of something **:** a history, exposition, or description presenting the outlines only ⟨competent ~*s* of the literatures of India, China, and Japan —*Times Lit. Supp.*⟩ ⟨continue his illustrated ~ of the music of southern Africa —*London Calling*⟩ — see SURVEY COURSE **3 a :** the process of surveying an area of land or water **:** the operation of finding and delineating the contour, dimensions, and position of any part of the earth's surface whether land or water ⟨a topographic and hydrographic ~ of a locality —C.H.Deetz⟩ **b :** a measured plan and description of a portion of an area or of a road or line through an area obtained by surveying **c :** an organization (as a government agency) engaged in surveying **4 :** something that is surveyed: **a** *archaic* **:** a delineation of a scene **:** VIEW **b :** PROSPECT **syn** see COMPENDIUM

sur·vey·able \(,)sər'vāəbəl\ *adj* **:** capable of being surveyed

survey agent *n* **:** a local agent (as of a fire insurance company) who is not authorized to write policies but must send applications directly to the company

sur·vey·al \(,)sə(r)'vā(ə)l\ *n* -s **:** the action of surveying **:** SURVEY ⟨her ~ of the room —Speed Lamkin⟩

sur·vey·ance \-āən(t)s\ *n* -s **1** *archaic* **:** SURVEY ⟨the expenses of ~ and sale —*American*⟩ **2 :** SURVEILLANCE

survey course *n* **:** a course treating briefly the chief topics of one or several allied broad fields of knowledge

surveyed *past of* SURVEY

sur·vey·ing \(,)sər'vāiŋ, sə'-\ *n* -s [ME, fr. gerund of *surveyen* to survey] **:** the action or occupation of one that surveys; *specif* **:** a branch of applied mathematics that teaches the art of determining the area of any portion of the earth's surface, the lengths and directions of the bounding lines, and the contour of the surface and of accurately delineating the whole on paper — see GEODETIC SURVEYING, HYDROGRAPHIC SURVEYING, PLANE SURVEYING

surveying sextant *n* **:** a light sextant with a large scale used in hydrographic surveying

survey meter *n* **:** an instrument sensitive to ionizing radiations used in prospecting for radioactive deposits

survey number *n* **:** a serial number for antimalarial drugs

sur·vey·or \(,)sər'vāər; sə'vāə(r, sə̄'-, səi'-\ *n* -s [ME *surveyour*, fr. MF *surveiour*, fr. *surveer* to look over, survey + *-our* -or — more at SURVEY] **1 :** one acting as an overseer or superintendent: as **a :** a government official having the functions of superintendence, administration, or inspection over a usu. specified area of responsibility (as a department or office) ⟨~ of highways⟩ **b :** one having oversight of the lands and boundaries of an estate **2** *Brit* **:** ARCHITECT; *esp* **:** one in charge of construction — see QUANTITY SURVEYOR **3 :** one that surveys land and other surfaces **:** one that practices the art of surveying **4 :** one that takes a view and esp. a mental view of something **:** one that examines, contemplates, or beholds ⟨some recent ~*s* of the present scene —H.W.Baehr⟩ **5 a :** one that views and examines with the purpose of ascertaining the condition, quantity, or quality of something ⟨the ~ inspected the damaged ship⟩ **b** (1) **:** a customs officer who ascertains the contents of casks and the quantity of dutiable liquors **:** GAUGER (2) **:** a customs officer formerly carrying out measures for ascertaining the quantity, condition, and value of merchandise brought into a port **6 a :** one that inspects and tallies lumber in cargo lots **b :** one that marks and tallies lumber as it comes from the saw **7 :** one that makes a survey

surveyor general *n*, *pl* **surveyors general** *or* **surveyor generals :** a principal or superintending surveyor: as **a :** an official having general oversight (as over an area, department, or function) ⟨*surveyor general* of army purchases during World War I⟩ ⟨*surveyor general* of the king's manors⟩ **b :** a U.S. government official in charge of the survey of public lands in a particular area (as a state)

surveyor's compass *or* **surveyor's dial** *n* **:** an instrument used in surveying for measuring horizontal angles — compare CIRCUMFERENTOR 1, SEMICIRCUMFERENTOR

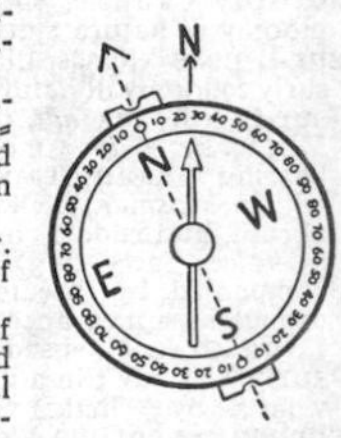

surveyor's compass

surveyor's cross *n* **:** a simple instrument made of two bars forming a right-angled cross with sights at each end and used in setting out right angles in surveying

sur·vey·or·ship \-,ship\ *n* [ME, fr. *surveyour* + *-ship*] **:** the office of surveyor

surveyor's level *n* **:** a level consisting of a telescope and a spirit level mounted on a tripod, revolving on a vertical axis, and having leveling screws provided for adjustment — compare DUMPY LEVEL, Y LEVEL

surveyor's measure *n* **:** a system of measurement having the surveyor's chain as a unit and used in land surveying — compare CHAIN 1c(1)

surveyor's rod *n* **:** LEVELING ROD

surveys *pres 3d sing of* SURVEY, *pl of* SURVEY

¹sur·view \sə(r)'vyü\ *n* [ME *survewe* inspection, survey, fr. MF *surveue*, fr. fem. of *surveu*, past part. of *surveer* to survey] *archaic* **:** SURVEY

²surview \"\ *vt*, *archaic* **:** to take a general or overall view of **:** view as a whole

sur·vi·grous \sə(r)'vigrəs\ *adj* [*sur-* + *vigorous*] *chiefly South & Midland* **:** extremely vigorous **:** very active, enterprising, or fierce

sur·viv·abil·i·ty \sə(r),vīvə'biləd·ē\ *n* **:** the quality or state of being survivable

sur·viv·able \sə(r)'vīvəbəl\ *adj* **1 :** capable of surviving **2 :** resulting in or permitting survival ⟨~ accidents⟩

sur·viv·al \sə(r)'vīvəl\ *n* -s *often attrib* [*survive* + *-al*] **1 a :** the action of living longer than another person or beyond something (as a time, event, development, or condition) ⟨the wife's ~ of her husband⟩ ⟨the ~ of the soul after death⟩ **b :** the continuance of something (as a custom) after the end of the period or the cessation of the conditions in which it had significance **c :** the continuation of life or existence in the presence of or despite usu. difficult conditions ⟨the biological needs of ~ and reproduction —Flanders Dunbar⟩ ⟨problems of ~ in arctic conditions⟩ **2 a :** one that survives or remains after others of its kind have disappeared : one that continues to exist after the cessation of something : a surviving individual or remnant ⟨~s of classical sculpture which . . . existed in Byzantium —O. Elfrida Saunders⟩ **b :** a culture trait remaining from former times but with diminished significance or with a function or utility meaningful only in terms of past history **c :** a linguistic feature that has escaped extinction or has resisted change

sur·viv·al·ism \-īvə,lizəm\ *n* -s **:** an attitude, policy, or practice based on the primacy of survival as a value ⟨the trend is away . . . from aggressive expansionism toward realistic ~ —Frank Gorrell⟩

survival kit *n* **:** a compact package of emergency equipment including food and other items that vary with climatic factors in the operational area for use by aircrew members who have descended in isolated or primitive territory

survival of actions : the continuance of proceedings in law despite the death of one or both of the parties involved

survival of the fittest : NATURAL SELECTION

survival value *n* **:** utility (as of one or more characters or qualities of an organism) in the struggle for existence

sur·viv·ance \sə(r)ˈvīvən(t)s\ *n* -s [F, fr. MF, fr. *survivant,* after such pairs as MF *abundant: abundance*] **1 :** SURVIVAL **2 :** the right of succession (as to an office or estate) of a survivor nominated before the death of the incumbent or holder

sur·viv·ant \sə(r)ˈvīvənt\ *adj* [MF, pres. part. of *survivre* to survive] *archaic* **:** continuing to survive **:** surviving something

sur·vive \sə(r)ˈvīv\ *vb* -ED/-ING/-S [ME *surviven,* fr. MF *survivre,* fr. L *supervivere,* fr. *super-* + *vivere* to live — more at QUICK] *vi* **1 :** to remain alive or in existence (as after another's death, or a time, event, disaster, or development, or the end of a condition) **:** live on **:** continue to exist or function ⟨pioneer methods of husbandry still ~ —E.C.Higbee⟩ ⟨men trained to ~ under severe conditions —*Boy Scout Handbk.*⟩ ⟨numerous . . . eighteenth-century houses ~ —*Amer. Guide Series: N.Y. City*⟩ ~ *vt* **1 :** to live beyond the life or existence of **:** live longer than ⟨only his son *survived* him⟩ **2 :** to continue to exist or live after (as a time or event) **:** outlast the end of (as a condition or development) ⟨other important leaders *survived* the explosion —*Current Biog.*⟩ ⟨one in a million of these childish talents ~s puberty —Aldous Huxley⟩ ⟨one of the few schools to ~ the 1857 panic —*Amer. Guide Series: Minn.*⟩ **3 :** to continue to exist, function, or compete despite (as a condition or development) ⟨ferries have *survived* the competition of the tunnels —*Amer. Guide Series: N.J.*⟩ ⟨one of the few Democrats . . . to ~ a Republican sweep —*Current Biog.*⟩ ⟨fishes are known to ~ conditions well below freezing-point —W.H.Dowdeswell⟩ **syn** see OUTLIVE

sur·viv·er \-īvə(r)\ *n* -s *archaic* **:** SURVIVOR

surviving *adj* **:** remaining alive or in existence ⟨some ~ friend of my youth —W.B.Yeats⟩ ⟨the only ~ frontier blockhouse in Pennsylvania —*Amer. Guide Series: Pa.*⟩

sur·vi·vor \sərˈvīvər, səˈvīvə(r\ *n* -s **:** one that survives: **a :** one that outlives another **:** one remaining alive after another's death **b :** one of two or more legally designated persons (as joint tenants or holders of a joint interest) who outlives one or more of the others **c :** one living through a time, event, or development marked by the death of others ⟨interviewed ~s of the air raid⟩ **d :** one continuing to exist, function, or compete after others have ceased to do so ⟨~s of the first heat⟩ ⟨only ~ of six newspapers founded in the 19th century⟩

sur·vi·vor·ship \-,ship\ *n* **1 :** the legal right of the survivor of two or more persons having joint interests in an estate or other property to take the interest of any of the number dying ⟨when more than two survive, the survivors receive the decedent's share subject to similar ~ in those left⟩ — see PRESUMPTION OF SURVIVORSHIP **2 :** the state or condition of being a survivor **:** SURVIVAL

survivorship annuity *n* **:** an annuity payable to a designated person in the event he survives an insured person or other designated beneficiary of the annuity

sus \ˈsəs\ *n, cap* [NL, fr. L, swine, hog — more at SOW] **:** a genus of mammals that is the type of the family Suidae and in former classifications comprised all or most of the swine but is usu. restricted to a few typical Eurasian and East Indian forms and the domestic breeds — see BEARDED PIG, CRESTED PIG, WILD BOAR

su·san \ˈsüzᵊn\ *n* -s [*lazy susan*] **:** LAZY SUSAN

su·san·nite \süˈza,nīt\ *n* -s [modif. of G *suzannit,* fr. *Susanna* mine, Leadhills, Scotland, where it was discovered + G *-it* -ite] **:** LEADHILLITE

sus·cept \səˈsept\ *n* -s [prob. fr. ¹*susceptible*] **:** an organism upon or in which another organism is or may become parasitic — compare HOST

sus·cep·tance \səˈseptən(t)s\ *n* -s [*susceptibility* + *-ance* (as in *conductance*)] **:** the ratio of the effective current to the effective electromotive force in an alternating-current circuit multiplied by the sine of the phase difference between current and electromotive force

sus·cep·ti·bil·i·ty \sə,septəˈbiləd·ē, -lətē, -i\ *n* -ES [ML *susceptibilitat-, susceptibilitas,* fr. LL *susceptibilis* susceptible + L *-itat-, -itas* -ity] **1 :** the quality or state of being susceptible **:** capability of or capacity for being acted upon, impressed, affected, or moved ⟨~ of a city to a submarine attack⟩ ⟨~ of a metal to corrosion⟩; *specif* **:** the state of being sensitive or predisposed (as to a pathogen, familial disease, drug) **:** SENSITIVITY, IDIOSYNCRASY 2b ⟨the ~ of a plant to a virus⟩ ⟨a test for ~ to scarlet fever⟩ — compare RESISTANCE, SPECIES SPECIFICITY **2 a :** a susceptible temperament, nature, or constitution **:** the character of being sensitive, affectible, impressionable, emotional ⟨the ~ of various social groups to Communist doctrine —Sidney Hook⟩ or esp. amorous ⟨his ~ to women interfered with his impartial judgment⟩ **b susceptibilities** *pl* **:** FEELINGS, SENSIBILITIES ⟨the mere thought of the enormity did outrage to her moral *susceptibilities* —Arnold Bennett⟩ ⟨when present at a ceremonial, the utmost care must be taken not to do or say anything to offend the *susceptibilities* of the people —*Notes & Queries on Anthropology*⟩ **3 a :** the ratio of the magnetization in a substance to the corresponding magnetizing force **b :** the ratio of the electric polarization to the electric intensity in a polarized dielectric

¹**sus·cep·ti·ble** \səˈseptəbəl\ *adj* [LL *susceptibilis,* fr. L *susceptus* (past part. of *suscipere* to take up, undertake, admit, fr. *sus-* — var. of *sub-* up — + *-cipere,* fr. *capere* to take) + *-ibilis* -ible — more at SUB-, HEAVE] **1 :** of such a nature, character, or constitution as to admit or permit **:** capable of submitting successfully to an action, process, or operation — used with *of* or *to* followed by an action noun or a verbal noun ⟨a theory ~ of proof⟩ ⟨this problem is . . . ~ to solution M.V.Vishniak⟩ ⟨impulses . . . ~ of control —Abram Kardiner⟩ ⟨several . . . contributors have initials ~ of being mistaken for mine —Elinor Wylie⟩ **2 a :** having such a constitution or temperament as to be open, subject, or unresistant to some stimulus, influence, or agency **:** easily influenced or affected through some trait (as weakness, pliability, sensitiveness, naïveté, or amorousness) — usu. used with *to* ⟨the snow was damp and ~ to clear impression —W.H.Wright⟩ ⟨a city ~ to air attack⟩ ⟨he became ~ to the influences of the sea —*Times Lit. Supp.*⟩ ⟨he is still ~, but not excessively so, to the attractions of other women —Anthony Quinton⟩ ⟨the foibles of the health faddists are particularly ~ to satire —Arthur Knight⟩ ⟨even the most autocratic of industries is in some degree ~ to public opinion —S.H.Adams⟩ **b** (1) **:** having little resistance to a specific infectious disease **:** capable of being infected (2) **:** predisposed to develop a noninfectious disease ⟨~ to diabetes⟩ (3) **:** abnormally reactive to various drugs **c :** capable of affecting as much as being affected, of conceiving, feeling, arousing, or bringing forth ⟨the subject is hardly ~ of high poetry —Richard Garnett †1906⟩ **3 :** easily influenced, affected, or moved **:** IMPRESSIONABLE, RESPONSIVE ⟨at 32,500 feet ~ individuals may develop symptoms after a few minutes —H.G.Armstrong⟩ ⟨with all the fervency of her palpitant and ~ twelve years, she was infatuated with a man thirty years her senior —S.H.Adams⟩ ⟨landslides can be prevented by proper ditch drainage of ~ areas —*Amer. Guide Series: Tenn.*⟩ ⟨far from a rake, though of a warm and ~ temperament —C.B.Nordhoff & J.N.Hall⟩ **syn** see LIABLE

²**susceptible** \"\ *n* -s **:** one who is susceptible (as to a disease) ⟨the usual classification of persons into ~s and immunes is a purely artificial and inexact one —G.W.Anderson & Margaret Arnstein⟩

sus·cep·ti·ble·ness *n* -ES [¹*susceptible* + *-ness*] **:** SUSCEPTIBILITY

sus·cep·ti·bly \-blē, -li\ *adv* **:** in a susceptible manner

sus·cep·tion \səˈsepshən\ *n* -s [L *susception-, susceptio,* fr. *susceptus* (past part. of *suscipere* to take up) + *-ion-, -io* -ion — more at SUSCEPTIBLE] **:** a taking upon or to oneself **:** RECEPTION, ASSUMING, ASSUMPTION

sus·cep·tive \səˈseptiv, -tēv\ *adj* [LL *susceptivus,* fr. L *susceptus* + *-ivus* -ive] **1 :** RECEPTIVE **2 :** SUSCEPTIBLE — **sus·cep·tive·ness** *n* -ES — **sus·cep·tiv·i·ty** \(,)sə,sepˈtivəd·ē\ *n* -ES

sus·ci·tate \ˈsəsə,tāt\ *vt* -ED/-ING/-S [L *suscitatus,* past part. of *suscitare* to stir up, rouse — more at RESUSCITATE] **:** EXCITE, ROUSE, ANIMATE

sus·ci·ta·tion \,=ˈtāshən\ *n* -s [LL *suscitation-, suscitatio,* fr. L *suscitatus* (past part. of *suscitare* to rouse, stir up) + *-ion-, -io* -ion] **:** the act of suscitating or the condition of being suscitated

¹**su·si·an** \ˈsüzēən\ *also* **su·si·a·ni·an** \ˌsüzēˈānēən\ *n* -s [*Susian* fr. L *Susiani* (pl.) inhabitants of Susa or of Susiana, fr. Gk *Sousianē* Susiana, province of the ancient Persian empire roughly coextensive with Elam, fr. *Sousa,* its capital; *Susianian* fr. Gk *Sousianē* + E *-ian*] **1** *cap* **:** a native or inhabitant of Susa or Susiana **2** *usu cap* **:** ELAMITE

²**susian** \"\ *also* **susianian** \"\ *adj, usu cap* **:** of, relating to, or characteristic of the ancient Persian province Susiana or to its capital Susa

sus·lik \ˈsəslik\ *or* **sous·lik** \ˈsüs-\ *n* -s [Russ *suslik;* akin to Bulg *súsel* ground squirrel, Czech *sysel,* Pol *susel;* all prob. fr. the root of OBulg *sysati* to hiss, of imit. origin] **1 :** any of several rather large short-tailed ground squirrels (genus *Citellus*) of eastern Europe or northern Asia with hairy feet and grayish black often more or less spotted pelage **2 :** the pelt or fur of a suslik

susp *abbr* suspend

¹**sus·pect** \(ˈ)səˈspekt\ *adj* [ME, fr. MF, fr. L *suspectus,* fr. past part. of *suspicere* to suspect — more at ⁴SUSPECT] **1 :** regarded with suspicion **:** DISTRUSTED, SUSPECTED ⟨the ~ drugs were removed from the market —Vivian Boardman⟩ ⟨religion has been academically ~ —George Hedley⟩ ⟨the idea of independence was ~ —E.S.Atiyah⟩ **2 :** having the nature or status of a suspicious person or thing **:** provocative or worthy of suspicion **:** SUSPICIOUS ⟨hold one ~ until his innocence is proved⟩ ⟨treat all innovation as ~ —A.T.Quiller-Couch⟩ ⟨he has been ~ to many members of his own party —*Time*⟩

²**suspect** \ˈ=,=\ *n* -s **:** one who is suspected; *esp* **:** one suspected of a crime or of being infected ⟨question a murder ~⟩ ⟨examine a tuberculous ~⟩

³**suspect** \=ˈ=\ *n* -s [ME, fr. ML *suspectus* act of suspecting, fr. L, act of looking up at, fr. *suspectus,* past part. of *suspicere* to look up at, suspect] *archaic* **:** the act of suspecting or the condition of being suspected **:** SUSPICION, APPREHENSION

⁴**suspect** \"\ *vb* -ED/-ING/-S [ME *suspecten,* fr. L *suspectare,* intens. of *suspicere* to look up at, regard with awe, suspect, fr. *sub-* from below, up + *specere* to look, look at — more at SUB-, SPY] *vt* **1 :** to have doubts of **:** be dubious or suspicious about **:** DISTRUST ⟨~s the motives of the salesman of goods or of ideas —Louis Wirth⟩ ⟨~ loud, unaccustomed noises as possible sources of danger —Elaine W. Gould⟩ **2 :** to imagine (one) to be guilty or culpable on slight evidence or without proof ⟨~ one of a theft⟩ ⟨~ one of giving false information⟩ ⟨no one had hitherto ~*ed* him of statecraft —John Buchan⟩ **3 :** to imagine to be or be true, likely, or probable **:** have a suspicion, intimation, or inkling, of **:** SURMISE ⟨we never ~ the disease because the attack amounts to nothing more than a bad headache —*Monsanto Mag.*⟩ ⟨when I know that he is honest and ~ that he is right —H.L.Mencken⟩ ⟨detective stories, which, however bad, I always enjoy since I never ~ the solution —H.J.Laski⟩ **4** *obs* **a :** to expect with dread **:** have an apprehension of **b :** RESPECT, NOTE, HEED ~ *vi* **:** to imagine something to be true or likely **:** be suspicious

sus·pect·able \səˈspektəbəl\ *adj* **:** that may be suspected

suspected *adj* [fr. past part. of ⁴*suspect*] **:** that one suspects or has a suspicion of **:** believed guilty, likely, or doubtful ⟨a ~ person⟩ ⟨a ~ infection⟩ ⟨a ~ story⟩ — **suspect·ed·ly** *adv* — **suspected·ness** *n* -ES

sus·pect·er \səˈspektə(r)\ *n* -s **:** one that suspects

sus·pend \səˈspend\ *vb* -ED/-ING/-S [ME *suspenden,* fr. OF *suspendre* to hang up, interrupt, fr. L *suspendere,* fr. *sus-* (var. of *sub-* up) + *pendere* to cause to hang, weigh — more at SUB-, PENDANT] *vt* **1 :** to debar or cause to withdraw temporarily from any privilege, office, or function **:** subject to suspension ⟨~ a student from school for disciplinary reasons⟩ ⟨~ a member of a club⟩ ⟨was ~*ed* from the army for a year —H.E.Scudder⟩ ⟨condemned him and ~*ed* him from the ministry —A.C.McGiffert⟩ **2 a :** to cause (as an action, process, practice, use) to cease for a time **:** stop temporarily ⟨~ publication of a magazine⟩ ⟨~ bus service⟩; *sometimes* **:** to stop permanently **:** DISCONTINUE **b :** STAY ⟨~ a hearing⟩ **c :** to set aside or make temporarily inoperative ⟨ready and able to ~ their personal values for the sake of magically collective ones —E.H.Erikson⟩ ⟨credit controls were relaxed and ~*ed* —C.L.James⟩ ⟨not a detached period in which the moral standards he adheres to at home can be temporarily ~*ed* —Scott Hershey & Harry Tennant⟩ ⟨article 140 provided that the constitutional court might ~ laws which violated the constitution —C.J.Friedrich⟩ ⟨the general ~*ed* constitutional guarantees for forty-five days —*Current Biog.*⟩ **d :** to cause to be intermitted or interrupted (as in motion or execution) ⟨they ~*ed* their oars to listen⟩ **3 :** to defer till later **:** POSTPONE; *usu* **:** to withhold for a time on specified conditions ⟨~ sentence on a convicted man⟩ **4 :** to hold in an undetermined or undecided state awaiting fuller information ⟨~ judgment until further knowledge is attainable —M.R.Cohen⟩ ⟨you ~ both belief and disbelief —T.S.Eliot⟩ ⟨expression was ~*ed* as she sought his mood, to know what to conform to —Louis Auchincloss⟩ **5 a :** HANG ⟨~*ing* his linen to dry on the frame of the wagon —Van Wyck Brooks⟩ ⟨the garment of primitive man was usually a simple robe that covered the body and was ~*ed* from the shoulders —Morris Fishbein⟩ ⟨~*ed* from his neck was a medallion —R.H.Brown⟩ ⟨the exterior walls instead of supporting the roof, are ~*ed* from it —*Amer. Fabrics*⟩; *esp* **:** to hang so as to be free on all sides except at the point of support **:** cause to depend ⟨~ a ball by a thread⟩ ⟨~ a chandelier from a ceiling⟩ **b :** to cause to be upheld or to be kept from falling or sinking by some invisible support (as buoyancy) ⟨dust ~*ed* in the air⟩ ⟨particles ~*ed* in water⟩ **c :** to support (the upper part of a vehicle) on the wheels or axles by springs or other devices **6 :** to hold riveted in attention **:** keep fixed or lost (as in wonder or contemplation) ⟨man . . . is forever ~*ed* in a floating world of action and contemplation —Richard Eberhart⟩ **7 :** to keep waiting in suspense or indecision **8 :** to make contingent or dependent on or upon **:** CONDITION **9 :** to hold (a musical note or tone) over into the following chord ~ *vi* **1 :** to cease temporarily from operation or activity ⟨the magazine ~*ed*⟩ ⟨the school ~*ed* for lack of finances⟩ **2 :** to stop payment or fail to meet obligations or engagements — used of a business or a bank **3** *obs* **a :** to suspend judgment **b :** to have an apprehension or a suspicion **4 a :** HANG ⟨baleen plates ~*ing* from the upper jaw —*Alaska Sportsman*⟩ **b :** to become held in suspension ⟨fine particles that ~ readily in water⟩ **syn** see DEFER, EXCLUDE — **suspend payments :** to cease paying debts or obligations — used of a business or a bank

suspended *adj* [fr. past part. of *suspend*] **1 :** temporarily debarred, inactive, inoperative **:** held in abeyance ⟨~ officials⟩ ⟨~ construction⟩ ⟨a ~ bank⟩ **2 :** held in suspension **:** HUNG, PENDENT ⟨there are few natural waters which do not contain at least a small amount of ~ matter such as silt, mud, small plant and animal forms —*Manufacture of Bottled Carbonated Beverages*⟩ ⟨a ~ fireplace⟩

suspended animation *n* **:** temporary suspension of the vital functions (as in persons nearly drowned) ⟨each case of *suspended animation* requires certain fundamental knowledge by the physician as to different methods of resuscitation —*Medical Physics*⟩

suspended cadence *n* **:** DECEPTIVE CADENCE

suspended ceiling *n* **:** a ceiling suspended from the floor or roof construction above

suspended cymbal *n* **:** CRASH CYMBAL

suspended joint *n* **:** a rail joint coming between two railroad ties — compare SUPPORTED JOINT

sus·pend·er \səˈspendə(r)\ *n* -s **1 a :** one that suspends **b** *Scots law* **:** the party that prays the court for a suspension **2 :** a device by which something may be suspended: as **a :** one of two supporting bands of elastic, leather, or cloth, worn across the shoulders and fastened at the waistline to trousers, a skirt, or belt — usu. used in pl. and often with *pair* ⟨a pair of ~s⟩ **b** *Brit* **:** GARTER **c :** a support (as a hanger or hook) for an electric cable **3 :** something (as a basket of flowers) suspended

suspenders 2a

suspender belt *n, Brit* **:** GARTER BELT

sus·pend·ible \səˈspendəbəl\ *adj* **:** capable of being suspended

¹**sus·pense** \səˈspen(t)s\ *n* -s [ME, fr. MF, fr. fem. of *suspens* suspended, in doubt, hesitant, fr. L *suspensus,* fr. past part. of *suspendere* to suspend] **1 a :** the state of being suspended **:** temporary cessation **:** SUSPENSION ⟨asks for ~ of judgment —*Manchester Guardian Weekly*⟩ **b :** the state in which a temporary cessation of one's legal right exists **2 a :** mental uncertainty **:** ANXIETY, APPREHENSION ⟨the thought of the ~ and terror that my absence must engender in my loved ones —Elinor Wylie⟩ ⟨the ~ which was more terrible than any certainty —Ellen Glasgow⟩ **b :** pleasant excitement as to a decision or outcome ⟨a novel of ~⟩ **3 :** the state or character of being undecided, not decided, or doubtful **:** lack of certainty **:** INDECISIVENESS ⟨our next strategic move was still in ~ —Sir Winston Churchill⟩

²**suspense** \"\ *adj* [ME, fr. MF *suspens* — more at ¹SUSPENSE] **1 :** waiting for the outcome **:** held in suspension **:** SUSPENDED, WITHHELD **2 :** HESITANT, CAUTIOUS

suspense account *n* **:** an account for the temporary entry of charges or credits pending determination of their ultimate disposition — often used of doubtful accounts receivable

sus·pense·ful \-)sfəl\ *adj* **:** full of suspense **:** marked by suspense ⟨as ~ as a ghost story⟩ ⟨a ~ drama⟩ ⟨this convention has been moderately ~ —R.H.Rovere⟩ ⟨after a ~ pause, everybody stood up —F.J.Warburg⟩

sus·pen·sion \səˈspenchən\ *n* -s [LL *suspension-, suspensio,* fr. L *suspensus* (past part. of *suspendere* to suspend) + *-ion-, -io* -ion] **1 :** the act of suspending or the state or period of being suspended, interrupted, or abrogated ⟨his business duties forced the ~ of his hobbies —*Current Biog.*⟩ ⟨an actress under ~ from a moving-picture studio for failing to report to work⟩: as **a :** temporary forced withdrawal from the exercise of office, powers, prerogatives, privileges as a member or communicant ⟨~ may be employed to remove an apparently seriously objectionable boy or girl from school —H.R.Douglass⟩ ⟨a rash of police ~s takes place because of alleged shakedowns —R.E.Merriam⟩ **b :** temporary withholding (as of belief, decision, or judgment) **c :** temporary remission of action or execution (as of a law, regulation, or rule) **d** *Scots law* (1) **:** a judicial remedy to prevent a threatened injury or to stop an unlawful proceeding brought in the Bill Chamber before a lord ordinary who may require caution before granting emergency relief and who then hears the case on its merits — called also *suspension and interdict* (2) **:** a petition brought in the Bill Chamber by a prisoner before a lord ordinary to satisfy him that the imprisonment is illegal — called also *suspension and liberation* **e** (1) **:** the holding over of one or more musical tones of a chord into the following chord, thus producing a momentary discord and suspending the concord which the ear expects; *specif* **:** such a dissonance which resolves downward (2) **:** the tone thus held over — compare RETARDATION 5 **f :** a penalty by which a cleric is forbidden wholly or in part to exercise the power of orders or office or to enjoy the fruits of his benefice **g :** stoppage of payment of obligations or engagements **:** FAILURE — used esp. of a business or a bank **h :** a rhetorical device whereby the hearer is kept in suspense over what is to follow or over the inference or conclusion to be drawn ("eye hath not seen, ear hath not heard . . ." is a ~) **i :** an abbreviation (as *IHS* for ΙΗΣΟΥΣ Jesus) consisting of the first letter or the first part of a word accompanied by a special mark indicating the omission of the rest **:** an abbreviation (as *ppt* for *precipitate*) consisting of the first letter or part of a word and the first letter or part of the second or third syllable of the word **2 a :** the act of hanging or the state of being hung ⟨the simple stake was employed for the impalement as well as for the ~ of those under sentence —Victor Schultze⟩ **b** (1) **:** the state of a substance when its particles are mixed with but undissolved in a fluid or solid ⟨dust particles in ~ in air⟩ ⟨silt in ~ in water⟩ ⟨droplets in ~ in a gas⟩ (2) **:** a substance in this state ⟨a ~ of fine sand in water⟩ (3) **:** a two-phase system consisting of a finely divided solid dispersed in a solid, liquid, or gas — compare DISPERSION 4b, EMULSION 2a, SOLUTION 2b(1) **3 :** something suspended ⟨the swinging bridge, a ~ of steel cables with stone towers and a wooden walkway —*Amer. Guide Series: Minn.*⟩ **4 a :** a device by which something (as a magnetic needle) is suspended ⟨a bifilar ~⟩ **b :** the system of springs and other devices supporting the upper part of a vehicle on the axles ⟨independent front-wheel ~ has entirely replaced the rigid front axle on American cars —Joseph Heitner⟩ **c :** the act, process, or manner in which the pendulum or torsion balance of a timepiece is suspended

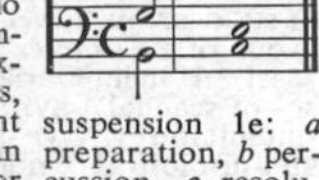

suspension 1e: *a* preparation, *b* percussion, *c* resolution

suspension bridge *n* **:** a bridge that has its roadway suspended from two or more cables usu. passing over towers and securely anchored at the ends, that has cables consisting of wire rope, eyebars, or parallel wires wrapped spirally with wire to protect them and hold them in position, and that usu. has the floor system made rigid by longitudinal stiffening trusses — see BRIDGE illustration

suspension feeder *n* **:** an animal that feeds on material (as planktonic organisms) suspended in water and that usu. has various structural modifications for straining out its food

suspension periods *or* **suspension points** *n pl* **:** usu. three spaced periods used to mark an omission of a word or group of words from a written context — compare ELLIPSIS 3

sus·pen·sive \səˈspen(t)siv, -)sēv *also* -)səv\ *adj* [ML *suspensivus,* fr. L *suspensus* (past part. of *suspendere*) + *-ivus* -ive] **1 :** stopping temporarily **:** tending or having the power to suspend **:** effecting suspension **:** SUSPENDING **2 :** characterized by suspense, suspended judgment, or indecisiveness ⟨a ~ novel⟩ **3 :** characterized by physical or rhetorical suspension **:** manifesting suspension ⟨~ sentences⟩ ⟨a ~ veto⟩

suspensive condition *n, Roman, civil, & Scots law* **:** a condition depending upon an uncertain event which must be fulfilled before an obligation arises **:** CONDITION PRECEDENT

sus·pen·sive·ly \-)sə̇vlē, -li\ *adv* **:** in a suspensive manner

sus·pen·sive·ness \-)sivnəs\ *n* -ES **:** the quality or state of being suspensive

suspensive veto *n* **:** a veto by which a law is merely suspended until reconsidered by the legislature and becomes a law if repassed by an ordinary majority

sus·pen·soid \səˈspen(t),sȯid\ *n* -s [ISV *suspension* + *colloid*] **1 :** a colloidal system in which the dispersed particles are solid — not used scientifically; compare EMULSOID 1 **2 :** a lyophobic sol (as a gold sol)

sus·pen·sor \səˈspen(t)sə(r)\ *n* -s [NL, lit., one that suspends, fr. L *suspensus* + *-or*] **1 :** SUSPENSORIUM **2 a :** a group or chain of cells that is produced from the zygote of a heterosporous plant and serves to push the embryo which arises at its extremity deeper into the embryo sac and into contact with the food supply of the megaspore **b :** one of the two hyphae in fungi of the order Mucorales that bear gametangia at their tips and later support the zygospore

sus·pen·so·ri·al \(ˌ)sə,spenˈsōrēəl\ *adj* [NL *suspensorium* + E *-al*] **:** SUSPENSORY 3

sus·pen·so·ri·um \(,)sə,spen'sōrēəm\ *n, pl* **suspenso·ria** \-ēə\ [NL, fr. LL, instrument for suspending, fr. L *suspensus* (past part. of *suspendere* to suspend) + *-orium*] : something that suspends a body part; *specif* : the bony or cartilaginous element or series of elements that in most vertebrates below mammals connects the lower jaw with the cranium

¹sus·pen·so·ry \sə'spen(t)s(ə)rē, -ri\ *adj* [L *suspensus* + E *-ory*] **1 a** : SUSPENDED **b** : fitted or serving to suspend ⟨a ~ ligament⟩ **2** : temporarily leaving undetermined : SUSPENSIVE 1, SUSPENDING **3** [NL *suspensorium* (n.)] : belonging to a suspensorium

²suspensory \"\ *n* -ES : something that suspends or holds up; *specif* : a band or pouch for supporting a part (as the scrotum)

suspensory ligament *n* : a ligament or fibrous membrane suspending an organ or part: as **a** : an annular fibrous membrane of the eye continuous with the hyaloid membrane and attached to the ciliary body by its outer border and to the capsule of the crystalline lens by its inner border holding the lens in place — see EYE illustration **b** : the falciform ligament of the liver **c** : a strong ligament in the foot of the horse arising from the carpal or tarsal bones and the upper part of the cannon bone, passing down and after dividing being attached to the two sesamoid bones of the fetlock and giving off a downward prolongation on each side of the great pastern bone to unite with the border of the extensor tendon

¹sus·pi·cion \sə'spishən\ *n* -S [ME, alter. (influenced by L *suspicion-, suspicio* suspicion, fr. *suspicere* to suspect + *-ion-, -io* -ion) of *suspecion*, fr. MF *sospeçon* suspicion (influenced in meaning by L *suspicion-, suspicio*), fr. LL *suspection-, suspectio* act of looking up at, awe, fr. L *suspectus* (past part. of *suspicere* to look up at, regard with awe) + *-ion-, -io* -ion — more at SUSPECT] **1 a** : the act or an instance of suspecting : imagination or apprehension of something wrong or hurtful without proof or on slight evidence ⟨in the inspection and interrogation of applicants the following points should lead to a ~ of tuberculosis —H.G.Armstrong⟩ **b** : the mental uneasiness aroused in one who suspects : MISTRUST, DOUBT ⟨he succeeded in dispelling their ~*s* and won their confidence —L.R.Hafen⟩ ⟨an independent, he was regarded with ~ by both parties —W.C.Ford⟩ ⟨the intentions of other nations were viewed with great caution, if not ~ —Theodore Hsi-En Chen⟩ ⟨her weakness for peanuts was balanced by a dark ~ of certain other common vegetables —R.K.Leavitt⟩ **c** : the state of being suspected ⟨protected from ~ by her complete lack of conventional attractiveness —Gerald Bullett⟩ ⟨relieved of his post on ~ of Communist sympathies —Madaline Nichols⟩ ⟨college teams, the amateur standing of which is not always above ~ —*Amer. Guide Series: N.Y.*⟩ ⟨came under the ~ of having been implicated in the revolution —H.S.Reichle⟩ **2** : INKLING, INTIMATION, HINT ⟨there had after all been nothing but whispered ~*s*, old wives' tales, fables invented by men —Sherwood Anderson⟩ ⟨not to have had the least ~ of the approaching marriage⟩ **3** : a slight touch : a mere trace : SUGGESTION ⟨never allow even a ~ of rust to appear on or in your rifle —*Hunter's Encyclopedia*⟩ ⟨just a ~ of light in the east —Hamlin Garland⟩ ⟨without a ~ of dizziness⟩ ⟨without a ~ of scandal⟩ **syn** see UNCERTAINTY

²suspicion \"\ *vt* -ED/-ING/-S *chiefly substand* : SUSPECT

sus·pi·cion·al \-nᵊl\ *adj* [¹*suspicion* + *-al*] : of or relating to suspicion esp. the abnormal suspicion suggesting paranoid mechanisms

sus·pi·cion·less \-nləs\ *adj* : having or showing no suspicion

sus·pi·cious \sə'spishəs\ *adj* [ME *suspicious, suspecious*, fr. MF *suspicieus, suspecious*, fr. L *suspiciosus*, fr. *suspicion-, suspicio* suspicion + *-osus* -ous] **1** : arousing or tending to arouse suspicion : QUESTIONABLE, SUSPECTED ⟨thinking the circumstances in which the watch was offered for sale somewhat ~ —Samuel Butler †1902⟩ ⟨haven't seen any *suspicious*-looking strangers around here —Lyle Saxon⟩ ⟨the patrol officer should constantly observe all ~ cars on his beat —R.L.Anderson⟩ ⟨he rises rapidly, and with almost ~ ease, to progressively important jobs —Hobe Morrison⟩ ⟨an X-ray diagnosis of a ~ tuberculous lesion was made —*Jour. of Pediatrics*⟩ ⟨have had one ~ death (suicide?) in a patient who was scheduled to start treatment —J.L.Fetterman⟩ **2** : suspecting or inclined to suspect : given or prone to suspicion ⟨the unsophisticated native is often ~ of all strangers —*Notes & Queries on Anthropology*⟩ ⟨puritanism was always ~ of anything that made for physical comfort —*Amer. Guide Series: Mass.*⟩ ⟨very ~ of one who did not complain about having to doctor the numerous ailments in the manuscripts he receives —E.S.McCartney⟩ ⟨be a little bit ~ next time you hear or read some argument for keeping taxes down —K.F. Zeisler⟩ ⟨in captivity the vervet is at first very timid and ~ —James Stevenson-Hamilton⟩ **3** : manifesting, expressing, or indicative of suspicion ⟨the countryman answered, with a ~ flash of a pair of cunning eyes —A. Conan Doyle⟩ ⟨who was now proceeding with a ~ briskness to prepare the evening meal —T.B.Costain⟩ ⟨the doors and windows were closed, and a ~ look was on everything —T.B.Thorpe⟩ ⟨no government can invite help and then adopt a prying, ~, inquisitorial attitude to those who accept the invitation —*Orient Bk. World*⟩ — **sus·pi·cious·ly** *adv* — **sus·pi·cious·ness** *n* -ES

sus·pi·ra·tion \,səspə'rāshən\ *n* -S [ME, fr. L *suspiration-, suspiratio*, fr. *suspiratus* (past part. of *suspirare* to sigh) + *-ion-, -io* -ion] : a long deep breath : SIGH ⟨little ~*s* of awe and astonishment —Tennessee Williams⟩

sus·pire \sə'spī(ə)r, -īə\ *vb* -ED/-ING/-S [ME *suspiren*, fr. L *suspirare* to draw a deep breath, sigh, fr. *sub-* + *spirare* to breathe — more at SPIRIT] *vi* **1** : to draw a long breath : SIGH, RESPIRE ⟨the patient began to ~ —Ellery Sedgwick⟩ ⟨like two fish ... suspended, and *suspiring* in a golden, liquid atmosphere —Hervey Allen⟩ **2** : to long for something — used with *for* or *after* ~ *vt* : to utter or give forth with a breath or sigh ⟨I have caught myself *suspiring*, "Ah, those were the days!" —J.S.Redding⟩

sus·pir·i·ous \sə'spirēəs\ *adj* [L *suspiriosus*, fr. *suspirium* deep breath, sigh (fr. *suspirare*) + *-osus* -ous] : breathing heavily : SIGHING

sus·que·han·na \¦səskwə¦hanə\ *n, pl* **susquehanna** *or* **susquehannas** *usu cap* **1** : an Iroquoian people of the Susquehanna River valley **2** : a member of the Susquehanna people

susquehanna salmon *n, usu cap 1st S* [fr. the *Susquehanna* river, central New York, Pennsylvania & Maryland] : WALLEYE 4

¹sus·sex \'səsiks\ *adj, usu cap* [fr. *Sussex*, county of southern England] : of or from the county of Sussex, England : of the kind or style prevalent in Sussex

²sussex \"\ *n* **1** *usu cap* : an English breed of dark red beef cattle similar to the Devon but larger and with incurving horns **2** *usu cap* : an English breed of domestic fowls of the meat type with single combs and usu. speckled or red plumage **3** : SUSSEX SPANIEL **4** -ES : an animal of a Sussex breed

sus·sex·ite \-k,sīt\ *n* -S [*Sussex*, county of northern New Jersey + E *-ite*] : a mineral $MnBO_2OH$ isomorphous with szaibelyite consisting of a borate of manganese and occurring in white fibrous veins (hardness 3, sp. gr. 3.4)

sussex spaniel *n* [¹*sussex*] **1** *usu cap both Ss* : a British breed of short-legged short-necked long-bodied spaniel of rather large size with a flat or slightly wavy golden liver coat **2** *usu cap 1st S & sometimes cap 2d S* : a dog of the Sussex Spaniel breed

sus·sul·ta·to·ry \sə'səltə,tōrē\ *adj* [It *sussultare* to leap up, heave (fr. L *subsultare*, fr. *sub-* up + *-sultare*, fr. *saltare* to leap) + E *-tory* (as in *successatory*) — more at SUB-, SALTANT] : characterized by up-and-down vibrations of large amplitude — used of an earthquake; compare SUCCUSSATORY

sus·sul·to·ri·al \¦səsəl¦tōrēəl\ *adj* [It *sussultorio* heaving, vibrating up and down (fr. *sussultare* to heave + *-orio* -ory, fr. L *-orius*) + E *-al*] : having the nature of or resulting from a sussultatory earthquake shock

sus·tain \sə'stān\ *vb* -ED/-ING/-S [ME *susteinen, sustenen*, fr. OF *sustenir*, fr. L *sustinēre* to hold up, sustain, fr. *sus-* (var. of *sub-* up) + *-tinēre* (fr. *tenēre* to hold) — more at SUB-, THIN] *vt* **1** : to give support (as military support) to : uphold by aiding or backing up : furnish relief to ⟨if the director be ~*ed* in the general endeavor to make the observatory useful —Cleveland Abbe⟩ ⟨they had behind them no great organization such as that which ~*ed* French and his colleagues —F.W.Crofts⟩ ⟨the officer witnesses ... with a record of service to their country to ~ them —H.W.Baldwin⟩ **2** : to provide for the support or maintenance of : supply with sustenance : NOURISH ⟨plant life ~*s* the living world —D.C.Peattie⟩ ⟨commitment of trained men to the machines that ~ war —C.W.deKiewiet⟩ ⟨the sort of defense which our economy can ~ —W.F.Knowland⟩ ⟨settlements along the seacoast ... are ~*ed* by the fishing trade —*Amer. Guide Series: N.J.*⟩ ⟨preached as he never preached before, ~*ing* himself with lemon juice and vegetables —*Time*⟩ **3 a** : to cause to continue (as in existence or a certain state or in force or intensity) : to keep up esp. without interruption, diminution, or flagging : MAINTAIN, PROLONG ⟨found it difficult to ~ an interest in their talk —L.C.Douglas⟩ ⟨the sort of writing which early established and has long ~*ed* his reputation —Bliss Perry⟩ ⟨policies which they said would be needed to ~ prosperity —Fritz Sternberg⟩ ⟨the civil war period was lived at a high tension that could not be ~*ed* —H.L.Matthews⟩ ⟨dissatisfaction with the work of the legislatures ~*s* the efforts of those critics —A.N.Holcombe⟩ ⟨difficult for even the most attentive and genuinely musical listener to ~ maximum attention every minute —Hunter Mead⟩ ⟨too fatigued to ~ a consecutive conversation —Lucien Price⟩ **b** (1) : to allow (a musical tone) to sound without dying away as long as the rhythm will permit (2) : to play (a musical composition or part) in legato style **4 a** : to bear up from or as if from below : support the weight of : hold up : PROP ⟨bones are the solid elements of structure that ~ the body —Morris Fishbein⟩ ⟨pins suitable for ~*ing* kilts —Ashley Halsey⟩ **b** : to carry or withstand (a weight or pressure) ⟨the dam ... could not ~ the heavy head of water —*Amer. Guide Series: Minn.*⟩ ⟨beam ... had to be much thicker in order to ~ even the same weight —S.F.Mason⟩ **5** : to prevent (as one's mind or spirit) from sinking or giving way : buoy up ⟨the scientist ... is ~*ed*, as are the religious, by a profound and unshakable faith —P.B. Sears⟩ ⟨excitement ~*ed* me —Polly Adler⟩ ⟨hope that had ~*ed* them —Frank Yerby⟩ ⟨~ the morale of the civilian population —R.D.W.Connor⟩ ⟨I read history to ~ myself in the violent confusions of these years —Ralph Bates⟩ ⟨comfort and ~ the parents —Agnes S. Turnbull⟩ **6** : ENDURE: as **a** : to submit to without failing or yielding : bear up under ⟨I couldn't ~ such an act —Rex Ingamells⟩ ⟨a man bravely ~*ing* the burden of fear —*Time*⟩ ⟨he would wonder whether he could ever again ~ a year's teaching —Lucien Price⟩ **b** : to bear as an affliction : to bear with suffering ⟨the tremendous nervous shock which has been ~*ed* —H.G.Armstrong⟩ ⟨~*ed* a concussion of the brain —Allan Nevins⟩ **c** : SUFFER, RECEIVE, UNDERGO ⟨must be prepared to ~ heavy losses —Bruce Bliven b. 1889⟩ ⟨the walls of its building bear bullet scars ~*ed* in a riot —*Amer. Guide Series: N.Y. City*⟩ **7 a** : to support as true, legal, or just; *sometimes* : CONTEND **b** : to allow or admit as valid ⟨the court ~*ed* the motion⟩ **8** : to support by adequate proof : ESTABLISH, CORROBORATE, CONFIRM ⟨testimony that ~*s* our contention⟩ ⟨a thesis which no one ... could conceivably ~ —*Times Lit. Supp.*⟩ **9** : to act the part of (a character) ⟨no reason why she should not have ~*ed* both roles —Anthony Powell⟩ ⟨directing that no letter or message be received on any occasion whatsoever from the enemy ... but such as should be directed to them in the characters they respectively ~*ed* —H.E.Scudder⟩ ~ *vi* : BEAR, MAINTAIN ⟨beyond a country's capacity to ~, it recommended grants rather than loans —*Americas*⟩ **syn** see EXPERIENCE, SUPPORT

sus·tain·able \-nəbəl\ *adj* : capable of being sustained

sus·tained \sə'stānd\ *adj* [fr. past part. of *sustain*] : maintained at length without interruption, weakening, or losing in power or quality : PROLONGED, UNFLAGGING ⟨~ reasoning⟩ ⟨~ comedy⟩ ⟨~ flight⟩ ⟨~ performance⟩ ⟨~ verse⟩ ⟨~ piece of music⟩ — **sus·tained·ly** \-nədlē, -nd-\ *adv*

sustained yield *n* : a recurrent increment of a biological resource (as timber or fish) such that the portion removed by one harvest is replaced by growth or reproduction before another harvest occurs — compare SELECTION 3b

sus·tain·er \sə'stānə(r)\ *n* -S [ME *susteinere*, fr. *susteinen* to sustain + *-ere* -er] **1** : one that sustains **2** : SUSTAINING PROGRAM

sustaining *adj* [fr. pres. part. of *sustain*] **1 a** : serving to sustain **b** : aiding in the support of an organization through a special fee ⟨a ~ member paying $25 annually⟩ **2** : of or relating to a sustaining program ⟨a ~ feature⟩ ⟨~ time⟩ — **sus·tain·ing·ly** *adv*

sustaining pedal *n* **1** : DAMPER PEDAL **2** : SOSTENUTO PEDAL

sustaining program *also* **sustaining show** *n* : a radio or television program that is paid for by a station or network and has no commercial sponsor

sus·tain·ment \sə'stānmənt\ *n* -S [*sustain* + *-ment*] : the act of sustaining : MAINTENANCE, SUPPORT

sus·te·nance \'səstənən(t)s\ *n* -S [ME, fr. OF, fr. *sustenir* to sustain + *-ance*] **1 a** : means of support, maintenance, or subsistence : LIVING ⟨it is chiefly through his equipment that man acts on and reacts to the external world, draws ~ therefrom —V.G.Childe⟩ ⟨there is neither tolerance nor ~ of his intended calling —F.C.Neff⟩ **b** (1) : FOOD, REFRESHMENTS ⟨trooping off the ladies as soon as they had taken their ~ —George Meredith⟩ (2) : NOURISHMENT ⟨countries in which children are in desperate need of physical ~ to remain alive —Mark Starr⟩ **2 a** : the act of sustaining or the state of being sustained **b** : a supplying or being supplied with the necessaries of life ⟨money for ~ of the homeless⟩ **3** : something that gives support, endurance, or strength **syn** see LIVING

sus·te·nant \-nənt\ *adj* [back-formation fr. *sustenance*] : SUSTAINING

sus·ten·tac·u·lar \¦səstən¦takyələ(r)\ *adj* [NL *sustentaculum* + E *-ar*] : serving to support or sustain

sustentacular cell *n* **1** : one of the branching connective-tissue cells of the spleen **2** : SERTOLI CELL

sus·ten·tac·u·lum \,səstən'takyələm\ *n, pl* **sustentacu·la** \-lə\ [NL, fr. L, prop, support, fr. *sustentare* (intens. of *sustinēre* to hold up) + *-culum*, suffix denoting an instrument — more at SUSTAIN] : a body part that supports or suspends another organ or part

sus·ten·ta·tion \,səstən'tāshən\ *n* -S [ME, fr. MF, fr. L *sustentation-, sustentatio* act of holding up, fr. *sustentatus* (past part. of *sustentare*) + *-ion-, -io* -ion] **1** : the act of sustaining or the state of being sustained: as **a** : MAINTENANCE, UPKEEP ⟨taxes for the ~ of a state college⟩ **b** : PRESERVATION, CONSERVATION ⟨the ~ of peace in a nation⟩ **c** : maintenance of life, growth, courage, morale **d** : provision with sustenance ⟨gave seeds ... and nectar of flowers for the ~ of His small birds —W.H.Hudson †1922⟩ **e** : physical support : a holding up or state of being held up **2** : something that sustains or provides sustenance : SUPPORT

sustentation fund *n* : a fund of a religious body (as the Presbyterian) for the more adequate support of its ministers

sus·ten·ta·tive \'səstən,tād·iv, sə'stentəd-\ *adj* [L *sustentatus* + E *-ive*] **1** : serving to sustain : relating to or giving sustentation ⟨~ action⟩ ⟨~ food⟩ **2** : serving to support or bind together body parts ⟨~ tissue⟩

sus·ten·tion \sə'stenchən\ *n* -S [fr. *sustain*, after such pairs as E *retain: retention*] : the act or instance of sustaining : SUSTENTATION

sus·ten·tor \sə'stentə(r)\ *n* -S [NL, fr. L *sustentus* (past. part. of *sustinere* to hold up) + *-or* — more at SUSTAIN] : one of two hooks on the posterior part of a butterfly pupa forming the cremaster

¹su·su \'sü(,)sü\ *n* -S [Bengali *susuk*, fr. Skt *śiśuka*, lit., baby, baby creature, fr. *śiśu* baby, child; fr. its being confused with the crocodile and believed to eat babies; akin to Gk *kyein* to be pregnant — more at CAVE] : a blind cetacean (*Platanista gangetica* or *Susu gangetica*) about eight feet long resembling a dolphin, inhabiting the larger rivers of India, and having a long, slender, slightly spatulate beak, many teeth, triangular pectoral fins, and a rudimentary ridgelike dorsal fin

²susu \"\ *n, pl* **susu** *or* **susus** *usu cap* **1 a** : a West African people of the Mali and Guinea republics and the area along the northern border of Sierra Leone **b** : a member of such people **2** : a Mande language of the Susu people

³susu \"\ *n* -S [Dobuan, lit., mother's milk; prob. akin to Malay *susu* breast, milk] : a Dobuan kinship group consisting of a woman, her brother, and her children but exclusive of her husband and her brother's children

su·su·hu·nan \,süsü'hü,nän\ *n* -S *sometimes cap* [Malay, fr. Old Jav *suhun* supporting on the head] **1** : a title of the former emperor of Java **2** : the ruler of the principality of Surakarta in Java

su·sur·rant \sə'sərənt\ *adj* [L *susurrant-, susurrans*, pres. part. of *susurrare* to whisper, murmur, fr. *susurrus* whisper] : WHISPERING, MURMURING ⟨~ voices⟩

su·sur·ra·tion \,süsə'rāshən\ *n* -S [ME, fr. LL *susurration-, susurratio*, fr. L *susurratus* (past part. of *susurrare* to whisper) + *-ion-, -io* -ion] **1** : the act of one that whispers or murmurs ⟨~ alone could not alter the proportionate emphasis of vowel over consonant —John Updike⟩ **2** : WHISPERING, MURMUR ⟨a mild ~ was audible —G.A.Wagner⟩

su·sur·rous \sə'sərəs\ *adj* [L *susurrus*, fr. *susurrus* whisper] : full of whispering sounds : RUSTLING ⟨the night was filled with a slow, sad, ~ rustle, like the wind fingering the pines —R.P.Warren⟩

su·sur·rus \"\ *n* -ES [L, whisper, murmur, hum — more at SWARM] : a whispering, rustling, or muttering sound ⟨river moving with a rich ~ below the ... pavement —Victor Canning⟩ ⟨a light ~ of conversation that seemed no more than the soughing of a faint wind —Donn Byrne⟩ ⟨the confused cries of the newspaper critics and the ~ of popular repetition that follows —T.S.Eliot⟩

su·sy-q \'süzē'kyü\ *n, usu cap S&Q* [origin unknown] : a dance step in which the hips and legs are swung sharply to one side while the shoulders and arms are bent forward and swung toward the opposite side with the clasped hands extended forward

su·taio \sə'tī(,)ō\ *n, pl* **sutaio** *or* **sutaios** *usu cap* **1** : an Indian people of southwestern South Dakota allied with the Cheyenne **2** : a member of the Sutaio people

sute \'süt\ *n* -S [ME, fr. *sute, siute* retinue, suite, suit — more at SUIT] : a flock of mallards

su·ter·berry \'süd·ə(r)- — *see* BERRY\ *n* [*suter* (of unknown origin) + *berry*] : a prickly ash (*Zanthoxylum americanum*)

suth·er·land·shire \'səthərlənd,shi(ə)r, -,shər\ *or* **suth·er·land** *adj, usu cap* [fr. *Sutherlandshire* or *Sutherland*, Scotland] : of or from the county of Sutherland, Scotland : of the kind or style prevalent in Sutherland

su·tile \'sütᵊl\ *adj* [L *sutilis* sewn together, fr. *sutus* (past part. of *suere* to sew) + *-ilis* -ile — more at SEW] *archaic* : done by stitching ⟨~ pictures which imitate tapestry —Samuel Johnson⟩

sut·ler \'sətlə(r)\ *n* -S [obs. D *soeteler* (now *zoetelaar*), fr. LG *suteler, sudeler* cook, sloppy cook, sloppy worker, fr. MHG *sudelen* to do sloppy work, to dirty; akin to OHG *siodan* to seethe — more at SEETHE] : a provisioner to an army post esp. when established in a shop on the post ⟨~ on the army post of frontier days before it had its own full-fledged quartermaster services —C.F.Kraenzel⟩

sut·lery \-lərē\ *n* -ES *archaic* : a sutler's occupation, stock, or shop

su·to \'süd·(,)ō\ *n, pl* **suto** *or* **sutos** *usu cap* **1** : BASUTO 1 **2** : SOTHO

su·tra \'sü·trə\ *also* **sut·ta** \'sůd·ə\ *n* -S [Skt *sūtra* thread, string of rules, aphorisms; akin to Skt *sīvyati* he sews — more at SEW] **1** *Brahmanism* : a precept, aphorism, or collection of brief rules produced generally in the period 500–200 B.C. **2** *Buddhism* : one of the narrative parts of the Buddhist canonical literature; *esp* : the dialogues of the Buddha **3** *Jainism* : any of various scriptures; *esp* : a scripture dealing with the life of the founder of Jainism

sut·tee *or* **sa·ti** \,sə'tē, '=,=\ *n* -S [Skt *satī*, lit., good woman, fem. of *sat, sant* existing, true, good — more at SOOTH] **1** : the act or custom of a Hindu widow willingly cremating herself or being cremated on the funeral pile of her husband as an indication of her devotion to him **2** : a woman cremated in this way

¹sut·tle \'səd·ᵊl\ *adj* [alter. of *subtle*] *of weight* : remaining after the tare is deducted

²suttle \"\ *n* -S : the weight that remains after the tare is deducted

³suttle \"\ *vi* -ED/-ING/-S [back-formation fr. *suttler*] *archaic* : to act as a sutler

suttler *obs var of* SUTLER

suttlety *obs var of* SUBTLETY

su·tur·al \'süchərəl\ *adj* [NL *suturalis*, fr. L *sutura* seam + *-alis* -al] : of, relating to, or in a suture or seam ⟨a ~ dehiscence⟩; *esp* : CONNECTIVE — **su·tur·al·ly** \-rəlē\ *adv*

sutural bone *n* : WORMIAN BONE

¹su·ture \'süchə(r)\ *n* -S [MF & L; MF, fr. L *sutura* seam, suture, fr. *sutus* (past part. of *suere* to sew) + *-ura* -ure — more at SEW] **1 a** (1) : a strand or fiber (as of silk, nylon, cotton, catgut, wire) used to unite parts (as tissues, nerves, or blood vessels) of the human or an animal body ⟨incisions were ... closed with stainless steel ~*s* —*Yr. Bk. of General Surgery*⟩ (2) : the material used for sutures ⟨silk is the most widely used nonabsorbable ~ at the present time —A.A.Stonehill⟩ **b** : a stitch made with a suture ⟨my right arm was bandaged to my side so as not to open the ~*s* —Laurence Oliphant⟩ **c** : the act or process of sewing with sutures ⟨fixation of mandibular fragments by direct bone ~ —*Internat'l Congress of Military Medicine*⟩ ⟨nerve ~ has not been the most dramatic accomplishment of this ... metal —F.G.Slaughter⟩ **d** : a seam whereby two edges of a cut or incision in a human or animal body are brought together so that they may ultimately unite **2 a** : a uniting of parts ⟨~ with glue is convenient —John Smith †1679⟩ **b** : the seam or seamlike line along which two things or parts have been united ⟨here and there ... we detect the ~*s* —J.D.Coleridge⟩ **3 a** : the line of union in an immovable articulation (as between the bones of the skull); **b** : an immovable articulation : SYNARTHROSIS **4 a** : the line or furrow formed at the junction of two adjacent parts; *often* : a line of dehiscence ⟨the ventral ~ of a legume⟩ **b** : the crease on the surface of various fruits (as the peach) **5 a** : the line at which the elytra of a beetle meet and are sometimes confluent **b** : a more or less impressed or otherwise distinguishable line of union (as between closely united sclerites of an arthropod or between the whorls of a univalve shell) **c** : the commonly more or less undulated or plicated line of junction of a septum of a cephalopod's shell with the wall of the shell — compare LOBE 2b, SADDLE 4b(2)

²suture \"\ *vt* -ED/-ING/-S **1** : to unite the parts of by means of a suture ⟨~ a wound⟩ **2** : to secure or fasten with sutures ⟨needles were *sutured* in place —J.B.Howell & J.M.Riddell⟩

su·tured \-(r)d\ *adj* [¹*suture* + *-ed*] **1** : CONSERTAL ⟨grains that form the ~ mosaic —*Jour. of Geol.*⟩ **2** : having or marked by a suture ⟨wavy septal lines that indicate the characteristically ~ Ammonites —W.E.Swinton⟩

suture needle *n* : SURGICAL NEEDLE

su·us et ne·ces·sa·ri·us he·res \'süə,set,nekə'sarēəs'hā,rās\ *n* [L, lit., own and necessary heir] : a family heir including a slave in the paternal power of a decedent at the latter's death who by Roman law becomes sui juris and succeeds to the decedent's property by intestacy or by will

su·us he·res \,süəs'hā,rās\ *n, pl* **sui here·des** \'süē'hā'rā-,dās\ [L, lit., own heir] **1** *Roman law* : an heir (as a wife, son, daughter or slave) under the paternal power of the decedent at the latter's death **2** *Roman law* : an heir in the family of the decedent at his death who becomes sui juris on succeeding to the decedent's property

su·wan·nee chicken \sə'wōnē, -wänē\ *n, usu cap S* [fr. *Suwannee*, river in Georgia and Florida] : an edible Florida river terrapin (*Pseudemys concinna suwannensis*)

suwarro *var of* SAGUARO

su·ze·rain \'süzərən, -zə,rān *sometimes* 'səz-\ *n* -S [F, fr. *sus* above, up, upon (fr. L *susum, sursum* up, upwards, fr. *sub-* up + *versum*, neut. of *versus*, past part. of *vertere* to turn) + *-erain* (as in *souverain* sovereign, fr. OF *soverain*) — more at SUB-, WORTH, SOVEREIGN] **1** : a superior lord to whom fealty is due : a feudal lord : OVERLORD **2** : a dominant state exercising varying degrees of control over a vassal state with regard to its foreign relations but allowing it sovereign authority in its internal affairs

su·ze·rain·ship \-n,ship\ *n* : SUZERAINTY

su·ze·rain·ty \-ntē, -ti\ *n* -ES [F *suzeraineté*, fr. *suzeraine* (fem. of *suzerain*) + *-té* -ty] : the dominion, authority, or relation of a suzerain with regard to the subject person or state esp. in the matter of control over the foreign affairs of such a state : OVERLORDSHIP

SV *abbr* **1** safety valve **2** sailing vessel **3** [L *Sanctitas Vestra*] Your Holiness **4** sluice valve **5** [L *spiritus vini*] spirit of wine **6** stop valve **7** *often not cap* [L *sub verbo* or *sub voce*] under the word **8** summer visitor **9** surface vessel

svab·ite \'sfä,bīt, 'svä-\ *n* -s [Sw *svabit*, fr. Anton *Svab* †1768 Swed. mining official + Sw *-it* -ite] : a mineral $Ca_5F(AsO_4)_3$ consisting of fluoride-arsenate of calcium that is at least partially isomorphous with apatite, hedyphane, and mimetite

svan *also* **svane** \'sfän, 'svän\ *or* **swan** \'swän\ *n, pl* **svan** *or* **svans** *usu cap* [Russ *Svan, Svanets*] **1 :** one of the Kartvelian or Georgian peoples of the Caucasus dwelling on the upper course of the Ingur river **2 :** a member of one of the Svan peoples

svan·berg·ite \'sfän,bər,gīt, 'svä-\ *n* -s [Sw *svanbergit*, fr. Lars F. *Svanberg* †1878 Swed. chemist + Sw *-it* -ite] : a mineral $SrAl_3(PO_4)(SO_4)(OH)_6$ consisting of a basic phosphate and sulfate of strontium and aluminum that is isomorphous with beudantite, corkite, hinsdalite, and woodhouseite

sva·ne·tian \sfä'nēshən, svä-\ *n* -s *usu cap* [Russ *Svanets* Svan + E *-ian*] **1 :** SVAN **2 :** the South Caucasic language of the Svan people

[1]**sva·ra·bhak·ti** \,sf|ärə'bäktē, ,sv|, ,sw|, -'bak-, |ərə'bək-, -ti\ *n* -s [Skt, lit., part of a vowel, fr. *svara* sound, vowel (fr. *svarati* he sounds, resounds) + *bhakti* division, portion, fr. *bhajati* he grants, allots — more at SWARM, BAKSHEESH] : the introduction of a vowel sound in Sanskrit esp. between *r* or *l* and a following consonant; *also* : a similar phenomenon in other languages

[2]**svarabhakti** \¦==¦==\ *also* **sva·ra·bhak·tic** \¦==¦=tik\ *adj* : of, relating to, or used in svarabhakti ⟨a ~ vowel⟩

svar·ga *or* **swar·ga** \'sf|ärgə, 'sv|, 'sw|, |ər-\ *n* -s [Skt *svarga*; akin to Skt *svarati* it shines — more at SWELTER] : a Hindu heaven

svastika *var of* SWASTIKA

svc *abbr* service

sve·co·fen·ni·an \¦sfekō¦fenēən, ¦svek-\ *adj, usu cap* [NL *Svecofennia* Sweden and Finland + E *-an*] : of, relating to, or constituting a division of the Precambrian — see GEOLOGIC TIME table

sved·berg \'sfed,bərg, 'sve-\ *or* **svedberg unit** *n* -s *often cap S* [after The *Svedberg* b1884 Swed. chemist, its formulator] : a unit of time amounting to 10^{-13} second that serves in measuring the sedimentation velocity of a protein solution or other colloidal solution in an ultracentrifuge for use in an equation for determining the molecular weight of a protein

svelte *also* **svelt** \'sfelt, 'sve-\ *adj* -ER/-EST [F, fr. It *svelto*, fr. past part. of *svellere* to pull out, stretch out, modif. (influenced by *s-*, fr. L *ex-* [1]ex-) of L *evellere* to pull out, fr. *e-* [1]ex- + *vellere* to pull — more at VULNERABLE] **1 a :** SLENDER, TRIM, LITHE ⟨her figure is ~⟩ ⟨she . . . looked . . . very ~ in a trim dark suit —Morris Gilbert⟩ ⟨a darting minnow with its ~ shadow beneath it —C.E.Craddock⟩ **b :** having clean lines : SMOOTH, SLEEK ⟨~ knitted bathing suits —*Fortune*⟩ **2 :** URBANE, SOPHISTICATED, SUAVE ⟨has spoken in his usual ~ accents —Nathaniel Peffer⟩ ⟨this is cold praise . . . and if there were no more to say we should have here only another ~ artist of the deep freeze —Dudley Fitts⟩ ⟨a ~ monthly magazine . . . for Italians all over the world —Horace Sutton⟩

svelte·ly *adv* : in a svelte manner

svelte·ness *n* -ES : the quality or state of being svelte

sven·ga·li \sfen'gälē, sve-, -'gal-, -li\ *n* -s *usu cap* [fr. *Svengali*, maleficent hypnotist in the novel *Trilby* (1894) by George du Maurier †1896 Brit. artist and novelist] : one who attempts usu. with evil intentions to persuade or force another to do his bidding

sverd·lovsk \'sferd,lȯlfsk, 'sve-, ¦vzk, =¦=, '=¦=l\ *adj, usu cap* [fr. *Sverdlovsk*, U.S.S.R.] : of or from the city of Sverdlovsk, U.S.S.R. : of the kind or style prevalent in Sverdlovsk

sve·tam·ba·ra \s(h)wā'tämbərə\ *n* -s *cap* [Skt *śvetāmbara*, lit., having white clothes, fr. *śveta* white + *ambara* garment — more at WHITE] : a major Jain sect whose members clothe themselves and their sacred images in white and in contrast to the Digambaras assert that women can attain salvation

SVP *abbr* [F *s'il vous plaît*] if you please

SVR *abbr* [L *spiritus vini rectificatus*] rectified spirit of wine

SVT *abbr* [L *spiritus vini tenuis*] proof spirit of wine

svy *abbr* survey

sw *abbr* **1** swatch **2** swell organ **3** switch

SW *abbr* **1** salt water **2** seawater **3** senior warden **4** *often not cap* sent wrong **5** shelter warden **6** shipper's weight **7** short wave **8** social work **9** southwest; southwestern **10** *often not cap* specific weight **11** stock width

[1]**swab** *or* **swob** \'swäb *also* -wȯb\ *n* -s [prob. fr. obs. D *swabbe*, fr. MD; akin to LG *swabber* mop] **1 a** (1) : a mop used esp. aboard a naval vessel (2) : an absorbent bundle (as of rags) used for cleaning or for applying a substance to a surface ⟨dip the ~ . . . in clean ammonia water, and rub the carpet face hard with it —Emily Holt⟩ **b** (1) : a wad of absorbent material (as cotton) wound around one end of a small stick and used for applying medication or for removing material from an area ⟨~s used for applications in the treatment of . . . conditions of the nose —D.W.Maurer & V.H.Vogel⟩ (2) : a specimen taken with a swab ⟨a throat ~⟩ **c :** [1]PATCH 7b **d :** a hemp brush used in founding esp. for holding water, moistening mold joints, spraying on edges, or spreading blacking on dry-sand molds **2 a :** a useless or contemptible person ⟨considered it out of the question that a little ~ of his age could have the sense to appreciate her —*Blue Bk.*⟩ **b :** [3]GOB **c** *Brit* : a naval officer's epaulet **3 :** a loosely fitting plunger with an internal check valve that is run on a cable and used for lifting fluids from a drilled well

swabs 1b(1)

[2]**swab** *or* **swob** \"\ *vt* **swabbed** *or* **swobbed; swabbed** *or* **swobbed; swabbing** *or* **swobbing; swabs** *or* **swobs** [partly fr. ME *swabben* to sway; akin to obs. D *zwabben* to sway, LG *swabber* mop, *swabben* to splash, sway, flap; prob. all of imit. origin; partly back-formation fr. *swabber*] **1 a :** to clean with or as if with a swab : wipe up : MOP ⟨~ the decks⟩ ⟨got the towel and *swabbed* off the plates —Wallace Stegner⟩ ⟨*swabbing* down the boat's hull⟩ ⟨*swabbed* up the . . . rich beef gravy with . . . crusty French bread —H.A.Sinclair⟩ **b :** to apply medication to with a swab ⟨cleanse the wound and ~ it with iodine⟩ **c :** to use a swab in applying (medication) ⟨~ iodine over the wound⟩ **2 :** to draw out (liquid) from an oil well with a swab

swab·ber \-bə(r)\ *n* -s [prob. fr. ME *swab* to sway + *-er*] **1 :** one that swabs: as **a :** a worker who swabs dope onto tanned hides **b :** a worker who swabs mud from a screen at the bottom of an oil well to reestablish the flow of oil **2 :** SAILOR **3 :** SWAB 2a

swab·bers \-bə(r)z\ *n pl* [origin unknown] : the ace of hearts, jack of clubs, and ace and deuce of trumps formerly entitling the holder to a share of the stakes in whist

swab·bie *also* **swab·by** \-bē\ *n, pl* **swabbies** [[1]swab + *-ie* or *-y*] *slang* : [3]GOB ⟨*swabbies* who haven't seen any action —Hansford Martin⟩

swabbing *n* -s [fr. gerund of [2]*swab*] : the material removed from tissue (as of a lesion) by means of a swab — usu. used in pl.

[1]**swa·bi·an** *or* **sua·bian** \'swābēən\ *adj, usu cap* [*Swabia* or *Suabia* (Schwaben), duchy in medieval Germany + E *-an* (adj. suffix)] **1 :** of, relating to, or characteristic of Swabia **2 :** of, relating to, or characteristic of the Swabians

[2]**swabian** *or* **suabian** \"\ *n* -s [*Swabia* or *Suabia* + E *-an* (n. suffix)] **1** *cap* : a native or inhabitant of Swabia: **a :** one of a people living in the former German duchy of Swabia **b :** a native or inhabitant of the German province of Swabia **2** *usu cap* : a High German dialect of Swabia

swab stick *n* : a stick used for swabbing: as **a :** a stick with fibers frayed at one end used to clean a drill hole for a blasting charge **b :** SWAB 1b(1)

[1]**swack** \'swak\ *n* -s [ME (Sc) *swak*, of imit. origin] *chiefly Scot* : a hard blow : WHACK

[2]**swack** \"\ *adj* [LG *swak* supple, pliant, weak, fr. MLG; akin to MD *swac* pliant, MLG *swacken* to rock, reel — more at SWAG] *chiefly Scot* : LITHE, NIMBLE

swacked \-kt\ *adj* [prob. fr. Sc dial. *swacked*, past part. of *swack* to drink deeply, perh. fr. ME (Sc) *swakken* to fling, dash, strike] *slang* : DRUNK, PLASTERED ⟨may come home late and be too ~ to remember —George Sklar⟩

[1]**swad** *n* -s [prob. of Scand origin; akin to Norw dial. *svadde* big stout fellow, *sodde* slow heavy fellow] *obs* : BUMPKIN, LOUT

[2]**swad** \'swäd *also* -wȯd\ *n* -s [perh. back-formation fr. [2]*swaddie*] *dial Eng* : POD, SHELL

[3]**swad** \"\ *n* -s [prob. fr. [1]*swad*] : SOLDIER

[4]**swad** \"\ *n* -s [perh. alter. of [1]*squad*] *slang* : a group of individuals : BUNCH ⟨a thick ~ of plants —*Westralian Farmers Co-Op. Gazette*⟩

[1]**swad·dle** \'swädᵊl *also* -wȯd-\ *vt* **swaddled; swaddled; swaddling** \-d(ᵊ)liŋ\ **swaddles** [ME *swadelen, swathelen*, prob. alter. (influenced by *swathen* to swathe) of *swedelen, swethelen* to swaddle, fr. *swethel* swaddle, fr. OE *swethel, swæthel*; akin to MD *swadel* swaddle, OHG *swedil* swaddle, MLG *swede* bandage — more at SWATHE] **1 a :** to wrap (an infant) with swaddling clothes ⟨the baby is tightly *swaddled* in long strips of material holding its legs straight and its arms down by its sides —Patrick Mullahy⟩ **b :** to wrap completely or almost completely : SWATHE, ENVELOP ⟨had they *swaddled* the head in clothes . . . would it have ceased to bleed —Glenway Wescott⟩ ⟨an elderly lady *swaddled* in sealskin started a conversation with us —*New Yorker*⟩ **2 :** to restrain protectively or in a confining manner : RESTRICT ⟨his mother ~s him with demure gentilities —Charles Lee⟩ ⟨liturgical style ~s all improprieties —Samuel Yellen⟩ **3** *archaic* : BEAT, THRASH

[2]**swaddle** \"\ *n* -s **1 :** SWADDLING CLOTHES **1 2** *archaic* : BANDAGE

swad·dler \-d(ᵊ)lə(r)\ *n* -s [[2]*swaddle* + *-er*; prob. fr. the frequent mention made by the preachers in their sermons to the swaddling clothes in which the infant Jesus lay (Lk 2:7)] *chiefly Irish* : a Methodist preacher; *broadly* : PROTESTANT

[1]**swaddling** *n* -s [ME *swadeling, swatheling* act of swaddling, fr. gerund of *swadelen, swathelen* to swaddle] **1 :** SWADDLING CLOTHES — usu. used in pl. ⟨changed the ~s on a baby —R.P. Warren⟩ **2 :** BANDAGING — usu. used in pl. ⟨in case the fracture be next to the knee from below, then use no ~s over the knee —A.L.Fox⟩

[2]**swaddling** *adj* [[1]*swaddling*; prob. fr. the frequent mention made by the preachers in their sermons to the swaddling clothes in which the infant Jesus lay (Lk 2:7)] *Brit* : PROTESTANT; *esp* : METHODIST ⟨swearing he would have none of their ~ prayers —John Wesley⟩

swaddling band *n* [ME *swadeling band*] : SWADDLING CLOTHES — usu. used in pl. ⟨the *swaddling bands* by which in darker times the human body was compressed —W.E.Channing⟩ ⟨stifled and strangled in the *swaddling bands* of mediocrity —*Nineteenth Century & After*⟩

swaddling clothes *n pl* **1 a :** narrow strips of cloth wrapped around an infant to restrict movement **b :** limitations or restrictions imposed upon the immature or inexperienced ⟨Assyrian sculpture must have freed itself from its Babylonian *swaddling clothes* —A.L.Frothingham & O.S.Tonks⟩ **2 :** a period of immaturity ⟨I have never seen him since I was in *swaddling clothes* —G.P.R.James⟩

swad·dy \'swädi\ *n* -ES [[3]*swad* + *-y* (dim. suffix)] *Brit* : SOLDIER

swa·de·shi \swä'dāshē, -deshē\ *n* -s *often cap* [Skt *svadeśin* native, national, fr. *sva* one's own + *deśa* country — more at SUICIDE, DESI] : a movement for national independence in India boycotting foreign goods and encouraging the use of domestic products — compare KHADDAR, SWARAJ

[1]**swag** \'swag, -aa(ə)g,-aig\ *vb* **swagged; swagged; swagging; swags** [prob. of Scand origin; akin to Norw *svaga* to sway, *svagga* to walk unsteadily, ON *sveggja* to cause to sway, veer, swag; akin to MLG *swacken* to rock, reel, OHG *swingan* to swing — more at SWING] *vi* **1 a :** to sway heavily or unsteadily ⟨their shutters ~ —Joseph Mitchell⟩ **b :** to swing or tip out of line : [6]LURCH, TILT ⟨a sudden crosscurrent caused the ship to ~⟩ ⟨trees *swagging* from constant strong winds⟩ **c :** to waver in making a decision : VACILLATE **2 :** to hang heavily from or as if from weight : DROOP, SAG ⟨his heavy sensual face *swagged* —W.J.Locke⟩ ⟨the moon *swagged* in the air —Allen Tate⟩ ~ *vt* **1 :** to cause to sway or lurch ⟨*swagged* the rowboat until it capsized⟩ **2 :** to cause to sag ⟨the snow was starting to ~ down the old roof⟩ **3 a :** to adorn (as clothing) with swags ⟨a taffeta skirt blows out below the *swagged* hipline —*Harper's Bazaar*⟩ **b :** to arrange (as drapery) with swags ⟨the *swagged* plush curtains —Marcia Davenport⟩

[2]**swag** \"\ *n* -s **1** *obs* : a blustering person **2 :** an irregular swaying movement : LURCH ⟨yawed to the deep inner ~ of the river —R.P.Warren⟩ **3 :** a heavy fall : THUD **4 a :** a representation (as of urns or fruit or draperies) used to decorate furniture, walls, pewter, or brass : FESTOON ⟨the carven ~s of Renaissance decoration —*Britain Today*⟩ **b :** a suspended cluster (as of branches or flowers) ⟨great ~s of lilac and laburnum spill over ancient, weathered walls —*advt*⟩ ⟨decking his premises . . . with ~s of mammoth royal-purple ermine tails —Mollie Panter-Downes⟩; *esp* : a cluster of evergreen branches arranged as a decoration for a doorway and used esp. at Christmas ⟨a pine ~ . . . trimmed with kumquats and bells —Frederic Morley⟩ **c** (1) : a decorative drapery that is fastened at two points so that the middle hangs in crescent-shaped folds — compare VALANCE (2) : a decorative draped fold (as on a dress) ⟨dramatic ~s of draping marking the slim skirt —*advt*⟩ **d :** something resembling such a swag esp. in curved outline ⟨our rocks stand midway between two ~s of this uneven high-water line —Peter Mayne⟩ **5 a :** goods acquired by unlawful means : BOOTY, LOOT ⟨the ~ from this and other forms of graft —F.L.Allen⟩ **b :** valuable articles or goods ⟨will find the equitable division of the ~ . . . a problem —Horace Sutton⟩ **c :** MONEY, LUCRE ⟨any listener who may lose out on ~ being offered by another network —Saul Carson⟩ **6 :** a large quantity or amount ⟨watched them putting away great ~s and wedges . . . of starch —Elizabeth Taylor⟩ ⟨spent a big ~ of ratepayers' money —*Sydney (Australia) Bull.*⟩ **7 :** a depression in the earth often filled with water ⟨two brothers . . . were drowned while bathing in an old colliery ~ —*Pall Mall Gazette*⟩ **8** *chiefly Austral* : a pack of personal belongings carried esp. by a swagman

[3]**swag** \"\ *adj* : SAGGING, LAX ⟨men with ~ watch chains —H.E.Bates⟩ ⟨an unsuccessful poet, ~ in mind as in belly —Christopher Morley⟩

swag-bellied \'=¦==\ *adj* : having a large protruding stomach ⟨a grimy, *swag-bellied* drudge —F.T.Bullen⟩

[1]**swage** \'swāj\ *vb* -ED/-ING/-S [ME *swagen*, fr. OF *souagier*, fr. (assumed) VL *suaviare, -suaviare*, fr. L *suavis* sweet — more at SWEET] *vt*, *archaic* : ASSUAGE ⟨quench my flames, and ~ these scorching fires —Francis Quarles⟩ ~ *vi, obs* : DECREASE, ABATE ⟨would swell and ~, according to the tides —Cotton Mather⟩

[2]**swage** \", -wej\ *n* -s [ME, fr. MF *souaige, souage*] **1** *obs* : a decorative border of grooving or molding (as on a candlestick) **2 :** any of several variously shaped or grooved tools: as **a :** a tool used by metalworkers to shape material to a desired form **b :** a tool used to set the teeth of a circular or band saw **c :** a tool used to form bullets **d :** a tool used to straighten damaged casing or pipe in a drilled oil well

swage; *1* bottom, *2* top

[3]**swage** \"\ *vt* -ED/-ING/-S : to shape by or as if by means of a swage: as **a :** to stretch or taper (metal or plastic) by high speed hammering **b :** to form (a bullet) with a swage **c :** SWAGE-SET **d :** to shape to the form of a model, cast, or die by compressive force ⟨porcelain teeth . . . soldered to gold plates *swaged* to fit the mouth —F.L.Hise⟩ **e :** to weld by pressure or hammering ⟨bushings . . . *swaged* on preformed . . . stainless steel wire rope —*Industrial Equipment News*⟩ **f :** to fuse (a strand of suture silk) onto the end of a suture needle

swage block *n* : a perforated cast-iron or steel block with grooved sides that is used in heading bolts and swaging bars of various sizes by hand

swage bolt *n* : a bolt with indentations swaged in its body by means of which it is gripped in masonry

swag·er \'swājə(r), -wej-\ *n* -s [[3]*swage* + *-er*] **1 :** one that swages **2 :** SWAGE

swage-set \'=,=\ *vt* [fr. *swage-set*, adj.] : to broaden the tips of (a saw tooth) to a width greater than the thickness of the saw

swagged *past of* SWAG

[1]**swag·ger** \'swagə(r), -waig-\ *vb* **swaggered; swaggered; swaggering** \-g(ə)riŋ\ **swaggers** [prob. fr. [1]*swag* + *-er* (as in *batter*)] *vi* **1 a :** to conduct oneself in an arrogant or superciliously pompous manner ⟨allowed . . . to ~ and bluster and take the limelight without a word of reproach —Margaret Mead⟩; *esp* : to walk with an air of overbearing self-confidence ⟨buccaneers ~*ed* down the filthy streets —H.E.Rieseberg⟩ **b :** to move with a swinging motion ⟨three or four elephants, loaded with hay, ~*ed* down the crowded street —L.C. Stevens⟩ **c** *Scot* : STAGGER, LURCH **2** *obs* **a :** QUARREL **b :** GRUMBLE **3 :** to talk in a boastful manner : BRAG ⟨talks little of his experience and I ask him why he doesn't ~ more —O.W.Holmes †1935⟩ ~ *vt* : to force by argument or threat : BULLY, BROWBEAT ⟨will strive either to cheat or to ~ you out of your money —Sir Walter Scott⟩

[2]**swagger** \"\ *n* -s **1 a :** an act or instance of swaggering ⟨his stride was majestic — just short of a ~ —Roark Bradford⟩ ⟨insisted, with a prideful ~ —Harry Hansen⟩ **b :** arrogant or conceitedly self-assured behavior ⟨the ~ of the brothers threatened further trouble —Hamlin Garland⟩ ⟨had driven to the opera with the real ~ of the aristocrat —Victoria Sackville-West⟩ **c :** ostentatious display or bravado : FANFARONADE ⟨these overtures are dazzling still for their ~ and dash —Irving Kolodin⟩ **2 :** a self-confident mental or intellectual outlook : COCKINESS ⟨the throng so full of ~ and youth —Osbert Sitwell⟩ ⟨poetry with all the American ~ left in —Louise Bogan⟩

[3]**swagger** \"\ *adj* **1 :** marked by elegance or showiness : FASHIONABLE, SMART, POSH ⟨~ youths in yellow gloves —Arnold Bennett⟩ ⟨a ~ wedding at eleven —Bruce Marshall⟩ **2** *of a coat* : flaring loosely and fully from the shoulder line ⟨familiar ~ trench coat —Lois Long⟩

[4]**swagger** *n* -s [[3]*swagger*] : a coat that flares loosely from the shoulder

[5]**swagger** \"\ *n* -s [[2]*swag* + *-er*] *chiefly Austral* : TRAMP

swag·ger·er \-gərə(r)\ *n* -s : one that swaggers

swaggering *adj* : of, relating to, or having the characteristics of one that swaggers ⟨a more ~ mood than usual —W.L. Shirer⟩ — **swag·ger·ing·ly** *adv*

swagger stick *n* : a short light stick typically capped at both ends with metal or covered with leather and intended for carrying in the hand (as by military officers)

swag·gie \-gē\ *n* -s [*swagman* + *-ie*] *chiefly Austral* : a traveler who carries his personal belongings in a pack

swagging *pres part of* SWAG

swaging *pres part of* SWAGE

swag·man \-gmən\ *also* **swags·man** \-gzmən\ *n, pl* **swagmen** *also* **swagsmen** [*swagman* fr. [2]*swag* + *man*; *swagsman* fr. *swags* (poss. of [2]*swag*) + *man*] *chiefly Austral* : VAGRANT; *esp* : one who carries a swag when traveling **syn** see VAGABOND

swa·go bass \'swä(,)gō-\ *n* [alter. of *Oswego bass*] : SMALLMOUTH BLACK BASS

swags *pres 3d sing of* SWAG, *pl of* SWAG

swa·hi·li \swä'hēlē, -li\ *n, pl* **swahili** *or* **swahilis** *usu cap* [Ar *sawāḥil* (pl. of *sāḥil* coast) + *-īy* belonging to] **1 a :** a Bantu-speaking people of Zanzibar and the adjacent coast **b :** a member of such people **2 :** a Bantu language of East Africa spoken orig. in Zanzibar and the adjacent coast that is a trade and governmental language over much of East Africa and in the Congo — see KINGWANA

swain \'swān\ *n* -s [ME *swain, swayne, swein* boy, servant, fr. ON *sveinn*; akin to OE *swān* herdsman, peasant, swain, OHG *swein* herdsman, swain, *giswīo* brother-in-law, Lith *svaine* sister-in-law, L *suus* one's own — more at SUICIDE] **1** *obs* : BOY, MAN **2 :** one who lives and works in the country : RUSTIC, PEASANT ⟨the sluggish clod, which the rude ~ turns with his share —W.C.Bryant⟩; *specif* : SHEPHERD **3 :** a male admirer or suitor ⟨the many ~s . . . besieging her from every noon to every midnight —Upton Sinclair⟩ **4 :** one having a freehold within a forest

swain·ish \-nish\ *adj* : unrefined in manner or attitude : BOORISH

swainling *n* -s *obs* : a young swain

swainmote *var of* SWANIMOTE

swain·so·na \swān'sōnə\ *n* [NL, fr. Isaac *Swainson* †1806 Eng. gardener] **1** *cap* : a genus of Australian herbs and subshrubs (family Leguminosae) having odd-pinnate leaves and racemes of small variously colored flowers with orbicular standard and twisted wings **2** -s : any plant of the genus *Swainsona* — see DARLING PEA

swain·son pea \'swān(t)sən-\ *n, usu cap S* [after Isaac *Swainson* †1806] : a plant of the genus *Swainsona*

swainson's hawk *also* **swainson hawk** *n* [after William *Swainson* †1855 Eng. naturalist] : a large variable but typically grayish brown to dusky brown hawk (*Buteo swainsoni*) that breeds from Alaska throughout most of western No. America, winters chiefly in the Argentine to which it migrates in large flocks, and feeds on small rodents and large insects

[1]**swale** \'swā(ə)l\ *n* -s [AF *swayl*] *chiefly dial* : BOARD, PLANK, LATH; *also* : PLANKING

[2]**swale** \"\ *var of* SWEAL

[3]**swale** \"\ *n* -s [ME, shade, shady place, prob. of Scand origin; akin to ON *svalr* cool, fresh, *svala* to cool, chill; akin to OE *swelan* to burn, be burned — more at SWELTER] **1** *chiefly dial* **a :** a shady place : SHADE **b :** COOLNESS **2 :** a low-lying stretch of land: as **a :** a small meadow or swamp **b :** an elongated depression in land that is at least seasonally wet or marshy, is usu. heavily vegetated, and is normally without flowing water **c :** a shallow depression in an undulating glacial moraine **d :** a low area between two ridges of a beach or sandspit

[4]**swale** \"\ *vi* -ED/-ING/-S [prob. fr. [1]*sway* + *-le*] : to move with a swaying motion : WAVER

swale·dale \'swā(ə)l,dā(ə)l\ *n* [fr. *Swaledale*, upland vale in Yorkshire, England, where it is bred] **1** *usu cap* : a British breed of hardy mutton type hill sheep producing a very long but coarse fleece **2** -s *often cap* : a sheep of the Swaledale breed

swal·ing·ly *adv* : in a swaling manner

swal·let \'swälət\ *n* -s [[3]*swallow* + *-et*] *dial Eng* : an underground stream; *also* : an opening through which a stream disappears underground

swal·lo \'swä(,)lō\ *n* -s [Malay (Minangkabau) *suala*] : TREPANG

[1]**swal·low** \'swä(,)lō, -lə *also* 'swȯ(-; -ləw, -lō + V; *dial, or NE+V*, -lər\ *n* -s [ME *swalwe, swalowe*, fr. OE *swealwe, swealewe*; akin to OHG *swalawa* swallow, ON *svala* swallow, Russ *solovei* nightingale] **1 :** any of numerous small long-winged passerine birds (family Hirundinidae) that are noted for their graceful flight and regular migrations, have a short bill with a wide gape, small weak feet, plumage usu. iridescent above, and often a deeply forked tail, occur in all parts of the world except New Zealand and polar regions, and feed on insects caught on the wing — see BANK SWALLOW, BARN SWALLOW, MARTIN **2 :** any of several swifts (as the chimney swift) that superficially resemble swallows — see SEA SWALLOW, WOOD SWALLOW

[2]**swallow** \"\ *vb* -ED/-ING/-S [ME *swalowen, swelewen*, fr. OE *swelgan*; akin to OHG *swelgan, swelahan* to swallow, ON *svelgja*] *vt* **1 a :** to take through the esophagus into the stomach : receive into the body through the mouth and throat ⟨~*ing* pint after pint of strong old ale —G.G.Carter⟩ **b :** to eat hurriedly without careful chewing : gulp down ⟨~*ed* his lunch and rushed out⟩ **2 a :** to cause to disappear : envelop completely : ENGULF, DEVOUR ⟨admire the view before the night ~*ed* it —Claud Cockburn⟩ ⟨history is big enough to ~ us too —H.J.Muller⟩ — often used with *up* ⟨wished the floor . . . would open and ~ her up —*Fortnight*⟩ **b :** to cause to become insignificant or unnoticeable : DISPLACE ⟨in danger of being ~*ed* by the world —R.W.Southern⟩ — usu. used with *up* ⟨had been ~*ed* up by the fame of the man he later came to be —Virginia D. Dawson & Betty D. Wilson⟩ ⟨the theory of electromagnetism ~*ed* up the theory of light —A.N.White-

head⟩ **c :** to cause to become engrossed **:** occupy completely — usu. used with *up* **3 a :** to absorb eagerly or easily (as with the mind) ⟨could not ~ books like oysters —Francis Biddle⟩ **b :** to grasp fully **:** COMPREHEND ⟨her head could not ~ it —R.A.W.Hughes⟩ **c :** to seize for oneself **:** APPROPRIATE ⟨feared that his . . . neighbors . . . would ~ him and his people —A.P.Ryan⟩ — often used with *up* ⟨city after city was ~*ed up* —G.G.Coulton⟩ **4 :** to accept readily without question ⟨city fathers who couldn't quite ~ the idea of being ruled by a 17-year-old girl —C.M.L.Beuf⟩; *esp* **:** to believe implicitly and often naïvely ⟨~*ed* his every remark as gospel —Rex Ingamells⟩ ⟨his talks were listened to with openmouthed attention and duly ~*ed* whole —Polly Adler⟩ **5 :** to make a retraction of **:** RECANT ⟨offered the opportunity of ~*ing* their views and fading away without harsher punishment —*Time*⟩ **6 :** to put up with **:** accept submissively **:** ENDURE ⟨~*ed* an injustice which others would not have tolerated —R.G.Adams⟩ **7 :** to refrain from expressing or showing **:** REPRESS ⟨pride was ~*ed* and the government retreated —J.H.Plumb⟩ ⟨~*ed* a smile —Hamilton Basso⟩ **8 :** to utter (as words) indistinctly through failure to open the mouth wide enough ⟨~*ed* so many of his words that he might as well have been singing in Esperanto —Robert Evett⟩ **~** *vi* **1 :** to receive something into the body through the mouth and throat ⟨finished chewing and ~*ed*⟩ **2 :** to perform the action characteristic of swallowing something esp. under emotional stress ⟨~*ed* hard and turned away —F.V.W.Mason⟩ **syn** see EAT — **swallow the anchor :** to retire from life at sea ⟨*swallowed the anchor* and stayed ashore —A.E.Marten⟩

³**swallow** \"\ *n* -s [ME *swalowe, swelowe,* fr. OE *geswelg* gulf, abyss; akin to MHG *swalch* abyss, gullet, ON *svelgr* whirlpool, swallower, *svelgja* to swallow] **1 a** *archaic* **:** a deep opening in the earth **:** CHASM, ABYSS **b** *archaic* (1) **:** a deep body of water (2) **:** WHIRLPOOL **c** *or* **swallow hole** *chiefly Brit* **:** SINK 5 **2 a :** a passage connecting the mouth to the stomach **b :** a part (as the pharynx, throat, esophagus) of this passage **3 a :** a capacity for swallowing **:** APPETITE ⟨measures the honesty and understanding of mankind by a capaciousness of their ~ —Henry Fielding⟩ **b :** a capacity for believing ⟨he believes with the aid of those who have a bigger ~ —Leo Stein⟩ **4 a :** an instance of swallowing **:** GULP ⟨ate the canapé in one ~⟩ **b :** an amount that can be swallowed at one time ⟨took a ~ of brandy to clear his head⟩ **5 :** an aperture in a block on a ship between the sheave and frame through which the rope reeves

swal·low·able \-ˌləwəbəl, -ˌlōəb-\ *adj* **:** capable of being swallowed **:** fit for swallowing

swallow bug *n* **:** any of various hairy blood-sucking bugs (genus *Oeciacus*) that are closely related to the bedbug and usu. feed on swallows and other wild birds but may also attack poultry and occas. man

swallow dive *n, chiefly Brit* **:** SWAN DIVE

swal·low·er \-ləwə(r), -lōə(-\ *n* -s **1 :** one that swallows **2 :** GLUTTON

swallow fish *n* [¹*swallow;* fr. the resemblance of its long gill-fins to a pair of long wings] **:** SAPPHIRINE GURNARD

swallow fork *n* [so called fr. its resemblance to the fork of a swallow's tail] **:** an earmark on an animal made by a triangular cut removing the tip of the ear — see EARMARK illustration

swallow hawk *n* **:** SWALLOW-TAILED KITE

swallowlike \ˈ==,=\ *adj* **:** resembling a swallow esp. in swiftness

swal·low·ling \-ˌləliŋ, -ˌlōl-\ *n* -s **:** a young swallow

swallow plover *n* **:** PRATINCOLE

swallow roller *n* **:** a broad-billed roller of the genus *Eurystomus*

swallows *pl of* SWALLOW, *pres 3d sing of* SWALLOW

swallow shrike *also* **swallow flycatcher** *n* **:** WOOD SWALLOW

swallowtail \ˈ==,=\ *n* [¹*swallow* + *tail;* partly trans. of F *queue d'aronde;* partly trans. of G *schwalbenschwanz*] **1 :** a forked and tapering tail (as of a swallow) **2 :** something resembling the tail of a swallow: as **a :** BROADHEAD 2 **b :** DOVETAIL **c :** an outwork with converging sides, whose front forms a reentrant angle **d :** a pennant tapering to a double point **e** *also* **swallowtail coat :** TAILCOAT **3** *also* **swallowtail butterfly :** any of various large butterflies of *Papilio* and related genera that have the border of the hind wing produced into a taillike process and are brightly colored with black and yellow commonly predominating — see BLACK SWALLOWTAIL, TIGER SWALLOWTAIL, ZEBRA SWALLOWTAIL

swallow-tailed \ˈ==¦=\ *adj* **1 :** marked by a deeply forked tail like that of a swallow ⟨a *swallow-tailed* dress suit⟩ **2 :** DOVETAILED 2

swallow-tailed duck *n* **:** OLD-SQUAW

swallow-tailed flycatcher *n* **:** SCISSORTAIL

swallow-tailed gull *n* **:** SABINE'S GULL

swallow-tailed kite *or* **swallow-tailed hawk** *n* **:** a graceful No. American kite (*Elanoides forficatus*) of the central and southern U.S. that is white with the back, wings, and deeply forked tail black

swallow-tailed moth *n* **:** a European moth (*Ourapteryx sambucaria*) having taillike lobes on the hind wings

swallow-tailed skipper *n* **:** a skipper butterfly (*Urbanus proteus*) of the eastern U.S. that is black with greenish reflections and has a long taillike process on each hind wing

swallow thorn *n* [alter. of *sallow thorn*] **:** SEA BUCKTHORN

swallow-wing \ˈ==,=\ *n* **:** a So. American barbet of the genus *Chelidoptera*

swallowwort \ˈ==,=\ *n* [¹*swallow* + *wort;* partly trans. of D *zwaluwenkruid;* partly trans. of G *schwalbenwurtz;* fr. the form of the pods suggesting a swallow with outspread wings] **1 :** CELANDINE 1 **2 :** any of several plants of the family Asclepiadaceae: as **a :** SOMA **b** (1) **:** BLACK SWALLOWWORT (2) **:** WHITE SWALLOWWORT **c :** BUTTERFLYWEED 1

swam [ME (past), fr. OE *swamm* (past)] *past and chiefly dial past part of* SWIM

swa·mi *also* **swa·my** \ˈswämē, -mi *also* -wȯm-\ *n, pl* **swamis** *or* **swamies** [Hindi *svāmī*, fr. Skt *svāmin* owner, lord, fr. *sva* one's own — more at SUICIDE] **1 a** *archaic* **:** a Hindu idol **b** *often cap* (1) **:** MASTER, LORD — used as a form of respectful address to a Hindu religious teacher or monk (2) **:** an initiated member of a Hindu religious order **2 :** one that resembles or emulates a swami **:** PUNDIT, SEER ⟨that modern ~, the quiz show contestant —*Shakespeare Newsletter*⟩ ⟨amateur theosophists, ~*s*, faith healers and founders of new cults in Manhattan —*Time*⟩

¹**swamp** \ˈswamp\ *adj* [ME (Sc) *swampe* distended, swollen, hollow] *chiefly Scot* **:** THIN, SLENDER

²**swamp** \ˈswämp, -wȯmp\ *n* -s *often attrib* [alter. (prob. influenced by LG *swampen* to quake & MHG *swamp* sponge, fungus) of ME *sompe* swamp, fr. MD *somp* morass, pool; akin to MHG *sumpf* marsh, OE *swamm* sponge, fungus, OHG *swamp* sponge, ON *svöppr*, Goth *swamms* sponge, Gk *somphos* spongy, porous] **1 a :** wet spongy land saturated and sometimes partially or intermittently covered with water **:** water-logged imperfectly drained land unsuitable for agriculture without artificial drainage; *esp* **:** such land supporting a natural vegetation predominantly of shrubs and trees and often intergrading into grassy marsh on the one hand and wet forest on the other — compare BOG **b :** a tract of swamp **2 :** a low spot in a coal deposit — compare SUMP

³**swamp** \"\ *vb* -ED/-ING/-S *vt* **1 :** to fill with or as if with water **:** INUNDATE, SUBMERGE ⟨the boat would probably be ~*ed* as soon as it hit the water —R.S.Porteous⟩ ⟨the land is completely ~*ed* by a mantle of ice —H.I.Drever & P.J. Wyllie⟩ **2 a :** to swallow up **:** overwhelm numerically or by an excess of something **:** ENGULF, FLOOD ⟨the creation of sufficient peers to ~ the opposition in the Lords —K.B. Smellie⟩ ⟨he was ~*ed* in misgivings —Marcia Davenport⟩ ⟨suddenly ~*ed* with orders —Harry Levine⟩ ⟨songs and slogans . . . ~*ed* the country —Dorothy B. Goebel⟩ **b :** to beat decisively or destroy completely **:** DEFEAT, RUIN ⟨the sailors ~*ed* the Springhill squad 13–6 —*Crowsnest*⟩ ⟨an organization of saboteurs . . . was promptly ~*ed* before it could get going —R.E.Danielson⟩ **3 a :** to clear out; *esp* **:** to open a passageway by removing underbrush or trees ⟨by ox-sled in the summer of 1824, ~*ing* a road as he came —*Amer. Guide Series: N.H.*⟩ — usu. used with *out* ⟨crews . . . ~*ed* out small landing strips by hand so that larger planes could come in with grading equipment —H.W.Richardson⟩ **b :** to trim off the branches of (a felled tree) to facilitate skidding **:** LIMB **~** *vi* **:** to become inundated or submerged **:** FLOOD, SINK ⟨ore ships will be filled with sea water until they nearly ~ —*Newsweek*⟩ ⟨a wild-sage smell ~*s* in through doors and windows —H.W.Stoke⟩ **syn** see OVERPOWER

swamp angel *n* **1 :** a person living in or frequenting a swampy region **2 :** HERMIT THRUSH

swamp apple *n* **:** a large white or pink slightly acid edible gall on the swamp azalea caused by a fungus (*Exobasidium vaccinii*)

swamp ash *n* **:** any of several ashes usu. found in swamps: as **a :** a water ash (*Fraxinus caroliniana*) **b :** RED ASH **c :** BLACK ASH 1

swamp azalea *n* **:** a common azalea (*Rhododendron viscosum*) growing in swamps throughout the eastern U.S. and having fragrant white flowers with a clammy corolla — called also *clammy azalea, swamp honeysuckle, white honeysuckle*

swamp bay *n* **1 :** a low and often shrubby tree (*Persea pubescens*) of the southeastern U.S. with pale green lanceolate leaves and pale creamy yellow flowers followed by blackish drupes **2 :** SWEET BAY 2

swamp beggar-ticks *n pl but sing or pl in constr* **:** an American beggar-ticks (*Bidens connata*) common in wet pastures and meadows

swamp·ber·ry \ˈ=-— *see* BERRY\ *n* **:** DWARF RASPBERRY

swamp birch *n* **1 :** YELLOW BIRCH **2 :** WESTERN PAPER BIRCH **3 :** a dwarf birch (*Betula pumila*)

swamp blackberry *n* **:** a dewberry (*Rubus hispidus*) of the eastern U.S.

swamp blackbird *n* **:** REDWING BLACKBIRD

swamp black gum *n* **:** BLACK GUM 1b

swamp blueberry *n* **:** HIGHBUSH BLUEBERRY

swamp box *n* **:** SWAMP MAHOGANY

swamp broom *n* **:** an Australian plant (*Viminaria denudata*) of the family Leguminosae resembling broom

swamp buggy *n* **:** a vehicle used to negotiate swampy terrain: as **a :** MARSH BUGGY **b :** an amphibious tractor **c** *also* **swamp glider :** a flat-bottomed boat driven by an airplane propeller

swamp bulrush *n* **:** a bulrush (*Scirpus etuberculatus*) of eastern No. America having the culm sharply 3-angled esp. above

swamp buttercup *n* **:** a common No. American perennial herb (*Ranunculus septentrionalis*) of low wet places with thick fibrous roots, elongate often trailing or spreading branches, mostly ternate leaves, and bright yellow flowers

swamp cabbage *n* **1 :** SKUNK CABBAGE 1 **2 :** CABBAGE PALMETTO

swamp candle *n* **:** a loosestrife (*Lysimachia terrestris*) with spikes of yellow flowers found in swamps or wet places — usu. used in pl.

swamp cat *n* **:** a wildcat of the Nile delta and adjacent swamps that is prob. a variety of the Kaffir cat

swamp cedar *n* **1 :** SOUTHERN WHITE CEDAR **2 :** an American arborvitae (*Thuja occidentalis*)

swamp chestnut oak *n* **:** BASKET OAK

swamp cottonwood *n* **:** a No. American poplar (*Populus heterophylla*) with resinous buds, large rounded crenate leaves, brown bark and brownish wood — called also *black cottonwood, downy poplar, swamp poplar*

swamp cypress *n* **1 :** either of two trees of the genus *Taxodium:* **a :** a bald cypress (*Taxodium distichum*) **b :** AHUEHUETE **2 :** SOUTHERN WHITE CEDAR

swamp deer *n* **:** a large yellowish brown deer (*Cervus duvaucelli*) of India having in the normal adult male six points on each antler and being in the young and sometimes also the adults spotted with white

swamp dock *n* **:** a common American dock (*Rumex verticillatus*)

swamp dogwood *n* **1 :** SILKY CORNEL **2 :** POISON SUMAC **3 :** HOP TREE **4 :** BUTTONBUSH

swamp elm *n* **:** an American elm (*Ulmus americana*)

swamp·er \ˈswämpə(r), -wȯm-\ *n* -s **1 :** an inhabitant of swamps or lowlands or one familiar with swampy terrain ⟨a guide, fisherman, expert on plant and animal life, crack shot — in short, a real ~ —R.E.Smallman⟩ **2 a :** one that slashes a path (as for skidding or hauling logs) or who trims the limbs and large knots from felled tree trunks — called also *busher, gutterman* **b :** GOPHERMAN **c :** BULL COOK **d :** one that works at the log deck of a woodworking establishment to trim and cut logs for the head saw **3 a :** a general assistant **:** HANDYMAN, HELPER ⟨works as a farm laborer, as a ~ on a truck, as a casual laborer around town —August Hollingshead⟩ ⟨the ~ . . . polished the brass spittoons for nothing, in exchange for the privilege of panning the sawdust in front of the bar —Klondy Nelson⟩; *esp* **:** a worker who performs heavy cleaning duties ⟨a ~ was brooming the night's debris out of Groot's saloon —H.G.Evarts⟩ **b :** a worker in a metal mine who helps load, haul, and unload ore and rock **c :** a rear brakeman

swamp evergreen *n* **:** a common club moss (*Lycopodium lucidulum*) with shining foliage and erect branches

swamp fever *n* [so called fr. its prevalence in low-lying and poorly drained areas] **1 :** LEPTOSPIROSIS **2 :** INFECTIOUS ANEMIA

swamp globeflower *n* **1 :** an American globeflower (*Trollius laxus*) **2 :** BUTTONBUSH

swamp gooseberry *n* **1 :** a No. American prickly shrub (*Ribes lacustre*) of low wet places **2 :** the reddish fruit of the swamp gooseberry

swamp grape *n* **:** FOX GRAPE

swamp gum *n* **1 :** any of various Australian gum trees (esp. *Eucalyptus regnans* and *E. ovata*) **2 :** BLACK GUM 1

swamp hare *n* **:** SWAMP RABBIT 1

swamp harrier *also* **swamp hawk** *n* **:** a harrier (*Circus approximans*) of Australia and neighboring islands that frequents open or marshy regions

swamp-haw \ˈ=,=\ *n* **:** any of several viburnums; *esp* **:** WITHE ROD

swamp hellebore *n* **:** an American hellebore (*Veratrum viride*)

swamphen \ˈ=¦=\ *n* **:** any of various birds (family Rallidae) that frequent swamps: as **a :** COOT 4 **b :** GALLINULE

swamp hickory *n* **1 :** BITTERNUT **2 :** WATER HICKORY

swamp honeysuckle *n* **:** SWAMP AZALEA

swamp hook *n* **:** a large hook on the end of a chain used for skidding or rolling logs

swampier *comparative of* SWAMPY

swampiest *superlative of* SWAMPY

swamp·i·ness \-pēnəs, -pin-\ *n* -ES **:** the quality or state of being swampy

swamping *n* -s [fr. gerund of ³*swamp*] **1 :** an act or instance of submerging or overwhelming ⟨numerical ~ of the natives —A.L.Kroeber⟩ ⟨the ~ of a girl's personality by the subtle influence of her parents' home —J.C.Powys⟩ **2 :** the work performed by a swamper

swamping ax *n* **:** DOUBLE-BIT AX

swampland \ˈ=,=\ *n* **:** SWAMP 1

swamp laurel *n* **1 :** a laurel (*Kalmia polifolia*) of bogs of cooler parts of No. America with pale leaves that are glaucous beneath and small purple flowers **2 :** SWEET BAY **3 :** LOBLOLLY BAY 1

swamp lily *n* **1 :** ATAMASCO LILY **2 :** a white-flowered crinum (*Crinum americanum*) of the southern U.S. **3 :** LIZARD'S-TAIL **4 :** TURK'S-CAP LILY b

swamp loosestrife *n* **:** a woody perennial marsh herb (*Decodon verticillatus*) of the family Lythraceae of eastern No. America having opposite or whorled lanceolate leaves and magenta flowers in axillary clusters — called also *swamp willow*

swamp magnolia *n* **:** SWEET BAY 2

swamp mahogany *n* **1 :** a small to medium-sized Australian eucalypt (*Eucalyptus robusta*) that grows esp. on tidal flats and yields a reddish straight-grained damp-resistant lumber **2 :** a tropical Australian tree (*Tristania suaveolens*) that yields a reddish hardwood of firm even texture that is used esp. for flooring and is highly resistant to damp and insect attack — called also *swamp box*

swamp mallow *n* **:** a rose mallow (*Hibiscus moscheutos*)

swamp maple *n* **:** any of several maples found in moist lowlands: as **a :** RED MAPLE **b :** SILVER MAPLE **c :** CALIFORNIA BOX ELDER

swamp milkweed *or* **swamp silkweed** *n* **:** a No. American milkweed (*Asclepias incarnata*) with lanceolate leaves and crimson or purple flowers

swamp moss *n* **:** SPHAGNUM

swamp oak *n* **1 :** a leafless Australian shrub (*Viminaria denudata*) of the family Leguminosae resembling broom and having small orange-yellow flowers and a one-seeded pod **2 :** a beefwood (*Casuarina glauca*) **3 :** any of several American oaks (as the pin oak, basket oak, or swamp white oak) that thrive in wet soils

swamp oat grass *n* **:** an oat grass of the genus *Trisetum*

swamp ore *n* **:** BOG IRON ORE

swamp owl *n* **:** SHORT-EARED OWL

swamp partridge *n* **:** SPRUCE GROUSE

swamp pheasant *n* **:** an Australian coucal (*Centropus phasianinus*)

swamp pine *n* **:** any of several pines that prefer or endure moist situations: as **a :** LONGLEAF PINE **b :** CARIBBEAN PINE **c :** LOBLOLLY PINE 1 **d :** BISHOP PINE

swamp pink *n* **1 a :** SWAMP AZALEA **b :** PINXTER FLOWER **2 :** a grass pink (*Calopogon pulchellus*) **3 :** a rare bog herb (*Helonias bullata*) of the eastern U.S.

swamp poplar *n* **:** SWAMP COTTONWOOD

swamp post oak *n* **:** OVERCUP OAK

swamp potato *n* **:** SWAN POTATO

swamp privet *n* **:** an American shrub (*Forestiera acuminata*) with opposite leaves and small axillary flowers

swamp quail *n* **1 :** a quail (*Coturnix ypsilophorus*) of Australia, Tasmania, and New Guinea that is reddish brown and grayish with V-shaped black bars beneath **2 :** a painted quail (*Coturnix chinensis*) of southern Asia and Australasia

swamp rabbit *n* **1 :** a large big-headed short-furred rabbit (*Sylvilagus aquaticus*) of moist lowlands in the Mississippi valley and southeastern U.S. that is closely related to but larger and darker than the cottontail — called also *canecutter, swamp hare* **2 :** MARSH HARE

swamp rattler *n* **:** MASSASAUGA a

swamp red bay *n* **:** SWAMP BAY 1

swamp robin *n* **1 :** CHEWINK **2 :** any of several thrushes; *esp* **:** WOOD THRUSH 1

swamp rose *n* **:** either of two wild roses (*Rosa carolina* and *R. palustris*) of the eastern U.S. that clamber over bushes in swamps

swamp rose mallow *n* **:** ROSE MALLOW 1

swamps *pl of* SWAMP, *pres 3d sing of* SWAMP

swamp sassafras *n* **:** SWEET BAY 2

swamp saxifrage *n* **:** a No. American saxifrage (*Saxifraga pennsylvanica*) bearing greenish flowers

swamp spanish oak *n, usu cap 2d S* **:** a pin oak (*Quercus palustris*)

swamp sparrow *n* **:** a common sparrow (*Melospiza georgiana*) of eastern No. America that lives in swampy places and is related to the song sparrow but distinguished by the absence of streaks on the underparts

swamp spleenwort *n* **:** a narrow-leaved spleenwort (*Asplenium pycnocarpon*) found in moist places in eastern No. America

swamp spruce *n* **:** BLACK SPRUCE 1

swamp squawweed *n* **:** GOLDEN RAGWORT

swamp sumac *n* **:** POISON SUMAC

swamp sunflower *n* **1 :** SNEEZEWEED 1a **2 :** a sunflower (*Helianthus angustifolius*) of eastern No. America found in wet bogs and having narrow leaves

swamp tea *n* **1 :** LABRADOR TEA a **2 :** any of several Australian or Tasmanian shrubs or trees of the genus *Melaleuca; esp* **:** a tea tree (*M. squarrosa*)

swamp thistle *n* **:** a No. American thistle (*Cirsium muticum*) with large purple flower heads

swamp tupelo *n* **:** TUPELO 1

swamp turnip *n* **:** JACK-IN-THE-PULPIT

swamp warbler *n* **:** any of several No. American warblers (as the prothonotary, the blue-winged, and the golden-winged) inhabiting swampy places

swampweed \ˈ=,=\ *n* **:** a small Australian fleshy-leaved creeping herb (*Selliera radicans*) of the family Goodeniaceae

swamp white cedar *n* **:** SOUTHERN WHITE CEDAR

swamp white oak *n* **1 :** a large flaky-barked oak (*Quercus bicolor*) of the eastern U.S. resembling white oak but having smaller leaves with fewer lobes and heavy strong wood that is used in construction **2 :** OVERCUP OAK **3 :** BASKET OAK

swamp willow *n* **1 :** a black willow (*Salix nigra*) **2 :** SWAMP LOOSESTRIFE

swamp willow herb *n* **:** a low bog herb (*Epilobium palustre*) of the north temperate zone with opposite oblong leaves, small whitish pink flowers, and long slender pods

swampwood \ˈ=,=\ *n* **1 :** LEATHERWOOD 1a **2 :** BUTTONBUSH

swampy \-pē,-pi\ *adj* -ER/-EST [²*swamp* + -*y*] **:** consisting of or resembling a swamp **:** water-logged and poorly drained

swampy cree *n, usu cap S&C* **1 :** an Algonquian people comprising the Maskegon and the Monsoni formerly inhabiting swampy regions of Manitoba and Ontario from Lake Winnipeg and Lake of the Woods to the Moose river and Hudson Bay and sometimes classed with the Cree people and sometimes with the Chippewa **2 :** a member of the Swampy Cree people

swamy *var of* SWAMI

¹**swan** \ˈswän *also* -wȯn\ *n, pl* **swans** *also* **swan** *often attrib* [ME, fr. OE; akin to MD *swane* swan, MHG *swan*, ON *svanr* swan, OE *swinsian* to make music, *swinn* music, melody; perh. fr. the legendary belief that the swan sings before it dies — more at SOUND] **1 :** any of various heavy-bodied very long-necked aquatic birds related to but larger than the geese, constituting a distinct subfamily of the family Anatidae, having usu. pure white plumage when adult, walking awkwardly, flying strongly when once started, and being graceful swimmers — see BLACK SWAN, MUTE SWAN, TRUMPETER SWAN, WHOOPER SWAN **2 a :** one that resembles or is likened to a swan ⟨the accused are all ~*s* and the blackness of guilt is thrown upon the witnesses —Miles Prance⟩ **b :** one who makes music of the melodic sweetness traditionally ascribed to the dying song of a swan **:** BARD, SINGER ⟨sweet ~ of Avon —Ben Jonson⟩

²**swan** \"\ *vi* **swanned; swanned; swanning; swans :** to wander aimlessly or sweep majestically **:** DALLY, SAIL ⟨such vehicles . . . would hamper operations if they started *swanning* about in the midst of a swirling, hit-and-run tank fight —Russell Hill⟩ ⟨professional delegates, *swanning* with practiced appreciation from one . . . convention to another —James Cameron⟩ ⟨aircraft equipped with loudspeakers *swanned* low over the forest with a new message —*Time*⟩

³**swan** \"\ *vb* **swanned; swanned; swanning; swans** [perh. euphemism for *swear*] *vi, dial* **:** DECLARE, SWEAR ⟨we're goin' to miss her, I ~ —J.C.Lincoln⟩ **~** *vt, dial* **:** SURPRISE ⟨said he'd be *swanned* . . . and took on like there was no predicting what a school education would do for a clerk —Frederick Way⟩

⁴**swan** *usu cap, var of* SVAN

swan animalcule *n* [¹*swan*] **:** any of various ciliate protozoans having a necklike extension of the body

swan boat *n* **:** a small pedal boat usu. for children or sightseers pedaled by an operator who sits aft in a large model of a swan ⟨*swan boats*, like those of Boston, carry visitors through the canals —Merrill Folsom⟩

swan dive *n* **:** a front dive executed with the trunk extended, head back, back arched, and arms spread sideways at shoulder height until the dive is nearly completed when they are brought together above the head to form a straight line with the body as the diver enters the water

swanflower \ˈ=,=\ *n* **:** any of several plants having flowers whose shape suggests the neck of a swan; *esp* **:** an orchid of the genus *Cycnoches* — called also *swanneck*

¹**swang** [ME, fr. OE] *chiefly dial past of* SWING

²**swang** \ˈswaŋ\ *n* -s [prob. blend of ²*swamp* and E dial. *wang* field (fr. ME *wang, wong*) — more at WONG] *dial Eng* **:** low wet grassy land **:** SWAMP

swan goose *n* **:** a swanlike goose; *specif* **:** CHINESE GOOSE

swanherd \ˈ=,=\ *n* [ME, fr. ¹*swan* + *herd*] **:** a herdsman of swans ⟨the royal ~ of England⟩

swan-hopper \ˈ=,häpə(r)\ *n* [by alter.] **:** SWAN-UPPER

swan-hopping \-piŋ\ *n* -s [by alter.] **:** SWAN-UPPING

swan·i·mote \ˈswänə,mōt\ *also* **swain·mote** \ˈswān,m-\ *or* **swan·mote** \ˈswän,m-\ *n* -s [ME *swanimot*, fr. (assumed) OE *swāngemōt*, fr. OE *swān* herdsman, peasant + *gemōt* judicial assembly, gemot — more at SWAIN, GEMOT] **:** a court formerly held before foresters, verderers, and other forest offi- try offenses against vert and venison and to hear grievances against forest officers

1swank \'swaŋk\ *adj* [MLG or MD *swanc* supple, pliant; akin to MHG *swank* supple, movable, swaying, OE *swancor* slender, supple, OHG *swenken* to fling, hurl, *swingan* to swing — more at SWING] *Scot* **:** full of life or energy **:** ACTIVE

2swank \", -waiŋk\ *vb* -ED/-ING/-S [perh. fr. MHG *swanken* to sway, swag; akin to MD *swancen* to sway, *swanc* supple, pliant] *vi* **:** to show off **:** behave ostentatiously **:** SWAGGER, STRUT ⟨he ~*ed* around . . . in white suits —Saul Bellow⟩ — often used with *it* ⟨he likes to slum and likes to ~ it too —*Newsweek*⟩ ~ *vt* **1 :** to doll up ⟨the roof as a whole was ~*ed* and gabled to madness —F.L.Wright⟩ **2 :** SNUB ⟨afraid to ~ an old acquaintance —Al Hine⟩

3swank \"\ *n* -S **1 :** arrogance or ostentation of dress or manner **:** PRETENTIOUSNESS, SWAGGER ⟨give his wife some diamond bracelets for ~ —J.B.S.Haldane⟩ ⟨a group of Briticisms which have connotations of ~ for Americans —Thomas Pyles⟩ **2 :** ELEGANCE, STYLE ⟨a prep school of considerable ~ —R.L.Taylor⟩

4swank \" *or* **swanky** \-kē,-ki\ *adj* -ER/-EST **1 :** characterized by showy display **:** OSTENTATIOUS, PLUSHY ⟨a new sport-model car, a big ~ sky-blue job, with wire wheels —F.B. Gipson⟩ **2 :** fashionably elegant **:** LUXURIOUS, SMART ⟨homes in the ~, well-kept Prado residential district —June W. Brown⟩ ⟨linen, nonchalant and ~ and cut with demure . . . simplicity —Lois Long⟩

swank·er \-kə(r)\ *n* -S [*2swank* + *-er*] *chiefly Brit* **:** one that swaggers or puts on airs

swank·i·ly \-kəlē, -li\ *adv* **:** in a swank manner

swank·i·ness \-kēnəs, -kin-\ *n* -ES **:** the quality or state of being swank

swank·ing \'swaŋkən, -kiŋ\ *adj* [*1swanky* + *-ing*] *chiefly Scot* **:** STRAPPING

1swanky *also* **swank·ie** \-ki\ *n, pl* **swankies** [of LG or D origin; akin to MLG & MD *swanc* supple, pliant — more at SWANK] *Scot* **:** an active alert strapping fellow

2swanky \" *or* **swank·ey** \"\ *n, pl* **swankies** *or* **swankeys** [*swank* of unknown origin + *-y*] *dial Brit* **:** inferior ale, beer, or cider

swanlike \'ˌ=ˌ=\ *adj* **:** resembling a swan or its long neck **:** GRACEFUL, SINUOUS ⟨~ movement⟩ ⟨a ~ neck⟩

swan maiden *n* [trans. of G *schwanenjungfrau*] **:** a maiden of Germanic mythology held to be able to transform herself into a swan by the use of a magical object (as a ring or a cloak of swan feathers)

swanmark \'ˌ=ˌ=\ *n* **:** a mark of ownership cut on the upper mandible of a swan

swan mussel *n* **:** a common European freshwater mussel (*Anodonta cygnea*)

swan–neck *also* **swan's neck** \'ˌ=ˌ=\ *n* **1 :** something (as a piece of pipe or railing) having a gooseneck or an ogee curve: as **a :** GOOSENECK a **b :** a bend in a handrail of a stair consisting of a ramp terminating in a knee **c :** one of the S-shaped cornices of a scroll pediment **2** *usu* **swanneck :** SWANFLOWER — **swan–necked** \'ˌ=ˌ=\ *adj*

swanned *past of* SWAN

swan·nery \'swänərē *also* -wȯn-\ *n* -ES [*1swan* + *-ery*] **:** a place where swans are bred or kept

swanning *pres part of* SWAN

swan·ny \-nē\ *adj, archaic* **:** SWANLIKE; *also* **:** full of swans

swan orchid *n* **:** a swanflower of the genus *Cycnoches*

swan pan *var of* SUAN PAN

swan potato *n* [alter. of *swamp potato*] **:** a plant of the genus *Sagittaria* having tubers used as food: as **a :** a common arrowhead (*S. latifolia*) of wet lands of the U.S. and southern Canada with starchy tubers once used extensively by the Indians **b :** a similar common Old World arrowhead (*S. sagittifolia*) that is sometimes cultivated in Japan and China

swan river daisy *n, usu cap S&R* [fr. *Swan River*, Western Australia] **:** an Australian annual herb (*Brachycome iberidifolia*) much cultivated for its flower heads with bluish, violet, rose, white, or variegated rays

swan river everlasting *n, usu cap S&R* [fr. *Swan River*, Western Australia] **:** an Australian everlasting (*Helipterum manglesii*)

swans *pl of* SWAN, *pres 3d sing of* SWAN

swans·combe man \'swänzkəm-\ *n, usu cap S* [fr. *Swanscombe*, Kent, England, where the remains were found] **:** a prehistoric man known from the left parietal and an occipital bone found in middle Pleistocene Thames gravels in association with Acheulean artifacts and coeval fauna and prob. representing an early form of Homo sapiens antedating Neanderthal man

swans·down \'swänzˌdau̇n *also* -wȯn-\ *n* [*swan's* (gen. of *1swan*) + *down*] **1 :** the soft downy feathers of the swan esp. when used as trimming on articles of dress ⟨she was wrapped in grey satin edged with ~ —Victoria Sackville-West⟩ **2 :** a heavy cotton flannel with a thick nap on the face made with sateen weave

swan·sea \-nz|ē, -n(t)s|, |i\ *adj, usu cap* [fr. *Swansea*, Wales] **:** of or from the city of Swansea, Wales **:** of the kind or style prevalent in Swansea

swan shot *n* **:** a large size of shot used in hunting wildfowl and other small game

swan·skin \-nzˌkin, -nˌsk-\ *n* **1 :** the skin of a swan with the down or feathers on it **2 :** any of various fabrics resembling flannel and having a soft nap or surface

swan song *n* [trans. of G *schwanenlied*] **1 :** a song of great sweetness formerly thought to be uttered by the swan just before its death **2 :** a farewell appearance or final act or pronouncement ⟨the *swan song* of a chivalry which died in the century before —*New Republic*⟩ ⟨before turning over the gavel, delivered his *swan song* as chairman of the board⟩; *specif* **:** the last work (as of an author or composer)

swan spectrum \-nz|p-, -n|sp-\ *n, usu cap 1st S* [after William *Swan* †1894 Eng. physicist] **:** the spectrum of the blue cone in a Bunsen burner when operating strongly caused by the excitation of carbon compounds; *also* **:** a similar spectrum observed in some vacuum-tube discharges

swan–upper \-ˌnəpə(r)\ *n* -S [*swan-upping* + *-er*] **:** an official who cuts a mark of ownership on the upper mandible of a swan

swan–upping \-piŋ\ *n* -S **1 :** the practice or process of marking young swans for the owners **2 :** an annual expedition for the purpose of swan-upping on the English Thames

1swap *also* **swop** \'swäp *also* -wȯp\ *vb* **swapped** *also* **swopped; swapped** *also* **swopped; swapping** *also* **swopping; swaps** *also* **swops** [ME *swapen*, *swappen* to strike, hit, hurl, throw, of imit. origin] *vt* **1** *chiefly dial* **:** to cause to strike or fall against something by throwing, moving, or flinging **:** BANG **2** [so called fr. the practice of striking hands in closing a business deal] **a :** to give in exchange **:** EXCHANGE, BARTER ⟨offered to ~ 250,000 tons of rice a year for 50,000 tons of rubber —Tom Fitzsimmons⟩ ⟨~ notes on progress in their particular fields —F.L.Allen⟩ **b** *obs* **:** to make or agree to (a bargain) ~ *vi* **1** *archaic* **:** to move swiftly and with violent force **:** SWOOP, POUNCE **2 :** to make an exchange **:** engage in trading

2swap \"\ *adv, chiefly dial* **:** at a blow **:** quickly and forcefully

3swap \"\ *n* -S [ME, fr. *swapen* to swap] **1** *chiefly dial* **:** BLOW, STROKE **2 :** the act or process of exchanging one thing for another **:** EXCHANGE, BARTER, TRADE ⟨stock ~⟩

swape \'swāp\ *n* -S [ME *swaipe* lever, swivel, prob. of Scand origin; akin to ON *sveipr* fold, *sveipa* to sweep, swoop — more at SWOOP] **1** *dial Eng* **:** a pole or bar used as a lever or swivel **2** *dial Eng* **:** a long steering oar used by keelmen on the Tyne

swap hook *n, dial Eng* **:** REAPING HOOK

swap·per \'swäpə(r), -wȯp-\ *n* -S **:** one that swaps

swapping *adj* [ME, striking, flapping, fr. pres. part. of *swappen* to strike, throw] *dial* **:** very big **:** HUGE

swa·raj \swə'rāj\ *n* -ES [Skt *svarāj* self-ruling, *svārājya* independent rule, fr. *sva* one's own + *rājya* rule — more at SUICIDE, RAJ] **:** political independence **:** national or local self-government **:** HOME RULE — compare KHADDAR, SWADESHI

swa·raj·ist \-jəst\ *n* -S **:** a member of a political party in British India advocating swaraj

1sward \'swȯ(ə)rd, -ō(ə)d\ *n* -S [ME, fr. OE *sweard*, *swearth* skin, hide, rind; akin to OFris *swarde* scalp, MD *swaerde* skin, hide, MHG *swart* skin, hide, fur, rind, W *gweryd* sward, earth, soil, OIr *feronn*, *ferann* land, field, L *operire* to cover — more at WEIR] **1** *archaic* **:** SKIN, RIND **2 a** (1) **:** the grassy surface of land **:** the part of the soil which is filled with the roots of grass **:** TURF, SOD (2) **:** a portion of ground covered with sward **:** GREENSWARD **b :** a growth or structure (as reindeer moss or a fungus) that resembles sward

2sward \"\ *vt* -ED/-ING/-S **:** to produce sward upon **:** cover with sward

sware [ME *swar*, alter. of *swoor*, fr. OE *swōr*] *archaic past of* SWEAR

1swarf \'swȯ(ə)rf, -wärf\ *n* [ME *swarff*, prob. of Scand origin; akin to ON *svarfa* to sweep, swerve — more at SWERVE] *Scot* **:** SWOON

2swarf \"\ *vi, chiefly Scot* **:** SWOON

3swarf \'swȯ(ə)rf, -ō(ə)f\ *n* -S [of Scand origin; akin to ON *svarf* file dust, *sverfa* to file — more at SWERVE] **1 :** fine metallic particles removed by a cutting or grinding tool; *specif* **:** chippings and shavings from soft iron castings used as a reducing agent in various chemical syntheses **2 :** the continuous thread of wax or lacquer produced in cutting the grooves of an original phonograph record

swarga *var of* SVARGA

1swarm \'swȯ(ə)rm, -ō(ə)m\ *n* -S [ME, fr. OE *swearm*; akin to OHG *swaram* swarm, ON *svarmr* tumult; prob. akin to ON *svarra* to swarm, MLG *swirren* to whir, buzz, L *susurrus* hum, murmur, OSlav *svirati* to whistle, Skt *svarati* he sounds, resounds] **1 :** a great number of honeybees emigrating together from a hive in company with a queen to start a new colony elsewhere; *also* **:** a colony of honeybees settled in a hive **2 a :** a great often overwhelming number usu. in motion and esp. migratory **:** a dense moving crowd or throng ⟨a ~ of butterflies⟩ ⟨a ~ of meteorites⟩ ⟨a ~ of local peasants crowded around our roped-off space —Christopher Rand⟩; *specif* **:** a horde seeking a new home ⟨a ~ of barbarians erupted from the steppes⟩ **b** *archaic* **:** a group of eels **c :** an aggregation of free-floating or free-swimming unicellular organisms — usu. used of zoospores **d :** a considerable number of similar geologic features or phenomena occurring close together in space or time ⟨a ~ of dikes⟩ ⟨an earthquake ~⟩ **e :** an aggregation of molecules (as those responsible for cybotactic effects) in a liquid — compare CYBOTAXIS

2swarm \"\ *vb* -ED/-ING/-S [ME *swarmen*, fr. *1swarm*] *vi* **1 a** *of bees* **:** to collect together and depart from a hive in a body to form a new colony — compare AFTERSWARM **b :** to escape in a swarm (as from a sporangium) usu. with a typical vibrating movement **:** move about actively previous to or following such escape **2 a :** to migrate, move, or assemble in a crowd **:** throng together **:** move in throngs ⟨rural population ~*ed* into the industrial towns —Roger Burlingame⟩ ⟨customers ~*ed* before the . . . meat counters —Clyde Hostetter⟩ **b :** to occur or exist in great numbers **:** be extremely numerous ⟨venomous species ~*ed* among the grass tussocks —C.L.Barrett⟩ **c :** to hover about or move irresistibly in the manner of a bee in a swarm ⟨had taken place . . . with monseigneur ~*ing* within a yard or two —Charles Dickens⟩ ⟨the little boy . . . just ~*ing* around me —William Faulkner⟩ **d :** to cover or infuse an area ⟨the exhilaration ~*ing* over my face —Allen Tate⟩ ⟨this tropical jungle ~*s* over the slopes of a mountain —Lawrence & Sylvia Martin⟩ **3 :** to contain a vast number and esp. moving throngs **:** be alive **:** TEEM ⟨the big blue station wagon . . . forced its way down the ~*ing* boulevard —Barnaby Conrad⟩ — usu. used with *with* ⟨gently rolling fields . . . ~*ing* with wild Canada geese —*Amer. Guide Series: Md.*⟩ ~ *vt* **1 :** to fill with a swarm **:** cause to teem ⟨myriads of small marine insects that ~*ed* the ocean —H.J.Wolfe⟩ ⟨men will ~ the decks —T.O.Heggen⟩ **2 :** to induce (a colony of bees) to swarm

3swarm \"\ *vb* -ED/-ING/-S [origin unknown] *vi* **:** to engage in climbing esp. hand over hand **:** SHIN ⟨two little tads . . . having a good time ~*ing* over the logs —Helen Eustis⟩ ⟨~ up a mast⟩ ~ *vt* **:** to climb up **:** MOUNT

swarm·er \-mə(r)\ *n* -S [*2swarm* + *-er*] **1 :** one that swarms **:** a member of a swarm **2 :** a hive of bees ready to swarm **3 :** SWARM SPORE

swarming *n* -S [fr. gerund of *2swarm*] **1 :** emigration or movement in a swarm **2 :** a period of motility esp. in ciliate spores

swarm spore *also* **swarm cell** *n* [*1swarm*] **:** any of various minute motile sexual or asexual spores: as **a :** ZOOSPORE **b :** PLANOGAMETE

swart \'swȯ(ə)rt\ *adj* [ME, fr. OE *sweart*; akin to OHG *swarz* black, ON *svartr*, Goth *swarts* black, L *sordes* dirt, *sordēre* to be dirty] **1 a :** of a dark color, complexion, or cast **:** BLACKISH, SWARTHY **b** *archaic* **:** producing a swarthy complexion **:** causing to tan **2 :** BANEFUL, MALIGNANT

swart·back \'swȯrtˌbak\ *n* [alter. (influenced by Norw *svartbak* swartback) of earlier *swarthback*, fr. ME *suerthbak*, fr. ON *svartbakr*, fr. *svartr* black + *bak* back — more at BACK] **:** GREAT BLACK-BACKED GULL

1swarth \'swȯ(ə)rth, -wärth\ *n* -S [ME, fr. OE *swearth* skin, hide, rind — more at SWARD] **1** *dial* **:** SKIN, RIND **2 :** SWARD 2

2swarth \"\ *vi, chiefly dial* **:** to produce sward

3swarth \"\ *n* -S [alter. (influenced by *1swarth*) of *1swath*] *dial* **:** a crop of grass for hay

4swarth \'swȯ(ə)rth\ *adj* [alter. of *1swart*] **:** SWART, SWARTHY

5swarth \'swȯ(ə)rth, -wärth\ *var of* SWARF

swarth·i·ness \'swȯ(r)thēnəs, -th-, |in-\ *n* -ES **:** the quality or state of being swarthy

swarthy \|ē, |i\ *adj* -ER/-EST [alter. of obs. *swarty*, fr. *swart* + *-y*] **:** possessing or being a dark color, complexion, or cast **:** DUSKY

swart·kranz ape–man *or* **swart·krans man** \'sfärtˌkränz, 'svä-\ *n, usu cap S* [fr. *Swartkranz* or *Swartkrans*, region near Johannesburg, So. Africa, where the remains were found] **:** a large extinct southern African australopithecine (*Homo erectus capensis*) known from skulls, teeth, and other fossil skeletal remains and having a flat face and brow with weak supraorbital crest, a well-developed sagittal crest, a distinctly manlike jaw and teeth, and a brain capacity surpassing that of any recent ape and possibly that of Java man — compare KROMDRAAI APE-MAN

swart·rut·ter \'swȯ(r)tˌrəd·ə(r)\ *n* -S [alter. (influenced by D *swartruiter* black rider) of G *schwartze rotte*, lit., black gang] **:** a member of any of various 16th and 17th century marauding bands in the Netherlands who blackened their faces and wore black garb

swart·zia \'swȯ(r)tsēə\ *n, cap* [NL, fr. Olof *Swartz* †1818 Swed. botanist + NL *-ia*] **:** a genus of tropical trees (family Leguminosae) with racemose irregular flowers of which the corolla is often reduced to a single petal or absent — see WAMARA

swartz·ite \-tˌsīt\ *n* -S [George K. *Swartz* †1949 Am. geologist + E *-ite*] **:** a mineral $CaMg(UO_2)(CO_3)_3.12H_2O$ consisting of a hydrous carbonate of calcium, magnesium, and uranium and occurring as clusters of tiny prismatic green crystals

1swash \'swäsh, -wȯsh\ *n* -ES [prob. imit.] **1 a** (1) **:** a body or mass of dashing splashing water (2) *or* **swash channel :** a narrow sound or channel of water lying within a sandbank or between a sandbank and the shore **b** (1) **:** a dashing or splashing of water against or upon something; *specif* **:** the rush of water up a beach from a breaking wave (2) **:** the sound made by the swash of water **c :** a bar over which the sea washes or an area covered by shallow seawater **d :** a slushy sloppy condition of the ground **2 a :** one that swaggers and blusters **:** SWASHBUCKLER **b :** blustering noise or behavior **:** SWAGGER **3 :** a heavy or resounding blow on or from a yielding substance

2swash \"\ *vb* -ED/-ING/-ES *vi* **1 :** to act in a blustering and bullying manner **:** put on or present an air of swaggering bravado **:** SWAGGER **2 :** to make a noise by or as if by clashing a sword on a sword or shield **3 :** to make violent noisy movements; *also* **:** to move or wander violently or erratically ⟨whole tribes and peoples have ~*ed* back and forth between Europe and Asia —Waldemar Kaempffert⟩ **4 a** *of a liquid* **:** to move or become moved back and forth or around and around with a splashing sound ⟨water ~*ed* throatily in a gourd —Oliver LaFarge⟩ **b :** to move within a liquid **:** cause a liquid to splash or become washed around or back and forth ⟨the intruder . . . ~*ing* through the pond —Mary McCarthy⟩ ~ *vt* **1 :** to cause (a liquid) to splash about or dash upon something ⟨~ water in a pail⟩ **2 :** to cause a liquid to splash forcefully upon ⟨buckets to ~ the decks with water —H.A. Chippendale⟩

3swash \"\ *adj* [fr. obs. *swash* slanting, of unknown origin] **:** having one or more strokes ending in an extended flourish ⟨the ~ letters *A R P N*⟩

swash·buck·le \'swäshˌbəkəl, -wȯsh-\ *vi* -ED/-ING/-S [back-formation fr. *swashbuckler*] **1 :** to play the swashbuckler **:** affect in the manner of a swashbuckler **2 :** to compose or consist of a tale filled with the adventures of swashbucklers

swash·buck·ler \-k(ə)lə(r)\ *n* -S [*2swash* + *buckler*] **1 :** a boasting violently active soldier, adventurer, or ruffian **:** a blustering daredevil **:** SWAGGERER, BRAVO **2 a :** a novel, play, or esp. movie dealing with the adventures of a swashbuckling hero and usu. having a setting in a romantic past era or exotic locale **b :** a writer of or actor in a swashbuckler

swash·buck·ler·ing \-ləriŋ\ *adj* **:** SWASHBUCKLING

swash·buck·ling \-k(ə)liŋ, -klēŋ\ *adj* [fr. *swashbuckler*, after such pairs as E *wrestler: wrestling*, adj.] **1 :** acting in the manner of a swashbuckler **2 :** characteristic of, marked by, or done by swashbucklers ⟨~ rovers from all points of the compass came to the island principality —*Amer. Guide Series: Texas*⟩ ⟨~ historical novel⟩ ⟨gawky uncertainty and ~ juvenility —T.D.Clark⟩

swash bulkhead *n* [*1swash*] **:** a transverse or longitudinal baffle in a tank aboard a ship to check excessive movement of liquid contents

swash·er \'swäshə(r), -wȯsh-\ *n* -S [*2swash* + *-er*] **:** SWASHBUCKLER

swashing *adj* [fr. pres. part. of *2swash*] **1 :** SWASHBUCKLING **2 a :** forcefully accompanied by a clashing sound **:** RESOUNDING ⟨~ blow —Shak.⟩ **b :** SPLASHING

swash mark *n* **:** a fine line or tiny ridge of sandy debris left on a beach by the swash at its farthest reach

swash plate *n* [fr. obs. *swash* slanting, of unknown origin] **1 :** a revolving circular plate set obliquely on a shaft and acting as a cam to give a reciprocating motion to a rod in a direction parallel to the shaft **2** [*1swash*] **:** SWASH BULKHEAD

swash–turned \'ˌ=ˌ=\ *adj* [fr. obs. *swash* slanting] **:** turned in a spiral pattern ⟨a *swash-turned* baluster⟩

swashway \'ˌ=ˌ=\ *n* [*1swash* + *way*] **:** SWASH 1a(2)

swashy \'swäshē, -wȯshē\ *adj* -ER/-EST [*1swash* + *-y*] **1 :** WET, WATERY **2 :** WEAK, INSIPID

swas·ti·ka *also* **svas·ti·ka** *or* **swas·ti·ca** \'sw|ästəkə, -tēkə, *chiefly Brit* |as-; *sometimes* =ˈstēkə *or* (')sf| *or* (')sv|\ *n* -S [Skt *svastika*, fr. *svasti* welfare, fr. *su-* well + *asti* he is; fr. the belief that it brings good luck — more at IS] **1 :** a symbol or ornament in the form of a Greek cross with the arms bent at right angles all in the same rotary direction or any of numerous variant forms of this symbol or ornament — called also *fylfot*; compare GAMMADION, HAKENKREUZ — see GAMMADION illustration **2 :** a swastika with arms extended clockwise

swastika

1swat *also* **swot** \'swä|t *also* -wȯ|; *usu* |d.+V\ *vb* **swatted; swatted; swatting; swats** [alter. of *1squat*] *vi* **1** *dial Eng* **:** SQUAT **2 :** to hit or hit out at an object or to flail about with the arms as if attempting to strike an object ⟨an old woman with a rolled mat *swatted* at her smartly —Esther Warner⟩ ~ *vt* **:** to strike or hit with a quick, heavy slapping blow usu. with a club, bat, or swatter ⟨~ a person over the head with an umbrella⟩ ⟨~ a ball hard⟩ **syn** see STRIKE

2swat *also* **swot** \"\ *n* -S **1 :** a vigorous or crushing blow ⟨gave him a ~ on the rear end to help him along —Shirley A. Grau⟩ **2 :** a long hit in baseball; *esp* **:** HOME RUN

3swat \"\ [ME (past), alter. of *swatte*, fr. OE *swǣtte*; ME (past part.), fr. OE *geswǣtt*] *dial past of* SWEAT

4swat \"\ *Brit var of* SWOT

5swat \" *or* **swa·ti** \-ˌād·ē, -ȯd·ē\ *n, pl* **swat** *or* **swats** *or* **swati** *or* **swatis** *usu cap* **1 :** a Muslim people of northern West Pakistan **2 :** a member of the Swat people

1swatch \'swäch *also* -wȯch\ *n* -ES [origin unknown] **1** *chiefly dial* **:** an owner's tally or tag attached to cloth sent to a dyer **2 a** (1) **:** a sample piece or patch (as of fabric, leather, or paper) (2) **:** a collection of samples esp. when issued by a single manufacturer **b :** something that serves as a typical act, instance, or member **:** a characteristic specimen ⟨a quick glance at a ~ of dialogue . . . is usually enough to identify one of his stories —John Woodburn⟩ **3 :** PATCH ⟨white ~*es* of hair ringing the sides and back of his head —Carson Wyatt⟩ ⟨irregular ~*es* of planted land —Josephine Pinckney⟩ ⟨his face . . . spotted with ~*es* of purple-red —Norman Mailer⟩ **4 :** a small number collected or clustered together or considered as a unit ⟨impressive ~*es* of canceled stamps —D.S.Boyer⟩ ⟨many of my own ~ of alumni have passed away —Christopher Morley⟩

2swatch \" *or* **swatchway** \'ˌ=ˌ=\ *n, pl* **swatches** *or* **swatchways** [perh. alter. of *1swash*] *Brit* **:** SWASH 1a(2)

1swath \'swä|th *also* -wȯ| *or* |th\ *or* **swathe** \-wāth\ *n, pl* **swaths** \|thz, |ths\ *or* **swathes** [ME *swath*, fr. OE *swæth*, *swathu* footstep, track, trace; akin to OFris *swethe* limit, boundary, MD *swat* swath, MHG *swade*] **1 a** (1) **:** the whole sweep of a scythe or a machine in mowing or cradling (2) **:** the path or the breadth of a path cut in one course **b :** a windrow of cut grain or grass left by a scythe or mowing machine **c :** a crop or row of grass or grain ready for reaping or haying **2 :** a long broad strip or belt ⟨the wide ~ of a firebreak —Victor Canning⟩ ⟨a ~ of land three blocks long —Lewis Mumford⟩ **3 :** a stroke of or as if of a scythe ⟨integrating factors which have survived the ~ of time —W.W.Taylor⟩ **4 :** a collection or a space emptied of a collection destroyed as if by a scythe ⟨chain stores cut great ~*s* in the jobbing business —*Amer. Guide Series: Minn.*⟩

2swath \'swath\ *dial Eng var of* SWARD

swathboard \'ˌ=ˌ=\ *n* [*1swath* + *board*] **:** a slanting board attached to the outer end of the cutter bar of a mower to force the cut grass into a narrower swath so as to leave a cleared strip for the mower wheel when cutting the next swath

1swathe \'swāth *also* -wȯth *sometimes* -wāth *or* -wäth *or* -wȯth\ *vt* -ED/-ING/-S [ME *swathen*, fr. OE *swathian*; akin to ON *svatha* to swathe, MLG *swede* bandage, W *chwidr* wild, foolish, Lith *svaigti* to become dizzy; basic meaning: turning, turn] **1 :** to bind, wrap, or swaddle with a swathe ⟨legs . . . *swathed* from the knee to the ankle in rough strips —Edna S. V. Millay⟩ **2 a :** to wrap or cover tightly or thoroughly in enveloping clothing or material ⟨a figure, *swathed* in black from head to foot —T.B.Costain⟩ ⟨the barge was still *swathed* in sheets —Michael Reynolds⟩ **b :** to put clothes or an article of clothing on ⟨*swathed* myself in the apron —Carolyn Hannay⟩ **3 :** to envelop, surround, or cover over in the manner of a swathe ⟨the whole stage is *swathed* in ever-changing light —E.R.Bentley⟩ ⟨fog ~*s* the river⟩

2swathe \'swāth\ *or* **swath** *like* 1SWATH\ *n* -S **1 :** a band used in wrapping or enveloping: as **a** *archaic* **:** SWADDLING CLOTHES — often used in pl. **b :** a surgical bandage **2 :** an enveloping medium

swath·er \'swä|thə(r), |th- *also* -wȯ| *sometimes* -wāth-\ *n* -S [*1swath* + *-er*] **1 :** an implement with a long cutter bar for cutting grain and seed crops and dropping them into a windrow for curing before gathering and threshing **2 :** an attachment to a mower which turns the swath into a windrow behind the mower wheels

swathing band *for pronunc see* 1SWATHE\ *n* [ME, fr. *swathing* (fr. gerund of *swathen* to swathe) + *band*] **1 swathing bands** *pl* **:** SWADDLING CLOTHES **2** *obs* **:** BANDAGE

swathing clothes *or* **swathing clouts** *n pl* [ME] *obs* **:** SWADDLING CLOTHES

1swa·tow \'swä;tau̇\ *n* -S *usu cap* **:** the Chinese dialect of Swatow, China, and vicinity

2swatow \"\ *adj, usu cap* [fr. *Swatow*, city in southeastern China] **:** of or from the city of Swatow, China **:** of the kind or style prevalent in Swatow

1swats \'swats\ *n pl* [prob. fr. OE *swātan*, pl., beer + E *-s* (pl. suffix); perh. akin to OE *swēte* sweet — more at SWEET] *Scot* **:** DRINK; *esp* **:** new ale ⟨reaming ~ that drank divinely —Robert Burns⟩

2swats *pl of* SWAT, *pres 3d sing of* SWAT

1swat·ter \'swätər\ *vi* [prob. fr. G dial. *schwattern*, *schwadern* to splash, spill, scatter, of imit. origin] *chiefly Scot* **:** to splash about

2swat·ter \ˈswäd·ə(r), |tə- *also* -wȯ|\ *n* -s [ˈswat + -er] **:** one that swats: as **a :** a device for killing insects usu. consisting of a flat piece of perforated rubber or plastic or fine-meshed wire netting attached to a handle — called also *flyswatter* **b :** a heavy hitter in baseball

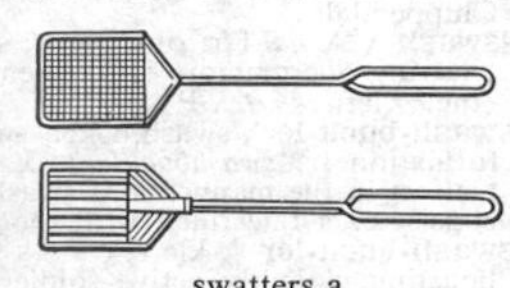
swatters a

swatting *pres part of* SWAT

s wave *n, usu cap S* **:** SHEAR WAVE

swa·ver \ˈswāvə(r)\ *vi* [ME *swaveren,* perh. of Scand origin; akin to Norw dial. *sveiva* to swing, ON *sveifla* to swing, spin, *svifa* to rove, ramble, drift — more at SWIVEL] *dial Brit* **:** STAGGER

1sway \ˈswā\ *vb* -ED/-ING/-S [alter. (prob. influenced by MLG *swāien* to sway) of earlier *swey* to fall, go down, swoon, fr. ME *sweyen, sweghen* to go down, swoon, go, move, prob. of Scand origin; akin to ON *sveigja* to bow, bend, sway, *sveigr* switch (flexible twig), *svigna* to bend, give way; akin to MLG *swāien* to sway, OE *swathian* to swathe — more at SWATHE] *vi* **1 a** (1) **:** to move or become moved in usu. slow and rhythmic back and forth oscillations **:** swing esp. with suppleness or grace from or as if from a base or pivot ⟨singing to us, ~*ing* to the rhythm —O.S.J.Gogarty⟩ ⟨the redbird . . . lit on a tall white iris, making it ~ gently —Clarissa F. Cushman⟩ (2) **:** to move forward while swaying from side to side ⟨caravans of camels, ~*ing* with their padded feet across the desert —L.P.Smith⟩ **b** (1) **:** to become rocked by weight, pressure, or applied force esp. into a permanent new position ⟨the earthquake caused the wall to ~ to the right⟩ (2) **:** to move gently from an upright to a leaning position ⟨~*ed* over and actually leaned his head on her shoulder —Joseph Conrad⟩ **2 a :** to hold sway **:** act as ruler or governor **b :** to be a deciding or prevailing influence ⟨distinguish what motive actually ~*ed* with him —Abraham Tucker⟩ **3 a :** to approach with hostile intentions **b** *obs* **:** to move in a specified direction **4 :** to alternate regularly between one point, position, or opinion and another ⟨the battle has ~*ed* backwards and forwards with incredible fury —Sir Winston Churchill⟩ ⟨the industry continues to ~ between extravagancy and bankruptcy —Andrew Buchanan⟩ **~** *vt* **1 a :** to cause to sway **:** set to swinging, rocking, nodding, oscillating, or vacillating ⟨~*ed* her head from side to side with worry —Winifred Bambrick⟩ **b :** to cause to bend downward to one side ⟨the pillars were ~*ed* three inches by the blast⟩ **c :** to cause to turn aside **:** DEFLECT, DIVERT **d :** to hoist or erect esp. by throwing the weight of the body on a halyard or other rope — often used with *up* ⟨~*ed* up her topmast —Kenneth Roberts⟩ **2 a** (1) **:** to be the legitimate wielder of (a symbol of authority) ⟨reign . . . true heir, and his full scepter ~ —John Milton⟩ (2) **:** to possess or exercise authority, control, guidance, or sovereignty over **:** GOVERN, RULE ⟨with a bloody hand he ~*s* a nation —Lord Byron⟩ **b** *archaic* **:** to make use of (an implement); *also* **:** to play upon (an instrument) **3 a :** to cause (as a person or his opinions) to vacillate **b :** to exert a guiding or controlling influence upon **:** determine or help to determine a course of action, viewpoint, or decision of (as a person) or the manner or direction of (as a course of action) ⟨man's reason is imperfect, and may be ~*ed* by his physical and social environment —Herbert Agar⟩ ⟨many men are ~*ed* by nicknames and catchwords —A.W.Long⟩ ⟨a presidential aspirant should be able to ~ vast audiences with his eloquence —V.L.Albjerg⟩ **c :** to deflect from an accustomed or chosen object ⟨a determination from which he could not be ~*ed* —T.B.Costain⟩ **syn** see AFFECT, SWING

2sway \"\ *n* -s [alter. (influenced by 1*sway*) of ME *sweyh, sweigh,* fr. *sweyen, sweghen* to swoon, go, move] **1 a** *obs* **:** a rotating motion about an axis **b** (1) **:** the action or an instance of swaying or of being swayed **:** an oscillating, fluctuating, swinging, nodding, or sweeping motion ⟨an easy ~ to the lurch of the ship —F.W.Crofts⟩ (2) **:** the sweep, force, or momentum of something swaying or being swayed ⟨the ~ of battle —John Milton⟩ (3) **:** an inclination or deflection caused by or as if by swaying **2 a :** a preponderating force or pressure **:** a controlling influence ⟨the personal element . . . should have little . . . ~ in determining the limits of legislative power —B.N.Cardozo⟩ ⟨scientists . . . under the ~ of a naturalistic optimism —W.R.Inge⟩ **b :** sovereign power **:** DOMINION, RULE ⟨the endeavor of the civil regime to extend its ~ to these islands —V.G.Heiser⟩ ⟨breaking down the ~ of the hereditary chiefs —Tom Marvel⟩ ⟨the region was under the ~ of great empires —David Mitrany⟩ **c :** the ability to exercise influence or authority or apply preponderating pressure **:** DOMINANCE ⟨classicism with its stateliness and promise of stability held ~ —Carl Bridenbaugh⟩ ⟨the idea once held ~ that the floor of the sea . . . was without life —R.E.Coker⟩ **3 :** grace of form, figure, carriage, or action ⟨his presence and social ~ —E.H.Collis⟩ **syn** see POWER

swayback \ˈ≈ˌ≈\ *n* **1 :** an abnormally hollow condition or sagging of the back found esp. in horses; *also* **:** a back so shaped — opposed to *camelback* **2 :** LORDOSIS **3 :** a copper-deficiency disease of young or newborn lambs that is marked by demyelination of the brain resulting in weakness, staggering gait, and collapse and is almost universally fatal but is readily preventable by copper supplementation of the diet of the pregnant ewe

swaybacked *also* **swayback** \ˈ≈ˌ≈\ *adj* **1 :** having or afflicted with swayback — opposed to *camelback* **2 a :** having or being a part with a concave center ⟨two cabins end to end . . . with a ~ roof over both —Emmett Gowen⟩ **b :** characterized by unevenness of quality, direction, or intention ⟨his performance follows a curiously ~ course —John Mason Brown⟩

sway bar *n* [2*sway*] **1 :** a bar attached to the hounds in the rear of the front axle of a wagon so as to slide on the reach as the axle is swung in turning **2 :** a steel bar placed near and parallel to an axle of an automotive vehicle to prevent excessive sway in turning

sway brace *n* **:** a brace to prevent swaying

swayed *adj* [fr. past part. of 1*sway*] **:** SWAYBACKED

sway·er \ˈswāə(r), -we(ə)r, -weə\ *n* -s **:** one that sways

swaying *n* -s [fr. gerund of 1*sway*] **:** a hollowing or sagging esp. as a result of swayback

sway·ing·ly *adv* **:** in a swaying manner **:** with swaying

sway·less \ˈswāləs\ *adj* **:** not capable of being swayed

sway pole *n* **:** a long pole or bar (as at a well) that can be pivoted for lifting or hanging

sways *pres 3d sing of* SWAY, *pl of* SWAY

swa·zi \ˈswäzē\ *n, pl* **swazi** *or* **swazis** *usu cap* **1 a :** a Bantu people of Swaziland **b :** a member of the Swazi people **2 :** a Bantu language of the Swazi people closely related to Zulu and Xhosa with which it forms the Ngoni group

swa·zi·land \-zēˌland\ *adj, usu cap* [fr. *Swaziland,* country in southern Africa] **:** of or from the country of Swaziland **:** of the kind or style prevalent in Swaziland

SWB *abbr* short wheelbase

swbd *abbr* switchboard

swchmn *abbr* switchman

SWD *abbr* sliding watertight door

swd *abbr* **1** sewed **2** sideward

sweal \ˈswēl, *esp before pause or consonant* -ēəl\ *vb* -ED/-ING/-S [ME *swailen, sweilen, swelen,* partly fr. OE *swelan* (vi) to burn; partly fr. OE *swǣlan* (vt) to cause to burn — more at SWELTER] *vi* **1** *chiefly dial, of a candle* **:** to melt away **:** GUTTER **2** *chiefly dial* **:** to waste away **~** *vt, chiefly dial* **:** BURN

1swear \ˈswe(ə)r, ˈswa(ə)(ə)r, ˈsweə, ˈswa(ə)ə\ *vb* **swore** \ˈswō(ə)r, ˈswȯ(ə)r, ˈswōə, ˈswȯ(ə)\ *or archaic* **sware** *pronounced like* SWEAR\ **sworn** \ˈswō(ə)rn, ˈswȯ(ə)n\ **swearing; swears** [ME *sweren,* fr. OE *swerian;* akin to OHG *swerien, swerren* to swear, ON *sverja* to swear, *svara* to answer, Goth *swaran* to swear, Oscan *sverrunei* (dat.) speaker, and perh. to OE *swearm* swarm — more at SWARM] *vt* **1 :** to utter or take solemnly (an oath) ⟨the queen ~*s* the oath at the high altar —*Newsweek*⟩ **2 a :** to solemnly declare or assert as true **:** affirm with an oath ⟨*swore* Monday to the banking committee he didn't yet know why he was fired —*Wall Street Jour.*⟩ ⟨a *sworn* affidavit⟩ **b :** to make a solemn promise of **:** pledge sacredly ⟨*swore* to uphold the Constitution⟩ **c :** to assert or promise emphatically or earnestly **:** ASSEVERATE ⟨~*s* that such action will cause the meat to shrivel in the cooking —*Amer. Guide Series: N.C.*⟩ ⟨*swore* to pay the money back soon⟩ **3 a :** to put to an oath **:** administer an oath to ⟨~ the witness⟩ ⟨*swore* him to secrecy⟩ **b :** to bind by a formal oath to the proper performance of a duty, function, or office esp. in connection with the law ⟨*swore* the jury⟩ ⟨two years later he was *sworn* to the bar —*Time*⟩ **4** *obs* **:** to invoke the name of (a sacred being) in an oath ⟨now by Apollo, King, thou *swear'st* thy gods in vain —Shak.⟩ **5 :** to bring into a specified or implied state by swearing ⟨*swore* himself into a fit of apoplexy⟩ ⟨*swore* his life away⟩ **~** *vi* **1 a :** to make a solemn promise or statement of intention **:** vow ⟨stay, sir, do not promise — do not ~ —Robert Browning⟩ **b :** to utter a solemn declaration with an appeal to God or a god for the truth of what is stated **:** affirm solemnly by something regarded as sacred **2 :** to give evidence or state under oath or to subscribe under the penalties of perjury **3 :** to use profane, blasphemous, or obscene language **:** CURSE ⟨not in the habit of ~*ing* even in his thoughts —LeRoy Smith⟩

syn AFFIRM, ASSEVERATE, DEPOSE, TESTIFY: to SWEAR is to give a solemn pledge, esp. before a court, often with an appeal to God or by laying one's hand on the Bible ⟨I do solemnly *swear* (or affirm) that I will faithfully execute the office of president of the United States —*U.S. Constitution*⟩ ⟨would have to make a statement and *swear* to it —Margaret Deland⟩ To AFFIRM is to state solemnly and with conviction, esp. before a court although without reference to God or like gestures ⟨must annually *affirm* his belief in a fundamentalist interpretation of the Scriptures —*Amer. Guide Series: Tenn.*⟩ ⟨the National Grange has again *affirmed* its conviction that the farmers' best hope for the future is in self-help —*Christian Science Monitor*⟩ To ASSEVERATE is to affirm earnestly and emphatically ⟨*asseverating* her innocence, and the innocence of her governess —Edith Sitwell⟩ ⟨*asseverated* that he had there become a mighty horseman —Osbert Sitwell⟩ To DEPOSE is to make a statement, as an affidavit or deposition, in writing or under oath ⟨the witness *deposed* that she had seen the man fire the shot⟩ ⟨the policeman called by the prosecutor's servant *deposed* to finding the prosecutor bruised and bleeding —Arthur Morrison⟩ To TESTIFY is to give evidence, often on the witness stand or in a deposition and usu. under oath or under penalties of perjury, or as if in such circumstances ⟨the following June he *testified* in favor of a Congressional bill providing for military advice and assistance to China —*Current Biog.*⟩ ⟨he offered affidavits from various individuals, including his parish priest, *testifying* to his good character —John Warner⟩

— swear at 1 : to use violent language to **:** CURSE ⟨*swore at* him for being late⟩ **2 :** to be out of harmony with **:** clash with ⟨a trailing lavender negligee that *swore at* her bright red hair —C.M.Smith⟩ **— swear by 1 :** to take an oath by ⟨*swear by* the saints⟩ ⟨*swear by* Apollo, the physician⟩ ⟨*swear by* my faith⟩ **2 :** to be sure of the existence of **:** be barely positive of — used in the phrase *enough to swear by* **3 :** to place great confidence in **:** trust implicitly ⟨the doctor has only just begun practice, but his patients *swear by* him⟩ **— swear for :** to answer for **:** GUARANTEE ⟨his friends will *swear for* his integrity⟩ **— swear off :** to vow to abstain from **:** RENOUNCE ⟨has *sworn off* drinking⟩ ⟨since his illness, he has had to *swear off* tennis⟩ **— swear the peace against :** to make oath that one is under actual fear of death or bodily harm from another in order to compel the accused to find sureties that he will keep the peace

2swear \"\ *n* -s **1 :** OATH ⟨do you think I would stand here and say that ~ and tell a story —Carson McCullers⟩ **2 :** a swearword or a fit of swearing ⟨finally the butler's suave voice . . . provoked a full-bodied ~ —*McClure's*⟩

swear·er \ˈswerə(r), ˈswa(ə)r-\ *n* -s [ME *swerere,* fr. *sweren* to swear + *-ere* -er] **1 :** one that takes an oath **2 :** one that uses swearwords **:** one given to swearing

swearer-in \ˈ≈≈ˌ≈\ *n, pl* **swearers-in** [*swear in* + *-er*] **:** one who administers an oath; *esp* **:** one who administers an oath of office

swear in *vt* **:** to induct into office by administration of an oath

swearing *pres part of* SWEAR

swear out *vt* **:** to procure (a warrant for arrest) by making a sworn accusation ⟨*swore* a warrant *out* against him⟩

swears *pres 3d sing of* SWEAR, *pl of* SWEAR

swearword \ˈ≈ˌ≈\ *n* **:** a profane or obscene oath or word **:** EXPLETIVE ⟨we strove after the most dreadful words we knew, and they were our father's ~*s* —Eden Phillpotts⟩

1sweat \ˈswet, *usu* -ed·+V\ *vb* **sweat** \"\ *or* **sweated** \-ed·əd, -etəd\ *or dial* **swat** \ˈswät, *also* -wȯt; *usu* -äd·+V\ **sweat** *or* **sweated** *or dial* **swat; sweating; sweats** [ME *sweten,* fr. OE *swǣtan,* fr. *swāt* sweat; akin to OFris & OS *swēt* sweat, OHG *sweiz,* ON *sveiti,* L *sudor* sweat, *sudare* to sweat, Gk *hidrōs* sweat, Skt *svidyati, svedate* he sweats] *vi* **1 a :** to excrete moisture in visible quantities through the openings of the sweat glands **:** PERSPIRE **b :** to labor in such a manner as to cause perspiration **:** work hard **:** DRUDGE ⟨some can absorb knowledge, the more tardy must ~ for it —T.S.Eliot⟩ ⟨now the machines do all the ~*ing* —A.H.Raskin⟩ ⟨grunt and ~ under a weary life —Shak.⟩ **2 a** (1) **:** to emit or exude moisture ⟨green plants ~ when closely packed⟩ ⟨cheese in ripening ~*s*⟩ (2) **:** to exude oil or other liquid ⟨a varnish that ~*s*⟩ (3) **:** to exude nitroglycerin — used of dynamite in which nitroglycerin separates from its adsorbent **b :** to gather surface moisture in beads as a result of condensation ⟨stones ~ at night⟩ ⟨the glass is ~*ing*⟩ **c** (1) **:** FERMENT — used esp. of tobacco or cacao beans (2) **:** PUTREFY — used esp. of hides **3 a** *archaic* **:** to suffer an infliction or penalty **b :** to undergo anxiety or mental or emotional distress ⟨grieve and ~ to think of all the time we have let go by and fear disappointments still —O.W.Holmes †1935⟩ **4 :** to become exuded through pores or a porous surface **:** OOZE ⟨the surplus moisture will ~ out⟩ ⟨the oil coat may ~ through this varnish⟩ **~** *vt* **1 :** to emit or seem to emit from pores **:** EXUDE ⟨the flowers ~ dew⟩ **2 a :** to manipulate or move by hard physical effort ⟨two sooty men intently occupied in ~*ing* a tire on the wheel —Cliff Farrell⟩ ⟨machine gunners ~*ed* their weapons up the hill —Georg Meyers⟩ **b :** to produce by hard work or drudgery ⟨~*ed* out one novel after another⟩ ⟨stood in front of her cookstove ~*ing* up supper —P.E.Green⟩ **3 a :** to get rid of or lose by or as if by sweating or being sweated — usu. used with *away* or *off* ⟨~*ed* away three pounds in the steam room⟩ **b :** to reduce the excess weight or bulk of by or as if by sweating — used with *down* ⟨novel about the peacetime army, ~*ed* down to a fine, muscular picture —*Time*⟩ **4 :** to make wet with perspiration ⟨the white shirt and pants he had bought himself . . . were ~*ed* through —Vicki Baum⟩ **5 a :** to cause to excrete moisture from the skin ⟨his physicians ~*ed* him⟩ **b :** to drive hard **:** OVERWORK ⟨he ~*ed* his crew unmercifully, to prepare them for any emergency⟩ **c :** to exact work from at low wages and under unfair or unhealthful conditions ⟨the good employers would have either to ~ the workers like the bad ones, or else be driven out of business —G.B.Shaw⟩ **d** *slang* **:** to give the third degree to ⟨advise ~*ing* her with everything the police have got —J.M. Cain⟩ **6 :** to cause to exude or lose moisture: as **a :** to dry thoroughly (as wood in a charcoal pit) **b :** to subject to fermentation (as tobacco leaves or cacao beans) **c :** to putrefy (sheepskins or hides) by exposing to warm, humid air so as to loosen the wool or hair **7 :** to extract something valuable from by unfair or dishonest means **:** BLEED, FLEECE; *specif* **:** to remove particles of metal from (a coin) by abrasion **8 a** (1) **:** to heat (as solder) so as to melt and cause to run esp. between surfaces to unite them ⟨~ soft solder into seams⟩ (2) **:** to unite by such means ⟨~ a gold pen to an iridium point⟩ **b** (1) **:** to heat so as to extract an easily fusible constituent ⟨~ bismuth ore⟩ (2) **:** to extract (oil and low-melting material) by heating a substance ⟨~ oil out of crude paraffin wax⟩ (3) **:** to cause (as paraffin wax) to sweat ⟨scale wax that has been further ~*ed* to specific melting point ranges —J.B. Tuttle⟩ **c :** to expose (citrus fruit) to a high temperature to hasten the coloring **d :** to apply heat to **:** STEAM ⟨~ the finely chopped onions in half the butter until tender —*Food & Cookery Rev.*⟩ **9 :** to hoist, haul, or set (as a sail or rope) as flat or taut as possible — usu. used with *up* **— sweat blood :** to work or worry intensely ⟨in preparing speeches each *sweats blood* in his own way —Stewart Cockburn⟩

2sweat \"\ *n* -s [ME *swet, sweet,* fr. *sweten* to sweat] **1 :** hard work **:** DRUDGERY ⟨the engines . . . saved wages and they saved ~, but they killed prices —Thomas Wood †1950⟩ **2 :** the fluid excreted from the sweat glands of the skin **:** PERSPIRATION ⟨in the ~ of your face you shall eat bread —Gen 3:19 (RSV)⟩ **3 :** moisture issuing from or gathering in drops on the surface of any substance or object ⟨~ formed on the cold pitcher⟩ ⟨the ~ of hay in a stack⟩ **4 a** (1) **:** the condition of one sweating or sweated ⟨he was in a ~ from fear⟩ ⟨apples spoiled by ~⟩ (2) **:** a spell of sweating ⟨a good ~ and a cold shower to freshen you up⟩ **b :** abnormally profuse sweating in some conditions or diseases — often used in pl. ⟨soaking ~*s*⟩ **c :** an exercise given a horse before a race **5 :** something that induces or promotes perspiration **:** SUDORIFIC **6 :** a sweating process; *specif* **:** a natural fermentation that takes place during the aging of tobacco and makes it more aromatic and pliable **7 :** a state of worry or impatience ⟨the average audience is in such a ~ to learn about the future —W.L.Gresham⟩ **8 :** CHUCK-A-LUCK **9 :** SWEATBAND 1 **10** *chiefly Brit* **:** SOLDIER — used esp. in the phrase *old sweat* ⟨real old ~*s* with tattooed arms —John Masters⟩ **— no sweat** *slang* **:** with little or no difficulty **:** EASILY ⟨anybody can land on the new deck, *no sweat* —Frank Harvey⟩

sweatband \ˈ≈ˌ≈\ *n* **1 :** a usu. leather band used as a lining around the inner edge of a hat or cap to prevent perspiration damage **2 :** a band of material tied around the head to absorb perspiration

sweat bee *n* **:** any of numerous small short-tongued bees; *esp* **:** a bee of the genus *Halictus*

sweat board *n* **:** a strip of wood fastened to the inboard surface of a ship's frame to prevent cargo from coming in contact with the shell plating

sweatbox \ˈ≈ˌ≈\ *n* **1 :** a device for sweating something (as hides in tanning, dried figs, raisins) **2 :** a room, place, enclosure, or procedure in which one is made to sweat; *esp* **:** a narrow box in which a prisoner is placed for punishment

sweat cloth *n* **:** a cloth layout used for dice games by early American gamblers; *also* **:** any of several games played on such a layout

sweated *adj* **:** of, subjected to, or produced under a sweating system ⟨~ labor⟩ ⟨~ goods⟩

sweat·er \ˈswed·ə(r), -etə-\ *n* -s **1 :** one that sweats esp. as a result of exertion or hard work **2 a :** SUDORIFIC **b :** an exertion or job that causes sweating **3 a :** a heavy woolen garment worn esp. by athletes after exercise or to induce sweating **b :** a knitted or sometimes crocheted elastic jacket or pullover made in various styles and of various materials and usu. having ribbing around the neck, cuffs, and lower edge **4 :** one who operates a sweatshop or employs sweated labor **5 a :** one that brings about sweating (as of tobacco or hides) **b :** a large shallow pan or stack of such pans or a small tank in which paraffin is sweated

sweat·ered \-ə(r)d\ *adj* **:** covered with a sweater ⟨hunched his thin, ~ shoulders —Ralph Robin⟩ **:** wearing a sweater ⟨a familiar ~ figure sprawled in a lawn chair —A.J.Liebling⟩

sweater girl *n* **:** a girl with a shapely bust

sweater man *or* **sweat man** *n* **:** a petroleum worker who operates equipment for sweating oil from slack wax

sweat·ful \ˈswetfəl\ *adj* **:** accompanied by or producing sweating **:** SWEATY ⟨the ~ practice sessions which mold the mighty football teams —Al Dewlen⟩

sweat gland *n* **:** a simple tubular gland of the skin that secretes perspiration, that in man is widely distributed in nearly all parts of the skin, and that consists typically of an epithelial tube extending spirally from a minute pore which opens on the surface of the skin into the deeper layer of the dermis or into the subcutaneous tissues where it ends in a convoluted tuft

sweathouse \ˈ≈ˌ≈\ *n* **1 :** a hut, lodge, or cavern heated by steam from water poured on hot stones and used esp. by American Indians for ritual or therapeutic sweating **2 :** a place used for sweating (as tobacco)

sweat·i·ly \ˈswe|d·ᵊlē, |tᵊl, |ᵊli, |əl-\ *adv* **:** in a sweaty manner **:** PERSPIRINGLY, LABORIOUSLY ⟨try, though not too ~, to entertain —Clifton Fadiman⟩

sweat·i·ness \|ēnəs, |in-\ *n* -ES **:** the quality or state of being sweaty

sweating *pres part of* SWEAT

sweating house *n* **:** SWEATHOUSE

sweating iron *n* **:** SWEAT SCRAPER

sweating plant *n* **:** BONESET 1

sweating sickness *n* **1 :** MILIARY FEVER **2 :** a febrile disease of southern African calves that is marked by profuse sweating, loss of hair and scaling of the skin, salivation, and more or less erosive inflammation of the mouth and that is probably due to thiamine deficiency but may represent an infective process

sweating system *n* **:** a system of employing labor (as in sweatshops) for long hours at low wages and often under unsafe or unsanitary conditions

sweat joint *n* **:** a soldered joint

sweat·less \ˈswetləs\ *adj* **:** being without sweat

sweat lodge *n* **:** SWEATHOUSE 1

sweat out *vt* **1 :** to endure, wait for, or wait through the course of (something beyond one's control) ⟨all they could do was to close their ranks, make the best speed they could, and *sweat* it *out* to the end —Nicholas Monsarrat⟩ ⟨these officers ate out of a mess kit and *sweated out* the same chow line I did —C.E.Fread⟩ **2 :** to work one's way painfully or tediously through (as a problem or situation) or to (as a solution or objective) ⟨a sprinkling of older men and women, experienced teachers, who are *sweating out* a master's degree —D.J.Lloyd⟩

sweat pants *n pl* **:** pants having a drawstring waist and elastic cuffs at the ankle that are worn esp. by athletes in warming up

sweatproof \ˈ≈ˌ≈\ *adj* **:** resistant to sweat

sweat room *n* **:** SWEATHOUSE 2

sweats *pres 3d sing of* SWEAT, *pl of* SWEAT

sweat scraper *n* **:** a flexible metal blade or curved rod used to sweep lather and soil from a sweating horse

sweat shirt *n* **:** a collarless long-sleeved pullover made of cotton jersey with a smooth-finished face and a heavily napped back

sweatshop \ˈ≈ˌ≈\ *n* **:** a usu. small manufacturing establishment employing workers under unfair and unsanitary conditions

sweat suit *n* **:** an exercise suit consisting of a sweat shirt and sweat pants

sweatweed \ˈ≈ˌ≈\ *n* **:** MARSHMALLOW 1a

sweat suit

sweaty \ˈswed·ē, -etē, -i\ *adj* -ER/-EST [ME *swety,* fr. *swet* sweat + *-y*] **1 a :** causing sweat by extreme heat ⟨a ~ day⟩ **b :** LABORED ⟨how ~ and clumsy he can make an honest argument look —R.E.Garis⟩ **2 :** moist, stained, or odorous with sweat ⟨homesteaders clutching their ~ bills and coins —Harriot B. Barbour⟩ ⟨even through the ~ football togs . . . you could still smell the flowers —A.M. Latimer⟩

swede \ˈswēd\ *n* -s [LG *Swede* (fr. MLG *Swēde*) or D *Zweed,* fr. MD *Swede;* akin to OE *Swēon* Swedes, OSw *Svear, Sviar,* ON *Svíar*] **1** *cap* **a :** a native or inhabitant of Sweden **b :** a person of Swedish descent **2** *or* **swede turnip** *sometimes cap S* [so called fr. its having been introduced into Scotland from Sweden] **:** RUTABAGA

swe·den \ˈswēdᵊn\ *adj, usu cap* [fr. *Sweden,* country in northwestern Europe occupying the eastern part of the Scandinavian peninsula] **:** of or from Sweden **:** of the kind or style prevalent in Sweden **:** SWEDISH

1swe·den·bor·gian \ˌswēdᵊnˈbȯrj(ē)ən *also* -rgēən\ *n* -s *usu cap* [Emanuel *Swedenborg* (Svedberg) †1772 Swed. scientist, philosopher, and religious writer + E *-ian*] **:** one who holds the doctrines of the New Jerusalem Church based on the teachings of Swedenborg who claimed to have direct intercourse with the spiritual world through his spiritual senses, who affirmed that Jesus Christ as comprehending all the fullness of godhead is the one and only God, and who held that there is a spiritual or symbolic sense to the Scriptures

which God revealed through him and which enabled him to see the correspondence between natural and spiritual things
²swedenborgian \"\ *adj, usu cap* **:** of or relating to Swedenborg or his doctrines
swe·den·bor·gian·ism \-ə,nizəm\ *n* -s *usu cap* **:** the doctrines taught by Swedenborg
swe·den·bor·gite \'==,bȯr,gīt\ *n* -s [G *swedenborgit*, fr. Emanuel *Swedenborg* + G *-it* -ite] **:** a mineral $NaBe_4SbO_7$ consisting of an oxide of sodium, beryllium, and antimony found at Langban, Sweden
swedge *var of* SWAGE
¹swed·ish \'swēdish, -dēsh\ *adj, usu cap* [*Swede* + *-ish*] **1 a :** of, relating to, or characteristic of Sweden **b :** of, relating to, or characteristic of the Swedes **2 :** of, relating to, or characteristic of the Swedish language
²swedish \"\ *n* -ES *cap* **:** the North Germanic language spoken in Sweden and a portion of Finland — see INDO-EUROPEAN LANGUAGES table
swedish box *n, usu cap S* **:** a piece of gymnastic apparatus used for vaulting and consisting of a series of rectangular frames that are graded in size to fit one on top of the other
swedish clover *n, usu cap S* **:** ALSIKE CLOVER
swedish fiddle *n, usu cap S* **1** *slang* **:** CROSSCUT SAW **2** *slang* **:** a large bow saw esp. for cutting pulp
swedish fly *n, usu cap S* **:** FRIT FLY
swedish green *n, usu cap S* **:** SCHEELE'S GREEN
swedish iron *n, usu cap S* **:** wrought iron of high quality made in Sweden
swedish jib *n, usu cap S* **:** GENOA JIB
swedish juniper *n, usu cap S* **:** a columnar juniper with nodding twigs that is a horticultural variety (*Juniperus communis suecica*) of the common juniper — compare IRISH JUNIPER
swedish lilywood *n, usu cap S* **:** birch burl veneer from northern Europe
swedish massage *n, usu cap S* **:** massage together with Swedish movements
swedish movements *n pl, usu cap S* **:** a system of active and passive exercise of different muscles and joints of the body first devised in Sweden
swedish nightingale *n, usu cap S* **:** REDWING 1
swedish punsch *or* **swedish punch** \-'pənch\ *n, usu cap S* [*punsch* fr. Sw, punch, fr. G, fr. E ⁴*punch*] **:** a sweet yellow-colored liqueur from Sweden consisting of arrack flavored with various aromatic substances — called also *arrack punsch, caloric punsch*
swedish sumac *n, usu cap S* **:** a tanning extract prepared from the leaves of the bearberry
swedish turnip *n, usu cap S* **:** RUTABAGA
¹sweel \'swē(ə)l\ *vt* [prob. fr. ME *swedelen* — more at SWADDLE] *Scot & Irish* **:** SWADDLE
²sweel \"\ *vb* [of Scand origin; akin to Norw dial. *svela, svila* to whirl, run around] *chiefly Scot* **:** SWIRL
swee·ney layout \'swēnē, -ni-\ *n, usu cap S* [fr. the name *Sweeney*] **:** EASTERN ROLL
swee·ny *also* **swee·ney** \'swēnē, -ni\ *or* **swin·ney** \'swinē, -ni\ *n* -ES [by folk etymology fr. PaG *schwinne*, fr. *schwinne* to waste away, vanish, fr. OHG *swintan* — more at SWINDLE] **:** an atrophy of the shoulder muscles of a horse; *broadly* **:** any muscular atrophy of a horse
¹sweep \'swēp\ *vb* **swept** \'swept\ **swept; sweeping; sweeps** [ME *swepen*; akin to OE *swāpan* to sweep — more at SWOOP] *vt* **1 a :** to brush away or off **:** remove from a surface with or as if with a broom or brush ⟨sent with broom before to ~ the dust behind the door —Shak.⟩ ⟨*swept* the crumbs from the table⟩ **b :** to cut with vigorous swings (as of a sword or scythe) ⟨the grain *swept* down by the reapers⟩ **c :** to destroy completely **:** wipe out — usu. used with *away* ⟨everything she loved, everything she cherished, might be *swept* away overnight —Louis Bromfield⟩ **d :** to remove with a single continuous forceful action ⟨*swept* the books off the desk⟩ ⟨*swept* the curtains aside⟩ ⟨as the train passes the net ~*s* the pouch from the arm —F.H.Briant⟩ **:** drive or carry away forcibly ⟨*swept* him away into a far corner of the hall —W.J.Locke⟩ **e :** to drive or carry along with irresistible force ⟨the boy and the girl had been *swept* well out of his reach and were bobbing along —Charles Price⟩ ⟨a wave of protest that *swept* the opposition into office⟩ **2 a :** to clean by vigorous and continuous brushings **:** remove particles of dirt or other matter from the surface of with a broom or brush ⟨~ the floor⟩ ⟨~ the street⟩ ⟨~ out the kitchen⟩ **b :** to clear by repeated and forcible blows, strokes, or gusts **c :** COMMAND ⟨artillery placed to ~ the whole field⟩ **d :** to range over destructively or violently **:** SCOUR ⟨a darkling plain *swept* with confused alarms of struggle and flight —Matthew Arnold⟩ ⟨fire *swept* the business district —*Amer. Guide Series: Md.*⟩ ⟨bucking heavy seas that *swept* the deck —Walter Hayward⟩ **e** (1) **:** to achieve quick and irresistible influence or domination over ⟨a great wave of fear *swept* the country⟩ ⟨archery, croquet, roller skating and then lawn tennis *swept* the country —F.R.Dulles⟩ (2) **:** to win all the games or contests of or on ⟨the team *swept* the series⟩ ⟨the crew *swept* the river⟩ (3) **:** to win an overwhelming victory in ⟨*swept* the elections⟩ **3 :** to gather together into one heap or in one place **:** COLLECT ⟨a fine mesh net narrowing . . . to the mouth of a glass tube into which the organisms are *swept* —W.H.Dowdeswell⟩ ⟨*swept* the two groups together —Elmer Davis⟩ **:** gather in ⟨~ his winnings into his pocket⟩ **4 a :** to touch or come in contact with (a surface) as if with a brush ⟨his fingers *swept* the strings of the guitar⟩ ⟨the innkeeper bowed so that his skirt *swept* the floor —Nora Waln⟩ **b :** to move along or across with a swift continuous action **:** pass over ⟨the active areas may emit streams that ~ the earth with each rotation of the sun —C.T.Elvey⟩ ⟨broad rolling open heights, *swept* by clean mountain winds —*Amer. Guide Series: Vt.*⟩ **c :** to brush over the bottom of (a body of water) **:** DRAG ⟨*swept* the river with a dragnet⟩ **d :** to brush over the surface of (as a plant) with a net to gather insects **e :** to clear (a body of water) of mines ⟨*swept* the channel⟩ **5 a** *archaic* **:** to execute (as a curtsy) with a sweep ⟨*swept* the prettiest little curtsy ever seen —W.M.Thackeray⟩ **b :** to trace or describe the curve of (as a line or circle) **c :** to cover the entire extent of in one's field of vision or perception **:** make a broad survey of ⟨*swept* the sky with his binoculars —K.M.Dodson⟩ ⟨his keen dark eyes *swept* the room —Robert Brennan⟩ **d :** to move round or about so as to cover a wide circle or extent ⟨*swept* the binoculars slowly from right to left, from left to right —Fred Majdalany⟩ **6 a** *archaic* **:** to carry so as to brush the ground ⟨like a peacock ~ along his tail —Shak.⟩ **b :** to cause to move lightly over or along a surface ⟨*swept* his brush across the canvas⟩ ⟨*swept* her fingers over the strings of the harp⟩ **7 :** to clear away snow in front of (an advancing curling stone) **8 :** to produce (as music) by a brushing movement of the fingers along the strings of an instrument ⟨~*ing* a wail from his instrument —Katharine N. Burt⟩ **9 :** to form (a mold) by shaping the surface of the sand or loam with a template or strickle instead of using a pattern **:** STRIKE, STRICKLE — often used with *up* **~** *vi* **1 a :** to clean a surface with or as if with a broom **:** do the work of cleaning or brushing ⟨a new broom ~*s* clean⟩ **b :** to move over the surface or extent of something with swiftness, force, or devastating effect ⟨a hurricane *swept* over the island, razing all the buildings —*Amer. Guide Series: La.*⟩ ⟨a thin and watery beam of light *swept* across the dewy grass —Robertson Davies⟩ ⟨such rage and despair had *swept* over her as she had never before known —F.M.Ford⟩ **:** go, pass, or move swiftly or forcefully ⟨she *swept* to her feet like a dancer —Paul Roche⟩ ⟨when the front doors were opened, the children *swept* in —*N.Y. Times*⟩ **2 :** to move with dignity or stateliness ⟨his formidable wife *swept* past him to greet us —Maurice Cranston⟩ **3 :** TRAIL ⟨heard the trailing garments of the night ~ through her marble halls —H.W.Longfellow⟩ **4 a :** to move in a wide curve ⟨our frantic horses *swept* round an angle of the road —Thomas De Quincey⟩ ⟨when the sun ~*s* across the sky at the lowest altitude —S.M.Spencer⟩ **b :** to extend in a curve or long stretch ⟨her penciled eyebrows ~ in wide arcs over her long-lashed eyes —Jossleyn Hennessy⟩ ⟨brush-covered rangelands ~ to distant horizons —*Amer. Guide Series: Texas*⟩ **5 :** to clear the ice of snow in the path of an advancing curling stone by brushing with a broom — **sweep one off one's feet :** to gain immediate and unquestioning support, approval, or acceptance by a person ⟨his courtship *swept her off her feet*⟩ — **sweep the board** *or* **sweep the table 1 :** to win all the bets on the table **2 :** to win everything in sight **:** excel all competitors
²sweep \"\ *n* -s [ME *swepe*, fr. *swepen*, v.] **1 :** something that sweeps or works with a sweeping motion: as **a :** a hand water-raising device consisting of a long pole or timber pivoted to the top of a tall post and used to raise and lower a bucket — compare PICOTAH, SHADOOF **b :** BALLISTA **c** (1) **:** the lever arm of a circular horsepower machine to which a horse is hitched (2) **:** a triangular-shaped cultivator blade with a curved face that cuts off weeds under the soil surface between crop rows (3) **:** a wide heavy triangular blade used for subsurface tillage (4) **:** BUCK RAKE **d :** a windmill sail **e** (1) **:** a long oar used in boats or small vessels to propel or steer them (2) **:** a wire or rope stretched between two ships following parallel courses with the center of the wire being allowed to sag below the surface at set depths to drag for obstructions (as rocks, mines) **f :** STRICKLE 3 **2 a :** the act, action, or an instance of sweeping **:** a clearing out or away with or as if with a broom ⟨giving the room a good ~⟩ ⟨a clean ~ of all the holdovers from the old administration⟩ **b :** the removal from the table in one play in casino of all the cards by pairing or combining **c :** an overwhelming or decisive victory in a political contest ⟨could distinguish no landslides, no ~ in favor of either party —Christopher Serpell⟩ **d** (1) **:** a winning of all the games or contests in a series competition ⟨their ~ of this crucial series clinched the pennant for them⟩ (2) **:** a capture of all the prizes at stake in a contest or competition ⟨another week saw her complete a ~ of the sport's three highest titles —*Current Biog.*⟩ ⟨made a surprising clean ~ of all the delegates —*Current History*⟩ **e :** a military, naval, or air action (as a patrol, reconnaissance, or attack) ranging over a particular sector ⟨there were full-dress artillery and aerial ~*s* all day and night —Irwin Shaw⟩ ⟨patrol ships dispersed enemy small craft in inshore ~*s* —*N.Y.Times*⟩ **f :** a minesweeping operation **3 a :** a continuous and forceful forward movement (as of waves or wind) ⟨is entirely open to the unobstructed ~ of waves —P.E.James⟩ ⟨caught the full ~ of a rising southeast wind that dotted the lake with whitecaps —Joseph Millard⟩ ⟨the slow ~ of a glacier —Douglas Stewart⟩ **b :** a course, progress, or activity marked by force, drive, or continuity along a broad front ⟨the great ~*s* of western migration —Russell Lord⟩ ⟨the ~ of economic evolution seems at first sight to have passed the professions by —R.M.MacIver⟩ ⟨the symphony has passages of ~ and power⟩ **c** (1) **:** a usu. swift motion or movement describing an arc or a circle **:** a curving or circular course ⟨the lemon-and-white pointer went off on great ~*s* that settled the question about her running —*Newsweek*⟩ ⟨the impatient ~ of a hand —R.G.Thomas⟩ (2) **:** a systematic search of the sky with a telescope (as in a visual search for comets) (3) **:** an end run in football **d :** the compass of a sweeping movement, course, or progress **:** SCOPE ⟨the whole area lay within the ~ of the telescope⟩ ⟨was interested in the whole ~ of cultural history —R.B.West⟩ **e :** a broad unbroken area or extent often in a wide curve ⟨a vast ~ of sage and mesquite, dotted with dozens of kinds of cactus —*Amer. Guide Series: Texas*⟩ ⟨a majestic ~ of flesh on either side of a small blunt nose —William Faulkner⟩ **f :** a series of buildings or rooms **4 :** a curving or flowing line or contour ⟨the ~ of the arch⟩ ⟨the ~ of the draperies⟩: as **a** (1) **:** a curved wall, stairway, or section of a building ⟨the entire front is a ~ of large glass panes —*Ford Times*⟩ (2) **:** a curved section of scenery **b :** a curved driveway in front of a house or public building ⟨the driver took the gravel ~ magnificently and turned off out the gate —Elizabeth Bowen⟩ **c :** a gradual bend (as in a log or piling) **5 :** something that is swept up; *specif* **:** the sweepings of a workshop where precious metals are processed — usu. used in pl. ⟨when some walls and floors were dismantled during renovations, approximately $67,000 in gold ~*s* was recovered —F.W.Taber⟩ **6 :** CHIMNEY SWEEP 1 **7 :** SWEEPSTAKES **8 :** any of several small dark-colored Australian percoid food and game fishes of the family Scorpididae **9 a :** the radius of the curve to which a piece (as a spring leaf or fender) is shaped **b :** ARCH, CAMBER **c :** obliquity of an aeronautical member with respect to a significant reference plane as measured in degrees; *specif* **:** obliquity of a wing with reference to the plane of symmetry of an aircraft — see SWEEPBACK, SWEEPFORWARD **d :** a rapid and wide horizontal deflection of a cathode-ray beam that causes the spot to move across the screen (as in an oscilloscope or a television receiver) **syn** see RANGE

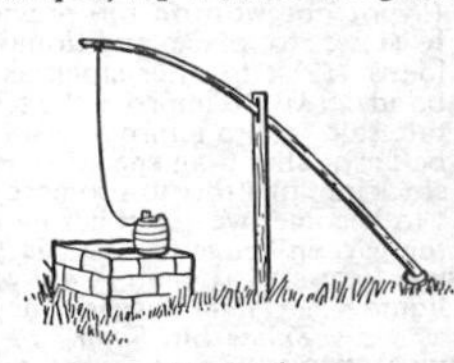
sweep 1a

³sweep \"\ *adv* **:** with a sweep
sweep·age \-pij, -pēj\ *n* -s **:** REFUSE ⟨by its strong, arched and labyrinthine roots collects the ~ of the fresh water —Marjory S. Douglas⟩
sweepback \'=,=\ *n* -s [fr. *sweep back*, v.] **:** a positive sweep in which the outer portion of an aeronautical member (as a wing) is downstream from the inner portion
sweep check *n* **:** the act or an instance of checking an opposing puck carrier in ice hockey by laying the stick flat on the ice and detaching the puck with a long, circular motion
sweep–chimney \'=;==\ *n* [¹*sweep* + *chimney*] *dial* **:** CHIMNEY SWEEP
sweep circuit *n* **:** an oscillatory circuit esp. designed to control the sweep in an oscilloscope or television cathode-ray tube
sweep cultivator *n* **:** a cultivator using sweeps to till the soil
sweep·dom \'swēpdəm\ *n* -s [²*sweep* + *-dom*] **:** the community of chimney sweeps
sweep·er \-pə(r)\ *n* -s [ME *swepare*, fr. *swepen* to sweep + *-are, -ere* -er] **1 :** a device that cleans by sweeping ⟨lawn ~⟩ **2 :** one that sweeps; *specif* **:** one whose work is cleaning an object or area by sweeping **3 :** MINE SWEEPER
sweepforward \'=;==\ *n* -s [fr. *sweep forward*, v.] **:** a negative sweep in which the outer portion of an aeronautical member (as a wing) is upstream from the inner portion
sweep generator *or* **sweep oscillator** *n* **:** an oscillator or signal generator to produce sweep signals

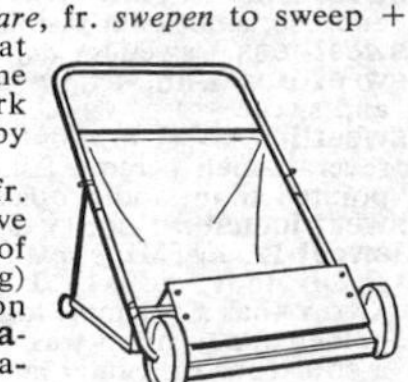
sweeper for a lawn

sweep hand *n* **:** SWEEP-SECOND
¹sweep·ing \'swēpiŋ, -pēŋ\ *n* -s [ME *sweping*, fr. gerund of *swepen* to sweep] **1 :** the act or action of one that sweeps ⟨gave the room a good ~⟩ **2 sweepings** *pl* **:** things collected by sweeping **:** REFUSE, RUBBISH ⟨contaminated by ~*s*, fly, and trash —M.R.Harden⟩
²sweeping *adj* [fr. pres. part. of ¹*sweep*] **1 a :** moving or extending in a wide curve or over a wide area ⟨threw the end of the cigar, with a large ~ gesture, into the fire —Arnold Bennett⟩ ⟨has many old white houses and a ~ view of the river valley —*Amer. Guide Series: N.H.*⟩ **b :** having a curving line or form ⟨the robe lies smoothly on the upper part of the body, and falls into ~ folds below —O. Elfrida Saunders⟩ **2 a :** on a large scale **:** wide-ranging **:** EXTENSIVE ⟨voted ~ election reforms —Andrew Morsund⟩ ⟨the expense . . . had made ~ economies necessary —T.B.Costain⟩ ⟨won a ~ victory⟩ **b :** INDISCRIMINATE, WHOLESALE ⟨this condemnation of an entire age sounds even more ~ than the indictment of a nation —William Anderson⟩ ⟨~ charges⟩ ⟨~ generalizations⟩ — **sweep·ing·ly** *adv* — **sweep·ing·ness** *n* -ES
sweeping score *n* **:** a line passing through the center of the tee at right angles to the length of a curling rink — see CURLING illustration
sweep mill *n* **:** a farm feed mill actuated by a circular sweep operated by horses
sweep net *n* **1** *or* **sweep seine :** a large fishing net usually paid out around an arc of a circle from a boat and then hauled ashore **2 :** a bag-shaped net with a handle used by entomologists for catching insects by sweeping it over vegetation
sweep of the tiller : a circular frame on which the tiller of a ship travels
sweep rake *n* **:** BUCK RAKE
sweeps *pres 3d sing of* SWEEP, *pl of* SWEEP
sweep–second \'=;==\ *n* **:** a second hand on a timepiece mounted concentrically with the other hands and read on the minute dial; *also* **:** a timepiece with such a second hand — called also *center-second*
sweep smelter *n* **:** one that smelts sweeps to regain the metals
sweep·stakes \'swēp,stāks\ *n pl but usu sing in constr, also* **sweep·stake** \-āk\ [ME *swepestake* one who wins all the stakes in a game, fr. *swepen* to sweep + *stake* stake (prize) — more at SWEEP, STAKE] **1 a :** a race or contest in which the entire prize is or may be awarded to the winner; *specif* **:** a horse race in which the stakes to be distributed are made up at least in part of the entry fees or other money contributed by three or more of the owners of horses entered **b :** a race, contest, or competition ⟨the presidential ~*s*⟩ ⟨the literary ~*s*⟩ ⟨a winning entry in the spring lingerie sales ~*s* —*Lingerie Merchandising*⟩ **2 :** any of various lotteries or contests for prizes
sweepstick \'=,=\ *n* **:** the part of a loom that connects the picking arm to the picker stick
sweepswinger \'=,==\ *n* **:** a member of a racing crew **:** OARSMAN
sweepup \'=,=\ *n* -s [fr. *sweep up*, v.] **:** CLEANUP
sweepwasher \'=,==\ *n* **:** one that extracts the residuum of precious metals from gold and silver sweeps
sweepy \'swēpē, -pi\ *adj* -ER/-EST **:** sweeping in motion, line, or force ⟨a magnificent avenue of ~ Australian pines —Horace Sutton⟩
sweer \'swēr, 'swi(ə)r\ *adj* [ME *swer, swere*, fr. OE *swǣr, swǣre*, lit., heavy — more at SERIOUS] **1** *Scot & dial Eng* **:** SLOW, INDOLENT **2** *Scot & dial Eng* **:** RELUCTANT, LOATH
swee·swee \'swē,swē\ *n* -s [imit.] **:** SPOTTED SANDPIPER
¹sweet \'swēt, *usu* -ēd·+V\ *adj* -ER/-EST [ME *swete, sweete*, fr. OE *swēte*; akin to OS *swōti, suoti* sweet, OHG *suozi*, ON *sætr* sweet, L *suadis* pleasant, sweet, Gk *hēdys* sweet, Skt *svādu*] **1 a :** marked by or arising from graciousness, kindness, or sympathy ⟨not often that a mind so attractive goes with a character so ~ as his —H.J.Laski⟩ ⟨her ~ personality⟩ **b :** not intemperate or extreme **:** EVEN, MODERATE ⟨~ reasonableness —Matthew Arnold⟩ **c :** CHARMING, NICE — often used as a generalized term of approval ⟨that's very ~ of her⟩ **2 a :** pleasing to the taste **:** indicating or inducing (as by stimulation with disaccharides) the one of the four basic taste sensations that is usu. felt as pleasing and agreeable — compare BITTER, SALT, SOUR **b** (1) *of a beverage* **:** containing a perceptible quantity of sugar or other sweetening ingredient **:** not dry (2) *of wine* **:** retaining a portion of natural sugar often through arrested fermentation effected either by pasteurization or by the addition of grape brandy ⟨a ~ sherry⟩ **c :** CLOYING, SACCHARINE ⟨the flaw in her book is the ~ side, the Pollyanna note, that fatal emphasis on the happy ending —Rosemary Benét⟩ **d :** mildly seasoned **:** not pungent ⟨~ pickles⟩ **3 a :** pleasing to the mind or the feelings **:** arousing agreeable or delightful emotions **:** ATTRACTIVE ⟨the ~*est* privilege that any writer can ask —Irving Kolodin⟩ ⟨the pleasant smell overcame him like ~ sleep —O.E.Rölvaag⟩ **b :** pleasing to the smell **:** FRAGRANT ⟨the valleys are ~ with the fragrance of orange blossoms —*Amer. Guide Series: Ariz.*⟩ ⟨the ~ smell of new-cut boards —Sherwood Anderson⟩ **c** (1) **:** pleasing to the ear **:** gently harmonious **:** not raucous or disturbing **:** MELODIOUS ⟨the angelic, disembodied voices . . . were incredibly pure and ~ —John Steinbeck⟩ ⟨the bell sounds as ~ today as it ever did —*New Yorker*⟩ (2) **:** of or relating to jazz performed typically without improvisation, having a moderate and smoothly pleasing tempo, tone color, harmony, and rhythm, and often imitating the qualities of symphonic or salon music — compare HOT **d :** pleasing to the eye **:** not bold or violent in color or line **:** SOFT ⟨flower motifs and emblems, all printed in ~ colors —Charles Rosner⟩ ⟨remembered the ~ lines of her arms —Walter O'Meara⟩ **e :** PRETTY, FETCHING ⟨a ~ young thing⟩ ⟨a ~ face⟩ **4 :** much loved **:** DEAR ⟨then pardon him, ~ father, for my sake —Shak.⟩ ⟨~*est* love, I do not go, for weariness of thee —John Donne⟩ **5 a :** having the taste or odor belonging to the original sound state of something **:** not sour, rancid, decaying, or stale **:** WHOLESOME ⟨put the bottle in the stream to keep the milk ~⟩ ⟨here was the pinch of mystery that kept the legend ~ —John Rosselli⟩ **b :** not salt or salted **:** FRESH ⟨~ water⟩ ⟨a ~ spring⟩ ⟨~ butter⟩ **c** *of land* **:** suitable in composition to production of crops **:** neutral or alkaline **:** not dank or acid — opposed to *sour* **d :** free from noxious gases and odors ⟨~ crude oil⟩ ⟨~ mine air⟩ **e :** free from excess of acid, sulfur, or corrosive salts **f :** free from malodorous sulfur compounds (as hydrogen sulfide or mercaptans) — used esp. of natural gas, petroleum, and petroleum distillates ⟨gas or oil is sour or ~, but you wouldn't find the sweet as tasty as that —Harry Botsford⟩ **6 a :** easily managed **:** SMOOTH-RUNNING ⟨a ~ ship⟩ **b :** managing or acting easily and smoothly **:** SKILLFUL ⟨for a high-up man like him he was a ~ hand at weeding —Edward Sheehy⟩ ⟨a ~ pilot⟩ ⟨a ~ fielder⟩ **c** *of an archery bow* **:** easy to the hand **:** drawing smoothly and releasing without kicking **d** *of glass* **:** easily workable **7 a :** agreeable or obedient to oneself or itself alone ⟨pleaded to be allowed to descend upon a community in my own ~ way —Cornelia Parker⟩ ⟨takes its own ~ time as it rolls lackadaisically across the prairie —Green Peyton⟩ **b :** FINE, GREAT, TERRIFIC — used as an intensive ⟨it would be a ~ gag to use mass communications in order to denounce them —J.B.Priestley⟩ ⟨one ~ inferiority complex —Harvey Breit⟩
syn ENGAGING, WINNING, WINSOME, DULCET: SWEET, applied to things other than those tasted, is a term of general commendation for what pleases, attracts, or charms, usu. in a mild way ⟨twilight, *sweet* with the smell of lilac and freshly turned earth —Corey Ford⟩ ⟨pleased at this sudden return to *sweet* reasonableness —C.G.D.Roberts⟩ ⟨has been very *sweet*. He wants to help, but of course there's nothing he can do —Louis Auchincloss⟩ ENGAGING may indicate power to attract favorable attention, sometimes by intriguing or charming characteristics ⟨affectionate, cheerful, happy, his sweet and *engaging* personality drew all men's love —H.O.Taylor⟩ ⟨the most *engaging* human beings who ever harbored a sly smile —Charlton Laird⟩ WINNING may suggest power to delight, charm, placate, or enamor ⟨a quiet, self-possessed, and gracious young lady, of singularly *winning* manners, and clear and resolutely honest eyes —William Black⟩ ⟨simple as a child, with his gentle, *winning* voice and grave smile —Van Wyck Brooks⟩ WINSOME may suggest any engaging quality; it may call up notions of blended comeliness, cheer, childlike nature, and open candor ⟨remembered her childlike look, and *winsome* fanciful ways, and shy tremulous grace —Oscar Wilde⟩ DULCET may apply to something gratifying, soothing, bland, and sweet ⟨the voice . . . *dulcet* as the hum of heavy honeybees amid orange blossoms —Herman Wouk⟩
— **sweet on :** strongly attracted to **:** in love with ⟨he's been *sweet on* her for years⟩
²sweet \"\ *vt* -ED/-ING/-S [ME *sweten*, fr. OE *swētan*; akin to MLG *sæten* to sweeten, MD *soeten*, OHG *suozen*; causative-denominative fr. the root of E ¹*sweet*] **:** SWEETEN
³sweet \"\ *adv* -ER/-EST [ME *swete, sweete*, fr. *swete, sweete*, adj.] **:** SWEETLY ⟨how ~ the moonlight sleeps upon this bank —Shak.⟩
⁴sweet \"\ *n* -s [ME *swete, sweete*, fr. *swete, sweete*, adj.] **1 :** something that is sweet to the taste: as **a :** a food (as a candy or preserve) having a high sugar content — usu. used in pl. ⟨filling up on candy and other ~*s* —Carl Binger⟩ ⟨can cross the street and readily buy ~*s* at a store —Jane Nickerson⟩ **b sweets** *pl, Brit* **:** sweetened wines and cordials **c** *Brit* **:** a sweet dish served at the end of a meal **:** DESSERT **d** *Brit* **:** CANDY ⟨put a large ~ in her cheek —Elizabeth Taylor⟩ ⟨this is done by swallowing, or by chewing a ~ or gum —*Before You Take Off*⟩ **e :** SWEET POTATO **2 :** a sweet taste sensation ⟨they see and smell and have their palates both for ~ and sour —Shak.⟩ **3 :** a pleasant or gratifying experience, possession, or state **:** something that delights or deeply satisfies ⟨precious ~*s* which older writers have coveted and gained —Sinclair Lewis⟩ ⟨the ~*s* of life⟩ ⟨the ~*s* of office⟩ **4 :** BELOVED, DARLING, SWEETHEART ⟨you can always talk to me, you ~ —Susan Ertz⟩ **5 a** *archaic* **:** sweet smell **:** FRAGRANCE ⟨the scent . . . makes

faint with too much ~ —P.B.Shelley⟩ **b sweets** *pl, archaic* **:** things having a sweet smell ⟨a wilderness of ~*s* —John Milton⟩
sweet acacia *n* **:** HUISACHE
sweet almond *n* **:** an almond that produces sweet edible seeds and forms a distinct variety (*Prunus amygdalus dulcis*) of the common almond; *also* **:** the edible seed of this tree — compare BITTER ALMOND
sweet almond oil *n* **:** ALMOND OIL 1a
sweet alyssum *also* **sweet alison** *n* **:** a perennial European herb (*Lobularia maritima*) having clusters of small fragrant white flowers
sweet amber *n* **:** TUTSAN
sweet–and–sour \'⸗⸗'⸗\ *adj* **:** seasoned with sugar and vinegar or lemon juice ⟨*sweet-and-sour* tongue⟩
sweet anise *n* **:** a sweet cicely (*Osmorhiza longistylis*)
sweet archangel *n* **:** RED ARCHANGEL
sweet ash *n* **:** WILD CHERVIL
sweet bag *n, archaic* **:** a small bag containing a scented or aromatic substance **:** SACHET
sweet balm *n* **1 :** LEMON BALM **2 :** a Canary Island mint (*Cedronella triphylla*) with ternate leaves
sweet balsam *n* **:** a balsamweed (*Gnaphalium obtusifolium*)
sweet basil *n* **:** a common basil (*Ocimum basilicum*)
sweet bay *n* **1 :** LAUREL 1 **2 :** an American magnolia (*Magnolia virginiana*) abundant along the Atlantic coast and in the southern states that has glaucous leaves and rather small globose fragrant white flowers **3 :** RED BAY
sweet bean *n* **:** HONEY LOCUST 1
sweetbells \'⸗,⸗\ *n pl* **:** an eastern No. American deciduous shrub (*Leucothoe racemosa*) with pinkish flowers in long racemes
sweet·berry \'⸗- — *see* BERRY\ *n* **:** SHEEPBERRY 1
sweet betty *n, usu cap B* [*betty* fr. the name *Betty*] **:** SOAPWORT 1
sweet billy *n, usu cap B* [*billy* fr. the name *Billy*] **1 :** SWEET WILLIAM 1 **2 :** the European goldfinch
sweet birch *n* **:** a common birch (*Betula lenta*) of the eastern U.S. that has a spicy brown bark containing a volatile oil, hard dark-colored wood used for furniture and cabinetwork, and erect fruiting aments — called also *black birch, cherry birch*
sweet–birch oil \'⸗,⸗-\ *n* **1 :** BIRCH OIL 2 **2 :** METHYL SALICYLATE
sweet brake *n* **:** MALE FERN
sweetbread \'⸗,⸗\ *n* **1 :** the thymus of a young animal (as a calf) used for food **2 :** BEEF BREAD
sweetbrier *also* **sweetbriar** \'⸗,⸗\ *n* **:** any of several closely related and similar Old World roses (esp. *Rosa eglanteria*) which have stout recurved prickles, small glandular-serrate leaves, and white to deep rosy pink single flowers followed by scarlet fruits, which are sometimes cultivated or used in hybridization, and some of which are naturalized outside their normal range (as in No. America) — called also *eglantine*
sweet broom *n* **1 :** a white-flowered fragrant shrub (*Cytisus fragrans*) of Teneriffe that is cultivated for ornament **2** *also*
sweet broomweed : BROOMWEED 1
sweet bubby *n* **:** CAROLINA ALLSPICE
sweet buckeye *n* **:** an often cultivated tall buckeye (*Aesculus octandra*) of the central U.S. that has yellow or red flowers and soft white wood
sweet bush *n* **:** SWEET FERN 2
sweet calabash *n* **:** a West Indian passionflower (*Passiflora maliformis*) with edible fruit about the size of an apple
sweet calamus *or* **sweet cane** *n* **1 :** SWEET FLAG **2 a :** SUGARCANE **b :** a grass (*Andropogon aromaticus*) of northwestern India that has leaves that are aromatic when bruised or broken
sweet cassava *n* **:** a cassava (*Manihot dulcis*) with roots that are used as a vegetable and herbage that is used for stock feed
sweet cherry *n* **1 :** a rather tall pyramidal Eurasian tree (*Prunus avium*) with reddish brown bark, white flowers, and fruits that are often small and bitter in the wild but have been developed under cultivation into large heart-shaped to globular sweet-flavored cherries — called also *gean, mazzard;* compare SOUR CHERRY **2 :** the fruit of the sweet cherry
sweet chervil *n* **:** a tall perennial sweet cicely (*Osmorhiza longistylis*) with sweet anise-flavored roots that is widely distributed in open moist woodlands of eastern and central No. America
sweet chestnut *n* **:** SPANISH CHESTNUT
sweet chocolate *n* **:** chocolate that contains added sugar
sweet cicely *n* **1 :** a European herb (*Myrrhis odorata*) having white flowers and an aromatic root **2 :** any of various herbs of an American genus (*Osmorhiza*) related to *Myrrhis* that typically have thick fleshy roots and grow in moist woodlands; *esp* **:** SWEET CHERVIL
sweet cider *n* **:** CIDER 1
sweet clover *n* **:** a tall erect annual or biennial legume of the genus *Melilotus* that is grown extensively esp. for hay and soil improvement — called also *melilot;* see WHITE SWEET CLOVER, YELLOW SWEET CLOVER
sweet clover disease *n* **:** a hemorrhagic diathesis of sheep and cattle feeding on improperly cured sweet clover containing excess quantities of dicoumarol
sweetclover weevil \'⸗,⸗⸗-\ *n* **:** a small brownish gray weevil (*Sitona cylindricollis*) that is native to Europe but now widespread in the central part of No. America and that as an adult feeds on and defoliates sweet clover while its larvae feed on the roots
sweet coltsfoot *n* **:** any of several herbs of the genus *Petasites* (as *P. fragrans* of Europe and *P. sagittatus* of No. America)
sweet corn *n* **:** an Indian corn that is grown in many horticultural varieties, is variously considered a distinct species (*Zea saccharata* or *Z. rugosa*), a subspecies (*Z. mays rugosa*), or a specific mutation of dent corn, and is distinguished esp. by kernels containing a high percentage of sugar in the milk stage when they are suitable for table use but later becoming horny, translucent, and wrinkled — compare FIELD CORN, GREEN CORN
sweet–corn wilt *n* **:** STEWART'S DISEASE
sweet cup *n* **:** any of several passionflowers or their fruits: as **a :** SWEET CALABASH **b :** JAMAICA HONEYSUCKLE
sweet–curd \'⸗,⸗\ *adj, of cheese* **:** made of curd formed with rennet from cow's milk set sweet and cooked rapidly to a very firm consistency
sweeted *past of* SWEET
sweet elder *n* **:** AMERICAN ELDER
sweet elm *n* **:** SLIPPERY ELM 1
sweet·en \'swēt°n\ *vb* **sweetened; sweetened; sweetening** \-t(°)niŋ\ **sweetens** [¹*sweet* + *-en*] *vt* **1 a :** to add sugar or other sweetening to ⟨~ the cereal⟩ ⟨~ the coffee⟩ **b :** to make more pleasant to the ear **:** make softer or more melodious ⟨the roaring river fills all the arching way with . . . reverberating music, which is ~*ed* at times by the ouzel —John Muir †1914⟩ **c :** to make more pleasant to the smell **:** add fragrance to ⟨the piny aroma of the greenwoods, ~*ed* by the fragrance of laurel and azalea —*Amer. Guide Series: Conn.*⟩ **2 a :** to make amiable and pleasant in disposition **:** free from harshness **:** REFINE ⟨religion . . . did not ~ her old age —George Santayana⟩ **b :** to soften the mood or attitude of **:** APPEASE, MOLLIFY ⟨now they thought it was time to ~ the people, and deliver them from their burthens —Lucy Hutchinson⟩ ⟨wants to ~ up U.S. opinion —*Time*⟩ **c :** to make amenable or obliging by friendly attentions or gifts **:** soften up ⟨brought in business because he got around, and ~*ed* contacts —J.P. Marquand⟩ ⟨had to . . . ~ dealers with beer, wrangle with claims agents —Saul Bellow⟩ **3 a :** to make agreeable or delightful **:** add a pleasant quality to ⟨pastimes and sports . . . ~*ed* the voyage and prevented arguments and quarrels —David Garnett⟩ ⟨suddenly cut off from all that ~*ed* life for her —Edith Wharton⟩ **b :** to lessen the unpleasant quality or effect of **:** make less painful or trying **:** LIGHTEN ⟨the most important single function of the humor is to ~ the instruction —Rebecca P. Parkin⟩ ⟨invariably ~*ed* his violence with wit —J.J.Mallon⟩ **c :** to make soft or mellow (as a line of tin) **4 :** to make fresh and wholesome **:** CLEANSE, PURIFY ⟨all the perfumes of Arabia will not ~ this little hand —Shak.⟩ **5 :** RELIEVE, SOLACE ⟨charity which ~*s* giver and recipient in equal measure —Roy Lewis & Angus Maude⟩ **6 :** to free from a harmful or undesirable quality or substance: as **a :** to reduce the acidity of (soil) by applying lime **b :** to deprive (as sea water) of salt **c :** to neutralize acid in by the use of an alkali **d :** to treat (as gasoline) so as to remove or make inoffensive sulfur or sulfur compounds that are malodorous and corrosive **e :** to purify esp. by fumigating or filtering **7 :** to make more valuable or attractive: as **a :** to add poker chips to (a pot not won on the previous deal) prior to another deal **b** (1) **:** to place additional securities as collateral for (a loan) (2) **:** to offer stock as a bonus to the purchaser of (a bond) (3) **:** to improve the terms of (a security issue) to facilitate sale **c :** to improve (as a grade of lumber) by including a better quality than specified **d :** to add new goods to (present stock) in an effort to promote sales — often used with *up* **~** *vi* **:** to become sweet ⟨set her mother's milk pails upside down on the garden hedge to ~ —Mary Webb⟩
sweet·en·er \-t(°)nə(r)\ *n* -s **:** one that sweetens ⟨a low-calorie liquid ~ —*Time*⟩ ⟨urges concessions on minor fiscal questions as ~*s* —*Times Lit. Supp.*⟩
sweetening *n* -s **1 :** the act or process of making sweet ⟨methods for the cleaning and ~ of cider barrels⟩ **2 a :** something that sweetens **b** *South & Midland* **:** something used to sweeten food and drink ⟨poured me coffee with lots of cream and ~, just the way I like it best —Helen Eustis⟩ — see LONG SWEETENING, SHORT SWEETENING
sweeter *comparative of* SWEET
sweetest *superlative of* SWEET
sweet fennel *n* **1 :** FLORENCE FENNEL **2 :** FENNEL
sweet fern *n* **1 a :** any of several shield ferns of the genus *Dryopteris* **b :** a common polypody (*Polypodium vulgare*) **2 :** a small No. American shrub (*Comptonia peregrina*) of the family Myricaceae having sweet-scented or aromatic fernlike leaves **3** *dial Eng* **:** SWEET CICELY
sweetfish \'⸗,⸗\ *n* **:** AYU
sweet flag *n* **:** a perennial marsh herb (*Acorus calamus*) having long leaves and a pungent rootstock — called also *calamus*
sweet gale *n* [*gale* fr. ME *gale, gayl* sweet gale — more at FERNGALE] **:** a bog shrub (*Myrica gale*) found throughout the north temperate zone and having bitter-tasting fragrant leaves — called also *Scotch gale*
sweet goldenrod *n* **:** BLUE MOUNTAIN TEA
sweet grass *n* **1 :** any of various grasses of sweet flavor or odor: as **a :** MANNA GRASS **b** (1) **:** a slender fragrant perennial widely distributed holy grass (*Hierochloe odorata*) that is sometimes used in basketry — called also *Seneca grass, vanilla grass* (2) **:** any of various other holy grasses **c** *southern Africa* **:** any of various grasses (as members of the genera *Panicum* and *Themeda*) that are relished by stock **2** *dial Eng* **a :** WOODRUFF **b :** EELGRASS 1 **3 :** SWEET FLAG
sweet gum *n* **1 a :** a No. American tree (*Liquidambar styraciflua*) with palmately lobed leaves, corky branches, and hard wood — see TREE illustration **b :** heartwood of the sweet gum tree or the reddish brown lumber sawed from it and sometimes used as an imitation of mahogany and Circassian walnut — called also *bilsted, gum, red gum, satin walnut* **2 :** the balsam produced by the sweet gum tree
sweet gum scale *n* **:** a scale (*Diaspidiotus liquidambaris*) that feeds on sweet gum
¹**sweetheart** \'⸗,⸗\ *n* [ME *swete hert,* fr. *swete* sweet + *hert* heart — more at SWEET, HEART] **1 :** DARLING — often used as a term of endearment **2 :** one who is loved **:** LOVER ⟨she married . . . an old ~ —W. F. De Morgan⟩ ⟨saw the face of his ~, his wife —Zane Grey⟩ **3 a :** AMERICAN ORPINE **b sweethearts** *pl* **:** the cleavers (*Galium aparine*)
²**sweetheart** \"\ *vb* -ED/-ING/-S *vi* **:** to have a sweetheart **:** make love ⟨boys your age ought to be ~*ing* —Richard Church⟩ **~** *vt* **:** COURT, WOO
sweetheart agreement *or* **sweetheart contract** *n* **:** an agreement between an employer and a labor union on terms favorable to the employer and often arranged by a union official without the participation or approval of the union members
sweetheart neckline *n* **:** a neckline for women's clothing that is high in back and low in front where it is scalloped to resemble the top of a heart
sweetheart rose *n* **:** any of various small roses (as a polyantha rose)
sweet herb *n* **:** a fragrant herb cultivated for culinary purposes — usu. used in pl.
sweet horsemint *n* **:** DITTANY 3
sweet·ie \'swēd·ē, -ētē, -i\ *n* -s [¹*sweet* + *-ie*] **1** *Brit* **:** CANDY, SWEET — usu. used in pl. ⟨can't get ~*s* for all this money —Samuel Butler †1902⟩ **2 :** SWEETHEART ⟨in his wanderings he had been lucky enough to marry a true-blue ~ —James Thurber⟩

sweetheart neckline

sweetie pie *n* **:** SWEETHEART
sweet·ing \'swēd·iŋ, -ētiŋ, -ēŋ\ *n* -s [ME *sweting,* fr. *swete* sweet + *-ing*] **1** *archaic* **:** SWEETHEART ⟨trip no further, pretty ~; journeys end in lovers meeting —Shak.⟩ **2 :** a sweet apple ⟨planted a little garden and some ~ apple trees —*Amer. Guide Series: R.I.*⟩
sweet·ish \'swēd·ish, -ētish, -ēsh\ *adj* **1 :** somewhat sweet ⟨emitted a ~ scent —H.G.Wells⟩ **2 :** sickeningly or unpleasantly sweet ⟨a new ~ reek that clutches horribly at your throat —John Dos Passos⟩
sweet jav·ril \-'javrəl\ *also* **sweet jar·vil** \-'järvəl, -'jáv-\ *n, pl* **sweet javrils** *also* **sweet jarvils** [*javril, jarvil* alter. of *chervil*] **:** a perennial herb (*Osmorhiza claytoni*) with aromatic roots, decompound leaves, and small white flowers in loose umbels
sweet john *n, usu cap J* [*john* fr. the name *John*] *archaic* **:** a narrow-leaved sweet william
sweetleaf \'⸗,⸗\ *n* **:** a small tree (*Symplocos tinctoria*) of southern U.S. with herbage and bark that yield a yellow dye
sweetleaf family *n* **:** SYMPLOCACEAE
sweet lemon *n* **:** any of several lemons having fruit with a sweet and usu. somewhat insipid pulp
sweet·less \'swētləs\ *adj* **:** having no sweets or sweetening
sweet·ling \-liŋ, -lēŋ\ *n* -s **1 :** DARLING **2 :** something small and sweet
sweetlips \'⸗,⸗\ *n pl but sing or pl in constr, Austral* **:** any of several small percoid fishes of the genus *Lethrinus* having a pointed snout and protrusible mouth; *specif* **:** SCAVENGER 4c
sweet locust *n* **:** HONEY LOCUST 1a(1)
¹**sweet·ly** *adv* [ME *sweteliche, swetely,* fr. *swete* sweet + *-liche -ly* -ly (adv. suffix)] **1 :** AGREEABLY, COMFORTABLY, PLEASANTLY ⟨has a ~ simple logic at first glance —Stuart Chase⟩ ⟨so golden and ~ hot it was —John Galsworthy⟩ **2 a** *archaic* **:** in a courteous or kindly manner **:** GRACIOUSLY **b :** in an affectionate or loving manner ⟨spoke ~ to him⟩ **3 :** with sweetness **:** in a manner sweet to the senses ⟨churches whose bells pealed so ~ —*Lamp*⟩ **4 :** CHARMINGLY ⟨she was indeed ~ fair —George Meredith⟩ **5 :** FINELY, GREATLY — used as an intensive ⟨will have to pay ~ for it⟩ **6 :** in an easy manner **:** SMOOTHLY ⟨the rope running ~ between us —Wynford Vaughan-Thomas⟩ ⟨the paper was coming off ~ now —Edna Ferber⟩
²**sweetly** \"\ *adj* [*sweet* + *-ly* (adj. suffix)] *archaic* **:** SWEET ⟨flowers which smelt so ~ —Thomas Hardy⟩
sweet magnolia *n* **:** SWEET BAY 2
sweet maize *n* **:** SWEET CORN
sweet marjoram *n* **:** an aromatic European herb (*Majorana hortensis*) with dense spikelike flower clusters — compare WILD MARJORAM
sweet marten *n* **:** the European pine marten
sweet mary *n, usu cap M* [*mary* fr. the name *Mary*] **1 :** a balm (*Melissa officinalis*) **2 :** OSWEGO TEA **3 :** COSTMARY 1
sweet mash *n* **:** a grain mash (as for distillation into whiskey) produced by the use of freshly developed yeast
sweetmeat \'⸗,⸗\ *n* [ME *swete mete,* fr. *swete* sweet + *mete* food — more at SWEET, MEAT] **1 :** a food rich in sugar — usu. used in pl. ⟨sit down to supper at a table which is literally covered with ~*s* —*Irish Digest*⟩: as **a :** a candied or crystallized fruit **b :** CANDY, CONFECTION **2 :** the first coat of japanning or varnish applied in making patent leather **3 :** a slipper limpet (*Crepidula fornicata*) of the American coast
sweet myrtle *n* **:** SWEET FLAG
sweet·ness \'swētnəs\ *n* -ES [ME *swetnes, sweetnes,* fr. OE *swētnes,* fr. *swēte* sweet + *-nes* -ness — more at SWEET] **1 :** something sweet **:** a sweet substance, sound, or feeling **2 :** the quality or state of being sweet
sweetness and light *n* **1 :** a harmonious combination of beauty and intelligence ⟨declared that the ideal of culture was *sweetness and light*⟩ **2 :** mild reasonableness **:** AMIABILITY ⟨suddenly dropped his threatening tone and became all *sweetness and light*⟩
sweet niter *n* **:** ETHYL NITRITE SPIRIT
sweet oil *n* **:** a mild edible oil: as **a :** OLIVE OIL **b :** rape oil or similar oils when used as food
sweet olive *n* **:** an evergreen Asiatic shrub or small tree (*Osmanthus fragrans*) used for ornament and having leaves entire or with small teeth and the corolla divided nearly to its base
sweet orange *n* **:** an orange (*Citrus sinensis*) that is prob. native to southern China or other parts of southeastern Asia, has a fruit with a pithy central axis, and is the source of the widely cultivated table and juice oranges; *also* **:** a cultivated orange derived from this species and usu. having fruit with relatively thin skin and a sweet juicy edible pulp — compare SOUR ORANGE
sweet orange oil *n* **:** ORANGE OIL a
sweet pea *n* **:** a garden plant (*Lathyrus odoratus*) native to southern Europe but widely used as an ornamental and having slender climbing stems, pinnate leaves with narrow leaflets, and large very fragrant blue, purple, red, pink, salmon, or white flowers
sweet pepper *n* **1 :** any of various large capsicum fruits that contain little if any capsaicin, are characterized by mild flavor, usu. have distinctly thick walls, and vary in form from oblong to bell-shaped or somewhat rounded — called also *bell pepper, green pepper;* compare HOT PEPPER **2 :** the plant (*Capsicum frutescens grossum*) that bears sweet peppers
sweet pepperbush *n* **:** a plant of the genus *Clethra* (esp. *C. alnifolia*) with fragrant flowers
sweet–pickle \'⸗'⸗⸗\ *vt* **:** to cure (as meat) by soaking in or injecting with a solution of common salt and sugar with sometimes the addition of nitrates or spice
sweet pinesap *n* **:** a plant of the genus *Monotropsis* — called also *pygmy-pipes;* compare CAROLINA BEECHDROPS, INDIAN PIPE
sweet plum *n* **:** BURDEKIN PLUM
sweet potato *n* **1 a :** a tropical vine (*Ipomoea batatas*) widely cultivated in warm regions and in the U.S. as far north as New Jersey that is related to the morning glory and has variously shaped leaves and purplish flowers **b :** the large, thick, sweet and farinaceous tuberous root of the sweet potato vine that is cooked and eaten as a vegetable — compare YAM **2 :** OCARINA
sweet–potato beetle *n* **:** any of several tortoise beetles of the genera *Coptocycla* and *Cassida* (esp. *Cassida bivittata*) that are destructive to the leaves of the sweet potato and related plants
sweet–potato flea beetle *n* **:** a chrysomelid beetle (*Chaetocnema confinis*) that feeds on corn and other crop plants
sweet–potato hornworm *or* **sweet–potato sphinx** *n* **:** a No. American hawkmoth (*Agrius cingulatus*) whose larva feeds on sweet potato foliage
sweet–potato scurf *n* **:** a scurf disease of sweet potatoes caused by a fungus (*Moniliochaetes infuscans*)
sweet–potato weevil *or* **sweet–potato borer** *n* **:** a bluish-black weevil (*Cylas formicarius*) with a red prothorax whose larva bores in sweet-potato tubers
sweet–potato worm *n* **:** a worm that is the larva of the sweet-potato sphinx
sweet reed *n* **1 :** an Indian reed (*Cinna arundinacea*) **2** *Africa* **:** SORGO
sweet–roast \'⸗'⸗\ *vt* **:** DEAD-ROAST
sweet rocket *n* **:** DAME'S VIOLET
sweet roll *n* **1 :** COFFEE ROLL **2 :** ³BUN 1a
sweetroot \'⸗,⸗\ *n* **1 :** LICORICE **2 :** an Australian timber tree (*Alyxia buxifolia*) of the family Apocynaceae **3 :** SWEET FLAG
sweet rush *n* **1 :** SWEET FLAG **2 :** CAMEL GRASS **3 :** a rush of the genus *Cyperus*
sweets *pres 3d sing of* SWEET, *pl of* SWEET
sweet scabious *n* **1 :** an Old World herb (*Scabiosa atropurpurea*) naturalized in America **2 :** DAISY FLEABANE **3 :** SKEVISH
sweet–scented \'⸗'⸗⸗\ *adj* **:** having a fragrant scent or smell — often used in vernacular names of plants to distinguish particular species or varieties ⟨*sweet-scented* cedar⟩
sweet–scented shrub *or* **sweet shrub** *n* **:** CAROLINA ALLSPICE
sweet sedge *n* **1 :** SWEET FLAG **2 :** YELLOW IRIS
sweetshop \'⸗,⸗\ *n* [⁴*sweet* + *shop*] *chiefly Brit* **:** a candy store
sweetsop \'⸗,⸗\ *n* **1 :** a tropical American tree (*Annona squamosa*) **2 :** the sweet pulpy fruit of the sweetsop that has a thick green scaly rind and shining black seeds — called also *anon, custard apple, sugar apple;* compare SOURSOP
sweet sorghum *n* **:** SORGO
sweet spire *n* **:** VIRGINIA WILLOW
sweet spirit of nitre *or* **sweet spirits of nitre :** ETHYL NITRITE SPIRIT
sweet sultan *n* **1 :** either of two annual Eurasian herbs (*Centaurea moschata* and *C. imperialis*) cultivated for their variously colored and fragrant flower heads **2 :** BLESSED THISTLE 1
sweet sumac *n* **:** FRAGRANT SUMAC
sweet su·san \-'süz°n\ *n, usu cap 2d S* [*susan* fr. the name *Susan*] **:** LOBEL'S CATCHFLY
¹**sweet–sweet** \'⸗'⸗\ *adj* [imit.] **:** CHIRPING
²**sweet–sweet** \"\ *n* **:** a chirping sound
sweet talk *n* **:** BLANDISHMENT, SOFT SOAP ⟨was so accustomed to flattery and elaborate *sweet talk* that she would think she were being insulted if addressed with ordinary courtesy —Budd Schulberg⟩
sweet–talk \'⸗'⸗\ *vb* [*sweet talk*] *vt* **:** BLANDISH, CAJOLE, COAX ⟨manages somehow to *sweet-talk* the showgirl into a moonlight supper at his apartment —John McCarten⟩ **~** *vi* **:** to use blandishments or flattery
sweet tangle *n* **:** a large seaweed (*Laminaria saccharina*) common along coasts and having fronds that contain a large quantity of sugar and are used in preparing a syrup
sweet thorn *n* **:** a tree (*Acacia karroo*) of southern Africa that has straight white thorns and drooping branches
sweet tooth *n* [ME *swete toth,* fr. *swete* sweet + *toth* tooth — more at SWEET, TOOTH] **:** a craving or fondness for sweet food ⟨can never get enough cake to satisfy his *sweet tooth*⟩
sweet trefoil *n* **:** BLUE MELILOT
sweet tussock *n* **:** a forage grass (*Poa bulbosa*) of Argentina
sweetveld \'⸗,⸗\ *n* **:** African veld that is not markedly acid in soil reaction and is characterized by production in the presence of adequate moisture of palatable grazing of predominantly annual grasses
sweet vernal grass *n* **:** a slender European grass (*Anthoxanthum odoratum*) that is often planted with other grasses for its fragrance and has narrow spikelike panicles in early spring — called also *vernal grass*
sweet viburnum *n* **:** SHEEPBERRY 1
sweet violet *n* **:** a common cultivated violet (*Viola odorata*) of Eurasia and northern Africa that is the source of many of the commercially developed violets — called also *garden violet*
sweet walnut *n* **:** SHAGBARK HICKORY
sweet water *n* **1 :** a dilute solution of glycerol (*sweet water* from the hydrolysis of fats may contain 10 to 25 percent of glycerol) **2 :** a sugar solution; *esp* **:** one obtained by recovery of waste sugar during refining
sweet white violet *n* **:** a stemless violet (*Viola blanda*) of eastern No. America that has fragrant white flowers with purple veins
sweet william *n, sometimes cap S & often cap W* [*william* fr. the name *William*] **1 a :** a widely cultivated Eurasian pink (*Dianthus barbatus*) with small white to deep red or sometimes purple flowers that are often showily spotted, banded, or mottled and are borne in rather large flat bracteate heads at the end of erect stalks **b :** BUTTON PINK **2 :** any of several sharks of Pacific and southern seas having rank inedible flesh **3 :** a deep pink that is bluer and lighter than average coral (sense 3b), bluer and less strong than fiesta, and yellower and less strong than begonia
sweet william catchfly *n, sometimes cap W* **:** LOBEL'S CATCHFLY
sweet wilson *n, usu cap W* [*wilson* fr. the name *Wilson*] **:** EARLY SAXIFRAGE
sweetwood \'⸗,⸗\ *n* **1 :** a laurel (*Laurus nobilis*) **2 :** any of various chiefly tropical American trees of the family Lauraceae: as **a :** a tree of the genus *Ocotea* — compare STINKWOOD **b :** a tree of the genus *Nectandra* — compare BEBEERU **c :** a

small or medium-sized Jamaican tree (*Licaria triandra* or *Acrodiclidium jamaicense*) with easily worked greenish yellow wood **3 :** LICORICE 1,2a

sweetwood bark *n* **:** CASCARILLA

sweet woodruff *n* **:** a small European sweet-scented herb (*Asperula odorata*) sometimes used in perfumery

sweetwort \ˈ=,=\ *n* **:** an unfermented malt infusion

sweety \ˈswēd·ē, -ētē, -i\ *Brit var of* SWEETIE 1

sweir \ˈswēr, ˈswi(ə)r\ *var of* SWEER

swe·ko·man \ˌsvākōˌmän\ *n* -s *usu cap* [Sw *svekoman*, fr. *sveko-* Swedish, Sweden (fr. NL or ML *Sueco-*, fr. *Suecia* Sweden, fr. OSw *Svēar* Swedes) + *-man* maniac — more at SWEDE, FENNOMAN] **:** a Finn supporting the use of Swedish esp. as the official language against the Fennomans

[1]**swell** \ˈswel\ *vb* **swelled; swelled** \-ld\ *or* **swol·len** \ˈswōlən *also* -ln\ **swelling; swells** [ME *swellen*, fr. OE *swellan*; akin to OS & OHG *swellan* to swell, ON *svella*, Goth ufs*walleins* inflation, conceit] *vi* **1 a :** to increase in volume **:** grow larger or bulkier **:** expand by internal pressure or growth **:** fill out **:** DILATE ⟨if I walked a hundred yards my ankles ~*ed* up —*Sydney* (*Austral.*) *Bull.*⟩ ⟨eight of my berries quickly disappeared, and the cheeks of the little vagabond ~*ed* —John Burroughs⟩ ⟨mucilaginous materials which ~ when water is added —Morris Fishbein⟩ **b :** to rise above or extend beyond a level, surface, or border ⟨up from the horizon ~*ed* a supernatural light —O.E.Rölvaag⟩ ⟨it is in this length of the river that it ~*s* to gigantic size —Tom Marvel⟩ **c :** to have a form that curves outward or upward **:** DISTEND, BULGE, PROTRUDE ⟨a comfortable paunch ~*ed* out beneath the buttons of his dinner jacket —Hamilton Basso⟩ ⟨the green slope ~*ed* upward to the pear orchard —Ellen Glasgow⟩ **2 a :** to become filled with pride and arrogance **:** become puffed up ⟨~*s* with pride and importance as he struts up and down —Martin Turnell⟩ **b :** to behave or speak in a pompous, blustering, self-important manner ⟨the diver crew will ~ around on the boat talking about different jobs they have been on —Richard Bissell⟩ **c :** to play the swell **:** behave as a man of fashion ⟨looked down on so much sheer ~*ing* around —*Newsweek*⟩ **3 a :** to develop and grow in the consciousness as if seeking an outlet ⟨the unseen grief that ~*s* with silence in the tortured soul —Shak.⟩ **b :** to become distended with emotion **:** become affected with a powerful feeling ⟨her heart ~*ed* with a suffocating sense of resentment —Anne D. Sedgwick⟩ **4 a :** to become augmented in force, intensity, degree, numbers, or value ⟨job opportunities ~*ed* hugely in government —Daniel Bell⟩ ⟨the credit union's capital ~*ed* to $110,000 —Frank Hamilton⟩ **b :** to become gradually louder **:** rise to a peak of loudness or sonority ⟨the cries ~*ed* and died away —John Galsworthy⟩ ⟨the organ ~*ed* to a climax⟩ **~** *vt* **1 :** to affect with a powerful or expansive emotion **:** INFLATE ⟨it ~*s* me to joyful madness —Walt Whitman⟩ ⟨he is *swollen* with pride⟩ **2 a :** to increase the volume or size of **:** cause to fill out or expand ⟨warm summer water . . . will quickly ~ the planks and so close the seams —C.D.Lane⟩ ⟨a hide . . . is put through a liming process that ~*s* it and loosens the hair —*Amer. Guide Series: Pa.*⟩ **b :** to cause (as a body of water) to become higher, wider, or more turbulent ⟨rivers *swollen* by rain⟩ ⟨ten thousand springs and creeks and a dozen lesser rivers run . . . to ~ the Sacramento —Julian Dana⟩ ⟨another little crop to ~ the flood of misery —Nevil Shute⟩ **3 a :** to increase in quantity, value, intensity, or degree **:** AUGMENT ⟨some large federal installation or project greatly ~*ed* the school population —*N.Y.Times*⟩ ⟨nobles, landed gentry, merchants . . . ~*ed* the demand for country houses —Bernard Smith⟩ **b :** to augment gradually in loudness (as a musical tone) ⟨the pealing anthem ~*s* the note of praise —Thomas Gray⟩ **syn** see EXPAND

[2]**swell** \ˈ"\ *n* -s **1 a :** the condition of being swollen **:** BULGE, PROTUBERANCE ⟨this causes too much ~ in the back of the book —Laurence Town⟩ ⟨a green bodice which fitted so snugly that the ~ of her breasts was accentuated —T.B. Costain⟩ **b** (1) **:** a rounded elevation or hill; *esp* **:** a long rounded ridge on a sea floor ⟨the mid-Atlantic ~⟩ (2) **:** a tract of rising ground (3) **:** a very broad anticlinal structure **c :** ENTASIS **d :** a local enlargement or thickening in a vein or ore deposit **e :** FLIPPER 2d **2 a :** a long relatively low wave or an unbroken series of such waves **b :** a slow rhythmic heaving or rolling action or process ⟨the thing rolls on its antique springs with a slow, disquieting ~ —Mollie Panter-Downes⟩ ⟨that sustained impressiveness, that booming ~, which becomes so intolerable —F.R.Leavis⟩ **3 a :** the act, action, or process of swelling **:** an increase in volume, size, force, or intensity ⟨a ~ in population⟩ ⟨there is little dramatic ~ into the tragic power that the end of the story demands —Edgar Johnson⟩ **b** (1) **:** a gradual increase and decrease of the loudness or volume of a musical sound; *also* **:** a sign <> indicating a swell (2) **:** a device used in a harpsichord or pipe or reed organ for governing the loudness of tones by opening or closing the cover or set of louvers over a box or chamber enclosing the sounding strings, vibrators, or pipes (3) **:** SWELL BOX (4) **:** SWELL ORGAN (5) **:** SWELL PEDAL **4 a** *archaic* **:** an impressive, pompous, or fashionable air or display **:** DASH ⟨a new necktie, nice shirts — you can imagine I cut quite a ~ —Walt Whitman⟩ **b :** a person dressed in the height of fashion **:** FASHION PLATE ⟨sketched himself as a . . . ~, in a top hat, a white silk scarf, and a chesterfield —Janet Flanner⟩ ⟨see quite a young ~ come out in the latest fashion —Patricia M. Johnson⟩ **c :** a person of high social position **:** NOB ⟨a tony street where all the ~*s* lived —J.T.Farrell⟩ **d :** a specialist or person of outstanding achievement in a particular field **:** EXPERT, MASTER ⟨a real ~ on birds —H.J.Laski⟩ ⟨an agreeable melodist and a terrific ~ at orchestration —Arnold Bennett⟩ **5 :** a small lever connected with the shuttle protector in the shuttle box of a loom

[3]**swell** \ˈ"\ *adj* -ER/-EST [[2]*swell* (person dressed in fashion)] **1 :** smartly dressed or turned out **:** STYLISH ⟨I am too shabby . . . only ~ people go to the park —Oscar Wilde⟩ **:** socially prominent **:** DISTINGUISHED ⟨had a lot of ~ social connections —Wilson Collison⟩ **2 :** suitable for or characteristic of swells **:** FASHIONABLE, TIP-TOP ⟨staying at the ~*est* hotel in town⟩ **3 :** EXCELLENT, GREAT, WONDERFUL — used as a generalized term of enthusiasm or approval ⟨makes a ~ impression and is hired —W.H.Whyte⟩ ⟨she was a really ~ girl —W.F.Jenkins⟩ ⟨it's a miracle . . . I feel perfectly ~ —W.S. Maugham⟩

swellbelly \ˈ=,==\ *n* **:** GLOBEFISH; *esp* **:** a common fish (*Sphoeroides maculatus*) of the Atlantic coast of No. America

swell box *n* **:** a box or chamber in an organ that contains the reeds or a set of pipes and has shutters that open or shut usu. by means of a pedal in order to regulate the volume of musical tone

swell–butted \ˈ=;==\ *adj*, *of a tree* **:** greatly enlarged at the base — compare KNEE 3c

swell dash *n* **:** DIAMOND DASH

swell·dom \ˈsweldəm\ *n* -s [[2]*swell* + *-dom*] **:** the world of fashion **:** high society ⟨was taken up by ~, whose practically unanimous verdict was that she was a charming addition to their circle —*Lincoln* (*Nebr.*) *Evening News*⟩

swelled *adj* **1 :** ENLARGED, INFLATED **2 :** having a bulge or curve ⟨a ~ column⟩ ⟨the ~ front of the desk⟩

swelled head *n* **1 a :** BIGHEAD 1a **b :** BIGHEAD 1c **2 :** an exaggerated opinion of oneself **:** SELF-CONCEIT ⟨risk the chance of your getting a *swelled head* and tell you what I think of your efforts —A.H.Gibbs⟩ — **swelled–headed** \ˈ=;==\ *adj* — **swelled–head·ed·ness** *n* -ES

swell·er \ˈswelə(r)\ *n* -s **:** one that swells

swellfish \ˈ=,=\ *n* **:** GLOBEFISH

swell front *n* **:** a front (as of a chest of drawers or a house) rounded out in a convex curve

swellhead \ˈ=,=\ *n* **1 a :** INFECTIOUS SINUSITIS **b :** BIGHEAD 1b **2 :** one who has a swelled head **:** a conceited person — **swellheaded** \ˈ=;==\ *adj* — **swell·head·ed·ness** *n* -ES

[1]**swell·ing** \ˈsweliŋ, -lēŋ\ *n* -s [ME, fr. gerund of *swellen* to swell] **1 :** something that is swollen **:** BULGE, PROTUBERANCE; *specif* **:** an abnormal bodily protuberance or localized enlargement ⟨a neoplastic ~⟩ **2** *archaic* **:** conceited feeling or behavior **:** excessive pride **3 a** *archaic* **:** the action of rising above a level or surface **b :** the act or process of dilating or the condition of having become dilated **:** EXPANSION ⟨experienced agreeable ~*s* of virtue —Mary Austin⟩

[2]**swelling** \ˈ"\ *adj* [fr. pres. part. of *swellen* to swell] **1 :** increasing in volume, amount, or force **:** filling out **:** ENLARGING, RISING ⟨the ~ bubble⟩ ⟨the ~ sails⟩ ⟨the ~ tide⟩ ⟨the ~ roar of the crowd⟩ **2 :** having a bulging or curving form; *specif* **:** having a gently rising contour ⟨eastward rise the ~ foothills —*Amer. Guide Series: Oregon*⟩ **3 a :** inflated with conceit **:** OVERWEENING ⟨prizefighters — ~ in triumph —Bergen Evans⟩ **b :** marked by intensity of feeling **:** EXPANSIVE ⟨the ~ sense of great things impending —F. Tennyson Jesse⟩ **c :** inflated in style or manner **:** BOMBASTIC, POMPOUS ⟨a ~ speech⟩ ⟨a ~ scene⟩ — **swell·ing·ly** *adv*

swell·ish \ˈswelish, -lēsh\ *adj* [[2]*swell* + *-ish*] **:** STYLISH, SWELL — **swell·ish·ness** *n* -ES

swell mob *n* [[2]*swell*] *Brit* **:** a group of criminals who dress fashionably and act with seeming respectability

swell–mobsman \ˈ=;==\ *n*, *Brit* **:** a criminal (as a pickpocket) who dresses fashionably and conducts himself with seeming respectability for professional purposes

swell organ *n* **:** a division in a pipe organ in which the pipes are enclosed in a swell box

swell pedal *n* **:** a pedal that operates an organ swell usu. by working a balanced lever mechanism that opens or shuts the louvers of the swell box

swell piece *n* **:** a flat piece (as of wood) with a convex outer face

swells *pres 3d sing of* SWELL, *pl of* SWELL

swell shark *n* **:** any of several short, wide-bodied sharks of the family Scyliorhinidae that take in air when caught and swell up; *esp* **:** a shark (*Cephaloscyllium uter*) of the California coast

swelltoad \ˈ=,=\ *n* **:** GLOBEFISH

swelt \ˈswelt\ *vb* -ED/-ING/-S [ME *swelten* — more at SWELTER] *vi* **1** *dial* **a :** DIE, PERISH **b :** FAINT, SWOON **2** *dial* **:** to become oppressed by heat **:** SWELTER, SUFFOCATE **~** *vt* **1** *dial* **:** to cause to die **2** *dial* **:** to overpower with or as if with heat **:** BROIL, SCORCH

[1]**swel·ter** \ˈsweltə(r)\ *vb* **sweltered; sweltered; sweltering** \-t(ə)riŋ, -l·triŋ\ **swelters** [ME *sweltren*, *swelteren*, freq. of *swelten* to die, faint, be overcome by heat, fr. OE *sweltan* to die, perish; akin to OS *sweltan* to die, OHG *swelzan* to burn up (with passion), ON *svelta* to die, starve, be hungry, Goth *swiltan* to die, and prob. to OE *swelan* to burn, MLG *swelen* to smolder, Gk *heilē*, *eilē*, *helē* heat of the sun, sunshine, Lith *svilti* to singe, Skt *svarati* it lights up, shines] *vi* **1 a :** to be faint from heat **:** become oppressed or excessively uncomfortable with heat **:** perspire profusely **:** SWEAT ⟨an explorer who has ~*ed* in the jungle and frozen in the far north⟩ **b :** to become exposed to excessive heat ⟨a land that ~*s* for most of the year⟩ **2** *archaic* **:** WALLOW, WELTER **3** *archaic* **:** to become exuded **~** *vt* **1 :** to oppress with heat **:** make faint with heat **:** cause to sweat profusely ⟨amphitheater which sheltered and ~*ed* the last . . . convention —Phyllis Battelle⟩ **2** *archaic* **:** EXUDE ⟨~*ed* venom —Shak.⟩

[2]**swelter** \ˈ"\ *n* -s **1 :** a state of oppressive heat ⟨the officers ate in a ~, sweat dripping from their hands and faces —Norman Mailer⟩ **2 :** WELTER ⟨the immense sweeps and ~*s* of the whirl —E.A.Poe⟩ **3 :** an excited or overwrought state of mind **:** SWEAT ⟨for all the bitter cold and my thin gown and us being far from the fire, I was all in a ~ —Mary Webb⟩

[1]**sweltering** *adj* **:** oppressively hot **:** causing or marked by excessive sweating or faintness ⟨a ~ day⟩ ⟨a ~ room⟩ ⟨watch the players battle their ~ way through matches lasting a couple of hours —Mollie Panter-Downes⟩

[2]**sweltering** *adv* **:** SWELTERINGLY

swel·ter·ing·ly *adv* **:** to a sweltering degree ⟨the sun came ~ in on us through the glass roof —Robert Lynd⟩

swel·try \ˈswel·trē, -ri\ *adj* -ER/-EST [[1]*swelter* + *-y*] **:** SWELTERING, SULTRY

swept *adj* [fr. past part. of [1]*sweep*] **:** possessing sweep ⟨the ~ wing of the airplane⟩

swept–back \ˈ=;=\ *adj* [fr. past part. of *sweep back*, v.] **:** possessing sweepback

swept–forward \ˈ=;==\ *adj* [fr. past part. of *sweep forward*, v.] **:** possessing sweepforward

sweptwing \ˈ=;=\ *adj* **:** having swept wings; *specif* **:** having swept-back wings

swer·tia \ˈswərsh(ē)ə, -rd·ēə\ *n*, *cap* [NL, fr. Emanuel *Swert* (Sweert), 17th cent. Du. botanist + NL *-ia*] **:** a small genus of herbs (family Gentianaceae) found chiefly in the western U.S. and having thick, bitter roots, opposite or whorled leaves, and dull-colored flowers — see GREEN GENTIAN

[1]**swerve** \ˈswərv, ˈswəv, ˈswəiv\ *vb* -ED/-ING/-S [ME *swerven*, fr. OE *sweorfan* to file away, polish, wipe, rub, scour; akin to OFris *swerva* to creep, OS *swerban* to wipe off, OHG *swerban* to wipe off, ON *sverfa* to file, *svarfa* to sweep, swerve, Goth af*swairban* to wipe off, W *chwerfu* to whirl, turn around, Gk *syrein* to drag, Russ *sverbet'* to itch; basic meaning: to turn] *vi* **1 :** to move from a straight line or course **:** turn aside **:** become deflected **:** DEVIATE ⟨*swerving* to avoid two errand boys on bicycles —Robert Graves⟩ ⟨the bull *swerved* to meet this new opponent —Francis Birtles⟩ ⟨the highway ~*s* south —*Amer. Guide Series: Fla.*⟩ **2 :** to become deflected from a fixed or right course of action, conduct, or belief **:** shift one's position or allegiance **:** WAVER ⟨had never *swerved* from what she conceived to be her duty —A.J.Kennedy⟩ **3** *archaic* **:** to give way **:** YIELD, TOTTER **~** *vt* **:** to turn aside **:** cause to turn from a straight course **:** cause to deviate ⟨~ the car⟩ ⟨~ a ball⟩ ⟨do not let your apprehension of what the judges may say ~ you from saying what you think —C.P. Curtis⟩

syn SWERVE, VEER, DEVIATE, DEPART, DIGRESS, and DIVERGE can mean, in common, to turn aside from a straight line or a defined course. SWERVE may suggest a physical, mental, or moral turning from a given course, usu. by an abrupt shift of direction ⟨the highway now skirts the lake shore . . . and again *swerves* inland —*Amer. Guide Series: Vt.*⟩ ⟨the driver of the motorcar *swerved* the other way but could not avoid the cab —Eric Linklater⟩ ⟨*swerved* and veered like a gull —John Dos Passos⟩ ⟨not to *swerve* from the path of duty or righteousness⟩ VEER, applying commonly to the change in the course of a wind or ship and often suggesting frequent turning or a series of turnings in the same direction, implies a change or a series of changes of direction or course under an external influence comparable to the wind ⟨the wind suddenly *veered* and drove the waters of the Gulf in mountainous waves upon them —*Amer. Guide Series: La.*⟩ ⟨his thought, *veering* and tacking as the winds blew —V.L.Parrington⟩ ⟨drift with every current of opinion and *veer* like a weathercock with every breeze of fashion —S.J.Brown⟩ ⟨literary men *veer* between the extremes of a contempt for the masses and a glorification of the people —H.J.Muller⟩ DEVIATE implies a turning aside from a customary, allotted, or prescribed course, suggesting a swerving from what is the norm, the law, the standard, or the proper procedure or course ⟨if he diminishes his speed by a fraction of a second or *deviates* a hair's breadth from the prescribed and never-changing movements of his hands —C.H.Grandgent⟩ ⟨anyone who *deviates* from that faith —V.M.Hancher⟩ ⟨has never *deviated* from the belief that the basis of a good cartoon is caricature —*Current Biog.*⟩ DEPART usu. signifies little more than leaving a given path, usu. figurative ⟨one point in which the definition of virtue and vice given above *departs* from tradition and from common practice —Bertrand Russell⟩ ⟨the design of the center departs somewhat from that of the newer buildings —*Amer. Guide Series: Minn.*⟩ ⟨forced by circumstances to *depart* from the principles of his own logic —W.P.Webb⟩ DIGRESS implies a departure from the subject of one's discourse whether intentional or from general lack of a sense of coherence ⟨*digress* a moment from a main point of discussion to consider a pressing tangential problem⟩ ⟨an irritating habit of *digressing* and never getting back to the main point of a story⟩ DIVERGE, often used in the sense of DEPART, usu., however, suggests a separation of one, usu. a main, path into two or more leading in different directions ⟨the absolute prohibition of all ideas that *diverge* in the slightest from the accepted platitudes —H.L.Mencken⟩ ⟨*diverged* from the path, and got before them on the left flank —George Meredith⟩ ⟨proceeded along the road together till they reached the town, and their paths *diverged* —Thomas Hardy⟩ ⟨a year later the careers of the brothers, so far linked together, *diverged* —*Current Biog.*⟩

[2]**swerve** \ˈ"\ *n* -s **1 :** the act, process, or an instance of swerving ⟨with a dexterous ~ he rounded the yawl about —Frederick Way⟩ **2 :** side-to-side curve of a bowled cricket ball before it pitches; *esp* **:** such curve induced by finger spin

swerved *past of* SWERVE

swerve·less \ˈ=ləs\ *adj* **:** UNSWERVING

swerv·er \ˈswərvər, ˈswəvə(r, ˈswəivə(r\ *n* -s **:** one that swerves

swerves *pres 3d sing of* SWERVE

swerving *pres part of* SWERVE

swev·en \ˈswevən\ *n* -s [ME, fr. OE *swefn* sleep, dream, vision — more at SOMNOLENT] *archaic* **:** DREAM, VISION

swg *abbr* switching

SWG *abbr* standard wire gauge

swich \ˈswich\ *chiefly dial var of* SUCH

swid·den \ˈswidᵊn\ *n* -s [E dial., burned clearing, prob. fr. ON *svithinn*, past part. of *svītha* to burn, singe] **:** an impermanent agricultural plot produced by cutting back and burning off vegetative cover — called also *kaingin*; compare MILPA

swie·te·nia \swēˈtēnēə\ *n*, *cap* [NL, fr. Gerard van *Swieten* †1772 Du. botanist and physician in Austria + NL *-ia*] **:** a small genus of tropical trees (family Meliaceae) having seeds winged above and anthers borne between the teeth of the stamen tube — see MAHOGANY

[1]**swift** \ˈswift\ *adj* -ER/-EST [ME, fr. OE; akin to OE *swīfan* to revolve, wend, sweep — more at SWIVEL] **1 :** moving or capable of moving with great speed **:** characterized by rapidity of motion **:** rapidly running, flying, flowing ⟨the ~ flight of an arrow⟩ ⟨making . . . a man a ~ runner, a nimble climber, a strong swimmer —J.G.Frazer⟩ ⟨the river's too deep to ford and too ~ to swim —Willa Cather⟩ **2 a :** taking place, done, or concluded within a very short time ⟨northers sometimes bring a ~ change from sunshine to howling blizzards —*Amer. Guide Series: Texas*⟩ ⟨shot a ~ smile toward him in that instant⟩ ⟨the ~ achievement of goals in half the projected time⟩ **b :** changing abruptly in character **:** SUDDEN ⟨the plains end, and with a ~ dramatic uprise the world of the mountains begins —Wynford Vaughan-Thomas⟩ **3 a :** quick in execution or accomplishment **:** speedy in action or performance ⟨better to be ~ and casual than to be slow and thorough —Ellen Glasgow⟩ ⟨must not search for penetrating or subtle characterization but rather for ~ and arresting caricature —William Peden⟩ **b :** quick to respond **:** READY, ALERT, PROMPT ⟨in her youth and prime . . . ~ in affection, and ~*er* still for vengeance —William Baucke⟩ ⟨afraid of rousing his ~ and terrible anger⟩ ⟨I will be a ~ witness against the sorcerers —Mal 3:5 (RSV)⟩ **syn** see FAST

[2]**swift** \ˈ"\ *adv* -ER/-EST [ME, fr. [1]*swift*] **:** SWIFTLY ⟨~ to its close ebbs out life's little day —Henry Lyte⟩ — often used in combination ⟨*swift*-flowing⟩

[3]**swift** \ˈ"\ *n* -s [[1]*swift*] **1 :** one that is swift: as **a :** any of several lizards (as the pine lizard and others of the genus *Sceloporus*) that run swiftly **b :** the rapid current of a stream **2 a :** a reel for winding yarn or thread usu. collapsible for removal or application of the skein **b :** one of the large cylinders covered with card cloth that carry forward the material in a carding machine; *also* **:** a similar cylinder in other machines **c :** a tapering reel revolved on a vertical spindle and used for uncoiling wire **3 :** any of numerous small plainly colored birds constituting the family Apodidae that are related to the hummingbirds and goatsuckers but superficially much resemble swallows, that have very long narrow wings, weak feet, and a short bill with a wide gape, that spend most of their time on the wing and when they alight usu. cling to some vertical surface, that feed on insects taken on the wing, and that have nests cemented together with their sticky saliva and often attached by saliva to some vertical surface (as the inside of a hollow tree or the wall of a building, cave, or cliff); *specif* **:** a common European bird (*Apus apus* syn. *Micropus apus*) noted for its shrieking notes, having a somewhat forked tail, and nesting chiefly in crevices about the eaves of buildings or on cliffs — compare CHIMNEY SWIFT, SWIFTLET **4 :** the sail of a windmill **5** *or* **swift moth :** GHOST MOTH **6** *also* **swift fox :** KIT FOX

[4]**swift** \ˈ"\ *vt* -ED/-ING/-S [ME *swiften*, prob. of Scand origin; akin to ON *svipta* to sweep off, reef, *svīfa* to ramble, turn, drift — more at SWIVEL] *Brit* **:** SWIFTER

swift·en \ˈswiftən\ *vi* -ED/-ING/-S [[1]*swift* + *-en*] **:** to move swiftly or more swiftly **:** HASTEN

[1]**swift·er** \ˈswiftə(r)\ *n* -s [[4]*swift* + *-er*] **1 :** the forward or after shroud of a lower mast — see SHIP illustration **2 :** a rope confining the capstan bars in their sockets while the capstan is being turned **3 :** a rope encircling a boat or ship longitudinally to strengthen or protect the sides

[2]**swifter** \ˈ"\ *vt* **swiftered; swiftered; swiftering** \-t(ə)riŋ\ **swifters :** to tauten, secure, or protect with a swifter or other line; *specif* **:** to tauten (slack standing rigging) by bringing the shrouds closer together with a swiftering line — often used with *in* ⟨~ in the shrouds⟩

[3]**swifter** \ˈ"\ *n* [[3]*swift* + *-er*] **:** a worker at a swift (sense 2); *esp* **:** WINDER

swiftering line *n* [*swiftering* (gerund of [2]*swifter*) + *line*] **:** a line used to swifter in rigging

swiftest *superlative of* SWIFT

swiftfoot \ˈ=,=\ *n*, *pl* **swiftfoots** [[1]*swift* + *foot*] **:** a European courser (*Cursorius cursor*)

swift·i·an \ˈswiftēən\ *adj*, *usu cap* [Jonathan *Swift* †1745 Eng. satirist + E *-ian*] **:** of, relating to, or characteristic of Jonathan Swift or his writings; *specif* **:** satirizing with bitter often savage irony the weakness and corruption of the human race ⟨a *Swiftian* satire⟩ ⟨*Swiftian* morality⟩

swift·let \ˈ=lət\ *n* -s [[3]*swift* + *-let*] **:** a swift of the genus *Collocalia*; *specif* **:** a swift (*C. inexpectata*) of eastern Asia that produces the edible bird's nest

swift·ly \ˈswiftlē, -li\ *adv*, *sometimes* -ER/-EST [ME, fr. OE *swiftlīce*, fr. [1]*swift* + *-līce* -ly] **:** in a swift manner ⟨early novels had ~ established him as an important new figure —*London Calling*⟩

swift·ness \-f(t)nəs\ *n* -ES [ME *swiftnes*, fr. OE, fr. [1]*swift* + *-nes* -ness] **1 :** the quality or state of being swift **:** SPEED, CELERITY ⟨the ~ of a lizard catching a fly —Vicki Baum⟩ **2 :** the fact of being swift ⟨when ~ of action was indispensable to surprise⟩

[1]**swig** \ˈswig\ *n* -s [origin unknown] **1 :** LIQUOR **2 :** a quantity drunk at one time **:** DRAFT, DRINK, PULL ⟨many ~*s* out of his father's decanter of whiskey —Hamilton Basso⟩

[2]**swig** \ˈ"\ *vb* **swigged; swigged; swigging; swigs** *vt* **:** to drink in long drafts **:** GULP ⟨fancy *swigging* a liqueur like beer —C.D.Lewis⟩ **~** *vi* **:** to take a swig **:** DRINK — **swig·ger** \-gə(r)\ *n* -s

[3]**swig** \ˈ"\ *vb* **swigged; swigged; swigging; swigs** [origin unknown] *vi* **1 :** to pull at right angles on the bight of a tackle or rope fast at one end to a weight to be raised and at the other passing through a block or around something and then to let go quickly and simultaneously take in the slack — usu. used with *off* **2 :** SWAY, ROCK; *also* **:** SWASH **~** *vt* **1 :** to hoist or set up taut (as a sail) by swigging off on a halyard or tackle — usu. used with *up* ⟨~ up a racing mainsail⟩ **2 :** to haul taut (as a rope, tackle) by swigging off on

[4]**swig** \ˈ"\ *n* -s **1 :** a tackle whose ropes run at a considerable angle **2 :** an act of swigging off on a tackle

swig·gle \ˈswigəl\ *vb* -ED/-ING/-S [by alter.] *dial* **:** SWIG

swile \ˈswīl\ *n* -s [origin unknown] **:** [1]SEAL

[1]**swill** \ˈswil\ *vb* -ED/-ING/-S [ME *swilen*, fr. OE *swillan*, *swilian* to wash out, rinse, gargle; perh. akin to OE *swelgan* to swallow — more at SWALLOW] *vt* **1 :** WASH, DRENCH, RINSE ⟨~*ed* my hands in the enamel bowl on the washhouse table —E.L.Thomas⟩; *esp* **:** to wash by flushing with water ⟨the amount of water used for ~*ing* cowsheds and pigsties should not be more than is necessary —C.B.Palmer⟩ ⟨a pint of bitter would ~ the dryness of the barley off his lips —G.A.Wagner⟩ **2 :** to supply abundantly or fill with (as an intoxicant) ⟨~*ing* themselves with ale —George Eliot⟩ **3 a :** to drink great drafts of **:** GUZZLE ⟨were ~*ing* down gin . . . and talking with loud jocosity —Bruce Marshall⟩ **b :** to devour greedily ⟨dogs who ~ their food from the ground —Norman Kelman⟩ **4 :** to pour (a liquid) freely ⟨~ out drinks⟩ **5 :** to cause

(liquid) to swish in a container — used with *about* or *around* ⟨~*s* a little hot water around in the pot before steeping the tea⟩ **6** [²*swill*] **:** to feed (as a pig) with swill **~** *vi* **1 :** to drink or eat freely, greedily, or to excess; *esp* **:** to drink liquor in large drafts or to excess ⟨as bad as the rest of them — ~*ing* in taverns . . . in planting time —Clements Ripley⟩ **2 :** to flow in a free, forcible, or turbulent manner **:** SWASH ⟨a wave ~*ed* along the steps —Haldane Macfall⟩

²swill \"\ *n* -s **1 a** (1) **:** a semiliquid food for animals (as swine) composed of the animal or vegetable refuse of kitchens, markets, or stores, mixed with water or skimmed or sour milk **:** SLOP, WASH (2) **:** a hog ration made of distillery slop **b :** food refuse **:** GARBAGE **2 :** something suggestive of slop or garbage **:** something evoking disgust **:** HOGWASH, REFUSE ⟨dismissed the whole literary production of his rival as ~⟩ ⟨treated them shabbily like ~⟩ **3 :** an act or instance of swilling: as **a :** a draft of liquor **b :** the swash of a liquid ⟨heard the ~ of the flood waters⟩

³swill \"\ *n* -s [ME *sqwill, swill*] **:** a large shallow basket roughly made (as of unpeeled willow) and used esp. in England for fish (as to transfer them from boat to shore or to measure them)

swillbowl \ˈ≈,≈\ *n* [¹*swill* + *bowl*] **:** DRUNKARD

swill·er \ˈswilə(r)\ *n* -s **:** one that swills

swilling *n* -s [fr. gerund of ¹*swill*] **1 :** the act or process of one that swills **2** *obs* **:** swill for hogs **3 swillings** *pl* **:** dirty liquid from washing

swill milk *n* [²*swill*] **:** milk given by cows fed on swill (as from a distillery)

¹swim \ˈswim\ *vb* **swam** \ˈswam, -aa(ə)m\ *also chiefly dial* **swimmed** \ˈswimd\ *or* **swum** \ˈswəm\ **swum** *also chiefly dial* **swam** *or* **swimmed; swimming; swims** [ME *swimmen*, fr. OE *swimman;* akin to OHG *swimman* to swim, ON *svimma*, Goth *swumfsl* swimming pool] *vi* **1 :** to move or propel oneself progressively in water by natural means (as by strokes of the hands and feet or by movements of the fins, flippers, or tail) **2 :** to move with a motion like that of swimming **:** slip or glide smoothly and quietly **:** FLOAT ⟨a cloud *swam* slowly across the moon⟩ **3 a :** to float on the surface of or rise to the top of a liquid **:** not sink ⟨oil ~*s* on water⟩ **b :** to overcome or surmount difficulties **:** not go under ⟨sink or ~, live or die, survive or perish —Daniel Webster⟩ **4 :** to become immersed or flooded **:** become surrounded or covered or filled with or as if with a liquid ⟨the meat ~*s* in gravy⟩ ⟨his heart *swam* with joy⟩ ⟨he ~*s* in riches⟩ **5 :** to appear to move unsteadily before the eyes **:** REEL ⟨sat down again as the room began to ~ crazily around her⟩ **6 :** to be dizzy **:** have an unsteady or reeling sensation ⟨feels faint and his head ~*s*⟩ **~** *vt* **1 a :** to move over, cover, or cross by propelling oneself through water ⟨~ a stream⟩ ⟨~ a mile⟩ **b :** to execute (a stroke) in swimming **2 a :** to cause or compel to swim or float ⟨~ a horse across a river⟩ **b :** to make float or permit floating of in or on the surface of a liquid ⟨immerse the eggs in enough water to ~ the light ones⟩ **3 :** to subject (one) to ordeal by water **4 :** to bring to a specified state by swimming **5 :** to compete with in a swimming match — **swim against the stream :** to move counter to or work against the prevailing or popular current (as in religion or politics)

²swim \"\ *n* -s **1 :** a smooth gliding motion **2 :** SWIM BLADDER **3 :** an act or period of swimming ⟨took a ~ in the bay⟩ ⟨back from his early morning ~⟩ **4 :** a temporary forgetfulness, dizziness, or unconsciousness **:** SWOON **5 a :** a part of a stream or other water frequented by fish **b :** the current trend of affairs ⟨that manufacturers slow to make the design change would be out of the ~⟩ **:** the thick of fashionable activity — usu. used in the phrase *in the swim* ⟨spent his vacation at a popular resort to be in the ~⟩ **6 :** a square flat overhanging bow on a barge (as formerly in the east of England)

³swim \"\ *adj* **:** of, concerned with, or used in or for swimming ⟨~ lessons⟩ ⟨~ show⟩ ⟨~ trunks⟩

swim bladder *n* **:** the air bladder of a fish

swim fin *n* **:** FLIPPER 1b

swim·mable \ˈswiməbəl\ *adj* **:** that can be swum

swim·mer \-mə(r)\ *n* -s [ME, fr. *swimmen* to swim + *-er*] **1 :** one that swims **2 :** a body part (as a specialized appendage) used in swimming

swim·mer·et *also* **swim·mer·ette** \ˌswiməˈret\ *n* -s [*swimmer* + *-et, -ette*] **:** one of a series of small unspecialized appendages under the abdomen of many crustaceans that are best developed in some decapods and are used in some cases for swimming but usu. for carrying eggs

swimmer's itch *n* **:** SCHISTOSOME DERMATITIS

swim·mi·ly \ˈswiməlē, -li\ *adv* **:** in a swimmy manner

swim·mi·ness \-mēnəs, -min-\ *n* -ES **:** the quality or state of being swimmy

¹swim·ming \ˈswimiŋ, -mēŋ\ *n* -s [ME, fr. gerund of *swimmen* to swim] **1 :** the act, art, or sport of swimming and diving **2 a :** VERTIGO, DIZZINESS **b :** blurred or dazzled vision (as in dizziness)

²swimming *adj* [fr. pres. part. of ¹*swim*] **1 a :** that swims **:** capable of or habituated to swimming ⟨a ~ bird⟩ **b** [¹*swimming*] **:** adapted to or used in or for swimming ⟨a ~ stroke⟩ ⟨a ~ lash⟩ **2 :** filled or flooded with or as if with water ⟨~ eyes⟩ **3 :** being in or affected by a state of vertigo or dizziness ⟨a ~ brain⟩

swimming bath *n, Brit* **:** SWIMMING POOL

swimming bell *n* **:** a bell-shaped swimming organ in some siphonophores composed of a greatly modified zooid without mouth or tentacles and serving to propel the colony by its rhythmical contractions **:** NECTOPHORE, NECTOCALYX

swimming bladder *n* **1 :** the air bladder of a fish **2 :** PNEUMATOCYST

swimming crab *n* **:** any of numerous marine crabs esp. of the family Portunidae that have some of the joints of one or more pairs of legs flattened and fringed so as to serve as fins

swimming funnel *n* **:** a large forwardly directed tube in cephalopods opening just behind and below the neck through which the water from the mantle cavity is discharged with the animal being able to swim backward by suddenly expelling water through it

swimming hole *n* **:** a comparatively deep place in a stream locally used for swimming

swim·ming·ly *adv* [*swimming* (pres. part. of ¹*swim*) + *-ly*] **:** in the easy, smooth, or steadily progressive manner of one swimming; *esp* **:** PROSPEROUSLY, SUCCESSFULLY ⟨in spite of one or two minor mishaps everything was going ~ —P.L.Fermor⟩

swimming plate *n* **:** one of the platelike rows of fused cilia forming the combs of a ctenophore

swimming pool *also* **swim pool** *n* **:** a pool suitable for swimming; *esp* **:** a tank (as of concrete or plastic) made for swimming

swimming pool

swimming sandpiper *n* **:** PHALAROPE

swimming stone *n* **:** FLOATSTONE 1

swim·my \ˈswimē, -mi\ *adj* -ER/-EST [¹*swim* + *-y*] **1 :** verging on, causing, or affected by dizziness or giddiness **:** tending toward vertigo ⟨~ with the local cider —Clemence Dane⟩ **2** *of vision* **:** BLURRED, UNSTEADY ⟨had red patches on his cheeks and his eyes were ~ —Greville Texidor⟩

swim ring *n* **:** an inflated ring of rubber or plastic material that a person may take into the water and hold onto for buoyancy

swimsuit \ˈ≈,≈\ *n* **:** BATHING SUIT; *esp* **:** MAILLOT

swin·burn·ian \(ˈ)swinˌbərnēən, -bən-, -bəia-, -nyən\ *adj, usu cap* [Algernon Charles *Swinburne* †1909 Eng. poet + E *-ian*] **:** of, relating to, or having the characteristics of Swinburne or his writings ⟨*Swinburnian* rhythms⟩

¹swin·dle \ˈswindᵊl\ *vb* **swindled; swindled; swindling** \-d(ᵊ)liŋ\ **swindles** [back-formation fr. *swindler*] *vi* **:** to obtain money or property from one by fraud or deceit **:** practice imposture for gain **~** *vt* **:** to deprive of money or property by fraud or deceit ⟨~ the unwary with fakes⟩ **syn** see CHEAT

²swindle \"\ *n* -s **1 :** the act or process of swindling or defrauding **2 :** an instance of swindling **:** FRAUD

swin·dle·able \-d(ᵊ)ləbəl\ *adj* **:** that can be swindled **:** GULLIBLE

swin·dler \-d(ᵊ)lə(r)\ *n* -s [G *schwindler* giddy person, fantastic schemer, fr. *schwindeln* to be dizzy, fr. OHG *swintilōn*, freq. of *swintan* to diminish, vanish, become unconscious; akin to OE *swindan* to languish, vanish, OIr *a-sennad* finally] **:** one that swindles **:** CHEAT, SHARPER

swindle sheet *n, slang* **:** EXPENSE ACCOUNT

swin·dling·ly *adv* [*swindling* (pres. part. of ¹*swindle*) + *-ly*] **:** in a swindling manner

swine \ˈswīn\ *n, pl* **swine** *often attrib* [ME, fr. OE *swīn;* akin to OHG *swīn* swine, ON *svīn*, Goth *swein*, L *suinus* of swine, *sus* swine, hog — more at SOW] **1 :** any of various animals that constitute the family Suidae and comprise stout-bodied short-legged omnivorous mammals with a thick skin usu. covered with coarse bristles, a rather long mobile snout, small tail, and two functional and except in peccaries two nonfunctional hoofed digits; *specif* **:** a domesticated member of the species (*Sus scrofa*) that includes the European wild boar — usu. used collectively **2 :** a contemptible person

swine back *n* **:** HOGBACK

swine–backed \ˈ≈;≈\ *adj* [*swine back* + *-ed*] **1 :** having a hog-back **2 :** convexly curved ⟨a *swine-backed* bow⟩

swine belt *n* **:** an area in the north-central U.S. in which hog raising is a major farm enterprise and which is more or less coextensive with the corn belt

swine–chopped \ˈ≈;≈\ *adj, of a dog* **:** having an overshot jaw

swine cress *or* **swine's–cress** \ˈswīnz+,-\ *n, pl* **swine's–cresses :** a cress of the genus *Coronopus* — called also *wart cress*

swine dysentery *n* **:** an acute infectious hemorrhagic dysentery of swine that is possibly a severe form of necrotic enteritis

swine erysipelas *n* **:** a destructive contagious disease of various mammals and birds that is caused by a bacterium (*Erysipelothrix rhusiopathiae*) that may occur in an acute highly fatal septicemic form or take a chronic course marked by endocarditis, arthritis, or urticaria, and that is of esp. economic importance in swine and domesticated turkeys — called also *erysipelas;* see DIAMOND SKIN DISEASE, ERYSIPELOID

swine fever *n* **:** HOG CHOLERA

swineherd \ˈ≈,≈\ *n* [ME, fr. OE *swȳnhyrde*, fr. *swīn* swine + *hyrde* herd] **:** one who tends swine

swineherd's disease \ˈ≈,≈-\ *also* **swineherder's disease** \ˈ≈,≈-\ *n* **:** LEPTOSPIROSIS

swine influenza *n* **:** an acute contagious febrile disease of swine marked by severe coughing and inflammation of the upper respiratory tract, sometimes passing into bronchopneumonia but rarely fatal, and caused by interaction of a specific virus introduced by the swine lungworm and a bacterium (*Hemophilus suis*) related to that of human influenza

swinelike \ˈ≈,≈\ *adj* **:** resembling swine

swine·man \ˈ≈mən\ *n, pl* **swinemen :** one in charge of or specializing in the raising of swine

swinepipe \ˈ≈,≈\ *n* **:** REDWING 1

swine plague *n* **:** hemorrhagic septicemia of swine with symptoms resembling those of hog cholera but commonly complicated by pneumonia

swine pox *n* **1** *obs* **:** CHICKENPOX ⟨found her up and merry as it did not prove the smallpox but the *swine pox* —Samuel Pepys⟩ **2 :** a mild virus disease of young pigs marked by fever, loss of appetite, dullness, and production of skin lesions suggestive of those of smallpox and caused by either of two unrelated viruses, one of which is related to the viruses of smallpox and cowpox

swin·ery \ˈswīn(ə)rē, -ri\ *n* -ES [*swine* + *-ery*] **1 :** a place where swine are kept **2 :** a swinish condition or action **3 :** a group of swine

swine's–feather \ˈ≈,≈≈\ *also* **swine's–pike** \ˈ≈,≈\ *n, pl* **swine's–feathers** *also* **swine's–pikes** [trans. of G *schweinsfeder;* so called fr. its being originally used as a hunting weapon] **:** a stake or spear resembling a bayonet formerly fixed in a musket rest or placed in the ground to hinder cavalry

swine's–grass \ˈ≈,≈\ *n, pl* **swine's–grasses :** KNOTGRASS 1

swine's–succory \ˈ≈,≈≈≈\ *n, pl* **swine's–succories 1 :** CHICORY **2 :** LAMB SUCCORY

swinestone \ˈ≈,≈\ *n* [trans. of G *schweinstein;* so called fr. its unpleasant odor] **:** a black bituminous limestone that usu. emits a fetid smell when rubbed

swinesty \ˈ≈,≈\ *n* **:** PIGSTY

swine typhoid *n* **:** NECROTIC ENTERITIS

¹swing \ˈswiŋ\ *vb* **swung** \ˈswəŋ\ *also chiefly dial* **swang** \ˈswaŋ, -aiŋ\ **swung; swinging; swings** [ME *swingen* to strike, beat, fling, hurl, rush, fr. OE *swingan* to strike, beat, fling oneself, rush; akin to OHG *swingan* to fling, rush, Goth *afswaggwjan* to make doubtful; basic meaning: to move with a rotating motion] *vt* **1 a :** to cause (something grasped or attached at one point) to move vigorously through a wide circle or arc **:** wield with a sweep or flourish ⟨charged the rival gang ~*ing* clubs and knives⟩ ⟨~ an axe⟩ ⟨~ a bat⟩ ⟨~ a scythe⟩ ⟨went for each other ~*ing* their fists⟩ ⟨jumped aside when the porcupine *swung* his tail⟩ **b** (1) **:** to cause (something suspended) to sway to and fro ⟨troops that marched and *swung* their arms in time with their song⟩ (2) **:** to give (a person) a ride in something (as a swing, hammock) that sways to and fro **c** (1) **:** to cause to turn on an axis **:** make rotate or pivot ⟨a gust that *swung* the door to⟩ (2) **:** to cause to face or move in another direction ⟨grasp him by the shoulder and ~ him around⟩ ⟨~ the gun towards them and fire⟩ ⟨~ the car into a side road⟩ (3) **:** to execute a swing with (in a square dance partner) ⟨~ your partner once around⟩ **d** (1) **:** to turn (a ship or airplane) to successive compass points (as the cardinal and quadrantal points) in order to ascertain and correct or record magnetic compass deviations by comparing on each heading the compass bearing of an object (as a distant landmark, the sun, a mark on an airport swinging base) with its known true magnetic bearing ⟨a tabulation of the deviation on different headings is made from the data obtained by ~*ing* ship —*Bluejackets' Manual*⟩ (2) **:** to ascertain the deviation of (an airplane compass) by so swinging the airplane usu. on a swinging base **2 :** to attach (as from an overhead support or by hinges) so as to permit swaying or turning **:** cause to hang **:** SUSPEND ⟨~ a hammock between nearby trees⟩ **3 :** to convey by suspension from a support ⟨huge cranes that ~ cargo up over the ship's side and into the hold⟩ **4** *of a lathe or lathe centers* **:** to be capable of holding for turning ⟨a lathe that ~*s* 12 inches⟩ **5 a** (1) **:** to exercise a determining influence on **:** influence decisively ⟨whether the labor vote will ~ the presidential election⟩ ⟨a lobby that ~*s* a lot of votes in the legislature⟩ (2) **:** to cause to change in attitude, loyalty, or outcome ⟨~ a bat-hater from fear and disgust to avid interest —R.K.Plumb⟩ (3) **:** to cause to rally or conform ⟨can ~ 20,000 workers behind the party line —C.H.Arke⟩ **b :** to succeed in doing, making, or having **:** bring about **:** MANAGE, ACCOMPLISH ⟨whether he is man enough to ~ the job⟩ ⟨~ the sale by entertaining the customer⟩ ⟨sure he can ~ a new car on his income⟩ **c :** to exert or be able to exert — used with *weight* ⟨got the job through a friend who ~*s* a lot of weight in city politics⟩ **6** [²*swing*] **:** to play or sing (as a melody) in the style of swing music ⟨~ a folk song⟩ **~** *vi* **1 a :** to move freely to and fro (as in suspension from an overhead support) ⟨the pendulum ~*s* with great regularity⟩ ⟨a basket ~*s* from her arm⟩ **b :** to ride in a swing **2 a :** to die by hanging ⟨was caught spying and made to ~ for it⟩ **b :** to hang freely from a support **:** be in suspension ⟨gray Spanish moss, ~*ing* from live oak and cypress —*Amer. Guide Series: La.*⟩ **3 :** to turn on or as if on an axis **:** move in or describe a circle or arc: as **a :** to move with the wind or tide around a single anchor or mooring ⟨a ship *swung* in the roadstead, awaiting cargo —Carleton Mitchell⟩ **b :** to go in a sweeping curve ⟨~*s* around the corner with a squeal of tires⟩ ⟨a plane that *swung* low over the field and nosed up again⟩ ⟨the highway ~*s* north around the end of the mountain —G.R.Stewart⟩ **c :** to turn on a hinge or pivot ⟨doors that ~ open automatically⟩ **d :** to turn in place **:** face a different direction **:** WHEEL ⟨she *swung* on a high heel and walked away —Wilson Collison⟩ **e :** to convey oneself from one point to another by swaying or pivoting on a fixed support ⟨~ aboard the train as it pulls out⟩ ⟨put one foot in the stirrup and ~ up into the saddle⟩ ⟨monkeys that ~ from limb to limb through the jungle⟩ **f :** to turn about with a partner in dancing **:** execute a swing ⟨gents ~ in and ladies ~ out⟩ **4 a :** to sound with or have a steady pulsing rhythm ⟨likes verses that ~⟩ **b** [²*swing*] **:** to play or sing with a lively compelling rhythm ⟨pomps . . . of life chronicled in ~*ing* hymnbook rhythms —*Brit. Bk. News*⟩; *specif* **:** to play swing music ⟨this band ~*s* more than anything since the bop era began —W.C.Herman⟩ **c :** to dance in swing or jazz style **5 :** to shift or fluctuate from one condition, form, position, or object of attention or favor to another (as an opposite) ⟨~ constantly from optimism to pessimism and back —Sinclair Lewis⟩ ⟨leading newspapers . . . *swung* against him —S.P. Brewer⟩ **6 a :** to move along with free, swaying movements ⟨a cocky, swaggering bunch of Americans *swung* along the jungle trail —Dave Richardson⟩ ⟨long Pacific rollers ~*ing* in rank after rank —Thomas Wood †1950⟩ **b :** to start up in a smooth vigorous manner ⟨minutemen who were ready to ~ into action against the British at a moment's notice —*Amer. Guide Series: Mass.*⟩ ⟨heard the musicians ~ into their first tune —Earl Hammer⟩ ⟨haul up the prisoning anchor, ~ out upon the tide —Bertha Runkle⟩ **7 :** to hit or aim at something with a sweeping arm movement ⟨a fast ball that the batter *swung* at and missed⟩ ⟨told the boxer to go into the ring *swinging*⟩ ⟨thinking I was being held up, I *swung* on him with all I had —H.A.Chippendale⟩ ⟨mounts his gun to his shoulder quickly but smoothly, ~*s* on the target . . . touches the trigger while the gun is still in motion —*Amer. Rifleman*⟩ **8 :** to ascertain the deviation of a magnetic ship or airplane compass by swinging the ship or plane **9 :** to make a circuit **:** take a side trip ⟨promised to ~ by and pick them up⟩ **:** take a tour ⟨*swung* through his district campaigning⟩ **10 :** to change direction in skiing by a swing

syn SWAY, OSCILLATE, VIBRATE, FLUCTUATE, PENDULATE, WAVER, UNDULATE: SWING implies a movement back and forth or in one direction of something attached at one side or one end ⟨*swing* like a pendulum⟩ ⟨the door *swung* open⟩ ⟨*swing* a lasso around your head⟩ SWAY implies a back and forward or teetering movement, usu. of an upright object esp. flexible or unsteady ⟨the bamboos at the corner of the house *swayed* slowly under a gentle night wind —Pearl Buck⟩ ⟨*sway* to the rhythm of the music⟩ ⟨the chimney *swayed* under the shock of the explosion⟩ OSCILLATE suggests the swinging of a pendulum, implying a movement, usu. rapid, between two points, poles, or conditions ⟨an *oscillating* reed⟩ ⟨it is clear that Bohemianism has continuously *oscillated* between the poles of escape and revolt —Harry Levin⟩ ⟨*oscillating* between humility and hatred —Francis Golffing⟩ VIBRATE, sometimes interchangeable with OSCILLATE, usu. implies a motion like the pulsating of a string on a musical instrument when plucked or struck or a periodic motion in alternating directions ⟨a car *vibrating* with the irregularity of the motor's explosions⟩ ⟨the ultrasonic, or high frequency, waves *vibrate* so fast they can't be heard by the human ear —Boyd Wright⟩ ⟨on summer evenings when the air *vibrated* with the song of insects —Sherwood Anderson⟩ FLUCTUATE implies constant irregular alternations suggestive of the movements of waves ⟨food prices *fluctuate* according to the law of supply and demand⟩ ⟨a handsome, confused and narcissistic woman who continually *fluctuates* between coldness and torturing kindness —Jean Garrigue⟩ ⟨causes the respiration, pulse, and blood pressure of the test subject to *fluctuate* widely from the normal —H.G.Armstrong⟩ PENDULATE, rare, is close to OSCILLATE, suggesting a swinging between two extremes or a similar constant change ⟨*pendulated* between extremes —John Cournos⟩ WAVER stresses an unsteady or uncertain swinging ⟨a reed *wavering* in the wind⟩ ⟨*waver* between love and hate⟩ UNDULATE suggests a steady gentle fluctuation as of a continuous rolling or rippling sea ⟨the great serpent drew back like a flash, and turning, *undulated* slowly away —William Beebe⟩ ⟨the country round with its *undulating* meadows —S.P.B.Mais⟩ ⟨blue hills, *undulating* like waves —*Amer. Guide Series: Ark.*⟩

syn WAVE, FLOURISH, BRANDISH, SHAKE, THRASH: SWING indicates regular oscillation back and forth or continuous rotation around ⟨*swinging* his arms as he walked⟩ ⟨*swinging* the pail over his head⟩ WAVE implies undulating, fluttering, or streaming motion without rhythmical regularity, as in signaling, warning, or greeting ⟨*wave* to an acquaintance⟩ ⟨*waved* his hand⟩ ⟨*wave* a flag⟩ ⟨the guard laughed and *waved* him through the gate —A.W.Long⟩ ⟨you cannot *wave* a wand over the country and say "Let there be Socialism": at least nothing will happen if you do —G.B.Shaw⟩ FLOURISH may imply triumph, bravado, or ostentation in waving or swinging ⟨rushed into my room *flourishing* a handsome volume —M.R.Cohen⟩ ⟨*flourishing* his cane as he strolled along⟩ SHAKE may but does not always imply forceful or violent motion or movement ⟨*shake* a rug⟩ ⟨*shake* a tree to bring down the fruit⟩ ⟨*shake* your fist in another's face⟩ BRANDISH usu. involves a shaking or waving with menace or threat ⟨*brandishing* their swords⟩ ⟨striking what appeared to them to be most belligerent attitudes, *brandishing* his machete —Thomas Barbour⟩ THRASH suggests the action of a flail in threshing grain; it may apply to any vigorous swinging or beating ⟨on a blanket on the nursery floor and watched him proudly while he *thrashed* his sturdy arms and legs —Marcia Davenport⟩ **syn** see in addition HANDLE

— **swing round the circle 1 :** to cover all points of a topical outline **2 :** to hold in turn all the various positions or conflicting beliefs ⟨had *swung round the circle* of theories and systems . . . without finding relief —A.V.G.Allen⟩ **3 :** to make a tour of a constituency to deliver speeches and explain one's policies — used of a political candidate — **swing the lead** [fr. the feeling that the task of sounding with the lead is a comparatively light assignment for a sailor] *Brit* **:** MALINGER

²swing \"\ *n* -s **1 :** an act or instance of swinging **:** swinging movement: as **a** (1) **:** a stroke or blow delivered with a sweeping arm movement ⟨the basic techniques of golf — stance, grip, and ~ —*Official Sports Guide*⟩ ⟨a batter with a powerful ~⟩; *specif* **:** a round-arm blow in boxing ⟨knocked out . . . with a right ~ —P.J.Cunningham⟩ (2) **:** a sweeping or rhythmic movement of the body or a bodily part ⟨dismounted with an easy ~⟩ ⟨the machinelike ~ of the bodies of the plant setters —Sherwood Anderson⟩ (3) **:** a square dance figure variously executed in which two dancers join arms or hands and dance around a point between them — see WALTZ SWING (4) **:** jazz dancing in moderate tempo with a peculiar lilting syncopation — see JITTERBUG (5) **:** a skiing turn executed by a rhythmical crouch-spring-crouch succession of movements combined with a simultaneous rotation and inward leaning of the body and a turning of both skis (6) **:** a gymnastic movement in which the body describes an arc forward or backward around the point of support **b** (1) **:** the regular movement of a freely suspended object (as a pendulum) along an arc and back **:** the action of swinging to and fro from a fixed point or on a fixed axis (2) **:** steady movement to and fro between wide limits **:** back and forth sweep ⟨the ~ of the tides⟩ ⟨the rains follow the sun in its annual ~ north and south —Tom Marvel⟩ (3) **:** the horizontal motion of a boom or shovel — compare CROWD, HOIST **c** (1) **:** steady pulsing rhythm (as in poetry or music) ⟨a perfect metrical ~ of the modern kind should have been attained by one poet —George Saintsbury⟩ (2) **:** a steady vigorous movement characterizing an activity or creative work ⟨his ~ and gusto, his abundant detail, and the swift excitement of his narrative —*Times Lit. Supp.*⟩ — often used in the phrase *go with a swing* ⟨the small, informal evening party will go with a ~ at home —Agnes M. Miall⟩ **d** (1) **:** a trend toward a high or low point in a fluctuating cycle of interest rates, prices, or any business activity ⟨industrialized nations have been subjected to periodic ~*s* of prosperity and depression —Asher Achinstein⟩ (2) **:** an often periodic shift from one condition, form, position, or object of attention or favor to another (as an opposite) ⟨manic depressive ~*s*⟩ ⟨in a wave of . . . straining for novelty, with constant ~*s* of style from one extreme to the other —Thomas Munro⟩ ⟨the ~ to diesels on U.S. railroads —*Time*⟩ **2 a** (1) *obs* **:** an impulsion from within **:** natural bent or bias **:** INCLINATION (2) **:** an indulgence of one's natural bent or bias **:** FLING ⟨letting youth have its ~⟩ (3) **:** liberty of action **:** free scope **:** LICENSE, REIN ⟨given full ~ in the conduct of the business⟩ **b** *archaic* **:** controlling au-

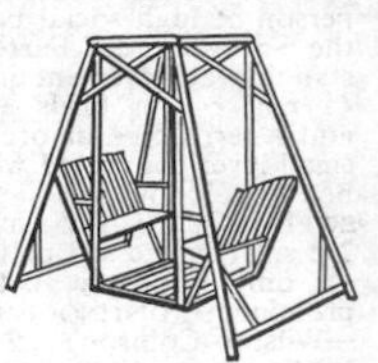

lawn swing 5a

thority : ruling power c (1) : the driving power of something swung or hurled ⟨the ~ of a battering ram against a wall⟩ (2) : steady vigorous advance : driving speed ⟨a train approaching at full ~⟩ 3 a : the progression of an activity, process, or phase of existence : COURSE, PROGRESS — usu. used in the phrase *in full swing* ⟨when the work is in full ~ this summer some fifteen thousand men . . . will be engaged on the highway —Harold Griffin⟩ b : the normal round or pace of activities ⟨will take you a couple of days . . . to get into the ~ of things —Richard Joseph⟩ c : a state of vigorous activity ⟨got production into full ~ after a slow start⟩ — usu. used in the phrase *in full swing* ⟨animated conversation was still in full ~ in the small hours —Enid McLeod⟩ 4 a : the arc or range through which something swings : the distance between the outer limits to which something swings ⟨a pendulum with a 3-inch ~⟩ b : the capacity of a turning lathe measured in the U.S. by the diameter of the largest object that can be turned on it and in England by half this measurement 5 : any of various objects that swing freely from or on a support: as a : an apparatus for recreation consisting of a seat suspended from a support (as by a looped rope or two chains) b : an amusement park ride in which the rider is mechanically revolved on a vertical or oblique plane in a suspended seat or compartment c : the movable part of a swing bridge d : the swingable part of a logging boom by means of which the boom is opened or closed e : SWINGBACK 6 : a curving course or outline: as a : a course from and back to a point or place : a circular tour (as of a political candidate) b : the curvature of the outer side of a shoe sole 7 : the lateral margins of a herd of cattle being driven : the sides of a trail herd; *also* : SWINGMEN 8 *or* **swing music** : music usu. modified and arranged for a large commercial dance band characterized by a lively insistent rhythm, a basic melody often submerged in improvisation, and a collective use of syncopated rhythms — compare JAZZ 9 : a score in contract bridge resulting from a swing hand 10 : an interval in a continuous work period during which a regular worker or shift takes a recess and a relief worker or alternate shift carries on : BREAK — **swing around the circle** : a tour about the country for political campaigning (as by a presidential candidate) ⟨whistle-stopped in 43 of the 50 states in his *swing around the circle*⟩

[3]swing \"\ *adj* [in sense 1, fr. [1]*swing*; in other senses, fr. [2]*swing*] 1 a : hinged or pivoted so as to permit swinging into a desired position or in either direction ⟨a ~ handle⟩ ⟨a ~ sash⟩ b : HANGING, SUSPENDED ⟨a ~ lamp⟩ 2 : of, belonging to, or used as a swing ⟨a ~ rope⟩ 3 : of, performing, or performed in the style of musical swing ⟨~ fans⟩ ⟨~ musicians⟩ ⟨~ tunes⟩ 4 : that may swing often decisively either way on an issue or in an election ⟨the candidate's need to attract the ~ vote⟩ ⟨the court's ~ man — whose vote is often decisive in close cases —*Newsweek*⟩ 5 : relieving other workers as needed : RELIEF ⟨a ~ chef⟩

swing·able \ˈswiŋəbəl\ *adj* : that can be swung — **swing·ably** \-blē\ *adv*

[1]swingback \ˈ=,=\ *n* [[3]*swing* + *back*, n.] 1 : a pivoting back for some cameras that allows the film or plateholder to be tilted for correcting or distorting the perspective in a photograph or for shifting the focal plane so as to bring oblique objects into focus 2 : swayback of lambs

[2]swingback \"\ *n* -s [fr. the phrase *swing back*, fr. [1]*swing* + *back*, adv.] : a movement of reaction (as a return to favor or influence of a political party)

swing bar *n* [[3]*swing*] : a pivoted or hinged bar (as a whippletree)

swing beam *also* **swing bolster** *n* : a crosspiece sustaining a railroad-car body so suspended that it may have an independent lateral motion

swingboat \ˈ=,=\ *n* : one of a group of boat-shaped commercial amusement swings (as at a British fair) having facing seats and propelled by the riders

swing bolt *n* : EYEBOLT

swing bridge *also* **swing drawbridge** *n* : a drawbridge that

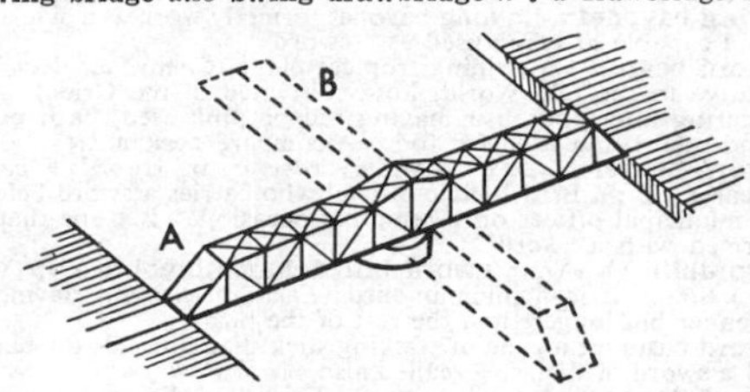

swing bridge: *A* closed; *B* open

opens and closes to river craft by rotating around a central pier — called also *swivel bridge*; compare LIFT BRIDGE

swing credit *n* : a credit provided for in the terms of an international trade agreement permitting trade to be unbalanced to a stated extent in either direction without settlement during the term of the agreement

swingdevil \ˈ=,==\ *n* : a common European swift

swing door *or* **swinging door** *n* : a door that can be pushed open from either side and that swings to when released ⟨the *swing door* between the pantry and dining room⟩ ⟨push through the *swinging doors* of a waterfront dive⟩

[1]swinge \ˈswinj\ *vt* **swinged; swinged; swingeing; swinges** [ME *swengen* to shake, move violently, fr. OE *swengan*; akin to OE *swingan* to beat, fling oneself, rush — more at SWING] 1 *chiefly dial* : BEAT, SCOURGE, THRASH ⟨the young dogs — ~ them to the labor —Robert Burns⟩ 2 *obs* : REVOLVE, WHIRL 3 *obs* : to swing (a tail) violently : LASH

[2]swinge *n* -s 1 *obs* : POWER, AUTHORITY 2 *obs* : freedom of action : SWING 2a(3) 3 *obs* : driving power : IMPETUS

[3]swinge \ˈswinj\ *vt* **swinged; swinged; swingeing; swinges** [alter. of *singe*] *dial* : SINGE, SCORCH ⟨a-*swingeing* the pinfeathers off that gobbler — Frances Gaither⟩

[1]swinge·ing *or* **swing·ing** \-njiŋ, -jēŋ\ *adj* [fr. pres. part. of [1]*swinge*] *chiefly Brit* : superlative in size, amount, or character : very large or good : WHOPPING, CAPITAL ⟨the ~ penalty . . . though dropped to half to secure payment, stopped the trade for a time —John Craig⟩ ⟨Parliament asserted its "Loyal Devotion to his Royal Person" in ~ terms —Nicholas Monsarrat⟩

[2]swingeing *or* **swinging** \"\ *adv*, *chiefly Brit* : to a swingeing degree : SUPERLATIVELY, VERY ⟨we reckon the time's coming when we'll want it ~ bad —P.L.Ford⟩

[1]swing·er \ˈswiŋə(r)\ *n* -s [[1]*swing* + *-er*] : one that swings

[2]swing·er \ˈswinjə(r)\ *n* -s [[1]*swinge* + *-er*] 1 : one that swinges 2 : a swingeing example or instance : WHOPPER

swing ferry *n* [[3]*swing*] : a ferryboat operated by a cable and the river current

swing front *n* : a pivoting front for some cameras that allows the lens to be tilted with respect to the camera axis for correcting or distorting the perspective in a photograph

swing gate *n* : a gate that swings in either direction and closes when released

swing-glass \ˈ=,=\ *n* : CHEVAL GLASS

swing hammer crusher *n* : HAMMER MILL 2

swing hand *n* : a deal in a contract bridge tournament in which a choice of bids or plays results or may result in a large gain (as 500 points or more) for one side

swingier *comparative of* SWINGY

swingiest *superlative of* SWINGY

[1]swing·ing \ˈswiŋiŋ, -ēŋ\ *n* -s [fr. gerund of [1]*swing*] 1 : the action or act of one that swings 2 a : variation in frequency of a transmitted radio wave that may be observed either as a variation in the beat frequency in beat reception or as a variation in received signal intensity b : FADING

[2]swinging \"\ *adj* [fr. pres. part. of [1]*swing*] 1 : that swings : characterized by swing or a swing ⟨a ~ flower basket⟩ ⟨a ~ pace⟩ 2 *of a livestock brand* : suspended from a horizontal quarter circle — see BRAND illustration

swinging bar *n* [[2]*swinging*] : SWING BAR

swinging base *n* : a permanent circular turntable at an airplane factory or airport marked with the cardinal and quadrantal points of the compass for swinging an airplane to ascertain compass deviation

swinging boom *n* : LOWER BOOM

swinging buoy *n* [[1]*swinging*] : one of a group of buoys used in swinging ship

[1]swing·ing·ly \ˈswiŋiŋlē, -jēŋ-, -li\ *adv* [[1]*swingeing, swinging* + *-ly*] *chiefly Brit* : SWINGEING

[2]swing·ing·ly \ˈswiŋiŋlē, -li\ *adv* [[2]*swinging* + *-ly*] : in a swinging manner : with a swinging movement

swinging play *n* : a game similar to a dance in which participants swing each other by the hands or waist to the music of ballad-singing — see PLAY-PARTY

swinging post *n* [[2]*swinging*] : GATEPOST

swinging ring *n* : a gymnastic ring usu. made of metal covered with leather or rubber and suspended so as to swing freely at the end of a rope

swing jack *n* [[3]*swing*] : TRAVERSING SCREW JACK

swing joint *n* : a pipe joint so constructed that the parts joined are movable either so that one of the parts may be rotated relative to the other or so that one of the parts in addition to being rotatable relative to the other may be moved about its own axis — called also respectively *single swing joint, double swing joint*

swing knife *n* : SWINGLE 1

[1]swin·gle \ˈswiŋgəl\ *n* -s [ME *swingel, swengil*, fr. MD *swinghel, swenghel* instrument for beating flax, swipe; akin to OE *swingell* whip, rod, blow, *swingan* to strike, beat — more at SWING] 1 : a wooden instrument like a large knife that is about two feet long, has one thin edge, and is used for beating and cleaning flax : SCUTCHER 2 a : the swiple of a flail b : a cudgel resembling a flail 3 : a lever resembling a spoke and used for turning the barrel in wire drawing or the roller of a plate press

[2]swingle \"\ *vt* **swingled; swingled; swingling** \-g(ə)liŋ\ **swingles** [ME *swinglen*, fr. MD *swinghelen*, fr. *swinghel* swingle] : to clean by beating with a swingle : separate away the coarse and woody parts of : SCUTCH

swing leaf *n* [[3]*swing*] : one of two swinging doors or casements of a double door or window

swinglebar \ˈ==,=\ *n* [[1]*swingle* + *bar*] *Brit* : WHIFFLETREE

swing leg *n* [[3]*swing*] : a hinged leg without stretcher that supports the drop leaf of a table

swingle staff *n* : SWINGLE 1

swingletail \ˈ==,=\ *or* **swingletail shark** *n* : THRESHER SHARK

swin·gle·tree \ˈswiŋgəl·(,)trē, -l·tri\ *n* [[1]*swingle* + *tree*] : WHIFFLETREE

swingling tow *also* **swingle tow** *n* [*swingling tow* fr. *swingling* (gerund of [2]*swingle*) + *tow*; *swingle tow* fr. [2]*swingle*] : coarse flax separated by swingling and hatcheling

swing·man \ˈ=mən\ *n*, *pl* **swingmen** [in sense 1, fr. [2]*swing*; in other senses, fr. [3]*swing*] 1 *or* **swing rider** : one of usu. two cowboys riding at each side of a trail herd behind the point men and ahead of the flank riders or the tail riders to prevent straying and keep other cattle out 2 : ROUNDSMAN 3 3 : a superintendent of a dairy route

swing music *n* : SWING 8

swing-over \ˈ=,==\ *n* -s [fr. the phrase *swing over*, fr. [1]*swing* + *over*] : a marked shift of opinion or favor ⟨the *swing-over* to conservatism displayed in the four recent by-elections —*Economist*⟩

swing pipe *n* [[3]*swing*] : a discharge pipe on a tank the extended intake end of which can be raised (as to drain only a floating layer)

swing plate *n* : a plate that may be swung about a pivot and clamped

swing plow *n* 1 : a plow without a fore wheel under the beam 2 : SWIVEL PLOW

swing port *n* : a port with a hinged cover in the gunwale of a ship

swing room *n* [[2]*swing*] : a room in which postal employees temporarily off duty may spend their time

swings *pres 3d sing of* SWING, *pl of* SWING

swing saw *n* [[3]*swing*] : a circular saw on a swinging frame

swing shift *n* 1 a : the shift usu. from 4 p.m. to midnight b : the workers working the swing shift between the day and night shifts in a factory operating 24 hours a day 2 : a group of workers in a factory operating seven days a week that mans the place as needed to permit the regular shift workers to have one or more free days per week

swing shifter *n* [*swing shift* + *-er*] : a worker on a swing shift

swing sickness *n* [[2]*swing*] : MOTION SICKNESS

swing·stock \ˈswiŋ+,-\ *n* [[2]*swingle* + *stock*] : a timber against the blunt top edge of which flax is laid to be swingled

swing-swang \ˈswiŋ,swaŋ, -aiŋ\ *n* -s [redupl. of [2]*swing*] : a swing backward and forward (as of a pendulum)

swing team *n* : the middle pair of a 6-mule or 6-horse team — compare LEADER, WHEELHORSE

swing tool *n* [[3]*swing*] : a device swung on centers so as to yield to unequal pressure in which delicate work (as parts of a watch) is held to be polished

swingy \ˈswiŋē, -iŋi\ *adj* -ER/-EST [[1]*swing* + *-y*] 1 : marked by swing : SWINGING 2 : offering more resistance to a sliding stone — used of ice in curling

swin·ish \ˈswīnish, -nēsh\ *adj* [*swine* + *-ish*] : of, suggesting, or befitting swine; *esp* : characterized by grossness or gluttony : BEASTLY, SENSUAL ⟨the aristocratic contempt of the Federalists for that same ~ multitude —V.L.Parrington⟩ — **swin·ish·ly** \-nəshlē, -nēsh-, -li\ *adv* — **swin·ish·ness** \-nishnəs, -nēsh-\ *n* -ES

[1]swink \ˈswiŋk\ *vi* -ED/-ING/-S [ME *swinken*, fr. OE *swincan*; akin to OE *swingan* to fling oneself, rush — more at SWING] *archaic* : LABOR, TOIL, SLAVE

[2]swink \"\ *n* -s [ME, labor, trouble, affliction, fr. OE *swinc*, fr. *swincan* to swink] *archaic* : LABOR, DRUDGERY

swinney *var of* SWEENY

swi·no·mish \swəˈnōmish\ *n*, *pl* **swinomish** *or* **swinomishes** *usu cap* 1 a : a Salishan people of Whidbey island and the lower Skagit river valley, Washington b : a member of such people 2 : a dialect related to Skagit

swint *var of* SUINT

[1]swipe \ˈswīp\ *n* -s [prob. alter. of [2]*sweep*] 1 *dial chiefly Brit* : a pole or bar used as a lever or swivel : SWAPE: as a : SWEEP 1a b : a starting lever for a portable engine 2 : a strong sweeping blow or stroke (as with a bat or club or paw of an animal) 3 : a long drink : DRAFT 4 : one who takes care of horses : GROOM 5 : a progression of two or more chords sung (as by a barbershop quartet) on a single syllable 6 : resource material (as clippings, tear sheets, brochures) from outside sources filed for use in advertising or fashion design

[2]swipe \"\ *vb* -ED/-ING/-S [partly alter. of [1]*sweep*; partly fr. [1]*swipe*] *vi* 1 : to cut, strike, or hit with a sweeping motion — often used with *at* ⟨~s away at the punching bag —Gertrude Samuels⟩ 2 : to drink a mug of liquor at one draft ~ *vt* 1 : to give a swipe to : strike or wipe with a sweeping motion ⟨an upper wing tore loose and *swiped* the cockpit going past —L.S.Jamieson⟩ 2 : SNATCH, PILFER ⟨caught *swiping* watermelons from a farmer's patch⟩ **syn** see STEAL

swip·er \-pə(r)\ *n* -s : one that swipes

swipes \ˈswīps\ *n pl* [origin unknown] *Brit* : poor, thin, or spoiled beer : small beer; *also* : BEER

swi·ple *or* **swip·ple** \ˈswipəl\ *n* -s [ME *swepyl, swipylle*, fr. *swepen* to sweep] : the part of a flail that strikes the grain in threshing : SWINGLE

[1]swirl \ˈswərl, *esp before pause or consonant* ˈswər·əl; ˈswəl, ˈswəil\ *n* -s [ME (Sc); prob. of imit. origin] 1 a : a whirling mass or motion (as of water, air, dust) : EDDY, VORTEX b : a state of whirling confusion ⟨a ~ of voices⟩ ⟨~ of events⟩ 2 : a spiraling shape or mark (as on fur or in the grain of wood) suggesting an eddy : CONVOLUTION ⟨icing . . . spread in rich creamy ~s —Patricia Benn⟩ 3 : an act or instance of swirling ⟨filled my glass . . . and gave it a gentle ~ to spread the bouquet —Joseph Wechsberg⟩ ⟨the ~ and splash of pickerel —*Amer. Guide Series: Maine*⟩

[2]swirl \"\ *vb* -ED/-ING/-S *vi* 1 a : to move with an eddying or whirling motion ⟨water that heaved and ~ed and gurgled as the ferries slid in and out —Thomas Wood †1950⟩ b : to flow turbulently as if in eddies : pass in whirling confusion ⟨a topic about which there has ~ed much talk and few facts —C.R.Rogers⟩ 2 : to have a twist or convolution ⟨prefers back hair . . . luxuriant enough to ~ snugly across the back —Lois Long⟩ ~ *vt* : to cause to swirl ⟨~ed the brandy around in the huge goblet —J.B.Benefield⟩ **syn** see TURN

swirl·er \ˈswərlər; ˈswələ(r, ˈswəil-\ *n* -s : one that swirls

swirl·ing·ly *adv* [*swirling* (pres. part. of [2]*swirl*) + *-ly*] : in a swirling manner

swirly \ˈswərlē, ˈswəl-, ˈswəil-, -li\ *adj* -ER/-EST [[1]*swirl* + *-y*] 1 *Scot* : KNOTTED, TWISTED 2 : having a swirling motion, shape, or marking ⟨a ~ full skirt for country dancing⟩ : full of eddies ⟨the ~ water of the rapids⟩

[1]swish \ˈswish\ *vb* -ED/-ING/-ES [imit.] *vi* : to move, pass, swing, or whirl with the sound of a swish : make the sound of a swish ⟨~ed before me in a tight dress —Raymond Chandler⟩ ⟨could hear cars ~ing past on the main road —Elizabeth Taylor⟩ ⟨windshield wipers ~ing —John McCarten⟩ ~ *vt* 1 : to move, pass, swing, or agitate with or as if with the sound of a swish : WHISK ⟨the saddled horse ~ing its tail —James Courage⟩ ⟨sipping water and ~ing it about in the mouth —F.A.Geldard⟩ 2 : to cut or remove with or as if with a swish — used with *off* ⟨~ off the tops of weeds with a sickle⟩ 3 : to strike or lash with a swish : FLOG

[2]swish \"\ *n* -ES [imit.] 1 *also* **swish-swish** \ˈ=,=\ a : a prolonged hissing sound (as produced by a whip rapidly cutting the air) ⟨the slow, steady ~ of scythes —S.H.Holbrook⟩ ⟨a far-off ~ of surf —S.E.Morison⟩ ⟨~ of tires —William Faulkner⟩ ⟨poplars swayed and tossed with a roaring ~ —Harvey Breit⟩ b : a light sweeping or brushing sound (as of a long or full silk skirt in motion) ⟨the ~ of drawing paper being unrolled —Angus McGugan⟩ ⟨the ~ of a mop —Virginia Woolf⟩ 2 : a movement accompanied by the sound of a swish ⟨tails swung rhythmically except for occasional sudden ~es at flies —Elizabeth Janeway⟩ 3 : a flogging birch or cane : SWITCH ⟨smarting under recent applications of the ~ —George Meredith⟩ 4 [[5]*swish*] : SMARTNESS, FASHIONABLENESS 5 [[1]*swish*; fr. his effeminate gait and gestures] *slang* : HOMOSEXUAL; *esp* : a male homosexual

[3]swish \"\ *adv* [imit.] : with a swish ⟨one day when the foliage all went ~ with autumn —Robert Frost⟩

[4]swish \"\ *n* -ES [origin unknown] : sun-dried earth used in West Africa as a building material

[5]swish \"\ *adj* [E dial., of unknown origin] : SMART, FASHIONABLE ⟨a ~ gown⟩ ⟨a ~ automobile⟩

swish·er \-shə(r)\ *n* -s : one that swishes : FLOGGER

swish·ing·ly *adv* [*swishing* (pres. part. of [1]*swish*) + *-ly*] : in a swishing manner or with a swishing sound

swishy \ˈswishē, -shi\ *adj* -ER/-EST [[2]*swish* + *-y*] 1 : producing a swishing sound : characterized by swishing sounds or movements ⟨~ fabrics⟩ 2 *slang* : characterized by or inclined to homosexuality

[1]swiss \ˈswis\ *n* -ES *see sense 1* [in sense 1, fr. MF *Suisse*, fr. MHG *Swizer*, — more at SWITZER; in other senses fr. [2]*swiss*] 1 *pl* **swiss** *cap* a : a native or inhabitant of Switzerland b : one that is of Swiss descent 2 *often cap* : any of various fine sheer fabrics of cotton made in Switzerland; *esp* : DOTTED SWISS 3 *or* **swiss cheese** *usu cap S* : a hard cheese characterized by elastic texture, mild nutlike flavor, and large holes that form during ripening

[2]swiss \"\ *adj*, *usu cap* 1 : of, relating to, or characteristic of Switzerland 2 : of, relating to, or characteristic of the people of Switzerland

swiss blue *n*, *often cap S* : a grayish blue that is redder and less strong than electric, redder and duller than copenhagen, and redder and deeper than Gobelin

swiss catchfly *n*, *usu cap S* : a rare catchfly (*Silene vallesia*) of the European Alps with long-peduncled white flowers

swiss chard *n*, *usu cap S* : CHARD

swiss cheese plant *n*, *usu cap S* [so called fr. the sometimes perforated leaves] : CERIMAN

swisser *n* -s *cap* [modif. (influenced by [1]*swiss*) of MHG *Swizer* — more at SWITZER] *obs* : SWISS

swiss guard *n*, *usu cap S* [so called fr. the fact that each member must be a native Swiss] : one of a small body of soldiers serving as a bodyguard for the pope of the Roman Catholic Church

swiss·ing \ˈswisiŋ, -sēŋ\ *n* -s [origin unknown] : a calendering process for cotton fabrics that produces a smooth compact texture

swiss mountain pine *n*, *usu cap S* : a prostrate shrub or low pyramidal tree (*Pinus mugo*) of central Europe with short bright green leaves

swiss pine *also* **swiss stone pine** *n*, *usu cap 1st S* : a tall Eurasian pine (*Pinus cembra*) having dark green leaves in bundles of five, short spreading branches, and cones usu. less than four inches in length and yielding cedar nuts and a resinous exudate

swiss roll *n*, *usu cap S* : JELLY ROLL

swiss steak *n*, *usu cap 1st S* : a slice of round steak into which flour is pounded on both sides and which is then browned in fat and smothered in onions, tomatoes, and other vegetables and seasonings

swiss tea *n*, *usu cap S* : an infusion of the herbage of any of several plants of the genus *Achillea* (as *A. atrata, A. moschata*, or *A. nobilis*)

[1]switch \ˈswich\ *n* -ES [perh. fr. MD *swijch* bough, branch, twig] 1 : a slender flexible whip, rod, or twig ⟨a riding ~⟩ 2 [[2]*switch*] : an act of switching : the action or office of one who switches: as a : a blow with a switch b : a turn of a switch c : a changing or switching from one (as an investment) to another d : a reversal or distinct variation of a familiar or usual mode or situation : a decided or unexpected change from the usual e : a shift to another suit than that previously led by one's side in bridge 3 : a tuft of long hairs at the end of the tail of an animal (as a cow or ox) — see COW illustration 4 a : a device made usu. of two movable rails, necessary connections, and operating parts and designed to turn a locomotive or train from a track on which it is running to another track b : a railroad sidetrack 5 : a device for making, breaking, or changing the connections in an electrical circuit 6 : a heavy strand of usu. long cut hair fastened at one end and used in addition to a person's own hair for some hairdresses

[2]switch \"\ *vb* -ED/-ING/-ES *vt* 1 a : to strike, beat, whip, or flog with or as if with a switch ⟨lower branches of the hornbeam ~ing the back of his head —J.C.Powys⟩ b : to stir up, drive away, or spur on or as if with a switch ⟨horses contentedly ~ing flies —B.A.Williams⟩ 2 a : SWING, WHISK, LASH ⟨~ a cane⟩ ⟨horse ~es his tail⟩ b : to jerk or pull with a jerk ⟨the rope may be ~ed out of your hand⟩ 3 a : to turn aside : DIVERT, SHIFT, CHANGE ⟨~ methods⟩ ⟨~ places⟩ ⟨~ one's vote⟩ ⟨~ the talk to another subject⟩ b : to dispose of (one issue of securities) and invest the proceeds in another c *of a produce exchange* : to transfer a futures contract from one month to another 4 a : to turn from one railroad track to another : transfer by a switch : SHUNT b : to move (cars) to different positions on the same track within terminal areas 5 a : to shift to another electrical circuit by means of a switch b : to operate an electrical switch so as to turn off or on ⟨~ off a current⟩ ⟨~ on a light⟩ ~ *vi* 1 : to move by or as if by being swung or lashed from side to side ⟨the cat's tail ~ing⟩ ⟨her black hair in a long thick braid ~ing to the speed of the . . . hoofs —Edna Ferber⟩ 2 : to move off or on as if on a spur track 3 a : to change or shift things, places, methods, actions, or directions b : to lead a suit other than that which one's side previously led in a card game

switch angle *n* : the angle formed by the switch and stock rails of a railroad track at the point of juncture as measured between the gage lines

[1]switchback \ˈ=,=\ *n* -s [[2]*switch* + *back* (adv.)] 1 : a zigzag road or trail in a mountainous region ⟨roads which today's tourists climb in easy ~s —*Ford Times*⟩; *specif* : an arrangement of zigzag railroad tracks for surmounting the grade of a steep hill 2 *or* **switchback railway** *Brit* : ROLLER COASTER

[2]switchback \ˈ=,=\ *adj* 1 : of or relating to a switchback : attained by means of switchbacks ⟨~ curves⟩ ⟨a long ~ descent —Stephen Bone⟩ 2 : resembling a switchback (as in shape or variety of levels) ⟨accident . . . explains his hero's ~ career —*Information Please Almanac*⟩

[3]switchback \ˈ=,=\ *vi* : to ride on or move as if on a switchback : zigzag in ascending or descending ⟨a trail that ~ed through rock and pine —Dan Cushman⟩ — **switchbacker** \ˈ=,==\ *n* -s

switchblade knife \'=,=-\ *or* **switchblade** *n* **:** a pocketknife having the blade spring-operated so that pressure on a release catch causes it to fly open

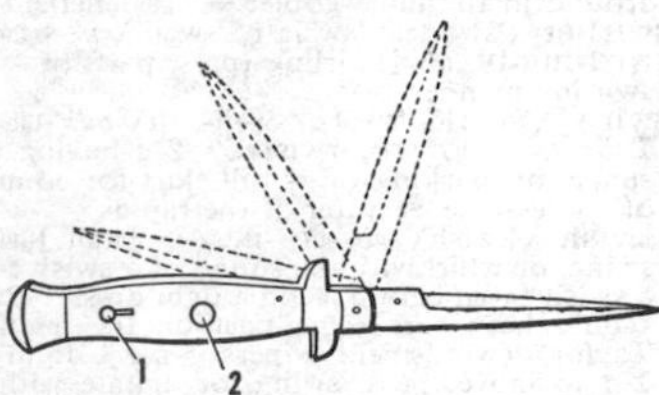
switchblade knife: *1* lock, *2* catch release

switch·board \'=,=\ *n* **:** an apparatus consisting of a panel, an assembly of panels, or a frame on which are mounted insulated switching, measuring, controlling, and protective devices with buses and connections so arranged that a number of circuits may be connected, combined, controlled, measured, and protected
switch box *n* **:** a metal box containing the working parts of an electrical switch
switch cane *n* **:** a grass (*Arundinaria tecta*) of watery or moist locations esp. in the southern U. S.
switched *adj* [fr. past part. of ²*switch*] **:** CONFOUNDED, DASHED — used in mild imprecation or exclamation of surprise ⟨I'll be ~⟩
switch·el \'swichəl\ *n* -s [origin unknown] **:** a drink made of molasses or sometimes honey or maple syrup, water, and sometimes rum and usu. flavored with ginger and vinegar
switch engine *n* **:** a railroad engine usu. of the total-adhesion type that is used for switching — compare ROAD ENGINE
switch·er \'swichə(r)\ *n* -s **:** one that switches: as **a :** SWITCHMAN **b :** SWITCH ENGINE **c :** a petroleum worker who controls the flow of oil from wells to tanks to pipelines according to proration — called also *switchman* **d :** a television technician who operates the equipment that cuts, fades, or dissolves from one picture to another and regulates the brightness of the image
switch·er·oo \ˌswichəˈrü\ *n* -s [alter. of ¹*switch*] *slang* **:** a reversal or surprising variation of a familiar or expected action or manner **:** SWITCH ⟨would work one ~ on the traditional presentation —W.L.Gresham⟩ ⟨life keeps pulling hilarious ~*s* on his fiction-bred expectations —Anthony Boucher⟩
switches *pl of* SWITCH, *pres 3d sing of* SWITCH
switchgear \'=,=\ *also* **switcher gear** *n* **:** the aggregate of switching facilities for a power station or transforming station
switch grass *n* [alter. of *quitch grass*] **:** a panic grass (*Panicum virgatum*) of the western U. S. that is used for hay
switch-hit \'=,=\ *vi* [back-formation fr. *switch-hitter*] **:** to bat right-handed against a left-hander and left-handed against a right-handed pitcher in baseball
switch-hitter \'=,==\ *n* **:** a baseball player who can bat either left-handed or right-handed
switch hook *n* **:** a hook provided with an insulating handle for opening and closing disconnecting switches
switch-horn \'=,=\ *n* **1 :** a simple unbranched horn on a stag **2 :** a stag bearing switch-horns
switching *pres part of* SWITCH
switching limits *n pl* [*switching* (gerund of ²*switch*) + *limits*] **:** boundaries for a railroad terminal area
switching yard *n* **:** YARD 3c
switch-ivy \'=,==\ *n* [¹*switch*] **:** DOG LAUREL
switchkeeper \'=,==\ *n* **:** SWITCH TENDER
switch key *n* **:** a key used for locking or unlocking manually operated railroad switches
switch knife *n* **:** SWITCHBLADE KNIFE
switch lamp *n* **:** a lamp for indicating by the color of its light whether a railroad switch is open or closed
switch line *or* **switch position** *n* **:** a defensive military position that is oblique to the front, connects other positions of a defensive system, and is designed to prevent hostile penetrations from being exploited to the flanks
switch lock *n* **:** a manual or automatic locking device for assuring that a switch remains in proper position prior to and during the passage of a train
switch·man \'=mən\ *n, pl* **switchmen 1 :** one who tends a switch **:** one employed in switching (as in a classification yard) **2 :** one who tests and repairs telephone or telegraph central-office equipment **3 :** SWITCHER c
switchover \'=,==\ *n* -s [²*switch* + *over*] **:** CHANGEOVER
switch plant *n* [¹*switch*] **:** a plant (as a broom) lacking true foliage leaves but with green twigs replacing them functionally
switch plate *n* **:** the metal plate in front of an electrical switch box through which the plugs or tumblers protrude
switch plug *n* **:** a combination of a switch and a plug attached to a flexible cord for use with an electric appliance (as an electric iron)
switch point *or* **switch rail** *n* **:** POINT RAIL
switch sorrel *n, Jamaica* **:** AKEAKE 1
switch stand *n* **:** a stand near a railroad track to which is pivoted a lever for the manual operation of switches or of movable center points

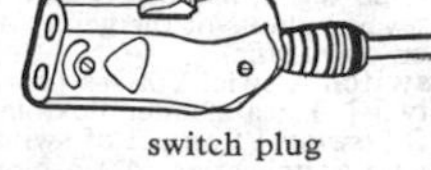
switch plug

switchtail \'=,=\ *n* **1 :** a smooth dogfish (*Mustelus canis*) **2 :** SHOVELNOSE STURGEON
switch tender *n* **:** one that tends and operates a railroad switch; *esp* **:** a railroad yardman who throws track switches
switch tie *n* **:** a railroad crosstie of extra length for use at turnouts or crossovers
switch tower *n* **:** a small tower containing the controls for working railroad switches and signals
switchyard \'=,=\ *n* **1 :** a place where railroad cars are switched from one track to another and where trains are made up **2 :** an area that is usu. enclosed by fence and that embraces the gear of a switching station of a power system
swith *or* **swithe** \'swith\ *adv* [ME, strongly, very much, quickly, fr. OE *swīthe* strongly, very much, fr. *swīth* strong; akin to MHG *swinde* strong, quick, ON *svinnr* quick, wise, Goth *swinths* strong, healthy — more at SOUND] *chiefly dial* **:** INSTANTLY, QUICKLY
¹**swith·er** \'swith̲ə(r)\ *vi* [origin unknown] *dial chiefly Brit* **:** DOUBT, WAVER, HESITATE
²**swither** \"\ *n* **1** *dial chiefly Brit* **:** INDECISION, DOUBT **2** *dial chiefly Brit* **:** FLURRY, PANIC
³**swither** \"\ *vi* [imit.] *dial chiefly Brit* **:** WHIZ, RUSH
switz·er \'switsə(r)\ *n* -s *cap* [MHG *Swizer*, fr. *Swiz* Switzerland] **:** SWISS
switz·er·land \'switsə(r)lənd\ *adj, usu cap* [fr. *Switzerland*, federal republic in central Europe] **:** of or from Switzerland **:** of the kind or style prevalent in Switzerland **:** SWISS
swive \'swīv\ *vb* -ED/-ING/-S [ME *swiven*, fr. OE *swīfan* to revolve, wend, sweep — more at SWIVEL] *vt, archaic* **:** to copulate with **~** *vi, archaic* **:** COPULATE
¹**swiv·el** \'swivəl\ *n* -s *often attrib* [ME *swivel, swevill;* akin to OE *swīfan* to revolve, wend, sweep, OHG *sweibōn, swebēn* to move freely, MHG *swibelen* to reel, waver, ON *svīfa* to ramble, drift, turn, *sveifla* to swing in a circle, MLG *swāien* to sway — more at SWAY] **1 :** a part that pivots freely on or as if on a headed bolt or pin: as **a :** a compound chain link having one end that turns on a headed bolt or pin **b :** a loom attachment made for guiding additional shuttles over limited areas and used in weaving small spot designs, esp. dots **c :** a part of the toolhead of a machine (as a planer, shaper, or radial drill) that can be rotated and clamped so as to hold the tool at a desired angle **d :** a swivel connection placed between the hose from the slush pumps and the drill stem in rotary drilling **e :** a revolving link used on terminal tackle to prevent twisting of a fishing line **2 :** SWIVEL GUN

swivel 1a in a chain

²**swivel** \"\ *vb* **swiveled** *or* **swivelled; swiveled** *or* **swivelled; swiveling** *or* **swivelling** \-v(ə)liŋ\ **swivels** *vt* **1 :** to turn on or as if on a swivel ⟨~ one's eyes in various directions⟩ **2 :** to provide with or secure by a swivel **~** *vi* **:** to swing or turn on or as if on a swivel ⟨~*ed* around in his chair to face the door⟩ ⟨an odd gust ~*ed* around the corner —Liam O'Flaherty⟩
swivel bridge *n* **:** SWING BRIDGE
swivel chain *n* **:** a chain having a swivel attached to or linked into it
swivel chair *n* **:** a chair that swivels on its base
swivel gun *n* **:** a usu. small gun fixed on a swivel (as on a stanchion or a wall) so that it can be rotated horizontally and vertically
swivel-hip \'==,=\ *vi* [back-formation fr. *swivel-hipped*] **:** to move or turn with a twisting motion of the hips ⟨the crowd *swivel-hipped* out of the way at the last moment, and the car sliced through the narrow corridor —H.W.Young⟩ ⟨the brunette came *swivel-hipping* out to the curb —Ray Brennan⟩
swivel-hipped \ˌ==ˈ=\ *adj* **:** moving with or characterized by movement with a twisting motion of the hips
swivel hips *n pl but sing in constr* **:** a trampoline stunt consisting of a seat drop followed by a ½ twist to another seat drop
swivel hook *n* **:** a hook secured by means of a swivel
swivel joint *n* **:** a joint with packed swivel to permit rotational motion of one part relative to another
swivel plow *n* **:** a plow having a reversible moldboard making the plow capable of throwing the furrow either to the right or to the left
swivel saw *n* **:** a pruning saw so made that the blade can be loosened, turned at an angle, and tightened in this position
swivel table *n* **:** a table of a machine tool that may be swiveled to and clamped in any of various positions
swivel union *n* **:** a union for connecting machine parts that permits relative rotation of the connected parts
swivel vise *n* **:** a vise that can be swiveled in one plane — compare UNIVERSAL VISE
swivel weaving *n* **:** weaving on a loom provided with a swivel
swiv·et *also* **swiv·vet** \'swivət, *usu* -əd·+V\ *n* -s [origin unknown] **:** a state of extreme agitation **:** TIZZY, FRENZY, SWEAT — usu. used in phrase *in a swivet*
swiz *or* **swizz** \'swiz\ *n, pl* **swizzes** [origin unknown] *Brit* **:** SWINDLE
¹**swiz·zle** \'swizəl\ *n* -s [origin unknown] **:** a cocktail consisting of a spirituous liquor, lime or lemon juice, bitters, and sugar churned in ice in a pitcher until the surface is frothed and served strained ⟨rum ~⟩ ⟨gin ~⟩
²**swizzle** \"\ *vb* **swizzled; swizzled; swizzling** \-z(ə)liŋ\ **swizzles** *vi* **:** to drink esp. to excess **:** GUZZLE **~** *vt* **:** to mix or stir with or as if with a swizzle stick
swiz·zler \-z(ə)lə(r)\ *n* -s **:** one that swizzles; *specif* **:** SWIZZLE STICK
swizzle stick *n* **1 :** a pronged stick made of wood, metal, or plastic and used to stir mixed drinks **2 :** a round or thin flat stick without prongs used to stir mixed drinks

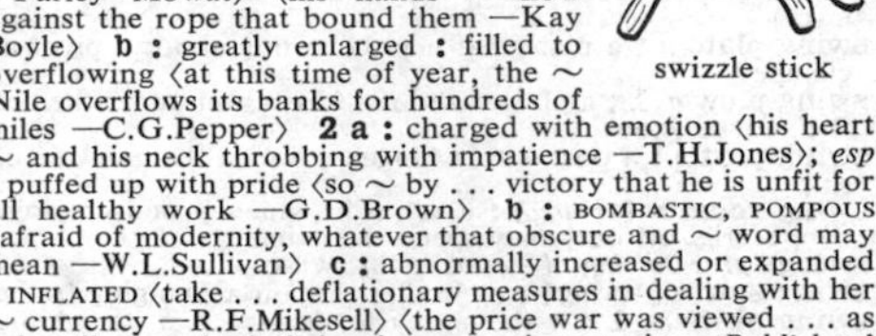
swizzle stick

SWL *abbr* **1** short wave listener **2** sulfite waste liquor
swob *var of* SWAB
swol·len \'swōlən *also* -ln\ *adj* [ME, fr. past part. of *swellen* to swell] **1 a :** protuberant or abnormally distended (as by injury or disease) **:** BULGING, PUFFY ⟨elongate in shape, small, flat or ~, usually with smooth shells —Joyce Allan⟩ ⟨the ~ continuity of curving space —Farley Mowat⟩ ⟨his hands ~ now against the rope that bound them —Kay Boyle⟩ **b :** greatly enlarged **:** filled to overflowing ⟨at this time of year, the ~ Nile overflows its banks for hundreds of miles —C.G.Pepper⟩ **2 a :** charged with emotion ⟨his heart ~ and his neck throbbing with impatience —T.H.Jones⟩; *esp* **:** puffed up with pride ⟨so ~ by . . . victory that he is unfit for all healthy work —G.D.Brown⟩ **b :** BOMBASTIC, POMPOUS ⟨afraid of modernity, whatever that obscure and ~ word may mean —W.L.Sullivan⟩ **c :** abnormally increased or expanded **:** INFLATED ⟨take . . . deflationary measures in dealing with her ~ currency —R.F.Mikesell⟩ ⟨the price war was viewed . . . as primarily a method of cleaning out ~ inventories —*Publishers' Weekly*⟩ ⟨the turgid, ~ city, with its acute job shortages —Frances Keene⟩
swollen-headed \ˌ==ˈ==\ *adj* **:** having a swelled head **:** ARROGANT, CONCEITED
swollen shoot *or* **swollen shoot disease** *n* **:** a virus disease of cacao characterized by mosaic and shedding of leaves, dwarfing and mottling of pods, and esp. by shortening and swelling of the internodes of the stem and of the roots
¹**swoon** \'swün\ *vb* -ED/-ING/-S [ME *swowenen, swounen*, prob. back-formation fr. *swowening, swouning* swoon — more at SWOONING] *vi* **1 a :** to suffer partial or total loss of consciousness **:** FAINT ⟨perhaps he fell asleep, perhaps he ~*ed* . . . who could say —Upton Sinclair⟩ **b :** to become enraptured **:** go into ecstasies ⟨the ladies were ~*ing* with joy —Frederick Way⟩ ⟨a man . . . whose mind ~*ed* with apocalyptic splendors —Bernard De Voto⟩ **2 :** to drift languidly or die away **:** FLOAT, FADE ⟨soar and swoop and ~ and glide again —Robert Gibbings⟩ ⟨the noise ~*ed* away, the trees were shrouded in a midnight hush —Gwyn Jones⟩ **~** *vt* **:** to cause to swoon
²**swoon** \"\ *n* -s [ME *swoune, swoun* fr. *swounen* to swoon] **1 a :** a partial or total loss of consciousness **:** SYNCOPE ⟨when I wakened from the ~ —Sheridan Le Fanu⟩ **b :** a state of bewilderment or ecstasy **:** DAZE, RAPTURE ⟨sat in a floating ~ of . . . erotic longing —William Faulkner⟩ **2 a :** a state of suspended animation **:** TORPOR ⟨left the author . . . in a kind of moral and intellectual ~ —*Times Lit. Supp.*⟩ **b** *obs* **:** a deep sleep **3 :** a languorous drift ⟨the orchestra goes Neapolitan in a ~ of strings —Claudia Cassidy⟩
swoon·er \-nə(r)\ *n* -s **:** one that swoons or causes swooning
¹**swoon·ing** \-niŋ, -nēŋ\ *n* -s [ME *swowening, swouning*, fr. *iswowen, swoun* being in a swoon (fr. OE *geswōgen* in a swoon, lifeless) + *-ing*] *archaic* **:** SWOON ⟨even disagreeable smells will sometimes occasion ~*s* —William Buchan⟩
²**swooning** *adj* [fr. pres. part. of ¹*swoon*] **:** characterized by languor or loss of consciousness — **swoon·ing·ly** *adv*
¹**swoop** \'swüp\ *vb* -ED/-ING/-S [alter. of ME *swopen* to sweep, fr. OE *swāpan* to sweep, swing, drive, rush; akin to OHG *sweifan* to swing around, coil, ON *sveipa* to sweep, swoop, wrap up, *swatha* to swathe — more at SWATHE] *vi* **1 a** *obs* **:** to move haughtily esp. in trailing robes **b :** to move rapidly or graze in passing **:** BRUSH, SWEEP ⟨~*ed* by the table and glanced at the papers that lay there —John Steinbeck⟩ ⟨the wind will be ~*ing* up . . . from the lake —J.J.Godwin⟩ **2 a :** to make a sudden attack **:** DESCEND, POUNCE ⟨arming and preparing to ~ —Dorothy Thompson⟩ — usu. used with *down* ⟨wind and snow ~*ed* down upon him —Robert Murphy⟩ ⟨fixed newcomers with an eagle eye, ~*ed* down upon them and demanded their names —*Amer. Guide Series: R.I.*⟩ **b :** to plunge suddenly or move in a sweeping arc **:** DIP, VEER ⟨seagulls and cranes wheel and ~ —*Geog. School Bull.*⟩ ⟨ladies in tights . . . ~*ing* through the air over our heads —Mary Deasy⟩ ⟨boat ~*ed* to the rise and fall of the waves —R.S.Porteous⟩ **c :** to come down **:** ALIGHT, DROP ⟨~*ed* down before the fire —F.C.Burnand⟩ ⟨in little more than an hour one may ~ down from winter to summer —John Muir †1914⟩ **~** *vt* **1 a :** to dislodge or remove abruptly **:** carry off **:** SWEEP ⟨the whirlwind's blast . . . ~*s* the haycocks off the lea —William Tennant⟩ ⟨British Intelligence . . . ~*ed* him off to London —J.P.O'Donnell⟩ **b :** to seize or capture unexpectedly **:** CATCH, SNATCH ⟨~*ed* her off the swing into his arms —Helen Howe⟩ **c :** to draw in **:** SWALLOW, SUCK ⟨~*ed* in a hot swallow, then aired his mouth —Helen Rich⟩ **2 :** to describe a sweeping arc with ⟨storks ~ white streaks . . . against the luminous blue —Claudia Cassidy⟩
²**swoop** \"\ *n* -s **:** an act or instance of swooping: as **a :** the swift plummeting of a bird on its prey **:** POUNCE, STOOP ⟨even as the fish's head fell from the crocodile's munching mouth there was a ~ of white wings —Francis Birtles⟩ **b :** a concentrated effort or attack **:** EXERTION, STROKE ⟨baggage can . . . be pushed off onto the pier in one ~ —*N.Y.Times*⟩ ⟨all my pretty chickens and their dam at one fell ~ —Shak.⟩ **c :** a sudden incursion **:** DESCENT, GRAB ⟨a ~ of security officers on a Communist espionage ring —Whittaker Chambers⟩ ⟨bring evacuees out . . . ships in as few ~*s* as possible —*Time*⟩ **d :** an undulating line or movement **:** DIP, FESTOON ⟨swallows . . . fluttered in graceful ~*s* in and out —Nora Waln⟩ ⟨the ~ and curl of the road up . . . from the plain —John Connell⟩
swoop·er \-pə(r)\ *n* -s **:** one that swoops
swoopstake *adv* [irreg. (influenced by ¹*swoop*) fr. *sweepstake*] *obs* **:** in the manner of a sweepstake **:** INDISCRIMINATELY
¹**swoosh** \'swüsh\ *vb* -ED/-ING/-ES [imit.] *vi* **1 :** to make a rushing sound ⟨something ~*ed*, and six sprinklers sent up watery bouquets —Ellery Queen⟩ **2 a :** to move with a rushing or rustling sound ⟨a car ~*ed* by . . . in a sucking swirl of dust —Gordon Woodward⟩ ⟨his date ~*ed* down the stairway in a taffeta evening gown⟩ **b :** to gush out **:** EDDY, SWIRL ⟨water ~*ing* from the town pump —Willie S. Ethridge⟩ ⟨the ~*ing* cloud of powder shown at right —*Life*⟩ **~** *vt* **:** to discharge or transport with a rushing sound ⟨the experimental rocket ship . . . expected to ~ a man into space —*Springfield (Mass.) Union*⟩
²**swoosh** \"\ *n* -ES **1 :** an act or instance of swooshing **:** GUSH ⟨spectacular flashes and ~*es* from the new weapons —*Newsweek*⟩ ⟨skirt fullness is concentrated in a ~ at the back —*Women's Wear Daily*⟩; *specif* **:** a rushing sound ⟨multiple jet engines audible as a sibilant ~ . . . gone almost as quickly as the planes themselves —H.E.Salisbury⟩ **2 :** a swift movement accompanied by a rushing sound ⟨first jet airliner to span the North Atlantic in a nonstop ~ —Frederick Graham⟩ ⟨whipped out a razor and made a violent ~ in the neighborhood of the other's neck —Alan Barth⟩
swop *var of* SWAP
swope \'swōp\ *archaic var of* SWOOP
¹**sword** \'sō(ə)rd, -ȯ(ə)rd, -ōəd, -ȯ(ə)d\ *n* -s *often attrib* [ME *swerd, sword*, fr. OE *sweord;* akin to OHG *swert* sword, ON *sverth*, Av *xvara* wound; basic meaning: to cut, stab] **1 a :** a weapon with a long blade for cutting or thrusting set in a hilt usu. terminating in a pommel and often having a tang or a protective guard where the blade joins the handle — see BROADSWORD, CUTLASS, ÉPÉE, ESTOC, RAPIER, SABER, SMALLSWORD; compare BAYONET, DAGGER, FOIL, KNIFE, SCIMITAR **b :** a sword worn as one of the side arms of ceremonial regalia or displayed as a symbol of honor or authority ⟨a ceremonial ~ with the Queen's cipher on the blade and hilt —René Lecler⟩ ⟨had the diamonds removed from the ~ of honor . . . and made into a necklace —R.A.H.N.Hood⟩ **2 a** (1) **:** an instrument of destruction **:** a militant force ⟨avarice . . . hath been the ~ of our slain kings —Shak.⟩ ⟨tempering . . . conscience until it should become a ~ with which to do effective battle against the vicious majority —Roy Lewis & Angus Maude⟩ (2) **:** a combative spirit **:** struggle as a means of achieving a worthwhile objective ⟨I have not come to bring peace, but a ~ —Mt 10:34 (RSV)⟩ ⟨this younger senator, whose ~ is not yet sheathed in pragmatism —Marya Mannes⟩ **b :** military prowess **:** war esp. as a means of settling disputes ⟨hireling combatants sold their ~*s* . . . to the best bidder —Sir Walter Scott⟩ ⟨the pen is mightier than the ~ —E.G.Bulwer-Lytton⟩ **3 :** coercive power or jurisdiction ⟨the magistrate . . . bears the ~ of justice by the consent of the whole community —William Blackstone⟩ ⟨to the Church belong both ~*s*, the spiritual and . . . the temporal —C.H.McIlwain⟩ **4 :** something that resembles a sword: as **a :** SWINGLE 1 **b :** the beak of the swordfish **c :** one of the end bars by which the lay of a handloom is suspended, or one of the uprights supporting the lay of a power loom — **at swords' points** *adv* **:** displaying mutual hostility **:** ready to fight **:** ANTAGONISTIC ⟨at the height of the quarrel when the two groups were *at swords' points*⟩
²**sword** \"\ *vt* -ED/-ING/-S **1 :** to arm with a sword **2 :** to wound or kill with or as if with a sword
sword-and-buckler *adj* \ˌ=ˈ==\ *archaic* **:** marked by or suggestive of braggadocio **:** SWASHBUCKLING ⟨lived in a ruffling time, so he loved *sword-and-buckler* men —Robert Naunton⟩
sword arm *n* [so called fr. its being the arm that wields the sword] **:** the right arm
sword bayonet *n* **:** a long bayonet formerly worn as a side arm and capable of being used as a sword
sword bean *n* **:** a twining tropical plant (*Canavalia gladiata*) native to the Old World, long cultivated in the Orient, and bearing long pods usu. having red or pink seed, both pods and seed being used for food — compare JACK BEAN
sword-bearer \'=,==\ *n* [ME *swordberer*, fr. ¹*sword* + *berer* bearer] **1 :** a British civic official who carries a sword before a municipal officer on ceremonial occasions **2 :** one that is armed with a sword
swordbill \'=,=\ *or* **sword-billed hummingbird** \'=ˌ=-\ *n* **:** a So. American hummingbird (*Ensifera ensifera*) having a slender bill longer than the rest of the bird
sword cane *n* **:** a cane or walking stick that conceals the blade of a sword or dagger — called also *sword stick*
sword dance *n* **1 :** a ceremonial English and west European folk dance executed by men in a ring by performing evolutions with a sword in the right hand and the tip of a neighbor's sword in the left and joining in figures in which the swords are brandished **2 :** a dance performed over or around swords without touching them; *esp* **:** the Scottish Highland solo dance performed in the angles formed by two swords or a sword and scabbard crossed on the ground **3 :** any male solo dance performed with the flourishing of a sword or saber
sword dancer *n* **:** one that performs or participates in a sword dance
sword dollar *n* **:** the Scottish silver ryal of James VI having a sword on the reverse
sword·er \'sōrdər, 'sȯr-, 'sōədə, 'sȯ(ə)də\ *n* -s [¹*sword* + *-er*] *archaic* **:** SWORDSMAN, CUTTHROAT
sword fern *n* **:** any of several ferns with long narrow more or less sword-shaped fronds: as **a :** a tropical fern (*Nephrolepis exaltata*) from which the Boston fern has been developed **b :** GIANT HOLLY FERN
swordfish \'=,=\ *n* [ME *swerd fyssh*, fr. *swerd* sword + *fyssh*, *fish* fish] **1 a :** a very large and widely distributed oceanic fish *Xiphias gladius*) that constitutes the family Xiphiidae, has the bones of the upper jaw consolidated into a long rigid swordlike beak, the dorsal fin high and without distinct spines, the ventral fins absent, and the adult destitute of teeth, sometimes attains a weight of 600 pounds, and is highly valued as a food and sport fish — called also *broadbill, espada, espadon* **b** (1) **:** MARLIN (2) **:** SAILFISH **2 :** a synchronized swimming stunt executed from a prone position with the back arched and the head and one foot above water and the other knee bent in which the head is submerged and the hands propel the body toward the feet while the extended leg is raised above the water until the body is overbalanced onto the back after which the bent leg is straightened
swordfisherman \'=,===\ *n* [blend of *swordfish* and *fisherman*] **:** one that is engaged in swordfishing
swordfishing \'=,==\ *n* [blend of *swordfish* and *fishing*] **:** fishing for swordfish
sword grass *n* **1 :** any of various grasses or sedges having leaves with a sharp or toothed edge: as **a** *Austral* **:** CUTTING GRASS **b :** any of several other Australian grasses of the genus *Cladium* **2 :** a plant having more or less sword-shaped leaves: as **a :** REED CANARY GRASS **b :** the common bulrush **3 :** a European spurry (*Spergularia segetalis*)
sword knot *n* **1 :** a leather thong attaching the hilt of a sword to the wrist to prevent its loss if forced out of the hand **2 :** an ornamental cord or tassel tied to the hilt
sword·less \'=ləs\ *adj* **:** lacking a sword
swordlike \'=,=\ *adj* **:** resembling a sword
sword lily *n* **:** GLADIOLUS
swordman *n, pl* **swordmen** [ME *swerdman*, fr. *swerd* sword + *man*] **1** *obs* **:** SWORDSMAN 1 **2** *obs* **a :** a soldier armed with a sword **b :** a military man **:** WARRIOR ⟨worthy fellows, and like to prove most sinewy *swordmen* —Shak.⟩
sword mat *n* [so called fr. the wooden sword used in weaving it] **:** a mat of closely woven rope yarns used as chafing gear on a ship
sword of dam·o·cles \-'damə,klēz\ *often cap S & usu cap D* [so called fr. the sword suspended by a single hair over the head of Damocles, guest at a sumptuous banquet given by Dionysius the Elder †367 B.C. Greek tyrant of Syracuse, as a reminder of the insecurity of a tyrant's happiness] **:** an impending disaster ⟨unaware of the *Sword of Damocles* hanging

over her, she pursued her own way . . . casually and cheerfully —Olive H. Prouty⟩

sword-plant \ˈs,=\ *n* **:** any of several plants of the genus *Sagittaria*

swordplay \ˈ=,=\ *n* **1 a :** the art or skill of wielding a sword esp. in fencing **b :** an exhibition of swordsmanship **2 :** something that resembles a fencing duel ⟨some very pretty diplomatic ~ —*Economist*⟩

swordplayer \ˈ=,==\ *n* [*swordplay* + *-er*] *archaic* **:** one skilled in swordplay

swords *pl of* SWORD, *pres 3d sing of* SWORD

sword sedge *n* **:** an Australian sedge (*Lepidosperma gladiatum*) that is important as a sand binder and yields a paper material similar to papyrus

sword service *n* **:** military service owed to a liege lord by his vassal

sword side *n* **:** the father's side of a family — compare DISTAFF

swords·man \-dzmən\ *n, pl* **swordsmen** [*swords-* (fr. genitive of ¹*sword*) + *man*] **1 :** one skilled in swordplay; *esp* **:** a saber fencer **2** *archaic* **:** a military man; *specif* **:** a soldier armed with a sword

swordsman·ship \ˈ==,ship\ *n* [*swordsman* + *-ship*] **:** SWORDPLAY 1

sword stick *n* **:** SWORD CANE

sword sucker *n* **:** a vigorous shoot arising from the rootstock of a banana plant and frequently used for replanting

sword-swallower \ˈ=,===\ *n* **:** a performer who pretends to swallow a sword or some other rigid object — **sword-swallowing** \ˈ=,===\ *n*

swordswoman \ˈ=,==\ *n, pl* **swordswomen** [*swords-* (fr. genitive of ¹*sword*) + *woman*] **:** a woman fencer

swordtail \ˈ=,=\ *n* **1 :** KING CRAB 1 **2 a :** any of various bugs (genus *Uroxiphus*) found on forest trees **b :** a long-horned grasshopper (genus *Conocephalus*) having a long swordlike ovipositor **3 :** any of several small Central American topminnows (genus *Xiphophorus*): as **a :** a fish (*X. helleri*) in which the lower lobe of the tail of the male is greatly prolonged and brightly colored and which is often kept in the tropical aquarium and is bred in many color varieties **b :** HELLERI 2

swordweed \ˈ=,=\ *n* [so called fr. its sword-shaped pods] **:** a senna (*Cassia occidentalis*)

swore [ME *swoor*, fr. OE *swōr*] *past of* SWEAR

sworl \ˈswȯr(-ə)l\ *chiefly dial var of* SWIRL

sworn \ˈswō(ə)rn, ˈswȯ(ə)n\ *adj* [ME *sworen, sworn*, fr. past part. of *sweren* to swear] **1 a :** bound by an oath **:** AVOWED ⟨now my ~ friend, and then mine enemy —Shak.⟩; *specif* **:** pledged by an oath of chivalry to share each other's fortunes, good or bad — used formerly of companions in arms ⟨according to an early tradition became his ~ brother —F.M.Stenton⟩ **b :** serving under an official oath of office ⟨~ jury⟩ ⟨all loads of gravel . . . are to be accompanied by weight slips signed by ~ weighers —*Springfield (Mass.) Union*⟩ **c :** certified under oath **:** ATTESTED ⟨~ evidence⟩ ⟨the ~ outlay . . . was $128,300 —S.H.Adams⟩ **2 :** as firmly established as if bound by oath **:** CONFIRMED, INVETERATE ⟨a ~ conservative⟩

¹**swot** \ˈswä|t *also* -wȯ|; *usu* |d·+V\ *n* -s [alter. of ²*sweat*] **1** *Brit* **:** one given to swotting **:** a student who has few interests besides studying **:** GRIND **2** *Brit* **:** hard work

²**swot** \"\ *vi* **swotted; swotted; swotting; swots** *Brit* **:** to study hard and constantly **:** GRIND — compare BONE

³**swot** *var of* SWAT

swot·ter \|d·ə(r), |tə-\ *n* -s *Brit* **:** ¹SWOT 1

¹**swound** \ˈswaund, ˈswünd\ *n* -s [ME, alter. of *swoun* swoon] *archaic* **:** SWOON

²**swound** \"\ *vi* -ED/-ING/-S *archaic* **:** SWOON

¹**swow** \ˈswau\ *dial var of* SOUGH

²**swow** \"\ *vi* [prob. fr. *swear* + *vow*] *dial* **:** SWEAR — usu. used in the phrase *I swow* as a mild oath

SWP *abbr* safe working pressure

s wrench *n, cap S* **:** a wrench with an S-shaped handle

swtg *abbr* switching

swum [ME *swummen* (past pl. & past part.), fr. OE *swummon* (past pl.), *geswummen* (past part.)] *past part. & chiefly dial past of* SWIM

S wrench

swung [ME *swungen* (past pl. & past part.), fr. OE *swungon* (past pl.), *geswungen* (past part.)] *past of* SWING

swung dash *n* [*swung* + *dash*; fr. its reversal of direction] **:** a character ~ used in printing to conserve space by representing part or all of a previously spelled-out word

swy \ˈswī\ *n* -s [modif. of G *zwei* two, fr. OHG — more at TWO] *Austral* **:** TWO-UP

sx *abbr* **1** sacks **2** simplex

sxn *abbr* section

sy \ˈsī\ *n* -s [by shortening & alter.] *chiefly dial* **:** SCYTHE

-sy \sē, si\ *n suffix* -ES [¹*-s* + *-y*] **:** small one **:** one affectionately regarded ⟨mop*sy*⟩ ⟨pop*sy*⟩

sy *abbr* **1** sticky **2** supply

SY *abbr* square yard

sya·gush \ˈsyä,güsh\ *n* -ES [Per *siyāh-gōsh*, lit., black ear, fr. *siyāh* black (fr. MPer) + *gōsh* ear, fr. OPer *gausha-*; akin to Av *gaosha-* ear, Skt *ghoṣa* noise] **:** CARACAL

syb·a·rite \ˈsibə,rīt, *usu* -īd·+V\ *n* -s [L *Sybarita*, fr. Gk *Sybaritēs*, fr. *Sybaris*, ancient Greek city in southern Italy + Gk *-itēs* -ite] **1** *cap* **:** a native or resident of the ancient city of Sybaris noted for its love of luxury and pleasure **2** *often cap* **:** a person devoted to luxury and pleasure **:** VOLUPTUARY ⟨laid aside this Spartan temperance for the ostentatious luxury of a *Sybarite* —T.B.Macaulay⟩

syb·a·rit·ic \ˈ==ˈrid·ik, -itik, -ēk\ *adj* [L *Sybariticus*, fr. Gk *Sybaritikos*, fr. *Sybaritēs* + *-ikos* -ic] **1** *usu cap* **a :** of, relating to, or characteristic of ancient Sybaris **b :** of, relating to, or characteristic of the people of Sybaris **2 :** marked by or given to luxury or voluptuous living ⟨take his rest in ~ grandeur that eclipses the splendor of a sultan's harem —Green Peyton⟩ ⟨the . . . basically ~ boy became a strong, aggressive, Spartan adult —G.W.Johnson⟩ **syn** see SENSUOUS

syb·a·rit·i·cal \-ə̇kəl\ *adj, often cap* [L *Sybariticus* + E *-al*] **:** SYBARITIC

syb·a·rit·i·cal·ly \-k(ə)lē\ *adv* **:** in a sybaritic manner **:** with sybaritic luxury

syb·a·rit·ish \-ˈrīd·ish\ *adj, often cap* **:** SYBARITIC

syb·a·rit·ism \ˈ===,rīd-,izəm, -,rī,tiz-\ *n* -s **:** the quality or state of being sybaritic ⟨lapsed into the ~ of sheer sensation —T.R.Weiss⟩ ⟨sensual to the point of ~ —R.R. Von Abele⟩

sybil *often cap, var of* SIBYL

sy·bo *or* **sy·bow** \ˈsī,bō\ *Scot var of* CIBOL

syc·a·mine \ˈsikə,mīn, -,mən\ *n* -s [L *sycaminus*, fr. Gk *sykaminos*, of Sem origin; akin to Heb *shiqmāh* mulberry tree, sycamore] **:** MULBERRY 1a

syc·a·more *also* **syc·o·more** \ˈsikə,mō(ə)r, -mȯ(ə)r, -ōə, -ȯ(ə)\ *n* -s [ME *sicamour, sicomour*, fr. MF *sicamor*, fr. L *sycomorus*, fr. Gk *sykomoros*, prob. modif. (influenced by Gk *sykon* fig & *moron* mulberry) of a Sem word akin to Heb *shiqmāh* sycamore — more at MULBERRY] **1** *or* **sycamore fig** *also* **sycomore fig :** a tree (*Ficus sycomorus*) of Egypt and Asia Minor that is the sycamore of Scripture, is useful as a shade tree, and has sweet and edible fruit similar but inferior to the common fig and leaves resembling those of the mulberry — called also *mulberry fig* **2 :** a Eurasian maple (*Acer pseudoplatanus*) having long racemes of showy yellow flowers that is widely planted as a shade tree **3 a :** ²PLANE; *esp* **:** a very large spreading tree (*Platanus occidentalis*) of eastern and central No. America with 3- to 5-lobed broadly ovate leaves — see TREE illustration **b :** the variably colored and sometimes variegated hard tough elastic wood of a sycamore — called also *lacewood*

sycamore anthracnose *n* **:** a disease of the sycamore caused by an ascomycetous fungus (*Gnomonia veneta*) and characterized by leaf and twig blight

sycamore lace bug *n* **:** a tingid bug (*Corythucha ciliata*) that is a serious pest on sycamores in No. America

sycamore maple *n* **:** SYCAMORE 2

syce \ˈsīs\ *n* -s [Hindi *sā'is*, fr. Ar *sā'is* (colloq. *sāyis*] **:** a groom or attendant esp. in India

sy·cee \ˈsīˈsē\ *n* -s [Chin (Cant) *sai sz*, lit., fine threads, fine silk] **:** silver money formerly used in China and made in the form of ingots measured by weight and usu. stamped — see SHOE

sy·cet·ta \sə̇ˈsed·ə\ *n, cap* [NL, fr. *Sycon* + It *-etta*, dim. suffix (fr. LL *-ita*, fem. of *-itus*)] **:** a genus (the type of the family Sycettidae) of primitive sycon sponges with the flagellated chambers opening directly into the paragaster

sy·cet·ti·dae \sə̇ˈsed·ə,dē\ *n pl, cap* [NL, fr. *Sycetta*, type genus + *-idae*] **:** a widely distributed family of calcareous sycon sponges — see SYCETTA, SYCON

sych·no·car·pous \ˌsiknəˈkärpəs\ *adj* [Gk *sychnos* plentiful, frequent + E *-carpous*] *of a plant* **:** able to produce fruit repeatedly **:** PERENNIAL

sy·con \ˈsī,kän\ *n* [NL, fr. Gk *sykon* fig — more at FIG] **1** *cap* **:** a genus of calcareous sponges (family Sycettidae) having typical sycon structure **2** -s **a :** any sponge of the genus *Sycon* **b :** a sponge or sponge larva in which the flagellated layer is restricted to more or less tubular outpouchings of the paragastric wall that are indirectly connected with the incurrent canals through lateral pores — compare ASCON, LEUCON — **sy·co·noid** \ˈsīkə,nȯid\ *adj or n*

sy·co·nes \sīˈkō(,)nēz\ *n pl, cap* [NL, fr. pl. of *Sycon*] *in some classifications* **:** a group comprising the sycon sponges: **a :** a group coextensive with Syconosa **b :** a suborder of Syconosa

sy·co·ni·um \-ˈnēəm\ *n, pl* **syco·nia** \-ēə\ [NL, fr. Gk *sykon* fig + NL *-ium*] **:** a collective fleshy fruit in which the ovaries are borne within an enlarged succulent concave or hollow receptacle (as in the fig)

sy·co·no·sa \ˌsīkəˈnōsə, -ōzə\ *n pl, cap* [NL, fr. *Sycon* + L *-osa* (neut. pl. of *-osus* -ous)] **:** an order of Calcispongiae comprising simple syconoid sponges and others derived from this type

syco·phan·cy \ˈsikəfənsē, -nsi *sometimes* ˈsīk-\ *n* -ES [L *sycophantia*, fr. Gk *sykophantia*, fr. *sykophantēs* + *-ia* -y] **1 :** the spreading of slanderous accusations **:** DEFAMATION; *esp* **:** the informing practiced in ancient Athens **2 a :** base or obsequious flattery **:** TOADYING ⟨as deplorable as the bootlicking ~ which they displayed —R.L.Riggs⟩ ⟨there has ever been and ever will be found ~ on the side of power —F.W. Robertson⟩ **b :** the characteristic of a servile flatterer or toady ⟨had seen the straightforwardness of many boys from the bush turn into whining ~ when they came to the coast —Esther Warner⟩

¹**syco·phant** \-fənt *sometimes* -,fant *or* -,faa(ə)nt\ *n* -s [L *sycophanta*, fr. Gk *sykophantēs*, fr. *sykon* fig + *-phantēs* (fr. *phainein* to reveal, show, make known); perh. fr. the use of the gesture of the fig in denouncing a culprit — more at FANCY] **1 :** a slandering accuser **:** DEFAMER; *esp* **:** one of a group of talebearers of ancient Athens **2 :** a base or servilely attentive flatterer and self-seeker **:** TOADY ⟨the ~s were gone, for the outgoing president had nothing to give —W.A.White⟩ ⟨her children entrusted to the care of court ~s —Ann F. Wolfe⟩ ⟨is surrounded by a group of arrogant military ~s —*New Republic*⟩ **3** *obs* **:** LIAR, DECEIVER **syn** see PARASITE

²**sycophant** \"\ *vb* -ED/-ING/-S *vt, obs* **:** to traduce or flatter in the manner of a sycophant ~ *vi, obs* **:** to act the sycophant

³**sycophant** \"\ *adj* **:** SYCOPHANTIC

syco·phan·tic \ˈ==ˈfantik, -faan-, -tēk\ *adj* [Gk *sykophantikos*, fr. *sykophantēs* + *-ikos* -ic] **:** of, relating to, or characteristic of a sycophant: **a :** FAWNING, OBSEQUIOUS ⟨some . . . have been chosen rather for their ~ talents than for their intellectual acumen —Ezra Pound⟩ ⟨creeps his ~ way along the bureaucratic path to knighthood —C.J.Rolo⟩ ⟨peacocking about on the lawn, among an imported bevy of ~ females —Osbert Sitwell⟩ **b :** SLANDEROUS, DEFAMATORY

syco·phan·ti·cal \-tə̇kəl, -tēk-\ *adj* [Gk *sykophantikos* + E *-al*] **:** SYCOPHANTIC

syco·phan·ti·cal·ly \-k(ə)lē, -li\ *adv* **:** in a sycophantic manner **:** by or with sycophancy

syco·phant·ish \ˌ==ˈfantish, -ˈfaan-, ˈ==,fən-\ *adj* **:** SYCOPHANTIC — **syco·phant·ish·ly** *adv*

syco·phant·ism \ˈ==,fən,tizəm, -,fan-, -,faan-\ *n* -s **:** SYCOPHANCY

syco·phant·ize \ˈ==(,)=,tīz\ *vi* -ED/-ING/-S [¹*sycophant* + *-ize*] *archaic* **:** to play the sycophant

syco·phant·ly *adv* [³*sycophant* + *-ly*] **:** SYCOPHANTICALLY

sy·co·sis \sīˈkōsə̇s\ *n, pl* **syco·ses** \-ō,sēz\ [NL, fr. Gk *sykōsis*, fr. *sykon* fig + *-ōsis* -osis] **:** a chronic inflammatory disease involving the hair follicles esp. of the bearded part of the face and marked by papules, pustules, and tubercles perforated by hairs with crusting

sycr *abbr* **1** synchronize **2** synchronizer

syden·ham's chorea \ˈsidᵊnəmz-, ˈsidᵊn,hamz-\ *n, usu cap S* [after Thomas *Sydenham* †1689 Eng. physician] **:** chorea following infection (as rheumatic fever) and occurring usu. in children and adolescents

sydenham's laudanum *n, usu cap S* [after T. *Sydenham*] **:** either of two opium preparations: **a :** WINE OF OPIUM **b :** tincture of opium with saffron

syd·ney \ˈsidnē, -ni\ *adj, usu cap* [fr. *Sydney*, New So. Wales, Australia] **:** of or from Sydney, the capital of New So. Wales **:** of the kind or style prevalent in Sydney

sydney blue gum *n, usu cap S* **:** a large Australian gum tree (*Eucalyptus saligna*) having bark with a bluish cast

sydney golden wattle *n, usu cap S* **:** a golden wattle (*Acacia longifolia*) with willowy branches

syd·ney·ite \ˈsidnē,īt\ *n* -s *cap* [*Sydney*, Australia + E *-ite*] **:** a native or resident of Sydney, Australia

sydney peppermint *n, usu cap S* **:** a peppermint gum (*Eucalyptus piperita*)

syd·none \ˈsid,nōn\ *n* -s [*Sydney*, Australia (where this type of compound was discovered) + E *-one*] **:** any of a class of heterocyclic compounds that contain a ring composed of two carbon atoms, two nitrogen atoms, and a fifth atom (as oxygen) and have an oxo or similar group, that are resonance hybrids of several ionic states and have large dipole moments, and that are obtainable in various ways (as by dehydration of *N*-nitroso-*N*-phenyl-glycine by acetic anhydride)

¹**sye** *var of* SIE

²**sye** *vi* [ME *syen*, fr. OE *sīgan*; akin to OS & OHG *sīgan* to sink, fall, ON *sīga* to sink, slide, *sīa* to strain, filter — more at SACK (wine)] *obs* **:** SINK, FALL, DESCEND

³**sye** *var of* SY

sy·e·nite \ˈsīə,nīt\ *n* -s [L *Syenites* (*lapis*), fr. *Syenites* of Syene (fr. Syene, ancient city in Egypt + L *-ites* -ite) + *lapis* stone] **1** *archaic* **:** a variety of granite anciently quarried at Syene in Upper Egypt in which biotite is substituted for or accompanied by hornblende **2 :** a phanerocrystalline intrusive igneous rock composed of dominant alkaline feldspar with or without subordinate plagioclase and without notable quartz or nepheline

sy·e·nit·ic \ˌ==ˈnid·ik\ *adj* **:** of, relating to, or containing syenite

sy·e·no·diorite \ˌ==,nō+\ *n* [*syenite* + *-o-* + *diorite*] **:** a plutonic rock composed of acid plagioclase, less orthoclase, and a ferromagnesian mineral — compare GRANODIORITE

sy·e·no·gabbro \"+\ *n* [*syenite* + *-o-* + *gabbro*] **:** a plutonic rock composed of basic plagioclase, less orthoclase, and a dark mineral (as augite)

¹**syke** *var of* SIKE

²**syke** \ˈsīk\ *n* -s [ME (northern dial.), small stream, rill, fr. OE *sīc* — more at SIKE] **:** FOUNTAIN 4

syl *or* **syll** *abbr* syllable

syl·la·ba an·ceps \ˌsiləbəˈän,keps, -an,ke-,-an,se-\ *n* [L, lit., doubtful syllable] **:** a syllable occurring at the end of a sentence or verse in a metrical scheme whose short or long quantity is obscured by the terminal pause; *specif* **:** such a syllable occurring in the rhythms of ancient verse wherever there is a diaeresis or serving as a terminal demarcation at the end of a verse or between asynartetic cola

syl·la·bar·i·um \ˌsiləˈba(a)rēəm, -ber-, -bär-\ *n, pl* **syl·labar·ia** \-rēə\ [NL] **:** SYLLABARY

syl·la·bary \ˈsilə,berē, -ri\ *n* -ES [NL *syllabarium*, fr. L *syllaba* syllable + *-arium* -ary — more at SYLLABLE] **:** a table or listing of syllables; *specif* **:** a series or set of written characters each one of which is used to represent a syllable — distinguished from ALPHABET; compare CUNEIFORM, KANA

syllabi *pl of* SYLLABUS

¹**syl·lab·ic** \sə̇ˈlabik, -bēk\ *adj* [LL *syllabicus*, fr. Gk *syllabikos*, fr. *syllabē* syllable + *-ikos* -ic — more at SYLLABLE] **1 :** of, relating to, or denoting syllables ⟨~ accent⟩ ⟨~ characters⟩ **2 :** constituting a syllable or the nucleus of a syllable: **a** *of a consonant* **:** not accompanied in the same syllable by a vowel ⟨\n\ is ~ in \ˈbätᵊnē\ *botany*, nonsyllabic in \ˈbätnē\⟩ **b** *of a vowel* **:** having vowel quality more prominent than that of another vowel in the syllable ⟨the first vowel of a falling diphthong, as \ȯ\ in \ȯi\, is ~⟩ **3 :** consisting of or using syllabic characters or a syllabary ⟨the Eskimos of the eastern arctic have a system of ~ writing —*Sat. Eve. Post*⟩ **4 :** characterized by distinct enunciation or separation of syllables ⟨~ utterance⟩ ⟨~ tunes⟩ — see SYLLABIC MELODY **5 :** forming or comprising a type of verse distinguished primarily by count of syllables rather than by rhythmical arrangement of accents or quantities — compare QUANTITATIVE

²**syllabic** \"\ *n* -s **1 :** a syllabic sign or character ⟨some signs . . . were used in the sense of an alphabet; some signs were employed as ~s; others were ideographic —Stanley Wernyss⟩ **2 :** a syllabic sound or utterance ⟨when two or more ~s occur . . . one can clearly hear different degrees of articulatory force —Stanley Newman⟩

-syl·lab·ic \sə̇ˈlabik, -bēk\ *adj comb form* [F *-syllabique*, fr. *-syllabe* -syllabic (fr. L *-syllabus*, fr. Gk *-syllabos*, fr. *syllabē* syllable) + *-ique* -ic — more at SYLLABLE] **:** having or relating to syllables of a (specified) kind or number ⟨ambi*syllabic*⟩ ⟨hepta*syllabic*⟩ ⟨impari*syllabic*⟩

syl·lab·i·cal \sə̇ˈlabə̇kəl, -bēk-\ *adj* [LL *syllabicus* + E *-al*] *archaic* **:** SYLLABIC

syl·lab·i·cal·ly \-k(ə)lē, -li\ *adv* **:** in, with, or by syllables

syl·lab·i·cate \sə̇ˈlabə,kāt, *usu* -ād·+V\ *vt* -ED/-ING/-S [back-formation fr. *syllabication*] **:** SYLLABIFY

syl·lab·i·ca·tion \=,==ˈkāshən\ *n* -s [ML *syllabication-*, *syllabicatio*, fr. *syllabicatus* (past part. of *syllabicare* to form into syllables, fr. LL *syllabicus* syllabic) + L *-ion-, -io* -ion] **:** the act, process, or method of forming or dividing words into syllables

syl·la·bic·i·ty \ˌsiləˈbisəd·ē\ *n* -ES **:** the state of being or the power of forming a syllable ⟨~ determined also by manner of articulation —Leonard Bloomfield⟩ ⟨the patterns of ~ are significant in determining the morpheme boundaries and junctures —E.A.Nida⟩

syllabic melody *or* **syllabic song** *n* **:** a song (as a Gregorian chant) in which each syllable has but one note — compare MELISMATIC

syl·lab·ic·ness \sə̇ˈlabiknə̇s, -bēk-\ *n* -ES **:** SYLLABICITY

syl·lab·i·fi·ca·tion \sə̇,labəfə̇ˈkāshən\ *n* -s [L *syllaba* syllable + E *-i-* + *-fication*] **:** SYLLABICATION

syl·lab·i·fy \=ˈ=bə,fī\ *vt* -ED/-ING/-ES [L *syllaba* + E *-ify*] **:** to form or divide into syllables

syl·la·bism \ˈsilə,bizəm\ *n* -s [ISV *syllab-* (fr. L *syllaba* syllable) + *-ism*] **1 :** the use or development of syllabic characters ⟨a polysyllabic language did not lend itself so readily as the Chinese monosyllabic to ~ —Edward Clodd⟩ **2 :** SYLLABICATION

syl·la·bize \-,bīz\ *vt* -ED/-ING/-S [ML *syllabizare*, fr. Gk *syllabizein*, fr. *syllabē* syllable + *-izein* -ize] **1 :** SYLLABIFY **2 :** to utter (as verse) with distinct articulation of separate syllables

¹**syl·la·ble** \ˈsiləbəl\ *n* -s [ME *sillable*, fr. MF *sillabe*, fr. L *syllaba*, fr. Gk *syllabē*, fr. *syllambanein* to gather together, put together, combine in pronunciation, fr. *syn-* + *lambanein* to take, grasp — more at LATCH] **1 :** a unit of spoken language that is next bigger than a speech sound and consists of one or more vowel sounds alone (as \ī\ and \ə\ in \īleftində\ *I left India*) or of a syllabic consonant alone (as \ᵊn\ in \wīdᵊn\ *widen*) or of either accompanied by one or more consonant sounds preceding or following (as \stāt\ in \stātmənt\ *statement* or \ᵊnd\ in \wīdᵊnd\ *widened* **2 :** one or more letters (as *syl, la,* and *ble*) in a word (as *syl·la·ble*) usu. set off from the rest of the word by a centered dot or a hyphen and roughly but often not exactly corresponding to the syllables of spoken language and treated as helps to the ascertainment of pronunciation or as markers of places where a word may be hyphenated at the end of a written or printed line **3 :** a monosyllabic word considered with reference to its meaning ⟨those awful ~s, hell, death, and sin —William Cowper⟩ **4 :** the smallest conceivable expression or unit of something **:** JOT ⟨kept a diary for years, but never entered in it a ~ that had to do with his official life —H.G.Dwight⟩ ⟨towns of gold can never countervail the least sentence or ~ of wit —R.W.Emerson⟩ ⟨as if the past had resolved itself into this tiny esoteric pattern and that I could grasp it in an instant of time, and interpret its every single ~ as briefly —Walter de la Mare⟩ **5 a :** SYLLABLE NAME **b :** SOL-FA SYLLABLES ⟨to sing by ~⟩

²**syllable** \"\ *vt* **syllabled; syllabled; syllabling** \-b(ə)liŋ\ **syllables 1 :** to give a number or arrangement of syllables to (a word or verse) ⟨some uncouth poet scarcely able to ~ his words —Virginia Woolf⟩ ⟨long unbroken sentences . . . filled with poly*syllabled* abstract nouns —*Times Lit. Supp.*⟩ **2 :** to express or utter in or as if in syllables ⟨tongues that ~ men's names —John Milton⟩ ⟨where the birds talked with words too sad and strange to ~ —J.C.Ransom⟩

syllable name *n* **:** the name of a given musical tone in solmization — compare SOL-FA SYLLABLES

syl·la·bub *or* **sil·la·bub** \ˈsilə,bəb\ *n* -s [origin unknown] **1 :** a drink or dessert made by curdling milk or cream with wine or other acid **2 :** a dessert that is made by beating to a froth sweetened milk or cream sometimes with added whites of eggs, is flavored with wine or liquor, and is served as a drink when thin or when thick is often poured over cake or fruit — compare WHIP

syl·la·bus \-,bəs\ *n, pl* **sylla·bi** \-,bī\ *or* **syllabuses** [LL, alter. (influenced by Gk *syllambanein*) of L *sillybus* label for a book, fr. Gk *sillybos*] **1 :** a compendium or summary outline of a discourse, treatise, course of study, or examination requirements **:** a series of abstracts **:** ABSTRACT, EPITOME ⟨drew up in consultation a definite scheme or ~ of the intended course —Edward Jenks⟩ ⟨preparing a complete historical and geographic ~ for each tour —*Current Biog.*⟩ **2 :** HEADNOTE 2 **3** *or* **syllabus of errors :** a collection of propositions condemned as erroneous by the Roman Catholic Church **syn** see COMPENDIUM

syl·lep·sis \sə̇ˈlepsə̇s\ *n, pl* **syllep·ses** \-p,sēz\ [L, fr. Gk *syllēpsis*, fr. the stem of *syllambanein* to gather together, put together + *-sis* — more at SYLLABLE] **1 :** the use of a word (as an adjective or verb) in grammatical agreement with only one of two nouns by which it is governed ⟨the verb in "I remain well and my wife also" is an example of ~⟩ **2 :** the use of a word in the same grammatical relation to two adjacent words in its literal sense with one and a metaphorical sense with the other ⟨"the tank fired, and the bridge and many hopes sank" is an example of ~⟩ — compare ZEUGMA

syl·lep·tic \-ptik\ *also* **syl·lep·ti·cal** \-tə̇kəl\ *adj* [fr. *syllepsis*, after such pairs as E *prolepsis: proleptic, proleptical*] **:** of, relating to, or involving a syllepsis — **syl·lep·ti·cal·ly** \-k(ə)lē\ *adv*

¹**syl·lid** \ˈsiləd\ *or* **syl·lid·i·an** \sə̇ˈlidēən\ *adj* [*syllid* fr. NL *Syllidae; syllidian* fr. NL *Syllidae* + E *-ian*] **:** of or relating to the Syllidae

²**syllid** \"\ *or* **syllidian** \"\ *n* -s **:** a worm of the family Syllidae

syl·li·dae \ˈsilə,dē\ *n pl, cap* [NL, fr. *Syllis*, type genus + *-idae*] **:** a large family of small free-swimming polychaete worms related to the Nereidae but usu. reproducing by asexual budding

syl·lis \ˈsiləs\ *n* [NL] **1** *cap* **:** the type genus of Syllidae **2** -ES **:** any worm of the genus *Syllis*

syl·lo·ge \ˈsilə(,)jē\ *n* -s [Gk *syllogē*, fr. *syllegein* to collect, fr. *syn-* + *legein* to collect, gather — more at LEGEND] **:** COLLECTION, COMPENDIUM

syl·lo·gism \-,jizəm\ *n* -s [ME *silogisme*, fr. MF, fr. L *syllogismus*, fr. Gk *syllogismos*, fr. *syllogizesthai* to infer, syllogize, fr. *syn-* + *logizesthai* to calculate — more at ANTILOGISM] **1 :** a deductive logical scheme or analysis of a formal argument that consists of a major premise, a minor premise, and a conclusion and that may be used either to prove a conclusion by showing that it follows from known premises or to test the truth of premises by showing what follows from them (as in "every virtue is laudable; kindness is a virtue; therefore kindness is laudable") — compare FIGURE table **2 :** explication of the relations of ideas esp. in accordance with syllogistic principles : DEDUCTIVE METHOD ⟨a man knows first, and then he is able to prove syllogistically; so that ~ comes after knowledge —John Locke⟩ — compare INDUCTION 2 **3 :** a subtle, specious, or crafty argument, piece of reasoning, or method of attaining one's end ⟨blithely accepts the perilous ~ that the end justifies the means —C.B.Davis⟩

syl·lo·gist \-jəst\ *n* -S [fr. *syllogism*, after such pairs as E *atheism: atheist*] : one who applies or is skilled in syllogistic reasoning

¹syl·lo·gis·tic \¦==¦jistik, -tēk\ *adj* [L *syllogisticus*, fr. Gk *syllogistikos*, fr. (assumed) *syllogistos* (verbal of *syllogizesthai*) + *-ikos* -ic] : of, relating to, or consisting of a syllogism ⟨~ reasoning⟩

²syllogistic \"\ *n, pl* **syl·lo·gis·tics** \-ks\ *sometimes sing in constr* **1 :** the branch of logic dealing with the syllogism **2 :** syllogistic reasoning ⟨views on abstraction . . . and his ~*s* —E.W.Beth⟩ ⟨knowledge was to be a ~, or at least rational and jointed —H.O.Taylor⟩

syl·lo·gis·ti·cal \¦==¦jistəkəl, -tēk-\ *adj* [L *syllogisticus* + E *-al*] **1 :** SYLLOGISTIC **2 :** given to reasoning by or dealing in syllogisms — **syl·lo·gis·ti·cal·ly** \-k(ə)lē, -li\ *adv*

syl·lo·gi·za·tion \,siləjə'zāshən, -,jī'z-\ *n* -S [ML *syllogization-, syllogizatio*, fr. LL *syllogizatus* (past part. of *syllogizare*) + L *-ion-, -io* -ion] : the act or process of syllogizing

syl·lo·gize \'silə,jīz\ *vb* -ED/-ING/-S [ME *sylogysen*, fr. LL *syllogizare*, fr. Gk *syllogizesthai* to infer, syllogize — more at SYLLOGISM] *vi* : to reason or infer by means of syllogisms : argue deductively ⟨can scarcely be said to ~; whatever he knows he knows all at once —Frank Thilly⟩ ⟨this thinking and *syllogizing* . . . this running over and over of hypothesis and surmise and supposition —L.P.Smith⟩ ~ *vt* : to deduce (something) by syllogism ⟨~*s* his moral laws⟩

sylph \'silf\ *n* -S [NL *sylphus*] **1 :** an imaginary or elemental being inhabiting the air and being mortal but soulless — compare UNDINE **2 :** a slender woman or girl of light and graceful carriage **3 :** any of several brilliant So. American hummingbirds (as *Aglaiocercus kingi*) having a long forked tail

sylph·ic \-fik\ *adj* : of, relating to, or resembling a sylph

¹sylph·id \-fəd\ *n* -S [F *sylphide*, fr. *sylphe* sylph (fr. NL *sylphus*) + *-ide* -id] : a young or diminutive sylph

²sylphid \"\ *adj* : SYLPHIC

sylphlike \'=,=\ *adj* : resembling a sylph : SYLPHIC

Syl·phon \'sil,fän\ *trademark* — used for a thin-walled tubular bellows used in temperature and pressure regulators, bellows seals, and expansion joints

syl·va \'silvə\ *n* -S [L *silva, sylva* forest, grove] **1 :** SILVA **2** *archaic* : a collection of poems, anecdotes, or literary pieces — used chiefly as a title

¹syl·van *or* **sil·van** \'silvən\ *n* -S [L *silvanus, sylvanus*, fr. *Silvanus, Sylvanus*, god of woods and trees, fr. *silva, sylva* forest + *-anus* -an (n. suffix)] **1 :** a deity or spirit frequenting groves or woods **2 :** a person, animal, or bird living in or frequenting the woods or forest

²sylvan *also* **silvan** \"\ *adj* [ML *silvanus, sylvanus*, fr. L *silva, sylva* + *-anus* -an (adj. suffix)] **1 a :** living or located in the woods or forest ⟨a group of ~ beings —J.G.Frazer⟩ ⟨still others, swamp and ~ types mainly, never leave their native haunts —V.M.Ehlers & E.W.Steel⟩ **b :** of, relating to, or characteristic of the woods or forest ⟨owned the whole mountain, led a ~ life there —Vincent Sheean⟩ ⟨some such ~ instrument of music —Nathaniel Hawthorne⟩ **2 a :** made, shaped, or formed of woods or trees ⟨living in a ~ bower⟩ ⟨an unbroken expanse of ~ vegetation⟩ **b :** abounding in woods, groves, or trees : WOODY, WOODED ⟨through which wind ~ drives and paths edged with laurel —*Amer. Guide Series: Conn.*⟩ ⟨a ~ setting for the Singing Tower —*Amer. Guide Series: Fla.*⟩

³sylvan *var of* SILVAN

syl·vaner \sil'vänər, -van-\ *n* -S *usu cap* [G *sylvaner, silvaner*, prob. fr. L *Sylvanus, Silvanus*, god of woods and trees + G *-er*] **1 a :** a German white wine grape **b :** a Rhine wine made from such grapes **2 a :** a California wine grape resembling the German Sylvaner **b :** a wine made from such grapes

syl·van·ite *also* **sil·van·ite** \'silvə,nīt\ *n* -S [F *sylvanite*, fr. *sylvane* sylvanite (fr. *Transylvania*, its locality) + *-ite*] : a mineral $(Au,Ag)Te_2$ consisting of a gold silver telluride, having a steel gray, silver white, or brass yellow color, and often occurring in implanted crystals resembling written characters (hardness 1.5–2 sp. gr. 7.9–8.3) — called also *graphic tellurium* — **syl·van·it·ic** \¦==¦nid·ik\ *adj*

syl·vat·ic \(')sil¦vad·ik\ *adj* [L *silvaticus, sylvaticus* — more at SAVAGE] **1 :** SYLVAN ⟨the ~ Indians who occupied the extreme western parts of the provinces —J.A.Cosculluela⟩ **2 :** occurring in wild animals ⟨in its ~ form it is endemic among wild rodents on the west coast —*Jour. Amer. Med. Assoc.*⟩ ⟨~ yellow fever —*Ecology*⟩

sylvatic plague *n* : a plague of which wild rodents and their fleas are the reservoirs and vectors and which is widely distributed in western No. and So. America though rarely affecting man

syl·ves·trene \sil've,strēn\ *n* -S [ISV *sylvestr-* (fr. NL *sylvestris* — specific epithet of *Pinus sylvestris*, the species of pine from which it is derived —, fr. L, sylvan) + *-ene*] : a liquid terpene hydrocarbon $C_{10}H_{16}$ or mixture of two isomeric terpenes occurring in dextrorotatory, levorotatory, and inactive racemic forms and obtained as the dihydrochloride of the dextrorotatory form by treating either of the carenes or oil fractions containing them with hydrogen chloride; 1, 8- or 6,8-*meta*-menthadiene

syl·ves·tri·an \(')sil¦vestrēən\ *adj* [L *silvestris, sylvestris* sylvan (fr. *silva, sylva* forest, grove) + E *-an*] : SYLVAN ⟨~ gods —John Gay⟩

syl·via \'silvēə\ *n* [NL, fr. the name *Sylvia*, often used as a nickname for a robin] **1** *cap* : the type genus of warblers of the formerly extensive family Sylviidae restricted to the European whitethroat, the blackcap, and related forms **2** -S : any warbler of the genus *Sylvia*

syl·vi·an aqueduct \'silvēən-\ *n, usu cap S* [*sylvian* fr. *Sylvius* (Jacques Dubois) †1555 Fr. anatomist + E *-an*] : AQUEDUCT OF SYLVIUS

sylvian fissure *n, usu cap S* : LATERAL FISSURE

syl·vi·col·i·dae \,silvē'kälə,dē\ [NL, fr. *Sylvicola*, type genus (fr. L, adj., inhabiting the forest, fr. *silvi-, sylvi-* — fr. *silva, sylva* forest — + *-cola* inhabitant) + *-idae* — more at -COLOUS] *syn of* PARULIDAE

¹syl·vic·o·line \sil'vikə,līn, -,lən\ *adj* [NL *Sylvicola* + E *-ine*] : of or relating to the Parulidae

²sylvicoline \"\ *n* -S : a warbler of the family Parulidae

sylvics *var of* SILVICS

sylviculture *var of* SILVICULTURE

syl·vid \'silvəd\ *n* -S *usu cap* [L *silva, sylva* forest + E *-id*] : an early American Indian of a physical type characterized by marked dolichocephaly and found esp. in the forested eastern part of No. America — compare CENTRALID, PACIFID

¹syl·vi·id \'silvēəd, -ē,id\ *adj* [NL *Sylviidae*] : of or relating to the Sylviidae

²sylviid \"\ *n* -S : a bird of the family Sylviidae

syl·vi·idae \sil'vīə,dē\ *n pl, cap* [NL, fr. *Sylvia*, type genus + *-idae*] : a family of small 10-primaried oscine passerine birds related to the thrushes and consisting of the Old World or true warblers and the kinglets and gnatcatchers of America

syl·vil·a·gus \sil'viləgəs\ *n* [NL *silvi-, sylvi-* (fr. *silva, sylva* woods) + Gk *lagōs* hare] **1** *cap* : a genus of mammals (family Leporidae) comprising the cottontail and related New World rabbits **2** -S : any rabbit of the genus *Sylvilagus*

syl·vin·ite \'silvə,nīt\ *n* -S [*sylvin* + *-ite*] : rock that contains chiefly potassium chloride though in an impure state

syl·vite \'sil,vīt\ *also* **syl·vin** \-vən\ *or* **syl·vine** \-vən, -,vēn\ *n* -S [*sylvite* alter. of *sylvine; sylvin, sylvine* fr. F *sylvine*, fr. NL (*sal digestivus*) *Sylvii*, lit., digestive salt of Sylvius + F *-ine*] : a mineral KCl consisting of native potassium chloride and occurring in colorless cubes or crystalline masses like rock salt but having a sharper taste (hardness 2, sp. gr. 1.98)

¹sym- — see SYN-

²sym- *or* **s-** *comb form* [symmetrical] *usu ital* : symmetrical — in names of organic compounds ⟨*sym*-dichloro-ethylene⟩ ⟨*s*-dichloro-ethylene⟩

sym *abbr* **1** symbol; symbolic **2** symmetrical **3** symphony

sym-allylene \'sim+\ *n* [²*sym-* + *allylene*] : ALLENE 1

symar *var of* SIMAR

sym·bal·lo·phone \sim'bälə,fōn\ *n* [Gk *symballein* to throw together, compare + E *-o-* + *-phone* — more at SYMBOL] : a double stethoscope having two chest pieces for the comparison of sounds in the body heard through the earpieces

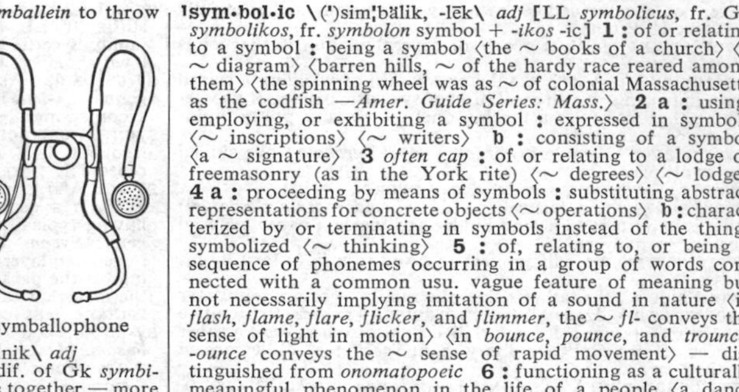

symballophone

sym·bat·ic \(')sim¦bad·ik\ *adj* [ISV, fr. Gk *symbatikos* tending or leading to agreement, fr. *symbat-* (verbal stem of *symbainein* to come to an agreement, fr. *syn-* + *bainein* to walk, come) + *-ikos* -ic — more at COME] *of two related variables* : increasing or decreasing together though not necessarily in direct proportion

sym·bi·on \'simbī,än, -bē,-\ *n* -S [NL, fr. Gk *symbiōn* (pres. part. of *symbioun*) or fr. Gk *symbion*, neut. of *symbios* living together — more at SYMBIOSIS] : SYMBIONT — **sym·bi·on·ic** \¦==¦änik\ *adj*

sym·bi·ont \'==,änt\ *n* -S [prob. fr. G, modif. of Gk *symbiount-, symbiōn*, pres. part. of *symbioun* to live together — more at SYMBIOSIS] : an organism living in symbiosis; *usu* : the smaller member of a symbiotic pair of dissimilar size as opposed to the larger host — **sym·bi·on·tic** \¦==¦äntik\ *adj*

sym·bi·on·ti·cism \,==¦äntə,sizəm\ *n* -S [*symbiontic* + *-ism*] : SYMBIOSIS

sym·bi·ose \'simbī,ōs, -bē,-\ *vi* -ED/-ING/-S [back-formation fr. NL *symbiosis*] : to associate symbiotically

sym·bi·o·sis \,simbī'ōsəs, -bē'-\ *n, pl* **symbio·ses** \-'ō,sēz\ [NL, modif. (influenced by Gk *symbiōsis*) of G *symbiose*, fr. Gk *symbiōsis* state of living together, fr. *symbioun* to live together, fr. *symbios* living together, fr. *syn-* + *bios* life, mode of life — more at QUICK] **1 a :** the living together in more or less intimate association or even close union of two dissimilar organisms (as in parasitism, mutualism, or commensalism) — compare HELOTISM **b :** the intimate living together of two dissimilar organisms in any of various mutually beneficial relationships; *often* : MUTUALISM **2 :** mutual cooperation between persons and groups in a society esp. when ecological interdependence is involved

sym·bi·ote \'simbī,ōt, -bē,-\ *also* **sym·bi·ot** \-,ät\ *n* -S [F *symbiote*, fr. Gk *symbiōtēs* companion, partner, fr. *symbioun* to live together] : SYMBIONT

sym·bi·ot·ic \¦==¦äd·|ik, ät|, |ēk\ *also* **sym·bi·ot·i·cal** \|əkəl\ *adj* [*symbiotic* fr. NL *symbiosis* + ISV *-otic; symbiotical* fr. *symbiotic* + *-al*] : relating to, characterized by, living in, or resulting from a state of symbiosis — compare FREE-LIVING, PARASITIC — **sym·bi·ot·i·cal·ly** \|ək(ə)lē\ *adv*

sym·bi·ot·ics \,=='äd·iks\ *n pl but sing in constr* [fr. *symbiotic*, after such pairs as E *economic: economics*] : a field of study dealing with symbiosis

symbiotic saprophytism *n* : the association of a saprophytic plant with a symbiotic fungus (as a mycorrhiza)

sym·bi·o·tism \'simbīə,tizəm, -bēə,-\ *n* -S [*symbiotic* + *-ism*] : SYMBIOSIS

sym·bleph·a·ron \sim'blefə,rän\ *n* -S [NL, fr. *syn-* + Gk *blepharon* eyelid] : adhesion between an eyelid and the eyeball (as from a burn)

¹sym·bol \'simbəl\ *n* -S [in sense 1, fr. LL *symbolum* baptismal creed, fr. LGk *symbolon*, lit., token, sign, fr. Gk; in other senses, fr. L *symbolus, symbolum* token, sign, fr. Gk *symbolon* token of identity (verified by comparing its other half), sign, symbol, fr. *symballein* to throw together, compare, contribute, fr. *syn-* + *ballein* to throw — more at DEVIL] **1 :** an authoritative summary of faith or doctrine : a creedal formulary : CREED **2 :** something that stands for or suggests something else by reason of relationship, association, convention, or accidental but not intentional resemblance; *esp* : a visible sign of something (as a concept or an institution) that is invisible ⟨the lion is the ~ of courage⟩ ⟨the cross was always one of the ~*s* of Christianity —E.S.Holden⟩ ⟨a flock of sheep is not the ~ of a free people —*New Republic*⟩ ⟨shop windows are full of festive ~*s*: cats and candles, witches and brooms, pumpkins and grotesque masks —Lucy Embury⟩ ⟨a heritage is at any moment a selection of ~*s* out of the past —Max Lerner⟩ **3 :** an arbitrary or conventional sign (as a character, a diagram, a letter, or an abbreviation) used in writing or printing relating to a particular field (as mathematics, physics, chemistry, music, or phonetics) to represent operations, quantities, spatial position, valence, direction, elements, relations, qualities, sounds, or other ideas or qualities : SIGN ⟨the usual ~*s* for crossroads, stores, and churches on rural maps —*Amer. Guide Series: Minn.*⟩ **4 a** (1) **:** a formal unit of expression (as a term, proposition, or formal argument) that represents an abstract thought capable of being dealt with as a unit (2) **:** a conventionally adopted character in logic **b :** a conventional or nonnatural sign depending for its meaning on an interpretant — contrasted with *icon* and *index* **5 :** an object or act that represents a repressed complex through unconscious association rather than through objective resemblance or conscious substitution **6 :** an act, sound, or material object having cultural significance and the capacity to excite or objectify a response ⟨there must be some ~*s* around which interaction can be organized —W.F. Whyte⟩

syn SYMBOL, EMBLEM, ATTRIBUTE, TYPE can signify, in common, a visible thing that stands for or suggests something invisible or intangible. SYMBOL and EMBLEM are often used interchangeably but may be distinguished by the fact that SYMBOL can apply to anything that serves as an outward sign of something else, usu. spiritual or immaterial ⟨the key *symbols* are the lilac which stands for the new birth in the spring of the year, the drooping star which stands for death, and the bird whose song embraces birth and death indifferently, and so inspires the poet that he becomes the bird —J.C.Ransom⟩ ⟨the present law is spiteful, and . . . has become a *symbol* of dissension and bitterness —A.E.Stevenson †1965⟩ ("Dr. Livingstone, I presume", a phrase whose casualness made it a *symbol* everywhere of British aplomb —*Amer. Guide Series: Ark.*⟩ ⟨language consists of *symbols*⟩ EMBLEM usu. applies to pictorial representation of or something standing as a pictorial or picturelike symbol and is often used of a pictorial device found on a shield or banner intended to serve as a chosen symbol of the character or history of the nation, royal line, or organization that has adopted it ⟨the national *emblem* of the Future Farmers of America is significant and meaningful in every detail . . . made up of five symbols: the owl, the plow, and the rising sun, within the cross section of an ear of corn which is surmounted by the American eagle —*Future Farmers of America*⟩ ⟨his *emblem* was a butterfly with a sting in its tail — a sting he attempted to keep in constant use —*Time*⟩ ⟨the American eagle, *emblem* of the U.S.⟩ ⟨the *emblem* of the U.S.S.R., the sickle around an arm and hammer⟩ ⟨the cold teapot, the emptied cups, *emblems* of hospitality —Joseph Conrad⟩ ATTRIBUTE, a term in painting and sculpture, applies to an object usu. associated with a representation of a character or personified abstraction and serving to identify it ⟨the *attribute* of Fortune, a turning wheel⟩ ⟨the scales and blindfold, the *attribute* of Justice⟩ TYPE, in this connection occurring chiefly in theological use, applies to a person or thing prefiguring or foreshadowing something or someone to come and serving as his or its symbol until the reality appears, often implying a divine dispensation whereby a person, event, or experience prefigures a spiritual or immaterial reality ⟨allegory was also called on to justify, as against educated pagans, certain acts of that heroic but peccant *type* of Christ, David, the son of Jesse —H.O.Taylor⟩ **syn** see in addition CHARACTER

²symbol \"\ *vb* **symboled** *or* **symbolled; symboled** *or* **symbolled; symboling** *or* **symbolling** \-b(ə)liŋ\ **symbols** *vt* : to visualize by means of a symbol : SYMBOLIZE ~ *vi* : to employ symbols ⟨man has the power to ~⟩

³symbol \"\ *n* -S [L *symbola*, fr. Gk *symbolē*, fr. *symballein* to throw together, contribute] : something that is thrown into a common fund : CONTRIBUTION

sym·bol·gram \-l,gram\ *n* [¹*symbol* + *-gram*] **1 :** an artistic combination of symbols usu. of American Indian origin that expresses the ambitions and desires of its designer **2 :** a personally symbolic design (as of a camp fire girl)

¹sym·bol·ic \(')sim¦bälik, -lēk\ *adj* [LL *symbolicus*, fr. Gk *symbolikos*, fr. *symbolon* symbol + *-ikos* -ic] **1 :** of or relating to a symbol : being a symbol ⟨the ~ books of a church⟩ ⟨a ~ diagram⟩ ⟨barren hills, ~ of the hardy race reared among them⟩ ⟨the spinning wheel was as ~ of colonial Massachusetts as the codfish —*Amer. Guide Series: Mass.*⟩ **2 a :** using, employing, or exhibiting a symbol : expressed in symbols ⟨~ inscriptions⟩ ⟨~ writers⟩ **b :** consisting of a symbol ⟨a ~ signature⟩ **3** *often cap* : of or relating to a lodge of freemasonry (as in the York rite) ⟨~ degrees⟩ ⟨~ lodge⟩ **4 a :** proceeding by means of symbols : substituting abstract representations for concrete objects ⟨~ operations⟩ **b :** characterized by or terminating in symbols instead of the things symbolized ⟨~ thinking⟩ **5 :** of, relating to, or being a sequence of phonemes occurring in a group of words connected with a common usu. vague feature of meaning but not necessarily implying imitation of a sound in nature ⟨in *flash, flame, flare, flicker*, and *flimmer*, the ~ *fl-* conveys the sense of light in motion⟩ ⟨in *bounce, pounce*, and *trounce*, *-ounce* conveys the ~ sense of rapid movement⟩ — distinguished from *onomatopoeic* **6 :** functioning as a culturally meaningful phenomenon in the life of a people ⟨a dance ritual with ~ rather than abstract, mimetic, or purely personal importance⟩

²symbolic \"\ *n* -S **1 :** something that is symbolic — usu. used with *the* ⟨the ~ may lose itself in unintelligibility —John Dewey⟩ **2** [G *symbolik*, fr. *symbol* creed (fr. LL *symbolum*) + *-ik* -ics, fr. Gk *-ikē*, fem. of *-ikos* -ic] : SYMBOLICS 1

sym·bol·i·cal \-lәkәl, -lēk-\ *adj* [LL *symbolicus* of a symbol + E *-al*] : marked by symbolism : SYMBOLIC, ALLEGORICAL, EMBLEMATIC ⟨~ language⟩ ⟨whether art is ~, poetic or imitative —Herbert Read⟩

sym·bol·i·cal·ly \-äləkə)lē, -älēk-, -)li\ *adv* [*symbolical* + *-ly*] : in a symbolic manner : ALLEGORICALLY, EMBLEMATICALLY ⟨the primitive was alleged not to think logically, but mystically and ~ —W.E.Moore⟩

sym·bol·i·cal·ness *n* -ES [*symbolical* + *-ness*] : the quality or state of being symbolic ⟨the ~ of an act⟩

symbolic books *or* **symbolical books** *n pl, often cap S&B* : books containing creeds or confessions of faith of a church ⟨the *Symbolic Books* of Orthodoxy⟩

symbolic delivery *n* : the delivery of property by means of a token (as a key or a bankbook)

symbolic equation *n* : a mathematical equation declaring the equivalence of a group of operations

symbolic language *n* : a language that employs symbols either extensively or exclusively; *esp* : one that has been artificially constructed for the purpose of precise formulations (as in symbolic logic, mathematics, or chemistry) — compare CALCULUS 3

symbolic logic *n* : a science of developing and representing logical principles by means of symbols for the purpose of providing an exact canon of deduction based on primitives, postulates, and formation and transformation rules — called also *mathematical logic;* see ALGEBRA OF CLASSES, ALGEBRA OF RELATIONS, CALCULUS OF INDIVIDUALS, COMBINATORY LOGIC, FUNCTIONAL CALCULUS, PROPOSITIONAL CALCULUS

sym·bol·ic·ly *adv* [¹*symbolic* + *-ly*] : SYMBOLICALLY

sym·bol·ics \sim'bäliks\ *n pl but sing in constr* [¹*symbol* + *-ics*] **1 :** historical theology dealing with Christian creeds and confessions of faith : SYMBOLISM **2 :** the study of ancient symbols and ceremonies

symbolic theology *n* [*symbolics*] : a branch of theology that deals with the doctrinal differences of churches as found in creeds

sym·bol·ism \'simbə,lizəm\ *n* -S [¹*symbol* + *-ism*] **1 :** the practice or art of using symbols esp. by investing things with a symbolic meaning or by expressing the invisible, intangible, or spiritual, by means of visible or sensuous representations: as **a :** the use of conventional or traditional signs (as the nimbus) in the representation esp. of divine beings and spirits in order to indicate qualities, powers, degrees, or other attributes **b :** artistic imitation or invention that is not an end in itself but a method of revealing or suggesting immaterial, ideal, or otherwise intangible truth or states and ranges in form from the allegorization of nature or life to the presentation of ideas, emotions, or states of mind through concatenations of sound (as in music or poetry), arrangements of lines and planes (as in painting and sculpture), or contrasts or blendings of color (as in painting) — compare IMAGISM **2 :** the theological study of religious creeds and confessions of faith : SYMBOLICS **3 :** a system of symbols or representations

¹sym·bol·ist \-ləst\ *n* -S [¹*symbol* + *-ist*] **1 a** *often cap* : one who regards the elements of the Eucharist as symbols and not as the body and blood of Christ **b :** one who advocates or employs symbolism in religious worship **2 :** one who employs symbols or symbolism **3 :** one skilled in the interpretation or explication of symbols **4** [F *symboliste*, fr. *symbole* symbol (fr. L *symbolus, symbolum*) + *-iste* -ist] *usu cap* : one of a group of writers and artists (as in France after 1880) who are reactionists against realism and the theories and practices of the Parnassians and who concern themselves with general truths instead of actualities, exalt the metaphysical and the mysterious, and aim to unify and blend the arts and the functions of the senses — compare DECADENT 2 **5 :** a logician who advocates or employs symbolic logic

²symbolist \"\ *adj* : of, relating to, or characteristic of symbolists

sym·bol·is·tic \¦simbə¦listik, -tēk\ *adj* [*symbolist* + *-ic*] : of, relating to, or characteristic of symbolists : executed by or in the manner of a symbolist : employing or marked by symbolism : SYMBOLIC ⟨~ poetry⟩ ⟨~ methods⟩ — **sym·bol·is·ti·cal·ly** \-tək(ə)lē\ *adv*

sym·bol·iza·tion \,simbələ'zāshən, -bə,lī'-\ *n* -S **1 :** the act or process of symbolizing : symbolical representation or an instance of it : SYMBOLISM **2 :** symbolic representation of a repressed complex (as in dreams) **3 :** the capacity of man in distinction to infrahuman beings to develop a system of meaningful symbols

sym·bol·ize \'simbə,līz\ *vb* -ED/-ING/-S *see -ize in Explan Notes, vi* **1** [MF *symboliser*, fr. ML *symbolizare* to express by a symbol, to be alike in quality, fr. L *symbolus, symbolum* symbol + LL *-izare* -ize] *archaic* : to be alike (as in qualities, properties, or principles) : become united : HARMONIZE, AGREE, CONCUR **2** [¹*symbol* + *-ize*] : to use symbols or symbolism ⟨the Middle Ages, with their constant tendency to ~ —Lewis Mumford⟩ ~ *vt* [ML *symbolizare* to express by a symbol] **1 :** to serve as a symbol of : stand for : TYPIFY ⟨the wedding ring ~*s* unending love⟩ **2 :** to represent, express, or identify by a symbol ⟨streets of a populated place need not be *symbolized* —*Topographic Surveying*⟩ ⟨talking ~*s* experience —Stuart Chase⟩

sym·bol·iz·er \-zə(r)\ *n* -S : one that symbolizes : SYMBOLIST

symbolled *past of* SYMBOL

symbolo- *comb form* [Gk *symbolon*] : sign : symbol ⟨*symbololatry*⟩

sym·bo·log·i·cal \¦simbə¦läjəkəl\ *adj* : of, relating to, or characteristic of symbology — **sym·bo·log·i·cal·ly** \-jək(ə)lē\ *adv*

sym·bol·o·gist \sim'bäləjəst\ *n* -S : a specialist in symbology

sym·bol·o·gy \-jē, -ji\ *n* -ES [*symbolo-* + *-logy*] **1 :** the art of expression by symbols **2 :** the study or interpretation of symbols

sym·bo·lo·phobia \¦simbə(,)lō+\ *n* [NL, fr. *symbolo-* + *phobia*] : fear that one's acts or speech may contain symbolic meanings

symbols *pl of* SYMBOL, *pres 3d sing of* SYMBOL

symbol train *n* : MANIFEST 4

sym·branch \'sim,braŋk\ *n* -S [NL *Symbranchii*] : a fish of the order Symbranchii

sym·bran·chia \sim'braŋkēə\ [NL, fr. *sym-* + *-branchia*] *syn of* SYMBRANCHII

¹sym·bran·chi·ate \-ēət, -ē,āt\ *adj* [NL *Symbranchia* + E *-ate*] : of or relating to the Symbranchii

²symbranchiate \"\ *n* -S : SYMBRANCH

sym·bran·chi·dae \sim'braŋkə,dē\ [NL, alter. of *Synbranchidae*] *syn of* SYNBRANCHIDAE

sym·bran·chii \sim'braŋkē,ī\ *n pl, cap* [NL, alter. of *Symbranchia*] : an order of teleost tropical fishes resembling the true eels (order Apodes) but having the maxillaries and

premaxillaries well developed and the pectoral arch joined to or near the skull
sym·bran·choid \sim'braŋ,kȯid\ *adj* [NL *Symbranchus* (syn. of *Synbranchus*, type genus of the Synbranchidae, fr. *syn-* + L *branchia* gill) + E *-oid* — more at BRANCHIA] **:** resembling or related to the Synbranchidae
sym·me·lus \'siməlǝs\ *n, pl* **symme·li** \-mə,lī\ [NL, fr. *syn-* + *-melus*] **:** SIRENOMELUS
sym·metallic \¦sim+\ *adj* [*syn-* + *-metallic* (as in *bimetallic*)] **:** of or relating to symmetallism ⟨~ coins⟩
sym·met·al·lism \(')sim¦med·ᵊl,izəm\ *n* -s [*syn-* + *-metallism* (as in *bimetallism*)] **:** a system of coinage in which the unit of currency consists of a particular weight of an amalgam of two or more metals (as gold and silver)
sym·met·ri·cal \sə'me·trəkəl, -rēk-\ *or* **sym·met·ric** \-rik, -rēk\ *adj* [*symmetry* + *-ical* or *-ic*] **1 :** having or involving symmetry **:** exhibiting symmetry **:** exhibiting correspondence in size and shape of parts **:** BALANCED, REGULAR ⟨the human body is ~⟩ ⟨crystals are often ~⟩ ⟨a ~ garden⟩ ⟨a ~ grouping⟩ **2 :** having corresponding points whose connecting lines are bisected by a given point or perpendicularly bisected by a given line or plane — used of geometrical figures **3 a :** being of such nature that the terms may be interchanged without altering the value, character, or truth — used esp. of mathematical relations, functions, and equations ⟨$c=f(a+b)$ is ~ with respect to *a* and *b* but not generally with respect to *a* and *c*⟩ **b :** COMMENSURABLE **4 a** *of a shoot or other plant part* **:** capable of division by a longitudinal plane into similar halves — compare ACTINOMORPHIC, ZYGOMORPHIC **b** *of a flower* **:** having the same number of members in each whorl of floral leaves — compare REGULAR 2c **5 :** affecting corresponding parts simultaneously and similarly ⟨~ gangrene of the legs⟩ **6 :** exhibiting symmetry in the structural formula; *esp* **:** relating to derivatives in which groups are substituted symmetrically in the molecule ⟨~ dichloro-ethylene ClCH=CHCl⟩ ⟨~ or 1,3,5-trinitro-benzene⟩
symmetrical diphenyl-urea *n* **:** CARBANILIDE
symmetrical lens *n* **:** a simple or compound lens whose optical properties are unaltered when the axis is rotated through 180 degrees
sym·met·ri·cal·ly \-rək(ə)lē, -rēk-, -li\ *adv* [*symmetry* + *-ically* (as in *geometrically*)] **:** in a symmetrical manner ⟨~ placed windows⟩ ⟨highly cultivated and ~ developed persons —C.W.Eliot⟩
sym·met·ri·cal·ness *n* -ES **:** the quality or state of being symmetrical **:** SYMMETRY
sym·me·tri·za·tion \,simə·trə'zāshən\ *n* -s [*symmetrize* + *-ation*] **:** the action of making symmetrical
sym·me·trize \'simə,trīz\ *vt* -ED/-ING/-S [*symmetry* + *-ize*] **:** to make symmetrical **:** reduce to symmetry
sym·me·tro·pho·bia \,simə·trə'fōbēə\ *n* [NL, fr. E *symmetry* + NL *-o-* + *-phobia*] **:** a characteristic asymmetry (as in ancient Egyptian architecture and in Japanese design) implying an aversion to symmetry
sym·me·try \'simə·trē, -ri\ *n* -ES [L *symmetria*, fr. Gk, commensurability, proportion, symmetry, fr. *symmetros* commensurate, suitable, symmetrical (fr. *syn-* + *metron* measure) + *-ia* -y — more at MEASURE] **1 a** *obs* **:** mutual relationship of parts (as in size, arrangement, or measurements) **:** PROPORTION **b :** due or balanced proportions **:** beauty of form or arrangement arising from balanced proportions ⟨with order, ~, and taste unblest —Robert Burns⟩ **2 :** correspondence in size, shape, and relative position of parts that are on opposite sides of a dividing line or median plane or that are distributed about a center or axis **:** an arrangement or external form (as in a body, a design, or a grouping) marked by bilateral conformity or geometrical regularity — see BILATERAL SYMMETRY, RADIAL SYMMETRY **3 :** the property of being symmetrical **4 :** the property of a crystal of having two or more directions that are alike in physical and crystallographic respects because of identity of atomic structure in the directions concerned or mirror-image relations along such directions
sym·minct \'simiŋkt\ *adj* [modif. of Gk *symmeiktos*, *symmiktos* mixed together, fr. *symmeignynai*, *symmignynai* to mix together, fr. *syn-* + *meignynai*, *mignynai* to mix — more at MIX] **:** composed of material that has not been segregated into separate layers of fine and coarse particles ⟨~ clay⟩ ⟨~ varve⟩
sym·pa·thec·to·mize \,simpə'thektə,mīz\ *vt* -ED/-ING/-S **:** to perform a sympathectomy on
sym·pa·thec·to·my \-təmē\ *n* -ES [ISV *sympath-* (fr. ²*sympathetic*) + *-ectomy*] **:** the surgical interruption (as by resection of a ganglion or plexus) of sympathetic nerve pathways
¹**sym·pa·thet·ic** \¦simpə¦thed·ik, -et|, |ēk\ *adj* [NL *sympatheticus*, fr. Gk *sympatheia* sympathy + *-ētikos* (as in *pathētikos* pathetic)] **1 :** existing or operating through a real or assumed affinity, interdependence, or mutual association in which the condition of one thing influences sometimes in an occult way that of a separate unrelated thing ⟨cut hair and nails are supposed by primitive man to remain in a ~ relation with their original owner —J.G. Frazer⟩ ⟨the ~ exhilaration of so many people's cheerfulness —Nathaniel Hawthorne⟩ **2 a :** of such nature or character that coexistence, accord, or association is feasible or satisfying **:** not discordant or antagonistic ⟨antipathetic to the law of community living, but ~ to the law of survival —Agnes N. Keith⟩ ⟨~ to slum-clearance programs⟩ **b :** appropriate to one's mood, inclinations, or disposition **:** having qualities leading to kindly acceptance, gratification, appreciation, or pleasurable association ⟨meekness was not a quality that she found ~ —Helen Howe⟩ ⟨found a ~ medium in wood engraving —Herbert Read⟩ **c :** marked by kindly or pleased appreciation ⟨in general the treatment of the subject is ~ rather than hostile —W.L.Sperry⟩ **3 :** given to, marked by, or arising from sympathy, compassion, friendly fellow feelings, and sensitivity to others' emotions ⟨when you are cold and critical, instead of ~ —Nathaniel Hawthorne⟩ ⟨a ~ gesture⟩ **4 :** favorably inclined **:** showing attitudes or preferences in harmony **:** APPROVING, FAVORING ⟨those more ~ to your ways or views —M.R.Cohen⟩ ⟨not ~ to the idea of a sales tax⟩ **5 :** showing empathy **:** exhibiting ready comprehension of others' mental states **:** led by disposition or intuition to a warm friendly appreciative interest in others ⟨though some considered her arrogant and forbidding, I found her personality ~ —Edmund Wilson⟩ **6 a :** of or relating to the sympathetic nervous system **b :** mediated by or acting on the sympathetic nerves **7 :** relating to musical tones produced by means of sympathetic vibration (as from a resonator or resonance cavity) ⟨~ tones⟩ or so tuned as to sound by sympathetic vibration rather than by being struck, plucked, or bowed ⟨~ string⟩ **syn** see CONSONANT, TENDER
²**sympathetic** \"\ *n* -s **:** a sympathetic structure; *esp* **:** SYMPATHETIC NERVOUS SYSTEM
sym·pa·thet·i·cal \|əkəl\ *adj* [NL *sympatheticus* + E *-al*] *archaic* **:** SYMPATHETIC
sym·pa·thet·i·cal·ly \|ək(ə)lē, |ēk-, -li\ *adv* [*sympathetical* + *-ly*] **:** in a sympathetic manner or mood **:** by reason of sympathy esp. through counteraction, consonance, or interdependence ⟨write ~⟩ ⟨the crisis must ~ affect all nations⟩ ⟨the characters are brilliantly observed but not ~ understood —M.R.Ridley⟩
sympathetic chain *n* **:** either of the ganglionated longitudinal cords of the sympathetic nervous system
sympathetic clock *n* **:** a clock synchronized from a master clock
sympathetic ink *n* **:** SECRET INK
sympathetic magic *n* **:** magic based on the assumption that a person or thing can be supernaturally affected through its name or an object (as a nail paring, image, or dancer) representing it **:** CONTAGIOUS MAGIC — compare IMITATIVE MAGIC
sympathetic nerve *n* **:** a nerve of the sympathetic nervous system
sympathetic nervous system *n* **1** *archaic* **:** AUTONOMIC NERVOUS SYSTEM **2 :** the part of the autonomic nervous system that contains chiefly adrenergic fibers and tends to depress secretion, decrease the tone and contractility of smooth muscle, and cause the contraction of blood vessels and that consists essentially of preganglionic fibers arising in the thoracic and upper lumbar parts of the spinal cord and passing through delicate white rami communicantes to ganglia located in a pair of ganglionated cords situated one on each side of the vertebral column or to more peripheral ganglia or ganglionated plexuses and postganglionic fibers passing typically through gray rami communicantes to spinal nerves with which they are distributed to various end organs — compare PARASYMPATHETIC NERVOUS SYSTEM
sym·pa·thet·ic·ness *n* -ES **:** the quality of being sympathetic
sympathetico- *comb form* [*sympathetic* (*nervous system*)] **1 :** sympathetic ⟨*sympathetico*mimetic⟩ **2 :** sympathetic and ⟨*sympathetico*adrenal⟩
sym·pa·thet·i·co·adrenal \¦simpə¦thed·ə(,)kō+\ *adj* [*sympathetico-* + *adrenal*] **:** of, relating to, or made up of sympathetic nervous and adrenal elements ⟨~ system⟩
sym·pa·thet·i·co·lyt·ic \¦simpə¦thed·əkə¦lid·ik\ *adj* [*sympathetico-* + *-lytic*] **:** SYMPATHOLYTIC
sym·pa·thet·i·co·mimetic \¦simpə¦thed·ə(,)kō+\ *adj or n* [*sympathetico-* + *mimetic*] **:** SYMPATHOMIMETIC
sympathetic ophthalmia *n* **:** inflammation in an uninjured eye as a result of injury and inflammation of the other
sym·pa·thet·i·co·to·nia \,simpə,thed·əkə'tōnēə\ *n* -s [NL, fr. *sympathetico-* + *-tonia*] **:** SYMPATHICOTONIA — **sym·pa·thet·i·co·ton·ic** \¦==¦===¦tänik\ *adj*
sympathetic powder *n* **:** a powder held by alchemists to be a sovereign cure for a wound even if applied merely to blood from it or to the weapon inflicting it
sympathetic strike *n* **:** a strike in which the strikers make no demands on their own employers but try to bring pressure against the employers of other workers on strike — called also *sympathy strike*
sympathetic system *n* **:** SYMPATHETIC NERVOUS SYSTEM
sympathetic vibration *n* **:** a vibration produced in one body by the vibrations of exactly the same period in a neighboring body
sym·pa·thet·o·blast \,simpə'thed·ə,blast\ *n* [*sympathetic* + *-o-* + *-blast*] **:** a cell destined to become a sympathetic neuron
sympathico- *comb form* [NL *sympathicus*, fr. *sympathia* sympathy + *-icus* -ic] **:** sympathetic ⟨*sympathico*tonia⟩
sym·path·i·co·blast \sim'pathəkō,blast\ *n* [ISV *sympathico-* + *-blast*] **:** SYMPATHETOBLAST
sym·path·i·co·lyt·ic \sim¦pathəkō¦lid·ik\ *adj* [ISV *sympathico-* + *-lytic*] **:** SYMPATHOLYTIC
sym·path·i·co·mimetic \sim¦pathə(,)kō+\ *adj* [ISV *sympathico-* + *mimetic*] **:** SYMPATHOMIMETIC
sym·path·i·co·to·nia \sim,pathəkō'tōnēə\ *n* -s [NL, fr. *sympathico-* + *-tonia*] **:** a condition characterized by domination of body functioning by the sympathetic nervous system and characterized by gooseflesh, vascular spasm, and abnormally high blood pressure — **sym·path·i·co·ton·ic** \=¦===¦tänik\ *adj*
sym·path·i·co·trop·ic cell \sim¦pathəkō-¦träpik-\ *n* [ISV *sympathico-* + *-tropic*] **:** any of various large epithelioid cells found in intimate association with unmyelinated nerve fibers in the ovary and testis esp. of the fetus
sym·pa·thin \'simpəthən\ *n* -s [ISV *sympath-* (fr. ¹*sympathetic*) + *-in*] **:** a neurohormone secreted by the sympathetic nerve endings and acting as chemical mediator to the various organs ⟨noradrenaline . . . and adrenaline . . . were identified with the ~s —*U.S. Dispensatory*⟩
sym·pa·thism \'simpə,thizəm\ *n* -s [*sympathy* + *-ism*] **:** the presence of like sensations or emotions in two or more persons
sym·pa·thize \'simpə,thīz\ *vb* -ED/-ING/-S *see -ize in Explan Notes* [MF *sympathiser*, fr. *sympathie* sympathy (fr. L *sympathia*) + *-iser* -ize] *vt* **1** *obs* **:** to experience in common **2** *obs* **:** to answer to **:** correspond to **:** MATCH **3** *obs* **:** to represent, express, conceive, or contrive with sympathetic imagination or art **~** *vi* **1 :** to suffer or be affected (as through affinity, association, or interdependence) **:** react or respond in sympathy ⟨a good eye often ~s with the diseased eye⟩ **2 :** to be in keeping, accord, harmony, or agreement **:** be like **:** resemble in nature or disposition **3 a :** to share in suffering or grief **:** experience compassion or pity **:** COMMISERATE — often used with *with* ⟨~ with a friend in trouble⟩ **b :** to express such sympathy — often used with *with* **4 :** to be in sympathy intellectually **:** understand through fellow feeling **:** be favorably impressed ⟨~ with one's insurgency⟩ ⟨~ with a proposal⟩
sym·pa·thiz·er \-zə(r)\ *n* -s **:** one that sympathizes **:** one that acts or reacts in sympathy ⟨strikers and their ~s⟩
sym·pa·thiz·ing·ly *adv* [*sympathizing* (pres. part. of *sympathize*) + *-ly*] **:** in a sympathizing manner
sympatho- *comb form* [NL *sympathicus* — more at SYMPATHICO-] **:** sympathetic ⟨*sympatho*lytic⟩
sym·pa·tho·blast \'simpəthō,blast\ *n* [ISV *sympatho-* + *-blast*] **:** SYMPATHETOBLAST
sym·pa·tho·lyt·ic \¦simpəthō¦lid·ik\ *adj* [ISV *sympatho-* + *-lytic*] **:** tending to oppose the physiological results of sympathetic nervous activity or of sympathomimetic drugs — used chiefly of chemical substances and their effects; compare PARASYMPATHOLYTIC, SYMPATHOMIMETIC
sym·pa·tho·mimetic \¦simpə(,)thō+\ *adj* [ISV *sympatho-* + *mimetic*] **:** simulating sympathetic nervous action in physiological effect **:** ADRENERGIC 2 — used esp. of various amines related to adrenaline or of their effects; compare PARASYMPATHOMIMETIC, SYMPATHOLYTIC
sym·pa·thy \'simpəthē, -thi\ *n* -ES [L *sympathia* state of feeling in common, fr. Gk *sympatheia*, fr. *sympathēs* having common feelings, sympathetic (fr. *syn-* + *pathos* feelings, emotion, experience) + *-ia* -y — more at PATHOS] **1** *archaic* **:** correspondence in qualities, properties, or disposition **:** mutual suitability **:** CONCORD ⟨you are not young, no more am I; go to then, there's ~ —Shak.⟩ **2 a :** an affinity, association, or relationship between persons or things or between persons and things wherein whatever affects one similarly affects the other ⟨steel prices have advanced in this district in ~ with rising prices elsewhere⟩ ⟨the magical ~ . . . supposed to exist between a man and any severed portion of his person, as his hair or nails —J.G.Frazer⟩ **b :** mutual or parallel susceptibility or a condition brought about by it ⟨there is a purely physical ~: a very young child will cry because a brother or sister is crying —Bertrand Russell⟩ **c :** unity or harmony in action or effect ⟨the most felicitous unity of general design . . . for every part is in complete ~ with the scheme as a whole —Edwin Benson⟩ **3 a :** inclination to think or feel alike **:** emotional or intellectual accord ⟨~ is as essential as love in marriage⟩ ⟨though not a member of the Society of Friends, I am in ~ with their aims⟩ **b :** feeling of loyalty **:** tendency to favor or support **:** active interest ⟨always identified in ~ with the laboring classes —E.S. Bates⟩ — often used in pl. ⟨radical *sympathies*⟩ ⟨republican *sympathies*⟩ ⟨they were Philadelphians, Quaker in their religious *sympathies* —Lucien Price⟩ **4 a :** the act or capacity of entering into or sharing the feelings or interests of another **:** the character or fact of being sensitive to or affected by another's emotions, experiences, or esp. sorrows **b :** the feeling or mental state brought about by such sensitivity **:** the expression or demonstration of this feeling ⟨have ~ for the poor⟩ ⟨seek ~ from a friend⟩ ⟨a boy goes for ~ and companionship to his mother and sisters, not often to his father —A.C.Benson⟩ **5 :** the correlation existing between bodies capable of communicating their vibrational energy to one another through some medium

syn PITY, COMPASSION, COMMISERATION, CONDOLENCE, RUTH, EMPATHY: SYMPATHY is the most general term, ranging in meaning from friendly interest or agreement in taste or opinion to emotional identification, often accompanied by deep tenderness ⟨in immediate *sympathy* with my desire to increase my . . . knowledge —David Fairchild⟩ ⟨*sympathies* were . . . with the Roman Stoics —Havelock Ellis⟩ ⟨satire had its roots not in hatred but in *sympathy* —Bliss Perry⟩ PITY has the strongest emotional connotation; the emotion may be one of tenderness, love, or respect induced by the magnitude of another's suffering or of fellowship with the sufferer ⟨*pity* is the feeling which arrests the mind in the presence of whatsoever is grave and constant in human sufferings and unites it with the human sufferer —James Joyce⟩ ⟨*pity* that made you cry . . . not for this person or that person who is suffering, but . . . for the very nature of things . . . out of *pity* comes the balm which heals —William Saroyan⟩ PITY may suggest a tinge of contempt for one who is inferior whether because of suffering or from inherent weakness; there is also a frequent suggestion that the effect if not the purpose of pity is to keep the object in a weak or inferior state ⟨*pity* for the man who could think of nothing better —T.S.Eliot⟩ ⟨the parents of a crippled child should give him understanding and challenge rather than *pity*⟩ COMPASSION orig. meant fellowship in suffering between equals; now it denotes imaginative or emotional sharing of the distress or misfortune of another or others who are considered or treated as equals; it implies tenderness and understanding as well as an urgent desire to aid and spare ⟨one of his neighbor women cooked a chicken and brought it in to him out of pure *compassion* —Willa Cather⟩ ⟨with understanding, with *compassion* (so different from pity) she shows the sordid impact . . . on the lives of the natives —Sarah Campion⟩ ⟨when Jesus came in his gentleness with his divine *compassion* —Robert Bridges †1930⟩ but while COMPASSION suggests a greater dignity in the object than PITY often does, it also implies a greater detachment in the subject ⟨as a priest he regards all history from that eminence of spiritual objectivity which is called *compassion* —W.F.Albright⟩ COMMISERATION and CONDOLENCE agree in placing the emphasis on expression of a feeling for another's affliction, rather than on the feeling itself. COMMISERATION denotes a spontaneous and vocal expression, often one made in public or by a crowd ⟨there was a murmur of *commiseration* as Charles Darnay crossed the room . . . the soft and compassionate voices of women —Charles Dickens⟩ CONDOLENCE denotes a formal expression of sympathy esp. for the loss of a relative through death and refers strictly to an observance of etiquette without any implication as to the underlying feeling ⟨a *condolence* call⟩ ⟨they received many *condolences*⟩ RUTH denotes softening of a stern or indifferent disposition ⟨look homeward, Angel, now, and melt with *ruth* —John Milton⟩ EMPATHY, of all the terms here represented, has the least emotional content; it describes a gift, often a cultivated gift, for vicarious feeling, but the feeling need not be one of sorrow; thus EMPATHY is often used as a synonym for some senses of SYMPATHY as well as in distinction from SYMPATHY ⟨what he lacks is not *sympathy* but *empathy*, the ability to put himself in the other fellow's place —G.W. Johnson⟩ EMPATHY is frequently employed with reference to a nonhuman object (as a literary character, an idea, culture, or work of art) ⟨a fundamental component of the aesthetic attitude is *sympathy*, or — more accurately — *empathy*. In the presence of any work of art . . . the recipient . . . must surrender his independent and outstanding personality, to identify himself with the form or action presented by the artist —Herbert Read⟩
sympathy strike *n* **:** SYMPATHETIC STRIKE
sym·pat·ric \(')sim¦pa·trik, -pā-\ *adj* [*syn-* + Gk *patra* fatherland (fr. *patēr* father) + E *-ic* — more at FATHER] **:** occupying or taking place in the same area ⟨a ~ distribution of two species⟩; *specif* **:** capable of occupying the same range without loss of identity due to interbreeding ⟨~ species kept apart by physiologic isolation⟩ — compare ALLOPATRIC — **sym·pat·ri·cal·ly** \-rək(ə)lē\ *adv* — **sym·pa·try** \'simpə·trē\ *n* -ES
sym·pet·a·lae \sim'ped·ᵊl,ē\ [NL, fr. *syn-* + *-petalae*] *syn of* METACHLAMYDEAE
sym·pet·a·lous \(')sim¦ped·ᵊləs\ *adj* [*syn-* + *-petalous*] **1 :** GAMOPETALOUS **2 :** characteristic of the Metachlamydeae — **sym·pet·a·ly** \sim'ped·ᵊlē\ *n* -ES
sym·pha·lan·gus \,sim(p)fə'laŋgəs\ *n, cap* [NL, fr. *syn-* + *phalang-*, *phalanx*] **:** a genus of gibbons comprising the siamang
sym·phile \'sim,fīl\ *n* -s [prob. back-formation fr. *symphily*] **:** an insect (as any of various beetles) living as a guest in the nest of a social insect (as an ant or termite) by which it is fed and guarded for its secretions which are used as food — called also *myrmecoxene, true guest*
sym·phil·ic \(')sim¦filik\ *adj* [*symphily* + *-ic*] **:** of, relating to, or characterized by symphily
¹**sym·phi·lid** *also* **sym·phy·lid** \'sim(p)fələd\ *adj* [NL *Symphyla* + E *-id*] **:** of or relating to the Symphyla
²**symphilid** *also* **symphylid** \"\ *n* -s **:** an arthropod of the class Symphyla and esp. of the genus *Scutigerella* — see GARDEN CENTIPEDE
sym·phi·lism \'sim(p)fə,lizəm\ *n* -s [*symphily* + *-ism*] **:** SYMPHILY
sym·phi·lous \'sim(p)fələs\ *adj* [*symphily* + *-ous*] **:** SYMPHILIC
sym·phi·ly \-lē\ *n* -ES [G *symphilie*, fr. Gk *symphilia* mutual friendship, fr. *syn-* + *philia* friendship — more at PHILIA] **:** commensalism with mutual benefit or attraction (as between some ants or termites and various guest insects that live in their nests) — compare SYNECHTHRY, SYNOECY
sym·phog·e·nous \(')sim¦fäjənəs\ *adj* [Gk *symphyesthai* to grow together + E *-o-* + *-genous* — more at SYMPHYSIS] **:** arising through the interweaving and compacting of hyphal branches (as in the development of some pycnidia) — compare MERISTOGENOUS
sym·pho·nette \¦sim(p)fə¦net\ *n* -s [*symphony* + *-ette*] **:** a symphony orchestra reduced in personnel and typically playing ensemble and salon music in addition to the standard orchestral literature
sym·pho·nia \sim'fōnēə\ *n* -s [L — more at SYMPHONY] **1 :** concord of sounds; *esp* **:** musical harmony **2** [LL, a kind of musical instrument, fr. L, concord of sounds] **:** any of various musical instruments (as the bagpipe and hurdy-gurdy) of the medieval period **3 :** SYMPHONY 2a, 2d, 2e
sym·phon·ic \(')sim¦fänik, -nēk\ *adj* [*symphony* + *-ic*] **1 :** relating to harmony of sound **:** HARMONIOUS, SYMPHONIOUS ⟨the ~ hum of a million insects —Jack Kerouac⟩ **2 :** relating to or characteristic of a symphony or symphony orchestra ⟨~ form⟩ ⟨~ music⟩ **3 :** suggestive of a symphony esp. in form, interweaving of themes, or harmonious arrangement ⟨a ~ drama⟩ ⟨a ~ novel⟩ ⟨a ~ flower arrangement⟩
sym·phon·i·cal·ly \-nək(ə)lē, -nēk-, -li\ *adv* [obs. *symphonical* (fr. *symphony* + *-ical*) + *-ly*] **:** in a symphonic form, style, or manner
symphonic ballet *n* **:** ballet emphasizing patterns rather than story
symphonic poem *n* [trans. of G *symphonische dichtung*] **:** an extended musical composition for a symphony orchestra differing from a symphony in being less restricted in form and based on a definite literary subject or a program, being usu. in one continuous movement, and having one or more principal themes
sym·pho·ni·ous \(')sim¦fōnēəs, -nyəs\ *adj* [*symphony* + *-ous*] **:** agreeing esp. in sound **:** producing harmonies **:** ACCORDANT, HARMONIOUS — **sym·pho·ni·ous·ly** *adv*
sym·pho·nist \'sim(p)fənəst\ *n* -s [*symphony* + *-ist*] **:** a composer of symphonies
sym·pho·nize \-fə,nīz\ *vi* -ED/-ING/-S *see -ize in Explan Notes* [*symphony* + *-ize*] **:** to play or sound together in or as if in a symphony **:** ACCORD, AGREE, HARMONIZE
sym·pho·ny \'sim(p)fənē, -ni\ *n* -ES [ME *symphonie*, fr. OF, fr. L *symphonia*, fr. Gk *symphōnia*, fr. *symphōnos* agreeing in sound, concordant (fr. *syn-* + *phōnē* voice, sound) + *-ia* -y — more at BAN] **1 :** a consonance or harmony of sounds ⟨night was a ~ of sounds —Guy Fowler⟩ **2 a :** an instrumental musical passage in a vocal composition **b :** SINFONIA 1 **c :** an instrumental movement in a choral work ⟨the Pastoral *Symphony* in Handel's *Messiah*⟩ **d :** an elaborate instrumental composition usu. in sonata form for full orchestra **e :** a work of similar proportions for organ **f :** SYMPHONY ORCHESTRA **3 a :** consonance or harmony of color (as in a painting) **b :** a pictorial composition or other arrangement marked by consonance or harmony of color **4 :** something that in its harmonious complexity or variety suggests a symphonic composition ⟨barren wastelands burst out in a fleeting ~ of wild flowers —Gladwin Hill⟩
symphony band *n* **:** CONCERT BAND
symphony orchestra *n* **:** a large orchestra with well-proportioned instrumentation presenting musical programs usu. made up of symphonic works and other compositions of serious artistic worth
sym·pho·ri·car·pos \,sim(p)fərə'kär,päs\ *n* [NL, fr. Gk *symphora* act of gathering or collecting (fr. *sympherein* to bring together, fr. *syn-* + *pherein* to bear, carry) + NL *-i-* + Gk *karpos* fruit; fr. the clustering of the fruit — more at BEAR, HARVEST] **1** *cap* **:** a small genus of No. American shrubs (family Caprifoliaceae) having bell-shaped flowers in axillary

racemes succeeded by fleshy white or red 2-seeded berries — see CORALBERRY, SNOWBERRY **2** *pl* **symphoricarpos :** any plant of the genus *Symphoricarpos*

sym·phy·la \'sim(p)fələ\ *n pl, cap* [NL, fr. *syn-* + Gk *phylē* kind, species, tribe; fr. their combining characteristics of both insects and myriopods — more at PHYL-] **:** a small class of minute progoneate arthropods that with the exception of the garden centipede are rarely seen and of no economic importance

sym·phy·lan \-lən\ *adj or n* [NL *Symphyla* + E *-an*] **:** SYMPHILID

symphylid *var of* SYMPHILID

sym·phy·note \'sim(p)fə,nōt\ *adj* [Gk *symphyēs* grown together (fr. *symphyesthai* to grow together) + *nōton* back — more at SYMPHYSIS] **:** having the valves cemented together at the back ⟨the ~ shells of some freshwater mussels⟩

sym·phy·ple·o·na \,sim(p)fə'plēənə\ *n pl, cap* [NL *symphy-* (fr. Gk *symphyēs* grown together) + *-pleona* (fr. Gk *plein* to swim) — more at FLOW] **:** a suborder of Collembola comprising collembolans with a nearly spherical body in which the segmentation is obscure or lacking — compare ARTHROPLEONA

sym·phys·e·al *also* **sym·phys·i·al** \(')sim¦fizēəl\ *adj* [*symphysial* fr. NL *symphysis* + E *-al; symphyseal*, alter. (influenced by Gk *symphyseōs*, gen. of *symphysis*) of *symphysial*] **1 :** of or relating to symphysis **2 :** having or relating to a mesial position between elements commonly in symphysis

symphyseal height *n* **:** the distance from the gnathion to a point between the two middle incisors of the lower jaw

sym·phys·i·on \sim'fizē,än\ *n* -S [NL, fr. *symphysis* + *-ion* (as in *gnathion*)] **1 :** the upper end of the symphysis of the jaw at the outer surface — see CRANIOMETRY illustration **2 :** the middle point in the upper border of the pubic arch

sym·phy·si·ot·o·my \,sim(p)fəzē'ädəmē\ *n* -ES [NL *symphysis* + E *-o-* + *-tomy*] **:** the operation of dividing the pubic symphysis to facilitate childbirth

sym·phy·sis \'sim(p)fəsəs\ *n, pl* **symphy·ses** \-fə,sēz\ [NL, fr. Gk, state of growing together, symphysis, fr. *symphyesthai* to grow together, middle of *symphyein* to make grow together, fr. *syn-* + *phyein* to make grow, bring forth — more at BE] **1 :** an immovable or more or less movable articulation of various bones in the median plane of the body — see PUBIC SYMPHYSIS, SYMPHYSIS MENTI **2 :** a symphysis (as of a joint between the bodies of vertebrae) in which the bony surfaces are connected by pads of fibrocartilage without a synovial membrane

symphysis menti *n* [NL, lit., symphysis of the chin] **:** the median articulation of the two bones of the lower jaw

symphysis pubis *n* [NL, lit., symphysis of the pubes] **:** PUBIC SYMPHYSIS

sym·phy·so·dac·tyl·ia \,sim(p)fəsōdak'tilēə\ *n* -S [NL, fr. *symphysis* + *-o-* + *-dactylia*] **:** fusion of two or more fingers or toes

sym·phy·ta \'sim(p)fədə\ [NL, fr. Gk, neut. pl. of *symphytos* grown together] *syn of* CHALASTROGASTRA

sym·phyt·ic \(')sim¦fid·ik\ *adj* [Gk *symphytos* grown together (fr. *symphyein* to make grow together) + E *-ic* — more at SYMPHYSIS] **:** formed by fusion **:** being a symphysis — **sym·phyt·i·cal·ly** \-d·ək(ə)lē\ *adv*

sym·phy·tum \'sim(p)fədəm\ *n, cap* [NL, fr. Gk *symphyton*, neut. of *symphytos* grown together] **:** a genus of Old World perennial herbs (family Boraginaceae) having coarse hairy entire leaves, yellow, blue, or purple flowers in one-sided racemes, and four obliquely ovoid nutlets — see COMFREY

sym·plasm \'sim,plazəm\ *n* [ISV *syn-* + *-plasm*] **1 :** COENOCYTE **2 :** an amorphous mass made up of numerous intimately fused bacteria — **sym·plas·mic** \(')sim¦plazmik\ *adj*

sym·plast \'sim,plast\ *n* -S [ISV *syn-* + *-plast*] **:** COENOCYTE — **sym·plas·tic** \(')sim¦plastik\ *adj*

symplastic growth *n* **:** growth in a group of cells without either movement of the cells or new contacts between them and accompanied by mutual adjustment between all the cells — compare GLIDING GROWTH, INTRUSIVE GROWTH

¹sym·plec·tic \(')sim¦plektik\ *adj* [Gk *symplektikos* of intertwining, fr. *symplektos* (verbal of *symplekein* to plait together, intertwine, fr. *syn-* + *plekein* to plait) + *-ikos* -ic — more at PLY] **1 :** relating to or being an intergrowth of two different minerals (as in ophicalcite, myrmekite, or micropegmatite) **2 :** relating to or being a bone between the hyomandibular and the quadrate in the mandibular suspensorium of many fishes that unites the other bones of the suspensorium

²symplectic \"\ *n* -S **:** the symplectic bone

sym·ple·site \'simplə,sīt\ *n* -S [G *symplesit*, fr. Gk *syn-* + *plēsiazein* to bring near, come near, associate with (fr. *plēsios* near) + G *-it* -ite; fr. its being found in association with other minerals — more at PLESI-] **:** a mineral $Fe_2(AsO_4)_3.8H_2O$ consisting of a hydrous iron arsenate and occurring in small blue to bluish-green monoclinic crystals and in radiated aggregates (hardness 2.5, sp. gr. 3)

sym·plo·ca·ceae \,simplə'kāsē,ē\ *n pl, cap* [NL *Symplocos*, type genus + *-aceae*] *in some classifications* **:** a family coextensive with the genus *Symplocos*

sym·plo·cos \'simplə,käs\ *n* [NL, fr. LGk *symplokos* entwined, fr. *symplekein* to plait together — more at SYMPLECTIC] **1** *cap* **:** a large genus of trees and shrubs (family Styracaceae) having flowers with the calyx tube adnate to the 5-celled ovary which becomes a fleshy indehiscent fruit and numerous stamens inserted on the corolla and being widely distributed in all continents except Europe and Africa — see SWEETLEAF; SYMPLOCACEAE **2** *pl* **symplocos** *also* **symplocoses :** any plant of the genus *Symplocos*

sym·po·di·al \(')sim¦pōdēəl\ *adj* [NL *sympodium* + E *-al*] **1 a :** characteristic of or simulating a sympodium **b :** CYMOSE **2 :** shifting in line of direction or development in the manner of a sympodium — used esp. of social phenomena — **sym·po·di·al·ly** \-ələ̄\ *adv*

sym·po·dite \'simpə,dīt\ *n* -S [*syn-* + *-podite*; fr. its more or less consolidated segments] **:** PROTOPODITE

sym·po·di·um \sim'pōdēəm\ *n, pl* **sympo·dia** \-ēə\ [NL, fr. *syn-* + Gk *podion* small foot, base — more at PEW] **:** an apparent main axis (as in the grapevine) not developed from a terminal bud but made up of successive secondary axes each of which represents one fork of a dichotomy the other fork of which is of weaker growth or suppressed entirely — compare MONOPODIUM

¹sym·po·si·ac \sim'pōzē,ak\ *n* -S [back-formation fr. obs. *symposiacs* (pl.) table conversation, fr. L *Symposiaca* (title given to the *Symposium* of Plutarch †*ab*120 A.D. Greek writer), fr. neut. pl. of *symposiacus* of a symposium] *archaic* **:** SYMPOSIUM

²symposiac \"\ *adj* [L *symposiacus*, fr. Gk *symposiakos*, fr. *symposion* symposium] **:** of, relating to, or similar to a symposium

sym·po·si·arch \sim'pōzē,ärk\ *n* -S [Gk *symposiarchos*, fr. *symposion* symposium + *archos* leader — more at ARCHI-] **:** one who presides over a symposium

sym·po·si·ast \-,ast\ *n* -S [Gk *symposiazein* to take part in a symposium, fr. *symposion* symposium; after such pairs as Gk *enthousiazein* to be inspired: E *enthusiast* — more at ENTHUSIASM] **1 :** BANQUETER **2 :** one who contributes to a symposium

sym·po·si·um \sim'pōzēəm *sometimes* -ōzh(ē)əm\ *n, pl* **sympo·sia** \-zēə, -zh(ē)ə\ *or* **symposiums** [L, fr. Gk *symposion*, fr. *sympinein* to drink together, fr. *syn-* + *pinein* to drink — more at POTABLE] **1 a :** a drinking party; *esp* **:** one following a banquet and providing music, singing, and conversation **b :** a banquet or other social gathering at which there is free interchange of ideas **2 a :** a meeting at which several speakers deliver short addresses on related topics or on various aspects of the same topic **b :** a collection of opinions on a subject; *esp* **:** one assembled and published by a periodical **c :** DISCUSSION

symp·tom \'sim(p)təm\ *n* -S [LL *symptomat-, symptoma*, fr. Gk *symptōmat-, symptōma* chance occurrence, property that goes with something, symptom, fr. *sympiptein* to fall together, meet with, occur by chance, fr. *syn-* + *piptein* to fall — more at FEATHER] **1 a :** subjective evidence of disease or physical disturbance observed by the patient ⟨headache is a ~ of many diseases⟩ ⟨visual disturbances may be a ~ of retinal arteriosclerosis⟩ — contrasted with *sign* **b :** an evident reaction to a pathogen by a plant — contrasted with *sign* **2 a :** something that indicates the existence of something else ⟨volcanoes . . . are ~s of some kind of internal disorder in the earth —Howel Williams⟩ ⟨sedition is often the ~ and not the cause of serious unrest —Zechariah Chafee⟩ ⟨describe the ~s which accompany a maladjustment between people and the land —P.E. James⟩ **b :** a slight indication **:** TRACE ⟨not a ~ of a draught disturbs the air —Thomas Hardy⟩ **syn** see SIGN

symp·to·mat·ic \¦sim(p)tə¦mad·ik, -at|, |ēk\ *adj* [LL *symptomat-, symptoma* symptom + E *-ic*] **1 a :** being a symptom of a disease ⟨gummas ~ of syphilis⟩ ⟨excessive drinking ~ of a psychiatric disturbance⟩ **b :** having the characteristics of a particular disease but arising from another cause ⟨~ epilepsy resulting from brain injury⟩ — opposed to *idiopathic* or *essential* **2 :** according to, concerned with, or affecting symptoms ⟨~ treatment⟩ **3 :** CHARACTERISTIC, INDICATIVE ⟨his behavior was ~ of his character⟩ ⟨changes in the vegetation were ~ of greater geographical changes —W.E.Swinton⟩ ⟨personality formation is ~ of both individual and social institutions —Abram Kardiner⟩ — **symp·to·mat·i·cal·ly** \|ək(ə)lē, |ēk-, -li\ *adv*

symptomatic anthrax *n* **:** BLACKLEG 1

symp·tom·a·tize \'sim(p)təmə,tīz\ *vt* -ED/-ING/-S *see -ize in Explan Notes* [Gk *symptōmat-, symptōma* symptom + E *-ize*] **:** to be symptomatic of

symp·to·mat·o·log·ic \,sim(p)tə¦mad·ᵊl¦äjik\ *or* **symp·to·mat·o·log·i·cal** \-jəkəl\ *adj* [*symptomatology* + *-ic* or *-ical*] **:** SYMPTOMATIC — **symp·to·mat·o·log·i·cal·ly** \-jək(ə)lē\ *adv*

symp·tom·a·tol·o·gy \,sim(p)təmə'täləjē, -ji\ *n* -ES [NL *symptomatologia*, fr. Gk *symptōmat-, symptōma* symptom + *-o-* + L *-logia* -logy] **1 :** a branch of medical science that treats of symptoms of diseases **2 :** the symptoms of a disease in a given case taken as a whole

symptom complex *n* **:** a group of symptoms occurring together and characterizing a particular disease **:** SYNDROME

symp·tom·ize \'sim(p)tə,mīz\ *vt* -ED/-ING/-S *see -ize in Explan Notes* [*symptom* + *-ize*] **:** SYMPTOMATIZE

symp·tom·less \'sim(p)təmləs\ *adj* **:** exhibiting no symptoms ⟨a ~ infection⟩

symp·to·mol·o·gy \,sim(p)tə'mäləjē, -ji\ *n* -ES [*symptom* + *-o-* + *-logy*] **:** SYMPTOMATOLOGY

sym·pus \'simpəs\ *n* -ES [NL, fr. Gk *sympous* with feet together, fr. *syn-* + *pous* foot — more at FOOT] **:** SIRENOMELUS

syn \'sin\ *adj* [*syn-*] **:** CIS — opposed to *anti*; compare SYN- 3

syn- *or* **sym-** *prefix* [*syn-* fr. ME *sin-, syn-*, fr. OF, fr. L *syn-*, fr. Gk, fr. *syn* with, together with, by means of, at the same time as, alter. of *xyn*; *sym-* fr. ME *sim-, sym-*, fr. MF, fr. L *sym-*, fr. Gk, fr. *syn-*] **1 :** with **:** along with **:** together ⟨*syn*cline⟩ ⟨*syn*genesis⟩ **2 :** at the same time ⟨*syn*anthesis⟩ **3** *syn-* **:** CIS- 3 — used esp. of chemical structures in which the atoms or groups on the same side of the molecule are attached to carbon-to-nitrogen or nitrogen-to-nitrogen double bonds ⟨sodium *syn*-benzene-diazoate⟩; opposed to *anti-* (sense 7); see BENZALDOXIME **4 :** like **:** associated ⟨*syn*type⟩

syn *abbr* **1** synchronize; synchronized; synchronizing **2** synergist **3** synonym; synonymous **4** synthetic

syn·a·del·phite \,sinə'del,fīt\ *n* -S [G *synadelphit*, fr. Gk *synadelphos* one that has a brother or sister (fr. *syn-* + *adelphos* brother) + G *-it* -ite — more at -ADELPHOUS] **:** a mineral $(Mn,Mg,Ca,Pb)(AsO_4)(OH)_5$ composed of a basic arsenate of manganese often with other elements (as magnesium, calcium, lead) and occurring in black prismatic crystals and grains (hardness 4.5, sp. gr. 3.5)

synaeresis *var of* SYNERESIS

synaesthesia *var of* SYNESTHESIA

syn·aes·the·sis \,sinəs'thēsəs\ *n* -ES [Gk *synaisthēsis* joint sensation, joint perception, fr. the stem of *synaisthanesthai* to perceive simultaneously, to share in perception (fr. *syn-* + *aisthanesthai* to perceive) + *-sis* — more at AUDIBLE] **:** harmony of different or opposing impulses produced by a work of art ⟨~ of thought and feeling in philosophical poetry⟩ ⟨~ of anxiety and calmness in a tragedy⟩ — compare SYNESTHESIA

synaesthetic *var of* SYNESTHETIC

syn·a·gog·al \¦sinə¦gägəl, -nē¦g- *sometimes* -¦gȯg- *or* **syn·a·gog·i·cal** \-¦gäjəkəl, -¦gäg- *sometimes* -¦gȯgə- *also* **syn·a·gogu·al** *like* SYNAGOGAL\ *adj* **:** of, relating to, or performed in a synagogue ⟨~ ritual⟩ ⟨~ music⟩ ⟨~ worship⟩

syn·a·gogue *or* **syn·a·gog** \'sᵊᵊ,gäg *sometimes* -,gȯg\ *n* -S [ME *synagoge*, fr. OF, fr. LL *synagoga*, fr. Gk *synagōgē* assembly, place of assembly, synagogue, fr. *synagein* to bring together, draw together, fr. *syn-* + *agein* to lead, drive — more at AGENT] **1 a** (1) **:** a Jewish local community under religious and more or less civil jurisdiction (2) **:** a local assembly of Jews organized chiefly for public worship **b :** the building or place of assembly used by Jewish communities primarily for religious worship **2 :** the Jewish religion or communion

syn·al·lag·mat·ic *or* **sin·a·lag·mat·ic** \¦sinə¦lag¦mad·ik, sə¦naləg-\ *adj* [Gk *synallagmatikos* of a contract, fr. *synallagmat-, synallagma* contract, covenant (fr. *synallassein* to enter into a contract, fr. *syn-* + *allassein* to change, exchange, barter, fr. *allos* other) + *-ikos* -ic — more at ELSE] **:** imposing reciprocal obligations and characterized by mutual rights and duties **:** BILATERAL ⟨~ contract⟩ — sometimes distinguished from *commutative*; compare COMMUTATIVE CONTRACT

syn·a·loe·pha *or* **syn·a·le·pha** \,sinə'lēfə\ *n* -S [NL, fr. Gk *synaloiphē, synalifē*, fr. *synaleiphein* to clog up, coalesce, unite two syllables into one, fr. *syn-* + *aleiphein* to anoint, besmear; akin to GK *lipos* fat — more at LEAVE] **:** the blending into one syllable of two vowels of adjacent syllables (as by crasis, synaeresis, synizesis, elision); *esp* **:** a contraction of syllables by obscuring or suppressing a vowel or diphthong at the end of a word before another vowel or diphthong (as in *th' army*, for *the army*)

syn·anastomosis \¦sin, sən+\ *n* [NL, fr. *syn-* + *anastomosis*] **:** an anastomosis involving several vessels

syn·an·ce·ja \,sinən'sējə\ *n, cap* [NL, irreg. fr. Gk *synankeia* place where two glens meet, meeting of waters, fr. *syn-* + *ankos* bend, glen + *-eia* -y — more at ANGLE] **:** a genus (the type of the family Synancejidae) of scorpion fishes comprising the stonefishes

syn·an·gial \sə'nanj(ē)əl\ *adj* [NL *synangium* + E *-al*] **:** of, relating to, or being a synangium

syn·an·gi·um \-jēəm\ *n, pl* **synan·gia** \-j(ē)ə\ [NL, fr. *syn-* + *-angium*] **1 :** the peripheral part of an arterial trunk from which the branches arise in a lower vertebrate — compare PYLANGIUM **2 :** a sorus (as in ferns of the family Marattiaceae) made up of sporangia variously united or cohered into a compound structure

syn·an·tec·tic \¦sinən-¦tektik, -i,nan-\ *or* **syn·an·tet·ic** \-ed·ik\ *adj* [*synantectic* alter. of *synantetic*; *synantetic* fr. (assumed) Gk *synantetos* (verbal of Gk *synantan* to meet, encounter, fr. *syn-* + *antan* to meet face to face, fr. *anta* opposite) + E *-ic*; akin to Gk *anti* against — more at END] **:** formed by the reaction of two other minerals — compare CORONA 2h

syn·an·thae \sə'nan(t)(,)thē\ [NL, fr. Gk *synanthein* to bloom together, fr. *syn-* + *anthein* to bloom, fr. *anthos* flower — more at ANTHOLOGY] *syn of* CYCLANTHALES

syn·an·thous \sə'nan(t)thəs\ *adj* [in sense 1, fr. *syn-* + *-anthous*; in sense 2, fr. Gk *synanthein* + E *-ous*] **1 :** exhibiting synanthy **2 :** having flowers and leaves which appear at the same time

syn·an·thy \'si,nan(t)thē, sə'na-\ *n* -ES [*syn-* + *-anthy*] **:** coalescence of normally separate flowers

syn-anti isomerism \(')ᵊ¦ᵊ(,)ᵊ-\ *n* [*syn-* + *anti-*] **:** cis-trans isomerism in compounds (as oximes, diazoates, and azo compounds) containing one or more carbon-to-nitrogen or nitrogen-to-nitrogen double bonds — compare BENZALDOXIME

syn·a·phea \sinə'fēə\ *also* **syn·a·pheia** \-fē(y)ə, -fīə\ *n* -S [Gk *synapheia*, lit., combination, union, fr. *synaphēs* united, connected (fr. *syn-* + *-aphēs*, fr. *haptein* to fasten) + *-ia* -y — more at APSIS] **:** continuous metrical regularity (as in a group of anapestic verses) such that syllables at the end of one line may form part of a foot completed by syllables at the beginning of the next line

syn·aposematic \¦sin, sən+\ *adj* [*syn-* + *aposematic*] **:** relating to protective mimicry in which defenseless species resemble others having special means of defense

syn·ap·o·sema·tism \,si,napə'sēmə,tizəm, sə,n-, -'sem-\ *n* -S **:** the occurrence or possession of synaposematic mimicry

¹syn·apse \'si,naps, sə'n-\ *n, pl* **synaps·es** \-psəz\ [NL *synapsis*, fr. Gk, contact, point of juncture, fr. *synaptein* to join together (fr. *syn-* + *haptein* to fasten) + *-sis* — more at APSIS] **1 a :** the locus at which the nervous impulse passes from the axon of one neuron to the dendrites of another having the form of an actual boundary between the two nerve fibers or possibly only a surface of contact and constituting the polarizing and selective element typical of most of the nervous systems of the higher animals **b :** the function of affording such communication between neuron processes **2 :** SYNAPSIS 1

²synapse \"\ *vi* -ED/-ING/-S **:** to form a synapse or come together in synapsis ⟨nerve endings ~ in the ganglia⟩

¹syn·ap·sid \sə'napsəd\ *adj* [NL *Synapsida*] **:** of or relating to the Synapsida

²synapsid \"\ *n* -S **:** a reptile or fossil of the subclass Synapsida

syn·ap·si·da \-psədə\ *n pl, cap* [NL, fr. *synapsis* + *-ida*] **:** a subclass of Reptilia comprising extinct reptiles of the Pennsylvanian, Permian, and Triassic, having a single pair of lateral temporal openings in the skull, and usu. held to be ancestral to the true mammals — compare ICTIDOSAURIA, THERAPSIDA

syn·ap·sis \-psəs\ *n, pl* **synap·ses** \-p(,)sēz\ [NL — more at SYNAPSE] **1 :** the process of association of homologous chromosomes with chiasma formation that is characteristic of the first meiotic prophase and that provides the mechanism for crossing-over **2 :** SYNAPSE 1

syn·ap·te \sē,näp'tē\ *n, pl* **synap·tai** \-tā\ [MGk *synaptē*, fr. fem. of *synaptos*] **:** a series of supplicatory prayers in the Eastern Orthodox Church that are in the form of a litany

syn·ap·tic \sə'naptik\ *also* **syn·ap·ti·cal** \-təkəl\ *adj* [fr. NL *synapsis*, after such pairs as E *prolepsis: proleptic, proleptical*] **:** of, relating to, or communicated by a synapse or synapsis ⟨~ transmission⟩ ⟨~ delay⟩ — **synaptically** *adv*

synaptic nervous system *n* **:** a nervous system in which functional contact is through synapses — distinguished from *nerve net*

syn·ap·tic·u·la \,si,nap'tikyələ, sə,n-\ *n, pl* **synapticu·lae** \-,lē, -,lī\ [NL, fr. Gk *synaptos* joined together (fr. *synaptein* to join together) + NL *-i-* + L *-cula*, fem. dim. suffix — more at SYNAPSE] **:** SYNAPTICULUM

syn·ap·tic·u·lar \¦si,nap¦tikyələ(r), sə¦n-\ *or* **syn·ap·tic·u·late** \-lət\ *adj* [NL *synapticulum* + E *-ar* or *-ate*] **:** of, relating to, or constituting a synapticulum

syn·ap·tic·u·lum \,si,nap'tikyələm, sə,n-\ *n, pl* **synapticu·la** \-lə\ [NL, fr. Gk *synaptos* + NL *-i-* + L *-culum*, neut. dim. suffix] **:** one of numerous conical or cylindrical calcareous processes that extend between and unite the adjacent septa of some corals

¹syn·ap·tid \sə'naptəd\ *adj* [NL *Synaptidae*] **:** of or relating to the Synaptidae

²synaptid \"\ *n* -S **:** a sea cucumber of the family Synaptidae

syn·ap·ti·dae \-tə,dē\ *n pl, cap* [NL, fr. *Synapta*, type genus (fr. Gk *synaptē*, fem. of *synaptos* joined together) + *-idae*] **:** a widely distributed family (order Apoda) of sea cucumbers lacking a respiratory tree, having the water-vascular system greatly reduced, and being mostly littoral but including some forms found in very deep waters

syn·ap·tol·o·gy \,si,nap'täləjē, sə,n-\ *n* -ES [Gk *synaptos* joined together + E *-o-* + *-logy*] **:** the scientific study of neural synapses

syn·ap·to·sau·ria \sə,naptə'sȯrēə\ *n pl, cap* [NL, fr. Gk *synaptos* + NL *-sauria*] **:** a subclass of Reptilia comprising Permian and Mesozoic typically aquatic or amphibious reptiles with temporal openings high on the roof of the skull and including the orders Protorosauria and Sauropterygia — **syn·ap·to·sau·ri·an** \ᵊ¦ᵊᵊ¦ᵊrēən\ *adj*

syn·aptychus \¦sin, sən+\ *n* [NL, fr. *syn-* + *aptychus*] **:** an operculum of two parts united in the median line (as in some ammonites)

synarchism *usu cap, var of* SINARQUISM

syn·ar·chy \'sinərkē, -,närkē\ *n* -ES [Gk *synarchia*, fr. *synarchein* to rule jointly with (fr. *syn-* + *archein* to rule, begin) + *-ia* -y — more at ARCHI-] **:** joint rule **:** joint sovereignty

syn·ar·tet·ic \¦si,när¦ted·ik, -,nər-\ *adj* [fr. (assumed) Gk *synartētos* (verbal of *synartan* to join together) + E *-ic* — more at ASYNARTETIC] **:** consisting of or relating to a succession of cola not separated by diaeresis **:** metrically continuous — opposed to *asynartetic*

syn·ar·thro·dia \¦si,när¦thrōdēə\ *n* -S [NL, fr. *syn-* + *arthrodia*] **:** SYNARTHROSIS

syn·ar·thro·di·al \-ēəl\ *adj* [NL *synarthrodia* + E *-al*] **:** of, relating to, or being a synarthrosis — **syn·ar·thro·di·al·ly** \-ēəlē\ *adv*

syn·ar·thro·sis \-ōsəs\ *n, pl* **synarthro·ses** \-ō,sēz\ [NL, fr. Gk *synarthrōsis*, fr. *syn-* + *arthrōsis* arthrosis — more at ARTHROSIS] **:** an immovable articulation in which the bones are united by intervening fibrous connective tissues

syn·as·try \sə'nastrē, 'si,nas-, 'sinəs-\ *n* -ES [LL *synastria*, fr. Gk, fr. *syn-* + *astr-* + *-ia* -y] **:** concurrence of starry position or influence upon two persons **:** similarity of condition or fortune prefigured by astrology

syn·ax·a·rion \,sē,näk'sär(,)yō(n), ,si,nak'sa(a)rēən\ *or* **syn·ax·a·ry** \sə'naksərē *or* **syn·ax·a·ri·um** \,si,nak'sa(a)rēəm\ *n, pl* **synaxa·ria** \-är(,)yä, -äryə, -a(a)rēə\ *or* **synaxaries** [*synaxarion* fr. MGk, fr. *synaxis* + *-arion* -ary (fr. L *-arium*); *synaxary, synaxarium* fr. ML *synaxarium*, fr. MGk *synaxarion*] **:** a short narrative of the life of a saint or exposition of a feast included in the Menaion and read in religious services of the Eastern Orthodox Church; *also* **:** a liturgical book containing such narratives

syn·ax·a·rist \sə'naksərəst\ *n* -S [*synaxarion* + *-ist*] **:** the author of a synaxarion

syn·ax·is \sə'naksəs *or esp in sense 2* 'sēnək(,)sēs\ *n, pl* **synax·es** \-ak(,)sēz, -ək(,)sēs\ [LL, fr. LGk, fr. Gk *synagein* to bring together, draw together + *-sis* — more at SYNAGOGUE] **1 :** an assembly met for worship; *esp* **:** a congregation in the early Church gathered for a liturgical service **2 :** an early part of the divine liturgy of the Eastern Orthodox Church

syn·branch \'sin,braŋk\ *adj* [NL *Synbranchus*] **:** of or relating to Synbranchidae

syn·bran·chi·dae \sin'braŋkə,dē\ *n pl, cap* [NL, fr. *Synbranchus*, type genus (fr. *syn-* + L *branchia* gill) + *-idae*] **:** a family (suborder Synbranchoidea) of tropical freshwater and brackish water elongated fishes

syn·bran·chii \-kē,ī\ [NL, fr. *Synbranchus*] *syn of* SYMBRANCHII

syn·bran·choi·dea \,sin,braŋ'kȯidēə\ *n pl, cap* [NL, fr. *Synbranchus*, genus of synbranch fishes + *-oidea*] **:** a suborder of Symbranchii coextensive with the family Synbranchidae

¹sync *also* **synch** \'siŋk\ *n* -S [by shortening] **:** SYNCHRONIZATION, SYNCHRONISM ⟨sound track out of ~ with the actors' lips⟩

²sync \"\ *vb* **synced** \-ŋkt\ **synced** \"\ **syncing** \-ŋkiŋ\ **syncs** [by shortening] **:** SYNCHRONIZE ⟨each changeover should be noted on the film . . . for convenience in later playback ~*ing* —*Cinematographer*⟩

³sync \"\ *adj* [¹*sync*] **:** relating to or having to do with synchronization **:** SYNCHRO

sync *abbr* synchronism; synchronizing; synchronous

syn·carida \(')sin, -iŋ+\ *n pl, cap* [NL, fr. *syn-* + *Carida*] **:** a division of Malacostraca coextensive with Anaspidacea

syn·car·pous \(')sin¦kärpəs, -iŋ¦k-\ *adj* [*syn-* + *-carpous*] **:** having the carpels of the gynoecium united in a compound ovary — opposed to *apocarpous*

syn·car·py \'ᵊ,ᵊpē\ *n* -ES [*syncarpous* + *-y*] **:** a syncarpous state or quality

syncaryon *var of* SYNKARYON

¹syn·categorematic \¦si|n, sə|, |ŋ+\ *adj* [LL *syncategoremat-, syncategorema* + E *-ic*] **:** not capable of standing alone as a term in a proposition **:** having significance only in conjunction with another expression ⟨*left* and *up* are ~ terms⟩ ⟨punctuation marks are ~ signs⟩ — opposed to *categorematic* — **syn·categorematically** \"+\ *adv*

²syncategorematic \"\ *n* -S **:** a syncategorematic word or sign

syn·cat·e·go·reme \sən'kad·əgə,rēm, saŋ'k-; ,sinkə'tegə,rēm, ,siŋk-\ *n, pl* **syncatego·rema·ta** \ᵊ¦ᵊᵊᵊ'remədə, ᵊᵊ,ᵊᵊ-, -'rēm-\ [LL *syncategorema*, fr. LGk *synkatēgorēma*, fr. Gk *synkatēgorein* to predicate jointly, fr. *syn-* + *katēgorein* to predicate — more at CATEGORY] **:** a syncategorematic term

syn·cel·lus \sən'seləs\ *n, pl* **syncel·li** \-e,lī\ [ML, fr. MGk *synkellos*, fr. LGk, cell mate, fr. Gk *syn-* + LGk *kella* cell, fr. L *cella* — more at CELL] **:** a diocesan official in the Eastern Church serving usu. as the secretary and chaplain of a bishop or metropolitan

syn·ceph·a·lus \sən'sefələs\ *n, pl* **syncepha·li** \-fə,lī\ [NL, fr. *syn-* + *-cephalus*] **:** a twin fetus having the two heads fused

syn·cerebral \(ˌ)sin, sən+\ *adj* [NL *syncerebrum* + E *-al*] **:** relating to or having a syncerebrum

syn·cerebrum \"+\ *n* [NL, fr. *syn-* + *cerebrum*] **:** a brain (as of an insect) consisting of several segments

synch *abbr* synchronize; synchronized; synchronizing

syn·chi·site \'siŋkə,sīt, -ink-\ *n* -s [irreg. fr. Gk *synchysis* mixture, confusion (fr. *synchein* to pour together, confound, confuse — fr. *syn-* + *chein* to pour — + *-sis*) + E *-ite* — more at FOUND] **:** a mineral (Ce,La)Ca$(CO_3)_2$F related to parisite and consisting of a fluoride and carbonate of calcium, cerium, and lanthanum

syn·chon·dro·sial \ˌsin,kän'drōzh(ē)əl, -iŋ,k-\ *adj* [NL *synchondrosis* + E *-al*] **:** of, relating to, or being a synchondrosis — **syn·chon·dro·sial·ly** \-əlē\ *adv*

syn·chon·dro·sis \ˌ=ˌ='drōsəs\ *n, pl* **synchondro·ses** \-ō,sēz\ [NL, fr. Gk *synchondrōsis*, fr. *syn-* + *chondr-* + *-ōsis* -osis] **:** an immovable skeletal articulation in which the union is cartilaginous

syn·chon·drot·o·my \-'drädəmē\ *n* -ES [ISV *synchondro-* (fr. NL *synchondrosis*) + *-tomy*] **:** SYMPHYSIOTOMY

syn·chorial \(')si|n, sə|, |ŋ+\ *adj* [*syn-* + *chorial*] **:** having a common placenta — used of twin or multiple fetuses

¹syn·chro \'sin(ˌ)krō, -iŋ(-\ *n* -s [*synchronous*] **:** SELSYN

²synchro \"\ *adj* [*synchro-*] **:** adapted to synchronization ⟨~ camera shutter⟩; *specif* **:** SYNCHROMESH

synchro- *comb form* [*synchronized & synchronous*] **:** synchronized **:** synchronous ⟨*synchro*flash⟩ ⟨*synchro*mesh⟩

synchro-cyclotron \ˌ=(ˌ)=+\ *n* [*synchro-* + *cyclotron*] **:** a modified cyclotron that achieves greater energies for the charged particles by compensating for the variation in mass that the particles experience with increasing velocity

synchroflash \'=ˌ=ˌ=\ *adj* [*syncro-* + *flash*] **:** employing or produced with a synchronizing mechanism that fires a flash lamp the instant the camera shutter opens ⟨~ photography⟩

¹synchromesh \'=ˌ=ˌ=\ *adj* [*synchro-* + *mesh*] **:** designed for effecting synchronized shifting of gears ⟨~ automobile transmission⟩ ⟨~ construction⟩

²synchromesh \"\ *n* **:** a synchromesh gear or gear system

syn·chro·nal \'siŋkrənᵊl, -ink-\ *adj* [LL *synchronus* synchronous + E *-al* — more at SYNCHRONOUS] **:** SYNCHRONOUS

syn·chro·ne·ity \ˌ=='nēəd·ē\ *n* -ES [*synchronous* + *-eity* (as in *spontaneity*)] **:** the state of being synchronous **:** SYNCHRONISM ⟨theory of glacial ~ over the northern hemisphere —S.A.Cain⟩

syn·chron·ic \(')si|n|'kränik, sə|n|'k-, |ŋ|, -änēk\ *also* **syn·chron·i·cal** \-änəkəl, -änēk-\ *adj* [LL *synchronos* synchronous + E *-ic*, *-ical*] **1 :** SYNCHRONOUS **2 a** [F *synchronique*, fr. LL *synchronos* + F *-ique* -ic, -ical] **:** DESCRIPTIVE 4 ⟨~ grammar⟩ — contrasted with *diachronic* **b :** concerned with the complex of events existing in a limited time period (as the present) and ignoring historical antecedents ⟨the functionalist emphasis upon institutional interrelationships has resulted in a ~ view of society⟩ — contrasted with *diachronic* **3** *of taxa* **:** occurring in the same segment of geologic time **:** CONTEMPORANEOUS — compare ALLOCHRONIC — **syn·chron·i·cal·ly** \-änək(ə)lē, -änēk-, -li\ *adv*

syn·chro·nic·i·ty \ˌsiŋkrə'nisəd·ē, -ink-\ *n* -ES **:** SYNCHRONISM 1

syn·chro·nism \'siŋkrə,nizəm, 'sink-\ *n* -s [LL *synchronos* synchronous + E *-ism*] **1 :** the quality or fact of being synchronous or simultaneous **:** concurrence of acts, events, or developments in time **:** coincident movement or existence **:** SIMULTANEOUSNESS ⟨find a general ~ in the secular and religious phases of lyric growth —H.O.Taylor⟩ **2 :** chronological arrangement of historical events and personages so as to indicate coincidence or coexistence; *also* **:** a table showing such concurrences ⟨in that book were . . . ~*s* of the kings of Ireland with the kings and emperors of the world —*Irish Digest*⟩ **3 a :** a representation in the same picture of two or more events which occurred at different times **b :** historical accuracy in detail in period architecture or interior decoration **4 a :** the state of having the same period or the same period and phase **b :** the condition of excessive rolling obtaining when a ship's rolling period is equal to the wave period or to one half the wave period **5 :** the concurrence in time of the picture image and the corresponding sound during projection on a motion-picture or television screen

syn·chro·nis·tic \ˌ=='nistik\ *adj* [LL *synchronos* + E *-istic*] **:** relating to, manifesting, or involving synchronism **:** SYNCHRONOUS — **syn·chro·nis·ti·cal** \-tə̇kəl\ *adj* — **syn·chro·nis·ti·cal·ly** \-tə̇k(ə)lē\ *adv*

syn·chro·ni·za·tion \ˌ==nə'zāshən, -ˌnī-\ *n* -s **:** the act or result of synchronizing **:** concurrence of events or motions in respect to time

syn·chro·nize \'=ˌ=,nīz\ *vb* -ED/-ING/-S *see -ize in Explan Notes* [LL *synchronos* synchronous + E *-ize*] *vi* **1 :** to happen or take place at the same time **:** be synchronous ⟨the voyages of discovery *synchronized* with the emergence of a capitalist economy —H.J.Laski⟩ ⟨action and sound must ~ perfectly⟩ ~ *vt* **1 :** to represent or arrange (events) so as to indicate coincidence or coexistence ⟨~ events of biblical and classical history⟩ **2 :** to cause to agree in time ⟨~ two watches⟩ **:** make synchronous in operation ⟨~ troop movements and artillery fire⟩ ⟨~ factory operations⟩ **3 a :** to make (dialogue, music, or sound effects) exactly simultaneous with the action shown in a motion picture **b :** to maintain a time interlock throughout (a television system) so that the scanning beams in the studio and the receiver move together **c :** to adjust (a camera shutter) so that a flashbulb fires at the instant the shutter opens

synchronized shifting *n* **:** a changing from one speed gear to another in a motor vehicle through a transmission employing a device by which both gears are brought to the same speed before the shift can be made

synchronized swimming *n* **:** exhibition swimming in which the movements of one or more swimmers are synchronized with a musical accompaniment so as to form changing patterns in the manner of dancers

syn·chro·niz·er \-zə(r)\ *n* -s **:** one that synchronizes **:** a device to indicate, produce, or maintain synchronous motion: as **a :** a regulator for a system of clocks **b :** a device for synchronizing the firing of a flashbulb with the opening of the camera shutter

syn·chron·o·graph \sin'kränə,graf, siŋ'k-, -gráf\ *n* [*synchronous* + *-o-* + *-graph*] **:** an automatic telegraph in which the alternating current which transmits the signals is regulated by a perforated paper ribbon traveling in synchronism with the generator

syn·chronological \(ˌ)si|n, sə|, |ŋ+\ *adj* **:** showing simultaneous occurrence or existence ⟨~ table of historical events⟩

syn·chronology \ˌsin, ˌsiŋ+\ *n* [*syn-* + *chronology*] **:** systematic arrangement of synchronous events

syn·chron·o·scope \sən'kränə,skōp, səŋ'k-\ *n* [*synchronous* + *-o-* + *-scope*] **:** SYNCHROSCOPE

syn·chro·nous \'siŋkrənəs, -ink-\ *adj* [LL *synchronos*, fr. Gk, fr. *syn-* + *chronos* time] **1 :** happening, existing, or arising at the same time ⟨having their beginning at different times, although their endings were ~ —*Encyc. Americana*⟩ ⟨recovery was ~ with therapy —*Jour. Amer. Med. Assoc.*⟩ **2 :** recurring or operating at exactly the same periods **:** marked by strict and exact coincidence in time, rate, or rhythm ⟨the ~ action of a bird's wings in flight⟩ ⟨~ in step with clocks⟩ **3 :** involving or indicating synchronism ⟨~ account of World War II⟩ **4 :** having the same period; *also* **:** having the same period and phase ⟨~ vibrations⟩ ⟨~ oscillations⟩ **syn** see CONTEMPORARY

synchronous clock *n* **:** ELECTRIC CLOCK e

synchronous condenser *n* **:** a synchronous phase advancer; *usu* **:** an overexcited synchronous motor equipped with damper windings to facilitate starting and to prevent surging and hunting — called also *rotary condenser*

synchronous converter *n* **:** a synchronous machine that converts from alternating to direct current or vice versa — called also *rotary converter*

syn·chro·nous·ly *adv* **1 :** at the same time **:** SIMULTANEOUSLY, CONTEMPORANEOUSLY **2 :** at the same speed or frequency

synchronous machine *n* **:** a dynamoelectric machine (as a generator or motor) that has a constant magnetic field and an armature which receives or delivers alternating current in synchronism with the motion of the machine and at a frequency equal to the product of the number of pairs of poles and the speed of the machine in revolutions per second — compare ALTERNATOR, CONVERTER b, MOTOR 4, RECTIFIER 3, SYNCHRONOUS CONVERTER

synchronous motor *n* **:** an electric motor having a speed that is strictly proportional to the frequency of the operating current

synchronous speed *n* **:** a definite speed for an alternating-current machine that is dependent on the frequency of the supply circuit because the rotating member passes one pair of poles for each alternation of the alternating current

synchronous telegraph *n* **:** MULTIPLE SYNCHRONOUS TELEGRAPH

syn·chro·ny \'siŋkrənē, -ink-\ *n* -ES [*synchronous* + *-y*] **1 :** synchronous or simultaneous occurrence **2 :** synchronistic arrangement or treatment; *specif* **:** synchronic linguistics — contrasted with *diachrony*

synchros *pl of* SYNCHRO

syn·chro·scope \-rə,skōp\ *n* [*synchro-* + *-scope*] **:** any of several devices for showing whether two associated machines or moving parts are operating in synchronism with each other or for giving an indication of their relative phase; *esp* **:** an instrument that permits the pilot of a multiengine airplane to synchronize the engines so as to prevent disagreeable beats and vibration

synchro-shutter \ˌsin(ˌ)krō, -iŋ(-+\ *n* [*synchro-* + *shutter*] **:** a camera shutter containing an electrical switching device to fire a flashbulb at the instant the shutter opens

synchro-sunlight \"+\ *adj* [*synchro-* + *sunlight*] **:** relating to the use of flash lamps as a supplement to daylight exposure

syn·chro·tron \'siŋkrə,trän, -ink-\ *n* -s [*synchro-* + *-tron*] **:** an apparatus for imparting very high speeds to charged particles (as electrons, protons) by means of a combination of a high-frequency electric field (as in the cyclotron) and a low-frequency magnetic field (as in the betatron)

synchs *pl of* SYNC

syn·chyt·ri·um \sən'ki·trēəm, səŋ'k-\ *n, cap* [NL, fr. *syn-* + Gk *chytrion* small earthen pot, dim. of *chytra* earthen pot — more at CHYTRA] **:** a genus (the type of the family Synchytriaceae of the order Chytridiales) of simple parasitic fungi having no mycelium but a unicellular thallus that at maturity functions either as single resting sporangia or as a sorus of sporangia surrounded by a common membrane — see POTATO WART

syncing *pres part of* SYNC

syn·clastic \(')si|n, sə|, |ŋ+\ *adj* [*syn-* + Gk *klastos* broken + E *-ic* — more at CLASTIC] **:** curved toward the same side in all directions — used of a surface (as of a sphere) that in all directions around any point bends away from a tangent plane toward the same side; opposed to *anticlastic*

¹syn·cli·nal \(')si|n|'klīnᵊl, sə|n|'k-, |ŋ|\ *adj* [*syn-* + Gk *klinein* to lean + E *-al* — more at LEAN] **1 :** inclined down from opposite directions so as to meet **2 :** having or relating to a folded rock structure in which the sides or limbs dip toward a common line or plane ⟨~ fold⟩ ⟨~ axis⟩ — opposed to *anticlinal* — **syn·cli·nal·ly** \-'lē\ *adv*

²synclinal \"\ *n* -s **:** SYNCLINE

synclinal valley *n* **:** a valley produced by or coinciding in position with a synclinal fold

syn·cline \'sin,klīn, 'siŋ,k-\ *n* -s [back-formation fr. ¹*synclinal*] **:** a trough of stratified rock in which the beds dip toward each other from either side — compare ANTICLINE

syn·clin·i·cal \-klinəkəl\ *adj* [*syncline* + *-ical*] **:** SYNCLINAL

syn·cli·nore \'siŋklə,nō(ə)r, -ink-\ *n* -s [NL *synclinorium*] **:** SYNCLINORIUM

syn·cli·no·ri·al \ˌ=='nōrēəl\ *or* **syn·cli·no·ri·an** \-ēən\ *adj* [NL *synclinorium* + E *-al* or *-an*] **:** relating to or resembling a synclinorium

syn·cli·no·ri·um \ˌ=='rēəm\ *n, pl* **synclino·ria** \-ēə\ [NL, fr. ISV *syncline* + NL *-orium*] **:** a compound flexure of the earth's crust having the form of an inverted anticlinorium

syn·clit·ic \(')si|n|'klid·ik, sə|n|'k-, |ŋ|\ *adj* [fr. (assumed) Gk *synklitos* (verbal of Gk *synklinein* to lean together, fr. *syn-* + *klinein* to lean) + E *-ic* — more at LEAN] **:** parallel to the axis of the pelvis — used of the planes of the fetal head in labor; compare ENCLITIC

syn·co·pal \'siŋkəpəl, -ink-\ *adj* [*syncope* + *-al*] **:** of, relating to, or characterized by syncope ⟨~ attack⟩

syn·co·pate \'siŋkə,pāt, -ink-, *usu* -ād·+V\ *vt* -ED/-ING/-S [ML *syncopatus*, past part. of *syncopare*, fr. LL *syncope*, *syncopa*] **1 a :** to shorten by syncope ⟨~ *suppose* to *s'pose*⟩ **:** produce by syncope ⟨*bewild'ring* is *syncopated* from *bewildering*⟩ **b :** to omit (a sound or letter) in the interior of a word ⟨~ the *o* of *policeman*⟩ **c :** to cut short **:** CLIP, ABBREVIATE **2 :** to modify or affect (musical rhythm) by syncopation

syncopated *adj* [ML *syncopatus* + E *-ed*] **1 :** marked by or exhibiting syncopation ⟨~ rhythm⟩ ⟨~ melody⟩ ⟨poetry using many ~ forms of words⟩ **2 :** cut short **:** ABBREVIATED, ABRIDGED ⟨correct the ~ calendar of memory —Dixon Wecter⟩ ⟨cleared his throat . . . producing a small, ~ noise —Dorothy Parker⟩

syncopated counterpoint *n* **:** counterpoint in which one note is added to each note of the cantus firmus after a fixed rhythmic interval

syncopated perforation *n* **:** INTERRUPTED PERFORATION

syn·co·pa·tion \ˌ=='pāshən\ *n* -s [ML *syncopation-*, *syncopatio*, fr. *syncopatus* + L *-ion-*, *-io* -ion] **1 :** SYNCOPE 2 **2 a :** a temporary displacement or shifting of the regular metrical accent in a musical composition occurring typically when a tone is begun on an unaccented beat and continued through the following accented beat or when a tone begins after the commencement of a beat and is continued into the following beat **3 :** a rhythm or dance step in syncopated time ⟨shoes scuffing ~*s* on the cement sidewalk —Booth Tarkington⟩

syncopation 2

syn·co·pa·tive \'=ˌ=,pād·iv\ *adj* **:** relating to syncopation ⟨all sorts of ~ subtleties that are quite foreign to European music —Aaron Copland⟩

syn·co·pa·tor \-ād·ə(r)\ *n* -s **:** one that uses syncopation; *esp* **:** a player of jazz music

syn·co·pe \'siŋkə(ˌ)pē, -ink-, -ˌpi\ *n* -s [LL, fr. Gk *synkopē*, fr. *synkoptein* to chop up, cut short, fr. *syn-* + *koptein* to strike, cut off — more at CAPON] **1 :** a partial or complete temporary suspension of respiration and circulation due to cerebral ischemia and characterized by sudden pallor, coldness of the skin, and partial or complete unconsciousness **:** FAINT, SWOON **2 a :** the loss of one or more sounds or letters in the interior of a word (as in *di'mond* for *diamond* or *fo'c'sle* for *forecastle*) — compare APHAERESIS, APOCOPE, CONTRACTION, HYPHAERESIS **b :** a form resulting from such a loss of sounds or letters **3 :** suppression or omission of a short syllable within a metrical foot or measure usu. with compensating protraction of an adjacent long **4** *obs* **:** SYNCOPATION 2

syn·craniate \(')si|n, sə|, |ŋ+\ *adj* [*syn-* + *craniate*] **:** relating to or having a skull with which certain vertebral elements are fused ⟨the skulls of amniotes are considered to be ~⟩ — opposed to *archaecraniate*

syn·cranium \"+\ *n* [NL, fr. *syn-* + *cranium*] **:** a syncraniate skull

syn·cran·te·ri·an \ˌsin,kran·'tirēən, ˌsiŋ,k-\ *also* **syn·cran·ter·ic** \-terik\ *adj* [*syn-* + Gk *krantēres* wisdom teeth + E *-ian* or *-ic*] **:** having the teeth in a continuous row — compare DIACRANTERIAN

syn·cret·ic \(')si|n|'kred·ik, sə|n|'k-, |ŋ|\ *adj* [*syncretism* + *-ic*] **1 :** characterized or brought about by syncretism **:** aiming at or making for syncretism **:** SYNCRETISTIC ⟨~ religious sect⟩ **2 :** having absorbed the functions of one or more other grammatical cases ⟨the Latin ablative is a ~ case⟩

syn·cre·tion \sən'krēshən, səŋ'k-\ *n* -s [*syncretic* + *-ion*] **:** an instance of syncretism **:** act of syncretizing

syn·cre·tism \'siŋkrə,tizəm, 'sink-\ *n* -s [NL *syncretismus*, fr. Gk *synkrētismos* federation of Cretan cities, fr. *synkrētizein* to unite against a common enemy] **1 :** the reconciliation or union of conflicting (as religious) beliefs or an effort intending such; *specif* **:** a movement of a Lutheran party in the 17th century led by George Calixtus seeking the union of Protestant sects with each other and with the Roman Catholic Church **2 :** flagrant compromise in religion or philosophy **:** eclecticism that is illogical or leads to inconsistency **:** uncritical acceptance of conflicting or divergent beliefs or principles **3 :** the developmental process of historical growth within a religion by accretion and coalescence of different and often orig. conflicting forms of belief and practice through the interaction with or supersession of other religions **4 :** the union or fusion into one of two or more orig. different inflectional forms

¹syn·cre·tist \-rəd·əst\ *n* -s [fr. *syncretism*, after such pairs as E *fatalism: fatalist*] **:** one who advocates or promotes syncretism

²syncretist \"\ *adj* **:** SYNCRETISTIC

syn·cre·tis·tic \ˌ=krə'tistik\ *adj* **:** of or relating to syncretism or syncretists ⟨~ writings⟩ ⟨~ adaptation of faith⟩

syn·cre·tize \'=ˌ=,tīz\ *vb* -ED/-ING/-S [NL *syncretizare*, fr. Gk *synkrētizein* to unite against a common enemy (as did the Cretans), fr. *syn-* + *Krēt*, *Krēs* Cretan + *-izein* -ize] *vi* **1 :** to become fused or united **2 :** to favor or practice syncretism ~ *vt* **:** to attempt to unite and harmonize (as conflicting principles) esp. without critical examination or real logical unity

syncrisis *n* [LL, fr. Gk, combination, comparison, fr. *synkrinein* to combine, compare (fr. *syn-* + *krinein* to separate, judge) + *-sis* — more at RIDDLE] *obs* **:** comparison of contraries or opposites

syn·cryp·ta \sin'kriptə, siŋ'k-\ *n, cap* [NL, fr. *syn-* + Gk *kryptē*, fem. of *kryptos* hidden — more at CRYPT] **:** a genus of biflagellate free-swimming flagellates (order Chrysomonadina) occurring as spheroidal colonies and sometimes causing in water supplies odors suggestive of overripe cucumbers

syn·cryp·tic \(')=ˌkriptik\ *adj* [*syn-* + *cryptic*] **:** of, relating to, or being a protective resemblance in appearance in which basically unlike organisms are similar (as in color) often through a common adaptation to their environment; *also* **:** exhibiting such resemblance ⟨~ species⟩ — compare SYNTECHNIC

syncs *pl of* SYNC, *pres 3d sing of* SYNC

syn·cyte \'sin,sīt\ *n* -s [NL *syncytium*] **:** SYNCYTIUM

syn·cy·tial \(')sin'sishəl, sən's-\ *adj* [NL *syncytium* + E *-al*] **:** of, relating to, or constituting syncytium ⟨~ tissue⟩

syn·cy·tio·trophoblast \sən'sishē(ˌ)ō+\ *n* [NL *syncitium* + *-o-* + E *trophoblast*] **:** SYNTROPHOBLAST

syn·cy·tium \sən'sish(ē)əm\ *n, pl* **syncy·tia** \-ə\ [NL, fr. *syn-* + *cyt-* + *-ium*] **1 :** a multinucleate mass of protoplasm resulting from fusion of cells (as in the plasmodium of a slime mold) **2 :** COENOCYTE 1

syn·cy·toid \'sinsə,tȯid\ *adj* [NL *syncytium* + E *-oid*] **:** of, relating to, or resembling a syncytium

synd *abbr* syndicate

¹syn·dac·tyl *or* **syn·dac·tyle** \(')sin'daktᵊl, sən'd-\ *adj* [F *syndactyle*, fr. *syn-* + Gk *daktylos* finger] **:** having two or more digits wholly or partly united — see SYNDACTYLISM

²syndactyl *or* **syndactyle** \"\ *n* -s **:** a syndactyl bird or mammal

syn·dac·ty·la \ˌ='daktələ\ *n pl, cap* [NL, fr. *syn-* + *-dactyla* (fr. Gk *daktylos* finger)] *in some classifications* **:** a primary division of Marsupialia comprising forms in which the second and third pedal digits are bound together into a single double-nailed toe and being approximately equal to Diprotodontia

syn·dac·tyl·ia \ˌsin,dak'tilēə\ *n* -s [NL, fr. ISV ¹*syndactyl* + NL *-ia*] **:** SYNDACTYLISM

syn·dac·tyl·ic \ˌsin,dak'tilik\ *or* **syn·dac·ty·lous** \(')sin'daktələs, sən'd-\ *adj* [F *syndactyle* + E *-ic*, *-ous*] **:** SYNDACTYL

syn·dac·ty·lism \ˌ='daktə,lizəm\ *n* -s **:** the state of being syndactyl **:** a union of two or more digits that is normal in many birds (as kingfishers, motmots, bee eaters, or hornbills) in which some of the toes are united and in some mammals (as the kangaroos and some other marsupials) and occurs in man as a familial anomaly marked by webbing of two or more fingers or toes

syn·dac·ty·ly \(')sin'daktəlē, sən'd-\ *n* -ES **:** SYNDACTYLISM

syn·de·re·sis \ˌsində'rēsəs\ *or* **syn·te·re·sis** \-ntə-\ *n* -ES [ML, fr. Gk *syntērēsis* preservation, fr. *syntērein* to preserve (fr. *syn-* + *tērein* to guard, observe) + *-sis*; akin to Gk *tinein* to pay — more at PAIN] **1 :** inborn knowledge of the primary principles of moral action — distinguished from *syneidesis* **2 :** the essence, ground, or center of the soul that enters into communion with God **:** the spark or emanation of divinity in the soul

syn·de·sis \'sindəsəs\ *n* -ES [NL, fr. Gk, action of binding together, fr. *syndein* to bind together + *-sis* — more at ASYNDETON] **:** SYNAPSIS 1

syndesm- *or* **syndesmo-** *comb form* [Gk *syndesmos*, fr. *syndein* to bind together] **:** ligament ⟨*syndesm*osis⟩ **:** connection **:** contact ⟨*syndesmo*chorial⟩

syn·des·mo·chorial \(ˌ)sin'dezmə+\ *adj* [*syndesm-* + *chorial*] *of a placenta* **:** having fetal epithelium in contact with maternal submucosa (as in ruminants) — compare ENDOTHELIOCHORIAL, EPITHELIOCHORIAL, HEMOCHORIAL

syn·des·mo·sis \ˌsin,dez'mōsəs\ *n, pl* **syndesmo·ses** \-ō,sēz\ [NL, fr. *syndesm-* + *-osis*] **:** an articulation in which the contiguous surfaces of the bones are rough and are bound together by an interosseous ligament

syn·des·mot·ic \ˌ=ˌ='mäd·ik\ *adj* [fr. NL *syndesmosis*, after such pairs as NL *hypnosis: E hypnotic*] **:** relating to or marked by syndesmosis

syn·det \'sin,det\ *n* -s [*synthetic detergent*] **:** DETERGENT c

syn·det·ic \(')sin'ded·ik, sən'de-\ *adj* [Gk *syndetikos*, fr. *syndetos* bound together + *-ikos* -ic — more at ASYNDETON] **:** CONNECTING, CONNECTIVE, INTERCONNECTED ⟨~ pronoun⟩; *also* **:** marked by a conjunctive ⟨~ relative clause⟩ — **syn·det·i·cal·ly** \-ed·ək(ə)lē\ *adv*

syn·dic \'sindik, -dēk\ *n* -s [F, fr. LL *syndicus*, fr. Gk *syndikos* court assistant, advocate, fr. *syn-* + *dikē* right, judgment — more at DICTION] **1 :** an officer of government invested with different powers (as magisterial or mayoral) in different countries **2 :** an agent of a corporation (as a university) or of a body of men engaged in a business enterprise **3 a :** an advocate, agent, or attorney for a city, university, or corporate body **b :** one appointed to manage an estate as a trustee **c** *Louisiana* **:** the assignee of a bankrupt **4 :** one of various officials in cities of ancient Greece having duties similar to those of a judge or advocate

syn·di·cal \-dəkəl, -dēk-\ *adj* [F, fr. *syndic* + *-al*] **1 :** of or relating to a syndic or to a committee that assumes the powers of a syndic **2 :** of or relating to syndicalism ⟨~ organization of capital and labor⟩

syn·di·cal·ism \-kə,lizəm\ *n* -s [F *syndicalisme*, fr. (*chambre*) *syndicale* trade union (fr. *chambre* chamber + *syndicale*, fem. of *syndical*) + *-isme* -ism] **1 :** a revolutionary political movement that aims by the general strike and direct action of labor unions to overthrow parliamentary democracy and establish a corporate society with general control in the hands of trade unions and workers' cooperatives — called also *anarcho-syndicalism*; compare CRIMINAL SYNDICALISM, MARXISM **2 :** TRADE UNIONISM

¹syn·di·cal·ist \-ləst\ *n* -s [F *syndicaliste*, fr. (*chambre*) *syndicale* + *-iste* -ist] **:** an advocate or adherent of syndicalism

²syndicalist \"\ *or* **syn·di·cal·is·tic** \ˌ==kə'listik, -tēk\ *adj* **:** relating to or advocating syndicalism

¹syn·di·cate \'sində,kāt, *usu* -ād·+V\ *vb* -ED/-ING/-S [in sense 1, fr. ML *syndicatus*, past part. of *syndicare*, fr. LL *syndicus* syndic; in other senses, fr. ²*syndicate* — more at SYNDIC] *vt* **1** *obs* **:** CENSURE, JUDGE **2 :** to subject to or bring under the control of a syndicate ⟨~ a mining enterprise⟩ ⟨~ a bond issue⟩ **:** combine into or manage as a syndicate ⟨~ a number of newspapers⟩ **3 a :** to sell (as an article or a cartoon) for publication through a syndicate ⟨a *syndicated* feature in the Sunday supplement⟩ **b :** to sell (as an article or a cartoon) for publication in many newspapers or periodicals at once ⟨never able to ~ his column widely —G.S.Perry⟩ ~ *vi* **:** to unite to form a syndicate — **syn·di·ca·tion** \ˌ=='kāshən\ *n* -s

²syn·di·cate \'sindəkət, -dēk-, *usu* -kəd·+V\ *n* -s [F *syndicat*, fr. *syndic* + *-at* -ate] **1 a :** the office or jurisdiction of a syndic **b :** a council, committee, or body of syndics **2 :** an association of persons officially authorized to undertake some duty or to negotiate some business **3 a :** a group of persons or concerns who combine under a usu. temporary agreement to carry out a particular transaction ⟨~ of investment houses for underwriting a bond issue⟩ ⟨~ of real estate men formed to buy an office building⟩ **b :** CARTEL 4 **c :** a loose association of racketeers in control of organized crime (as the policy racket, bookmaking, prostitution) **4 :** a business concern that sells to the press materials (as special articles, photographs, or comic strips) for publication in a number of newspapers or periodicals simultaneously **5 :** a group of newspapers under one management **:** a newspaper chain

syn·di·ca·tor \-də,kād·ə(r), -ātə-\ *n* -s **:** one that syndicates **:** one that manages or operates a syndicate

syn·diploidy \(ˈ)sin, sən+\ *n* [*syn-* + *diploidy*] **:** doubling of the gametic chromosome number by reassociation of the daughter groups of meiotic chromosomes at any time after the first meiotic metaphase

syn·drome \ˈsin,drōm *sometimes* -,drəm *or* -drə(,)mē *or* -drəmi\ *n* -s [NL, fr. Gk *syndromē* act of running together, combination, syndrome, fr. *syn-* + *-dromē* (fr. *dramein* to run) — more at DROMEDARY] **1 :** a group of symptoms or signs typical of a disease, disturbance, condition, or lesion in animals or plants ⟨shoulder-arm ~⟩ ⟨~ of genetic abnormalities⟩ ⟨starvation ~⟩ ⟨schizophrenia . . . is a ~ related to a variety of etiological factors —Leopold Bellak & Elizabeth Willson⟩ **2 :** a set of concurrent things **:** CONCURRENCE ⟨a word possesses a ~ of meanings —*English Jour.*⟩ — **syn·drom·ic** \(ˈ)sin¦drōmik, -räm-, -mēk\ *adj*

syn·dy·oc·er·as \,sindēˈäsərəs\ *n, cap* [NL, fr. Gk *syndyo* two together (fr. *syn-* + *dyo* two) + NL *-ceras* — more at TWO] **:** a genus of extinct ungulates from the Miocene of Nebraska related to *Protoceras* and having a skull with two pairs of horns curving toward each other

syn·dyo·tac·tic *or* **syn·dio·tac·tic** \¦sindēō¦taktik, sən¦dīə¦t-\ *adj* [ISV *syndyo* (fr. Gk) + *-tactic*] **:** having or relating to a regular alternation of differences in stereochemical structure in the repeating units of a polymer — compare ISOTACTIC

[1]**syne** \(ˈ)sīn\ *adv* [ME (northern dial.) *syne, seyne,* prob. fr. ON *sīthan,* fr. *sīth* since — more at SINCE] **1** *chiefly Scot* **:** NEXT, THEN **2** *chiefly Scot* **:** LATER **3** *chiefly Scot* **:** since then **:** AGO ⟨got a shot at me two days ~ —John Buchan⟩

[2]**syne** \"\ *conj* [ME (northern dial.) *syne, seyne,* fr. *syne, seyne,* adv.] *Scot* **:** SINCE

[3]**syne** \"\ *prep* [[1]*syne*] *Scot* **:** SINCE

syn·ec·do·che \səˈnekdə(,)kē\ *n* -s [L, fr. Gk *synekdochē,* fr. *syn-* + *ekdochē* interpretation, fr. *ekdechesthai* to receive from another, understand in a certain way, fr. *ek, ex* out of, from + *dechesthai* to take, accept, receive; akin to Gk *dokein* to seem good — more at EX-, DECENT] **:** a figure of speech by which a part is put for the whole (as *fifty sail* for *fifty ships*), the whole for a part (as *the smiling year* for *spring*), the species for the genus (as *cutthroat* for *assassin*), the genus for the species (as *a creature* for *a man*), or the name of the material for the thing made (as *willow* for *bat*) — compare METONYMY

syn·ec·doch·ic \¦si,nekˈdäkik, sə¦n-\ *or* **syn·ec·doch·i·cal** \-äkəkəl\ *adj* [Gk *synekdochikos,* fr. *synekdochē* + *-ikos* -ic, -ical] **:** expressed by or implying a synecdoche — **syn·ec·doch·i·cal·ly** \-äkək(ə)lē\ *adv*

syn·ec·do·chism \səˈnekdə,kizəm\ *n* -s [*synecdoche* + *-ism*] **1 :** the use of synecdoche **:** an instance of such use **2 :** the use in sympathetic magic of a part of an object as representing the whole — compare MAGIC 1a

syn·echia \səˈnekēə, -ˈnēk-; ,sinəˈkīə\ *n, pl* **synechiae** \-kē,ē, -ˈkī,ē\ [NL, fr. Gk *synecheia* continuity, coherence, fr. *synechēs* holding together, continuous (fr. *synechein* to hold together, fr. *syn-* + *echein* to have, hold) + *-ia* -y — more at SCHEME] **:** an adhesion of parts; *specif* **:** a disease of the eye in which the iris adheres to the cornea or to the capsule of the crystalline lens

syn·e·chism \ˈsinə,kizəm\ *n* -s [Gk *synechismos* continuity, fr. *synechizein* to make continuous, fr. *synechēs* continuous + *-izein* -ize] **:** a principle in philosophy holding continuity (as of hypotheses) to be of prime importance

syn·ech·thran \səˈnekthrən\ *n* -s [*synechthry* + *-an*] **:** an insect (as a beetle) living as an unwelcome guest among other insects (as ants)

syn·ech·thry *or* **syn·ec·thry** \ˈsi,nekthrē, sə¦n-\ *n* -ES [*syn-* + Gk *echthros* enemy + E *-y;* perh. akin to Gk *ex* from, out of — more at EX-] **:** hostile commensalism — compare SYMPHILY, SYNOECY

syn·ecologic *or* **syn·ecological** \(¦)sin+\ *adj* **:** of, relating to, or involving synecology — **syn·ecologically** \"+\ *adv*

syn·ecology \¦sin+\ *n* [G *synökologie,* fr. *syn-* + *ökologie* ecology] **:** a branch of ecology that deals with the structure, development, and distribution of ecological communities in relation to environment — compare AUTECOLOGY

syn·ec·pho·ne·sis \,si,nekfəˈnēsəs, sə,n-\ *n, pl* **synecphoneses** \-ē,sēz\ [NL, fr. Gk *synekphōnēsis,* fr. *synekphōnein* to utter together (fr. *syn-* + *ekphōnein* to utter, pronounce, fr. *ek, ex* out of, from + *phōnein* to speak, utter, fr. *phōnē* sound, voice) + *-sis* — more at EX-, BAN] **:** contraction of two syllables into one **:** SYNIZESIS, SYNERESIS

syn·edra \səˈnēdrə, səˈned-, ˈsinəd-\ *n, cap* [NL, fr. Gk *synedros* sitting together, fr. *syn-* + *-edros* (fr. *hedra* seat) — more at SIT] **:** a large genus related to *Fragilaria* and comprising elongated linear or commonly needle-shaped solitary or loosely colonial diatoms that may cause earthy odors in water supplies

syn·edri·al *or* **syn·edri·an** \səˈnēdrēəl, -ned-\ *adj* [*synedrion* + *-al, -an*] **:** of or relating to the Sanhedrin

syn·edri·on \-rēən\ *or* **syn·edri·um** \-rēəm\ *n, pl* **syn·edria** \-rēə\ *usu cap* [Gk *synedrion* — more at SANHEDRIN] **:** SANHEDRIN

syn·ei·de·sis \,si,nīˈdēsəs\ *n, pl* **syneide·ses** \-ē,sēz\ [ML, fr. Gk *syneidēsis,* lit., consciousness, awareness, fr. *syneidenai* to have knowledge of something, be aware of something (fr. *syn-* + *eidenai* to know) + *-sis* — more at WIT] **:** the capacity to apply general principles of moral judgment to particular cases — distinguished from *synderesis*

sy·ne·ma \səˈnēmə\ *n, pl* **sy·nema·ta** \-nēməd·ə, -nem-\ [NL, irreg. fr. *syn-* + Gk *nēma* thread — more at NEEDLE] **:** the column of united filaments in a monadelphous flower

syn·ener·gy \səˈnenərjē, ˈsinə,nər-\ *n* [*syn-* + *energy*] *archaic* **:** SYNERGY

syn·en·tog·nath \,sinənˈtäg,nath, səˈnentəg-\ *n* -s [NL *Synentognathi*] **:** a fish of the order Synentognathi

syn·en·tog·na·thi \,sinənˈtägnə,thī\ *n pl, cap* [NL, fr. *syn-* + *ent-* + *-gnathi* (fr. Gk *gnathos* jaw) — more at GNATH-] **:** an order of fishes having spineless fins, united lower pharyngeal bones, and the lateral line forming a ridge along the lower lateral part of the body that includes the needlefishes, sauries, flying fishes, and halfbeaks — **syn·en·tog·na·thous** \¦==¦==-,thəs\ *adj*

syn·eph·rine \səˈnefrən, -,frēn\ *n* -s [*syn-* + epi*nephrine*] **:** a crystalline sympathomimetic amine $C_9H_{13}NO_2$ isomeric with phenylephrine

syn·er·e·sis *or* **syn·aer·e·sis** \səˈnerəsəs, -nir-, *esp in sense 2* ÷ ,sinəˈrēsəs\ *n, pl* **synere·ses** *or* **synaere·ses** \-ə,sēz, -ē,sēz\ [LL *synaeresis,* fr. Gk *synairesis,* lit., contraction, fr. *synairein* to seize and bring together, shorten, contract (fr. *syn-* + *hairein* to seize, take) + *-sis* — more at HERESY] **1 a :** the union or drawing together into one syllable of two vowels ordinarily separated in pronunciation (as \ˈsēst\ for \ˈsē-əst\ *seest*) — opposed to *diaeresis* **b :** SYNIZESIS 1 **2 :** the separation of liquid from a gel caused by contraction ⟨~ if carried further . . . results in coagulation —J.W.McBain⟩ — compare COAGULATION 1, IMBIBITION 2a

syn·er·get·ic \¦sinər¦jed·ik\ *adj* [Gk *synergētikos,* fr. (assumed) *synergētos* (verbal of *synergein* to work with, cooperate, fr. *synergos* working together, fr. *syn-* + *ergon* work) + *-ikos* -ic — more at WORK] **:** SYNERGIC

syn·er·gia \səˈnərj(ē)ə\ *n* -s [NL — more at SYNERGY] **:** SYNERGY, SYNERGISM

syn·er·gic \səˈnərjik, (ˈ)si¦n-\ *also* **syn·er·gi·cal** \-jəkəl\ *adj* [NL *synergicus,* fr. *synergia* + L *-icus* -ic, -ical] **:** working together **:** COOPERATING, COOPERATIVE ⟨~ muscles⟩ — **syn·er·gi·cal·ly** \-jək(ə)lē\ *adv*

syn·er·gid \səˈnərjəd, ˈsinər-\ *n* -s [NL *synergida,* fr. Gk *synergein* to work together, cooperate + NL *-ida* (fr. L *-ides,* patronymic suffix)] **:** one of the two small cells lying near the micropylar end of the embryo sac in seed plants constituting with the egg the egg apparatus — **syn·er·gi·dal** \səˈnərjədᵊl\ *adj*

syn·er·gi·da \səˈnərjədə\ *n, pl* **synergi·dae** \-,dē\ [NL] **:** SYNERGID

syn·er·gism \ˈsinər,jizəm\ *n* -s [NL *synergismus,* fr. Gk *synergos* working together + L *-ismus* -ism] **1 :** an ancient theological doctrine holding that in regeneration there is cooperation of divine grace and human activity ⟨this form of ~ is technically known as semi-Pelagianism, but it is much older than the semi-Pelagians, being essentially the view of the Church, both east and west, ever since Irenaeus —A.C. McGiffert⟩ — compare MONERGISM **2 :** cooperative action of discrete agencies (as drugs or muscles) such that the total effect is greater than the sum of the two or more effects taken independently — opposed to *antagonism*

syn·er·gist \-jəst\ *n* -s [NL *synergista,* fr. Gk *synergos* + L *-ista* -ist] **1 :** one who holds the doctrine of synergism **2 a :** an agent that increases the effectiveness of another agent when combined with it: as **a :** a drug that acts in synergism with another **b :** a substance (as piperonyl butoxide) that increases the effectiveness of an insecticide or other pesticide **c :** a substance that increases the activity of an antioxidant; *esp* **:** such a substance (as phosphoric acid) that is not an antioxidant by itself **3 :** an organ (as a muscle) that acts in concert with another to enhance its effect — compare AGONIST

syn·er·gis·tic \¦sinər¦jistik\ *also* **syn·er·gis·ti·cal** \-təkəl\ *adj* **1 :** of or relating to the doctrine of synergism ⟨~ controversy⟩ **2 a :** having the capacity to act in synergism ⟨~ drug⟩ ⟨~ muscle⟩ ⟨~ action⟩ — compare INCOMPATIBLE **b :** of, relating to, or resembling synergism ⟨a ~ reaction⟩ ⟨a ~ effect⟩ — **syn·er·gis·ti·cal·ly** \-tək(ə)lē\ *adv*

syn·er·gize \ˈsinər,jīz\ *vb* -ED/-ING/-S [*synergy* + *-ize*] *vi* **:** to act as synergists **:** exhibit synergism **:** COOPERATE, COORDINATE ~ *vt* **:** to increase the activity of (a substance)

syn·er·gy \ˈsinərjē\ *n* -ES [NL *synergia,* fr. Gk *synergos* working together + L *-ia* -y — more at SYNERGETIC] **:** combined action or operation (as of muscles or nerves); *specif* **:** SYNERGISM 2

syn·er·ize \ˈsinə,rīz\ *vi* -ED/-ING/-S [*syneresis* + *-ize*] **:** to undergo syneresis ⟨clots of another type . . . ~ readily, become dense with loss of fluid —E.J.Cohn⟩

syn·esis \ˈsinəsəs\ *n* -ES [NL, fr. Gk, union, intelligence, fr. *synienai* to bring together, perceive, understand (fr. *syn-* + *hienai* to send) + *-sis* — more at JET] **:** a construction in which one or more forms make agreement or reference not according to the requirements of syntax but according to the sense of the passage (as *anyone* and *them* in "if anyone calls, tell them I am out")

syn·es·the·sia *or* **syn·aes·the·sia** \,sinəsˈthēzh(ē)ə\ *n* [NL, fr. *syn-* + *-esthesia, -aesthesia* (as in *anesthesia, anaesthesia*)] **:** a concomitant sensation; *esp* **:** a subjective sensation or image of a sense (as of color) other than the one (as of sound) being stimulated — compare CHROMESTHESIA, PHONISM, PHOTISM

syn·es·thete \ˈsinəs,thēt, səˈnes-\ *n* -s [back-formation fr. *synesthetic*] **:** one who experiences synesthesia ⟨no two ~s agree on the correspondence between the colors and the pitches —R.J.Williams⟩

syn·es·thet·ic *or* **syn·aes·thet·ic** \¦sinəs¦thed·ik\ *adj* [fr. NL *synesthesia, synaesthesia,* after such pairs as NL *anesthesia:* E *anesthetic, anaesthetic*] **:** relating to or experiencing synesthesia ⟨~ response to music⟩ **:** involving more than one of the senses ⟨~ metaphor⟩

synezesis *var of* SYNIZESIS

syn·game·on \sinˈgamēən, siŋˈg-, -gām-\ *n* -s [NL, fr. Gk *syngameon, syngamoun,* neut. of *syngameōn, syngamōn,* pres. part. of *syngamein* to marry together, fr. *syngamos* united in wedlock, connected by marriage] **:** the members of a population capable of exchanging genes directly or indirectly

syn·ga·mi·a·sis \,siŋgəˈmīəsəs, ,sing-\ *or* **syn·ga·mo·sis** \-ˈmōsəs\ *n, pl* **syngamia·ses** \-ī,ə,sēz\ *or* **syngamo·ses** \-ō,sēz\ [NL, fr. *Syngamus* + *-iasis* or *-osis*] **:** infestation with or disease caused by roundworms of the genus *Syngamus* **:** GAPES

syn·gam·ic \(ˈ)si|n¦gamik, sə|n|ˈg-, |ŋ|\ *adj* [Gk *syngamos* + E *-ic*] **:** relating to or involving sexual reproduction

[1]**syn·gam·id** \sənˈgaməd, səŋˈg-; ˈsiŋgəm-, -ing-\ *adj* [NL *Syngamidae* family of nematode worms, fr. *Syngamus,* type genus + *-idae*] **:** of or relating to the genus *Syngamus* or family Syngamidae

[2]**syngamid** \"\ *n* -s **:** a nematode of the genus *Syngamus* or family Syngamidae

syn·ga·mus \ˈsiŋgəməs, -ing-\ *n, cap* [NL, fr. Gk *syngamos* united in wedlock, connected by marriage, fr. *syn-* + *-gamos* -gamous] **:** a genus (coextensive with the strongyloid family Syngamidae) of nematode worms parasitic in the trachea or esophagus of various birds and mammals — see GAPEWORM, GULLET WORM

syn·ga·my \-mē\ *n* -ES [ISV *syn-* + *-gamy*] **:** sexual reproduction by union of gametes — compare HOLOGAMY

syn·ge·ne·sio·transplantation \,sinjə¦nēzē(,)ō+\ *n* [irreg. fr. Gk *syngenēs* inborn, related, cognate (fr. *syn-* + *-genēs,* fr. *gignesthai* to be born) + E *transplantation* — more at KIN] **:** a graft of material or tissue between closely related individuals of the same species — compare HOMOGRAFT

syn·ge·ne·sious \¦sinjə¦nēzh(ē)əs\ *adj* [NL *Syngenesia,* a class in the Linnaean system (fr. *syn-* + *-genesia*) + E *-ous*] **:** united by the anthers ⟨~ stamens⟩ **:** having stamens so united

syn·genesis \(ˈ)sin, sən+\ *n* [NL, fr. *syn-* + *genesis*] **1 :** sexual reproduction; *specif* **:** derivation of the zygote from both paternal and maternal substance — contrasted with *ovism* and *spermism* **2 :** ENCASEMENT 1b **3 :** community of origin **:** blood relationship

syn·ge·net·ic \¦sinjə¦ned·ik\ *also* **syn·gen·ic** \(ˈ)sin¦jenik, sən¦j-\ *adj* [*syn-* + *genetic* or *genic*] **1 :** of, relating to, or formed by syngenesis **2 :** formed at the same time as the enclosing rock — used of ore deposits; compare EPIGENETIC

syn·ge·nite \ˈsinjə,nīt\ *n* -s [G *syngenit,* fr. Gk *syngenēs* related + G *-it* -ite; fr. its relationship to polyhalite] **:** a mineral $K_2Ca(SO_4)_2.H_2O$ consisting of a hydrous calcium potassium sulfate and occurring in colorless or white tabular crystals (hardness 2.5, sp. gr. 2.6)

syng·natha \ˈsiŋnəthə\ [NL, fr. *syn-* + *-gnatha*] *syn of* CHILOPODA

syng·na·thid \-thəd\ *n* -s [NL *Syngnathidae*] **:** a fish of the family Syngnathidae

syng·nath·i·dae \siŋˈnathə,dē\ *n pl, cap* [NL, fr. *Syngnathus,* type genus + *-idae*] **:** a family of fishes (order Solenichthyes) having an elongate tubular snout, lacking the pelvic and first dorsal fins, and comprising the sea horse and pipefishes

[1]**syng·na·thoid** \ˈsiŋnə,thȯid\ *adj* [NL *Syngnathus* + E *-oid*] **:** resembling or related to the Syngnathidae

[2]**syngnathoid** \"\ *n* -s **:** a syngnathoid fish

syng·na·thous \ˈsiŋnəthəs\ *adj* [in sense 1, fr. *syn-* + *-gnathous;* in sense 2, fr. NL *Syngnathus* + E *-ous*] **1 :** having the jaws drawn out into a tubular snout **2 :** of or relating to the Syngnathidae

syng·na·thus \"\ *n, cap* [NL, fr. *syn-* + *-gnathus*] **:** the type genus of Syngnathidae comprising various typical pipefishes

syn·go·ni·um \sinˈgōnēəm, siŋˈg-\ *n, cap* [NL, fr. *syn-* + *gon-* + *-ium*] **:** a genus of climbing shrubs (family Araceae) native to Central and So. America and used as ornamental house plants esp. for their velvety foliage

syn·graph \ˈsin,graf, -iŋ,g-, -răf\ *n* [L *syngraphus,* fr. Gk *syngraphos* something written down, decree, contract, fr. *syngraphein* to write down, draw up a contract, fr. *syn-* + *graphein* to write — more at CARVE] **:** a written statement or contract signed and often sealed by all the parties thereto; *specif* **:** an indenture corresponding to the chirograph of common law

syn·hexyl \(ˈ)sin, sən+\ *n* [*syn-* + *hexyl*] **:** a compound derived from dibenzo-pyran that is said to have a euphoriant action more powerful than that of cannabis and is used experimentally in the treatment of depressive mental states

syn·i·ze·sis \,sinəˈzēsəs\ *n* -ES [in sense 1, fr. LL, fr. Gk *synizēsis,* lit., collapse, fr. *synizein* to collapse (fr. *syn-* + *hizein* to sit, sit down) + *-sis;* akin to Gk *hezesthai* to sit; in sense 2, NL, fr. Gk *synizēsis* — more at SIT] **1 :** contraction of two syllables into one by uniting in pronunciation two adjacent vowels (as when the *ee* of *eleemosynary* is pronounced as one syllable) or by making a high vowel before another vowel consonantal (as in \ˈrōmyō\ for \ˈrōmē,ō\ *Romeo*) **:** SYNECPHONESIS — compare SYNERESIS 1a **2** *or* **syn·eze·sis** \"\ **a :** the massing of the chromatin of the nucleus preceding the maturation division **b :** SYNAPSIS — not used technically

syn·kary·on *also* **syn·kari·on** *or* **syn·cary·on** \(ˈ)si|n|¦karē,än, -ēən, sə|n|ˈk-, |ŋ|\ *n* -s [NL, fr. *syn-* + Gk *karyon* nut — more at CAREEN] **:** a cell nucleus formed by the fusion of two preexisting nuclei **:** a zygote nucleus — compare FERTILIZATION, PRONUCLEUS — **syn·kar·y·on·ic** \(¦)=¦==¦änik\ *adj*

syn·ka·tath·e·sis \,sinkəˈtathəsəs, -iŋk-\ *n* -ES [Gk, lit., approval, assent, fr. the stem of *synkatatithenai* to agree entirely with (fr. *syn-* + *katatithenai* to put down, put an end to, settle, fr. *kata-* cata- + *tithenai* to put, place) + *-sis* — more at DO] **:** acceptance or endorsement of a presentation or idea as true or valid — used of a Stoic doctrine analogous to the modern view of judgment

syn·ki·ne·sia \¦sin,kīˈnēzh(ē)ə, -iŋ,k-, -,kəˈn-\ *n* -s [NL, fr. *syn-* + *-kinesia*] **:** SYNKINESIS

syn·ki·ne·sis \-ˈnēsəs\ *n* [NL, fr. *syn-* + *kinesis*] **:** involuntary movement in one part when another part is moved **:** an associated movement

syn·ki·net·ic \-¦ned·ik\ *adj* [*syn-* + *kinetic*] **:** relating to or involving synkinesis

syn·les·ti·dae \sənˈlestə,dē\ *n pl, cap* [NL, fr. *Synlestes,* type genus (irreg. fr. *syn-* + Gk *lēistēs* robber) + *-idae* — more at LESTOBIOSIS] **:** a family of primitive mostly tropical damselflies

syn·ne·ma \səˈnēmə\ *n, pl* **syn·nema·ta** \-nēməd·ə, -nem-\ [NL, fr. *syn-* + Gk *nēma* thread — more at NEEDLE] **:** a coremium having tightly compacted hyphae

syn·neu·ro·sis \¦sinyə¦rōsəs, ¦sinn(y)ə-\ *n* [NL, fr. Gk *synneurōsis,* fr. *syn-* + *neuron* sinew + *-osis* — more at NERVE] **:** SYNDESMOSIS

syn·od \ˈsinəd\ *n* -s [ME, fr. LL *synodus* synod, conjunction of heavenly bodies, fr. LGk & Gk; LGk *synodos* synod, fr. Gk, assembly, meeting, conjunction of heavenly bodies, fr. *syn-* + *hodos* way, journey — more at CEDE] **1 :** an ecclesiastical council **:** a formal meeting to consult and decide on church matters **2 :** a church governing or advisory body: as **a :** an official meeting of clerical and lay deputies from the dioceses within a province of the Protestant Episcopal Church **b :** a Presbyterian judicatory ranking in authority above a presbytery but below the general governing body and composed of the members or of delegates from all the presbyteries within its bounds **c :** any of the courts above the classes in various Reformed Churches **d :** a denominational body of clerical and lay delegates representing the congregations within a region ⟨each of the 33 synods of the Evangelical and Reformed Church⟩ **e :** the entire body of a church or denomination — see GENERAL SYNOD, HOLY SYNOD **3 :** the ecclesiastical district governed by a synod ⟨commended to all churches within the bounds of that ~⟩ **4 a :** COUNCIL, ASSEMBLY **b :** CONVENTION, MEETING

[1]**syn·od·al** \-dᵊl\ *adj* [ME *synodall,* fr. LL *synodalis,* fr. *synodus* + L *-alis* -al] **:** of, relating to, of the nature of, or constituting a synod — **syn·od·al·ly** \-ᵊlē\ *adv*

[2]**synodal** \"\ *n, pl* **synodals** \-ᵊlz\ *or* **syn·o·da·lia** \,sinəˈdālyə\ [ML *synodale,* fr. LL, decree made by a synod, fr. neut. of *synodalis*] **1 :** a constitution made in a provincial or diocesan synod **2 :** a tribute in money formerly paid to the bishop or archdeacon at the time of his visitation by every parish priest of the Church of England

syn·od·al·ist \ˈsinədᵊləst\ *n* -s **:** a member of a synod

[1]**syn·od·i·cal** \səˈnädəkəl, (ˈ)si¦n-\ *or* **syn·od·ic** \-dik\ *adj* [LL *synodicus,* fr. LGk & Gk; LGk *synodikos* of a synod, fr. Gk, of a meeting, of a conjunction, fr. *synodos* + *-ikos* -ic, -ical] **1 :** SYNODAL **2 :** relating to conjunction; *esp* **:** relating to the period between two successive conjunctions of the same celestial bodies (as the moon and the sun) — **syn·od·i·cal·ly** \-dək(ə)lē\ *adv*

[2]**synodical** \"\ *n* -s *usu cap* **:** a women's auxiliary organization associated with a synod and composed of delegates from the presbyterials within its bounds

synodic month *also* **synodical month** *n* **:** the average period of recurrence of the phases of the moon (as from new moon to new moon) equal to 29 days, 12 hours, 44 minutes, and 2.8 seconds of mean solar time — called also *lunar month*

syn·odi·con \səˈnädə,kän, sənōthēˈkōn\ *n* -s [LGk *synodikon,* fr. neut. of *synodikos*] **:** a letter, decree, or other document emanating from a synod in the Eastern Orthodox Church; *specif* **:** an instrument of appointment to a high ecclesiastical office (as of a bishop)

synodic period *n* **:** the time between two successive conjunctions of a planet with the sun

syn·od·ist \ˈsinədəst\ *n* -s [*synod* + *-ist*] **:** one who supports a synod or council; *esp* **:** one who upholds the jurisdiction of a synod in preference to that of a pope or patriarch

syn·odon·ti·dae \,sinəˈdäntə,dē\ *n pl, cap* [NL, fr. *Synodont-, Synodus,* type genus (fr. *syn-* + *-odont-, -odus*) + *-idae*] **:** a family of fishes (order Iniomi) comprising the lizard fishes

syn·ods·man \ˈsinədzmən\ *n, pl* **synodsmen** **1 :** a lay member of a synod **2 :** a churchwarden's assistant **:** SIDESMAN

syn·oe·cete \səˈnē,sēt\ *or* **syn·oe·kete** \-nē,kēt\ *n* -s [Gk *synoiketēs* fellow lodger, fr. *synoikein* to live together (fr. *synoikos* dwelling in the same house, fr. *syn-* + *oikos* house) + *-tēs,* agent suffix — more at VICINITY] **:** an ant or termite guest tolerated with indifference by the host

syn·oe·cious \səˈnēshəs\ *adj* [in sense 1, fr. *syn-* + *-oecious* (as in *dioecious*); in sense 2, fr. *synoecy* + *-ous*] **1 :** exhibiting monoecism **2 :** exhibiting or relating to synoecy — **syn·oe·cious·ly** *adv* — **syn·oe·cious·ness** *n* -ES

syn·oe·cism \səˈnē,sizəm\ *also* **syn·oi·cism** \-nȯi,kizəm, -nȯi,si-\ *n* -s [Gk *synoikismos* wedlock, act of combining into one city-state, fr. *synoikizein*] **1 :** a joining together **:** UNION; *specif* **:** a uniting of several towns or villages into one community (as in ancient Greece) **2 :** the condition of being synoecious

syn·oe·cize \-nē,sīz\ *vt* -ED/-ING/-S [Gk *synoikizein* to give in wedlock, combine into one city-state, unite, fr. *synoikos* dwelling in the same house + *-izein* -ize] **:** to join (diverse things) together; *esp* **:** to form into a large community by synoecism

syn·oe·cy \səˈnēsē, ˈsi,n-\ *also* **syn·oe·ky** \-nēkē\ *n* -ES [Gk *synoikia* body of people living together, community, fr. *synoikos* dwelling together + *-ia* -y] **:** SYNOECISM: **a :** commensalism in which the guests are indifferently tolerated by their hosts — compare SYMPHILY, SYNECHTHRY **b :** association between two species benefiting the one without harm to the other **c :** MONOECISM

syn·oi·cous \səˈnȯikəs\ *adj* [Gk *synoikos* dwelling together] **:** having archegonia and antheridia in the same involucre ⟨~ moss⟩ — compare AUTOICOUS, DIOICOUS, MONOICOUS, PAROICOUS, SYNOECIOUS

syn·o·nym \ˈsinə,nim\ *n* -s [ME *sinonyme,* fr. L *synonymum,* fr. Gk *synōnymon,* fr. neut. of *synōnymos* synonymous — more at SYNONYMOUS] **1 :** a word having the same meaning as another word: as **a :** one of two or more words of the same language and grammatical category having the same or nearly the same essential or generic meaning and differing only in connotation, application, or idiomatic use **:** one of two or more words having essentially identical definitions ⟨nonscientific writers are free to use a variety of ~s to express the same idea in subtly different ways —Aldous Huxley⟩ ⟨a determined repetition of the same word, where it occurred often in a passage, instead of hunting about for a ~ or periphrasis —Robert Graves⟩ — compare ANTONYM **b :** one of two or more words that have one or more senses in common **c :** one of two or more expressions any one of which can in accordance with the rules of the language be substituted in a statement for each of the others without changing the meaning of the statement **2 :** a name that suggests another through real or supposed association **:** a symbolic or figurative name **:** METONYM ⟨the name of the street was . . . the local ~ for poverty —Nadine Gordimer⟩ **3 :** one of two or more names for the same thing in different languages or localities ⟨whose name, Minerva, suggested the Greek ~, Athena —*Amer. Guide Series: Vt.*⟩ **4 :** a taxonomic name (as of a species or genus) rejected as being incorrectly applied or incorrect in form or spelling or rejected in favor of another because of evidence of the priority of that other ⟨declared a ~ because another name had been applied to the same type specimen four years earlier⟩ — compare HOMONYM, NOMENCLATURE

syn·o·nym·at·ic \ˌsinəˌniˈmad·ik\ *adj* [*synonym* + *-atic* (as in *idiomatic*)] **:** of or relating to synonymy

syn·o·nyme \ˈsinəˌnim\ *archaic var of* SYNONYM

syn·o·nym·ic \ˌsinəˈnimik\ *or* **syn·o·nym·i·cal** \-mə̇kəl\ *adj* [*synonym* + *-ic*, *-ical*] **:** of, relating to, composed of, or characterized by synonyms ⟨~ relations between classical and other words in English —W.K.Wimsatt⟩

syn·o·nym·i·con \ˌsinəˈnimə̇ˌkän\ *n* -S [*synonym* + *-icon* (as in *lexicon*)] **:** a lexicon of synonyms

syn·o·nym·ics \ˌ==ˈ=miks\ *n pl but usu sing in constr* **:** the scientific or theoretical treatment of synonyms **:** SYNONYMY

syn·on·y·mist \sə̇ˈnänəmə̇st\ *n* -S **:** one who lists, studies, or discriminates synonyms

syn·o·nym·i·ty \ˌsinəˈnimə̇d·ē\ *n* -ES **:** the quality or fact of being synonymous **:** identity of meaning or significance ⟨commonly assumed ~ of homelessness, vagrancy (and all equivalent terms) with alcoholic addiction —Robert Straus & R.G.McCarthy⟩

syn·on·y·mize \sə̇ˈnänəˌmīz\ *vb* -ED/-ING/-S *vt* **1 :** to give or analyze synonyms of (a word) **:** provide (as a dictionary) with synonymies **2 :** to demonstrate (a taxonomic name) to be a synonym **:** place in synonymy ~ *vi* **:** to use synonyms **:** express an idea variously by means of synonyms

syn·on·y·mous \sə̇ˈnänəməs\ *adj* [ML *synonymus*, fr. Gk *synōnymos*, fr. *syn-* + *onyma*, *onoma* name — more at NAME] **1 :** having the character of a synonym **:** alike or nearly alike in meaning ⟨*glad* is ~ with *joyful*⟩ **:** capable of being substituted for another word or expression in a statement without essentially changing the statement's meaning **2 :** having the same connotations, implications, or reference **:** suggesting the same thing — usu. used with *with* ⟨Newark has become virtually ~ in the public mind with long-distance air travel —*Amer. Guide Series: N.J.*⟩ ⟨believed that lack of knowledge of English is ~ with stupidity —C.S.Stine⟩ — **syn·on·y·mous·ly** *adv* — **syn·on·y·mous·ness** *n* -ES

syn·on·y·my \-mē, -mi\ *n* -ES [*synonym* + *-y*] **1 a :** the study or discrimination of synonyms or of words which may be confused in meaning **b :** a list or collection of synonyms or words of similar meaning often defined and discriminated from each other **2 :** the scientific names that have been used in different publications to designate a species or other taxonomic group; *also* **:** a list of these names specifying by date the books and authors employing them **3** [LL *synonymia* synonym, synonymousness, fr. Gk *synōnymia* synonym, fr. *synōnymos* synonymous + *-ia* -y] **:** the quality or fact of being synonymous **:** SYNONYMOUSNESS, SYNONYMITY

syn·op·sis \sə̇ˈnäpsə̇s\ *n, pl* **synop·ses** \-pˌsēz\ [LL, fr. Gk, general view, estimate, synopsis, fr. *synopsesthai* to be going to have a general view, be going to comprehend (fr. *syn-* + *opsesthai* to be going to see) + *-sis* — more at OPTIC] **1 :** a brief orderly outline affording a quick general view (of a treatise or narrative) **:** a condensed statement **:** ABSTRACT ⟨~ of a scientific report⟩ ⟨~ of the week's news⟩ **2 a :** a brief outline summarizing the action of a proposed screen play or television script **b :** a summary of a completed film (as for cataloging in a film library) **3 :** a conjugation by one person and number **syn** see ABRIDGMENT

sy·nop·size \-pˌsīz\ *vt* -ED/-ING/-S [LGk *synopsizein*, fr. Gk *synopsis* + *-izein* -ize] **1 :** to make a synopsis of **:** give the essential points of **:** summarize briefly ⟨~ a novel⟩ **2 :** EPITOMIZE ⟨this changing taste of Americans is *synopsized* in the advertisements of bookstores —J.D.Hart⟩

[1]**syn·op·tic** \-ptik, -ptēk\ *also* **syn·op·ti·cal** \-ptə̇kəl, -ptēk-\ *adj* [Gk *synoptikos*, fr. *synoptos* (verbal of *synopsesthai*) + *-ikos* -ic, -ical] **1 :** affording a general view of a whole ⟨~ presentation of a physical theory⟩ **2 :** manifesting or characterized by comprehensiveness or breadth of view ⟨~ genius of Shakespeare⟩ **3 a :** affording, presenting, or taking the same or common view **b** *often cap* **:** of or relating to the first three Gospels of the New Testament as being distinguished from the fourth by their many agreements in subject, order, and language ⟨the *synoptic* Gospels⟩ ⟨*synoptic* sayings⟩ **4 :** relating to or displaying atmospheric and weather conditions as they exist simultaneously over a broad area ⟨~ study of polar air masses⟩ ⟨~ chart⟩ — **syn·op·ti·cal·ly** \-ptə̇k(ə)lē, -ptēk-, -li\ *adv*

[2]**syn·op·tic** \"\ *n* -S *often cap* **:** any of the synoptic Gospels

synoptic meteorology *n* **:** a branch of meteorology that uses synoptic weather observations and charts for the diagnosis, study, and forecasting of weather

syn·op·tist \sə̇ˈnäptə̇st\ *n* -S *often cap* [[2]*synoptic* + *-ist*] **:** an author of one of the synoptic Gospels

syn·op·to·phore \-təˌfō(ə)r\ *n* -S [Gk *synoptos* + E *-phore*] **:** an instrument for diagnosing imbalance of eye muscles and treating them by orthoptic methods

syn·or·chism \sə̇ˈnȯ(r)ˌkizəm, ˈsiˌn-\ *also* **syn·or·chi·dism** \-kəˌdizəm\ *n* -S [*syn-* + *-orchism* or *-orchidism*] **:** partial or complete fusion of the testes

syn·orogenic \(ˌ)sin, sən+\ *adj* [*syn-* + *orogenic*] **:** formed or occurring during an orogenic movement ⟨~ plutonism⟩

syn·os·tose \ˈsinəˌstōs, -ˌnäˌs-, -ōz, səˈnäˌs-\ *vt* -ED/-ING/-S [back-formation fr. *synostosis*] **:** to unite by synostosis

syn·os·to·sis \ˌsiˌnäˈstōsə̇s\ *also* **syn·os·te·osis** \(ˌ)siˌnästēˈōsə̇s, səˌn-\ *n, pl* **synosto·ses** *also* **synoste·oses** \-ōˌsēz\ [*synostosis*, NL, fr. *syn-* + *-ostosis*; *synosteosis*, NL, fr. *syn-* + *oste-* + *-osis*] **:** union of two or more separate bones to form a single bone; *also* **:** the union so formed (as at an epiphyseal line) — compare ANKYLOSIS

syn·os·tot·ic \ˌsiˌnäˈstäd·ik\ *adj* [fr. NL *synostosis*, after such pairs as NL *hypnosis*: E *hypnotic*] **:** of, affected by, or marked by synostosis — **syn·os·tot·i·cal·ly** \-d·ə̇k(ə)lē\ *adv*

syn·o·vec·to·my \ˌsinəˈvektəmē\ *n* -ES [ISV *synov-* (fr. *synovial membrane*) + *-ectomy*; orig. formed as F *synovectomie*] **:** surgical removal of a synovial membrane

syn·o·via \sə̇ˈnōvēə\ *n* -S [NL] **:** a transparent viscid lubricating fluid that contains a substance resembling mucin and is secreted by the synovial membranes of articulations, bursae, and tendon sheaths

syn·ovi·al \-ēəl\ *adj* [NL *synovia* + E *-al*] **1 :** of or relating to synovia **:** secreting synovia **2 :** occurring in or affected by synovitis — **syn·ovi·al·ly** \-ēəlē\ *adv*

synovial capsule *n* **:** the completely closed cavity containing synovia formed by the smooth cartilages covering the articular surfaces of the bones and the surrounding capsular ligament in freely movable joints

synovial fluid *n* **:** SYNOVIA

synovial joint *n* **:** DIARTHROSIS

synovial ligament *n* **:** one of the folds of the synovial membrane resembling ligaments and occurring in various joints (as the knee)

synovial membrane *n* **:** the dense connective-tissue membrane often produced into folds or villi and partially covered with patches of flattened cells that lines the ligamentous surfaces of articular capsules, sheaths of tendons where free movement is necessary, and bursae and that secretes the synovia

syn·ovi·o·ma \sə̇ˌnōvēˈōmə\ *n, pl* **synoviomas** *or* **synovioma·ta** \-məd·ə\ [NL, fr. *synovia* + *-oma*] **:** a tumor of a synovial membrane

syn·ovi·tis \ˌsinəˈvīd·ə̇s\ *n* -ES [NL, fr. *synovia* + *-itis*] **:** inflammation of a synovial membrane usu. with pain and swelling of the joint

syn·pel·mous \(ˈ)sinˈpelməs, sənˈp-\ *adj* [irreg. fr. *syn-* + Gk *pelma* sole of the foot + E *-ous* — more at FELL] **:** having the two main flexor tendons of the toes blended above the divisions which go to each digit ⟨~ foot of a bird⟩

syn·rhabdosome \(ˈ)sin, sən+\ *n* [irreg. fr. *syn-* + *rhabdosome*] **:** a colony of graptolites made up of rhabdosomes

syn·sacrum \"+\ *n* [NL, fr. *syn-* + *sacrum*] **:** a solidly fused series of vertebrae in the pelvic region in birds, dinosaurs, and pterosaurs comprising usu. the last rib-bearing or thoracic vertebra, the two sacral vertebrae, and a varying number of caudal vertebrae — compare SACRUM

synscp *abbr* synchroscope

syn·semantic \ˈsin+\ *adj* [*syn-* + *semantic*] **:** AUXILIARY, DEPENDENT, INCOMPLETE, SYNCATEGOREMATIC ⟨a ~ expression⟩ ⟨~ sign⟩

syn·sepalous \(ˈ)sin, sən+\ *adj* [*syn-* + *-sepalous*] **:** GAMOSEPALOUS

syn·tac·tic \(ˈ)sinˈtaktik, sənˈt-, -aktēk\ *or* **syn·tac·ti·cal** \-aktə̇kəl, -tēk-\ *adj* [NL *syntacticus*, fr. Gk *syntaktikos* putting together, composing, fr. *syntaktos* (verbal of *syntassein* to put in order, arrange, fr. *syn-* + *tassein* to put in order, arrange) + *-ikos* -ic, -ical — more at TACTICS] **:** of, relating to, or according to the rules of syntax or syntactics — **syn·tac·ti·cal·ly** \-tə̇k(ə)lē, -tēk-, -li\ *adv*

syntactical aphasia *n* **:** the loss of power to form grammatical constructions

syntactic construction *n* **:** a grammatical construction having only free forms as immediate constituents and having no formal characteristics identifying it as a compound (as "he went to school") — compare MORPHOLOGICAL CONSTRUCTION

syntactic definition *n* **:** DEFINITION 4b(1)

syn·tac·ti·cian \ˌsinˌtakˈtishən\ *n* -S **:** a grammarian who specializes in syntax **:** an authority on syntax

syn·tac·tics \sənˈtaktiks, -aktēks\ *n pl but sing or pl in constr* **:** a theory that deals with the formal relations between signs or expressions in abstraction from their signification and their interpreters — compare PRAGMATICS, SEMIOTIC

syn·tagm \ˈsinˌtam\ *or* **syn·tag·ma** \sənˈtagmə\ *n, pl* **syn·tagms** \-amz\ *or* **syntag·mas** \-gməz\ *or* **syntag·ma·ta** \-gməd·ə\ [Gk *syntagma*, fr. *syntassein* to put in order, arrange — more at SYNTACTIC] **1 :** a systematic collection of writings **2 :** a syntactic unit **:** a word or phrase that has syntactic relation

syn·tag·mat·ic \ˌsinˌtagˈmad·ik\ *adj* [Gk *syntagmatikos*, fr. *syntagmat-*, *syntagma* + *-ikos* -ic] **1 :** relating to or being a syntagm **2 :** SYNTACTIC

syn·tal·i·ty \sənˈtaləd·ē\ *n* -ES [*syn-* + *-tality* (as in *mentality*)] **:** the inferred behavioral tendencies of a group acting as a group that correspond to personality in an individual

syn·tan \ˈsinˌtan\ *n* [*synthetic* + *tan*] **:** any of a class of synthetic tanning materials that are sulfonated condensation products of aromatic compounds with formaldehyde or some other aldehyde

syn·tax \ˈsinˌtaks\ *n* -ES [F or LL; F *syntaxe*, fr. LL *syntaxis*, fr. Gk, fr. the stem of *syntassein* to put in order, arrange + *-sis* — more at SYNTACTIC] **1 :** connected system or order **:** orderly arrangement **:** harmonious adjustment of parts or elements **2 a :** sentence structure **:** the arrangement of word forms to show their mutual relations in the sentence **b :** the part of grammar that treats of the expression of predicative, qualifying, and other word relations according to established usage in the language under study — compare MORPHOLOGY **3 a :** SYNTACTICS **b :** the area of syntactics dealing specifically with the formal properties of languages or calculi — called also *logical syntax*

syn·tax·ic \sənˈtaksik\ *adj* [*syn-* + *-taxic* (as in *parataxic*)] **:** characterized by or relating to a mode of experience or symbolic behavior that relates symbols and referents, speech and action, subject and object in a sequentially logical and interpersonally or publicly verifiable manner — compare PROTOTAXIC

syn·tax·is \sənˈtaksə̇s\ *n* [LL] **1** *archaic* **:** SYNTAX **2** [NL, fr. Gk, arrangement, syntax] **:** ARTICULATION 2a

syntax language *n* **:** a metalanguage used to refer to the syntactic properties of a language under study

syn·technic \(ˈ)sin, sən+\ *adj* [*syn-* + *technic*] **:** of, relating to, or being a similarity in behavior of unlike organisms due to adaptation to a common environment; *also* **:** exhibiting such similarity — compare SYNCRYPTIC

syn·tec·tic \(ˈ)sinˈtektik, sənˈt-\ *also* **syn·tec·ti·cal** \-ektə̇kəl\ *adj* [Gk *syntēktikos* able to liquefy, liquefactive, fr. *syntēktos* (verbal of *syntēkein* to dissolve, liquefy, fr. *syn-* + *tēkein* to melt) + *-ikos* -ic, -ical — more at THAW] **:** of, relating to, or produced by syntexis **:** melting or wasting away

syn·telome \(ˈ)sin, sən+\ *n* [*syn-* + *telome*] **:** a group of fused telomes

syn·te·no·sis \ˌsintəˈnōsə̇s\ *n* -ES [NL, fr. *syn-* + *teno-* + *-sis*] **:** articulation by tendons

synteresis *var of* SYNDERESIS

syn·tex·is \sənˈteksə̇s\ *n* -ES [Gk *syntēxis* liquefaction, fr. *syntēkein* to dissolve, liquefy + *-sis*] **:** the generation and augmentation of magma by melting and assimilation of crustal rocks

syn·ther·mal \(ˈ)sin, sən+\ *adj* [*syn-* + *thermal*] **:** maintained at equal temperatures — used of two or more bodies whose temperatures may or may not be varying

syn·the·sis \ˈsin(t)thəsə̇s\ *n, pl* **synthe·ses** \-thəˌsēz\ [L, fr. Gk, lit., action of putting together, fr. the stem of *syntithenai* to put together (fr. *syn-* + *tithenai* to put, place) + *-sis* — more at DO] **1 :** a loose garment of ancient Rome sometimes worn in place of the more formal toga **2 a :** composition or combination of parts or elements so as to form a whole ⟨~ of those arts . . . completely blended to achieve . . . performance at its finest —Miles Kastendieck⟩ **b :** the production of a chemical compound by the union of elements or simpler compounds or by the degradation of a complex compound esp. by laboratory or industrial methods ⟨~ of water from hydrogen and oxygen⟩ ⟨~ of ascorbic acid from glucose⟩ ⟨~ of phthalic anhydride by oxidation of naphthalene⟩; *broadly* **:** the artificial production of a substance — contrasted with *analysis*; compare BIOSYNTHESIS, PHOTOSYNTHESIS, REACTION **c :** the combining of often varied and diverse ideas, forces, or factors into one coherent or consistent complex; *also* **:** the complex so formed ⟨a *summa* is a ~ of the philosophy of an age⟩ ⟨only political parties can produce the ~ or compromise of interest necessary to make representative government work —D.D.McKean⟩ **3 a :** deductive reasoning from general principles or causes to particular instances or effects **b :** the combination of separate elements of sensation or thought into a whole (as of simple into complex conceptions or of species into genera) **c** *Hegelianism* **:** the combination of the partial truths of a thesis and its antithesis into a higher stage of truth — compare DIALECTIC **4 :** the combination of radical and modifying elements into single words (as Latin *patri* to the father) **:** frequent and systematic use of inflected grammatical forms — contrasted with *analysis*; compare POLYSYNTHESISM

synthesis gas *n* **:** a gas used in synthesis; *esp* **:** a mixture composed essentially of hydrogen and carbon monoxide often in a ratio of 2 to 1, produced by various methods (as by the action of steam with or without oxygen on coal or lignite, by the action of steam or oxygen on methane or natural gas, or by enrichment of blue gas with hydrogen), and used chiefly in the synthesis of methanol and ammonia, in the Fischer-Tropsch process, and in the oxo process — compare PRODUCER GAS

syn·the·sist \-thəsə̇st\ *n* -S [blend of *synthesis* and *-ist*] **:** one who employs synthesis or follows synthetic methods **:** SYNTHESIZER

syn·the·size \-thəˌsīz\ *vb* -ED/-ING/-S *see -ize in Explan Notes* [blend of *synthesis* and *-ize*] *vt* **1 :** to combine or put together by synthesis **:** form into a whole **:** deal with synthetically ⟨*synthesizing* the teachings of modern dynamic psychiatry and religion —*advt*⟩ ⟨does not examine one aspect of the war but attempts to ~ the whole situation —Peter Ritner⟩ **2 :** to produce by synthesis ⟨~ alizarin⟩ ~ *vi* **:** to make a synthesis **:** proceed or function synthetically ⟨*synthesizing* tradition of masculine reason —J.C.Powys⟩

syn·the·siz·er \-zə(r)\ *n* -S **:** one that synthesizes ⟨~ of scattered results of investigations⟩; *esp* **:** an instrument used in scientific synthesis ⟨electronic ~ for reproducing speech sounds⟩

syn·the·tase \ˈsin(t)thəˌtās, -āz\ *n* -S [[1]*synthetic* + *-ase*] **:** an enzyme that catalyzes the union of two molecules with concurrent breakdown of a pyrophosphate bond in a triphosphate (as ATP) ⟨glutamine ~⟩

[1]**syn·thet·ic** \(ˈ)sinˈthed·ik, sənˈth-, ¦ēk\ *also* **syn·thet·i·cal** \¦ə̇kəl, ¦ēk-\ *adj* [Gk *synthetikos* skilled in putting together, component, fr. *synthetos* put together, compounded, composed (fr. *syntithenai* to put together) + *-ikos* -ic, -ical — more at SYNTHESIS] **1 a :** relating to or involving synthesis ⟨limnology is essentially a ~ science composed of elements . . . which extend well beyond the limits of biology —P.S.Welch⟩ **b :** not analytic ⟨the ~ aspects of a philosophy⟩ **2 a :** attributing to a subject a predicate that is not contained in the essence of that subject **b :** having the truth determined by observation or the facts of experience **c :** not resulting in a contradiction upon being negated **3** *of a language* **:** characterized by synthesis **:** INFLECTIONAL ⟨Sanskrit, Greek, Latin, and Turkish are ~ languages⟩ — contrasted with *analytic* **4 a :** of, relating to, or being a taxonomic category retained for reasons of convenience but not regarded as constituting a natural unit **b :** of, relating to, or being a group deliberately produced by combining genes in a manner unlikely to occur in nature ⟨a ~ tetraploid variety produced by colchicine⟩ **5** *of an organ stop* **:** composed of two or more pipes for each tone ⟨~ clarinet⟩ **6 a :** produced by artificial processes either from relatively simple substances or from naturally occurring sometimes complex substances **:** MAN-MADE ⟨~ quartz⟩ ⟨~ indigo⟩ ⟨natural and ~ dyes⟩ ⟨~ plastics⟩ — compare SEMISYNTHETIC **b :** devised, arranged, or fabricated for special situations to imitate or replace usual realities ⟨~ diet⟩ ⟨~ mock-up for pilots' ground training⟩ **:** employing or concerning such devices or fabrications instead of actualities ⟨~ flight instruction⟩ **c :** patently produced or maintained by special effort and therefore often forced, constrained, distorted, or simulated **:** not natural or spontaneous **:** SPURIOUS, FACTITIOUS ⟨no comfort I could have offered that wouldn't have sounded ~ —Norman Cousins⟩ ⟨producing ~ books to suit fancied trends —John Farrar⟩ **7** *of cubist art* **:** involving the composing of pictorial objects without the restrictions of natural appearances or relations — opposed to *analytical*; compare CUBISM **syn** see ARTIFICIAL

[2]**synthetic** \"\ *n* -S **:** something produced by synthesis rather than natural growth; *esp* **:** a yarn or fabric (as nylon) made by chemical synthesis usu. of hydrocarbons

syn·thet·i·cal·ly \¦ə̇k(ə)lē, ¦ēk-, -li\ *adv* **:** in a synthetic manner ⟨what followed is so confused in my memory, so transposed and foreshortened, that I can only describe it ~ —Christopher Isherwood⟩ **:** by synthetic means or methods ⟨producing drugs ~⟩

synthetic ammonia process *n* **:** any of several processes (as the Haber process or the Claude process) for the manufacture of ammonia from nitrogen and hydrogen under conditions of high temperature and pressure in the presence of a catalyst (as a promoted iron catalyst) — compare NITROGEN FIXATION 1

synthetic a priori *n* **:** a synthetic judgment or proposition that is known to be true on a priori grounds; *specif* **:** one that is factual but universally and necessarily true ⟨the Kantian conception that the basic propositions of geometry and physics are *synthetic a priori*⟩

synthetic detergent *n* **:** DETERGENT c

synthetic fiber *n* **:** any of various man-made textile fibers including usu. those made from natural materials (as rayon and acetate from cellulose or regenerated protein fibers from zein or casein) as well as fully synthetic fibers (as nylon or acrylic fibers) — compare POLYMER

synthetic geometry *n* **:** elementary or projective geometry as distinguished from analytic geometry

synthetic iron oxide *n* **:** a pigment that is produced from an iron salt (as copperas) by precipitation or calcination under controlled conditions and is often purer than natural iron oxides

syn·thet·i·cism \sənˈthed·əˌsizəm, -etə,-\ *n* -S **:** synthetic principles or method

synthetic judgment *n* **:** a judgment that attributes to a subject a predicate not contained in the essence or connotation of that subject — compare ANALYTIC JUDGMENT

synthetic medium *n* **:** a culture medium consisting only of known mixtures of chemical compounds (as salts, sugars)

synthetic philosophy *n* **:** SPENCERIANISM

synthetic photograph *n* **:** a combination picture in which a photograph of a staged scene is combined with other photographs to represent a scene unavailable for direct photography — called also *composograph*

synthetic resin *n* **:** a resinlike product made by polymerization or condensation **:** RESIN 2a; *sometimes* **:** a resinlike product made by chemical modification of a natural substance **:** RESIN 2b — distinguished from *natural resin*

synthetic rubber *n* **:** any of various products (as GR-S, neoprene, butyl rubber, or nitrile rubber) that resemble natural rubber more or less closely esp. in physical properties and ability to be vulcanized, that are made usu. by polymerization of butadiene, isoprene, or similar unsaturated hydrocarbons or by copolymerization of such hydrocarbons with styrene, isobutylene, acrylonitrile, or other polymerizable compounds, and that have uses similar to those of natural rubber but are superior for some applications and inferior for others and are often used in combination with natural rubber **:** RUBBER 2b — compare ELASTOMER

synthetic seniority *n* **:** SUPERSENIORITY

syn·the·tism \ˈsin(t)thəˌtizəm\ *n* -S *often cap* [Gk *synthetos* put together, composed + E *-ism* — more at SYNTHETIC] **:** an art theory current in France about 1890 that a painting is to be considered a formal arrangement of color on a flat surface before it is a particular representation — compare NABI

syn·the·tist \-ˌtə̇st\ *n* -S [[1]*synthetic* + *-ist*] **1 :** SYNTHESIST **2** *often cap* **:** an advocate of synthetism

syn·the·tize \-ˌtīz\ *vt* -ED/-ING/-S *see -ize in Explan Notes* [[1]*synthetic* + *-ize*] **:** SYNTHESIZE

syn·thol \ˈsinˌthȯl, -ˌthōl\ *n* -S [[1]*synthetic* + *-ol*] **:** a synthetic motor fuel made by heating water gas or synthesis gas under pressure in the presence of a catalyst and containing chiefly alcohols, fatty acids, and ketones or chiefly hydrocarbons — compare FISCHER-TROPSCH PROCESS

syn·thro·non \ˈsin(t)thrəˌnän, ˈsenthrōnȯn\ *or* **syn·thro·nus** \ˈsin(t)thrənəs\ *or* **syn·thro·nos** \ˈsin(t)thrəˌnäs, ˈsenthrōnōs\ *n, pl* **synthro·ni** \ˈsin(t)thrəˌnī\ *also* **synthro·noi** \ˈsin(t)thrəˌnȯi, ˈsenthrənē\ [MGk *synthronon*, *synthronos*, fr. Gk *syn-* + *thronos* throne — more at FIRM] **:** a structure in a church combining the bishop's throne and clergy stalls placed behind the altar against the east wall and now found chiefly in Eastern churches

syn·tone \ˈsinˌtōn\ *n* -S [back-formation fr. *syntonic*] **:** a person of syntonic constitution or temperament

syn·ton·ic \(ˈ)sin¦tänik, sənˈt-\ *adj* [Gk *syntonos* being in harmony with + E *-ic*] **1 :** possessing a temperament normally responsive and adaptive to one's social or interpersonal environment — compare CYCLOTHYMIC **2 :** of or relating to resonance; *esp* **:** having the same resonant frequency — **syn·ton·i·cal·ly** \-ə̇nə̇k(ə)lē\ *adv*

syntonic comma *n* **:** the difference in pitch between two tones respectively four perfect fifths and two octaves plus a major third from a given tone represented by the ratio of 81:80 — called also *comma syntonum*

syn·to·ni·za·tion \ˌsintənə̇ˈzāshən, -ˌnīˈz-\ *n* -S **:** the act or result of syntonizing

syn·to·nize \ˈsintəˌnīz\ *vt* -ED/-ING/-S [*syntony* + *-ize*] **:** to put (two or more radio instruments or systems) in resonance **:** TUNE

syn·to·nous \ˈsintənəs\ *adj* [Gk *syntonos* being in harmony] **:** SYNTONIC

syn·to·ny \-nē\ *n* -ES [Gk *syntonia* agreement, fr. *syntonos* being in harmony (fr. *syn-* + *tonos* voice, pitch) + *-ia* -y — more at TONE] **1 :** the state of being normally responsive to and in harmony with the environment **2 :** RESONANCE 1b(2)

syn·trope \ˈsinˌtrōp\ *n* -S [*syn-* + *-trope*] **:** a syntropic part or appendage — opposed to *antitrope*

syn·troph·ic \(ˈ)sin¦träfik, sənˈt-\ *adj* [ISV *syn-* + *-trophic*] **:** associated or mutually dependent upon one another with reference to food supply ⟨~ cells⟩

syn·tro·phism \ˈsin·trəˌfizəm\ *n* [*syntrophic* + *-ism*] **:** mutual dependence (as of different strains of bacteria) for the satisfaction of nutritional needs **:** syntrophic state

syn·trophoblast \(ˈ)sin, sən+\ *n* [*syn-* + *trophoblast*] **:** the outer syncytial layer of the trophoblast that actively invades the uterine wall forming the outermost fetal component of the placenta — **syn·trophoblastic** \(ˈ)sin, sən+\ *adj*

syn·trop·ic \(ˈ)sin, sən+\ *adj* [*syn-* + *-tropic*] **:** repeated symmetrically without being reversed ⟨~ ribs⟩ — opposed to *antitropic*

syn·tro·py \ˈsin·trəpē\ *n* -ES [*syn-* + *-tropy*] **:** the quality or state of being syntropic

syn·type \ˈsinˌtīp\ *n* [*syn-* + *type*] **1 :** a member of a taxonomic type series when no holotype is designated **2 :** PARATYPE 1, ISOTYPE 1b(1) — **syn·typ·ic** \(ˈ)sin¦tipik, sənˈt-\ *adj*

syn·ura \səˈn(y)u̇rə\ *n, cap* [NL, fr. *syn-* + *-ura*] **:** a genus of biflagellate free-swimming flagellates (order Chrysomona-

dina) occurring in spheroidal colonies and producing odors and sometimes oily fishy flavors in water supplies
syn·usia \sə'n(y)üzh(ē)ə, -zēə\ *n, pl* **syn·usi·ae** \-z(h)ē,ē\ [NL, fr. Gk *synousia* social intercourse, society, company, fr. *synous-* (part. stem of *syneinai* to come together, assemble, gather, fr. *syn-* + *einai* to be) + *-ia* -y — more at IS] **:** a structural unit of a major ecological community characterized by relative uniformity of life-form or of height and usu. constituting a particular stratum of that community ⟨the herbaceous ~ of open forest⟩ — **synusial** *adj*
syph \'sif\ *n* -s [by shortening] **:** SYPHILIS
sy·pha·cia \sī'fāshēə\ *n, cap* [NL, irreg. fr. L *sipho, siphon* tube, pipe + *-acea*, fem. of *-aceus* -aceous — more at SIPHON] **:** a genus of nematode worms (family Oxyuridae) including a species (*S. obvelata*) normally parasitic in the cecum and colon of rodents and rarely in man
syphil- *or* **syphilo-** *comb form* [NL, fr. *syphilis*] **:** syphilis ⟨*syphilology*⟩ ⟨*syphiloma*⟩
syph·i·lid \'sifələd\ *n* -s [NL *syphilides*, fr. *syphilis* + *-ides* -id] **:** a syphilitic id
syph·i·lis \'sif(ə)ləs\ *n* -ES [NL, after *Syphilus*, the supposed first sufferer from the disease and the hero of the poem *Syphilis sive Morbus Gallicus* (1530), by Girolamo Fracastoro †1553 Ital. physician, astronomer, and poet] **:** a chronic, contagious, usu. venereal, and often congenital disease caused by a spirochete (*Treponema pallidum*) and characterized by a clinical course in three stages continued over many years and lesions that may involve many organs and tissues of the body — see PRIMARY SYPHILIS, SECONDARY SYPHILIS, TERTIARY SYPHILIS
¹syph·i·lit·ic \,sifə¦lid·ik, -lit|, |ēk\ *adj* [NL *syphiliticus*, fr. *syphilis* + L *-iticus* -itic] **:** of, relating to, or infected with syphilis
²syphilitic \"\ *n* -s **:** a person infected with syphilis
syph·i·li·za·tion \,sifələ'zāshən\ *n* -s [F *syphilisation*, fr. *syphiliser* + *-ation*] **1 :** the condition of being infected with syphilis **2 :** the act or process of inoculating with the spirochete (*Treponema pallidum*)
syph·i·lize \'sifə,līz\ *vt* -ED/-ING/-s [F *syphiliser*, fr. *syphil-* + *-iser* -ize] **1 :** to inoculate with syphilis **2 :** to introduce syphilis among
syph·i·lo·derm \'sifəlō,dərm\ *or* **syph·i·lo·der·ma** \,==-'dərmə\ *n, pl* **syphiloderms** \-mz\ *or* **syphiloder·ma·ta** \,===='dərməd·ə\ [NL *syphiloderma*, fr. *syphil-* + *-derma*] **:** SYPHILID
syph·i·log·ra·pher \,sifə'lägrəfə(r)\ *n* -s [*syphilography* + *-er*] **:** one who writes scientifically about syphilis
syph·i·log·ra·phy \-fē\ *n* -ES [*syphil-* + *-graphy*] **:** the scientific description of syphilis
syph·i·loid \'sifə,lȯid\ *adj* [*syphil-* + *-oid*] **:** resembling syphilis ⟨~ infection⟩
syph·i·lo·log·ic \'sifəlō¦läjik\ *adj* **:** relating to or concerning syphilis ⟨~ practice⟩
syph·i·lol·o·gist \,sifə'läləjəst\ *n* -s **:** a physician who specializes in the diagnosis and treatment of syphilis
syph·i·lol·o·gy \-jē\ *n* -ES [*syphil-* + *-logy*] **:** a branch of medicine that deals with syphilis
syph·i·lo·ma \,sifə'lōmə\ *n, pl* **syphilomas** *or* **syphilomata** [NL, fr. *syphil-* + *-oma*] **:** a syphilitic tumor **:** GUMMA — **syph·i·lom·a·tous** \,==¦lämәd·əs, -¦lōm-\ *adj*
syph·i·lo·phobe \'sifəlō,fōb\ *n* -s [NL, fr. *syphil-* + *-phobe*] **:** one afflicted with syphilophobia
syph·i·lo·phobia \,sifə(,)lō+\ *n* [NL, fr. *syphil-* + *phobia*] **:** abnormal dread of syphilis or fear of being infected with it
syph·i·lo·psychosis \"+\ *n* [NL, fr. *syphil-* + *psychosis*] **:** a mental disorder resulting from syphilis of the brain
syph·i·lo·therapy \"+\ *n* [*syphil-* + *therapy*] **:** the treatment of syphilis ⟨~ with penicillin⟩
syphon *var of* SIPHON
syr *abbr* syrup
¹syr·a·cu·san \,sirə¦kyüzᵊn, -üsᵊn\ *also* **syr·a·cu·si·an** \-üzēən, -üsēən, -üzhən, -üshən\ *adj, usu cap* [*Syracuse*, Sicily & *Syracuse*, N.Y. + E *-an, -ian*] **:** of or belonging to the ancient city of Syracuse, Sicily, or to the city of Syracuse, N.Y.
²syracusan \"\ *also* **syracusian** \"\ *n* -s *cap* **:** a native or resident of Syracuse, Sicily, or Syracuse, N.Y.
syr·a·cuse \'==,kyüs (*usual local pronunc*), -üz, *locally also* 'ser-\ *adj, usu cap* [fr. *Syracuse*, N.Y.] **:** of or from the city of Syracuse, N.Y. ⟨a *Syracuse* industry⟩ **:** of the kind or style prevalent in Syracuse
syracuse watch glass *or* **syracuse dish** *n, usu cap S* **:** a small circular flat-bottomed dish of thick glass with a shallow depression used in biology (as for staining, culturing, and various phases of microtechnic)
sy·ren \'sīrən\ *chiefly Brit var of* SIREN
Syr·ette \sə'ret\ *trademark* — used for an injection unit comprising a small collapsible tube fitted with a hypodermic needle and containing a single dose of a medicinal agent
syr·ia \'sirēə\ *adj, usu cap* [fr. *Syria*, country in southwestern Asia] **:** of or from Syria **:** of the kind or style prevalent in Syria **:** SYRIAN
¹syr·i·ac \'sirē,ak\ *adj, usu cap* [L *syriacus* Syrian, fr. Gk *syriakos*, fr. *Syria*] **1 :** of, relating to, or written in Syriac **2 :** using or versed in Syriac
²syriac \"\ *n* -s *cap* **1 :** ARAMAIC **2 a :** a literary language based on an eastern Aramaic dialect and used as the literary and liturgical language by several Eastern churches **b :** a form of Aramaic spoken by eastern Christian communities
syriac alphabet *n, usu cap S* **:** an alphabet of Aramaic origin used for writing Syriac
syr·i·a·cism \'sirēə,sizəm\ *n* -s *usu cap* **:** a form of expression peculiar to Syriac
¹syr·i·an \'sirēən\ *n* -s [ME *sirien*, fr. MF, fr. *Syrie* Syria + MF *-en* -an] *usu cap* **1 :** a native or inhabitant of Syria **2 :** a member of a Syrian church
²syrian \"\ *adj, usu cap* **1 a :** of or relating to ancient Syria **b :** of or relating to the territory now included in Syria and Lebanon **c :** of or relating to the Republic of Syria or the Syrian Region of the United Arab Republic **2 :** of, relating to, or being one of the Eastern churches originating in Byzantine or Persian Syria, using Syriac liturgies, and including the Jacobite church and the Nestorian church
syrian bear *n, usu cap S* **:** a silvery or yellowish gray Syrian brown bear (*Ursus arctos syriacus*)
syrian grass *n, usu cap S* **:** JOHNSON GRASS
syrian hamster *n, usu cap S* **:** GOLDEN HAMSTER
syrian hyrax *n, usu cap S* **:** the common hyrax (*Procavia syriaca*) of Asia Minor that is the cony of the Old Testament
syrian juniper *n, usu cap S* **:** an evergreen tree (*Juniperus drupacea*) of Greece and Asia Minor with a brownish or bluish edible fruit covered with a bloom
syrian rue *n, usu cap S* **:** AFRICAN RUE
syrian tobacco *n, usu cap S* **:** a wild tobacco (*Nicotiana rustica*) formerly supposed to yield the tobacco produced in Syria
syrian wild ass *n, usu cap S* **:** HEMIPPE
syr·i·asm \'sirē,azəm\ *n* -s *usu cap* [*Syriac* + *-asm* (as in *enthusiasm*)] **:** SYRIACISM
syring- *or* **syringo-** *comb form* [Gk, panpipe, fistula, tube, fr. *syring-, syrinx* — more at SYRINGE] **:** tube **:** fistula ⟨*syringadenous*⟩
sy·rin·ga \sə'riŋgə\ *n* [NL, fr. Gk *syring-, syrinx*] **1** *cap* **:** a genus of Old World shrubs or low trees (family Oleaceae) having purple, white, or sometimes pink flowers with a cylindrical tube and four spreading lobes that are borne in terminal usu. thyrsoid panicles and are followed by winged seeds and comprising the widely cultivated lilacs **2** -s **:** MOCK ORANGE 1
syr·ing·ad·e·nous \,siriŋ¦adᵊnəs\ *adj* [*syring-* + *aden-* + *-ous*] **:** of or relating to the sweat glands
¹sy·ringe \sə'rinj *also* 'sirənj *or* 'si,rinj, *in rapid speech often* 'srinj\ *n* -s [ME *syring*, fr. ML *syringa, siringa*, fr. LL, injection, fr. Gk *syring-, syrinx* panpipe, fistula, tube; akin to Gk *sōlēn* channel, pipe, OSlav *tulŭ* quiver, Skt *tūṇa, tūṇī* quiver, *tūṇava* flute] **1 :** a device used to inject fluids into or withdraw them from the body or its cavities: as **a :** a device consisting of a nozzle of varying length and a compressible rubber bulb and used for injection or irrigation ⟨ear ~⟩ ⟨vaginal ~⟩ **b :** an instrument that consists of a glass barrel fitted with a plunger and a hollow needle and is used for the injection of medicines or for aspiration of fluid from body cavities ⟨hypodermic ~⟩ **c :** a device that operates by gravity, consists of a reservoir of rubber, glass, or enamelware fitted with a long rubber tube ending with an exchangeable nozzle, and is used for irrigation of the vagina or bowel — called also *fountain syringe* **2 :** SYRINGIUM

syringe 1a

²syringe \"\ *vb* -ED/-ING/-s *vt* **1 :** to irrigate (a part of the body) by means of a syringe **2 a :** to spray (plants) with a fine powerful spray of water usu. directed at the lower surface of the foliage to dislodge insects **b :** to spray (a greenhouse) with a fine mist of water usu. from an overhead spray system primarily to help maintain humidity **~** *vi* **1 :** to use a syringe **2 :** to spray a plant or greenhouse with water
sy·rin·ge·al \sə'rinjēəl\ *adj* [NL *syring-, syrinx* + E *-eal* (as in *laryngeal*)] **:** of or relating to the syrinx ⟨~ muscles⟩
sy·ringe·ful *pronunc at* SYRINGE +,fu̇l\ *n* -s **:** the amount a syringe can hold
sy·rin·gic acid \sə'rinjik-\ *n* [ISV *syringin* + *-ic*] **:** a crystalline phenolic acid $HO(CH_3O)_2C_6H_2COOH$ obtained by decomposition esp. of syringin and prepared by acid hydrolysis of the trimethyl ether of gallic acid
sy·rin·gin \-jən\ *n* -s [F *syringine*, fr. NL *Syringa* (generic name of *Syringa vulgaris*) + F *-ine*] **:** a crystalline glucoside $C_{17}H_{24}O_9$ found esp. in the bark of a lilac (*Syringa vulgaris*) and of privets that on hydrolysis yields glucose and methoxyconiferyl alcohol
sy·rin·gi·um \sə'rinjēəm\ *n* -s [NL, fr. *syring-* + *-ium*] **1 :** a muscular tubular organ connected with the mouth parts of hemipterous insects and used for the ejection of a poisonous salivary secretion **2 :** a tubular organ on the body of some insect larvae from which an offensive fluid can be ejected
sy·rin·go·bul·bia \sə,riŋgō'bəlbēə\ *n* -s [NL, fr. *syring-* + L *bulbus* onion, bulb + NL *-ia* — more at BULB] **:** the presence of abnormal cavities in the medulla oblongata
sy·rin·go·my·e·lia \sə,riŋgō,mī'ēlēə\ *n* -s [NL, fr. *syring-* + *-myelia*] **:** a chronic progressive disease of the spinal cord characterized by the presence of long cavities in the substance of the spinal cord with sensory disturbances, muscle atrophy, and spasticity — **sy·rin·go·my·el·ic** \=¦===¦elik\ *adj*
sy·rin·goph·i·lus \,siriŋ'gäfələs\ *n, cap* [NL, fr. *syring-* + *-philus*] **:** a genus of parasitic mites that live inside the quills of bird feathers in Europe and No. America
syr·inx \'siriŋks, -rēŋks\ *n, pl* **sy·rin·ges** \sə'rin,jēz\ *or* **syrinxes** [in sense 1a, fr. Gk; in sense 2, fr. LL, fr. Gk; in other senses, fr. NL, fr. Gk — more at SYRINGE] **1 a :** PANPIPE **b :** a mouthpiece attached to the aulos **2 :** a tunnel-shaped rock-cut passage of ancient Egypt esp. when in a burial vault **3 :** the vocal organ of birds that is a special modification of the lower part of the trachea or of the bronchi or of both — called also *lower larynx* **4 :** a tube formed from modified deltidial plates and surrounding the pedicle in some extinct brachiopods
syr·i·ol·o·gist \,sirē'äləjəst\ *n* -s *usu cap* [*Syria* + E *-o-* + *-logy* + *-ist*] **:** an archaeologist specializing in Syrian remains
syr·ma \'sərmə\ *n, pl* **syrmas** \-məz\ *or* **syrma·ta** \-məd·ə\ [Gk, fr. *syrein* to drag — more at SWERVE] **:** a trailing robe worn by tragic actors of ancient Greece
syr·ni·um \'sərnēəm\ [NL, fr. Gk *syrnion*, a bird of ill omen] *syn of* STRIX b
syro- *comb form, usu cap* [L, fr. Gk, fr. *Syros* Syrian] **1 :** Syria or Syrians ⟨*Syro*phile⟩ **2 :** Syrian and ⟨*Syro*-Egyptian⟩ ⟨*Syro*-Iraqi⟩ **3 :** Syriac and ⟨*Syro*-Aramaic⟩
sy·ro-aramaic \,sī(,)rō, ¦si(,)rō+\ *n* -s *cap S&A* [*Syro-* + *Aramaic*] **:** Syriac and Aramaic considered as a single language
sy·ro-hittite \"+\ *adj, usu cap S&H* [*Syro-* + *Hittite*] **:** of or relating to the esp. glyptic art and the archaeological remains characteristic of northern Syria and eastern Asia Minor
¹sy·ro·phoenician \"+\ *adj, usu cap* [*Syrophoenicia*, ancient Roman province in southwestern Asia + E *-an*] **1 :** of or relating to the Roman province of Syrophoenicia **2 :** of or relating to Syrophoenicians
²syrophoenician \"\ *n* -s *cap* **:** a native or inhabitant of Syrophoenicia
¹syr·phid \'sərfəd\ *adj* [NL *Syrphidae*] **:** of or relating to the Syrphidae
²syrphid \"\ *n* -s **:** a fly of the family Syrphidae **:** SYRPHUS FLY
syr·phi·dae \-fə,dē\ *n pl, cap* [NL, fr. *Syrphus*, type genus + *-idae*] **:** a large and widely distributed family of cyclorrhaphous dipterans — see SYRPHUS FLY
syr·phus fly \'sərfəs-\ *or* **syrphid fly** *n* [*syrphus* fr. NL *Syrphus* genus of dipterous flies, fr. Gk *syrphos* gnat] **:** any of numerous active day-flying flies that constitute the family Syrphidae, frequent flowers and feed on nectar, vary greatly in form and coloration but generally have a spurious longitudinal vein near the middle of each wing, often mimic bees or wasps and have the abdomen banded with yellow, and produce larvae which feed on decaying organic matter or are predaceous on plant lice — called also *flowerfly*; compare HOVER FLY, RAT-TAILED LARVA
syr·tis \'sərd·əs\ *or* **syrt** \'sərt\ *n, pl* **syr·tes** \-rd·(,)ēz, -r,tēz\ *or* **syrts** [L *Syrtis* (fr. Gk), either of two inlets of the Mediterranean sea on the coast of northern Africa (Gulf of Gabès and Gulf of Sidra), known in classical times for their quicksands] *archaic* **:** QUICKSAND, BOG
¹syr·up *or* **sir·up** \'sər·əp, 'sirəp *sometimes* 'sə-rəp *or* 'serəp *or rapid* 'sərp\ *n* -s [ME *sirop, sirup*, fr. MF *sirop*, fr. ML *syrupus, sirupus*, fr. Ar *sharāb* drink, wine, coffee, syrup, fr. *shariba* to drink] **1 a :** a thick sticky liquid consisting of a concentrated solution of sugar and water with or without the addition of a flavoring agent ⟨lemon ~⟩ ⟨chocolate ~⟩ or medicinal substance ⟨~ of codeine⟩ or of sugar and juice of a fruit or herb — compare CORN SYRUP **b :** the concentrated juice of a fruit or plant ⟨apple ~⟩; *specif* **:** the evaporated juice of the sugar cane as it occurs just prior to crystallization of the sugar in the process of manufacturing cane sugar — compare MAPLE SYRUP, SORGHUM 2 **2 :** cloying sweetness or sentimentality ⟨fancy blended with ~ and eroticism and having almost nothing to do with facts —Iris Barry⟩ ⟨children's theater . . . production . . . was, for sophisticated adults at least, pretty much tricks and ~ —Henry Hewes⟩ **3 :** a light to moderate olive brown — called also *antique* **4 :** a synthetic resin or plastic in the form of a liquid or solution ⟨partially polymerized casting ~⟩
²syrup *or* **sirup** \"\ *vt* -ED/-ING/-s **:** to add syrup to (as fruit in canning)
syr·up·er *or* **sir·up·er** \-pə(r)\ *n* -s **1 :** one that bottles syrup or that places a fixed amount of syrup in a bottle prior to the addition of plain or carbonated water **2 :** one that fills containers of canned goods with syrup
syrup pan *n* **:** a large evaporating pan usu. containing a series of alternating baffles in which the juice of sugar cane or sorghum is boiled into syrup
syr·upy *or* **sir·upy** \-pē, -pi\ *adj* **1 :** resembling syrup in appearance or quality ⟨~ color⟩ ⟨coffee . . . thick and ~ —Hugh MacLennan⟩ **2 :** cloyingly sweet or sentimental ⟨promptly cover the taste of defeat with ~ new daydreams —Katharine Scherman⟩ ⟨when a ~ mood is on him and his wife, they spend a deplorable amount of time clutching at and kissing each other —John McCarten⟩; *esp* **:** excessively sweet and melodious **:** DULCET ⟨theater organ music, ~ sweet —Rumer Godden⟩ ⟨slender fingers would draw out the ~ music from the strings —Osbert Sitwell⟩
syr·ye·ni·an \sə'r'yēnēən\ *also* **syr·yan** \'sir,yan, + sər'y-\ *n, pl* **syryenian** *or* **syryenians** *cap* [*Syryenian* irreg. fr. Russ *Zyryanin* Zyrian + E *-an*; *Syryan* modif. of Russ *Zyryanin*] **:** ZYRIAN
sys *pl of* SY
sys *abbr* system
sys·sar·co·sis \,sisär'kōsəs\ *n, pl* **syssarco·ses** \-ō,sēz\ [NL, fr. Gk *syssarkōsis* fact of being overgrown with flesh, fr. *syssarkousthai* to be overgrown with flesh also (fr. *syn-* + *sarkousthai*, passive of *sarkoun* to make fleshy, grow fleshy, fr. *sark-, sarx* flesh) + *-sis* — more at SARCASM] **:** the junction of two or more bones by means of attached muscles (as the scapula with the thorax or the hyoid with the mandible and sternum)
sys·sel \'sisəl\ *n* -s [Dan, fr. Icel *sȳsla* business, work, activity, syssel, fr. ON; akin to OE *sūsl* misery, torment, torture, *sēoslig* afflicted, ON *sȳsl* eager, painstaking, *sjūkr* sick — more at SICK] **:** an Icelandic administrative district
syst *abbr* system
sys·tal·tic \sə'stȯltik, -tal-\ *adj* [Gk *systaltos* (verbal of *systellein* to contract) + E *-ic* — more at SYSTOLE] **:** marked by regular contraction and dilatation **:** PULSING ⟨the ~ action of the heart⟩ ⟨flux and reflux of ~ tides —V.P.Watkins⟩
sys·tem \'sistəm\ *n* -s [LL *systema*, fr. Gk *systēma*, fr. *synistanai* to bring together, combine, fr. *syn-* + *histanai* to cause to stand — more at STAND] **1 a :** a complex unity formed of many often diverse parts subject to a common plan or serving a common purpose **b :** an aggregation or assemblage of objects joined in regular interaction or interdependence **:** a set of units combined by nature or art to form an integral, organic, or organized whole **:** an orderly working totality **:** a coherent unification ⟨the notion implicit in the word *universe* expresses an act of faith, for it projects ~ far beyond the evidence⟩ **c :** a group of bodies (as the solar system) moving together in an interrelated pattern or under the influence of related forces or attractions **d :** the related body organs that cooperate in performing one of the fundamental vital functions **e :** a group of related natural objects or forces ⟨a weather ~⟩ ⟨rivers of the continental drainage ~⟩ **f :** a group of devices or artificial objects forming a network or used for a common purpose ⟨a nationwide dial telephone ~⟩ ⟨an express highway ~⟩ ⟨a ~ of public parks⟩ ⟨a hot air heating ~⟩ ⟨the electrical ~s of automobiles grew steadily more elaborate⟩ **g :** a major division of rocks usu. larger than a series and including all formations deposited or otherwise formed during a period or an era ⟨the Silurian ~⟩ **h :** a group of freight or passenger transportation lines or services operating under common management and usu. covering several routes ⟨a national airfreight ~⟩ **2 a :** the body considered as a functional unit ⟨toxins from a focal lesion pervading the whole ~⟩ **b :** one's whole affective being ⟨a few hard knocks will get that cockiness out of his ~⟩ **3 a :** the structure or whole formed by the essential principles or facts of a science or branch of knowledge or thought **:** an organized or methodically arranged set of ideas, theories, or speculations **b** (1) **:** the content of laws, doctrines, ideas, or principles belonging to a philosophy, a religion, or a form of government **:** an orderly scheme of thought or constitutions (2) **:** a particular philosophy, religion, or political order ⟨a positivistic ~⟩ ⟨a collectivist ~⟩ ⟨the capitalist ~⟩ (3) **:** a form of social, economic, or other organization or practice ⟨a tenant farmer ~⟩ ⟨a managed currency ~⟩ **c :** HYPOTHESIS **d :** TREATISE **e :** coherent or harmonious arrangement, pattern, or form **:** ORDERLINESS, REGULARITY ⟨began to plan how she would . . . bring ~ out of confusion —Ellen Glasgow⟩ **f :** a particular classification, notation, or other formal arrangement or scheme ⟨a biological taxonomic ~⟩ ⟨a ~ of musical notation⟩ ⟨a Vigenère ~ of cryptography⟩ **4** *Eng law* **:** method or design as shown by other acts of a defendant similar to that charged of which evidence is admissible to rebut or negative a defense of accident, mistake, or ignorance or to prove a course of conduct **5 a :** a sequence of syllables, feet, cola, periods, lines, or strophes so related together as to present a relatively discrete and bounded rhythmic pattern or figure **b :** a series with fixed limits in classical prosody: (1) **:** a group of two or more periods (2) **:** a group of verses in the same measure **6 a :** a musical interval in ancient Greek music regarded as a compound of two lesser ones **b :** a classified series of tones (as a mode or scale) **c :** the collection of staffs which form a full score **7 :** a group of zooids in a compound ascidian arranged about a cloacal cavity which serve for them in common and into which the atrial orifices of all open **8 :** an assemblage of substances that is in or tends toward equilibrium, that may be homogeneous or heterogeneous and if the latter may be classed by the number of phases, and that may also be classed by the number of components or the number of variables ⟨a two-phase ternary ~⟩ ⟨univariant and bivariant ~s⟩ — see PHASE RULE **9 :** an organized or established procedure or method or the set of materials or appliances used to carry it out ⟨a business office ~⟩ **10 :** an organization or network for the collection and distribution of information, news, or entertainment **:** a communications industry ⟨a financial news ~⟩ ⟨a radio broadcasting ~⟩ ⟨a telephone ~⟩ **11 :** either of the two sets of four rows of squares that extend across the checkerboard from the black squares in the king row **12 :** an organized society or social situation regarded as hampering, stifling, or stultifying ⟨had always loved that effort to beat the ~ —J.P.Marquand⟩ ⟨it's the ~, and I'm caught —Morley Callaghan⟩ **13 :** a method or scheme of betting by which a gambler tries to assure himself of greater winnings than luck or chance would afford ⟨invented a new ~ at roulette —D.G.Gerahty⟩
syn SCHEME, NETWORK, COMPLEX, ORGANISM, ECONOMY: SYSTEM may imply that the component units of an aggregate exist and operate in unison or concord according to a coherent plan for smooth functioning ⟨amid a *system* where the classic principles of capitalism still work successfully —H.J.Laski⟩ ⟨comprehend all experience in a closed *system* —W.R.Inge⟩ ⟨it does not form an independent *system*, like the universe: it exists as an element in human culture —Lewis Mumford⟩ SCHEME may stress an overall design for the interrelation of components, often a design carefully calculated ⟨the cheerful, sanguine, courageous *scheme* of life, which was in part natural to her and in part slowly built up —Havelock Ellis⟩ ⟨our complex system, presenting the rare and difficult *scheme* of one general government, whose action extends over the whole —John Marshall⟩ ⟨the Newtonian *scheme* of the universe does not banish God from the universe —*Times Lit. Supp.*⟩ NETWORK suggests a system with interconnection or intercrossing at salient points sometimes involved but susceptible to analysis or control ⟨a *network* of abandoned narrow-gage logging roads penetrates the wooded areas —*Amer. Guide Series: Mich.*⟩ ⟨even the lowliest savages live in a social world characterized by a complex *network* of traditionally conserved habits, usages, and attitudes —Edward Sapir⟩ COMPLEX stresses an elaborate interweaving, interconnection and interrelationship of components difficult to trace ⟨for these ancestors of ours, in one half of their thoughts and acts, were still guided by a *complex* of intellectual, ethical, and social assumptions of which only medieval scholars can today comprehend the true purport —G.M. Trevelyan⟩ ⟨this *complex* of conditions which taxes the terms upon which human beings associate and live together is summed up in the word *culture* —John Dewey⟩ ⟨modern science, with infinite effort, has discovered and announced that man is a bewildering *complex* of energies —Henry Adams⟩ ORGANISM literally applies only to systems having life; figuratively, it suggests analogies to biological systems ⟨not because of an interest in the individual himself as a matured and single *organism* of ideas but in his assumed typicality for the community as a whole —Edward Sapir⟩ ⟨the Church grew, like any other *organism*, by responding to its environment —W.R.Inge⟩ ECONOMY implies a system concerned with needs and their regulation and fulfillment by individual, species, household, business, or government ⟨the plantation *economy*, with its base in slavery, was not conducive to the growth of industrial enterprise —*Amer. Guide Series: N.C.*⟩ ⟨the principle may operate successfully in the close *economy* of a good family, or even within a small religious community —J.A.Hobson⟩ **syn** see in addition METHOD
sys·tem·at·ic \,sistə¦mad·|ik, -at|, |ēk\ *also* **sys·tem·at·i·cal** \|əkəl, |ēk-\ *adj* [*systematic* fr. LL *systematicus*, fr. Gk *systēmatikos*, fr. *systēmat-, systēma* system + *-ikos* -ic; *systematical* fr. LL *systematicus* + E *-al*] **1 a :** expounding a subject or covering a field thoroughly according to an orderly scheme or plan ⟨~ study of market movements and consumer demand —F.H.Boland⟩ ⟨a ~ treatise⟩ ⟨a ~ scholar⟩ **b :** reduced to or presented or formulated as a coherent body of ideas or principles **:** offering or constituting a complete scheme, outline, or classification ⟨~ philosophical thought⟩ **c :** marked by or manifesting system, method, or orderly procedure **:** following or observing a plan **:** METHODICAL, REGULAR ⟨~ examination of the terrain was begun —*Amer. Guide Series: Pa.*⟩ ⟨as a workman he was ~⟩ **2 :** of or relating to classification esp. in the sciences ⟨the ~ name of a chemical⟩ **:** TAXONOMIC ⟨~ botany⟩ **3 :** SYSTEMIC **4 a :** of, relating to, or constituting a group of two or more periods in classical prosody **b :** of, relating to, or constituting a group of verses in the same classical measure **syn** see ORDERLY
sys·tem·at·i·cal·ly \|ək(ə)lē, |ēk-, -li\ *adv* **:** in a systematic manner

systematic error *n* **:** a statistical error that persists and cannot be considered as due entirely to chance — opposed to *random error*

sys·tem·a·ti·cian \\ˌsistəmə'tishən\\ *n* -s **:** SYSTEMATIST ⟨hence the word *theology* is not to be defined solely as the ~*s* do —G.E.Wright⟩

sys·tem·at·ic·ness *n* -ES **:** the quality or state of being systematic

sys·tem·at·ics \\ˌsistə'mad·\|iks, -at\|, \|ēks\\ *n pl but sing in constr* **1 :** the science of classification **:** classificatory method **:** ORGANIZATION ⟨his genius was not for ~ but for penetrating fragments —Maurice Natanson⟩ **2 :** a system of classification; *usu* **:** the classification and study of organisms with regard to their natural relationships **:** TAXONOMY — compare BIOSYSTEMATY **3 :** an organizational scheme or structure **:** FORM, HIERARCHY, PLAN ⟨a highly theoretical assumption about the ~ of a culture —Abraham Edel⟩

systematic theology *n* **:** constructive theology **:** a branch of theology that attempts to reduce all religious truth to statements forming a self-consistent and organized whole

sys·tem·a·tism \\'sistəmə,tizəm\\ *n* -s [fr. *systematize*, after such pairs as *organize: organism*] **:** the practice of system-building or an addiction to it

sys·tem·a·tist \\'sistəməd·əst\\ *n* -s [LL *systemat-*, *systema* system + E *-ist*] **1 :** a maker or follower of a system **2 :** a classifying scientist **:** TAXONOMIST

sys·tem·a·ti·za·tion \\ˌsistəməd·ə'zāshən, -mətə'-, -məˌtī'-\\ *n* -s **:** the act or practice of systematizing

sys·tem·a·tize \\'sistəməˌtīz\\ *vb* -ED/-ING/-S *see -ize in Explan Notes* [LL *systemat-*, *systema* system + E *-ize*] *vt* **:** to make into a system **:** arrange methodically **:** reduce to order **:** CLASSIFY, METHODIZE, ORGANIZE ⟨the great historic efforts to ~ the law⟩ ~ *vi* **:** to form a system **:** ORGANIZE ⟨cultures differ in their ability to ~ —A.L.Kroeber⟩ **syn** see ORDER

sys·tem·a·tiz·er \\-zə(r)\\ *n* -s **:** one that systematizes ⟨he was a ~ and an innovator of methods resulting in great economies —W.J.Ghent⟩

sys·tem·a·ty \\sə'stemad·ē\\ *n* -ES [*systematic* + *-y*] **:** systematic classification **:** TAXONOMY

sys·temed \\'sistəmd\\ *adj* **:** operating as or made into a system **:** ordered systematically

1**sys·tem·ic** \\sə'stemik, -mēk\\ *adj* [*system* + *-ic*] **:** of, relating to, or common to a system: as **a :** affecting the body generally — distinguished from *local* ⟨~ death⟩ ⟨~ wilt in plants⟩ **b :** supplying those parts of the body that receive blood through the aorta rather than the pulmonary artery **c :** being a pesticide which as used is harmless to a plant or higher animal but when absorbed into the sap or blood stream makes the whole organism toxic to pests (as aphids, mites, or cattle grubs)

2**systemic** \\"\\ *n* -s **:** a systemic pesticide

sys·tem·i·cal·ly \\-mək(ə)lē, -mēk-, -li\\ *adv* **:** in a manner affecting the body as a whole

systemic arch *n* **:** any branchial arch that persists in the adult **:** AORTIC ARCH

systemic circulation *n* **:** the passage of arterial blood from the left auricle of the heart through the left ventricle, the systemic arteries, and the capillaries to the organs and tissues that receive much of its oxygen in exchange for carbon dioxide and its return via the systemic veins to enter the right auricle and participate in the pulmonary circulation — used of man and other animals with a complete double circulation

systemic heart *n* **:** the part of the heart propelling blood through the systemic circulation; *specif* **:** the left auricle and ventricle of higher vertebrates — compare PULMONARY HEART

sys·tem·ist \\'sistəməst\\ *n* -s [*system* + *-ist*] **:** SYSTEMATIST

sys·tem·iza·tion \\ˌsistəmə'zāshən, -təˌmī'-\\ *n* -s **:** SYSTEMATIZATION

sys·tem·ize \\'sistəˌmīz\\ *vt* -ED/-ING/-S [*system* + *-ize*] **:** to reduce to system **:** SYSTEMATIZE

sys·tem·less \\'sistəmləs\\ *adj* **:** devoid of system, order, or structure

systems *pl of* SYSTEM

sys·to·le \\'sistə(ˌ)lē, -ˌli\\ *n* -s [Gk *systolē*, lit., contraction, fr. *systellein* to contract, fr. *syn-* + *stellein* to set up, place, send — more at STALL] **1 :** the shortening in verse of a syllable naturally or by position long (as for metrical convenience) — opposed to *ectasis*, *diastole* **2** [NL, fr. Gk *systolē*] **:** a rhythmically recurrent contraction: as **a :** the contraction of the heart by which the blood is forced onward and the circulation kept up **b :** the contraction of a rhythmically pulsating contractile vacuole — **sys·tol·ic** \\sə'stälik, -lēk\\ *adj*

systolic pressure *n* [*systole* + *-ic*] **:** the highest arterial blood pressure of a cardiac cycle occurring immediately after systole of the left ventricle of the heart — compare DIASTOLIC PRESSURE

sys·tyle \\'siˌstīl\\ *n* -s [L *systylos*, fr. Gk, having columns close together, fr. *syn-* + *stylos* column, pillar — more at STEER] **:** an intercolumniation of two diameters — see INTERCOLUMNIATION ILLUSTRATION

syz·y·get·ic \\ˌsizəˌjed·ik\\ *adj* [*syzygy* + *-etic*] **:** of, relating to, or constituting a syzygy **:** SYZYGIAL — **syz·y·get·i·cal·ly** \\-d·ək(ə)lē\\ *adv*

sy·zyg·i·al \\sə'zijēəl\\ *adj* [*syzygy* + *-al*] **:** of or relating to a syzygy

sy·zyg·i·um \\-ēəm\\ *n, pl* **syzyg·ia** \\-ēə\\ [NL, alter. of LL *syzygia*] **:** SYZYGY

syz·y·gy \\'sizəjē, -ji\\ *n* -ES [LL *syzygia*, fr. Gk, lit., state of being yoked together, fr. *syzygos* yoked together, united (fr. *syn-* + *zygon* yoke) + *-ia* -y — more at YOKE] **1 :** the nearly straight-line configuration of three celestial bodies (as the sun, moon, and earth during a solar or lunar eclipse) in a gravitational system **2 :** a group of two coupled feet in Greek or Latin prosody: **a :** DIPODY **b** (1) **:** a combination of two differing feet (2) **:** a foot of four syllables (as the Ionic) **3 :** a pair of correlatives, opposites, or otherwise related things; *esp* **:** a pair of gnostic aeons male and female ⟨the ~ of Man and Church⟩ **4 a** (1) **:** the immovable union and partial concrescence of two joints of an arm of a crinoid to form a single segment (2) **:** the segment so formed **b :** temporary end-to-end union of gregarines — compare PRIMITE, SATELLITE

szai·bel·yite \\sā'belˌyīt\\ *n* -s [G *szajbelyit*, fr. Stephan *Szailbely* †1855 Hungarian mine surveyor + G *-it* -ite] **:** a mineral $MgBO_2OH$ consisting of a magnesium borate that occurs in nodular masses of white acicular crystals

szcze·cin \\'shchetsēn\\ *adj, usu cap* [fr. *Szczecin*, Poland] **:** of or from the city of Szczecin, Poland **:** of the kind or style prevalent in Szczecin

sze·ged \\'seˌged\\ *adj, usu cap* [fr. *Szeged*, Hungary] **:** of or from the city of Szeged, Hungary **:** of the kind or style prevalent in Szeged

szek·ler \\'seklə(r)\\ *or* **szek·el** \\'sekəl\\ *n* -s *cap* [*szekler* fr. G, fr. Hung *Székely*, fr. *székel* to reside; *szekel* fr. Hung *Székely*] **1 :** a member of the Transylvanian branch of the Magyar race **2 :** the Hungarian dialect of the Szeklers written in its own runic alphabet

szi \\'sē\\ *n, pl* **szi** *or* **szis** *usu cap* **:** a member of a people found mainly in the Sadon area of the Burma-China frontier and closely related to or identical with the Maru

szmik·ite \\'smiˌkīt\\ *n* -s [G *szmikit*, fr. Ignaz *Szmik*, 19th cent. Hung. mining official + G *-it* -ite] **:** a mineral $MnSO_4.H_2O$ consisting of a hydrous manganese sulfate isomorphous with kieserite and szomolnokite

szo·mol·nok·ite \\sə'mälnəˌkīt\\ *n* -s [G *szomolnokit*, fr. *Szomolnok* (Smolnik), Czechoslovakia + G *-it* -ite] **:** a mineral $FeSO_4.H_2O$ consisting of a hydrous ferrous sulfate isomorphous with kieserite and szmikite

T t t t 𝔗

¹t \'tē\ *n, pl* **t's** *or* **ts** \'tēz\ *often cap, often attrib* **1 a :** the 20th letter of the English alphabet **b :** an instance of this letter printed, written, or otherwise represented **c :** a speech counterpart of orthographic *t* (as *t* in *tie, sty, bat, hatpin, later,* or French *tu*) **2 :** a printer's type, a stamp, or some other instrument for reproducing the letter *t* **3 :** someone or something arbitrarily or conveniently designated *t* esp. as the 19th or when j is used for the 10th the 20th in order or class **4 a :** something having the shape of the letter T **b** [by shortening] **:** T FORMATION — **to a T** *adv* [short for *to a tittle*] **:** to perfection ⟨suits me *to a T*⟩

²t *abbr, often cap* **1** table **2** [It *tace*] be silent **3** tackle **4** taken **5** taper **6** tare **7** target **8** teaspoon **9** technical; technician **10** telephone **11** teletype **12** temperature **13** tempo **14** temporal **15** temporary **16** [L *tempore*] in the time of **17** tenor **18** tense **19** tension **20** tensor **21** terminal; termination **22** territorial; territory **23** tertiary **24** testament **25** thickness **26** thief **27** thread **28** tied **29** time; times **30** toe **31** tome **32** [L *tomus*] volume **33** ton **34** tooth **35** top **36** town; township **37** trace **38** trainer **39** transcription **40** transformer **41** transit **42** transition; transitional **43** transitive **44** tread **45** triangle **46** trillo **47** [LL *Trinitas*] the Trinity **48** triple **49** tropical **50** trotter **51** troy **52** true **53** tun **54** Turkish **55** tutti

³t *symbol* **1** *cap* absolute temperature **2** *ital* meridian angle **3** *cap* octodecimo **4** *cap* tritium **5** *usu ital* triton

t- \ˌtərt\ *abbr, usu ital* [tertiary] tertiary — esp. in names of organic chemical radicals ⟨*t*-butyl⟩

¹t' \tə\ *prep* [by contr.] **:** TO ⟨*t'* abandon⟩ ⟨*t'* engrave⟩

²t' \tə *before a consonant,* t *before a vowel*\ *definite article* [by contr.] *dial* **:** THE ⟨*t'* other⟩ ⟨*t'* bottle⟩ ⟨*t'* heart⟩

't \t\ *pron* [by contr.] **:** IT ⟨'twill do⟩ — not often in formal use

¹ta \'tä\ *dial var of* TAKE

²ta \'tə\ *chiefly dial var of* TO

³ta \"\ *pron* [by alter.] **:** THOU, YOU ⟨what was ~ doin in theer —Alfred Ollivant⟩

⁴ta \'tä\ *n* [baby talk] *dial Brit* **:** THANKS

⁵ta \tə\ *definite article* [by alter.] *dial chiefly Scot* **:** THE

TA *abbr* **1** table of allowances **2** target area **3** tax agent **4** telegraphic address **5** territorial army **6** *often not cap* [L *testantibus actis*] as the acts show **7** toxin-antitoxin **8** traffic agent; traffic auditor **9** transit authority

Ta *symbol* tantalum

taaffe·ite \'tä,fīt\ *n* -s [Count Edward Charles Richard *Taaffe* b1898 Irish gemmologist born in Bohemia who first found it as a faceted gem + E *-ite*] **:** a rare mineral $BeMgAl_4O_{16}$ consisting of oxide of beryllium, magnesium, and aluminum and resembling mauve-colored spinel

taal \'täl\ *n, cap* [Afrik, fr. D, speech, language, fr. MD *tale;* akin to OE *talu* speech — more at TALE] **:** AFRIKAANS — usu. used with *the*

ta·a·nith es·ther *or* **ta·a·nit esther** \ˌtäə'nēt(h)e'ster\ *n, pl* **taanith esthers** *or* **taanit esthers** *usu cap T&E* [Heb *ta'ănīth esthēr*] **:** FAST OF ESTHER

¹tab \'tab, -aa(ə)b\ *n* -s *often attrib* [origin unknown] **1 a :** a short flap, loop, or other device projecting from an object to facilitate its identification or grasping: as (1) **:** the piece of leather to which a saddle girth is secured (2) *dial Eng* **:** the tip of a shoelace (3) **:** a small hand grip ⟨swung the musette around front and pulled open the ~s on it —R.O. Bowen⟩; *specif* **:** PULL STRAP (4) **:** a small lettered guide affixed to the bottom of the notch of a thumb index or projecting from the edge of a page (5) **:** a projection from a card used as an aid in filing (6) **:** a margin on a stamp or sheet of stamps bearing an ornamentation or a descriptive or advertising inscription **b** (1) **:** the collar insignia of a British army officer (2) *Brit* **:** STAFF OFFICER **c** (1) **:** *dial chiefly Eng* **:** a shoe latchet (2) **:** a small strap or flap fastening (as for a coat) stitched to a garment at one end and buttoned at the loose end (3) **:** a projecting metal strip or a key fitting into a slot (as for securing a roller to its mandrel) **d :** a small insert, addition, or remnant ⟨license plate ~⟩ ⟨shoe . . . reinforced at the toe and heel by metal ~s —William Duber⟩ **e** *dial Eng* **:** DAB ⟨boys, as they followed the path above, could toss ~s of turf down her chimney —A.T. Quiller-Couch⟩ **f :** APPENDAGE, EXTENSION: as (1) **:** a small pendant or projecting part of a garment ⟨~s . . . are favorite trimmings, used at necklines —*Women's Wear Daily*⟩; *esp* **:** one of a series of pendants forming a decorative border or edge (2) *or* **tab·leau** \'ta,blō, ₌'₌\ [*tableau* fr. ¹*tableau*] **:** a narrow framed or unframed drop used esp. for masking offstage spaces (3) **:** TAG 3d(1) **g :** a piece of leather with two finger holes and a slot for the arrow shaft worn by an archer to protect the drawing fingers **h :** a small auxiliary airfoil hinged to a control surface (as to the trailing edge of an aileron, rudder, or elevator) to help stabilize an airplane in flight — called also *trim tab* **2** [partly short for ¹*table;* partly fr. sense 1] **a :** an itemized account or close surveillance **:** TALLY, WATCH ⟨keep close ~s on both American and British publications —Bennett Cerf⟩ ⟨difficult to keep a ~ on the nefarious activities of these people —R.G.Menzies⟩ ⟨a color styling service . . . keeps ~s on mass-market trends in color —*Dun's Rev.*⟩ **b :** a creditor's statement **:** BILL, CHECK ⟨few merchants could afford to throw out all their fixtures and foot the ~ for a . . . new floor setup —E.B.Weiss⟩ ⟨big spending, which includes . . . picking up the ~, as well as big tipping —John Bainbridge⟩ **c :** an incurred expense or market value **:** COST, PRICE ⟨45 cents a pound, the ~ at which the industry . . . hope butter will move quickly onto dinner tables —*Wall Street Jour.*⟩ ⟨the ~ for superhighways may run as high as 3 million dollars a mile —*Changing Times*⟩ **3** [by shortening] **a :** TABLOID ⟨farm ~s that sometimes go out with larger dailies —Lois M. Miller⟩ ⟨~ show, specializing in brief revues —R.L.Taylor⟩ **b :** TABULATOR ⟨for typing tables, first set ~s to space the columns evenly⟩ ⟨run data cards through a ~⟩ **c :** TABLET ⟨two boxes of heat ~s —Paul Gallico⟩

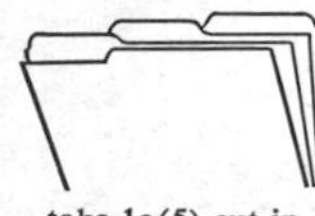
tabs 1a(5) cut in thirds

²tab \"\ *vt* **tabbed; tabbed; tabbing; tabs 1 :** to furnish or ornament with tabs ⟨when these cards are removed from the active list, they are *tabbed* according to group —*Amer. Business*⟩ ⟨cuffed neckline is looped and *tabbed* at the side —*Fashion Digest*⟩ **2 :** to single out **:** NAME, DESIGNATE, IDENTIFY ⟨the $14 million *tabbed* . . . for aid to school districts —*Fortnight*⟩ ⟨listeners have her *tabbed* as a chanteuse of the whispering school —*Los Angeles (Calif.) Times*⟩ ⟨someone once *tabbed* me the critic's critic —Ralph de Toledano⟩ **3** [by shortening] **:** TABULATE ⟨*tabbing* up ballots —*Time*⟩ ⟨~ all lines except the first . . . and double-space —H.H.Smith & A.C.Lloyd⟩

tab *abbr* **1** [NL *tabella*] lozenge **2** table **3** tabulate; tabulated

ta·baco *also* **ta·bac·co** \tə'ba(,)kō\ *archaic var of* TOBACCO

ta·ba·li·an \tə'bālēən\ *n* -s *usu cap* [*Tabal* the Tabalians + E *-an*] **:** a member of a Hittite cultural group living north of the Taurus mountains in southern Turkey and comprising 24 kingdoms in the second millennium B.C.

¹tab·a·nid \'tabənəd\ *adj* [NL *Tabanidae*] **:** of or relating to the Tabanidae

²tabanid \"\ *n* -s **:** a fly of the family Tabanidae

ta·ban·i·dae \tə'banə,dē\ *n pl, cap* [NL, fr. *Tabanus,* type genus + *-idae*] **:** a very large and important family of Diptera comprising the horseflies and deerflies whose females suck blood and sometimes transmit disease (as loaiasis) to human beings

ta·ba·nu·co *or* **ta·bo·nu·co** \ˌtäbə'nü(,)kō\ *n* -s [AmerSp, prob. fr. Taino] **:** CANDLEWOOD 1e

ta·ba·nus \tə'bānəs\ *n, cap* [NL, fr. L, horsefly] **:** the type genus of Tabanidae comprising various horseflies and greenbottle flies

tab·ard \'tabə(r)d\ *n* -s [ME, fr. OF *tabart*] **1 :** a tunic with or without short sleeves worn by a knight over his armor and emblazoned with his arms **2 a :** the official cape or coat of a herald made with or without short sleeves and emblazoned with his lord's arms **b :** the official surcoat of an officer of arms emblazoned with the royal arms ⟨dressed as heralds, with ~ and trumpet, looking for all the world like the knaves in a pack of cards —Victoria Sackville-West⟩ **3 :** a rectangular silk pendant bearing special emblems and attached to the bugles or trumpets of a military organization

tab·ard·ed \-dəd\ *adj* **:** wearing a tabard

Ta·bas·co \tə'ba(,)skō\ *trademark* — used for a pungent condiment sauce made from capsicum berries

tabasco mahogany *n, usu cap T* [fr. *Tabasco,* state in Mexico] **:** HONDURAS MAHOGANY

tab·a·sheer *also* **tab·a·shir** \ˌtabə'shi(ə)r\ *n* -s [Hindi *tabāshīr,* fr. Per] **:** a siliceous concretion in the joints of the bamboo valued in the East Indies as a medicine

¹tab·ber \'tabə(r)\ *dial Eng var of* TABOR

²tabber \"\ *n* -s [²*tab* + *-er*] **:** one that tabs; *specif* **:** a worker who makes or attaches tabs (as for identification, strengthening, or ornament)

tabbinet *var of* TABINET

¹tab·by \'tabē, -bi\ *n* -ES [F *tabis,* fr. MF *atabis,* fr. ML *attabi,* fr. Ar *'attābī,* fr. Al-*'Attābīya,* quarter in Baghdad where it was orig. made] **1 a** *archaic* (1) **:** a plain silk taffeta esp. with a moiré finish (2) **:** a dress of this fabric **b** (1) **:** PLAIN WEAVE ⟨~ is used for more purposes than any other weave —Harriette Brown⟩ (2) **:** a fabric in plain weave **2** [²*tabby*] **a :** a domestic cat having a gray or tawny coat striped and mottled with black and with the individual hairs variously banded and barred **b :** a domestic cat; *esp* **:** a female cat ⟨*tabbies* and toms⟩ **3 a :** a prying woman **:** BUSYBODY, GOSSIP ⟨some old *tabbies* would begin asking questions —Helen Eustis⟩ **b** *chiefly Brit* **:** SPINSTER 3

²tabby \"\ *adj* **1 a :** made of tabby ⟨a ~ waistcoat⟩ **b :** of or relating to tabby ⟨a ~ weave⟩ **2 a :** striped and mottled with black or with another color darker than the ground color **:** BRINDLED ⟨a ~ cat⟩ ⟨white with a ~ saddle on his back —Ngaio Marsh⟩ — compare MACKEREL **b :** DOMESTIC ⟨turn a ~ cat into a tiger —*Newsweek*⟩

³tabby \"\ *n* -ES [Gullah *'tabi,* of African origin; akin to Wolof *tabax* wall of a house made of sand, lime, or mud, Hausa *ta'bo* mud, Kongo *ntaba* muddy place] **:** a cement made of lime, sand or gravel, and oyster shells and used chiefly along the coast of Georgia and So. Carolina in the 17th and 18th centuries — compare TABIA, TAPIA

tab·e·bu·ia \ˌtabə'büyə\ *n, cap* [NL, fr. Tupi *tabebuya,* a tree, fr. *tacyba* ant + *bebuya* wood] **:** a large genus of tropical American shrubs and trees (family Bignoniaceae) having the calyx at first closed and differing from *Tecoma* chiefly in having digitate instead of pinnate leaves

ta·bel·la \tə'belə\ *n, pl* **tabel·lae** \-e,lē\ [NL, fr. L, tablet] **:** a medicated lozenge or tablet

tab·el·lar·ia \ˌtabə'la(a)rēə\ *n, usu cap* [NL, fr. fem. of L *tabellarius* relating to tablets, fr. *tabella* tablet + *-arius* -ary] **:** a genus of pinnate diatoms (family Tabellariaceae) united in zigzag often fixed colonies and often causing in water odors suggestive of fish or geraniums

ta·bel·lion \tə'belyən\ *n* -s [LL *tabellion-, tabellio,* fr. L *tabella* tablet, writing, document, dim. of *tabula* board — more at TABLE] **1 :** a scrivener under the Roman Empire with some notarial powers **2 :** an official scribe or notary public esp. in England and New England in the 17th and 18th centuries

¹tab·er·na·cle \'tabə(r),nakəl\ *n* -s [ME, fr. OF, fr. LL *tabernaculum* (trans. of Heb *ōhel mō'ēd*), fr. L, tent, dim. of *taberna* hut — more at TAVERN] **1 a** *often cap* **:** a portable sanctuary consisting of a rectangular wooden framework covered with curtains and carried by the Israelites during their wanderings of the Exodus as a holy dwelling place for their God and as a place for worship — called also *tent of meeting* **b :** a dwelling place **:** HABITATION — used formerly of the body as the temporary abode of the soul ⟨true image of the Father . . . enshrined in fleshly ~ —John Milton⟩ **c** *archaic* **:** a temporary shelter **:** HUT, TENT ⟨a place wherein to pitch their ~ and pursue their fortune —J.H.Burton⟩ **2 a :** a canopied niche or recess usu. framed by columns or pilasters and having a corbel or bracket (as for a statue) — compare BALDACHIN **b :** an ecclesiastical receptacle for the consecrated elements of the Eucharist; *esp* **:** an ornamental locked box resting on the middle of the altar and containing the pyx **3 a :** a temporary place of worship **:** one not conforming to traditional church architecture; *esp* **:** a meetinghouse with a large assembly hall ⟨Mormon ~⟩ **b :** a building or shelter used predominantly for evangelistic services ⟨the camp meeting is held each year . . . under a big open-air ~ —Green Peyton⟩ **4 a :** a boxlike support above deck in which the heel of a mast is stepped and pivoted so that it can be lowered to rest on the deck (as for negotiating a low bridge) **b :** a similar device in an open boat fitted from keel to thwart

²tabernacle \"\ *vb* **tabernacled; tabernacled; tabernacling** \-k(ə)liŋ\ **tabernacles** [ML *tabernaculare* (trans. of Gk *skēnoun* to pitch tent, encamp), fr. LL & L *tabernaculum*] *vi* **:** to take up temporary residence **:** SOJOURN; *esp* **:** to inhabit a physical body ⟨the Logos has become flesh, and has *tabernacled* among men —S.A.Cook⟩ ~ *vt, archaic* **:** to deposit in a tabernacle **:** ENSHRINE

tabernacle mirror *n* **:** CONSTITUTION MIRROR

tabernacle work *n* **1 :** ornamental usu. pierced tracery (as in the carved canopies over niches or stalls in churches) **2 :** architectural design characterized by the use of tabernacles

tab·er·nac·u·lar \ˌtabə(r)ˈnakyələ(r)\ *adj* [LL *tabernaculum* + E *-ar*] **:** of or characterized by tabernacle work ⟨cloisters . . . fronted with ~ or open work —Thomas Warton †1790⟩

ta·ber·nae·mon·ta·na \tə,bərnēmän'tānə\ *n* [NL, fr. J. T. *Tabernaemontanus* (Latin name of J. T. Müller) †1590 Ger. botanist] **1** *cap* **:** a large genus of tropical trees and shrubs (family Apocynaceae) having cymose flowers and a fleshy fruit **2** -s **:** any plant of the genus *Tabernaemontana*

ta·ber·nan·thine \ˌtabə(r)'nan(t),thēn, -ˌthən\ *n* -s [NL *Tabernanthe* (genus name of the plant *Tabernanthe iboga*) — fr. a native name in central Africa — + E *-ine*] **:** a bitter crystalline alkaloid $C_{20}H_{26}N_2O$ isomeric with ibogaine and occurring with it

ta·bes \'tā,bēz\ *n, pl* **tabes** [L — more at THAW] **1 :** wasting accompanying a chronic disease **2** [NL, fr. L] **:** TABES DORSALIS — **ta·bes·cent** \tə'besᵊnt\ *adj*

tabes dorsalis *n* [NL, dorsal tabes] **:** syphilis involving the posterior columns of the spinal cord and sensory nerve trunks, characterized by wasting, and marked by paroxysmal attacks of pain, functional disturbances of organs (as the stomach or larynx), incoordination of voluntary movements, loss of reflexes, and disorders of sensation, nutrition, and vision — called also *locomotor ataxia*

ta·bet \'tābət\ *n* -s [origin unknown] *Scot* **:** sense of feeling **:** SENSATION — often used in pl.

¹ta·bet·ic \tə'bed·ik\ *adj* [ISV *tab-* (fr. NL *tabes*) + *-etic*] **:** resembling, having the nature of, or affected with tabes dorsalis

²tabetic \"\ *n* -s **:** one who is affected with tabes dorsalis

tabetic crisis *n* **:** a paroxysmal attack of pain occurring in tabes dorsalis

ta·bet·i·sol \tə'bed·ə,sȯl, -säl\ *n* -s [L *tabēre* to melt + E connective *-i-* + *-isol* (as in *pergelisol*)] **:** unfrozen ground above, within, or below the pergelisol

ta·bet·less \'tābətləs\ *adj* [*tabet* + *-less*] **1** *Scot* **:** NUMB ⟨~ fingers had to be thawed —James Colville⟩ **2** *Scot* **:** SENSELESS, FOOLISH

ta·bia \'täbyə\ *n* -s [prob. alter. of *tapia*] **:** a building material composed of earth, lime, and pebbles rammed into place between forms and found very durable in rainless areas and esp. in building the castles of the northern Sahara — compare ³TABBY

tab·id \'tabəd\ *adj* [L *tabidus,* fr. *tabēre* to waste away, melt — more at THAW] *archaic* **:** TABETIC

tab index *n* **:** an index consisting of projecting tabs — compare STEP INDEX

tab·i·net *or* **tab·bi·net** \'tabə,net\ *n* -s [*tabinet* fr. obs. E *tabine,* a fabric, prob. tabby (prob. fr. ¹*tabby* + *-ine*) + E *-et; tabbinet* alter. (influenced by ¹*tabby*) of *tabinet*] **:** a silk and worsted fabric similar to poplin and usu. given a moiré finish

tab·la·ture \'tabləˌchů(ə)r, -ˌchüə, -ˌchə(r)\ *n* -s [MF, prob. fr. (assumed) NL *tabulatura,* fr. ML *tabulatus* tablet, fr. L *tabula* record, document, writing tablet + *-atus* -ate] **1 a :** an early instrumental musical notation indicating by letters and other signs the string, fret, key, or finger to be used instead of the tone to be sounded **b :** tonic sol-fa notation **c :** TABULATUR 1 **2** *archaic* **a :** a tablet (as a gravestone) bearing an inscription **b :** a work of art **:** PAINTING, PICTURE **c :** pictorial representation **d :** a verbal image **:** DESCRIPTION **3 :** division into plates or tables with intervening spaces ⟨the ~ of the cranial bones⟩

¹ta·ble \'tābəl\ *n* -s [ME, fr. OE *tabule* & OF *table;* both fr. ML & L; ML *tabula* table, fr. L, board, tablet, writing tablet, record, document, list; perh. akin to OHG *dili, dilla* plank, plank floor — more at THILL] **1 a** *obs* **:** a flat slab (as of wood or stone) ⟨the inner part of the temple is . . . covered with great ~s of porphyry —Thomas Washington⟩ **b** (1) **:** TABLET 1a(1) ⟨leave a ~ in the middle of the panel —Fiske Kimball⟩ ⟨write the vision, and make it plain upon ~s, that he may run that readeth it —Hab 2:2 (AV)⟩ (2) **:** a set of laws inscribed on tablets ⟨the Twelve *Tables* of Roman law⟩ ⟨~s of the decalogue⟩ **c** *obs* (1) **:** TABLET 1b ⟨asked for a writing ~, and wrote . . . his name —Lk 1:63 (AV)⟩ (2) **:** an indelible record ⟨the everlasting ~s of right reason —Richard Bentley †1742⟩ **2 a** (1) **tables** *pl* **:** BACKGAMMON (2) **:** one of the two leaves of a backgammon board or either half of a leaf ⟨white's inner ~ is opposite black's inner ~⟩ ⟨play into the home ~⟩ **b :** a game board **3 a** (1) **:** a piece of furniture consisting of a smooth flat slab fixed on legs or other support and variously used (as for eating, writing, working, or playing games) (2) **:** an operating or examining table ⟨put the patient on the ~⟩ (3) **:** an official bench or rostrum ⟨the original of the letter . . . must be delivered at the ~ by the member who makes the complaint —T.E.May⟩ **b** (1) **:** a supply or regular source of food or the manner of its preparation **:** BOARD, FARE ⟨their farms were better and their ~s more bountiful than most —R.H.Shryock⟩ ⟨spent his teens . . . as a poor relation at the ~ of his mother's family —*Amer. Guide Series: N. Y.*⟩ ⟨the ~ the landlady set was really something special and we ate all we could hold —Emmett Kelly⟩ (2) **:** an act or instance of assembling to eat **:** MEAL, SITTING ⟨sit down to ~ with an ambassador —Agnes M. Miall⟩ ⟨if visitors can see into the kitchen while at ~, no doubt they will offer to help with the washing up —G.F.Lawson⟩ ⟨still hoping . . . he'll get to eat at the first ~ —F.B.Gipson⟩ **c** (1) **:** a group of people (as diners, committeemen, or players in a game) assembled at or as if at a table ⟨the ~ then spoke of . . . how bracing the air was —James Joyce⟩ ⟨a ~ of aldermen⟩ ⟨a ~ of bridge⟩ ⟨a famous poker ~, which challenged all comers —Harvey Fergusson⟩ (2) **:** a legislative or negotiating session ⟨an ill-armed victor lacks power at the peace ~ —F.E.Hill⟩ **4 a :** the altar or altar rail at which communicants receive Holy Communion **b :** EUCHARIST 1a **5 a :** a flat usu. raised band or projecting ledge on a wall **:** STRINGCOURSE, WATER TABLE **b** *archaic* **:** PANEL 3b(2) **6 a :** a tabular arrangement of data ⟨results of this survey are given in ~s in the appendix⟩; *specif* **:** a systematic arrangement (as of numerical values) usu. in parallel rows or columns for ready reference ⟨~ of weights and measures⟩ ⟨~ of logarithms⟩ ⟨multiplication ~⟩ **b :** a condensed enumeration **:** LIST, SYNOPSIS ⟨~ of contents⟩ ⟨~ of organization⟩ ⟨offer his little ~ of oppositions and . . . let it stand —Carlos Baker⟩ **7 :** something that resembles a table esp. in having a plane surface: as **a** (1) **:** the principal facet at the top of a brilliant — see BRILLIANT illustration (2) **:** TABLE DIAMOND **b** (1) **:** TABLELAND (2) **:** LEVEL — see WATER TABLE **c** *obs* (1) **:** PICTURE (2) **:** the surface on which a picture is painted (3) **:** a plane of perspective **d** (1) **:** the external or internal layer of compact bone of the skull separated by cancellous diploe (2) **:** the flat worn upper surface of a tooth (as of a horse) **e** *archaic* **:** a large round sheet of crown glass **f :** a flat or short prismatic crystal **g** (1) **:** a flat plate in a machine tool that is often movable and is usu. provided with T slots on its upper surfaces to which work can be fastened while it is being processed (2) **:** a concentrating table (as for washing or screening coal ore) **:** settling trough **:** RUN **h :** a long flat-bottomed slightly inclined trough down which a slurry of starch and gluten flows slowly so that the heavier starch particles settle out while the gluten runs off **i :** BELLY 5f — **on the table** *adv* **:** in plain sight **:** in a fully revealed position ⟨put your cards *on the table*⟩ ⟨the editors do an excellent job in putting both sides *on the table* —Benjamin Fine⟩ — **under the table** *adv* **1 :** into a stupor ⟨drink a man *under the table*⟩ ⟨five minutes' serious thought about the eruption of eternity into time puts me *under the table* —Stuart Chase⟩ **2 :** under the counter **:** SECRETLY ⟨buy your liquor *under the table* —J.H. Allen⟩ ⟨strategic requirements for tin will be the major consideration *under the table* during the coming negotiations —*Economist*⟩

²table \"\ *adj* [ME, fr. ¹*table*] **1** *obs* **:** of or relating to backgammon ⟨your ~ players, and other gamesters —James Mabbe⟩ **2 a :** of, relating to, or used on a table ⟨~ mat⟩ ⟨~ lamp⟩ ⟨~ model⟩ ⟨gambling-license holders must pay a ~ tax to the state —J.F.McDonald⟩ **b :** raised or processed for table use **:** suitable for human consumption ⟨~ bird⟩ **3 :** resembling a table **:** having a plane surface ⟨~ rock⟩ ⟨~ reef⟩ ⟨*table*-jawed tweezers⟩ **4 :** TABULAR ⟨~ matter⟩ ⟨~ work⟩ **5 :** of, relating to, or mounted on the table of a machine ⟨~ vise⟩ ⟨tool has more teeth in cutters allowing for increased ~ feed per minute —*Steel*⟩

³table \"\ *vb* **tabled; tabled; tabling** \-b(ə)liŋ\ **tables** [ME *tablen,* fr. ¹*table*] *vt* **1 :** to enter on a table **:** TABULATE ⟨quarterly distribution . . . is as *tabled* below —T.J.Grayson⟩ **2 :** to provide with food **:** FEED ⟨*tabled* in midmorning they ate sour pickles —Thomas Wolfe⟩ **3 a** *Brit* **:** to place on the agenda **:** submit for discussion ⟨research groups prepare the draft bills *tabled* by . . . parliamentary representatives —Barbara & Robert North⟩ **b :** to lay on the table ⟨the hydroelectric project has been *tabled,* revived, *tabled* again —E.W. Smith⟩ **c :** to put on a table ⟨ale, for which he too used to ~ his twopence —Thomas Carlyle⟩ ⟨florists *tabled* a large . . assortment of cut flowers —*Gardeners' Chronicle*⟩ **4 a** *archaic* **:** ⁴SCARF 1 **b :** to strengthen (a sail) by making a broad hem on the edges attached to the boltrope **5 :** to wash or screen on a table ⟨~ ground ore⟩ **6 :** to sediment (starch) by use of a table ~ *vi, archaic* **:** to take food **:** BOARD, EAT

¹tab·leau \'ta,blō, ₌'₌\ *n, pl* **tab·leaux** \-ō(z)\ *also* **tableaus** \-ōz\ [F, fr. MF *tablel,* dim. of *table*] **1 a :** a graphic description or visualization **:** IMAGE, PICTURE ⟨a popular writer . . . presenting winsome *tableaux* of old-fashioned literary days and ways —J.D.Hart⟩ ⟨thirteen *tableaux* . . . using one permanent frame —*Spectator*⟩ **b :** a striking effect or artistic grouping **:** ARRANGEMENT, SCENE ⟨the whole house party grouped in a welcoming ~ —Osbert Lancaster⟩ ⟨a series of window *tableaux* planned and executed by . . . interior designers —*Antiques*⟩ **c** *or* **tableau vi·vant** \-vē'väⁿ\ *pl* **tableaux vivants** \"\ [F, lit., living picture] **:** a sustained pose **:** a static depiction usu. presented on a stage with participants in appropriate costume ⟨a series of *tableaux* called "Grecian Statues", accompanied by explanatory song —*Amer. Guide Series: Wash.*⟩ ⟨stood with outstretched hand . . . in what seemed an endlessly-held ~ —Hartley Howard⟩ **2 a** *archaic* **:** an official list **:** TABLE ⟨official *tableaux* of rank —*Harper's*⟩ **b :** a large alphabet square in cryptography **3 :** the part of a solitaire layout on which building is usu. done

²tableau *var of* TAB

tableau curtain *n* **:** a stage curtain that opens in the center and has its sections drawn upward as well as to the side in order to produce a draped effect

tableau curtain

table–board \'₌₌,₌\ *n* **1 :** a gaming table **2** *chiefly dial* **a :** TABLE 3a(1) **b :** TABLETOP **3 :** board without room ⟨find *table-board* at some of the neighboring houses —W.D.Howells⟩

table book *n* **1** *archaic* **:** TABLET 1c ⟨found in the dead man's

pocket a *table book*, wherein were entered . . . names —Samuel Pepys⟩ **2 :** a book customarily displayed on a table ⟨this was the age of . . . lavish and heavy *table books* —J.M.Wells⟩
table chair *n* **:** CHAIR TABLE
table clock *n* **:** an early mainspring-driven clock with a horizontal dial
tablecloth \ˈ⸗⸗,⸗\ *n* [ME, fr. *table* + *cloth*] **1 :** a covering spread over a dining table before the places are set **2** *archaic* **:** an ornamental cover for a table — compare SCARF 3
table-cut \ˈ⸗¦⸗\ *adj* **1 :** cut with a table — used of a gem **2 :** cut individually **:** CUSTOM-MADE — used of gloves
table cut *n* **:** a style of cutting gems in which the table is wider than the culet and joins the girdle in beveled edges — compare STEP CUT; see CUT illustration
ta·ble d'hôte \ˌtäbəlˈdōt, ˌtab-, ˌtab-\ *n, pl* **table d'hôtes** \-ˈdōt(s)\ [F, lit., host's table] **1 :** a meal (as in a hotel) served to all guests at a stated hour and a fixed price **2 :** a complete meal of several courses (as appetizer, entrée, dessert, and beverage) offered at a fixed price — compare A LA CARTE
table diamond *n* **:** a relatively flat diamond of table cut
table dormant *n* [ME, dormant table, fr. MF] **:** the first permanent type of table to replace the movable board on trestles in the medieval period
ta·ble·ful \ˈtābəl,fu̇l\ *n, pl* **tablefuls** *or* **tablesful** \-l,fu̇lz, -lz,fu̇l\ **:** as much or as many as a table can hold or accommodate ⟨a ~ of dishes⟩ ⟨a ~ of guests⟩
table garden *n* [so called fr. its supplying vegetables to the owner's table] **:** KITCHEN GARDEN
table-hop \ˈ⸗⸗,⸗\ *vi* **:** to move from table to table (as in a restaurant) visiting with friends ⟨customers *table-hopped*, called out greetings from across the room —*Omnibook*⟩ — **table-hop·per** \-pə(r)\ *n*
ta·ble·land \ˈtābəl,(l)and\ *n* **:** a broad level elevated area **:** PLATEAU, MESA
table linen *n* **:** linen (as tablecloths and napkins) for use at the table
ta·ble·man \ˈtābəlmən\ *n, pl* **tablemen** [ME] **1** *obs* **:** a piece used in playing backgammon **2 :** one who works at or tends a table: as **a :** a worker who lays out and marks marble slabs for cutting **b :** an operator of a machine for cutting bricks or tiles from a column of moist clay **c :** one who tends the tables where ore is concentrated
table mountain *n* **:** a mountain with a flat top
table-mountain pine *n* **:** a pine (*Pinus pungens*) distinguished by spine-tipped knobby cone scales — called also *hickory pine, prickly pine, yellow pine*
table rapping *or* **table tapping** *n* **:** SPIRIT RAPPING
table roll *n* **:** any of a series of small rolls that support and hold level the wire of a fourdrinier machine
tables *pl of* TABLE, *pres 3d sing of* TABLE
table salt *n* **:** salt for use at the table and in cooking; *esp* **:** SALT 1a
table settle *n* **:** a settle having a back hinged so that it can be let down on the arms
tablespoon \ˈ⸗⸗,⸗\ *n* **1 :** a large spoon usu. used for serving — see SPOON illustration **2 :** TABLESPOONFUL
ta·ble·spoon·ful \ˈ⸗⸗ˌspün,fu̇l *sometimes* -pün-\ *n, pl* **tablespoonfuls** *also* **tablespoonsful** \-n,fu̇lz, -nz,fu̇l\ **1 :** an amount equal to the capacity of one tablespoon **:** enough to fill a tablespoon **2 :** a unit of measure used esp. in cookery equal to one level tablespoonful or 4 fluidrams
table stake *n* **1 :** a stake that a player places on the table at the start of a poker game or deal as the amount he is willing to bet and that may not be changed after the deal begins **2 table stakes** *pl* **:** poker in which the betting limit for a player is the amount remaining in his table stake
table stone *n* **:** DOLMEN
¹**tab·let** \ˈtablət, *usu* -əd·+V\ *n* -s [ME *tablett, tablette*, fr. MF *tablete*, dim. of *table* — more at TABLE] **1 a** (1) **:** a flat surface, slab, or plaque suited for or bearing an inscription ⟨cuneiform ~s⟩ ⟨~s . . . range in size from small nameplates and directional signs to large memorials and honor rolls —*Sweet's Catalog Service*⟩ (2) *archaic* **:** a relatively thin flat panel containing a picture or engraving ⟨knew not when to take his hand from the ~ which he was painting —Vicesimus Knox⟩ **b :** a thin slab (as of clay) or one of a set of portable leaves or sheets (as of ivory or wax-coated wood) used for writing ⟨behind the throne stood . . . the scribe, inscribing the judgments with a pointed tool on ~s of clay —Nora B. Kubie⟩ ⟨two ~s fastened together with string . . . could form a closed letter which the recipient, after smoothing over the wax, could return with his answer —F.G.Kenyon⟩ **c :** a collection of sheets of paper usu. of the same size laid together and glued at one edge and usu. having a front cover — compare PAD 7 **d :** something that resembles a tablet: as (1) **:** a flat piece of an inflexible material (as an ornamental tile for a fireplace) (2) **:** PANEL 3f(3) (3) **:** a key controlling a stop on an electronic organ ⟨by . . . depressing any one of the stop ~s a tonal combination is set up —R.L.Eby⟩ **2 a :** a compressed or molded block of a solid material **:** CAKE, BAR ⟨a ~ of soap⟩ **b :** a small mass of medicated material usu. in the shape of a disk or flat square ⟨aspirin ~⟩ — compare PILL **c** *chiefly Brit* **:** a small patty or lozenge of candy ⟨almond ~⟩ ⟨lemon ~⟩ **3 a :** a table-cut gem **b :** a tabular crystal **4 a :** a horizontal coping stone **b :** TABLE 5a
²**tablet** \"\ *vt* **tableted** *or* **tabletted; tableted** *or* **tabletted; tableting** *or* **tabletting; tablets 1 a :** to provide or mark with a tablet **b :** to inscribe on a tablet **2 :** to form into a tablet
table talk *n* **:** informal conversation at or as if at a dining table; *esp* **:** the social conversation of a celebrity recorded for publication
tablet-arm chair *also* **tablet chair** *n* **:** a chair with one arm that is broadened to serve as a writing surface

tablet-arm chair

table tennis *n* **:** a table game resembling lawn tennis played with wooden paddles and a small hollow celluloid or plastic ball — see RACKET illustration
table tipping *or* **table tilting** *or* **table turning** *n* **:** the lifting or manipulation of a table during a séance attributed to the agency of spirits
¹**tabletop** \ˈ⸗⸗,⸗\ *n* **1 :** the top of or as if of a table ⟨the ~ of a road vehicle is about 3′6″ above the ground —*Materials Handling in the Wool Industry*⟩ **2 :** a photograph of small objects or a miniature scene arranged on a table ⟨~s are popular for Christmas cards —*Amer. Photography*⟩ — distinguished from *still life*
²**tabletop** \"\ *adj* **1 :** forming or designed for use on a flat working surface ⟨~ water heater⟩ ⟨~ can opener⟩ **2 :** of or relating to small models in a miniature setting ⟨~ photography⟩
tablet tea *n* **1 :** a small brick of choice tea **2 :** tea dust pressed into a small tablet for making one cup or into smaller tablets so that several are needed to infuse a cup of tea — compare BRICK TEA
tablet triturate *n* **:** a small tablet made by molding fine moistened powder containing a medicinal and a diluent (as a sugar)
table viewer *n* [so called fr. being small enough to operate on a table] **:** a small projector incorporating its own rear projection screen, optics, and illumination for viewing transparencies (as 35mm slides)
tableware \ˈ⸗⸗,⸗\ *n* **:** china, glassware, silver, and other utensils used for setting a table or serving food and drink — compare FLATWARE, HOLLOW WARE
table wine *n* **:** a wine of not more than 14 percent alcohol by volume that is red (as Burgundy or claret), white (as chablis or Rhine wine), or rosé and usu. served with food; *esp* **:** one that is still — called also *light wine, natural wine;* compare DESSERT WINE, SPARKLING WINE
tabling *n* -s [ME, fr. gerund of *tablen* to table — more at TABLE] **1** *archaic* **:** TABULATION **2 a :** ¹COPING **b :** TABLE 5a **c :** the formation of a horizontal joint by placing various stones in a course so they will extend into the next course to prevent slippage **3** *archaic* **:** BOARD 4c **4 :** a broad hem along the edges of a sail to which the boltrope is secured
tab·li·num \təˈblīnəm\ *n, pl* **tabli·na** \-nə\ [L, contr. of *tabulinum*, fr. *tabula* record, writing tablet, tablet, board + *-inum* (neut. of *-inus* -ine) — more at TABLE] **:** a room or alcove between the atrium and the peristyle of a Roman house for storing the family records on tablets
ta·bli·ta \täˈblēd·ə\ *n* -s [AmerSp, dim. of Sp *tabla* tablet, board, fr. L *tabula*] **:** a headdress in the form of a colored panel or plaque decorated with feathers and symbolic designs and worn by Pueblo Indian women in ceremonial dances
¹**tab·loid** \ˈta,blȯid\ *adj* [fr. *Tabloid*, a trademark applied to a concentrated form of drugs and chemicals] **1 a :** greatly condensed or shortened **:** CAPSULE ⟨provides in ~ form the evolution of the orchestra by families of instruments —William Schuman⟩ **b :** consisting of abbreviated episodes ⟨~ musical⟩ **2 a :** characterized by sensationalism **:** LURID, VULGAR ⟨the sensation-mongering ~ press —Robert Eisler⟩ ⟨feeding its ~ hungers . . . on more local horrors —John Mason Brown⟩ **b :** of, relating to, or resembling a tabloid (as in size or format) ⟨a ~ machine . . . takes the double 32-page signatures, gives them the final fold —P.R.Russell⟩ ⟨conservative-appearing ~ newspapers . . . published weekly in small towns —T.F. Barnhart⟩
²**tabloid** \"\ *n* -s **1 :** a short item or episode **:** BRIEF, SYNOPSIS ⟨provides in the form of a . . . ~ the concentrated essence of science —*Saturday Rev.*⟩ **2 a :** a newspaper of small format usu. presenting the news in concise form ⟨there is about these American ~s a terseness and finality which leave nothing to be said —Eric Partridge⟩; *esp* **:** a small profusely illustrated newspaper characterized by sensationalism ⟨it was a ~, and the headlines were a mixture of war news, recent murders, and scandals —Caroline Slade⟩ **b :** a publication resembling a tabloid in size or format ⟨most company ~s, like company magazines, are monthly —K.C.Pratt⟩ **c :** DIGEST, SUMMARY ⟨a 28-page ~ containing complete texts of all . . . regulations, interpretations, and directions issued through November —*Jour. of Accountancy*⟩
tab·loid·ism \-ȯi,dizəm\ *n* -s **:** the journalistic style and characteristics of a tabloid newspaper ⟨to astound the world with the new is the very essence of ~ —Oscar Cargill⟩
tabo- *comb form* [NL, fr. L *tabes* — more at THAW] **:** progressive wasting **:** tabes ⟨*tabo*phobia⟩
tabonuco *var of* TABANUCO
¹**ta·boo** *or* **ta·bu** \təˈbü, taˈ- *sometimes* ˈta¦bü\ *adj* [Tongan *tabu*] **1 :** set apart as venerable or as charged with a dangerous supernatural power **:** forbidden to profane use or contact **:** SACRED, INVIOLABLE ⟨the sacred or ~ animal of a neighboring people —L.E.Fuller⟩ ⟨~ grounds — the home only of spirit hosts awaiting the return of the ancient worship —I.L.Idriess⟩ ⟨the person of the tribal chief is ~⟩ **2 :** banned on grounds of morality or taste or as constituting a risk **:** outlawed by common consent **:** DISAPPROVED, PROSCRIBED ⟨many obscene and sacred words are ~ because the name is regarded as the equivalent of the object —Daniel Katz⟩ ⟨a ~ list containing 300,000 songs —Leonard Allen⟩ ⟨many of the cows are tubercular, so fresh milk is strictly ~ —*Infantry Jour.*⟩
²**taboo** *or* **tabu** \"\ *n* -s [Tongan *tabu*] **1 a :** a prohibition instituted for the protection of a cultural group or as a safeguard against supernatural reprisal ⟨~ on using . . . a dead person's name —J.B.Casagrande⟩ ⟨Great Spirit set the whirlwinds blowing . . . as a punishment to those who, breaking the ~, had taught the white men how to snare salmon —*Amer. Guide Series: Oregon*⟩ — called also *kapu, tapu* **b** (1) **:** an act or object avoided as sacrosanct (2) **:** the quality or state of being taboo ⟨fishes are spread out on the floor . . . until the women pour water over them to free them from ~ —Margaret Mead⟩ **2 :** a prohibition imposed by social usage or as a protective measure **:** BAN, RESTRAINT ⟨subject to all the conventional ~s of her age, her sex and her pleasant place in the Victorian sun —Florence Bullock⟩ ⟨control of behavior by the inner ~s of moral sense —R.L.Jenkins⟩ ⟨rigid ~s about older men doing heavy work —*N. Y. State Legislative Committee on Problems of the Aging*⟩ **3 :** belief in or observance of taboos **:** CONVENTION, SUPERSTITION ⟨the man of the tribe, ruled by totem and ~ —Dorothy Thompson⟩ ⟨social repressions lead to . . . folklore, religion, and ~ —Thomas Munro⟩
³**taboo** *or* **tabu** \"\ *vt* **tabooed** *or* **tabued; tabooed** *or* **tabued; tabooing** *or* **tabuing; taboos** *or* **tabus 1 a :** to set apart as sacrosanct esp. by marking with a ritualistic symbol **:** exclude from profane use or contact ⟨names of sacred chiefs and gods are ~*ed*, and may not be spoken —J.G.Frazer⟩ **b :** to avoid or ban on grounds of morality or taste or as constituting a danger **:** PROSCRIBE, SHUN ⟨you will do, or ~, what your culture calls for —L.A.White⟩ ⟨provoke . . . wrath by discussing ~*ed* subjects —Lucy M. Montgomery⟩ **2** *archaic* **:** to curtail the use of **:** put off limits ⟨that sacred enclosure of respectability was ~*ed* to us —J.R.Lowell⟩ ⟨splendid couches ~*ed* against the reception of wearied feet —T.E.Hook⟩
ta·bo·paralysis \¦tā(,)bō+\ *n* [NL, fr. *tabo-* + *paralysis*] **:** TABOPARESIS
ta·bo·paresis \"+\ *n* [NL, fr. *tabo-* + *paresis*] **:** paresis occurring with tabes, and esp. tabes dorsalis
¹**ta·bor** *also* **ta·bour** \ˈtābə(r)\ *n* -s [ME, fr. OF *tabor*, perh. modif. of Per *tabīr* drum] **:** a small drum with one head of soft calfskin used as an accompaniment to a pipe or fife, both being played by the same person — compare TABRET, TAMBOURINE
²**tabor** *also* **tabour** \"\ *vb* -ED/-ING/-S [ME *tabouren*, fr. *tabor, tabour*] *vi, dial* **:** to beat on or as if on a drum ~ *vt, archaic* **:** to strike or tap repeatedly
ta·bor·er *also* **ta·bour·er** \-bərə(r)\ *n* -s [ME *tabourer*, fr. *tabor, tabour* + *-er*] **:** one that plays on the tabor
tab·o·ret *or* **tab·ou·ret** \ˌtabəˈret, ˈtabərət\ *n* -s [F *tabouret*, lit., small drum, fr. MF, dim. of *tabour* drum, tabor, fr. OF *tabor*] **1 a :** a cylindrical seat or stool without arms or back **b :** a small portable stand (as for holding a potted plant) **2 :** a small cabinet often on casters for making supplies readily available in a working area

taboret

tab·o·rin \ˈtabərən\ *also* **tab·o·rine** \¦tabəˈrēn\ *n* -s [MF *tabourin*, fr. OF *tabor* + *-in* -ine] **:** TABRET
ta·bor·ite \ˈtäbə,rīt\ *n* -s *usu cap* [*Tábor*, town south of Prague in the former kingdom of Bohemia (now a province of western Czechoslovakia) founded in 1420 as a Taborite stronghold by Jan Ziska †1424 Bohemian Hussite leader + E *-ite*] **:** a member of the radical wing of the Hussites rejecting everything without direct biblical warrant except war (as waged fiercely under Ziska)
tabor pipe *n* **:** PIPE 1a(1)
tab·ret \ˈtabrət\ *n* -s [ME *taberet*, fr. *tabor, tabour* + *-et*] **:** a small tabor — called also *taborin*
¹**ta·briz** \təˈbrēz\ *adj, usu cap* [fr. *Tabriz*, Iran] **:** of or from the city of Tabriz, Iran **:** of the kind or style prevalent in Tabriz
²**tabriz** \"\ *n, pl* **tabriz** *usu cap* [fr. *Tabriz*, city in northwestern Iran] **:** a Persian rug usu. having a cotton warp, firm wool pile, medallion design and usu. tied with a Sehna knot
tabs *pl of* TAB, *pres 3d sing of* TAB
tabucki grass *var of* TAMBOOKIE GRASS
tab·u·la \ˈtabyələ\ *n, pl* **tabu·lae** \-yə,lē\ [NL, fr. L, board, tablet] **:** one of the transverse septa found in the calyculi of various corals and hydroids
tab·u·la·ble \ˈtabyələbəl\ *adj* [¹*tabulate* + *-able*] **:** capable of being tabulated
tab·u·lar \ˈtabyələ(r)\ *adj* [L *tabularis* relating to boards, fr. *tabula* board + *-aris* -ar] **1 a :** having a plane surface **:** resembling a slab **:** FLAT, LAMINAR ⟨a ~ root system⟩ ⟨~ plateaus, cliff-bound mesas —C.O.Dunbar⟩ ⟨~ deposits . . . of magnetite and hematite —A.M.Bateman⟩ **b** (1) **:** having two parallel faces that predominate — used of a crystal (2) **:** composed of thin platelike crystals ⟨a ~ mineral⟩ **2 a** (1) **:** of, relating to, or arranged in a table ⟨~ logarithms⟩ ⟨data summarized in ~ form⟩; *specif* **:** set up in rows and columns ⟨printers' rates for ~ work⟩ (2) **:** used in setting up a table ⟨~ key⟩ **b :** derived from or computed by means of a table ⟨~ value⟩ — **tab·u·lar·ly** *adv*
tabula ra·sa \-ˈräsə, -ˈräzə\ *n, pl* **tabulae ra·sae** \-ˈrä,sī, -ˈrä,zē\ [L] **:** a smoothed tablet or blank slate — used esp. of the mind before receiving outside impressions ⟨came into this world with a mind innocent and blank, a *tabula rasa* —*Times Lit. Supp.*⟩; see LOCKEANISM
tabular berg *or* **tabular iceberg** *n* **:** BARRIER BERG
tabular difference *n* **:** the difference between two consecutive numbers in a table sometimes printed in the table (as in the last column of a table of logarithms)
tabular spar *n* [so called fr. appearing sometimes in tabular twinned crystals] **:** WOLLASTONITE
tabular standard *n* **:** a sliding scale to regulate the amount of money to be paid in discharge of a debt designed to assure the creditor of a definite amount of purchasing power rather than a fixed sum in currency that may have changed in value — compare INDEX NUMBER
tab·u·la·ta \ˌtabyəˈläd·ə\ *n pl, cap* [NL, fr. neut. pl. of *tabulatus* tabulate] *in some classifications* **:** an artificial group of stony corals (as of the genus *Favosites*) including those having tubular calicles divided into chambers by transverse septa
¹**tab·u·late** \ˈtabyə,lāt, *usu* -ād·+V\ *vb* -ED/-ING/-S [L *tabula* board, tablet + E *-ate* — more at TABLE] *vt* **:** to put into tabular or summary form ⟨~ the results of a poll⟩ ~ *vi* **1 :** CONDENSE, SUMMARIZE **2** [back-formation fr. *tabulator*] **a :** to set a tabulator stop **b :** to move the carriage of a typewriter to a designated point by depressing the tabulator bar or key
²**tab·u·late** \-yələt, -yə,lāt\ *adj* [NL *tabulatus*, fr. *tabula* + L *-atus* -ate] **:** having tabulae
tab·u·lat·ed \-yə,lād·əd\ *adj* [in sense 1, fr. L *tabulatus* boarded (fr. *tabula* board + *-atus* -ate) + E *-ed;* in sense 2, fr. past part. of ¹*tabulate*] **1** *archaic* **:** TABULAR 1 **2 a :** reduced to tabular or synoptic form ⟨~ statistics⟩ **b :** derived from a table ⟨~ altitude⟩
tabulating machine *n* **:** TABULATOR b
tab·u·la·tion \ˌtabyəˈlāshən\ *n* -s [¹*tabulate* + *-ion*] **1 :** the act or process of tabulating ⟨the ~ of results⟩ **2 :** a result of tabulating **:** TABLE ⟨his aim was to gain international acceptance for this ~ —Roger Burlingame⟩
tab·u·la·tor \ˈtabyə,lād·ə(r), -ātə-\ *n* -s [¹*tabulate* + *-or*] **:** one that tabulates: as **a :** a typist or clerk who makes tabulations **b :** a business machine for tabulating data; *esp* **:** one that sorts and selects information from a series of marked or perforated cards fed into it — compare PUNCH CARD **c :** a device on an office machine (as a typewriter or biller) having stops that can be set for tabular work
ta·bu·la·tur \ˌtäbəlaˈtu̇(ə)r\ *n* -s *usu cap* [G, prob. fr. (assumed) NL *tabulatura* musical notation — more at TABLATURE] **1 :** the system of rules for poetic and musical composition established by the Meistersinger **2 :** TABLATURE 1a
ta·bun \ˈtä,bün\ *n* -s *often cap* [G] **:** a liquid organic phosphorus ester $(CH_3)_2NP(CN)O(OC_2H_5)$ that acts as a nerve gas
ta·bun man \täˈbün-\ *n, usu cap T* [fr. *Tabun*, cave at the mouth of the Wadi Mughara on the slopes of Mt. Carmel in northwestern Palestine, where the remains were found] **:** a fundamentally Neanderthaloid strain of Palestine man known from a female skeleton and a large male mandible with well-developed chin
tabus *pl of* TABU, *pres 3d sing of* TABU
ta·but \täˈbüt\ *n* -s [Ar *tābūt*] **:** a bier or tomb found in Muslim countries
tac *abbr* tactical
tac·a·ma·hac \ˈtak(ə)mə,hak\ *also* **tac·a·ma·haca** \ˌ⸗(ə)⸗ˈhakə, -ˈhäkə\ *or* **tac·ma·hack** \ˈtak(ə)mə,hak\ *or* **tak·a·maka** \ˌtakəˈmakə\ *n* -s [Sp *tacamahaca, tacamaca*, fr. Nahuatl *tecamaca*] **1 :** an aromatic oleoresin used in ointments and plasters and for incense: as **a :** the product of any of several tropical trees of the genera *Protium* (esp. *P. heptaphyllum* and *P. altissimum*) and *Bursera* — compare ELEMI b **b :** the product of either of two East Indian trees (*Calophyllum inophyllum* and *C. tacamahaca*) **c :** the resinous exudate of the balsam poplar **d :** GALIPOT **2 :** a tree yielding tacamahac; *esp* **:** BALSAM POPLAR
ta·ca·na \təˈkänə\ *n, pl* **tacana** *or* **tacanas** *usu cap* [Sp, of AmerInd origin] **1 a :** a group of peoples of Bolivia, Brazil, and Peru **b :** a member of any of such peoples **2 :** the language family of the Tacana peoples — **ta·ca·nan** \-nən\ *adj, usu cap*
tac·ca \ˈtakə\ *n, cap* [NL, fr. Malay *takah*, lit., notched] **:** a small genus (the type of the family Taccaceae) of tropical herbs having creeping rootstocks, basal compound leaves, and small umbellate flowers — see PIA
tac·ca·ce·ae \taˈkāsē,ē\ *n pl, cap* [NL, fr. *Tacca*, type genus + *-aceae*] **:** a family of tropical herbs (order Liliales) comprising only *Tacca* and the monotypic genus *Schizocapsa* and having regular flowers with six stamens and a one-celled ovary — **tac·ca·ceous** \(ˈ)taˈkāshəs\ *adj*
t account *n, cap T* **:** a simplified form of account usu. for demonstration or instruction that consists of a horizontal line for the heading and a vertical line separating debits and credits and forms a T shape
tace *var of* TASSE
ta·cet \ˈtā,ket, ˈtāsət\ *v imper* [L, 3d pers. sing. pres. indic. of *tacēre* to be silent — more at TACIT] **:** be silent — used as a direction in music for a part to be silent through a movement or a section
tachanun *var of* TAHANUN
ta·char·dia \təˈshärdēə\ [NL, fr. Gui *Tachard* †1712 Fr. Jesuit missionary in East Indies and Siam + NL *-ia*] *syn of* LACCIFER
¹**tache** \ˈtash\ *n* -s [ME *teche, tache*, fr. MF, stain, spot, of Gmc origin; akin to OS *tēkan* sign — more at TOKEN] *chiefly Scot* **:** STAIN, BLEMISH
²**tache** \"\ *vt* -ED/-ING/-S [ME *tassen, tatchen*, fr. MF *tacher*, fr. OF *techier, tachier*, fr. *teche, tache* stain, spot] *chiefly Scot* **:** to stain, blemish, or tarnish esp. with respect to character and reputation
³**tache** \ˈtach\ *also* **tach** \"\ *n, pl* **taches** [ME, fr. MF *tache* nail, fastening, of Gmc origin; akin to MD *tac* pointed instrument, sharp point — more at TACK] **:** BUCKLE, CLASP ⟨couple the curtains together with the ~s —Exod 26:6 (AV)⟩
tache noire \(ˈ)tash¦nwär, ¦⸗ nä¦w-\ *n, pl* **taches noires** \-r(z)\ [F, lit., black spot] **:** a small dark-centered ulcer that appears at the site of a tick bite and is the primary lesion of boutonneuse fever
tach·e·om·e·ter \ˌtakēˈäməd·ə(r)\ *n* [F *tachéomètre*, irreg. fr. Gk *tachys* swift (gen. masc. sing. *tacheos*) + F *-mètre* -meter — more at TACHY-] **:** TACHYMETER
tach·i·na fly \ˈtakənə-\ *n* [NL *Tachina*, genus of flies — more at TACHINIDAE] **:** any of numerous bristly usu. grayish or black flies comprising the family Tachinidae
tach·i·nar·ia \ˌtakəˈna(a)rēə\ *n pl, cap* [NL, fr. *Tachina* + *-aria*] *in some classifications* **:** a group coextensive with the family Tachinidae
¹**tach·i·nid** \ˈtakənəd\ *adj* [NL *Tachinidae*] **:** of or relating to the Tachinidae
²**tachinid** \"\ *n* -s **:** a fly of the family Tachinidae
ta·chin·i·dae \taˈkinə,dē, təˈk-\ *n pl, cap* [NL, fr. *Tachina*, type genus (fr. Gk *tachinos* swift, fleet, fr. *tachos* speed + *-inos* -ine) + *-idae* — more at TACHO-] **:** a large family of specialized two-winged flies that have bare aristae, are active flyers, and produce larvae which are parasitic in caterpillars and other insects and are important factors in the natural control of various noxious insects — see TACHINA FLY
ta·chis·to·scope \təˈkistə,skōp\ *n* [ISV *tachisto-* (fr. Gk *tachistos*, superl. of *tachys* swift, fleet) + *-scope;* orig. formed as G *tachistoskop*] **:** an apparatus for the brief exposure of visual stimuli that is used in the study of learning, attention, and perception ⟨worked with a ~ to accelerate the pupils' reading⟩
ta·chis·to·scop·ic \⸗¦⸗⸗ˈskäpik\ *adj* **:** of, relating to, or conducted by a tachistoscope ⟨~ training⟩ ⟨~ presentation⟩
ta·chis·to·scop·i·cal·ly \-pək(ə)lē\ *adv* **:** by means of a tachistoscope ⟨exposed ~⟩
tacho- *comb form* [ISV, fr. Gk *tachos* speed; akin to Gk *tachys* swift — more at TACHY-] **:** speed ⟨*tacho*gram⟩
tach·o·gram \ˈtakə,gram\ *n* [ISV *tacho-* + *-gram*] **:** an autographic record of a registering tachometer
tach·o·graph \-raf, -räf\ *n* [ISV *tacho-* + *-graph*] **1 :** a recording or registering tachometer **2 :** TACHOGRAM
ta·chom·e·ter \taˈkäməd·ə(r), təˈk-\ *n* [*tacho-* + *-meter*] **1 :** a device for indicating speed of rotation **2 :** a part of a chronograph dial that gives the speed of an object
tach·o·met·ri·cal·ly \¦takə¦me·trək(ə)lē\ *adv* [fr. *tachometer*, after such pairs as E *meter: metrically*] **:** by means of a tachometer

ta·chom·e·try \ta'kämə·trē, tə'k-\ *n* -ES [*tacho-* + *-metry*] : measurement with a tachometer

tachy- *comb form* [Gk, fr. *tachys;* perh. akin to OIr *daingen* strong, firm, OSlav *dęgŭ* strength] : swift : rapid : accelerated ⟨*tachy*cardia⟩ ⟨*tachy*genesis⟩ ⟨*tachy*lyte⟩ ⟨*tachy*meter⟩

tachy·auxesis \¦takē+\ *n* [NL, fr. *tachy-* + *auxesis*] : allometric growth characterized by acceleration of a part in comparison with the body as a whole — compare BRADYAUXESIS — **tachy·auxetic** \"+\ *adj*

tachy·car·dia \¦takə̇¦kärdēə\ *n* -S [NL, fr. *tachy-* + *-cardia*] : relatively rapid heart action whether physiological (as after exercise) or pathological — compare PAROXYSMAL TACHYCARDIA

tachy·genesis \¦takə̇+\ *n* [NL, fr. *tachy-* + L *genesis*] **1** : acceleration of development by the shortening of ancestral stages during embryonic development — compare BRADYGENESIS, LIPOGENESIS **2** : SALTATORY EVOLUTION

tachy·genetic \"+\ *or* **tachy·gen·ic** \"+¦jenik\ *adj* [*tachy-* + *-genetic* or *-genic*] : of, relating to, or exhibiting tachygenesis

tachy·glos·sal \¦takə̇¦gläsəl, -lȯs-\ *or* **tachy·glos·sate** \-sə̇t, -,sāt\ *adj* [NL *Tachyglossus* + E *-al* or *-ate*] : TACHYGLOSSID

[1]**tachy·glos·sid** \-,sə̇d\ *adj* [NL *Tachyglossidae*] : of or relating to the Tachyglossidae

[2]**tachyglossid** \"\ *n* -S : a mammal of the family Tachyglossidae : ECHIDNA

tachy·glos·si·dae \,==ˈ=sə,dē\ *n pl, cap* [NL, fr. *Tachyglossus*, type genus + *-idae*] : a family of mammals (order Monotremata) consisting of the genera *Tachyglossus* and *Zaglossus* and comprising the echidnas

tachy·glos·sus \-səs\ *n, cap* [NL, fr. *tachy-* + Gk *glōssa* tongue — more at GLOSS] : the type genus of Tachyglossidae including all the Australian echidnas — compare ZAGLOSSUS

tachy·graph \'takə̇,graf, -raf\ *n* [F *tachygraphe*, fr. Gk *tachygraphos*, fr. *tachy-* + *-graphos* (fr. *graphein* to write) — more at CARVE] **1** : TACHYGRAPHER **2** : a tachygraphic writing

ta·chyg·ra·pher \ta'kigrəfə(r), tə'k-\ *or* **ta·chyg·ra·phist** \-fə̇st\ *n* -S [*tachygraphy* + *-er* or *-ist*] : one skilled in tachygraphy : STENOGRAPHER; *esp* : an ancient Greek or Roman notary

tachy·graph·ic \¦takə̇¦grafik\ *or* **tachy·graph·i·cal** \-fə̇kəl\ *adj* [*tachygraphy* + *-ic* or *-ical*] : of or relating to tachygraphy

tachy·graph·i·cal·ly \-fə̇k(ə)lē\ *adv* : in a tachygraphic manner : by means of tachygraphy

tachy·graph·om·e·ter \,==,gra'fämәd·ə(r), -ra'f-\ *n* [blend of *tachymeter* and *grapho-*] : a tachymeter with alidade for surveying

tachy·graph·om·e·try \-mə·trē\ *n* -ES [blend of *tachymetry* and *grapho-*] : measurement with a tachygraphometer

ta·chyg·ra·phy \ta'kigrəfē, tə'k-\ *n* -ES [Gk *tachygraphein* to write shorthand (fr. *tachygraphos* tachygrapher) + E *-y* — more at TACHYGRAPH] **1** : the art or practice of rapid writing : SHORTHAND, STENOGRAPHY; *esp* : the rapid writing or shorthand of the ancient Greeks and Romans **2 a** : cursive writing **b** : the abbreviated form of Greek and Latin used in the Middle Ages

tachy·hy·drite \,takə̇'hī,drīt\ *also* **tach·y·drite** \'takə̇,drīt\ *n* -S [modif. of G *tachhydrit*, blend of *tachy-* and *hydr-* + *-it* -ite] : a mineral $CaMg_2Cl_6.12H_2O$ consisting of a hydrous chloride of calcium and magnesium

tachy·lyte *also* **tachy·lite** \'takə̇,līt\ *n* -S [*tachylyte* fr. G *tachylyt*, fr. *tachy-* + Gk *lytos* soluble, fr. *lyein* to unbind, release, dissolve; *tachylite* alter. (influenced by *-lite*) of *tachylyte* — more at LOSE] : BASALT GLASS

ta·chym·e·ter \ta'kimәd·ə(r), tə'k-\ *n* [ISV *tachy-* + *-meter*] **1** : an instrument for determining quickly the distances, bearings, and elevations of distant objects in surveying; *esp* : a transit or theodolite with stadia hairs **2** : a speed indicator

tachy·met·ric \¦takə̇¦me·trik\ *adj* : of, relating to, or determined by tachymetry

ta·chym·e·try \ta'kimə·trē, tə'k-\ *n* -ES [F *tachymétrie*, fr. *tachy-* + *-métrie* -metry] : measurement with the tachymeter

tachy·phy·lac·tic \¦takə̇fə̇¦laktik\ *adj* [fr. NL *tachyphylaxis*, after such pairs as NL *prophylaxis:* E *prophylactic*] : of or relating to tachyphylaxis

tachy·phy·lax·is \,===ˈlaksə̇s\ *n, pl* **tachyphylax·es** \-k,sēz\ [NL, fr. *tachy-* + *-phylaxis* (as in *prophylaxis*)] : diminished response to later increments in a sequence of applications of a physiologically active substance (as the diminished pressor response that follows repeated injections of renin)

tachy·pnea *also* **tachy·pnoea** \,takə̇(p)'nēə\ *n* -S [NL, fr. *tachy-* + *-pnea, -pnoea*] : increased rate of respiration — **tachy·pne·ic** \¦==¦nēik\ *adj*

tachy·scope \'takə̇,skōp\ *n* [ISV *tachy-* + *-scope;* orig. formed as G *tachyskop*] : an early animated-picture machine in which glass photographic transparencies mounted on the periphery of a large rotating wheel are viewed through an aperture with a flashing light source serving as the illuminant

ta·chys·ter·ol \ta'kistə,rōl, tə'k-, -rōl\ *n* [*tachy-* + *sterol*] : an oily liquid alcohol $C_{28}H_{43}OH$ isomeric with ergosterol that is formed by ultraviolet irradiation of ergosterol or lumisterol and that on further irradiation yields vitamin D_2 — compare DIHYDROTACHYSTEROL

tachy·tel·ic \¦takə̇¦telik\ *adj* : of or relating to tachytely

tachy·tely \'==,telē\ *n* -ES [*tachy-* + Gk *tel*os end, consummation, degree of completion, state of maturity + E *-y* — more at WHEEL] : evolution at a relatively rapid rate tending to result in speedy differentiation and fixation of new types — compare BRADYTELY, HOROTELY

tac·it \'tasə̇t, *usu* -ə̇d·+V\ *adj* [F or L; F *tacite*, fr. L *tacitus* silent, fr. past part. of *tacēre* to be silent, to pass over in silence; akin to OS *thagon*, *thagian* to be silent, OHG *dagēn*, ON *thegja*, Goth *thahan* to be silent, and perh. to W *tagu* to choke, OIr *tachtaid* he chokes] **1 a** *archaic* : not speaking : SILENT ⟨a man rather ~ than discursive —Thomas Carlyle⟩ **b** : expressed or carried on without words or speech : UNSPOKEN, WORDLESS ⟨the blush was a ~ answer —Bram Stoker⟩ ⟨wooed her with ~ patient worship —George Eliot⟩ ⟨occasioned ~ rejoicing among the men —A.J.Liebling⟩ **2 a** : implied or indicated but not actually expressed : IMPLICIT ⟨~ consent⟩ ⟨a ~ assumption⟩ ⟨a ~ warning⟩ ⟨notions . . . some ~, some openly expressed —Fred Rodell⟩ ⟨enjoys the ~ support . . . of the inhabitants —*New Statesman & Nation*⟩ **b** (1) : arising without express contract or agreement — compare CONVENTIONAL 1a (2) : arising by operation of law ⟨a ~ mortgage⟩ — compare LEGAL

tac·i·te·an \¦tasə¦tēən, ta'sid·ē-\ *adj, usu cap* [fr. Cornelius *Tacitus* † *ab* A.D.117 Rom. statesman and historian + E *-ean*] : of or relating to the historian Tacitus or resembling his style or writings (as in terseness or studied lack of parallelism) ⟨his discourse . . . was couched on this occasion in *Tacitean* brevity —Norman Douglas⟩

tacit hypothec *or* **tacit hypothecation** *n* : MARITIME LIEN

tac·it·ly *adv* : in a tacit manner: as **a** : without speaking : SILENTLY ⟨held his look, ~ assuring him that she valued it fully —Helen Howe⟩ **b** : by unexpressed agreement, allowance, or understanding : IMPLICITLY, ACQUIESCENTLY ⟨~ consenting to whatever violence must be done —K.K.Darrow⟩ ⟨~ permitted by the judges to practise —H.D.Hazeltine⟩ ⟨phenomena . . . ~ recognized since time immemorial —Ralph Linton⟩ **c** : without acknowledgment ⟨borrowed extensively but ~ from these . . . volumes —J.T.Krumpelmann⟩

tac·it·ness *n* -ES : the quality or state of being tacit : SILENCE, QUIET ⟨inward ~ of mind —Walter Pater⟩

tacit relocation *n, civil & Scots law* : a renewal of a lease arising by operation of law from a failure of both landlord and tenant to discover properly their intention to have the lease dissolved at the expiration of its term

tac·i·turn \'tasə,tərn, -,tə̄n, -,təin\ *adj* [F or L; F *taciturne*, fr. L *taciturnus*, fr. *tacitus*] **1** : habitually silent : temperamentally disinclined or reluctant to talk or converse : LACONIC, RETICENT ⟨a brooding and ~ man, he said nothing till others had their say —G.D.Brown⟩ **2** : marked by a lack of expressiveness or amiability : DOUR ⟨from self-revealing sociability to ~ misanthropy —Aldous Huxley⟩ ⟨a ~ and iron-bound visage —Charles Dickens⟩ **syn** see SILENT

tac·i·tur·ni·ty \,==ˈ=əd·ē, -ətē, -i\ *n* -ES [ME *taciturnite*, fr. MF or L; MF *taciturnité*, fr. L *taciturnitat-*, *taciturnitas*, fr. *taciturnus* + *-itat-*, *-itas* -ity] **1** : the quality or state of being taciturn: **a** : inclination to spare, curt, or laconic speech : RETICENCE ⟨the ~ and the short answers which gave so much offense —T.B.Macaulay⟩ **b** : lack of expressiveness : RESERVE ⟨tight-lipped they endure their fates and we are the losers from their numb ~ —Anthony Quinton⟩ **2** *Scots law* **a** : such failure to assert a legal right as implies that there has been satisfaction or abandonment of it **b** : the plea of mora and taciturnity setting up such failure

tac·i·turn·ly *adv* : in a taciturn manner: as **a** : RETICENTLY **b** : SILENTLY

[1]**tack** \'tak\ *n* -S *often attrib* [ME *tak;* akin to MLG *tacke* pointed instrument, sharp point, MD *tac*] **1 a** *obs* : a small hooked, knobbed, or pointed device of metal for fastening one thing to another: as (1) : BUCKLE (2) : a hook fitting into an eye (3) : NAIL **b** : a small short sharp-pointed nail usu. having a broad flat head; *esp* : one for affixing a light object or material to a solid surface ⟨a carpet ~⟩ ⟨a thumb ~⟩ **c** : a strip binding stalks (as to a wall) in gardening **d** : an ear on a pipe for fastening it (as to a wall) **2** *chiefly dial* : the ability to hold on, last, or endure : STABILITY, ENDURANCE **3 a** : a rope to hold in place the forward lower corner of a course on a sailing ship — compare SHEET **b** : a rope for hauling the outer lower corner of a studding sail to the end of the boom **c** : the lower forward corner of a fore-and-aft sail **d** : the corner of a sail to which a tack is fastened (as the weather clew of a square sail) **4 a** : the direction of a ship with respect to the trim of her sails ⟨the starboard ~⟩ ⟨the port ~⟩ **b** : the run of a sailing ship on one tack ⟨the ship sailed well on that last ~⟩ **c** : a change when close-hauled from the starboard to the port tack or vice versa ⟨made two ~*s* in rounding the point⟩ **d** : a zigzag movement on land ⟨watched for openings and got through the dense crowd in a series of ~*s*⟩ **e** : a course or method of action; *esp* : one sharply divergent from that previously taken or followed ⟨go off on the wrong ~⟩ ⟨try a new ~⟩ ⟨kept changing the ~ of your questions —B.V.Dryer⟩ **5 a** : a tying or fastening esp. of a temporary kind **b** : any of various usu. temporary stitches: as (1) : TAILOR'S TACK (2) : BAR TACK **c** *Brit* : a supplement or rider esp. to a parliamentary bill **d** : a short deposit for holding the sections of a joint in place in welding **6 a** : the quality or state of sticking or adhering : ADHESIVENESS, STICKINESS ⟨the ~ of a paint⟩ ⟨the ~ of ink⟩ ⟨tape with good ~⟩ **b** : the property of raw rubber or compounded rubber stock of adhering firmly when layers are pressed together **7** : stable gear

[2]**tack** \"\ *vb* -ED/-ING/-S [ME *takken*, fr. *tak*, n.] *vt* **1 a** : to cause to join or hold together : ATTACH ⟨~ on a fragment of black cloth for an eye —*Farmer's Weekly* (*So. Africa*)⟩; *esp* : to nail, pin, or affix with tacks ⟨~*ing* down a stairway carpet⟩ ⟨~ a notice on a bulletin board⟩ ⟨~*ing* upholstery⟩ **b** *archaic* : to join in matrimony : HITCH 2c ⟨~ me first; my love is waiting —R.B.Sheridan⟩ **c** : to join (things that are separated) by a linking part : CONNECT ⟨islands ~*ed* together by . . . bridges —John Evelyn⟩ ⟨at this common point . . . the two routes may be ~*ed* —S.H.Lynne⟩ **2** : to attach or join slightly or only at separated points for a temporary purpose: as **a** : to join (two pieces of metal) by drops of solder **b** : to stitch together lightly (two pieces of cloth) : BASTE ⟨~ the pleat in position at the hemline⟩ **3 a** : to add, attach, or join as a usu. inappropriate or arbitrary complement : LINK, TIE ⟨themes loosely and rather aimlessly ~*ed* together⟩ — usu. used with *to* or *on* ⟨a weak, spotty piece of music ~*ed* to an absurd, garish drama —Alfred Frankenstein⟩ ⟨~*ed* on to escape a banal conclusion —Anthony Quinton⟩ **b** (1) : to add or attach to as a supplement : ANNEX — usu. used with *on* or *onto* ⟨~*ed* it on as an afterthought⟩ ⟨~ an extra dollar onto the price⟩ ⟨one large studio with three . . . little rooms ~*ed* onto it —Aldous Huxley⟩ (2) : to add (a rider) to a parliamentary bill : APPEND — usu. used with *to*, *on*, or *onto* ⟨a provision . . . ~*ed* to a supply bill —T.E.May⟩ ⟨get the measure through the legislature by ~*ing* it onto an appropriation bill⟩ **4 a** *Eng law* : to unite or join (securities given at different times) so as to prevent a person having intermediate securities or rights from claiming a title to redeem or otherwise discharge one or more prior ones without also redeeming or discharging one or more subsequent ones united to the prior ones **b** : to add on (a period of disability or adverse possession by one person to that of another immediately preceding or following and in privity with him) **5 a** : to change the direction of (a sailing ship) when sailing close-hauled by putting the helm alee and shifting the sails so that it will come up into the wind and then fall off on the other side until it proceeds at about the same angle to the wind as before **b** : to navigate (a sailing ship) by a series of tacks ⟨often he had ~*ed* a monstrous ship of the line in heavy weather —C.S. Forester⟩ — compare WEAR ~ *vi* **1 a** : to change the direction of a sailing ship **b** : *of a sailing ship* : to move in a different direction through the shifting of the helm to leeward so that the wind strikes the sails from the other side ⟨~*ed* along smoothly with the onshore breeze —H.H.Martin⟩ **2 a** : to follow a zigzag course : [5]ANGLE 2 ⟨rode scornfully on, ~*ing* from side to side —Angela Thirkell⟩ **b** : to modify abruptly (as a policy or an attitude) esp. for reasons of expediency : SHIFT ⟨~*ing* temporarily in her aggressive designs but hoping to push on directly again later⟩ **3** : to associate oneself with or follow closely after a person : tag along ⟨thought you wouldn't mind my ~*ing* on to you —C.S.Lewis⟩ — **tack down wind** : to sail before the wind in a series of alternate reaches to starboard and port with sheets in instead of in a direct straight course with boom off and spinnaker set

[3]**tack** \"\ *n* -S [ME *tak*, fr. *taken* to take — more at TAKE] **1** *chiefly Scot* : a contract by which the use of something is set or let for hire : LEASE **2** *chiefly Scot* : pasture land hired usu. by the week, month, or quarter **3** *chiefly Scot* : a catch of fish : HAUL, TAKE

[4]**tack** \"\ *n* -S [origin unknown] *dial Eng* : a distinctive flavor esp. when unpleasant

[5]**tack** \"\ *n* -S [origin unknown] : STUFF ⟨we should be jawing about . . . some such ~ —D.H.Lawrence⟩; *esp* : FOODSTUFF ⟨salt junk and weevily ~ give way to soggy baker's bread —E.J.Schoettle⟩

tack and half tack *n* : a long tack followed by a short one in sailing

tack board *n* : a usu. cork board for tacking up notices and display materials (as charts or maps) : BULLETIN BOARD ⟨each classroom has . . . *tack boards* —*Springfield* (*Mass.*) *Daily News*⟩

tack bumpkin *n* : BUMPKIN a

tack claw *n* : a small hand tool with a handle and slightly bent bifurcated end for removing tacks

tack claw

tack duty *n* [[3]*tack*] *Scots law* : rent under a lease

tack·er \'takə(r)\ *n* -S [[2]*tack* + *-er*] **1** : one that tacks: as **a** : one that fastens wet hides onto boards to dry in leather working **b** : one that joins metal parts temporarily by welding at a number of spots along the edges **c** : a sewer that makes bar tacks **d** : one that joins, marks, or sews with tacking stitches **e** : one that staples or sews padding to the innersprings of mattresses **f** : a device incorporating a strong spring made tense and then released by a trigger and used for the rapid driving of staples fed from a reservoir chamber **2** *Brit* : one seeking to secure passage of a legislative measure by appending it to a money bill

[1]**tack·et** \'takə̇t\ *n* -S [ME *taket*, fr. *tak* tack + *-et*] *dial Brit* : HOBNAIL

[2]**tacket** \"\ *vt* -ED/-ING/-S *dial Brit* : to strengthen or fasten with tackets

tacketing gut *n, Brit* : bookbinder's gut

tack·ety \-ə̇ti\ *adj, chiefly Scot* : HOBNAILED ⟨~ boots⟩

tack·ey *var of* [3]TACKY

tack hammer *n* : a lightweight hammer that has usu. one magnetized face and is used for holding and driving tacks

tackier *comparative of* TACKY

tackies *pl of* TACKY

tackiest *superlative of* TACKY

tack·i·fi·er \'takə,fī(ə)r\ *n* -S : a tackifying agent

tack·i·fy \-fī\ *vt* -ED/-ING/-ES [*tacky* + *-fy*] : to improve the tack of (as rubber) : make tacky

tack·i·ness \'takēnə̇s, -kin-\ *n* -ES : the quality or state of being tacky : STICKINESS, ADHESIVENESS ⟨the ~ of unvulcanized rubber⟩

tacking *pres part of* TACK

[1]**tack·le** \'takəl, *by seamen often* 'tāk-\ *n* -S *often attrib* [ME *takel;* akin to MLG & MD *takel* ship's rigging, and perh. to E [1]*tack*] **1** : a collection, set, or complement of the equipment, apparatus, or materials designed for use in a particular activity : PARAPHERNALIA, GEAR ⟨sports ~ was rationed —Tom Clarke⟩ ⟨so undignified, using father's shaving ~ —Dodie Smith⟩: as **a** : equipment for fishing **b** : an archer's equipment **c** : harness for a horse **2 a** : a ship's rigging; *specif* : a ship's purchase (as an arrangement of lines and blocks) in which the line runs through more than one block **b** : an assemblage of ropes and pulleys arranged to gain mechanical advantage for hoisting and pulling : PURCHASE 4a(2) — compare BURTON 1; see PULLEY illustration **3** [[2]*tackle*] **a** : the act or an instance of tackling ⟨he made key ~*s* and ran to several first downs —*N.Y.Times*⟩ **b** : one of two players on each side of the center and between guard and end in the line in football ⟨played as right ~ early in the season and left ~ in later games⟩ **syn** see EQUIPMENT

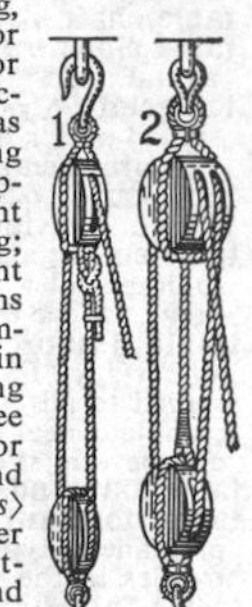

tackles 2b: *1* gun, *2* luff

[2]**tackle** \"\ *vb* **tackled; tackled; tackling** \-k(ə)liŋ\ **tackles** *vt* **1 a** : to attach or secure with or as if with tackle; *specif* : HARNESS — often used with *up* ⟨~ the horse up for plowing⟩ **b** : to harness a horse to (as a coach) **2 a** : to seize, take hold of, or grapple with esp. with the intention of stopping or subduing ⟨a wrestler ~*s* his opponent⟩ ⟨dive in and ~ the creature —*Amer. Guide Series: Fla.*⟩ **b** : to seize and throw down or stop (an opposing player with the ball) in U.S. or rugby football ⟨*tackled* the ball carrier and brought him down a yard from the goal line⟩ **c** : to obstruct or interfere with (an opponent dribbling or playing the ball) so as to bring about loss of possession of the ball (as in soccer or field hockey) **3 a** : to set about dealing with (as a difficult problem or a formidable task) : come to grips with : take on ⟨~ the problem of disarmament —Gordon Dean⟩ ⟨~ a steep ascent that lay before me —R.L.Stevenson⟩ **b** : to approach (a person) esp. with the expectation of encountering hostility or resistance ⟨planned to ~ the boss for a raise⟩ ⟨proceeded to ~ him on the subject —*Irish Digest*⟩ **c** : to attack (food) ⟨the most elaborate dinner I ever *tackled* —W.A.White⟩ ~ *vi* : to tackle an opposing player (as in football)

tackle block *n* : BLOCK 4a

tackle board *or* **tackle post** *n* : a board, post, or frame at the end of a rope walk that supports the spindles or whirls for twisting the yarns

tack·led \'takəld, 'tāk-\ *adj* [[1]*tackle* + *-ed*] : made of tackle or ropes ⟨cords made like a ~ stair —Shak.⟩

tackle fall *n* : the rope or cable of a tackle to which force is applied

tackle-house \'==,=\ *n* : a house or building having a tackle used in lading or unlading ships

tack·ler \-k(ə)lə(r)\ *n* -S : one that tackles: as **a** *Brit* : LOOMFIXER **b** *Brit* : an attendant of a machine for making paper bags **c** : one that tackles an opponent in a sport (as wrestling or football) ⟨shook off half a dozen ~*s* to crash over the goal line —*N.Y.Times*⟩

tackline \'=,=\ *n* : a short piece of line used to separate flags in a signal hoist

tack·ling \'tak(ə)liŋ, 'tāk-\ *n* -S [ME *takling*, fr. gerund of *taklen* to furnish with tackle, fr. *takel*, n.] **1** : furniture of the masts and yards of a ship (as rigging or cordage) : TACKLE 2a **2 a** : a collection of equipment or apparatus used in a particular activity : TACKLE 1 ⟨fishing ~⟩ **b** : the harness of a draft animal **3 a** : the act or skill of making a tackle in football **b** : the act or skill of taking or attempting to take possession of the ball from an opponent in soccer or field hockey

tack pin *n* : BELAYING PIN

tack rag *n* : a cloth for picking up dust before painting

tack rivet *n* : a temporary rivet for securing pieces during riveting

tack room *n* : a room in or attached to a stable for the storage and maintenance of riding tack (as saddles and bridle) and often of stud records or for the display of prizes or other honors of the stable

tacks *pl of* TACK, *pres 3d sing of* TACK

tacks·man \'taksmən\ *n, pl* **tacksmen** [fr. poss. of [3]*tack* + *man*] *Scots law* : LESSEE

tackweed \'=,=\ *n* : PUNCTURE VINE

tack-weld \'=,=\ *vt* [back-formation fr. *tack welding*] : to fasten (two pieces of metal) together by welding them at various isolated points

tack weld *n* [*tack-weld*] **1** : a joint or fastening secured by tack welding **2** : one of the small welded points in a joint that has been tack-welded

[1]**tacky** \'takē, -ki\ *adj* -ER/-EST [[2]*tack* + *-y*] : barely sticky to the touch : ADHESIVE: as **a** : having a quality of adhering, clinging, or binding ⟨~ varnish⟩ ⟨~ ink⟩ ⟨keeps rubber rollers and blankets ~ —*Graphic Arts Monthly*⟩ **b** : characterized by tack

[2]**tacky** \"\ *n* -ES *chiefly Brit* : SNEAKER, TENNIS SHOE — usu. used in pl.

[3]**tacky** \"\ *n* -ES [origin unknown] **1** *chiefly South* : a small pony or inferior horse **2** *chiefly South* : an inferior or low-class person : POOR WHITE ⟨the ditch-edge child of some sharecropping sandhill ~ —William Humphrey⟩

[4]**tacky** \"\ *adj* -ER/-EST **1 a** : having the characteristics of or suitable for a low-class person : COMMON ⟨a poor-white and untidy person . . . he in short, was ~ —J.B.Cabell⟩ ⟨stigmatized as ~ —A.P.Hudson⟩ **b** : marked by shabbiness or signs of neglect : DOWN-AT-HEEL, SEEDY ⟨the neighborhood was really getting very ~ —Walter Karig⟩ ⟨a ~ boardinghouse —*New Yorker*⟩ **2 a** : marked by lack of style or good taste : ridiculously unbecoming : OUTMODED, DOWDY ⟨~ knitted garments modeled on dumpy hausfrau types —*Newsweek*⟩ ⟨that pasty fat girl with those ~ pigtails —Carson McCullers⟩ ⟨looked God-awful ~ for a woman who was supposed to be a good designer —Hollis Alpert⟩ **b** : marked by cheap showiness : FLASHY, GAUDY ⟨a ~ costume⟩ ⟨sumptuously ~ countess who inhabits a cellar —*Time*⟩

tacky party *n* [[4]*tacky*] : a party at which the guests wear tacky clothes and prizes are awarded for the tackiest costume

tacmahack *var of* TACAMAHAC

ta·co \'tä(,)kō\ *n* -S [MexSp, fr. Sp, bung, drink of wine, snack, perh. of Gmc origin; akin to E [1]*tack*] : a sandwich made of a tortilla rolled up with or folded over a filling and usu. fried

ta·co·ma \tə'kōmə\ *adj, usu cap* [fr. *Tacoma*, Wash.] : of or from the city of Tacoma, Wash. : of the kind or style prevalent in Tacoma

ta·co·man \-mən\ *n* -S *cap* [*Tacoma*, Wash. + E *-an*] : a native or resident of Tacoma, Wash.

ta·con·ic \tə'känik\ *adj, usu cap* [fr. *Taconic* range, mountains in northeastern U.S.] : of or relating to mountain-making movements in northeastern No. America near the close of the Ordovician period — see GEOLOGIC TIME table

tac·o·nite \'takə,nīt\ *n* -S [*Taconic* range + E *-ite*] : a flintlike rock containing granules of iron oxide; *specif* : this rock when high enough in iron content to become commercially valuable as an ore

tact \'takt\ *n* -S [F, fr. L *tactus* sense of touch, fr. *tactus*, past part. of *tangere* to touch — more at TANGENT] **1 a** *archaic* : the sense of touch : FEELING ⟨sight is a very refined ~ —Joseph Le Conte⟩ **b** : a sensitive touch : SKILL ⟨must not be set to do work of a practical nature until he has shown ~ —Katharine S. Woods⟩ **2** : sensitive mental or aesthetic perception : a nice feeling for refinements or subtle values : SENSITIVITY, TASTE ⟨the Venetians as a school were from the first endowed with exquisite ~ in their use of color —Bernhard Berenson⟩ ⟨precision and ~ of interpretation —Martin Price⟩ **3** : a keen sense of what to do or say in a difficult or delicate situation in order to maintain good relations with others or avoid offense : CONSIDERATENESS, DIPLOMACY, DELICACY ⟨without the ~ to perceive when remarks were untimely —Thomas Hardy⟩ ⟨~ is an inestimable quality in a secretary —Harold

Croft⟩ ⟨his editing is a marvel of unobtrusive ~ —*N. Y. Herald Tribune Bk. Rev.*⟩

syn ADDRESS, POISE, SAVOIR FAIRE: TACT implies both skill and considerateness in dealings with others and esp. delicacy or sympathetic understanding in observing the feelings of others ⟨his vicar, who had so much *tact* with the natives, so much sympathy with all their shortcomings —Willa Cather⟩ ⟨hoping however that the matter would be handled with sufficient delicacy and *tact* to avoid breaking up the committee —A.L.Funk⟩ ⟨more than sufficient *tact* never to discuss either whiskeys or sermons in the wrong place —Arnold Bennett⟩ ADDRESS is more general than TACT in suggesting a good impression when meeting strangers or in handling new or difficult situations, often implying adroitness or suavity ⟨tall, well formed, of remarkably fine *address*, ready in decision and prompt in action, a gentleman of heart and intellect whom both teachers and children respected —H.N.Sherwood⟩ ⟨if he expresses his judgments cogently and aims them with sufficient *address* at the critical conscience —F.R.Leavis⟩ POISE suggests a self-possession or equanimity that is preserved even under the stress of embarrassing or upsetting situations ⟨the appearance of self-possession or *poise* that comes from an habitual attention to what is graceful and becoming —D.C.Hodges⟩ ⟨recovers its dignity and *poise* and becomes once more a stately avenue of a waterborne commerce —Tom Marvel⟩ SAVOIR FAIRE carries the idea of a worldly experience that gives the skilled ability to handle all situations with tact and poise ⟨to her relief he took it with the *savoir faire* of a man of the world —*MacLean's Mag.*⟩ ⟨its technical know-how needs to be supplemented in the political field by some European *savoir faire* —Percy Winner⟩

tact·ful \ˈtaktfəl\ *adj* **:** showing tact: as **a :** marked by considerateness and appreciation of the feelings of others **:** DIPLOMATIC ⟨his ~ skill in negotiations —Vera M. Dean⟩ ⟨a ~ verdict . . . which awarded each claimant a similar amount —*Amer. Guide Series: Mass.*⟩ **b :** unobtrusively sympathetic and perceptive **:** SENSITIVE ⟨a ~ editor⟩ **c :** skillfully appropriate **:** FITTING ⟨the action in relation to the camera is always ~ —Parker Tyler⟩

tact·ful·ly \-fəlē, -li\ *adv* **:** in a tactful manner: as **a :** CONSIDERATELY, DIPLOMATICALLY ⟨terminate the acquaintance ~ —Agnes M. Miall⟩ **b :** with skillful appropriateness **:** ADROITLY ⟨an almost slangy everyday speech, ~ used to relieve the modern ear —Leslie Rees⟩

tact·ful·ness \-fəlnəs\ *n* -ES **:** the quality or state of being tactful **:** DIPLOMACY, SENSITIVITY ⟨the ~ demanded of a labor-management mediator⟩

¹tac·tic \ˈtaktik, -aktēk\ *adj* [NL *tacticus*, fr. Gk *taktikos* of order, of tactics, fit for arrangement — more at TACTICS] **1** *archaic* **:** of or relating to military or naval tactics **:** TACTICAL **2 a :** of or relating to arrangement or order **b :** regular in structure of repeating units in a polymer **3** [Gk *taktikos*] **:** of, relating to, or showing biological taxis

²tactic \ˈ\ *n* -S [NL *tactica*, fr. Gk *taktikē*, fr. fem. of *taktikos*] **1 :** TACTICS **2 a :** a method of employing troops, ships, or aircraft in combat ⟨for taking such heavily fortified centers, encirclement is the customary ~ —Anna L. Strong⟩ **b :** a device or expedient for accomplishing an end **:** MANEUVER ⟨a delaying ~⟩ ⟨using the ~ of surprise⟩ ⟨a ~ for splitting the opposition⟩ ⟨set up a row of straw men and then knock them down . . . a standard ~ of the doctrinaire —Roderick Stephens⟩ ⟨think up six ~*s* to get that person to change the habit —Bennett Cerf⟩ ⟨the politician's ~*s* are determined by the way that your vote may be won —Volta Torrey⟩

³tactic \ˈ\ *adj* [*tact* + *-ic*] **:** of or relating to touch **:** TACTUAL

-tac·tic \ˌtaktik, -aktēk\ *adj comb form* [Gk *taktikos*] **1 :** having an arrangement or pattern of ⟨chaeto*tactic*⟩ **2 :** showing orientation or movement directed by a (specified) force or agent ⟨geo*tactic*⟩ ⟨photo*tactic*⟩ **3 :** having an arrangement or pattern of a (specified) kind ⟨homo*tactic*⟩

tac·ti·cal \ˈtaktəkəl, -aktēk-\ *adj* [Gk *taktikos* + E *-al*] **1 :** of or relating to military tactics (as of air, sea, or ground forces): as **a :** involving actions or means (as equipment or plans) that are distinguished from those of strategy by being of less importance to the outcome of a war or of less magnitude or by taking place or going into effect at a shorter distance from a base of operations **b** *of an air force* (1) **:** designed for use in the battle area including air-to-air and air-to-surface action (2) **:** of or relating to air attack on the enemy in the battle line in support of friendly ground forces **c :** of or relating to combat functions or units as distinguished from those concerned with support or administration **d :** of or relating to the activities concerned with military drill as distinguished from the activities concerned with training on a training base **2 a :** of or relating to tactics generally **:** designed to achieve a given purpose ⟨made a ~ error⟩ ⟨regard such negotiations as ~ maneuvers —R.H.S.Crossman⟩: as (1) **:** of or relating to the planning or execution of small-scale actions as part of a larger purpose ⟨the big gains . . . count, not the little ~ advances —*Nation's Business*⟩ ⟨played excellent ~ tennis⟩ (2) **:** made or carried out with only a limited or immediate end in view **:** designed to gain a temporary advantage **:** SHORT-RANGE, OPPORTUNISTIC ⟨~ decisions⟩ ⟨think . . . they are merely forming a ~ alliance —Edmond Taylor⟩ ⟨~, makeshift policies —Joel Carmichael⟩ (3) **:** designed as a necessary or prudent temporary adjustment to unfavorable conditions **:** EXPEDIENT ⟨has only made a ~ withdrawal, not given up —Claire Sterling⟩ **b :** marked by skill in tactics **:** adroit in planning or maneuvering to accomplish a purpose **:** POLITIC ⟨a ~ statesman⟩ ⟨their ~ treatment of American politics —D.W.Brogan⟩ **3 :** of or relating to tactics, tagmemes, or taxemes in linguistics

tactical diameter *n* **:** the perpendicular distance between a ship's course when the helm is put hard over and its course when she has turned through 180 degrees

tac·ti·cal·ly \-aktək(ə)lē, -tēk-, -li\ *adv* **1 :** in a tactical manner ⟨handled his Army Corps ~ —*Current History*⟩ **2 :** in terms of or with regard to tactics ⟨finds it ~ convenient to encourage the spread of this belief —G.F.Hudson⟩ **3 :** with regard to the study of tactics in linguistics ⟨~ equivalent to two or more morphemic categories —W.L.Wonderly⟩

tactical radius *n* **:** the distance an aircraft can fly and return to its base with its load under existing weather conditions and fill other operating requirements of a particular mission

tactical range *n* **:** the distance that an aircraft can fly in one general direction under combat conditions — compare RANGE

tactical unit *n* **:** an organization of troops designed to function as a single unit in combat; *specif* **:** the organizational unit (as an infantry battalion or a cavalry squadron) in any arm of the service upon which the tactical instruction of that particular arm is based

tac·ti·cian \takˈtishən\ *n* -S [F *tacticien*, fr. *tactique* tactics, after such pairs as F *mathématique* mathematics: *mathématicién* mathematician] **:** one versed in tactics **:** a skillful maneuverer ⟨the wily ~, with a keen eye for electioneering advantage —Alexander Brady⟩; *specif* **:** one skilled in military tactics ⟨a brilliant ~ in armored warfare with a poor grasp of the grand strategy⟩

tac·tic·i·ty \takˈtisədē\ *n* -ES **:** the quality or state of being stereochemically tactic

tac·tics \ˈtaktiks, -aktēks\ *n pl* [NL *tactica*, pl., fr. Gk *taktika*, fr. neut. pl. of *taktikos* of order, of tactics, fit for arranging, fr. *taktos* (verbal of *tassein, tattein* to arrange, order, place in battle formation) + *-ikos* -ic; akin to TochA *tāśśi* commanders, Lith *patogus* comfortable, respectable, Latvian *patāgs* comfortable; basic meaning: to arrange] **1** *usu sing in constr* **a :** the science and art of disposing and maneuvering troops, ships, or aircraft in relation to each other and the enemy and of employing them in combat ⟨strategy wins wars; ~ wins battles —*Plane Talk*⟩ ⟨~ . . . requires concentration of troops —S.O.Fuqua⟩ **b :** the art or skill of employing available forces with an end in view ⟨devising . . . a ~ of power —John Buchan⟩ **2** *usu pl in constr* **:** a system or mode of procedure **:** METHOD ⟨the bullying ~ of the prosecuting attorney⟩ ⟨their ~ demoralize the industry —*N.Y.Times*⟩ **3** *sing or pl in constr* **:** the study of the grammatical relations within a language including morphology and syntax; *esp* **:** the study of the structure of combinations of morphemes into larger constructions as to order, selection of allomorphs, agreement, and concurrent stress, pitch, and rhythm patterns

¹tac·tile \ˈtaktᵊl, -k,tīl, -k(,)til\ *adj* [F or L; F, fr. L *tactilis*, fr. *tactus* (past part. of *tangere* to touch) + *-ilis* -ile — more at TANGENT] **1 :** perceptible by the touch **:** capable of being felt or touched **:** TANGIBLE ⟨~ qualities⟩ ⟨slide rule for sightless individuals employs ~ symbols —*Scientific Monthly*⟩ **2 a :** of or relating to the sense of touch **:** TACTUAL ⟨~ sensitivity⟩ ⟨~ sensuality⟩ ⟨the ~ sensations he gets manipulating the controls —Herbert Mitgang⟩ **b :** having the sense of touch **:** used in touching ⟨fingers ~ as antennae —Marcia Davenport⟩ ⟨~ organs⟩ **c :** affecting the sense of touch ⟨~ anesthesia⟩ **3 :** depending on the sense of touch (as for orientation) ⟨corals and sea anemones have an almost purely ~ contact with their environment⟩ **4 :** appealing by synesthesia to the sense of touch ⟨how extraordinarily ~ the verses are —Dudley Fitts⟩

²tactile \ˈ\ *n* -S **:** one whose prevailing mental imagery is tactile rather than visual, auditory, or motor — compare AUDILE, MOTILE, VISUALIZER

tactile cell *n* **:** one of the oval nucleated cells that are situated in close contact with the expanded ends of nerve fibers in the deeper layers of the epidermis and dermis of some parts of the body and prob. serve a tactile function

tactile corpuscle *n* **:** one of the numerous minute bodies in the skin and some mucous membranes that usu. consist of a group of cells enclosed in a capsule, contain nerve terminations, and are held to be end organs of touch

tactile disk *n* **:** MERKEL'S CELL

tactile hair *n* **:** a hair or hairlike structure sensitive to touch occurring in various groups of animals

tactile receptor *n* **:** an end organ that responds to light touch

tac·til·ist \ˈtaktələst, -k,tīl-\ *n* -S **:** a painter emphasizing tactile values

tac·til·i·ty \takˈtilədē, -lətē, -i\ *n* -ES **:** the quality or state of being tactile: as **a :** the capability of being felt or touched **:** TANGIBILITY **b :** responsiveness to stimulation of the sense of touch **:** tactile sensitivity

tac·tion \ˈtakshən\ *n* -S [L *taction-, tactio*, fr. *tactus* (past part. of *tangere* to touch) + *-ion-, -io* -ion — more at TANGENT] **:** the act of touching **:** TOUCH, CONTACT ⟨being roused by some external ~ upon the organs of speech and hearing —Jonathan Swift⟩

tac·tism \ˈtak,tizəm\ *n* -S [ISV *tact-* (fr. Gk *taktos*, verbal of *tassein, tattein* to arrange, order) + *-ism* — more at TACTICS] **:** TAXIS 2

tac·tite \ˈtak,tīt\ *n* -S [L *tactus* (past part. of *tangere* to touch) + E *-ite* — more at TANGENT] **:** a contact-metamorphosed carbonate rock (as limestone) containing crystalline silicate minerals (as garnet, diopside, or vesuvianite)

tact·less \ˈtak(t)ləs\ *adj* **:** marked by a lack of tact: as **a :** INCONSIDERATE, UNDIPLOMATIC ⟨~, forever lugging in disagreeable truths —V.L.Parrington⟩ **b :** BLUNT ⟨the canals are sewers and, in ~ truth, they smell —Claudia Cassidy⟩ **c :** INEPT ⟨their ~ handling of the situation —E.E.Shipton⟩

tact·less·ly *adv* **:** in a tactless manner

tact·less·ness *n* -ES **:** the quality or state of being tactless

tac·toid \ˈtak,tȯid\ *n* -S [ISV *tact-* (fr. Gk *taktos*, verbal of *tassein, tattein* to arrange, order) + *-oid* — more at TACTICS] **:** an elongated particle (as in vanadium pentoxide sol, tobacco mosaic virus, myosin, or fibrin) that appears as a spindle-shaped body under the polarizing microscope and occurs in a tactosol — compare COACERVATE

tac·tom·e·ter \takˈtäməd·ə(r)\ *n* [L *tactus* sense of touch + E *-o-* + *-meter* — more at TACT] **:** an instrument for testing and measuring the acuteness of the sense of touch

tac·tor \ˈtaktə(r)\ *n* -S [NL, fr. LL, one that touches, fr. L *tactus* (past part. of *tangere* to touch) + *-or* — more at TANGENT] **:** a tactile organ (as an antenna or a tactile corpuscle)

tac·to·receptor \ˌtak(ˌ)tō+\ *n* [L *tactus* sense of touch + E *-o-* + *receptor*] **:** TACTILE RECEPTOR

tac·to·sol \ˈtaktə,sȯl, -sōl\ *n* [ISV *tacto-* (fr. Gk *taktos*) + *sol*; orig. formed as G *taktosol*] **:** a sol containing tactoids arranged spontaneously on aging in parallel order

tacts *pl of* TACT

tac·tu·al \ˈtakchəwəl, -ksh-\ *adj* [L *tactus* sense of touch + E *-al*] **:** of or relating to the sense or the organs of touch **:** derived from or producing the sensation of touch **:** TACTILE ⟨a ~ sense⟩ ⟨~ tests⟩ ⟨the ~ luxury of stroking human hair —F.R. Leavis⟩

tac·tu·al·ly \-wəlē\ *adv* **:** in a tactual manner **:** by means of touch ⟨test a fabric ~⟩

ta·cu·ba·ya \ˌtäkü¦bīə\ *adj, usu cap* [fr. *Tacubaya*, Mexico] **:** of or from the city of Tacubaya, Mexico **:** of the kind or style prevalent in Tacubaya

tad \ˈtad\ *n* -S [prob. fr. E dial., toad, fr. ME *tade, tadde, tode* — more at TOAD] **:** BOY ⟨film . . . that will give any ~ his fill of action —John McCarten⟩

ta·dar·i·da \təˈdarədə\ *n, cap* [NL] **:** a nearly cosmopolitan genus of small brown free-tailed bats of the family Molossidae — see POCKETED BAT

tad·dick \ˈtadik\ *South var of* TODDICK 2

tadjik *usu cap, var of* TAJIK

tad·pole \ˈtad,pōl\ *n* -S [ME *taddepol*, fr. *tade, tadde, tode* toad + *pol* head — more at TOAD, POLL] **1 :** a larval amphibian; *specif* **:** a frog or toad larva that at hatching has a rounded body with a long fin-bordered tail and external gills soon replaced by internal gills and that subsequently undergoes a metamorphosis in which limbs and lungs are developed, adult body proportions are attained, and the tail and gills are lost **2 :** a minute tadpole-shaped larva of an ascidian **3** *usu cap* **:** MISSISSIPPIAN — used as a nickname

tadpole madtom *n* **:** a common widely distributed madtom (*Schilbeodes mollis*)

tadpole shrimp *n* **:** a notostracan crustacean esp. of the genus *Triops*

tadzhik *usu cap, var of* TAJIK

¹tae \tə, (ˈ)tā\ *Scot var of* TO

²tae \ˈtā\ *Scot var of* TOE

taedium *var of* TEDIUM

tae·di·um vi·tae \ˌtēdēəmˈvī,tē, -mˈvē,tī; ˌtīdēəmˈwē,tī\ *n* [L] **:** weariness or loathing of life **:** intense discontent

tae·gu \(ˈ)ta¦gü, (ˈ)tī¦gü\ *adj, usu cap* [fr. *Taegu*, Korea] **:** of or from the city of Taegu, Korea **:** of the kind or style prevalent in Taegu

tae·jon \(ˈ)ta¦jän, (ˈ)tī¦j-\ *adj, usu cap* [fr. *Taejon*, Korea] **:** of or from the city of Taejon, Korea **:** of the kind or style prevalent in Taejon

tael *or* **tale** \ˈtā(ə)l\ *n* -S [Pg *tael*, fr. Malay *tahil*, a weight, tael, prob. fr. Hindi *tolā* weight of a sicca rupee, fr. Skt *tulā* balance, scale, weight — more at TOLERATE] **1 :** any of various units of weight of eastern Asia; *esp* **:** LIANG **2 :** any of various Chinese units of value based on the value of a tael weight of silver — see HAIKWAN TAEL, KUPING TAEL

taen- *or* **taeni-** *or* **taenio-** *comb form* [L *taenia*] **1 :** ribbon **:** fillet ⟨*taeni*ate⟩ ⟨*taenio*donta⟩ **2 :** tapeworm ⟨*taeni*asis⟩ ⟨*taeni*cide⟩ ⟨*taeni*fuge⟩

tae·nia \ˈtēnēə, -nyə\ *n* [L, fr. Gk *tainia*; akin to Gk *teinein* to stretch — more at THIN] **1** *pl* **taenias :** an ancient Greek fillet **2** *also* **te·nia** \ˈtēnēə, -nyə\ *pl* **taeni·ae** \-nē,ē\ *or* **taenias** *also* **tenias :** a band on a Doric order separating the frieze from the architrave **3** *also* **tenia** *pl* **taeniae** *or* **taenias** *also* **tenias** [NL, fr. L] **:** a band of nervous tissue or muscle **4 a** *also* **tenia** *pl* **taenias** *also* **tenias :** TAPEWORM **b** *cap* [NL, fr. L] **:** a genus (the type of the family Taeniidae) of cyclophyllidean tapeworms including the common beef and pork tapeworms of man and numerous other forms usu. occurring as adults in the intestines of carnivores and as larvae in various ruminants

tae·nia·ci·dal *also* **te·nia·ci·dal** \ˌtēnēə¦sīdᵊl, -nyə-\ *adj* [*taeniacide, teniacide* + *-al*] **1 :** destroying tapeworms **2 :** of, relating to, or being a taeniacide

tae·nia·cide *also* **te·nia·cide** \ˈtēnēə,sīd, -nyə-\ *n* -S [*taeniacide* fr. *taenia* + *-cide*; *teniacide* alter. of *taeniacide*] **:** an agent that destroys tapeworms

taenia co·li \ˌ=(=)=ˈkō,lī\ *n, pl* **taeniae coli** [NL, lit., band of the colon] **:** any of three external longitudinal muscle bands of the large intestine

tae·ni·a·da \tēˈnīədə; ˌtēnēˈädə, -ˈādə\ [NL, irreg. fr. *Taenia* + *-ida*] *syn of* CESTOIDEA

tae·ni·a·dea \ˌtēnēˈādēə\ [NL, irreg. fr. *Taenia* + *-idea*] *syn of* CYCLOPHYLLIDEA

tae·nia·fuge *also* **te·nia·fuge** \ˈtēnēə,fyüj, -nyə-\ *n* -S [*taeniafuge* fr. *taenia* + *-fuge*; *teniafuge* alter. of *taeniafuge*] **:** a tapeworm expellant

tae·nia·rhyn·chus \ˌ=(=)=ˈriŋkəs\ *n, cap* [NL, fr. *Taenia* + *-rhynchus*] *in some classifications* **:** a genus of tapeworms comprising the beef tapeworm of man

tae·ni·a·sis *also* **te·ni·a·sis** \tēˈnīəsəs\ *n* -ES [NL, fr. *taen-* + *-iasis*] **:** infestation with or disease caused by tapeworms

tae·ni·ate \ˈtēnē,āt, -nēət\ *adj* [*taen-* + *-ate*] **:** longitudinally striped

tae·nid·i·al \tēˈnidēəl\ *adj* [NL *taenidium* + E *-al*] **:** of, relating to, or having the characteristics of a taenidium ⟨~ ridges⟩

tae·nid·i·um \-dēəm\ *n, pl* **taenid·ia** \-dēə\ [NL, fr. Gk *tainidion* small ribbon, dim. of *tainia*] **:** a spiral sclerotized fiber that stiffens the walls of the tracheae of insects

¹tae·ni·id \ˈtēnēəd\ *adj* [NL *Taeniidae*] **:** of or relating to the Taeniidae

²taeniid \ˈ\ *n* -S **:** a tapeworm of the family Taeniidae

tae·ni·idae \tēˈnīə,dē\ *n pl, cap* [NL, fr. *Taenia*, type genus + *-idae*] **:** a large family of tapeworms (order Cyclophyllidea) including numerous worms of medical or veterinary importance — see TAENIA 4b

taenio- — see TAEN-

tae·nio·bran·chia \ˌtēnēōˈbraŋkēə\ [NL, fr. *taen-* + *-branchia*] *syn of* THALIACEA

tae·ni·odont \ˈtēnēə,dänt\ *n* -S [NL *Taeniodonta*] **:** a mammal or fossil of the order Taeniodonta

tae·ni·odon·ta \ˌ===ˈdäntə\ *n pl, cap* [NL, fr. *taen-* + *-odonta*] **:** an order of No. American Paleocene and Eocene mammals related to the edentates but distinguished by molars with roots and enamel

tae·ni·odon·tia \-ˈdänch(ē)ə\ [NL, fr. *taen-* + *-odontia* (irreg. fr. *odont-, odōn* tooth) — more at TOOTH] *syn of* TAENIODONTA

tae·nio·glos·sa \ˌtēnēəˈgläsə, -lȯsə\ *n pl, cap* [NL, fr. *taen-* + *-glossa*] **:** a large suborder of Pectinibranchia comprising marine and freshwater gastropod mollusks in which the odontophore is long and narrow and usu. bears seven teeth in each transverse row — compare HETEROPODA, PLATYPODA — **tae·nio·glos·sate** \-sət, -,sāt\ *adj or n*

tae·ni·oid \ˈtēnē,ȯid\ *adj* [*taen-* + *-oid*] **:** resembling or related to the Taeniidae

tae·nio·in·ei \ˌtēnēōˈinē,ī\ [NL, fr. *Taenia*] *syn of* ¹CESTOIDEA

tae·ni·op·ter·is \ˌtēnēˈäptərəs\ *n, cap* [NL, fr. *taen-* + *-pteris*] **:** a genus of fossil ferns or cycad ferns found in Mesozoic or Late Paleozoic strata and characterized by ribbon-shaped pinnae and usu. pinnately arranged veins or veinlike structures

tae·nio·some \ˈtēnēə,sōm\ *n* -S [NL *Taeniosomi*] **:** a fish of the suborder Taeniosomi

tae·nio·so·mi \ˌ===ˈsō,mī\ *n pl, cap* [NL, fr. *taen-* + *-somi* (fr. Gk *sōma* body) — more at SOMA] *in some classifications* **:** a suborder of Allotriognathi containing the oarfishes and dealfishes

tae·nio·so·mous \¦===¦sōməs\ *adj* [NL *Taeniosomi* + E *-ous*] **:** of, relating to, or resembling the Taeniosomi

tae·nio·thrips \ˈtēnēə,thrips\ *n, cap* [NL, fr. *taen-* + *thrips*] **:** a widely distributed genus of thrips — see GLADIOLUS THRIPS, PEAR THRIPS

tae·nite \ˈtē,nīt\ *n* -S [G *tänit*, fr. *tän-* taen- + *-it* -ite] **:** a mineral consisting of a nickel-iron alloy that forms with kamacite the mass of most meteoric iron

taen·sa \ˈten,sȯ, täˈen-\ *n, pl* **taensa** *or* **taensas** *usu cap* [fr. *Taensas*, a village of the Taensa people] *cap* **1 a :** a Natchesan people of northeastern Louisiana **b :** a member of such people **2 :** the language of the Taensa people

TAF *abbr* tactical air force

taf·fe·ta \ˈtafəd·|ə, -fət|\ *also* **taf·fe·ty** \|ē, |i\ *or* **taf·fa·ta** \|ə\ *n, pl* **taffetas** *also* **taffeties** *or* **taffatas** [ME, *taffeta, taffata*, fr. MF *taffetas*, fr. OIt *taffettà*, fr. Turk *tafta*, fr. Per *tāftah* woven, spun, fr. *tāftan* to spin] **1 :** a crisp plain-woven fabric with a fine cross rib and a smooth lustrous surface on both sides that is woven of various fibers (as silk, linen, rayon) and used esp. for women's clothing **2 :** a yellow greaseproof film of cellulose used as a covering (as for greased areas or moist surgical dressings)

taffeta weave *n* **:** PLAIN WEAVE

taf·fe·tized \-fə,tīzd\ *adj, of cloth* **:** having a crisp finish ⟨standout value among ~ cottons —*Women's Wear Daily*⟩

taff·rail \ˈtafrəl; ˈta,frāl, ˈtaf,f-\ *also* **taf·fer·el** \ˈtaf(ə)rəl\ *n* -S [*taffrail* alter. (influenced by *rail*) of *tafferel*; *tafferel* fr. D *tafereel*, fr. MD, picture, fr. OF *tablel* picture, tableau — more at TABLEAU] **1 :** the upper flat part of the stern of a wooden ship often ornamented with carvings **2 :** a rail around the stern of a ship

taffrail log *n* **:** a log that is mounted on the taffrail of a ship and consists of a rotator, log line, and recording device — compare HARPOON LOG

¹taf·fy \ˈtafē, ˈtaif-, -fi *also* ˈtaaf-\ *n* -ES [origin unknown] **1 :** a candy made usu. of molasses or brown sugar boiled until caramelized and pulled until porous and light-colored **2 :** insincere flattery or wheedling ⟨just giving him ~ . . . but he did not know —G.H.Devol⟩ **3 :** WALNUT BROWN

²taffy \ˈ\ *n* -ES *usu cap* [modif. of W *Dafydd* David, a common Welsh Christian name] *slang* **:** WELSHMAN

taffy pull *n* **:** a social gathering at which taffy is made

ta·fia \ˈtafēə\ *n* -S [F, fr. West Indian Creole, alter. of *ratafia*] **:** an inferior rum made esp. from distilled sugarcane juice in the West Indies

¹tag \ˈtag, -aa(ə)-, -ai-\ *n* -S [ME *tagge*, prob. of Scand. origin; akin to Sw & Norw *tagg* barb, prickle; perh. akin to MLG *tacke* pointed instrument, sharp point — more at TACK] **1 :** a loose hanging piece of cloth **:** TATTER, RAG **2 :** a metal or plastic ferrule on an end of a shoelace for facilitating passage through an eyelet **3 :** a piece of material hanging from or attached to something: as **a :** a loop, knot, or tassel on a garment ⟨their long-plumed hats and . . . endless ~*s* and aiglets and rosettes —Austin Dobson⟩ **b :** a large lock of soiled and matted wool **c :** a strip of parchment attached to a deed for bearing a seal **d** (1) **:** a shred of flesh or muscle (2) **:** a small abnormal projecting piece of tissue esp. when potentially or actually neoplastic in character **e :** a shred of metal adhering to a casting **4 :** the tip of an animal's tail; *specif* **:** the white tip of a fox's tail **5 a :** material added as ornamentation or explanation to something written or spoken ⟨~*s* provided a moral framework for the play —Muriel C. Bradbrook⟩ **b** (1) **:** a brief quotation used for rhetorical emphasis or sententious effect ⟨in the great days of . . . empire building, Latin ~*s* were on the lips of the builders —D.W.Brogan⟩ ⟨dotes on . . . spellbinding oratory stuffed with big words . . . and Latin ~*s* —*Newsweek*⟩ ⟨famous Popian ~ —Donald Davie⟩ (2) **:** a hackneyed saying or quotation **:** CLICHÉ, SAW ⟨the trite ~ . . . that wars are declared by the wicked and fought by the virtuous —Herbert Agar⟩ ⟨could hardly open his mouth without using one or other of his ~*s* —Samuel Butler †1902⟩ **c :** TAGLINE 1 **d :** a rhyming end of a line of verse **e :** a closing usu. improvised phrase in a jazz piece — compare CODA **f :** a recurrent characteristic verbal expression ⟨characters with mannerisms and ~*s* of speech parade through the novel —E.R. Davis⟩ **g :** a word or phrase acting as an interrogative increment to a question ⟨the ~ *isn't it* in "it's fine, isn't it?"⟩ **6 a** (1) **:** a marker made usu. of cardboard, plastic, or metal and used for identification or classification ⟨a ~ pinned to his lapel, bearing his name and destination —*Current Biog.*⟩ ⟨a string shipping ~ slipped through a loop in the handle is used instead of the gummed label —Elizabeth Golterman⟩ — see DOG TAG, LICENSE PLATE, PRICE TAG (2) **:** TAGBOARD **b :** a word or phrase used as an often superficial description or identification **:** LABEL, EPITHET ⟨to the name of murderess would be added the ~ of ingrate —Grace Metalious⟩ ⟨*social behaviorist* is the ~ that has remained on him —Maurice Natanson⟩ **7 :** a small piece of tinsel or other bright material encircling the shank of the hook at the end of the body of an artificial fly — see FLY illustration **8 :** a detached fragmentary piece of something **:** VESTIGE ⟨the few ~*s* and oddments I was able to hold on to, and treasure up in memory —Thomas Wood †1950⟩ **9 :** a document notifying an automobile owner of having committed a traffic violation : TICKET ⟨been putting ~s on the car at twenty-minute intervals —Erle Stanley Gardner⟩ **10** : LABEL 9

²tag \"\ *vb* **tagged; tagged; tagging; tags** [ME *taggen*, fr. *tagge*, n.] *vt* **1** : to provide or mark with or as if with a tag: as **a** : to supply with an identifying marker ⟨took a week to ~ every item in the store⟩ **b** (1) : to provide with a verbal tag ⟨~s his speeches with poetry —*Examiner*⟩ (2) : to provide with a name or epithet : LABEL, IDENTIFY, BRAND ⟨one might ~ this book traditional —William Nicoll⟩ ⟨the trick is always to ~ the other fellow as . . . left-wing —T.H.White b. 1915⟩ ⟨study of what have perhaps loosely been *tagged* as guilt patterns —Abraham Edel⟩ ⟨~ with an unfavorable word the pursuit of human desires —F.L.Mott⟩ **c** : to put a ticket on for a traffic violation ⟨cars *tagged* for obstructing traffic —J.C.Ingraham⟩ **2 a** *obs* : to fasten together : CONJOIN **b** : to link together esp. with rhymes **3** : to attach as an addition : JOIN, APPEND ⟨*tagged* to our name all the opprobrious epithets the English language supplies —Thomas Campbell⟩ ⟨the general theory . . . *tagged* on at the end seems a little forced —Rayner Heppenstall⟩ **4** : to clear (a sheep) of tags of wool **5** : to follow closely and persistently : DOG, TAIL, TRAIL ⟨~s his big brothers around —John Bird⟩ ⟨a huge hammerhead shark . . . was *tagging* me —H.A.Chippendale⟩ **6** : to hold responsible for something : SADDLE ⟨is *tagged* with the . . . defeat —Gordon Harrison⟩: as **a** : to charge with a violation of the law ⟨was *tagged* by . . . Michigan cops for driving through a stop signal —*Best True Fact Detective*⟩ ⟨was *tagged* for . . . assault —Burt Woolis⟩ **b** : to charge (a pitcher) with defeat in baseball ⟨made two more runs in the eighth to ~ him with his first setback of the season⟩ **7** : to fix the price of ⟨decided to ~ the picture at $100⟩ **8 a** : LABEL 2 ⟨~ penicillin molecules with radioactive sulfur as a tracer⟩ **b** : to distinguish (as a part of a living organism or the organism as a whole) by introducing a labeled atom ⟨the donors' red cells became *tagged* by the radioactive iron atoms in the hemoglobin molecules of the red cells —R.D. Evans⟩ ~ *vi* : to keep close : stay close at hand ⟨first honeymoon I ever knew where a mother-in-law *tagged* —W.A. White⟩ ⟨*tagged* after her, glancing over her shoulder —Hamilton Basso⟩ ⟨inclined to crash parties or ~ onto older groups —Elizabeth Bowen⟩ ⟨two unarmed launches *tagged* behind —Joseph Millard⟩ ⟨a spaniel *tagging* at their heels —Corey Ford⟩ **syn** see FOLLOW

³tag \"\ *n* -s [origin unknown] **1** : a game in which one player chases the others and tries to touch one to make him it **2** : an act or instance of tagging a runner in baseball ⟨put the ~ on him as he slid into third⟩

⁴tag \"\ *vt* **tagged; tagged; tagging; tags 1 a** : to touch in or as if in a game of tag ⟨runs . . . around the outside of the circle and ~s another as he goes —Ruth McIntire⟩ **b** : to put out (a runner in baseball) by a touch with the ball or the gloved hand in which the ball is held — often used with *out* ⟨*tagged* him out on a steal of home⟩ **2 a** : to hit solidly : STRIKE ⟨*tagged* his opponent on the jaw twice in the first round⟩ ⟨was almost *tagged* by passing cars —James Thurber⟩ **b** : to hit (a baseball) with a bat ⟨*tagged* the first pitch to deep right center⟩ **3** [partly fr. ⁴*tag*; partly fr. ²*tag*] : to choose esp. for a special purpose : SELECT, PICK ⟨peacetime equipment . . . would be *tagged* for civil defense use —R.W.Stokley⟩ ⟨two years at the forestry school . . . before the Army *tagged* him —Nard Jones⟩ **4** : to make a hit or a run off (a pitcher) in baseball ⟨was *tagged* for six hits and three runs in the second inning and lost his fourth game of the season⟩

TAG *abbr* the adjutant general

ta·ga·bi·li \ˌtägəˈbēlē\ *n, pl* **tagabili** *or* **tagabilis** *usu cap* [Cebuan, fr. Tagabili *Tabili*] **1 a** : a people of southern Mindanao in the Philippines **b** : a member of such people **2** : an Austronesian language of the Tagabili people

ta·ga·kao·lo \ˌtägəˈkau̇(ˌ)lō\ *n, pl* **tagakaolo** *or* **tagakaolos** *usu cap* **1 a** : a people of southwestern Mindanao in the Philippines **b** : a member of such people **2** : an Austronesian language of the Tagakaolo people

ta·gal \təˈgäl\ *n* -s [prob. fr. Sp *tagalo* Tagalog] : a straw braid made from Manila hemp and used for hats

ta·ga·la \təˈgälə\ *n* -s *usu cap* [Sp, fem. of *tagalo* Tagalog, fr. Tag *Tagalog*] : a subgroup of Austronesian languages of the Philippines — used in former classifications

tag alder *n* [¹*tag*] : any of several American alders: as **a** : SPECKLED ALDER **b** : RED ALDER 1

ta·ga·log \təˈgäləg, -gȧl-, -ˌlȯg, -ˌläg\ *n, pl* **tagalog** *or* **tagalogs** *usu cap* [Tag] **1 a** : a people of central Luzon in the Philippines **b** : a member of such people **2** : an Austronesian language of the Tagalog people

tag along *vi* [²*tag*] : to follow another's lead : go in company with another ⟨the biggest first and the smallest *tagging along* frantically in the rear —Alan Moorehead⟩ ⟨got in by *tagging along* with the assistant D.A. and posing as his aide —*Current Biog.*⟩

tagalong \ˈ⸗⸗ˌ⸗\ *n* -s [*tag along*] : one that persistently and often annoyingly follows the lead of another ⟨felt honored to be a ~ tolerated by the older boys —Jay Edwards⟩

tag and rag *n* : RAG, TAG, AND BOBTAIL ⟨shout of *tag and rag*, and march of rank and file —Robert Southey⟩

ta·gan·rog \ˈtagənˌrälg, ˈtäg-, -rȯ|, |k, ˌ⸗⸗ˈ⸗\ *adj, usu cap* [fr. *Taganrog*, U.S.S.R.] : of or from the city of Taganrog, U.S.S.R. : of the kind or style prevalent in Taganrog

ta·ga·sas·te \ˌtägəˈsästē\ *n* -s [Sp] : a shrub (*Cytisus proliferus*) of the Canary islands that yields cattle fodder

ta·ga·tose \ˈtagəˌtōs *also* -ōz\ *n* -s [alter. of *galactose*] : a crystalline sugar $C_6H_{12}O_6$ of the ketohexose class found naturally in the D-form (as in gum from a West African tree *Sterculia setigera*) and also obtainable from galactose by treatment with dilute alkali

ta·gaur \təˈgau̇(ə)r\ *n, pl* **tagaur** *or* **tagaurs** *usu cap* **1** : an Indo-European people living in the central Caucasus and speaking an Ossetic dialect **2** : a member of the Tagaur people

tag·ba·nu·wa \ˌtägˌbänəˈwä\ *also* **tag·ba·nua** *n, pl* **tagbanuwa** *or* **tagbanuwas** *also* **tagbanua** *or* **tagbanuas** *usu cap* **1 a** : a people of Palawan in the Philippines **b** : a member of such people **2** : an Austronesian language of the Tagbanuwa people

tagboard \ˈ⸗ˌ⸗\ *n* [¹*tag* + *board*] : strong cardboard used esp. for making tags

tag dance *n* [³*tag*] : a ballroom dance in which a man may cut in on a couple by touching the other man on the shoulder

tag day *n* [¹*tag*] : a day on which contributions are solicited (as for a charity) and small tags are given in return

tag end *n* [¹*tag*] **1** : the last part of something : TAIL END ⟨born at the *tag end* of the eighteenth century —S.H.Adams⟩ ⟨at the *tag end* of nearly every long . . . party —John Cheever⟩ **2** : a miscellaneous or random fragment of something — usu. used in pl. ⟨*tag ends* of memories bob up unexpectedly —*Dial*⟩

tage·tes \taˈjēˌtēz, təˈjed·(ˌ)ēz\ *n* [NL, prob. after *Tages*, an ancient Etruscan deity] **1** *cap* : a genus of strong-scented tropical American herbs (family Compositae) having opposite pinnatifid leaves and showy heads of flowers with yellow or orange rays — see MARIGOLD 1b **2** *pl* **tagetes** \"\ any plant of the genus *Tagetes*

tag·e·tone \ˈtajəˌtōn\ *n* -s [NL *Tagetes* (genus name of *Tagetes minuta*) + E *-one*] : a pale yellow oily unsaturated ketone $C_{10}H_{16}O$ obtained from a So. American marigold (*Tagetes minuta*)

tagged \ˈtagd, -aa(ə)-,-ai-\ *adj* [ME, fr. *tagge* tag + *-ed* — more at TAG] : having, bearing, or marked with a tag or label; *esp* : matted into tags (as of wool)

tagged atom *n* : a radioactive isotope or isotope of unusual mass useful as a tracer

tag·ger \-gə(r)\ *n* -s : one that tags

tagging *pres part of* TAG

tag·gy \-gē,-gi\ *adj* -ER/-EST [¹*tag* + *-y*] : full of or matted into tags (as of wool)

tagh·lik \ˈtäglik\ *n, pl* **taghlik** *or* **taghliks** *usu cap* **1** : a people of western Tibet **2** : a member of the Taghlik people

tag·i·lite \ˈtägəˌlīt, təˈgi,l-\ *n* -s [G *tagilith*, fr. (*Nizhni*) *Tagil*, Sverdlovsk region, U.S.S.R., its locality + G *-lith* -lite] : a mineral $Cu_2(PO_4)(OH).H_2O$ consisting of a hydrous basic copper phosphate and occurring in bright green reniform masses (hardness 3–4, sp. gr. 4.1)

ta·gish \təˈgash\ *n, pl* **tagish** *or* **tagishes** *usu cap* [fr. *Tagish* lake, B.C., Canada] **1 a** : an Athapascan people of Yukon Territory and British Columbia **b** : a member of such people **2** : a language of the Tagish people

ta·glia·ri·ni \ˌtalyəˈrēnē\ *n* -s [It, fr. *tagliare* to cut (fr. LL *taliare*) + *-ini* (pl. of *-ino* -ine, fr. L *-inus*) — more at TAILOR] : an alimentary paste in flat ribbon form

tag line *n* [¹*tag*] **1 a** : a final line (as in a play, story, joke); *esp* : one that serves to clarify a point or create a dramatic effect ⟨always hesitated before delivering the *tag line* that stunned the audience⟩ **b** : a reiterated phrase identified with an individual, group, or product : SLOGAN, CATCHWORD ⟨song lyrics, jokes . . . and performers' *tag lines* became . . . part of the whole country's stock of knowledge —Joe Laurie⟩ ⟨never wrote a *tag line* that didn't sell⟩ **2** : a cable running from a crane boom to a bucket for steadying the bucket

ta·glio·ni \talˈyōnē\ *n* -s [after Filippo *Taglioni* †1871 Ital. ballet master] : an overcoat worn in the early 19th century

taglock \ˈ⸗ˌ⸗\ *n* [¹*tag* + *lock*] : a matted or tangled lock of hair or wool : DAGLOCK

tag·ma \ˈtagmə\ *n, pl* **tagma·ta** \-məd·ə\ [NL, fr. Gk *tagma* arrangement, order, row, fr. *tassein*, *tattein* to arrange — more at TACTICS] : a compound body section of an arthropod resulting from embryonic fusion of two or more somites (as the cephalothorax of a spider) or consisting of two or more distinguishable segments (as the thorax of an insect)

tag·man \ˈtagˌman, -ˌmən\ *n, pl* **tagmen** [¹*tag* + *man*] : a construction worker who handles the guide lines on loads to be hoisted or lowered

tag match *n* [³*tag*] : a wrestling match between two tag teams

tag·meme \ˈtagˌmēm, ˈtaig-\ *n* -s [Gk *tagma* arrangement, order, row + E *-eme*] **1** : a constituent of a meaningful grammatical relation that cannot be analyzed into smaller meaningful features and that may be marked by features of word order, selection of allomorphs, agreement with finite verb forms, and elaboration by preceding adjectival modifiers **2** : the class of grammatical forms that function in a particular grammatical relation

tag·mo·sis \tagˈmōsəs\ *n, pl* **tagmo·ses** \-ōˌsēz\ [NL, irreg. fr. *tagma* + *-osis*] : division of the arthropod body into tagmata

¹tagrag \ˈ⸗ˌ⸗\ *n* [¹*tag* + *rag*] **1** : RAGTAG **2** : a loosely connected tag

²tagrag \"\ *adj* : SHABBY ⟨clad in the ~ garb of democracy —William Taylor †1836⟩

³tagrag *adv, obs* : in a mob : HELTER-SKELTER

tag, rag, and bobtail *or* **tagrag and bobtail** *n* : a motley group : RABBLE, CANAILLE ⟨all the *tagrag and bobtail* of the town —J.G.Frazer⟩

tag·rag·gery \ˈtaˌgragərē\ *n* -ES [¹*tagrag* + *-ery*] : a heterogeneous collection of people or things

tags *pl of* TAG, *pres 3d sing of* TAG

tag team *n* [³*tag*] : a team composed of two professional wrestlers who spell one another during a match

ta·gua \ˈtägwə\ *n* -s [AmerSp, fr. Araucan] **1** : IVORY PALM **2** : IVORY NUT 1

ta·guan \ˈtäˌgwän\ *n* -s [native name in Philippines] : a large East Indian flying squirrel (*Petaurista petaurista*)

tag up *vi* [⁴*tag*] : to touch a base in baseball before running after a fly ball is caught ⟨*tagged up* and scored after an outfield fly⟩

ta·ha \ˈtä(ˌ)hä\ *n* -s [Zulu *taka*] : a So. African weaverbird (esp. *Euplectes taha*) with black and yellow plumage in the male

ta·ha·nun *or* **ta·cha·nun** \ˈtäkˌnün\ *n, pl* **tahanu·nim** *or* **tachanu·nim** \ˌtäk(ˌ)nüˈnēm\ *usu cap* [LHeb *taḥănūn*, fr. Heb *ḥannēn* to beg for grace, fr. *ḥēn* grace] : a prayer for grace recited in the daily morning and afternoon synagogue service

ta·ha·rah \täˈhärä\ *n, pl* **taha·roth** *or* **taha·rot** \tähäˈrōt(h), -ōs\ [Heb *ṭāhārāh*, lit., purification, fr. *ṭāhēr* to be clean, be pure] : a ceremony in the Jewish religion of washing a corpse before burial

¹ta·hi·tian \təˈhēshən *also* täˈh- *or* taˈh- *or* -ēd·|ēən *or* -ēt| *or* |iən\ *adj, usu cap* [fr. *Tahiti*, island in the southern Pacific + E *-an*] **1 a** : of, relating to, or characteristic of Tahiti **b** : of, relating to, or characteristic of the Tahitians **2** : of, relating to, or characteristic of the Tahitian language

²tahitian \"\ *n* -s *cap* **1** : a native or inhabitant of Tahiti **2** : the Polynesian language of the Tahitian people

ta·hi·ti orange *or* **tahiti lime** \-hēd·|ē-, -hēt|, |i-\ *n, usu cap T* [fr. *Tahiti*, island in the southern Pacific] : PERSIAN LIME

tahl·tan \ˈtältən\ *n, pl* **tahltan** *or* **tahltans** *usu cap* **1 a** : an Athapaskan people of northwestern British Columbia and southern Alaska **b** : a member of such people **2** : a language of the Tahltan people

ta·hoe trout \ˈtäˌhō-, ˈtäˌhō-\ *n, usu cap 1st T* [fr. Lake *Tahoe* on the California-Nevada boundary] : a large cutthroat trout (*Salmo clarkii henshawi*) found in Lake Tahoe and neighboring regions

ta·ho·ka daisy \təˈhōkə-\ *n, usu cap T* [fr. *Tahoka*, Texas] : an aster (*Aster tanacetifolius*) of the southern U.S. and Mexico that has pinnatifid leaves and flower heads with lavender-blue rays and golden-yellow centers and is widely cultivated as an ornamental

ta·ho·na \təˈhōnə\ *n* -s [Sp, fr. Ar *ṭāḥūna* mill] : ARRASTRA

tahr *or* **thar** \ˈtär\ *n* -s [Nepali *thār*] : a Himalayan beardless wild goat (*Hemitragus jemlaicus*) having short thick recurving horns and a dark reddish brown mane; *also* : a closely related and similar goat (*H. hylocrius*)

tah·sil \täˈsē(ə)l\ *n* -s [Hindi *taḥsīl*, fr. Ar, collection of revenue] : a district administration or revenue subdivision in India

tah·sil·dar \ˌtäsēlˈdär\ *n* -s [Hindi *taḥsīldār*, fr. Per, fr. Ar *taḥsīl* + Per *-dār* having] : a revenue officer in India

¹tai \ˈtī\ *n, pl* **tai** *usu cap* : a widespread group of peoples in south China and southeast Asia associated ethnically with valley paddy-rice culture and including various groups (as the Burma Shan, the Chinese Chungchia, the valley dwellers of Laos, and the dominant people of Thailand) — compare THAI

²tai \"\ *n, pl* **tai** [Jap] : any of several Pacific porgies of *Pagrus* or a related genus; *esp* : RED TAI

ta·i·a·ha \ˈtäēəˌhä\ *n* -s [Maori] : a long light staff or club adorned with a band of red feathers or dog's hair that is carried by Maori chiefs as a sign of authority and used as a two-handed striking weapon

tai-chinese \ˈ⸗ˌ⸗ˈ⸗\ *adj, usu cap T&C* : of or relating to the Tai and Chinese language groups jointly

tai·chung \ˈtīˈchu̇ŋ\ *adj, usu cap* [fr. *Taichung*, Formosa] : of or from Taichung, Formosa : of the kind or style prevalent in Taichung

tai·ga \tīˈgä, -ˈgȧ, ˈtīgə\ *n* -s [Russ *taĭga*, of Turkic origin; akin to Teleut *taiga* rocky, mountainous terrain, Turk *dağ* mountain] **1** : swampy coniferous forest of Siberia beginning where the tundra ends **2** : moist subarctic forest of Europe and No. America dominated by spruces and firs

taiglach *var of* TEIGLACH

tai·gle \ˈtāgəl\ *vb* [ME *tagilen*, *tangilen* — more at TANGLE] **1** *Scot & dial Eng* : CATCH, ENTRAP **2** *Scot & dial Eng* : DELAY, HINDER, FATIGUE **3** *Scot & dial Eng* : DRAG, TRAIL, LOITER

¹tail \ˈtāl, *esp before pause or consonant* -āəl\ *n* -s *often attrib* [ME, fr. OE *tægel*, *tægl*; akin to OHG *zagal* tail, ON *tagl* horse's tail, Goth *tagl* hair, OIr *dúal* lock of hair, and perh. to Skt *daśā* fringe of a garment, wick] **1 a** : the part of the vertebrate body posterior to the portion containing the body cavity: (1) : a rather slender more or less elongated process that arises from the trunk of many mammals immediately above the anus, contains the caudal vertebrae, and is often variously modified as a support, a balancer, or a grasping organ — see COCCYX; see COW illustration (2) : the uropygium of a bird with its attached feathers; *sometimes* : the feathers alone of this part ⟨the peacock spreads his splendid ~⟩ — see BIRD illustration (3) : the caudal fin and caudal peduncle of a fish; *sometimes* : CAUDAL FIN (4) : the portion of the body of a limbless reptile behind the vent **b** : any of various backwardly directed and usu. posterior processes on the body of an invertebrate animal **2** : something resembling an animal's tail in shape or position : a hindmost part or something that trails behind : a terminal appendage or rear end: as **a** : the luminous train of a comet **b** : a stroke or loop at the bottom of a letter (as *g* or *y*) of the alphabet usu. extending below the line **c** : one of the narrow prolongations of the hind wings of some butterflies and moths **d** : one of the slender stringy tips of some swollen roots (as of beets or turnips) **e** : a rudder or vane that turns a windmill to face the wind **f** : a braid of hair or a long switch or pigtail ⟨her woolly hair was braided in sundry little ~s —Harriet B. Stowe⟩ **3** : a train or company of attendants : RETINUE **4 tails** *pl* **a** : TAILCOAT **b** : full evening dress for men ⟨came downstairs resplendent in ~s and white tie —Joseph Wechsberg⟩ **c** : the skirt, hem, or train of a gown or other long garment ⟨his raincoat . . . kept slipping and he trod on its ~ —John Buchan⟩ **5 a** : BUTTOCKS ⟨sits on his ~ at a desk —Frances & Richard Lockridge⟩ **b** *slang* : SEXUAL INTERCOURSE — usu. considered vulgar **6 a** : something that trails or follows in time or place : the back, last, lower, or inferior part of something : the part opposed to the head, superior part, front, or beginning : END, EXTREMITY, REAR, CONCLUSION **b** : the concluding part of a word, sentence, or discourse ⟨at the ~ of their conversation —Harriet Martineau⟩ **c** : a part that occurs or appears last ⟨seemed to tire toward the ~ of the evening⟩ **d** : the rear of a vehicle or of a traveling mechanism or implement ⟨tumbled out at the ~ of the cart —Roger Fry⟩ ⟨in the private cabin in the ~ of the ship —W.L.Worden⟩ **e** : the rear end of a procession (as a marching army) **f** : the reverse of a coin — see HEAD OR TAIL **g** : the part of a millrace downstream from the wheel : the downstream section of a pool or river **h** : the outermost or underwater part of a projecting bank or bar **i** : one end of a molecule regarded as opposite to the head — used esp. of monomers as they are joined in polymers **7 a** : the residuum or refuse part left after a process (as milling, ore dressing, or distilling) : DREGS, TAILINGS **b** : the lowest grade of flour derived in milling from a final treatment of the impure stocks **8** : a sprout of barley **9 a** : the group standing hindmost in accomplishment, value, or skill (as in a political party, a society, a team, or in a herd or flock) **b** *also* **tail end** : the members of a cricket team who are not played primarily as batsmen and who go in to bat towards the end of the innings **10** : a horsetail formerly used in Turkey as a mark of rank ⟨a pasha of two ~s⟩ **11** : any of various parts of bodily structures that are terminal: as **a** : the distal tendon of a muscle **b** : the slender left end of the human pancreas **c** : the common convoluted tube that forms the lower part of the epididymis **12** : the stem of a written or printed musical note **13** : a police or other spy who follows or keeps watch on someone : DETECTIVE, INVESTIGATOR, OPERATIVE, SHADOW ⟨his ~ might be anything from a private dick to a G-man —Erle Stanley Gardner⟩ **14 a** : the exposed lower end of a slate, tile, or rafter **b** : TAILING 4 **15** *naut* : a rope spliced around a block with long ends by which it may be lashed to something **16** : an augment (as the additional lines of a tailed sonnet) added to a recognized prosodic form — see TAIL RHYME **17** : TAIL FLY **18 a** : the blank space below the printed part of a page or the corresponding part of the form from which the page is printed **b** : FOOT 9d **19** : ⁶JET 3 **20** *or* **tail unit** *or* **tail group** : the rear part of an airplane consisting of horizontal and vertical stabilizing surfaces to which are attached movable surfaces for longitudinal and directional control : EMPENNAGE **21** : the trail left by one who is going forward in or as if in flight ⟨let the guy pass me to get him off my ~⟩ ⟨had a posse on his ~⟩

²tail \"\ *vb* -ED/-ING/-S *vt* **1** : to fasten by or at the tail, stern, or rear : connect end to end : string out ⟨~*ed* weak words endlessly one to another⟩ **2** : to drag, grasp, or pull by the tail ⟨~*ed* a badger that the dog had drawn out⟩ **3 a** : to remove the tail of (an animal) : DOCK **b** : to cut off the stringy ends of ⟨top and ~ the green beans —Dione Lucas⟩ **4 a** : to make or furnish with a tail ⟨~*ed* a kite for his young son⟩ **b** : to follow or be drawn behind like a tail ⟨~*ed* the champion to take second place⟩ **5** : to fasten an end of (a tile, brick, or timber) into a wall or other support **6** *Austral* : to act as herdsman of (sheep or cattle) : DRIVE, HERD **7** : to follow (someone) for purposes of surveillance : keep under observation : TRAIL, WATCH ⟨all the afternoon, the detectives ~*ed* the two men —Joel Sayre⟩ ~ *vi* **1** : to ground stern first — used with *aground* **2** : to form or move in a straggling line : stretch out in a loose, irregular, or widely spaced column or file ⟨with some hundred more ~*ing* out in single file to join them —N.J.Berrill⟩ **3 a** : to diminish gradually : grow progressively smaller, fainter, or more scattered : approach an end : SUBSIDE ⟨her voice ~*ed* off into hesitant silence⟩ ⟨the airy rain had ~*ed* away into the soft, moist blackness —Mervyn Wall⟩ **b** : to blend or merge gradually ⟨a beach ~*ed* out into the shallows —Nelson Hayes⟩ **4** : to break the surface of water with the tail while feeding on the bottom or in weeds **5** : to become built into a wall or other support so as to be held by the end — used of a timber, tile, or brick **6** : to swing or lie with the stern in a named direction — used of a ship at anchor ⟨the ship ~*ed* toward the shore⟩ ⟨a liner ~*ed* downriver⟩ **7** : to follow or mix closely with : TAG ⟨found it pleasanter to ~ along with the crowd he knew⟩ **syn** see FOLLOW

³tail \"\ *adj* [ME *taille*, *tayle*, fr. AF *taylé*, fr. OF *taillié*, past part. of *taillier* to cut, shape, fix, limit — more at TAILOR] : limited as to tenure : ABRIDGED, CURTAILED, ENTAILED, REDUCED — compare ESTATE TAIL, FEE TAIL

⁴tail \"\ *vt* -ED/-ING/-S [ME *taylen*, *taillen*, fr. AF *tayler*, fr. OF *taillier* to cut, shape, limit] : to limit or encumber with an entail : grant in tail

⁵tail \"\ *n* -s [ME *tayle*, *taille*, fr. MF *taille*, fr. OF, fr. *taillier*] **1** *obs* : TALLY 1a **2** : the state or condition of entailment : LIMITATION, ABRIDGMENT

tailback \ˈ⸗ˌ⸗\ *n* : the offensive football back who lines up farthest from the line of scrimmage

tailband \ˈ⸗ˌ⸗\ *n* : FOOTBAND

tail barley *n* : brewer's screenings of barley

tail bay *n* **1 a** : the bay of a framed floor or roof which is next to the end wall so that its joists rest one end on the wall and the other on a girder **b** : the space between a wall and the nearest girder of a floor — compare CASE BAY **2** : the part of a canal lock below the lower gates

tail beam *n* : TAILPIECE 4

tail block *n* : a pulley block with a loose tail of rope for attaching it

tailboard \ˈ⸗ˌ⸗\ *n* : the tailgate esp. of a wagon — called also *endgate*

tailbone \ˈ⸗ˌ⸗\ *n* **1** : a caudal vertebra **2** : COCCYX ⟨walking bent over, one hand on his ~ like an old man —Shelby Foote⟩

tail boom *n* : ²BOOM 7

tail bud *n* : a knob of embryonic tissue not divided into germ layers that arises at the primitive knot and contributes to the formation of the posterior part of the vertebrate body

tailcoat *n* : a coat with tails; *esp* : a man's full-dress coat with satin-faced lapels, waist-length fronts that do not close, and two long tapering skirts at the back resembling the tail of a swallow — called also *claw hammer*; compare EVENING DRESS

tailcoat

tail·coat·ed \ˈ⸗ˌkōd·əd\ *adj* [*tailcoat* + *-ed*] : wearing a tailcoat ⟨~ headwaiters⟩

tail cone *n* : the exhaust tube of a jet engine

tail coverts *n pl* : the feathers that cover the bases of the tail quills — see BIRD illustration

tailcup lupine *n* : a lupine (*Lupinus caudatus*) of the northwestern U.S. having the calyx lobes reflexed

tail down *vt* : to roll (logs) down a skidway (as for loading)

tailed \ˈtā(ə)ld\ *adj* [ME, fr. *tail* + *-ed*] **1** : having a tail **2** [fr. past part. of ²*tail*] : deprived of a tail

tailed pepper *n* **1** : CUBEB 1a **2** : JAVA PEPPER

tailed rhyme *var of* TAIL RHYME

tailed sonnet *n* : a sonnet augmented by additional lines that are arranged systematically and are often shorter than the basic line of the sonnet proper — compare CURTAL SONNET, TAIL RHYME

tail end *n* [ME *tailende*, fr. *tail* + *ende* end — more at END] **1 :** RUMP, BEHIND, BUTTOCKS ⟨sitting around the house on his *tail end* —Shirley A. Grau⟩ **2 :** the hindmost end **:** the part opposite to the head or inferior to the rest ⟨watched the *tail end* of the company move out —James Jones⟩ **3 :** the concluding period ⟨the *tail end* of a cabinet meeting —A.M.Schlesinger b. 1917⟩ **4 :** TAIL 9b

tail·end·er \'=ˈendə(r)\ *n* -s [*tail end* + *-er*] **:** one at the tail end (as in a competition)

[1]**tail·er** \'tālə(r)\ *n* -s [[2]*tail* + *-er*] **1 :** one that tails: as **a :** SHADOW 10b ⟨combined all the attributes of a successful ~ — iron legs and arches, the considerable acting ability a man must have to make himself unnoteworthy, and a sixth sense of anticipation —Joel Sayre⟩ **b :** one that follows; *esp* **:** one that rounds up or drives on the stragglers of a herd **c :** one that removes products from the discharge end of a machine (as a lathe, wrapping machine, or wet machine) **2 a :** a fish that tails **b :** a device that closes a metal loop around the tail of a fish (as a salmon) and is used in landing it

[2]**tailer** \"\ *n* -s [alter. of [1]*tailor*] **:** BLUEFISH 1

tailer-down \'==ˈ=\ *n* -s [*tail down*, v. + *-er*] **:** TAILER-IN

tailer-in \'==ˈ=\ *n* -s [*tail in*, v. + *-er*] **:** a worker who rolls logs with cant hook or peavey to a place convenient for loading or stacking

tail fan *n* **:** the fanlike swimming organ formed by the last pair of pleopods and the telson in some decapod crustaceans

tail-female \'=ˈ=,=\ *n* [[5]*tail* (limitation) + *female* (adj.)] **:** the maternal ancestral line esp. of a thoroughbred horse

tail fin *n* **1 :** CAUDAL FIN **2 :** FIN 2c(3)

tailfirst \'=¦=\ *adv* **:** with the hinder part foremost **:** BACKWARD ⟨a coon comes down a tree headfirst for most of the way . . . then finishes the descent ~ —E.B.White⟩

tailflower \'=,=\ *n* **:** an aroid of the genus *Anthurium*

tail fly *n* **:** the fly at the end of a fishline leader — called also *end fly*

tailforemost \'=ˈ=,=\ *adv* **:** TAILFIRST

[1]**tailgate** \'=,=\ *n* **1 :** a gate at the rear: as **a :** the lower gate of a canal lock **b :** a board or gate at the rear end of a vehicle that can be removed or let down for convenience in loading **c :** a heavy wooden panel pivoted to the end of a railroad freight car to form an incline from the car bottom to the rails that is used in loading **2** [so called fr. the custom of seating trombonists at the rear end of trucks carrying jazz bands in parades] **:** a style of jazz trombone playing (as the playing of Dixieland in ensemble) characterized by slides to and from long sustained tones, smears and glissandi, and the playing of improvised countermelodies and rhythms often in a nonlegato manner extending through the entire range of the instrument

[2]**tailgate** *vi* **:** to drive too close to another vehicle for safety ~ *vt* **:** to follow (another vehicle) too close for safety

tail grape *n* **:** any of various tropical woody vines constituting a genus (*Artabotrys*) of the family Annonaceae and having solitary or clustered flowers borne on a woody often hooked peduncle that functions as a tendril; *esp* **:** an eastern Asian vine (*A. odoratissimus* or *A. uncinatus*) that is sometimes cultivated for its very fragrant inconspicuous reddish brown flowers and showy inedible golden yellow pear-shaped fruits

tail group *n* **:** TAIL 20

tailhead \'=,=\ *n* **:** the base of an animal's tail — see COW illustration

tail-heavy \'=,==\ *adj* **:** having a nose that tends to rise when the longitudinal control is released in level flight ⟨a *tail-heavy* airplane⟩ — compare NOSE-HEAVY

tail house *n* **1 :** a housing for the tension carriage in an endless-rope mine hoisting system **2 :** a building in which are placed the discharge ends of the condensing apparatus used in petroleum distillation

tailing *n* -s [fr. gerund of [2]*tail*] **1 :** the act of one that tails ⟨the ~ of people is a normal part of detective and intelligence work⟩ **2 :** inferior or refuse material separated as residue in processing — usu. used in pl.: as **a :** stones that tail over the largest openings of the screen of a stone crusher **b :** the lighter inferior coffee berries floated away in washing **c :** the gangue and other refuse material resulting from the washing, concentration, or treatment of ground ore ⟨the ~*s* of the silver mines of those times are being worked over for the tin that was then discarded —Marrion Wilcox⟩ — compare CONCENTRATE, HEAD, MIDDLING **3 :** the last part of something **4 :** the part of a projecting stone or brick inserted in a wall **5 :** a blur or other break in impression in textile printing **6 tailings** *pl* **:** the lighter and coarser particles (as bran or fibrous or flaked endosperm) that tail over the sieves of a purifier while the heavier middlings pass through **7 tailings** *pl* **:** GRUFFS **8 tailings** *pl* **:** the parts (as of crude spirit) that come over last in fractional distillation **:** FOOTS **9 :** a reused tanning liquor **10 :** short lengths of yarn or fabric — usu. used in pl.

tail joist *n* **:** TAILPIECE 4

tail-kidney \'=¦==\ *n* **:** METANEPHROS

tail lamp *n* **:** TAILLIGHT

taille \'tī, 'tā(ə)l\ *n* -s [F, fr. OF, fr. *taillier* to cut, shape, fix, limit, tax — more at TAILOR] **1 a :** an imposition or tax formerly levied by a French king or seigneur on his subjects or on lands held of or under him **b :** a royal or a national tax in 15th century France from which the lords and later the clergy and others were exempt — compare CORVÉE, GABELLE, TALLAGE **2** *obs* **:** the shape of the bust **:** BUILD, FIGURE, FORM **3 a :** a middle voice or tenor in early choral music **b :** a part to be performed on the tenor viol, the viola, or the English horn

tail·less \'tā(ə)lləs\ *adj* **:** having no tail — **tail·less·ly** *adv* — **tail·less·ness** *n* -ES

tailless airplane *n* **:** an aircraft consisting of a single wing without conventional fuselage or tail, housing cargo and personnel within the wing structure, and achieving stability and control by means of vertical external surfaces mounted on the wing tips or booms attached to the wing

tailless whip scorpion *n* **:** an arachnid of the family Tarantulidae

tail·leur *R* tä'yər, tal'-, +V -'yər·; –*R* -'yə̄, + *vowel in a word following without pause* -'yər· *or* -'yə̄ *also* 'yə̄r\ *n* -s [F, lit., cutter, tailor, fr. OF] **1 :** the dealer in a card game **2 :** a woman's tailored costume; *esp* **:** a suit for town wear

tail·lie \'tāli\ *n* -s [ME — more at TAILZIE] *Scots law* **:** TAILZIE

taillight \'=,=\ *n* **:** a usu. red light mounted at the rear esp. of an automotive vehicle as a warning to following traffic

taillike \'=,=\ *adj* **:** resembling a tail

tail louse *n* **:** a widely distributed sucking louse (*Haematopinus quadripertusus*) that is an ectoparasite on cattle on the tail of which the adults congregate

tail-male \'=ˈ=\ *n* [[5]*tail* (limitation) + *male* (adj.)] **:** the male ancestral line esp. of a thoroughbred horse

tail of the eye : the outer corner of the eye ⟨out of the *tail of his eye*, he glanced at his only passengers —Agnes S. Turnbull⟩

[1]**tai·lor** \'tālə(r)\ *n* -s [ME *taillour*, fr. OF *tailleur*, lit., one that cuts, fr. *taillier* to cut (fr. LL *taliare*, fr. L *talea* twig, stick, cutting) + *-eur* -or; akin to Gk *talis* marriageable girl, *tēlis* fenugreek, Lith *attolas, atolas* rowen, and perh. to ON *thöll* young pine tree; basic meaning: growing thing] **1 :** one whose occupation or business is making or altering men's or women's outerwear (as suits and coats) **2 a** *or* **tailor herring :** FALL HERRING **b** (1) **:** BLUEFISH 1 (2) **:** a closely related Australian fish

[2]**tailor** \"\ *vb* -ED/-ING/-S *vi* **1 :** to do the job or carry on the business of a tailor **2 :** to adapt to tailoring ⟨a material that ~*s* well⟩ ~ *vt* **1 a :** to make or fashion as the work of a tailor ⟨~*ed* him several suits⟩ **b :** to make or adapt to suit a special need or purpose ⟨this striking force that can ~ its power to meet the demands of the moment —H.H.Martin⟩ ⟨~*ed* a new cartridge to the new gun —W.W.Stout⟩ ⟨failed to ~ the manners of his ego to those prevailing in the environment he invaded —Thomas Sugrue⟩ **2 :** to fit with clothes **:** make clothes for ⟨the best tailors ~*ed* him⟩ **3 :** to fit or style (women's garments or items of interior decor) with trim, straight lines and finished handwork like that of a tailor's work on men's garments

[3]**tailor** \"\ *n* -s [by folk etymology] **:** [1]TELLER 2b

tailorbird \'==,=\ *n* **:** any of numerous Asiatic, East Indian, and African warblers (family Sylviidae) that stitch leaves together to support and hide their nests; *esp* **:** a common garden-frequenting bird (*Orthotomus sutorius*) of southern and eastern Asia that is yellowish green above and white below and has a long tapering tail

tai·lor·dom \-(r)dəm\ *n* -s **1 :** tailors as an occupational group **:** the trade or domain of tailors **2 :** TAILORING

tailored *adj* **1 :** made by a tailor **2 a :** fashioned or fitted to resemble a tailor's work **b :** having trim, simple, straight lines ⟨~ curtains⟩ **3 :** MADE-TO-ORDER **4 a :** having the look of one fitted by a custom tailor **:** well turned out ⟨she has the ~ look —John Mason Brown⟩ **b :** appearing well cared for **:** STYLISH, TRIM ⟨a well-*tailored* neighborhood —*Time*⟩

tailored gardenia *n* **:** a gardenia removed from the peduncle, wired, and supported by a collar of stapled foliage

tai·lor·ess \'tālərəs\ *n* -ES **:** a woman tailor

tailor-fashion \'==,==\ *adv* (*or adj*) **:** CROSS-LEGGED 1 ⟨sat down *tailor-fashion* in a place of honor —F.G.Slaughter⟩

tailoring *n* -s **1 a :** the business or occupation of a tailor **b :** the work or workmanship of a tailor ⟨the kind of ~ which goes by the name of ready-made —Irving Kolodin⟩ **2 :** the making or adapting of something to suit a particular purpose ⟨the ~ of history books to fit the party line of the moment had for some time been an established practice —Sergius Yakobson⟩ **3 :** a rounding off of the corners of grooved rolls of iron and steel to prevent fins from forming on the bars in rolling

tai·lor·ism \'tālə,rizəm\ *n* -s **1 :** the labor, employment, or product of a tailor **2 :** a tailor's mannerism

tai·lor·ize \-,rīz\ *vb* -ED/-ING/-S *vi* **:** to do the work of a tailor **:** behave as a tailor ~ *vt* **:** to reduce to a tailor's status **:** treat as a tailor **:** DEGRADE, DEMORALIZE

[1]**tailor-made** \¦==¦=\ *adj* [[1]*tailor* + *made*] **1 a :** made by a tailor or with a tailor's care and style ⟨a *tailor-made* suit⟩ **b :** marked by trimness of fit, simplicity of line and ornament, and fine finish — used of women's garments **c :** having the appearance of one turned out by a good tailor ⟨a *tailor-made* man⟩ **2 :** made or fitted esp. to a particular use or purpose **:** MADE-TO-ORDER ⟨the wage provisions of its agreement are *tailor-made* for that company's circumstances —R.A.Lester⟩ ⟨his music is *tailor-made* to the requirements and conditions of a specific time and place —Abraham Veinus⟩ ⟨a *tailor-made* fuel with special characteristics —*Ethyl News*⟩ **3 :** factory-made rather than hand-rolled — used of cigarettes

[2]**tailor-made** \"\ *n* -s **1 :** a woman's tailor-made garment **2 :** a factory-made cigarette

tailor-make \¦==¦=\ *vt* [back-formation fr. [1]*tailor-made*] **:** to make or adapt to a particular use or purpose or to the needs of an individual — opposed to *mass-produce*

tailor muscle *also* **tailor's muscle** *n* **:** SARTORIUS

tailor's chair *n* **:** a seat with back rest but no legs used by tailors at work

tailor's chalk *n* **:** a thin flat piece of hard chalk or soapstone used by tailors and seamstresses for making temporary marks on cloth

tailor's cushion *n* **:** a tailor's ham

tai·lor·ship \'tālə(r),ship\ *n* **:** the trade or work of a tailor **:** TAILORING

tailor's tack *n* **:** a basting stitch taken with a double thread through two pieces of fabric and then cut apart with large loops being left in each piece for marking seam lines and perforations

tailor warbler *n* **:** a tailorbird (*Orthotomus sutorius*)

tai·lory \'tālərē\ *n* -ES [ME *taillourie*, fr. *taillour* tailor + *-ie* -y — more at TAILOR] **1 :** the work or business of a tailor **2 :** clothing made by a tailor

tail over *vt* **:** to pass (material that will not go through) over a sieve in milling

tailpiece \'=,=\ *n* **1 :** a subsidiary part at the lower or rear end **:** a piece added on at the end **:** APPENDAGE ⟨the ~ of a crustacean⟩ ⟨the ~ of a musical composition⟩ **2 :** a triangular piece (as of ebony) between which and the pegs the strings of a stringed musical instrument are stretched **3 :** the part of a telescope containing the adjusting device for the eyepiece **4 :** a relatively shorter beam or rafter tailed in a wall and supported by a header **5 :** a piece for transmitting motion from the hub of a lock to the latch bolt **6 :** an ornament placed below the text matter of a page (as at the end of a chapter) — compare HEADPIECE

tailpin \'=,=\ *n* **1 :** the tailstock center in a lathe **2 :** a pin projecting from the body of a large stringed musical instrument (as a cello) to raise it off the floor when being played

tailpipe \'=,=\ *vt* **:** to tie a tin can to the tail of (a dog)

tail pipe *n* **1 :** the suction pipe of a pump **2 :** the pipe discharging into the atmosphere the exhaust gases from the muffler of an automotive engine **3 :** the part of a jet engine that carries the exhaust gases rearward and discharges them through a nozzle

tail-pipe burner *n* **:** AFTERBURNER

tail plane *n* **:** the horizontal tail surfaces of an airplane including the stabilizer and the elevator

tail print *n* **:** a core print carried to the top of a foundry mold so that the pattern may be molded in one box

tailrace \'=,=\ *n* **1 :** a race for conveying water away from a point of industrial application (as a waterwheel or turbine) after use — called also *afterbay;* compare HEADRACE, MILLRACE **2 :** the channel in which mine tailings are floated off

tail rhyme *also* **tailed rhyme** *n* **:** a verse form in which rhymed lines (as couplets or triplets) are followed by a line of different usu. shorter length which does not rhyme with the couplet or triplet

tail-rhyme stanza *also* **tail-rhymed stanza** \'=,=-\ *n* **:** a stanza consisting of rhymed couplets or triplets with tails that rhyme with each other

tail rider *n* **:** one of usu. two cowboys who keep a herd of cattle moving from the rear **:** one that rides drag — compare SWINGMAN

tail rod *n* **:** a continuation of a piston rod or valve rod through the back cylinder cover or valve chest (as of a steam engine or an air compressor)

tail rope *n* **:** a rope attached to the rear part or end of something: as **a :** a rope fastened to the tail of a mine car or train to haul it back empty after unloading or to brake its speed on a downgrade **b :** the rope beneath either of two counterbalancing cages in a mine shaft

tails *pl of* TAIL, *pres 3d sing of* TAIL

tail set *n* **:** a device used to hold the tail of a gaited saddlehorse in the desired cocked position

tail shaft *n* **:** the after section of a ship's propeller shaft extending through the stern tube

tail sheet *n* **:** a strip of larger-mesh bolting cloth used at the tail end of a sieve to sift out coarser stock in milling

tail skid *n* **:** a yielding support on which the tail of an airplane rests when on the ground

tail slide *n* **:** the tailfirst slide rearward and downward that some airplanes may be made to take after being brought into a stalling position by a steep climb

tailspin \'=,=\ *n* **1 :** [2]SPIN 2a ⟨the airplane went into a ~⟩ **2 :** a collapse into mental or emotional depression or confusion ⟨the sight of it had nearly sent him into a ~ —Jean Stafford⟩ **3 :** a state of disordered or depressed activity **:** CHAOS, DEMORALIZATION ⟨an abrupt falling off in foreign trade may send the economy into a ~ —*Atlantic*⟩

tail spindle *n* **:** the tailstock spindle in a lathe

tailstock \'=,=\ *n* **:** the adjustable or sliding head of a lathe containing the dead center

tail surface *n* **:** a stabilizing surface or a control surface in the tail of an airplane

tail tackle *n* **1 :** WATCH TACKLE **2 :** LUFF TACKLE

tail tree *n* **:** the spar tree farthest from the power source in a cable logging rig

tail trimmer *n* **:** a trimmer placed along a wall to receive the ends of joists

tail twisting *n* **1 :** the twisting of an animal's tail usu. as a means of torture **2 :** HARASSMENT, ABUSE

tail unit *n* **:** TAIL 20

tail up *vt* [[1]*tail*] *West* **:** to lift (an animal) out of a bog by the tail; *also* **:** to twist the tail as a means of forcing (a benumbed animal) to rise

tail-wagging \'=,==\ *n* **:** TEMPO TURN

[1]**tail·ward** \'tā(ə)lwə(r)d\ *adj* [[1]*tail* + *-ward*] **:** located at or directed toward the rear **:** REARWARD

[2]**tailward** \"\ *or* **tail·wards** \-dz\ *adv* **:** to the rear **:** REARWARD

tail water *n* **1 :** water in a tailrace **2 :** water below a dam or waterpower development

tail wheel *n* **:** an auxiliary wheel on which the rear of an airplane rests or taxis on the ground

tail wind *n* **:** a wind having the same general direction as the course of an airplane or a ship in motion ⟨a stout *tail wind* was giving a friendly boost —W.D.Patterson⟩

[1]**tail·zie** \'tāl(y)i\ *n* [alter. (*ȝ* being taken as *z*) of earlier *tailȝie*, fr. ME *taillie, tailyie, tailȝie*, fr. MF *tailliee*, fr. fem. of *taillié*, past part. of *taillier* to cut, shape, fix, limit — more at TAILOR] *Scots law* **:** ENTAIL

[2]**tailzie** \"\ *vt* -ED/-ING/-S *Scots law* **:** ENTAIL

tai·men \'tī,men\ *n* -s [Russ *taĭmen'*, fr. Finn *taimen*] **:** a giant trout (*Salmo taimen* or *S. fluviatilis*) of the rivers of northern Asia

[1]**tai·nan** \'tīnən\ *adj, usu cap* [*Taino* + *-an*] **:** of or relating to the Taino or their language

[2]**tai·nan** \'tī'nän\ *adj, usu cap* [fr. *Tainan*, Formosa] **:** of or from the city of Tainan on the island of Formosa, China **:** of the kind or style prevalent in Tainan

tai·ni·o·lite \'tīnēō,līt\ *n* -s [*tainio-* (fr. Gk *tainia* band) + *-lite;* akin to Gk *teinein* to stretch — more at THIN] **:** a mineral $KLiMg_2Si_4O_{10}F_2$ consisting of a silicate and fluoride of potassium, lithium, and magnesium of the mica group

tai·no \'tī(,)nō\ *n, pl* **taino** *or* **tainos** *usu cap* [Sp, of AmerInd origin] **1 a :** an extinct aboriginal Arawakan people of the Greater Antilles and the Bahamas, esp. of Hispaniola **b :** a member of such people **2 :** the language of the Taino people

[1]**taint** \'tānt\ *vb* -ED/-ING/-S [ME *taynten*, fr. AF *teinter*, fr. MF *teint*, past part. of *teindre* to color, dye, fr. L *tingere* — more at TINGE] *vt* **1** *obs* **:** to touch with color **:** TINGE, TINT **2** *obs* **:** to apply balm or ointment to (a wound or sore spot) **:** ANOINT **3** [influenced in meaning by obs. *taint* to attaint, fr. ME *taynten*, fr. MF *ataint*, past part. of *ataindre* to accuse, convict, attain — more at ATTAIN] **a :** to touch or affect slightly with something bad or undesirable ⟨to aid openly would be to . . . ~ his memory —S.H.Adams⟩ ⟨directed toward the purge from the public service rolls of those ~*ed* with fascism —Taylor Cole⟩ **b :** to affect with putrefaction **:** make noxious or poisonous **:** ROT ⟨the meat was ~*ed*⟩ **c :** to contaminate morally **:** CORRUPT, DEFILE, DEPRAVE, STAIN ⟨all the lighter kinds of literature were deeply ~*ed* by the prevailing licentiousness —T.B.Macaulay⟩ ~ *vi* [influenced in meaning by obs. *taint* to attaint] **1** *obs* **:** to become weak **:** lose courage ⟨I cannot ~ with fear —Shak.⟩ **2** *archaic* **:** to become affected with putrefaction or corruption **:** ROT **syn** see CONTAMINATE

[2]**taint** \"\ *n* -s [MF *teint*, fr. past part. of *teindre*] **1** *obs* **:** COLOR, HUE, TINGE **2** [influenced in meaning by [3]*taint*] **a :** a spot or stain of something bad (as of dishonor or disgrace) **:** BLEMISH ⟨some ineradicable ~ of impropriety attached in their minds to any association with the stage —Mary Austin⟩ ⟨the river that I know washes from all ~ of sin —Rudyard Kipling⟩ **b :** a germ, source, or cause of corruption **:** a contaminating influence **:** a rotting or depraving force ⟨remembered his bouts with the bottle and were afraid that the ~ had been passed on to me —Hamilton Basso⟩

[3]**taint** \"\ *n* -s [MF *atainte* — more at ATTAINT] **:** ATTAINT 1

tain·ter gate *or* **tain·tor gate** \'tāntə(r)-\ *n* [after Jeremiah B. *Tainter*, 19th cent. Am. inventor] **:** RADIAL GATE

taint·less \'tāntləs\ *adj* [[2]*taint* + *-less*] **:** having no taint **:** CLEAN, IMMACULATE, PURE — **taint·less·ly** *adv* — **taint·less·ness** *n* -ES

tain·ture \'tānchə(r)\ *n* -s [MF *teinture*, fr. L *tinctura* — more at TINCTURE] **:** DEFILEMENT, STAIN, TAINT

taintworm \'=,=\ *n* [[2]*taint* + *worm*] **:** a worm or larva parasitic on mammals

tai nua \'tīnü'ä\ *n, pl* **tai nua** *or* **tai nuas** *usu cap T&N* **1 :** a Tai people closely related to the Laotians of Laos **2 :** a member of the Tai Nua people

[1]**tai·pan** \'tī,pan\ *n* -s [Chin (Pek) *tai*[4] *pan*[1]] **:** the head of a foreign house of business in China **:** a great merchant

[2]**taipan** \"\ *n* -s [native name in Australia] **:** an exceedingly venomous elapid snake (*Oxyuranus scutellatus*) of northern Australia and the Pacific islands

tai·pei *or* **tai·peh** \'tī¦pā, -¦bā\ *adj, usu cap* [fr. *Taipei*, Formosa] **:** of or from Taipei, the capital of Formosa, China **:** of the kind or style prevalent in Taipeh

tai·ping \'tī¦piŋ\ *n* -s *usu cap* [Chin (Pek) *t'ai*[4] *p'ing*[2] peaceful] **:** a Chinese insurgent taking part in a rebellion (1848–65) against the Manchu dynasty

ta·i·po \'täē,pō\ *n* -s [Maori *taepo*] *NewZeal* **:** a demon, devil, or other specter appearing at night

taira *var of* TAYRA

ta·i·ro·na \,täē'rōnə\ *n, pl* **tairona** *or* **taironas** *usu cap* [Sp, of AmerInd origin] **1 :** an extinct Chibchan people of northern Colombia **2 :** a member of the Tairona people

taisch \'tāsh, 'tīsh\ *n* -ES [ScGael *taibhis, taibhse;* akin to IrGael *taidhbhse* ghost, OIr *taidbsiu* to show] *Scot* **:** an apparition of a person about to die

[1]**tait** \'tāt\ *var of* TATE

[2]**tait** \"\ *n* -s [native name in Australia] **:** HONEY POSSUM

[1]**tai·ver** \'tāvər\ *var of* TAVER

[2]**taiver** \"\ *n* -s [prob. of Scand origin; akin to Norw & Dan dial. *tave* rag; akin to ON *thefja* to stir, *thōf* act of beating cloth, Gk *tapeinos* low, humble, abject] *Scot* **:** SHRED, TATTER — usu. used in pl.

tai·vert \-rt\ *var of* TAVERT

tai·wan \(')tī¦wän\ *adj, usu cap* [fr. *Taiwan* (Formosa), island in the China Sea] **:** FORMOSA

[1]**tai·wan·ese** \(¦)tī¦wä¦nēz, -ēs\ *adj, usu cap* [*Taiwan* + E *-ese*] **1 :** of, relating to, or characteristic of the island of Taiwan **2 :** of, relating to, or characteristic of the people of Taiwan

[2]**taiwanese** \"\ *n, pl* **taiwanese** *cap* **:** a native or inhabitant of Taiwan

tai·wa·nia \tī'wänēə\ *n, cap* [NL, fr. *Taiwan* + NL *-ia*] **:** a genus of coniferous trees (family Pinaceae) having leathery triangular leaves that are incurved at the apex

tai·yu·an \'tīyü¦än\ *adj, usu cap* [fr. *Taiyuan*, China] **:** of or from the city of Taiyuan, China **:** of the kind or style prevalent in Taiyuan

taj \'täzh, 'täj\ *n* -ES [Ar *tāj*, fr. Per, crown, crest, cap] **:** a cap worn in Muslim countries; *esp* **:** a tall cone-shaped cap worn by dervishes

ta·jik *or* **ta·djik** *or* **ta·dzhik** \tä'jik, -'jēk\ *n, pl* **tajik** *or* **tajiks** *or* **tadjik** *or* **tadjiks** *or* **tadzhik** *or* **tadzhiks** *usu cap* **:** a member of a people of old Iranian blood and speech bearing resemblance to Europeans and dispersed among the populations of Afghanistan and Turkistan

ta·jiki \-kē\ *n* -s *usu cap* **:** the Iranian language of the Tajik people

ta·jin \tä'hēn\ *adj, usu cap* [MexSp *Tajín*, a pyramidal monument found near Papantla, Vera Cruz, Mexico, constructed by the Totonacs, fr. Nahuatl, thunder] **:** of or relating to the extinct culture of the Totonacs near the present state of Vera Cruz, Mexico, and characterized by the use of double outlines in design and of stone ax blades shaped like human faces

tak·able *or* **take·able** \'tākəbəl\ *adj* **:** capable of being taken ⟨would take . . . whatever was ~ —*Harper's*⟩

Taka-Diastase \¦takə, ¦täkə+\ *trademark* — used for an enzyme preparation obtained usu. as a yellowish white hygroscopic powder by growing a mold (*Aspergillus oryzae*) on wheat bran and used chiefly as a starch digestant

ta·ka·he \tə'kī\ *n* -s [Maori] **:** NOTORNIS 2

takamaka *var of* TACAMAHAC

ta·ka·mat·su \¦täkə¦mät(,)sü\ *adj, usu cap* [fr. *Takamatsu*, city of Shikoku Island, Japan] **:** of or from the city of Takamatsu, Japan **:** of the kind or style prevalent in Takamatsu

ta·ka·oka \tə'käōkə, -'kaůkə\ *adj, usu cap* [fr. *Takaoka*, city of central Japan] **:** of or from the city of Takaoka, Japan **:** of the kind or style prevalent in Takaoka

[1]**take** \'tāk\ *vb* **took** \'tůk, *dial* 'tək\ *or dial* **tak·en** \'tākən *sometimes* -kᵊŋ\ **taken** \"\ *or dial* **took** *or chiefly Scot* **tane** \'tān\ **taking; takes** [ME *taken*, fr. OE *tacan*, fr. ON *taka;* akin to MD *taken* to take, Goth *tekan* to touch] *vt* **1 :** to get into one's hands or into one's possession, power, or control by force or stratagem: as **a :** to seize or capture physically (as men, munitions, works, or territory in war, a person charged with an offense, or a piece of property by legal process) ⟨*took* 300 of the enemy's men and a dozen of his cannon⟩ ⟨believed they could ~ the fort in about three days⟩ ⟨was *taken* by the police within three hours of the crime⟩ ⟨*took* the town and

carried off what wine and oil it contained —C.L.Jones⟩ **b** (1) **:** to get possession of (as fish or game) by killing or capturing ⟨eighty percent of the whales today are *taken* in the Antarctic —Mary H. Vorse⟩ ⟨the nets by which the bats were to be *taken* —R.L.Ditmars & A.M.Greenhall⟩ ⟨*took* many nice fish —Alexander MacDonald⟩ ⟨had never more than three or four pellets in them . . . for he *took* them upon the very edge of the shot pattern —William Humphrey⟩ ⟨proclamation governing the *taking* of upland game birds and deer —*N. Dak. Hunting Regulations*⟩ — sometimes used to include acts in attempt to kill or capture ⟨the word ~ as used in this Act means hunt, shoot, pursue, lure, kill, destroy, capture, trap or ensnare, or to attempt so to do —*Illinois Game & Fish Codes*⟩ (2) **:** to seize as prey ⟨tales of children *taken* by tigers⟩ **c :** to capture or secure (as an opponent's piece in chess or card in bridge) in order to remove from play ⟨*took* his opponent's queen on the fourth move⟩; *also* **:** to serve to capture ⟨planned to let his rook ~ the knight⟩ ⟨ace ~*s* the king⟩ **d :** to seize or destroy (property) for public purposes **:** acquire title by eminent domain **:** CONFISCATE **e** (1) **:** to catch or field (as a batted ball) in baseball or cricket ⟨~ it on the fly⟩ ⟨*took* it on the first hop⟩ (2) **:** to catch (a batsman) out in cricket ⟨was *taken* in the slips⟩ **2 a :** to lay or get hold of with arms, hands, or fingers or with a hand or an instrument **:** GRASP, GRIP ⟨~ the ax by the handle⟩ ⟨~ the book in your right hand⟩ ⟨always *took* his hand when they crossed the street⟩ ⟨*took* his sleeve to guide him⟩ ⟨*took* him by the shoulders and shook him soundly⟩ ⟨dentist *took* the tooth in his forceps⟩ ⟨*took* the child in her arms to comfort it⟩ ⟨~ the railing as you go down⟩ **b :** to catch hold upon (as by contact or adhesion) ⟨sound of a ship *taking* the ground⟩ ⟨oars rhythmically *taking* the water⟩ **3 a :** to catch, seize, or attack through the effect of a sudden force or influence: as (1) **:** to seize or attack so as to have an effect upon ⟨was *taken* with a fit of laughing⟩ ⟨was suddenly *taken* with a need for companionship⟩ ⟨liked to work as the humor *took* him⟩ ⟨toward morning he was *taken* with frenzy and leaped from bed —J.A.Michener⟩ ⟨seemed to be *taken* with a great restlessness —S.H.Holbrook⟩ (2) **:** to strike or affect so as to cause to be in a particular condition ⟨was *taken* ill⟩ ⟨found himself *taken* hoarse⟩ ⟨was *taken* down with pneumonia⟩ (3) **:** to attack through magical or supernatural forces **:** cast a spell on **:** use malign influence over ⟨blasts the tree and ~*s* the cattle —Shak.⟩ **b :** to catch or come upon (as a person) in a particular situation or action ⟨question *took* him unprepared⟩ ⟨was *taken* unawares⟩ ⟨tried to ~ him napping⟩ ⟨*took* him in the very act⟩ **c :** to strike or hit (as a person) usu. in or on a specified part ⟨a straight left-hander that *took* him on the broad chin —Arthur Morrison⟩ ⟨*took* the boy a smart box on the ear⟩ **d** (1) **:** to capture or gain the approval or liking of **:** CAPTIVATE, CHARM, DELIGHT ⟨performance that seemed to have *taken* the fancy of the crowd⟩ — usu. used with *with* ⟨was much *taken* with him at their first meeting⟩ ⟨so *taken* with the decorations that she decided to copy them⟩ or sometimes with *by* ⟨quite *taken* by their concern for his comfort⟩ (2) **:** to catch and hold (as the attention, interest, regard) often for only a short time ⟨*took* his attention momentarily⟩ ⟨kind of thing that ~*s* one's eye⟩ **4 a :** to get into one's hand or one's hold or possession by a physical act of simple transference ⟨I ~ my pen in hand⟩ ⟨*took* his hat and coat and left⟩ ⟨reached over and *took* a piece of bread⟩ ⟨*took* a cigar and lit it⟩ ⟨*took* the youngster on her lap⟩ ⟨*took* a stake and pounded it in the ground⟩ **b** (1) **:** to introduce or receive into one's body (as by eating, drinking, or inhaling) ⟨had *taken* no food for three days⟩ ⟨~ a glass of water⟩ ⟨~ snuff⟩ ⟨~*s* the smoke into his lungs⟩ ⟨~ one tablet after each meal⟩ ⟨*took* poison⟩ ⟨killed himself by *taking* gas⟩ ⟨communed with spirits while *taking* tobacco and a narcotic herb —J.H.Steward⟩ ⟨label reading "this medicine is not to be *taken* internally"⟩ ⟨*took* his bottle well and had gained back to birth weight —E.F.Patton⟩ (2) **:** to expose oneself to (as sun or air) for pleasure or for physical benefit ⟨*taking* the sun on the beach before the little teahouse —Hamilton Basso⟩ ⟨piers . . . where families in the neighborhood could ~ the river air in warm weather —Brooks Atkinson⟩ (3) **:** to partake of (as a meal) **:** EAT, DRINK ⟨the audience would ~ tea there —Virginia Woolf⟩ ⟨*took* supper with an English earl —F.B.Gipson⟩ ⟨residents are required to ~ their meals in the houses —*Official Register of Harvard Univ.*⟩ ⟨~*s* dinner about six⟩ **5 a** (1) **:** to bring or receive into a relation or connection ⟨*took* his son into the firm⟩ ⟨wouldn't ~ me into his confidence⟩ ⟨~*s* a few private pupils⟩ ⟨was reduced to *taking* lodgers⟩ ⟨time he *took* a wife⟩ ⟨the stupid bride he means to ~ —Carl Van Doren⟩ ⟨*took* a squaw to wife —Burges Johnson⟩ ⟨serve you right if she *took* a lover —Guy McCrone⟩ (2) **:** to receive into one's household for provision and care or to adopt ⟨*took* her dead brother's youngest child⟩ ⟨married children arranged to ~ their father a month at a time⟩ ⟨agreed to ~ a war orphan⟩ **b :** to copulate with **6 :** to transfer into one's own keeping **:** enter into or arrange for possession, ownership, or use of: **a :** APPROPRIATE ⟨*took* the umbrella to keep it from being lost or stolen⟩ ⟨if nobody wants this, I'll ~ it⟩ ⟨found that somebody had *taken* his hat⟩ ⟨accused me of *taking* his camera⟩ ⟨had been *taking* money out of the till for months⟩ **b** (1) **:** to obtain or secure for use (as by lease, subscription, or contract) ⟨~ a cottage for the summer⟩ ⟨~ a box at the opera⟩ ⟨family ~*s* several magazines⟩ ⟨~ two quarts of milk every other day⟩ (2) **:** to obtain by purchasing **:** BUY ⟨spent an hour looking around but didn't ~ anything⟩ ⟨finally decided to ~ a blue serge suit⟩ ⟨wanted to ~ the ranch house but his wife wouldn't agree⟩ ⟨salesman tried to persuade him to ~ the convertible⟩ **7 :** to adopt or lay hold of for oneself or as one's own **:** ASSUME: as **a** (1) **:** to invest oneself with (as a property or an attribute) ⟨butter often ~*s* the flavor of substances near it⟩ ⟨fog *took* ghostly shapes⟩ ⟨ancient Greek gods often *took* the likeness of a human being⟩ ⟨unconsciously he *took* color from his environment —V.L.Parrington⟩ ⟨~ different shapes on different occasions —Curtis Bok⟩; *also* **:** to assume a property or attribute of ⟨the plaster *took* the mold in perfect detail⟩ (2) **:** to assume as a badge or symbol (as of a function or an office) ⟨~ the veil of a nun⟩ ⟨asked him to ~ the gavel⟩ ⟨had *taken* the throne at twenty⟩ **b :** to charge oneself with (as a duty, obligation, or task) **:** UNDERTAKE ⟨~ office⟩ ⟨~ service under a foreign flag⟩ ⟨~ the responsibility for keeping order⟩ ⟨each teacher must ~ the study hall once every week⟩; *specif* **:** to assume responsibility for checking the effectiveness of (a player on an opposing team) on a given play ⟨our right end ~*s* defensive fullback —A.E. Neale⟩ **c** (1) **:** to subject oneself to **:** bind oneself by ⟨~ a vow⟩ ⟨~ a pledge⟩ ⟨~ my oath he hasn't grown an inch —*New Yorker*⟩ ⟨*took* oath as president on December 1st —Virginia Prewett⟩ (2) *obs* **:** to make oneself responsible for the truth of (as a statement) **:** AFFIRM, SWEAR — used with *it* ⟨*took*'t upon mine honor thou hadst it not —Shak.⟩ **d** (1) **:** to undertake and perform or exercise ⟨~ the role of the villain⟩ ⟨*took* an important part in the negotiations⟩ ⟨the teacher who *took* the third grade last year⟩ ⟨~ soprano⟩ ⟨had to ~ three sections of freshman English⟩ ⟨curate *took* the early morning service⟩ (2) **:** to give or impose upon oneself (as special or added responsibility) as part of or in the course of something undertaken or done — used chiefly in the phrase *take pains* or *take the trouble* ⟨man who is willing to ~ the trouble to do good work⟩ ⟨have *taken* pains with the documentation —Van Wyck Brooks⟩ ⟨*took* no pains to soften their footsteps —Jean Stafford⟩ ⟨few of our statesmen can have *taken* so little pains to keep themselves in the public eye —G.M. Young⟩ **e :** to adopt (as another's part or side) as one's own **:** align or ally oneself with ⟨knew that his mother would ~ his side⟩ — often used in the phrase *take sides* ⟨members *take* sides against each other in all public affairs —A.C.Whitehead⟩ **f :** to adopt or advance as one's fundamental point of argument or defense ⟨a point well *taken*⟩ ⟨*took* his stand on judicial incorruptibility⟩ **g :** to assume as if rightfully one's own or as if granted **:** arrogate to oneself ⟨~ the credit⟩ ⟨~ the liberty of disagreeing⟩ ⟨*took* my consent for granted⟩ ⟨~ leave to protest⟩ **h :** to have or assume as a proper part of or accompaniment to itself **:** be formed or used with ⟨~*s* an accent on the last syllable⟩ ⟨~*s* an *s* in the plural⟩ ⟨transitive verbs ~ an object⟩ ⟨~*s* the objective case⟩ ⟨plural noun ~*s* a plural verb⟩ **8 a :** to secure by winning in competition **:** WIN ⟨*took* six tricks in a row⟩ ⟨*took* the fight by a knockout⟩ ⟨*took* first place in the broad jump⟩ ⟨*took* the Latin prize for two years⟩ ⟨was lucky to ~ one game out of four⟩ ⟨*took* first-class honors in history —*Current Biog.*⟩ ⟨*took* ribbons for his vegetables —*Lamp*⟩ **b :** to win over (as an opponent) **:** BEAT, DEFEAT ⟨*took* him in straight sets⟩ ⟨bragged that he could ~ the new marshal —J.W.Schaefer⟩ **9 :** to pick out **:** CHOOSE, SELECT ⟨was told to ~ the road bearing left at the fork⟩ ⟨was sure he *took* the middle course if there was one⟩ ⟨let him ~ his pick⟩ ⟨~ any number from one to ten⟩ **10 :** to adopt, choose, or avail oneself of for use **:** have recourse to and use ⟨~ the first opportunity⟩ ⟨*took* every means he could think of⟩ ⟨was forced to ~ severe measures⟩: as **a :** to have recourse to as an instrument for doing something ⟨had *taken* his belt to the disobedient boy⟩ ⟨nothing to do with the weeds but ~ a scythe to them⟩ **b :** to use as a means of transportation or progression ⟨could ~ the subway to work⟩ ⟨*took* a freighter to Europe⟩ ⟨usually *took* the car⟩ ⟨he ~*s* airplanes, but his wife won't fly —Philip Hamburger⟩ ⟨insisted on *taking* a taxi all the way —Christopher Isherwood⟩; *also* **:** to go aboard or mount (as something providing such transportation) **:** BOARD ⟨always *took* the train at the main station⟩ ⟨had *taken* horse and ridden into the fields —J.H.Wheelwright⟩ ⟨just before I *took* ship at New York for Sweden —Sinclair Lewis⟩ ⟨~*s* the train every morning at 6:45⟩ **c :** to have recourse to (as a place) esp. for safety or refuge ⟨~ shelter⟩ ⟨~ sanctuary⟩ ⟨~ harbor⟩ ⟨had one look at the bear and then *took* the nearest tree⟩ ⟨could often ~ refuge from his humiliation in a sort of dignity —Elizabeth Bowen⟩ ⟨~ cover behind prejudices and theories —Roger Fry⟩ **d :** to enter upon or into in order to go along or through ⟨wished he could ~ a paved road⟩ ⟨every single plane . . . fit to ~ the air —Ira Wolfert⟩ ⟨readying the boat to ~ the water⟩ **e** (1) **:** to proceed to occupy (as a place or position) ⟨~ a seat in the rear⟩ ⟨*took* the nearest chair⟩ ⟨*took* his place in the procession⟩ ⟨was unwilling to ~ the center of the stage⟩ ⟨always ready to ~ the spotlight⟩ ⟨*took* the chair in the absence of the regular chairman⟩ (2) **:** to use up (as space by filling or time by consuming) ⟨~ enough time to be sure⟩ ⟨doesn't ~ much room⟩ ⟨*took* a long time to dry out⟩ (3) **:** NEED, REQUIRE ⟨~*s* a size nine shoe⟩ ⟨job *took* more attention than he could give⟩ ⟨*took* two men to keep the tub filled —H.A.Chippendale⟩ ⟨a good long letter (*took* two postage stamps) —Walt Whitman⟩ ⟨*took* the baroque age to invent, and to respect, the . . . periwig —Gilbert Highet⟩ ⟨getting to the right place at the right time . . . ~*s* a bit of doing —Nevil Shute⟩ **11 a :** to obtain by deriving from a source **:** DRAW ⟨~*s* its title from the name of the hero⟩ ⟨family probably *took* its name from the place where it lived⟩ ⟨*took* his design from natural rock formations⟩ ⟨~*s* his good looks from his mother⟩ ⟨*took* his text from the Old Testament⟩ ⟨*took* his subject from his own experience⟩: as (1) **:** to extract and use over again (as for quoting or adapting) **:** BORROW ⟨*took* his plot from an old folk tale⟩ ⟨retorted with a line *taken* verbatim from Shakespeare⟩ ⟨our habit of *taking* words from other languages —Thomas Pyles⟩ (2) **:** to obtain from a natural source ⟨coal used is imported . . . while the limestone is *taken* from the company's own quarries —N.R. Heiden⟩ **b** (1) **:** to obtain as the result of a special procedure (as of observation, examination, or inquiry) **:** ASCERTAIN ⟨~ the temperature⟩ ⟨~ the dimensions of a room⟩ ⟨tailor *took* his measurements⟩ ⟨~ a census⟩ ⟨*took* the opinion of the group⟩; *also* **:** to carry out (a procedure yielding such a result) **:** CONDUCT ⟨~ an observation of the sun⟩ ⟨~ a test of its efficiency⟩ ⟨~ a poll⟩ ⟨~ a vote⟩ (2) **:** to get in writing **:** write down ⟨~ notes⟩ ⟨~ the attendance⟩ ⟨~ minutes of a meeting⟩ ⟨~ an inventory⟩ ⟨~ a copy of a will⟩ — often used with *down* ⟨~ down a speech in shorthand⟩ ⟨*took* down the principal points⟩ ⟨sent for a stenographer to ~ down his confession⟩ (3) **:** to get by drawing or painting or esp. by photography **:** make or execute a picture of **:** represent or portray in any artistic form; *esp* **:** to take a photograph of **:** PHOTOGRAPH ⟨likes to ~ pictures⟩ ⟨~ a snapshot⟩ ⟨*took* the children in their party clothes⟩ (4) **:** to get by transference from one surface to another (as by means of ink) ⟨~ a proof⟩ ⟨~ a person's fingerprints⟩ ⟨~ rubbings of ancient brasses⟩ ⟨worked out a way of *taking* the carved impression from the stone —Roger Burlingame⟩ **12 :** to receive or accept whether willingly or reluctantly (as something given, offered, proposed, or administered) ⟨wouldn't ~ my hand when I offered it⟩ ⟨taught her not to ~ candy from strangers⟩ ⟨*took* the present but didn't seem pleased with it⟩ ⟨wouldn't ~ no for an answer⟩ ⟨~ a bribe⟩ ⟨~ a bet⟩ ⟨was told to ~ it or leave it⟩ ⟨shipped it through the Canal and I *took* delivery on it here this afternoon —Robert Carson⟩: as **a :** to receive when bestowed or tendered (as an office, an honor, a degree, a prize) ⟨was on hand to ~ an honorary doctorate⟩ ⟨has been trained to ~ salutes on state occasions —*Star Weekly*⟩ **b** (1) **:** to submit to **:** ENDURE, UNDERGO ⟨*took* his punishment like a man⟩ ⟨~ a blow without flinching⟩ ⟨is *taking* treatments⟩ ⟨physician told him he ought to stay for six months and ~ the cure —*College English*⟩ ⟨the mauling his corps *took* in the peach orchard —R.M.Lovett⟩ ⟨seeing men die and *taking* three wounds in his own body —Dixon Wecter⟩ **:** put up with ⟨don't have to ~ anything from him, or to stand his bad manners —Willa Cather⟩ ⟨after *taking* twenty years of living in these cramped quarters —Henry Hewes⟩ — often used with *it* ⟨for people who can ~ it like pioneers, here is a new frontier —W.P.Webb⟩ ⟨she deserved the accolade of the modern generation — she could ~ it —*New Republic*⟩ (2) **:** to undergo without yielding **:** resist successfully **:** WITHSTAND ⟨~*s* hard usage⟩ ⟨specifications may require the glass . . . to ~ an impact blow of 6 to 9 ft. lbs. —E.B.Shand⟩ ⟨~*s* extremes of weather beautifully⟩ **c** (1) **:** to accept as true **:** BELIEVE ⟨had to ~ his word for it⟩ ⟨you can ~ it from me that he is not here⟩ (2) **:** to accept for guidance **:** FOLLOW ⟨~ a warning⟩ ⟨~ a hint⟩ ⟨~ a suggestion⟩ ⟨please ~ my advice⟩ (3) **:** to accept with the mind in a specified way ⟨~ a situation calmly⟩ ⟨*took* the joke in earnest⟩ ⟨*took* it ill of them⟩ ⟨would ~ it kindly if we could answer at once⟩ (4) **:** to accept without objection or opposition ⟨~ things as they come⟩ ⟨ready to ~ the consequences of his act⟩ ⟨~ the bad along with the good⟩ **d :** to indulge in and enjoy ⟨was *taking* his ease on the porch⟩ ⟨hoped to be able to ~ a brief vacation⟩ ⟨*took* a five-minute break for coffee⟩ ⟨time to ~ a rest⟩ **e :** to receive or accept as a return (as in payment, compensation, or reparation) ⟨agreed to ~ a thousand dollars in complete settlement of the claim⟩ ⟨wouldn't ~ less than a hundred a week⟩ ⟨wants more but would probably ~ less⟩ **f** (1) *obs* **:** to exact (as a promise or an oath) of another (2) **:** to accept the tender of (as a promise or an oath) (3) **:** to accept (as an oath, an affidavit, or a deposition) in a legal capacity (as by administering or witnessing) **g :** to admit (a male animal) in copulation **:** be covered by **h :** to respond to (bait or a lure) by seizing ⟨bonefish will ~ a fly during a strong wind —R.R.Camp⟩ ⟨*taking* feathered lures and spinning stuff —*Sports Illustrated*⟩ **i :** to accept a bet offered by ⟨ready to ~ all comers⟩ **j :** to deliberately make no attempt to hit (a pitched ball) ⟨manager signaled him to ~ the next pitch⟩ **13 a** (1) **:** to permit to enter **:** let in **:** ADMIT ⟨liable to ~ a great deal of water over the bow in bad weather —D.W. Pye⟩ ⟨seams had opened and the boat was ~*ing* water fast⟩ (2) **:** to have room for **:** ACCOMMODATE ⟨shelf just ~*s* the books⟩ ⟨harbor is so badly silted it can ~ only small craft —Christopher Rand⟩ ⟨suitcase wouldn't ~ another thing⟩ ⟨runway . . . long enough to ~ any of the biggest airliners of tomorrow —A.J.Cathrein⟩ ⟨largest canals ~ barges of more than a thousand tons —Alice Mutton⟩ **b :** to be affected injuriously by (as a disease) **:** CATCH, CONTRACT ⟨~ cold⟩ ⟨*took* the measles⟩ ⟨one of the sorrels *took* colic and died —J.F.Dobie⟩ ⟨their liability to ~ the blight —H.E.Laffer⟩ **:** be seized by ⟨~ a fit⟩ ⟨~ fright⟩ **c :** to absorb or become impregnated with (as dye) **:** be affected by (as polish) ⟨cloth that ~*s* dye well⟩ ⟨surface will not ~ paint⟩ ⟨granite ~*s* a high polish⟩ ⟨won't ~ a shine, no matter how long you wear it —Clarence Woodbury⟩ **d :** to receive into itself: (1) *obs* **:** CONTAIN, INCLUDE (2) *Scot* **:** to close in upon and submerge ⟨giantess who was so big the Sound of Mull *took* her only knee-deep —Alastair Borthwick⟩ **14 a** (1) **:** to receive into the mind **:** APPREHEND, COMPREHEND, UNDERSTAND ⟨his hearers were slow to ~ his meaning⟩ ⟨object of the writer will be . . . to make the reader ~ his meaning readily and precisely —Ernest Gowers⟩ ⟨event was so unusual and unexpected that we did not know how to ~ it —R.M.Lovett⟩ ⟨~ a remark as it was intended⟩ (2) **:** to apprehend the meaning of (a person) ⟨if I ~ you correctly⟩ ⟨in the other scenes we have no difficulty in *taking* him as we are meant to ~ him —F.R.Leavis⟩ **b :** to regard or look upon **:** CONSIDER, SUPPOSE ⟨we ~ this to be your final offer⟩ ⟨~ it as settled⟩ ⟨I ~ it that you approve⟩ ⟨hoped he would not be *taken* as absolutely committed⟩ ⟨does not wish people to ~ his fictions as novels —Carlos Lynes⟩ ⟨the type *taken* as normal in English political writing —D.W. Brogan⟩ ⟨canon law may be *taken* to include theology —H.O. Taylor⟩ ⟨do not ~ me as urging that it ought to be done —F.S. Mitchell⟩ **c :** to accept, consider, or reckon as being or as equal to ⟨*taking* a stride at the usual 30 inches⟩ ⟨reports by . . . untrained observers are all *taken* at a hundred percent of their face value —M.R.Cohen⟩ **d :** to feel or begin to feel or experience (as a state of mind) ⟨~ pleasure⟩ ⟨*took* delight in perversity —G.W.Brace⟩ ⟨*took* an immediate dislike to the newcomer⟩ ⟨saw no reason to ~ offense⟩ ⟨~ a little reasonable umbrage —C.E.Montague⟩ ⟨~*s* satisfaction in inertly orthodox generalities —F.R.Leavis⟩ ⟨*took* pride in his work⟩ ⟨nurse their griefs . . . seem, in fact, almost to ~ a delight in brooding over them —H.A.Overstreet⟩ **e** (1) **:** to form and adopt in the mind or with the will ⟨~ a resolution⟩ ⟨~ a grave view of a situation⟩ ⟨was here that the real decisions on policy were *taken* —J.H.Plumb⟩ ⟨whenever he *took* a notion he wanted something, he bought it —Margaret Cousins⟩ ⟨*taking* harsh judgments of his contemporaries —S.L.A.Marshall⟩ (2) **:** to form with the mind or will and exercise or display in action ⟨~*s* pity on all suffering creatures⟩ ⟨had *taken* no further heed of her existence —W.J.Locke⟩ **15 a :** to convey, lead, carry, remove, or cause to go along to another place, the direction of movement being away from the place from which the action is regarded: as (1) **:** to cause (as a person) to go along with one to a place ⟨~ the baby to the park⟩ ⟨*took* his girl to the prom⟩ ⟨promised to ~ the whole family to dinner⟩ ⟨this bus will ~ you into town⟩; *also* **:** LEAD ⟨this line ~*s* us directly to the city⟩ ⟨fine road ~*s* you through the forest —Tom Marvel⟩ ⟨to climb it would ~ us in the wrong direction —D.L.Busk⟩ (2) **:** to bear with one to a place or person ⟨~ your father's slippers to him⟩ ⟨~ the dishes to the kitchen⟩ ⟨*took* a plentiful lunch with them but brought most of it back⟩ (3) **:** to require or induce to go ⟨business *took* him west⟩ ⟨an appointment that *took* him into town⟩ ⟨neighbor whose employment ~*s* him on periodic trips across the country —Sidney Alexander⟩ **b :** to lead, convey, or remove in thought or mind ⟨seeking interests that would ~ him out of himself⟩ ⟨journey *took* his mind away from his troubles⟩ **c :** to convey to a higher or lower degree ⟨last-minute touchdown *took* the score to 57⟩ ⟨heavy selling in the afternoon *took* the list lower⟩ **d** *archaic* **:** to give (oneself) up or over **:** BETAKE, COMMIT, DEVOTE **16 a :** to remove or obtain by removing **:** ABSTRACT ⟨~ eggs from a nest⟩ ⟨~ the cream off the milk⟩ ⟨you can ~ a cork out of one of those bottles⟩ **b** (1) **:** to put an end to (as life or one's life) ⟨the right of the state to ~ human life⟩ ⟨*took* his own life in a fit of despondency⟩ (2) **:** to remove by death **:** deprive of life **:** cause to die ⟨was *taken* in his prime⟩ ⟨those who have been *taken* hence⟩ ⟨a mother whose only child had recently been *taken*⟩ ⟨a cruel fate *took* him from us⟩ **c** (1) **:** DEDUCT, SUBTRACT ⟨~ two from four⟩ ⟨*took* ten percent off the bill for cash⟩ ⟨celebrates his fiftieth birthday, give or ~ a few months, with this selection —Carlos Baker⟩ (2) **:** to carry away **:** WITHDRAW ⟨never *took* his eyes from hers⟩ ⟨gave him kicks that *took* the laugh off his face —Claud Cockburn⟩ **17 :** to undertake and make (as a movement) or do or perform (as an act or an action) ⟨~ a walk⟩ ⟨~ a look⟩ ⟨~ aim⟩ ⟨~ a trip⟩ ⟨~ a turn around the block⟩ ⟨~ two steps forward⟩ ⟨stopped two or three times to ~ a sounding —Nevil Shute⟩ ⟨able to ~ such action by air, naval, or land forces as may be necessary —Vera M. Dean⟩: as **a :** to direct and make a specified motion (as a blow) ⟨*took* a swing at a policeman⟩ ⟨tested the pillow by *taking* a poke at it⟩ **b :** to set in motion (as a lawsuit) **:** INSTITUTE ⟨~ proceedings⟩ ⟨~ legal action⟩ **c :** to put or set forth **:** RAISE ⟨~ an objection⟩ ⟨be fired . . . if an important reader or advertiser *took* exception to something he said —*Phoenix Flame*⟩ ⟨might ~ exception to his representative having a meal with casteless persons —Dillon Ripley⟩ **d :** BID, SAY ⟨~ adieu⟩ ⟨~ a last farewell⟩ **18** *archaic* **:** to assume or resume (as a discourse) at a point of leaving off **19 a :** to apply oneself to and treat or deal with ⟨~ first things first⟩ ⟨doctor was sure he had *taken* the disease in time⟩ ⟨~ the problems one by one⟩ ⟨next let us ~ the Peloponnesian War⟩ ⟨if he be summoned to court, his case is *taken* in a language he does not understand —Stuart Cloete⟩ **b** (1) **:** to deal with, consider, or view in a particular relation ⟨*taken* together, the details were quite significant⟩ ⟨*taking* one thing with another, decided they had not done badly⟩ (2) **:** to consider as an instance ⟨to illustrate, ~ ancient Greece⟩ **c :** to apply oneself to the study of or the acquisition of skill in ⟨~ fancy dancing⟩ ⟨~ music lessons⟩; *specif* **:** to study (as a subject or course) at an educational institution ⟨*took* English 21 last year⟩ ⟨is *taking* both French and German⟩ **20 :** to apply oneself to getting through or past or to surmounting (as a hedge or a hurdle) **:** succeed in clearing (as a difficulty or an obstacle) ⟨~ two stairs at a time⟩ ⟨*took* the corner on two wheels⟩ ⟨was *taking* fences at the age of six⟩ ⟨*took* the puddle in an easy leap⟩ ⟨*took* an exit at three times the posted limit —Hugh Sherwood⟩ ⟨sort of hill which any car can ~ with ease —F.G. Kay⟩ **21 :** to impose upon **:** CHEAT, SWINDLE ⟨how can the amateur collector be sure he isn't being *taken* —*New Orleans (La.) Times-Picayune*⟩ ⟨*taken* for over a hundred thousand dollars on shakedowns alone —F.B.Gipson⟩ ⟨girl who would ~ me for a lot of money —Merle Miller⟩ ~ *vi* **1 :** to obtain possession: as **a :** CAPTURE ⟨the queen in chess ~*s* at any distance in a straight line⟩ ⟨the symbol *x*, read "~*s*", indicates a capture —*New Complete Hoyle*⟩ **b :** to receive property under law as one's own **:** receive the title to property ⟨he ~*s* as heir⟩ ⟨was entitled, as a society with a lawful object, to ~ under a charitable bequest —Eduard Jenks⟩ **c** *of a fish* **:** to seize a lure or bait **:** rise to bait **:** BITE ⟨salmon *took* that morning, though halfheartedly —B.A.Williams⟩ ⟨will ~ in clear water⟩ ⟨tench, who stop *taking* soon after breakfast —T.H. White b. 1906⟩ **2 :** to lay hold **:** CATCH, ENGAGE, HOLD ⟨high-velocity harpoon is fired. If this strikes and ~*s*, an explosive charge goes off inside the animal's rib cage —I.T.Sanderson⟩ **3 a :** to establish a take esp. by uniting or growing — used of living things (as plant or surgical grafts) ⟨with any experienced surgeon some 90 percent of the grafts ~ —*Lancet*⟩ **b :** STRIKE 17a **4 a** (1) **:** to betake oneself **:** strike out **:** set out **:** GO, PROCEED ⟨~ after a purse snatcher⟩ ⟨~ down the street and around the corner⟩ ⟨~ across a field⟩ ⟨~ over the hill⟩ (2) *chiefly dial* **:** to take its course or run or lead (as of a road or river) ⟨road turns here and ~*s* over the hill⟩ **b** *chiefly dial* — used as an intensifier or often simply redundantly with a following verb ⟨*took* and swung at the ball but missed⟩ ⟨*took* and grabbed his hat and ran⟩ ⟨*took* and cried everytime anybody looked at her⟩; compare GO **5 a :** to have the natural or intended effect or action **:** take effect **:** ACT, OPERATE ⟨an expensive lesson in caution; it could only be hoped that it would ~⟩: as (1) **:** to catch hold **:** get hold ⟨wick was dry and the sparks didn't ~⟩ (2) *of a plan* **:** to work out or turn out successfully **:** SUCCEED ⟨fanciful schemes without a chance of *taking*⟩ ⟨where retirements are often announced but seldom ~ —*Springfield (Mass.) Union*⟩ (3) *of a vaccine or vaccination* **:** to produce a take **b :** to show the natural or intended effect (as of fire or cold) **:** become affected (as by adherence or absorption) in the expected or desired way ⟨dry fuel ~*s* readily⟩ ⟨she had never *taken* after his first vaccination⟩ **6 :** CHARM, CAPTIVATE: **a :** to exert a spell ⟨no planets strike, no fairy ~*s*, nor witch hath power to charm —Shak.⟩ **b :** to prove taking or attractive **:** gain a favorable reception **:** win popular favor ⟨the play *took* greatly and was still drawing big audiences —W.A.Darlington⟩ ⟨book had not yet *taken* with the general reader⟩ **7 :** DETRACT — used with *from* ⟨a few minor irritations that *took* only slightly from their general satisfaction⟩ **8 :** to be or admit of being affected: as **a :** to be seized or attacked in a specified way **:** BECOME, FALL ⟨died suddenly in 1820, *taking* ill on his way home —Isobel Hutchison⟩ ⟨*took* sick⟩ ⟨*took* pretty surly —*Punch*⟩ **b :** to be capable of being moved in a specified way **:** COME ⟨top ~*s* off⟩ ⟨toy clock with varicolored plastic works that ~ apart for reassembly by the child⟩ ⟨table ~*s* apart for packing⟩ ⟨gadget ~*s* to pieces for cleaning⟩ **c :** to adhere or become absorbed ⟨ink that ~s well on cloth⟩ **d :** to admit of being photographed ⟨colors that ~ well⟩ ⟨~s best highlighted against a dark background⟩

syn SEIZE, GRASP, CLUTCH, SNATCH, GRAB: TAKE is a general term without very specific connotation and applicable to the notion of coming to hold or possess, momentarily or longer, by physical action of the hand or in any other way ⟨*take* the book from the shelf⟩ ⟨a city *taken* by the enemy⟩ ⟨*take* a cottage for the summer⟩ SEIZE suggests sudden and forcible taking, often the taking or apprehending of something elusive or difficult by quick, opportune action ⟨they *seize* all the cattle and other property left behind by the fugitives in their haste —J.G.Frazer⟩ ⟨the Breton *seized* more than he could hold; the Norman took less than he would have liked —Henry Adams⟩ ⟨the character . . . is difficult to *seize*, for it comprised qualities hardly ever combined in one man —Hilaire Belloc⟩ GRASP implies a firm quick laying hold and tightening fingers around, a taking or seizing likened to such an action, or a similar effective comprehension ⟨she *grasped* him by the arm, driving her fingers deep into the flesh —R.P.Warren⟩ ⟨determined to *grasp* all they could for Pennsylvania, Colonial officials tricked the Indians —*Amer. Guide Series: Pa.*⟩ ⟨understood the words I heard, but couldn't seem to *grasp* their meaning —Kenneth Roberts⟩ CLUTCH may suggest increased suddenness, force, or firmness in taking hold, apprehending, or attempting to take hold ⟨with an agonized cry, she *clutches* his shoulders and drags herself to her feet —G.B. Shaw⟩ ⟨straws were straws, and the frailer they were the harder she *clutched* them —George Meredith⟩ ⟨flung himself forward with the others, desperately *clutching* at the precious escaping fish —A.J.Cronin⟩ SNATCH stresses suddenness of motion without indicating a forceful retention and may suggest stealthy or ready promptness in action ⟨many too are killed by their stronger companions in their desperate attempts to *snatch* their share of food —James Stevenson-Hamilton⟩ ⟨tried to keep hold of the plate which the school teacher tried to *snatch* away and for a few minutes they struggled laughing —Sherwood Anderson⟩ GRAB typically suggests rude rough forceful action, often in indifference to or violation of the rights of others ⟨could apparently *grab* Silesia by force of arms —Stringfellow Barr⟩ ⟨the more adventurous hastened to California with a pocketful of paper to *grab* rich mineral and timber lands —*Amer. Guide Series: Minn.*⟩ **syn** see in addition ATTRACT, RECEIVE

— **take a bow 1 :** to bow in acknowledging applause (as in a theater) **2 :** to accept credit or recognition (as for an accomplishment) ⟨high time we *took a bow* for what we have been able to do well —Nard Jones⟩ ⟨*take the bows* with the burdens —J.S.Dickey⟩ — **take account of :** to take into account — **take a chance** *or* **take one's chances :** to leave an outcome entirely to chance **:** trust one's fortunes in a particular venture to mere chance ⟨*take a chance* on the weather remaining fair⟩ ⟨Pilgrims . . . preferred to *take their chances* with the Indians —Leslie Thomas⟩ — **take a dare 1 :** to be dared to do something and attempt it **2 :** to be dared to do something and not to attempt it — **take a dive** *of a boxer* **:** to pretend to be knocked out esp. in a fixed fight — **take advantage of 1 :** to make use of for one's own benefit **:** use to advantage **:** profit by ⟨extends his examination . . . to *take advantage of* modern methods of diagnosis —Morris Fishbein⟩ ⟨feels we are not *taking* proper *advantage of* our opportunity —R.A.Smith⟩ **2 :** impose upon **:** ABUSE, EXPLOIT ⟨was always good to people . . . and there was those that *took advantage of* him —Nigel Balchin⟩ ⟨not above *taking advantage of* another's weakness⟩ — **take after 1 :** to take as an example **:** FOLLOW ⟨she is going to *take after* her grandmother —Elizabeth Taylor⟩ **2 :** to resemble in features, build, character, or disposition ⟨*takes after* his mother's side of the family⟩ ⟨*takes after* his father in everything except his eyes⟩ ⟨sons all *took after* him, if only at a distance —G.G.Coulton⟩ — **take against** *chiefly Brit* **:** take sides against **:** OPPOSE **:** feel dislike for or disapproval of ⟨nodded to the unknown guest; *took against* him —Virginia Woolf⟩ ⟨whether I was right or wrong, I *took* faintly *against* him —William Plomer⟩ — **take a joke :** to endure a joke at one's own expense — **take alarm 1 :** to heed a warning of danger **2 :** to become alarmed — **take amiss :** to impute a wrong motive or a bad meaning or intention to **:** take offense at ⟨afraid a refusal will be *taken amiss* —Dorothy Barclay⟩ ⟨don't *take* it *amiss* if his counsels are not pleasant —Richard Ginder⟩ — **take apart 1 :** to separate part from part or into parts **:** DISASSEMBLE, DISMANTLE, DISMEMBER **:** treat as if to dismember by force **:** rough up ⟨*take* a town *apart*⟩ **2 :** to analyze or dissect esp. in order to discover or reveal a weakness, flaw, or fallacy ⟨dislikes the dictum . . . and in this small book he *takes* it *apart* skillfully and ruthlessly —G.W.Johnson⟩ ⟨specialists in sports who *take* the various games and sponsors *apart*, but seldom bother to reassemble them —*Phoenix Flame*⟩ ⟨*takes* the ordinary American citizen *apart* in a most callous fashion —G.W. Johnson⟩ **3 a :** to subject to treatment intended to disorganize ⟨chances are that some opposing congressman will . . . *take* the witness *apart* —J.R.Fitzpatrick⟩ **b :** to treat roughly or harshly in any way **:** tear into ⟨isn't like an ordinary election campaign where you can *take* your opponent *apart* —*Time*⟩ ⟨*took* wives *apart* for the way they play poker —T.S. Geisel⟩ — **take a powder** *or* **take a runout powder** *slang* **:** to leave hurriedly **:** skip out **:** DECAMP, FLEE ⟨not likely to cross you up or *take a powder* on you —W.L.Gresham⟩ ⟨*taking a powder* and leaving everything up in the air —George Sklar⟩ ⟨*took a powder* for Paris accompanied by a beautiful blond mistress —Mike Stern⟩ ⟨*took a runout powder* this morning —Clayton Rawson⟩ — **take a reef 1 :** to reduce sail by reefing **2 :** to proceed more cautiously (as by curtailing expenses or activities) — **take arms :** to commence war or hostilities — **take breath :** to stop (as from working) in order to rest — **take care :** to be careful **:** exercise caution or prudence ⟨difference between *taking* due *care* and striking blindly in a wave of hysteria —Vannevar Bush⟩ **:** be watchful ⟨shall *take care* that the laws be faithfully executed —*U. S. Constitution*⟩ or provident or solicitous ⟨have *taken care* to assemble a good cast —Edward Sackville-West & Desmond Shawe-Taylor⟩ ⟨life *takes care* that we all learn the lesson thoroughly —Roger Fry⟩ — **take care of 1 a :** to attend to the needs, operation, or treatment of ⟨*takes care of* a ten-room house without help⟩ ⟨is home *taking care of* a sick child⟩ ⟨each operator can *take care of* three machines⟩ ⟨family doctor who had been *taking care of* them for 20 years⟩ **b :** to provide for ⟨five dollars should *take care of* unavoidable tips⟩ ⟨has his aged parents to *take care of*⟩ ⟨little steamers *take care of* transportation —Samuel Van Valkenburg & Ellsworth Huntington⟩ **2 a :** to deal with ⟨a change in the draft law to *take care of* draftees who refuse to answer loyalty questions —*Newsweek*⟩ ⟨a clerk *takes care of* routine inquiries⟩ **b :** to dispose of ⟨*take care of* the rubbish⟩ ⟨ordinary ventilation will automatically *take care of* the excess carbon dioxide —H.G. Armstrong⟩ ⟨the "longest lake entirely within New England" (that *takes care of* Lake Champlain) —R.S.Monahan⟩ **c** (1) **:** FIX ⟨could be counted on to *take care of* a traffic ticket⟩ ⟨the cops were well *taken care of;* the joint was running wide open —W.L.Gresham⟩ (2) **:** KILL ⟨they take another inmate . . . and they tell him to *take care of* me and they'll take good care of him for it —*Workers Defense Bull.*⟩ — **take charge 1 :** to assume care, custody, command, or control ⟨*take charge* of an office⟩ ⟨*take charge* of a neighbor's children⟩ ⟨*took charge* of operations in the western sector⟩ ⟨was sent to the new division to *take charge*⟩ **2 a :** to get out of control ⟨anchor chain *took charge* and ran out⟩ ⟨should a ladder which is being raised or lowered *take charge* —*Fire Service Drill Bk.*⟩ **b** *of a ship* **:** to come up into the wind in spite of the helmsman — **take counsel :** CONSULT, DELIBERATE ⟨when a student decides to become a musician, let him first *take counsel* with himself —S.A.Koussevitzky⟩ ⟨*taking counsel* of his own thought, not overtolerant of those who differed with him —V.L. Parrington⟩ ⟨you have *taken counsel* of your ambition —Abraham Lincoln⟩ — **take croquet :** to croquet a ball — **take effect 1 :** to become operative ⟨any alteration of the charter . . . shall *take effect* when ratified —Vera M. Dean⟩ — compare EFFECT 10 **2 :** to produce a result esp. as expected or intended **:** be effective ⟨fired four shots, all *taking effect* —D.D.Martin⟩ — **take example :** to use as an example or warning — **take fire :** to catch fire ⟨sulfur and quicklime, which *took fire* when exposed to moisture —Tom Wintringham⟩ ⟨small number of students *take fire* from these courses —*New Republic*⟩ ⟨immense crowds of people *took fire* and came alive under their leadership —John Reed⟩ — **take five** *or* **take ten :** to take a five or ten minute intermission (as in a rehearsal of actors or musicians or on a march or work detail) **:** take a short break — **take for :** to suppose to be; *esp* **:** to suppose mistakenly to be **:** mistake for ⟨was often *taken for* a German because of his fair hair⟩ ⟨a car which could be *taken for* a custom sports model —*Lamp*⟩ ⟨strangers often *took* her *for* her own daughter⟩ ⟨naturally disliked being *taken for* a fool⟩ — **take from the table :** to call up (as a parliamentary report or motion) for consideration from the table of the presiding officer — **take guard :** to place the bat at guard in cricket — **take heart :** to gain courage or confidence **:** become encouraged — **take hold 1 a :** GRASP, GRIP, SEIZE ⟨*take hold* of a railing⟩ ⟨*took hold* and hung on tight⟩ **b :** to establish a hold on or over ⟨felt hate *take hold* of my whole body —Edita Morris⟩ ⟨a second conviction *took hold* of him —T.B.Costain⟩ ⟨story . . . *takes hold* of a reader from the first —Walter Havighurst⟩ **c :** to assume management or control **:** take in hand and deal with **:** take charge ⟨there was a new overseer . . . and he was *taking hold*, fast —Laura Krey⟩ ⟨women who *take hold* of things and aren't afraid of work —Ellen Glasgow⟩ ⟨administration fails to *take hold* of and solve the big problems —F.D.Roosevelt⟩ **2** [ME *taken hold*, fr. *taken* to take + *hold*] **:** to become attached or established ⟨once the glue dries and *takes* firm *hold* —Emily Holt⟩ **:** take effect **:** catch on ⟨theory *took hold* because the future was with it —W.P.Webb⟩ ⟨idea . . . does not seem to have *taken hold* very widely —Elmer Davis⟩ — **take into account** *or* **take into consideration :** to make allowance for (as in passing judgment) ⟨judge *took* the boy's age *into account*⟩ — **take into camp :** take in **:** DECEIVE, DUPE, TRICK ⟨straightforward, modest manner *took into camp* everybody he met —Bennett Cerf⟩ — **take into one's head :** to conceive as a sudden notion **:** be seized with an idea or form a sudden resolve ⟨*took* it *into his head* to open a small shop of his own⟩ — **take in vain** [ME *taken in vain*] **:** to use (a name) profanely or without proper respect — **take issue :** to adopt an opposed or contrary view or position **:** take up the opposite side **:** join issue **:** DISPUTE ⟨*took issue* with reports which charged the army with laxness —*Current Biog.*⟩ — **take it in snuff :** to become angry or offended — **take it on the chin :** to undergo complete defeat, failure, or frustration **:** endure punishment, abuse, or suffering — **take it or leave it :** accept or reject unconditionally — **take it out of :** to exact satisfaction or a penalty from ⟨threatened to *take it out of* the boy's hide⟩ **:** take the energy out of ⟨hot summer *took it out of* him as never before⟩ — **take kindly to :** to feel a natural attraction toward or an inclination or willingness to accept or adopt — **take lying down :** to endure (as an injury, an affront) passively or submissively — **take notice :** to look about one with attention ⟨as we approach, the black ducks begin to *take notice* —Wyman Richardson⟩ — **take notice of 1 :** to perceive especially **:** observe or treat with special attention ⟨isn't likely she'd ever *take* any *notice of* me —J.D. Beresford⟩ **2 :** to comment or remark upon ⟨papers *took notice of* his promotion⟩ — **take oath :** to swear with solemnity or in a judicial manner — **take one at one's word :** to understand and accept one's statement as literally true ⟨when he said he wanted to be left alone, we *took him at his word* and went away⟩ — **take one's death :** to expose oneself to death (as by catching cold or a disease) — **take one's life in one's hands :** to risk one's life deliberately — **take one's medicine :** to submit to punishment **:** accept unpleasant consequences of one's acts — **take one's time** *or* **take one's own time :** to be leisurely about doing something — **take order** *archaic* **:** to take suitable measures **:** make arrangements ⟨whiles I *take order* for mine own affairs —Shak.⟩ — **take orders 1 :** to receive directions or commands **2 :** to enter the Christian ministry by ordination (as to the priesthood) — **take or leave 1 :** to accept or reject solely according to one's judgment or inclination often of the moment ⟨a singer I can *take or leave* —Charles Miller⟩ ⟨imply that peace is something we Americans can *take or leave* —R.J.Bunche⟩ **2 :** to give or take ⟨left an estate of $100,000,000, *take or leave* a few dollars —Lucius Beebe⟩ — **take part** [ME *taken part*] **:** JOIN, PARTICIPATE, SHARE ⟨able to play games and *take part* in conversation —R.A.Hall b. 1911⟩ ⟨opportunity to *take part* in a practical solution of the social problem —R.M.Lovett⟩ — **take place :** HAPPEN, OCCUR ⟨died before the marriage could *take place* —O. Elfrida Saunders⟩ ⟨music *takes place* in time and painting in space —C.W.H. Johnson⟩ ⟨heard a conversation *taking place* in the next room⟩ — **take possession :** to get into one's possession by an act of one's own **:** enter into possession ⟨*take possession* of a new house⟩ ⟨doing the Lord's work by *taking possession* of the Promised Land —A.J.Toynbee⟩ ⟨had bought a car but hadn't yet *taken possession*⟩ **:** affect, sway, or dominate to the exclusion of all else ⟨idiotic slogan . . . *took possession* of his brain —Dorothy Sayers⟩ — **take root 1 :** to send forth roots **:** become rooted **2 :** to become fixed or established as if by sending forth roots ⟨colony has *taken root* and become a city —Tom Marvel⟩ ⟨free public education had been slow to *take root* —Jerome Ellison⟩ ⟨expectation *takes root* that American military forces will be available against any aggressor —A.O.Wolfers⟩ ⟨the price . . . of never having been allowed to *take root* in any community —F.R.Leavis⟩ — **take shape :** to assume a definite or distinctive form ⟨idea which was *taking shape* almost frightened him by its novelty —Marcia Davenport⟩ ⟨vision of a railway network covering the whole country was beginning to *take shape* —O.S.Nock⟩ ⟨our American universities . . . had not really *taken shape* much before 1910 —Harlan Hatcher⟩ — **take silk** *Brit* **:** to become a king's or queen's counsel — **take stage** *or* **take the stage :** to center attention upon oneself (as by moving to an important position on the stage) — **take the bull by the horns :** to face up to and grapple with a difficulty — **take the cake :** to carry off the prize orig. in a cakewalk **:** rank first ⟨*takes the cake* for sheer weight of national holidays — twenty-seven —*New Yorker*⟩ ⟨for . . . pure cheek that *takes the cake* —*Sydney* (*Australia*) *Bull.*⟩ — **take the count 1** *of a boxer* **:** to remain down while the referee completes a count of ten seconds **:** be counted out **2 :** to go down in defeat ⟨always had the willingness to *take the count* if I'm wrong —Hollis Alpert⟩ — **take the cross** [ME *taken the croice*, fr. *taken* to take + *the* + *croice*, *cros* cross] **:** to take a vow to fight the enemies of Christianity (as by entering upon a crusade) — **take the field 1 :** to go upon the playing field (as of a football team) **2 :** to enter upon a military campaign — **take the floor 1 :** to rise (as in a meeting or a legislative assembly) to make a more or less formal address, to make a motion, or for some similar purpose **2 :** to stand up to dance — **take the road :** to begin traveling; *specif* **:** to engage on a round of theatrical performances from town to town — **take the rue** *Scot* **:** REPENT — **take the wind out of one's sails 1 :** to sail to windward of a sailing vessel and so cut off the wind **2 :** to frustrate by anticipating (as in argument) or by forestalling (as in action or movement) — **take the word** *also* **take up the word :** to begin to speak — **take the words out of one's mouth :** to utter the exact words about to be used by another — **take time by the forelock :** to make prompt use of something **:** not let slip an opportunity — **take to** [ME *taken to*] **1 :** to take in hand **:** take charge of **:** care for ⟨charladies who *take to* their gentlemen —F.A.Swinnerton⟩ ⟨long to make pets of them all, but . . . their mothers *take to* them —Rachel Henning⟩ **2 :** to betake oneself to **:** have recourse to (as a place or a means of progression) ⟨*take to* the lifeboats⟩ ⟨bird *took to* flight⟩ ⟨*take to* the woods⟩ ⟨*took to* the parlor sofa and let everyone wait on her —Rosemary Benét⟩ **3 :** to begin to apply or devote oneself to (as a practice, habit, occupation) ⟨*take to* begging⟩ ⟨*take to* drink⟩ ⟨women who seem to *take to* the dressmaking and millinery trades by instinct —Mary Austin⟩ ⟨develop howls or *take to* biting visitors —Robert Littell⟩ **4 :** to adapt oneself to **:** respond to ⟨*took* so well *to* animal bait —Richard Semon⟩ ⟨never been milked by a woman . . . don't know how they'll *take to* it —Ellen Glasgow⟩ ⟨young stock *took* most readily *to* the concentrates —*Sydney* (*Australia*) *Bull.*⟩ ⟨home rulers would not *take* kindly *to* any suggestion of a centralized state —V.L.Parrington⟩ **5 :** to conceive a liking for ⟨*took to* the stranger at first sight⟩ ⟨nice to anybody she happens to *take to* —Kenneth Roberts⟩ — **take to one's heels :** to run away **:** FLEE — **take to task 1** *obs* **:** to undertake as one's special work **:** challenge to a feat **:** deal with **2 :** to call to account for a shortcoming **:** REPROVE ⟨is right in *taking to task* the historians for slighting this important development —C.V.Woodward⟩ — **take wake :** to let one's boat fall into the wake of another — **take water 1 :** to enter the water — used of a waterfowl **2 :** to ship water (as in a rough sea) — **take with** [ME *taken with* to accept, fr. OE *tacan with*, fr. *tacan* to take + *with*] **1** *Scot* **a :** to be pleased with **:** LIKE **b :** to put up with **2** *Scot* **:** ADMIT, CONFESS, ACKNOWLEDGE **3** *archaic* **:** to take the part or side of **:** agree with **:** side with **4** *dial* **:** to become affected by (as fire or water)

[2]**take** \ˈtāk\ *n* -s **1 :** an act or the action of taking (as by seizing, accepting, or otherwise coming into possession): as **a :** an act or the action of killing, capturing, or catching (as game or fish) ⟨the hunting ~ and other causes of mortality to pheasant eggs —*Sports Illustrated*⟩ **b** *chiefly Brit* **:** the action of leasing land (as for farming or mining) **c :** an action of accepting something (as by way of compromise) — compare GIVE-AND-TAKE **d** (1) **:** the capture of a chessman (2) **:** a position in which capture can be made — used with *on* ⟨White has left his queen on ~⟩ **e** (1) **:** the uninterrupted photographing or televising of a single scene or part of a scene (2) **:** the making of a sound recording ⟨session opened with the second ~ of the first part of the concerto —Murray Schumach⟩ **2 :** something that is taken: **a :** the amount of money received (as from a business venture, a sale, an admission charge, an enforced contribution): as (1) **:** the sum total taken in esp. from particular sources ⟨was fixing to increase the state's ~ on mutuel betting —J.G. Forrest⟩ ⟨the farmer's ~ last year⟩ ⟨the tax ~⟩ ⟨~ has lagged behind the increased outgo —Harlow Shapley⟩ ⟨a box-office ~ which yearly declined —Kaspar Monahan⟩ ⟨the 1956 ~ from tourism —*Newsweek*⟩ ⟨crowds became larger, and the ~ greater —Carey McWilliams⟩ (2) **:** a percentage of total receipts deducted or reserved (as the amount of a racing bet deducted by the state and the track owners) **:** CUT ⟨gambling ~ helps pay for the state's roads —Jack Goodman⟩ ⟨2.17 percent, the syndicate's net ~ on the issue —John Brooks⟩ (3) **:** a criminal's haul **b :** the number or quantity (as of animals, fish, or pelts) taken at one time **:** CATCH, HAUL ⟨a catch of four cows and an oil ~ of more than a hundred barrels —H.A.Chippendale⟩ ⟨yearly ~ of cottontail rabbits . . . runs into the millions —*Amer. Guide Series: Mich.*⟩ **c** (1) *chiefly Brit* **:** a piece of land taken by lease **:** HOLDING (2) **:** oil taken or bought from a lease **d** (1) **:** an installment of copy given to a compositor for typesetting; *esp* **:** a section of a running newspaper or wire service story sent to the pressroom in sections (2) **:** the type set from such copy **e** (1) **:** a passage to be taken down or an amount taken down at one time (as in shorthand) or transcribed (as on a typewriter) ⟨the high-speed ~*s* in this course have been taken from the *Congressional Record* —C.I.Blanchard & C.E.Zoubek⟩ (2) **:** a section or installment (as of an article, a speech) arbitrarily chosen (as for convenience in reading, recording, translation) ⟨prepared speech, translated in short ~*s* —W.V.Shannon⟩ ⟨an informal anthology in short ~*s* —William Miller⟩ ⟨might be wisest to read them in short ~*s* —*New Yorker*⟩ **f** (1) **:** a scene or part of a scene filmed or televised at one time without stopping the camera and with or without a sound recording ⟨usually a cutter receives hundreds of ~*s* of scenes —Andrew Buchanan⟩; *also* **:** the photography of a scene sequence identified by photographing a scene number on a take board (2) **:** a sound recording made during a single recording period usu. seven or eight minutes in length ⟨hundreds of feet of tape contain dozens of ~*s* —*N.Y. Times*⟩; *often* **:** a trial recording **3 a :** something that takes effect: as (1) *obs* **:** a magic spell (2) **:** taking quality **:** CHARM **b :** something (as a play or song) that becomes popular **4 :** an action or a result of taking effect: **a :** reaction of vaccinia indicating successful introduction of virus into the skin and its multiplication ⟨should be vaccinated again and again, if necessary, until there is a ~ —Benjamin Spock⟩ **b :** a successful union (as of a graft) ⟨skin grafting . . . resulted in a complete ~ —*Science News Letter*⟩ **5 :** an act or the action of taking something in mentally (as by a show of understanding) **:** REACTION, RESPONSE ⟨gave my name to the uniformed maid — whose ~, as I announced myself, was something to behold —Polly Adler⟩ ⟨the lovable baby with the big feet and the slow ~ —Robert Hatch⟩ ⟨no stage gasp or actor's ~ —Otis Ferguson⟩ ⟨would strike the committee, in a giant delayed ~ —Russell Maloney⟩ — compare DOUBLE TAKE — **on the take** *adv* (*or adj*) **:** alert to, in search of, or in pursuit of an opportunity to take or take advantage of another ⟨the big fish will be *on the take* in the water —Alec Robertson⟩

takeable *var of* TAKABLE

take about *vt* **:** to escort publicly to various places (as of entertainment)

take-all \ˈ=,=\ *n* -s **:** a destructive disease of cereal grasses caused by a fungus (*Ophiobolus graminis*) and characterized by foot rot and partially filled or empty heads and by bleaching of stalks, leaves, and heads — called also *whiteheads*

take-apart \ˈ==,=\ *adj* [*take apart*] **:** constructed so as to be readily taken apart and reassembled **:** TAKEDOWN ⟨*take-apart* toys⟩

take away *vb* [ME *taken away*, fr. *taken* to take + *away*] *vt* **1 :** to bear off to another place **:** carry away ⟨drop in . . . and *take away* an armful of their publications —Richard Joseph⟩ ⟨would allow foreign investors . . . to *take away* their capital gains —W.B.Preston⟩ **2 a :** REMOVE, SEPARATE ⟨*took* geometry *away* from its subject matter of lengths, areas, and volumes —S.F.Mason⟩ ⟨improved the house by *taking* the front porch *away*⟩ **b :** SUBTRACT ⟨*take away* six from nine⟩ **3 a :** to cause deprivation of ⟨*take* the right to vote *away*⟩ ⟨if support is suddenly *taken away* from an infant —H.A.Overstreet⟩ **b :** DETRACT ⟨without desiring to *take away* anything from the . . . production showing —*Securities Outlook*⟩ ~ *vi* **1 :** to clear away a meal from the table ⟨younger children had the task of *taking away*⟩ **2 :** to derogate or detract (as from merit or effect) often to a specified extent **:** lessen reputation ⟨these new elements have constantly *taken away* from the sea . . . until little but mediocrity remains —E.J.Schoettle⟩ — **take it away** — used as a cue or signal to begin a radio or television broadcast and equivalent to *you're on the air* — **take one's breath away :** to make one breathless from excitement or emotion or from astonishment or amazement

take back *vt* **1 :** RETURN ⟨*take* that jar *back* and get the right brand —*Phoenix Flame*⟩ **2 :** to resume possession of: **a :** to accept the return of ⟨store willingly *takes back* anything it sells⟩ **b :** REPOSSESS ⟨stories of . . . furniture *taken back* because of failure to meet payments —E.S.Hoyt⟩ **3 :** to permit to come back ⟨had been fired twice and both times *taken back*⟩ **4 :** RETRACT, WITHDRAW ⟨would neither apologize nor *take back* what he had said⟩ **5 :** to lead or draw back in thought to an earlier time ⟨*took* me *back* to when I was about twenty —Walter de la Mare⟩ ⟨there's nothing like music for *taking* you *back* —Mary Deasy⟩

take board *n* **:** SLATE 3b

take down *vb* [ME *taken down*, fr. *taken* to take + *down*] *vt* **1 a :** to pull down or to pieces (as a building, a scaffold) **:** cut down (as a tree) **b** (1) **:** to take apart or to pieces (as a motor) **:** DISASSEMBLE ⟨*take* a rifle *down*⟩ (2) **:** DISTRIBUTE ⟨*take* standing type *down*⟩ **2 :** to take from a higher to a lower place or level: as **a** (1) **:** SWALLOW ⟨*took* the dose *down* with a grimace⟩ (2) **:** SUBMERGE ⟨*take* a submarine *down* in a practice dive⟩ **b :** to conduct or escort to a place on a lower level ⟨*take* a lady *down* to dinner⟩ **c** (1) **:** to lower the spirit or vanity of **:** ABASE, HUMBLE ⟨had two methods of *taking* men *down:* babying them and harping on their faults —Edmund Wilson⟩ ⟨whippersnapper needs to be *taken down* a bit⟩ (2) **:** to reduce in strength **:** lay low ⟨was *taken down* with fever⟩ (3) *dial Eng* **:** to reduce in flesh **:** EMACIATE **d :** to reduce (as light or sound) in intensity ⟨signals the electrician to *take* the houselights *down* —Henning Nelms⟩ **3 :** to remove from a shelf or a hook ⟨*took down* his navy blue suit from the wardrobe —D.M.Davin⟩ ⟨*took* the family Bible *down*⟩ **4 a :** to write down ⟨notes *taken down* in shorthand⟩ ⟨no stenographers in Athens to *take down* what Demosthenes said —Max Eastman⟩ ⟨*take* a name *down*⟩ **b :** to record by mechanical means ⟨a wire recorder that was *taking down* the bebop music —Chandler Brossard⟩ ⟨this particular performance . . . was *taken down* in the Rome Opera House —Douglas Watt⟩ ~ *vi* **1 :** to become seized or attacked esp. by illness ⟨*took down* with typhoid fever⟩ ⟨man . . . who was bearing most of the fitting-out expense *took down* sick —J.F.Dobie⟩ ⟨youngsters always *took down* with notions —H.L.Davis⟩ **2 :** to admit of being taken down ⟨hospital could set up in four hours and *take down* in two, they boasted —A.J.Liebling⟩ ⟨doubles *take down* into a shorter package than most pumps —Warren Page⟩

1takedown \ˈ⸗ˌ⸗\ *adj* [*take down*] **:** constructed so as to be readily taken apart ⟨a ~ rifle⟩ ⟨~ style⟩

2takedown \"\ *n* -s [*take down*] **1 :** the action or an act of taking down: as **a :** the action of humiliating esp. by deceiving **b :** DISASSEMBLY ⟨~ of an engine⟩ ⟨easy ~ for cleaning and oiling⟩ **c :** the act of bringing one's opponent in amateur wrestling under control to the mat from a standing position for a score of 2 points — compare ESCAPE, REVERSAL **2 :** one that takes down or humiliates (as by deception) **3 :** something (as a rifle or shotgun) having takedown construction

take-home pay *also* **take-home** \ˈ⸗ˌ⸗-\ *n* -s **:** the remainder of a person's gross salary or wages after deduction usu. at the source of salary payment of such items as income tax withholding, retirement insurance payments, and union dues

take in *vb* [ME *taken in*, fr. *taken* to take + *-in*] *vt* **1 a :** to allow to enter **:** ADMIT ⟨ship was *taking* water *in*⟩ **b :** to bring or draw in from outside ⟨air compressor . . . is used to *take in* atmospheric air, compress it, and force it into the cabin —H.G. Armstrong⟩ ⟨tankers . . . *taking in* cargoes of finished oil products —Martin Chisholm⟩ **2 a :** to carry or conduct within doors or into a room; *specif* **:** to escort (a lady) from a drawing room into dinner **b :** to take into custody **:** take to a police station as a prisoner ⟨going to have to *take* you *in* for attempted homicide —Ellery Queen⟩ **3 :** to draw into a smaller compass **:** reduce the extent of (as by shortening or tightening) ⟨*take in* a slack line⟩: **a :** FURL ⟨*take* a sail *in*⟩ **b :** to make (a garment) smaller by making seams, darts, and tucks larger ⟨dress needed to be *taken in* a bit⟩ **4 a :** to receive as a guest or inmate ⟨inn gladly *takes in* children⟩ ⟨widow had started *taking* a few lodgers *in*⟩ **b :** to give shelter to ⟨*take in* a stray dog⟩ **5 :** to receive in payment or as proceeds of a venture ⟨store *takes* a lot of money *in* each day⟩ ⟨compare notes on how much each has *taken in* on his pitch —W.L.Gresham⟩ **6 a** *chiefly Brit* **:** to receive (as a periodical) regularly ⟨*takes in* four daily papers —Christopher Isherwood⟩ **b :** to receive (work) into one's house to be done for pay ⟨*take in* washing⟩ ⟨sisters *took* a little plain sewing *in*⟩ ⟨*take in* typing jobs⟩ **7 :** to take (land) into possession **:** ANNEX, ENCLOSE, FENCE; *also* **:** to take under cultivation ⟨soil was usually exhausted in two or three years, when fresh land was *taken in* —Mary Tew⟩ **8 a :** to encompass within its limits **:** COMPRISE, EMBRACE, INCLUDE ⟨that expansiveness of view which *takes in* all the discrepant factors —H.A.Overstreet⟩ ⟨ban will *take in* fifty-eight miles of curb space —*N.Y.Times*⟩ ⟨in this day of the guided missile . . . the real world we live in *takes in* the whole earth —Herbert Bracker⟩ **b** (1) **:** to include in an itinerary or visit **:** explore or visit in seeing the sights ⟨can also *take in* some of the notable architectural monuments —Paul Henissart⟩ ⟨is *taking in* the sights of the World's Fair —*Newsweek*⟩ (2) **:** ATTEND ⟨*take in* a movie⟩ ⟨read more history or *take in* more plays —W.H.Whyte⟩ **9 a :** to receive into the mind **:** COMPREHEND, UNDERSTAND ⟨paused a few seconds to *take* the situation *in* —Rex Ingamells⟩ ⟨was pleased at the . . . way his mind was *taking in* impressions and interpreting them —Irwin Shaw⟩ ⟨stood motionless as though trying to *take in* the meaning of her words —Agnes S. Turnbull⟩ ⟨cannot easily *take in* new ideas —*Atlantic*⟩ **b :** to take note of ⟨in the second before she spoke . . . she had *taken in* the expensive hat and coat —Ruth Park⟩ **:** observe keenly ⟨seemed to *take* him all *in* anew before answering —S.H.Adams⟩ **:** PERCEIVE ⟨*took in* the special possibilities open to a monarch for extortion —Francis Hackett⟩ **10 :** to impose upon **:** CHEAT, DECEIVE, TRICK ⟨prides himself . . . that he will not be *taken in* by anybody —Louis Wirth⟩ ⟨*taken in* by a spurious document —G.C.Sellery⟩ ⟨couldn't lie convincingly enough to *take* a child *in*⟩ ⟨even the most experienced eye may be *taken in* on certain occasions —Henry Wynmalen⟩ ~ *vi* **:** COMMENCE, OPEN ⟨school *takes in* at nine and lets out at three⟩ — **take in with** *obs* **:** to take sides with **:** agree with **:** make terms with

take-in \ˈ⸗ˌ⸗\ *n* -s [*take in*] **1 :** an act of taking in (as by cheating or deceiving someone or by bringing something in) **2 :** one that takes in someone; *esp* **:** FRAUD **3 :** a number or quantity taken in

ta·kel·ma \təˈkelmə\ *n, pl* **takelma** *or* **takelmas** *usu cap* **1 a :** an Indian people of southwestern Oregon **b :** a member of such people **2 :** a Takilman language of the Takelma people

1taken [ME (past part.)] *past part or dial past of* TAKE

2ta·ken \ˈtākən *sometimes* -kᵊŋ\ *dial var of* TOKEN

take off *vb* [ME *taken of*, fr. *taken* to take + *of* off] *vt* **1 :** to remove from a position on something or the condition of being attached to or part of something (as by lifting, pulling, cutting, or breaking off or by subtracting or deducting) ⟨*took* his shoes *off* and put on his slippers⟩ ⟨chinook winds . . . *took off* as much as a foot of snow in 24 hours —E.B.Crane⟩ ⟨gave up trying to drive a car after *taking off* a fender —T.P.Whitney⟩ ⟨preparation *takes* paint *off* in one application⟩ ⟨system for *taking off* honey —Guy Diemer⟩: as **a :** RELEASE ⟨*take* the brake *off*⟩ **b :** DISCONTINUE, WITHDRAW ⟨play was *taken off* after three performances⟩ ⟨company announced that it would *take* two evening trains *off*⟩ **c :** to pick up and take along (as from a ship or an island) ⟨put in to *take* some stranded seamen *off*⟩ ⟨steamer calls once a week to *take off* mail⟩ **d** (1) **:** to take or allow as a discount ⟨*take* 10 percent *off* for cash⟩ (2) **:** to except, omit, or withhold from service owed or from time being spent or usu. spent in a particular way (as at one's occupation) ⟨looking for any excuse to *take* an hour *off* —Lillian Hellman⟩ ⟨*took* two weeks *off* in August⟩ ⟨usually played golf on Sunday but decided to *take* that Sunday *off*⟩ ⟨*took* a few minutes *off* to rest⟩ **2 :** to remove the burden of ⟨*take off* a tax⟩ ⟨promised to *take* the restrictions *off*⟩ **3 :** to put an end to **:** do away with ⟨turn up the furnace long enough to *take* the chill *off*⟩ ⟨poured in a small jug of raw cream — this, as they said, *took off* the greasiness —Paul Jennings⟩ **4 :** to take the life of ⟨disease appeared . . . and without respect of persons or neighborhoods, *took off* young and old —*Amer. Guide Series: Del.*⟩ ⟨pneumonia *took* him *off* in his prime⟩ **5 :** to drink down ⟨*took* a pint of beer *off* without lowering his glass⟩ **6 a :** to copy from an original **:** REPRODUCE ⟨*take off* a hundred copies⟩ **b :** to make a likeness of **:** PORTRAY ⟨*took off* his head and shoulders in charcoal⟩ **c :** to imitate esp. so as to parody or burlesque **:** MIMIC ⟨mannerisms that his critics delighted in *taking off*⟩ **d :** to take down from a receiving apparatus ⟨*take off* a telegram⟩ **7 a :** to measure off or estimate in determining requirements (as of materials in building) ⟨in *taking off* glass . . . even inches are used to describe the sizes —*Building, Estimating & Contracting*⟩ **b :** to calculate (as a quantity) with a calculating machine ⟨*take off* a total⟩ **c :** PREPARE ⟨*take off* a trial balance⟩ **8 a :** to lead away ⟨was *taken off* by the police⟩ **b :** to betake (oneself) from a place ⟨*takes* himself *off*, then telegraphs home for money —Elizabeth Bowen⟩ ~ *vi* **1 a :** to cause lessening or subtraction (as from the value of something) **:** DETRACT **:** take away **b** *of a tide, storm, or wind* **:** to grow less **:** ABATE, DECREASE **2 a :** to start off or away often suddenly **:** set out **:** DEPART, LEAVE ⟨*took off* in a radio command car —Bill Davidson⟩ ⟨*took off* without comment, stamping down the steps —R.O.Case⟩ ⟨*took off* downriver —Bernard De Voto⟩ **b** (1) **:** to branch off (as from a main stream or stem) ⟨pike *taking off* straight east is the Ramona Freeway —Ralph Friedman⟩ ⟨occasionally . . . *takes off* from reality, and then he is at his best —*Time*⟩ (2) **:** to take or have origin **:** DERIVE, ORIGINATE, STEM ⟨*takes off* from something observed or remembered —David Daiches⟩ **c** *of a jumper, hurdler, or vaulter* **:** to begin a leap or spring **d** *of an airplane, rocket, or bird* **:** to leave the surface of the land or water **:** begin flight **e :** to play a solo in jazz music that is characterized by wild improvisation and usu. a fast rhythmic beat **f :** to take a narcotic drug ⟨ritual of *taking off* was over and the drug was in his head —Hal Ellson⟩ **3 :** to be removable ⟨top *takes off* easily⟩

takeoff \ˈ⸗ˌ⸗\ *n* -s *often attrib* [*take off*] **1 :** something that detracts **:** DRAWBACK **2 :** an imitation esp. in the way of caricature **:** the action or an instance of mimicking **:** BURLESQUE, PARODY ⟨one of his ~*s* is on a young Southern novelist —Hollis Alpert⟩ ⟨a ~ on the conventional college song —Stewart Alsop⟩ ⟨musical comedy ~ on the Westerns —Arthur Knight⟩ ⟨competition started as a ~ on the traditional races —*Buick Mag.*⟩ **3 a :** a rise or leap esp. from the ground in making a jump or flight **:** a start in leaping or hurdling, in making an ascent in an aircraft, or in the launching of a rocket ⟨~ was done without any of your springboards —Edward Bass⟩ ⟨other birds need a long ~ run —*Time*⟩ ⟨had been test-fired twice . . . and that in each case it had blown up, or been detonated, soon after ~ —John Brooks⟩; *specif* **:** an action of beginning flight in which an aircraft is accelerated from rest to the condition of normal flight ⟨~ had been normal⟩ ⟨~ distance⟩ ⟨it was the ~ and the landing which he loved best —Louis Bromfield⟩ ⟨~ time⟩ **b :** an action of starting out or setting out ⟨everybody made a scram ~ for a foxhole —Ira Wolfert⟩ ⟨~ hour for the armored cars —Joseph Alsop⟩ ⟨severity with which you drive your car (sudden stops, quick ~*s*, fast cornering) —Walt Woron⟩ ⟨book . . . has a long, slow ~, although the materials are interesting —Edmund Fuller⟩ ⟨statesmen are elderly and slow on the ~ —Upton Sinclair⟩ **4 a :** a spot at which one takes off or may take off ⟨cars are arriving at the ~ —Bert Pierce⟩ ⟨can be climbed onto and used as a ~ for a higher leap —A.L.Kroeber⟩; *specif* **:** the spot or an object (as a rubber or board) from which a jumper, vaulter, or hurdler rises in leaping ⟨sketch of their pit showing two high jump ~*s* —*Athletic Jour.*⟩ ⟨~ board⟩ **b :** a starting point **:** point of departure **:** base of operations ⟨the ~ point of the real revolution of industrialization —H.R.Lieberman⟩ ⟨study of filter cigarettes published nearly seven months ago . . . became the ~ for a new campaign this week —*Advertising Age*⟩ **5 :** an action of removing something ⟨package is positioned horizontally to allow a better ~ —S.B.Bradley⟩ ⟨chemical and physical treatments of rayon, from the ~ at the spinning machine to the final product —F.C.Hahn⟩; *specif* **:** the skinning process in leather manufacturing **6 :** the action of estimating or measuring an amount of material needed (as in building) **:** quantity survey ⟨plumbing ~⟩ ⟨~ man⟩ **7 :** a device, mechanism, or part by means of which something is led or drawn off (as to another place, for another purpose) ⟨~*s* to houses are loops that return to the mains —W.R.Moore⟩; *specif* **:** a mechanism for transmission through which the power of an engine or vehicle may be taken off to operate some other mechanism ⟨two power ~*s* at the front of the motor —Bernard Gladstone⟩ ⟨rear ~ can provide either a belt drive . . . or a shaft drive —*Country Life*⟩ ⟨~ power from his tractor —*Ethyl News*⟩

take on *vb* [ME *taken on*, fr. *taken* to take + *on*] *vt* **1 a :** to invest or clothe oneself with **:** DON ⟨dry facts of history *take on* flesh and blood —V.L.Parrington⟩ **b :** ADD ⟨had been *taking* flesh *on*⟩ ⟨*took on* five pounds in one month⟩ **c :** to take aboard ⟨train stops only to *take on* through passengers⟩ ⟨put in to *take* water and provisions *on*⟩ **:** LOAD ⟨*take* cargo *on*⟩ **2 a :** to begin to perform or deal with **:** UNDERTAKE ⟨*take* a new job *on*⟩ ⟨didn't realize what a responsibility he had *taken on* —L.C.Douglas⟩ ⟨was *taking on* quite a contract —Russell Lord⟩ ⟨I'd just *taken on* a dealership for milking machines —C.A.Lindbergh b. 1902⟩ **b :** to undertake or engage with as or as if an opponent **:** accept the challenge of ⟨*taking on* the powerful in behalf of the poor and the weak —P.H.Douglas⟩ ⟨*took on* the wild boar, the water buffalo, the rhinoceros . . . and he conquered them all —James Thurber⟩ ⟨she and two sister subs *took on* a seventeen-ship convoy —E.L.Beach⟩ ⟨funks riding the black colt but *takes* it *on* to please his dad —Leslie Rees⟩ ⟨*took on* all comers in the boxing booth attached to the circus —G.E.Odd⟩ **3 a :** ENGAGE, HIRE ⟨company was *taking* workmen *on*⟩ ⟨*take on* a bookkeeper⟩ **b :** to accept in a relationship ⟨doctor was not *taking on* any new patients⟩ ⟨talked him into *taking* me *on* as a client⟩ ⟨wife . . . worked in a war plant but *took on* one man after another —W.L.Gresham⟩ **4 a :** to assume or acquire (as an appearance or quality) as or as if one's own ⟨can act . . . in the old-fashioned sense of *taking on* the complete being and personality of a wide variety of characters —Faubion Bowers⟩ ⟨green through all the winter, it now *takes on* every shade of color —Norman Douglas⟩ ⟨had begun to *take on* that wasted appearance which is characteristic of unused muscles —Grace Reiten⟩ ⟨*taking on* the slowness of a tidal stream —Julian Dana⟩ ⟨riddle of church and state has *taken on* fresh urgency —W.L.Sperry⟩ ⟨disease *took on* epidemic character —C.L. Jones⟩ ⟨familiar features . . . appear in a different perspective, *take on* another meaning —W.P.Webb⟩ **b :** ADOPT ⟨foreign dynasties in China have always submitted to the superior culture of the Chinese and have *taken on* their language —Edward Sapir⟩ ⟨threw in with the Indians, *taking on* their dress and manners —F.B.Gipson⟩ ⟨soon *took on* new ways of life —Kemp Malone⟩ **5** *Scot* **:** to get into debt for **:** obtain on credit ~ *vi* **1 a :** to show one's feelings esp. of grief or anger in a demonstrative way **:** behave or talk excitedly or extravagantly **:** make a great fuss ⟨*took on* about it as though he had lost a child —Sherwood Anderson⟩ ⟨dressed as an old lady and they cried and *took on* something terrible until I removed my wig —Bob Hope⟩ **b :** to put on airs **:** behave in a proud or haughty manner **2 a :** to engage oneself for service esp. by enlisting or reenlisting in military service **b :** to begin to associate or consort **:** take up **3 :** to find acceptance; *esp* **:** to become popular **:** make a hit **:** catch on ⟨song *took on* overnight⟩ ⟨idea somehow failed to *take on*⟩

take out *vb* [ME *taken out*, fr. *taken* to take + *out*] *vt* **1 :** to remove from within (as from a receptacle, a place, enclosing bounds or limits, a set or composite) ⟨had his tonsils *taken out*⟩ ⟨*took* his pen *out* and signed on the spot⟩ ⟨*took* the melodrama *out* of the rescue scenes and substituted pathos —M.W.Fishwick⟩ ⟨nurse *took out* the supper trays and the lights in the ward were turned off —Carson McCullers⟩: as **a** (1) **:** DEDUCT, SEPARATE ⟨*took* his commission *out* before turning over the proceeds⟩ (2) **:** EXCEPT, EXCLUDE, OMIT ⟨21 working days, *taking out* weekends and holidays⟩ (3) **:** WITHDRAW, WITHHOLD ⟨some land will be *taken out* of spring wheat and flaxseed —*Successful Farming*⟩ **b :** to draw out by cleansing ⟨a preparation for *taking* stains *out*⟩ **c :** to find release for **:** give vent to **:** EXPEND — usu. used with *on* ⟨*take out* their resentments on one another —J.W.Aldridge⟩ ⟨*take out* their wanderlust on geographic magazines —T.H.Robsjohn-Gibbings⟩ **d :** to get rid of or put an end to (as an obstacle, an opponent) **:** ELIMINATE ⟨second ball *takes out* all the remaining pins —*Beginning Bowling*⟩ ⟨main job was to *take out* enemy airfields —Walter Millis⟩ ⟨needed to have some of the conceit *taken out* of him⟩ **2** *obs* **:** COPY **3 :** to lead or carry forth (as into the open air, from a private to a public place, into society) ⟨*took* the dog *out* for a run⟩ ⟨mother liked to be *taken out* for dinner occasionally⟩ ⟨perfect weather for *taking* the baby *out*⟩ ⟨prettiest girl he had ever *taken out* on the dance floor⟩: as **a :** ESCORT ⟨not a puzzle to her that men seldom wanted to *take* her *out* —Aurelia Levi⟩ **b :** CONDUCT ⟨the next year he *took out* his first road company —W.B.Shaw⟩ **4 :** to take as an equivalent **:** obtain or receive the value of in another form — used with *in* ⟨part of the mill-workers' pay is *taken out* in houses —Sinclair Lewis⟩ ⟨*took* what remained of the debt *out* in goods⟩ **5 a :** to obtain (as by application) from the proper authority ⟨*take out* a summons⟩ ⟨*take out* a charter⟩ ⟨forgot to *take* a new dog license *out*⟩ ⟨new Socialist peers have followed tradition and *taken out* coats of arms —*N. Y. Herald Tribune*⟩ ⟨applied to *take out* citizenship⟩ **b :** to arrange for (insurance) ⟨your age at the time you *take out* your annuity —*advt*⟩ **6 :** to overcall (as one's bridge partner or his bid) in a denomination that is different or to bid over (as a double or redouble by partner) when the intervening opponent has passed, doubled, or redoubled ~ *vi* **:** to start on a course **:** set out **:** strike out ⟨wagons were *taking out*, some of them to face . . . miles of country road —William Faulkner⟩ ⟨saw the tracers of his machine guns *taking out* after them —Ira Wolfert⟩ ⟨trail *took out* across a long undulating grass prairie —H.L.Davis⟩ ⟨*take out* for home⟩ — **take it out on :** to expend anger, vexation, or frustration in harassment of ⟨*taking it out on* one another because of their hopeless dissatisfaction —Leslie Rees⟩

takeout \ˈ⸗ˌ⸗\ *n* -s [*take out*] **1 :** the action or an act of taking out; *specif* **:** a bridge bid that takes a partner out of a bid, double, or redouble after the intervening opponent has passed ⟨a forcing ~⟩ **2 :** a usu. automatic device for taking something out (as a finished article from a press or mold) **3 :** something taken out ⟨the state's ~ from racetrack receipts⟩ or prepared for taking out ⟨restaurant did a brisk trade in ~*s*⟩: as **a :** the minimal number or value of poker chips a player may buy from the banker at one time or the usual number or value of such chips **:** STACK **b :** a special article (as a biographical sketch, a background study) printed to fill completely successive pages or columns for easy removal ⟨a huge (39-page) and handsome Mexican ~ —*Time*⟩ ⟨a meaty ~ on the profitable doings of the famous five-and-tens —*Fortune*⟩

takeout double *n* **:** INFORMATORY DOUBLE

take over *vt* **:** to assume control or possession of esp. from or after another **:** succeed to the management of **:** assume charge of or responsibility for ⟨officers . . . preparing to *take over* the administration of occupied territories —Bernard Bloch⟩ ⟨a perfect handbook . . . on how to *take over* and use an honest nationalist government —R.A.Smith⟩ ⟨*took* the family business *over* when he was thirty⟩ ⟨automation is *taking* us *over* —John Lear⟩ ⟨*took over* the furniture of the previous tenant⟩ **:** ADOPT, BORROW ⟨Christianity *took over* this aspect of Platonism —Bertrand Russell⟩ ⟨Romans continued to *take over* from the Greeks not only their philosophy but their more practical arts —Benjamin Farrington⟩ ~ *vi* **1 :** to assume control or possession esp. by succeeding or supplanting another **:** take charge ⟨told his assistant to *take over* for him⟩ ⟨placed two loaded pistols on the president's desk and told all who had tarried to listen that he was *taking over* —*New Republic*⟩ **2 :** to displace another **:** become dominant ⟨saw a new point of view *taking over* —W.H.Hale⟩ ⟨the home is vanishing and the business office is *taking over* —Eric Sevareid⟩ ⟨the late twenties, when the movies *took over* —Arthur Miller⟩ ⟨now his emotional nature *took over* —H.A.McHugh⟩ ⟨transplanted tropical flowers and plants *take over* completely —Steve Trumbull⟩

take-over \ˈ⸗ˌ⸗⸗\ *n* -s [*take over*] **:** the action or an act of taking over **:** assumption of management, control, ownership, or possession ⟨Communist Party here aims for a gradual legal *take-over* of the democratic machinery —George Weller⟩ ⟨have been preparing the ground for the *take-over* —*Atlantic*⟩ ⟨best, perhaps only, hope for blocking a Red *take-over* —*Newsweek*⟩ ⟨the presidential *take-over* —Drew Pearson⟩

tak·er \ˈtākə(r)\ *n* -s [ME, fr. *taken* to take + *-er*] **:** one that takes (as by seizing, removing, accepting, receiving) ⟨our ~*s* of the West were nomads of fixed and gentle habits —Russell Lord⟩ ⟨United States was a heavy ~ of copper —R.G.Woolbert⟩ ⟨fish . . . are often free ~*s* there —J.E.Hutton⟩: **a :** one that captures or seizes **:** CATCHER, CAPTOR ⟨these natives were the fur ~*s* —Julian Dana⟩ **b** *obs* **:** one that takes wrongfully **:** PILFERER, ROBBER, THIEF **c** (1) **:** one that takes possession esp. of land (2) **:** one that takes a lease of property **:** LESSEE, TENANT **d :** one that takes by collecting, receiving, removing, or recording ⟨ticket ~⟩ ⟨assiduous ~*s* of notes⟩ ⟨a ~ of dictation, maker of appointments, mailer of reminders —Helen Waterman⟩ ⟨one inventory ~ counts the units and a second puts down the count —H.S.Noble⟩; *specif* **:** a worker who carries or moves leather from one place or process to another in the hide house, beamhouse, or tan house **e :** one that accepts something offered (as a bet, a dare or challenge, merchandise, assistance, an opportunity) ⟨odds were five to three with no ~*s*⟩ ⟨if he was hunting a feud, he had no ~*s* who dared to quip about his kilt —Ashley Halsey⟩ ⟨call money offered at 2⅝ percent without attracting ~*s* —*Financial Times (London)*⟩ ⟨a creative mathematician . . . peddling lessons to no ~*s* —E.T. Bell⟩ ⟨section of the table given over to tea and raisin cakes had had no ~*s* —*New Yorker*⟩

taker-down \ˈ⸗⸗ˈ⸗\ *n* -s **:** one that takes something down esp. as a part of the process of manufacture; *specif* **:** a worker who takes down galvanized sheets from the cooling racks for sorting and sending — called also *drier-down*

taker-in \ˈ⸗⸗ˈ⸗\ *n* -s **:** one that takes in: as **a :** CHEAT, DECEIVER, SWINDLER **b :** LICKER-IN **c :** a boy (as an apprentice) who carries articles of glassware to the annealing oven

taker-off \ˈ⸗⸗ˈ⸗\ *n* -s **:** one that takes something off esp. in withdrawing or carrying away as part of a process (as of manufacture) ⟨worked as a *taker-off* in a brickyard⟩ ⟨attachment . . . saves labor, by dispensing with the work of the *taker-off* —John Southward⟩

takes *pres 3d sing of* TAKE, *pl of* TAKE

take up *vb* [ME *taken up*, fr. *taken* to take + *up*] *vt* **1 a :** to pick up ⟨*took up* the morning paper and left the room⟩ ⟨*take up* longhandled nets and go forth into the salt marshes —Hugh Cave⟩ **:** LIFT, RAISE ⟨*take* her *up* tenderly —Thomas Hood †1845⟩ **b :** to remove by lifting or pulling up from a settled position ⟨*took* the carpets *up* each spring⟩ ⟨city was *taking* the old streetcar tracks *up*⟩ ⟨noise of workers *taking up* the street⟩ **c :** to pick up with the intention of using ⟨first time he had *taken up* his pen in days⟩ ⟨private gentlemen who had *taken up* arms against the king —H.E.Scudder⟩ ⟨*take up* the life of some eminent public man . . . often an autobiography —G.M. Young⟩ **d :** to allow to mount **:** take aboard ⟨train stops on signal to *take up* passengers⟩ **2 :** to carry or conduct to a higher place **3 :** to take into possession **:** assume possession of ⟨chartered or, as they then called it, *taken up* for the voyage —*Manchester Guardian Weekly*⟩ ⟨told that all available accommodation was *taken up* —*Farmer's Weekly (So. Africa)*⟩: as **a :** to begin to occupy (land) ⟨new industries to start . . . and new land to *take up* —F.D.Roosevelt⟩ ⟨have *taken up* the fertile plains and valleys —A.L.Kroeber⟩ ⟨first *taken up* for sheep in 1882, it was abandoned twenty years later —George Farwell⟩ **b :** to buy up ⟨scalpers *took* all available tickets *up*⟩ **c :** to borrow at interest ⟨arranged to *take up* a new loan⟩ **d :** to pay the amount of (as a note or loan) **:** pay in full for (as stock bought on a margin) **e :** to gather in ⟨*take up* a collection⟩ ⟨*take up* contributions⟩ **f :** to remove from the possession of another **:** take away ⟨has his license *taken up* by the policeman who issues the summons —*N.Y.Times*⟩ ⟨authorization from the attorney general to *take up* the alien's border-crossing identification card —*U.S.Code*⟩ **4 :** to receive, accept, or adopt for the purpose of assisting **:** lend one's favor or support to **:** proceed to patronize ⟨is *taken up* by the daughter of the college's athletic director —K.S.Davis⟩ ⟨rabble-rousing broadcaster . . . who was *taken up* by rich men and conservative politicians —Elmer Davis⟩ ⟨amazed at the suddenness with which you will be *taken up* by the best people —*New Republic*⟩ ⟨the universities were *taking* him *up* —*Times Lit. Supp.*⟩ **5 a :** to take or accept as one's own (as a belief, idea, practice) **:** come to use, do, or believe in **:** ADOPT ⟨*took up* the practice of walking to work⟩ ⟨*took up* the use of toothbrush, nail file, clothes brush —Dixon Wecter⟩ ⟨outline style also was *taken up* and modified by the Court artists —O.Elfrida Saunders⟩ ⟨Latin accentual verse did not *take up* the principle of regularity —H.O.Taylor⟩ **b :** to invest oneself with **:** take on oneself **:** ASSUME ⟨ready to *take up* an active and aggressive attitude to any . . . problem —J.H.Plumb⟩ ⟨no suggestion in his work . . . that corruption is an affectation *taken up* in order to astonish the bourgeoisie —Roger Fry⟩ **c :** to receive into itself or upon its surface and hold **:** SORB ⟨the elastic roller thus *takes up* the color from the pores of the wood —*Scribner's*⟩ ⟨plants generally *take up* nitrogen as nitrates —C.B. Palmer⟩ ⟨invading yeast was *taken up* by the phagocytic cells —*Immunity*⟩ **6 a :** to enter upon (as a business, profession, subject of study) ⟨*took up* his father's trade⟩ ⟨disliked the subject and wished he had not *taken* it *up*⟩ ⟨is thinking of *taking up* the violin⟩ ⟨town . . . has *taken up* art in its old age —S.T.Williamson⟩ **:** engage in ⟨passengers streamed off . . . to *take up* their daily chores —H.A.Smith⟩ **b :** to take in hand **:** proceed to deal with ⟨effect is to compel Congress to *take up* one industrial situation at a time —T.W.Arnold⟩ ⟨expected his case to be *taken up* at the next session⟩ **c :** concern oneself or itself with ⟨his next lecture would *take up* early Christian art⟩ ⟨*takes up* again a situation he dealt with . . . more than forty years —Paul Pickrel⟩ **d :** to make (as a cause) one's own concern **:** ESPOUSE, SUPPORT ⟨a reputation for *taking up* unpopular causes⟩ **7 :** to check or interrupt by dissent or reproof **:** REBUKE, REPRIMAND ⟨author should not *take up* his reviewer on matters of judgment —Patric Dickinson⟩ ⟨before she could *take* him *up* for it the door . . . opened —H.L.Davis⟩ **8 a :** to proceed to occupy (as a place or position) **:** establish oneself in ⟨restored emperor *took up* his residence at the "eastern capital" —F.A.Ogg & Harold Zink⟩ ⟨was invited to *take up* his abode in the town —*Amer. Guide Series: R.I.*⟩ ⟨*took up* quarters in an abandoned schoolhouse⟩ ⟨studied in Italy, returning to *take up* a canonry —S.F.Mason⟩ ⟨would return ready and equipped to *take up* jobs —*Lamp*⟩ **b :** to occupy (as space, time) entirely or exclusively and often so as to obstruct **:** fill up ⟨only exit was *taken up* with two bicycles and a baby carriage⟩ ⟨spoken programs . . . *take up* more than 70 percent of our radio time —*Americas*⟩ ⟨afternoons that are not *taken up* with baptisms or visits —Frank Hamilton⟩ ⟨darkness . . . which *takes up* the largest area in his pictures —C.W.H. Johnson⟩ **c :** to engage (as a person, the mind, the attention) fully **:** ENGROSS, EMPLOY ⟨had been reading it to himself, and . . . seemed all *taken up* with it —Dorothy C. Fisher⟩ ⟨ideas, interests, and occupations that *take up* the attention of the community —Edward Sapir⟩ ⟨is too much *taken up* with the children —Rachel Henning⟩ **9 a :** to constrict (as an artery) by tying up **b :** to pull up or pull in (as by drawing or winding) so as to tighten or to shorten ⟨*take up* the slack in a rope⟩ ⟨*take up* stirrup leathers⟩ ⟨*take* a brake cable *up*⟩ **c :** to gather or pull together and make fast ⟨*take* a dropped stitch *up*⟩ **d :** to remove looseness from (as by adjustment of parts) ⟨*take up* lost motion in a machine bearing⟩ **10 :** to take into custody **:** ARREST, SEIZE ⟨had been *taken up* for crap shooting —R.M. Lovett⟩ ⟨Jews were also *taken up* in the streets and trams —*Manchester Guardian Weekly*⟩ **11 :** ACCEPT; *esp* **:** to respond favorably to (as a bet, challenge, proposal or the one offering it) ⟨men threaten a strike and . . . he invites them to try running the company . . . they *take* him *up* —Robert Hatch⟩ ⟨bragging kid who made a pass at me . . . was scared half to death when I *took* him *up* on it —James Jones⟩ **12 :** to begin again (as something left off) or take over from another ⟨your turn to *take up* the tale —John Buchan⟩ ⟨another band *took up* the tune —Elsie Singmaster⟩ ⟨secretary had now joined us and *took up* the discussion —Oscar Handlin⟩ **:** RESUME ⟨*took* the story *up* again where she had left off⟩ ⟨should *take up* life vigorously again —H.A.Overstreet⟩ **13** *Scot* **:** COMPREHEND, UNDERSTAND **:** to get the point of (as a joke, an allusion) **:** APPRECIATE ~ *vi* **1** *dial* **:** to come to a stop **:** restrain oneself; *esp* **:** to stop short in some bad practice **2** *of weather* **:** CLEAR **3 a :** to make a beginning esp. where another has left off ⟨practitioner is often required to *take up* where the theorist . . . is obliged to leave off —K.W.Thompson⟩ **b** *of a school* **:** to begin a session **4 a :** to become shortened **:** draw together **:** SHRINK **b :** to close up of itself (as of a leak) — **take up for :** take the part or side of **:** stand up for **:** side with ⟨had nobody to *take up for* him⟩ — **take up the cudgels :** to engage vigorously in a defense (as of a person, a principle) esp. in argument or debate — usu. used with *for* ⟨will gladly *take up the cudgels* for you, if you'll just send in your arguments —*Wilson Library Bull.*⟩ — **take up the hatchet :** to make or declare war **:** begin warlike activity ⟨induce the Indians to *take up the hatchet* for England —R.C.Downes⟩ — **take up with 1 :** to become interested or absorbed in ⟨*taking up with* forbidden science, listening to forbidden propaganda —H.A.Overstreet⟩ **2 :** to begin to associate with ⟨found myself *taking up with* someone who turned out to be more plausible than trustworthy —*Harper's*⟩; *esp* **:** to begin to keep company with **:** CONSORT ⟨a nice girl who *takes up with* a not so nice boy —F.H.Bennett⟩ ⟨*takes up with* many sorts of women —*Newsweek*⟩ **3 a :** to assent to **:** agree with **:** ADOPT, ESPOUSE ⟨not one to *take up* readily *with* new ideas —L.C.Douglas⟩ **b** *obs* **:** to receive or accept without opposition **:** put up with

take–up \ˈ⸗,⸗\ *n* -s [*take up*] **1 :** the action or an act of taking up (as by gathering or contraction, reeling in, absorption, compensation or adjustment) ⟨bottom edge should be slightly curved and wider than the top to allow for *take-up* in draping —Mary B. Picken⟩ ⟨liner plate reversible and adjustable for wear *take-up* —*Jaeger Dewatering Pumps*⟩ ⟨nylon fibers and fabrics have a very low water *take-up* —R.S.Horsfall & L.G. Lawrie⟩ ⟨selenium — soil and plant *take-up* of, from spraying orange groves —*Jour. of Amer. Pharmaceutical Assoc.*⟩ **2 :** UPTAKE 2a **3 :** any of various devices for tightening or drawing in: as **a :** a device in a sewing machine for drawing up the slack thread as the needle rises in completing a stitch **b :** a sometimes automatic device for taking up slack in the belt of an elevator or belt conveyor **c** *or* **take–up motion :** an automatic motion in a loom for rolling up the cloth as it is woven **d :** a device for winding photographic film upon a reel, core, or spool **e :** a device or piece of equipment used in shopwork to take up slack or to remove looseness (as from wear of parts) ⟨screw *take-up*⟩ ⟨brake cable *take-up*⟩ **4 a :** decrease in length of yarns when twisted or plied **b :** decrease in length of warp yarn in a cloth compared with original length of yarn on the beam

tak·haar \ˈtak,här, ˈtä,kär, ˈtä-\ *n* -s [Afrik, lit., unkempt person, fr. *tak* branch, bough (fr. MD *tac* sharp point, branch) + *haar* hair, fr. MD *haer;* akin to OE *hǣr* hair — more at TACK, HAIR] *southern Africa* **:** a backveld Boer

takh·ta·djy \ˈtäktə,jē\ *n, pl* **takhtadjy** *or* **takhtadjies** *usu cap* **1 :** a Turkish-speaking and mostly Muslim people of the Anatolian plateau **2 :** a member of the Takhtadjy people

ta·kil·man \təˈkilmən\ *n* -s *usu cap* [irreg. fr. *takelma* + *-an*] **:** a language family of the Penutian phylum in Oregon comprising only the Takelma language

ta·kin \ˈtäˈkēn, ˈtä,k-\ *n* -s [Mishmi] **:** a large heavily built goat antelope (*Budorcas taxicolor*) of Tibet related to the musk-oxen

¹taking *n* -s [ME, fr. gerund of *taken* to take] **1 a :** SEIZURE ⟨had a ~, which he took calmly, simply bidding us hold him upside down by his ankles —J.J.Chapman⟩ **b** *obs* **:** a seizure or attack from a malevolent influence **:** BLIGHT **2 a** *chiefly Scot* **:** an unfavorable state or condition **:** PLIGHT ⟨his head and his stomach were in a very sad ~ —C.E.Abernethy⟩ **b :** a state of violent agitation and distress ⟨put him in a great ~ . . . grew as white as a napkin —John Buchan⟩ **3 :** something taken or received: as **a takings** *pl* **:** receipts esp. of money ⟨in those days the ~s of a popular play were much less —W.S.Maugham⟩ ⟨~s did not cover expenses⟩ ⟨gross ~s⟩ **b :** a catch or take of fish or animals **c :** a holding of land for mining

²taking *adj* [fr. pres. part. of ¹*take*] **1 :** that takes the fancy **:** ALLURING, ATTRACTIVE, CAPTIVATING, PLEASING ⟨book has a very ~ period flavor —*Times Lit. Supp.*⟩ ⟨knew she would be a ~ girl; how lovely, I did not guess —George Meredith⟩ ⟨something inexpressibly ~ in his manner —Douglas Jerrold⟩ **2 :** CONTAGIOUS, INFECTIOUS, CATCHING

tak·ing·ly *adv* **:** in a taking manner **:** ATTRACTIVELY, ENGAGINGLY

tak·ing·ness *n* -ES **:** the quality of being taking **:** ATTRACTIVENESS

taki–taki \ˈ;täkē;täkē\ *n* -s *usu cap both Ts* [Taki-Taki, by modif. & redupl., fr. E ²*talk*] **:** an English-based pidgin language of Surinam — called also *Ningre-Tongo*

tak·ka·nah \ˈtäˈkä(,)nä\ *n, pl* **takka·noth** *or* **takka·not** \-,nōs; ,⸗ˈnōt(h), -ōs\ [LHeb *taqqānāh*] **:** a rabbinic ordinance initiating a practice not directly based on biblical authority or oral tradition and promulgated to meet the needs of the times or circumstances

ta·ko·sis \təˈkōsəs, taˈk-\ *n* -ES [NL, fr. Gk *tak-* (akin to Gk *tēkein* to melt) + NL *-osis* — more at THAW] **:** a bacterial wasting disease of goats that is marked by diarrhea, pneumonic symptoms, and emaciation and is often fatal

ta·krou·ri \təˈkrürē\ *n* -s [origin unknown] **:** the chopped tops of cannabis used by addicts for smoking

takt \ˈtäkt\ *n* -s [G, time in music, measure, fr. L *tactus* touch, sense of touch — more at TACT] **1 :** a beat or pulse in music **2 :** MEASURE 4c(1) **3 :** TEMPO

taku \ˈta(,)kü, ˈtä(-\ *n, pl* **taku** *or* **takus** *usu cap* **1 :** a Tlingit people on Taku river and inlet, Stevens Channel, and Gastineau Channel, Alaska **2 :** a member of the Taku people

¹ta·la \ˈtälə\ *n* -s [Sp, fr. Quiche *tara*] **:** a timber tree (*Celtis tala*) of Argentina; *also* **:** the yellowish gray hard wood of this tree

²tala \ˈ"\ *n* -s [Mongolian, open country] **:** a broad structural basin formed by subsidence or warping

ta·laing \täˈlīŋ\ *n* -s *usu cap* [Burmese] **:** ³MON

talaisim *pl of* TALIS

ta·la·je \təˈlähā\ *n* -s [AmerSp, fr. Nahuatl *tlalaxin*] **:** a tick (*Ornithodoros talaje*) of the American tropics that infests horses, man, and other mammals

ta·lak \təˈläk\ *n* -s [Ar *ṭalāq*] **:** a Muhammadan divorce that is effected by the simple act of the husband's rejecting the wife

ta·la·man·ca \,täləˈmäŋkə\ *n, pl* **talamanca** *or* **talamancas** *usu cap* **1 a :** a Chibchan people of central Costa Rica **b :** a member of such people **2 :** a language of the Talamanca people

tal·a·poin \ˈtalə,pȯin, -pwan\ *n* -s [F, Buddhist monk, talapoin (fr. its fancied resemblance to a Buddhist monk), fr. Pg *talapão* (pl. *talapões*) Buddhist monk, fr. Mon *tala poi* our lord (title of respect)] **:** a western African monkey (*Cercopithecus talapoin*) that is the smallest of the guenons and is olivaceous above and whitish beneath with a black face and yellowish whiskers

ta·la·ri \ˈtälarē\ *n* -s [Ar *ṭalari*, fr. G *taler* taler — more at DOLLAR] **:** an old silver coin of Ethiopia last minted in 1904

ta·lar·ia \təˈla(a)rēə\ *n pl* [L, fr. neut. pl. of *talaris*, fr. *talus* ankle, heel + *-aris* -ar] **:** winged shoes fastened to the ankles and chiefly used as an attribute of the god Hermes or Mercury of classical mythology

tala·ve·ra \,taləˈverə\ *n* -s *usu cap* [fr. *Talavera* de la Reina, commune of central Spain where it originated] **:** colorful glazed and decorated earthenware of Spanish or Spanish colonial origin

ta·la·yot \təˈlä,yōt\ *n* -s [Catalan, fr. Ar *ṭalāʼiʻ* advance guard] **:** one of the prehistoric corbelled stone towers of the Balearic islands resembling the nuraghe of Sardinia

tal·bot \ˈtȯlbət, ˈtal-\ *also* **talbot dog** *or* **talbot hound** *n* -s *usu cap T* [prob. fr. *Talbot*, name of a Norman family in England] **:** a large heavy mostly white hound with pendulous ears and drooping flews that is thought to be ancestral to the bloodhound and some other modern breeds; *also* **:** a figure representing such a dog esp. as a heraldic device

talbot's law *n, usu cap T* [prob. after W. H. F. *Talbot* †1877] **:** a principle in optics: when two or more colors or degrees of brightness are alternately presented (as on a rotating sector disk) to the eye, there is a frequency of recurrence beyond which flicker ceases and the effect of the combination appears to be uniform

tal·bo·type \ˈtȯlbə,tīp, ˈtal-\ *n* [W. H. F. *Talbot* †1877 Eng. pioneer in photography + E *type*] **:** CALOTYPE

talc \ˈtalk, ˈtaük\ *n* -s [MF *talc* or ML *talcum*, fr. Ar *ṭalq*] **1 :** mica of muscovite; *also* **:** a thin sheet of such mineral **2 a :** a mineral $Mg_3Si_4O_{10}(OH)_2$ consisting of a basic magnesium tetrasilicate that is usu. whitish, greenish, or grayish with a soapy feel and occurs in foliated, granular, or fibrous masses (hardness 1, sp. gr. 2.6–2.9) — compare STEATITE **b :** TALCUM POWDER

tal·ca gum \ˈtalkə-\ *or* **tal·co gum** \-l(,)kō-\ *n* [by alter.] **:** TALHA GUM

talc·er \-kə(r)\ *n* -s [*talc* + *-er*] **:** SOAPSTONER

talcky \-kē\ *adj* [*talc* + *-y*] **:** TALCOSE

talco– *comb form* [*talcum*] **:** talc and ⟨*talco*chlorite⟩ **:** talcose and ⟨*talco*micaceous⟩

talc·ose \ˈtal,kōs\ *adj* [*talcum* + *-ose*] **:** of, relating to, or containing talc

talc·ous \ˈtalkəs, ˈtaük-\ *adj* [*talc* + *-ous*] **:** composed of or resembling talc

tal·cum \-kəm\ *n* -s [ML, fr. Ar *ṭalq*] **:** TALC 2

talcum powder *n* **1 :** powdered talc **2 :** a toilet powder composed of perfumed talc or talc and some mild antiseptic

¹tale \ˈtāl, *esp before pause or consonant* -āəl\ *n* -s [ME, talk, narrative, list, fr. OE *talu;* akin to OHG *zala* number, ON *tala* talk, number, Goth *talzjan* to instruct, and prob. to L *dolus* guile, deceit, Gk *dolos*] **1** *obs* **:** RELATION, DISCOURSE, TALK **2 a :** a series of related events or facts told or presented usu. to justify or clarify something **:** explanatory statement **:** ACCOUNT ⟨this error was due to a ~ of misfortunes piling up simultaneously —Frank Debenham⟩ ⟨a similar ~ of lack of communication between administrators and students —M.J. Herskovits⟩ ⟨multiple-factor analysis has much the same ~ to tell —William Stephenson⟩ ⟨thereby hangs a ~ —Shak.⟩ **b** (1) **:** a report of a secret or confidential matter — often used in pl. ⟨dead men tell no ~s⟩ ⟨telling ~s out of school⟩ (2) **:** idle talk or rumor **:** SLANDER ⟨the person who listens to gossip makes no free and generous effort to understand . . . the person about whom the ~ is told —H.A.Overstreet⟩ **c :** an account, enumeration, or category common to two or more persons or things ⟨the disputants ultimately found themselves in the same ~⟩ **3 a :** a narrative of some event or sequence of actual, legendary, or fictitious events usu. imaginatively composed with intent to entertain or amuse **:** STORY ⟨~s based on folklore, legends of great men and small —Jane G. Mahler⟩ ⟨it is essential . . . to know whether a given ~ is regarded as historical fact or fiction —W.R.Bascom⟩ ⟨the ~ goes back to the time when he was still a buck private —Marion Hargrove⟩ **b :** an untrue or inaccurate relation of events, incidents, or facts **:** FALSEHOOD ⟨the prince of literary rogues, who always preferred the ~ to the truth —Sir Winston Churchill⟩ ⟨sheer tall ~s spun by a moralist who was also a comic poet —Margaret Marshall⟩ **4 a :** a reckoning or enumeration by numbers **:** COUNT, TALLY ⟨as he admitted them to the fold . . . cast away one pebble at a time from his pile until the ~ was complete —J.A.N.Friend⟩ ⟨when the short ~ of English dead is rendered —L.G.Pine⟩ **b :** a number of things taken in the aggregate **:** SUM, TOTAL ⟨find pride, impatience, unreasonableness . . . all the unpleasant if effective ~ of traits of the successful technician of revolution —Crane Brinton⟩ **c :** a recorded accounting or declaration ⟨repaired to the treasury where each handed over his ~ of 70 pieces —John Craig⟩

²tale \ˈ"\ *vt* -ED/-ING/-S **:** to count, enumerate, or tell out (something) by number

³tale *var of* TAEL

talebearer \ˈ⸗,⸗⸗\ *n* [¹*tale* + *bearer*] **:** one that officiously or maliciously spreads gossip, scandal, or idle rumors **:** GOSSIP

¹talebearing \ˈ⸗,⸗⸗\ *n* **:** the act or habit of spreading gossip ⟨a reputation for ~⟩

²talebearing \ˈ"\ *adj* **:** given to talebearing ⟨my ~ neighbor⟩

taleisim *pl of* TALIS

tal·ent \ˈtalənt\ *n* -s [ME *talent, talente;* in sense 1, fr. OE *talente*, fr. L *talenta*, pl. of *talentum* unit of weight or money, fr. Gk *talanton* balance, pair of scales, unit of weight or money; akin to L *tollere* to lift up — more at TOLERATE; in sense 2, fr. OF *talent* inclination, desire, disposition, fr. ML *talentum*, perh. fr. L, unit of weight or money; in remaining senses fr. ME, unit of money; fr. the parable of the talents in Mt 25: 14–30] **1 a :** any of several ancient units of weight (as a Babylonian unit equal to 3600 shekels, a unit equal to 3000 shekels used in Palestine and Syria, and a Greek unit equal to 6000 drachmas) **b :** a unit of value equal to the value of a talent of gold or silver **c** *obs* **:** WEALTH, RICHES, ABUNDANCE **2 a** *archaic* **:** a characteristic feature, aptitude, or disposition of a person or animal **b** *obs* **:** an evil disposition or attitude **:** PASSION, ANGER **3 :** the abilities, powers, and gifts bestowed upon a man **:** natural endowments ⟨the stewardship of your time, ~, and treasure⟩ ⟨the ~s which God has given you as a divine trust⟩ **4 a :** a special innate or developed aptitude for an expressed or implied activity usu. of a creative or artistic nature ⟨the possessor of rare ~ as a pianist —Arthur Krock⟩ ⟨mental characteristics . . . connected with mathematical ~ —C.R.Fish⟩ ⟨the American mind with its great ~ for satire —J.B.Priestley⟩ ⟨credits the ladies . . . with a great ~ for intrigue —A.M.Young⟩ ⟨has no ~ for metaphysical speculation —J.W.Beach⟩ ⟨a man with a ~ for ingratitude and unsociability —T.S.Eliot⟩ ⟨man's industrious and senseless ~ for involving himself in the superfluous —James Boyd⟩ — often used in pl. ⟨students with ~s in music find both recreation and training —*Bull. of Bates Coll.*⟩ ⟨opportunity for the exercise of his political ~s —C.L.Becker⟩ **b :** general intelligence or mental power **:** ABILITY ⟨the labors of many scholars of ~, and some few of genius, had brought new technique to lexicography —R.W.Chapman⟩ ⟨~ is a wishy-washy thing unless . . . solidly founded on honest hard work —E.G. Coleman⟩ ⟨this task calls for . . . sheer imaginative ~ —R.D. Altick⟩ **5 a :** a person of talent usu. in a specific branch of activity ⟨he was a minor ~, but authentic —Malcolm Cowley⟩ ⟨the most . . . significant ~s in contemporary writing —Richard Watts⟩ ⟨younger ~s came to the fore —Hans Kohn⟩; *collectively* **:** a number of persons of talent in a usu. specified field or activity ⟨argued with an immense array of legal ~ —D.W. Brogan⟩ ⟨competing . . . for top-grade scientific ~ —Vannevar Bush⟩ ⟨methods of recruiting athletic ~ —Robert Rice⟩ **b :** one that is talented or skilled in a performing art ⟨one of Hollywood's most luminous ~s —Seymour Peck⟩ ⟨one of our big spontaneous musical ~s —Arthur Berger⟩; *collectively* **:** those engaged in a performing art ⟨the succession of new, worthwhile ~ was augmented by . . . a young baritone —Irving Kolodin⟩ ⟨the young ~ . . . caromed off to Hollywood —W.I. Nichols⟩ ⟨staging the show with local ~⟩ **syn** see GIFT

tal·ent·ed \-təd\ *adj* [*talent* + *-ed*] **:** having talent **:** possessing special aptitude **:** mentally gifted **:** ACCOMPLISHED ⟨a ~ musician⟩ ⟨our most ~ and successful chronicler of the upper middle class —Taliaferro Boatwright⟩ ⟨~ young actors⟩

tal·ent·less \-tləs\ *adj* **:** lacking talent

talent scout *n* **:** a person engaged in discovering and recruiting people of talent for a specialized field or activity ⟨a *talent scout* . . . saw him in the leading role —*Current Biog.*⟩ ⟨acting as a *talent scout* who brings into the firm many new authors —Hellmut Lehmann-Haupt⟩ ⟨oil firms have *talent scouts* constantly out searching for new dealers —W.C.Oursler⟩ ⟨is a full-time player *talent scout* for the Lions —Tommy Devine⟩

talent show *n* **:** a show or entertainment consisting of a series of individual performances (as singing, playing, dancing) by amateur or aspirant performers who may be selected for special recognition or advancement as performing talent ⟨the winners . . . compete in the intercollegiate *talent show* —*Springfield (Mass.) Daily News*⟩ ⟨annual all-community *talent show* —*Future*⟩

ta·ler *also* **tha·ler** \ˈtälə(r)\ *n* -s [G — more at DOLLAR] **:** any one of numerous large silver coins issued by various German states from the 15th to the 19th centuries and varying considerably in weight and fineness **:** a German dollar

¹tales *pl of* TALE, *pres 3d sing of* TALE

²ta·les \ˈtā(,)lēz\ *n, pl* **tales** [ME, fr. the ML phrase *tales de circumstantibus* such (persons) of the bystanders; fr. the use of the phrase in the writ summoning them] **1** *tales pl* **:** persons added to a jury usu. from those in or about the courthouse to make up a deficiency in the available number of jurors regularly summoned **2 :** a judge's writ or order summoning the tales

tales·man \ˈtālzmən, ˈtā(,)lēz-\ *n, pl* **talesmen** [*tales* + *man*] **:** a person summoned as one of the tales added to a jury

tale–teller \ˈ⸗,⸗⸗\ *n* **1 :** one who tells tales or stories **2 :** TALEBEARER, TELLTALE

tal·ha gum \ˈtalhə-\ *or* **talh gum** \ˈtal-\ *n* [fr. native name of *Acacia stenocarpa* in Sudan] **:** a brittle commercial gum arabic obtained from two north African acacias (*Acacia stenocarpa* and *A. seyal*) — called also *Suakin gum, talca gum*

¹tali *pl of* TALUS

²ta·li \ˈtälē\ *n* -s [Tamil *tāli*] **:** a gold piece tied about a bride's neck by the bridegroom in India and worn during his life

³tali \ˈ"\ *n* -s [origin unknown] **:** SISSOO

tal·i·era \,taleˈerə\ *n* -s [Bengali *tāliera*, fr. Skt *tālī*, fr. *tāla* palmyra palm, of Dravidian origin; akin to Kanarese *tāṛ* palm] **:** BOOK PALM

tal·i·grade \ˈtalə,grād\ *adj* [NL *tal*us ankle, ankle bone + E *-i-* + *-grade*] **:** bearing the weight on the outer side of the foot in walking

taling *pres part of* TALE

ta·li·num \təˈlīnəm\ *n, cap* [NL, fr. native name of one species in Senegal] **:** a genus of chiefly American herbs (family Portulacaceae) having ephemeral variously clustered flowers with 2 sepals and 10 stamens — see ROCK PINK

tal·i·on \ˈtalēən\ *n* -s [ME *talioun* legal retaliation, punishment in kind, fr. L *talion-, talio;* prob. akin to MIr *taile* pay, W *tal*] **:** LEX TALIONIS

tal·i·pes \ˈtalə,pēz\ *n* [NL *taliped-, talipes*, fr. L *talus* ankle, ankle bone + *ped-, pes* foot — more at FOOT] **:** CLUBFOOT 1a

tal·i·pot \ˈtalə,pät\ *n* -s [Bengali *tālipōt* palm leaf, fr. Skt *tālī* book palm + *pattra* feather, leaf; akin to Skt *patati* he flies — more at TALIERA, FEATHER] **1** *or* **talipot palm :** a showy fan palm (*Corypha umbraculifera*) of Ceylon, the Philippines, and the Malabar coast having a trunk 60 to 100 feet high and bearing a crown of gigantic fan-shaped leaves that are used as umbrellas and fans and when cut into strips as a substitute for writing paper — see BUNTAL, OLLA **2 :** a starch obtained from the talipot palm

ta·li·say \təˈlē,sī\ *n* -s [Tag] **:** JAVA ALMOND

ta·lishi \təˈlishē\ *n* -s *usu cap* **:** one of the Caspian languages

tal·is·man \ˈtaləsmən, -əzm-\ *n, pl* **talismans** [F *talisman* or Sp *talismán* or It *talismano*, fr. Ar *ṭilsam*, fr. MGk *telesma*, fr. Gk, consecration, fr. *telein* to complete, initiate into the mysteries, fr. *telos* end — more at WHEEL] **1 :** an object cut or engraved with a sign or character under various superstitious observances or influences of the heavens and thought to act as a charm to avert evil and bring good fortune ⟨the stone had become a . . . ~ on which the fertility of their crops depended —Edward Clodd⟩ **2 :** something that produces extraordinary or apparently magical or miraculous effects ⟨truth is a ~ of which the charm never fails —Arnold Bennett⟩ ⟨her pride . . . as the sort of ~ that would save her from every kind of ill —Hugh Walpole⟩ ⟨representative government is . . . not in itself a ~ —W.C.Brownell⟩

tal·is·man·ic \ˌ;taləˈsmanik, -əzˈm-, -nēk\ *or* **tal·is·man·i·cal** \-nəkəl, -nēk-\ *adj* **:** of, relating to, or having the properties of a talisman **:** MAGICAL ⟨~ signs⟩ ⟨the ~ power of driving away snakes —Norman Lewis⟩ ⟨the book turns out to have a ~ effect on the fortunes of the family —Robert Lynd⟩ — **tal·is·man·i·cal·ly** \-nək(ə)lē\ *adv*

talith *or* **talit** *or* **talis** *var of* TALLITH

tal·i·tol \ˈtalə,tȯl, -tōl\ *n* -s [*talose* + *-itol*] **:** a crystalline polyhydroxy alcohol $C_6H_{14}O_6$ formed by reduction of talose

¹talk \ˈtȯk\ *vb* -ED/-ING/-S [ME *talken;* akin to Fris *talken* to talk, OE *talu* tale — more at TALE] *vt* **1 :** to deliver or express in speech **:** SAY, UTTER ⟨to say that . . . is to ~ very little sense —Charlton Laird⟩ ⟨the vice-president ~*ed* what . . . was sensible enough —O.W.Holmes †1935⟩ **2 a :** to make the subject of conversation or discourse **:** CONSIDER, DISCUSS ⟨~*ed* books till the small hours —H.J.Laski⟩ ⟨~ the day's news —Paul Engle⟩ ⟨never . . . ~s personalities —Elmer Davis⟩ — often used with *over* ⟨~*ed* it over with his family —W.L.Gresham⟩ ⟨suggest . . . that the three of us ~ the situation over —H.B. Safford⟩ **b :** to speak confidently or boastfully of without matching the words with performance ⟨~s a good, enlightened prolabor line which . . . turns out to be window dressing —*New Republic*⟩ ⟨they don't just ~ a good game, they play it —Charles Price⟩ **3 :** to use (a language) for conversing or communicating **:** SPEAK ⟨to ~ the language well is still the indispensable accomplishment of a gentleman —E.G.Bulwer-Lytton⟩ ⟨the peculiar French patois that he ~*ed* —Aaron Copland⟩ ⟨~*ed* Italian fluently and French like a Frenchman —G.M.Trevelyan⟩ **4 a :** to bring to a specified state by talking ⟨~*ed* herself hoarse answering queries over the phone —Jane Woodfin⟩ ⟨~*ed* him deaf, dumb, and blind⟩ ⟨~ the economy into a recession —*New Republic*⟩ **b :** to persuade, influence, or affect by talking ⟨could ~ the university into giving me money enough —Oliver LaFarge⟩ ⟨his own weak effort to ~ himself out of what he had already decided to do —W.F.Davis⟩ ~ *vi* **1 a :** to express, communicate, or exchange ideas or thoughts by means of spoken words **:** CONVERSE ⟨had supper and ~*ed* until very late —Bruce Siberts & W.D.Wyman⟩ ⟨stood outside . . . in little groups ~*ing* —Louis Bromfield⟩ — often used with *to* or *with* ⟨~s to the children when they come to see him⟩ ⟨out ~*ing* with the neighbors⟩ **b :** to convey information or communicate with signs or with sounds made as if by talking ⟨30 deaf mutes, their faces alight . . . when they ~ —W.F.McDermott⟩ ⟨ahead of him two flickers were ~*ing* —Steve Frazee⟩ ⟨a rawhide drum started ~*ing* in measured beats —F.B.Gipson⟩ ⟨on the flying bridge . . . the light began to ~ to us —Vincent McHugh⟩ ⟨how to choose the book that's going to ~ to him in a way he finds enjoyable —Horace Sutton⟩ **c :** to make sounds or noises that are suggestive of talking ⟨a bracing wind . . . ~s menacingly of storm and stress and shipwreck —Alfred Buchanan⟩ ⟨a gun was ~*ing* . . . filling the night with battle uproar —Alan LeMay⟩ **2 a :** to use the faculty of speech **:** utter or make the sound of words ⟨~ in human language better than many a parrot —Morris Gilbert⟩ ⟨most hard-of-hearing people . . . ~ very loud —Eleanor B. Simmons⟩ ⟨this is a microphone . . . you ~ straight into it —Jane Woodfin⟩ **b :** to speak idly or incessantly to no purpose **:** PRATE, CHATTER ⟨all the while she ~*ed*, saying trivial, idiotic things —Louis Bromfield⟩ ⟨foolish and perverse, banal, intolerably ~*ing* on and on —H.O.Taylor⟩ ⟨and Congress ~*ed* —*Economist*⟩ **c :** to speak to the point **:** say something worthwhile ⟨now you're ~*ing*⟩ **:** carry weight ⟨money ~*s*⟩ **3 a :** to transmit a speculation or rumor usu. about another **:** GOSSIP — often used with *about* ⟨she does not ~ about others behind their backs⟩ **b :** to reveal secret or confidential information usu. concerning unlawful acts or practices ⟨he ~*ed* and revealed much valuable information to the F.B.I. —J.M.Wolfe⟩ ⟨cash-on-the-side payments . . . are oftentimes difficult to ascertain unless the buyer ~*s* —M.B.Clinard⟩ **4 :** to give a talk **:** LECTURE ⟨he ~*s* on the radio and to community groups⟩ **syn** see SPEAK — **talk at :** to speak to (a person) urgently or unremittingly ⟨goes into company not to contradict but to *talk at* you —William Hazlitt⟩ ⟨whenever she could get me into a corner, she *talked at* me —Gladys Schmitt⟩ — **talk big :** to talk boastfully or bombastically ⟨here was an unknown . . . who *talked big* but could he deliver —Neal Stanford⟩ ⟨people have come to country towns, *talked big* or tried to organize fantastic schemes —P.E.Curtiss⟩ — **talk of** *or* **talk about :** to refer to or deliberate (something) **:** PONDER, CONTEMPLATE ⟨*talk of* the devil and he'll appear⟩ ⟨a $20 million office structure the state *talks of* building —*New Englander*⟩ ⟨it is *about* the bet on yourself that I want to *talk* —J.S.Dickey⟩ ⟨the stability statesmen *talk about* would be possible —E.M.Forster⟩ — **talk one's head off :** to talk to one volubly and unremittingly ⟨are shy at first, but once they get to know you, they'll *talk your head off*⟩ — **talk one's way :** to obtain passage through or in a restricted place by talking or persuasion ⟨would *talk his way* into monasteries, ask to see the library —Gilbert Highet⟩ ⟨once *talking his way* past a detective who stopped him —Al Spiers⟩ — **talk sense :** to voice rational, logical, or sensible thoughts or ideas ⟨at a time for greatness . . . we owe it to the people to *talk sense* —A.E. Stevenson †1965⟩ — **talk through one's hat :** to voice irrational, illogical, or erroneous statements ⟨unless we test it, our talk of . . . economic aid and government propaganda will be *talking through our hats* —*Wall Street Jour.*⟩ — **talk to** *Midland* **:** COURT, WOO — **talk to death :** to prevent passage of (a legislative bill) by unlimited discussion or filibuster ⟨rule 22 . . . allows . . . senators to *talk to death* any civil rights measure —*Economist*⟩ ⟨reports persisted today that friends . . . might try to *talk to death* a resolution proposing his censure, on which the Senate opens formal debate tomorrow —*Springfield (Mass.) Daily News*⟩

²talk \"\ *n* -s [ME, fr. *talken* to talk] **1 a :** the act of talking **:** SPEECH, CONVERSATION ⟨an opportunity to . . . enjoy a bit of ~ —Margaret Jones⟩ ⟨asked the question . . . with apparent intention only of keeping ~ going —Gilbert Parker⟩ **b :** an instance or period of such speech or conversation ⟨expects to have a long ~ with his old friend⟩ ⟨stops to have ~*s* with people he knows⟩ **2 a :** the utterance of words **:** ARTICULATION ⟨writers . . . whose ear for the vernacular is so accurate that they can bring a whole stratum of society to life by the ~ of their characters —Amy Loveman⟩ ⟨it is difficult to understand them because of their strange ~⟩ **b :** pointless or fruitless discussion **:** VERBIAGE, CHATTER ⟨meeting produced little but ~ —*Time*⟩ ⟨a man who has had his dinner is never a revolutionist: his politics are all ~ —G.B.Shaw⟩ ⟨the drowning of one's mental disturbances in brave ~ —W.J.Reilly⟩ **3 :** a formal or prearranged discussion, negotiation, or exchange of views usu. of a political nature **:** CONFERENCE, MEETING ⟨latest bid for Big Four ~*s* on a . . . peace treaty —*Current History*⟩ ⟨sent word to . . . come in for ~*s* at Fort King —Marjory S. Douglas⟩ **4 a :** the making of often speculative statements or comment **:** MENTION, REPORT ⟨much ~ of the atomic bomb —C.G.McAleer⟩ ⟨~ of acquiring a large amount of surplus war material —A.H.Lybyer⟩ ⟨all the ~ we hear about quality being adversely affected —Bruce Payne⟩ **b :** RUMOR, GOSSIP ⟨only telling you the ~ in our neighborhood —Mary R. Rinehart⟩ ⟨a lot too much ~ going on —S.H.Adams⟩ **5 :** the topic of interested comment, conversation, or gossip ⟨it was the ~ not only of the town but of the country —Edward Bok⟩ ⟨by evening of that day the project had become the ~ . . . of the whole community —L.B.Salomon⟩ ⟨a pert young daughter . . . whose adventures were common ~ —L.C.Douglas⟩ **6 a :** an analysis or discussion formally prepared for public presentation **:** SPEECH, LECTURE ⟨at the first American Writers' Congress . . . he gave a ~ on "The Tradition of American Literature" —C.I.Glicksberg⟩ ⟨broadcasts a weekly inspirational ~ called "The Art of Living" —Bernard Kalb⟩ **b :** written analysis or discussion presented in an informal or conversational manner ⟨here is timeless old England . . . given in such lists and such ~ as only this writer can command —*N. Y. Herald Tribune Bk. Rev.*⟩ ⟨wrote a book called *Talks to Teachers*⟩ **7 :** communicative sounds or signs resembling or functioning as talk ⟨heard a scuffle and then a good deal of pheasant ~ up a hill among some huge boulders —Dillon Ripley⟩ ⟨lake ships use a whistle ~ that consists of 450 different signals —H.F.Unger⟩ ⟨occasional slang signs with which a deaf person . . . intersperses his ~ —J.S.Long⟩

talk·abil·i·ty \ˌtȯkəˈbiləd·ē\ *n* **:** the quality or state of being talkable

talk·able \ˈtȯkəbəl\ *adj* **1 :** capable of being talked about ⟨fishing is always a ~ subject⟩ **2 :** disposed to friendly conversation ⟨a ~ person has the gift . . . of being interesting, charming, delightful, in the most offhand and various modes of utterance —Henry Van Dyke⟩

talk around *vt* **:** to talk over ⟨*talked* most of them *around* . . . and kept the wagon train moving down the trail —A.M. Schlesinger b. 1917⟩

talk·a·thon \ˈtȯkəˌthän\ *n* -s [¹*talk* + *-athon* (as in *marathon*)] **:** a protracted session of public discussion or speech-making: as **a :** FILIBUSTER 2a ⟨had not yet decided whether they would conduct a ~ against the bill —*Wall Street Jour.*⟩ **b :** a campaigning device in which a candidate answers telephoned queries on radio or television for a period of many hours ⟨waged one of the most vigorous campaigns . . . through his radio ~*s* —Graham Hovey⟩

talk·a·tive \ˈtȯkəd·|iv, -ət|\ *adj* [¹*talk* + *-ative*] **:** given to or filled with talking **:** LOQUACIOUS, GARRULOUS ⟨was now, especially when fortified with liquor, as ~ as might be —W.M. Thackeray⟩ ⟨this is a ~ town and you are the last person it will spare —O.S.J.Gogarty⟩ ⟨for the first time in all these ~ weeks, people appeared to have nothing much to say, whether they approved of the decision or not —Mollie Panter-Downes⟩ ⟨a ~ book⟩

syn TALKATIVE, LOQUACIOUS, GARRULOUS, and VOLUBLE all apply to one given to talking; TALKATIVE usu. stresses only a readiness to engage in talk but may suggest a disposition to enjoy conversation ⟨told a number of his best Indian stories; for he was extremely *talkative* in man's society —W.M. Thackeray⟩ ⟨his wife was considerably younger . . . and *talkative* where he was monosyllabic —Dorothy Sayers⟩ LOQUACIOUS commonly implies fluency and ease in speech or an unusual talkativeness ⟨talks in a rapid and persuasive fashion (he is described as *loquacious* and good-natured) —*Current Biog.*⟩ ⟨the briskness of the mountain atmosphere, or some other cause, made everybody so *loquacious* —Nathaniel Hawthorne⟩ GARRULOUS usu. stresses an unchecked, rambling, often foolish, sometimes tedious, talkativeness ⟨this delightfully *garrulous* volume of memoirs —*Books of the Month*⟩ ⟨the Italian quarter, noisy, *garrulous*, good-natured, and vital —*Amer. Guide Series: Mass.*⟩ ⟨did most of the talking: he was a *garrulous* young man —T.O.Heggen⟩ ⟨the glories of silent appreciation were shattered by *garrulous* nothings —William Beebe⟩ ⟨a *garrulous* old man⟩ VOLUBLE suggests a free, easy, often seemingly endless loquacity ⟨a *voluble* man, given to telling anecdotes —Jean Stafford⟩ ⟨was to placate *voluble* voters who came in to complain —Sinclair Lewis⟩ ⟨was very *voluble*, repeating, with increased circumlocutory detail and reference to what he had said to Dick and Dick to him, the account he had originally given to the police —Dorothy Sayers⟩

talk·a·tive·ly \|əvlē\ *adv* **:** in a talkative manner **:** with much talking

talk·a·tive·ness \|ivnəs\ *n* -ES **:** the quality or state of being talkative

talk away *vt* **:** to consume or pass (as time) in talking ⟨*talking* the long night hours *away*⟩

talk back *vi* [¹*talk* + *back*, adv.] **:** to speak in answer usu. to a command or admonishment in a flippant or impertinent manner — usu. used with *to* ⟨her children *talk back* to her —*Saturday Rev.*⟩ ⟨a young man should not *talk back* to his superiors⟩ ⟨soldiers are taught not to *talk back* to superior officers⟩

talk-back \ˈ=,=\ *n* -s [fr. the phrase *talk back*, fr. ¹*talk* + *back*, adv.] **:** a two-way radio system providing esp. for one receiving instructions or directions to speak back to the instructor; *esp* **:** such a system set up between a broadcasting studio and its control room

talk down *vt* **1 :** to overcome or silence by superior argument or by loud and insistent talking ⟨burst out with attacks on the play . . . but they had their facts wrong and were *talked down* —Elmer Davis⟩ ⟨tries to argue back but his opponent vociferously *talks* him *down*⟩ **2 :** to disparage or belittle by talking ⟨endeavored to interrupt and then to *talk down* all hymns —Haldane Macfall⟩ ⟨in boosting his own products he never *talks* theirs *down*⟩ **3 :** to bring an airplane in for a blind landing by means of instructions radioed to the pilot by a ground observer who watches the approach of the craft by means of radar ⟨the ground control radar operator *talked* the . . . pilot *down* the landing approach to the runway —A.M. Johnston⟩ ~ *vi* **:** to speak in a condescending or oversimplified fashion with the false assumption that the listener is altogether ignorant of the matter involved — usu. used with *to* ⟨tired of being *talked down* to and are rightly insulted by being treated most of the time as . . . morons —John Mason Brown⟩ ⟨in teaching him he never *talked down* to him, indulged or flattered him; he treated him as a man and an equal —Elizabeth Goudge⟩

talked *past of* TALK

talk·ee-talk·ee \ˈtȯkēˈtȯkē\ *n* -s [West Indies Pidgin E, by modif. & redupl. fr. E ²*talk*] **1 :** broken speech; *esp* **:** corruption of speech due to unfamiliarity with its words, idioms, or pronunciation **2 :** idle chatter **:** PRATTLE

talk·er \ˈtȯkə(r)\ *n* -s [ME, fr. *talken* + *-er*] **:** one that talks; *specif* **:** a man trained and equipped to transmit orders or communications to the crew of a naval vessel by telephone or the PA

talkfest \ˈ=,=\ *n* -s [²*talk* + *-fest*] **1 :** an informal gathering for general talk or discussion **2 :** a protracted discussion or debate of a matter of public concern ⟨new ~*s* may break out in Congress over the measure to set up a private atomic industry —*Wall Street Jour.*⟩ ⟨the village branches of all these . . . organizations were called together for endless ~*s* —Joseph Alsop⟩

talk·ie \ˈtȯkē, -ki\ *n* -s [¹*talk* + *movie*] **:** a sound motion picture

talk in *vt* [¹*talk* + *in*] **:** to talk down (sense 3) ⟨had to *talk* me *in* when the . . . windshield iced over on one of my early rocket flights —Arthur Murray⟩

talking *pres part of* TALK

talking book *n* **:** a phonograph recording of a reading of a book or magazine that is designed chiefly for the use of the blind

talking chief *n* **:** a Polynesian and esp. a Samoan noble or title-holder who speaks and acts for a high chief in official, social, and economic matters

talking film *also* **talking picture** *n* **:** TALKIE

talking machine *n* **:** PHONOGRAPH

talking point *n* [*talking* (fr. gerund of ¹*talk*) + *point*] **1 :** a point, fact, or development that lends support for an argument or proposal ⟨provided the Revolutionary leaders in Philadelphia with a *talking point* in urging the establishment of a navy —*Amer. Guide Series: Maine*⟩ ⟨one of the greatest *talking points* in the argument —*Jour. of the History of Ideas*⟩ **2 :** a feature or argument of use in selling ⟨yarns . . . are the *talking points* of some interesting new fabrics —*Women's Wear Daily*⟩

talking-to \ˈ==,=\ *n* -s **:** DRESSING DOWN, LECTURE ⟨came down and gave me a tremendous *talking-to* —Rebecca West⟩ ⟨thought I would give him a *talking-to* in a nice way —Mary S. Watts⟩

talk out *vt* **1 :** FILIBUSTER ⟨the arguments by which it has been *talked out* of existence —Stephen Spender⟩ **2 :** to clarify or settle (as a problem) by oral expression or discussion ⟨meet . . . to discuss knotty problems and *talk* them *out* to a point of mutual understanding —C.E.Wilson⟩ ⟨the caseworker . . . encourages her to *talk out* her anxieties which have been critically restricting —Gertrude Samuels⟩

talk over *vt* **:** to change the mind or opinion of (a person) by talking ⟨is very good at *talking* opponents *over* to his viewpoint⟩

talks *pres 3d sing of* TALK, *pl of* TALK

talk up *vt* **:** to discuss in a favorable fashion **:** COMMEND, PROMOTE, ADVOCATE ⟨enthusiast had been *talking up* the game —F.S.Blanchard⟩ ⟨organizing crews to ring doorbells and *talk up* loans —N.M.Clark⟩ ⟨sponsoring and . . . *talking up* a so-called right-to-work bill —P.F.Healy⟩ ~ *vi* **:** to speak up plainly or directly ⟨if you do not talk down to a child, it will assuredly *talk up* to you —Wilson Follett⟩ ⟨*talks up* in the evening . . . talking bolder than he sometimes feels —Meridel Le Sueur⟩

talky \ˈtȯkē, -ki\ *adj* -ER/-EST [¹*talk* + *-y*] **1 :** given to talking **:** TALKATIVE ⟨a rather ~ lawyer . . . who likes to dilate upon the distinction between business and the professions —*New Yorker*⟩ **2 :** abounding in or containing too much talk: reaching a level no higher than talk ⟨when a play is ~, the talk must be purposeful, or it will be dull —M.M.Smith⟩ ⟨his book is bold and ~ and generally fuzzy, an excellent example of the axiom that good intentions are not enough —Walter Bernstein⟩

talky-talky \ˈ==ˈ==\ *adj* **:** TALKY 2 ⟨a rather loose, flat, *talky-talky* idiom —Dorothy Van Ghent⟩

¹tall \ˈtȯl\ *adj* -ER/-EST [ME, ready, handsome, brave, prob. fr. OE *getæl* quick, ready; akin to OHG *gizal* quick, Goth *untals* disobedient, uninstructed, *talzjan* to instruct — more at TALE] **1** *obs* **:** BRAVE, BOLD, COURAGEOUS ⟨spoke like a ~ fellow that respects his reputation —Shak.⟩ **2** *obs* **:** comely of feature **:** HANDSOME **3** *obs* **:** READY, QUICK, DEXTEROUS ⟨swear to the prince thou art a ~ fellow of thy hands —Shak.⟩ **4 a :** high in stature **:** of greater than average height among others of a kind or class ⟨was ~ — about six feet in height —H.N.Fowler⟩ ⟨the giraffe, ~*est* of animals⟩ **b :** of a specified stature or height ⟨stands five feet one inch ~ and weighs 97 pounds —*Current Biog.*⟩ **5 a :** of a considerable or great height **:** elevated above the ground **:** LOFTY ⟨the shade of the ~ young pines —Corey Ford⟩ ⟨the ~ clouds of deep July —C.G.Glover⟩ ⟨command of a ~ and gallant ship —S.E. Morison⟩ ⟨a ~ cavernous room —Ben Hecht⟩ ⟨hit a ~ fly to the outfield⟩ ⟨a ~ hill⟩ ⟨climbing a ~ fence⟩ **b :** of unusual length from bottom to top **:** LONG ⟨wears ~ hats to add to her height —*Current Biog.*⟩ ⟨a ~, cool lemonade —Ray Bradbury⟩ ⟨unusual page sizes, including ~ books —*Publishers' Weekly*⟩ **c :** of a distinctly higher growing variety or species of plant ⟨two types of lima beans — dwarf and ~ —*New Zealand Jour. of Agric.*⟩ **6 a :** large or formidable in amount, extent, or degree ⟨think £10,000 rather a ~ price —M.V.Reidy⟩ ⟨saving anything is a ~ order today —*advt*⟩ ⟨got to . . . do some ~ growing —*Adult Leadership*⟩ ⟨will have some ~ explaining to do —*New Republic*⟩ ⟨had to do some ~ riding to keep 'em together —Will James⟩ ⟨a ~ problem that has been a long time growing —H.R.Isaacs⟩ **b :** grandiloquent, high-flown, or affected in style or subject matter ⟨indulging in ~ talk about the vast mysteries of life —W.A.White⟩ ⟨~ talk, empty talk, the stuff dreams are made of —H.G.Evarts⟩ ⟨placing a number of ~, opaque words . . . betwixt your own and the reader's conception —Laurence Sterne⟩ **c :** unusual, incredible, or fanciful in conception or invention **:** IMPROBABLE ⟨~ tales they are . . . the man who shot five bears with one bullet —*Amer. Guide Series: Maine*⟩ ⟨the talk grew ~, and it only took a few makings to roll up a good story —Meridel Le Sueur⟩ ⟨spin ~ yarns about frontier life —E.S.Clifton⟩ **syn** see HIGH

²tall \"\ *adv* **:** in a tall manner ⟨the entrance makes you walk ~ —Claudia Cassidy⟩ ⟨renewing faith, we shall stand ~ again —Isabel Tudeen⟩ ⟨two books about fighting — rather savage persons talking ~ in both — but how different in manners —O.W.Holmes †1935⟩

tal·lage \ˈtalij\ *n* -s [ME *taillage, taliage, tallage*, fr. OF *taillage*, fr. *taillier* to cut, limit, tax + *-age* — more at TAILOR] **1 :** a toll, fee, or render paid by a feudal tenant to his lord apparently in commutation of a render in kind or services **2 :** an impost or due levied by a lord upon his tenants sometimes of definite amount according to local custom or the terms of tenure; *specif* **:** a tax or compulsory aid levied occas. by the Norman kings on their demesne lands and royal boroughs or cities

tal·la·has·see \ˌtaləˈhasē, -si\ *adj, usu cap* [fr. *Tallahassee*, capital of Florida] **:** of or from Tallahassee, the capital of Florida **:** of the kind or style prevalent in Tallahassee

tall·ate \ˈtäˌlāt\ *n* -s [*tall* (*oil*) + *-ate*] **:** a metallic soap made from tall oil

tall bellflower *n* **:** an annual or biennial herb (*Campanula americana*) of eastern No. America bearing long leafy spikes of blue or white flowers

tall blueberry *or* **tall bilberry** *n* **:** HIGHBUSH BLUEBERRY

tall blue lettuce *n* **:** a No. American annual or biennial herb (*Lactuca spicata*) bearing mostly pinnatifid leaves and small blue or white flower heads in large clusters

tallboy \ˈ=,=\ *n* [¹*tall* + *boy*] **1 :** a tall-stemmed drinking glass **2 a :** HIGHBOY **b :** CHEST-ON-CHEST **c** *Brit* **:** CLOTHESPRESS

tall buttercup *or* **tall crowfoot** *or* **tall field buttercup** *n* **:** a perennial European buttercup (*Ranunculus acris*) widely naturalized esp. in eastern No. America and having a short thick rootstock and long petioled rosette leaves that are 5- to 7-parted with linear toothed segments

tall case clock *n* **:** a tall narrow floor clock equipped with a pendulum, striking mechanism, chimes, and sometimes a device for showing the month, day, and phases of the moon — compare GRANDFATHER CLOCK

tall clock *n* **:** GRANDFATHER CLOCK

tall coneflower *n* **:** a No. American herb (*Rudbeckia laciniata*) from which the golden glow is derived

tall copy *n* **:** an esp. good copy of a book with ample margins at the tops and bottoms of the pages

tall cupflower *n* **:** a shrubby Chilean herb (*Nierembergia frutescens*) used as an ornamental and having bluish white tubular flowers

tall drink *n* **:** a mixed drink served in a tall glass

tal·le·ga·lane \ˈtaləgəˌlān\ *or* **tal·le·ga·lene** \-ˌlēn\ *or* **tal·ly·ga·lone** \-ˌlōn\ *n* -s [fr. native name in Australia] **:** a sand mullet (*Myxus elongatus*) or a related Australian fish

taller *comparative of* TALL

tallest *superlative of* TALL

tal·let \ˈtalət\ *n* -s [W *taflawd* loft, roof, fr. ML *tabulata* boarded platform, flooring, fr. fem. of L *tabulatus* floored, boarded, fr. *tabula* board, tablet + *-atus* -ate] **1** *dial Eng* **:** HAYLOFT **2** *dial Eng* **:** ATTIC

tall fescue *or* **tall fescue grass** *n* **:** MEADOW FESCUE

tall grama *n* **:** a No. American grama grass (*Bouteloua curtipendula*) having flower spikes arranged in slender one-sided racemes

tallgrass \ˈ=,=\ *n* **:** any of various grasses (as members of the genus *Andropogon*) that are characterized by tall stature and are prominent chiefly in periods and areas of abundant moisture — compare SHORTGRASS

tallied *past of* TALLY

tallies *pl of* TALLY, *pres 3d sing of* TALLY

tal·lin *or* **tal·linn** \ˈtalən, ˈtäl-\ *adj, usu cap* [fr. *Tallin* or *Tallinn*, capital of Estonia] **:** of or from Tallin, the capital of Estonia **:** of the kind or style prevalent in Tallin

tall·ish \ˈtȯlish, -lēsh\ *adj* **:** somewhat or rather tall

tal·lith *or* **tal·lit** *or* **tal·lis** *also* **ta·lith** *or* **ta·lit** *or* **ta·lis** \ˈtäləs, ˈtal-, ˈtal-, -ət(h)\ *n, pl* **tal·li·thim** *or* **tal·li·tim** *or* **tal·li·sim** \ˌtäləˈsēm, -ˈt(h)ēm\ *or* **tal·lei·sim** \tä'lāsəm\ *also* **ta·li·thim** *or* **ta·li·tim** *or* **ta·li·sim** \ˌtäləˈsēm, -ˈt(h)ēm\ *or* **ta·lei·sim** *or* **ta·lai·sim** \tä'lāsəm\ [Heb *ṭallīth* cover, sheet, cloak, fr. Aram. *ṭĕlal* to cover] **:** a woolen or silk rectangular or square shawl with fringes at the 4 corners and black or blue stripes at the ends that is worn over the head or round the shoulders by orthodox and conservative Jewish men and boys over 13 usu. during the morning prayers — called also *prayer scarf;* see ZIZITH; compare ARBA KANFOTH

tall larkspur *n* **:** a slender herb (*Delphinium exaltatum*) of the central U.S. bearing a dense raceme of blue or purple flowers

tall meadow rue *n* **:** a meadow rue (*Thalictrum polygamum*) bearing white or purplish flowers

tall·ness *n* -ES **:** the quality or state of being tall

tall oat grass *or* **tall meadow oat** *n* **:** a perennial Eurasian grass (*Arrhenatherum elatius*) resembling the oat and introduced into No. America for use as forage esp. in moist soils

tall oil \ˈtäl-\ *n* [part trans. of G *tallöl*, part trans. of Sw *tallolja*, fr. *tall* pine (akin to ON *thöll* young pine tree) + *olja* oil — more at TAILOR] **:** a by-product from the manufacture of chemical pulp that is obtained from the black liquor as a dark odorous liquid before refining, that contains principally resin acids and fatty acids (as oleic acid and linoleic acid) with some sterols and other nonacid compounds, and that is used chiefly in making paint, varnish, and other coatings, driers and drying oils, emulsions, lubricants, and soaps

tal·lo·te \tä(l)ˈyōd·ē\ *n* -s [Sp *talayote*, a kind of gourd, fr. Nahuatl *tlalayotli*, fr. *tlalli* earth + *ayotli* gourd] **:** CHAYOTE

¹tal·low \ˈta(ˌ)lō, -lə; -ləw *or* -ˌlō+V\ *n* -s *often attrib* [ME *talgh, talow;* akin to MD *talch* tallow, ON *tólgr*] **1 :** animal fat **:** SUET **2 a :** the rendered fat of cattle and sheep that is white and almost tasteless when pure, that is in general harder than grease with a titer of above 40°C, that is composed of glycerides of fatty acids containing a large proportion of palmitic acid and stearic acid, and that is used chiefly in making soap, glycerol, margarine, candles, and lubricants **b :** any of various fats (as from other animals or from plants) resembling beef and mutton tallow — compare WAX MYRTLE

²tallow \"\ *vb* -ED/-ING/-S [ME *taloghen, talowen*, fr. *talgh, talow* tallow] *vt* **:** to grease or smear with tallow ~ *vi* **:** to produce or yield tallow

tallow bayberry *or* **tallow shrub** *n* **:** WAX MYRTLE

tallow drop *n* **:** a style of cutting a precious stone so that one or both sides are dome-shaped

tallow-faced \ˈ=,=\ *adj* **:** having a sickly pale or yellow complexion

tal·low·i·ness \ˈtaləw|ēnəs, -lō|, |in-\ *n* -ES **:** the quality or state of being tallowy

tallow nut *n* **1 :** FALSE SANDALWOOD **2 :** the fruit or seed of the false sandalwood

tallow oil *n* **:** an animal oil obtained by pressing tallow and used chiefly as a lubricant esp. when mixed with minerals oils — compare OLEO OIL, OLEOSTEARIN

tallow pot *n* **:** a locomotive fireman

tallow-top \ˈ==,=\ *n* **:** a precious stone cut rounded in front and flat in the back — **tallow-topped** \ˈ==,=\ *adj*

tallow tree *n* **1 :** CHINESE TALLOW TREE **2 :** CANDLENUT 2

tallowweed \ˈ==,=\ *n* **:** an annual herb (*Actinea linearifolia*) of the family Compositae used to fatten cattle in the southwestern U.S.

tallowwood \ˈ==,=\ *n* **1 a :** an Australian gum tree (*Eucalyptus microcorys*) having stringy bark and hard wood and containing an oily principle and a gum rich in tannin **b :** a related tree (*E. affinis*) **2 :** FALSE SANDALWOOD

tal·lowy \ˈtaləw|ē, -lō|, |i\ *adj* [ME *talwy*, fr. *talow* tallow + *-y*] **1 :** of the nature of or like the substance of tallow **:** SEBACEOUS **2 :** similar to tallow in color or complexion ⟨the moon . . . throwing its ~ light along the lawns —Richard Church⟩ ⟨behind his ~ mask and goggle eyes —F.M.Ford⟩ **3 :** CAPPY

tall redtop *n* **:** a No. American perennial grass (*Triodia flava*) with spreading purplish panicles

tall sisymbrium *n* **:** TUMBLE MUSTARD

tall speedwell *n* **:** CULVER'S ROOT

tall thistle *n* **:** a coarse prickly herb (*Cirsium altissimum*) of the eastern U.S. with large usu. solitary heads of purplish flowers

tall timber *n* **:** the rural or sparsely settled districts **:** BACKWOODS ⟨a prize contest that seemed very corny to sophisticates but . . . wowed booklovers in the *tall timber* —Bennett Cerf⟩

tall wheatgrass *n* **:** a European grass (*Agropyron elongatum*) introduced into the U.S. as a pasture and forage crop

tall white lettuce *n* **:** a tall perennial herb (*Prenanthes alba*) with large panicles of drooping greenish yellow or yellowish white flower heads

tallwood *var of* TALWOOD

¹tal·ly \ˈtalē, -li\ *n* -ES [ME *taly, talye*, fr. ML *talea, tallia*, fr. L *talea* stick, twig, cutting — more at TAILOR] **1 :** a visible device for recording or accounting esp. business transactions: as **a** : a usu. square wooden rod or stick notched with marks representing numbers and split lengthwise through the notches so that each of two bargaining parties may have a record of a transaction and of the amount of money due or paid; *specif* : such a cloven stick formerly used by the English Exchequer as a record of government transactions **b** : any of various primitive devices or wooden sticks used for marking or counting **c** : any of various bookkeeping forms or sheets serving to record or check accounts, sales, or shipments **d** : a mechanical counter held in the hand and operated with a button or lever **e** : a tag or label used to mark or classify plants, trees, or goods **f** : a card or folder that designates a bridge player's starting position and provides space for recording his score **2 a** : a reckoning or recorded account of something ⟨a daily ~ of accidents should be kept —Theodore Loveless⟩ ⟨game warden keeps ~ on the creel —*Amer. Guide Series: Conn.*⟩ ⟨been out on the range . . . helping with the fall ~ —W.V.T. Clark⟩ ⟨a ~ of mixed blessings —Dixon Wecter⟩ **b** : a score or point made (as in a game) ⟨a record ~ of 263 for 72 holes —*Current Biog.*⟩ ⟨drove in the first . . . ~ in the opening inning —*N.Y. Times*⟩ ⟨the ~ coming on a 15-yard pass —*N.Y. Times*⟩ **c** : a record of the number of pieces and the grades of lumber **3 a** : a half, part, or entity that agrees or corresponds to an opposite or companion member : COMPLEMENT, COUNTERPART ⟨one twin is the ~ of the other⟩ **b** : the state or fact of correspondence or agreement ⟨will find again the ~ between proportion and thought —*Edinburgh Rev.*⟩ **4 a** : a usu. specified number or lot taken as a whole : TOTE **b** : a number or division used as a unit of computation **c** : the last of a specified unit or number **5** *dial Eng* : COMPANIONATE MARRIAGE 2

²**tally** \"\ *vb* -ED/-ING/-ES *vt* **1 a** : to mark (as a number) on or as if on a tally : TABULATE, RECORD ⟨~ the election returns as they are reported⟩ ⟨*tallied* a deficit of . . . $1000 —*Future*⟩ ⟨*tallies* some 10,000 automobile miles a year —*Time*⟩ ⟨ideas and methods . . . impossible to ~ on a balance sheet —*Nation's Business*⟩ **b** : to list or check off (a cargo, load, or shipment) by items ⟨the mates supervising the loading and ~*ing* the cargo⟩ **c** : to supply (a bale or shipment) with a label or distinguishing mark **d** : to grade and record the number of pieces (as of lumber) **e** : to register or cause to be registered (a point or score) in a game or contest ⟨some means of ~*ing* the scores —C.J.Erasmus⟩ ⟨~*ing* 269 for 72 holes and prize money —*Current Biog.*⟩ ⟨*tallied* five TD's and two field goals —Eddie Beachler⟩ **2** : to make a count of (something) : RECKON, TOTAL ⟨~ your expenses for the day —Winston Brebner⟩ ⟨can ~ among his followers . . . three or four democratic senators —R.L.Neuberger⟩ ⟨those men are waiting to ~ . . . cattle —S.E.White⟩ ⟨try to ~ the bloody price exacted for this crime —O.T.Lanham⟩ — sometimes used with *out* or *up* ⟨when we *tallied* out the herd, every cow was counted —S.E.Fletcher⟩ ⟨~ up the *for* and *against* —C.C.Furnas⟩ ⟨when the intelligence reports were finally *tallied* up —Lou Stoumen⟩ **3** : to cause to correspond or complement : MATCH ⟨the far-fetched imagery, the insistent anecdote . . . are *tallied* by an equal amount of pains and forethought —Sacheverell Sitwell⟩ ~ *vi* **1 a** : to make a tally by or as if by tabulating a number or record ⟨if an error is made in ~*ing*, the results of computations will be wrong —Lester Guest⟩ ⟨at that time they *tallied* close to $110 billion —W.H.Anderson⟩ ⟨the quarterly and annual ~*ing* of payrolls —A.J.Caruso⟩ **b** : to register a point or score in a game or contest ⟨*tallied* on a 34-yard burst through tackle —*N.Y. Times*⟩ ⟨the first time . . . over a five-year span that they had not *tallied* —Louis Effrat⟩ **2** : to balance or correspond in complementary fashion ⟨calculated values of the centripetal force and the gravitational force did not ~ —S.F.Mason⟩ ⟨so completely did the two ghosts . . . ~ in their particularity —Sacheverell Sitwell⟩ — often used with *with* ⟨representation must ~ with thing represented —R.M.Weaver⟩ ⟨this family doctrine *tallied* so little with the manifest circumstances —H.G.Wells⟩ **syn** see AGREE

³**tally** \"\ *vt* -ED/-ING/-ES [origin unknown] : to haul aft (as a sheet)

tally board *n* **1** : a board used as a tally sheet **2** : a board attached to the tail block of a rope sent out to a ship in distress containing instructions for using the apparatus

tally clerk *n* : TALLYMAN

tallygalone *var of* TALLEGALANE

¹**tal·ly·ho** \ˌtalēˈhō\ *n* -S [prob. fr. F *taïaut*, cry used to excite hounds in deer hunting, fr. OF *taho, tielau*] **1 a** : the cry sounded by hunters upon sighting the fox as it breaks from cover — usu. used interjectionally **b** : a call transmitted by radio by a fighter pilot upon sighting an enemy plane — usu. used interjectionally **2** [after the *Tally-ho*, name of a coach formerly plying between London and Birmingham] : a four-in-hand coach **3** : a dark grayish yellowish brown that is very slightly deeper than lama or bison and slightly lighter than Congo

²**tallyho** \ˈ=ˌ=ˌ=\ *vi* -ED/-ING/-S : to utter the cry *tallyho* ⟨our combat patrols ~*ed* on the 200 . . . planes —Fletcher Pratt⟩

tal·ly·man \ˈtalēmən, -lim-\ *n, pl* **tallymen** [¹*tally* + *man*] **1** *Brit* : one who keeps a tally shop or sells goods on the installment plan **2** : one who tallies, checks, or keeps an account or record; *esp* : a worker who keeps a tally of information (as of quantity or weight) needed for records concerning production, shipping, or receipt of goods

tally sheet *also* **tally card** *n* : a sheet on which a tally or account is kept often in tabular form

tal·ly·wag \ˈtalēˌwag\ *n* -S [origin unknown] : a sea bass (*Centropristes striatus*) of the Atlantic coast

tal·ma \ˈtalmə\ *n* -S [after François-Joseph *Talma* †1826 Fr. actor] : a large cape or short full cloak of the 19th century

tal·mi gold \ˈtalmē-\ *n* [G *talmigold*] : a brass made to resemble gold and sometimes gold-plated and used for trinkets or costume jewelry

tal·mouse \talˈmüs\ *n, pl* **talmous·es** \-üs(əz)\ [F] : a pastry shell with a filling of cheese

tal·mud \ˈtälˌmu̇d, ˈtalməd\ *n* -S *usu cap* [LHeb *talmūdh*, lit., instruction, fr. Heb *lāmadh* to learn] : the authoritative body of Jewish law and tradition developed on the basis of the scriptural law after the closing of the Pentateuchal text about 400 B.C., incorporated in the Hebrew Mishnah and the Aramaic Gemara, and represented in one edition completed in Palestine in the 4th century A.D. and another longer and more authoritative edition completed in Babylon in the 5th century A.D. — see AMORA, SABORA; compare HAGGADA, HALAKAH

tal·mud·ic \(ˈ)tal¦m(y)üdik, (ˈ)täl-, (ˈ)tál-, -məd-, -mu̇d-, -dēk\ *also* **tal·mud·i·cal** \-dəkəl, -dēk-\ *adj, often cap* **1** : of, relating to, or characteristic of the Talmud ⟨~ literature⟩ ⟨~ studies⟩ ⟨~ lore⟩ **2** : of or relating to the period in which the Talmud was compiled ⟨the ~ age⟩ ⟨~ sages⟩

tal·mud·ism \ˈtälˌmu̇ˌdizəm, ˈtalməˌd-\ *n* -S *often cap* [*talmud* + *-ism*] : the teachings of the Talmud; *also* : adherence to such teachings

tal·mud·ist \-ˌdəst\ *n* -S *often cap* [*talmud* + *-ist*] **1** : one of the compilers of the Talmud **2** : one who is versed in, accepts, or practices the teachings and law of the Talmud

talmud torah *n, pl* **talmud torahs** *usu cap both Ts* [NHeb *talmūdh tōrāh*, lit., study of or instruction in the Torah] : a communal religious school for instruction of children in Hebrew, Scriptures, Talmud, and Jewish history —compare ²HEDER

ta·lo \ˈtä(ˌ)lō\ *n* -S [Samoan; akin to Tahitian *taro*] : TARO

talo- *comb form* [L *talus* ankle, anklebone] : astragalar and ⟨*talo*fibular⟩ ⟨*talo*tibial⟩

tal·on \ˈtalən\ *n* -S [ME, fr. MF, heel, spur, fr. (assumed) VL *talon-, talo*, fr. L *talus* ankle, anklebone, heel] **1 a** *obs* : the hinder part of a hoof **b** : the claw of an animal; *esp* : the claw of a bird of prey — usu. used in pl. ⟨the hawk seizes its prey in its sharp ~*s*⟩ **c** : a finger of the human hand ⟨led . . . around the contorted wrist to a sinewy ~ that had been a thumb —Earle Birney⟩ **2** : a part or object shaped like or suggestive of a heel or claw: as **a** : an ogee molding — see INVERTED TALON **b** : the shoulder of the bolt of a lock on which the key acts to shoot the bolt **c** : the crushing region of the crown of an upper molar posterior to the trigon — compare TRITUBERCULY **3 a** : cards laid aside in a pile in a game of solitaire that may or may not be used again in the game **b** : STOCK 17a **4** : a certificate attached to various bonds and exchangeable for an extra set of coupons

talon 1b of a hawk

ta·lo·navicular \¦tā(ˌ)lō+\ *adj* [*talo-* + *navicular*] : of or relating to the talus and the navicular of the tarsus

tal·oned \-nd\ *adj* [*talon* + *-ed*] : having or provided with talons ⟨these creatures with ~ fingers fought —Hugh Walpole⟩

ta·lon·ic acid \təˈlänik-\ *n* [ISV *talon-* (irreg. fr. *galactonic acid*) + *-ic*; orig. formed as G *talonsäure*] : a crystalline acid $HOCH_2(CHOH)_4COOH$ formed by oxidation of talose but more readily obtained by heating galactonic acid with pyridine

tal·on·id \ˈtalənəd\ *n* -S [*talon* + *-id* (structural element)] : the crushing region of a lower molar tooth usu. better developed than the corresponding talon

tal·ose \ˈtaˌlōs\ *n* -S [ISV *tal-* (in *talonic acid*) + *-ose*] : a rare sugar $C_6H_{12}O_6$ of the aldohexose class obtained indirectly from galactose or formed by reduction of talonic acid

tal·pa \ˈtalpə\ *n, cap* [NL, fr. L, mole] : a genus (the type of the family Talpidae) that comprises the common Old World moles

tal·pa·co·ti \ˌtalpəˈkōd·ē\ *n* -S [NL, of AmerInd origin] : a So. American ground dove (*Columbigallina talpacoti*)

tal·pa·ta·te *or* **tal·pe·ta·te** \ˌtälpəˈtäd·ē\ *n* -S [AmerSp *tepetate, talpetate*, fr. Nahuatl *tepetatl*, fr. *tetl* stone + *petatl* mat] **1** : a rock of superficial origin formed by the cementing action of calcium carbonate on sand, soil, or volcanic ash and equivalent in part to caliche or calcrete **2** : rather poor thin soil consisting of partly decomposed volcanic ash more or less consolidated

talpi- *comb form* [L *talpa*] : mole ⟨*talpi*form⟩

¹**tal·pid** \ˈtalpəd\ *adj* [NL *Talpidae*] : of or relating to the Talpidae

²**talpid** \"\ *n* -S : a mole of the family Talpidae

tal·pi·dae \ˈtalpəˌdē\ *n pl, cap* [NL, fr. *Talpa*, type genus + *-idae*] : a family of insectivores (superfamily Soricoidea) including all moles except the golden and marsupial moles — see TALPA

tal·poid \ˈtalˌpȯid\ *adj* [NL *Talpa* + E *-oid*] : like or related to the Talpidae

tal qual \ˈtälˈkwäl\ *abbr* [L *talis qualis* such as] just as they come

tal·tush·tun·tu·de \ˌtältu̇shtu̇nˈtüdā\ *n, pl* **taltushtuntude** *or* **taltushtuntudes** *usu cap* **1** : an Athapaskan people on Galise creek, a tributary of the Rogue river in southwestern Oregon **2** : a member of the Taltushtuntude people

ta·luk \täˈlu̇k\ *or* **ta·lu·ka** *also* **ta·loo·ka** \-kə\ *n* -S [Urdu *ta'alluq* estate, fr. Ar] **1** : an hereditary estate in India **2** : a collectorate or administrative subdivision comprising an Indian revenue district

¹**ta·lus** \ˈtāləs\ *n* -ES [F, fr. L *talutium* slope indicating presence of gold under the soil, prob. of Iberian origin] **1** : a slope formed esp. by an accumulation of rock debris **2** : rock debris at the base of a cliff or slope chiefly as the result of gravitational roll or slide; *also* : a mass of such debris

²**talus** \"\ *n, pl* **ta·li** \-ā,lī\ [NL, fr. L, ankle, anklebone, heel] **1** : the astragalus of man bearing the weight of the body and with the tibia and fibula forming the ankle joint **2 a** : the entire ankle esp. of man **b** : a part in birds and insects corresponding to the ankle

talus glacier *n* [¹*talus*] : ROCK STREAM

tal·wood *or* **tall·wood** \ˈtȯlˌwu̇d\ *n* [ME, part trans., part modif. of OF *bois de tail*] : wood cut up for firewood

ta·lysh·in \təˈlishən\ *or* **ta·lyshe** \-shē\ *n, pl* **talyshin** *or* **talyshins** *or* **talyshe** *or* **talyshes** *usu cap* **1 a** : a people of the region around Lenkoran, Azerbaidzhan **b** : a member of such people **2** : a dialect related to Talishi

tam \ˈtam, -aa(ə)m\ *n* -S [by shortening] : TAM-O'-SHANTER

tam·abil·i·ty *or* **tame·abil·i·ty** \ˌtāməˈbiləd·ē\ *n* : capacity for being tamed

tam·able *or* **tame·able** \ˈtāməbəl\ *adj* : capable of being tamed — **tam·able·ness** *n* -ES

tamachek *usu cap, var of* TAMASHEK

ta·ma·le \təˈmälē, -mál-, -li\ *n* -S [MexSp *tamales*, pl. of *tamal* tamale, fr. Nahuatl *tamalli*] : ground meat seasoned with chili or other filling, rolled up in cornmeal dough, wrapped in corn husks, and steamed

ta·man·dua \təˈmandəˌwä, -njə-, ˌ=ˈ==ˈwə\ *n* [Pg *tamanduá*, fr. Tupi, lit., ant-catcher, fr. *taixi* ant + *mondé* to catch] **1** -S **a** : a prehensile-tailed arboreal anteater (*Tamandua tetradactyla*) of Central and So. America that is smaller than the ant bear and much more variable in marking, being sometimes gray striped with black and sometimes straw-colored and unstriped **b** : an edentate anteater **2** *cap* [NL, fr. Pg *tamanduá*] : a genus comprising the tamandua

ta·ma·noir \ˌtamənˈwär\ *n* -S [F, of Cariban origin; akin to Galibi *tamanoa* ant bear, Acawai *tamanowa*; akin to Tupi *tamanduá* tamandua] : ANT BEAR

ta·ma·nu \təˈmä(ˌ)nü\ *n* -S [Tahitian & Samoan] **1** : POON **2** : a heavy green resin derived from the poon

tam·ar \ˈtamə(r)\ *adj* [Ar *tamr* dried date] : of, relating to, or constituting the last of four recognized stages in the ripening of the date in which it is dried sufficiently to prevent spoiling — compare KHALAL, KIMRI, RUTAB

ta·ma·ra \təˈmärə\ *n* -S [origin unknown] : a powdered mixture of cinnamon, cloves, and coriander, anise, and fennel seeds used as a condiment esp. in Italy

tam·a·rack \ˈtaməˌrak\ *n* -S [origin unknown] **1 a** (1) : any of several American larches; *esp* : a larch (*Larix laricina*) of northern U.S., Canada, and Alaska — called also *American larch, black larch* (2) : the wood of the tamarack **b** or **tamarack pine** : LODGEPOLE PINE **2** : MUMMY BROWN 2b

ta·ma·rau \ˌtaməˈrau̇\ or **tim·a·rau** \ˌtim-\ *also* **tam·a·rao** \ˌtaməˈrau̇\ *n* -S [Tag *tamaráw, timaraw*] : a small dark hairy water buffalo (*Bubalus mindorensis* or *Anoa mindorensis*) of the Philippine island of Mindora

tam·a·ri·ca·ce·ae \ˌtamərəˈkāsēˌē\ *n pl, cap* [NL, fr. *Tamaric-, Tamarix*, type genus + *-aceae*] : a family of chiefly desert and often heathlike shrubs or trees (order Parietales) widely distributed in warm regions and having narrow entire leaves and flowers with five stamens and a one-celled ovary — **tam·a·ri·ca·ceous** \¦==¦==¦kāshəs\ *adj*

tam·a·rin \ˈtamərən, -ˌran\ *n* -S [F, fr. Galibi] : any of numerous small So. American marmosets of the genus *Leontocebus* having elongate canine teeth, silky fur, and long nonprehensile tail, and running about like squirrels rather than leaping from branch to branch — see PINCHE, SILKY TAMARIN

tam·a·rind \ˈtamərənd, -ˌrind\ *also* **tam·a·rin·do** \ˌ==ˈrin(ˌ)dō\ *n* -S [Sp & Pg *tamarindo*, fr. Ar *tamr hindī*, lit., Indian date, fr. *tamr* dried date + *hindī* of India, fr. *Hind* India; akin to OPers *Hindu* India — more at INDIA] **1 a** : a widely cultivated tropical tree (*Tamarindus indica*) of the family Leguminosae with hard yellowish wood that is used in turnery and pinnate leaves and red-striped yellow flowers that are eaten in India and are also used as mordants in dyeing **b** : the fruit of the tamarind tree that has an acid pulp used for preserves and made into a cooling laxative drink and seeds that are cooked and also ground into meal **2** : any of various trees resembling the tamarind ⟨bastard ~⟩ ⟨native ~⟩

tam·a·risk \ˈtamərəsk, -ˌrisk\ *n* -S [ME *tamarisc*, fr. LL *tamariscus*, fr. L *tamaric-, tamarix*] : a shrub or tree of the genus *Tamarix*

tamarisk family *n* : TAMARICACEAE

tamarisk gall *n* : a gall that is formed on a tamarisk (*Tamarix articulata*) and yields tannin

tam·a·rix \ˈtaməˌriks\ *n* [NL, fr. L, tamarisk] **1** *cap* : a large genus (the type of the family Tamaricaceae) of shrubs or small trees that are natives of the eastern Mediterranean region and tropical Asia and have minute scalelike leaves and feathery racemes of small white or pinkish flowers with free stamens and 3 to 4 styles **2** -ES : any shrub or tree of the genus *Tamarix*

tamarix family *n* : TAMARICACEAE

tam·a·ru·gite \ˌtaməˈrüˌgīt\ *n* -S [G *tamarugit*, fr. *tamarugal* (fr. Pampa del *Tamarugal*, desert plateau in northern Chile, its locality) + *-it* -ite] : a mineral $NaAl(SO_4)_2.6H_2O$ that is a hydrous sulfate of sodium and aluminum isostructural with amarillite

ta·mas \ˈtəməs\ *n* -ES [Skt, darkness — more at TEMERITY] : the inertia or dullness that constitutes one of the three gunas of Sankhya philosophy — compare RAJAS, SATTVA

tam·a·shek *also* **tam·a·chek** \ˈtaməˌshek\ *n* -S *usu cap* : the Berber language of the Tuareg people spoken in the central and southern Sahara

ta·mau·li·pec \təˈmau̇ləˌpek\ *n, pl* **tamaulipec** *or* **tamaulipecs** *usu cap* **1 a** : an Indian people of northeastern Mexico **b** : a member of such people **2** : a Coahuiltecan language of the Tamaulipec people

tambac *var of* TOMBAC

tam·ber \ˈtambə(r), ˈtaam-\ *n* -S [by alter.] : TIMBRE

¹**tam·bo** \ˈtam(ˌ)bō\ *n* -S *often cap* [short for ¹*tambourine*] : an end man in a minstrel show who often plays the tambourine — compare BONES

²**tam·bo** \", ˈtäm-\ *n* -S [AmerSp, fr. Quechua *tánpu* army camp, storehouse, inn] **1** : an Inca inn or way station on the highroads of ancient Peru **2** : a wayside tavern in modern Peru, Ecuador, and Bolivia

tam·boo·kie \tamˈbu̇kē, -bu̇kē\ *also* **tambookie thorn** *n* -S [Afrik *tamboekie*, fr. *Tamboekie* Kaffir of the Tembu tribe, prob. fr. *Tamboe* Tembu + *-kie* (fr. D *-kje*, dim. suffix)] **1** : a southern African shrub or small tree (*Erythrina acanthocarpa*) with spiny fruit **2** : the extremely light wood of the tambookie

tambookie grass \"-\ *or* **ta·bucki grass** \təˈbu̇kē-\ *n, usu cap T* [trans. of Afrik *tamboekiegras*] : any of several southern African grasses; *esp* : a grass (*Sorghum verticilliflorum*) growing to a height of six or eight feet and used for thatching and in making paper

tam·bor \ˈtamˌbȯ(ə)r, ˌ=ˈ=\ *n* -S [Sp, drum, fr. Ar *ṭanbūr*] **1** : any of several puffers **2** : a red rockfish (*Sebastodes ruberrimus*) of the Pacific coast

tam·bo·ri·to \ˌtämbəˈrēd·(ˌ)ō\ *n* -S [AmerSp, lit., little drum, fr. Sp, dim. of *tambor* drum] : a modern Panamanian couple dance with intricate footwork

¹**tam·bour** \ˈtamˌbu̇(ə)r, ˌ=ˈ=\ *n* -S *often attrib* [F, drum, fr. MF, fr. Ar *ṭanbūr*, modif. (influenced by *ṭunbūr*, a lute) of Per *tabīr*] **1** *also* **tam·bor** \-bȯ(ə)r\ **a** : ¹DRUM 1 **b** : DRUMMER 1 **2 a** : ¹DRUM 4a(1) **b** : ¹BELL 5e **c** : a circular wall (as one supporting a dome) **d** : a sloping buttress or projection (as in court tennis or fives) for deflecting a ball that strikes it **3 a** : an embroidery frame; *esp* : a set of two interlocking hoops between which cloth is stretched before stitching **b** : the embroidery made on a tambour frame; *esp* : embroidery consisting of looped stitches similar to chain stitch and worked with a fine hook **c** : TAMBOUR LACE **4** : a shallow metallic cup or drum with a thin elastic membrane supporting a writing lever used singly or in groups to transmit and register arterial pulsations, blood pressure, respiratory movements, peristaltic contractions, and other slight motions (as of speech) **5** : a rolling top or front (as of a desk) composed of narrow half-round strips of wood glued on canvas

²**tambour** \"\ *vb* -ED/-ING/-S *vt* : to embroider (cloth) with tambour ~ *vi* : to work at a tambour frame — **tam·bour·er** \-ūrə(r)\ *n* -S

tam·bou·ra *or* **tam·bu·ra** \tamˈbu̇rə\ *n* -S [Per *ṭambūra*] : an Asiatic musical instrument of the lute type but without frets used only to produce a drone accompaniment to singing

tambour clock *n* : a clock enclosed in an upright drum-shaped case with an extended base

tambour clock

tambour de basque \-dəˈ=\ *n* [F, lit., Basque drum] : TAMBOURIN 1a

tam·bou·rin \ˈtambərən, ¦==¦ran\ *n* -S [Prov, dim. of *tambour* drum, fr. Ar *ṭanbūr*] **1 a** : a long narrow drum used in Provence **b** : an Egyptian bottle-shaped drum **2 a** : a lively old Provençal dance orig. with tambourin accompaniment **b** : music written for or in the quick duple measure of a tambourin dance usu. with a drone bass on the tonic or dominant

¹**tam·bou·rine** \¦tambə¦rēn, ¦taam-\ *n* -S [MF *tambourin*, dim. of *tambour* drum — more at TAMBOUR] **1** : a small drum; *esp* : a shallow one-headed drum with loose metallic disks or jingles at the sides that is played by shaking, striking with the hand, or rubbing with the thumb : TIMBREL **2** : a mostly white African wild dove (*Tympanistria tympanistria*) whose wings and tail are black-tipped and which has a distinctive resonant note

tambourines

²**tambourine** \"\ *vi* -ED/-ING/-S : to play on the tambourine

tam·bou·rin·ist \-nəst\ *n* -S : one who plays on the tambourine

tambour lace *n* : a lace made in a tambour frame by embroidering or darning designs on machine-made net

tam·bu·ti *also* **tam·boo·ti** \tamˈbüd·ē\ *or* **tam·bo·ti** \-bōd·ē\ *n* -S [Afrik *tamboetie*, fr. *Tamboe* Tembu + *-tie*, dim. suffix] : a southern and eastern African deciduous tree (*Spirostachys africanus*) of the family Euphorbiaceae with foliage that turns red in fall and hard slightly fragrant wood that is golden yellow in the sapwood and black in the heartwood and is used locally for furniture and cabinetwork

tam·bov \(ˈ)tam¦bȯf, -ȯv\ *adj, usu cap* [fr. *Tambov*, U.S.S.R.] : of or from the city of Tambov, U.S.S.R. : of the kind or style prevalent in Tambov

tam·bu·rel·lo \ˌtämbəˈre(ˌ)lō, ˌtam-\ *n* -S [It, lit., little drum, dim. of *tamburo* drum, fr. Ar *ṭanbūr* — more at TAMBOUR] : a modification of pallone that is played with a ball and rackets like battledores

tam·bu·rit·za *also* **tam·bou·rit·za** \tämˈbu̇rətsə\ *n* -S [Serb *tamburitza*, fr. *tambur* drum, fr. It *tamburo*] : one of a family of plucked stringed musical instruments of Yugoslavia similar to the guitar in shape and the mandolin in sound

tam·bu·ro·ne \ˌtämbəˈrōnē\ *n* -S [It, lit., large drum, aug. of *tamburo* drum] : BASS DRUM

¹**tame** \ˈtām\ *adj* -ER/-EST [ME, fr. OE *tam*; akin to OFris *tam* tame, OHG *zam*, ON *tamr*; all fr. a prehistoric verb represented by OE *temian* to tame, OHG *zemmen*, ON *temja*, Goth *gatamjan*, L *domare*, Gk *damnanai* to tame, Skt *damayati* he tames] **1 a** : reduced from a state of native wildness : made tractable and useful to man : DOMESTICATED ⟨~ cattle gone wild —Hart Stilwell⟩ **b** : maintained or displayed to serve the purposes of another : permitted to exist as a harmless specimen of its kind ⟨our ~ firebrand —Dorothy Sayers⟩ ⟨the new ~ sultan —Janet Flanner⟩ **c** : brought under control : HARNESSED ⟨on the day the control structures are completed . . . the mighty Mississippi should be a pretty ~ and useful river —A.W.Baum⟩ **2 a** : not having or showing the qualities (as ferocity or shyness) characteristic of a wild state ⟨the chipmunks . . . are so ~ they beg for food —*Amer. Guide Series: Calif.*⟩ **b** : made docile and submissive : MEEK, SUBDUED ⟨no colt will bear it, or he's a ~ beast —George Meredith⟩ **3** : CULTIVATED ⟨the yield of ~ blueberries runs from 150 to 1200 quarts per acre —J.M.White⟩ **4** : lacking in spirit, zest, or interest : DULL, MILD, INSIPID ⟨struck out for himself and refused to live the ~ easy life —Frank Sargeson⟩ ⟨a little ~ wood which rambled up from the village —Audrey Barker⟩ ⟨a ~ book⟩ ⟨a ~ campaign⟩

syn SUBDUED, SUBMISSIVE: TAME, in relation to persons and their actions and utterances, suggests domination by others, often with voluntary surrender, or a marked docility and timidity, and lack of independence, assertiveness, exuberance, or wildness ⟨the *tamest*, the most abject creatures that we can possibly imagine: mild, peaceable, and tractable, they seem to have no will or power to act but as directed by their masters —William Bartram⟩ ⟨*tame* acquiescence in tradition and routine —Irving Babbitt⟩ SUBDUED generally implies a loss of vehemence, intensity, or force; in reference to people it suggests the quietness or meekness of one dependent, chastised, broken, or timorous ⟨*subdued* voices⟩ ⟨there were seamen going about routine duties, but they performed them in a *subdued*, soundless manner as though they were officiating at church —C.B.Nordhoff & J.N.Hall⟩ ⟨their next meeting displayed her quieter: *subdued* as one who had been set thinking

—George Meredith⟩ SUBMISSIVE implies deferring to the will of another and yielding and humbly obeying ⟨a people, gentle, *submissive*, prompt to obey, and accustomed, as were the Egyptians, to the inexorable demands of tyranny —Agnes Repplier⟩ ⟨in the *submissive* way of one long accustomed to obey under coercion, he ate and drank what they gave him —Charles Dickens⟩

²tame \"\ *vb* -ED/-ING/-S [ME *tamen*, fr. *tame*, adj.] *vt* **1 a :** to reduce from a wild to a domestic state **:** make gentle or tractable **:** DOMESTICATE ⟨~ a lion⟩ **b :** to subject to cultivation ⟨small valleys and plains that have been *tamed* and worked into precise patterns by generations of farmers —Patrick O'Donovan⟩ **c :** to bring under control **:** make manageable or usable ⟨roads blasted in the solid rock, wild streams dammed and *tamed* —John Muir †1914⟩ ⟨~ the atom⟩ ⟨the sources have been *tamed* in a masterly fashion —M.M. Postan⟩ **2 :** to deprive of spirit, courage, or resistance **:** HUMBLE, SUBDUE ⟨*tamed* the populace with shiploads of . . . wheat —T.H.Fielding⟩ **3 :** to tone down **:** SOFTEN ⟨in revising the play, he has *tamed* it⟩ ~ *vi* **:** to become tame ⟨the manatees *tamed* quickly —*Natural History*⟩ ⟨a roughneck frontiersman who ~*s* down at the end —Walter Havighurst⟩

³tame \"\ *vt* -ED/-ING/-S [ME *tamen*, short for *atamen*, fr. MF *atamer* to attack, fr. LL *attaminare*, fr. L *ad-* + *taminare* to violate (akin to L *tangere* to touch) — more at TANGENT] **1** *dial Eng* **:** to cut into **:** PIERCE; *esp* **:** BROACH **2** *dial Eng* **:** PRUNE

tameable *var of* TAMABLE

tame cat *n* **:** one who allows himself to be used or controlled by another **:** a person completely subordinate to another

tame hay *n* **:** hay cut from cultivated grasses

ta·mein \tə'mīn, -mān\ *n* -S [Burmese *thameiṅ*] **:** a draped skirt worn by Burmese women

tame·less \'tāmləs\ *adj* **:** not tamed or not capable of being tamed ⟨~ and swift and proud —P.B.Shelley⟩ — **tame·less·ly** *adv* — **tame·less·ness** *n* -ES

tame·ly *adv* **:** in a tame manner **:** MEEKLY ⟨people who ~ allow slavery to be imposed on them —Kenneth Roberts⟩

tame·ness *n* -ES **:** the quality or state of being tame

tame pasture *n* **:** pasture land sown to cultivated grasses or legumes

tam·er \'tāmə(r)\ *n* -S **:** one that tames

tamest *superlative of* TAME

tami·as \'tāmēəs, 'tam-\ *n, cap* [NL, fr. Gk, dispenser, steward; akin to Gk *temnein* to cut — more at TOME] **:** a genus of ground squirrels comprising the chipmunks of eastern No. America and sometimes extended to include the western No. American and the Old World chipmunks commonly placed in *Eutamias*

tam·il \'taməl, 'təm-,'tām-\ *n, pl* **tamil** *or* **tamils** *usu cap* **1 :** a Dravidian language of Madras state in southern India and of northern and eastern Ceylon **2 :** a Tamil-speaking person or a descendant of Tamil-speaking ancestors **3 :** a script customarily used for writing Tamil

¹ta·mil·ian \tə'milēən\ *also* **ta·mil·ic** \-lik\ *adj, usu cap* **1 :** of or relating to Tamil or the Tamils **2 :** DRAVIDIAN

²tamilian \"\ *n* -S *usu cap* **1 :** TAMIL **2 :** DRAVIDIAN

tami·ops \'tāmē,äps, 'tam-\ *n, cap* [NL, fr. *Tamias* + *-ops*] **:** a genus of striped arboreal squirrels of southeastern Asia resembling the chipmunks but having tufted ears and a short slender thinly-haired tail

tam·is \'tamē, məs\ *n, pl* **tam·ises** \-mēz,-məsəz\ [F, fr. OF, prob. of Celt origin; akin to Bret *tamouez* strainer] **:** a strainer made of worsted cloth in a plain open weave

tam·mann's rule \'tamənz-, 'tä,mänz-\ *n, usu cap T* [after Gustav *Tammann* †1938 Ger. chemist] **:** a rule in metallurgy: in binary alloys a less fusible metal dissolves more of a more fusible metal in the solid phase than the more fusible does of the less fusible

tam·ma·ny \'tamənē, -ni\ *adj, usu cap* [fr. *Tammany* Hall, headquarters of the Tammany Society, a political organization orig. founded as a fraternal society in New York City that between 1865 and 1871 under the political boss William M. Tweed †1878 obtained control of the city and plundered it of millions of dollars, fr. *Tammany* Society, after *Tamanend fl* 1682–1700 Delaware Indian chief] **:** of, relating to, or constituting a group or organization exercising or seeking municipal political control by methods often associated with corruption and bossism

tam·ma·ny·ism \-nē,izəm, -ni,iz-\ *n* -S *usu cap* [*Tammany* Hall + E *-ism*] **:** the political principles or practices attributed to or associated with Tammany Hall

tam·ma·ny·ite \-,īt\ *n* -S *usu cap* [*Tammany* Hall + E *-ite*] **:** an adherent of Tammany Hall or of Tammanyism

tam·ma·ny·ize \-,īz\ *vt* -ED/-ING/-S *often cap* [*Tammany* Hall + *-ize*] **:** to bring under Tammany rule or the domination of Tammanyism

tam·mar \'tamə(r)\ *n* -S [native name in Australia] **:** DAMA PADEMELON

tam·mie no·rie *or* **tam·my norie** \,tami'nōri\ *n* [prob. fr. *Tammie* or *Tammy* (alter. of *Tommy*, nickname for the name *Thomas*) + *Norie*, prob. dim. of the feminine name *Nora*, short for *Honora*] *Scot* **:** PUFFIN 1

tam·muz *also* **ta·muz** \'tä(,)müz\ *n* -ES *usu cap* [Heb *Tammūz*] **:** the 10th month of the civil year or the 4th month of the ecclesiastical year in the Jewish calendar — see MONTH table

¹tam·my \'tamē\ *n* -ES [prob. by shortening and alter. fr. obs. E *tamin* estamin, fr. obs. F *estamine* — more at ESTAMIN] **:** a plain-woven often glazed cloth of fine worsted or woolen and cotton formerly used for dresses, curtains, and linings

²tammy \"\ *n* -ES [prob. by shortening and alter. fr. *tamis*] **:** a strainer made of tammy cloth

³tammy \"\ *vt* -ED/-ING/-ES **:** to strain through a tammy

ta·mo \'tä(,)mō\ *n* -S [Jap] **:** JAPANESE ASH 2

¹tamo·nea \tə'mōnēə, ,tamə'nēə\ *n* -S [NL] **:** a flower or plant of the genus *Miconia*

²tamonea \"\ [NL] *syn of* MICONIA

tam-o'-shanter \'tamə,shantə(r), -shaan-, ,==='==\ *n, pl* **tam-o'-shanters** [after *Tam o' Shanter*, hero of the poem of that name (1789) by Robert Burns †1796 Scot. national poet] **:** a woolen cap of Scottish origin that is made with a tight headband and a very wide flat circular crown usu. with a pompon in the center — compare BONNET

tam-o'-shanter

¹tamp \'tamp, -aa(ə)-,-ai-\ *vb* -ED/-ING/-S [prob. fr. F *tamponner* to stop up, plug, fr. MF, fr. *tampon, tapon* plug, fr. (assumed) OF *taper* to stop up, of Gmc origin; akin to OE *tæppa* tap — more at TAP] *vt* **1 :** to fill up (a drill hole) above a blasting charge with material (as clay, earth, sand) **2** [partly fr. F *tamponner* to stop up; partly fr. F *étamper* to punch, strike, stamp, fr. OF *estamper*, of Gmc origin; akin to OHG *stampfōn* to stamp — more at STAMP] **a :** to drive in or down by a succession of light or medium blows **:** COMPACT ⟨~*ed* some more tobacco into my pipe —H.G. Evarts⟩ ⟨~*ed* the earth⟩ ⟨~*ed* the wet concrete⟩ **b :** to put a cover on ⟨these rivalries are usually ~*ed* down by the code that has governed the army —T.H.White b. 1915⟩ **3 :** to fill in or pack round tightly ⟨took out his pipe and began to ~ it —Dilys Laing⟩ ~ *vi* **:** to pack or consolidate loose material by ramming **syn** see PACK

²tamp \"\ *n* -S **:** a tool for tamping ⟨a pipe-smoker's knife, complete with a reamer, a ~, and a regular blade —*New Yorker*⟩

tam·pa \'tampə, -aam-,-aim-\ *adj, usu cap* [fr. *Tampa*, Fla.] **:** of or from the city of Tampa, Fla. ⟨a *Tampa* cigar⟩ **:** of the kind or style prevalent in Tampa

tam·pala \tam'palə\ *n* -S [native name in India] **:** an annual potherb (*Amaranthus tricolor*) native to the Orient that is cultivated for its tender stems and for its often variegated leaves which resemble spinach in taste — see JOSEPH'S COAT

¹tam·pan \'tam,pan\ *n* -S [native name in southern Africa] **:** any of various argasid ticks; *esp* **:** CHICKEN TICK

²tam·pan \'tampən, -aam-,-aim-\ *n* -S *cap* [*Tampa*, Fla. + E *-an*] **:** a native or resident of Tampa, Fla.

tam·pa·ni·an \(')tam¦pānēən\ *adj, usu cap* [Kota *Tampan*, locality in northern Malaya where the tools were found + E *-an*] **:** of or belonging to a Lower Paleolithic cultural development in Malaya characterized by choppers flaked on one surface only

¹tam·per \'tampə(r), -aam-,-aim-\ *vb* **tampered; tampered; tampering** \-p(ə)riŋ\ **tampers** [prob. fr. MF *temprer* to mix, meddle, blend, temper — more at TEMPER] *vi* **1 :** to deal secretly **:** carry on underhand or improper negotiations **:** bring improper influence to bear (as by bribery or intimidation) — used with *with* ⟨charged that the defense attorney had ~*ed* with the witnesses⟩ **2 a :** to interfere so as to weaken or change for the worse — used with *with* ⟨as old customers themselves, they would not ~ with the place's traditions or staff —*Newsweek*⟩ ⟨could not easily ~ with the privileges of the nobility —D.W.Brogan⟩ **b :** to busy oneself rashly **:** try foolish or dangerous experiments — used with *with* ⟨is far from innocent in her own ~*ing* with his sensibilities —James Gray⟩ **3** *archaic* **:** to work secretly for some end **:** PLOT, SCHEME ~ *vt* **:** to alter for an improper purpose or in an improper way ⟨here, perhaps, is the most objectionable aspect of . . . ~*ing* the texts: his bland presumption —Richard Hanser⟩ **syn** see MEDDLE

²tamp·er \"\ *n* -S [¹*tamp* + *-er*] **:** one that tamps: as **a :** one that prepares for blasting by filling the hole in which the charge has been placed **b :** a round wooden stick or metal bar used to pack tamping in a drill hole **c :** a tool or machine for compacting concrete by tamping **d :** a mass of material used to delay a nuclear reaction and prevent the escape of neutrons

tamper c

tam·pe·re \'tampərə, 'täm-\ *adj, usu cap* [fr. *Tampere*, Finland] **:** of or from the city of Tampere, Finland **:** of the kind or style prevalent in Tampere

tam·per·er \'tampərə(r), -aam-,-aim-\ *n* -S **:** one that tampers

tam·pi·can \tam'pēkən, taam-\ *n* -S *cap* [*Tampico*, seaport in eastern Mexico + E *-an*] **:** a native or resident of Tampico, Mexico

tam·pi·co fiber *also* **tampico hemp** \-pē(,)kō-\ *n, usu cap T* [fr. *Tampico*, Mexico] **:** ISTLE b

tampico jalap *n, usu cap T* [fr. *Tampico*, Mexico] **:** the dried root of a Mexican morning glory (*Ipomoea simulans*) or the powdered drug containing a resin prepared from it

tamping *n* -S [fr. gerund of ¹*tamp*] **1 :** the act or an instance of tamping; *specif* **:** the act of filling up a hole preparatory to blasting **2 :** the material used in tamping

tamping bar *n* **:** a long-handled metal bar with a wide flat head for tamping the ballast under railroad ties

tamping pick *n* **:** a pick built with a wide flat head on one end for driving ballast under railroad ties

tam·pi·on \'tampēən, 'täm- *or* **tom·pi·on** \'täm-\ *n* -S [ME *tampion, tampine, tampon*, fr. MF *tampon, tapon* — more at TAMP] **:** something that stops an opening **:** PLUG: as **a** *archaic* **:** a wooden plug used as wadding for a gun **b :** a wooden plug used to close the muzzle of a gun not in use **c :** a metal or canvas cover for the muzzle of a gun

¹tam·pon \'tam,pän, -,pən\ *n* -S [F, fr. MF *tampon, tapon* plug] **1 :** a plug of cotton or other material introduced into a natural or artificial body cavity to arrest hemorrhage, absorb secretions, or fill a defect **2 :** an ink dabber sometimes used in gravure **3 :** a 2-headed drumstick sometimes used in playing the bass drum

²tampon \"\ *vt* -ED/-ING/-S [prob. fr. F *tamponner* — more at TAMP] **:** to plug with a tampon

tam·pon·ade \,tampə'nād\ *or* **tam·pon·age** \'==,nij\ *n* -S [²*tampon* + *-ade* or *-age*] **1 :** the use of tampons to stop bleeding **2 :** CARDIAC TAMPONADE

tamps *pres 3d sing of* TAMP, *pl of* TAMP

tamrac pine *var of* TAMARACK PINE

tam-tam \'tam,tam, 'təm,təm\ *n* -S [Hindi *ṭamṭam*] **1 :** TOM-TOM **2 :** GONG; *esp* **:** one of a tuned set as used in a gamelan orchestra

ta·mu·re \tə'mürē\ *n* -S [Maori] **:** ³SNAPPER 3c

ta·mus \'tāməs\ *n, cap* [NL, prob. fr. L *tamnus*, a vine] **:** a genus of tuberous-rooted vines (family Dioscoreaceae) with twining stems, cordate leaves, and flowers in axillary racemes

tamuz *usu cap, var of* TAMMUZ

tam·worth \'tam(,)wərth\ *n* [fr. *Tamworth*, borough in Staffordshire, England, where the breed was developed] **1** *usu cap* **:** a breed of large long-bodied red swine of the bacon type originated in Ireland but largely developed in England **2** -S *often cap* **:** an animal of the Tamworth breed — called also *Irish grazier*

¹tan \'tan, -aa(ə)n\ *vb* **tanned; tanned; tanning; tans** [ME *tannen*, fr. MF *tanner*, fr. ML *tannare*, fr. *tannum, tanum* tanbark, prob. of Celt origin; akin to Ir *tana* thin, Corn *tanow*] *vt* **1 a** (1) **:** to convert (skin) into leather by impregnation with an infusion of tree bark, mineral salts, or some other form of tannin or a substitute (2) **:** to convert (collagen or other protein) to leather or a similar product **b :** to apply a mixture (as of oak bark and coloring matter) to (as a sail) for preservative or hardening purposes **2 :** to make tan or brown (as by exposure to the rays of the sun) ⟨~ the skin⟩ **3 :** to thrash soundly **:** BEAT, WHIP ⟨would have *tanned* my hide if they had caught me rambling around —Louis Armstrong⟩ **4 :** to make (the gelatin layer of a photographic material) selectively insoluble in water by chemical treatment or by the action of light ~ *vi* **:** to get or become tanned ⟨a man's skin ~*s* more deeply —J.F.Stanwell-Fletcher⟩

²tan \"\ *n* -S [F, fr. OF, fr. ML *tanum*] **1 :** TANBARK 1 **2 a :** a tanning material **b :** the active tanning agent (as tannin) in such a material **3 :** a brown color imparted to the skin by exposure to the sun or weather ⟨hands covered with ~⟩ **4 a :** a variable color averaging a light yellowish brown that is redder, lighter, and stronger than khaki, deeper and slightly yellower than walnut brown, and yellower and slightly paler than cinnamon **b :** LEATHER 4 **5 tans** *pl* **:** tan-colored articles of clothing; *esp* **:** SHOES ⟨school superintendents were freshening their ~*s* . . . and looking up timetables —*Newsweek*⟩

³tan \"\ *adj, sometimes* **tanner**; *sometimes* **tannest** **1 :** of, relating to, or used for tan or tanning **2 :** of the color tan

⁴tan \'dän\ *n, pl* **tan** [Chin (Pek) *tan*¹] **:** a Chinese unit of weight **:** PICUL

⁵tan \'tän\ *n, pl* **tan** [Jap] **:** a Japanese unit of land area equal to ¼ acre

⁶tan \'dän\ *n, pl* **tan** *or* **tans** *usu cap* [short for *tanka*] **:** one of a boat-dwelling people distantly related to the Li whose boats form compact colonies in the river esp. at Canton and Foochow, China — called also *Tanka*

tan *abbr* tangent

¹ta·na \'tänə\ *n, cap* [Malay (*tupai*) *tanah* ground shrew, fr. *tupai* shrew, squirrel + *tanah* ground] **:** a small genus of Bornean and Sumatran tree shrews with a long muzzle bearing an extended nose pad

²tana *often cap, var of* TANNA

tan·a·ce·tin \,tanə'sētᵊn\ *n* -S [ISV *tanacet-* (fr. NL *Tanacetum*, genus name of the tansy *Tanacetum vulgare*) + *-in*] **:** the bitter principle $C_{11}H_{16}O_4$ of the common tansy

tan·a·ce·tum \-ēd·əm\ *n, cap* [NL, fr. ML, tansy] **:** a genus of chiefly Old World strong-scented herbs (family Compositae) having usu. dissected foliage and small discoid flower heads in flat-topped corymbs — see TANSY 1a

ta·nach \tä'näk\ *n, cap* [MHeb *tnk*, abbr. of Heb *tōrāh, nĕbhī'īm, kĕthūbhīm* Pentateuch, Prophets, Hagiographa] **:** the Hebrew Scriptures

tan·a·ger \'tanəjə(r), -nēj-\ *n* -S [NL *tanagra*, fr. Pg *tangará*, fr. Tupi] **:** any of numerous American passerine birds (family Thraupidae) having brightly colored males, being mainly unmusical, and chiefly inhabiting woodlands — see SCARLET TANAGER, WESTERN TANAGER

¹tan·a·gra \'tanəgrə, tə'nagrə\ *n, cap* [NL] **:** a genus of small fruit-eating tropical American tanagers having variegated coloring and short tails and broad gapes — see EUPHONIA

²tanagra \"\ *n* -S [fr. *Tanagra*, town in the ancient republic of Boeotia, east central Greece] **1** *or* **tanagra figurine** *usu cap T* **:** one of many small terra-cotta statuettes often representing people of fashion discovered in ancient tombs principally in Boeotia and highly prized by collectors **2** *often cap* **:** CASTILIAN BROWN

ta·nag·ri·dae \tə'nagrə,dē\ [NL, fr. *Tanagra* + *-idae*] *syn of* THRAUPIDAE

tan·a·ida·cea \,tanēə'dāshēə\ *n pl, cap* [NL, fr. *Tanaid-, Tanais*, genus of crustaceans (fr. L *Tanais* the river Don, fr. Gk *Tanaïs*) + *-acea*] **:** a small order of malacostracan crustaceans (division Peracarida) often included in the Isopoda and intermediate in character between that order and the Cumacea

tanaim *pl of* ²TANA

ta·nai·na \tə'nīnə\ *n, pl* **tanaina** *or* **tanainas** *usu cap* **1 a :** an Athapaskan people of the area around Cook Inlet, southern Alaska **b :** a member of such people **2 :** the language of the Tanaina people

ta·na·la \tə'nälə\ *n, pl* **tanala** *or* **tanalas** *usu cap* **:** one of a forest people in southeastern Madagascar prob. more directly descended from the aboriginal inhabitants than are the bulk of the island's peoples

tan·a·na \'tanə,nȯ\ *n, pl* **tanana** *or* **tananas** *usu cap* **1 a :** an Athapaskan people of the Tanana and Yukon river valleys, Alaska, near their confluence **b :** a member of such people **2 :** the language of the Tanana people

ta·nan·a·rive \tə'nanə,rēv\ *adj, usu cap* [fr. *Tananarive*, capital of the Malagasy Republic] **:** of or from Tananarive, the capital of the Malagasy Republic **:** of the kind or style prevalent in Tananarive

tanbark \'=,=\ *n* [²*tan* + *bark*] **1 a :** a bark rich in tannin bruised or cut into small pieces and used in tanning **b** (1) **:** spent tanbark used as a covering (as for a circus ring or racetrack) (2) **:** a surface covered with tanbark **2 :** a light to moderate brown that is slightly redder than suede and very slightly redder than mocha bisque — called also *Algerian*

tanbark beetle *n* **1 :** the adult of the tanbark borer **2 :** a small black boring beetle (*Stephanopachys substriatus*) that infests hemlock tanbark

tanbark borer *n* **:** a borer that is the larva of a cerambycid beetle (*Phymatodes testaceus*) and feeds beneath the bark of various trees

tanbark oak *n* **:** an oak that yields tanbark: as **a :** an evergreen oak (*Lithocarpus densiflora*) of the Pacific coast area differing from the typical oaks esp. in having erect staminate catkins **b :** CHESTNUT OAK c **c :** a black oak (*Quercus velutina*)

tanbark tree *n* **:** HEMLOCK 2a

tan bay *n* **:** LOBLOLLY BAY 1

tan·bur \'tan,bu̇(ə)r, ='=\ *n* -S [Per *ṭambūr*] **:** TAMBOURA

¹tan·chel·mi·an \(')tan¦kelmēən, -aŋ¦k-\ *adj, usu cap* [*Tanchelm* †1115? Flemish heretic + E *-an*] **:** of or relating to Tanchelm who denounced the church and the sacraments and led an armed revolt

²tanchelmian \"\ *n, usu cap* **:** a follower of Tanchelm

T and A *abbr* tonsillectomy and adenoidectomy

tan·dan \'tandən\ *n* -S [native name in Australia] **:** an Australian freshwater catfish (*Tandanus tandanus*)

tan·da·va \'tändəvə\ *n* -S [Skt *tāṇḍava*] **:** the energetic and virile dance type of India — contrasted with *lasya*

¹tan·dem \'tandəm, -aan-\ *n* -S [L, at length, at last (taken to mean "lengthwise"), fr. *tam* so, so much, as (akin to Gk *to* that) + *-dem* (demonstrative suff.) — more at THAT] **1 a** (1) **:** a 2-seated carriage drawn by horses harnessed one before the other (2) **:** a team harnessed in this manner **b :** TANDEM BICYCLE **c :** TANDEM AIRPLANE **d :** a vehicle (as a trailer or truck) having close-coupled pairs of axles **2 :** a group of two or more arranged or following one behind the other **:** two or more used or acting in conjunction ⟨a more persuasive . . . ~ could not be found, nor two men with more sincerity —Darrell Berrigan⟩ — **in tandem** *adv* **1 :** in a tandem arrangement ⟨tugging two supply-laden sleds *in tandem* —*Time*⟩ **2 :** in partnership ⟨the majority party will be functioning *in tandem* with the minority party —Elmo Roper⟩

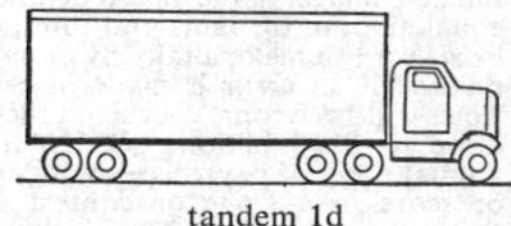
tandem 1d

²tandem \"\ *adv* [L, adv., at length] **:** one after or behind another ⟨horses driven ~⟩

³tandem \"\ *adj* **:** consisting of two arranged one behind the other ⟨a ~ arrangement of engine cylinders⟩

tandem airplane *n* **:** an airplane having two or more sets of wings of about the same area placed one in front of the other on the same level

tandem bicycle *n* **:** a bicycle for two or more persons on which the riders sit one behind another

tandem cart *n* **:** a 2-wheeled vehicle having seats back to back with the front one somewhat elevated

tandem compound *n* **:** a tandem compound steam engine or turbine

tandem engine *n* **:** a steam engine having two or more steam cylinders in line with a common piston rod

tandem hitch *n* **:** a hitch in which two or more animals are placed in line tail to head or two rows of several animals abreast are placed one row ahead of the other

tandem method *n* **:** a method of improving livestock by breeding animals selected for excellence in one quality (as milk production) and neglecting other qualities until that chosen is considered adequately fixed in the strain when another quality may be selected and bred into the strain — compare TOTAL SCORE METHOD

tandem mill *n* **:** a rolling mill with several stands in succession

tandem office *n* **:** a telephone central office or switchboard used entirely for the interconnection of telephone exchanges that reduces the number of trunk circuits

tandem roller *n* **:** a steam or gasoline driven roller in which the weight is divided between two heavy iron rolls one behind the other

T and G *abbr* **1** tongue and groove **2** tongued and grooved

tan disease *n* [²*tan*; fr. the brownish patches] **:** a condition of roots or woody stems caused by excessive moisture in which brownish or white granular or woolly patches consisting of dead cells form on the surface

T and O *abbr* taken and offered

tandour *var of* TENDOUR

¹tane *chiefly Scot past part of* TAKE

²tane \'tān\ *Scot & dial Eng var of* ¹TONE

ta·ne·ka·ha \,tänə'kä(,)hä\ *n* -S [Maori] **:** CELERY-TOPPED PINE

¹tang \'taŋ, -aiŋ\ *n* -S [ME *tang, tange*, of Scand origin; akin to ON *tangi* point, spit of land, tang of a knife; perh. akin to ON *tunga* tongue — more at TONGUE] **1 a** *dial* (1) **:** a serpent's tongue (2) **:** STING, PANG **b** *Scot & dial Eng* **:** something having a sharp projecting point: as (1) **:** a tine of a stag's horn (2) **:** a prong of a fork (3) **:** a buckle tongue (4) **:** the tongue of a Jew's harp **2 a :** a piece that forms an extension from the blade or analogous part of an instrument (as a table knife or fork, file, chisel, or sword) and connects with the handle and that may be a thin flat plate on each side of which a rounded piece is secured to form the handle or that may be a tapered piece inserted into the haft or handle — see FILE illustration **b :** a butt and stem of a prehistoric arrowhead made to fit into a shaft **c :** the strip or plate sometimes extending from the receiver or frame of a firearm by which it is secured to the stock **3 a** (1) **:** a sharp distinctive flavor that lingers on the tongue **:** a taste of something extraneous to the thing itself that may produce an unpleasant response ⟨a cheese with the ~ of garlic⟩ ⟨cider with the ~ of the cask⟩ ⟨meals . . . retain the unmistakable ~ of country cooking —*Amer. Guide Series: Ind.*⟩ (2) **:** a particularly pungent odor ⟨the ~ of peat fires —*Holiday*⟩ ⟨an afternoon full of . . . the ~ of mown grass —J.C.Trewin⟩ **b :** something having the effect of a sharp taste in the mouth or a pungent odor ⟨treated murder as a joke with a ~ to it —Graham Greene⟩ ⟨her prose is a cidery flowing of sweetness

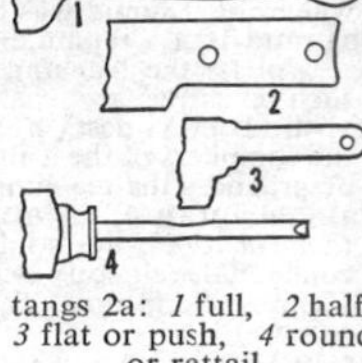

tangs 2a: *1* full, *2* half, *3* flat or push, *4* round or rattail

and ~ —Charles Lee⟩ **4 a :** a faint suggestion **:** noticeable trace **:** SMATTERING — usu. used with *of* ⟨kindness is seasoned with the ~ of humor —Elliott Dobson⟩ ⟨will find himself getting a ~ of enjoyment out of it —S.C.Pepper⟩ **b :** a distinguishing characteristic that sets apart or gives a special individuality ⟨nothing in contemporary England quite to match . . . the American ~ —Howard M. Jones⟩ ⟨give the place a definite grass-roots ~ —D.F.Malcolm⟩ **5 :** SURGEONFISH **6** *Scot & dial Eng* **:** a low projecting cape or narrow strip of land **7 :** JET 3 **8 :** a ship's mast fitting to which stays and shrouds are attached **9 :** a diamond cutter's stand for holding the dop in constant position with reference to the surface of the skeif so as to cut and polish the stone **syn** see TASTE

²tang \"\ *vt* -ED/-ING/-S [ME *tangen*, fr. *tang, tange*, n.] **1** *dial Eng* **:** STING **2 :** to furnish with a tang **3 :** to affect with or as if with a tang ⟨evergreen forests ~*ed* with salt air —*Amer. Guide Series: Oregon*⟩ ⟨breeze blows . . . ~*ed* with flowers —Amy Lowell⟩

³tang \"\ *n* -S [of Scand origin; akin to Dan & Norw *tang* seaweed, ON *thang* kelp, tangleweed] **:** any of various large coarse seaweeds; *esp* **:** a rockweed of the genus *Fucus* — compare BLADDER WRACK 1; see PRICKLY TANG

⁴tang \"\ *vb* -ED/-ING/-S [imit.] *vt* **1 :** to cause to ring or sound loudly ⟨~*ing* the spoon on the shovel —Flora Thompson⟩ **2 :** to utter with a tang ⟨let thy tongue ~ arguments of state —Shak.⟩ ~ *vi* **:** to make a harsh ringing sound

⁵tang \"\ *n* -S [imit.] **:** a sharp twanging sound (as of a single stroke on metal or of the plucking of a string) **:** TWANG

⁶tang \'täŋ\ *adj, usu cap* [*Tang, T'ang*, Chin. dynasty (A.D. 618–907), fr. Chin (Pek) *t'ang²*] **:** of, relating to, or having the characteristics of the period of the Tang dynasty and esp. of the art forms developed during that period ⟨*Tang* pottery⟩

tan·ga *also* **tang·ka** *or* **tan·ka** *or* **tan·kah** \taŋ'gä, -ŋ'kä\ *n* -S [Hindi *ṭaṅgā*] **:** any of various Eastern coins: as **a :** a former silver coin of India corresponding to the rupee **b :** an old debased silver coin of Tibet **c :** a bronze coin of Portuguese India and corresponding in value to 1/16 rupia

tan·ga·le \täŋ'gälē\ *n, pl* **tangale** *or* **tangales** *usu cap* **1 :** a people of the Bauchi district of northern Nigeria **2 :** the language of the Tangale people

tan·ga·lung \taŋ'gäləŋ\ *n* -S [Malay *tĕnggalong*] **:** a long-muzzled civet (*Viverra tangalunga*) that is dark gray with longitudinal black stripes more or less broken into spots and is widely distributed in the East Indies

tang·an·tang·an \ˌtaŋˌänˈtäŋˌän\ *n* -S [Tag] **:** CASTOR-OIL PLANT

tan·gan·yi·ka \ˌtaŋgən'yēkə, ˌtaŋg-, ˌtaiŋg-, -gə'nē-\ *adj, usu cap* [fr. *Tanganyika*, territory in eastern Africa] **:** of or from Tanganyika **:** of the kind or style prevalent in Tanganyika

¹tan·gan·yi·kan \-ēkən\ *adj, usu cap* [*Tanganyika*, eastern Africa + E *-an*] **1 :** of, relating to, or characteristic of Tanganyika **2 :** of, relating to, or characteristic of the people of Tanganyika

²tanganyikan \"\ *n* -S *cap* [*Tanganyika* + E *-an* (n. suffix)] **:** a native or inhabitant of Tanganyika

tan·gar·i·dae \tan'garəˌdē, taŋ'g-\ [NL, fr. Pg *tangará* tanager + NL *-idae* — more at TANAGER] *syn of* THRAUPIDAE

tanga·ro·an \ˌtäŋ(g)ə'rōən, ˌtaŋ-\ *n* -S *usu cap* [*Tangaroa*, Polynesian deity + E *-an*] **:** one of an ethnic group or late wave of conquering Polynesians

tang chisel *n* [¹*tang*] **:** a chisel in which the shank tapers to a point and is driven into a handle

tanged \'taŋd, -aiŋd\ *adj* **:** having or equipped with a tang ⟨~ flint daggers⟩

tan·ge·lo \'tanjəˌlō\ *n* -S [blend of *tangerine* and *pomelo*] **1 :** a hybrid between a tangerine or mandarin orange and either a grapefruit or shaddock **2 :** the fruit of the tangelo

tan·gem·on \tan'jemən\ *n* -S [blend of *tangerine* and *lemon*] **1 :** a hybrid between the tangerine and the lemon **2 :** the fruit of the tangemon

tan·gen·cy \'tanjənsē, 'taan-, -si\ *n* -ES **:** the quality or state of being tangent

tang end *n* **:** a projection on the end of a rod used to strengthen the joint between the rod and a pipe

¹tan·gent \'tanjənt, 'taan-\ *adj* [L *tangent-, tangens*, pres. part. of *tangere* to touch; akin to Gk *tetagōn* having seized, OE *thaccian* to stroke, touch gently] **1 a :** touching at a single point ⟨a straight line ~ to a curve⟩ **b** (1) **:** having a common tangent line at a point — used of two curves in a plane, two space curves, or a surface and a space curve (2) **:** having a common tangent plane at a point — used of two surfaces **2 a :** diverging from an original purpose or course **:** ERRATIC ⟨much of his work is chaotic and distorted by ~ obsessions —Tennessee Williams⟩ **b :** CONTIGUOUS **:** being in agreement ⟨subject matter ~ to the country's growth in those years —M.F.Milton⟩

²tangent \"\ *n* -S [NL *tangent-, tangens*, fr. L, pres. part. of *tangere* to touch] **1 a :** TANGENT LINE **b :** the ordinate of any point on the terminal side of an angle divided by the nonzero abscissa of this point with the vertex coinciding with the origin of a plane rectangular coordinate system and the initial side of the angle coinciding with the positive x-axis — abbr. *tan* **2 :** a course abruptly deviating from that previously pursued **:** DIGRESSION, IRRELEVANCY ⟨avoid wandering off on ~*s* —J.F.Wharton⟩ ⟨his critics . . . went off at a ~ —Saul Carson⟩ **3 :** a small upright flat-ended metal pin at the inner end of a clavichord key that strikes the string to produce the musical tone and fixes the pitch by damping the string **4 :** a piece of straight railroad track

tan·gen·tal \'tanjəntᵊl, (')tan'jen-\ *adj* **:** TANGENTIAL

tangent arc *n* **:** a halo that touches a circular halo

tangent-cut \ˈ≈ˌ≈\ *adj* **:** TANGENT-SAWED

tangent galvanometer *n* **:** a galvanometer consisting of a very small magnetic needle in the center of a large vertical circular coil of wire through which electric current is passed and whose plane is in the magnetic meridian with the intensity of the current being proportional to the tangent of the angle of deflection of the needle

tan·gen·tial \(')tan'jenchəl, -aan'-\ *adj* **1 :** of, relating to, or of the nature of a tangent **:** being in the direction of a tangent **2 a :** acting along or lying in a tangent **b :** arranged or having parts arranged like tangents **3 a :** deviating widely and sometimes erratically **:** DIVERGENT ⟨the discussion method . . . is time-consuming and alarmingly ~ —R.C.Snyder⟩ **b :** touching lightly or in the most tenuous way **:** INCIDENTAL ⟨no place . . . for political controversy save in occasional ~ comment —W.R.Benét⟩

tangential creep *n* **:** slow horizontal movement of material composing the earth's crust

tangential force *n* **:** a force that acts on a moving body in the direction of a tangent to the curved path of the body

tan·gen·tial·ly \-chəlē, -li\ *adv* **:** in a tangential manner **:** at a tangent ⟨the vapors enter the trap ~ —*Modern Chem. Processes*⟩ ⟨a few of the times great figures come into the story, but only ~ —Jean S. Untermeyer⟩

tangential motion *n* **:** proper motion of a star corrected for the effect of distance and expressed in linear units usu. kilometers per second and being that component of the star's motion with respect to the solar system that is at right angles to the line of sight

tangential stress *n* **:** a force acting in a generally horizontal direction; *esp* **:** a force that produces mountain folding and overthrusting

tangent line *n* [trans. of NL *linea tangens*] **:** a line at a fixed point *P* of a curve that is the limit approached by the secant *PQ* as *Q* approaches *P* along the curve

tan·gent·ly \'tanjəntlē\ *adv* **:** TANGENTIALLY

tangent plane *n* **:** the plane through a point of a surface that contains the tangent lines to all the curves on the surface through the same point

tangent-saw \ˈ≈ˌ≈\ *vt* **:** to saw (a log) lengthwise by parallel cuts in regular succession — compare QUARTERSAW

tangent screw *n* **1 :** a worm that works tangentially on a worm wheel to which it imparts an endless motion **2 :** a very fine screw giving a tangential movement for making the final adjustment to an instrument of precision (as a surveyor's transit)

tangent sight *n* **:** a rear sight for a firearm that has the graduations corresponding to the tangents of the angles of elevation and that is usu. graduated to read in yards of range

tangent spoke *n* **:** a tension spoke of a bicycle or similar wheel secured tangentially to the hub

tan·ger·e·tin \ˌtanjə'rētᵊn\ *n* -S [²*tangerine* + *-etin* (as in *fisetin*)] **:** a crystalline flavone $C_{20}H_{20}O_7$ obtained from the peel of tangerines

¹tan·ger·ine \ˌtanjə'rēn, ˌtaan-\ *adj, usu cap* [*Tanger* (Tangier), seaport in Morocco + E *-ine*] **:** of, relating to, or from Tangier

²tangerine \"\ *n* -S [*Tanger* (Tangier), Morocco + E *-ine* (n. suffix)] **1** *cap* **:** a native or inhabitant of Tangier **2 a** (1) **:** any of various cultivated citrus fruits that have deep orange to almost scarlet skin and pulp and are the only mandarins grown on a large scale in the U.S. and southern Africa — distinguished from *mandarin* (2) **:** MANDARIN 4b(1) **b :** a tree producing tangerines **:** MANDARIN 4a **3 a :** a variable color ranging from moderate reddish orange to vivid or strong orange **b :** *of textiles* **:** a strong reddish orange

tangfish \ˈ≈ˌ≈\ *n* [³*tang* + *fish*] *dial Brit* **:** HARBOR SEAL

tanghan *var of* TANGUN

tan·ghin \'taŋgən\ *n* -S [F, fr. Malagasy (*voa*) *tanging*] **1 :** a virulent poison derived from the kernels of the ordeal tree of Madagascar **2 :** ORDEAL TREE 1

tan·ghin·ia \tan'ginēə, taŋ'g-\ *n, cap* [NL, fr. Malagasy *tanging* + NL *-ia*] **:** a genus of Madagascan trees (family Apocynaceae) having evergreen oblanceolate leaves clustered at the ends of the branches and terminal cymes of small white flowers — see ORDEAL TREE 1

tan·ghinin \tan'ginən, taŋ'g-; 'taŋgənən\ *n* -S [ISV *tanghin*- (fr. NL *Tanghinia*, genus name of the ordeal tree *Tanghinia venenifera*) + *-in*] **:** a poisonous bitter crystalline compound constituting the active principle of the ordeal tree

¹tangi \'taŋē, 'täŋē\ *n* -S [Maori, lit., to mourn, cry] **:** a Maori funeral rite; *also* **:** a lamentation or dirge that accompanies it

²tan·gi \(')täŋ'gē\ *n* -S [Per *tangī* narrowness, fr. *tang* narrow] *India* **:** a narrow gorge

tan·gi·bil·i·ty \ˌtanjə'bilədˌē, ˌtaan-, -lətē, -i\ *n* -ES **:** the quality or state of being tangible

¹tan·gi·ble \'tanjəbəl, 'taan-\ *adj* [LL *tangibilis*, fr. L *tangere* to touch + *-ibilis* -ible — more at TANGENT] **1 a :** capable of being touched **:** able to be perceived as materially existent esp. by the sense of touch **:** PALPABLE, TACTILE ⟨a ~ separable thing, like . . . salt or bread —Sinclair Lewis⟩ **b :** substantially real **:** MATERIAL ⟨the conquest of a territory meant a ~ advantage to the conqueror —Norman Angell⟩ ⟨a ~ gain in money —Wessie Connell⟩ **2 :** capable of being realized by the mind **:** conceived or thought of as definable or measurable ⟨I have never been in a community where happiness was so ~ —Arthur Langford⟩ ⟨the motives of action are quite ~ and the tales reflect actual situations —H.O.Taylor⟩ **3 :** constituting or consisting of a corporeal item capable of being appraised at an actual or approximate value ⟨~ assets⟩ **syn** see PERCEPTIBLE

²tangible \"\ *n* -S **:** something that is tangible: as **a :** a tangible asset **b :** a piece of tangible property

tan·gi·ble·ness *n* -ES **:** TANGIBILITY

tangible property *n* **:** property (as real estate) having physical substance apparent to the senses; *sometimes* **:** intangible property (as stocks, bonds, notes) involved in a government's exercise of its police or taxing power

tan·gi·bly \'tanjəblē, 'taan-, -bli\ *adv* **:** in a tangible manner ⟨virtue is ~ rewarded —J.D.Hart⟩

¹tan·gier \(')tan'ji(ə)r, -aan-, -iə\ *also* **tan·giers** \-i(ə)rz, -iəz\ *adj, usu cap* [fr. *Tangier, Tangiers*, Morocco] **:** of or from the city of Tangier, Morocco **:** of the kind or style prevalent in Tangier **:** TANGERINE

²tangier \"\ *n, often cap* [fr. *Tangier, Tangiers*, seaport in Morocco] **:** OCHER ORANGE

³tangier *comparative of* TANGY

tangier pea *also* **tangier peavine** *n, usu cap T* **:** a wild pea (*Lathyrus tingitanus*) of northern Africa resembling the sweet pea and having showy but odorless flowers and pods without wings

tangiest *superlative of* TANGY

tangile *var of* TANGUILE

tan·gil·in \tan'gilən\ *n* -S [Malay *tĕnggiling*, fr. *giling* roll; fr. its characteristic of rolling itself into a ball] **:** an East Indian pangolin (*Manis javanica*)

tanging *pres part of* TANG

tan·gi·pa·hoa \ˌtanjəpə'hō, ˌtanchp-\ *n, pl* **tangipahoa** *or* **tangipahoas** *usu cap* **1 :** an extinct Muskhogean people of southeastern Louisiana **2 :** a member of the Tangipahoa people

tangka *var of* TANGA

tang·khul \'täŋˌkül\ *n, pl* **tangkhul** *or* **tangkhuls** *usu cap* **:** one of a Naga people on the eastern slopes of the Manipur hills

¹tan·gle \'taŋgəl, 'taiŋ-\ *vb* **tangled; tangled; tangling** \-g(ə)liŋ\ **tangles** [ME *tangilen, tagilen*, prob. of Scand origin; akin to Sw dial. *taggla* to disarrange, tangle] *vt* **1 :** to involve so as to hamper, obstruct, or embarrass ⟨lost in a growing institutionalism, and *tangled* in a hopeless controversy —F.K.Stamm⟩ **2 :** to seize and hold in or as if in a snare **:** ENTRAP ⟨he was *tangled* by his own lies⟩ **3 a :** to unite or knit together in confusion **:** interweave or interlock in a manner almost impossible to unravel **b :** to mix inextricably ⟨economics and literature had become so . . . *tangled* —May L. Becker⟩ ⟨father's business affairs are greatly *tangled* —P.B.Kyne⟩ ~ *vi* **1 :** to engage in conflict **:** become involved in argument or altercation **:** have a set-to ⟨opposing lawyers *tangled* heatedly over . . . constitutional guarantees —*N.Y. Times*⟩ ⟨only a few planes dared to . . . ~ with the allied fleets —*Newsweek*⟩ **2 :** to become entangled **:** INTERTWINE ⟨the streets of Santa Cruz wind and ~ —V.S. Pritchett⟩

²tangle \"\ *n* -S **1 a :** a tangled twisted condition or mass **:** a knot of threads or something similar (as hairs, branches, vines) united confusedly or so interwoven as not to be easily disengaged **:** RAVEL, SNARL ⟨a stretch of back road that . . . now is a ~ of weeds and wild grasses —A.W.Turnbull⟩ **b :** something resembling a tangle in appearance ⟨became lost in the ~ of streets along the waterfront⟩ ⟨an interminable ~ of waterless ravines —S.H.Howard⟩ ⟨the old wharf with its ~ of sails and boats and people —Vicki Baum⟩ **2 a :** a complicated jumbled aggregation **:** a highly involved often confused state or condition ⟨in a hopeless ~ of conflicting allegiances —Gordon Merrick⟩ ⟨the formerly open . . . border is now a ~ of red tape —J.S.Roucek⟩ ⟨works amid a forbidding ~ of technical regulations and restrictions —*Lamp*⟩ **b :** a state of perplexity or complete bewilderment ⟨his brain got all in a ~ and he could make a beginning nowhere —Liam O'Flaherty⟩ **3 :** a bar or frame to which short lengths of chain bearing bundles of various material (as frayed rope or cotton waste) are attached and which is dragged over the sea bottom to entangle and catch animals (as starfish) **4 :** a serious altercation **:** ARGUMENT, CONFLICT ⟨felt she was not to blame for the ~ with her neighbor⟩ ⟨unwillingness . . . to trust an armed Germany has been a factor in every European political ~ for several hundred years —G.W.Johnson⟩

³tangle \"\ *also* **tangleweed** \ˈ≈≈ˌ≈\ *n* -S [*tangle* of Scand origin; akin to Norw *tongull* tangle, ON *thöngull* tangle, *thang* kelp, tangle, Dan *tang* seaweed — more at TANG] **:** a large seaweed; *esp* **:** either of two seaweeds (*Laminaria saccharina* or *L. digitata*)

⁴tangle \"\ *n* -S [prob. fr. ²*tangle;* influenced in meaning by ¹*dangle*] **:** something that is pendulous: as **a** *Scot* **:** a hanging icicle **b** *Scot* **:** a lock of hair

tangleberry \ˈ≈≈ˌ≈\ — *see* BERRY\ *n* [⁴*tangle* + *berry*] **:** DANGLEBERRY

tanglebush \ˈ≈≈ˌ≈\ *n* [²*tangle* + *bush*] **:** a spiny branching spreading forestiera (*Forestiera neomexicana*) of the western and southwestern U.S.

tangled *adj* [fr. past part. of ¹*tangle*] **1 :** existing in or giving the appearance of a state of utter disorder **:** JUMBLED, SNARLED **:** thickly intertwined ⟨the ~ path which led beneath the ruined walls —Sheila Rowlands⟩ ⟨around us loom the ~ masses of peaks —P.A.Moore⟩ ⟨twenty miles of ~ traffic —Claudia Cassidy⟩ **2 :** exceedingly complex **:** very involved ⟨laws had failed to resolve the ~ case —*N.Y. Times*⟩ ⟨a simplification of ~ customs rules —*Newsweek*⟩

tanglefish \ˈ≈≈ˌ≈\ *n* [⁴*tangle* + *fish;* fr. its lean slender shape] **:** a pipefish (*Syngnathus acus*) of Europe

tanglefoot \ˈ≈≈ˌ≈\ *n, pl* **tanglefoots** [¹*tangle* + *foot*] **1 :** strong drink; *esp* **:** a cheap whiskey **2 a :** HEATH ASTER **b :** DEERWEED

tanglehead \ˈ≈≈ˌ≈\ *n* **:** a perennial grass (*Heteropogon contortus*) of worldwide distribution that is used as a forage grass in the southwestern U.S. and has long tangled flexuous awns

tangle-legs \ˈ≈≈ˌ≈\ *n pl but sing or pl in constr* **:** HOBBLEBUSH

tan·gle·ment \'taŋgəlmənt, 'taiŋ-\ *n* -S **:** a tangled condition **:** a state of being embroiled or confused ⟨great issues in our drama . . . serve as the background for individual human ~*s* —S.L.Weaver⟩

tangle net *n* **:** GILL NET

tangleroot \ˈ≈≈ˌ≈\ *n* **:** an abnormal condition of the pineapple in which the main roots wind around the rootstock instead of growing out into the soil

tangle-tail \ˈ≈≈ˌ≈\ *n* **:** a stonecrop (*Sedum acre*)

tanglewrack \ˈ≈≈ˌ≈\ *n* [³*tangle* + *wrack*] **:** ³TANGLE

tan·gly \'taŋg(ə)lē, 'taiŋ-, -li\ *adj* -ER/-EST **:** full of tangles or knots **:** ENTANGLED, INTRICATE, SNARLY

¹tan·go \'taŋ(ˌ)gō, 'taiŋ-\ *n* -S [AmerSp, Negro drum dance, Negro dance and festival, tango, prob. of Niger-Congo origin; akin to Ibibio *tamgu* to dance] **1 a :** a ballroom dance of Spanish-American origin in 2/4 time characterized by posturing, frequent pointing positions, and a great variety of steps **b :** the music for the tango or a composition marked by similar syncopation shown typically as a dotted eighth note, sixteenth note, and two eighth notes **2 :** a variety of bingo

²tango \"\ *vi* -ED/-ING/-S **:** to dance the tango

³tango \"\ *usu cap* — a communications code word for the letter *t*

tan·gor \'tanˌjȯ(ə)r, 'taŋˌgȯ-\ *n* -S [blend of *tangerine* and *orange*] **1 :** a hybrid between the mandarin orange and the sweet orange usu. having large deeply colored and easily peeled fruit ⟨temple oranges are usu. considered to be ~*s*⟩ **2 :** the fruit of a tangor

tan·go·receptor \ˌtaŋ(ˌ)gō+\ *n* [*tango-* (fr. L *tangere* to touch) + *receptor* — more at TANGENT] **:** a receptor for the sense of touch

tang peep *n* **:** a peep sight mounted on the tang of the receiver of a gun

tan·gram \'taŋgrəm, -ang-, -anˌgram\ *n* [perh. fr. Chin (Pek) *t'ang²* Chinese + E *-gram*] **:** a Chinese puzzle made by cutting a square of thin material into five triangles, a square, and a rhomboid which are capable of recombination in many different figures

tangram

¹tangs \'taŋz\ *Scot & dial Eng var of* TONGS

²tangs *pl of* TANG, *pres 3d sing of* TANG

tangue \'taŋ\ *n* -S [Malagasy *tàndeke*] **:** TENREC

tang·ui·le *or* **tang·i·le** \'täŋəlē\ *n* -S [Tag *tangili*] **1 :** a Philippine mahogany (*Shorea polysperma*) with reddish brown wood **2 :** the wood of tanguile — called also *red lauan*

tang·uing·ue \täŋ'iŋē\ *also* **tang·ui·gue** \täŋ'ēgē\ *n* -S [Tag *tanguingi*] **:** SPANISH MACKEREL 1c

tan·guis cotton \'täŋˌgwēs-\ *n, usu cap T* [AmerSp *tangüis*] **:** a white-fibered Peruvian cotton with a staple length of 1 to 1¼ inches

tan·gun \'täŋgən\ *or* **tan·gum** \-gəm\ *also* **tan·ghan** \-gən\ *n* -S [Hindi *ṭāgan, ṭāghan*] **:** a small strong usu. piebald pony of Tibet and Bhutan

tan·gut \(')tän'güt\ *n* -S *usu cap* [fr. *Tangut*, ancient region in northwestern China] **:** a Tibetan esp. of the west central province of Tsinghai in China

tangy \'taŋē, 'taiŋ-, -ŋi\ *adj, sometimes* -ER/-EST [¹*tang* + *-y*] **:** having or suggestive of a tang ⟨the rich ~ scent of pine needles —Ysabel Rennie⟩ ⟨told in ~ 18th century English —Bernardine Kielty⟩

tanh *abbr* hyperbolic tangent

tan·ha \'tən(ˌ)hä\ *n* -S [Pali *taṇhā*, fr. Skt *tṛṣṇā* thirst, desire, fr. *tṛṣyati* he thirsts — more at THIRST] *Buddhism* **:** an intense desire for life

tan house *n* [ME *tanhous*, fr. *tannen* to tan + *hous* house — more at TAN, HOUSE] **:** a tannery building for tanning vats or drums

tan·ia *or* **tan·ier** *or* **tan·nia** *or* **tan·nier** *or* **tan·ya** *also* **tan·yah** \'tanēə(r), -nyə(r)\ *n* -S [F *tannie*, perh. modif. (influenced by *tanaisie* tansy, fr. OF *tanesie*) of a word of Arawakan, Cariban, or Tupian origin; akin to Arawak *taya* taro, Calinago *tâia*, Tupi *taiá* — more at TANSY] **:** any of several aroids having edible farinaceous roots: as **a :** TARO 1 **b :** YAUTIA a

ta·ni·ko \'tänə(ˌ)kō\ *n* -S [Maori] **1 :** a Maori ornamental border of a mat **2 :** a type of weaving with colored yarns used commonly for headdresses and bodices worn in Maori dances and for belts

tan·ist \'tanəst, 'thȯn-\ *n* -S [IrGael *tānaiste* second, second person in rank, tanist] **:** the lord or proprietor elected under the system of tanistry

tan·ist·ry \-trē\ *or* **tan·is·tria** \ta'nistrēə, thȯ'n-\ *n, pl* **tanistries** *or* **tanistrias** [*tanistry* fr. *tanist* + *-ry; tanistria* fr. NL, fr. *tanista* tanist (fr. IrGael *tānaiste*), after E *tanistry*] **:** an early Irish law of succession by which the heir or successor of a chief or king is appointed during the lifetime of the reigning chief, is not necessarily his oldest son, is generally the worthiest and wisest of the male relatives of the chief, and is elected by the people from among the eligible candidates but because of resultant bloody wars and feuds between families declared illegal by a decision of the Anglo-Irish judges in the first year of James I

ta·nite \'täˌnīt\ *adj, usu cap* [*Tanis*, ancient city in the Nile delta, Lower Egypt + E *-ite*] **:** of or relating to ancient Tanis in Egypt or the kings of the XXIst and XXIIId dynasties making it their capital

tan·jong \'tänˌjȯŋ\ *n* -S [Malay, cape, headland, promontory] **:** CAPE, POINT

¹tank \'taŋk, -aiŋk\ *n* -S [Pg *tanque*, short for *estanque*, fr. *estancar* to stop a flow, dam, stanch, fr. (assumed) VL *stanticare* to cause to stand, stanch — more at STANCH] **1 a** *India* **:** a pool of water **:** LAKE, RESERVOIR **b** *dial* **:** a small lake **:** POND, POOL; *esp* **:** a pond built as a water supply **c :** a basin where experimental models of ships are tested ⟨submarine ~⟩ **2 a :** a usu. large artificial receptacle used for holding, transporting, or storing liquids ⟨gasoline ~⟩ ⟨fish ~⟩ ⟨oil ~⟩ **b :** a compartment in a ship for holding water, oil, or liquids **c :** a container in or attached to an airplane for carrying fuel; *esp* **:** one that is auxiliary or droppable and used to increase range or to carry napalm **3** [so called fr. the fact that during its orig. secret manufacture in England the hull was referred to as a water tank] **:** a full-track enclosed armored vehicle that usu. mounts a cannon and automatic weapons and has excellent cross-country mobility, armor protection, fire power, and the capability of shock action — compare ARMORED CAR **4 :** TANK FURNACE **5 :** a container for a photographic solution **6 :** a congregate prison cell or enclosure used esp. for receiving prisoners

²tank \"\ *vt* -ED/-ING/-S **1 :** to subject to some operation in a tank; *specif* **:** to treat (as animal refuse) in a closed tank with steam and hot water to extract fat **2 :** to cause to flow into a tank **:** store in a tank

³tank \"\ *n* -S [imit.] *dial chiefly Eng* **:** KNOCK, HIT, BANG

⁴tank \'täŋk\ *n, pl* **tank** [Hindi *ṭāk*, fr. Skt *ṭaṅka* stamped coin] **:** an Indian unit of weight for pearls equal to about 0.15 ounce

¹tan·ka \'dänˈgä\ *n, pl* **tanka** *or* **tankas** *usu cap* [Chin (Cant) *taánka*, lit., egg people] **:** ⁶TAN

²tanka *or* **tankah** *var of* TANGA

³tan·ka \'täŋkə\ *n* -S [Jap] **:** a Japanese fixed form of verse of five lines the first and third of which have five syllables and the others seven — compare HOKKU

⁴tanka \"\ *n* -S [Tibetan *thaṅka*] **:** a Tibetan religious painting mounted on brocade for use as a processional banner

tank·age \'taŋkij, -aiŋ-, -kēj\ *n* -s **1 :** the capacity or contents of a tank **2 :** a by-product of slaughterhouses or rendering plants that consists of animal residues (as meat scrap, blood, and bone) cooked and usu. freed of fat and gelatine and dried and that is used in feeds and fertilizers — see DIGESTER TANKAGE, GARBAGE TANKAGE **3 a :** the act or process of putting or storing in tanks **b :** fees charged for storage in tanks

tan·kard \-ŋkə(r)d\ *n* -s [ME] **1 :** a tall one-handled drinking vessel; *esp* **:** a mug of silver or pewter with a lid **2 :** a drink served in a tankard ⟨we can give you cold meat and a ~ —Charles Lamb⟩

tank barge *n* **:** a barge equipped with tanks for transporting liquids

tank car *n* **:** a railroad car for transporting liquids or gases in bulk

tank circuit *n* **1 :** an oscillatory radio circuit associated with the output circuit of a tube generator which absorbs the generator ouput in the form of energy impulses of high value and short duration and in turn delivers its output to an antenna **2 :** a tuned circuit connected in the plate circuit of a tube generator **3 :** an absorption circuit

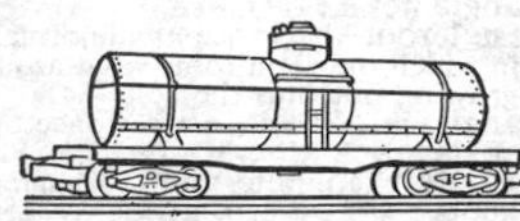
tank car

tank destroyer *n* **:** a highly mobile lightly armored vehicle that is usu. constructed on a half track or a tank chassis and mounts a cannon

tank dome *n* **:** the vertical chamber on the top of a tank car

tank·doz·er \'=,dōzə(r)\ *n* [¹*tank* + bull*dozer*] **:** a tank with a bulldozer blade attached

tank drama *n* **1 :** a melodrama having as its chief sensation the use of a tank of water usu. in representing a rescue from drowning **2 :** a spectacular sensational play; *esp* **:** one with cheap or claptrap effects **3 :** drama suitable for or played in tank towns

tanked *adj* [fr. past part. of *tank* (in *tank up*)] **:** DRUNK

tank engine *n* **:** TANK LOCOMOTIVE

tank·er \'taŋkə(r), -aiŋ-\ *n* -s **1 a :** a steel cargo boat fitted with tanks for the carrying of oil, molasses, or other liquid in bulk **b :** a vehicle on which a tank is mounted to carry liquids (as water, gasoline, milk, chemicals) — see TANK TRAILER, TANK TRUCK, TANK WAGON **c :** a cargo airplane fitted with large fuel tanks inside its fuselage for transporting fuel to advance air bases or for use in aerial refueling **2 :** one that tends to tanks **3 a :** a member of the armored branch of the armed forces **b :** a member of a military tank crew **4** [prob. fr. ¹*tank* + *-er;* fr. his taking a dive] **:** a boxer who goes down easily esp. in a fixed fight

tan·ker·a·bo·gus \,taŋkərə'bōgəs\ *n* -ES [prob. fr. *tanker* (alter. of *tantara*) + *bogus*, alter. of *bogey*] *dial Eng* **:** BOOGEYMAN

tank·er·man \'taŋkə(r)mən, 'taiŋ-\ *n, pl* **tankermen :** a seaman who is a qualified member of a crew of a tanker

tank·ette \(')taŋ¦ket\ *n* -s [¹*tank* + *-ette*] **:** a small military tank

tank farm *n* **:** a continuous area used exclusively for the field storage of oil in tanks; *esp* **:** such an area with all of the tanks and equipment

tank farming *n* **:** HYDROPONICS

tank furnace *n* **:** a hearth or basin into one end of which a batch is shoveled and from the other end of which melted glass is drawn

tanking *pres part of* TANK

tank iron *n* **:** plate iron thinner than boiler plate and thicker than sheet iron or stovepipe iron

tan·kle \'taŋkəl\ *n* -s [short for *tinkle-tankle*, redupl. of *tinkle*] **:** a sound louder and less acute than a tinkle

tank locomotive *n* **:** a locomotive having compartments for carrying its own fuel and water and not needing a tender

tank·man \'taŋkmən, 'taiŋ-\ *n, pl* **tankmen 1 :** a worker who tends tanks or vats in which an industrial operation is carried out **2 :** TANKER 3 **3 :** an attendant in an aquarium who takes care of the fish and aquatic plants and their tanks

tank runner *n* **:** PHEASANT-TAILED JACANA

tanks *pl of* TANK, *pres 3d sing of* TANK

tankship \'=,=\ *n* **:** TANKER 1

tank-stock \'=,=\ *n* **:** lumber from heartwood of California redwood, western red cedar, and other trees that has close grain and high decay resistance and is well suited for wood= tank construction

tank table *n* **:** a table that has a tank-shaped top and is suitable for collecting oil cast in it

tank top *n* **:** INNER BOTTOM

tank town *n* **1 :** a town at which trains stop for water **2 :** an insignificant small town ⟨a kind of tent show playing the *tank towns* —Thomas Pyles⟩

tank trailer *n* **:** a truck-drawn trailer equipped and used as a tanker

tank trap *n* **:** a natural or artificial obstacle of sufficient width and depth and with steep sides to stop military tanks

tank truck *n* **:** a truck equipped and used as a tanker

tank up *vi* **:** to stuff oneself with food or drink ⟨*tank up* on breakfast —G.S.Perry⟩ ⟨*tanked up* on beer —J.V.Fox⟩; *esp* **:** to drink liquor to excess

tank wagon *n* **:** a horse-drawn wagon equipped and used as a tanker

tan·ling \'tanliŋ\ *n* -s [³*tan* + *-ling*] **:** one tanned by the sun

tann- *or* **tanno-** *comb form* [F, fr. *tannin, tanin* — more at TANNIN] **:** tan **:** tannin **:** tanning substance ⟨*tanno*gen⟩ ⟨*tann*ase⟩ ⟨*tanno*meter⟩

tan·na *also* **ta·na** \'tä(,)nä\ *n, pl* **tanna·im** *also* **tana·im** \,tänä'im, -nä'ēm\ *often cap* [Heb *tannā'* teacher, tanna, fr. Aram *tĕnā* to repeat, teach] **:** one of the rabbis of Palestine during the first two centuries A.D. whose interpretations of biblical law and Hebrew oral tradition are recorded in the Mishnah, Tosephta, and other works together with their parables and homiletic comments on Scripture — compare AMORA, SABORA

tan·nage \'tanij\ *n* -s [¹*tan* + *-age*] **:** the act, process, or result of tanning

tan·na·ite \'tänə,īt\ *n* -s *often cap* [Heb *tannā'* + E *-ite*] **:** TANNA

tan·na·it·ic \,tänə¦id-ik\ *also* **tan·na·ic** \tä'nä,ik\ *adj, often cap* [*tannaitic* fr. *tannaite* + *-ic; tannaic* fr. *tanna* + *-ic*] **:** of or relating to the tannaim

tan·nase \'ta,nās, -āz\ *n* -s [ISV *tann-* + *-ase*] **:** an enzyme that accelerates the hydrolysis of a tannin

tan·nate \-nāt\ *n* -s [F, fr. *tann-* (fr. *tannin, tanin*) + *-ate*] **:** a compound (as a salt) of a tannin

tanned *adj* [ME, partly fr. past part. of *tannen* to tan hides & partly fr. OE *getanned*, fr. past part. of *tannian* to tan hides, prob. fr. ML *tannare* — more at TAN] **1 :** treated or colored by tanning **2 :** made tawny or brown by exposure to the sun **:** covered with tan

¹**tan·ner** \'tanə(r), 'taan-\ *n* -s [ME, fr. OE *tannere*, fr. *tannian* to tan hides + *-ere* -er] **:** one that tans hides

²**tanner** *comparative of* TAN

³**tan·ner** \'tanə(r)\ *n* -s [origin unknown] *Brit* **:** SIXPENCE

tanner's bark *n* **:** TANBARK

tanner's sumac *or* **tanning sumac** *n* **:** a European sumac (*Rhus coriaria*) widely grown in Sicily for use in tanning and dyeing

tanner's wool *n* **:** ²SLIPE

tan·nery \'tanərē, 'taan-, -ri\ *n* -ES **1 :** a place where the work of tanning is carried on **2 :** the art or process of tanning

tannery fungus *n* **:** a slime mold (*Fuligo septica*) common on tanbark

tannest *superlative of* TAN

tannia *or* **tannier** *var of* TANIA

tan·nic \'tanik, -nēk\ *adj* [F *tannique*, fr. *tann-* + *-ique* -ic] **:** of or relating to tan **:** derived from or resembling tan or a tannin

tannic acid *n* **1 :** GALLOTANNIN **2 :** TANNIN 1b

tan·nide \'ta,nīd, -,nəd\ *n* -s [*tann-* + *-ide*] **:** a substance that whether it is a tannin or not gives microchemical tannin reactions and that may occur in the same plant cells with alkaloids sometimes combined with them

tan·nif·er·ous \(')ta¦nif(ə)rəs\ *adj* [*tann-* + *-iferous*] **:** yielding or containing tannin

tan·nin \'tanən\ *n* -s [F *tannin, tanin*, fr. *tanner* to tan hides (fr. MF) + *-in* — more at TAN] **1 a :** GALLOTANNIN **b :** any of a group of soluble astringent complex phenolic substances including gallotannin that are widely distributed in plants and are obtained commercially from various sources (as powdered gallnuts, shredded tara, quebracho wood, chestnut wood, wattle, sumac, valonia), that precipitate gelatin and albumin from solution and tan skin and hides, that also precipitate many alkaloids and most basic dyes, that form bluish black or greenish black colors or precipitates with ferric salts, that have been classified on the basis of behavior with acids or enzymes as either hydrolyzable to water-soluble products or as condensed yielding phlobaphenes, and that are used chiefly in tanning, dyeing, and making ink and in medicine as astringents and formerly in the treatment of burns — compare ELLAGITANNIN, TEA TANNIN **2 :** a substance that has a tanning effect as determined by its adsorption by hide powder **:** TAN 2b

tan·nined \-ənd\ *adj* **:** impregnated or treated with tannin

tanning *n* -s [ME, fr. gerund of *tannen* to tan] **1 :** the art or process by which a skin is tanned **2 :** a browning esp. of the skin by exposure to sun **3 :** a usu. severe whipping ⟨when his father got home he'd get a good ~⟩

tanning drum *n* **:** a revolving wood or metal container used for tumbling hides in the tanning process

tanning extract *n* **:** an extract that may be liquid, semisolid, or solid and that is made from tanniferous material (as oak bark, sumac leaves and twigs, or quebracho wood) for use in tanning

tan·nish \'tanish\ *adj* [³*tan* + *-ish*] **:** somewhat tan

tanno- — see TANN-

¹**tan·noid** \'ta,nȯid\ *adj* [*tann-* + *-oid*] **:** resembling the tannins

²**tannoid** \"\ *n* -s **:** a tannoid substance

tan·nom·e·ter \ta'nämət-ə(r)\ *n* [*tann-* + *-meter*] **1 :** an apparatus for determining the strength of a tanning liquor by drawing it through hide and measuring its resulting loss in density **2 :** BARKOMETER

tannu-tuvan \,tanü'tüvən\ *n* -s *cap both Ts* [*Tannu-Tuva*, former name of the Tuva Autonomous Region + E *-an*] **:** a native or inhabitant of the Tuva Autonomous Region, U.S.S.R. — called also *Tuvinian*

ta·no \'tä(,)nō\ *n* -s *usu cap* **1 :** a group of former pueblos lying south of Santa Fe, New Mexico **2 :** an Indian of any of the Tano pueblos

ta·noa \tə'nōə\ *n* -s [Samoan, Tongan, & Fijian] **:** a bowl used in western Polynesia and Fiji for kava

tan oak *n* **:** TANBARK OAK a

¹**ta·no·an** \'tänəwən\ *adj, usu cap* [*tano* + E *-an* (adj. suffix)] **1 :** of or relating to the Tanos **2 :** of or relating to Tanoan

²**tanoan** \"\ *n* -s *usu cap* [*tano* + E *-an*] **:** a language family of New Mexico including Tewa, Tiwa, and Towa

tan pit *n* **:** TAN VAT

tan·que·lin·i·an \,taŋkə'linēən, ,taŋ-\ *n* -s *usu cap* [*Tanquelin* (Tanchelm) †1115? Flemish heretic + E *-an*] **:** TANCHELMIAN

tanrec *var of* TENREC

tan ride *n* **:** a riding track covered with tan

tan rot *n* **:** a disease of strawberries caused by a fungus (*Pezizella lythri*) and characterized by somewhat sunken tan-colored areas in the fruit that lift out readily

tans *pres 3d sing of* TAN, *pl of* TAN

tan spud *n* **:** a spud used for stripping bark from trees

tan·sy *also* **tan·sey** \'tanzē, 'taan-, -zi\ *n, pl* **tansies** *or* **tanseys** [ME *tansy, tanesey*, fr. OF *tanesie*, fr. ML *athanasia* medicine to prolong life, tansy, fr. Gk, immortality, fr. *a-* ²a- + *-thanasia* (fr. *thanatos* death) — more at THANAT-] **1 a :** a plant of the genus *Tanacetum; esp* **:** a common herb (*T. vulgare*) with a strong aromatic odor and a very bitter taste **b :** any of various other plants: as (1) **:** SILVERWEED a (1) (2) **:** TANSY RAGWORT **2 :** a tansy-flavored cake or pudding

tansy mustard *n* **:** an herb of the genus *Descurainia; esp* **:** a No. American herb (*D. pinnata*) that resembles a cress but has leaves like those of a tansy

tansy oil *n* **:** a yellow poisonous essential oil obtained from the leaves and tops of the common tansy

tansy ragwort *n* **:** a common ragwort (*Senecio jacobaea*) with pinnatifid leaves and compact clusters of yellow flower heads that is native to Europe, No. Africa, and western Asia but has been introduced in No. America, New Zealand, and Australia and in some areas is a dangerous and aggressive weed and toxic to cattle when consumed in quantity

tan·ta \'täntə\ *adj, usu cap* [fr. *Tanta*, Egypt] **:** of or from the city of Tanta, Egypt **:** of the kind or style prevalent in Tanta

tantal- *or* **tantalo-** *also* **tantali-** *comb form* [Sw, fr. NL *tantalum*] **:** tantalum ⟨*tantali*ferous⟩

tan·ta·late \'tant³l,āt, -³lət\ *n* -s [ISV *tantal*ic + *-ate*] **:** a salt of a tantalic acid

tan·ta·le·an \,tant³l'ēən, (')tan·¦talē-\ *or* **tan·ta·li·an** \(')tan·¦talē-\ *adj, usu cap* [L *tantaleus* of or relating to Tantalus (fr. *Tantalus*, mythical king) + E *-an*] **:** of or relating to Tantalus **:** ELUSIVE, TANTALIZING

tan·tal·ic \(')tan·¦talik\ *adj* [ISV *tantal-* + *-ic*] **:** of, relating to, or derived from tantalum

tantalic acid *n* **:** any of several weakly acidic hydrated forms $Ta_2O_5.nH_2O$ of tantalum pentoxide that react with alkalies to yield salts

tan·ta·lite \'tant³l,īt\ *n* -s [Sw *tantalit*, fr. NL *tantalum* + Sw *-it* -ite] **:** a mineral $(FeMn)(TaCb)_2O_6$ consisting of a heavy iron-black oxide of iron, manganese, tantalum, and columbium that is isomorphous with columbite (hardness 6, sp. gr. up to 7.3)

tan·ta·li·za·tion \,tant³lə'zāshən, ,taan-, -³l,ī'z-\ *n* -s **:** the act or process of tantalizing ⟨a girl with an infinite capacity for ~ —H.T.Moore⟩

tan·ta·lize \'tant³l,īz, 'taan-\ *vb* -ED/-ING/-s *see -ize in Explan Notes* [*Tantalus*, in Greco-Roman mythology the king of Phrygia who for his sins was condemned to stand in Tartarus up to his chin in water that receded whenever he stooped to drink and under some branches of fruit that likewise receded whenever he tried to grasp them (fr. L, fr. Gk *Tantalos*) + E *-ize*] *vt* **:** to tease or torment by presenting something to the view and exciting desire but continually frustrating the expectations by keeping it out of reach ⟨anchors, dots, and arrows on the rocks . . . have long *tantalized* treasure hunters —*Amer. Guide Series: Oregon*⟩ ⟨*tantalized* by dreams of being . . . his country's savior —John Buchan⟩ ⟨~ their publishers by submitting synopses that sparkle —Bennett Cerf⟩ ~ *vi, obs* **:** to suffer in a manner resembling Tantalus **syn** see WORRY

tan·ta·liz·er \-zə(r)\ *n* -s **:** one that tantalizes

tantalizing *adj* **:** possessing a quality that arouses or stimulates desire or interest **:** mockingly or enticingly out of reach **:** teasingly provocative ⟨for me it remained a ~ puzzle —Herbert Passin⟩ ⟨smiled his lazy ~ smile —P.B.Kyne⟩ ⟨thick shrubs make it impossible to get more than a ~ glimpse of this beautiful house —S.P.B.Mais⟩

tan·ta·liz·ing·ly \'==,==, ,==¦==\ *adv* **:** in a tantalizing manner ⟨a ~ slim chance of survival in the courts —Wenzell Brown⟩ ⟨illuminate an era of human life and of nature so ~ recent and so utterly destroyed —John Collier b.1884⟩

tan·ta·lum \'tant³ləm\ *n* -s [NL, fr. *Tantalus*, mythical king condemned to stand up to his chin in water that receded whenever he stooped to drink; fr. its incapacity to absorb acid] **:** a lustrous platinum-gray hard ductile metallic element that has a very high melting point, that is chiefly pentavalent and is resistant to attack by most chemicals except hydrofluoric acid, that occurs combined in tantalite, columbite, and other rare minerals almost always associated with niobium, that is extracted usu. by the formation and reduction of a complex potassium tantalum fluoride, and that is used chiefly in making corrosion-resistant chemical apparatus and processing equipment, in electrolytic capacitors and rectifiers, in surgery as suture wire and bone-repair plates, and in alloys — symbol *Ta;* see ELEMENT table

tantalum carbide *n* **:** a very high-melting heavy dark yellow or brown crystalline compound TaC that is one of the hardest substances known, that is made by heating carbon with tantalum or tantalum pentoxide at high temperatures, and that is used in the cutting edges of high-speed tools, in dies, and in wear-resisting parts

tantalum gauze *or* **tantalum mesh** *n* **:** a flexible netting of tantalum wire used esp. in the repair of large hernias and other body defects

tantalum lamp *n* **:** an incandescent lamp with tantalum filament

tantalum oxide *n* **:** an oxide of tantalum; *esp* **:** the crystalline pentoxide Ta_2O_5 obtained by igniting tantalum in air or oxygen and used in making optical glass and tantalum carbide

¹**tan·ta·lus** \'tant³ləs, 'taan-\ [NL, fr. *Tantalus*, mythical king] *syn of* MYCTERIA

²**tantalus** \"\ *n* -ES [after *Tantalus* — more at TANTALIZE] **:** a locked case or cellaret for wines and liquors having the contents visible but not obtainable without a key

tantalus

tantamount \'tantə,maunt\ *adj* [obs. E *tantamount*, n., something equivalent, fr. *tant amount*, v., to amount to as much, fr. AF *tant amunter*, fr. OF *tant* so much, as much (fr. L *tantum*, fr. neut. of *tantus* so great, fr. *tam* so, so much, as) + *amounter* to ascend, add up to; akin to Skt *tat*, neut. demonstrative pron. — more at THAT, AMOUNT] **:** equivalent in value, significance, or effect ⟨refusal to prolong the truce . . . would be ~ to a threat —*Current Biog.*⟩ **syn** see SAME

tan·tara \tan·'tarə, -'tärə; 'tantərə\ *also* **tan·ta·rara** \,tantə'rarə, -'rärə\ *or* **tar·an·tara** \,tarən'tarə, -tärən-, -n'tärə; tə'rantərə\ *or* **tar·a·tan·tara** \,tarə,tan'tarə, -'tär,t-, -'tärə; ,=='tantərə\ *n* -s [*tantara, tantarara, tarantara* by shortening & alter. fr. L *taratantara*, of imit. origin] **1 a :** the blare of a trumpet or horn **b :** FANFARE **2 :** a sound resembling a trumpet call ⟨the ~ of growing winds —Gene Fowler⟩

tan·ta·ra·bo·bus \,tantərə'bōbəs\ *n* -ES [prob. fr. *tantara* + *bobus*, alter. of *bogey*] *dial Eng* **:** BOOGEYMAN

tan·ti \'təntē\ *n* -s [Skt, weaver, fr. *tanoti* he stretches, weaves — more at THIN] **:** one of a Hindu caste of weavers of Assam and Bengal

tan·tième \tän·tyem\ *n* -s [F, fr. *tant* so much + *-ème* thing, unit, -eme] **:** a percentage or proportional share esp. of profits or earnings; *also* **:** BONUS

¹**tan·tivy** \(')tan·¦tivē\ *adv* [origin unknown] **:** in a headlong dash **:** at a gallop ⟨for three weeks U.S. tabloids went ~ after her . . . diary —*Time*⟩

²**tantivy** \"\ *n* -ES **1 :** a rapid gallop or ride **:** rushing movement **:** impetuous rush **2** *usu cap* [so called fr. a cartoon published in 1680–81 in England that depicted a number of Tory clergymen mounted upon the Church of England and riding tantivy to Rome behind the duke of York] **:** an English Royalist or Tory esp. of the last quarter of the 17th century **3 :** the blare of a horn ⟨the fanfare and ~ of the bugles were stilled —Frank Sullivan⟩

³**tantivy** \"\ *adj* [²*tantivy*] **:** having the demeanor of a Tantivy

tan·to \'tän·(,)tō\ *adv* [It, fr. L *tantum* — more at TANTAMOUNT] **:** MUCH **:** so much ⟨allegro non ~ (brisk, but not too much so)⟩

tan·tra \'tən·trə\ *n* -s *often cap* [Skt, lit., warp, essential part, doctrine, fr. *tanoti* he stretches, weaves — more at THIN] **1 :** a Hindu religious writing of the less ancient fourth class of shastras containing mystical teachings (as that the natural processes of creation and destruction rather than being illusory manifest the active conscious energy of divine spirit to be worshiped as a goddess wife of a Vedic god who attains his highest power in union with her) and ritual instructions including magical incantations, gestures, and diagrams (as for healing illness, averting evil), largely supplanting the Vedas, and forming esp. the scriptures of the Shakta sects **2 :** one of a body of related Buddhist treatises of similar character

tan·tric *or* **tan·trik** \-rik\ *adj, often cap* [Skt *tāntrika*, fr. *tantra* + *-ika*, adj. suffix — more at -Y] **1 :** of or relating to the tantras or Tantrism ⟨the gross *Tantric* rites connected with the worship of Kali —A.C.Bouquet⟩ **2 :** having the character of a tantra or Tantrism ⟨~ Buddhism⟩

tan·trism \'tən,trizəm\ *n* -s *usu cap* [*tantra* + *-ism*] **1 :** SHAKTISM **2 :** a school of Mahayana Buddhism originating in northern India and formative in Lamaism and Shingon that incorporates Hindu and pagan elements (as pantheistic mysticism, spells, the worship of female divinities) and teaches that the individual can realize his essential Buddhahood and obtain earthly benefits by theurgic practices (as mantra, mudra, erotic rites)

tan·trist \'tən·trəst\ *n* -s *usu cap* **:** a follower of Tantrism

tan·trum \'tan·trəm, 'taan-,'tain-\ *n* -s [origin unknown] **:** a burst of ill humor **:** a fit of bad temper ⟨a brief outburst of ~ at a children's tea party —Richard Joseph⟩ ⟨~s that used to flare up after the chimpanzees had made the wrong choice and had been denied food —G.W.Gray b.1886⟩

tan vat *n* **:** a vat in which hides steep in liquor with tan

tanwood \'=,=\ *n* **:** wood yielding a tanning extract

tany- *comb form* [NL, fr. Gk, long, stretched out — more at THIN] **:** stretched out ⟨*Tany*stomata⟩ ⟨*Tany*gnathus⟩

tanya *also* **tanyah** *var of* TANIA

tanyard \'=,=\ *n* [³*tan* + *yard*] **:** the section or portion of a tannery housing tanning vats

tany·lo·bous \,tanə¦lōbəs\ *adj* [NL, fr. *tany-* + *lobus*] **:** having or being an elongated prostomium set off by a groove and overlapping the first true segments in the form of a tonguelike process ⟨an annelid worm with a ~ prostomium⟩

tan·yo·sho pine \tän'yō(,)shō-\ *n* [*tanyosho* fr. Jap, umbrella pine] **:** a low-growing broad-headed ornamental pine that is a variety (*Pinus densiflora umbraculifera*) of the Japanese red pine — called also *umbrella pine*

tany·sto·ma·ta \,tanə'stōməd·ə\ *n pl, cap* [NL, fr. *tany-* + *-stomata*] *in some classifications* **:** a division of dipterous insects in which the proboscis is large and contains lancelike mandibles and maxillae — compare HORSEFLY, ROBBER FLY

tany·stoma·tous \¦==¦stäməd·əs, -tōm-\ *adj* [NL *Tanystomata* + E *-ous*] **:** of or relating to the Tanystomata

tany·stome \'==,stōm\ *n* -s [F, fr. *tany-* + *-stome*] **:** an insect of the division Tanystomata

tan·za·nia \¦tanzə¦nēə\ *adj, usu cap* [fr. *Tanzania*, country in eastern Africa] **:** of or from the country of Tanzania **:** of the kind or style prevalent in Tanzania

tan·za·ni·an \-ēən\ *n* -s *cap* [*Tanzania*, Africa + E *-an*] **:** a native or inhabitant of Tanzania — **tanzanian** *adj, usu cap*

¹**tao** \'tau̇, 'dau̇\ *n* -s [Chin (Pek) *tao⁴*, lit., way] **1** *Taoism* **a :** the unitary first principle from which all existence and all change in the universe spring **:** the unconditioned unnameable source of all reality that transcends being and nonbeing by standing above and beyond all distinctions **b :** the eternal order of the universe **2** *Confucianism* **a :** the right way of life **:** the path of virtuous conduct **b :** the principles that govern each separate category of existence **c :** the universal criterion of right and wrong **:** TRUTH **d :** the ultimate principle of universal reality **:** cosmic reason

²**tao** \'tau̇\ *n* -s [Tag, person, man] *Philippines* **:** MAN, PEASANT

taoi·seach \'thēshək\ *n* -s [IrGael, lit., leader, chief] *Irish* **:** PRIME MINISTER

tao·ism \'tau̇,izəm, 'dau̇-\ *n* -s *cap* [¹*tao* + *-ism*] **:** a religion and philosophy of China traditionally founded by Lao-tzu in the 6th century B.C. and orig. teaching conformity to the Tao by unassertive action and retirement from the world for a pristine simplicity but later becoming a highly syncretistic religion greatly concerned with obtaining longevity and immortality often by magical means

¹**tao·ist** \-əst\ *or* **tao·is·tic** \(')=¦istik\ *adj, usu cap* [¹*tao* + *-ist* or *-istic*] **:** of or relating to Taoism

²**taoist** \"\ *n* -s *cap* [¹*tao* + *-ist*] **:** an adherent of Taoism

taos \'tau̇s\ *n, pl* **taos** *usu cap* **1 a :** a Tanoan people occupying a pueblo in New Mexico **b :** a member of such people **2 :** the language of the Taos people

tao-ti·eh \¦tau̇tē¦ā\ *n* -s [Chin (Pek) *t'ao¹- t'ieh⁴*] **:** an often conventionalized figure of a mythical animal's face appearing as a decorative motive on very ancient objects of Chinese art and possibly intended as a warning against gluttony

[1]tap \'tap\ n -s [ME *tappe*, fr. OE *tæppa*; akin to MD *tappe* tap, OHG *zapho*, ON *tappi* tap, OE *ātimplian* to provide with nails, MLG *timpe* tip and prob. to OHG *zumpfo* penis, Av *duma* tail] **1 a :** a plug for stopping a hole (as in a cask) **:** SPIGOT **b :** a device consisting of a spout and valve that is attached to the end of a pipe to control the flow of a liquid or gas **:** FAUCET, COCK ⟨turn on the ~ of a hydrant⟩ **c :** CORPORATION COCK **2 a** (1) **:** liquor drawn through a tap (2) *archaic* **:** a particular kind or quality of liquor ⟨liquor of the same ~⟩ **b :** a quantity of a liquid (as molten metal from a furnace) run out at one time **c :** the procedure of removing fluid (as from a body cavity) ⟨a spinal ~⟩ **3** [by shortening] **:** TAPROOM **4** [by shortening] **:** TAPHOLE **5 a :** a tool for forming an internal screw thread (as in a nut) consisting of a hardened tool-steel male screw grooved longitudinally so as to have cutting edges — see BOTTOMING TAP, HAND TAP, MACHINE TAP, PIPE TAP **b :** NUT 3 **6** *slang* **:** a request for a loan or gift **7 a :** a connection to an electric coil making it possible to place only part of the coil in circuit **b :** a wire brought from a winding to which connections may be made **c :** a current tap **d :** an intermediate point where an electrical connection may be made **8 :** the action or an instance of wiretapping ⟨put a ~ on the suspect's telephone —Joel Sayre⟩ — **on tap 1 :** ready to be drawn ⟨ale *on tap*⟩ **2 :** broached or furnished with a tap **3 :** on hand **:** AVAILABLE ⟨other sports and entertainment facilities are *on tap* —Richard Joseph⟩ ⟨doesn't have to think: the newspapers are always *on tap* —Henry Miller⟩ **4 :** offered for sale continuously and not limited as to amount that can be purchased — used esp. of government securities ⟨savings bonds are sold *on tap*⟩

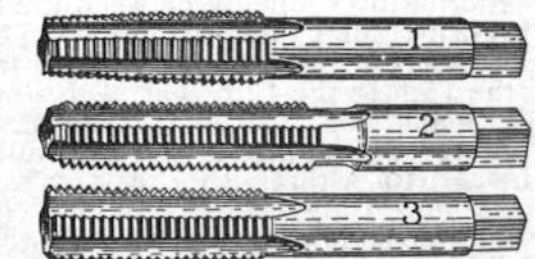
taps 5a: *1* taper, *2* second, *3* bottoming

[2]tap \"\ vb **tapped; tapped; tapping; taps** [ME *tappen*, fr. OE *tæppian*; akin to MD *tappen* to draw off, tap, OHG *zepfo*; denominative fr. the root of E [1]*tap*] vt **1 :** to furnish with a tap ⟨~ a bolt⟩ **2 :** to let out or cause to flow by piercing or by drawing a plug from the containing vessel ⟨~ a liquor⟩ **3 a :** to pierce so as to let out or draw off a fluid **:** draw off or drain off fluid or gas from ⟨~ a cask⟩ ⟨~ the abdomen⟩ ⟨~ a rubber tree⟩ ⟨~ a blast furnace⟩ **b :** to open up (anything) so as to extract something **:** draw from ⟨several railways ~ the region —C.L.White & G.T.Renner⟩ ⟨~ new sources of energy⟩ **4 :** to remove the taproot from **5 :** to form a female screw in by means of a tap ⟨~ a nut⟩ — distinguished from *thread* **6 :** to get money from as a loan or gift **7 :** to connect (a street gas or water main) with a local supply (as at a house) by a corporation cock **8 a :** to connect or cut in (an electrical circuit) on another circuit **b :** to cut in on (a telephone or telegraph wire) to get messages, information, or evidence **9 :** to bet in a game of poker played for table stakes all the money in the possession of (oneself) or an amount equaling all the money in the possession of (an opponent) whichever is the lesser amount **~** *vi* **:** to tap oneself or an opponent in game of poker played for table stakes

[3]tap \"\ adj [fr. the phrase (*on*) *tap*] **:** offered for sale continuously and not in a fixed total amount ⟨a ~ issue of government bonds⟩ — see TAP BOND

[4]tap \"\ vb **tapped; tapped; tapping; taps** [ME *tappen*; partly fr. MF *taper* to strike with the flat of the hand, of Gmc origin; akin to MHG *tāpe* paw, blow dealt with the paw; partly of Scand origin; akin to Sw dial. *tāpa* to tap, ON *tæpta*; akin to MLG *tappen* to tug, pluck, ON *tapa* to lose, bring to an end, destroy and prob. to OHG *teilen* to divide, Skt *dayate* he apportions — more at DEAL, TIDE] vt **1 :** to strike lightly esp. with a slight sound **:** rap lightly and repeatedly ⟨*tapped* a typewriter all morning⟩ ⟨*tapped* me on the shoulder with his forefinger⟩ ⟨~ a bell with a hammer⟩ ⟨~ a brick into place⟩ ⟨had *tapped* him to sleep with a blackjack —Erle Stanley Gardner⟩ **2 :** to give one or more light usu. audible blows with ⟨~ a pencil on the table⟩ **3 :** to produce by striking repeatedly with light blows ⟨a woodpecker *tapped* a hole in the tree⟩ — often used with *out* ⟨~ out a telegraph message⟩ ⟨~ out a paragraph on a typewriter⟩ **4 :** to repair by putting a tap on ⟨~ shoes⟩ **5 :** SELECT, DESIGNATE ⟨was *tapped* for police commissioner⟩; *specif* **:** to elect to membership in a particular organization (as a fraternity) **6 :** to divert (a basketball) to a player of one's own side or into the basket by a tap with the fingertips **:** TIP **~** *vi* **1 :** to strike lightly but audibly **:** RAP ⟨moths *tapped* and blurred at the window screen —R.P.Warren⟩ **2** *of a hare or rabbit* **:** to drum with the feet **3 :** to walk with light but audible steps ⟨*tapped* off on nonchalant heels —LaSelle Gilman⟩ **4 :** TAP-DANCE

[5]tap \"\ n -s [ME *tape, tappe*, fr. *tappen* to tap] **1 a :** a light usu. audible blow **:** a light rap **b :** the sound of a light blow ⟨the ~ of ivy on the pane —Virginia Woolf⟩ **c :** one of several drumbeats on a snare drum played usu. at a rapid speed **d :** a striking of the ball with the fingertips in basketball ⟨gained the opening ~⟩ **e :** FLAP 6 **2 :** a partial sole put on over the worn sole of a shoe **:** HALF SOLE — called also *tap sole* **3 :** a slight amount ⟨didn't do a ~ of work⟩ ⟨without a ~ of work or fuss by your client —*Empire State Architect*⟩ **4 taps** \'taps\ *pl* **a :** a small metal plate for attaching to the sole or heel of a shoe esp. to make a clicking sound (as in tap dancing) — compare CLEAT 2a **b :** TAP SHOE **c :** a step (as in tap dancing) in which the ball or the toes of one foot are touched lightly to the floor so as to make a sound **d :** TAP DANCE ⟨~ lessons⟩ **5 :** a solid hit in the pocket that leaves a lone bowling pin standing

[6]tap \'təp\ n -s [Hindi, fr. Skt *tapa* heat, fr. *tapati* it gives out heat — more at TEPID] **1** *India* **:** HEAT **2** *India* **:** MALARIAL FEVER 1 **3** *India* **:** PENANCE

[7]tap \'tap\ n -s [by shortening] **:** TAPADERO

[1]ta·pa *also* **tap·pa** \'täpə\ n -s [Marquesan & Tahitian *tapa*] **1 :** the bark of the paper mulberry or of an Hawaiian tree (*Pipturus albidus*) **2** *or* **tapa cloth :** a coarse cloth made in the Pacific islands from the pounded bark of the paper mulberry, breadfruit, and other plants, usu. decorated with geometric patterns, and still used as clothing and covering in isolated islands but elsewhere worn only on festive occasions, exchanged ceremonially, used as a house ornament, or sold to foreigners

[2]tapa \"\ n -s [Sp, fr. *tapar* to stop up, cover, fr. *tapa* cover, lid, of Gmc origin; akin to OE *tæppa* tap — more at TAP] **:** SNACK

ta·pa·chu·la \,täpə'chülə\ *or* **ta·pa·chul·tec** \-'chül,tek\ n, *pl* **tapachula** *or* **tapachulas** *or* **tapachultec** *or* **tapachultecs** *usu cap* [MexSp, fr. Nahuatl] **1 a :** a Zoquean people of the Mexico-Guatemala border region **b :** a member of such people **2 :** the language of the Tapachula people

tap·a·co·lo \,tapə'kō(,)lō *or* **tap·a·cu·lo** \-'kü(,)lō\ n -s [AmerSp *tapaculo*, lit., one that covers its backside, fr. Sp *tapar* to cover + *culo* backside, fr. L *culus* — more at CULET] **1 :** a small plainly colored clamatorial terrestrial bird (*Scelorchilus albicollis*) of the family Rhinocryptidae of Chile and Argentina having short rounded wings and short tail carried erect **2 :** any of several birds related to the tapacolo — see TURCO

tap·a·de·ro \,tapə'de(,)rō\ *or* **tap·a·de·ra** \-rə\ n -s [AmerSp, fr. Sp, cover, plug, fr. *tapar* to cover, stop up] *West* **:** a leather hood covering the stirrup of a stock saddle and used esp. to protect the boot when riding through brush

tap bolt *n* **:** a headed bolt used without a nut for screwing into a hole — called also *cap screw, tap screw;* see BOLT illustration

tap bond *n* **:** a government security of an issue unlimited in total amount and offered for sale for an unspecified period — called also *tap issue*

tap borer *n* **:** an implement for boring tapholes

tap box *n* **1 :** CHINESE TEMPLE BLOCK **2 :** JUNCTION BOX **3 :** an enclosure for a corporation cock

tap changer *n* **:** an apparatus or accessory for usu. automatically changing transformer taps to regulate system voltage

tap dance *n* **:** a step dance esp. in a difficult syncopated rhythm that is tapped out audibly with the feet or parts of the feet (as the toes or heels) often by means of clogs or of specially made hard-soled shoes

tap-dance \'⸗,⸗\ vi [*tap dance*] **:** to perform a tap dance

tap dancer *n* **:** one that performs a tap dance **:** one proficient in tap dancing

tap drill *n* **:** a drill for drilling a hole of exact diameter for tapping

[1]tape \'tāp\ n -s [ME *tape, tappe*, fr. OE *tæppe* narrow strip of cloth; prob. akin to OFris *tapia* to tug, unravel, pluck, MLG *tappen* — more at TAP (touch)] **1 a :** a narrow fabric of natural or artificial fibers usu. woven singly in plain or twill weaves esp. in widths of less than 8 inches and used esp. for string, binding esp. on clothing and carpets, wicks, and with or without special finishes for medical and industrial purposes **b :** any of the woven cotton bands sewn across the backbone of a book and attached to the covers **c :** the narrow belt that turns each of the spindles on a ring spinner **d :** one of the endless flexible fabric bands on which sheets travel (as in the delivery of some cylinder presses and in some folding machines) **e :** ADHESIVE TAPE **f :** FRICTION TAPE **2 :** RED TAPE **3 :** a piece of light string stretched breast-high above the finishing line to aid the judges in determining the winner of a race **4 :** a narrow limp or flexible strip or band (as of paper, plastic, or metal): as **a :** TICKER TAPE **b :** MASKING TAPE **c :** MAGNETIC TAPE ⟨record a program on ~⟩ **5 a :** a graduated steel ribbon used by surveyors in place of a chain **b :** TAPE MEASURE **c :** a specially calibrated flexible rule for measuring the circumference and diameter of railroad-car wheels **6** [by shortening] **:** TAPEWORM **7 :** TAPE RECORDING

[2]tape \"\ vb -ED/-ING/-S vt **1 :** to furnish with tape **:** fasten, tie, bind, cover, or support with tape (as adhesive tape or friction tape) ⟨the sprain cases had all been *taped* up —Earle Birney⟩: as **a :** to bind or finish (an edge) with tape ⟨~ the seams of a leather jacket⟩ **b :** to join the sections of (a book) with tape **2 a :** to measure with a tape **b :** GIRTH 3 **3 :** to widen (a pelt) by leathering — compare LET OUT **4** *chiefly Brit* **:** to size up **:** figure out **:** CLASSIFY ⟨you had this world all *taped* —Ernest Hemingway⟩ ⟨afraid you've got all this *taped* out wrong —Agatha Christie⟩ **5 :** to record on magnetic tape ⟨~ a TV program⟩ ⟨a *taped* interview⟩ **~** *vi* **1 :** MEASURE **2 :** to stick threads together during the slashing operation in textile manufacture

tape condenser *n* **:** a device that receives the wide fiber web from a woolen card, divides it, and rubs each section into a sliver

tape grass *n* **:** a submerged aquatic plant (*Vallisneria spiralis*) with long ribbonlike leaves — called also *celery, eelgrass, water celery, wild celery*

tape-grass family \'⸗,⸗-\ *n* **:** VALLISNERIACEAE

tape guide *n* **:** a rod of sapphire, glass, or hardened steel in a magnetic recorder that is used to force the tape to move in a precisely defined path

ta·pei·no·ce·phal·ic \tə,pīnōsə'falik, -pān-\ adj [F *tapinocéphale* (fr. Gk *tapeinos* low + F *-céphale* -cephalic) + E *-ic*] **:** having a low skull with a breadth-height index of less than 79 due to synostosis of the great wings of the sphenoid with the frontal bone — **ta·pei·no·ceph·a·lism** *n* -s — **ta·pei·no·ceph·a·ly** \-lē\ *n* -ES

ta·pei·no·cra·nic \⸗'⸗⸗¦krānik\ adj [G *tapeinokran* (fr. Gk *tapeinos* low + *kranion* cranium) + E *-ic*] **:** having a low skull flattened in front with a cranial breadth-height index of less than 92 — **ta·pei·no·cra·ny** \⸗'⸗⸗,krānē\ *n* -ES

tape·less \'tāpləs\ *adj* **:** being without tape **:** operated or done without the use of tape

tapeline \'⸗,⸗\ *n* [[1]*tape* + *line*] **:** TAPE MEASURE

tape machine *n* **1** *Brit* **:** TICKER b **2 :** TAPE RECORDER

tape·man \'tāpmən\ *n, pl* **tapemen :** CHAINMAN 4

tape measure *n* **:** a narrow strip of a strong but limp or flexible material (as cloth or steel) that is marked off in units of length (as inches or centimeters) for measuring

tape primer *n* **:** a primer for some percussion locks consisting of bits of priming compound sealed in a paper tape

tape punch *n* **:** a device for recording symbols in tape by perforating individual holes or combinations of holes

[1]ta·per \'tāpə(r)\ n -s [ME *taper, tapre*, fr. OE *taper, tapor*] **1 a :** a usu. slender wax candle **b :** a long waxed wick used esp. as a spill **c :** any feeble light or source of light **2 a :** a tapering form or figure (as a spire) **b :** gradual diminution of thickness, diameter, or width in an elongated object often expressed in inches per foot, inches per inch, or by numbers ⟨the ~ of a tree trunk⟩ ⟨glass tubing with extremely accurate bore or ~ —C.J.Phillips⟩ ⟨the ~ of a file⟩ **c :** a gradual decrease **3 :** a trowel used by molders in founding **4 :** DRAFT 17a,b **5 :** a taper wire used esp. to splice electric cables

[2]taper \"\ adj [ME *tapre*, fr. *taper, tapre*, n.] **1 :** regularly narrowed toward a point **:** CONICAL, PYRAMIDAL ⟨~ fingers⟩ — see LEG illustration **2 :** GRADUATED, SCALED ⟨~ freight rates⟩

[3]taper \"\ vb **tapered; tapered; tapering** \-p(ə)riŋ\ **tapers** [[1]*taper*] vi **1 :** to become gradually smaller toward one end ⟨a stick that ~s to a point⟩ ⟨a wall ~ing from a thickness of three feet at the bottom to two feet at the top⟩ **2 :** to grow gradually less **:** DIMINISH ⟨as . . . defense demands ~ed, prices started down —*Time*⟩ ⟨sparse subarctic forest which ~s northward to the treeless tundra —Jim Wright⟩ — often used with *down* ⟨the way that a news story is written — beginning with the most important and ~ing down to the least important —T.F.Barnhart⟩; see TAPER OFF **~** *vt* **1 :** to make or cause to taper ⟨~ a stick to a point⟩ **2 :** to cut and thin (the hair) so that the ends are invisibly blended

[4]tap·er \'tāpə(r)\ n -s [[1]*tape* + *-er*] **1 :** a worker who applies tape (as to seal, label, protect, decorate, or strengthen objects) by hand or by machine **2 :** a device for dispensing or applying tape

tape reading *n* **:** the study and interpretation of transactions as printed on the ticker tape for indications of price trends

tape-record \'⸗⸗,⸗\ vt [back-formation fr. *tape recording*] **:** to make a tape recording of ⟨*tape-record* a speech⟩

tape recorder *n* **:** a magnetic recorder using magnetic tape

tape recording *n* **:** magnetic recording on magnetic tape; *also* **:** a recording made by this process

tapered *adj* [fr. past part. of [3]*taper*] **:** TAPER

ta·per·er \'tāp(ə)rə(r)\ n -s [ME, fr. [1]*taper* + *-er*] **1 :** one who bears a candle (as in a religious procession) **2 :** one that tapers

taper file *n* **:** a file with converging edges — distinguished from *blunt file*

ta·per·ing·ly *adv* **:** in a tapering fashion

ta·per·ness \'tāpə(r)nəs\ *n* -ES **:** the quality or state of being taper

taper off *vi* **1 :** to become taper **:** TAPER **2 :** to stop gradually **:** cease little by little ⟨the organization *tapered off* in about a year —G.B.Oxnam⟩ **~** *vt* **:** to make or cause to taper **:** decrease gradually ⟨if not retire, at least *taper off* the amount of time given to work —Lynn White⟩ ⟨use in *tapering off* morphine and opium addicts —D.W.Maurer & V.H.Vogel⟩

taper pin *n* **:** a tapered rod of metal or hardwood used as a dowel to locate one part with reference to another or to secure two parts together by driving into a tapered hole passing through both parts

taper pipe thread *n* **:** pipe thread formed with a slightly tapering diameter to secure a firm and leakproof joint

taper reducer sleeve *or* **taper sleeve** *n* **:** a sleeve that is tapered both externally (as to fit a specified socket) and internally (as to receive the tapered shank of a drill) — called also *reducer sleeve, shell socket*

taperstick \'⸗⸗,⸗\ *n* [[1]*taper* + *stick*] **:** a candlestick for holding small tapers

taper tool *n* **:** TURRET TAPER TOOL

tapes *pl of* TAPE, *pres 3d sing of* TAPE

tap·es·tried \'tapəstrēd, -rid\ *adj* [*tapestry* + *-ed*] **1 :** covered or decorated with or as if with tapestry ⟨chairs with wooden backs and arms and ~ seats —Sally Benson⟩ ⟨terraces of limestone, ~ with velvet moss —*Amer. Guide Series: Oregon*⟩ **2 :** woven or depicted in tapestry ⟨~ scenes from legend⟩

tap·es·try \-trē, -tri\ *n* -ES [ME *tapistry, tapstery*, modif. of MF *tapisserie*, fr. *tapisser* to furnish with a carpet, cover with tapestry (fr. OF *tapis, tapiz* carpet, carpeting, fr. Gk *tapēt-, tapēs* carpet, rug, prob. of Iranian origin) + *-ie* -y; akin to Per *tābīdan* to turn, spin; akin to Lith *tempti* to stretch — more at TEMPORAL] **1 a :** a heavy handwoven textile for hangings, curtains, and upholstery made either by the low-warp or high-warp method and usu. with a wool, linen, or cotton warp and with wool, silk, and metal threads in the weft with the warp threads set out on the loom for the width of the fabric and the weft threads loosely inserted by hand over and under the warp threads and pressed down to cover the warp threads completely and characterized by complicated pictorial designs that are the same on both sides except for the ends of threads showing on the back as a result of the weft threads being used not from selvage to selvage but only in the limited area of each separate color and being joined to other weft threads by interlocking or dovetailing or left unjoined leaving a slit — see GOBELIN **b :** a nonreversible conventionalized imitation of tapestry made usu. of wool, cotton, and rayon on a jacquard loom and used chiefly for upholstery **c :** embroidery on canvas resembling the woven tapestry ⟨needlepoint ~⟩ **2 :** TAPESTRY CARPET

tapestry beetle *n* **:** CARPET BEETLE b

tapestry brussels *n, usu cap B* **:** BRUSSELS CARPET 2

tapestry carpet *n* **:** a carpet (as tapestry Brussels or tapestry velvet) in which the designs are printed in colors on the threads before the fabric is woven; *esp* **:** a carpet the threads of which are printed before even the warp is formed and which is often used in place of real tapestry for hangings

tapestry moth *n* **:** CARPET MOTH

tapestry needle *n* **:** a short needle with a long eye and a blunt point

tapestry red *n* **:** a dark red that is yellower, less strong, and slightly darker than cranberry and yellower and paler than average garnet or average wine

tapestry velvet carpet *n* **:** a velvet carpet made like tapestry Brussels but having the pile longer and cut so that the surface resembles that of Wilton carpet

tapestry weave *n* **1 :** a weave used for handmade tapestry **2 :** a machine method of weaving tapestry having weft threads running from selvage to selvage **3 :** a hand or machine weave for rugs that have warp threads completely covered by weft threads

tapestry-woven \'⸗⸗⸗¦⸗⸗\ *adj* **:** having a tapestry weave

ta·pe·tal \tə'pēdᵊl\ *adj* [NL *tapetum* + E *-al*] **:** of or relating to a tapetum

ta·pe·te \tə'pēd·ē\ *n* -s [NL, fr. L, carpet, tapestry] **:** TAPETUM 1

tape thermometer *n* **:** a small thermometer attached temporarily to a steel measuring tape for the purpose of indicating the temperature of the tape

tap·e·ti *or* **tap·i·ti** \'tapəd·ē\ *n* -s [Tupi] **:** a small So. American rabbit (*Sylvilagus braziliensis*)

ta·pe·to·retinal \tə¦pēd·ō+\ *adj* [NL *tapetum* + E *-o-* + *retinal*] **:** of, relating to, or involving both tapetum and retina

ta·pe·tum \tə'pēd·əm\ *n, pl* **tape·ta** \-d·ə\ [NL, fr. L *tapete* carpet, tapestry, fr. Gk *tapēt-, tapēs* carpet, rug — more at TAPESTRY] **1 :** the layer of nutritive cells that invests the sporogenous tissue in the sporangium of higher plants and that is broken down and digested during development of the spores **2 a :** any of various membranous layers or areas esp. of the choroid and retina of the eye; *specif* **:** a layer in the choroid chiefly of nocturnal mammals that reflects light and is made up of several layers of flattened cells covered by a zone of doubly refracting crystals **b :** a layer of nerve fibers derived from the corpus callosum and forming part of the roof of each lateral ventricle of the brain — called also *tapetum lu·ci·dum* \-'lüsədəm\

tapeworm \'⸗,⸗\ *n* [[1]*tape* + *worm*] **:** a worm (subclass Cestoda) that is parasitic as an adult in the alimentary tract of vertebrates including man and as larva in a great variety of vertebrates and invertebrates, that typically consists of an attachment organ usu. with suckers, grooves, hooks, or other devices for adhering to the host's intestine followed by an undifferentiated growth region from which buds off a chain of segments of which the anterior members are little more than blocks of tissue, the median members have fully developed organs of both sexes, and the posterior members are degenerated to egg-filled sacs, that has no digestive system and absorbs food through the body wall, and that has a nervous system consisting of ganglia and commissures in the scolex and longitudinal cords extending the length of the strobila — see BEEF TAPEWORM, FISH TAPEWORM, PORK TAPEWORM; compare ECHINOCOCCUS

tapeworm plant *n* **:** CENTIPEDE PLANT

taph·e·pho·bia \,tafə'fōbēə\ *n* [NL, fr. Gk *taphē* burial, grave (akin to Gk *thaptein* to inter, bury) + NL *phobia* — more at EPITAPH] **:** fear of being buried alive

tap holder *n* **:** a device (as a chuck or grip) for holding or floating a tap (as in a screw machine or turret lathe) when tapping holes

taphole \'⸗,⸗\ *n* **:** a hole for a tap; *specif* **:** a hole at or near the bottom of a furnace or ladle through which molten metal, matte, or slag can be tapped

taph·ria \'tafrēə\ [NL, fr. Gk *taphrē* trench, ditch + NL *-ia*] *syn of* TAPHRINA

ta·phri·na \ta'frīnə, tə'f-, -rēnə\ *n, cap* [NL, fr. Gk *taphrē* trench, ditch (akin to Gk *taphos* tomb) + NL *-ina* — more at EPITAPH] **:** a genus (the type of the family Taphrinaceae) of parasitic fungi that produce asci in a superficial hymenium having an indeterminate margin and cause leaf curling and malformations like blisters on various vascular plants — see LEAF CURL, PLUM POCKET

taph·ri·na·ce·ae \,tafrə'nāsē,ē\ *n pl, cap* [NL, fr. *Taphrina*, type genus + *-aceae*] **:** a small family of ascomycetous fungi (order Taphrinales) with thin-walled chlamydospores — see TAPHRINA — **taph·ri·na·ceous** \¦⸗⸗'nāshəs\ *adj*

taph·ri·na·les \-'nā(,)lēz\ *n pl, cap* [NL *Taphrina* + *-ales*] **:** an order of parasitic fungi (subclass Hemiascomycetes) in which chlamydospores produced from the hyphae each germinate to form a single ascus

ta·pia \'täpyə\ *n* -s [Sp] **:** a building material made chiefly of clay or earth; *esp* **:** puddled adobe — compare PISÉ, TABBY

ta·pi·eté \,täpēā'tā\ *n, pl* **tapieté** *or* **tapietés** *usu cap* [Sp, fr. Guarani] **1 :** a Guaranian people of Bolivia **2 :** a member of the Tapieté people

tap-in \'⸗,⸗\ *n* -s [fr. *tap in*, v.] **:** TIP-IN

taping *pres part of* TAPE

tap·i·no·ma \,tapə'nōmə\ *n, cap* [NL, fr. Gk *tapeinos* low, humble + NL *-oma*] **:** a genus of small ants with a noticeably pungent odor

tap·i·o·ca \,tapē'ōkə\ *n* -s [Pg & Sp, fr. Tupi *typyóca*, fr. *ty* juice + *pýa* heart, pith + *ocó* to be removed] **1 :** a preparation of cassava starch processed into granular, flake, pellet, or flour form and used as a food in bread or as a thickening agent in liquid foods, as puddings, soups, or juicy pies, or industrially as a size or adhesive **2** *or* **tapioca plant :** CASSAVA 1

tapioca fish *n* **:** ESCOLAR

tap·i·o·lite \'tapēə,līt\ *n* -s [Sw *tapiolit*, fr. *Tapio*, Finnish god of the forests + Sw *-lit* -lite; fr. its being found in the village of Sukula in Finland] **:** a mineral $FeTa_2O_6$ that consists of oxide of iron and tantalum and is isomorphous with mossite and polymorphous with tantalite

ta·pir \'tāpə(r) *sometimes* tə'pi(ə)r *or* -iə *or* 'tä,pi-\ *n, pl* **tapir** *or* **tapirs** [Tupi *tapiira*] **:** any of several large perissodactyl ungulates (family Tapiridae) that inhabit So. and Central America, Malaya, and Sumatra, have a heavy sparsely hairy body, the snout prolonged into a short mobile proboscis, a rudimentary tail, stout legs, and four front and three hind toes, are chiefly nocturnal, shy, and gentle, and frequent heavy forests in the vicinity of water — see INDIAN TAPIR

tapir (Malayan)

ta·pi·ra·na \ˌtäpəˈränə\ *n, pl* **tapirana** [Pg, fr. *tapir*, fr. Tupi *tapiira*] : ³ANTA 1a

ta·pi·ra·pé \ˌtäpərəˈpā\ *n, pl* **tapirapé** *or* **tapirapés** *usu cap* [Sp, fr. Guarani] **1 a :** a Guaranian people of the northeastern part of Mato Grosso state, Brazil **b :** a member of such people **2 :** the language of the Tapirapé people

¹ta·pir·id \ˈtāpərəd, təˈpirəd\ *adj* [NL *Tapiridae*] **:** of or relating to the Tapiridae

²tapirid \"\ *n* -s **:** an ungulate of the family Tapiridae

ta·pir·i·dae \təˈpirəˌdē\ *n pl, cap* [NL, fr. *Tapirus*, type genus + *-idae*] **:** a family of ungulate mammals (suborder Ceratomorpha) that comprises the tapirs and extinct related forms

ta·pir·id·i·an \ˌtāpəˈridēən\ *adj or n* [NL *Tapiridae* + E *-an*] **:** TAPIRID

ta·pir·ine \ˈtāpəˌrīn, təˈpi,r-, -ˌrən\ *adj* [NL *Tapirus* + E *-ine*] **:** of or relating to the genus *Tapirus*

ta·pi·ro \təˈpi(ˌ)rō\ *n, pl* **tapiro** *or* **tapiros** *usu cap* **1 :** a Negrito people inhabiting the northern part of Netherlands New Guinea **2 :** a member of the Tapiro people

¹ta·pir·oid \ˈtāpəˌrȯid, təˈpi,r-\ *adj* [NL *Tapiroidea*] **:** of or relating to the Tapiroidea

²tapiroid \"\ *n* -s **:** a tapiroid mammal

ta·pi·roi·dea \ˌtāpəˈrȯidēə\ *n pl, cap* [NL, fr. *Tapirus* + *-oidea*] *in some classifications* **:** a superfamily of perissodactyl mammals comprising the tapirs and extinct related forms — compare CERATOMORPHA

tap·i·rus \ˈtapərəs\ *n, cap* [NL, fr. Tupi *tapiira* tapir] **:** a genus (the type of the family Tapiridae) of ungulates comprising the tapirs

tap·is *n* -ES [MF, fr. OF *tapis, tapiz* carpet, carpeting — more at TAPESTRY] *obs* **:** tapestry or a similar material used esp. for hangings, floor coverings, and tablecloths — **on the tapis** \(ˈ)taˈpē, (ˈ)täˈpē, ˈtāpəs, ˈtapəs\ *adv (or adj)* [trans. of F *sur le tapis*] *archaic* **:** under consideration ⟨two more large jobs *on the tapis* —J.D.Beresford⟩ ⟨another wedding is *on the tapis* —D.D.Martin⟩

ta·pis·se·rie \ˌtäpēsrē\ *n, pl* **tapisseries** \"\ [ME, fr. MF — more at TAPESTRY] **:** TAPESTRY 1

ta·pis·sier \täpēsyā\ *n, pl* **tapissiers** \"\ [F, fr. OF, fr. *tapis, tapiz* carpet + *-ier* -er] **:** a dealer in or maker of tapestries

tap issue *n* **:** TAP BOND

tapiti *var of* TAPETI

taplash \ˈ=,=\ *n* [¹*tap* + *lash* (onslaught of water)] **1** *dial* **:** the washings or dregs of a cask or glass of liquor **2** *dial* **:** poor or weak liquor; *esp* **:** weak or stale beer

tap·let \ˈtaplət\ *n* -s [¹*tap* + *-let*] **:** a small tap; *specif* **:** an insulating block usu. of porcelain provided with screw terminals for connection of electrical circuits where there is no change in the size of wire

tap line *n* [¹*tap*] **:** INDUSTRIAL RAILROAD

tap·man \ˈ=ˌmən\ *n, pl* **tapmen 1 :** one who taps a blast furnace **2 :** TAPPER-OUT 2

ta·poa \təˈpōə\ *n* -s [native name in New South Wales, Australia] **:** a Tasmanian phalanger (*Trichosurus fuliginosus*)

tap off *vi* **:** to start a play in basketball from the center circle by tapping a jump ball toward a player of one's own side

tap–off \ˈ=,=\ *n* -s [*tap off*] **:** TIP-OFF

ta·po·sa \təˈpōsə\ *n, pl* **taposa** *or* **taposas** *usu cap* **1 :** an extinct Muskogean people of the Yazoo river valley, Mississippi **2 :** a member of the Taposa people

ta·pote·ment \təˈpōtmənt\ *n* -s [F, fr. *tapoter* to tap (fr. MF, fr. *taper* to strike with the flat of the hand) + *-ment* — more at TAP (strike, touch)] **:** percussion in massage

tap out *vi* [²*tap*] **:** to bet all one has

tappa *var of* TAPA

tap·pable \ˈtapəbəl\ *adj* [²*tap* + *-able*] **:** capable of being tapped **:** fit for tapping — **tap·pable·ness** *n* -ES

tapped *past of* TAP

¹tap·per \ˈtapə(r)\ *n* -s [⁴*tap* + *-er*] **:** one that makes a sound of tapping or that performs an operation by lightly striking: as **a :** a telegraph key; *specif* **:** a double-contact key that makes one contact and breaks another by one movement **b :** a tapping device (as a bell) for sound signaling **c :** a worker who taps holes in watch parts with a hand press or powered machine **d :** TAP DANCER

²tapper \"\ *n* -s [²*tap* + *-er*] **:** one that applies or makes taps or draws by tapping: **a :** a worker who taps by hand or machine esp. to make or open holes **b :** one that taps a blast furnace, cask, storage bin, or other container to let the contents out **c :** one that taps trees to remove or draw sap ⟨rubber ~⟩ **d :** a machine for tapping nuts **e :** a worker who makes screw threads (as in nuts, pipes, or machine parts) **f :** a worker who makes uniform the width of ring shanks by compressing the soldered joints between dies

tapper–out \ˈ==ˈ=\ *n, pl* **tappers–out 1 :** one that taps something out **2 :** an iron or steel worker who keeps clean the slag taphole of a furnace in which billets are heated — called also *tapman*

tapper tap *n* **:** a tap designed primarily for use in a nut-tapping machine and usu. having a short thread length and a long shank that is smaller than the minor diameter of the thread to provide a space on the shank for the tapped nuts to accumulate

tap·pet \ˈtapət, *usu* -əd·+V\ *n* -s [⁴*tap* + *-et*] **1 :** a lever or projection moved by some other piece (as a cam) or intended to tap or touch something else to cause a particular motion (as in forms of steam-engine or internal-combustion-engine valve gear or in a stamp battery for crushing ore) **2** *Brit* **:** a cam for moving the heddles in some forms of power loom

tappet motion *n* **:** a valve motion (as in a steam pump) worked by tappets

tappet rod *n* **:** a rod carrying or actuating a tappet (as for opening or closing the valves in a steam or internal-combustion engine)

tappet wrench *n* **:** a wrench with an open-end jaw at each end of a long thin handle

tap·pie·too·rie \ˌtapiˌtüri\ *n* -s [*tappie* (dim. of *tap*, var. of ¹*top*) + *toorie*] *Scot & Irish* **:** TOORIE

tapping *n* -s [fr. gerund of ²*tap*] **1 :** the act, process, or means by which something is tapped **2 :** PARACENTESIS

tapping drill *n* **1 :** TAP DRILL **2 :** a machine for tapping nuts

tapping hole *n* **:** a hole made smaller than the nominal size of a screw or pipe to allow for tapping

tapping key *n* **:** a light flexible metallic strip provided with contacts so that when it is momentarily pressed an electric circuit is made or broken and when it is released the opposite effect is automatically produced

tapping screw *n* **:** a hardened screw that cuts threads in the pieces it secures and that is used in materials which would otherwise require a separate tapping operation or the use of a nut

tap·pit hen \ˈtapət-\ *n* [*tappit* fr. *tap* (var. of ¹*top*) + *-it*] **1** *Scot* **:** a crested hen **2** *Scot* **:** a drinking vessel with a knob on the lid

tap·poon \taˈpün\ *n* -s [Sp *tapón* stopper, fr. *tapar* to stop up — more at TAPA] **:** a piece of wood or sheet metal fitted into a ditch to dam up the water so as to overflow a field

tappit hen 2

tap rivet *n* **:** SCREW RIVET

taproom \ˈ=,=\ *n* **:** a room where liquors are kept on tap **:** BARROOM

¹taproot \ˈ=,=\ *n* [¹*tap* + *root*] **1 :** a root having a prominent central portion, growing vertically downward, and giving off small lateral roots in succession — compare FIBROUS ROOT **2 :** one that resembles a taproot in having a deep-lying central position in any line of growth or development ⟨intuitive faculty of going to the ~ of his subject —H.W.Wells⟩ ⟨principle which has been the ~ of the American belief in education —W.R.Steckel⟩ ⟨bosses and machines have sprung from the same ~ —Louise Young⟩ **3 :** the first recognized female ancestor of a horse and esp. of a Thoroughbred

²taproot \"\ *vi* **:** to put forth a taproot

¹taps *pl of* TAP, *pres 3d sing of* TAP

²taps \ˈtaps\ *n pl but usu sing in constr* [prob. alter. of obs. *taptoo* tattoo — more at TATTOO] **1 :** the last bugle call at night blown as a signal that all unauthorized lights are to be put out ⟨~ was sounded⟩ — compare TATTOO **2 :** a similar call blown as part of the final honors at military funerals and sometimes at memorial services

tapsal–teerie \ˌtapsəlˈtēri\ *adv* [by alter.] *Scot* **:** TOPSY-TURVY

tap screw *n* **:** TAP BOLT

tap shoe *n* **:** a shoe worn esp. for tap-dancing and having a hard sole or a sole and heel to which taps have been attached

tap sole *n* **:** ⁵TAP 2

tap·ster \ˈtapstə(r)\ *n* -s [ME, fr. OE *tæppestre* female tapster, barmaid, fr. *tæppere* tapster, barkeeper (fr. *tæppa* tap + *-ere* -er) + *-estre* -ster — more at TAP] **:** one employed to dispense liquors in a barroom

¹tap-tap \ˈ=ˈ=\ *n* [redupl. of ⁵*tap*] **:** a series of taps or their sound ⟨steady *tap-tap* of typewriters —*Manchester Guardian Weekly*⟩

²tap-tap \"\ *vi* **:** to make a sound of repeated tapping **:** move with a sound of tapping ⟨her shoes were *tap-tapping* on the tessellated floor —W.G.Hardy⟩ ⟨dark plane-tree leaves *tap-tapped* at the window —John Galsworthy⟩

ta·pu \ˈtäˌpü\ *n* -s [Maori] **:** TABOO

ta·pu·ya \təˈpüyə\ *n, pl* **tapuya** *or* **tapuyas** *usu cap* [Pg, fr. Tupi, savage, Tapuya] **:** a non-Tupi Amerind people of southern or central Brazil

tap water *n* **:** ordinary water from a tap or faucet that has not been distilled or otherwise specially purified

tap wrench *n* **:** a wrench for turning a tap

ta·qi·ya *or* **ta·qi·yah** \təˈkēyə\ *n* -s [Ar *taqīyah*, lit., self-protection] **:** the principle of practicing the dissimulation of outward conformity permitted Muslims in a hostile or persecuting non-Muslim environment for the sake of their personal safety

tap wrench

taq·lid \taˈklēd\ *n* -s [Ar *taqlīd*, lit., winding round; fr. the custom of honoring one by girding him with a sword] *Islam* **:** uncritical and unqualified acceptance of a traditional orthodoxy or of an authoritarian code of a particular religious teacher

¹tar \ˈtär, ˈtȧ(r\ *n* -s [ME *tarr, terr*, fr. OE *teoru*; akin to MLG *tere* tar, MD *tar, terre*, ON *tjara*, tar, Goth *triu* tree, wood — more at TREE] **1 a :** any of various dark brown or black bituminous usu. odorous viscous liquids or semiliquids that are obtained by the destructive distillation of wood, coal, peat, shale, and other organic materials and yield pitch on distillation ⟨road ~*s*⟩ — see COAL TAR, WATER-GAS TAR, WOOD TAR **b :** a substance resembling tar in appearance and formed by chemical change ⟨~*s* in tobacco smoke⟩ **2** [short for *tarpaulin*] **:** SEAMAN, SAILOR ⟨salt ~*s*⟩ **3 :** STUFFING, GIMP ⟨going to whale the ~ out of you —Helen Eustis⟩ ⟨has scared the ~ out of solid citizens all over the world —Stuart Chase⟩

²tar \"\ *or* **tarre** \"\ *vt* **tarred; tarred; tarring; tars** *or* **tarres** [ME *terren, tarren*, fr. OE *tyrwan, tirgan* to irritate, upset, provoke; akin to MLG *tergen, targen* to incite, irritate, Norw dial. *terga* to tease, Russ *dërgat'* to pluck, pull, tear, OE *teran* to tear — more at TEAR] **:** to urge into action **:** INCITE — usu. used with *on* ⟨other assistants, *tarring* them on, as the rabble does when dogs fight —Thomas Carlyle⟩ ⟨portions and parcels of the past who still guide us and ~ us on —O.S.J.Gogarty⟩

³tar \"\ *vt* **tarred; tarring; tars** [ME *tarren, terren*, fr. *tarr, terr* tar] **1 :** to cover or overspread with tar ⟨boarded walls which had once been *tarred* but were now mellowed —Margery Allingham⟩ **2 :** to smear or defile as if with tar **:** TAINT, STAIN ⟨rendered ineffective by *tarring* as stooges of the outside —James Still⟩ — often used with *with* ⟨~ the Democrats with the stick of secession —H.S.Commager⟩ ⟨the humble things with which he was *tarred* were pulling him down —Oliver La Farge⟩ — **tar and feather :** to smear (a person) with tar and cover with feathers as a punishment or indignity ⟨*tarred and feathered* them and rode them out of town on a rail⟩ — **tar with the same brush :** to mark or stain with the same fault or characteristic ⟨author and hero tended to melt into one . . . were *tarred with the same brush* —William Troy⟩

⁴tar \"\ *n* -s [Per] **:** an oriental lute

¹tara *var of* TARO

²tara \ˈtärə, ˈtarə\ *n* -s [AmerSp, fr. Quechua *tára*] **:** any of various plants of the genus *Caesalpinia* (esp *C. tinctoria*) that yield tannin

ta·ra·boo·ka \təˈräbəkə, ˌtarəˈbükə\ *n* -s [Ar *darābukkah*] **:** DARABUKKA

¹tara·ca·hi·tian \ˌtarəkəˈhēshən\ *adj, usu cap* [*Tara*humara + *Cahita* + E *-an* (adj. suffix)] **:** of, relating to, or characteristic of the Taracahitian peoples or their languages

²taracahitian \"\ *n* -s *usu cap* [*Tara*humara + *Cahita* + E *-an* (n. suffix)] **1 a :** a group of peoples of Mexico including the Acaxee, Baciroa, Cahita, Concho, Cora, Opata, and Tarahumara **b :** a member of any of the peoples of the Taracahitian group **2 :** a language family comprising the languages of the Taracahitian peoples

tar acid *n* **:** any of the phenols (as phenol, cresols, xylenols) obtained from tar and esp. coal tar — compare CRESYLIC ACID

tar–acid oil *n* **:** an oil containing usu. 10 to 55 percent of tar acids obtained by distilling coal tar or by dissolving tar acids in coal-tar oils — compare CARBOLIC OIL

tar·a·did·dle *also* **tar·ra·did·dle** \ˌtarəˈdidᵊl\ *n* -s [origin unknown] **1 :** a minor falsehood **:** FIB ⟨not only told her ~ about having hunted . . . she even came near believing it —George Orwell⟩ ⟨all the idle rumors and ~*s* heard in the . . . country —R.G.Howarth⟩ **2 :** pretentious nonsense **:** insincere or false matter ⟨some stale and fantastic ~ on the theme of espionage, which is worked to death —*Foreign Affairs*⟩ ⟨declares a ringing hail and farewell to the hero with all the domestic and military ~ —*Time*⟩ ⟨accustomed to so much ~ and so-called aesthetic interpretation in the field of music . . . that we are likely to shy away —William Howell⟩

tar·a·hu·ma·ra \ˌtarəhüˈmärə\ *also* **tar·a·hu·ma·re** \-ˈärē\ *or* **tar·a·hu·mar** \ˌ===ˈmär\ *n, pl* **tarahumara** *or* **tarahumaras** *also* **tarahumare** *or* **tarahumares** *or* **tarahumar** *or* **tarahumars** *usu cap* [Sp *Tarahumara, Tarahumare*, fr. Tarahumara *Ralámari*, lit., foot runners] **1 a :** a Taracahitian people of southern Sonora and Chihuahua, Mexico **b :** a member of such people **2 :** the language of the Tarahumara people

ta·rai·re *also* **ta·rai·ri** \təˈrīrē\ *n* -s [Maori] **1 :** a New Zealand timber tree (*Beilschmiedia tarairi*) of the family Lauraceae **2 :** the light easily worked wood of the tairiri

tar·a·ki·hi \ˌtarəˈkēhē\ *or* **ter·a·ki·hi** \ˌter-\ *n* -s [Maori] **:** a morwong (*Dactylopagrus macropterus*)

tar·a·mel·lite \ˌtarəˈmeˌlīt\ *n* -s [It, fr. Torquato *Taramelli* †1922 Ital. geologist + It *-ite*] **:** a mineral $BaFe_5Si_{10}O_{31}$ consisting of a barium iron silicate and occurring in brownish red radially fibrous aggregates (hardness 5.5, sp. gr. 3.9)

tar·a·na·ki \ˌtarəˈnäkē\ *adj, usu cap* [fr. *Taranaki*, New Zealand] **:** of or from the provincial district of Taranaki, New Zealand **:** of the kind or style prevalent in Taranaki provincial district

tar·a·na·kite \ˌ==ˈ=ˌkīt\ *n* -s [*Taranaki*, provincial district in New Zealand, its locality + E *-ite*] **:** a mineral $K_2Al_6(PO_4)_6(OH)_2.18H_2O$(?) consisting of a basic hydrous phosphate of aluminum and potassium in compact clayey masses

ta·ran·chi \təˈränchē\ *n, pl* **taranchi** *or* **taranchis** *usu cap* [Jagatai *Taranči*, lit., farmer] **:** a Turkic people of mixed Iranian origin living in Kazakh Republic U.S.S.R. **2 :** a member of the Taranchi people

tarantara *var of* TANTARA

ta·ran·tass \ˌtarənˈtäs\ *n* -ES [Russ *tarantas*, fr. Kazan Tatar *taryntas*] **:** a low four-wheeled carriage used in Russia

tar·an·tel·la \ˌtarənˈtelə\ *or* **tar·en·telle** \ˌ==ˈtel\ *n* -s [*tarantella* fr. It, fr. *Taranto*, seaport in southern Italy often associated with the dancing mania of tarantism + It *-ella*; *tarentelle* fr. F, fr. It *tarantella*] **1 :** a vivacious folk dance of southern Italy in ⁶⁄₈ time usu. performed by couples shaking tambourines **2 :** music suited to the tarantella or in its presto sextuple measure (as ⁶⁄₈ or in early examples quadruple) usu. alternating suddenly between the major and the minor modes

tar·an·tism \ˈtarənˌtizəm\ *n* -s [NL *tarantismus*, fr. *Taranto*, seaport in southern Italy where tarantism was common from the 15th to the 17th cent. + L *-ismus* -ism] **:** a dancing mania or malady of late medieval Europe popularly regarded as being caused by the bite of the tarantula

ta·ran·to \ˈtärənˌtō, ˈtar-; təˈran(ˌ)tō\ *adj, usu cap* [fr. *Taranto*, Italy] **:** of or from the city of Taranto, Italy **:** of the kind or style prevalent in Taranto

ta·ran·tu·la \təˈranch(ə)lə, -raan-, -ntᵊlə\ *n* [ML, fr. OIt *tarantola*, fr. *Taranto*, seaport in southern Italy] **1** *pl* **tarantulas** \-ləz\ *also* **tarantu·lae** \-chəˌlē, -tᵊlˌē\ **:** a European wolf spider (*Lycosa tarentula*) regarded as the cause of tarantism **2** *pl* **tarantulas** *also* **tarantulae a :** a spider of the suborder Mygalomorphae; *esp* **:** any of various large hairy spiders of the family Theraphosidae that are typically rather sluggish and though capable of biting sharply are not significantly poisonous to man **:** BIRD SPIDER **b :** a large spider — not used technically **3** *cap* [NL, fr. ML] **:** a genus (the type of the family Tarantulidae) of whip scorpions

tarantulas: *A* tarantula 1; *B* an American tarantula 2a

tarantula hawk *or* **tarantula killer** *n* **:** a large wasp of the genus *Pepsis* (family Pompilidae); *esp* **:** any of several solitary wasps of the southwestern U.S. that capture tarantulas as food for their young

¹ta·ran·tu·lid \-ch(ə)ləd, -tᵊləd\ *adj* [NL *Tarantulidae*] **:** of or relating to the Tarantulidae

²tarantulid \"\ *n* -s **:** a scorpion of the family Tarantulidae

tar·an·tu·li·dae \ˌtarənˈt(y)üləˌdē\ *n pl, cap* [NL, fr. *Tarantula*, type genus + *-idae*] **:** a family of whip scorpions (order Pedipalpida) that lack the caudal prolongation of other forms and have an extremely long slender first pair of legs

tar·a·pa·ca·ite \ˌtarəpəˈkäˌīt\ *n* -s [Sp *tarapacaita*, fr. *Tarapacá*, province in northern Chile, its locality + Sp *-ita* -ite] **:** a mineral consisting of a native potassium chromate and occurring in Chilean nitrate deposits

ta·ras·can \təˈraskən, -räs-\ *n* -s *usu cap* [Sp *Tarasco* + E *-an*] **1 :** TARASCO **2 :** a language family of the state of Michoacán, Mexico

ta·ras·co \-(ˌ)skō\ *n, pl* **tarasco** *or* **tarascos** *usu cap* [Sp] **1 a :** a people of the state of Michoacán, Mexico **b :** a member of such people **2 :** the language of the Tarasco people

ta·ra·ta *also* **ta·ra·tah** \təˈrädə\ *n* -s [Maori *tarata*] **:** a small evergreen tree (*Pittosporum eugenioides*) of New Zealand having white bark and fragrant corymbs of pale yellow flowers — called also *white mapau*

taratantara *var of* TANTARA

tara vine \ˈtärə-, ˈtarə-\ *n* [*tara* fr. Jap] **:** BOWER ACTINIDIA

ta·rax·a·cum \-ksəkəm\ *n* [NL, fr. Ar *tarakhshaqūn* wild chicory] **1** *cap* **:** a genus of chiefly weedy nearly cosmopolitan scapose perennial herbs (family Compositae) having long tap roots, toothed or pinnatifid leaves, usu. yellow flower heads, and achenes with a simple pappus — see DANDELION, KOK-SAGHYZ **2** -s **:** the dried rhizome and roots of the dandelion (*T. officinale*) used as a bitter and laxative

ta·rax·e·in \təˈraksēən\ *n* -s [Gk *taraxis* confusion (fr. *tarassein* to trouble, confuse) + E *-ein* (as in *protein*); akin to Gk *thrassein, thrattein* to trouble, disturb — more at DARK] **:** a substance isolable from the blood of schizophrenic persons, capable of inducing transitory schizophrenic symptoms in normal individuals, and believed to act upon a specific enzyme

tar·ba·gan \ˌtärbəˈgan\ *n* -s [Russ, fr. Teleut] **:** a pale or reddish gregarious bobac inhabiting the grassy steppes of central Asia

tar base *n* **:** any of the organic bases (as aniline, pyridine, or quinoline) obtained esp. from coal tar or ammonia liquor — compare PYRIDINE BASE

tar·boosh *also* **tar·bush** *or* **tar·boush** \(ˈ)tärˈbüsh, -bu̇sh\ *n* -ES [Ar *ṭarbūsh*] **:** a red hat similar to the fez used alone or as part of a turban and worn esp. by Muslim men in countries of the eastern Mediterranean

tar·bou·ka \tärˈbükə\ *n* -s [Ar *darbūkkah*] **:** DARABUKKA

tarbrush \ˈ=,=\ *n* [¹*tar* + *brush*] **1 :** a brush for applying tar **2 :** colored or Negro blood ⟨everyone's brothers under the skin, but there's no ~ in my family —Michael Williams⟩ ⟨very complicated, this color business . . . you might, you know, have a touch of the ~ yourself —Eleanor Early⟩ ⟨has a dash of the ~ in her⟩

tarbrush

tarbush \ˈ=,=\ *n* [¹*tar* + *bush*] **1 :** YERBA SANTA **2 :** any of several California shrubs of the genus *Chamaebatia* **3 :** a sticky shrub (*Flourensia cernua*) of the family Compositae native to the southwestern U.S. and Mexico

tar·butt·ite \ˈtärbəˌtīt\ *n* -s [Percy C. *Tarbutt*, 20th cent. Australian mine director + E *-ite*] **:** a basic zinc phosphate $Zn_2PO_4(OH)$ in clusters of colorless or pale yellow, brown, red, or green triclinic crystals

tar·da·men·te \ˌtärdəˈmentē\ *adv* [It, fr. *tardare* to slow down, retard, fr. L, to make slow, delay, fr. *tardus* slow — more at TARDY] **:** SLOWLY — used as a direction in music

tar·dan·do \tärˈdän(ˌ)dō\ *adv (or adj)* [It, fr. L *tardandum*, gerund of *tardare* to delay] **:** RITARDANDO

tar·de·noi·sian \ˌtärdᵊnˈȯizhən, -ˈȯizēən, -ˈwäzēən\ *adj, usu cap* [Fère-en-*Tardenois*, town in northeastern France where the implements were found + E *-an*] **:** of or belonging to an early Mesolithic culture characterized by small flint implements of geometrical form and regarded by some authorities as the northward advance of the Capsian culture contemporaneous with the Azilian culture

tar·di·gra·da \tärˈdigrədə, ˌtärdəˈgrädə\ *n pl, cap* [NL, fr. neut. pl. of L *tardigradus* slow-moving] **1** *in former classifications* **:** an order of mammals equivalent to the Bradypodidae **2 :** a division of Arthropoda comprising microscopic creatures that live in water or damp moss, resemble arachnids in having four pairs of legs, lack mouth appendages and circulatory and respiratory organs, and have a pair of styliform piercing organs connected with the pharynx

¹tar·di·grade \ˈtärdəˌgrād\ *adj* [F, fr. L *tardigradus*, fr. *tardus* slow + *gradus* step — more at TARDY, GRADE] **1 :** moving or stepping slowly **:** SLOW-PACED, SLUGGISH **2** [NL *Tardigrada*] **:** of or relating to the Tardigrada

²tardigrade \"\ *or* **tar·di·grad** \-ˌgrad\ *n* -s [NL *Tardigrada*] **:** an arthropod of the division Tardigrada

tar·di·ly \ˈtärdᵊlē, ˈtäd-, -dəl, |i\ *adv* **1 :** in an unhurried manner **:** at a slack pace **:** SLOWLY ⟨glaciers move ~⟩ ⟨coming toward us ~⟩ **2 :** after the expected, hoped for, or proper time **:** LATE ⟨notice of aggression . . . came so ~ that aid with whatever force was available could not be given —C.L.Jones⟩ ⟨to the fireman, all homes are firetraps when an outbreak is ~ discovered —P.W.Kearney⟩

tar·di·ness \-dēnəs, -din-\ *n* -ES **:** the quality or state of being tardy ⟨looked at the program which, as a result of ~ on my part, listed no topics for this address —F.M.Hechinger⟩

tar distillate *n* **:** a fraction in petroleum refining containing heavy oils and paraffin

tar·dive \ˈtärdiv\ *adj* [F, fem. of *tardif*, fr. MF, tardy] **:** tending to or characterized by lateness esp. in development or maturity ⟨~ syphilis develops after the second year —E.R. Pund⟩

tar·do \'tär(,)dō\ *adj* [It, fr. L *tardus*] **:** SLOW — used as a direction in music

tar drum *n* **:** a separator used in petroleum distilling for condensing the heavier vapors

¹**tar·dy** \'tärdē, 'tȧd-, -di\ *adj* -ER/-EST [alter. (influenced by -*y*, adj. suffix) of earlier *tardif*, fr. MF, fr. (assumed) VL *tardivus*, fr. L *tardus* slow + -*ivus* -ive; prob. akin to Gk *terēn* soft, tender — more at TENDER] **1 a :** moving with slow pace, motion, or progress **:** SLUGGISH ⟨she could not wait for the ~ operations of her ambassadress —W.M.Thackeray⟩ ⟨where the vulgar dialects were *tardiest* in taking distinctive form —H.O. Taylor⟩ ⟨ten years is a long . . . courtship, and she summons courage to spur her ~ swain —Seamus Kelly⟩ **b :** acting, occurring, or developing after the expected, hoped for, or proper time **:** DELAYED, DILATORY, LATE ⟨is often an hour ~ at school⟩ ⟨~ in recognizing that the barbiturates are just as dangerous as the opiates —D.W.Maurer & V.H.Vogel⟩ ⟨the intellectuals were somewhat ~ . . . what they discovered was what the public everywhere had long known —John Mason Brown⟩ **2** *obs* **:** off guard **:** UNPREPARED, REMISS

syn LATE, BEHINDHAND, OVERDUE: TARDY applies to failure to arrive at a time set, sometimes through lack of punctuality, negligence, or tendency to dawdle, sometimes through unavoidable delay ⟨*tardy* arrivals at the play slowing down the first act⟩ ⟨a number of *tardy* children rebuked by the principal⟩ LATE centers attention on the fact of not arriving on time; it may or may not imply blame ⟨*late* for school⟩ ⟨persons coming *late* were seated in the balcony⟩ ⟨docked for being *late*⟩ BEHINDHAND applies to the situation of persons who have fallen into arrears or whose development, progress or action is slower than normal ⟨*behindhand* in his mortgage payments⟩ ⟨in a big house . . . one is always *behindhand*. The days aren't long enough —George Moore⟩ OVERDUE may refer to what has been due and left unpaid or undone, to what has been expected or scheduled but lacks arrival or completion, or to what might logically or suitably have occurred or appeared a long time before ⟨an *overdue* bill⟩ ⟨an *overdue* library book⟩ ⟨small chance of search planes even though we were a week *overdue* — L.A.Viereck⟩ ⟨the valuable work of this branch of chemistry received long *overdue* recognition —J.H.Kuney⟩ ⟨legislative reforms are long *overdue*⟩

²**tardy** *adv, archaic* **:** TARDILY ⟨too swift arrives as ~ as too slow —Shak.⟩

¹**tare** \'ta(a)(ə)r, 'te|, |ə\ *n* -S [ME; prob. akin to MD *tarwe* wheat, Gaulish *dravoca* darnel, Gk *daratos*, a bread, Lith *dirva* field, Skt *dūrvā* panic grass, OE *teran* to tear — more at TEAR] **1 a :** the seed of a vetch **b :** any of several vetches (esp. *Vicia sativa* and *V. hirsuta*) **2 tares** *pl* **:** an injurious weed of grainfields esp. of Biblical times that is usu. held to be the darnel ⟨while men slept, his enemy came and sowed ~*s* among the wheat —Mt 13:25(AV)⟩ **3 tares** *pl* **:** a bad or undesirable element or growth that endangers the well-being of what is good or desirable ⟨though . . . generally condemned by the Church . . . these ~*s* did manage at all times to flourish amidst the orthodox wheat —G.G.Coulton⟩ ⟨the bitter ~*s* of the past were exorcised —Sylvia Berkman⟩ ⟨the critic . . . should endeavor to discipline his personal prejudices and cranks — ~*s* to which we are all subject —T.S.Eliot⟩

²**tare** \"\ *n* -S [ME, fr. MF, fr. OIt *tara*, fr. Ar *ṭarḥa* that which is removed, fr. *ṭaraḥa* to remove, reject] **1 a :** the weight of a container or vehicle that is deducted from the gross weight to obtain the net weight — see ACTUAL TARE **b :** a deduction from the gross weight of a substance and its container made in allowance for the weight of the container — see AVERAGE TARE; compare TARE WEIGHT **2 a :** COUNTERWEIGHT; *esp* **:** an empty receptacle similar to one being used as a container used to counterpoise any change in weight of the container due to temperature, moisture, or other conditions ⟨the best ~ is made of the same material as the apparatus —A.A.Benedetti-Pichler⟩ **b :** the weight of a container used as a deduction esp. in laboratory weighing operations **3 :** soil or similar waste material adhering to sugar beets ⟨the percentage of ~ for a load is estimated from a sample⟩

³**tare** \"\ *vt* -ED/-ING/-S **:** to ascertain or mark the tare of **:** weigh so as to determine the tare ⟨the weight on one beam being used to ~ the bottle or jar while the other weight is left free —E.F.Cook & E.W.Martin⟩ ⟨allow the mercury to flow into a *tared* vessel and divide the net weight —*Science*⟩

⁴**tare** \"\ *usu cap* — a communications code word for the letter *t*

tare grass *n* **1 :** TARE 2 **2 :** TUFTED VETCH **3 :** DARNEL

tarekat *var of* TARIQA

tare man *n* **1 :** a worker who estimates the percentage of tare in a load of sugar beets by weighing a sample before and after cleaning **2 :** a textile worker who handles wool and identifies the types

ta·rente \tə'ränt\ *n* -S [F, fr. *Tarente* Taranto, seaport in southern Italy] **:** a gecko (*Tarentola mauritanica*) of southern Europe and adjacent regions that is found esp. among old ruins

tarentelle *var of* TARANTELLA

¹**tar·en·tine** \'tarən,tīn, -,tēn; tə'rentᵊn\ *adj, usu cap* [L *tarentinus*, fr. *Tarentum* Taranto (fr. Gk *Tarant-*, *Taras*) + -*inus* -ine] **1 :** of, relating to, or characteristic of Tarentum, a Greek city of ancient Italy **2 :** of, relating to, or characteristic of the people of Tarentum

²**tarentine** \"\ *n* -S *cap* **:** a native or inhabitant of Tarentum

ta·ren·to·la \tə'rentᵊlə\ *n* [NL, fr. It dial. *tarantola* salamander, fr. OIt, tarantula, fr. *Taranto*, seaport in southern Italy] **1** -S **:** TARENTE **2** *cap* **:** a widely distributed genus of Old and New World geckos including the tarente

tares *pl of* TARE, *pres 3d sing of* TARE

tare vetch *n* **:** ¹TARE 1

tare weight *n* **:** the officially accepted weight of an empty car, vehicle, or container that when subtracted from gross weight yields the net weight of cargo or shipment upon which charges can be calculated — compare ²TARE

tarflower \'=,=\ *n* [¹*tar* + *flower*] **:** an evergreen undershrub (*Bejaria racemosa*) of the family Ericaceae of the southern U.S. bearing pinkish white racemose flowers and bristly hairy twigs

¹**targe** \'tärj\ *n* -S [ME, fr. OF — more at TARGET] *archaic* **:** a light shield or buckler carried esp. by footmen and archers

²**targe** \'tärj\ *vt* -ED/-ING/-S [origin unknown] **1** *chiefly Scot* **:** to question in some detail **:** INTERROGATE **2** *chiefly Scot* **:** to keep in order or under strict watch **3** *chiefly Scot* **:** BEAT, SCOLD

¹**tar·get** \'tärgət\ *n* -S *often attrib* [ME, fr. MF *targette*, dim. of OF *targe* light shield, of Gmc origin; akin to OHG *zarga* frame, border, ON *targa* shield; prob. akin to MIr *dremm* group of people, Bret *dramm* bundle, Arm *trc̣ak* bundle of wood, and perh. to Gk *drassesthai* to grasp] **1 a :** a small circular shield or buckler **b :** such a target or its replica used as a heraldic device **2 a :** a butt or mark to shoot at in practice or competition or for testing the accuracy of a firearm or the force of a projectile: as (1) **:** a series of concentric circles of specified size marked on a paper or wooden surface with a bull's-eye at the center (2) **:** a circular mat of straw four feet in diameter covered by a canvas face painted with five concentric circles and mounted on a tripodal stand for use in archery — see PRINCE'S RECKONING **b** (1) **:** a target marked or penetrated by the shots fired at it to make a score (2) **:** the score made in target shooting ⟨shot the high ~ for the day⟩ (3) **:** CLAY PIGEON (4) **:** the section or part of a person or animal regarded as the object to be hit (as in hunting or fencing) **c :** something (as an airplane or ship, installation or area) that is or may be fired at as a military objective ⟨directly over the ~ . . . gave the order to drop the ash cans and a floating flare to mark the point of attack —John Hersey⟩ ⟨must be used to obtain the required results upon hostile ~*s* —H.P.Rand⟩ **3 :** something that is or may be aimed at: as **a :** a person or thing that is made the object of derogatory remarks or critical comment ⟨the colonists . . . made him their chief ~ of scorn —Stanley Pargellis⟩ ⟨was making herself a ~ for ridicule —Virginia Woolf⟩ ⟨in some ways the textbook makes an even more satisfactory ~ than the teacher —V.M. Rogers⟩ ⟨his social criticism . . . remains primarily moral — its principal ~ is human nature —C.J.Rolo⟩ **b :** a person or thing that is made the object of an action, political movement, or other development designed usu. to affect or change ⟨investors . . . might become a favored ~ for unfair action on the part of foreign governments —M.A.Heilperin⟩ ⟨might direct such investigations to ~*s* like corruption or inefficiency — Christopher Serpell⟩ ⟨this area was the constant ~ of enemy propaganda —H.I.Poleman⟩ ⟨the peninsula . . . is not an easy ~ for economic development —Marion Wilhelm⟩ **c :** a goal (as a date, figure, production level, or quota) set or proposed for achievement ⟨with the ~ for land collection set at 50 million acres by 1957 —Vera M. Dean⟩ ⟨the ~ of the air route . . . was 85,000 tons per month —G.C.Marshall⟩ ⟨the week-end adjournment ~ was abandoned —J.D.Morris⟩ ⟨officers whose initial ~ was the rapid establishment of law and order — *Current History*⟩ **4 :** a visible signal or device used to mark or identify something: as **a :** a railroad day signal attached to a switch stand that indicates by its position, shape, color, or shape and color combined whether the switch is open or closed **b :** the vane or sliding sight on a surveyor's leveling staff **c :** an indicator to show that an electrical relay has functioned — compare DROP 3f **5 a :** the metallic surface usu. of a platinum or tungsten anode upon which the stream of cathode rays within an X-ray tube is focused **b :** a body, surface, or substance bombarded with nuclear particles **c :** the fluorescent material on which the desired patterns or pictures are produced in television, radar, and other electronic devices **6 :** the standard or original object or thought that is to be recognized or affected through psychokinesis, telepathy, or clairvoyance **:** STIMULUS-OBJECT

²**target** \"\ *vt* -ED/-ING/-S **1 a :** to make a target of ⟨is already ~*ed* as the first victim —*Newsweek*⟩ ⟨the fires were smothered to keep . . . planes from ~*ing* the oil fields —*Nat'l Geographic*⟩ **b :** to set forth or determine as a goal or mark to be achieved ⟨coal production . . . was ~*ed* for 100 million tons in 1955 — *Newsweek*⟩ ⟨if zooming costs had not prevented . . . the bargain price originally ~*ed* —*Forbes*⟩ **2 :** to signal (as the position of a railroad switch) by means of a target **3 :** to determine by experiment the firing data necessary for aiming and firing (a firearm) accurately ⟨traded rifles . . . and I ~*ed* the thing —W.C.Tuttle⟩ **4 :** to direct toward a target

target cell *or* **target corpuscle** *n* **:** an atypical red blood cell with a peripheral ring and central mass of hemoglobin-containing cytoplasm separated by a relatively hemoglobin-free ring

target date *n* **:** the date set for an event or for the completion of a project, goal, or quota ⟨the *target date* for the invasion . . . was set —F.D.Roosevelt⟩ ⟨would not set a *target date* for accomplishment of the plan —Stanley Levey⟩ ⟨here and there the *target dates* may have to be changed —Van McDougall⟩

tar·ge·teer *also* **tar·ge·tier** \,tärgə'ti(ə)r\ *n* -S **1 :** one armed with a target or shield **2 :** SIGHTER 1

target gland *or* **target organ** *n* **:** an endocrine organ of which the functional activity is controlled by a tropic fraction of the pituitary secretion

target lamp *or* **target lantern** *n* **:** a lamp or lantern for use at a railroad switch target

tar·get·man \'tärgət,man\ *n, pl* **targetmen :** one who uses a railroad target in signaling

target of opportunity : a military target on which fire or attack is unplanned and which is attacked upon favorable presentation or unexpected discovery or appearance — usu. used in pl. ⟨was permitted to engage any *targets of opportunity* which I might see —*Coast Artillery Jour.*⟩ ⟨this company was held in reserve for . . . attacking *targets of opportunity* — *Infantry Jour.*⟩

target pistol *n* **:** a pistol made esp. for target shooting

target practice *n* **:** practice in shooting at targets

target range *n* **:** RANGE 5a(3)

target rifle *n* **:** a rifle made esp. for target shooting

target rod *n* **:** a leveling rod that has an adjustable target

target spot *n* **1 :** a disease (as early blight of tomato and potato) characterized by lesions having concentric markings resembling a target **2 :** a target-spot lesion

tar·ghee \'tär(,)gē\ *n* [fr. *Targhee* Pass, southwestern Montana, near Dubois, Idaho, where the breed originated] **1** *usu cap* **:** an American breed of sheep developed by intercrossing Lincolns and Rambouillets to produce a hardy range sheep with good mutton conformation and a heavy fleece of moderately fine wool **2** -S *often cap* **:** a sheep of the Targhee breed

targing *pres part of* TARGE

tar·gum \'tär,güm, -güm\ *n, pl* **tar·gums** \-mz\ *or* **tar·gu·mim** \,=='mēm\ *usu cap* [LHeb *targūm*, fr. Aram, translation, interpretation] **:** an Aramaic translation or paraphrase of a portion of the Old Testament

tar·gum·ic \(')=¦=ik\ *adj, often cap* **:** of or relating to the Targums

tar·gum·ist \'=,=əst\ *n* -S *usu cap* **1 :** the writer or translator of a Targum **2 :** a specialist in the Targums

tarheel \'=,=\ *also* **tar·heel·er** \"ə(r)\ *n* -S *usu cap* [*tarheel* fr. ¹*tar* + *heel*; *tarheeler* fr. *Tarheel* State, nickname for North Carolina + E -*er*] **:** a North Carolinian — used as a nickname

ta·ri \(')tä¦rē\ *n* -S [It *tarì*] **:** a small medieval coin struck in Italy, Sicily, and Malta; *also* **:** a corresponding unit of value

tar·i·ana \,tarē'anə, -'änə\ *n, pl* **tariana** *or* **tarianas** *usu cap* **1 a :** an Arawakan people of northwestern Brazil **b :** a member of such people **2 :** the language of the Tariana people

target rods

¹**tar·iff** \'tarəf *also* 'ter-\ *n* -S [It *tariffa*, fr. Ar *ta'rīfa*, *ta'rīf*, fr. *'arifa* to inform, make known] **1** *also* **ta·rif·fa** \tə'rifə, -rēfə\ *archaic* **:** an arithmetic or multiplication table **2 :** a schedule, system, or scheme of duties imposed by a government on imported or exported goods for the production of revenue, for the artificial fostering of home industries, or as a means of coercing foreign governments to grant reciprocity privileges — compare PROTECTION, FREE TRADE **3 :** a listing or scale of rates or charges for a business or a public utility: as **a :** a published schedule of rates, ratings, or charges with associated rules, regulations, routes, and information issued by carriers or their agents and filed with a public regulatory agency **b :** a schedule of rates or charges of a hotel, motel, or lodging house ⟨rooms and meals at ~*s* well below comparable accommodations elsewhere —Lucius Beebe⟩ **c :** a schedule of postal rates or charges ⟨the flat rate principles on which the postal ~ is based —A.J.Bruwer⟩ **4 :** the duty or rate of duty imposed in a tariff ⟨the ~ on wool⟩ ⟨a ~ of two cents a pound⟩ **5 :** a charge or fee set as the cost of goods or service **:** PRICE ⟨creating a market in shells . . . and modifying the ~ according to the supply —Arnold Bennett⟩ ⟨excellent workmanship at not too high a ~ —*Fashion Digest*⟩ ⟨the stiff ~ of 15 bucks that the fraternity was charging —Martin Dibner⟩ ⟨keep the tickets on a par with the ~ in the unofficial stands —Horace Sutton⟩

²**tariff** \"\ *vt* -ED/-ING/-S **:** to levy a tariff or set a price on (goods or service)

tar·iff·less \'tarəfləs *also* 'ter-\ *adj* **:** being without or not subject to a tariff ⟨wants a single, ~ European market —F.R. Kuh⟩

tariff wall *n* **:** a rate or scale of custom duties designed to check the flow of imports

ta·rin *also* **te·rin** \tə'ran\ *n* -S [F, prob. of imit. origin] **:** the European siskin

taring *pres part of* TARE

ta·ri·qa *also* **ta·ri·qah** \tə'rēkə\ *or* **ta·ri·qat** \-kət\ *n* -S [Ar *ṭarīqah*, *ṭarīqat*, lit., way] **1 :** the Sufi path of spiritual development involving stages of meditation and contemplation leading to intimate communion with the deity **2** *or* **ta·re·kat** \-kət\ **:** a Muslim religious brotherhood; *esp* **:** a religious fraternity of Muslim mystics

ta·rir·ic acid \tə'ririk-\ *n* [ISV *tariri-* (fr. NL *Tariri*, fr. AmerSp *tariri*, a plant of the genus *Picramnia*, of AmerInd origin) + -*ic*] **:** a crystalline acetylenic fatty acid $CH_3(CH_2)_{10}$-C≡C$(CH_2)_4$COOH that is isomeric with linoleic acid and occurs as a glyceride in the oil of the seeds of several plants of the genus *Picramnia*

tar·ka·ni \'tär'känē\ *also* **tar·ka·la·ni** \,tärkə'länē\ *n, pl* **tarkani** *or* **tarkanis** *also* **tarkalani** *or* **tarkalanis** *usu cap* **1 :** one of a group of Pathan hill people of Durani descent that live west of the Panjkora river in northern West Pakistan **2 :** a member of the Tarkani people

tar·khan \'tär,kän\ *n* -S [Osmanli & Jagatai *Tarchan*, fr. OTurk *Tarkan*, a privileged class] **:** a member of a low Muslim caste of artisans of Upper India

tar·la·tan \'tärlətᵊn, -lətən\ *also* **tarle·ton** \", -ltən\ *n* -S [F *tarlatane*, *tarnatane*] **:** a sheer cotton fabric in open plain weave usu. heavily sized for stiffness and used for dresses, costumes, dust covers, trimmings, and some industrial purposes

tar·mac \'tär,mak\ *n* -S [short for *tarmacadam*] **:** a tarmacadam road, apron, or runway

Tar·mac \"\ *trademark* — used for a bituminous binder for surfacing roads

tarmacadam \¦==¦==\ *n* [¹*tar* + *macadam*] **1 :** a pavement constructed by spraying or pouring a tar binder over courses of crushed stone in situ and then consolidating with a power roller **2 :** a material of tar and aggregates mixed in a plant and shaped on the roadway

tarn \'tärn\ *n* -S [ME *tarne*, *terne*, of Scand origin; akin to ON *tjörn* small lake; akin to Skt *dara* hole in the ground, OE *teran* to tear — more at TEAR] **:** a small steep-banked mountain lake or pool; *specif* **:** one in a basin produced by glacial erosion or deposition

tar·nal \'tärnᵊl, 'tȧn-\ *adv (or adj)* [alter. of *eternal*] *dial* **:** DAMNED — used as a mild imprecation ⟨paid a ~ high price for it —C.G.Loomis⟩ ⟨fire is a cruel, ~ thing —Conrad Richter⟩ — **tar·nal·ly** \-ᵊlē, -ᵊli\ *adv, dial*

¹**tar·na·tion** \(')tär¦nāshən, (')tȧ¦n-\ *adv (or adj)* [alter. (influenced by *tarnal*) of *darnation*] *dial* **:** DAMNED — used as a mild imprecation ⟨so ~ still there you began listening for something —Esther Forbes⟩ ⟨so ~ old —Josephine Y. Case⟩ ⟨some ~ fool'll be going over —Della Lutes⟩

²**tarnation** \"\ *n* -S *dial* **:** DAMNATION — used as a mild imprecation ⟨where in ~ is she at —Frederick Way⟩ ⟨what in ~'*s* pemmican —F.W.V.Mason⟩

¹**tar·nish** \'tärnish, 'tȧn-, -nēsh, *esp in pres part* '-nəsh\ *vb* -ED/-ING/-S [MF *terniss-*, stem of *ternir* to tarnish, prob. of Gmc origin; akin to OHG *ternen*, *tarnen* to hide — more at DERN] *vt* **1 :** to diminish, dull, or destroy the luster of esp. by or as if by air, dust, or dirt **:** SOIL, STAIN ⟨polishing the ~*ed* spoons⟩ ⟨the mist settling down and ~*ing* the great plague of silver —William Beebe⟩ ⟨a ~*ed* tidewater creek —Berton Roueché⟩ ⟨~*ed* marigold stalks —J.C.Powys⟩ **2 a :** to detract from the good or desirable quality of **:** VITIATE, SPOIL ⟨the brightest of its ideas grow ~*ed* —H.V.Gregory⟩ ⟨reciting some plain facts . . . which somewhat ~*ed* the latter's eulogies —V.L.Parrington⟩ ⟨had ~*ed* himself, filled his mind with corruption —Oscar Wilde⟩ **b :** to bring disgrace or cast doubt upon (one's name or reputation) **:** TAINT, SULLY ⟨am not worried that the . . . name will be ~*ed* by my association with the governor —F.D.Roosevelt⟩ ⟨the belief that some uranium stocks . . . could ~ the reputation of American business — *Wall Street Jour.*⟩ ~ *vi* **1 :** to become dull, discolored, or stained in appearance ⟨silver ~*es* quickly if left uncared-for⟩ **2 a :** to undergo a lowering in quality **:** DISSIPATE, DETERIORATE ⟨the bright hopes of the Liberation have ~*ed* rapidly —Stanley Karnow⟩ ⟨in contact with the seamy realities . . . the dream soon ~*es* —L.C.Stevens⟩ **b :** to grow less in prestige or esteem **:** DIMINISH ⟨his reputation may have ~*ed* somewhat among . . . the population —J.H.Huizinga⟩ ⟨have allowed his justly bright fame . . . to —C.R.Anderson⟩

²**tarnish** \"\ *n* -ES **1 a :** the condition of being tarnished **:** STAIN, SOIL, BLEMISH ⟨~ on silver⟩ **b :** the altered luster or surface color of a mineral or metal caused either by slight alteration or a thin film of deposition **2 :** the condition of being lowered in quality, worth, or esteem **:** DEBASEMENT, DETERIORATION ⟨time and circumstance brought a ~ to the glory —R. T. La Piere⟩ ⟨bright as that reputation long was, it is beginning to show ~ —V.L.Parrington⟩

tar·nish·able \-shəbəl\ *adj* **:** likely to undergo tarnishing

tarnished plant bug *n* **:** a common and widespread mirid bug (*Lygus lineolaris*) that is destructive to many kinds of plants by sucking the sap from buds, leaves, and fruits and causing decline and disfigurement (as catfacing of peaches) and by carrying diseases (as fire blight of pears) — see STOPBACK

tarnishproof \¦==¦=\ *adj* **:** incapable of tarnishing ⟨the most ~ preconceived picture of Paris —P.E.Deutschman⟩

taro \'tä(,)rō, 'ta(a)(,)-, 'te(,)-, 'tȧ(,)-\ *n* -S *also* **tara** \-rə\ *n* -S [Tahitian & Maori *taro*] **1 :** an aroid (*Colocasia esculenta*) of the Pacific islands that is grown throughout the tropics for its edible starchy tuberous rootstocks and in temperate regions for ornament — called also *dalo*; compare ELEPHANT'S EAR **2 :** the rootstock of the taro plant that serves as a food staple in the tropics — called also *eddo*; see POI

ta·ro·ga·to \'tärōgə,tō\ *n* -S [Hung *tárogató*] **:** a Hungarian musical instrument consisting of a wooden pipe with a clarinet reed at the mouthpiece and a globular bell similar to that of an English horn

tar oil *n* **:** any of various oils obtained from tar (as coal tar or pine tar) usu. by distillation

ta·rok *also* **ta·roc** *or* **ta·rock** \tə'räk\ *n* -S [obs. It *tarocco* (now *tarocchi*, pl. of obs. *tarocco*), fr. OIt] **:** an old and popular card game of central Europe played with a pack containing the 22 tarots plus 40, 52, or 56 cards equivalent to modern playing cards

ta·rot \(')ta¦rō\ *n, pl* **tarots** \-ō(z)\ [MF, fr. OIt *tarocco*] **1 :** any of a set of 22 pictorial playing cards used for fortune-telling and serving as trumps in tarok **2** *tarots pl* **:** TAROK

tarp \'tärp, 'tȧp\ *n* -S [by shortening] **:** TARPAULIN

tar·pan \(')tär¦pan\ *n* -S [Russ, fr. Kirghiz] **:** a small swift dun-colored horse once found wild in Europe and parts of Asia but now extinct in its pure wild form and confined to herds which have been reestablished esp. in Poland

tar paper *n* **:** a heavy paper coated or impregnated with tar for use esp. in building

¹**tar·pau·lin** \tär'pȯlən, tȧ'p-, '=,pələn, *chiefly in substand speech* ='pōlyən *or* -ōlēən\ *n* -S [earlier *tarpauling*, *tarpawling*, prob. fr. ¹*tar* + *-pauling*, *-pawling* covering, fr. *paule*, *pawl*, *pall* cloth, covering, fr. ME *pall* — more at PALL] **1 :** a piece or sheet of waterproofed canvas or other waterproof material used for covering or protecting goods, vehicles, athletic fields, or other exposed objects **2 :** SAILOR

²**tarpaulin** \"\ *vt* -ED/-ING/-S **:** to cover with a tarpaulin ⟨the ~*ed* shelter which housed the car and the truck —Jon Godden⟩

tarpaulin muster *n* [so called fr. its being formerly collected by having the crew toss their money into a tarpaulin] **:** a pooling of funds for common use esp. by seamen

tar·pe·ian \(')tär¦pē(y)ən\ *adj, usu cap* [L *tarpeius* (fr. *Tarpeius*, cliff or rock on the Capitoline hill, prob. fr. *Tarpeia*, legendary Roman maiden) + E -*an*] **:** of, relating to, or being a cliff or rock of the Capitoline hill in Rome used in ancient times for hurling condemned criminals to their deaths

tar·pon \'tärpən, 'tȧp- *sometimes* -,pän\ *n, pl* **tarpon** *or* **tarpons** [origin unknown] **1 a :** a marine fish (*Tarpon atlanticus* or *Megalops atlanticus*) that is closely related to the tenpounder, is common in the Gulf of Mexico off the coast of Florida, has an elongate and compressed body with large scales brilliantly silvery on the sides and belly, reaches a length of about six feet and a weight of 200 pounds, and is noted as a sport fish **b :** a smaller related fish (*Megalops cyprinoides*) of the Indo-Pacific area — called also *oxeye* **2** *southern Africa* **:** the common bonefish (*Albula vulpes*)

tar·pum \-,pəm, -pᵊm\ *n* -S [by alter.] **:** TARPON 1

tar putty *n* **:** a mixture of tar and lampblack

tar·quin·i·an \(')tär¦kwinēən\ *adj, usu cap* [L *tarquinius* (fr. *Tarquinius* Tarquin, any one of a succession of legendary Roman kings of the 6th and 5th centuries B.C., prob. fr. *Tarquinii* Tarquinia, ancient Roman town in central Italy that was the birthplace of the first Tarquin king) + E -*an*] **:** of or relating to the legendary Tarquin kings of ancient Rome noted esp. for their tyranny

tarradiddle *var of* TARADIDDLE

tar·ra·gon \ˈtarə͵gän, -͵gən\ *n* -s [earlier *taragon*, fr. MF *targon*, fr. ML *tarcon*, *tarchon*, fr. Ar *ṭarkhūn*] **1** : a small European perennial wormwood (*Artemisia dracunculus*) grown for its pungent aromatic foliage that is used in making pickles and vinegar **2** : the foliage of tarragon **3** : a moderate yellowish green that is yellower and stronger than average almond green and yellower and duller than malachite green or verdigris

tar·ra·go·na \͵tarəˈgōnə\ *n* -s [fr. *Tarragona*, Spanish portlike wine, fr. *Tarragona*, region in northeastern Spain where it is produced] : IRON-OXIDE RED

tarragon oil *n* : an aromatic essential oil obtained from tarragon and used chiefly as a flavoring material — called also *estragon oil*

tarras *var of* TRASS

tar·ra·tine *also* **tar·ra·teen** \ˈtarə͵tēn\ *n* -s *usu cap* : ABNAKI

tarre *var of* TAR

tarred *past of* TAR

tar·ri·ance \ˈtarēən(t)s *also* ˈter-\ *n* -s **1** : the act of tarrying : PUTTING OFF, DELAY ⟨the day was too far advanced to admit of further ~ —Susan E. Ferrier⟩ **2** : a temporary stay in a place : SOJOURN ⟨after two days ~ there, returned —Alfred Tennyson⟩ **3** *obs* : the act of waiting usu. in anticipation

tar·ri·etia \͵tarēˈēsh(ē)ə\ *n, cap* [NL, fr. native name in Java] : a small genus of chiefly eastern Asian and Australian timber trees (family Sterculiaceae)

tar·ri·ness \ˈtärēnəs, ˈtär-, -rin-\ *n* -ES : the quality or state of being tarry

tarring *pres part of* TAR

¹tar·ry \ˈtarē, -ri *also* ˈter-\ *vb* -ED/-ING/-ES [ME *tarien*] *vt* **1** *obs* : to cause (as a person) to stay or wait : DELAY, HINDER **2** : to wait for or in expectation of ⟨sitting down to ~ their return⟩ ~ *vi* **1 a** : to delay or be tardy in acting or doing : PROCRASTINATE, DAWDLE ⟨the men ~ about marriage —Jack Lusby⟩ ⟨we could not ~ if we wanted to be there on time⟩ **b** : to stay or linger in expectation of a person or an event : WAIT ⟨not ~*ing* long before the door is opened⟩ **2 a** *archaic* : to remain or continue in a state or condition **b** : to abide or stay in or at a place : SOJOURN ⟨no reason to ~ in this town —Elmer Davis⟩ ⟨over the island a horrid stillness *tarried* —Jean Stafford⟩ **syn** see STAY

²tarry \"\ *n* -ES [ME *tary*, fr. *tarien*] : STAY, SOJOURN ⟨make some little ~ in this town —J.G.Whittier⟩

³tar·ry \ˈtärē, ˈtär-, -ri\ *adj* -ER/-EST [¹*tar* + -*y*] **1** : of, resembling, or having the characteristics of tar ⟨the room had a ~, stuffy odor from the fire —Kenneth Roberts⟩ **2** : consisting of or covered with or as if with tar : TARRED ⟨~ deposits are found in the cylinders —Malcolm McLaren⟩

tarrying irons *n pl* : TIRING IRONS

tarry stool *n* : an evacuation from the bowels having the color of tar caused by hemorrhage in the stomach or upper intestines or by drugs (as iron or bismuth)

tars *pl of* TAR, *pres 3d sing of* TAR

tars- *or* **tarso-** *comb form* [NL, fr. *tarsus*] **1** *usu tarso-* : tarsus ⟨*tarso*phyma⟩ ⟨*tarsal*gia⟩ ⟨*tars*ectomy⟩ **2** *usu tarso-* : tarsal and ⟨*tarso*orbital⟩ ⟨*tarso*tibial⟩

¹tar·sal \ˈtärsəl, ˈtäs-\ *adj* [NL *tarsalis*, fr. *tarsus* + L -*alis* -al] **1** : of or relating to the tarsus **2** : being or relating to plates of dense connective tissue that serve to stiffen the eyelids of man and many animals

²tarsal \"\ *n* -s : a tarsal part (as a bone or cartilage)

tarsal arch *n* : either of two arterial loops: **a** : a superior loop near the free margin of the upper or lower eyelid **b** : an inferior loop in this region

tar·sale \tärˈsa(͵)lē, -sä(, -sā(-\ *n, pl* **tarsa·lia** \-lēə\ [NL, fr. neut. sing. of *tarsalis*] : one of the bones or cartilages of the tarsus; *esp* : one of those articulating with the metatarsals

tarsal gland *n* : MEIBOMIAN GLAND

tarsal pad *n* : a flat pad on the tarsus of an insect

tar sand *n* : a natural impregnation of sand or sandstone with petroleum from which the lighter portions have escaped

tarsi *pl of* TARSUS

tar·sia \ˈtärsēə, ═ˈ══\ *n* -s [It, fr. Ar *tarṣīʿ*] : INTARSIA 1

tar·si·er \ˈtärsē͵ā, -ēər\ *n* -s [F, fr. *tarse* tarsus (fr. NL *tarsus*) + -*ier* -er] : any of several closely related nocturnal arboreal mammals of the genus *Tarsius* of the East Indies that are related to the lemurs, that are about the size of a small squirrel with soft grayish brown fur, slender legs, a tufted tail, and very large goggle eyes, and that have adhesive disks on the fingers and toes and very long proximal tarsal bones

tar·si·idae \tärˈsīə͵dē\ *n pl, cap* [NL, fr. *Tarsius*, type genus + -*idae*] : a family of lower primates (suborder Prosimii) that is coextensive with the genus *Tarsius*

tar·si·i·for·mes \͵tärsēəˈfȯr(͵)mēz\ *n pl, cap* [NL, fr. *Tarsius* + -*iformes*] : a subgroup of Prosimii equivalent to Tarsioidea

¹tar·si·oid \ˈtärsē͵ȯid\ *adj* [in sense 1, fr. NL *Tarsioidea*; in sense 2, fr. *tarsier* + -*oid*] **1** : of or relating to the Tarsioidea ⟨a ~ prosimian⟩ **2** : resembling or resembling that of a tarsier ⟨a ~ stage of development⟩

²tarsioid \"\ *n* -s : a tarsioid primate : TARSIER

tar·si·oi·dea \͵tärsēˈȯidēə\ *n pl, cap* [NL, fr. *Tarsius* + -*oidea*] *in some classifications* : a suborder or lesser division of primate mammals comprising the tarsier and extinct related mammals that are often placed with the lemurs in Prosimii

tar·si·pes \ˈtärsə͵pēz\ *n, cap* [NL *Tarsiped-*, *Tarsipes*, fr. *tarsus* + L *ped-*, *pes* foot — more at FOOT] : a genus of marsupial mammals (family Phalangeridae) consisting of the honey possum

tar·si·us \ˈtärsēəs\ *n, cap* [NL, fr. *tarsus*; fr. the length of the tarsal bones] : a genus (the type of the family Tarsiidae) comprising the tarsiers

tarso- — see TARS-

tar·so·mere \ˈtärsə͵mi(ə)r\ *n* -s [*tars-* + -*mere*] : one of the movable subsegments of the insect tarsus

tar·so·metatarsal \¦tär(͵)sō+¦══-\ *adj* [in sense 1, fr. *tars-* + *metatarsal*; in sense 2, fr. NL *tarsometatarsus* + E -*al*] **1** : of or relating to the tarsus and metatarsus ⟨~ articulations⟩ **2** : of or relating to the tarsometatarsus

tar·so·metatarsus \"+¦══͵══\ *n* [NL, fr. *tars-* + *metatarsus*] : the large bone of the shank of a bird consisting of the fused metatarsal bones united with the end of the distal tarsal elements; *also* : the segment of the limb this structure supports

¹tar·so·ne·mid \͵tärsəˈnēməd\ *adj* [NL *Tarsonemidae*] : of or relating to the Tarsonemidae

²tarsonemid \"\ *n* -s : a mite of the family Tarsonemidae

tar·so·nemi·dae \͵tärsəˈnemə͵dē, -nēm-\ *n pl, cap* [NL, fr. *Tarsonemus*, type genus + -*idae*] : a family of small soft-bodied usu. pale-colored mites including some that suck the juices of plants and others that are predaceous on insects and other minute animals

tar·so·ne·mus \-nēməs\ *n, cap* [NL, fr. *tars-* + -*nemus* (fr. Gk *nēma* thread) — more at NEEDLE] : the type genus of Tarsonemidae

tar·sor·rha·phy \tärˈsȯrəfē\ *n* -ES [*tars-* + -*rrhaphy*] : the operation of suturing the eyelids together entirely or in part

tar spot *n* [¹*tar*] **1 a** : a leaf-blotch disease of maple, willow, or oak caused by fungi of the genus *Rhytisma* that produce raised black stromatic cushions on the foliage **b** : one of the spots produced **2** : a disease of many grasses caused by a fungus (*Phyllacora graminis*) and resembling the tar spot of trees

tar still *n* : a still in which tar or similar material is distilled: as **a** : a still in which the heavy residuum from the first distillation in petroleum refining is rectified — compare CRUDE STILL **b** : an apparatus for testing esp. tars and asphalt

tar·sus \ˈtärsəs\ *n, pl* **tar·si** \-͵sī, -(͵)sē\ [NL, fr. Gk *tarsos* frame of a wickerwork, flat basket, flat of the foot, ankle, edge of the eyelid; akin to Gk *tersesthai* to become dry — more at THIRST] **1 a** : the part of the foot of a vertebrate between the metatarsus and the leg : ANKLE **b** : the small bones that support this part of the limb **2** : TARSOMETATARSUS **3** : the distal part of the limb of an arthropod: **a** : the part of the limb of an insect distal to the tibia and usu. consisting of four or five segments and bearing two claws often with a pulvillus at the end **b** : the distal segment of the foot of a spider **4** : the plate of strong dense fibrous connective tissue that forms the supporting structure of the eyelid

¹tart \ˈtär|t, ˈtä|, *usu* |d·+V\ *adj* -ER/-EST [ME, fr. OE *teart* sharp, severe; akin to MHG *traz*, *truz* spite, hostility, stubbornness, MD *torten* to defy, challenge and prob. to OE *teran* to tear — more at TEAR] **1 a** : agreeably acid, sharp, or piquant to the taste : ACIDULOUS, PUNGENT ⟨a ~, fiery applejack —*N. Y. Times*⟩ ⟨soup ~ with quantities of fresh watercress —*Amer. Guide Series: N. Y. City*⟩ **b** : possessing a sharp or mildly acrid odor ⟨the ~ smell of rainy grass —V.S.Pritchett⟩ **2** : marked by a biting, acrimonious, or cutting quality : CAUSTIC ⟨his ~ deflations of the more boastful accounts —H.A.Larrabee⟩ ⟨insert ~ rejoinders to the opposition's noisy interjections —Guy Eden⟩ ⟨a short, ~, scathing laugh —Mary McCarthy⟩ ⟨a sort of ~ but not sour cheerfulness —Arnold Bennett⟩ ⟨was decidedly ~ in his admonitions —A.T. Quiller-Couch⟩ **syn** see SOUR

²tart \"\ *n* -s [ME *tarte*, fr. MF] **1** : a small pie or shell of pastry containing jelly, custard, or fruit and often having no top crust **2** : a wanton or loose girl or woman; *esp* : PROSTITUTE ⟨morals was what kept you out of going to bed . . . with some ~ or other —Richard Llewellyn⟩

tart *abbr* **1** tartar **2** tartaric

tar·ta·go \ˈtärd·ə͵gō\ *n* -s [Sp *tártago*] : PHYSIC NUT

¹tar·tan \ˈtärtᵊn, ˈtät-\ *n* -s [prob. fr. MF *tiretaine* linsey-woolsey] **1** : a plaid textile design of Scottish origin consisting of stripes of varying width and color against a solid ground and usu. patterned to designate a distinctive clan **2 a** : a twilled woolen fabric with a tartan design **b** : any of various imitative fabrics in other fibers with woven or printed designs **3** : a garment of cloth with a tartan design ⟨the ~ was thrown over the shoulder —*Botany Call O' The Clans*⟩

²tartan \"\ *also* **tar·tana** \-ˈtanə, ═ˈtänə\ *or* **tartane** \(ˈ)═¦tan\ *n* -s [F *tartane*, fr. It *tartana*] : a coasting vessel having one mast carrying a large lateen sail and a bowsprit with stay-sail or jib and used in the Mediterranean

¹tar·tar \ˈtär|d·ər, ˈtä|d·ə(r, |tə-\ *n* -s [ME *tartre*, *tartar*, fr. MF & ML; MF *tartre*, fr. ML *tartarum*] **1** : a substance consisting essentially of cream of tartar found in the juice of grapes and deposited in wine casks together with yeast and other suspended matters as a pale or dark reddish crust or sediment; *esp* : a recrystallized product yielding cream of tartar on further purification — compare ¹ARGOL, ³LEE **2 a** : an incrustation deposited from a liquid **b** : an incrustation on the teeth consisting of salivary secretion, food residue, and various salts (as calcium carbonate or phosphate)

²tartar \"\ *n* -s [ME *Tartre*, fr. MF *Tartare*, prob. fr. ML *Tartarus*, modif. (influenced by L *Tartarus* the infernal regions) of Per *Tātār* — more at TATAR] **1** *cap* : a native or inhabitant of Tatary of Mongolic or Turkic origin **2** *usu cap* : TATAR 2 **3** *often cap* : a person of irritable, violent, or intractable temper **4** : a person or thing that when grasped or tackled proves unexpectedly formidable ⟨had caught a ~, a fish too heavy even for his strength —Bud Jackson⟩ ⟨raillery seems to be a proper rod . . . but great caution and skill are necessary in the use of it or you may happen to catch a ~ —Earl of Chesterfield⟩

³tartar \"\ *adj, usu cap* **1** : of, relating to, or characteristic of the region of Tatary extending indefinitely from the Sea of Japan to the Dnieper river **2** : of, relating to, or characteristic of the Tartars

tartarated *var of* TARTRATED

tar·tar·ean \(ˈ)tär¦ta(a)rēən\ *adj, usu cap* [L *tartareus* (fr. Gk *tartareios*, fr. *Tartaros* Tartarus) + E -*an*] : of or relating to Tartarus : INFERNAL ⟨the *Tartarean* gloom in which he found himself —Edith Sitwell⟩

tartar emetic *n* : a poisonous efflorescent crystalline salt that has a sweetish metallic taste and is used chiefly in dyeing as a mordant, in poisoned baits as an insecticide, and in medicine as an expectorant and in the treatment of tropical diseases and formerly as an emetic — called also *antimony potassium tartrate*

tar·tar·e·ous \-ēəs\ *adj* [NL *tartareus*, fr. ML *tartarum* tartar + L -*eus* -eous] : consisting of or resembling tartar

tartar horse *n, usu cap T* [³*tartar*] : TARPAN

¹tar·tar·ian \tärˈta(a)rēən\ *n* -s *usu cap* [ME *Tartarien*, fr. MF, fr. ML *Tartarus* + MF -*ien* -ian] *archaic* : TARTAR 1

²tartarian \(ˈ)═¦══\ *adj, usu cap* : TARTAR

tartarian aster *n, usu cap T* : a commonly cultivated late-blooming Siberian herb (*Aster tataricus*) often growing seven feet high and having very long basal leaves and blue to purple flower heads

tartarian buckwheat *n, usu cap T* : a buckwheat (*Fagopyrum tataricum*) introduced from Asia and distinguished by slender racemes of flowers and fruit with obtuse often corrugated angles — compare COMMON BUCKWHEAT

tartarian dogwood *n, usu cap T* : a tall Asiatic shrub (*Cornus alba*) sometimes cultivated as an ornamental and having opposite leaves, bluish white or whitish fruit, and often bright red twigs

tartarian honeysuckle *n, usu cap T* : a widely cultivated Asiatic bush honeysuckle (*Lonicera tatarica*) with cordate-ovate leaves and white to pink flowers

tartarian lamb *n, usu cap T* : SCYTHIAN LAMB

tartarian oat *n, usu cap T* : SIDE OAT

¹tar·tar·ic \(ˈ)tär¦tarik (ˈ)tä¦t-, -ärēk *also* -¦ter-\ *adj* [ISV ¹*tartar* + -*ic*; orig. formed as F *tartarique*] : of, relating to, derived from, or resembling tartar or tartaric acid

²tartaric \"\ *adj, usu cap* [²*tartar* + -*ic*] : TARTAR

tartaric acid *n* : a strong dicarboxylic acid HOOC(CHOH)$_2$COOH occurring in four optically isomeric crystalline forms; 2,3-dihydroxy-succinic acid: **a** : a dextrorotatory or R(+)-tartaric acid that is widely distributed in plants and esp. in fruits (as grapes and mountainash) both free and combined as salts, that is usu. obtained from tartar, and that is used chiefly in effervescent beverages and pharmaceutical preparations, in desserts and candies, in photography, in making salts and esters, and as a sequestrant **b** : a levorotatory or L(−)-tartaric acid obtained usu. by resolving the racemic acid **c** : RACEMIC ACID **d** : an internally compensated optically inactive meso acid obtained usu. as the crystalline monohydrate by heating the other forms with alkali

tar·ta·rin \ˈtärd·ərən\ *n* -s [F, prob. fr. *Tartarie* Tatary, indefinite region in Asia and Europe inhabited by Tatars (fr. ML *Tartaria*) + F -*in*] : SACRED BABOON

tar·tar·ish \ˈtärd·ərish\ *adj* : tending to form a tartar

tar·tar·ize \ˈtärd·ə͵rīz\ *vt* -ED/-ING/-S **1** : to impregnate or combine with tartar : subject to the action of tartar **2** : to rectify with cream of tartar

tartarized antimony *n* : TARTAR EMETIC

tar·tar·ly \ˈtärd·ərlē\ *adj* : of, relating to, or resembling the manner of a Tartar : FEROCIOUS, ROUGH ⟨literature . . . needs the savage and ~ note, even the astringence of insult —Clifton Fadiman⟩

tar·tar·ous \ˈtärd·ərəs\ *adj* : containing, consisting of, or resembling tartar : due to or derived from tartar

tar·tar sauce *or* **tar·tare sauce** \͵tär|d·|ər-, ͵tä|d·|ə-, |t|\ *n* [F *sauce tartare*] : a sauce made of mayonnaise dressing with chopped pickles, olives, capers, and parsley and usu. served with fish

tar·ta·rus \-rəs\ *n* -ES *usu cap* [L, fr. Gk *Tartaros*] **1** : the infernal regions of ancient mythology — compare ELYSIUM, HADES **2** : a place suggestive of Tartarus : HELL

tar·ta·ry buckwheat \ˈtärd·ərē-\ *n, usu cap T* [*tartary* fr. *Tartary* (Tatary), indefinite region in Asia and Europe inhabited by Tatars, fr. ME *Tartarie*, fr. MF, fr. ML *Tartaria*] : TARTARIAN BUCKWHEAT

tartar yeast *n* : a deposit of yeast cells, tartar, and other substances formed during the fermentation of grape juice in wine manufacture

tartemorion *var of* TETARTEMORION

tarter *comparative of* TART

¹tar·tes·sian \tärˈtesēən, -eshən\ *adj, usu cap* [L *tartessius* (fr. *Tartessus*, ancient kingdom on the southwestern coast of Spain) + E -*an* (adj. suffix)] **1** : of, relating to, or characteristic of ancient Tartessus, Spain **2** : of, relating to, or characteristic of the people of Tartessus

²tartessian \"\ *n* -s *cap* [L *Tartessii* the inhabitants of Tartessus + E -*an* (n. suffix)] : a native or inhabitant of ancient Tartessus

tartest *superlative of* TART

tar·tine \(ˈ)tär¦tēn\ *n* -s [F, fr. *tarte* tart, fr. MF] : a slice of bread spread with butter and usu. preserves or jam

tar·ti·ni's tone \tärˈtēnēz-\ *n, usu cap 1st T* [after Giuseppe *Tartini* †1770 Ital. violinist and composer] : COMBINATION TONE

tart·ish \ˈtärd·ish\ *adj* : somewhat tart ⟨a ~ taste⟩ — **tart·ish·ly** *adv*

tart·let \ˈtärtlət\ *n* -s : a small tart

tart·ly *adv* : in a tart manner; *esp* : with asperity ⟨was ~ called to account by . . . party spokesmen —F.A.Ogg & Harold Zink⟩

tart·ness *n* -ES : the quality or state of being tart ⟨behind her ~ lay a large tolerant humor —John Buchan⟩

tartr- *or* **tartro-** *comb form* [F, fr. *tartre* tartar, fr. MF — more at TARTAR] : tartar : tartaric acid ⟨*tartr*amide⟩

tar·tram·ic acid \(ˈ)tär¦tramik-\ *n* [ISV *tartr-* + -*am* + -*ic*] : a syrupy acid HOOC(CHOH)$_2$CONH$_2$ made by the action of aqueous ammonia on a tartaric ester : the half amide of tartaric acid

tar·tra·mide \ˈtär·trə͵mīd, -məd\ *n* [ISV *tartr-* + *amide*] : a crystalline compound H$_2$NCO(CHOH)$_2$CONH$_2$ made by the action of alcoholic ammonia on a tartaric ester : the amide of tartaric acid

tar·trate \ˈtar͵trāt\ *n* -s [ISV *tartr-* + -*ate*] : a salt or ester of tartaric acid

tar·trat·ed \-ād·əd\ *also* **tar·tar·at·ed** \ˈtärd·ə͵rā-\ *adj* [*tartr-* or ¹*tartar* + -*ate* + -*ed*] **1** : containing tartar **2** : derived from tartar **3** : combined with tartaric acid

tartrated antimony *n* : TARTAR EMETIC

tar·tra·zine \ˈtär·trə͵zēn, -zən\ *n* [ISV *tartr-* + *azine*] : a yellow pyrazolone acid dye used chiefly in dyeing wool and silk, in making organic pigments, and in coloring foods and drugs — see DYE table I (under *Acid Yellow 23*)

tar·tron·ic acid \(ˈ)tär·¦tränik-\ *n* [F *tartronique*, fr. *tartr-* + -*onique* (as in *malonique* malonic)] : a crystalline hydroxy acid HOCH(COOH)$_2$ obtained by reducing mesoxalic acid and by hydrolysis of bromo-malonic acid; hydroxy-malonic acid

tarts *pl of* TART

tar·tuffe *or* **tar·tufe** \(ˈ)tär¦tu̇f, -¦tüf\ *n* -s *usu cap* [F, fr. *Tartufe*, hypocritical hero of the play *Tartufe* (1669) by Molière (Jean Baptiste Poquelin) †1673 Fr. playwright] : a hypocritical pretender to religion; *broadly* : HYPOCRITE

tar·tuf·fery *or* **tar·tuf·fer·ie** \═ˈ═ərē\ *n, pl* **tartufferies** *usu cap* [F *tartufferie*, fr. *tartuffe* + -*rie* -ry] : the character or behavior of a Tartuffe : HYPOCRISY ⟨his chronicle of evasions, face-saving absurdities, and bureaucratic *Tartufferies* —Anthony West⟩

tar·tuf·fism \═ˈ═͵izəm\ *n* -s *usu cap* : TARTUFFERY

tar·u·ma \͵tarəˈmä\ *n, pl* **taruma** *or* **tarumas** *usu cap* **1 a** : an Arawakan people of southern British Guiana **b** : a member of such people **2** : the language of the Taruma people

Tar·via \ˈtärvēə\ *trademark* — used for a viscid surfacing and binding material for roads that is made from coal tar

tar-water \ˈ═͵══\ *n* : a cold infusion of tar in water formerly regarded as a cure-all

tarweed \ˈ═͵═\ *n* [¹*tar* + *weed*; fr. their stickiness and heavy smell] **1** : any of various California resinous glandular plants esp. of the genera *Madia* and *Grindelia* **2** : MOUNTAIN MISERY **3** : FIDDLE-NECK 2

tar·whine \ˈtär͵(h)wīn\ *n* -s [origin unknown] *Austral* : either of two sea breams (family Sparidae): **a** : SILVER BREAM 1 **b** : a closely related fish (*Rhabdosargus australis*)

tarwood \ˈ═͵═\ *n* [¹*tar* + *wood*] : a New Zealand silver pine (*Dacrydium colensoi*) of conical habit with long slender flexuous branches

tar·zan \ˈtärzᵊn, ˈtäz- *also* -͵zan *or* -͵zaa(ə)n\ *n* -s *usu cap* [fr. *Tarzan*, hero of the adventure stories of Edgar Rice Burroughs †1950 Am. writer] : a strong agile person of heroic proportions and bearing ⟨a chimpanzee can easily run away . . . and once in the trees, no human *Tarzan* is half a match for it —Weston La Barre⟩

TAS *abbr* true air speed

ta·sa·ji·llo \͵täsəˈhē(͵)(y)ō\ *n* -s [MexSp, dim. of *tasajo*] : an arborescent prickly pear (*Opuntia leptocaulis*) of the southwestern U. S. and Mexico with slender cylindrical joints and greenish yellow flowers

ta·sa·jo *also* **tas·sa·jo** \təˈsä(͵)hō\ *n* -s [Sp *tasajo*, fr. OSp, piece of meat; akin to Pg *tossalho* large piece of something to eat] **1** : jerked meat; *esp* : jerked beef **2** [MexSp, fr. Sp] : any of several cacti of the southwestern U. S. and Mexico; *esp* : CHOLLA

tas·bih \ˈtäz͵bē\ *n* -s [Ar] : a Muslim rosary or set of 33, 66, or 99 prayer beads used in reciting the 99 titles of Allah and in meditation

tas-de-charge \͵tädəˈshärzh\ *n* -s [F *tas de charge*, lit., pile for the burden] : the portion of a group of vault ribs that occurs just above the spring where the ribs are still joined together

tash *var of* TACHE

ta·shi lama \ˈtäshē-\ *or* **te·shu lama** \ˈtā(͵)shü-\ *n, usu cap T&L* [*tashi*, *teshu* fr. *Tashi* (*Lunpo*), *Teshu* (*Lunpo*), monastery in Tibet presided over by the Panchen Lamas] : PANCHEN LAMA

tash·kent *or* **tash·kend** \(ˈ)tash¦kent, (ˈ)täsh-\ *adj, usu cap* [fr. *Tashkent* (*Tashkend*), U. S. S. R.] : of or from the city of Tashkent, U. S. S. R. : of the kind or style prevalent in Tashkent

tash·lik *or* **tash·lich** \ˈtäshlik\ *n* -s [Heb *tashlīkh* thou will cast (as in Mic 7:19), 2d sing. imperf. of *hishlīkh* to cast] : a symbolic propitiatory rite that is celebrated by Orthodox Jews traditionally on the afternoon of Rosh Hashanah and that consists in assembling along the banks of a running stream, reciting Micah 7:18–20 and penitential prayers, and shaking one's garments as if casting one's sins into the water to be washed or swept away

¹ta·si·an \ˈtäsēən\ *adj, usu cap* [(*Deir*) *Tasa*, village in Upper Egypt, type site of the Tasian culture + E -*ian*] : of or relating to a predynastic neolithic culture of Upper Egypt earlier than the Badarian

²tasian \"\ *n* -s *usu cap* : one of the ancient Egyptian people who produced the Tasian culture

¹task \ˈtask, ˈtaa(ə)sk, ˈtaisk, ˈtäsk\ *n* -s [ME *taske*, *tasque*, fr. ONF *tasque*, fr. (assumed) VL *tasca* task, remuneration, alter. of *taxa*, fr. L *taxare* to touch, feel, rate, compute — more at TAX] **1 a** : a specific piece or amount of work usu. assigned by another and often required or expected to be finished within a certain time ⟨the ~*s* that were set for chemistry at last year's examination for the school-leaving certificate of the high schools —*Jour. of Chem. Education*⟩ ⟨a novel . . . I had once read as a school holiday ~ —Adrian Bell⟩ **b** : something that has to be done or needs to be done and usu. involves some difficulty or problem ⟨Greece . . . passed on to Macedon and thence to Rome that ~ of reconciling the individual and the class with the whole —G.L.Dickinson⟩ : something hard or unpleasant to do ⟨deciphering some people's handwriting is quite a ~⟩ **c** : the job allotted to someone as his duty or to some inanimate thing as its proper function ⟨forecasting is . . . one of the most important ~*s* of the statistician in business —M.K.Adler⟩ ⟨every inch of material . . . from crypt to vault . . . had its ~ —Henry Adams⟩ **2** *obs* : TAX, IMPOST **3** : subjection to adverse criticism : REPRIMAND — used in the expressions *to take*, *call*, or *bring one to task* **4** : the performance that is required of the subject in a psychological experiment or test and that is usu. made known to a human subject by verbal instructions **5** : a definite usu. operational objective assigned to a unit or group of units in the armed forces **6** : a set of actions performed to accomplish a specific purpose whose accomplishment is one of the duties though usu. not the only duty of an employee holding a particular position

syn DUTY, ASSIGNMENT, JOB, STINT, CHORE: TASK refers to a specific piece of work or service usu. imposed by authority or circumstance, sometimes undertaken voluntarily ⟨some person or some organization whose *task* it is to realize the daydreams of the masses —Aldous Huxley⟩ ⟨the spirit in which judge or advocate is to look upon his *task* —B.N.Cardozo⟩ DUTY is likely to indicate work, service, or conduct enjoined on a person because of his rank, status, occupation, or affiliation; it is likely in most uses to suggest obligation, often moral ⟨it is emphatically the province and *duty* of the judicial department to say what the law is —John Marshall⟩ ⟨some of the military branches having a preferred status . . . had higher pay scales for less dangerous *duties* —Kingsley Davis⟩ ASSIGNMENT suggests a specific amount of work or sort of service assigned authoritatively ⟨it is not our *assignment* to settle specific questions of territories —H.S.Truman⟩ JOB is a general term wide in suggestion ranging from voluntary undertaking of some signal service down to an assigned bit of menial work ⟨a *job* that suffers from some relative poverty in charm, such as totting up endless small sums at a desk or feeding coal in at the door of a furnace —C.E.Montague⟩ STINT stresses carefully or equitably measured or timed apportionment of work ⟨took to doing "German Romance" as my daily work, ten pages daily my *stint* —Thomas Carlyle⟩ CHORE is likely to suggest minor routine activity necessary for continuing satisfactory operating, as of farm or office ⟨leisure after the *chores* and happy meeting places where the farmer and his family might play —Roger Burlingame⟩

²task \"\ *vt* -ED/-ING/-S [ME *tasken*, fr. *taske, tasque,* n.] **1** *obs* **:** TAX **2 :** to impose a task upon **:** assign a definite amount of business, labor, or duty to ⟨there ~ thy maids, and exercise the loom —John Dryden⟩ **3 a** *obs* **:** REPRIMAND **b** *archaic* **:** ACCUSE, CHARGE — often used with *with* ⟨too impudent to ~ me with those errors —Francis Beaumont & John Fletcher⟩ **4 a :** to oppress with great labor **:** keep busy at or as if at a task **:** BURDEN ⟨~*s* his mind with details⟩ **b :** to test as by the imposition of a burden

task-and-bonus system \'ˌ=ˌ=-\ *n* **:** a system of incentive wage payment whereby a worker receives a guaranteed hourly rate and for accomplishing or bettering a set task a bonus that is a percentage of his hourly rate for the time allowed for the task

task·er \-kə(r)\ *n* -S [ME, fr. *taske, tasque,* n. + *-er*] **1** *chiefly dial* **:** one that performs a task; *specif* **:** a laborer (as a thresher or reaper) at piecework **2 :** one that imposes a task **:** TASKMASTER

task force *n* **1 :** a temporary grouping of armed forces units under one commander for the purpose of accomplishing a definite usu. operational objective (as taking an island from an enemy) ⟨a *task force* of over 50 naval vessels⟩ ⟨a small *task force* that might, say, . . . blow up an atomic stockpile —*New Yorker*⟩ ⟨a *task force* to test military equipment under polar conditions —Frank Illingworth⟩ **2 a :** a group of persons with various specialties that is charged with investigating a particular problem (as in industry or government) and with formulating proposals for its solution and that frequently is part of a larger group dealing with a complex of related problems ⟨the commission promptly secured the service of three hundred experts, who were assigned to twenty-four research committees called *task forces* —B.D.L.Nash & Cornelius Lynde⟩ **b :** any group of persons charged with the accomplishment of a definite objective ⟨a courtroom *task force* that tore the state's case to shreds —G.A.Morran⟩

task group *n* **1 :** a part of a naval task force **2 :** TASK FORCE 2

taskmaster \'ˌ=ˌ=\ *n* **:** one that imposes a task or burdens another with labor **:** one whose duty is to assign tasks **:** OVERSEER

task·mas·ter·ship \'ˌ=ˌ==ˌship\ *n* **:** the status or position of a taskmaster

taskmistress \'ˌ=ˌ=\ *n* **:** a female taskmaster

tasks *pl of* TASK, *pres 3d sing of* TASK

tasksetter \'ˌ=ˌ==\ *n* **:** one that sets a task: **a :** one that sets the tasks of workers by designating the output to be attained or the time to be consumed and that also usu. determines the pay rate when an incentive plan is used **b :** a worker whose rate of output on a specified task is used as a standard for other workers

tasksetting \'ˌ=ˌ==\ *n* **:** performance of the duties of a tasksetter

task time *n* **:** the time set in an incentive wage system as proper for the performance of an industrial operation by a worker

task unit *n* **:** a part of a naval task group

taskwork \'ˌ=ˌ=\ *n* [ME *taske werke*] **1 :** PIECEWORK **2 :** hard work

tas·let \'taslət\ *n* -S [*tasse* + *-let*] **:** TASSE

tas·ma·nia \taz'mānēə, -nyə\ *adj, usu cap* [fr. *Tasmania*, island in the southern Pacific] **:** of or from the island or the state of Tasmania **:** of the kind or style prevalent in Tasmania **:** TASMANIAN

¹tas·ma·ni·an \-ən\ *n* -S *cap* [*Tasmania* + E *-an*] **1 :** a native or inhabitant of Tasmania; *specif* **:** one of the extinct aborigines of Tasmania **2 :** any of several languages of the Tasmanian aborigines

²tasmanian \"\ *adj, usu cap* **:** of or belonging to Tasmania

tasmanian blue gum *n, usu cap T* **:** a blue gum (*Eucalyptus globulus*)

tasmanian devil *n, usu cap T* **:** a powerful carnivorous burrowing marsupial (*Sarcophilus harrisii*) formerly widely distributed in Australia but now limited to the wilder parts of Tasmania that is about the size of a large cat or badger, has a black coat marked with white on the chest, and in many of its habits resembles the raccoon

tasmanian dodge *n, usu cap T* **:** a device used to cast fraudulent ballots in an election that usu. involves the theft of an unmarked ballot by one voter, its delivery to the person buying votes for marking outside the polling place, and its deposit in the ballot box by another voter who in turn steals a new ballot to continue the process

tasmanian myrtle *n, usu cap T* **:** an Australian evergreen tree (*Nothofagus cunninghamii*)

tasmanian oak *n, usu cap T* **:** any of several Australian trees of the genus *Eucalyptus* (esp. *E. obliqua*)

tasmanian sassafras *n, usu cap T* **:** SASSAFRAS 3a(1)

tasmanian wolf *also* **tasmanian tiger** *n, usu cap 1st T* **:** a carnivorous dasyurid marsupial (*Thylacinus cynocephalus*) formerly common in Australia but now limited to the remoter parts of Tasmania that is doglike in appearance and somewhat larger than a fox and has a smooth grayish brown pelt conspicuously cross-striped with black on the hinder half of the back and the base of the tapering tail

tas·ma·nite \'tazməˌnīt\ *n* -S [*Tasmania*, its locality + E *-ite*] **1 :** a compound of carbon, hydrogen, oxygen, and sulfur in minute reddish brown scales in shale **2 :** a light-colored shaly coal that is composed largely of the compound tasmanite and yields a large quantity of petroleum on dry distillation — called also *combustible shale*

tas·ma·noid \'tazməˌnȯid\ *adj, usu cap* [*Tasmania* + E *-oid*] **:** of, belonging to, or constituting an ethnic group of northern Queensland that is characterized by pygmy build, round skulls, and curly hair

tass \'tas\ *n* -ES [MF *tasse*, fr. Ar *ṭass, ṭassah*, fr. Per *tast*] **1** *chiefly Scot* **:** a drinking cup or bowl **2** *chiefly Scot* **:** a small drink esp. of liquor

tassajo *var of* TASAJO

tasse \'tas\ *or* **tace** \", 'tās\ *n* -S [perh. fr. MF *tasse* purse, pouch, fr. MHG *tasche* pouch, pocket, fr. OHG *tasca*; akin to OS *dasga* pouch, MD *tassche, tessche*; all fr. (assumed) VL *tasca* task, remuneration, money pouch — more at TASK] **:** one of a series of overlapping metal plates in a suit of armor that form a short skirt covering the part of the body just below the waist — see ARMOR illustration

¹tas·sel \'tasəl, 'taas-, 'tais-, 'tás- *also* 'täs- *or* 'tòs-\ *n* -S [ME, clasp, tassel, fr. OF, fr. (assumed) VL *tassellus*, alter. of L *taxillus* small die, dim. of (assumed) OL *taxlus* (whence L *talus* ankle, anklebone, die)] **1 :** a pendent ornament used on clothing, curtains, and other articles that is made by laying parallel a bunch of cords or threads of even length and fastening the bunch at one end **2 :** something resembling or felt to resemble a tassel: as **a :** the male inflorescence of some plants esp. at the top of a stalk of corn — compare SILK **b :** the beard of a male turkey **3 :** a pendant of woolen yarn worn on an archer's belt and used for wiping arrows

tassel 1

²tassel \"\ *vb* **tasseled** *or* **tasselled; tasseled** *or* **tasselled; tasseling** *or* **tasselling** \-s(ə)liŋ\ **tassels** [ME *tasselen*, fr. *tassel*, n.] *vt* **:** to adorn with or as if with tassels **:** attach tassels to ~ *vi* **:** to put forth inflorescences ⟨when the corn begins to ~⟩ — often used with *out*

³tassel *var of* TIERCEL

⁴tassel *var of* TORSEL

tassel bush *n* **1 :** a shrub (*Garrya elliptica*) of the Pacific coast of the U.S. **2 :** BEAR BRUSH

tas·sel·er \-s(ə)lə(r)\ *n* -S **:** a worker who makes tassels

tasselfish \'ˌ=ˌ=\ *n* **1 :** any of several threadfins **2** *Africa* **:** any of several croakers of the family Sciaenidae

tassel flower *n* **1 :** a tropical Asiatic annual herb (*Emilia sagittata*) sometimes cultivated for its small tassel-shaped heads of scarlet flowers **2 :** PRAIRIE CLOVER **3 :** any of several plants of the genus *Brickellia*; *esp* **:** a perennial herb (*B. umbellata*) of the western U. S. **4 :** LOVE-LIES-BLEEDING 1

tassel-gentle *var of* TERCEL GENTLE

tassel grass *n* **:** an aquatic herb of the genus *Ruppia*; *esp* **:** TASSEL PONDWEED

tassel hyacinth *n* **:** a grape hyacinth (*Muscari comosum monstrosum*) that bears only sterile flowers which are bluish violet with a fringed corolla and are borne in loose clusters on a branched scape

tasselled crab *n* **:** a small dull brown or gray hairy crab (*Pilumnus fissifrons*) common on Australian seashores

tassel plant *n* **:** BAY CEDAR 2

tassel pondweed *n* **:** a marine tassel grass (*Ruppia maritima*)

tas·sely *or* **tas·sel·ly** \-s(ə)lē\ *adj* **:** decorated with tassels **:** resembling a tassel

tas·set \'tasət\ *n* -S [*tasse* + *-et*] **:** TASSE

tas·sie \'tasī\ *n* -S [*tass* + *-ie*] *chiefly Scot* **:** a small cup

tastable *var of* TASTEABLE

¹taste \'tāst\ *vb* -ED/-ING/-S [ME *tasten* to touch, examine by touch, test, feel, taste, fr. OF *taster*, fr. (assumed) VL *tastare*, alter. of *taxitare*, freq. of L *taxare* to touch — more at TAX] *vt* **1** *obs* **a :** TOUCH **b :** TEST **2 :** to become acquainted with by experience **:** gain firsthand knowledge of **:** FEEL, UNDERGO ⟨~ . . . the privations of modern warfare —Earle Birney⟩ ⟨*tasted* the sweet delights of office —J.H.Plumb⟩ **3 a :** to ascertain the flavor of by taking a small quantity into the mouth ⟨*tasted* the tea and then added more sugar⟩; *specif* **:** to test the quality of (a food or drink) by the taste ⟨~ wine⟩ **b :** to test the quality of as if by tasting ⟨the rare ability to ~ a sentence before he writes or utters it —E.R.Murrow⟩ **4 a** (1) **:** to eat or drink esp. in small quantities ⟨the first food he has *tasted* since yesterday morning⟩ (2) **:** to experience to a slight extent ⟨have at least *tasted* these evils —J.C.Powys⟩ **b :** to consume a sample of (food or drink prepared for another) in order to test whether poison is present **5 :** to perceive, recognize, or experience by or as if by the sense of taste **6 :** to impart a flavor to **:** FLAVOR **7** *chiefly dial* **:** to make a pleasant taste in (the mouth) **:** please (a person) by an agreeable taste **8** *archaic* **:** LIKE, APPRECIATE, ENJOY **9** *obs* **:** to copulate with **10 :** SMELL 1a ~ *vi* **1 :** to exercise the sense of taste **:** distinguish flavors **2 a** (1) **:** to eat or drink a part **:** eat or drink a little **:** eat or drink even a little — often used with *of* ⟨~ of these conserves —Shak.⟩ ⟨food whereof we wretched seldom ~ —John Milton⟩ (2) **:** to have a limited experience or portion — often used with *of* ⟨age but ~*s* of pleasures, youth devours —John Dryden⟩ **b :** to consume a sample of food or drink prepared for another and thereby test whether poison is present **3 :** to ascertain the flavor or quality of something by or as if by taking a small quantity into the mouth — often used with *of* **4 :** to have perception, experience, or enjoyment **:** PARTAKE — often used with *of* ⟨~ of nature's bounty⟩ ⟨the valiant never ~ of death but once —Shak.⟩ **5 a :** to have a certain flavor when applied to the taste organs **:** excite a particular sensation by which the specific quality or flavor is distinguished ⟨the milk ~*s* sour⟩ ⟨a liquid that ~*s* like vinegar⟩ ⟨the salad ~*s* of garlic⟩ **b :** to have a particular quality that is perceived as if by taste ⟨when will life ~ clean again —Laurence Binyon⟩ — **taste blood :** to experience a new and keen pleasure esp. as a result of defeating an opponent

²taste \"\ *n* -S [ME *tast* touch, action of touching, testing, tasting, taste, fr. OF, fr. *taster*] **1** *obs* **:** TEST **2 a** *obs* **:** the act of tasting with or as if with the mouth **b :** a small amount tasted or eaten **c :** a small or tiny amount **:** BIT, SAMPLE; *esp* **:** a small sample of an experience ⟨a ~ of high life —Robert Westerby⟩ **3 a :** the power of perceiving flavor **:** gustatory sensation or the capacity for it **b :** the one of the special senses that is concerned with the perception and distinguishing of the sweet, sour, bitter, or salty quality of a dissolved substance, is mediated by the taste buds of the tongue, is conducted centrally by the glossopharyngeal and lingual nerves, and is coordinated esp. by centers in the posteroventral nuclei of the thalamus **4 :** the objective sweet, sour, bitter, or salty quality of a dissolved substance as perceived by the sense of taste **5 a :** a sensation produced by the stimulation of the sense of taste **:** the total blend of sensations that is obtained from a substance in the mouth and that typically consists not only of sensations produced by stimulating the sense of taste but also of sensations produced by stimulating the sense of touch and esp. the sense of smell **:** FLAVOR ⟨the ~ of an orange⟩ **b :** the distinctive quality of an experience esp. with reference to the emotion that it consists of or arouses ⟨the flat ~ of another disillusionment —C.J.Rolo⟩ — often used with *in one's mouth* ⟨his attempt to cheat me left a bad ~ in my mouth⟩ **6 a :** individual preference **:** LIKING, RELISH, FONDNESS, INCLINATION ⟨a ~ for music⟩ ⟨the note of sadness . . . which the poets were to find so much more to their ~ than the note of gladness —Henry Adams⟩ ⟨expensive ~*s*⟩ ⟨walking too fast for my ~⟩ ⟨all ~*s* are legitimate, and it is not necessary to account for them —Virgil Thomson⟩ ⟨not a historian by training or ~ —D.W.Brogan⟩ **b :** preference or liking in food or drink ⟨a ~ for rare beef⟩ ⟨season to ~⟩ **7 a :** the power or practice of discerning and enjoying whatever constitutes excellence esp. in the fine arts and belles lettres **:** critical judgment, discernment, or appreciation ⟨~ is nothing but sensibility to the different degrees and kinds of excellence in the works of art or nature —William Hazlitt⟩ ⟨establishing sound canons of literary ~ —*Encyc. Americana*⟩ ⟨the laws of ~ differ . . . widely in different nations —W.H.Prescott⟩ ⟨a well developed and cultivated . . . musical ~ —P.H.Lang⟩ **b :** manner indicative of such discernment or appreciation **:** aesthetic quality **:** style of artistic production or of any behavior capable of being judged on an aesthetic basis ⟨a pleasant room upstairs, Victorian in its ~ —R.M.Stern⟩ ⟨the chapters on . . . courtship and conquest are thoroughly engrossing and written with ~ —J.M.Flagler⟩ ⟨her book is a minor miracle of . . . good ~ —Lon Tinkle⟩ ⟨people who mock educational deficiencies of others show bad ~ —David Minsberg⟩

syn TASTE, SAPIDITY, FLAVOR, SAVOR, TANG, RELISH, and SMACK can signify in common that property of a substance that makes it perceptible to the gustatory sense; TASTE merely indicates the property ⟨the *taste* of cherries⟩ ⟨the *taste* of castor oil⟩ ⟨there was the cold *taste* of fear in his mouth —Gordon Merrick⟩ SAPIDITY implies a highly perceptible taste as opposed to blandness ⟨cook all *sapidity* out of the food⟩ FLAVOR suggests both taste and smell acting together ⟨the *flavor* of coffee⟩ ⟨the tart *flavor* of quinces⟩ ⟨the strong *flavor* of ripe muskmelons⟩ SAVOR usu. stresses a sensitivity of palate in detection of flavor, esp. delicate or pervasive ⟨the *savor* of roast pheasant and a good dry wine⟩ ⟨the *savor* of aristocracy about a man⟩ TANG applies chiefly to a sharp, penetrating, often pungent, savor, flavor, or odor ⟨the *tang* of outdoor cooking⟩ ⟨the *tang* of saltwater spray —Frank Waters⟩ RELISH and SMACK are close to SAVOR and usu. connote enjoyment, SMACK often suggesting a flavor that is added to or different from one characteristic of a substance ⟨the *relish* of wine —David Hume †1776⟩ ⟨a *smack* of pepper in a stew⟩

³taste \"\ *n* -S [origin unknown] **:** a narrow thin silk ribbon

taste·able *also* **tast·able** \-təbəl\ *adj* **:** capable of being tasted

taste bud *also* **taste bulb** *or* **taste goblet** *n* **:** an end organ mediating the sensation of taste, lying chiefly in the epithelium of the tongue and esp. in the walls of the vallate papillae, and consisting of a conical or flask-shaped mass made up partly of supporting cells and partly of neuroepithelial sensory cells that terminate peripherally in short hairlike processes which project into the pore in the overlying epithelium and by which communication with the mouth cavity is effected

taste cell *n* **:** a neuroepithelial cell that is located in a taste bud and is the actual receptor of the sensation of taste — called also *gustatory cell*

taste cup *n* **:** a sensillum in insects that has a gustatory function

tasted \ˌtāstəd\ *adj* **:** having such a taste — used in combinations ⟨pleasant-*tasted*⟩ ⟨sweet-*tasted*⟩

taste·ful \'tāstfəl\ *adj* **1 :** TASTY 1a **2 :** having, exhibiting, or conforming to good taste ⟨~ simplicity⟩ ⟨~ furniture⟩ ⟨a ~ artisan⟩ — **taste·ful·ly** \-fəlē, -li\ *adv* — **taste·ful·ness** *n* -ES

taste hair *n* **:** the hairlike termination of a neuroepithelial cell in a taste bud

taste·less \'tāstləs\ *adj* **1 :** having no sense of taste **:** unable to distinguish flavors **2 a :** having no taste **:** INSIPID ⟨~ vegetables⟩ **b :** arousing no interest **:** DULL, UNINTERESTING ⟨the tale comes to a flat and ~ end, despite some tension in the last chapters —R.C.Carpenter⟩ **3 :** not having or not exhibiting good taste **:** lacking in critical discernment **:** not being in good taste ⟨coarse and ~ luxury —F.W.Farrar⟩ — **taste·less·ly** *adv* — **taste·less·ness** *n* -ES

taste panel *n* **:** a group of persons having the joint duty to taste a product in order to determine factors relating to its flavor

tast·er \'tāstə(r)\ *n* -S [ME, fr. *tasten* to taste + *-er*] **1 :** one that tastes: as **a :** a person that has the duty of tasting food or drink prepared for another person (as a king) and thereby testing whether poison is present **b :** a person employed to sample a food product or beverage to determine its quality and taste appeal before it is offered for sale to the public **c :** a person able to taste the chemical phenylthiourea **2 :** a device used in tasting or sampling something: as **a :** a shallow metal cup used in tasting wine **b :** a fluted tool for taking a sample of cheese or butter **3 a :** a small amount esp. of food or drink taken as a sample **:** TASTE **b** *Brit* **:** a serving of ice cream in a shallow glass dish

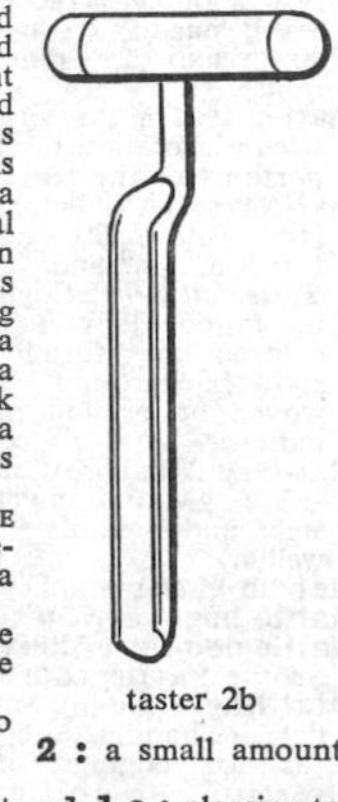

taster 2b

tastes *pres 3d sing of* TASTE, *pl of* TASTE

tast·i·ly \'tāstəlē, -li\ *adv* **1 :** in a tasteful manner ⟨~ decorated⟩ **2 :** in a tasty manner ⟨~ cooked⟩

tast·i·ness \-tēnəs, -tin-\ *n* -ES **1 :** the quality or state of being tasteful **2 :** the quality or state of being tasty

tasting *n* -S [ME, fr. gerund of *tasten* to taste] **1 :** the act of one that tastes **2 :** a small amount **:** SAMPLE

¹tasty \'tāstē, -ti\ *adj* -ER/-EST [²*taste* + *-y*] **1 a :** pleasing to the taste **:** SAVORY ⟨a ~ pie⟩ **b :** strikingly attractive or interesting ⟨the *tastiest* irony in a book full of ironies —Geoffrey Moore⟩ ⟨gusto and detail that make ~ reading —A.L.Coleman⟩; *esp* **:** arousing interest by being risqué ⟨some ~ bits of gossip⟩ **2 :** TASTEFUL 2 **syn** see PALATABLE

²tasty \"\ *n* -ES **:** something good to eat **:** GOODY — usu. used in pl.

¹tat \'tat\ *vb* **tatted; tatted; tatting; tats** [perh. of imit. origin] *vt, chiefly dial* **:** to touch lightly ~ *vi, chiefly dial* **:** PAT ⟨he stood, frowned, *tatted* at his moustache —Elizabeth Bowen⟩

²tat \'tät\ *n* -S [Hindi *ṭāṭ*] **:** a coarse fabric (as matting) esp. as stretched on a frame and used for the withering of tea leaves

³tat \'tat\ *n* -S [by shortening] **:** ⁵TATTOO

⁴tat *also* **tatt** \"\ *vb* **tatted; tatted; tatting; tats** *also* **tatts** [back-formation fr. *tatting*] *vi* **:** to work at tatting ~ *vt* **:** to make by tatting

⁵tat \'tät\ *n* -S *usu cap* [Russ, fr. Turk] **1 a :** an agricultural people living in scattered groups throughout Transcaucasia and possibly allied to the Tajiks **b :** a member of such people **2 :** the Iranian language of the Tat people

TAT *abbr* **1** thematic apperception test **2** toxin-antitoxin

ta–ta \(')tä¦tä\ *interj* [origin unknown] **:** GOOD-BYE

ta·ta·ju·ba \ˌtätə'zhübə\ *n* -S [Pg] **:** the yellow brown heavy durable wood of a Brazilian tree (*Bagassa guianensis*) of the family Moraceae that is used for furniture and heavy construction work

ta·ta·mi \tə'tämē\ *n, pl* **tatami** *or* **tatamis** [Jap] **:** straw matting used as a floor covering in a Japanese home

ta·tar \'täd·ə(r), -ätə-\ *n* -S *usu cap* [Per *Tātār*, of Turkic origin; akin to Kazan Tatar & Turk *Tatar*] **1 :** a member of one of the numerous chiefly Turkic peoples prob. originating in Manchuria and Mongolia and now found mainly in the Tatar republic of the U.S.S.R., the north Caucasus, Crimea, and sections of Siberia — see GOLDEN HORDE **2 :** the Turkic language of any of the Tatar peoples

ta·tar·i·an \tä'ta(a)rēən, -'ter-, -'tär-\ *also* **ta·tar·ic** \-'tarik\ *adj, usu cap* **:** TURKIC

tatarian honeysuckle *n, usu cap T* **:** TARTARIAN HONEYSUCKLE

ta·tar·ize \'täd·əˌrīz, -ätə-\ *vt* -ED/-ING/-S *often cap* **:** to make Tatarian

tatar of the volga *usu cap T&V* **:** KAZAN TATAR

tatar sable *n, usu cap T* **:** KOLINSKY 1b

ta·tau·pa \ˌtətȯpə\ *n* -S [Pg, fr. Tupi] **:** a So. American tinamou (*Crypturellus tataupa*)

tat·beb \'tatˌbeb\ *n* -S [F, modif. of Egypt *tebtebti* (two) sandals, soles of the feet] **:** an ancient Egyptian sandal

tate \'tāt\ *n* -S [perh. of Scand origin; akin to Icel *tæta* tuft, tatter, fiber; akin to ON *tō* tuft of grass, tuft of wool — more at TOW] **1** *dial Brit* **:** a small piece (as of wool or hay) **2** *dial Brit* **:** a lock of hair

ta·ter \'tād·ə(r)\ *n* -S [by shortening & alter.] *dial* **:** POTATO

ta·tha·ga·ta \tə,tägə'tə\ *n* -S [Skt *tathāgata*, fr. *tathā* thus + *gata* gone, come, arrived, fr. *gamati* he goes — more at COME] *Buddhism* **:** an enlightened one **:** a finder of truth **:** one who has attained perfection

ta·tha·ga·ta·gar·bha \tə,tägə,tə'gərbə\ *n* -S [Skt *tathāgatagarbha*, fr. *tathāgata* + *garbha* womb — more at DOLPHIN] *Buddhism* **:** the eternal and immutable matrix of all reality **:** the womb of the absolute and the essence of Buddhahood

ta·tha·ta \'təd·əˌtä\ *n* -S [Pali *tathatā*, fr. *tathā* thus, fr. Skt; akin to Skt *tad*, neut. demonstrative pron. — more at THAT] **:** SUCHNESS 2

ta·tian·ist \'tāsh(ē)ənəst\ *n* -S *usu cap* [*Tatian*, 2d cent. A.D. Christian writer + E *-ist*] **:** ENCRATITE

ta·tie \'tād·ē\ *n* -S [by shortening & alter.] *dial* **:** POTATO

tatoo *var of* TATTOO

ta·tou *also* **ta·tu** \tə'tü\ *n* -S [F *tatou* & Pg *tatú, tatu*, fr. Tupi & Guarani *tatú, tatu*] **:** ARMADILLO; *esp* **:** GIANT ARMADILLO

tat·ou·ay \'tatüˌā, ˌtätü'ī\ *n* -S [Sp *tatuay*, fr. Guarani *tatu ai*, lit., worthless armadillo; fr. the inedibility of the flesh] **:** a large armadillo (*Cabassous unicinctus*) of tropical So. America that has 12 or 13 movable bands or plates around the body

tatou peba *n* **:** PEBA

tat·pur·u·sha \tat'pürəshə, ˌtət-\ *n* -S [Skt *tatpuruṣa*, lit., his servant (a compound of this type), fr. *tad-, tat-* that one (fr. *tad*, neut. demonstrative pron.) + *puruṣa* man, servant] **1 :** a class of compound words having as first constituent a noun or noun stem that modifies the second constituent by standing in the relation to it of possessor (as in *sheepskin*), thing possessed (as in *motorboat*), object of action (as in *shoemaker*), location or habitat (as in *tree toad*), agent (as in *man-made*), instrument (as in *landlocked*), or any of numerous other relations **2 :** a compound word belonging to the tatpurusha class — see ¹DEPENDENT 2f

¹tats \'tats\ *n pl* [origin unknown] *slang* **:** DICE; *esp* **:** false dice

²tats *pres 3d sing of* TAT, *pl of* TAT

tatt *var of* TAT

tat-tat-tat \(')tat¦tat¦tat\ *also* **tat-tat-tat** \ˌtat,tat¦tat\ *n* -S [imit.] **:** RAT-A-TAT

tatted *past of* TAT

¹tat·ter \'tad·ə(r), -atə-\ *n* -S [ME *tater, tatter*, of Scand origin; akin to ON *tǫturr* tatter, rag; akin to OE *tætteca* rag, tatter, OHG *zotta* matted hair, tuft — more at TOD] **1 a :** a part torn and left hanging **:** RAG, SHRED ⟨tear a passion to ~*s* —Shak.⟩ ⟨a stand of ragged gums that drip their ~*s* of gray bark on to the gravelly paths —T.A.G.Hungerford⟩ **b tatters** *pl* **:** tattered clothing **:** RAGS ⟨the tramp was dressed in ~*s*⟩ **2** *archaic* **:** TATTERDEMALION ⟨a scarecrow ~ of a man —William Goyen⟩ **3** *also* **tat·ter·er** \-ərə(r)\ **:** one that collects waste with a cart or barrow **:** a rag gatherer

²tatter \"\ *vb* -ED/-ING/-S *vt* **:** to tear into shreds **:** to make ragged ~ *vi* **:** to become ragged

³tat·ter \'tatə(r)\ *vi* -ED/-ING/-S [imit.] *dial Brit* **:** BUSTLE, HURRY

⁴tat·ter \'tad·ə(r)\ *n* -S [⁴*tat* + *-er*] **:** one that makes tatting

tat·ter·de·ma·lion \ˌtad·ə(r)də'mālyən, -atə(-, -dē'-, -'mal-, -lēən\ *n* -S [¹*tatter* + *-demalion*, of unknown origin] **:** a person dressed in ragged clothing : one who is disreputable in appearance : RAGAMUFFIN, SCARECROW

²tatterdemalion \"\ *adj* **1 a** : ragged or disreputable in dress or appearance ⟨~ and careless in dress, with unpolished boots, baggy trousers, and shapeless dark cloth cap —Vernon Leonard⟩ **b** : being in a decayed state or condition : BROKEN-DOWN, DILAPIDATED ⟨the old ~ farmhouse —Theodore Dreiser⟩ **2** : BEGGARLY, DISREPUTABLE ⟨the most ~ party ever seen in American politics —H.L.Mencken⟩

tat·tered \ˈtad·ə(r)d, -atə-\ *adj* [ME *tatered*, fr. *tater* + *-ed*] **1** : wearing ragged clothes ⟨a ~ barefoot boy⟩ **2** : torn in shreds : RAGGED ⟨going about in shirts which have become ~ shreds in their struggles —E.H.Spicer⟩ ⟨a ~ book⟩ **3 a** : BROKEN-DOWN, DILAPIDATED ⟨decaying houses along ~ paved streets —P.B.Martin⟩ ⟨~ cottages —Jane Austen⟩ **b** : DISRUPTED, SHATTERED ⟨a ~ remnant of its former strength⟩ ⟨~ conventions⟩

tatter leaf *n* : a virus disease of sweet cherries marked by severe laceration resulting from the dropping out of necrotic portions of the leaves

tat·ter·sall \ˈtad·ə(r),sȯl, -atə-, -ˌsəl\ *or* **tattersall check** *n* -s [fr. *Tattersall's* horse market, London, England, after Richard *Tattersall* †1795 English horseman, its founder] **1** : a pattern of colored lines forming squares of solid background **2** : a fabric woven or printed in a tattersall pattern

tattersall 1

tat·tery \ˈtad·ərē\ *adj* [¹*tatter* + *-y*] : RAGGED, TATTERED ⟨worn steps and ~ roofs —Richard Llewellyn⟩

tat·tie \ˈtatī\ *n* -s [by shortening & alter.] *Scot* : POTATO

tattie bogle *n*, *Scot* : a scarecrow in a potato field

tattie doo·lie \-ˈdülī\ *n* [Sc *doolie* scarecrow, of imit. origin] *Scot* : TATTIE BOGLE

¹**tat·ting** \ˈtad·|iŋ, -at|, |ēŋ\ *n* -s [origin unknown] **1** : a delicate handmade lace (as for edgings, insertion, or doilies) formed usu. by looping and knotting with a single cotton thread and a small shuttle to make varied designs of rings and semicircles **2** : the act or process of making tatting

tatting 1

²**tatting** *pres part of* TAT

¹**tat·tle** \ˈtad·ᵊl, -atᵊl\ *vb* **tattled; tattled; tattling** \-d·ᵊliŋ, -t(ᵊ)liŋ\ **tattles** [MD *tatelen*; akin to MLG *tatelen* to babble, tattle, ME, MD, & MLG *tateren*] *vi* **1** : to talk idly or meaninglessly : CHATTER, PRATE ⟨the voice of the boy *tattled* endlessly over the piece he was learning to say —Elizabeth M. Roberts⟩ **2** : to tell tales or secrets : be a talebearer : BLAB ⟨*tattled* on her estranged husband —*Springfield (Mass.) Union*⟩ ~ *vt* : to utter or disclose in gossip or chatter ⟨~ tales⟩

²**tattle** \"\ *n* -s **1** : idle talk : CHATTER ⟨endless ~ about dress —Guy McCrone⟩ **2** : GOSSIP, TALEBEARING ⟨snaps his fingers at ~ —George Meredith⟩

tat·tler \ˈtad·ᵊlə(r), -at(ᵊ)lə-\ *n* -s **1** : TATTLETALE **2** : any of various slender long-legged shorebirds (as the willet, yellowlegs, and redshank) of the family Scolopacidae that have a loud and frequently uttered call

tattletale \ˈ⸗⸗,⸗\ *n* [¹*tattle* + *tale*] : one that tattles : INFORMER, TATTLER, TELLTALE ⟨the inescapable odium of the ~ —Dixon Wecter⟩ ⟨small things like these are often big ~s about human character —Laura Z. Hobson⟩

tattletale gray *n* : a grayish white : OFF-WHITE

¹**tat·too** *also* **ta·too** \(ˈ)taˈtü\ *n* -s [alter. of earlier *taptoo*, fr. D *taptoe*, fr. the imperative phrase *tap toe!* taps shut!, fr. *tap* tap of a keg (fr. MD *tappe*) + *toe*, to, shut, fr. MD; akin to OE *tō* to — more at TAP, TO] **1 a** : a call or signal sounded (as on a bugle or drum) shortly before taps as notice to soldiers or sailors to repair to quarters **b** : an evening entertainment given by troops usu. in the form of outdoor military exercises with music ⟨the evening was not yet over, for the splendid military ~ and massed bands rounded out an unforgettable day —J.W.Davies⟩ **2** : a usu. rapid rhythmic beating or rapping ⟨the hoofs of his horse beat a soft ~ on the roads —Sherwood Anderson⟩ ⟨the running gear beat a ~ against the masts —H.A.Chippendale⟩ — see DEVIL'S TATTOO

²**tattoo** *also* **tatoo** \"\ *vb* -ED/-ING/-S *vt* : to beat or rap rhythmically on : drum on ⟨dragged him out, face up, his head lolling back, his slack heels ~*ing* the pavement —Nathaniel Burt⟩ ~ *vi* : to give a series of rhythmic taps ⟨~*ed* on a door —Elizabeth Bowen⟩

³**tattoo** *also* **tatoo** \"\ *n* -s [modif. of Tahitian *tatau*] **1** : the act of tattooing or the fact of being tattooed ⟨~ . . . consists of pricking pigment into the skin —*Notes & Queries on Anthropology*⟩ ⟨facial ~ with conspicuous curvilinear patterns . . . was common —R.H.Lowie⟩ **2** : an indelible mark or figure fixed upon the surface of the body by the insertion of pigment under the skin or by the production of scars

⁴**tattoo** *also* **tatoo** \"\ *vt* -ED/-ING/-S **1 a** : to mark or color (the skin) by pricking in coloring matter so as to form indelible marks or figures or by production of scars **b** : to mark the skin with (a tattoo) ⟨~*ed* a flag on his chest⟩ **2** : to mark permanently ⟨his entire body is ~*ed* with souvenirs of the first bomb —W.M.Hitzig⟩

⁵**tat·too** \ˈta(ˌ)tü, ˈtə(-\ *n* -s [Hindi *ṭaṭṭū*] : a native-bred pony of India

tat·too·er \(ˈ)taˈtüə(r)\ *or* **tat·too·ist** \-üəst\ *n* -s : one that makes a business of forming or removing tattoos

tattooing *n* -s **1** : the act or practice of marking the skin with tattoos **2** : a tattoo or a set of tattoos

tatts *pres 3d sing of* TATT

¹**tat·ty** \ˈtad·|ē, -at|, |ī\ *adj* [perh. akin to OE *tættec* rag, tatter — more at TATTER] **1** *dial Brit* : SHAGGY **2** : CHEAP, INFERIOR — used as a generalized term of disapproval ⟨the street . . . seemed immensely long and wide, but rather dirty and ~ —Geoffrey Cotterell⟩ ⟨the ~ climax . . . seems an inexcusable last resort —*Time*⟩

²**tatty** *also* **tattie** *n*, *pl* **tatties** [Hindi *ṭaṭṭī*] *India* : a mat or screen of fibers in a door or window kept wet to cool the air

¹**tatu** *var of* TATOU

²**ta·tu** \ˈtä(ˌ)tü\ [NL, fr. Pg *tatú*, *tatu* armadillo — more at TATOU] *syn of* DASYPUS

³**ta·tu** \ˈtä(ˌ)tü\ *n*, *pl* **tatu** *or* **tatus** *usu cap* [Pomo] : HUCHNOM

ta·tu·a·su \tə,tüəˈsü\ *n* -s [Pg *tatuaçu*, *tatuaçú*, fr. Tupi *tatú asú*, lit., giant armadillo] : GIANT ARMADILLO

ta·tu·ki·ra \ˌtätüˈkērə\ *n* -s [Pg *tatuquira*] : a small So. American biting fly of the genus *Phlebotomus* that is believed to carry leishmaniasis

ta·tu·sia \təˈtüzēə, -üsēə\ [NL, modif. of Tupi *tatú* armadillo] *syn of* DASYPUS

tau \ˈtaů, ˈtȯ\ *n* -s [Gk, of Sem origin; akin to Heb *tāw* sign, cross, taw (letter)] **1 a** : the 19th letter of the Greek alphabet — symbol Τ or τ; see ALPHABET table **b** : ⁴TAW **2** : a T-shaped mark or object (as a St. Anthony's cross, a pastoral staff, or an ankh)

tau·ba·da \taůˈbädə\ *n* -s [Papuan] *Austral* : MASTER

tau cross *n* **1** : a T-shaped cross sometimes having expanded ends and foot : SAINT ANTHONY'S CROSS 1 **2** : CRUX COMMISSA 1

tau cross

tau·fer \ˈtoifə(r)\ *n* -s *usu cap* [G *täufer* one that baptizes, fr. OHG *toufāri*, fr. *toufen* to baptize + *-āri* -er — more at DOPE] : DUNKER

¹**taught** \ˈtȯt, *usu* -ȯd·+V\ [ME *taghte*, *taughte* (past), *taght*, *taught*, *ytaght*, *ytaught* (past part.), fr. OE *tǣhte*, *tāhte* (past), *tǣht*, *tāht*, *getǣht*, *getāht* (past part.) — more at TEACH] *past of* TEACH

²**taught** \"\ *adj* [ME *taght*, *taught*, fr. *taght*, *taught*, past part.] **1** : INSTRUCTED ⟨he is badly ~⟩ **2** : conveyed by instruction ⟨a ~ tradition of hewing to principles —*Nation's Business*⟩

tauhid *var of* TAWHID

tau·la \ˈtaůlə\ *n* -s [Catal, lit., table, fr. ML *tabula* — more at TABLE] : an ancient massive crude stone structure of unknown use but suggesting a table, platform, or altar that is found esp. in the Balearic islands

taung·thu \ˈtaůŋ,tü\ *n*, *pl* **taungthu** *or* **taungthus** *usu cap* **1 a** : a Karen people of eastern Burma **b** : a member of such people **2** : the Karen language of the Taungthu people

¹**taunt** \ˈtȯnt, ˈtänt, ˈtant\ *vb* -ED/-ING/-S [fr. obs. E *taunt* to tease, perh. fr. MF *tenter*, *tanter* to try, tempt — more at TEMPT] *vt* **1 a** : to reproach in a mocking or insulting manner : jeer at : UPBRAID ⟨at last he ~*ed* me beyond endurance —G. B.Shaw⟩ ⟨took no part in the revivals and usually teased and ~*ed* those who did —J.M.Hunt⟩ **b** *obs* : to make the subject of censure or reproach : cast in one's teeth ⟨~ my faults —Shak.⟩ **2** : to drive or accomplish by taunting : PROVOKE ⟨~*ed* him into losing his temper⟩ ~ *vi* : to utter taunts ⟨~ away —Robert Browning⟩ **syn** see RIDICULE

²**taunt** \"\ *n* -s **1** : a bitter or sarcastic reproach, insult, or challenge ⟨calmly ignored the ~*s* of his enemy⟩ **2** *archaic* : one who is taunted : an object of scornful reproach ⟨will make them . . . a reproach, a byword, a ~, and a curse —Jer 24:9 (RSV)⟩

³**taunt** \"\ *adj* [origin unknown] : very tall — used esp. of the masts of a ship

taunt·er \-tə(r)\ *n* -s : one that taunts

taunt·ing·ly *adv* : in a taunting manner

taun·ton turkey \ˈtäntᵊn-, ˈtȯntᵊn-, ˈtäntᵊn-, ˈtantᵊn-\ *n*, *usu cap 1st T* [fr. *Taunton*, Mass.] : ²ALEWIFE 1a

taupe \ˈtōp\ *n* -s [F, lit., mole, fr. L *talpa*] **1** : a brownish gray that is paler and slightly yellower than chocolate, duller and slightly redder than mouse gray, and duller and slightly redder than castor **2** : MOLE 4a

taupe brown *n* : a variable color averaging a grayish reddish brown that is yellower and paler than liver brown

taupe gray *n* : a dark purplish gray that is redder and lighter than slate, redder, lighter, and stronger than charcoal, and bluer and darker than pigeon

taupe rose *n* : ROSE TAUPE

tau·pou *also* **tau·po** \taůˈpō\ *n* -s [Samoan *taupo*] : a ceremonial hostess selected by a high chief of a Samoan village from the young girls of his household, elevated to a high rank, and charged with the formal reception and entertainment of visitors

taur- *or* **tauri-** *or* **tauro-** *comb form* [taur-, tauri- fr. L, fr. *taurus*; tauro- fr. LL, fr. Gk, fr. *tauros* — more at STEER] **1** : bull ⟨*taurodont*⟩ ⟨*tauricide*⟩ ⟨*tauromorphic*⟩ **2** : taurine ⟨*taurocholic*⟩

tau·ra·co \ˈtaůrə,kō\ *n*, *cap* [NL, alter. of *Touraco*, fr. F *touraco*] : a genus of touracos including those with feathered nostrils

tau·ra·nga \taůˈräŋgə\ *n* -s [Maori] *NewZeal* : BUSH SICKNESS

tau·re·an *or* **tau·ri·an** \ˈtȯrēən\ *adj* [*taurean* fr. L *taureus* taurine (fr. *taurus* bull) + E *-an*; *taurine* fr. *taur-* + *-ine*] : TAURINE

tau·ri \ˈtȯ,rī\ *n pl*, *usu cap* [L, fr. Gk *Tauroi*] : an ancient people of the southern Crimea

tau·ric \ˈtȯrik\ *adj* [*taur-* + *-ic*] : TAURINE

¹**tau·rine** \ˈtȯ,rīn, -ȯrən\ *adj* [L *taurinus*, fr. *taur-* + *-inus* -ine] **1** : of or relating to a bull : BOVINE **2** : of or relating to the common ox (*Bos taurus*) as distinguished from the zebu (*B. indicus*)

²**tau·rine** \ˈtȯ,rēn, -ȯrən\ *n* -s [ISV *taur-* + *-ine*; fr. its having been discovered in the bile of cattle] : a crystalline compound $H_2NCH_2CH_2SO_3H$ of neutral reaction that occurs esp. in invertebrates (as in the juices of muscles) that is obtained by the hydrolysis of taurocholic acid or the decarboxylation of cysteic acid, that is synthesized usu. by reaction of sodium isethionate and aqueous ammonia under heat and pressure, and that is used in making various surface-active agents; 2-amino-ethanesulfonic acid

tau·ris·cite \ˈtȯrə,sīt\ *n* -s [G *tauriszit*, fr. L (*Pagus*) *Tauriscorum* Canton Uri, Switzerland, its locality + G *-it* -ite] : a mineral $FeSO_4.7H_2O$ that is a hydrous ferrous sulfate sometimes considered isomorphous with epsomite

tau·ro·bo·li·um \ˌtȯrəˈbōlēəm\ *also* **tau·rob·o·ly** \tȯˈräbəlē\ *n*, *pl* **taurobolia** \-ˈbōlēə\ *also* **taurobolies** [LL *taurobolium*, fr. Gk *taurobolion*, fr. *tauros* bull + *-bolion* (fr. *ballein* to throw) — more at STEER, DEVIL] : a ceremony in the cult of certain Mediterranean deities (as Cybele and Mithras) in which worshipers were baptized with the blood of a sacrificed bull — compare CRIOBOLIUM

tau·ro·cho·late \ˌtȯrəˈkō,lāt, -ˈkä,-\ *n* -s [ISV *taurocholic* + *-ate*] : a salt or ester of taurocholic acid

tau·ro·cho·lic acid \ˌ⸗⸗ˈkōlik-, -ˌkälik-\ *n* [ISV *taur-* + *cholic acid*] : a deliquescent crystalline acid $(HO)_3C_{23}H_{36}CONHCH_2CH_2SO_3H$ that occurs in the form of the sodium salt in the bile of man, of carnivorous animals, and of the ox and a few other herbivorous animals and that on hydrolysis yields taurine and cholic acid

tau·ro·dont \ˈtȯrə,dänt\ *adj* [*taur-* + *-odont*] : having the pulp cavities of the teeth very large and the roots reduced — used esp. of a primitive fossil man

tau·ro·dont·ism \-nt,izəm, -n,ti-\ *n* -s : a dental condition marked by the enlargement of the pulp cavities and the reduction of the roots

tau·ro·ka·thap·sia \ˌtȯrəkəˈthapsēə\ *n pl but sing in constr* [Gk, fr. *tauros* + *kathaptos* (verbal of *kathaptein* to fasten upon, attack, fr. *kata-* cata- + *haptein* to fasten) + *-ia* -y — more at APSIS] : an ancient Cretan sport in which a performer grasps the horns of a bull and somersaults over him

tau·ro·ma·chi·an \ˌtȯrəˈmākēən\ *or* **tau·ro·mach·ic** \-ˈmakik\ *adj* [*tauromachian* fr. *tauromachy* + *-an*; *tauromachic* fr. Sp *tauromáquico*, fr. *tauromaquia* + *-ico* -ic (fr. L *-icus*)] : of or relating to tauromachy

tau·rom·a·chy \tȯˈräməkē\ *n* -ES [Sp *tauromaquia*, fr. Gk *tauromachia*, fr. *taurus* + *-machia* -machy] **1** : the art or practice of bullfighting **2** : BULLFIGHT

tau·ro·ma·quia \ˌtaůrōˈmäkēə\ *n* -s [Sp] : TAUROMACHY

tau·ro·mor·phic \ˌtȯrəˈmȯrfik\ *adj* [*taur-* + *-morphic*] : shaped in the form of a bull : resembling a bull ⟨the ~ vases of the Minoan culture⟩

tau·rot·ra·gus \tȯˈrä·trəgəs\ *n*, *cap* [NL, fr. *taur-* + Gk *tragos* he-goat] : a genus of large African antelopes consisting of the elands

¹**tau·rus** \ˈtȯrəs\ *n* -ES *usu cap* [ME, fr. L, lit., bull — more at STEER] : the second sign of the zodiac — see SIGN table; ZODIAC illustration

²**taurus** \"\ [NL, fr. L, bull] *syn of* BOS

tau·ryl \ˈtȯrəl\ *n* -s [*taur-* + *-yl*] : the univalent acid radical $H_2NCH_2CH_2SO_2$— of taurine

tau-sa·ghyz \ˈtaůsəˈgēz\ *n* -ES [Russ *tau-sagyz*, fr. Turki *tau-sağız*, fr. *tau* mountain + *sağız* gum, rubber] : a perennial yellow-headed herb (*Scorzonera tau-saghyz*) of the family Compositae that is native to the Kazakh republic of the U. S. S. R., bears leafy rosettes, and is cultivated for its rubber-containing roots

¹**taut** \ˈtȯt, *usu* -ȯd·+V\ *adj* -ER/-EST [ME *tought*; prob. akin to OE *togian* to draw, drag — more at TOW] **1 a** : tightly drawn : tensely stretched : not slack ⟨the flesh seemed smoothed back, even painfully ~ —R.P.Warren⟩ ⟨a piece of strong fabric about one yard square, kept ~ by a wooden frame —W.H.Dowdeswell⟩ **b** : HIGH-STRUNG, TENSE ⟨her nerves were ~ as bowstrings —O.E.Rölvaag⟩ ⟨strain our already ~ nerves a little further —W.F.Hambly⟩ **2** : SEVERE, STRICT ⟨is reputed to drive pretty ~ bargains —G.S.Perry⟩ **3 a** : kept in proper order or condition : well disciplined ⟨sailormen prefer a happy ship to a ~ ship, where strict discipline is the only diet —A.R.Griffin⟩ ⟨each team had brought a small but ~ cheering section of its own —A.J.Liebling⟩ **b** : not loose or flabby : FIRM, TRIM ⟨a figure that was slender, ~, and graceful —Aline B. Saarinen⟩ ⟨the ~, economical style contains more than meets the casual eye —*Time*⟩ **syn** see TIGHT

²**taut** \ˈtȯt\ *vt* -ED/-ING/-S [origin unknown] *Scot* : TANGLE

taut *abbr* tautological; tautology

taut- *or* **tauto-** *comb form* [LL, fr. Gk, fr. *tautos* identical, fr. *to auto* the same, fr. *to*, neut. definite article + *auto* (neut. of *autos*) same — more at THAT, AUT-] : same ⟨*tautomerism*⟩ ⟨*tautonym*⟩

taut·en \ˈtȯtᵊn\ *vb* -ED/-ING/-S [¹*taut* + *-en*] *vt* : to make taut ⟨~ your canvas again and resume your cruise —*All Hands*⟩ ~ *vi* : to become taut ⟨the skin of her cheeks ~*ed* —G.A. Wagner⟩

taut helm *n* : WEATHER HELM

taut·ly *adv* : in a taut manner

taut·ness *n* -ES : the quality or state of being taut

tau·to·chrone \ˈtȯd·ə,krōn\ *n* -s [F, fr. *taut-* + Gk *chronos* time] : a curve which is a cycloid under a horizontal base and down which the time of descent under gravity from every point to the lowest point is the same

tau·tog *or* **tau·taug** \ˈtȯˈtȯg, -ˈtäg\ *n* -s [Narraganset *tautauog*, pl. of *taut*, *tautau*] : a common food and sport fish (*Tautoga onitis*) of the family Labridae that is found along the Atlantic coast of the U. S. and in the adult is black with greenish gray blotches — called also *blackfish*, *oysterfish*

tau·to·log·i·cal \ˌtȯd·ᵊlˈäjəkəl, -ȯtᵊl-, -jēk-\ *also* **tau·to·log·ic** \-jik, -jēk-\ *adj* : of, relating to, or marked by tautology : TAUTOLOGOUS — **tau·to·log·i·cal·ly** \-jək(ə)lē, -jēk-, -lī\ *adv*

tau·tol·o·gism \tȯˈtälə,jizəm\ *n* -s : the use or an instance of tautology

tau·tol·o·gist \-jəst\ *n* -s : one who uses tautology

tau·tol·o·gize \-lə,jīz\ *vi* -ED/-ING/-S : to practice tautology

tau·tol·o·gous \-ləgəs\ *adj* [Gk *tautologos*, fr. *taut-* + *logos* word, speech — more at LEGEND] **1** : TAUTOLOGICAL **2 a** : ANALYTIC **b** : true in terms of the sentential connectives of a truth table **c** : true purely by virtue of the meanings of component terms — **tau·tol·o·gous·ly** *adv*

tau·tol·o·gy \tȯˈtäləjē, -ji\ *n* -ES [LL *tautologia*, fr. Gk, fr. *tautologos* + *-ia* -y] **1 a** (1) : needless or meaningless repetition in close succession of an idea, statement, or word : PLEONASM, REDUNDANCY ⟨a certain ~ in describing any act of society as social —*Foreign Affairs*⟩ (2) : an instance of such repetition ⟨the phrase "a beginner who has just started" is a ~⟩ ⟨a speech full of *tautologies*⟩ **b** : a tautologous statement **2** : repetition of an act or experience ⟨the ~ of two drunken brawls in the same scene⟩

tau·to·mer \ˈtȯd·əmə(r)\ *n* -s [ISV *taut-* + *-mer*] : one of the forms of a tautomeric compound

tau·to·mer·ic \ˌtȯd·əˈmerik\ *adj* [ISV *taut-* + *-meric*] **1** : characterized by or relating to tautomerism ⟨~ equilibrium⟩ **2** : taking part in tautomerization ⟨the enolic or the ~ hydrogen atom —G.W.Wheland⟩

tau·tom·er·ism \tȯˈtämə,rizəm\ *n* -s [*taut-* + *-merism*] : the phenomenon shown by a compound of behaving in chemical reactions as though the atoms in its molecule were arranged in more than one way expressible by different structural formulas, the two or more interconvertible isomeric forms not necessarily being isolable — called also *dynamic isomerism*; see ANIONOTROPY, CATIONOTROPY, DESMOTROPISM, KETO-ENOL TAUTOMERISM; compare ISOMERISM, RESONANCE 5

tau·tom·er·iza·tion \tȯ,tämərəˈzāshən\ *n* -s : the process of tautomerizing

tau·tom·er·ize \tȯˈtämə,rīz\ *vb* -ED/-ING/-S [*tautomer* + *-ize*] *vi* : to become changed into a tautomeric form ~ *vt* : to cause to change into a tautomeric form

tau·tom·ery \-mərē\ *n* -ES [ISV *taut-* + *-mery*] : TAUTOMERISM

tau·to·met·ric \ˌtȯd·əˈme·trik\ *also* **tau·to·met·ri·cal** \-rəkəl\ *adj* [*taut-* + *metric*, *metrical*] : equal or identical in metrical structure, arrangement, or position

tau·to·nym \ˈtȯd·ə,nim, -ōtə-, -ōtᵊn,im\ *n* -s [*taut-* + *-onym*] : a taxonomic binomial in which the generic name and specific epithet are alike and which is in common use in zoology esp. to designate a common or typical form but is forbidden to botanical taxonomists under the International Code of Botanical Nomenclature ⟨*Mephitis mephitis* is a ~ designating a common No. American skunk⟩ — **tau·to·nym·ic** \ˌ⸗⸗ˈnimik, ˌ⸗⸗ˈimik\ *or* **tau·ton·y·mous** \(ˈ)tȯˈtänəməs\ *adj* — **tau·ton·y·my** \tȯˈtänəmē\ *n* -ES

tau·toph·o·ny \tȯˈtäfənē\ *n* -ES [MGk *tautophōnia*, fr. *tautophōnos* sounding identical, fr. Gk *taut-* + *-phōnos* (fr. *phōnein* to sound, fr. *phōnē* voice, sound) + *-ia* -y — more at BAN] : repetition of the same sound

tau·to·syllabic \ˌtȯd·(ˌ)ō+\ *adj* [*taut-* + *syllabic*] : belonging to the same syllable

tau·to·zonal \"+\ *adj* [*taut-* + *zonal*] : belonging to the same zone — **tau·to·zonality** \"+\ *n*

tave \ˈtāv\ *vi* [ME *taven*, prob. of Scand origin; akin to Norw *tava* to toil fruitlessly] *dial Brit* : to thrash or toss wildly : STRUGGLE

ta·ver \ˈtāvər\ *vi* [freq. of *tave*] **1** *Scot* : ROAM, WANDER **2** *Scot* : to talk foolishly : BABBLE

¹**tav·ern** \ˈtavə(r)n\ *n* -s *often attrib* [ME *taverne*, fr. OF, fr. L *taberna* hut, booth, shop, inn, tavern, alter. of (assumed) *traberna*, fr. *trabs*, *trabes* beam, roof — more at THORP] **1 a** *obs* : a shop for selling and drinking wine **b** : an establishment where alcoholic liquors are sold to be drunk on the premises **2** : a house where travelers or other transient guests are accommodated with rooms and meals : INN

²**tavern** \"\ *vi* -ED/-ING/-S : to frequent a tavern

tavern car *n* : LOUNGE CAR

tav·ern·er \-nə(r)\ *n* -s [ME *taverner*, fr. MF *tavernier*, fr. OF, fr. *taverne* + *-ier*] **1** : one that keeps a tavern **2** *obs* : one that frequents taverns

tav·ern·less \-nləs\ *adj* : having no tavern

tavern table *n* : a type of small table with oval or rectangular top and four turned legs used as a service table in the taproom of 18th century taverns

tavern table

tavern token *n* : a token issued as change by a tavern keeper

ta·vert \ˈtāvərt\ *adj* [Sc *tavert*, past part. of *taver*] **1** *Scot* : TIRED, FATIGUED **2** *Scot* : CONFUSED, STUPID

tav·gi \ˈtävˈgē\ *n*, *pl* **tavgi** *cap* **1** : NGANASANI **2** : the Uralic language of the Nganasani people — see URALIC LANGUAGES table

tav·is·tock·ite \ˈtavə,stä,kīt\ *n* -s [*Tavistock*, Devonshire, England + E *-ite*] : a mineral $Ca_3Al_2(PO_4)_3(OH)_3$ consisting of a basic calcium aluminum phosphate and occurring in minute white crystals

¹**taw** \ˈtȯ\ *vt* -ED/-ING/-S [ME *tawen*, fr. OE *tawian*; akin to OHG *zouwen* to prepare, ON *tæja*, *týja* to help, Goth *taujan* to do, make, L *bonus* good — more at BOUNTY] **1** *archaic* : to prepare or dress (as hemp by beating) for use **2** : to convert (skin) into white leather (as for gloves) by mineral tanning with alum, salt, and other agents (as an emulsion of egg yolk) **3** *archaic* : BEAT, SCOURGE

²**taw** \"\ *n* -s [origin unknown] **1 a** : a marble to be used as a shooter **b** : RINGTAW **2 a** *also* **tawline** \ˈ⸗,⸗\ : the line from which players shoot at marbles **b** : the starting line in any game or sport (as racing) **3** : a square-dance partner **4** : a sum of money invested : STAKE

³**taw** \"\ *vi* -ED/-ING/-S : to shoot a marble

⁴**taw** *or* **tav** \ˈtä|f, ˈtȯ|, |v\ *also* **thau** \ˈt(h)aů\ *n* -s [Heb *tāw*, lit., sign, cross] **1** : the 23d letter of the Hebrew alphabet — symbol ת; see ALPHABET table **2** : the letter of the Phoenician or of any of various other Semitic alphabets corresponding to Hebrew taw

TAW *abbr*, *often not cap* twice a week

ta·wa \ˈtäwə, ˈtaůə\ *n* -s [Maori] : a New Zealand evergreen tree (*Beilschmiedia tawa*) of the family Lauraceae with slender branches and graceful foliage resembling that of the willow and white straight-grained wood used chiefly for rough work (as clothespins)

ta·wa·sa \təˈwäsə\ *n*, *pl* **tawasa** *usu cap* **1 a** : a Muskogean people of northwestern Florida **b** : a member of such people **2** : the language of the Tawasa people — compare MUSKOGEE

taw·dri·ly \ˈtȯdrəlē, ˈtäd-\ *adv* : in a tawdry manner : so as to be tawdry ⟨a ~ papered room⟩ ⟨~ dressed⟩

taw·dri·ness \-rēnəs, -rin-\ *n* -ES : the quality or state of being tawdry

¹**taw·dry** \-rē, -ri\ *n* -ES [*tawdry (lace)*] : cheap showy finery

²**tawdry** \"\ *adj* -ER/-EST : cheap and gaudy in appearance or quality : tastelessly showy ⟨she was festooned with flags, but she appeared rather ~ . . . for her white hull was streaked with rust and she had a general air of dishevelment —*New Yorker*⟩ **syn** see GAUDY

tawdry lace *n* [alter. of earlier *St. Audrey's lace,* after *St. Audrey* (Etheldreda or Æthelthryth) †679 queen of Northumbria who founded an abbey at Ely; fr. the tradition that she died of a throat tumor inflicted as a punishment for her fondness for necklaces] *obs* **:** a woman's tie of lace worn about the neck

¹taw·er \'tȯ(ə)r, 'tȯə\ *n* -s [ME, fr. *tawen* to taw + *-er*] **:** one that taws skins **:** a dresser of white leather

²tawer \"\ *n* [³*taw* + *-er*] **:** one that shoots marbles

taw·ery \'tȯ(ə)rē\ *n* -es [¹*taw* + *-ery*] **:** a place where skins are tawed

ta·whai \'tä,hwī\ *n* -s [Maori] **:** RED BIRCH 3

taw·hid *or* **tau·hid** \tȯ'hēd\ *n* [Ar *tawḥīd* unity] **1 :** the Muslim doctrine of the radical unity of God **2** *Sufism* **:** the union of the individual soul with God

taw·ie \'tȯ·i\ *adj* [prob. fr. ¹*taw* + *-ie* (alter. of *-y*)] *Scot* **:** TRACTABLE

taw·kee \'tȯkē\ *also* **taw·kin** \-kən\ *n* -s [of Algonquian origin; akin to Delaware *p'tuckquen* it is round, Natick *pĕtŭkqui*] **1 :** GOLDEN CLUB **2 :** an arrow arum (*Peltandra virginica*)

tawn·i·ly \'tȯnᵊlē, 'tän-, -nəl-\ *adv* **:** in a tawny shade

tawn·i·ness \-nēnəs\ *n* -es **:** the quality or state of being tawny

¹tawny \-nē, -ni\ *adj* -ER/-EST [ME *taune, tawny,* fr. MF *tanné,* past part. of *tanner* to tan — more at TAN] **:** of the color tawny ⟨walking along the ~ sands⟩ ⟨~ squares of ripened grain —*Amer. Guide Series: Oregon*⟩ ⟨~ lion⟩ ⟨black . . . dog with ~ points —Irving Bacheller⟩

²tawny \"\ *n* -es [ME *taune, tawny,* fr. *taune, tawny,* adj.] **1 :** a brownish orange to light brown that is slightly redder than sorrel — compare TENNÉ **2 :** a tawny-colored cloth or garment **3** *archaic* **a :** a brown-skinned person **b :** AMERICAN INDIAN

tawny birch *n* **:** SANDSTONE 2

tawny bunting *n* **:** SNOW BUNTING

tawny–coat *n, obs* **:** an ecclesiastical apparitor

tawny eagle *n* **1 :** a brownish eagle (*Aquila rapax*) with varied purplish and rufous feathers on the back found in Africa and parts of Asia and rarely in Europe **2 :** an eagle of the Indian peninsula that is smaller than but usu. considered a variety (*Aquila rapax vindiana*) of the African tawny eagle

tawny–moor \'==,=\ *n, archaic* **:** a dark-skinned native of a non-European land

tawny owl *n* **1 :** a common owl (*Strix aluco* syn. *Syrnium aluco*) of Europe and northern Africa related to the barred owl of America and having no ear tufts, the upper parts reddish brown with blackish vermiculations, and the underparts buffy, streaked, and barred with brown **2** *usu cap T&O* **:** an assistant adult leader of a pack of brownie scouts in the Girl Guide movement in Britain, Canada, and various other countries and formerly in the U.S.

tawny port *n* **1 :** a port wine consisting of a blend of several vintages matured in wood so that it loses some of its original color and acquires a brownish tinge **2 :** a wine lighter in color and body than standard port and made from grapes not as rich in color

tawny thrush *n* **:** VEERY

¹taw·pie *or* **taw·py** \'tȯpē, -pi\ *n, pl* **tawpies** [of Scand origin; akin to Norw *tåpe* simpleton, Dan *tåbe,* Sw *tåp*; akin to ON *tæpta* to tap — more at TAP] *chiefly Scot* **:** a foolish or awkward young person

²tawpie *or* **tawpy** \"\ *adj* **:** FOOLISH, SENSELESS

taws *also* **tawse** \'tȯz\ *n pl but sing or pl in constr* [prob. fr. pl. of obs. *taw* tawed leather, thong, fr. ¹*taw*] *Brit* **:** a whip consisting of a strap or thong of leather slit into two or more strips at the end

taw–sug \'tȯ'süg\ *n, pl* **taw–sug** *or* **taw–sugs** *usu cap T&S* [Taw-Sug, fr. *taw* person + *sug, sulúg* current] **1 a :** a Moro people of the Sulu Archipelago **b :** a member of such people **2 :** an Austronesian language of the Taw-Sug people

tawt \'tät\ *Scot var of* ²TAUT

¹tax \'taks\ *vt* -ED/-ING/-ES [ME *taxen,* fr. MF & ML; MF *taxer,* fr. ML *taxare* to tax, assess, fr. L, to touch, feel, rate, compute, censure, freq. of *tangere* to touch — more at TANGENT] **1 a** *archaic* **:** to place a value upon **:** estimate the worth of or fix the price of **b :** to assess, fix, or determine judicially the amount of ⟨~ the costs of an action in court⟩ **2 :** to make subject to the payment of a tax **:** levy a charge on; *esp* **:** to exact money from for the support of government **3** *obs* **:** to enter in a list ⟨a decree . . . that all the world should be ~*ed* —Lk 2:1 (AV)⟩ **4 a :** to call to account **:** take to task **:** CHARGE, ACCUSE ⟨ran to grandfather and ~*ed* him with his falsehoods —W.H.Hudson †1922⟩ **b :** CENSURE ⟨~*es* science for being unable . . . to give us moral directives —Bernard Rosenberg⟩ — usu. used with *with* **5 :** to place under onerous and rigorous demands ⟨every muscle is ~*ed,* and every nerve strained —John Burroughs⟩ ⟨it may ~ the highest wisdom of the race to preserve civilization at all —F.N.Robinson⟩ **syn** see BURDEN

²tax \"\ *n* -ES *often attrib* [ME, fr. *taxen,* v.] **1 a** (1) **:** a usu. pecuniary charge imposed by legislative or other public authority upon persons or property for public purposes **:** a forced contribution of wealth to meet the public needs of a government —compare CUSTOM 3, DEATH TAX, EXCISE, INCOME TAX, INDIRECT TAX, INHERITANCE TAX, SINGLE TAX (2) **:** DIRECT TAX ⟨the Congress shall have the power to lay and collect ~*es,* duties, imposts, and excises —*U.S. Constitution*⟩ (3) *Brit* **:** a levy (as on income) paid to the national government — compare RATE 3b (5) **b :** a sum levied on the members of an organization to defray its expenses **2 :** a heavy charge or demand exacted **:** BURDEN, STRAIN ⟨the grinding duties of this position . . . proved too great a ~ on the strength of even so robust a man —A.W.Long⟩

tax- *or* **taxo-** *also* **taxi-** *comb form* [*tax-* fr. Gk *taxis*; *taxo-* fr. F, fr. Gk *taxis*; *taxi-* fr. F, fr. Gk, fr. *taxis* — more at TAXIS] **:** arrangement ⟨*taxaspidean*⟩ ⟨*taxeme*⟩ ⟨*taxidermy*⟩ ⟨*taxology*⟩

taxa *pl of* TAXON

tax·abil·i·ty \,taksə'biləd·ē\ *n* **:** the quality or state of being taxable

¹tax·able \'taksəbəl\ *adj* [ME, fr. *taxen* to tax + *-able*] **1 :** capable of being taxed **:** liable by law to the assessment of taxes **2 :** that may be legally charged by a court against the plaintiff or defendant in a suit ⟨~ costs⟩ **3** *obs* **:** CENSURABLE **4 :** used as the basis of a tax computation ⟨the ~ year⟩ ⟨~ horsepower⟩ — **tax·able·ness** *n* -ES — **tax·a·bly** \-blē, -li\ *adv*

²taxable \"\ *n* -s **:** one that is liable to a tax **:** a subject for taxation, whether property, person, corporation, or other legal entity

tax·a·ce·ae \tak'sāsē,ē\ *n pl, cap* [NL, fr. *Taxus,* type genus + *-aceae*] **:** a family of mostly evergreen trees and shrubs (order Coniferales) distinguished from the Pinaceae by dioecious flowers, commonly fleshy fruit, and an embryo with but two cotyledons — **tax·a·ceous** \(')tak¦sāshəs\ *adj*

tax·ad \'tak,sad\ *n* -s [NL *Taxus* + E *-ad*] **:** a tree or shrub of the family Taxaceae

tax·am·e·ter \tak'samədə(r)\ *n* [G, irreg. fr. ML *taxa* charge, assessment, tax (fr. *taxare* to assess, tax) + G *-meter* — more at TAX] **:** TAXIMETER

tax·as·pid·e·an \,taksə¦spidēən\ *adj* [*tax-* + *aspid-* + *-ean*] **:** having or being a tarsus of a bird with the scales of its hind side rectangular and arranged in regular rows

tax·a·tion \tak'sāshən\ *n* -s [ME *taxacioun,* fr. MF *taxation,* fr. ML *taxation-, taxatio,* fr. L, evaluation, appraisal fr. *taxatus* (past part. of *taxare*) + *-ion-, -io* -ion] **1 :** the action of taxing: as **a :** the imposing of taxes on the subjects of a state by government or on the members of a corporation or company by the proper authority **b :** the act of assessing judicially (as a bill of costs) **2 :** an amount assessed or obtained by taxation **:** TAX **3 :** a system of raising revenue by the imposition of compulsory contributions — see DOUBLE TAXATION

tax·a·tion·al \-shənᵊl\ *adj* **:** of or relating to taxation

tax·a·tor \tak'sād·ə(r)\ *n* -s [ME *taxatour,* fr. ML *taxator,* fr. *taxatus* (past part. of *taxare* to tax, assess) + L *-or* — more at TAX] **:** TAXOR

tax bond *n* **:** a government bond made receivable in payment of taxes

tax book *n* **:** TAX LIST

tax cart *or* **taxed cart** *n* **:** a spring cart formerly subject to a small tax in England

tax certificate *n* **:** the certificate issued to the purchaser of land at a tax sale certifying to the sale and the payment of the consideration therefor and entitling the purchaser upon certain conditions and at a certain time thereafter to a deed or instrument of conveyance of the land to be executed by the proper officer

tax deed *n* **:** a deed in the form required by statute evidencing the statutory rights and title acquired by the grantee as purchaser of the property described at its sale for nonpayment of a tax — compare TAX CERTIFICATE, TAX SALE, TAX TITLE

taxeater \'=,==\ *n* **:** a person deriving support from public funds

taxed *past of* TAX

tax·eme \'tak,sēm\ *n* -s [*tax-* + *-eme*] **:** a minimum grammatical feature of selection (as the occurrence of the noun *actor* before *-ess* in *actress*), of order (as the fact that *actr-* precedes *-ess* in *actress*), of stress (as the occurrence of one main stress on the first syllable in *actress*), of pitch (as the interrogative final pitch when *Actress?* is an entire utterance constituting a question), or of phonetic modification (as the change of *actor* to *actr-* before *-ess*) — **tax·e·mic** \(')tak¦sēmik\ *adj*

tax·e·op·o·da \,taksē'äpədə\ *n pl, cap* [NL, fr. Gk *taxis* arrangement, order, regularity (gen. *taxeōs*) + NL *-poda*] *in former classifications* **:** an order of chiefly taxeopodous mammals comprising the Proboscidea, Condylarthra, Hyracoidea, and sometimes others

tax·e·op·o·dous \¦==¦äpədəs\ *adj* [irreg. fr. Gk *taxis* + E *-podous*] **:** having each or most of the tarsal or carpal bones of one row articulating with only one bone of the other row — used esp. of an ungulate mammal; opposed to *diplarthrous*

tax·er \'taksə(r)\ *n* -s [¹*tax* + *-er*] **:** one that taxes

taxes *pl of* TAXIS *or of* TAX, *pres 3d sing of* TAX

-taxes *pl of* -TAXIS

¹tax–exempt \¦=¦=\ *adj* [²*tax* + *exempt*] **1 :** exempted from a tax **2 :** bearing interest free from a federal or state income tax ⟨*tax-exempt* securities⟩

²tax–exempt \"\ *n* -s **:** a tax-exempt bond

tax–free \'=¦=\ *adj* **:** TAX-EXEMPT

¹taxi \'taksē, -si\ *n, pl* **taxis** *also* **taxies** [short for *taxicab*] **1 :** TAXICAB **2 :** a similarly operated boat or airplane

²taxi \"\ *vb* **taxied; taxied; taxiing** *or* **taxying; taxis** *or* **taxies** *vi* **1 :** to ride in a taxicab **:** go by taxicab **2 a** *of an airplane* **:** to go at low speed along the surface of the ground or water (as when maneuvering into position for takeoff or parking) ⟨the plane comes in and ~*s* up to its place —C.B. Palmer b. 1910⟩ **b :** to operate an airplane on the ground under its own power ⟨a pilot ~*s* to the warmup apron and holds there for several minutes before taking off —*Civil Air Regulations*⟩ ~ *vt* **1 :** to transport by or as if by taxi ⟨the last visiting novelist has been safely ~*ed* to his . . . hotel —*Saturday Rev.*⟩ **2 :** to cause (an airplane) to taxi ⟨the aircraft captain . . . ~*s* the plane . . . across the airport to the terminal —Richard Thruelsen⟩

³taxi \"\ *n* -s [²*taxi*] **:** an act or action of taxiing

taxi- — see TAX-

-tax·ia \'taksēə\ *n comb form* -s [NL, fr. Gk — more at -TAXY] **:** -TAXIS 1 ⟨hetero*taxia*⟩

tax·i·arch \'taksē,ärk\ *n* -s [Gk *taxiarchos, taxiarchēs,* fr. *taxis* + *archos, -archēs* -arch] **:** a commander of an ancient Greek taxis

tax·ic \'taksik\ *adj* [NL *taxis* + E *-ic*] **:** of, relating to, or involving a taxis

taxi·cab \'taksē,kab, -si,-, -kaa(ə)b\ *n* [*taxi*meter *cab*] **:** a chauffeur-driven automobile available on call to carry a passenger between any two points (as within a city) for a fare determined by a taximeter, zone system, or flat rate

taxi dance hall *n* **:** a dance hall catering to men and providing taxi dancers as partners

taxi dancer *n* [¹*taxi*; fr. the fact that such dancers are hired like taxis for a short period of time] **:** a girl employed by a dance hall, café, or cabaret to dance with patrons who pay a certain amount for each dance or period of time

tax·id·ea \tak'sidēə\ *n, cap* [NL, fr. ML *taxus* badger (of Gmc origin; akin to OHG *dahs* badger) + NL *-idea* — more at TECHNICAL] **:** a genus of mammals (family Mustelidae) consisting of the American badger

tax·i·der·mic \¦taksə¦dərmik, -dəm-, -dəim- -mēk\ *also* **tax·i·der·mal** \-məl\ *adj* **:** of or relating to taxidermy

tax·i·der·mist \'==,məst\ *n* -s **:** one who practices taxidermy

tax·i·der·my \-mē, -mi\ *n* -es [*tax-* + *derm-* + *-y*] **:** the art of preparing lifelike representations of animals by stuffing the skin or usu. by fashioning a wooden or plaster model on which the skin of the specimen (as a bird or mammal) is mounted or by molding and painting a plastic replica of the specimen (as a fish or reptile)

-taxies *pl of* -TAXY

tax·i·fo·lin \,taksə'fōlən\ *n* [NL *taxifolia* (specific epithet of *Pseudotsuga taxifolia,* fr. *tax-* + *-folia,* fr. L *folium* leaf) + E *-in* — more at BLADE] **:** a crystalline pentahydroxy flavanone $C_{15}H_7O_2(OH)_5$ that occurs naturally esp. in the heartwood of Douglas fir, may be prepared from quercetin by reduction with sodium hydrosulfite, and yields quercetin on oxidation; dihydro-quercetin

taximan \'=mən\ *n, pl* **taximen** [¹*taxi* + *man*] *chiefly Brit* **:** the operator of a taxi **:** taxi driver

tax·i·me·ter \'taksē,mēd·ə(r), -si,- -ētə-\ *n* [F *taximètre,* modif. of G *taxameter* — more at TAXAMETER] **:** an instrument for use in a hired vehicle (as a taxicab) for automatically showing the fare due

tax·ine \'tak,sēn, -ksən\ *n* -s [ISV *tax-* (fr. NL *Taxus*) + *-ine*] **:** a bitter poisonous alkaloid $C_{37}H_{51}NO_{10}$ obtained as an amorphous powder from the leaves, shoots, and seeds of the English yew

taxing *adj* [fr. pres. part. of ¹*tax*] **:** that taxes **:** ONEROUS, WEARING — **tax·ing·ly** *adv*

tax in kind : a tax payable in goods or services instead of money

tax·in·o·my \tak'sinəmē\ *n* -es [by alter.] **:** TAXONOMY

taxiplane \'==,=\ *n* [¹*taxi* + *plane*] **:** an airplane used as a public vehicle for hire

¹tax·is \'taksəs\ *n, pl* **tax·es** \-k,sēz\ [Gk, lit., arrangement, order, fr. *taktos* (verbal of *tassein* to arrange, order) + *-sis* — more at TACTICS] **1 :** the manual restoration of a displaced body part; *specif* **:** the reduction of a hernia manually **2** [NL, fr. *-taxis*] **a :** reflex movement by a freely motile and usu. simple organism that is translational or sometimes merely orientational and that constitutes a positive or negative response to a source of stimulation (as a light or a temperature or chemical gradient) — compare KINESIS, TROPISM **b :** a reflex reaction involving such movement **3 :** a unit (as a company, battalion) of varying size in an ancient Greek army

²taxis *pl of* TAXI, *pres 3d sing of* TAXI

-tax·is \'taksəs\ *n comb form, pl* **-tax·es** \-k,sēz\ [NL, fr. Gk *taxis*] **1 :** arrangement **:** order ⟨homo*taxis*⟩ **2 :** taxis (sense 2) ⟨chemo*taxis*⟩ ⟨helio*taxis*⟩ ⟨thermo*taxis*⟩

taxi stand *n* **:** a place where taxis may park awaiting hire **:** CABSTAND

taxi strip *n* **:** TAXIWAY

tax·ite \'tak,sīt\ *n* -s [G *taxit,* fr. *tax-* + *-it* -ite] **:** volcanic rock of clastic or schlieric appearance due to the aggregation of flows of different colors, textures, granularity, or mineral composition **:** EUTAXITE, ATAXITE — **tax·it·ic** \(')tak¦sid·ik\ *adj*

taxi track *n, Brit* **:** TAXIWAY

taxiway \'==,=\ *n* **:** a usu. paved strip for taxiing (as from the terminal to the end of the runway) at an airport

tax·less \'taksləs\ *adj* **:** free from taxation **:** UNTAXED — **tax·less·ly** *adv* — **tax·less·ness** *n* -ES

tax lien *n* **:** a statutory charge on property for taxes due giving the taxing authority a security interest therein

tax list *or* **tax roll** *n* **:** a document maintained by a public officer (as an assessor) listing taxable persons or property or both within a taxing district and often also the tax assessed on each — called also *tax book*

taxo- — see TAX-

tax·o·di·a·ce·ae \tak,sōdē'āsē,ē\ *n pl, cap* [NL, fr. *Taxodium,* type genus + *-aceae*] **:** a family of coniferous trees or rarely shrubs that are sometimes included in Pinaceae but are distinguished by flat or peltate cone scales lacking bracts and each producing 2 to 9 seeds and by dimorphic leaves or none — **tax·o·di·a·ceous** \=¦==¦āshəs\ *adj*

tax·o·di·ine \tak'sōdē,īn\ *or* **tax·o·di·oid** \-ē,ȯid\ *adj* [NL *Taxodium* + E *-ine* or *-oid*] **:** of or relating to *Taxodium* or the Taxodiaceae

tax·o·di·um \-ōdēəm\ *n* [NL, fr. *Taxus* + *-odium* (fr. Gk *-odos* -ode)] **1** *cap* **:** a small genus of tall deciduous trees (family Taxodiaceae) having drooping branches, spirally arranged linear leaves, and globose cones with thick woody scales — see AHUEHUETE, BALD CYPRESS **2** -s **:** any tree of the genus *Taxodium*

¹tax·o·dont \'taksə,dänt\ *adj* [NL *Taxodonta*] **:** of or relating to the Taxodonta

²taxodont \"\ *n* -s **:** a mollusk of the order Taxodonta

tax·o·don·ta \,==¦däntə\ *n pl, cap* [NL, fr. *tax-* + *-odonta*] *in some classifications* **:** an order of Lamellibranchia comprising bivalve mollusks with the hinge teeth numerous and unspecialized and the adductor muscles both present and equally developed

tax·ol·o·gy \tak'säləjē\ *n* -es [*tax-* + *-logy*] **:** TAXONOMY 1

tax·on \'tak,sän\ *n, pl* **taxa** \-ksə\ *also* **taxons** [ISV, back-formation (influence of *etymon*) fr. *taxonomy*] **1 :** a taxonomic group or entity **2 :** the name applied to a taxonomic group in a formal system of nomenclature

tax·o·nom·ic \¦taksə¦nämik, -mēk\ *also* **tax·o·nom·i·cal** \-məkəl, -mēk-\ *adj* **:** of or relating to or having the character of taxonomy

tax·o·nom·i·cal·ly \-mək(ə)lē\ *adv* **:** from a taxonomic standpoint **:** with regard to taxonomy

tax·on·o·mist \tak'sänəməst\ *n* -s **:** a specialist in taxonomy

tax·on·o·my \-mē, -mi\ *n* -es [F *taxonomie,* fr. *tax-* + *-nomie* -nomy] **1 :** the study of the general principles of scientific classification **:** SYSTEMATICS **2 :** the systematic distinguishing, ordering, and naming of type groups within a subject field **:** CLASSIFICATION; *specif* **:** orderly classification of plants and animals according to their presumed natural relationships forming a basic biological discipline involving during its Linnaean period the firm establishment of binomial nomenclature and acceptance of the static concept of fixity of the species, during its Darwinian period the dynamic concept of speciation by natural selection, and during its modern Mendelian epoch an expansion to include study of the mechanisms underlying speciation and related processes (as radiation, variation) — compare BIOSYSTEMATY, CYTOTAXONOMY, DETERMINE 5b

tax·or \'taksə(r)\ *n* -s [ME *taxour* assessor, fr. AF, fr. OF *taxer* to tax + AF *-our* -or — more at TAX] **:** one of two former officers at the older British universities empowered to regulate the prices of students' lodgings and food

taxpayer \'=,==\ *n* **1 :** one that pays or is liable to pay a tax **2 :** a temporary building erected to earn something to meet the taxes on the land

tax sale *n* **:** a sale (as at public auction) conducted by an officer of the taxing authority of specific property for nonpayment of a tax due from its owner and granting to the purchaser a tax title

tax stamp *n* **1 :** a stamp marked on or affixed to a taxable item as evidence that the tax has been paid **2 :** POSTAL TAX STAMP

tax title *n* **:** the right or title acquired by a purchaser of property at a tax sale being subject to redemption by the delinquent owner for a specified time, sometimes granting immediate possession and the title that the owner had, sometimes granting only the right upon compliance with statutory requirements to acquire that owner's title or a new paramount title in fee simple absolute, and often requiring confirmation by a court decree

tax·us \'taksəs\ *n* [NL, fr. L, yew] **1** *cap* **:** a small genus (the type of the family Taxaceae) comprising the yews and including ornamental trees and shrubs having stiff somewhat petioled linear leaves spirally arranged, a fruit consisting of a fleshy aril enclosing a hard seed, and poisonous juice — see GROUND HEMLOCK, JAPANESE YEW **2** *pl* **taxus :** any plant of the genus *Taxus*

taxwise \'=,=\ *adv* [²*tax* + *-wise*] **:** with respect to a tax or taxation

-taxy \'taksē, -si\ *n comb form* -ES [Gk *-taxia,* fr. *taktos* (verbal of *tassein* to arrange, order) + *-ia* -y — more at TACTICS] **:** -TAXIS ⟨epi*taxy*⟩ ⟨pleio*taxy*⟩

taxying *pres part of* TAXI

tay \'tā\ *dial var of* **tea**

ta·ya·ci·an \tə'yāsēən\ *adj, usu cap* [F *tayacien,* fr. *Tayac,* its type site near Les Eyzies in southwestern France + F *-ien* -ian] **:** of or belonging to a stage of culture intermediate between the Clactonian and the Mousterian characterized by poorly made planoconvex flake tools

ta·yal \tə'yäl\ *also* **ata·yal** \,äd·ə'yäl\ *n, pl* **tayal** *or* **tayals** *usu cap* **1 :** a Malaysian people on Formosa **2 :** a member of the Tayal people

ta·yas·su \tə'ya(,)sü\ *n, cap* [NL, fr. Pg *taiaçu, taiaçú* white-lipped peccary, fr. Tupi] **:** a genus (the type of the family Tayassuidae) of American wild swine comprising the living peccaries and having a complex stomach, a gland on the back, and three toes on the hind feet — compare SUIDAE

¹ta·yas·su·id \-asəwəd\ *adj* [NL *Tayassuidae,* family of wild swine, fr. *Tayassu,* type genus + *-idae*] **:** of or relating to the genus *Tayassu* or family Tayassuidae

²tayassuid \"\ *n* -s **:** a swine of the genus *Tayassu* or family Tayassuidae **:** PECCARY

tay·lor·ism \'tālə,rizəm\ *n* -s *usu cap* [Frederick W. *Taylor* †1915 Am. engineer + E *-ism*] **1 :** the methods of factory management first developed and advocated by Frederick W. Taylor **2 :** SCIENTIFIC MANAGEMENT

tay·lor·ite \'tālə,rīt\ *n* -s [W. J. *Taylor* †1864 Am. mineral chemist + E *-ite*] **:** a mineral $(K,NH_4)_2SO_4$ consisting of a potassium ammonium sulfate and occurring in compact white lumps in the guano beds of the Chincha islands, Peru

tay·lor system *also* **taylor plan** \'tālə(r)-\ *n, usu cap T* [after F. W. *Taylor*] **:** TAYLORISM 1; *specif* **:** DIFFERENTIAL PIECE-RATE SYSTEM

taylor–white process \'=='(h)wīt-\ *n* [after F. W. *Taylor* & Maunsel B. *White* †1912 Am. engineers] **:** a process invented about 1899 for heat-treating high-speed steels

tay·ra *also* **tai·ra** \'tīrə\ *n* -s [Pg *taira* & Sp *taira, tayra,* fr. Tupi] **:** a long-tailed mustelid mammal (*Galera barbara*) of So. and Central America that resembles the No. American fisher in size but has short fur and is black with a grayish head

taz·et·tine \'tazə,tēn, -zətən\ *n* -s [NL *tazetta* (specific epithet of *Narcissus tazetta*) + E *-ine*] **:** a crystalline alkaloid $C_{18}H_{21}NO_5$ obtained chiefly from the bulbs of the polyanthus narcissus

taze·well \'taz,wel, -wəl\ *n* -s *usu cap* [fr. *Tazewell,* county in Ill.] **:** a substage of the Wisconsin glacial stage; *also* **:** the drift of such substage

ta·zia \tə'zēə\ *n* -s [Ar *ta'zīyah,* lit., mourning for the dead] **1 :** a Muslim passion play celebrated by the Shi'a in Muharram **2 :** a replica of the tomb of Husain the martyred son of Muhammad carried in processions during the Shi'ite festival of Muharram

taz·za \'tätsə\ *n* -s [It, cup, mug, basin, fr. Ar *ṭass, ṭassah* — more at TASS] **:** an ornamental receptacle (as a cup or vase) with a large flat shallow bowl resting on a pedestal or pillar and often having handles

tazza

tb *abbr* tablespoon; tablespoonful

TB \'tē'bē\ *n* -s [fr. *TB,* abbr. for *tubercle bacillus*] **:** TUBERCULOSIS

TB *abbr* **1** tariff bureau **2** technical bulletin **3** telegraph bureau **4** time base **5** times at bat **6** torpedo boat **7** torpedo bomber **8** total bases **9** traffic bureau **10** trial balance **11** tubercle bacillus

Tb *symbol* terbium

TBA *abbr* **1** table of basic allowances **2** tires, batteries, and accessories **3** to be announced

t bandage *n, cap T* **:** a bandage shaped like the letter T and used chiefly about the waist or perineum to hold a dressing in place

TB and S *abbr* top, bottom, and sides

t bar *or* **t beam** *cap T, or* **tee bar** *or* **tee beam** *n* **:** a metal bar or beam having a cross section of the form of the letter T

t-bar lift \ˈ=,=-\ *or* **t-bar** *n, cap T* **:** a ski lift in which two skiers at a time lean against a bar suspended in the center while being pulled uphill

TBB *abbr* tenor, baritone, bass

t-beam bridge \ˈ=,=-\ *n, cap T* **:** a reinforced-concrete bridge consisting of a floor slab monolithic with the supporting beams so that a cross section resembles a series of T beams

t bevel *n, cap T* **:** BEVEL 2

TBL *abbr* through bill of lading

tblspn *abbr* tablespoon; tablespoonful

TBM *abbr* temporary bench mark

t bolt *cap T, also* **tee bolt** *n* **1 :** a bolt having a crosspiece for a head **2 :** a bolt with a head of square or rectangular shape intended to fit a T slot

t-bone \ˈ=,=\ *also* **t-bone steak** *n, cap T* **:** a small beefsteak from the thin end of the short loin containing a T-shaped bone and a small piece of tenderloin — compare PORTERHOUSE; see BEEF illustration

TB-1 *or* **TB 1-698** *n* [G, fr. *TB + 1-698,* its laboratory code number; fr. its use in the treatment of tuberculosis] **:** THIACETAZONE

T bolt

TBP *abbr* true boiling point

tbr *abbr* timber

tbs *abbr* tablespoon; tablespoonful

TBS \ˌtē,bē'es\ *abbr or n* -s [*talk between ships*] **:** a short range radio system that is used for communication within naval task forces

tbsp *abbr* tablespoon; tablespoonful

t-budding \ˈ=,==\ *n, cap T* **:** SHIELD BUDDING

TBW *abbr* to be withheld

tc *abbr* **1** tical **2** tierce

TC *abbr* **1** tank corps **2** tariff circular; tariff commission **3** teachers college **4** technical college **5** temporary constable **6** tennis club **7** terra-cotta **8** thermocouple **9** till countermanded **10** top of column **11** total chances **12** touring club **13** town clerk; town councillor **14** traffic commissioner; traffic consultant **15** training center; training circular **16** transportation corps **17** turret captain

Tc *symbol* technetium

TCA *abbr or n* -s [*trichloroacetic acid*] **:** trichloroacetic acid or one of its derivatives (as the sodium salt)

t cart *n, cap T* **:** an open wagon with two seats and a T-shaped body

tce *abbr* terrace

tcham·bu·li \chäm'bülē\ *n, pl* **tchambuli** *or* **tchambulis** *usu cap* **1 :** a people of the Sepik district, Territory of New Guinea **2 :** a member of the Tchambuli people

tcha·viche \chə'vēsh\ *n* -s [F, fr. NL *tschawytscha* (specific epithet of *Onchorhyncus tschawytscha*), fr. Russ *chavycha*] **:** KING SALMON

tche·by·cheff inequality \chəbə'shȯf-\ *n, usu cap T* [after Pafnuty L. *Tchebycheff* †1894 Russ. mathematician] **:** an inequality that gives an upper limit to the probability that a variable will assume a value more than a specified number of standard deviations away from its mean

tche·func·te \chə'fu̇ŋktə\ *adj, usu cap* [fr. *Tchefuncte* State Park, La.] **:** of or relating to a culture of Louisiana of about A.D. 500–900 characterized by conical burial mounds, circular structures, and coiled pottery with linear punctate ornamentation

tcher·vo·nets *or* **tcher·vo·netz** \chər'vônəts\ *var of* CHERVONETS

tchet·vert \'chetvə(r)t\ *var of* CHETVERT

tchi *usu cap, var of* TWI

tchr *abbr* teacher

t connection *n, cap T* **:** a connection of two coils (as of a transformer) diagrammatically as a letter T chiefly used for transforming two-phase systems into three-phase systems and vice versa — called also *Scott connection;* compare DELTA CONNECTION

t connector *n, cap T* **:** an electrical binding post consisting of three posts forming the three arms of a letter T

TCP *abbr* traffic control post

tcr *abbr* tracer

TCS *abbr* traffic control station

t-cushion \ˈ=,==\ *n, cap T* **:** a square cushion for an upholstered chair having front extensions to fit around the arms in T shape

TD \ˈtē'dē\ *n* -s [fr. *TD,* initials stamped on a common make of clay pipe] **:** a clay pipe

TD *abbr or n* -s [*touchdown*] touchdown

TD *abbr* **1** tank destroyer **2** [IrGael *Teachta Dala*] member of parliament **3** telegraph department **4** telephone department **5** temporary disability; temporary duty **6** territorial decoration **7** time deposit **8** tons per day **9** total depth **10** tractor-drawn **11** traffic director **12** treasury decision; treasury department

T-cushion

TDE \ˌtē,dē'ē\ *abbr or n* -s [*tetrachloro-diphenyl-ethane*] **:** DDD

tdm *abbr* tandem

TDN *abbr* total digestible nutrients

TDS *abbr* **1** *often not cap* [L *ter die sumendum*] to be taken three times a day **2** time, distance, speed

TDY *abbr or n* -s temporary duty

te *var of* TEE

TE *abbr* **1** table of equipment **2** topographical engineer **3** trailing edge

Te *symbol* tellurium

[1]**tea** \ˈtē\ *n* -s [Chin (Amoy) *t'e;* akin to Chin (Pek) *ch'a²* tea] **1 a :** a shrub (*Camellia sinensis*) cultivated from antiquity in China and now in Japan, India, Ceylon, Sumatra, Java, and other countries and having lanceolate leaves and fragrant white flowers **b :** the leaves, leaf buds, and internodes of this plant prepared and cured for the market by several recognized methods, classed according to method of manufacture (as green, black, or oolong) and graded according to leaf size (as congou, orange pekoe, pekoe, souchong) — see GUNPOWDER TEA, HYSON **c :** an aromatic beverage that is prepared from cured tea leaves by infusion with boiling water, has mild stimulant and tonic properties due to the alkaloid caffeine, and is capable of being strongly astringent from the presence of tannin **2 a** (1) **:** any of numerous plants somewhat resembling tea in appearance or properties (2) **:** an infusion prepared from their leaves and used medicinally or as a beverage — used usu. with qualifying adjective or attributive; see ABYSSINIAN TEA, BREAST TEA, LABRADOR TEA, SAGE TEA **b :** TEA ROSE **c** *slang* **:** MARIJUANA **3 a :** light refreshments usu. including tea with bread and butter sandwiches, crackers, cookies, served in late afternoon **b :** a formal social occasion (as a reception) at which tea and other refreshments are served **c** *Brit* **:** a light late afternoon or evening meal **:** SUPPER **4 :** a grayish yellow green to pale green that is lighter than Surrey green **5** *chiefly Brit* **:** something or someone that suits one's taste or preference ⟨an odd pair, I shouldn't have thought she was at all his ~⟩ — compare CUP OF TEA

[2]**tea** \"\ *adj* **1 :** of or relating to tea or the tea plant ⟨~ plantation⟩ **2 :** dealing in tea ⟨~ merchant⟩ **3 :** used for or in connection with tea ⟨~ urn⟩

[3]**tea** \"\ *vb* -ED/-ING/-s *vi* **:** to drink tea or take a light meal ~ *vt* **:** to entertain with a tea

tea bag *n* **:** a cloth or filter paper bag holding a measured amount of tea for making an individual serving of tea

tea ball *n* **:** a perforated metal ball that holds tea leaves and is used for making tea in cups or in a teapot

tea ball

tea basket *n, Brit* **:** a lunch basket or picnic hamper

tea·berry \ˈtē- — *see* BERRY\ *n* [[1]*tea + berry;* fr. the use of its dried leaves to make a substitute for tea] **1 :** CHECKERBERRY 1a **2 :** CREEPING SNOWBERRY

tea biscuit *n, Brit* **:** a short or sweet biscuit served with afternoon tea **:** CRACKER, COOKIE

teaboard \ˈ=,=\ *n* **:** a tray for serving tea

tea borer *n* **:** a borer that is the larva of a moth (*Zeuzera coffeae*) of the family Cossidae and bores into the stems and branches of coffee, tea, and sandal

teabowl \ˈ=,=\ *n* **:** a teacup having no handle

tea·boy \ˈtē,bȯi\ *n, Irish* **:** MANSERVANT

tea bread *n* **:** sweetened bread or buns to be eaten with tea

tea broom *n* **:** an Australian tea tree (*Leptospermum scoparium*)

tea caddy *n* **:** CADDY 1a

tea cake *n* **1** *Brit* **:** a light flat cake **2 :** COOKIE

tea cart *n* **:** a dinner wagon used in serving tea or light refreshments

teach \ˈtēch\ *vb* **taught** \ˈtȯt, *usu* -ȯd·+V\ **taught; teaching; teaches** [ME *techen,* fr. OE *tǣcan* to show, instruct; akin to OE *tācen, tācn* sign, token — more at TOKEN] *vt* **1** *obs* **:** SHOW, GUIDE, DIRECT **2 a :** to cause to know a subject ⟨all children are *taught* the three R's⟩ ⟨*taught* his sons a trade⟩ **b :** to cause to know how to do something **:** show how ⟨my father is ~*ing* me to drive⟩ **c :** to accustom to some action or attitude ⟨should ~ students to think for themselves⟩ ⟨have been *taught* respect for the self-made man⟩ **d :** to make (one) know the disagreeable consequences of some action ⟨I'll ~ you to come home late⟩ **3 :** to direct as an instructor **:** guide the studies of **:** conduct through a course of studies **:** give instruction to ⟨the most active mind that I have ever *taught*⟩ **4 a :** to impart the knowledge of ⟨~ algebra⟩ **b :** to present in a classroom lecture or discussion ⟨have *taught Hamlet* many times⟩ **c :** to instruct in the rules, principles, or practice of ⟨~ music⟩ ⟨~ dancing⟩ **5 a :** to direct, instruct, or train by precept, example, or experience ⟨that same prayer does ~ us all to render the deeds of mercy —Shak.⟩ ⟨had *taught* himself to view the war as one of God's processes —R.M.Weaver⟩ **b :** to seek to make known and accepted **:** IMPLANT, PREACH ⟨the philosopher *taught* purity, moderation, and self-containment⟩ ⟨the culture which *taught* despising of the body —H.A.Overstreet⟩ ⟨experience ~*es* us that our powers are limited⟩ **6 :** to conduct instruction regularly in ⟨*taught* school for several years before her marriage⟩ ~ *vi* **1 a :** to provide instruction, guidance, or discipline **:** act or become employed as a teacher ⟨has *taught* in the public schools for many years⟩ **b :** to propound a doctrine **:** demonstrate a lesson or moral ⟨a work that ~*es* without becoming overly moralistic⟩ **2 :** to be capable of exposition or explanation ⟨a book that ~*es* easily⟩

syn INSTRUCT, EDUCATE, TRAIN, DISCIPLINE, SCHOOL, COACH, TUTOR: TEACH is a general term for causing one to acquire knowledge or skill, usu. with the imparting of necessary incidental information and the giving of incidental help and encouragement ⟨*teach* a child to read⟩ ⟨*teaching* him algebra⟩ ⟨*taught* the boys how to swim⟩ INSTRUCT may suggest methodical, continuing, or formal teaching ⟨*instruct* the men in safety procedures⟩ ⟨*instructing* students in military drill⟩ EDUCATE may apply to more pretentious processes of teaching and instruction designed to ensure full development of the capacities of a more intelligent person ⟨a school designed to *educate* candidates for the ministry⟩ ⟨a program to *educate* the leaders of tomorrow⟩ TRAIN may suggest methodical, thorough instruction and guidance with a specific end in mind until rapid and successful execution of duties and tasks is assured ⟨a *trained* anesthetist⟩ ⟨officers' *training* schools⟩ ⟨a *trained* radio actress⟩ DISCIPLINE calls attention to subordination to a master or subjection to control, sometimes one's own ⟨well-*disciplined* cadets⟩ ⟨*disciplined* party workers⟩ ⟨one must not let one's thoughts run on like this: one must *discipline* one's mind —Victoria Sackville-West⟩ SCHOOL, often interchangeable with others in this set, perhaps more often has suggestions of TRAIN although it lacks the specificity of this latter word ⟨the growing demand by industry for able people *schooled* in engineering and business administration —*Report of General Motors Corp.*⟩ ⟨with division, corps, and Army staffs *schooled* in the same language, practices, and techniques —W.P. Corderman⟩ ⟨*schooled* himself to accept her will, in this as in other matters, as absolute and unquestionable —Thomas Hardy⟩ COACH is likely to refer to training with demonstration and practice in some specialized, often extracurricular activity ⟨*coaching* football⟩ ⟨was *coaching* the school play⟩ TUTOR usu. applies to teaching on an individual basis in some specialized subject ⟨*tutoring* him in mathematics⟩ ⟨special *tutoring* sessions for those deficient⟩ ⟨the enemies of this faith know no god but force, no devotion but its use. They *tutor* men in treason —D. D.Eisenhower⟩

teach·abil·i·ty \ˌtēchə'biləd·ē\ *n* **1 :** suitability for use in teaching ⟨illustrations increase the ~ of a textbook⟩ **2 :** ability to learn by instruction **:** TEACHABLENESS

teach·able \ˈtēchəbəl\ *adj* **1 a :** capable of being taught ⟨whether virtue was ~ or not⟩ **b :** apt and willing to learn **:** DOCILE ⟨a ~ pupil⟩ ⟨the ~ humility essential to learning —G.B.Oxnam⟩ **2 :** favorable to teaching **:** making for easy teaching ⟨choosing the ~ moment⟩ ⟨a ~ text⟩ — **teach·able·ness** *n* -ES — **teach·ably** \-blē\ *adv*

teach·er \ˈtēchə(r)\ *n* -s [ME *techer,* fr. *techen* to teach + *-er*] **1 :** one that teaches or instructs ⟨nature was his only ~⟩; *esp* **:** one whose occupation is to instruct ⟨a ~ at the local high school⟩ ⟨a driving ~⟩ **2 a :** a religious instructor or preacher often not regularly ordained in a Congregational church **b :** a member of the Aaronic priesthood of the Mormon Church of the grade between deacon and priest

teach·er·age \-chərij\ *n* -s [*teacher + -age* (as in *parsonage*)] **:** a residence provided for teachers

teacher bird *also* **teacher** *n* [imit.] **1 :** OVENBIRD **2 2 :** RED-EYED VIREO

teach·er·less \-chə(r)ləs\ *adj* **:** lacking a teacher

teachers college *n* **:** a college for the training of teachers usu. offering a full four-year course and granting a bachelor's degree — compare NORMAL SCHOOL

teachers' council *n* **:** a representative assembly chosen from the teaching staff of a school system that makes recommendations to the superintendent of schools and to the board of education

teach·er·ship \-(r),ship\ *n* [*teacher + -ship*] **:** a teaching position

teacher's pet *n* **1 :** a pupil who has won his teacher's special favor **2 :** one who has ingratiated himself with an authority **:** FAVORITE

teach·ery \-chərē\ *adj* [*teacher + -y*] **:** suggestive of a teacher

tea chest *n* **1 :** CADDY 1a **2 :** a square wooden case usu. lined with sheet lead or tin and used for exporting tea

[1]**teaching** *n* -s [ME *teching,* fr. gerund of *techen* to teach] **1 :** the act, practice, or profession of teaching ⟨~ requires intelligence, maturity, and devotion⟩ ⟨many young people will go into ~⟩ **2 :** something that is taught **:** INSTRUCTION, DOCTRINE ⟨you have had excellent ~⟩ ⟨the ~*s* of Confucius⟩

[2]**teaching** *adj* [fr. pres. part. of *teach*] **:** that teaches ⟨~ profession⟩ ⟨~ doctor⟩

teaching aid *n* [[1]*teaching*] **:** printed material (as a picture or map) or other device (as a record player or gyroscope) used by a teacher to fortify or enliven classroom instruction ⟨audio-visual *teaching aids*⟩

teaching elder *n* [[2]*teaching*] **:** a minister in the Presbyterian Church — compare ELDER 4b

teaching fellow *n* **:** a resident student at a graduate school who is granted free tuition and maintenance in return for assisting with teaching or laboratory duties

teaching hospital *n* [[1]*teaching*] **:** a hospital that is affiliated with a university medical school and provides the means for medical education to students, interns, and residents and sometimes postgraduates

teachy \ˈtēchē\ *adj* [*teach + -y*] **:** DIDACTIC, SCHOOLMASTERISH

tea clipper *n* **:** a clipper built for tea trade (as from China to London)

tea cloth *n* **:** a small tablecloth

tea cozy *n* **:** a cozy for keeping tea warm

tea crab *n* **:** an Asiatic crab tree (*Malus hupehensis*) used as an ornamental and having branches growing wide in a fan shape and pink flowers that turn to white

teacup \ˈ=,=\ *n* **:** a cup with a handle and usu. of less than 8-oz. capacity used commonly with a saucer for hot beverages

tea·cup·ful \ˈ=,=,fu̇l\ *n, pl* **teacupfuls** *or* **teacupsful** \-p,fu̇lz, -ps,fu̇l\ [*teacup + -ful*] **:** as much as a teacup can hold **:** enough to fill a teacup

tea dance *n* **:** a dance held in the late afternoon

tea dust glaze *n* **:** a brown or greenish brown Chinese ceramic glaze flecked with green

teaed *past of* TEA

tea·ette \(ˈ)tē¦et\ *n* -s [[1]*tea + -ette*] **:** TEA MAKER

tea family *n* **:** THEACEAE

tea fight *n* **:** TEA PARTY 1

tea garden *n* **1 :** a public garden where tea and other refreshments are served **2 :** a tea plantation

tea gown *n* **:** a semiformal gown of fine materials in graceful flowing lines worn esp. for afternoon for entertaining at home

tea green *n* **:** a grayish yellow green that is yellower and paler than average sage green and yellower and lighter than palmetto — called also *Queen Anne green*

tea hound *n* **:** a man who frequents teas ⟨assumption that . . . every diplomat is a *tea hound* —*Wall Street Jour.*⟩

teahouse \ˈ=,=\ *n* **:** a public house or restaurant where tea and other refreshments are sold

teaing *pres part of* TEA

[1]**teak** \ˈtēk\ *n* -s [Pg *teca,* fr. Malayalam *tēkka*] **1 a :** a tall East Indian timber tree (*Tectona grandis*) of the family Verbenaceae now planted in West Africa and tropical America for its wood **b :** the hard strong durable yellowish brown wood of teak that is highly resistant to insect attack and to warping and is used esp. for shipbuilding **2 :** any of several trees resembling teak or having wood used in place of teakwood: as **a** (1) **:** AUSTRALIAN TEAK **a** (2) **:** FLINDOSA **b :** an Australian timber tree (*Dissiliaria baloghioides*) of the family Euphorbiaceae **c :** AFRICAN OAK 1 **d** *NewZeal* **:** PURIRI **e :** IROKO **f :** RHODESIAN MAHOGANY **3 a :** EBONY 4 **b** *or* **teak brown :** SIENNA BROWN

[2]**teak** \"\ *adj* **:** of or relating to teak **:** made of teakwood

teakettle \ˈ=,==\ *n* **:** a covered kettle with a fixed handle or bail and spout for boiling water

tea knife *n* **:** a small table knife used esp. for pastry

teakwood \ˈ=,=\ *n* **1 :** TEAK 1b **2 :** SOOT BROWN

teakettle

teal \ˈtēl, *esp before pause or consonant* -ēəl\ *n, pl* **teal** *or* **teals** [ME *tele;* akin to MD *teling, teelingh* teal] **1 a :** any of several small short-necked river ducks of Europe and America belonging to the genus *Anas* or esp. formerly placed in *Nettion* and *Querquedula* and including the garganey and related birds and the blue-winged and cinnamon teals which both have a light blue area on the forepart of the wing — compare GREENWING **b :** any of several other small wild ducks (as *Aythya novae-seelandiae* and *Stictonetta naevosa*) of New Zealand and Australia **2 :** a variable color averaging a dark greenish blue that is greener, lighter, and stronger than teal duck or teal blue and greener and less strong than drake

teal blue *n* **:** a variable color averaging a dark greenish blue that is bluer and duller than average teal, duller and slightly greener than drake, and greener, lighter, and stronger than teal duck

teal duck *n* **1 :** TEAL **2 :** a dark greenish blue that is bluer and duller than average teal, averaging teal blue, drake, or duckling

tea lead *n* **:** a metal alloy used to line tea chests

tea·less \ˈtēləs\ *adj* [[1]*tea + -less*] **:** lacking or deprived of tea

tealgrass \ˈ=,=\ *n* [*teal + grass;* fr. its being considered an important food for teal] **:** a love grass (*Eragrostis hypnoides*) of the central U. S.

teal gray *n* **:** a dark bluish gray that is greener and lighter than smoke blue

teal green *n* **:** a variable color averaging a dark bluish green that is bluer, lighter, and stronger than invisible green (sense 2) or pine tree

teall·ite \ˈtē,līt\ *n* -s [J. J. Harris *Teall* †1924 Eng. geologist + E *-ite*] **:** a mineral $PbSnS_2$ consisting of a sulfide of tin and lead and occurring in black metallic flexible folia (hardness 1–2, sp. gr. 6.4)

[1]**team** \ˈtēm\ *n* -s [ME *teme, tem,* fr. OE *tēam* offspring, lineage, group of draft animals; akin to OFris *tām* bridle, progeny, lineage, OHG *zoum* rein, bridle, ON *taumr,* OE *tēon* to draw, pull — more at TOW] **1** *obs* **:** LINEAGE, RACE **2 :** a group of animals having something in common: as **a :** a brood of young animals (as pigs or ducks) **b :** a number of animals moving together **c :** a flock of birds flying together **d :** a matched group of animals for exhibition **e** *Austral* **:** a group of rams used together on a flock of ewes **3 a :** two or more horses, oxen, or other draft animals harnessed to the same vehicle (as a coach, wagon, sled) or to the same plow or other implement **b** (1) **:** draft animals with their harness and attached vehicle (2) **:** a single animal used for labor and service often with harness and vehicle **c :** a wagon, carriage, or other drawn vehicle ⟨a horse and ~⟩ **4 :** a number of persons associated together in work or activity: as **a :** a number of persons selected to contend on one side in a match (as in cricket, football, rowing, or a debate) **b :** a group of workmen each completing one of a set of operations **:** CREW, GANG ⟨~ of riveters⟩ ⟨~ of divers⟩ **c :** a group of specialists or scientists functioning as a collaborative unit ⟨the diagnostic ~ of psychiatrist, clinician, and social worker in a child guidance clinic⟩ **5 :** a person of extraordinary ability or energy ⟨he's a whole ~ by himself⟩ **6** *old Eng law* **a :** an action to authenticate a claim (as to purchased goods) by summoning a seller to court **b :** a right or franchise of holding a court into which persons out of the jurisdiction may be vouched as warrantors (as where a purchaser vouches his seller as warrantor to prove that goods were not stolen) — used usu. in the phrase *toll and team*

[2]**team** \"\ *vb* -ED/-ING/-s *vt* **1 :** to yoke or join in a team ⟨one horse and one cow which were ~*ed* to a crude plow —R. A.Billington⟩ **2 :** to convey or haul with a team ⟨~ lumber⟩ ~ *vi* **1 :** to drive a team or motortruck **:** be a teamster **2 :** to form a team **:** join forces or efforts ⟨~*ed* together in a defensive alliance⟩ — often used with *up* ⟨Communist tactics of ~*ing* up with hot-blooded nationalism —Tillman Durdin⟩

[3]**team** \"\ *adj* **:** of, belonging to, or performed by a team ⟨~ horse⟩ ⟨~ game⟩ ⟨~ effort⟩

tea maker *n* **:** a perforated covered spoon that holds tea leaves and is used in brewing tea in a cup

tea·man \ˈtēmən\ *n, pl* **teamen :** a dealer in tea; *esp* **:** a tea buyer

team boat *n* **:** a paddle boat propelled by horses

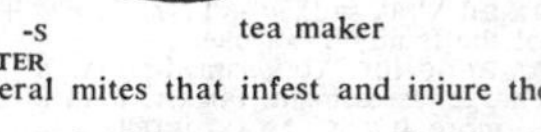

tea maker

team·er \ˈtēmə(r)\ *n* -s [[1]*team + -er*] **:** TEAMSTER

tea mite *n* **:** any of several mites that infest and injure the tea plant

teamland \ˈ=,=\ *n* [ME *teme lond,* fr. *teme* team + *lond* land] *Old Eng law* **:** PLOWLAND 1

team·man \ˈtēmmən\ *n, pl* **teammen :** TEAMSTER

teammate \ˈ=,=\ *n* **:** a fellow member of a team **:** PARTNER

team of four : four bridge players in two partnerships entered as a unit in a tournament or other contest

tea mosquito *n* **:** a capsid bug of the genus *Helopeltis* (esp. *H. theivora*) that feeds on the tea plant and causes a stem canker resembling a fungus disease

team play *n* **1 :** collective play with mutual assistance of team members ⟨skillful *team play* in hockey⟩ **2 :** cooperative effort ⟨need for *team play* in time of war —Christopher La Farge⟩

teams·man \ˈtēmzmən\ *n, pl* **teamsmen** [*teams-* (fr. genitive of [1]*team*) + *man*] **:** TEAMSTER

team·ster \ˈtēmztə(r), -m(p)st-\ *n* -s [[1]*team + -ster*] **:** one who drives a team or motortruck esp. as an occupation

team track *n* **:** a siding with public access on which freight cars are placed for loading or unloading by shippers and consignees

teamwork \ˈ=,=\ *n* **:** work done by a number of associates with usu. each doing a clearly defined portion but all sub-

ordinating personal prominence to the efficiency of the whole ⟨~ of a football eleven⟩ ⟨the smoothly coordinated ~ of a crack gun crew⟩
team yard *n* : a railroad yard having team tracks
tea oil *n* **1** : a fragrant essential oil obtained from black tea **2** : TEA-SEED OIL
tea oil tree *n* : SASANQUA
tea olive *n* : any of several cultivated Asiatic shrubs of the genus *Osmanthus*
tea party *n* [³*tea* + *party*] **1** : an afternoon social gathering at which tea is served **2** [so called fr. the Boston Tea Party, name facetiously applied to the occasion in 1773 when a group of citizens threw a shipment of tea into Boston harbor in protest against the tax on imports] : an exciting disturbance or proceeding : SKIRMISH
teapot \ˈ=,=\ *n* : a vessel with a spout in which tea is brewed and from which it is served
tea·poy *or* **te·poy** \ˈtē,pȯi\ *n* -s [Hindi *tipāī*, fr. Skt *tri* three + *pāda* foot; akin to Skt *pad* foot — more at THREE, FOOT] **1** : an ornamental stand with three legs **2** : a stand for a tea service : TEA TABLE

teapot

¹**tear** \ˈti(ə)r, ˈtiə\ *n* -s [ME *ter, tere, tear*, fr. OE *tēar, tæhher, teagor;* akin to OHG *zahar* tear, ON *tār*, Goth *tagr*, OL *dacruma*, L *lacrima*, Gk *dakry*] **1 a** : a drop of the clear saline fluid secreted normally in small amount by the lacrimal gland, diffused between the eye and the eyelids to moisten the parts and facilitate their motion, and passed ordinarily through the nasolacrimal duct into the nose **b tears** *pl* : a secretion of profuse tears that overflow the eyelids and dampen the face **2 tears** *pl* **a** : an act of weeping ⟨break into ~*s*⟩ ⟨found the child in ~*s* over her broken doll⟩ **b** : an act of grieving **3 a** : a transparent drop of fluid or hardened fluid matter (as resin) **b** : RUPERT'S DROP **4** : undissolved material or a partially vitrified bit of clay in glass
²**tear** \"\ *vb* -ED/-ING/-S [ME *teren*, fr. *ter, tere*, tear] *vi* : to fill with tears : shed tears ⟨eyes ~*ing* in the November wind —Saul Bellow⟩ ~ *vt* : to cause to flow or fill with tears ⟨sudden pity ~*ed* his sight⟩
³**tear** \ˈta(a)(ə)r, ˈte(ə)r, |ə\ *vb* **tore** \ˈtō(ə)r, ˈtȯ(ə)r, -ōə, -ȯ(ə)\ *or archaic* **tare** \ˈta(a)(ə)r, ˈte|, |ə\ **torn** \ˈtō(ə)rn, ˈtȯ(ə)rn, -ōən, -ȯ(ə)n\ *or archaic* **tare; tearing; tears** [ME *teren*, fr. OE *teran*; akin to OHG *zeran* to destroy, Goth *gatairan* to tear, destroy, Gk *derein* to skin, flay, Skt *dṛṇāti* he tears, bursts] *vt* **1 a** : to divide (as a piece of fabric or paper) forcefully or violently into parts ⟨~ a letter in half⟩ **b** : to make a rent in ⟨~ a coat on a nail⟩ **c** : to wound by slashing or lacerating ⟨~ the skin⟩ **d** : to shatter or destroy usu. as if by tearing ⟨~ the place apart⟩ ⟨the explosion *tore* the town to pieces⟩ **2 a** : to split or disrupt emotionally and violently by presenting with a compulsory choice between unacceptable or equally pressing alternatives ⟨*torn* between love and hate⟩ ⟨*torn* by conflicting loyalties⟩ **b** : disrupt or throw into confusion by violent oppositions as between parties or factions ⟨*torn* by factional disputes and religious dissension⟩ **c** : to affect violently as if by lacerating ⟨*torn* by doubts⟩ ⟨*torn* by anarchy⟩ ⟨thunderbolt *tore* the heavens⟩ **3 a** : to pull, wrench, or remove by force or violent means ⟨~ a weapon from the agent's grasp⟩ ⟨~ a glove away from a dog⟩ ⟨*tore* out his hair by the roots⟩ ⟨~ some pages out of a book⟩ ⟨~ a cover off a box⟩ **b** : to force as if by pulling or wrenching ⟨tried to ~ his eyes from the scene⟩ ⟨try to ~ your thoughts from the past⟩ ⟨a reply *torn* from the heart⟩ **4** : to cut (a hole, a path) by violent means ⟨~ a hole in the wall⟩ ⟨the flood *tore* a . . . gorge through the township —*Amer. Guide Series: Vt.*⟩ ~ *vi* **1** : to divide, separate, or develop breaks or rents on being subjected to pulling, laceration, snagging ⟨this cloth ~*s* easily⟩ ⟨the stocking *tore* when it caught on the nail⟩ **2** : to run, move, or act with great speed, impetus, or force or without restraint or check ⟨automobiles . . . in which the rich could ~ noisily along —F.L.Allen⟩ ⟨*tore* up the stairs two steps at a time⟩
syn RIP, REND, SPLIT, CLEAVE, RIVE: TEAR implies a forcible, somewhat crude, pulling or wrenching part from part, as of a fabric, or pulling or wrenching away, usu. so that ragged or irregular edges result ⟨*tear* a newspaper in half⟩ ⟨a Roman citizen was *torn* to pieces by the infuriated populace of Thebes —Agnes Repplier⟩ ⟨*tear* a photograph out of an album⟩ RIP implies a less crude, often purposeful, pulling part from part, as of a fabric in a rapid, uninterrupted action often along a straight line, grain, or seam or so that more or less straight edges result ⟨the woman *ripped* the pages out of the book, neatly, one by one⟩ REND is more rhetorical than RIP or TEAR and suggests greater violence than either ⟨*rend* your hearts and not your garments —Joel 2:13 (RSV)⟩ ⟨the black volume of clouds . . . *rent* asunder by flashes of lightning —Washington Irving⟩ CLEAVE implies very forceful, often violent, cutting into or separation of part from part, as of a substance more solid than fabric ⟨struck the final blow, *cleaving* the archbishop's skull —E.V.Lucas⟩ ⟨Norse vessels *cleaving* the channel with high and figured prows —Will Durant⟩ SPLIT suggests a more precise though forceful cutting or separation of part from part than CLEAVE, usu. along a grain or seam or between layers ⟨*split* a log for firewood⟩ ⟨mines opened, forests planted, and racks *split* —William Wordsworth⟩ RIVE suggests an action similar to SPLIT or CLEAVE but rougher, more violent ⟨the oak was struck and *riven* by lightning —George Santayana⟩ ⟨even in the days of the *riven* atom —Vannevar Bush⟩ **syn** see in addition RUSH
—tear at : LACERATE ⟨the sight of her grief *tore at* his heart⟩ **—tear into** : to attack without caution or restraint ⟨*tore into* his opponent with head down and fists flying⟩ ⟨*tore into* him with a fearful tongue-lashing⟩ **—tear it** *chiefly Brit* : to bring an end (as to one's hopes or expectations) : make continuation impossible ⟨discovered that I bored her to tears, which *tore it* for me —H.A.Vachell⟩ **—tear one's hair** : to pull or pluck one's hair as an expression of grief, rage, frustration, desperation, anxiety; *also* : to feel or display such an emotion ⟨*tearing his hair* over a pile of bills⟩
⁴**tear** \"\ *n* -s **1** : the act of tearing : damage from being torn — used chiefly in the phrase *wear and tear* **2 a** : a hole or flaw made by tearing : RENT ⟨mending a ~ in her skirt⟩ **b** : a crack in a casting **3 a** : a tearing pace : violent rush : FLURRY ⟨the train went by at a ~⟩ **b** : a state of headlong urgency or eagerness : great hurry ⟨why are you in such a ~ to get home⟩ **c** : SPREE ⟨go on a ~⟩
⁵**tear** \"\ *adj* [ME *teer, tere, ter*, fr. MD *teder, teer* tender, delicate; akin to OE *tieder* weak, delicate] *obs* : DELICATE, DAINTY, FINE
⁶**tear** \"\ *n* -s [ME *teer*, fr. *teer* delicate, fine] **1** *archaic* : something (as flax or hemp) of the finest quality **2** : the proportion of top to noil in combing wool
tear·able \ˈta(a)rəbəl, ˈter-\ *adj* [³*tear* + *-able*] : capable of being torn : readily torn — **tear·able·ness** *n* -ES
tear·age \-rij\ *n* -s [⁶*tear* + *-age*] : amount of or allowance for removal of short fiber in wool combing
tear around *vi* **1** : to go about in excited or angry haste **2** : to lead a wild or disorderly life ⟨when is he going to stop *tearing around* and settle down⟩
tear away *vt* [³*tear*] : to remove (as oneself) reluctantly ⟨several hours before he could *tear* himself *away* from the party⟩
tearaway \ˈ=,=,=\ *n* -s [*tear away*] *chiefly Brit* : one that acts or moves with impetuosity or speed ⟨at his best, man is a patchy deadly old ~ —Bryan MacMahon⟩ ⟨a great ~ chestnut horse —T.E.Hook⟩
tear bag *n* [¹*tear*] : TEARPIT
tear-blanket \ˈ=,=,=\ *n* [³*tear* + *blanket*] : HERCULES'-CLUB
tear bomb *n* [¹*tear*] : a bomb charged with tear gas
tear bottle *n* : LACHRYMATORY
tear-coat \ˈ=,=\ *n* [³*tear* + *coat*] : HERCULES'-CLUB
tear down *vt* **1 a** : to cause to decompose or disintegrate : DESTROY **b** : VILIFY, DENIGRATE ⟨*tear down* a reputation⟩ **2** : to take apart : DISASSEMBLE ⟨*tear* an engine *down* for overhaul⟩
teardown \ˈ=,=\ *n* -s [*tear down*] : DISASSEMBLY
¹**teardrop** \ˈ=,=\ *n* [¹*tear* + *drop*] **1** : ¹TEAR 1a **2** : something shaped like a dropping tear; *specif* : a pendent gem on an earring or necklace
²**teardrop** \"\ *adj* : PEAR-DROP

teardrop on an earring

tear duct *n* : LACRIMAL DUCT
teared *past of* TEAR
tear·er \ˈta(a)rə(r), ˈter-\ *n* -s [³*tear* + *-er*] **1** : one that tears or rends; *specif* : one who tears cloth from bolts for the making of handkerchiefs, sheets, or other specified articles **2** : one that rushes or blusters : something that violently attracts attention ⟨that storm was a ~⟩
tear fault *n* [⁴*tear*] : a fault occurring in the rocks above a low-angle thrust fault and striking approximately at right angles to the strike of the thrust fault
tear·ful \ˈtirfəl, ˈtiəf-\ *adj* [¹*tear* + *-ful*] **1** : flowing with or accompanied by tears : WEEPING ⟨~ entreaties⟩ **2** : causing tears ⟨fine sense of the grim and the ~ —T.L.Peacock⟩ — **tear·ful·ly** \-f(ə)lē, -li\ *adv* — **tear·ful·ness** *n* -ES
tear gas *n* : a solid, liquid, or gaseous substance that on dispersion in the atmosphere blinds the eyes with tears but does not damage them and that is used chiefly in dispelling mobs — called also *lacrimator*
tear gland *n* : LACRIMAL GLAND
tear grass *n* : JOB'S TEARS 2
tear·i·ly \ˈtirəlē\ *adv* : in a teary manner : with tears or weeping
¹**tearing** *adj* [fr. pres. part. of ³*tear*] **1** : causing continuing or repeated pain or distress : HARROWING ⟨~ headache⟩ ⟨~ cough⟩ **2** : HASTY, VIOLENT, FURIOUS ⟨~ hurry⟩ ⟨~ rage⟩ **3** *chiefly Brit* : SPLENDID, IMPRESSIVE ⟨~ success⟩
²**tearing** *n* -s [fr. gerund of ²*tear*] : abnormal watering of the eyes occurring as a reaction to local conditions (as conjunctivitis) or because of obstruction of the lacrimal passages ⟨~ from the eye and nose-blowing —M.F.A.Montagu⟩
tea ring *n* [³*tea*] : a yeast-raised coffeecake baked in ring form
tearing strength *n* [*tearing* (gerund of ³*tear*) + *strength*] : the property of paper or fabric that is measured by the force required to tear it
tearjerker \ˈ=,=,=\ *n* [¹*tear* + *jerker*] : an extravagantly pathetic story, play, film, or radio or television program
tear-jerking \ˈ=,=,=\ *adj* [¹*tear* + *jerking*] : excessively or deliberately pathetic : SENTIMENTAL ⟨*tear-jerking* plot⟩ ⟨*tear-jerking* appeals for donations⟩
tear·less \ˈtirləs, ˈtiəl-\ *adj* [¹*tear* + *-less*] : shedding no tears : free from tears — **tear·less·ly** *adv* — **tear·less·ness** *n* -ES
tear-off \ˈ=,=\ *n* -s [fr. the phrase *tear off*] : part of a piece of paper intended to be removed by tearing usu. along a marked line (as a row of dashes)
tear off *vt* [³*tear*] : to compose rapidly ⟨*tore off* a whole play in three weeks⟩ ⟨just time to *tear off* a letter home⟩
tea·room \ˈtē,rüm, -rům\ *n* : a public dining room or small restaurant with service and decor designed primarily for a feminine clientele — **tea·roomy** \-mē\ *adj*
tea rose *n* **1** : any of numerous tender or half-hardy hybrid garden bush roses descended chiefly from a Chinese rose (*Rosa odorata*) and valued esp. for their abundant large usu. tea-scented blossoms — see HYBRID TEA **2** *or* **tea-rose pink** **a** : a variable color averaging a light yellowish pink that is yellower and stronger than average shell pink (sense 1) and yellower and slightly lighter than average baby pink **b** *of textiles* : a strong yellowish pink that is redder and paler than average salmon
tearpit \ˈ=,=\ *n* [¹*tear* + *pit*] : a sebaceous gland that opens beneath the lower eyelid of most deer and antelope, that can be controlled in its opening voluntarily, and that secretes a waxy odorous substance — called also *lacrimal sinus*
tears *pl of* TEAR, *pres 3d sing of* TEAR
tear sac *n* : TEARPIT
tear sheet *n* [³*tear*] : a sheet torn from a publication usu. to send as proof of insertion to an advertiser whose advertisement appears on it
tear shell *n* [¹*tear*] : an artillery shell charged with tear gas
tearstain \ˈ=,=\ *n* **1** : a spot or streak left by tears **2** : a reddish or reddish green streaking of citrus fruits that occurs in some diseases (as anthracnose or melanose) or is caused by attacks of the rust mite
tear streak *n* : TEARSTAIN 2
tear strip *n* [³*tear*] : the scored band in a can or added narrow ribbon in a wrapper or on a fiber box that provides an easy and defined way of opening
¹**teart** \ˈti(ə)rt\ *adj* [alter. of *tart*] **1** *dial Eng* : TART, SOUR **2** *of soil or herbage* : containing excessive quantities of molybdenum — **teart·ness** *n* -ES
²**teart** \"\ *n* -s : scouring of cattle on pastures in parts of England containing excess molybdenum
tear tape *n* [³*tear*] : a strong tape glued to the inside of a shipping container with one end protruding so that the container is readily opened by pulling out the tape
tearthumb \ˈ=,=\ *n* [³*tear* + *thumb*; fr. the minute prickles on the stem] : any of several plants of the genus *Polygonum* having prickly stems
tear up *vt* [³*tear*] **1** : to damage, remove, or effect an opening in (as a floor surface) ⟨*tear* the street *up* to repair a sewer⟩ **2** : destroy by tearing : tear to pieces ⟨*tear* a letter *up*⟩ ⟨*tear up* an agreement⟩
teary \ˈtirē, -ri\ *adj* -ER/-EST [ME *tery*, fr. *ter* tear + *-y*] **1 a** : wet or stained with tears : TEARFUL **b** : consisting of tears or drops like tears **2** : provocative of tears : PATHETIC ⟨~ story⟩
teas *pl of* TEA, *pres 3d sing of* TEA
teas·able \ˈtēzəbəl\ *adj* : capable of being teased — **teas·able·ness** *n* -ES
tea scrub *n* : a scrub formed by the Australian tea tree; *also* : the tree itself
¹**tease** *also* **teaze** \ˈtēz\ *vb* -ED/-ING/-S [ME *tesen, teesen*, fr. OE *tǣsan*; akin to OHG *zeisan* to pluck, tease] *vt* **1 a** : to disentangle and lay parallel by combing or carding ⟨~ wool⟩ **b** : to scratch (cloth) so as to raise a nap : TEASEL **2** : to tear in pieces; *esp* : to separate (a tissue or specimen) into minute shreds for microscopic examination **3** : ³RUFF 3 **4 a** : to disturb or annoy by persistent irritating or provoking action ⟨an unpleasant thought seemed to ~ him like a wasp: he moved his head slightly to avoid it —Christopher Isherwood⟩ — or tantalizing elusiveness ⟨curiosity to know more about living things . . . has *teased* man's mind for centuries —Joel Turner⟩ **b** : to attempt to provoke anger, resentment, or confusion in esp. for sport : GOAD, TORMENT ⟨a cheap cleverness put on to worry and ~ the simple philistine —J.C.Powys⟩ **c** : to annoy or disturb with petty persistent requests : PESTER, IMPORTUNE ⟨the children have been *teasing* me all day to be allowed to go out⟩; *also* : to obtain by repeated coaxing **d** : to coax or persuade into acquiescence esp. by persistent small efforts ⟨relieved to be in a house where the family did not ~ him to break the promise —Dorothy C. Fisher⟩ **5** : to tantalize or baffle by arousing desire in without the intention of satisfying it; *specif* : to determine the presence of estrus in (a female domestic animal) by approach to or contact with a male ~ *vi* : to engage in tormenting, tantalizing, provoking, or importuning **syn** see WORRY
²**tease** *also* **teaze** \"\ *n* -s **1** : act of teasing or state of being teased ⟨most parodies are little more than literary ~*s* —Michael Swan⟩ **2** : one that teases or torments ⟨a cruel ~ when the comic spirit was riding him —J.W.Beach⟩ **3** *slang* : MONEY ⟨a mere national dearth of ~ may have seemed a redundant misfortune —A.J.Liebling⟩
³**tease** \"\ *vt* -ED/-ING/-S [alter. (influenced by ¹*tease*) of ME *taysen, teisen*] *archaic* : to urge on : DRIVE, ROUSE ⟨did ~ their horses homeward with convulsed spur —John Keats⟩
⁴**tease** *also* **teaze** \"\ *vt* -ED/-ING/-S [F *tiser*, short for *attiser* to feed or stir up (a fire), fr. (assumed) VL *attitiare*, fr. L *ad-* + *titio* firebrand] : to operate or stoke (a glass-melting furnace)
tea-seed oil *n* : a fatty oil resembling olive oil obtained from the seeds of the sasanqua and used chiefly as an edible oil, as a hair oil, and in soap — called also *tea oil*
teasehole \ˈ=,=\ *n* [⁴*tease* + *hole*] : the opening in a glass-making furnace for fuel
¹**tea·sel** *also* **tea·sle** *or* **tea·zel** *or* **tea·zle** \ˈtēzəl\ *n* -s [ME *tesel, tasel*, fr. OE *tǣsel*; akin to OHG *zeisila* teasel, OE *tǣsan* to tease — more at TEASE] **1** : a plant of the genus *Dipsacus* (esp. *D. fullonum* and *D. sylvestris*) — see FULLER'S TEASEL, WILD TEASEL **2 a** : a flower head of the fuller's teasel covered with firm finely hooked bracts and used when dried to raise a nap on woolen cloth **b** : a wire substitute for the fuller's teasel
²**teasel** \"\ *vt* **teaseled** *or* **teaselled; teaseled** *or* **teaselled; teaseling** *or* **teaselling** \-z(ə)liŋ\ **teasels** : to nap (cloth) with teasels
tea·sel·er *also* **tea·sel·ler** \-z(ə)lə(r)\ *n* -s [ME *teselere*, fr. *tesel* teasel + *-ere* -er] : GIGGER
teasel family *n* : DIPSACACEAE
teasel gourd *n* : HEDGEHOG GOURD
teaselwort \ˈ=,=,=\ *n* : a plant of the family Dipsacaceae
tease·ment \ˈtēzmənt\ *n* -s [¹*tease* + *-ment*] : an act of teasing
tease out *vt* [¹*tease*] : to obtain by disentangling or freeing with or as if with a pointed instrument ⟨isolated striated muscle fibers can be *teased out* from muscles —*Medical Physics*⟩ ⟨delicately *teasing out* the embryos from a little deer mouse —D.C.Peattie⟩
¹**teas·er** \ˈtēzə(r)\ *n* -s [ME *teser*, fr. *tesen* to tease + *-er*] **1** : a textile worker or a textile machine that teases fiber or cloth **2** : something difficult to dispose of, solve, or decide about : something not easily either grasped or dismissed ⟨whether to accept the offer was a ~⟩ ⟨riddles, conundrums, ~*s*⟩ **3 a** : one that annoys, torments, or tantalizes **b** : a woman who provokes or encourages sexual advances but evades or refuses intercourse **c** : a male animal used for identifying females in heat; *also* : a cow in heat used to stimulate a bull for semen collection for artificial insemination **d** : STRIPTEASER **4 a** : an object without hooks towed astern of a boat to attract fish **b** : an advertisement meant to arouse curiosity sometimes by withholding part of the material information **5** [so called fr. its habit of chasing other birds and forcing them to disgorge their prey] : JAEGER **6** : a border, curtain, or canvas-covered framework suspended parallel to and just behind the proscenium arch in order to establish the height of the actual proscenium opening and to conceal the upper part of the stage **7** : one of two coils or transformers forming a T connection
²**teaser** *also* **teaz·er** \"\ *n* -s [F *tiseur*, fr. *tiser* to tease — more at TEASE (stoke)] : an operator or fireman of a glass-melting furnace
tea service *n* : a set of china or metalware for service at table: **a** : a set of china consisting of a teapot, sugar bowl, creamer, sometimes a coffeepot, and usu. plates, cups, and saucers — compare COFFEE SERVICE **b** : a set of metalware consisting of a teapot, sugar bowl, creamer, sometimes a coffeepot, and usu. waste bowl, kettle, and tray

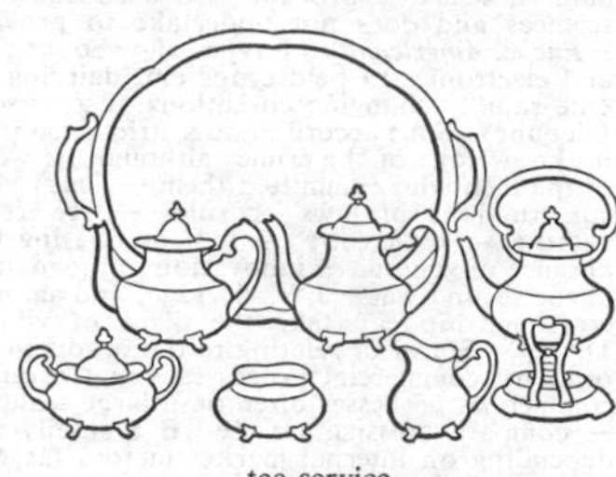
tea service

tea set *n* **1** : TEA SERVICE **2** : a china set consisting of teapot, sugar bowl, creamer, cups and saucers, and dessert plates
tease up *vt* [¹*tease*] : to improve or bring into being by small changes or touches ⟨*tease up* a picture⟩
tea shop *n* **1** *chiefly Brit* : TEAROOM **2** *Brit* : LUNCHROOM, CAFÉ
teas·ing·ly *adv* [*teasing* (pres. part. of ¹*tease*) + *-ly*] : in a teasing manner ⟨threatened ~ to throw her in the pond⟩ : ANNOYINGLY, TEASINGLY ⟨~ elusive significance in his remarks⟩
teasing needle *n* [*teasing* (gerund of ¹*tease*) + *needle*] : a tapering needle mounted in a handle and used for teasing tissues or other objects for microscopic examination
teaspoon \ˈ=,=\ *n* **1** : a small commonly silver spoon suitable for stirring and sipping tea or coffee and having a standard capacity of one third of a tablespoon — see SPOON illustration **2** : TEASPOONFUL
tea·spoon·ful \ˈ=,spün,fu̇l *sometimes* -pün-\ *n, pl* **teaspoonfuls** *or* **teaspoonsful** \-n,fu̇lz, -nz,fu̇l\ [*teaspoon* + *-ful*] **1** : as much as one teaspoon can hold : enough to fill a teaspoon **2** : a unit of measure used esp. in cookery and pharmacy equal to one level teaspoonful or 1⅓ fluid drams
teasy \ˈtēzē\ *adj* -ER/-EST [¹*tease* + *-y*] : inclined to tease : IRRITATING, ANNOYING
teat \ˈtit, ˈtēt, *usu* |d.+V\ *n* -s [ME *tete, tet*, fr. OF *tete, tette*, of Gmc origin; akin to OE *tit, titt* teat, MHG *zitze*] **1** : the protuberance through which milk is drawn from the udder or breast of a mammal : NIPPLE, MAMMILLA, DUG — see COW illustration **2** *Brit* : NIPPLE 2a **3 a** : a small projecting part on a countersink or counterbore to guide it in a drilled hole **b** : a nib or projection on a leaf spring
tea table *n* **1** : a table used or spread for tea; *specif* : a small table for serving afternoon tea **2** : the place of gathering or company at tea ⟨favorite topics at the *tea table*⟩
tea tannin *n* : a tannin found in green tea leaves and in green tea and in oxidized form in black tea
teataster \ˈ=,=,=\ *n* : an expert who judges or grades tea by tasting a standard brew
teat canal *n* : the channel in a teat through which milk passes
teat cup *n* : the part of a milking machine that covers the teat of a cow
teat·ed \|d.əd\ *adj* [*teat* + *-ed*] : having teats; *often* : having functional teats ⟨a three-*teated* cow⟩
teatfish \ˈ=,=\ *n* [so called fr. the shape of the tentacles] : TREPANG
tea-things \ˈ=,=\ *n pl* : articles used for serving tea
teatime \ˈ=,=\ *n* : the customary time for tea : late afternoon or early evening ⟨long past ~⟩ ⟨traffic at ~ was heavy⟩
tea tortrix *n* : a small Indian moth (*Homona coffearia*) whose larva feeds on the leaves of tea, coffee, and other plants
tea towel *n* : DISH TOWEL
tea tray *n* : a tray that accommodates a tea service
tea tree *n* [¹*tea* + *tree*] **1** : TEA 1a **2** [so called fr. the use of their leaves as a substitute for tea] **a** : any of various Australian shrubs or trees of the genus *Leptospermum* (esp. *L. scoparium*) or the genus *Melaleuca* (esp. *M. squarrosa*) forming dense thickets **b** : AFRICAN TEA TREE
tea-tree oil *n* : an essential oil obtained fr. the leaves and terminal branches of various tea trees (sense 2a); *esp* : a light yellow oil obtained from an Australian tree (*Melaleuca alternifolia*) and used as a germicide
tea trolley *n, chiefly Brit* : TEA WAGON
tea wagon *n* : a small table on wheels used in serving tea and light refreshments
tea yellows *n pl but usu sing in constr* : a sulfur deficiency disease of tea characterized by chlorosis of the leaves
teaze *var of* TEASE
teazel *or* **teazle** *var of* TEASEL
teb·bad \ˈte,bad\ *n* -s [perh. fr. Per *tab* fever + *bād* wind, fr. MPer *vāt*; akin to Av *vāta-* wind, Skt *vāta* — more at WIND] : a sandstorm
teb·bit \ˈtebət\ *var of* TABET
te·bel·di \təˈbeldē\ *n* -s [Ar dial. *tabaldi*; prob. of Berber origin] : BAOBAB
te·bet *also* **te·beth** *or* **te·vet** *or* **te·veth** \tāˈvāth, ˈtā,ves\ *n* -s *usu cap* [Heb *Ṭēbhēth*] : the 4th month of the civil year or the 10th month of the ecclesiastical year in the Jewish calendar — see MONTH table

tea wagon

tebu *usu cap, var of* TIBBU
tec \ˈtek\ *n* -s [by shortening] *slang* : DETECTIVE
tec *abbr* technical; technician; technology

te·ca·li \ˌtäkäˈlē\ *n* -S [Sp *tecali,* fr. *Tecali,* village in Puebla, Mexico] : ALABASTER 1
tech *or* **techn** *abbr* technical; technically; technician; technology
teched *or* **tetched** \ˈtecht\ *adj* [alter. of *touched*] : mentally unbalanced : somewhat deranged
techiness *var of* TETCHINESS
techinnah *var of* TEHINNAH
tech·ne \ˈteknē\ *n* -S [Gk *technē* — more at TECHNICAL] : ART, SKILL; *esp* : the principles or methods employed in making something or attaining an objective — compare UNDERSTANDING
tech·ne·ti·um \tekˈnēshēəm\ *n* -S [NL, fr. Gk *technētos* artificial (fr. *technasthai* to devise by art, fr. *technē* art) + NL *-ium* — more at TECHNICAL] : a crystalline radioactive metallic element that resembles rhenium and manganese chemically and that was obtained as the first synthetic element by bombarding molybdenum with deuterons or neutrons and later as one of the fission products of uranium — symbol *Tc;* see ELEMENT table
¹tech·nic \ˈteknik, -nēk\ *adj* [Gk *technikos*] : TECHNICAL
²technic \"\, *in sense 2 also* (ˈ)tekˈnēk\ *n* -S **1** : a technical term or detail : TECHNICALITY **2** [trans. of F *technique*] **a** : TECHNIQUE 1 ⟨glaring defects both in sonority and recording ~ —*Scribner's*⟩ — often used in pl. but sing. or pl. in constr. ⟨literary ~*s* . . . depends on reproducing experiments from life —*Contemporary Rev.*⟩ **b** : TECHNIQUE 2a ⟨various ~*s* have been developed for increasing the consumption of oxygen —Morris Fishbein⟩ **3 technics** *pl but sing or pl in constr* : TECHNOLOGY 2a, 2b(1) ⟨modern ~*s* is giving man a sense of power —Bertrand Russell⟩
¹tech·ni·cal \ˈteknəkəl, -nēk-\ *adj* [Gk *technikos* of art, skillful, practical (fr. *technē* art, craft, practical skill + *-ikos* -ic) + E *-al;* akin to Gk *tektōn* carpenter, builder, Skt *takṣan* carpenter, *takṣati* he forms, constructs, L *texere* to weave, construct, OHG *dehsa* hatchet, *dahs* badger] **1 a** : having special usu. practical knowledge esp. of a mechanical or scientific subject ⟨the construction of the thermonuclear weapon was a great challenge to the ~ people of this country —Edward Teller⟩ **b** : marked by or characteristic of specialization ⟨highly ~ matters hardly suitable for popular lecturing —William James⟩ ⟨~ language⟩ **2** : of or relating to a particular subject ⟨outlined his ~ qualifications for the office of comptroller⟩; *esp* : of or relating to a practical subject that is organized on modern scientific principles ⟨is a college of liberal arts and sciences and does not undertake to provide a ~ training —*Encyc. Americana*⟩ ⟨all types of ~ books ranging from radio and electronics to field crops and dairying —*Saturday Rev.*⟩ ⟨the rapidly changing conditions of a ~ society —Reinhold Niebuhr⟩ **3 a** : according to a strict legal interpretation ⟨had no knowledge of the crimes although he was in ~ command of the men who committed them —*Time*⟩ **b** : created by the constructions of laws or rules — see TECHNICAL FELONY, TECHNICAL KNOCKOUT **4** : of or relating to technique ⟨the absence of genuine ~ innovation in the majority of the novels of the second war —J.W.Aldridge⟩ ⟨no amount of ~ skill and craftsmanship can take the place of vital interest —John Dewey⟩ **5** : of or relating to the production of chemicals by ordinary commercial processes; *esp* : produced by ordinary commercial processes often on a large scale ⟨~ sulfuric acid⟩ — compare COMMERCIAL 1e **6** : chiefly resulting from or depending on internal market factors (as price changes and volume) rather than fundamental economic considerations ⟨the late burst of demand . . . yesterday was interpreted by most analysts as confirming their forecasts that the market is due for a ~ rally —C.J.Elia⟩ — **tech·ni·cal·ly** \-nək(ə)lē, -nēk-, -li\ *adv* — **tech·ni·cal·ness** *n* -ES
²technical \"\ *n* -S : TECHNIC 1
technical estoppel *n* : an estoppel by record or by deed : a common law or legal estoppel
technical felony *n* : a felony that usu. results in imprisonment for life or for an indeterminate sentence when an offender has been convicted of designated serious offenses for three or some other specified number of times
technical foul *n* **1** : a foul in basketball caused by one who is not playing **2 a** : a player foul in basketball that involves no contact with an opponent **b** : a player foul that involves unsportsmanlike contact with an opponent when the ball is not in play
tech·ni·cal·ism \-kəˌlizəm\ *n* -S : addiction to technicality
tech·ni·cal·ist \-ləst\ *n* -S : one addicted to technicality
tech·ni·cal·i·ty \ˌteknəˈkaləd·ē, -lətē, -i\ *n* -ES **1** : the quality or state of being technical ⟨~ in the presentation would defeat the major purpose —R.E.Coker⟩ **2** : something that is technical: as **a** : a detail that has meaning only for the specialist ⟨finally caught him in a legal ~ —Dorothy C. Fisher⟩ **b** : a technical word or phrase
tech·ni·cal·iza·tion \ˌteknəkələˈzāshən\ *n* -S [*technicalize* + *-ation*] : the action of making technical
tech·ni·cal·ize \ˈteknəkəˌlīz\ *vt* -ED/-ING/-S [¹*technical* + *-ize*] : to make technical
technical knockout *n* : a knockout ruled by the referee when a boxer is unable or is declared to be unable (as because of injury) to continue the fight
technical sergeant *n* : a noncommissioned officer in the air force just below a master sergeant and above a staff sergeant
technical traverse *n* : a legal traverse preceded by an inducement
tech·ni·cian \tekˈnishən\ *n* -S [¹*technic* + *-ician*] **1** : a specialist in the technical details of a subject: as **a** : a technical expert ⟨a scholarly ~ . . . who is of service to the management side of industry but not of it —Alfred Kazin⟩ **b** : one who has learned the practical technical details and special techniques of an occupation ⟨skilled electrical ~*s* are needed to keep this equipment in good running condition —*Best True Fact Detective*⟩ **2** : one who has acquired the technique of an art or other area of specialization ⟨a superb ~ and a musician of integrity —Irving Kolodin⟩ ⟨the ~ had finally become the artist —*Newsweek*⟩ ⟨an excellent ~ at every level of politics —T.H.White b. 1915⟩
tech·ni·cist \ˈteknəsəst\ *n* -S [¹*technic* + *-ist*] : TECHNICIAN
tech·ni·cize \ˈteknəˌsīz\ *vt* -ED/-ING/-S [¹*technic* + *-ize*] : TECHNICALIZE
tech·ni·col·o·gy \ˌteknəˈkäləjē\ *n* -ES [Gk *technikos* + E *-logy*] : TECHNOLOGY
technics *pl of* TECHNIC
tech·ni·cum *or* **tech·ni·kum** \ˈteknəkəm\ *n* -S [Russ or G; Russ *tekhnikum,* fr. G *technikum,* fr. Gk *technikon,* neut. of *technikos* technical] : a technical school esp. in the U.S.S.R.
tech·nique \(ˈ)tekˈnēk\ *n* -S [F, fr. *technique* technical, fr. Gk *technikos* — more at TECHNICAL] **1** : the way in which technical details are treated: as **a** : the manner in which a creative artist (as a writer or painter) uses the technical elements of his art to express himself ⟨where ~ is deficient, characterization cannot but suffer —E.R.Bentley⟩ **b** (1) : the manner in which a musician, dancer, or athlete uses basic physical movements in performance ⟨will specialize in ~ and improvisation for teenage and professional dancers —*Dance Observer*⟩ (2) : the ability of a musician, dancer, or athlete to use basic physical movements effectively ⟨a clarinetist of very limited ~ —John Hammond⟩ **c** (1) : a body of technical methods used in scientific research ⟨every science has its own special ~ a considerable part of which serves chiefly to prevent error —R.W.Murray⟩ (2) : the ability to use such methods effectively **2 a** : a technical method of accomplishing a desired aim ⟨the ~ of establishing linguistic families . . . is too difficult to be gone into here —Edward Sapir⟩; *esp* : a particular technical method ⟨used a ~ involving radioactive carbon to measure photosynthesis —E.F.Thompson⟩ **b** : METHOD, WAY, MANNER ⟨the usual fishing ~ is to loll around quietly in a small boat —*Buick Mag.*⟩ ⟨young women whose ~ is faulty are prone to meet failure and disillusionment —C.W.Cunningham⟩
techno- *comb form* [Gk, fr. *technē* — more at TECHNICAL] **1** : art : craft ⟨*technography*⟩ **2** : technical : technological ⟨*technocracy*⟩ ⟨*technoculture*⟩ **3** : applied ⟨*technopsychology*⟩
tech·noc·ra·cy \tekˈnäkrəsē, -si\ *n* -ES [*techno-* + *-cracy*] **1** : government by technicians; *specif* : management of society by technical experts **2** *often cap* : a movement flourishing in the early 1930s and advocating replacement of the capitalist price system as the basis of industrial production and distribution by a system of control by technicians aiming primarily at production to the limit of industrial capacity **3** : TECHNOLOGY 2b ⟨the ~ of destruction has become greater and more terrible —E.L.Beach⟩
tech·no·crat \ˈteknəˌkrat\ *n* -S [*techno-* + *-crat*] **1** *often cap* : an adherent of technocracy **2** : a technical expert; *esp* : one exercising managerial authority
tech·no·crat·ic \ˌteknəˈkrad·ik\ *adj* [*techno-* + *-cratic*] : of, relating to, or having the characteristics of technocracy ⟨illusions to which a ~ culture is already too prone —Reinhold Niebuhr⟩ ⟨under a ~ as under a capitalist arrangement, the efficiency of machines as well as of human beings would have economic significance only in terms of production of values —A.L.Harris⟩
tech·nog·ra·phy \tekˈnägrəfē\ *n* -ES [ISV *techno-* + *-graphy*] : the description of arts and crafts esp. with reference to their ethnic distribution and historical development
tech·no·log·ic \ˌteknəˈläjik\ *adj* [*technology* + *-ic*] : TECHNOLOGICAL ⟨inject an element of ~ unemployment in an industry —*Science News Letter*⟩
tech·no·log·i·cal \-jəkəl, -jēk-\ *adj* [*technology* + *-ical*] **1** : of, relating to, or characterized by technology ⟨~ advances⟩ ⟨~ reasons⟩ ⟨a ~ civilization⟩ **2** : resulting from improvement in technical processes that increases the productivity of machines and eliminates manual operations or the operations done by older machines ⟨~ unemployment⟩ — **tech·no·log·i·cal·ly** \-jək(ə)lē, -jēk-, -li\ *adv*
tech·nol·o·gist \tekˈnäləjəst\ *n* -S [*technology* + *-ist*] : a specialist in technology
tech·nol·o·gy \-jē, -ji\ *n* -ES [Gk *technologia* systematic treatment, fr. *techno-* + *-logia* -logy] **1** : the terminology of a particular subject : technical language **2 a** : the science of the application of knowledge to practical purposes : applied science ⟨the great American achievement has been . . . less in science itself than in ~ and engineering —Max Lerner⟩ **b** (1) : the application of scientific knowledge to practical purposes in a particular field ⟨studies are also made of polymeric materials to dental ~ —*Report: Nat'l Bureau of Standards*⟩ (2) : a technical method of achieving a practical purpose ⟨a ~ for extracting petroleum from shale⟩ **3** : the totality of the means employed by a people to provide itself with the objects of material culture
-tech·ny \ˌteknē, -ni\ *n comb form* -ES [F *-technie,* fr. Gk *technē* art, craft + F *-ie* -y — more at TECHNICAL] : technical specialization ⟨hydro*techny*⟩ ⟨metallo*techny*⟩
techy *var of* TETCHY
tecno- *comb form* [Gk *tekno-,* fr. *teknon* — more at THANE] : child ⟨*tecnology*⟩ ⟨*tecnogenesis*⟩
te·co \ˈtā(ˌ)kō\ *n, pl* **teco** *or* **tecos** *usu cap* [Sp cuitla*teco* cuitlatec] : CUITLATEC
te·coma \təˈkōmə\ *n* [NL, fr. MexSp *tecomasuchil,* fr. Nahuatl *tecomaxochitl,* fr. *tecomatl* clay pot + *xochitl* flower] **1** *cap* : a genus of tropical American shrubs and trees (family Bignoniaceae) having large showy flowers with a 5-toothed calyx, a nearly regular corolla, and four perfect stamens **2** -S : any plant of the genus *Tecoma* or the related genus *Campsis; esp* : TRUMPET CREEPER
tecs *pl of* TEC
tecta *pl of* TECTUM
tec·tal \ˈtektəl\ *adj* [NL *tectum* + E *-al*] : of or relating to the tectum
¹tec·ti·branch \ˈtektəˌbraŋk\ *adj* [NL *Tectibranchia*] : of or relating to the Tectibranchia
²tectibranch \"\ *n* -S : a mollusk of the suborder Tectibranchia
tec·ti·bran·chia \ˌ==ˈbraŋkēə\ *n pl, cap* [NL, fr. L *tectus* covered (fr. past part. of *tegere* to cover) + NL *-i-* + *-branchia* — more at THATCH] : a suborder of Opisthobranchia comprising gastropod mollusks (as bubble shells and sea hares) in which the gill is usu. situated on one side of the back and protected by a fold of the mantle — compare PTEROPODA — **tec·ti·bran·chi·an** \ˌ==ˈbraŋkēən\ *adj or n* — **tec·ti·bran·chi·ate** \-ēət, -ēˌāt\ *adj or n*
tec·ti·bran·chi·a·ta \ˌ==ˌbraŋkēˈäd·ə\ [NL, fr. L *tectus* + NL *-i-* + *branchi-* + *-ata*] *syn of* TECTIBRANCHIA
¹tec·ti·form \ˈtektəˌfȯrm\ *adj* [NL *tectiformis,* fr. L *tectum* roof + *-iformis* -iform — more at TECTUM] : shaped like a roof
²tectiform \"\ *n* -S : a design found (as at Font-de-Gaume, Dordogne, France) in the cave art of paleolithic man assumed to represent a dwelling
tec·to·fu·gal \(ˈ)tekˈtäfyəgəl\ *adj* [NL *tectum* + *-o-* + E *-fugal*] : passing out of the tectum
tec·to·gene \ˈtektəˌjēn\ *n* -S [ISV *tecto-* (fr. Gk *tektainein* to frame, build, fr. *tektōn* carpenter, builder) + *-gene* — more at TECHNICAL] : a long narrow downward fold of the earth's crust that is postulated as an early phase in the process of the formation of a mountain range or an island arc — **tec·to·gen·ic** \ˌ==ˈjenik\ *adj*
tec·to·na \tekˈtōnə\ *n, cap* [NL, perh. fr. Gk *tektōn* carpenter; fr. its use in carpentry] : a small genus of trees (family Verbenaceae) of India, Malaysia, and the Philippines having entire woolly leaves and paniculate cymes of small white or bluish flowers — see TEAK
tec·ton·ic \(ˈ)tekˈtänik\ *adj* [LL *tectonicus,* fr. Gk *tektonikos* of a builder or carpenter, skilled in building, fr. *tektōn* carpenter, builder + *-ikos* -ic — more at TECHNICAL] : of or relating to tectonics: as **a** : ARCHITECTURAL, ARCHITECTONIC **b** : of or relating to the deformation of the earth's crust, the forces involved in or producing such deformation, and the resulting rock structures and external forms — **tec·ton·i·cal·ly** \-nək(ə)lē\ *adv*
tec·ton·ics \tekˈtäniks\ *n pl but usu sing in constr* [fr. *tectonic,* after such pairs as *economic: economics*] **1** : the science or art of construction (as of a building) both in relation to use and to artistic design : ARCHITECTONICS **2 a** : geological structural features as a whole **b** : a branch of geology concerned with structure esp. with folding and faulting **c** : DIASTROPHISM
tec·ton·ism \ˈtektəˌnizəm\ *n* -S [ISV *tecton-* (fr. *tectonic*) + *-ism*] : DIASTROPHISM
tec·ton·ite \-ˌnīt\ *n* -S [ISV *tecton-* + *-ite*] : a rock that has undergone differential movement of its component parts and in consequence still retains a coherent fabric
tec·tono·physicist \tekˈtä(ˌ)nō, ˈtektə(ˌ)nō +\ *n* : a specialist in tectonophysics
tec·tono·physics \"+\ *n pl but sing in constr* [*tectonic* + *-o-* + *physics*] : a branch of geophysics that deals with the forces responsible for movements in and deformation of the earth's crust
tec·tono·sphere \tekˈtänəˌsfi(ə)r, ˈtektənō,-\ *n* [ISV *tectonic* + *-o-* + *sphere*] : the zone within the earth in which crustal movements originate
tec·to·ri·al \(ˈ)tekˈtōrēəl, -tȯr-\ *adj* [L *tectorius* (fr. *tectus* — past part. of *tegere* to cover — + *-orius* -ory) + E *-al* — more at THATCH] : forming a covering : resembling a roof
tectorial membrane *n* [NL *tectorium* + E *-al*] : MEMBRANE OF CORTI
tec·to·ri·din \tekˈtōrədən\ *n* -S [*tectorum* (specific epithet of *Iris tectorum*) (fr. L, gen. pl. of *tectum* roof, house, building) + *-idin* — more at TECTUM] : a crystalline isoflavone glucoside $C_{22}H_{22}O_{11}$ found esp. in the rhizomes of an Asiatic iris (*Iris tectorum*)
tectorigenin *n* -S [*tectoridin* + *-genin*] : a crystalline phenolic isoflavone $CH_3OC_{15}H_6O_2(OH)_3$ obtained by hydrolysis of tectoridin
tec·to·ri·um \tekˈtōrēəm, -tȯr-\ *n, pl* **tecto·ria** \-ēə\ [NL, fr. L, cover, covering, fr. neut. of *tectorius* of or forming a covering] : MEMBRANE OF CORTI
tec·to·silicate \ˈtek(ˌ)tō+\ *n* [L *tectum* roof, building + E *-o-* + *silicate* — more at TECTUM] : a polymeric silicate in which the silicon-oxygen tetrahedral groups are linked by sharing all of their oxygen atoms with other such groups so as to form a three-dimensional structure or network — compare CYCLOSILICATE
tec·to·sphere \ˈtektəˌsfi(ə)r\ *n* [Gk *tēktos* molten (fr. *tēkein* to melt) + E *sphere* — more at THAW] : ASTHENOSPHERE
tec·to·spinal \ˈtek(ˌ)tō+\ *adj* [NL *tectum* + E *-o-* + *spinal*] : extending from the tectum of the midbrain to the spinal cord — used esp. of a tract of nerve fibers connecting these parts
tec·to·spon·dy·li \ˌtektōˈspändəˌlī\ *n pl, cap* [NL, prob. fr. L *tectum* roof + NL *-o-* + *-spondyli*] *in some classifications* : an order or other division of elasmobranch fishes typically having tectospondylic vertebrae and comprising the spiny dogfishes and related forms and the angelfish (genus *Squatina*) and formerly also the rays and sawfishes — compare BATOIDEI, CYCLOSPONDYLI
tec·to·spon·dyl·ic \ˌtektōˌspänˈdilik\ *also* **tec·to·spon·dy·lous** \-ndələs\ *adj* [NL *Tectospondyli* + E *-ic, -ous*] : having more than one calcified cylinder surrounding the notochord in each vertebral centrum ⟨~ sharks⟩ — see TECTOSPONDYLI; compare CYCLOSPONDYLIC
tec·tri·cial \(ˈ)tekˈtrishəl\ *adj* [NL *tectric-, tectrix* + E *-ial*] : of or relating to a tectrix
tec·trix \ˈtektriks\ *n, pl* **tectri·ces** \-rəˌsēz, tekˈtrīˌsēz\ [NL *tectric-, tectrix,* fem. of L *tector* one that covers, fr. *tectus* (past part. of *tegere* to cover) + *-or*] : COVERT 3
tec·tum \ˈtektəm\ *n, pl* **tec·ta** \-tə\ [NL, fr. L, roof, dwelling, building, fr. neut. of *tectus,* past part. of *tegere* to cover — more at THATCH] : a bodily structure resembling or serving as a roof; *specif* : the dorsal part of the midbrain including the corpora quadrigemina — called also *tectum me·sen·ceph·a·li* \-ˌmesᵊnˈsefəˌlī\
ted \ˈted\ *vt* **tedded; tedded; tedding; teds** [fr. (assumed) ME *tedden;* akin to OHG *zetten* to spread, ON *tethja* to manure, Gk *dateisthai* to divide, *daiesthai* to divide, distribute — more at TIDE] : to spread out in order to dry : SCATTER ⟨where are the blithe and jocund to ~ the hay? —John Betjeman⟩
te·da \ˈtādə\ *n, pl* **teda** *or* **tedas** *usu cap* : TIBBU
ted·der \ˈtedə(r)\ *n* -S : one that teds; *specif* : a machine for stirring and spreading hay to hasten drying and curing
ted·dy \ˈtedē, -di\ *n, pl* **teddies** *sometimes sing in constr* [origin unknown] : CHEMISE 2
teddy bear *n, sometimes cap T* [fr. *Teddy,* nickname of Theodore Roosevelt †1919 26th U. S. president; fr. a cartoon depicting the president sparing the life of a bear cub while hunting] : a stuffed toy bear

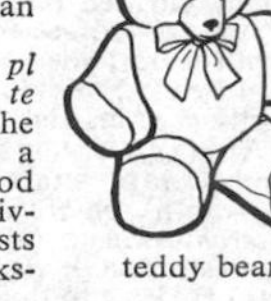
teddy bear

teddy boy *n, usu cap T & often cap B* [fr. *Teddy,* nickname for Edward] : a young British hoodlum who affects Edwardian dress
te de·um \(ˈ)tāˈdāəm, (ˈ)tēˈdēəm\ *n, pl* **te deums** *usu cap T&D* [ME, fr. LL *te deum laudamus* thee, God, we praise, the opening words of the hymn] **1 a** : a hymn of thanksgiving and praise to God **b** : an expression of praise or thanksgiving **2** : a religious service that consists chiefly of a hymn of praise and thanksgiving
tedge \ˈtej\ *n* -S [origin unknown] : ²INGATE
tediosity *n* [*tedious* + *-ity*] *obs* : TEDIOUSNESS
te·di·ous \ˈtēdēəs, ˈtējəs\ *adj* [ME, fr. LL *taediosus,* fr. L *taedium* tedium + *-osus* -ous] **1** : tiresome because of slowness, continuance, or prolixity ⟨a ~ public ceremony⟩ **2** *archaic* : SLOW, DILATORY **3** : tiresome because of dullness ⟨rather ~ fellows who substituted fustian for creative thought —V.L.Parrington⟩
te·di·ous·ly *adv* : in a tedious manner ⟨lengthily and ~ interrogated —Glenway Wescott⟩
te·di·ous·ness *n* -ES : the quality or state of being tedious
te·di·ou·some \ˈtēdēəsəm, ˈted-\ *adj* [*tedious* + *-some*] *chiefly Scot* : TEDIOUS
te·di·um *also* **tae·di·um** \ˈtēdēəm\ *n* -S [L *taedium* irksomeness, disgust, fr. *taedēre* to disgust, weary] **1** : the quality or state of being tedious : TEDIOUSNESS ⟨incessant recurrence without variety breeds ~ —J.L.Lowes⟩ **2** : a tedious period of time ⟨long ~*s* of strained anxiety —H.G.Wells⟩
¹tee \ˈtē\ *n* -S [ME] **1** *also* **te** \"\ : the letter *t* **2** : something that is shaped like a capital T: as **a** : a short piece of pipe that has a lateral outlet and is used to connect a line of pipe with a pipe at a right angle to the line — see BRANCH illustration **b** : a short piece of iron fastened at its middle to the end of a chain, passed through a hole, and turned crosswise to secure the chain **c** : T BAR **d** : WIND TEE **3** : the mark aimed at in various games (as curling) — see CURLING illustration **4** : a lattice weave in basketry in which upright and horizontal rods are twined together — **to a tee** *adv* : PRECISELY, EXACTLY ⟨suits me to a tee⟩

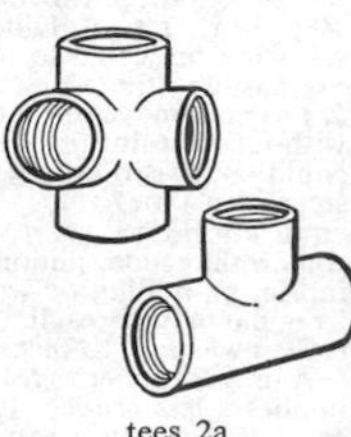
tees 2a

²tee \"\ *vt* **teed; teed; teeing; tees** : to connect or secure by means of a tee
³tee \"\ *n* -S [back-formation fr. earlier *teaz* (taken as pl.), of unknown origin] **1 a** (1) : a small artificial elevation of dirt on which a golf ball is placed before being struck at the beginning of play on a hole (2) : a peg with a concave top used to raise a golf ball before striking it at the beginning of play on a hole **b** : a device for holding a football in position so that it can be kicked off the ground **2** : the area from which a golf ball is struck at the beginning of play on a hole
⁴tee \"\ *vt* **teed; teed; teeing; tees 1** : to place (as a ball) on or as if on a tee — often used with *up* **2** : PREPARE, ARRANGE — usu. used with *up* ⟨an offensive was being *teed* up —Fred Majdalany⟩
tee bar *var of* T BAR
tee beam *var of* T BEAM
tee bolt *var of* T BOLT
tee–bulb \ˈ=,=\ *adj* [¹*tee* + *bulb*] : BULB-TEE
tee·dle \ˈtēdᵊl\ *vb* [prob. imit.] *Scot* : to sing by humming
teed off *adj* [prob. fr. past part. of *tee off*] : ANNOYED, ANGRY ⟨was *teed off* because the chief had me type his spares inventory —N.T.Kenney⟩
tee–hee *var of* TEHEE
tee hinge *var of* T HINGE
tee–hole \ˈ=,=\ *n* [fr. gerund of ⁴*tee*] *dial Eng* : the entrance to a beehive
teeing ground *n* [fr. gerund of ⁴*tee*] : ³TEE 2
tee iron *var of* T IRON
tee joint *also* **tee connection** *n* [¹*tee*] : an electrical connection used for joining a branch conductor to a main conductor where the main conductor continues beyond the branch
teel *var of* TIL
teel oil *n* : SESAME OIL
¹teem \ˈtēm\ *vb* -ED/-ING/-S [ME *temen, teamen,* fr. OE *tīeman, tǣman, tȳman;* akin to OE *tēam* offspring — more at TEAM] *vt, archaic* : to bring forth : give birth to : PRODUCE ⟨the even mead . . . conceives by idleness and nothing ~*s* but hateful docks —Shak.⟩ ~ *vi* **1** *obs* **a** : to bring forth offspring : give birth **b** : to become pregnant : CONCEIVE ⟨if that the earth could ~ with woman's tears, each drop she falls would prove a crocodile —Shak.⟩ **2 a** : to be marked by fertility : become filled to overflowing : ABOUND, SWARM — usu. used with *with* ⟨the inland lakes ~ with pike —*Amer. Guide Series: Mich.*⟩ ⟨this sprawling boisterous capital which ~*s* with color and historic interest —A.J.Mathers⟩ **b** : to be present in such large quantity as to cause overflowing ⟨a score of plans were ~*ing* in his mind —Edna Ferber⟩
²teem \"\ *vb* -ED/-ING/-S [ME *temen,* fr. ON *tœma;* akin to OE *tōm* empty, OHG *zuomig,* ON *tōmr*] *vt* **1** *archaic* : EMPTY **2** : POUR; *specif* : to pour (molten metal) into a mold ~ *vi* : POUR; *esp* : to rain in torrents
teem·er \-mə(r)\ *n* -S : one that teems; *specif* : a workman who controls the rate at which stainless steel is poured into molds
teem·ful \-mfəl\ *adj* [¹*teem* + *-ful*] : PRODUCTIVE, FRUITFUL — **teem·ful·ness** *n* -ES
teem·ing·ly *adv* [*teeming* (pres. part. of ¹*teem*) + *-ly*] : in a teeming manner
teem·ing·ness *n* -ES : the state or quality of being teeming
teemless *adj* [¹*teem* + *-less*] *obs* : BARREN
teems \ˈtēmz\ *n pl* [pl. of E dial. *teem* large quantity, fr. ¹*teem*] *dial Brit* : LOT 9
¹teen \ˈtēn\ *n* -S [ME *tene,* fr. OE *tēona* injury, anger, grief; akin to OFris *tiona* injury, OS *tiono,* ON *tjōn,* and perh. to Gk *daiein* to kindle, burn up, Skt *dunoti* he burns, distresses] **1** *obs* : INJURY, DAMAGE, HURT **2** *chiefly Scot* : IRRITATION,

ANGER **3** *archaic* **:** GRIEF, MISERY, AFFLICTION ⟨with public toil and private ~ thou sank'st alone —Matthew Arnold⟩
²teen \"\ *var of* TIND
³teen \"\ *adj* [*-teen* (as in *thirteen*)] **:** TEENAGE ⟨about the beginning of the ~ period —John Ruskin⟩
teen·age \'ˌ=\ *adj* [*-teen* (as in *thirteen*) + *age*] **:** of, being, or relating to people in their teens
teen-aged \'ˌ=\ *adj* [*-teen* (as in *thirteen*) + *aged*] **:** TEENAGE
teen·ag·er \'tēˌnājə(r)\ *n* -s [*teenage* + *-er*] **:** a person in his teens
teename *var of* TO-NAME
teen·er \'tēnə(r)\ *n* -s [*-teen* (as in *thirteen*) + *-er*] **:** TEENAGER
teens \'tēnz\ *n pl* [*-teen* (as in *thirteen*)] **1 :** the numbers 13 to 19 inclusive; *specif* **:** the years 13 to 19 in a lifetime ⟨in his ~⟩ or in a particular century **2 :** TEENAGERS ⟨the ~ want fun and glamour —*Parents' Mag.*⟩
teens·ter \'tēnztə(r), -n(t)st-\ *n* -s [*teens* + *-ster*] **:** TEENAGER
teen·sy *also* **teent·sy** \'tēn(t)sē\ *adj* -ER/-EST [alter. of *teeny*] **:** TINY ⟨just a ~ keg of whiskey —A.B.Guthrie⟩
teen·sy-ween·sy *also* **teent·sy-weent·sy** *or* **teen·sie-ween·sie** \ˌtēn(t)sēˈwēn(t)sē\ *adj* [alter. of *teeny-weeny*] **:** TINY ⟨another *teensy-weensy* martini —Merle Miller⟩
teen·ty \'tēntē\ *adj* -ER/-EST [alter. of *teeny*] **:** TINY ⟨the least little ~ hands —Mary S. Watts⟩
tee·ny \'tēnē, -ni\ *adj* -ER/-EST [alter. (influenced by *weeny*) of *tiny*] **:** TINY ⟨cheated just a ~ bit⟩ **syn** see SMALL
tee·ny-wee·ny *also* **tee·nie-wee·nie** \ˌtēnēˈwēnē\ *adj* [*teeny* + *weeny*] **:** TINY ⟨even a pair of *teeny-weeny* rubber gloves in the kitchen —V.V.Nabokov⟩
tee off *vi* [⁴*tee*] **1 :** to drive from a tee **2 :** BEGIN, START ⟨the book *tees off* with a discussion of bitterness —*Holiday*⟩ **3 :** to hit hard ⟨*teed off* on the new pitcher's first delivery and sent it over the center-field wall —Bennett Cerf⟩ **4 :** to make an angry denunciation **:** SCOLD — often used with *on* ⟨*teed off* on the selection committee in an ill-tempered article —*Time*⟩
teepee *var of* TEPEE
tee·ple·ite \'tēpəˌlīt\ *n* -s [John E. *Teeple* †1931 Am. chemist + E *-ite*] **:** a mineral $NaBO_2Cl.2H_2O$ consisting of hydrous chloride and borate of sodium
tees *pl of* TEE, *pres 3d sing of* TEE
tee shirt *var of* T-SHIRT
tee slot *var of* T SLOT
tee square *var of* T SQUARE
teest \'tēst\ *n* -s [origin unknown] **:** a small anvil
tees·water \'tēz+ˌ-\ *n* [*Tees*, river of northern England + *water*] **1** *usu cap* **:** an extinct British breed of cattle believed to have been the principal stock from which the Shorthorns are derived **2** -s *often cap* **:** an animal of the Teeswater breed
teetee *var of* TITI
¹tee·ter \'tēd·ə(r), -ētə-\ *vb* -ED/-ING/-S [alter. of earlier *titter*, fr. ME *titeren* to totter, reel, sway; akin to OHG *zittarōn* to shiver, shake, ON *titra* to twinkle, shiver, Gk *apodidraskein* to run away, *dramein* to run, Skt *drāti* he runs — more at DROMEDARY] *vi* **1 a :** to move unsteadily: as (1) **:** to progress (as by walking) unsteadily ⟨~*ed* across the half-finished bridge —Burgess Scott⟩ (2) **:** to move unsteadily before or as if before falling **:** WOBBLE ⟨stood on chairs and ~*ed* on stepladders —John Dos Passos⟩ **b** (1) **:** to waver precariously **:** show signs of possible impending failure ⟨for the next few days the attack would ~ from enemy counterattacks —Norman Mailer⟩ — often used with *on* ⟨is always ~*ing* on the edge of catastrophe —Charles Hamblett⟩ (2) **:** to oscillate unsteadily esp. in a dangerous position ⟨a passive type who ~s between conformity and revolt —R.N.Denney⟩ **2 :** SEESAW ⟨took the little girl to the park so that she could ~⟩ ~ *vt* **:** SEESAW ⟨~*ed* his chair and sighed —G.A.Chamberlain⟩
²teeter \"\ *n* -s **1** [so called fr. the teetering movements of its tail] **:** SPOTTED SANDPIPER **2 :** an act of teetering **3 :** SEESAW 2b **4 :** a transverse rolling or rocking in a spring suspension **:** UNDULATION
teeterboard \'==ˌ=\ *n* [¹*teeter* + *board*] **1** *also* **teetering board :** SEESAW 2b **2 :** a board placed on a raised support in such a way that a person standing on one end of the board is thrown into the air if another person jumps on the opposite end
teetertail \'==ˌ=\ *n* [¹*teeter* + *tail*] **:** SPOTTED SANDPIPER
¹tee·ter-tot·ter \'tēd·ə(r),tād·ə(r), 'tētə(r),tätə(r)\ *vi* [alter. of E dial. *titter-totter*, game of seesawing, fr. obs. *titter* to teeter + *totter* — more at TEETER] **:** SEESAW
²teeter-totter \"\ *n* -s **:** SEESAW
tee·tery \'tēd·ərē\ *adj* [¹*teeter* + *-y*] **:** TOTTERY
teeth *pl of* TOOTH
teethe \'tēth\ *vb* -ED/-ING/-S [back-formation fr. *teething*] *vi* **:** to cut one's teeth **:** grow teeth ~ *or* **teeth** \'tēth\ *vt, chiefly Scot* **:** to provide (as a comb or harrow) with teeth
teeth·er \-thə(r)\ *n* -s [*teethe* + *-er*] **:** an object (as a teething ring) designed for a baby to chew on safely during teething
teeth·i·ly \'tēthəlē\ *adv* [¹*teethy* + *-ly*] *chiefly Scot* **:** IRRITABLY, CROSSLY
teeth·ing \'tēthiŋ, -thēn\ *n* -s [*teeth* + *-ing*] **1 :** the first growth of teeth **2 :** the phenomena accompanying the growth of teeth through the gums

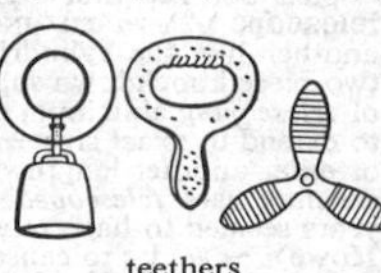
teethers

teething ring *n* **:** a ring usu. of rubber or plastic for a teething infant to bite on
teeth·less \'tēthləs\ *adj* **:** having no teeth
teethridge \'=ˌ=\ *n* **:** the inner surface of the gums of the upper front teeth
¹teethy \'tēthi\ *adj* [ME *tethee*, perh. fr. *tethen* to teethe (fr. *teth, teeth* teeth) + *-ee -y*; fr. the irritability of teething infants] *chiefly Scot* **:** IRRITABLE, CROSS
²teethy \'tēthē, 'tēthē\ *adj* -ER/-EST [*teeth* + *-y*] **:** TOOTHY
¹tee·to·tal \'tē¦tōd·ᵊl, -ōtᵊl\ *adj* [*total* + *total* (*abstinence*)] **1 a :** of or relating to total abstinence from alcoholic drinks ⟨the ~ movement was strong in the state capital —S.H.Adams⟩ **b :** totally abstaining from alcoholic drinks ⟨the stale joke of a ~ spinster getting drunk and amorous —E.R.Bentley⟩ **2 :** TOTAL, COMPLETE, ABSOLUTE ⟨rest in ~ peace —Della Lutes⟩ — **tee·to·tal·ly** \-ᵊlē\ *adv*
²teetotal \"\ *vi* **:** to advocate or practice teetotalism
tee·to·tal·er *or* **tee·to·tal·ler** \-ᵊlə(r)\ *n* -s **:** one that practices or advocates total abstinence from alcoholic drinks
tee·to·tal·ism \-ᵊlˌizəm\ *n* -s [¹*teetotal* + *-ism*] **:** the principle or the practice of complete abstinence from alcoholic drinks
tee·to·tal·ist \-ᵊləst\ *n* -s [¹*teetotal* + *-ist*] **:** one who advocates or practices teetotalism
¹tee·to·tum \(')tē¦tōd·əm, -ōtəm\ *n* -s [¹*tee* + L *totum* all, the whole, fr. neut. of *totus* whole, entire; fr. the letter *T* inscribed on one side as an abbr. of *totum* (take) all] **1 :** a small top inscribed with letters and used in playing put-and-take; *also* **:** PUT-AND-TAKE **2 :** a small top
²teetotum \"\ *vi* -ED/-ING/-S **:** to spin like a teetotum
tee·vee \'tē'vē\ *n* -s [¹*tee* + *vee;* fr. the abbr. *TV*] **:** TELEVISION
teff \'tef\ *also* **teff grass** *n* -s [Amharic *ṭēf*] **:** an economically important African cereal grass (*Eragrostis abyssinica*) used for its grain which yields a white flour of good quality and as a forage and hay crop
te·fil·lin *or* **te·phil·lin** *also* **tfil·lin** \tə'filən *also* -lēm\ *n pl but sometimes sing in constr* [LHeb *tĕphillīn*, fr. Aram, attachments; akin to Heb *tāphēl* whitewash, mortar] **:** the phylacteries worn by Jews
teg *also* **tegg** \'teg\ *n* -s [origin unknown] **1 :** a doe in its second year **2 a** *chiefly Brit* **:** a sheep in its second year **b :** the fleece cut from a sheep in its second year
TEG *abbr, often not cap* top edges gilt
teg·e·nar·ia \ˌtejə'na(a)rēə\ *n, cap* [NL] **:** a genus of spiders related to *Agalena*
teg·e·tic·u·la \ˌtejə'tikyələ\ *n, cap* [NL, fr. L, little mat, dim. of *teget-, teges* covering, mat, fr. *tegere* to cover — more at THATCH] **:** a genus of moths (family Tineidae) that includes the yucca moth
teg·men \'tegmən\ *n, pl* **tegmi·na** \-mənə\ [NL, fr. L *tegmen, tegumen*, covering, cover, fr. *tegere* to cover] **:** INTEGUMENT, COVERING: as **a :** ENDOPLEURA **b** (1) **:** one of the elytra of a beetle (2) **:** one of the thickened forewings of various orthopterans **c** *or* **tegmen tympani :** a thin plate of bone that covers the middle ear and separates it from the cranial cavity
teg·men·tal \(')teg¦mentᵊl\ *adj* [L & NL *tegmentum* + E *-al*] **1 :** of or relating to an integument **2 :** of, relating to, or associated with a tegmentum esp. of the brain
teg·men·tum \teg'mentəm\ *or* **teg·u·men·tum** \-gyə'-\ *n, pl* **tegmen·ta** *or* **tegumen·ta** \-tə\ [NL, fr. L, covering, integument — more at TEGUMENT] **:** COVERING: as **a :** the part of the cerebral peduncles above the substantia nigra formed of longitudinal white fibers with arched transverse fibers and gray matter **b** (1) **:** the outer covering of scales on a leaf bud (2) **:** one of these scales **c :** the outer layer of a plate of a chiton — compare ARTICULAMENTUM
tegu *var of* TEJU
te·gua \'tāgwə\ *n* -s [Keresan] **:** an ankle-high rawhide moccasin of the southwestern U. S. and Mexico
te·gu·ci·gal·pa \tə¦güsə¦galpə\ *adj, usu cap* [fr. *Tegucigalpa*, capital of Honduras] **:** of or from Tegucigalpa, the capital of Honduras **:** of the kind or style prevalent in Tegucigalpa
te·guex·in \tə'gweksən\ *n* -s [NL *teguixin* (specific epithet of *Tupinambis teguixin*, genus of lizards), fr. Nahuatl *tecoixin, tecuixin*] **:** a bluish black teju (*Tupinambis teguixin*) with pale or whitish yellow spots on the back
teg·u·la \'tegyələ\ *n* [NL, fr. L, tile — more at THATCH] **1** *pl* **tegu·lae** \-yəˌlē\ **a :** one of a pair of small scalelike sclerites of the mesothorax of some insects (as of the orders Hymenoptera and Lepidoptera) that cover the bases of the forewings **b :** a patagium of a lepidopterous insect **c :** the alula of a dipterous insect **2** *cap* **:** a widely distributed genus of turban shells sometimes used for food
teg·u·lar \-yələ(r)\ *adj* [L & NL *tegula* + E *-ar*] **1 :** of, relating to, or resembling a tile **2 :** of or relating to a tegula — **teg·u·lar·ly** *adv*
teg·u·ment \'tegyəmənt\ *n* -s [ME, fr. L *tegmentum, tegumentum*, fr. *tegere* to cover + *-mentum*, -ment — more at THATCH] **:** INTEGUMENT — **teg·u·men·tal** \ˌtegyə'mentᵊl\ *adj*
teg·u·men·tary \¦==¦mentərē, -ri\ *adj* [*tegument* + *-ary*] **:** of, relating to, or consisting of an integument **:** serving as a covering ⟨the reduction of the ~ tissues goes very far in some seeds —A.J.Eames & L.H.MacDaniels⟩
te·gu·ri·um *or* **tu·gu·ri·um** \tə'gyürēəm\ *n, pl* **teguria** *or* **tuguria** [LL, covering, shrine, fr. L, hut, cottage, perh. fr. *tegere* to cover] **:** a roof over an altar or a sarcophagus usu. supported by light columns and often pointed
¹te·hee *or* **tee-hee** \'tē'hē\ *n* -s [ME *te he*, of imit. origin] **:** a laugh in a high voice — often used interjectionally
²tehee *or* **tee-hee** \"\ *vi* **teheed** *or* **tee-heed; teheed** *or* **tee-heed; teheeing** *or* **tee-heeing; tehees** *or* **tee-hees :** to laugh in a high voice esp. in superficial amusement or derision **:** TITTER
te·hin·nah *or* **te·chin·nah** \tə'kinə\ *n, pl* **tehin·noth** *or* **tehin·not** *or* **techin·noth** *or* **techin·not** \təkiˈnōt(h)\ [Yiddish *tekhine*, fr. LHeb *tăhanūn* prayer for grace — more at TAHANUN] **1 :** a prayer in Yiddish used by Jewish women only **2 :** a book of tehinnoth
teh·ran *or* **te·he·ran** \ˌtāə'ran, ˌteə-, -ˌ'rän *sometimes* tə'ran *or* tā'- *or* -'rän\ *adj, usu cap* [fr. *Tehran, Teheran*, capital of Iran] **:** of or from Tehran, the capital of Iran **:** of the kind or style prevalent in Tehran
te·huan·te·pec·er \tə'wäntəˌpekə(r)\ *n* -s *usu cap* [Gulf of *Tehuantepec*, inlet of the Pacific, southeastern Mexico + E *-er*] **:** a violent north wind that brings an inflow of cold air to Central America and esp. to regions around the Gulf of Tehuantepec
te·huel·che \tə'welchē\ *n, pl* **tehuelche** *or* **tehuelches** *usu cap* [Araucanian, lit., people of the southeast] **1 a :** a Chonan people of southern Argentina **b :** a member of such people **2 :** the language of the Tehuelche people — **te·huel·che·an** \-ēən\ *adj, usu cap*
teian \'tē(y)ən\ *adj, usu cap* [L *teius* (fr. Gk *tēios*, fr. *Tēos, Teōs* Teos, ancient Greek city of Asia Minor) + E *-an*] **:** of or relating to Teos ⟨produce his dainty translations of the *Teian* bard —Thomas Walsh⟩
teich·mann's crystal \'tīkmənz-\ *n, usu cap T* [after L. K. *Teichmann*-Stawiarski †1895 Ger. anatomist] **:** one of the crystals of hemin obtainable from hemoglobin and useful as a test for blood **:** BLOOD CRYSTAL
teig·lach *also* **taig·lach** *or* **teig·lech** \'tāgləḳ, 'tīg-\ *n pl but sing or pl in constr* [Yiddish *teyglekh*, dim. of *teyg* dough, fr. MHG *teig, teic*, fr. OHG *teic* — more at DOUGH] **:** small pieces of dough boiled in honey
¹teiid \'tē(y)əd\ *adj* [NL *Teiidae*] **:** of or relating to the Teiidae
²teiid \"\ *n* -s **:** a lizard of the family Teiidae
teiidae \'tē(y)əˌdē\ *n pl, cap* [NL, fr. *Teius*, type genus (fr. Pg *tejú, teiú* teju) + *-idae* — more at TEJU] **:** a family of mostly tropical American lizards (as the tejus of So. America and the race runner of the western U. S.) having a flat elongate scaly tongue that ends in two long smooth points
teil tree \'tē(ə)l-\ *also* **teil** *n* -s [F dial. *teil*, fr. OF, fr. L *tilia*] **:** LINDEN 1a
teind \'tēnd\ *n* -s [ME *tend, teind*, fr. *tende, tend, teind* tenth; akin to OHG *zehanto* tenth, ON *tīundi;* Goth *taihunda*, Gk *dekatos;* all fr. a prehistoric IE adjective fr. the source of OE *tīen* ten] **1** *chiefly Scot* **:** TITHE **2 :** the part of the estates of the Scottish laity that can be assessed for the stipend of the clergy of the established church
teind·able \-dəbəl\ *adj* [Sc *teind* to assess tithes (fr. ME *tenden, teinden*, fr. *teind*) + *-able*] *Scot* **:** TITHABLE
teind boll *n, Scot* **:** a boll of grain accepted as tithe
teind court *n, usu cap T&C* **:** a court for the control of teinds consisting of the judges of the Court of Session
tein·ite \'tāˌnīt\ *n* -s [*Teine*, name of a mine in Hokkaido, Japan + E *-ite*] **:** a mineral $Cu_{13}(SO_4)_3(TeO_4)_{10}.26H_2O$ consisting of hydrous sulfate and tellurate of copper
teist·ie \'tīsti, 'tēs-\ *Scot var of* TYSTIE
teize \'tēz\ *archaic var of* TEASE
te·ja·no \tā'hä(ˌ)nō\ *n* -s [Sp, fr. *Tejas* Texas + *-ano* -an, fr. L *-anus*] *Southwest* **:** TEXAN
te·ji·dae \'tejəˌdē, 'tej-\ [NL, fr. *Tejus*, genus of lizards (fr. Pg *tejú, teiú* teju) + *-idae*] *syn of* TEIIDAE
te·ju \tə'zhü\ *also* **te·gu** \-'gü\ *n* -s [Pg *tejú, tetú*, fr. Tupi & Guarani *tejú, teyú*] **:** any of several large blackish So. American lizards of the genus *Tupinambis* (family Teiidae) that have yellow or white bands across the back, grow to a length of about three feet, often raid hen roosts, and are hunted as pests and for their flesh which is regarded as a delicacy
te·ki·ah \tə'kēə\ *n, pl* **teki·oth** *or* **teki·ot** \təkē'ōt(h)\ *or* **tekiahs** [Heb *tĕqī'āh*] **:** one of the long deep calls sounded on the shofar as prescribed in the Jewish ritual for Rosh Hashanah and Yom Kippur — compare TERUAH
te·kint·si \tə'kin(t)sē\ *n, pl* **tekintsi** *or* **tekintsis** *usu cap* **:** ¹TEKKE
¹tek·ke \'tek,kē\ *n, pl* **tekke** *or* **tekkes** *usu cap* **1 :** a Turkoman people living on the frontiers of Iran, Afghanistan, and the Turkmen S.S.R. **2 :** a member of the Tekke people
²tekke *n, pl* **tekkes** *also* **tekke** [Turk] **:** a dervish monastery
tek·non·y·mous \(')tek¦nänəməs\ *adj* **:** of or relating to teknonymy — **tek·non·y·mous·ly** *adv*
tek·non·y·my \tek'nänəmē\ *n* -ES [Gk *teknon* child + E *-onymy* — more at THANE] **:** the custom of naming the parent after the child
tek·tite \'tek,tīt\ *n* -s [ISV *tekt-* (fr. Gk *tēktos* molten, fr. *tēkein* to melt) + *-ite* — more at THAW] **:** a glassy body of probably meteoritic origin and of rounded but indefinite shape found esp. in Czechoslovakia, Indonesia, and Australia
¹tel- *or* **tele-** *also* **telo-** *comb form* [NL, fr. Gk *tēl-, tēle-* far, far off, distant, fr. *tēle* — more at PALE-] **1 :** distant **:** at a distance **:** over a distance ⟨*telegram*⟩ ⟨*telegnosis*⟩ ⟨*telekinesis*⟩ ⟨*telesthesia*⟩ ⟨*television*⟩ ⟨*telodynamic*⟩ **2 a :** telegraph ⟨*teletape*⟩ ⟨*teletypewriter*⟩ **b :** television ⟨*telecamera*⟩ **c :** telephoto ⟨*telelens*⟩ **d :** telecommunication ⟨*teleman*⟩
²tel- *or* **telo-** *also* **tele-** *comb form* [ISV, fr. Gk *tel-, telo-*, fr. *telos* end, consummation, completeness — more at WHEEL] **1 :** end ⟨*telangiectasia*⟩ ⟨*teloblast*⟩ ⟨*telemetacarpal*⟩ **2 :** complete **:** mature ⟨*Telanthera*⟩ ⟨*Telanthropus*⟩
tel *abbr* **1** telegram **2** telegraph; telegraphic; telegraphy **3** telephone; telephony
TEL *abbr* tetraethyl lead
te·la \'tēlə\ *n, pl* **te·lae** \-ˌlē\ [NL, fr. L, web — more at TOIL] **:** an anatomical tissue or layer of tissue: as **a :** a fold of pia mater roofing a ventricle of the brain **b :** a layer of loose connective tissue separating layers of other tissues — **te·lar** \-lə(r)\ *adj*
telaesthesia *var of* TELESTHESIA
telaesthetic *var of* TELESTHETIC
te·la·ku·cha \tə'läkəˌchä\ *n* -s [Bengali *telākucā*] **:** IVY GOURD
tel·a·mon \'teləˌmän, -ˌmən\ *n, pl* **telamo·nes** \ˌ=='mō(ˌ)nēz\ [L, fr. Gk *telamōn* bearer, supporter, fr. the stem of *tlēnai* to bear — more at TOLERATE] **1 :** a male figure used like a caryatid as a supporting column or pilaster **:** ATLAS 4 **2** [NL, fr. L] **:** an accessory outgrowth of the cloacal wall forming part of the copulatory apparatus of various male nematode worms
tel·ang \'te,lanj\ *adj* [by shortening] **:** TELANGIECTATIC ⟨a ~ bovine liver⟩
tel·an·gi·ectasia *or* **tel·an·gi·ectasis** \tə¦lanjē, te¦l-+\ *n, pl* **telangiectasias** *or* **telangiectases** [NL, fr. ²*tel-* + *angi-* + *ectasia* or *ectasis*] **1 :** an abnormal dilatation of capillary vessels and arterioles that often forms an angioma; *specif* **:** a pathological state of the bovine liver in which dilated capillaries form small angiomas and there is excessive storage of vitamin A **2 :** a hereditary abnormality inherited as a simple dominant and characterized by bleeding into the tissues and mucous surfaces because of the abnormal fragility of the capillaries — **tel·an·gi·ectatic** \"+\ *adj*
tel·an·thera \tə'lan(t)thərə, te'l-\ *n* [NL, fr. ²*tel-* + *-anthera*] **1** *cap* **:** a genus of tropical herbs or shrubs (family Amaranthaceae) that is commonly included in the genus *Alternanthera* from which it may be distinguished by the presence of five stamens and five staminodia united into a tube and that comprises plants with inconspicuous whitish flowers and showy brightly colored foliage which are often used for carpet bedding **2** -s **:** ALTERNANTHERA 2
tel·an·thro·pus \tə'lan(t)thrəpəs, te'l-; ˌte,lan'thrōp-\ *n, cap* [NL, fr. ²*tel-* + *-anthropus*] **:** a genus of southern African fossil hominids that is based on an incomplete lower jaw and associated teeth and is held to comprise forms intermediate in some respects between the australopithecines and true man
tel·au·to·gram \te'lȯd·əˌgram\ *n* [ISV *telautograph* + *-gram*] **:** a message or other facsimile transmitted and recorded by a TelAutograph device
Tel·Au·to·graph \-raf, -räf\ *trademark* — used for a facsimile telegraph for reproducing graphic matter by means of a transmitter in which the motions of a pencil are communicated by levers to two rotary shafts that produce variations in current in two separate circuits and by means of a receiver in which these variations are utilized by electromagnetic devices and levers to move a pen as the pencil moves
tel aviv \ˌtelə¦vēv\ *adj, usu cap T&A* [fr. *Tel Aviv*, Israel] **:** of or from the city of Tel Aviv, Israel **:** of the kind or style prevalent in Tel Aviv
tel aviv·ian \ˌtelə'vēvēən, -vēvyən\ *n* -s *cap T&A* [*Tel Aviv*, Israel + E *-ian*] **:** a native or resident of Tel Aviv, Israel
¹tele \'telē\ *n* -s [Gk *tēle* far, far off, distant — more at PALE-] **:** mutual feeling or psychic affinity between two or more people
²tele \'telē, -lə\ *n* -s [by shortening] **:** TELEVISION
¹tele- — see ¹TEL-
²tele- *or* **teleo-** *comb form* [NL, fr. Gk *teleio-, teleo-*, fr. *teleios, teleos*, fr. *telos* end, consummation, completeness — more at WHEEL] **:** complete **:** perfect ⟨*teleodont*⟩ ⟨*Teleocephali*⟩
³tele- — see ²TEL-
tele·binocular \ˌtelə+\ *n* [¹*tel-* + *binocular*] **:** a stereoscopic instrument for determining various eye defects, measuring visual acuity or fusion of images, and conducting orthoptic training
tel·e·blem \'teləˌblem\ *n* -s [¹*tel-* + *-blem* (as in *periblem*)] **:** UNIVERSAL VEIL
tele·camera \¦telə +\ *n* [¹*tel-* + *camera*] **:** a television camera
¹tele·cast \'telə+ˌ-\ *n* -s [¹*tel-* + broad*cast*] **:** a broadcasting or a program broadcast by television
²telecast \"\ *vb* **telecast** *also* **telecasted; telecast** *also* **telecasted; telecasting; telecasts :** to broadcast by television
tele·cast·er \"ə(r)\ *n* -s **:** a television broadcaster
tele·cen·tric \ˌtelə¦sen·trik\ *adj* [¹*tel-* + *-centric*] **:** of or relating to a telecentric lens
telecentric lens *n* **:** a lens system in which either the entrance pupil or the exit pupil is at infinity and which is used in optical measuring devices to eliminate parallax between an image and the scale for its measurement
tele·cine \ˌtelə¦sinē\ *n* [¹*tel-* + *cine*] **:** a televised motion picture ⟨~ equipment⟩ ⟨a ~ program⟩ ⟨~ transmission⟩
tele·communication \ˌtelə+\ *n* [ISV ¹*tel-* + *communication*] **1 :** communication at a distance (as by cable, radio, telegraph, telephone, or television) **2 :** the science that deals with telecommunication ⟨study ~⟩ — usu. used in pl.
tele·control \"+\ *n* [¹*tel-* + *control*] **:** remote control utilizing radio, wire transmission line, or sound waves
tele·course \'telə+ˌ-\ *n* [¹*tel-* + *course*] **:** a course of study conducted over television
teledendron *var of* TELODENDRION
tel·e·du \'teləˌdü\ *n* -s [Malay *tĕledu*] **:** a small carnivorous mammal (*Mydaus meliceps*) of the mountains of Java and Sumatra resembling the badger and like the skunk secreting an offensive fluid which it can expel a short distance and being blackish brown with a yellowish white stripe down the back — called also *Javanese skunk*
tel·e·fer·ic \ˌteləˈferik\ *also* **tel·e·fe·rique** \ˌteləfə'rēk\ *n* -s [*teleferic* fr. It *teleferica*, fem. of *teleferico* of telpherage, fr. F *téléphérique*, fr. *téléphérage* telpherage (alter. of *telpherage*, fr. E *telpherage*) + *-ique* -ic; *teleferique* fr. F *téléférique*, fr. It *teleferica*] **:** TELPHER
tele·film \'telə+ˌ-\ *n* [¹*tel-* + *film*] **:** a motion picture produced for televising
teleg *abbr* **1** telegram **2** telegraph; telegraphic; telegraphy
te·le·ga \tə'legə, təl'ye-\ *n* -s [Russ] **:** a 4-wheeled springless wagon used by the Russians
tel·e·gen·ic \ˌtelə¦jenik\ *adj* [¹*tel-* + *-genic*] **:** eminently suitable for broadcast by television; *esp* **:** having an appearance and manner that are markedly attractive to television viewers — **tel·e·gen·i·cal·ly** \-nək(ə)lē\ *adv*
tel·eg·no·sis \ˌtelə¦nōsəs, ˌte,leg'n-\ *n* -ES [NL, fr. ¹*tel-* + *-gnosis*] **:** knowledge of distant happenings obtained by occult or unknown means **:** CLAIRVOYANCE — **tel·egnos·tic** \¦=(ˌ)=¦nästik\ *adj*
te·leg·o·ny \tə'legənē\ *n* -ES [ISV ¹*tel-* + *-gony*] **:** the supposed carrying over of the influence of a sire to the offspring of subsequent matings of the dam with other males — compare SATURATION
¹tel·e·gram \'teləˌgram, -raa(ə)m, *South also* -ˌgrəm\ *n* [¹*tel-* + *-gram*] **:** a message by telegraph; *esp* **:** one sent at the regular daytime rate
²telegram \"\ *vb* **telegrammed; telegrammed; telegramming; telegrams :** TELEGRAPH
tel·e·gram·mat·ic \ˌteləgrə¦mad·|ik, -ˌgra¦m-, -at|, |ēk\ *adj* [*telegram* + *-atic* (as in *epigrammatic*)] **:** TELEGRAMMIC
tel·e·gram·mic \-ˌ¦gramik\ *adj* **:** relating to or resembling a telegram **:** LACONIC, BRIEF ⟨scribbled her ~ poems on torn-off newspaper margins and old envelopes —J.T.Winterich⟩
¹tel·e·graph \'teləˌgraf, -raa(ə)f, -raif, -räf\ *n, often attrib* [F *télégraphe*, fr. *télé-* ¹*tel-* + *-graphe* -graph] **1 a :** an apparatus for communication at a distance by means of preconcerted signals; *broadly* **:** an apparatus, system, or process for communication at a distance other than the ordinary ones of speech and letter writing — compare SEMAPHORE **b :** an electrical apparatus consisting essentially of a wire that forms a complete circuit, a source of current, a transmitter by which the circuit can be made or broken at will, and a receiver that is affected by every make and break so that an audible or visual indication is given (as by deflection of a pointer, marks made on a moving tape, or sharp clicks) — compare PRINTER 2b **c :** an electrical or mechanical apparatus that is used on a ship for issuing or repeating orders from and to the bridge **2 :** TELEGRAM **3 :** a device (as an elevated board or frame-

work) on which information can be displayed (as for the benefit of spectators at a game or race) **4** : an inclined trough, chute, or similar device through which coal or other material slides to a lower level **5** : TELEGRAPH STAMP

²telegraph \"\ *vb* -ED/-ING/-S *vt* **1 a** : to send or communicate by or as if by telegraph ⟨~ news⟩ ⟨~ congratulations⟩ ⟨sensory nerves which immediately ~ to the brain the sensations experienced by them —T.D.Buchanan⟩ ⟨the kiss from her full, pouty lips ~*ed* itself to his toes —T.W.Duncan⟩ **b** : to send a telegram to **c** : to send (as flowers or money) by means of a telegraphic order **2** : to display (as a score) on a telegraph board **3 a** : to make known by signs : SIGNAL ⟨a look about him which ~*ed* bad news —Niven Busch⟩ ⟨a jaw that ~*ed* to every movie villain that here was a man who would take no foolishness —Emmett Kelly⟩ **b** : to reveal unknowingly and in advance the intention with respect to (as a blow, move, or pitch) ⟨swung, but he ~*ed* it and the other ducked easily —G.A.Wagner⟩ ~ *vi* **1** : to send a telegram : communicate or signal by telegraph **2** : to telegraph something

telegraph block *n* : a block with many small sheaves used in making nautical flag signals

telegraph blue *n* : a grayish purple that is bluer and darker than mauve gray, bluer and duller than average orchid gray, and bluer and paler than average rose mauve

telegraph board *n* : TELEGRAPH 3

telegraph cable *n* : a telegraphic cable of several conducting wires enclosed by an insulating and protecting material so as to bring the wires into compact compass for use on poles or to form a strong cable impervious to water to be laid under ground or under water

telegraph editor *n* : an editor who handles the copy that comes into a newspaper or news periodical office by wire

te·leg·ra·pher \tə'legrəfə(r); 'telə,grafə(r), -raaf-, -raif-, -räf-\ *n* -S [¹*telegraph* + *-er*] : one that sends and receives telegraphic messages : telegraphic operator

tel·e·graph·ese \,telə,gra¦fēz, -raa¦f-, -rai¦f-, -rä¦f-, -ēs\ *n* -S [¹*telegraph* + *-ese*] : language characterized by the terseness and elliptical expressions that are common in telegrams ⟨~ style . . . is distinguished by its omission of articles, relatives, connectives, personal, demonstrative and other pronouns, and auxiliary verbs —Richard Hoggart⟩ ⟨in vivid ~ which combined pithy comment with a tart humor —*Notes & Queries*⟩

tel·e·graph·ic \¦telə¦grafik, -fēk\ *adj* [¹*telegraph* + *-ic*] **1** : of or relating to the telegraph ⟨a ~ machine⟩ : made or communicated by a telegraph ⟨a ~ report⟩ ⟨~ news⟩ **2** : communicated over a distance as if by telegraph ⟨stopped in answer to a ~ glance from his companion⟩ **3** : having the style of a telegram; *esp* : SHORT, CONCISE, TERSE ⟨with ~ economy of words —F.S.Mitchell⟩ ⟨the author's ~ style with its verbless sentences and one-lined paragraphs —Grace Frank⟩ **4** : being a place for the receipt of telegrams ⟨my ~ address while I am away from home⟩ — **tel·e·graph·i·cal·ly** \-fək(ə)lē, -fēk-, -li\ *adv*

telegraphic transfer *n, chiefly Brit* : CABLE TRANSFER

te·leg·ra·phist \tə'legrəfəst; 'telə,grafəst, -raaf-, -raif-, -räf-\ *n* -S [F *télégraphiste*, fr. *télégraphe* + *-iste* -ist] : one skilled in telegraphy : TELEGRAPHER

te·leg·ra·phone \tə'legrə,fōn\ *n* [Dan *telegrafon*, fr. *tele-* ¹tel- + *-grafon* (blend of *graf-* graph- and *-fon* -phone)] : an early magnetic recorder

tel·e·graph·o·scope \,telə'grafə,skōp\ *n* [¹*telegraph* + *-o-* + *-scope*] : an early device for transmitting pictures over a telegraph circuit

telegraph plant *n* : an East Indian tick trefoil (*Desmodium gyrans*) whose lateral leaflets jerk up and down like the arms of a semaphore and also rotate on their axes

telegraph stamp *n* : a stamp for use as evidence that charges on a telegram have been paid

te·leg·ra·phy \tə'legrəfē, -fi\ *n* -ES [¹*tel-* + *-graphy*] **1 a** : the use or operation of a telegraph apparatus or system esp. of the electric telegraph for transmitting or receiving communications **b** : the occupation of one who specializes in such use or operation ⟨railroad ~⟩ **c** : a system of communication by telegraph and esp. electric telegraph **2** : the transmission of intelligence or information over a distance as if by telegraph ⟨mental ~⟩

telegu *usu cap, var of* TELUGU

tel·ei \'te(,)lā\ *n, pl* **telei** *or* **teleis** *usu cap* **1 a** : a Papuan people on Bougainville, Solomon islands **b** : a member of such people **2** : the language of the Telei people

tele·ki·ne·sis \,teləkə'nēsəs, -,kī-\ *n, pl* **telekine·ses** \-ē,sēz\ [NL, fr. ¹*tel-* + *-kinesis*] : the apparent production of motion in objects (as by a spiritualistic medium) without contact or other physical means — **tele·ki·net·ic** \¦==(,)=¦ned·ik\ *adj*

tele·lens \'telə+,-\ *n* [¹*tel-* + *lens*] : a telephoto lens

tele·man \'telē,man\ *n, pl* **telemen** [¹*tel-* + *man*] : a petty officer (as in the U.S. Navy) who performs clerical, coding, and communications duties

tel·e·mark \'telə,märk\ *n* -S *sometimes cap* [Norw, fr. *Telemark*, region in southern Norway] : a turn in which the ski that is to be on the outside of the turn is advanced considerably ahead of the other ski and then turned inward at a steadily widening angle until the actual turn

tele·mechanic \¦telə+\ *adj* [ISV ¹*tel-* + *mechanic*] : being or relating to a device for operating mechanisms at a distance — **tele·mechanically** \"+\ *adv*

tele·metacarpal \"+\ *adj* [²*tel-* + *metacarpal*] : having the terminal parts of the first and fifth metacarpals vestigial (as various deers)

tele·meteorograph \"+\ *n* [ISV ¹*tel-* + *meteorograph*; prob. orig. formed as F *télémétéorographe*] : an apparatus recording meteorological phenomena at a distance from the measuring apparatus (as by electricity or compressed air); *esp* : an apparatus recording conditions at many distant stations at a central office — **tele·meteorographic** \"+\ *adj* — **tele·meteorography** \"+\ *n* -ES

¹tele·me·ter \'telə,mēd·ə(r)\ *n* [ISV ¹*tel-* + *-meter*] **1** : an instrument (as a telescope with a micrometer for measuring the apparent diameter of an object whose dimensions are known or a telescope with stadia hairs) for measuring the distance of an object from an observer : RANGE FINDER **2** : an electrical apparatus for measuring a quantity (as pressure, radiation intensity, speed, temperature), transmitting the result to a distant station, and there indicating or recording the quantity measured : an automatic radio transmitter (as in a rocket) that broadcasts measurements of such quantities — **tele·met·ric** \¦==¦me·trik\ *adj* — **tele·met·ri·cal·ly** \-rək(ə)lē\ *adv* — **te·lem·e·try** \tə'lemə·trē\ *n* -ES

²telemeter \"\ *vb* -ED/-ING/-S *vt* : to transmit (the measurement of a quantity) by telemeter ⟨rocket-powered research models ~ heating data obtained on flights through the atmosphere —*Report: Nat'l Advisory Committee for Aeronautics*⟩ ~ *vi* : to telemeter the measurement of a quantity ⟨a new ~*ing* device was developed for transmitting scientific and operating information from high-flying rockets back to ground observation stations —G.R.Henninger⟩

tele·microscope \¦telə+\ *n* [NL *telemicroscopium*, fr. ¹*tel-* + *microscopium* microscope — more at MICROSCOPE] : a microscope with a long-focus objective that may be used either as a low-power microscope or as a reading telescope

tele·mor·phic \¦telə¦mȯrfik\ *adj* [¹*tel-* + *-morphic*] : having an effect at a distance from its point of origin or location ⟨~ plant hormones⟩

tele·motor \'telə+,-\ *n* [ISV ¹*tel-* + *motor*] : a hydraulic device by which the movement of the wheel on a ship's bridge operates the steering gear at the stern

tel·en·ce·phal·ic \(¦)te¦lensə¦falik\ *adj* [NL *telencephalon* + E *-ic*] : of or relating to the telencephalon

tel·encephalon \¦tel+\ *n* [NL, fr. ²*tele-* + *encephalon*] : the anterior subdivision of the forebrain comprising the cerebral hemispheres and associated structures

te·len·get *also* **te·len·git** \tə'leŋgət\ *n, usu cap* : TELEUT

te·len·o·mus \tə'lenəməs\ *n, cap* [NL] : a large and widespread genus of minute serphoid wasps (family Scelionidae) having larvae that are parasitic in the eggs of various insects

teleo- — see TELE-

tele·objective \¦telē+\ *n* [ISV ¹*tel-* + *objective*] : a telephoto lens

tel·eo·ceph·ali \,telēō'sefə,lī *sometimes* ,tēl-\ *n pl, cap* [NL, fr. ²*tele-* + *-cephali*] *in some classifications* : a division of teleost fishes including those having the typical number of cranial and opercular bones, separate anterior vertebrae, and no mesocoracoid (as the perches and pike) — **tel·eo·ceph·a·lous** \¦==¦==lәs\ *adj*

tel·e·oc·er·as \,==¦äsərəs\ *n, cap* [NL, fr. ²*tele-* + *-ceras*] : a genus of short-legged rhinoceroses from the American Upper Miocene and Lower Pliocene having a small nasal horn

tel·eo·des·ma·cea \,==_ō,dez'māshēə\ *n pl, cap* [NL, fr. ²*tele-* + *desm-* + *-acea*] *in some classifications* : a large group comprising bivalve mollusks with well-developed cardinal teeth in the hinge and being nearly equivalent to the order Eulamellibranchia — **tel·eo·des·ma·cean** \¦===,=¦māshən\ *adj or n* — **tel·eo·des·ma·ceous** \-shəs\ *adj*

tele·odont \'telēə,dänt *sometimes* 'tēl-\ *adj* [²*tele-* + *-odont*] : having large mandibles — used of an insect (as various stag beetles); compare PRIODONT

tel·e·o·log·i·cal \¦==ə¦läjəkəl, -jēk-\ *or* **tel·e·o·log·ic** \-jik, -jēk\ *adj* [*teleology* + *-ic*, *-ical*] : of or relating to teleology; *specif* : having the nature of or relating to, design, purpose, final intention, or cause — **tel·e·o·log·i·cal·ly** \-jək(ə)lē, -jēk-, -li\ *adv*

teleological argument *n* : ARGUMENT FROM DESIGN

teleological ethics *n pl but sing or pl in constr* : a theory of ethics (as utilitarianism or ethical egoism) according to which the rightness of an act is determined by its end

teleological idealism *n* : an idealistic philosophy that endeavors to reconcile the ethicoreligious idealism of Fichte with the stricter critical idealism of Kant

tel·e·ol·o·gism \,=='älə,jizəm\ *n* -S [*teleology* + *-ism*] : belief in or acceptance of teleology

tel·e·ol·o·gist \-jəst\ *n* -S [*teleology* + *-ist*] **1** : one that specializes in or believes in the actuality of teleology **2** : an advocate of a doctrine of teleology

tel·e·ol·o·gy \-jē, -ji\ *n* -ES [NL *teleologia*, fr. *teleo-* (irreg. fr. Gk *telos* end) + L *-logia* -logy — more at WHEEL] **1 a** : the philosophical study of evidences of design in nature — compare MECHANISM **b** : the doctrine or belief that ends are immanent in nature (as in vitalism and holism) **c** : a metaphysical doctrine explaining phenomena and events by final causes **2** : the fact or the character of being directed toward an end or shaped by a purpose — used of natural processes or of nature as a whole conceived as determined by final causes or by the design of a divine Providence and opposed to purely mechanical determinism or causation exclusively by what is temporally antecedent **3** : the use of design, purpose, or utility as an explanation of any natural phenomenon **4** : ENTELECHY

tel·eo·mitosis \¦telēō+\ *n, pl* **teleomitoses** [NL, fr. ²*tele-* + *mitosis*] : KARYOKINESIS

tel·e·op·tile \,=='äptəl, -,tīl\ *n* -S [²*tele-* + *-ptile*] : a mature feather — compare NEOSSOPTILE

tel·eo·roentgenogram \¦telēō *sometimes* ¦tēl-\ *also* **tele·roentgenogram** \-lə+\ *n* [ISV ²*tele-* + *roentgenogram*] : an X-ray photograph taken at a distance of usu. six feet with resultant practical parallelism of the rays and production of shadows of natural size

tel·eo·roentgenography \"+\ *also* **tele·roentgenography** \"+\ *n* [ISV ²*tele-* + *roentgenography*] : the act, science, or practice of making teleroentgenograms

tel·eo·saur \'telēə,sȯ(ə)r *sometimes* 'tēl-\ *n* -S [NL *Teleosaurus*] : a teleosaurian reptile

¹tel·eo·sau·ri·an \¦===¦sȯrēən\ *adj* [NL *Teleosaurus* + E *-ian*] : of or relating to the genus *Teleosaurus* or family Teleosauridae

²teleosaurian \"\ *n* -S : TELEOSAUR

tel·eo·sau·rus \,===sȯrəs\ *n, cap* [NL, fr. ²*tele-* + *-saurus*] : a genus (the type of the family Teleosauridae) of crocodilian reptiles of the Jurassic having a long and slender snout like a gavial and platycelous vertebrae

¹tel·e·ost \'telē,äst *sometimes* 'tēl-\ *adj* [NL *Teleostei*] : relating to or having the characteristics of the Teleostei

²teleost \"\ *n* -S : one of the Teleostei

tel·e·os·te·an \¦==¦ästēən\ *adj or n* [NL *Teleostei* + E *-an*] : TELEOST

tel·e·os·tei \,=='==,ī\ *n pl, cap* [NL, fr. ²*tele-* + *-ostei* (fr. Gk *osteon* bone) — more at OSSEOUS] *in some classifications* : a subclass or other division of fishes nearly or exactly equivalent to Teleostomi

tel·e·os·to·mate \¦==¦ästəmāt\ *adj* [NL *Teleostomi* + E *-ate*] : TELEOSTOMOUS

tel·eo·stome \'==_ə,stōm\ *n* -S [NL *Teleostomi*] : one of the Teleostomi : a true fish

tel·e·os·to·mi \,=='ästə,mī\ *n pl, cap* [NL, fr. ²*tele-* + *-stomi*] : a class or sometimes a subclass that contains all existing jawed fishes except the Chondrichthyes or sometimes the Chondrichthyes and Choanichthyes, that is characterized by membrane bones developed in connection with and entering into the structure of the jaws, cranium, pectoral arch, and opercular apparatus, gill arches bearing filamentous gills, and no claspers on the ventral fins, and that includes the ganoids and teleosts and is further characterized by the hyostylic suspensorium, bony fin rays, and lack of cerebral hemispheres — **tel·eo·sto·mi·an** \¦===¦stōmēən\ *or* **tel·eo·stom·ic** \¦===¦stämik\ *or* **tel·e·os·to·mous** \¦==¦ästəməs\ *adj*

tel·e·ot·ro·cha \,telē'ä·trəkə *sometimes* ,tēl-\ *n* [NL, fr. ²*tele-* + *-trocha*] *var of* TELOTROCHA

¹tel·e·path \'telə,path\ *vb* -ED/-ING/-S [back-formation fr. *telepathy*] *vt* : to communicate by telepathy ~ *vi* : to practice telepathy

²telepath \"\ *n* -S [back-formation fr. *telepathy*] : TELEPATHIST

tel·e·path·ic \¦==¦pathik, -thēk\ *adj* [*telepathy* + *-ic*] : of or relating to telepathy : supposedly transferred or communicated by telepathy — **telepathically** \-thək(ə)lē, -thēk-, -li\ *adv*

te·lep·a·thist \tə'lepəthəst\ *n* -S [*telepathy* + *-ist*] **1** : a believer in telepathy **2** : one supposedly having telepathic power

te·lep·a·thize \-,thīz\ *vb* -ED/-ING/-S [*telepathy* + *-ize*] *vt* : to affect telepathically ~ *vi* : to practice telepathy

te·lep·a·thy \-,thē, -thi\ *n* -ES [¹*tel-* + *-pathy*] : apparent communication from one mind to another other than through the channels of sense : THOUGHT TRANSFERENCE

¹tel·e·phone \'telə,fōn\ *n* [¹*tel-* + *-phone*] **1** : an instrument for reproducing sounds esp. articulate speech at a distance: as **a** : a device in which the voice or sound causes in a thin diaphragm vibrations that are directly transmitted along a wire or string connecting it to a similar diaphragm thus reproducing the sound **b** : an apparatus consisting of a transmitter (as a microphone) for converting sound esp. of the human voice into electrical impulses or varying electrical current for transmission by wire, a receiver for reproducing the original sounds from such transmitted varying electrical current, and usu. a switch and a signaling device **2** : any of various devices (as a sound-signaling device or a speaking tube) resembling or suggesting the telephone

telephones 1

²telephone \"\ *vi* : to communicate by telephone : call on the telephone ~ *vt* **1** : to send (as a message) by telephone **2** : to speak to (a person) by telephone : call on the telephone

telephone book *n* : a book listing names, addresses, and telephone numbers of telephone subscribers

telephone booth *n* : an enclosure (as for a public or widely= used telephone) intended to insure privacy for one telephoning

telephone box *n, Brit* : a public telephone booth

telephone exchange *n* : a central office in which the wires of telephones may be connected to permit conversation

telephone number *n* : a number assigned to a telephone instrument and used by a person to call that telephone

tel·e·phon·er \-nə(r)\ *n* -S : one that telephones

telephone receiver *n* : a device (as in a telephone) for converting electric impulses or varying current into sound

telephone theory *n* : a theory in physiology: the perception of pitch depends on the frequency of the nerve impulses induced by sounds of different pitch — compare PLACE THEORY

telephone transmitter *n* : TRANSMITTER a(1)

tel·e·phon·ic \¦==¦fänik, -nēk\ *adj* [¹*tel-* + *phonic*] **1** : conveying sound to a distance **2** [*telephone* + *-ic*] : of or relating to the telephone : carried or conveyed by telephone — **tel·e·phon·i·cal·ly** \-nək(ə)lē, -nēk-, -li\ *adv*

tel·e·phon·ist \'==,fōnəst, tə'lefən-\ *n* -S [¹*telephone* + *-ist*] : one who uses or operates a telephone; *specif* : a switchboard operator in a telephone exchange

tel·e·phon·itis \,telə,fō'nīd·əs\ *n* -ES [¹*telephone* + *-itis*] : marked fondness for or obsession with telephoning ⟨afflicted with the ~ . . . common to all teen-agers —J.S.Qualey⟩

te·leph·o·ny \tə'lefənē, 'telə,fōnē\ *n* -ES [ISV ¹*tel-* + *-phony*] : the use or operation of an apparatus for transmission of sounds between widely removed points; *specif* : the use of a telephone employing electrical variations or a system of such telephones for such transmission with or without connecting wires — compare RADIOTELEPHONY

¹tele·photo \¦telə+\ *adj* [by shortening] : TELEPHOTOGRAPHIC ⟨a ~ effect⟩; *specif* : being a camera lens system designed to give a usu. large image of a distant object

²telephoto \"\ *n* : a telephoto lens

Telephoto \"\ *trademark* — used for an apparatus for transmitting photographs electrically or for a photograph so transmitted

tele·photograph \¦telə+\ *n* [¹*tel-* + *photograph*] : a photograph taken with a camera having a telephoto lens

tele·photographic \"+\ *adj* [ISV ¹*tel-* + *photographic*] : of, relating to, or being the process of telephotography

telephotographic lens *n* : a telephoto lens

tele·photography \¦telə+\ *n* [ISV ¹*tel-* + *photography*] **1** : PHOTOTELEGRAPHY **2** : the photography of distant objects in more enlarged form than is possible by the ordinary means usu. by a camera provided with a telephoto lens or mounted in place of the eyepiece of a telescope so that the real or a magnified image falls on the sensitive plate

tele·photometer \"+\ *n* [¹*tel-* + *photometer*] : a photometer used to measure the illumination of distant objects

tele·plasm \'telə+,-\ *n* [ISV ¹*tel-* + *-plasm*] : ECTOPLASM — **tele·plasmic** \¦telə+\ *adj*

tele·play \'telə+,-\ *n* [¹*tel-* + *play*] : a play written for or presented on television

tele·port \"+,-\ *vt* [¹*tel-* + *port* (to carry)] : to move (an object or oneself) without physical contact by psychokinesis — **tele·por·ta·tion** \¦==,pōr¦tāshən, -,pȯr-, pər-\ *n* -S

tele·printer \'telə+,-\ *n* [¹*tel-* + *printer*] : TELETYPEWRITER

Tele·Promp·Ter \"+\ *trademark* — used for a device for unrolling a magnified script in front of a speaker on television

tel·e·ran \'telə,ran\ *n* -S [*television-radar navigation*] : a system of aerial navigation in which ground radar scans the area about an airport and the results are televised so that the pilot of an airplane sees the positions of all craft in the vicinity superimposed upon a map of the area

tel·er·gic \(')te¦lərjik\ *or* **tel·er·gi·cal** \-jəkəl\ *adj* : of or relating to telergy — **tel·er·gi·cal·ly** \-jək(ə)lē\ *adv*

tel·er·gy \'te(,)lərjē\ *n* -ES [¹*tel-* + *-ergy*] : a hypothetical action of one person's thought and desire upon the brain of another person by the transmission of some unknown form of energy

teles *pl of* TELE

¹tel·e·scope \'telə,skōp\ *n, often attrib* [NL *telescopium*, fr. Gk *tēleskopos* far-seeing (fr. *tēle-* ¹tel- + *skopos* watcher) + L *-ium* — more at SCOPE] **1 a** : an optical instrument usu. tubular in shape for viewing distant objects by means of the refraction of light rays through a lens or the reflection of light rays by a concave mirror so that the rays enter an opening and converge to form an image seen through a magnifying eyepiece — compare CASSEGRAINIAN TELESCOPE, GALILEAN TELESCOPE, HERSCHELIAN TELESCOPE, REFLECTOR, REFRACTOR, TERRESTRIAL TELESCOPE **b** : TELESCOPE SIGHT **c** : any of various tubular magnifying optical instruments (as for reading the scale on a galvanometer or for use in a bronchoscope) ⟨a bronchoscopic ~⟩ ⟨a cystoscopic ~⟩ **d** : RADIO TELESCOPE **2** *or* **telescope bag** : a traveling bag consisting of two parts of which the larger fits over the smaller **3** : TELESCOPE GOLDFISH **4** : something that telescopes or that is telescoped ⟨rigged the ~ steel bait rod first —Hugh Fosburgh⟩

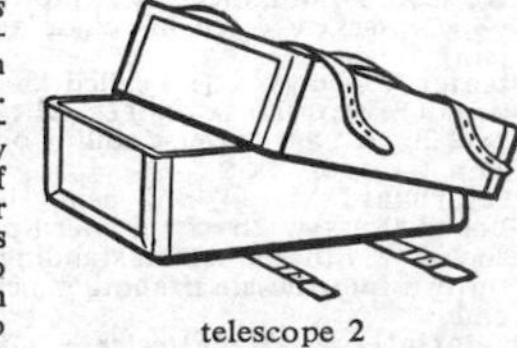
telescope 2

²telescope \"\ *vb* -ED/-ING/-S *vi* **1** : to slide or pass one within another like the cylindrical sections of a hand telescope ⟨a two-piece knockdown support, designed for the tent and made of *telescoping* aluminum tubes —Sheila Hibben⟩ ⟨both rods ~ to extend to exact size —*Spiegel's Catalog*⟩ : force a way into or enter another lengthwise as the result of collision ⟨the two sleeping cars *telescoped*⟩ **2** : to become telescoped ⟨those years seemed to have *telescoped*, like time in a dream —Helen Howe⟩ ~ *vt* **1** : to cause to telescope ⟨the front and end cars that took the shock of the impact were *telescoped* —Howard Austin⟩ ⟨from the river side the three parts of the building appear to be *telescoped* into each other —*Amer. Guide Series: Md.*⟩ **2** : to combine, coalesce, or run together in order to shorten or simplify : COMPRESS, CONDENSE ⟨the rules of good cooking cannot be *telescoped* into a single sentence or even paragraph —J.L.Evans⟩ ⟨the book arbitrarily ~*s* time and space, and as arbitrarily extends them —Phoebe Adams⟩ ⟨~ a century of industrial history into a decade —G.L.Arnold⟩ ⟨*telescoped* into a brief span experiences that represented chronologically many times that number of years —Stella Center⟩ ⟨if an evolutionary development may be verbally *telescoped* into an event —A.L.Kroeber⟩ ⟨one can ~ the seasons and witness four weeks of spring's advance in the space of seven days —I.R.Barnes⟩; *specif* : to combine (words) by omitting part of one or more of the components ⟨~ two words (like *infanticipate*, from *infant* and *anticipate*) —*Word Study*⟩ : form (as a word or title) by such combining

telescope box *n* : a two-piece box in which the sides of one part fit over those of the other

telescope eye *n* : an eye on a retractile stalk (as in land snails)

telescope fly *n* : any of various acalyptrate two-winged flies with eyes on very long stalks that constitute *Diopsis* and a few related genera of Africa and Asia

telescope goldfish *n* : a goldfish of a breed characterized by a very short thick body, a large and double tail fin, and protuberant eyes — see CELESTIAL TELESCOPE

telescope jack *n* : a lifting jack whose male screw is a telescope screw in which another male screw works with the two screws having threads of unequal pitch or opposite direction so that the effect is similar to that produced by a differential screw

telescope sight *or* **telescopic sight** *n* : a telescope on a firearm for use as a sight

telescope table *n* : EXTENSION TABLE

telescope word *n* : BLEND d

tel·e·scop·ic \¦telə¦skäpik, -pēk\ *also* **tel·e·scop·i·cal** \-pəkəl, -pēk-\ *adj* [¹*telescope* + *-ic*, *-ical*] **1 a** : of or relating to a telescope ⟨the ~ tube⟩ : performed by a telescope ⟨a ~ observation⟩ **b** : suitable for magnifying distant objects : used in a telescope ⟨a ~ lens⟩ **2** : seen or discoverable only by a telescope ⟨~ stars⟩ **3** : able to discern objects at a distance : FARSEEING, FAR-REACHING ⟨a ~ eye⟩ ⟨~ vision⟩ ⟨a historian with a ~ view of the vagaries of man throughout civilization —*Harper's*⟩ **4** : having the power of movement (as extension) by joints sliding one within another like the tube of a hand telescope ⟨~ shock absorbers⟩ ⟨a ~ vertical antenna⟩ ⟨a ~ landing gear⟩; *esp* : constructed of concentric tubes or other parts that fit one within another ⟨a ~ drinking cup⟩ ⟨a ~ box⟩ — **tel·e·scop·i·cal·ly** \-pək(ə)lē, -pēk-, -li\ *adv*

tele·screen \'telə+,-\ *n* [¹*tel-* + *screen*] : the screen of a television receiver

tele·seism \ˈteləˌsīzəm\ *n* -s [¹*tel-* + *-seism*] **:** an earth tremor caused by an earthquake in a part of the world remote from the recording station — **tele·seismic** \ˌtelə+\ *adj*

tele·seismology \"+\ *n* [¹*tel-* + *seismology*] **:** seismology dealing with records obtained at long distances — compare ENGYSSEISMOLOGY

tel·e·sis \ˈteləsəs\ *n, pl* **tele·ses** \-ləˌsēz\ [NL, fr. Gk, event, fulfillment, fr. *telein* to complete, fulfill (fr. *telos* end) + *-sis* — more at WHEEL] **:** progress intelligently planned and directed **:** the attainment of desired ends by the application of intelligent human effort to the means

tel·es·mat·ic \ˌteləzˈmad·ik\ *or* **tel·es·mat·i·cal** \-d·əkəl\ *adj* [MGk *telesmat-, telesma* + E *-ic*] *archaic* **:** TALISMANIC — **tel·es·mat·i·cal·ly** \-d·ək(ə)lē\ *adv, archaic*

tel·esme \ˈteˌlezəm\ *n* -s [MGk *telesma* — more at TALISMAN] *archaic* **:** TALISMAN

tel·es·ta·cea \ˌteləˈstāshēə\ *n pl, cap* [NL, fr. *Telesto,* genus of Coelenterata (fr. Gk *telestos* fulfilled, fr. *telein* to fulfill) + *-acea*] **:** a small order of alcyonarian coelenterates sometimes included in the Alcyonacea and having colonies that consist of long axial polyps with lateral polyps as side branches

tele·stereoscope \ˌtelə+\ *n* [ISV ¹*tel-* + *stereoscope;* orig. formed as G *telestereoskop*] **:** a binocular telescope; *esp* **:** one in which the distance between the objectives is greater than the interocular distance and which is used to obtain enhanced impressions of relief in distant objects

tel·esthesia *or* **tel·aesthesia** \ˌtel+\ *n* [NL, fr. ¹*tel-* + *esthesia, aesthesia*] **:** an impression similar to a sense impression and supposedly received at a distance without the normal operation of the organs of sense — **tel·esthetic** *or* **telaesthetic** \"+\ *adj*

te·les·tial glory \təˈles(h)chəl, (ˈ)teˈl|, -stēəl\ *n* [*telestial* fr. ¹*tel-* + *-estial* (as in *celestial*)] **:** the lowest of three Mormon degrees or kingdoms of glory attainable in heaven — compare CELESTIAL GLORY, TERRESTRIAL GLORY

te·les·tic \təˈlestik\ *adj* [Gk *telestikos,* fr. *telestos* (verbal of *telein* to fulfill, initiate into mysteries or sacred rites) + *-ikos* -ic] **:** MYSTICAL

te·les·tich \təˈlestik, ˈteləˌs-\ *n* -s [²*tel-* + Gk *stichos* line — more at STICH] **:** a poem in which the consecutive final letters of the lines spell a name — compare ACROSTIC 1a

tele·tape \ˈtelə+ˌ-\ *n* [¹*tel-* + *tape*] **:** a tape perforated in accordance with the telegraph code by a special typewriter and run through a telegraph transmitter to obtain a higher speed of transmission

tele·therapy \ˌtelə+\ *n* [¹*tel-* + *therapy*] **:** the treatment of diseased tissue with high-intensity radiation (as gamma rays from radioactive cobalt)

tele·thermometer \"+\ *n* [ISV ¹*tel-* + *thermometer*] **:** an apparatus for indicating the temperature of a distant point (as by a thermoelectric circuit and a galvanometer) — **tele·thermometry** \"+\ *n*

tele·thermoscope \"+\ *n* [¹*tel-* + *thermoscope*] **:** TELETHERMOMETER

tel·e·thon \ˈteləˌthän\ *n* -s [¹*tel-* + *-thon* (as in *marathon*)] **:** a television program lasting several hours; *esp* **:** one for soliciting money for a specific fund

tele·transcription \ˌtelə+\ *n* [¹*tel-* + *transcription*] **:** KINESCOPE 2

Tele·type \ˈtelə+ˌ-\ *trademark* **1** — used for a teletypewriter **2 :** a message sent by a Teletype machine

Tele·typesetter \ˌtelə+\ *trademark* — used for an apparatus for the automatic operation of a keyboard slugcasting machine consisting essentially of a separate keyboard that perforates a tape which is fed either into an attachment to the slugcasting machine or into a sender that transmits electrical impulses telegraphically to any number of reperforators with the perforated tape causing the slugcasting machine to set type by automatic operation of the keyboard

tele·typesetting \"+\ *n* **:** the process of setting type with a Teletypesetter apparatus

tele·typewriter \"+\ *n* [¹*tel-* + *typewriter*] **:** a printing telegraph recording like a typewriter and capable of being used over practically any telephonic communication system

tele·typist \"+\ *n* [¹*tel-* + *typist*] **:** one that operates a teletypewriter

tel·e·ut \ˈteleˌüt, ˌ==ˈ=\ *n, pl* **teleut** *or* **teleuts** *usu cap* **1 a :** a group of nomadic Altaic Tatar peoples of the Altai plateau, West Siberia Region, that are Mongolian in type and Buddhist in religion — called also *Telenget* **b :** a member of any of such peoples **2 :** the Turkic language of the Teleut peoples

teleut- *or* **teleuto-** *comb form* [Gk *teleutē,* fr. *telos* end — more at WHEEL] **:** completion ⟨*teleuto*spore⟩

te·leu·to·sorus \təˈlüd·ə, təlˈyü·+\ *n, pl* **teleutosori** [NL, fr. *teleut-* + *-sorus*] **:** TELIUM

te·leu·to·spore \=ˈ==+\ *n* [ISV *teleut-* + *-spore*] **:** TELIOSPORE — **te·leu·to·spor·ic** \=ˌ==+ˈspōrik\ *or* **te·leu·to·sporiferous** \=ˌ==+\ *adj*

tele·view \ˈtelə+ˌ-\ *vi* [¹*tel-* + *view*] **:** to observe or watch by means of a television receiver — **tele·viewer** \" + ˌ-\ *n*

tel·e·vise \ˈteləˌvīz\ *vb* -ED/-ING/-S [back-formation fr. *television*] *vt* **:** to pick up and usu. to broadcast (as a baseball game, meeting, movie, news event, scene, or speaker) by television ~ *vi* **:** to broadcast by television

tel·e·vi·sion \ˈteləˌvizhən *sometimes* ˌ==ˈ==\ *n* [F *télévision,* fr. *télé-* ¹tel- + *vision*] **1 :** the transmission and reproduction of transient images of fixed or moving objects; *specif* **:** an electronic system of transmitting such images together with sound over a wire or through space by apparatus that converts light and sound into electrical waves and reconverts them into visible light rays and audible sound **2** -s **:** a television receiving set **3 a :** the television broadcasting industry ⟨after the Vice President's initial blast at ~, network executives were quick to respond —Robert Goralski⟩ **b :** television as a medium of communication — **tel·e·vi·sion·al·ly** \ˌ==ˈvizhənˀlē, -zhnəlē\ *adv* — **tel·e·vi·sion·ary** \-zhəˌnerē\ *adj*

television receiver *or* **television set** *n* **:** a television receiving set

television transmitter *n* **:** a television transmitting set

television tube *n* **:** KINESCOPE 1

tel·e·vi·sor \ˈ==ˌvīzə(r) *sometimes* ˌ==ˈ==\ *n* -s [*televise* + *-or*] **1 :** a television transmitting or receiving apparatus **2 a :** a television broadcaster **b :** one that uses a television receiver

tele·visual \ˌtelə+\ *adj* [fr. *television,* after such pairs as E *vision: visual*] **1 :** of or relating to television **2 :** TELEGENIC

tele·writer \ˈtelə+ˌ-\ *n* [¹*tel-* + *writer*] *chiefly Brit* **:** a Tel-Autograph device

tel·fair·ia \telˈfa(a)rēə\ *n, cap* [NL, fr. Charles *Telfair* †1833 Ir. naturalist + NL *-ia*] **:** a genus of tropical African vines (family Cucurbitaceae) having very long shoots which may exceed 45 feet, purplish flowers, and immense gourds — see OYSTER NUT

telfer *var of* TELPHER

¹tel·ford \ˈtelfə(r)d\ *adj* [after Thomas *Telford* †1834 Scot. civil engineer] **:** being or relating to a road pavement having a surface of small stone rolled hard and smooth and distinguished from macadam road by its firm foundation of large stones with fragments of stone wedged tightly in the interstices

²telford \"\ *n* -s **:** a telford road

tel·ford·ize \-fə(r)ˌdīz\ *vt* -ED/-ING/-S [¹*telford* + *-ize*] **:** to furnish (a road) with a telford pavement

telg *abbr* telegram

tel·harmonium \ˌtel+\ *n* [NL, fr. ¹*tel-* + *harmonium*] **:** an instrument for producing music at a distant point via telephone wire by means of alternating currents of electricity controlled by an operator who plays on a keyboard

te·li \ˈtālē\ *n, pl* **teli** *or* **telis** [Hindi *telī* oilmaker, fr. Skt *taila* sesame oil, fr. *tila* sesame] **:** a member of a low Hindu caste of characteristically oil makers and merchants

te·lial \ˈtēlēəl, -lyəl\ *adj* [NL *telium* + E *-al*] **:** of or relating to a telium

telic \ˈtelik, ˈtēl-\ *adj* [Gk *telikos* final, fr. *tel-* ²tel- + *-ikos* -ic] **1 :** tending toward an end **:** PURPOSIVE, TELEOLOGICAL ⟨the writing is always ~, never a mere stream of consciousness —R.D.Ellmann⟩ ⟨the mind . . . becomes ~, thus enabling mankind to pass from passive to active evolutionary processes, and from natural to human or social evolution —J.Q.Dealey⟩ ⟨a linguistic change is not ~: it does not work for the benefit of the system; on the contrary it disrupts it —R.S.Wells⟩ **2 :** PERFECTIVE 2 — contrasted with *atelic* — **teli·cal** \-ləkəl\ *adj* — **teli·cal·ly** \-lək(ə)lē\ *adv*

te·lin·ga \təˈliŋgə\ *n* -s *usu cap* [of Dravidian origin; akin to Tamil *teliṅkam* Telugu country; fr. the employment of Telugus as sepoys] **:** SEPOY

telinga potato *n, usu cap T* **:** PUNGAPUNG

te·lio·sorus \ˌtēlēō+\ *n, pl* **teliosori** [NL, fr. *telium* + *-o-* + *-sorus*] **:** TELIUM

te·lio·spore \ˈ===+ˌ-\ *n* [*telium* + *-o-* + *spore*] **:** one of the thick-walled one- or more-celled chlamydospores developed in the final stage in the life cycle of rust fungi and within which nuclear fusion occurs prior to development of the promycelium — see TELIUM — **te·lio·spor·ic** \ˌ===ˈspōrik\ *adj*

te·lio·spo·re·ae \ˌ===ˈspōrēˌē\ *n pl, cap* [NL, fr. ISV *teliospore*] *in some classifications* **:** a subclass of fungi (class Basidiomycetes) including the rusts and smuts (orders Uredinales and Ustilaginales) and characterized by the production of a teliospore or a comparable body in which the diploid nucleus is produced — compare EUBASIDIAE, HETEROBASIDIAE

te·li·um \ˈtēlēəm\ *n, pl* **te·lia** \-lēə\ [NL, fr. ²*tel-* + *-ium*] **:** an aggregation of teliospores often stalked and either forming a subcuticular or subepidermal cushion or rupturing the host tissue to form an open sorus — compare AECIUM

¹tell \ˈtel\ *vb* **told** \ˈtōld\ **told; telling; tells** [ME *tellen* (past *tolde,* past part. *told*), fr. OE *tellan* (past — northern & Midland dial. — *talde,* past part. — northern & Midland dial. — *getald*); akin to OHG *zellen* to count, tell (past *zalta,* past part. *gizalt*), ON *telja* (past *talthi,* past part. *talithr*); causative-denominative fr. the root of E ¹*tale*] *vt* **1 :** to mention one by one or piece by piece **:** COUNT, NUMBER, RECKON ⟨~ the stars, if thou be able to number them —Gen 15:5 (AV)⟩ ⟨walked round the walls and *told* the towers —Rose Macaulay⟩ ⟨all *told* there were 27 public schools —C.L.Jones⟩: as **a :** to count in keeping track of decades of rosary prayers — used in the phrase *to tell one's beads* **b** *obs* **:** to calculate the total amount or value of **2 a :** to relate in detail **:** NARRATE, RECOUNT ⟨one of her recipes . . . ~*s* how to make maple syrup dumplings —Rose Feld⟩ ⟨~*ing* a boastful story —J.V. Allen⟩ ⟨dancers *told* ancient legends with tradition's rhythms and gestures —*Nat'l Geographic*⟩ **b :** SAY, UTTER ⟨to ~ you the truth, I don't really remember —Lenard Kaufman⟩ ⟨a man in high position utters an accusation or ~*s* a lie —Gilbert Seldes⟩ ⟨give me a chance to ~ Kit good-by —Hamilton Basso⟩ **3 a :** to make known **:** DISCLOSE, DIVULGE ⟨~ the news⟩ ⟨~ your name⟩ **:** REVEAL, MANIFEST ⟨fossils ~ much about the past⟩ ⟨more than words, his movements, gestures *told* his evident delight in ballet —Cyril Cusack⟩ ⟨followed suit with an ungainly stiffness which *told* how much at sea he felt —T.B.Costain⟩ **b :** to express in words ⟨cannot ~ how sorry I am⟩ **4 a :** to give information to **:** report to **:** INFORM ⟨I'll ~ him as soon as he comes⟩ ⟨~ executives and employees of our policies and plans —Milton Hall⟩ ⟨*told* his listeners about his vacation —*Current Biog.*⟩ **b :** to give information on **:** REPORT ⟨he said all of it in a flat, business voice that *told* you nothing more or less than the words said —Wirt Williams⟩ ⟨no book could really ~ you what a hell of a feeling it was —Gwyn Thomas⟩ ⟨nobody could ~ her anything —Edith Sitwell⟩ ⟨the victim's subconscious generally ~*s* him something is wrong as soon as the prowler enters —Rufus Jarman⟩ ⟨his eyes *told* him that the walls were festooned with flowers —T.B.Costain⟩ **c :** to inform positively **:** assure emphatically ⟨he did not do it, I ~ you⟩ ⟨we are distinctly *told* that he did not buy it —Douglas Carruthers⟩ **5 :** ORDER, REQUEST, DIRECT ⟨*told* her to wait⟩ **6 :** to discern so as to report **:** ascertain by observing **:** find out **:** DECIDE, RECOGNIZE ⟨how if it is unpublished can you ~ that it is a masterpiece —John Barkham⟩ ⟨the patrol officer can ~ whether things are normal or abnormal —R.L.Anderson⟩ ⟨usually one couldn't ~ much about the writer from the letter of a not very well-educated woman —Elizabeth Goudge⟩ ⟨management can ~, by its own observation, whether a man is capable of leadership —Bruce Payne⟩ ~ *vi* **1 :** to give an account **:** make a report ⟨wrote an article ~*ing* of his experiences⟩ ⟨the twelve contributors ~ of modern man —F.E.Hill⟩ **2 :** to state positively **:** decide definitely **:** SAY ⟨who can ~⟩ ⟨you can't ~ about drunks —S.H.Holbrook⟩ **3 :** to act as a talebearer **:** INFORM — usu. used with *on* or *of* ⟨the sister *told* on him, though he tried to shush her —John Dollard⟩ ⟨never *told* on each other, no matter what happened —C.T.Jackson⟩ ⟨I'll get even with you if you ever ~ on me —*Inside Detective*⟩ **4** *dial Eng* **:** TALK, CHAT **5 :** to take effect **:** have a marked effect **:** be of account ⟨events of the past two or three weeks were beginning to ~ on her nerves —Edna Ferber⟩ ⟨the influence of the school had begun to ~ —Robert Littell⟩ ⟨a great many garments of the highest quality and all designed for overseas markets where quality ~*s* —D.E.Keir⟩ ⟨the long hours, the close confinement, and the strain of having to stand behind a counter from eight o'clock in the morning till eight o'clock at night was beginning to ~ upon her —J.C.Snaith⟩ **6 :** to serve as evidence or indication **:** be significant — usu used with *of* ⟨the calculating look in his eyes that *told* of his Norman blood —T.B.Costain⟩ ⟨the arid sands that ~ of desert days will still show angled stones that forgotten winds have carved —W.E.Swinton⟩ **7 :** to stand forth clearly **:** become apparent, evident, or known ⟨evidence that you were riding at a race meeting will ~ strongly against you in the subsequent police proceedings —*Punch*⟩ ⟨he remains so disfigured that appearances will always ~ against him —Dixon Wecter⟩ **syn** see COUNT, REVEAL

²tell \"\ *n* -s *dial* **:** something that is told **:** TALK, TALE, ACCOUNT ⟨have a ~ with you —Eden Phillpotts⟩

³tell \"\ *n* -s [Ar *tall*] **:** HILL, MOUND; *specif* **:** an ancient mound in the Middle East composed of remains of successive settlements — compare TEPE

tell down *vt, Scot* **:** to pay down

tel·len \ˈtelən\ *n* -s [modif. of NL *Tellina*] **:** TELLIN

¹tell·er \ˈtelə(r)\ *n* -s [ME, fr. *tellen* to tell + *-er*] **1 :** one that relates or communicates **:** INFORMER, NARRATOR, DESCRIBER ⟨a story based on the ~'*s* actual experiences⟩ **2 a :** a device or apparatus that announces **:** ANNUNCIATOR **b** *dial Eng* **:** one of the strokes made by a church bell in tolling for a death **3 :** one that reckons or counts: as **a :** one appointed to count votes (as in a legislative body, public meeting, assembly) ⟨those for and those against a motion pass between ~*s,* and the affirmative and negative vote is counted separately —Alice F. Sturgis⟩ **b :** a member of a bank's staff concerned with the direct handling of money received by or paid out by the institution ⟨a paying ~⟩ ⟨a receiving ~⟩ ⟨a savings ~⟩

²tel·ler \"\ *dial Eng var of* TILLER

tel·li·cher·ry bark \ˈteləˌcherē-\ *n, usu cap T* [fr. *Tellicherry,* seaport in Madras state, India] **:** the bitter bark of any of several East Indian or African trees of the family Apocynaceae (as *Wrightia zeylanica, Holarrhena antidysenterica* or *H. africana*) used esp. in folk medicine as a remedy for dysentery

tellicherry pepper *n, usu cap T* **:** a superior grade of Indian pepper characterized by exceptional richness of body and fullness of flavor

tellies *pl of* TELLY

tel·li·ma \ˈteləmə\ *n, cap* [NL, anagram of *Mitella,* genus of plants allied to *Tellima,* fr. L, headband, dim. of *mitra* headband, turban — more at MITER] **:** a genus of hardy herbaceous perennials (family Saxifragaceae) of western No. America that have palmately lobed leaves and long racemes of small nodding 5-petaled flowers — see FALSE ALUMROOT

tel·lin \ˈtelən\ *n* -s [NL *Tellina*] **:** a mollusk of the family Tellinidae **:** SUNSET SHELL

tel·li·na \təˈlīnə, -lēnə\ *n* [NL, fr. Gk *tellinē,* a shellfish] **1** *cap* **:** a genus (the type of the family Tellinidae) of marine bivalve mollusks having the siphons long and separate, the foot and labial palpi very large, and the shell thin, delicate, and often showily colored **2** -s **:** any mollusk of the genus *Tellina* **:** SUNSET SHELL

tel·li·na·cea \ˌteləˈnāshēə\ *n pl, cap* [NL, fr. *Tellina* + *-acea*] **:** a suborder or other division of Eulamellibranchia comprising usu. rather small and bottom-dwelling mollusks with separate siphons, a large strong foot, and often brightly colored shells and including the sunset shells, surf clams, and wedge shells

telling *adj* [fr. pres. part. of *tell*] **1 :** producing a marked effect **:** EFFECTIVE, IMPRESSIVE, STRIKING ⟨a ~ attack, made with skill and shrewd insight —V.L.Parrington⟩ ⟨delivered ~ blows in the interests of toleration and freedom —M.R. Cohen⟩ ⟨describes in her deft and ~ phrases the teacher-town relationship —E.A.Weeks⟩ ⟨paragraphs, packed with ~ detail —Benjamin Farrington⟩ ⟨a ~ piece of satire —A.L.Vogelback⟩ ⟨advocated with ~ effect better measures for the equipment of the soldiers —C.A.Duniway⟩ ⟨he made a ~ picture standing alert —John Muir †1914⟩ **2 :** REVEALING, EXPRESSIVE ⟨many of the most ~ pages in her story —E.K.Brown⟩ ⟨a ~ study of the corrosive effects of snobbery and ostracism on the human spirit —Paul Pickrel⟩ **syn** see VALID

tell·ing·ly *adv* **:** in a telling manner ⟨gesture at times speaks more ~ than tongues —Geoffrey Jefferson⟩

tel·lin·i·dae \təˈlinəˌdē\ *n pl, cap* [NL, fr. *Tellina,* type genus + *-idae*] **:** a family of marine bivalve mollusks (suborder Tellinacea) comprising the sunset shells

tell off *vt* **1 :** to number and set apart; *esp* **:** to detail for special duty **:** count off **:** ASSIGN ⟨*told off* a detail and put them to opening a trench —J.F.Dobie⟩ ⟨men were *told off* for household duties —*Amer. Guide Series: Mich.*⟩ ⟨trains *told off* for the use of British soldiers —Robert Keable⟩ ⟨*told off* to make a speech —A.P.Herbert⟩ **2 :** to reprove severely **:** DENOUNCE, REPRIMAND, SCOLD ⟨when she increases her nagging, I lose patience and *tell* her *off* quite brutally —Rex Ingamells⟩ ⟨his growing disgust boils over, he *tells off* the boss —Hobe Morrison⟩ ⟨in a mood to be *told off,* and they embraced most warmly the writers who scolded hardest —J.H. Jackson⟩

tells *pres 3d sing of* TELL, *pl of* TELL

¹telltale \ˈ=ˌ=\ *n* [¹*tell* + *tale* (after the phrase *tell tales*)] **1 :** one who officiously gives information of the private concerns of others **:** one who tells what should be withheld **:** TALEBEARER, INFORMER **2 :** something that serves to disclose something else or give information **:** HINT, INDICATION **3 :** a device for indicating or recording something: as **a :** a device for keeping a check on employees (as factory hands, drivers, check takers); *esp* **:** TIME CLOCK **b** (1) **:** a mechanical attachment to a ship's steering wheel that shows the position of the helm or rudder (2) **:** a compass in the cabin where the captain can see it (3) **:** a wind direction indicator in the form of a ribbon or similar piece of material **c :** a small overflow pipe that indicates by dripping when a tank is full **d :** a strip of metal on the front wall of a racquets or squash court to a height of from 2 to 2½ feet above the ground over which the ball must be hit **e :** a device serving as a warning on a railroad: as (1) **:** a row of long strips (as of rope) hung from a bar over the tracks to warn freight brakemen of their approach to a low overhead bridge (2) **:** a low fender placed near a hole in the permanent way to warn trackwalkers and others **4 :** TATTLER 2

²telltale \"\ *adj* **1 :** officiously telling what one should hold secret or in confidence **:** INFORMING, TALEBEARING **2 :** disclosing or indicating something often of a private or secret nature **:** BETRAYING, REVEALING ⟨there was only that ~ patch of oil on the water to mark where he had disappeared —*Oxford Bk. of English Talk*⟩ ⟨scanning each vein of rock for the ~ glint of yellow metal —R.A.Billington⟩ ⟨a hair-brush can be a ~ thing when a fellow begins to lose his hair —Valentine Williams⟩ ⟨months of ~ psychological preparation must precede an aggressive war —M.W.Straight⟩ **3 a :** being any of various devices for giving warning or keeping a watch or record ⟨a ~ indicator in the bureau, calling attention of the management only in case a bell has rung —J.R.Stuart⟩ ⟨a ~ panel of lights indicating everything from motor heat to whether the stewardess shut the door —H.G.Armstrong⟩ **b :** being a process or operation by which such a device warns or records ⟨a ~ operation⟩ — **tell·tale·ly** *adv*

³telltale \"\ *vt* -ED/-ING/-S [²*telltale*] **:** to perform a telltale operation on ⟨~ forgings to determine whether there is sufficient stock for finishing⟩

telltruth \ˈ=ˌ=\ *n* [¹*tell* + *truth* (after the phrase *tell the truth*)] *archaic* **:** one who tells the truth **:** a frank and honest person

tellur- *or* **telluri-** *or* **telluro-** *comb form* [L *tellur-, tellus* earth — more at THILL] **1 :** earth ⟨*tellur*ian⟩ ⟨*telluro*meter⟩ **2 :** tellurium ⟨*tellur*ic⟩ ⟨*telluri*ferous⟩ ⟨*telluro*bismuthite⟩ **3** *usu telluro-* **:** containing bivalent tellurium usu. in place of oxygen ⟨*telluro*cyanic acid HTeCN⟩ — compare THI-

tel·lu·rate \ˈtelyəˌrāt\ *n* -s [*tellur-* + *-ate*] **:** a salt or ester of telluric acid

¹tel·lu·ri·an \təˈlu̇rēən, tel, |lˈyu̇-\ *adj* [*tellur-* + *-ian*] **:** of, relating to, or characteristic of the earth ⟨the newly discovered ~ genus —T.H.Huxley⟩ ⟨great collective forces of instinct, resentment and ~ inspiration —Jacques Maritain⟩

²tellurian \"\ *n* -s **:** a dweller on the earth

³tellurian \"\ *or* **tel·lu·ri·on** \"\ *n* -s [*tellurian* modif. of NL *tellurion; tellurion,* NL, fr. *tellur-* + Gk *-ion,* dim. suffix] **:** an apparatus to illustrate the causation of day and night by the rotation of the earth on its axis and the dependence of the seasons on the sun's declination

tel·lu·ric \-rik\ *adj* [*tellur-* + *-ic*] **1 :** of, relating to, or containing tellurium — used esp. of compounds in which this element has a higher valence than in tellurous compounds **2 :** of or relating to the earth **:** proceeding from the earth **:** TERRESTRIAL ⟨we have lived too long in the ~ cavern —Eugene Jolas⟩ ⟨an apology for men enmeshed in ~ forces —Roger Bastide⟩ ⟨how are we, as ~ clods, to know what you are talking about —Herbert Mirschel⟩

telluric acid *n* **:** an acid containing hexavalent tellurium: as **a :** a very weak acid H_6TeO_6 that is a good oxidizing agent and is obtainable in two crystalline forms and as a tetrahydrate by oxidizing tellurium or tellurium dioxide — called also *orthotelluric acid* **b :** a polymerized acid $(H_2TeO_4)_n$ obtainable in a syrupy mixture by heating orthotelluric acid; poly-meta-telluric acid — called also *allo-telluric acid*

telluric line *n* **:** any of the absorption lines or bands added to the spectrum of a heavenly body by various substances in the earth's atmosphere ⟨the *telluric lines* of nitrogen, oxygen, water vapor⟩

tel·lu·ride \ˈtelyəˌrīd\ *n* -s [ISV *tellur-* + *-ide*] **:** a binary compound of tellurium usu. with a more electropositive element or radical ⟨metal ~*s* are sometimes regarded as alloys⟩

tel·lu·rif·er·ous \ˌtelyəˈrif(ə)rəs\ *adj* [ISV *tellur-* + *-ferous*] **:** containing or yielding tellurium

tel·lu·rite \ˈtelyəˌrīt\ *n* -s [*tellur-* + *-ite*] **1 :** a salt of tellurous acid **2 :** a mineral TeO_2 that consists of tellurium dioxide and occurs sparingly in tufts of white or yellowish crystals

tel·lu·ri·um \təˈlu̇rēəm, tel, |lˈyu̇-\ *n* -s [NL, fr. *tellur-* + *-ium*] **1 :** a semimetallic element that is related to selenium and sulfur and resembles them chemically, that is known either in a silvery white brittle crystalline form having a metallic luster but conducting electricity poorly or in a dark amorphous form of variable properties, that burns in air with a greenish blue flame to yield the crystalline dioxide, that is found native but more often combined esp. with metals in tellurides (as sylvanite) associated with sulfides and selenides, that is obtained usu. as a by-product in the electrolytic refining of copper and also as a fission product of uranium, and that is used chiefly in the rubber industry as a secondary vulcanizing agent and in metallurgy in iron castings and in copper, lead, and other alloys — symbol *Te;* see ELEMENT table **2 :** a place for the care and exhibition of selected flora and fauna (as in a school for instruction purposes)

tel·lu·rized \ˈtelyəˌrīzd\ *adj* [*tellur-* + *-ize* + *-ed*] **:** combined with or containing tellurium

tel·lu·ro·bismuthite \ˌtelyə(ˌ)rō, təˈlu̇(ˌ)rō, tel, |lˈyu̇-+\ *n* [*tellur-* + *bismuthite*] **:** a mineral Bi_2Te_3 consisting of bismuth telluride and found as irregular plates or foliated masses

tel·lu·ro·ni·um \ˌtelyəˈrōnēəm\ *n* -s [NL, fr. *tellur-* + *-onium* (as in *sulfonium*)] **:** a univalent cation TeH_3^+ or radical H_3Te analogous to sulfonium

tel·lu·rous \ˈtelyərəs; təˈlu̇r-, tel, |lˈyu̇-\ *adj* [ISV *tellur-* + *-ous*] **:** of, relating to, or containing tellurium — used esp. of compounds in which this element has a lower valence than in telluric compounds

tellurous acid *n* **:** a very weak unstable acid H_2TeO_3 containing tetravalent tellurium and known in solution and in the form of salts

tel·ly \'teli\ *n* -ES [by shortening & alter.] *chiefly Brit* : TELEVISION: as **a** : television considered as a source of entertainment — usu. used with *the* ⟨a merciful relief from the mediocre twaddle on the ~ —*The People*⟩ **b** : a television receiver ⟨turn the ~ on —William Sansom⟩

tel·ma·tol·o·gy \,telmə'tälәjē\ *n* -ES [Gk *telmat-*, *telma* stagnant water, marsh + E *-o-* + *-logy;* akin to Gk *stalassein* to let drop, drip — more at STALE] : a branch of physiography treating of wet lands (as peat bogs or swamps)

1telo- — see 2TEL-

2telo- — see 1TEL-

telo·blast \'tēlə,blast, 'tel-\ *n* -S [ISV 2*tel-* + *-blast*] : one of the large cells that produce lines of smaller cells at the growing end of many embryos (as of most annelids) — **telo·blas·tic** \¦==¦blastik\ *adj*

1telo·cen·tric \¦==¦sen·trik\ *adj* [ISV 2*tel-* + *-centric*] : having the form of a straight rod due to the terminal position of the centromere ⟨a ~ chromosome⟩ — compare METACENTRIC

2telocentric \"\ *n* : a telocentric chromosome

telo·den·dri·on \,=='dendrēən\ *also* **tele·den·dron** *or* **telo·den·dron** \,=='dendrən\ *n, pl* **telo·den·dria** \-rēə\ [*telodendrion*, NL, fr. 2*tel-* + Gk *dendrion* small tree, dim. of *dendron* tree; *teledendron*, *telodendron*, NL, fr. 2*tel-* + *-dendron* — more at DENDR-] : the terminal arborization of a nerve fiber — used orig. of dendrites but now esp. of the main arborization of an axon

telo·dynamic \¦tēlō, ¦telō+\ *adj* [ISV 1*tel-* + *dynamic*] : relating to the transmission of power to a distance esp. by a system of ropes or cables and pulleys

telo·go·nia \,=lə'gōnēə\ *n pl, cap* [NL, fr. 2*tel-* + *-gonia* (fr. Gk *gonos* offspring, procreation, genitals) — more at GON-] *in some classifications* : an order of Nematoda comprising forms in which new germ cells originate only at the distal end of the gonad — compare HOLOGONIA — **telo·gonic** \¦==¦gänik -¦gōn-\ *adj*

telo·lecithal \¦tēlō, ¦telō+\ *adj* [2*tel-* + Gk *lekithos* yolk of an egg + E *-al*] : having the yolk large in amount and concentrated at one pole — used of an egg; compare CENTROLECITHAL

telome \'tē,lōm *also* 'te,l-\ *n* -S [ISV 2*tel-* + *-ome;* orig. formed as G *telom*] : a basic unit of structure in vascular plants: **a** : a terminal branchlet having a distal sporangium and a vascular supply **b** : the simplest most fundamental unit of the plant body whether terminal or not — compare MESOME — **te·lomic** \tē'lōmik, te'l-, -läm-\ *adj*

tel·o·mer \'teləmə(r)\ *n* -S [2*tel-* + *-mer*] : the product of telomerization

telo·mere \'tēlə,mi(ə)r, 'tel-\ *n* -S [ISV 2*tel-* + *-mere*] : a chromosome end regarded as a specialized self-perpetuating structure

tel·o·mer·iza·tion \,teləmərə'zāshən, -,rī'z-\ *n* -S [*telomer* + *-ize* + *-ation*] : a chemical reaction involving addition of fragments of one molecule (as of an alcohol, acetal, or chloroform) to the ends of a polymerizing olefin system ⟨~ of carbon tetrachloride with styrene in the presence of acetyl peroxide forms the telomer $Cl[CH(C_6H_5)CH_2]_nCCl_3$⟩

telome theory *n* : a theory in botany: the entire plant body can be interpreted in terms of telomes whether single, with or without sporangia, or variously modified (as in being fused to serve as leaves or other organs)

telo·mit·ic \¦==¦mid·ik\ *adj* [2*tel-* + *mit-* + *-ic*] : TELOCENTRIC

teloogoo *usu cap, var of* TELUGU

te·lo·pea \tə'lōpēə\ *n, cap* [NL, fr. Gk *tēlōpos* seen from afar, fr. *tēl-* 1tel- + *-ōpos* (akin to Gk *ōps* eye, face) — more at EYE] : a genus of Australian shrubs and trees (family Proteaceae) notable for their showy scarlet tetramerous flowers which have a common involucre at the base of the clusters and which are followed by capsules with winged seeds — see WARATAH

telo·phase \'tēlə, 'telə+,-\ *n* [ISV 2*tel-* + *phase;* orig. formed in G] : the final stage of mitosis in which the new nuclei are differentiated and which is usu. accompanied by cytoplasmic division to form new daughter cells — **telo·phasic** \¦==+\ *adj*

telo·phragma \¦==+\ *n, pl* **telophragmata** [NL, fr. 2*tel-* + Gk *phragma* fence — more at PHRAGMA] : KRAUSE'S MEMBRANE

te·lop·o·dite \tə'läpə,dīt\ *n* -S [2*tel-* + *-podite*] : the part of the arthropod limb distal to the coxa

te·los \'tē,läs, 'te,l-\ *n, pl* -ES [Gk — more at WHEEL] : an ultimate end or object

telo·spo·rid·ia \,tēlōspə'ridēə, ,tel-\ *n pl, cap* [NL, fr. 2*tel-* + *-sporidia*] : a subclass of Sporozoa comprising parasitic protozoans that form spores without polar capsules or filaments which contain one or more infective sporozoites and including the orders Gregarinida, Coccidia, and Haemosporidia — **telo·spo·rid·i·an** \¦===¦=dēən\ *adj or n*

telo·syn·ap·sis \¦==sə¦napsəs\ *n* [NL, fr. 2*tel-* + *synapsis*] : end-to-end union of chromosomes in synapsis — compare PARASYNAPSIS — **telo·syn·ap·tic** \-ptik\ *adj* — **telo·syn·ap·tist** \-ptəst\ *n*

telo·syndesis \¦tēlō, ¦telō+\ *n* [NL, fr. 2*tel-* + *syndesis*] : TELOSYNAPSIS

telo·taxis \"+\ *n* [NL, fr. 2*tel-* + *taxis*] : a taxis in which an organism orients itself in respect to a stimulus (as a light source) as though that were the only stimulus acting on it

telo·trema·ta \,==·'tremәd·ə, -rēm-\ *n pl, cap* [NL, fr. 2*tel-* + Gk *trēmata*, pl. of *trēma* hole — more at THROW] : an order of brachiopods having the opening for the peduncle shared by both valves in earlier stages but usu. confined to one in later stages and more or less limited below by a pair of deltidial plates and having spiral arms that are supported by calcareous bars, loops, or spirals — **telo·tremate** \,=='=mәt\ *n* -S — **telo·trema·tous** \¦==¦=məd·əs\ *adj*

telo·troch \'==,träk\ *n* -S [NL *telotrocha*] **1 a** : the preanal tuft of cilia in a trochophore larva **b** : a ciliated girdle at the hinder end of an actinotrocha or of the tornaria of hemichordates **2** : TELOTROCHA

te·lot·ro·cha \tə'lä·trəkə\ *n, pl* **telotro·chae** \-,kē\ [NL, fr. 2*tel-* + *-trocha*] : a larva of various annelids having a preoral and a posterior circlet or tuft of cilia — **te·lot·ro·chal** \-,kəl\ *adj* — **te·lot·ro·chous** \-kəs\ *adj*

telo·troph \'tēlə·,träf, 'tel-, -rȯf\ *n* -S [2*tel-* + Gk *trophos* feeder — more at TROPH-] : a growing vegetative form of some sporozoans that does not engage in schizogony

telo·troph·ic \¦==·¦träfik\ *adj* : ACROTROPHIC

telo·type \'tēlə,tīp, 'tel-\ *n* [1*tel-* + *-type*] **1** : a printing telegraph **2** : an automatically printed telegram

tel·pher *also* **tel·fer** \'telfə(r)\ *n* -S [*telpher* irreg. fr. 1*tel-* + Gk *pherein* to bear; *telfer* alter. of *telpher* — more at BEAR] : a light car suspended from and running on aerial cables; *esp* : one automatically propelled by electricity

tel·pher·age *also* **tel·fer·age** \-fərij\ *n* -S **1** : a system of automatic electric transportation; *esp* : an automatic electric system in which the cars are hung from and run on wire cables suspended in the air **2** : a telpher system operated by other than electric power

telpher carrier *n* : the carriage, car, bucket, or other unit container used in a telpher conveyor system

tel·pher·man \'telfə(r)mən\ *n, pl* **telphermen** : a telpher operator

tel·puch·cal·li \,tel,püch'kälē\ *n, pl* **telpuchcalli** [Sp *telpuchcali*, *telpuchcalli*, fr. Nahuatl *telpuchcalli*] : an Aztec school for boys giving instruction in civil and military arts including crafts, history, and religious practices — distinguished from *calmecac*

tel·son \'telsən, -,sän\ *n* -S [NL, fr. Gk, boundary, limit, prob. fr. *telos* end — more at WHEEL] : the terminal segment of the body of an arthropod or segmented worm or of a crustacean (as the lobster) where it forms the middle lobe of the tail — **tel·son·ic** \(')tel¦sänik\ *adj*

tel·u·gu *or* **tel·e·gu** *also* **tel·oo·goo** \'telə,gü\ *n, pl* **telugu** *or* **telugus** *or* **telegu** *or* **telegus** *also* **teloogoo** *or* **teloogoos** *usu cap* **1 a** : the largest group of people in Andhra, India **b** : a member of such people **2 a** : the Dravidian language of the Telugu people **b** : the script usu. employed in writing this language

telvsn *abbr* television

tel·yn \'telən\ *n* -S [W, fr. MW; akin to OCorn *telein* harp, Bret *telenn*] : an old Celtic harp

TEM \¦tē,ē¦em\ *abbr or n* -S : TRIETHYLENEMELAMINE

te·ma \'tāmə\ *n* -S [It, theme (in general), fr. L *thema* — more at THEME] : THEME 4a

te·ma·cha \'tāmə,chä, tā'mächə\ *n* -S [Per *tamākhra* joke, humor] : a Persian comic or farcical interlude performed by traveling players

tem·a·dau \,temə'dau̇\ *n, pl* **temadau** *or* **temadaus** [native name in Borneo] : a Bornean banteng

te·ma·la·ca·tl \,tāmələ'käd·ᵊl\ *n* -S [Nahuatl, lit., spindle stone, fr. *tetl* stone + *malacatl* spindle] : a spindle-shaped stone in Aztec sacrificial rites to which an inadequately armed captive was attached while allowed ostensibly to defend himself against his executioners — called also *spindle stone*

tem·be \'tembē\ *n, pl* **tembe** *or* **tembes** *usu cap* **1** : a people that is a northern Malay branch of the Sakai **2** : a member of the Tembe people

tem·blor \'temblə(r), 'tem,blȯ(ə)r, -ȯ(ə)\ *or* **trem·blor** \'trem-\ *or* **trem·bler** \-mblə(r)\ *n* -S [*temblor* fr. Sp, trembling, earthquake, fr. *temblar* to tremble, quiver, fr. ML *tremulare; tremblor* alter. of *trembler; trembler* modif. (influenced by E *tremble*) of Sp. *temblor* — more at TREMBLE] : EARTHQUAKE ⟨deposits of sand and mud . . . periodically dislodged by submarine ~*s* —F.J.Pettijohn⟩

tem·bu \'tem(,)bü\ *n, pl* **tembu** *or* **tembus** *usu cap* **1** : a Bantu-speaking people of Tembuland in southern Africa **2** : a member of the Tembu people

tem·e·nos \'temə,näs\ *n, pl* **teme·ne** \-,nē\ [Gk, piece of land cut off as an official or sacred domain, temenos, fr. *temnein* to cut — more at TOME] : a temple enclosure or court in ancient Greece : a sacred precinct

tem·er·ar·i·ous \¦temə¦ra(a)rēəs, -¦rer-\ *adj* [L *temerarius*, fr. *temere* by chance, rashly + *-arius* -ary — more at TEMERITY] **1** : marked by temerity : rashly or presumptuously daring : RECKLESS, BRASH ⟨how often we have been cowardly and hung back, or ~ and rushed unwisely in —R.L.Stevenson⟩ **2** *archaic* : happening by chance : FORTUITOUS ⟨principles . . . not merely casual and ~ —James Harris⟩ **syn** see ADVENTUROUS

tem·er·ar·i·ous·ly *adv* : in a temerarious manner : RASHLY, FOOLHARDILY ⟨~ criticized the board chairman in open meeting⟩

tem·er·ar·i·ous·ness *n* -ES : the quality or state of being temerarious : TEMERITY

te·mer·i·ty \tə'merəd·ē, -rətē, -i\ *n* -ES [ME *temeryte*, fr. L *temeritas*, fr. *temere* by chance, rashly + *-itas* -ity; akin to OS *thim* dark, OHG *demar* darkness, *dinstar* dark, ON *thām* mugginess, OIr *temel* darkness, L *tenebrae*, Skt *tamas;* basic meaning: dark] : unreasonable or foolhardy contempt of danger or opposition : reckless and often presumptuous boldness : rash venturesomeness ⟨a private with the ~ to speak up against the sergeant's bullying⟩ ⟨the author's intellectual ~ is colossal —Rubin Gotesky⟩

syn HARDIHOOD, AUDACITY, NERVE, EFFRONTERY, CHEEK, GALL: TEMERITY suggests a boldness or courage in forward action or gesture arising from contempt of danger or from lack of due consideration of chances of failure, rebuff, or defeat ⟨he impetuously brushed aside the legalistic twaddle of the lawyers . . . and they frowned on such *temerity* —C.G. Bowers⟩ ⟨tenth-rate critics and compilers, for whom any violent shock to the public taste would be a *temerity* not to be risked —Matthew Arnold⟩ HARDIHOOD indicates a determined resolution or self-confidence in bold gestures that may involve defiance or insolence ⟨glowering in sullen suspense between *hardihood* and fear —John Galsworthy⟩ ⟨the reviewers . . . were staggered by my *hardihood* in offering a woman of forty as a subject of serious interest —Arnold Bennett⟩ AUDACITY suggests a daring boldness with an openly expressed disdain of prudence, restraint, convention, or authority ⟨the supreme *audacity* of looking into her soul —Victoria Sackville-West⟩ ⟨the *audacity* . . . in offering battle against forces ten times his own⟩ NERVE indicates an assured, cool boldness which may offend by being presumptuous ⟨you had the *nerve* to ask me to marry you —Barnaby Conrad⟩ EFFRONTERY suggests flagrant or flaunted insolence that is rude and presumptuous ⟨had the *effrontery* to pose as the avenger of outraged morality —G.B.Shaw⟩ ⟨unable to endure the cool *effrontery* of a Yankee schoolmaster's dabbling in affairs peculiarly English —H.R.Warfel⟩ CHEEK suggests impudent or insolently flaunted self-assurance ⟨I've never allowed anyone to talk to me as you do . . . you have the *cheek* of the devil himself —Hartley Howard⟩ GALL is most extreme in suggesting a brazen boldness likely to irritate or enrage ⟨some have only one attribute, a colossal *gall* —Stanley Walker⟩

tem·es·cal *or* **tem·as·cal** \,temə'skal\ *n* -S [MexSp *temascal*, fr. Nahuatl *temazcalli*, fr. *tema* to bathe + *calli* house] : a sweathouse of Mexican or Central American Indians

tem·minck's stint \'temiŋks-\ *n, usu cap T* [after Conrad J. *Temminck* †1858 Du. naturalist] : a very small Old World sandpiper (*Pisobia temminckii* or *Calidris temminckii*) that is largely gray with sparse white markings on wings and tail

tem·ne \'temnē\ *or* **tim·ne** \'tim-\ *n, pl* **temne** *or* **temnes** *or* **timne** *or* **timnes** *usu cap* **1 a** : a people of the interior of Sierra Leone in western Africa **b** : a member of the Temne people **2** : a West-Atlantic language of the Temne people

tem·no·spon·dy·li \,temnō'spändə,lī\ *n pl, cap* [NL, fr. Gk *temnein* to cut + NL *-o-* + *-spondyli* — more at TOME] *in some classifications* : a suborder of Stegocephalia including parts of the orders Embolomeri and Rhachitomi and sometimes the Stereospondyli

tem·no·spon·dy·lous \¦==¦spändələs\ *adj* [NL *Temnospondyli* + E *-ous*] **1** : RHACHITOMOUS — opposed to *stereospondylous* **2** : of or relating to the Temnospondyli

tem·o·ra \'temərə\ *n, cap* [NL] : a genus of marine copepods important as fish food in northern waters

temp \'temp\ *n* -S [by shortening] **1** : TEMPERATURE **2** : TEMPO

temp *abbr* **1** temperance **2** template **3** temporal **4** temporary **5** [L *tempore*] in the time of

tem·pe \'tempē\ *n* -S *usu cap* [L, fr. *Tempe*, a beautiful valley in ancient Thessaly, fr. Gk *Tempē*] : a place (as a valley, glen, or rustic retreat) of great natural beauty and charm

tem·pe·an \-ēən\ *adj* : of, relating to, or resembling a Tempe

1tem·per \'tempə(r)\ *vb* **tempered**; **tempered**; **tempering** \-p(ə)riŋ\ **tempers** [ME *tempren*, *temperen*, fr. OE & OF; OE *temprian* & OF *temprer*, fr. L *temperare* to mix, blend, regulate, restrain oneself, abstain, prob. fr. *tempor-*, *tempus* period of time, fitting time, season, time (in general) — more at TEMPORAL] *vt* **1 a** : to dilute, qualify, or soften (as something strong, harsh, or excessive) by the addition or influence of something else : make temperate : MODERATE, SEASON ⟨~ wine with water⟩ ⟨~ justice with mercy⟩ ⟨enthusiasm ~*ed* with a touch of skepticism⟩ ⟨~*s* the wind . . . to the shorn lamb —Laurence Sterne⟩ ⟨the breeze . . . ~*ed* the August sun —Arnold Bennett⟩ ⟨his firmness must always be ~*ed* with tact and shrewdness —R.M.Dawson⟩ **b** : to make suitable for : adapt to : ADJUST, MODIFY — usu. used with *to* ⟨officers . . . ~ their actions to outside political whimsy —T.H.White b.1915⟩ ⟨stick to these few principles and ~ them to suit your taste —Betty Fisk⟩ **c** *archaic* : to mix (ingredients) in suitable proportions : prepare by combining : COMPOUND, BLEND ⟨a confection after the art of the apothecary, ~*ed* together —Exod 30:35 (AV)⟩ ⟨importuned me to ~ poisons for her —Shak.⟩ **2** *archaic* **a** : to exercise control over : GOVERN, RESTRAIN ⟨Jove ~*s* the fates of human race above —Alexander Pope⟩ **b** : to cause to be well disposed : MOLLIFY ⟨~*ed* and reconciled them both —Richard Steele⟩ **3** : to bring (a substance or material) to a suitable state (as of consistency or workability) by mixing in or adding a usu. liquid ingredient: as **a** (1) : to mix (clay) with water and knead to a uniform texture (2) : to add an aplastic material (as grog or sand) to (clay) **b** : to mix oil with (colors) in making paint ready for use **c** : to moisten (as sand for molding) to a proper consistency and stir thoroughly **d** : to dampen or remove moisture from (grain) to secure the best grinding **e** : to make (leather) uniformly moist and soft for further processing **4 a** (1) : to soften (hardened steel or cast iron) by reheating at a temperature well below that from which previous quenching for hardening was done (2) : to harden and reheat (steel or cast iron) or to harden alone esp. in oil — not used technically **b** : to anneal or toughen (glass) by a process of gradually heating and cooling **5** : to make stronger and more resilient through hardship : TOUGHEN ⟨the hammerblows of fate seemed not to weaken but to ~ her strength —John Buchan⟩ **6 a** : to put in tune with : ATTUNE ⟨to which the birds ~*ed* their matin lay —P.B.Shelley⟩ ⟨our ears are ~*ed* to harsh sounds —Ronald Bottrall⟩ **b** : to adjust the pitch of (a note, chord, instrument) to a temperament ~ *vi* : to produce satisfactory temper — used of metallic alloys which can be treated to give the desired physical properties **syn** see MODERATE

2temper \"\ *n* -S [ME *tempre*, fr. *tempren*, v.] **1 a** *archaic* : the state of any compound substance resulting from the mixture of ingredients; *esp* : a suitable proportion or balance of qualities : a middle state between extremes : MEAN, MEDIUM ⟨virtue is . . . a just ~ between propensities any one of which, if indulged to excess, becomes vice —T.B.Macaulay⟩ **b** *archaic* : a particular mixture of elements or characteristics : CHARACTER, QUALITY ⟨the ~ of the land you design to sow —John Mortimer⟩ ⟨a man of such a feeble ~ —Shak.⟩ **c** : characteristic tone : TREND, TENDENCY ⟨the ~ of the times⟩ ⟨the general ~ of his view —Alan Gewirth⟩ ⟨literary circles which foster certain modes and ~*s* of form and emotion —W.S.B.Braithwaite⟩ ⟨the ~ of English literature at the turn of the century —*Times Lit. Supp.*⟩ **d** : high quality of mind or spirit : COURAGE, METTLE ⟨no trumpet calls . . . to keep our ~ at its keenest —R.W.Livingstone⟩ ⟨not of the ~ of which martyrs are made —Ellen Glasgow⟩ **2** : the state of a substance with respect to certain desired qualities (as hardness, elasticity, or workability): as **a** (1) : the degree of hardness or resiliency given steel by tempering (2) : the color of steel after tempering : TEMPER COLOR **b** : the condition of relative dryness (as of grain) proper for treatment in processing **c** : the feel and relative solidity of leather **3** : a substance added to or mixed with something else to modify the properties of the latter: as **a** : any of various mixtures of metals added to another metal in making an alloy **b** : the carbon content of steel that affects its hardening properties **c** : the moisture content of foundry sand **d** : aplastic material (as grog or sand) added to clay to reduce shrinkage upon drying and firing **4 a** *obs* : atmospheric conditions : CLIMATE ⟨the changeful ~ of the skies —John Dryden⟩ **b** *archaic* : TEMPERATURE **5 a** : a characteristic or habitual cast of mind or state of feeling : DISPOSITION ⟨a calm ~⟩ ⟨a sunny ~⟩ ⟨an occupation that suited his ~⟩ ⟨the man of mercurial ~ —William McDougall⟩ ⟨that reverence towards fact which constitutes . . . the scientific ~ —Bertrand Russell⟩ **b** : calmness of mind : COMPOSURE, EQUANIMITY ⟨keep me in ~; I would not be mad —Shak.⟩ — used esp. in the expressions *keep one's temper*, *lose one's temper*, and *out of temper* ⟨kept his ~ despite the provocation⟩ ⟨failed to get the witness to lose her ~⟩ ⟨are you out of ~ because you let those men put something over on you —Ellen Glasgow⟩ **c** : state of feeling or frame of mind at a particular time : HUMOR, MOOD ⟨had they been in a ~ to judge fairly —T.B. Macaulay⟩ ⟨kept the populace . . . in good ~ —R.M.French⟩ ⟨she was . . . in a gay, frolicsome ~ —W.H.Hudson †1922⟩ **d** : heat of mind or emotion : proneness to anger : PASSION ⟨a man with a ~ to beware of⟩ ⟨a display of ~⟩ ⟨as the strike dragged on, ~*s* flared on all sides —Mary K. Hammond⟩ ⟨threw down the cloth in a ~ —*Irish Digest*⟩ **syn** see DISPOSITION, MOOD

tem·pera *also* **tem·po·ra** \'tempərə\ *n* -S *often attrib* [It *tempera* temper (of metals), distemper (in music), tempera, fr. *temperare* to temper, fr. L — more at TEMPER] : a process of painting in which an albuminous or colloidal medium is employed as a vehicle instead of oil — compare 4DISTEMPER

tem·per·able \'tempərəbəl\ *adj* [ME, fr. *tempren*, *temperen* to temper + *-able*] : capable of being tempered

temperality *n* -ES *obs* : physical condition ⟨now you are in an excellent good ~ —Shak.⟩

tem·per·a·ment \'temp(ə)rəmənt, -pərm-\ *n* -S [ME, fr. L *temperamentum*, fr. *temperare* to mix, blend, regulate + *-mentum* -ment — more at TEMPER] **1** *obs* **a** : the state (as of a substance, body, or organism) with respect to the mixture or balance in due proportions of its elements, qualities, or parts : CONSTITUTION, MAKEUP ⟨the best founded commonwealths . . . have aimed at a certain mixture or ~, partaking the several virtues of each other state —John Milton⟩ **b** : COMPLEXION 1b **2 a** : the peculiar or distinguishing mental or physical character of a person as determined according to medieval physiology by the relative proportions of the humors in his body — compare 1HUMOR 1b ⟨the choleric, melancholic, phlegmatic, and sanguine ~*s*⟩ **b** : characteristic or habitual inclination, frame of mind, or mode of emotional response ⟨a nervous ~⟩ ⟨the artistic ~⟩ ⟨the poetic ~⟩ ⟨buoyant and expansive in ~⟩ ⟨the mind of a dreamer joined to the ~ of a soldier —John Buchan⟩ ⟨the ~ of an animal shown by its gait and carriage⟩ **c** : extremely high sensibility; *esp* : excessive sensitiveness or irritability often accompanied by impatience or lack of restraint : TEMPER ⟨always having ~ and making trouble —*This Week Mag.*⟩ ⟨dropped his racket during a rare display of ~ —Harry Gordon⟩ **3** *archaic* **a** : CLIMATE **b** : TEMPERATURE 5 **4** *archaic* **a** : the act or process of tempering or modifying : ADJUSTMENT, COMPROMISE ⟨any ~ that can be found in things . . . so disputable —John Milton⟩ **b** : middle course : MEAN ⟨a judicious ~, which the reformers would have done well to adopt —Henry Hallam⟩ **5 a** : the system or process of slightly modifying the musical intervals of the pure scale to produce a set of compromise tones consisting of 12 fixed tones to the octave and thus permit modulations without the use of an inconveniently large number of distinctions in pitch **b** : the adjustment so made **syn** see DISPOSITION

tem·per·a·men·tal \¦temp(ə)rə¦mentᵊl, -pər¦-\ *adj* **1** : of, relating to, or arising from temperament : CONSTITUTIONAL ⟨~ peculiarities⟩ ⟨~ indifference to neatness and order —G. W.Johnson⟩ **2 a** : marked by excessive sensitivity and sudden impulsive and often explosive changes of mood : HIGH-STRUNG, EXCITABLE ⟨a ~ opera singer⟩ ⟨~, argumentative and full of rowdy spirits —Stanley Walker⟩ **b** : marked by erratic, unpredictable behavior : CAPRICIOUS, FICKLE ⟨this parasite . . . proved to be a most ~ performer; sometimes it would and sometimes it would not —C.C.Furnas⟩ ⟨that beautiful, but ~ instrument, the flute —Osbert Lancaster⟩

tem·per·a·men·tal·ly \-ᵊlē, -ᵊli\ *adv* : in, by, or according to temperament : in nature or disposition : CONSTITUTIONALLY ⟨~ a conservative⟩ ⟨~ unable to appreciate irony⟩ ⟨a time that was ~ unfriendly to . . . historical criticism —R.E.Spiller⟩

tem·per·ance \'temp(ə)rən(t)s, -pərn-\ *n* -S *often attrib* [ME *temperaunce*, fr. L *temperantia*, fr. *temperant-*, *temperans* (pres. part. of *temperare* to mix, blend, regulate, restrain oneself, abstain) + *-ia* -y — more at TEMPER] **1 a** : moderation in action, thought, or feeling : RESTRAINT ⟨the cardinal virtues of prudence, justice, ~, and fortitude⟩ ⟨public opinion . . . its ~ or caprice —A.E.Stevenson †1965⟩ ⟨compositions marked by ~, serious reflection, and expert writing —*New Yorker*⟩ **b** : habitual moderation in the indulgence of the appetites or passions : SELF-CONTROL ⟨preaches ~ in the enjoyment of the pleasures of bed and table⟩ ⟨his own . . . perfect ~ had in it a fascinating power —Walter Pater⟩; *specif* : moderation in or abstinence from the use of intoxicating drink : SOBRIETY ⟨~ in those days was generally understood to mean total abstinence —John Lardner⟩ **2 a** *obs* : the proper mixture or proportion of elements or qualities; *esp* : the combination producing the desired state of a substance : CONSISTENCY ⟨boiled until they come unto a soft ~ —Edward Topsell⟩ **b** : mildness of weather or climate : TEMPERATENESS ⟨this island . . . must needs be of subtle, tender, and delicate ~ —Shak⟩.

tem·per·ate \'temp(ə)rət, *usu* -əd+V\ *adj* [ME *temperat*, fr. L *temperatus*, fr. past part. of *temperare*] **1** : marked by moderation : keeping or existing in the middle ground between extremes: as **a** : keeping or held within limits : not extreme or excessive : MILD ⟨expressing ~ satisfaction with his results —R.W.Firth⟩ **b** : moderate in indulgence of appetite or desire : SELF-CONTROLLED, CONTINENT ⟨singularly ~ . . . noted for his scant indulgence in meat, drink, or sleep —J.R.Green⟩ **c** : moderate in or abstemious from the use of intoxicating liquors ⟨not as ~ as he might have been but never a drunkard⟩ **d** : marked by an absence or avoidance of extravagance, violence, or extreme partisanship : RESTRAINED, DISPASSIONATE ⟨~ language⟩ ⟨rare indeed is such ~ and rational discussion of crucial problems —C.A.Baylis⟩ **e** : having duly limited power : CONSTITUTIONAL — used of a monarchy or ruler ⟨our loyal passion for our ~ kings —Alfred Tennyson⟩ **f** : existing as a prophage in infected cells and rarely causing lysis ⟨~ bacteriophages⟩ **2 a** : having a moderate climate ⟨a ~ region⟩ ⟨the ~ zones⟩ **b** : found in or associated with a moderate climate ⟨a ~ plant⟩ ⟨~ insects⟩ **c :** of or relating to a point (as the 66° F reading on a thermometer) marking a moderate temperature **3 :** TEMPERED — used of a musical interval or scale **syn** see SOBER

tem·per·ate·ly *adv* [ME *temperatly*, fr. *temperat* + *-ly*] **:** in a temperate manner: as **a :** without extravagance **:** DISPASSIONATELY ⟨these preferences are ~ . . . stated —Agnes Repplier⟩ **b :** with restraint ⟨~ used the privileges of his office —A.T. Quiller-Couch⟩ **c :** without overindulgence **:** ABSTEMIOUSLY ⟨indulge ~ in cocktails⟩

tem·per·ate·ness *n* -ES [ME *temperatnes*, fr. *temperat* + *-nes* -ness] **:** the quality or state of being temperate **:** MODERATION: as **a** *obs* **:** TEMPERANCE 1b **b :** SELF-RESTRAINT ⟨an effective ~ in debate⟩ **c :** mildness of climate ⟨the ~ of the weather⟩

temperate rain forest *n* **:** woodland of temperate but usu. rather mild climatic areas with heavy rainfall usu. including numerous kinds of trees and being distinguished from tropical rain forest by the presence of a dominant tree (as the podocarpus forests of New Zealand)

temperate zone *n, often cap T&Z* **:** the area or region between the tropic of Cancer and the arctic circle or between the tropic of Capricorn and the antarctic circle

tem·per·a·ture \R ˈtempə(r)ˌchu̇(ə)r, -p(ə)rəl, ˌchər *sometimes* ˌ·ˌtyu̇(ə)r *or* ˌtu̇(ə)r *or* ˈtem(p)chər; *-R* ˈtempə(r)ˌchu̇ə, -p(ə)rəl, ˌchə *sometimes* ˌ·ˌtyu̇ə *or* ˌtu̇ə *or* ˈtem(p)chə\ *n* -S *often attrib* [L *temperatura*, fr. *temperatus* (past part. of *temperare* to mix, blend, regulate, restrain oneself, abstain) + *-ura* -ure — more at TEMPER] **1** *archaic* **:** a mixture or blending of elements **:** COMPOSITION, CONSTITUTION ⟨beings of our make and ~ —John Bonnycastle⟩ **2** *obs* **a :** a proper middle course **:** a mean between extremes **:** COMPROMISE, MODERATION **b :** mildness of climate **:** TEMPERATENESS **3** *archaic* **a :** COMPLEXION 1b **b :** TEMPERAMENT 2a **c :** TEMPERAMENT 2b **4 :** TEMPER 2a **5 a :** degree of hotness or coldness measured on one of several arbitrary scales based on some observable phenomenon (as the expansion of mercury) **:** the degree of a material substance that is a linear function of the kinetic energy of the random motion of its molecules **:** the degree of a vacuum that depends upon the density of the radiant energy within it — compare ABSOLUTE ZERO, HEAT **b :** the degree of heat that is natural to the body of a living being, that in invertebrates and cold-blooded vertebrates approximates that of the environment, and that in warm-blooded vertebrates fluctuates in a narrow range characteristic of the kind of animal and largely independent of the environment ⟨man's normal oral ~ of about 98.6° F⟩ **c :** abnormally high body heat ⟨running a ~⟩ **:** a feverish condition ⟨had a ~ for three days⟩ **d :** relative state of emotional warmth **:** level of interest **:** INTENSITY ⟨aware of a change in the ~ of our friendship —Christopher Isherwood⟩ ⟨the low ~ of competition —V.O. Key⟩

temperature coefficient *n* **:** a numerical value indicating the relation between a change in temperature and a simultaneous change in some other property (as solubility); *specif* **:** the factor α in the equation $R_t = R_o(1+\alpha t)$ in which R_t equals the resistance of a conductor at $t°$ centigrade and R_o equals its resistance at 0° centigrade

temperature curve *n* **:** a graph recording changes in temperature over given periods of time

temperature gradient *n* **:** the rate of change of temperature with displacement in a given direction (as with increase of height) — compare LAPSE RATE

temperature inversion *n* **:** an increase of temperature with height through a layer of air

temperature scale *n* **1 :** the scale of degrees on a thermometer **2 :** a system of reckoning temperature ⟨the centigrade *temperature scale*⟩ ⟨the Kelvin *temperature scale*⟩ ⟨the international *temperature scale*⟩

temperature sensation *n* **:** a sensation of warmth or cold mediated respectively by warm spots and cold spots of the skin

temperature sense *n* **:** the largely cutaneous sense that responds to stimulation by warmth and cold

temperature spot *n* **:** one of many points on the skin that are selectively sensitive either to warmth or to cold

temperature wave *n* **:** a wave in which the propagated disturbance is a variation of temperature and of which the velocity is ordinarily very small except in the case of liquid helium II where the wave speed approaches that of sound — compare SECOND SOUND

temper color *n* **:** any of the colors varying from very pale yellow to very dark blue that are assumed by a smooth surface of steel as a result of reheating, are due to thin films of oxide, and correspond to definite temperatures

tem·pered \ˈtempə(r)d\ *adj* [ME *tempred, tempered*, fr. past part. of *tempren, temperen* to temper — more at TEMPER] **1 a :** having the elements or qualities mixed in proper or satisfying proportions **:** TEMPERATE ⟨this finely ~ air —G.B.Shaw⟩ ⟨has a wonderfully ~ mind —H.J.Laski⟩ **b :** qualified, lessened, or diluted by the mixture or influence of an additional ingredient **:** MODERATED ⟨a pale gleam of ~ sunlight fell through the leaves —W.H.Hudson †1922⟩ ⟨plea . . . for a guided and ~ experimentalism —P.H.Douglas⟩ **2 :** treated by tempering **:** brought to the desired state (as of hardness, flexibility, or resiliency) ⟨~ steel⟩ ⟨~ glass⟩ **3 :** having a specified temper — used in combination ⟨bad-*tempered*⟩ ⟨ill-*tempered*⟩ ⟨short-*tempered*⟩ ⟨even-*tempered*⟩ **4 :** conformed to esp. equal temperament — used of a musical interval, intonation, semitone, or scale

tem·per·er \ˈtempərə(r)\ *n* -S [¹*temper* + *-er*] **:** one that tempers: as **a :** one who mitigates or soothes **b :** one whose work is tempering (as metal, leather, chocolate) **c :** a machine in which materials (as lime or cement) are mixed with water

tempering *pres part of* TEMPER

tem·per·ish \-rish\ *adj* [²*temper* + *-ish*] **:** inclined to show temper **:** easily angered **:** IRASCIBLE ⟨a beefy, ~ customer, stubborn and cocksure —Arthur Mayse⟩

temper pin *n, chiefly Scot* **:** the regulating pin of a spinning wheel

tempers *pres 3d sing of* TEMPER, *pl of* TEMPER

temper screw *n* **1 :** a screw link to which the rope of a rope-drilling apparatus is attached so that the drill may be fed and slightly turned at each stroke **2 :** a setscrew used for adjusting

tem·per·some \-pə(r)səm\ *adj* [²*temper* + *-some*] **:** marked by displays of temper **:** HOTHEADED ⟨used to humoring a ~ man —Mary Webb⟩

tem·pery \-pərē\ *adj* [²*temper* + *-y*] **:** marked by quick temper or irritability **:** TOUCHY ⟨she had ~ ways —H.E.Giles⟩

tempes *pl of* TEMPE

¹**tem·pest** \ˈtempəst\ *n* -S [ME *tempeste, tempest*, fr. OF *tempeste*, fr. (assumed) VL *tempesta*, alter. of L *tempestas* period of time, season, weather, storm, fr. *tempus* time — more at TEMPORAL] **1 a :** an extensive violent wind; *esp* **:** one accompanied by rain, hail, or snow **:** a furious storm ⟨a real ~ blowing that had been rising for two or three days —Mary Webb⟩ **b** *dial* **:** THUNDERSTORM **2 :** a violent commotion or agitation **:** TUMULT, UPROAR ⟨a ~ of applause⟩ ⟨a ~ of tears⟩ ⟨a political ~⟩ ⟨raised a ~ of derision —T.B.Macaulay⟩ ⟨seek frantically for anchors amid the ~*s* of our time —Ben Bradford⟩ **3** *archaic* **a :** a noisy confused throng **b :** a fashionable assembly or reception **:** ²ROUT 4

²**tempest** \"\ *vb* -ED/-ING/-S [ME *tempesten*, fr. MF *tempester*, fr. *tempeste*, n.] *vt* **1 :** to raise commotion in **:** stir up **:** AGITATE ⟨the huge dolphin ~*ing* the main —Alexander Pope⟩ **2** *archaic* **:** to disturb by emotional outbursts **:** UPSET ⟨his house is ~*ed* by female eloquence —Thomas Campbell⟩ ~ *vi* **:** to cause a commotion like a tempest **:** RAGE, STORM ⟨she ~*ed* out —W.D.Howells⟩

tem·pes·ti·cal \(ˈ)temˈpestəkəl\ *adj* [¹*tempest* + *-ical*] *dial* **:** STORMY

tempest in a teapot : a great commotion about a matter of small importance ⟨her anger was unreasonable, a *tempest in a teapot* —E.A.McCourt⟩

tem·pes·tive \(ˈ)temˈpestiv\ *adj* [L *tempestivus*, fr. *tempestus* period of time, season (fr. *tempus* time) + *-ivus* -ive — more at TEMPORAL] *archaic* **:** occurring at a proper time or season **:** OPPORTUNE, TIMELY

tempest-tossed *or* **tempest-tost** \ˈ==ˌ=\ *adj* **:** tossed about or agitated violently **:** thrown into confusion **:** OVERWHELMED ⟨when upon life's billows you are *tempest-tossed* —Johnson Oatman⟩ ⟨send these, the homeless, *tempest-tossed*, to me —Emma Lazarus⟩

tem·pes·tu·ous \(ˈ)temˈpes(h)chəwəs\ *adj* [L *tempestuosus*, fr. *tempestus* + *-osus* -ous] **1 :** of, involving, or resembling a tempest **:** WINDY, WILD ⟨~ weather⟩ ⟨~ seas⟩ ⟨a wild, ~ evening, when the wind screamed and rattled against the windows —A. Conan Doyle⟩ **2 :** marked by violent disturbance **:** TURBULENT, STORMY ⟨an actress of ~ disposition⟩ ⟨a ~ debate⟩ ⟨~ ovations⟩ ⟨their ~ life together —Al Hine⟩ ⟨the rapidity of his ~ thoughts —Liam O'Flaherty⟩

tem·pes·tu·ous·ly *adv* **:** in a tempestuous manner **:** VIOLENTLY, STORMILY ⟨stirring the atmosphere ~⟩ ⟨those ~ beautiful moments which one had been so freely theirs —B.A.Williams⟩

tem·pes·tu·ous·ness *n* -ES **:** the quality or state of being tempestuous **:** STORMINESS, WILDNESS ⟨the ~ of the sea⟩ ⟨a time of violence and ~⟩

tempi *pl of* TEMPO

¹**tem·plar** \ˈtemplə(r)\ *n* -S [ME *templere, templer*, fr. OF *templier*, fr. ML *templarius*, fr. L *templum* temple + *-arius* -ary — more at TEMPLE] **1** *usu cap* **:** a member of a religious military order established about 1118 in Jerusalem, widespread in Europe, and suppressed by the Council of Vienne in 1312 **2 :** a barrister or student of law having chambers in the Temple, London **3** *usu cap* **:** KNIGHT TEMPLAR 2 **4** *sometimes cap* **:** GOOD TEMPLAR

²**templar** \"\ *adj* [L *templaris*, fr. *templum* + *-aris* -ar] **:** of or relating to a temple

tem·plary \-lərē\ *n* -ES *usu cap* [ME *templarie*, fr. ML *templarius*] **1** *obs* **:** ¹TEMPLAR 1 **2** [¹*templar* + *-y*] **:** the membership or realm of an organization of Templars

¹**tem·plate** *or* **tem·plet** \ˈtemplət, *usu* -əd·+V\ *n* -S [*template* alter. (influenced by *plate*) of *templet*; *templet* prob. fr. F, temple (device in a loom), dim. of *temple*] **1 :** a short piece placed horizontally in a wall under a girder or other beam to distribute its weight or pressure (as over a door or window frame) **2 :** a pattern or guide of any of various kinds used in manufacturing: as **a :** a usu. thin metal pattern used in laying out and scribing a work piece **b :** a metal pattern followed by the tracer of an automatic machine in guiding the cutting tool to produce a desired profile **c :** a chart showing the standard form against which machined parts are checked in an optical comparator **d :** any of various locating devices (as for placing rivets or applying airplane trim) **e :** a full-size wooden mold or paper pattern used in making ship hull parts of steel plate or wood **f :** a gage or pattern for checking dimensions, locations, or contours (as on castings) **g :** a pattern used in lettering **h :** a pattern used by a tailor or dressmaker in cutting a part to shape or in locating buttonholes **i :** ²OVERLAY 2f **3** *usu templet* **:** a bezel in a cut gem **4 :** ⁵LUTE 2 **5 :** a framed workbench for making theatrical flats

²**template** *also* **templet** \"\ *vt* -ED/-ING/-S **:** to mark or lay off the pattern or position of with a template ⟨he *templated* the rivet holes⟩

template excavator *n* **:** an excavator in which a small scoop moves back and forth along the underside of a vertical steel template having the form of the cross section of the ditch to be excavated

¹**tem·ple** \ˈtempəl\ *n* -S *often attrib* [ME, fr. OE & OF; OE *templ, tempel* & OF *temple*, fr. L *templum* space for observation marked out by the augur, consecrated place, shrine, temple; prob. akin to L *tempus* period of time — more at TEMPORAL] **1 :** an edifice dedicated to the worship of a deity **:** an edifice held to be a residing place of a deity **2** *often cap* **:** one of three successive buildings for Hebrew worship in ancient Jerusalem built respectively by Solomon, Zerubbabel, and Herod the Great **3 :** a usu. large imposing edifice for public worship **4 :** a place in which the divine presence specially resides ⟨the ~ of his body —Jn 2:21(RSV)⟩ ⟨you are God's ~ —1 Cor 3:16(RSV)⟩ **5 :** a building constructed, dedicated, and used for the administration of Mormon sacred ordinances to and for the living and to the living in behalf of the dead (as baptism for the dead, the endowment, and sealing in marriage) **6 :** SYNAGOGUE **7 a :** a local lodge of any of various fraternal orders or the building housing it **b :** a building housing labor organizations **8 a :** a building devoted to a particular purpose or focusing on activity of a special kind ⟨movie ~*s*⟩ ⟨financial ~*s*⟩ **b :** the structure of thought, value, or belief that enshrines the spirit or essence of something ⟨a belief that is the cornerstone of the ~ of Christian faith⟩ ⟨the ~ of man's historic achievement⟩ **c :** the center or focus of something prized or valued ⟨a ~ of domesticity⟩

²**temple** \"\ *vt* -ED/-ING/-S **:** to build or devote a temple to **:** provide with a temple

³**temple** \"\ *n* -S [ME, fr. MF, fr. (assumed) VL *tempula*, alter. (influenced by L *-ula*, fem. dim. suffix) of L *tempora*, pl. of *tempus* temple; prob. akin to L *tempus* period of time — more at TEMPORAL] **1 :** the area on each side of the head of man and some other mammals back of the eye and forehead, above the zygomatic arch, and in front of the ear **2 :** one of the side supports of a pair of glasses jointed to the bows and passing on each side of the head **3 :** the posterior or upper part of the gena of an insect

⁴**temple** \"\ *n* -S [ME *tempylle*, fr. MF *temple*, prob. fr. L *templum* temple (sanctuary), small timber] **:** a device (as a flat wooden bar with small pins at each end or nippers through which selvage must pass) in a loom for keeping the web stretched transversely

templed \-ld\ *adj* [¹*temple* + *-ed*] **1 :** supplied with temples or churches **2 :** enclosed in a temple

templelike \ˈ==ˌ=\ *adj* **:** resembling a temple

¹**temple mound** *n* **1 :** a mound forming the foundation of a temple (as in Mayan and Aztec architecture) — compare TEOCALLI **2 :** a truncated American Indian mound believed to have been the site of an altar or rude temple

²**temple mound** *adj, usu cap T&M* [¹*temple mound*] **:** of or belonging to a culture of the southern and southeastern U. S. about 1300–1700 characterized by pyramidal mounds built as platforms for temples and by village-states, shell-tempered polychrome pottery, and intensive hoe agriculture

¹**templet** *var of* TEMPLATE

²**tem·plet** \ˈtemplət\ *n* -S [F — more at TEMPLATE] **:** ⁴TEMPLE

³**templet** \"\ *n* -S [¹*temple* + *-et*] **:** a small temple

tem·ple·to·nia \ˌtempəlˈtōnēə\ *n, cap* [NL, fr. John *Templeton* †1825 Irish botanist + NL *-ia*] **:** a genus of Australian shrubs (family Leguminosae) having simple leaves and red or yellow flowers with a reflexed standard and narrow wings — see CORALBUSH

temple tree *n* **:** a tree grown in temple gardens; *esp* **:** PAGODA TREE c(1)

¹**tem·po** \ˈtem(ˌ)pō\ *n, pl* **tem·pi** \-pē\ *or* **tempos** [It, time, tempo, fr. L *tempus* time — more at TEMPORAL] **1 :** rate of rhythmic recurrence or movement; *specif* **:** the rate of speed of a musical piece or passage indicated by one of a series of directions associated conventionally with speed (as largo, presto, allegro) and often by an exact metronome marking ⟨the symphonies were set forth very authoritatively and occasionally in ~*s* more deliberate than some I have heard —Winthrop Sargeant⟩ **2 :** rate of motion or activity **:** PACE ⟨the campaign ~ stepped up —*Newsweek*⟩ ⟨staccato dance *tempi*⟩ ⟨increased sales and production ~ —*Wall Street Jour.*⟩ ⟨after dawn the ~ of the town slowed down —H.E.Rieseberg⟩ **3 :** a turn to move in chess in relation to one's opponent's turns ⟨gain a ~ when the opponent makes a useless move⟩

²**tempo** \"\ *n* -S [Jap] **:** an old oval bronze coin of Japan having a square hole in the center coined in the first half of the 19th century

¹**tempora** *pl of* TEMPUS

²**tempora** *var of* TEMPERA

¹**tem·po·ral** \ˈtemp(ə)rəl\ *adj* [ME, fr. L *temporalis*, fr. *tempor-, tempus* period of time, fitting time, season, time (in general) + *-alis* -al; akin to ON *thambr* swollen, thick, Lith *tempti* to stretch, and prob. to L *tendere* to stretch — more at THIN] **1 a :** of or relating to time as opposed to eternity **:** TEMPORARY, TRANSITORY ⟨~ matters of but fleeting moment —F.D.Roosevelt⟩ **b :** of or relating to earthly life as contrasted with heavenly **:** TERRESTRIAL ⟨the same actual, prosaic, uninspired regard which he turned upon ~ matters —Hilaire Belloc⟩ **c** [ME, fr. ML *temporalis*, fr. L] **:** of or relating to lay or secular concerns as opposed to clerical or sacred **:** CIVIL, POLITICAL ⟨~ courts⟩ ⟨~ power⟩ — see LORD TEMPORAL **2 a :** of or relating to the quantity of syllables (as in Greek and Latin verse) **b :** of or relating to grammatical tense **:** expressive of a distinction of time **3 :** of or relating to time as distinguished from space or to a particular time **:** CHRONOLOGICAL ⟨music is a ~ art —Hunter Mead⟩ ⟨all the external events of which we are aware are recorded as spatial and ~ patterns of excitation in the sense organs —E.D.Adrian⟩ **syn** see PROFANE

²**temporal** \"\ *n* -S [ME, fr. *temporal*, adj.] **:** something temporal, secular, or material **:** TEMPORALITY — usu. used in pl. ⟨its ~*s* provided the church's revenue⟩

³**temporal** \"\ *n* -S [MF, fr. *temporal*, adj.] **:** a temporal part (as a bone, muscle, or scale)

⁴**temporal** \"\ *adj* [MF, fr. LL *temporalis*, fr. L *tempor-, tempus* temple (of the head) + *-alis* -al — more at TEMPLE] **1 :** of or relating to the temples or the sides of the skull behind the orbits **2 :** of or relating to the temporal bone **3** *of a scale of a reptile* **:** lying behind the postoculars and between the parietals and supralabials

temporal arch *n* [⁴*temporal*] **:** a bony bar extending from the upper jaw to the quadrate in some turtles

temporal artery *n* [⁴*temporal*] **:** any of several arteries supplying the sides of the head: **a :** any of the branches of the internal maxillary artery that supplies the temporal muscle — called also *deep temporal artery* **b :** SUPERFICIAL TEMPORAL ARTERY **c :** any of three branches of the superficial temporal artery — called also respectively *anterior temporal artery, middle temporal artery, posterior temporal artery*

temporal augment *n* [¹*temporal*] **:** the lengthening of an initial vowel in past tenses of Greek and Sanskrit verbs

temporal bone *n* [⁴*temporal*] **:** a compound bone of the side of the human skull whose four principal parts are the squamous, petrous, and tympanic portions and the mastoid process

temporal convolution *or* **temporal gyrus** *n* [⁴*temporal*] **:** any of three major convolutions of the external surface of the temporal lobe of the cerebrum that are ordered approximately horizontally as a superior, a middle, and an inferior convolution

tem·po·ra·le \ˌtempəˈrä(ˌ)lē\ *n* -S [ML, fr. L, neut. of *temporalis* temporal (of time) — more at TEMPORAL] **:** a part of the breviary and missal that contains the daily offices of the ecclesiastical year — compare SANCTORALE

temporal fascia *n* [⁴*temporal*] **:** a broad fascia covering the temporal muscle and attached below to the zygomatic arch

temporal fossa *n* [⁴*temporal*] **:** one of the broad fossae on the sides of the skull of higher vertebrates behind the orbit lodging muscles for raising the lower jaw that in man is separated from the orbit by the zygomatic bone and greater wing of the sphenoid lying mostly above the zygomatic arch and is occupied by the temporal muscle

tem·po·ral·is \ˌtempəˈraləs, -ˈrāl-, -ˈräl-\ *n* -ES [NL, fr. LL, temporal (of the temple) — more at TEMPORAL] **:** TEMPORAL MUSCLE

tem·po·ral·ism \ˈtemp(ə)rəˌlizəm\ *n* -S [¹*temporal* + *-ism*] **:** a philosophical doctrine that emphasizes the ultimate reality of time and temporal things as contrasted with doctrines which reduce the temporal to a manifestation of the eternal — compare ETERNALISM

tem·po·ral·ist \-ˌləst\ *n* -S [¹*temporal* + *-ist*] **1 :** an adherent of the doctrine of temporalism **2 :** one who emphasizes the temporal element in analyzing the rhythmic structures of verse

tem·po·ral·is·tic \ˌ;temp(ə)rəˈlistik\ *adj* **:** of or relating to temporalism or temporalists

tem·po·ral·i·ty \ˌtempəˈraləd·ē, -lətē, -i\ *n* -ES [in sense 1, fr. ME *temporalite*, fr. ML *temporalitas*, fr. *temporalis* temporal (secular) + L *-itas* -ity; in sense 2, fr. LL *temporalitas*, fr. L *temporalis* temporal (of time) + *-itas* -ity — more at TEMPORAL] **1 a :** civil or political as distinguished from spiritual or ecclesiastical power or authority **b :** ecclesiastical properties or revenues — often used in pl. **2 a :** temporary or transitory quality **:** relation to time and the world rather than to eternity, transcendence, or spirit ⟨we cannot afford to be too self-conscious about the ~ of our attitudes —H.J.Muller⟩ **b :** concern with time, process, and overt mundane events as more real or significant than timeless or eternal forms, structures, or patterns (as ideas or institutions) **:** emphasis on change rather than permanence **c :** position, extension, or duration in time — distinguished from *spatiality*

tem·po·ral·ize \ˈtemp(ə)rəˌlīz\ *vt* -ED/-ING/-S [¹*temporal* + *-ize*] **1 :** to place or define in time relations **2 :** SECULARIZE

temporal lobe *n* [⁴*temporal*] **:** a large lobe of each cerebral hemisphere situated below the lateral fissure and in front of the occipital lobe and containing the middle cornu of the lateral ventricle

tem·po·ral·ly \-rəlē, -li\ *adv* [ME, fr. ¹*temporal* + *-ly*] **1 :** in regard to or with concern for temporal things **:** in earthly life **2 :** with regard to time

temporal muscle *n* [⁴*temporal*] **:** a large muscle in the temporal fossa serving to raise the lower jaw and in man being composed of fibers that arise from the surface of the temporal fossa and converge to an aponeurosis which contracts into a thick flat tendon inserted into the coronoid process of the mandible

temporal nerve *n* [⁴*temporal*] **:** any of several nerves derived from the facial and mandibular nerves and supplying the structures of the temporal region

tem·po·ral·ness *n* -ES [¹*temporal* + *-ness*] **:** the quality or state of being temporal

temporal pattern *n* [¹*temporal*] **:** the unitary impression produced by a succession of stimuli (as in a melody or rhythm)

temporal punishment *n* **:** a punishment for sin that according to Roman Catholic doctrine may be expiated in this world or if not sufficiently expiated here will be exacted in full in purgatory

temporal ridge *or* **temporal line** *n* [⁴*temporal*] **:** any of four nearly parallel curved ridges or lines situated two on each side of the skull and chiefly on the parietal bone

temporals *pl of* TEMPORAL

temporal sign *n* [¹*temporal*] **:** an indicator of the position or relations in time of something perceived

temporal sulcus *n* [⁴*temporal*] **:** any of the sulci between temporal convolutions

tem·po·ral·ty \ˈtemp(ə)rəltē, -ti\ *n* -ES [ME *temporalte*, fr. MF *temporalité*, fr. ML *temporalitat-, temporalitas* — more at TEMPORALITY] **1 a** *obs* **:** TEMPORALITY 1a **b :** TEMPORALITY 1b **2 :** lay persons (as lords temporal and commons) **:** LAITY — distinguished from *spirituality*

temporal vein *n* [⁴*temporal*] **:** any of several veins draining the temporal region: as **a :** a large vein on each side of the head formed by anterior and posterior tributaries from the scalp and adjacent parts receiving a middle tributary from the temporal muscle and uniting with the internal maxillary vein to form the posterior facial vein — called also *superficial temporal vein* **b :** one of the veins arising from behind the temporal muscle and emptying into the pterygoid plexus — called also *deep temporal vein*

tem·po·rar·i·ly \ˌ;tempəˈrerəlē, -li\ *adv* **1 :** for a brief period **:** during a limited time **:** BRIEFLY ⟨a power failure ~ darkened the town⟩ **2 :** in time **:** in relation to time **:** TEMPORALLY ⟨a ~ punctiform occurrence . . . must necessarily be counted as one event —H.A.C.Dobbs⟩

tem·po·rar·i·ness \ˈ==ˌrerēnəs, -ˌrerin-\ *n* -ES **:** the quality or state of being temporary

¹**tem·po·rary** \-ˌrerē, -reri\ *adj* [L *temporarius*, fr. *tempor-, tempus* period of time, fitting time, season, time (in general) + *-arius* -ary — more at TEMPORAL] **1 a :** lasting for a time only **:** existing or continuing for a limited time **:** IMPERMANENT, TRANSITORY ⟨insisted on the entirely ~ quality of any victory over nature —David Riesman⟩ **b** *obs* **:** bearing the marks of a particular time **:** deriving interest from or having relation to a restricted period or special era **:** DATED, EPHEMERAL — distinguished from *universal* **2** *obs* **a :** of or relating to man's present life on earth **:** MUNDANE, TEMPORAL **b :** occurring in or related to time rather than eternity

²**temporary** \"\ *n* -ES **:** someone or something serving for a limited time only ⟨the others were *temporaries* like me —Tom Weir⟩ ⟨the wartime *temporaries* . . . will be replaced by 75 permanent homes —*Springfield (Mass.) Union*⟩

temporary alimony *n* **:** ALIMONY PENDENTE LITE

temporary annuity *n* **:** an annuity payable for a limited time only; *usu* **:** TEMPORARY LIFE ANNUITY

temporary chairman *n* **:** the chairman chosen by the national committee of a political party to preside at the opening of a national convention

temporary duty *n* **:** military service away from one's assigned organization usu. for a limited period of time

temporary hardness *n* **:** the portion of the total hardness of water that is removable by boiling whereby the soluble bicarbonates of calcium and magnesium are converted into the corresponding insoluble carbonates and are precipitated — distinguished from *permanent hardness*

temporary life annuity *n* **:** an annuity payable for a life not extending beyond a specified date

temporary partial disability *n* **:** disability resulting from an injury that temporarily impairs a worker's earning capacity

temporary star *n* **:** NOVA

temporary total disability *n* **:** disability resulting from an injury that temporarily destroys a worker's earning capacity

temporary wilting *n* **:** wilting from which a plant will recover by reduction of the transpiration rate and without addition of water to the soil

tem·po·ri·za·tion \ˌtempərə̇ˈzāshən, -pəˌrīˈ-\ *n* -s **:** the act, policy, or practice of temporizing

tem·po·rize \ˈtempəˌrīz\ *vb* -ED/-ING/-S *see -ize in Explan Notes* [MF *temporiser*, fr. ML *temporizare* to pass the time, fr. L *tempor-, tempus* time + *-izare* -ize — more at TEMPORAL] *vi* **1 :** to act to suit the time or occasion **:** adapt to a situation **:** bow to practical necessities **2 :** to make terms or work out a compromise with someone or between parties **3 :** to draw out discussions or negotiations so as to gain time **:** put off decisive action ⟨you'd have to ~ until you found out how she wanted to be advised —Mary Austin⟩ **~** *vt* **:** EXTEMPORIZE

tem·po·riz·er \-zə(r)\ *n* -s **:** one that temporizes **:** TRIMMER, TIMESERVER

tem·po·riz·ing·ly *adv* **:** in a temporizing manner

temporo- *comb form* [⁴*temporal*] **:** temporal and ⟨*temporo*maxillary⟩ ⟨*temporo*frontal⟩

tem·po·ro·mandibular \ˈtempə(ˌ)rō+\ *adj* [*temporo-* + *mandibular*] **:** relating to or joining the temporal bone and the mandible

tem·po·ro·maxillary \"+\ *adj* [*temporo-* + *maxillary*] **:** relating to or situated in the region of the temporal bone or area and the upper jaw

tem·po·ro·spatial \"+\ *adj* [*temporo-* + *spatial*] **:** of, relating to, or occurring in both time and space

tempos *pl of* TEMPO

tempo turn *n* **:** a parallel-ski turn of wide radius executed without breaking speed — called also *high-speed turn, parallel turn, tail-wagging*

¹**temps** \ˈtäⁿ\ *n, pl* **temps** \"\ [F, lit., time, fr. L *tempus* — more at TEMPORAL] **:** a ballet movement or part of a step without change of weight

²**temps** *pl of* TEMP

tempt \ˈtem(p)t\ *vt* -ED/-ING/-S [ME *tempten*, fr. OF *tempter, tenter*, fr. L *temptare, tentare* to touch, feel, attack, attempt, urge, excite, tempt; *temptare* akin to L *tempus* time; *tentare* fr. *tentus*, past part. of *tendere* to stretch, strive, try — more at TEMPORAL, THIN] **1 :** to entice to do wrong by promise of pleasure or gain **:** allure into evil **:** SEDUCE **2 a** *obs* **:** to put to the test **:** make trial of **:** PROVE ⟨God did ~ Abraham —Gen 22:1 (AV)⟩ **b :** to make presumptuous trial of **:** PROVOKE ⟨you have agreed together to ~ the Spirit of the Lord —Acts 5:9 (RSV)⟩ ⟨~*ed* Providence by driving at excessive speed⟩ **c :** to risk the disfavor of (fate or fortune) **:** incur the chance of loss or injury from (adverse fortune) **3 :** to induce to do something **:** attract or allure to an act **:** INCITE, PERSUADE, PROMPT ⟨laughter that I should be ~*ed* to call ironic —E.K. Brown⟩ ⟨~*s* him to forget the obvious —A.L.Kroeber⟩ ⟨~*ed* thousands of new commuters into the state —*Amer. Guide Series: N. J.*⟩ ⟨~*ed* the young man into kissing her —Sherwood Anderson⟩ **4 :** to venture on **:** risk the dangers of ⟨~*ed* the hardships of a strange land⟩ **syn** see LURE

tempt·able \-təbəl\ *adj* **:** capable of being tempted

temp·ta·tion \tem(p)ˈtāshən\ *n* -s [ME *temptacioun*, fr. OF *temptation, tentation*, fr. LL *temptation-, temptatio, tentation-, tentatio*, fr. L *temptatus, tentatus* (past part. of *temptare, tentare*) + *-ion-, -io* -ion] **1 a :** the act of tempting or the state of being tempted esp. to evil **:** ALLUREMENT, ENTICEMENT, SEDUCTION ⟨it is a ~ to abandon hopes of which the realization seems distant and difficult —Bertrand Russell⟩ **b :** something tempting **:** a cause or occasion of enticement ⟨view it, and lay the bright ~ down —John Dryden⟩ **2 :** TESTING, TRIAL **3** *obs* **:** a severely trying experience **:** a painful affliction

temp·ta·tion·al \(ˈ)tem(p)ˌtāshənᵊl\ *adj* **:** of, relating to, or offering temptation **:** ALLURING

temp·ter \ˈtem(p)tə(r)\ *n* -s [ME, fr. *tempten* to tempt + *-er*] **1 :** one that tempts or entices **2** *often cap* **:** DEVIL 1 ⟨when he was on his knees, the *Tempter* would come —R.H.Bainton⟩

tempting *adj* [ME, fr. pres. part. of *tempten* to tempt] **:** ALLURING, ENTICING — **tempt·ing·ly** *adv* — **tempt·ing·ness** *n* -ES

tempt·ress \-trə̇s\ *n* -ES **:** a female tempter

tem·pu·ra \ˌtempəˈrä\ *n* -s [Jap, fried food] **:** fritters of sea food and vegetables fried in deep fat

tem·pus \ˈtempəs\ *n, pl* **tempo·ra** \-pərə\ [L, time — more at TEMPORAL] **:** the unit of time in mensural music

tem·pus de·li·be·ran·di \ˈtempəsdə̇ˌlibəˈrandē, -nˌdī\ *n* [L, time for deliberating] *Roman, civil, & Scots law* **:** the time formerly permitted to an heir to decide whether to accept an inheritance — compare JUS DELIBERANDI

TEMs *pl of* TEM

¹**temse** \ˈtemz\ *n* -s [ME *temse*, fr. OE *temes;* akin to MLG *tēmes, tēmse* sieve, MD *teems*, G dial *zims* sieve, OHG *zimissa* bran] *dial chiefly Brit* **:** SIEVE

²**temse** \"\ *vb* -ED/-ING/-S [ME *temsen*, fr. OE *temsian, temesian*, fr. *temes*, n.] *dial chiefly Brit* **:** SIFT

temsebread \ˈ\,ˌ\ *n, dial Eng* **:** bread made of sifted flour

¹**ten** \ˈten\ *adj* [ME, fr. OE *tīen, tȳn, tēn;* akin to OHG *zehan* ten, ON *tīu*, Goth *taíhun*, L *decem*, Gk *deka*, Skt *daśa*] **:** being one more than nine in number ⟨~ years⟩ — see NUMBER table

²**ten** \"\ *pron, pl in constr* [ME *tene, ten*, fr. OE *tīene, tȳne tēne*, fr. *tīen, tȳn, tēn*, adj.] **:** ten countable persons or things not specified but under consideration and being enumerated ⟨~ are here⟩ ⟨~ were found⟩

³**ten** \"\ *n* -s [ME *tene, ten*, fr. OE *tīene, tȳne, tēne*, fr. *tīene, tȳne tēne*, pron.] **1 :** twice five **:** five times two **2 a :** ten units or objects ⟨a total of ~⟩ **b :** a group or set of ten ⟨arranged by ~*s*⟩ **3 a :** the numerable quantity symbolized by the arabic numerals 10 **b :** the letter X **4 :** 10 o'clock — compare BELL table, TIME illustration **5 :** the tenth in a set or series: as **a :** a playing card marked to show that it is tenth in a suit **b :** an article of clothing of the tenth size ⟨wears a ~⟩ **6 :** something having as an essential feature ten units or members **7 a :** a ten-shilling note **b :** a ten-pound note **c :** a ten-dollar bill **8 :** the number occupying the position two to the left of the decimal point in the arabic notation (as 6 in the number 2968) — usu. used in pl. **9 a :** a short rest period (as of ten minutes) **:** BREAK ⟨the captain halted the company and ordered them to take ~⟩

ten *abbr* **1** tenement **2** tenor **3** tenuto

ten'a \ˈtenə\ *n, pl* **ten'a** *usu cap* **:** KOYUKON

ten·a·bil·i·ty \ˌtenəˈbiləd·ē *chiefly Brit* -ətē, *also* ˌtēn-, -i\ *n* **:** the quality or state of being tenable

ten·a·ble \ˈtenəbəl *chiefly Brit also* ˈtēn-\ *adj* [F, capable of being held, fr. OF, fr. *tenir* to hold (fr. L *tenēre*) + *-able* — more at THIN] **1 a :** capable of being defended against attack **:** DEFENSIBLE ⟨their position was no longer ~ and they retreated to the main line of defense⟩ **b :** capable of being maintained against argument or objection **:** REASONABLE ⟨a ~ assumption⟩ ⟨a ~ theory⟩ ⟨a ~ guess⟩ **2** *archaic* **:** capable of being retained or kept under control ⟨if you have hitherto concealed this sight, let it be ~ in your silence still —Shak.⟩ **3 :** capable of being occupied or used ⟨has been appointed . . . to the chair of public health, ~ at the London School of Hygiene and Tropical Medicine —*Science*⟩ ⟨the scholarships will be ~ for a full, four-year college course —*College English*⟩ — **ten·a·ble·ness** \-bəlnə̇s\ *n* -ES — **ten·a·bly** \-blē, -li\ *adv*

ten·ace \ˈteˌnās, teˈnās, ˈtenə̇s\ *n* -s [modif. (influenced by F *tenace* tenacious, fr. L *tenac-, tenax*) of Sp *tenaza*, lit., forceps, pincers, prob. fr. L *tenacia*, neut. pl. of *tenac-, tenax* tenacious] **:** a combination in one hand in bridge and other card games of two high or relatively high cards once separated in rank (as ace and queen) with an opponent holding the intervening card — see MAJOR TENACE, MINOR TENACE

te·na·cious \tə̇ˈnāshəs *also* teˈn-\ *adj* [L *tenac-, tenax* tending to hold fast (fr. *tenēre* to hold) + E *-ious* — more at THIN] **1 a :** having parts or elements strongly adhering to each other **:** not easily pulled apart **:** COHESIVE, TOUGH ⟨her ships provided a slender, but very ~, link between East and West —R.W. Southern⟩ ⟨a ~ metal⟩ **b :** tending to adhere to another substance **:** ADHESIVE, STICKY, VISCOUS ⟨slippers stuck fast in the ~ yellow clay and were nearly dragged off my feet —Mary S. Broome⟩ ⟨~ sputum⟩ **2 a :** holding fast or tending to hold fast **:** persistent in maintaining or adhering to something valued or habitual (as an opinion, purpose, way of life) ⟨a mind not gifted to discover truth but ~ to hold it —T.S. Eliot⟩ ⟨here . . . men are slow of speech, ~ of opinion, and averse . . . to innovation of any sort —C.B.Nordhoff & J.N. Hall⟩ **b :** RETENTIVE ⟨combined an encyclopedic knowledge with a ~ memory —C.M.Fuess⟩ **3 :** not yielding **:** OBSTINATE, STUBBORN ⟨men are more ~ dieters than women —*Newsweek*⟩ ⟨the transition to a new theory is seldom easy; old ideas are apt to be ~ —J.B.Conant⟩ **syn** see STRONG

te·na·cious·ly *adv* **:** in a tenacious manner

te·na·cious·ness *n* -ES **:** the quality or state of being tenacious **:** TENACITY

te·nac·i·ty \ə̇ˈnasəd·ē, -ətē, -i\ *n* -ES [L *tenacitat-, tenacitas*, fr. *tenac-, tenax* tenacious + *-itat-, -itas* -ity] **1 a :** the quality or state of holding fast **:** DETERMINATION, FIRMNESS, PERSISTENCE ⟨the stubborn ~ with which its landowners have clung to their homes —*Amer. Guide Series: La.*⟩ ⟨maintained this conviction with a fearless ~ —Russell Kirk⟩ **b :** PERSISTENCY, RETENTIVENESS ⟨~ of memory⟩ ⟨the chief distinguishing feature is their ~ of life —C.R.A.Martin⟩ **2 a :** the quality or state of being cohesive **:** tensile strength **:** COHESIVENESS: as (1) **:** resistance of a mineral to deformation (as breaking, crushing, bending) (2) **:** resistance of a textile fiber, filament, or yarn to strain or breaks **:** BREAKING STRENGTH **b :** ADHESIVENESS, GLUTINOUSNESS ⟨clay of the most extraordinary ~ —O.S.Nock⟩ **syn** see COURAGE

ten·a·cle \ˈtenə̇kəl\ *n* -s [LL *tenaculum* instrument for holding] **1** *obs* **:** a stalk of a plant **2 tenacles** *pl* **:** the tentacles by which some plants (as ivies) attach themselves in climbing

te·nac·u·lum \tə̇ˈnakyələm\ *n, pl* **tenacu·la** \-ələ\ *or* **tenaculums** [NL, fr. LL, instrument for holding, fr. L *tenēre* to hold + *-aculum*, suffix denoting instrument] **1 :** a slender sharp-pointed hook attached to a handle and used mainly in surgery for seizing and holding parts (as arteries) **2 :** an adhesive structure: as **a :** a pair of partially fused appendages on the third abdominal segment of a collembolan which holds the furcula in place **b :** the claspers of a shark or a chimaera

tenaculum 1

te·naille \təˈnā(ə)l, -nī\ *n* -s [MF, lit., forceps, pincers, fr. LL *tenacula*, pl. of *tenaculum* instrument for holding] **:** an outwork in the main ditch between two bastions of a fortification

te·nail·lon \tənäyōⁿ\ *n, pl* **tenaillons** \-ōⁿ(z)\ [F, fr. *tenaille*] **:** a work constructed on each side of a ravelin to increase its strength, procure additional ground beyond the ditch, or cover the shoulders of the bastions

te·na·im *or* **tna·im** \təˈnä(y)ə̇m, -ēm; təˌnäˈēm\ *also* **tnoy·im** \tə̇ˈnȯi(y)ə̇m, -ēm\ *n pl but sing or pl in constr* [Yiddish *tnoyim*, fr. LHeb *tĕnā'im*, fr. pl. of *tĕnā'ī* agreement] **1 :** formal prenuptial conditions or agreement made at a Jewish betrothal ceremony **2 :** a Jewish social function announcing an engagement

ten·an·cy \ˈtenənsē, -si\ *n* -ES [*tenant* + *-cy*] **1 a :** a holding of an estate or a mode of holding an estate **:** the temporary possession of something that belongs to another **:** TENURE; *specif* **:** a temporary occupancy (as of land, a house, an office) usu. for a specified period under the terms of a lease **b :** the period of a tenant's occupancy or possession **2 :** the possession or occupation of a position or place ⟨the ~ of a university lectureship —Yakov Malkiel⟩ ⟨a minuscule jail now in ~ of spiders —Idwal Jones⟩

tenancy at sufferance : a tenancy that arises in an estate when a tenant under a lawful demise holds over after his estate is ended — compare ESTATE AT SUFFERANCE

tenancy at will : a tenancy of an estate that is terminable at the will of either party and that may be created by oral declaration or by deed — compare ESTATE AT WILL

tenancy by the entirety *or* **tenancy by entireties :** a tenancy in which husband and wife are seized of the whole estate but without power of severing — compare JOINT TENANCY

tenancy by the rod *or* **tenancy by the verge :** COPYHOLD

tenancy from year to year : a tenancy in which the property is held for a year and upon the condition that the tenancy cannot be determined by either party alone except at the end of any number of entire years from the time of its beginning

tenancy in common : the tenancy of those who hold lands or other property in common — compare JOINT TENANCY

¹**ten·ant** \ˈtenənt\ *n* -s [ME *tenaunt, tenant*, fr. MF *tenant*, fr. pres. part. of *tenir* to hold — more at TENABLE] **1 a :** one who holds or possesses real estate or sometimes personal property (as an annuity) by any kind of right (as in fee simple, in common, in severalty, for life, for years, or at will) **b :** one who has the occupation or temporary possession of lands or tenements the title of which is in another; *specif* **:** one who rents or leases (as land or a house) from a landlord **2 :** one that has possession of a place **:** DWELLER, INHABITANT, OCCUPANT ⟨it is the ~*s* of this upper gallery who . . . make all the noise and uproar —Eugene Burr⟩ ⟨grass is the best possible ~ for our far-spread domain of retired and resting lands —C.E.Wilson⟩

²**tenant** \"\ *vb* -ED/-ING/-S *vt* **:** to hold, occupy, or possess as a tenant **:** INHABIT ⟨won some measure of relief by being allowed to ~ the bogs —*Irish Digest*⟩ ⟨broad and pleasant meadow . . . ~*ed* by the summer camps of the shepherds — Douglas Carruthers⟩ **~** *vi* **:** to occupy a place as a tenant

ten·ant·able \-təbəl\ *adj* **:** capable of being tenanted

tenant at sufferance : one who has a tenancy at sufferance

tenant at will : one who has a tenancy at will

tenant by copy of court roll *or* **tenant by the verge :** COPYHOLDER

tenant by curtesy initiate : a husband who holds a potential interest in an estate by curtesy initiate

tenant by the entirety : one who has a tenancy by the entirety

tenant farmer *n* **:** a farmer who works land owned by another and pays rent either in cash or in shares of produce — compare MÉTAYER

tenant hair *var of* TENENT HAIR

tenant in capite *or* **tenant in chief :** a feudal tenant holding immediately of his lord and esp. of the crown

tenant in common : one who has a tenancy in common

tenant·less \ˈ=ˌləs\ *adj* **:** having no tenants **:** UNOCCUPIED, UNTENANTED

tenantlike \ˈ=,=\ *adj* [¹*tenant* + *like*] **:** conforming to the rights and obligations of a tenant

tenant right *n, Brit* **:** the beneficial interest that remains in the tenant after the expiration of his lease and that includes various legal and customary rights (as the right to claim compensation for improvements not exhausted at the expiration of the lease, the right to claim fixity of tenure on condition of paying the former rent or some rent not arbitrarily fixed by the landlord)

ten·ant·ry \ˈtenəntrē, -ri\ *n* -ES [ME, fr. ¹*tenant* + *-ry*] **1 :** property rented out to tenants ⟨made . . . a neat village of brick buildings . . . for his own appropriate little ~ with rents at a guinea a year —G.E.Fussell⟩ **2 a :** the condition or state of occupying as a tenant **:** TENANCY ⟨ended his ~ of the estate⟩ **b :** the condition, state, or system of being occupied by a tenant ⟨survey his . . . lands for ~ —J.C.Fitzpatrick⟩ **3 :** the body of tenants ⟨urban mechanics and laborers, the ~ of New York — S.E.Morison & H.S.Commager⟩ ⟨the empty shacks perched upon them rot and tumble about their ~ of field rats and spiders —Edward Kimbrough⟩

tenant·ship \ˈ=,ship\ *n* [¹*tenant* + *-ship*] **:** TENANCY

ten-cent \(ˈ)=ˈ=\ *adj* [*ten* + *cent*] **:** CHEAP, CONTEMPTIBLE, SORRY ⟨what a cheap, insecure, *ten-cent* snob —Hamilton Basso⟩

ten-cent store *n* [*ten* + *cent* + *store*] **:** FIVE-AND-TEN

tench \ˈtench\ *n, pl* **tench** *or* **tenches** [ME, fr. MF *tenche*, fr. LL *tinca*] **:** a European and western Asiatic freshwater cyprinoid fish (*Tinca tinca*) that is related to the dace and ide, is noted for its ability to survive for some time outside its normal watery environment, sometimes approaches a weight of eight pounds, and is a locally important table fish

¹**tend** \ˈtend\ *vb* -ED/-ING/-S [ME *tenden*, short for *attenden* to attend] *vi* **1** *archaic* **:** to give ear **:** LISTEN ⟨~ to the master's whistle —Shak.⟩ **2 :** to pay attention **:** apply oneself ⟨you mind your business, and I'll ~ to mine —Evelyn Barkins⟩ **3 :** to act as an attendant or servant **:** SERVE, WAIT ⟨never closed an eye watching and ~*ing* in his house —Walter Macken⟩ **4** *obs* **:** to be waiting **:** AWAIT ⟨the time invites you, go, your servants ~ —Shak.⟩ **~** *vt* **1** *archaic* **:** to attend as a servant **:** accompany in order to render service ⟨had I not four or five women once that ~*ed* me —Shak.⟩ **2** *chiefly dial* **:** to be present at **:** ATTEND **3 a :** to apply oneself to the care of **:** care for the wants of **:** minister to **:** watch over ⟨~*ed* him and ministered to his wants like an angel —C.B.Fairbanks⟩ ⟨~*ing* the destitute mothers and children —Winston Churchill⟩ **b :** to have or take charge of as a caretaker or overseer ⟨a likely little citizen who . . . ~*s* the family sheep —Irene Smith⟩ **c :** CULTIVATE, FOSTER ⟨rice which has been specially planted and ~*ed* —J.G.Frazer⟩ **d :** to manage the operations of or do the necessary work connected with **:** MIND ⟨~*ed* his textile mills —T.D.Parrish⟩ ⟨quit to ~ an open hearth —*Time*⟩ ⟨~ store⟩ ⟨~ bar⟩ ⟨~ the fire⟩ **4** *archaic* **:** be attentive to **:** listen to ⟨the stars that ~ thy bidding —John Keats⟩ — **tend out on** *dial* **:** to attend or attend to

²**tend** \"\ *vi* -ED/-ING/-S [ME *tenden*, short for *intenden*, *entenden* to intend] *dial* **:** INTEND, PURPOSE

³**tend** \"\ *vb* -ED/-ING/-S [ME *tenden*, fr. MF *tendre* to stretch, stretch out, direct oneself toward a place, tend, fr. L *tendere* — more at THIN] *vi* **1 a :** to direct one's course or become moved in a particular direction ⟨saw far in the north the misty outlines of the shore towards which they were ~*ing* — William Black⟩ **b :** to undergo change or development in a particular direction or toward a particular goal ⟨the ideal toward which evolution continually ~*ed* —Roscoe Pound⟩ ⟨the symptoms — where they were ~*ing*, where they were bound to end — disturbed him —J.G.Cozzens⟩ **c :** to extend in a certain direction ⟨the foot of each sail is ~*ing* aft at quite an angle —*All Hands*⟩ **2 a :** to have an inclination to a particular quality, aspect, or state ⟨modern hive design ~*s* to simplicity —F.D.Smith & Barbara Wilcox⟩ ⟨many marine invertebrates ~ towards transparency or a bluish coloration —W.H.Dowdeswell⟩ **b :** to have an inclination toward a particular belief, feeling, or attitude ⟨he ~*s* to deny the moral content in human affairs —Norman Cousins⟩ ⟨painters ~ to rejoice in the commonplace —David Sylvester⟩ **3 :** to exert activity or influence in a particular direction **:** serve as a means **:** CONDUCE ⟨the reduction of reserve requirements will ~ to ease business borrowing —*Nation's Business*⟩ ⟨not true that any advance in the scale of culture inevitably ~*s* to the preservation of society —A.N.Whitehead⟩ **4** *of a ship* **:** to swing with the tide or wind while anchored **~** *vt* **1 :** to manage (an anchored vessel) so as to prevent fouling of the cable **2 :** to stand by (as a rope) in readiness to prevent fouling or other mischance ⟨has a lifeline round him which is ~*ed* inboard —*Manual of Seamanship*⟩

⁴**tend** \"\ *n* -s **:** the angle made by the line of a ship's keel and the direction of the anchor cable when the ship is swinging at anchor ⟨signaling with a flashlight the ~ of the chain to the bridge —Chesley Wilson⟩

ten·dai \ˈtenˌdī\ *n* -s *cap* [Jap, fr. Chin (Pek) *t'ien¹ t'ai²* t'ien t'ai, fr. *T'ien¹ T'ai²*, mountain in Chekiang province, eastern China, where the doctrine was first formulated] **:** a Japanese Buddhist sect founded in the 9th century A.D. by Dengyo Daishi that is the doctrinal equivalent of the Chinese T'ien T'ai sect

tend·ance \ˈtendən(t)s\ *n* -s [short for *attendance*] **1 a :** the act of looking after someone or something **:** the giving of attention **:** watchful care **:** MINISTRATION ⟨fidelity and patience and unselfish ~ gently rendered by a domestic angel —A.C. Benson⟩ **b :** service done to gain favor **:** service or homage to the gods for divine favor ⟨needs and values associated with rites of ~ —H.E.Barnes & H.P.Becker⟩ **2** *archaic* **:** persons in attendance **:** RETINUE

tend·ant \-dənt\ *adj* [by shortening] *archaic* **:** ATTENDANT

ten-day fern *n* **:** a widely distributed tropical fern (*Polystichum adiantiforme*) in which the ultimate pinnae of the large fronds resemble those of the maidenhair

tend·ence \-dən(t)s\ *n* -s [ML *tendentia*] **:** TENDENCY ⟨the sedan developed a ~ to overheat —N.F.Busch⟩

tendencious *var of* TENDENTIOUS

tend·en·cy \ˈtendənsē, -si\ *n* -ES [ML *tendentia*, fr. L *tendent-, tendens* (pres. part. of *tendere* to tend) + *-ia* -y] **1 a :** direction or course toward a place, object, effect, or result **:** BIAS, INCLINATION ⟨regarded political economy as a science of *tendencies* only —R.H.Hutton⟩ ⟨that ~ in art which has been called abstract —Herbert Read⟩ **b :** a proneness to or readiness for a particular kind of thought or action **:** DRIVE, PROPENSITY, SET ⟨disliked the ~ of amateur diplomats to burst into print —H.G.Dwight⟩ ⟨my instinctive ~ has always been to temperance —Havelock Ellis⟩ **c :** a presumptive course of future behavior in continuation of observed acts and attitudes **2 a :** the designed and purposeful trend of something written or said **:** AIM ⟨an evident ~ on the part of the writers to enlarge on the blessings of nature —R.H.Brown⟩ **b :** deliberate but indirect advocacy (as in speech or writing) of a particular point of view ⟨a policy at once plausible and insidious, temporizing and yet thick with ~ —Francis Hackett⟩

syn TENDENCY, TREND, DRIFT, TENOR, CURRENT can mean a movement in a particular direction or of a particular character or the direction or character of such a movement. TENDENCY usu. implies an inherent or acquired inclination to move in a given direction, literally or figuratively, sometimes suggesting something opposable and alterable with great difficulty in the long run ⟨the whole *tendency* of evolution is towards a diminishing birthrate —Havelock Ellis⟩ ⟨a *tendency* toward lower prices for some equipment —*Nation's Business*⟩ ⟨the revolutionary oil is designed to decrease the *tendency* of engines to knock —*Report: Union Oil Co. of Calif.*⟩ ⟨has not escaped that *tendency* to violence —G.B.Shaw⟩ ⟨the *tendency* to moralize — Bliss Perry⟩ TREND is a general direction maintained despite minor deviations, differing from TENDENCY in usu. implying a direction more subject to change ⟨by *trend* is meant a persistent general movement in the direction of some distant goal as yet undefined or only vaguely held —C.A.Dawson & W.E. Gettys⟩ ⟨the national *trend* toward corporate control and mass production —*Amer. Guide Series: Ind.*⟩ ⟨a *trend* toward a favorable balance of trade —R.E.Scott⟩ ⟨the *trend* of his mind was historical —H.N.Fowler⟩ DRIFT adds to TREND the idea of a slowness and seeming indirection, often a meandering or uncertain quality, often a direction the objective of which is not overt or obvious to a quick view ⟨a more general process of internal migration that involved both regional shifts and a *drift* to the cities —Oscar Handlin⟩ ⟨vigorous protest against the *drift* toward revolution —H.J.Thornton⟩ ⟨saw the *drift* of the fellow's intentions —Rafael Sabatini⟩ ⟨the *drift* and meaning of the story —Gilbert Parker⟩ TENOR is very close to DRIFT but applies more commonly and specif. to the import of statements or documents and suggests more certainty and clearness ⟨the whole *tenor* of the teaching of Jesus —W.F.Hambly⟩ ⟨the general *tenor* or direction of the talks — Bernard Smith⟩ ⟨one frightening aspect of the *tenor* of the times —V.M.Rogers⟩ CURRENT implies a movement or course more clearly defined and of more distinct identity and some substance ⟨the *current* of opinion and the whole drift of feeling —W.C.Brownell⟩ ⟨the very central *current* of the evolution of medieval Latin poetry —H.O.Taylor⟩ ⟨he has not . . . changed the *current* of our constitutional law —M.R.Cohen⟩

tend·ent \-dənt\ *adj* [alter. (influenced by L *tendent-, tendens*, pres. part. of *tendere* to tend) of earlier *tendant*, fr. ME, fr. MF, pres. part. of *tendre* to tend] **:** DIRECTED, INCLINED

ten·den·tial \ten'denchəl\ *adj* [ML *tendentia* tendency + E *-al*] : TENDENTIOUS — **ten·den·tial·ly** \-chəlē, -li\ *adv*

ten·den·tious *also* **ten·den·cious** \ten'denchəs\ *adj* [ML *tendentia* tendency + E *-ous*] **1** : marked by a tendency in favor of a particular point of view : motivated by an intent to promote a particular cause : BIASED ⟨under the cloak of objective reporting the reporter can be as ~ as the writer who openly expresses his own opinion —*Times Lit. Supp.*⟩ ⟨distinguish between verifiable fact and ~ assertion —D.M.Potter & T.G.Manning⟩ **2** : having or conforming to a particular tendency ⟨the most recalcitrant, ~, and subtly variable of all animal species —Melville Jacobs & B.J.Stern⟩ — **ten·den·tious·ly** *adv* — **ten·den·tious·ness** *n* -ES

ten·denz \ten'dents\ *n, pl* **tendenz·en** \-ntsən\ [G, lit., tendency, fr. ML *tendentia*] : a dominating point of view or purpose influencing the structure and content of a literary work : LEANING ⟨scarcely a week went by without a new magazine of some unearthly ~ or other appearing on the stands —H.L.Mencken⟩

[1]**ten·der** \'tendə(r)\ *adj* -ER/-EST [ME, fr. OF *tendre*, fr. L *tener* tender, young; prob. akin to Sabine *tereno-* soft, Gk *terēn* soft, tender, *teru* weak, delicate, Skt *taruṇa* tender, young] **1 a** : having a soft or yielding texture : easily broken, cut, or damaged : not hard or tough : not resistant : DELICATE, FRAGILE ⟨that remarkable ~ limestone which is the island's chief treasure —J.P.O'Donnell⟩ ⟨the ruthless flint doth cut my ~ feet —Shak.⟩ ⟨its eggs are extremely frail and ~ —Richard Semon⟩ **b** : easily chewed : SUCCULENT ⟨small buttered ears of the ~*est* white corn —Mary McCarthy⟩ **c** *of wool* : having a weak staple lacking in tensile strength **2 a** : physically weak : not able to endure hardship ⟨they're a thought too young and ~ for the work at hand . . . it's bitter cold up at the front now —Rudyard Kipling⟩ **b** : not fully developed or grown : IMMATURE, YOUNG ⟨blight so agreeable a myth in its ~ stage —V.L.Parrington⟩ ⟨children of ~ years⟩ **c** : incapable of resisting cold : not hardy ⟨as the climate grows more severe toward the interior of the continent, many of the more ~ species drop out —*Boy Scout Handbk.*⟩ **d** *dial chiefly Brit* : in feeble health **3** : marked by, responding to, or expressing the softer emotions : FOND, LOVING ⟨the security that goes with a ~ relationship —Abram Kardiner⟩ ⟨for the moment she was ~ with regrets —Sherwood Anderson⟩ ⟨the sweet things of life, the fastidious and ~ things, the gentle approaches —Richard Church⟩ **4 a** : showing care or thoughtful consideration : careful to keep from harm or injury : SOLICITOUS ⟨a ~ and consistent regard for the rights of states —C.A. & Mary Beard⟩ ⟨a ~ and far-reaching solicitude could not always save the Egyptian cat from harm —Agnes Repplier⟩ **b** : highly susceptible to impressions or emotions : IMPRESSIONABLE ⟨thinking to quiet your ~ conscience with this pitiful stratagem —T.L.Peacock⟩ **c** : showing care to avoid or prevent : CAUTIOUS, WARY ⟨did not want to take blame to herself, and was most ~ of throwing any on her husband —Jane Austen⟩ **5 a** : soft in action or movement ⟨a ~ wind stirred the water —Elinor Wylie⟩ **b** : appropriate or conducive to a delicate or sensitive constitution or character : not rough, harsh, or severe : GENTLE, MILD ⟨~ breeding⟩ ⟨~ irony⟩ **c** : delicate or soft in quality or tone ⟨looked out on the long and ~ dawn of the flatlands —Meridel Le Sueur⟩ ⟨sounds of many contrasting kinds: harsh as well as mellow, brilliant as well as ~ —Robert Donington⟩ **6** *obs* : DEAR, PRECIOUS ⟨whose life's as ~ to me as my soul —Shak.⟩ **7 a** : sensitive to the touch ⟨a ~ scar⟩ : painful on palpation ⟨a ~ palpable kidney⟩ ⟨a ~ spleen⟩ **b** : sensitive to injury or insult : easily offended : TOUCHY ⟨a peerage was protection for ~ pride —J.M. Barzun⟩ **c** : demanding careful and sensitive handling : TICKLISH ⟨they both felt that the situation was extremely ~ and critical —W.M.Thackeray⟩ **d** *of a ship* : inclined to heel over easily under sail : somewhat crank ⟨the bricks were not good ballast because they were too light and the boat was very ~ —H.A.Calahan⟩

syn RESPONSIVE, COMPASSIONATE, SYMPATHETIC, WARM, WARMHEARTED: TENDER may indicate an inclination to gentle emotions like love or kindliness or cherishing, affectionate, or gentle solicitude ⟨his mother was very *tender* with him —D.H. Lawrence⟩ ⟨a *tender* laugh of benevolence —W.M.Thackeray⟩ RESPONSIVE indicates a ready inclination to respond or react impressionably to others' emotions, esp. warmer ones, or to conditions or circumstances facing one ⟨she took up life, and became alert to the world again, *responsive*, like a ship in full sail, to every wind that blew —Rose Macaulay⟩ COMPASSIONATE describes a disposition easily moved to pity, mercy, or tolerance of others ⟨one who cherishes the ideal of tolerance may enfold Fascists in the mantle of *compassionate* understanding —H.J.Muller⟩ ⟨love was unfailing in *compassionate* word and deed —H.O.Taylor⟩ SYMPATHETIC is somewhat wider than *compassionate* in indicating a disposition to share another's emotions, esp. his sorrows, but also his interests and ways of thought ⟨cynicism found no echo in the large and *sympathetic* temper —J.R.Green⟩ ⟨the sailors themselves were *sympathetic* . . . but the masters (the hunters and the captain) were heartlessly indifferent —Jack London⟩ ⟨a temper so *sympathetic* and responsive was immensely influenced by others as well as inclined to influence them —Gamaliel Bradford⟩ WARM indicates a ready capacity for love, affection, or interest, with more heartiness, cordiality, or fervor, and less softness and gentleness than indicated by TENDER ⟨a perfect gentleman, unaffected, *warm*, and obliging —Jane Austen⟩ ⟨the *warm* courage of national unity —F.D.Roosevelt⟩ WARMHEARTED may describe a warm personality oriented toward well-wishing, generosity, or sympathy ⟨Arizonans are *warmhearted* and hospitable —*Amer. Guide Series: Ariz.*⟩ ⟨the idea of sharing poverty and privation in company with the beloved object is . . . far from being disagreeable to a *warmhearted* woman —W.M.Thackeray⟩

[2]**tender** \"\ *vb* **tendered; tendered; tendering** \-(ə)riŋ\ **tenders** [ME *tendren*, fr. [1]*tender*] *vt* **1** : to make tender : SOFTEN, WEAKEN ⟨the ~*ed* areas to which leaks are due —*Manual of Firemanship (Gt. Brit.)*⟩ **2** *archaic* : to regard or treat with tenderness ⟨which name I ~ as dearly as my own —Shak.⟩ **3** : to weaken (textile fibers or fabrics) esp. in the process of bleaching, dyeing, or printing ~ *vi* : to become tender ⟨the dyed cotton is liable to ~ on prolonged storage —C.M.Whittaker & C.C.Wilcock⟩

[3]**tender** *n* -S [[1]*tender*] *obs* : CONSIDERATION, REGARD

[4]**tend·er** \'tendə(r)\ *n* -S [ME, fr. *tenden* to tend, attend to + *-er*] : one that tends : one that takes care of a person or thing: as **a** (1) : a ship employed to attend other ships (as to supply them with provisions and other stores, to transport catches of fish to the market) (2) : a boat or small steamer for communication between shore and a larger vessel (3) : a warship that provides logistic support ⟨a destroyer ~⟩ ⟨seaplane ~⟩ **b** : a vehicle attached to a locomotive for carrying a supply of fuel and water **c** *or* **tender truck** : an auxiliary fire-fighting vehicle; *esp* : one carrying hose and special equipment

[5]**ten·der** \'tendə(r)\ *vb* **tendered; tendered; tendering** \-d(ə)riŋ\ **tenders** [MF *tendre* to stretch out, offer — more at TEND] *vt* **1** : to proffer in satisfaction of an obligation or condition arising from a relationship between parties ⟨~ the amount of rent⟩ **2 a** : to present for acceptance : offer freely : PROFFER ⟨~*ed* his resignation⟩ ⟨~*ed* his advice⟩ ⟨~*ed* a banquet to their colleague on retirement⟩ **b** : to offer for sale ⟨~ stock⟩ ~ *vi* : to make a tender for a contract : make a bid — often used with *for* ⟨contractors who propose ~*ing* for this scheme —*Scotsman*⟩ **syn** see OFFER

[6]**tender** \"\ *n* -S **1** : a proffer of money, property, or services in satisfaction of an obligation or condition arising from a relationship between parties **2** : an offer or proposal made for acceptance ⟨honored him by the ~ of some important appointment —J.D.Hicks⟩: as **a** : an offer of a bid for a contract ⟨became as exhilarated as if his ~ for building a mansion had been accepted —Flora Thompson⟩ **b** : an offering of securities for bidding **c** *Scots law* : an offer of compromise settlement made during litigation **3** : something that may be offered in payment; *specif* : MONEY ⟨no State shall . . . make anything but gold and silver coin a ~ in payment of debts —*U.S.Constitution*⟩

ten·der·abil·i·ty \,tend(ə)rə'biləd·ē, -ətē, -i\ *n* : the quality or state of being tenderable

ten·der·able \'tend(ə)rəbəl\ *adj* [[5]*tender* + *-able*] : capable of being tendered; *specif* : of a quality or grade acceptable for delivery in settlement of a futures contract

tender annual *n* [[1]*tender*] : an annual (as the tomato or squash) not able to withstand cold and injured by the first frost — compare HARDY ANNUAL

ten·der·er \'tend(ə)rə(r)\ *n* -S [[5]*tender* + *-er*] : one that tenders

tenderest *superlative of* TENDER

tenderfoot \'==,=\ *n, pl* **tenderfeet** *also* **tenderfoots** *often attrib* [[1]*tender* + *foot*] **1 a** : a newcomer in a comparatively rough or newly settled region; *esp* : one not hardened to frontier or outdoor life **b** : an inexperienced beginner : NEOPHYTE ⟨political ~⟩ ⟨business ~⟩ **2** : the first rank in the rising scale of ranks in the Boy Scouts of America or the Girl Scouts of America — compare FIRST CLASS, SECOND CLASS

tenderfooted \¦==¦==\ *adj* [[1]*tender* + *footed*] : TIMID

tendergreen \'==,=\ *n* [[1]*tender*] : a mustard (*Brassica perviridis*) prob. of eastern Asiatic origin that is used as a vegetable for its swollen root crown and edible foliage — called also *spinach mustard*

tenderhearted \¦==¦==\ *adj* [[1]*tender* + *hearted*] : easily moved to love, pity, or sorrow : susceptible to the softer emotions : COMPASSIONATE, IMPRESSIONABLE ⟨a noble ~ creature, who sympathizes with all the human race —W.M.Thackeray⟩ — **tenderheartedly** \¦==¦===\ *adv* — **tenderheartedness** \¦==¦===\ *n* -ES

tender-heft·ed \¦==¦heftəd\ *adj* [[1]*tender* + *heft* (alter. of *haft* handle) + *-ed*] *archaic* : TENDERHEARTED ⟨thy *tender-hefted* nature shall not give thee o'er to harshness —Shak.⟩

tendering *n* -S [fr. gerund of [2]*tender*] : a lessening of the strength of cloth or yarn; *esp* : a weakening caused by acids during manufacture

ten·der·iza·tion \,tendərə'zāshən, -,rī'z-\ *n* -S : the process of tenderizing

ten·der·ize \'==,rīz\ *vt* -ED/-ING/-S [[1]*tender* + *-ize*] : to make tender; *specif* : to make (meat or meat products) tender by applying any process or substance that breaks down connective tissue without impairment of flavor or nutritive quality

ten·der·iz·er \-zə(r)\ *n* -S : a device or substance that tenderizes — compare PAPAIN

ten·der·ling \'tendə(r)liŋ, -lēŋ\ *n* -S [[1]*tender* + *-ling*] **1** *archaic* **a** : one who has been coddled : one who is weak or effeminate **b** : a little child **2** : one of the budding antlers of a deer

tenderloin \'==,=\ *n* [[1]*tender* + *loin*] **1** : a strip of tender meat consisting of the psoas muscle on each side of the vertebral column : a fillet of beef or pork — compare CHATEAUBRIAND, FILET MIGNON, TOURNEDOS **2** [so called fr. its making possible a luxurious diet for a corrupt policeman] : a district of a city largely devoted to vice and other forms of lawbreaking that encourage political or police corruption ⟨the dives and shady ~*s* of the underworld —H.E.Barnes & N.K.Teeters⟩

ten·der·ly *adv* [ME, fr. [1]*tender* + *-ly*] : in a tender manner

tender-minded \¦==¦==\ *adj* [*tender* + *minded*] : tending toward or characterized by idealism, optimism, and dogmatism; *esp* : reluctant to face unpleasant facts or to test assumptions by observation and experience

ten·der·ness \'tendə(r)nəs\ *n* -ES [ME *tendernes*, fr. [1]*tender* + *-nes* -ness] : the quality or state of being tender

tender-nosed \¦==¦=\ *adj* [*tender* + *nosed*] : KEEN-SCENTED ⟨only the most persistent and *tender-nosed* hounds can make anything of scent on these occasions —Muriel Bowen⟩

tender of amends [[6]*tender*] : an offer of satisfaction for a wrong or breach of contract that serves when sufficient to stop the further accruing of interest and to impose on the plaintiff liability for subsequent costs in the action

tender of issue : a form of words in a pleading by which a party offers to refer the question raised upon it to the appropriate mode of decision

tenders *pres 3d sing of* TENDER, *pl of* TENDER

ten·di·do \ten'dē(,)dō, -ē(,)t͟hō\ *n* -S [Sp, fr. past part. of *tender* to stretch out, fr. L *tendere* — more at THIN] : one of several tiers of seats at a bullring that are located above the ringside rows — compare BARRERA

tending *pres part of* TEND

ten·di·ni·tis *or* **ten·do·ni·tis** \,tendə'nīd·əs\ *n* -ES [*tendinitis* fr. NL, fr. *tendin-*, *tendo* tendon + *-itis; tendonitis* alter. (influenced by *tendon*) of *tendinitis*] : inflammation of a tendon (as in the elbow, shoulder, or knee)

ten·di·nous \'tendənəs\ *adj* [NL *tendinosus*, fr. *tendin-*, *tendo* tendon + L *-osus* -ous] **1 a** : relating to a tendon **b** : like or resembling a tendon **2** : consisting of tendons : SINEWY

tendinous arch *n* : a thickened fascial arch through which pass vessels or nerves or both; *esp* : one in the pelvic fascia giving origin to fibers of muscles of the pelvic opening

tendinous ring of zinn \-'zin, -tsin\ *usu cap Z* [after Johann G. *Zinn* †1759 Ger. physician and botanist] : a fibrous membrane surrounding the optic foramen and serving as a common origin for the rectus muscles of the eye

ten·di·ped·id \¦tendə¦pedəd\ *adj or n* [NL *Tendipedidae*] : CHIRONOMID

ten·di·ped·i·dae \,=='pedə,dē\ [NL, fr. *Tendiped-*, *Tendipes*, genus of two-winged flies (fr. L *tendere* to stretch + *-i-* + *-ped-*, *-pes* -ped) + *-idae* — more at THIN] *syn of* CHIRONOMIDAE

ten·do \'ten,dō\ *n, pl* **tendi·nes** \-,də,nēz\ [NL *tendin-*, *tendo*, alter. of ML *tendon-*, *tendo*] : TENDON 1

ten·don \'tendən\ *n* -S [ML *tendon-*, *tendo*, fr. L *tendere* to stretch — more at THIN] **1** : a tough cord or band of dense specialized irregularly arranged white fibrous connective tissue that unites a muscle with some other part, transmits the force which the muscle exerts, and is continuous with the connective tissue epimysium and perimysium of the muscle and when inserted into a bone with the periosteum of the bone — see APONEUROSIS **2** : FRENULUM 2

tendon of achilles *usu cap A* [trans. of NL *tendo Achillis*] : ACHILLES' TENDON

ten·don·ous \'tendənəs\ *adj* [*tendon* + *-ous*] : TENDINOUS

tendon reflex *n* : a reflex act (as a knee jerk) in which a muscle is made to contract by a blow upon its tendon

tendon sense *n* : a sense adjunct to the muscle sense and mediated by receptors on or near the tendons

tendon spindle *n* : a sensory end organ in a tendon

ten·dour *also* **tan·dour** *or* **ten·door** \(')ten¦dů(ə)r, (')tan-\ *n* -S [Turk *tandır*, fr. Ar *tannūr*, fr. Aram *tannūra*, fr. Akkadian *tinūru*] : a table or seat with a brazier of coals under it that is used for warmth in some countries of southwestern Asia

ten·do·vaginal \¦tendō+\ *adj* [NL *tendovaginalis*, fr. *tendo* tendon + L *vagina* sheath + *-alis* -al — more at VAGINA] : of or relating to a tendon and its synovial sheath

ten·dre \'täⁿdrə\ *n* -S [F, fr. *tendre*, adj., tender — more at TENDER] *archaic* : a tender regard : LOVE

ten·dresse \täⁿ'dres\ *n, pl* **tendresses** \"\ [F, fr. MF, fr. *tendre* tender] **1** : tender feeling : FONDNESS ⟨suppose I have some ~ for hidden weakness —Anthony West⟩ **2** : LOVE ⟨it was a strange ~ . . . I was never once alone with her —Alec Waugh⟩

[1]**ten·dril** \'tendrəl\ *n* -S [perh. modif. of MF *tendron* tendril, alter. (influenced by *tendron* tender bud, cartilage) of *tendon* tendon, tendril, fr. ML *tendon-*, *tendo* tendon] **1** : a portion or the whole of a leaf, stipule, or stem that is modified into a slender spirally coiling sensitive organ serving to attach a plant (as a peavine or grapevine) to its support and to assist it in climbing **2 a** : something resembling a tendril ⟨her hair hung in loose, vivid ~*s* around her face —Laura Krey⟩ ⟨~*s* of mist were curling over the edges of the meadow —P.A. Brodeur⟩ **b** : something that clings like a tendril ⟨was aware of each ~ of her being seeking some substance to which it might cling —Helen Howe⟩

[2]**tendril** \"\ *adj* **1** : of, relating to, or like a tendril **2** : TENDRILED

ten·driled *or* **ten·drilled** \-ld\ *adj* [[1]*tendril* + *-ed*] : having tendrils

ten·dril·if·er·ous \¦tendrə¦lif(ə)rəs\ *adj* [[1]*tendril* + *-iferous*] : bearing tendrils

ten·dril·lar \'tendrələ(r)\ *adj* [[1]*tendril* + *-ar*] : TENDRILOUS

ten·dril·ly \-lē\ *adj* [[1]*tendril* + *-y*] : TENDRILOUS

ten·dril·ous \-drələs\ *adj* [[1]*tendril* + *-ous*] **1** : TENDRILED **2** : resembling a tendril

ten·dron \'tendrən\ *n* -S [ME, fr. MF, fr. OF *tendre* tender, soft] **1** *archaic* : a young shoot, sprout, or bud **2** **tendrons** *pl, archaic* : pieces of tender cartilage from the bones situated at the extremity of a breast of veal

tends *pres 3d sing of* TEND, *pl of* TEND

ten·du \täⁿ'd(y)ü\ *adj* [F, fr. past part. of *tendre* to stretch, stretch out, fr. MF — more at TENDER (to offer)] : extended in a taut manner — used of a leg in ballet

-tene \,tēn\ *n comb form* -S [L or Gk; L *taenia* ribbon, band, fr. Gk *tainia* — more at TAENIA] : stage of meiotic prophase characterized by (such) chromosomal filaments ⟨diplo*tene*⟩ ⟨pachy*tene*⟩

ten·e·brae \'tenə,brā, -,brī, -(,)brē\ *n pl but sing or pl in constr, often cap* [ML, fr. L, darkness — more at TEMERITY] : a church service observed during the final part of Holy Week in commemoration of the sufferings and death of Christ with the public chanting of psalms and the progressive extinguishing of all candles until only one remains burning behind or under the altar

ten·e·bres·cence \,=='bresᵊn(t)s\ *n* -S [L *tenebrae* darkness + E *-escence*] : an absorption of light (as induced in a crystal by irradiation with X rays) that is not intrinsic to the material involved

ten·e·brif·ic \¦==¦brifik\ *adj* [L *tenebrae* + E *-i-* + *-fic*] **1** : GLOOMY ⟨it brightens the ~ scene —Robert Burns⟩ **2** : causing gloom or darkness ⟨a ~ time —Robert Browning⟩

[1]**te·neb·ri·o·nid** \tə'nebrēənəd\ *adj* [NL *Tenebrionidae*] : of or relating to the Tenebrionidae

[2]**tenebrionid** \"\ *n* -S : a beetle of the family Tenebrionidae

te·neb·ri·on·i·dae \=,=='änə,dē\ *n pl, cap* [NL, fr. *Tenebrion-*, *Tenebrio*, type genus (fr. L, one who shuns light, fr. *tenebrae* darkness) + *-idae*] : a large family of heteromerous firm-bodied mostly dark-colored vegetable-feeding beetles esp. characteristic of arid regions and often with the hind wings vestigial and functionless and with larvae that are usu. hard cylindrical worms — see DARKLING BEETLE, MEALWORM

te·neb·ri·ous \=='=rēəs\ *adj* [by alter.] : TENEBROUS

ten·e·brism \'tenə,brizəm\ *n* -S *often cap* [L *tenebrae* darkness + E *-ism*] : a style of painting typically associated with the Italian painter Caravaggio and his followers of the late 16th and early 17th centuries that submerges most of the forms depicted in shadow but dramatically illuminates the remaining forms by a concentrated beam of light usu. coming from an identifiable source

[1]**ten·e·brist** \-,brəst\ *n* -S *often cap* [L *tenebrae* + E *-ist*] : one who adheres to or uses tenebrism

[2]**tenebrist** \"\ *adj* : marked by, using, or constituting tenebrism ⟨perhaps the glare in his ~ canvases is a bit too strong —Stuart Preston⟩

ten·e·brose \-,brōs\ *adj* [L *tenebrosus* — more at TENEBROUS] : TENEBROUS

ten·e·bros·i·ty \,=='bräsəd·ē, -sətē, -i\ *n* -ES [ML *tenebrositat-*, *tenebrositas*, fr. L *tenebrosus* dark + *-itat-*, *-itas* ity] : DARKNESS ⟨switches off the light, calls for the first slide, and talks for three quarters of an hour in Stygian ~ —*Lancet*⟩

ten·e·bro·so \¦tenə¦brō(,)sō, -)zō\ *adj* [It, lit., dark, fr. L *tenebrosus*] : TENEBRIST; *specif* : of or relating to the painting of Caravaggio and his immediate followers

ten·e·brous \'tenəbrəs\ *adj* [ME, fr. MF *tenebreus*, fr. L *tenebrosus*, fr. *tenebrae* (pl.) darkness + *-osus* -ous — more at TEMERITY] **1 a** : shut off from the light : DARK, MURKY ⟨a ~ cave⟩ ⟨a ~ forest⟩ **b** : TENEBRIST **2** : hard to understand : MYSTERIOUS, OBSCURE ⟨a ~ affair⟩ ⟨a ~ theory⟩ **3** : GLOOMY ⟨moderates our ~ and fantastical imaginations —Rose Macaulay⟩ — **ten·e·brous·ness** *n* -ES

1080 *also* **ten-eighty** \(')te¦nād·|ē, -āt|, |i\ *n, pl* **1080s** *also* **ten-eighties** [so called fr. its laboratory serial number] : SODIUM FLUOROACETATE

ten·e·ment \'tenəmənt\ *n* -S [ME, fr. MF, fr. ML *tenementum*, fr. L *tenēre* to hold + *-mentum* -ment — more at THIN] **1 a** : something that is held by tenure : land or any of various forms of incorporeal property (as an inheritable estate, an estate for life, or an estate for years) treated like land that is held by a person of another or as owner : HOLDING **b** : a freehold estate in a corporeal or an incorporeal hereditament as distinguished from a less estate (as an estate for a term of years) **2 a** : a house used as a dwelling : RESIDENCE **b** : a single room or set of rooms for use by one tenant or family : APARTMENT, FLAT ⟨a vacant second-floor ~ —*Springfield (Mass.) Union*⟩ **c** *Scot* : an edifice of several houses separately tenanted **d** : TENEMENT HOUSE ⟨the bare flat at the top of an ugly ~ —Marjorie Earl⟩ **3 a** : DWELLING, HABITATION ⟨whole roads and ~*s* of experience poorly mapped —C.D.Lewis⟩ **b** : a human body in which the soul is held to have a temporary dwelling place ⟨beholds man trapped in the ~ of flesh —C.I. Glicksberg⟩

ten·e·men·tal \¦==¦mentᵊl\ *adj* : of or relating to a tenement : held by or leased to tenants

ten·e·men·ta·ry \¦==¦mentərē, -n·trē, -ri\ *adj* [*tenement* + *-ary*] : consisting of tenements : TENEMENTAL

ten·e·ment·ed \'tenəmentəd\ *adj* [*tenement* + *-ed*] **1** : leased to tenants : containing separate dwelling units ⟨~ houses⟩ **2** : consisting of tenement houses ⟨born in the teeming and ~ . . . section —*Reporter*⟩

tenement house *n* : a dwelling house divided into separate apartments for rent to families : APARTMENT BUILDING; *esp* : one meeting minimum standards of sanitation, safety, and comfort and occupied by poorer families usu. in a large city

te·nen·das \tə'nen,das\ *n* -ES [L, accus. pl. fem. of *tenendus*; fr. *tenendas praedictas terras* the aforesaid lands to be held, a phrase of the clause] *Scots law* : TENENDUM

te·nen·dum \-ndəm\ *n* -S [L, to be held, neut. of *tenendus*, gerundive of *tenēre* to hold; fr. the first word of the clause — more at THIN] : a clause formerly used in a deed to designate the kind of tenure vested in the grantee — compare HABENDUM

tenent *n* -S [L, they hold, 3d sing. pres. indic. of *tenēre* to hold] *obs* : TENET

tenent hair *or* **tenant hair** *n* [L *tenent-*, *tenens*, pres. part. of *tenēre* to hold] : a hair much more swollen at the tip than the base, sometimes secreting an adhesive fluid, growing in tufts on the feet of many spiders and insects, and enabling them to move freely on smooth or vertical surfaces

ten·er·al \'tenərəl\ *adj* [L *tener* tender, young + E *-al* — more at TENDER] : of, relating to, or constituting a state of the imago of an insect immediately after molting during which it is soft and immature in coloring

ten·er·a·men·te \,tenərə'mentē, -men·(,)tā\ *adv* [It, fr. *tenero* tender, fr. L *tener*] : TENDERLY — used as a direction in music

ten·er·iffe lace \'tenə,rif-, -rēf-\ *n, usu cap T* [fr. *Teneriffe*, *Tenerife*, one of the Canary islands] : a handmade or machine-made lace with spider-web designs that is used for insertion and edging

te·nes·mus \tə'nezməs *also* -nes-\ *n* -ES [L, fr. Gk *teinesmos*, fr. *teinein* to stretch, strain — more at THIN] : a painful and distressing but ineffectual urge to evacuate the rectum or urinary bladder

ten·et \'tenət *Brit often* 'tēn-; *usu* -əd·+V\ *n* -S [L, he holds, 3d sing. pres. indic. of *tenēre* to hold; fr. its use in NL to introduce an account of the opinion of an individual or sect — more at THIN] **1** : a principle, dogma, belief, or doctrine generally held to be true; *esp* : one held in common by members of an organization, group, movement, or profession ⟨the two great ~*s* of the physical sciences, observation and deduction —M.A.Pei⟩ ⟨rare to find a design so boldly original in conception transgressing so few architectural ~*s* —W.M. Emery⟩ **2** *archaic* : a personal opinion **syn** see DOCTRINE

ten·e·te·hara \,tenətə'härə, -harə\ *n, pl* **tenetehara** *or* **teneteharas** *usu cap* **1 a** : a Tupian people of the state of Maranhão, Brazil **b** : a member of such people **2** : the language of the Tenetehara people

[1]**ten·fold** \'=¦fōld\ *adj* [ME, fr. [1]*ten* + *-fold*] **1** : having 10 parts or aspects **2** : being 10 times as large, as great, or as many as some understood size, degree, or amount ⟨a ~ increase⟩

[2]**tenfold** \"\ *adv* : to 10 times as much or as many : by ten times ⟨increased ~⟩

ten-foot·er \'=¦fůd·ə(r)\ *n* [*ten* + *foot* + *-er*] : a small building or ell ten feet square; *specif* : one formerly used for shoemaking on some New England farms

ten-gallon hat \'=¦==-\ *n* [so called fr. its great size] : COWBOY HAT

teng·ger·ese \ˌteŋgəˈrēz, -ēs\ *n, pl* **tenggerese** *or* **tenggereses** *usu cap* [Jav *Těnggěr* Tenggerese (fr. *těnggěr* high-level land, plateau) + E *-ese*] **1 :** an Indonesian people inhabiting the mountain regions of eastern Java **2 :** a member of the Tenggerese people

tenia *var of* TAENIA

teniacide *var of* TAENIACIDE

teniafuge *var of* TAENIAFUGE

teniasis *var of* TAENIASIS

te·nien·te \tānˈyentē\ *n* -S [Sp, fr. L *tenent-, tenens,* pres. part. of *tenēre* to hold — more at THIN] **:** a local official in Latin America and the Philippines

te·ni·no \təˈnē,nō\ *n, pl* **tenino** *or* **teninos** *usu cap* **1 :** a Shahaptian people of the Columbia river valley of northern Oregon **2 :** a member of the Tenino people

ten–in–one ration \ˌ==ˈ=-\ *n* **:** a packaged field ration (as of the U. S. Army) intended to feed ten men for one day

te·nio \təˈnē,ō\ *n* -S [Sp *teniu*] **1 :** a timber tree (*Weinmannia trichosperma*) of southern So. America **2 :** the rosy-brown wood of the tenio that resembles that of the sweet birch

Ten·ite \ˈteˌnīt\ *trademark* — used for any of various thermoplastic molding compositions made from a cellulose ester

ten·nant·ite \ˈtenən‧,tīt\ *n* -S [Smithson *Tennant* †1815 Eng. chemist + E *-ite*] **:** a mineral $(Cu,Fe)_{12}As_4S_{13}$ that consists of a blackish lead-gray sulfide of iron, copper, arsenic, and sulfur and is isomorphous with tetrahedrite

ten·ne \ˈtenē\ *n* -S [MF *tenné,* alter. of *tanné,* past part. of *tanner* to tan — more at TAN] **1** *also* **tenney** *or* **tenny** \"\ **:** the heraldic color orange or orange-tawny **2 :** TAWNY

ten·ner \ˈtenə(r)\ *n* -S [¹*ten* + *-er*] **1 :** a ten-pound note **2 :** a ten-dollar bill

¹**ten·nes·se·an** *or* **ten·nes·see·an** \ˌtenəˈsēən\ *adj, usu cap* [*Tennessee,* state of U.S.A. + E *-an*] **1 :** of, relating to, or characteristic of the state of Tennessee **2 :** of, relating to, or characteristic of the people of Tennessee

²**tennessean** *or* **tennesseean** \"\ *n, cap* **:** a native or resident of Tennessee

ten·nes·see \ˌtenəˈsē\ *adj, usu cap* [fr. *Tennessee,* southeast central state of U.S.A., fr. the *Tennessee* river, fr. Cherokee *Tanasi,* name of a village] **:** of or from the state of Tennessee ⟨a *Tennessee* county⟩ **:** of the kind or style prevalent in Tennessee **:** TENNESSEAN

tennessee walker *n, usu cap T&W* **:** TENNESSEE WALKING HORSE

tennessee walking horse *n* **1** *usu cap T&W&H* **:** an American breed of large easy-gaited saddle horses that is largely of Standardbred and Morgan ancestry **2** *usu cap T & sometimes cap W&H* **:** a horse of the Tennessee Walking Horse breed — called also *Plantation walking horse*

tennessee warbler *n, usu cap T* **:** a small olive-green white-breasted warbler (*Vermivora peregrina*) of No. America that nests in Canada and winters in northern So. America

ten·nis \ˈtenəs\ *n* -ES *often attrib* [ME *tenys, teneys, tenetz,*

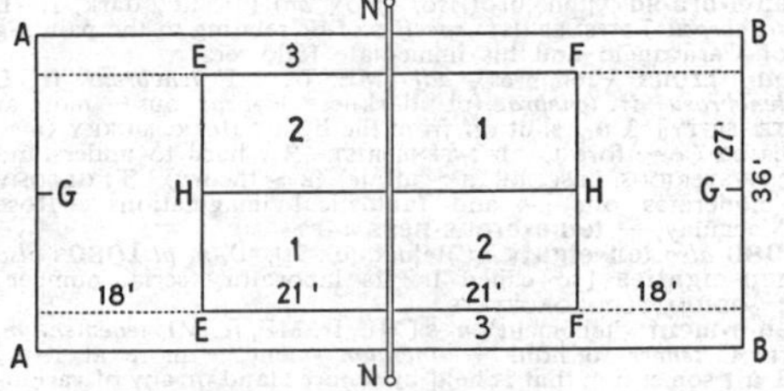

tennis court laid out for doubles: base lines *AA, BB;* sidelines *AB, AB;* service lines *EE, FF;* service sidelines *EF, EF;* center marks *G, G;* center service lines or half-court lines *HH;* net *NN; 1, 1,* right service courts; *2, 2,* left service courts; *3, 3* alleys

prob. fr. AF *tenetz,* 2d pers. pl. imper. of *tenir* to hold — more at TENABLE] **1 :** COURT TENNIS **2 :** a typically outdoor game that is played with rackets and a light elastic ball by two players or pairs of players on a level court divided by a low net and that is scored in points, games, and sets — called also *lawn tennis;* see RACKET illustration

tennis ball *n* **:** a ball used in tennis that is made of rubber covered with felt and weighs about two ounces

tennis elbow *n* **:** inflammation and pain over the outer side of the elbow involving the lateral epicondyle of the humerus and usu. resulting from excessive or violent twisting movements of the hand

tennis shoe *n* **:** a light shoe worn esp. in playing tennis and generally made of canvas with a rubber sole — compare SNEAKER

tennis shoes

ten·nisy \ˈtenəsē\ *adj* [*tennis* + *-y*] **:** devoted to tennis

ten·no \ˈte(ˌ)nō, =ˈ=\ *n, pl* **tenno** *or* **tennos** *often cap* [Jap *tennō*] **:** an emperor of Japan regarded as a religious leader and held to be an incarnation of the divine — compare MIKADO

ten·ny·so·nian \ˌtenəˈsōnēən, -nyən\ *adj, usu cap* [Alfred, Lord *Tennyson* †1892 Eng. poet + E *-ian*] **:** of, relating to, or having the characteristics of the poet Tennyson or his writings ⟨it had been produced specifically as an exercise in *Tennysonian* art —*Atlantic*⟩

teno- *comb form* [irreg. fr. Gk *tenont-, tenōn* tendon; akin to Gk *teinein* to stretch — more at THIN] **:** tendon ⟨*teno*plasty⟩ ⟨*teno*tomy⟩

te·noch·ca \təˈnächkə\ *n, pl* **tenochca** *or* **tenochcas** *usu cap* [MexSp, fr. *Tenochtitlán,* ancient name of Mexico City] **:** AZTEC 1

te·no·de·sis \ˌtenəˈdēsəs, -ˈdes-; təˈnädəsəs\ *n, pl* **tenode·ses** \-ˌsēz\ [NL, fr. *teno-* + *-desis*] **:** the operation of suturing the end of a tendon to a bone ⟨*tenodeses* or transplantations of the tendons alone —*Jour. Amer. Med. Assoc.*⟩

¹**ten·on** \ˈtenən\ *n* -S [ME, fr. OF, fr. *tenir* to hold — more at TENABLE] **:** a projecting member in a piece of wood or other material for insertion into a mortise to make a joint; *esp* **:** one passing entirely through the piece in which a mortise is cut — compare TUSK TENON; see LEWIS illustration

²**tenon** \"\ *vb* -ED/-ING/-S *vt* **1 :** to unite or hold in place by or as if by a tenon **2 :** to cut or fit for insertion in a mortise ~ *vi* **:** to become fixed in place by means of a tenon

ten·on·er \-nə(r)\ *n* -S **:** one that tenons

tenon's capsule \təˈnōⁿz-, ˈtenənz-\ *n, usu cap T* [after Jacques-René *Tenon* †1816 Fr. anatomist] **:** a thin connective-tissue membrane ensheathing the eyeball behind the conjunctiva

tenon's space *n, usu cap T* [after Jacques-René *Tenon*] **:** a lymph space between Tenon's capsule and the sclerotic coat of the eye that is traversed by strands of reticular tissue and by the optic nerve and ocular muscles

tenon tooth *n* **:** a fine saw tooth for cutting tenons

¹**ten·or** \ˈtenə(r)\ *n* -S [ME *tenour, tenor,* fr. OF, fr. L *tenor,* act of holding on, uninterrupted course, fr. *tenēre* to hold — more at THIN] **1 a :** the course of thought that is held to through a discourse, speech, or piece of writing **:** the general drift of something spoken or written **:** INTENT, PURPORT, SUBSTANCE ⟨the ~ of the book is expressed in the introduction —J.B.Griffin⟩ **b :** an exact copy of a writing set forth in the words and figures of it **:** TRANSCRIPT **c :** the concept, object, or person meant in a metaphor **:** the latent aspect of a metaphorical statement — compare VEHICLE 2b **2 a** (1) **:** a melodic line that usu. forms the cantus firmus in medieval polyphony (2) **:** the voice part next to the lowest in four-part harmony **b :** the highest natural adult male voice **c :** a person who sings the tenor part or an instrument that plays it **d :** the main reciting note in plainsong psalmody **e :** the lowest of a set of church bells used in change ringing **3 :** a continuance in a course, movement, or activity **:** PROCEDURE, TREND ⟨kept the noiseless ~ of their way —Thomas Gray⟩ ⟨earth and sun will continue the even ~ of their ways for an inconceivably long period —K.F.Mather⟩ **4 :** habitual condition **:** CHARACTER, NATURE, STAMP ⟨this success would look like chance, if it were not perpetual, and always of the same ~ —John Dryden⟩ **5 :** the time between the date of issue or acceptance of a note or draft and the maturity date — compare USANCE **6 :** the percentage or average amount of metal or mineral in an ore **syn** see TENDENCY

²**tenor** \"\ *adj* **:** of or relating to the tenor or the tenor part in music ⟨~ singer⟩ ⟨~ quality⟩

tenor clef *n* [so called fr. the fact that such a staff is most convenient for writing notes within the tenor voice range] **:** the C clef when it is on the fourth line of the staff — see CLEF illustration

te·no·re \tāˈnōr(ˌ)ā, -ō(ˌ)rā\ *n, pl* **teno·ri** \-ōr(ˌ)ē, -ō(ˌ)rē\ [It, fr. L *tenor* act of holding, uninterrupted course — more at TENOR] **:** TENOR

ten·or·ist \ˈtenərəst\ *n* -S [*tenor* + *-ist*] **:** one who sings tenor or plays a tenor instrument

ten·o·rite \ˈtenə,rīt\ *n* -S [It *tenorite,* fr. M. *Tenore* †1861 Ital. botanist + It *-ite*] **:** a mineral CuO that is a native cupric oxide occurring in minute steel-gray or iron-gray scales or black earthy masses — compare MELACONITE

tenor·less \ˈ==ləs\ *adj* **:** having no tenor **:** lacking intent or substance

ten·or·man \ˈ==ˌman, -mən\ *n, pl* **tenormen :** one who plays the tenor saxophone

ten·or·oon \ˌtenəˈrün\ *n* -S [²*tenor* + *bassoon*] **1 :** a tenor bassoon that is pitched a fifth higher than the standard bassoon **2 :** an incomplete stop found in an old pipe organ

tenor violin *n* **1 :** VIOLA **2 :** any of several instruments intermediate between the viola and the violoncello; *specif* **:** VIOLOTTA

ten·o·synovitis \ˌtenō+\ *n* [NL, fr. *teno-* + *synovitis*] **:** inflammation of a tendon sheath that is usu. a result of trauma or infection

ten·o·tome \ˈtenə,tōm\ *n* -S [*teno-* + *-tome*] **:** a slender narrow-bladed surgical instrument mounted on a handle

te·not·o·mist \təˈnädəməst\ *n* -S [*tenotomy* + *-ist*] **:** one who performs a tenotomy

te·not·o·mize \-ˌmīz\ *vt* -ED/-ING/-S [*tenotomy* + *-ize*] **:** to perform a tenotomy on

te·not·o·my \-mē\ *n* -ES [*teno-* + *-tomy*] **:** surgical division of a tendon

ten·our \ˈtenə(r)\ *chiefly Brit var of* TENOR

ten·pence *Brit* ˈtenpən(t)s, *US* " *or* ˈ=ˌpen-\ *n, pl* **tenpence** *or* **tenpences** [¹*ten* + *pence*] **1 :** the sum of ten usu. British pennies **2 :** a token representing ten pennies or a coin worth ten pennies

¹**ten·pen·ny** \-pənē, -ni; -ˌpenē\ *adj* [¹*ten* + *penny*] **:** amounting to, worth, or costing tenpence

²**tenpenny** \"\ *n* **1 :** a tenpenny token or coin **2** *Scot* **:** a child's reader formerly costing tenpence

tenpenny nail *n* [so called fr. its original price per hundred] **:** a nail 3 inches long

ten–percent·er \ˈtenpə(r)ˈsentə(r)\ *n* -S [*ten percent* + *-er;* fr. the rate of his commission] *slang* **:** an actor's agent

tenpin \ˈ=ˌ=\ *n* **1 :** a bottle-shaped bowling pin 15 inches high **2 tenpins** *pl but sing in constr* **:** a bowling game using ten tenpins and a large ball 27 inches in circumference and allowing each player to bowl two balls in each of ten frames — compare CANDLEPINS, DUCKPINS

7 8 9 10
4 5 6
2 3
1

arrangement of pins in tenpins

ten·pound·er \ˈ=ˈpaündə(r)\ *n* [*ten pounds* + *-er*] **1 :** a large silvery food and sport fish (*Elops saurus*) that has a somewhat compressed body resembling that of a herring, is closely related to the tarpon, and is prob. cosmopolitan in warm seas **2** *Brit* **:** a voter occupying property valued at ten pounds' annual income

ten·rec \ˈtenˌrek\ *n* [F *tanrac, tanrec, tenrec,* fr. Malagasy *tràndraka, tàndraka*] **1** *also* **tanrec** \ˈtan,-\ -S **:** any of numerous small often spiny insectivorous mammals of the family Tenrecidae of Madagascar; *esp* **:** a tailless insectivore (*Tenrec ecaudatus*) that breeds prolifically and feeds chiefly on earthworms — compare RICE TENREC **2** *cap* [NL, fr. F *tenrec*] **:** the type genus of the family Tenrecidae

Ten·rec·i·dae \tenˈresə,dē\ *n pl, cap* [NL *Tenrec,* type genus + *-idae*] **:** a family of insectivores comprising the tenrecs and with the West African otter shrew, the West Indian alamiqui, and extinct related forms often constituting a distinct superfamily of Insectivora

ten–ring \ˈ=ˌ=\ *n* [so called fr. its value in scoring] **:** the center ring of a paper target used in small-bore riflery

tens *pl of* TEN

¹**tense** \ˈten(t)s\ *n* -S [ME *tens, tense* time, tense, fr. MF *tens,* fr. L *tempor-, tempus* — more at TEMPORAL] **1 :** a distinction of form in a verb to express past, present, or future time or duration of the action or state it denotes **2 a :** a set of inflectional forms of a verb that express distinctions of time — see PAST TENSE, PRESENT TENSE **b :** a particular inflectional form of a verb expressing a specific time distinction ⟨used the wrong ~ of the verb⟩ **3 :** the part of the meaning of a verb form that consists of the expression of a time distinction **4 :** a verb phrase that includes a tense auxiliary

²**tense** \"\ *vt* -ED/-ING/-S **:** to provide with a tense ⟨a *tensed* statement⟩

³**tense** \"\ *adj* -ER/-EST [L *tensus,* fr. past part. of *tendere* to stretch — more at THIN] **1 :** stretched tight **:** made taut **:** RIGID ⟨the skeletal musculature involuntarily becomes ~ —H.G.Armstrong⟩ **2 a :** feeling or showing nervous tension **:** under mental or emotional strain **:** JITTERY ⟨~, taciturn, sensitive, given to worry —A.L.Kroeber⟩ **b :** causing strain **:** inducing tension ⟨the riffles get rougher and navigating is a bit ~ —*Buick Mag.*⟩ ⟨no game is *tenser* than solemn tournament billiards: cold-blooded concentration and steady nerves are demanded —*Time*⟩ **c :** charged with tension **:** marked by strain or suspense ⟨the air was ~ with complaint and constraint —L.C.Douglas⟩ ⟨the first eleven pages . . . have a ~ and gripping power —A.H.MacCormick⟩ **3** *of a speech sound* **:** produced with the muscles involved in a relatively tense state ⟨the vowels \ē\ and \ü\ in contrast with the vowels \i\ and \u̇\ are ~⟩ — compare LAX **syn** see STIFF, TIGHT

⁴**tense** \"\ *vb* -ED/-ING/-S *vt* **:** to make tense ⟨held my mouth open to ~ my eardrums —Christopher Morley⟩ ~ *vi* **:** to become tense ⟨*tensed* like a coiled rattler —Jack McLarn⟩ — often used with *up*

tense auxiliary *n* [¹*tense*] **:** an auxiliary verb (as *be, have*) used to form a compound tense of another verb

tense·less \ˈ=ləs\ *adj* **:** not having a tense or tenses — **tense·less·ly** *adv* — **tense·less·ness** *n* -ES

tense·ly *adv* [³*tense* + *-ly*] **:** in a tense manner ⟨the sound we had been waiting ~ to hear —H.L.Merillat⟩ ⟨stretched ~ over the drumhead⟩

tense·ness *n* -ES **:** the quality or state of being tense

ten·ser *or* **ten·sor** \ˈten(t)sə(r)\ *n* -S [ME *tenser,* fr. MF *tense, tence* protection (fr. OF, fr. *tenser, tencer* to defend, protect) + ME *-er*] **:** a noncitizen resident of an English city formerly required to pay for license to trade in the city

ten·si·bil·i·ty \ˌten(t)səˈbilədē\ *n* -ES **:** the quality or state of being tensible ⟨the nonelastic nature of the arthropod cuticula gives the body wall but little ~ —R.E.Snodgrass⟩

ten·si·ble \ˈten(t)səbəl\ *adj* [LL *tensibilis,* fr. L *tensus* (past part. of *tendere*) + *-ibilis* -ible] **:** capable of being extended — **ten·si·ble·ness** \-bəlnəs\ *n* -ES — **ten·si·bly** \-blē\ *adv*

ten·sile \ˈten(t)səl, -nˌsil, -n(ˌ)sīl\ *adj* [NL *tensilis,* fr. L *tensus* (past part. of *tendere* to stretch) + *-ilis* -ile — more at THIN] **1 :** capable of tension **:** DUCTILE ⟨is made of highly ~ steel alloy —Sam Pollock⟩ **2 :** of or relating to tension ⟨~ pull⟩ ⟨~ stress⟩ — **ten·sile·ly** \-əl(l)ē, -īll, -il(l)ē, |i\ *adv* — **ten·sile·ness** \-əlnəs, -īln-, -iln-\ *n* -ES — **ten·sil·i·ty** \tenˈsilәd·ē, -lətē, -i\ *n* -ES

tensile strength *n* **:** resistance to rupture under tension **:** BREAKING STRENGTH, COHESIVENESS; *specif* **:** the greatest longitudinal stress (as pounds per square inch) a substance can bear without tearing apart — compare COMPRESSIVE STRENGTH

ten·sim·e·ter \tenˈsimәd·ә(r)\ *n* [*tension* + *-meter*] **:** an instrument for measuring gas or vapor pressure **:** MANOMETER

ten·si·om·e·ter \ˌten(t)sēˈämәd·ә(r)\ *n* [*tension*] **1** *or* **ten·som·e·ter** \tenˈsäm-\ [³*tense*] **:** a device for measuring tension (as of fabric, yarn, or structural material) **2 :** an instrument for determining the moisture content of soil **3 :** an instrument for measuring the surface tension of liquids — **ten·sio·met·ric** \-sēōˈme·trik\ *adj* — **ten·si·om·e·try** \-sēˈämә·trē, -ri\ *n*

¹**ten·sion** \ˈtenchәn\ *n* -S *often attrib* [MF or L; MF *tension,* fr. L *tension-, tensio,* fr. *tensus* (past part. of *tendere* to stretch) + *-ion-, -io* -ion — more at THIN] **1 a :** the act or action of stretching or the condition or degree of being stretched to stiffness **:** TAUTNESS ⟨to install the belt, slip it over the pulleys and adjust its ~ —H.F.Blanchard & Ralph Ritchen⟩ **b :** STRESS ⟨arterial ~⟩ ⟨muscular ~⟩ **c :** a momentary state of muscular tautness in dance technique that inevitably resolves into relaxation **2 a :** either of two balancing forces causing or tending to cause extension **b :** the stress resulting from the elongation of an elastic body — contrasted with *compressive stress* **c** *archaic* **:** PRESSURE **3 a :** inner unrest, striving, or imbalance **:** a feeling of psychological stress often manifested by increased muscular tonus and by other physiological indicators of emotion ⟨went back to bed and dropped asleep suddenly with the release of ~ —Mary Austin⟩ ⟨~*s* distort personality —Bruce Bliven b. 1889⟩ **b :** a state of latent hostility or opposition between individuals or groups (as classes, races, nations) ⟨there is bitter ~ between them —Bernard De Voto⟩ ⟨a lessening of minority-group ~*s* —J.A.Morris b. 1904⟩ ⟨mob insanity explodes when ~ reaches the flash point —*New Republic*⟩ **c :** a balance maintained in an artistic work (as a poem, painting, musical composition) between opposing forces or elements **:** a controlled dramatic or dynamic quality ⟨the ~ which makes his sonata . . . so compelling —Stephen Spender⟩ ⟨the poetry of Dryden and Pope is characterized by the ~ between its constituent elements —F.W.Bateson⟩ **4 :** ELECTRIC POTENTIAL **5 :** any of various devices in textile manufacturing machines or sewing machines that are used to control the tautness and movement of thread or material passing through **syn** see BALANCE, STRESS

²**tension** \"\ *vt* **tensioned; tensioned; tensioning** \-ch(ә)niŋ\ **tensions :** to subject to tension **:** tighten to a desired degree **:** TAUTEN ⟨this must be heavily ~*ed,* almost to the breaking point —Albert Thompson & Sigfrid Bick⟩ ⟨cut the wire off and ~*ed* and dead-ended it —W.W.Haines⟩

ten·sion·al \-chәnᵊl, -chnәl\ *adj* **:** of, relating to, or resulting from tension ⟨manufacturers and distributors of ~ steel —*Economist*⟩ ⟨is not religion essentially a ~ relation between God and man —Georges Florovsky⟩

tension element *n* **:** a flexible link (as an endless belt with its pulleys) for transmitting tension only — compare PRESSURE ELEMENT

ten·sion·er \-ch(ә)nә(r)\ *n* -S [²*tension* + *-er*] **:** ¹TENSION 5

tension·less \ˈ==lәs\ *adj* **:** free from tension

tension man *n* **:** a worker who keeps newsprint feeding through a web press at the proper tension

tension pulley *n* **:** a pulley over which a belt is caused to pass in order to keep it taut

tension rod *n* **:** a metal rod used as a tension member

tension wood *n* **:** a reaction wood formed on the upper side of tree branches and leaning trunks and characterized by narrower and thinner walled wood and fiber elements, excessive longitudinal shrinkage, and tendency to collapse on drying — compare COMPRESSION WOOD

tension zone *n* **:** ECOTONE

ten·si·ty \ˈten(t)sәd·ē, -sәtē, -i\ *n* -ES [ML *tensitat-, tensitas,* fr. L *tensus* tense + *-itat-, -itas* -ity] **:** TENSENESS ⟨with a sudden ~ of which he had never suspected her —A.J.Cronin⟩

ten·sive \ˈten(t)siv, -sēv *also* -sәv\ *adj* [F *tensif,* fr. MF, fr. L *tensus* (past part. of *tendere* to stretch) + MF *-if* -ive] **:** of, relating to, or causing tension

ten·son \ˈten(t)sәn\ *also* **ten·so** \-nˌsō\ *or* **ten·zon** \-nzәn\ *n* -S [*tenson* fr. F, fr. MF *tençon, tenson,* fr. Prov *tensoun; tenzon* fr. It *tenzone,* fr. Prov *tensoun; tenso* fr. Prov *tensoun, tenso* quarrel, contest, tenson, fr. L *tension-, tensio* tension — more at TENSION] **:** a lyric poem of dispute composed by Provençal troubadours in which two opponents speak alternate stanzas, lines, or groups of lines usu. identical in structure — compare DÉBAT, PARTIMEN

¹**ten·sor** \ˈten(t)sә(r), -nˌsȯ(ә)r\ *n* -S [NL, fr. L *tensus* (past part. of *tendere* to stretch) + *-or* — more at THIN] **1** *or* **tensor muscle :** a muscle that stretches a part or makes it tense **2 :** a generalized vector with more than three components each of which is a function of the coordinates of an arbitrary point in space of an appropriate number of dimensions

²**tensor** *var of* TENSER

ten·so·ri·al \(ˈ)tenˈsōrēәl, -sȯr-\ *adj* [NL *tensor* + E *-al*] **:** of, relating to, or characteristic of a tensor

ten–spot \ˈ=ˌ=\ *n* [¹*ten* + *spot*] **1 :** a ten-dollar bill **2 :** a playing card with ten spots

ten–strike \ˈ=ˌ=\ *n* **1 :** a strike in tenpins **2 :** a highly successful stroke or achievement **:** a smashing success ⟨three months ago I thought that at last I had written a *ten-strike* —Bernard De Voto⟩

¹**tent** \ˈtent\ *n* -S *often attrib* [ME *tente, tent,* fr. OF *tente,* fr. L *tenta,* fem. of *tentus,* past part. of *tendere* to stretch — more at THIN] **1 :** a collapsible shelter of canvas or other material stretched and sustained by poles, usu. made fast by ropes attached to pegs hammered into the ground, and used for camping outdoors (as by soldiers or vacationers) or as a temporary building (as for a theatrical performance) — see FLY TENT, PUP TENT, SIBLEY TENT, WALL TENT **2 :** ABODE, DWELLING, HABITATION ⟨others among the great who are admissible into the ~*s* of the mighty —J.T.Farrell⟩ ⟨moved with the smart clientele, pitching his ~ in the resorts during the proper seasons —E.O.Hauser⟩ **3 :** something that resembles a tent or that serves as a shelter ⟨the pale, silky-looking ~*s* of the . . . mountains —Cid R. Sumner⟩ ⟨the ~ of free enterprise —*Wall Street Jour.*⟩: as **a** *Scot* **:** a wooden pulpit for open-air preaching **b :** HUT, SHACK **c :** a local organization of the Rechabites **d :** the web of a tent caterpillar **e :** a canopy or airtight chamber placed over the head and shoulders of a patient to retain vapors or oxygen during administration

²**tent** \"\ *vb* -ED/-ING/-S *vi* **1 :** to reside for the time being **:** make a temporary abode **:** LODGE ⟨the blue skies with the leisurely clouds ~*ing* among them —J.H.Wheelwright⟩ **2 :** to live in a tent ⟨~*ed* in the state park for a week⟩ ~ *vt* **1 :** to cover with or as if with a tent ⟨the rich brocade in which she was ~*ed* —John Mason Brown⟩ ⟨~*ed* his head with his hands —Warren Eyster⟩ **2 :** to lodge in tents ⟨~*ed* his men on top of the hill⟩

³**tent** \"\ *n* -S [ME, short for *attent* attention, intention, expectation, fr. OF *attente,* fr. L *attenta,* fem. of *attentus,* past part. of *attendere* to attend] *dial chiefly Brit* **:** ATTENTION, HEED, CARE

⁴**tent** \"\ *vt* -ED/-ING/-S [ME *tenten,* fr. ³*tent*] **1** *chiefly Scot* **:** to pay attention to **:** HEED **2** *chiefly Scot* **:** to attend to **:** care for **:** watch over **:** TEND **3** *chiefly Scot* **:** OBSERVE, WATCH

⁵**tent** \"\ *n* -S [ME *tent, tente,* fr. MF *tente,* fr. OF, fr. *tenter* to try, tempt, test, probe — more at TEMPT] **1** *obs* **:** a probe for searching a wound ⟨the ~ that searches to the bottom of the worst —Shak.⟩ **2 :** a roll of lint or linen or a conical or cylindrical piece of sponge or other absorbent formerly used chiefly to dilate a natural canal, to keep open the orifice of a wound, or to absorb discharges

⁶**tent** \"\ *vt* -ED/-ING/-S **1** *obs* **:** PROBE ⟨~ him to the quick —Shak.⟩ **2** *archaic* **:** to keep open or treat with a surgical tent

⁷**tent** \"\ *n* -S [Sp *tinto,* fr. *tinto* dark red, fr. L *tinctus,* past part. of *tingere* to wet, dye — more at TINGE] **:** a very dark red sweet Spanish wine

tent·a·bil·i·ty \ˌtentәˈbilәd·ē\ *n* [irreg. fr. *temptable* + *-ity*] **:** the quality or state of being temptable

ten·ta·cle \ˈtentәkәl, -tēk-\ *n* -S [NL *tentaculum,* fr. L *tentare* to touch, feel, attempt + *-culum,* suffix denoting an instrument — more at TEMPT] **1 :** any of various elongate flexible simple or branched processes that are usu. tactile or prehensile or both in function but sometimes have other functions (as respiration or locomotion) and that are borne by animals chiefly on the head or about the mouth: as **a :** one of the arms of a cephalopod, crinoid, or polyp **b :** one of the fleshy processes sometimes bearing eyes on the head of a gastropod mollusk or many worms — see SNAIL illustration **c :** one of the threadlike processes bearing stinging cells that depend from the margin of the umbrella of many jellyfishes **d :** one of the tubular suctorial processes of a suctorian **e :** one of the numerous small ciliated processes borne on the arms of a brachiopod or the lophophore of a bryozoan **2 a :** something that acts like a tentacle in grasping or feeling out **:** FEELER, TENDRIL ⟨these ~*s* of organized crime and corruption —R.E.Merriam⟩ ⟨in every experience we touch the world through some particular ~ —John Dewey⟩ **b :** a sensitive hair or emergence (as one of the gland-tipped insect-catching hairs on the leaves of the sundew)

ten·ta·cled \-kəld\ *adj* [*tentacle* + *-ed*] **:** having tentacles ⟨influences which reach . . . like ~ weeds —*Newsweek*⟩

ten·tac·u·lar \(ˈ)tenˌtakyələ(r)\ *adj* [NL *tentaculum* + E *-ar*] **1 :** of, relating to, or resembling tentacles ⟨matted beards that seemed ~ as the arms of an octopus —Osbert Sitwell⟩ **2 :** equipped with tentacles **:** acting by means of tentacles ⟨his ~ mind poking into everything —Amy Lowell⟩ ⟨the ~ organization of modern society —*Times Lit. Supp.*⟩

ten·tac·u·la·ta \tenˌtakyəˈlād·ə, -lād·ə\ *n pl, cap* [NL, fr. neut. pl. of *tentaculatus* tentaculate] **:** a class of Ctenophora comprising forms with tentacles that are retractile into sheaths and that may be long and pinnate (as in members of the orders Cydippida and Platyctenea), small and unbranched (as in members of the order Cestida), or present only in the immature stage (as in members of the order Lobata)

ten·tac·u·late \ˈ=ˌ==lət\ *adj* [NL *tentaculatus*, fr. *tentaculum* + L *-atus* -ate] **1 :** having tentacles **2 :** of or relating to the Tentaculata

ten·tac·u·lat·ed \-ˌlād·əd\ *adj* [NL *tentaculatus* + E *-ed*] **:** TENTACLED

ten·tac·u·lif·era \=ˌ==ˈlif(ə)rə\ [NL, fr. *tentaculum* + *-i-* + L *-fera*, neut. pl. of *-fer*] *syn of* SUCTORIA

ten·tac·u·lif·er·ous \=ˌ==ˈlif(ə)rəs\ *adj* [NL *tentaculum* + E *-iferous*] **:** bearing tentacles

ten·tac·u·lite \=ˈ==ˌlīt\ *n* -s [NL *Tentaculites*] **:** a fossil or individual of the genus *Tentaculites* or family Tentaculitidae

ten·tac·u·li·tes \=ˌ==ˈlīd·(ˌ)ēz\ *n, cap* [NL, fr. *tentaculum* + *-ites*] **:** a genus of small conical fossil shells found abundantly in some Paleozoic rocks and often made the type of the family Tentaculitidae

ten·tac·u·lit·i·dae \-ˈlid·əˌdē\ *n pl, cap* [NL, fr. *Tentaculites*, type genus + *-idae*] **:** a family of shelled Paleozoic invertebrates (group Conulariida) — see TENTACULITES

ten·tac·u·lo·cyst \=ˈ==ˌlō+\ *n* [NL *tentaculum* + *-o-* + E *cyst*] **:** one of the sense organs situated on the margin of the umbrella of many jellyfishes, consisting of a greatly modified and reduced tentacle containing a cavity with lithites, and often being sunk in a pit or enclosed in a pouch

ten·tac·u·loid \-ˌlȯid\ *adj* [NL *tentaculum* + E *-oid*] **:** resembling a tentacle

ten·tac·u·lo·zooid \=ˈ==ˌlō+\ *n* [NL *tentaculum* + *-o-* + E *zooid*] **:** a zooid of a colonial polyp that is adapted to act as a tentacle

ten·tac·u·lum \=ˈ==ləm\ *n, pl* **tentacu·la** \-lə\ [NL — more at TENTACLE] **1 a :** TENTACLE 1 **b :** VIBRISSA **2 :** HAPTERON, HOLDFAST

ten·ta·dero \ˌtentəˈde(ˌ)rō\ *n* -s [Sp, corral where young bulls are tested, fr. *tentado* (past part. of *tentar* to touch, feel, try, fr. L *tentare*), fr. L *tentatus*, past part. of *tentare* — more at TEMPT] **:** TIENTA

tent·age \ˈtentij, -tēj\ *n* -s [¹*tent* + *-age*] **:** a collection or supply of tents **:** tent facilities or equipment ⟨are equipped with sufficient ~ for sheltering patients —C.M.Walson⟩

ten·ta·tion \tenˈtāshən\ *n* -s [L *tentation-*, *tentatio*, fr. *tentatus* (past part. of *tentare* to feel, attempt, tempt) + *-ion-*, *-io* -ion] **1** *archaic* **:** TEMPTATION **2 :** a mode of adjusting or operating by successive steps, trials, or experiments

¹**ten·ta·tive** \ˈtentəd·iv, -ətiv\ *adj* [ML *tentativus*, fr. L *tentatus* (past part. of *tentare* to feel, attempt tempt) + *-ivus* -ive — more at TEMPT] **1 a :** of the nature of an experiment or hypothesis **:** offered, undertaken, or arrived at as a first step **:** PROVISIONAL ⟨for him all questions are open, all assumptions ~ —Walter Moberly⟩ **b :** offered or given for the time being **:** subject to change or withdrawal **:** not final ⟨a ~ program⟩ ⟨a ~ acceptance⟩ ⟨a ~ refusal⟩ **2 :** HESITANT, UNCERTAIN ⟨a sort of ~, almost apologetic smile —R.P. Warren⟩ ⟨~ made his voice ~ —Jean Stafford⟩ ⟨his speech is jerky and ~ —Walter Bernstein⟩ — **ten·ta·tive·ly** \-əvlē, -li\ *adv* — **ten·ta·tive·ness** \-ivnəs\ *n* -ES

²**tentative** \ˈ"\ *n* -s **:** a tentative undertaking, experiment, or offer ⟨the few surviving scraps of notes . . . are crammed with story ~*s* —Jay Leyda⟩

tent bed *n* [¹*tent*] **:** FIELD BED

tent caterpillar *n* **:** any of several gregarious caterpillars that construct on trees large silken webs into which they retreat when at rest — see EASTERN TENT CATERPILLAR, FOREST TENT CATERPILLAR; compare FALL WEBWORM, WEBWORM

tent club *n* **:** a club devoted to the sport of pigsticking

tent·ed \ˈtentəd\ *adj* [¹*tent* + *-ed*] **1 a :** covered with tents **:** containing tents ⟨the ~ field⟩ **b :** sheltered by or provided with a tent ⟨the ~ soldiers⟩ **2 :** shaped like a tent ⟨~ arch⟩ ⟨~ ice⟩

tented wagon *n* **:** COVERED WAGON

¹**ten·ter** \ˈtentə(r)\ *n* -s [ME *teyntur*, *tayntour*, *taynter*, perh. modif. (influenced by MF *teindre* to dye) of ML *tentura*, fr. L *tentus* (past part. of *tendere* to stretch) + *-ura* -ure — more at THIN] **1 :** a frame or endless track with hooks or clips along two sides that is used for drying and stretching cloth **2** *archaic* **:** TENTERHOOK — **on the tenters** *archaic* **:** on tenterhooks ⟨I have seen him stretched *on the tenters* to keep thee in countenance —Samuel Richardson⟩

²**tenter** \ˈ"\ *vt* -ED/-ING/-S [ME *teynteren*, fr. *teyntur*, *taynter* tenter] **:** to hang or stretch on or as if on a tenter

³**tent·er** \ˈtentə(r)\ *n* -s [⁴*tent* + *-er*] **1** *Brit* **:** one that has charge of something; *specif* **:** one that tends a machine in a factory **2** *Brit* **:** HELPER 2

⁴**tenter** \ˈ"\ *n* -s [²*tent* + *-er*] **:** one that lives in or occupies a tent ⟨they slept in better style than ~*s* —Gordon Webber⟩

ten·ter·er \ˈtentərə(r)\ *n* -s [²*tenter* + *-er*] **:** one that tenters (as cloth)

tenterhook \ˈ==ˌ=\ *n* [ME *tentourhok*, *tayntyrhok*, fr. *taynter*, *tayntour* tenter + *hok* hook] **1 :** a sharp hooked nail used esp. for fastening cloth on a tenter **2 :** something that serves as a means or device for stretching or straining — **on tenterhooks :** in a state of uneasiness, strain, or suspense ⟨the new men are frankly *on tenterhooks*, for they have a career at stake —Roy Lewis & Angus Maude⟩ ⟨puts his readers right *on tenterhooks* —W.G.Rogers⟩

¹**tenth** \ˈten(t)th\ *adj* [ME *tenthe*, alter. (influenced by *ten*) of *tethe*, fr. OE *tēotha*; akin to OS *tegotho* tenth, MLG *tegede*; all fr. a prehistoric WGmc ordinal whose first element is the source of OE *tien*, *tȳn*, *tēn* ten and whose second element is the source of OE *-otha*, *-tha* -th — more at TEN, -TH] **1 :** being number 10 in a countable series ⟨the ~ day⟩ — see NUMBER table **2 :** being one of 10 equal parts into which something is divisible ⟨a ~ share of the money⟩

²**tenth** \ˈ"\ *n, pl* **tenths** \-n(t)s, -n(t)ths\ [ME *tenthe*, fr. *tenthe*, adj.] **1 :** number 10 in a countable series ⟨the ~ of the month⟩ **2 :** the quotient of a unit divided by 10 **:** one of 10 equal parts of something ⟨one ~ of the total⟩ **3 a :** a tax of one tenth levied on the personal property of a subject and granted to the English sovereign from 1272 to 1624 **b :** a tenth part of the annual profit of every Anglican benefice paid from 1534 to 1703 to the crown and after 1703 into a special fund to aid needy churches or augment church livings **4 a :** a musical interval embracing an octave and a third **b :** a note or tone at this interval **c :** an organ stop sounding a tenth above the normal pitch of the digitals played upon **5 :** a unit of capacity for wine equal to one tenth of a U.S. gallon; *also* **:** a bottle holding this quantity of wine

³**tenth** \ˈ"\ *adv* [¹*tenth*] **1 :** in the tenth place **2 :** with nine exceptions ⟨the nation's ~ largest city⟩

tenth card *n* **:** a card in cribbage (as a face card or a ten) counting ten points

tenth cranial nerve *or* **tenth nerve** *n* **:** VAGUS NERVE

tenth·ly *adv* [¹*tenth* + *-ly*] **:** in the tenth place

tenthmeter \ˈ=ˌ==\ *n* [²*tenth* + *meter* (unit)] **1 :** a metric unit of length equal to one ten millionth of a millimeter ⟨one meter equals 10^{10} ~*s*⟩ **2 :** ANGSTROM a

tenth-rate \ˈ=ˈ=\ *adj* **:** most inferior **:** of the lowest character or quality ⟨the way he had done his research, his lack of critical sense, his taking his professor's evidence — that wasn't even second-rate, it was *tenth-rate* —C.P.Snow⟩

¹**ten·thred·i·nid** \tenˈthredənəd\ *adj* [NL *Tenthredinidae*] **:** of or relating to the Tenthredinidae

²**tenthredinid** \ˈ"\ *n* -s **:** a sawfly of the family Tenthredinidae

ten·thre·din·i·dae \ˌten(t)thrəˈdinəˌdē\ *n pl, cap* [NL *Tenthredin-*, *Tenthredo*, type genus (fr. Gk *tenthrēdōn*, a kind of wasp) + *-idae*] **:** a family of Hymenoptera comprising all the sawflies or now more commonly including various typical sawflies — see TENTHREDINOIDEA

ten·thre·di·noi·dea \ˌten(t)thrədəˈnȯidēə\ *n pl, cap* [NL, fr. *Tenthredin-*, *Tenthredo* + *-oidea*] **:** a superfamily (suborder Chalastogastra) of hymenopterous insects comprising the sawflies and being coextensive with Tenthredinidae in its broadest use

tent·i·form \ˈtentəˌfȯrm\ *adj* [¹*tent* + *-iform*] **:** resembling or building a nest that resembles a tent in form ⟨~ leaf miners⟩

ten·til·lum \tenˈtiləm\ *n, pl* **tentil·la** \-lə\ [NL, fr. L *tentare* to feel + *-illum*, dim. suffix — more at TEMPT] **:** a branch of a tentacle; *esp* **:** one of the contractile branches that are rich in nematocysts and that occur on the tentacles of various siphonophores

tenting *pres part of* TENT

¹**tent·less** \ˈ=ˌləs\ *adj* [³*tent* + *-less*] *Scot* **:** CARELESS, HEEDLESS

²**tentless** \ˈ"\ *adj* [¹*tent* + *-less*] **:** having no tent **:** being without means of shelter

tentmaker \ˈ=ˌ==\ *n* **1 :** one that makes tents **2 :** any of numerous moths whose gregarious larvae spin communal nests usu. in trees

tentmate \ˈ=ˌ=\ *n* **:** one that occupies the same tent

tent of meeting : TABERNACLE 1a

ten·to·ri·al \(ˈ)tenˈtōrēəl, -tȯr-\ *adj* [NL *tentorium* + E *-al*] **:** of, relating to, or involving the tentorium

tentorial ridge *n* **:** a bony ridge on the inner surface of the skull that marks the attachment of the tentorium

tentorial sinus *n* **:** STRAIGHT SINUS

ten·to·ri·um \tenˈtōrēəm\ *n, pl* **tento·ria** \-rēə\ [NL, fr. L, tent, fr. *tentus* (past part. of *tendere* to stretch) + *-orium*] **1** *or* **tentorium ce·re·bel·li** \-ˌserəˈbeˌlī\ [*tentorium cerebelli*, fr. NL, lit., tentorium of the cerebellum] **:** an arched fold of dura mater covering the upper surface of the cerebellum, supporting the occipital lobes of the cerebrum, having its posterior and lateral border attached to the skull and its anterior border free, and in some forms (as the cat) being completely ossified **2 :** the internal chitinous skeleton of an insect's head formed usu. of two or three paired apodemes arising from the chitinous head capsule

tent pegging *n* [*tent peg* + *-ing*] **:** a sport originating in India of riding a horse at a charging pace and endeavoring to uproot on the point of a lance a tent peg in the ground

tents *pl of* TENT, *pres 3d sing of* TENT

tent shell *n* **:** LIMPET

tent slide *or* **tent slip** *n* **:** a device used to adjust the tension of a guy rope of a tent — called also *rope key*

tent stitch *n* **:** a short stitch slanting to the right that is used in embroidery and canvas work to form even lines of solid background — compare GROS POINT, PETIT POINT

tent stitch

ten-twenty-thirty \ˈ=ˈ==ˈ==\ *or* **ten-twent-thirt** \ˈ=ˈtwentˈthərt\ *n* [so called fr. the prices in cents of seats] **:** a cheap and typically melodramatic theatrical entertainment; *also* **:** a theater or touring company offering such entertainment

tent worm *n* **:** TENT CATERPILLAR

tenty *also* **tent·ie** \ˈtentī\ *adj* [³*tent* + *-y*] *Scot* **:** ATTENTIVE, CAREFUL, WATCHFUL

te·nue \tənˈü\ *n, pl* **tenues** \ˈ"\ [F, fr. fem. of *tenu*, past part. of *tenir* to hold, fr. OF — more at TENABLE] **1 :** BEARING, CARRIAGE, DEPORTMENT ⟨the sacrifices made in the sacred name of ~ . . . the smiles amiably exchanged in public between mortal enemies —Victoria Sackville-West⟩ **2 :** mode of dress ⟨the long black coat with the lavender trousers and mauve vest that must have been his ~ when he married his first wife —*Young's Mag.*⟩

ten·u·i·ros·ter \ˌtenyəwēˈrästə(r)\ *n* -s [NL, sing. of *Tenuirostres*] **:** a bird of the Tenuirostres

ten·u·i·ros·tres \-ˌäˌstrēz\ *n pl, cap* [NL, fr. L *tenuis* thin + *rostrum* beak — more at THIN, ROSTRUM] *in former classifications* **:** an unnatural group of mostly passerine birds (as hummingbirds, sunbirds, honey eaters, nuthatches) having slender bills

ten·u·is \ˈtenyəwəs\ *n, pl* **tenu·es** \-əˌwēz\ [ML, lit., thin, slight, trans. of Gk *psilos* bare, unaspirated — more at PSIL-] **:** an unaspirated voiceless stop

te·nu·i·ty \teˈn(y)üəd·ē, təˈn-, -üətē, -i\ *n* -ES [L *tenuitat-*, *tenuitas*, fr. *tenuis* thin, slight + *-itat-*, *-itas* -ity] **1 :** lack of substance **:** MEAGERNESS, POVERTY ⟨as far as the ~ of my understanding would hold out —Laurence Sterne⟩ **2 :** lack of thickness **:** SLENDERNESS, THINNESS ⟨the ~ of a hair⟩ **3 :** lack of density **:** rarefied quality or state **:** RARITY ⟨in studying the upper atmospheric region it is helpful to bear in mind its high ~ —S.K.Mitra⟩ **4 :** lack of intensity or vigor **:** FAINTNESS, FEEBLENESS ⟨speak with a shrill yet sweet ~ of voice —Nathaniel Hawthorne⟩

ten·u·lin \ˈtenyələn\ *n* -s [NL *tenuifolium* (specific epithet of *Helenium tenuifolium*) (fr. L *tenuis* thin + *folium* leaf) + *-lin* (as in *helenalin*) — more at BLADE] **:** a crystalline sesquiterpenoid lactone $C_{17}H_{22}O_5$ obtained from plants of the genus *Helenium* (as *H. tenuifolium*)

ten·u·ous \ˈtenyəwəs\ *adj* [L *tenuis* thin, slight, tenuous — more at THIN] **1 :** not dense **:** having a thin consistency **:** RARE ⟨as ~ as a comet's trail —A.M.Young⟩ **2 :** not thick **:** SLENDER, SLIM ⟨lowering himself down rocky ravines with a ~ nylon rope —*Sydney (Australia) Bull.*⟩ ⟨write it in ~, trailing letters —P.M.Hollister⟩ **3 a :** having little substance or strength **:** FLIMSY, INSIGNIFICANT, WEAK ⟨a ~ idealism lost touch with reality —Laurence Binyon⟩ ⟨the ~ character of his physical strength —E.H.Blashfield⟩ **b :** not firmly based or supported ⟨the seeds sprout slowly, and take ~ root —Fred Rodell⟩ ⟨~ growth that will wither beneath the hot winds of summer —George Farwell⟩ **c :** not definite, sharp, or clear-cut **:** HAZY, VAGUE ⟨impossible to analyze all the ~ influences at work —*Amer. Guide Series: Mich.*⟩ **syn** see THIN

ten·u·ous·ly *adv* **:** in a tenuous manner

ten·u·ous·ness *n* -ES **:** the quality or state of being tenuous

¹**ten·ure** \ˈtenyə(r)\ *also* -ˌnyů(ə)r *or* -üə\ *n* -s [ME, fr. OF *teneüre*, *tenure*, fr. ML *tenitura*, fr. (assumed) VL *tenitus* (past part. of L *tenēre* to hold) + L *-ura* -ure — more at THIN] **1 a** (1) **:** the act or right of holding property esp. real estate ⟨land ~ is a leading political issue in many parts of the world⟩ (2) *Eng law* **:** the holding of an estate of a superior **b :** the manner of holding property **:** the title and conditions by which property is held ⟨~ by knight service⟩ ⟨~ by fee simple absolute⟩ **2 :** ESTATE, HOLDING ⟨like most Old English leaseholds, the ~*s* . . . created were limited to three lives —F.M.Stenton⟩ **3 a :** the act, action, or a means of holding something **:** GRASP, HOLD ⟨the uncertain ~ which mere military demonstrations in force gave her over a proud people —John Buchan⟩ ⟨hope that you will hold your place in company by a nobler ~ —Earl of Chesterfield⟩ ⟨trousers held, apparently, by a very insecure ~ —Rachel Henning⟩ **b :** manner, condition, or term of holding something ⟨the great limitations just indicated affect the ~ of this power —C.H.McIlwain⟩ ⟨spends his ~ of office fighting for time to assess facts and to think —Dorothy Fosdick⟩ **c :** a status granted usu. after a probationary period to one holding a position esp. as a teacher and protecting him from dismissal except for serious misconduct or incompetence determined by formal hearings or trial **:** permanent tenure

²**ten·ure** \ˈtenyə(r)\ [ME, alter. of *tenour* tenor] *archaic var of* TENOR

tenure by free alms : FRANKALMOIGN

tenure in chivalry : tenure by knight service

ten·u·ri·al \teˈnyůrēəl, təˈn-\ *adj* [¹*tenure* + *-ial*] **:** of or relating to tenure ⟨this ~ revolution never degenerated into a scramble for land —F.M.Stenton⟩ — **ten·u·ri·al·ly** \-ēlē\ *adv*

te·nu·to \təˈnüd·(ˌ)ō\ *adv (or adj)* [It, fr. past part. of *tenere* to hold, fr. L *tenēre* — more at THIN] **:** in a manner so as to hold a tone or chord firmly to its full value — used as a direction in music; compare STACCATO

ten-week stock \ˈ=ˌ=-\ *n* **:** any of several garden stocks that constitute a variety (*Matthiola incana annua*) of the common stock and that bloom from seed during the summer and fall of their first season of growth — compare BROMPTON STOCK

tenzon *var of* TENSON

te·o·cal·li \ˌtēōˈkalē, ˌtāəˈkälē\ *n* -s [Nahuatl, fr. *teotl* god + *calli* house] **:** an ancient temple of Mexico or Central America usu. built upon the summit of a truncated pyramidal mound; *also* **:** the mound itself

te·o·pan \ˈtāōˌpän, ˌ==ˈ=\ *n* -s [Nahuatl, fr. *teotl* god + *pan* place] **:** the precincts of an ancient temple of Mexico **:** a walled enclosure containing a teocalli and other buildings devoted to religious uses

te·o·sin·te \ˌtāəˈsintē\ *also* **te·o·cen·tli** \-sentlē\ *or* **te·o·cin·tle** \-sintlē\ *n* -s [Nahuatl *teocentli*, fr. *teotl* god + *centli* ear of corn] **:** a large annual grass (*Euchlaena mexicana*) that is native to Mexico and Central America, is sometimes regarded as the progenitor of Indian corn, and is grown esp. for fodder in many warm countries

te·o·ti·hua·can \ˌtāōˌtēwəˈkän\ *adj, usu cap* [fr. *Teotihuacán*, town of central Mexico noted for its Toltec ruins] **:** of or belonging to the Toltec period of Nahuatl culture in Mexico characterized by temple building and the establishment of gods such as Tlaloc and Quetzalcoatl

te·pa \ˈtāpə\ *n* -s [fr. native name in Chile] **1 :** a So. American timber tree (*Laurelia serrata*) of the family Monimiaceae **2 :** the wood of the tepa

te·pa·che \təˈpächē\ *n* -s [Sp, fr. Nahuatl *tepiatl*, fr. *tepitl* a kind of corn + *atl* water] **:** any of several Mexican drinks; *specif* **:** an intoxicating beverage made from pulque and coarse sugar with timbe used to retard fermentation

te·pal \ˈtēpəl, ˈtep-\ *n* -s [F *tépale*, alter. (influenced by *sépale* sepal, fr. NL *sepalum*) of *pétale* petal, fr. NL *petalum* — more at SEPAL, PETAL] **:** any of the modified leaves making up a perianth

te·pa·nec \ˌtepəˈnek\ *or* **te·pa·neca** \ˌ==ˈnekə\ *n, pl* **tepanec** *or* **tepanecs** *or* **tepaneca** *or* **tepanecas** *usu cap* **1 :** a Nahuatl people of the Valley of Mexico **2 :** a member of the Tepanec people

te·pa·ry bean \ˈtepərē-\ *n* [origin unknown] **:** an annual twining bean (*Phaseolus acutifolius latifolius*) native to southwestern U.S. and Mexico but cultivated for its resistance to drought and heat and having roundish white, yellow, brown, or bluish black edible seeds

te·pe \ˈtepē\ *n* -s [Turk, hill, summit] **:** an artificial mound — used in place names; compare ³TELL

te·pe·ca·no \ˌtepāˈkä(ˌ)nō\ *n, pl* **tepecano** *or* **tepecanos** *usu cap* [MexSp, fr. Nahuatl *tepetl* mountain + *aco* on top of] **1 a :** a Piman people of the northern part of the state of Jalisco, Mexico **b :** a member of such people **2 :** the language of the Tepecano people

te·pee *or* **ti·pi** *also* **tee·pee** \ˈtē(ˌ)pē, ˌpi\ *n* -s [Dakota *tipi* tent, fr. *ti* to dwell + *pi* to use for] **:** an American Indian conical tent used esp. by the Plains tribes and consisting of a covering usu. of skins spread over a frame of poles — compare LODGE 8a

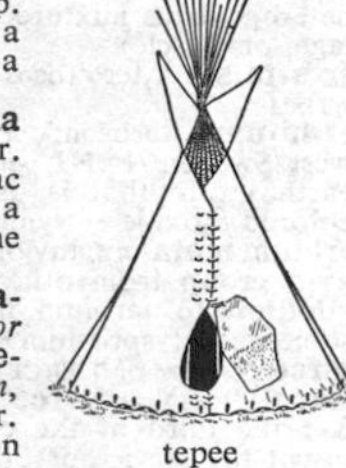

tepee

te·pe·hua \təˈpā(ˌ)wä\ *n, pl* **tepehua** *or* **tepehuas** *usu cap* [MexSp, prob. fr. Nahuatl *Tepehuan*] **1 a :** a Totonac people of southeastern Mexico **b :** a member of such people **2 :** the language of the Tepehua people

te·pe·huan \ˌtepəˈwän\ *or* **te·pe·hua·ne** \ˌ==ˈwänē\ *n, pl* **tepehuan** *or* **tepehuans** *or* **tepehuane** *or* **tepehuanes** *usu cap* [MexSp *Tepehuán*, *Tepehuane*, fr. Nahuatl *Tepehuan*, fr. *tepetl* mountain + *huan* at the junction of] **1 a :** a Piman people of Durango and adjacent states in northwestern Mexico **b :** a member of such people **2 :** the language of the Tepehuan people

te·pe·ta·te \ˌtepəˈtädē\ *n* -s [MexSp, fr. Nahuatl *tepetatl*, fr. *tetl* stone + *petatl* matting] **:** CALICHE

te·pex·pán man \ˌtepəˈspän-\ *n, usu cap T* [fr. *Tepexpán*, village of central Mexico] **:** an extinct man that is known from a fossilized skeleton found in the Valley of Mexico and attributed to the late Pleistocene and that was probably coeval with Folsom man

tephillin *var of* TEFILLIN

te·phrit·i·dae \təˈfridəˌdē\ [NL, fr. *Tephritis*, genus of two-winged flies (fr. Gk *tephros* ash gray) + *-idae*] *syn of* TRYPETIDAE

teph·ro·ite \ˈtefrōˌīt\ *n* -s [G *tephroit*, fr. Gk *tephros* ash gray + G *-it* -ite] **:** a mineral Mn_2SiO_4 that consists of Manganese silicate and is isomorphous with olivine

te·phro·sia \təˈfrōzh(ē)ə, teˈf-\ *n, cap* [NL, fr. Gk *tephros* ash gray, fr. *tephra* ashes; fr. the appearance of its foliage — more at DAY] **:** a genus of herbs or undershrubs (family Leguminosae) having odd-pinnate leaves, white or purplish flowers, and flat legumes

teph·ro·sin \ˈtefrəsən\ *n* -s [NL *Tephrosia* + ISV *-in*] **:** a crystalline compound $C_{23}H_{22}O_7$ that is obtained from the leaves of a leguminous plant (*Tephrosia vogelii*) and from the roots of derris and cube and that is isomeric with toxicarol; hydroxy-deguelin

tep·id \ˈtepəd\ *adj* [L *tepidus*, fr. *tepēre* to be moderately warm; akin to Skt *tapati* it gives out heat, *tapas* heat, OIr *tess* heat] **1 :** moderately warm **:** LUKEWARM ⟨a ~ bath⟩ ⟨a ~ pool⟩ **2 a :** lacking in passion, force, or animation **:** DULL, LIFELESS ⟨grave and precise in manner, courteous and ~ —Arnold Bennett⟩ ⟨was so ~ and had so few resources and so little initiative —George Santayana⟩ **b :** marked by an absence of enthusiasm or conviction **:** HALFHEARTED ⟨had only a ~ interest in public health —A.W.Long⟩ ⟨still enjoys a measure of ~ praise —T.S.Eliot⟩ — **tep·id·ly** *adv* — **tep·id·ness** *n* -ES

te·pi·dar·i·um \ˌtepəˈda(a)rēəm\ *n, pl* **tepidar·ia** \-rēə\ [L, fr. *tepidus* tepid + *-arium*] **:** a warm room of the ancient Roman thermae used to sit in

te·pid·i·ty \təˈpidəd·ē, -dətē, -i\ *n* -ES [LL *tepiditat-*, *tepiditas*, fr. L *tepidus* tepid + *-itat-*, *-itas* -ity] **:** the quality or state of being tepid **:** LUKEWARMNESS

tep·o·nax·tle *or* **tep·o·naz·tli** *or* **te·po·naz·tli** \ˌtepəˈnästlē\ *n* -s [MexSp & Nahuatl; MexSp *teponaxtle*, fr. Nahuatl *teponaztli*] **:** a Mexican slit-drum of Aztec origin

tepoy *var of* TEAPOY

TEPP \ˌtēˌēˌpēˈpē\ *abbr or n* -s [*tetraethyl pyrophosphate*] **:** TETRAETHYL PYROPHOSPHATE

tep·ti·ar \ˈteptēˌär\ *n, pl* **teptiar** *or* **teptiars** *usu cap* **1 :** a Tatar people of central Asia related to the Kazaks and Bashkirs **2 :** a member of the Teptiar people

te·qui·la \təˈkēlə\ *n* -s [Sp, fr. *Tequila*, district of Jalisco state, west central Mexico] **1 :** a Mexican century plant (*Agave tequilana*) much cultivated as one of the chief sources of mescal **2** *also* **te·quil·la** \ˈ"\ **a :** a Mexican liquor made by redistilling mescal — compare SOTOL **b :** MESCAL

te·quis·tla·tec \təˈkistləˌtek\ *n, pl* **tequistlatec** *or* **tequistlatecs** *usu cap* **1 a :** an Indian people of southern Oaxaca, Mexico **b :** a member of such people **2 :** the Tequistlatecan language of the Tequistlatec people — called also *Chontal*

te·quis·tla·tec·an \=ˌ==ˈ=ən\ *n, pl* **tequistlatecan** *or* **tequistlatecans** *usu cap* [*tequistlatec* + *-an*] **:** a language family of the Hokan stock in Mexico comprising only the Tequistlatec language

ter- *comb form* [L, fr. *ter* three times; akin to Gk & Skt *tris* three times, L *tres* three — more at THREE] **1 :** three times, threefold, thrice, three ⟨*ter*centenary⟩ **2 :** TRI- 4 — esp. in names of organic compounds to denote tripling of a radical or molecule ⟨*ter*phenyl⟩

ter *abbr* **1** terrace **2** terrazzo **3** territory **4** tertiary

ter·a·con·ic acid \ˌterəˌkänik-\ *n* [ISV *terebic* + *itaconic*] **:** a crystalline dicarboxylic acid $C_7H_{10}O_4$ that is obtainable by the distillation of terebic acid and that is a dimethyl homologue of itaconic acid; isopropylidene-succinic acid

ter·a·cryl·ic acid \ˌterə¦krilik-\ *n* [ISV *terpenylic* + *acrylic*] : an unsaturated liquid acid $C_7H_{12}O_2$ obtained by distillation of terpenylic acid; 3,4-dimethyl-3-penten-oic acid

ter·a·glin \ˈterəglən\ *n* -s [fr. native name in Australia] : GEELBEC 2

te·rai \təˈrī\ *also* **terai hat** *n* -s [fr. *Tarai*, a swampy lowland belt of northeastern India] : a double felt sun hat with wide turned brim worn esp. in subtropical regions

terai

terakihi *var of* TARAKIHI

te·rap \təˈrap\ *n* -s [Malay *tĕrap*] **1** : a tall Malayan tree (*Artocarpus kunstleri*) **2** : a coarse fiber from the bark of the terap

ter·aph \ˈterəf\ *n, pl* **tera·phim** \ˈterəˌfim *also* -fēm *sometimes* ˌ==ˈ=\ [Heb *tĕrāphīm* (pl. in form but sing. in meaning)] : an image representing a primitive household god among the ancient Jews and other Semitic peoples and later used in divination and as a talismanic figure

ter·as \ˈterəs\ *n, pl* **tera·ta** \-rədə\ [NL *terat-, teras*, fr. Gk, marvel, monster] : an organism (as a fetus) that is grossly abnormal in structure due to genetic or developmental causes : MONSTER

terat *abbr* teratology

terat- *or* **terato-** *comb form* [Gk, fr. *terat-, teras* marvel, portent, monster; akin to Lith *keras* enchantment, Skt *kṛtyā* action, enchantment, *karoti* he does, acts, and perh. to ON *skars* monster, *skyrsi* portent, Skt *āścarya* marvelous — more at KARMA] : monster ⟨*teratism*⟩ ⟨*teratology*⟩

ter·a·tism \ˈterəˌtizəm\ *n* -s [*terat-* + *-ism*] **1** : anomaly of organic form and structure : MONSTROSITY **2** : love of the marvelous : worship of monsters ⟨man's pathetic struggle up from ~ through animism and taboo and magic to our present day —*Saturday Rev.*⟩

ter·a·to·genesis \ˌterətō+\ *n* [NL, fr. *terat-* + L *genesis*] : production of monstrous growths or fetuses

ter·a·to·gen·ic \¦terətō¦jenik\ *also* **ter·a·to·genetic** \-(ˌ)tōjə¦nedik\ *adj* [ISV *terat-* + *-genic* or *-genetic*] : tending to cause developmental malformations and monstrosities — **ter·a·to·ge·nic·i·ty** \-(ˌ)tōjə¦nisədē\ *n* -ES

¹ter·a·toid \ˈterəˌtȯid\ *adj* [ISV *terat-* + *-oid*] **1** : abnormal in formation ⟨~ tumor⟩ **2** : characteristic of a teratoma

²teratoid \"\ *n* -s : TERATOMA

ter·a·to·log·i·cal \ˌterətə¦läjəkəl, -rədəl¦ä-\ *adj* [*teratology* + *-ical*] : relating to abnormality of organic growth or structure ⟨~ specimen⟩ : belonging to teratology ⟨~ publications⟩

ter·a·tol·o·gist \ˌterəˈtäləjəst\ *n* -s [ISV *teratology* + *-ist*] : a student of teratology

ter·a·tol·o·gy \-jē\ *n* -ES [Gk *teratologia*, fr. *terat-* + *-logia* -logy] **1 a** : fantastic mythmaking or storytelling in which prodigies and monsters play a large part **b** : a collection of such stories **2** [ISV *terat-* + *-logy*] : the study of malformations, monstrosities, or serious deviations from the normal type in growing organisms : study of the nature and origin of terata

ter·a·to·ma \ˌterəˈtōmə\ *n, pl* **teratomas** \-məz\ *or* **tera·toma·ta** \-mədə\ [NL, fr. *terat-* + *-oma*] : a tumor derived from more than one embryonic layer and made up of a heterogeneous mixture of tissues (as epithelium, bone, cartilage, or muscle)

ter·a·to·sis \ˌterəˈtōsəs\ *n* -ES [NL, fr. *terat-* + *-osis*] : TERATISM

ter·bi·um \ˈtərbēəm\ *n* -s [NL, fr. *Ytterby*, village of southwest Sweden + NL *-ium*] : a metallic element of the rare-earth group that is usu. trivalent but is tetravalent in its colored dioxide — symbol *Tb*; see ELEMENT table

terbium metal *n* : any of a group of rare-earth metals separable as a group from other metals occurring with them and in addition to terbium including europium, gadolinium, and sometimes dysprosium — compare YTTRIUM METAL

¹terce *obs var of* TIERCE

²terce \ˈtərs\ *or* **tierce** \ˈti(ə)rs\ *n* -s [ME — more at TIERCE] **1** : the third of the canonical hours beginning at 9 a.m.; *also* : the service or office for that hour **2** *Scots law* : the widow's right corresponding to the common-law dower

tercel *var of* TIERCEL

terce·let \ˈtərslət\ *n* -s [ME, fr. MF, fr. *tercel* tiercel + *-et* — more at TIERCEL] : TIERCEL

tercel gentle *or* **tassel-gentle** \ˈ==ˈ==\ *n* [ME *tercel gentil*, fr. *tercel* tiercel + *gentil* gentle] : a trained male falcon

¹ter·centenary \(¦)tər, ¦tə, ˌtə+\ *adj* [*ter-* + *centenary*] : relating to a 300th anniversary or its celebration

²tercentenary \"\ *n* : a 300th anniversary or its celebration

ter·centennial \¦tər, ¦tə+\ *adj or n* [*ter-* + *centennial*] : TERCENTENARY

ter·centesimal \"+\ *adj* [*ter-* + *centesimal*] : based on the number 300 ⟨~ scale⟩

terc·er \ˈtərsər\ *n* -s [²*terce* + *-er*] *Scots law* : a widow entitled to terce

ter·ce·ron \¦tərsə¦rōn\ *n* -s [AmSp *tercerón*, fr. Sp *tercero* third, fr. L *tertiarius* containing a third part; fr. his being third in descent from a Negro — more at TERTIARY] : QUADROON

ter·cet \ˈtərsət\ *or* **tier·cet** \ˈtirsət\ *n* -s [It *terzetto* tercet, terzetto, fr. dim. of *terzo* third, fr. L *tertius* — more at THIRD] : a unit or group of three lines of verse: **a** : one of the three-line stanzas linked by rhyme in terza rima **b** : one of the two groups of three lines forming the sestet in an Italian sonnet

ter·chloride \¦tər+\ *n* [*ter-* + *chloride*] : TRICHLORIDE

ter·cio \ˈtersēˌō\ *or* **ter·cia** \-ēə\ *n* -s [Sp *tercio*, fr. *tercio* third (adj.), fr. L *tertius* — more at THIRD] : a Spanish or Italian infantry regiment of the 16th and 17th centuries

ter·diurnal \¦tər+\ *adj* [*ter-* + *diurnal*] : occurring three times per day ⟨~ variation of atmospheric pressure⟩

ter·e·bel·la \ˌterəˈbelə\ *n, cap* [NL, fr. dim. of L *terebra* borer, gimlet — more at TEREBRA] : a genus of tube-forming marine polychaete worms with horseshoe-shaped preoral lobe, many filamentous tentacles, several pairs of segmental gills, and reduced parapodia that is type of a family Terebellidae of nearly cosmopolitan distribution — **ter·e·bel·lid** \¦==¦=ləd\ *adj or n* — **ter·e·bel·loid** \-ˌlȯid\ *adj or n*

ter·e·bel·li·dae \ˌ==ˈbeləˌdē\ *n pl, cap* [NL, fr. *Terebella*, type genus + *-idae*] : a large family of marine burrowing or tube-forming polychaete worms with often showy filamentous anterior gills and usu. a long thick body

ter·e·bene \ˈterəˌbēn\ *n* -s [F *térébène*, fr. *térébinthe* terebinth (fr. MF) + *-ène* -ene] : a liquid mixture of terpenes that is formed by the action of sulfuric acid on turpentine (sense 2) and distillation with steam, that consists chiefly of dipentene and terpinenes, that resinifies on exposure to air and light, and that is used chiefly as an expectorant

ter·e·ben·thene \ˌ==ˈbenˌthēn\ *n* -s [F *térébenthène*, irreg. (influenced by *térébenthine* turpentine, fr. MF *terebentine*) fr. L *terebinthus* terebinth + F *-ène* -ene — more at TURPENTINE] : levorotatory alpha-pinene

te·re·bic acid \təˈrebik-, -rēbik-\ *n* [L *terebinthus* terebinth + E *-ic*] : a crystalline lactonic acid $C_7H_{10}O_4$ obtained esp. by the oxidation of turpentine oil; dimethyl-paraconic acid

ter·e·binth \ˈterəˌbin(t)th\ *n* -s [ME *therebinthe, terebynt*, fr. MF *therebinte, terebinthe*, fr. L *terebinthus* — more at TURPENTINE] **1** *or* **terebinth tree** : a small European tree (*Pistacia terebinthus*) yielding Chian turpentine **2** *obs* : the resin yielded by the terebinth

ter·e·bin·tha·ce·ae \ˌterəbənˈthāsēˌē\ *n pl, cap* [NL, fr. *Terebinthus*, type genus (fr. L, terebinth) + *-aceae*] *in some classifications* : a family of plants coextensive with the Anacardiaceae

ter·e·bin·thi·nate \ˌterəˈbin(t)thəˌnāt\ *adj* [NL *terebinthinatus*, fr. *terebinthina* turpentine, fr. L, fem. of *terebinthinus* of the terebinth — more at TURPENTINE] : relating to, containing, or resembling turpentine (as in odor)

ter·e·bin·thine \¦terə¦bin(t)thən\ *adj* [L *terebinthinus* of the terebinth] : TEREBINTHINATE

tere·bra \təˈrēbrə, ˈterəb-\ *n* [L, borer, gimlet, fr. *terere* to rub, grind + *-bra*, suffix denoting an instrument — more at THROW] **1** *pl* **terebras** \-brəz\ *or* **terebrae** \-ē(ˌ)brē; -ə(ˌ)brē, -əˌbrī\ : a device used by the ancient Romans for starting a breach in a fortified wall **2** [NL, fr. L, borer] **a** : the boring ovipositor of a hymenopterous insect **b** *cap* : a genus of marine gastropods (suborder Stenoglossa) having a long tapering spire and being the type of a family Terebridae comprising the auger shells **c** -s : AUGER SHELL — **tere·bral** \təˈrēbrəl, ˈterəb-\ *adj*

¹tere·brant \təˈrēbrənt, ˈterəb-\ *adj* [NL *Terebrantia*] : of or relating to the Terebrantia

²terebrant \"\ *n* -s : an insect of the suborder Terebrantia

ter·e·bran·tia \ˌterəˈbranchēə\ *n pl, cap* [NL, fr. L, neut. pl. of *terebrant-, terebrans*, pres. part. of *terebrare* to bore, fr. *terebra* borer, gimlet] **1** : a suborder or other division of Hymenoptera including insects (as sawflies, horntails, and various parasitic hymenoptera) that have a boring ovipositor — compare ACULEATA **2** : a suborder of hairy-winged Thysanoptera in which the females have a serrated ovipositor

tere·bra·tel·la \ˌtəˌrēbrəˈtelə, ˌterəb-\ *n, cap* [NL, fr. L *terebratus* (past part. of *terebrare* to bore) + *-ella*] : a cosmopolitan genus of articulate brachiopods (family Terebratulidae) that includes a common species (*T. transversa*) of the western coast of No. America

ter·e·brat·u·la \ˌterəˈbrachələ\ *n* [NL, fr. L *terebratus* + *-ula*] **1** *cap* : a genus of articulate brachiopods with arms borne by a calcareous loop and a short peduncle projecting through the shell that is type of a family Terebratulidae **2** *pl* **terebratulas** \-ləz\ *or* **terebratu·lae** \-ˌlē\ : a brachiopod of the genus *Terebratula* : LAMP SHELL — **ter·e·brat·u·lar** \¦==¦==lə(r)\ *adj* — **ter·e·brat·u·line** \-ˌlīn, -lən\ *adj*

¹ter·e·brat·u·lid \¦==¦==ləd\ *adj* [NL *Terebratulidae*] : of or relating to the Terebratulidae

²terebratulid \"\ *n* -s : a brachiopod or fossil of the family Terebratulidae

ter·e·bra·tu·li·dae \ˌterəbrəˈtüləˌdē, -brəˈtyü-\ *n pl, cap* [NL *Terebratula*, type genus + *-idae*] : a large family of living and extinct brachiopods usu. placed with a few related forms in a distinct superfamily or suborder of the order Telotremata — see TEREBRATULA

¹ter·e·brat·u·loid \-ˌlȯid\ *adj* [NL *Terebratula* + E *-oid*] : related to or resembling the Terebratulidae

²terebratuloid \"\ *n* -s : a terebratuloid brachiopod or fossil

te·reb·ri·dae \təˈrebrəˌdē\ *n pl, cap* [NL, fr. *Terebra*, type genus + *-idae*] : a family of chiefly tropical marine snails (group Toxoglossa) with slender tall-spired shells of many whorls — see AUGER SHELL

¹ter·e·din·id \ˌterə¦dinəd, təˈredənˈn-\ *adj* [NL *Teredinidae*] : of or relating to the Teredinidae

²teredinid \"\ *n* -s : a mollusk of the family Teredinidae : SHIPWORM

ter·e·din·i·dae \ˌterəˈdinəˌdē\ *n pl, cap* [NL, fr. *Teredin-, Teredo*, type genus + *-idae*] : a family of marine bivalve mollusks (order Eulamellibranchia) that live in burrows (as in wood or clay) which they rasp out with their small trilobed shells and line with a calcareous secretion, are very destructive to marine wooden constructions (as ships and wharves), and are vermiform with very long siphons united through most of their length — see BANKIA, SHIPWORM, TEREDO; compare PHOLAS

te·re·do \təˈrē(ˌ)dō\ *n* [L *teredin-, teredo* worm that bores wood, fr. Gk *terēdon-, terēdōn*; akin to Gk *tetrainein* to bore through, pierce — more at THROW] **1** *pl* **teredos** \-ōz\ *or* **te·red·i·nes** \-redənˌēz\ : SHIPWORM **2** *cap* [NL *Teredin-, Teredo*, fr. L, worm that bores wood] : a genus of mollusks that contains the typical shipworms and is type of a family Teredinidae — compare BANKIA

¹te·re·fah *or* **tre·fah** *or* **tre·fa** \təˈrāfə, ˈtrā-, -(ˌ)fä\ *n, pl* **tere·foth** *or* **tere·fot** *or* **tre·foth** *or* **tre·fot** \-(ˌ)fōt(h), -ˌfōs\ [Heb *tĕrēphāh*, fr. *ṭāraph* to tear, rend] **1** : the meat of animals killed accidentally or by beasts of prey and forbidden to the Israelites as food **2** : a food, food product, or utensil that is not ritually clean or prepared according to Jewish law and is thus prohibited as unfit for Jewish use

²terefah *or* **terefa** *var of* TREF

ter·ek \ˈterək\ *n* -s [fr. *Terek*, river of southeast Soviet Russia, Europe] : a sandpiper (*Xenus cinerea*) of the Old World breeding in the far north of eastern Europe and Asia and migrating to southern Africa and Australia and frequenting rivers

te·re·na \təˈrānə\ *also* **te·re·no** \-(ˌ)nō\ *n, pl* **terena** *or* **tereno** *usu cap* **1 a** : an Arawakan people of southern Mato Grosso, Brazil **b** : a member of such people **2** : the language of the Terena people

te·ren·tian \təˈrenchən, teˈr-\ *adj, usu cap* [L *Terentianus*, fr. P. *Terentius* Afer (Terence) †159 B.C. Roman playwright + L *-anus* -an] : of or relating to Terence or having qualities (as refinement and poetic finish) like those of his comedies

ter·eph·thal·ate \ˌteˌrefˈthaˌlāt, -lət; təˈrefthəˌlāt\ *n* -s [ISV *terephthalic* + *-ate*] : a salt or ester of terephthalic acid

ter·eph·thal·ic acid \¦teˌre¦fthalik-, ¦terə¦\ *n* [ISV *terebene* + *phthalic*] : a crystalline dicarboxylic acid $C_6H_4(COOH)_2$ that is much less soluble and much higher melting than phthalic acid, that has been obtained by oxidation of turpentine but is usu. made by oxidation of *para*-xylene, and that is used chiefly in the synthesis of polyesters for textile fibers or film by reaction with ethylene glycol; *para*-benzene-dicarboxylic acid

teres \ˈtiˌrēz, ˈteˌr-\ *n, pl* **ter·e·tes** \ˈterəˌtēz\ [NL *teret-, teres*, fr. L, smooth, rounded — more at TERETE] : an elongated cylindrical anatomical structure; *usu* : either of two muscles arising from the scapula and inserting on the humerus, one arising chiefly from the lower third of the axillary border and inserting on the bicipital groove, the other chiefly from the upper two thirds of the same border and passing behind the long head of the triceps to insert on the great tubercle of the humerus — called also respectively *teres major, teres minor*

te·re·sian \təˈrēzhən\ *n* -s *usu cap* [*Teresa, Theresa* †1582 Span. saint + E *-ian*] : a barefooted Carmelite of the reformed order established in the 16th century by St. Teresa of Ávila

terete \təˈrēt, (ˈ)teˌr-\ *adj* [L *teret-, teres* smooth, well turned, rounded; akin to L *terere* to rub — more at THROW] : approximately cylindrical but usu. tapering at one or both ends ⟨a ~ seedpod⟩ ⟨the ~ body form of a barracuda⟩

ter·fez \tə(r)ˈfez\ *n, pl* **terfez** [F, fr. NL *Terfezia*] : the edible fruit of a fungus (genus *Terfezia*) of the desert regions of Africa, Asia, and southern Europe

ter·fez·ia \-zēə\ *n, cap* [NL, fr. Tuareg *tarfest, tĕrfest* (fr. Ar *tirfās, tirfāsh* truffle) + NL *-ia*] : a genus of fungi (family Tuberaceae) resembling truffles and having subterranean tuberous ascocarps and in some classifications comprising a distinct family

ter·gal \ˈtərgəl\ *adj* [L *tergum* back + E *-al*] : relating to a tergum; *sometimes* : DORSAL

ter·gant \ˈtərgənt\ *also* **ter·gi·ant** \-rjēənt\ *adj* [L *tergum* back + E *-ant* (as in *rampant*)] : showing the back ⟨arms showing an eagle ~⟩

ter·gif·er·ous \(ˌ)tərˈjif(ə)rəs\ *adj* [L *tergum* + E *-iferous*] : DORSIFEROUS

ter·gite \ˈtərˌjīt\ *n* -s [ISV *terg-* (fr. L *tergum*) + *-ite*] : the dorsal plate or dorsal portion of the covering of a metameric segment of an articulate animal; *esp* : one on the abdomen — compare NOTUM

¹ter·gi·ver·sant \¦tərjə¦vərsᵊnt, (ˌ)tərˈjiv- *sometimes* (ˌ)tərˈgi-\ *adj* [L *tergiversant-, tergiversans*, pres. part. of *tergiversari* to tergiversate] : TERGIVERSATING

²tergiversant \"\ *n* -s : TERGIVERSATOR

ter·giver·sate \ˈtərjəvərˌsāt, ˌ=ˈ==ˌ=; (ˌ)tərˈjivər-, *sometimes* (ˌ)tərˈgi-\ *vi* -ED/-ING/-S [L *tergiversatus*, past part. of *tergiversari* to turn the back, shuffle, shift, evade, fr. *tergum* back + *versare* to turn, freq. of *vertere* to turn — more at WORTH] **1** : to practice tergiversation : become a renegade : APOSTATIZE **2** : to use subterfuges : SHUFFLE, EQUIVOCATE

ter·gi·ver·sa·tion \ˌtərjə(ˌ)vərˈsāshən; (ˌ)tərˌjivə- *sometimes* (ˌ)tərˌgi-\ *n* -s [L *tergiversation-, tergiversatio* evasion, fr. *tergiversatus* + *-ion-, -io* -ion] **1** : desertion of a cause, party, or religious faith : reversal of opinion or policy ⟨a policy of utility is apt to fluctuate, and between 1868 and 1875 there were some extraordinary ~s —A.M.Young⟩ **2** : evasion of straightforward action or clearcut statement of position : EQUIVOCATION, AMBIGUITY ⟨while we trust the human mind I think we have carefully to scrutinize its ~s —H.J.Laski⟩ ⟨humanism depends very heavily . . . on the ~s of the word *human* —T.S.Eliot⟩

ter·gi·ver·sa·tor \ˈtərjə(ˌ)vərˌsādər, ˌ==ˈ=ˌ==; (ˌ)tərˈjivər- *sometimes* (ˌ)tərˈgi-\ *n* -s [L, fr. *tergiversatus* + *-or*] : one that tergiversates : TURNCOAT, RENEGADE

ter·gi·ver·sa·to·ry \¦tərjə¦vərsəˌtōrē; (ˌ)tərˈjivər- *sometimes* (ˌ)tərˈgi-\ *adj* [LL *tergiversatorius*, fr. L *tergiversatus* + *-orius* -ory] : displaying or practicing tergiversation ⟨~ political career⟩

ter·gi·verse \ˈtərjəˌvərs\ *vi* -ED/-ING/-S [L *tergiversari*] : TERGIVERSATE

ter·gum \ˈtərgəm\ *n, pl* **ter·ga** \-gə\ [L; in senses 2 & 3 fr. NL, fr. L, back] **1** : the back of an animal **2** : TERGITE, NOTUM **3** : one of the dorsal plates of the operculum of a barnacle

-te·ria \ˈtirēə\ *n comb form* -s [*cafeteria*] : place having self-service ⟨grocet*eria*⟩

terin *var of* TARIN

ter·lin·gua·ite \(ˌ)tərˈlingwəˌīt\ *n* -s [*Terlingua*, Brewster co., Texas + E *-ite*] : a mineral Hg_2ClO consisting of a mercuric oxychloride and occurring in yellow monoclinic crystals (hardness 2–3, sp. gr. 8.7)

¹term \ˈtərm, ˈtōm, ˈtəim\ *n* -s [ME *terme*, fr. OF, fr. L *terminus* boundary, limit, end; akin to Gk *termōn* boundary, end, *termat-, terma* boundary, end, turning post, Skt *tarati* he crosses over, overcomes, and perh. to Gk *tormos* hole, socket, pivot] **1 a** *archaic* : a bound or limit in space **b** : END, TERMINATION ⟨the age of liberalism had reached its ~, and had been replaced by a totalitarian regime —*Times Lit. Supp.*⟩ **2 a** : a limited or definite extent of time : the time for which something lasts : DURATION, TENURE ⟨~ of five years in prison⟩ ⟨during the ~ of an insurance policy⟩ ⟨president's second ~⟩ ⟨borrowing for a long ~⟩ **b** (1) **terms** *pl, obs* : MENSTRUATION (2) : parturition at the normal period : time at which a pregnancy of normal length terminates ⟨continued to develop to ~ but was stillborn⟩ — often used with *full* ⟨a healthy calf born at full ~⟩ **3 a** : a time or date fixed or agreed upon for an action or as a boundary between periods **b** : a time fixed for the payment of rents or interest — compare QUARTER DAY **c** : the day on which a working period ends **d** (1) : the whole period for which an estate is granted (2) : the estate or interest held by one for a term **e** : a space of time granted to a debtor for discharging his obligation **f** : the time for which a court is held or is open for the trial of cases and during which the powers of the court incidental to actual settlements for the hearing of cases may be validly exercised — see EASTER TERM, HILARY TERM, MICHAELMAS TERM, TRINITY TERM **4** : one of several divisions of the year in a school, college, or university representing a continuous period during which instruction is regularly given to students — compare QUARTER 4b, SEMESTER 2; see CANDLEMAS TERM, HILARY TERM, MARTINMAS TERM, MICHAELMAS TERM, TRINITY TERM, WHITSUN TERM **5** : one of the unequal divisions of the 30 degrees of a sign allocated in astrology to each of the planets as an essential dignity **6 a** : a member of an expression connected with another member by a plus or minus sign **b** : any of the members composing a ratio or proportion **c** : any or each of a series or sequence ⟨~s of a geometrical progression⟩ **d** : one of a set of frequencies assigned one for each state to an atomic system such that the frequencies of the light emitted are differences between the members of the set **7** : a substantive word or phrase used as the subject or predicate of a proposition or standing as one member of a relation; *esp* : one of the three substantive elements of a syllogism each of which appears twice — see MAJOR TERM, MIDDLE TERM, MINOR TERM **8 a** : a word or expression that has a precisely limited meaning in some uses or is peculiar to a science, art, profession, trade, or special subject ⟨technical ~⟩ ⟨legal ~⟩ **b terms** *pl* : diction of a specified kind ⟨described in glowing ~s⟩ ⟨praised in the highest ~s⟩ ⟨talking of marriage in vague ~s, not actually proposing⟩ **9 terms** *pl* : propositions, limitations, or provisions stated or offered for the acceptance of another and determining (as in a contract) the nature and scope of the agreement : CONDITIONS ⟨~s of a sale⟩ ⟨credit granted on liberal ~s of repayment⟩ ⟨~s of a will⟩ **10 terms** *pl* **a** : mutual relationship : relative position : FOOTING — usu. used with *on* or *upon* ⟨remained on good ~s with his neighbors⟩ ⟨fight on even ~s⟩ **b** : AGREEMENT, CONCORD ⟨came to ~s after long bargaining⟩ **11** : a boundary post or stone; *esp* : a quadrangular pillar often tapering downward and adorned on the top with the figure of a head or upper part of the body — called also *terminal figure*; compare HERM, TERMINUS 2b **syn** see CONDITION, WORD — **at term** *adv* : at the end of a definite or stipulated period of time — **in terms of** *prep* : with respect to, in relation to, or in ways of thought belonging to (a particular category) : in comparison with ⟨a conception of nature *in terms of* human politics —William Empson⟩ ⟨tends to think of everything *in terms of* money⟩

term 11

²term \"\ *vt* -ED/-ING/-S **1** *obs* : EXPRESS, STATE, PHRASE **2** : to apply a term to : CALL, NAME ⟨determined to overcome what she ~*ed* her own selfishness —Agnes S. Turnbull⟩ ⟨normal collector who in some circles would be ~*ed* naive —Reginald Kell⟩

term *abbr* **1** terminal **2** termination

ter·ma·gan·cy \ˈtərməgənsē, ˈtōm-, ˈtəim-, -si\ *n* -ES [*termagant* + *-cy*] : the quality or state of being termagant : habitual bad temper : scolding disposition

¹ter·ma·gant \-gənt *sometimes* -ˌgant *or* -ˌgaa(ə)nt\ *n* -s [ME *Tervagant, Termagant*, imaginary Muslim deity represented in medieval mystery plays as a boisterous character] **1** *obs* : a brawling boisterous turbulent person **2** : an overbearing, quarrelsome, scolding, or nagging woman : SHREW, VIRAGO ⟨matrimonial adventures of an extremely rich and bullying ~ —*Saturday Rev.*⟩

²termagant \"\ *adj* : TUMULTUOUS, TURBULENT, BOISTEROUS ⟨life . . . wrecked by a ~ mother —*Newsweek*⟩ — **ter·ma·gant·ly** *adv*

ter·ma·gant·ish \-ˌgantish, -ˌgaan-, -gən-, -tēsh\ *adj* [¹*termagant* + *-ish*] : resembling a termagant : SHREWISH

term attendant *n* [¹*term* + *attendant*, adj.] : ATTENDANT TERM

term day *n* [ME *terme day*, fr. *terme* term + *day*] **1** : a day that is set as a term (as a Scottish quarter day) or is a day in a term (as of the sitting of a court) **2** : one of a series of special days designated by scientists for making synoptic magnetic, meteorological, or other physical observations

ter·men \ˈtərmən\ *n, pl* **termi·na** \-mənə\ [NL *termin-, termen*, fr. L, end, boundary; akin to L *terminus* end, boundary — more at TERM] : the outer margin of a triangularly shaped wing of an insect

term·er \ˈtərmər; ˈtōmə(r, ˈtəimə(r\ *n* -s [¹*term* + *-er*] **1** *obs* : one resorting to London only during the law term or fashionable season **2** : a person serving for a specified term (as in prison) ⟨first ~⟩ ⟨life ~⟩

ter·mes \ˈtər(ˌ)mēz\ *n, cap* [NL *Termit-, Termes*, fr. L *termit-, termes, tarmit-, tarmes* worm that eats wood; akin to Gk *tetrainein* to bore through, pierce — more at THROW] : the type genus of the family Termitidae

term fee *n* : a fee by the term chargeable to a suitor or by law fixed and taxable in the costs of a case for each or any term it is in court

ter·mi·na·bil·i·ty \ˌtərmənəˈbilədē, ˌtōm-, ˌtəim-, -lətē, -i\ *n* -ES : the quality or state of being terminable ⟨~ of an annuity at the death of an annuitant⟩

ter·mi·na·ble \ˈ===bəl\ *adj* [ME, fr. *terminen* to termine + *-able*] : capable of being terminated or bounded : discontinuing after a definite period : subject to termination ⟨institutions . . . to fit the fact that marriage is a ~ institution —Margaret Mead⟩ ⟨~ bond⟩ — **ter·mi·na·ble·ness** \-nəs\ *n* -ES — **ter·mi·na·bly** \-blē, -bli\ *adv*

¹ter·mi·nal \ˈtərmənᵊl, ˈtōm-, ˈtəim-, -mnəl\ *adj* [L *terminalis*, fr. *terminus* boundary, end + *-alis* -al — more at TERM] **1 a** : of or relating to an end, extremity, boundary, or terminus ⟨~ pillar⟩ **b** : growing at the end of a branch or stem ⟨~ bud⟩ — compare LATERAL **c** : of or relating to either end of a transport line ⟨~ airport⟩ ⟨freight pickup is a ~ service⟩ ⟨~ charge⟩ **2 a** : of or relating to a fixed period of time : occurring in a term or each term ⟨~ examinations⟩ ⟨~ payments⟩ **b** : relating to or constituting a term in a proposition or equation ⟨~ quantity⟩ **c** : occurring at or contributing to the end of life

⟨~ pneumonia⟩ ⟨~ cancer⟩ **3 a :** occurring at or constituting the end of a closed series **:** CONCLUDING, FINAL ⟨~ syllable⟩ **:** ULTIMATE ⟨~ problems⟩ **b** *of an educational institution or program* **:** constituting an entity that is limited but complete **:** leading to an end which may but need not be a step to further education ⟨the modern junior college, besides preparing some of its students for the four-year college, has a ~ curriculum⟩ **c :** at or near the end of a chain of atoms constituting a molecule ⟨a ~ hydroxyl group⟩ ⟨~ bonds⟩ **syn** see LAST

²**terminal** \"\ *n* -s **1 :** a part that forms the end **:** END, EXTREMITY, TERMINATION **2 :** a letter, sound, syllable, or word, forming a termination **3 :** a terminating and usu. ornamental detail **:** FINIAL **4 :** a device attached to the end of a wire or cable or to a piece of electrical apparatus for convenience in making connections — see LIGHTNING ARRESTER illustration **5 :** an apical growth on a plant **6 a :** either end of a carrier line (as a railroad, trucking or shipping line, or airline) with classifying yards, dock and lighterage facilities, management offices, storage sheds, and freight and passenger stations **b :** a freight or passenger station that is central to a considerable area or serves as a junction at any point with other lines **c :** a town or city at the end of a carrier line **:** TERMINUS

terminal arborization *n* **:** a multiple branching at the end of a nerve fiber

terminal board *n* **:** an insulating slab (as on a switchboard) on which electric terminals are mounted

terminal company *n* **:** a company or organization whose business is the operation of a railroad terminal

terminal cutting *n* **:** a stem cutting consisting of a portion of a stem or branch with a terminal bud

terminal figure *or* **terminal statue** *n* **:** TERM 11

terminal filament *n* **:** the distal part of an insect ovariole

¹**ter·mi·na·lia** \ˌtərməˈnālēə, -lyə\ *n, cap* [NL, fr. L *terminalis* terminal + NL *-ia*] **:** a large genus of tropical trees and shrubs (family Combretaceae) having entire leaves clustered at the ends of the branches and small apetalous flowers in loose spikes — see MALABAR ALMOND, MYROBALAN 1

²**terminalia** \"\ *n pl* [NL, fr. L, neut. pl. of *terminalis* terminal] **:** the terminal elements of a part; *esp* **:** the final segments of the insect abdomen modified to form the external genitalia

ter·mi·na·li·a·ce·ae \ˌtərməˌnālēˈāsēˌē\ [NL, fr. *Terminalia* + *-aceae*] *syn of* COMBRETACEAE

ter·mi·nal·iza·tion \ˌtərmənᵊləˈzāshən, -ᵊlˌīˈz-\ *n* -s [¹*terminal* + *-ization*] **:** the movement of transverse bonds between paired chromosomes in meiosis from their points of origin toward the ends of the chromosomes

terminal juncture *n* **:** an intonation pattern signaling the end of an utterance or a break between utterances

terminal leave *n* **:** a final leave consisting of accumulated unused leave granted to a member of the armed forces just prior to his separation or discharge from service

ter·mi·nal·ly \ˈtərmənᵊlē, ˈtəm-, ˈtəim-, -mnəl, ǀi\ *adv* [¹*terminal* + *-ly*] **1 :** at each term: by the term ⟨rent to be paid ~⟩ **2 :** at the end ⟨bear leaves laterally or ~⟩

terminal market *n* **:** a central marketing place for a farm product (as grain, livestock) received from scattered or outlying shipping points and sold through a public exchange

terminal moraine *n* **:** a moraine deposited by a glacier at its end when the ice is at its maximum extent — compare END MORAINE

terminal parenchyma *n* **:** parenchyma occurring as a more or less continuous layer at the outer boundary of a growth ring

terminal pedestal *n* **:** GAINE

terminal reserve *n* **:** the reserve for an insurance policy at the close of a year after net premiums for the year have been received and death claims paid

terminal sclereid *n* **:** any of various diversely branched or lobed sclereids found singly or in groups esp. at the ends of veinlets in leaves

terminal shoe *n* **:** an appliance for permitting the transfer of a telpher carrier from a track to the cable without jar or impact

terminal side *n* **:** the straight line that is revolved about a point on another straight line in forming a trigonometric figure

terminal sinus *n* **:** a circular blood sinus bordering the area vasculosa of the vertebrate embryo

terminal velocity *n* **:** the limiting uniform velocity attained by a falling body when the resistance of the air has become equal to the force of gravity

terminal voltage *n* **:** the voltage at the terminals of an electrical device (as a battery or a generator)

¹**ter·mi·nate** \ˈtərməˌnāt, ˈtəm-,ˈtəim-, *usu* -ād-+V\ *vb* -ED/-ING/-S [L *terminatus*, past part. of *terminare* to set bounds, limit, fr. *terminus* boundary, limit, end — more at TERM] *vt* **1 a :** to bring to an ending or cessation in time, sequence, or continuity **:** CLOSE ⟨~ a conference⟩ ⟨benediction *terminated* the service⟩ **b :** to form the ending or conclusion of ⟨his acceptance *terminated* the interview⟩ **c :** to end formally and definitely (as a pact, agreement, contract) ⟨his employment with the company was *terminated*⟩ ⟨the age at which the youth of each nation ~*s* full-time education —J.B.Conant⟩ **d :** to bring or deliver (a passenger, a freight shipment) to destination **e :** to discontinue the employment of **:** DISCHARGE **2 :** to set a limit to in space **:** serve as an ending, boundary, limit, dividing line ⟨the gallery was *terminated* by folding doors —Jane Austen⟩ **3 a** *archaic* **:** to perfect with finishing touches **b** *archaic* **:** to express or describe in terms ⟨censuring or rather *terminating* my own soul —R.W.Emerson⟩ **c** *obs* **:** to direct or destine to something as object or end **~** *vi* **1 a :** to come to an end in space or extent **:** extend only to a point, line, surface, or other limit **b :** to find or reach a terminus ⟨a railroad line *terminating* at a seaport⟩ **2 a :** to come to an end in time **:** cease to be ⟨the coalition . . . *terminated* with the danger from which it had sprung —T.B.Macaulay⟩ **b :** to become nil or void after reaching a term or limit **:** EXPIRE ⟨Italian sovereignty over Trieste *terminated* upon the coming into force of the Treaty of Peace —*Amer. Jour. of Internat. Law*⟩ **3 a :** to form an ending or final part ⟨words that properly ~ in an obscure vowel —C.H. Grandgent⟩ ⟨chair legs *terminating* in ball-and-claw feet⟩ ⟨the two imposing towers at the facade ~ in pale blue tile domes — *Amer. Guide Series: Mich.*⟩ ⟨his thoughts always *terminated* in regret⟩ **b :** to have an indicated outcome or result ⟨the fight *terminated* with the champion winning⟩ **syn** see CLOSE

²**ter·mi·nate** \-nət, *usu* -əd-+V\ *adj* [L *terminatus*, past part. of *terminare*] **1 :** coming to an end or capable of ending **:** LIMITED, LIMITABLE **2 :** expressed or expressible in a finite number of figures ⟨~ decimal⟩ ⟨~ number⟩ **3 :** indicating an action as a whole ⟨~ aspect of a verb⟩

terminating building and loan association *or* **terminating society** *n* **:** a savings and loan association whose members have provided by their articles of association that upon their shares all attaining the value specified in the articles that value shall be paid to the shareholders and the society dissolved

terminating decimal *n* [*terminating* (pres. part. of ¹*terminate*) + *decimal*] **:** a terminate decimal

ter·mi·na·tion \ˌtərməˈnāshən, ˌtəm-, ˌtəim-\ *n* -s [ME, fr. L *termination-, terminatio* act of setting bounds, determining, fr. *terminatus* (past part. of *terminare* to set bounds, determine) + *-ion-, -io* -ion — more at TERMINATE] **1** *obs* **:** the act of determining **:** DECISION **2** *obs* **:** WORD, TERM **3 a :** end in time or existence **:** CLOSE, CESSATION, CONCLUSION ⟨~ of life⟩ ⟨~ of the middle ages⟩ **b :** a limit in space or extent **:** BOUND, EXTREMITY ⟨~ of a route⟩ ⟨~ of a cave⟩ ⟨~ of a journey⟩ **c :** the ending of a word **:** a final syllable or letter; *esp* **:** the part added to a stem in inflection **:** ENDING, SUFFIX **4 :** the act of terminating **:** act of setting bounds or bringing to an end or concluding ⟨after the ~ of hostilities⟩ ⟨voluntary ~ of an agreement⟩ **5 :** OUTCOME, RESULT ⟨a dispute brought to a satisfactory ~⟩ **syn** see END

ter·mi·na·tion·al \¦==¦nāshənᵊl, -shnəl\ *adj* [*termination* + *-al*] **1 :** of, relating to, or forming a termination ⟨~ accentuation⟩ **2 :** formed by inflectional suffixes ⟨~ comparison of adjectives⟩ — compare PERIPHRASTIC

¹**ter·mi·na·tive** \ˈtərməˌnād·iv, ˈtəm-,ˈtəim-, -m(ə)nəl, \t\, \ēv *also* \əv\ *adj* [ME, fr. ML *terminativus*, fr. L *terminatus* + *-ivus* -ive] **1 a :** tending or serving to put an end to or set a limit to something **b :** coming to an end **:** ENDING ⟨contracts ~ with the cessation of hostilities⟩ **2 a :** relating to a verb or a verbal form which expresses the action as complete or denotes the end or completion of the action — compare PERFECTIVE 2 **b :** denoting direction toward ⟨~ case of a noun⟩ — **ter·mi·na·tive·ly** \|əvlē, -li\ *adv*

²**terminative** \"\ *n* -s **:** the terminative case or a form in the terminative case

ter·mi·na·tor \-məˌnād·ə(r), -ātə-\ *n* -s [LL, fr. L *terminatus* + *-or*] **1 :** one that terminates **2 :** the dividing line between the illuminated and the unilluminated part of the moon's or a planet's disk **:** the dividing line between day and night as observed from a distance

ter·mi·na·to·ry \-m(ə)nəˌtōrē\ *adj* [L *terminatus* + E *-ory*] **:** TERMINAL, TERMINATING

ter·mine \ˈtərmən\ *vb* -ED/-ING/-S [ME *terminen*, fr. OF *terminer*, fr. L *terminare* — more at TERMINATE] **1** *obs* **:** BOUND, LIMIT, TERMINATE **2 :** DETERMINE

terming *pres part of* TERM

ter·mi·nism \ˈtərməˌnizəm\ *n* -s [*terminist* + *-ism*] **:** the doctrine of the terminists; *specif* **:** OCKHAMISM

ter·mi·nist \-nəst\ *n* -s [NL *terminista*, fr. ML *terminus* term, period + L *-ista* -ist] **1 :** one who maintains that God has fixed a certain term for the probation of individual persons during which period and no longer they have the offer of grace **2 :** OCKHAMIST — **ter·mi·nis·tic** \¦==¦nistik\ *adj*

ter·mi·nize \ˈtərməˌnīz\ *vt* -ED/-ING/-S [ML *terminus* term + E *-ize*] **:** to supply (as a science) with nomenclature ⟨conceptions that owe their present definiteness . . . to felicitous *terminizing* —*Popular Science Monthly*⟩ ⟨the industrious *terminizing* of a cherished colleague —C.F.Talman⟩

ter·mi·no·log·i·cal \¦tərmənᵊl¦äjəkəl, ¦təm-, ¦təim-, -mnə¦lä-, -jēk-\ *adj* **:** relating to terminology ⟨~ convenience⟩ ⟨pure ~ dispute⟩ — **ter·mi·no·log·i·cal·ly** \-k(ə)lē, -li\ *adv*

terminological platonism *n, often cap P* **:** PLATONISM 5

ter·mi·nol·o·gy \ˌ=məˈnäləjē, -ji\ *n* -ES [ML *terminus* term, expression, word (fr. L, boundary, limit, end) + E *-o-* + *-logy* — more at TERM] **1 :** the technical or special terms or expressions used in a business, art, science, or special subject **2 :** nomenclature as a field of study

term insurance *n* **:** insurance for a specified period providing for no payment to the insured except upon losses during the period and becoming void upon its expiration

ter·mi·nus \ˈtərmənəs, ˈtəm-,ˈtəim-\ *n, pl* **termi·ni** \-ˌnī, -ˌnē\ *or* **terminuses** [L — more at TERM] **1 :** final goal of a journey or an endeavor **:** finishing point **:** END; *also* **:** starting point ⟨obliged to be born separately, and to die separately, and, owing to these unavoidable *termini* —E.M.Forster⟩ **2 a :** TERM 11 **b :** a post or stone marking a boundary **3 a :** either end of a transportation line, travel route, pipe line, tunnel, canal **b :** the station or the town or city at such a place **:** TERMINAL **4 :** EXTREMITY, TIP ⟨~ of a glacier⟩ ⟨~ of a peninsula⟩ **5 :** that end of a line representing a vector quantity which indicates the sense of the vector and is commonly identified by an arrowhead **:** the end of a vector that is not the origin **syn** see END

terminus ad quem \-ˌadˈkwem\ *n* [NL, lit., limit to which] **1 :** a goal, object, or course of action, motion, or purpose **:** DESTINATION, END, PURPOSE **2** *also* **terminus an·te quem** \-ˌantē-\ [*terminus ante quem* fr. NL, lit., limit before which] **:** a time or date established or chosen as the end of a time period **:** the later of two limiting points in time

terminus a quo \-ˌäˈkwō\ *n* [NL, lit., limit from which] **1 :** starting point of line of action or of a journey **:** point of origin **2** *also* **terminus post quem** \-ˌpōst-\ [*terminus post quem* fr. NL, lit., limit after which] **:** a time or date established or chosen as the beginning of a time period **:** the earlier of two limiting points in time

ter·mi·tar·i·um \ˌtərməˈterēəm\ *n, pl* **termitar·ia** \-ēə\ [NL, fr. *Termit-, Termes* genus of termites + L *-arium*] **:** a termites' nest

ter·mi·tary \ˈtərməˌterē\ *n* -ES [*termite* + *-ary*] **:** TERMITARIUM

ter·mite \ˈtərˌmīt, ˈtəˌm-, ˈtəiˌm-, *usu* -īd-+V\ *n* -s [NL *Termit-, Termes* genus of termites — more at TERMES] **:** any of numerous pale-colored soft-bodied social insects of the order Isoptera that live in colonies each consisting of distinct forms (as queen, male, wingless sterile workers and soldiers) that show incomplete metamorphosis, build or tunnel out large nests, and feed on wood and that include some (as *Reticulitermes flanipes* in U.S. and *R. lucifugus* in Europe) which are very destructive to wooden structures and trees

termite-proof \¦=¦=¦=\ *adj* [*termite* + *proof*] **:** constructed or treated so as to prevent entrance of termites

ter·mit·ic \¦tərˈmid·ik\ *or* **ter·mit·al** \ˈ=ˌmīd·ᵊl\ *adj* [*termite* + *-ic* or *-al*] **:** of, relating to, or produced by termites

¹**ter·mi·tid** \ˈtərməd·əd, -ˌmīd·əd\ *adj* [NL *Termitidae*] **:** of or relating to the Termitidae

²**termitid** \"\ *n* -s **:** a termite of the family Termitidae

ter·mit·i·dae \ˌtərˈmid·əˌdē\ *n pl, cap* [NL, fr. *Termit-, Termes*, type genus + *-idae*] **:** a family of termites including the most highly specialized forms characterized by having 4-jointed tarsi and a simple radial vein in the wings

termito- *comb form* [NL *Termit-, Termes*] **:** termite ⟨*termitophagous*⟩

ter·mitol·o·gist \ˌtərməˈtäləjəst, ˌtərˌmīdˈä-\ *n* -s [*termito-* + *-logist*] **:** one who studies termites

ter·mi·to·phile \ˌtərˈmid·əˌfīl\ *n* -s [ISV *termito-* + *-phile*] **:** an insect normally living in association with termites in their nests — **ter·mitoph·i·lous** \¦tərmə¦täfələs, -ˌmīd·¦ä-\ *adj*

term·less \ˈtərmləs\ *adj* **1 :** having no term or end **:** BOUNDLESS, UNENDING ⟨~ grief⟩ **2 :** UNCONDITIONED, UNCONDITIONAL ⟨~ peace⟩

term loan *n* **:** a loan extended by banks or insurance companies to corporations with provision for serial repayment generally for a period of from 5 to 15 years

¹**term·ly** \ˈtərmlē\ *adv* [ME *termely*, fr. *terme* term + *-ly*] *archaic* **:** by the term **:** PERIODICALLY

²**termly** \"\ *adj* [¹*term* + *-ly*] *archaic* **:** occurring every term

term of art *archaic* **:** a word or phrase having a specific signification in a particular art, craft, or department of knowledge **:** a technical term

term of reference *chiefly Brit* **:** a defined or assigned task or field of activity or inquiry ⟨numerous royal commissions . . . whose *terms of reference* concerned farming and farm workers —G.E.Fussell⟩

ter·molecular \¦tər+\ *adj* [*ter-* + *molecule* + *-ar*] **:** TRIMOLECULAR ⟨~ reaction⟩

ter·mon \ˈtərmən\ *n* -s [MIr *termonn* church lands, sanctuary, fr. L *terminus* boundary — more at TERM] **:** land belonging to a religious house in Ireland **:** church land exempt from secular taxation

ter·mone \ˈtərˌmōn\ *n* -s [*determining* + *hormone*] **:** a sex-determining hormone or chemical substance

ter·mor \ˈtərmər\ *n* -s [ME *termurre*, fr. AF *termer*, fr. OF *terme* term + AF *-er*] **:** one who has an estate for a term of years or for life

term paper *n* **:** a major written assignment in a school or college course representative of a student's achievement during a term

term policy *n* **:** a property insurance policy issued for a period of usu. three to five years at a reduced rate

term rate *n* **:** the reduced rate that applies to a term policy

terms *pl of* TERM, *pres 3d sing of* TERM

term settlement *n* **:** a reckoning (as on the London stock exchange) between buyers and sellers occurring periodically instead of daily

terms of trade : the ratio between the prices of two countries participating in international trade

termtime \ˈ=ˌ=\ *n* [ME *terme tyme*, fr. *terme* term + *tyme* time] **1 :** the time during a university, college, school, or legal term **2** *chiefly Scot* **:** TERM 3a

term-trotter \ˈ=ˌ==\ *n, Brit* **:** one who attends a college or a law court for an occasional term but not regularly

¹**tern** \ˈtərn, ˈtən, ˈtəin\ *n* -s [of Scand origin; akin to ON *therna* tern, and prob. to OE *stearn*, a bird, prob. tern — more at STARLING] **:** any of numerous sea birds of *Sterna* and related genera that are smaller and slenderer in body and bill than typical gulls, have narrower wings and often forked tails, and are more graceful and dashing in flight — called also *sea swallow*

²**tern** \"\ *adj* [L *terni* (pl.) three each; akin to L *tres* three — more at THREE] **:** TERNATE

³**tern** \"\ *n* -s **1 :** something that consists of three things or numbers together **:** TRIO, TRIPLET **2** *also* **tern schooner** [F *terne*, fr. L *terni* three each] **:** a 3-masted schooner

tern 2

ter·na \ˈternə, ˈtər-\ *n* -s [NL, fr. L, neut. pl. of *terni* three each] **:** a list of three nominees for institution into a Roman Catholic benefice or bishopric presented to the pope or other authority

ter·nar *or* **ter·ner** \ˈtərnər\ *n* -s [L *ternarius* ternary] **:** a university student assigned to the third and lowest social rank and required to pay the lowest fees — compare SECONDER

¹**ter·na·ry** \ˈtərnərē\ *adj* [ME, fr. L *ternarius*, fr. *terni* three each + *-arius* -ary] **1 a :** consisting of or based on three **:** proceeding by threes ⟨~ method of counting⟩ **b :** having three elements, parts, or divisions **:** THREEFOLD, TRIPLE **c :** arranged in threes ⟨~ petals⟩ **2 a :** using three as the base ⟨~ numeration⟩ ⟨~ logarithm⟩ **b :** involving three variables ⟨~ form⟩ **3 :** consisting of an alloy of three elements **4 :** containing, consisting of, or relating to three different parts (as elements, atoms, radicals or components) ⟨sulfuric acid is a ~ acid⟩ ⟨~ liquid mixtures⟩ **5 :** relating or belonging to a crystal system in which 3-sided forms occur **6 :** third in series, order, or rank

²**ternary** *n* -ES [ME, fr. ¹*ternary*] *obs* **:** a set or group of three

ternary form *n* **1 :** a musical form (as a rondo) in which the principal subject appears three or more times **2 :** a song form in which the third part is a repetition of the first with a contrasting section in the middle

ternary steel *n* **:** a steel of iron and carbon alloyed with one other metal

ternary system *n* **:** a physical-chemical system having three components

ter·nate \ˈtərˌnāt, -nət\ *adj* [NL *ternatus*, fr. ML, past part. of *ternare* to treble, fr. L *terni* three each — more at TERN] **1 :** arranged in threes ⟨~ leaves⟩ **2 :** composed of three leaflets or subdivisions ⟨a compound ~ leaf⟩ — **ter·nate·ly** *adv*

ternati- *comb form* [NL *ternatus* ternate] **:** ternately ⟨*ternati-pinnate*⟩

¹**terne** \ˈtərn\ *also* **terneplate** \ˈ=ˌ=\ *n* -s [*terne*, short for *terneplate*, prob. fr. F *terne* dull (fr. MF, fr. *ternir* to tarnish) + E *plate* — more at TARNISH] **:** sheet iron or steel coated with an alloy of about 4 parts lead to 1 part tin

²**terne** \"\ *vt* -ED/-ING/-S **:** to coat with an alloy of tin and lead ⟨*terned* steel plates⟩

terner *var of* TERNAR

tern·ery \ˈtərnərē\ *n* -ES [¹*tern* + *-ery*] **:** a place where terns breed gregariously

tern foot *n* [²*tern*] **:** a foot (as of a chair) formed of three scrolls or carved lines

ter·ni·dens \ˈtərnəˌdenz\ *n, cap* [NL, fr. L *terni* three each + *dens* tooth — more at TERN, TOOTH] **:** a genus of nematode worms (family Strongylidae) parasitic in the intestine of various African apes and monkeys and occas. in man

ter·ni·on \ˈtərnēən, -ēˌän\ *n* -s [L *ternion-, ternio*, fr. *terni* three each] *archaic* **:** a set or group of three **:** TRIAD, TRIO

tern·let \ˈtərnlət\ *n* -s [¹*tern* + *-let*] **:** any of various small terns

ter·nov·skite \tərˈnóf,skīt, -nȯvz,k-\ *n* -s [Russ *ternovskit*, fr. *Ternovskiĭ*, name of a mine in Krivoi Rog, southeast central Ukraine, U.S.S.R. + Russ *-it* -ite] **:** a mineral $Na_2(Mg,Fe)_3Fe_2Si_8O_{22}(OH)_2$ consisting of a basic silicate of sodium, magnesium, and iron of the amphibole group

tern schooner *var of* TERN

tern·stroe·mia \ˌtərnˈstrēmēə, -strōm-\ *n, cap* [NL, fr. Christopher *Ternström* †1746 Swed. botanist + NL *-ia*] **:** a large genus of chiefly tropical American trees and shrubs (family Theaceae) having bracteate flowers with free sepals and petals slightly coherent at the base

tern·stroe·mi·a·ce·ae \ˌ=ˌ==ˈāsēˌē\ [NL, fr. *Ternstroemia* + *-aceae*] *syn of* THEACEAE

terp \ˈte(ə)rp\ *n, pl* **terps** \-ps\ *or* **terpen** \ˈterpən\ [Fris, fr. OFris, village; akin to OE *thorp* village — more at THORP] **:** a large artificial mound in the Netherlands (as in Friesland) providing a site or refuge for a prehistoric settlement in a seasonally flooded area

ter·pa·di·ene \¦tərpə¦dīˌēn\ *n* -s [*terpane* + *-diene*] **:** MENTHADIENE

ter·pane \ˈtərˌpān\ *n* -s [ISV *terp-* (fr. G *terpentin*) + *-ane*] **:** MENTHANE; *esp* **:** the para isomer

ter·pene \-ˌpēn\ *n* -s [ISV *terp-* (fr. G *terpentin* turpentine, fr. ML *terbentina*) + *-ene* — more at TURPENTINE] **1 a :** any of a class of isomeric hydrocarbons $C_{10}H_{16}$ (as myrcene, limonene, or pinene) that are found in many essential oils esp. from conifers, that have also been synthesized in many cases, that are usu. classified according to the absence or presence of one or more rings in the molecule as acyclic, monocyclic, bicyclic, or tricyclic, and that are used chiefly as solvents and as intermediates in organic synthesis **:** MONOTERPENE ⟨~*s* and sesquiterpenes⟩ **b :** any of a large class of hydrocarbons $(C_5H_8)_n$ including the monoterpenes and also hemiterpenes, sesquiterpenes, diterpenes, triterpenes, and polyterpenes that are found esp. in essential oils, resins, and balsams, that are regarded in general as structurally constituted of branched five-carbon units (as in isoprene and 2-methyl-butane), and that are also classifiable according to the absence or presence of rings in the molecule **2 :** any of various compounds derived from terpene hydrocarbons or closely related to them; *esp* **:** a naturally occurring oxygenated derivative (as geraniol, citral, camphor, or abietic acid) — compare TERPENOID

ter·pene·less \ˈtərˌpēnləs\ *adj* **:** free or relatively free from terpenes and esp. monoterpenes usu. as a result of processing (as extraction with solvents or distillation in a vacuum) ⟨~ essential oils⟩

terpene resin *n* **:** any of various pale amber transparent thermoplastic polyterpene resins

ter·pe·nic \¦tər¦pēnik\ *adj* [*terpene* + *-ic*] **:** relating to, containing, or derived from a terpene

¹**ter·pe·noid** \ˈtərpəˌnȯid\ *adj* [*terpene* + *-oid*] **:** resembling a terpene in molecular structure

²**terpenoid** \"\ *n* -s **:** any of a class of compounds that are characterized by an isoprenoid structure like that of the terpene hydrocarbons and that often include these hydrocarbons as well as oxygenated derivatives (as alcohols, aldehydes, ketones, or acids) and hydrogenated derivatives (as menthane) — compare CAROTENOID, STEROID, TERPENE 2

ter·pe·nyl·ic acid \¦tərpə¦nilik-\ *n* [ISV *terpene* + *-yl* + *-ic*] **:** a crystalline lactonic acid $C_8H_{12}O_4$ obtained esp. by the oxidation of turpentine (sense 2)

ter·phenyl \¦tər+\ *n* [ISV *ter-* + *phenyl*] **:** any of three isomeric crystalline hydrocarbons $C_6H_5C_6H_4C_6H_5$ that contain three benzene rings linked in ortho, meta, and para positions, that are obtained usu. along with biphenyl from benzene, and that are used chiefly as industrial heat transfer media; *also* **:** a mixture of two or all three of these hydrocarbons

ter·pin \ˈtərpən\ *n* -s [ISV *terpene* + *-in*] **:** a crystalline saturated terpenoid glycol $C_{10}H_{18}(OH)_2$ that is known in cis and trans forms and is obtained readily in the form of terpin hydrate — called also *1,8-terpin*

ter·pi·nene \-pəˌnēn\ *n* -s [ISV *terpin* + *-ene*] **:** any of three liquid isomeric monocyclic terpene hydrocarbons $C_{10}H_{16}$ obtained usu. in mixtures of the alpha and gamma isomers (as by isomerization of pinene, alpha-phellandrene, or dipentene with sulfuric acid): as **a :** the isomer that has an odor like that of lemons and is the principal component of the mixtures and that occurs in coriander oil, chenopodium oil, and other essential oils; 1,3-*para*-mentha-diene — called also *alpha-terpinene* **b :** the isomer that occurs in coriander oil, lemon oil, and other essential oils; 1,4-*para*-menthadiene — called also *crithmene, gamma-terpinene*

ter·pin·e·ol \ˌtərˈpinēˌōl, -ˌōl\ *n* -s [ISV *terpine*, *terpin* + *-ol*] **:** any of three fragrant isomeric unsaturated low-melting crystalline terpenoid alcohols $C_{10}H_{17}OH$ or a viscous liquid commercial mixture containing them obtained from terpin or terpin hydrate by dehydration and used chiefly in perfumes, in soap, in denaturing alcohol, and as a solvent: **a :** the isomer that is the principal component of the commercial mixture, that has an odor of lilacs, that occurs in many essential oils in three optically isomeric forms and in the form of esters, that is obtained also from pine oil by distillation or from pinene by hydration, and that is used chiefly in perfumes; 1-*para*-menthen-8-ol — called also *alpha-terpineol* **b :** an isomer having an odor of hyacinths — called also *beta-terpineol* **c :** an isomer having an odor of lilacs similar to that of alpha-terpineol — called also *gamma-terpineol*

terpin hydrate *n* **:** an efflorescent crystalline or powdery compound $C_{10}H_{18}(OH)_2.H_2O$ formed from *cis*-terpene by absorption of water, obtained usu. from turpentine oil or alpha-pinene by hydration with dilute acids or from pine oil by steaming the residual rosin, and used as an expectorant for a cough and as an intermediate in making terpineol

ter·pi·nol \ˈtərpə,nōl, -nȯl\ *n* -s [ISV *terpin* + *-ol*] **1 :** TERPIN **2 :** TERPINEOL; *esp* **:** the commercial liquid mixture

ter·pin·o·lene \,tər'pinᵊl,ēn\ *n* -s [ISV *terpinol* + *-ene*] **:** a liquid monocyclic terpene hydrocarbon $C_{10}H_{16}$ reported in a few essential oils and obtained synthetically (as in the manufacture of terpineol); 1,4(8)-*para*-menthadiene

ter·pi·nyl \ˈtərpənᵊl, -,nil\ *n* -s [ISV *terpin* + *-yl*] **:** a univalent radical $C_{10}H_{17}$ derived from terpineol and esp. alpha-terpineol

terpinyl acetate *n* **:** a fragrant liquid ester $CH_3COOC_{10}H_{17}$ found in several essential oils, made synthetically (as by reaction of alpha-terpineol or alpha-pinene with acetic anhydride), and used in perfumes and soaps

ter·polymer \ˈtər+\ *n* [*ter-* + *polymer*] **:** a product of the polymerization of three different polymerizing substances — compare COPOLYMER

terp·sich·o·re \,tərp'sikə(,)rē, tōp-,təip-, -kəri\ *n* -s [after *Terpsichore*, the muse of choral dance and song] **:** DANCING, CHOREOGRAPHY — **terp·si·cho·re·an** \,=,sikə'rēən, ,=,səkə'r-, ,=sə'kōr-\ *adj*

terr *abbr* **1** terrace **2** territorial; territory

ter·ra al·ba \,terə'albə, -rə'öl-\ *n* [NL, lit., white earth] **:** any of several white mineral substances: as **a :** gypsum ground for a pigment **b :** kaolin used esp. as an adulterant of paints **c :** BURNT ALUM **d :** MAGNESIA 3a **e :** BLANC FIXE

terra car·i·o·sa \,==,karē'ōsə, -ōzə\ *n* [L, lit., rotten earth] **:** ROTTENSTONE

¹ter·race \ˈterəs\ *n* -s [MF *terrasse, terrace* pile of earth, platform, terrace, fr. OProv *terrassa*, fr. *terra* earth, fr. L *terra* earth, land, country; akin to OIr *tīr* territory, *tīr* dry, L *torrēre* to dry, parch — more at THIRST] **1 a :** a colonnaded porch or promenade **:** GALLERY, PORTICO ⟨shops in arcade and along a covered ~ —*Architectural Rev.*⟩ **b :** a flat roof or open platform **:** BALCONY, DECK ⟨the dining ~ looks out upon the tumbling, rushing waters —*Ford Times*⟩ **c :** a relatively level paved or planted area adjoining a building and in formal settings often surrounded by a balustrade ⟨the court side . . . shelters a formal English ~ and garden —*Amer. Guide Series: Mich.*⟩ **2 a :** a raised embankment with the top leveled for walking **b :** a horizontal or gently sloping ridge or offset made in a hillside to conserve moisture or to minimize erosion ⟨built his ~*s* with a moldboard plow; uses them as guides for his contour rows —*Farm Journal*⟩ — compare STEP TERRACE **c :** something that resembles a terrace ⟨the pyramid . . . had five ~*s* —E.H.Short⟩ ⟨stood on a status ~ with some below and others above him —John Dollard⟩ **3 a :** a level and ordinarily rather narrow plain usu. with a steep front bordering a river, a lake, or the sea **:** a topographic bench — compare ALLUVIAL TERRACE, KAME TERRACE, MARINE TERRACE, ROCK TERRACE, STREAM TERRACE **b :** STRUCTURAL TERRACE **4 a :** a row of houses or apartments situated on raised ground or a sloping site **b :** a group of row houses ⟨street after street exactly alike, lined with . . . ~*s* —Talbot Hamlin⟩ **c :** MEDIAN STRIP **d :** STREET

²terrace \"\ *vb* -ED/-ING/-S *vt* **1 :** to make into a terrace or supply with terraces ⟨farms long ago *terraced* by the Inca Indians —Russell Lord⟩ ⟨planted and *terraced* the . . . estate —Alva Johnston⟩ **2 :** to provide (a building) with a terrace; *esp* **:** to design (a structure) with offsets ~ *vi* **:** to occupy a terrace ⟨olive trees *terracing* in steps dug out of rock —Richard Llewellyn⟩

³terrace \"\ *adj* **1 :** of or relating to a terrace ⟨~ roof⟩ ⟨~ farmer⟩ ⟨depositional ~ plains —H.N.Fisk⟩ **2 :** having or forming a terrace ⟨~ apartment⟩

⁴terrace *var of* TRASS

ter·raced \ˈterəst\ *adj* [partly fr. ¹*terrace* + *-ed*; partly fr. past part. of ²*terrace*] **:** formed into or provided with or as if with a terrace

ter·ra·ceous \(ˈ)te'rāshəs\ *adj* [L *terra* earth + E *-aceous*] **:** EARTHEN

ter·rac·er \ˈterəsə(r)\ *n* -s [²*terrace* + *-er*] **:** a machine used for constructing terraces or wide channels for surface drainage

ter·rac·ette \,terə'set\ *n* -s [¹*terrace* + *-ette*] **:** CATSTEP

ter·rac·i·form \te'rasə,fórm, ˈterəs-\ *adj* [¹*terrace* + *-iform*] **:** having the form of a terrace

terracing *n* -s [fr. gerund of ²*terrace*] **1 :** a terraced structure or contour ⟨there are more miles of ~ in Georgia and Alabama today than in any other states —Louis Bromfield⟩ **2 :** the formation of terraces ⟨~ occurs . . . as a result of shrinkage of the glacier —R.F.Flint⟩ ⟨wind and soil erosion . . . should be checked by ~ —Welles Hangen⟩

terra-cotta \,terə'kädə, -ätə\ *n, pl* **terra-cottas** [It *terra cotta*, lit., baked earth] **1 a :** a usu. low-fired and typically reddish unglazed ceramic material (as the earthenware of many primitive potters); *also* **:** an object (as a bowl or figurine) of such material ⟨Greek *terra-cottas*⟩ **b :** a usu. hard-fired glazed or unglazed ceramic architectural material often pressed or cast in ornamental forms and used esp. for decorative facing and tiles **2 a :** a brownish orange that is redder and deeper than spice, leather, or gold pheasant **b** *of textiles* **:** a moderate to strong reddish brown

terra-cotta lumber *n* **:** a very porous earthenware that is easy to pierce or cut and will hold nails driven into it

ter·ra dam·na·ta \,terə,dam'näd·ə\ *n* [NL, lit., condemned earth] **:** CAPUT MORTUUM 1

ter·rae fil·i·us \,te(,)rē'filēəs, -,rī'f-\ *n, pl* **terrae fil·ii** \-ē'filē,ī, -ī'filē,ē\ [L, lit., son of the earth] **1** *archaic* **:** a person of lowly birth **2 :** a student (as at Oxford University) formerly appointed to deliver a satirical oration — compare PREVARICATOR 4

ter·ra fir·ma \,terə'fərmə, -fōmə,-fəimə\ *n* [NL, lit., solid land] **1 a** *obs* **:** CONTINENT, MAINLAND **b** *archaic* **:** Italian peninsular territories formerly controlled by Venice **2 :** dry land **:** solid ground

¹ter·rain \tə'rān *also* (ˈ)te'r-\ *n* -s [F, land, ground, modif. of L *terrenum* — more at TERRENE] **1** *archaic* **:** a geographical location **:** SPOT **2 a** (1) **:** a geographical area **:** REGION, TERRITORY ⟨explosions . . . spread a large amount of ash over the surrounding ~ —*Report: Smithsonian Institution*⟩ (2) **:** a piece of earth **:** GROUND ⟨bump along the ~ right up to the clubhouse —W.B.Furlong⟩ **b :** the physical features of a tract of land **:** CONTOUR, TOPOGRAPHY ⟨analysis of ~ in aerial photos in different seasons —Ragnar Thoren⟩ **c :** a physical environment of various kinds ⟨a ~ of water that covered almost four million square miles —Wirt Williams⟩ **d :** an area devoted to a specified activity ⟨the entire Union became a racing and breeding ~ —John Hervey⟩ **3 :** TERRANE 1 **4 a :** a defined range of subject matter **:** field of knowledge ⟨travel lightly but skillfully over the whole ~ of economics —S.E.Harris⟩ **b :** a sphere of action **:** ARENA ⟨transferred the ~ of theological controversy from the learned tractate to the popular pamphlet —Helen Sullivan⟩

²terrain \"\ *adj* [alter. (influenced by ¹*terrain*) of ¹*terrene*] **:** TERRESTRIAL, TOPOGRAPHIC

ter·ra in·cog·ni·ta \÷,terə,in,käg'nēd·ə *also* ,==ən'kägnəd·ə\ *n, pl* **ter·rae incogni·tae** \,te,rī . . . nē,tī, -nə,tī\ [L] **:** unknown territory **:** an unexplored country or field of knowledge

ter·ra ja·pon·i·ca \,terəjə'pänəkə\ *n* [NL, lit., Japanese earth] **1 :** GAMBIER **2 :** CATECHU

ter·ral \te'räl\ *n* -s [Sp, fr. *tierra* earth, land (fr. L *terra*) + *-al* (fr. L *-alis*) — more at TERRACE] **:** a land breeze

ter·ra lem·nia \,terə'lemnēə\ *n* [L, lit., Lemnian earth] **1** *usu cap L* **:** LEMNIAN BOLE **2** *often cap L* **:** BOLE 3

ter·ra·ma·ra \,terə'märə\ *n, pl* **terrama·re** \-ärē\ [It, mound of crumbling earth (such as found in terramara settlements), terramara, prob. fr. *terra* earth (fr. L) + It dial. *mara* marl, alter. of It *marna*, fr. OF *marne*, alter. of *marle* — more at TERRACE, MARL] **:** a late Neolithic or early Bronze Age lake dwelling or settlement of northern Italy known from remains found in mounds of the Po valley

ter·ra mi·rac·u·lo·sa \,terəmə,rakyə'lōsə\ *n* [NL, lit., miraculous earth] **:** ²BOLE 1

Ter·ra·my·cin \,terə'mīsᵊn\ *trademark* — used for oxytetracycline

ter·rane \tə'rān, (ˈ)te;r-\ *n* -s [alter. of ¹*terrain*] **1 a :** a rock formation or group of formations **b :** the area or surface over which a particular rock or group of rocks is prevalent **2 :** TERRAIN 2a

ter·ra·nean \tə'rānēən, te'r-, -ānyən\ *adj* [L *terra* earth + E *-anean* (as in *subterranean*)] **:** of or relating to the earth

ter·ra·neous \-ēəs,-yəs\ *adj* [L *terra* + E *-aneous* (as in *subterraneous*)] — more at TERRACE] **:** TERRESTRIAL, TERRANEAN

terra nul·li·us \,terənə'lēəs, -'nùlē-\ *n* [NL, lit., nobody's land] **:** territory not annexed by any nation ⟨the greater portion of Antarctica . . . is still *terra nullius* —L.M.Gould⟩

ter·ra or·ella·na \,terə,órə'lānə, -órə(l)'yä-\ *n* [NL, lit., earth of Orellana (Francisco de Orellana †1549 Span. soldier and explorer)] **:** ANNATTO 2a

ter·ra·pe·ne \,terə'pēnē\ *n, cap* [NL, fr. obs. E *terrapine, terrapene* terrapin] **:** a genus comprising the box tortoises

ter·ra·pin \ˈterəpən, 'tar-\ *n* -s [obs. E *terrapine*, of Algonquian origin; akin to Delaware *torope* turtle] **1 a :** any of various edible No. American turtles of the family Testudinidae living in fresh or brackish water; *esp* **:** DIAMONDBACK TERRAPIN — see RED-BELLIED TERRAPIN, YELLOW-BELLIED TERRAPIN **b :** any of various other esp. freshwater turtles **2 :** a moderate brown that is redder, lighter, and stronger than coffee, lighter, stronger, and slightly redder than chestnut brown, and yellower, lighter, and stronger than auburn — called also *feuille* **3** *usu cap* **:** a Marylander — used as a nickname

diamondback terrapin

terrapin scale *n* **:** a small brownish convex soft scale (*Lecanium nigrofasciatum*) that is very destructive to several cultivated trees (as peach, plum, and apple) — called also *peach lecanium*

ter·ra pon·der·o·sa \,terə,pändə'rōsə\ *n* [NL, lit., heavy earth] *archaic* **:** BARITE

terra poz·zu·o·li \-,pätsə'wólē\ *n* [It *terra* earth (fr. L) + *Pozzuoli*, commune of Campania, southern Italy] **:** BOLE 3

terra pu·tu·ra \,==,pə'türə, -pyə'tyürə\ *n* [NL] *Old Eng law* **:** land subject to puture

terr·aqueous \(ˈ)ter, ,tər +\ *adj* [L *terra* earth + E *aqueous* — more at TERRACE] **:** consisting of land and water ⟨cover . . . more than half of the ~ globe —Malcolm Cowley⟩

ter·rar \ˈterər, -e,rär\ *n* -s [ML *terrarius*, fr. L *terra* land + *-arius* -ary; fr. his handling the income from and disbursements for the lands belonging to the house] **:** a bursar of a religious house

ter·rar·i·um \tə'rerēəm\ *n, pl* **terrar·ia** \-ēə\ *or* **terrariums** [NL, fr. L *terra* earth + *-arium* (as in *aquarium*)] **1 :** a vivarium for terrestrial animals **2 :** a fully enclosed wholly or predominantly glass container (as a Wardian case) for the indoor cultivation of moisture-loving plants; *also* **:** a planting in such a container **:** GLASS GARDEN

ter·ra ro·sa \,terə'rōzə, -ōsə\ *n* [NL, lit., gnawed earth] **:** RED OCHER

terra ros·sa \-'rōsə, -'räsə\ *n* [It, lit., red earth] **:** red shallow residual clayey soils formed from hard limestone and occurring in the Mediterranean climate and in limited areas in southern Australia

terra si·en·na \,==,sē'enə\ *n* [modif. of It *terra di Siena*] **:** RAW SIENNA 2

terra sig·il·la·ta \,==,sigə'lād·ə, -,sijə'lād·ə\ *n* [ML, lit., stamped earth] **1 :** BOLE 3 **2 :** ancient Roman pottery of red or occas. black body adorned with figures; *esp* **:** ARRETINE WARE

ter·rasse \te'räs\ *n* -s [F, fr. MF] **:** TERRACE

ter·ra ver·de \,terə'ver(,)dā\ *n* [It, lit., green earth] **:** TERRE VERTE

ter·raz·zo \tə'ra|(,)zō, -räl, |t(,)sō, |_zə, |tsə\ *n* -s [It, terrace, terrazzo, perh. fr. OProv *terrassa* terrace — more at TERRACE] **1 :** a mosaic flooring made by embedding small pieces of marble or granite in freshly placed mortar and after hardening grinding and polishing the surface **2 :** a surface (as a border or counter top) of mosaic and mortar either precast or cast-in-place

terre à terre \,terə'te(ə)r\ *adj* [F, lit., earth to earth] **1 a :** performed on or close to the ground or floor **:** performed with little elevation ⟨*terre à terre* dancing⟩ **b :** performing with the feet close to the ground ⟨*terre à terre* dancer⟩ **2 :** lacking in imagination **:** MATTER-OF-FACT, PROSAIC

ter·rel·la \tə'relə\ *n* -s [NL, small earth or planet, spherical magnet, fr. L *terra* earth + *-ella* — more at TERRACE] **:** a spherical magnet used to simulate the magnetic properties of the earth

ter·rell grass \ˈterəl-\ *n, usu cap T* [fr. the proper name *Terrell*] **:** a coarse American lyme grass (*Elymus virginicus*) used in some districts for pasturage

¹ter·rene \(ˈ)te;rēn, tə'r-\ *adj* [ME, fr. L *terrenus* of earth, of the earth, fr. *terra* earth — more at TERRACE] **1 :** of or relating to this world or life **:** MUNDANE ⟨by what devotion call down the notice of these eyes to so ~ a being as himself —R.L. Stevenson⟩ **2** *archaic* **a :** consisting of or resembling earth **:** EARTHY **b :** encountered on land rather than water **:** TERRESTRIAL **syn** see EARTHLY

²terrene \"\ *n* -s [L *terrenum* land, ground, fr. neut. of *terrenus* of earth] **:** a land area **:** EARTH, TERRAIN

ter·rene·ly *adv* **:** in an earthly manner **:** MUNDANELY

terre·plein \ˈterə,plān\ *n* -s [MF, fr. OIt *terrapieno*, fr. ML *terraplenum*, fr. the phrase *terrā plenus* filled with earth, full of earth, fr. L *terrā* (abl. sing. of *terra* earth) + *plenus* full — more at TERRACE, FULL] **1 a :** the level space behind the parapet of a rampart where guns are mounted **b :** the level at which a battery is placed whether above or below ground **2 :** an embankment of earth with a broad level top

¹ter·res·tri·al \tə'restrēəl, te'r-, *prob by r-dissimilation or/and on the analogy of "celestial"* ÷-es(h)chəl *or* -estēəl\ *adj* [ME, fr. L *terrestris* of the earth, of land (fr. *terra* earth, land) + ME *-al* — more at TERRACE] **1 a :** of or relating to the earth or its inhabitants **:** EARTHLY, GLOBAL ⟨the nearest thing to an angelic being that treads this ~ ball —J.B.Martin⟩ ⟨funneling an inadequate supply of U. S. dollars into the large ~ dollar deficit —*Economist*⟩ **b :** mundane in scope or character **:** EARTHBOUND, PROSAIC ⟨that philosophy is essentially ~, not . . . cosmic —J.L.Lowes⟩ ⟨self-taught from childhood, he developed an immense ~ practicality —Alfred Kreymborg⟩ **2** *obs* **:** consisting of or resembling soil **:** EARTHY **3 a :** of or relating to land as distinct from air or water ⟨~ transportation⟩ ⟨sedimentary material of ~ origin —*Jour. of Geol.*⟩ **b** (1) **:** living on or in or growing from the land ⟨~ plants⟩ ⟨~ birds⟩ — distinguished from *amphibious, aquatic, arboreal, epiphytic* (2) **:** of or relating to terrestrial organisms ⟨~ habits⟩ **4** *astron* **:** belonging to the same class with the earth **syn** see EARTHLY

²terrestrial \"\ *n* -s **:** an inhabitant of land or of the earth ⟨this orchid is one of the ~*s*⟩

terrestrial deposit *n* **1 :** a sedimentary deposit made on land above tidal reach as a result of the activity of glaciers, wind, rainwash, and streams **2 :** a sedimentary deposit formed by springs or by underground water in cavities of rocks

terrestrial equator *n* **:** EQUATOR 2

terrestrial glory *n* **:** the second of three Mormon degrees or kingdoms of glory attainable in heaven — compare CELESTIAL GLORY, TELESTIAL GLORY

terrestrial latitude *n* **:** latitude on the earth — compare ASTRONOMICAL LATITUDE, GEOCENTRIC LATITUDE, GEOGRAPHICAL LATITUDE

terrestrial longitude *n* **:** longitude on the earth

ter·res·tri·al·ly \-ēəlē, -li\ *adv* [¹*terrestrial* + *-ly*] **1 :** in an earthly manner **:** MUNDANELY, TEMPORALLY ⟨~ transient⟩ **2 :** to a land environment ⟨~ adapted⟩ **3 :** by contact with the earth or its atmosphere ⟨a ~ oxidized meteor⟩

terrestrial magnetism *n* **1 :** the magnetism of the earth **2 :** a branch of geophysics that deals with the phenomena of the earth's magnetic condition

terrestrial meridian *n* **:** MERIDIAN 4a

terrestrial planet *n* **:** one of the four inner planets of the solar system ⟨Mercury, Venus, Earth, and Mars are the *terrestrial planets*⟩ — compare MAJOR PLANET

terrestrial pole *n* **:** ⁴POLE 1b

terrestrial telescope *n* **:** a refracting telescope for viewing terrestrial objects through an eyepiece that consists of three or four lenses so arranged that the final image is right side up — compare ASTRONOMICAL TELESCOPE, FIELD GLASS, SPYGLASS

ter·ret *also* **ter·rit** \ˈterət\ *n* -s [ME *toret, teret*, fr. MF *toret*, fr. OF, dim. of *tor* circuit] **:** one of the rings on the top of a harness pad through which the reins pass

terre-tenant *or* **ter·ten·ant** \ˈter-,tenənt, 'tər-\ *n* [ME *teretenaunt*, fr. AF *terre tenant*, fr. OF *terre* land (fr. L *terra*) + *tenant* holding, fr. pres. part. of *tenir* to hold, fr. L *tenēre* — more at TERRACE, THIN] **:** one who has the actual possession of land **:** the occupant of land; *often* **:** one other than a judgment debtor owning an interest in the debtor's land after the lien of the judgment creditor attached thereto

terrets on harness pad

terre verte \(ˈ)ter¦ve(ə)rt\ *n* [F, lit., green earth] **1 :** GREEN EARTH 2 **2 :** the variable color of terre verte pigment, which averages a grayish green that is bluer, lighter, and stronger than slate green, bluer and duller than average reseda (sense 2a), and yellower and duller than average blue spruce (sense 2a) — called also *Bohemian earth, cyprian earth, green earth, green ocher, holy green, Italian green, permanent green, Tyrol green, Verona green*

ter·ri·bi·li·ta \,terə¦bēlə'tä\ *n* -s [It *terribilità*, lit., terribleness, fr. LL *terribilitat-, terribilitas*, fr. L *terribilis* terrible + *-itat-, -itas* -ity] **:** an effect or expression of powerful will and immense angry force (as in the work of Michelangelo)

¹ter·ri·ble \ˈterəbəl\ *adj* [ME, fr. MF, fr. L *terribilis*, fr. *terrēre* to frighten + *-ibilis* -ible — more at TERROR] **1 a :** exciting extreme alarm **:** FRIGHTENING, TERRIFYING ⟨the instantly cataclysmic effect of these ~ new weapons —J.C. Slessor⟩ ⟨the ~ powers of the Inquisition —J.H.Randall⟩ **b :** overwhelmingly tragic ⟨a human being devoid of hope is the most ~ object in the world —Victor Heiser⟩ **c :** formidable in nature **:** commanding respect **:** AWESOME, IMPOSING ⟨courage of those sailors . . . made the flag of England ~ on the seas —T.B.Macaulay⟩ ⟨a choice . . . which affected so many other lives was a ~ responsibility —John Mason Brown⟩ **d :** requiring extreme effort or fortitude **:** DIFFICULT, LABORIOUS ⟨a ~ ordeal⟩ ⟨a ~ task⟩ **2 :** extreme in degree **:** GREAT, INTENSE ⟨~ anxiety⟩ ⟨the artist's ~ and all-consuming dedication to his work —David Sylvester⟩ **3 a :** defective or injurious in nature **:** BAD, DESTRUCTIVE ⟨the road got bumpier . . . and the land on either side of it was in ~ shape —Emily Hahn⟩ ⟨the rainy season finds its ~ climax . . . in the crashing impact of a hurricane —Marjory S. Douglas⟩ **b :** strongly repulsive **:** DISREPUTABLE, OBNOXIOUS ⟨people . . . live in that ~ old shack —Peggy Bennett⟩ ⟨musk . . . smells simply ~ by itself —D.W.Dresden⟩ **4 a :** tending to appall **:** DREADFUL, SHOCKING ⟨blend of ~ sentimentality and brassy sophistication —Wolcott Gibbs⟩ ⟨gave the beggar . . . my own quarter, so what's so ~ —Mary Barrett⟩ **b :** of very poor quality **:** AWFUL, PUNK ⟨Italian painting, when it is bad, can be really ~ —R.M. Coates⟩ ⟨bought a drink of ~ whiskey —Herbert Asbury⟩ **syn** see FEARFUL

²terrible \"\ *adv* **:** to an extreme degree **:** VERY, TERRIBLY ⟨a ~ brave man —John Buchan⟩ ⟨a ~ cold night⟩

³terrible \"\ *n* -s **:** a terrible person or thing

ter·ri·ble·ness *n* -ES **:** the quality or state of being terrible

ter·ri·bly \-blē,-bli\ *adv* [¹*terrible* + *-ly*] **1 :** in a formidable or frightening manner **:** AWESOMELY, TERRIFYINGLY ⟨the ~ glittering advance of a tidal wave⟩ ⟨the fear is ~ mutual —Hal Lehrman⟩ **2 a :** to a superlative degree **:** EXTREMELY, INTENSELY ⟨it is ~ difficult to translate poetry —Gilbert Highet⟩ ⟨the reaction of a ~ sincere spirit to something . . . sham and sophisticated —Herbert Read⟩ ⟨an eighty-five cent dinner that was ~ good and quick —Mary McCarthy⟩ **b :** to an excruciating or shocking extent **:** APPALLINGLY ⟨wars . . . aggravated matters ~ —E.B.George⟩ ⟨the story is ~ involved —Roger Fry⟩ ⟨played pinochle, and . . . cheated ~ —Edita Morris⟩

ter·ric·o·lae \te'rikə,lē, tə'r-, -,lī\ *n pl, cap* [NL, fr. L, pl. of *terricola* earth dweller, fr. *terri-* (fr. *terra* earth) + *-cola*] *in some esp former classifications* **:** a group of Oligochaeta comprising mainly the more terrestrial oligochaete worms — compare LIMICOLAE, NEOLIGOCHAETA

ter·ric·o·lous \-ləs\ *or* **ter·ri·cole** \ˈterə,kōl\ *also* **ter·ric·o·line** \te'rikə,līn, tə'r-, -,lən\ *adj* [*terricole* fr. L *terricola* earth dweller; *terricolous, terricoline* fr. L *terricola* + E *-ous* or *-ine*] **:** TERRESTRIAL 3b

¹ter·ri·er \ˈterēə(r), *chiefly dial* 'tar-\ *n* -s [F, fr. MF, fr. ML (*liber*) *terrarius*, lit., book relating to land, fr. L *liber* book + ML *terrarius* of earth, of land — more at LEAF] **1 :** a register (as in a book or roll) of English real property: **a :** one listing the names of vassals or tenants with details of their holdings, services, and rents **:** RENT-ROLL **b :** one in which the lands of a private person or of a corporation are described by site, boundaries, and acreage; *esp* **:** one detailing the real property of a parish church **2** *obs* **:** an inventory of property or goods

²terrier \"\ *n* -s [F (*chien*) *terrier*, lit., earth dog, fr. *chien* dog (fr. L *canis*) + *terrier* of earth, fr. ML *terrarius* of earth, of land, fr. L *terra* earth, land + *-arius* -ary — more at HOUND, TERRACE] **:** any of various usu. small and rather low-built dogs (as an airedale, fox terrier, schnauzer) kept chiefly as pets but orig. used by hunters to dig for small furred game and engage the quarry underground or drive it out of its hole — compare BULLTERRIER; see FOX TERRIER illustration

terries *pl of* TERRY

ter·rif·ic \tə'rifik, -fēk\ *adj* [L *terrificus*, fr. *terrēre* to frighten + *-i-* + *-ficus* -fic — more at TERROR] **1 a :** exciting fear or awe **:** TERRIBLE, TERRIFYING ⟨the ~ destruction . . . visited upon the country —I.M.Price⟩ ⟨~, serrated outcrops of naked rock —Douglas Carruthers⟩ **b :** very bad **:** AWFUL, FRIGHTFUL ⟨might well have passed at three hearts . . . with his ~ distribution —*Springfield (Mass.) Daily News*⟩ ⟨covering up a ~ literary scandal for one of his clients —Robert Cantwell⟩ **2 a :** of an extraordinary nature **:** ASTOUNDING, TREMENDOUS ⟨can read the most involved books at the ~ rate of 600 pages a day —Bernard Eaton⟩ ⟨the ~ heat exploded ammunition in the wing guns —O.O.Jensen⟩ **b :** exceptionally strong or violent **:** POWERFUL, SEVERE ⟨punched him . . . in the stomach, short ~ jabs —Raymond Chandler⟩ ⟨sad to see . . . the damage done by this ~ winter —Georgina Grahame⟩ ⟨the impact of thirty million aliens is a ~ test of any culture —G.W. Johnson⟩ **3 :** unusually fine or gratifying **:** exciting admiration or enthusiasm **:** MAGNIFICENT, MARVELOUS ⟨a ~ view . . . all the way to the Black Mountains of Wales, some fifty miles distant —Richard Joseph⟩ ⟨told him that the piece would be a great success in the concert hall and ~ on records —Moses Smith⟩ **syn** see FEARFUL

ter·rif·i·cal·ly \-fək(ə)lē, -fēk-, -li\ *adv* [*terrific* + *-ally*] **:** to a terrific degree or extent

terrified *adj* [fr. past part. of *terrify*] **1 :** filled with intense fear or apprehension ⟨the men were ~ . . . and wanted to retreat out of harm's way —C.S.Forester⟩ **2 :** filled with anxiety or worry ⟨has no faith in her powers of attraction, and she's ~ of being thought ridiculous —Constance Walsh⟩ **syn** see AFRAID

ter·ri·fy \ˈterə,fī\ *vt* -ED/-ING/-ES [L *terrificare*, fr. *terrificus* terrific] **1 a :** to fill with terror **:** frighten greatly ⟨sermons . . . providing a sanction for other men to ~ the imaginations of ill-balanced persons —V.L.Parrington⟩ ⟨the prospect of nuclear warfare *terrifies* the population⟩ **b :** to drive or impel by menacing **:** SCARE ⟨the gunman's threats ~ her into handing over the money⟩ **c :** DETER, INTIMIDATE ⟨book . . . so technical as to ~ the average reader —Anthony Boucher⟩ ⟨museums and galleries ~ us —Clive Bell⟩ **2** *dial Brit* **:** to cause trouble to **:** HARASS, TORMENT **syn** see FRIGHTEN

terrifying *adj* [fr. pres. part. of *terrify*] **1 :** causing terror or apprehension **:** FRIGHTENING ⟨the most ~ things he met on his travels were the marching ants of Tanganyika —*Irish Digest*⟩ ⟨ascent of a ~ icefall —Raymond Holden⟩ ⟨his ~ insistence upon appalling and merciless retribution —W.L.Sullivan⟩ **2 :** of a formidable nature **:** AWESOME, TREMENDOUS ⟨the ~ formality . . . of the great drawing rooms of Paris —Elinor Wylie⟩ ⟨a ~ and voracious erudition —Morris Watnick⟩ ⟨take a ~ leap to the unimaginable range of temperatures . . . in the universe —Gerard Piel⟩ — **ter·ri·fy·ing·ly** \\'==,===, ,=='===\\ *adv*

ter·rig·e·nous \\tə'rijənəs, te'r-\\ *adj* [L *terrigena* earthborn (fr. *terri-* — fr. *terra* earth — + *-gena* — akin to L *gignere* to beget) + E *-ous* — more at TERRACE, KIN] **:** formed by the erosive action of rivers, tides, and currents — used of an ocean bottom ⟨~ deposits drape the continental shelves . . . and trail downward to the abysses —F.C.Lane⟩

ter·rine \\tə'rēn, (')te¦r-\\ *n* -s [F — more at TUREEN] **1 a :** TUREEN **b :** a usu. earthenware dish (as a casserole) in which foods are cooked and served **2 :** an earthenware jar containing a table delicacy (as goose liver) and sold with its contents

territ *var of* TERRET

¹**ter·ri·to·ri·al** \\¦terə¦tōrēəl, -ȯr-\\ *adj* [L *territorialis* of a territory, fr. *territorium* territory + *-alis* -al] **1 a :** of or relating to the immediate vicinity **:** LOCAL **b :** serving outlying areas **:** REGIONAL ⟨the ~ minister and the district worker —W. G.Blaikie⟩ **2 a :** of or relating to a territory ⟨~ government⟩ ⟨~ regiment⟩ ⟨~ delegate⟩ ⟨protested violations of its ~ air by planes of a foreign power —*Springfield (Mass.) Union*⟩ ⟨two states have been admitted to the Union without having passed through the ~ stage —J.E.Stoner⟩ **b :** of or relating to private property ⟨the soil of Italy was fast passing into the hands of a few ~ magnates —J.A.Froude⟩ **3 a :** of or relating to an assigned or preempted area ⟨the line of . . . command extends, in its simplest terms, from general to chief of the staff to ~ commanders —Don Pitt⟩ ⟨although some animals appear to have no discernible ~ demands, most . . . are territory-conscious —L.W.Wing⟩ **b :** exhibiting territoriality ⟨a ~ species⟩ ⟨strongly ~ birds⟩ — **ter·ri·to·ri·al·ly** \\-ēəlē, -li\\ *adv*

²**territorial** \\"\\ *n* -s **1 :** a territorial military unit; *esp* **:** HOME RESERVE **2 :** a member of a territorial military unit

territorial gold *n* **:** PRIVATE GOLD

ter·ri·to·ri·al·ism \\,==¦==ə,lizəm\\ *n* -s [¹*territorial* + *-ism*] **1 :** LANDLORDISM 2 **2 :** the principle established by the Peace of Augsburg in 1555 providing for compulsory conformity of all the inhabitants of a territory of the Holy Roman Empire to the Lutheranism or Roman Catholicism established by their ruler or for their emigration **3** *often cap* **:** a doctrine, theory, or movement among the Jews seeking to establish the settlement of the Jews on an autonomous basis in any suitable and available part of the world — compare ZIONISM **4 :** TERRITORIALITY 2

ter·ri·to·ri·al·ist \\-¸ləst\\ *n* -s [¹*territorial* + *-ist*] **:** one that practices or advocates territorialism

ter·ri·to·ri·al·i·ty \\,==,=='aləd.ē, -ətē, -i\\ *n* -ES [¹*territorial* + *-ity*] **1 :** territorial status **2 a :** persistent attachment to a specific territory **b :** the pattern of behavior associated with the defense of a male animal's territory

ter·ri·to·ri·al·iza·tion \\,==,===ələ'zāshən, -ə,lī'z-\\ *n* -s [*territorialize* + *-ation*] **:** the act or process of organizing into territories

ter·ri·to·ri·al·ize \\,terə'tōrēə,līz, -'tȯr-\\ *vt* -ED/-ING/-s *see -ize in Explan Notes* **:** to reduce to the status of a territory **:** organize on a territorial basis

territorial jurisdiction *n* **:** the sovereign jurisdiction that a state has over the land within its boundary limits, over its inland and territorial waters and to a reasonable extent over the airspace above and subsoil below in such land and waters, and over all persons and things within those areas subject to its control (as on its vessels or on aircraft over the high seas) — compare EXTRATERRITORIALITY

territorial law *n* **:** law applying alike to all persons regardless of their nationality or citizenship within a given territory — distinguished from *personal law*

territorial reserve *n* **:** HOME RESERVE

territorial sea *n* **:** the part of territorial waters subject to the jurisdiction of a coastal state usu. extending from mean low water mark on the shore or from the seaward limit of a bay or mouth of a river a marine league or 3 geographical miles outward to the open sea — compare INLAND WATER

territorial style *n, usu cap T* **:** the architectural style resulting from the influences of eastern U. S. settlers on the Indian and Spanish building techniques of New Mexico

territorial waters *n pl* **:** the waters under the territorial jurisdiction of a nation or state including both inland waters and marginal sea as measured from mean low-water mark or from the seaward limit of a bay or river mouth

ter·ri·to·ri·an \\,=='==ən\\ *n* -s *usu cap* [*territory* + *-an*] **:** an inhabitant of the Northern Territory of Australia

ter·ri·to·ry \\'terə,tōrē, -ōri, -ȯr-\\ *n* -ES [ME, fr. L *territorium* land around a town, district, territory, prob. fr. *terri-* (fr. *terra* land) + *-torium* (as in *praetorium*) — more at TERRACE] **1 a :** a geographical area belonging to or under the jurisdiction of a political authority ⟨defeated the German armies on their home ~ —C.E.Black & E.C.Helmreich⟩ ⟨out-of-town police . . . questioned him about several similar murders in their *territories* —E.D.Radin⟩ **b :** an administrative subdivision of a country ⟨the 15 republics of the U. S. S. R. are divided into 128 *territories* and regions⟩ **c :** an organized portion of a country not yet admitted to statehood ⟨Minnesota became a ~ in 1849 —*Amer. Guide Series: Minn.*⟩ ⟨Mexico is divided into 29 states, 1 federal district . . . and 2 *territories* —*Statesman's Yr. Bk.*⟩ **d :** a geographical area (as a colonial possession) dependent upon an external government but having some degree of autonomy ⟨the status of France's third North African ~ will be challenged —Mario Rossi⟩ — compare TRUST TERRITORY **e** *Scots law* **:** the district subject to the jurisdiction of a court or judge **:** JURISDICTION **2 a** (1) **:** a geographical area of indeterminate extent **:** REGION, TRACT ⟨in Virginia . . . there were large *territories* of unsettled lands —R.B.Taney⟩ (2) **:** LAND, TERRAIN ⟨without their mustangs Texas cowboys could never have covered so much ~ —S.E. Fletcher⟩ (3) **:** an area of specified potential ⟨some of the state's best fish and game ~ —*Amer. Guide Series: Vt.*⟩ ⟨huge accumulations of . . . clouds that made perfect ambush ~ for pilots —Ira Wolfert⟩ **b :** an area of knowledge or special interest **:** FIELD, GROUND ⟨the large adjoining *territories* of social and economic history —Franz Philipp⟩ ⟨that question covers a lot of ~ —*Magazine of Wall Street*⟩ **c :** a specified area (as of the body) ⟨stuck soda straws up each nostril . . . while we poured plaster over his surrounding facial ~ —Beverly Smith⟩ **3 :** an assigned or preempted area: as **a :** the area defended by an athletic team ⟨a brilliant 52-yard dash . . . moved Ohio State from deep in its own ~ into striking position —*N. Y. Times*⟩ **b :** a geographic area to which a salesman or distributor confines his commercial activities **c :** the largest administrative unit of the Salvation Army usu. comprising a country or group of countries **d :** an area usu. including the nesting or denning site and a variable foraging range that is preempted by an individual male (as a bird or mammal) and defended against the intrusion of rival individuals — compare HOME RANGE **syn** see FIELD

territory wool *n* [so called fr. the former territorial status of the states in which it was produced] **:** wool produced esp. in Montana, Wyoming, Idaho, Utah, Nevada, Colorado, and Washington

ter·ron \\tə'rōn\\ *n, pl* **terro·nes** \\-nēz\\ [MexSp *terrón*, fr. Sp, clod, lump of earth, fr. L *terra* earth, fr. L *terra*] **:** a block of sun-dried sod used as a construction brick in the Rio Grande valley ⟨heavy clay with abundant fine grass roots makes the best ~*es* —A.A.Lindsey⟩

¹**ter·ror** \\'terə(r)\\ *n* -s *often attrib* [ME *terrour*, fr. MF *terreur*, fr. L *terror*, fr. *terrēre* to frighten; akin to Gk *trein* to flee from fear, be afraid, Skt *trasati* he trembles, is afraid] **1 a :** a state of intense fright or apprehension **:** stark fear ⟨disquietude had developed into fright; fright . . . into ~ —Emile Gaboriau⟩ ⟨every beast . . . jarred out of tranquillity into ~, was spending its strength in flight —F.D.Davison⟩ **b :** TERRIBLENESS ⟨the dramatic, apocalyptic ~ of concentrated bombing attacks —Anthony West⟩ ⟨the blizzard broke in all its ~ —O.E.Rolvaag⟩ **2 a :** one that inspires fear **:** THREAT, SCOURGE ⟨horse thieves and murdering ruffians who were the ~ of the border —E.V.Buckholder⟩ **b :** a frightening aspect ⟨while withdrawal from opiates is never a pleasant experience, its ~*s* have probably been exaggerated —D.W.Maurer & V.H. Vogel⟩ **c :** a cause of anxiety **:** WORRY ⟨it was the ~ of my life that he might catch a chill —Ernest Beaglehole⟩ **d :** an appalling person or thing; *esp* **:** ²BRAT 2 ⟨a little ~ at two and a half —May Sherwin⟩ **3 :** REIGN OF TERROR ⟨reports that the Germans are increasing their ~ in occupied regions —Walter Bernstein⟩ **syn** see FEAR

²**terror** \\"\\ *vt* -ED/-ING/-s **:** FRIGHTEN

ter·ror·ful \\-fəl\\ *adj* **:** full of terror **:** TERRIFYING

ter·ror·ism \\'terə,rizəm\\ *n* -s [F *terrorisme*, fr. L *terror* + F *-isme* -ism] **1 :** the systematic use of terror as a means of coercion ⟨the opening stage of a well-planned campaign of political ~ —Heinz Eulan⟩ — compare REIGN OF TERROR **2 :** an atmosphere of threat or violence ⟨study the effects on children of ~ in TV shows⟩

ter·ror·ist \\'terərəst\\ *n* -s [F *terroriste*, fr. L *terror* + F *-iste* -ist] **1 :** an advocate or practitioner of terror as a means of coercion; *esp* **:** JACOBIN 2a **2 :** one who panics or causes anxiety **:** ALARMIST — **ter·ror·is·tic** \\¦terə¦ristik\\ *adj*

ter·ror·iza·tion \\,terərə'zāshən, -erə,rī'z-\\ *n* -s **:** the act or process of terrorizing

ter·ror·ize \\'terə,rīz\\ *vb* -ED/-ING/-s *see -ize in Explan Notes* [¹*terror* + *-ize*] *vt* **1 :** to fill with terror or anxiety **:** SCARE **2 :** to coerce by threat or violence ⟨~ the members of that union into helpless submission —T.W.Arnold⟩ ~ *vi* **:** to excite fear **:** rule by intimidation **syn** see FRIGHTEN

ter·ror·less \\'terə(r)ləs\\ *adj* **:** holding no terrors

ter·rour *n* [ME] *archaic* **:** TERROR

ter·ry \\'terē, -ri\\ *n* -ES *often attrib* [perh. modif. of F *tiré*, past part. of *tirer* to draw, fr. OF — more at TIRADE] **1 :** the loop forming the pile in uncut pile fabrics — compare ⁸PILE 2 **2** *or* **terry cloth :** a soft absorbent usu. cotton fabric characterized by loops in allover or pattern effects on one or both sides and made in various weights (as for towels, bathrobes, sportswear, spreads)

ter·ry clock \\'terē-, -ri-\\ *n, usu cap T* [after Eli *Terry* †1852 Am. clock manufacturer] **:** PILLAR AND SCROLL

ter·sanctus \\'tər, 'ter+\\ *n* -ES *often cap* [NL, lit., thrice holy (trans. of LGk *trisagios*), fr. L *ter* three times + *sanctus* holy — more at TER-, SAINT] **1 :** SANCTUS **2** *often cap* **:** any hymn or invocation praising God as the thrice-holy deity

terse \\'tərs, 'təs, 'təis\\ *adj* [L *tersus* clean, neat, fr. past part. of *tergēre* to rub off, wipe; akin to Goth *thairko* hole, Gk *trōglē* hole, cave, L *terere* to rub — more at THROW] **1 a** *archaic* **:** freed of debris or roughness **:** CLEAN, BURNISHED ⟨enamored of this street . . . 'tis so polite and ~ —Ben Jonson⟩ **b :** smoothly elegant **:** POLISHED, REFINED ⟨clinging, with a true instinct for style, to what is ~ and elliptic —C.E.Montague⟩ ⟨the more lapidary and ~ this subject the better it is suited for symphonic elaboration —P.H.Lang⟩ **2 :** devoid of superfluity **:** BRIEF, CONCISE ⟨his answers were very clipped and ~ —Raymond Boyle⟩ ⟨occasional ~ volleys of rifle fire —H.E.Bates⟩ ⟨keep the copy short, ~ and easy to read —*Printers' Ink*⟩ **syn** see CONCISE

terse·ly *adv* **:** in a terse manner **:** BRIEFLY

terse·ness *n* -ES **:** the quality or state of being terse **:** BREVITY, POLISH

ter·sulfide \\¦tər+\\ *n* [*ter-* + *sulfide*] **:** TRISULFIDE

tert- \\¦tərt\\ *comb form, usu ital* [*tertiary*] **:** tertiary — esp. in names of organic chemical radicals ⟨*tert*-butyl⟩

tertenant *var of* TERRE-TENANT

tertia *var of* TERCIO

¹**ter·tial** \\'tərshəl\\ *adj* [L *tertius* third + E *-al*; fr. the fact that tertials form the third row of feathers] **1 :** of, relating to, or constituting the flight feathers borne on the basal joint of a bird's wing — compare PRIMARY 2c **2 :** of, relating to, or constituting some of the innermost secondaries when different from the others or the scapular feathers — not used technically

²**tertial** \\"\\ *n* -s **:** a tertial feather

¹**ter·tian** \\'tərshən\\ *adj* [in sense 1, fr. ME *tercian (fever)* tertian fever, part trans. of L *tertiana febris*, fr. *tertiana* (fem. of *tertianus* of the third) + *febris* fever; fr. its recurring every third day; in other senses fr. L *tertianus* of the third, fr. *tertius* third + *-anus* -an — more at THIRD] **1 :** recurring at approximately 48-hour intervals — used chiefly of vivax malaria — compare QUARTAN **2 :** of or relating to a tertiary or to tertianship **3 :** relating to the mean tone system of musical temperament in which the major thirds are perfectly in tune

²**tertian** \\"\\ *n* -s [L *tertianus* of the third] **1** [ME *tercian*, fr. L *tertiana*, fr. *tertiana febris*] **:** a tertian fever; *specif* **:** VIVAX MALARIA **2** [ME *tercian*, fr. L *tertianus* of the third] **:** an old unit of liquid capacity equal to ⅓ tun **3 :** a third-year student in arts (as at Aberdeen University) **4** *or* **tertian father** *usu cap T&F* **:** a Jesuit during tertianship **5 :** a compound organ stop composed of two ranks of open metal pipes tuned a major third apart

ter·tian·ship \\-,ship\\ *n* [²*tertian* + *-ship*] **:** a third period of novitiate or training undertaken by a Jesuit after ordination

¹**ter·tiary** \\'tərshē,erē, 'təsh-, 'təish-, -eri *also* -shər-\\ *n* -ES [in sense 1, fr. ML *tertiarius*, fr. L, of or containing a third; in other senses fr. ²*tertiary*] **1 :** a member of a monastic third order after the first order of monks and the second order of nuns composed of men and women of the laity who take no more than simple vows, who may remain outside of a monastery and hold property, and yet who follow to some degree a portion of a monastic rule ⟨Franciscan and Dominican *tertiaries*⟩ **2 :** a tertial feather **3** *usu cap* **:** the Tertiary period or system of rocks **4 :** TERTIARY COLOR **5 a :** a lesion of tertiary syphilis **b :** TERTIAN 1

²**tertiary** \\"\\ *adj* [L *tertiarius* of or containing a third, fr. *tertius* third + *-arius* -ary — more at THIRD] **1 a :** third in order or importance **:** preceded by two others ⟨a ~ characteristic⟩ ⟨a few transformers are provided . . . with a ~ winding —J.B.Gibbs⟩ ⟨a ~ cambium develops around a number of the secondary elements —Ernst Artschwager⟩ **b :** of or relating to a monastic third order **c :** of or relating to education following the secondary level whether at a college or university or at an intermediate institution **d :** of or relating to the service industries (as distribution, transportation, domestic service) compared with agriculture or manufacturing **e :** of, relating to, or constituting the third strongest of the three or four degrees of stress recognized by most linguists ⟨the third syllable in *basketball's fun* carries the ~ stress⟩ **f :** TERTIAL **2** *usu cap* **:** of or relating to the time interval between the close of the Mesozoic era and the beginning of the Quaternary period during which the Alps, Caucasus, Himalayas, and other high mountains were formed, the Cordilleran system from Alaska to Cape Horn was developing, and the dominant land life was mammalian — see GEOLOGIC TIME table **3 :** characterized by replacement in the third degree **:** resulting from the substitution of three atoms or groups in a molecule ⟨a ~ salt⟩ ⟨~ phosphates⟩; *esp* **:** being or characterized by a carbon atom united by three valences to chain or ring members ⟨~ butyl $(CH_3)_3C$⟩ — compare PRIMARY 5, SECONDARY 2e **4 :** occurring or being in the third stage ⟨~ lesions of syphilis⟩

tertiary alcohol *n* **:** an alcohol characterized by the group ≡COH consisting of a carbon atom holding the hydroxyl group and attached by its other three valences to other carbon atoms in a chain or ring

tertiary amine *n* **:** an amine (as trimethylamine, dimethylaniline, or nicotine) having three organic substituents attached to the nitrogen atom

tertiary amyl alcohol *n* **:** a secondary pentyl alcohol $CH_3CH_2C(OH)(CH_3)_2$ having a camphoraceous odor, a burning taste, and hypnotic properties that can be made by hydrating amylene (sense a) and that is used chiefly as a solvent; 2-methyl-2-butanol — called also *amylene hydrate*

tertiary color *n* **:** a color produced by mixing two secondary colors

tertiary quality *n* **:** the quality of a thing as an object of evaluation — compare PRIMARY QUALITY, SECONDARY QUALITY

tertiary syphilis *n* **:** the third stage of syphilis developing soon or late after the disappearance of the secondary symptoms and marked by ulcers in and gummas under the skin and commonly involvement of the skeletal, cardiovascular, and nervous systems

ter·ti·um quid \\,tərshēəm'kwid, ,tərd·ē-, ,terd·ē-\\ *n* [LL, lit., third something, trans. of Gk *triton ti*] **1 :** a middle course or intermediate component **:** something that escapes classification with either of two mutually exclusive and supposedly exhaustive categories but shares elements of both ⟨God occupies merely an external relation, as a *tertium quid*, to mind and matter —James Martineau⟩ ⟨where there are two systems of law and two orders of courts, there must obviously be some *tertium quid* to deal with conflicts of law and jurisdiction — Ernest Baker⟩ **2 :** a third party of ambiguous status ⟨once upon a time there was a man and his wife and a *tertium quid* — Rudyard Kipling⟩

ter·tul·lian·ist \\(,)tər'təlēənəst, -'tül-, -lyən-\\ *n* -s *usu cap* [*Tertullian* †A.D.230? Latin ecclesiastical writer + E *-ist*] **:** a follower of Tertullian of Carthage

te·ru·ah \\tə'rüə, -ü(,)ä\\ *n, pl* **teru·oth** *or* **teru·ot** \\-ü,ōt(h), -ōs\\ *or* **teruahs** [Heb *tĕrū'āh* shout or blast of war, fr. *rūa'* to raise a shout, give a blast] **:** one of the calls composed of a series of staccato blasts followed by a longer high note and blown on the shofar as prescribed in the Jewish ritual on certain festivals and at certain ceremonies — compare TEKIAH

ter·u·tero \\,terü'te(,)rō\\ *or* **ter·u·teru** \\-(,)rü\\ *n* -s [Sp, fr. Guarani *teruteru*, of imit. origin] **:** a So. American lapwing (*Belonopterus chilensis cayennensis*) similar to the common lapwing but having a short hind toe and a spur on the bend of the wing

ter·valence *also* **ter·valency** \\¦tər+\\ *n* [*ter-* + *valence*, *valency*] **:** TRIVALENCE

tervalent \\"+\\ *adj* [*ter-* + *valent*] **:** TRIVALENT

ter·za ri·ma \\,tertsə'rēmə\\ *n* [It, lit., third rhyme] **:** a verse form consisting of tercets usu. in iambic pentameter in English poetry in which the second line of each rhymes with the first and third lines of the next ⟨Dante's *Divina Commedia* is written in *terza rima*⟩

ter·zet·to \\tert'sed·(,)ō\\ *or* **ter·zet** \\(')tert¦set\\ *n, pl* **terzet·tos** \\-d·(,)ōz\\ *or* **terzets** \\-ts\\ *also* **terzet·ti** \\-d·(,)ē\\ [It *terzetto* — more at TERCET] **:** a musical composition for three voices **:** TRIO

ter·zi·na \\tert'sēnə\\ *n, pl* **terzinas** \\-nəz\\ *or* **terzi·ne** \\-nā\\ [It] **:** TRIPLET 1

tes *pl of* TE

tesch·e·mach·er·ite \\'teshə,makə,rīt\\ *n* -s [Frederick E. *Teschemacher* †1863 Eng. chemist + E *-ite*] **:** a mineral consisting of an acid ammonium carbonate occurring in yellowish to white crystals in beds of guano (hardness 1.5, sp. gr. 1.4)

te·schen disease \\'teshən-\\ *n, usu cap T* [fr. *Teschen* (Cieszyn), region on the border of Poland and Czechoslovakia where it was first recognized] **:** a severe virus encephalomyelitis of swine marked by lesions of the central nervous system and by varying degrees of systemic paralysis and in many respects resembling human poliomyelitis but prob. not closely related etiologically

te·shu·bah *or* **te·shu·vah** \\'chüvə, tə'shüvə, -(,)vä\\ *n* [LHeb *tĕshūbhāh*, fr. Heb, return] **:** REPENTANCE

teshu lama *usu cap T&L, var of* TASHI LAMA

tes·la coil \\'teslə-\\ *or* **tesla transformer** *n, usu cap T* [after Nikola *Tesla* †1943 Am. electrician and inventor] **:** an air-core transformer for high-frequency alternating or oscillating electrical currents

tesla current *n, usu cap T* [after Nikola *Tesla* †1943] **:** a high-frequency oscillating current of medium voltage used in therapeutic treatment

te·so \\'tā(,)sō\\ *n, pl* **teso** *or* **tesos** *usu cap* **1 a :** a Nilo-Hamite people of eastern Uganda **b :** a member of such people **2 :** a Nilotic language of the Teso people

te·so·ta \\tə'sōd·ə\\ *n* -s [NL (specific epithet of *Olneya tesota*), fr. AmerSp, ironwood] **:** DESERT IRONWOOD 1

tessara- *or* **tessera-** *also* **tessar-** *comb form* [L, fr. Gk *tessara, tessera*, neut. of *tessares, tesseres, tettares* four — more at FOUR] **:** four ⟨*tessara*glot⟩ ⟨*tessera*decade⟩

tes·sa·ra·ce \\'tesərə,sē\\ *n* -s [*tessara-* + *-ace*] **:** a tetrahedral summit

tes·sa·ra·con·ter \\,tesərə'käntə(r)\\ *n* -s [Gk *tessarakontērēs*, fr. *tessarakonta, tesserakonta* forty, fr. *tessara-* + *-konta* (akin to L *-ginti* in *viginti* twenty) — more at VICENARY] **:** a galley with forty banks of oars

tes·sa·ra·glot \\'===,glät\\ *adj* [*tessara-* + *-glot*] **:** using or containing four languages

tes·sel·la \\tə'selə\\ *n* -s [L, small die, dim. of *tessera*] **:** TESSERA 2a

tes·sel·lar \\'tesələ(r)\\ *adj* **:** formed of or resembling tesserae

tes·sel·la·ta \\,tesə'läd·ə, -äd·ə\\ [NL, fr. L, neut. pl. of *tessellatus* checkered, tessellated] *syn of* PALAEOCRINOIDEA

¹**tes·sel·late** *also* **tes·se·late** \\'tesə,lāt, *usu* -ād·+V\\ *vt* -ED/-ING/-s [LL *tessellatus*, past part. of *tessellare* to pave with tiles, fr. L *tessella* small die] **1 :** to decorate with or as if with tesserae **:** make a mosaic of ⟨~ a floor⟩ **2** *archaic* **:** to fit into or as if into a mosaic ⟨this meaning is vague . . . impossible to ~ into any formal scheme —F.W.Farrar⟩

²**tes·sel·late** *also* **tes·se·late** \\-ələt, -ə,lāt, *usu* -d·+V\\ *adj* [L *tessellatus*, fr. *tessella* + *-atus* -ate] **:** TESSELLATED

tes·sel·lat·ed *also* **tes·se·lat·ed** \\-,lād·əd\\ *adj* [L *tessellatus* + E *-ed*] **1 :** of, relating to, or resembling mosaic ⟨a ~ pavement⟩ **2 :** having a checkered appearance **:** MOTTLED, RETICULATED

tessellated epithelium *n* **:** PAVEMENT EPITHELIUM

tessellated scale *n* **:** a soft flattened dark brown scale (*Eucalymnatus tessellatus*) marked with pale lines that infests a variety of tropical plants and that occurs commonly in greenhouses

tes·sel·la·tion \\,tesə'lāshən\\ *n* -s [LL *tessellatus* (past part. of *tessellare* to pave with tiles) + E *-ion*] **1 :** an act or instance of tessellating **:** state of being tessellated ⟨~ of a counter top⟩ ⟨~ of a leaf blade⟩ **2 :** a careful juxtaposition of elements into a coherent pattern **:** MOSAIC ⟨a ~ of important sentences from this book —D.A.Stauffer⟩

tes·sera \\'tesərə\\ *n, pl* **tesser·ae** \\-ə,rē, -rī\\ [L, perh. fr. Gk *tessares, tesseres, tettares* four; fr. its being four-cornered — more at FOUR] **1 a :** a small tablet or die (as of wood, bone, or ivory) used by the ancient Romans as a ticket, tally, voucher, or means of identification ⟨*tesserae* . . . served as tokens for the distribution of corn —R.L.Poole⟩ **b :** an identifying card or password ⟨showed him the ~ with photograph and identification —Ernest Hemingway⟩ **2 a :** a small piece (as of marble, glass, or tile) cut usu. with a square or rectangular face and used in mosaic work ⟨inlaid with shining *tesserae* of blue glass —Norman Douglas⟩ **b :** something that is likened to a piece of mosaic ⟨*tesserae* cemented together with brief comment and explanation —*Times Lit. Supp.*⟩ **3 :** a small rectangular plate of bone (as in the carapace of the armadillo)

tes·ser·act \\'tesə,rakt\\ *n* -s [Gk *tesseres* four + *aktis* ray — more at ACTIN-] **:** the four-dimensional analogue of a cube

tes·ser·al \\-sərəl\\ *also* **tes·su·lar** \\-syələ(r)\\ *adj* [*tesseral* fr. *tessera* + *-al*; *tessular* fr. (assumed) NL *tessula* (dim. of L *tessera*) + E *-ar*] **1 :** of, relating to, or resembling a tessera **:** TESSELLAR **2 :** having or constituting an isometric system **:** REGULAR ⟨a ~ crystal⟩

tes·ser·ate \\-ərət, -,rāt *usu* -d·+V\\ *also* **tes·ser·at·ed** \\-,rād·əd\\ *adj, archaic* **:** TESSELLATED

tes·si·tu·ra \\,tesə'türə\\ *n* -s [It, lit., texture, fr. L *textura* — more at TEXTURE] **:** the general range of a melody or voice part; *specif* **:** the part of the register in which most of the tones of a melody or voice part lie ⟨wrote always with the colors and ~*s* of instruments and voices clear in his mind — *Times Lit. Supp.*⟩

¹**test** \\'test\\ *n* -s [ME, vessel in which metals were assayed, cupel, fr. MF, fr. L *testum* earthen vessel; akin to L *testa* piece of burned clay, earthen pot, shell, Av *tashta* cup, L *texere* to construct, weave — more at TECHNICAL] **1 a** *chiefly Brit* **:** CUPEL **b** (1) **:** an act or process that reveals inherent qualities (as of character) **:** TRIAL ⟨needs to put his thinking to the ~ of research experience —*Jour. of Social Studies*⟩ ⟨a fiberless man disintegrating before ~ —Leslie Rees⟩ (2) **:** the procedure of submitting an empirical statement to observational or experimental conditions designed either to negate or confirm it (3) **:** the procedure of submitting an analytical statement to such either generally recognized or specifically stipulated

operations as will either prove or disprove it — compare PROOF (4) **:** something that serves as a basis for evaluation **:** CRITERION, TOUCHSTONE ⟨insisted that the correct ~ of any social system . . . was the type of man it tended to produce —H.D.Gideonse⟩ ⟨the best ~ of a travel book is a place the reader has also been —Gerald Sykes⟩ **c :** an ordeal or oath required as proof of conformity with a set of beliefs ⟨no religious ~ shall ever be required as a qualification to any office or public trust under the United States —*U.S.Constitution*⟩ **2 a :** a procedure or reaction used to identify or characterize a substance or constituent ⟨the iodine ~ for starch⟩ — compare ¹ASSAY 1d(1) **b :** the reagent used in such a test **c :** a positive result obtained in such a test **d :** a procedure for determining the performance characteristics (as of a product or machine) ⟨abrasion ~⟩ ⟨shakedown ~⟩ **e :** a diagnostic procedure for determining the nature of a condition or disease or for revealing a change in a function ⟨eye ~⟩ **f :** an instance or result of testing: as (1) **:** TEST MATCH (2) **:** an oil well drilled to test the possibilities of an undeveloped area (3) **:** AUDITION, SCREEN TEST (4) **:** minimum tensile strength as determined by test ⟨a fishing line of 20 pound ~⟩ **3 a :** a technique for measuring objectively an individual's personal characteristics, potentialities, or accomplishments esp. by comparing his behavior in response to standard stimuli or situations with the behavior of others against whom the particular technique is said to have been standardized — compare BATTERY 7a(1), INTELLIGENCE TEST, INVENTORY 5, ⁷SCALE 8 **b :** an examination to determine factual knowledge or mental proficiency esp. given to students during the course of a school term and covering a limited part of the year's work — compare ACHIEVEMENT TEST

²**test** \"\ *vb* -ED/-ING/-S *vt* **1 a** *chiefly Brit* **:** to subject (as gold or silver) to cupellation **:** ASSAY **b :** to put to the proof **:** TRY, VALIDATE ⟨a strategy of restraint would . . . ~ the patience and self-control of Americans —H.W.Baldwin⟩ ⟨the constant ~*ing* of hypotheses by empirical data —*Amer. Polit. Sci. Rev.*⟩ ⟨~ a court ruling by appeal to a higher court⟩ — often used with *out* ⟨~ out a formula⟩ **c :** to require a doctrinal oath of ⟨you shall not ~ or examine any prophet who speaks in the spirit —E.J.Goodspeed⟩ **2 a :** to examine or analyze (a substance) by the use of a reagent ⟨~ a solution with litmus paper⟩; *esp* **:** to examine for the presence of a substance ⟨~ a salt for calcium⟩ **b :** to determine the attributes or performance characteristics of ⟨enough samples must be ~*ed* to show how the product performs —*Mech. Engineering*⟩ **c :** to examine for disease or physical defect ⟨~ a tumor⟩ ⟨~ the reflexes⟩ **3 :** to explore the aptitudes, attitudes, knowledge, or skills of (as a student or a job applicant) by means of tests ⟨they have been trade ~*ed* by the adjutant, who . . . interviewed each —H.H.Arnold & I.C.Eaker⟩ ~ *vi* **1 a :** to undergo a test ⟨actors . . . best suited to the roles for which they ~*ed* —*Christian Herald*⟩ ⟨the great turboprop . . . was still ~*ing* —*Newsweek*⟩ **b :** to achieve a rating on the basis of tests ⟨the eyesight of different peoples may ~ the same —Ruth Benedict⟩ ⟨this same group when seniors . . . ~*ed* to a median of 70 —Angell Mathewson⟩ **2 :** to apply a test as a means of analysis or diagnosis — used with *for* ⟨use colored blocks to ~ for mechanical aptitude⟩ ⟨use the scratch technique in ~*ing* for allergies⟩ **syn** see PROVE

³**test** \"\ *adj* **1 :** of, relating to, or constituting a trial, proof, or criterion **2 a :** subjected to, used for, or revealed by testing ⟨~ group⟩ ⟨summaries of ~ data⟩ ⟨twelve medium-sized, geographically scattered ~ cities are trying to discover ways of coordinating and expanding adult education —F.M.Hechinger⟩ **b :** employed in determining attributes or performance characteristics (as of a product or machine) ⟨~ dive⟩ ⟨~ apparatus⟩ ⟨questions . . . carefully prepared and given a ~ run with a selected guinea-pig group —R.D.Haun & Leo Herbert⟩

⁴**test** \"\ *n* -S [ME, fr. L *testis* — more at TESTAMENT] **1** *obs* **:** EVIDENCE, WITNESS **2** *Scot* **:** WILL, TESTAMENT

⁵**test** \"\ *vb* -ED/-ING/-S [L *testari*, fr. *testis* witness] *vi*, *Scot* **:** to make a will ~ *vt* **1** *archaic* **:** to date and sign (as a writ) **:** ATTEST **2** *Scot* **:** to bear witness to **:** AUTHENTICATE

⁶**test** \"\ *n* -S [L *testa* shell — more at TEST (trial)] **:** the external shell or other hard or firm covering of many invertebrates (as foraminiferans, mollusks, many echinoderms, and crustaceans); *esp* **:** the thick outer covering of the body of a tunicate secreted by the mantle but containing cells which have emigrated into it, varying in consistency in different forms from leathery or cartilaginous to soft and gelatinous, and in compound ascidians usu. forming a solid mass in which the zooids are embedded

test *abbr* **1** testament; testamentary **2** testator

tes·ta \'testə\ *n, pl* **tes·tae** \-eˌstē, -stī\ *also* **testa** [NL, fr. L, shell — more at TEST] **:** the hard external coating or integument of a seed — called also *episperm*

test·abil·i·ty \ˌtestəˈbiləd·ē, -ətē, -i\ *n* **:** susceptibility to testing

¹**test·able** \'testəbəl\ *adj* [L *testabilis*, fr. *testari* to be a witness, make a will] + *-abilis* -able] **1 :** qualified (as by being legally capable) to bear witness or make a will **2 :** disposable by will

²**testable** \"\ *adj* [²*test* + *-able*] **:** capable of being tested **:** CONFIRMABLE

tes·ta·cea \teˈstāsh(ē)ə\ *n pl, cap* [NL, fr. L, neut. pl. of *testaceus* covered with a shell] **:** an order of Rhizopoda containing forms (as of the genera *Arcella* and *Difflugia*) with an external test — **tes·ta·cean** \(ˈ)ₛ;ₛshən\ *adj or n*

tes·ta·ceous \(ˈ)ₛ;ₛshəs\ *adj* [L *testaceus* consisting of bricks, covered with a shell, fr. *testa* piece of burned clay, brick, shell + *-aceus* -aceous] **1** *obs* **:** of, relating to, or made of earthenware **2 a :** having a shell ⟨a ~ protozoan⟩ **b :** consisting of shell or calcareous material ⟨stone . . . of a pale reddish brick color, and a ~ composition —Mark Van Doren⟩ **3 :** of any of the several light colors of bricks, averaging the color pheasant

tes·ta·cy \'testəsē, -si\ *n* -ES [¹*testate* + *-cy*] **:** the state or circumstance of being testate

tes·ta·ment \'testəmənt\ *n* -S [ME, fr. LL & L; LL *testamentum* covenant, Scripture (trans. of Gk *diathēkē* covenant), fr. L, last will, fr. *testari* to be a witness, make a will (fr. *testis* witness) + *-mentum* -ment; L *testis* akin to Oscan *trstus* witnesses; both fr. a prehistoric Italic compound whose first and second constituents respectively are akin to L *tres* three and to L *stare* to stand; fr. the witness standing by as a third party in a litigation — more at THREE, STAND] **1 a :** the written record of a compact **:** COVENANT, SCRIPTURE ⟨ancient ikons and ~*s* —A.R.Williams⟩ **b** *usu cap* **:** either of two main divisions of the Bible ⟨discusses the measure of unity between the *Testaments* —*British Book News*⟩ **2 a :** a tangible proof or tribute **:** EVIDENCE, WITNESS ⟨this capital teems with ~*s* to the tragic miscalculations . . . of U.S. policy —John Osborne⟩ ⟨a ~ to the skilled men who have penetrated the ocean of air —J.A.Michener⟩ **b :** an expression of conviction **:** AFFIRMATION, CREDO ⟨the ~ of a man in a high state of indignation —E.B. White⟩ ⟨works . . . published as a political ~ —S.E.Morison⟩ **3 :** an instrument in writing by which a person declares his intent as to the disposal of his estate and effects after his death **:** WILL

tes·ta·men·tal \ˌₛₛˈmentᵊl\ *adj* [LL *testamentalis*, fr. L *testamentum* will + *-alis* -al] **:** of or relating to a testament **:** TESTAMENTARY

tes·ta·men·ta·ry \ˌtestəˈmentərē, -n·trē, -ri\ *adj* [ME, fr. LL *testamentarius*, fr. L *testamentum* will + *-arius* -ary] **1 :** of or relating to a will or testament or the administration of a will ⟨letters ~⟩ ⟨~ witnesses⟩ **2 :** bequeathed by will **:** given by or expressed in a testament ⟨~ heirlooms⟩ **3 :** done or appointed by or founded on a testament or will ⟨a ~ donation⟩

testamentary capacity *n* **:** the mental competence necessary for making a will

testamentary guardian *n* **1** *Brit* **:** a person appointed by deed or will by a father to act as guardian of his minor child **:** a guardian by statute **2 :** a person named in a will to serve as guardian **:** STATUTORY GUARDIAN

testamentary succession *n* **:** succession determined in accordance with the provisions of a lawful will and the applicable rules of law

testamentary trust *n* **:** a trust created by the terms of a will — compare LIVING TRUST

testament dative *n, pl* **testaments dative** *Scots law* **:** confirmation by the sheriff of one's right upon giving security to execute a will when not designated executor in the will

tes·ta·men·tum \ˌtestəˈmentəm\ *n, pl* **testamen·ta** \-ntə\ [L] **:** TESTAMENT

tes·ta·mur \teˈstāmə(r)\ *n* -S [L, we are witnesses, 1st pers. pl. pres. indic. of *testari* to be a witness; fr. the opening phrase of the certificate] *Brit* **:** a certificate that an examination held esp. by a university has been passed

¹**tes·tate** \'teˌstā|t, -stə|, *usu* |d+V\ *adj* [ME, fr. L *testatus*, past part. of *testari* to be a witness, make a will] **1 :** having made and left a will ⟨a person dying ~⟩ — opposed to *intestate* **2 :** disposed of in a will ⟨~ property⟩

²**testate** \"\ *n* -S [L *testatus*, past part. of *testari*] **1** *obs* **:** WITNESS, TESTIMONY **2 :** a testate person **:** TESTATOR

³**testate** \"\ *adj* [⁶*test* or *testa* + *-ate*, adj. suffix] **:** having a firm external covering **:** covered with a test or testa

tes·ta·tion \teˈstāshən\ *n* -S [LL *testation-, testatio*, fr. L *testatus* (past part.) + *-ion-, -io* -ion] **1** *obs* **:** AFFIRMATION, TESTAMENT **2 :** the act or power of disposing of property by testament or will

tes·ta·tor \'teˌstād·ə(r), -ātə-, ₛˈₛₛ\ *n* -S [ME *testatour*, fr. AF, fr. LL *testator*, fr. L *testatus* (past part. of *testari* to be a witness, make a will) + *-or* — more at TESTAMENT] **1 :** a person who leaves a will or testament in force at his death **2** *obs* **:** one that testifies **:** WITNESS

tes·ta·trix \teˈstā·triks, 'ₛ,ₛₛ\ *n, pl* **testatri·ces** \teˈstā·trəˌsēz, ˌtestəˈtrī(ˌ)sēz\ [LL, fem. of *testator* — more at -TRIX] **:** a female testator

tes·ta·tum \teˈstād·əm, -ātəm\ *n, pl* **testa·ta** \-ād·ə, -ātə\ [NL, fr. neut. of L *testatus*, past part. of *testari*] **1 :** the portion of the ordinary purchase deed that contains the statement of the consideration, the words incorporating covenants for title, and the operative words **2 :** TESTATUM CAPIAS

testatum ca·pi·as \-ˈkāpēəs\ *or* **testatum capias ad satis·fa·ci·en·dum** \-ˌad,sad·ə,sfāshēˈendəm\ *n* [NL, lit., take the writ (for satisfying)] **:** a supplementary writ sometimes issued by a court of one county to the sheriff of another when an ordinary capias has been returned without action

test–bed \'ₛ,ₛ\ *n* **:** a support often in or on a vehicle (as an airplane or submarine) for an engine while it is being tested

test board *n* **:** a paperboard for shipping containers that must test up to specific requirements (as for resistance to puncture)

test case *n* **1 :** a representative case whose outcome is likely to serve as a precedent for decisions in future or pending cases involving similar points of law **2 :** a proceeding usu. in the form of a suit for injunction brought by agreement or on an understanding of the parties to obtain a decision as to the constitutionality of a statute

¹**test check** *n* **:** an auditing procedure based on selective and systematic sampling

²**test check** *vt* **:** to verify by means of a test check

¹**testcross** \'ₛ,ₛ\ *n* [³*test* + *cross*] **:** a cross between a recessive homozygote and the corresponding dominant to determine whether the latter is heterozygous or homozygous

²**testcross** \"\ *vt* **:** to subject to a testcross

tes·te \'te(ˌ)stē\ *n* -S [L, abl. of *testis* witness — more at TESTAMENT] **1 :** the witnessing or concluding clause of a writ or other precept **2 :** WITNESS — often used to indicate that what immediately follows is named as authority for what precedes

¹**tested** *adj* [fr. past part. of ²*test*] **1 :** subjected to test **:** TRIED, PROVEN ⟨a ~ combat veteran⟩ ⟨time-*tested* principles⟩ **2 :** certified by examination; *esp* **:** pronounced free of disease as a result of testing ⟨tuberculin-*tested* cattle⟩

²**tes·ted** \'te(ˌ)stēd\ *adj* [*teste* + *-ed*] **:** having the teste duly attached — used of a legal precept (as a writ or deed)

test·ee \(ˈ)teˈstē\ *n* -S [¹*test* + *-ee*] **:** one who takes an examination

¹**tes·ter** \'testə(r), 'tēs-\ *n* -S [ME *testere* headpiece, tester, fr. MF *testiere* headpiece, head covering, fr. *teste* head (fr. LL *testa* skull, fr. L, shell) + *-iere* -er — more at TEST (trial)] **1 a :** the frame on which the canopy of a bed rests **b :** the canopy of a bed including the frame and its hangings **2 :** BALDACHIN; *esp* **:** a canopy suspended from the ceiling over an altar or pulpit

bed frame with tester 1a

²**tes·ter** \'testə(r)\ *n* -S [modif. (influenced by *-er*) of MF *testart* teston, fr. *teston* + *-art* -ard — more at TESTON] **:** TESTON c

³**test·er** \'testə(r)\ *n* -S [²*test* + *-er*] **:** one that tests: as **a :** ASSAYER **b :** one whose work is testing the quality and conformance to specifications of products by visual examination, by means of testing instruments, or through laboratory tests **c :** a piece of testing apparatus **d :** one that serves as a control ⟨endosperm strains crossed with . . . ~*s* for all 10 chromosomes —*Amer. Naturalist*⟩ **e :** one who administers an examination

tester bed *n* **:** a four-poster of moderate height with a canopy supported on a frame

testes *pl of* TESTIS

test–fire \'ₛ,ₛ\ *vt* **:** to subject to a firing test ⟨*test-fire* a gun⟩

test–fly \'ₛ,ₛ\ *vt* **:** to subject to a flight test ⟨*test-fly* an experimental plane⟩

test glass *n* **:** a small often footed glass for holding a liquid to be tested

tes·ti·car·di·nes \ˌtestəˈkardᵊnˌēz\ [NL, fr. L *testa* shell + NL *cardines* — more at TEST] *syn of* ARTICULATA

tes·ti·cle \'testəkəl, -tēk-\ *n* -S [ME *testicule*, fr. L *testiculus*, dim. of *testis* — more at TESTIS] **:** a male genital gland usu. with its enclosing membranes **:** TESTIS

tes·tic·u·lar \(ˈ)teˈstikyələ(r)\ *adj* [L *testiculus* + E *-ar*] **1 :** of, relating to, or derived from the testes **2 :** TESTICULATE

tes·tic·u·late \-lə|t, -ˌlā|, *usu* |d+V\ *or* **tes·tic·u·lat·ed** \-ˌlād·əd, -ātəd\ *adj* [*testiculate* fr. NL *testiculatus*, fr. L *testiculus* testicle + *-atus* -ate; *testiculated* fr. NL *testiculatus* + E *-ed*] **1 :** resembling a testis **:** ovate and solid **2 :** having two tubers shaped like testes — used of an orchid

testier *comparative of* TESTY

testiest *superlative of* TESTY

tes·ti·fi·er \'testəˌfī(ə)r, -īə\ *n* -S **:** one that testifies **:** WITNESS; *esp* **:** a religious proselyte

tes·ti·fy \-ˌfī\ *vb* -ED/-ING/-ES [ME *testifien*, fr. L *testificari*, fr. *testis* witness + *-ficare* -fy — more at TESTAMENT] *vi* **1 a :** to make a statement based on personal knowledge or belief **:** bear witness ⟨I can ~ as to the vital influences that reading had upon our thinking —C.R.Woodward⟩ ⟨of such enormous importance was the birth of a child in the imperial family that there must be many witnesses . . . to ~ to having seen the birth —P.I.Wellman⟩ ⟨the Quakers had long been ~*ing* against the abuses —H.S.Canby⟩ **b :** to serve as evidence **:** constitute a proof ⟨renaissance of the trade fair *testifies* to the rapid recovery of European economies —*Modern Industry*⟩ ⟨shattered gateways . . . ~ to the existence of a population at this remote spot —Norman Douglas⟩ ⟨two major works . . . ~ to his industry as well as to his high standards of scholarship —L.P.Kirwan⟩ **2 :** to express a personal conviction ⟨suffered the worst and emerged to ~ without rancor to the dignity of the spirit —Gordon Harrison⟩; *esp* **:** to affirm one's regeneration by the grace of God ⟨hear reformed sinners ~ —Green Peyton⟩ **3 :** to make a solemn declaration under oath for the purpose of establishing a fact (as in a court) **:** give testimony according to the law of legal procedure ⟨a neighbor *testified* against the accused man —B.L.K.Henderson⟩ ⟨called to ~ before a congressional fact-finding committee⟩ ~ *vt* **1 a :** to support the truth of (a statement) **:** bear witness to (a fact) **:** ATTEST ⟨everyone who has ever worked in the editorial sanctum will ~ that her story . . . has the true ring of experience —*Atlantic*⟩ ⟨the college demands a letter ~*ing* that the student is of good moral character —W.A.Lunden⟩ **b :** to serve as evidence of **:** PROVE ⟨thy breath shall ~ thou livest —Shak.⟩ ⟨that it is of no recent date is *testified* by the age of the tree whose roots surrounded it —*Amer. Guide Series: Minn.*⟩ **2** *archaic* **a :** to make known (a personal conviction) **:** AFFIRM, PROFESS ⟨~ their faith therein openly and aloud —P.E.F.W.Smythe⟩ **b :** to give evidence of **:** SHOW ⟨could not better ~ my respect for your sister —Charles Dickens⟩ **3 :** to declare under oath before a tribunal or officially constituted public body **syn** see SWEAR

tes·ti·ly \'testəlē, -li\ *adv* **:** in a testy manner

¹**tes·ti·mo·nial** \ˌtestəˈmōnēəl, -nyəl\ *adj* [ME, fr. LL *testimonialis*, fr. L *testimonium* witness, evidence + *-alis* -al] **1 :** of, relating to, or constituting testimony ⟨a ~ letter from a satisfied customer⟩ **2 :** expressive of appreciation or esteem ⟨~ dinner⟩

²**testimonial** \"\ *n* -S [ME, fr. LL *testimonialis* (of testimony)] **1 :** something that serves as evidence **:** PROOF, TESTIMONY ⟨it is a remarkable ~ to the truth of these statistics that . . . the percentages should agree so closely —G.G.Coulton⟩ ⟨the layout . . . is a ~ to the designers' ingenuity in mastering a difficult site —*Amer. Guide Series: N.Y. City*⟩ **2 a :** a certified statement **:** AFFIDAVIT, WARRANT; *specif* **:** an endorsement of a product or service usu. solicited from a celebrity by the supplier for advertising purposes **b :** a character reference **:** letter of recommendation ⟨selected what seemed to me from the ~*s* to be the two best men —F.W.Crofts⟩ **c :** a public profession of the healing or uplifting effect of religious experience upon the life of an individual ⟨numerous ~*s* were offered during the revival meeting⟩ **3 :** an expression of appreciation **:** token of esteem **:** TRIBUTE ⟨a ~ planned in his honor —*Springfield (Mass.) Daily News*⟩ ⟨as a ~ to his war service, he was . . . made the recipient of a sword of superb workmanship —C.D.Rhodes⟩

tes·ti·mo·nial·ize \-əˌlīz\ *vt* -ED/-ING/-S **:** to honor with a testimonial

testimonial of the great seal : the quarter seal of Scotland

tes·ti·mo·ni·um \ˌtestəˈmōnēəm\ *n, pl* **testimoniums** \-ēəmz\ *or* **testimo·nia** \-ēə\ [L, witness, evidence] **1** *archaic* **:** TESTIMONIAL 2b **2 :** the final or authenticating clause of an instrument that typically begins "In witness whereof" and furnishes such information as when it was signed and before what witnesses

tes·ti·mo·ny \'testəˌmōnē, -ni, *US also & Brit usu* -mən-\ *n* -ES [ME, fr. LL & L; LL *testimonium* Decalogue, tablets of the Decalogue (trans. of Heb *'ēdhūth*, lit., witness, testimony), fr. L, witness, evidence, fr. *testis* witness — more at TESTAMENT] **1 a :** the tablets inscribed with the Mosaic law or the ark containing them ⟨you shall put into the ark the ~ which I shall give you —Exod 25:16 (RSV)⟩ ⟨encamp around the tabernacle of the ~ —Num 1:53 (RSV)⟩ **b :** the word of God as contained in the Scriptures ⟨enriched the book with a number of *testimonies* from the Old Testament —*Interpreter's Bible*⟩ **2 a :** firsthand authentication of a fact **:** EVIDENCE, WITNESS ⟨that he was impressive in bearing was . . . the common ~ of all who met him —W.J.Ghent⟩ ⟨the ~ of the great geologist . . . confirmed the new thesis —R.W.Murray⟩ ⟨eruptions . . . bear vivid ~ to this upward concentration of gas in a magma column —Howel Williams⟩ **b :** something that serves as an outward sign **:** PROOF, SYMBOL ⟨his own unpretentious clarity is . . . ~ to his discipline —Irwin Edman⟩ ⟨the new library, which he hopes will remain a ~ to his brief career as acting president —F.J.Hoffman⟩ **c :** a solemn declaration usu. made orally by a witness under oath in response to interrogation by a lawyer or authorized public official ⟨power to administer oaths and take ~ —*Harvard Law Rev.*⟩ ⟨~ before a grand jury is secret —Brian Gilbert⟩ **3 a :** an open acknowledgement **:** PROFESSION; *specif* **:** TESTIMONIAL 2c ⟨there is no ordained ministry; services consist of prayer, ~, and readings —F.S.Mead⟩ **b** *archaic* **:** an expression of disapproval **:** PROTEST ⟨uplifting her voice in many a ~ against it —Elizabeth C. Gaskell⟩ **4 :** a written attestation **:** CERTIFICATE

testimony meeting *n* **:** EXPERIENCE MEETING ⟨telling in a *testimony meeting* about her husband's conversion —*Sunday School Times*⟩

test indicator *n* **:** a sensitive gauge (as a dial gauge) combined with an adjustable mount for testing the accuracy of machined work

tes·ti·ness \'testēnəs, -tin-\ *n* -ES **:** the quality or state of being testy

¹**testing** *n* -S [fr. gerund of ²*test*] **:** an act or process of subjecting to test **:** EXAMINATION, TRIAL ⟨the ~ of 50 million children . . . for tuberculosis —Paul Harris⟩ ⟨laboratories concerned . . . with commercial ~ —*Science*⟩

²**testing** *adj* [fr. pres. part. of ²*test*] **1 :** of, relating to, or used for demonstration or experiment ⟨~ procedure⟩ ⟨~ ground⟩ **2 :** requiring maximum effort or ability ⟨confronted with a most difficult and ~ problem —Ernest Bevin⟩ ⟨felt out of practice for severe rock climbing and wanted something less ~ —Tom Weir⟩ — **test·ing·ly** *adv*

testing clause *n*, *Scots law* **:** TESTIMONIUM 2

tes·tis \'testəs\ *n, pl* **tes·tes** \-eˌstēz\ [L, witness, testis; perh. fr. its being evidence of maleness — more at TESTAMENT] **1 :** a male reproductive gland that usu. consists largely of convoluted tubules from the epithelium of which spermatozoa develop, that corresponds to the ovary of the female and in craniate vertebrates is usu. paired and developed from the genital ridges of the embryo, and that in most mammals descends into the scrotum before the attainment of sexual maturity and in many cases before birth **2 :** either of the inferior corpora quadrigemina

test lamp *n* **:** a portable lamp in socket with free leads to connect to various points of a faulty circuit to locate a defect (as a blown fuse)

test lead *n* **:** lead free from silver and often finely granulated for use in a metallurgical process (as cupellation)

test match *n* **1 :** any of a series of championship cricket matches played between teams representing Australia and England — compare ³ASH 6 **2 :** a championship game or series (as of cricket or rugby) played between teams representing different countries

test meal *n* **:** a meal of definite composition and quantity given to excite gastric secretion and so furnish material to withdraw for examination

tes·to \'te(ˌ)stō\ *n* -S [It, lit., text, fr. L *textus* — more at TEXT] **1 :** the libretto of a musical composition **2 :** a narrator or soloist in a musical performance

test oath *n* **:** an oath required of an applicant or candidate for public employment or political office to determine his fitness

tes·ton \'testən, -ˌstän\ *or* **tes·toon** \(ˈ)teˈstün\ *n* -S [MF *teston*, fr. OIt *testone*, aug. of *testa* head, fr. LL, skull; fr. the fact that the obverse type on the testone was a head — more at TESTER] **:** any of several old European coins: as **a :** TESTONE 1 **b :** a French silver coin of the 16th century worth between 10 and 14½ sous **c :** a shilling of Henry VII of England decreasing in value to ninepence, then to sixpence in Shakespeare's time **d :** TOSTÃO

tes·to·ne \teˈstō(ˌ)nā\ *n* -S [OIt] **1 :** an Italian silver coin of the 15th and 16th centuries **2 :** TOSTÃO

tes·tos·ter·one \teˈstästəˌrōn\ *n* -S [*testis* + *-o-* + *sterol* + *-one*] **:** an androgenic hormone that is a crystalline hydroxy steroid ketone $C_{19}H_{28}O_2$, is obtained esp. from the testes of bulls or synthetically (as from cholesterol or diosgenin), and is used in medicine chiefly in the form of esters (as the propionate)

test paper *n* **1 :** paper (as litmus paper) cut usu. in strips and saturated with an indicator or other reagent that changes color in testing for various substances **2 :** a writing admitted as a standard for comparison of handwriting

test pattern *n* **:** a fixed picture broadcast by a television station to assist viewers in adjusting their receivers

test pilot *n* **:** a pilot who specializes in putting new or experimental airplanes through maneuvers designed to test them (as for strength or controllability) by producing strains in excess of normal

test pit *n* **:** a shallow shaft sunk in ore or overburden to determine the existence, grade, or extent of a mineral deposit

test record *n* **:** a phonograph record containing recordings of various tones of accurately controlled frequency and intensity and used for testing phonographs and pickups

tests *pl of* TEST, *pres 3d sing of* TEST

test solution *n* **:** a solution used in chemical testing

test tube *n* **:** a tube for simple tests that is usu. a plain tube of thin glass closed at one end but sometimes has a foot, bulb, graduated scale, or other modification

test-tube \(ˈ)=¦=\ *adj* [*test tube*] **1 :** developed or produced in or as if in a test tube ⟨*test-tube* fabrics⟩ **2 :** produced by artificial insemination ⟨a *test-tube* calf⟩ ⟨testimony . . . that there were about 20,000 *test-tube* babies in the United States —Morris Ploscowe⟩

test type *n* **:** any of the printed letters or characters on an eye chart ⟨a typeface carefully chosen for use as *test type*⟩

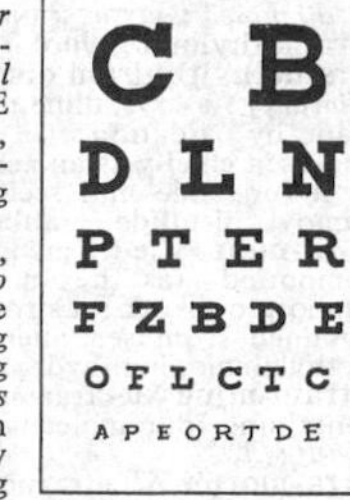

test type

tes·tu·di·nal \(ˈ)te¦st(y)üdᵊnəl\ *or* **tes·tu·di·nar·i·ous** \(¦)te-¦st(y)üdᵊn¦a(a)rēəs\ *adj* [*testudinal* fr. L *testudin-, testudo* tortoise + E *-al; testudinarious* fr. L *testudin-, testudo* + E *-arious* (as in *arbitrarious*)] **:** of, relating to, or resembling a tortoise or tortoise shell

tes·tu·di·nar·ia \(,)=,==ˈa(a)rēə\ *n, cap* [NL, fr. L *testudin-, testudo* tortoise + NL *-aria;* fr. the surface of the rootstock often becoming cracked into pieces resembling tortoise shells] *in some classifications* **:** a small genus of southern African desert vines that is characterized by huge edible rootstocks growing partly above ground and by seeds winged only at the apex and that is usu. included in the genus *Dioscorea*

tes·tu·di·na·ta \(,)=,==ˈäd·ə, -ˈād·ə\ *n pl, cap* [NL, fr. *Testudin-, Testudo* + *-ata*] **:** an order or other division of Reptilia comprising the turtles and tortoises and being distinguished by a trunk more or less enclosed in a shell of bony dermal plates that is usu. covered externally with horny shields and in nearly all cases firmly united with some of the vertebrae, ribs, and sternum, and by jaws that are toothless and sheathed

¹**tes·tu·di·nate** \(ˈ)=¦=ət, -ˌāt\ *adj* [NL *Testudinata*] **:** of or relating to the Testudinata

²**testudinate** \"\ *n* -s **:** a reptile of the order Testudinata

tes·tu·di·nes \teˈst(y)üdᵊn,ēz\ [NL, pl. of *Testudin-, Testudo*] *syn of* TESTUDINATA

tes·tu·din·i·dae \ˌtest(y)üˈdinə,dē\ *n pl, cap* [NL, fr. *Testudin-, Testudo,* type genus + *-idae*] **:** a family of turtles comprising carnivorous freshwater and herbivorous terrestrial forms that usu. have a strong thick convex carapace, broad plastron, and club-shaped feet in which the toes are firmly bound together so that the claws alone are evident — compare EUROPEAN TORTOISE, PAINTED TURTLE

tes·tu·do \teˈstü(,)dō\ *n* [NL, fr. L, tortoise, tortoise shell, vault; akin to L *testa* shell — more at TEST (trial)] **1** *cap* **:** a genus (the type of the family Testudinidae) of turtles comprising the typical land tortoises but formerly including all turtles — compare GIANT TORTOISE **2** -s **:** a protective screen (as a cover of overlapping shields held overhead or a shed wheeled up to a wall) used by an attacking force in ancient Rome **3** -s **:** an ancient Greek lyre believed to have been made of a tortoise shell **4** -s **:** an arched ceiling or vault esp. when surbased

tes·ty \ˈtestē, -ti\ *adj* -ER/-EST [ME *testif,* fr. AF, heady, headstrong, fr. OF *teste* head (fr. LL *testa* skull) + *-if* -ive — more at TESTER] **1 :** having a quick temper **:** easily annoyed **:** IRRITABLE, WASPISH ⟨a ~ man, given to incalculable fits of temper —Adrienne Koch⟩ ⟨became ~ when a long-winded doctor of divinity overprayed the time allotted to him on a commencement program —A.W.Long⟩ **2 :** marked by or indicative of impatience or ill humor **:** CAUSTIC, EXASPERATED ⟨a somewhat ~ emphasis on contemporary barbarians —H. A.Finch⟩ ⟨made ~ noises with her tongue —Nigel Dennis⟩ **syn** see IRASCIBLE

te·su·que \təˈsükē\ *n, pl* **tesuque** *or* **tesuques** *usu cap* **1 :** a Tanoan people occupying a pueblo in New Mexico **2 :** a member of the Tesuque people

tet *var of* TETH

tetan- *or* **tetano-** *comb form* [NL, fr. Gk, fr. *tetanos* — more at TETANUS] **:** tetanus ⟨*tetano*genic⟩ ⟨*tetani*form⟩

tet·a·nal \ˈtetᵊnəl *sometimes* -tnəl\ *adj* [*tetan-* + *-al*] **:** relating to or derived from tetanus ⟨~ antitoxin⟩

te·tan·ic \teˈtanik\ *adj* [NL *tetanicus,* fr. Gk *tetanikos* suffering from tetanus, fr. *tetanos* tetanus + *-ikos* -ic] **1 :** of or relating to tetanus or tetany ⟨a ~ condition⟩ **:** constituting tetanus or tetany ⟨~ contraction⟩ **2 :** producing or tending to produce tetanus or tetany ⟨~ toxin⟩ — **te·tan·i·cal·ly** \-nək(ə)lē\ *adv*

te·tan·i·form \-nə,fȯrm\ *adj* [ISV *tetan-* + *-iform;* orig. formed as F *tétaniforme*] **:** resembling tetanus or tetany

tet·a·ni·za·tion \ˌtetᵊnəˈzāshən, -ᵊn,īˈz-\ *n* -s [ISV *tetanize* + *-ation*] **:** the induction of muscular tetanus; *also* **:** tetanized condition of muscle

tet·a·nize \ˈtetᵊn,īz\ *vt* -ED/-ING/-s [ISV *tetan-* + *-ize*] **:** to induce tetanus in ⟨~ a muscle⟩

tet·a·no·gen·ic \ˌtetᵊnō¦jenik\ *adj* [*tetan-* + *-genic*] **:** producing tetanus

tet·a·noid \ˈtetᵊn,ȯid\ *adj* [ISV *tetan-* + *-oid*] **:** resembling tetanus or tetany ⟨~ spasms⟩

tet·a·no·lysin \¦tetᵊnō+\ *n* [ISV *tetan-* + *lysin*] **:** a hemolytic toxin produced by the tetanus bacillus

tet·a·no·spas·min \ˌ===ˈspazmən\ *n* -s [ISV *tetan-* + *spasm* + *-in*] **:** TETANUS TOXIN

tet·a·nus \ˈtetᵊnəs *sometimes* -tnəs\ *n* -ES [ME, fr. L, fr. Gk *tetanos,* fr. *tetanos* rigid, stretched, fr. *teinein* to stretch — more at THIN] **1 a :** an acute infectious disease characterized by tonic spasm of voluntary muscles and esp. of the muscles of the jaw and caused by the specific toxin produced by the tetanus bacillus which is usu. introduced through a wound — see LOCKJAW **b** *or* **tetanus bacillus :** the bacterium (*Clostridium tetani*) that causes tetanus **2 :** prolonged contraction of a muscle resulting from a series of motor impulses following one another too rapidly to permit intervening relaxation of the muscle — compare CONTRACTURE

tetanus toxin *or* **tetanal toxin** *n* **:** a crystalline unstable neurotoxin produced by the tetanus bacillus and held to be the cause of the tetanic convulsions of tetanus — called also *tetanospasmin*

tet·a·ny \ˈtet(ᵊ)nē, -ni\ *n* -ES [ISV *tetan-* + *-y;* prob. orig. formed as F *tétanie*] **:** a condition of physiologic mineral imbalance (as abnormal calcium metabolism) characterized by intermittent tonic spasm of the voluntary muscles and associated with deficiencies of parathyroid secretion or other disturbances

tetart- *or* **tetarto-** *comb form* [ISV, fr. Gk, fr. *tetartos;* akin to Gk *tettares, tessares* four — more at FOUR] **:** one fourth ⟨*tetarto*hedral⟩

te·tar·te·mo·ri·on \təˌtärd·əˈmōrē,än, -ēən\ *also* **tar·te·mo·ri·on** \ˌtärd·əˈ-\ *n* -s [*tetartemorion* fr. Gk *tetartēmorion,* fr. *tetartē* one fourth (fr. fem. of *tetartos*) + *morion* part, portion, dim. of *moros* part (akin to Gk *meros* part); *tartemorion* fr. Gk *tartēmorion,* short for *tetartēmorion* — more at MERIT] **:** a small coin struck in Athens and several small city-states of the Greeks **:** a quarter obol

te·tar·to·cone \təˈtärd·ə,kōn\ *also* **tet·ar·cone** \ˈted·ə(r)-,kōn\ *n* [*tetartocone* fr. *tetart-* + *cone; tetarcone* contr. of *tetartocone*] **:** the posterior medial cusp of an upper molar tooth

te·tar·to·co·nid \təˌtärd·əˈkōnəd\ *also* **tet·ar·co·nid** \ˌted·ə(r)ˈkōnəd\ *n* [*tetartocone, tetarcone* + *-id*] **:** the posterior medial cusp of a lower molar tooth

te·tar·to·he·dral \tə¦tärd·ō¦hēdrəl\ *adj* [*tetart-* + *-hedral*] **1** *of a crystal* **:** having one fourth the number of planes required by complete symmetry — compare HOLOHEDRAL **2 :** having the symmetry appropriate to a tetartohedral form — **te·tar·to·he·dral·ly** \-drəlē, -li\ *adv*

te·tar·to·he·drism \-ˈhē,drizəm\ *n* -s [*tetartohedral* + *-ism*] **:** the quality of crystallizing tetartohedrally

te·tar·to·he·dron \-ˌdrən\ *n, pl* **tetartohe·drons** \-drənz\ *or* **tetartohe·dra** \-drə\ [NL, fr. *tetart-* + *-hedron*] **:** a tetartohedral form

te·tar·toid \təˈtär,tȯid\ *n* -s [*tetart-* + *-oid*] **:** a 12-faced solid belonging to the tetartohedral group of the isometric system and having faces corresponding to one fourth of those of the hexoctahedron

te·tar·toi·dal \¦te,tär¦tȯidᵊl, tə¦tä-\ *adj, of a crystal* **:** having symmetry that produces a tetartoid **:** having three inverse tetrad axes and four triad axes of symmetry

tetched *var of* TECHED

tetch·i·ly \ˈtechəlē, -li\ *adv* **:** in a tetchy manner

tetch·i·ness *also* **tech·i·ness** \-chēnəs, -chin-\ *n* -ES **:** the quality or state of being tetchy

tetchy *or* **techy** \ˈtechē, -chi\ *adj* -ER/-EST [perh. fr. obs. E *tetch* habit, quality, bad habit (fr. ME *tecche, tache,* fr. MF *teche, tache* stain, spot, fr. OF) + E *-y* (adj. suffix) — more at TACHE] **:** irritably or peevishly sensitive **:** TOUCHY ⟨the ~ manner of two women living in the same house —Elizabeth Taylor⟩ ⟨a ~ traveler at best —*New Yorker*⟩ ⟨a ~ situation⟩ ⟨a ~ question⟩ **syn** see IRASCIBLE

tête \ˈtāt\ *n* -s [F, head, fr. MF *teste* — more at TESTER (canopy)] **:** a high elaborately ornamented style of woman's hairdress or wig worn esp. in the latter half of the 18th century

¹**tête-à-tête** \¦täd·ə¦tāt, ¦tāt·ə- (+V *usu* -ə¦täd·), ÷-ə¦tā *sometimes* ¦tēd·ə¦tēt, ¦tēt·ə- (+V *usu* -ə¦tēd·)\ *n, pl* **tête-à-têtes** \-āts,-āz,-ēts\ *also* **têtes-à-têtes** \"\ [F, lit., head to head] **1 :** a private conversation or familiar interview between two persons without the presence of a third person **2 :** a short sofa or other piece of furniture intended to seat two persons esp. so that they face each other **:** CONVERSATION CHAIR 2

²**tête-à-tête** \"\ *adv* [F] **:** FACE-TO-FACE, PRIVATELY, FAMILIARLY

³**tête-à-tête** \"\ *adj* **:** being face-to-face ⟨find yourself *tête-à-tête* with one member of the assembly —Agnes M. Miall⟩ **:** PRIVATE ⟨a *tête-à-tête* home dinner —*New Yorker*⟩

tête-bêche \(ˈ)tāt¦bāsh\ *adj* [F, n., pair of inverted stamps, fr. *tête* head + *bêche,* short for obs. F *bechevet* double bedhead, fr. F *bes-* (fr. L *bis-*) + *chevet* bedhead, chevet — more at CHEVET] **:** of or relating to a pair of stamps inverted in relation to one another either as the result of an error in printing or intentionally so printed ⟨a set of bicolor *tête-bêche* triangular stamps —A.H.Murphey⟩

teth *also* **tet** \ˈtāt, -āth, -ās, -et, -eth, -es\ *n* -s [Heb *ṭēth*] **1 :** the 9th letter of the Hebrew alphabet — symbol ט; see ALPHABET table **2 :** the letter of the Phoenician or of any of various other Semitic alphabets corresponding to Hebrew teth

¹**teth·er** \ˈteth̲ə(r)\ *n* -s [ME *tethir, tedir,* prob. of Scand origin; akin to ON *tjōthr* tether, Sw *tjuder;* akin to MD *tuder* tether, OHG *zeotar* pole of a wagon and perh. to OHG *zogōn* to pull — more at TOW] **1 :** something (as a rope or chain) by which an animal is fastened so that it can range or feed only within the radius allowed **2 :** something (as a rope or cable) used in a way suggesting a tether **3 :** the limit of one's strength or resources **:** SCOPE ⟨poverty-stricken farmer is at his last ~ —Leslie Rees⟩ — used esp. in the phrase *the end of one's tether*

²**tether** \"\ *vt* **tethered; tethered; tethering** \-th̲(ə)riŋ\ **tethers** [ME *tediren,* fr. *tethir, tedir* tether] **1 a :** to fasten or restrain (an animal) with a rope or chain ⟨~ a cow to graze⟩ ⟨grove was full of ~*ed* teams —William Faulkner⟩ **b :** to fasten so as to allow a short radius of movement ⟨~ a boat⟩ ⟨toddlers, ~*ed* for safety —*Nat'l Geographic*⟩ ⟨balloon was ~*ed* by a string to the doorknob —Joseph Mitchell⟩ ⟨threads should be firmly ~*ed* at one end —Peggy Tearle⟩ **2 :** to limit the effectiveness or activity of **:** BIND ⟨~ one's plans to one's resources⟩

tetherball \ˈ==,=\ *n* **:** a game which is played by two contestants with rackets and a ball suspended by a string from an upright pole and in which the object of each contestant is to wrap the string around the pole by striking the ball in a direction opposite to the other

tether-devil \¦==¦==\ *n* **:** a bittersweet (*Solanum dulcamara*)

¹**teth·y·id** \ˈtethēəd\ *adj* [NL *Tethyidae*] **:** of or relating to the Tethyidae

²**tethyid** \"\ *n* -s **:** an ascidian or a mollusk of the family Tethyidae

te·thy·i·dae \təˈthīə,dē\ *n pl, cap* [NL; in sense 1, fr. *Tethyum,* type genus + *-idae;* in sense 2, fr. *Tethys,* type genus + *-idae*] **1 :** a family of simple ascidians with tough leathery often brightly colored tests, large branchial sacs, and several lateral longitudinal folds — see TETHYUM **2 :** a family of mollusks (suborder Tectibranchia) including the sea hares — see TETHYS

te·thys \ˈtēthəs\ *n, cap* [NL, fr. L *Tethys,* wife of Oceanus and mother of sea nymphs and deities, fr. Gk *Tēthys*] **:** a genus (the type of the family Tethyidae) of large often conspicuously colored sluglike marine mollusks having a pair of lateral swimming lobes on the foot and four tentacles, occurring chiefly in the warmer seas, and including forms that emit a purple fluid when disturbed — see SEA HARE

te·thy·um \ˈtēthēəm\ *n, cap* [NL, fr. Gk *tēthyon* sea squirt, fr. *Tēthys,* wife of Oceanus] **:** a genus (the type of the family Tethyidae) of large muscular simple ascidians sometimes used for food

te·ti·o·thal·ein sodium \tə¦tīō¦thalēən-, -ăl-, -,lēn-\ *n* [*tetiothalein* fr. *tetraiodophenolphthalein,* fr. *tetra-* + *-iod-* + *phenol* + *phthalein*] **:** the disodium salt of iodophthalein

te·ton \ˈtē,tän, -tᵊn\ *n, pl* **teton** *or* **tetons** *usu cap* **1 a :** a western division of the Dakota peoples — see BRULÉ, MINICONJOU, OGLALA, SIHASAPA, TWO KETTLE **b :** a member of such division **2 :** a dialect of Dakota

tet·ra \ˈte·trə\ *n* -s [short for NL *Tetragonopterus,* genus of tetras in former classifications, fr. LL *tetragonum* square + NL *-pterus* — more at TETRAGONAL] **:** any of numerous small brightly colored So. American characin fishes often bred in the tropical aquarium — see NEON TETRA

tetra- *or* **tetr-** *comb form* [ME, fr. LL, fr. L, fr. Gk; akin to Gk *tettares, tessares* four — more at FOUR] **1 :** four **:** having four **:** having four parts ⟨*tetra*carpellary⟩ ⟨*tetra*partite⟩ ⟨*tetra*tomic⟩ **2 :** containing four atoms, radicals, or groups (of a specified kind) ⟨*tetra*boric⟩ ⟨*tetr*acid⟩

tet·ra·acetate \¦te·trə+\ *n* [*tetra-* + *acetate*] **:** an acetate containing four acetate groups

tetraacid *var of* TETRACID

tet·ra·basic \¦te·trə+\ *adj* [ISV *tetra-* + *basic*] **1 :** having four hydrogen atoms capable of replacement by basic atoms or radicals — used of acids (as hypophosphoric acid) **2 :** containing four atoms of a univalent metal or their equivalent — used of salts **3 :** having four basic hydroxyl groups **:** able to react with four molecules of a monoacid — used of bases and basic salts — **tet·ra·basicity** \"+\ *n* -ES

tet·ra·borate \"+\ *n* [ISV *tetrabor-* (in *tetraboric acid*) + *-ate*] **:** a salt or ester of tetraboric acid

tet·ra·boric acid \"+-\ *n* [ISV *tetra-* + *boric*] **:** a dibasic acid $H_2B_4O_7$ containing four atoms of boron in the molecule, formed by heating ordinary boric acid, and known esp. in the form of salts (as borax)

tet·ra·brach \ˈte·trə,brak\ *n* -s [Gk *tetrabrachys,* fr. *tetra-* + *brachys* short — more at BRIEF] **:** a word or foot of four short syllables in classical prosody

¹**tet·ra·branch** \ˈte·trə,braŋk, -aiŋk\ *adj* [NL *Tetrabranchia*] **:** of or relating to the Tetrabranchia

²**tetrabranch** \"\ *n* -s **:** a tetrabranch mollusk or fossil **:** NAUTILOID

tet·ra·bran·chia \ˌ==ˈbraŋkēə, -aiŋ-\ *n pl, cap* [NL, fr. *tetra-* + *-branchia*] **:** a subclass or order of Cephalopoda including among existing forms only the genus *Nautilus,* differing from the remaining existing cephalopods in having four gills, four auricles to the heart, and a large chambered external shell, and including many extinct forms — see AMMONOIDEA, NAUTILOIDEA; compare DIBRANCHIA

tet·ra·branchiata \"+\ [NL, fr. *tetra-* + *branchiata*] *syn of* TETRABRANCHIA

tet·ra·branchiate \¦==+\ *adj or n* [NL *Tetrabranchiata*] **:** TETRABRANCH

tetrabrom- *or* **tetrabromo-** *comb form* [ISV *tetra-* + *brom-*] **:** containing four atoms of bromine — in names of chemical compounds ⟨*tetrabromo*ethylene⟩; compare BROM-

tet·ra·bromide \¦te·trə+\ *n* [*tetrabrom-* + *-ide*] **:** a bromide containing four atoms of bromine

tet·ra·bro·mo \¦te·trə¦brō(,)mō\ *adj* [*tetrabrom-*] **:** containing four atoms of bromine

tet·ra·bro·mo·ethane \¦==¦=(,)=+\ *n* [ISV *tetrabromo-* + *ethane*] **:** either of two isomeric heavy liquid compounds $C_2H_2Br_4$; *esp* **:** the heavy yellowish liquid symmetrical isomer $CHBr_2CHBr_2$ used chiefly in separating minerals and as a solvent

tet·ra·bro·mo·phenolphthalein \"+\ *n* [*tetrabrom-* + *phenolphthalein*] **:** a dye $C_{20}H_{10}Br_4O_4$ used in the form of its disodium salt in X-ray examination esp. of the gall bladder

tet·ra·caine \ˈte·trə,kān\ *n* -s [*tetra-* + *procaine*] **:** a crystalline basic ester $C_{15}H_{24}N_2O_2$ closely related chemically to procaine and used chiefly in the form of its hydrochloride as a local anesthetic

tet·ra·carbonyl \¦te·trə+\ *n* [*tetra-* + *carbonyl*] **:** a compound containing four carbonyl groups combined with a metal

tet·ra·carboxylic \"+\ *adj* [*tetra-* + *carboxylic*] **:** containing four carboxyl groups in the molecule

tet·ra·cene \ˈte·trə,sēn\ *n* -s [alter. of *tetrazene*] **:** a yellow solid compound $(H_2N_2C)NHNHN{=}N(CN_2H_2)NHNO$ made by reaction of amino-guanidine and nitrous acid and used as an explosive in priming compositions for cartridges and in combination with lead azide to reduce the flash point of the latter — called also *tetrazene*

te·trac·er·us \təˈtrasərəs\ *n, cap* [NL, fr. *tetra-* + *-cerus*] **:** a genus of Asiatic ruminant mammals consisting of the four-horned antelope of India

tetrachlor- *or* **tetrachloro-** *comb form* [ISV *tetra-* + *chlor-*] **:** containing four atoms of chlorine — in names of chemical compounds; compare CHLOR- ⟨*tetrachloro*phthalic anhydride⟩

tet·ra·chloride \¦te·trə+\ *n* [*tetrachlor-* + *-ide*] **:** a chloride (as carbon tetrachloride) containing four atoms of chlorine

tet·ra·chlo·ro \¦te·trə¦klōr(,)ō, -ō(,)rō\ *adj* [*tetrachlor-*] **:** containing four atoms of chlorine

tet·ra·chlo·ro·ethane \"+ *also* **tet·ra·chlor·ethane** \¦==-,klōr+\ *n* [ISV *tetrachlor-* + *ethane*] **:** either of two isomeric heavy liquid compounds $C_2H_2Cl_4$; *esp* **:** the symmetrical isomer $CHCl_2CHCl_2$ that forms toxic vapors with an odor similar to that of chloroform, that is made from acetylene and chlorine, and that is used chiefly as a nonflammable solvent of medium volatility and in making trichloroethylene and tetrachloroethylene

tet·ra·chlo·ro·ethylene \¦te·trə¦klōr(,)ō, -ō(,)rō+\ *n* [ISV *tetrachlor-* + *ethylene*] **:** a heavy mobile nonflammable liquid compound $CCl_2{=}CCl_2$ made in various ways (as by treating penta-chloro-ethane with lime or by heating carbon tetrachloride) and used chiefly in dry cleaning and dry-cleaning soaps, in degreasing metals, as a solvent for rubber, tar, and other organic materials, and as an anthelmintic — called also *perchloroethylene*

tet·ra·chlo·ro·methane \"+\ *n* [ISV *tetrachlor-* + *methane*] **:** CARBON TETRACHLORIDE

tet·ra·chord \ˈte·trə,kȯrd, -ō(ə)d\ *n* [Gk *tetrachordon* unit of four tones, fr. neut. of *tetrachordos* four-stringed, fr. *tetra-* + *-chordos* stringed (fr. *chordē* string) — more at YARN] **1 :** a musical instrument with four strings **2 :** the basic unit of analysis in ancient Greek music consisting of a diatonic or disjunct series of four notes or tones with an interval of a perfect fourth between the first and last and distinguished by the relative position of the half step or steps or quarter tone or tones in the series **3 :** the musical interval of a perfect fourth

tet·ra·cho·ric \¦te·trə¦kōrik\ *adj* [*tetra-* + *chori-* + *-ic;* fr. the correlation involving a fourfold table] **:** of, relating to, or being a method of statistical correlation between variables that do not admit of exact measurement

tet·ra·chot·o·mous \ˌ==ˈkäd·əməs\ *adj* [Gk *tetracha* in four parts (fr. *tetra-* + *-cha,* as in *dicha* in two) + E *-tomous* (as in *dichotomous*) — more at DICH-] **:** regularly dividing by fours **:** having a quadruple arrangement ⟨~ peduncles⟩

tet·ra·chromatic \"+\ *adj* [*tetra-* + *chromatic*] **1 :** having four colors **2 :** dependent upon or sensitive to four primary colors

te·trach·ro·nous \təˈtrakrənəs\ *adj* [Gk *tetrachronos,* fr. *tetra-* + *-chronos* -chronous] **:** TETRASEMIC

¹**te·trac·id** \təˈtrasəd\ *also* **tet·ra·acid** \¦te·trə+\ *adj* [*tetra-* + *acid* (adj.)] **1 :** able to react with four molecules of a monobasic acid or two of a dibasic acid to form a salt or ester — used esp. of bases **2** [²*tetracid*] **:** containing four hydrogen atoms replaceable by basic atoms or radicals — used esp. of acid salts

²**tetracid** \"\ *also* **tetraacid** \"\ *n* [*tetra-* + *acid* (n.)] **:** an acid having four acid hydrogen atoms

¹**tet·ra·coc·cus** \ˌte·trəˈkäkəs\ *n* [NL, fr. *tetra-* + *-coccus*] **:** a micrococcus occurring in square groups of four

²**tetracoccus** \"\ [NL] *syn of* GAFFKYA

³**tetracoccus** \"\ [NL] *syn of* MICROCOCCUS

tet·ra·co·lon \ˌte·trəˈkōlən, -ˌlän\ *n* [L, fr. Gk *tetrakōlon,* neut. of *tetrakōlos* of four members, of four limbs, fr. *tetra-* + *-kōlos* limbed (fr. *kōlon* limb) — more at CALK] **:** a period of four cola in classical prosody

tet·ra·cor·al \ˌ==ˈkȯrəl, -kär-\ *n* [NL *Tetracoralla*] **:** one of the Tetracoralla

tet·ra·co·ral·la \ˌ==kəˈralə\ *n pl, cap* [NL, fr. *tetra-* + L *coralla*] *in some classifications* **:** a subclass or other group of Paleozoic corals in which the septa when present are usu. in multiples of four and of which many are solitary and cornucopia-shaped and sometimes attain large size

tet·ra·coralline \¦==+\ *adj* [NL *Tetracoralla* + E *-ine*] **:** of or relating to the Tetracoralla

tet·ra·co·sane \ˈte·trəkə,sān\ *n* -s [*tetra-* + *eicosane*] **:** a solid paraffin hydrocarbon $C_{24}H_{50}$; *esp* **:** the normal hydrocarbon $CH_3(CH_2)_{22}CH_3$ obtained from coal tar

tet·ra·co·sa·no·ic acid \¦==¦kōsə¦nōik-\ *n* [*tetracosanoic* fr. *tetracosane* + *-oic*] **:** LIGNOCERIC ACID

tet·ra·covalent \¦==+\ *adj* [*tetra-* + *covalent*] **:** sharing four covalent bonds with other atoms or characterized by such sharing ⟨~ nitrogen⟩

¹**tet·ract** \ˈte,trakt\ *adj* [*tetra-* + *-act*] *of a sponge spicule* **:** having four rays

²**tetract** \"\ *n* -s **:** a 4-rayed sponge spicule

te·trac·tine \təˈtrak,tin, -ˌtən\ *n* -s [*tetra* + *-actine*] **:** TETRACT

¹**te·trac·ti·nel·lid** \tə¦traktə¦neləd\ *also* **te·trac·ti·nel·li·dan** \-lədən\ *adj* [*tetractinellid* fr. NL *Tetractinellida; tetractinellidan* fr. NL *Tetractinellida* + E *-an*] **:** of or relating to the Tetractinellida

²**tetractinellid** \"\ *n* -s **:** a sponge of the subclass Tetractinellida

te·trac·ti·nel·li·da \ˌ=,==ˈnelədə\ *n pl, cap* [NL, fr. *Tetractina,* a division of sponges in some classifications (fr. *tetra-* + *-actina* -actine) + *-ella* + *-ida*] *in some classifications* **:** a subclass or other division of Demospongiae comprising sponges with siliceous 4-rayed spicules or sometimes with desmas or without spicules

te·trac·ti·nel·line \ˌ=¦==¦ne,līn, -ˌlən\ *adj* [NL *Tetractinellida* + E *-ine*] **:** TETRACTINELLID

tet·ra·cyanoauric acid \¦te·trə+-\ *n* [*tetra-* + *cyanoauric*] **:** CYANOAURIC ACID

tet·ra·cyclic \¦==+\ *adj* [ISV *tetra-* + *cyclic*] **1** *of a flower* **:** having four whorls of floral organs **2 :** containing four usu. fused rings in the molecular structure

tet·ra·cy·cline \ˌte·trəˈsī,klēn, -ˌklən\ *n* -s [ISV *tetracyclic* + *-ine*] **1 :** a yellow crystalline broad-spectrum antibiotic $C_{22}H_{24}N_2O_8$ derived from an octa-hydro-naphthacene, produced by a soil actinomycete (*Streptomyces viridifaciens*), or prepared from chlortetracycline by catalytic reduction, and administered usu. in the form of its hydrochloride **2 :** any of various derivatives of tetracycline (as chlortetracycline or oxytetracycline)

¹**tet·rad** \ˈte,trad\ *n* -s [Gk *tetrad-, tetras* group of four, four; akin to Gk *tettares, tessares* four — more at FOUR] **1 :** a group or arrangement of four **:** something composed of four parts **:** QUATERNION: as **a :** a tetravalent element, atom, or radical **b :** a group of four cells arranged usu. in the form of a tetrahedron and produced by the successive divisions of a mother cell — compare SPORE MOTHER CELL **c :** an arrangement of chromosomes by fours in the first meiotic prophase due to precocious longitudinal splitting of paired homologous chromosomes **2 :** TETRALOGY 3

²**tetrad** \"\ *adj* **:** FOURFOLD — used esp. of an axis of symmetry ⟨a ~ axis requires that every aspect of the crystal be repeated at 90 degree intervals during rotation about the axis⟩

¹**tet·ra·dactyl** \¦te·trə+\ *adj* [Gk *tetradaktylos*] **:** TETRADACTYLOUS — **tet·ra·dac·tyl·i·ty** \¦==,dakˈtiləd·ē\ *n* -ES — **tet·ra·dactyly** \¦==+\ *n* -ES

²**tetradactyl** \"\ *n* -s **:** a tetradactylous animal

tet·ra·dac·ty·lous \¦==ˈdaktələs\ *adj* [Gk *tetradaktylos,* fr. *tetra-* + *daktylos* finger, toe] **:** having four digits ⟨a ~ animal⟩

tet·ra·decane \"+\ *n* [ISV *tetra-* + *decane*] : a paraffin hydrocarbon $C_{14}H_{30}$; *esp* : the normal liquid hydrocarbon $CH_3(CH_2)_{12}CH_3$ that is a liquid of high boiling point and freezes at 5°C

tet·ra·decanoic acid \"+-\ *n* [*tetradecane* + *-oic*] : MYRISTIC ACID

tet·ra·de·cap·o·da \ˌ⁼⁼dəˈkapədə\ [NL, fr. *tetra-* + *deca-* + *-poda*] *syn of* ARTHROSTRACA

tet·ra·decyl \ˈ⁼⁼+\ *n* [ISV *tetra-* + *decyl*] : an alkyl radical $C_{14}H_{29}$ derived from a tetradecane; *esp* : the normal radical $CH_3(CH_2)_{12}CH_2$—

tetradecyl alcohol *n* : a higher aliphatic alcohol $C_{14}H_{29}OH$; *esp* : the normal waxy alcohol $CH_3(CH_2)_{12}CH_2OH$ obtained from spermaceti or made by hydrogenation of myristic acid or one of its esters

te·trad·ic \teˈtradik\ *adj* [Gk *tetradikos*, fr. *tetrad-*, *tetras* tetrad, four + *-ikos* -ic] : of or relating to a tetrad : taking the form of a tetrad

tet·rad·ite \ˈte·trəˌdīt\ *n* -s *usu cap* [NL *Tetradites*, fr. LGk *Tetraditēs*, a heretic, fr. Gk *tetrad-*, *tetras* tetrad, four + *-itēs* -ite] : one holding that there are four persons in God ⟨the epithet of *Tetradite* has historically been applied to Nestorians and Origenists among others⟩

tet·ra·drachm \ˈte·trəˌdram, -aa(ə)m\ *also* **tet·ra·drach·ma** \ˌ⁼⁼ˈdrakmə\ *n* [*tetradrachm* fr. Gk *tetradrachmon*, fr. *tetra-* + *drachmē* drachma; *tetradrachma* alter. (influenced by L *drachma*) of L *tetradrachmum*, fr. Gk *tetradrachmon* — more at DRACHMA, DRAM] : an ancient Greek silver coin worth four drachmas — **tet·ra·drach·mal** \ˌ⁼⁼ˈdrakməl\ *adj*

tet·ra·drach·mon \ˌ⁼⁼ˈdrakˌmän\ *n, pl* **tetradrach·ma** \-kmə\ [Gk] : TETRADRACHM

tet·ra·dym·ia \ˌte·trəˈdimēə\ *n, cap* [NL, fr. *tetra-* + *-dymia*] : a genus of low rigid tomentose shrubs (family Compositae) having alternate entire leaves, head with concave overlapping bracts, and terete achenes

te·trad·y·mite \təˈtradəˌmīt\ *n* -s [LGk *tetradymos* fourfold, fr. Gk + *didymos* twin; fr. its occurrence in compound twin crystals — more at -DYMUS] : a mineral Bi_2Te_2S consisting of a telluride and sulfide of bismuth, sometimes containing selenium, being pale steel gray in color and of a metallic luster, and occurring usu. in foliated masses (hardness 1.5–2, sp. gr. 7.2–7.6)

tet·ra·dy·nam·ia \ˌ⁼⁼dīˈnamēə, -dəˈ-, -nām-\ *n pl, cap* [NL, fr. *tetra-* + Gk *dynamis* power + NL *-ia* — more at DYNAMIC] *in former classifications* : a class of higher plants comprising all plants having tetradynamous stamens

tet·ra·dy·nam·i·an \ˌ⁼⁼⁼ˈmēən\ *adj* [NL *Tetradynamia* + E *-an*] : of or relating to the Tetradynamia

tet·ra·dy·nam·i·ous \-mēəs\ *adj* [NL *Tetradynamia* + E *-ous*] : TETRADYNAMIAN

tet·ra·dyna·mous \ˈ⁼⁼ˈdīnəməs, -din-\ *adj* [ISV *tetradynam-* (fr. *tetra-* + Gk *dynamis* power) + *-ous*] : having six stamens four of which are longer than the others ⟨the Cruciferae are ~⟩

tet·ra·eth·oxy·silane \ˌte·trəˌeˈthäksē+\ *n* [*tetra-* + *eth-* + *oxy-* + *silane*] : ETHYL SILICATE

tet·ra·ethyl \ˈte·trə+\ *adj* [ISV *tetra-* + *ethyl*] : containing four ethyl groups in the molecule

tetraethylammonium \ˈ⁼⁼ˈ⁼⁼⁼ˈ⁼⁼⁼\ *n* [*tetraethyl* + *ammonium*] : the quaternary ammonium ion $(C_2H_5)_4N^+$, containing four ethyl groups; *also* : a salt of this ion (as the deliquescent crystalline chloride used as a ganglionic blocking agent)

tetraethyl lead *n* : a heavy oily poisonous liquid compound $Pb(C_2H_5)_4$ that is insoluble in water but soluble in gasoline and other organic solvents, that is made usu. by the action of ethyl chloride on a sodium-lead alloy, and that is used as an antiknock agent — abbr. *TEL*

tetraethyl orthosilicate *n* : ETHYL SILICATE

tetraethyl pyrophosphate *n* : a mobile hygroscopic corrosive liquid ester $(C_2H_5)_4P_2O_7$ that is a powerful anticholinesterase and is used as an insecticide and parasympathomimetic agent — abbr. *TEPP*; compare HEXAETHYL TETRAPHOSPHATE

tetraethylthiuram disulfide \ˈ⁼⁼ˈ⁼⁼⁼ˈ⁼⁼⁼-\ *n* [*tetraethyl* + *thiuram*] : a cream-colored crystalline compound $[(C_2H_5)_2NCS]_2S_2$ used in the treatment of alcoholism and in the vulcanization of rubber; bis(diethyl-thiocarbamoyl) disulfide — called also *disulfiram*

tet·ra·fluoride \ˈte·trə+\ *n* [*tetra-* + *fluoride*] : a fluoride containing four atoms of fluorine

tet·ra·flu·or·o·ethylene \ˌte·trəˌflüərō+\ *n* [*tetra-* + *fluor-* + *ethylene*] : a flammable gaseous fluorocarbon $CF_2{=}CF_2$ used in making polytetrafluoroethylene resins — abbr. *TFE*

te·trafossate \ˈ⁼⁼+\ *adj* [*tetra-* + *fossate*] *of a tapeworm* : having four bothridia

te·trag·e·nous \təˈtrajənəs\ *adj* [*tetra-* + *-genous*] : growing in square groups of four ⟨~ bacteria⟩

te·trag·o·nal \təˈtragənᵊl, -raig-\ *adj* [LL *tetragonalis*, fr. *tetragonum* square, quadrangle (fr. Gk *tetragōnon*, fr. neut. of *tetragōnos* tetragonal, fr. *tetra-* + *-gōnos* -cornered, -angled, fr. *gōnia* corner, angle) + L *-alis* -al — more at -GON] **1** : having four angles or sides ⟨the parallelogram, square, and rhombus are ~ figures⟩ — see SCALENOHEDRON illustration **2** : of, relating to, or characteristic of the tetragonal system — **te·trag·o·nal·ly** \-nᵊlē, -ˈli\ *adv* — **te·trag·o·nal·ness** *n* -ES

tetragonal system *n* : a crystal system (as in the right square prism) characterized by three axes at right angles of which only the two lateral axes are equal — compare RHOMBOHEDRAL SYSTEM; see CRYSTAL SYSTEM illustration

tetragonal tristetrahedron *n* : DELTOHEDRON

tet·ra·go·nia \ˌte·trəˈgōnēə\ *n, cap* [NL, fr. Gk *tetragōnia* spindle tree, fr. *tetragōnos* tetragonal + *-ia* -y] : a genus of fleshy herbs or undershrubs (family Aizoaceae) of wide distribution having yellow or reddish apetalous flowers and a winged or quadrangular nut or drupe — see NEW ZEALAND SPINACH

tet·ra·go·ni·a·ce·ae \ˌ⁼⁼ˌgōnēˈāsēˌē\ [NL, fr. *Tetragonia* + *-aceae*] *syn of* AIZOACEAE

tet·ra·gram \ˈte·trəˌgram, -raa(ə)m\ *n* [MGk *tetragrammon*, fr. neut. of LGk *tetragrammos* having four letters, fr. Gk *tetra-* + *-grammos* (fr. *gramma* letter)] : a word of four letters : TETRAGRAMMATON

tet·ra·gram·ma·ton \ˌ⁼⁼ˈgramətən, -ədən, -ətᵊn *also* -əˌtän\ *n, pl* **tetragramma·ta** \-mətə, -ədə *sometimes* -əˌtä *or* -əˌtà\ *often cap* [ME *Tetragramaton*, fr. Gk *tetragrammaton*, fr. neut. of *tetragrammatos* having four letters, fr. *tetra-* + *grammat-*, *gramma* letter — more at GRAM] : the Hebrew word of the four letters יהוה constituting a divine proper name which the Jews out of reverence or for fear of desecration ceased to pronounce about three centuries B.C. and for which they substituted *Adonai* or *Elohim* and being variously transliterated without indication of the vocalization usu. by *YHWH, YHVH, JHVH, JHWH*, or *IHVH* and with vowels usu. by *Jehovah, Yahweh, Jahveh, Jahweh, Yahveh, Jahve, Jahwe, Yahvè*, or *Yahwe* — compare BLASPHEMY

tet·ra·graph \ˈte·trəˌgraf\ *n* [*tetra-* + *-graph*] : a cluster of four successive letters in cryptography — **tet·ra·graph·ic** \ˈ⁼⁼ˈgrafik\ *adj*

tet·ra·gyn·ia \-ˈjinēə\ *n pl, cap* [NL, fr. *tetra-* + *-gynia*] *in former classifications* : a class of higher plants comprising those with four styles or pistils

tet·ra·gyn·i·an \ˈ⁼⁼ˈjinēən\ *adj* [NL *Tetragynia* + E *-an*] : of or relating to the Tetragynia

tet·ra·gy·nous \ˈ⁼⁼ˈjīnəs, -ˈgī-\ *adj* [*tetra-* + *-gynous*] : having four pistils or carpels

tet·ra·he·dral \ˈ⁼⁼ˈhēdrəl\ *adj* [NL *tetrahedron* + E *-al*] **1** : of or relating to a tetrahedron : having or made up of four sides **2 a** : having the form of the regular tetrahedron **b** : relating to a tetrahedron or the system of hemihedral forms to which the tetrahedron belongs **c** : having the symmetry of a tetrahedron — **tet·ra·he·dral·ly** \-drəlē, -li\ *adv*

tetrahedral angle *n* : a polyhedral angle of four faces

tetrahedral coordination *n* : the state of being surrounded by four atoms whose centers are at the corners of a tetrahedron

tetrahedral hypothesis *n* : a hypothesis in geology: the earth's assumed original spherical form giving a minimum surface for a given volume tended as the earth shrank to develop into a tetrahedron giving a maximum surface for a given volume with the continents as the edges and the ocean basins as the sides

tetrahedral kite *n* : a kite shaped like a tetrahedron

tet·ra·he·drite \ˌ⁼⁼ˈhēˌdrīt\ *n* -s [G *tetraëdrit*, fr. LGk *tetraedros* having four faces + G *-it* -ite] : a fine-grained gray mineral $(Cu,Fe)_{12}Sb_4S_{13}$ that is isomorphous with tennantite, consists of a sulfide of copper, iron, and antimony and often also contains zinc, lead, mercury, or silver, occurs in characteristic tetrahedral crystals and also in massive form, and is often a valuable ore of silver and is also worked for copper (hardness 3–4, sp. gr. 4.4–5.1)

tet·ra·he·dron \ˌ⁼⁼ˈhē|drən *sometimes* |ˌdrän *or chiefly Brit* ˈhe|\ *n, pl* **tetrahedrons** *or* **tetrahe·dra** \-drə\ [NL, fr. LGk *tetraedron*, neut. of *tetraedros* having four faces, fr. Gk *tetra-* + *hedra* seat, face — more at SIT] **1** : a polyhedron of four faces **2** : an object having the form of or suggesting a tetrahedron: as **a** : CALTROP 2a **b** : three logs or lengths of steel bolted or lashed together and used as an obstacle **c** : a large concrete block of tetrahedral shape used esp. in constructing or strengthening revetments — compare TETRAPOD 3 **d** : a large wind-indicating device used on airfields and consisting of a frame covered with airplane cloth and pivoted so that the pointed end indicates the wind direction

tet·ra·hex·a·he·dral \ˈ⁼⁼ˌheksəˈhēdrəl\ *adj* [NL *tetrahexahedron* + E *-al*] : of, relating to, or being a tetrahexahedron

tet·ra·hexahedron \ˌte·trə+\ *n* [NL, fr. *tetra-* + *hexahedron*] : a form of the isometric system bounded by 24 congruent isosceles-triangular faces with four to each face of the cube

tetra-hexahedron

tetrahydr- *or* **tetrahydro-** *comb form* [ISV *tetra-* + *hydr-*] : combined with four atoms of hydrogen — in names of chemical compounds ⟨*tetrahydride*⟩ ⟨*tetrahydronaphthalene*⟩

tet·ra·hydrate \ˈ⁼⁼+\ *n* [*tetra-* + *hydrate*] : a chemical compound with four molecules of water — **tet·ra·hydrated** \"+\ *adj*

tet·ra·hy·dric \ˈ⁼⁼ˈhīdrik\ *adj* [ISV *tetra-* + *-hydric*] : TETRAHYDROXY — used esp. of alcohols and phenols

tet·ra·hy·dride \ˌ⁼⁼ˈhīˌdrīd, -ˌdrəd\ *n* [*tetrahydr-* + *-ide*] : a binary compound of an element or radical with four atoms of hydrogen

tet·ra·hy·dri·do·borate \ˈ⁼⁼ˈhīdrədō+\ *n* [*tetrahydride* + *-o-* + *borate*] : BOROHYDRIDE — used in the system of nomenclature adopted by the International Union of Pure and Applied Chemistry

tet·ra·hy·dro \ˌ⁼⁼ˈhīˌdrō\ *adj* [*tetrahydr-*] : combined with four atoms of hydrogen

tet·ra·hy·dro·benzene \ˈ⁼⁼ˈ⁼⁼+\ *n* [*tetrahydr-* + *benzene*] : CYCLOHEXENE

tet·ra·hy·dro·borate \"+\ *n* [*tetrahydr-* + *borate*] : BOROHYDRIDE

tet·ra·hy·dro·furan \"+\ *n* [ISV *tetrahydr-* + *furan*] : a flammable liquid heterocyclic ether C_4H_8O resembling ethyl ether that is made by hydrogenation of furan and is used as a solvent and as an intermediate in the manufacture of nylon

tet·ra·hy·dro·furfuryl alcohol \"+-\ *n* [*tetrahydr-* + *furfuryl*] : a high-boiling liquid $(C_4H_7O)CH_2OH$ made by catalytic hydrogenation of furfural and used as a solvent and in the preparation of esters

tet·ra·hy·dro·naphthalene \"+\ *n* [ISV *tetrahydr-* + *naphthalene*] : an oily liquid hydrocarbon $C_{10}H_{12}$ obtained by partial hydrogenation of naphthalene in the presence of a catalyst and used chiefly as a solvent (as for paints and lacquers) — called also *1,2,3,4-tetrahydronaphthalene*

tet·ra·hy·droxy \ˈ⁼⁼hīˈdräksē\ *adj* [*tetrahydroxy-*] : containing four hydroxyl groups in the molecule

tetrahydroxy- *comb form* [ISV *tetra-* + *hydroxy-*] : containing four hydroxyl groups — in names of chemical compounds ⟨*tetrahydroxy*anthraquinone⟩

tetraiod- *or* **tetraiodo-** *comb form* [*tetra-* + *iod-*] : containing four atoms of iodine — in names of chemical compounds ⟨*tetraiodo*fluorescein⟩; compare IOD-

tet·ra·iodide \ˈ⁼⁼+\ *or* **te·tri·odide** \təˈtrīəˌdīd, -ˌdəd\ *n* [*tetra-* + *iodide*] : an iodide containing four atoms of iodine

tet·ra·iodo \ˈte·trəˈī(ˌ)ō(ˌ)dō, ˈīəˌdō\ *adj* [*tetraiod-*] : containing four atoms of iodine in the molecule

tet·ra·iodo·phenolphthalein \ˈ⁼⁼⁼ˈ⁼(ˌ)⁼+, ˈ⁼⁼ˈ⁼⁼ˌ⁼+\ *n* [ISV *tetraiod-* + *phenolphthalein*] : IODOPHTHALEIN

tet·ra·kai·dec·a·he·dron \ˌte·trəˌkīˌdekəˈhēdrən\ *n* [NL, fr. LGk *tetrakaidekaedron*, fr. Gk *tetrakaideka* fourteen (fr. *tetra-* + *kai* and + *deka* ten) + *-edron* -hedron — more at TEN] : a 14-sided figure having 6 quadrilateral and 8 hexagonal faces

tetrakis- *comb form* [Gk, fr. *tetrakis*; akin to Gk *tettares, tessares* four — more at FOUR] : four times : quadrupled — esp. in complex chemical expressions ⟨*tetrakis*-(2-hydroxyethyl)⁼ ammonium chloride $(HOCH_2CH_2)_4NCl$⟩

tet·ra·kis·azo \ˈte·trəkəs+\ *adj* [*tetrakis-* + *azo*] : containing four azo groups in the molecule ⟨~ dyes⟩

tet·ra·kis·hexahedron \"+\ *n* [NL, fr. *tetrakis-* + *hexahedron*] : TETRAHEXAHEDRON

tet·ra·lem·ma \ˌte·trəˈlemə\ *n* -s [*tetra-* + *dilemma*] : an argument analogous to a dilemma but presenting four alternatives in the premisses

Tet·ra·lin \ˈte·trələn\ *trademark* — used for tetrahydronaphthalene

te·tral·o·gy \-te·ˈtraləjē, -ral-, -ji\ *n* -ES [Gk *tetralogia*, fr. *tetra-* + *-logia* -logy] **1** : a group of four dramatic pieces including three tragedies and one satyric piece or sometimes four tragedies represented consecutively on the Attic stage at the Dionysiac festival **2** : a series of four connected works (as dramas, operas, or novels) **3** : a group of four symptoms that are characteristic of a disease; *specif* : TETRALOGY OF FALLOT

tetralogy of fal·lot \-(ˈ)faˈlō\ *usu cap F* [after E. L. A. *Fallot* †1911 Fr. physician who orig. described it] : a congenital abnormality of the heart characterized by pulmonic stenosis, an opening in the interventricular septum, malposition of the aorta over both ventricles, and hypertrophy of the right ventricle

tet·ra·lone \ˈte·trəˌlōn\ *n* -s [ISV *tetralin* + *-one*] : either of two ketones $C_{10}H_{10}O$ derived from tetrahydronaphthalene

tet·ra·loph·odon \ˌ⁼⁼ˈläfəˌdän\ *n, cap* [NL, fr. *tetra-* + *loph-* + *-odon*] : a genus of Pliocene mastodons having a very short lower jaw and long straight upper tusks

¹tet·ra·lophodont \ˈte·trə+\ *adj* [ISV *tetra-* + *lophodont*] **1** *of a molar tooth* : having four crests or ridges **2** : having tetralophodont molars

²tetralophodont \"\ *adj* [NL *Tetralophodont-, Tetralophodon*] : of or relating to the genus *Tetralophodon*

³tetralophodont \"\ *n* : a mastodon of the genus *Tetralophodon*

tet·ra·mer \ˈte·trəmə(r)\ *n* -s [*tetra-* + *-mer*] : a polymer formed from four molecules of a monomer

te·tram·era \teˈtramərə\ [NL, fr. neut. pl. of *tetramerus* tetramerous] *syn of* PSEUDOTETRAMERA

te·tram·er·al \-mərəl\ *also* **tet·ra·mer·ic** \ˌte·trəˈmerik\ *adj* [NL *tetramerus* tetramerous + E *-al*] : TETRAMEROUS

te·tram·er·es \teˈtraməˌrēz\ *n, cap* [NL, fr. Gk *tetramerēs* having four parts] : a genus of nematode worms (family Spiruridae) parasitic in the proventriculus of gallinaceous birds including domestic fowls

te·tram·er·ism \-əˌrizəm\ *n* -s : the quality or state of being tetramerous

te·tram·er·ous \-ərəs\ *adj* [NL *tetramerus*, fr. Gk *tetramerēs*, fr. *tetra-* + *-merēs* (fr. *meros* part) — more at MERIT] : having or characterized by the presence of four parts: **a** *of a flower* : having the parts arranged in sets of four or multiples of four — often written *4-merous* **b** : having four or apparently only four joints in each of the tarsi ⟨~ beetles⟩

tet·ra·metaphosphate \ˌte·trə+\ *n* [*tetra-* + *metaphosphate*] : a cyclic tetrameric metaphosphate [as sodium tetrametaphosphate $(NaPO_3)_4$]

¹te·tram·e·ter \teˈtramədə(r), -ətə-\ *n* [Gk *tetrametron*, fr. neut. of *tetrametros* of four measures] : a line of four measures consisting either of four dipodies (as in classical iambic, trochaic, and anapaestic verse) or four feet (as in modern English verse)

²tetrameter \"\ *adj* [LL, fr. Gk *tetrametros*, fr. *tetra-* + *-metros* (akin to Gk *metron* measure, meter) — more at MEASURE] : consisting of four dipodies or four metrical feet

tet·ra·methyl \ˈte·trə+\ *adj* [ISV *tetra-* + *methyl*] : containing four methyl groups in the molecule

tetramethylammonium \ˈ⁼⁼ˈ⁼⁼⁼ˈ⁼⁼\ *n* [*tetramethyl* + *ammonium*] : the quaternary ammonium ion $(CH_3)_4N^+$ containing four methyl groups — see TETRAMINE 2

tet·ra·methylene \"+\ *n* [ISV *tetra-* + *methylene*] **1** : a bivalent radical $-CH_2CH_2CH_2CH_2-$ containing four methylene groups **2** : CYCLOBUTANE

tetramethylene cyanide *or* **tetramethylene dicyanide** *n* : ADIPONITRILE

tetramethylenediamine \ˈ⁼⁼ˈ⁼⁼,⁼⁼ˈ⁼⁼\ *n* [ISV *tetramethylene* + *diamine*] : PUTRESCINE

tetramethylene glycol *n* : BUTANEDIOL b

tetramethylthiuram disulfide \ˈ⁼⁼ˈ⁼⁼⁼ˈ⁼⁼-\ *n* [*tetramethyl* + *thiuram*] : a crystalline irritating compound $[(CH_3)_2NCS]_2S_2$ made by oxidation of a salt of dimethyl-dithiocarbamic acid and used chiefly as an accelerator of rubber vulcanization and as a fungicide and seed disinfectant; bis-(dimethyl-thiocarbamoyl) disulfide — abbr. *TMTD*; called also *thiram*

tet·ra·mine \ˈte·trəˌmēn, -ˌmən\ *n* [*tetra-* + *amine*] **1** : a compound (as hexamethylenetetramine) containing four amino groups **2** : a strong toxic unstable base $(C_2H_5)_4NOH$ obtained from sea anemones or made synthetically; tetramethylammonium hydroxide

te·tram·mine \teˈtramən\ *n* [*tetra-* + *ammine*] : an ammine containing four molecules of ammonia — compare CUPRAMMONIUM 1

tet·ra·morph \ˈte·trəˌmȯrf\ *n* [Gk *tetramorphon*, neut. of *tetramorphos* of four shapes, fr. *tetra-* + *-morphos* -morphous] : a representation of the four attributes of the Evangelists in a winged figure standing on winged fiery wheels with the wings covered with eyes — **tet·ra·mor·phic** \ˈ⁼⁼ˈmȯrfik\ *adj*

tet·ra·mor·phism \ˌ⁼⁼ˈmȯrˌfizəm\ *n* -s [*tetra-* + *-morphism*] : the property of crystallizing in four distinct forms — compare POLYMORPHISM

tet·ra·mor·phous \ˈ⁼⁼ˈmȯrˈfəs\ *adj* [*tetra-* + *-morphous*] : relating to or characterized by tetramorphism

te·tran·dria \teˈtrandrēə\ *n pl, cap* [NL, fr. *tetra-* + *-andria*] *in former classifications* : a class of higher plants comprising those with four stamens

te·tran·dri·an \-drēən\ *adj* [NL *Tetrandria* + E *-an*] : of or relating to the Tetrandria

te·tran·drous \-drəs\ *adj* [ISV *tetra-* + *-androus*] : having four stamens

tet·ra·nitrate \ˈte·trə+\ *n* [*tetra-* + *nitrate*] : a chemical compound containing four nitrate groups

tetranitro- *comb form* [ISV *tetra-* + *nitr-*] : containing four nitro groups — in names of chemical compounds

tet·ra·ni·tro·aniline \ˈte·trəˈnīˌtrō+\ *n* [*tetranitro-* + *aniline*] : a powerful explosive $C_6H(NO_2)_4NH_2$ obtained as a yellow crystalline solid by nitrating aniline

tet·ra·ni·tro·methane \"+\ *n* [ISV *tetranitro-* + *methane*] : a volatile toxic liquid compound $C(NO_2)_4$ made usu. by the action of nitric acid on acetic anhydride and used chiefly in very powerful liquid explosive mixtures

tet·ra·nuclear \ˈte·trə+\ *adj* [*tetra-* + *nuclear*] : containing four nuclei ⟨~ cyanine dyes⟩ — compare TETRACYCLIC 2

tet·ra·nucleotide \"+\ *n* [*tetra-* + *nucleotide*] : a nucleotide consisting of four mononucleotides in combination

¹te·tran·y·chid \teˈtranəkəd, ˈte·trəˈnik-\ *adj* [NL *Tetranychidae*] : of or relating to the Tetranychidae

²tetranychid \"\ *n* -s : a mite of the family Tetranychidae : RED SPIDER

tet·ra·nych·i·dae \ˌte·trəˈnikəˌdē\ *n pl, cap* [NL, fr. *Tetranychus*, type genus + *-idae*] : a family of medium-sized soft⁼ bodied mites that have the movable chela of each chelicera modified into a long piercing organ, tenent hairs on the claws, and no genital suckers, that feed on plants and usu. spin silken webs over the foliage, and that comprise the economically important red spiders

te·tran·y·chus \teˈtranəkəs\ *n, cap* [NL, fr. *tetra-* + Gk *-onychos* -clawed (fr. *onych-*, *onyx* claw) — more at NAIL] : a genus (the type of the family Tetranychidae) of mites — see PACIFIC MITE

tet·rao \ˈte·trəˌō, -rēˌō\ *n, cap* [NL, fr. L, heath cock, moorfowl, fr. Gk *tetraōn* — more at TURTLE (turtledove)] : a genus (the type of the family Tetraonidae) of grouses now restricted to the capercaillie and closely related forms

te·tra·odon \teˈtrāəˌdän\ *n, cap* [NL, fr. *tetra-* + *-odon*] : a genus (the type of the family Tetraodontidae) of tropical marine fishes

¹te·tra·odont \-ˌdänt\ *adj* [NL *Tetraodontidae*] : of or relating to the Tetraodontidae

²tetraodont \"\ *n* -s : a fish of the family Tetraodontidae

te·tra·odon·ti·dae \ˌte·trəōˈdäntəˌdē, -rēō-\ *n pl, cap* [NL, fr. *Tetraodont-, Tetraodon*, type genus + *-idae*] : a family of tropical marine fishes comprising the puffers and with the ocean sunfishes and a few other related forms constituting a distinct suborder of the Plectognathi — see GLOBEFISH

tetraodontoxin *var of* TETRODOTOXIN

tet·ra·on·i·dae \ˌte·trəˈänəˌdē\ *n pl, cap* [NL, fr. *Tetraon-, Tetrao*, type genus + *-idae*] : a variously limited family of birds (order Galliformes) that is usu. restricted to those grouses which have the tarsi and nostrils feathered

tet·ra·phosphate \ˈte·trə+\ *n* [ISV *tetra-* + *phosphate*] **1** : a substance similar to a metaphosphate glass — used chiefly commercially **2** : a fertilizer made by heating ground phosphate rock principally with carbonates of calcium, magnesium, and sodium carbonates

¹tet·ra·phyl·lid \ˈ⁼⁼ˈfiləd\ *adj* [NL *Tetraphyllidea*] : of or relating to the Tetraphyllidea

²tetraphyllid \"\ *n* -s : a tapeworm of the order Tetraphyllidea

tet·ra·phyl·lid·ea \ˌ⁼⁼fəˈlidēə\ *n pl, cap* [NL, fr. *tetra-* + *phyll-* + *-idea*] : an order of Cestoda comprising tapeworms parasitic in elasmobranch fishes and distinguished by a scolex having four bothridia and sometimes also hooks or suckers for attachment to the host

tet·ra·phyl·lid·e·an \ˈ⁼⁼fəˈlidēən\ *adj* [NL *Tetraphyllidea* + E *-an*] : TETRAPHYLLID

tet·ra·pla \ˈte·trəplə\ *n* -s *often cap* [NL, fr. neut. pl. of Gk *tetraplous, tetraploos* fourfold, fr. *tetra-* + *-plous, -ploos* -fold (as in *diploos* twofold, double) — more at DOUBLE] : a polyglot book with four texts in parallel columns — compare HEXAPLA, OCTAPLA

tet·ra·ple·gia \ˌ⁼⁼ˈplēj(ē)ə\ *n* -s [NL, fr. *tetra-* + *-plegia*] : QUADRIPLEGIA

¹tet·ra·ploid \ˈte·trəˌplȯid\ *adj* [ISV *tetra-* + *-ploid*] : fourfold in appearance or arrangement; *specif* : having or being a chromosome number that is four times the monoploid number ⟨a ~ cell⟩ — compare POLYPLOID — **tet·ra·ploi·dic** \ˈ⁼⁼ˈplȯidik\ *adj*

²tetraploid \"\ *n* -s : a tetraploid individual

tet·ra·ploi·dy \ˈ⁼⁼ˌplȯidē\ *n* -ES [ISV ¹*tetraploid* + *-y*] : the condition of being tetraploid

¹tet·ra·pod \ˈte·trəˌpäd\ *n* -s [NL *tetrapodus*, fr. Gk *tetrapod-*, *tetrapous* four-footed] **1** : a four⁼ footed animal : QUADRUPED — used chiefly of higher terrestrial vertebrates **2** : a four-footed bottom section (as of a pedestal table) **3** : a large reinforced concrete object having four arms and used esp. for protecting breakwaters from wave damage — compare TETRAHEDRON 2c

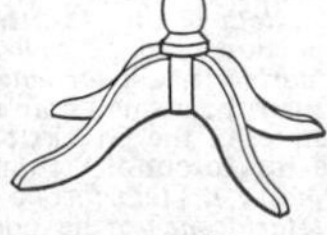
tetrapod 2

²tetrapod \"\ *also* **te·trap·o·dous** \teˈtrapədəs\ *adj* [*tetrapod* fr. Gk *tetrapod-, tetrapous*, fr. *tetra-* + *pod-*, *pous* foot; *tetrapodous* fr. Gk *tetrapod-, tetrapous* + E *-ous* — more at FOOT] : having four feet or walking appendages

¹te·trap·o·da \teˈtrapədə\ *n pl, cap* [NL, fr. neut. pl. of Gk *tetrapodos* four-footed, fr. *tetrapod-, tetrapous*] : a division of butterflies including those with only two pairs of perfect legs

²tetrapoda \"\ *n pl, cap* [NL, fr. Gk, neut. pl.] *in former classifications* : a division of vertebrates including all forms above fishes

te·trap·o·dal \-dᵊl\ *adj* [¹*tetrapod* + *-al*] **1** : TETRAPOD ⟨~ reptiles⟩ **2** : constituting one of four supporting legs ⟨pottery consisting of vessels with ~ supports⟩

te·trap·o·dy \-dē\ *n* -ES [Gk *tetrapodia*, fr. *tetrapod-, tetrapous* four-footed + *-ia* -y] : a unit of four metrical feet

tet·ra·polar \ˈte·trə+\ *adj* [*tetra-* + *polar*] : having four poles ⟨certain abnormal mitotic figures are ~⟩ — **tet·ra·polarity** \"+\ *n*

te·trap·ter·an \te'traptərən\ *adj* [Gk *tetrapteros* + E *-an*] *of an insect* : having four wings

te·trap·ter·on \-ə,rän\ *n* -s [NL, fr. neut. of Gk *tetrapteros* having four wings] : a four-winged insect

te·trap·ter·ous \-_rəs\ *adj* [Gk *tetrapteros*, fr. *tetra-* + *-pteros* -pterous] : TETRAPTERAN

te·trap·tu·rus \,te,trap't(y)ůrəs\ *n, cap* [NL, fr. *tetra-* + *pter-* + *-urus*] : a genus of large vigorous marine fishes (family Istiophoridae) comprising the spearfishes (sense 1)

tet·rap·tych \te'traptik\ *n* -s [Gk *tetraptychon*, neut. of *tetraptychos* fourfold, fr. *tetra-* + *-ptychos* (akin to Gk *ptychē* fold, layer)] : an arrangement of pictures in four parts (as for an altarpiece)

tet·ra·pylon \¦te·trə+\ *n, pl* **tetrapyla** [Gk, fr. *tetra-* + *pylōn* gateway — more at PYLON] : an edifice having four gates or portals (as one marking the intersection of two thoroughfares in an ancient Roman city)

tet·ra·radiate \¦te·trə+\ *adj* [*tetra-* + *radiate*, adj.] : having four principal radii of symmetry ⟨a ~ sponge spicule⟩

¹**tetrarch** \'te,trärk, 'tē,-\ *n* -s [ME, fr. LL *tetrarcha*, fr. L *tetrarches*, fr. Gk *tetrarchēs*, fr. *tetra-* (akin to Gk *tettares*, *tessares* four) + *-archēs* ¹-arch — more at FOUR] **1** : a governor of the fourth part of an ancient province (as in the Roman Empire) **2** : a subordinate prince or petty king **3** : any of four officials or directors jointly in control

²**tetrarch** \"\ *adj* [*tetra-* + *-arch*] : having four xylem groups — used of a stele

tetrarch·ate \-r,kāt\ *n* -s [¹*tetrarch* + *-ate*] : TETRARCHY

te·trar·chic \(')te¦trärkik, (')tē¦t-, tə¦t-\ *also* **te·trar·chi·cal** \-rkəkəl\ *adj* [*tetrarchic* fr. Gk *tetrarchikos* of a tetrarch, fr. *tetrarchēs* tetrarch + *-ikos* -ic; *tetrarchical* fr. Gk *tetrarchikos* + E *-al*] : of or relating to a tetrarchy or a tetrarch

¹**tetrarchy** \'te,trärkē, 'tē,-\ *n* -ES [ME *tetrarchie*, fr. L *tetrarchia*, fr. Gk, fr. *tetrarchēs* tetrarch + *-ia* -y] **1** : the district, office, or jurisdiction of a tetrarch **2 a** : rule by four persons jointly **b** : the four rulers of a tetrarchy

²**tetrarchy** \"\ *n* -ES [²*tetrarch* + *-y*] : the state of having four xylem strands or groups

tet·ra·rhyn·chid·ea \,te·trə(,)riŋ'kidēə\ *or* **tet·ra·rhyn·choi·dea** \-'kȯidēə\ [NL, fr. *Tetrarhynchus*, genus of tapeworms (fr. *tetra-* + *-rhynchus*) + *-idea* or *-oidea*] *syn of* TRYPANORHYNCHA

tet·ra·rhyn·chid·e·an \¦==(,)=¦kidēən\ *or* **tet·ra·rhyn·choid** \¦==¦riŋ,kȯid\ *adj or n* [*tetrarhynchidean* fr. NL *Tetrarhynchidea* + E *-an*; *tetrarhynchoid* fr. NL *Tetrarhynchoidea*] : TRYPANORHYNCHAN

tet·ra·saccharide \¦te·trə+\ *n* [ISV *tetra-* + *saccharide*] : any of a class of carbohydrates (as stachyose) that yield on complete hydrolysis four monosaccharide molecules

tet·ra·selenodont \"+\ *adj* [*tetra-* + *selenodont*] : relating to or having molar teeth with four crescentic crests or ridges

tet·ra·seme \'te·trə,sēm\ *n* -s [back-formation fr. *tetrasemic*] : a tetrasemic foot (as a tetrabrach or a spondee)

tet·ra·se·mic \¦==¦sēmik\ *or* **tet·ra·seme** \'==,sēm\ *adj* [*tetrasemic* fr. Gk *tetrasēmos* of four time units (fr. *tetra-* + *-sēmos*, fr. *sēmeion* unit of time, mark, sign, fr. *sēma* sign) + E *-ic*; *tetraseme* fr. Gk *tetrasēmos* — more at SEMANTICS] : consisting of or of the length of four morae in classical prosody

tet·ra·silicate \¦te·trə+\ *n* [ISV *tetra-* + *silicate*] : a silicate (as talc) containing four atoms of silicon in the molecule

tet·ra·skele *also* **tet·ra·scele** \'te·trə,skēl\ *n* -s [NL, fr. Gk *tetraskelēs* four-legged, fr. *tetra-* + *-skelēs* (fr. *skelos* leg) — more at CYLINDER] : TETRASKELION

tet·ra·skel·i·on \,te·trə'skelēən, -ē,än\ *n, pl* **tetraskelions** \-nz\ *or* **tetraskel·ia** \-ēə\ [NL, dim. of *tetraskele*] : a figure (as the swastika) composed of four arms radiating from a center and bent in the same direction — compare TRISKELION

tet·ra·sodium pyrophosphate \¦te·trə+-\ *n* [*tetra-* + *sodium*] : SODIUM PYROPHOSPHATE b

tet·ra·so·mat·ic \¦==sō¦mad·ik\ *adj* [*tetrasomaty* + *-ic*] : of or relating to tetrasomaty

tet·ra·som·a·ty \¦==¦sōməd·ē\ *n* -ES [*tetra-* + *somat-* + *-y*] : polysomatic octoploidy — compare POLYSOMATY

tet·ra·some \'==,sōm\ *n* -s [*tetra-* + *-some*] : an association (as in a polyploid) of four homologous chromosomes in the meiotic prophase — compare BIVALENT, TETRAD

¹**tet·ra·so·mic** \¦==¦sōmik\ *adj* [*tetra-* + *-somic*] : having one or a few chromosomes tetraploid in otherwise diploid nuclei due to nondisjunction — **tet·ra·so·my** \'==,sōmē\ *n* -ES

²**tetrasomic** \"\ *n* -s : a tetrasomic individual

tet·ra·spo·ra·les \,==spə'rā(,)lēz\ *n pl, cap* [NL, fr. *Tetraspora*, genus of green algae (fr. *tetra-* + *-spora*) + *-ales*] : an order of green algae having vegetative cells that are immobile but capable of changing temporarily into a motile stage and that form colonies that are not filamentous and are often amorphous

tet·ra·spo·ran·gi·ate \¦==¦ranjēət, -ē,āt\ *adj* [NL *tetrasporangium* + E *-ate*] : of, relating to, or being a tetrasporangium

tet·ra·sporangium \"+\ *n* [NL, fr. *tetra-* (in ISV *tetraspore*) + *sporangium*] : a sporangium producing tetraspores

tet·ra·spore \'==,spō(ə)r\ *n* [ISV *tetra-* + *spore*] : one of the haploid asexual spores in the red algae developed meiotically and commonly in groups of four from the diploid tetrasporangia and germinating to produce the haploid gametophytic plants — compare CARPOSPORE — **tet·ra·spor·ic** \¦==¦spōrik\ *adj* — **tet·ra·spor·ous** \¦te·trə¦spōrəs, tə'trasp̄ərəs\ *adj*

tet·ra·spo·rif·er·ous \¦==,spə¦rif(ə)rəs\ *adj* [*tetraspore* + *-iferous*] : bearing tetraspores

tet·ra·spo·ro·phyte \¦==¦spōrə,fīt\ *n* [*tetraspore* + *-o-* + *-phyte*] : a plant bearing tetraspores

tet·ras·ter \(')te¦trastə(r)\ *n* -s [NL, fr. *tetra-* + *-aster*] : a mitotic figure characterized by four astral poles instead of the more usual two and in an embryo usu. resulting from abnormal polyspermy

tet·ra·stich \'te·trə,stik\ *n* -s [L *tetrastichon*, fr. Gk, neut. of *tetrastichos* of four lines, fr. *tetra-* + *stichos* line, verse — more at STICH] : a prosodic unit or stanza of four lines — **te·tras·ti·chal** \tə'trastəkəl\ *adj* — **tet·ra·stich·ic** \¦te·trə¦stikik\ *adj*

te·tras·ti·chous \te'trastəkəs\ *adj* [LL *tetrastichus* of four lines, of four rows, fr. Gk *tetrastichos*] **1** : ranked by fours **2** : arranged in four vertical rows — used esp. of the inflorescence of a grass or of its constituent parts

te·tras·ti·chus \-kəs\ *n, cap* [NL, fr. Gk *tetrastichos* of four lines] : a genus of minute chalcid flies that contains numerous hyperparasites and is sometimes made the type of a distinct family

tet·ra·sto·on \,te·trə'stō,än, te'trastə,wän\ *n, pl* **tetra·stoa** \-stōə, -stəwə\ [Gk, fr. neut. of *tetrastoos* having four porticoes, fr. *tetra-* + *stoa* portico — more at STOIC] : a courtyard enclosed by four porticoes

¹**tet·ra·style** \'te·trə,stīl\ *n* [LL *tetrastylon*, fr. L, neut. of *tetrastylos* having four pillars, fr. Gk, fr. *tetra-* + *stylos* pillar — more at STEER] : a building or portico having four columns in front — **tet·ra·styl·ic** \¦==¦stilik\ *or* **tet·ra·sty·lous** \¦==¦stīləs\ *adj*

²**tetrastyle** \"\ *adj* : marked by columniation with four columns across the front — compare DISTYLE

tet·ra·substituted \¦==+\ *adj* [*tetra-* + *substituted*] : having four substituent atoms or groups in the molecule

tet·ra·sulfide \"+\ *n* [*tetra-* + *sulfide*] : a binary compound of an element or radical with four atoms of sulfur

tet·ra·syllabic \¦==+\ *or* **tet·ra·syllabical** \"+\ *adj* [Gk *tetrasyllabos* (fr. *tetra-* + *-syllabos*, fr. *syllabē* syllable) + E *-ic* or *-ical* — more at SYLLABLE] : having four syllables

tet·ra·the·ism \¦==(,)thē,izəm\ *n* [*tetra-* + *-theism*] : a doctrine that there are three persons in the Godhead and a divine essence constituting their common origin and that is interpreted as being a belief in four Gods

tet·ra·thi·o·nate \,==¦thīə,nāt\ *n* [ISV *tetrathion-* (in *tetrathionic acid*) + *-ate*] : a salt of tetrathionic acid

tet·ra·thionic acid \¦==+-\ *n* [ISV *tetra-* + *thionic*; orig. formed as F *tétrathionique*] : the thionic acid $H_2S_4O_6$ containing four atoms of sulfur in the molecule

tet·ra·thyridium \"+\ *n* [NL, fr. *tetra-* + *thyridium*] : a modified cysticercus resembling an elongated plerocercoid with a scolex invaginated at one end

tet·ra·tom·ic \¦te·trə¦tämik\ *adj* [ISV *tetra-* + *atomic*] **1** : consisting of four atoms : having four atoms in the molecule **2** : having four replaceable atoms or radicals

tet·ra·ton·ic \¦==¦tänik\ *adj* [Gk *tetratonos* having four tones (fr. *tetra-* + *tonos* tone) + E *-ic* — more at TONE] **1** : consisting of four musical tones ⟨~ scale⟩ **2** : relating to the tetratonic scale

tet·ra·valence \¦te·trə+\ *or* **tet·ra·valency** \"+\ *n* [*tetravalence* ISV, fr. *tetravalent*, after such pairs as E *present: presence*; *tetravalency* fr. *tetravalent*, after such pairs as E *president: presidency*] : the quality or state of being tetravalent ⟨the ~ of the carbon atom⟩

¹**tet·ra·valent** \"+\ *adj* [ISV *tetra-* + *valent*] **1** : having a valence of four **2** : QUADRUPLE — used of homologous chromosomes when four are present and associate in synapsis

²**tetravalent** \"\ *n* -s : a tetravalent chromosome group

te·trax·i·al \te'traksēəl\ *also* **te·trax·ile** \-k,sīl\ *adj* [*tetra-* + *axial* or *axile*] : having four axes

te·trax·on \te'traksän\ *n* -s [*tetra-* + Gk *axōn* axle, axis — more at AXIS] : a tetraxial sponge spicule

tet·rax·o·nia \,te,trak'sōnēə\ [NL, fr. *tetra-* + *axonia*] *syn of* DEMOSPONGIAE

tet·rax·o·nid \te'traksənəd, -,nid\ *adj or n* [NL *Tetraxonida*] : TETRACTINELLID

tet·rax·on·i·da \,te,trak'sänədə\ [NL, fr. *tetra-* + Gk *axōn* axis + NL *-ida*] *syn of* TETRACTINELLIDA

tetraz- *or* **tetrazo-** *comb form* [ISV *tetra-* + *az-*] : containing four atoms of nitrogen — in names of chemical compounds ⟨*tetrazole*⟩

tet·ra·zene \'te·trə,zēn\ *n* -s [ISV *tetraz-* + *-ene*] **1** : either of two hypothetical isomeric hydrides of nitrogen $HN{=}NNH{-}NH_2$ or $H_2NN{=}NNH_2$ known in the form of organic derivatives (as tetracene) **2** : TETRACENE

tet·ra·zine \'te·trə,zēn, -,zən\ *n* -s [ISV *tetraz-* + *-ine*] **1** : any of three isomeric parent compounds $C_2H_2N_4$ that may be regarded as benzene with four methylidyne groups replaced by nitrogen atoms; *esp* : the symmetrical or 1,2,4,5-isomer forming very volatile unstable purple-red crystals **2** : any of various derivatives of the tetrazines

tet·ra·zo \-,zō\ *adj* [*tetraz-*] **1** : containing four atoms of nitrogen in the molecule; *esp* : DISAZO **2** : TETRAKISAZO

tet·ra·zole \'te·trə,zōl\ *n* -s [ISV *tetraz-* + *-ole*] : a crystalline acidic parent compound CH_2N_4 containing a ring composed of one carbon atom and four nitrogen atoms; *also* : any of various derivatives of this compound — compare PENTYLENETETRAZOL

tet·ra·zo·li·um \,==¦zōlēəm\ *n* -s [NL, fr. ISV *tetrazole* + NL *-ium*] : a univalent ion $CH_3N_4^+$ or radical CH_3N_4 analogous to ammonium and derived from tetrazole; *also* : any of various derivatives of this ion ⟨~ salts are redox indicators —*Science*⟩ — compare FORMAZAN

tetrazolium chloride *n* **1** : the hydrochloride of tetrazole **2** : TRIPHENYLTETRAZOLIUM CHLORIDE

te·traz·o·lyl \te'trazə,lil\ *n* -s [*tetrazole* + *-yl*] : the univalent radical CHN_4 derived from tetrazole

tet·ra·zooid \¦te·trə+\ *n* [*tetra-* + *zooid*] : one of the first four blastozooids formed from the precocious stolon of the cyathozooid of a member of the genus *Pyrosoma*

te·traz·o·ti·za·tion \te,trazəd·ə'zāshən, -zə,tī'z-\ *n* -s : the process of tetrazotizing

te·traz·o·tize \=¦=ə,tīz\ *vt* -ED/-ING/-S [*tetra-* + *-azotize* (as in *diazotize*)] : to diazotize doubly : convert (as an aromatic diamine) into a disazo compound ⟨benzidine is *tetrazotized* for making a benzidine disazo dye⟩

¹**te·trig·id** \te'trijəd\ *adj* [NL *Tetrigidae*] : of or relating to the Tetrigidae

²**tetrigid** \"\ *n* -s : an insect of the family Tetrigidae

te·trig·i·dae \-jə,dē\ *n pl, cap* [NL, fr. *Tetrig-*, *Tetrix*, type genus + *-idae*] : a family of saltatorial insects (order Orthoptera) comprising the grouse locusts and having the pronotum greatly lengthened

tetriodide *var of* TETRAIODIDE

tet·ri·tol \'te·trə,tȯl, -tōl\ *n* -s [*tetrose* + *-itol*] : any of the tetrahydroxy alcohols $HOCH_2(CHOH)_2CH_2OH$ (as erythritol) obtainable by reducing the corresponding tetrose

tet·rix \'te·triks\ *n, cap* [NL, modif. (influenced by Gk *tetrix*, a bird, perh. pipit) of Gk *tettix* cicada, of imit. origin — more at TURTLE (turtledove)] : a genus of small very active usu. dark-colored grouse locusts

te·trobol \te'träbəl, -rōb-\ *also* **te·trob·o·lon** \-räbəlän\ *n, pl* **tetrobols** \-bəlz\ *also* **tetrobo·la** \-bələ\ [Gk *tetrōbolon* fr. neut. of *tetrōbolos* of four obols, fr. *tetra-* + *obolos* obol — more at OBOL] : a silver coin of ancient Greece worth four obols

tet·rode \'te,trōd\ *n* -s [*tetra-* + *-ode*] : a vacuum tube with four electrodes, a cathode, an anode, a control grid, and an additional grid or other electrode

tet·rodon \'te·trə,dän\ [NL, fr. *tetra-* + *-odon*] *syn of* TETRAODON

tet·ro·dont \-nt\ *adj or n* [NL *Tetrodontidae*] : TETRAODONT

tet·ro·don·ti·dae \,==¦däntə,dē\ [NL, fr. *Tetrodont-*, *Tetrodon* + *-idae*] *syn of* TETRAODONTIDAE

tet·ro·do·toxin \¦te·trədō+\ *or* **tet·ra·odon·toxin** \¦te·trəō-,dän+\ *n* [*tetrodotoxin* ISV *tetrodo-* (fr. NL *Tetrodon*) + *toxin*; *tetraodontoxin* fr. NL *Tetraodon* + *toxin*] : a poisonous compound $C_{16}H_{31}NO_{16}$(?) obtained from Japanese fugus

te·trolic acid \te'trälik-, -trōl-\ *n* [ISV *tetr-* + *-ol* + *-ic*] : a crystalline acetylenic acid $CH_3C{\equiv}CCOOH$ obtained synthetically; methyl-propiolic acid

te·tron·ic acid \te'tränik-\ *n* [ISV *tetron-* (fr. *tetra-* + connective *-on-*) + *-ic*] : a crystalline enolic lactone $C_4H_4O_3$ that has acidic properties and is the parent compound of acidic compounds obtained by the fermenting action of a mold (*Penicillium charlesii*) from spoiled corn

tet·rose \'te,trōs *also* -ōz\ *n* -s [ISV *tetra-* + *-ose*] : any of a class of monosaccharides $C_4H_8O_4$ (as erythrose or threose) containing four carbon atoms

te·trox·a·late \te'träksə,lāt\ *n* [*tetra-* + *oxalate*] : a complex acid oxalate (as potassium tetroxalate) made by adding one equivalent of base to four equivalents of oxalic acid

te·trox·ide \-k,sīd\ *n* [ISV *tetra-* + *oxide*] : an oxide containing four atoms of oxygen

tet·ryl \'te·trəl\ *n* -s [ISV *tetra-* + *-yl*] : a pale yellow crystalline explosive $(NO_2)_3C_6H_2N(CH_3)NO_2$ obtainable by nitrating dimethylaniline or methylaniline and used esp. as a detonator; methyl-picryl-nitramide — called also *trinitrophenylmethylnitramine*

tet·ter \'ted·ə(r), -etə-\ *n* -s [ME *tetere*, fr. OE *teter* — more at DARTROSE] **1** : any of various vesicular skin diseases (as ringworm, eczema, and herpes) **2** *dial* : PIMPLE, PUSTULE, BLISTER, ULCER

tetterwort \'==,=\ *n* [ME *teterwort*, fr. *tetere* tetter + *wort*] : a plant used to treat tetter: as **a** *Eng* : CELANDINE **b** : BLOODROOT

tet·ti·gel·li·dae \,ted·ə'jelə,dē\ *n pl, cap* [NL, fr. *Tettigella*, type genus (fr. Gk *tettig-*, *tettix* cicada + L *-ella*) + *-idae*] : a family of insects (suborder Homoptera) consisting of the true leafhoppers — compare JASSIDAE

tet·tig·i·dae \te'tijə,dē\ [NL, fr. *Tettig-*, *Tettix* + *-idae*] *syn of* TETRIGIDAE

¹**tet·ti·go·ni·id** \¦ted·ə¦gōnēəd\ *adj* [NL *Tettigoniidae*] : of or relating to the Tettigoniidae

²**tettigoniid** \"\ *n* -s : an insect of the family Tettigoniidae : LONG-HORNED GRASSHOPPER

tet·ti·go·ni·idae \,==gə'nīə,dē\ *n pl, cap* [NL, fr. *Tettigonia*, type genus (fr. L *tettigonia* leafhopper, fr. Gk *tettigonion*, dim. of *tettig-*, *tettix* cicada) + *-idae*] : a large family of insects (order Orthoptera) having long slender antennae and four-segmented tarsi and comprising the long-horned grasshoppers

tet·tix \'ted·iks\ [NL, fr. Gk, cicada, of imit. origin] *syn of* TETRIX

teu·cri·um \'t(y)ükrēəm\ *n, cap* [NL, fr. Gk *teukrion* germander, perh. fr. *Teukros* Teucer, first king of Troy] : a large widely distributed genus of herbs (family Labiatae) having flowers with four exserted stamens, a short corolla tube, and a prominent lower lip — see GERMANDER 1

teuk \'t(y)ük\ *n* -s [imit.] *dial Eng* : REDSHANK 1

teu·thid·i·dae \t(y)ü'thidə,dē\ *n pl, cap* [NL, fr. *Teuthid-*, *Teuthis*, type genus + *-idae*] : a family of marine fishes comprising the surgeonfishes that are distinguished by a bony plate or spine on the side of the tail, teeth resembling incisors, and fine scales resembling shagreen and with the Moorish idols constituting a distinct suborder of Percomorphi

teu·this \'t(y)üthəs\ *n, cap* [NL, fr. LL, squid, fr. Gk] : the type genus of Teuthididae

teu·ton \'t(y)üt°n\ *n* -s *cap* [L *Teutoni*, *Teutones*, pl.] **1** : a member of an ancient prob. Germanic or Celtic people first appearing in history as allies of the Cimbri **2** : a member of one of the peoples speaking a language of the Germanic branch of the Indo-European family of languages; *esp* : GERMAN

¹**teu·ton·ic** \t(y)ü¦tänik, -nēk\ *adj, usu cap* [L *teutonicus*, fr. *Teutoni*, *Teutones* Teutons + *-icus* -ic] : of, relating to, or having the characteristics of the Teutons; *esp* : ¹GERMANIC 1 ⟨formidable volumes, *Teutonic* in their thoroughness —*Times Lit. Supp.*⟩ — **teu·ton·i·cal·ly** \-nək(ə)lē, -nēk-, -li\ *adv, usu cap*

²**teutonic** \"\ *n* -s *cap* : GERMANIC

teutonic knight *n, usu cap T&K* : a knight of a powerful religious military order founded at Acre in 1190 as a brotherhood of German crusaders

teu·ton·ism \'t(y)üt°n,izəm\ *n, usu cap* [NL *teutonismus*, fr. L *Teutoni* + *-ismus* -ism] : GERMANISM ⟨the style is stilted and marred by *Teutonisms* —John Layard⟩ ⟨prejudice in favor of *Teutonism* —W.Z.Ripley⟩

teu·ton·ist \-_°nəst\ *n* -s *usu cap* : GERMANIST

teu·ton·i·za·tion \,t(y)üt°nə'zāshən, -°n,ī'z-\ *n* -s *often cap* : GERMANIZATION

teu·ton·ize \'t(y)üt°n,īz\ *vt* -ED/-ING/-S *often cap* : GERMANIZE ⟨keep their eyes . . . on a *Teutonized* Europe —*Blackwood's*⟩ ⟨~s his phrases for a scholarly effect⟩

tevet *or* **teveth** *usu cap, var of* TEBET

¹**tew** \'t(y)ü\ *vb* -ED/-ING/-S [ME *tewen*, alter. of *tawen* — more at TAW] *vt* **1** *obs* : to work (leather) by beating or kneading **2** *obs* : to prepare for some purpose **3** *obs* : BEAT, BELABOR ~ *vi* **1** *chiefly dial* : to work hard **2** *dial* : FUSS, WORRY

²**tew** \"\ *n* -s *chiefly dial* : a state of worried agitation or excitement : STEW ⟨my wife was always in a ~ about the danger —W.D.Howells⟩

³**tew** *vt* -ED/-ING/-S [prob. alter. of ¹*tow*] *obs* : PULL, HAUL

te·wa \'tāwə, 'tēwə\ *n, pl* **tewa** *or* **tewas** *usu cap* **1 a** : any of several Tanoan peoples of New Mexico and northeastern Arizona **b** : a member of any of such peoples **2** : a language of the Tewa peoples

tew·el \'t(y)üəl\ *n* -s [ME, shaft, vent, tewel, fr. MF *tuel*, *tuyau* pipe, tube, prob. of Gmc origin; akin to MD & MLG *tute* pipe, tube] *archaic* : ANUS, RECTUM — used chiefly of a horse

¹**tex·an** \'teksən\ *also* **tex·i·an** \-sēən\ *adj, usu cap* [*Texas* state + E *-an* (adj. suffix)] **1** : of, relating to, or characteristic of Texas **2** : of, relating to, or characteristic of Texans

²**texan** \"\ *also* **texian** \"\ *n* -s *cap* [*Texas* state + E *-an* (n. suffix)] : a native or resident of the state of Texas

¹**tex·as** \'teksəs, *esp by Texans* -əz\ *adj, usu cap* [fr. *Texas*, state in the southwestern U.S., fr. AmerSp, a confederation of Indians allied against the Apache, fr. Caddo *techas* allies] : of or from the state of Texas ⟨a *Texas* ranch⟩ : of the kind or style prevalent in Texas : TEXAN

²**texas** \"\ *n, pl* **texas** *or* **texases** [AmerSp, a confederation of Indians, prob. Hasinai] **1** *usu cap* : HASINAI **2** [fr. *Texas* state; fr. the practice on Mississippi steamboats of naming the cabins after the states, the officers' cabins being the largest] : a structure on the awning deck of a steamer containing the officers' cabins and having the pilothouse in front or on top

texas adelia *n, usu cap T* : SWAMP PRIVET

texas bedbug *n, usu cap T* : CONENOSE

texas bluegrass *n, usu cap T* : a vigorous forage grass (*Poa arachnifera*) of the southern U.S. that resembles Kentucky bluegrass but has stems that are less flattened

texas brown-eyed susan *n, usu cap T&S* : a bristly annual herb (*Rudbeckia bicolor*) of the southern U.S. that has ray flowers darker toward the center of the head

texas buckeye *or* **texan buckeye** *n, usu cap T* : SPANISH BUCKEYE

texas buckthorn *n, usu cap T* : LOTE

texas catclaw *n, usu cap T* : a tall shrub or small to large tree (*Acacia wrightii*) with many short spines and dense foliage that yields firewood and is a locally important honey plant in parts of the southwestern U.S. — called also *tree cat's-claw*

texas fever *or* **texas cattle fever** *n, usu cap T* : an infectious disease of cattle transmitted by the cattle tick and caused by a protozoan (*Babesia bigemina*) that multiplies in the blood and destroys the red blood cells — called also *blackwater*, *splenetic fever*; see RED WATER 1a; compare ICTEROHEMATURIA

texas fever tick *n, usu cap T* : a cattle tick (*Boophilus annulatus*)

texas fly *n, usu cap T* : HORN FLY

texas independence day *n, usu cap T&I&D* : March 2 that is observed as the anniversary of the declaration of independence of Texas from Mexico in 1836 and also as the birthday of Sam Houston

texas leaf-cutting ant *n, usu cap T* : a leaf-cutting ant (*Atta texana*) that is sometimes a destructive defoliator in Texas and Louisiana

texas leaguer *n* [*Texas* (baseball) *League* + E *-er*] : a fly in baseball that falls too far out to be caught by an infielder and too close in to be caught by an outfielder

texas longhorn *n, usu cap T* : LONGHORN 2b

texas millet *n, usu cap T* : an annual weedy grass (*Panicum texanum*) used for hay

texas nighthawk *n, usu cap T* : a largely gray black-striped goatsucker (*Chordeiles acutipennis texensis*) of the southwestern U.S. and parts of Mexico

texas palmetto *n, usu cap T* : a tall palm (*Sabal texana*) of southern Texas and Mexico whose leaves are used for thatching and chair seats

texas pea *n, usu cap T* : a perennial bushy herb (*Astragalus nuttallianus*) of the southwestern U. S. that yields forage

texas plume *n, usu cap T* : STANDING CYPRESS

texas ranger *n, usu cap T&R* : a member of a mounted police force in Texas

texas red oak *also* **texas oak** *n, usu cap T* : a usu. small to medium-sized oak (*Quercus texana*) of dry Texas uplands having a reddish brown bark, deeply lobed leaves, and usu. solitary short-stalked biennial acorns

texas root rot *n, usu cap T* : COTTON ROOT ROT

texas sage *n, usu cap T* : a perennial herb (*Salviastrum texanum*) of the family Labiatae having tufted hairy stems and blue flowers in close panicles

texas snakeroot *n, usu cap T* : a birthwort (*Aristolochia reticulata*) of the southwestern U. S. that resembles the Virginia snakeroot in its medicinal properties

texas sparrow *n, usu cap T* : a finch (*Arremonops rufivirgatus*) of southern Texas and Mexico that is olive green above with inconspicuous rufous stripes on the head and yellow on the wings

texas star *n, usu cap T* **1** : an annual Texan herb (*Lindheimera texana*) of the family Compositae sometimes cultivated for its rather showy radiate yellow heads **2** : PRAIRIE SABBATIA

texas steer *n, usu cap T* : a small side-branded steer hide

texas tender *n* : a waiter in the texas of a steamboat

texas thistle *n, usu cap 1st T* **1** : BASKET FLOWER 1 **2** *or* **texas nettle** : BUFFALO BUR

texas tower *n, usu cap 1st T* [²*texas*] : a radar-equipped platform supported on caissons sunk in the ocean floor and forming part of an offshore warning system against air attack

texas umbrella tree *n, usu cap 1st T* : an ornamental tree that has a crowded often flattened crown and is a horticultural variety (*Melia azedarach umbraculiformis*) of the china tree

¹**text** \'tekst\ *n* -s [ME, fr. MF *texte*, fr. OF, fr. ML *textus* text, passage, Scripture, fr. L, texture, tissue, structure, context, fr. past part. of *texere* to construct, weave — more at TECHNICAL] **1 a** (1) : the original written or printed words and form of a literary work ⟨apologize for . . . methods of softening or otherwise changing the ~ of the letters —J.S. Bassett⟩ ⟨no room to print full ~s of important speeches in Congress —Herbert Agar⟩ (2) : an edited or emended copy of the wording of an original work ⟨the ~ that was printed showed the results of an editor's blue pencil⟩ ⟨prepared a new ~ of the Shakespearean comedies⟩ **b** : a work containing such text ⟨pleased with the autographed ~ the young poet had given him⟩ ⟨the revised ~ did not sell as well as its predecessor⟩ **2 a** : the main body of printed or written matter

on a page exclusive of headings, running title, footnotes, illustrations, or margins **b :** the principal part of a book exclusive of the front and back matter ⟨use roman numerals in preliminary pages, arabic in ~⟩ **c :** the printed score of a musical composition ⟨strictly observed the ~ of the preludes and fugues and resisted individual interpretation⟩ **3 a** (1) **:** a verse or passage of Scripture chosen esp. for the subject of a sermon or for authoritative support (as in a question of doctrine) ⟨these outlines . . . and Scriptural ~*s* will be excellent supplementary material in the preparation of sermons —*Lenten & Easter Cat.*⟩ ⟨then, mustering ~*s* to justify his course . . . proceeded to baptize himself —George Willison⟩ (2) **:** a passage from an authoritative source providing an introduction or basis (as for an essay, speech, or lecture) ⟨one brief phrase which might form the ~ to an exhaustive treatise —Bernard Groom⟩ ⟨uses that ~ . . . as the point of departure —A.T.Weaver⟩ **b :** something providing a chief source of information or authority ⟨my ~ for this chapter is . . . any good daily newspaper —Weston La Barre⟩ ⟨Confucianism provided, in the main, the ~ for the cultivation of feudal loyalty —A.M.Young⟩ **c :** TEXTBOOK ⟨a ~ in chemistry, designed for use in a high school —*Chemistry at Work*⟩ ⟨included three Greek plays on the list of ~*s* for his humanities course⟩ **4 a :** TEXT HAND **b :** a type considered suitable for printing running text **5 a :** a subject on which one writes or speaks **:** THEME, TOPIC ⟨writers who hold forth glibly on that ~ —Douglas Bush⟩ **b :** the form and substance of something written or spoken ⟨the ~ of the appeal was a closely reasoned, eloquent and occasionally rhetorical argument against slavery —Martha Gruening⟩ ⟨the ~ of their conversation consists . . . of a recital of the exact order of action which is habitual on such an expedition —E.D.Chapple & C.S.Coon⟩ **6 :** the words of something (as a poem, libretto, scriptural passage, folktale) set to music ⟨in all vocal compositions a complete ~ for every voice part is given in the music —Carl Parrish & J.F.Ohl⟩ ⟨many hundred ~*s* and tunes of English-Canadian folk songs —*Report:* (*Canadian*) *Royal Commission on Nat'l Development*⟩

2text *vt*, *obs* **:** to write in large letters

text bible *n*, *usu cap B* **:** an edition of the Bible published with an unannotated text

textbook \\'=,=\\ *n*, *often attrib* **:** a book used in the study of a subject: as **a :** a book containing a usu. systematic presentation of the principles and vocabulary of a subject ⟨preparing a comprehensive ~ on geomorphology⟩ **b :** a book recording the historical development of a subject ⟨criticized an art history ~ for its sketchy treatment of the Florentine artists⟩ **c :** a collection of writings by various authors dealing with a specific subject ⟨a ~ of literary criticism by contemporary British and American authors⟩ **d :** a literary work relevant to the study of a subject ⟨among the suggested ~*s* were several novels written during the period⟩

textbookish \\'=,==\\ *adj* **:** of, relating to, or having the characteristics of a textbook ⟨has tied all the strands of his plot together in a slightly ~ fashion —*Amer. Scholar*⟩ ⟨except for a few all too brief interludes, the style is heavy and ~ —*Nation*⟩

text-critical \\'=¦===\\ *adj* **:** of, relating to, or having the characteristics of textual criticism esp. of the Scriptures ⟨*text-critical* study . . . makes it clear that the Hebrew text has suffered little corruption —Robert Gordis⟩

text edition *n* **:** an edition prepared for use esp. in schools and colleges — compare TRADE EDITION

text hand *n* **:** a style of handwriting marked by the use of large letters

tex·tile \\'tek,stīl, -kstᵊl, -k(,)stil\\ *n* -s *often attrib* [L, fr. neut. of *textilis* woven, fr. *textus* (past part.) + *-ilis* -ile] **1 :** CLOTH 1a; *esp* **:** a woven or knit cloth **2 :** a fiber, filament, or yarn used in the making of cloth

textile cone *n* **:** a showy but extremely venomous cone shell (*Conus textile* or *Darioconus textile*) having a cylindrical ovate shell that is pearly white blotched and reticulated with orange brown and marked with wavy dark brown tracery — called also *cloth-of-gold cone*

textile red WR-263 *n*, *usu cap T&R* **:** an organic pigment — see DYE table I (under *Pigment Red 23*)

textile screw pine *n* **:** a Polynesian screw pine (*Pandanus tectorius*) — called also *lauhala*

textile tissue *n* **:** TWISTING PAPER

text letter *n*, *obs* **:** a large calligraphic letter

tex·tu·al \\'tekschəwəl, -chəl\\ *adj* [ME *textuel*, fr. AF, fr. OF *texte* text + *-el* -al — more at TEXT] **:** of, relating to, or based on the text of something ⟨his management of ~ questions in his own edition of Shakespeare —Elizabeth Morrow⟩ ⟨the ~ image, the rose, appears and reappears —Austin Warren⟩ ⟨sought to extract a meaning from the ~ reading⟩

textual critic *n* **:** a practitioner of textual criticism

textual criticism *n* **1 :** the study of a literary work that aims to establish the original text ⟨those . . . who have given themselves to the *textual criticism* of the New Testament —B.W. Bacon⟩ ⟨*textual criticism* of Shakespearean tragedies⟩ — compare LOWER CRITICISM **2 :** a critical study of literature emphasizing a close reading and analysis of the text ⟨subjected several modern poems to concentrated *textual criticism*⟩ — compare NEW CRITICISM

tex·tu·al·ism \\-ə,lizəm\\ *n* -s **:** rigid adherence to a text of the Scriptures

tex·tu·al·ist \\-ˌləst\\ *n* -s **:** one who is a close student of the text of the Scriptures

tex·tu·al·ly \\-ch(əw)əlē, -li\\ *adv* **1 :** in or with regard to the text of something ⟨references implied but not expressed ~⟩ ⟨unacquainted with the Koran ~ —J.E.Merrill⟩ **2 :** VERBATIM ⟨rules . . . which reproduce ~ provisions of the charter —*U.N. General Assembly Rules of Procedure*⟩

1tex·tu·ary \\-chə,werē\\ *n* -ES [ML *textus* + E *-ary* (n. suffix)] **:** one who is well informed on the Bible or in biblical scholarship

2textuary \\"\\ *adj* [ML *textus* + E *-ary* (adj. suffix)] **:** TEXTUAL

tex·tur·al \\'tekschərəl\\ *adj* **:** of, relating to, or marked by texture ⟨based upon the ~ and physical characteristics . . . of the rock fragments —*Jour. of Geology*⟩ ⟨her skin had undergone a ~ change —Thomas Hardy⟩

1tex·ture \\'tekschə(r)\\ *n* -s [L *textura* web, texture, fr. *textus* (past part. of *texere* to weave) + *-ura* -ure — more at TECHNICAL] **1 a :** something composed of closely interwoven elements ⟨nor the spider entangle the heedless fly in his ~ —Abraham Tucker⟩; *specif* **:** a woven cloth ⟨took up from the couch the great purple-and-gold ~ that covered it —Oscar Wilde⟩ **b :** the structure formed by the threads of a fabric ⟨the open ~ of mesh⟩ **2 a :** the essential part of something **:** SUBSTANCE, NATURE ⟨not a mere exercise in metaphysics: for him it is . . . the very ~ of action —Irving Howe⟩ ⟨musical theater, American in its quality and ~ —Rouben Mamoulian⟩ **b :** an identifying quality **:** CHARACTER ⟨the distinctive ~ of Mediterranean culture —Morris Watnick⟩ ⟨by the cigars they smoke, and the composers they love, ye shall know the ~ of men's souls —John Galsworthy⟩ **3 a :** the size and organization of small constituent parts of a body or substance ⟨cellular ~ of a plant stem⟩ ⟨a soil is fine or coarse in ~ according to the relative proportions of fine and coarse particles present —C.F.Marbut⟩ **b :** the visual or tactile surface characteristics and appearance of something ⟨the ~*s* and shapes of people's well-kept-up places showed cold-washed and brilliant —Edmund Wilson⟩ ⟨nubby ~ of tweed⟩ ⟨a photography that transmutes the ~*s* of earth and water, woods, and grasses —Arthur Knight⟩ ⟨scrawl calligraphic convolutions over the painted surface . . . to give it ~ —David Sylvester⟩ **c :** the characteristic consistency esp. of a liquid or semiliquid ⟨thinning baby's cereal with formula . . . makes the ~ more familiar —*advt*⟩ ⟨the finished product, made of glue and glycerin, has a rubbery ~ —*Saturday Rev.*⟩ **d :** GRAIN 6a ⟨the ~ varies with different woods and rate of growth —Thomas Corkhill⟩ **4 a :** the smaller features of a rock that depend on the size, shape, arrangement, and distribution of the component minerals ⟨the ~ of the unaltered rock varies, ranging from porphyritic . . . to seriate —*Economic Geology*⟩ — compare STRUCTURE **b :** a composite of the elements of prose or poetry ⟨all these words . . . meet violently to form a ~ impressive and exciting —John Berryman⟩ ⟨the ~ of the internal monologue derives its richness and stiffness from a continuous thread of quotation —Harry Levin⟩ **c :** a pattern of musical sound created by tones or lines played or sung together ⟨the harmonic ~ constantly suggested tonality to my ear —Irving Kolodin⟩ ⟨is sung by each voice in turn so that another parallel melodic line is added to the ~ —Norman Demuth⟩ **5 a :** a basic scheme or structure **:** FABRIC ⟨closely inwoven with the ~ of rational experience —W.R.Inge⟩ ⟨believed that character was the pervasive ~ of personality —Doris F. Bernays⟩ **b :** the overall structure of something incorporating all or most of its parts **:** BODY ⟨lessons . . . yet to become absorbed into the ~ of contemporary society —F. H.A.Micklewright⟩ ⟨once a theme . . . assumes importance it tends to recur and become integrated into the ~ of the play —E.A.Armstrong⟩

2texture \\"\\ *vt* -ED/-ING/-S **1 :** to make by or as if by weaving ⟨a bright faultless vision *textured* out of mere sunbeams —Jane W. Carlyle⟩ **2 a :** to form with a texture ⟨walled with opaque glass . . . *textured* into little cubes —Lewis Mumford⟩ **b :** to give a texture to ⟨carpets *textured* with patterns in high and low pile⟩

texture·less \\'==ˌləs\\ *adj* **:** lacking a texture

texture paint *n* **:** a paint of heavy consistency and coarse grain consisting usu. of gypsum and sand with water-thinned binder and used for creating a rough patterned effect on a wall

tex·tus \\'tekstəs\\ *n*, *pl* **textus** [ML & L — more at TEXT] **1 :** a text of the Bible **2 :** TISSUE

textus re·cep·tus \\-rə'septəs, -rē'-\\ *n* [NL, lit., received text] **:** the generally accepted text of a literary work (as the Greek New Testament)

text writer *n* **:** one who writes textbooks relating esp. to law

TF *abbr* **1** task force **2** territorial force **3** *often not cap* till forbidden **4** *often not cap* to fill **5** *often not cap* to follow

TFE *abbr or n* -S tetrafluoroethylene

tfillin *var of* TEFILLIN

t formation *n*, *cap T* **:** an offensive football formation in which the fullback lines up behind the center and quarterback and one halfback is stationed on each side of the fullback

tfr *abbr* transfer

tg *abbr* **1** telegram **2** telegraph

TG *abbr* **1** task group **2** tollgate **3** *often not cap* type genus

TGB *abbr*, *often not cap* tongued, grooved, and beaded

tgl *abbr* toggle

tgt *abbr* target

1-th — see 1-ETH

2-th \\th, *usu with preceding epenthetic* t *after some consonants and in* eighth; *often* t *after some consonants or/and before the plural ending* s, *as in* sixth(s), ninths\\ *or* **-eth** \\əth\\ *adj suffix* [ME *-the, -te, -ethe*, fr. OE *-tha, -ta, -otha, -etha;* akin to OHG *-do, -to* -th, ON *-di, -ti*, Goth *-da, -ta*, L *-tus*, Gk *-tos*, Skt *-tha*] — used in forming ordinal numbers ⟨ten*th*⟩ ⟨twenti*eth*⟩

3-th \\th, *usu with preceding epenthetic* p, t, *or* k *after some consonants; often* t *before the plural ending* s, *as in* widths\\ *n suffix* -s [ME *-the, -th*, fr. OE *-thu, -th;* akin to OHG *-ida*, suffix forming abstract nouns, ON *-th*, Goth *-itha*, L *-ta*, Gk *-tē*, Skt *-tā*] **1 :** act or process ⟨spil*th*⟩ **2 :** state or condition ⟨bread*th*⟩ ⟨green*th*⟩ ⟨wid*th*⟩

th *abbr* **1** thoroughbred **2** threshold

-th *symbol* [2*-th*] — used after figures (as 4, 5, 6, 7, 8, 9) to indicate ordinal numbers ⟨May 4*th*⟩ ⟨44*th* Street⟩

TH *abbr* **1** true heading **2** two hands

Th *symbol* thorium

th' \\th\\ *definite article* [ME, short for *the*] **:** THE — used sometimes before words beginning with a vowel sound

1tha \\thə\\ *dial var of* THEE

2tha \\"\\ *dial var of* THOU

3tha \\"\\ *dial var of* THY

thack *also* **thak** \\'thak\\ *dial var of* THATCH

thack·er \\-kə(r)\\ *dial var of* THATCHER

1thack·er·ay·an \\'thakərēən\\ *adj*, *usu cap* [William M. *Thackeray* †1863 Eng. novelist + E *-an* (adj. suffix)] **:** of, relating to, or characteristic of W.M.Thackeray or his writings ⟨digressing in obsolete *Thackerayan* fashion —J.B.Cabell⟩ ⟨*Thackerayan* asides —H.L.Mencken⟩

2thackerayan \\"\\ *n* -s *usu cap* [William M. *Thackeray* †1863 + E *-an* (n. suffix)] **:** an authority on or devotee of Thackeray

1thae \\'thā\\ *chiefly Scot var of* THOSE

2thae \\"\\ *chiefly Scot var of* THESE

thai \\'tī\\ *n*, *pl* **thai** *or* **thais** *cap* **1** *or* **thai·land·er** \\'tī-,landə(r)\\ -s **:** a native or inhabitant of Thailand or one of his descendants **2 :** the language of the Thai **:** the official language of Thailand — called also *Siamese* **3 :** a group of languages including Thai, Lao, Shan, Khamti, and Ahom and considered by some to belong to the Sino-Tibetan language group

thai·land \\'tī,land *sometimes* -ˌlənd\\ *adj*, *usu cap* [fr. *Thailand*, country in southeast Asia] **:** of or from Thailand **:** of the kind or style prevalent in Thailand **:** SIAMESE

thairm \\'thārm\\ *n* -s [ME *therm, tharm* gut, fr. OE *thearm* — more at DERMA (beef casing)] *dial chiefly Scot* **:** CATGUT; *esp* **:** a fiddle string

tha·is \\'thāəs\\ *n*, *cap* [NL, after *Thais*, 4th cent. B.C. Greek hetaera, fr. L, fr. Gk *Thaïs*] **:** a widely distributed genus that comprises marine snails with a rough thick shell sometimes ornamented with tubercles and is sometimes made the type of a distinct family but is usu. placed in Muricidae — see DOG WHELK, PURPURA

tha·kur \\'tä,ku̇(ə)r\\ *n* -s *usu cap* [Hindi *ṭhākur*, fr. Skt *ṭhakkura*] **:** a member of the Kshatriya caste among the Hindus

thalam- *or* **thalamo-** *comb form* [NL, fr. *thalamus*] **1 :** thalamus ⟨*thalam*encephalon⟩ ⟨*thalamo*fugal⟩ **2 :** thalamic and ⟨*thalamo*cortical⟩

thal·a·men·ce·phal·ic \\¦thalə¦mensə¦falik\\ *adj* [NL *thalamencephalon* + E *-ic*] **:** DIENCEPHALIC

thal·a·men·ceph·a·lon \\,thaləmən'sefə,län\\ *n* -s [NL, fr. *thalam-* + *encephalon*] **:** DIENCEPHALON

tha·lam·ic \\thə'lamik, -mēk\\ *adj* [NL *thalamicus*, fr. *thalamus* + L *-icus* -ic] **:** of, relating to, or involving the thalamus — **tha·lam·i·cal·ly** \\-mək(ə)lē\\ *adv*

thalamic radiation *n* **:** any of several large bundles of nerve fibers connecting the thalamus with the cerebral cortex by way of the internal capsule

thal·a·mite \\'thalə,mīt\\ *n* -s [Gk *thalamitēs*, fr. *thalamos* chamber, hold of a ship + *-itēs* -ite] **:** the outermost of the three rowers to a bench on a trireme sitting somewhat in advance and below the other two — compare THRANITE, ZYGITE

thal·a·mo·cele *or* **thal·a·mo·coele** \\'thaləmō,sēl\\ *n* -s [*thalam-* + *-cele, -coele*] **:** the third ventricle of the brain

thal·a·mo·cortical \\¦thalə(,)mō+\\ *adj* [*thalam-* + *cortical*] **:** of, relating to, or connecting the thalamus and the cerebral cortex

thal·a·mof·u·gal \\¦thalə¦mäfyəgəl\\ *adj* [*thalam-* + *-fugal*] **:** passing out of the thalamus

thal·a·mo-olivary \\¦thalə(,)mō+\\ *adj* [*thalam-* + *olivary*] **:** relating to or connecting the thalamus and the inferior olivary body

thal·a·moph·o·ra \\,thalə'mäfərə\\ [NL, fr. Gk *thalamos* chamber + NL *-phora*] *syn of* FORAMINIFERA

thal·a·mot·o·my \\,thalə'mäd·əmē\\ *n* -ES [*thalam-* + *-tomy*] **:** a surgical operation involving electrocoagulation of areas of the thalamus and thereby interrupting pathways of nervous transmission through the thalamus for relief of certain mental disorders

thal·a·mus \\'thaləməs\\ *n*, *pl* **thala·mi** \\-lə,mī\\ [NL, fr. Gk *thalamos* room, woman's apartment, bridal chamber; perh. akin to Gk *tholos* rotunda — more at DALE] **1 :** the largest subdivision of the diencephalon consisting chiefly of an ovoid mass of nuclei in each lateral wall of the third ventricle and being divisible into an anterior and medial group of nuclei that constitutes the paleothalamus, is concerned with primitive correlations in connection with the corpus striatum but not the cerebral cortex, and is a center for the crude perception of pain and the affective qualities of other sensations and a lateral group of nuclei that constitutes the neothalamus and serves as the great relay station of somatic sensory and optic paths to the cerebral cortex with which it is connected by the thalamic radiation **2 :** RECEPTACLE 3b **3** *or* **tha·la·mi·um** \\thə'lāmēəm\\ -s [*thalamus* fr. L, fr. Gk *thalamos; thalamium*, NL, dim. of L *thalamus*] **:** an inner room or bower in classic architecture usu. for the women of the family

thal·arc·tos \\tha'lärk,täs\\ *n*, *cap* [NL, irreg. fr. Gk *thalassa* sea + *arktos* bear — more at ARCTIC] **:** a genus of bears consisting of the polar bear — compare URSUS

thalass- *or* **thalasso-** *comb form* [Gk, fr. *thalassa, thalatta*] **:** sea ⟨*thalass*emia⟩ ⟨*thalasso*meter⟩

tha·las·sal \\thə'lasəl\\ *adj* [*thalass-* + *-al*] **:** THALASSIC

thal·as·sarc·tos \\,thalə'särk,täs\\ [NL, fr. *thalass-* + Gk *arktos* bear] *syn of* THALARCTOS

thal·as·se·mia \\,thalə'sēmēə\\ *also* **thal·ass·anemia** \\¦thaləs+\\ *n* -s [NL, fr. *thalass-* + *-emia* or *anemia*] **:** a familial hypochromic anemia characterized by microcytic anemia, splenomegaly, and changes in the bones and skin and occurring esp. in children of Mediterranean parents

tha·las·si·an \\thə'lasēən\\ *n* -s [*thalass-* + *-ian*] **:** SEA TURTLE

tha·las·sic \\thə'lasik, -sēk\\ *adj* [F *thalassique*, fr. *thalass-* + *-ique* -ic] **1 :** of or relating to the sea or ocean **2 :** of or relating to seas or gulfs as distinguished from oceans ⟨deposits of sediment in gulfs and seas rather than in the oceans proper are known as ~ deposits —*Scientific Monthly*⟩

1tha·las·si·nid \\thə'lasənəd\\ *adj* [NL *Thalassinidea*] **:** of or relating to the Thalassinidea

2thalassinid \\"\\ *n* -s **:** a crustacean of the subtribe Thalassinidea

tha·las·si·nid·ea \\thə,lasə'nidēə\\ *n pl*, *cap* [NL, fr. *Thalassina*, genus of crustaceans (fr. *thalass-* + *-ina*) + *-idea*] **:** a subtribe of Anomura including small crustaceans with a thin flexible carapace, long soft abdomen, and unsymmetrical chelae that burrow in sand or mud along seashores — compare GHOST SHRIMP — **tha·las·si·nid·e·an** \\=¦==¦nidēən\\ *n or adj* — **tha·las·si·noid** \\thə'lasə,nȯid\\ *adj*

thal·as·soch·e·lys \\,thalə'säkələs\\ [NL, fr. *thalass-* + Gk *chelys* tortoise — more at CHELYS] *syn of* CARETTA

thal·as·soc·ra·cy \\,thalə'säkrəsē\\ *n* -ES [Gk *thalassokratia*, fr. *thalass-* + *-kratia* -cracy] **:** maritime supremacy ⟨insecurity of the seas . . . which followed the collapse of the Mycenaean ~ —*Interpreter's Bible*⟩

tha·las·so·crat \\thə'lasə,krat\\ *n* -s [fr. *thalassocracy*, after such pairs as E *democracy: democrat*] **:** one who has maritime supremacy

thal·as·sog·ra·pher \\,thalə'sägrəfə(r)\\ *n* -s [*thalassography* + *-er*] **:** a specialist in thalassography

tha·las·so·graph·ic \\thə¦lasə¦grafik\\ *or* **tha·las·so·graph·i·cal** \\-fəkəl\\ *adj* **:** of or relating to thalassography

thal·as·sog·ra·phy \\,thalə'sägrəfē\\ *n* -ES [ISV *thalass-* + *-graphy*] **:** oceanography esp. relating to seas and gulfs

thal·as·som·e·ter \\,thalə'säməd·ə(r)\\ *n* [ISV *thalass-* + *-meter*] **:** TIDE GAGE

thale-cress \\'thā(ə)l'kres\\ *n* [after Johann *Thal* †1583 Ger. physician] **:** MOUSE-EAR CRESS

tha·len·ite \\'thälə,nīt\\ *n* -s [F *thalénite*, fr. T. R. *Thalén* †1905 Sw. physicist + F *-ite*] **:** a mineral $Y_2Si_2O_7$ or $2Y_2Si_2O_7.H_2O$ consisting of an yttrium silicate and occurring in flesh-red monoclinic crystals possibly isomorphous with thortveitite (hardness 6.5, sp. gr. 4.2)

thaler *var of* TALER

tha·le·sian \\thā'lēzhən\\ *adj*, *usu cap* [*Thales* †546 B.C. Gk philosopher and scientist + E *-ian*] **:** of, relating to, or typical of the Grecian Thales or his nature philosophy according to which water is the basic stuff of the physical universe — compare MILESIAN

tha·lia \\'thālēə\\ *n*, *cap* [NL, fr. Gk, abundance, fr. the stem of *thallein* to sprout, grow, thrive + *-ia* -y; akin to Arm *dalar* green, fresh, Alb *dal* I come forth, and perh. to W *dail* leaves, MIr *duille;* basic meaning: to blossom, bloom] **1 :** a small genus of American mostly aquatic herbs (family Marantaceae) with broad long-stalked basal leaves, terminal panicles of bracted purple flowers, and globose capsules **2 :** a genus of pelagic tunicates commonly regarded as a subgenus of *Salpa*

tha·li·a·cea \\,thālē'āshēə\\ *n pl*, *cap* [NL, fr. *Thalia* + *-acea*] **:** a small order of tunicates consisting of various aberrant free-swimming pelagic forms (as of the genera *Salpa* and *Doliolum*) — **tha·li·a·cean** \\¦==¦āshən\\ *n or adj*

tha·li·an \\thə'līən\\ *adj*, *sometimes cap* [*Thalia*, ancient Greek Muse of comedy (fr. L, fr. Gk *Thaleia*) + E *-an*] **:** of or relating to comedy **:** COMIC

tha·lic·trum \\thə'liktrəm\\ *n* [NL, fr. L, meadow rue, fr. Gk *thaliktron*] **1** *cap* **:** a large widely distributed genus of herbs (family Ranunculaceae) comprising the meadow rues and having ternately decompound leaves, small polygamous or unisexual apetalous flowers, and fruit consisting of several achenes **2** -s **:** any plant of the genus *Thalictrum*

thall- *or* **thalli-** *or* **thallo-** *comb form* [NL, fr. Gk *thall-*, *thallo-*, fr. *thallos* — more at THALLUS] **1 :** a young shoot **:** thallus ⟨*Thallo*phyta⟩ ⟨*thall*ium⟩ ⟨*thalli*form⟩ **2 :** thallium ⟨*thall*ic⟩

thal·lic \\'thalik\\ *adj* [ISV *thall-* + *-ic*] **:** of, relating to, or containing thallium — used esp. of compounds in which this element is trivalent; compare THALLOUS

thal·lif·er·ous \\thə'lif(ə)rəs\\ *adj* [*thall-* + *-ferous*] **:** containing or yielding thallium

thal·li·form \\'thalə,fȯrm\\ *adj* [*thall-* + *-form*] **:** having the form of a thallus

1thal·line \\'tha,līn, -alən\\ *adj* [*thall-* + *-ine*] **:** consisting of or constituting a thallus

2thal·line \\'tha,lēn, -alən\\ *n* -s [ISV *thall-* + *-ine;* fr. the green color it forms with oxidizing agents] **:** a crystalline base $CH_3OC_9H_9NH$ derived from quinoline, forming a green color with oxidizing agents, and formerly used in the form of salts as an antipyretic

thal·li·um \\'thalēəm\\ *n* -s [NL, fr. *thall-* + *-ium;* fr. the bright green line in its spectrum] **:** a sparsely but widely distributed metallic element that resembles tin in appearance but on exposure to air readily forms a gray and then brown-black coating of oxide, that is malleable like lead but a little softer, that occurs combined in a few minerals (as crookesite and lorandite) and in smaller amounts in various other minerals and in plants, that is usu. obtained from flue dusts from pyrites burners or from lead and zinc smelters and refiners, that is very poisonous and principally univalent but sometimes trivalent in its compounds, and that forms alloys but is used chiefly in the form of compounds (as the sulfide in photoelectric cells) — symbol *Tl;* see ACTINIUM SERIES, THORIUM SERIES, URANIUM SERIES; ELEMENT table

thallium sulfate *n* **:** a poisonous crystalline salt Tl_2SO_4 used chiefly as a rodenticide and insecticide — called also *thallous sulfate*

thal·lo·gen \\'thaləjən\\ *n* -s [*thall-* + *-gen*] **:** a plant in which growth is not restricted to an apical growing point **:** THALLOPHYTE — compare ACROGEN — **thal·lo·gen·ic** \\¦thalə¦jenik\\ *or* **thal·log·e·nous** \\thə'läjənəs\\ *adj*

thal·loid \\'tha,lȯid\\ *adj* [*thall-* + *-oid*] **:** of, relating to, resembling, or consisting of a thallus

thal·loph·y·ta \\thə'läfəd·ə\\ *n pl*, *cap* [NL, fr. *thall-* + *-phyta*] *in some classifications* **:** a primary division of the plant kingdom that consists of plants with single-celled sex organs or with many-celled sex organs of which all cells give rise to gametes, that is now commonly considered to be a heterogeneous assemblage, and that when recognized comprises the Algae and Fungi — compare EUMYCETES

thal·lo·phyte \\'thalə,fīt\\ *n* -s [NL *Thallophyta*] **:** a plant belonging to the Thallophyta — **thal·lo·phyt·ic** \\¦==¦fid·ik\\ *adj*

thal·lose \\'tha,lōs\\ *adj* [*thall-* + *-ose*] **:** THALLOID

thal·lo·spore \\'thalə,spō(ə)r, -pȯ(ə)r\\ *n* [ISV *thall-* + *-spore*] **:** a spore not abstricted from a conidiophore; *esp* **:** a spore (as a blastospore) developing by septation or budding of hyphal cells

thal·lous \\'thaləs\\ *adj* [*thall-* + *-ous*] **:** of, relating to, or containing thallium — used esp. of compounds in which this element is univalent; compare THALLIC

thallous sulfate *n* **:** THALLIUM SULFATE

thal·lus \\'thaləs\\ *n*, *pl* **thal·li** \\-a,lī\\ *or* **thalluses** [NL, fr. L, young shoot, green stalk, fr. Gk *thallos*, fr. *thallein* to sprout — more at THALIA] **:** a plant body that is characteristic of the thallophytes, that does not grow from an apical point, shows no differentiation into distinct tissue systems (as vascular tissue) or members (as stems, leaves, or roots) or is composed of members resembling and performing many of the functions of but not homologous with those of the higher plants, and that may be simple or branched, may consist of filaments or plates of cells, and may vary widely in form and size from microscopic one-celled plants to complex foliated or arborescent forms (as in some of the larger marine algae)

thal·po·sis \thal'pōsəs\ *n, pl* **thalpo·ses** \-ō,sēz\ [NL, fr. Gk *thalpos* heat, warmth (fr. *thalpein* to heat) + NL *-osis;* perh. akin to *thallein* to sprout — more at THALIA] **:** the warmth sense **:** warmth sensation

thal·pot·ic \(')thal¦päd·ik\ *adj* **:** of, relating to, or having a sense of warmth

thal·weg \'täl,veg, -vāk\ *n* -S [G *talweg* (formerly spelled *thalweg*), fr. *tal* valley (fr. OHG) + *weg* way, path, fr. OHG — more at DALE, WAY] **1 a :** a line following the lowest part of a valley whether under water or not **b :** the line of continuous maximum descent from any point on a land surface or one crossing all contour lines at right angles **c :** subsurface water percolating beneath and in the same direction as a surface stream course **2 :** the middle of the chief navigable channel of a waterway which constitutes a boundary line between states

tha·ma·kau \¦thämə¦kau̇\ *n* -S [Fiji] **:** a large outrigger canoe used in the Fiji islands

thames barge \'temz-\ *n, usu cap T* [fr. the *Thames* river, England] **:** a round-bowed transom-sterned broad-beamed freight boat usu. having a sprit mainsail and small gaff mizzen that can be lowered to pass under bridges and plying the coast and rivers of southern England

thames measurement *n, usu cap T* **:** a British measurement of tonnage esp. for yachts ⟨small vessel of . . . 36 tons *Thames measurement* —*Times Lit. Supp.*⟩

tha·min \'thä,min\ *also* **tha·meng** \-meŋ\ *n* -S [Burmese *thamin, thamañ*] **:** a deer (*Cervus eldi*) of Burma, Siam, and the Malay peninsula having antlers with long curved brow tines

thamn- *or* **thamno-** *comb form* [Gk, fr. *thamnos;* akin to Gk *thama* frequent, often, *tithenai* to place, put — more at DO] **:** bush **:** shrub ⟨*thamno*phile⟩

tham·nid·i·um \tham'nidēəm\ *n, cap* [NL, fr. *thamn-* + *-idium*] **:** a genus (the type of the family Thamnidiaceae) of molds related to the typical bread molds and characterized by branched sporangiophores and sporangia consisting of a large terminal one with a columella and smaller lateral sporangioles without columella — compare WHISKER 2c

tham·ni·um \'thamnēəm\ *n* -S [NL, fr. Gk *thamnion* small bush, dim. of *thamnos* bush] **:** the branched or fruticose thallus of various lichens (as of the genus *Cladonia*)

tham·no·phile \'thamnə,fīl\ *n* -S [NL *Thamnophilus*] **:** ANT-SHRIKE

tham·noph·i·line \tham'näfə,līn\ *adj* [NL *Thamnophilus* + E *-ine*] **:** of or relating to the genus *Thamnophilus*

tham·noph·i·lus \-fələs\ *n, cap* [NL, fr. *thamn-* + *-philus*] **:** a genus of Neotropical hook-billed antbirds (family Formicariidae) consisting of the antshrikes

tham·no·phis \'thamnəfəs\ *n, cap* [NL, fr. *thamn-* + *-ophis*] **:** a genus of American colubrid snakes comprising the garter snake

tham·no·tet·tix \,thamnō'ted·iks\ *n, cap* [NL, fr. *thamn-* + Gk *tettix* cicada, of imit. origin] **:** a genus of leafhoppers including some that transmit virus diseases (as yellows) to many plants

¹tha·mu·dic \thə'müdik\ *adj, usu cap* [*Thamud*, an ancient people of Arabia (fr. Ar *Thamūd*) + E *-ic*] **:** of or relating to various old Semitic inscriptions in characters resembling the Sabaean

²thamudic \"\ *n* -S *usu cap* **:** a form of North Arabic that is known from inscriptions from the fifth century B.C. to the fourth century A.D.

¹than \thən, then, (')than, *rapid sometimes* ən *or* ᵊn (*after* t, d, s, *or* z) *or* n (*as in one pronunciation*, ,bed·ə(r)'nathə(r)z, *of* "better than others")\ *conj* [ME *thanne, thonne, than, thenne, then*, fr. OE *thanne, thonne, thænne;* akin to OFris *than*, OS *thanna, thanne*, than, OHG *thanne, thanna, denne;* all fr. a prehistoric WGmc conj. derived fr. an adv. represented by OE *thanne, thonne, thænne* then — more at THEN] **1 a** — used as a function word to indicate that what immediately follows is the second member or the member taken as point of departure in a comparison expressive of inequality; used with comparative adjectives and comparative adverbs ⟨he is older ~ I⟩ ⟨deer can run faster ~ cows⟩ ⟨easier said ~ done⟩ ⟨arrived earlier ~ usual⟩ ⟨paid more ~ necessary⟩ ⟨knows better ~ to start a quarrel⟩ ⟨I regard him more highly ~ to suspect him⟩ ⟨has more ~ doubled his output⟩ ⟨he deceived us worse ~ if he had told us an outright lie⟩ ⟨he resolved, rather ~ yield, to die with honor —Samuel Butler †1680⟩ ⟨lemurs . . . are nearly related to the true monkeys, ~ which they are a more primitive type —James Stevenson-Hamilton⟩ **b** — used as a function word to indicate difference of kind, manner, or identity; used with some adjectives and adverbs that express diversity and with some words derived from them ⟨other woe ~ ours —John Keats⟩ ⟨anywhere else ~ at home⟩ ⟨he could hardly have behaved otherwise ~ he did⟩ ⟨others ~ the four who hold the . . . center of his stage —Carl Van Doren⟩ ⟨the task of education is not different for gifted children ~ for others —Elise Martens⟩; sometimes considered substandard except with *other, else,* and their derivatives, though use with *different* and *differently* is of long standing and found in many reputable authors; compare ¹DIFFERENT 1 **2 :** rather than — usu. used only after *prefer, preferable,* and *preferably,* and sometimes considered substandard even there ⟨I preferred to be called a coward ~ fight —John Reed⟩ **3 :** other than ⟨we have no alternative ~ to follow the sense of our own experience —K.L. Patton⟩ **4 :** WHEN ⟨had barely left the lift at the bottom ~ the lift bell started to ring —David Masters⟩ — used esp. after *scarcely* and *hardly* ⟨hardly had the birds dropped ~ she jumped into the water and retrieved them —G.G.Carter⟩

²than \"\ *prep* **:** in comparison with **:** by way of superiority or inferiority to — used by speakers on all educational levels and by many reputable writers with the objective case form of the following pronoun when the first term in the comparison is the subject of a verb or the predicative complement after a copulative verb though disapproved by some grammarians except in the phrase *than whom* ⟨they were both somewhat taller ~ her —Anthony Trollope⟩ ⟨man, ~ whom nothing could be more miserable —Jeremy Taylor⟩

tha·na \'tänə\ *n* -S [Hindi *thānā*, fr. Skt *sthāna* place, fr. *tiṣṭhati* he stands — more at STAND] **1 :** a military post in India during the British occupation **2 :** an Indian police station **:** police division serving as a unit of Indian local administration

tha·na·dar \,tänə'där\ *n* -S [Hindi *thānādār*, fr. *thānā* + Per *-dār* having] **:** the chief officer of a thana

than·age \'thānij\ *n* -S [ME, fr. ML *thanagium, thenagium*, fr. ME *theyn, thayn* + ML *-agium* (fr. OF *-age*) — more at THANE] **1 :** the land held by a thane **2 :** the rank or office of a thane

thanat- *or* **thanato-** *comb form* [Gk, fr. *thanatos;* akin to Skt *adhvanīt* it vanished and prob. to L *fumus* smoke — more at FUME] **:** death ⟨*thanat*oid⟩ ⟨*thanato*logy⟩

than·a·to·coe·nose \,thanətō'sē,nōs\ *or* **than·a·to·coe·no·sis** \-tōsə'nōsəs\ *n, pl* **thanatocoeno·ses** \-sə'nō,sēz\ [NL *thanatocoenosis*, fr. *thanat-* + Gk *koinōsis* sharing — more at BIOCENOSE] **:** an assemblage of organisms or their parts brought together (as by deposition from flowing water) in nature after death

than·a·toid \'thanə,tȯid\ *adj* [*thanat-* + *-oid*] **:** resembling death **:** DEATHLY

than·a·to·log·i·cal \¦thanətə¦läjəkəl\ *adj* **:** of or belonging to thanatology

than·a·tol·o·gy \,thanə'täləjē\ *n* -ES [*thanat-* + *-logy*] **:** the description or study of the phenomena of somatic death

than·a·to·mania \¦thanə(,)tō+\ *n* [NL, fr. *thanat-* + *mania*] **1 :** suicidal mania **2 :** death by autosuggestion

than·a·to·phid·ia \,thanətə'fidēə\ *n pl* [NL, fr. *thanat-* + *Ophidia*] **:** venomous snakes

than·a·to·pho·bia \,thanətə'fōbēə\ *n* [NL, fr. *thanat-* + *phobia*] **:** fear of death ⟨thus he showed how Epicurus tried to rid the mind of ~ —O.S.J.Gogarty⟩

than·a·tos \'thanə,täs\ *n* -ES *usu cap* [Gk, death — more at THANAT-] **:** instinctual destructiveness **:** DEATH INSTINCT — contrasted with *Eros*

than·a·to·sis \,thanə'tōsəs\ *n* -ES [NL, fr. *thanat-* + *-osis*] **:** a state that in some respects resembles shock, is characterized by cessation of all voluntary activity and usu. by assumption of a posture suggestive of death, and occurs in various insects (as beetles) when disturbed

than·a·tot·ic \¦==¦täd·ik\ *adj* [*Thanatos* + *-otic*] **:** of or belonging to Thanatos

thane *or* **thegn** \'thān\ *n* -S [*thane* fr. ME *theyn, thayn*, fr. OE *thegn;* *thegn* fr. OE; akin to OS & OHG *thegan* warrior, freeman, thane, ON *thegn* freeman, thane, Gk *teknon* child, *tiktein* to give birth to, beget, Skt *takman* offspring, child; basic meaning: to beget, bear] **1 :** a retainer or free servant of a lord; *specif* **:** one holding lands from the king or other superior in Anglo-Saxon England and performing military and various other governmental services **2 a :** one holding land of a Scottish king **b :** the chief of a Scottish clan **c :** a Scots peer or noble

thane·dom *or* **thegn·dom** \-ndəm\ *n* -S [ME *thayndom*, fr. *theyn, thayn* thane + *-dom*] **:** THANAGE

thane·hood *or* **thegn·hood** \-n,hu̇d\ *n* **1 :** thanes as a class **2 :** the rank or office of a thane

thane·land *or* **thegn·land** \-n,land, -nlənd\ *n* **:** land granted to a thane by his feudal superior

thane·ship *or* **thegn·ship** \-n,ship\ *n* **:** THANAGE

than·ess \-nəs\ *n* -ES [*thane* + *-ess*] **:** the wife of a Scottish thane

¹thank \'thaŋk, 'thaiŋk\ *n* -S [ME *thank, thonk*, fr. OE *thanc, thonc* thought, will, mercy, favor, pleasure, gratitude; akin to OHG *thank, dank* memory, thought, gratitude, ON *thökk* gratitude, Goth *thanks* gratitude, L *tongēre* to know, Alb *tângë* resentment, Toch A *tuṅk-* love, Toch B *taṅkw;* basic meaning: to think, feel] **1 thanks** *pl* **:** kindly or grateful thoughts **:** GRATITUDE ⟨express my ~*s*⟩ **2** *obs* **:** worthiness to be thanked **:** MERIT, CREDIT ⟨if ye do good to them which do good to you, what ~ have ye? —Lk 6:33 (AV)⟩ **3 a :** an expression of gratitude **:** acknowledgment esp. by words of a benefit received from or offered by another ⟨never a ~ was accorded any for always battling . . . the foemen —W.B. Smith & Walter Miller⟩ — usu. used in pl.; often used in pl. in an utterance containing no verb and serving as an ordinarily courteous and somewhat informal expression of gratitude ⟨~*s*⟩ ⟨many ~*s*⟩ ⟨~*s* a lot⟩ ⟨~*s* for helping me⟩ ⟨no, ~*s*⟩ **b thanks** *pl* **:** an expression of gratitude to God in the form of a short prayer before or after a meal — used esp. in the phrases *give thanks* and *return thanks* — **no thanks to :** not as a result of any benefit conferred by ⟨I am feeling better now, *no thanks to* you⟩ — **thanks to :** with the help of ⟨*thanks to* his stepmother . . . he secured a good education —W.A.Robinson⟩ **:** owing to ⟨it took us a couple of days to get there, *thanks to* fog —D.B. Putnam⟩

²thank \"\ *vb* -ED/-ING/-S [ME *thanken, thonken*, fr. OE *thancian, thoncian;* akin to OHG *thankōn, danchōn* to thank, ON *thakka;* denominative fr. the root of E ¹*thank*] *vt* **1 a :** to express gratitude to **:** acknowledge esp. by words a benefit received from or offered by ⟨~*ed* her uncle for the birthday present⟩ — used in the phrase *thank you* with a first person subject or without any subject as the most polite formula for expressing gratitude on the part of the speaker or writer or the group to which he belongs ⟨~ you very much for the loan⟩ ⟨I ~ you for your music —Shak.⟩; used in such phrases as *thank God, thank goodness, thank heaven* usu. without any subject to express gratitude or more often only pleasure or satisfaction on the part of the speaker or writer ⟨~ God nobody was killed in the wreck⟩ ⟨the beds are all made, ~ goodness⟩ **b :** to hold responsible **:** give the credit or blame to ⟨whether we eat the food directly as the plant stored it or indirectly after some animal has converted it into meat or milk, we still have to ~ the plant for it —J.B.Robson⟩ ⟨had only his inexperience to ~ for his failure to get ahead⟩ **c :** REQUEST — used esp. after *will* or *'ll* to imply forced courtesy or barely veiled hostility ⟨I'll ~ you to open the window⟩ ⟨I will ~ you to mind your own business⟩ **d :** to feel gratitude to ⟨a textbook that thousands of teachers will ~ the author for writing⟩ **2 :** to express gratitude for ⟨ten thousandfold the favor I shall ~ —Robert Browning⟩ ~ *vi* **:** to express gratitude — **thank one's stars** *or* **thank one's lucky stars :** to congratulate oneself on one's good fortune **:** consider oneself fortunate

thank·ee *or* **thanky** \-kē\ *also* **thank·ye** \-kyē\ *interj* [alter. of *thank you*] — used to express gratitude

thank·er \-kə(r)\ *n* -S **:** one that thanks

thank·ful \-kfəl\ *adj, sometimes* **thankfuller**; *sometimes* **thankfullest** [ME, fr. OE *thancful* thoughtful, contented, thankful, fr. *thanc* thought, pleasure, gratitude + *-ful*] **1 :** conscious of benefit received and kindly disposed toward the benefactor **:** GRATEFUL ⟨a ~ heart⟩ **2 :** expressive of thanks or gratitude ⟨~ service⟩ **3 :** well pleased **:** GLAD ⟨I was ~ they could not see my face, for I was blushing —Paul Roche⟩ — **thank·ful·ly** \-fəlē, -li\ *adv* — **thank·ful·ness** *n* -ES

thank·less \-kləs\ *adj* **1 :** not expressing or feeling gratitude **:** UNGRATEFUL ⟨how sharper than a serpent's tooth it is to have a ~ child —Shak.⟩ **2 :** not obtaining thanks **:** not likely to obtain thanks **:** UNAPPRECIATED ⟨a ~ task⟩ — **thank·less·ly** *adv* — **thank·less·ness** *n* -ES

thank offering *n* **:** an offering made as an expression of thanks

thanks *pl of* THANK, *pres 3d sing of* THANK

thanksgiver \'=,==\ *n* **:** one that gives thanks

thanksgiving \(')=¦==\ *n* **1 :** the act of giving thanks **:** acknowledgment of favors or benefits ⟨hymns of high ~ —John Keble⟩ **2 :** an utterance (as a prayer) that is often in a set form of words and that expresses gratitude esp. for divine mercies ⟨in the ~ before meat —Shak.⟩ **3 a :** a public acknowledgment or celebration of divine goodness and mercies **b** *usu cap* **:** a day appointed for such celebration: as (1) **:** THANKSGIVING DAY a (2) **:** THANKSGIVING DAY b

thanksgiving day *n, usu cap T&D* **:** a day appointed for giving thanks for divine goodness and mercies: as **a :** the fourth Thursday in November observed as a legal holiday in the U.S. **b :** the second Monday in October observed as a legal holiday in Canada

thankworthy \'=,==\ *adj* [ME, fr. *thank* + *worthy*] **:** worthy of thanks or gratitude **:** MERITORIOUS

thank-you \'=,=\ *n* -S [fr. the phrase *thank you*] **:** a polite expression of one's gratitude as by saying "thank you"

thank-you-ma'am \'==,=\ *n* -S [prob. so called fr. the fact that such rough spots cause a passenger in a vehicle to double over in a way reminiscent of the bow formerly prescribed as an adjunct of an expression of thanks to a woman] **:** a bump or depression in a road; *specif* **:** a small ridge or hollow made across a road esp. on a hillside to cause water to run off

thap·sia \'thapsēə\ *n* [NL, fr. L, a poisonous plant, fr. Gk, fr. *Thapsos*, town and peninsula in Sicily] **1** -S **:** a plant of the genus *Thapsia;* esp **:** DEADLY CARROT **2** *cap* **:** a small genus of herbs (family Umbelliferae) of the Mediterranean region having the flowers in compound umbels without involucres and the fruit broadly winged

thap·sic acid \'thapsik-\ *n* [NL *Thapsia* (genus name of the deadly carrot *Thapsia garganica*) + E *-ic*] **:** a crystalline dicarboxylic acid $HOOC(CH_2)_{14}COOH$ found in the roots of the deadly carrot and the wax of a juniper (*Juniperus sabina*); hexadecane-dioic acid

¹thar \'thär\ *dial var of* THERE

²thar *var of* TAHR

tharf \'thärf\ *adj* [ME *therf, tharf* unleavened, fr. OE *theorf;* akin to OHG *derb* unleavened, ON *thjarfr* unleavened, insipid, OE *starian* to stare — more at STARE] *dial Brit* **:** HEAVY, STIFF, UNBENDING

tharf·cake \'thärf,kāk\ *n* [ME *therfcake*, fr. *therf* unleavened + *cake*] *dial Eng* **:** a cake made of unleavened flour or meal dough rolled thin and baked

thar·gé·lia \thär'gēlēə, -'jēl-\ *n* -S *usu cap* [Gk *Thargēlia*, pl.] **:** an ancient Athenian and Ionian festival celebrated in May in honor of Apollo

thar·par·kar \(')thär¦pärkər\ *n* [fr. *Thar (and) Parkar*, district in Pakistan] **1** *usu cap* **:** an Indian breed of pale gray humped dairy cattle with lyrate horns **2** -S *often cap* **:** an animal of the Tharparkar breed

tha·ru \'tä(,)rü\ *n* -S *usu cap* **:** a member of a valley-dwelling people of Mongol origin in Nepal

¹tha·si·an \'thāsh(ē)ən\ *n* -S *cap* [*Thasos*, island in Aegean sea + E *-ian*] **:** a native or inhabitant of the island of Thasos in the Aegean sea

²thasian \"\ *adj, usu cap* **:** of or relating to Thasos

thas·pi·um \'thaspēəm\ *n, cap* [NL, irreg. fr. *Thapsia*] **:** a small genus of herbs (family Umbelliferae) found in eastern No. America that have yellow flowers and have fruit with all the ribs prominently winged

¹that \'that, *usu* -ad·+V\ *pron, pl* **those** \'thōz\ [ME, fr. OE *thæt*, neut. demonstrative pron. & definite article; akin to OHG *thaz, daz*, neut. demonstrative pron. & definite article, ON *that*, neut. demonstrative pron., Goth *thata*, neut. demonstrative pron. & definite article, L *istud*, neut. demonstrative pron., Gk *to*, neut. demonstrative pron. & definite article, Skt *tad*, neut. demonstrative pron. & adj.] **1 a :** the person, thing, or idea pointed to, mentioned, or understood from the situation **:** the one indicated ⟨who is ~⟩ ⟨~ is my father⟩ ⟨what kind of tree is ~⟩ ⟨~ is a maple⟩ ⟨*those* are my sisters talking to the man in the corner⟩ ⟨*those* are violets⟩ ⟨he wanted to become a professional writer but ~ was no easy matter⟩ — often used as subject of a form of the verb *be*, usu. the contracted third person singular present indicative *'s*, in expressions indicating or implying that the person mentioned in the predicate is following or is expected shortly to follow an approved course of action ⟨hold the pen like this, ~*'s* a good girl⟩ ⟨take your medicine, ~*'s* a good boy⟩ ⟨~*'s* the boy⟩; sometimes used disparagingly of a person who has been mentioned by name or otherwise circumstantially identified ⟨the boy who sits across from my daughter in history class offered to take her to the football game but she refused him and told her friends she wouldn't be seen in public with ~⟩ **b** *Scot* **:** the following thing — used to point forward to a noun clause occurring later in the sentence **c :** the time just mentioned **:** the action or event just mentioned viewed with reference to the time of its occurrence — used after any of various prepositions ⟨he will not be there until eleven o'clock, and I expect to get there before ~⟩ ⟨read to the end of the chapter, and after ~ he went to bed⟩ **d :** the one specified as follows **:** the kind specified as follows **:** the thing specified as follows — used before a modifying expression other than a clause, esp. a prepositional phrase or a participle with or without a modifier or an adjective with or without a modifier ⟨one of the first major tasks confronting the pioneer was ~ of clearing some land —W.M.Kollmorgen⟩ ⟨the symptoms of the disease . . . sounded a good deal like *those* of polio —*Time*⟩ ⟨the purest water is ~ produced by distillation⟩ ⟨the organism that causes Malta fever . . . is closely related to ~ responsible for brucellosis —S.A.Waksman⟩ **e :** the blow just being dealt **:** the insult or injury just being inflicted — used in the expression *take that* **f :** a settled matter **:** something about which no further action can be taken — used in the predicate after a form of the verb *be* with *that* (sense 1a) as subject ⟨I won't sell it for less than fifty dollars and that is ~⟩ **g :** a person, thing, idea, or group of the indicated kind **:** such a one **:** such ones **:** such a thing ⟨when you want something you can't have it, and by the time you can have it you've stopped wanting it, but ~*'s* life⟩ ⟨wily and destructive —~*'s* foxes for you⟩ **2 a** (1) **:** the one farther away **:** the one less immediately under observation or discussion ⟨*those* are elm trees and these are maples⟩ ⟨~ is porcelain and this is plastic⟩ — contrasted with *this* (2) **:** the former ⟨two principles in human nature reign; self-love, to urge, and reason, to restrain; nor this a good, nor ~ a bad we call —Alexander Pope⟩ — contrasted with *this* **b :** another thing — sometimes contrasted with *this* ⟨talking about this and ~⟩; sometimes used as second member of a three-part series with *this* as the first member and *the other* as the third ⟨buying this, ~, or the other⟩ **3 a** — used as a function word after *and* to indicate emphatic repetition of the idea expressed by a previous word or phrase which is not necessarily a noun or noun equivalent ⟨he shall pay . . . , and ~ soundly —Shak.⟩ ⟨he was helpful, and ~ to an unusual degree⟩ **b** — used as a function word immediately before or immediately after a word group consisting of either a verbal auxiliary or a form of the verb *be* preceded by either *there* or a personal pronoun subject to indicate emphatic repetition of the idea expressed by a previous verb or predicate noun or predicate adjective ⟨is he capable? He is ~⟩ ⟨he told the whole truth; ~ he did⟩ **4 a :** the one **:** the thing **:** the kind **:** SOMETHING, ANYTHING — used as antecedent to a relative pronoun ⟨recognize the truth of ~ which is true⟩ ⟨one of *those* who introduced into the United States the results of foreign . . . scholarship —H.N.Fowler⟩ or in a like function with reference to a relative adverb ⟨the senses are ~ whereby we experience the material world⟩ or to a relative clause containing no relative pronoun or relative adverb ⟨what's ~ you say⟩ **b** *those pl* **:** some persons — used as antecedent to a relative pronoun ⟨there are *those* who think that the time has now come for a further step —*Report: (Canadian) Royal Commission on Nat'l Development*⟩ — **all that 1 a :** everything of the kind indicated ⟨tact, discretion, and *all that*⟩ ⟨he made an eloquent speech, but his hearers were unconvinced for *all that*⟩ **b :** more things of the same kind ⟨a store where you can get cabbage and carrots and *all that*⟩ **2 :** the extreme degree or quantity that has been indicated or implied — used in negative comparisons after *as* ⟨not as cold as *all that*⟩ — **and that :** and more things of the same kind **:** and so forth ⟨blow all their money on tarts and cards, on getting tight *and that* —Robert Westerby⟩ — **at that 1 :** in spite of what has been said or implied **:** taking everything into consideration ⟨we might be worse off *at that*⟩ **2 :** in addition to what has already been said **:** into the bargain **:** BESIDES ⟨a bridge built on stilts, and weak stilts *at that* —O.S.Nock⟩ **3 :** in the state or form indicated ⟨we left it *at that*⟩ — **that is** *or* **that is to say :** the following or immediately preceding word or word group may express the intended meaning more understandably or more accurately than a previous word or word group — used to introduce or accompany an explanation or correction

²that \"\ *adj, pl* **those** \"\ [ME, fr. OE *thæt*, neut. demonstrative pron. & definite article — more at ¹THAT] **1 a :** being the person, thing, or idea pointed to, mentioned, or understood from the situation **:** being the one indicated ⟨~ dog⟩ ⟨*those* houses⟩ **b :** being the one specified or singled out — used interchangeably with the definite article *the* but usu. expressing slightly greater emphasis; used almost exclusively before nouns having a following modifier (as a phrase or clause) ⟨three o'clock in the afternoon, ~ last moment when the sun's intensity may be felt —A.N.Lytle⟩ ⟨~ little understood . . . subject of bird migration —F.C.Lincoln⟩ ⟨*those* topics that lie outside the scope of this book —Fred Hoyle⟩ **c :** the well known **:** being the one about whom or about which further comment is unnecessary ⟨*those* little steamers that are Venice's street cars —Claudia Cassidy⟩ ⟨one of *those* election bets⟩ — often used disparagingly ⟨*those* feet of his⟩ ⟨~ brother of yours⟩ **d :** SUCH **:** such a **:** so great a ⟨~ gentleness . . . as I was wont to have —Shak.⟩ ⟨perplexed his mind to ~ degree that he was fain . . . to scratch his head —Charles Dickens⟩ **2 a :** the farther away **:** the less immediately under observation or discussion ⟨this chair or ~ one⟩ — contrasted with *this* **b :** the other **:** ANOTHER — sometimes contrasted with *this* ⟨we argued it this way and we argued it ~ way —Lilian Balch⟩; sometimes used as second member of a three-part series with *this* as the first member and *the other* as the third ⟨this, ~, and the other way⟩ — **that way 1 :** in the manner indicated **:** as indicated ⟨what makes him act *that way*⟩ **2 a :** in or into the condition indicated ⟨a very successful man and it is easy to see how he got *that way*⟩ **b :** in a lovesick condition ⟨those two are *that way* about each other⟩ ⟨Texans are *that way* about quarter horses —*Time*⟩

³that \thə|t, (')tha| *sometimes* ,the|, *usu* |d·+V\ *conj* [ME, fr. OE *thæt*, fr. *thæt*, neut. demonstrative pron. — more at ¹THAT] **1 a** (1) — used as a function word to introduce a subordinate clause that is a noun equivalent, esp. the subject or object of a verb, the predicate nominative after a copulative verb, or the substantive expression anticipated by the expletive *it* occurring as grammatical subject or object of a verb ⟨~ many historic houses . . . are rapidly disappearing for lack of care has been emphasized by several organizations —*Report: (Canadian) Royal Commission on Nat'l Development*⟩ ⟨courts declare ~ they have nothing to do with theoretic economics —M.R. Cohen⟩ ⟨the idea is ~, without ruining the sport, you want to protect the participants —Charles Oldfather⟩ ⟨it is interesting ~ so many of the books which have really stirred things up . . . have been small books —A.J.Nock⟩ ⟨he made it clear ~ he did not desert⟩ (2) — used as a function word to introduce a subordinate clause anticipated by the expletive *it* occurring as subject of a form of the copulative verb *be* when what follows the copulative verb is an adverb or adverbial phrase logically modifying the verb of the clause introduced by *that* ⟨it was there ~ I first met her⟩ ⟨it was almost as if in entreaty or reproach ~ she put her next question —Walter de la Mare⟩ (3) — used as a function word to introduce a subordinate clause that is joined as complement or modifier to a noun or adjective or is in apposition with a noun ⟨we are certain ~ this is true⟩ ⟨the certainty ~ this is true⟩ ⟨the fear ~ something unpleasant may happen⟩ ⟨the fact ~ you are here⟩ **b** (1) — used as a function word to introduce a subordinate clause that is the object of a preposition; usu. interpreted as being joined with the preposition to form a compound subordinating conjunction; used currently and frequently in only a few combinations, esp. *but that, except that, in that, notwithstanding that*, and *save that*, and occurring as an archaism in a few others, esp. *after that, before that, for that, till that*, and *until that* ⟨some of his earlier writings . . . have become classics in ~ they are read by most students professionally interested in anthropology —D.G.Mandelbaum⟩ ⟨if we sin wilfully after ~ we have received the knowledge of the truth —Heb 10:26 (AV)⟩ (2) — used as a function word to introduce a subordinate clause that is in absolute construction with a participle; often interpreted as being joined with the participle to form a compound subordinating conjunction ⟨men and women . . . could yet live in an ideal society provided ~ they were governed by a hard-living intellectual minority —Maurice Cranston⟩ **c** — used as a function word to introduce an exclamatory clause expressing a strong emotion esp. of surprise or sorrow or indignation; sometimes preceded by an interjection or other short exclamation ⟨oh Lord! ~ ever I lived to see this day⟩ ⟨~ it should come to this!⟩ ⟨alas! ~ all we loved of him should be . . . as if it had not been —P.B. Shelley⟩ **2 a** — used as a function word to introduce a subordinate clause expressing purpose or desired result ⟨cutting down expenses ~ her son might inherit an unencumbered estate —W.B.Yeats⟩; often preceded by *so* or *in order* and sometimes by *to the end* **b** — used as a function word to introduce an exclamatory clause expressing a wish; sometimes preceded by an interjection or other short exclamation ⟨oh, ~ the world could be persuaded of the truth of that maxim —W.S.Gilbert⟩ **3 a** — used as a function word to introduce a subordinate clause expressing a reason or cause ⟨rejoice ~ you are lightened of a load —Robert Browning⟩; often used with *should* in the clause which it introduces ⟨I am sorry ~ you should think so⟩ **b** — used as a function word after *not* to introduce a clause making a statement that is understood to be not true and therefore impossible to be taken as the reason or basis for an immediately preceding or following statement ⟨she ignored my suggestion — not ~ I care⟩ ⟨not ~ it matters, but the shirts aren't back from the laundry yet⟩ **4 a** — used as a function word to introduce a subordinate clause expressing consequence, result, or effect ⟨are of sufficient importance ~ they cannot be neglected —Hannah Wormington⟩; often preceded by *so* or *such* ⟨he gazed so long ~ both his eyes were dazzled —Alfred Tennyson⟩ **b** — used as a function word after a question or negative statement to introduce a clause expressing an appropriate consequence of what is being questioned or denied ⟨am I a dog, ~ you come to me with sticks —1 Sam 17:43 (RSV)⟩ ⟨I am not a doormat, ~ you should walk all over me⟩ **c** — used as a function word to introduce a negative subordinate clause after a negative main clause and to indicate that what is denied in the subordinate clause is the inevitable result or invariable accompaniment of what is denied in the main clause ⟨I can't speak, ~ you don't try to insult me —Douglas Jerrold⟩ **5** *archaic* — used as a function word at the beginning of the second of two subordinate clauses in parallel construction to replace the conjunction which introduces the first such clause ⟨when he had carried Rome and ~ we looked for no less spoil than glory —Shak.⟩ **6** — used as a function word after a subordinating conjunction without modifying its meaning ⟨if ~ thy bent of love be honorable —Shak.⟩; used currently and frequently in only a few combinations, esp. *now that* **7 a** — used as a function word to introduce a subordinate clause modifying an adverb or adverbial expression ⟨will go anywhere ~ he is invited⟩ ⟨the more ~ doubts assailed me . . . the louder I apologized —Eugene Lyons⟩ **b** *obs* — used as a function word to introduce a subordinate clause that is the equivalent of a sentence adverb modifying the entire main clause ⟨thou hast well done ~ thou art come —Acts 10:33 (AV)⟩ — **for all that** *conj* **:** in spite of the fact that **:** ALTHOUGH ⟨I don't trust him, *for all that* so many people consider him reliable⟩

⁴that \"\ *pron* [ME, fr. OE *thæt*, neut. relative pron., fr. *thæt*, neut. demonstrative pron. — more at ¹THAT] **1 a** — used as a function word to introduce a restrictive relative clause and to serve as a substitute within that clause for the substantive modified by that clause; used in any grammatical relation within the relative clause except that of a possessive or the object of a preceding preposition ⟨a court jester ~ fell in love with a queen —M.I.Seiden⟩ ⟨the cow ~ started the Chicago fire —L.A.White⟩ ⟨another conclusion ~ emerges clearly from this . . . statement —*Times Lit. Supp.*⟩ ⟨this ideal theater . . . ~ he discerns —Stark Young⟩ ⟨those beliefs ~ demonstrate they are trustworthy —J.L.Childs⟩ ⟨the responsibilities ~ literature owes to itself —Harry Levin⟩ ⟨a subject ~ most Americans probably think nothing need be said about —J.W.Clark b. 1907⟩ ⟨thoughtful journalist and conscientious citizen ~ he was, he did not look with any satisfaction on that little story —F.L.Mott⟩; sometimes used after *so* or *such* with the implication that the action or state expressed in the clause introduced by *that* is a real or appropriate consequence of what is expressed by the phrase containing *so* or *such* ⟨who is here so base ~ would be a bondman —Shak.⟩ **b** — used as a function word to introduce a nonrestrictive relative clause and to serve as a substitute within that clause for the substantive modified by that clause; used in any grammatical relation within the relative clause except that of a possessive or the object of a preceding preposition ⟨out of the forty thousand who were within the walls eight hundred only, ~ had fled at the first sound of the attack, made their way to the camp —J.A.Froude⟩ ⟨it was his specialty, ~ he never liked to do when there was a crowd —James Jones⟩ **2 a :** at which **:** in which **:** on which **:** by which **:** with which **:** to which — used not only to serve within its restrictive relative clause as a substitute for the substantive modified by that clause but also additionally to express a relation of conformity, agreement, or identity esp. in reference to time ⟨each year ~ the lectures were given⟩ ⟨I will drink no more of the fruit of the vine, until that day ~ I drink it new in the kingdom of God —Mk 14:25 (AV)⟩ ⟨work in the arts is significant in the measure ~ it has submitted to discipline —*General Education in a Free Society*⟩ ⟨this author has never been neglected to the same extent ~ some of his contemporaries have been⟩ ⟨treated with the same respect ~ others are⟩ **b :** according to what **:** to the extent of what — used after a negative ⟨has never been here ~ I know of⟩ ⟨have never met him ~ I can recall⟩ **3 a** *archaic* **:** that which — used to introduce a relative clause with no expressed antecedent ⟨~ thou doest, do quickly —Jn 13:27 (AV)⟩ **b** *obs* **:** the person who **:** persons who — used to introduce a relative clause with no expressed antecedent ⟨I am ~ I am —Exod 3:14 (AV)⟩ ⟨there be ~ can rule Naples as well as he —Shak.⟩

⁵that \'t͟hat, *usu* -ad·+V\ *adv* [ME, fr. *that*, adj.] **1** *dial* **:** to such an extent — used as modifier of a following adjective or adverb followed in turn by a clause that completes the meaning ⟨I'm ~ tired I can hardly walk⟩ **2 a :** to the extent that has already been indicated ⟨it is a hot day . . . when boys devote themselves principally to conversation and this day was ~ hot —Booth Tarkington⟩ **b :** to the extent that is being indicated by some nonlinguistic reference (as a gesture) ⟨a nail about ~ long⟩ **3** *dial* **:** EXTREMELY ⟨she'll be ~ pleased when I tell her the news⟩

⁶that \"\ *n* -s [¹*that*] **1 :** one of the members and usu. the second of a pair or series ⟨civilization, they agree, faces an inexorable alternative, either this or that; but their thises are irreconcilable and even their ~s are not the same —*Saturday Rev.*⟩ — sometimes used with an initial capital to stand for a proper name which is not mentioned ⟨Squire This and Farmer *That* whom he had known since boyhood —Max Peacock⟩; contrasted with *this* **2 :** an existent thing quite apart from whatever may be known or stated about it **:** the substratum of an entity in abstraction from all of its qualities — compare ⁴WHAT 2b

that·away \'t͟had·ə,wā, -atə,-\ *adv* [alter. of the phrase *that way*] **1** *dial* **:** in that direction **2** *dial* **:** in that manner **:** like that

¹thatch \'thach\ *vb* -ED/-ING/-ES [ME *thecchen, thacchen*, fr. OE *theccan* to cover, conceal; akin to OE *thæc* roof, OHG *dah* roof, *decchen, decken* to cover, ON *thak* roof, thatch, *thekja* to cover, L *tegere* to cover, *tegula* tile, Gk *stegein* to cover, shelter, *stegos, egos* roof, Skt *sthagati* he covers] *vt* **:** to roof or cover with or as if with thatch **:** make of thatch ~ *vi* **:** to cover something with thatch **:** make something (as a roof) of thatch

²thatch \"\ *n* -ES [ME *thacche*, fr. *thecchen, thacchen* to thatch] **1 a :** a plant material (as rushes, reeds, palm leaves, or esp. straw) arranged in a thick mat with the individual parts parallel and sloping so as to shed water and used as a sheltering cover esp. of a house ⟨a house with a roof of ~ —Fiske Kimball⟩ ⟨we all went about in thatched-straw raincoats and peaked ~ hats —Nora Waln⟩ **b :** a sheltering cover (as a house roof) made of such material **2 :** something resembling the thatch of a house ⟨the cool spring that flowed out from under a bank into a ~ of dark watercress —Willa Cather⟩; *esp* **:** the hair of one's head ⟨a man with a cap on his white ~ —Eudora Welty⟩ **3 :** THATCH PALM

thatch·er \-chə(r)\ *n* -S [ME *thaccher*, fr. *thacchen, thecchen* to thatch + *-er*] **:** one that thatches

thatch grass *n* **:** any of various usu. tall coarse grasses or occas. other plants that are used or suitable for use in thatching; *esp* **:** any of several South African grasses of the genus *Hyparrhenia*

thatch·ing \-chiŋ\ *n* -S [ME *thecchyng*, fr. gerund of *thecchen, thacchen* to thatch] **1 :** the act or art of covering with thatch **2** [²*thatch* + *-ing*] **:** THATCH 1a

thatch palm *also* **thatch tree** *n* **:** any of various palms (as the nipa) whose leaves are used in thatching; *esp* **:** any of several tropical American palms esp. of the genera *Thrinax, Sabal*, or *Inodes* — see SILVER THATCH

¹that'n \'t͟hatᵊn\ *adv* [irreg. fr. ¹*that*] *dial chiefly Eng* **:** in that way

²that'n \"\ [by alter.] *dial* **:** that one

that·ness *n* -ES [¹*that* + *-ness*] **1 :** the condition of being an existent thing apart from whatever may be known or stated about that thing **2 :** resemblance to or affinity with one of the members and usu. the second of a pair or series ⟨metaphor . . . brings out the thisness of a that, or the ~ of a this —K.D. Burke⟩

thau *var of* TAW

thau·ma·site \'thȯmə,sīt\ *n* -S [ISV *thaumas-* (fr. Gk *thaumasios* wondrous, fr. *thauma* miracle, wonder) + *-ite* — more at THEATER] **:** a white mineral $Ca_4Al_6Si_6O_{24}(SO_4,CO_3,Cl_2)$ consisting of a basic silicate, carbonate, and sulfate of calcium (hardness 3.5, sp. gr. 1.88)

thau·ma·tol·o·gy \,thȯmə'täləjē\ *n* -ES [ISV *thaumato-* (fr. Gk, fr. *thaumat-, thauma* miracle, wonder) + *-logy* — more at THEATER] **:** doctrine, discussion, or study of the performing of miracles

thau·ma·trope \'thȯmə,trōp\ *n* -S [Gk *thauma* miracle, wonder + E *-trope*] **:** an optical instrument or toy that shows the persistence of an impression upon the eye and that consists of a card having on its opposite faces different designs that appear to the eye combined in a single picture when the card is whirled rapidly round a diameter by the strings that hold it — **thau·ma·trop·i·cal** \;==;träpəkəl\ *adj*

thau·ma·turge \'thȯmə,tərj, -təj, -təij\ *also* **thau·ma·turg** \-rg\ *n* -S [F & NL; F *thaumaturge*, fr. NL *thaumaturgus*, fr. Gk *thaumatourgos* working miracles, fr. *thaumat-, thauma* miracle + *-ourgos* working (akin to Gk *ergon* work) — more at THEATER, WORK] **:** a performer of miracles (as a saint or magician)

thau·ma·tur·gic \;==;tərjik, -təj-, -təij-\ *also* **thau·ma·tur·gi·cal** \-jəkəl, -jēk-\ *adj* [NL *thaumaturgicus*, fr. *thaumaturgus* + L *-icus* -ic, -ical] **1 :** performing miracles **2 :** of, connected with, or dependent on thaumaturgy

thau·ma·tur·gist \'==,tərjəst, -təj-, -təij-\ *n* -S **:** a performer of miracles; *esp* **:** MAGICIAN

thau·ma·tur·gus \,==ˈtərgəs\ *n, pl* **thaumatur·gi** \-r,jī\ [NL] **:** a performer of miracles

thau·ma·tur·gy \'==,tərjē, -təj-, -təij-, -ji\ *n* -ES [Gk *thaumatourgia*, fr. *thaumatourgos* + *-ia* -y] **1 :** the performance of miracles **2 :** HOCUS-POCUS 3 ⟨any metaphysics which portrays reality as something strangely unfamiliar or beyond the ordinary grasp, stamps itself as ~, and is false upon the face of it —C.I.Lewis⟩ **syn** see MAGIC

thau·me·to·poea \,thȯmətō'pēə\ *n, cap* [NL, prob. irreg. fr. *thaumat-, thauma* miracle + *-o-* + *-poiia* (fr. *poiein* to make) — more at POET] **:** a genus of chiefly palaearctic notodontid moths comprising the processionary moths

¹thaw \'thȯ\ *vb* **thawed** *or dial* **thew** \'thü\ **thawed** \-ōd\ *also archaic* **thawn** \-ōn\ **thawing; thaws** [ME *thawen*, fr. OE *thawian*; akin to MD *dooyen, douwen* to thaw, OHG *douwen, dōan, dewen*, ON *theyja* to thaw, L *tabes* wasting disease, *tabēre* to waste away, melt, *tabescere* to melt gradually, decay, Gk *tēkein* to melt, Ossetic *thayun* to thaw, melt, Arm *t'anam* I moisten; basic meaning: to melt] *vt* **1 a :** to cause (something frozen) to go into a liquid state ⟨~*ing* the ice⟩ **b :** to rid of stiffness, hardness, numbness, ice, or other effect of cold by warming ⟨held his hands close to the fire to ~ them out⟩ ⟨~*ing* frozen vegetables⟩ **2 :** to rid of cold aloofness or hostility **:** cause to grow gentle or genial ⟨the convivial crowd soon ~*ed* him out⟩ **3 :** to nullify or cause to disappear as if by melting ⟨she can unlock the clasping charm, and ~ the numbing spell —John Milton⟩ **4 :** to bring into a condition in which adjustments, adaptations, or modifications are possible ⟨broke through the static repose of the Aristotelian system, and, so to speak, ~*ed* its frozen logic —P.E.More⟩ **5 :** to activate or change in a manner that reverses the effect of a legislative, administrative, or economic freeze ⟨~*ing* out the frozen assets⟩ ~ *vi* **1 a :** to go from a frozen to a liquid state (as of ice or snow) **:** MELT **b :** to become free of stiffness, hardness, numbness, ice, or other effect of cold as a result of being warmed ⟨the ground has ~*ed* out⟩ **2 :** to be warm enough to melt ice and snow — used with *it* in reference to the weather ⟨it is ~*ing* today⟩ **3 :** to abandon aloofness, reserve, or hostility **:** grow gentle or genial **:** UNBEND **4 :** to become mobile, active, or susceptible to change ⟨in medieval times property and people were all frozen, but with the opening of the Great Frontier both ~*ed* out and began to flow and mingle —W.P.Webb⟩

²thaw \"\ *n* -S [ME *thawe*, fr. *thawen*, v.] **1 a :** the action, fact, or process of thawing **b :** a warmth of weather sufficient to thaw ice or snow **:** period when the weather is so warm as to thaw ice or snow ⟨a January ~⟩ **2 :** the action or process of becoming less aloof, less hostile, or more genial **3 :** reversal, weakening, or termination of a legislative, administrative, or economic freeze

thaw house *also* **thawing house** *n* **:** a small building fitted and equipped for thawing frozen dynamite

thaw·less \-ōləs\ *adj* **:** never thawing

thawy \-ōi, -ōē\ *adj* -ER/-EST **:** characterized by thawing **:** tending to thaw

ThD *abbr or n* -S [NL *theologiae doctor*] **:** a doctor of theology

thd *abbr* **1** thread **2** thunderhead

thdr *abbr* thunder

¹the *before consonants & esp South before vowels also* t͟hə, *before vowels* t͟hē *or* t͟hi, *in sense 1r often* 't͟hē\ *definite article* [ME, fr. OE *thē*, masc. demonstrative pron. & definite article, alter. (influenced by the oblique cases — as *thæs*, gen., & *thǣm*, dat. — & by *thæt*, neut. demonstrative pron. & definite article) of *sē*; akin to ON *sā*, masc. demonstrative pron. & adj., Goth *sa*, masc. demonstrative pron. & definite article, Gk *ho*, masc. demonstrative pron. & definite article, Skt *sa*, masc. demonstrative pron. & adj. — more at THAT] **1 a** — used as a function word to indicate that a following noun or noun equivalent refers to someone or something previously mentioned or clearly understood from the context or the situation ⟨if anyone offers you a dollar for that picture, take ~ dollar⟩ ⟨put ~ cat out⟩ ⟨this is a good shirt but ~ sleeves are too long⟩; sometimes used archaically before the relative pronoun *which* ⟨a foolish quest, ~ which to gain and keep he sacrificed all rest —Lord Byron⟩; found in obsolete usage as recently as the 17th century before the relative pronoun *whom* ⟨your mistress, from ~ whom I see there's no disjunction to be made —Shak.⟩ **b** — used as a function word before an abstract noun; obsolete except with a very few nouns with which it appears in certain set constructions, in some of which it has some particularizing force ⟨a fight to ~ finish⟩ ⟨portrayed to ~ life⟩ ⟨~ truth is that I was absent⟩ ⟨that's ~ truth⟩ ⟨that's ~ bunk⟩ ⟨to keep ~ peace⟩ **c** — used as a function word to indicate that a following noun or noun equivalent refers to someone or something that is unique or is thought of as unique or exists as only one at a time ⟨~ Lord⟩ ⟨~ Messiah⟩ ⟨~ devil⟩ ⟨~ sun⟩ ⟨~ earth⟩ ⟨~ universe⟩ ⟨~ Pope⟩ ⟨~ Dalai Lama⟩; often used with some kinds of geographical names, esp. of rivers ⟨~ Hudson⟩, oceans ⟨~ Atlantic⟩, seas ⟨~ Adriatic⟩, and groups (as of islands or mountains) that have a plural name but a distinctive identity ⟨~ Azores⟩ ⟨~ Alps⟩; often used with names of literary or artistic works ⟨~ *Jungle Book*⟩ ⟨~ Mona Lisa⟩ ⟨~ Moonlight Sonata⟩ **d** — used as a function word before nouns that designate natural phenomena or points of the compass ⟨~ night is cold⟩ ⟨~ heat is intense⟩ ⟨~ wind came from ~ east⟩ ⟨~ clouds look threatening⟩ **e** — used as a function word before some esp. rather old-fashioned or nontechnical names of diseases ⟨~ palsy⟩ ⟨~ measles⟩ ⟨~ piles⟩ ⟨~ flu⟩ ⟨~ pox⟩ **f** — used as a function word before a title or a class name to designate the particular holder of that title or the particular member of that class that is most familiar to the speaker or writer by reason of the nation or culture of which he is a member ⟨~ President⟩ ⟨~ Congress⟩ ⟨~ Civil War⟩ ⟨~ west coast⟩ ⟨~ Renaissance⟩ **g** (1) *Brit* — used as a function word before the name of a day of the week to indicate reference to the next ensuing day so named in the period immediately under consideration ⟨five days later, on ~ Sunday —David Masters⟩ (2) — used as a function word before a noun denoting time to indicate reference to that which is present or immediate or is under consideration ⟨news of ~ hour⟩ ⟨best movie of ~ week⟩ ⟨he was at a loss for ~ moment⟩ ⟨in ~ future⟩ (3) *chiefly Scot* — used as a function word immediately before any of several nouns denoting divisions of time, esp. *day, night, morn*, and *year*, to form phrases with an adverbial function corresponding in meaning to standard English *today, tonight, tomorrow, this year* **h** — used as a function word before names of some parts of the body or of the clothing as an equivalent of a possessive adjective indicating that the part in question belongs to a person previously mentioned ⟨led her by ~ hand⟩ ⟨grabbed him by ~ collar⟩ or to the speaker or writer or the person addressed ⟨how's ~ arm today⟩ ⟨~ ankle is better today, thanks⟩; sometimes used in a similar way before nouns denoting a family, a member of a family, an ailment from which the speaker or writer or the person addressed is known to have been suffering, or some other aspect of an individual person's situation in life ⟨he's going on a trip and taking ~ family along⟩ ⟨I suppose you'll have to consult ~ wife⟩ ⟨how's ~ cough⟩ ⟨~ headache is better, thanks⟩ ⟨you've been lucky enough to rate a four-week vacation from ~ job —Richard Joseph⟩ **i** (1) — used as a function word before a title or a personal name to designate a person of eminence or widespread reputation, esp. as a man of high rank, a figure of great historical importance, a singer, an actress, or a courtesan ⟨Robert ~ Bruce⟩ ⟨~ Siddons⟩ ⟨~ Duse⟩ ⟨~ Pompadour⟩; sometimes used somewhat disparagingly in reference to a person of only very local or restricted prominence (2) — used as a function word before the surname of an Irish or Scottish clan to indicate reference to the chief of the clan ⟨~ Mackintosh⟩ **j** — used as a function word before the name of an art, artistic movement, craft, branch of learning, profession, sport, or other branch of human endeavor or proficiency; used in standard English only in a very limited number of such combinations ⟨~ opera⟩ ⟨~ cinema⟩ ⟨~ rococo⟩ ⟨~ law⟩ ⟨~ hunt⟩ **k** (1) **:** EACH, EVERY — used after prepositions ⟨eighty crackers to ~ package⟩ (2) — used as a function word in prepositional phrases esp. with *by* to indicate that the noun in the phrase serves as a basis for computation ⟨sold by ~ dozen⟩ ⟨rented by ~ month⟩ ⟨dying by ~ hundreds⟩ **l** — used as a function word before the proper name of a ship or a well-known building (as a theater or movie house well known at least in the city where it is located) ⟨~ Mayflower⟩ ⟨~ Bijou⟩ **m** — used as a function word before the name of a language; obsolete except in contexts that indicate translation from an original language ⟨translated from ~ German⟩ **n** — used as a function word before a gerundial verbal noun to indicate reference to an immediate instance ⟨will cause the meat to shrivel in ~ cooking —*Amer. Guide Series: N.C.*⟩ **o** — used as a function word before a noun derived without affixation from a verb expressing an action or state that has duration in time and after the preposition *upon* or usu. *on* to indicate a single continuous involvement in such an action or state ⟨on ~ move⟩ ⟨on ~ prowl⟩ or the temporal point of termination of such involvement ⟨caught the ball on ~ fly⟩ **p** (1) — used as a function word before a date consisting only of a numeral denoting a year; obsolete except before *1715* or its contraction *'15* in reference to the Jacobite uprising of that year or to the year itself as marked by that uprising and before *1745* or its contraction *'45* in reference to the Jacobite uprising of that year or to the year itself as marked by that uprising ⟨he was not out in ~ 1715 —W.M.Parker⟩ ⟨the commencement of the rising of ~ '15 —Leslie Smith⟩ (2) — used as a function word before the plural form of a numeral that is a multiple of ten to denote a particular decade of a century or of a person's life ⟨American life in ~ twenties⟩ ⟨a man somewhere in ~ sixties⟩ **q** — used as a function word before the name of a commodity or any familiar appurtenance of daily life to indicate reference to the individual thing, part, or supply thought of as at hand ⟨too fond of ~ booze⟩ ⟨looking out of ~ window⟩ ⟨talked to him on ~ telephone⟩ **r** — used as a function word to designate one of a class as the best, most typical, or most worth singling out ⟨this is ~ life⟩ ⟨an author who even in his own lifetime was widely regarded as ~ novelist⟩; sometimes used before a personal name to denote the most prominent bearer of that name ⟨became acquainted with a mathematician who was named Einstein but was not ~ Einstein⟩; sometimes used with the plural form of a family name to denote the most prominent branch of the family ⟨on his father's side he was, to be sure, a Guzmán but not one of ~ Guzmáns —D.C.Peattie⟩; often marked in speech by full stress or in writing by special typography (as italics) **s :** ENOUGH ⟨I would have liked to write a letter instead of a postcard, but I didn't have ~ time⟩ **t** (1) — used as a function word before a proper name denoting a particular character in a dramatic work or before a common noun denoting a particular role in a dramatic work to refer to the one playing that character or filling that role ⟨in this performance a singer who has not appeared here before was ~ Figaro⟩ ⟨threw rotten eggs at ~ villain⟩ (2) — used as a function word before a noun denoting a particular role in a real-life situation to refer to the one filling that role ⟨I'm no fool; you're ~ fool⟩ ⟨in 1914, by contrast with 1898, England and France were ~ belligerents and America was ~ neutral⟩ **2 a** (1) — used as a function word with a noun modified by an adjective or by an attributive noun to limit the application of the modified noun to that specified by the adjective or by the attributive noun ⟨~ right answer⟩ ⟨~ privileged classes⟩ ⟨~ English language⟩ ⟨~ greatest difficulty⟩ ⟨~ third time⟩ ⟨~ Boston road⟩ ⟨~ seafood industry⟩ ; sometimes used with the adjective following the article-noun combination and itself either unmodified or more often modified ⟨~ church militant⟩ ⟨~ man most suitable for the job⟩; often used in conventional epithets ⟨~ Venerable Bede⟩ ⟨~ White House⟩ including some in which the article and the adjective both follow the noun ⟨Peter ~ Great⟩ ⟨Elizabeth ~ Second⟩; used also in constructions containing an additional modifier (as a subordinate clause, prepositional phrase, or infinitive phrase) as well as an adjective or an attributive noun ⟨~ usual excuses that everybody gives⟩ ⟨~ seafood industry of this country⟩ ⟨~ wrong way to do it⟩ (2) — used as a function word before an absolute adjective that is equivalent in meaning to a noun modified by an adjective, including virtually all absolute occurrences of superlative adjectives or ordinal numbers ⟨use the white buttons and not ~ black⟩ ⟨he and she are both very intelligent, but her responses are ~ quicker⟩ ⟨nothing but ~ best⟩ ⟨he is to arrive on ~ sixth⟩ **b** — used as a function word before a noun to limit its application to that specified by a noun esp. a proper name in apposition ⟨~ poet Wordsworth⟩; often used before a title consisting of a generic term followed by a limiting appositive ⟨~ Lord Chief Justice⟩; sometimes used with the limiting term first esp. in conventional epithets ⟨William ~ Conqueror⟩ **c** — used as a function word before a noun to limit its application to that specified by a succeeding element in the sentence, esp. a subordinate clause, prepositional phrase, or infinitive phrase ⟨~ flowers that bloom⟩ ⟨~ John Maclean who was interred at Itchingfield —W.M.Parker⟩ ⟨~ days of our youth⟩ ⟨~ man in the iron mask⟩ ⟨~ London of Elizabeth I⟩ ⟨~ right to vote⟩; often used before a title consisting of a generic term followed by a limiting prepositional phrase ⟨~ Duke of York⟩ **3 a** (1) — used as a function word before a singular noun denoting a human being, an animal, a plant, or a precious stone to indicate that the noun is to be understood generically and not individually ⟨helpful hints for ~ beginner⟩ ⟨courtesy distinguishes ~ gentleman⟩ ⟨~ dog was domesticated in prehistoric times⟩ ⟨hunt ~ wild ox⟩ ⟨cultivation of ~ potato⟩ ⟨~ diamond is a form of carbon⟩; used with *man* or *woman* only in explicit contrast with another noun denoting a human being ⟨the child is father of ~ man —William Wordsworth⟩ or when *man* or *woman* is the object of the verb *act* or *play;* used also with a noun other than *man* or *woman* occurring as object of the verb *act* or *play* ⟨play ~ knave⟩ ⟨play ~ martyr⟩ ⟨act ~ fool⟩ (2) — used as a function word before a singular substantivized adjective denoting a human being to indicate generic rather than individual application ⟨let ~ wicked forsake his way —Isa 55:7 (RSV)⟩ **b** — used as a function word before a noun denoting the body, the mind, the soul, or any part, attribute, or function of any of them, to indicate generic rather than individual application ⟨~ mind is clearest when ~ body is in good health⟩ ⟨good for ~ soul⟩ ⟨~ hand is quicker than ~ eye⟩ ⟨pleasing to ~ appetite⟩ ⟨a product of ~ imagination⟩ **c** — used as a function word before a noun denoting an object (as an implement, weapon, or musical instrument) to indicate generic rather than individual application ⟨invention of ~ wheel⟩ ⟨users of ~ bow and arrow⟩ ⟨playing ~ piano⟩ ⟨the writing is close, analytic, sharply focused on ~ significant detail —William Barrett⟩ **d** *archaic* — used as a function word before the name of a day of the week to indicate reference to that day as one that recurs week after week ⟨on ~ Sunday he goes perhaps to church —T.B.Macaulay⟩ **e** — used as a function word before a singular substantivized adjective to indicate an abstract idea ⟨an essay on ~ sublime⟩ ⟨to recognize and enjoy ~ beautiful⟩ **4 a** — used as a function word before a singular noun denoting a group to indicate reference to the group as a whole ⟨~ elite⟩ ⟨~ aristocracy⟩ ⟨~ rabble⟩ **b** — used as a function word before a substantivized adjective to indicate inclusive reference to a group so characterized ⟨blessed are ~ merciful —Mt. 5:7 (AV)⟩ ⟨the land of ~ free —F.S.Key⟩ **c** — used as a function word before a plural noun denoting a group to indicate reference to the group as a whole ⟨~ Greeks⟩ ⟨~ newspapers⟩

²**the** \before consonants & esp South before vowels also thə, before vowels thē or thi\ *adv* [ME *the, thi,* fr. OE *thē, thȳ* by that, because of that, instrumental of *thæt,* neut. demonstrative pron. — more at THAT] **1** : than before : than otherwise — used before a comparative ⟨I am none ~ wiser for attending that lecture⟩ ⟨instead of quieting down, they talked all ~ louder⟩ ⟨pulled his cot alongside the window, ~ better to lean his chin on the sill —Ethel Anderson⟩ **2 a** : by how much : to what extent — used before a comparative as one of the members, usu. the first member, of the correlative pair *the . . . the . . .* ⟨~ sooner the better⟩ ⟨~ harder you work, the sooner you will finish⟩ **b** : by that much : to that extent — used before a comparative as one of the members, usu. the second member, of the correlative pair *the . . . the . . .* ⟨the sooner ~ better⟩ **3** : so as to exceed all others — used before a superlative ⟨of all my books I like this ~ best —Charles Dickens⟩

³**the** \"\ *prep* [¹*the*] : in, to, or for each : for every ⟨ten dollars ~ bottle⟩

the- or **theo-** *comb form* [ME *theo-,* fr. LL, fr. L, god, fr. Gk *the-, theo-* god, God, fr. *theos;* perh. akin to MHG *getwās* ghost, Lith *dvasia* spirit, *dvasas* spirit, breath — more at DUST] **1 a** : God ⟨*the*ism⟩ ⟨*theo*centric⟩ **b** : god ⟨*theo*mancy⟩ **2 a** : theological and ⟨*theo*astrological⟩ **b** : theology and ⟨*theo*mythology⟩

thea \'thēə\ *n, cap* [NL, fr. *thea* tea, fr. the source of E ¹*tea*] *in some classifications* : a genus comprising evergreen shrubs with pediceled flowers and persistent sepals that are now usu. placed in the genus *Camellia* and include the tea plant of commerce

the·a·ce·ae \thē'āsē,ē\ *n pl, cap* [NL, fr. *Thea,* type genus + *-aceae*] : a family of trees and shrubs (order Parietales) having alternate undivided leaves, large regular pentamerous flowers, and a fleshy or capsular fruit and being mainly tropical but widely distributed — compare ¹CAMELLIA, ²GORDONIA, STEWARTIA

the·a·ceous \-'āshəs\ *adj* [NL *Theaceae* + E *-ous*] : of or relating to the Theaceae

t-head \'=,=\ *adj, cap T* **1** : having the intake and exhaust valves in compartments of the block on opposite sides of the cylinder ⟨a *T-head* gasoline engine⟩ **2** : having a cross member at the head end of a longitudinal one ⟨a *T-head* pier⟩

t-head toggle *n, cap T* : a toggle (as a rod or screw) with a piece pivoted near its end that turns transversely and prevents withdrawal after the toggle has been inserted through a hole

the·an·dric \thē'andrik\ *adj* [LGk *theandrikos,* fr. *theandros* God-man (fr. Gk *the-* + *-andros* -androus) + Gk *-ikos* -ic] : of or relating to the divine and human or their union or joint operation ⟨one and the same Christ, working both the divine and the human actions by one ~ operation —B.J.Kidd⟩

the·an·throp·ic \,thēən'thräpik, -pēk\ *adj* [*theanthropos* + *-ic*] **1 a** : believed to embrace or to be a god in man **b** : being both divine and human ⟨Jesus Christ's ~ nature⟩ **2** : partaking of the natures of a god and of man — used of a sacrificial victim

the·an·thro·pism \thē'an(t)thrə,pizəm\ *n* -s [*theanthropos* + *-ism*] **1** : a state of being God and man; *esp* : the union of the divine and human natures in Christ **2 a** : the ascription of human attributes to the Deity, or to a polytheistic deity : ANTHROPOMORPHISM **b** : belief in the incarnation of deity in human form or in the divinity of a mortal

the·an·thro·pist \-pəst\ *n* -s [*theanthropos* + *-ist*] : a defender of theanthropism or believer in it

the·an·thro·pol·o·gy \thē,an(t)thrə'päləjē\ *n* -ES [*theanthropos* + *-logy*] : THEANTHROPISM

the·an·thro·poph·a·gy \-äfəjē\ *n* -ES [*theanthropos* + *-phagy*] : the practice of eating a god-man

the·an·thro·pos \,thēən'thrō,päs\ *n* [LGk *theanthrōpos,* fr. Gk *the-* + *anthrōpos* man — more at ANTHROP-] : a man incarnating or believed to incarnate God or a god : GOD-MAN

the·an·thro·pos·o·phy \thē,an(t)thrə'päsəfē\ *n* -ES [*theanthropos* + *-sophy*] : a system of belief concerning theanthropism

the·an·thro·py \thē'an(t)thrəpē\ *n* -ES [*theanthropos* + *-y*] : THEANTHROPISM

the·arch·ic \thē'ärkik\ *adj* [LGk *thearchikos,* fr. *thearchia* + Gk *-ikos* -ic] **1** : of or relating to the rule of God : divinely sovereign or supreme : THEOCRATIC **2** : of or relating to a system of deities

the·ar·chy \'thē,ärkē\ *n* -ES [LGk *thearchia,* fr. Gk *the-* + *-archia* -archy] **1** : a political system based on government of men by God : divine sovereignty : THEOCRACY ⟨in the Hindu ~ there are two powerful and rival goddesses among manifold others —Rumer Godden⟩ **2** : a system or hierarchy of deities

theat *abbr* theater; theatrical

the·a·ter or **the·a·tre** \'thēəd·ə(r), 'thiə|, |tə *sometimes* 'thē,ā| or thē'ā|\ *n* -s [ME *theatre,* fr. MF, fr. L *theatrum,* fr. Gk *theatron,* fr. *theasthai* to see, view (fr. *thea* action of seeing, sight) + *-tron,* suffix denoting means, instrument, or place; akin to Gk *thauma* wonder, miracle — more at -TRON] **1 a** : an outdoor structure for dramatic performances or spectacles in ancient Greece and Rome including a stage with associated buildings and usu. semicircular tiers of unroofed seats **b** : a building for dramatic performances in modern

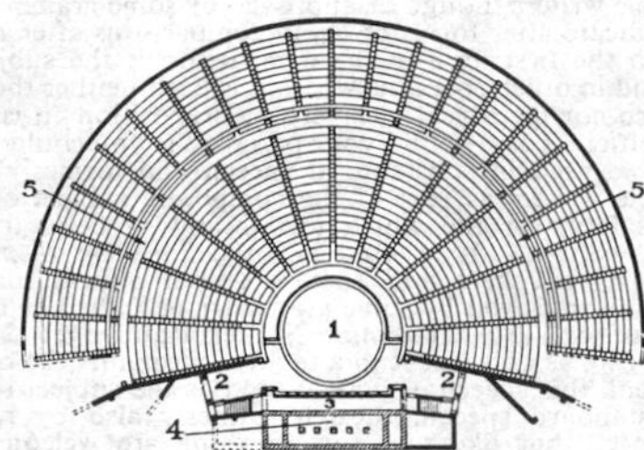

theater 1a: plan of Greek theater: *1* orchestra, *2* parodos, *3* proscenium, *4* skene, *5* diazoma

times usu. including a stage with side wings and flies and with dressing rooms for actors and an auditorium often with balconies and boxes : PLAYHOUSE **c** *obs* : a theater stage **d** : a theater audience : HOUSE ⟨the ~ applauded him warmly⟩ **e** : a building for the showing of motion pictures **f** : a company of performers which presents plays or dances **2** : something resembling a theater in form or use: as **a** : a place rising by steps or gradations ⟨shade above shade, a woody ~ of stateliest view —John Milton⟩ **b** : a room often with rising tiers of seats for lectures, surgical demonstrations, or other assemblies or exhibitions ⟨the hospital has . . . a clinic ~ for student instruction —*Amer. Guide Series: Md.*⟩ **c** *usu theatre, Brit* : a hospital operating room **3** *obs* : a comprehensive outline or view : CONSPECTUS — used chiefly in book titles **4 a** : a place or sphere that is the scene of dramatic events or significant action ⟨the ~ of public life⟩ ⟨this was the ~ of . . . the most stupendous financial fiasco in the history of the world —F.J.Haskin⟩ **b** : the scene of a public ceremony (as a temporary platform) ⟨the cathedral crossing became the coronation ~⟩ **5** *obs* : EXAMPLE, EXHIBITION, SPECTACLE **6 a** : written dramatic literature : PLAYS ⟨the ~ of Eugene O'Neill⟩ ⟨the ~ of 19th century France⟩ **b** : dramatic performance or representation : drama as an active art ⟨naïveté was the keynote to the American ~ —Otis Skinner⟩ **c** : dramatic aptitude or effectiveness : skillful depiction of character or of the conflict or interplay of persons ⟨this is pure ~ —Cecile Starr⟩ ⟨the play makes lively ~⟩ ⟨the weakest ~ in the play⟩

the·a·ter·go·er \-,gō(ə)r, -ōə\ *n* : PLAYGOER

the·a·ter·go·ing \-ōiŋ\ *n* : attendance at theaters

theater-in-the-round \'=====\ *n* : ARENA THEATER

theater of operations : the part of a theater of war in which active operations are conducted including a combat zone and a communications zone

theater of war : the entire land, sea, and air area that is or may become involved directly in war operations and includes the theater of operations and the zone of the interior

the·a·tine \'thēətən\ *n* -s *usu cap* [NL *Theatinus,* fr. L *Teatinus* inhabitant of Chieti, fr. *Teate* Chieti, Italy + *-inus* -ine; fr. the fact that one of the founders of the congregation was Giovanni P. Caraffa †1559 Ital. prelate, archbishop of Chieti and later Pope Paul IV] : a member of a Roman Catholic congregation of regular clerics established in 1524 in Italy to elevate clerical and lay morality and to combat Lutheranism

the·a·tral \'thēə·trəl\ *adj* [F *théâtral,* fr. L *theatralis,* fr. *theatrum* + *-alis* -al] : of or relating to theater or drama

theatre sister *n, Brit* : an operating-room nurse

the·at·ric \thē'a·trik, thi'-\ *adj* [LL *theatricus*] : THEATRICAL

¹**the·at·ri·cal** \thē'a·trəkəl, thi'-, -rēk-\ *adj* [LL *theatricus* (fr. Gk *theatrikos,* fr. *theatron* theater + *-ikos* -ic) + E *-al* — more at THEATER] **1** : of or relating to the theater or to the acting or presentation of plays ⟨a ~ jack-of-all-trades —Claudia Cassidy⟩ ⟨made no objection to his son's ~ ambitions —*Collier's Yr. Bk.*⟩ **2** : marked by pretense or artificiality : not genuine : UNREAL ⟨a ~ evangelist whose staged confessions and railings against sin are . . . hypocritical —Nona B. Brown⟩ **3 a** : having the qualities of a stage play or of an actor's performance : DRAMATIC, HISTRIONIC ⟨active virtue . . . is therefore ~, consciously dramatic, the wearing of a mask —W.B. Yeats⟩ **b** : marked by extravagant display or exhibitionism : SHOWY, SPECTACULAR ⟨a ~ bow —Michael McLaverty⟩ ⟨one of the most ~ figures in public life —J.K.Howard⟩

²**theatrical** \"\ *n* -s **1 theatricals** *pl* : the performance and presentation of plays ⟨forbid ~s and other secular amusements in churches and churchyards —K.S.Latourette⟩ ⟨amateur ~s⟩ ⟨student ~s⟩ **2 theatricals** *pl* **a** : the arts of acting and stagecraft : DRAMATICS **b** : theater properties or memorabilia **3** : a professional actor ⟨an eminent ~ —*Times Lit. Supp.*⟩ **4 theatricals** *pl* : showy or extravagant gestures or actions ⟨the addition of exaggerated ~s continued the steady deterioration of this ancient and once popular sport —*Collier's Yr. Bk.*⟩

theatrical gauze *n* : a transparent open-mesh gauze of cotton or linen with a stiff finish for use in theatrical costumes and scenery and in curtains

the·at·ri·cal·ism \-kə,lizəm\ *n* -s : stage mannerisms, methods, or practices : EXHIBITIONISM, SHOWINESS, STAGINESS ⟨a display of moody ~ —Bosley Crowther⟩

the·at·ri·cal·i·ty \thē,a·trə'kaləd·ē\ *n* -ES : the quality or state of being theatrical (as in action, appearance, or style) ⟨a gesture of large ~ and little meaning —Frederic Morton⟩

the·at·ri·cal·iza·tion \thē,a·trəkələ'zāshən\ *n* -s : the act of theatricalizing or the state of being threatricalized

the·at·ri·cal·ize \thē'a·trəkə,līz\ *vt* -ED/-ING/-S [¹*theatrical* + *-ize*] **1** : to adapt to the theater : make theatrical : DRAMATIZE **2** : to display in showy fashion : make flashy

the·at·ri·cal·ly \thē'a·trək(ə)lē, thi'-, -rēk-, -li\ *adv* : in a theatrical manner ⟨~ talented students⟩ ⟨its green-lit fumes rose ~ against the enormous cheap-gaudy nightscape —Christopher Isherwood⟩

the·at·ri·cal·ness *n* -ES : the quality or state of being theatrical

the·a·tri·cian \,thēə·'trishən\ *n* -s : a specialist or technician in theater arts

the·at·ri·cism \thē'a·trə,sizəm\ *n* -s : THEATRICALISM

the·at·rics \thē'a·triks, thi'-, -rēks\ *n pl* [*theatric* + *-s*] **1** : ²THEATRICAL 1 ⟨amateur ~⟩ **2** : staged or contrived effects ⟨a tale of high adventure — heightened not by studio ~ but by one's sense of being an immediate participant —Arthur Knight⟩

theatro- *comb form* [Gk, fr. *theatron* — more at THEATER] : theater ⟨*theatro*mania⟩

the·a·troc·ra·cy \,thēə·'träkrəsē\ *n* -ES [Gk *theatrokratia,* fr. *theatro-* + *-kratia* -cracy] : government by the people assembled in their theater (as in the Athenian democracy)

the·at·ro·graph \thē'a·trə,graf, -räf\ *n* [*theatro-* + *-graph*] : an early motion picture projector

theave \'thēv, 'thāv\ *n* -s [ME *theyve*] *dial Eng* : a young ewe; *esp* : one that has not yeaned

¹**the·ba·ic** \thə'bāik\ *adj, usu cap* [L *Thebaicus,* fr. Gk *Thēbaikos,* fr. *Thēbai, Thēbē* Thebes, ancient city in Upper Egypt + *-ikos* -ic] : of or relating to Thebes in Egypt

²**thebaic** \"\ *n* -s *usu cap* : SAHIDIC

the·ba·ine \'thēbə,ēn, thə'bā,ēn, -āən\ *n* -s [NL *thebaia* Egyptian opium produced at Thebes (fr. L *Thebae* Thebes, fr. Gk *Thēbai*) + E *-ine*] : a poisonous crystalline alkaloid $C_{19}H_{21}NO_3$ found in opium in small quantities, related chemically to morphine and codeine, and possessing a sharp bitter taste and a tetanic action like strychnine

¹**the·ban** \'thēbən\ *adj, usu cap* [ME, fr. L *Thebanus* adj. & n., fr. *Thebae* Thebes, city in ancient Greece and in Upper Egypt (fr. Gk *Thēbai*) + *-anus* -an] : of or relating to ancient Thebes, Egypt, or Thebes, Greece

²**theban** \"\ *n* -s *cap* [ME, fr. L *Thebanus*] : a native or inhabitant of Thebes

the·be·sian vessel *also* **thebesian vein** *or* **thebesian channel** \thə'bēzhən-\ *n, sometimes cap T* [fr. Adam C. *Thebesius* †1732 Ger. anatomist + E *-an*] : any of the minute veins of the heart wall that drain directly into the cavity of the heart

thec- or **theci-** or **theco-** *comb form* [NL, fr. *theca*] : theca ⟨*theci*ferous⟩ ⟨*thec*itis⟩ ⟨*Theco*somata⟩

the·ca \'thēkə\ *n, pl* **the·cae** \-ē(,)sē\ [NL, fr. L, case, cover — more at TICK] **1** : SAC, CAPSULE, SPORE CASE: as **a** : the capsule of a moss **b** : the pollen sac of an anther **2** : an enveloping sheath or case: as **a** : the cuticular case of an insect larva **b** : the sheath of dura mater enclosing the spinal cord **c** : the layer of dense stroma surrounding a Graafian follicle **d** : HYDROTHECA **e** : the calcareous wall of a coral calyculus **f** : the test of a testate protozoan or rotifer **g** : the dorsal cup of the calyx of a crinoid

-theca \"\ *n comb form, pl* **-thecae** \"\ [NL, fr. L *theca*] : sheath or covering of a (specified) type ⟨gono*theca*⟩ ⟨myxo*theca*⟩

the·cal \'thēkəl\ *adj* [*thec-* + *-al*] : of or relating to a theca

the·ca·moe·bae \,thēkə'mē(,)bē\ *or* **the·cam·oe·baea** \thə-,kamē'bēə\ [NL, fr. pl. of *Thecamoeba* genus of Rhizopoda, fr. *thec-* + *Amoeba*] *syn of* TESTACEA

the·ca·ta \thə'kād·ə\ [NL, fr. *thec-* + *-ata*] *syn of* LEPTOMEDUSAE

the·cate \'thē,kāt\ *adj* [*thec-* + *-ate*] : having a theca : TESTATE

the·cial \'thēsh(ē)əl, -sēəl\ *adj* [NL *thecium* + E *-al*] : of or relating to a thecium

the·ci·um \'thēs(h)ēəm\ *n, pl* **the·cia** \-)ēə\ [NL, fr. Gk *thēkion* small case, small chest, dim. of *thēkē* case, chest — more at TICK] : HYMENIUM

-thecium \"\ *n comb form, pl* **-thecia** \"\ [NL, fr. Gk *thēkion* small case, small chest] : small containing structure ⟨endo*thecium*⟩

thec·la \'theklə\ [NL, prob. fr. the name *Thecla*] *syn of* STRYMON

¹**the·co·dont** \'thēkə,dänt\ *adj* [*thec-* + *-odont*] : having the teeth inserted in sockets in the alveoli

²**thecodont** \"\ *n* -s : a thecodont animal; *esp* : a thecodont reptile

the·co·don·tia \,thēkə'dänchə\ *n pl, cap* [NL, fr. *thec-* + *-odontia*] : an order of Reptilia comprising various generalized diapsid Triassic forms presumably on the common ancestral line of the dinosaurs, crocodiles, and birds

the·coid \'thē,kȯid\ *adj or n* [NL *Thecoidea*] : EDRIOASTEROID

the·coi·dea \thə'kȯidēə\ [NL, fr. *thec-* + *-oidea*] *syn of* EDRIOASTEROIDEA

¹**the·coph·o·ra** \thə'käf(ə)rə\ [NL, fr. *thec-* + *-phora*] *syn of* LEPTOMEDUSAE

²**thecophora** \"\ *n pl, cap* [NL, fr. *thec-* + *-phora*] *in some classifications* : a suborder of Testudinata including all recent turtles except the leatherback — **the·coph·o·ran** \-rən\ *adj or n*

the·coph·o·roi·dea \thə,käfə'rȯidēə\ [NL, fr. *Thecophora* + *-oidea*] *syn of* THECOPHORA

the·co·so·ma·ta \,thēkə'sōməd·ə\ *n pl, cap* [NL, fr. *thec-* + *-somata*] *in some classifications* : a division of Pteropoda comprising pteropods with a shell — compare GYMNOSOMATA — **the·co·so·ma·tous** \-d·əs\ *adj*

thé dansant \tādäⁿsäⁿ\ *n, pl* **thés dansants** \"\ [F] : TEA DANCE

¹**thee** \(ˌ)thē, thi\ *pron, objective case of* THOU [ME, fr. OE *thē* — more at THOU] **1** : ¹THOU: **a** *archaic* — used esp. in biblical, ecclesiastical, solemn, or poetical language, and to some extent in the speech of Friends esp. among themselves, in contexts where the objective case form of an inflected pronoun is the one to be expected esp. as indirect object of a verb ⟨the land . . . which he sware unto thy fathers to give ~ —Exod 13: 5 (AV)⟩ or as personal object of an impersonal verb ⟨do what seemeth ~ good —1 Sam 1: 23 (AV)⟩ or as object of a preposition ⟨sweet land of liberty, of ~ I sing —Samuel Francis Smith⟩ or as direct object of a verb ⟨I take ~ at thy word —Shak.⟩ **b** — used by reputable writers occas. from the 14th to the 17th centuries, in many British dialects down to the present day, and in the prevailing usage of the speech of Friends esp. among themselves, in contexts where the nominative case form of an inflected pronoun is the one to be expected esp. as subject of a verb ⟨don't think I am afraid of such a fellow as ~ art —Henry Fielding⟩ or in the predicate after a form of the verb *be* ⟨proud . . . that I am not ~ —Shak.⟩; in the usage of Friends and in many British dialects usu. accompanied by the third person singular form of a verb of which it is the subject ⟨~ still thinks of going to Canada —Harriet B. Stowe⟩ **2** *archaic* : THYSELF — used reflexively as indirect object of a verb ⟨get ~ a sword —Shak.⟩ or object of a preposition ⟨when Thou tookest upon *Thee* to deliver man —*Te Deum Laudamus*⟩ or direct object of a verb ⟨thou bearest ~ like a king —Shak.⟩

²**thee** \'thē\ *n* -s : ³THOU

³**thee** \"\ *vb* **thee'd; thee'd; theeing; thees** *vt* : to address as *thee* ~ *vi* : to use *thee* in address

⁴**thee** *vi* [ME *theen,* fr. OE *thēon;* akin to OHG *dihan* to thrive, Goth *theihan* to increase, progress — more at TIGHT] *obs* : THRIVE, PROSPER ⟨well mote ye ~ —Edmund Spenser⟩

theek \'thēk\ *vt* -ED/-ING/-S [ME *theken,* perh. of Scand origin; akin to ON *thekja* to cover, thatch — more at THATCH] *Scot* : THATCH, COVER

Thee·lin \'thēlən\ *trademark* — used for a preparation of estrone

thee·lol \-ē,lōl, -ē,lōl\ *n* -s [ISV *theel*in + *-ol*] : ESTRIOL

theet·see \'thētsē\ *n* -s [Burmese *thitse*] : BLACK-VARNISH TREE

thee·zan tea \'thēzⁿn-\ *n* [fr. NL *theezans* (specific epithet of *Sageretia theezans*), prob. fr. NL *Thea*] : a Chinese shrub (*Sageretia theezans*) with edible fruit and leaves that are often used in place of tea

theft \'theft\ *n* -s [ME *thiefthe, thefthe, thefte, thifte,* fr. OE *thīefth, thēofth, thȳfth;* akin to OFris *thiūvethe, thiūfthe* theft, OS *thiubda,* ON *thȳfth, thȳft;* derivative fr. the stem of E *thief*] **1 a** : the act of stealing; *specif* : the felonious taking and removing of personal property with intent to deprive the rightful owner of it **b** : an instance of such an act **2** : the taking of property unlawfully (as by robbery, embezzlement, fraud) ⟨has just ruled that ~ from a spouse is possible —*Jour. of the Amer. Judicature Society*⟩ **3** *obs* : something that is stolen ⟨if the ~ be certainly found in his hand alive . . . he shall restore double —Exod 22: 4 (AV)⟩

theft·bote \'theft,bōt\ *n* -s [alter. of *thefbote,* fr. ME, fr. *thef* thief + *bote* compensation — more at THIEF, BOOT (help)] *old Eng & Scots law* : the offense of agreeing to receive stolen goods or a compensation from a thief whether by the owner by way of composition or by a judge as an inducement for conniving at the escape of the thief from punishment

theft insurance *n* : insurance against loss or damage caused by the unlawful taking of property

theftproof \'=,=\ *adj* : safe from theft : resistant to thieves ⟨~ strongbox⟩ ⟨~ lock⟩

thef·tu·ous \'thefchəwəs\ *adj* [alter. (influenced by *-uous*) of ME *thiftwis,* fr. *thifte* theft + *wis, wise* wise — more at THEFT, WISE] : THIEVISH — **thef·tu·ous·ly** *adv*

the·gith·er \thə'githər\ *Scot var of* TOGETHER

thegn *var of* THANE

thegn·ly *adj* [trans. of OE *thegnlīc*] : of, relating to, or befitting a thane

thei·le·ria \thī'lirēə\ *n* [NL, fr. Sir Arnold *Theiler* †1936 Eng. veterinary bacteriologist born in Switzerland + NL *-ia*] **1** *cap* : a genus of parasitic protozoans (family Babesiidae) that includes the parasite of east coast fever of cattle and is sometimes variously treated either as a subgenus of *Babesia* or as type of a separate family **2** *pl* **thei·le·ri·ae** \-ē,ē\ *also* **theilerias** : any organism of the genus *Theileria* — **thei·le·ri·al** \-rēəl\ *adj*

thei·le·ri·a·sis \,thīlə'rīəsəs\ *or* **thei·le·ri·o·sis** \,thī,lirē-'ōsəs\ *n* -ES [NL, fr. *Theileria* + *-iasis* or *-osis*] : infection with or disease caused by a theileria; *esp* : EAST COAST FEVER

the·ine \'thē,ēn, 'thēən\ *n* -s [NL *theina,* fr. *thea* tea + *-ina* -ine; fr. its occurrence in tea — more at THEA] : CAFFEINE

¹**their** [ME, fr. ON *theirra, theira,* gen. pl. demonstrative & personal pron.; akin to ON *that,* neut. demonstrative pron. — more at THAT] *obs possessive of* ¹THEY

²**their** \thər, (ˌ)the(ə)r, (ˌ)tha(ə)r, |ə\ *adj* [ME, fr. *their,* pron.] **1 a** : of or belonging to them or themselves as possessors : due to them : inherent in them : associated or connected with them ⟨~ furniture⟩ ⟨~ rights⟩ ⟨~ neighbors⟩ **b** : of or relating to them or themselves as authors, doers, givers, or agents : effected by them : experienced by them as subject : that they are capable of ⟨~ verses⟩ ⟨~ confidence in you⟩ ⟨responsible for ~ being here⟩ ⟨doing ~ utmost⟩ **c** : of or relating to them or

themselves as object of an action **:** experienced by them as object ⟨~ defeat⟩ ⟨~ being seen⟩ **d :** that they have to do with or are supposed to possess or to have knowledge or a share of or some special interest in ⟨they know ~ algebra⟩ ⟨they like ~ leisure⟩ **e :** that is esp. significant for them **:** that brings them good fortune or prominence — used with *day* or sometimes with other words indicating a division of time ⟨the twins had a wonderful birthday party; this certainly was ~ day⟩ **2 :** his or her **:** HIS, HER — used with a singular antecedent that is indefinite or that does not specify gender ⟨anyone in ~ senses —W.H.Auden⟩ ⟨we shall be pleased to send a free specimen copy . . . to a friend or relative on receipt of ~ address —*London Calling*⟩ **3** *obs* — used after a plural or collective noun or a group of two or more nouns to indicate a possessive case relation ⟨in the father, mother, and governess *their* absence —*The Lives of Women Saints*⟩ **4** *archaic* **:** of those — used esp. as antecedent to a relative pronoun ⟨nor better was ~ lot who fled —Sir Walter Scott⟩

theirn \ˈthe(ə)rn, ˈtha(ə)|, |ən\ *pron* [by alter. (influence of *mine, thine, hisn*)] *dial* **:** THEIRS

[1]**theirs** \ˈthe(ə)rz, ˈtha(ə)|, |əz\ *pron* [ME *theirs, theires,* fr. *their* + *-s, -es* -'s] **1 :** their one **:** their ones — used without a following noun as a pronoun equivalent in meaning to the adjective *their* ⟨bought his car the same day his neighbors bought ~⟩ ⟨our customs are not like ~⟩; often used after *of* to single out one or more members of a class belonging to or connected with certain persons not including the one speaking or writing nor the one being addressed ⟨a friend of ~⟩ ⟨some shrubs of ~⟩ or merely to identify something or someone as belonging to or connected with certain persons not including the one speaking or writing nor the one being addressed without any implication of membership in a more extensive class ⟨that dog of ~⟩ ⟨those flashy clothes of ~⟩ **2 :** something belonging to them **:** what belongs to them ⟨they are determined to get ~⟩ **3 :** his or hers **:** HIS, HERS — used with a singular antecedent that is indefinite or that does not specify gender ⟨I will do my part if everybody else will do ~⟩

[2]**theirs** *adj, obs* **:** [2]THEIR 1 — used as the first of two possessive adjectives modifying the same noun

their·selves \thərˈselvz, the(ə)r-, tha(ə)r-, -eu̇vz\ *pron* [obs. E *theirself* themselves (fr. ME, fr. *their* + *self*) + E *-es*] *substand* **:** THEMSELVES

the·ism \ˈthēˌizəm\ *n* -s [*the-* + *-ism*] **1 :** belief in the existence of a god or gods; *specif* **:** belief in the existence of one God who is viewed as the creative source of man, the world, and value and who transcends and yet is immanent in the world ⟨Christian ~⟩ — opposed to *atheism;* distinguished from *pantheism* and *polytheism* **2 :** a system of thought founded on the belief in one or more gods ⟨these philosophies, which are usually called ~s, view all of life as a divinely ordered sequence —J.R. Everett⟩

-the·ism *when immediately preceded by stress* thēˌizəm *or* ˈth-, *when immediately preceded by nonstress* (ˌ)th- *or* ˈth-\ *n comb form* -s [MF *-théisme,* fr. *thé-* the- + *-isme* -ism] **:** belief in (such) a god or (such or so many) gods ⟨pan*theism*⟩ ⟨zoo*theism*⟩

the·ist \ˈthēəst\ *n* -s [*the-* + *-ist*] **:** a believer in theism

-the·ist *when immediately preceded by stress* thēəst *or* ˈth-, *when immediately preceded by nonstress* (ˌ)th- *or* ˈth-\ *n comb form* -s [MF *-théiste,* fr. *thé-* the- + *-iste* -ist] **:** one that believes in (such) a god or (such or so many) gods ⟨hylo*theist*⟩ ⟨mono*theist*⟩ — **-the·is·tic** \thēˈistik, -tēk\ *adj comb form*

the·is·tic \thēˈistik, -tēk\ *also* **the·is·ti·cal** \-tə̇kəl, -tēk-\ *adj* **:** of or relating to theism or a theist **:** believing in theism — **the·is·ti·cal·ly** \-tə̇k(ə)lē, -tēk-, -li\ *adv*

theistic naturalism *n* **:** PROCESS PHILOSOPHY

theistic naturalist *n* **:** an advocate of religious naturalism; *specif* **:** a Protestant Christian theologian who utilizes process philosophy as a framework for interpreting the Christian faith

the·la·zia \thə̇ˈlāzēə\ *n, cap* [NL, fr. Gk *thēlazein* to suckle, suck (fr. *thēlē* nipple) + NL *-ia* — more at FEMININE] **:** a genus of nematode worms that comprises various eye worms and is the type of the family Thelaziidae

thel·a·zi·a·sis \ˌthelə̇ˈzīəsə̇s\ *n* -ES [NL, fr. *Thelazia* + *-iasis*] **:** infestation with or disease caused by roundworms of the genus *Thelazia*

thel·a·zi·idae \ˌthelə̇ˈzīəˌdē\ *n pl, cap* [NL, fr. *Thelazia,* type genus + *-idae*] **:** a family of spiruroid nematode worms containing various forms of medical or veterinary importance — see THELAZIA

thel·em·ite \ˈtheləˌmīt\ *n* -s [F *thélémite,* fr. Abbaye de *Thélème,* imaginary abbey with the motto "Do as you please" in *Gargantua* (1535) by François Rabelais †1553 Fr. satirist + F *-ite*] **:** one who does as he pleases; *esp* **:** LIBERTINE

thel·e·pho·ra·ce·ae \ˌthelə̇fəˈrāsēˌē\ *n pl, cap* [NL, fr. *Thelephora,* type genus (fr. Gk *thēlē* teat, nipple + NL *-phora*) + *-aceae* — more at FEMININE] **:** a family of fungi (order Agaricales) having leathery or membranous sporophores with smooth or corrugated basidial surfaces

the·lig·o·num *also* **the·lyg·o·num** \thə̇ˈligənəm\ [NL, fr. L *thelygonon,* any of several plants of the genera *Mercurialis* and *Crucianella,* fr. Gk *thēlygonon,* fr. *thēlys* female + *-gonon* (fr. the stem of *gignesthai* to be born) — more at FEMININE, KIN] *syn of* CYNOCRAMBE

the·li·on \ˈthēlēˌän\ *n* -s [NL, fr. Gk *thēlē* nipple, teat + NL *-ion,* dim. suffix] **:** the central point of the nipple

thel·o·don·ti·dae \ˌthelə̇ˈdäntə̇ˌdē\ *n pl, cap* [NL, fr. *Thelodont-, Thelodus,* type genus + *-idae*] **:** a family of Devonian and Silurian ostracoderms that is included among the Heterostraci or isolated in the order Coelolepida

thel·o·dus \ˈthelədə̇s\ *n, cap* [NL, fr. Gk *thēlē* nipple + NL *-odus*] **:** a genus of Silurian and Devonian ostracoderms (family Thelodontidae) that have small dermal tubercles consisting of dentine and enamel

thel·phu·sa \thelˈfyüsə\ *n, cap* [NL] **:** a genus (the type of the family Thelphusidae) of freshwater crabs living in or on river banks in warm countries — **thel·phu·si·an** \(ˈ)thelˈfyüsēən, -üshən\ *adj or n*

thely- *comb form* [Gk *thēly-,* fr. *thēlys* — more at FEMININE] **:** female ⟨*thely*genic⟩

thel·y·gen·ic \ˌthelə̇ˈjenik\ *adj* [*thely-* + *-genic*] **:** producing female offspring solely or predominantly

[1]**the·lyph·o·nid** \thə̇ˈlifənə̇d\ *adj* [NL *Thelyphonidae*] **:** of or relating to the Thelyphonidae

[2]**thelyphonid** \"\ *n* -s **:** a whip scorpion of the family Thelyphonidae

thel·y·phon·i·dae \ˌthelēˈfänəˌdē\ *n pl, cap* [NL, fr. *Thelyphonus,* type genus (fr. *thely-* + Gk *phonos* murder) + *-idae* — more at PHOENICIAN] **:** a widely distributed family of tailed whip scorpions

thel·y·to·cia \ˌthelēˈtōshēə\ *n* -s [NL, fr. Gk *thēlytokia* condition of bearing females] **:** THELYTOKY

the·lyt·o·kous \thə̇ˈlid·əkəs\ *also* **thel·y·ot·o·kous** \ˌthelēˈäd·əkəs\ *adj* [Gk *thēlytokos* bearing females] **:** producing only females ⟨~ parthenogenesis⟩

the·lyt·o·ky \-kē\ *also* **thel·y·ot·o·ky** \ˌ==ˈäd·əkē\ *n* -ES [Gk *thēlytokia* condition of bearing females, fr. *thēlytokos* bearing females (fr. *thēly-* thely- + *-tokos,* fr. *tiktein* to bear) + *-ia* -y — more at THANE] **:** parthenogenesis in which only female offspring are produced — compare ARRHENOTOKY

[1]**them** \(th)əm, ᵊm, (ˌ)them\ *pron, objective case of* THEY [ME *them;* partly fr. *tham,* fr. OE *thǣm, thām,* dat. pl. demonstrative pron. & definite article; partly fr. *theim,* fr. ON, dat. pl. demonstrative & personal pron.; akin to OE *thæt,* neut. demonstrative pron. & definite article — more at THAT] **1 :** [1]THEY 1, 3: **a** — used as indirect object of a verb ⟨men . . . who, as the fields and woods have given ~ birth, will build their savage fortunes only there —William Wordsworth⟩ **b** — used as object of a preposition ⟨to provide for organizing, arming, and disciplining the militia, and for governing such part of ~ as may be employed in the service of the United States —*U.S.Constitution*⟩ **c** — used as direct object of a verb ⟨you do not have to understand someone in order to love ~ —Lawrence Durrell⟩ ⟨they say things are going from bad to worse, but for my part, let ~ say what they like⟩ **d** — used in comparisons after *than* and *as* when the first term in the comparison is the direct or indirect object of a verb or the object of a preposition ⟨would hurt us as much as ~⟩ ⟨giving you better terms than ~⟩ ⟨easier for you than ~⟩ **e** — used in absolute constructions esp. together with a prepositional phrase, adjective, or participle ⟨~ being my friends, I did as they asked⟩ **f** — used by speakers on all educational levels and by many reputable writers though disapproved by some grammarians in the predicate after forms of *be,* in comparisons after *than* and *as* when the first term in the comparison is the subject of a verb, and in other positions where it is itself neither the subject of a verb nor the object of a verb or preposition ⟨it is ~⟩ ⟨we are as efficient as ~⟩ ⟨did your parents say you could go? Not ~⟩ **g** — used in substandard speech and formerly also by reputable writers as part of the compound subject of a verb ⟨your safety, for the which myself and ~ bend their best studies —Shak.⟩ **h** — used like the adjective *their* with a gerund by speakers and writers on all educational levels though disapproved by some grammarians ⟨whether there are any objections to ~ smoking —Noreen Routledge⟩ **2 :** THOSE — used esp. as antecedent to a relative pronoun ⟨the best of ~ that speak this speech —Shak.⟩; used as the subject of a verb in substandard speech, though formerly also by reputable writers ⟨~ that like that sort of thing are welcome to it⟩ **3 :** THEMSELVES — used reflexively as indirect object of a verb ⟨a folk that had founded ~ homes round wintry Dodona —W. B.Smith & Walter Miller⟩ or object of a preposition ⟨people that have their wits about ~⟩ or archaically as direct object of a verb ⟨like bride and groom devesting ~ for bed —Shak.⟩

[2]**them** \ˈthem\ *adj, substand* **:** THOSE ⟨take ~ dirty boots off —Helen Eustis⟩ ⟨~ box pleats . . . is the latest thing —Ellen Glasgow⟩

the·ma \ˈthēmə\ *n, pl* **thema·ta** \-məd·ə\ [L — more at THEME] **1 :** a topic or subject of discourse or of a written dissertation **:** THESIS **2 :** THEME 6 **3 :** THEME 4

the·mat·ic \(ˈ)thēˈmad·|ik, thə̇ˈ-, -at|, |ēk\ *adj* [Gk *thematikos,* fr. *themat-, thema* theme + *-ikos* -ic] **1 a :** of or relating to the stem of a word **b** *of a vowel* **:** being the last part of a word stem before an inflectional ending **2 :** of or relating to a melodic subject ⟨~ development⟩ ⟨~ catalog of a composer's works⟩ **3 :** of, relating to, or constituting a topic of discourse or a subject of artistic or cultural expression ⟨~ analysis of a poem⟩ ⟨~ approach to the study of a primitive society⟩ — **the·mat·i·cal·ly** \|ə̇k(ə)lē, |ēk-, -li\ *adv*

thematic apperception test *n* **:** a projective technique widely used in clinical psychology wherein personality, psychodynamic, and diagnostic assessments are based on the subject's verbal responses to a series of black-and-white pictures — abbr. *TAT*

thematic verb *n* **:** a verb whose present tense stem ends in the varying thematic vowel *e:o,* (as Latin *seque, sequo*)

thematic vowel *n* **:** a vowel ending the stem of a noun or verb but not belonging to the root; *esp* **:** the varying *e:o* (as in Latin nominative *servos,* vocative *serve* slave) — compare GRADE 4

the·ma·tist \ˈthēməd·əst\ *n* -s [L *themat-, thema* + E *-ist*] **:** one who composes themes

[1]**theme** \ˈthēm\ *n* -s [ME *teme, theme,* fr. OF & L; OF *teme,* fr. L *thema,* fr. Gk, lit., something laid down, that which is laid down, fr. *tithenai* to place, set, lay down — more at DO] **1 a :** a subject or topic on which one speaks or writes ⟨~ of rags to riches⟩ ⟨economic ~*s*⟩ **b :** a proposition for discussion or argument ⟨stressed the ~ of equal rights for all⟩ **c :** a subject of fictional or artistic representation ⟨waterfalls are from very early times a favorite ~ for the painter —Laurence Binyon⟩ ⟨guilt and its punishment is the constant ~ of the dramas of Aeschylus —G.L.Dickinson⟩ **d :** an idea, ideal, or orienting principle that is dominant or persistent in a popular or tribal culture and often effective in controlling and activating belief and conduct in a specific direction — compare ETHOS, GESTALT **2 :** STEM 4a **3 :** a written exercise required of a student commonly at frequent regular intervals in a composition course ⟨weekly ~⟩ ⟨research ~⟩ **4 a :** a melodic subject of a musical composition or movement **b :** a short melody constituting the basis of variation, development, or other repetition with modification **c :** a visual motif or figure that forms by repetition, contrast, or variation a component of design in any of the graphic or plastic arts **5 :** HOROSCOPE **6 :** an administrative division of the Byzantine Empire **7 :** SIGNATURE 9

[2]**theme** \"\ *vt* -ED/-ING/-S **:** to give a topic, subject, or text to **:** furnish with or direct toward a theme — used chiefly in past part. ⟨*themed* to making things out of wood, the book is written in clear, simple terms —*Toys and Novelties*⟩

theme and variations *n* **:** a standard form of musical composition consisting of a simple usu. harmonized melody presented first in its original unadorned form then repeated several or many times with varied treatment so based on the theme that at least some semblance of its general melodic or harmonic form is evident

theme·less \-mlə̇s\ *adj* **:** lacking a theme

them·er \-mə(r)\ *n* -s **:** one that sets or provides a theme

theme song *n* **1 :** a melody recurring so often in a musical or dramatic performance that it characterizes the production or one of its principal characters **2 :** an assertion or complaint repeated so often as to be regarded as characteristic of its user **3 :** SIGNATURE 9

the·mis·tian \thə̇ˈmis(h)chən\ *n* -s *usu cap* [*Themistius,* 6th cent. deacon of Alexandria, founder of the sect + E *-an*] **:** AGNOETE

them·selves \thəmˈselvz, them-, -eu̇vz, *South often* -e(ə)vz\ *pron pl* [obs. E *themself* themselves (fr. ME *thamself, theimself, themself,* fr. *tham, theim, them* them + *self*) + E *-es*] **1 :** those identical ones that are they **:** the selves that belong to them **:** the selves that are theirs — used (1) reflexively as object of a preposition or direct or indirect object of a verb ⟨they keep their plans to ~⟩ ⟨nations that govern ~⟩ ⟨they are getting ~ an incinerator⟩; (2) for emphasis in apposition with *they, who, which, that,* or a noun ⟨they ~ were surprised⟩ ⟨some who ~ were very busy nevertheless took the time to help others⟩ ⟨postcards which ~ supply the skeleton of the message —Randall Jarrell⟩ ⟨people that enjoy a game of bridge ~⟩ ⟨the teachers ~ were as glad as the pupils when the school year ended⟩; (3) for emphasis instead of nonreflexive *them* as object of a preposition or direct or indirect object of a verb ⟨their combined salaries support their children and ~⟩; (4) for emphasis instead of *they* or instead of *they themselves* as predicate nominative ⟨there is someone they can always depend on and that is ~⟩ or in comparisons after *than* or *as* ⟨they envied us though we were as poor as ~⟩ or as part of a compound subject ⟨to get their education as ~ or their neglectful government might see fit —S.A.Allibone⟩ or archaically or dialectally as only subject of a verb ⟨some . . . can render no ill services, in recompense for what ~ required —William Wordsworth⟩; (5) in absolute constructions ⟨~ bankrupt morally and economically, the landowners have sought to prevent and retard government intervention —Mario Einaudi⟩ **2 :** their normal, healthy, or sane condition ⟨both persons involved in the accident were in a state of shock for a time but soon came to ~⟩ **:** their normal, healthy, or sane selves ⟨after a good night's rest they were ~ again⟩ **3 :** HIMSELF, HERSELF — used with a singular antecedent that is indefinite or that does not specify gender ⟨nobody can call ~ oppressed —Leonard Wibberley⟩

[1]**then** \(ˌ)then *sometimes* than\ *adv* [ME *thanne, than, thenne, then,* fr. OE *thanne, thonne, thænne;* akin to OHG *thanne, thanna, denne* then, ON *thā,* Goth *than* then, OE *thæt,* neut. demonstrative pron. & definite article — more at THAT] **1 :** at that time **:** at the time mentioned or specified ⟨the situation as it ~ was⟩ ⟨science as it was ~ taught⟩ **2 :** soon after that **:** immediately after that **:** next in order of time ⟨walked to the door, ~ turned⟩ ⟨first left, ~ right⟩ ⟨~ came the thunder⟩ — used often to imply a causal or other relation to the preceding ⟨come closer, ~ I won't have to shout⟩ **3 a :** following next after this in order of position, narration, enumeration ⟨a hill, ~ a river valley, ~ another hill⟩ **b :** in addition **:** BESIDES ⟨and ~ there is the interest to be paid⟩ **4 a :** in that case **:** under those circumstances ⟨keep it, ~, if you want to⟩ ⟨if he didn't take it, ~ who did⟩ ⟨hurry, ~, if you're coming with us⟩ ⟨what if there should be a fire, what ~⟩ — used after *but* to qualify or offset a preceding statement ⟨it's true he lost the race, but ~ he never really expected to win it⟩ **b :** according to that **:** as may be inferred ⟨you did go, ~, after all⟩ ⟨your mind is made up, ~⟩ **c :** by way of summing up **:** as it appears ⟨these, ~, are the things you must do⟩ ⟨the cause of the accident, ~, seems to be established⟩ **d :** as a necessary or logical consequence **:** CONSEQUENTLY ⟨if the angles are equal, ~ their complements are equal⟩ — **and then some :** with much more in addition **:** at the very least ⟨would need all his luck *and then some*⟩

[2]**then** *conj* [ME *thanne, than, thenne, then,* fr. *thanne, than, thenne, then,* adv.] *obs* **:** at the time that **:** WHEN

[3]**then** \ˈthen\ *n* -s [ME *thanne, than, thenne, then,* fr. *thanne, than, thenne, then,* adv.] **:** that time **:** that moment ⟨till ~, who knew the force of those dire arms —John Milton⟩ ⟨we should get there long before ~⟩ ⟨they were friends from ~ on⟩

[4]**then** \"\ *adj* [[1]*then*] **:** existing, acting at, or belonging to the time mentioned ⟨the ~ current of opinion⟩ ⟨the ~ secretary of state⟩

[5]**then** \thən, (ˌ)then\ *dial var of* THAN

then·a·bouts \ˈthenəˌbau̇ts\ *adv* [[1]*then* + *-abouts* (as in *thereabouts*)] **:** near that time **:** about then

then·a·days \-ˌdāz\ *adv* [[1]*then* + *-adays* (as in *nowadays*)] **:** at that time **:** in those days

then and there *adv* **:** on the spot **:** IMMEDIATELY ⟨decided *then and there* to give up the trip and go home⟩

[1]**the·nar** \ˈthēˌnär, -nȧ(r\ *n* -s [NL, fr. Gk; akin to OHG *tenar* palm of the hand — more at DEN] **1 a** *or* **thenar eminence :** the ball of the thumb **b** *or* **thenar muscle :** the intrinsic musculature of the thumb **2 :** PALM 2a; *sometimes* **:** [1]SOLE 1a

[2]**thenar** \"\ *also* **the·nal** \-ēnᵊl\ *adj* [*thenar* fr. NL *thenar; thenal* fr. NL *thenar* + E *-al*] **:** of, relating to, involving, or constituting the thenar ⟨~ neuritis⟩

the·nard·ite \thə̇ˈnärˌdīt\ *n* -s [F *thénardite,* fr. Baron Louis J. *Thénard* †1857 French chemist + F *-ite*] **:** a mineral Na_2SO_4 consisting of native anhydrous sodium sulfate and occurring in white or brownish crystals, masses, or crusts often in connection with salt lakes

the·nard's blue \thə̇ˈnärdz-\ *n, usu cap T* [after Baron L. J. *Thénard*] **1 :** COBALT BLUE 1a **2 :** COBALT BLUE 2

thence \ˈthen(t)s *also* ˈthe-\ *adv* [ME *thannes, thennes,* fr. *thanene, thonene, thenene, thanne, thenne* from that place (fr. OE *thanon, thonan, thonon*) + *-s,* adv. suffix; akin to OFris *thana* from that place, OS & OHG *thanan, thanana,* ON *thanan* from that place, *thā* then — more at THEN] **1 :** from that place ⟨proceeding ~ directly to college⟩ — often used with *from* ⟨timed . . . the farther walk from ~ to the entrance to the docks —F.W.Crofts⟩ **2 a** *archaic* **:** not there **:** ELSEWHERE **b :** away from there — used chiefly in statements of distance ⟨the church stood two miles ~⟩ **3** *archaic* **:** from that time **:** THENCEFORTH **4 :** from that fact or circumstance **:** THEREFROM ⟨atomic formulas and all compounds ~ constructible —W.V.Quine⟩ ⟨a natural conclusion follows ~⟩

thenceafter \(ˈ)=ˈ==\ *adv* **:** after that time **:** AFTERWARD

thenceforth \(ˈ)=ˈ=\ *adv* [ME *thennes forth*] **:** from that time forward **:** THEREAFTER ⟨in the island which was ~ to be their home —Kemp Malone⟩

thenceforward *also* **thenceforwards** \(ˈ)=ˈ==\ *adv* [ME *thens forward*] **:** onward from that place or time **:** THENCEFORTH

thencefrom \(ˈ)=ˈ=\ *adv, archaic* **:** from that place **:** THENCE

then-clause \ˈ=ˌ=\ *n* **:** the conclusional clause of a conditional sentence — compare IF-CLAUSE

then·ness \ˈthennə̇s\ *n* -ES **:** the quality or state of having existence in past time ⟨feel a difference between nowness and ~⟩ or a specified past time ⟨thereness and ~ of a particular event⟩

the·no·ic acid \thə̇ˈnōik-\ *n* [*thiophene* + *-o-* + *-ic*] **:** either of two isomeric crystalline acids C_4H_3SCOOH made from thiophene; thiophene-carboxylic acid

then·o·yl \ˈthenəˌwil\ *n* -s [*thenoic (acid)* + *-yl*] **:** either of the two radicals C_4H_3SCO— of the thenoic acids

then·yl \ˈthenᵊl\ *n* -s [*thiophene* + *-yl*] **:** the radical $C_4H_3SCH_2$— derived from methyl-thiophene by removal of a hydrogen atom from the methyl group — compare BENZYL, THIENYL

theo- — see THE-

theo *abbr* **1** theology **2** theoretical

the·o·bro·ma \ˌthēəˈbrōmə\ *n, cap* [NL, fr. *the-* + Gk *brōma* food, fr. *bibrōskein* to devour — more at VORACIOUS] **:** a genus of tropical American trees (family Sterculiaceae) having large simple leaves, small flowers with inflexed petals borne on the old wood, and large fleshy fruits — see CACAO

theobroma oil *n* **:** COCOA BUTTER

the·o·bro·mine \-ōˌmēn, -ōmə̇n\ *n* -s [NL *Theobroma* + ISV *-ine*] **:** a feebly basic bitter crystalline compound $C_7H_8N_4O_2$ that is the principal base of cacao beans and chocolate, is found in small amounts elsewhere (as in kola nuts and tea), and is also made synthetically, that is isomeric with theophylline and is closely related to caffeine, and that is used in the form of salts and other derivatives as a diuretic, myocardial stimulant, and vasodilator; 3,7-dimethyl-xanthine

the·o·cen·tric \ˌthēōˈsen·trik\ *adj* [*the-* + *-centric*] **:** assuming God as the center **:** having God as the central interest and ultimate concern ⟨a ~ view of the world⟩ — **the·o·cen·tric·i·ty** \ˌ==sen·ˈtrisəd·ē\ *n*

the·o·cen·trism \ˌ==ˈsen·ˌtrizəm\ *or* **the·o·cen·tri·cism** \-trəˌsizəm\ *n* -s **:** theocentric beliefs

the·oc·ra·cy \thēˈäkrəsē, -si\ *n* -ES [Gk *theokratia,* fr. *the-* + *-kratia* -cracy] **1 a :** government of a state by the immediate direction or administration of God **b :** government or political rule by priests or clergy as representatives of God **2 :** a state governed by God or by religious officials

the·oc·ra·sy \"\ *or* **the·o·cra·sia** *also* **the·o·kra·sia** \ˌthēəˈkrāzh(ē)ə\ *n, pl* **theocrasies** *or* **theocrasias** [LGk *theokrasia,* fr. Gk *the-* + *-krasia* (fr. *kras-* — stem of *kerannynai* to mix — + *-ia* -y) — more at CRATER] **1 :** a fusion or mixture of different deities in the minds of worshipers ⟨the ~ of divinities of East and West⟩; *also* **:** the identification of formerly separate deities ⟨the ~ of Zeus and Helios in the invocation of Zeus-Helios as one god⟩ **2 :** an intimate union of the soul with the One or God in contemplation

the·o·crat \ˈthēəˌkrat\ *n* -s [*the-* + *-crat*] **1 :** one who rules in or lives under a theocratic form of government **2 :** one who favors a theocratic form of government

the·o·crat·ic \ˌ==ˈkrad·|ik, -at|, |ēk\ *adj* **:** of, relating to, or being a theocracy ⟨a ~ state⟩ — **the·o·crat·i·cal·ly** \|ə̇k(ə)lē, |ēk-, -li\ *adv*

the·oc·ri·te·an \thēˌäkrəˈtēən\ *also* **the·oc·ri·tan** \thēˈäkrətᵊn\ *adj, usu cap* [*Theocritus,* 3d cent. B.C. Greek pastoral poet + E *-ean, -an*] **:** of, relating to, or in the manner of the poet Theocritus **:** IDYLLIC, PASTORAL, BUCOLIC ⟨a *Theocritean* idyl⟩ ⟨*Theocritean* simplicity⟩

theo·democracy \ˌthē(ˌ)ō+\ *n* [*the-* + *democracy*] **:** a community governed by the people according to the revealed will of deity

the·od·i·ce·an \thēˌädəˈsēən\ *adj* **1 :** of or relating to theodicy **2 :** having the character of a theodicy

the·od·i·cy \thēˈädəsē\ *n* -ES [modif. of F *théodicée,* fr. *théo-* the- + Gk *dikē* right, judgment — more at DICTION] **1 :** vindication of the justice of God esp. in ordaining or permitting natural and moral evil **2 :** an area of philosophy that treats of the nature and government of God and the destiny of the soul **:** NATURAL THEOLOGY

the·od·o·lite \thēˈädᵊlˌīt\ *n* -s [NL *theodelitus,* perh. modif. of E *the alidade* — more at ALIDADE] **:** a surveyor's instrument for measuring horizontal and usu. also vertical angles that consists of a telescope mounted so as to swivel vertically in supports secured to a revolvable table carrying a vernier for reading horizontal angles and usu. includes also a graduated arc or circle for altitudes and a horizontal compass — compare TRANSIT 4 — **the·od·o·lit·ic** \=ˌ==ˈlid·ik\ *adj*

the·o·dore \ˈthēəˌdō(ə)r, -dȯ(ə)r\ *n* -s [by folk etymology fr. Sp *fiador*] **:** FIADOR

[1]**the·o·do·sian** \ˌthēəˈdōsh(ē)ən\ *adj, usu cap* **1** [*Theodosius* I †395 A.D. Roman emperor + E *-an,* adj. suffix] **:** of or relating to Theodosius the Great under whom the Roman state undertook to enforce Christianity and orthodoxy **2** [*Theodosius* II †450 A.D. Eastern Roman emperor + E *-an,* adj. suffix] **:** of or relating to Theodosius II or the Theodosian Code promulgated during his reign codifying imperial constitutions issued since the reign of Constantine I and including laws banning paganism and penalizing heresy

[2]**theodosian** \"\ *n* -s *usu cap* **1** [*Theodosius* †*ab* 538 A.D. patriarch of Alexandria + E *-an,* n. suffix] **:** a follower of Theodosius of Alexandria the leader of the Monophysites in the 6th century **2** [*Theodosius,* 16th cent. Russ. monk + E *-an,* n. suffix] **:** a follower of the Russian monk Theodosius

who preached in Lithuania in 1525 against idolatry and founded a sect practicing prayer for purification of articles acquired from unbelievers

the·o·do·tian \ˌthēə'dōshən\ *n* -s *usu cap* [*Theodotus fl* 190 A.D. Byzantine tanner and religious teacher who founded dynamic monarchianism + E *-ian*] **:** a follower of Theodotus of Constantinople

the·o·dy \'thēədē\ *n* -ES [modif. (influenced by *the-*) of It *teodia*, fr. *te-* the- (fr. LL *theo-*) + *-odia* (as in *melodia* melody, fr. LL) — more at MELODY] **:** a hymn praising God

the·o·gon·ic \ˌthēə'gänik\ *adj* **:** of or relating to theogony

the·og·o·nist \thē'ägənəst\ *n* -s **:** an authority on theogony

the·og·o·ny \-nē, -ni\ *n* -ES [Gk *theogonia*, fr. *the-* + *-gonia* (fr. the stem of *gignesthai* to be born + *-ia* -y) — more at KIN] **:** the generation or genealogy of the gods **:** a branch of theology or mythology that deals with the origin and descent of the deities

the·ol·a·try \thē'älə·trē\ *n* -ES [*the-* + *-latry*] **:** worship of a god

the·ol·o·gas·ter \thē'äləˌgastə(r), ˌ=ˌ==ˈ==\ *n* -s [NL, fr. L *theologus* theologue + *-aster*] **:** a shallow theologian; *esp* **:** one who pretends to possess great theological knowledge

the·ol·o·gate \thē'äləgət, -ləˌgāt\ *n* -s [*theologue* + *-ate*] **:** SEMINARY 2b(2)

the·ol·o·ger \thē'äləjə(r)\ *n* -s [*theology* + *-er*] **:** THEOLOGIAN

the·o·lo·gian \ˌthēə'lōjən *sometimes* -jēən\ *n* -s [MF *theologien*, fr. *theologie* theology (fr. LL *theologia*) + *-en* -an — more at THEOLOGY] **1 :** a specialist in theology **:** a professor of or writer on theology or divinity **2 :** a candidate for Roman Catholic priesthood engaged in his theological course of study

the·o·log·i·cal \ˌthēə'läjəkəl, -jēk-\ *also* **the·o·log·ic** \-jik, -jēk\ *adj* [*theological* fr. MF *theologique* or LL *theologicus* + E *-al; theologic* fr. MF *theologique*, fr. LL *theologicus*, fr. *theologia* + L *-icus* -ic] **1 :** of, relating to, or emphasizing theology ⟨~ principles⟩ ⟨~ systems⟩ ⟨a religious outlook more ~ than devotional⟩ **2 :** preparing for a religious vocation (as for the ministry, priesthood, or rabbinate or for religious education in church and school) ⟨~ students⟩ ⟨~ education⟩ ⟨a ~ school⟩

the·o·log·i·cal·ly \-jək(ə)lē, -jēk-, -li\ *adv* **1 :** in a theological manner ⟨dealt with the problem of evil ~ rather than philosophically⟩ **2 :** from the standpoint of theology **:** as regards theology ⟨examined the ministerial candidate and found him ~ sound⟩

theological virtue *n* **:** one of the three basic spiritual graces faith, hope, and charity often held in Christian ethics to be created by God in the redeemed man and to perfect the natural virtues by giving them harmony and fulfillment in the service of God — called also *supernatural virtue*

theologico- *comb form* [NL, fr. LL *theologicus*] **:** theological and ⟨*theologico*philosophical⟩ ⟨*theologico*political⟩

the·ol·o·gism \thē'äləˌjizəm\ *n* -s [fr. *theologize*, after such pairs as E *criticize: criticism*] **1 :** theological speculation **2 :** the act or process of subsuming other disciplines under theology **:** excessive extension of theological presuppositions or authority

the·ol·o·gist \-jəst\ *n* -s [NL *theologista*, fr. LL *theologia* theology + L *-ista* -ist] **:** THEOLOGIAN 1

the·ol·o·gize \-ləˌjīz\ *vb* -ED/-ING/-S [ML *theologizare*, fr. LL *theologia* + *-izare* -ize] *vi* **:** to theorize or speculate on theological subjects ⟨~ from a biblical basis⟩ ~ *vt* **:** to make theological **:** treat in a theological manner **:** give a religious character or theological significance to ⟨~ wit and good humor⟩ ⟨~ astrology⟩

the·o·lo·gou·me·non \ˌthēəlō'gümə,nän\ *or* **the·o·lo·gu·me·non** *n, pl* **theologume·na** *or* **theologume·na** \-mənə\ [NL, fr. Gk *theologoumenon*, neut. of *theologoumenos*, pres. passive part. of *theologein* to discourse on the gods, talk about God, fr. *theologos* theologue] **:** a theological statement or concept in the area of individual opinion rather than of authoritative doctrine

the·o·logue \'thēəˌlȯg *also* -läg\ *n* -s [L *theologus*, fr. Gk *theologos*, fr. *the-* + *-logos* (fr. *legein* to speak) — more at LEGEND] **1 :** THEOLOGIAN **2** *or* **the·o·log** \"\ **:** a student preparing for full-time work in religion **:** a theological student

the·ol·o·gy \thē'äləjē, -ji\ *n* -ES [ME *theologie*, fr. LL *theologia*, fr. L, study of the heathen gods, fr. Gk, fr. *the-* + *-logia* -logy] **1 :** rational interpretation of religious faith, practice, and experience: as **a :** the analysis, application, and presentation of the traditional doctrines of a religion or religious group — see APOLOGETICS, DOGMATIC THEOLOGY, NATURAL THEOLOGY, SYSTEMATIC THEOLOGY; compare PRACTICAL THEOLOGY **b :** the study of God and his relation to man and the world **:** a branch of systematic theology dealing with the arguments for the existence of God, the divine nature and attributes, and the doctrines of the Trinity, creation, and Providence — compare CHRISTOLOGY, ESCHATOLOGY, SOTERIOLOGY **c** (1) **:** the analytical and historical study of religious beliefs ⟨historical ~⟩ ⟨exegetical ~⟩ ⟨comparative ~⟩ — compare PATROLOGY, SYMBOLICS (2) **:** descriptive study of concepts relating to matters of ultimate concern ⟨a ~ of culture⟩ **d :** the interpretation of religious beliefs in relation to contemporary thought and life **e :** an inquiry that seeks an adequate interpretation of matters of ultimate concern **2 a :** a coherent body of theological doctrine **:** a theological theory or system ⟨a ~ of atonement⟩ ⟨the normative status of Thomist ~⟩; *specif* **:** the doctrine of God **b** (1) **:** a body of theological opinion distinguished by some characteristic emphasis, method, or association ⟨the ~ of the Word of God⟩ ⟨the ~ of paradox⟩ ⟨Calvinist ~⟩ (2) **:** the group of theologians sharing such a viewpoint ⟨the task of present-day liberal ~⟩ **c :** the sum of the beliefs held by an individual or group regarding matters of religious faith or of ultimate concern **:** the ideational element in religion ⟨the vagueness of the average man's ~⟩ **3 :** a course of Roman Catholic seminary study usu. requiring four years and including Scripture, church history, homiletics, canon law, and moral and dogmatic theology

the·om·a·chist \thē'äməkəst\ *n* -s [*theomachy* + *-ist*] **:** one who resists God or the gods or the divine will

the·om·a·chy \-kē\ *n* -ES [LL *theomachia*, fr. Gk, fr. *the-* + *-machia* -machy] **1** *obs* **:** opposition to God or the gods or the divine will **2 :** a battle or strife among the gods

the·o·man·cy \'thēəˌman(t)sē\ *n* -ES [*the-* + *-mancy*] **:** divination by the responses of oracles supposed to be divinely inspired

theo·mania \ˌthē(ˌ)ō+\ *n* [NL, fr. *the-* + *mania*] **:** religious madness in which the patient believes that he is the Deity or is inspired — **theo·maniac** \"+\ *n*

theo·monism \"+\ *n* [*the-* + *monism*] **:** metaphysical monism holding that one divine spirit governs the universe **:** theistic spiritualism

the·o·mor·phic \ˌthēə'mȯrfik\ *adj* [Gk *theomorphos* (fr. *the-* + *morphē* form) + E *-ic* — more at FORM] **:** having divine form **:** formed in the image of deity **:** endued with a divine aspect ⟨the Christian emphasis on the ~ conception of man rather than the anthropomorphic conception of God⟩

the·o·mor·phism \ˌthēə'mȯ(r)ˌfizəm\ *n* -s [*the-* + *-morphism*] **:** representation or conception of something or someone in the form of deity **:** the condition of being formed in the image of God

the·on·o·mous \thē'änəməs\ *adj* [*the-* + *-nomous* (as in *autonomous*)] **:** governed by God **:** subject to God's authority — compare AUTONOMOUS, HETERONOMOUS — **the·on·o·mous·ly** *adv*

the·on·o·my \-mē\ *n* -ES [G *theonomie*, fr. *theo-* the- + *-nomie* -nomy] **:** government by God **:** divine rule; *also* **:** the state of being subject to God's authority and rule ⟨are told . . . to return to Christianity, to ~ —R.K.Bultmann⟩

the·o·pan·tism \ˌthēə'panˌtizəm\ *n* -s [*the-* + Gk *pant-, pas* all, every + E *-ism* — more at PAN-] **:** the mystical doctrine that God is the sole reality — compare PANTHEISM

the·o·pas·chite \ˌthēə'paˌskīt\ *n* -s *usu cap* [ML *theopaschita*, fr. LGk *theopaschitēs*, fr. Gk *the-* + *paschein* to experience, suffer + *-itēs* -ite — more at PATHOS] **:** one holding that in Christ's passion God suffered; *specif* **:** an adherent of a sixth century sect of Monophysites — compare PATRIPASSIAN

theo·pathetic \ˌthē(ˌ)ō+\ *or* **the·o·path·ic** \ˌthēə'pathik\ *adj* [*the-* + *pathetic* or *-pathic*] **:** of or relating to theopathy; *esp* **:** of, relating to, or associated with intense absorption in religious devotion

the·op·a·thy \thē'äpəthē\ *n* -ES [*the-* + *-pathy*] **:** experience or capacity for experience of the divine illumination; *esp* **:** intense absorption in religious devotion

the·oph·a·gous \thē'äfəgəs\ *also* **the·o·phag·ic** \ˌthēə'fajik\ *adj* [*theophagous* fr. *the-* + *-phagous; theophagic* fr. *theophagy* + *-ic*] **:** of, relating to, or practicing theophagy

the·oph·a·gy \thē'äfəjē\ *n* -ES [*the-* + *-phagy*] **:** the sacramental eating of a god typically in the form of an animal, image, or other symbol as a part of a religious ritual and commonly for the purpose of communion with or the receiving of power from the god

the·o·phan·ic \ˌthēə'fanik\ *also* **the·oph·a·nous** \thē'äfənəs\ *adj* [*theophany* + *-ic* or *-ous*] **1 :** of, relating to, or characterized by theophany **2 :** that constitutes a theophany

¹the·oph·a·ny \thē'äfənē\ *n* -ES [ML *theophania*, fr. LGk *theophaneia*, fr. Gk *the-* + *-phaneia* (as in *epiphaneia* appearance, manifestation) — more at EPIPHANY] **1 :** a physical presentation or personal manifestation of a deity to an individual **:** a brief appearance of Deity ⟨the glorious ~ in which Jehovah will avenge himself of his adversaries —R.H.Pfeiffer⟩ **2 :** something manifesting or revealing deity ⟨in earlier Hebrew traditions angels had often been direct *theophanies* —George Santayana⟩ ⟨an enchanted world where every living thing was a ~ —Evelyn Underhill⟩

²theophany \"\ *n* -ES [LL *theophania*, fr. LGk, pl., fr. Gk, pagan festival at which statues of gods were shown, fr. *the-* + *-phania* (fr. the stem of *phainein* to show + *-ia*, neut. pl. of *-ios*, adj. suffix) — more at FANCY] *Eastern Church* **:** EPIPHANY

the·o·phil·an·throp·ic \ˌthēōˌfilən'thräpik\ *adj* [F *théophilanthropique*, fr. *théophilanthropie* + *-ique* -ic] **:** of or relating to theophilanthropism or the theophilanthropists

theo·phi·lan·thro·pism \ˌthēōfə'lan(t)thrəˌpizəm\ *n* [F *théophilanthropisme*, fr. *théophilanthropie* + *-isme* -ism] **:** the doctrines or tenets of the theophilanthropists

the·o·phi·lan·thro·pist \-pəst\ *n* [*theophilanthropy* + *-ist*] **:** a member of a deistic society established in Paris during the period of the Directory aiming to institute in place of Christianity, which had been officially abolished, a new religion affirming belief in the existence of God, in the immortality of the soul, and in virtue

the·o·phi·lan·thro·py \-pē\ *n* [F *théophilanthropie*, fr. *théo-* the- + *philanthropie* philanthropy, fr. LL *philanthropia*] **:** THEOPHILANTHROPISM

theo·phobia \ˌthē(ˌ)ō+\ *n* [NL, fr. *the-* + *phobia*] **1 :** dread of the wrath of God **2 :** a phobia of which God is the object

the·o·phor·ic \ˌthēə'fȯrik, -fär-\ *or* **the·oph·o·rous** \thē'äfərəs\ *adj* [*theophoric* fr. Gk *theophoros* theophoric (fr. *the-* + *-phoros* -phorous) + E *-ic; theophorous* fr. Gk *theophoros*] **:** derived from or bearing the name of a god

the·o·phras·ta·ce·ae \ˌthēəfra'stāsēˌē\ *n pl, cap* [NL, fr. *Theophrasta*, type genus (after *Theophrastus*, who wrote treatises on botany) + *-aceae*] **:** a family of mainly tropical trees and shrubs (order Primulales) distinguished from Myrsinaceae mainly by staminodia in the flowers — **the·o·phras·ta·ceous** \ˌ===stāshəs\ *adj*

the·o·phras·tian \ˌthēə'fras(h)chən\ *adj, usu cap* [*Theophrastus* †*ab* 287 B.C. Greek philosopher and scientist + E *-ian*] **1 :** of or relating to the philosopher Theophrastus or his writings on natural philosophy **2 :** treated in the manner of Theophrastus in his sketches of character types ⟨*Theophrastian* characters⟩

the·o·phyl·line \ˌthēə'fiˌlēn, -ilən\ *n* -s [ISV *theo-* (fr. NL *thea* tea) + *phyll-* + *-ine*] **:** a feebly basic bitter crystalline compound $C_7H_8N_4O_2$ that is extracted from tea leaves but is usu. made synthetically, that is isomeric with theobromine and closely related to caffeine, and that is used in medicine often in the form of derivatives or combinations with other drugs chiefly as a muscle relaxant in asthma, as a vasodilator, and as a diuretic; 1,3-dimethyl-xanthine

theophylline ethylenediamine *n* **:** AMINOPHYLLINE

the·op·neust \'thēäpˌn(y)üst\ *or* **the·op·neus·tic** \ˌ==ˈn(y)üstik\ *adj* [*theopneust* fr. Gk *theopneustos*, fr. *the-* + (assumed) *pneustos*, verbal of *pnein* to breathe; *theopneustic* fr. Gk *theopneustos* + E *-ic* — more at SNEEZE] **:** given by inspiration of the Spirit of God **:** divinely inspired

theor *abbr* theorem

the·or·bist \thē'ȯrbəst\ *n* -s **:** a player on a theorbo

the·or·bo \-r(ˌ)bō\ *n* -s [modif. of It *tiorba, teorba*, prob. fr. Venetian dial. *tiorba, tuorba* traveling bag, fr. Slovenian *torba*, fr. Turk, bag; fr. its having been carried by wandering mendicants] **:** an obsolete 17th century musical instrument like a large lute but having two necks with two sets of pegs, the upper carrying long bass strings used for open tones **:** ARCHLUTE

theorbo

the·o·rem \'thēərəm, 'thi(ə)r- *sometimes* 'thēr-\ *n* -s [LL *theorema*, fr. Gk *theōrēma* sight, spectacle, theory, theorem, fr. *theōrein* to look at, behold, contemplate, consider, fr. *theōros* spectator, fr. *thea* sight, view — more at THEATER] **1 a :** a statement in mathematics that has been proved or whose truth has been conjectured **b :** a rule or statement of relations (as the binomial theorem) expressed in a formula or by symbols **c :** a formula, proposition, or statement in logic deduced from a set of axioms **2 :** an idea accepted or proposed as a demonstrable truth and often forming part of a general theory **:** PROPOSITION, THEORY ⟨an arms policy based on the ~ that the best defense is offense⟩ **syn** see PRINCIPLE

the·o·re·mat·ic \ˌthēərə'madˌik\ *adj* [Gk *theōrēmatikos*, fr. *theōrēmat-, theōrēma* + *-ikos* -ic] **1 :** of, relating to, or comprised in a theorem **2 :** consisting of theorems — **the·o·re·mat·ical·ly** \-d·ək(ə)lē\ *adv*

theorem of py·thag·o·ras \-pə'thagərəs, -pī'-, -thaig-\ *usu cap P* [after *Pythagoras*, 6th cent. B.C. philosopher and mathematician] **:** PYTHAGOREAN THEOREM

the·o·re·tic \ˌthēə'red·ik\ *or* **the·o·ret·ics** \-ks\ *n, pl* **theoretics** [LL *theoretica*, fr. fem. of *theoreticus*] **:** the speculative part of an art or science **:** THEORY

the·o·ret·i·cal \ˌ==ˈred·əkəl, -etl, |ēk-\ *also* **the·o·ret·ic** \|ik, |ēk\ *adj* [LL *theoreticus*, fr. Gk *theōrētikos*, fr. *theōrētos* (verbal of *theōrein* to look at, behold, contemplate, consider) + *-ikos* -ic, -ical — more at THEOREM] **1 a :** of, relating to, or having the character of theory — compare APPLIED, PRACTICAL **b :** depending on or confined to theory **:** terminating in theory or speculation **:** SPECULATIVE ⟨~ learning⟩ ⟨~ mechanics⟩ — compare DESCRIPTIVE **2 :** addicted to speculative thought **:** given to theorizing; *also* **:** having the ability to theorize **3 :** of or relating to abstract knowledge as contrasted with practical knowledge (as moral intuitions or religious beliefs) **:** CONTEMPLATIVE, INTELLECTUAL — compare PRACTICAL REASON **4 :** existing only in theory **:** HYPOTHETICAL, FICTITIOUS

the·o·ret·i·cal·ly \|ək(ə)lē, |ēk-, -li\ *adv* **1 :** with reference to theory ⟨the most conservative ~ of the . . . British chemists —S.F.Mason⟩ **:** in a theoretical way ⟨it is quite possible to enjoy flowers . . . without knowing anything about plants ~ —John Dewey⟩ **2 :** according to an ideal or assumed set of facts or principles **:** in theory **:** HYPOTHETICALLY ⟨the absolute . . . vacuum ~ involves an area in which no atomic particles are present —T.A.Dickinson⟩ ⟨a task that would ~ take a man equipped with pencil and paper 800 years —Robert Bendiner⟩

theoretical reason *n* **:** reason leading to cognition **:** the capacity to grasp the universal in the particular — contrasted with *practical reason*

the·o·re·ti·cian \ˌthēərə'tishən\ *n* -s **1 :** THEORIST ⟨attracted foreign scientists, chiefly young ~*s* —F.D.Rasetti⟩ ⟨dismiss professors as eggheads and ivory-domed ~*s* —L.L.Snyder⟩ **2 :** one who bases practice on theory ⟨his emphasis upon the craft of composition places him among the ~*s* —Norman Demuth⟩

theoretico- *comb form* [*theoretical*] **:** theoretical and ⟨*theoretico*practical⟩

theoretic virtue *n, Aristotelianism* **:** one of the intellectual virtues of understanding, science, and wisdom

¹the·o·ric \'thēərik\ *or* **the·o·rique** \ˌthēə'rēk\ *n* -s [ME *theorique*, fr. MF, fr. LL *theorice*, fr. fem. of *theoricus*] **1** *archaic* **:** SPECULATION, THEORY — sometimes used in pl. **2 :** a device used in early modern astronomy for calculating positions of bodies

²the·or·ic \thē'ȯrik, -'ärik\ *or* **the·or·i·cal** \-rəkəl\ *adj* [MF *theorique*, fr. LL *theoricus*, fr. Gk *theōria* theory + L *-icus* -ic, -ical] **1** *obs* **:** THEORETICAL **2** [Gk *theōria* act of viewing + E *-ic*] **:** of or relating to an ancient Greek public spectacle — **the·or·i·cal·ly** \-rək(ə)lē\ *adv*

the·o·ri·cian \ˌthēə'rishən\ *n* -s [F *théoricien*, fr. *théorique*, after such pairs as F *mathématique* mathematic: *mathématicien* mathematician] **:** THEORIST

the·o·rist \'thēərəst, 'thi(ə)r- *sometimes* 'thēr-\ *n* -s [*theory* + *-ist*] **:** one who theorizes **:** a person given to speculative thought **:** one who formulates theories (as to account for perceived phenomena)

the·o·ri·za·tion \ˌthēərə'zāshən\ *n* -s **:** an act or product of theorizing **:** formation of a theory **:** SPECULATION

the·o·rize \'thēəˌrīz\ *vb* -ED/-ING/-S *see -ize in Explan Notes* [ML *theorizare*, fr. LL *theoria* + *-izare* -ize] *vi* **:** to form a theory or theories **:** form opinions solely by theory ~ *vt* **1 :** to formulate a theory about **2 :** to postulate (something stated) as a step in the formulation of a theory

the·o·riz·er \-zə(r)\ *n* -s **:** one that theorizes

the·o·ry \'thēərē, 'thi(ə)r-, -ri *sometimes* 'thēr-\ *n* -ES [LL *theoria*, fr. Gk *theōria* act of viewing, contemplation, consideration, theory, fr. *theōrein* to look at, behold, contemplate, consider + *-ia* -y — more at THEOREM] **1** *archaic* **:** imaginative contemplation of reality **:** direct intellectual apprehension **:** INSIGHT ⟨nor can I think I have the true ~ of death when I contemplate a skull —Sir Thomas Browne⟩ **2 a :** a belief, policy, or procedure proposed or followed as the basis of action **:** a principle or plan of action ⟨educational system, based on the ~ that men learn better from actual experience than from books —*Amer. Guide Series: Mich.*⟩ ⟨wanted to kill him, presumably on the ~ that dead men tell no tales —D.D.Martin⟩ ⟨the hedonistic ~ of ethics⟩ **b :** an ideal or hypothetical set of facts, principles, or circumstances ⟨the days when law and order was more of a ~ than a fact —Seth Agnew⟩ — often used in the phrase *in theory* ⟨the failure in practice of what looked so promising in ~⟩ **3 a** (1) **:** the body of generalizations and principles developed in association with practice in a field of activity (as medicine, music) and forming its content as an intellectual discipline **:** pure as distinguished from applied art or science ⟨spent two years . . . in the study of ~ and piano —W.T.Upton⟩ ⟨made a distinct contribution to museum ~ and practice —R.F.Bach⟩ (2) **:** the coherent set of hypothetical, conceptual, and pragmatic principles forming the general frame of reference for a field of inquiry (as for deducing principles, formulating hypotheses for testing, undertaking actions) ⟨the importance of ~ if research is to be significant and its findings are to be cumulative —Pendleton Herring⟩ ⟨anthropological ~⟩ ⟨contributions to the ~ of knowledge⟩ (3) **:** a body of mathematical theorems presenting a clear, rounded, and systematic view of a subject ⟨~ of equations⟩ ⟨~ of probability⟩ — see THEORY OF NUMBERS **b :** abstract knowledge ⟨necessary . . . in designing retaining walls to be guided by experience rather than by ~ —G.T.Snelling⟩ ⟨the period of transition from ~ to practice in the study of shorthand —J.R.Gregg⟩ **c** (1) **:** a field of intellectual inquiry ⟨literary critics badly need the sort of foundation that such . . . inquiries as ~ of signs and ~ of value could give them —P.B.Rice⟩ (2) **:** a systematic analysis, elucidation, or definition of a concept ⟨study the philosophers' conflicting *theories* of right⟩ — see COHERENCE THEORY **4 :** a judgment, conception, proposition, or formula (as relating to the nature, action, cause, or origin of a phenomenon or group of phenomena) formed by speculation or deduction or by abstraction and generalization from facts ⟨her ~ of the relationship of order to disorder in the language of poetry —Archibald MacLeish⟩ ⟨the wave ~ of light⟩ ⟨the ~ that the individual recapitulates the development of the race⟩ ⟨the gesture ~ of the origin of language⟩ ⟨the emotive ~ of value judgments⟩: as **a :** a hypothetical entity or structure explaining or relating an observed set of facts ⟨the Freudian ~ of the superego⟩ ⟨the Greek ~ of the atom⟩ **b :** a working hypothesis given probability by experimental evidence or by factual or conceptual analysis but not conclusively established or accepted as a law ⟨the ~ of relativity⟩ ⟨the ~ that compounds in dilute solutions obey the same laws that apply to gases⟩ ⟨the ~ of radioactive decay⟩ ⟨a ~ of exchange rates which is merely a special case of the general theory of exchange and markets —K.E.Boulding⟩ **5 :** something taken for granted esp. on trivial or inadequate grounds **:** CONJECTURE, SPECULATION, SUPPOSITION ⟨her ~ that the house was once occupied by spies⟩

theory of epigenesis : a theory in biology: development involves differentiation of an initially undifferentiated entity

theory of exchange : a theory in physics: when thermal radiation occurs from one body to another, it also takes place in the opposite direction, and therefore the question as to whether or not the temperature of either body will change depends upon whether the body gains more energy than it loses or loses more than it gains

theory of games : a method of applying mathematical logic to determine which of several available strategies is likely to maximize one's gain or to minimize one's loss in a game, a business situation, or a military problem in which one's opponent or opponents also can choose between several strategies — called also *game theory*

theory of internal relations : the doctrine that all relations are internal and every part of reality is intrinsically related to every other part

theory of numbers : a theory dealing with properties of integers

theory of signs : SEMIOTIC

theory of types : a rule in symbolic logic: the arguments for which a propositional function is significant are restricted to some one type

the·o·soph \'thēəˌsäf\ *n* -s [F *théosophe*, fr. ML *theosophus*] **:** THEOSOPHIST 1

the·os·o·pher \thē'äsəfə(r)\ *n* -s [ML *theosophus* (fr. LGk *theosophos*, fr. Gk *the-* + *sophos* clever, wise, skilled) + E *-er*] **:** THEOSOPHIST

the·o·soph·i·cal \ˌthēə'säfəkəl, -fēk-\ *also* **the·o·soph·ic** \-fik, -fēk\ *adj* **:** of or relating to theosophy — **the·o·soph·i·cal·ly** \-fək(ə)lē, -fēk-, -li\ *adv*

the·os·o·phism \thē'äsəˌfizəm\ *n* -s [*theosophy* + *-ism*] **:** belief in theosophy

the·os·o·phist \-ˌfəst\ *n* -s [*theosophy* + *-ist*] **1 :** an adherent of theosophy **2** *usu cap* **:** a member of a theosophical society

the·os·o·phis·tic \thēˌäsə'fistik\ *also* **the·os·o·phis·ti·cal** \-təkəl\ *adj* **:** THEOSOPHICAL

the·os·o·phize \thē'äsəˌfīz\ *vi* -ED/-ING/-S [*theosophy* + *-ize*] **:** to speculate theosophically

the·os·o·phy \-əfē, -fi\ *n* -ES [ML *theosophia*, fr. LGk, fr. Gk *the-* + *sophia* wisdom — more at -SOPHY] **1 :** a body of doctrine relating to deity, cosmos, and self and held to rest on direct intuitions of supersensible reality by preternaturally perceptive individuals and to give a wisdom superior to that of historical religion or empirical philosophy or science by which the initiate can master nature and guide his destiny **:** a system of often occult and esoteric thought presented as a means of individual salvation and sometimes associated with mysticism, pantheism, or magic — compare BOEHMENISM, GNOSTICISM, NEOPLATONISM, SWEDENBORGIANISM **2** *usu cap* **:** a syncretistic system of theosophy following chiefly Hindu philosophies and associated with a movement originating in the U.S. in 1875, aiming to serve through its societies as the nucleus of a universal brotherhood of man and to guide the individual toward perfect wisdom through the study of world literature on the laws of the universe and through the development under the esoteric teachings of mahatmas of his latent inner senses responsive to the invisible cosmos, and teaching physical and spiritual evolution (as of the soul through reincarnations); *also* **:** the modern movement promulgating this theosophy

theo·to·kion \ˌthēō'tōˌkyȯn, -ˌtō'kēˌȯn\ *n, pl* **theoto·kia** \-(ˌ)kyä, -'kē(ˌ)ä\ [MGk, fr. LGk *theotokos* bearer of God (epithet of the Virgin Mary), fr. Gk *the-* + *-tokos* (fr. *tiktein* to bear, beget) — more at THANE] **:** a hymn of the Eastern Church ascribing praise to the Virgin Mary as the Mother of God and forming the final troparion of a canonical ode

the·ow \ˈthā(ˌ)ō\ *n* -s [OE *thēow;* akin to OHG *thiomuoti* servant's disposition, humility, *thionōn* to serve, ON *thjōna* to serve, Goth *thius* servant, and perh. to OIr *techid* he flees, Skt *takti* he hurries; basic meaning: to run] **:** a British slave of Anglo-Saxon times

ther- *or* **thero-** *comb form* [Gk *thēr-, thēro-,* fr. *thēr* — more at FIERCE] **:** wild beast ⟨*Thero*morpha⟩ ⟨*ther*odont⟩

ther·a·peu·sis \ˌtherəˈpyüsəs\ *n, pl* **therapeu·ses** \-üˌsēz\ [NL, fr. Gk, treatment, fr. *therapeuein* to attend, treat] **:** therapeutic treatment **:** THERAPEUTICS ⟨high pressure oxygen as a means of ~ in CO poisoning —*Science*⟩ ⟨isolation of vitamin K . . . an important advance in ~ —*Surgery, Gynecology & Obstetrics*⟩

ther·a·peu·tae \ˌtherəˈpyü(ˌ)tē\ *n pl, cap* [NL, fr. Gk *therapeutai,* pl. of *therapeutēs* attendant, worshiper, medical attendant, fr. *therapeuein* to attend] **:** ascetics of both sexes held to have dwelt anciently near Alexandria and described by Philo as devoted to contemplation and meditation

ther·a·peu·tant \-ütᵊnt\ *n* -s [¹*therapeutic* + *-ant*] **:** a healing or curative agent or medicine ⟨plant ~*s*⟩ ⟨spraying ~*s* on elms is much easier and cheaper —*Agric. Chemicals*⟩

¹**ther·a·peu·tic** \ˌ;therəˈpyüd·ik, -üt|, |ēk\ *also* **ther·a·peu·ti·cal** \|ōkəl, |ēk-\ *adj* [*therapeutic* fr. Gk *therapeutikos,* fr. *therapeutos* (verbal of *therapeuein* to attend, worship, treat medically, fr. *theraps* attendant) + *-ikos* -ic; *therapeutical* fr. Gk *therapeutikos* + E *-al*] **:** of or relating to the treatment of disease or disorders by remedial agents or methods **:** CURATIVE, MEDICINAL ⟨~ diet⟩ ⟨~ dose⟩ ⟨~ approach to criminality⟩ — **ther·a·peu·ti·cal·ly** \|ōk(ə)lē, |ēk-, -li\ *adv*

²**therapeutic** \"\ *n* -s *usu cap* [NL *therapeut*ae + E *-ic*] **:** one of the Therapeutae

therapeutic abortion *n* **:** abortion induced when pregnancy constitutes a threat to the mother's life

therapeutic nihilism *n* **:** skepticism regarding the worth of therapeutic agents esp. in a particular disease

therapeutic positivism *n* **:** positivism that undertakes to remedy the ambiguities, paradoxes, and perplexities of traditional philosophical and esp. metaphysical problems by employing logical analysis to disclose the linguistic confusions that give rise to them

ther·a·peu·tics \ˌtherəˈpyüd·iks, -üt|, |ēks\ *n pl but sing or pl in constr* [trans. of LL *therapeutica,* fr. Gk *therapeutika,* fr. neut. pl. of *therapeutikos* therapeutic] **:** a branch of medical science that treats of the application of remedies for diseases **:** THERAPY — often used in combination ⟨electro*therapeutics*⟩ ⟨chemo*therapeutics*⟩

therapeutic shock *n* **:** SHOCK THERAPY

therapeutic test *n* **:** a test to aid in diagnosis of an undiagnosed disease by giving the specific remedy for the disease suspected ⟨use of liver extract as a *therapeutic test* for suspected pernicious anemia⟩

ther·a·peu·tist \ˌtherə|pyüd·əst, -ütə-\ *n* -s [*therapeutic* + *-ist*] **:** THERAPIST

ther·a·pho·sa \ˌtherəˈfōsə, -ōzə\ *n, cap* [NL, fr. Gk *theraphion,* dim. of *thēr, thērion* wild beast, animal, monster — more at FIERCE] **:** the type genus of the family Theraphosidae including a rare African spider (*T. blondi*) that is the largest of spiders with a body length of over three inches and a leg span of nearly 10 inches

ther·a·phose \ˈtherəˌfōs, -ōz\ *n* -s [NL *Theraphosa*] **:** a spider of the genus *Theraphosa*

¹**ther·a·pho·sid** \ˌ;therə|fōsəd, -ōzəd\ *adj* [NL *Theraphosidae*] **:** of or relating to the Theraphosidae

²**theraphosid** \"\ *n* -s **:** a spider of the family Theraphosidae **:** BIRD SPIDER

ther·a·pho·si·dae \ˌtherəˈfōsəˌdē, -ōzə-\ *n pl, cap* [NL, fr. *Theraphosa,* type genus + *-idae*] **:** a family of very large chiefly tropical spiders with four spinnerets and the eight eyes in a compact group — see BIRD SPIDER, EURYPELMA, TARANTULA, THERAPHOSA

ther·a·pist \ˈtherəpəst\ *n* -s [*therapy* + *-ist*] **1 :** a physician concerned with treatment of disease **2 :** one trained in applying occupational or physical measures in the treatment or rehabilitation of patients ⟨occupational ~⟩

ther·a·pon \ˈtherəˌpän\ *n* [NL, fr. Gk *therapont-, therapōn* attendant; akin to Gk *theraps* attendant] **1** *cap* **:** a genus of small silvery Indo-Pacific percoid fishes — see SILVER PERCH **2** -s **:** any fish of the genus *Therapon*

¹**the·rap·sid** \thəˈrapsəd\ *adj* [NL *Therapsida*] **:** of or relating to the Therapsida

²**therapsid** \"\ *n* -s **:** a reptile of the order Therapsida

the·rap·si·da \-sədə\ *n pl, cap* [NL, fr. Gk *theraps* attendant + NL *-ida*] **:** an order of Reptilia comprising Permian and Triassic reptiles (subclass Synapsida) that are held to be the ancestors of the mammals

ther·a·py \ˈtherəpē, -pi\ *n* -ES [NL *therapia,* fr. Gk *therapeia* attendance, medical treatment, fr. *therapeuein* to attend, treat + *-ia* -y — more at THERAPEUTIC] **1 :** treatment of disease in animals or plants by therapeutic means ⟨specific ~⟩ ⟨surgical ~⟩ ⟨dance ~⟩ — often used in combination ⟨chemo*therapy*⟩ ⟨syphilo*therapy*⟩ ⟨hydro*therapy*⟩ **2 :** PSYCHOTHERAPY **3 a :** treatment of the maladjusted (as prisoners, social agency clients) through a program of clinical, custodial, or casework services in order to further their restoration to society **b :** a force working to relieve a social tension ⟨recreation activities provide a form of community ~⟩ ⟨a human relations program as ~ for workers⟩

ther·a·va·da \ˌtherəˈvädə\ *n* -s *usu cap* [Pali *theravāda,* lit., doctrine of the elders, fr. *thera* elder (fr. *thera* old, venerable, fr. Skt *sthavira* stout, old, venerable) + *vāda* speech, doctrine, fr. Skt, fr. *vadati* he speaks — more at STEER] **:** HINAYANA

ther·a·va·din \-dᵊn\ *n* -s *usu cap* [Pali *theravādin,* fr. *theravāda* Hinayana] **:** an adherent of Hinayana

ther·blig \ˈthər(ˌ)blig\ *n* -s [anagram, after Frank B. *Gilbreth* †1924 Am. engineer] **1 :** one of the manual, visual, or mental elements into which an industrial manual operation may be analyzed in time and motion study **2 :** a symbol devised for representing a therblig in writing or notation

¹**there** \(ˈ)tha(ə)|(ə)r, (ˈ)the|, |ə, *adv* [ME *ther, there, thar, thare,* fr. OE *thǣr, thēr, thār;* akin to OHG *dār* there, ON & Goth *thar,* Skt *tarhi* then, OE *thæt* that — more at THAT] **1 a :** in or at that place **:** in or at a place other than that of the speaker — opposed to *here* ⟨stand over ~ until I call you⟩ ⟨put it ~ on that table⟩ ⟨please go home and stay ~⟩ **b :** in or at a place indicated, referred or pointed to, described, or qualified ⟨~, where the roads meet⟩ ⟨for where your treasure is, ~ will your heart be also —Mt 6:21 (AV)⟩ — used to call attention to something ⟨~ goes the dinner bell⟩ ⟨~ he comes now⟩ or point to with approval ⟨~'s glory for you⟩; often used interjectionally ⟨~, look at that⟩ ⟨~, that must be his car now stopping outside⟩ **2 :** to or into that place **:** THITHER — used after verbs of motion or direction ⟨time to go ~ and back⟩ ⟨seldom go ~ any more⟩ ⟨when she got ~ the cupboard was bare —*Mother Goose*⟩ **3 :** at that point of time in a continuing action or progress ⟨stop right ~ before you say any more⟩ **4 :** in that matter **:** in that respect **:** in relation to that ⟨to sleep, perchance to dream: aye, ~'s the rub —Shak.⟩ ⟨just ~ is where I disagree with you⟩ **5** — used interjectionally to express satisfaction ⟨~, that's finished at last⟩ ⟨~, I told you so⟩ or approval ⟨~, that should be enough scrubbing⟩ or encouragement or sympathy ⟨~ now, it's not really that bad, is it⟩ or spitefulness or defiance ⟨I'm not sorry I said it, so ~⟩ — **get there :** to achieve one's object **:** SUCCEED — **have been there :** to know at first hand ⟨her hold on actuality is everywhere firm. She *has been there* — she knows —L.O.Coxe⟩ — **in there :** continuing the fight or the struggle **:** not quitting or flagging in effort ⟨plain people . . . will be *in there* fighting for peace and freedom —G.P.Musselman⟩ ⟨a revue that . . . involved the services of a bunch of people who were always *in there* trying —Wolcott Gibbs⟩

²**there** \(ˌ)tha(ə)|r, (ˌ)the|, |ə, *in sense 1 often* thə(r)\ *pron* [ME *ther, thar,* fr. OE *thǣr,* fr. *thǣr,* adv.] **1** — used as a function word to introduce a sentence or clause in which the subject follows the verb ⟨~ shall come a time⟩ ⟨~ shall be weeping and gnashing of teeth —Lk 13:28 (AV)⟩ ⟨~ are many things to be considered⟩ ⟨~ is no telling when he'll be home⟩ **2** — used as an indefinite substitute for a name ⟨hi ~⟩ ⟨well, hello ~⟩ ⟨say ~, do you have the time⟩

³**there** *like* ¹THERE\ *n* -s [¹*there*] **1 :** that place or position — opposed to *here* ⟨there is no here and no ~ . . . in pure space —James Ward⟩ **2 :** that point ⟨I'll get everything ready and you take it from ~⟩

⁴**there** \"\ *adj* [¹*there*] **1 a** — used for emphasis esp. after a demonstrative pronoun ⟨I'd rather take those ~⟩ or after a noun modified by a demonstrative adjective ⟨those men ~ can tell you⟩ **b** *substand* — used for emphasis after a demonstrative adjective but before the noun modified ⟨I wouldn't vote for that ~ fellow for anything⟩ **2 :** EXISTENT, PRESENT ⟨nothing is more imperiously ~ for observation and study than the tactics —K.D.Burke⟩ ⟨prosperity was ~ and almost every civilian shared in it —*Time*⟩ ⟨the pain was still ~ when he woke up⟩ **3 a :** DEPENDABLE, RELIABLE ⟨he's always right ~ when you need him⟩ **b :** fully conscious **:** fully aware ⟨an hour that I lay there . . . I was ~ in the head by that time —J.M. Cain⟩

there·abouts \ˈ==ˌbau̇ts, ˌ==ˈ=\ *or* **there·about** \-t\ *adv* [*thereabout* fr. ME *ther aboute,* fr. OE *thǣr abūtan,* fr. *thǣr* there + *abūtan* about; *thereabouts* fr. ME *ther aboutes,* fr. *ther aboute* + *-s* (as in *dayes* days)] **1 :** near that place **:** in the neighborhood ⟨film set in the Mojave desert and the mountains *thereabout* —*Sydney (Australia) Bull.*⟩ ⟨stayed there or ~ for several days⟩ **2 a :** near that time or date ⟨got home at six o'clock or ~⟩ ⟨vignettes seen through the French illustrations of the 1850's or ~ —Irving Kolodin⟩ **b :** near that number **:** near that degree **:** near that quantity ⟨living in Wessex, off and on, for thirty years or *thereabout* —H.M.Tomlinson⟩ **3** *usu thereabout, archaic* **:** about that **:** in connection with that ⟨they were much perplexed *thereabout* —Lk 24:4 (AV)⟩

thereafter \(ˈ)=ˈ==\ *adv* [ME *therafter,* fr. OE *thǣr æfter,* fr. *thǣr* there + *æfter* after] **1 :** after that ⟨died that year, and his wife died soon ~⟩ **:** from then on **:** THENCEFORTH ⟨~ he wrote only occasionally⟩ **2** *archaic* **:** according to that **:** ACCORDINGLY

thereagainst \ˌ==ˈ=\ *adv* [ME *there agenst,* fr. ¹*there* + *agenst* against] **:** against that **:** against it **:** on the contrary

thereamong \ˌ==ˈ=\ *adv* [ME, fr. ¹*there* + *among*] **:** among them **:** among that

thereanent \ˌ==ˈ=\ *adv* [¹*there* + *anent*] **:** with reference to that matter, subject, or affair

thereat \(ˈ)=ˈ=\ *adv* [ME, fr. OE *thǣr æt,* fr. *thǣr* there + *æt* at] **1 :** at that place or point ⟨wide is the gate, and many there be which go in ~ —Mt 7:13 (AV)⟩ **2 :** at that occurrence or event **:** upon that **:** on that account ⟨ridiculously soon at his ease, and much astonished ~ —Donn Byrne⟩

thereaway \ˈ==ˌ=\ *adv* [ME *there away,* fr. ¹*there* + *away*] *chiefly dial* **:** APPROXIMATELY, THEREABOUTS ⟨Oriental matters which were landed . . . from China and ~ —C.F.Saunders⟩

therebeside \ˌ==ˈ=\ *adv* [ME *there beside,* fr. ¹*there* + *beside*] *archaic* **:** by the side of that

therebetween \ˌ==ˈ=\ *adv* [¹*there* + *between*] **:** in the space between

thereby \(ˈ)=ˈ=\ *adv* [ME *therby,* fr. OE *thǣrbī,* fr. *thǣr* there + *bi* by] **1 :** by that ⟨judges in every state shall be bound ~ —*U.S.Constitution*⟩ **:** by that means **:** in consequence of that ⟨paid cash, ~ avoiding interest charges⟩ **2 :** connected with that **:** with reference to that ⟨~ hangs a tale —Shak.⟩ **3** *chiefly Scot* **:** beside that **:** near by **:** about that **:** BESIDE, THEREABOUTS

therefor \(ˈ)=ˈ=\ *adv* [ME *therfor, therfore, therefor, therefore* for that, for that reason, fr. *ther, there* there + *for, fore* for] **1 :** for that **:** in return for that ⟨reasons ~⟩ ⟨issued bonds ~⟩ ⟨when the need ~ no longer exists⟩ ⟨substituting ~ a more general term⟩ **2 :** THEREFORE

¹**there·fore** *R* ˈtha(ə)rˌfō(ə)r, ˈther,f-, -fó(ə)r; *–R* ˈtha(ə)əˌfōə, ˈtheə,f-, ˈtha(ə),f-, -fó(ə), + V" *or* -fō(ə)r *or* -fó(ə)r; *sometimes* -ˌfə(r)\ *adv* [ME *therfor, therfore, therefor, therefore* for that, for that reason] **1** *obs* **:** THEREFOR **2** *archaic* **:** THEN, ACCORDINGLY ⟨hear ye ~ the parable of the sower —Mt 13:18 (AV)⟩ **3 :** for that reason **:** because of that **:** on that ground **:** to that end **:** CONSEQUENTLY, HENCE ⟨lost the wager; ~ they must pay⟩ ⟨A is greater than B, and B is greater than C, ~ A is greater than C⟩

²**therefore** \"\ *n* -s **:** a proved proposition **:** an argumentative conclusion **:** a logical implication

therefrom \(ˈ)=ˈ=\ *adv* [ME *therfrom,* fr. *ther* there + *from*] **:** from that **:** from it ⟨public opinion and a policy . . . deriving ~ —Frank Gorrell⟩ ⟨had a pretty good script going for him — but what a movie he has made ~ —Judith Crist⟩

therein \(ˈ)=ˈ=\ *adv* [ME *therin,* fr. OE *thǣrin,* fr. *thǣr* there + *in*] **1 :** in or into that place **:** in or into that thing ⟨the box and the jewels found ~⟩ **2 :** in that particular **:** in that respect **:** in such matter ⟨~ our letters do not well agree —Shak.⟩

thereinafter \ˌ==ˈ==\ *adv* [*therein* + *after*] **:** in the following part of that matter (as writing, document, or speech)

thereinbefore \ˌ=(ˌ)==ˈ=\ *adv* [*therein* + *before*] **:** in the preceding part of that matter (as writing, document, or book)

thereinto \(ˌ)=+\ *adv* [¹*there* + *into*] *archaic* **:** into that or into it ⟨let them not enter ~ —Lk 21:21 (AV)⟩

ther·e·min \ˈtherəmən *sometimes* ˈter-\ *n* -s [after Leo *Theremin b*1896 Russ. engineer & inventor] **:** a purely melodic instrument of the electronic family typically played by moving the right hand between two projecting electrodes with the left hand controlling dynamics and articulation — **ther·e·min·ist** \-mənəst, -ˌmin-\ *n* -s

there·ness \ˈtha(ə)|(ə)rnəs, ˈthe|, |ən-\ *n* -ES [¹*there* + *-ness*] **:** the condition of being there in position **:** presence in a place distinguishably there not here; *also* **:** real existence ⟨things are really there . . . capture the ~ of them —Charles Hopkinson⟩

thereof \(ˈ)=ˈ= *sometimes* -ˈäf\ *adv* [ME *therof,* fr. OE *thǣrof,* fr. *thǣr* there + *of*] **1 :** of that or of it ⟨in the day that thou eatest ~, thou shalt . . . die —Gen 2:17 (AV)⟩ ⟨problem and the solution ~⟩ **2 :** from that cause **:** from that particular **:** THEREFROM ⟨more good ~ shall spring —John Milton⟩

thereon \(ˈ)=ˈ=\ *adv* [ME *theron,* fr. OE *thǣron,* fr. *thǣr* there + *on*] **1 :** on that **:** on it ⟨text and commentary ~⟩ **2** *archaic* **:** after or as a result of some specified thing **:** THEREUPON

thereout \(ˈ)=ˈ=\ *adv* [ME *theroute,* fr. OE *thǣrūt,* fr. *thǣr* there + *ūt* out] *archaic* **:** out of that **:** THEREFROM

thereover \ˌ==ˈ==\ *adv* [ME *ther over,* fr. OE *thǣrofer,* fr. *thǣr* there + *ofer* over] **:** over that **:** ABOVE **:** in a superior position

there·right \(ˈ)=ˈrīt\ *adv* [ME *ther riht,* fr. OE *thǣr rihte,* fr. *thǣr* there + *rihte* right] *dial Eng* **:** FORTHWITH, STRAIGHTWAY

theres *pl of* THERE

therethrough \(ˈ)=ˈ=\ *adv* [ME *ther thurh,* fr. *ther* there + *thurh* through] **1 :** through that **:** in or through a specified opening **2 :** in consequence **:** because of that **:** THEREBY

thereto \(ˈ)=ˈ=\ *adv* [ME *therto,* fr. OE *thǣrtō,* fr. *thǣr* there + *tō* to] **1 :** to that ⟨with all the appurtenances fitting ~⟩ **2** *archaic* **:** BESIDES, MOREOVER, ALSO

there·to·fore \ˈtha(ə)r|d·əˌfō(ə)r, ˈthe|, |ə|, |tə, -fó(ə)r, -fōə, -fó(ə), ˌ==ˈ=\ *adv* [ME *ther tofore,* fr. *ther* there + *tofore* before — more at HERETOFORE] **:** up to that time **:** until then **:** before then ⟨~ obscure community —Robert Rice⟩ ⟨new knowledge produced powerful techniques for smashing the ~ indestructible atom —Barry Commoner⟩

there·toward \(ˈ)=+\ *adv* [ME *thertoward,* fr. *ther* there + *toward*] **:** toward it

thereunder \(ˈ)=ˈ==\ *adv* [ME *therunder,* fr. OE *thǣrunder,* fr. *thǣr* there + *under*] **:** under that ⟨heading and the items listed ~⟩ ⟨acreage with . . . mineral wealth lying ~ —*U.S.Code*⟩

there·until \(ˌ)=+\ *adv* [¹*there* + *until*] **:** up to that time **:** THERETOFORE

there·unto \"+\ *adv* [ME *therunto,* fr. *ther* + *unto*] **1** *archaic* **:** unto that **:** THERETO, BESIDES **2** *obs* **:** in addition to that **:** BESIDES

thereupon \ˈ==ˌ=, ˌ==ˈ=\ *adv* [ME *ther upon,* fr. *ther* there + *upon*] **1 :** upon that **:** on that matter **:** THEREON **2 :** on account of or in consequence of that **:** THEREFORE **3 :** immediately after that **:** at once **:** without delay

¹**the·rev·id** \thəˈrevəd, ˈtherəv-\ *adj* [NL *Therevidae*] **:** of or relating to the Therevidae

²**therevid** \"\ *n* -s **:** a two-winged fly of the family Therevidae **:** STILETTO FLY

the·rev·i·dae \thəˈrevəˌdē\ *n pl, cap* [NL, fr. *Thereva,* type genus (fr. Gk *thēreuein* to hunt, fr. *thēr* wild animal) + *-idae* — more at FIERCE] **:** a family of chiefly holarctic brachycerous two-winged flies constituted by the stiletto flies

therewhile *also* **therewhilst** \(ˈ)=ˈ=\ *adv* [*therewhile* fr. ME *ther whyle,* prob. fr. OE *thǣre hwīle* in that time, fr. *thǣre* (dat. sing. fem. of *sē, sēo, thæt* that) + *hwīle,* dat. sing. of *hwīl* while, time; *therewhilst* alter. (influenced by *whilst*) of *therewhile* — more at THAT] *obs* **:** in the meantime **:** WHILST

therewith \(ˈ)=ˈ=\ *adv* [ME *therwith,* fr. OE *thǣrwith,* fr. *thǣr* there + *with*] **1 :** with that ⟨I have learned in whatsoever state I am, ~ to be content —Phil 4:11(AV)⟩ **2** *archaic* **:** THEREUPON, FORTHWITH

there·with·al \ˈ=wəˌthȯl, -ˌthȯl, ˌ==ˈ=\ *adv* [ME *ther withal,* fr. *ther* there + *withal*] **1** *archaic* **:** BESIDES, MOREOVER **2 :** with that **:** at the same time **:** THEREWITH ⟨thy slanders I forgive; and ~ remit thy other forfeits —Shak.⟩ **3 :** at the same time **:** THEREUPON

therewithin \ˌ==ˈ=\ *adv* [ME *ther within,* fr. *ther* there + *within*] *archaic* **:** within that

the·ria \ˈthirēə, ˈthēr-\ *n pl, cap* [NL, fr. Gk *thēria,* pl. of *thērion* wild animal — more at TREACLE] *in some classifications* **:** a subclass of Mammalia comprising the higher mammals and including the Pantotheria, Metatheria, and Eutheria and excluding the Prototheria and Allotheria — **the·ri·an** \-ən\ *n or adj*

-theria \"\ *n comb form* [NL, fr. Gk *thēria,* pl. of *thērion*] **:** beasts **:** animals — in names of higher taxa of mammalian forms ⟨Proto*theria*⟩

¹**the·ri·ac** \ˈthirēˌak\ *n* -s [NL *theriaca*] **1 :** THERIACA **2 :** CURE-ALL

²**theriac** \"\ *also* **the·ri·a·cal** \thəˈrīəkəl\ *adj* **:** ANTIDOTAL, MEDICINAL

the·ri·a·ca \thəˈrīəkə\ *n* -s [NL, fr. L, antidote against poison — more at TREACLE] **1** *or* **theriaca an·drom·a·chi** \-anˈdräməˌ(ˌ)kē\ *usu cap A* [*theriaca Andromachi* fr. NL, lit., antidote of Andromachus (Greek physician of the emperor Nero)] **:** an antidote to poison consisting typically of about 70 drugs pulverized and reduced with honey to an electuary — called also *Venice treacle* **2** *Brit* **:** TREACLE, MOLASSES

the·ri·an·throp·ic \ˌ;thirē;an;thräpik\ *adj* [Gk *thērianthrōpos* beast-man (fr. *thēri-* therio- + *anthrōpos* man, human being) + E *-ic* — more at ANTHROP-] **1 :** combining human and animal form ⟨~ deity⟩ **2 :** relating to religions in which the deities worshiped are partly human and partly animal in form

the·ri·an·thro·pism \ˌ==ˈan(t)thrəˌpizəm\ *n* -s [*therianthropic* + *-ism*] **:** the conception of or belief in therianthropic deities

the·ri·at·rics \ˌthirēˈa·triks\ *n pl but sing or pl in constr* [*ther-* + *-iatrics*] **:** the science of veterinary medicine

¹**the·rid·i·id** \thəˈridēəd, ¦therəˈdīəd\ *adj* [NL *Theridiidae*] **:** of or relating to the Theridiidae

²**theridiid** \"\ *n* -s **:** a spider of the family Theridiidae

ther·i·di·idae \ˌtherəˈdīəˌdē\ *n pl, cap* [NL, fr. *Theridion,* type genus (fr. Gk *thēridion,* dim. of *thēr* wild beast) + *-idae* — more at FIERCE] **:** a family of spiders that spin netlike webs and have usu. a small globose body and slender legs

therio- *comb form* [Gk *thērio-, thēri-,* fr. *thērion* — more at TREACLE] **:** wild animal **:** beast ⟨*therio*latry⟩ ⟨*therio*mimicry⟩

the·ri·odont \ˈthirēəˌdänt\ *n* -s [NL *Theriodontia*] **:** a reptile of the suborder Theriodontia

¹**the·ri·odon·tia** \ˌthirēəˈdänch(ē)ə\ *n pl, cap* [NL, fr. Gk *thēri-* therio- + NL *-odontia*] **:** a group of extinct reptiles usu. considered a suborder of Therapsida but sometimes classified as a separate order that are characterized by teeth which are differentiated into incisors, prominent canines, and molars with numerous cusps and that are known mostly from skulls found in the Permian and Triassic formations of southern Africa

²**theriodontia** \"\ *or* **the·ri·odon·ta** \ˌthirēəˈdäntə\ [NL, fr. Gk *thēri-* therio- + NL *-odontia* or *-odonta*] *syn of* PELYCOSAURIA

the·ri·ol·a·try \ˌthirēˈäləˌtrē\ *n* -ES [*therio-* + *-latry*] **:** worship of animals or theriomorphic divinities

the·rio·morph \ˈthirēəˌmȯrf\ *n* [Gk *thēriomorphos* shaped like an animal, fr. *thērio-* therio- + *morphē* shape, form — more at FORM] **:** an artifact (as a vase) shaped in animal form

the·rio·mor·phic \ˌ;===ˈmȯrfik\ *adj* [Gk *thēriomorphos* + E *-ic*] **:** having an animal form ⟨~ gods⟩ ⟨~ stage in the development of the divinity —*Modern Language Rev.*⟩

the·rio·mor·phism \ˌ===ˈmȯrˌfizəm\ *n* -s [Gk *thēriomorphos* + E *-ism*] **1 :** the conception or representation of deity in animal form **2 :** ascription of animal characteristics to man — compare ANTHROPOMORPHISM

the·rio·mor·phize \ˌ===ˌfīz\ *vt* -ED/-ING/-S [Gk *thēriomorphos* + E *-ize*] **:** to represent or conceptualize (something) in animal form ⟨in Assyrian history the forces of nature were *theriomorphized* —*Times Lit. Supp.*⟩

-the·ri·um \ˈthirēəm, ˈthēr-\ *n comb form* [NL, fr. Gk *thērion* — more at TREACLE] **:** beast **:** animal — in generic names of extinct mammalian forms ⟨Mega*therium*⟩ ⟨Titano*therium*⟩

therm \ˈthərm, ˈthōm, ˈthəim\ *n* -s **1** [MF *thermes* (pl.), fr. L *thermae* hot springs, public baths, fr. Gk *thermai,* fr. pl. of *thermē* heat, fr. *thermos* hot — more at WARM] *archaic* **:** a public bathing establishment **2** [Gk *thermos* hot, or *thermē* heat] **:** any of several units of quantity of heat: as **a :** CALORIE b(1) **b :** CALORIE a **c :** 1000 kilogram calories **d :** 100,000 British thermal units

therm- *or* **thermo-** *comb form* [Gk, fr. *thermē* heat] **1 :** heat ⟨*thermo*acoustic⟩ ⟨*thermo*chemistry⟩ **2 :** thermoelectric ⟨*thermo*pile⟩

-therm \ˌ=ˈ=\ *n comb form* -s [Gk *thermē* heat, fr. *thermos* hot] **1** [prob. fr. F *-therme,* fr. Gk *thermē* heat] **a :** plant accustomed to a (specified) type of heat ⟨mega*therm*⟩ ⟨micro*therm*⟩ ⟨xero*therm*⟩ **b :** animal having a (specified) body temperature ⟨ecto*therm*⟩ ⟨endo*therm*⟩ **2 :** thermic line ⟨isobathy*therm*⟩

therm *abbr* thermometer

ther·mae \ˈthərˌmē\ *n pl* [L — more at THERM] **:** a public bathing establishment esp. in ancient Greece or Rome

¹**ther·mal** \ˈthərməl, ˈthōm-, ˈthəim-\ *adj* [Gk *thermē* heat + E *-al*] **1** [L *therm*ae hot springs + E *-al* — more at THERM] **:** of or relating to hot springs or geysers ⟨~ regions⟩ ⟨health resort with natural ~ waters —*advt*⟩ **2 :** of, relating to, or caused by heat **:** WARM, HOT ⟨~ requirements of a room —Herman Nelson⟩ ⟨~ burns⟩ **3 :** of or relating to a state of matter that depends upon its temperature alone ⟨~ movements of molecules⟩ **4 :** having translational speeds and energies of the order of those due to thermal agitation ⟨~ neutrons⟩

²**thermal** \"\ *n* -s **:** a rising body of warm air

thermal agitation *n* **:** the ceaseless random motion of molecules or other small component particles of a substance that is associated with heat

thermal ammeter *n* **:** a hot-wire ammeter

thermal analysis *n* **:** the study of transition processes (as from one allotropic form to another) or of chemical changes in a substance as indicated by abrupt evolution or absorption of heat accompanying such processes

thermal barrier *n* **:** a limit to unlimited increase in airplane or rocket speeds imposed by aerodynamic heating that without adequate provisions for cooling the exposed surfaces will result in loss of strength and eventual melting of the metal skin — called also *heat barrier*

thermal belt *n* **:** a well-defined zone on the sides of many valleys where frost damage is at a minimum that is due to the adiabatic compression and consequent heating of the cold air flowing down the hill or mountain sides into the valley

thermal black *n* **:** a carbon black made by thermal decomposition of hydrocarbons (as natural gas and acetylene) in preheated furnaces — called also *furnace thermal black;* compare ACETYLENE BLACK

thermal capacity *n* **:** HEAT CAPACITY

thermal conduction *n* **:** the transmission of heat energy by conduction (as through the bottom of a kettle)

thermal conductivity *n* **1 :** capability of conducting heat **2 :** the quantity of heat that passes in unit time through a unit area of plate whose thickness is unity when its opposite faces differ in temperature by one degree

thermal converter *n* **:** a thermoelectric hot-wire alternating-current ammeter

thermal cracking *n* **:** cracking of petroleum or similar oils by means of heat and pressure alone — distinguished from *catalytic cracking;* compare PYROLYSIS

thermal cutout *n* **:** a protective device for automatically opening an overloaded electrical circuit because of excessive rise of temperature

thermal death point *n* **:** the temperature at which all organisms of a culture will be killed by heat either instantaneously or within an arbitrary brief finite period

thermal diffusion *n* **:** an effect wherein a temperature gradient in a gaseous or liquid mixture tends to cause a separation of the heavy components from the light

thermal diffusivity *n* **:** DIFFUSIVITY 2

thermal efficiency *n* **:** the ratio of the heat utilized by a heat engine to the total heat units in the fuel consumed

thermal electromotive force *n* **:** THERMOELECTROMOTIVE FORCE

thermal energy *n* **:** energy in the form of heat

thermal equator *n* **1 :** the region of the earth enclosed within the annual isotherms of 80° including the northern part of So. America and the greater part of Africa and India **2 :** the middle line of the thermal equator belt

thermal equilibrium *n* **:** a state of a system in which all parts are at the same temperature

thermal expansion *n* **:** increase in linear dimensions of a solid or in volume of a fluid because of rise in temperature

thermal head *n* **:** temperature difference responsible for a flow of heat or for convection

thermal inertia *n* **:** the degree of slowness with which the temperature of a body approaches that of its surroundings and which is dependent upon its absorptivity, its specific heat, its thermal conductivity, its dimensions, and other factors

thermal insulation *n* **1 :** the process of insulating against transmission of heat **2 :** material of relatively low heat conductivity used to shield a volume against loss or entrance of heat by radiation, convection, or conduction

thermal ionization *n* **:** ionization of a gas or vapor produced by subjecting it to a high temperature

ther·mal·iza·tion \\ˌthərmələˈzāshən, -ˌlīˈz-\\ *n* -S **:** the action or process of thermalizing

ther·mal·ize \\ˈ==,līz\\ *vt* -ED/-ING/-S [ˈ*thermal* + *-ize*] **:** to change the effective speed of (a particle) to a thermal value ⟨~ a neutron⟩

ther·mal·ly \\ˈthərməlē, ˈthōm-, ˈthəim-, -li\\ *adv* **:** in a thermal manner **:** by means of heat **:** with respect to thermal qualities

thermal metamorphism *n* **:** THERMOMETAMORPHISM

thermal noise *n* **:** radio-receiver or amplifier noise due to thermal agitation of the free electrons in the circuit and the tubes — called also *Johnson noise;* compare SHOT EFFECT

thermal radiation *n* **:** quantized electromagnetic radiation excited by thermal agitation of molecules or atoms and having a range including infrared, visible light, and ultraviolet

thermal resistance *n* **:** the resistance of a body to the flow of heat

thermals *pl of* THERMAL

thermal shock *n* **:** a large and rapid change of temperature considered esp. with respect to its effects upon living organisms or structural parts

thermal spring *n* **:** a spring whose water issues at a temperature higher than the mean temperature of the locality where the spring is situated — compare HOT SPRING

thermal stress *n* **:** stress in a body or structure due to inequalities of temperature

thermal transpiration *or* **thermal effusion** *n* **:** transpiration of gas through a capillary tube between enclosures orig. at the same pressure but at different temperatures wherein the movement is from the cooler to the warmer chamber

thermal unit *n* **:** a unit for the comparison or calculation of quantities of heat — see BRITISH THERMAL UNIT; compare CALORIE

therm·antidote \\ˌthərm+\\ *n* [*therm-* + *antidote*] **:** a device used in India for circulating and cooling the air and consisting essentially of a kind of rotating wheel fitted in a window and encased in wet tatties

ther·mate \\ˈthər,māt\\ *n* -S [fr. *Thermit,* a trademark + E *-ate*] **:** a mixture of aluminum powder, powdered iron oxide, and other substances (as barium nitrate) to accelerate burning that forms the standard filling for incendiary bombs

therm·el \\ˈthər,mel\\ *n* -S [*therm-* + *electric*] **:** a thermoelectric thermometer

therm foot \\ˈthərm,=\\ *n* [fr. obs. E *therm* pillar with tapering rectangular base, alter. (influenced by *herm*) of E ¹*term*] **:** SPADE FOOT

-ther·mia \\ˈthərmēə, ˈthōm-, ˈthəim-\\ *or* **-ther·my** \\ˌ=mē, -mi\\ *n comb form, pl* **-thermias** *or* **-thermies** [NL *-thermia,* fr. Gk *thermē* heat + L *-ia* -y — more at THERM] **:** state of heat **:** generation of heat ⟨dia*thermy*⟩ ⟨hypo*thermia*⟩

ther·mic \\ˈthərmik\\ *adj* [Gk *thermē* heat + E *-ic*] **:** of or relating to heat **:** due to heat **:** THERMAL ⟨~ energy⟩ ⟨~ reaction⟩ — **ther·mi·cal·ly** \\-mək(ə)lē\\ *adv*

thermic anomaly *n* **:** the difference of the mean temperature of a place from the normal temperature of its latitude

thermic fever *n* **:** fever caused by heatstroke

ther·mi·dor \\ˈthərmə,dȯ(ə)r; ˈthōmə,dȯ(ə), ˈthəim-, + V " *or* -dȯ(ə)r\\ *n* -S *usu cap* [F *Thermidor,* month of the Fr. revolutionary calendar beginning July 19; fr. the overthrow of Robespierre which took place in that month in 1794] **:** a moderate counterrevolutionary stage following an extremist stage of a revolution and usu. characterized often through the medium of a dictatorship by an emphasis on the restoration of order, a relaxation of tensions, and some return to patterns of life held to be normal

ther·mi·do·re·an *also* **ther·mi·do·ri·an** \\ˌ==ˈdōrēən, -ˈdȯr-\\ *adj, usu cap* [F *thermidorien,* fr. *Thermidor* + *-ien* -ian] **:** of, relating to, or having the characteristics of a Thermidor

therm·ion \\ˈthərm +\\ *n* -S [ISV *therm-* + *ion*] **:** an electrically charged particle emitted by an incandescent substance

therm·ion·ic \\ˌthər,mīˈänik, -ˌmē¦ä-\\ *adj* [ISV *thermion* + *-ic*] **:** of, relating to, or characteristic of thermions ⟨~ cathode⟩ ⟨~ properties⟩ — **therm·ion·i·cal·ly** \\-nək(ə)lē\\ *adv*

thermionic current *n* **:** an electric current due to the directed movements of thermions (as in the electric discharge through a vacuum tube with the cathode incandescent)

thermionic emission *n* **:** emission of particles (as electrons) from materials at high temperatures due to the heat energy imparted to them — compare FIELD EMISSION, PHOTOEMISSION

therm·ion·ics \\ˌ=(ˌ)=ˈäniks\\ *n pl but usu sing in constr* [fr. *thermionic,* after such pairs as E *economic: economics*] **:** a branch of physics dealing with thermionic phenomena and devices

thermionic tube *n* **:** an electron tube in which electron emission is produced by the heating of an electrode

therm·is·tor \\(ˈ)thərˈmistər\\ *n* -S [*thermal resistor*] **:** an electrical resistor made of a material whose resistance varies sharply in a known manner with the temperature

Ther·mit \\-ˌmət\\ *trademark* — used for a mixture of aluminum powder and powdered iron oxide that when caused to react by strong heating evolves a great deal of heat and yields alumina and a white-hot molten mass of metallic iron and that is used in welding and in incendiary bombs

therm leg \\ˈthərm,=\\ *n* [fr. obs. E *therm* pillar with tapering rectangular base — more at THERM FOOT] **:** a tapered furniture leg that is square in section

thermo- — see THERM-

ther·mo·ammeter \\ˌthər(ˌ)mō+\\ *n* [*therm-* + *ammeter*] **:** a thermoelement in circuit with a sensitive voltmeter for measuring small currents

ther·mo·analysis \\"+\\ *n* [*therm-* + *analysis*] **:** THERMAL ANALYSIS

ther·mo·bacterium \\"+\\ *n* [NL, fr. *therm-* + *bacterium*] **:** any of various thermoduric lactobacilli often considered to constitute a subgenus (*Thermobacterium*) of the genus *Lactobacillus*

ther·mo·balance \\"+\\ *n* [*therm-* + *balance*] **:** a balance designed esp. for weighing bodies at high temperatures

ther·mo·barograph \\"+\\ *n* [ISV *therm-* + *barograph*] **:** an instrument for recording simultaneously the pressure and temperature of a gas **:** a combined thermograph and barograph

ther·mo·barometer \\"+\\ *n* [ISV *therm-* + *barometer*] **1 :** HYPSOMETER **2 :** a siphon barometer adapted to be used also as a thermometer

ther·mo·cautery \\"+\\ *n* [ISV *therm-* + *cautery*] **:** ACTUAL CAUTERY

ther·mo·chemical \\"+\\ *adj* [*thermochemistry* + *-ical*] **:** of, relating to, or obtained by thermochemistry — **ther·mo·chemically** \\"+\\ *adv*

ther·mo·chemist \\"+\\ *n* [back-formation fr. *thermochemistry*] **:** one trained in or engaged in thermochemistry

ther·mo·chemistry \\"+\\ *n* [*therm-* + *chemistry*] **1 :** a branch of chemistry that deals with the relations existing between heat and chemical reaction or physical changes of state — compare ENDOTHERMIC, EXOTHERMIC, HEAT OF REACTION **2 :** the thermochemical properties of a substance ⟨~ of rocket fuels⟩

ther·mo·chro·mic \\¦thərmə¦krōmik\\ *adj* [*thermochromism* + *-ic*] **:** of, relating to, or exhibiting thermochromism

ther·mo·chro·mism \\ˈthərmə,krō,mizəm\\ *n* [*therm-* + *chrom-* + *-ism*] **:** the phenomenon of reversible change of color of a substance with change of temperature (as the change of mercuric oxide from nearly colorless on being cooled by liquid air to red at room temperature and to black on being heated)

ther·mo·clin·al \\¦thərmə¦klīnᵊl\\ *adj* **:** of, relating to, or constituting a thermocline

ther·mo·cline \\ˈ==,klīn\\ *n* -S [*therm-* + *-cline*] **1 :** a temperature gradient; *esp* **:** one marking sharp change **2 :** a layer of water in a thermally stratified lake or other body of water separating an upper warmer lighter oxygen-rich zone from a lower colder heavier oxygen-poor zone; *specif* **:** a stratum in which temperature declines at least one degree centigrade with each meter increase in depth

ther·mo·coagulation \\¦thər(ˌ)mō+\\ *n* [*therm-* + *coagulation*] **:** surgical coagulation of tissue by the application of heat (as from a high-frequency current)

ther·mo·couple \\ˈthərmə +,-\\ *n* [*therm-* + *couple*] **:** a device for measuring temperature in which two electrical conductors of dissimilar metals (as copper and iron) are joined at the point where heat is to be applied and the free ends are connected to an electrical measuring instrument (as an ammeter) which by registering the amount of thermoelectric current being produced at the juncture of the dissimilar conductors indicates the temperature at that point

ther·mo·current \\¦thərmō+\\ *n* [*therm-* + *current*] **:** a thermoelectric current

ther·mo development \\¦thər(ˌ)mō-\\ *n* [*therm-* + *development*] **:** TIME AND TEMPERATURE METHOD

ther·mo·diffusion \\¦thər(ˌ)mō+\\ *n* [ISV *therm-* + *diffusion*] **:** THERMAL DIFFUSION

¹**ther·mo·du·ric** \\¦thərmō¦d(y)u̇rik\\ *adj* [*therm-* + L *durare* to last + E *-ic* — more at DURE] **:** able to survive high temperatures; *specif* **:** able to survive pasteurization — used of microorganisms ⟨~ organisms in dairy equipment⟩

²**thermoduric** \\"\\ *n* -S **:** a thermoduric microorganism

ther·mo·dynamic *also* **ther·mo·dynamical** \\¦thərmə+\\ *adj* [*therm-* + *dynamic, dynamical*] **:** of or relating to thermodynamics **:** caused or operated by force due to the application of heat ⟨~ principles⟩ — **ther·mo·dynamically** \\"+\\ *adv*

thermodynamic cycle *n* **:** a succession of processes in a substance which involve changes esp. in temperature, pressure, density, and entropy, which result in the return of the substance to its original condition, and in which the substance acts in general as a means of transformation of energy — compare CARNOT CYCLE

thermodynamic efficiency *n* **:** the ratio of work output to heat-energy input in a heat-engine cycle or of heat energy removal to work input in a refrigeration cycle

thermodynamic equilibrium *n* **:** a state of a physical system in which it is in mechanical, chemical, and thermal equilibrium and in which there is therefore no tendency for spontaneous change

ther·mo·dy·nam·i·cist \\ˌthərmō,dīˈnaməsəst *sometimes* -ˌdə-ˈn-\\ *n* -S **:** a specialist in thermodynamics

thermodynamic potential *n* **:** a quantity of energy that along with other defining quantities determines the condition of a thermodynamic mechanism

ther·mo·dynamics \\¦thərmə +\\ *n pl but sing or pl in constr* [*therm-* + *dynamics*] **1 :** a branch of physics that deals with the mechanical action or relations of heat **2 :** thermodynamic processes and phenomena

thermodynamic scale *n* **:** the Kelvin scale

thermodynamic system *n* **:** an aggregation of atoms, molecules, colloidal particles, or larger bodies that constitute an isolated group

ther·mo·elastic \\¦thər(ˌ)mō+\\ *adj* [*therm-* + *elastic*] **:** of or relating to a thermodynamic aspect of elastic deformation

ther·mo·electric \\"+\\ *adj* [*therm-* + *electric*] **:** of or relating to a class of phenomena involving relations between the temperature and the electrical condition in a metal or in contacting metals

thermoelectric constant *n* **:** either of two constants characteristic of any metal that enter into the expressions for the thermoelectric power of the metal and for the electromotive forces of thermocouples utilizing it

thermoelectric inversion *n* **:** reversal in direction of a current produced by a thermocouple when the difference of temperature is increased beyond a neutral point

ther·mo·electricity \\¦thər(ˌ)mō+\\ *n* [*therm-* + *electricity*] **:** electricity involved in thermoelectric phenomena; *specif* **:** electricity accumulated or put in motion by thermoelectric action

thermoelectric power *n* **:** rate of change of the thermoelectromotive force of a thermocouple with temperature ⟨the *thermoelectric power* of a given metal is that of a couple formed of that metal with lead, the *thermoelectric power* of lead being taken arbitrarily as zero⟩

thermoelectric series *n* **:** a series of conductors arranged in the order of their thermoelectric powers

ther·mo·electromotive force \\¦thər(ˌ)mō+. . .-\\ *n* [*therm-* + *electromotive force*] **:** electromotive force in a circuit composed of dissimilar conductors that is produced because of its not being at a uniform temperature throughout — compare PELTIER EFFECT, THOMSON EFFECT

ther·mo·electron \\¦thər(ˌ)mō+\\ *n* [*therm-* + *electron*] **:** an electron released in thermionic emission — **ther·mo·electronic** \\"+\\ *adj*

ther·mo·element \\"+\\ *n* [*thermo*couple + *element*] **:** a device for measuring small currents consisting of a wire heating element and a thermocouple in electrical contact with it — compare THERMOAMMETER

ther·mo·for process \\ˈthərmə,fō(ə)r-\\ *n, often cap T* [*therm-* + *reforming*] **:** a catalytic cracking process in which the catalyst is passed by gravity through the oil or oil vapors in a tall reactor

ther·mo·galvanometer \\¦thər(ˌ)mō+\\ *n* [*thermo*element + *galvanometer*] **:** a thermoammeter for small currents usu. consisting of a thermoelement and a direct-current galvanometer

ther·mo·genesis \\¦thərmō+\\ *n* [NL, fr. *therm-* + *genesis*] **:** the production of heat esp. in the body (as by oxidation)

ther·mo·gen·ic \\¦thərmə¦jenik\\ *adj* [*therm-* + *-genic*] **:** of or relating to the production of heat **:** producing heat

ther·mo·gram \\ˈthərmə,gram\\ *n* [*therm-* + *-gram*] **:** the trace or record made by a thermograph

¹**ther·mo·graph** \\-,graf, -ˌräf\\ *n* [ISV *therm-* + *-graph*] **:** a self-recording thermometer

²**thermograph** \\"\\ *vt* [back-formation fr. *thermography*] **:** to produce by thermography ⟨a ~*ed* business card⟩

ther·mog·ra·pher \\(ˌ)thərˈmägrəfər\\ *n* -S **:** one that thermographs **:** one engaged in thermography

ther·mo·graph·ic \\¦thərmə¦grafik\\ *adj* **1 :** relating to, obtained by, or used in a thermograph ⟨~ process⟩ ⟨~ paper⟩ **2 :** of or used in thermography ⟨a ~ process⟩ ⟨~ inks⟩ — **ther·mo·graph·i·cal·ly** \\-fək(ə)lē\\ *adv*

ther·mog·ra·phy \\(ˌ)thərˈmägrəfē\\ *n* -ES [*therm-* + *-graphy*] **1 :** a process of writing or printing involving the use of heat; *esp* **:** a raised printing process in which matter printed by letterpress is dusted with powder and heated to make the lettering rise **2 :** a technique for detecting and measuring variations in the heat emitted by various regions of the body and transforming them into visible signals that can be recorded photographically (as for diagnosing abnormal or diseased underlying conditions); *also* **:** a similar technique used elsewhere (as on engines)

ther·mo·hardening \\¦thərmō+\\ *adj* [*therm-* + *hardening*] **:** THERMOSETTING

ther·mo·hydrometer \\¦thər(ˌ)mō+\\ *n* [*therm-* + *hydrometer*] **:** a hydrometer enclosing a thermometer to indicate the temperature of the liquid under test

ther·mo·junction \\¦thərmō+\\ *n* [*therm-* + *junction*] **:** a junction of two dissimilar conductors used to produce a thermoelectric current **:** one junction of a thermocouple

ther·mo·labile \\"+\\ *adj* [ISV *therm-* + *labile*] **:** unstable when heated; *specif* **:** subject to loss of characteristic properties on being heated to or above 55° C — used esp. of immune bodies, enzymes, and vitamins; opposed to *thermostable*

ther·mo·lability \\¦thər(ˌ)mō+\\ *n* **:** the quality or state of being thermolabile

ther·mo·luminescence \\"+\\ *n* [ISV *therm-* + *luminescence;* orig. formed as G *thermolumineszenz*] **:** phosphorescence developed in a previously excited substance (as quartz) upon gentle heating — called also *thermophosphorescence* — **ther·mo·luminescent** \\"+\\ *adj*

ther·mol·y·sis \\(ˌ)thərˈmäləsəs\\ *n* [ISV *therm-* + *-lysis;* orig. formed as G *thermolyse*] **:** the dissipation of heat from the living body

ther·mo·lyt·ic \\¦thərmə¦lid·ik\\ *adj* [fr. *thermolysis,* after such pairs as E *analysis: analytic*] **:** of or relating to thermolysis ⟨~ mechanisms of the body⟩

ther·mo·magnetic \\¦thər(ˌ)mō+\\ *adj* [*therm-* + *magnetic*] **1 :** of or relating to the effects of heat upon the magnetic properties of substances **2 :** of or relating to the effects of a magnetic field upon thermal conduction (as in the Righi-Leduc effect)

ther·mo·mechanical \\"+\\ *adj* [*therm-* + *mechanical*] **:** designed for or relating to the transformation of heat energy into mechanical work

ther·mo·metamorphic \\"+\\ *adj* [*therm-* + *metamorphic*] **:** of or relating to thermometamorphism

ther·mo·metamorphism \\"+\\ *n* [*therm-* + *metamorphism*] **:** metamorphism in rocks due to heat but not the result of dynamic action or volcanic emanations

ther·mom·e·ter *R* thə(r)ˈmäməd·ər, -ämətər, *-R* thəˈmäm-əd·ə(r, -ämətə(r\\ *n* [F *thermomètre,* fr. Gk *thermē* heat + F *-o-* + *-mètre* -meter — more at THERM] **1 :** an instrument for determining temperature usu. by means of a scale graduated directly in temperature units and consisting typically of (1) a device having a bimetallic element whose expansion or contraction indicates a change in temperature or (2) a glass bulb attached to a fine tube of glass with a numbered scale etched on or fastened to it and containing a liquid (as mercury or colored alcohol) that is sealed in and rises and falls with changes of temperature and that indicates the temperature by the number corresponding to the top of the column of liquid — see DRY-BULB THERMOMETER, GAS THERMOMETER, RESISTANCE THERMOMETER, REVERSING THERMOMETER, WET-BULB THERMOMETER **2 :** one that serves as a precise indicator of a position on a scale ⟨retail sales as a business ~⟩ ⟨letters to the editor — a ~ of public opinion⟩

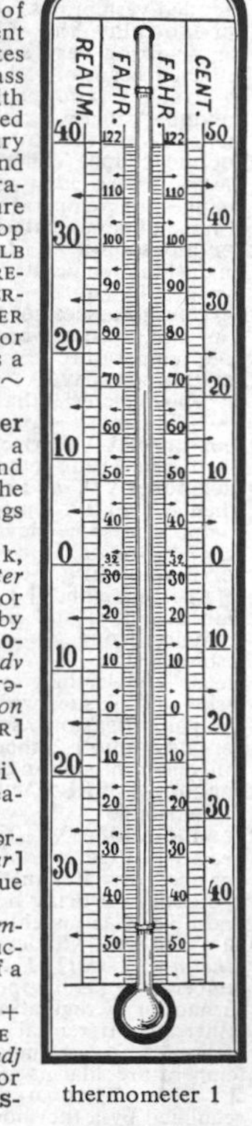

thermometer 1

thermometer screen *or* **thermometer shelter** *n* **:** a structure that shelters a thermometer from direct sunlight and other conditions that would cause the thermometer to give erroneous readings of the free air temperature

ther·mo·met·ric \\¦thərmə¦me·trik, ¦thōm-, ¦thəim, -·trēk\\ *adj* [*thermometer* + *-ic*] **:** of or relating to a thermometer or thermometry **:** made or ascertained by means of a thermometer — **ther·mo·met·ri·cal·ly** \\-·trək(ə)lē, -rēk-, -li\\ *adv*

ther·mo·met·ro·graph \\ˌthərməˈme·trə,graf, -ˌräf\\ *n* [*therm-* + Gk *metron* measure + E *-graph* — more at METER] **:** THERMOGRAPH

ther·mom·e·try \\thə(r)ˈmäm·ə·trē, -·tri\\ *n* -ES [ISV *therm-* + *-metry*] **:** the measurement of temperature

ther·mo·molecular pressure \\¦thər(ˌ)mō+. . .-\\ *n* [*therm-* + *molecular*] **:** the pressure difference developed due to thermal transpiration

ther·mo·motive \\¦thərmə +\\ *adj* [*therm-* + *motive*] **:** of or relating to the production of motion by heat — used esp. of a hot-air engine

ther·mo·motor \\"+\\ *n* [*therm-* + *motor*] **:** HEAT ENGINE, HOT-AIR ENGINE

ther·mo·nas·tic \\¦thərmə¦nastik\\ *adj* [*thermonasty* + *-ic*] **:** of, relating to, or caused by thermonasty — **ther·mo·nas·ti·cal·ly** \\-stək(ə)lē\\ *adv*

ther·mo·nas·ty \\ˈ==,nastē\\ *n* -ES [ISV *therm-* + *-nasty*] **:** a nastic movement that is associated with changes in temperature

ther·mo·na·trite \\ˌthərməˈnā·,trīt\\ *n* -S [ISV *therm-* + *natron* + *-ite;* orig. formed as G *thermonatrit;* fr. its being produced by the action of heat on natron] **:** a mineral $Na_2CO_3{\cdot}H_2O$ consisting of native hydrous sodium carbonate and found in some lakes and alkali soils

ther·mo·neutral \\¦thərmō+\\ *adj* [*therm-* + *neutral*] **:** characterized by thermoneutrality ⟨a ~ environment⟩ **:** not tending to alter thermal relationships (as of an organism)

ther·mo·neutrality \\¦thər(ˌ)mō+\\ *n* [*therm-* + *neutrality*] **:** a state of thermal balance between an organism and its environments such that bodily thermoregulatory mechanisms are inactive

ther·mo·nuclear \\"+\\ *adj* [ISV *therm-* + *nuclear*] **1 :** of or relating to the transformations in the nucleus of atoms of low atomic weight (as hydrogen) that require an extraordinarily high temperature for their inception — used of the fusion of elements of low atomic weight into elements of higher atomic weight (as in the hydrogen bomb or in the sun) ⟨~ reaction⟩ ⟨~ weapon⟩ **2 :** of, utilizing, or relating to a thermonuclear bomb ⟨~ explosion⟩ ⟨~ war⟩ ⟨~ attack⟩

ther·mo·period \\¦thərmō+\\ *n* [*therm-* + *period*] **:** the period of exposure of a plant to a particular temperature; *specif* **:** the period characteristic of the diurnal alternation of day and night temperature when both period and temperature are at or near the optimum for the induction of various activities (as growth or flowering) — compare PHOTOPERIOD — **ther·mo·periodic** \\¦thər(ˌ)mō+\\ *adj*

ther·mo·pe·ri·od·ism \\ˌthərmōˈpirēə,dizəm\\ *also* **ther·mo·pe·ri·o·dic·i·ty** \\-,pirēəˈdisəd·ē\\ *n* [*thermoperiodism* fr. *thermoperiod* + *-ism; thermoperiodicity* fr. *thermoperiodic* + *-ity*] **:** the sum of the responses of an organism to appropriately fluctuating temperatures — compare PHOTOPERIODISM

¹**ther·mo·phile** \\ˈthərmə,fīl\\ *also* **ther·mo·phil** \\-,fil\\ *adj* [ISV *therm-* + *-phil*] **:** of, relating to, or being a thermophile

²**thermophile** \\"\\ *also* **thermophil** \\"\\ *n* -S **:** an organism growing at a high temperature (as various bacteria that thrive at 122–131° F) — compare PSYCHROPHILE

ther·mo·phil·ic \\¦thərmə¦filik\\ *or* **ther·moph·i·lous** \\(ˌ)thərˈmäfələs\\ *adj* [*therm-* + *-philic* or *-philous*] **:** THERMOPHILE

ther·moph·i·ly \\(ˌ)thərˈmäfəlē\\ *n* -ES [ISV *therm-* + *-phily*] **:** the ability of an organism to grow at a high temperature

ther·mo·phone \\ˈthərmə,fōn\\ *n* [ISV *therm-* + tele*phone*] **1 :** a portable telethermometer using a telephone in connection with a differential thermometer **2 :** a telephone involving heat effects (as changes in temperature) due to pulsations of the line current in a fine wire connected with the receiver diaphragm

ther·mo·phosphor \\¦thərmə+\\ *n* [*therm-* + *phosphor*] **:** a substance that exhibits thermoluminescence

ther·mo·phosphorescence \\¦thər(ˌ)mō+\\ *n* [*therm-* + *phosphorescence*] **:** THERMOLUMINESCENCE

ther·mo·phyte \\ˈthərmə,fīt\\ *n* -S [*therm-* + *-phyte*] **:** a plant that requires or thrives best at elevated temperatures

ther·mo·pile \\-,pīl\\ *n* [*therm-* + *pile* (heap)] **:** an apparatus consisting of a number of thermoelectric couples (as of antimony and bismuth or of copper sulfide and German silver) combined so as to multiply the effect and used to generate electric currents for various purposes and also in a very sensitive form for determining intensities of radiation due esp. to its heating effect

¹**ther·mo·plas·tic** \\¦thərmə¦plastik\\ *adj* [*therm-* + *plastic*] **:** having the property of softening or fusing when heated and of hardening and becoming rigid again when cooled ⟨~

synthetic resins) ⟨~ materials can be remelted and cooled time after time without undergoing any appreciable chemical change —J.S.Campbell⟩ — distinguished from *thermoset* and *thermosetting* — **ther·mo·plas·tic·i·ty** \,==,pla'stisəd-ē\ *n*

²**thermoplastic** \"\ *n* : a thermoplastic material (as gutta-percha, cellulose acetate, or polyethylene)

ther·mo·polymerization \¦thər(,)mō+\ *n* [*therm-* + *polymerization*] : polymerization effected with heat

ther·mo·prene \'thərmə,prēn\ *n* [*therm-* + *-prene* (as in *neoprene*)] : any of various tough thermoplastic cyclized rubbers

ther·mop·sis \(,)thər'mäpsə̇s\ *n, cap* [NL, fr. Gk *thermos* lupine + NL *-opsis*] : a genus of American and Asiatic showy herbs (family Leguminosae) having trifoliolate stipulate leaves and yellow or purple racemose flowers — see BUSH PEA

ther·mo·radiography \¦thər(,)mō+\ *n* [*therm-* + *radiography*] : conversion of a pattern of radiant heat into an image for viewing or recording (as by photography)

ther·mo·receptor \¦thərmō+\ *n* [*therm-* + *receptor*] : a sensory end organ that is stimulated by heat or cold

ther·mo·reduction \"+\ *n* [*therm-* + *reduction*] : reduction at high temperatures

ther·mo·regulation \"+\ *n* [ISV *therm-* + *regulation*] **1** : the maintenance or regulation of temperature; *specif* : the maintenance of a particular temperature of the living body **2** : the physiological mechanisms concerned with the maintenance of steady body temperature in an environment with a fluctuating temperature

ther·mo·regulator \"+\ *n* [ISV *therm-* + *regulator*] : a device for the regulation of temperature : THERMOSTAT

ther·mo·regulatory \"+\ *adj* [*therm-* + *regulatory*] : serving to maintain a body at a particular temperature whatever its environmental temperature ⟨the ~ mechanisms of warm-blooded vertebrates⟩

ther·mo·relay \¦thər(,)mō+\ *n* [*therm-* + *relay*] : a device for detecting very small optical-lever deflections in which a reflected beam of radiation falls on a sensitive thermocouple so arranged as to measure very small deflections

ther·mos \'thərməs, 'thōm-, 'thəim-\ *n* -ES [fr. *Thermos*, a trademark] : VACUUM BOTTLE

ther·mo·scope \'thərmə,skōp\ *n* [NL *thermoscopium*, fr. *therm-* + *-scopium* -scope] : an instrument for indicating changes of temperature by the accompanying changes in volume of some material (as a gas)

ther·mo·scop·ic \¦==¦skäpik\ *adj* [*thermoscope* + *-ic*] : distinguishing temperature differences — **ther·mo·scop·i·cal·ly** \-pək(ə)lē\ *adv*

ther·mo·senescence \¦thərmō+\ *n* [*therm-* + *senescence*] : an aging process consisting of prolonged maintenance at a high temperature

ther·mo·sensitive \"+\ *adj* [*therm-* + *sensitive*] : relating to or being a material that is in one or more ways sensitive to heat ⟨~ adhesives⟩ ⟨~ papers⟩

¹**ther·mo·set** \'thərmə,set\ *n* [*therm-* + *set* (become solid)] : a thermosetting material before or after curing

²**thermoset** \"\ *adj* : relatively incapable of softening or fusing when heated : THERMOSETTING ⟨a truly ~ material may decompose at some elevated temperature but will not soften —R.R.McGregor⟩ — compare THERMOPLASTIC

ther·mo·set·ting \-ed-iŋ\ *adj* [*therm-* + *setting*, pres. part. of *set* (become solid)] : having the property of becoming permanently hard and rigid when heated or cured : capable of changing from a plastic or fusible state to an infusible or insoluble state by a chemical reaction effected by heat or other means and leading to a complex high polymer ⟨the phenol resins and plastics were the original synthetic ~ materials⟩ — compare THERMOPLASTIC

ther·mo·siphon \¦thərmō+\ *n* [*therm-* + *siphon*] : an arrangement of siphon tubes for assisting circulation in a liquid

ther·mo·stability \¦thərmō+\ *n* : the quality of being thermostable

ther·mo·stable \"+\ *adj* [*therm-* + *stable*] : stable when heated — used esp. of a substance (as an immune substance, enzyme, or vitamin) that does not lose its characteristic properties on being heated to moderate temperatures ⟨are ~ and do not act as antigens —*Science*⟩

¹**ther·mo·stat** \'thərmə,stat, 'thōm-, 'thəim-, *usu* -ad·+V\ *n* -s [*therm-* + *-stat*] **1 a** : an automatic device for regulating temperature (as by opening or closing the damper of a heating furnace or by regulating supply of gas) and commonly utilizing either the differential expansion of solids or the vapor pressure of liquids **b** : a similar device esp. for actuating fire or low-temperature alarms or for controlling automatic sprinklers **2** : a piece of apparatus (as a constant-temperature chamber) regulated by a thermostat

²**thermostat** \"\ *vt* **thermostated** *or* **thermostatted**; **thermostated** *or* **thermostatted**; **thermostating** *or* **thermostatting**; **thermostats** : to provide with or control by a thermostat ⟨a ~*ed* heating system⟩

ther·mo·stat·ic \¦==¦stad·|ik, -at|, |ēk\ *adj* [*thermostat* + *-ic*] : of or relating to a thermostat : controlled by a thermostat

ther·mo·stat·i·cal·ly \|ək(ə)lē, |ēk-, -li\ *adv* : by means of a thermostat ⟨recorded by a glass dilatometer placed in a ~ controlled high-pressure vessel—D.W.van Krevelen & Johannes Schuyer⟩

ther·mo·stimulation \¦thər(,)mō+\ *n* [*therm-* + *stimulation*] : stimulation (as of a nerve) by means of heat

ther·mo·stromuhr \¦thərmə+\ *n* [ISV *therm-* + *stromuhr*] : a stromuhr that measures the rate of blood flow in an intact blood vessel by determining the amount of heating of the blood as indicated by a sensitive galvanometer when a radio-frequency current is passed through the vessel between thermocouples so that the amount of heating is inversely proportional to the rate of flow

ther·mo·tactic \¦thərmō¦taktik\ *adj* [*therm-* + *-tactic*] : characterized by or exhibiting thermotaxis : of or relating to thermotaxis

ther·mo·tax·is \-aksə̇s\ *n* [NL, fr. *therm-* + *-taxis*] **1** : a taxis in which a temperature gradient constitutes the directive factor **2** : the regulation of body temperature

ther·mo·therapy \¦thərmō+\ *n* [ISV *therm-* + *therapy*] : treatment of disease by heat (as by hot air, hot baths, or diathermy)

ther·mo·tolerant \"+\ *adj* [*therm-* + *tolerant*] : THERMODURIC

ther·mo·trop·ic \¦thərmō¦träpik\ *adj* [ISV *therm-* + *-tropic*] : manifesting thermotropism : characterized by thermotropism

ther·mot·ro·pism \(,)thər'mä·trə,pizəm\ *n* [ISV *therm-* + *-tropism*] : a tropism in which a temperature gradient determines the orientation

-ther·mous \¦thərməs, -¦thōm-, -¦thəim-\ *adj comb form* [Gk *-thermos*, fr. *thermē* heat — more at THERM] : having (such) heat ⟨homo*thermous*⟩ ⟨xero*thermous*⟩

ther·mo·well \'thərmō+,-\ *n* [*thermometer* + *well*] : a tube or tubular opening provided expressly for the insertion of a thermometer

therms *pl of* THERM

-therms *pl of* -THERM

-thermy — see -THERMIA

thero- — see THER-

the·ro·dont \'thirə,dänt\ *n* -s [*ther-* + *-odont*] : THERIODONT

the·rol·o·gy \thi'räləjē\ *n* -ES [NL *therologia*, fr. *ther-* + *-logia* -logy] : MAMMALOGY

the·ro·morph \'thirə,mȯrf\ *n* [NL *Theromorpha*] : PELYCOSAUR

the·ro·mor·pha \,thirə'mȯrfə\ [NL, fr. *ther-* + *-morpha*] *syn of* PELYCOSAURIA

the·ro·phyte \'thirə,fīt\ *n* -s [ISV *thero-* (fr. Gk *theros* summer) + *-phyte*; akin to Gk *thermos* hot — more at WARM] : an annual plant that overwinters as a seed

¹**the·ro·pod** \-,päd\ *adj* [NL *Theropoda*] : of or relating to the Theropoda

²**theropod** \"\ *n* -s [NL *Theropoda*] : a dinosaur of the suborder Theropoda

the·rop·o·da \thi'räpədə\ *n pl, cap* [NL, fr. *ther-* + *-poda*] : a suborder of Saurischia that comprises carnivorous digitigrade dinosaurs having premaxillary teeth, small forelimbs, and simple slender pubic bones meeting in a symphysis and walking on their hind legs — see COMPSOGNATHUS, MEGALOSAURUS

the·rop·o·dous \-dəs\ *adj* [NL *Theropoda* + E *-ous*] : THEROPOD

thesaurer *n* -s [ME, fr. LL *thesaurarius*, fr. L, of treasure, fr. *thesaurus* treasure + *-arius* -ary] *obs* : TREASURER

the·sau·rus \thə̇'sȯrəs\ *n, pl* **thesau·ri** \-,rī\ *or* **thesau·ruses** [NL, fr. L, treasure, store, collection, fr. Gk *thēsauros*] **1 a** : a book containing a store of words or of information about a particular field or set of concepts; *specif* : a dictionary of synonyms **b** : a collection of concepts or words constituting the contents of a thesaurus ⟨must employ only the ~ of Chinese rhetoric —H.H.Hart⟩ ⟨indicated by . . . use of such terms as *ostensible, emulative, conspicuous*, and the rest of his beautifully ironic ~ —David Riesman⟩ **2** : TREASURY, STOREHOUSE

these [ME *thes, these* (pl. of *this*, pron. & adj.), fr. OE *thæs* (pl. of *thes*, pron. & adj., this) — more at THIS] *pl of* THIS

the·sis \'thēsə̇s, *in sense 3* " *or* 'thes-\ *n, pl* **the·ses** \-(,)sēz\ [L, fr. Gk, act of placing, act of laying down, position, proposition, downbeat of the foot in keeping time, fr. *tithenai* to put, place, lay down — more at DO] **1 a** : a claim put forward : STATEMENT, PROPOSITION; *specif* : a position or proposition that a person (as a candidate for scholastic honors) advances and maintains or offers to maintain by argument **b** : an affirmation or proposition to be proved or one advanced without proof esp. in contrast with a negation: as (1) : the proposition or point of view defended by an argument (2) : ASSUMPTION, POSTULATE (3) : the consequent of a hypothetical proposition (4) *Kantianism* : the affirmative member of one of the antinomies or paradoxes of reason (5) *Hegelianism* : the proposition or conception representing the first and least adequate stage of developing thought — compare ANTITHESIS, SYNTHESIS **2** : a dissertation embodying results of original research and esp. substantiating a specific view: as **a** : a substantial paper written by a candidate for an academic degree under the individual direction of a professor **b** : a paper written by an undergraduate desirous of achieving honors or distinction **3 a** (1) [LL, fr. Gk, act of placing; fr. the lowering of the voice] : the lighter or unstressed part of a poetic foot esp. in accentual verse (2) : the heavier or longer part of a poetic foot esp. in quantitative verse **b** : the accented part of a musical measure : DOWNBEAT — compare ARSIS **syn** see DISCOURSE

thesis novel *n* : a novel that advances, illustrates, or defends a thesis ⟨a *thesis novel* directed against the corruption of the clergy —E. G. Du Cal⟩

thesis play *n* : a play that advances, illustrates, or defends a thesis

the·si·um \'thēsēəm, thə̇'sīəm\ *n, cap* [NL, fr. L *thesium, thesion* bastard toad flax, fr. Gk *thēseion*, prob. fr. neut. of *thēseios* of Theseus, fr. *Thēseus* Theseus, mythological Greek hero] : a large genus of Old World root-parasitic herbs of the family Santalaceae with small linear or scalelike leaves and diclinous flowers — see BASTARD TOADFLAX

thes·mo·pho·ria \,thezmə'fōrēə\ *n* -s *usu cap* [L (pl.), fr. Gk, fr. *thesmophoros* giving laws (epithet of Demeter), fr. *thesmos* law, ordinance (fr. *tithenai* to put, lay down) + *-phoros* -phore — more at DO] : a festival of Demeter as Thesmophoros or of Demeter and Kore celebrated by women and having as its essential ceremony the casting of pigs into chasms of the earth and the bringing up of their decaying flesh to be mixed with seed to insure fertility — **thes·mo·pho·ri·an** \¦==¦==ən\ *adj, usu cap* — **thes·mo·phor·ic** \¦==¦fȯrik\ *adj, usu cap*

thes·mo·thete \'thezmə,thēt\ *n* -s [Gk *thesmothetēs*, fr. *thesmos* law + *thetēs* one who sets, lays down, fr. *tithenai* to put, lay down] : LAWGIVER, LEGISLATOR; *specif* : one of the six ancient Athenian junior archons

thes·o·cyte \'thesə,sīt\ *n* -s [Gk *thesis* act of laying down, deposit + E *-o-* + *-cyte* — more at THESIS] : an amoebocyte containing ergastic inclusions

thes·pe·sia \-'spēzh(ē)ə\ *n, cap* [NL, fr. Gk, fem. of *thespesios* marvelous, divine, lit., told by a god; akin to Gk *theos* god and to *enepein, ennepein* to tell, speak — more at THE-] : a small genus of tropical trees (family Malvaceae) having undivided leaves and large bracted flowers with a nearly simple style and 5-celled ovary — see PORTIA TREE

thes·pe·sius \-zh(ē)əs\ *n, cap* [NL, fr. Gk *thespesios* marvelous] : a genus of Upper Cretaceous No. American ornithischian dinosaurs related to *Hadrosaurus*

¹**thes·pi·an** \'thespēən\ *adj* [*Thespis*, 6th cent. B.C. Greek poet and reputed originator of the actor's role in drama + E *-an*, adj. suffix] **1** *usu cap* : of or relating to Thespis **2** *often cap* : relating to the drama : DRAMATIC ⟨a movie director getting excellent ~ cooperation —H.E.Clurman⟩

²**thespian** \"\ *n* -s *sometimes cap* [*Thespis* + E *-an*, n. suffix] : ACTOR

¹**thes·sa·lian** \the'sālēən, -lyən\ *adj, usu cap* [L *Thessali*us of Thessaly, fr. *Thessalia* Thessaly, district of east central Greece + E *-an*] **1** : of or relating to Thessaly **2** : of or relating to the people of Thessaly

²**thessalian** \"\ *n* -s *cap* **1** : a native or inhabitant of Thessaly **2** : an Aeolic dialect of ancient Greek used by the Thessalians

¹**thes·sa·lo·nian** \¦thesə¦lōnyən, -ōnēən\ *adj, usu cap* [irreg. fr. *Thessalonica*, seaport city of west central Macedonia (now *Salonika*) + E *-an*] : of or relating to ancient Thessalonica, Macedonia

²**thessalonian** \"\ *n* -s *cap* : a native or resident of Thessalonica

the·ta \'thād-ə, -ātə *also* 'thē-\ *n* -s [Gk *thēta*, of Sem origin; akin to Heb *ṭēth* teth] : the eighth letter of the Greek alphabet — symbol Θ or θ; see ALPHABET table

thet·ic \'thed·ik\ *adj* [Gk *thetikos* fit for placing, of a thesis, positive, fr. *thetos* (verbal of *tithenai* to put, place, lay down) + *-ikos* -ic — more at DO] **1** *or* **thet·i·cal** \-d·ə̇kəl\ : laid down : PRESCRIBED, POSITIVE, ARBITRARY **2 a** : constituting a poetic thesis ⟨a ~ syllable⟩ **b** : beginning with a thesis ⟨~ line⟩ ⟨~ measure⟩ — **thet·i·cal·ly** \-d·ə̇k(ə)lē\ *adv*

the·tin \'thēt°n\ *also* **the·tine** \", -ē,tēn\ *n* -s [*thio-* + *betaine*] : any one of a class of sulfonium carboxylates that are analogous to the betaines ⟨dimethyl-*thetin*, $(CH_3)_2S^+CH_2COO^-$⟩

the·ur·gic \(')thē¦ərjik\ *or* **the·ur·gi·cal** \-jə̇kəl\ *adj* [*theurgic* fr. LL *theurgicus*, fr. LGk *theourgikos*, fr. *theourgos* wonder-worker, divine worker (fr. Gk *the-* + *-ourgos* worker, fr. *-o-* + *ergon* work) + Gk *-ikos* -ic; *theurgical* fr. LL *theurgicus* + E *-al* — more at WORK] : of or relating to theurgy : MAGICAL

the·ur·gist \'thē(,)ərjə̇st\ *n* -s [*theurgy* + *-ist*] : WONDER-WORKER, MAGICIAN

the·ur·gy \-jē\ *n* -ES [LL *theurgia*, fr. LGk *theourgia*, fr. *theourgos* wonder-worker + Gk *-ia* -y] **1 a** : the art or science of compelling or persuading a god or beneficent supernatural power to do or refrain from doing something; *specif* : an occult art in which the operator by means of self-purification and discipline, sacred rites, and knowledge of divine signatures in nature is held to be capable of evoking or utilizing the aid of divine and beneficent spirits **b** : a human act, process, power, or state of supernatural efficacy or origin; *also* : theurgic acts **2** : a divine work : MIRACLE

the·ve·tia \thə̇'vēsh(ē)ə\ *n, cap* [NL, fr. André *Thévet* †1592 Fr. traveler and author + NL *-ia*] : a genus of tropical American trees and shrubs (family Apocynaceae) having alternate entire leaves and large cymose flowers with a campanulate corolla that has overlapping lobes

the·ve·tin \thə̇,vēt°n, 'thevətə̇n\ *n* -s [NL *Thevetia* + ISV *-in*] : a poisonous crystalline cardiac glycoside $C_{42}H_{66}O_{18}$ obtained esp. from the seeds of the yellow oleander that yields on hydrolysis glucose, digitalose, and a sterol — compare DIGITOXIN

¹**thew** \'th(y)ü\ *n* -s [ME, custom, habit, personal quality, virtue, fr. OE *thēaw*; akin to OS *thau* custom, habit, OHG *kathau* discipline, and prob. to L *tuēri* to observe, protect — more at TUITION] **1 thews** *pl, archaic* : mental or moral qualities, traits, or customs **2 a** : MUSCLE, SINEW ⟨broad of shoulder and great of ~ —Frank Yerby⟩ — usu. used in pl. **b** (1) : muscular power or development (2) : STRENGTH, VITALITY ⟨the naked ~ and sinew of the English language —G.M.Hopkins⟩

²**thew** *dial past of* THAW

thewed \¦th(y)üd\ *adj* [ME, fr. ¹*thew* + *-ed*] **1** *obs* : MANNERED, BEHAVED **2** : furnished with thews ⟨buxom, deep-breasted, strong-*thewed*, fit to be mates and mothers of big men — Bernard DeVoto⟩

thew·less \'th(y)üləs\ *var of* THOWLESS

¹**they** \(¦)thā, *before* "re" *or* "are" *usu* (,)the\ *pron, pl in constr* [ME, fr. ON *their*, masc. pl. demonstrative & personal pron.; akin to ON *that*, neut. demonstrative pron. — more at THAT] **1 a** : those ones — used as nominative third person pronoun serving as the plural of *he*, the plural of *she*, or the plural of *it*, or referring to a group of two or more individuals that are not all of the same sex ⟨your sons are popular because ~ dance well⟩ ⟨ask your wife and daughter what ~ think about it⟩ ⟨we are so used to matches that we can hardly imagine what life was like before ~ were invented⟩ ⟨today is my neighbors' wedding anniversary but I don't know what presents ~ are giving each other⟩; often used with an antecedent that is singular in form but collective in meaning ⟨even if the unofficial minority voted solidly against a government measure — a rare circumstance because ~ were divided by mutual jealousies —W.T. Stace⟩ ⟨if industry is to do this important job ~ must understand not only what the men think —E.R.Smith⟩; sometimes in poetry and in substandard speech used pleonastically together with a noun or group of nouns as subject of a verb ⟨the olives ~ were not blind to Him —Sidney Lanier⟩ ⟨my father and mother ~ told me not to do it⟩; compare HE, IT, SHE **b** : he or she : ¹HE 2 — used with an indefinite singular antecedent ⟨everyone tries to make the person ~ love just like themselves —H.D.Skidmore⟩ ⟨no person has a right to any coat of arms (or crest) unless ~ are the "heir-male" for the time being —Thomas Innes⟩ ⟨the liability for damages lies against whoever is knowingly involved in such sale whether or not ~ receive any part of the consideration —*U.S.Code*⟩ **2** : THOSE — used esp. as antecedent to a relative pronoun ⟨blessed are ~ that mourn —Mt 5:4 (AV)⟩ ⟨the mothers who kept score did a fine job but ~ who did the umpiring left much to be desired —*Deerfield (Wisc.) Independent*⟩ **3** : ¹PEOPLE 1a : unspecified persons and esp. those responsible for a particular act, practice, or decision ⟨curiosity killed a cat, ~ say⟩ ⟨~ are going to hold the commencement exercises outdoors if the weather permits⟩ ⟨he's as lazy as ~ come⟩ ⟨at Nedroma ~ think they can make a prodigious crop rise from the earth by inviting the tallest worker to stretch himself at full length in the first furrow —J.G.Frazer⟩ **4** *dial chiefly Eng* : THEM — used emphatically as object of a verb or preposition ⟨good enough for the likes of ~⟩

²**they** \"\ *adj* [ME, fr. *they*, pron.] *dial Eng* : THOSE ⟨its ~ deserters that commit half the crimes —Rose Macaulay⟩ ⟨if you fetches out ~ hedges, master . . . I'll not work for 'ee no more —C.G.Glover⟩

³**they** \"\ *n* -s [¹*they*] : a group of unspecified persons or forces of which the speaker or writer is not a member; *esp* : such a group held to be responsible for acts or decisions that impose unwelcome restrictions on the speaker or writer ⟨the same ~ we always mean, . . . authority, the gods, fate, circumstances —Ralph Ellison⟩

⁴**they** \"\ *pron* [by alter.] *substand* : ²THERE 1 ⟨~'s music in the twitter of the bluebird and the jay —J.W.Riley⟩ ⟨~ wasn't a house nowhere in sight —Helen Eustis⟩

⁵**they** \"\ *adj* [by alter.] *substand* : ²THEIR ⟨the kids was sleeping all together in ~ bed over in the corner —Ralph Ellison⟩

thi- *or* **thio-** *comb form* [ISV, fr. Gk *thei-, theio-* sulfur, brimstone, fr. *theion*; prob. akin to Gk *thyein* to rage, seethe — more at DUST] : containing sulfur ⟨*thi*amine⟩; *esp* : containing bivalent sulfur usu. in place of oxygen ⟨*thio*cyanic⟩ ⟨*thio*ether⟩ — compare SULF- c

THI *abbr* time handed in

¹**thia-** *or* **thi-** *comb form* [ISV, fr. *thi-* + *-a-*] : containing sulfur in place of carbon or regarded as in place of carbon usu. in place of the methylene group $-CH_2-$ ⟨*thia*cyclohexane⟩ ⟨*thia*diazole⟩ ⟨*thi*azole⟩ — compare AZA-, OXA-

²**thia-** *comb form* : THI- ⟨*thia*chroman⟩

thi·acet·azone \,thīə'sed·ə,zōn\ *n* -s [*thi-* + *acet-* + *az-* + *-one*] : a bitter pale yellow crystalline tuberculostatic drug $C_{10}H_{12}N_4OS$; *para*-acetamido-benzaldehyde thiosemicarbazone

thia·diazole \¦thīə+\ *n* [*thia-* + *diazole*] : any of four isomeric heterocyclic parent compounds $C_2H_2N_2S$ containing a ring composed of two carbon atoms, two nitrogen atoms, and one sulfur atom; *also* : a derivative of any of these

thi·al \'thī,al\ *n* -s [ISV *thi-* + *-al*] : THIOALDEHYDE

thi·al·dine \thī'al,dēn, -,də̇n\ *n* [ISV *thi-* + *ald-* + *-ine*] : a crystalline heterocyclic compound $CH_3CH{=}(SCHCH_3)_2{=}NH$ formed by action of ammonia and hydrogen sulfide on acetaldehyde; *broadly* : a compound similarly derived from another aldehyde

thi·ami·nase \thī'amə,nās, 'thīəm-, -āz\ *n* [ISV *thiamine* + *-ase*] : an enzyme or any of a group of enzymes that promote the destruction of thiamine in the body and are found esp. in raw freshwater fish and in raw clams, crustaceans, and starfish

thi·amine \'thīəmə̇n; 'thīə,mēn, -,mə̇n\ *also* **thi·amin** \-,mə̇n\ *n* [*thiamine* alter. (influenced by *amine*) of *thiamin*, fr. *thi-* + *-amin* (as in *vitamin*)] **1** *also* **thiamine chloride** : the antineuritic member of the vitamin B complex that is an amino hydroxy quaternary ammonium water-soluble salt $[C_{12}H_{17}N_4OS]Cl$ containing a thiazole ring and a pyrimidine ring, that occurs widely both free (as in the germs of cereals and hulls of grain) and combined (as in yeast and in animal tissues like liver, kidneys, and heart) but is usu. synthesized commercially, that functions in the body as cocarboxylase and is essential for conversion of carbohydrate to fat and for normal nervous action and that is used in nutrition (as in vitamin preparations and in enriching flour and bread) and in medicine in treating thiamine deficiency — called also *vitamin* B_1 **2** *or* **thiamine base** : the cation $[C_{12}H_{17}N_4OS]^+$ of thiamine chloride ⟨~ mononitrate is used similarly to thiamine hydrochloride⟩

thia·naph·thene \,thīə¦naf,thēn, ÷ -ap,th-\ *n* -s [¹*thia-* + *naphth-* + *-ene*] : a crystalline heterocyclic compound C_8H_6S that has an odor like that of naphthalene and is found in lignite tar — called also *benzothiophene*

thi·an shan sheep \tē'än,shän-\ *n, usu cap T & 1st S* [*Thian Shan* (Tien Shan), mountain chain in central Asia] : MARCO POLO SHEEP

thian shan stag *n, usu cap T & 1st S* : a very large deer (*Cervus eustephanus*) of the Tien Shan mountains of western China related to the maral and the American wapiti

thi·an·threne \thī'an,thrēn\ *n* -s [ISV *thi-* + *-anthrene*] : a crystalline heterocyclic parent compound $C_{12}H_8S_2$ that is regarded as anthracene in which the two middle methylidyne groups are replaced by sulfur atoms and that is made by the action of sulfur chloride on benzene in the presence of aluminum chloride and in other ways

thi·ara \thī'a(a)rə\ *n, cap* [NL] : a genus of freshwater snails that is the type of the family Thiaridae and that includes several forms which are intermediate hosts of medically important trematodes

thi·ar·i·dae \-'arə,dē\ *n pl, cap* [NL, fr. *Thiara*, type genus + *-idae*] : a family of Old World operculate freshwater snails (suborder Taenioglossa) — see HUA, SEMISULCOSPIRA, THIARA

thi·a·sine \'thīə,sēn, -,sə̇n\ *n* -s [irreg. fr. *thi-*] : ERGOTHIONEINE

thi·a·zine \'thīə,zēn, -,zə̇n\ *n* [ISV *thi-* + *azine*] : any of several parent compounds C_4H_5NS or their derivatives containing a ring composed of four carbon atoms, one sulfur atom, and one nitrogen atom; *also* : any of various derivatives of them — see AZINE 1; compare PHENOTHIAZINE

Thiazine \"\ *trademark* — used for a dyestuff; see DYE table I (under *Direct Red 45*)

thi·a·zole \'thīə,zōl\ *n* [ISV *thi-* + *azole*] **1** : a basic liquid parent compound C_3H_3NS that has an odor resembling that of pyridine and that is analogous in structure to oxazole with sulfur in place of oxygen — compare STRUCTURAL FORMULA **2** : any of various derivatives of thiazole or benzothiazole

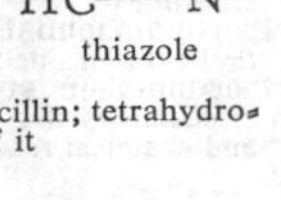

thiazole

thi·a·zol·idine \,thīə'zōlə,dēn, -zäl-, -,də̇n\ *n* -s [ISV *thiazole* + *-idine*] : a basic liquid saturated heterocyclic compound C_3H_7NS whose ring is present in the structure of penicillin; tetrahydrothiazole; *also* : any of various derivatives of it

thi·az·o·line \thī'azə,lēn, -ˌlən\ *n* -s [ISV *thiazole* + *-ine*] **:** any of three basic heterocyclic compounds C_3H_5NS; dihydro-thiazole; *also* **:** any of various derivatives of them

thi·a·zol·sul·fone \ˌthīə,zōl'səl,fōn, -zōl-\ *n* [prob. irreg. fr. *thiazole* + *sulfone*] **:** a crystalline antibacterial drug $C_9H_9N_3O_2S_2$ used orally in treating leprosy; 2-amino-5-sulfanilyl-thiazole

¹**thibet** *usu cap, var of* TIBET

²**thi·bet** *also* **ti·bet** \tə'bet, *usu* -ed+V\ *n* -s [*Thibet* (*Tibet*), country in central Asia where the wool was originally produced] **1 :** a fine woolen fabric formerly used for dresses **2 :** a suiting and coating fabric usu. of wool and finished with a soft smooth heavily-felted face

thi·ble \'thībəl, 'thib-\ *var of* THIVEL

¹**thick** \'thik\ *adj* -ER/-EST [ME *thikke*, fr. OE *thicce;* akin to OHG *dicki* thick, ON *thykkr*, OIr *tiug*] **1 a :** having or being of relatively great depth or extent from one surface to its opposite ⟨a ~ plank⟩ ⟨a ~ neck⟩ ⟨a ~ book⟩ **b :** heavily built **:** BURLY, THICKSET ⟨that ~ man . . . is as fine as a needle —Joseph Conrad⟩ ⟨a slow, closemouthed man, ~ in the shoulders and muscled like a bull —H.G.Evarts⟩ **2 a :** close-packed with units or individuals **:** densely massed or tightly filled **:** CRAMMED, CROWDED ⟨the air was ~ with snow⟩ ⟨a ~ forest⟩ ⟨libel suits were ~ in the air —Dorothy C. Fisher⟩ **b :** occurring in large numbers in a limited area or in close succession **:** NUMEROUS, FREQUENT ⟨in that canyon the fossils were particularly ~ —D.B.Putnam⟩ **c :** holding much solid matter in suspension or solution **:** dense or viscous in consistency ⟨a ~ syrup⟩ **d :** foul or heavy with fumes **:** heavy with dust or other foreign matter **:** CLOSE 6, IMPURE, STUFFY — used of the air **e :** dense with particles **:** having drops or specks close together ⟨~ fog⟩ ⟨~ smoke⟩ **f :** marked by haze, fog, or mist enough to obstruct or reduce vision ⟨~ weather⟩ ⟨a ~ day⟩ **g :** impenetrable to the eye **:** GROSS, PROFOUND — used of night or darkness **h :** showing massive concentration **:** UNRELIEVED ⟨serves in place of a slower and ~*er* naturalism —*N.Y.Times*⟩ ⟨one of the ~*est* concentrations of heavy industry in the world —Sam Pollock⟩ **i :** extreme in intensity **:** SHEER, UTTER ⟨~ silence⟩ **3 :** measuring in thickness ⟨a log 12 inches ~⟩ ⟨a coin 1 mm. ~⟩ **4 a :** marked by huskiness or hoarseness **:** imperfectly articulated **:** INDISTINCT, MUFFLED, GUTTURAL, ROUGH ⟨plays his part with a ~ accent —Henry Hewes⟩ **b :** marked by rich and close harmony esp. in the lower register — used of a musical score **5 a :** dull of hearing or sight **b :** dull or slow of mind or apprehension **:** not acute or keen **:** OBTUSE, STUPID ⟨you're obtuse, that's all; just plain ~ —Jean Kerr⟩ **6** *obs* **:** lined up one behind another **:** DEEP ⟨a guard of spies ten ~ —Ben Jonson⟩ **7 :** associated on close or familiar terms **:** INTIMATE ⟨the two were ~ as thieves for months⟩ **8 :** exceeding bounds of propriety or fitness **:** past toleration or endurance **:** EXCESSIVE, EXTRAVAGANT, EXTREME, GROSS ⟨called it a bit ~ to be fired out of hand in that way⟩ ⟨laid his flattery on ~⟩ **syn** see CLOSE, FAMILIAR, STOCKY

²**thick** \"\ *n* -s [ME *thikke*, fr. *thikke*, adj.] **1 :** the most crowded or most fully occupied part **:** the densest concentration ⟨we came around a turn into the ~ of a mob of yelling people —Mollie Panter-Downes⟩ ⟨wide-reaching branches and a ~ of leaves —Padraic Colum⟩ **2 :** the most intense or most active part or stage ⟨the ~ of battle⟩ ⟨major producers . . . are in the ~ of this trend —*Wall Street Jour.*⟩ **3 a :** the part of greatest thickness ⟨the ~ of the thumb⟩ **b :** THICKET **c :** a dense or stupid person ⟨you must think I'm a right ~ —Brendan Behan⟩

³**thick** \"\ *adv* -ER/-EST [ME *thicke*, fr. OE *thicce;* akin to OHG *dicco* often; both fr. a prehistoric WGmc adv. fr. the root of OE *thicce*, adj. — more at ¹THICK] **:** THICKLY ⟨misfortunes came ~ and fast⟩ — often used in combination ⟨*thick*-starred⟩ ⟨*thick*-swarming⟩

⁴**thick** \"\ *vb* -ED/-ING/-S [ME *thikken*, fr. OE *thiccian*, fr. *thicce*, adj.] *archaic* **:** to make, be, or become thick **:** THICKEN

thick and thin *n* [ME *thikke and thinne*, fr. *thikke*, n., thick + *and* + *thinne*, n., thin] **:** every difficulty and obstacle **:** all hindrances and obstructions — used esp. in the phrase *through thick and thin* ⟨stand by her shoulder to shoulder through *thick and thin* —Gustave Weigel⟩ ⟨had been his friend through *thick and thin*⟩

thick-and-thin \ˌ=='=\ *adj* [*thick and thin*] **1 :** having one sheave thicker than the other and taking two ropes of differing size — used of a tackle block; compare FIDDLE BLOCK **2 :** ready to go through thick and thin **:** unreservedly or blindly loyal or devoted ⟨a *thick-and-thin* friend⟩ **3 :** having regularly or irregularly spaced sections thicker than the rest — used of yarns

thick and threefold *adv (or adj)* **:** in rapid succession **:** THICKLY, CONTINUOUSLY, FREQUENTLY

thick-billed murre *or* **thick-billed guillemot** \'=,=-\ *n* **:** a widely distributed murre (*Uria lomvia*) with a rather short distinctly thick bill

thick-billed parrot *n* **:** a parrot (*Rhynchopsitta pachyrhyncha*) of northern Mexico and southwestern U. S. that is green marked with red

thick china *n* [perh. so called fr. the resemblance of the coating to the glaze of chinaware] **:** a coated paperboard similar to railroad board but lighter in weight

thick·en \'thikən\ *vb* **thickened; thickened; thickening** \-k(ə)niŋ\ **thickens** [ME *thiknen*, fr. *thikke*, adj., thick + *-nen* -en] *vt* **1 a :** to make thick, dense, or viscous in consistency ⟨~*s* gravy with flour⟩ **b :** to make close or compact **:** fill up the openings or interstices of ⟨~*s* platoon fires and turn back any enemy counterattack —*Combat Forces Jour.*⟩ **2 :** to make stronger **:** CONFIRM, INTENSIFY ⟨this may help to ~ other proofs —Shak.⟩ **3 a :** to increase the thickness of **:** add to the depth or diameter of ⟨the years had ~*ed* the man's figure⟩ **b :** BROADEN ⟨the strokes *m* and *n* are halved and ~*ed* to indicate a following *d* —*Pitman Shorthand*⟩ **4 :** BLUR, OBSCURE ⟨alcohol had ~*ed* his speech⟩ ~ *vi* **1 a :** to become dense (as in consistency or texture) **:** grow thick or compact ⟨the mist ~*ed*⟩ **b :** to become concentrated in numbers, mass, or frequency **:** gather in a crowd or dense aggregation ⟨the Indians . . . were ~*ing* in Kentucky again —Rebecca Caudill⟩ ⟨all through the café the groups of players had ~*ed* —Winifred Bambrick⟩ **2 :** to grow blurred, obscure, or dark **:** become foggy or misty ⟨his speech ~*ed* as he drank on⟩ ⟨the weather ~*ed*⟩ **3 :** to increase in mass or measurement **:** grow broader or bulkier ⟨her tall straight figure had ~*ed* —Ellen Glasgow⟩ **4 :** to become more profound, intense, or intricate **:** grow complicated or keen ⟨the plot ~*s*⟩

thick·en·er \-k(ə)nə(r)\ *n* -s **:** one that thickens: as **a :** an apparatus for the sedimentation and collection of suspended solids in industrial liquids **b :** a mechanical device for removing part of the water from slush pulp

thickening *n* -s **1 :** the act of making or becoming thick ⟨underwent a gradual ~⟩ **2 :** something used to thicken (as flour in a gravy) **3 :** a thickened part or place

thicker *comparative of* THICK

thickest *superlative of* THICK

thick·et \'thikət, *usu* -əd+V\ *n* -s [fr. (assumed) ME *thikket*, fr. OE *thiccet*, fr. *thicce*, adj., thick] **1 :** a dense and usu. circumscribed growth of shrubbery or small trees **:** COPPICE ⟨~*s* of sumac, blackberries, and poison ivy —Nathaniel Burt⟩ **2 :** something likened to a thicket for density or impenetrability **:** TANGLE ⟨the myriad ~*s* and morasses of superstition —Alan Gregg⟩ ⟨ghost-written sources have built an impenetrable ~ around the truth —E.R.May⟩

thick·et·ed \-əd·əd, -ətəd\ *adj* **:** dotted or covered with thickets **:** abounding in thickets ⟨~ hills⟩

thick·ety \-əd·ē, -ət|, |i\ *adj* **:** full of thickets

thickhead \'=,=\ *n* **1 a :** WHISTLER 1b(1) **b :** a thick-knee (*Burhinus capensis*) of southern Africa **2 :** a stupid person **:** BLOCKHEAD **3 :** BLUETONGUE 1

thickheaded \'='==\ *adj* **1 :** having a thick head — used esp. in names of animals **2 :** dull of intellect **:** STUPID — **thick·head·ed·ly** *adv* — **thick·head·ed·ness** *n* -ES

thickheaded fly *n* **:** any of various flies comprising the family Conopidae, having a more or less elongate and sometimes pedicellate abdomen and a large head broader than the thorax, and being parasitic as larvae on other insects (as wasps)

thick·ish \'thikish, -kēsh\ *adj* **:** rather thick

thick-knee \'=,=\ *n* **:** STONE CURLEW 1; *esp* **:** a stone curlew of the genus *Burhinus*

thick lead *n* **:** a printer's lead of 3 points thickness

thicklips \'=,=\ *n pl but sing in constr* **:** one with thick lips

thick·ly *adv* [ME *thikkely*, fr. *thikke*, adj., thick + *-ly*] **:** in a thick manner

thickneck \"\ *n* **:** SCALLION 3

¹**thick·ness** *n* -ES [ME *thiknesse*, fr. OE *thicnes*, fr. *thicce*, adj., thick + *-nes* -ness] **1 :** the quality or state of being thick **2 :** the smallest of three dimensions ⟨the length, width, and ~ of a sheet of paper⟩ ⟨the length, height, and ~ of a wall⟩ ⟨the length, circumference, and ~ of a log⟩ **3 a :** viscous consistency ⟨boiled to the ~ of honey⟩ **b :** the condition of being smoky, foul, or foggy — used of the air **4 a :** roughness or harshness of breathing **b :** dullness of hearing **c :** a blurring or indistinctness of speech **5 :** the thick part of something ⟨this winding stair had been constructed in the ~ of the castle wall —Sax Rohmer⟩ **6 :** density of aggregation **:** CONCENTRATION ⟨the relative ~ of population in any given area —Edward Sapir⟩ **7 :** dullness of mind or perception **:** STUPIDITY ⟨made up my mind to forgive your ~ —Anne Green⟩ **8 :** LAYER, PLY, SHEET ⟨the number of ~*es* of boxboard was reduced from 244 to 60 —*Paper Trade Jour.*⟩ ⟨a single ~ of canvas⟩ **9 :** fullness of content or meaning **:** FIRMNESS, SOLIDITY, VOLUMINOUSNESS ⟨that forgotten moral ~ for which so many of us were sick —Herbert Gold⟩

²**thickness** \"\ *vt* -ED/-ING/-ES **1 :** to make uniform in thickness (as flooring planks) **2 :** to cover or coat in thicknessing

thickness gage *n* **:** FEELER 3

thicknessing *n* -s **1 :** a method of making a mold for a plaster cast or a metal casting in which a temporary thickness of wax or other material is put on the pattern or part of the unfinished mold and run out by heat or otherwise removed after it has been used to complete the mold **2 :** the thickness of wax or other material used in thicknessing

thickness piece *n* **:** a board or narrow flat used to outline a door or window in theatrical scenery and suggest the thickness of a wall

thickness ratio *n* **:** the ratio of the maximum thickness of an airfoil to the chord at that station

thick register *n* **:** CHEST REGISTER

thicks *pl of* THICK, *pres 3d sing of* THICK

¹**thickset** \'='=\ *adj* [ME *thikke sette*, fr. *thikke*, adv., thick + *sette*, *sett*, adj., set] **1 :** closely placed **:** densely planted **:** growing thickly ⟨a ~ wood⟩ **2 :** set or studded thickly or abundantly ⟨~ trees⟩ **3 :** having a thick body **:** BURLY **syn** see STOCKY

²**thickset** \"\ *n* **:** something thickset: as **a :** a cotton fabric with a short dense pile; *esp* **:** a durable corduroy for working clothes **b :** THICKET

thick shellbark *n* **:** BIG SHELLBARK

thickskin \'=,=\ *adj* **:** THICK-SKINNED

thick-skinned \'='=\ *adj* **1 :** having a thick skin **:** PACHYDERMATOUS **2 :** CALLOUS, INSENSITIVE ⟨there was a force in him that . . . subdued even a *thick-skinned*, conceited boy —Virginia Woolf⟩ ⟨being a *thick-skinned* man, he had no conception of how galling such remarks could be —C.B.Nordhoff & J.N. Hall⟩

thickskull \'=,=\ *n* **:** a dull-witted person **:** BLOCKHEAD

thickskulled \'='=\ *adj* **1 :** having a thick skull **2 :** dull of apprehension **:** slow to learn **:** INSENSITIVE, STUPID

thick-sown \'='=\ *adj* **:** sown closely together **:** thickly set **:** STUDDED ⟨speech *thick-sown* with French phrases⟩

thick space *n* **:** THREE-EM SPACE

thick stuff *n* **:** sided ship's timber more than 4 inches thick and less than 12

thick-tailed ray \'=,=-\ *n* **:** a ray of the suborder Sarcura

thick wind \'=,=\ *n* **:** a chronic defect of respiration in the horse due to obstruction of the respiratory passages (as by nasal polyps or deformed bones) — compare ROARING 2 — **thick-wind·ed** \'='windəd\ *adj*

thick-witted \'='==\ *adj* **:** dull or slow of mind **:** DENSE, STUPID — **thick-wit·ted·ly** *adv* — **thick-wit·ted·ness** *n* -ES

thief \'thēf\ *n, pl* **thieves** \-ēvz\ [ME *theef*, fr. OE *thēof;* akin to OHG *diob* thief, ON *thjōfr*, Goth *thiubs* thief, Lith *tupėti* to squat, crouch] **1 a :** one who steals esp. stealthily or secretly **:** one who commits theft or larceny **b** *archaic* **:** FREEBOOTER, ROBBER **c** *dial Brit* **:** SCOUNDREL, RASCAL, SCAMP **2 :** something that takes possession by stealth ⟨procrastination is the ~ of time⟩ **3** *also* **thief tube :** a device for taking a sample esp. of a liquid from a receptacle at any specified depth below the surface

thief ant *n* **:** any of several minute ants (esp. *Solenopsis molesta*) that nest near the galleries of other ants from which they steal food

thief·dom \'thēfdəm, -ftəm\ *or* **thieve·dom** \-ēvdəm\ *n* -s **1 :** THIEVES **2 :** the domain of thieves

thieftaker \'=,==\ *n, Brit* **:** a person who apprehends thieves or highwaymen

thief vault *n* **:** a vault over a piece of gymnastic apparatus executed from a one-foot takeoff in which both feet are thrust forward and over and the hands are placed on the apparatus as the body passes over it

thie·la·via \thē'lāvēə\ *n, cap* [NL, fr. F. von *Thielaw*, 19th cent. Ger. botanist + NL *-ia*] **:** a genus of fungi of the family Aspergillaceae but sometimes placed in the family Perisporiaceae having spherical brown perithecia and conidia that are endogenous and conidia that are borne in chains — see ROOT ROT

thie·la·vi·op·sis \(ˌ)thē,lāvē'äpsəs\ *n, cap* [NL, fr. *Thielavia* + *-opsis*] **:** a form genus of fungi (family Aspergillaceae) having conidia dark in color, borne in chains, and arising both endogenously and exogenously

thi·enyl \'thīə,nil\ *n* -s [ISV *thiophene* + *-yl*] **:** either of two univalent isomeric radicals C_4H_3S derived from thiophene by removal of a hydrogen atom from either the alpha or 2-position or the beta or 3-position

thieve \'thēv\ *vb* -ED/-ING/-S [fr. *thief*, after such pairs as E *grief: grieve*] *vi* **:** to practice or engage in theft **:** steal something **:** subsist by theft ~ *vt* **1 :** to take by theft **:** STEAL **2** *or* **thief :** to extract by means of a thief ⟨~ a sample of oil⟩ **syn** see ROB

thieve·less \'thēvləs\ *adj* [perh. alter. of *thowless*] *Scot* **1 :** LISTLESS **2 :** cold of manner or demeanor

thiev·ery \'thēv(ə)rē, -ri\ *n* -ES **1 :** the act, practice, or an instance of stealing **:** THEFT **2** *archaic* **:** something stolen

thieves' kitchen *n, Brit* **:** a slum or other area harboring thieves where children are easily led into crime

thieves' latin *n, usu cap L* **:** the cant of thieves

thiev·ing·ly *adv* [*thieving* (pres. part. of *thieve*) + *-ly*] **:** by means of theft

thiev·ish \'thēvish, -vēsh\ *adj* [ME *thevysch*, *thefyisch*, fr. *thef*, *theef* thief + *-ysch*, *-ish* -ish] **1** *obs* **:** infested by thieves ⟨bid me . . . walk in ~ ways —Shak.⟩ **2 a :** given to stealing ⟨~ magpies⟩ **b :** of, relating to, or characteristic of a thief **:** STEALTHY, SLY — **thiev·ish·ly** *adv* — **thiev·ish·ness** *n* -ES

thig \'thig\ *vb* **thigged; thigged; thigging; thigs** [ME *thiggen*, of Scand origin; akin to OSw *thiggia* to beg; akin to OE *thicgan* to accept, receive, OHG *diggen* to ask for, W *teg* beautiful, Lith *tėkti* to extend, suffice] *Scot* **:** BEG

thig·ger \-gə(r)\ *n* -s [ME(Sc) *thiggar*, fr. ME *thiggen* to beg + *-ar*, *-er*, *-ere* -er] *Scot* **:** BEGGAR

thigh \'thī\ *n* -s [ME *thigh*, *thie*, fr. OE *thēoh*, *thīoh;* akin to OHG *dioh* thigh, ON *thjō* buttock, MIr *tōn* buttocks, OSlav *tukŭ* fat, Skt *tavīti* he is strong — more at THUMB] **1 a :** the proximal segment of the vertebrate hind limb extending from the hip to the knee and supported by a single large bone — compare FEMUR **b :** the segment of the leg immediately distal to the thigh in a bird or in a quadruped in which the true thigh is obscured by skin or feathers or by its position in relation to the trunk — see COW illustration **c :** the femur of the leg of an insect **2 :** something resembling or covering a thigh ⟨the ground . . . fell back from the ~ of his moldboard —Stuart Cloete⟩ ⟨rubbed his oily hands on the ~*s* of his pants —Thomas Anderson⟩

thighbone \'=,=\ *n* [ME *the bane*, fr. *the*, *the*, *thigh*, *thie* thigh + *bane*, *boon*, *bon* bone] **:** FEMUR

thigh boot *n* **:** a boot whose upper part covers the thigh

thigmo- *comb form* [NL, fr. Gk *thigma* touch (fr. *thinganein* to touch, handle) + NL *-o-;* akin to L *fingere* to shape — more at DOUGH] **:** touch ⟨*thigmo*receptor⟩

thig·mo·cyte \'thigmə,sīt\ *n* -s [*thigmo-* + *-cyte*] **:** a blood cell of a crustacean that plays an important role in blood clotting

thig·mo·receptor \ˌthig(,)mō+\ *n* [*thigmo-* + *receptor*] **:** a sensory end organ responding to simple touch

thig·mo·tac·tic \ˌthigmə'taktik\ *adj* [fr. NL *thigmotaxis*, after such pairs as NL *hypotaxis:* E *hypotactic*] **:** STEREOTACTIC

thig·mo·tax·is \-'taksəs\ *n* [NL, fr. *thigmo-* + *-taxis*] **:** STEREOTAXIS

thig·mo·trop·ic \ˌthigmə'träpik\ *adj* [*thigmo-* + *-tropic*] **:** STEREOTROPIC

thig·mot·ro·pism \thig'mä trə,pizəm\ *n* [ISV *thigmo-* + *-tropism*] **:** STEREOTROPISM

thik \(ˌ)thik\ *pron* [ME *thike*, alter. of *thilke*] *dial Brit* **:** that same **:** THIS, THAT

thilk \(ˌ)thilk\ *pron* [ME *thilke*, fr. ¹*the* + *ilk*, *ilke* same — more at ILK] *obs* **:** that same **:** THIS, THAT

¹**thill** \'thil\ *n* -s [ME *thille*, perh. fr. OE, plank, thin board; akin to OHG *dili*, *dilla* plank, plank floor, ON *thili* plank, wainscot, *thilja* plank, planking, L *tellus* earth, Gk *tēlia* table, board, Skt *tala* surface, level] **:** the shaft of a vehicle

²**thill** \"\ *n* -s [ME, fireclay] **1** *dial Brit* **:** the floor of a coal mine **2** *dial Brit* **:** a thin stratum of fireclay

thill·er \'thilə(r)\ *n* -s **:** THILL HORSE

thill horse *n* [ME *thil horse*, fr. *thil*, *thille* thill + *hors*, *horse* horse] **:** a horse that goes between the shafts and supports them

thim·ble \'thimbəl\ *n* -s [ME *thymbyl*, prob. alter. of OE *thȳmel* thumbstall, fr. *thūma* thumb — more at THUMB] **1 a :** a cuplike cover made usu. of metal or plastic with a pitted surface and used to protect the end of a finger when pushing a needle through material **2 :** a more or less thimble-shaped apparatus, appendage, or fixture: as **a :** a tubular distance piece through which a bolt or pin passes (as a socket in a door-lock escutcheon plate to receive the knob spindle) **b :** a fixed or movable ring, tube, or lining **c :** a tubular cone for expanding a flue tube **d :** a circular wall box **e :** a metal socket for fixing a lead pipe to stoneware **f :** a ring of thin metal formed with a grooved outer edge so as to fit within an eye (as in a rope, sail, or rope splice) and protect it from chafing **g :** a short section of metal tubing fastened to the underside of a muzzle-loader for holding a ramrod **h :** a small tapering cup with a projecting arm used as a support for plates during firing in a kiln **i :** a thimble-shaped cup or shell (as of filter paper or fritted glass) for containing material to be extracted by solvents esp. in chemical analysis ⟨extraction ~*s*⟩ **3 :** THIMBLEFUL **4 a :** a foxglove (*Digitalis purpurea*) **b thimbles** *pl* **:** HAREBELL 1

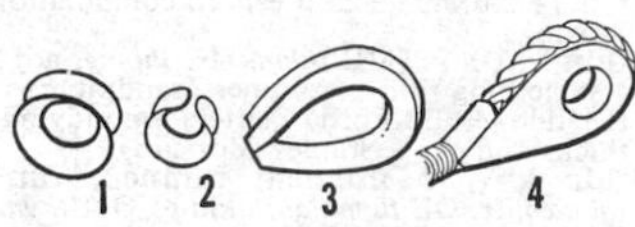

thimbles 2f: *1* round welded, *2* round open, *3* heart-shaped open, *4* solid

thimble and pea *n, Brit* **:** THIMBLERIG 1

thim·ble·berry \'thimbəl— *see* BERRY\ *n* **:** any of several American raspberries or blackberries having thimble-shaped fruit (esp. *Rubus occidentalis*, *R. parviflorus*, and *R. argutus*)

thimble chamber *n* [so called fr. its shape and size] **:** an ionization chamber for measuring roentgens

thimble-eye \'==,=\ *n* **1 :** CHUB MACKEREL **2 :** an eye in a plate used esp. as a deadeye

thimbleflower \'==,==\ *n* **1 :** a self-heal (*Prunella vulgaris*) **2 :** a foxglove (*Digitalis purpurea*) **3 :** a gilia (*Gilia capitata*) with lavender blue flowers in dense heads

thim·ble·ful \'thimbəl,fu̇l\ *n* -s **:** as much as a thimble will hold **:** a very small quantity

thimble lily *n* **1 :** an Australian plant (*Blandfordia nobilis*) cultivated for its ornamental racemose flowers **2 :** a lily (*Lilium bolanderi*) of western U.S. that is used as an ornamental and has whorled leaves and red-purple flowers with darker spots

¹**thim·ble·rig** \'thimbəl,rig\ *n* **1 :** a sleight-of-hand trick that is often practiced as a swindling operation (as at a fair) and that is played with three small cups shaped like thimbles and a small ball or pea that is so quickly shifted from under one cup to under another that the person watching is often misled — compare SHELL GAME **2 :** THIMBLERIGGER

²**thimblerig** \"\ *vt* **1 :** to swindle by thimblerig **2 :** to cheat by trickery — **thim·ble·rig·ger** \-gə(r)\ *n*

thimbleweed \'==,=\ *n* [so called fr. the conical receptacle] **1 :** CONEFLOWER a **2 :** any of various anemones: as **a :** WOOD ANEMONE a **b :** a common No. American anemone (*Anemone cylindrica*) with silky leathery sepals and crimson styles **c :** a similar plant (*A. riparia*) of northern No. America with white to red petaloid sepals **d :** an anemone (*A. virginiana*) of the eastern and central U.S. with variable often pubescent leathery or petaloid green to reddish or pure white sepals **3 :** PRAIRIE CLOVER

thi·mero·sal \thī'mərə,sal, -'mer-\ *n* -s [prob. fr. *thi-* + *mercury* + *-o-* + *salicylate*] **:** a cream-colored crystalline organic mercurial $C_9H_9HgNaO_2S$ used in medicine and surgery as an antiseptic and germicide and also as a biological preservative; sodium (ethyl-mercuri)-thio-salicylate

¹**thin** \'thin\ *adj* **thinner; thinnest** [ME *thinne*, fr. OE *thynne;* akin to OHG *dunni* thin, ON *thunnr*, L *tenuis* thin, Gk *tany-* long, stretched out, Skt *tanu* thin, OE *thennan* to stretch out, OHG *dennen* to stretch, ON *thenja*, Goth *ufthanjan*, L *tendere* to stretch, *tenēre* to hold, Gk *teinein* to stretch, Skt *tanoti* he stretches] **1 a :** having little extent from one surface to its opposite ⟨~ paper⟩ ⟨~ layer of paint⟩ ⟨~ slice of meat⟩ ⟨~ coin⟩ **b :** measuring little in cross section or diameter ⟨~ rope⟩ ⟨~ rod⟩ **2 :** not dense in arrangement or distribution **:** not compactly set or disposed ⟨~ stand of trees⟩ ⟨a ~ rain was falling⟩ ⟨his hair was ~ and lank⟩ **3 :** not well fleshed **:** not filled out **:** not plump or fat **:** SPARE, LEAN, SKINNY ⟨~ lips⟩ ⟨long ~ figure⟩ **4 a :** more fluid or rarefied than usual, normal, or average ⟨~ syrup⟩ ⟨~ batter⟩ ⟨~ air of the high mountains⟩ **b :** having less than the usual number of persons ⟨~ congregation⟩ ⟨~ attendance at a meeting⟩ **c :** few in number **:** not abundant **:** SCARCE **d :** scantily occupied, supplied, or provided ⟨~ assortment of goods on the counter⟩ ⟨~ ranks of volunteers⟩ **e** *of a market* **:** characterized by a paucity of bids or offerings so that transactions tend to be few and difficult to effect **5 a :** wanting substance, strength, or richness from lack of a usual constituent **:** WEAK, UNSATISFYING ⟨~ broth⟩ ⟨~ wine⟩ ⟨~ diet⟩ **b** *of soil* **:** POOR, INFERTILE **6 a :** lacking in solidity, substance, or force **:** UNSUBSTANTIAL, INADEQUATE ⟨novel with a ~ plot⟩ **b :** UNBELIEVABLE, UNCONVINCING ⟨~ excuse⟩ **c :** not up to expectations **:** disappointingly poor or hard ⟨have a ~ time of it⟩ **7 a** *of a voice* **:** wanting in fullness and resonance **:** somewhat feeble and shrill ⟨nearly soundless laughter ~ as a bat's cry —Elinor Wylie⟩ **b** *of harmony* **:** lacking richness of texture **c** *of reproduced sound* (1) **:** having prominent treble and weak bass tones (2) **:** having a narrow range of overtones **d** *of a speech sound* **:** FRONT 2 **8 a** *of light* **:** wanting in radiance ⟨~ winter sunshine⟩ **b** *of a color* **:** lacking in intensity or brilliance **:** DULL **9 a :** easily seen through or penetrated **:** TRANSPARENT, FLIMSY ⟨~ pretext⟩ ⟨~ disguise⟩ **b :** ready to snap or give way ⟨his patience was wearing ~⟩ **10** *of a photographic negative or print* **:** lacking sufficient density or contrast ⟨overexposure produces ~ images —E.F.Brewer⟩

syn THIN, SLENDER, SLIM, SLIGHT, TENUOUS, and RARE can mean, in common, not broad, thick, abundant, or dense. THIN implies comparatively little extension between two surfaces ⟨a *thin* board⟩ ⟨a *thin* layer of frosting⟩ or a comparatively small diameter of a cylindrical or roughly cylindrical object in proportion to its length ⟨a *thin* pole⟩ ⟨a *thin* wire⟩ and it implies also a comparative lack of flesh or substance giving a thing fullness, richness, or density ⟨a *thin* face⟩ ⟨a *thin* soup⟩ ⟨*thin* hair⟩ ⟨a play that is pretty *thin* in plot⟩ SLENDER chiefly implies leanness or spareness without suggesting gauntness or lankiness, usu. connoting gracefulness and good proportions ⟨*slender* hands⟩ ⟨a *slender* figure⟩ and is similar to THIN though implying, not strongly, a meagerness or scantiness ⟨*slender* success in an enterprise⟩ ⟨*slender* advice⟩ ⟨a *slender* chance of success⟩ SLIM is much like SLENDER when applied to persons or animals, though suggesting more fragility, gauntness, or lack of flesh than grace or good proportion ⟨very *slim* children⟩ and it is like SLENDER in extended meaning, though stressing meagerness and scantiness more strongly ⟨a *slim* chance of

recovery⟩ ⟨a *slim* pay envelope⟩ SLIGHT stresses smallness rather than thinness, seldom suggesting height or length as do SLENDER and, sometimes, SLIM ⟨a *slight* woman of very small frame⟩ and in application to things, it is often derogatory, applying to what is inappreciable or inadequate ⟨a *slight* difference in age between two men⟩ ⟨a very *slight* imaginative quality in a book⟩ ⟨a *slight* compensation for great effort⟩ TENUOUS implies extreme thinness ⟨a *tenuous* thread⟩ ⟨the *tenuous* filament of a spider's web⟩ or sheerness ⟨a *tenuous* and almost fully transparent fabric⟩ and its most common extended use implies an extreme lack of density, solidity, or substance ⟨*tenuous* mists along the road⟩ ⟨a mind given to *tenuous* ideas⟩ ⟨a *tenuous* grasp of a difficult subject⟩ RARE is applied chiefly to air or gases and implies tenuousness or lack of density ⟨the extremely *rare* atmosphere of the stratosphere⟩
— **into thin air** *adv* : without a trace : UTTERLY, COMPLETELY ⟨his whole fortune suddenly vanished *into thin air*⟩ — **on thin ice** *adv (or adj)* : in a position or situation requiring wariness, dexterity, or tact if trouble or embarrassment is to be avoided : on dangerous ground — **out of thin air** : out of nothing : without substantial basis, precedent, or evidence ⟨create stories *out of thin air*⟩ ⟨arbitrary authority which sets up standards *out of thin air* —A.T.Weaver⟩

2thin \"\ *adv* **thinner; thinnest** [ME *thinne*, fr. *thinne*, adj., thin] : THINLY — used esp. in combinations ⟨*thin*-clad⟩ ⟨*thin*-flowing⟩

3thin \"\ *n* -s [ME *thinne*, fr. *thinne*, adj., thin] : a thin part : something thin or thinner ⟨sandpipers running in the ~ of the tide —F.M.Ford⟩ ⟨letters embodying sharply contrasted thicks and ~s —Stanley Morison⟩

4thin \"\ *vb* **thinned; thinned; thinning; thins** [ME *thinnen*, fr. OE *thynnian*; akin to ON *thynna* to thin; causative fr. the root of E 1*thin*] *vt* : to make thin or thinner : **a :** to reduce in thickness or depth : ATTENUATE **b :** to make less dense or viscous : make more fluid : RAREFY ⟨~ glue with alcohol⟩ **c :** to make less strong or less rich : make weak : cause to lose vigor, force, or effectiveness : DILUTE ⟨~ wine with water⟩ ⟨the ballad, with its old religious, military, or tragic contents, was *thinned* out into the sentimental popular song —Lewis Mumford⟩ **d :** to make lean or slender : cause to lose flesh ⟨*thinned* by weeks of privation⟩ **e :** to make less crowded or less populated — used often with *out* **f :** to remove surplus plants or trees from (a bed, nursery, woodland) so as to improve the growth of the rest; *also* : to take out (as superfluous buds or shoots) : PRUNE **g :** to reduce the bulk of (hair) by spaced cutting with specially notched shears ~ *vi* **1 :** to grow or become thin or thinner : become less thick, dense, or crowded ⟨his hair is *thinning*⟩ — used often with *down* or *out* or *off* ⟨the limestone layer *thinned* out and soon came to an end⟩ ⟨toward the city limits the houses began to ~ out⟩ ⟨the stream had *thinned* down to a mere trickle⟩ **2 :** to become weak, ineffective, or less urgent ⟨this desire ~s out —M.L.Anshen⟩

syn ATTENUATE, EXTENUATE, DILUTE, RAREFY: THIN is a general term indicating reduction in thickness, density, weight, intensity, strength, or concentration ⟨*thinning* paint⟩ ⟨*thinning* the trees in a woodlot⟩ ⟨the crowd *thinned* a little⟩ ⟨the *thinning* ranks of true cowboys —*Amer. Guide Series: Texas*⟩ ⟨the lines of magnetic and electric force *thinned* out geometrically with the square of the distance from their origin —S.F.Mason⟩ ATTENUATE may indicate thinning by mechanical or chemical means or thinning accompanied by enervation, enfeeblement, or other weakening ⟨*attenuate* wire by drawing it out⟩ ⟨the powerful frame *attenuated* by spare living —Charles Dickens⟩ ⟨the apparent brightness of the stars as we see them, with their light *attenuated* by distance and the cosmic haze —G.W.Gray b. 1886⟩ ⟨illusions which science can *attenuate* or destroy —J.W.Krutch⟩ EXTENUATE may sometimes mean to emaciate; it usu. suggests a diminution of significance and effect ⟨the whole tendency of modern thought and modern opinion and modern manners is to *extenuate* the responsibility of human nature —Compton Mackenzie⟩ DILUTE indicates a weakening of concentration by addition of a weakening, neutralizing, or counteracting agency ⟨*dilute* the paint with turpentine⟩ ⟨acid *diluted* with water⟩ ⟨explosives in nuclear weapons, when *diluted*, provide the fuel required for most peaceful atom products —*New Republic*⟩ ⟨the strength of passionate emotion is *diluted* to the languor of interminable sentimentality —R.A. Hall b. 1911⟩ ⟨the pioneer spirit has been *diluted* by new race mixtures, its confidence shaken by new social trends —*Amer. Guide Series: Minn.*⟩ RAREFY indicates a thinning in density, sometimes, with reference to matters intellectual or emotional, by refining and eliminating all dross or by imparting a tenuous or even nebulous quality ⟨*rarefied* mountain air⟩ ⟨these claims are argued in the *rarefied* atmosphere of academic discussion —M.S.Handler⟩ ⟨a civilization so *rarefied* that it is almost decadent —Santha Rama Rau⟩

thin-boiling starch \ˈ=,==-\ *n* : SOLUBLE STARCH

1thine [ME *thin*, fr. OE *thīn*, gen. of *thū, thu* thou; akin to OHG *dīn* (gen. of *dū, du* thou), ON *thīn* (gen. of *thū* thou), Goth *theina* (gen. of *thu* thou) — more at THOU] *obs possessive of* 1THOU

2thine \(ˌ)thīn\ *adj* [ME *thin*, fr. OE *thīn* — more at THY] *archaic* : THY — used esp. before a word beginning with a vowel or *h* ⟨give every man ~ ear, but few thy voice —Shak.⟩ ⟨a true report which I heard . . . of ~ acts —2 Chron 9:5 (AV)⟩ ⟨peace be to ~ helpers —1 Chron 12:18 (AV)⟩

3thine \"\ *pron, sing or pl in constr* [ME *thin*, fr. OE *thīn*, adj., thy — more at THY] : something belonging to thee ⟨all that I have is ~ —Lk 15:31 (AV)⟩ : thy one or thy ones — used without a following noun as a pronoun equivalent in meaning to the adjective *thy* ⟨not my will, but ~, be done —Lk 22:42 (AV)⟩ ⟨mine eyes, even sociable to the show of ~, fall fellowly drops —Shak.⟩; often used after *of* to single out one or more members of a class belonging to or connected with the one that is being addressed ⟨thou too, desert stream! no pool of ~ . . . did e'er reflect the stately virgin's robe —S.T.Coleridge⟩ or merely to identify something or someone as belonging to or connected with the one that is being addressed without any implication of membership in a more extensive class ⟨what means that hand upon that breast of ~ —Shak.⟩ ⟨those linen cheeks of ~ —Shak.⟩; used archaically esp. in biblical, ecclesiastical, solemn, or poetic language and still surviving to some extent in ordinary usage in the speech of Friends esp. among themselves; compare YOURS

1thing \ˈthiŋ\ *n* -s [ME, fr. OE, thing, assembly, reason; akin to OHG *ding* thing, assembly, reason, ON *thing* object of value, assembly, parliament, Goth *theihs* time, and prob. to Gk *teinein* to stretch — more at THIN] **1 a :** a matter of concern : AFFAIR ⟨let's get this ~ over with quickly⟩ ⟨several ~s to attend to⟩ **b things** *pl* : state of affairs in general or within a specified or implied sphere ⟨~s are getting better⟩ ⟨that wouldn't change ~s between us⟩ ⟨how are ~s going at the office⟩ **c :** a particular state of affairs : SITUATION, COMPLICATION ⟨try to look at this ~ from another viewpoint⟩ **d :** EVENT, CIRCUMSTANCE ⟨that shooting was a terrible ~⟩ ⟨a lucky ~ no one was lost in the fire⟩ **2 a :** DEED, ACT, ACCOMPLISHMENT — used commonly as cognate object of *do* ⟨expects to do great ~s⟩ ⟨that was a mean ~ to do to your brother⟩ ⟨a ~ worth doing is worth doing well⟩ **b :** a product of work or activity ⟨likes to make ~s with his hands⟩ **c :** the end or aim of effort or activity ⟨the ~ is now to get well⟩ ⟨liked to put first ~s first⟩ **3 a :** whatever exists or is conceived to exist as a separate entity or as a distinct and individual quality, fact, or idea : a separable or distinguishable object of thought ⟨there is a name for every ~⟩ **b :** the real or actual essence or substance as distinguished from its appearances or from a name, word, or symbol that stands for it : REALITY ⟨in talking of *its* appearances we appear to distinguish the ~ from the appearances —A.J.Ayer⟩ ⟨a philosopher who deals with words and not ~s⟩ — compare THING-IN-ITSELF **4 a :** an entity that can be apprehended or known as having existence in space or time as distinguished from what is purely an object of thought ⟨virtue is not a ~, but an attribute of a ~⟩ **b :** an inanimate object as distinguished from a living being **c things** *pl* : POSSESSIONS, GOODS ⟨assemble the inhabitants, their cattle, and their ~s⟩ **d :** whatever may be possessed or owned or be the object of a right — distinguished from *person* **e :** an article of clothing ⟨haven't a ~ to wear to the party⟩ ⟨some new ~s for Easter⟩ ⟨time to put on your ~s and come to dinner⟩ ⟨get your outdoor ~s⟩ **f things** *pl* : equipment or utensils esp. for a particular purpose ⟨bring in the tea ~s⟩ **g things** *pl* : personal belongings : EFFECTS ⟨packed his ~s and left⟩ ⟨his ~s are always lying around⟩ **5 :** an object or entity that cannot or need not be precisely designated ⟨what's that ~ in your left hand⟩ ⟨do you ever use this ~⟩ ⟨what does that round ~ on the end of the motor do⟩ ⟨churches . . . turned into mosques . . . or used for army stores and ~s —Rose Macaulay⟩ **6 a :** DETAIL, QUALITY, POINT, PARTICULAR ⟨worrying over every little ~⟩ ⟨the ~ I don't like about this plan⟩ ⟨the important ~ to remember in night driving⟩ **b :** a material or substance (as food, drink, medicine) of a specified kind ⟨avoid sweet or starchy ~s⟩ **7 :** something that is said, told, or thought ⟨say the right ~⟩ ⟨think hard ~s of a person⟩: **a :** a written or spoken discourse ⟨that any ~ of mine is fit to live —P.B.Shelley⟩ **b :** a witty retort or story : JEST ⟨got off some good ~s in his speech⟩ **c :** IDEA, NOTION ⟨says the first ~ that comes into his head⟩ **d :** a piece of news or information ⟨couldn't get a ~ out of him⟩ ⟨refused to tell me a ~ about what he was doing⟩ **8 :** BEING, INDIVIDUAL ⟨not a living ~ was to be seen on that rocky expanse⟩ — used often in pity ⟨poor little ~⟩ or contempt ⟨how could you ever speak to that vile ~⟩ or reproach ⟨you selfish ~, you⟩ or affection ⟨she's a pretty little ~⟩ **9 :** an artistic composition (as a piece of music) ⟨has written many popular ~s for small bands⟩ **10 a :** way of acting or behaving ⟨always tried to do the decent ~⟩; *esp* : the proper, right, desirable, required, or fashionable way of behaving, talking, dressing — used with *the* ⟨rolled-up blue jeans were the ~ then among the teen-agers⟩ **b** *chiefly Brit* : one in normal health and good spirits — used with *the* ⟨you've seemed nervous and not quite the ~ ever since the reception —Margery Allingham⟩ **11 :** an irrational fear of or strong prejudice concerning something : a mild obsession or phobia ⟨she has this ~, lately, about driving at night⟩ — **a thing or two :** something worth knowing or telling : something proving equality or superiority in knowledge ⟨knows *a thing or two* about finance⟩; *also* : words of blunt advice or reproach ⟨if he does it again I'll certainly tell him *a thing or two*⟩ — **first thing** *adv* : before anything else : right away : IMMEDIATELY ⟨I'll get that letter off *first thing*⟩ ⟨promised to call *first thing* in the morning⟩ — **good thing :** a profitable investment, enterprise, or transaction ⟨made a *good thing* out of stamp collecting⟩ ⟨put him onto a *good thing* in the stock market⟩; *also* : information leading to such a transaction — **of all things** *adv* : least appropriately : with the least degree of logical justification : most surprisingly ⟨people still call it, *of all things*, a system of free, individual initiative —Max Ascoli⟩ — **sure thing :** something safe to wager on : something certain to take place : a contestant certain to win

2thing \ˈthiŋ(g), -ŋk\ *also* **ting** \ˈtiŋ\ *n* -s *usu cap* [*thing* fr. ON & Icel; Icel *thing* assembly, parliament, fr. ON; *ting* fr. Norw, Dan, & Sw, fr. or akin to ON *thing* — more at 1THING] : a legislative or judicial assembly in Iceland and other Scandinavian countries

thing·a·bob \ˈthiŋə,bäb\ *or* **thing·a·ma·bob** \ˈthiŋəm(ə)-,bäb\ *n* -s [by alter.] : THINGUMBOB

t hinge *cap T, or* **tee hinge** *n* : a hinge having the appearance of a letter T when opened : a strap hinge of which one leaf is replaced by a butt

T hinge

thing·hood \ˈthiŋ,hu̇d\ *n* **1 :** the quality or state of being a thing : objective existence : THINGNESS ⟨reducing human life to ~ —C.J. Rolo⟩ **2 :** something that constitutes a thing as such ⟨~ must also include objective change —C.I.Lewis⟩

thing in action : CHOSE IN ACTION

thing·i·ness \-ŋēnəs\ *n* -ES : the quality or state of being thingy

thing-in-itself \ˈ=ˈ=ˈ=\ *n, pl* **things-in-themselves** [trans. of G *ding an sich*] : an ultimate reality unqualified by the subjective modes of human perception and thought : a metaphysical reality — compare NOUMENON, PHENOMENON 2a(4)

thing·ish \ˈthiŋish\ *adj* : THINGY

thing-language \ˈ=,==\ *n* : a language whose terms refer to spatiotemporal things and events and their physical attributes — contrasted with *sense-datum language;* compare PHYSICAL LANGUAGE

thinglike \ˈ=,=\ *adj* : like a physical object : lacking consciousness or will — **thing·like·ness** *n*

thing·man \ˈthiŋmən\ *n, pl* **thingmen** [trans. of ON *thingmathr*] : a member of a Scandinavian legislative or judicial assembly; *specif* : HOUSECARL

thing·ness \ˈthiŋnəs\ *n* -ES : the fact, quality, or condition of objective existence : objective reality

things personal *n pl* : PERSONAL PROPERTY

thing·stead \ˈthiŋz,ted, -ŋ,st-\ *n* [2*thing* + *stead*] : the place where a Scandinavian assembly is held

thing·um \ˈthiŋəm\ *n* -s [irreg. fr. 1*thing*] : THINGUMBOB

thing·um·a·jig *or* **thing·a·ma·jig** \ˈthiŋəmə,jig\ *n* -s [irreg. fr. *thingum*] : something which is hard to classify or whose name is not known ⟨a patented ~ that prevents salt from caking —Sheila Hibben⟩

thing·um·bob *or* **thing·um·a·bob** \ˈthiŋəm(ə),bäb\ *n* -s [irreg. fr. *thingum*] : something whose specific name or designation has been forgotten or is not known ⟨mysterious electrical ~s that go off with a bang —*Literary Rev.*⟩

thing·um·my \ˈthiŋəmē\ *n* -ES [irreg. fr. *thingum*] : THINGUMBOB, THINGUMAJIG ⟨promise . . . that you will . . . not invent anything other than a silent burglar ~ —A.J.Coutts⟩

thingy \ˈthiŋē\ *adj* [1*thing* + -*y*] **1 :** of, relating to, or having the characteristics of things : REAL, MATERIAL **2 :** concerned with or devoted to real things or practical matters

thinite \ˈthī,nīt, ˈthi,n-\ *adj, usu cap* [*Thinis* (This), ancient city in central Upper Egypt + E -*ite*, n. suffix] : of or relating to the period of culture in Egypt during the First and Second Dynasties from 3000 B.C. to 2778 B.C., characterized by the stereotyping of forms and relative dimensions of statues and reliefs

1think *vi* **thought; thought; thinking; thinks** [ME *thinken* (past *thoughte*), fr. OE *thyncan* (past *thūhte*, past part. *gethūht*); akin to OHG *dunken* to seem (past *dūhta*, past part. *gidūht*), ON *thykkja* (past *thōtti*, past part. *thōtt*), Goth *thunkjan* (past *thūhta*), L *tongēre* to know] *obs* : SEEM, APPEAR — usu. used impersonally ⟨him *thought* that in his depth of sleep he saw a soldier armed —Thomas Heywood⟩; compare METHINKS

2think \ˈthiŋk\ *vb* **thought** \ˈthȯt, *usu* -ȯd·+V\ *or dial* **thunk** \ˈthəŋk\ **thought** *or dial* **thunk; thinking; thinks** [ME *thenken* (past *thoughte*, past part. *thought, ythought*), fr. OE *thencan* (past *thōhte*, past part. *gethōht*); akin to OHG *denken* to think (past *dāhta*, past part. *gidāht*), ON *thekkja* to perceive (past *thātti*), Goth *thankjan* to deliberate (past *thāhta*), L *tongēre* to know — more at THANK] *vt* **1 a :** to form or have (as a thought) in the mind ⟨few people think accurately — and ~ things not words —O.W.Holmes †1935⟩ ⟨"an evil bird," he *thought* —Louis Bromfield⟩ ⟨ashamed to ~ how easily we capitulate —R.W.Emerson⟩ **b** *dial chiefly Brit* : FEEL 2b ⟨men should ~ shame to be less heroic —Gilbert Highet⟩ **2 :** to have in one's mind as an intention or desire : INTEND, HOPE ⟨*thought* to return early⟩ ⟨yet manhood remained to act the thing I *thought* —P.B.Shelley⟩ **3 a** (1) **:** to have as an opinion : BELIEVE ⟨*thought* the question might arise —F.J. Haskin⟩ ⟨a fine performance, he *thought*⟩ (2) **:** to have as an opinion without sufficient basis in fact ⟨comes to ~ that the prison is the world —J.B.Priestley⟩ ⟨we know, or ~ we know, . . . the critical method —T.S.Eliot⟩ ⟨was first *thought* to have drowned —*Time*⟩ **b :** to regard as : take for : CONSIDER ⟨may adjourn them to such time as he shall ~ proper —*U.S. Constitution*⟩ ⟨~ it not unfair to suggest —Virgil Thomson⟩ ⟨put a copy on order . . . if you ~ it your kind of book —*Times Lit. Supp.*⟩ **4 a :** to reflect on : PONDER ⟨these deeds must not be *thought* after these ways —Shak.⟩ ⟨~ what their children would be —E.T.Thurston⟩ — often used with *over* ⟨said he would ~ the matter over⟩ **b :** to determine by reflecting ⟨was ~*ing* what to do next⟩ — often used with *out* ⟨parents must ~ out for themselves what this means to their own young —Dorothy Barclay⟩ **5 :** to call to mind : REMEMBER ⟨*thought* to ask him the trick of it —Anne S. Mehdevi⟩ **6 :** to create or devise by thinking ⟨the Almighty . . . *thought* the archetypes of all things and devised their variations —William James⟩ — usu. used with *out* or *up* ⟨remain calm and ~ out a solution —James Hewitt⟩ ⟨*thought* up a caption that exactly covered the whole idea —William Murrell⟩ **7 a** *obs* : SUSPECT ⟨he, ~*ing* no harm, agreed —Daniel Defoe⟩ **b :** EXPECT ⟨*thought* to find him at home⟩ **8 :** to believe to exist ⟨there be who ~ not God at all —John Milton⟩ **9 :** to bring (as into a specified position or condition) by thinking ⟨a novelist has *thought* . . . characters into existence —Bernard DeVoto⟩ ⟨learned to ~ his feelings by way of French symbolism —Harold Rosenberg⟩ **10 a** (1) **:** to center one's thoughts on : have one's mind full of ⟨talks and ~s nothing but airplanes⟩ (2) **:** to be imbued with the thoughts and the ways of thinking that are characteristic of a people or a group ⟨many white men . . . were ~*ing* black and advocating absolute equality between the two races —*Cape Times*⟩ **b :** to bring before one's mind clearly (as by imagining or recalling) : form a mental picture of ⟨found it difficult to ~ infinity⟩ **11 :** to subject to the processes of logical thought esp. in order to reach a conclusion — usu. used with *out* or *through* ⟨wanted to be left alone to ~ things out —Victoria Sackville-West⟩ ⟨always ~s the problems through before acting⟩ ~ *vi* **1 a :** to exercise the powers of judgment, conception, or inference as distinguished from simple sense perception ⟨it is the power to ~ which makes us human —Vicki Baum⟩ **b** (1) **:** to exercise the powers of thought with regard to a particular matter ⟨would do well to ~ again —J.F. Golay⟩ ⟨will ~ twice before he risks another defeat —L.C. Douglas⟩ — often used with a preposition (as *about, of,* or *on*) ⟨the American child is taught to ~ about each situation as it comes up —Margaret Mead⟩ (2) **:** to call an idea (as of a possible solution or a device) to mind by mental effort — usu. used with *of* ⟨the best plan they could ~ of was to leave⟩ **2 a :** to have the mind engaged in reflection : MEDITATE — usu. used with a preposition (as *about, of, on,* or *upon*) ⟨enabled me to ~ with tender affection upon her loyalty and devotion —*Nashville Tennessean*⟩ **b** (1) **:** to have something (as a plan) in the mind — usu. used with *of* or *about* ⟨the department is ~*ing* of opening new message centers —Armand Schwab⟩ (2) **:** to consider the suitability (as of a person under consideration for a vacant position) — usu. used with *of* ⟨*thought* of him for the presidential nomination⟩ **3 a** (1) **:** to have a thought in the mind : have a thought come into the mind — usu. used with *of* ⟨*thought* of his old home when he saw the house⟩ (2) **:** to have or form a particular idea : REGARD — usu. used with *of* and *as* ⟨will ~ of himself as a partner —Thomas Munro⟩ ⟨was to ~ of nothing as being his own —K.S.Latourette⟩ **b :** to have an opinion — usu. used with *of* and an adverb or an adverbial phrase that indicates the kind of opinion ⟨*thought* well of him —Carol L. Thompson⟩ ⟨~s a great deal of his physician —Walt Whitman⟩ ⟨~s nothing of his brother⟩ **4 :** to have consideration, regard, or concern — usu. used with *of* ⟨a man must ~ of his family, his realm, his empire —Francis Hackett⟩ **5 :** to be aware (as of the future) : EXPECT, SUSPECT ⟨may strike when you least ~⟩ — sometimes used with *for* ⟨will get along better than he ~s for —Walt Whitman⟩

syn SPECULATE, REFLECT, REASON, DELIBERATE, COGITATE: THINK is a general term, nearly always capable of being substituted for any of the following terms. SPECULATE is often used in reference to thought, logical and analytic or not, on that on which certainty is impossible or unlikely ⟨what caused the Mound Builder culture . . . to die out? We can only *speculate* —R.W.Murray⟩ ⟨in times of peace the specialists of war . . . may only *speculate* about the effect of new weapons —S.L.A. Marshall⟩ REFLECT is likely to suggest an unhurried contemplative consideration involving recall and reexamination ⟨she could *reflect* in long, sane meditations above the uneasy sea of her pain —Arnold Bennett⟩ ⟨the standpoint of the man who did not criticize or *reflect*, but accepted simply —G.L.Dickinson⟩ REASON indicates careful attention to rational or logical thought sequences, to orderly thought processes from evidence or premise to conclusion ⟨Lincoln's way with any problem was to examine it from all sides and *reason* it out intellectually —Ruth P. Randall⟩ ⟨perhaps a close study of the behavior of very young children . . . may provide some valuable hints, but it seems dangerous to *reason* from such experiments —Edward Sapir⟩ ⟨found himself *reasoning* in a circle⟩ DELIBERATE implies a pondering with careful thought, unhurried procedure, and fair consideration of various aspects ⟨a nationwide representative assembly, with power to *deliberate* although not actually to make laws —F.A.Ogg & Harold Zink⟩ ⟨the future relations of the two countries could now be *deliberated* on with a hope of settlement —J.A.Froude⟩ COGITATE indicates deep, intent, sometimes labored thinking ⟨*cogitating* over the problem for hours⟩ ⟨*cogitated* about the question a noticeable time before answering⟩

syn CONCEIVE, IMAGINE, FANCY, REALIZE, ENVISAGE, ENVISION: THINK, often general and not specific, may indicate merely the mental harboring of an idea; it may imply conscious mental effort to achieve a definite picture or clear impression ⟨helpful to *think* of two economic systems operating simultaneously throughout rural parts of the Northeast —P.E.James⟩ ⟨found church a very good place for *thinking* her love affairs into their right proportion —Sheila Kaye-Smith⟩ CONCEIVE may imply forming an idea and nurturing and developing it to serviceable fullness as a concept ⟨for the poem Coleridge *conceived* in theory as well as evolved in practice a quantitative metric —W.R. Parker⟩ ⟨now *conceived* a plan of returning to France and obtaining a force to conquer Canada —J.C.Fitzpatrick⟩ IMAGINE may imply the process of free mental visualization or pictorialization that is often vivid, relatively unguided, and unchecked by rationality ⟨a marvelously *imagined* description of the state of blessed souls —H.O.Taylor⟩ ⟨by burning or otherwise destroying the image he *imagines* that he kills his foe —J.G.Frazer⟩ ⟨could *imagine* easily original plots for stories or plays, but never received any impulse to write them —G.W.Russell⟩ FANCY, often interchangeable with IMAGINE, may imply a dreamy, indulgent fondness for unguided contemplation of the unreal ⟨*fancied* he saw them take each other's hands and dance a strange and monstrous dance, the dance of the Annihilation of All Life —J.C.Powys⟩ ⟨who *fancied* she had been transferred to a fairy palace —William Black⟩ REALIZE suggests a vividness of conception or imagination whereby a grasp is attained of the significance of the matter being thought about ⟨saw a tin lamp burning kerosene, and *realized* its possibilities —Allan Nevins⟩ ⟨burning with the passion of infinitely *realized* and therefore eternally restless love —W.L.Sullivan⟩ ENVISAGE and ENVISION may imply a clarity of conception or imagination with clear-cut detail ⟨had a flair for *envisaging* the possible molecular structures of compounds —S.F.Mason⟩ ⟨*envisaged* the flat land beyond the Alps in Lombardy as he later *envisaged* Catalonia beyond the Pyrenees and the right bank of the Middle Rhine, not as country to be conquered but as a belt of protection beyond a frontier —Hilaire Belloc⟩ ⟨includes the territories *envisioned* by the tsarist planners of 1914–16 as part of the Russian empire —D.J.Dallin⟩ ⟨the approaching truck driver tramped down hard; brakes squealed; the photographer momentarily *envisioned* a smashed truck and mangled driver —G.R.Stewart⟩ ⟨those early predictors who *envisioned* great ports in the shores of Lake Pontchartrain —*Amer. Guide Series: La.*⟩
— **think better of :** to reconsider and make a better decision ⟨started to protest but *thought better of* it —Irwin Shaw⟩ — **think long** *dial Brit* : LONG, YEARN — **think much** *obs* : to consider serious or burdensome ⟨*thought* not *much* to clothe his enemies —John Milton⟩

3think \"\ *n* -s **1 :** an act of thinking ⟨has to make up his mind in a deep hard ~ —Jerome Ellison⟩ ⟨if he thinks he can fool me, he has another ~ coming⟩ **2 :** something (as an idea or opinion) that is thought ⟨let's exchange ~s⟩

4think \"\ *adj* **1 :** of or relating to thinking: as **a :** used for thinking **b :** appealing to the mind ⟨a new ~ film⟩ **2 :** of or relating to think pieces ⟨a frequently quoted ~ columnist⟩

1think·able \ˈthiŋkəbəl\ *adj* **1 :** capable of being thought about ⟨concepts that are easy enough to be ~⟩ **2 :** capable of being made actual : conceivably possible ⟨nationalism was at this time scarcely ~ —*Times Lit. Supp.*⟩ — **think·able·ness** \-nəs\ *n* -ES — **think·ably** \-blē,-bli\ *adv*

²**thinkable** \"\ *n* -S : one that is thinkable ⟨wants to discover if there are any intuitively presented ~*s* —Norman Malcolm⟩

think·er \'thiŋkə(r)\ *n* -S [ME *thenkare,* fr. *thenken* to think + *-are, -er, -ere* -er — more at THINK] : one that thinks: as **a** : one that thinks in a specified way ⟨a superficial ~⟩ **b** : one that has special capacity for thinking : one that devotes himself to study and thought rather than to action : PHILOSOPHER ⟨widely known as an original ~ and a distinguished teacher —R.G.Cole⟩ **c** : MIND, BRAIN

¹**thinking** *n* -S [ME *thenkinge,* fr. gerund of *thenken* to think] **1** : the action of using one's mind to produce thoughts ⟨~ is mainly . . . performed with words and other symbols —J.B.S. Haldane⟩ ⟨plain living and high ~⟩ **2 thinkings** *pl* : THOUGHTS, MEDITATIONS ⟨full of ~*s* about his people at home —Mark Twain⟩ ⟨speak to me as to thy ~*s* —Shak.⟩ **3 a** : OPINION, JUDGMENT ⟨is to my ~ the highest point that poetry has ever reached —T.S.Eliot⟩ **b** : the kind of thought that belongs (as to a period, group, or person) ⟨in modern ~ the emotion is viewed as a response —J.E.Anderson⟩ ⟨the traditions of economic ~⟩

²**thinking** *adj* [fr. pres. part. of ²*think*] **1** : having or using the ability to think ⟨admires his high-*thinking* offspring —*Newsweek*⟩ **2** : marked by use of the intellect : THOUGHTFUL, RATIONAL ⟨~ people throughout the country were concerned with social justice —Mary H. Vorse⟩ — **think·ing·ness** *n* -ES

thinking cap *n* : a state or mood in which one thinks ⟨put on your *thinking caps* —Zane Grey⟩

think·ing·ly *adv* : in a thinking manner; *esp* : with awareness ⟨~ abandoned the dog⟩

thinking-machine \'==,=\ *n* : COMPUTER a

thinking part *n* : a theatrical role that has no lines to be spoken : silent part

think piece *n* : a news article consisting chiefly of background material, generalized observations, and personal opinion and analysis as distinguished from direct factual news reporting — compare DOPE STORY

thinks *pres part of* THINK, *pl of* THINK

think-so \'=,=\ *n* -S [fr. the phrase *think so*] : an unsupported opinion

thin lead *n* : a 1-point or 1½-point printer's lead

thin·ly *adv* [ME *thynnelich,* fr. *thynne, thinne* thin + *-lich, -liche* -ly] : in a thin manner : INSUFFICIENTLY ⟨~ disguised⟩ SPARSELY ⟨~ clad⟩ ⟨~ settled⟩

thinned *past of* THIN

¹**thinner** *comparative of* THIN

²**thin·ner** \'thinə(r)\ *n* -S [⁴*thin* + *-er*] : one that thins: as **a** : a volatile liquid (as turpentine) used esp. to thin paint, lacquer, and cement to the desired consistency — compare DILUENT a **b** : one that adds thinners and driers to paste mixtures to make liquid paint or varnish **c** : one that pulls out superfluous plants or picks off superfluous buds or fruit to improve the crop

thin·ness \'thinnəs\ *n* -ES [ME *thinnesse,* fr. OE *thynnes,* fr. *thynne* thin + *-nes* -ness] : the quality or state of being thin

thinnest *superlative of* THIN

thinning *pres part of* THIN

thinning shears *n pl* : shears with a serrate blade for thinning hair

thin·nish \'thinish, -nēsh\ *adj* : somewhat thin : inclined to thinness ⟨~ arms⟩ ⟨~ humor⟩

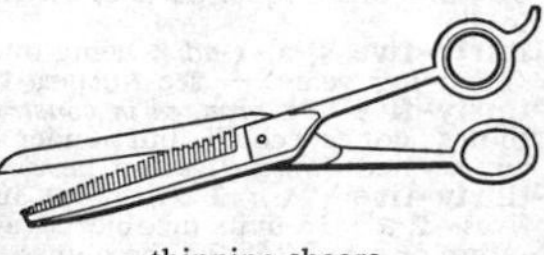
thinning shears

thino·cor·i·dae \,thinə'kȯrə,dē, ,thīn-\ *n pl, cap* [NL, fr. *Thinocorus,* type genus + *-idae*] : a family of So. American birds (suborder Charadrii) comprising the seed snipes

thi·noc·o·rus \thə'näkərəs, thī'n-\ *n, cap* [NL, fr. Gk *thin-, this* shore, sandbank + NL *-o-* + *-corus* (irreg. fr. Gk *korys* helmet); perh. akin to Gk *thyein* to rage, seethe — more at DUST, CORYTHOSAURUS] : the type genus of the family Thinocoridae

thin register *n* : HEAD REGISTER

thin rind *n, usu cap T&R* [prob. so called fr. its use as a bacon breed] : ¹HAMPSHIRE 1

thins *pl of* THIN, *pres 3rd sing of* THIN

thin section *n* : a section of rock 0.02 to 0.03 millimeters thick cemented for study between clear glass plates

thin-shell concrete *n* : thin reinforced usu. precast concrete forming arched or domed roofs esp. over large unpartitioned areas

thin-skinned \'=;=\ *adj* **1** : having a thin skin or rind ⟨*thin-skinned* orange⟩ **2** : readily or unduly susceptible to criticism or insult : SENSITIVE, TOUCHY

thin-skinned·ness \'='skin(d)nəs\ *n* -ES : the quality or state of being thin-skinned

thin space *n* **1** : FOUR-EM SPACE **2** : FIVE-EM SPACE

thin stroke *n* : HAIRLINE 2c(1)

thin-wall conduit *n* : light steel tubing for enclosing electric wiring — compare RIGID CONDUIT

thio \'thī(,)ō\ *adj* [*thi-*] : relating to or containing sulfur esp. in place of oxygen

thio- — see THI-

thio·acetal \¦thī(,)ō+\ *n* [*thi-* + *acetal*] : MERCAPTAL

thio·acetic acid \"+. . .-\ *n* [*thioacetic* ISV *thi-* + *acetic*] : a pungent liquid acid CH_3COSH made by heating acetic acid with phosphorus pentasulfide and used as a chemical reagent

thio acid *n* [ISV *thio* + *acid*] : an acid in which oxygen is partly or wholly replaced by sulfur

thio·alcohol \¦thī(,)ō+\ *n* [ISV *thi-* + *alcohol*] : an aliphatic mercaptan (as ethyl mercaptan)

thio·aldehyde \"+\ *n* [ISV *thi-* + *aldehyde*] : a compound having the general formula RCHS that is an aldehyde in which oxygen is replaced by sulfur and that in general is readily polymerizable — called also *thial*

thio·amide \"+\ *n* [ISV *thi-* + *amide*] : an amide of a thio acid; *esp* : an amide having the general formula $RCSNH_2$ and made usu. by the reaction of an amide of a carboxylic acid with phosphorus pentasulfide or by addition of hydrogen sulfide to a nitrile

thio·antimonate *also* **thio·antimoniate** \"+\ *n* [ISV *thi-* + *antimonate, antimoniate*] : a salt or ester containing pentavalent antimony and sulfur in the acid portion of the molecule — see SCHLIPPE'S SALT

thio·an·ti·mo·nite \¦thī(,)ō'antəmə,nīt\ *n* [*thi-* + *antimony* + *-ite*] : a salt or ester containing trivalent antimony and sulfur in the acid portion of the molecule — see CROCUS OF ANTIMONY

thio·arsenate \¦thī(,)ō+\ *n* [ISV *thi-* + *arsenate*] : a salt (as sodium thioarsenate Na_3AsS_4) or ester containing pentavalent arsenic and sulfur in the acid portion of the molecule and obtainable from arsenic pentasulfide

thio·arsenite \"+\ *n* [ISV *thi-* + *arsenite*] : a salt (as sodium thioarsenite Na_3AsS_3) or ester containing trivalent arsenic and sulfur in the acid portion of the molecule and obtainable in the case of the salts from arsenic trisulfide

thio·bacillus \"+\ *n* [NL, fr. *thi-* + *bacillus*] **1** *cap* : a genus of small rod-shaped bacteria (family Thiobacteriaceae) that live in water, sewage, and soils, derive energy from oxidation of sulfides, thiosulfates, or elemental sulfur, and obtain carbon from carbon dioxide, bicarbonates, or carbonates in solution **2** *pl* **thiobacilli** : any member of the genus *Thiobacillus*

thio·bacteriaceae \"+\ *n pl, cap* [NL, fr. *Thiobacterium,* genus of sulfur bacteria in some classifications + *-aceae*] : a family of coccoid to rod-shaped free-living bacteria (order Pseudomonadales) that oxidize sulfur compounds as a source of energy usu. with the deposit of free sulfur and may or may not require an organic source of carbon — see THIOBACILLUS; compare NITROBACTERIACEAE

thio·bacteriales \"+\ *n pl, cap* [NL, fr. *Thiobacterium* + *-ales*] *in some classifications* : an order of bacteria of various shapes usu. containing either sulfur granules or bacteriopurpurin or both, usu. thriving best in the presence of hydrogen sulfide, and comprising the families Achromatiaceae, Beggiatoaceae, and Rhodobacteriaceae

thio·bacterium \"+\ *n, pl* **thiobacteria** *often cap* [NL, fr. *thi-* + *bacterium*] : SULFUR BACTERIUM

thio·carbamide \¦thī(,)ō +\ *n* [ISV *thi-* + *carbamide*] : THIOUREA

thio·carbamoyl *or* **thio·carbamyl** \"+\ *n* [*thi-* + *carbamoyl, carbamyl*] : the univalent radical NH_2CS— that is carbamoyl in which oxygen is replaced by sulfur — called also *thiuram*

thio·carbanilide \"+\ *n* [ISV *thi-* + *carbanilide*] : a crystalline compound $CS(NHC_6H_5)_2$ made by reaction of aniline and carbon disulfide and used chiefly as an accelerator for the vulcanization of rubber and as an intermediate in organic synthesis — called also *diphenylthiourea*

thio·carbimide \"\ *n* [*thi-* + *carbimide*] : ISOTHIOCYANATE, MUSTARD OIL 2b

thio·carbonate \"+\ *n* [*thi-* + *carbonate*] : a salt or ester of a thiocarbonic acid

thio·carbonic acid \"+. . .-\ *n* [*thiocarbonic* ISV *thi-* + *carbonic*] : an acid derived from carbonic acid by replacement of oxygen by sulfur: as **a** : TRITHIOCARBONIC ACID **b** : XANTHIC ACID 2

thio·carbonyl \"+\ *n* [ISV *thi-* + *carbonyl*] : the bivalent radical >CS that is carbonyl in which oxygen is replaced by sulfur

thiochem sulfur yellow R \'thīō,kem-\ *n, usu cap T&S&Y* [*thiochem* fr. *thi-* + *-chem* (prob. fr. *chemical*)] : a sulfur dye — see DYE table I (under *Sulfur Yellow 1*)

thio·chrome \'thīə,krōm\ *n* [ISV *thiamine* + *-o-* + *-chrome*] : a yellow crystalline tricyclic alcohol $C_{12}H_{14}N_4OS$ found in yeast, formed by oxidation of thiamine, and giving a blue fluorescence under ultraviolet light that serves as the basis of a method of determining thiamine

thi·oc·tic acid \(')thī¦äktik-\ *n* [*thioctic* fr. *thi-* + *octa-* + *-ic*] : alpha or oxidized lipoic acid — called also *6,8-thioctic acid*

thiocyan- *or* **thiocyano-** *comb form* [ISV *thi-* + *cyan-*] : thiocyanogen : containing the thiocyanogen radical — esp. in names of organic compounds; compare ISOTHIOCYAN-

¹**thio·cyanate** \¦thī,ō+\ *n* [ISV *thiocyan-* + *-ate,* n. suffix] : a salt or ester of thiocyanic acid

²**thiocyanate** \"\ *vt* -ED/-ING/-S [*thiocyan-* + *-ate,* v. suffix] : to introduce the thiocyanogen radical into (a chemical compound) esp. with replacement of hydrogen — **thio·cy·a·na·tion** \,===sīə'nāshən\ *n* -S

thiocyanato- *comb form* [¹*thiocyanate* + *-o-*] : THIOCYAN- — esp. in names of inorganic acids and salts and of coordination complexes ⟨potassium *thiocyanato*chromate $K_3Cr(SCN)_6$⟩

thio·cyanic acid \¦thī(,)ō +. . .-\ *n* [*thiocyanic* ISV *thi-* + *cyanic*] : an unstable liquid acid HSCN or HNCS of strong odor that is usu. obtained by distilling a thiocyanate salt with dilute sulfuric acid and that polymerizes readily — see ISOTHIOCYANIC ACID

thio·cyanide \¦thīō+\ *n* [*thiocyan-* + *-ide*] : THIOCYANATE

thio·cyano \¦thī(,)ō+\ *adj* [*thiocyan-*] : relating to, containing, or being the thiocyanogen radical — used esp. of organic compounds

thio·cyanogen \"+\ *n* [*thi-* + *cyanogen*] **1** : a univalent radical —SCN present in thiocyanic acid and other simple and complex thiocyanates **2** : an unstable liquid compound $(SCN)_2$ that is obtained by the action of halogens on thiocyanates and that polymerizes readily (as to a red or an orange solid)

thiocyanogen value *or* **thiocyanogen number** *n* : a measure of unsaturation (as of an oil or fat) expressed usu. as the number of grams or percentage of iodine equivalent to the thiocyanogen absorbed by 100 grams of the substance and serving as a supplement to the iodine number because thiocyanogen adds to double bonds to a different extent from the usual reagents for determining iodine number ⟨the *thiocyanogen value* . . . is thus different from the ordinary iodine value in that it differentiates between oleic, linoleic, and linolenic groups —T.P.Hilditch⟩

thio·diglycol \¦thīō+\ *n* [ISV *thi-* + *diglycol*] : a hygroscopic liquid glycol $(HOCH_2CH_2)_2S$ that is made from ethylene oxide and hydrogen sulfide, that yields mustard gas on reaction with hydrochloric acid, and that is used as a solvent esp. for dyes; bis-(2-hydroxyethyl sulfide)

thio·diphenylamine \¦thī(,)ō+\ *n* [ISV *thi-* + *diphenylamine*] : PHENOTHIAZINE

thio·ether \¦thīō+\ *n* [ISV *thi-* + *ether*] : SULFIDE 2

thio·flavine *also* **thio·flavin** \"+\ *n, often cap T* [ISV *thi-* + *flavin, flavine*] : either of two yellow thiazole dyes used as biological stains as well as in dyeing or making organic pigments — see DYE table I (under *Basic Yellow 1* and *Direct Yellow 7*)

thio·gly·colate *also* **thio·gly·col·late** \,thīō'glīkə,lāt, -,glī-'käl,āt\ *n* [ISV *thioglycol-, thioglycoll-* (fr. *thioglycolic acid thioglycollic acid*) + *-ate*] : a salt or ester of thioglycolic acid : a mercapto-acetate

thio·glycolic acid *also* **thio·glycollic acid** \¦thīō+. . .-\ *n* [*thioglycolic, thioglycollic* ISV *thi-* + *glycolic, glycollic* (in *glycolic acid, glycollic acid*)] : an ill-smelling liquid mercapto acid $HSCH_2COOH$ analogous to the hydroxy acid glycolic acid that is made usu. by reaction of chloroacetic acid and hydrogen sulfide, that is a sensitive reagent for ferric iron (as by the formation of an intense red color in ammoniacal solution), and that is used chiefly in the form of its ammonium salt in setting cold waves and in the form of the calcium and other alkaline salts as depilating agents — called also *mercaptoacetic acid;* not used systematically

-thio·ic \¦thī¦ōik\ *adj comb form* [ISV *thi-* + *-ic*] : containing one atom of sulfur replacing one oxygen atom in the molecule of an acid ⟨phospho*rothioic* acid⟩ ⟨octane*thioic* acid C_7H_{15}-COSH⟩

thio·indigo \¦thī(,)ō+\ *n* [ISV *thi-* + *indigo*] **1** : a red vat dye $C_{16}H_8O_2S_2$ like indigo in chemical structure except for replacement of both imino groups by sulfur atoms — see DYE table I (under *Vat Red 41*) **2** : any of several vat dyes derived from or closely related to thioindigo — see DYE table I

thio·indigoid \"+\ *adj* [*thioindigo* + *-oid*] : related to or resembling thioindigo esp. in chemical structure and dyeing properties

thioindigoid dye *also* **thioindigoid** *n* : any of a class of vat dyes characterized by the same chromophore as indigo (sense 1b) but with sulfur instead of an imino group as an auxochrome — compare INDIGOID DYE

thioindigo red B *n, usu cap T&R* : THIOINDIGO 1

thio·ketone \¦thīō+\ *n* [*thi-* + *ketone*] : a compound that is a ketone in which oxygen is replaced by sulfur and which in general is readily polymerizable (as in the general formula RCSR) — called also *thione*

Thi·o·kol \'thīə,kōl, -kȯl\ *trademark* — used for any of a series of polysulfide rubbers or closely related liquid polymers or water-dispersed latices

thi·ol \'thī,ōl, -,ȯl\ *n* -S [ISV *thi-* + *-ol*] **1** : MERCAPTAN **2** : the mercapto group — **thi·ol·ic** \(')=¦ikˋ\ *adj*

thiolic acid *n* [*thiolic* fr. *thiol* + *-ic*] : a thio acid in which the mercapto group is present — compare THIONIC ACID 2

¹**thion-** *comb form* [ISV, fr. Gk *theion* — more at THI-] : sulfur ⟨*thionic*⟩

²**thion-** *or* **thiono-** *comb form* [*thion-* ISV, fr. Gk *theion* sulfur; *thiono-* ISV, fr. Gk *theion* + ISV *-o-*] : containing sulfur doubly bound to another atom (as in the thiocarbonyl group) ⟨*thiono*thiolic⟩

thio·naph·thene \,thīō'naf,thēn, ÷ -ap,th-\ *n* [ISV *thi-* + *naphth-* + *-ene*] : THIANAPHTHENE

¹**thi·o·nate** \'thīə,nāt, -,nət\ *n* -S [ISV *thion-* (fr. *thionic acid*) + *-ate,* n. suffix] : a salt or ester of a thionic acid

²**thi·o·nate** \-,nāt\ *vt* -ED/-ING/-S [¹*thion-* + *-ate,* v. suffix] : to combine with sulfur or introduce sulfur into (an organic compound) esp. in making sulfur dyes — **thi·o·na·tion** \,thīə'nāshən\ *n* -S

thi·one \'thī,ōn\ *n* -S [*thi-* + *-one*] : THIOKETONE

thi·one·ine \thī'ōnē,ēn, -ī'än-, -nēən\ *n* -S [by shortening] : ERGOTHIONEINE

thi·on·ic \(')thī¦änik\ *adj* [ISV ¹*thion-* + *-ic*] : relating to or containing sulfur

thionic acid *n* [*thionic* ISV ¹*thion-* + *-ic*] **1** : any of a series of unstable acids of the general formula $H_2S_nO_6$ in which the number of atoms of sulfur in the molecule varies from 2 to 6 — compare DITHIONIC ACID, POLYTHIONIC ACID **2** [*thionic* ISV ²*thion-* + *-ic*] : a thio acid in which sulfur doubly bound to another atom (as in the thiocarbonyl group) is present — compare THIOLIC ACID

Thi·o·nine \'thīə,nēn, -,nən\ *trademark* — used for a dark crystalline basic dye of the thiazine class that is the parent compound of methylene blue and is used chiefly as a biological stain

thi·o·ni·um \thī'ōnēəm\ *n* -S [NL, fr. *thi-* + *-onium*] : SULFONIUM

-thionium \"\ *n comb form* -S [NL, fr. *thi-* + *-onium*] : onium compound containing sulfur and usu. another element (as nitrogen) besides carbon in a ring ⟨phenaza*thionium*⟩

thi·o·nyl \'thīən³l, -,nil\ *n* -S [ISV ¹*thion-* + *-yl;* orig. formed in G] : the bivalent radical or cation >SO of sulfurous acid : SULFINYL — used esp. in names of inorganic compounds

thionyl chloride *n* : a volatile fuming corrosive liquid compound $SOCl_2$ usu. made commercially by oxidation of sulfur dichloride with sulfur trioxide or sulfuryl chloride and used chiefly in making acyl chlorides from carboxylic acids and alkyl chlorides or alkyl sulfites from alcohols

thio·pen·tal \,thīō'pen,tal, -tȯl\ *n* -S [*thi-* + *penta-* + *-al*] : a barbiturate $C_{11}H_{18}N_2O_2S$ that is a sulfur analogue of pentabarbital and is used in the form of its yellowish white powdery sodium derivative as an intravenous anesthetic of short duration and also in psychotherapy

thio·pen·tone \-tōn\ *n* [*thi-* + *penta-* + *-one*] *Brit* : THIOPENTAL

thi·o·phen \'thīəfən, -,fen\ *chiefly Brit var of* THIOPHENE

thi·o·phene \'thīə,fēn\ *n* -S [ISV *thi-* + *phene*] : a liquid compound C_4H_4S that is analogous to furan and pyrrole in its heterocyclic structure and resembles benzene both physically and chemically except for its greater reactivity, that is found in small amounts (as up to 0.5 percent by weight) in benzene from coal tar unless it has been removed by treatment with sulfuric acid, that is usu. made commercially from butane and sulfur at high temperature, and that is used chiefly in organic synthesis (as of antihistaminic drugs) — see INDOPHENIN; compare STRUCTURAL FORMULA

thiophene

thi·oph·e·nine \thī'äfə,nēn, ¦thīəfə¦nēn\ *n* -S [ISV *thiophene* + *-ine*] : either of two amines $(C_4H_3S)NH_2$ structurally resembling aniline but stable only when acidified to form salts; amino-thiophene

thio·phenol \¦thīō+ \ *n* [ISV *thi-* + *phenol*] **1** : a mobile liquid mercaptan C_6H_5SH with a smell like garlic and with acid properties somewhat stronger than those of phenol that may be formed by the action of phosphorus pentasulfide on phenol but that is better synthesized by reduction of benzenesulfonyl chloride — called also *phenyl mercaptan* **2** : an aromatic mercaptan (as thiophenol)

thio·phosgene \¦thīō+\ *n* [ISV *thi-* + *phosgene*] : a red ill-smelling liquid compound $CSCl_2$ obtainable (as by reaction with hydrogen sulfide at high temperature) from carbon tetrachloride; thiocarbonyl chloride

thio·phosphate \"+\ *n* [ISV *thi-* + *phosphate*] : a salt or ester of a thiophosphoric acid

thio·phosphite \"+\ *n* [*thi-* + *phosphite*] : a salt or ester of a thiophosphorous acid

thio·phosphoric acid \"+. . .-\ *n* [*thiophosphoric* fr. *thi-* + *phosphoric*] : any of a series of acids derived from the phosphoric acids by replacement of one or more atoms of oxygen with sulfur; *esp* : the mono-thio orthophosphoric acid H_3PO_3S obtained as a concentrated solution at low temperature or in the form of salts and esters

thio·phosphorous acid \"+. . .-\ *n* [*thiophosphorous* fr. *thi-* + *phosphorous*] : any of a series of acids derived from the phosphorous acids by replacement of one or more atoms of oxygen with sulfur

thio·phosphoryl \"+\ *n* [*thi-* + *phosphoryl*] : the usu. trivalent radical PS that is phosphoryl in which oxygen is replaced by sulfur — compare SULFOCHLORIDE 1

thi·o·plast \'thīə,plast\ *n* -S [ISV *thi-* + *-plast*] : any of various rubberlike materials made from an alkali polysulfide and an organic dihalide : POLYSULFIDE RUBBER

thio·rho·da·ce·ae \,thīərō'dāsē,ē\ *n pl, cap* [NL, fr. *thi-* + *rhod-* + *-aceae*] : a family of purple sulfur bacteria (suborder Rhodobacteriinae) using hydrogen sulfide as a hydrogen donor in their metabolism and accumulating molecular sulfur as a metabolic by-product

thio·semicarbazide \¦thī(,)ō+\ *n* [*thi-* + *semicarbazide*] : a crystalline compound $H_2NCSNHNH_2$ that is the analogue of semicarbazide in which oxygen is replaced by sulfur

thio·semicarbazone \"+\ *n* [*thi-* + *semicarbazone*] : any of a class of compounds analogous to semicarbazones and formed by the action of thiosemicarbazide on an aldehyde or ketone; *esp* : THIACETAZONE

thio·sin·amine \,thīōsə'namən, -ō'sinə,mēn\ *n* [ISV *thi-* + *sin-* (fr. L *sinapis* mustard) + *amine* — more at SINAPIS] : ALLYLTHIOUREA

thio·spirillum \¦thīō+\ *n* [NL, fr. *thi-* + *Spirillum*] **1** *cap* : a genus of spiral purple sulfur bacteria (family Thiorhodaceae) motile by means of polar flagella and common in mud and stagnant water **2** *pl* **thiospirilla** : any bacterium of the genus *Thiospirillum*

thio·sulfate \¦thīə +\ *n* [ISV *thi-* + *sulfate*] : a salt or ester of thiosulfuric acid; *esp* : SODIUM THIOSULFATE

thiosulfato- *comb form* [*thiosulfate* + *-o-*] : containing the bivalent radical S_2O_3 characteristic of thiosulfates — esp. in names of coordination complexes ⟨sodium *thiosulfato*aurate (I) $Na_3Au(S_2O_3)_2$⟩

thio·sulfonic acid \¦thīə +. . .-\ *n* [*thiosulfonic* fr. *thi-* + *sulfonic*] : any of a series of unstable acids of the general formula RSO_2SH derived from sulfonic acids by replacement of oxygen by sulfur and known only in the form of salts and esters

thio·sulfuric acid \"+. . .-\ *n* [*thiosulfuric* fr. *thi-* + *sulfuric*] : an unstable acid $H_2S_2O_3$ derived from sulfuric acid by replacement of one oxygen atom by sulfur and known only in solution or in the form of salts and esters

thio·thrix \'thīə,thriks\ *n, cap* [NL, fr. *thi-* + *-thrix*] : a genus of bacteria (family Beggiatoaceae) consisting of nonmotile ensheathed attached filaments differentiated into a base and a tip

thio·uracil \¦thīō+\ *n* [ISV *thi-* + *uracil*] : a bitter crystalline compound $C_4H_4N_2OS$ that depresses the function of the thyroid gland; 2-mercapto-pyrimidin-4-ol; *also* : any of several of its derivatives (as methylthiouracil or propylthiouracil)

thio·urea \"+\ *n* [ISV *thi-* + *urea*] : a bitter crystalline compound $CS(NH_2)_2$ that is analogous to urea with the oxygen replaced by sulfur and resembles urea in chemical properties, that is obtained by heating ammonium thiocyanate or by adding hydrogen sulfide to cyanamide, and that is used chiefly in the separation of hydrocarbons (as various liquid normal paraffin hydrocarbons from branched-chain hydrocarbons), in organic synthesis, and esp. formerly in synthetic resins

thiouronium *var of* THIURONIUM

thio·xanthone \¦thīō+\ *n* [ISV *thi-* + *xanthone*] : a yellow crystalline ketone $C_6H_4(CO)(S)C_6H_4$ that is the sulfur analogue of xanthone

thir \.thər, (¦)thi(ə)r, (¦)thü(ə)r\ *pron* [ME (northern dial.), perh. irreg. fr. ME ¹*this*] *dial Brit* : THESE ⟨~ breeks o' mine, my only pair —Robert Burns⟩

thi·ram \'thī,ram\ *n* -S [prob. alter. of *thiuram*] : TETRAMETHYLTHIURAM DISULFIDE — used esp. of the fungicide and seed disinfectant

¹**third** \'thərd, 'thəd, 'thəid\ *adj* [ME *thirde, thridde,* fr. OE *thirdda, thridda;* akin to OHG *dritto* third, ON *thrithi,* Goth *thridja,* L *tertius,* Gk *tritos,* Skt *tṛtīya;* derivative fr. the root of OE *thrīe, thrēo* three — more at THREE] **1 a** : being number three in a countable series ⟨the ~ day⟩ — abbr. *3d* or *3rd;* see NUMBER table **b** (1) : being next to the second in place or time ⟨~ in line for promotion⟩ (2) : ranking next to the second of a grade or degree in authority or precedence ⟨~ mate⟩ **c** : being a type of grammatical declension or conjugation conventionally placed third in a standard arrangement of the types **d** : being the forward speed or gear next higher than second in an automotive vehicle **2 a** : being one of three equal parts into which anything is divisible ⟨a ~ share of the money⟩

b : being the last in each group of three in a series — often preceded by *every* ⟨take out every ~ card⟩ **3 :** other than the two known, mentioned, or participating ⟨there cannot be a ~ person in a secret⟩ **4 :** being between 2.51 and 3.50 on the magnitude scale — used of the magnitude of a star

²third \"\ *n* -s [ME *thridde,* fr. *thirde, thridde,* adj.] **1 :** number three in a countable series ⟨the ~ of the month⟩ **2 :** the quotient of a unit divided by three : one of three equal parts of something ⟨one ~ of the total⟩ **3 thirds** *pl* **a :** the third part of the personal estate of a deceased husband which by the common-law statute of distribution and by some local statutes goes after various conditions have been fulfilled absolutely to the widow upon the husband's dying intestate and leaving a child or descendant **b :** a widow's dower **c :** a widow's statutory right to share in her deceased husband's estate and esp. in his personalty **d** *Scots law* **:** the third part of the revenues of the ecclesiastical benefices taken in 1562 and 1567 and later by the king into his hands and appropriated to the support of the acting clergy **4 a :** a musical interval embracing three diatonic degrees **b :** a tone at this interval; *specif* **:** the third note or tone of a scale : MEDIANT **c :** the harmonic combination of two tones a third apart **5 :** an article of merchandise (as coarse flour) of a third grade or quality or inferior to seconds — usu. used in pl. **6 :** the price formerly paid by a student entering a British university for the furniture in his rooms being commonly two thirds of that paid by the previous tenant **7 :** THIRD BASE **8 :** the third gear or speed of an automotive vehicle **9 :** TIERCE 4 **10 :** one having authority or precedence next below that of a person (as a mate) ranking second in a grade or degree

³third \"\ *adv* [¹*third*] **1 :** in the third place **2 :** with two exceptions ⟨the nation's ~ largest city⟩

⁴third \"\ *vt* -ED/-ING/-S [ME(Sc) *thridden,* fr. ME *thirde, thridde,* adj., third] **1 :** to divide into three parts **2 :** to follow a seconder in supporting (as a motion)

third angle *n* **:** an angle of the Great Triangle formed on the palm by the intersection of the lines of Head and Mercury that when clear, well-pointed, and even is usu. held by palmists to indicate quickness of intellect, individuality, and good health — called also *middle angle;* compare FIRST ANGLE, SECOND ANGLE

third base *n* **1 :** the base that must be touched third by a base runner in baseball **2 :** the player position for defending the area of the infield around third base

third baseman *n* **:** the baseball player stationed at the third-base position — see BASEBALL illustration

third-best \ˈ=ˌ=\ *adj* [ME(Sc) *thrid best,* fr. ME *thirde, thridde, thrid* third + *best*] **:** next to second-best in quality or excellence

third·borough \ˈthərd,=(,)=\ *n* [ME *thridborro,* prob. by folk etymology (influence of ME *thirde, thridde, thrid* third) fr. *frithborg* frankpledge — more at FRITHBORH] **:** a former English peace officer esp. of a tithing

third class *n* **:** the third and usu. next below the second class in a classification: as **a :** a class of U.S. mail comprising printed matter exclusive of regularly issued periodicals and merchandise less than 16 ounces in weight and not sealed against inspection; *also* **:** a similar class of Canadian mail with different weight limits **b :** the least expensive class of accommodations (as on a railroad train) — compare TOURIST CLASS

¹third-class \ˈ=ˌ=\ *adj* [*third class*] **:** of or relating to a class, rank, or grade next below the second

²third-class \ˈ=ˌ=\ *adv* **:** by a third-class conveyance **:** with third-class accommodations ⟨travel *third-class*⟩

third cranial nerve *or* **third nerve** *n* **:** OCULOMOTOR NERVE

third day *n, usu cap T* **:** TUESDAY — used chiefly by the Friends

third deck *n* **:** LOWER DECK 1b — see DECK illustration

third degree *n* **1 :** MASTER MASON 2a **2 :** the subjection of a prisoner to mental torture (as continuous questioning over excessively long periods) or physical torture (as restriction to a meager diet or deprivation of sleep) in an effort to wring a confession from him

¹third-degree \ˈ==ˌ=\ *adj* [fr. the phrase *third degree*] **:** of a degree next to the second; *specif* **:** of a degree of criminal culpability or seriousness second after first-degree ⟨*third-degree* arson⟩

²third-degree \"\ *vt* [*third degree*] **:** to administer the third degree to ⟨the police beat prisoners and *third-degree* them —*Newsweek*⟩

third-degree burn *n* **:** a burn characterized by destruction of the skin through the depth of the derma and possibly into underlying tissues, loss of fluid, and sometimes shock if the burned area is extensive

third dimension *n* **1 :** thickness or depth esp. when it is the quality that confers solidity on an object ⟨the image on the paper seems to have a *third dimension*⟩ **2 :** a quality that confers reality or lifelikeness ⟨night sounds that stick in the mind and give a *third dimension* to the memory —Adie Suehsdorf⟩ — **third-dimensional** *adj*

third estate *n* **:** the third of the traditional political orders; *specif* **:** the commons

third eyelid *n* **:** NICTITATING MEMBRANE

third floor *n* **:** THIRD STORY

third force *n* **:** a grouping (as of political parties or nations) intermediate between two opposing political forces

third-generation \ˌ=ˌ==ˈ==\ *adj* [fr. the phrase *third generation*] **1 :** being a member of the third generation of a family to be born in the U.S. ⟨a *third-generation* American⟩ **2 :** being a member of the second generation of a family to be born in the U.S.

third hand *n* **1 :** the third person to own or sell a used article **2 :** a thirdhand source (as of information) **3 :** the third player to have the right to bid in bridge **:** the third player to play to any trick **4 a :** a workman who helps the backtender at the dry end of a paper machine **b :** one who under the direction of a second hand supervises a section of workers in a textile mill **c :** a factory worker who assists operators or fixers of machines

¹thirdhand \ˈ=ˌ=\ *adj* [*third hand*] **1 :** received from or through two intermediaries ⟨~ information⟩ **2 a :** used or worn by two previous owners **:** bought or acquired after being used by two others ⟨a ~ stove⟩ **b :** dealing in thirdhand merchandise

²thirdhand \"\ *adv* **:** at third hand

third house *n* [so called fr. its relation to the two houses of which many legislatures are composed] **:** a legislative lobby

third·ings \ˈthərdiŋz\ *n pl* [*thirding* (gerund of ⁴*third*) + *-s,* n. pl. suffix] **:** a heriot consisting of the third part of the corn or grain growing on the ground at the tenant's death

third inversion *n* **:** a seventh chord with the seventh in the bass — see SEVENTH CHORD illustration

third law of thermodynamics : LAW OF THERMODYNAMICS 3

third·ly *adv* **:** in the third place

third man *n* **1 :** an off side fielding position in cricket usu. near the boundary and roughly in line with third slip and the striker; *also* **:** a player fielding in this position — see CRICKET illustration **2** [trans. of Gk *tritos anthrōpos*] **:** a logical paradox in which the attempt to pass from one thing to another or to relate one conception to another reveals the necessity of a third and intervening thing or conception and hence leads to an infinite regress

third mortgage *n* **:** a mortgage given or recorded after two others have been previously given on the same property with a lien subordinate to the first two given or recorded

third·ness *n* -ES **:** a fundamental category in Peircean philosophy consisting of the connecting bond between firstness and secondness and expressive of law, generality, purpose, and habit

third order *n* [trans. of ML *tertius ordo;* fr. the partial resemblance to an order of monks or an order of nuns] **:** a group affiliated with a Roman Catholic religious order and comprising men and women devoted to a special rule of pious living usu. without vows

third-order reaction *n* [*third-order* fr. the phrase *third order*] **:** a chemical reaction in which the rate of reaction is proportional to the concentration of each of three reacting molecules — compare ORDER OF A REACTION

third party *n* **1 :** a person other than the principals ⟨a *third party* to a divorce proceeding⟩ ⟨insurance against injury to *third parties*⟩ **2 a :** a major political party operating over a limited period of time in addition to two other major parties in a political unit (as a nation or state) normally characterized by a two-party system **b :** MINOR PARTY

third-party \ˈ=ˌ=\ *adj* [*third party*] **:** of, involving, or referring to a third party ⟨*third-party* insurance⟩ ⟨the *third-party* vote⟩

third person *n* **1 a :** a set of linguistic forms (as verb forms, pronouns, and inflectional affixes) referring to someone or something that is neither the speaker or writer of the utterance in which they occur nor the one to whom that utterance is addressed ⟨Latin *videt* "he sees" is in the *third person* singular⟩ ⟨English *they* is a nominative plural pronoun of the *third person*⟩ **b :** a linguistic form belonging to such a set ⟨English *is* and *goes* are *third person*⟩ **2 :** reference of a linguistic form to someone or something that is neither the speaker or writer of the utterance in which it occurs nor the one to whom that utterance is addressed ⟨the Latin verb ending *-t* that marks the *third person*⟩

third personal *adj* **:** of or belonging to the third person ⟨a *third personal* pronoun⟩

third rail *n* **:** a metal rail through which current is led to the motors of an electric locomotive — compare RUNNING RAIL

third-rate \ˈ=ˌ=\ *adj* [fr. the phrase *third rate*] **:** of third quality or value **:** less than second rate in excellence or worth

third-rat·er \ˈ=ˈrād·ə(r), -āta-\ *n* **:** one that is third-rate

third reading *n* **1 :** the stage in the British legislative process following the report stage and usu. providing for debate on the reported text of a bill before a vote on its final disposition **2 :** the stage in the U.S. legislative process which follows the second reading and in which an engrossed bill is read usu. by title only before a vote on its final disposition

thirds *pl of* THIRD, *pres 3d sing of* THIRD

third sex *n* **:** HOMOSEXUALS

third slip *n* **:** a fielding position in cricket near to and on the off side of second slip; *also* **:** a player fielding in this position

third story *n* **1 :** the second story above the ground floor **2** *Brit* **:** the third story above the ground floor

third ventricle *n* **:** the median unpaired ventricle of the brain bounded by parts of the telencephalon and diencephalon — see BRAIN illustration

third water *n* **:** the quality or luster next below second water — used of a gem (as a diamond or pearl)

third way *n* **:** economic and political development distinct from or esp. midway between the paths proposed by two extremes

¹thirl \ˈthər(·ə)l\ *n* -s [ME, fr. OE *thyrel,* fr. *thurh* through — more at THROUGH] *dial* **:** HOLE, PERFORATION, OPENING

²thirl \"\ *vt* -ED/-ING/-S [ME *thirlen,* fr. OE *thyrlian,* fr. *thyrel,* n.] **1** *dial Brit* **:** PIERCE, PERFORATE, DRILL **2** *dial Brit* **:** to pierce with emotion : THRILL

³thirl \"\ *vt* -ED/-ING/-S [alter. of Sc *thrill,* fr. ME (Sc) *thrillen* to subject to thirlage, enslave, fr. *thril* thrall, alter. of ME *thral* — more at THRALL] **1** *Scots & old Eng law* **:** to subject to thirlage **2** *chiefly Brit* **:** to tie down **:** confine in course of action : RESTRICT

⁴thirl \"\ *n* -s **1** *Scot* **:** THIRLAGE **2** *Scot* **:** SUCKEN

thirl·age \ˈthərlij\ *n* -s [alter. of Sc *thrillage* thralldom, fr. ME (Sc), fr. *thril* thrall + ME *-age*] **:** a feudal servitude, right, or service binding the tenants of a sucken to carry the grain produced there to a particular mill for grinding and to pay the agreed or customary dues; *also* **:** the dues so exacted — compare OUTSUCKEN

thirl·ing \-liŋ\ *n* -s [fr. gerund of ²*thirl*] **:** a cross hole or short passage between breasts or headings in a coal mine usu. for ventilation

¹thirst \ˈthərst, ˈthə̄st, ˈthəist\ *n* -s [ME, alter. (prob. influenced by *thirsten* to thirst) of *thurst,* fr. OE; akin to OHG *durst* thirst, ON *thorsti,* Goth *thaurstei* thirst, L *torrēre* to dry, parch, Gk *tersesthai* to become dry, Skt *tṛṣyati* he thirsts] **1 a :** a sensation of dryness in the mouth and throat associated with a desire for liquids; *also* **:** the bodily condition (as of dehydration) that induces this sensation **b :** a desire for potable liquids or to drink **2 :** an ardent desire **:** CRAVING, LONGING ⟨the home folks' ~ for news of its armies —Bruce Catton⟩ ⟨the ~ for new and up-to-date vehicles —F.L.Allen⟩ **3** *or* **thirstland** \ˈ=ˌ=\ **:** a waterless tract (as a desert)

²thirst \"\ *vi* -ED/-ING/-S [ME *thirsten,* fr. OE *thyrstan;* akin to OHG *dursten* to thirst, ON *thyrsta;* denominative fr. the root of OE *thurst,* n., thirst] **1 :** to feel thirsty **:** suffer thirst **2 :** to have a vehement desire **:** CRAVE ⟨a savage, unprincipled brute who ~*ed* to overturn a society . . . not to his advantage —J.H.Plumb⟩ ⟨adventurers ~*ing* for excitement —Waldemar Kaempffert⟩ ⟨~ after every conceivable form of achievement —Ernest Nagel⟩ **syn** see LONG

thirst·er \-stə(r)\ *n* -s [ME *thristere,* fr. *thristen, thirsten* to thirst + *-ere* -er] **:** one that is thirsty

thirst·i·ly \-stəlē, -li\ *adv* **:** with thirst **:** on account of thirst ⟨drink ~⟩ ⟨we wait ~ for each new poem —Kenneth Clark⟩

thirst·i·ness \-stēnə̇s, -stin-\ *n* -ES **:** the quality or state of being thirsty

thirsting *n* -s **:** the sensation of thirst; *also* **:** CRAVING, LONGING

thirst·less \-stlə̇s\ *adj* **:** having no thirst

thirst·less·ness *n* -ES **:** the quality or state of being thirstless

thirst out *vt* **:** to conquer, expel, or gain control of by causing to thirst ⟨will turn off the water . . . with their dams and *thirst us out* —Mary Lindsay⟩

thirsty \ˈthərstē, ˈthə̄s-,ˈthəis-, -sti\ *adj* -ER/-EST [ME, fr. OE *thyrstig, thurstig;* akin to OHG *durstag* thirsty; both fr. a prehistoric WGmc adjective whose first constituent is represented by OE *thurst* thirst and whose second constituent is represented by OE *-ig* -y] **1 a :** feeling thirst **:** experiencing a desire for drink **b :** deficient in moisture : DRY, PARCHED, ARID ⟨a dry and ~ land, where no water is —Ps 63:1 (AV)⟩ **c :** able to take in large quantities of liquid or moisture **:** highly absorbent ⟨the water sinks rapidly into the ~ ground —P.E. James⟩ **2 :** having a strong desire **:** LONGING, AVID ⟨~ for some contact with the natural world —Fairfield Osborn⟩

¹thir·teen \(ˈ)thər|(t)ˈtēn, (ˈ)thə̄|, (ˈ)thəi| *sometimes* |d·|ēn\ *adj* [ME *thirttene, thr[e]ttene,* fr. OE *thrēotīne, thrēotȳne, thrēotēne* (akin to OHG *drīzehan,* ON *threttān*), fr. *thrīe, thrēo* three + *-tīene, -tȳne, -tēne* (fr. *tīen, tȳn, tēn* ten) — more at THREE, TEN] **:** being one more than 12 in number ⟨~ years⟩ — see NUMBER table

²thirteen \"\ *pron, pl in constr* [ME *threttene,* fr. OE *thrēotȳne,* fr. *thrēotīne, thrēotȳne, thrēotēne,* adj.] **:** thirteen countable persons or things not specified but under consideration and being enumerated ⟨~ are here⟩ ⟨~ were found⟩

³thirteen \"\ *n* -s [ME *thrittene,* fr. *thirttene, threttene, thrittene,* adj.] **1 :** 10 and three **2 a :** 13 units or objects ⟨a total of ~⟩ **b :** a group or set of 13 **3 :** the numerable quantity symbolized by the arabic numerals 13 **4** [so called fr. the fact that it was once worth thirteen copper pence in Irish money] *chiefly Irish* **:** an English shilling **5 :** the 13th in a set or series; *esp* **:** an article of clothing of the 13th size

thir·teen·er \-nə(r)\ *n* -s **1 :** THIRTEEN 4 **2 :** the card of a suit left after 12 are played

thirteen-lined ground squirrel *also* **thirteen-lined gopher** \ˌ=ˌ=ˈ=-\ *n* **:** a widely distributed western No. American burrowing squirrel (*Citellus tridecemlineatus*) that is grayish brown and marked with a series of longitudinal white lines more or less broken into discrete spots — called also *leopard squirrel, striped ground squirrel*

¹thir·teenth \-n(t)th\ *adj* [ME *threttenthe,* alter. (influenced by *threttene* thirteen) of *thrett[e]the,* fr. OE *thrēotēotha* (akin to ON *threttāndi* thirteenth), fr. *thrēotīne, thrēotȳne, thrēotēne* thirteen + *-otha, -tha* -th] **1 :** being number 13 in a countable series ⟨the ~ day⟩ — see NUMBER table **2 :** being one of 13 equal parts into which anything is divisible ⟨a ~ share of the money⟩

²thirteenth \"\ *n, pl* **thirteenths** \-n(t)s, -n(t)ths\ **1 :** number 13 in a countable series ⟨the ~ of the month⟩ **2 :** the quotient of a unit divided by 13 **:** one of 13 equal parts of anything ⟨one ~ of the total⟩ **3 :** a tax in medieval England comprising the 13th part of the value of movables or of an annual rent **4 a :** the musical interval comprising an octave and a sixth **b :** a note or tone at this interval

¹thir·ti·eth \ˈthər|d·|ēə̇th, ˈthə̄|, ˈthəi|, |t|, |iə̇th\ *adj* [ME *thrittithe,* fr. OE *thrītigotha* (akin to ON *thrituganḋi*), fr. *thrītig* thirty + *-otha, -tha* -th] **1 :** being number 30 in a countable series ⟨the ~ day⟩ — see NUMBER table **2 :** being one of 30 equal parts into which anything is divisible ⟨a ~ share of the money⟩

²thirtieth \"\ *n* -s **1 :** number 30 in a countable series ⟨the ~ of the month⟩ **2 :** the quotient of a unit divided by 30 **:** one of 30 equal parts of anything ⟨one ~ of the total⟩

thirt·over \ˈthər,tōvər, ˈth̲-\ *var of* THWARTOVER

¹thir·ty \ˈthər|d·|ē, ˈthə̄|, ˈthəi|, |t|, |i\ *adj* [ME *thirty, thritty,* fr. OE *thrītig,* fr. *thrītig,* n., group of 30, fr. *thrīe, thrēo* three + *-tig* group of 10 — more at THREE, EIGHTY] **:** being one more than 29 in number ⟨~ years⟩ — see NUMBER table

²thirty \"\ *pron, pl in constr* [ME *thirty, thritty,* fr. OE *thrītig,* fr. *thrītig,* n. & adj.] **:** 30 countable persons or things not specified but under consideration and being enumerated ⟨~ are here⟩ ⟨~ were found⟩

³thirty \"\ *n* -ES [ME *thritty,* fr. OE *thrītig,* fr. *thrītig,* adj.] **1 :** three tens **:** twice 15 **:** five times six **:** six fives **2 a :** 30 units or objects ⟨a total of ~⟩ **b :** a group or set of 30 ⟨arranged by *thirties*⟩ **3 :** the numerable quantity symbolized by the arabic numerals 30 **4 thirties** *pl* **a :** the numbers 30 to 39 inclusive ⟨a score in the *thirties*⟩ ⟨low grades in the *thirties*⟩ **b :** the members of a series or set of successive numbers that end in 30 to 39 inclusive ⟨the *thirties* of the preceding century⟩ ⟨lives in the *thirties* in the next block⟩ **c :** the portion of a continuum lying between 30 and 40 on a scale of measurement or segmentation ⟨temperatures in the *thirties* tomorrow⟩ ⟨a man in his *thirties*⟩ ⟨dresses selling in the *thirties*⟩ ⟨in the latitude of the *thirties*⟩ **5 :** the 30th in a set or series; *esp* **:** an article of clothing of the 30th size ⟨wears a ~⟩ **6 :** something having as an essential feature 30 units or members **7 a :** a mark or sign of completion ⟨"Thank you, Mr. President" the traditional ~ closing press conferences —*Ethyl News*⟩ **b :** END, CONCLUSION ⟨had ~ written on their earthly life —*Trade Compositor*⟩ **8 :** the second point scored by a side in tennis **9 :** a 30 caliber machine gun — usu. written .30

¹thirty-eight \ˌ=ˈ=\ *adj* **:** being one more than 37 in number ⟨*thirty-eight* years⟩ — see NUMBER table

²thirty-eight \"\ *pron, pl in constr* **:** 38 countable persons or things not specified but under consideration and being enumerated ⟨*thirty-eight* are here⟩ ⟨*thirty-eight* were found⟩

³thirty-eight \"\ *n* **1 :** eight and 30 **:** 19 times two **2 a :** 38 units or objects ⟨a total of *thirty-eight*⟩ **b :** a group or set of 38 **3 :** the numerable quantity symbolized by the arabic numerals 38 **4 :** the 38th in a set or series **5 :** a 38 caliber pistol — usu. written .38

¹thirty-eighth \ˌ==ˈ=\ *adj* **1 :** being number 38 in a countable series ⟨the *thirty-eighth* day⟩ — see NUMBER table **2 :** being one of 38 equal parts into which anything is divisible ⟨a *thirty-eighth* share of the money⟩

²thirty-eighth \"\ *n* **1 :** number 38 in a countable series **2 :** the quotient of a unit divided by 38 **:** one of 38 equal parts of anything ⟨one *thirty-eighth* of the total⟩

¹thirty-fifth \ˌ==ˈ=\ *adj* **1 :** being number 35 in a countable series ⟨the *thirty-fifth* day⟩ — see NUMBER table **2 :** being one of 35 equal parts into which anything is divisible ⟨a *thirty-fifth* share of the money⟩

²thirty-fifth \"\ *n* **1 :** number 35 in a countable series **2 :** the quotient of a unit divided by 35 **:** one of 35 equal parts of anything ⟨one *thirty-fifth* of the total⟩

¹thirty-first \ˌ==ˈ=\ *adj* **1 :** being number 31 in a countable series ⟨the *thirty-first* day⟩ — see NUMBER table **2 :** being one of 31 equal parts into which anything is divisible ⟨a *thirty-first* share of the money⟩

²thirty-first \"\ *n* **1 :** number 31 in a countable series ⟨the *thirty-first* of the month⟩ **2 :** the quotient of a unit divided by 31 **:** one of 31 equal parts of anything ⟨one *thirty-first* of the total⟩

¹thirty-five \ˌ==ˈ=\ *adj* **:** being one more than 34 in number ⟨*thirty-five* years⟩ — see NUMBER table

²thirty-five \"\ *pron, pl in constr* **:** 35 countable persons or things not specified but under consideration and being enumerated ⟨*thirty-five* are here⟩ ⟨*thirty-five* were found⟩

³thirty-five \"\ *n* **1 :** five and 30 **:** five times seven **:** seven fives **2 a :** 35 units or objects ⟨a total of *thirty-five*⟩ **b :** a group or set of 35 **3 :** the numerable quantity symbolized by the arabic numerals 35 **4 :** a gambling game for from two to five players in which the pot is won by the player who holds cards of the same suit totaling 35 or more points in value

¹thir·ty·fold \ˌ=ˈ=ˌfōld\ *adj* [ME *thrittifold,* fr. OE *thrītigfeald,* fr. *thrītig* thirty + *-feald* -fold] **1 :** having 30 parts or aspects **2 :** being 30 times as large, as great, or as many as some understood size, degree, or amount ⟨a ~ increase⟩

²thirtyfold \"\ *adv* **:** to 30 times as much or as many **:** by 30 times ⟨brought forth fruit, some an hundredfold, some sixtyfold, some ~ —Mt 13:8 (AV)⟩

¹thirty-four \ˌ==ˈ=\ *adj* **:** being one more than 33 in number ⟨*thirty-four* years⟩ — see NUMBER table

²thirty-four \"\ *pron, pl in constr* **:** 34 countable persons or things not specified but under consideration and being enumerated ⟨*thirty-four* are here⟩ ⟨*thirty-four* were found⟩

³thirty-four \"\ *n* **1 :** four and 30 **:** 17 times two **2 a :** 34 units or objects ⟨a total of *thirty-four*⟩ **b :** a group or set of 34 **3 :** the numerable quantity symbolized by the arabic numerals 34

¹thirty-fourth \ˌ==ˈ=\ *adj* **1 :** being number 34 in a countable series ⟨the *thirty-fourth* day⟩ — see NUMBER table **2 :** being one of 34 equal parts into which anything is divisible ⟨a *thirty-fourth* share of the money⟩

²thirty-fourth \"\ *n* **1 :** number 34 in a countable series **2 :** the quotient of a unit divided by 34 **:** one of 34 equal parts of anything ⟨one *thirty-fourth* of the total⟩

thir·ty·ish \ˈ==ish\ *adj* **:** approaching or being about 30 years old

¹thirty-nine \ˌ==ˈ=\ *adj* **:** being one more than 38 in number ⟨*thirty-nine* years⟩ — see NUMBER table

²thirty-nine \"\ *pron, pl in constr* **:** 39 countable persons or things not specified but under consideration and being enumerated ⟨*thirty-nine* are here⟩ ⟨*thirty-nine* were found⟩

³thirty-nine \"\ *n* **1 :** nine and 30 **:** three times 13 **2 a :** 39 units or objects ⟨a total of *thirty-nine*⟩ **b :** a group or set of 39 **3 :** the numerable quantity symbolized by the arabic numerals 39

¹thirty-ninth \ˌ==ˈ=\ *adj* **1 :** being number 39 in a countable series ⟨the *thirty-ninth* day⟩ — see NUMBER table **2 :** being one of 39 equal parts into which anything is divisible ⟨a thirty-ninth share of the money⟩

²thirty-ninth \"\ *n* **1 :** number 39 in a countable series **2 :** the quotient of a unit divided by 39 **:** one of 39 equal parts of anything ⟨one *thirty-ninth* of the total⟩

¹thirty-one \ˌ==ˈ=\ *adj* **:** being one more than 30 in number ⟨*thirty-one* years⟩ — see NUMBER table

²thirty-one \"\ *pron, pl in constr* **:** 31 countable persons or things not specified but under consideration and being enumerated ⟨*thirty-one* are here⟩ ⟨*thirty-one* were found⟩

³thirty-one \"\ *n* **1 :** one and 30 **2 a :** 31 units or objects ⟨a total of *thirty-one*⟩ **b :** a group or set of 31 **3 :** the numerable quantity symbolized by the arabic numerals 31 **4** [trans. of F *trente et un*] **:** any of various games played with cards, dice, or numbers in which the winner is the player whose score equals or most nearly approaches 31

thirty-one order *n* **:** a train order for which the engineer or other member of a train crew must sign — compare *nineteen order*

¹thirty-second \ˌ==ˈ==\ *adj* **1 :** being number 32 in a countable series ⟨the *thirty-second* day⟩ — see NUMBER table **2 :** being one of 32 equal parts into which anything is divisible ⟨a *thirty-second* share of the money⟩

²thirty-second \"\ *n* **1 :** number 32 in a countable series **2 :** the quotient of a unit divided by 32 **:** one of 32 equal parts of anything ⟨one *thirty-second* of the total⟩

thirty-second note *n* **:** a musical note with a three-flagged stem having the time value of one thirty-second of a whole note — called also *demisemiquaver*

thirty-second notes

thirty-second rest *n* **:** a rest equal in time value to a thirty-second note

¹thirty-seven \ˌ==ˈ=\ *adj* **:** being one more than 36 in number ⟨*thirty-seven* years⟩ — see NUMBER table

²thirty-seven \"\ *pron, pl in constr* **:** 37 countable persons or things not specified but under consideration and being enumerated ⟨*thirty-seven* are here⟩ ⟨*thirty-seven* were found⟩

³thirty-seven \"\ *n* **1 :** seven and 30 **2 a :** 37 units or objects ⟨a total of *thirty-seven*⟩ **b :** a group or set of 37

3 : the numerable quantity symbolized by the arabic numerals 37

1**thirty-seventh** \¦==¦==\ *adj* **1 :** being number 37 in a countable series ⟨the *thirty-seventh* day⟩ — see NUMBER table **2 :** being one of 37 equal parts into which anything is divisible ⟨a *thirty-seventh* share of the money⟩

2**thirty-seventh** \"\ *n* **1 :** number 37 in a countable series **2 :** the quotient of a unit divided by 37 **:** one of 37 equal parts of anything ⟨one *thirty-seventh* of the total⟩

1**thirty-six** \¦==¦=\ *adj* **:** being one more than 35 in number ⟨*thirty-six* years⟩ — see NUMBER table

2**thirty-six** \"\ *pron, pl in constr* **:** 36 countable persons or things not specified but under consideration and being enumerated ⟨*thirty-six* are here⟩ ⟨*thirty-six* were found⟩

3**thirty-six** \"\ *n* **1 :** six and 30 **:** three times 12 **:** four times nine **:** three dozen **:** six sixes **:** the square of six **2 a :** 36 units or objects ⟨a total of *thirty-six*⟩ **b :** a group or set of 36 **3 :** the numerable quantity symbolized by the arabic numerals 36 **4 :** the 36th in a set or series; *esp* **:** an article of clothing of the 36th size ⟨wears a *thirty-six*⟩

1**thirty-sixth** \¦==¦=\ *adj* **1 :** being number 36 in a countable series ⟨the *thirty-sixth* day⟩ — see NUMBER table **2 :** being one of 36 equal parts into which anything is divisible ⟨a *thirty-sixth* share of the money⟩

2**thirty-sixth** \"\ *n* **1 :** number 36 in a countable series **2 :** the quotient of a unit divided by 36 **:** one of 36 equal parts of anything ⟨one *thirty-sixth* of the total⟩

1**thirty-third** \¦==¦=\ *adj* **1 :** being number 33 in a countable series ⟨the *thirty-third* day⟩ — see NUMBER table **2 :** being one of 33 equal parts into which anything is divisible ⟨a *thirty-third* share of the money⟩

2**thirty-third** \"\ *n* **1 :** number 33 in a countable series **2 :** the quotient of a unit divided by 33 **:** one of 33 equal parts of anything ⟨one *thirty-third* of the total⟩

thirty-thirty \¦==¦==\ *n* **:** a rifle that fires a 30 caliber cartridge having a 30 grain powder charge — usu. written .30-30

1**thirty-three** \¦==¦=\ *adj* **:** being one more than 32 in number ⟨*thirty-three* years⟩ — see NUMBER table

2**thirty-three** \"\ *pron, pl in constr* **:** 33 countable persons or things not specified but under consideration and being enumerated ⟨*thirty-three* are here⟩ ⟨*thirty-three* were found⟩

3**thirty-three** \"\ *n* **1 :** three and 30 **:** three times 11 **2 a :** 33 units or objects ⟨a total of *thirty-three*⟩ **b :** a group or set of 33 **3 :** the numerable quantity symbolized by the arabic numerals 33 **4 :** a microgroove phonograph record designed to be played at 33⅓ revolutions per minute — usu. written 33

1**thirty-two** \¦==¦=\ *adj* **:** being one more than 31 in number ⟨*thirty-two* years⟩ — see NUMBER table

2**thirty-two** \"\ *pron, pl in constr* **:** 32 countable persons or things not specified but under consideration and being enumerated ⟨*thirty-two* are here⟩ ⟨*thirty-two* were found⟩

3**thirty-two** \"\ *n* **1 :** two and 30 **:** four times eight **2 a :** 32 units or objects ⟨a total of *thirty-two*⟩ **b :** a group or set of 32 **3 :** the numerable quantity symbolized by the arabic numerals 32 **4 :** the 32d in a set or series; *esp* **:** an article of clothing of the 32d size ⟨wears a *thirty-two*⟩ **5 :** a 32 caliber pistol — usu. written .32

thirty-two-foot octave \ˌ=='=ˌ=-\ *n* **:** SUBCONTRAOCTAVE

thirty-two-foot pitch *n* **:** the pitch of a 32-foot stop on a pipe organ

thirty-two-foot stop *n* **:** a pipe-organ stop sounding pitches two octaves lower than the notes indicate — compare EIGHT-FOOT STOP

thirty-two·mo \ˌ=='=ˌmō\ *n* [*thirty-two* + *-mo*] **:** the size of a piece of paper cut 32 from a sheet; *also* **:** paper or a page of this size — abbr. *32mo;* symbol *32°*; see BOOK tables

thirty-year man *n* **:** an enlisted man who plans to complete thirty years of military service

1**this** \(¦)this, ˌthəs\ *pron, pl* **these** \(¦)thēz\ [ME *this,* pron. & adj. (pl. *thes, these, thos, those*), fr. OE *thes* (masc.), *thēos* (fem.), *this* (neut.), pron. & adj. (pl. *thǣs, thās*); akin to OHG *dese, desēr* this, ON *thessi;* all fr. a prehistoric NGmc-WGmc pronoun whose first constituent is akin to OE *thæt* (neut. demonstrative pron. & definite article) and whose second constituent is prob. akin to OE *sē* (masc. demonstrative pron. & definite article) — more at THAT, THE] **1 a** (1) **:** the person, thing, or idea that is present or near in place, time, or thought or that has just been mentioned ⟨~ is the twelfth of August⟩ ⟨*these* are my hands⟩ ⟨~ is a warmer welcome than I was expecting⟩ ⟨the plan has only two faults, but *these* are so serious that they may outweigh its merits⟩ — often used with a general reference to something stated or implied in the previous context but without particular reference to a noun or noun equivalent in that context ⟨in so far as those habits did change gradually over the century, ~ was thought to be due to a thing called progress —Christopher Hollis⟩ ⟨what he had to teach is far from clear, and ~ despite the fact that his prose style is extolled . . . for its marvelous simplicity —Irving Kristol⟩; often used in reference to a person as subject of a form of the verb *be* esp. in performing an introduction ⟨~ is my sister⟩ ⟨*these* are my sons⟩ (2) **:** what is stated in the following or the not yet completed phrase, clause, or discourse ⟨let me tell you ~: I have had feeling of my cousin's wrongs —Shak.⟩ ⟨a queer problem ~, of causing a character . . . to step out of the page —*Countryman*⟩ ⟨the demonstratives may, and ~ in most languages . . . hold up their nouns to censure or to blame —M.E.B.Charnley⟩ **b :** the present time **:** this time ⟨expected him to return before ~⟩ ⟨the time 'twixt ~ and supper —Shak.⟩ **c :** this place ⟨take yourself from ~, young fellow, or I'll maybe add a murder to my deeds today —J.M. Synge⟩ **2 a** (1) **:** the nearer one **:** the one more immediately under observation or discussion ⟨~ is iron and that is tin⟩ ⟨*these* are sparrows and those are robins⟩ — contrasted with *that* (2) **:** the latter — contrasted with *that* **b :** one thing — sometimes contrasted with *that;* sometimes used as first member of a 3-part series with *that* as the second member and *the other* as the third

2**this** \"\ *adj, pl* **these** [ME, fr. OE *thes, thēos, this*] **1 a :** being the person, thing, or idea that is present or near in place, time, or thought, or that has just been mentioned ⟨~ man sitting beside me is the one who made the highest bid⟩ ⟨~ book is mine⟩ ⟨~ moment⟩ ⟨entertaining a great deal *these* days⟩ ⟨one of the most memorable experiences I had in Europe ~ summer⟩ ⟨he is to enter college ~ fall⟩ ⟨*these* United States⟩ — used before a noun denoting a part of a day to indicate reference to the present day ⟨got up early ~ morning⟩ ⟨expecting to dine out with some friends ~ evening⟩; used before a noun denoting a day of the week to indicate reference to the next ensuing day so named ⟨going to make a business trip ~ Monday⟩; sometimes used before a noun denoting a person to form a phrase referring to the writer or speaker ⟨~ reviewer⟩ ⟨~ commentator⟩; sometimes used archaically before a combination of possessive adjective plus noun ⟨in ~ our country⟩, where the standard and fully current construction instead has the noun followed by *of* plus the corresponding possessive pronoun ⟨in ~ country of ours⟩ **b :** constituting the immediately following part of the present utterance or writing ⟨~ commandment we have from him, that he who loves God should love his brother also —1 Jn 4:21 (RSV)⟩ **c :** that is well known or much talked about esp. as being recent or in vogue ⟨~ existentialism⟩ ⟨*these* satellites⟩ — sometimes used disparagingly **d :** constituting the immediate past or the immediate future — used with expressions denoting a length of time ⟨after being friends all *these* years⟩ ⟨dinner has been waiting ~ half hour⟩ ⟨may your husband live *these* fifty years —R.B.Sheridan⟩ **e** (1) *these pl, obs* **:** SUCH ⟨under *these* hard conditions as this time is like to lay on us —Shak.⟩ (2) *these pl* **:** constituting such a number — used in the same construction with *many* ⟨the products of a technically adequate adjustment to reality constitute *these* many proofs of human potency —Weston La Barre⟩ **f :** being one not previously mentioned ⟨I was waiting for the bus and ~ old man came along and asked me for a dime⟩ ⟨gave me a light from ~ big lighter off the table —J.D.Salinger⟩ **2 a :** the nearer at hand **:** the more immediately under observation or discussion ⟨~ car or that one⟩ — contrasted with *that* **b :** a certain **:** ONE, SOME — sometimes contrasted with *that* ⟨turn his ship ~ way and that —C.S.Forester⟩; sometimes used as first member of a 3-part series with *that* as the second member and *the other* as the third ⟨~, that, or the other business —F.D.Roosevelt⟩

3**this** \"\ *adv* [ME, fr. 1*this*] **1** *obs* **:** in this way **:** THUS **2 :** to the degree or extent indicated by something immediately present **:** as this ⟨didn't expect to have to wait ~ long⟩ ⟨the fact that a novel about present-day Formosa could be quite ~ interesting seems odd —Margaret Parton⟩

4**this** \'this\ *n, pl* **thises** *or* **thisses** [1*this*] **:** one of the members and usu. the first of a pair or series — sometimes used with an initial capital to stand for a proper name which is not mentioned ⟨Lady *This* running an antique shop, and Madam That selling hats —*Spectator*⟩; contrasted with *that*

this and that *n* **1 :** one thing and another ⟨weighing *this and that* —*New Yorker*⟩ **2 :** a number of heterogeneous or pertinent things ⟨filling with cheese and a little chopped *this and that* —Anne Parrish⟩

this·a·way \'thisəˌwā\ *adv* [alter. of the phrase *this way*] *dial* **:** in this manner or direction

this·ness \'thisnə̇s\ *n* -ES [trans. of ML *haecceitas*] **:** the quality in a thing of being here and now or such as it is **:** the concrete objective reality of a thing **:** HAECCEITY

this·sen \'thisᵊn\ *adv* [irreg. fr. 1*this*] *dial Eng* **:** in this way **:** SO — sometimes used in the phrase *a thissen*

this·tle \'thisəl\ *n* -S [ME *thistel,* fr. OE; akin to OHG *distil* thistle, ON *thistill,* and perh. to Skt *tejate* it is sharp — more at STICK] **1 a** (1) **:** any of various prickly plants of the family Compositae and esp. of the genera *Carduus, Cirsium,* and *Onopordon* that are often segregated in the separate family Carduaceae — see SCOTCH THISTLE (2) **:** any of various similar plants of other sections of the family Compositae — see SOW THISTLE **b :** any of various prickly plants of families other than Compositae — usu. used with a qualifying adjective; see RUSSIAN THISTLE **2** *usu cap* **:** membership in the Scottish Order of the Thistle **3 :** COBALT VIOLET 2

thistle

thistlebird \'==ˌ=\ *n* **:** GOLDFINCH

thistle butterfly *n* **:** PAINTED LADY 1

thistle crown *n* **:** a gold coin of four shillings issued 1604 to 1612 by James I of England and having a Scotch thistle on the obverse

thistle cup *n* **:** a metal cup made esp. in 17th century Scotland and shaped somewhat like a thistle

thistle dollar *n* **:** a Scottish coin of the reign of James VI worth two marks and having a thistle on the reverse

thistledown \'==ˌ=\ *n* **:** the pappus from the ripe flower head of a thistle

thistle family *n* **:** CARDUACEAE, COMPOSITAE

thistle finch *n* **:** GOLDFINCH 1

thistlelike \'==ˌ=\ *adj* **:** resembling a thistle

thistle poppy *n* **:** PRICKLY POPPY

thistle saffron *n* **:** SAFFLOWER 1

thistle sage *n* **:** an annual woolly herb (*Salvia carduacea*) of the western U. S. yielding considerable honey

thistle-shaped \'==ˌ=\ *adj* **:** suggesting the rounded swollen base of a typical flower head of a thistle

thistle tube *n* **:** a funnel tube usu. of glass with a bulging top and flaring mouth

this·tly \'this(ə)lē\ *adj* **1 :** resembling a thistle **:** PRICKLY, THORNY ⟨the contemplation of various ~ matters —John Woodburn⟩ **2 :** consisting of or abounding in thistles ⟨a weedy and ~ field⟩

this world *n* [ME, fr. OE *thēos worold*] **:** the world known to living men; the world of here and now — compare *otherworld*

this-world·li·ness \'=¦===\ *n* [*this-worldly* + *-ness*] **:** interest in, concern with, or devotion to things of this world

this-world·ly \'=¦==\ *adj* [*this world* + *-ly*] **:** characterized by or manifesting this-worldliness ⟨the struggle between *this-worldly* and otherworldly values —George Orwell⟩

1**thith·er** \'thithə(r) *also* 'thi-\ *adv* [ME *thither, thider,* fr. OE *thider,* prob. alter. (influenced by *hider* hither) of *thæder;* akin to ON *thathra* there, Skt *tatra* there, to that place; all fr. a prehistoric IE adverb whose first constituent is akin to OE *thæt* (neut. demonstrative pron. & definite article) and whose second constituent is represented by OE *-der* (in *hider*) — more at THAT, HITHER] **1 :** to that place **:** THERE ⟨I shall go ~ to claim my reward —Allen Upward⟩ ⟨in transit ~ —W.P.Webb⟩ — compare HITHER **2** *obs* **:** to that end

2**thither** \"\ *adj* **:** being on the other and farther side **:** more remote **:** FARTHER ⟨the ~ bank of a stream⟩ ⟨on the ~ side of forty⟩ — compare HITHER

thitherto \¦==¦tü\ *adv* [ME *thider to,* fr. *thider* thither + *to*] **:** until that time **:** up to a past time specified or implied ⟨an approach to ~ unknown truth —G.W.Johnson⟩

thith·er·ward \'==ˌwə(r)d\ *also* **thith·er·wards** \-dz\ *adv* [*thitherward* fr. ME *thiderward,* fr. OE *thiderweard,* fr. *thider* thither + *-weard* -ward; *thitherwards* fr. ME *thiderwardes,* fr. OE *thiderweardes,* fr. *thiderweard* + *-es* -s] **:** toward that place **:** THITHER

thit·ka \'thitkə\ *n* -S [native name in Burma] **:** BURMA MAHOGANY

thi·u·ram \thī'yu̇rəm, 'thīyəˌram\ *n* -S [perh. irreg. fr. *thiourea* + *-amyl* (as in *carbamyl*)] **1 a :** THIOCARBAMOYL — used esp. in names of sulfides **b :** any of several organic derivatives of this radical R_2NCS— **2 :** any of several thiuram sulfides (as tetraethylthiuram disulfide and tetramethylthiuram disulfide)

thi·u·ro·ni·um \ˌthīyə'rōnēəm\ *also* **thio·uro·ni·um** \ˌthīōyə'r-\ *n* -S [*thiur-* (as in *thiuram*) or *thiour-* (as in *thiourea*) + *-onium*] **:** the cation $[HSC(NH_2)_2]^+$ resulting from addition of a proton to thiourea; *esp* **:** any of its derivatives formed by adding organic halides to thiourea

thivel \'thīvəl, 'thiv-,'thēv-\ *n* -S [ME *thyvelle*] *dial Brit* **:** a stick or spatula for stirring porridge or other food

thixo·trop·ic \¦thiksə·¦träpik\ *adj* **:** of, relating to, or exhibiting thixotropy ⟨~ ink⟩ ⟨mayonnaise, a good example of a ~ fluid —*Technical News Bull.*⟩

thix·ot·ro·py \thik'sä·trəpē\ *n* -ES [ISV *thix-* (fr. Gk *thixis* action of touching, fr. *thinganein* to touch, handle) + *-o-* + *-tropy;* akin to L *fingere* to shape — more at DOUGH] **:** the property exhibited by various gels (as bentonite or paint containing pigment) of becoming fluid when shaken, stirred, or otherwise disturbed and of setting again to a gel when allowed to stand **:** a reversible gel-sol transformation under isothermal shearing stress followed by rest — compare FALSE BODY, RHEOPEXY

thk *abbr* thick

thlas·pi \'thlaˌspī, -ˌspē\ *n, cap* [NL, fr. L, shepherd's purse, fr. Gk] **:** a genus of herbs (family Cruciferae) native to temperate regions and distinguished by the sessile often orbicular pod with two or more seeds in each cell — see PENNYCRESS

thling·cha·din·ne \ˌthliŋchə'dinə, -nē\ *n, pl* **thlingchadinne** *or* **thlingchadinnes** *usu cap* [Déné, lit., dog flank] **:** DOGRIB

1**tho** *var of* THOUGH

2**tho** \'thō\ *n, pl* **tho** *or* **thos** *usu cap* **1 :** a Tai people of northern Tonkin and adjoining parts of the Chinese provinces of Yunnan and Kwangsi **2 :** a member of the Tho people

thocht \'thäkt\ *chiefly Scot var of* THOUGHT

1**thoft** \'thäft\ *n* -S [ME *thofte,* fr. OE; akin to MLG *ducht* rower's bench, OHG *dofta,* ON *thopta* rower's bench, and prob. to Lith *tupėti* to squat, crouch — more at THIEF] *dial Brit* **:** a rower's bench

2**thoft** \"\ *dial Eng var of* THOUGHT

1**thole** \'thōl\ *vb* -ED/-ING/-S [ME *tholen,* fr. OE *tholian* — more at TOLERATE] *chiefly dial* **:** to endure esp. with patience or in silence **:** SUFFER, BEAR

2**thole** \"\ *also* **thow·el** \'thōəl\ *n* -S [ME *tholle* peg, fr. OE *thol* peg, thole for an oar; akin to MLG *dolle* thole for an oar, ON *thollr* peg, Gk *tylos* callus, knob, Skt *tavīti* he is strong — more at THUMB] **:** PEG, PIN; *specif* **:** a wooden or metal pin set in pairs in the gunwale of a boat to serve in place of an oarlock

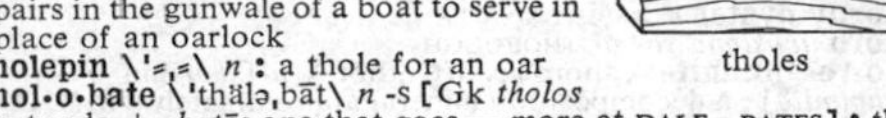

tholes

tholepin \'=ˌ=\ *n* **:** a thole for an oar

thol·o·bate \'thäləˌbāt\ *n* -S [Gk *tholos* rotunda + *-batēs* one that goes — more at DALE, -BATES] **:** the base of a dome

tho·loid \'thōˌlȯid\ *n* -S [Gk *tholos* + E *-oid,* n. suffix] **:** a rounded dome-shaped mass of lava rising above the surface of a lava flow or crater floor

tho·los \'thōˌläs\ *or* **tho·lus** \-ōləs\ *n, pl* **tho·loi** \-ōˌlȯi\ *or* **tho·li** \-ōˌlī\ [Gk & L; L *tholus* rotunda, tholos, fr. Gk *tholos*] **1 :** a round building of classical Greek date and style **2 :** a circular tomb of beehive shape approached by a horizontal passage in the side of a hill

tho·mae·an *or* **tho·me·an** \tō'mēən, thō'-\ *n* -S [prob. fr. (assumed) NL *thomaeus* of or belonging to Thomas (fr. LL *Thomas* Thomas, one of Jesus' twelve apostles) + E *-an*] *usu cap* **:** a member of the Mar Thoma Church in southwestern India that claims the apostle Thomas as its founder

thom·as \'täməs\ *n* -ES *usu cap* **:** DOUBTING THOMAS

thom·as-gil·christ process \'täməs'gilkrə̇st-\ *or* **thomas process** *n, usu cap T&G* [after Sidney G. *Thomas* †1885 and Percy C. *Gilchrist* †1935 Eng. metallurgists who invented it] **:** the basic Bessemer process

thom·as·ing \'täməsiŋ\ *n* -S [*Thomas,* one of Jesus' twelve apostles + E *-ing*] *Brit* **:** begging from house to house on St. Thomas' Day, Dec. 21

thom·as·ite \'täməˌsīt\ *n* -S *usu cap* [John *Thomas* †1871 Am. physician and religious leader + E *-ite*] **:** CHRISTADELPHIAN

thomas meal *n, usu cap T* [after Sidney G. *Thomas* †1885 Eng. metallurgist] **:** basic slag ground for use as a fertilizer

thomas precession *n, usu cap T* [after L. H. *Thomas* b1903 Am. physicist (born in England) who discovered it] **:** a precessional motion of the spin axis of an orbital electron caused by the interaction between the electron spin and the electric field of the nucleus

thomas slag *or* **thomas phosphate** *n, usu cap T* [after Sidney G. *Thomas* †1885 Eng. metallurgist] **:** BASIC SLAG

thomas splint *n, usu cap T* [after Hugh Owen *Thomas* †1891 Eng. surgeon] **:** a metal splint for fractures of the arm or leg that consists of a ring at one end to fit around the upper arm or leg and two metal shafts extending down the sides of the limb in a long U with a crosspiece at the bottom where traction is applied

Thomas splint

1**tho·mi·sid** \'thōməsə̇d\ *adj* [NL *Thomisidae*] **:** of or relating to the Thomisidae

2**thomisid** \"\ *n* -S [NL *Thomisidae*] **:** a crab spider of the family Thomisidae

tho·mis·i·dae \thō'misəˌdē\ *n pl, cap* [NL, fr. *Thomisus,* type genus (irreg. fr. Gk *thōminx* cord, string) + *-idae;* fr. their drawing single threads — more at FUNICULUS] **:** a widely distributed family of spiders that spin no webs, usu. have the first two pairs of legs much longer than the last two pairs, and comprise the crab spiders

tho·mism \'tōˌmizəm *sometimes* 'täˌ-\ *n* -S *usu cap* [prob. fr. (assumed) NL *thomismus,* fr. *Thomas* Aquinas †1274 Ital. scholastic theologian + L *-ismus* -ism] **1 :** the system of St. Thomas Aquinas teaching that philosophy and theology have separate spheres with one seeking truth through the agency of reason and the other through that of revelation but reaching conclusions that support each other, that all knowledge begins with sense perception from the data of which the intellect abstracts universals and on the basis of these proceeds through deduction and induction to science or knowledge of things in their causes and thence to knowledge of ultimate causality and the conclusion that the universe is the creation of an infinite uncreated Being, that everything in nature is composed of matter and form with the potentiality of the former being brought to actuality by the latter, that everything that is natural is good in itself and a cause of evil only when used for ends other than those for which it was created or beyond the limits prescribed by sound reason or divine law, and that because of his rational nature man is compelled by necessity to seek the highest good **2 :** a theological theory deriving from Thomas Aquinas that explains the relation between efficacious grace and free will as a free determination of the will accomplished by virtue of a divine physical premotion — compare MOLINISM

1**tho·mist** \-ˌmə̇st\ *n* -S *usu cap* [ML *thomista,* fr. *Thomas* Aquinas + L *-ista* -ist] **:** an adherent of St. Thomas Aquinas or of Thomism

2**thomist** \"\ *or* **tho·mis·tic** \tō'mistik\ *adj, usu cap* [*thomist* fr. 1*thomist; thomistic* fr. NL *thomisticus,* fr. ML *thomista* Thomist + L *-icus* -ic] **:** of or relating to Thomism or Thomists

tho·mite \'tōˌmīt, 'thō-\ *n* -S *usu cap* [*Thomas,* one of Jesus' twelve apostles + E *-ite*] **:** THOMAEAN

tho·mo·mys \'thōməˌmis\ *n, cap* [NL, fr. Gk *thōmos* heap + NL *-mys;* fr. the heaps of earth thrown out along the burrows; akin to Gk *tithenai* to place, set — more at DO] **:** a genus of rodents (family Geomyidae) comprising the pocket gophers of western No. America

thomp·son \'täm(p)sən\ *n, pl* **thompson** *or* **thompsons** *usu cap* [*Thompson* river, southern British Columbia, Canada] **1 a :** a Salishan people of the Fraser river valley, British Columbia **b :** a member of such people **2 :** the language of the Thompson people

thompson river indian *n, usu cap T&R&I* **:** THOMPSON 1b

thompson submachine gun *n, usu cap T* [after John T. *Thompson* †1940 Am. army officer who invented it in collaboration with John Blish †1921 Am. naval officer] **:** a light portable automatic weapon fed from a magazine or drum and provided with a pistol grip and a buttstock for firing from the shoulder

thom·sen·o·lite \'täm(p)sənəˌlīt\ *n* -S [Julius *Thomsen* †1909 Dan. chemist + E *-o-* + *-lite*] **:** a mineral $NaCaAlF_6.H_2O$ consisting of a hydrous fluoride of aluminum, calcium, and sodium and occurring in small white prismatic monoclinic crystals on cryolite

thom·son coefficient \'täm(p)sən-\ *n, usu cap T* [after William *Thomson* (Baron Kelvin) †1907 Brit. mathematician and physicist] **:** the Thomson electromotive force per degree of temperature

thomson effect *or* **thomson heat** *n, usu cap T* **:** a redistribution of temperature differences along an otherwise homogeneous strip of metal due to an electric current passing through it — called also *Kelvin effect;* see THOMSON ELECTROMOTIVE FORCE

thomson electromotive force *n, usu cap T* **:** a difference of electric potential associated with difference of temperature between different parts of an otherwise homogeneous strip of metal inferred from the Thomson effect

thom·so·ni·an \täm'sōnēən\ *adj, usu cap* [James *Thomson* †1748 Scot. poet + E *-an*] **:** of, relating to, or having the characteristics of James Thomson or his writings ⟨*Thomsonian* blank verse⟩

thom·son·ite \'täm(p)səˌnīt\ *n* -S [Thomas *Thomson* †1852 Scot. chemist + E *-ite*] **:** a mineral $NaCa_2Al_5Si_5O_{20}.6H_2O$ of the zeolite family consisting of a hydrous silicate of aluminum, calcium, and sodium, occurring generally in masses of a radiated structure or rarely in distinct orthorhombic crystals, and being snow-white when pure (hardness 5–5.5)

thomson process *n, usu cap T* [after Elihu *Thomson* †1937 Am. electrician and inventor] **:** a process of electric welding in which heat is developed by a large current passing through the metal

thomson's gazelle *n, usu cap T* [after Joseph *Thomson* †1895 Scot. explorer] **:** an East African gazelle (*Gazella thomsoni*) that is the smallest of the gazelles

thomson's hypothesis *n, usu cap T* [after Sir George Paget *Thomson* b1892 Eng. physicist] **:** a theory in physics: an atom consists of a large number of electrons held together by a mass with a positive charge equal to the sum of the negative charges of the electrons

1**thon** \'thän\ *pron* [alter. (influenced by 1*this* and 1*that*) of *yon,* pron.] *chiefly Scot* **:** the one yonder **:** 1THAT

2**thon** \"\ *adj, chiefly Scot* **:** being the one yonder **:** 2THAT

thon·der \'thändə(r)\ *adv or adj* [by alter. (influenced by *thon*)] *chiefly Scot* **:** YONDER

thon·draki \thän'draˌkī\ *also* **thon·drak·i·ans** \-akēənz\ *or* **thon·dra·cians** \-rāshənz\ *n pl, cap* [*thondraki* prob. fr. (assumed) MGk *thondrakoi,* fr. *Thondrak,* town in Armenia that was the headquarters of Smbat, 9th cent. Armenian theologian;

thondrakians, thondracians fr. *Thondrak* + E *-ans* (pl. of *-an*, n. suffix)] **:** a group of Armenian Paulicians founded by Smbat of Thondrak in the 9th century

[1]**thong** \'thȯŋ *also* 'thäŋ\ *n* -s [ME *thong, thwong, thwang*, fr. OE *thwang, thwong;* akin to MLG *dwenge* ferrule, ON *thvengr* thong, latchet, OE *gethwinglod* fastened up, OHG *dwingan* to oppress, overcome, compel, ON *thvinga* to oppress, burden, Av *thwązjaiti* he becomes distressed] **1 a :** a strap or strip of leather or hide used as a whiplash or a rein **b :** a strap or strip esp. of leather or hide used for fastening something (as a snowshoe or sandal) **2 :** a root cutting

[2]**thong** \"\ *vt* -ED/-ING/-S [ME *thongen*, fr. *thong*, n.] **1 :** to furnish or fasten with a thong **2 :** to lash with a thong

thon·ga \'täŋgə\ *n, pl* **thonga** *or* **thongas** *usu cap* **:** RONGA

thong seal *n* [so called fr. the use of its hide for leather lines] **:** BEARDED SEAL

thon·nier \tō'nyā\ *n* -s [F, fr. *thon* tuna — more at TUNNY] **:** a Breton sailing boat used in fishing for tuna

thon·zyl·a·mine \thän'zilə,mēn, -,mən\ *n* [prob. fr. *methoxy-* + *benzyl* + *amine*] **:** an antihistaminic drug $C_{16}H_{22}N_4O$ derived from pyrimidine and used in the form of its crystalline hydrochloride

[1]**tho·oid** \'thō,ȯid\ *adj* [Gk *thōs* jackal + E *-oid;* akin to L *faunus* faun — more at FAUN] **:** resembling a wolf — used of a wolf, dog, or jackal as distinguished from the foxes or alopecoid members of the genus *Canis*

[2]**thooid** \"\ *n* -s **:** a thooid canine

thorac- *or* **thoraci-** *or* **thoraco-** *comb form* [F *thorac-*, fr. LGk *thōrak-*, fr. Gk *thōrak-*, *thōrako-* corslet, fr. *thōrak-*, *thōrax* corslet, chest — more at THORAX] **1 :** chest **:** thorax ⟨*thoracodynia*⟩ ⟨*thoracoplasty*⟩ **2 :** thoracic and ⟨*thoracispinal*⟩ ⟨*thoracolumbar*⟩

tho·ra·cen·te·sis \,thōrəsen'tēsə̇s, ,thȯr-\ *n, pl* **thoracenteses** \-ē,sēz\ [NL, fr. *thora-* (fr. L *thorax* chest, thorax) + *centesis*] **:** aspiration of fluid from the chest (as in empyema)

thoraces *pl of* THORAX

tho·rac·ic \thə'rasik, thō'ra-, thȯ'ra-, -sēk\ *adj* [F *thoracique*, fr. LGk *thōrakikos*, fr. Gk *thōrak-*, *thōrax* corslet, chest + *-ikos* -ic] **1 :** of, relating to, located within, or involving the thorax **2** *of a pelvic fin* **:** placed under the corresponding pectoral fin and connected with the pectoral girdle

tho·rac·i·ca \-sə̇kə\ *n pl, cap* [NL, fr. *thoracica*, neut. pl. of *thoracicus* thoracic, fr. LGk *thōrakikos*] **:** a division of Cirripedia including barnacles that have six thoracic segments usu. bearing six pairs of cirri

tho·rac·i·cal \-kəl\ *adj* [*thoracic* + *-al*] *archaic* **:** THORACIC

thoracic aorta *n* **:** the part of the aorta extending beyond the arch and lying in the thorax

thoracic artery *n* **:** any of several branches of the axillary artery supplying the pectoral muscles, walls of the thorax, axilla, and adjacent parts

thoracic cage *n* **:** RIB CAGE

thoracic cavity *n* **:** the division of the body cavity of a warm-blooded vertebrate lying anterior to or above the diaphragm, bounded peripherally by the wall of the chest, and containing the heart and lungs

thoracic choke *n* **:** obstruction of the thoracic part of the esophagus of horses or cattle resulting in choking or asphyxia due to pressure on the trachea

thoracic duct *n* **:** the main trunk of the system of lymphatic vessels lying along the front of the spinal column, extending from a dilatation behind the aorta and opposite the second lumbar vertebra up through the thorax where it turns to the left and opens into the left subclavian vein, and receiving chyle from the intestine and lymph from the abdomen, the lower limbs, and the entire left side of the body

thoracic nerve *n* **1 :** any of several nerves arising from the brachial plexus and supplying chiefly muscles of the walls of the thorax **2 :** a spinal nerve emerging just below a thoracic vertebra

tho·rac·i·co·acromial \thə'rasə(,)kō+\ *adj* [*thoracic* + *-o-* + *acromial*] **:** of, relating to, or lying between the thorax and the acromial process of the scapula

thoracicoacromial artery *n* **:** a short branch of the axillary artery supplying the deltoid, pectoral, and serratus anterior muscles

tho·rac·i·co·lumbar \"+\ *or* **tho·ra·co·lumbar** \'thōrə(,)kō, 'thȯrə(,)kō+\ *adj* [*thoracicolumbar* fr. *thoracic* + *-o-* + *lumbar; thoracolumbar* fr. *thorac-* + *lumbar*] **:** of, relating to, arising in, or involving the thoracic and lumbar regions; *often* **:** SYMPATHETIC ⟨~ nerve fibers⟩

thoracic vertebra *n* **:** any of the vertebrae dorsal to the thoracic region and characterized by articulation with the ribs ⟨there are 12 *thoracic vertebrae* in man⟩ — called also *dorsal vertebra*

tho·raci·spinal \thə'rasə+\ *adj* [*thorac-* + *spinal*] **:** of or relating to the thoracic part of the spinal column or cord

tho·ra·co·dorsal \'thōrə(,)kō, 'thȯrə(,)kō+\ *adj* [*thorac-* + *dorsal*] **:** of, relating to, or lying in the dorsal aspect of the thorax

tho·ra·co·dyn·ia \,thōrəkə'dinēə, ,thȯr-\ *n* -s [NL, fr. *thorac-* + *-odynia*] **:** pain in the chest

tho·ra·cop·a·gus \,thōrə'käpəgəs, ,thȯr-\ *n, pl* **thoracopaguses** \-sə̇z\ *or* **thoracopa·gi** \-pə,jī\ [NL, fr. *thorac-* + *-pagus*] **:** Siamese twins joined at the thorax

tho·ra·co·plas·ty \'thōrəkō,plastē, 'thȯr-\ *n* -ES [ISV *thorac-* + *-plasty*] **:** the surgical operation of removing or resecting one or more ribs so as to obliterate the pleural space and collapse a diseased lung (as to accomplish immobilization) — compare COLLAPSE THERAPY

tho·ra·co·scope \thə'rākə,skōp, -'rak-\ *n* [ISV *thorac-* + *-scope*] **:** an instrument fitted with a lighting system and telescopic attachment, designed to permit visual inspection within the chest cavity and treatment under visual control, and inserted through a puncture in the chest wall in an intercostal space — **tho·ra·co·scop·ic** \=¦==¦skäpik\ *adj*

tho·ra·cos·tei \,thōrə'kästē,ī, ,thȯr-\ *n pl, cap* [NL, fr. *thorac-* + *-ostei* (fr. Gk *osteon* bone) — more at OSSEOUS] *in some classifications* **:** an order comprising fishes with the body more or less completely covered by bony plates and the pharyngeal bones and other structures about the head more or less undeveloped and including the sticklebacks, pipefishes, and sea horses

tho·ra·cos·to·my \,thōrə'kästəmē, ,thȯr-\ *n* -ES [ISV *thorac-* + *-stomy*] **:** surgical opening of the chest (as for drainage)

tho·ra·cos·tra·ca \,thōrə'kästrəkə, ,thȯr-\ [NL, fr. *thorac-* + *-ostraca*] *syn of* PODOPHTHALMIA

tho·ra·cot·o·my \,thōrə'käd·əmē, ,thȯr-\ *n* -ES [ISV *thorac-* + *-tomy*] **:** surgical incision of the chest wall

tho·rax \'thōr,aks, -ȯr-\ *n, pl* **thoraxes** \-sə̇z\ *or* **tho·ra·ces** \'thōrə,sēz, -ȯr *also* thə'rā,s-\ [ME, fr. L, corslet, chest, fr. Gk *thōrax;* perh. akin to Skt *dhārayati* he holds, carries, keeps — more at FIRM] **1 :** the part of the body of man and other mammals situated between the neck and the abdomen and supported by the ribs, costal cartilages, and sternum; *also* **:** THORACIC CAVITY **2** [NL, fr. L] **a :** a portion of the insect body that is the middle of the three chief divisions of the body and that consists of three segments each commonly bearing a pair of legs and the last two each usu. bearing a pair of wings in the adult **b :** the corresponding part of a crustacean or arachnid usu. fused with the head to form a cephalothorax **c :** the anterior division of the body of a zooid of a compound ascidian comprising the branchial sac and surrounding atrium **d :** an anterior differentiated part of the body behind the head of many tubicolous polychaete worms **3 :** BREASTPLATE, CUIRASS, CORSLET; *esp* **:** the breastplate worn by the ancient Greeks

tho·reau·lite \'thōrō,līt\ *n* -s [F, fr. Jacques *Thoreau* b1886 Belg. mineralogist + F *-lite*] **:** a mineral $SnTa_2O_7$ consisting of an oxide of tin and tantalum

tho·reau·vi·an \thə'rōvēən\ *adj, usu cap* [Henry David *Thoreau* †1862 Am. writer + E *-v-* (as in *peruvian*) + *-an*] **:** of, relating to, or having the characteristics of Thoreau or his writings ⟨often wanted to go and live a *Thoreauvian* life —Charles Poore⟩

tho·ria \'thōrēə\ *n* -s [NL, fr. *thorium* + *-a*] **:** THORIUM OXIDE

tho·ri·a·nite \-ēə,nīt\ *n* -s [*thoria* + connective *-n-* + *-ite*] **:** a strongly radioactive mineral ThO_2 that is an oxide of thorium isomorphous with uraninite and often contains rare-earth metals

tho·ri·ate \-ē,āt\ *vt* -ED/-ING/-S [*thoria* + *-ate*] **:** to impregnate (an electron-tube cathode) with thoria in order to increase the thermionic emission

thor·ic \'thōrik, 'thär-, 'thȯr-\ *adj* [ISV *thor-* (fr. NL *thorium*) + *-ic*] **:** of, relating to, or containing thorium

tho·rif·er·ous \thə'rif(ə)rəs\ *adj* [*thorium* + *-iferous*] **:** containing or yielding thorium

tho·rite \'thōr,īt\ *n* -s [Sw *thorit*, fr. NL *thorium* + Sw *-it* -ite] **:** a rare mineral $ThSiO_4$ that is a brown to black or sometimes orange-yellow thorium silicate resembling zircon but usu. metamict (sp. gr. 4.5–5.4)

tho·ri·um \'thōrēəm, 'thȯr-\ *n* -s [NL, fr. *Thor*, Norse god of thunder + NL *-ium*] **:** a radioactive tetravalent metallic element that occurs combined in minerals (as monazite and thorite) and usu. associated with rare earths and principally as the isotope of mass number 232 having a half-life of 1.39×10^{10} years and emitting alpha particles to form mesothorium 1, that is obtained by reduction of its compounds as a pyrophoric gray powder or a heavy malleable metal changing from silvery white to dark gray or black in air, and that is used chiefly with tungsten or nickel electrodes in gas-discharge lamps and for conversion to fissionable uranium of mass number 233 by the absorption of neutrons and gamma rays — symbol *Th;* see ACTINIUM SERIES, THORIUM SERIES, URANIUM SERIES; ELEMENT table

thorium emanation *n* **:** THORON

thorium nitrate *n* **:** an oxidizing salt $Th(NO_3)_4$ obtained as a deliquescent crystalline mass by extraction of monazite sand in a series of steps and used chiefly in producing thorium oxide by ignition in the manufacture of incandescent gas mantles

thorium oxide *or* **thorium dioxide** *n* **:** a refractory crystalline compound ThO_2 obtained usu. as a dense white powder by igniting thorium nitrate and used chiefly in incandescent gas mantles, in crucibles and refractories, in silica-free optical glass, and in catalysts — called also *thoria*

thorium series *n* **:** a radioactive series beginning with thorium of mass number 232 and ending with thorium D which is the nonradioactive isotope of lead of mass number 208: thorium, at. no. 90 → mesothorium 1, at. no. 88 (syn. radium 228) → mesothorium 2, at. no. 89 (syn. actinium 228) → radiothorium, at. no. 90 (syn. thorium 228) → thorium X, at. no. 88, (syn. radium 224) → thoron, at. no. 86 (syn radon 220) → thorium A, at. no. 84 (syn. polonium 216) → thorium B, at. no. 82 (syn. lead 212) [or astatine 216] → thorium C, at. no. 83 (syn. bismuth 212) → thorium C′, at. no. 84 (syn. polonium 212) [or thorium C″, at. no. 81 (syn. thallium 208)] → thorium D, at. no. 82 (syn. lead 208)

[1]**thorn** \'thȯ(ə)rn, -ȯ(ə)n\ *n* -s *often attrib* [ME, fr. OE; akin to OHG *dorn* thorn, ON *thorn*, Goth *thaurnus* thorn, Skt *tṛṇa* grass, blade of grass] **1 a :** a woody plant bearing briers, prickles, spines, or other sharp impeding process **b :** a plant of the genus *Crataegus*: as (1) **:** HAWTHORN (2) **:** PEAR HAW **c :** the wood of a thorn; *esp* **:** the tough hard wood of a hawthorn or blackthorn **d :** a growth or thicket of thorn **2 a :** a sharp rigid process on a plant; *specif* **:** a short, indurated, sharp-pointed, and leafless branch developed from a bud in a manner typical to a leafy branch — compare PRICKLE, SPINE **b :** any of various sharp spinose structures on an animal (as the spines of a sea urchin's test) **c :** something that affects like a thorn (as by pricking, stinging, or hurting) **:** a cause of irritation or source of distress ⟨had been a nagging ~ to her husband through 40 years of marriage⟩ **3** [ME, runic letter þ, thorn (plant), thorn (process on a plant), fr. OE] **:** the runic letter þ used in Old English and Middle English for either of the sounds of Modern English *th* (as in *thin, then*) and in Icelandic in early use for either of the same two sounds but in modern use only for *th* as in *thin* — see ANGLO-SAXON ALPHABET; compare EDH

[2]**thorn** \"\ *vt* -ED/-ING/-S [ME *thornen*, fr. *thorn*, n.] **1 :** to cause to be thorny; *esp* **:** to provide (as a newly set hedge) with a protection of thorny brush **2 :** to prick with or as if with a thorn **:** ANNOY, IRRITATE, HARASS

thorn apple *n* **1 a :** the fruit of a hawthorn **:** HAW **b :** a plant that produces thorn apples **2 :** a plant of the genus *Datura; esp* **:** JIMSONWEED

thornback \'=,=\ *n* [ME *thornebakk*, fr. *thorne, thorn* thorn + *bakk, bak* back] **1 a :** any of various rays having spines on the back **b :** THREE-SPINED STICKLEBACK **2 :** a large European spider crab (*Maja squinado*) **3** *archaic* **:** SPINSTER 3

thornback ray *n* **:** a common European ray (*Raja clavata*) having several large curved spines on the back and tail

thornbill \'=,=\ *n* **1 :** any of several small brilliant So. American hummingbirds of the genera *Ramphomicron* and *Chalcostigma* that have a long slender sharp bill and feed on honey, insects, and the juice of sugarcane **2 :** any of several small Australian warblers of the genus *Acanthiza*

thornbush \'=,=\ *n* [ME *thorn busk*, fr. [1]*thorn* + *bush, busk* bush] **1 :** any of various spiny or thorny shrubs or small trees: as **a :** [1]THORN 1b **b :** WHITETHORN 3 **c :** any of various shrubby and thorny African or Australian acacias **2 :** a low growth of thorny shrubs esp. of dry tropical regions (as in southern Africa and parts of Brazil) — compare THORN FOREST

thorned \-nd\ *adj* **:** having or abounding in thorns or thornbushes **:** THORNY

thorn forest *n* **:** a tropical xerophytic savanna woodland commonly dominated by small thorny trees

thorn–headed worm \'=,==-\ *n* **:** ACANTHOCEPHALAN

thorn hedge *n* **:** a hedge of thornbushes; *esp* **:** a hawthorn hedge — **thorn–hedged** \'=,=\ *adj*

thorn·i·ly \'thȯ(r)nᵊlē, -nᵊli, -nəl-\ *adv* **:** so as to be thorny **:** in the manner of a thorn

thorn·i·ness \-nēnə̇s, -nin-\ *n* -ES **:** the quality or state of being thorny

thorn·less \'thȯrnlə̇s\ *adj* **:** free from thorns — **thorn·less·ness** *n* -ES

thorn·let \-lə̇t\ *n* -s **:** a minute thorn

thornlike \'=,=\ *adj* **:** resembling a thorn esp. in sharpness or irritating quality

thorn locust *n* **:** HONEY LOCUST

thorn needle *n* **:** a phonograph needle made of cactus spine

thorn oyster *n* **:** SPINY OYSTER

thorn palm *n* **:** any of various palms (as of the genera *Bactris, Acrocomia*, and *Astrocaryum*) with spiny trunks; *also* **:** any of various hook climbers (as of the genera *Desmoncus* and *Calamus*)

thorn plum *n* **1 :** THORN APPLE 1 **2 :** a rough or spiny American wild plum

thorn poppy *n* **:** PRICKLY POPPY

thorntail \'=,=\ *n* **:** any of several Neotropical hummingbirds of the genus *Popelairia; esp* **:** a hummingbird (*P. conversii*) whose tail is deeply forked with the outer feathers slender and pointed

thorn tree *n* [ME *thorne tree*, fr. *thorne, thorn* thorn + *tree*] **:** any of various thorny or spiny trees: as **a :** HAWTHORN **b :** HONEY LOCUST **c** *Africa* **:** a spiny arborescent acacia

thorny \'thȯrnē, -ȯ(ə)n-, -ni\ *adj* -ER/-EST [ME, fr. OE *thornig*, fr. [1]*thorn* + *-ig* -y] **1 :** full of thorns or spines or thornbushes **:** rough or thick with thorns **:** SPINY, BRAMBLY ⟨a ~ bush⟩ ⟨~ ground⟩ **2 a :** beset with trials, vexations, obstacles, or other difficulties ⟨the steep and ~ way to heaven —Shak.⟩ **b :** sharp as a thorn **:** keenly distressing **:** STABBING ⟨~ cares⟩ **c :** as difficult to handle as a thorny branch or a thornbush **:** bristling with perplexities, points of controversy, or other conflicting elements ⟨the ~ question of states' rights⟩

thorny acacia *n* **:** any of various notably thorny acacias or closely related plants (as a honey locust)

thorny amaranth *n* **:** an amaranth (*Amaranthus spinosus*) having a pair of divergent spines at most of its leaf nodes

thorny–backed eel \'==,=-\ *n* **:** SPINY EEL

thorny coral *n* **:** BLACK CORAL

thorny devil *n* **:** MOLOCH 2b

thorny–headed worm \'==,==-\ *n* **:** ACANTHOCEPHALAN

thorny lobster *n* **:** SPINY LOBSTER

thorny locust *n* **:** HONEY LOCUST

thorny oyster *n* **:** SPINY OYSTER

thoro *nonstand var of* THOROUGH

tho·ro·gummite \,thōrə'gə,mīt, ,thȯr-\ *n* [*thorium* + *-o-* + *gummite*] **:** a decomposition mineral approximately $Th_2(UO_2)Si_3O_{11}.3H_2O$ that is a hydrous silicate of thorium and uranium

tho·ron \'thōr,än, 'thȯ,rän\ *n* -s [NL, fr. *thor-* (fr. *thorium*) + *-on*] **:** a heavy radioactive gaseous isotope of the group of inert gases that is isotopic with radon and actinon, is formed by disintegration of thorium, emits alpha rays, and has a half-life of less than a minute (mass number 220) — called also *thorium emanation;* see THORIUM SERIES

Tho·ro·trast \'thōrə,trast\ *trademark* — used for a suspension of thorium oxide used as a radiopaque medium

[1]**thor·ough** \'thər·(,)ō, 'thər·ə, 'thə·(,)rō, 'thə·rə *sometimes* 'thō(,)rō *or* -,rə; -r·əw *or* --rəw *or* -,rō +V\ *prep* [ME *thorugh, thorw, thorow*, fr. OE *thuruh, thurh*, prep. & adv. — more at THROUGH] *archaic* **:** THROUGH ⟨~ the fog it came —S.T. Coleridge⟩

[2]**thorough** \"\ *adv* [ME *thorugh, thorw, thorow*, fr. OE *thuruh, thurh*, prep. & adv.] **1** *archaic* **:** THROUGH ⟨the plowshare drawn ~ —A.C.Swinburne⟩ **2** *dial chiefly Brit* **:** THOROUGHLY ⟨a ~ good sort —Virginia Woolf⟩

[3]**thorough** \"\ *adj, sometimes* -ER/-EST [ME *thorow*, fr. *thorugh, thorw, thorow*, adv.] **1 :** marked by completeness: as **a** (1) **:** carried through to completion esp. with full attention to details **:** COMPLETE ⟨a ~ search⟩ ⟨drastic ~ intensive reform —J.G. Harrison⟩ (2) **:** marked by attention to many details ⟨the very ~ description of the country —G.F.Hudson⟩; *esp* **:** marked by sound systematic attention to all aspects and details ⟨completed ~ courses in mathematics —H.H.Arnold & I.C.Eaker⟩ ⟨his ~ grasp of economic matters —Alexander Brady⟩ (3) **:** complete in all respects ⟨the performance is a ~ delight —Brooks Atkinson⟩ **b** (1) **:** characterized by mastery (as of a profession or an art) ⟨a ~ musician⟩ (2) **:** having all the typical qualities ⟨were both ~ children of the Renaissance —Gamaliel Bradford⟩ (3) **:** careful about all details ⟨is not brilliant but he is very ~ —O.W.Holmes †1935⟩ **2 :** passing through — **thor·ough·ly** \-r·əlē --rə-, -li\ *adv* — **thor·ough·ness** *n* -ES

[4]**thorough** \"\ *n -s usu cap* **:** a thorough policy or action; *esp* **:** a thorough and tyrannical political policy (as in 17th century England)

thorough–band \'==,=\ *n* **:** PERPEND 1

thorough bass *n* **:** CONTINUO

thorough–bind \'==,=\ *vt* **:** to bind with a perpend

thor·ough·brace \-r·ə,brās, --rə,-\ *n* **1 :** one of several leather straps supporting the body of a carriage and serving as springs **2 :** a vehicle (as a stagecoach) that is supported on thoroughbraces

[1]**thor·ough·bred** \-,bred\ *adj* **1 a :** thoroughly trained or skilled ⟨a ~ soldier who weighs all contingencies⟩ **b :** THOROUGH, COMPLETE, GENUINE ⟨a ~ sailor —Herman Melville⟩ **2 :** bred from the best blood through a long line **:** PUREBLOOD, PUREBRED — used of domestic animals **3** [[2]*thoroughbred*] *a usu cap* **:** of, relating to, or being a member of the breed of horses called Thoroughbred **b** (1) **:** having characteristics resembling those of a Thoroughbred **:** GRACEFUL, ELEGANT, CULTIVATED, ARISTOCRATIC ⟨more ~ or fairer fingers —Lord Byron⟩ ⟨a beautifully . . . ~ piece of work moving with . . . conscious but quiet assurance —M.R.Ridley⟩ (2) **:** FIRST-CLASS ⟨the stability and accuracy of the ~ sports car —*Country Life*⟩ — **thor·ough·bred·ness** *n* -ES

[2]**thoroughbred** \"\ *n* **1** *usu cap* **a :** an English breed of light speedy horses kept chiefly for racing and originating from crosses between English mares of uncertain ancestry and Arabian stallions imported about the end of the 17th century **b** -s **:** a horse of this breed **2** -s **:** a purebred or pedigreed animal **3** -s **:** one that has characteristics resembling those of a Thoroughbred: as **a :** a thoroughbred person **b :** a first-class vehicle

[1]**thor·ough·fare** \-,fa(a)(ə)r, -,fe(, |ə\ *n* [ME *thoruhfare*, fr. *thoruh, thorugh, thorw, thorow* through + *fare* passage — more at THOROUGH, FARE] **1 :** a way or place through which there is passing: as **a** *archaic* **:** a town through which considerable traffic passes **b** (1) **:** a street that goes through from one street to another (2) **:** an unobstructed way open to the public (3) **:** an important street or highway **c** (1) **:** a waterway (as a river or strait) used for travel or shipping (2) **:** a waterway usu. without flowage between two bodies of water (as lakes) **2 a :** the action of passing through **:** PASSAGE, TRANSIT ⟨hell and this world, one realm, one continent of easy ~ —John Milton⟩ **b :** the conditions necessary for passing through ⟨a streetcar came, jerked to a stop just at the bumper, and clanged for ~ —Margaret Avison⟩

[2]**thoroughfare** \"\ *vt* **:** to pass through ⟨those slits that *thoroughfared* the older town —J.R.Lowell⟩

thoroughfoot \'==,=\ *vt* -ED/-ING/-S **:** to straighten (twisted rope) by coiling

thoroughgoing \'==¦==\ *adj* **:** marked by thoroughness or zeal **:** going the full length **:** THOROUGH, EXTREME ⟨the most ~ democrat of his generation —V.L.Parrington⟩ ⟨reconstruction will require ~ cooperation between industry and labor —F.D. Roosevelt⟩ — **thor·ough·go·ing·ly** *adv* — **thor·ough·go·ing·ness** *n* -ES

thorough light *n* **1 thorough lights** *pl, archaic* **:** windows on opposite sides of a room **2** *archaic* **:** a light that passes through

thorough–paced \'==¦=\ *adj* **1 :** thoroughly trained **:** ACCOMPLISHED ⟨a *thorough-paced* politician⟩ **2 :** THOROUGH, COMPLETE ⟨only a *thorough-paced* rotter would have made such a suggestion —Margaret Kennedy⟩ ⟨his reforms were too *thorough-paced* —*Times Lit. Supp.*⟩

thoroughpin \'==,=\ *n* [so called fr. the appearance of the swelling as if a peg were sticking through the leg and causing the skin to bulge on each side] **:** a synovial dilatation just above the hock of the horse on both sides of the leg and slightly anterior to the hamstring tendon that is often associated with lameness

thoroughsped \'==¦=\ *adj* **:** THOROUGH-PACED

thoroughstem \'==,=\ *n* **:** a boneset (*Eupatorium perfoliatum*)

[1]**thorough–stitch** \'==,=\ *adv* [prob. fr. the phrase *thorough stitch* fr. [1]*thorough* + *stitch*, n.] *archaic* **:** all the way through ⟨obliged to go *thorough-stitch* with it —Bernard Mandeville⟩

[2]**thorough–stitch** \"\ *or* **thorough–stitched** \'==,=\ *adj* [*thorough-stitch* fr. [1]*thorough-stitch; thorough-stitched* fr. [1]*thorough-stitch* + *-ed*] *archaic* **:** THOROUGHGOING ⟨his book may properly be considered . . . a *thorough-stitched* digest and regular institute —Laurence Sterne⟩

thoroughwax \'==,=\ *n* [[2]*thorough* + *wax*, v.; trans. of G *durchwachs;* fr. the fact that the stem appears as if growing through the leaves] **1 :** HARE'S-EAR 1 **2 :** a boneset (*Eupatorium perfoliatum*)

thoroughwort \'==,=\ *n* -s **:** BONESET 1

thorp *also* **thorpe** \'thȯrp\ *n* -s [ME *thorp, throp*, fr. OE; akin to OHG *dorf* village, ON *thorp* village, Goth *thaurp* landed property, L *trabs, trabes* beam, timber, roof, Gk *teramna* house, Latvian *trā̃ba* house] *archaic* **:** VILLAGE, HAMLET

thort·veit·ite \(')tȯ(r)t¦vī,tīt, (')thȯ-\ *n* -s [G *thortveitit*, fr. Olaus *Thortveit*, 20th cent. Norw. mineralogist + G *-it* -ite] **:** a mineral $(Sc,Y)_2Si_2O_7$ consisting of scandium yttrium silicate and occurring in slender grayish-green orthorhombic crystals (hardness 6–7, sp. gr. 3.6)

thor·y·bes \'thōrə,bēz\ *n, cap* [NL] **:** a genus of skipper butterflies with broad wings

[1]**thos** \'thäs\ *n, cap* [NL, fr. L, jackal, fr. Gk *thōs;* akin to L *faunus* faun — more at FAUN] *in some classifications* **:** a genus that is now usu. considered a subgenus of *Canis* and that includes the Asiatic and African jackals and sometimes the American coyotes

[2]**thos** *pl of* THO

those [ME *thos, those*, fr. *thos, those* these (pl. of *this*, pron. & adj.), fr. OE *thās* (pl. of *thes*, pron. & adj., this) — more at THIS] *pl of* THAT

[1]**thou** \'thau̇\ *pron* [ME, fr. OE *thū, thu* (dat. & acc. *thē*); akin to OHG *dū, du* thou (dat. *dir*, acc. *dih*), ON *thū* (dat. *thēr*, acc. *thik*), Goth *thu* (dat. *thus*, acc. *thuk*), L *tu* (dat. *tibi*, acc. *te*), Gk *sy* (dat. *soi*, acc. *se*), Skt *tvam* (dat. *te*, acc. *tvā*)] *archaic* **:** the one that is being addressed — used as a nominative pronoun of the second person singular esp. in biblical, ecclesiastical, solemn, or poetic language ⟨~ shalt have no other gods before me —Exod 20:3 (AV)⟩ ⟨be ~ our guide while life shall last —Isaac Watts⟩ ⟨~ wast not born for death, immortal bird —John Keats⟩; used in Middle English and in early modern English at least into the 17th century as the appropriate form of address to an intimate friend or a person of lower social status than the speaker and hence adopted by the early Friends as the universal form of address to one person

in accordance with their belief in the equality of all persons before God; compare THEE, THINE, THY, YE, YOU

²thou \"\ vb -ED/-ING/-S [ME *thouen*, fr. *thou*, pron.] vt : to address as *thou* ~ vi : to use *thou* in address

³thou \"\ n -S [¹*thou*] : the person or self of the one that is being addressed ⟨in thinking I am related to general truth, to ideas, not to the ~ of my neighbor —Emil Brunner⟩

⁴thou \'thau̇\ n, pl **thou** *or* **thous** [short for ¹*thousand*] : a thousand of anything: as **a** : a thousand pounds **b** : a thousand dollars

thou *abbr* thousand

¹though *also* **tho** \'t͟hō\ *adv* [ME *though, thogh*, adv. & conj., of Scand origin; akin to ON *thō* nevertheless, yet; akin to OE *thēah* nevertheless, yet, though, OHG *doh* nevertheless, yet, though, Goth *thauh* then as a result] : HOWEVER, NEVERTHELESS — used at the end or in the middle of a sentence ⟨continued to eat at the hotel ~ —Sloan Wilson⟩

²though *also* **tho** \(ˈ)t͟hō\ *conj* [ME *though, thogh*, adv. & conj.] **1 a** : in spite of the fact that : WHILE ⟨~ they know the war is lost, they continue to fight —Bruce Bliven b. 1889⟩ ⟨the earliest fishes, ~ remarkable, have close resemblances to some modern forms —W.E.Swinton⟩ **b** : in spite of the possibility that : even if ⟨~ he slay me, yet will I trust in him —Job 13:15 (AV)⟩ ⟨~ they may all ultimately fail, they do try —Harry Roskolenko⟩ **2** *obs* : THAT, IF ⟨no marvel, my lord, ~ it affrighted you —Shak.⟩ ⟨this book, ~ only forty pages, is quite difficult to read⟩

¹thought [partly fr. ME *thoughte* (past of *thinken* to seem, (assumed) ME *ythought* (past part. of *thinken*), fr. OE *thūhte* (past of *thyncan*), *gethūht* (past part. of *thyncan*); akin to OHG *dūhta* seemed (past of *dunken*), *gidūht* seemed (past part. of *dunken*), ON *thōtti* (past of *thykkja*), *thōtt* (past part. of *thykkja*), Goth *thūhta* (past of *thunkjan*); partly fr. ME *thoughte* (past of *thenken* to think), *thoughte*, *ythought* (past part. of *thenken*), fr. OE *thōhte* (past of *thencan*), *gethōht* (past part. of *thencan*); akin to OHG *dāhta* thought (past of *denken*), *gidāht* thought (past part. of *denken*), ON *thātti* perceived (past of *thekkja*), Goth *thāhta* deliberated (past of *thankjan*)] *past of* THINK

²thought \'thȯt, *usu* -ȯd·+V\ n -S [ME, fr. OE *thōht, gethōht*; OE *thōht* akin to MHG *dāht* thought; derivative fr. the root of OE *thencan* to think; OE *gethōht* akin to MD *gedacht* thought; both fr. a prehistoric WGmc word whose first constituent is represented by OE *ge-* (perfective, associative, and collective prefix) and whose second constituent is derived fr. the root of OE *thencan* — more at CO-, THINK] **1 a** (1) : the action or process of thinking : mental concentration on ideas as distinguished from sense perceptions or emotions : the arranging of ideas in the mind ⟨a philosophy of life filled with deep ~ —William Clark⟩ ⟨there must be ~ and care even in such a task as the delivery of milk —William Feather⟩ (2) : MEDITATION, REFLECTION ⟨a very necessary off day with only swimming and lazy ~ —Elyne Mitchell⟩ **b** : serious consideration : ATTENTION, CARE, REGARD ⟨gave no ~ at all to the opportunities the river landing offered —*Amer. Guide Series: Minn.*⟩ ⟨built with some ~ for the officers and crew —Alan Dixon⟩ **c** : RECOLLECTION, MIND ⟨I and my brother are not known; yourself so out of ~ . . . cannot be questioned —Shak.⟩ **2 a** (1) : the faculty or power of thinking; *esp* : the ability to think logically ⟨the course will deal . . . with ~ directed toward problems of human relations —*Official Register of Harvard Univ.*⟩ (2) : use of the ability to think logically ⟨a situation that calls for swift sure ~ —*N.Y. Herald Tribune Bk. Rev.*⟩ **b** : the power to conceive or realize : CONCEPTION, IMAGINATION ⟨beauty beyond ~⟩ **3** : something that is thought: as **a** (1) : an individual product of thinking : IDEA ⟨have to wait for the occasional genius or the occasional lucky ~ —A.N.Whitehead⟩ ⟨the central ~ of the paragraph⟩ (2) : an individual act of thinking ⟨too familiar to give a ~ to —John Buchan⟩ ⟨a fearful person needs . . . ~*s* of courage —W.J.Reilly⟩ (3) : an idea that stimulates thinking or supplies material for reflection ⟨concluded his sermon with what he called a ~ for the day⟩ (4) : a more or less clearly defined intention or plan ⟨the ~ behind the campaign is to win decisively⟩ — often used in negative constructions ⟨had no ~ of becoming a minister —H.E.Starr⟩ (5) : HOPE, EXPECTATION ⟨beset by lung trouble, he gave up ~ of a college education —L.A.Weigle⟩ ⟨an experiment undertaken . . . without ~ of a strict financial return —W.B.Fisher⟩ (6) : OPINION, BELIEF ⟨a change has been made . . . but with tests, in the ~ of many, too mechanical and absolute —B.N.Cardozo⟩ **b** (1) : whatever is in one's mind : IDEAS, OPINIONS ⟨if he disliked anything one said or did, he spoke all his ~ —W.B. Yeats⟩ (2) : the product of careful and reasoned consideration ⟨those of us who like . . . more ~ in our music —Virgil Thomson⟩ (3) : the intellectual product or the organized views and principles (as of a particular period, place, group, or individual) : PHILOSOPHY ⟨it is only in criticism that the ~ of an era becomes articulate —C.I.Glicksberg⟩ ⟨modern scientific ~⟩ **4** *archaic* : SORROW, GRIEF, TROUBLE **5** : ³BIT 3c — used only in the adverbial phrase *a thought* ⟨slapped him a ~ too heartily on the back —Noel Coward⟩ **syn** see IDEA

thought control n **1** : the practice by a totalitarian government of attempting (as by propaganda) to prevent subversive and other undesired ideas from being received and competing in the minds of the people with the official ideology and policies **2** : the use by a group or institution of authoritarian techniques similar in nature and purpose to governmental thought control

thought·ed \'thȯd·əd, -ȯtəd\ *adj* : having thoughts — usu. used in combination ⟨high-*thoughted*⟩

thoughten *adj* [irreg. fr. ¹*thought*] *obs* : having specified thoughts ⟨be you ~ for that I came with no ill intent —Shak.⟩

thought experiment n [prob. trans. of G *gedankenexperiment*] : an imaginary experiment worked through with ideal apparatus under ideal conditions but with no violation of the basic laws of physics : GEDANKENEXPERIMENT

thought·ful \'thȯtfəl\ *adj* [ME, fr. ²*thought* + *-ful*] **1** : marked by thought: as **a** : absorbed in calm reflective thought : MEDITATIVE ⟨looked ~ for a moment and went away —Dashiell Hammett⟩ **b** : characterized by careful reasoned thinking ⟨a ~ person, slow to act, who enjoys analyzing, interpreting, and patiently summarizing —W.J.Reilly⟩ ⟨a ~ book on a serious subject —L.E.Seltzer⟩ **c** : having thoughts : MINDFUL, HEEDFUL ⟨became ~ about his personal religion and joined the church —H.K.Rowe⟩ **d** : marked by consideration for others : CONSIDERATE ⟨a ~ generous man⟩ **2** *obs* : suffering from anxiety or sorrow : SAD, MELANCHOLY — **thought·ful·ly** \-fəlē, -li\ *adv* — **thought·ful·ness** n -ES

thought·less \'thȯtləs\ *adj* **1** : marked by absence of thought: as **a** : marked by failure to think before acting : CARELESS, RASH ⟨the ~ victim of an unnecessary accident⟩ **b** : marked by failure to keep in mind : HEEDLESS ⟨easy to fault them, to call them . . . ~ of tomorrow and God —A.B.Guthrie⟩ **c** (1) : marked by a deficiency of thought : showing lack of intelligence : STUPID ⟨a ~ housing boom which contains the seeds of its own undoing —*New Republic*⟩ (2) : devoid of thought : INSENSATE ⟨the ~ forces of nature —Bertrand Russell⟩ **d** : marked by lack of consideration for others : INCONSIDERATE ⟨is horribly ~ and seems to take a real delight in giving me pain —Oscar Wilde⟩ **2** *archaic* : free from trouble or care ⟨every ~ nest —William Blake⟩ — **thought·less·ly** *adv* — **thought·less·ness** n -ES

thought·let \-lət\ n -S : a small or inconsequential thought

thought-out \'ˌ=ˌ=\ *adj* [fr. *thought out*, past part. of the phrase *think out*] : produced or arrived at through careful and thorough consideration ⟨a coherent and deeply *thought-out* philosophy of life —E.V.Rostow⟩

thought-read \'=ˌ=\ *vt* **1** : to determine the unspoken thoughts of (a person) by observation of facial expressions or by telepathy ⟨easily *thought-read* his friend⟩ **2** : to determine (the unspoken thoughts) of a person by observation of facial expressions or by telepathy ⟨*thought-read* the commander's plans⟩ — **thought-reader** \'=ˌ=\ n

thought transference n : the transference of thought from one mind to another; *specif* : TELEPATHY ⟨every sort of psychical investigation . . . , conducting experiments in *thought transference* —W.H.Salter⟩

thoughtway \'=ˌ=\ n : a way of thinking that is characteristic of a particular group (as a profession or social class), time, or culture ⟨a society dominated by scientific ~*s* —Ralph Pieris⟩

thoughty \'thȯd·ē\ *adj* [ME, fr. ²*thought* + *-y*] *chiefly dial* : THOUGHTFUL

thouing *pres part of* THOU

thou·let solution \(ˈ)thüˌlā\ n, *usu cap T* [after *J. Thoulet*, 19th cent. Fr. chemist] : SONSTADT SOLUTION

thous *pl of* THOU, *pres 3d sing of* THOU

¹thou·sand \'thau̇zᵊn(d)\ n, *pl* **thousands** *or* **thousand** [ME, fr. OE *thūsend*; akin to OHG *dūsunt* thousand, ON *thūsund*, Goth *thūsundi*; all fr. a prehistoric Gmc compound whose first constituent is akin to the first part of Lith *túkstantis* thousand and of Russ *tysyacha* thousand and to Skt *tavas* strong, *tavīti* he is strong, and whose second constituent is akin to OE *hund* hundred — more at THUMB, HUNDRED] **1** : 10 hundred; 100 times 10 — see NUMBER table **2 a** : 1000 units or objects ⟨a total of a ~⟩ ⟨a total of four ~⟩ **b** : a group or set of 1000 **3 a** : the numerable quantity symbolized by the arabic numerals 1000 **b** : the letter M **4** : the number occupying the position four to the left of the decimal point in the Arabic notation (as 2 in the number 2968) — usu. used in pl. **5** : a very large number ⟨had ~*s* of things to do before the guests arrived⟩ **6 a** : typeset matter equivalent to 1000 ems ⟨he keyboards five ~ an hour⟩ ⟨a piecework rate of $1 a ~⟩ **b** *Brit* : typeset matter equivalent to 1000 ens — **by the thousand** *or* **by the thousands** : in great numbers

²thousand \"\ *adj* [ME, fr. OE *thūsend*, fr. *thūsend*, n.] **1** : being 1000 in number ⟨a ~ years⟩ — usu. preceded by *a* or a numeral (as *one, four*) **2** : being very great in number ⟨a ~ questions⟩ — usu. preceded by *a* or a numeral (as *one, four*) **3** *obs* : THOUSANDTH

¹thou·sand·fold \ˈ=ˌ=ˌfōld\ *adv* [ME, fr. ¹*thousand* + *-fold*] : by 1000 times — usu. preceded by *a* or a numeral ⟨increased a ~⟩ ⟨the small sum spent upon his scientific genius would be returned to the nation ten ~ —*World's Work*⟩

²thousandfold \"\ *adj* [ME, fr. OE *thūsendfeald*, fr. *thūsend* thousand + *-feald* -fold] : being 1000 times as large, as great, or as many as some understood size, degree, or amount : very great — usu. preceded by *a* or a numeral (as *one, four*) ⟨and with a ~ reverberation —S.T.Coleridge⟩ ⟨a ~ increase⟩ — **thou·sand·fold·ly** *adv*

thousand-headed cabbage \'=ˌ=ˌ=-\ n : BRUSSELS SPROUTS

thousand-headed kale *also* **thousand-head kale** n : a tall many-branched leafy kale (*Brassica oleracea fruticosa*) that is used as green feed for cattle and poultry

thousand island dressing n, *usu cap T&I* [prob. fr. *Thousand Islands*, group of islands in the St. Lawrence river partly in New York state and partly in Ontario, Canada] : mayonnaise with various added seasoning and flavoring ingredients (as chili sauce, chopped green peppers, pickles, olives, and cream)

thousand-leaf \'=ˌ=ˌ=\ n : YARROW

thousand-legger \'=ˌ=ˌlegə(r)\ *also* **thousand-legged worm** \'=ˌ=ˌ=-\ n -S [*thousand-legger* fr. ²*thousand* + *leg* + *-er*; *thousand-legged worm* fr. *thousand-legged* (fr. ²*thousand* + *legged*) + *worm*] : MILLIPEDE ⟨as if a *thousand-legger* had scurried over his skin —Gladys Schmitt⟩

thousand-legs \'=ˌ=ˌ=\ n *pl but sing or pl in constr* : MILLIPEDE

thousand-miler \'=ˌ=ˌmīlə(r)\ n [²*thousand* + *mile* + *-er*] : a dark shirt (as worn by railroad men) that does not show dirt

thousand mothers n *pl but sing or pl in constr* : PICKABACK PLANT

¹thou·sandth \'thau̇zᵊn(t)th\ *adj* **1** : being number 1000 in a countable series — see NUMBER table **2** : being one of 1000 equal parts into which anything is divisible

²thousandth \"\ n -S \-ᵊn(t)s, -ᵊn(t)ths\ **1** : number 1000 in a countable series **2** : the quotient of a unit divided by 1000 : one of 1000 equal parts of anything

thousandweight \'=ˌ=ˌ=\ n : a unit equal to 1000 pounds

thow *or* **thowe** \'thō\ *chiefly Scot var of* THAW

thowel *var of* THOLE

thow·less \'thau̇ləs\ *adj* [ME *thowles, thewles* immoral, dissolute, fr. *thew* custom, moral quality + *-les* -less — more at THEW] *Scot* : FEEBLE, LAZY, SPIRITLESS

thowt \'thōt\ *dial Eng var of* THOUGHT

THP *abbr, often not cap* thrust horsepower

thr *abbr* **1** their **2** there **3** through

¹thra·cian \'thrāshən\ n -S *cap* [L *thracius*, adj., Thracian (fr. Gk *thraikios*, fr. *Thraikē* Thrace, region of the eastern Balkan peninsula, southeast Europe) + E *-an*, n. suffix] **1** : a native or inhabitant of Thrace **2** : the language of the Thracians generally assumed to be Indo-European but of uncertain position within the family

²thracian \"\ *adj, usu cap* [L *thracius*, adj., Thracian + E *-an*, adj. suffix] : of or relating to Thrace or the Thracians

thra·co-illyrian \ˈthrā(ˌ)kō+\ *adj, usu cap T&I* [*thraco-* (fr. Gk *thraiko-*, fr. *Thraikē* Thrace + Gk *-o-*) + *illyrian*] : of, relating to, or constituting a supposed subfamily of Indo-European languages comprising Thracian, Illyrian, and Albanian

thraco-phrygian \"+\ *adj, usu cap T&P* [*thraco-* + *phrygian*] : of, relating to, or constituting a tentative branch of the Indo-European language family to which are sometimes assigned various languages of the Balkans and Asia Minor not otherwise assignable

¹thrall \'thrȯl\ n -S [ME *thral*, fr. OE *thrǣl*, fr. ON *thrǣll*; prob. akin to OHG *drigil* servant, OE *thrāg* time, *thrǣgan* to run, Goth *thragjan* to run, OIr *traig* foot] **1 a** : a member of the lowest social class of ancient northern and esp. Scandinavian Europe existing either as an accident of birth or as a result of capture in a state of slavery to a master or lord : a servant slave : BONDMAN; *sometimes* : SERF **b** *archaic* : a person (as a captive held for ransom) deprived of liberty **c** : a person in moral or mental servitude : a person intangibly bound (as by a habit) **2** : the condition of a thrall: **a** : a state of complete absorption or servitude : SLAVERY ⟨the summer mountains could hold me in ~ with a subtle attraction of their own —Elyne Mitchell⟩ ⟨in the ~ of a habit⟩ **b** *archaic* : OPPRESSION, SUFFERING

²thrall \"\ *vt* -ED/-ING/-S [ME *thrallen*, fr. *thral*, n.] *archaic* : ENTHRALL, ENSLAVE

³thrall \"\ *adj* [ME *thral*, fr. *thral*, n.] *archaic* : ENSLAVED, SUBJUGATED, SUBJECT

⁴thrall \"\ n [origin unknown] *dial Eng* : a stand for barrels, milk pans, or cans

thrallborn \'=ˌ=\ *adj* : born in thralldom

thrall·dom *or* **thral·dom** \'thrȯldəm\ n -S [ME *thraldom*, fr. *thral* thrall + *-dom*] : the condition of a thrall : SLAVERY, BONDAGE ⟨from this world's ~ to the joys of heaven —Shak.⟩

thra·neen \'thrəˌnēn\ *var of* TRANEEN

¹thrang \'thraŋ\ *chiefly Scot var of* ³THRONG

²thrang \"\ *adv* [ME *thrange*, fr. *thrang* throng, adj.] *Scot* : BUSILY

thra·nite \'thrāˌnīt\ n -S [Gk *thranitēs*, fr. *thranos* bench + *-itēs* -ite; akin to Gk *thrēsasthai* to sit down — more at FIRM] : the rower highest and farthest back on a bench of three rowers on a trireme — compare THALAMITE

thrap \'thrap\ *vt* **thrapped; thrapped; thrapping; thraps** [by alter.] *chiefly dial* : FRAP 2

thrap·ple \'thrapəl\ n -S [alter. of *thropple*] *Scot* : THROAT, WINDPIPE — used esp. of the horse

¹thrash \'thrash, -raa(ə)sh, -raish, *dial* -räsh\ vb -ED/-ING/-ES [alter. of *thresh*] *vt* **1** : to separate the grain of (as a cereal grass) from the husks and straw by beating : THRESH 1 **2 a** : to beat soundly with or as if with a stick or whip : strike repeatedly : POUND, FLOG, DRUB ⟨~*ed* him well⟩ **b** : to defeat decisively or with severe losses : VANQUISH ⟨~ the visiting team⟩ **3** : to swing, beat, or strike in the manner of a rapidly moving flail ⟨~*ing* his arms from side to side⟩ ⟨~*ed* the water futilely with his oars⟩ **4** : to go over (as a problem) repeatedly usu. in search of a plan of action — usu. used with *over* but sometimes with *about* ⟨~*ed* the matter over once more without reaching a conclusion⟩; compare THRASH OUT **5** : to sail (a ship) to windward in a lively sea ~ *vi* **1** : to thresh grain **2** : to deal blows or strokes in the manner of one using a flail or whip ⟨~ at a hedge with his cane⟩ **3** : to move or stir about violently : toss about ⟨~ in bed with a high fever⟩ ⟨the ship ~*ed* against her anchor⟩ — compare THRESH **4** : to sail to windward in a fresh breeze **syn** see BEAT, SWING

²thrash \"\ n -ES : an act of thrashing: as **a** : an act of sailing to windward in a fresh breeze and a lively sea **b** : a method of moving the legs employed in the crawl and the backstroke

³thrash \'thrash\ n -ES [alter. of ⁵*rash*] *Scot* : RUSH

⁴thrash \"\ *dial var of* TRASH

¹thrash·er \'thrashə(r), -raash-, -raish-\ n -S [alter. of *thresher*] **1** : one that threshes something and esp. grain **2** : THRESHER 2 **3** : one that thrashes

²thrasher \"\ n -S [prob. alter. (influenced by ¹*thrasher*) of *thrush*] : any of numerous long-tailed birds of the American family Mimidae and esp. of the genus *Toxostoma* that resemble thrushes, are closely related to the mockingbird, and include notable singers and mimics — see BROWN THRASHER, CALIFORNIA THRASHER, CRISSAL THRASHER, CURVE-BILLED THRASHER, SAGE THRASHER

thrasherman *var of* THRESHERMAN

thrasher shark n : THRESHER 2

thrasher whale n : KILLER 3

thrashing n -S **1** : the act of one that thrashes **2** : a result of thrashing: as **a** : a batch of thrashed grain **b** : a severe or vicious beating : DRUBBING

thrashing machine n : THRESHING MACHINE

thrash out *vt* : to go over (as a problem or a disputed point) in detail with careful exploration of diverse views and possibilities for solution usu. in an attempt to reach an agreement between conflicting interests ⟨you'll have to *thrash out* that question among yourselves⟩

thra·son·i·cal \thrāˈsänəkəl\ *also* **thra·son·ic** \-nik\ *adj* [L *Thrason-*, *Thraso* Thraso, braggart soldier in the comedy *Eunuchus* by Terence †159 B.C. Roman playwright + E *-ical* or *-ic*] : of, relating to, like, or characteristic of Thraso : BRAGGING, BOASTFUL ⟨Caesar's ~ brag of "I came, saw, and overcame" —Shak.⟩ — **thra·son·i·cal·ly** \-nək(ə)lē\ *adv*

thrau·pi·dae \'thrȯpəˌdē\ n *pl, cap* [NL, fr. *Thraupis*, type genus (fr. Gk *thraupis*, a small bird) + *-idae*] : a family of passerine birds comprising the tanagers and closely related to Fringillidae

thrave \'thrāv\ n -S [ME *thrave, threve*, fr. OE *threfe*, of Scand origin; akin to ON *threfi* thrave, OSw *thravi*] **1** : any of various units of measure for unthreshed grain used locally in Great Britain; *esp* : a unit equal to 24 sheaves **2** : a goodly quantity or number

¹thraw \'thrȯ\ vb -ED/-ING/-S [ME *thrawen*, fr. OE *thrāwan*] *vt* **1** *chiefly Scot* : to cause to twist or turn **2** *chiefly Scot* : CROSS, THWART ~ *vi* **1** *chiefly Scot* : TWIST, TURN **2** *chiefly Scot* : to be in disagreement

²thraw \"\ n -S **1** *chiefly Scot* : TWIST, TURN **2** *chiefly Scot* : ILL HUMOR, ANGER

thra·wart \'thräwərt\ *adj* [ME (Sc), alter. of ME *froward* — more at FROWARD] **1** *chiefly Scot* : habitually disposed to opposition : STUBBORN, PERVERSE **2** *Scot* : CROOKED, TWISTED

thrawn \'thrän\ *adj* [ME (Sc) *thrawin*, fr. past part. of ME *thrawen* to cause to twist or turn] *chiefly Scot* : lacking in pleasing or attractive qualities: as **a** : PERVERSE, RECALCITRANT **b** : CROOKED, MISSHAPEN **c** : SULLEN, GLOOMY — **thrawn·ly** *adv, chiefly Scot*

thre- *or* **threo-** *comb form* [ISV, fr. *threose*] **1** : threose ⟨*thre*itol⟩ **2** *threo-, usu ital* : having the same stereochemical arrangement of two asymmetric carbon atoms as that found in threose ⟨*threo*-3-chloro-2-butanol⟩

¹thread \'thred\ n -S [ME *thred, threed*, fr. OE *thrǣd*; akin to OHG *drāt* wire, ON *thrāthr* thread; derivative fr. the root of OE *thrāwan* to cause to twist or turn — more at THROW] **1 a** : a filament, a group of filaments twisted together, or a filamentous length formed by spinning and twisting short textile fibers into a continuous strand **b** : a fine continuous strand made by plying two or more of these filament groups or lengths either with a tight twist and smooth finish (as for sewing or lace) or with a loose twist (as for embroidery) — compare CORD, ROPE **c** : a piece of thread; *esp* : a length for hand sewing **d** : YARN; *esp* : a warp or weft yarn in a woven fabric **2** : something felt to resemble a textile thread: as **a** : any of various natural filaments ⟨the ~*s* of a spider web⟩ ⟨byssus ~*s*⟩ **b** : a slender stream (as of water) **c** : the middle of a river **d** : a narrow line or streak (as of light or color) ⟨a ~ of lamplight escaped under the edge of the shade⟩ ⟨a quartz sparkling with fine ~*s* of gold⟩ **e** : SCREW THREAD **f** (1) : any of various manufactured filaments (as of glass, plastic, rubber, metal) (2) : a filament removed in the course of some process (as the cutting of the grooves of an original disc recording) **g** : the filament that forms when sugar boiled to 240° F is poured from a spoon **3** : something felt as drawn out or spun out or blended together like the filaments forming a textile thread: as **a** : the continuing course of a life : THREAD OF LIFE **b** : an ordered course (as that linking the elements of a discourse) : a line of reasoning, sequence of ideas, or train of thought ⟨lost the ~ of his argument⟩ **c** : CLEW 2b **d** : a continuing element that colors and modifies a whole ⟨a ~ of poetry marked all his writing⟩ **4** : a tenuous or feeble support that offers no real security : an extremely uncertain and problematical turn of events ⟨a life hanging by a ~⟩ **5** *obs* : KIND, QUALITY, NATURE **6** : a measure for cotton yarn that is equal to ¹⁄₈₀ lea or 1½ yards or 1.37 meters

²thread \"\ vb -ED/-ING/-S [ME *threden*, fr. *thred, threed*, n.] *vt* **1 a** : to pass a thread through the eye of (a needle) **b** : to arrange a thread, yarn, or lead-in piece in working position for use in (a particular machine or device) ⟨~ a bobbin⟩ ⟨~ the sewing machine⟩ **c** : to feed (an exposing or a projecting mechanism) with film : feed film into (a camera) **2 a** : to pass through in the manner of a thread ⟨~ a pipe with wire⟩ ⟨~ tubing in a vein⟩ ⟨streamlets ~*ing* the valley floor⟩ **b** : PIERCE, PENETRATE **c** : to make one's way through or between (as a narrow way or obstacles) ⟨peddlers ~*ing* the narrow alleys⟩; *also* : to make (one's way) usu. cautiously through a hazardous place or situation ⟨~*ed* his way through the legal entanglements⟩ **3** : to put or bring together by or as if by passing a thread through ⟨~ beads⟩ ⟨~*ed* several casual ideas into a charming essay⟩ **4 a** : to interweave with or as if with threads : INTERSPERSE ⟨dark hair ~*ed* with silver⟩ **b** : to cover with threads or a network of threads : screen with overlapping threads ⟨~ plants to protect them from destructive birds⟩ **5** : to form a screw thread or threads on or in; *specif* : to form an external thread on — distinguished from *tap* **6** : to carry (a web) from point to point through a papermaking machine ~ *vi* **1** : to thread or wind a way — usu. used with *through* ⟨~*ing* through narrow passages⟩ ⟨able to ~ but slowly through the intricate report⟩ **2** *of a boiling syrup* : to reach the thread stage : form a thread when poured from a spoon

³thread \"\ *adj* [¹*thread*] : relating to, made of, or resembling thread ⟨~ stockings⟩ ⟨*thread*-shaped⟩

thread angle n : ANGLE OF THREAD

thread bacterium n : ACTINOMYCETE

thread bar n : a threaded bar or rod

threadbare \'=ˌ=\ *adj, sometimes* -ER/-EST [ME *thredbare*, fr. *thred* thread + *bare*] **1 a** : worn to the point that the thread is visible : having the nap wholly or partly worn off ⟨~ clothes⟩ **b** : clad in threadbare clothing : SHABBY ⟨a neat but ~ clerk⟩ **2** : suggesting a threadbare fabric (as in poverty of invention, meanness, or shabbiness) : SCANTY, BARREN ⟨a ~ history⟩ **3** : having lost its freshness or bloom : lacking in novelty or interest : TRITE, HACKNEYED **syn** see TRITE

thread·bare·ness n -ES : the quality or state of being threadbare

thread blight n : a disease of cocoa, tea, citrus, and other woody plants in semitropical and tropical countries caused by basidiomycetous fungi of the genera *Pellicularia* and *Marasmius* that form filamentous strands of mycelium over the surface of leaves and twigs

thread cell n : NEMATOCYST

thread chaser n : a multiple point tool used typically as one of a set of four in a die head for cutting a screw thread

thread count n : COUNT 8b

thread·dle \'thredᵊl\ *var of* THREADLE

thread·ed \'thredəd\ *adj* : furnished with a thread ⟨a ~ needle⟩ — usu. used in combination ⟨double-*threaded*⟩

threaded glass *or* **thread glass** n : glass with a surface decoration of fine applied threads often of contrasting color or a surface appearance of being made up of fine threads

thread eel n : SNIPE EEL

thread·en \'thredᵊn\ *adj* [ME *threden*, fr. *thred* thread + *-en*] : made of thread

thread·er \ˈthredə(r)\ *n* -s : one that threads: as **a** : a worker who threads material into a machine or sets up a machine by threading **b** (1) : a device for threading a needle (2) : any of various devices for drawing a line through one or more narrow openings or channels **c** : a device for cutting a screw thread ⟨bolt and pipe ~s⟩

threader b(1)

thread escutcheon *n* : a small plate outlining an opening (as a keyhole)

threadfin \ˈ=,=\ *n* [so called fr. the filaments of the pectoral fin] **1** : a fish of the family Polynemidae **2** : a fish of the genus *Polymixia*

threadfish \ˈ=,=\ *n, pl* **threadfish** *or* **threadfishes** **1** : a small compressed deep-bodied carangid fish (*Alectis ciliaris*) having long filamentous streamers depending from its fins and being nearly cosmopolitan in warm seas **2** : THREADFIN 1

threadflower \ˈ=,=\ *n* **1** : any of various plants of the genus *Nematanthus* (family Gesneriaceae) having long slender peduncles to the crimson flowers **2** : a plant of the genus *Poinciana*

threadfoot \ˈ=,=\ *n* [so called fr. its threadlike leaves] : RIVERWEED

thread fungus *n* : a fungus causing dermatomycosis

thread gage *n* : a gage for measuring screw threads or for checking or determining the pitch, thread angle, or diameter of a screw thread

thread generator *n* : a machine in which screw threads (as of a worm) are produced by a cutter in the form of a helical pinion

thread herring *n* **1** : GIZZARD SHAD **2** : either of two herrings: **a** : a herring (*Opisthonema oglinum*) of the West Indies and east coast of the U. S. having the last ray of the dorsal fin long and slender **b** : a very similar fish (*O. libertate*) of the west coast of tropical America

thread gage

thread·i·ness \ˈthredēnəs\ *n* -ES : the quality or state of being thready

threading *n* -s [fr. gerund of ²*thread*] : DRAWING-IN

threading lathe *n* : a screw-cutting lathe having a control shaft that operates mechanisms which remove the tool from the work at the end of the cut and set it for the next operation

threading machine *n* : THREADER c

threading tool *n* : a tool for cutting screw threads

thread lace *n* : lace made of linen thread

threa·dle \ˈthredᵊl\ *vt* -ED/-ING/-S *dial Eng* : THREAD

threadleaf *also* **threadleaved** \ˈ=,=\ *adj* : having long slender leaves

threadleaf sedge *also* **threadleaved sedge** *n* : a sedge (*Carex filifolia*) of No. America with filiform or acicular leaves

thread-legged bug \ˈ=,=(=)-\ *n* : SPIDER BUG

thread·less \ˈthredləs\ *adj* : lacking thread or a thread ⟨a rambling ~ story⟩ ⟨a ~ connection between pipes⟩

thread·let \-lət\ *n* -s : a small thread : a delicate filament

threadlike \ˈ=,=\ *adj* : slender and elongated like a thread : FILAMENTOUS

thread-line fishing *n* : SPINNING

thread lungworm *n* : a slender widely distributed nematode worm (*Dictyocaulus filaria*) that parasitizes the air passages of the lungs of sheep

thread miller *n* : a milling machine on which screw threads are milled with a formed cutter or a hob

¹**thread-needle** \ˈ=,==\ *also* **thread-the-needle** \ˈ==,==\ *n* [*thread-needle* fr. ²*thread* + *needle*, n.; *thread-the-needle* fr. the phrase *thread the needle*] **1** : a children's game in which all join hands and the leader followed by the other players passes under the arched arms of those at the other end **2** : a country dance figure resembling the procession of the threadneedle game

²**thread-needle** \"\ *vi* **1** : to play or move as if playing threadneedle **2** : to execute the thread-needle figure in dancing

thread of life : the course of individual existence esp. as fabled in ancient times to be spun and cut by the Fates

thread paper *n* **1** : a strip of folded paper serving to hold skeins of thread in its divisions **2** : something and esp. a person as long and narrow as a thread paper

thread roller *n* : a roller designed to make threads (as on a screw)

threads *pl of* THREAD, *pres 3d sing of* THREAD

thread-waisted wasp \ˈ=,==-\ *n* : any of numerous wasps of the family Sphecidae having a very slender abdominal petiole

threadway \ˈ=,=\ *n* : a way (as in a nut) for a thread

threadworm \ˈ=,=\ *n* : a long slender nematode worm

thread-worn \ˈ=,=\ *adj* **1** : THREADBARE **2** : worn in the thread ⟨a *thread-worn* screw⟩

thready \ˈthredē, -di\ *adj* -ER/-EST [ME *thredy*, fr. *thred* thread + *-y*] **1** : consisting of or bearing fibers or threadlike elements ⟨a coarse ~ bark⟩ **2 a** : having the form or appearance of a thread : slenderly elongate : FILAMENTOUS ⟨~ prolongations of the lobes⟩ **b** : tending to form threads or to draw out into somewhat elastic strands : ROPY ⟨a thick ~ solution⟩; *also* : marked by such a tendency ⟨a ~ condition of the urine⟩ **3** : lacking in strength or fullness : deficient in body or vigor : THIN, SLIGHT ⟨a ~ voice⟩ — see THREADY PULSE **4** *of a fabric* : having a clear finish that allows all threads to be seen

thready pulse *n* : a scarcely perceptible and commonly rapid pulse that feels like a fine mobile thread under the palpating finger

¹**threap** \ˈthrēp\ *vb* -ED/-ING/-S [ME *threpen*, fr. OE *thrēapian*] *vt* **1** *chiefly Scot* : SCOLD, CHIDE **2** *chiefly Scot* : to assert to be : affirm or maintain persistently **3** *obs* : to urge the acceptance of : PRESS ~ *vi*, *chiefly Scot* : to talk contentiously : DISPUTE, WRANGLE

²**threap** \"\ *n* -s [ME *threp*, fr. *threpen*, v.] **1** *chiefly Scot* : the act of one who threaps : ACCUSATION **2** *chiefly Scot* : a debatable account : TRADITION, LEGEND, REPORT

threap down *vt*, *chiefly Scot* : to reduce to silence by vigorous or repeated assertion

threap·er \-pə(r)\ *n* -s *chiefly Scot* : one that asserts or argues pertinaciously

¹**threat** \ˈthret, *usu* -ed·+V\ *n* -s [ME *thret* threat, coercion, troop, fr. OE *thrēat* coercion, troop; akin to OE *thrēotan* to annoy, MHG *drōz* annoyance, OHG *driozan* to annoy, ON *thraut* hard task, *thrjōta* to fail, lack, Goth us*thriutan* to harass, persecute, L *trudere* to push, thrust, Russ *trud* labor] **1** : an indication of something impending and usu. undesirable or unpleasant ⟨the air held a ~ of rain⟩: as **a** : an expression of an intention to inflict evil, injury, or damage on another usu. as retribution or punishment for something done or left undone ⟨quieted at once on the teacher's ~ to keep them in after school⟩ **b** : expression of an intention to inflict loss or harm on another by illegal means and esp. by means involving coercion or duress of the person threatened ⟨~s inducing fear of bodily harm are often cause for legal action even in the absence of overt violence⟩ **2** : something that by its very nature or relation to another threatens the welfare of the latter ⟨the crumbling cliff was a constant ~ to the village below⟩ ⟨economic depressions constitute a major ~ to party hegemony —C.A.M.Ewing⟩

²**threat** \"\ *vb* -ED/-ING/-S [ME *threten*, fr. OE *thrēatian*, fr. *thrēat*, n.] *vt* **1** *obs* : to exert pressure upon : URGE, PRESS **2** *archaic* : THREATEN ~ *vi*, *archaic* : THREATEN

threat·en \ˈthretᵊn\ *vb* **threatened; threatened; threatening** \-t(ᵊ)niŋ\ **threatens** [ME *thretnen*, *thretenen*, fr. OE *thrēatnian* to force, fr. *thrēat* coercion + *-nian* -en] *vt* **1** : to utter threats against : promise punishment, reprisal, or other distress to ⟨~ trespassers with arrest⟩ **2** *archaic* : to charge under pain of punishment : WARN ⟨let us straitly ~ them, that they speak henceforth to no man in this name —Acts 4:17 (AV)⟩ **3** : to promise as a threat : hold out by way of menace or warning ⟨~ punishment to all trespassers⟩ **4 a** : to give signs of the approach of (something evil or unpleasant) : indicate as impending : PORTEND ⟨the sky ~s a storm⟩ **b** : to hang over as a threat : MENACE ⟨famine ~s the city⟩ **5** : to announce as intended or possible ⟨~ to buy a car⟩ ~ *vi* **1** : to utter or use threats or menaces **2** : to have a menacing appearance : portend evil ⟨though the seas ~ they are merciful —Shak.⟩

syn MENACE: THREATEN applies to the probable visitation of some evil or affliction; it may be used of attempts to dissuade by promising punishment or retribution ⟨most of them lived on the margin of survival, constantly *threatened* by famine and disease —Arthur Geddes⟩ ⟨another form of lying, which is extremely bad for the young, is to *threaten* punishments you do not mean to inflict —Bertrand Russell⟩ ⟨discredit completely all other forms of Christianity, denying any efficacy to their rites, and *threatening* all their members with eternal damnation —W.R.Inge⟩ MENACE may connote more deeply a dire, malignant, hostile, or fearful character or aspect ⟨the devastating weapons which are at present being developed may *menace* every part of the world —Clement Attlee⟩ ⟨the conviction that it was foreigners who *menaced* the American Way —Oscar Handlin⟩

threat·en·er \-t(ə)nə(r)\ *n* -s : one that threatens

threat·en·ing·ly *adv* : in a threatening manner : so as to provide or constitute a threat

threat·ful \ˈthretfəl\ *adj* : full of threats : THREATENING, MENACING — **threat·ful·ly** \-fəlē\ *adv*

threats action *n, Brit* : an action for damages and an injunction against one threatening without justification to sue for alleged infringement of patent rights

¹**three** \ˈthrē\ *adj* [ME *three*, *thre*, fr. OE *thrīe* (masc.), *thrēo* (fem. & neut.); akin to OHG *drī* (masc.) three, *drīo* (fem.), *driu* (neut.), ON *thrīr* (masc.), *thrjār* (fem.), *thrjū* (neut.), Goth *thrija* (neut.), L *tres* (masc. & fem.), *tria* (neut.), Gk *treis* (masc. & fem.), *tria* (neut.), Skt *tri*] : being one more than two in number ⟨~ years⟩ — see NUMBER table

²**three** \"\ *pron, pl in constr* [ME *three*, *thre*, fr. *three*, *thre*, adj.] : three countable persons or things not specified but under consideration and being enumerated ⟨~ are here⟩ ⟨~ were found⟩

³**three** \"\ *n* -s [ME *three*, *thre*, fr. *three*, *thre*, adj.] **1** : one more than two **2 a** : three units or objects ⟨a total of ~⟩ **b** : a group or set of three ⟨arranged by ~s⟩ **3 a** : the numerable quantity symbolized by the arabic numeral 3 **b** : the figure 3 **4** : three o'clock — compare BELL table, TIME illustration **5** : the third in a set or series: as **a** : a playing card marked to show that it is third in a suit **b** : a domino with three spots on one of its halves **c** : a die with three spots on the side uppermost **d** : an article of clothing of the third size

three-arm protractor *or* **three-armed protractor** \ˈ=,=-\ *n* : STATION POINTER

three-awn \ˈ=,=\ *also* **three-awn grass** *n* : a grass of the genus *Aristida*

three-ball \ˈ=,=\ *n* : STRAIGHT RAIL

three-ball match *n* : a golf match in which three players compete against one another with each playing his own ball

three-banded armadillo \ˈ=,==-\ *n* : an armadillo with a shell having three bands; *esp* : APAR

three-base hit \ˈ=,=-\ *or* **three-bag·ger** \ˈ=¦bagə(r), -¦baag-, -¦baig-\ *n* : a base hit that enables a batter to reach third base safely — called also *triple*

three birds *n pl but sing or pl in constr* [so called fr. the suggested resemblance of the shape of flower to three birds perched on the spur] **1** : a perennial toadflax (*Linaria triornithophora*) of Spain cultivated for its showy purple and yellow flowers **2** : NODDING CAP

three-card monte *n* : a gambling game in which the dealer shows three cards, then manipulates them by sleight-of-hand, throws them face down on a table, and invites persons to bet they can identify the location of a particular card

three-card poker *n* : poker in which each player's hand contains only three cards and the hands rank downward in the order three of a kind, three cards of the same suit in sequence, three cards of the same suit, three cards in sequence, pair, and high card

three-centered arch \ˈ=,==-\ *n* : an arch whose intrados curve is described from three centers

three-cent piece *n* : a silver coin worth three cents issued in the U. S. 1851–1873 or a nickel coin issued 1865–1889

three-charge rate *n* : a two-charge rate to which has been added a service charge

three-centered arch

three-circuit switch *n* : THREE-WAY SWITCH

three-color \ˈ=¦==\ *adj, of process printing* : using inks of 3 different colors

three-color photography *or* **three-color process** *n* : any of various processes of color photography wherein three primary colors (as blue-violet, green, and red in the additive process or magenta, yellow, and blue-green in the subtractive process) are used to produce the color of the subject photographed

three-color theory *n* : a theory of color vision that assumes three psychologically primary colors

three-corner \ˈ=¦==\ *adj* : THREE-CORNERED

three-cornered \ˈ=¦==\ *adj* [ME, fr. *three*, *thre* three + *cornered*] **1** : having three corners ⟨a *three-cornered* hat⟩ — see COCKED HAT **2** : involving a group or set of three ⟨the race ended in a *three-cornered* tie⟩

three-cornered constituency *n* : a constituency with three members to be returned at one election with each voter voting for only two candidates

three-cushion billiards *also* **three cushions** *n pl but usu sing in constr* : carom billiards in which the cue ball must touch one or more cushions three different times plus the two object balls to score a count

three-cushion carom *n* : THREE-CUSHION BILLIARDS

threed \ˈthrēd\ *dial Brit var of* THREAD

¹**3-D** \ˈthrē¦dē\ *adj* [*D* abbr. of *dimensional*] THREE-DIMENSIONAL

²**3-D** \ˈ=¦=\ *n* : the three-dimensional form or a picture produced in it

three-day fever *n* : a fever or febrile state lasting three days: as **a** : PHLEBOTOMUS FEVER **b** : DENGUE **c** *or* **three-day sickness** : an infectious disease of cattle esp. in Africa marked by fever, muscular rigidity, conjunctivitis, and nasal discharge, and usu. subsiding within two or three days — called also *ephemeral fever*

three-deck *or* **three-decked** \ˈ=¦=\ *adj* : having three decks

three-decker \ˈ=¦==\ *n* [*three-deck* + *-er*] **1 a** : a warship carrying guns on three decks **b** : a cargo or passenger ship with three full decks **2 a** : a structure having three floors, stories, or tiers: as (1) : the clerk's desk, reading desk, and pulpit proper arranged one above the other on three separate levels in some churches (2) : a sandwich made of three slices of bread and two fillings **b** : a book and esp. a novel in three volumes; *broadly* : an unusually long novel **3** : a thing of great importance, size, or eminence

three-dimensional \ˈ=¦=(=)=\ *adj* **1** : of or involving three dimensions ⟨*three-dimensional* space⟩ **2** : giving the illusion of depth or varying distances — used of a pictorial representation (as a photograph or a motion picture in which this illusion is enhanced by stereoscopic or other means) — compare TWO-DIMENSIONAL **3** : describing or being described in well-rounded completeness ⟨a *three-dimensional* analysis of multiple historical processes —L.L.Snyder⟩; *esp* : LIFELIKE ⟨the only book of the batch . . . that has *three-dimensional* characters —David Dempsey⟩ **4** : of, relating to, or involving military operations in three spheres (as land, sea, and air)

three-eighths blood *n* : a grade of wool next below half blood in a descending scale of fineness — compare BLOOD 7, HALF BLOOD 3

three-em space *n* : a space in printing that is ⅓ of an em in thickness

three farthings *n pl but sing or pl in constr* : an Elizabethan silver coin worth ¾ of an English penny

three-field system *or* **three-course system** *n* : a system of land cultivation under which the common land is divided into three parts of which one or two in rotation lie fallow in each year and the rest are cultivated

¹**three-fold** \ˈthrē¦fōld\ *adj* [ME *threfold*, fr. OE *thrēofeald*, fr. *thrīe*, *thrēo* three + *-feald* -fold] **1** : having three parts or aspects : TRIPLE ⟨a ~ purpose⟩ ⟨a ~ meaning⟩ **2** : being three times as large, as great, or as many as some understood size, degree, or amount ⟨a ~ increase⟩

²**threefold** \"\ *adv* [ME *threfolde*, fr. OE *thrēofealde*, fr. *thrēofeald*, adj.] : to three times as much or as many : THRICE : by three times ⟨increased ~⟩

threefold purchase *or* **threefold tackle** *n* : a tackle of two treble blocks

three-four \ˈ=¦=\ *or* **three-four time** *n* : the rhythmic content per measure as indicated ¾ in a musical composition consisting of three quarter notes or tones or their equivalent

three-fourths value clause *n* : an insurance policy provision limiting the insurer's liability to an amount not greater than three fourths of the cash value of the insured property but not exceeding the face of the policy often used to cause the insured to safeguard the property

three-gaited \ˈ=¦==\ *adj, of a horse* : trained to use the walk, trot, and canter

three-halfpence \ˈ=¦==\ *n, pl* **three-halfpence** *or* **three-halfpences** [ME *threhalpenys*, fr. *three*, *thre* three + *halpenys*, *halfpenys*, pl. of *halpeny*, *halfpeny* halfpenny] **1** : the sum of three halfpence : one penny halfpenny **2** : a small English silver coin of Queen Elizabeth I worth 1½ pennies; *also* : a silver coin struck under William IV and Queen Victoria for the colonies

three-halfpenny \ˈ=¦=(=)=\ *adj* : worth or costing three-halfpence

three-handed \ˈ=¦==\ *also* **three-hand** \ˈ=¦=\ *adj* : played or to be played by three players

three-high \ˈ=¦=\ *adj* : of or relating to a train of three rolls in a rolling mill set one above another

three-hol·er \ˈthrē¦hōlə(r)\ *n* [¹*three* + *hole* + *-er*] : a privy with three openings

three-hooped *adj, obs* : bound with three hoops

three-in-hand \ˈ==,=\ *n* **1** : a team of three horses driven by one person **2** : a vehicle drawn by a three-in-hand team

three in one *cap T&O* : TRINITY 1a(1)

three island ship *n* : a ship with a raised forecastle, midship structure, and poop

three jump *n* : a leap in figure skating from a forward outside edge of one foot to an outside back edge of the opposite foot with a one-half turn of the body in the air — called also *waltz jump*

three kings' day *n, usu cap T&K&D* [so called fr. the wise men (traditionally kings and three in number) that brought gifts to the infant Jesus (Mt 2:1–12)] : EPIPHANY

three-leaved arum \ˈ=,=-\ *n* : JACK-IN-THE-PULPIT

three-leaved hop tree *n* : HOP TREE

three-leaved indian turnip *n, usu cap I* : JACK-IN-THE-PULPIT

three-leaved ivy *n* : POISON IVY

three-leaved maple *n* : BOX ELDER

three-leaved stonecrop *n* : WILD STONECROP

three-legged \ˈ=¦=(=)\ *adj* : having three legs ⟨a *three-legged* stool⟩

three-legged race *n* : a race between contestants who run in pairs having the proximate legs bound together

three-lined potato beetle \ˈ=,=-\ *n* : a small yellow leaf beetle (*Lema trilineata*) with three black lines on each elytron whose larva feeds on the potato plant

three-line octave *n* [so called fr. the three accent marks of the symbol C‴ representing the second C above middle C] : the musical octave that begins on the second C above middle C — see PITCH illustration

three·ling \ˈthrēliŋ\ *n* -s [³*three* + *-ling*] : TRILLING

three-master \ˈ=¦==\ *n* -s [obs. E *three-mast*, adj., having three masts (fr. E ¹*three* + *mast*, n.) + E *-er*] : a 3-masted ship

three-men-in-a-boat \ˈ=,===ˈ=\ *n* : OYSTER PLANT 3

three-mile limit *n* : a limit of the marine belt of three miles included in the territorial waters of a state

three-minute glass *n* : a device similar to an hourglass used to measure 3-minute intervals and esp. to time the boiling of eggs

three of a kind : three cards of the same rank — see POKER illustration

three old cat \¦thrēə¦kat, ¦thrē,ōl¦k-\ *or* **three o'cat** \¦thrēə¦k-\ *n* : one old cat played with three batters

threep \ˈthrēp\ *var of* THREAP

three-part form *n* : TERNARY FORM

three·pence *Brit* ˈthripən(t)s *or* -rəp- *or* -rep- *or* -rŭp-, *US* " *or* -rē,pen·\ *n, pl* **threepence** *or* **threepences** **1** : the sum of three usu. British pennies **2** : a coin worth three pennies

three·pen·ny \-nē, -ni, -,pnē, -pni\ *adj* [ME *threpeny*, fr. *three*, *thre* three + *peny* penny] **1** : costing or worth threepence **2** : worth little : POOR, MEAN

threepenny bit *or* **threepenny piece** *n* : THREEPENCE 2

threepenny nail *n* [so called fr. the former price per hundred] : a nail 1⅛ inches long

three·pen·ny·worth \(ˈ)thrēˈpenē(,)wərth, -nərth\ *n* : the amount that a threepence buys

three-phase \ˈ=¦=\ *adj* : of, relating to, or operating by means of a combination of three circuits energized by alternating electromotive forces that differ in phase by one third of a cycle

¹**three-piece** \ˈ=¦=\ *adj* : consisting of or made in three pieces ⟨*three-piece* living room set⟩ ⟨a woman's *three-piece* suit⟩

²**three-piece** \ˈ=,=\ *n* : a three-piece outfit

three-piled *or* **three-pile** \ˈ=¦=\ *adj* **1** : having a pile of treble thickness **2** *obs* : of high rank, quality, or excellence

three-plier \ˈ=¦plī(ə)r\ *n* [*three-ply* + *-er*] : a three-ply rivet

three-ply \ˈ=¦=\ *adj* **1** : consisting of three distinct parts: as **a** : having three strands ⟨*three-ply* yarn⟩ **b** : having three layers interwoven ⟨*three-ply* cloth⟩ **c** : consisting of three veneers glued together with opposing grains **2** : passing through three thicknesses ⟨*three-ply* rivet⟩

three-point landing *n* : an airplane landing in which the two main wheels of the landing gear and the tail wheel or skid or nose wheel touch the ground simultaneously

three-point perspective *n* : linear perspective in which parallel lines along the width of an object meet at two separate points on the horizon and vertical lines on the object meet at a point on the perpendicular bisector of the horizon line

three-point problem *n* : the problem of locating the point of observation from the observed angles subtended by three known sides of a triangle either by mathematical calculation or by plotting with a station pointer

three-point switch *n* : THREE-WAY SWITCH

¹**three-quarter** *or* **three-quarters** \ˈ=¦==\ *adj* **1 a** : of, relating to, or being a painted portrait measuring 30 by 25 inches or one showing the figure down to the hips only **b** : of, relating to, or being a photographic portrait showing the figure about to the knees **2** : extending to three-quarters of the normal full length ⟨*three-quarter* coat⟩ ⟨*three-quarter* sleeve⟩

²**three-quarter** \"\ *n* **1 a** : a three-quarter-length portrait **b** : a three-quarter-face portrait **c** : three-quarter lighting of a face or figure **2** *or* **three-quarter back** : a player in rugby whose regular position is between the standoff half and the fullback

three-quarter binding *n* : a book binding in which the material (as leather) of the backbone and the corners is different from that of the sides and the material of the backbone extends upon the boards for one third of their width — compare FULL BINDING, HALF BINDING, QUARTER BINDING

three-quarter-bound *adj, of a book* : having a three-quarter binding

three-quarter-bred \ˈ=¦==,=\ *adj* : having three grandparents of the pure blood of one breed — used of a domestic animal

three-quarter-floating axle \ˈ=¦==-\ *n* : a live axle in which the outer ends of the axle shaft are supported by wheels forming a rigid unit with the shaft and depending on it for alignment

three-quarter nelson *n* : a wrestling hold in which a wrestler kneeling beside a prone opponent passes his far arm under the opponent's corresponding arm and behind his neck and grasps the wrist of his own near arm passed under his opponent's body from the near side — compare FULL NELSON, HALF NELSON, QUARTER NELSON

three-quarter time *n* : THREE-FOUR

three-quarter vamp *n* : a vamp extending from the inner side of the shank around the toe to the backseam

three-quarter view *n* : a representation of a head or figure posed about halfway between front and profile views

three-ridge \'ˌ=ˌ=\ *n* [so called fr. the three ridges on the shell] **:** a freshwater clam (*Amblema costata* syn. *Quadrula plicata*) of the Mississippi drainage system

three-ring circus *or* **three-ringed circus** \'ˌ=ˌ=-\ *n* **1 :** a circus with simultaneous performances in three rings **2 :** something wild, confusing, engrossing, or entertaining ⟨what a *three-ringed circus* that fellow is —Dorothy C. Fisher⟩

three r's *n pl, usu cap R* [so called fr. the facetiously used phrase *reading, 'riting, and 'rithmetic*] **1 :** the fundamentals taught in elementary school; *esp* **:** reading and writing and arithmetic **2 :** the fundamental skills in a field of endeavor

threes *pl of* THREE

threescore \'ˌ=ˌ=\ *adj* [ME *thre scoor,* fr. *three, thre* three + *scoor, scor* score] **:** being 60 in number

three-seeded mercury \'ˌ=ˌ==-\ *n* **:** a weedy herb of the genus *Acalypha* (esp. *A. virginica* of eastern No. America)

[1]**three·some** \'thrēsəm\ *n* -S [ME(Sc) *thresum,* fr. ME *three, thre* three + ME (northern dial.) *-sum* -some] **1 :** a group of three **:** TRIO **2 :** a golf match in which one person plays his ball against the ball of two others playing each stroke alternately

[2]**threesome** \"\ *adj* **:** performed or engaged in by three persons ⟨a ~ dance⟩

three-spined stickleback \'ˌ=ˌ=-\ *n* **:** a stickleback (*Gasterosteus aculeatus*) of fresh or brackish waters typically with three dorsal spines

three-spot \'ˌ=ˌ=\ *n* **:** a three in cards or dice

three-spot gourami *n* [so called fr. the spot at the body center, the spot at the caudal base, and the prominent eye] **:** a small gourami (*Trichogaster trichopterus*) of southeastern Asia introduced into other countries as an aquarium fish

[1]**three-square** \'ˌ=ˌ=\ *adj* [ME *thre sqware* having three equal sides, fr. *three, thre* three + *sqware, square* square] **:** having an equilateral triangular cross section — used esp. of a file

[2]**three-square** \'ˌ=ˌ=\ *n* **1** *also* **three-square rush** [so called fr. the triangular stems] **:** any of various rushes of the genus *Scirpus; esp* **:** CHAIRMAKER'S RUSH **2 :** a three-square file

three-step \'ˌ=ˌ=\ *n* **1 :** a dance characterized esp. by three steps in each movement **2 :** a skiing maneuver to attain speed on level ground consisting of two short steps followed by a glide

three-striper \'ˌ=ˌ==\ *n* **:** a commander in the U.S. Navy

three-syllable law *n* **:** a statement in grammar: in some languages (as Latin) the primary accent is limited to one of the last three syllables of a word

three-tailed porgy \'ˌ=ˌ=-\ *n* **:** a spadefish (*Chaetodipterus faber*)

three thorn acacia *also* **three-thorned acacia** \'ˌ=ˌ=-\ *n* **:** HONEY LOCUST

three-throw \'ˌ=ˌ=\ *adj* **1 :** THREE-WAY **2 :** having three cranks on the same shaft

three times three : three cheers repeated three times

three-toed plover \'ˌ=ˌ=-\ *n* **:** GOLDEN PLOVER

three-toed sloth *n* **:** a sloth of the genus *Bradypus* having three claws on each front foot

three-toed woodpecker *n* **:** any of several boreal woodpeckers of the genus *Picoides* in which the inner digit is lacking or vestigial

three-toes \'ˌ=ˌ=\ *n pl but sing or pl in constr* **:** GOLDEN PLOVER

three-toothed cinquefoil \'ˌ=ˌ=-\ *n* **:** CRYSTAL TEA 1

three-valued \'ˌ=ˌ==\ *adj* [trans. of G *dreiwertig,* trans. of Pol *trójwartościowej*] **:** possessing three truth values instead of the customary two of truth and falsehood

three-vol·um·er \'ˌ='välyəmə(r)\ *n* -S [[1]*three* + *volume* + *-er*] *Brit* **:** a 3-volume novel

three-way \'ˌ=ˌ=\ *adj* **1 :** allowing passage in any of three directions ⟨*three-way* intersection⟩ ⟨*three-way* valve⟩ **2 :** involving three participants ⟨a *three-way* profit split⟩ ⟨a *three-way* play-off⟩

three-way bulb *n* **:** an electric light bulb having two filaments of different wattage that can be lighted separately or together to give three levels of illumination

three-way cross *n* **:** the first generation obtained by crossing a simple hybrid with a third form

three-way lamp *n* **:** a lamp using a three-way bulb

three-way switch *n* **:** an electric switch having three terminals used to control a circuit from two different points

three-wheel·er \'ˌ='(h)wēlə(r)\ *n* [[1]*three* + *wheel* + *-er*] **:** a vehicle with three wheels: as **a :** TRICYCLE **b :** a motorcycle with a side car; *also* **:** a motorcycle with one front wheel and two rear wheels **c :** a 3-wheeled automobile

three-wire generator *n* **:** a direct-current generator with both slip rings and a commutator used for supplying current to a direct-current three-wire system whose neutral wire is connected to the center point of a high-reactance winding connected across the slip rings and whose two main conductors are connected to the commutator brushes

three-wire system *n* **:** a constant potential system of electric distribution in which lamps or other receiving devices are connected between either one of two main conductors and a third wire and motors and heavy duty appliances are usu. connected across the main conductors

thre·i·tol \'thrēə,tōl, -,tȯl\ *n* -S [*thre-* + *-itol*] **:** a sweet crystalline tetrahydroxy alcohol $HOCH_2(CHOH)_2CH_2OH$ known in three optically isomeric forms and formed by reduction of threose

threm·ma·tol·o·gy \,thremə'täləjē\ *n* -ES [Gk *thremmat-, thremma* nursling + E *-o-* + *-logy* — more at ATROPHY] **:** the science of breeding animals and plants under domestication

thre·node \'thrē,nōd, 'thre,-\ *n* -S [by alter. (influenced by *ode*)] **:** THRENODY — **thre·nod·ic** \thrə'nädik\ *adj*

thren·o·dist \'threnədəst\ *n* -S [*threnody* + *-ist*] **:** a writer of threnodies

thren·o·dy \-dē, -di\ *n* -ES [Gk *thrēnōidia,* fr. *thrēnos* threnody, dirge + *-ōidia* (fr. *aeidein* to sing); akin to Skt *dhraṇati* it sounds — more at DRONE, ODE] **:** a song, poem, composition, or speech of lamentation esp. for someone dead or something regarded as dead **:** DIRGE, ELEGY

thre·nos \'thrē,näs\ *also* **thre·nus** \-ēnəs\ *n, pl* **thre·noi** \-ē,nȯi\ *also* **thre·ni** \-ē,nī\ [*threnos* fr. Gk *thrēnos; threnus* fr. LL, fr. Gk *thrēnos*] **:** THRENODY; *esp* **:** a lyrical lament over a victim of the catastrophe in a tragedy

threo- — see THRE-

thre·on·ic acid \thrē'änik-\ *n* [*threonic* ISV *thre-* + *-onic*] **:** a syrupy or crystalline trihydroxy acid $HOCH_2(CHOH)_2COOH$ formed by oxidation of threose

thre·o·nine \'thrēə,nēn, -,nən\ *n* -S [prob. fr. *threon-* (as in *threonic acid*) + *-ine*] **:** a crystalline alpha-amino acid $CH_3CHOHCH(NH_2)COOH$ known in six optically isomeric forms; 2-amino-3-hydroxy-butyric acid; *esp* **:** the levorotatory L-form related to D-threose that is obtained by hydrolysis of various proteins (as casein and egg proteins) and is essential to normal nutrition

thre·ose \'thrē,ōs\ *n* -S [ISV *thre-* (prob. anagram of part of *erythr-*) + *-ose*] **:** a syrupy synthetic aldo-tetrose sugar $CH_2OH(CHOH)_2CHO$ that is the epimer of erythrose and is known in three optically isomeric forms

threpe \'thrēp\ *dial var of* THREAP

threp·tic \'threptik\ *adj* [Gk *threptikos* able to feed, fr. *threptos* (verbal of *trephein* to nourish, feed) + *-ikos* -ic — more at ATROPHY] **:** of or relating to the feeding or rearing of offspring esp. among ants or other social insects

[1]**thresh** \'thrash, -raa(ə)sh, -raish, -resh\ *vb* -ED/-ING/-ES [ME *thresshen,* fr. OE *threscan, therscan;* akin to OHG *dreskan* to thresh, ON *thriskja,* Goth *thriskan* to thresh, L *terere* to rub — more at THROW] *vt* **1 a :** to beat out grain or seed from (as wheat stalks) by treading, rubbing, striking with a flail, or by a threshing machine **b :** to beat off (as kernels of grain) **2 :** to go over (as a problem) again and again — often used with *over* ⟨~*ing* over the systems of the past —John Dewey⟩ ⟨continued to ~ the matter over in his mind —T.B.Costain⟩ **3 :** to strike repeatedly **:** THRASH ⟨the paddles . . . ~*ing* the black water —F. Tennyson Jesse⟩ ~ *vi* **1 :** to thresh grain **:** operate a flail or threshing machine **2** *of grain* **:** to undergo the threshing process **3 :** to strike with or as if with a flail or whip **4 :** to toss about — compare THRASH **syn** see BEAT

[2]**thresh** \"\ *n* -ES **1 :** the act of threshing grain **2 :** THRASH

[3]**thresh** \'thresh\ *n* -ES [alter. of [2]*resh*] *Scot* **:** [1]RUSH

thresh·er \'thrashə(r), -raash-, -raish-, -resh-\ *n* -S [ME *thressher,* fr. *thresshen* to thresh + *-er, -ere* -er] **1 :** one that threshes **:** a threshing machine or a person tending or operating a flail or a threshing machine **2** *also* **thresher shark :** a large shark (*Alopias vulpinus*) nearly cosmopolitan in distribution that is distinguished by the greatly elongated curved upper lobe of its tail with which it is said to thresh the water to round up the fish on which it feeds and that is highly regarded as a sport fish and in some areas used as food — called also *fox shark*

thresh·er·man *also* **thrash·er·man** \'ˌ==mən\ *n, pl* **thresher·men** *also* **thrashermen** [*thresher* or [1]*thrasher* + *man*] **:** one who makes a business of custom threshing

thresher whale *n* **:** KILLER 3

threshing floor *n* [ME *thresschinge flor,* fr. *thresschinge, thresshinge* (gerund of *thresschen, thresshen* to thresh) + *flor* floor] **:** ground or floor space for threshing or treading out grain

threshing machine *n* **:** a machine for separating grain or seeds from straw

[1]**thresh·old** \'thresh,(h)ōld\ *n* -S [ME *threshwold, thresshold,* fr. OE *threscwald, threscold,* akin to ON *threskjǫldr* threshold, OE *threscan, therscan* to thresh] **1 :** the plank, stone, or piece of timber or metal that lies under a door; *esp* **:** SILL **2 a :** GATE, DOOR **b** (1) **:** END, BOUNDARY; *specif* **:** the end of a runway (2) **:** the place or point of entering or beginning **:** ENTRANCE, OUTSET ⟨the ~ of an era of scientific and technological development —A.L.Nickerson⟩ ⟨on the ~ of adulthood —Frances Keene⟩ ⟨a hamlet on the ~ of a narrow valley —*Amer. Guide Series: Oregon*⟩ **3** [trans. of G *schwelle*] **:** the point at which a physiological or psychological effect begins to be produced (as the degree of stimulation of a nerve or nerve center which just produces a response or the concentration of sugar in the blood at which sugar just begins to pass the barrier of the kidneys and enter the urine) ⟨below the ~ of consciousness⟩ ⟨the ~ of pain⟩ ⟨a high renal clearance ~⟩ ⟨with an alteration of the physical environment some ecological ~*s* of the ecosystem or of certain of its components may be crossed and the system disrupted —J.R.Beerbower⟩

[2]**threshold** \"\ *adj* **1 :** resembling a threshold; *also* **:** suggesting a threshold in nature, use, or function **2 :** that constitutes a threshold ⟨a ~ voltage⟩ ⟨~ levels of sugar⟩

threshold exposure *n* **:** the least photographic exposure whose effect is discernible on development

threshold frequency *n* **:** the minimum frequency of radiation that will produce a photoelectric effect

thresh out *vt* **:** to thrash out

thres·ki·or·nith·i·dae \,thres̈kēō(r)'nithə,dē\ *n pl, cap* [NL, fr. *Threskiornith-, Threskiornis,* type genus (fr. Gk *thrēskeia* religion, worship + NL *-ornith-, -ornis* -ornis) + *-idae;* prob. akin to Skt *dhārayati* he holds, carries, keeps — more at FIRM] **:** a family of birds (order Ciconiiformes) consisting of the ibises and spoonbills or restricted to the former

threw *past of* THROW

[1]**thrib·ble** \'thribəl\ *adj* [[1]*three* + *-ble* (as in *double*)] *dial* **:** TRIPLE

[2]**thribble** \"\ *n* -S **:** a unit of pipe for drilling oil consisting of three lengths coupled together — compare FOURBLE

thrice \'thrīs\ *adv* [ME *thries,* fr. *thrie* three times (fr. OE *thriga, thriwa*) + *-es,* gen. sing. ending of nouns (functioning adverbially, as in *nedes* needs); akin to OFris *thria* three times, OS *thriuo, thriwo;* derivative fr. the root of OE *thrie* three — more at THREE, -S] **1 :** three times ⟨a cleaning woman ~ weekly should do —Waldo Frank⟩ ⟨bells . . . which ~ daily chime the Angelus —*Amer. Guide Series: Calif.*⟩ **2 a :** in a threefold manner or degree **b :** to a high degree **:** FULLY, REPEATEDLY — used as an intensive ⟨~ is he armed that hath his quarrel just —Shak.⟩

thrice-accented octave \'ˌ='ˌ==-\ *n* **:** THREE-LINE OCTAVE

thricecock \'ˌ=ˌ=\ *n* [prob. alter. of *thrush cock*] *dial Eng* **:** MISTLE THRUSH

thrid \'thrid\ *vb* **thridded** *also* **thrid; thridded** \-dəd\ *also* **thridden** \-dᵊn\ **thridding; thrids** [alter. of [2]*thread*] *vt* **:** THREAD ⟨woodpeckers . . . ~ the wildwood branches —Robinson Jeffers⟩ ~ *vi* **:** THREAD ⟨we ~ all the way among shoals —R.L.Stevenson⟩

thrift \'thrift\ *n* -S *often attrib* [ME, fr. ON, success, prosperity, fr. *thrifask* to thrive — more at THRIVE] **1 :** healthy and vigorous growth ⟨the first things noticed about infested sheep are dullness and lack of ~ —J.T.Lucker & A.O.Foster⟩ **2 :** good fortune **:** SUCCESS ⟨with excellent ~ he fixed his young affections upon the only child of a wealthy merchant —V.L.Parrington⟩ **3 :** savings accumulated through frugality **:** acquired or hoarded wealth **4 a :** careful management esp. of financial affairs **:** good husbandry **:** wise frugality in expenditure ⟨children should early be trained to value ~⟩ **b :** STINGINESS, MISERLINESS ⟨showed his ~ by refusing his daughter a college education⟩ **5** *chiefly Scot* **:** gainful occupation **:** useful employment **6 :** a plant of the genus *Armeria; esp* **:** a tufted scapose herb (*A. maritima*) of the seacoasts and mountains of the north temperate zone having heads of pink or white flowers — called also *cliff rose*

thrift account *n* **:** a savings account esp. in a commercial bank

thrift·i·ly \-tᵊlē, -tᵊli, -təl-\ *adv* [ME, fr. *thrifty* + *-ly*] **1** *obs* **:** in a proper or worthy manner ⟨hast sung well and ~ —Philip Sidney⟩ **2 :** with particular attention to the cost **:** ECONOMICALLY ⟨the houses were ~ built —William Petersen⟩

thrift·i·ness \-tēnəs, -tin-\ *n* -ES **:** the quality or state of being thrifty

thrift·less \-tləs\ *adj* [ME *thriftles* unsuccessful, not prosperous, fr. *thrift* + *-les* -less] **1 :** lacking usefulness or worth ⟨what ~ sighs —Shak.⟩ **2 :** incapable of frugal management **:** wasteful of money or resources **:** IMPROVIDENT ⟨a ~ character who never knew where his next meal was coming from⟩ — **thrift·less·ly** *adv*

thrift·less·ness *n* -ES **:** the quality or state of being thriftless ⟨blame their difficulties on their ~ —Bruno Lasker⟩

thrift society *n* **:** a voluntary association usu. unincorporated to promote thrift and for the collective investment of the savings of the members

thrifty \-tē, -ti\ *adj, sometimes* -ER/-EST [ME, fr. *thrift* + *-y*] **1 :** thriving by industry and frugality **:** increasing in wealth ⟨this is a ~ modern-looking town —Elihu Burritt⟩ **2 :** growing vigorously **:** THRIVING ⟨my flock is *thriftier* looking than a year ago —E.B.White⟩ ⟨the bean plants stood erect in ~ order —Pearl Buck⟩ **3 a :** given to or evincing thrift **:** characterized by economy and good management **:** PROVIDENT ⟨she had been a prudent and ~ wife to him —W.M.Thackeray⟩ ⟨~ farmers whose hard work made the limestone region . . . a huge wheat granary —Allan Nevins & H.S.Commager⟩ **b :** overly frugal **:** SAVING, SPARSE ⟨ginger cookies with which she was not too ~ when little girls passed by —Nancy Hale⟩ ⟨only to be regretted that the references to literature are so very ~ —*Philosophic Abstracts*⟩ **syn** see SPARING

[1]**thrill** \'thril\ *vb* -ED/-ING/-S [ME *thrillen,* alter. of *thirlen* to pierce — more at THIRL] *vt* **1** *obs* **a :** to perforate or penetrate with or as if with a pointed instrument **b :** to hurl (as a lance, spear) with strength **2 :** to cause to have a shivering or tingling sensation **:** produce excitement in **:** affect emotionally ⟨a spectacle which has ~*ed* and fascinated the human race —Barbara Buchman⟩ ⟨new gold rushes continued to ~ the prospectors —R.A.Billington⟩ **3 :** to cause to vibrate **:** affect so as to produce vibrations or quivering ⟨an earthquake ~*s* the land⟩ ~ *vi* **1** *obs* **:** PIERCE — usu. used with *through* **2 a :** to act, move, or pass in such a manner as to provoke a sudden wave of emotion ⟨a faint cold fear ~*s* through my veins —Shak.⟩ **b :** to experience an unexpected emotional reaction **:** feel a tingling or shivering sensation ⟨people ~ to gay and beautiful music —*London Calling*⟩ ⟨you'll ~ at seeing sights reminiscent of life two centuries ago —*advt*⟩ ⟨the humblest peasant can ~ with pride —M.R.Cohen⟩ **3 :** to move or act tremulously **:** seem to tremble **:** VIBRATE ⟨very rocks seem to ~ with life —John Muir †1914⟩ ⟨though a very old town . . . it ~*s* and reverberates with the romance of machinery —Arnold Bennett⟩

[2]**thrill** \"\ *n* -S **1 :** an instantaneous excitement **:** a tingling of or as if of the nerves produced by a sudden emotional reaction ⟨the pungent ~ of hate —M.R.Cohen⟩ ⟨her laughter contained a ~ of joy —Ellen Glasgow⟩ ⟨a ~ of anticipation —Guy Priest⟩ ⟨a little ~ of horror —W.S.Maugham⟩ **2 :** a tangible vibration or tremor (as of the land during an earthquake) **:** THROBBING **3 :** an abnormal fine tremor or vibration in the respiratory or circulatory systems felt on palpation **4 a :** a stirring, sensational, or exciting quality or element ⟨stories . . . that for sheer ~*s* rival gold prospecting —Ruth & Leonard Greenup⟩ **b :** THRILLER

[3]**thrill** *var of* TRILL

thrill·er \'thrilə(r)\ *also* **thriller-dill·er** \ˌ=='dilə(r)\ *n* -S [*thriller* fr. [1]*thrill* + *-er; thriller-diller* fr. *thriller* + *-diller* (as in *killer-diller*)] **:** one that produces thrills; *esp* **:** a work of fiction or drama designed to hold the interest by the use of a high degree of action, intrigue, adventure, or suspense

thrill·ful \'thrilfəl\ *adj* **:** full of thrills or excitement ⟨a small ~ boy, prepared to follow . . . the band —Stephen Crane⟩

thrilling *adj* **1 a** *obs* **:** PIERCING **b :** penetrating with cold **:** inducing shivering and shaking ⟨a ~ wind blew off the frozen lake⟩ **2 :** causing an instantaneous surge of emotion **:** producing tremulous excitement **:** deeply moving ⟨gave ~ hints of an unknown world —W.H.Downes⟩ ⟨~ narratives of Indian captivities became a favorite form of literature —A.F.Harlow⟩ ⟨a postcard . . . gave me ~ news —Christopher Morley⟩ **3 :** THROBBING, VIBRATING

thrill·ing·ly *adv* **:** in a thrilling manner

thrilly \-lē\ *adj* [[2]*thrill* + *-y*] **:** providing thrills **:** SENSATIONAL

[1]**thrim·ble** \'thrimbəl\ *vt* -ED/-ING/-S [origin unknown] *chiefly Brit* **:** to finger (as money) in a hesitating way

[2]**thrimble** \"\ *dial Eng var of* TREMBLE

thrin \'thrin\ *n* -S [alter. (influenced by *three*) of *twin*] *dial* **:** one of triplets **:** one of three

thri·nax \'thrī,naks\ *n, cap* [NL, fr. Gk, trident, three-pronged fork; fr. the shape of the leaves] **:** a genus of No. American fan palms with orbicular leaves cleft into many induplicate segments, smooth petioles, and monoecious flowers succeeded by small globose fruits — see THATCH PALM

thring \'thriŋ\ *vi* [ME *thringen,* fr. OE *thringan* — more at THRONG] *chiefly Scot* **:** to press or push ahead in or as if in a throng

[1]**thrin·ter** \'thrintə(r)\ *n* -S [[1]*three* + *winter*] *dial Brit* **:** a three-year-old sheep

[2]**thrinter** \"\ *adj, dial Brit* **:** being three years old

[1]**thrip** \'thrip\ *vt* **thripped; thripped; thripping; thrips** [imit.] **1** *obs* **:** to snap (the fingers) softly **2 :** to twitch slightly

[2]**thrip** \"\ *n, pl* **thrips** *or* **thrip** [back-formation] *chiefly Brit* **:** THRIPS

[1]**thrip·id** \'thripəd\ *adj* [NL *Thripidae*] **:** of or relating to the family Thripidae

[2]**thripid** \"\ *n* -S [NL *Thripidae*] **:** an insect of the family Thripidae **:** THRIPS

thrip·i·dae \'thripə,dē\ *n pl, cap* [NL, fr. *Thrip-, Thrips,* type genus + *-idae*] **:** a family of insects (order Thysanoptera) comprising the thrips

thrip·pence *like* THREEPENCE\ *also* **thrip** \'thrip\ *n* [*thrippence* alter. of *threepence; thrip* by shortening & alter. fr. *threepence*] **:** THREEPENCE

thrip·ple \'thripəl\ *n* -S [ME *therrepyll*] *Eng* **:** an extension frame or rail used on a vehicle usu. for hay

thrips \'thrips\ *n* [NL *Thrip-, Thrips,* fr. L *thrip-, thrips* woodworm, fr. Gk] **1 a** *cap* **:** a genus of insects that is the type of the family Thripidae **b** *pl* **thrips :** any of numerous insects (family Thripidae) that are of small often minute size, that have narrow broadly fringed wings with rudimentary nervures, asymmetrical mouth parts used for sucking, and tarsi ending in a peculiar bladderlike structure, and that feed mostly on plant juices and are often destructive pests — see ONION THRIPS, TOBACCO THRIPS **2** *pl* **thrips :** any of various small injurious insects; *esp* **:** GRAPE LEAFHOPPER

[1]**thrist** \'thrist\ *dial Brit var of* THIRST

[2]**thrist** \"\ *dial Brit var of* THRUST

thris·tle *or* **thris·sel** \'thrisəl\ *chiefly Scot var of* THISTLE

thrive \'thrīv\ *vi* **throve** \-rōv\ *or* **thrived** \-rīvd\ **thriv·en** \-rivən\ *also* **thrived; thriving; thrives** [ME *thriven,* fr. ON *thrifask,* prob. reflexive of *thrífa* to clutch, grasp] **1 :** to grow vigorously **:** become increasingly larger and healthier **:** physically improve ⟨sheep and goats ~ on uplands and rough, eroded regions —*Amer. Guide Series: Texas*⟩ ⟨the sparrow *thrived* under her care —Thomas Foster⟩ ⟨children seem to ~ even in city streets⟩ **2 :** to prosper outstandingly **:** gain in wealth or material possessions **:** advance successfully ⟨industry has never *thriven* under restrictions —L.D.Stamp⟩ ⟨the region *thrived* as steel and aircraft . . . establishments built up —Oscar Handlin⟩ **3 :** to achieve growth or progress toward one's own goal **:** flourish despite or because of circumstances or conditions ⟨creating an atmosphere in which injustice finds it harder to ~ —Lionel Trilling⟩ ⟨she ~*s* on the attention —Bradford Smith⟩ ⟨he *thrived* on opposition —*Sydney (Australia) Bull.*⟩ **syn** see SUCCEED

thrive·less \'thrīvləs\ *adj* **:** being without advantage **:** UNSUCCESSFUL

thriving *adj* **:** characterized by prosperity **:** successfully engaged in achieving a goal ⟨the city is now a ~ tourist center —Sam Pollock⟩ ⟨floral booths did a ~ business in orchids —Dorothy Kahn⟩ — **thriv·ing·ly** *adv*

-thrix \(,)thriks\ *n comb form* [NL *-trich-, -thrix,* fr. Gk *trich-, thrix* hair — more at TRICHINA] **1 :** one having (such) hair or hairlike filaments — in generic names of plants and animals ⟨Lago*thrix*⟩ ⟨Strepto*thrix*⟩ **2** *pl* **-tri·ches** \(·)trə,kēz\ *or* **-thrixes :** pathological condition of having (such) hair ⟨lepo*thrix*⟩ ⟨monile*thrix*⟩

thro \'thrü\ *prep* [ME *thro,* short for *throgh, through*] *archaic* **:** THROUGH ⟨stares ~ the window at a scrawl of boughs —Constance Carrier⟩

[1]**throat** \'thrōt, *usu* -ōd.+V\ *n* -S *often attrib* [ME *throte,* fr. OE *throte, throtu;* akin to OHG *drozza* throat, ON *throti* swelling, *thrūtna* to swell, OE *thrūtian*] **1 a** (1) **:** the part of the neck in front of the spinal column (2) **:** the passage through it to the stomach and lungs containing the pharynx and upper part of the esophagus, the larynx, and the trachea **b :** voice or the seat of the voice ⟨the nightingale poured out his ~ in song⟩ **2 :** something felt to resemble the throat esp. in being an entrance, a passageway, a constriction, or a narrowed part ⟨the ~ of a vase⟩ ⟨the narrow ~ of a stream⟩: as **a :** the part of a chimney (as of a house) between the portion of the funnel that contracts in ascending (as above a hearth) and the flue proper; *also* **:** a similar part of an industrial flue system (as of a metallurgical furnace) **b :** a groove or channel on the underside of a projection (as a stringcourse or coping) that prevents water from running back into the wall **c** (1) **:** the inside of a timber knee of a ship — compare BREECH (2) **:** the end of a gaff next to the mast (3) **:** the upper fore corner of a staysail or of a fore-and-aft sail (4) **:** the curved part of an anchor's arm where it joins the shank — see ANCHOR illustration **d :** the orifice of a tubular organ esp. of a plant; *usu* **:** the spreading upper part of the tube of a gamopetalous corolla or calyx **e :** a gullet or clearance space at the bottom of a sawtooth **f** (1) **:** the narrowest place between the wing rails of a railroad frog (2) **:** the curved space between the flange and tread of a car wheel (3) **:** the point at which a railroad line enters or leaves a yard and from which the yard tracks branch out — called also *choke point* **g :** a gap in the frame behind the tool in a punching, shearing, vertical-boring, or similar machine the depth of which limits the size of the work taken **h :** a short tube connecting larger tubes or a contracted section of a tube between expanded portions **i :** the opening in the vamp of a shoe at the instep — see SHOE illustration **j :** the part of a tennis racket between the head and the handle **k :** the minimum distance from the root of a fusion weld to its face **3** *obs* **:** a center of or capacity for destructive action **:** JAWS, MOUTH

[2]**throat** \"\ *vt* -ED/-ING/-S **1 a :** to utter in the throat **:** MUTTER ⟨~ threats⟩ **b :** to sing or enunciate in a throaty voice ⟨~*ing* her words huskily⟩ **2 :** to make or provide with a throat ⟨~ the underside of a stringcourse⟩

throatband \'ˌ=ˌ=\ *n* **1 :** THROATLATCH **2 :** NECKBAND

throat botfly *n* **:** a rusty reddish hairy botfly (*Gasterophilus nasalis*) that lays its eggs on the hairs about the mouth of the horse whence the larvae on hatching migrate and attach themselves to the walls of the stomach and intestine — called also *chin fly*

throat brail *n* **:** a brail running through a block at the throat of a gaff

throat·ed \'thrōd·əd, -ōtəd\ *adj* [ME *throted,* fr. *throte* throat + *-ed*] **:** having a throat — usu. used in combination ⟨choke-*throated*⟩ ⟨deep-*throated*⟩ ⟨white-*throated*⟩

throat halyard *n* **:** a line used to hoist the throat of a gaff

throat·i·ly \'thrōd·ᵊlē, -ōt, |ᵊli, |ōl-\ *adv* [*throaty* + *-ly*] **:** in a throaty manner **:** with a peculiar tonal quality caused by oral utterance with the throat constricted **:** GUTTURALLY ⟨wiped her red old eyes . . . and clucked ~ —Rudyard Kipling⟩

throat·i·ness \ēnəs, |in-\ *n* -ES **:** the quality or state of being throaty

throat·ing \'thrōd·iŋ\ *n* -S [¹*throat* + *-ing*] **:** a throated structure or area (as the throat beneath a stringcourse)

throatlash \'=,=\ *n* [¹*throat* + *lash*, alter. of ²*latch*] **:** THROATLATCH

throatlatch \'=,=\ *n* **1 :** a strap of a bridle or halter passing under a horse's throat — see BRIDLE illustration **2 a :** the portion of a horse's throat around which the throatlatch passes — see HORSE illustration **b :** a corresponding region on another animal ⟨the ~ of a fish⟩

throat·less \'thrōtləs\ *adj* **:** having no throat

throat microphone *n* **:** a small contact microphone or pickup held or fastened against the speaker's throat and actuated directly by the vibration of the larynx

throat plate *n* **1 :** THROAT SHEET **2 :** a flat plate holding the feed dog of a sewing machine

throat register *n* **:** a middle register of the clarinet extending from the written G above middle C to and including the B flat immediately above it

throatroot \'=,=\ *n* **1 :** a bennet (*Geum virginianum*) **2 :** WATER AVENS

throats *pl of* THROAT, *pres 3d sing of* THROAT

throat seizing *n* **:** a seizing in which the parts of a rope cross each other

throat sheet *n* **:** a boiler plate on a steam locomotive flanged to connect the cylindrical part of the boiler with the side sheets of the firebox or on some models with both the side and roof sheets

throatstrap \'=,=\ *n* **:** THROATLATCH 1

throat sweetbread *n* **:** THYMUS

throat track *n* **:** a track connecting ladder tracks with main tracks at a railway yard or station

throatwort \'=,=\ *n* **1 :** any of several bellflowers; *esp* **:** a European herb (*Campanula trachelium*) formerly used to treat sore throat **2 :** FOXGLOVE 1 **3 :** any of various figworts (as *Scrophularia nodosa* of Europe or *S. marylandica* of America) **4 :** a button snakeroot (*Liatris spicata*)

throaty \'thrōd·|ē, -ōt|, |i\ *adj* -ER/-EST [¹*throat* + *-y*] **1 a :** uttered with a hard quality caused by the sound coming from the throat rather than from the mouth **:** GUTTURAL **b :** relatively heavy, thick, and deep as if emitted from low in the throat ⟨an entrancing ~ laugh⟩ ⟨a rich ~ voice⟩ ⟨~ from her cold⟩ ⟨a cat's little ~ meow⟩ **2 :** having a large loose-hanging throat — used esp. of cattle or dogs

¹**throb** \'thräb\ *vi* **throbbed; throbbed; throbbing; throbs** [ME *throbben*, prob. of imit. origin] **1 a :** to pulsate with abnormal force or rapidity (as from fright, pain, or agitation) **:** PALPITATE ⟨her heart *throbbed* with sudden shock⟩ ⟨a finger *throbbing* from an infected cut⟩ **b :** to pulsate, vibrate, or beat in a normal rhythmic manner ⟨pulse *throbbing* steadily⟩ ⟨the engines *throbbed* quietly beneath the deck⟩ **2 :** to become moved strongly by or as if by emotion ⟨a spirit *throbbing* with desire⟩ ⟨the child *throbbed* with loneliness⟩ **syn** see PULSATE

²**throb** \"\ *n* -S **1 :** a single pulse of a pulsating movement or sensation (as of pain or violent emotion) ⟨a sudden ~ of pain⟩ ⟨each ~ of her heart⟩ **2 :** a rhythmic pulsation or beating ⟨a pulsating rhythm, like the ~ of . . . many machines in a big factory —W.T.C.King⟩

throb·ber \-bə(r)\ *n* -S **:** one that throbs; *esp* **:** one that is unduly emotional

throb·bing·ly *adv* [*throbbing* (pres. part. of ¹*throb*) + *-ly*] **:** in a throbbing manner **:** with a throb

throb·less \-bləs\ *adj* **:** free from throbs or throbbing **:** STATIC, QUIET, PLACID, UNEXCITING

¹**throe** \'thrō\ *n* -S [ME *throwe*, alter. (influenced by *throwen* to suffer, fr. OE *thrōwian* — akin to OE *thrāwu* threat, pang) of *thrawe*, fr. OE *thrāwu*, *thrēa* threat, punishment, pang; akin to OHG *drawa*, *drōa* threat, ON *thrā* pang, longing, Gk *trauma* wound, *tryein* to wear out, distress] **1 a throes** *pl* **:** the physical struggle and anguish accompanying parturition **:** labor pains **b :** the struggle and anguish immediately preceding death **:** a death struggle — usu. used in pl. **c :** a sudden spasm or pang (as of pain or emotion) ⟨forced from love's exultant ~ —James McAuley⟩ **2 throes** *pl* **:** a condition of struggle, anguish, disorder, or confusion characteristic of a transitional period (as the active phase of creation of some new thing) ⟨a state in the ~s of revolution⟩ ⟨a college . . . in the ~s of selecting a new president —W.S.Carlson⟩ ⟨air commerce is in the ~s of an essential transition —*Current Biog.*⟩ **syn** see PAIN

²**throe** \"\ *vb* -ED/-ING/-S *vt*, *obs* **:** to put in agony **:** cause to suffer ~ *vi* **:** to struggle in distress **:** be in agony

thromb- *or* **thrombo-** *comb form* [Gk *thrombos* lump, clot of blood, curd — more at ATROPHY] **1 a :** blood clot ⟨*thrombo*cyst⟩ **b :** associated with the clotting of blood ⟨*thrombin*⟩ ⟨*thrombo*stasis⟩ **2 :** marked by or associated with thrombosis ⟨*thrombo*angiitis⟩

throm·base \'thräm,bās\ *n* -S [ISV *thromb-* + *-ase*] **:** THROMBIN

throm·bas·the·nia \,thrämbəs'thēnēə\ *n* [NL, fr. *thromb-* + *asthenia*] **:** PSEUDOHEMOPHILIA

thrombi *pl of* THROMBUS

throm·bin \'thrämbən\ *n* -S [ISV *thromb-* + *-in*] **:** a proteolytic enzyme that is formed from prothrombin (as in blood plasma as needed), that facilitates the clotting of blood by promoting conversion of fibrinogen to fibrin, and that is used as a local hemostatic for capillary bleeding and also in binding tissues together after surgery — compare ANTITHROMBIN, FIBRIN FOAM

throm·bo·angiitis \¦thräm(,)bō+\ *n* [NL, fr. *thromb-* + *angiitis*] **:** inflammation of the lining of a blood vessel with thrombus formation

thromboangiitis ob·lit·er·ans \-ə'blid·ə,ranz\ *n* [NL, lit., obliterating thromboangiitis] **:** thromboangiitis of the small arteries and veins of the extremities and esp. the feet resulting in occlusion, ischemia, and gangrene — called also *Buerger's disease*

throm·bo·arteritis \¦thräm(,)bō+\ *n* [NL, fr. *thromb-* + *arteritis*] **:** inflammation of an artery with thrombus formation

throm·bo·blast \'thrämbə,blast\ *n* [*thromb-* + *-blast*] **:** an immature thrombocyte

throm·bo·cyte \-,sīt\ *n* -S [ISV *thromb-* + *-cyte*] **:** BLOOD PLATELET; *also* **:** a cell having a similar function in clotting (as a spindle cell of some lower vertebrates) — **throm·bo·cyt·ic** \¦==¦sid·ik\ *adj*

throm·bo·cy·to·pe·nia \,thrämbō,sīd·ō'pēnēə\ *n* -S [NL, fr. ISV *thrombocyte* + *-o-* + NL *-penia*] **:** persistent decrease in the number of blood platelets usu. associated with hemorrhagic conditions — compare PURPURA 1 — **throm·bo·cy·to·pe·nic** \¦==¦==¦pēnik\ *adj*

thrombocytopenic purpura *n* **:** PURPURA HEMORRHAGICA 1

throm·bo·cy·to·poi·e·sis \,==,==,pȯi'ēsəs\ *n* [NL, fr. ISV *thrombocyte* + *-o-* + NL *-poiesis*] **:** the production of blood platelets from megakaryocytes typically in the bone marrow

throm·bo·cy·to·sis \,thrämbō,sī'tōsəs\ *n*, *pl* **thrombocytoses** \-'tō,sēz\ [NL, fr. ISV *thrombocyte* + NL *-osis*] **:** increase and esp. abnormal increase in the number of blood platelets

throm·bo·em·bol·ic \¦thrämbōem¦bälik\ *adj* [ISV *thromb-* + *embol-* + *-ic*] **:** marked by or associated with thromboembolism ⟨a ~ syndrome⟩

throm·bo·embolism \¦thräm(,)bō+\ *n* [*thromb-* + *embolism*] **:** the blocking of a blood vessel by an embolus that has broken away from a thrombus at its site of formation

throm·bo·gen \'thrämbəjən\ *n* -S [ISV *thromb-* + *-gen*] **:** PROTHROMBIN

throm·bo·gen·ic \¦thrämbə¦jenik\ *adj* [ISV *thromb-* + *-genic*] **:** tending to produce a thrombus

throm·bo·kinase \¦thräm(,)bō+\ *n* [ISV *thromb-* + *kinase*] **:** THROMBOPLASTIN

throm·bon \'thrämbən\ *n* -S [*thrombocyte* + *-on* (as in *plankton*)] **:** the entire body of blood platelets and their precursors that constitute a distinct organ of the body

throm·bo·pe·nia \,thrämbō'pēnēə\ *n* -S [NL, fr. *thromb-* + *-penia*] **:** THROMBOCYTOPENIA — **throm·bo·pe·nic** \¦==¦pēnik\ *adj*

throm·bo·phlebitis \¦thräm(,)bō+\ *n* [NL, fr. *thromb-* + *phlebitis*] **:** inflammation of a vein with formation or presence of a thrombus and esp. one that is firmly attached to the vessel wall — compare PHLEBOTHROMBOSIS

throm·bo·plas·tic \¦thrämbō¦plastik\ *adj* [ISV *thromb-* + *-plastic*] **1 :** initiating or accelerating the clotting of blood usu. by converting prothrombin to thrombin **2 :** of, relating to, or constituting thromboplastin — **throm·bo·plas·ti·cal·ly** \-tək(ə)lē\ *adv*

throm·bo·plas·tin \,==¦plastən\ *n* -S [ISV *thromboplastic* + *-in*] **:** a complex substance that contains chiefly protein and various phosphatides, that is found in brain, lung, and other tissues and esp. in blood platelets, and that when released from disintegrating cells participates in the clotting of blood by promoting the conversion of prothrombin to thrombin; *also* **:** a tissue extract rich in this substance sometimes used as a local hemostatic

throm·bose \'thräm,bōz, -ōs\ *vb* -ED/-ING/-S [back-formation fr. *thrombosis*] *vt* **:** to affect with thrombosis ~ *vi* **:** to undergo thrombosis

throm·bo·sis \thräm'bōsəs\ *n*, *pl* **thrombo·ses** \-ō,sēz\ [NL, fr. Gk *thrombōsis* coagulation, clotting, fr. *thrombousthai* to become clotted, fr. *thrombos* clot] **1 :** the formation or presence of a blood clot within a blood vessel during life **2 :** a plant disease in which water conduction is interfered with by the growth of a parasite (as in wilt diseases)

throm·bot·ic \(')thräm¦bäd·|ik, -bät|, |ēk\ *adj* [fr. NL *thrombosis*, after such pairs as NL *narcosis*: E *narcotic*] **:** of, relating to, involving, or affected with thrombosis ⟨a ~ disorder⟩ ⟨~ changes⟩ ⟨a ~ patient⟩

throm·bus \'thrämbəs\ *n*, *pl* **throm·bi** \-m,bī\ [NL, fr. Gk *thrombos* lump, clot of blood, curd — more at ATROPHY] **:** a clot of blood formed within a blood vessel and remaining attached to its place of origin — compare EMBOLUS

¹**throne** \'thrōn\ *n* -S [ME, alter. (influenced by L *thronus*) of *trone*, fr. OF, fr. L *thronus*, fr. Gk *thronos* chair, throne — more at FIRM] **1 a :** a chair of state: as (1) **:** a royal seat on a dais with a canopy (2) **:** the ceremonial seat of a prince, bishop, or other high dignitary — see CATHEDRA (3) **:** the seat of a deity or superhuman power ⟨Satan's dark ~⟩ **b :** an elevated seat provided by an artist for his model **c** *slang* **:** TOILET SEAT **2 a :** sovereign or sometimes episcopal power and dignity **:** supreme rank or position **:** SOVEREIGNTY **b :** the one invested therewith **:** an exalted or dignified personage **3 thrones** *pl* **:** a high order of angels — see CELESTIAL HIERARCHY **4** *Eastern Church* **:** SANCTUARY 1b

²**throne** \"\ *vb* -ED/-ING/-S [ME *tronen*, *thronen*, fr. *trone*, *throne* throne] *vt* **:** to exalt to a throne **:** give sovereignty or dominion to **:** ENTHRONE ~ *vi* **:** to be in or to sit on a throne **:** be in power as if on a throne ⟨a kind of sanctuary in which she *throned* among his secret thoughts and longings —Edith Wharton⟩

throne·less \-nləs\ *adj* **:** lacking a throne

throne·let \-lət\ *n* -S **:** a little throne **:** an insignificant dominion

throne name *n* **:** the official name taken by a ruler and esp. an ancient Egyptian pharaoh on ascending the throne

throne room *n* **1 :** a formal audience room in which stands the throne of a sovereign **2 :** a place in which authority is actually centered

throne·ward \-nwə(r)d\ *adv* [¹*throne* + *-ward*] **:** toward a throne

¹**throng** \'thrȯŋ *also* 'thräŋ\ *n* -S [ME *thrang*, *throng*, fr. OE *gethrang*, *thrang*; akin to OE *thringan* to press, crowd, push ahead, OHG *dringan*, ON *thröngva*, Goth *threihan* to press, squeeze, Lith *trenkti* to jolt] **1 a :** a multitude of persons congregated into a close assemblage **b :** a goodly number assembled in fact or concept **:** HOST ⟨~s of ants joined the picnic⟩ ⟨a ~ of confused notions cluttering her brain⟩ **2 a :** a crowding together of many persons **b :** a pressing of activity (as in seasonal work) **:** PRESSURE ⟨this ~ of business —S.R.Crockett⟩ **3** *chiefly Scot* **:** DISTRESS, HARDSHIP **syn** see CROWD

²**throng** \"\ *vb* -ED/-ING/-S [ME *thrangen*, *throngen*, fr. *thrang*, *throng* throng] *vt* **1 a** *obs* **:** to press closely together or as if between opposing forces **:** COMPRESS, SQUEEZE **b** *archaic* **:** to gather together in one place **:** CROWD **2 :** to gather about and press upon so as to crush or jostle ⟨much people followed him, and ~*ed* him —Mk 5:24 (AV)⟩ **3 :** to fill closely by forcing or pressing into **:** PACK, JAM ⟨shoppers ~*ing* the streets⟩ ~ *vi* **1 :** to crowd together in great numbers **:** move, pass, go, or advance in multitudes ⟨commuters ~*ing* towards the station⟩ **2** *obs* **:** to press one's way against difficulties (as in forcing a way through a crowd)

³**throng** \'thräŋ\ *adj* [ME *thrang*, *throng*; akin to OE *thringan* to press, crowd] **1** *chiefly Scot* **:** closely packed **:** CROWDED **2** *chiefly Scot* **:** filled with or fully engaged in work **:** BUSY **3** *chiefly Scot* **:** closely associated **:** INTIMATE

¹**throp·ple** \'thräpəl\ *n* -S [ME *throppill*] *chiefly dial* **:** THROAT, WINDPIPE — used esp. of a horse; compare THROATLATCH

²**thropple** \"\ *vt* -ED/-ING/-S [alter. (influenced by ¹*thropple*) of ¹*throttle*] *chiefly Scot* **:** THROTTLE

thros·tle \'thräsəl\ *n* -S [ME *throstle*, *throstil*, fr. OE *throstle* — more at THRUSH] **1 :** ¹THRUSH 1; *specif* **:** SONG THRUSH **2 a :** an outmoded frame for spinning cotton from roving **b** *Brit* **:** a worsted spinning frame

throstle cock *n* [ME *throstilcok*, fr. *throstil* throstle + *cok* cock] **1 :** SONG THRUSH **2 :** MISTLE THRUSH

throt \'thrät\ *chiefly Scot var of* THROAT

¹**throt·tle** \'thräd·ᵊl, -ät³l\ *vb* **throttled; throttled; throttling** \-d·ᵊliŋ, -t(ᵊ)liŋ\ **throttles** [ME *throtelen*, *throtlen*, fr. *throte* throat] *vt* **1 a** (1) **:** to seize and compress the throat of so as to impede or check breathing; *broadly* **:** to impede or check the breathing of by any means **:** CHOKE (2) **:** to kill by such action **b :** to suppress or prevent or hinder expression, expansion, or other activity of by choking constriction **:** bring under severe check or control ⟨might not such regulation ~ the freedom of science —John Dewey⟩ **2** *obs* **:** to utter brokenly as if half suffocated **3 a :** to obstruct the flow of (as steam to an engine) esp. by a throttle valve **b :** to reduce the speed of (as an engine) by such means — often used with *down* ⟨*throttled* the car down to 20 miles an hour⟩ — compare GOVERN 2b ~ *vi* **:** to have the throat obstructed so as to be in danger of suffocation **:** CHOKE **syn** see SUFFOCATE

²**throttle** \"\ *n* -S [perh. alter. (influenced by ¹*throttle*) of ¹*thropple*] **1 a :** THROAT 1 **b :** TRACHEA 1 **2** [*throttle valve*] **a :** THROTTLE VALVE **b :** THROTTLE LEVER — **at full throttle :** with the throttle valve set at its widest opening **:** at full speed

throttlebottom \'==,==\ *n*, *usu cap* [after Alexander *Throttlebottom*, character in the musical comedy *Of Thee I Sing* (1932) by George S. Kaufman *b*1899 & Morris Ryskind *b*1895 Am. playwrights] **:** an innocuously inept and futile person in public office

throttlehold \'==,=\ *n* [¹*throttle* + *hold*] **:** a vicious, strangling, or stultifying control ⟨a ~ on the daily press⟩

throttle lever *n* **:** a pedal or lever that controls a throttle valve

throt·tle·man \'==mən\ *n*, *pl* **throttlemen** [²*throttle* + *man*] **:** one stationed at or in immediate control of a throttle valve

throt·tler \'thräd·ᵊlə(r)\ *n* -S **:** one that throttles

throttle valve *n* [¹*throttle* + *valve*] **:** a valve designed to regulate the supply of a fluid (as steam or gas and air) to an engine and operated by a handwheel, a lever, or automatically by a governor; *esp* **:** the valve in an internal-combustion engine incorporated in or just outside the carburetor and controlling the volume of vaporized fuel charge delivered to the cylinders

throttling bar *n* [*throttling* (fr. pres. part. of ¹*throttle*) + *bar*] **:** a bar of varying cross section that controls the flow of the liquid past the piston in some types of hydraulic recoil brakes

throttling governor *n* **:** an automatic governor on a throttle valve

¹**through** *also* **thru** \'thrü\ *prep* [ME *thurgh*, *thurh*, *thruh*, *through*, fr. OE *thuruh*, *thurh*; akin to OHG *duruh*, *durh* through, Goth *thairh*, L *trans* across, beyond, Skt *tiras* through, across, *tarati* he crosses over — more at TERM] **1 a** (1) — used as a function word to indicate penetration of or passage within, along, or across an object, substance, or space usu. from one side or surface to the opposite one ⟨sawed ~ the board⟩ ⟨put a bullet ~ his hat⟩ ⟨the oars cut ~ the water⟩ (2) — used as a function word to indicate passage from one side to another of an object by means of an opening or openings ⟨the party encountered the wire, and again crawled ~ it —P.W.Thompson⟩ ⟨walked ~ the gate⟩ (3) — used as a function word to indicate extension from one end or boundary (as of a place or area) to another ⟨a road ~ the desert⟩ ⟨a path ~ the woods⟩ **b** — used as a function word to indicate passage into and out of some treatment, handling, or process ⟨had probably been ~ half a dozen men's hands by now —C.S.Forester⟩ **c** (1) — used as a function word to indicate the transmission of light or vision by some opening or medium ⟨must conduct its observations ~ the restless, dust-filled, and moisture-laden atmosphere —J.G.Vaeth⟩ ⟨learned to look at trees ~ the eyes of a craftsman —W.F.Hambly⟩ ⟨looked ~ the window⟩ ⟨looked ~ the telescope⟩ (2) — used as a function word to indicate movement by way of a specified channel or passage ⟨went out ~ the kitchen⟩ ⟨walk across the platform, wait until a train pulls in, walk ~ this train to the next platform —A.C.Spectorsky⟩ **d** — used as a function word to indicate passage between or among the separate or separable units of something ⟨a broad highway ~ overhanging palms —Rex Moorfoot⟩ ⟨a big "whew" went ~ the audience —Dart Smith⟩ **e** (1) — used as a function word to indicate passage around or past an obstacle or impeding force ⟨took the shock of the man's shoulder without breaking stride, ran right ~ him —Irwin Shaw⟩ (2) **:** without stopping for **:** in disregard of **:** PAST ⟨drove ~ a red light⟩ ⟨went ~ a stop sign⟩ **f** — used as a function word to indicate the change in the quality of certain speech sounds consequent on the opening of the nasal passages ⟨speaks ~ the nose⟩ **g** — used as a function word to indicate the penetration of one sound by a fainter or more distant sound ⟨the radio whined so loud that it was a job to talk ~ it —Rose Macaulay⟩ **2 a** (1) **:** by means of **:** by the help or agency of ⟨he educated himself ~ correspondence courses —*Current Biog.*⟩ ⟨this idea is somewhat more difficult to present ~ statistics —N.R.Heiden⟩ (2) **:** by the intermediary of **:** in the person of ⟨speaking ~ the chairman of its committee on economic policy —*Collier's Yr. Bk.*⟩ ⟨speaking ~ an interpreter⟩ (3) — used as a function word to indicate passage by an intermediary or transmission at second hand ⟨a conception of politics derived ~ books⟩ ⟨has gotten his knowledge of the country ~ the reports of travelers⟩ (4) — used as a function word to indicate descent from or relationship by means of a specified individual or group of individuals ⟨the principal lines . . . are those ~ four celebrated stallions —Dennis Craig⟩ ⟨are related ~ their grandfather⟩ **b :** by reason of **:** on the basis of **:** because of ⟨farmers at first refused to use it ~ fear that it might poison the soil —*Amer. Guide Series: N.J.*⟩ **c :** as a result of ⟨now extinct ~ disease —R.N.Rudmose-Brown⟩ ⟨~ illness, he lost the use of his feet —Louise P. Kellogg⟩ **3 a :** along the entire expanse of **:** THROUGHOUT ⟨landmarks scattered ~ the pastoral countryside —Budd Schulberg⟩ **b** — used as a function word to indicate movement from point to point within a broad expanse or area ⟨felt the earth wheeling ~ infinity —F.M.Ford⟩ ⟨he'd fly ~ the air with the greatest of ease, this handsome young man on the flying trapeze —George Leybourne⟩ **c** — used as a function word to indicate movement within a specified environment or exposure to a specified set of conditions ⟨the drive . . . was ~ a radiant summer morning —Lucien Price⟩ ⟨didn't you know that she'd try to get it out of me, putting me ~ hell —Hamilton Basso⟩ **4 a :** during the entire period of ⟨all ~ the year⟩ ⟨~ life⟩ — sometimes used postpositively ⟨study the whole summer ~⟩ **b :** from the first to the last of (as an event, action, process) ⟨remained standing ~ the earthquake⟩ ⟨never rested ~ the entire campaign⟩ ⟨put him ~ his paces⟩ **c :** to and including ⟨estimated to cost $425 million for 1954 ~ 1957 —*Wall Street Jour.*⟩ **d** — used as a function word to indicate extension (as of an action or process) into and to the end of a specified period ⟨has decided to prolong his visit ~ the weekend⟩ ⟨will continue construction ~ the winter months⟩ **5 a** — used as a function word to indicate completion or exhaustion of something ⟨a rapid reader who has been known to go ~ three books in a morning —*Current Biog.*⟩ ⟨went straight ~ the brandy and even then had not had enough to drink —Jean Stafford⟩ ⟨went ~ a fortune in one year⟩ **b** (1) — used as a function word to indicate completion of a stage in a process or course of development ⟨passing ~ nature to eternity —Shak.⟩ ⟨many things only just ~ the prototype stage —Bertram Mycock⟩ (2) — used as a function word to indicate a specified quantity, extent, or angle of change or movement ⟨the heat required to raise one pound of water ~ 1° F. —S.F.Mason⟩ ⟨the airplane would roll or pitch very slowly ~ several degrees of rotation —H.G.Armstrong⟩ **c** — used as a function word to indicate achievement of a desired or successful outcome or result of a process, activity, or experience ⟨got ~ his final examinations⟩ ⟨got ~ the ordeal of his speech⟩ **d** — used as a function word to indicate satisfaction or completion of the requirements for acceptance or approval by a group or official body ⟨got his application ~ the committee⟩ ⟨got the bill ~ the legislature⟩

²**through** *also* **thru** \"\ *adv* [ME *thurgh*, *thurh*, *thruh*, *through*, fr. OE *thuruh*, *thurh*, prep.] **1 a :** from one end or side to the other by passing into the inner part or space ⟨jealousy pierced her ~⟩ **b :** over the whole distance **:** all the way to a destination ⟨always buy ~ to your farthest destination —Richard Joseph⟩ ⟨the next train goes ~ to New York⟩ **c :** in diameter ⟨a tree measuring twelve inches ~⟩ **2 a :** from beginning to end **:** along the whole of a planned or required course or process ⟨do you read books ~ —Samuel Johnson⟩ ⟨heard the speech ~ without interrupting⟩ **b :** to the very end **:** to completion, conclusion, or accomplishment ⟨were determined to see it ~ at whatever cost —D.W.Brogan⟩ ⟨think it ~⟩ ⟨follow ~⟩ **3 :** to the core **:** COMPLETELY, THOROUGHLY — used only following an adjective or participle ⟨the rain is over, but I am soaked ~ —Ellen Glasgow⟩ ⟨returned to the house chilled ~ by the exposure —H.E.Scudder⟩ ⟨wet ~⟩ **4 :** into the open **:** into perception ⟨when the strong emotion did actually break ~ —H.A.Overstreet⟩

³**through** *also* **thru** \"\ *adj* **1 a :** extending or passing from one end or surface to another ⟨a ~ mortise⟩ ⟨~ ventilation⟩ **b** (1) **:** admitting free or continuous passage **:** not interrupted or obstructed **:** DIRECT ⟨a ~ road⟩ ⟨a ~ route⟩ (2) **:** affording right of way **c :** at a point of issuance from a substance or channel ⟨that rain pepped things up . . . corn and beans are ~ —H.R.O'Brien⟩ **2 a :** going from point of origin to destination without change or reshipment and often involving more than one carrier ⟨~ train⟩ ⟨~ trailer⟩ **b :** of or relating to such movement ⟨a ~ rate⟩ ⟨a ~ bill of lading⟩ ⟨a ~ ticket⟩ **3 a :** arrived at completion or accomplishment ⟨the patient receives his treatment and then is ~ except for follow-up —*Jour. Amer. Med. Assoc.*⟩ ⟨is almost ~ with his studies⟩ **b :** having no further value, strength, or resources **:** no longer useful or wanted **:** done for **:** FINISHED ⟨nor can you ever be quite sure when a man is ~ —Elmer Davis⟩ ⟨you are ~, you're finished, your nerves are shot —Barnaby Conrad⟩ **c :** having no further concern **:** DONE ⟨he was ~ with school and he was ~ with family —John Dos Passos⟩ ⟨~ with gambling⟩ ⟨~ with drinking⟩

⁴**through** \"\ *n* -S [³*through*] **1 :** PERPEND 1 **2 throughs** *pl* **:** material that falls through something (as a screen or sieve); *specif* **:** the material that passes through a sieve during the process of milling flour

⁵**through** \'thrük\ *n* -S [ME *thrughe*, *throgh*, *through* coffin, through stone, fr. OE *thrūh* pipe, trough, coffin; akin to ON *thrō* trough] *chiefly Scot* **:** ¹THROUGH STONE

¹**through and through** *prep* [ME] **:** repeatedly through **:** in at one side and out the other side of ⟨thy slander hath gone *through and through* her heart —Shak.⟩

²**through and through** *adv* [ME] **1 :** in every possible way or aspect **:** to the fullest extent **:** THOROUGHLY ⟨was *through and through* a liberal, a democrat, and a republican —Oscar Handlin⟩ **2 :** all the way through **:** from one end to the other ⟨a thunderstorm that drenched them *through and through*⟩

through-and-through coal \'==='=-\ *n*, *Brit* **:** RUN OF MINE

through arch *n* **:** an arch through a heavy wall

through bolt *n* **:** a bolt passing through all the thicknesses or layers which it binds or in which it is fixed and made fast by a nut at the end opposite the head

through bond *n* **:** a transverse bond formed by a member that extends crosswise through the wall

through bridge *n* **1 :** a bridge in which the roadway or track passes between the supporting elements (as trusses, girders, or arches) — compare DECK BRIDGE **2 :** BOTTOM-ROAD BRIDGE

through check *n* **:** a check in a piece of timber extending all the way through from surface to surface

through–composed \'==ˈ=\ *adj* [trans. of G *durchkomponiert*] **:** having an individual musical setting for each stanza or strophe — used of a song or aria; compare STROPHIC

through cut *n* **:** a cut with excavated slopes on both sides of the roadway

throughfall \'=,=\ *n* **:** rainfall in a forest area that is not intercepted by the crown canopy and reaches the forest floor

throughfare *n* [by contr.] *obs* **:** THOROUGHFARE

through girder bridge *n* **:** a girder bridge in which the traffic passes between the girders

1**throughgoing** \'=,==\ *n* [2*through* + *going*, gerund of *go*] **1** *archaic* **:** EXAMINATION, OVERHAULING **2** *archaic* **:** REPRIMAND

2**throughgoing** \"\ *adj* [2*through* + *going*, pres. part. of *go*] **1 :** passing or extending all the way through **2** *archaic* **:** ENERGETIC

1**through·ith·er** \'thrü,ithə(r)\ *or* **through·oth·er** \-,əthə(r)\ *adv* [1*through* + *other*] *chiefly Scot* **:** in confusion **:** PROMISCUOUSLY

2**throughither** \"\ *or* **throughother** \"\ *adj, chiefly Scot* **:** CONFUSED, DISORDERLY, SCATTERBRAINED ⟨would turn out scientific, and him such a *throughither* laddie —John Buchan⟩

through·ly *adv* [ME, fr. 2*through* + *-ly*] **1** *archaic* **:** THOROUGHLY ⟨I'll be revenged most ~ for my father —Shak.⟩ **2** *archaic* **:** THROUGH AND THROUGH ⟨take this book; peruse it ~ —Christopher Marlowe⟩

1**throughout** \='=\ *adv* [ME *thurhout, throughout*, fr. *thurh, through* through (adv.) + *out*] **1 a :** in or to every part **:** from one end to the other **:** EVERYWHERE ⟨the second variety . . . is a light pink ~, with flecks of red —*Amer. Guide Series: Tenn.*⟩ **b :** as far as the edges or extremities of a heraldic field **2** *archaic* **:** right through to the end **:** COMPLETELY ⟨you may read a book ~ —L.R.McCalvin⟩ **3 :** during the whole time or action **:** from beginning to end ⟨the survey has ~ aimed at carrying out a large scientific program —G.deQ.Robin⟩

2**throughout** \"\ *prep* [ME *thurhout, throughout*, fr. *thurh, through* through (prep.) + *out*] **1 :** all the way from one end to the other of **:** in or to every part of ⟨all duties, imposts, and excises shall be uniform ~ the United States —*U.S.Constitution*⟩ **2 :** during the whole course or period of ⟨receiving a wound in one of his arms that troubled him ~ life —E.W. Parks⟩

3**throughout** \"\ *adj* [ME, fr. 1*throughout*] **:** extending to the edges of a heraldic field **:** ENTIRE — used postpositively ⟨a lozenge ~⟩

throughput \'=,=\ *n* **:** an amount of raw material put through processing or finishing operations in a specific time ⟨its initial daily ~ of 110,000 barrels —*Lamp*⟩ ⟨a ~ of about 500,000 birds a year —*Country Life*⟩

through rate *n* **1 :** a single transportation rate on an interline haul made up of two or more separately established rates **2 :** JOINT RATE

through retort *n* **:** a retort (as used for the distillation of mercury from cinnabar or for producing coal gas) with doors or mouthpieces at both ends that are closed during distillation

throughs *pl of* THROUGH

through shake *n* **:** a crack or fissure in timber that extends from side to side, edge to edge, or side to edge

through–shine \'=;=\ *adj* [ME, fr. OE *thurhscīne*, fr. *thurh* through + *scīnan* to shine — more at SHINE] **:** TRANSPARENT ⟨a *through-shine* glow of boyish vanity —George Biddle⟩

through station *n* **:** a railroad station whose tracks do not terminate at the station building but extend past it — compare STUB STATION

1**through stone** *n* [ME *throgh stone*, fr. *throgh* through + *stone* — more at THROUGH ⟨through stone⟩] *chiefly Scot* **:** a flat tombstone

2**through stone** *n* [3*through* + *stone*] **:** PERPEND 1

through street *n* **:** a street on which the through movement of traffic is given preference; *specif* **:** one at which traffic on all intersecting streets is required by law to stop or yield before entering or crossing except where traffic signal or officer control is employed

through switch *n* **:** a snap switch installed in a length of flexible cord

through traffic *n* **:** traffic initiated at and destined for points outside a local zone

through train *n* **:** a train usu. making a limited number of stops on which passengers may travel to a scheduled destination without changing to another train

through valley *n* **:** a depression or channel eroded across a divide by glacial ice or meltwater

throughway \'=,=\ *n* **1 :** THROUGH STREET **2 :** EXPRESSWAY

throve *past of* THRIVE

1**throw** \'thrō\ *vb* **threw** \'thrü\ *or dial* **throwed** \'thrōd\ *or* **trun** \'trən\ **thrown** \'thrōn\ *or dial* **throwed; throwing; throws** [ME *thrawen, throwen* to cause to twist, throw, fr. OE *thrāwan* to cause to twist or turn; akin to MD *draeyen* to cause to twist or turn, OHG *drāen*, L *terere* to rub, grind, *terebra* borer, gimlet, Gk *tetrainein* to bore through, pierce, *trēmat-, trēma* hole, *teirein* to oppress, distress, *tribein* to rub, grind; basic meaning: to rub with a twisting motion, bore] *vt* **1 a** (1) **:** to propel through the air by a forward motion of the hand and arm ⟨~ a baseball⟩ ⟨have no intention of ~*ing* bombs —J.B.Priestley⟩ (2) **:** to propel through the air with the hand and arm in an attempt to surpass competitors in an athletic contest ⟨~ the discus⟩ ⟨~ the javelin⟩ **b :** to propel through the air in any manner ⟨heavy rifles . . . able to ~ a bullet about five miles —Mari Sandoz⟩ ⟨a fire engine ~*ing* a stream of water⟩ ⟨satellite will be *thrown* into space —Courtney Sheldon⟩ **c :** to cast (a net, line hook, bait) in fishing **2 a** (1) **:** to cause to fall ⟨the wrestler easily *threw* his opponent⟩ (2) **:** to tackle (a ballcarrier) behind the line of scrimmage ⟨sometimes save our passer from being *thrown* for a loss —Norman Geske⟩ (3) **:** WEDGE 5 **b :** to cause to fall off **:** UNSEAT ⟨the horse *threw* his rider⟩ **c :** to get the better of **:** OVERCOME ⟨it was too formidable an enterprise for her but it didn't ~ her entirely —Douglas Watt⟩ **3 a :** to fling (oneself) in a precipitate manner ⟨just had time to ~ myself behind a small sofa —Patrick Campbell⟩ ⟨*threw* himself down on his knees like a miser who has found a . . . treasure —O.E.Rölvaag⟩ **b :** to drive or impel in a violent manner **:** DASH ⟨the ship was *thrown* on a reef⟩ **4 a** (1) **:** to cause to be in a particular position, condition, or situation **:** PUT ⟨*thrown* upon his own resources at the age of fifteen —D.E.Smith⟩ ⟨~*s* a subject out of balance with other ideas —C.E.Kellogg⟩ ⟨wage earners were *thrown* out of employment —W.J.Ghent⟩ ⟨a lot of yak-yak ~*s* me off my game —Willard Temple⟩ ⟨~*ing* her body backward at the shoulders like a young cadet —Scott Fitzgerald⟩ ⟨prepared to ~ open another room —David Garnett⟩ ⟨turned to ~ her arms round him —C.W.H.Johnson⟩ (2) **:** to put on hastily or carelessly **:** DON ⟨*threw* a coat over her shoulders and ran into the yard⟩ (3) **:** to put forcefully or roughly ⟨*threw* the chiefs of the opposition into prison —T.B.Macaulay⟩ (4) **:** to place or propel as if by a throw ⟨is not intended to . . . ~ any slur whatever on your firm —F.W.Crofts⟩ ⟨wants to ~ into a word every trace of meaning that it can hold —C.S.Kilby⟩ **b :** to move quickly **:** ADVANCE ⟨resolved to ~ his army across the river —J.W.Pratt⟩ **c :** to bring to bear **:** EXERT ⟨her influence was *thrown* upon the side of . . . the students —D.C.Peattie⟩ ⟨*threw* the weight of his paper against the movement —Broadus Mitchell⟩ **d :** to change into another form **:** CONVERT ⟨stories which they *threw* into crude stanzas —W.A.Neilson⟩ ⟨the necessity of ~*ing* confidential correspondence into cipher —Fletcher Pratt⟩ **e :** BUILD, CONSTRUCT ⟨the two concrete dams they *threw* across the stream bed to create reservoirs —F.J.Taylor⟩ ⟨*threw* his pontoon bridge across the river near this spot —*Amer. Guide Series: Tenn.*⟩ **f :** to bring into association ⟨his inclinations . . . naturally *threw* him into companionship with geologists —G.P.Merrill⟩ ⟨found himself *thrown* less with his queen and her sober intimates —Francis Hackett⟩ **g :** TIE ⟨~ a diamond hitch⟩ **5 a :** to form or shape on a potter's wheel ⟨smudging their smocks as they ~ the wet spinning clay —*Time*⟩ ⟨used the rotating wheel to ~ his pottery —*Times Lit. Supp.*⟩ **b :** to fashion or frame in a particular shape or manner **:** FORM ⟨*threw* his opinion into a neatly turned phrase⟩ **c :** CAST 4a (1) ⟨~ a bullet⟩ **d :** to form by digging or plowing ⟨plows . . . set for ~*ing* a ridge . . . 18 in. high —*Farmer's Weekly (So. Africa)*⟩ **6 a :** to deliver (a blow) in or as if in boxing ⟨*threw* . . . a tentative right to the expansive midriff of his towering opponent —L. W.T.Dovale⟩ **b :** to give (a salute) in a jaunty manner ⟨*threw* the marine on guard a nifty salute —J.A.Michener⟩ **7 a :** to twist two or more filaments of (as silk, rayon) into a thread or yarn **b :** to double and twist (singles) in the making of plied yarns **8 a :** to direct orally ⟨~*ing* a cheerful greeting to his secretary —Max Peacock⟩ ⟨paused for a moment and then *threw* an abrupt question at him —T.B.Costain⟩ **b :** to direct (as a look) in a hurried or cursory manner ⟨a glance that I had seen her ~ over her shoulder —Lord Dunsany⟩ ⟨*threw* a slight, easy look at his men and . . . walked out on the platform —Owen Wister⟩ **9 a** (1) **:** to make a cast of (dice) (2) **:** to make (a cast) at dice **b :** to play (a card) in a card game; *esp* **:** DISCARD **10 a :** to get rid of **:** divest or strip oneself of **:** cast off ⟨the snake ~*s* her enameled skin —Shak.⟩ ⟨his horse had *thrown* a shoe and he came up to the barn to draw out the nails —Erskine Caldwell⟩ ⟨one tank *threw* a track on a coconut log and went out of action —*Infantry Jour.*⟩ **b :** to free oneself from **:** DISLODGE, EJECT ⟨the fish leaps clear of the water trying to ~ the hook —Carlos Baker⟩ **c :** to give up as if by throwing away **:** ABANDON ⟨*threw* prudence to the wind and eloped —DeLancey Ferguson⟩ ⟨~*ing* all her moral teachings and inhibitions overboard —Ruth Park⟩ **11 a :** to send forth **:** PROJECT ⟨men . . . ~*ing* two burly shadows across the rocking chair —William Wiser⟩ ⟨fog ~*ing* the light back into his eyes —Harry Sylvester⟩ ⟨their effort ~*s* light on how the brain itself operates —Stuart Chase⟩ ⟨the light it ~*s* on the art movements of the time —O. Elfrida Saunders⟩ **b :** to give off **:** EMIT ⟨one of the planes began to ~ smoke⟩ **12 :** to make (oneself) dependent **:** commit (oneself) for help, support, or protection ⟨had *thrown* herself on their good nature —Ida A. R. Wylie⟩ ⟨you can . . . ~ yourselves on his mercy —John Buchan⟩ **13 a :** to cause to move or turn ⟨~ your mind back to the time when you saw melodrama of the now unfashionable kind —Daniel George⟩ **b :** to turn in a sudden or forceful manner ⟨was obliged to ~ his craft violently to avoid a collision —Walter O'Meara⟩ **14 a :** to give oneself up to unrestrainedly **:** give way to ⟨others ~ temper tantrums or pick fights —M.M. Hunt⟩ ⟨was able to get off the bus without ~*ing* a fit —J.D. Sheridan⟩ **b :** to apply freely or fully **:** DEVOTE ⟨dancing . . . with all the force and energy they could ~ into it —Meridel Le Sueur⟩ ⟨*threw* his whole physique into his conducting —Warwick Braithwaite⟩ **c :** to busy (oneself) in a zealous earnest manner ⟨*threw* themselves heartily into the preparations —Agnes S. Turnbull⟩ ⟨~*s* himself into his painting with furious energy —C.C.Walcutt⟩ **15 a :** to cast (a vote) in an election ⟨presidential votes . . . *thrown* for the Democratic candidate —James Bryce⟩ **b :** to send (an election) for final decision ⟨through lack of a popular majority the election was *thrown* into the legislature —W.A.Robinson⟩ **16 a** (1) **:** to give birth to **:** bring forth ⟨a fat sow . . . will not ~ large farrows —E.W.Lloyd⟩ (2) **:** SIRE, ENGENDER ⟨this ram is ~*ing* good stock —F.C.Stone⟩ **b :** PRODUCE, BEAR ⟨a field that ~*s* a good crop⟩ **17 :** to allow an opponent to win **:** lose intentionally or deliberately ⟨basketball players convicted of ~*ing* games —*Christian Science Monitor*⟩ ⟨~ a case . . . by remarks in court which will lay grounds for mistrials —D.D.McKean⟩ **18 a :** to move (a lever) so as to connect or disconnect parts of a clutch, machine, or switch **b :** to connect or disconnect (as a clutch, switch) by moving a lever **19 a :** to draw and aim (as a firearm) ⟨his finger was tight on the trigger as he *threw* the gun —R.J.Hogan⟩ — often used with *down* **b :** to make use of in a military attack ⟨*threw* everything they had against her: high-level bombs, dive bombers, and suicidal torpedo bombers —T.W.Lawson⟩ **20 :** to move (a typewriter carriage) to the left on completing a line by striking the line space lever **21 :** to give by way of entertainment **:** serve as host at ⟨had *thrown* one of his tremendous parties for the circus people —Alva Johnston⟩ **22 :** to engage in (as aimless talk) often as a means of passing the time ⟨sat around most of the afternoon ~*ing* the bull⟩ **23 :** to demand or obtain an advantage over a person by the assertion of (as superiority) ⟨sergeant . . . I have got to ~ rank at you —Bill Mauldin⟩ **24 :** to weigh out (a charge of powder) ~ *vi* **1 a :** to propel something through the air ⟨are taught the proper way to . . . field a ball and ~ —*Scholastic Coach*⟩ **b :** to have the capacity of propelling a missile ⟨the bazooka would have to ~ about eighty yards to reach the tank —Irwin Shaw⟩ **2 :** to fling oneself forcefully or violently **:** SPRING ⟨the black dog . . . *threw* at her —J.C.Atkinson⟩ **3 :** to cast dice **:** play at dice

syn TOSS, CAST, SLING, PITCH, HURL, FLING: THROW is the general term in this set and is very often interchangeable with the others; typically it indicates propelling through the air by distinctive movement of the bent arm followed by release of the object involved. TOSS may suggest less force, occasional aimlessness or lack of purpose, and an upward outward motion of the arm ⟨she rested on a log and *tossed* the fresh chips —Robert Frost⟩ In extended uses it may indicate light, easy throwing ⟨prevented Americans from *tossing* aside their global burdens —E.D.Canham⟩ CAST is a close synonym for *throw* but has been supplanted by the latter except in various special uses ⟨*cast* a net⟩ ⟨*casting* dice⟩ ⟨*cast* seed⟩ SLING may imply quick, sudden propulsion well aimed, as though accomplished with a sling ⟨*slung* an inkwell at a fellow senator in a congressional free-for-all —*Time*⟩ PITCH may suggest a definite, purposive aim to a specific spot or area ⟨*pitching* matchbooks at a crack for tomorrow's ration . . . was the favorite sport —James Jones⟩ ⟨possible for whole companies of grenadiers to run up to their enemy's lines and roll, bowl, or *pitch* their grenades among the legs of their opponents —Tom Wintringham⟩ HURL implies forceful impetus in the propulsion ⟨the wind picked the sand off the flinty, rolling ridges and *hurled* it in malicious bursts at you —Irwin Shaw⟩ ⟨electrons are *hurled* between cloud and cloud or between cloud and earth in long, branching flashes —Waldemar Kaempffert⟩ FLING stresses a certain force in throwing and may suggest unnecessary violence or random aimlessness brought about by strong emotion ⟨then he loathed his own beauty, and, *flinging* the mirror on the floor, crushed it into silver splinters beneath his heel —Oscar Wilde⟩ ⟨came racing up the path on his bicycle, *flung* it down in the yard and rushed straight into the farmhouse —George Orwell⟩

— **throw one's weight around** *or* **throw one's weight about :** to exercise influence or authority esp. to an excessive degree or in an objectionable manner ⟨began *throwing her weight around* the moment she was installed in her job —Bennett Cerf⟩ ⟨prickly with vanity and *throwing his weight about* as a young lieutenant —V.S.Pritchett⟩ — **throw together 1 :** to put together in a hurried and usu. careless manner ⟨an obviously profitable move to *throw together* six excerpts for a third suite —Arthur Berger⟩ **2 :** to bring into casual association ⟨were *thrown together* necessarily by a common interest —R.M.Lovett⟩

2**throw** \"\ *n* -s **1 a :** an act or instance of throwing, hurling, or flinging ⟨the catcher's ~ was high and the runner slid safely into second⟩ ⟨an underhand ~⟩ **b** (1) **:** an act of throwing dice (2) **:** the number or aggregate thrown ⟨a ~ of 7 or 11⟩ **c :** a method of throwing an opponent in wrestling or judo ⟨scissor-jump ~⟩ ⟨straight thigh ~⟩ **d** *chiefly Brit* (1) **:** an act of felling timber (2) **:** the quantity of trees felled **2 :** the distance that a missile is or may be thrown ⟨lived within a stone's ~ of the school⟩ **3 :** an undertaking that involves chance or danger **:** RISK, VENTURE ⟨has been marked by . . . a reckless ~ that failed —T.R.Ybarra⟩ **4 :** an instrument (as a potter's wheel) for turning **5 a :** the amount of vertical displacement up or down produced by a fault — compare DOWNTHROW, UPTHROW **b :** DISLOCATION b **6 a :** the extreme movement given or available to a pivoted or reciprocating piece by a cam, crank, or eccentric **:** TRAVEL, STROKE ⟨the ~ of a switch⟩ **b** (1) **:** the length of the radius of a crank or the virtual crank radius of an eccentric or cam (2) **:** CRANK WEB **7 a :** a lightweight flat cover (as a bedspread or afghan) that is casually draped or laid over something **b :** a woman's scarf or light wrap **8 :** the instantaneous deflection of a galvanometer needle or suspension when the instrument is used as a ballistic galvanometer **9 a :** the distance between a projector lens and the screen surface upon which an image is focused **b :** the distance between a loudspeaker and its audience **10 :** an object or individual regarded as a distinct member of a kind or class **:** UNIT, PIECE ⟨copies are to be sold at $5 a ~ —Harvey Breit⟩ **11 a :** 2SLING 2 **b :** the stipulated number of shots in a round of darts **12 :** a lever by means of which the binding of a ski is tightened

throw about *vi* **:** to go in a different direction **:** TACK

throw away *vt* **1 a :** to get rid of as worthless or unnecessary ⟨*threw away* a pair of old shoes⟩ **b :** DISCARD 1b **2 a :** to use in a foolish or wasteful manner **:** SQUANDER ⟨worked too hard for this money to *throw* it *away* —Kenneth Roberts⟩ **b :** to fail to take advantage of **:** WASTE ⟨the chance for a successful stand . . . was *thrown away* —Herbert Agar⟩ **3 :** to de-emphasize (as a line in a play) by casual delivery ⟨knows when to move upstage, when to modulate his voice, when to *throw away* a line —Harriet Van Horne⟩

throwaway \'==,=\ *n* -s [*throw away*] **:** something that is or is designed to be thrown away: as **a :** a handbill, pamphlet, advertising circular, newspaper, or shopping guide distributed free **b :** a line or segment of dialogue (as in a play) de-emphasized by casual delivery

throw back *vt* **1 :** to delay the progress or advance of **:** CHECK ⟨armies concentrated to . . . *throw back* the British striking forces —Tom Wintringham⟩ **2 :** to cause to rely **:** make dependent ⟨the Boston mind, *thrown back* upon itself, resumed its old colonial allegiance —Van Wyck Brooks⟩ **3 :** REFLECT ⟨pavements *throw back* the lights in wavy lines —Thomas Wood †1950⟩ ~ *vi* **:** to revert to an earlier type or phase; *specif* **:** to exhibit atavism ⟨the tendency of all varieties of pigeons to *throw back* —*Amer. Pigeon Jour.*⟩

throwback \'=,=\ *n* -s [*throw back*] **1 :** a reversal or backward deviation from a path or course **2 a :** reversion to an earlier type or phase; *specif* **:** ATAVISM **b :** an instance or product of such reversion ⟨have eliminated the sports and ~*s* and are getting a definite, consistent, and predictable type —*Fortune*⟩ ⟨a ~ to the heroic drama of Shakespearean times —Leslie Rees⟩ ⟨an aristocrat of the old line, a ~ to another century —W.A.White⟩ **3 :** FLASHBACK ⟨makes clever use of multiple-scene ~*s* and is . . . in every way a first-rate drama —*N.Y. Herald Tribune Bk. Rev.*⟩

throw by *vt* **:** to put aside **:** discard as worthless or unnecessary

throw–crook \'=,=\ *n* [1*throw* + *crook*] *chiefly Scot* **:** an instrument used for twisting rope from hay, straw, or hair

throw down *vt* [ME *throwen doun*, fr. *throwen* to throw + *doun* down] **1 :** to cause to fall **:** OVERTHROW ⟨if a tree is *thrown down* in a storm —J.G.Frazer⟩ **2 :** PRECIPITATE **3 :** to cast off **:** DISCARD, REJECT ⟨her beau's gone and *thrown* her *down* —William Faulkner⟩

throwdown \'=,=\ *n* -s [*throw down*] **:** an act or instance of a referee's putting a soccer ball in play by dropping it to the ground between two opposing players

throwed *dial past of* THROW

throw·er \'thrō(ə)r, -ōə\ *n* -s **:** one that throws: as **a :** a worker who forms pottery on a potter's wheel **b :** THROWSTER

throw in *vt* **1 :** to add as a gratuity or supplement ⟨compromised in the end by *throwing in* a cheap clock —Arthur Morrison⟩ **2 :** to introduce or interject in the course of something **:** CONTRIBUTE ⟨not a word wasted, not a sentiment capriciously *thrown in* —Matthew Arnold⟩ **3 :** DISTRIBUTE 3b(1) **4 a :** to cause (as gears) to mesh **b :** ENGAGE ⟨*throw in* the clutch⟩ ~ *vi* **1 :** to enter into association or partnership **:** JOIN ⟨agrees to *throw in* with a crooked ex-cop —*Newsweek*⟩ **2 :** DROP 2b(6) — **throw in one's hand 1 :** to signify withdrawal from the current hand of a card game by putting one's cards into the discard **2 :** to give up the struggle or contest **:** SURRENDER — **throw in one's lot with :** to join as an associate **:** share the fate of ⟨reluctant to *throw in their lot with* a new society —*Farmer's Weekly (So. Africa)*⟩ — **throw in the sponge** *or* **throw up the sponge** *or* **throw in the towel** [fr. the practice of a boxer's second of throwing a sponge or towel into the ring for his fighter to wipe his face, this being taken as an admission that they were no longer willing to continue the bout] **:** to abandon the struggle **:** acknowledge defeat **:** give up ⟨*throwing in the sponge* and failing to accomplish our mission —Glen Jacobsen⟩ ⟨when so many had *thrown up the sponge* and surrendered all faith in humanity —Van Wyck Brooks⟩ ⟨when the chaplain *throws in the towel* over your problem —*All Hands*⟩

throw–in \'=,=\ *n* -s [*throw in*] **1 :** an act or instance of throwing a ball in: as **a :** a throw made from the touchline in soccer to put the ball back in play after it has gone into touch **b :** a throw made by an outfielder in baseball to the infield **c :** a throw between the opposing ranks of players in polo with each team being on its own side of the line of the throw **d :** a throw made from outside the boundaries in basketball to put the ball back in play after it has gone out of bounds **2 :** an end play in bridge in which an opponent is forced to win a trick at a time when he must next make a lead disadvantageous to his side

throwing *pres part of* THROW

throwing–knife \'==,=\ *or* **throwing–iron** \'==,=(=)\ *n* [*throwing* (gerund of 1*throw*) + *knife* or *iron*] **:** a knifelike weapon often with several blades set at different angles that is used by some central African people for casting at an enemy or animal

throwing power *n* **:** the ability to deposit a plating of uniform depth on a surface of irregular shape

throwing–spear \'==,=\ *n* **:** a spear or spear-shaped object that is propelled with or without the help of a mechanical device

throwing–stick \'==,=\ *n* **1** *or* **throwing–board** \'==,=\ **:** a device for throwing a spear or dart consisting of a rod or board with a groove on the upper surface and a hook, thong, or projection at the rear end to hold the weapon in place until its release — called also *dart thrower, spear-thrower* **2 :** a wooden weapon in the form of a simple club or of an S-shaped, angular, or curved stick that is thrown by hand — compare WAR CLUB

throw lathe *n* **:** a small hand lathe

throw line *n* **1 :** a handline for fishing **2 :** a line indicating the throw of a crank or eccentric

thrown \'thrōn\ *adj* [fr. past part. of 1*throw*] *of a violin stroke* **:** performed with a loose grip so that the upper part of the bow is free to fall and rebound on the strings by its own weight ⟨~ staccato⟩

thrown–out \'=,=\ *adj* **:** inserted as a throw-out ⟨*thrown-out* maps⟩

thrown silk *n* **:** reeled silk that has been twisted or doubled and twisted into yarns

throw off *vt* **1 a :** to free oneself from **:** get rid of ⟨his only chance of *throwing off* the evil spell —Bill Beatty⟩ ⟨*throw off* his political masters and start a revolution —T.P.Whitney⟩ **b :** to cast off often in a hurried or vigorous manner **:** ABANDON, DISCARD ⟨*threw off* his coat and went to work⟩ ⟨*threw off* all sense of restraint⟩ **c :** to shake off **:** DIVERT ⟨wasn't to be *thrown off* by a false scent —*Blackwood's*⟩ **2 :** to make a start with in a hunt ⟨*throw off* thy ready pack —William Somerville⟩ **3 :** to give off **:** EMIT, EJECT ⟨mills *throwing off* . . . greenish clouds of smoke —*Amer. Guide Series: Conn.*⟩ **4 :** to produce in or as if in an offhand manner **:** execute with speed or facility ⟨some little scrap of tune that the composer had *thrown off* —James Hilton⟩ ⟨can *throw off* a criticism of eighteenth-century architecture or of the fad for whole-meal bread —*Times Lit. Supp.*⟩ **5 :** to remove (a man) from the backgammon board after all the men are home **6 a :** to cause to depart from an expected or desired course ⟨hidden assumptions *threw* the Newtonian calculations *off* just the smallest bit —T.H.Littlefield⟩ ⟨violation of form had *thrown* the whole story *off* —Alec Rackowe⟩ **b :** to cause to make a mistake or form a wrong impression **:** MISLEAD ⟨it had been her thick accent that had *thrown* me *off* —Richard Wright⟩ ~ *vi* **1 :** to begin hunting **2 :** to make derogatory comments **:** cast aspersions ⟨was constantly *throwing off* on the neighbors⟩

throw–off \'=,=\ *n* -s [*throw off*] **1 :** an act or instance of throwing off; *specif* **:** the start of a hunt **2 :** something that is thrown off **3 :** something that throws off: as **a** (1) **:** a device in a printing press for suspending impression without stopping the machine (2) : an automatic device in a machine tool to stop the feed **b :** DERAIL **4 :** the amount of cash generated by the operation of a business

throw out *vt* **1 a :** to remove from a place, office, or employment usu. in a sudden or unexpected manner ⟨your grooms . . . could perhaps *throw* me *out* —S.H.Adams⟩ ⟨be *thrown out* again as a result of some fresh change in the political landscape —A.J.Toynbee⟩ **b :** to get rid of as worthless or unnecessary ⟨people . . . won't *throw out* things fast enough to create new needs —K.D.Burke⟩ **2 :** to give expression to **:** UTTER ⟨*threw out* a remark . . . that utterly confounded him —Jean Stafford⟩ ⟨merely *throw out* these considerations to the House —Sir Winston Churchill⟩ **3 :** to dismiss from acceptance or consideration **:** REJECT ⟨a coerced confession . . . is sure to be *thrown out* —Charles Oldfather⟩ ⟨had *thrown out* certain specked ballots —E.F.Humphrey⟩ **4 :** to make visible or manifest **:** DISPLAY ⟨the signal was *thrown out* for the . . . fleet to prepare for action —Archibald Duncan⟩ **5 :** to leave behind **:** OUTDISTANCE ⟨had been unluckily *thrown out* and was riding fast to be in my place —Sir Walter Scott⟩ **6 :** to give forth from or as if from within **:** EMIT ⟨the radio *throwing out* a good tune —Anton Vogt⟩ ⟨an apple tree . . . *threw out* a sharp scent —Edith Sitwell⟩ **7 a :** to send out ⟨urged the general to *throw out* . . . Indian scouts into the woods —H.E.Scudder⟩ **b :** to cause to project **:** EXTEND ⟨this whitish house with . . . the wing *thrown out* at right angles —Virginia Woolf⟩ **8 :** to put out **:** CONFUSE, DISCONCERT ⟨automobiles in line blocking the road . . . *threw* the whole schedule *out* —F.D.Roosevelt⟩ ⟨anyone boorish . . . *threw* him *out* a little —Elizabeth Taylor⟩ **9 :** to cause to stand out **:** make prominent or clear ⟨the figures of . . . its greater men are *thrown out* plainly by their written works —H.O.Taylor⟩ **10 a :** to run out (a cricket batsman) by breaking the wicket with a direct throw of a fielded ball **b :** to make a throw that enables a teammate in baseball to put out (a base runner) **11 :** DISENGAGE ⟨*throw out* the clutch⟩

throw-out \\'ˌ\\ *n* -s [*throw out*] **1 :** an act or instance of throwing out **2 :** one that is rejected or discarded ⟨the attack on the government was led by envious *throw-outs* —George Orwell⟩ ⟨the *throw-outs* of ten generations, household rubbish made romantic by time —Richard Church⟩ **3 a :** a device for throwing a machine out of gear **b :** the mechanism or assemblage of mechanisms by which the driven and driving plates of a clutch in an automotive vehicle are separated **4 :** a book insert made in such a way that when unfolded its printed content is outside the edges of the book **5 :** BREAK 4f

throw over *vt* **1 :** to forsake despite bonds of attachment or duty **:** ABANDON ⟨*threw* her *over* for a girl from a wealthy family —Polly Adler⟩ **2 :** to refuse to accept **:** REJECT ⟨in his chapter on accent . . . *throws over* the ancient rules —H.O. Taylor⟩ ⟨carefully planned campaign to *throw over* the treaty —F.D.Roosevelt⟩

throw rug *n* **:** SCATTER RUG

throws *pres 3d sing of* THROW, *pl of* THROW

throw·ster \\'thrōstə(r)\\ *n* -s [ME *throwester*, fr. *throwen* to throw, twist + *-ster*] **:** one who throws silk or synthetic filaments

throw stick *n* **:** THROWING-STICK

throw up *vb* [ME *throwen up*, fr. *throwen* to throw + *up*] *vt* **1 :** to raise quickly or unexpectedly ⟨*throw up* the window⟩ **2 :** to give up **:** QUIT, RELINQUISH ⟨*threw up* a good job to devote his whole time to art —Herbert Read⟩ ⟨*throw* the whole thing *up* and do exactly what he wanted to do —Mary Deasy⟩ **3 :** to build in or as if in a hurried manner **:** construct hastily ⟨makeshift dwellings . . . were *thrown up* almost overnight —*Amer. Guide Series: N.Y. City*⟩ ⟨a breastwork was *thrown up* around the outskirts —*Amer. Guide Series: Minn.*⟩ **4 :** VOMIT ⟨if they are swallowed whole they may be *thrown up* —H.H.Miller⟩ **5 :** to bring forth **:** PRODUCE ⟨proves that Parliament can *throw up* leaders —Ernest Barker⟩ ⟨all the voluminous information *thrown up* by successive . . . investigations —S.F.Bemis⟩ **6 :** to make prominent or distinct esp. by contrast **:** cause to stand out ⟨white and yellow . . . help to *throw up* the other colors in the garden —Stuart Ogg⟩ **7 :** to mention repeatedly by way of reproach ⟨don't want that *thrown up* to me when I'm old and gray —Hamilton Basso⟩ ~ *vi* **1 :** VOMIT ⟨it was pretty hot . . . and she got sick and *threw up* —Don Ludlow⟩ **2** *of a hound* **:** to raise the head on losing the scent — **throw up one's hands :** to admit defeat ⟨the average conductor, faced with such a score, *throws up his hands* —Deems Taylor⟩

thru *var of* THROUGH

1thrum \\'thrəm\\ *n* -s [ME, fr. OE *-thrum* (as in *tungethrum* ligament of the tongue); akin to OS *thrumi* end part of a spear, OHG *drum* end part, fragment, ON *thrömr* edge, verge, brim, Gk *tramis* perineum, *termōn* boundary, end — more at TERM] **1 a** (1) **:** a fringe of warp threads left on the loom after the cloth has been removed (2) **:** one of these warp threads **b :** loom waste consisting of warp ends and test fabric pieces **c :** a short soft thread or tuft of threads **d :** a tuft or short piece of rope yarn used in thrumming canvas — usu. used in pl. **e :** something held to resemble a thrum **:** BIT, PARTICLE, SCRAP **2 a :** a hair, fiber, or threadlike leaf on a plant that resembles or is held to resemble a thrum **b :** a tuft, bundle, fringe, or other mass of such structures **3** *obs* **:** a ragged beggarly lout **4** *Brit* **:** THREEPENCE **:** a threepenny piece

2thrum \\"\\ *vt* **thrummed; thrummed; thrumming; thrums** **1 a :** to furnish with thrums **b :** to cover with tufts or pile **2** *obs* **:** to attire with or as if with a covering or fringe **:** CLOTHE, FRINGE **3 :** to insert short pieces of rope yarn or spun yarn in (a piece of canvas) to make a rough surface or a mat which can be wrapped about rigging to prevent chafing or used to stop a leak — **thrum caps** *obs* **:** to waste time in an idle or foolish occupation

3thrum \\"\\ *adj* **:** made of or woven from thrum ⟨in his ~ nightcap —Laurence Sterne⟩

4thrum \\"\\ *vb* **thrummed; thrummed; thrumming; thrums** [imit.] *vi* **1 :** to play idly on or as if on a stringed musical instrument by plucking or strumming with the fingers or by keys ⟨at night, with guitars, we *thrummed* and sang —Eve Langley⟩ ⟨~ on a mandolin⟩ ⟨~ on a table⟩ **2 a :** to sound with a repeated and often monotonous hum like a string or an instrument when strummed ⟨the blood *thrummed* in my ears —Rumer Godden⟩ **b :** to move accompanied by such a sound ⟨the wire ~*s* out steadily —*Science*⟩ **3 :** to repeat something over and over **:** to speak or read aloud monotonously ~ *vt* **1 :** to play (as a stringed musical instrument) in an idle or relaxed manner ⟨~*s* a preliminary chord or two —P.B.Kyne⟩ ⟨~ a guitar⟩ **2 :** to recite monotonously **:** repeat in a singsong voice **3 :** to strike with the fingers as if playing on a musical instrument **:** drum on ⟨~ the table⟩

5thrum \\"\\ *n* -s **1 :** an often monotonous sound made by thrumming ⟨across the plaza came the ~ of guitars —*Atlantic*⟩ ⟨~ of hoofs from the paddock —Elizabeth Bowen⟩ ⟨the ~ of the mighty engines⟩ **2 :** the purring of a cat

thrum·ble \\'thrəm(b)əl, -rům-\\ *var of* THRIMBLE

thrum-eyed \\'ˌ\\ *adj* **:** having the anthers exserted and visible at the throat of the corolla ⟨*thrum-eyed* flowers of various primulas⟩ — compare PIN-EYED

thrum·mer \\'thrəmə(r)\\ *n* -s [4*thrum* + *-er*] **:** one that thrums an instrument; *esp* **:** a strolling player

thrum·ming \\'thrəmiŋ, -mēŋ\\ *n* -s [1*thrum* + *-ing*] **:** a mass of tufts or short pieces of rope yarn used in thrumming canvas

thrum·my \\-mē, -mi\\ *adj* [1*thrum* + *-y*] **1 :** made of or with thrums ⟨a ~ cap⟩ **2 :** having a shaggy or downy surface ⟨~ flowers⟩

thrump \\'thrəmp\\ *n* -s [imit.] **:** a heavy and usu. repeated sound (as of motors, artillery, or marching men)

thrumwort \\'ˌ\\ *n* [1*thrum* + *wort*] **1 :** a love-lies-bleeding (*Amaranthus caudatus*) **2 :** STARFRUIT **3 :** a water plantain (*Alisma plantago-aquatica*)

1thrush \\'thrəsh\\ *n* -ES [ME *thrusche, thrusch*, fr. OE *thrysce;* akin to OE *throstle* thrush, OS *throsla*, OHG *droscala*, ON *thröstr*, L *turdus*, Russ *drozd*] **1 :** any of numerous small or medium sized passerine birds that constitute the widely distributed family Turdidae, include many excellent singers, are mostly of a plain color although many have spotted underparts and the young have the entire plumage spotted, have 10 primaries of which the first is spurious and booted tarsi, and feed esp. on worms and insect larvae or on fruits — see BLACKBIRD, FIELDFARE, GRAY-CHEEKED THRUSH, HERMIT THRUSH, MISTLE THRUSH, OLIVE-BACKED THRUSH, REDWING, ROBIN, SONG THRUSH, VARIED THRUSH, VEERY, WOOD THRUSH; BILL illustration **2 :** any of numerous birds of families other than Turdidae that are felt to resemble the true thrushes — usu. used with qualifier; see SHRIKE THRUSH, WATER THRUSH **3 :** CANARY 4 **4** *or* **thrush brown :** a grayish to moderate yellowish brown — called also *shagbark*

2thrush \\"\\ *n* -ES [prob. of Scand origin; akin to Dan & Norw *trøske* thrush, Sw *torsk*, Sw dial. *trosk* thrush; prob. akin to Sw dial. *trosk* growth, Norw dial. *trausk, trosk*] **1 a :** a mycotic disease of the upper digestive tract characterized by the formation of white plaques within the oral cavity often coalescing in a false membrane, occurring esp. in debilitated children and adults and in birds, and caused by infection with a fungus (*Candida albicans*) **b :** any of several oral disorders (as sore mouth of sheep) more or less resembling this mycotic disease **2 :** an inflammatory and suppurative affection of the feet in various animals; *specif* **:** a purulent degenerative state of the frog in the horse

thrush blackbird *n* **:** RUSTY BLACKBIRD

thrush fungus *n* [2*thrush*] **:** a fungus (*Candida albicans*) causing thrush

thrush lichen *or* **thrush moss** *n* [2*thrush*] **:** a lichen (*Peltigera apthosa*) held to cure thrush

thrushlike \\'ˌ\\ *adj* **:** resembling a thrush (as in song or appearance)

thrush nightingale *n* **:** a large nightingale (*Luscinia luscinia*) of eastern Europe

thrushy \\'thrəshē, -shi\\ *adj* -ER/-EST [2*thrush* + *-y*] **:** having or affected with thrush

1thrust \\'thrəst\\ *vb* **thrust; thrust; thrusting; thrusts** [ME *thrusten, thristen*, fr. ON *thrȳsta* to thrust, press; prob. akin to ON *thrjōta* to fail, lack — more at THREAT] *vt* **1 a :** to push or drive with physical force **:** exert force upon or against so as to move in a desired direction **:** DRIVE, FORCE, IMPEL, SHOVE ⟨~ his hand into his pocket⟩ ⟨~ the chair forward⟩ ⟨~ me suddenly from her —Kenneth Roberts⟩ ⟨a hen having medicine ~ down its throat —Andrew Buchanan⟩ **b :** to push, drive, or impel as if with physical force ⟨he ~ aside all precautionary advice⟩ ⟨poetry ~*s* the great passions of men before us —C.S.Kilby⟩ ⟨into his churning mind . . . one single idea ~ itself —Walter O'Meara⟩ **2 :** to cause to enter, pierce, or penetrate something or some place by or as if by pushing ⟨~ a dagger into her heart⟩ **3 :** to push forth into some place **:** extend in some direction **:** throw out in or as if in the process of growth **:** SPREAD ⟨a poplar ~*s* its rootlets far and wide⟩ ⟨mountains which ~ an arm eastward into the Great Plains —R.A.Billington⟩ ⟨prosperous cities had . . . ~ out suburbs —G.M.Trevelyan⟩ **4** *archaic* **:** to stab or pierce with a pointed weapon **5 a :** to put (as a person who is unwilling) forcibly into some course of action or position ⟨he was ~ into the leadership —*Irish Digest*⟩ ⟨~ into an atmosphere of superinduced excitement —R.M.Weaver⟩ **b :** to introduce often improperly or irrelevantly into some position **:** INTERPOLATE **6 a :** to intrude (as a person) into a position or upon one or more other persons **:** INTERPOSE **b :** to press, force, or impose the acceptance of (something) upon someone ⟨~ new responsibilities upon him⟩ ⟨some have greatness ~ upon 'em —Shak.⟩ ~ *vi* **1 a :** to push in **:** force an entrance or passage **b** (1) **:** to push forward **:** press onward or into a place ⟨railroads began to ~ into the buffalo country —C.C.Rister⟩ ⟨the determination of the United Nations forces . . . to ~ beyond the 38th parallel —*Current Biog.*⟩ ⟨with a whoop . . . the Indian ~ ashore —*McClure's*⟩ (2) **:** to ride forward of the field in hunting **:** ride too close to the hounds **c :** to push upward ⟨a rock said to ~ 200 feet above the water⟩ **2 :** to make a thrust, stab, or lunge with or as if with a pointed weapon ⟨~ at her with a knife⟩ **syn** see PUSH

2thrust \\"\\ *n* -s *often attrib* **1** *obs* **:** a crowd of people **:** PRESS, THRONG **2 a** (1) **:** an action of forcibly moving a pointed weapon (as a sword or dagger) in the direction of its length and usu. toward an objective **:** LUNGE (2) **:** the result of such an action **:** a stab made with a pointed weapon or an instrument of any kind ⟨a bayonet ~ in the . . . abdomen —Raymond Boyle⟩ **b :** an action held to resemble such a movement: as (1) **:** a verbal attack of greater or lesser intensity ⟨enliven their editorials with barbed ~*s* at their neighbors —*Amer. Guide Series: Minn.*⟩ ⟨hilarious . . . ~*s* at our sentimentality —John Mason Brown⟩ (2) **:** an attack or assault by military forces ⟨the enemy made a ~ deep into our position⟩ ⟨withstanding a sudden ~ by . . . 100 to 150 divisions —Patrick McMahon⟩ **3 :** a pushing or driving force: as **a :** a force causing breakdown of a mine-gallery roof under its superincumbent weight **b :** the sideways force or pressure of one part of a structure against another part; *esp* **:** a horizontal or diagonal outward pressure (as of an arch against an abutment or any member of the upper chord of a truss against its terminal joints) **c** (1) **:** the force that is exerted endwise through a propeller shaft (as of a ship or airplane) due to reaction of the water or air on the revolving blades or vanes of the propeller and that serves to drive the craft ahead (2) **:** the forwardly directed reaction force produced by a high-speed jet of fluid discharged rearwards from a nozzle or orifice (as in a jet airplane or a rocket) — called also *jet thrust* **d :** a compressive tangential stress in the earth's crust or the effect of such stress **:** THRUST FAULT **4 a :** the action of pushing, driving, or otherwise moving something by the exertion of physical force ⟨the glide of birch canoes and the ~ of . . . paddles —*Amer. Guide Series: Vt.*⟩ **b :** an instance of such movement by the exertion of force **5 a** (1) **:** an action of pushing forward into some place or in some direction ⟨helps him in his ~ for higher office —*Saturday Rev.*⟩ ⟨forward ~*s* in history have not always been the product of universal assent —*Saturday Rev.*⟩ (2) **:** a movement (as by a group of people) in a usu. specified direction ⟨the most westerly ~ of the English toward the Dutch settlement —*Amer. Guide Series: Conn.*⟩ **b :** an instance of pushing upward ⟨the upward ~ of the . . . skyscrapers —*Amer. Guide Series: N.Y. City*⟩ **c :** a quality marked by usu. forceful movement forward or upward ⟨Japanese walkers are silent, less full of ~ —Santha Rama Rau⟩ ⟨his performance has a ~ . . . that none of the other violinists brings to the music —H.C.Schonberg⟩ **d :** something (as a projection) that is thrust out or up ⟨~*s* . . . extrude at almost every section of the frontiers —Herbert Feis⟩ ⟨the most easterly ~ of the mountain range⟩ **6 :** a percussive movement of striking or shoving in modern dance **syn** see STRESS

thrust augmentation *n* **:** a process by which the thrust produced by a jet-propulsion engine may be increased temporarily over its normal value by some secondary means (as the burning of additional fuel in the tail pipe, or the injection of water into the engine inlet and the combustion chambers) which increases the mass flow, the velocity, or both

thrust augmentor *n* **:** AUGMENTOR

thrust bearing *or* **thrust block** *n* **:** a bearing to resist end thrust; *specif* **:** one provided with collars or horseshoe-shaped pieces or rollers which bear against corresponding collars on the shaft journal

thrust block *n* **:** a segment of the earth's crust moved along a thrust fault esp. at a low angle

thrust coefficient *n* **:** the thrust force of a jet-propulsion engine per unit of frontal area per unit of incompressible dynamic pressure

thrust·er \\'thrəstə(r)\\ *n* -s [1*thrust* + *-er*] **:** one that thrusts: as **a :** one that rides too close to the hounds in fox hunting **b :** one that intrudes himself or pushes himself forward **:** PUSHER ⟨a crude and awkward social ~⟩

thrust face *n* **:** BLADE FACE

thrust fault *n* **:** a reverse fault in which the angle between the horizontal and the plane is small — called also OVERTHRUST FAULT

thrust·ful \\'ˌfəl\\ *adj, Brit* **:** characterized by thrusting or an ability to thrust **:** FORCEFUL, AGGRESSIVE

thrust·ful·ness *n* -ES *Brit* **:** the quality or state of being thrustful

thrust hoe *n* **:** SCUFFLE HOE

thrust horsepower *n* **1 :** the actual horsepower delivered by the engine-propeller unit in an airplane and found less than brake horsepower because the propeller is never 100 percent efficient **2 :** the thrust of a jet engine or a rocket expressed in horsepower and found by multiplying thrust in pounds by speed of aircraft and dividing by 375

thrusting *pres part of* THRUST

thrust key *n* **:** PUSH KEY

thrust line *n* **:** a line located on a map by two points or one point and a direction and from which any point can be identified by giving a distance along the line from the base point and a distance perpendicular to the thrust line

Thrus·tor \\'thrəstə(r)\\ *trademark* — used for a hydraulic operating mechanism actuated by an electric motor

thrust plane *n* **:** the surface that is never strictly a plane along which dislocation has taken place in the case of a reverse or thrust fault

thrust plate *or* **thrust sheet** *n* **:** a geologic thrust block of great lateral extent

thrusts *pres 3d sing of* THRUST, *pl of* THRUST

thrust shaft *n* **:** the length of a propeller shaft provided with collars for resisting the end thrust of the propeller and held by the thrust bearing

thrust spoiler *n* **:** a device intended to reduce the thrust of a jet engine (as by deflecting the jet of exhaust gases)

thruway *var of* THROUGHWAY

thrym·sa \\'thrimzə, -msə\\ *n* -s [OE *thrymsa, thrimsa*, gen. pl., alter. (influenced by *thrīe* three) of *trymesa, trimesa*, gen. pl. of *trymes, trimes*, fr. LL *tremis*, a coin, fr. L *tres* three + *-mis* (as in *semis*) — more at THREE, SEMIS (coin)] **:** a 7th century gold coin and corresponding unit of value of Anglo-Saxon England

1thry·on·o·my·id \\thrīˌänəˈmīəd\\ *adj* [NL *Thryonomyidae*, family of rodents, fr. *Thryonomys*, type genus + *-idae*] **:** of or relating to the genus *Thryonomys* or to the family Thryonomyidae

2thryonomyid \\"\\ *n* -s **:** a thryonomyid rodent

thry·on·o·mys \\thrī'änəməs\\ *n, cap* [NL, fr. Gk *thryon* reed, rush + NL *-o-* + *-mys*] **:** a genus (coextensive with the family Thryonomyidae) of hystricomorph rodents comprising the African ground pigs

thsd *abbr* thousand

thu·cho·lite \\'th(y)ükəˌlīt\\ *n* -s [*Th* (symbol for *thorium*) + *U* (symbol for *uranium*) + *C* (symbol for *carbon*) + *H* (symbol for *hydrogen*) + *O* (symbol for *oxygen*) + *-lite*] **:** a bitumen containing uranium and thorium

thu·cyd·i·de·an \\(ˌ)th(y)üˌsidəˈdēən\\ *adj, usu cap* [*Thucydides* †*ab* 400 B.C. Greek historian + E *-an*] **1 :** of, relating to, or characteristic of the Greek historian Thucydides (as in compactness and precision of expression, historical accuracy, or philosophical breadth of view) **2 :** of, relating to, or resembling the device of putting appropriate speeches into the mouths of persons who appear in a history

1thud \\'thəd\\ *vi* **thudded; thudded; thudding; thuds** [prob. fr. ME *thudden* to thrust, push, fr. OE *thyddan*] **:** to move or strike so as to make a thud ⟨an uppercut that *thudded* like a mallet on wood —Donn Byrne⟩

2thud \\"\\ *n* -s **1** *Scot* **:** a tempest or gust of wind **:** WINDSTORM **2 a :** a blow or a series of repeated blows **b :** a dull sound like that produced by striking with or against a somewhat soft substance **:** THUMP ⟨the whistle and ~ of the bullets —Hanama Tasaki⟩ ⟨fell with the dull ~ of a sack of sand —Green Peyton⟩

thud·ding·ly *adv* **:** with thuds ⟨~ galloped across the floor —Sinclair Lewis⟩

thug \\'thəg\\ *n* -s [Hindi *ṭhag*, lit., thief, fr. Skt *sthaga* rogue, fr. *sthagati* he covers, conceals — more at THATCH] **1** *often cap* **:** one of a group of professional robbers and murderers in India characteristically strangling their victims **2 :** a person inclined or hired to treat another roughly, brutally, or murderously **:** GANGSTER, KILLER

thu·ga \\'th(y)ügə\\ *also* **thu·ya** \\-üyə\\ *n* -s [modif. of NL *thuja*] **:** THYINE WOOD

thug·gee \\'thəgē\\ *n* -s [Hindi *ṭhagī* robbery, fr. *ṭhag* thief — more at THUG] **:** murder and robbery by thugs

thug·gery \\'thəgərē, -ri\\ *n* -ES [*thug* + *-ery*] **1 :** THUGGEE **2 :** the behavior of a thug

thu·id·i·um \\th(y)ü'idēəm\\ *n, cap* [NL, fr. ML *thuia* + NL *-idium*] **:** a widely distributed genus of mosses (order Hypnobryales) with fernlike leaves — see FERN MOSS

thu·ja \\'th(y)üjə\\ *n* [NL, fr. ML *thuia*, a kind of cedar, fr. Gk *thyia*] **1 a** *cap* **:** a genus of evergreen shrubs and trees (family Pinaceae) having flat distichous branches and scalelike closely imbricated or compressed leaves **b** -s **:** any tree of the genus *Thuja; esp* **:** ARBORVITAE **2** -s **:** THUGA

thu·jane \\-ˌjān\\ *n* -s [ISV *thuj-* (fr. NL *Thuja*) + *-ane*] **:** a saturated bicyclic terpene hydrocarbon $C_{10}H_{18}$ that is the parent compound of thujene and thujone — called also *sabinane*

thuja oil *n* **:** a fragrant essential oil obtained from the leaves and twigs of arborvitae and used chiefly in scenting shoe polishes, floor waxes, and other technical preparations — called also *cedarleaf oil*

thu·ja·pli·cin \\-'plīsᵊn\\ *n* -s [NL *Thuja plicata* species of red cedar + E *-in*] **:** any of three isomeric crystalline compounds $C_3H_7C_7H_5O_2$ that are obtained esp. from the heartwood of the canoe cedar and possess the fungicidal properties that preserve this wood against decay **:** isopropyl-tropolone

thu·jene \\'th(y)üˌjēn\\ *n* -s [ISV *thuj-* (fr. NL *Thuja*) + *-ene*] **:** any of several unsaturated bicyclic terpene hydrocarbons $C_{10}H_{16}$ related to thujane: as **a :** an oily liquid obtained from various essential oils — called also *alpha-thujene, 3-thujene* **b :** SABINENE

thu·jic acid \\'th(y)üjik-\\ *n* [NL *Thuja* + E *-ic*] **:** a crystalline unsaturated acid $C_9H_{11}COOH$ containing a 7-membered ring and found in the heartwood of the canoe cedar

thu·jone \\-ˌjōn\\ *n* -s [ISV *Thuj-* (fr. NL *Thuja*) + *-one*] **:** a fragrant oily ketone $C_{10}H_{16}O$ derived from thujane, occurring in mixtures of dextrorotatory and levorotatory stereoisomeric forms in various essential oils (as thuja oil, wormwood oil, tansy oil), and used in making synthetic essential oils

thu·jop·sis \\th(y)ə'jäpsəs\\ *n, cap* [NL, fr. *Thuja* + *-opsis*] **:** a genus of Japanese evergreen trees (family Pinaceae) with irregular or whorled horizontal branches and leaves glossy green above and marked with a white band beneath — see HIBA ARBORVITAE

thu·jyl \\'th(y)üjəl\\ *n* -s [ISV *thuj*one + *-yl*] **:** a univalent radical $C_{10}H_{17}$ derived from thujyl alcohol

thujyl alcohol *n* **:** an alcohol $C_{10}H_{17}OH$ known in several stereoisomeric usu. syrupy liquid forms, found free or combined as esters in various essential oils (as wormwood oil), and formed by reduction of thujone

1thu·le \\'th(y)ülē, -li\\ *n* -s [fr. L *Thule, Thyle* (fr. Gk *Thoulē, Thylē*), a land represented as being six days' sail north of Britain and considered to be the northernmost part of the habitable world] **1** *usu cap* **:** the northernmost part of the habitable world **2** *often cap* **a :** a very distant mysterious or mythical region **b :** a remote goal or end

2thu·le \\'tülē, -li\\ *adj, usu cap* [fr. *Thule*, settlement in Greenland] **:** of or belonging to the Eskimo culture extending over arctic lands from Alaska to Greenland about A.D. 500–1400, characterized by the hunting of sea mammals and esp. of whales, winter semisubterranean houses of whalebone or wood, stone, and earth and summer tents, stone or earthenware lamps and pots, ground slate tools, and use of dog sleds

thu·lite \\'th(y)üˌlīt\\ *n* -s [L *Thule*, northernmost part of the habitable world + E *-ite*] **:** a mineral consisting of a rose-red variety of zoisite found in Tellemarken, Norway, and elsewhere and occas. cut for use in jewelry

thulite pink *n, often cap T* **:** a dark to deep purplish pink

thu·li·um \\-ˌlēəm\\ *n* -s [NL, fr. *Thule* + *-ium*] **:** a trivalent metallic element of the rare-earth group that occurs combined in rare minerals associated with granite or pegmatite veins and that forms pale green compounds resembling those of erbium, ytterbium, and lutetium in solubility — symbol *Tm;* see ELEMENT table

thu·luth \\'thüləth\\ *n* -s [Ar] **:** one of the chief forms of Arabic and Persian script

1thumb \\'thəm\\ *n* -s *often attrib* [ME *thoume, thoumbe, thombe*, fr. OE *thūma;* akin to OS & OHG *thūmo* thumb, ON *thumall* thumb of a glove, L *tumēre* to swell, Gk *saos, sōs* whole, sound, Skt *tavīti* he is strong; basic meaning: to swell] **1 a :** the short and thick first or most preaxial digit of the human hand differing from the other fingers in having but two phalanges and in having greater freedom of movement and being opposable to the other fingers : POLLEX **b :** the corresponding digit in any of various animals — see BAT illustration **2 :** the width of the thumb usu. equated with one inch **3 :** something resembling or suggesting a thumb (as in appearance, place, or function): as **a :** a thumb-shaped projection from a plant or tree **b :** a thumb-shaped pinnacle of rock **4 :** the part of a glove or mitten that covers the thumb — see GLOVE illustration **5 :** a convex molding : OVOLO **6 :** the large fixed branch of an arthropod's chela — **all thumbs** : extremely awkward or clumsy ⟨as an example of playwriting, it is *all thumbs,* echoes, and foolishness —John Mason Brown⟩ — **under the thumb of** *or* **under one's thumb :** under the influence of : in a state of subservience to ⟨is *under the thumb of* an excellent but stern mother —V.S.Pritchett⟩ ⟨had only to bring *under his thumb* the existing control points —*Wall Street Jour.*⟩

[2]**thumb** \"\ *vb* -ED/-ING/-S *vt* **1 :** to play (a musical instrument) with or as if with the thumbs **2 a :** to examine, feel, press, point at, attack, or sort by means of the thumb ⟨~*ed* the front door release —*Newsweek*⟩ ⟨~*ed* him in the eye⟩ **b :** to bring into a specified state by gesturing with or applying the thumb ⟨~*ed* a match afire on the packet —Thurston Scott⟩ ⟨~*ed* his hat off his forehead —Luke Short⟩ ⟨only twice have umpires ~*ed* him out of a game —*Newsweek*⟩ **3 a :** to leaf through (as a book or periodical) rapidly as in searching or examining ⟨~*ing* his billfold —Jerome Ellison⟩ ⟨anyone who has even ~*ed* leaves in that book will have noted it —Albert Hofstadter⟩ **b :** to read often, regularly, or repeatedly : REREAD ⟨I shall prize it and continue to ~ it —L.F.Ward⟩ **c :** to soil or wear by or as if by frequent or repeated thumbing ⟨a badly ~*ed* law book⟩ **4 :** to retard the speed of (a fishing reel) by pressure of the thumb on the line wound on the spool or by a mechanical device esp. in order to prevent a backlash **5 a :** to request or obtain (a ride) in a passing automobile by signaling with the thumb in the desired direction **b :** to signal (an approaching vehicle) with the thumb in asking a ride ⟨~*ed* the big trucks that started rolling —Jack Kerouac⟩ **c :** to make (one's way) by thumbing rides **~** *vi* **1 :** to turn over pages in searching or perusal ⟨~ through volumes . . . hunting for the answer —*Mech. Engineering*⟩ **2 :** to travel or make a trip by thumbing rides — **thumb one's nose 1 :** to point at with extended fingers and the thumb at one's nose as a gesture of derision, scorn, or defiance **2 :** to treat or regard with disdain ⟨*thumb their noses* at the collective wisdom of the ages —C.I.Glicksberg⟩

thumb-and-finger rule \ˈ=-ˈ==-\ *n* **:** either of two statements in electromagnetism: when the fingers of the right hand are bent so that the thumb points in the direction of the decrease in flux in a magnetic circuit, the fingers will point in the direction of the induced voltage in the electric circuit linked with the magnetic circuit; and when the fingers of the right hand are bent so that they follow the direction of the flow of current through a helical or coil conductor, the thumb will point in the direction of the flux through the helix or coil — compare LEFT-HAND RULE, RIGHT-HAND RULE

thumb-bolt \ˈ=,=\ *n* **:** a lock operated by a thumb turn

thumb bottle *n* **:** PHIAL

thumb box *n* **:** a small box that contains painting materials, a panel for mixing colors, and a small canvas or board and has a thumb hole or other device by which it can be held upon the thumb like a palette to make a small sketch usu. in oil

thumb cleat *n* **:** a small cleat with but one horn used on a yard or boom

thumb cut *n* **:** THUMB NOTCH 2

thumb down *vt* **:** to turn thumbs down on : REJECT ⟨*thumbed down* one request that it print the whole Bible, chapter by chapter —*Newsweek*⟩

thumb·er \ˈthəmə(r)\ *n* -S **1 :** one that thumbs rides : HITCHHIKER **2 :** a worker who sews thumbs in gloves or mittens

thumb flint *n* **:** a prehistoric often tiny flint tool shaped like a thumb and thought to be a scraper

[1]**thumbhole** \ˈ=,=\ *n* [[1]*thumb* + *hole*] **1 :** an opening in which to insert the thumb; *specif* **:** a semicircular cut in the sides or ends of a container to facilitate lifting the cover **2 :** a hole in a wind musical instrument opened or closed by the thumb

[2]**thumbhole** \"\ *vt* **:** to provide with a thumbhole

thumb·hol·er \-lə(r)\ *n* **:** a worker who makes thumbholes

thumbier *comparative of* THUMBY

thumbiest *superlative of* THUMBY

thumb index *n* **:** an index consisting of rounded thumb notches cut symmetrically on the fore edge of a book and tabs denoting the letters (as in a dictionary) or sections referred to beginning on the page that faces or forms the base of each notch

thumb-index \ˈ=ˈ==\ *vt* [*thumb index*] **:** to equip (a book) with a thumb index ⟨the main part of the book is a *thumb-indexed* directory listing ministries —*Times Lit. Supp.*⟩

thumbing *pres part of* THUMB

thumb knot *n* **:** OVERHAND KNOT; *also* **:** a loop knot made with an overhand knot

thumb·less \ˈ=ləs\ *adj* **1 :** having no thumb **2 :** CLUMSY

thumb·ling \ˈthəmliŋ, -lēŋ\ *n* -S [[1]*thumb* + *-ling*] **:** a very tiny thumb-sized person : MANIKIN

thumb knot

thumb lock *also* **thumb latch** *n* **:** a lock that can be released by pressure with the thumb

[1]**thumbmark** \ˈ=,=\ *n* [[1]*thumb* + *mark*] **1 :** an impression left by a thumb esp. when used as a mark of identification **2 :** a depression in the sides of a single comb of a fowl that is a defect in show birds

[2]**thumbmark** \"\ *vt* **:** to mark with the thumb; *also* **:** to take a thumbmark of (as for identification)

thumb mold *or* **thumb molding** *n* **:** a narrow convex molding on furniture having a profile in a flattened curve

[1]**thumbnail** \ˈ=,=, ,=ˈ=\ *n, often attrib* [[1]*thumb* + *nail*] **1 :** the nail of the thumb **2 :** something small, brief, or concise ⟨a ~ sketch⟩

[2]**thumbnail** \ˈ=,=\ *vt* **:** to make a thumbnail sketch of ⟨the minor characters have been methodically ~*ed* in conventional types —J.S.Shrike⟩ ⟨practically everybody anybody ever heard of is cited, ~*ed*, keelhauled, cuddled —*Time*⟩

thumb notch *n* **1 :** a notch of a size to admit the tip of a thumb cut in the outer edges of the pages of a book for the insertion of index letters or headings — compare THUMB INDEX **2 :** a half-moon cut in the sides of a slipcase to facilitate removal of the book — called also *thumb cut*

thumb nut *n* **:** a nut designed to be turned by thumb and finger: as **a :** WING NUT **b :** a nut with a knurled edge

thumb pad *n* **:** a fleshy pad over the inner metacarpal bone of various frogs and esp. of males in breeding condition

thumbpiece \ˈ=,=\ *n* **1 :** an appendage to a handle (as of a vessel) to afford a hold for the thumb **2 :** a part designed to be operated by the thumb or thumb and fingers: as **a :** a small inside knob for a night latch **b :** a small knob or button to operate a catch (as on a bracelet) **3** *dial* **:** a small amount of food

thumb pin *n* **:** THUMBTACK

thumb piston *n* **:** COMBINATION PISTON

thumb plane *n* **:** a very small carpenter's plane for use in a somewhat inaccessible place

thumb pot *n* **:** a flowerpot of the smallest size used esp. for starting seedlings (as of orchids)

[1]**thumbprint** \ˈ=,=\ *n* [[1]*thumb* + *print*] **:** an impression made by the thumb; *esp* **:** a print made by the inside of the first joint and showing its characteristic lineation — compare FINGERPRINT

[2]**thumbprint** \"\ *vt* **:** to take a thumbprint of

thumb ring *n* **1 :** a ring worn on the thumb **2 :** a ring (as on a bow or a sword guard) to receive or protect the thumb

thumbrope \ˈ=,=\ *n, dial Brit* **:** a rope made by twisting hay or straw round the thumb

thumb rule *n* **:** RULE OF THUMB

thumbs *pl of* THUMB, *pres 3d sing of* THUMB

[1]**thumbscrew** \ˈ=,=\ *vt* [[1]*thumb* + *screw,* v.] **:** to torture by use of the thumbscrew; *also* **:** to coerce by or as if by such torture

[2]**thumbscrew** \"\ *n* [[1]*thumb* + *screw,* n.] **1 :** a screw whose head is flattened at the side or knurled so that the screw may be turned by the thumb and forefinger — see SPOKESHAVE illustration **2 :** an instrument of torture for compressing the thumb by a screw

thumbs-down \ˈ=ˈ=\ *n* -S [fr. the imperative phrase *thumbs down*] **:** the act, process, or an instance of rejection, disapproval, or condemnation ⟨the government *thumbs-down* on penicillin for endocarditis was published —Paul de Kruif⟩

thumbstall \ˈ=,=\ *n* [[1]*thumb* + *stall*] **:** a protective covering for the thumb; *also* **:** any of various similar devices for other purposes (as a rubber cover for the thumb to aid in sorting mail)

thumb-sucker \ˈ=,==\ *n* **:** an infant or young child that habitually sucks a thumb

thumb-sucking \ˈ=,==\ *n* -S **:** the habit of sucking a thumb beyond the period of physiologic need

thumbs up *interj* — used to raise one's spirits or to express a hope of good fortune

[1]**thumbtack** \ˈ=,=\ *n* [[1]*thumb* + *tack*] **:** a short steel point with a broad flat head for pressing into a board by the thumb and used for temporary or quick securing of a light thin object (as a sheet of drawing paper)

[2]**thumbtack** \"\ *vt* **:** to fasten with a thumbtack

thumb turn *n* **:** a part designed to be turned by the thumb and finger

thumby \ˈthəmē\ *adj* -ER/-EST [[1]*thumb* + *-y*] **:** AWKWARD, CLUMSY

[1]**thump** \ˈthəmp\ *vb* -ED/-ING/-S [imit.] *vt* **1 a :** to strike or beat with or as if with something thick or heavy or so as to cause a dull sound ⟨his tail ~*ed* the ground —John & Ward Hawkins⟩ ⟨~*ing* the counter with his fist —Rearden Conner⟩ **b :** POUND, KNOCK, HAMMER **c :** CUDGEL, THRASH, WHIP ⟨~*ed* the indoctrination officer who tried to stop him —*Springfield (Mass.) Union*⟩ **2 :** to force or drive by repeatedly thumping **3 :** to defeat decisively **4 :** to strike against an object with a dull sound ⟨the old man ~*ed* his glass down on the bar and stalked out —G.G.Carter⟩ **5 :** to produce (music) mechanically or in a mechanical manner by means of repeated thumps — usu. used with *out* ⟨~ out a tune on the piano⟩ **~** *vi* **1 a :** to inflict or emit a thump : fall or hit so as to produce a dull sound ⟨the gorilla is just as likely to ~ upon the upper chest with his fists —Weston La Barre⟩ ⟨the drums ~*ed* and rolled again —Kenneth Roberts⟩ **b :** to move with heavy pounding sounds ⟨down the steps ~*ed* a crush of cheerful boys —Wilfred Goatman⟩ ⟨the convoy of trucks ~*ed* along for about thirty miles —Earle Birney⟩ **c :** to beat heavily ⟨his heart ~*ed* at the sight of her —T.B.Costain⟩ ⟨the radiators began to ~ —Berton Roueché⟩ **2 :** to vigorously advocate, endorse, or advertise a program, policy, candidate, or product ⟨got a couple of United States senators to ~ for him —*N.Y. Herald Tribune*⟩

[2]**thump** \"\ *n* -S **1 :** a blow or knock with or as if with something blunt or heavy ⟨the ~*s* and bumps of factory and warehouse activity —*Modern Industry*⟩; *also* **:** the sound made by such a blow ⟨the smooth rumble of wheels over rails broke into a series of rattling ~*s* —John Dos Passos⟩ **2 thumps** *pl but sing in constr* **a :** a dyspneic breathing that is marked by throbbing movements of the sides of the chest due to spasmodic contractions of the diaphragm analogous to those of hiccups in man, is esp. common in young pigs, and is associated with deficiency anemia or the passage of larval ascarid worms through the lungs **b :** a disease (as a nutritional anemia or verminous pneumonia) of young pigs of which thumps is a symptom **3 :** interference in a telephone circuit caused by the operation of telegraph or signaling circuits esp. if the interfering circuits are using the same lines

thump·er \ˈthəmpə(r)\ *n* -S **1 :** one that thumps **2 :** something extra large or great

thumping *adj* [fr. pres. part. of [1]*thump*] **:** impressively large, great, or excellent ⟨passed by a ~ seven-to-one majority —*Wall Street Jour.*⟩ ⟨the short story became a ~ two-volume novel —Thomas Mann⟩

thump·ing·ly *adv* **1 :** with a thump **2 :** in a thumping manner : IMPRESSIVELY, RESOUNDINGLY ⟨~ lost the national election —Philip Hamburger⟩

thun·ber·gia \,thənˈbərj(ē)ə\ *n* [NL, fr. Carl P. *Thunberg* †1828 Swed. botanist + NL *-ia*] **1** *cap* **:** a genus of herbs or twining woody vines (family Acanthaceae) native to the tropics of the Old World and having opposite leaves and large flowers succeeded by beaked capsules — see BLACK-EYED SUSAN 3, CLOCK VINE **2** -S **:** any plant of the genus *Thunbergia*

thun·berg lespedeza \ˈthən,bərg-\ *n* [after Carl P. *Thunberg*] **:** an Asiatic lespedeza (*Lespedeza thunbergii*) with long slender racemes of purple flowers that is used as an ornamental and is often found as an escape from cultivation in No. America

[1]**thun·der** \ˈthəndə(r)\ *n* -S [ME *thoner, thonder, thunder,* fr. OE *thunor;* akin to OS *thunar* thunder, OHG *thonar* thunder, ON *Thōrr* god of thunder, L *tonare* to thunder, Gk *stenein* to moan, groan, Skt *stanati, staniti, stanayati* it thunders, *tanyati* it resounds, roars] **1 a :** the loud and at a distance often rolling sound that follows a flash of lightning due to the sudden expansion of the air in the path of the discharge **b** *archaic* **:** a discharge of lightning : THUNDERBOLT ⟨six the ~ has smitten —P.B.Shelley⟩ **c** *archaic* **:** a peal of thunder : THUNDERCLAP ⟨a sullen ~ is rolled —Alfred Tennyson⟩ **d** *dial* **:** THUNDERSTORM **2 a :** a usu. threatening declamation or utterance whether bombastic or eloquent ⟨hurled his ~ over the terrified heads of mortals who had spoken in error —C.R.Tracy⟩ ⟨legal maneuvers, editorial ~, and political speech —J.B.Martin⟩ — often used in pl. **b :** great force, strength, violence, or energy ⟨their carefully cultivated air of benevolence . . . shattered by the ~ of a purge —*N. Y. Times*⟩ **3 :** a loud or noisy sound likened to thunder : BANG, RUMBLE ⟨the roaring ~ of big guns —*Amer. Guide Series: Vt.*⟩ ⟨the ~ of horses' hooves⟩ **4 —** used often interjectionally as a mild oath ⟨who in ~ are you⟩ ⟨by ~, I'll show you who's master —Max Peacock⟩

[2]**thunder** \"\ *vb* **thundered; thundered; thundering** \-d(ə)riŋ\ **thunders** [ME *thoneren, thonderen, thunderen,* fr. OE *thunrian,* fr. *thunor,* n.] *vi* **1 a :** to produce thunder **:** sound, rattle, or roar as the effect of a discharge of atmospheric electricity — usu. used impersonally ⟨it ~*ed* loudly⟩ **b :** to give forth a sound likened to thunder ⟨clarion notes of the trumpet ~*ed* through five expansive movements —*Lutheran Quarterly*⟩ **c :** to move, go, or progress with the accompaniment of loud reverberations suggesting thunder ⟨a huge white horse came ~*ing* into the yard —Zane Grey⟩ ⟨a mighty cataract ~*ed* into the ravine —*Amer. Guide Series: Minn.*⟩ **d :** to strike an object so as to produce a loud sound ⟨the general's fist ~*ed* on the table —Kenneth Roberts⟩ **2 :** to utter violent, loud, bombastic, or impressively phrased denunciation, warning, or threat ⟨~*ed* day in and day out on the "manifest destiny" of the United States —*Amer. Guide Series: Nev.*⟩ ⟨the preacher ~*ed* from the pulpit against corruption⟩ **~** *vt* **1 a :** to utter in or as if in a loud thundering tone esp. as a threat or warning ("woe unto you" he ~*ed* at these blind leaders —W.F.Hambly⟩ ⟨~*ed* out the words: "Seekest thou great things for thyself" —*Current Biog.*⟩ **b :** to express (as an emotion) in or as if in a loud thundering tone ⟨preachers had ~*ed* hatred of the South —Dixon Wecter⟩ **2 :** to strike so as to cause a sound likened to thunder

thunder-and-lightning \ˈ==ˈ==\ *adj, of apparel* **:** of strongly contrasting colors **:** of a startling color

thun·der·a·tion \,thəndəˈrāshən\ *interj* [*thunder* + *-ation*] — used as a mild oath

thunderball \ˈ==,=\ *n* **:** THUNDERBOLT 1b

thunderbird \ˈ==,=\ *n* **1 :** an Australian whistler (*Pachycephala pectoralis*) that in the male is marked with black and yellow and has a black crescent on the breast **2 a :** a mythical bird believed by American Indians to cause lightning and thunder that is frequently a supernatural eagle conceived as the spirit or god of thunder and rain **b :** a figure of a bird with outstretched wings common in aboriginal No. American art

thunder-blasted \ˈ==ˈ==\ *adj, archaic* **:** struck by lightning

[1]**thun·der·bolt** \ˈthəndə(r),bōlt\ *n* [ME *thonder-bolte*] **1 a :** a single discharge of lightning with the accompanying thunder **b** (1) **:** an imaginary elongated mass cast as a missile to earth in the lightning flash (2) **:** a stone or stone implement (as a hatchet or arrowhead) thought to be the material part of lightning; *broadly* **:** THUNDERSTONE 2 **2 a :** a person or thing likened to lightning in suddenness, effectiveness, or destructive power ⟨nuclear subs may hide under the polar ice cap, awaiting only a signal . . . to fire their ~*s* —*Newsweek*⟩ **b :** vehement threatening or censure : FULMINATION ⟨hurling ~*s* at the newspapers —E.D.Canham⟩ **3 :** a conventionalized representation of a thunderbolt; *specif* **:** a twisted bar with inflamed ends between two wings and with four jagged darts issuant from its center — used in heraldry

[2]**thunderbolt** \"\ *vt* -ED/-ING/-S *dial Brit* **:** to strike with a thunderbolt

thunderclap \ˈ==,=\ *n* [ME *thonder clappe*] **1 :** a clap of thunder **2 :** something likened to or suggesting a clap of thunder (as in suddenness, sound, or effect) ⟨a ~ of applause —*New Yorker*⟩

thundercloud \ˈ==,=\ *n* **1 :** a cloud charged with electricity and producing lightning and thunder **2 :** something threatening, gloomy, or expressive of anger ⟨turned a ~ face toward the struggling prisoners —Frank Yerby⟩

thundercrack \ˈ==,=\ *n* [ME *thunder-crakke*] **:** THUNDERCLAP

thunder egg *n* **:** chalcedony in rounded concretionary nodules

thun·der·er \ˈthənd(ə)rə(r)\ *n* -S [ME *thonderere,* fr. *thonderen* to thunder + *-ere* -er] **:** one that thunders ⟨a continuous editorial ~ against stream pollution —K.S.Dixon⟩

thunderfish \ˈ==,=\ *n* **1 :** WEATHERFISH; *esp* **:** a European fish (*Misgurnus fossilis*) **2 :** ELECTRIC CATFISH

thunderflower \ˈ==,==\ *n* **1** *dial Eng* **:** STITCHWORT **2** *dial Eng* **:** CORN POPPY **3** *dial Eng* **:** WHITE CAMPION a

thun·der·ful \ˈthəndə(r)fəl\ *adj* **:** charged or resounding with thunder

thunder god vine *n* **:** a perennial Chinese vine (*Tripterygium wilfordii*) of the family Celastraceae introduced into the U.S. for its possible use as a source of an insecticide

thunder-gust \ˈ==,=\ *n* **:** a thunderstorm with wind

thunderhead \ˈ==,=\ *n* **:** a rounded mass of cumulus cloud with shining white edges often appearing before a thunderstorm

[1]**thun·der·ing** \ˈthənd(ə)riŋ, -rēŋ\ *n* -S [ME *thondring,* fr. OE *thunring,* fr. *thunrian* to thunder + *-ing*] **:** THUNDER

[2]**thundering** *adj* [fr. pres. part. of [2]*thunder*] **:** awesome in virtue of impressive greatness, magnitude, or unusualness ⟨the ~ silence of what was left unsaid —A.E.Stevenson b. 1900⟩ ⟨a ~ success as a salesman —R.H.Rovere⟩ — **thun·der·ing·ly** *adv*

thun·der·less \ˈ==ləs\ *adj* **:** being without accompanying thunder

thunder lizard *n* **:** BRONTOSAUR

thunder mug *n, dial* **:** CHAMBER POT

thun·der·ous \ˈthənd(ə)rəs\ *adj* [[1]*thunder* + *-ous*] **1 :** producing thunder; *also* **:** making or accompanied by a noise like thunder **2 :** extremely remarkable or great esp. in ominousness ⟨world events of ~ import —F.D.Roosevelt⟩ — **thun·der·ous·ly** *adv*

thunderpeal \ˈ==,=\ *n* **:** THUNDERCLAP

thunder pumper *or* **thunderpump** \ˈ==,=\ *n* **1 :** AMERICAN BITTERN **2 :** FRESHWATER DRUM

thunders *pl of* THUNDER, *pres 3d sing of* THUNDER

thunder sheet *n* **:** a large galvanized iron sheet suspended from a rope in a theater and shaken or hit to produce a sound representing thunder, artillery, or explosions

thundershower \ˈ==,==\ *n* **:** a shower accompanied by lightning and thunder

thunder snake *n* **1 :** MILK SNAKE; *also* **:** any of various closely related snakes **2 :** a reddish colubrid ground snake (*Carphophis amoena*) of the eastern U.S.

thundersquall \ˈ==,=\ *n* **:** a squall attended with lightning and thunder

thunderstick \ˈ==,=\ *n* **:** BULL-ROARER

thunderstone \ˈ==,=\ *n* **1** *archaic* **:** THUNDERBOLT 1b(1) **2 :** any of various somewhat cylindrical or tapering stones (as a fossil belemnite shell, prehistoric stone implement, natural concretion, or meteorite) supposed to be a thunderbolt — compare FAIRY ARROW, THUNDERBOLT 1b(2)

thunderstorm \ˈ==,=\ *n* **:** a storm accompanied by lightning and thunder

thunderstorm cirrus *n* **:** FALSE CIRRUS

thunderstrike \ˈ==,=\ *vt* **1** *archaic* **:** to strike, blast, or injure by or as if by lightning **2 :** to strike dumb with or as if with something terrible : ASTONISH ⟨readers will be *thunderstruck* to learn —*Current Biog.*⟩

thunderstroke \ˈ==,=\ *n* **:** a stroke by or as if by lightning with the attendant thunder

thunderwood \ˈ==,=\ *n* **:** POISON SUMAC

thunderworm \ˈ==,=\ *n* [so called fr. its habit of leaving its burrows after thundershowers] **:** a small burrowing limbless lizard (*Rhineura floridana*) that resembles a worm and is native to Florida

thun·dery \ˈthənd(ə)rē, -ri\ *adj* **1 :** accompanied with or indicating thunder : THUNDEROUS **2 :** OMINOUS, THREATENING

thunge \ˈthənj, ˈthünj\ *n* -S [imit.] *dial Brit* **:** a loud hollow sound; *also* **:** a blow causing such a sound

[1]**thunk** \ˈthəŋk\ *dial past of* THINK

[2]**thunk** \"\ *n* -S [imit.] **:** a flat hollow sound ⟨heard the dull ~ of wood against wood —Brian Harwin⟩

thun·nus \ˈthənəs\ *n, cap* [NL, fr. L, tunny — more at TUNNY] **:** a genus of large marine fishes that comprises the typical tunas and is sometimes made the type of a separate family but is usu. included among the Scombridae

thur·be·ria \,thərˈbirēə\ *n* [NL, fr. George *Thurber* †1890 Am. botanist + NL *-ia*] **1** *cap, in some classifications* **:** a genus of shrubby herbs that are characterized by a 3-celled capsule and are usu. included in *Gossypium* **2** -S **:** WILD COTTON 2a

thurberia weevil *n, sometimes cap T* **:** a boll weevil (*Anthonomus grandis thurberiae*) that is native to Arizona and adjacent Mexico, feeds on a wild cotton (*Gossypium triloba*), and also attacks cultivated cotton in that region

thu·ri·ble \ˈth(y)u̇rəbəl, ˈthərə-\ *n* -S [ME *turrible,* fr. MF *thurible,* fr. L *thuribulum, turibulum,* fr. *thur-, thus, tur-, tus* incense (fr. Gk *thyos* incense, sacrifice, fr. *thyein* to sacrifice) + *-i-* + *-bulum,* suffix denoting an instrument — more at THYME] **:** a censer used in religious services

thu·ri·fer \-rəfə(r)\ *n* -S [NL, fr. L *thurifer, turifer,* adj., incense-burning, fr. *thur-, thus, tur-, tus* + *-ifer* -iferous] **:** one who carries a censer in an ecclesiastical rite

thu·rif·er·ous \th(y)əˈrif(ə)rəs\ *adj* [L *thurifer* + E *-ous*] **:** producing frankincense

thu·ri·fi·ca·tion \,th(y)u̇rəfəˈkāshən, ,thərə-\ *n* -S [ME *thurybycacyon,* fr. MF *thurification,* fr. ML *thurification-, thurificatio,* fr. LL *thurificatus* (past part. of *thurificare*) + L *-ion-, -io* -ion] **:** the act, process, or an instance of censing

thu·ri·fy \ˈ==,fī\ *vt* -ED/-ING/-ES [ME *thurifien,* fr. MF *thurifier,* fr. LL *thurificare,* fr. L *thur-, thus, tur-, tus* incense + *-ificare* -ify] **:** CENSE

thü·rin·ger \ˈth(y)u̇rənjə(r), ˈthərə-, ˈthirə-; ˈtiriŋə-, ˈtūeriŋə-\ *also* **thüringer sausage** *n, usu cap T* [*thüringer* fr. G *Thüringer*wurst, fr. *Thüringer* Thuringian (fr. *Thüringen* Thuringia) + *wurst* sausage; *thüringer sausage* part trans. of G *Thüringerwurst*] **:** a mildly seasoned fresh or smoked summer sausage

[1]**thu·rin·gian** \th(y)əˈrinj(ē)ən\ *n* -S *cap* [in sense 1, fr. L *Thuringi,* a Germanic people living in central Germany in ancient times + E *-an;* in sense 2, fr. *Thuringia,* region in Central Germany + E *-an*] **1 :** a member of an ancient Germanic people established in a kingdom near the center of Germany and overthrown by the Franks in the 6th century **2 :** a native or inhabitant of the kingdom, principality, region, or state of Thuringia

[2]**thuringian** \"\ *adj, usu cap* **1 :** of or relating to Thuringia or the Thuringians **2 :** of or relating to the Franconian dialect of the German language spoken in Thuringia

thu·rin·gite \th(y)əˈrin,jīt\ *n* -S [G *thuringit,* fr. *Thuringia* + G *-it* -ite] **:** a mineral $Fe_3(Si,Al)_2O_5(OH)_4$ of the chlorite family consisting of a basic aluminum iron silicate and occurring as an aggregation of minute scales with an olive-green color and pearly luster

[1]**thurl** \ˈthər(-ə)l\ *dial Eng var of* THIRL

[2]**thurl** \"\ *n* -S [perh. fr. E dial. *thirl, thurl* gaunt] **:** the hip joint in cattle — see COW illustration

thurm \ˈthərm\ *vt* -ED/-ING/-S [origin unknown] **:** to work (as a table leg or molding) with saw and chisel across the grain so as to produce patterns like those produced by turning

thur·nia \ˈthərnēə\ *n, cap* [NL, fr. Sir Everard F. Im *Thurn* †1932 Eng. botanist & explorer] **:** a small genus of herbs (family Juncaceae) related to and resembling the typical rushes and having heads of flowers on 3-angled stalks with long bracts and perianth parts that are all similar

thurs·day \ˈthərzdē, -ōz-, -əiz-, -di *also* -z(ˌ)dā\ *n* -s *usu cap* [ME *thuresday, thursday,* fr. OE *thuresdæg, thursdæg,* fr. ON *thōrsdagr;* akin to OE *thunresdæg* Thursday, OHG *Donares tag;* all fr. a prehistoric NGmc-WGmc compound formed fr. constituents represented by OHG *Donar,* the Germanic god of the sky (fr. *thonar, donar* thunder), and by OHG *tag* day; trans. of L *Jovis dies,* lit., day of Jupiter (the ancient Roman god of the sky and the planet Jupiter) — more at THUNDER, DAY] **:** the fifth day of the week **:** the day following Wednesday

thurs·days \-z\ *adv, usu cap* **:** on Thursday repeatedly **:** on any Thursday

1**thus** \ˈt͟həs\ *adv* [ME, fr. OE; akin to OS & OFris *thus,* MD *dus, dos* thus, OE *thæt,* neut. demonstrative pron. & definite article — more at THAT] **1 :** in this or that manner or way ⟨had lain exposed . . . and ~ had become extremely fragile —R.D. Altick⟩ ⟨I picture the process ~ —Anthony Harris⟩ **2 :** to this degree or extent **:** SO ⟨~ wise⟩ ⟨~ far⟩ **3 :** because of this or that **:** for this or that reason or cause **:** CONSEQUENTLY, HENCE ⟨there had been no coordinated building program; ~ examples of the worst and the best . . . will be found —*Amer. Guide Series: Minn.*⟩ **4 :** as an example ⟨people often fail to take precautions; ~, a man I knew was hurt in a car accident because he had not fastened his seat belt⟩

2**thus** \ˈthəs\ *n* -ES [ME, fr. L, incense — more at THURIBLE] **:** GUM THUS 2

1**thus and thus** *or* **thus and so** *adv* [*thus and thus* fr. ME] **:** in the manner explained esp. in detail **:** in this or that way

2**thus and thus** *or* **thus and so** *n* **:** an unspecified member of a group usu. not of persons **:** any one of several or of several possibilities

thu·shi \ˈtüshē\ *n, pl* **thushi** *or* **thushis** *usu cap* **1 :** a people of the Chechen group **2 :** a member of the Thushi people

thus·ly \ˈt͟həslē, -li\ *adv* **:** in this manner **:** to this degree **:** THUS ⟨he summoned his counselors and spoke ~ to them —*Congressional Record*⟩

thus·ness *n* -ES **1 :** the condition of being thus **2 :** SUCHNESS 2

thus·wise \ˈ≈ˌwīz\ *adv* [ME *thus wise*] **:** THUS, SO

thut·ter \ˈthəd·ə(r), -ətə-\ *vi* -ED/-ING/-S [imit.] **:** to make a dull, throbbing, or sputtering sound ⟨a light machine gun ~*ed* briefly —J.M.Moore b. 1890⟩

1**thu·ya** \ˈthüyə\ *syn of* THUJA

2**thuya** *var of* THUGA

thu·yop·sis \thüˈyäpsəs\ *syn of* THUJOPSIS

1**thwack** \ˈthwak\ *vb* -ED/-ING/-S [imit.] *vt* **1 a** (1) **:** to strike with or as if with something flat or heavy **:** BANG, WHACK (2) **:** to beat (a half-dried pantile) into shape **b :** to bring into a specified state by thwacking ⟨to modulate the voice was ~*ed* into them by a generation of firm-handed mothers —J.H. Wheelwright⟩ **2** *obs* **:** to fill to overflowing **:** PACK **3 :** to administer a stinging defeat, punishment, or rebuke to; *also* **:** to satirize severely ~ *vi* **:** to strike with a thwack ⟨her head ~*ed* against the sidewalk —Jonas Bayer⟩

2**thwack** \ˈ"\ *n* -s **:** a heavy blow with or as if with something flat or heavy **:** WHACK ⟨hitting the floor with a ~ —Mary Lasswell⟩; *also* **:** the sound of a thwack ⟨the crews worked silently except for the ~ of axhead against trees —R.G.Lillard⟩

thwack·er \-kə(r)\ *n* -s **:** one that thwacks; *specif* **:** a wooden implement with which a half-dried pantile is beaten to take out any warping

1**thwaite** \ˈthwāt\ *n* -s [of Scand origin; akin to ON *thveit* parcel of land; akin to OE *thwītan* to cut, cut off — more at WHITTLE] *dial* **:** a piece of land used as a meadow, field, or pasture; *specif* **:** forest land cleared and converted to tillage

2**thwaite** *or* **thwaite shad** *var of* TWAITE

1**thwart** \ˈthwȯ(ə)r|t, -ȯ(ə)|, *nautical often* ˈthȯ-; *usu* |d·+V\ *adv* [ME *thwert, thwart,* fr. ON *thvert,* fr. neut. of *thverr* transverse, oblique; akin to OE *thweorh* transverse, crooked, angry, OHG *dwerah, twerh* transverse, oblique, Goth *thwairhs* angry, L *torquēre* to twist — more at TORTURE] **:** THWARTLY, ATHWART

2**thwart** \ˈ"\ *adj* [ME *thwert, thwart,* fr. *thwert, thwart,* adv.] **1 :** situated or placed across something else **:** TRANSVERSE, OBLIQUE **2 :** PERVERSE, STUBBORN, INTRACTABLE ⟨reasoning that defies ~ time —*Times Lit. Supp.*⟩ — **thwartly** *adv*

3**thwart** \ˈ"\ *vb* -ED/-ING/-S [ME *thwerten, thwarten,* fr. *thwert, thwart,* adv.] *vt* **1 a :** to run counter to **:** OPPOSE, BAFFLE, CONTRAVENE ⟨I did not like to ~ her in her present mood —Rose Macaulay⟩ **b :** to oppose successfully: (1) **:** to defeat the hopes, aspirations or plans of ⟨attempted to seize the governorship . . . and was ~*ed* by the State Supreme Court —*New Republic*⟩ ⟨religious taboos have not succeeded in ~*ing* lovers —Waldemar Kaempffert⟩ (2) **:** to block or check the occurrence, performance, or completion of **:** prevent the development or fulfillment of ⟨to prohibit children from reaching them would be to ~ the reading habit —Eamon Ryan⟩ ⟨hesitated to ~ the whims of the king —J.H.Plumb⟩ **2 a** (1) **:** to move or pass through or across (2) *archaic* **:** to cross the path of **b** (1) *obs* **:** to lay across an object (2) *archaic* **:** to cause to be crossed by or as if by an overlying mark **c :** to place an obstruction across (as a passage) ~ *vi* **1 :** to be in opposition **:** CLASH, QUARREL **2** *archaic* **:** to go or extend in an oblique manner **syn** see FRUSTRATE

4**thwart** \ˈ"\ *prep* [ME, fr. *thwert, thwart,* adv.] *archaic* **:** ACROSS, ATHWART

5**thwart** \ˈ"\ *n* -s [3*thwart*] **1 :** OPPOSITION, OBSTRUCTION **2 a :** a rower's seat extending athwart a boat or canoe **b :** one of the short crosspieces secured to one or two of the uprights erected alongside a ship in process of construction to support the stages

thwart·ed·ly *adv* **:** in a thwarted manner

thwart·er \-ȯr|d·|ər, -ȯ(ə)|, |t|\ *n* -s **:** one that thwarts

thwartover \ˈ≈ˌ≈\ *adj* [ME *thwertover, thwartover,* fr. *thwert, thwart,* adv. + *over,* adv.] *dial chiefly Eng* **:** CONTRARY

thwartsaw *n* [ME *thwertsawe, thwartsawe,* fr. *thwert, thwart,* adj. + *sawe* saw] *obs* **:** CROSSCUT SAW

thwartship \ˈ≈ˌ≈\ *adj* [4*thwart* + *ship* (n.)] **:** lying or leading athwartship ⟨a ~ spar⟩

thwart·ships \-ps\ *adv* [4*thwart* + *ship* + *-s*] **:** ATHWARTSHIPS

thwartwise \ˈ≈ˌ≈\ *adv* (*or adj*) [2*thwart* + *-wise*] **:** in a transverse manner **:** CROSSWISE

thwit·tle \ˈthwid·ᵊl, -itᵊl\ *n* -s [ME *thwitel* — more at WHITTLE] *Brit* **:** KNIFE

thy \ˈt͟hī\ *adj* [ME *thy, thi, thin,* fr. OE *thīn,* gen. of *thū* thou — more at THINE] *archaic* **:** of, belonging to, or connected with thee or thyself as possessor, as author, doer, giver, or agent or as object of an action ⟨stretch out ~ rod —Exod 8:16(AV)⟩ ⟨~ slanders I forgive —Shak.⟩ ⟨so thou be chastened by ~ banishment —Alfred Tennyson⟩ — used esp. in biblical, ecclesiastical, solemn, or poetic language, and to some extent in the speech of Friends esp. among themselves; compare 1THEE, 1THOU, YOUR

thy·es·te·an \(ˈ)thīˈestēən\ *adj, usu cap* [*Thyestes,* ancient Greek legendary character who at a banquet unwittingly ate the flesh of his own sons (fr. L, fr. Gk *Thyestēs*) + E *-an*] **:** of or relating to the eating of human flesh **:** CANNIBAL

thy·iad \ˈthī(ˌ)yad, -(y)əd\ *n, pl* **thyiads** \-dz\ *or* **thy·ia·des** \ˈthī(y)əˌdēz, thīˈīəˌd-\ *usu cap* [L *Thyiad-, Thyias,* fr. Gk, fr. *thyein* to rage, seethe; akin to Gk *thymos* spirit, mind, courage — more at FUME] **:** a member of a group of ancient Greek women devoted to the orgiastic worship of Dionysus esp. as practiced on Mount Parnassus

thy·ine wood \ˈthī(y)ən-\ *n* [ME *tyyin, thyine, thina,* fr. LL *thyinus* of citron wood, fr. Gk *thyinos,* fr. *thyon, thya* thyine≈ wood] **:** the fragrant and ornamental wood of the sandarac tree (sense 1)

thy·la·cine \ˈthīləˌsīn, -ˌsən\ *n* -s [NL *Thylacinus*] **:** TASMANIAN WOLF

thy·la·ci·nus \ˌthīləˈsīnəs\ *n, cap* [NL, fr. Gk *thylakos* sack, pouch + L *-inus* -ine] **:** a genus of marsupial mammals (family Dasyuridae) consisting of the Tasmanian wolf

thy·la·co·leo \ˌthīləˈkōlēˌō\ *n, cap* [NL, fr. Gk *thylakos* sack + L *leo* lion — more at LION] **:** a genus (coextensive with the family Thylacoleontidae) of Pleistocene Australian marsupial mammals having a skull about the size of that of a lion, large tusks, and crushing molars

thy·lac·o·mys \thīˈlakəməs\ *n, cap* [NL, fr. Gk *thylakos* sack + NL *-mys*] **:** a genus of Australian marsupial mammals (family Peramelidae) comprising the rabbit bandicoots

thy·la·cy·nus \ˌthīləˈsīnəs\ *syn of* THYLACINUS

thy·la·ken·trin \ˌthīləˈken·trən\ *n* -s [*thylakentr-* (blend of Gk *thylakē* scrotum and *kentron* sharp point, goad) + *-in* — more at CENTER] **:** FOLLICLE-STIMULATING HORMONE

thy·log·a·le \thīˈlägə(ˌ)lē\ *n, cap* [NL, irreg. fr. Gk *thylakos* sack, pouch + *galeē, galē* weasel, ferret — more at GALEA] **:** a genus of marsupial mammals (family Macropodidae) comprising the scrub wallabies and pademelons

1**thym-** *or* **thymo-** *comb form* [ISV, fr. L *thymum* — more at THYME] **1 :** thyme ⟨*thymol*⟩ **2 :** thymol ⟨*thymo*quinone $CH_3C_6H_2(C_3H_7)O_2$⟩

2**thym-** *or* **thymo-** *comb form* [NL *thymus*] **:** thymus **:** of the thymus ⟨*thymo*privic⟩ ⟨*thym*ectomize⟩

3**thym-** *or* **thymo-** *comb form* [NL, fr. Gk, fr. *thymos* spirit, soul, mind — more at FUME] **:** soul **:** spirit **:** emotion ⟨*thymo*genic⟩ ⟨*thymo*tactic⟩

thy·mal·li·dae \thīˈmaləˌdē\ *n pl, cap* [NL, fr. *Thymallus,* type genus (fr. Gk *thymallos,* a salmonoid fish, prob. fr. *thymon* thyme; fr. the odor) + *-idae*] **:** a family of salmonoid fishes constituted by the graylings

1**thyme** \ˈtīm *sometimes* ˈthīm\ *n* -s [ME *thyme, tyme,* fr. MF *thym, tym,* fr. L *thymum,* fr. Gk *thymon,* fr. *thyein* to make a burnt offering, sacrifice; akin to L *fumus* smoke — more at FUME] **1 a :** a mint of the genus *Thymus; esp* **:** a common garden herb (*T. vulgaris*) used in seasoning and esp. formerly in medicine **b :** any of several other pungent aromatic herbs chiefly of the family Labiatae — usu. used with a qualifying term; see BASIL THYME **2 :** PITCH PINE 2

thyme 1a

2**thyme** \ˈ"\ *vt* -ED/-ING/-S **:** to cover or scent with thyme ⟨*thymed* breezes⟩

thyme camphor *n* **:** THYMOL

thy·mec·to·my \thīˈmektəmē\ *n* -ES [ISV 2*thym-* + *-ectomy*] **:** excision of the thymus

thyme dodder *n* **:** CLOVER DODDER

thyme·laea \ˌthiməˈlēə, ˌthim-\ *n, cap* [NL, fr. L, any of several plants of the genus *Daphne,* fr. Gk *thymelaia,* fr. *thymos* thyme + *elaia* olive] **:** a genus of European and Asiatic herbs and undershrubs (family Thymelaeaceae) having small sessile apetalous flowers with a calyx that has a spreading border and is usu. persistent

thyme·lae·a·ce·ae \ˌ≈≈≈ˈāsēˌē\ *n pl, cap* [NL, fr. *Thymelaea,* type genus + *-aceae*] **:** a family of tough-barked trees, shrubs, and herbs (order Myrtales) that are native to temperate climates chiefly of the Old World and have entire leaves, capitate apetalous flowers, and drupaceous or capsular fruits

thyme·lae·a·les \-ā(ˌ)lēz\ [NL, fr. *Thymelaea* + *-ales*] *syn of* MYRTALES

thym·e·le \ˈthimə(ˌ)lē\ *n* -s [LL *thymele, thymela,* fr. Gk *thymelē,* fr. *thyein* to make a burnt offering — more at THYME] **:** an ancient Greek altar; *esp* **:** a small altar of Dionysus standing in the middle of the orchestra of a theater — **thy·mel·ic** \(ˈ)thīˈmelik, thəˈm-\ *or* **thy·mel·i·cal** \-ləkəl\ *adj*

thyme-leaved sandwort \ˈ≈ˌ≈-\ *n* **:** a Eurasian annual sprawling weed (*Arenaria serpyllifolia*) naturalized throughout No. America and having opposite entire leaves and paniculate small white flowers

thyme-leaved speedwell *n* **:** a perennial decumbent herb (*Veronica serpyllifolia*) found throughout Eurasia and the New World and having small opposite leaves and blue flowers in short narrow racemes

thy·mel·i·ci \thīˈmeləˌsī\ *n pl* [L, fr. Gk *thymelikoi,* fr. pl. of *thymelikos* of a thymele, fr. *thymelē* + *-ikos* -ic] **:** a chorus that dances around the thymele in an ancient Greek theater

thyme oil *n* **:** a fragrant essential oil containing thymol and carvacrol that is obtained from various thymes and is used chiefly as an antiseptic in pharmaceutical and dental preparations, as a perfume esp. in soaps, and as a flavor in foods — compare ORIGANUM OIL

thymes *pl of* THYME, *pres 3d sing of* THYME

thymey *var of* THYMY

thymi *pl of* THYMUS

-thy·mia \ˈthīmēə\ *n comb form* -s [NL, fr. Gk, fr. *thymos* spirit, mind, courage + *-ia* — more at FUME] **:** (such) a condition of mind and will ⟨schizo*thymia*⟩

thy·mi·a·te·ri·on \ˌthimēəˈtirēən\ *n* -s [Gk *thymiatērion,* fr. *thymian* to smoke, burn incense, fr. (assumed) Gk *thymos* smoke (whence Gk *thymos* spirit) — more at FUME] **:** a vessel for burning incense esp. as used by the ancient Greeks

1**thy·mic** \ˈtīmik, ˈthī-\ *adj* [ISV 1*thym-* + *-ic*] **:** relating to or derived from thyme

2**thy·mic** \ˈthīmik\ *adj* [2*thym-* + *-ic*] **:** of, relating to, or involving the thymus

3**thy·mic** \ˈthīmik\ *adj* [3*thym-* + *-ic*] **:** of or relating to emotion or emotional lability

thy·mi·dine \ˈthīməˌdēn, -dən\ *n* -s [blend of *thymine* and *-id*] **:** a crystalline nucleoside $C_{10}H_{14}N_2O_5$ that is obtained by partial hydrolysis of deoxyribonucleic acid, yields on hydrolysis thymine and deoxyribose, and is a growth factor esp. for lactobacilli

thy·mi·dyl·ic acid \ˌthīməˈdilik-\ *n* [*thymid*ine + *-yl* + *-ic*] **:** either of two isomeric crystalline nucleotides $C_{10}H_{15}N_2O_8P$ obtained by partial hydrolysis of deoxyribonucleic acid **:** an ester of thymidine and orthophosphoric acid

thy·mine \ˈthīˌmēn, -mən\ *n* -s [G *thymin,* fr. *thym-* 2thym- + *-in* -ine] **:** a crystalline pyrimidine base $C_5H_6N_2O_2$ obtained by hydrolysis of deoxyribonucleic acid and from spermatozoa of fishes; 5-methyl-uracil

thymo- — see THYM-

thy·mo·centric \ˌthīmōˈsen·trik\ *adj* [3*thym-* + *-centric*] **:** oriented toward feeling and emotion rather than toward intellect and morality

thy·mo·cyte \ˈ≈≈ˌsīt\ *n* -s [ISV 2*thym-* + *-cyte*] **:** a cell of the thymus; *esp* **:** a thymic lymphocyte

thy·mol \ˈthīˌmȯl, -mōl\ *n* -s [ISV 1*thym-* + *-ol*] **:** a crystalline phenol $CH_3C_6H_3(C_3H_7)OH$ that has a pleasant aromatic odor and antiseptic properties, occurs naturally in thyme oil and other essential oils or is made synthetically (as from *meta*≈cresol and isopropyl alcohol or propylene), and is used chiefly as a fungicide and preservative and in pharmaceutical, dental, and toilet preparations; 5-methyl-2-isopropyl-phenol — compare CARVACROL

thymol blue *n* **:** a greenish crystalline compound $C_{27}H_{30}O_5S$ of the sulfonephthalein series derived from thymol and used as an acid-base indicator

thymolphthalein \ˌ≈ˌ≈ˈ≈≈≈\ *n* [ISV *thymol* + *phthalein*] **:** a crystalline compound $C_{28}H_{30}O_4$ analogous to phenolphthalein and likewise used as an acid-base indicator

thy·mo·ma \thīˈmōmə\ *n, pl* **thymo·mas** \-məz\ *or* **thy·mo·ma·ta** \-məd·ə\ [NL, fr. 2*thym-* + *-oma*] **:** a tumor that arises from the tissue elements of the thymus

thy·mo·nucleic acid \ˌthīˌmō+-\ *also* **thymus nucleic acid** *n* [ISV 2*thym-* + *nucleic*] **:** DEOXYRIBONUCLEIC ACID

1**thy·mus** \ˈthīməs\ *also* **thymus gland** *n, pl* **thymus·es** \-məsəz\ *or* **thy·mi** \-ˌmī\ *often attrib* [NL, fr. Gk *thymos* warty excrescence, thymus gland] **:** a glandular structure largely of lymphoid tissue that is present in the young of most vertebrates, arises from the epithelium of one or more embryonic branchial clefts, lies typically in the upper anterior part of the chest or at the base of the neck, tends to become vestigial in the adult, and is held to play a major role in cellular immunological responses — see SWEETBREAD

2**thymus** \ˈ"\ *n, cap* [NL, fr. Gk *thymos, thymon* thyme — more at THYME] **:** a large genus of Old World mints having small entire leaves and clustered purple 2-lipped flowers — see THYME

thymy *also* **thymey** \ˈtīmē, ˈthī-, -mi\ *adj* **thym·i·er; thym·i·est :** constituting or resembling thyme **:** abounding in or fragrant with thyme

thy·myl \ˈthīməl\ *n* -s [ISV 1*thym-* + *-yl*] **:** a univalent radical $C_{10}H_{13}$ derived from thymol

1**thyn·nid** \ˈthinəd\ *adj* [NL *Thynnidae*] **:** of or relating to the Thynnidae

2**thynnid** \ˈ"\ *n* -s **:** an insect of the family Thynnidae

thyn·ni·dae \-nəˌdē\ *n pl, cap* [NL, fr. *Thynnus,* type genus (fr. L *thynnus, thunnus* tunny) + *-idae* — more at TUNNY] **:** a family of aculeate hymenopterans confined mainly to Australia and having the females wingless and much smaller than the winged males

thyr- *or* **thyro-** *comb form* [*thyroid*] **1 :** thyroid ⟨*thyr*asthenia⟩ **2 :** thyroid and ⟨*thyro*arytenoid⟩

thy·ra·tron \ˈthīrəˌträn\ *n* -s [fr. *Thyratron,* a trademark] **:** a gas-filled 3-element hot cathode tube in which the grid controls only the start of a continuous current thus giving the tube a trigger effect

thyreo- *comb form* [ISV, fr. Gk *thyreoeidēs* — more at THYROID] **1 :** thyroid ⟨*thyreo*tomy⟩ **2 :** thyroid and ⟨*thyreo*cervical⟩

thy·re·o·cor·i·dae \ˌthīrēōˈkȯrəˌdē\ *n pl, cap* [NL, fr. *Thyreocoris,* type genus (fr. Gk *thyreos* oblong shield + *koris* bug) + *-idae;* akin to Gk *keirein* to cut — more at THYROID, SHEAR] **:** a family of true bugs including the negro bugs

thy·re·oid \ˈthīrēˌȯid\ *adj or n* [ISV, fr. Gk *thyreoeidēs* — more at THYROID] **:** THYROID

thy·re·o·trop·ic \ˌ≈≈ə·ˈträpik\ *adj* [*thyreo-* + *-tropic*] **:** THYROTROPHIC

thy·rid·i·al \thīˈridēəl\ *adj* [NL *thyridium* + E *-al*] **:** of, relating to, or being a thyridium

thy·rid·i·dae \-dəˌdē\ *n pl, cap* [NL, fr. *Thyrid-, Thyris,* type genus (fr. Gk *thyrid-, thyris* window, dim. of *thyra* door) + *-idae* — more at DOOR] **:** a family of small moths having the wings marked with translucent spots

thy·rid·i·um \-dēəm\ *n, pl* **thyrid·ia** \-ēə\ [NL, fr. Gk *thyridion* window, dim. of *thyra* door] **1 :** a pale spot in the wing vein of some insects esp. of the orders Hymenoptera and Trichoptera **2 :** one of a pair of oval pits on the second abdominal tergite of some hymenopterans

thy·ri·o·the·ci·um \ˌthīrēōˈthēs(h)ēəm\ *n, pl* **thyriothe·cia** \-s(h)ēə\ [NL, irreg. fr. Gk *thyreos* oblong shield + NL *-thecium* — more at THYROID] **:** an ascocarp so inverted that the generative hyphae are dependent

Thy·rite \ˈthīˌrīt\ *trademark* — used for an electrical resistance material consisting primarily of silicon carbide, having low resistance at high currents and high resistance at low currents, and used esp. in lightning arresters

thyro- — see THYR-

thy·ro·active \ˌthīrō+\ *adj* [*thyr-* + *active*] **1 :** capable of entering into the thyroid metabolism and of being incorporated into the thyroid hormone ⟨~ iodine⟩ **2 :** simulating the action of the thyroid hormone ⟨~ iodocasein⟩

thy·ro·arytenoid \ˈ"+\ *adj* [NL *thyroarytenoides,* fr. *thyr-* + *arytenoides* arytenoid — more at ARYTENOID] **:** connecting the thyroid and arytenoid cartilages of the larynx

thy·ro·ar·y·te·noi·de·us \ˌthīrōˌarəd·əˈnȯidēəs\ *also* **thy·ro·arytenoid** \ˌthīrō+\ *n* [NL *thyroarytenoideus,* fr. *thyroarytenoides*] **:** a muscle extending between the thyroid and arytenoid cartilages and serving to relax and shorten the vocal cords

thyroarytenoid fold *or* **thyroarytenoid ligament** *n* **:** any of four elastic ligaments of the larynx that are covered by folds of mucous membrane and arranged in a superior pair constituting the false vocal cords and an inferior pair forming the true vocal cords

thyroarytenoid muscle *n* **:** THYROARYTENOIDEUS

thy·ro·cervical \ˌ≈≈+\ *adj* [*thyr-* + *cervical*] **:** of or relating to the neck and the thyroid gland

thy·ro·colloid \ˈ"+\ *n* [*thyr-* + *colloid*] **:** the colloid substance within the vesicles of the thyroid gland

thy·ro·epiglottic \ˈ"+\ *adj* [ISV *thyr-* + *epiglottic*] **:** connecting the thyroid cartilage and epiglottis

thy·ro·genic \ˌthīrəˈjenik\ *or* **thy·rog·e·nous** \thīˈräjənəs\ *adj* [*thyr-* + *-genic* or *-genous*] **:** originating in or caused by activity of the thyroid

thy·ro·globulin \ˌthīrō+\ *n* [ISV *thyr-* + *globulin*] **:** an iodine≈containing protein that exhibits the general properties of the globulins, is obtained from the thyroid gland, and yields on hydrolysis thyroxine, diiodotyrosine, and related iodo amino acids in addition to amino acids found as constituents of most proteins

thy·ro·glossal \ˈ"+\ *adj* [*thyr-* + *glossal*] **:** of, relating to, or connecting the tongue and thyroid gland

thy·ro·hy·al \-ˈhīəl\ *n* -s [*thyr-* + *hy-* + *-al*] **:** the greater cornu of the hyoid bone; *also* **:** an embryonic skeletal element that becomes the greater cornu or in lower forms remains as a separate bone or cartilage

1**thy·ro·hyoid** \ˌthīrō+\ *also* **thy·ro·hyoidean** \ˈ"+\ *adj* [*thyr-* + *hyoid* or *hyoid* + *-an,* adj. suffix] **1 a :** connecting the thyroid cartilage of the larynx and the hyoid bone **b :** of, relating to, or associated with the thyrohyoid bone **2 :** of, relating to, or being the first branchial arch of the vertebrate embryo

2**thyrohyoid** \ˈ"\ *n* **:** a thyrohyoid part (as a muscle or a nerve)

thyrohyoid arch *n* **:** the third branchial arch of the vertebrate embryo of which the cartilage persists as the thyrohyal

1**thy·roid** \ˈthīˌrȯid\ *adj* [NL *thyroides,* fr. Gk *thyreoeidēs* shaped like a shield, thyroid, fr. *thyreos* shield shaped like a door (fr. *thyra* door) + *-eidēs* -oid — more at DOOR] **1** *of an anatomical part* **:** SHIELD-SHAPED — used almost exclusively of a cartilage in the larynx and an endocrine gland **2 a :** of, relating to, involving, or caused or produced by the thyroid gland ⟨a severe ~ insufficiency⟩ **b :** suggestive of a disordered and esp. a hyperactive thyroid ⟨~ eyes⟩ ⟨a tense ~ personality⟩ ⟨a somewhat ~ spinster —*Time*⟩

2**thyroid** \ˈ"\ *n* -s [NL *thyroides,* fr. *thyroides,* adj.] **1 a** *or* **thyroid gland :** a large endocrine gland of craniate vertebrates that arises as a median ventral outgrowth of the pharynx, lies in the base of the neck or anterior ventral part of the thorax, is often accompanied by lateral accessory glands sometimes more or less fused with the main mass, produces an iodine-containing hormone having a profound influence on growth and development and specifically stimulating the metabolic rate, and has complex interrelations with the pituitary and adrenal and possibly other endocrine glands — see CRETINISM, GOITER, HYPERTHYROIDISM, HYPOTHYROIDISM, THYROXINE; compare MYXEDEMA **b :** a body part (as an artery or nerve) associated with the thyroid gland or cartilage **2 :** a preparation of the thyroid gland of various food animals containing approximately 1/10 percent of iodine combined in thyroxine and used in treating thyroid disorders

thy·roi·dal \(ˈ)thīˈrȯidᵊl\ *adj* [2*thyroid* + *-al*] **1 :** THYROID 2 **2 :** resembling that of the thyroid hormone

thyroid artery *n* **:** either of two arteries supplying not only the thyroid gland but many muscles and other structures of the front of the neck

thyroid cartilage *n* **:** the chief cartilage of the larynx

thy·roid·ec·to·mize \ˌthīˌrȯiˈdektəˌmīz\ *vt* -ED/-ING/-S [*thyroidectomy* + *-ize*] **:** to subject to thyroidectomy

thy·roid·ec·to·my \-mē, -mi\ *n* -ES [ISV *thyroid* + *-ectomy*] **:** partial or complete excision of the thyroid gland

thyroid ganglion *n* **:** the middle of the three cervical ganglia of the sympathetic system of each side

thyroid hormone *n* **:** thyroxine or other closely related metabolically active compound (as triiodothyronine) that is stored in the thyroid gland in the form of thyroglobulin or circulates in the blood apparently bound to plasma protein

thy·roid·i·tis \ˌthīˌrȯiˈdīd·əs\ *n* [NL, fr. *thyroides* thyroid + *-itis*] **:** inflammation of the thyroid gland

thyroid vein *n* **:** any of several small paired veins carrying blood from the thyroid gland and other structures of the front of the neck

thy·ro·lac·tin \ˌthīrəˈlaktən\ *n* [*thyr-* + *lact-* + *-in*] **:** IODINATED CASEIN

thy·ro·nine \ˈthīrəˌnēn, -nən\ *n* -s [*thyr-* + *-on* + *-ine*] **:** a phenolic amino acid $HOC_6H_4OC_6H_4CH_2CH(NH_2)COOH$ of which thyroxine is a tetraiodo derivative; the *para*-hydroxy≈phenyl ether of tyrosine

thy·ro·protein \ˌthīrō+\ *n* [*thyr-* + *protein*] **:** any of various preparations made by iodinating proteins and having physiological activity similar to that of thyroxine and related iodinated protein constituents from the thyroid gland; *esp* **:** IODINATED CASEIN

thy·ros·tra·ca \thīˈrästrəkə\ *n pl, cap* [NL, fr. *thyro-* (fr. Gk *thyra* door, opening) + Gk *ostraka,* pl. of *ostrakon* shell —

more at DOOR, OYSTER] *in some esp. former classifications* **:** a subclass of Crustacea coextensive with Cirripedia — **thy·ros·tra·can** \ ˌ=ˈ=kən\ *adj or n*

thy·ro·toxic \ˌthīrōˈtäksik\ *adj* [*thyr-* + *-toxic*] **:** of, relating to, or affected with hyperthyroidism — **thy·ro·toxicity** \"+\ *n*

thy·ro·toxicosis \"+\ *n* [NL, fr. *thyr-* + *toxicosis*] **:** HYPERTHYROIDISM

thy·ro·trophic \ˌthīrəˈträfik, -trōf-\ *or* **thy·ro·trop·ic** \-ˈträp-\ *adj* [*thyr-* + *-trophic* or *-tropic*] **:** exerting or characterized by a direct influence on the secretory activity of the thyroid gland ⟨the ~ hormone of the anterior pituitary⟩ ⟨~ functions⟩ — **thy·ro·trophi·cal·ly** \-fək(ə)lē\ *adv*

thy·rot·ro·phin \thīˈrä·trəfən, ˌthīrəˈtrō\ *or* **thy·rot·ro·pin** \ˌpən\ *n* -s [*thyrotrophic, thyrotropic* + *-in*] **:** a hormone secreted by the anterior lobe of the pituitary body that regulates the formation and secretion of thyroid hormone and is used chiefly in the treatment of hypothyroidism due to pituitary deficiency

thy·rox·ine \thīˈräkˌsēn, -ˌsən\ *also* **thy·rox·in** \-ˌsən\ *n* -s [ISV *thyr-* + *ox-* + *-ine, -in*] **:** a crystalline iodine-containing phenolic amino acid $C_{15}H_{11}I_4NO_4$ that is the chief active principle of the thyroid gland, occurs there in the levorotatory L-form combined in thyroglobulin and in the blood apparently bound to plasma protein, is also made synthetically (as from diiodotyrosine), and is used esp. in the form of its soluble sodium salt in the treatment of hypothyroidism; tetraiodothyronine — compare THYROID HORMONE, TRIIODOTHYRONINE

thyrse \ˈthərs, -ōs, -əis\ *n* -s [NL *thyrsus*] **:** an inflorescence as in the lilac and horse chestnut in which the main axis is racemose and the secondary and later axes are cymose

thyr·soid \ˈthərˌsȯid\ *adj* [NL *thyrsus* + E *-oid*] **:** having somewhat the form of a thyrse ⟨a ~ panicle⟩

thyr·sus \-ˌsəs\ *n, pl* **thyr·si** \-ˌsī\ [L, fr. Gk *thyrsos*] **1 :** a staff surmounted by a pine cone or by a bunch of vine or ivy leaves with grapes or berries that is carried by Bacchus and by satyrs and others engaging in Bacchic rites **2** [NL, fr. L] **:** THYRSE

thysan- *or* **thysano-** *comb form* [NL, fr. Gk, fr. *thysanos*] **:** tassel **:** fringe ⟨*Thysanoptera*⟩ ⟨*Thysanura*⟩

thysa·no·car·pus \ˌthīsənōˈkärpəs, ˌthis-\ *n, cap* [NL, fr. *thysan-* + *-carpus*] **:** a small genus of slender annual herbs (family Cruciferae) that have pinnatifid basal leaves, entire stem leaves, small white flowers, and an ovate or orbicular one-seeded winged silicle and are widely distributed in dry upland areas of the Pacific coast of No. America — see FRINGEPOD

thysa·nop·ter \ˌthīsəˈnäptə(r), ˌthis-\ *n* -s [NL *Thysanoptera*] **:** THYSANOPTERON

thysa·nop·tera \-tərə\ *n pl, cap* [NL, fr. *thysan-* + *-ptera*] **:** an order of insects comprising the thrips and including various important plant pests — **thysa·nop·ter·an** \ˌ==ˈ=tərən\ *adj or n* — **thysa·nop·ter·ous** \-t(ə)rəs\ *adj*

thysa·nop·ter·ist \ˌ==ˈ=tərəst\ *n* -s [NL *Thysanoptera* + E *-ist*] **:** a specialist in the Thysanoptera

thysa·nop·ter·on \-təˌrän\ *n, pl* **thysanop·tera** \-tərə\ [NL, back-formation fr. *Thysanoptera*] **:** one of the Thysanoptera **:** THRIPS

thysa·no·so·ma \ˌ==nōˈsōmə\ *n, cap* [NL, fr. *thysan-* + *-soma*] **:** a genus of tapeworms (family Anoplocephalidae) including the common fringed tapeworm of ruminants

thysa·nu·ra \ˌ==ˈn(y)u̇rə\ *n pl, cap* [NL, fr. *thysan-* + *-ura*] **:** an order of wingless insects having setiform caudal appendages projecting as bristles and comprising the bristletails — **thysa·nu·ran** \ˌ==ˈ=rən\ *adj or n* — **thysa·nu·rous** \-rəs\ *adj*

thysa·nu·ri·form \ˌ==ˈ=rəˌfȯrm\ *adj* [NL *Thysanura* + E *-iform*] **:** CAMPODEIFORM

thy·self \thīˈself\ *pron* [ME, alter. (influenced by *thy* & *herself*) of *theeself*, fr. OE *thē selfum* & *thē selfne*, dat. & acc. respectively of *thū self* thou thyself — more at THOU, THEE, SELF] *archaic* **:** YOURSELF ⟨thou to ~ wast cruel —John Milton⟩ ⟨physician, heal ~ —Lk 4:23 (AV)⟩ ⟨do ~ no harm —Acts 16:28 (AV)⟩ ⟨thou ~ hast . . . shed a gleam —William Wordsworth⟩ ⟨thou hadst power ~ to keep this vow —Robert Herrick †1674⟩ ⟨he whom next ~ of all the world I loved —Shak.⟩ ⟨as if it were ~ that's here —William Wordsworth⟩ ⟨me than ~ more miserable —John Milton⟩ ⟨~ and thy belongings are not thine own —Shak.⟩ ⟨~ should govern Rome and me —Shak.⟩ ⟨thou . . . standest smiling in thy future grave, . . . ~ thy monument —Sidney Lanier⟩ — used esp. in biblical, ecclesiastical, solemn, or poetical language, and to some extent in the speech of Friends esp. among themselves

thy·sen \-ˈsen\ *pron* [by alter.] *dial Eng* **:** THYSELF

¹ti \ˈtē\ *n* -s [Tahitian, Marquesan, Samoan, & Maori] **1** *or* **ki** \ˈkē\ **:** any of several Asiatic and Pacific trees or shrubs of the genus *Cordyline*: as **a :** a medium-sized New Zealand tree (*C. australis*) having either a single trunk with a terminal tuft of elongated often varicolored leaves or a branching trunk with each branch similarly crowned and having very large panicles of tiny creamy white or bluish globose berries **b :** a variable woody plant (*C. terminalis*) with terminal tufts of elongated leaves that are used locally for thatching, clothing, and food wrappers and thick sweet roots that are used as food or as the base of an intoxicating beverage **2** [by shortening & alter.] **:** TEA TREE 2a

²ti \"\ *n* -s [alter. of *si*] **:** the seventh tone of the diatonic scale in solmization

³ti \"\ *n, pl* **ti** *or* **tis** *usu cap* **1 :** an early Tatar people related to the Hsiung-Nu **2 :** a member of the Ti people

Ti *symbol* titanium

¹ti·a·hua·na·can \ˌtēəwəˈnäkən\ *adj, usu cap* [*Tiahuanaco*, Bolivia + E *-an*, adj. suffix] **:** TIAHUANACO

²tiahuanacan \"\ *n* -s *usu cap* [*Tiahuanaco*, Bolivia + E *-an*, n. suffix] **:** one of the prehistoric peoples of Peru and Bolivia who produced the Tiahuanaco culture

ti·a·hua·na·co \-ä(ˌ)kō\ *adj, usu cap* [fr. *Tiahuanaco*, village in western Bolivia where remains of the culture were found] **:** of or relating to a culture of Peru, Bolivia, and contiguous areas from about 100 B.C. to A.D. 900 characterized by fine stone masonry and carving in stone, polychrome pottery, textiles (as tapestry) and bronze ornaments, weapons, and tools; *also* **:** of the stiff angular but dignified style of design found on these artifacts having as central motif an anthropomorphized demon figure often carrying a throwing-stick

ti·a·hua·na·coid \-äˌkȯid\ *adj, usu cap* [*Tiahuanaco*, Bolivia + E *-oid*] **1 :** EPIGONAL **2 :** resembling the style and symbolism of Tiahuanaco textile and pottery designs

ti·ang \(ˈ)tēˈaŋ\ *n* -s [Dinka] **:** TOPI; *esp* **:** a rather small purplish red black-marked Senegalese topi (*Damaliscus korrigum tiang*)

tiao \ˈdēˈau̇\ *n* -s [Chin (Pek) *tiao⁴*] **:** a string of former Chinese cash or a unit of value equivalent to it varying in amount in different times and localities and the cash often being units of account rather than actual coins

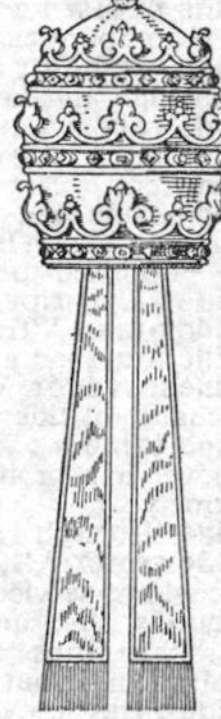
tiara 1b

tiaong \ˈtēˈau̇ŋ\ *n* -s [native name in the Philippines] **:** RED LAUAN

ti·ar \ˈtī(ə)r\ *archaic var of* TIARA

ti·ara \tēˈa(a)rə, -ˈerə, -ˈärə, -ˈärə *sometimes* tīˈa(a)- *or* tiˈe-\ *n* -s [L, fr. Gk *tiara, tiaras*] **1 a :** a headdress worn by the ancient Persians; *specif* **:** a high and erect royal tiara encircled with a diadem **b :** the pope's triple crown **2 :** a decorative band or semicircular ornament for the head often made of flowers, fabric, or metal for wear by women on formal occasions **3 a** *also* **ti·are** \tēˈa(a)(ə)r, -ˈel, |ə\ [*tiare* fr. F, tiara, fr. L *tiara*] **:** any of several fragrant-flowered shrubs of the genus *Gardenia* found in Pacific islands **b :** MITER 3

ti·a·rel·la \ˌtēəˈrelə, ˌtīə-\ *n, cap* [NL, fr. L *tiara* + *-ella*] **:** a small genus of No. American herbs (family Saxifragaceae) having mostly basal palmately lobed or divided leaves with long petioles and a slender raceme of delicate white flowers with a one-celled ovary and basal placentae — see FALSE MITERWORT

ti·ar·is \tēˈa(a)rəs\ *n, cap* [NL, fr. L *tiara*] **:** a genus of tropical American finches (family Fringillidae) often with bright yellow markings about the head — see GRASSQUIT

tib \ˈtib\ *n* -s [fr. *Tib*, nickname fr. the feminine name *Isabel*] **1** *obs* **:** GIRL, LASS; *also* **:** PROSTITUTE **2 :** the ace of trumps in gleek

tib·a·re·ni \ˌtibəˈrānē\ *n pl, usu cap* **:** one of numerous ancient peoples associated with iron making in the Armenian plateau

tib·bit \ˈtibət\ *var of* TABET

ti·bu *or* **tibu** \ˈti(ˌ)bü\ *n, pl* **tibbu** *or* **tibbus** *or* **tibu** *or* **tibus** *usu cap* **1 :** a Negroid people of the area around and in the Tibesti mountains northeast of Lake Chad in Africa **2 :** a member of the Tibbu people

ti·ber green \ˈtībə(r)-\ *n, often cap T* [fr. *Tiber*, river in central Italy] **:** a light yellowish green that is yellower and paler than apple green (sense 2), lighter and stronger than pistachio, and yellower and stronger than crayon green

ti·be·ri·an \(ˈ)tīˈbirēən, -bēr-\ *adj, usu cap* [L *tiberianus*, fr. *Tiberius* †A.D. 37 second emperor of Rome + *-anus* -an] **1 :** of, relating to, or resembling the Roman emperor Tiberius or his policies **2** [*Tiberias*, northern Palestine + E *-an*] **:** of or relating to the ancient city of Tiberias

¹tibet *var of* THIBET

²ti·bet *also* **thi·bet** \təˈbet, *usu* -ed.+V\ *adj, usu cap* [fr. *Tibet* (*Thibet*), country in central Asia] **:** of or from Tibet **:** of the kind or style prevalent in Tibet **:** TIBETAN

¹ti·bet·an \təˈbetᵊn\ *adj, usu cap* [*Tibet*, country in central Asia + E *-an*, adj. suffix] **1 :** of, relating to, or characteristic of Tibet **2 :** of, relating to, or characteristic of the people of Tibet

²tibetan \"\ *n* -s *cap* [*Tibet* + E *-an*, n. suffix] **1 a :** a member of the Mongoloid native race of Tibet that is modified in the west and south by intermixture with Indian peoples and in the east with Chinese typically being about five feet five inches in height and brachycephalic and having wavy hair, brown or hazel eyes, skin tawny brown to white, the beard scant, and the nose either flat or prominent **b :** a native or inhabitant of Tibet **2 :** the Tibeto-Burman language of the Tibetan people

tibetan mastiff *n, usu cap T* **:** a very large powerful rough-coated dog with small drooping ears, bushy tail, and black or black-and-tan hair that is native to central Asia

tibetan terrier *n, usu cap both Ts* [so called fr. its being found in parts of Asia, esp. India and China] **:** a breed of medium-sized terrier much resembling the old English sheepdog but having a curled, well-feathered tail; *also* **:** a dog of this breed — called also *chrysanthemum dog*

tibeto- *comb form, usu cap* [²*tibet* + *-o-*] **:** Tibetan and ⟨*Tibeto*-Chinese⟩ ⟨*Tibeto*-Himalayan⟩

¹tibeto-burman \təˈbed·(ˌ)ō+\ *n, cap T&B* **1 :** a language family of Asia including Tibetan, Garo, Bodo, Lushei, Kachin, Burmese, by some included in Sino-Tibetan **2 :** a member of a people speaking a Tibeto-Burman language

²tibeto-burman \"\ *adj, usu cap T&B* **1 :** of, relating to, or being Tibeto-Burman or a language belonging to Tibeto-Burman **2 :** of, relating to, or being Tibeto-Burmans

tibeto-burmese \təˈbed·(ˌ)ō+\ *n, cap T&B* **:** TIBETO-BURMAN

ti·bey \təˈbā\ *n* -s [AmerSp] **:** any of several plants of the genus *Isotoma* (family Lobeliaceae) the foliage of which is poisonous to cattle

tib·ia \ˈtibēə\ *n, pl* **tibi·ae** \-bēˌē, -bēˌī\ *also* **tibias** [L, shinbone, pipe, flute — more at SIPHON] **1 a :** the preaxial and in the usual position of the limb the inner and usu. the larger of the two bones of the vertebrate leg or hind limb between the knee and ankle articulating above with the femur and below with the talus and in many forms more or less fused with the accompanying fibula **b :** the fourth joint counting from the base of the leg of an insect that lies between the femur and tarsus **2 :** an ancient flute orig. fashioned from an animal's leg bone — used esp. in names of various labial wood pipe organ stops ⟨~ clausa⟩ ⟨~ plena⟩

tib·i·al \-bēəl\ *adj* [L *tibialis*, fr. *tibia* + *-alis* -al] **:** of, relating to, or located near a tibia

tibial artery *n* **:** either of the arteries of the lower leg formed by the bifurcation of the popliteal artery being a larger posterior that divides between the medial malleolus and heel into the two plantar arteries and a smaller anterior that passes forward between the bones

¹tib·i·ale \ˌtibēˈa(ˌ)lē, -ˈä(-, -ˈä(-\ *n, pl* **tibi·alia** \-ˈlēə\ [NL, fr. neut. of L *tibialis* tibial] **:** the most preaxial element of the proximal row of bones of the tarsus and in man prob. a part of the talus

²tibiale \"\ *n, pl* **tibialia** [NL] **:** TIBIAL POINT

tib·i·a·lis \-ˈləs\ *n, pl* **tibi·a·les** \-(ˌ)lēz\ [NL; in sense a, short for *tibialis anticus* anterior tibial (muscle), fr. *tibialis* tibial muscle (fr. L, tibial) + *anticus* anterior; in sense b, short for *tibialis posticus* posterior tibial (muscle), fr. *tibialis* + *posticus* posterior — more at ANTICUS, POSTICOUS] **:** either of two muscles of the calf of the leg: **a :** a muscle arising chiefly from the outer tuberosity and part of the shaft of the tibia and inserted by a long tendon into the first cuneiform and first metatarsal bones — called also *tibialis anterior, tibialis anticus* **b :** a deeply situated muscle arising from the tibia and fibula, interosseous membrane, and intermuscular septa and inserted by a tendon passing under the medial malleolus into the navicular and first cuneiform bones — called also *tibialis posterior, tibialis posticus*

tibial nerve *n* **:** the large nerve in the back of the leg that is a continuation of the sciatic and terminates at the medial malleolus in the lateral and medial plantar nerves

tibial pad *n* **:** a flexible pad on the tibia in some insects

tibial point *n* **:** the upper margin and edge of the interior prominence of the head of the tibia

tibial spur *n* **:** a spine or one of several spines borne on the distal end of the tibia of many insects **:** CALCAR

tibial vein *n* **:** either the anterior vein or the posterior vein accompanying the corresponding tibial arteries

tibio- *comb form* [NL, fr. L *tibia* shinbone — more at SIPHON] **1 :** fused tibia and ⟨*tibio*tarsus⟩ **2 :** tibial and ⟨*tibio*calcaneal⟩ ⟨*tibio*femoral⟩

tib·io·fibula \ˌtibēō+\ *n* [NL, fr. *tibio-* + *fibula*] **:** a bone resulting from fusion of the tibia and fibula (as in the tailless amphibia) — **tib·io·fibular** \"+\ *adj*

Ti·bi·one \ˈtē(ˌ)bēˌwən\ *trademark* — used for thiacetazone

tib·io·tarsal \ˈtibēō+\ *adj* [NL *tibiotarsus* + E *-al*] **:** of or relating to the tibiotarsus

tibio·tarsus \"+\ *n* [NL, fr. *tibio-* + *tarsus*; fr. some of the tarsal elements being fused into its lower end] **:** the tibia of a bird

tib·ou·chi·na \ˌtibəˈkīnə, -kēnə\ *n* [NL, fr. *tibouch* (fr. native name in Guiana) + *-ina*] **1** *cap* **:** a large genus of So. American shrubs or rarely herbs (family Melastomaceae) having entire 5- to 7-nerved leaves and trichotomous panicles of large purple flowers with a hairy calyx, 10 stamens, and a 5-celled ovary — see GLORY-BUSH, SPIDERFLOWER 2 **2** -s **:** any plant of the genus *Tibouchina*

ti·bour·bou \təˈbu̇r(ˌ)bü\ *n* -s [F, fr. Galibi] **:** a tropical American tree (*Apeiba tibourbou*) of the family Tiliaceae with yellowish flowers in lateral cymes, bark that yields jangada fiber, and an extraordinarily light wood that is used along the coast of Brazil for making jangadas

tibs *pl of* TIB

tibu *usu cap, var of* TIBBU

ti·bu·ron \ˌtibəˈrän, -rōn\ *n, pl* **tiburo·nes** \ˌ==ˈrō(ˌ)nēz\ [Sp *tiburón*, fr. Pg *tubarão*, prob. fr. Tupi *tubarám*] **:** any of various large voracious sharks of the West Indies and Central America

ti·bur·tine \ˈtībə(r)ˌtīn\ *adj, usu cap* [ME, fr. L *tiburtinus*, fr. *tiburt-*, *tiburs* of Tibur (fr. *Tibur*, region in ancient Latium corresponding to Tivoli, commune in central Italy) + *-inus* -ine] **:** of or relating to Tibur ⟨the *Tiburtine* sibyl⟩

tic \ˈtik\ *n* -s [F] **1 :** a convulsive motion of some muscles esp. of the face usu. resulting from nervous habit **:** TWITCHING **2 :** OBSESSION, FIXATION

ti·cal *or* **ti·kal** \təˈkäl, ˈtikəl, ˈtēkəl\ *n, pl* **ticals** *or* **tical** [Thai, fr. Malay *tikal*, a monetary unit] **1 a :** an old Thai monetary unit orig. used in designation of the value of uncoined silver **b :** an old Thai silver coin containing 15 grams of silver 0.900 fine **2 :** the basic monetary unit of modern Thailand **:** BAHT

tic dou·lou·reux \ˌtik,düləˈrü, -dül-, -ˈrər(·), -ˈrə, -ˈrā\ *n* [F, painful twitch] **:** TRIGEMINAL NEURALGIA

ti·chod·ro·ma \tīˈkädrəmə, təˈk-\ *n, cap* [NL, fr. Gk *teichos* wall + *dromos* act of running, racecourse — more at DOUGH, -DROM] **:** a genus of birds (family Certhiidae) consisting of the wall creeper

ticho·drome \ˈtīkəˌdrōm, ˈtik-\ *n* -s [NL *Tichodroma*] **:** WALL CREEPER

tichor·rhine \ˈtīkəˌrīn, ˈtik-\ *n* -s [NL *tichorhinus* (specific epithet of the woolly rhinoceros *Rhinoceros tichorhinus*), fr. Gk *teichos* wall + NL *-rhinus*; fr. the vertical bony septum forming a supporting wall for the nose] **:** WOOLLY RHINOCEROS

¹ti·ci·nese \ˌtichəˈnēz, -ēs\ *adj, usu cap* [*Ticino*, canton in the Lepontine Alps, Switzerland + E *-ese*, adj. suffix] **1 :** of, relating to, or characteristic of the canton of Ticino **2 :** of, relating to, or characteristic of the people of Ticino

²ticinese \"\ *n, pl* **ticinese** *cap* [*Ticino*, Switzerland + E *-ese*, n. suffix] **:** a native or inhabitant of Ticino

¹tick \ˈtik\ *n* -s [ME *tyke, teke*; akin to OE *ticia* tick, MHG *zeche* tick, MIr *dega* stag beetle, Arm *tiz* tick] **1 :** any of numerous arachnids that constitute the acarine superfamily Ixodoidea, are much larger than the closely related mites, are bloodsuckers which attach themselves to warm-blooded vertebrates to feed, are chiefly important as vectors of various infectious diseases of man and lower animals, and although the immature larva has but six legs, may be readily distinguished from an insect by the complete lack of external segmentation **2 :** any of various usu. wingless parasitic dipterous insects (as a bird tick, sheep ked, or bat fly)

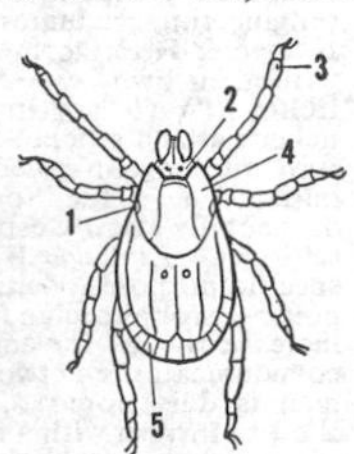

tick 2: *1* ocellus, *2* capitulum, *3* sense organ of tarsus, *4* shield, *5* festoon

²tick \"\ *n* -s [ME *tek*; akin to MHG *zic* light push, tick, Norw dial. *tikka* to push lightly, touch lightly and prob. to ME *teke* tick (arachnid)] **1 a** *obs* **:** a light touch **:** TAP **b** *Brit* **:** TAG **2 a** (1) **:** a light quick distinct audible tapping sound esp. in a rhythmic series ⟨the beating of the metronome . . . at 120 ~s per minute —R.S. Woodworth⟩; *also* **:** a series of such ticks ⟨the breathless ~ of the clock —Berton Roueché⟩ (2) **:** a pulsation or series of pulsations likened to the tick of a clock ⟨his heart gave a ~ —Marguerite Steen⟩ **b** *chiefly Brit* **:** the time taken or indicated by the tick of a clock **:** a very small interval of time **:** MOMENT, SECOND ⟨we'll be ready in a couple of ~s —Richard Llewellyn⟩ **3 a :** a dot, speck, dash, or check used to direct attention to something, to mark off an item (as on a list) as having been examined, to represent a point on a scale, or as a symbolic abbreviation ⟨making ~s in a mail-order catalogue on her lap with a pencil stub —Arthur Mayse⟩ ⟨had to start all over again, using the same letters with ~s to signify higher decimal orders —Lancelot Hogben⟩ ⟨the intervals on the scale are marked off by lines and ~s —C.F.Schmid⟩ **b :** a small spot of a different color on a furred or feathered creature — **on the tick** *or* **to the tick** *adv, chiefly Brit* **:** at a precise moment **:** exactly on the instant ⟨arrived at my destination *on the tick* —Adrian Bell⟩

³tick \"\ *vb* -ED/-ING/-S *vi* **1 a :** to make the sound of a tick or a continuous series of ticks ⟨listening to the clock ~⟩ **b :** to make a muted oscillating somewhat regular rumbling noise — used of an idling internal-combustion engine; *also* **:** IDLE 2 — usu. used with *over* **2 :** to take place in or be a measured or regular esp. temporal sequence ⟨meantime life in the ward ~*ed* away as usual —Earle Birney⟩ ⟨the telephone poles ~*ing* past —*Harper's*⟩ **3 :** to take place, come into existence, or arrive to the accompaniment of ticks ⟨the sports news has been ~*ing* in from places of which few Americans have ever heard —Horace Sutton⟩ **4 :** to act in or manifest an often unusual or inexplicable character **:** operate or function by or as if by a hidden clockwork mechanism ⟨persons who are ~*ing* along fine on one kidney —*Time*⟩ ⟨his mind kept ~*ing* on steadily —Ira Wolfert⟩ — often used in such phrases as *what makes one tick* ⟨knowledge about my fellow citizens and what makes them ~ —*Survey Graphic*⟩ ⟨shows what makes totalitarian society ~ —W.H.Chamberlin⟩ ⟨find out how and why a modern poet ~*ed* —Mary Barrett⟩ ~ *vt* **1 :** to mark with or as if with a written tick **:** CHECK ⟨~*ing* away in his mind the yards yet separating her from the onrushing . . . destroyer —E.L.Beach⟩ — usu. used with *off* ⟨dashing up and down with lists and ~*ing* off names —Anthony Carson⟩ ⟨~*ing* off small numbers with his fingers —J.A.N. Friend⟩ **2 :** to mark, note, count, give forth, measure, or announce by or as if by repeated ticking beats ⟨~*ing* off heroic couplets —H.R.Warfel⟩ ⟨his taxicab outside, ominously ~*ing* out the pence and minutes —Osbert Sitwell⟩ ⟨clockwork that ~s off the years and their changes —Rose Feld⟩ **3 :** to touch with a momentary sharp or glancing blow ⟨determining if the ball ~s the net on the serve —J.W.Bunn⟩ ⟨~*ed* the cat under the chin —Raymond Chandler⟩

⁴tick \"\ *n* -s [ME *tike, teke*, prob. fr. MD; akin to OHG *ziahha* pillowcase, tick; both fr. a prehistoric WGmc word borrowed fr. L *theca* cover, sheath, fr. Gk *thēkē*; akin to Gk *tithenai* to put, set — more at DO] **1 :** the fabric case usu. of ticking of a mattress, pillow, or bolster; *also* **:** a mattress consisting of a tick and its resilient filling **2 :** TICKING

⁵tick \"\ *n* -s [short for ¹*ticket*] **:** CREDIT, TRUST; *also* **:** a credit account ⟨ordered a suit of clothes on ~ —W.A.White⟩

⁶tick *vi* -ED/-ING/-S *obs* **:** to buy or sell on credit

tickbean \ˈ=ˌ=\ *n* [¹*tick* + *bean*] **:** any of various horsebeans having small seeds shaped like a tick

tickbird \ˈ=ˌ=\ *n* [¹*tick* + *bird*] **:** a bird (as the oxpecker or ani) that eats ticks infesting quadrupeds

tick-bite fever *n* **:** TICK FEVER

tick-borne *adj* **:** capable of being transmitted by the bites of ticks ⟨Rocky Mountain spotted fever is a *tick-borne* disease⟩

tick-borne fever *n* **:** a mild rickettsial disease of sheep transmitted by a tick (genus *Ixodes*), marked by fever, listlessness, and loss of condition, and persisting for about ten days

tick clover *n* **:** TICK TREFOIL

tickeater \ˈ=ˌ==\ *n* **:** TICKBIRD

ticked \ˈtikt\ *adj* [²*tick* + *-ed*] **1 :** marked or variegated with ticks **2** *of a hair* **:** banded with two or more colors

tick·en \ˈtikən\ *n* -s [alter. (influenced by *-en* as in *woolen*) of ¹*ticking*] *Brit* **:** TICKING

¹tick·er \ˈtikə(r)\ *n* -s [³*tick* + *-er*] **:** something that ticks or produces a ticking sound: as **a :** WATCH **b :** a telegraphic receiving instrument that automatically prints off stock quotations or news on a paper ribbon **c :** HEART ⟨I'm feeling better, but the old ~'s not so good —*Newsweek*⟩

²ticker *var of* TIKKER

tick·er·man \ˈtikə(r)mən, -ˌman\ *n, pl* **tickermen :** a worker who installs and repairs telegraphic tickers

ticker tape *n* **1 :** the paper ribbon on which a telegraphic ticker prints off its information **2 :** paper streamers (as ticker tape) and scraps (as confetti) thrown from upper-story windows usu. over a passing parade in honor of a celebrity

¹tick·et \ˈtikət, *usu* -əd.+V\ *n* -s *often attrib* [obs. F *etiquet* (now *étiquette*), fr. MF *etiquet, estiquet*, fr. *estiquer, estiquier* to attach, stick, fr. MD *steken* to stick; akin to OHG *stehhan* to stick — more at STICK] **1 a** *obs* **:** a short note or document in writing ⟨if your ~ had overtaken me . . . I had certainly returned —Richard Baker⟩ **b :** a document that serves as a certificate, license, or permit; *specif* **:** a master's, captain's, mate's, pilot's, or airman's certificate **c :** a written, typed, printed, stamped, or engraved notice, record, memorandum, or token: as (1) **:** a paper or card on an item giving information (as of its owner, identity, maker, or price) **:** TAG, LABEL ⟨tagged with a ~ giving the number of the machine, the operator, and the lot —Werner Von Bergen & H.R.Mauersberger⟩ ⟨examined the price on the ~⟩ (2) *obs* **:** PROMISSORY NOTE (3) *Brit* **:** VISITING CARD (4) **:** a summons or warning issued to an offender esp. of a traffic regulation ⟨parking ~⟩ **d** (1) **:** a certificate, evidence, or token of a right (as of admission to a place of assembly, of passage in a public conveyance, of debt, or of a chance) ⟨a theater ~⟩ ⟨a railroad ~⟩ ⟨a lottery ~⟩ ⟨a pawn ~⟩ (2) *Brit* : a library borrower's card **e** (1) : SLATE 4b ⟨the power of a popular president to carry his whole ~ to victory with him —W.H.Hessler⟩ ⟨some individuals vote the party ~ —L.W.Doob⟩ — see SPLIT TICKET, STRAIGHT TICKET (2) : a sheet of paper bearing the names of candidates for office (as of a political party or faction) and usu. used as a ballot ⟨the voter received the party ~ outside the polling place —H.R.Penniman⟩ **f** : a slip or card with ruled spaces on which is written a record of a transaction or undertaking or detailed instructions (as an order for specific repairs on some equipment) ⟨deposit ~⟩ ⟨sales ~⟩ ⟨the driver is required to make an entry on his trip ~ at each stop⟩ — compare DEPOSIT SLIP **2** : a sealed bid for ore to be sold **3** : a means to something desirable ⟨a used car is the ~ out of the bad living conditions —Warner Bloomberg⟩ ⟨good manners . . . are your ~ to popularity —*Girl Scout Handbk.*⟩ **4** : the suitable, correct, or desirable thing ⟨quick action, that's the ~ —T.B. Costain⟩ ⟨a little trip'll be just the ~ for you —Maritta Wolff⟩ **5** : a program or plan for a project, career, or intended course of life used esp. in such phrases as *write one's own ticket* ⟨engineering graduates . . . are writing their own job ~s —Ira Kamen & R.H.Dorf⟩ ⟨committees make their own rules and write their own ~s —*New Yorker*⟩

²ticket \"\ *vb* -ED/-ING/-S *vt* **1 a** : to classify or mark by a ticket : attach a ticket to : LABEL ⟨things in their proper place, ~*ed* and pigeon-holed —W.M.Dixon⟩ ⟨~*ed* only with the initials *A.J.* —Hamilton Basso⟩ **b** : to describe, characterize, or mentally classify esp. in a set phrase ⟨he's ~*ed* as a zealous reformer —*Kiplinger Washington Letter*⟩ **c** : to designate for a specific purpose, position, or destination ⟨a defense contract now ~*ed* for a foreign factory —G.E.Cruikshank⟩ ⟨most of the increase is ~*ed* for earthbound assets like bases, radar, and communications networks —*Newsweek*⟩ ⟨a promising young man is duly noted . . . and ~*ed* for future office —*Time*⟩ **2 a** : to furnish with a ticket : BOOK ⟨children . . . under twelve . . . cannot be ~*ed* unless accompanied by parent or guardian —Chicago, Milwaukee, St. Paul & Pacific RR⟩ **b** : to serve with a ticket ⟨~*ed* for backing out of a parking space into an oncoming car —*Time*⟩ ~ *vi* : to issue or check tickets

ticket agency *n* : a usu. independent agency selling transportation or theater and entertainment tickets

ticket agent *n* : one who acts as an agent of a transportation company to sell tickets for travel by train, boat, airplane, or bus; *also* : one who sells theater and entertainment tickets

ticket book *n* : a book having tickets authorizing a specified amount of travel or a specified number of trips between designated points used esp. for commuter travel

ticket day *n, Brit* : NAME DAY 2

tick·et·er \ˈtikəd·ə(r), -ətə-\ *n* -S : a worker who prepares labeling tickets or attaches them to goods

ticket gate *n, Brit* : an exit on a railway platform where passengers issuing from a train surrender their tickets

tick·et·less \ˈtikətləs\ *adj* : lacking a ticket : not requiring a ticket

ticket office *n* : an office of a transportation company, theatrical or entertainment enterprise, or ticket agency where tickets are sold and reservations made

ticket-of-leave \ˌ=ˈ=ˈ=\ *n, pl* **tickets-of-leave** *n* : a license or permit formerly given in the United Kingdom and the British Commonwealth to a convict under imprisonment to go at large and to labor for himself subject to certain specific conditions

ticket porter *n* : a licensed porter in the city of London

tickets *pl of* TICKET, *pres 3d sing of* TICKET

tickety-boo \ˌtikətiˈbü\ *adj* [¹*ticket* (sense 4) + *-y* + ¹*boo*] *Brit* : FINE, OKAY ⟨everything is going to be *tickety-boo* eventually —A.J.Liebling⟩

tick·ey *also* **tick·ie** *or* **ticky** \ˈtikē\ *n* -S [Afrik, prob. modif. of Pg *pataca* & F *patac* pataca (fr. Pg)] *Africa* : THREEPENCE

tick farcy *n* : EPIZOOTIC LYMPHANGITIS

tick fever *n* **1** : a febrile disease (as Rocky Mountain spotted fever) transmitted by the bites of ticks **2** : TEXAS FEVER

tick·i·ci·dal \ˌtikəˈsīdᵊl\ *adj* **1** : destroying or controlling ticks ⟨~ drugs⟩ **2** : of or relating to a tickicide

tick·i·cide \ˈtikə,sīd\ *n* -S [¹*tick* + *-i-* + *-cide*] : an agent used to kill ticks

tickier *comparative of* TICKY

tickiest *superlative of* TICKY

¹tick·ing \ˈtikiŋ, -kēŋ\ *n* -S [⁴*tick* + *-ing*] : a strong firm fabric of cotton or linen usu. twilled and striped used for upholstering, covering mattresses, pillows, or box springs, and in lighter weights for clothing

²ticking \"\ *n* -S [fr. gerund of ³*tick*] : ticks made by a clock, telegraph sounder, or other device ⟨telegraphic ~ is virtually a pure example of referential symbolism —Edward Sapir⟩

³ticking \"\ *n* -S [²*tick* + *-ing*] **1** : minute distinct color marks on a bird or mammal esp. on the tips of feathers — compare LACING **2** : the presence of longer guard hairs of a color unlike the body fur scattered throughout a fur **3** : the condition of having the individual hairs marked with several bands of distinct color usu. with the tip black — compare AGOUTI

¹tick·le \ˈtikəl\ *vb* **tickled; tickled; tickling** \-k(ə)liŋ\ **tickles** [ME *tikelen*; akin to OE *tinclian* to tickle and prob. to OE *citelian* to tickle, OHG *kizzilōn, kuzzilōn*, ON *kitla*] *vi* **1** *obs* : to feel excitement, tingling, or titillation : tingle or thrill with or as if with pleasure ⟨he with secret joy therefore did ~ inwardly in every vein —Edmund Spenser⟩ **2** : to have a tingling or restless sensation ⟨my back ~*s*⟩ **3** : to excite the surface nerves : cause a tickle ⟨that feather ~*s*⟩ ~ *vt* **1 a** (1) : to excite or stir up agreeably : awaken a sensation of pleasure in : furnish with esp. sensual gratification ⟨a piece of music . . . does more than ~ our sense of rhythm or color —Edward Sapir⟩ ⟨it ~*s* the sense of vicarious adventure —John Dolman⟩ ⟨intentional cheapening of her work to ~ the banal reader —Sinclair Lewis⟩ (2) : to excite or arouse from dormancy or to a higher degree : STIMULATE, ANNOY, PROVOKE ⟨it *tickled* all that is evil in me —O.W.Holmes †1935⟩ ⟨the self-esteem of the selected candidates was immensely *tickled* —Tom Marvel⟩ ⟨men have to be . . . *tickled* up by propaganda before they'll fight —Aldous Huxley⟩ **b** (1) : to excite amusement or merriment in : arouse the sense of humor of : AMUSE ⟨so excessively *tickled* by the jest that he couldn't forget it —Charles Dickens⟩ (2) : to provide with pleasure or enjoyment : make pleased ⟨how *tickled* they were . . . because they still had time to sell our rooms to four royalists —Christopher Morley⟩ **2 a** (1) : to touch (as a person or a part of the body) lightly with or as if with the fingers so as to excite the surface nerves and to cause uneasiness, laughter, or spasmodic movements ⟨the physical spasm which seizes children when they are *tickled* —Willa Cather⟩ (2) : to tease, torment, or pet by or as if by tickling ⟨the sound of the wrapping paper being torn away *tickled* his ears —N.A.Wasserman⟩ (3) : to bring into a specified state by or as if by tickling ⟨be *tickled* to death to see you⟩ ⟨all were *tickled* pink to be on land again⟩ **b** : to touch or stir gently ⟨the piano player *tickled* the keys⟩ **c** : to capture (a fish) by groping for it with the hands and sliding the fingers into its gills **3** : WHIP, CHASTISE, BEAT **syn** see PLEASE — **tickle it** *obs* : to bring to a desired end : complete successfully — **tickle the palm of** *or* **tickle in the palm 1** : BRIBE **2** : TIP

²tickle \"\ *n* -S **1** : something (as a touch) that tickles **2** : a tickling sensation **3** : the act or process of tickling

tickle grass *n* **1** : any of several grasses of the genus *Agrostis*; *esp* : ROUGH BENT **2** : WITCHGRASS 2

tick·len·burg \ˈtiklən,bərg\ *n* -S [fr. *Ticklenburg* (Tecklenburg), locality in northwestern Germany where it was orig. manufactured] : a coarse linen fabric

tick·ler \ˈtik(ə)lə(r)\ *n* -S **1** : a person or device that tickles ⟨tormented passersby with water pistols and ~*s*⟩ **2** : a device for jogging the memory; *specif* : a book, file, or set of memoranda kept as a reminder esp. by a business firm ⟨sales ~⟩ **3** *or* **tickler coil** : a feedback coil

tickler file *n* : a file that serves as a reminder and is arranged to bring matters to timely attention

tickles *pres 3d sing of* TICKLE, *pl of* TICKLE

tickleweed \ˈ=ˌ=\ *n* : AMERICAN HELLEBORE

tickling *pres part of* TICKLE

¹tick·lish \ˈtik(ə)lish, -lēsh\ *adj* [³*tickle* + *-ish*] **1** : sensitive to tickling **2 a** : easily disturbed emotionally : TOUCHY, OVERSENSITIVE ⟨employed to scare the dickens out of anyone who is ~ about atomic energy —*Newsweek*⟩ **b** : easily overturned or unbalanced : not affording security or support : UNSTEADY, UNSTABLE ⟨a canoe is the most ~ of navigable things —Herman Melville⟩ **3** : requiring delicate handling : DELICATE, NICE, CRITICAL ⟨hesitates to be explicit on so ~ a subject —*Publ's Mod. Lang. Assoc. of Amer.*⟩ ⟨the takeoff is twice as ~ as the landing —T.H.Fielding⟩ **4** : UNCERTAIN, UNRELIABLE, CHANGEABLE ⟨~ weather⟩ — **tick·lish·ly** *adv* — **tick·lish·ness** *n* -ES

²ticklish \"\ *adv* : TICKLISHLY

tick·ly \-k(ə)lē, -li\ *adj* -ER/-EST : TICKLISH

tick off *vt* **1** : to read off (an item in a list) : RECITE, ENUMERATE ⟨the commission *ticked off* six specific causes for the price spiral —*Wall Street Jour.*⟩ ⟨*ticking off* the appetizing aspects of summer —Jane Nickerson⟩ **2** : REPRIMAND, REBUKE ⟨wanted to *tick him off* a bit for letting me in for all this —P.G.Wodehouse⟩ **3** : to describe with succinct accuracy ⟨a period which it would be so difficult to *tick off* in a phrase —*Times Lit. Supp.*⟩

tick over *vi* : to come near to failure : FALTER ⟨when they have nothing to say their music *ticks over* dopingly —Charles Reid⟩

tick paralysis *n* : an ascending paralysis in man or lower animals caused by a neurotoxin secreted by some ticks (as *Dermocentor andersoni*) and injected into the host during feeding

tick pyemia *n* : staphylococcal pyemia of lambs due to bacteria introduced by tick bite

ticks *pl of* TICK, *pres 3d sing of* TICK

tickseed \ˈ=ˌ=\ *n* [¹*tick* + *seed*; fr. the shape of the seeds] **1** : COREOPSIS **2** : TICK TREFOIL

tickseed sunflower *n* : any of various large-rayed No. American plants of the genus *Bidens* (esp. *B. coronata* and *B. trichosperma*)

¹tick·tack *or* **tic·tac** \ˈtik,tak\ *n* -S [imit.] **1 a** : a repeated ticking or tapping noise like that made by a clock or watch ⟨the ~ of sleet on frosted windowpanes —Merle Crowell⟩ **b** : a contrivance to make a tapping or rattling sound (as on a window or door) operated from a distance esp. as a practical joke ⟨hold ~*s* up against their windows —John O'Hara⟩ **2** [modif. of MF *trictrac*] *obs* : TRICTRAC **3** *Brit* : secret signaling between bookmakers at a race

²ticktack *or* **tictac** \"\ *vb* -ED/-ING/-S **1** : to move or sound with a ticktack **2** *Brit* : to signal by ticktack

tick·tack·toe \ˌtik,takˈtō\ *also* **tick·tack·too** \-akˈtü\ *or* **tic-tac-toe** \-akˈtō\ *also* **tit-tat-toe** \ˌti(t),taˈ-\ *n* -S [fr. *tic-tac-toe* game formerly played in which the players with the eyes shut brought a pencil down on a slate marked with numbers and scored the number hit, fr. *tictac* + *toe*] : a game in which two players alternately put crosses and ciphers in compartments of a figure formed by two vertical lines crossing two horizontal lines and try to get a row of three crosses or three ciphers before the opponent does — called also *noughts-and-crosses*

tick·tick \ˈtik,tik\ *n* [redupl. of ²*tick*] : a repeated ticking sound

¹tick·tock *also* **tic·toc** \ˈtikˌtäk\ *n*-S [imit.] : a ticking sound made esp. by a large clock

²ticktock *also* **tictoc** \"\ *vi* -ED/-ING/-S : to make a sound like a ticktock

tick trefoil *n* [¹*tick*; fr. the sticky loments that adhere to clothing and the hair of animals] : any of various plants (genus *Desmodium*) characterized by trifoliolate leaves and rough sticky loments

tick typhus *n* : a disease that occurs in widely separated areas in Asia, Australia, Africa, Siberia, and Europe and is caused by the bite of a tick

tickweed \ˈ=ˌ=\ *n* **1** : PENNYROYAL 2 **2** : COREOPSIS

tick-worry \ˈ=ˌ==\ *n* : a generalized state of unease and irritability of cattle severely infested with ticks often leading to serious loss of energy and condition

¹ticky \ˈtikē, -ki\ *adj* -ER/-EST : affected or infested with or full of ticks

²ticky *var of* TICKEY

tic-polonga \ˌtikpəˈlōŋgə\ *n* -S [Sinhalese *tikpolan̄gā*, fr. *tik* spot + *polan̄gā* viper] : RUSSELL'S VIPER

tics *pl of* TIC

ticul \təˈkəl, ˈtik-,ˈtēk-\ *n, pl* **ticul** *or* **ticuls** [by alter.] : TICAL

¹tid \ˈtid\ *n* -S [alter. of ¹*tide*] **1** *chiefly Scot* : a right time or season esp. for an agricultural activity **2** *chiefly Scot* : MOOD, HUMOR

²tid \"\ *n* -S [by alter.] : a girl or young woman

TID *abbr, often not cap* [L *ter in die*] three times a day

ti·dal \ˈtīdᵊl\ *adj* [¹*tide* + *-al*] **1** : of or relating to tides : caused by tides : having tides : periodically rising and falling or flowing and ebbing ⟨~ waters⟩ **2** : moved or actuated by tides ⟨a ~ motor⟩ **3** : dependent (as in regard to the time of arrival or departure) upon the state of the tide ⟨a ~ steamer⟩ ⟨a ~ train run in connection with a tidal steamer⟩; *also* : navigable only at high tide ⟨a ~ harbor⟩ **4** : of, relating to, or constituting tidal air ⟨the ~ volume exhaled⟩ — **ti·dal·ly** \-dᵊlē, -li\ *adv*

tidal air *n* : the air that passes in and out of the lungs in an ordinary breath and averages 500 cubic centimeters in human adults

tidal amplitude *n* : the elevation of tidal high water above mean sea level

tidal basin *n* : a dock or basin communicating with tidal water usu. through lock gates or locks

tidal bore *n* : ⁴BORE

tidal box *n* : a hatching box used in fish culture with an automatic siphon that causes the level of the water in the box to rise and fall alternately

tidal breeze *n* : a light breeze (as in the Gulf of St. Lawrence) attributed to tidal action

tidal clock *n* : a clock showing the times of high and low water and the state of the tides at any time of day

tidal constant *n* : either of the two factors that when combined completely specify a simple tide and include the tidal amplitude and the tidal epoch

tidal current *n* : a current produced by tidal forces

tidal day *n* : TIDE DAY

tidal epoch *n* : the tidal constant that represents the time elapsing between the moon's meridian passage and the ensuing high tide

tidal flat *n* : essentially horizontal and commonly muddy or marshy land that is covered and uncovered by the rise and fall of tides

tidal friction *n* : the frictional effect of the tidal wave esp. in shallow waters lengthening the tidal epoch and tending to retard the rotational velocity of the earth and so increase very slowly the length of the day

tidal load *n* : variation of pressure in the earth due to the movement of the water caused by the tide or due to the stresses produced by the changing positions of the moon and sun relative to the earth

tidal marsh *n* : wet land regularly inundated by the backing up of adjoining streams through tidal action — compare TIDAL FLAT

tidal pool *n* : TIDE POOL

tidal river *n* : a river up the course of which the tides are noticeable for a considerable distance

tidal stream *n* **1** : TIDAL RIVER **2** *Brit* : TIDAL CURRENT

tidal theory *n* **1** : a theory of the evolution of a celestial body that is based on the action of tidal forces; *specif* : such a theory explaining the moon's evolution **2** : the theory of the present ocean tides

tidal watch *n* : a watch functioning like a tidal clock

tidal water *n* : TIDEWATER 1

tidal wave *n* **1** : TIDE WAVE **2 a** : an unusually high sea wave that sometimes follows an earthquake : SEISMIC SEA WAVE **b** : an unusual rise of water alongshore due to exceptionally strong winds **3** : an unexpected and intense reaction (as an overwhelming impulse, a burst of feeling, or a heavy majority vote)

tid·bit *or* **tit·bit** \ˈtid,bit, ˈtit,b-, *usu* -bid·+V\ *n* [perh. fr. *tit-* (as in *titmouse*) + *bit*] **1** : a delicate piece of anything eatable : a choice morsel of food **2** : a small and pleasing, interesting, or spicy bit (as of news or information)

tid·dle \ˈtidᵊl\ *vb* **tiddled; tiddled; tiddling** \-d(ᵊ)liŋ\ **tiddles** [origin unknown] *vi* **1** : POTTER, FIDGET **2** *chiefly NewEng* : SEESAW, TEETER ~ *vt, dial chiefly Eng* : to rear or care for with excessive solicitude : COSSET, PAMPER

tid·dle·dies \ˈtidᵊldēz, -diz\ *n pl* [origin unknown] : soft flexible ice or chunks of floating ice

tid·dle·dy·wink \ˈtidᵊl(d)ē,wiŋk, ˈtidlē,-, ˌ=(=)=ˈ=\ *n* [alter. of *tiddlywink*] **1 tiddledywinks** *pl but sing in constr* : a game the object of which is to snap small disks from a flat surface into a small container **2** : ⁴WINK

tid·dler \ˈtid(ᵊ)lə(r)\ *n* -S [prob. fr. E dial. *tiddly* little + *-er*] **1** *Brit* **a** : a small fish; *esp* : STICKLEBACK **b** *slang* : a small 4-man submarine used by the British in World War II **2** *Brit* : a small child **3** : a player at tiddledywinks

¹tid·dly *or* **tid·dley** \ˈtid(ᵊ)li\ *n, pl* **tiddlies** *or* **tiddleys** [prob. fr. E dial. *tiddly* little, alter. of *little*] *Brit* : an alcoholic drink

²tiddly *or* **tiddley** \"\ *adj* **1** *chiefly Brit* : somewhat intoxicated : DRUNK ⟨will make me ~ if I drink it all —Nathaniel Benchley⟩ **2** *chiefly Brit* : precisely arrayed and ordered : dressed up : SMART ⟨quite a busy time getting the ship ~ —*Crowsnest*⟩

tid·dly·wink \ˈtid(ᵊ)lē,wiŋk\ *n* [prob. fr. E dial. *tiddly* little + *wink*] **1** *dial Eng* : an unlicensed public house : BEERHOUSE **2** *or* **tid·dley·wink** \"\ : TIDDLEDYWINK

tid·dy \ˈtidē, -di\ *adj* [prob. alter. of *little*] *chiefly Brit* : TINY, TRIVIAL

¹tide \ˈtīd\ *n* -S *often attrib* [ME *tyde, tide* time, fr. OE *tīd*; akin to OFris & OS *tīd* time, OHG *zīt*, ON *tīthr* time, Gk *daiesthai* to distribute, divide, Skt *dayate* he apportions, *dāti* he cuts, divides, mows; basic meaning: to divide] **1 a** *obs* : a space of time : WHILE, PERIOD **b** *archaic* : a particular point in time : a definite moment : OCCASION **c** : fit or opportune time : OPPORTUNITY **d** (1) : an ecclesiastical anniversary or festival (2) : HOLIDAY; *also* : a holiday season as distinguished from the specific day on which the holiday is celebrated (3) *Brit* : a fair or merrymaking on a parish feast day **e** : a space of time (as between two high tides or during the height of a flood tide) at sea when the water level permits a particular activity to be carried out **2 a** (1) : the alternate rising and falling of the surface of the ocean and of gulfs, bays, estuaries, and other water bodies connected with the ocean that occurs twice a day over most of the earth and is caused by the gravitational attraction of the sun and moon occurring unequally on different parts of the earth — see DIRECT TIDE, EBB TIDE, FLOOD TIDE, NEAP TIDE, OPPOSITE TIDE, SPRING TIDE (2) : a similar but less marked rising and falling of an inland body of water (3) : EARTH TIDE (4) : ATMOSPHERIC TIDE **b** (1) : FLOOD TIDE ⟨the ship departed on the ~⟩ (2) : a specific instance of tide ⟨there was a ~ at 9:53 p.m.⟩ **c** : the mass of water moving in a tide ⟨sand castles covered by the ~⟩; *also* : TIDEMARK ⟨animals living between the ~*s*⟩ **3 a** : something that may turn, rise and fall, or decrease or increase like the tides of the sea ⟨a waning ~ of popular interest⟩ **b** : an extreme condition usu. of excellence or badness ⟨how our fortunes ever got to such a ~⟩ **4** : mobile water: as **a** : a flowing stream : CURRENT **b** : the waters of the ocean **c** : flood waters : the overflow of a flooding stream **syn** see FLOW

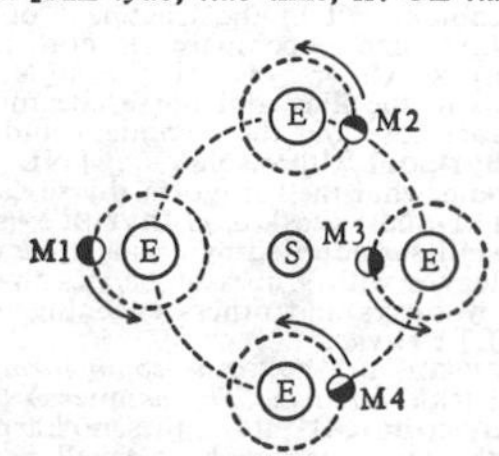

tides 2a(1): *M1* and *M3* position of moon at spring tides; *M2* and *M4* moon at neap tides

²tide \"\ *vb* -ED/-ING/-S *vi* **1** : to flow as or in a tide : surge to and fro : pour forth **2 a** : to drift with the tide esp. in navigating a ship into or out of an anchorage, harbor, or river **b** : to become carried : drift as if with a tide — usu. used with *on* or *onward* or *over* ⟨*tiding* on toward an uncertain fate⟩ ~ *vt* **1** : to transport or cause to float with or as if with the tide ⟨the sea *tiding* debris back to shore⟩ **2** : to proceed along (one's way) by taking advantage of tides

³tide \"\ *vi* [ME *tiden*, fr. OE *tīdan*; akin to OFris *tīdia* to proceed to, MD *tiden* to go, come, MLG *tiden* to hurry, strive, ON *titha* to long for, wish, *tīthr* time — more at ¹TIDE] *archaic* : BETIDE, HAPPEN, BEFALL

tide boat *n* : a small craft plying with the tides

tide crack *n* : a crack caused by the tide and separating the ice foot and sea ice along a frigid shore

tid·ed \ˈtīdəd\ *adj* [¹*tide* + *-ed*] : affected by or having tides ⟨~ waters⟩

tide day *n* : an interval occurring between the arrival of any two consecutive high waters of the direct tide or of the opposite tide at any given place and averaging 24 hours 51 minutes

tideflat \ˈ=ˌ=\ *n* : TIDAL FLAT

tide·ful \-fəl\ *adj* [ME, fr. *tyde, tide* + *-ful*] : flooded by the tide

tide gage *or* **tide register** *n* : a gage for showing the height of the tide; *esp* : one for registering its state continuously

tide gate *n* **1** : an opening through which water may flow freely when the tide sets in one direction but which closes automatically and prevents the water from flowing in the other direction **2** : a place where the tide runs with great velocity as if through a gate : TIDEWAY

tidehead \ˈ=ˌ=\ *n* : the inland limit of the tide

tide·land \ˈ=,land, -,laa(ə)nd, -ˌlənd\ *n* **1** : littoral land that is overflowed by the tide but exposed by low water **2** : land underlying the ocean, lying beyond the low tidemark, but being within a nation's territorial waters — often used in pl.

tideland spruce *n* : SITKA SPRUCE

tide·less \ˈtīdləs\ *adj* : having no tides ⟨a ~ sea⟩ — **tide·less·ness** *n* -ES

tide line *n* : TIDEMARK

tide lock *n* : a lock situated between an enclosed basin or a canal and the tidewater of a harbor or river when they are on different levels so that craft can pass either way at all times of the tide

tidemark \ˈ=ˌ=\ *n* **1** : a high-water or sometimes low-water mark left by tidal water or a flood ⟨between the ~*s*⟩; *also* : a mark placed to indicate this point **2** : the point to which something has attained or below which it has receded

tide mill *n* **1** : a mill operated by the tidal currents **2** : a mill for clearing lands from tidewater

tide over *vt* [²*tide*] **1** : to carry through or help along in the manner of a boat floated on a high tide ⟨food enough to *tide* us *over* until spring⟩ **2** : to provide money or supplies to ⟨willing to *tide over* his sister a little longer⟩

tide pool *n* : a pool left (as in a rock basin) by an ebbing tide — compare BEACH POOL

tide predictor *n* : a mechanical device for predicting the times of high and low tide

tide race *n* : a strong tidal current

tide rip *n* **1** : a rip due to opposing tides **2** : a swift tidal current

tide-rode \ˈ=ˌ=\ *adj* [¹*tide* + *rode*, chiefly dial. past part. of *ride*] : swung by the tide regardless of the wind when at anchor — opposed to *wind-rode*

tides *pl of* TIDE, *pres 3d sing of* TIDE

tides·man \ˈtīdzmən\ *n, pl* **tidesmen** : TIDEWAITER

tide staff *n* : a vertical graduated rod used as a tide gage

tidesurveyor \ˈ=(ˌ)=ˌ==\ *n* : an executive customs officer in charge of tidewaiters

tide table *n* : a table that indicates the height of the tide in a given harbor at different times of the day and night throughout one year

tide through *vt* [²*tide*] : to tide over (sense 1)

tidewaiter \ˈ=ˌ==\ *n* **1 a** : an officer in various preventive customs services who boards ships and watches the landing of goods **b** : any customs inspector working at dockside or aboard ships **2** : an English dock laborer who tows or warps ships in or out at full tide

tidewater \ˈ=ˌ==\ *n* **1** : water overflowing land at flood tide; *also* : water (as rivers and streams) affected by the ebb and flow of the tide **2** : land traversed by tidewater streams : low-lying coastal land ⟨the forests of ~ Virginia⟩

tidewater glacier *n* **:** a glacier that descends to the sea and usu. breaks off into icebergs
tide wave *n* **:** a rise and fall of water as the tide moves about the earth
tideway \ˈ=,=\ *n* **1 :** a channel in which the tide runs; *also* **:** a rush of tidal water through a channel or stream **2 :** a course or onrush suggestive of a tideway ⟨one of the remaining great ~*s* of urban retail business⟩
tide wheel *n* **:** a waterwheel operated by the tides
ti·di·ly \ˈtīdə̇lē, -li\ *adv* [ME, fr. *tidy* + *-ly*] **:** in a tidy manner **:** NEATLY
ti·di·ness \-dēnə̇s, -din-\ *n* -ES **:** the quality or state of being tidy
[1]**tid·ing** \ˈtīdiŋ, -dēŋ\ *n* -S [ME, fr. OE *tīdung*, fr. *tīdan* to happen + *-ung* -ing — more at TIDE] **1** *archaic* **:** EVENT, HAPPENING **2 :** an account of an event hitherto unknown or unreported **:** a piece of news **:** MESSAGE, NEWS, INTELLIGENCE — usu. used in pl. ⟨good ~*s*⟩
[2]**tid·ing** \ˈtīdiŋ, -dēŋ\ *n* -S [[1]*tide* + *-ing*] **:** a tidal flow or ebb; *also* **:** a progressing or drifting with the tide
tid·ley \ˈtid(ᵊ)li\ *n* -S [prob. fr. E dial. *tiddly* little — more at TIDDLY] *dial Eng* **:** WREN
ti·dol·o·gy \tīˈdäləjē, -ji\ *n* -ES [[1]*tide* + *-o-* + *-logy*] **:** the science or theory of tides
tids *pl of* TID
[1]**ti·dy** \ˈtīdē, -di\ *adj* -ER/-EST [ME, fr. *tyde, tide* time + *-y* — more at TIDE] **1 :** properly filled out **:** PLUMP, COMELY, HEALTHY ⟨a sleek, ~ beauty —*Current Biog.*⟩ **2 a** *obs* **:** DILIGENT, UPRIGHT, WORTHY, SKILLFUL **b :** adequately satisfactory **:** sufficiently good or pleasing to be acceptable **:** DECENT, FAIR ⟨a convenient and sufficiently ~ arrangement —*Times Lit. Supp.*⟩ ⟨got a ~ price for the property⟩ **c :** clever usu. to the point of being somewhat crafty **:** SHREWD ⟨hoped to play him some ~ little tricks —F.M.Ford⟩ **3** *obs* **:** occurring at a suitable time **:** TIMELY, SEASONABLE **4 a :** neat and orderly in appearance or habits **:** kept in good trim **:** well ordered and cared for ⟨a ~ person⟩ ⟨~ white houses⟩ **b :** maintaining neatness and order in things under one's charge ⟨a ~ housekeeper⟩ **c :** characterized by inherent neatness and order (as in formulation or function) **:** free from irregularity or slovenliness and often from any marked individuality **:** PRECISE ⟨a ~ handwriting⟩ ⟨~ thinking⟩ ⟨a ~ mind⟩ **5 :** not small in worth **:** comfortably large or valuable ⟨came into a ~ estate⟩ ⟨must have paid a ~ sum⟩ **syn** see NEAT
[2]**tidy** \"\ *vb* -ED/-ING/-ES *vt* **:** to put in proper order **:** make neat or tidy — often used with *up* ⟨~ up a room⟩ ~ *vi* **:** to make things tidy — usu. used with *up* ⟨~*ing* up after supper⟩
[3]**tidy** \"\ *n* -ES **:** any of various articles or devices intended to promote neatness or order: as **a :** a piece of fancywork used to protect the back, arms, or headrest of a chair or sofa from wear or soil **b :** a receptacle with pockets or compartments in which sewing materials, toilet articles, or odds and ends can be kept in order **c :** a perforated receptacle for draining small garbage at a sink

tidy c

[4]**tidy** \"\ *adv, chiefly dial* **:** TIDILY
tidytips \ˈ==,=\ *n pl but sing or pl in constr* **:** an annual California herb (*Layia platyglossa*) having yellow-rayed flower heads often tipped with white
[1]**tie** \ˈtī\ *n* -S [ME *teg, tey, tye*, fr. OE *tēag*; akin to ON *taug* rope, string, OE *tēon* to pull — more at TOW] **1 a :** something (as a line, chain, ribbon) in the form of a cord used for fastening, uniting, or drawing closed some material thing ⟨dainty pink ~*s* down the front of her robe⟩ ⟨ordered six cattle ~*s*⟩ ⟨the mouth of the sack was closed by a ~⟩: as (1) **:** SHOELACE (2) **:** [4]TYE (3) **:** STOP 4c(1) **b :** a structural element that serves to link other elements and usu. to reinforce the structure of which it is a part: as (1) **:** a beam, rod, or angle iron holding two pieces together **:** a tension member in a construction — compare STRUT (2) **:** one of the transverse supports to which railroad rails are fastened to keep them to line, gage, and grade and to cushion, distribute, and transmit the stresses of traffic through the ballast to the roadbed — called also *crosstie, sleeper* (3) **:** KEY 12a (4) **:** a fastening strip of leather, cord, or fabric attached to a book cover at its fore edge or to the open end of a portfolio (5) **:** a narrow strip left in the open part of a stencil to stiffen or hold together the design **2 :** something that serves as a connecting link usu. between discrete elements: as **a** (1) **:** a moral or legal obligation to someone or something typically constituting a restraining power, influence, or duty **:** a bond that constrains or restrains ⟨pledged by the ~*s* of common purpose⟩ ⟨unwilling to accept the ~*s* and responsibilities of family life⟩ (2) **:** a linking force that tends to unify **:** a shared and unifying relationship ⟨the ~*s* of race⟩ ⟨the strong ~ of community of interests⟩ ⟨there may or may not be a determinable ~ between race and language⟩ **b** (1) **:** a curved line that joins two musical notes indicating the same pitch and that is used to denote a single tone sustained through the time value of the two **:** BIND — compare SLUR 2a (2) **:** a connecting line in stroked notes **c** *Brit* **:** the obligation of a tied house to purchase its goods of a particular firm **d :** a connection between electric power systems by means of which each can interchange power with the other **3 a :** an equality in number (as of votes or scores) **b :** equality in a contest (as a race, election, or competition); *also* **:** a match or contest that ends in a draw **c** *Brit* **:** a deciding match played by those who tied in previous competition **d :** a match in a sports tournament in which the contestants are paired off two by two and the losers drop out until only one contestant is left as winner **4 :** a method or style of tying or knotting: as **a :** a method of connecting the harness cords in a jacquard loom to produce a desired pattern; *also* **:** the arrangement of cords thus produced **b :** an arrangement (as of loops or eyelets) for the lacing of a shoe **5 :** something that is knotted or is to be knotted when worn: as **a :** TIEWIG **b** *archaic* **:** a knot of hair **c :** NECKTIE **d :** a low laced shoe commonly without a tongue and with three or fewer pairs of eyelets — compare OXFORD **6 :** a depression over the spine near the middle of the back of developed cattle where the skin is bound down by connective tissue

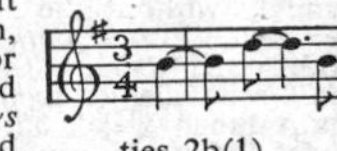

ties 2b(1)

[2]**tie** \"\ *vb* **tied** *or archaic* **tight; tied** *or archaic* **tight; tying** *or* **tieing; ties** [ME *tegen, teyen, tyen*, fr. OE *tiegan, tīgan*; akin to ON *teygja* to stretch out, draw; causative-denominative fr. the root of E [1]*tie*] *vt* **1 a :** to fasten, attach, bring together, close, or restrain by means of a tie (as a line, chain, ribbon) ⟨~ your horse to the tree⟩ ⟨her bonnet was *tied* on⟩ ⟨*tied* his bathrobe and went to the door⟩ ⟨vicious dogs should be *tied*⟩ ⟨~ off a bleeding artery⟩ ⟨~ a bundle⟩ **b** (1) **:** to form a knot or bow in (as a line) ⟨~ your scarf⟩ (2) **:** to form (as a knot) in the course of tying something ⟨wished she could ~ such a neat bow⟩ ⟨learned to ~ a square knot⟩ (3) **:** to make by tying constituent elements ⟨*tied* a daisy wreath⟩; *esp* **:** to make (artificial angling flies) by securing feathers, tinsel, and other parts to the shank of a fishhook **2 :** to bring together firmly as if tied by a rope **:** unite in some manner into a functional whole ⟨*tied* the addition into the older building⟩: as **a :** to unite in marriage **b :** to unite (as musical notes) by a tie **c :** to fix (a railroad track) in position with supporting ties; *also* **:** to provide (as a railroad line) with ties **d :** to join electrically (two power systems) in order that power may be interchanged **3 :** to restrain from independence or freedom of action or choice as if tied by a rope ⟨illness *tied* him to his bed⟩: as **a :** to constrain by or as if by authority, influence, agreement, or obligation ⟨*tied* to his job by a contract⟩ ⟨responsibilities that ~ one down⟩ **b** *obs* **:** to reduce to bondage **:** ENSLAVE **c :** to bind by gratitude for past favors **:** put under obligation **d** *obs* **:** to make (as a treaty) binding usu. by some formal act or attestation **4 a :** to make or have an equal score with in a contest or competition ⟨the home team *tied* the visitors⟩ **b :** to come up with something equal to or better than **:** EQUAL, BEAT ⟨can you ~ that⟩ **5 :** to cancel (a postage stamp) so that both cover and stamp receive a firm imprint giving the stamp added philatelic value on cover and making the cover proof against falsification as a philatelic item ⟨~ a stamp with a slogan cancellation⟩ ⟨a stamp *tied* to cover with a first-day cancellation⟩ ~ *vi* **1 :** to make a tie: as **a :** to make a bond or connection **b :** to make an equal score **:** EQUAL **c :** to pair one's vote **d :** ATTACH ⟨his answer ~*s* logically to the earlier discussion⟩ **e :** to close by means of a tie ⟨a wraparound that ~*s* at the waist⟩ **2 :** to stipulate in a loan contract between two countries that the borrowing country expend all or part of the loan on goods of the lending country — **tie a can to** *slang* **:** to get rid of — **tie by the leg :** to restrain as if by physical bonds **:** SHACKLE — **tie into 1 :** to attack with vigor ⟨*tied into* the job and was soon finished⟩: as **a** *slang* **:** to reprimand with severity ⟨the old lady really *tied into* me⟩ **b :** to consume voraciously ⟨*tied into* his dinner as if he hadn't eaten in a week⟩ **c :** to hit a pitched baseball hard ⟨*tied into* the ball for a home run⟩ **d :** to hit a baseball pitcher for a series of hits ⟨*tied into* him in the ninth for four runs⟩ **2 :** to get into one's possession **:** CATCH ⟨hoped to *tie into* a few good bass⟩ — **tie one on** *slang* **:** to get drunk — **tie one's hands :** to make one unable to act or to proceed in an action ⟨her secrecy *tied his hands*⟩ — **tie one's tongue :** to compel one to remain silent **:** constrain one to secrecy — **tie the knot :** to perform a marriage ceremony; *also* **:** to get married — **tie to :** to become associated with so as to depend on (as for protection or care) ⟨a man to *tie to*⟩
tie-and-dye \ˌ==ˈ=\ *also* **tie-dye** \ˈ=,=\ *n* **:** a hand method of textile printing characterized by tying portions of the fabric or yarn so that they will not absorb the dye — **tied-and-dyed** \ˌ==ˈ=\ *also* **tie-dyed** \ˈ=ˌ=\ *adj*
tieback \ˈ=,=\ *n* [fr. *tie back*, v.] **1 :** a decorative strip or device of cloth, cord, or metal for draping a curtain to the side of a window **2 :** a curtain with a tieback — usu. used in pl.

tieback 2

tie ball *n* **:** HELD BALL
tie bar *n* **1 :** a bar used as a tie rod **2 :** a rod between two railway switch rails to hold them to gage
tie beam *n* **:** a beam acting as a tie (as in a roof) — see ROOF illustration
tie breaker *n* **1 :** a circuit breaker placed on a tie line **2 :** a contest of exceptional difficulty used to select a winner from among contestants with tied scores in a previous contest
tie conductor *n* **:** a conductor used to join two power systems electrically
tied cottage *n, Brit* **:** a cottage maintained by an employer (as a farmer) for occupancy by an employee
tied house *n* **1** *Brit* **:** a business house that is under contract to buy of a particular firm; *esp* **:** a public house rented from or mortgaged to a brewery with or through whom the local proprietor is pledged to do all his liquor buying **2** *Brit* **:** TIED COTTAGE
tied image *n* **:** a memory image blended with and completing a sensory impression
tied island *n* **:** an island connected with the mainland by a tombolo
tied letters *n pl* **:** two or more characters constituting a ligature
tie-down \ˈ=,=\ *n* -S [fr. *tie down*, v.] **1 :** a fitting or a system of lines and fitting used to tie something (as an airplane, a horse's head, or a load of cargo) down in a desired position **2 :** the act of tying something down
tie dyeing *n* **:** TIE-AND-DYE
tie hack *n* **:** a faller and hewer of crossties
tie in *vt* **:** to bring into connection with something relevant **:** join in a unified whole ⟨*tie* a generating station *in* with a power system⟩: as **a :** to make the final connection of ⟨*tied in* the new branch pipeline⟩ **b :** to coordinate in such a manner as to produce balance and unity ⟨the illustrations were cleverly *tied in* with the text⟩ ⟨*tied in* his arguments to the previous discussion⟩ **c :** to use as a tie-in esp. in advertising ~ *vi* **1 :** to become tied in — usu. used with *with* or *to* **2 :** to join warp threads of one series to another **:** pull a new set of warp threads through the reed
[1]**tie-in** \ˈ=,=\ *n* -S [*tie in*] **:** something that ties in: as **a** (1) **:** an advertisement by a retail dealer that is placed near or coordinated with a related advertisement by a manufacturer (2) **:** an advertisement that is coordinated with some topical matter (as a specific holiday) (3) **:** an advertisement that fixes attention on an idea by presentation of two or more of its aspects (as by punning allusion) (4) **:** comment uniting in one advertisement two otherwise separate advertising items; *also* **:** similar comment in other than advertising writing **b :** the electrical joining of two power systems so that each can furnish power to the other **c :** an article or right to purchase that is only available under a tie-in arrangement **d :** an obscure or secret relation ⟨there is evidently some *tie-in* between delinquency and divorce⟩ ⟨suspected a *tie-in* between his assistant and the opposition⟩
[2]**tie-in** \ˈ=ˌ=\ *adj* [*tie in*] **:** allowed by a seller only on condition of attendant purchase of another product or fulfillment of an attendant agreement ⟨a *tie-in* sale⟩; *also* **:** involving the use of tie-in sales ⟨*tie-in* merchandising⟩
tieing *pres part of* TIE
tie line *n* **1 :** a string used for lining one end of track ties before laying rails when building a railroad track **2 :** a line measured on the ground to connect some object to a survey **3 :** a line connecting two power systems for interchange of power **4 :** a telephone line that directly connects two or more private branch exchanges **5 :** a straight horizontal line drawn on a phase diagram to join two points on curves giving the compositions of phases in equilibrium
tie·mann·ite \ˈtēmə,nīt\ *n* -S [G *tiemannit*, fr. W. *Tiemann*, 19th cent. Ger. scientist who discovered it + G *-it* -ite] **:** a mineral HgSe that is a native mercuric selenide and occurs commonly in dark gray or nearly black masses of metallic luster (sp. gr. 8.2–8.5)
tie mill *n* **:** a machine with four circular saws arranged to cut from a log two slabs, two boards, and a cant or a tie in a single operation
t'ien \ˈtēˌen, ˈtyen\ *n* -S *usu cap* [Chin (Pek) *t'ien*[1]] **1 :** the physical heaven **:** SKY **2 :** a controlling principle **:** DIVINITY
tiend \ˈtēnd\ *Brit var of* TEIND
tien·da \tēˈendə\ *n* -S [Sp, tent, awning, shop, fr. (assumed) VL *tenda*, alter. of L *tenta*, fem. of *tentus*, past part. of *tendere* to stretch — more at THIN] *chiefly Southwest* **:** a booth or shop where goods are sold **:** STORE
tien·ta \tēˈentə\ *n* -S [Sp, lit., test, probe, fr. *tentar* to touch, test, probe, fr. L *temptare, tentare* to touch, feel, attempt, tempt — more at TEMPT] **:** a test of the spirit and keenness of young bulls and heifers to determine their fitness for the ring or for breeding — called also *tentadero*
t'ien t'ai \ˈtēˈenˈtī, ˈtyenˈtī\ *n, usu cap 1st T & often cap 2d T* [Chin (Pek) *t'ien*[1] *t'ai*[2] — more at TENDAI] **:** a Chinese Buddhist sect founded in the 6th century A.D. that teaches a comprehensive doctrine of salvation for all based on sutras and the principle of the ultimate harmony of three levels of truth
tien·to \tēˈen(ˌ)tō\ *n* -S [Sp, lit., touch, fr. *tentar*] **:** a 16th century Spanish pipe-organ composition having strict imitative counterpoint and resembling the ricercar
tien·tsin \tēˈen(t)ˈsin, ˈtin(t)-\ *adj, usu cap* [fr. *Tientsin*, China] **:** of or from the city of Tientsin, China **:** of the kind or style prevalent in Tientsin
tientsin jute *n* **:** CHINGMA
tie off *vt* **1 :** to close by means of an encircling or enveloping tie ⟨*tie off* a bleeding vessel⟩ **2 :** to fasten (a fly line) to a pinrail in adjusting theatrical scenery
tie-on \ˈ=ˌ=\ *adj* [fr. *tie on*, v.] **:** fastened with ties or by tying on **:** designed to be used or worn tied on or over something else ⟨variations of a striped playsuit and a *tie-on* overskirt —*Women's Wear Daily*⟩
tie-out \ˈ=,=\ *n* -S [fr. *tie out*, v.] **1 :** a rope or cable anchorage **2 :** a batch of mail bundled and tied for dispatch to the post office that will deliver it
tiepin \ˈ=,=\ *n* **:** an ornamental straight pin often with a jeweled head and a sheath for the point that is used to hold the ends of a necktie in place
tie plate *n* **1 :** one of several narrow plates to space and strengthen deck beams of a ship — see SHIP illustration **2 :** a plate to distribute the pressure of a tie (as on a supporting beam) **3 :** a metal plate between a railroad rail and tie to assist in holding the rail to line and to protect the tie from mechanical wear
tie-plate \ˈ=,=\ *vt* [*tie plate*] **:** to furnish (as a railroad track) with tie plates
tie plug *n* **:** a small section of wood shaped like a spike and used for plugging a hole in a railroad tie left when a spike has been withdrawn
[1]**tier** \ˈti(ə)r, -iə\ *n* -S [MF *tire* order, rank, row — more at ATTIRE] **1 :** a row, rank, or layer of articles; *esp* **:** one of two or more rows arranged one above another ⟨~ upon ~ of huge casks⟩ ⟨built up neat ~*s* of firewood⟩ ⟨a window curtained with three ~*s* of ruffled net⟩ **2 a :** a row of guns or gun portholes (as in a warship or fort) **b** (1) **:** the ranges of the windings of a coiled cable; *also* **:** a layer of anchor chain (2) **:** the hollow space enclosed by a coil of cable (3) **:** CABLE TIER **c :** a row of moored or anchored ships **d :** a vertical layer of brickwork whose thickness is the width of a brick — called also *withe* **e** *Austral* **:** a mountain range **f :** a group of political or geographical divisions (as counties or states) that form a row across the map **g :** an antenna array consisting of rows of antenna elements placed one above another **3 a :** CLASS, CATEGORY ⟨the lowest ~ of society⟩ **b :** RANK 9

tiers 1 of window curtains

[2]**tier** \"\ *vb* -ED/-ING/-S *vt* **:** to place or arrange in tiers ~ *vi* **:** to rise in tiers ⟨cliffs ~*ing* along the margin of the valley⟩
[3]**ti·er** *also* **ty·er** \ˈtī(ə)r, -īə\ *n* -S [[2]*tie* + *-er*] **1 :** one that ties; *esp* **:** a worker that closes openings or binds articles by tying **2** *NewEng* **:** a child's pinafore fastened with ties
tier *abbr* tierce
tier·able \ˈtirəbəl\ *adj* [[2]*tier* + *-able*] **:** suitable for stacking ⟨~ goods⟩
[1]**tierce** *var of* TERCE
[2]**tierce** \ˈti(ə)rs\ *n* -S [ME *terce, tierce*, fr. MF, fr. fem. of *terz, ters, tiers*, adj., third, fr. L *tertius* — more at THIRD] **1** *obs* **:** THIRD 1 **2 a :** any of various units of liquid capacity equal to ⅓ pipe; *esp* **:** a unit equal to 42 wine gallons **b :** a cask of tierce capacity for wine or other commodities (as salted meat) **3 :** a sequence of three playing cards of the same suit **4 :** a fencing parry or guard position which defends the upper outside target and in which the hand is in a position of pronation at chest height and the tip of the blade is directed toward the opponent's eyes — compare SIXTE **5 a :** THIRD 4 **b :** the tone two octaves and a major third above a given tone **c :** an organ stop giving tones at this interval from the normal pitch of the digitals
[3]**tier·cé** \tirˈsā\ *adj* [F, fr. *tierce* third] **:** TIERCED
tierced \ˈti(ə)rst, ˈtiəst\ *adj* [F *tiercé* + E *-ed*] *heraldry* **:** divided into three parts of different tinctures or bearing different coats of arms — followed usu. by an indication of the direction of the direction of the lines of partition ⟨~ in bend⟩ ⟨~ in fess⟩ ⟨~ bendwise⟩
tierce de pic·ar·die \ˌtirsdəˈpikərdē\ *n, pl* **tierces de picardie** *usu cap P* [F] **:** PICARDY THIRD
tier·cel \ˈtirsəl\ *or* **ter·cel** \ˈtərs-\ *or* **tas·sel** \ˈtas-\ *n* -S [ME *tercel, tassel*, fr. MF *tercel, tiercel*, fr. (assumed) VL *tertiolus*, fr. dim. of L *tertius* third; perh. fr. the belief that every third egg in the nest produced a male — more at THIRD] **:** a male of various hawks (as the peregrine falcon and the goshawk)
tier·ce·ron \ˈtirsərən\ *n* -S [F, fr. MF, fr. *tierce* third] **:** one of the minor or intermediate ribs in Gothic vaulting that spring from the pier on each side of the main diagonal rib and therefore do not pass through the center of the vault
tiercet *var of* TERCET
tiered \ˈti(ə)rd, -iəd\ *adj* [[1]*tier* + *-ed*] **:** having or arranged in tiers, rows, or layers — used chiefly in combination ⟨triple-*tiered*⟩
tier·er \ˈtirə(r)\ *n* -S **:** one that tiers; *specif* **:** one of the sailors stationed in the cable tier of a ship to stow the chain or cable as it comes in
tier-in \ˌtiˌrin\ *n, pl* **tiers-in** [*tie in*, v. + *-er*] **:** a textile worker who ties in new warp threads
tiering *pres part of* TIER
tie rod *n* **1 :** a rod used as a connecting member or brace **:** TIE BAR — see BUCKSTAY illustration **2 :** a rod in the steering system of an automotive vehicle connecting one of the arms of each steering knuckle to the corresponding arm of the other
tier pole *n* **:** a horizontal pole in a tobacco barn on which the tobacco sticks are hung
tier·ra ca·lien·te \tēˌerəˌkalēˈentē\ *n, pl* **tierras calientes** [Sp, lit., hot land] **:** a region or zone of hot climate; *esp* **:** low-lying tropical land usu. below 2000 feet with continuous hot weather
tierra fria \=,==ˈfrēə\ *n, pl* **tierras frí·as** [Sp, lit., cold land] **:** a region or zone of cold climate; *esp* **:** tropical land of usu. above 6000 foot elevation in which the temperature is sharply modified by the elevation
tier ranger *n, Brit* **:** a waterfront thief
tier·ras \tēˈerəz\ *n pl* [Sp, pl. of *tierra* earth, land, fr. L *terra* — more at TERRACE] **:** fine material of earth or rock mixed with quicksilver ore
tierra tem·pla·da \-temˈplädə\ *n, pl* **tierras templadas** [Sp, lit., temperate land] **:** a region or zone of temperate climate; *esp* **:** tropical land of usu. from 2000 to 6000 foot elevation in which the temperature is modified by the elevation
tiers *pl of* TIER, *pres 3d sing of* TIER
tiers-argent \tēˌerˌzärˈzhäⁿ\ *n* [F, fr. *tiers* third + *argent* silver — more at TIERCE, ARGENT] **:** a silver alloy containing approximately one third of its weight of silver usu. alloyed with aluminum or German silver
tier shot *n* **:** grapeshot having the shot arranged in regular tiers separated by plates
tiers·man \ˈti(ə)rzmən, ˈtiəz-\ *n, pl* **tiersmen 1 :** one who arranges articles (as casks) in tiers **2** *Austral* **:** MOUNTAINEER
tier table *n* **:** a small table or stand with two or more usu. round tops arranged one above another
ties *pl of* TIE, *pres 3d sing of* TIE
ti-es \(ˈ)tēˌes\ *n* [Haitian Creole] **:** CANISTEL
-ties *pl of* -TY
tie scoring machine *n* **:** a portable power-operated machine provided with two circular saws designed to saw the face of railroad track ties to uniform width and depth as a guide for hand adz work to provide a proper bearing for rail or tie plates in relay track work
tie silk *n* **:** a usu. twilled silk fabric of firm resilient pliable texture and in solid color or with typically small stylized and bright design that is suitable for neckties and much used for blouses and accessories; *also* **:** a similar fabric of a material other than silk
tie tack *n* **:** an ornamented pin whose point holds a necktie to a shirt and fits into a receiving button or snap underneath
tie·tick \ˈtētə̇k\ *n* -S [imit.] *dial Brit* **:** MEADOW PIPIT; *also* **:** ROCK PIPIT
tie-tie \ˈ=,=\ *n* **:** one of several cords on a nautical hammock by which it may be tied in a roll; *broadly* **:** any of various lines or cords
tie up *vt* **1 :** to fasten or restrain with or as if with a tie **2 :** to cause to be in a hindered, impaired, or inoperative condition ⟨all week long . . . filibustering and Communist clamoring *tied up* the assembly —*Time*⟩ ⟨a strike that would *tie up* the port —C.P.Curtis⟩ **3 a :** to put in such a place or invest in such a manner as to make unavailable for other purposes ⟨*tie* your money *up* in stocks⟩ **b :** to subject (property) to such restrictions or bring into such condition that alienation or sale is impossible ⟨the will *tied up* the estate⟩ **4 :** to connect closely **:** LINK ⟨a striking window display *tied up* with an autographing party —*Publishers' Weekly*⟩ **5 a :** to keep busy **:** PREOCCUPY ⟨*tied up* in conference all day⟩ **b :** to preempt the use of ⟨*tied up* the phone for an hour⟩ ~ *vi* **1 a :** to make a boat secure ⟨we *tied up* . . . twenty-six hours after leaving —W.O.Douglas⟩ **b :** DOCK ⟨warships . . . *tie up* together —*N. Y. Herald Tribune*⟩ **2 a :** to establish a close relationship ⟨Christian counsels . . . *tie up* integrally with the civil law —Mary W. Hess⟩ **b :** to enter into a partnership ⟨*tie up* with other advertisers⟩

tie-up \'ˌ(ˌ)ˌ\ *n* -s [*tie up*] **1 :** something that is tied up or used in tying up: as **a** *obs* **:** TIEWIG **b :** TIE 4a **c :** a mooring place for a boat **d :** a cow stable esp. when forming an extension of a larger barn; *also* **:** a space for a single cow in a stable **2 :** the act or fact of tying up or the state of being tied up: as **a** (1) **:** a suspension of traffic or business (as by a strike or lockout of employees or a breakdown of machinery) (2) **:** enforced idleness of a train crew because of a rule or statutory provision on the maximum number of hours' work **b :** the tying up of harnesses in a plain or dobby loom **c :** a linking association **:** CONNECTION ⟨the close brain-eye *tie-up* —Weston La Barre⟩ ⟨political *tie-up* with gangsters⟩

tievine \'ˌˌ\ *n* **:** any of several bindweeds

tiewig \'ˌˌ\ *n* **:** a wig having the back hair tied with ribbon

¹tiff *vt* -ED/-ING/-S [ME *tiffen*, fr. OF *tifer, tiffer*] *obs* **:** to deck out **:** DRESS

²tiff \'tif\ *n* -s [origin unknown] **1** *archaic* **:** alcoholic liquor esp. when weak **:** small beer **2** *archaic* **:** a small draft of liquor (as punch)

³tiff \"\ *n* -s [origin unknown] **:** a slight fit of anger **:** an outburst of temper or spite **:** a petty quarrel ⟨in tizzies over ~*s* with boyfriends —Stanley Frank⟩ **syn** see QUARREL

⁴tiff \"\ *vi* **:** to be in a tiff or pet **:** quarrel in a small way **:** be peevish — usu. used with *with* ⟨~*ed* with friends and foes alike⟩

⁵tiff \"\ *vi* [back-formation fr. *tiffin*] *India* **:** to take tiffin **:** LUNCH

⁶tiff \"\ *n* [origin unknown] *chiefly Midland* **:** BARITE

¹tif·fa·ny \'tifənē, -ni\ *n* -ES [prob. fr. obs. F *tiphanie* Epiphany, fr. LL *theophania* — more at THEOPHANY] **1 :** any of several very thin transparent textiles: as **a :** a sheer silk gauze formerly used for clothing and trimmings **b :** a plain-weave open-mesh cotton fabric (as cheesecloth) **2 :** an article (as a sieve) made of tiffany

²tiffany \"\ *adj* **:** DELICATE, FILMY, FRAGILE ⟨a *tiffany*-winged fly⟩

³tiffany \"\ *adj, usu cap* [after Charles L. *Tiffany* †1902 Am. jeweler] *of a jewelry setting* **:** having long prongs to hold a gem

⁴tiffany \"\ *adj, usu cap* [after Louis C. *Tiffany* †1933 Am. artist] **:** exhibiting or characterized by irregular areas of translucent blended color due to the use of a glazing liquid over a suitably painted surface (as of a wall) ⟨a *Tiffany* effect⟩ ⟨the popularity of *Tiffany* finishes⟩ — compare SCUMBLE

tiffany glass *n, usu cap T* [after L. C. *Tiffany*] **:** American glassware made in the late 19th and early 20th century and often characterized by an iridescent surface

¹tif·fin \'tifən\ *n* -s [prob. alter. of *tiffing*, gerund of obs. *tiff* to drink, eat between meals, fr. ²*tiff*] **1 :** a midday meal **:** LUNCHEON **2 :** a moderate yellowish brown that is very slightly redder and deeper than mummy, redder and very slightly darker than Bismarck brown, and darker and slightly redder than maple sugar — called also *condor*

²tiffin \"\ *vi* -ED/-ING/-S **:** to take tiffin **:** LUNCH

ti·fi·nagh \tə'fēˌnäg\ *also* **ti·fi·nar** \-är\ *adj* [Tuareg *tifinagh* writing, writings] **:** of, relating to, or constituting a Libyan alphabet that is apparently descended from the Old Libyan or Numidian characters derived from the Punic cursive script and is still used by the Tuaregs

ti·flis \'tifləs *sometimes* tə'flēs\ *adj, usu cap* [fr. *Tiflis*, U.S.S.R.] **:** of or from the city of Tiflis, U.S.S.R. **:** of the kind or style prevalent in Tiflis

¹tift \'tift\ *vt* -ED/-ING/-S [ME *tiften*, perh. fr. *tift*, past part. of *tiffen* to tiff (deck out) — more at TIFF] *chiefly dial* **:** to put in order **:** make ready or array properly **:** ARRANGE

²tift \"\ *n* -s *chiefly Scot* **:** a particular state, condition, or mood

³tift \"\ *chiefly dial var of* TIFF

⁴tift \"\ *n* -s [prob. of imit. origin] *chiefly Scot* **:** a puff or gust of wind

¹tig \'tig\ *vb* **tigged; tigged; tigging; tigs** [ME *tiggen*] *vi* **1** *chiefly Scot* **a :** to poke or pat one in a playful manner **b :** to have dealings **:** MEDDLE, TAMPER — used with *with* **2** *dial* **:** ANNOY, TEASE, PESTER **~** *vi* **1 :** ⁴TAG **2** *Austral* **:** to touch for a loan

²tig \"\ *n* -s **1** *chiefly Scot* **:** a noticeable but not violent touch **:** PAT, POKE **2 :** the game of tag

tige \'tēzh\ *n* -s [F, stem, shaft, rod, pin, fr. L *tibia* shinbone, pipe, flute — more at SIPHON] **:** a steel pin in the breech of an early rifle against which the ball is hammered by the ramrod and expanded to fit the grooves

ti·gel·la \tə'jelə\ *or* **ti·gelle** \-'jel\ *n* -s [*tigella*, NL, fr. F *tigelle*; *tigelle* fr. F, dim. of *tige* stem, stalk] **:** a short or rudimentary stem; *specif* **:** the hypocotyl sometimes together with the plumule — **ti·gel·late** \-lət\ *adj*

ti·ger \'tīgə(r)\ *n, pl* **tigers** *also* **tiger** [ME *tigre*, fr. OE *tiger* & OF *tigre*, both fr. L *tigris*, fr. Gk, of Iranian origin; akin to Av *tighri-* arrow, *tighra-* pointed; akin to Skt *tejate* it is sharp — more at STICK] **1 a :** a large Asiatic carnivorous mammal (*Felis tigris*) having a tawny coat transversely striped with black, a long untufted tail that is ringed with black, underparts that are mostly white, and no mane, being typically slightly larger than the lion with a total length usu. of 9 to 10 feet but sometimes of more than 12 feet, living usu. on the ground, feeding mostly on larger mammals (as cattle), in some cases including man, and ranging from Persia across Asia to the Malay peninsula, Sumatra, and Java and northward to southern Siberia and Manchuria — compare BENGAL TIGER, SABER-TOOTHED TIGER **b :** any of several large felid mammals: as (1) *Africa* **:** LEOPARD (2) **:** JAGUAR (3) **:** COUGAR **c :** a domestic cat with a striped pattern **:** TIGER CAT **d** *Austral* **:** TASMANIAN WOLF **e :** TIGER SNAKE **f :** any of several strong vigorous aggressive fishes: as (1) **:** TIGER SHARK (2) *Africa* **:** a large grunt (*Pomadasys operculare*) of the Indian ocean that is highly esteemed as a sport and food fish (3) **:** a fish that is a hybrid between the muskellunge and pike **2 a :** a representation of a tiger usu. as a symbol or badge (as of an organization) **b** *often cap* **:** any of several organizations having a tiger as recognized emblem; *also* **:** a member of such an organization **3 a :** a person or sometimes an animal of fierce and bloodthirsty ways **b :** fierce tigerish quality or aspect ⟨aroused the ~ in his nature⟩ **c :** a person vigorously aggressive and usu. highly skilled in some activity (as a sport or military combat) **4** *Brit* **a :** a groom in livery; *esp* **:** a young or small groom who rides usu. standing on a platform at the rear of a vehicle (as a dogcart) driven by the person on whom he is in attendance **b :** a dissolute or vulgar fellow **:** SWAGGERER, BULLY, RAKE **5 a** (1) **:** BIG CAT (2) **:** LITTLE CAT **b** (1) **:** FARO (2) **:** FARO BANK **6 :** a loud cry often of the word *tiger* that terminates a round of enthusiastic cheering (as at a political or sports rally) **7** *slang* **:** BLIND TIGER

tiger

tiger barb *n* **:** a small vigorous eastern Asian barb (*Barbus sumatranus* or *B. tetragona*) sometimes kept in the tropical aquarium

tiger bass *n* **:** SMALLMOUTH BLACK BASS

tiger beetle *n* **:** any of numerous active rapid-flying carnivorous beetles constituting the family Cicindelidae and having larvae that live in tunnels in the soil

tiger bittern *n* **:** any of several So. and Central American herons of the genus *Tigrisoma* having plumage with much buff or chestnut vermiculated with black

tiger butterfly *n* **:** TIGER SWALLOWTAIL

tiger cat *n* **1 a :** any of various wildcats of moderate size and variegated coloration: as (1) **:** CLOUDED LEOPARD (2) **:** MARBLED CAT (3) **:** SERVAL (4) **:** OCELOT (5) **:** MARGAY **b** *Austral* **:** NATIVE CAT; *esp* **:** a large native cat (*Dasyurus maculatus*) with a white-spotted tail that is now largely restricted to Tasmania **2 :** a domestic cat with markings suggesting those of a tiger **:** a striped or sometimes blotched tabby cat

tiger cocoa *n* **:** PATASHTE

tiger cowry *n* **:** a large abundant cowry (*Cypraea tigris*) having a shell mottled and blotched with brown on an ivory or pale brown ground or sometimes with green on a paler green ground

ti·gered \'tīgə(r)d\ *adj* **:** striped or blotched usu. with a darker color

tigereye \'ˌˌˌ\ *n* -s **1** *also* **tiger's-eye** \'ˌˌˌ\ *pl* **tiger's-eyes :** a usu. yellow-brown chatoyant stone that is much used for ornament and is a silicified crocidolite in which the fibers embedded in quartz are changed to oxide of iron — compare HAWK'S-EYE **2 :** a ceramic glaze resembling in appearance the tigereye

tiger finch *n* **:** AVADAVAT

tiger fish *n* **:** any of various fishes that suggest a tiger usu. either in being extremely voracious or in being marked with black: as **a :** any of several vigorous predaceous freshwater sport fishes (genus *Hydrocyon*) widely distributed in African rivers **b :** CARIBE **c** *Africa* **:** a black-striped Indo-Pacific sea perch (*Therapon jarbua*)

tiger flathead *n* **:** a large vigorous flathead (*Neoplatycephalus macrodon*) of deep waters off the eastern coast of Australia that is an important market fish and is usu. taken by trawling

tigerflower \'ˌˌˌ\ *n* **:** a plant or flower of the genus *Tigridia*

tiger frog *n* **1 :** LEOPARD FROG **2 :** a large frog (*Rama tigrina*) of India and Malaysia

tiger heart *n* **:** a heart on the inside of which stripes of yellowish or white myocardium caused by fatty degeneration alternate with stripes of normal color so that tiger skin is simulated

ti·ger·ish \'tīg(ə)rish, -rēsh\ *adj* **:** of or relating to tigers **:** resembling a tiger usu. in sleek grace, voracity, ferocity, or vigorous intensity of action ⟨~ grace⟩ ⟨a ~ appetite⟩ ⟨a ~ fury⟩ ⟨worked with ~ concentration⟩ — **ti·ger·ish·ly** *adv* — **ti·ger·ish·ness** *n* -ES

ti·ger·ism \-gəˌrizəm\ *n* -s *archaic* **:** showy ostentation **:** SWAGGER

ti·ger·kin \'tīgə(r)kən\ *n* -s **:** a little tiger

tigerlike \'ˌˌˌ\ *adj* **:** having the ways or appearance of a tiger **:** resembling that of a tiger ⟨a ~ grace⟩

tiger lily *n* **1 a :** a common Asiatic garden lily (*Lilium tigrinum*) having nodding orange-colored flowers densely spotted with black and the perianth segment strongly reflexed **b :** any of various lilies (as *L. pardalinum* and *L. philadelphicum*) having similar spotted flowers **2** *usu* **tigerlily a :** a moderate to strong reddish orange that is redder and lighter than chrome scarlet **b :** a deep yellowish pink of a textile that is redder and deeper than candy pink

ti·ger·ling \'tīgə(r)liŋ, -lēŋ\ *n* -s **:** a little tiger

ti·ger·ly *adj* **:** TIGERISH, TIGERLIKE

tiger maple *n* **:** maple lumber with a distinct irregularly striped pattern resembling but bolder than curly maple

tiger mosquito *n* **:** YELLOW-FEVER MOSQUITO

tiger moth *n* **:** any of various stout-bodied long-winged moths (family Arctiidae) that are usu. of moderate size with bright or richly colored wings often intricately patterned and with larvae that are hairy caterpillars — compare WOOLLY BEAR

tigernut \'ˌˌ(ˌ)ˌ\ *n* **:** CHUFA

tiger pear *n* **:** a much-branched very spiny prickly pear (*Opuntia aurantiaca*) that is a troublesome weed esp. in Australia

tiger python *n* **:** INDIAN PYTHON

tiger rattlesnake *n* **:** a rather small yellow or tawny rattlesnake (*Crotalus tigris*) that is narrowly striped with black and occurs in mountainous deserts of western No. America

tiger salamander *n* **:** a widely distributed No. American salamander (*Ambystoma tigrinum*) that is brown or black above with vertical yellowish lateral blotches often running together ventrally

tiger's-claw \'ˌˌˌ\ *n, pl* **tiger's-claws :** a boring rod or rifling rod in which the tool is sheathed on entering the bore and is automatically thrust outward on the cutting stroke

tiger's-eye \'ˌˌˌ\ *var of* TIGEREYE

tiger shark *n* **:** a large very voracious gray or brown stocky-bodied shark that is often a man-eater, is nearly cosmopolitan esp. in warm seas, and is commonly held to constitute a single species (*Galeocerdo arcticus* or *G. cuvieri*) but is sometimes separated into two or more species

tiger shell *n* **:** TIGER COWRY

tiger's-jaw \'ˌˌˌ\ *n, pl* **tiger's-jaws :** a southern African fig marigold (*Faucaria tigrinum* syn. *Mesembryanthemum tigrinum*) having long ciliate teeth on the upturned leaf margins — compare CAT-CHOP

tiger's-mouth \'ˌˌˌ\ *n, pl* **tiger's-mouths :** any of several plants of the family Scrophulariaceae (as the foxglove, snapdragon, and toadflax)

tiger snake *n* **1 :** a widely distributed extremely venomous elapid snake (*Notechis scutatus*) of Australia and Tasmania that is predominantly brown with dark crossbars **2 :** an African boigid snake (*Tarbophis semiannulatus*)

tiger's-tail spruce \'ˌˌˌ-\ *or* **tigertail spruce** \'ˌˌˌ-\ *n* **:** a Japanese evergreen tree (*Picea polita*) that has rigid spiny leaves and is often cultivated for ornament

tiger swallowtail *n* **:** a widely distributed swallowtail butterfly (*Papilio glaucus*) of eastern No. America

tigerware \'ˌˌˌ\ *n* **:** stoneware characterized by a mottled glaze somewhat resembling the coat of a tiger and orig. produced in the Rhine valley

tiger weasel *n* **:** any of several heavily built Old World weasels closely related to the polecats but usu. held to comprise a separate genus (*Vormela*)

tiger wolf *n* **1 :** SPOTTED HYENA **2 :** TASMANIAN WOLF

tigerwood \'ˌˌˌ\ *n* **:** any of several showy striped or black-marked woods used in cabinetwork; *esp* **:** AFRICAN WALNUT

tigged *past of* TIG

tigging *pres part of* TIG

¹tight \'tīt, *usu* -īd·+V\ *adj* -ER/-EST [ME, alter. of *thight*, of Scand origin; akin to ON *thēttr* tight, close; akin to OE *metethīht* thick with food, MLG & MHG *dihte* close, thick, Goth *theihan* to increase, progress, MIr *tēcht* coagulated, Skt *tanakti* it causes to coagulate; basic meaning: thick, thicken] **1 :** of firm compact texture **:** DENSE, SOLID **2 :** so close in structure as not to permit passage of a liquid or gas **:** not slack or leaky **:** firm or solid in condition ⟨a ~ roof⟩: as **a :** proof or proofed against the entry or exit of something expressed or implied ⟨the ship was sound and ~⟩ ⟨a ~ cask⟩ — usu. used in combination (*gas*tight fitting) ⟨an *air*tight cover⟩ **b** (1) **:** impervious to moisture **:** WATERTIGHT (2) **:** not giving free passage to water ⟨~ clay soils are often wet and sour⟩ **c :** WET 11 **d :** impervious to the activity or effect of ⟨a hog-*tight* fence⟩ **3 a :** fixed firmly or securely in place so as to be difficult to move ⟨loosen a ~ jar cover⟩ ⟨a ~ sticking door⟩ ⟨the roots are very long and ~⟩ **b :** FAITHFUL, CONSTANT **4 :** not slack or loose: as **a :** firmly stretched, drawn, or set **:** TAUT ⟨a ~ drumhead⟩ ⟨the rope was ~ and firm⟩ **b :** fitting closely and usu. too closely (as for comfort or good taste) ⟨a ~ dress⟩ ⟨a painfully ~ shoe⟩ **c** *of the respiratory passages* **:** congested, constricted, or sometimes dehydrated so as to be partially occluded ⟨her throat was ~ with fear⟩ ⟨the ~ clogged nose of a bad head cold⟩ **d :** having the participants in close touch with one another ⟨a ~ formation in football⟩ **e :** excessively precise without breadth of treatment ⟨a work of art that is unduly harsh and ~ in treatment⟩ **5** *chiefly dial* **a :** marked by energetic competence **:** CAPABLE, ALERT, READY **b :** marked by shapely graceful form **:** COMELY **c** (1) **:** trim and tidy in dress (2) **:** neat and orderly in arrangement or design **:** SNUG **6 :** difficult to get through or out of or not readily coped with or circumvented **:** TRYING, EXACTING ⟨in a ~ corner for money⟩ ⟨a good man in a ~ situation⟩: as **a :** firm in control **:** designed to master and maintain order ⟨kept a ~ hand on all his affairs⟩ **b :** unwilling to part with money or other possessions **:** MISERLY; *often* **:** difficult to do business with because of this tendency ⟨perfectly honest but ~ in all his dealings⟩ **c :** evenly contested **:** CLOSE ⟨a ~ tennis match⟩ ⟨~ play in a game⟩ **7 :** packed or compressed to the limit **:** entirely full ⟨a ~ bale⟩: as **a :** full of liquor **:** INTOXICATED, DRUNKEN **b** *of language* **:** highly condensed and often to the point of loss of fluency ⟨a ~ literary style⟩ **c** *of printed matter* (1) **:** closely spaced ⟨a ~ line⟩ (2) **:** so full as to make insertion of additional matter difficult ⟨a ~ page⟩ (3) *of a line* **:** set to full measure and safe to lift **d :** having little space available for news usu. because of large volume of advertising to be accommodated ⟨a ~ edition of a newspaper⟩ **e :** FULL 12a **8 a :** scantily supplied or obtainable in proportion to demand **:** available only in inadequate amounts to meet existent needs ⟨~ money is delaying construction⟩ ⟨steel is very ~ just now⟩ — compare EASY 2f(2) **b :** characterized by such a scarcity ⟨a ~ labor market⟩ **9** *of lumber* **:** sound in every way and free from ring shakes and checks ⟨logs with ~ hearts⟩

syn TAUT, TENSE: TIGHT is likely to describe a snug binding together, a close drawing together of all parts, a confining constriction, or a cornering or squeezing together ⟨a *tight* coat⟩ ⟨forming *tight* ranks⟩ ⟨a *tight* roof⟩ ⟨shoelaces that were too *tight*⟩ ⟨in a *tight* position⟩ TAUT applies to what has been stretched or drawn out to the limit; in reference to persons TAUT may describe the effects of strain making a drain on nervous energy ⟨pulling the ropes *taut*⟩ ⟨her sails are loose, her tackles hanging, waiting men to seize and haul them *taut* —Amy Lowell⟩ ⟨their look of horror as they stared up at me, eyes and mouths open and faces *taut* —Norman Cousins⟩ TENSE calls attention strongly to a keyed-up, intent condition or to tension and strain ⟨signalman, *tense* and alert, awaited the word to flash out orders by blinker —Alexander Forbes⟩ ⟨yet she was, as always after a concert, *tense* and nervous, filled with a terrible energy which would not let her sleep until dawn —Louis Bromfield⟩ ⟨he is *tense*, jittery — a mass of jangled nerves — his fingers tremble as he lights one cigarette after another —S.N.Behrman⟩ **syn** see in addition DRUNK, STINGY

²tight \"\ *vt* -ED/-ING/-S **1** *obs* **:** to make tight and esp. watertight **2** *chiefly dial* **:** to put in order **:** TIDY — used with *up*

³tight \"\ *adv* -ER/-EST **1 :** TIGHTLY, FIRMLY, HARD ⟨holding ~ to the rail⟩ ⟨the door was shut ~⟩ **2** *chiefly dial* **:** SOUNDLY, VIGOROUSLY, THOROUGHLY ⟨fell ~ asleep⟩

⁴tight \"\ *n* -s **:** something that is tight: as **a** *slang* **:** a difficult or trying situation **:** a tight place ⟨pulled him out of a ~ —F. B.Gipson⟩ **b :** close forward play in rugby — often used with *the;* contrasted with *loose* ⟨packs which could hold their own with any, whether in the ~ or loose —O.L.Owen⟩ **c** (1) **:** a radio or television program that is barely held within time limits (2) **:** a television close shot made with a narrow angle lens

⁵tight *archaic past of* TIE

tight backbone *or* **tight back** *n* **:** a book backbone adhered solidly to the cover — compare HOLLOW BACK; see SPINE illustration

tight-cut *adj* **:** having little or no evident checking — used esp. of thin-cut veneer

tight·en \'tītᵊn\ *vb* **tightened; tightened; tightening** \-t(ᵊ)niŋ\ **tightens** ['*tight* + *-en*] *vt* **:** to make tight or tighter ⟨~ a belt⟩ ⟨~ economic controls⟩ ⟨~*s* his hand on a steering wheel⟩ — often used with *up* ⟨~ up a bolt⟩ **~** *vi* **:** to become tight or tighter ⟨money ~*ed* after the war⟩ ⟨the drying rawhide ~*ing* in the sun⟩: as **a :** to become tense ⟨muscles ~*ing* with fatigue⟩ **b :** to become more complete or adequate **:** IMPROVE ⟨controls gradually ~*ed*⟩ ⟨his act ~*ed* considerably⟩ — **tighten one's belt :** to practice rigid economy

tight·en·er \-t(ᵊ)nə(r)\ *n* -s **:** one that tightens; *often* **:** an idle pulley or a sprocket wheel pressed against a belt, band, rope, or chain to tighten it — called also *tightening pulley*

tighter *comparative of* TIGHT

tightest *superlative of* TIGHT

tightfisted \'ˌˌˌ\ *adj* **:** reluctant to part with money **:** wary about expenditures ⟨must be eagle-eyed and ~ about these expenditures —A.E.Stevenson †1965⟩ **syn** see STINGY

tight·ish \'tīd·|ish, 'tīt|, |ēsh\ *adj* ['*tight* + *-ish*] **1 :** somewhat tight **:** CLOSE-FITTING ⟨~ long sleeves pushed back over the wrist —D.C.Calthrop⟩ **2 :** somewhat difficult

tight joint *n* **:** a book joint against which the cover board is set snugly without the space or depression of the open joint — called also *smooth joint*

tight-knit \'ˌ'ˌ\ *adj* **:** closely and firmly integrated ⟨a *tight-knit* schedule⟩ ⟨a *tight-knit* organization⟩

tight-laced \'ˌ'ˌ\ *adj* **:** STRAITLACED

tight-leg *vi* **:** to grip a horse firmly with the legs without using the spurs in riding

tightlining \'ˌˌˌ\ *n* **:** a method of high-line logging in which the logs are lifted over obstructions by tightening on the haul-back

tight-lipped \'ˌ'ˌ\ *adj* **1 :** having the lips and mouth closed tight through determination or suppression of emotion ⟨*tight-lipped* throughout her ordeal⟩ **2 :** marked by accustomed or determined cautious reticence in speech **:** UNCOMMUNICATIVE ⟨*tight-lipped* friends keeping the matter secret⟩ **syn** see SILENT

tightlock \'ˌ'ˌ\ *adj* **:** of, relating to, or being a coupling device for cushioning the impact between railroad cars at starts or stops by taking up the slack

tight lock *n* **:** a disease of cotton caused by any of several fungi (esp. of the genus *Diplodia*) and characterized by failure of the affected locks to fluff and by discoloration and weakening of the fibers — **tight-locked** \'ˌ'ˌ\ *adj*

tight·ly *adv* **:** in a tight manner or state **:** so as to be tight

tight-mouthed \'ˌ'ˌ\ *adj* **:** CLOSEMOUTHED

tight·ness *n* -ES **:** the quality or state of being tight

¹tightrope \'ˌ'ˌ\ *n, often attrib* ['*tight* + *rope*] **1 :** a rope or wire stretched taut on which acrobats perform — compare HIGH WIRE, SLACK ROPE **2 :** a hazardous situation

²tightrope \"\ *vt* **:** to walk on or along as if on a tightrope ⟨*tightroped* the foundation and jumped clear of the gooseberry bushes —Wallace Stegner⟩ **~** *vi* **1 :** to walk, dance, or perform acrobatics on a tightrope **2 :** to move or progress as if on a tightrope

tights \'tīts\ *n pl* ['*tight* + *-s*] **1 :** close-fitting breeches usu. for men's formal wear (as in court dress) **2 :** skintight garments covering the body from the neck down or from the waist down and worn esp. for ease and display by dancers, acrobats, or gymnasts — compare LEOTARD

tight sap *n* **:** sapwood having close pores

tight scrummage *n* **:** a close formation of the forwards of each team in rugby

tight ship *n* **:** a ship with crew and officers working well together

tight side *n* **:** the concave face of a sheet of veneer — compare LOOSE SIDE

tight squeeze *n* **:** a passage or difficult situation that one barely manages to get through

tightwad \'ˌˌ\ *n* **:** a person who spends, lends, or gives away money grudgingly or not at all **:** a close or miserly person

tightwire \'ˌˌ\ *n* **:** a tightrope made of wire

tig·lal·de·hyde \tiˈglaldəˌhīd\ *n* [ISV *tiglic* + *aldehyde*] **:** a liquid compound C_4H_7CHO that has the odor of bitter almonds and is obtained by distilling guaiacum resin; α-methylcrotonaldehyde

tig·lic acid \'tiglik-\ *n* [ISV *tigl-* (fr. NL *tiglium*, specific epithet of *Croton tiglium*, fr. ML or NL, seed from a species of croton) + *-ic*] **:** a vesicant crystalline unsaturated acid $CH_3CH{=}C(CH_3)COOH$ that has a spicy odor, that is the stable stereoisomer of angelic acid and that occurs in the form of esters esp. in Roman chamomile oil and in croton oil; *trans-a*-methyl-crotonic acid

tiglic aldehyde *n* **:** TIGLALDEHYDE

ti·glon \'tīglən\ *n* -s [*tiger* + *lion*] **:** TIGON

ti·gnon \(')tēˌyōn\ *n* -s [LaF, fr. F, nape of the neck, chignon, fr. F dial. *tigne* moth, scalp disease, fr. L *tinea* moth, worm] **:** a madras handkerchief used esp. in Louisiana as a headdress

tig·num \'tignəm\ *n* -s [L, building material, beam — more at STAKE] **:** building material

ti·gog·e·nin \tə'gäjənən, tī'g-, -ˌnēn; ˌtīgə'jenən, ˌtig-\ *n* -s [blend of *tigonin* and *-gen*] **:** a crystalline steroid sapogenin $C_{27}H_{44}O_3$ obtained esp. by hydrolysis of tigonin

ti·gon \'tīgən\ *n* -s [*tiger* + *lion*] **:** a hybrid between a male tiger and a female lion — compare LIGER

ti·go·nin \tə'gōnən, tī'g-; 'tīgənən, 'tig-\ *n* -s [anagram of *gitonin*] **:** a steroid saponin obtained esp. from the leaves of either of two foxgloves (*Digitalis purpurea* and *D. lanata*)

ti·grai *or* **ti·gray** \tə'grī\ *n* -s *cap* **:** TIGRINYA

ti·gre \tə'grā\ *n* -s *cap* **:** a Semitic language of northern Ethiopia — see AFRO-ASIATIC LANGUAGES table

ti·gress \'tīgrəs\ *n* -ES [F *tigresse*, fr. *tigre* tiger + *-esse* -ess — more at TIGER] **:** a female tiger; *also* **:** a tigerish woman

ti·grid·ia \tī'gridēə\ *n, cap* [NL, fr. Gk *tigrid-, tigris* tiger + NL *-ia* — more at TIGER] **:** a small genus of Mexican and Central American plants (family Iridaceae) comprising the tigerflowers and having variegated evanescent flowers with spreading perianth segments and 2-parted style branches

ti·gri·gna \tə'grēnyə\ *n* -s *cap* **:** TIGRINYA

ti·grine \'tīgrən, -,grīn\ *adj* [L *tigrinus,* fr. *tigris* tiger + *-inus* -ine — more at TIGER] **:** of or relating to a tiger **:** resembling a tiger esp. in coloring

ti·gri·nya *also* **ti·gri·ña** \tə'grēnyə\ *n* -s *cap* **:** a Semitic language of northern Ethiopia — see AFRO-ASIATIC LANGUAGES table

ti·groid \'tī,grȯid\ *adj* [Gk *tigroeidēs,* fr. *tigris* tiger + *-oeidēs* -oid] **1 :** resembling a tiger esp in being striped or spotted **2 :** being or consisting of Nissl substance

tigroid granules *n pl* **:** NISSL BODIES

tigroid substance *n* **:** NISSL SUBSTANCE

ti·grol·y·sis \tī'gräləsəs\ *n* [NL, fr. *tigro-* (fr. E *tigroid body*) + *-lysis*] **:** loss of Nissl bodies or substance accompanying degenerative changes in nervous tissue

tigs *pres 3d sing of* TIG, *pl of* TIG

tigua *usu cap, var of* TIWA

tig·u·rine \'tigyə,rīn\ *adj or n, usu cap* [L *Tigurinus* of or constituting a district in ancient Helvetia generally identified with Zürich, Switzerland] **:** ZWINGLIAN

TIH *abbr* Their Imperial Highnesses

tikal *var of* TICAL

tike *var of* TYKE

ti·ki \'tēkē\ *n* -s [Maori & Marquesan] **1** *usu cap* **:** an embodiment of the male principle in Polynesian mythology often depicted as the first man or the superhuman creator of mankind **2 a :** a Polynesian wood or stone image set up as a temporary abode or embodiment of a god or other supernatural power but not worshiped as an idol **b :** a Maori image representing an ancestor that is usu. either large and of wood or small, often in the form of a pendant, and of greenstone ⟨a greenstone ~ which has been in her family for many generations —*Auckland (New Zealand) Star*⟩ — compare HEI-TIKI

ti·ki·ti·ki \¦tēkē¦tēkē\ *n* -s [Tag & Bisayan] **:** RICE POLISHINGS; *also* **:** an alcoholic extract of rice polishings used in the treatment of beriberi

tik·ka \'tikə\ *n* -s [Hindi *ṭīkā* spot, mark] **:** a leaf spot disease of the peanut esp. in India that is caused by an imperfect fungus (*Cercospora personata*)

tik·ker *or* **ticker** \'tikə(r)\ *n* -s [*tikker* alter. of [1]*ticker*] **:** a form of interrupter used in the early days of radio as a detector of continuous waves consisting of a rapidly rotating wheel and a fine wire brush with the current made and broken by momentary contacts between the brush and a continuous strip of conducting material in the rim of the wheel

tik·kun \'tikün\ *n* -s [NHeb *tiqqūn,* fr. MHeb, collection of excerpts from the Bible and Mishnah, fr. LHeb, arrangement, order] **:** a recital of prayers and excerpts from the Pentateuch, the Prophets, and rabbinic literature by observant Jews during the night on Shabuoth and Hoshana Rabbah

ti·kling \tə'kliŋ\ *n* -s [Tag *tikling*] *Philippines* **:** any of several rails; *esp* **:** a large slender rail (*Rallus philippensis*) that is olive brown with black spots above and has the underparts barred with black and white

tik·o·loshe *or* **tik·o·losh** \¦tikə¦läsh, -lōsh\ *n, pl* **tikoloshes** [Xosa *utikoloshe*] **:** a mischievous spirit in southern African folklore taking the form of a short little man, living in the water, and being friendly to children

ti·ko·pia \tə'kōpēə\ *n, pl* **tikopia** *or* **tikopias** *usu cap* [fr. *Tikopia,* one of the Solomon islands] **1 a :** a Polynesian people on Tikopia, Solomon islands **b :** a member of such people **2 :** the language of the Tikopia people

tikor \'tikər, 'tēk-, -,kō(ə)r\ *n* -s [Hindi *tīkhur*] **1 :** a starch or arrowroot made from the tubers of an East Indian herb (*Curcuma angustifolia*) **2 :** a plant that yields tikor

ti·kug \tə'küg\ *n* -s [native name in the Philippines] **:** a tall coarse Philippine sedge (*Scirpus grossus*) the stems of which are used in weaving baskets and mats

[1]**til** *var of* TILL

[2]**til** \'til, 'tē(ə)l\ *also* **teel** \'tē(ə)l\ *n* -s [Hindi *til,* fr. Skt *tila*] **:** SESAME

til·ak \'tilək\ *n* -s [Skt *tilaka;* perh. akin to Skt *tila* sesame] **:** an ornamental spot worn on the forehead chiefly by Hindus as a sectarian mark

ti·la·pia \tə'läpēə\ *n* [NL] **1** *cap* **:** a genus of African freshwater food fishes (family Cichlidae) in many respects resembling the American sunfishes **2** -s **:** any fish of the genus *Tilapia*

til·as·ite \'tilə,sīt\ *n* -s [Sw *tilasit,* fr. Daniel *Tilas* †1772 Swedish mining engineer + Sw *-it* -ite] **:** a mineral CaMg(AsO$_4$)F consisting of a magnesium calcium arsenate and fluoride and occurring in violet-gray granular masses (sp. gr. 3.3)

til·burg \'til,bərg\ *adj, usu cap* [fr. *Tilburg,* Netherlands] **:** of or from the city of Tilburg, Netherlands **:** of the kind or style prevalent in Tilburg

til·bury \'til,berē, -,b(ə)rē\ *n* -ES [after *Tilbury,* 19th cent. London coach builder] **:** a light two-wheeled carriage with an elaborate spring suspension system and with or without a top

til·de \'tildə\ *n* -s [Sp, fr. L *titulus* superscription, sign, title — more at TITLE] **1 :** a mark ~ placed esp. over the letter *n* (as in Spanish *señor* sir) to denote the sound \nʸ\ or over vowels (as in Portuguese *não* no) to indicate nasality **2 :** the mark ~ used in logic and mathematics as a modified *n* generally read "not" and serving to indicate negation or denial or occas. used as the sign for the biconditional connective

[1]**tile** \'tīl, *esp before pause or consonant* -īəl\ *n* -s *often attrib* [ME, fr. OE *tigel, tigele;* akin to OS *tiegla* tile, OHG *ziagala, ziagal,* ON *tigl;* all fr. a prehistoric WGmc-NGmc word borrowed fr. L *tegula* — more at THATCH] **1** *pl* **tiles** *or* **tile a :** a flat or curved piece of fired clay, stone, concrete, or other material used esp. for roofs, floors, or walls and often for such work of an ornamental nature — see ENCAUSTIC TILE, FACE TILE; compare BLOCK, BRICK **b :** a hollow or a semicircular and open earthenware or concrete drain (as a pipe or gutter) ⟨laying out underground ~ to drain fields —John Bird⟩; *also* **:** a piece used in constructing such a drain **c :** a hollow building unit made of burned clay or shale or of gypsum **2 :** TILING **3 :** a small flat piece of baked earth or earthenware used to cover vessels in which metals are fused **4 :** HAT; *esp* **:** a high silk hat **5 :** a thin piece of resilient material (as an asphalt composition, cork, linoleum, or rubber) used esp. for covering floors or walls **6 :** a flat usu. square ceramic plate used esp. as a coaster for hot dishes or as an ornament **7 :** a thin block used as a playing piece and usu. marked (as with letters or characters) for a particular game — **on the tiles** *or* **upon the tiles** *adv (or adj)* **:** on a debauch

tiles 1a

[2]**tile** \"\ *vb* -ED/-ING/-S [ME *tilen,* fr. *tile,* n.] *vt* **1 :** to cover with or as if with tiles ⟨~ a house⟩ ⟨~ a floor⟩ **2** *also* **tyle** \"\ **a :** to protect (as a lodge meeting) from intrusion **:** GUARD ⟨~ the door⟩ **b :** to bind or swear (a member of a secret society) to secrecy **3 a :** to install drainage tile in **b :** to drain by use of tile ~ *vi* **:** to install drainage tile

tile blue *n* **:** a grayish blue that is redder, lighter, and stronger than electric, greener and stronger than copenhagen, redder, stronger, and slightly lighter than Gobelin, and greener, lighter, and stronger than average shadow blue

tileboard \'=,=\ *n* **1 :** a board used in interior finishing and made from a large sheet of any of various materials having a decorative coating simulating a tiled surface **2 :** a thin large square piece (as of wood) often with beveled edges that is fitted together with other like pieces to cover ceilings or walls

tile cell *n* **:** one of the apparently empty upright ray cells found interspersed with the procumbent cells in the wood of various trees (as basswood) usu. in horizontal series

tiled \'tī(ə)ld\ *adj* [ME *tyled,* fr. past part. of *tilen, tylen* to tile] **1 a :** covered or roofed with or as if with tiles **:** furnished with tiles **b :** drained by tiles ⟨~ fields⟩ **2 :** IMBRICATED **3 :** protected from intrusion **:** barred to intruders ⟨a lodge meeting within ~ doors⟩

tile drain *n* **:** a drain made of tiles

tile-drain \'=,=\ *vt* [*tile drain*] **:** to drain by or furnish with a tile drain

tilefish \'=,=\ *n* [*tile-* (modif. of NL *Lopholatilus,* genus of fishes including the tilefish) + *fish*] **:** a large deepwater violet blanquillo (*Lopholatilus chamaeleonticeps*) more or less thickly covered with large round yellow spots and having a fleshy appendage on the back of the head

tile hanging *n* **:** application of tiles to a vertical surface (as a wall) by hanging the tiles on battens

tile hat *n* **:** a high silk hat ⟨white-whiskered ancient in *tile hat* —Lucius Beebe⟩

tile ore *n* **:** an earthy cuprite often mixed with iron oxide

tile pipe *n* **:** pipe made of cement or pottery and used esp. for drains, chimney pots, and linings for chimney flues

til·er \'tīlə(r)\ *n* -s [ME *tyler,* fr. *tile, tyle* + *-er*] **1 :** one that lays tiles **2** *also* **tyl·er** \"\ **:** a doorkeeper in a lodge of a secret society (as of Freemasons)

tile red *n* **1 :** a strong brown that is redder, lighter, and stronger than average russet and redder and paler than rust **2 :** a moderate reddish orange that is yellower and duller than crab apple and yellower and darker than flamingo

til·ery \'tīlərē, -ri\ *n* -ES [[1]*tile* + *-ery*] **1 :** a kiln or field where tiles are made or burned **2 :** the art of using tile for decorative effects in buildings

tileseed \'=,=\ *n* **:** an Australian tree of the genus *Geissois* (family Cunoniaceae) having imbricated seeds

til·ia \'tilēə\ *n, cap* [NL, fr. L, linden] **:** a genus (the type of the family Tiliaceae) of trees that are native in temperate regions and often planted as shade trees, that are distinguished by having cordate leaves, a winglike bract coalescent with the peduncle, indehiscent fruit with one or two seeds, and soft easily carved wood, and that have a strong hybridizing tendency — see BASSWOOD, LINDEN

til·i·a·ce·ae \,=='āsē,ē\ *n pl, cap* [NL, fr. *Tilia,* type genus + *-aceae*] **:** a family of herbs, shrubs, or trees (order Malvales) distinguished chiefly by the free stamens and 2-celled anthers — **til·i·a·ceous** \¦==¦āshəs\ *adj*

til·i·kum \'tiləkəm\ *var of* TILLICUM

til·ing \'tīliŋ, -lēŋ\ *n* -s [ME *tylynge,* fr. gerund of *tilen, tylen* to tile] **1 :** the act or work of one who tiles **2** [[1]*tile* + *-ing*] **a :** TILES **b :** a surface of tiles

[1]**till** *also* **til** \tᵊl (*often* dᵊl *after a vowel*), təl\ *prep* [ME, fr. OE *til;* akin to OFris & ON *til* to, till, OE *til* good, suitable — more at [3]TILL] **1** *chiefly Scot* **a :** to a place of arrival **:** through to **:** as far as ⟨~ an end⟩ **b :** to or toward a limit or goal ⟨changed ~ a dragon⟩ **c :** TO — used to introduce an indirect object or complement of various adjectives and nouns ⟨gie it ~ him⟩ ⟨aye kind ~ his ain⟩ **d :** AT, BY, FOR, OF, CONCERNING **2 :** throughout the interval extending to **:** during the whole time from the starting point up to **:** up or down to a specified time **:** UNTIL — used with an implication of termination or change at the time mentioned ⟨~ his return⟩ ⟨~ after four o'clock⟩ ⟨~ next week⟩ ⟨to live ~ ninety⟩ **3 :** at any time before or before the arrival, appearance, or beginning of — used after a negative expression with an implication that the action or condition began or is to begin at the specified time ⟨a refund which I did not get ~ ten years later⟩ **4 —** used as a function word indicating position before the clock hour ⟨five minutes ~ three⟩

[2]**till** *also* **til** \"\ *conj* [ME, fr. *till, til,* prep.] **1 :** throughout the interval extending to the (specified) time thereafter **:** up to the time when **:** UNTIL ⟨wait ~ I come⟩ — formerly used with *that* ⟨~ that a capable and wide revenge swallow them up —Shak.⟩ ⟨~ that we see our cheeks ale-dyed —Robert Herrick †1674⟩ **2 a** *dial* **:** BEFORE ⟨felt like a frost ~ morning —Conrad Richter⟩ **b :** previous to the time when **:** at any time before **:** unless at some future time — used after a negative statement or an injunction ⟨you'll never succeed ~ you concentrate your efforts⟩ **c** *chiefly dial* **:** up to or at the time when **:** WHEN — used in negative constructions ⟨scarcely reached home ~ the rain started⟩ **3** *dial* **:** in extent of time intervening before ⟨it seemed long ~ dawn came⟩ **4 :** continuously up to the point at which **:** for so long that **:** so that finally ⟨ran and ran ~ he could run no more⟩ **5** *chiefly dial* **:** WHILE ⟨enjoy the roses ~ they flourish —Thomas Wright⟩ **6** *dial* **:** THAN ⟨more ~ one can play⟩ **7** *dial* **:** in order that **:** so that ⟨can't write my name ~ you can read it —J.H.Stuart⟩

[3]**till** \'til\ *vt* -ED/-ING/-S [ME *tilien, tilen, tillen* to strive for, obtain, work, cultivate, fr. OE *tilian;* akin to OE *til* good, suitable, OHG *zil* goal, *zilōn* to hurry, ON *aldrtíli* death, Goth *gatils* suitable] **1 :** to turn or stir (as by plowing, harrowing, or hoeing) and prepare for seed **:** sow, dress, and raise crops from **:** CULTIVATE ⟨learned to ~ the soil —Eric Newton⟩ ⟨~*ed* the rocky land —E.W.Smith⟩ ⟨helping to ~ the fields —Will Irwin⟩ **2** *dial Eng* **:** PREPARE, SET ⟨~ a snare⟩ **3 a :** to improve by assiduous labor or study **:** foster the growth or development of **:** care for ⟨new ground, not adequately ~*ed* in any older book —Hugo Leichtentritt⟩ ⟨the president of a university in those days ~*ed* a very broad field —A.D.White⟩ ⟨whole broad field of liberty was being ~*ed* —W.H.Allison⟩ **b :** to make researches into **:** work upon ⟨~ a field of knowledge⟩

[4]**till** *vt* -ED/-ING/-S [ME *tullen, tillen,* fr. OE *-tyllan* (as in *fortyllan* to seduce, *betyllan* to allure); akin to OE *talu* talk, narrative, list — more at TALE] *obs* **:** ATTRACT, ENTICE, CHARM

[5]**till** \'til\ *n* -s [AF *tylle*] **1 a :** a box, drawer, or tray in a receptacle (as a cabinet or chest) used esp. for valuables **b :** a money drawer in or behind a counter or desk (as in a store or bank) **c :** a removable compartment fitting in the drawer of a cash register and used to hold or carry money ⟨gunmen . . . lifted $225 from the ~ —*Time*⟩ **d :** a place where money is kept for ready access ⟨bank . . . needs some cash in its ~ to meet day-to-day needs of customers for cash —*Federal Reserve System*⟩ **2 a :** the money contained in a till ⟨borrow from the ~⟩ **b :** a quantity or supply of ready money ⟨passion for a brimful ~ —E.O. Hauser⟩ ⟨amateur groups never forget the insistency of the ~ —Robertson Davies⟩ — compare TILL MONEY **3 :** one of the four spaces between projections above the platen of a hand press **4 :** TILL BASKET

till 1c

[6]**till** \"\ *vt* -ED/-ING/-S **:** to put (as money) in a till

[7]**till** \"\ *n* -s [prob. fr. G *tülle* socket, mouth of a pitcher, fr. OHG *tulli* socket for an arrowhead; akin to OHG *tuolla* small valley — more at DOLE] **:** a horizontal piece fitted between the main uprights in an early handpress and supporting the sleeve with the spindle and screws

[8]**till** \"\ *n* -s [origin unknown] **1** *chiefly Scot* **:** a hard unproductive usu. clay subsoil often containing stones and gravel **2 :** unstratified drift deposited by a glacier and consisting of clay, sand, gravel and boulders intermingled in any proportions **:** BOULDER CLAY

till·able \'tiləbəl\ *adj* [[3]*till* + *-able*] **:** capable of being tilled **:** ARABLE ⟨an acre of irrigated land is equivalent to 4 acres of nonirrigated, ~ land —O.W.Israelsen⟩

till·age \-lij, -lēj\ *n* -s [ME, fr. *tilien, tillen* to till + *-age*] **1 :** the operation, practice, or art of tilling land **:** the improving of land for agricultural purposes **2 a :** a place tilled or cultivated **:** cultivated land ⟨forests have . . . given place to ~ and pasture — John Buchan⟩ **b :** crops growing on tilled ground — **in tillage :** under cultivation ⟨forty acres *in tillage*⟩

til·la·mook \'tilə,mük\ *n, pl* **tillamook** *or* **tillamooks** *usu cap* [Chinook] **1 a :** a Salishan people of the Oregon coast **b :** a member of such people **2 :** a language of the Tillamook people **3** *or* **tillamook cheese** [fr. *Tillamook,* town and county in Oregon] **:** a cheddar cheese of crumbly texture and sharp flavor

til·lands·ia \tə'landzēə\ *n* [NL, fr. Elias *Tillands* †1693 Finnish botanist + NL *-ia*] **1** *cap* **:** a very large genus of chiefly epiphytic plants (family Bromeliaceae) confined to tropical and subtropical America and usu. bearing a rosette of narrow overlapping basal leaves that often hold a considerable quantity of water and spicate or paniculate flowers that have free perianth segments and are often subtended by colored bracts **2** -s **:** any plant of the genus *Tillandsia*

till basket *n* [[5]*till*] **:** a small rectangular basket for packing fruits or vegetables having its bottom and sides formed of two crossed pieces of veneer or of other material (as plastic or paperboard), usu. holding a pint or quart, and often fitting into a larger crate or other shipping container — compare BERRY BASKET, CLIMAX BASKET

[1]**till·er** \'tilə(r)\ *n* -s [ME *tiliere, tilier, tiler,* fr. *tilien, tilen tillen* to till + *-ere, -er* -er] **1 :** one that tills **:** HUSBANDMAN, CULTIVATOR, PLOWMAN **2 :** an implement for tilling ground

[2]**til·ler** \"\ *n* -s [ME *tiler* stock of a crossbow, fr. MF *telier,* lit., beam of a loom, fr. ML *telarium,* fr. L *tela* web + *-arium* -ary — more at TOIL] **1 :** a notched stick used to hold a bow drawn during its shaping **2 a :** a lever of wood or metal that is fitted to the rudderhead and used for turning the rudder from side to side and that in small boats is usu. turned by hand but in ships is moved by mechanical appliances, is usu. in the form of a quadrant extending on each side of the rudderhead perpendicular to the keel, and has a rope or chain leading forward from each end to the wheel or other steering device **b :** a bar used for steering a vehicle (as an automobile) **3 :** a handle shaped like a boat's tiller: as **a :** the upper handle of a pit saw **b :** a two-handled bar for turning the rope in rope drilling **4** *or* **tiller wheel :** a steering wheel controlling the rear wheels or trailer section of a vehicle (as a ladder truck)

[3]**til·ler** \"\ *vb* -ED/-ING/-S *vt* **:** to use a tiller in archery ~ *vi* **:** to shape (a bow) to correct curvature

[4]**til·ler** \"\ *n* -s [fr. (assumed) ME, fr. OE *telgor, telgra* branch, twig, shoot; akin to OHG *zelga* twig, ON *tjalga* thin twig, *telgja* to shape by hewing, L *dolare* to hew — more at CONDOLE] **1 :** a young timber tree **:** SAPLING **2 :** SPROUT, STALK; *esp* **:** one from the base of a plant or from the axils of its lower leaves — compare STOOL 4

[5]**til·ler** \"\ *vi* -ED/-ING/-S **:** to put forth tillers ⟨some wheats and ryes ~ freely⟩

tiller chain *n* [[2]*tiller*] **:** a chain leading forward from either end of the tiller to the wheel or other steering device

til·ler·man \'==mən\ *n, pl* **tillermen** [[2]*tiller* + *man*] **:** one in charge of a tiller

tiller rope *n* [[2]*tiller*] **1 :** a rope leading forward from either end of the tiller to the wheel or other steering device **2 :** rope that consists of 6 strands of 42 wires each of ordinary lay about a hemp center and that is suitable where great flexibility is required (as for signal pulls and steering lines, and in the operation of tillers and of elevator controlling devices)

til·let \'tilət\ *n* -s [ME *tyllete,* fr. MF *tellette, teilete, toilete* — more at TOILET] **:** a glazed fabric used formerly for wrapping and protecting fabrics

til·le·tia \tə'lēsh(ē)ə\ *n, cap* [NL] **:** a genus (the type of the family Tilletiaceae) of smuts distinguished by single-celled chlamydospores that form a promycelium with a terminal tuft of sporidia — see [2]BUNT; compare USTILAGO

til·le·ti·a·ce·ae \=,=shē'āsē,ē\ *n pl, cap* [NL, fr. *Tilletia,* type genus + *-aceae*] **:** a family of smuts (order Ustilaginales) that is distinguished from the Ustilaginaceae by the simple promycelium bearing the spores in an apical cluster and that includes numerous genera some of which (as *Tilletia* and *Urocystis*) contain economically important parasites of cultivated plants — compare USTILAGO — **til·le·ti·a·ceous** \=¦==¦āshəs\ *adj*

til·leul \tə'yər(-ə)l, -'yəl,-'yə̄l\ *or* **tilleul green** *n* -s [F *tilleul* linden, fr. (assumed) VL *tiliolus,* fr. L *tilia*] **:** a pale greenish yellow that is very slightly paler than primrose green

tilleul buff *n* **:** ALABASTER 2

til·ley·ite \'tilē,īt\ *n* -s [fr. the name *Tilley* + E *-ite*] **:** a mineral $Ca_5(Si_2O_7)(CO_3)_2$ consisting of a carbonate and silicate of calcium

til·li·cum \'tiləkəm\ *n* -s [Chinook jargon, fr. Chinook *tlxam* people] **1** *Northwest* **:** PERSON, FRIEND **2** *Northwest* **:** PEOPLE; *esp* **:** the common people of an Indian tribe as distinguished from the chiefs

tilling *pres part of* TILL

till·ite \'ti,līt\ *n* -s [[8]*till* + *-ite*] **:** rock formed of consolidated or lithified till

till money *n* [[5]*till*] **:** money kept by a bank on its premises to meet day-to-day cash requirements

[1]**til·lo·dont** \'tilə,dänt\ *adj* [NL *Tillodontia*] **:** of or relating to the Tillodontia

[2]**tillodont** \"\ *n* -s **:** a mammal or fossil of the order Tillodontia

til·lo·don·tia \,==¦dänch(ē)ə\ *n pl, cap* [NL, fr. Gk *tillein* to pluck, tear + NL *-odontia*] **:** a small order of Eocene mammals of No. America and Europe probably derived from insectivores but having resemblances to rodents or carnivores

till plain *n* [[8]*till*] **:** a level or rolling land area covered by ground moraine

tills *pl of* TILL, *pres 3d sing of* TILL

till sheet *n* [[8]*till*] **:** GROUND MORAINE

[1]**tilly** \'tilē, -li\ *adj* -ER/-EST [[8]*till* + *-y*] **:** composed of or having the character of till ⟨~ land⟩ ⟨~ clay⟩

[2]**til·ly** \'tilē, -li\ *n* -ES [IrGael *tuilleadh*] *Irish* **:** something added for good measure

til·ma \'tilmə\ *n* -s [MexSp, fr. Nahuatl *tilmatl*] *chiefly Southwest* **:** a simple cloak of Indian origin

til oil *n* [[2]*til*] **:** SESAME OIL

ti·lop·te·ri·da·les \tə,läptərə'dā(,)lēz\ *n pl, cap* [NL, fr. *Tilopterid-, Tilopteris,* genus of algae (fr. Gk *tilos* something plucked — fr. *tillein* to pluck — + *pteris* fern) + *-ales* — more at PTERIS] **:** an order of brown algae (class Isogeneratae) resembling those of the genus *Ectocarpus* but with the cells of the prostrate lower portion of the thallus arranged in transverse tiers

til seed *n* [[2]*til*] **:** the seed of sesame

til·sit \'tilzət\ *or* **til·set cheese** \-zət-\ *n* -s *usu cap T* [fr. *Tilsit,* East Prussia (now Sovetsk, U.S.S.R.)] **:** a cheese consisting of whole or skim milk and having a plastic body and a mild to slightly sharp flavor

til·sit·er \'tilzəd·ə(r)\ *n* -s *usu cap* [G, fr. *Tilsiter* of Tilsit, one from Tilsit, fr. *Tilsit*] **:** TILSIT

[1]**tilt** \'tilt\ *vb* -ED/-ING/-S [ME *tulten, tilten;* akin to OE *tealt* unstable, *tealtian, tealtrian* to totter, stumble, waver, MD *touteren* to tremble, Sw *tulta* to waddle, Norw dial. *tylta* to walk softly] *vt* **1 :** to cause to slope **:** INCLINE, SLANT, TIP ⟨~ a chair against a wall⟩ ⟨~*ed* sedimentary beds —*Jour. of Geol.*⟩ **2 :** to pour forth contents by tipping **:** empty or unload by inclining ⟨~ a cart⟩ **3 a :** to point or thrust in or as if in a tilt ⟨~ a lance⟩ **b :** to make a tilt or rush at **:** charge against ⟨~ an adversary⟩ **4 :** to hammer or forge with a tilt hammer ⟨~ a bar of iron⟩ **5 :** to rotate (a camera) about a horizontal axis that is at right angles to the lens axis so as to elevate or lower the viewing angle ~ *vi* **1 :** to move or shift so as to lean or incline **:** heel over **:** TIP, SLANT ⟨the board ~*ed* up when he stepped on it⟩ ⟨the tree ~*s* to the south⟩ **2 :** to move up and down **:** sway unsteadily **:** SEESAW, PITCH ⟨bird . . . ~*ing* among the leaves —Amy Lowell⟩ ⟨boats ~*ing* on the waves⟩ **3 a :** to engage in a combat with lances **:** ride or charge and thrust with a lance **:** JOUST **b :** to engage in an altercation or controversy **:** make an impetuous attack ⟨~ at wrongs⟩ **4 :** RUSH, BURST ⟨~ through the crowd⟩ ⟨~ into a room⟩ **5 :** to incline from a horizontal or vertical position ⟨roads that rise and dip and ~ past lively brooks —Frederick Nebel⟩ ⟨~*ing* strata⟩ **6 :** to tilt a camera — **tilt at windmills** [so called fr. the episode in *Don Quijote de la Mancha* in which Don Quixote battles with a windmill, thinking it a giant — more at DON QUIXOTE] **:** to fight imaginary enemies or illusory evils ⟨even though this rebellion may be a *tilting at windmills* —Rachel Frank⟩ ⟨viewed them as harmless literary eccentrics, *tilting at windmills* —Donald Davidson⟩

[2]**tilt** \"\ *n* -s **1 a** (1) **:** a military exercise on horseback in which two combatants (as knights in armor) charging with lances or similar weapons try to unhorse each other **:** JOUST (2) **:** a similar exercise in which an armed rider charges at a mark **b :** a tournament of tilts — compare QUINTAIN 2 **2 a :** an encounter in which opponents attack each other in a manner suggestive of that of tilting knights **:** ALTERCATION, DISPUTE ⟨had a sharp ~ with the manager⟩ ⟨fiery ~*s* against the evils of his day —Sarah G. Bowerman⟩ ⟨vocal ~*s* of legislators —T.C.Desmond⟩ **b :** SPEED — used esp. in the phrase *at full tilt* **3 a :** the act or fact of tilting **:** the state or position of being tilted **:** inclination from a vertical or horizontal position ⟨give a board a ~⟩ ⟨gave him a signal with a ~ of her gray head —Marcia Davenport⟩ **b :** a sloping surface ⟨warps, folds, or ~*s* that exist in rocks of the earth's crust —J.D.Forrester⟩ **4 :** BLACK-NECKED STILT **5 :** HELVE HAMMER **6 :** a contrivance used in fishing through the ice in which the tilting of a piece gives notice of the biting of a fish **7 :** any of various sports resembling or suggesting tilting with lances; *esp* **:** a water

sport in which the contestants stand on logs or in canoes or boats and thrust with poles **8 :** lack of parallelism between the plane of film in an aerial camera that is pointed downward and the plane of the ground — **at tilt :** ATILT ⟨lances *at tilt*⟩

³tilt \"\ *adj* [²*tilt*] **1 :** TILTED ⟨the ~ world returns from sun to ice —Philip Booth⟩ **2 :** that is emptied by tilting ⟨~ bucket⟩ ⟨~ pot⟩ ⟨~ wagon⟩

⁴tilt \"\ *n* -s [ME *teld, tild, telte* tent, canopy, fr. OE *teld;* akin to MLG & MD *telt* tent, OHG *zelt,* ON *tjald,* and perh. to L *dolare* to hew — more at CONDOLE] **1 :** a cloth covering or canopy (as of a cart, wagon, boat, or stall) ⟨bench under a little canvas ~ —J.G.Cozzens⟩ ⟨gaily colored ~*s* of the market stalls —*Courier (London)*⟩ **2** *Newfoundland & Labrador* **:** a log cabin or lean-to in which the logs are set upright

⁵tilt \"\ *vt* -ED/-ING/-s **:** to cover or provide with a tilt ⟨a ~*ed* jousting field⟩

tilt·able \ˈtiltəbəl\ *adj* **:** capable of being tilted

tiltboard \ˈ=,=\ *or* **tilt table** *n* **:** an apparatus for testing perception of bodily position by rotating a blindfolded person from horizontal to vertical or oblique positions

tilt cart *n* **:** a cart having a body that can be tilted for emptying

tilted *adj* **:** taken with an aerial camera having the film plane out-of-parallel with the ground plane

¹tilt·er \ˈtiltə(r)\ *n* -s [¹*tilt* + *-er*] **1 :** one that tilts: as **a :** JOUSTER **b :** a workman who operates a helve hammer **c :** a workman who tilts out coal **d :** a contrivance for emptying something (as a barrel or carboy) by tilting **e :** a contrivance for varying the pitch of something (as the slats of a venetian blind) **f :** TILT 6 **2 a :** SPOTTED SANDPIPER **b :** SOLITARY SANDPIPER **c :** AVOCET

²tilter \"\ *vi* -ED/-ING/-s [freq. of ¹*tilt*] **:** to swing up and down **:** SEESAW, TEETER

tilth \ˈtilth *also* -lth\ *n* -s [ME, fr. OE, fr. *tilian* to till + *-th* — more at TILL] **1 a :** the act, work, or occupation of tilling **:** cultivation of the soil **:** TILLAGE ⟨the ~ of the land⟩ **b :** mental or spiritual cultivation ⟨children without the ~ of kindness —Francis Hackett⟩ **2 :** cultivated land as distinguished from pasture, woodland, and waste land **:** PLOWLAND ⟨gradual extension of ~ drove the woods farther up the hills —Benjamin Farrington⟩ **3 :** the state of being tilled **:** condition when tilled ⟨land in good ~⟩ **4 a :** surface soil as prepared for sowing or planting **:** the depth of friable earth ⟨have never known the plow furrows break down so readily to a nice ~ —*Country Life*⟩ **b :** the state of aggregation of a soil ⟨a fine ~ is desirable —*New Zealand Jour. of Agric.*⟩

tilt hammer *n* **:** HELVE HAMMER

¹tilting *n* -s [fr. gerund of ¹*tilt*] **:** the action or sport of one who tilts **:** JOUSTING ⟨was killed at a ~ —*Notes & Queries*⟩

²tilting *adj* [fr. pres. part. of ¹*tilt*] **1 :** that tilts, causes to tilt, or may be tilted **:** rising and falling **:** SLANTING, SWAYING **2 :** used for or in tilting ⟨~ field⟩ ⟨~ lance⟩ ⟨~ spear⟩

tilting board *n, NewEng* **:** SEESAW 2b

tilting fillet *n* **:** ARRIS FILLET

tilting helmet *or* **tilting helm** *n* **:** a helmet of great size and strength worn at tilts — called also *jousting helmet*

tilting table *n* **:** a mechanically controlled table used in casting a horse

tiltmeter \ˈ=,==\ *n* **:** an instrument to measure tilting of the earth's surface

tilt mill *n* **:** a mill where metal (as steel) is tilted

tilt roof *n* **:** a roundheaded roof

tilts *pres 3d sing of* TILT, *pl of* TILT

tilt-top table \ˈ=,=-\ *n* **:** TIP-TOP TABLE

tilt-up \ˈ=,=\ *adj* [fr. *tilt up,* v.] **:** of or relating to a method of constructing concrete walls in which the slabs are cast in horizontal position and then tilted up into place ⟨*tilt-up* building⟩

tiltup \ˈ=,=\ *n* -s [fr. *tilt up,* v.] **:** TILT 6

tiltyard \ˈ=,=\ *or* **tilting yard** *n* **:** a yard or place for tilting

til·yer \ˈtilyə(r)\ *n* -s [Hindi *tiliyar, tilyar* starling, small speckled bird, fr. *til* speck, sesame seed, fr. Skt *tila*] **:** ROSE-COLORED STARLING

tim \ˈtim\ *adj* [alter. of ¹*toom*] *Scot* **:** EMPTY

ti·ma·lia \tə̇ˈmālyə, -lēə\ *n, cap* [NL, prob. fr. native name in India] **:** the type genus of Timaliidae formerly including many Old World babblers but now usu. restricted to a single form of India and Java

tim·a·li·idae \,timəˈlīə,dē\ *n pl, cap* [NL, fr. *Timalia,* type genus + *-idae*] **:** a family of passerine birds comprising usu. a variety of forms not all of which may be closely related but having as typical representatives a group of babblers that are commonly isolated in a distinct subfamily and are characterized by short rounded wings with large outer primary, a bill like that of a thrush, and unspotted young

ti·ma·li·ine \tə̇ˈmālēən, -ē,īn\ *also* **tim·a·line** \ˈtimə,līn\ *adj* [NL *Timalia* + E *-ine*] **:** of or relating to the genus *Timalia* or the family Timaliidae

ti·mar \tə̇ˈmär\ *n* -s [Turk *tımar* attendance, care, timar, fr. Per *tīmār* sorrow, care] **:** a Turkish fief formerly held under condition of military service

timarau *var of* TAMARAU

ti·mar·chy \ˈtī,märkē\ *n* -ES [Gk *timarchia,* fr. *timē* price, value, honor + *-archia* -archy — more at PAIN] **:** TIMOCRACY

ti·mar·i·ot \tə̇ˈmärēət, -mar-\ *n* -s [F, fr. It *timariota,* fr. NGk *timariōtēs,* fr. *timarion* timar, fr. Turk *tımar*] **:** one holding a timar

tim·bal *also* **tymbal** \ˈtimbəl\ *n* -s [F *timbale,* fr. MF, alter. (influenced by *cymbale* cymbal) of *tamballe,* modif. (influenced by *tambour* drum) of OSp *atabal* — more at CYMBAL, TAMBOUR, ATABAL] **1 :** KETTLEDRUM 1 **2 :** the vibrating membrane in the shrilling organ of a cicada

tim·bale \ˈtimbəl; timˈbäl, tamˈ-\ *n* -s [F, lit., kettledrum] **1 :** a creamy mixture (as of chicken, lobster, cheese, or fish) cooked in a drum-shaped mold or in individual molds or cups **2 :** a small pastry shell fried with a timbale iron and filled with a cooked timbale mixture or served with fruit sauce or dusted with powdered sugar — compare ROSETTE 9b

timbale iron *n* **:** an iron mold of varying design with a detachable handle used in making pastry shells for timbales

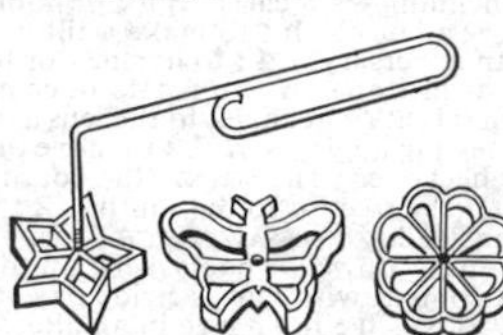
timbale irons

tim·be \ˈtimbē\ *n* -s [MexSp *timbe, timbre,* name of various trees, esp. *Acacia angustissima*] **:** the bark or root of any of several Mexican trees and shrubs (esp. *Acacia angustissima* and *Calliandra anomala*) used in the manufacture of tepache

¹tim·ber \ˈtimbə(r)\ *n* -s [ME *timber, timmer,* fr. OE *timber* house, building, building material, wood, trees; akin to OHG *zimbar* house, room, wood, ON *timbr* timber, L *domus* house, Gk *domos* house, *demein* to build, Skt *dama* house] **1 a** (1) **:** growing trees or their wood ⟨standing ~⟩ (2) *Eng law* **:** trees (as oak, ash, elm over 20 years old) that are part of a freehold and may not be cut by a life tenant **b :** a wooded area **:** FOREST ⟨the early settlers had clung to rivers and ~*s* —Carl Sandburg⟩ ⟨hid out in the big ~ —Vance Randolph⟩ **c :** a standing tree or its trunk — often used interjectionally as a shout of warning to those near a falling tree **2 :** wood used for or suitable for building (as a house or boat) or for carpentry or joinery ⟨the turner, who concentrated on chair making, had beech for his favorite ~ —Andrew Phelan⟩ ⟨tropical wet evergreen forest producing valuable ~*s* —S.H. Howard⟩ **3 a :** MATERIAL, STUFF ⟨believe it's best-seller ~ —Richard Mallett⟩ **b :** something that helps to form a person **:** individual character or one of its constituents ⟨in this testing . . . inner ~*s* begin to part at once, the stuff of which he is made begins at once to deteriorate —F.R.Leavis⟩ **c :** human material suitable for a particular position or status ⟨presidential ~⟩ ⟨management ~⟩ ⟨officer ~⟩ **d :** bony structure in a dog **4 :** something that is made of wood or is likened to a wooden object: as **a :** a wooden gate, fence, post, or rail required to be jumped by a horse ⟨take a pull on your horse, considerably easing your pace as you near the ~ —C.C.W.Aldin⟩ **b** *slang* **:** LEG ⟨hobbled out on my gouty ~*s* for a walk —C.B.Fairbanks⟩ **5 a** (1) **:** a comparatively large squared or dressed piece of wood ready for use or forming part of a structure ⟨roof ~*s*⟩ ⟨bridge ~*s*⟩ ⟨floor ~*s*⟩; *esp* **:** one that in technical specifications usu. is not less than 5 inches in least dimension — compare PLANK; see ROOF illustration (2) *Brit* **:** a piece of sawed wood that in technical specifications usu. has a thickness of at least 4½ inches and a width of at least 6 inches **b** *Brit* **:** ²LUMBER 2a **c :** a curving frame branching outward from the keel of a ship and bending upward in a vertical direction that is usu. composed of several pieces united **:** RIB 3b(1)

²timber \"\ *vb* **timbered; timbered; timbering** \-b(ə)riŋ\ **timbers** [ME *timbren,* fr. OE *timbran, timbrian;* akin to OHG *zimbarōn* to construct of wood, ON *timbra,* Goth *timrjan,* OE ¹*timber*] *vt* **1** *archaic* **:** to construct of wood **2 :** to frame, cover, or support with timbers ⟨the boards would suit admirably for ~*ing* cuts for drains —F.W.Crofts⟩ ~ *vi* **1 :** to cut timber ⟨a man ~*ing* in the wooded area —Don Browning⟩ **2 :** to provide timbers for support ⟨in all work in clay it was found advisable to ~ at once —*Military Engineer*⟩

³timber \"\ *adj* **1 :** formed of wood **:** WOODEN **2 :** of, relating to, or for timber **3** *Scot* **:** heavy as wood **:** DULL; *specif* **:** having no ear for music

⁴timber *var of* TIMBRE

timber and room *n* **:** ROOM AND SPACE

timber bar *n* **:** a crowbar having a working end that has a square section and ends in a right pyramid — called also *bridge bar*

timberbeast \ˈ==,=\ *n, slang* **:** LOGGER

timber beetle *n* **:** any of various beetles (as the ambrosia beetles) whose larvae bore deeply in the wood of trees

timber borer *n* **:** any of numerous insects whose larvae develop as borers in living or dead trees or in timbers

timber connector *n* **:** CONNECTOR 2e

timber cruiser *n* **:** CRUISER 4a

tim·ber-doo·dle \ˈ==,düd°l\ *n* [¹*timber* + *doodle* (in *cock-a-doodle-doo*), euphemism for *cock* (associated with *cock* penis)] **:** the American woodcock ⟨the long-billed ~*s* were whistling all over the place as the flight came in —*N.Y.Times*⟩

tim·bered \ˈtimbə(r)d\ *adj* [ME *timbred,* partly fr. ¹*timber* + *-ed;* partly fr. past part. of *timbren* to timber] **1 a :** furnished with, made of, or covered with timber ⟨one or two magnificently ~ old barns —Sinclair Lewis⟩ — often used in combination ⟨the waterlogged, rotten-*timbered,* barnacled old blubber hunter —H.A.Chippendale⟩ **b :** having walls framed by exposed timbers — compare HALF TIMBER **2 :** having a specified structure or constitution **:** BUILT, FORMED, MADE ⟨my arrows, too slightly ~ for so loud a wind —Shak.⟩ **3 :** covered with growing timber **:** WOODED ⟨sand hills whose thickly ~ ridges are clothed with loblolly pine, live oak, and holly —*Amer. Guide Series: N.C.*⟩ ⟨the hills, ~ up to their summits, formed an amphitheater —Anthony Trollope⟩

timber forest *n* **:** HIGH FOREST

timber grapple *n* **:** LUG HOOK

timber grouse *n* **:** a grouse (as the ruffed grouse) that inhabits woods — distinguished from *prairie chicken*

timberhead \ˈ==,=\ *n* **1 :** the top end of a ship's timber used above the gunwale (as for belaying ropes) **2 :** a bollard bolted to the deck where the end of a timber would come

timber hitch *n* **1 :** a knot that is made by passing the end of a line around an object and twisting it back on itself, is used to secure a line (as to a log or spar), and is often supplemented by a half hitch to aid in towing and lifting **2 :** a knot resembling a timber hitch that is used to form the lower loop of an adjustable bowstring — called also *bowyer's knot*

timber hitch 1

tim·ber·ing \ˈtimb(ə)riŋ\ *n* -s [ME, fr. ¹*timber* + *-ing*] **:** a set of timbers **:** TIMBERWORK; *specif* **:** one used for support (as of a roof or wall)

timberjack \ˈ==,=\ *n* **:** LOGGER

timber jumper *n* **:** a horse skilled in jumping over barriers (as fences or gates)

tim·ber·land \ˈ==,land\ *n* **:** land covered with forest and esp. with marketable timber

tim·ber·less \-ləs\ *adj* **:** having no timber **:** not wooded

timberline \ˈ==,=\ *n* **:** the upper limit of arboreal growth in mountains or in high latitudes ⟨all of the material included in the present study was obtained at ~ on the east slope . . . of the Rocky mountains —*Ecology*⟩

tim·ber·ling \-liŋ\ *n* -s [¹*timber* + *-ling*] *Brit* **:** a small tree

tim·ber·man \-mən\ *n, pl* **timbermen 1 :** LUMBERMAN **2 a :** a mine worker who frames and installs supporting timberwork **b :** a construction worker who cuts and puts together timbers and planking to form framing or supporting structures (as a retaining wall, trestle, or cofferdam) — called also *bracer*

timber mill *n* **:** a sawmill in which logs are cut into heavy timbers

timber mining *n* **:** ruthless cutting of timber with complete disregard for the future of the forests

timber rattlesnake *n* **:** a moderate-sized rattlesnake (*Crotalus horridus horridus*) that is widely distributed through the eastern half of the U. S., seeks rugged stony ground, and feeds largely on mice and other rodents — compare CANEBRAKE RATTLER

timber right *n* **:** ownership of standing timber without ownership of the land

timber rot *n* **1 :** a decay of lumber and building timbers; *specif* **:** one caused by a fungus (*Poria incrassata*) **2 :** a disease of various herbaceous plants caused by a fungus (*Sclerotinia sclerotiorum*) and marked by dry granular stem lesions near the ground and white mold on the surface

timbers *pl of* TIMBER, *pres 3d sing of* TIMBER

timber scribe *n* **:** a gouge for blazing trees

tim·ber·some \ˈtimbə(r)səm\ *var of* TIMORSOME

timber toe *n* **:** a wooden leg

timber-toed \ˈ==ˈ=\ *adj* [*timber toe* + *-ed*] **:** having a wooden leg ⟨*timber-toed* cripples stilted along —Herman Melville⟩

timber-topper \ˈ==,==\ *n* **:** HURDLER 2

timber wolf *n* **:** a large broad-headed heavy-muzzled wolf (*Canis lupus lycaon*) of northern No. America that is extinct over much of the eastern and southern parts of its range and that has a dense heavy coat of clear or brownish gray or sometimes brownish white usu. with blackish shadowing along the back

timberwork \ˈ==,=\ *n* **:** work made of timbers **:** a timber construction

timber worm *n* **:** a worm (as a timber borer) infesting timber

tim·bery \ˈtimb(ə)rē, -ri\ *adj* [¹*timber* + *-y*] **:** abounding in or characterized by timber ⟨the clean ~ look of her new house —P.H.Lowrey⟩

timbes *pl of* TIMBE

¹tim·bo \tēmˈbō, tim-, -bō\ *n* -s [Pg *timbó,* fr. Tupi] **1 :** an Amazonian woody vine (*Paullinia pinnata*) the bitter bark of which contains a fish poison **2 :** ³CUBE 2

²timbo \"\ *n* -s [Sp *timbó,* fr. Guarani] **1 :** a timber tree (*Enterolobium timbouva*) of Argentina **2 :** the easily worked red wood of timbo used for furniture and interior woodwork

¹tim·bre \ˈtambə(r), ˈtim-,ˈtaam-\ *n* -s [MF — more at ³TIMBRE] **:** the crest on a coat of arms

²timbre \"\ *also* **tim·ber** \"\ *vt* -ED/-ING/-s **:** to surmount and adorn with a heraldic timbre

³timbre \"\ *also* **timber** \"\ *n* -s [F *timbre,* fr. MF, bell struck by a hammer, crest of a helmet, armorial crest, fr. OF, drum, fr. MGk *tymbanon* kettledrum, alter. of Gk *tympanon* — more at TYMPANUM] **1 :** a quality of sound that depends chiefly on the presence or absence and the relative intensity of various overtones: as **a :** the resonance quality of a voiced speech sound by which the ear recognizes and identifies it **b :** the quality of tone distinctive of a singing voice or an instrument **2 :** distinctive character, quality, or tone ⟨that consciousness is clearly very closely related to the author's own personal ~ —F.R.Leavis⟩ ⟨the dance did not prove to be one of dark ~ —*Dance Observer*⟩ ⟨would have shamed them forever, had they had the ~ of his world in their characters —*Yale Rev.*⟩

tim·brel \ˈtimbrəl\ *n* -s [obs. E *timbre* tambourine (fr. ME, fr. OF, drum) + E *-el*] **:** a small hand drum or tambourine ⟨the shallow ~ . . . which itinerant jugglers carried—Curt Sachs⟩

tim·brelled \-ld\ *adj* [fr. past part. of obs. E *timbrel* to play upon or accompany with a timbrel, fr. E *timbrel,* n.] **:** played upon or accompanied with a timbrel ⟨there the ~ hymn rings to Osiris —W.L.Bowles⟩

¹time \ˈtīm\ *n* -s [ME *time, tyme,* fr. OE *tīma, tȳma;* akin to ON *tīmi* time, OE *tīd* time — more at TIDE] **1 a :** a period during which something (as an action, process, or condition) exists or continues **:** an interval comprising a limited and continuous action, condition, or state of being **:** measured or measurable duration ⟨no one had spoken to him all the ~ we were at lunch —Ernest Hemingway⟩ ⟨could not sleep, and after a ~ he rose —Louis Bromfield⟩ ⟨gone a long ~⟩ ⟨written in three hours' ~⟩ **b :** a period set apart in some specified or implied way from others ⟨a ~ to weep, and a ~ to laugh; a ~ to mourn, and a ~ to dance —Eccles 3:4 (AV)⟩ ⟨Saturday evenings, traditional shopping ~ for millworkers and farmers —*Amer. Guide Series: N. H.*⟩ **c** (1) **:** a period sufficiently or conveniently long ⟨just ~ to reach shelter before the storm broke⟩ ⟨there is no ~ here to trace the means by which these errors of planning were corrected —*Amer. Guide Series: N. Y.*⟩ (2) **:** LEISURE ⟨there was ~ for athletic sports and private reading —Lucien Price⟩ ⟨as much good music as he has ~ to listen to —*Report: (Canadian) Royal Commission on Nat'l Development*⟩ (3) **:** the length of the period required for or consumed in performing an action or going over a course ⟨the winner's ~ was just under four minutes⟩ ⟨the ~ of the train trip was two hours⟩ (4) *slang* **:** progress in winning favor or sexual acceptance ⟨two guys tried to beat each other's ~ around the women —Russell Thacher⟩ ⟨the guy . . . trying to make ~ with his secretary —Bennett Cerf⟩ **d :** a period or segment of the radio or television broadcasting day ⟨one of the first to insist on the sale of radio ~ for both sides of a controversial issue —C.C.Barry⟩ **2 a :** a point or period when something occurs **:** the moment of an event, process, or condition **:** OCCASION ⟨we were not twenty yards from the rocks, at the ~ that the ship passed abreast of them —Frederick Marryat⟩ ⟨from that ~ she was his tennis instructor and patron —*Current Biog.*⟩ **b :** an opportune, convenient, or suitable moment or period **:** a favorable opportunity or occasion ⟨biding his ~⟩ ⟨the ~ has come to sift and synthesize the findings of these works —Julian Towster⟩ ⟨notice in him any sense of ~*s* and occasions and the demands of social etiquette —L.P.Smith⟩ **3 :** an appointed, fixed, or customary moment or hour for something to happen, begin, or end ⟨spring came ahead of ~ this year⟩ ⟨a half-hour before edition ~ —William DuBois⟩: as **a :** the normal or expected moment or period of death ⟨you'll die before your ~ —W.J. Reilly⟩ **b :** the normal end of the period of gestation **:** the expected moment of childbirth ⟨when her ~ has come, counted by the moons, she betakes herself to a special little hut built for the women —Corinne Feeney⟩ **c :** a scheduled moment of arrival or departure ⟨asked for the ~ of the next northbound train⟩ **d** *Brit* **:** the legally fixed closing hour of a public house

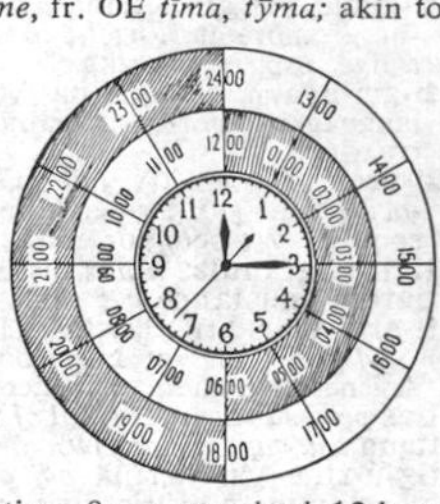
time 8c: a standard 12-hour dial surrounded by bands to show equivalent 24-hour time

4 a : a period associated with or characterized or dated by reference to a particular individual ⟨lived in the ~ of Elizabeth I⟩ ⟨one of the most popular writers of his ~⟩ **b** (1) **:** an historical period **:** AGE, ERA ⟨a fast moving ~ such as we are now in —T.K.Finletter⟩ ⟨geography could not fail to share in the mathematical advances of the ~ —Benjamin Farrington⟩ — often used in pl. ⟨ancient ~*s*⟩ ⟨modern ~*s*⟩ (2) **:** a division of geologic chronology **c :** conditions prevalent at present or in a specified or implied period of the past **:** state of things ⟨the ~ is out of joint —Shak.⟩ — usu. used in pl. ⟨refused to follow the trend of the ~*s* —Gerard MacGowan⟩ ⟨behind the ~*s*⟩ ⟨move with the ~*s*⟩ **d :** the present time — used with *the* ⟨many of the most important issues of the ~ —Brand Blanshard⟩ **5 :** a known, fixed, or anticipated period of existence or duration: as **a :** LIFETIME ⟨one man in his ~ plays many parts —Shak.⟩ **b :** a period of apprenticeship ⟨apprentices in the last year of their ~ —John Southward⟩ **c :** a term of military service ⟨had been enlisted for a short term only, and before the end of December . . . would have served their ~ —H.E.Scudder⟩ **d :** a prison sentence ⟨did ~ for lying about his bank accounts —P.F.Healy⟩ **6 a :** SEASON ⟨that ~ of year thou mayst in me behold —Shak.⟩ ⟨it's very hot for this ~ of year⟩ **b :** a point or portion of a day or year recurring periodically or established by routine — usu. used in combination ⟨dinner-*time*⟩ ⟨rest-*time*⟩ ⟨examination-*time*⟩ ⟨vacation-*time*⟩ **7 a :** a unit of duration as a basis for poetic meter; *esp* **:** MORA 2a **b :** rate of speed (as in marching, dancing, speaking) **:** TEMPO ⟨the woman dances regular ~ to the music —Chandler Brossard⟩ ⟨did this in slow ~, talking and laughing together —H.V.Morton⟩ **c** (1) **:** the grouping of the successive rhythmic beats or pulses as represented by a musical note taken as a time unit into measures or bars that are marked off by bar lines according to the position of the principal accent **:** METER, RHYTHM (2) **:** the rate or tempo at which a piece is performed **8 a :** a definite moment, hour, day, or year as indicated or fixed by a clock or calendar **:** a precise instant or date ⟨the ~ was midnight⟩ ⟨we do not know the exact ~ of his birth⟩ ⟨what ~ is it⟩ **b** (1) **:** a number that represents the duration of a process or condition or the interval elapsing between two events and that is obtained in effect by counting a series of arbitrarily chosen regularly recurrent events (as the swings of a pendulum) that take place during the interval to be measured (2) **:** a number (as on a clock dial or calendar) that marks the occurrence of a specified event as to hour or date and that is obtained by counting from a fiducial epoch (as that of a meridian passage of the sun or the birth of Christ) **c :** reckoning of time **:** a system of reckoning the lapse or progress of time — see SIDEREAL TIME, SOLAR TIME, STANDARD TIME **9 a :** one of a series of recurring instances or repeated acts or actions ⟨he took the stairs four at a ~ —*Phoenix Flame*⟩ ⟨a machine that can perform three operations at a ~⟩ ⟨been told that many ~*s*⟩ **b times** *pl* (1) **:** multiplied instances ⟨five ~*s* greater⟩ (2) **:** equal fractional parts of which an indicated number equal a comparatively greater quantity ⟨seven ~*s* smaller⟩ ⟨three ~*s* closer⟩ **c :** TURN ⟨got two hits out of three ~*s* at bat⟩ **10 a :** finite duration **:** the duration of one's life or of the material universe as contrasted with infinite duration ⟨~, that takes survey of all the world, must have a stop —Shak.⟩ **b :** FATHER TIME **11 a** *Platonism* **:** a reality that is an absolute flowing apart from the events filling it **b** *Aristotelianism* **:** the numerable aspect of motion **c** *Kantianism* **:** the a priori form of inner sensible intuitions that have no existence independently of the mind and are a subjective mode in which phenomena appear — see OBJECTIVE TIME, SUBJECTIVE TIME **12 a :** a person's experience during a specified period or on a particular occasion ⟨have the ~ of their lives putting on the yearly show —Louise Gerdts⟩ ⟨a good ~⟩ ⟨a hard ~⟩ **b :** a highly enjoyable or disagreeable experience ⟨had himself a ~ drinking beer from a glass in one hand, milk from a glass in the other —*Time*⟩ ⟨had a ~ with them; couldn't figure any way to get them out —W.L.Gresham⟩ **c** *slang* **:** CAROUSAL, SPREE ⟨still thought he might be out on a ~ —Ernest Hemingway⟩ **13 a :** the hours or days given to or due to be given to one's work ⟨make up ~⟩ **b :** a rate of pay fixed in terms of a unit of time (as an hour) ⟨paid him straight ~ for his overtime work⟩ **c :** amount of pay due esp. according to an hourly rate; *specif* **:** a final payment of wages due ⟨any cowboy who hit a horse over the head or spurred one in the shoulders was asking for his ~ —Ross Santee⟩ ⟨asked for his ~, but it was just a misunderstanding and was straightened out —E.C. Abbott & Helena Smith⟩ **14 :** the shutter setting on a camera for making a time exposure **15 a :** official suspension of play during a game or contest ⟨the umpire called ~⟩ **b :** a temporary official stopping of the clock during a game or portion of a game (as basketball or football) scheduled to end after a specific number of minutes of play **syn** see OPPORTUNITY — **at the same time :** HOWEVER, NEVERTHELESS ⟨this frightened, insecure, querulous man . . . must *at the same time* possess the qualities of authority and command —Arthur Knight⟩ — **at times** *adv* **:** at intervals **:** now and then ⟨*at times* he sleeps, *at times* he tosses restlessly⟩ — **for the time being**

: for the present : at the moment ⟨will take no action *for the time being*⟩ — **from time to time** : once in a while : OCCASIONALLY ⟨goes to the theater *from time to time*⟩ — **in good time** *adv* : in time — **in no time** *adv* : in the shortest possible time ⟨moved his fellows to a concerted attack, and *in no time* boulders were hurtling down the cliffs —*Amer. Guide Series: Minn.*⟩ — **in time** *adv* **1** : in due season : sufficiently early ⟨had they not been agreed upon *in time*, the states might have fallen asunder —Allan Nevins⟩ **2** : in the course of time : EVENTUALLY ⟨*in time* rose . . . to be general manager —*Current Biog.*⟩ **3** : in correct tempo ⟨has never learned to play *in time*⟩ **4** : on earth — used as an intensive ⟨why *in time* don't you come in the other room —Zona Gale⟩ — **on one's own time** : without being paid ⟨has done extra work *on his own time*⟩ — **on time** **1 a** : at the appointed time : PUNCTUALLY ⟨failed to arrive *on time* for his appointment⟩ **b** : on schedule ⟨the train is *on time*⟩ **2** : on the installment plan ⟨a portable typewriter he was buying *on time* —Hamilton Basso⟩ — **out of time** : not within the designated period : too late ⟨the appeal was filed *out of time*⟩ — **time and time again** : time and again

[2]**time** \"\ *vb* -ED/-ING/-S [ME *timen*, fr. [1]*time*] *vt* **1 a** : to arrange or set the time of : fix a time for : SCHEDULE ⟨*timed* his occasional calls to coincide with the hour of tea —Gertrude Atherton⟩ ⟨consciously *timed* that pause for dramatic effect —J.P.Marquand⟩ **b** : to regulate the speed or stops of (as a train) according to a timetable ⟨the train was *timed* to leave the station at 1:05 p.m.⟩ **c** : to adjust (as a watch) to keep correct time **2 a** : to set the tempo for ⟨the conductor *timed* the performance admirably⟩ **b** : to give a fixed or appropriate rhythm to ⟨gave a dragging tempo to the first movement, but *timed* the second movement effectively⟩ **c** : to regulate the moment, speed, or duration of for desired or maximum effect ⟨*timed* the exposure for two seconds⟩ ⟨*timed* his swing to hit the ball into right field⟩ **3** : to make coincident in time : cause to keep time with something ⟨*timed* his steps to the music⟩ **4 a** : to ascertain or record the time, duration, or rate of ⟨*timed* the horse in his last workout before the race⟩ **b** : to calculate or estimate the speed of ⟨*timed* the ball badly and missed it by a foot⟩ **5** : to dispose (as a mechanical part) so that an action occurs at a desired instant or in a desired way ⟨another factor which reduces distortion to a negligible value is the fact that the plate circuit is *timed* —L.E.Barton⟩ ~ *vi* : to keep or beat time : move in time ⟨beat, happy stars, *timing* with things below —Alfred Tennyson⟩

[3]**time** \"\ *adj* [[1]*time*] **1 a** : of or relating to time ⟨poetry, dance and music are ~ arts —J.M.Barzun⟩ ⟨a ~ salesman⟩ **b** : giving, recording, or marking time ⟨~ register⟩ **2** : timed to ignite or explode at a specific moment ⟨~ charge⟩ **3 a** : payable on a specified future day or a given length of time after presentation for acceptance **b** (1) : made with the understanding that extended terms will be given for settlement ⟨a ~ sale⟩ (2) : to be paid for in installments ⟨a ~ purchase⟩ : divided into installments ⟨a ~ payment⟩

time about *adv, chiefly Scot* : in turn : by turns : ALTERNATELY

time–advantage \ˈ⸗,⸗ˈ⸗⸗\ *n* : the accumulated time during which a wrestler is in a position of advantage over his opponent used as a limited basis of scoring in amateur bouts

time allowance *n* **1** : an allowance of time usu. in seconds per mile that is given a yacht in competition with one of a higher rating **2** : ALLOWED TIME 2

time and again *adv* : REPEATEDLY ⟨natural disasters recur *time and again* —O.N.Larsen⟩

time and a half *n* : payment of a worker (as for overtime or holiday work) at one and a half times his regular wage rate

time and motion study *or* **time–motion study** *n* : systematic observation, analysis, and measurement of the separate steps in the performance of a specific job for the purpose of establishing a standard time for each performance, improving procedures, and increasing productivity — called also *motion and time study, motion study, time study*

time and temperature method *n* : adjustment of the development time of a photographic negative in accordance with the developer solution temperature — called also *thermo development*

time at bat : AT BAT

time azimuth *n* : an observation by compass of the azimuth of a celestial body made at a specific time as a step in computing the compass error

time ball *n* : a large ball on a pole (as at an observatory) that is arranged to drop suddenly to mark a particular hour of day (as noon)

time base *n* : a part of an electronic circuit having a voltage varying accurately with time and used (as in radar) to provide range information or (as in television) to time the scanning operation

time belt *n* : TIME ZONE

time bet *n* : a provisional bet on a race made with a bookmaker that is invalid if the purchase time noted on the betting slip is later than the official start of the race

time bill *n* **1** : a bill of exchange payable at a definite future time **2** *Brit* : TIMETABLE

time–binding \ˈ⸗,⸗⸗\ *n* : the characteristically human activity of transmitting experience from one generation to another esp. through the use of symbols

time bomb *n* **1** : a bomb so constructed as to explode at a predetermined time **2** : something (as a situation, conflict, personality trait) that has a delayed explosive action ⟨too many administrators sit unknowingly on *time bombs* —H.F. & Katharine Pringle⟩

time book *n* : a book in which hours spent on a job by workers are recorded

time buyer *n* : a person employed by an advertising agency to select and arrange radio and television coverage for clients

time capsule *n* : a container holding historical records or objects representative of current culture that is deposited (as in the earth or in a cornerstone) for preservation until discovery by some future age

time card *n* **1** *usu* **timecard** : TIMETABLE ⟨despite a greatly speeded-up *timecard*, it hit every stop on schedule —B.A. Long & W.J.Dennis⟩ **2** : a card on which is kept a daily record of the time worked by an employee or the time of his arrival and departure

time chart *n* **1** : a chart showing the standard times in various

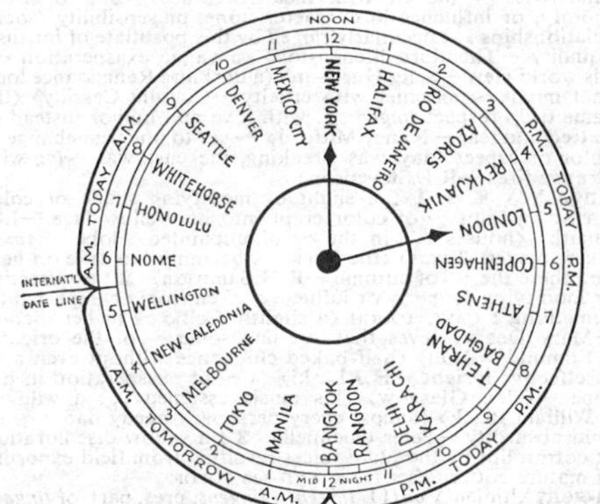

time chart

parts of the world with reference to a specified time at a specified place **2** : a table listing important events for successive years or groups of years within a particular historical period

time charter *n* : a contract for the cargo space of a manned ship for a specified period

time clerk *n* : TIMEKEEPER

time clock *n* : a clock with a device to record the times of arrival and departure of employees or the time at which a job is begun or completed — compare TELLTALE 3a

time constant *n* **1** : the time required for a current turned into a circuit under a steady electromotive force to reach to $\frac{e-1}{e}$ or 0.632 of its final strength (where *e* is the base of natural logarithms); *specif* : the ratio of the inductance of a circuit in henries to its resistance in ohms **2** : the relaxation time in the discharge of a capacitor that is equal to the product of the resistance in ohms of the discharging circuit and the capacity in farads of the condenser

time–consuming \ˈ⸗⸗,⸗⸗\ *adj* **1** : using or taking up a great deal of time ⟨the development of young clone selections from such seedling material had proved to be rather *time-consuming* —*Farmer's Weekly (So. Africa)*⟩ **2** : wasteful of time ⟨efforts to block legislation may take the form of speech-making, roll-calls, and other *time-consuming* tactics —W.S.Sayre⟩

time copy *n* : newspaper or periodical copy usu. set in type beforehand and that can be used at any time

timed *adj* [fr. past part. of [2]*time*] **1** : made to occur at or in a set time ⟨a ~ explosion⟩ ⟨a ~ examination⟩ **2** : done or taking place at a time of a specified sort ⟨a poorly ~ speech⟩ ⟨a propitiously ~ proposal⟩ ⟨ill-*timed*⟩

time deposit *n* : a bank deposit payable a specified number of days after deposit or after receipt by the bank of notice of withdrawal and considered by federal regulations as being any deposit payable after 30 days or after 30 days' notice

time depth *n* : a period of time during which a culture, language, or group of languages has been undergoing independent genetic development ⟨a language with a *time depth* of 5000 years⟩

timed fire *n* : target firing in which a given number of rounds are fired within a particular time limit

time draft *n* : a draft payable a specified number of days after date of the draft or presentation to the drawee

time error *n* : a systematic error in the comparison of magnitudes resulting from the fact that one magnitude follows the other in time

time–expired \ˈ⸗⸗,⸗\ *adj* : having completed a term of enlistment or military service ⟨fifteen hundred *time-expired* veterans had been discharged from the two regiments —Robert Graves⟩

time exposure *n* **1** : exposure of a photographic film for a definite time that is usu. more than one half second **2** : a photograph taken by time exposure

time fire *n* : artillery fire in which the projectile bursts or is intended to burst in air

time freight *n* : freight for movement on regularly scheduled trains providing expedited service and a guaranteed time of delivery; *also* : a train for handling such freight

time·ful \ˈtīmfəl\ *adj* [ME, fr. [1]*time* + *-ful*] *archaic* : SEASONABLE, TIMELY — **time·ful·ly** \-fəlē\ *adv*

time fuze *n* : a fuze that detonates a bursting charge after a definite interval of time has elapsed

time hit *n* : a hit made by a time thrust

time–honored \ˈ⸗,⸗⸗\ *adj* **1** : honored or entitled to honor because of age or long usage ⟨a deep respect for *time-honored* institutions —*New Republic*⟩ **2** : long established ⟨begun to undermine the *time-honored* position of the traditional holders of authority —H.W.Glidden⟩ ⟨a *time-honored* phrase⟩

time immemorial *n* **1 a** : a time beyond legal memory formerly fixed by English law as the beginning of the reign of Richard I in 1189 but modified in common law by various prescription acts **b** : a time going back beyond the memory of any person living **2** : time so long past as to be indefinite in history or tradition ⟨field forces from *time immemorial* have dealt with such offenses on the spot —R.H.Jackson⟩

timekeeper \ˈ⸗,⸗⸗\ *n* : one that keeps, measures, regulates, or determines the time: as **a** : TIMEPIECE **b** : one who keeps records of the time worked by employees (as for use in making up a payroll) **c** : one appointed to mark and announce the time of participants or the elapsed time in a race, game, or contest

timekeeping \ˈ⸗,⸗⸗\ *n* : the act, function, or process of keeping time

time killer *n* **1** : one who kills time : a person with time on his hands ⟨the reading room held many students, as well as a few *time killers*⟩ **2** : something that passes the time : DIVERSION ⟨made the experience full and memorable, made it an experience instead of a *time killer* —J.M.Barzun⟩

time killing *n* : the act or action of killing time

time lag *n* **1** : an interval of time between two related phenomena (as a cause and its effect) ⟨the *time lag* between the discovery of a scientific principle and its application —*Lamp*⟩ **2** : CULTURAL LAG ⟨have suffered a singular *time lag*, in bringing to the problems of today and tomorrow the elements of yesterday's thinking —Sidney Wallach⟩

time–lapse \ˈ⸗,⸗\ *adj* [fr. the n. *time lapse*] : of, relating to, or constituting a motion picture taken at a speed slower than normal but usu. projected at a normal speed so that a slow action (as the opening of a flower bud) appears to be speeded up : STOP-MOTION

[1]**time·less** \ˈtīmləs\ *adj* [[1]*time* + *-less*] **1** *archaic* : PREMATURE, UNTIMELY ⟨a pack of sorrows which would press you down . . . to your ~ grave —Shak.⟩ **2 a** : having no beginning or end : ETERNAL, INTERMINABLE, UNENDING ⟨nothing on dry land can match the ghastly war for survival which continues ceaselessly in a ~ night and seasonless year —F.G.Kay⟩ **b** : not restricted to a particular time or date : DATELESS ⟨much of what seems contemporary in popular fiction is fairly ~ —W.H.Whyte⟩ ⟨criticize him from the perspective of some ~ realism —D.R.Meyer⟩ **3** : not affected by time : AGELESS, CHANGELESS ⟨one of those ~ people who sometimes looked younger as they grew older —J.P.Marquand⟩ — **time·less·ly** *adv* — **time·less·ness** *n* -ES

[2]**timeless** \"\ *adv, archaic* : TIMELESSLY

tim·e·li·idae \,timəˈlīə,dē\ [NL, fr. *Timelia*, genus of babblers (prob. fr. native name in India) + *-idae*] *syn of* TIMALIIDAE

time limit *n* : a fixed period for doing or ending something; *specif* : a fixed amount of time allowed for a test with the object of measuring the amount of work an individual can accomplish in such time — contrasted with *amount limit*

time·li·ness \ˈtīmlēnəs, -lin-\ *n* -ES : the quality or state of being timely

time loan *n* : a loan with a definite maturity date — compare CALL LOAN

time lock *n* : a lock controlled by clockwork to prevent its being unlocked before a set time

[1]**time·ly** \ˈtīmlē, -li\ *adv* [ME *timliche, timely*, fr. OE *tīmlīce*, fr. *tīma* time + *-līce*, adv. suffix] **1** *archaic* : EARLY, SOON ⟨he did command me to call ~ on him —Shak.⟩ **2** : in time : OPPORTUNELY, SEASONABLY ⟨the present action was ~ brought within two years after his appointment —R.W.Starr⟩

[2]**timely** \"\ *adj* -ER/-EST [ME *timlich, timely*, fr. [1]*time* + *-lich, -ly* -ly, adj. suffix] **1 a** : done or occurring at a suitable time : OPPORTUNE ⟨if ~ treatment is available the patient has a good chance of recovery —*Nat'l Safety News*⟩ **b** : occurring at a normal or expected time ⟨I love my habits, the ~ routine and oscillation of the hours —L.P.Smith⟩ **c** : falling within a time prescribed by law or contract ⟨the plaintiff filed a ~ claim for refund —T.M.Madden⟩ **d** : appropriate to the times or the occasion ⟨a ~ book⟩ ⟨a ~ remark⟩ ⟨a ~ hogshead of home-brewed beer . . . served effectively as fire extinguisher —*Amer. Guide Series: Vt.*⟩ **2** *archaic* : ADVANCE, EARLY ⟨I know that he will presently be summoned . . . I have ~ information —Charles Dickens⟩ **syn** see SEASONABLE

time money *n* : money loaned or ready to be loaned for a specified period of time

time–motion study *var of* TIME AND MOTION STUDY

ti·meno·guy \tīˈmenə,gī\ *n* -ES [prob. fr. F *timon* tiller, helm + E *guy* — more at TIMONEER] : a rope stretched taut from a projecting obstacle to prevent rigging from chafing or fouling

time note *n* : a note payable at a specified time — compare DEMAND NOTE

time of day **1 a** : the time as indicated by the clock ⟨asked him what *time of day* it was⟩ **b** : the present time ⟨it is unnecessary at this *time of day* to argue that the world is round⟩ **2 a** : the state of the case : the true situation ⟨he's been here long enough to know the *time of day*⟩ **b** : the latest fashion ⟨has long set the *time of day* in . . . champagnes —*New Yorker*⟩

time on target : a concentration of artillery fire on a target in which the time of firing by each unit participating is so regulated that all the projectiles reach the target simultaneously

time·ous \ˈtīm(ē)əs, ˈtīmēəs\ *adj* [ME, fr. [1]*time* + *-ous*] : TIMELY ⟨has to give ~ notice to that effect —*Farmer's Weekly (So. Africa)*⟩ — **time·ous·ly** *adv*

time–out \ˈ⸗ˈ⸗\ *n* -S [fr. the phrase *to take time out*] **1** *usu* **time out** : a usu. brief suspension of activity or work : BREAK, INTERMISSION ⟨his eldest son died and he took *time out* to recover from the shock —*Newsweek*⟩ **2** : a brief period of suspension of play declared by an official in any of various organized sports (as for rest of players, treatment of an injured player, officials' conference)

time out of mind [ME] : TIME IMMEMORIAL

timepiece \ˈ⸗,⸗\ *n* : an instrument (as a clock or watch) for measuring time; *esp* : one that has no striking or chiming mechanism

timepleaser *n, obs* : TIMESERVER

time policy *n* : a marine insurance policy covering property for a specified period (as a year)

tim·er \ˈtīmə(r)\ *n* -S [[2]*time* + *-er*] **1** : one that measures, records, or regulates time: as **a** : TIMEPIECE; *esp* : a stopwatch for timing races or contests **b** : TIMEKEEPER **c** : a device in the ignition system of an internal-combustion engine that causes the spark to be produced in the cylinder at the correct time either by the interruption or by the closing of the primary circuit — compare DISTRIBUTOR **d** : one who determines the exposure time to be used to obtain a satisfactory print of each scene of a motion-picture negative **e** : one who corrects the escapement of timepieces **f** (1) : a device (as a clock) that indicates by means of an audible signal the end of the interval of time for which it is set (2) : a device for automatically starting or stopping a machine or other device at a given time or for automatically controlling the operating interval **2** [[1]*time* + *-er*] : one that does or serves in or for a specified time ⟨a first ~ in this office⟩ : one that has a specified relationship to time ⟨young-*timers* hep to the special needs of the holiday season —*advt*⟩

time rating *n* : the length of time a machine can carry a load without the specified conditions of load and temperature rise being exceeded

time recorder *n* : TIME CLOCK

[1]**times** \(ˌ)tīmz\ *prep* [ME, fr. pl. of [1]*time*] : multiplied by ⟨two ~ two is four⟩

[2]**times** \(ˌ)tīmz\ *adv* [fr. pl. of [1]*time*] *dial Eng* : many times : FREQUENTLY

time–saver \ˈ⸗,⸗⸗\ *n* : something that saves time

timesaving \ˈ⸗,⸗⸗\ *adj* : intended or serving to expedite something ⟨a ~ device⟩

time scale *n* : an arrangement of events used as a measure of the relative or absolute duration or antiquity of a period of history or geologic or cosmic time ⟨on the *time scale* of modern cosmology his brief and fevered existence seems a mere flash in the pan —*Times Lit. Supp.*⟩

time sense *n* : an ability to feel the lapse of time and to estimate and compare intervals esp. of short duration

time series *n* : a frequency distribution in which time is the independent variable

timeserver \ˈ⸗,⸗⸗\ *n* : one that shapes his behavior and ideas to fit the dominant pattern of his times or environment or to please his superiors : TEMPORIZER ⟨was in matters of principle inherently shifty, an opportunist and a ~ —S.H.Adams⟩

time service *n* : the determination and announcement of the precise time usu. conducted as a part of the work of an astronomical observatory, usu. based on transit observations of stars, and announced mainly by telegraphic and radio signals — compare TIME SIGNAL

[1]**timeserving** \ˈ⸗,⸗⸗\ *n* : the behavior or practice of a timeserver ⟨discourages energy and initiative in public office, and encourages ~ —L.K.Caldwell⟩

[2]**timeserving** \"\ *adj* : marked by or revealing a lack of independence or integrity : TEMPORIZING ⟨a mean, ~ little man, grovelling odiously before the wealthy people in the district —Peter Forster⟩ ⟨we cannot afford a ~ tameness —*Times Lit. Supp.*⟩ — **time·serv·ing·ness** *n* -ES

time sheet *n* **1** : a sheet for recording the time of arrival and departure of workers and for recording the amount of time spent on each job **2** : a sheet for summarizing hours worked by each worker during a pay period

time–shift \ˈ⸗,⸗\ *n* : a narrative method (as in a novel) that shifts back and forth in time from past to present instead of proceeding in strict chronological sequence

time sight *n* **1** : a set of observations for the determination of time that are usu. made with a transit instrument **2** : an observation by sextant of the altitude of a heavenly body to determine longitude by comparing the local time with Greenwich time

time signal *n* : a signal indicating an exact instant of time that is sent by telegraph or radio to regulate timepieces

time signature *n* **1** : a fraction that has a denominator indicating the kind of note (as a quarter note) taken as the time unit for the beat and a numerator indicating the number of these to the measure and that is placed at the beginning of a musical composition, movement, or section just after the key signature or at any point at which the meter changes to indicate the meter **2** : a symbol used to indicate the meter of a musical composition — compare [3]C 1

time spirit *n* [trans. of G *zeitgeist*] : ZEITGEIST

time stamp *n* : a clock-actuated device for recording time; *specif* : one for recording the date and time of day that letters or papers are received or sent out

time–stratigraphic \ˈ⸗,⸗⸗ˈ⸗⸗\ *adj* : of, relating to, or constituting rocks deposited during a specified time regardless of their composition, fossil content, or conditions of origin

time study *n* : TIME AND MOTION STUDY

time switch *n* : an electric switch that automatically operates at a set time

timetable \ˈ⸗,⸗⸗\ *n* **1** : a printed table showing times of departure and arrival (as of trains, buses, airplanes) from and at scheduled stopping points between two terminuses **2** : a schedule or plan listing or indicating the sequence in which things are to occur or be done and often the approximate or exact time of each ⟨a ~ that pinned the start and finish of each of this year's 133 events down to the minute —*Newsweek*⟩ ⟨determined resistance upset the ~ which had been set for the operation —H.L.Merillat⟩ **3** : a table showing the time value or relative duration of the various musical notes

time thrust *n* : a counterattack in fencing executed against and arriving in advance of the opponent's attack — compare STOP THRUST

time ticket *n* : TIME CARD 2

time train *n* : a train of wheels that drives the balance and escapement of a timepiece

time value *n* **1 a** : value measured by hours of labor **b** : value due to the date of receipt of goods or maturity of obligations **2** : the relative duration esp. of a musical note, tone, or rest

timework \ˈ⸗,⸗\ *n* : work paid for at a standard rate for the hour or the day — compare PIECEWORK

timeworker \ˈ⸗,⸗⸗\ *n* : a worker engaged on timework

timeworn \ˈ⸗,⸗\ *adj* **1** : worn or impaired by time ⟨its graceful, ~ residences of the plantation type —*Amer. Guide Series: Texas*⟩ **2 a** : AGE-OLD, ANCIENT ⟨based on ~ procedures and the collocated experience of the ages —F.C.Neff⟩ **b** : HACKNEYED, STALE ⟨a ~ joke⟩ ⟨a ~ expression⟩

time zone *n* : one of 24 longitudinal zones into which the world has been divided for establishing a regular sequence of time changes, which are each 15 degrees wide, and which each have as standard time throughout its area the time of its central meridian except where variations to maintain national or local uniformity are necessary

tim·id \ˈtiməd\ *adj, usu* -ER/-EST [L *timidus*, fr. *timēre* to be afraid, fear] **1** : lacking in courage or self-confidence : easily frightened or overawed ⟨~, silent, crouching under oppression —J.R.Green⟩ ⟨a ~ person would rather remain miserable than do anything unusual —Bertrand Russell⟩ **2 a** : marked by or revealing a lack of boldness or determination ⟨a ~ policy⟩ ⟨a ~ look⟩ ⟨their ~ love of established ways —V.L. Parrington⟩ **b** : HESITANT, TENTATIVE ⟨this intellectual life was ~, cautious and derivative —Van Wyck Brooks⟩ ⟨the darkness is broken by the ~ flare of a lamp or a candle —Lewis Mumford⟩

syn TIMOROUS: TIMID may stress lack of courage and venturesomeness and a tendency to cling to the safe, accustomed, undemonstrative, and unobtrusive ⟨meek, humble, *timid* persons, who accept things as they are, who tread in beaten paths, who are easily persuaded, who are cautious, prudent, and submissive —A.C.Benson⟩ ⟨in comparison with their fearlessness, their bold drawing, their dashing conception, their passion and action . . . how *timid* and conventional seemed his own friends —Edgar Johnson⟩ TIMOROUS may imply stronger influence of or domination by apprehension, fear, or terror causing one to shrink from independence or decision ⟨must have been a powerful, perhaps an insane, impulsion which drove the *timorous*, inconclusive Jesse, with his intuitive horror of guns, to send a bullet into his brain —S.H.Adams⟩ ⟨grew *timorous* and dejected, apprehending themselves to be haunted and possessed with vengeful spirits, on account of human blood that had been undeservedly spilt in this old town —William Bartram⟩

ti·mid·i·ty \tə'midəd·ē, -idətē, -i\ *n* -ES [L *timiditat-, timiditas*, fr. *timidus* timid + *-itat-, -itas* -ity] **:** the quality or state of being timid ⟨the animals have become so accustomed to motor traffic that they have quite lost their natural ~ —James Stevenson-Hamilton⟩ ⟨the ~ and conformity of the present day —C.V.Woodward⟩

tim·id·ly *adv* **:** in a timid manner

tim·id·ness *n* -ES [*timid* + *-ness*] **:** TIMIDITY

timing *n* -S [fr. gerund of ²*time*] **1 :** selection for maximum effect of the precise moment for beginning or doing something ⟨his bad luck or aim or ~ or whatever it was that caused him inevitably to be low man —Hamilton Basso⟩ ⟨the proper ~ of the operation in reference to the course of the disease —*Jour. Amer. Med. Assoc.*⟩: as **a :** the art or practice of regulating tempo (as in musical performance, utterance, dramatic action) so as to heighten the effectiveness of various moments by emphasis and of the whole by appropriate variations; *also* **:** the effect so produced ⟨often have to experiment with a comic scene, cutting it, changing its ~, before they can see how it works —*College English*⟩ **b :** the regulating of the speed of a motion, stroke, or blow so as to cause it to reach its maximum at the correct moment; *also* **:** the coordination of movements of body, arms, and hands to produce such effect **c :** coordination between a boxer's blows and the opportunities offered for attack **2 :** observation and recording of the elapsed time of an act, action, or process often by means of a stopwatch

timing gears *n pl* **:** the gear train with a two to one reduction through which the crankshaft drives the camshaft and thus controls valve timing in a four-stroke cycle internal-combustion engine

timing screw *n* **:** any of the adjustable screws in the rim of a watch balance that are used in timing the watch

timing valve *n* **:** an adjustable valve in a gas engine with hot tube ignition that automatically opens to permit a portion of the compressed explosive mixture to enter the ignition tube and so cause ignition at any desired point of the stroke — compare TIMER 1c

timing washer *n* **:** a small thin ring of metal (as gold or platinum) placed under the balance screws of a watch to slow the vibration period of the balance or to help poise it

ti·mis·ka·ming \tə'miskəmiŋ\ *adj, usu cap* [fr. *Timiskaming*, lake & district of southeast Ontario, Canada] **:** of or relating to a division of the Archeozoic — see GEOLOGIC TIME table

ti·mi·soa·ra \¦tēmēshə¦wärə, ¦tim-, -¦shwä-\ *adj, usu cap* [fr. *Timişoara*, city of southwest Romania] **:** of or from the city of Timisoara, Romania **:** of the kind or style prevalent in Timisoara

tim·ist \'tīməst\ *n* -S [¹*time* + *-ist*] **:** one that keeps time or is concerned with time

tim·mer \'timər\ *chiefly Scot var of* TIMBER

timne *usu cap, var of* TEMNE

ti·moc·ra·cy \tī'mäkrəsē\ *n* -ES [MF *tymocracie*, fr. ML *timocratia*, fr. Gk *timokratia* polity based on honor or wealth, fr. *timē* price, value, honor + *-kratia* -cracy — more at PAIN] **1** *Aristotelianism* **:** a stage of political development in which political and civil honors are distributed according to wealth **2** [Gk *timokratia*] *Platonism* **:** a stage of political development in which love of honor or glory is the ruling principle

ti·mo·crat·ic \¦tīmə¦krad·ik\ *or* **ti·mo·crat·i·cal** \-d·əkəl\ *adj* [*timocratic* fr. Gk *timokratikos*, fr. *timokratia* timocracy + *-ikos* -ic; *timocratical* fr. Gk *timokratikos* + E *-al*] **:** of, relating to, or representative of timocracy

timo·neer \¦timə¦ni(ə)r, ¦tim-\ *n* -S [F *timonier*, fr. MF, fr. *timon* tiller, helm (fr. — assumed — VL *timon-, timo*, alter. of L *temon-, temo* shaft of a wagon, beam of a plow, pole) + *-ier* -ary] **:** HELMSMAN ⟨teach him the trade of a ~ —W.S.Gilbert⟩

ti·mon·ism \'tīmə,nizəm\ *n* -S *usu cap* [*Timon*, 5th cent. B.C. Athenian misanthrope + E *-ism*] **:** MISANTHROPY ⟨expressive of a period of *Timonism* and despair in the author's life —*Times Lit. Supp.*⟩

tim·o·rese \¦timə¦rēz, -ēs\ *n, pl* **timorese** *cap* [*Timor*, island in southern Malay archipelago + E *-ese*] **:** a native or inhabitant of the island of Timor

timo·ro·so \,timə'rō(,)sō, ,tēm-, -rō(,)zō\ *adj (or adv)* [It, fr. ML *timorosus*] **:** HESITATING, TIMID — used as a direction in music

tim·o·rous \'tim(ə)rəs\ *adj* [ME, fr. MF *temoros, timoureus*, fr. ML *timorosus*, fr. L *timor* fear (fr. *timēre* to be afraid, fear) + *-osus* -ous] **1 a :** experiencing or showing fear or apprehension **:** AFRAID ⟨the tunny is ~ when coming in to spawn —Alan Villiers⟩ — sometimes used with *of* ⟨one is ~ of change, another dissatisfied with the present —B.N.Cardozo⟩ ⟨is occasionally unduly ~ of these rule-givers —Thomas Pyles⟩ **b :** fearful by nature or character **:** TIMID ⟨a ~ incompetent who was lucky to have good men under him —W.A.Swanberg⟩ **2 :** marked by or expressing timidity ⟨spoke little, and generally in a ~ tone, as though silence had been enjoined —Arnold Bennett⟩ **syn** see TIMID

tim·o·rous·ly *adv* **:** in a timorous manner

tim·o·rous·ness *n* -ES **:** the quality or state of being timorous

tim·or·some \'timə(r)səm\ *adj* [fr. *timorous*, after such pairs as E *cumbrous: cumbersome*] *chiefly dial* **:** TIMOROUS

ti·mo·te \tə'mōd·ē\ *n, pl* **timote** *or* **timotes** *usu cap* **1 a :** an Indian people or peoples of western Venezuela **b :** a member of such people **2 :** the language of the Timote people

tim·o·thy \'timəthē, -thi\ *or* **timothy grass** *n* -ES [prob. after *Timothy* Hanson, 18th cent. Am. farmer said to have introduced it from New England to the southern States] **:** a European grass (*Phleum pratense*) with long cylindrical spikes that is grown in northern U.S. and in Europe for hay — called also *herd's-grass*

timpan *var of* TYMPAN

tim·pa·ni \'timpə(,)nē, -,ni\ *n pl but sometimes sing in constr* [It, pl. of *timpano* kettledrum, fr. L *tympanum* drum — more at TYMPANUM] **:** a set of usu. two or three kettledrums played by one performer in an orchestra or band

tim·pa·nist \'timpənəst\ *n* -S [*timpani* + *-ist*] **:** one who plays the kettledrums **:** TYMPANIST

tim·u·cua \,timə'küə\ *n, pl* **timucua** *or* **timucuas** *usu cap* **1 a :** a possibly Muskogean people of central and northeastern Florida **b :** a member of such people **2 :** the language of the Timucua people

tim·u·cu·an \-üən\ *n, pl* **timucuan** *or* **timucuans** *usu cap* [*Timucua* + *-an*] **1 :** TIMUCUA 1 **2 :** a tentative language family comprising only the Timucua language and perhaps related to Muskogean

tim-whiskey \'tim,=,=\ *n* [*tim* (of unknown origin) + *whiskey*] **:** WHISKEY

¹**tin** \'tin\ *n* -S [ME, fr. OE; akin to OHG *zin* tin, ON *tin*] **1 :** a soft faintly bluish white lustrous low-melting metallic element that in this beta form exists as tetragonal crystals and is malleable and ductile at ordinary temperatures but changes gradually at low temperatures to a powdery gray cubic allotropic alpha form, that is bivalent and tetravalent in its compounds and is not oxidized by moist air, that occurs principally in the form of the dioxide cassiterite and various sulfides (as stannite), that is extracted by roasting and smelting with carbon, and that is used chiefly as a protective coating (as for steel and copper), in tinfoil, in collapsible tubes, and in soft solders, bronze, pewter, babbitt metals, type metals, and casting and other alloys — symbol *Sn*; see BLOCK TIN, FUSIBLE METAL, TERNE, TIN PEST, TINPLATE; ELEMENT table **2 :** a box, can, pan, or other vessel made of tinplate: **a :** any of various open tinplate sheets or pans used chiefly for baking ⟨drop the cookies on a greased ~⟩ ⟨pour the batter into a cake ~⟩ **b** *chiefly Brit* (1) **:** a vacuum-sealed can holding canned food ⟨a ~ of salmon⟩ ⟨open a ~ of tomatoes⟩ (2) **:** a tinplate container with cover or lid used for packaging biscuits, crackers, sweets, or tobacco **3 :** thin plates of iron or steel covered with tin **:** TINPLATE **4** *chiefly Brit* **:** CASH, MONEY ⟨pray them to advance the requisite ~ for ransom —H.C.Bunner⟩

²**tin** \"\ *adj* **1 :** of, relating to, or consisting of tin **2 :** of base or inferior material **:** SPURIOUS ⟨other narrow-minded little ~ gods —*N.Y. Times*⟩ ⟨the bright ~ divinity of the happy ending —Clifton Fadiman⟩

³**tin** \"\ *vt* **tinned; tinned; tinning; tins** [ME *tinnen*, fr. *tin*] **1 a :** to cover, coat, or plate (something) with tin **b :** to cover (as a soldering iron or the back of an electrotype shell) with solder or a tin alloy **2** *chiefly Brit* **:** to put up or pack in tins **:** CAN ⟨cannery workers ~ asparagus —*Nat'l Geographic*⟩ ⟨stopped to have lunch — tea and *tinned* food —Russell Hill⟩

⁴**tin** \"\ *n, pl* **tin** *or* **tins** *usu cap* **1 :** a people of the lower mountains of northeastern Thailand related to the Kha of Vietnam — called also *Khatin* **2 :** a member of the Tin people

ti·na·ja \tə'nä(,)hä\ *n* -S [Sp, aug. of *tina* jar, fr. L, wine jar] **1 :** a large porous water jar for cooling water by evaporation **2** *Southwest* **:** WATER POCKET, POTHOLE

ti·nam·i·dae \tə'namə,dē\ *n pl, cap* [NL, fr. *Tinamus*, type genus (fr. F *tinamou*) + *-idae*] **:** a family of large predominantly terrestrial birds (order Tinamiformes) comprising the tinamous

tin·a·mi·for·mes \,tinəmə'fȯr(,)mēz, tə,nam-\ *n pl, cap* [NL, fr. *Tinamus* + *-iformes*] **:** an order of birds (superorder Neognathae) coextensive with the family Tinamidae

tin·a·mine \'tinə,mīn, -,mən\ *adj* [*tinamou* + *-ine*] **:** of or relating to the tinamous

tin·a·mou \'tinə,mü\ *n* -S [F, fr. Galibi *tinamu*] **:** any of numerous birds that constitute the family Tinamidae, resemble gallinaceous birds in habits but are related to the ratite birds esp. in the structure of the palate though the sternum is deeply keeled, have a rudimentary tail without a pygostyle, and produce eggs with a peculiar enameled surface

ti·na process \¦tēnə-\ *n* [Sp *tina* jar, tub] **:** a process for amalgamation of silver ores in tubs

tin·cal \'tiŋkəl; 'tiŋ,kal, -kȧl, 'tin,k-\ *n* -S [Malay *tingkal*] **:** a mineral $Na_2B_4O_7.10H_2O$ consisting of a native borax formerly imported from Tibet and once the chief source of boric compounds

tin·cal·co·nite \tin'kalkə,nīt, tiŋ'k-\ *n* -S [*tincal* + Gk *konia* ashes, dust + E *-ite* — more at INCINERATE] **:** a mineral $Na_2B_4O_7.5H_2O$ consisting of sodium borate pentahydrate that is one of the principal ore minerals of borax and boron compounds — compare KERNITE

tin can *n* **1 :** a can or cup made of tin or similar metal **2** *slang* **:** DESTROYER 2

tin·chel \'tiŋkəl, 'tiŋkəl\ *n* -S [ScGael *timchioll* circuit, compass] *Scot* **:** a ring formed by hunters to drive or enclose deer

tin chloride *n* **:** a chloride of tin: as **a :** STANNIC CHLORIDE **b :** STANNOUS CHLORIDE

tinclad \'=,=\ *n* -S [²*tin* + *clad* (as in ²*ironclad*)] **:** a gunboat protected with light armor

tin cry *n* **:** the peculiar creaking noise made when a bar of tin is bent by twinning of the metal crystals

tin crystals *n pl but usu sing in constr* **:** stannous chloride dihydrate $SnCl_2.2H_2O$ used formerly as a mordant — called also *tin salt*

¹**tinct** \'tiŋ(k)t\ *adj* [L *tinctus*, past part. of *tingere* to tinge — more at TINGE] **:** TINGED, TINTED ⟨the blue in black, the green in gray is ~ —Edmund Spenser⟩

²**tinct** \"\ *n* -S [L *tinctus*, past part. of *tingere*] **:** TINCTURE, TINGE ⟨in the color or ~ lies the main difference between Irish and American glass —Dorothy Daniel⟩ ⟨new leaf and shadowy ~ —Wallace Stevens⟩

tinct *abbr* tincture

tinc·tion \'tiŋ(k)shən\ *n* -S [LL *tinction-, tinctio* act of dipping, fr. L *tinctus* (past part.) + *-ion-, -io* -ion] **:** the act or process of staining or dyeing; *also* **:** coloring matter

tinc·to·ri·al \(')tiŋk¦tōrēəl\ *adj* [L *tinctorius* of or relating to dipping (fr. *tinctus*, past part. + *-orius* -ory) + E *-al*] **:** of or relating to colors or to dyeing or staining **:** imparting a color ⟨has the greatest opacity and ~ strength of all white pigments —Andries Voet⟩ — **tinc·to·ri·al·ly** \-ēəlē\ *adv*

¹**tinc·ture** \'tiŋ(k)chə(r), -)sh-\ *n* -S [ME, fr. L *tinctura* act or instance of dyeing or tinging, fr. *tinctus* (past part. of *tingere* to tinge) + *-ura* -ure — more at TINGE] **1 a :** a substance that colors, dyes, or stains **:** PIGMENT, STAIN **b :** a color conveyed by or assumed from such a substance **:** HUE, TINT ⟨one dye of that ~ covered his clothes —Thomas Hardy⟩ ⟨all the ~*s* of the rainbow⟩ **2 a :** a characteristic or quality with which a person or thing is imbued or modified **:** TINGE, CAST ⟨both young men were Whigs of a radical ~ —*Current History*⟩ ⟨Protestantism has . . . a deep ~ of empiricism —A.N.Wilder⟩ **b :** a slight admixture or smattering of something **:** TOUCH, TRACE ⟨his followers were not altogether without a ~ of soldiership —T.B.Macaulay⟩ ⟨what he said had plausibility and perhaps a ~ of sincerity —Francis Hackett⟩ ⟨with a ~ of modern science added to . . . backwoods Calvinism —Carl Van Doren⟩ **3** *obs* **a :** an immaterial quintessential active alchemical principle capable of causing material and spiritual transmutations **b :** a chemical principle esp. when obtained by extraction; *also* **:** EXTRACT **4 :** a heraldic metal, color, or fur — usu. used in pl. ⟨the ~*s* of the armorial coat are carefully described⟩ **5 :** a solution of a medicinal substance (as a plant principle) in an alcoholic or hydroalcoholic menstruum or in a mixture of alcohol and ether

²**tincture** \"\ *vt* **tinctured; tinctured; tincturing** \-chəriŋ, -sh(ə)riŋ\ **tinctures 1 :** to tint or stain with a color **:** TINGE ⟨the islands were . . . so infused with the hues of the *tinctured* clouds —H.M.Tomlinson⟩ ⟨the blossom *tinctured* with deep green —*Parke-Bernet Galleries Cat.*⟩ **2 a :** to infuse or instill a physical property or entity in **:** IMPREGNATE ⟨the heavy traffic ~*s* the air with carbon monoxide⟩ ⟨the cytoplasm . . . is so *tinctured* by the products of the bacilli contained in it —*Amer. Jour. of Pathology*⟩ **b :** to imbue with a character or quality **:** AFFECT ⟨was not sure envy did not ~ his disdain —Waldo Frank⟩ ⟨*tinctured* political life with a similar monotony —Carleton Beals⟩ ⟨hardly ever spoke a sentence that was not *tinctured* . . . with his delightful and rare personality —Osbert Sitwell⟩

tincture press *n* **:** a cylindrical press used to express the menstruum adhering to the particles of a drug after extraction

tind \'tin(d), 'tīn\ *vb* -ED/-ING/-S [ME *tinden*, fr. (assumed) OE *tyndan*; akin to OE *tendan* to kindle — more at TINDER] *vt, dial Eng* **:** to set on fire **:** KINDLE, IGNITE ~ *vi, dial Eng* **:** to catch fire or become inflamed **:** BURN

tin·dal \'tindᵊl\ *n* -S [Hindi *tandail*] **:** a petty officer or supervisor of lascars or Indian workmen

tin·da·lo \'tində,lō\ *n* -S [Tag *tindalō*] **1 :** a timber tree (*Pahudia rhomboidea*) of the family Leguminosae of the Philippines having a hard valuable wood like that of the ipil **2 :** the wood of the tindalo

tin·der \'tində(r)\ *n* -S [ME, fr. OE *tynder, tyndre*; akin to OHG *zuntra* tinder, ON *tundr*; akin to OE *tendan* to kindle, OHG *zunten*, ON *tendra*, Goth *tandjan* to kindle, *tundnan* to burn] **1 :** an inflammable substance that readily takes spark or fire and is adaptable for use as kindling ⟨the woods are dry as ~⟩ — see ³PUNK **2 :** something that serves to incite, inflame, or spread abroad a movement, idea, or development ⟨men who are spiritually unfulfilled . . . are prey for the demagogue, ~ for the incendiary —C.T.Lanham⟩ ⟨the spark of your idea will . . . spread through the fresh ~ of new generations —L.J.Halle⟩ ⟨the human ~ that he writes about is best suited to kindle . . . wild mob rule —*Atlantic*⟩

tinderbox 1

tinderbox \'=,=\ *n* **1 a :** a metal box for holding tinder and usu. a flint and steel for striking a spark **b :** an object (as a building) or place containing highly inflammable material ⟨the old tenements are ~*es* ready to go up in flame⟩ ⟨region 5 of the U.S. forest service is America's touchiest ~ —Frank Cameron⟩ **2 :** a person or thing containing inflammatory or explosive potentialities esp. for strife or conflict ⟨the whole Caribbean region was a ~; only a spark was needed to set it off —H.B.Murkland⟩ ⟨events that were potentially the ~ of World War III —*Saturday Rev.*⟩

tinder fungus *n* **:** a fungus that is a source of punk; *esp* **:** a destructive pore fungus (*Fomes fomentarius*) that attacks the beech, elm, and various fruit trees and is used in making tinder and a pliant feltlike material

tin·dery \'tind(ə)rē, -ri\ *adj* **:** resembling tinder **:** highly inflammable or inflammatory ⟨covered with dry, ~ sea moss —Herman Melville⟩ ⟨described the . . . drought with a ~ phrase capable of kindling this page —*Nat'l Geographic*⟩ ⟨ahead in the ~ future —*Time*⟩

tin dichloride *n* **:** STANNOUS CHLORIDE

tin dioxide *n* **:** STANNIC OXIDE

¹**tine** \'tīn, 'tin\ *vt* [ME *tinen*, fr. OE *tȳnan*; akin to OE *tūn* enclosure, fence, village, town — more at TOWN] *dial Eng* **:** CLOSE, SHUT, ENCLOSE

²**tine** \'tīn\ *n* -S [ME *tind*, fr. OE; akin to OHG *zint* point, spike, tine, ON *tindr* and prob. to OHG *zinna* pinnacle] **1 :** one of a set of slender pointed projecting parts of an implement or a weapon **2 :** a pointed branch of a deer's antlers ⟨prongs are not indicative of age . . . but the number of ~*s* on the antlers —*Wyo. Wild Life*⟩

³**tine** \'tīn\ *vb* **tined** \'tīnd\ *or* **tint** \'tint\ **tined** *or* **tint; tining; tines** [ME *tinen, tynen*, of Scand origin; akin to ON *tȳna* to lose, destroy; akin to ON *tjōn* injury — more at TEEN] *vt, dial Brit* **:** LOSE, WASTE ~ *vi, dial Brit* **:** to become lost **:** PERISH

⁴**tine** \"\ *n* -S [perh. fr. ³*tine*; fr. the trouble or damage it causes] *dial Eng* **:** any of various plants (as vetches) having twining or clasping tendrils

tin·ea \'tinēə\ *n* [ME, fr. ML, fr. L, worm, moth] **1** -S **:** any of several fungous diseases of the skin of man and domestic animals **:** RINGWORM **2** *cap* [NL, fr. L, worm, moth] **:** the type genus of the family Tineidae

ti·nea bar·bae \,tinēə'bär,bē\ *n* [NL, tinea of the beard] **:** BARBER'S ITCH

ti·nea ca·pi·tis \-'kapəd·əs\ *n* [LL, lit., worm of the head] **:** an infection of the scalp caused by fungi of the genera *Trichophyton* and *Microsporum* and characterized by scaly patches penetrated by a few dry brittle hairs

ti·nea cor·po·ris \-'kȯ(r)pərəs\ *n* [NL, tinea of the body] **:** a fungous infection involving parts of the body not covered with hair

ti·nea cru·ris \-'krürəs\ *n* [NL, crural tinea] **:** a fungous infection involving the groin, perineum, and the perianal region

tin·e·al \'tinēəl\ *adj* **:** of, relating to, or being tinea ⟨a ~ rash⟩

ti·nea pe·dis \,tinēə'pedəs\ *n* [NL, tinea of the foot] **:** ATHLETE'S FOOT

tin ear *n* **1 :** CAULIFLOWER EAR **2 :** a deafened or insensitive ear ⟨motorists . . . have developed a glass eye and a *tin ear* for traffic safety programs —*Springfield (Mass.) Union*⟩ ⟨only at his best does he transcend a *tin ear* and color blindness —George Mayberry⟩

ti·nea ton·su·rans \,tinēə,tän'sürənz, -,ranz\ *n* [NL, fr. ML *tinea* + NL *tonsurans* (specific epithet of the parasitic fungus *Trichophyton tonsurans*), pres. part. of *tonsurare* to shear, clip, fr. ML, fr. L *tonsura* act of shearing, tonsure — more at TONSURE] **:** tinea capitis involving any portion of the hairy parts of domestic animals

tined \'tīnd\ *adj* [²*tine* + *-ed*] **:** having or furnished with tines

¹**tin·e·id** \'tinēəd\ *adj* [NL *Tineidae*] **:** of or relating to the Tineidae

²**tineid** \"\ *n* -S **:** a moth of the family Tineidae

ti·ne·idae \tə'nēə,dē\ *n pl, cap* [NL, fr. *Tinea*, type genus + *-idae*] **:** a family of small usu. dully colored moths (superfamily Tineoidea) comprising the common clothes moths and related insects and in former classifications including all or most of the Microlepidoptera

tin·e·ina \,tinē'īnə, -ē'ēnə\ *n pl, cap* [NL, fr. *Tinea* + *-ina*] *in some esp former classifications* **:** a group of small moths variously ranked and nearly coextensive with the modern superfamily Tineoidea — **tin·e·ine** \'tinē,īn, -ē,ēn\ *adj*

¹**tin·e·oid** \'tinē,ȯid\ *adj* [NL *Tineoidea*] **:** of or relating to the Tineoidea

²**tineoid** \"\ *n* -S **:** a moth of the superfamily Tineoidea

tin·e·oi·dea \,tinē'ȯidēə\ *n pl, cap* [NL, fr. *Tinea* + *-oidea*] **:** a superfamily of small moths comprising the majority of the Microlepidoptera (as the clothes moths, carpet moths, leaf miners) and having narrow simply veined wings broadly fringed with hairs

ti·ne·o·la \tə'nēələ, ,tinē'ōlə\ *n* [NL, fr. LL, small worm, small moth, dim. of L *tinea*] **1** *cap* **:** a genus of clothes moths including the webbing clothes moth **2** -S **:** any moth of the genus *Tineola*; *esp* **:** WEBBING CLOTHES MOTH

tines *pl of* TINE, *pres 3d sing of* TINE

tin fish *n, slang* **:** TORPEDO

tinfoil \'=,= *sometimes* '=,'=\ *n* [ME, fr. ²*tin* + *foil*] **1 :** a thin metal sheeting now usu. made of aluminum or tin-lead alloy **2 a :** FOIL 4a **b :** SILVER PAPER 2

¹**ting** \'tiŋ\ *vb* -ED/-ING/-S [ME *tingen*, of imit. origin] *vt* **:** to cause (as a bell) to make a ting ~ *vi* **:** to sound with or make a ting

²**ting** \"\ *n* -S **:** a high-pitched sound (as made by a light stroke on a small bell) ⟨the ~ of the bell at . . . table —Nathaniel Burt⟩

³**ting** *var of* THING

⁴**ting** \'diŋ\ *n* -S [Chin (Pek) *ting*³] **:** an ancient Chinese ceremonial vessel consisting of a deep bowl with usu. two handles supported on three legs

ting-a-ling \'tiŋə¦liŋ\ *n* -S [imit.] **:** the sound of a tinkling bell

¹**tinge** \'tinj\ *vb* **tinged; tinged; tingeing** *or* **tinging; tinges** [ME *tingen*, fr. L *tingere* to dip, moisten, tinge; akin to Gk *tengein* to wet, moisten, OHG *dunkōn, thunkōn* to dip] *vt* **1 a :** to color with a slight shade or stain **:** TINT ⟨kill plants that . . . will ~ the edge of the melting snow with early green —Allan Fraser⟩ ⟨the scarlet glare of the flames *tinged* her flesh with the color of rusty iron —Ellen Glasgow⟩ ⟨the sun . . . ~*ing* with colors of the rainbow the sandy beach —A.C. Whitehead⟩ **b :** to affect or modify with a slight odor or taste ⟨the roses ~ the air with their fragrance⟩ **2 :** to affect, modify, or influence in character, tone, or sensibility ⟨social relationships . . . peculiarly *tinged* by this postulate of intrinsic equality —Theodore Bienenstok⟩ ⟨a vague exasperation ~*s* his world view —Selig Harrison⟩ ⟨a darkling Renaissance look that might ~ mischief with cruelty —Claudia Cassidy⟩ ⟨the same deep respect *tinged* . . . with love and humor instead of hatred and fear —Nancy Mitford⟩ ~ *vi* **:** to undergo change in color or aspect ⟨day was breaking, the east was ~*ing* with strange fires —R.L.Stevenson⟩

²**tinge** \"\ *n* -S **1 :** a slight or modifying shade or color **:** TINT ⟨a faint ~ of color crept into her yellow face —J.C. Snaith⟩ ⟨houses . . . in the ~ of unpainted adobe —*Amer. Guide Series: Texas*⟩ ⟨the trees . . . beginning to take on here and there the ~*s* of autumn —R.H.Sampson⟩ **2 :** an affective or modifying property or influence taken from or imparted by something **:** CAST, TOUCH ⟨a slightly Celtic ~ in her diction —Mary Deasy⟩ ⟨eyes that . . . had some ~ of the oriental —Edmund Wilson⟩ ⟨half-baked eloquence without even a ~ of effective insight —H.J.Laski⟩ ⟨a ~ of exasperation in her tone —Ellen Glasgow⟩ ⟨his music assumed . . . a wild ~ —William Black⟩ ⟨almost every personal tragedy had a ~ of mild absurdity —Peter Quennell⟩ **3 :** a yellow discoloration of cotton lint by the plant juices resulting from field exposure of mature cotton after frost **syn** see COLOR

tin·gent \'tinjənt\ *adj* [L *tingent-, tingens*, pres. part. of *tingere* to tinge] *archaic* **:** having the power to tinge **:** COLORING

ting·gi·an *also* **tin·gui·an** \tiŋ'gē,än\ *n, pl* **tinggian** *or* **tinggians** *also* **tinguian** *or* **tinguians** *usu cap* **1 a :** a predominantly pagan people inhabiting western Luzon, Philippines **b :** a member of such people **2 :** the Austronesian language of the Tinggian people

¹**tin·gid** \'tinjəd\ *adj* [NL *Tingidae*] **:** of or relating to the Tingidae

²**tingid** \"\ *n* -S **:** a bug of the family Tingidae **:** LACE BUG

tin·gi·dae \'tinjə,dē\ *n pl, cap* [NL, fr. *Tingis*, type genus (of unknown origin) + *-idae*] **:** a family of bugs (order Hemiptera) containing the lace bugs

tin·git·i·dae \tin'jid·ə,dē\ [NL, fr. *Tingit-, Tingis*, genus of lace bugs + *-idae*] *syn of* TINGIDAE

tin glaze *n* **:** an opaque glaze made of an oxide of tin or tin ashes and used on pottery

tin-glaze \'=,=\ *vt* **:** to coat (pottery) with a tin glaze

1tin·gle \'tiŋgəl\ *n* -s [ME] **1 :** a small nail **:** TACK **2 :** a patch on a boat constructed to cover a hole or leak by overlapping

2tingle \"\ *vb* **tingled; tingled; tingling** \-g(ə)liŋ\ **tingles** [ME *tinglen*, alter. of *tinklen* to tinkle — more at TINKLE] *vi* **1 a :** to experience or feel a ringing, stinging, prickling, or thrilling sensation ⟨a great blast of his boat's whistle . . . made our ears ~ —R.P.Warren⟩ ⟨the blister on his right foot began to ~ —Fred Majdalany⟩ ⟨music that made . . . blood ~ —Sherwood Anderson⟩ ⟨like to weep, to laugh, to ~ with excitement, admiration, or fear —Rose Macaulay⟩ **b :** to cause such a sensation ⟨the trumpets ~ in his ears⟩ **2 :** to make a repeated light ringing or tinkling sound **:** TINKLE ⟨bells began to ~ above us —Ernest Beaglehole⟩ ⟨rain *tingled* steadily on the roof —Graham Greene⟩ ~ *vt* **1 :** to cause a thrilling, stinging, or pricking sensation in **:** STIR, STIMULATE ⟨an eagerness *tingled* him when he saw what he wanted —Alan Kapelner⟩ ⟨each is guaranteed . . . to ~ the brain —*advt*⟩ **2 :** to cause (a bell) to ring lightly **:** TINKLE

3tingle \"\ *n* -s **1 :** a tinkling sound **:** TINGLING **2 :** a tingling sensation or condition ⟨gave me a wincing ~ to see the deep marks of the murderously sharp talons —R.T.Bird⟩ ⟨feel the ~ of the hot blood of resentment mounting to our cheeks —B.N.Cardozo⟩ ⟨felt a ~ of excitement —Earle Birney⟩ ⟨was filled with a ~ of pleasure —Louis Auchincloss⟩

tingle-tingle \'tiŋgəl¦tiŋgəl\ *n* [fr. native name in western Australia] **:** STRINGYBARK

tin·gling·ly *adv* **1 :** in a manner that causes one to tingle ⟨his book is . . . ~ provocative —Donald Harrington⟩ **2 :** with tingling ⟨~ conscious of it —Christine Weston⟩

tin·gly \'tiŋg(ə)lē, -li\ *adj* **:** tingling or causing tingling

tings *pres 3d sing of* TING, *pl of* TING

ting·tang \'tiŋ,taŋ\ *n* [redupl. of *2ting*] **:** the alternating sound of two differently toned bells esp. in a clock that sounds the quarter and half hours on only two bells

tin hat *n* **:** a metal hat or helmet worn (as by a soldier or industrial worker) for protection

tinhorn \'=,=\ *n* [*2tin* + *horn*] **:** a pretentious or boastful person or gambler having little money, power, or ability ⟨the gambling places were . . . swarming with ~*s* . . . dockhands, traveling men —H.L.Davis⟩ ⟨those ~*s* that spend all they got on dress suits and haven't got a decent suit of underwear to their name —Sinclair Lewis⟩

tinier *comparative of* TINY

tinies *pl of* TINY

tiniest *superlative of* TINY

tin·i·kling \,tinə'kliŋ\ *n* -s [Tag, fr. *tikling* tikling] **:** BAMBOO DANCE

ti·ni·ly \'tīn³lē, -nəl|, |i\ *adv* **:** in the manner or condition of something tiny ⟨a miniature worm of train rolled ~ along the embankment —Bruce Marshall⟩

ti·ni·ness \'tīnēnəs, -īnin-\ *n* -ES **:** the quality or state of being tiny

tining *pres part of* TINE

1tink \'tiŋk\ *vi* -ED/-ING/-S [ME *tinken*, of imit. origin] **:** to make a tinkling sound **:** TINKLE ⟨no roar came . . . and no bell ~*ed* —F.M.Ford⟩

2tink \"\ *n* -s **:** the sound of a light object striking against a resonant metal **:** PLINK ⟨the crackling of the fire, the ~ of sparks in the stovepipe —Dorothy Thomas⟩ ⟨the wind caught a ~ of harness rings and a jingle of spur rowels —Tom Lea⟩

1tin·ker \'tiŋkə(r)\ *n* -s [ME *tinkere*, prob. fr. *tink* tinkle (of imit. origin) + *-ere* -er] **1 a :** a usu. itinerant repairman who mends kitchen or household utensils **b** *chiefly Irish* **:** GYPSY ⟨a story of wandering ~*s* and their struggle against the conventions of society —Paul Rotha⟩ **c :** an unskillful mender **:** BUNGLER **d :** TINNER 5 **2 :** TINKER MACKEREL **3 :** one that seeks to change, adjust, or improve often experimentally ⟨desire of every theatrical ~ and literary meddler —Richard Hanser⟩ ⟨social ~*s* —O.W.Holmes †1935⟩ ⟨all of us are . . . ~*s* of words —*Holiday*⟩

2tin·ker \"\ *vb* **tinkered; tinkered; tinkering** \-k(ə)riŋ\ **tinkers** *vi* **:** to work or act as or in the manner of a tinker; *esp* **:** to repair or adjust something in an unskilled or experimental manner ⟨the American likes to ~, and his passion for gadgets is notorious —H.S.Commager⟩ ⟨while he could read blueprints . . . he preferred to experiment and ~ —J.K. Galbraith⟩ ⟨even professionals have to ~ to make these sentences come out right —Milton Hall⟩ — often used with *with* or *at* ⟨spent . . . his spare time ~*ing* with machines —*Current Biog.*⟩ ⟨people ~ with their houses and keep adding to them —Mary H. Vorse⟩ ⟨the feeling they could also ~ with their social system and their psyches to reach a worldly paradise —J.D.Hart⟩ ⟨began to ~ at the wound in rather a clumsy way —Stephen Crane⟩ ⟨was always ~*ing* at verse —W.A. White⟩; sometimes used with *around* ⟨is not something that can be easily fixed merely by ~*ing* around with the curriculum —Norman Cousins⟩ ~ *vt* **:** to repair, adjust, or experiment with ⟨could expertly ~ pot, pan, or kettle —S.H.Adams⟩ ⟨they ~ everything, from decrepit hay rakes to railroad bridges —S.K.Farrington⟩ ⟨had ~*ed* their old car into shape —John Hermann⟩ — sometimes used with *up* ⟨~ up as many of the finished models as could be kept off the scrap heap —L.J.Carr⟩

tinkerbird \'=,=,=\ *n* **:** any of various barbets with a harsh ringing note: as **a :** COPPERSMITH 2 **b :** any of several small African barbets of the genus *Pogoniulus*

tin·ker·er *n* -s **:** one that tinkers

tinker mackerel *n* **:** a small or young mackerel; *esp* **:** CHUB MACKEREL

tinker's curse *or* **tinker's cuss** *n* [prob. so called fr. the reputation of tinkers as being given to idle profanity] *Brit* **:** TINKER'S DAMN

tinker's damn *or* **tinker's dam** *n* [*tinker's damn* prob. so called fr. the tinkers' reputation for blasphemy; *tinker's dam* prob. by folk etymology fr. *tinker's damn*; prob. fr. the use by tinkers of a small dam of dough or mud to confine solder used in patching holes in pans] **:** something absolutely worthless ⟨people who didn't give a *tinker's damn* about poetry were . . . interested —James Blish⟩ ⟨pointed out a federal system isn't worth a *tinker's damn* —H.J.Laski⟩ ⟨is too involved . . . to make us care a *tinker's dam* what happens —R.B.Morris⟩

tin·ker's root \¦tiŋkə(r)z-\ *or* **tinker's weed** *n* [*tinker* prob. fr. the name *Tinker*] **:** FEVERROOT

tin-kettling \(')tin'ket(³)liŋ\ *n* [fr. *tin kettle* + *-ing*] *Brit* **:** a mock serenade; *esp* **:** SHIVAREE

1tin·kle \'tiŋkəl\ *vb* **tinkled; tinkled; tinkling** \-k(ə)liŋ\ **tinkles** [ME *tinklen*, freq. of *tinken* to make a tinkling sound] *vi* **1 :** TINGLE **2 a :** to make or emit a tinkle ⟨bells from distant sheep ~ through dreamy air —Lord Dunsany⟩ ⟨drums beating and marimbas *tinkling* —Dan Wickenden⟩ **b :** to make a sound suggestive of a tinkle esp. while flowing or moving ⟨the brook *tinkled* —George Meredith⟩ ⟨a footfall *tinkled* suddenly, incredibly tiny —Elinor Wylie⟩ ⟨the chaffinches *tinkled* excitedly —Gerald Durrell⟩ **c :** RHYME, JINGLE ⟨frames it in tripping rhythms and absurdly *tinkling* rhymes —Louis Untermeyer⟩ **3 a :** to produce a sound of or suggestive of a tinkle ⟨she *tinkled* on the piano but was not allowed to join an orchestra —Virginia Woolf⟩ ⟨can sit . . . and ~ away at waltzes —Claudia Cassidy⟩ **b :** to talk idly or foolishly or in a light gay manner **:** CHATTER, PRATE ⟨skipping and *tinkling* through all the social events of the town —Dorothy Parker⟩ **4 :** URINATE — not often in polite use ~ *vt* **1 :** to sound or make known (the time) by a tinkle ⟨through the tumult the bells . . . *tinkled* the hour —Hugh Walpole⟩ — sometimes used with *out* ⟨a small ornate clock . . . that *tinkled* out the hours —Mary Deasy⟩ **2 a :** to cause to make the sound of or as if of a tinkle ⟨likes to ~ the piano keys⟩ ⟨~*s* his guitar at every opportunity⟩ **b :** to produce (a sound or tune) by tinkling ⟨sitting idly *tinkling* a tune on his harpsichord⟩ — sometimes used with *out* ⟨found a Jew's harp . . . and began to ~ out an Irish jig tune —Henry Lapham⟩

2tinkle \"\ *n* -s **1 a :** a series of short high ringing or clinking sounds ⟨from the engine room the ~ of bells —R.H.Davis⟩ ⟨the ~ of glassware —H.A.Sinclair⟩ **b :** a sound suggestive of a tinkle ⟨the high ~ of the harp —Willa Cather⟩ ⟨the high ~ of their laughter —Irwin Shaw⟩ ⟨after the ~ of accompaniment . . . he made the old songs roar —Virginia D. Dawson & Betty D. Wilson⟩ **2 :** a jingling sound effect achieved in light repetitious verse or in wordy empty prose ⟨the ~ of words is all that strikes the ears —William Mason⟩

tin·kler \'tiŋk(ə)lə(r)\ *n* -s [ME *tinkeler*, prob. alter. (influenced by *-len* -le) of *tinkere* tinker — more at TINKER] *dial Brit* **:** TINKER

tinkling *n* -s [fr. gerund of *1tinkle*] **1 :** a tinkle or succession of tinkles ⟨drowsy ~*s* lull the distant folds —Thomas Gray⟩ **2** [so called fr. its note] **:** a grackle (*Quiscolus niger crassirostris*) that is native to Jamaica, often associates with domestic cattle, and rids them of insects

tin·kling·ly *adv* **:** in a tinkling manner **:** with a tinkling sound

tin·kly \'tiŋk(ə)lē, -li\ *adj* [*2tinkle* + *-y*] **:** TINKLING

tinks *pres 3d sing of* TINK, *pl of* TINK

tin liquor *n* **:** a solution of stannous chloride used formerly as a mordant in dyeing

tin liz·zie \(')=¦lizē, -zi\ *n* [fr. *Tin Lizzie*, nickname for the Model T Ford automobile, fr. *tin* + *Lizzie*, nickname for *Elizabeth*] **:** a small and relatively inexpensive automobile ⟨they are in ancient *tin lizzies*, on motor scooters . . . in bicycle rickshas —Horace Sutton⟩

tin·man \'tinmən\ *n, pl* **tinmen 1 :** a maker of or worker in tinplate **:** TINSMITH **2 :** one who supervises the weighting of cloth or yarn with a tin solution — called also *tinner*

tinmouth \'=,=\ *n* [*2tin* + *mouth*] **:** BLACK CRAPPIE

tin·ne \'tinē\ *n, pl* **tinne** *or* **tinnes** *usu cap* [Athabascan, lit., people] **:** DÉNÉ

tinned *past of* TIN

tinnen *adj* [ME, fr. OE *tinen*, fr. *tin* + *-en*] *obs* **:** made or consisting of tin

tin·ner \'tinə(r)\ *n* -s **1 :** a tin miner **2 :** TINSMITH **3 :** one that tins metal articles **4 :** TINMAN 2 **5 :** one that makes or works with sheet metal

tin·nery \'tinərē\ *n* -ES [*1tin* + *-ery*] **:** a tin mine **:** TINWORKS

tin·nevel·ly senna \tə'nevəlē-, ¦tinə¦velē-\ *n, usu cap T* [fr. *Tinnevelly*, Madras, India] **:** senna from a cassia (*Cassia angustifolia*) — called also *Indian senna*

tin·ni·ent \'tinēənt\ *adj* [L *tinnient-, tinniens*, pres. part. of *tinnire* to ring, jingle, of imit. origin] **:** having a clear or ringing quality ⟨~ resonance of carillon music —P.D.Peery⟩ ⟨listened to the ting, ~ crackling of the coals —Mervyn Wall⟩

tin·ni·ly \'tin³lē, -nəl|, |i\ *adv* **:** in a tinny manner **:** with a tinny sound ⟨pots and pans . . . tinkling ~ as they jiggled and swung —Adria Langley⟩

tin·ni·ness \-nēnəs, -nin-\ *n* -ES **:** the quality or state of being tinny

tinning *n* -s [ME, fr. gerund of *tinnen* to tin — more at TIN] **1 :** the act or process of one who tins **2 :** a coating or lining of tin or tinfoil

tin·ni·tus \'tinətəs *also* tə'nīd·əs *or* -'nēd-\ *n* -ES [L, fr. *tinnitus*, past part. of *tinnire* to ring] **:** a ringing, roaring, hissing, or other sensation of noise in the ears that is purely subjective

tin·ny \'tinē, -ni\ *adj* -ER/-EST **1 :** of, abounding in, or yielding tin ⟨working a ~ lode⟩ **2 :** resembling or suggestive of tin: **a :** having the appearance of tin **:** LIGHT, FRAGILE, SHINY ⟨the cheap ~ doorknob —Maritta Wolff⟩ ⟨wears a ~ dollar watch⟩ ⟨drives a small ~ car⟩ **b :** lacking resonance or depth of tone **:** THIN, METALLIC, HARSH ⟨could hear a ~ voice asking querulously —Hartley Howard⟩ ⟨the ~ alarm clock —Woody Klein⟩ ⟨the ceaseless ~ tumult of the jukebox —John McNulty⟩ ⟨the noble trumpet in F had to be given up in favor of a ~ little instrument in a higher key —Ralph Vaughan Williams⟩ ⟨a ~ paraphrase of the best-known . . . peroration —D.S. Berkeley⟩ **c :** tasting or smelling of tin **3 :** lacking matter, substance, or profundity of utterance **:** EMPTY, WORDY, INSIGNIFICANT ⟨the slick, well constructed, but ~ novels written by the literary engineers of today —Hiram Haydn⟩ ⟨power to drown out the ~ words of tiny men —*Reporter*⟩ ⟨the voice began to ring a ~ untruth —William Sansom⟩

tin ore *n* **:** CASSITERITE

tin oxide *n* **:** either of two oxides of tin; *esp* **:** STANNIC OXIDE — compare STANNOUS OXIDE

tin-pan \'=¦=\ *or* **tin-panny** \'=¦panē\ *adj* [E dial. *tin-pan*, v., to shivaree, fr. E *tin pan*] **:** NOISY, HARSH, TINNY

tin pan alley *n, usu cap T&P&A* **1 :** a district used or occupied chiefly by composers or publishers of popular music **2 :** the body or realm of composers or publishers of popular music ⟨the E major study which *Tin Pan Alley* has brought to the populace in the form of a song —A.H.Dent⟩

tin pants *n pl* **:** trousers of stout material soaked in paraffin for waterproofing and worn esp. by lumbermen

tin pest *also* **tin plague** *n* **:** the transformation of ordinary white metallic tin into powdery gray tin in extremely cold weather

tinplate \'=¦=\ *n* [*2tin* + *plate*, n.] **:** thin sheet iron or steel coated with tin

tin-plate \"\ *vt* **:** to plate or coat (as a metal sheet) with tin

tin pot *n* **1 :** a pot made of tin or tinplate **2 :** the vessel holding the molten tin in the tin-plating process

tin-pot \'=,=\ *adj* [*tin pot*] **:** poor or paltry in quality **:** WRETCHED, INFERIOR ⟨this *tin-pot* town isn't the whole world —Hartley Howard⟩ ⟨when the *tin-pot* locomotive is unable to make the steepest grade, the passengers . . . pile out and push —E.A.Powell⟩ ⟨wasn't interested in his *tin-pot* politics —John Buchan⟩

tin putty *n* **:** PUTTY POWDER

tin pyrites *n* **:** STANNITE

tins *pl of* TIN, *pres 3d sing of* TIN

tin salt *n* **:** TIN CRYSTALS — sometimes used in pl.

1tin·sel \'tin(t)səl *sometimes* -nzəl\ *adj* [earlier *tinselle*, fr. MF *etincellé, estencelé*, past part. of *etinceller, estenceler* to ornament with sparkling colors, to sparkle, fr. *etincelle, estencele* spark] **1 a :** interwoven with or overlaid with gold, silver, or metallic thread **b :** made of or covered with tinsel **2 :** cheaply glittering or gaudy **:** showily pretentious **:** SPECIOUS, TAWDRY ⟨wanders through its massive moldering architecture and ~ gaieties —Cecil Sprigge⟩ ⟨surrounded by the ~ splendor of his parties —J.W.Aldridge⟩ ⟨a world . . . with shoddy emotions and ~ values —Max Lerner⟩

2tinsel \"\ *n* -s [MF *etincelle, estincelle, estencele* spark, glitter, spangle — more at STENCIL] **1 a :** a silk or silk and wool fabric formerly interwoven or overlaid with glittering metallic threads or strips usu. of gold, silver, or copper **b :** LAMÉ **2 a :** a thread, strip, or sheet of metal, paper, or plastic used to produce a glittering and sparkling appearance in fabrics, yarns, Christmas decorations, or advertising materials **b :** a yarn of various fibers covered or combined with a thread of tinsel and used for knitting, weaving, or embroidering **3 :** something superficially showy, attractive, or glamorous that actually has little real worth ⟨those austere spirits who . . . had scorned the fumes and ~ of the loud world —L.P.Smith⟩ ⟨the ~ and power of high office did not appeal —J.C.Fitzpatrick⟩ ⟨a superglamorous baggage of ~ . . . a major movie star —Nolan Miller⟩ **4 :** DEEP STONE

3tinsel \"\ *vt* **tinseled** *or* **tinselled; tinseled** *or* **tinselled; tinseling** *or* **tinselling; tinsels 1 :** to interweave, overlay, or adorn with or as if with tinsel ⟨can produce ~*ed* or velvet surfaces by flocking —*Publishers' Weekly*⟩ ⟨dew ~*ed* the leaves —Truman Capote⟩ ⟨a gaudy ~*ed* dragonfly —Haldane Macfall⟩ **2 :** to impart to or cover with a meretricious brightness or appearance ⟨enraptured by all the ~*ed* glamour —Arthur Knight⟩ ⟨her ~*ed* picture of high life . . . thrilled the drab Victorian maiden —Robert Halsband⟩

4tinsel \"\ *n* -s [*2tinsel*; fr. the delicate filament or flimmer] **:** a flagellum (as on the zoospores of some phycomycetes) having a central axis from which extend short lateral hairs — compare FLIMMER, WHIPLASH

tin·sel·ly \'tin(t)s(ə)lē, -li *sometimes* -nzəl-\ *adj* **:** TINSELED ⟨a ~ star stuck high on a tree —Edwin Honig⟩ ⟨encompassing . . . all sides of life, the tawdry and ~ as well as the tautly tragic —E.J.West⟩ ⟨his playing . . . is elegant, sometimes ~ —Joseph Kerman⟩

tinsel of the feu *Scots law* **:** forfeiture of the feu right for failure to pay feu duty for two entire years

tin·sel·ry \'tin(t)səlrē, -ri *sometimes* -nzəl-\ *n* -s **:** tinseled material, ornamentation, or appearance **:** pretentious display ⟨the complacency of show and tangled ~ . . . had all been subdued into dust —Sean O'Casey⟩

tin·sey *also* **tin·sy** \'tin(t)sē, -nzē\ *n, pl* **tinseys** *also* **tinsies** [by alter.] **:** *2*TINSEL

tinsmith \'=,=\ *n* [*2tin* + *smith*] **:** a worker who makes or repairs things of tin or other metal (as roofs, automobile equipment, kitchen utensils) — called also *tinman*

tin·smithy \'=,smithē, -ithē\ *n* **:** a tinsmith's workshop

tin soldier *n* **1 :** a toy soldier made of tin or other metal **2 :** one who plays at soldiering

tin spirit *n* **:** any of various solutions of tin salts used as mordants in dyeing — often used in pl.

tin spot *n* **:** a small hard white mass that is sometimes found in phosphor bronze, composed of an alloy of copper, tin, and phosphorus, frequently so hard as to be untouched by a file, and caused by excess of phosphorus

tinstone \'=,=\ *n* [*2tin* + *stone*] **:** CASSITERITE

tin stream *n* **:** an alluvial deposit of tin ore — usu. used in pl.

tin streaming *n* **:** the washing of tin from a tin stream

1tint *past of* TINE

2tint \'tint\ *n* -s [alter. (prob. influenced by It or Sp *tinta* tint fr. LL *tincta* inked stroke, fr. fem. of L *tinctus*, past part. of *tingere* to tinge) of *3tinct* — more at TINGE] **1 a :** a usu. slight or pale coloration **:** HUE ⟨colors as pure and delicate as the ~*s* of early morning —Willa Cather⟩ ⟨witch hazel and sumac add a variety of ~*s* —*Amer. Guide Series: Tenn.*⟩ ⟨dark it appeared, but the precise ~ was indeterminable —W.H.Hudson †1922⟩ ⟨own the familiar pink and blue ~*s* of his anger —Louis Auchincloss⟩ **b :** any of various lighter or darker shades of a color **:** TINGE ⟨in the western sky a certain greenish phosphorescent ~ —J.C.Powys⟩ ⟨a ~ of yellow was creeping up the rushes —Richard Jefferies⟩ **2 :** a variation of a color produced by adding white to it and characterized by a low saturation with relatively high lightness — compare SHADE 9a **3 :** a usu. slight modifying quality or characteristic of something ⟨in it there was no ~ of fear for . . . the integrity of art —Sean O'Casey⟩ ⟨the purposeful political ~ of international loans —Herbert Feis⟩ ⟨showing a ~ of jealousy⟩ **4 :** a shaded effect in engraving produced by fine parallel lines close together **5 :** a panel of light, solid, or screened color often serving as background for matter in another color printed on top of it **6 :** dye for the hair **syn** see COLOR

3tint \"\ *vb* -ED/-ING/-S *vt* **1 :** to impart or apply a tint to **:** COLOR, TINGE ⟨spring ~*ing* her orchards with pastel hues —*advt*⟩ ⟨a small but gaudily ~*ed* society of women —G.N. Shuster⟩ ⟨having her hair ~*ed*⟩ — compare DYE **2 :** to modify or alter the aspect of by imparting an affective quality or characteristic ⟨the scent of roses just ~*ed* the clear . . . air —H.G.Wells⟩ ⟨the story's . . . ~*ed* with all the high colorings of adventure —Henry Cavendish⟩ ⟨his cheerfulness ~*ed* with some healthy cynicism —Henri Peyre⟩ ~ *vi* **:** to acquire a tint or color ⟨leaves ~ in the fall of the year⟩

4tint \"\ *n* -s [perh. alter. of *5tent*] *dial Brit* **:** TASTE, FORETASTE, TRACE

tin tack *n, chiefly Brit* **:** a tin-plated tack

tin·ta·marre *also* **tin·ta·mar** \,tintə¦mär\ *n* -s [F *tintamarre*, fr. MF, fr. *tinter* to ring (fr. L *tinnitare*, freq. of *tinnire* to ring) + *-amarre*, of unknown origin] **:** a great confused noise **:** UPROAR, DIN ⟨I did not know . . . though I did guess by such a ~ and cough and sneeze —Sir Walter Scott⟩

tint block *n* **:** a block or plate from which a tint is printed

tint·er \'tintə(r)\ *n* -s **:** one that tints; *specif* **:** one that mixes in pigments to obtain paints of the desired color and shade

tin tetrachloride *n* **:** STANNIC CHLORIDE

tin·tic·ite \'tinti,kīt\ *n* -s [*Tintic* district, Utah, its locality + E *-ite*] **:** a mineral $Fe_3(PO_4)_2(OH)_3 \cdot 3H_2O$ consisting of a dense earthy to porcelaneous hydrous basic phosphate of iron

tinting *n* -s [fr. gerund of *3tint*] **1 :** the act or process of one that tints: as **a :** the act or manner of producing an engraved tint **b :** the uniform dyeing of the gelatin layer of a transparency, lantern slide, or motion-picture film **2 :** the engraved or colored tint produced by the act of one that tints

tinting strength *n* **:** the ability of a pigment to change the hue of another pigment; *esp* **:** the depth of color produced by mixing a pigment or dye with white

tin·tin·nab·u·lar \,tintə¦nabyələ(r)\ *adj* [L *tintinnabulum* bell + E *-ar*] **:** TINTINNABULARY

tin·tin·nab·u·lary \-,lerē\ *adj* [L *tintinnabulum* bell (fr. *tintinnare* to ring, jingle — fr. *tinnire*, of imit. origin — + *-bulum*, n. suffix) + E *-ary*] **:** of, relating to, or characterized by bells or their sounds ⟨has since enjoyed a . . . ~ fame as New York's Liberty Bell —*New Yorker*⟩

tin·tin·nab·u·la·tion \¦=,=¦=¦lāshən\ *n* -s [L *tintinnabulum* + E *-ation*] **1 :** the ringing or sounding of bells ⟨all the church bells . . . tolled his knell in a quivering, melancholy ~ —Janet Flanner⟩ **2 :** a jingling or tinkling sound as of bells ⟨the splashing and ~ of a hundred country-scented showers —Osbert Sitwell⟩

tin·tin·nab·u·lous \¦=¦=¦=ləs\ *adj* [L *tintinnabulum* + E *-ous*] **:** TINTINNABULARY ⟨bright ~ jewelry at ears and wrists —Audrey Barker⟩

tin·tin·nab·u·lum \,=='=ləm\ *n, pl* **tintinnabu·la** \-lə\ [L, bell] **:** a small tinkling bell

1tin·tin·nid \tin·'tinəd\ *adj* [NL *Tintinnidae*] **:** of or relating to the Tintinnidae

2tintinnid \"\ *n* -s **:** a ciliate of the family Tintinnidae

tin·tin·ni·dae \tin·'tinə,dē\ *n pl, cap* [NL, fr. *Tintinnus*, type genus (prob. fr. L *tintinnare* to ring) + *-idae*] **:** a large family that comprises loricate oligotrichous typically pelagic ciliates widely distributed in the seas and occas. found in fresh and brackish water and sometimes made coextensive with a suborder or other major division of Spirotricha

tintlaying \'=,==\ *n* **:** the laying of a tint by the benday process

tint·less \'tintləs\ *adj* **:** having no tints **:** lacking color

tint tool *n* **:** a fine graver used for cutting the parallel lines that produce tints

tintype \'=,=\ *n* [*2tin* + *type*] **:** FERROTYPE 1

tinware \'=,=\ *n* [*2tin* + *ware*] **:** articles esp. utensils made of tinplate

tin whistle *n* **:** PENNY WHISTLE

tin-white \'=¦=\ *adj* **:** bluish white

tinwork \'=,=\ *n* **1 :** work in tin; *also* **:** something made of tin **:** the part of a structure composed of tin **2 tinworks** *pl but sing or pl in constr* **:** an establishment where tin is smelted, rolled, or otherwise worked

1ti·ny \'tīnē, -ni\ *adj* -ER/-EST [alter. (influenced by *-y*, adj. suffix) of ME *tine* tiny] **:** very small or diminutive **:** MINUTE ⟨a ~ baby⟩ ⟨a ~ mountain town —R.M.Coates⟩ ⟨a ~ hangar on a small flying field —*Amer. Guide Series: Conn.*⟩ ⟨a ~ army —C.S.Forester⟩ ⟨a ~ fraction of the money —H.G.Rickover⟩ ⟨the ~ clink of hammer and chisel —Tom Marvel⟩ **syn** see SMALL

2tiny \"\ *n* -ES *chiefly Brit* **:** a young child **:** INFANT ⟨rich food upsets the digestion of *tinies* —*Farmer's Weekly (So. Africa)*⟩

tiny tim \'=¦tim\ *n* -s *usu cap both Ts* [fr. *Tiny Tim*, crippled little boy in the story *A Christmas Carol* (1843) by Charles Dickens †1870 Eng. novelist] **:** a yellow-flowered prairie herb (*Thymophylla aurea*) of the family Compositae

tin·zen·ite \'tinzə,nīt, 'tin(t)sə,-\ *n* -s [*Tinzen*, Switzerland + E *-ite*] **:** a mineral $CaMnAl(SiO_4)_2$ consisting of a silicate of manganese, aluminum, and calcium and occurring in yellow monoclinic crystals at Tinzen, Grisons, Switzerland

ti·o·non·ta·ti \,tīō'näntətē\ *n, pl* **tionontati** *or* **tionontatis** *usu cap* **1 :** an Iroquoian people of southern Ontario **2 :** a member of the Tionontati people

ti·ou *or* **ti·oux** \'tē(,)ü\ *n, pl* **tiou** *or* **tious** *or* **tioux** *usu cap* [F *Tioux*, fr. Tunica *Tiou*] **1 :** a Tunican people of northwestern Mississippi **2 :** a member of the Tiou people

1tip \'tip\ *n* -s [ME *tip, tippe;* akin to MHG *zipf* tip, MD *tip*, MLG *timpe* — more at TAP] **1 a :** the pointed or rounded end or extremity of something ⟨the ~ of his finger⟩ ⟨~ of the spear⟩ ⟨tracks . . . led over the ~ of the hill —Robert Lund⟩ ⟨the very ~ of the nose of the fuselage —H.G.Armstrong⟩ ⟨at the southern ~ of the island —*Amer. Guide Series: Maine*⟩ ⟨the yellow ~ of the sun —V.G.Heiser⟩ ⟨the ~*s* of their wings⟩ **b** *obs* **:** the highest or utmost point or extremity **:** CROWN, SUMMIT **2 a :** a small piece or part (as of a belt, shoe, cane, pen, or billiard cue) designed to serve as an end, cap, or point and made usu. of metal, leather, or other durable substance — see SHOE illustration **b :** the end of a feather or tail of fur used in trimming a hat; *specif* **:** a small ostrich plume **c** (1) **:** the piece or section of a jointed fishing rod farthest from the butt (2) **:** the terminal guide on the end of such a rod **d** (1) **:** FOOTHOLD 3 (2) **:** CAP 3a (3) **:** a short horseshoe made to reach only half round the hoof and worn to protect the crust **e** (1) **:** a thimble of leather used in archery for the protection of the drawing fingers (2) **:** PILE 4a **3 a :** a thin broad brush made of camel's or badger's hair and used in laying gold leaf (as in bookbinding) **b :** any insert pasted to the binding edge of a book or section **4 :** a triangular piece of beef cut from between the round and the sirloin and used for roasting or for steaks **5** *Austral* **:** the exposed weathered end of the fibers of wool on the sheep; *also* **:** an area or clump formed by the clotted ends of such fibers **6 tips** *pl* **:** a grade of tobacco comprising the top two or three leaves on a stalk

²tip \"\ *vt* **tipped; tipped** *also* **tipt; tipping; tips** [ME *tippen*, fr. *tip, tippe* tip] **1 a :** to attach a tip or point to or furnish a tip for ⟨the natives ~ their arrows with stone⟩ ⟨a summer settlement ~*s* the slender headland —*Amer. Guide Series: Maine*⟩ **b** (1) **:** to cover or adorn the tip of ⟨black wrought iron legs handsomely *tipped* with brass —*advt*⟩ ⟨*tipped* with gold-leaf trim —Frederick Way⟩ ⟨scales *tipped* with yellowish green above the back —P.M.Roedel⟩ (2) **:** to blend (furs) for improved appearance by brushing the tips of the hair with dye **2 :** to affix or paste (an insert) in a book at the binding margin — often used with *in* or sometimes with *into* or *on* ⟨one volume . . . with 105 full-color reproductions from photographs *tipped* in —*Yale Rev.*⟩ ⟨when plates are *tipped* on, they should be freed from the text —Edith Diehl⟩ **3 :** to remove the ends of (as living shoots) ⟨~ raspberries⟩ ⟨the cows' horns were *tipped* to prevent injury in shipping⟩

³tip \"\ *vb* **tipped; tipped** *also* **tipt; tipping; tips** [ME *tipen*] *vt* **1 a :** to cause to overturn or proceed downward **:** throw or cast down **:** UPSET — usu. used with *over* or *onto* ⟨the wind struck the car and nearly *tipped* it over —Ernest Hemingway⟩ ⟨the truck *tipped* its trailer onto the car⟩ **b :** to knock down (a bowling pin) otherwise than by direct impact of a bowl ⟨the bowled kingpin *tipped* three other pins⟩ **2 :** to turn (something) from a horizontal or vertical position to a slanting or inclined position **:** CANT, TILT ⟨*tipped* his head to one side —A.R.Wetjen⟩ ⟨neighborhood loafers *tipped* their chairs —S.T. Williamson⟩ ⟨were required to ~ their hats to the chemists —W.H.Whyte⟩ ⟨would eventually ~ the balance of power —*Time*⟩ **3** *chiefly dial* **:** to drink (liquor) esp. at one draft **4** *Brit* **:** to empty by tilting **:** DUMP ⟨a hole into which I had been *tipping* cinders —Francis King⟩ ⟨*tipped* it down gently off the spade onto the grass —*Punch*⟩ ~ *vi* **1 :** to become overturned or upset **:** TOPPLE — usu. used with *over* ⟨a canoe will sometimes ~ over quickly⟩ **2 :** to move from the vertical or horizontal **:** LEAN, SLANT ⟨the bench ~*s* on the uneven floor⟩ ⟨tall buildings ~ slightly in the wind⟩ — **tip the scales** *or* **tip the scale 1 :** to register weight on a scale or balance ⟨*tips the scales* at 210 pounds —*Current Biog.*⟩ **2 :** to shift the balance of fortune, influence, or power ⟨a blind world in which building and destroying successively *tip the scale* —W.L. Sperry⟩ ⟨Americans . . . *tipped the scales* decisively in two world wars —A.E.Stevenson †1965⟩ ⟨adding small gifts to *tip the scales* in my favor —Claudia Cassidy⟩

⁴tip \"\ *n* -s **1** *archaic* **:** the upsetting of a bowling pin by another that falls or rolls against it **2 :** the act or an instance of tipping **:** TILT ⟨the tower has a slight ~ to the south⟩ **3** *Brit* **a :** an elevated runway along which railroad cars or wagons can be run to have their contents tipped or dumped (as into a chute) at the end **b :** such a runway together with a crane that picks up a car or wagon and swings it bodily so that its contents can be tipped or dumped as desired — compare ⁴TIPPLE **4** *Brit* **:** a place for depositing something (as rubbish or garbage or material for embankments) by tipping or dumping **:** DUMP

⁵tip \"\ *n* -s [ME *tippe*; akin to LG *tippen* to tap] **:** the act or process of tipping **:** a light touch or blow **:** TAP ⟨giving him a ~ on the shoulder⟩

⁶tip \"\ *vb* **tipped; tipped** *also* **tipt; tipping; tips** *vt* **1 :** to strike lightly **:** TOUCH, TAP ⟨the sword *tipped* his shoulder —*Irish Digest*⟩ ⟨a baseball catcher sometimes ~*s* the batsman's bat illegally with his mitt⟩ **2 :** to hit (a baseball or cricket ball) a glancing blow with the edge or side of the bat ⟨the batter *tipped* the ball foul⟩ **3 :** to hit (as a basketball) lightly with the hand or fingers ⟨~*s* the ball to keep it rim high —*Scholastic Coach*⟩ — often used with *in* ⟨the forward *tipped* in another basket⟩ ~ *vi* **:** to move or proceed with mincing or light steps **:** TIPTOE ⟨*tipping* to the front windows, she closed them —J.B.Benefield⟩

⁷tip \"\ *vb* **tipped; tipped** *also* **tipt; tipping; tips** [perh. fr. ⁶*tip*] *vt* **1 :** GIVE, PRESENT ⟨be merry and ~ us a song⟩ ⟨*tipped* the head clerk a signal —Mark Twain⟩ **2 :** to give a tip or gratuity to ⟨the searchers, being *tipt* with half a crown, allowed us to proceed —Tobias Smollett⟩ ⟨*tipped* the servants liberally —W.F.DeMorgan⟩ ⟨~ them if they bring refreshments to your seat —Richard Joseph⟩ ~ *vi* **:** to bestow a tip or gratuity ⟨always ~*s* generously⟩ ⟨how much to ~ is a problem⟩ — **tip one the wink :** to give one a hint, suggestion, signal by or as if by a wink ⟨*tipped him the wink* as he passed, so he went over there —Richard Llewellyn⟩

⁸tip \"\ *n* -s **:** a gift or a usu. small sum of money tendered in payment or often in excess of prescribed or suitable payment for a service performed or anticipated ⟨cost 15 cents plus a 10-cent ~⟩ ⟨the redcaps had begun . . . to press for their interests in the question of ~*s* —*Current Biog.*⟩ ⟨at the entrance girl artists do portrait sketches for a ~ —*Amer. Guide Series: Fla.*⟩

⁹tip \"\ *n* -s [perh. fr. ⁷*tip*] **1 :** an item of expert or authoritative information imparted or sought for one's guidance ⟨take my ~ and do not venture in there without a guide —Fred Streeter⟩ ⟨wanted to pick up the ~*s* which experience had taught the pioneers —R.C.Snyder⟩ ⟨giving . . . useful ~*s* on all sorts of ways of spending the Christmas holidays —*N.Y.Times*⟩ **2 :** a piece of advance or confidential information given by or received from one thought to have access to special or inside sources **:** HINT, STEER: as **a :** a prediction concerning the expected change in the value or status of a stock, bond, or other security ⟨brokers . . . versed in the art of getting ~*s* and advance information of events likely to affect prices —Frederick Simpich †1950⟩ ⟨~*s* and rumors . . . send shares from quotations of a few cents up to thousands and down again —*Amer. Guide Series: Nev.*⟩ **b :** a forecast of the outcome or winner of a sporting event (as a horse or dog race) used chiefly for placing a bet ⟨through her I got that ~ on the horse race —Erle Stanley Gardner⟩ ⟨in one day you clean out half of what I had saved with your phoney ~*s* —*Ring*⟩ **c :** an advance notice or report concerning a newsworthy development of special interest to a reporter or a newspaper ⟨personnel frequently offer ~*s* or clues to news developments —*Banking*⟩ ⟨has been following obscure news ~*s* and developing stories of wide significance —*Current Biog.*⟩ ⟨even an hour's delay may mean the difference between ~ and fact —*Radio News*⟩

¹⁰tip \"\ *vt* **tipped; tipped; tipping; tips 1 a :** to impart a tip, a piece of information or advice, or a warning about often in a secret or confidential manner ⟨somebody was *tipping* their flights to the rebels —J.A.Phillips⟩ ⟨are you afraid I'll ~ the plot —Maurice Zolotow⟩ **b :** to make mention of as a prospective winner or a profitable investment ⟨has been *tipped* as council president⟩ ⟨practically nothing makes you look more foolish than *tipping* a loser —G.F.T.Ryall⟩ ⟨industrials are being *tipped* in the forecasts⟩ **2 :** to give a tip or private or confidential information to ⟨his wife . . . was *tipped* three days in advance and returned —*Newsweek*⟩ ⟨both had already been *tipped* to . . . keep top-secret documents face down on the desk —J.P.O'Donnell⟩ — often used with *off* ⟨a friend *tipped* him off that pianos were having a phenomenal sale —Green Peyton⟩ ⟨thousands . . . were *tipped* off in time to flee —T.H. Fielding⟩ — **tip one's hand :** to show one's hand ⟨the Justice department wouldn't *tip its hand* by saying its next move . . . would be —*Newsweek*⟩

¹¹tip \"\ *n* -s [perh. fr. ⁶*tip*] **:** a crowd gathered or attracted by a pitchman or barker ⟨the opening ~ consisted of all the roughnecks and loafers —G.A.Hamid⟩ ⟨for his horoscope pitch he often has his wife circulate among the ~ —W.L. Gresham⟩

ti palm *n* **:** ¹TI 1

tip and run *n*, *Brit* **:** a game similar to cricket in which a batsman is required to run each time he touches a bowled ball with his bat

tip-and-run \ˌ=ˌ=ˈ=\ *adj* [*tip and run*] *chiefly Brit* **:** characterized by bolting immediately upon striking ⟨a heavy bomb from a *tip-and-run* raider scored a direct hit —O.S.Nock⟩ ⟨sallied to make *tip-and-run* assaults —*Manchester Guardian Weekly*⟩

tip blight *n* **:** any of several diseases of plants characterized by death of terminal shoots: as **a :** a disease of balsam fir caused by a fungus (*Rehmielliopsis balsamae*) **b :** a virus disease of tomato

tipburn \ˈ=ˌ=\ *n* [¹*tip* + *burn*] **:** a disease of the potato, lettuce, and other cultivated plants characterized by burning or browning of the tips and margins of the leaflets and caused by loss of water due to excessive heat and sunshine — compare HOPPERBURN

tipcart \ˈ=ˌ=\ *n* [³*tip* + *cart*] **:** a cart whose body can be tipped on the frame to empty its contents

tipcat \ˈ=ˌ=\ *n* [⁶*tip* + *cat*] **:** a game in which one player using a bat strikes lightly a tapered wooden peg and as it flies up strikes it again to drive it as far as possible while fielders try to recover it; *also* **:** the peg used in this game

tip cheese *n* **:** a boy's game resembling tipcat

tip cutting *n* **:** TERMINAL CUTTING

tip–dye \ˈ=ˌ=\ *vt* **:** ²TIP 1b(2)

tip·ful \ˈtip¦fu̇l\ *adj* **:** BRIMFUL

tiph·ia \ˈtifēə\ *n* [NL, fr. Gk *tiphē* beetle + NL *-ia*] **1** *cap* **:** a genus (the type of the family Tiphiidae) of shining black wasps that includes a species (*T. vernalis*) of larval parasites of the Japanese beetle **2** -s **:** any wasp of the genus *Tiphia*

¹tiph·i·id \ˈtifēəd\ *adj* [NL *Tiphiidae*] **:** of or relating to the Tiphiidae

²tiphiid \"\ *n* -s **:** a wasp of the family Typhiidae

ti·phi·idae \təˈfīəˌdē\ *n pl*, *cap* [NL, fr. *Tiphia*, type genus + *-idae*] **:** a family of rather small slender usu. black and often hairy wasps that as larvae parasitize the grubs of various scarabaeid beetles — see TIPHIA

tipi *var of* TEPEE

¹tip–in \ˈ=ˌ=\ *n* -s [²*tip*] **:** ¹TIP 3b

²tip–in \"\ *n* -s [⁶*tip*] **:** a score made in basketball by deflecting the ball into the basket with the fingertips ⟨both guards trail the forward . . . for possible follow-up shots and *tip-ins* —G.K. Loveless⟩

tip–it *or* **tip·pit** \ˈtipət\ *n* -s [fr. the phrase *tip it*; fr. the command of the guesser when touching the other player's hand] **:** the game of up Jenkins sometimes played as a gambling game

tip·i·ti \ˈtipəd·ē, ¦tipə¦tē\ *n* -s [Pg, fr. Tupi *tapeti*] **:** an elastic plaited cylinder of jacitara palm bark used in expressing the juice from the root in making cassava

tip layering *also* **tip layerage** *n* **:** the propagation of plants by bending a stem to the ground and covering the tip with soil so that roots and new shoots may develop

ti·ple \ˈtē(ˌ)plā\ *n* -s [Sp, lit., soprano, treble, prob. alter. of *triple*, fr. L *triplus* triple — more at TRIPLE] **:** a soprano guitar

tip·less \ˈtipləs\ *adj* **:** marked by the absence of tips or gratuities ⟨a ~ hotel⟩

tip·man \ˈtipmən\ *n*, *pl* **tipmen** [³*tip* + *man*] **:** DUMPER 1c

tip moth *n* **:** any of several moths esp. of the family Olethreutidae whose larvae bore in the tips of branches of trees

¹tip–off \ˈ=ˌ=\ *n* -s [¹⁰*tip*] **:** an indication, hint, or warning of an otherwise unknown fact, development, or move **:** TIP, GIVEAWAY ⟨the only *tip-off* on his rank was the way the men addressed him —Dave Richardson⟩ ⟨the mysterious informer whose *tip-off* had brought them to witness the drug-running operation —Darrell Berrigan⟩ ⟨the production of certain . . . men's gloves or underwear might provide a *tip-off* on an impending military expedition —S.A.Rice & J.W.Kappel⟩ ⟨watch the blocking back for the *tip-off* as to where the play is going —A.J.Yunevich⟩

²tip–off \"\ *n* -s [⁶*tip*] **:** the act or an instance of putting the ball in play in basketball by a jump ball

tip–on \ˈ=ˌ=\ *n* -s [²*tip*] **:** ¹TIP 3b

ti·po·ni \ˈtēpənē\ *n* -s [Hopi *tiponi* idol or amulet seen only by owner] **:** a sacred badge of authority of the Hopi Indians usu. consisting of an ear of corn decorated with feathers or a valued stone and worn or displayed by a chief, priest, or religious society

tip–over \ˈ=ˌ==\ *n* -s [fr. *tip over*, v.] **:** a disease of egg plant caused by a fungus (*Phomopsis vexans*) and characterized by girdling of the stem of seedlings just above the soil line

tip·pa·ble \ˈtipəbəl\ *adj* [⁷*tip* + *-able*] **:** able to be tipped or to receive tips

tipped *past of* TIP

tip·pee \(ˈ)ti¦pē\ *n* -s [⁷*tip* + *-ee*] **:** one receiving or that receives a tip ⟨experienced ~*s* develop a pretty keen eye for what to expect —P.T.White⟩ ⟨standard ~*s* include hotel and railroad station porters . . . taxi drivers, doormen and delivery boys —*Wall Street Jour.*⟩

tip·per \ˈtipə(r)\ *n* -s **:** one that tips: as **a :** DUMPER 1c **b :** one whose work is making, fastening, or applying tips **c** *or* **tipper–in** \ˌ==ˈ=\ **:** a worker who tips pages into book or pamphlet signatures **d :** a worker who blocks felt hats **e :** a worker who picks and dresses poultry **f** *Brit* **:** a truck whose body tips for unloading **:** DUMP TRUCK

tip·pe·rary \ˌtipə¦re\|rē, ¦ra(a)|, -¦rā|, |ri\ *adj*, *usu cap* [fr. *Tipperary*, Ireland] **:** of or from County Tipperary, Ireland **:** of the kind or style prevalent in County Tipperary

tip·pet \ˈtipət, *usu* -əd·+V\ *n* -s [ME *tipet*, prob. fr. *tip, tippe* tip + *-et* — more at TIP (point)] **1 :** a long hanging end of cloth attached to a sleeve, cap, or hood and used esp. in the late medieval period — see LIRIPIPE **2 :** a shoulder cape of fur or cloth often with hanging ends worn esp. by women or by men as a garment of office **3 :** a scarf or band with long hanging ends worn over the robe or vestment esp. by Anglican or Episcopal clergymen **4** *Brit* **:** a hangman's rope **5 a :** a patagium of a lepidopteran **b :** a ruff of feathers on a bird **6 a :** a short length of fine gut, nylon, or horsehair used for securing a fly to the leader of a fishline **b :** a barb of a feather used as the tail of an artificial fly

tipping *pres part of* TIP

¹tip·ple \ˈtipəl\ *vb* **tippled; tippled; tippling** \-p(ə)liŋ\ **tipples** [back-formation fr. obs. E *tippler* barkeeper, fr. ME *tipler, tipeler*] *vt* **1 :** to drink (intoxicating liquor) esp. continuously in small amounts ⟨farmers, artisans, and tradesmen *tippled* the stiffer drink —W.H.Lyon⟩ **2** *archaic* **:** to spend or lose by tippling **:** SQUANDER ~ *vi* **:** to drink intoxicating liquor esp. by habit or to excess ⟨had been *tippling* all that morning —Hamilton Basso⟩ ⟨the managers are afraid to drink . . . and the ex-boxers are usually too broke to ~ —A.J.Liebling⟩

²tipple \"\ *n* -s **:** an intoxicating beverage **:** DRINK ⟨trying to forget him and seeking oblivion in ~ —Norman Douglas⟩ ⟨an old gentleman . . . whose only ~ was straight vodka —A.J. Liebling⟩

³tipple \"\ *vb* -ED/-ING/-S [freq. of ³*tip*] *vi*, *dial Eng* **:** TUMBLE, OVERTURN ~ *vt*, *dial Eng* **:** to cause to fall, upset, or overturn

⁴tipple \"\ *n* -s **1 a :** an apparatus by which loaded cars are emptied by tipping sometimes including an elevated runway or framework upon which the cars are run for tipping — compare ⁴TIP 3b **2 :** the place where tipping is done **:** TIP; *specif* **:** a coal-screening plant

tip·pler \ˈtip(ə)lə(r)\ *n* -s **:** one that tipples: as **a :** one that operates or works in a tipple **b :** ⁴TIPPLE 1 **c :** one of an English breed of pigeons similar to the tumblers but long-flying and commonly chocolate brown and white **d :** TUMBLER 3e

tippling house *n*, *archaic* **:** BARROOM

tip·ply \ˈtip(ə)lē, -li\ *adj* -ER/-EST [³*tipple* + *-y*] **:** ²TIPPY

¹tip·py \ˈtipē, -pi\ *adj* [¹*tip* + *-y*] **1** *Brit* **:** TIPTOP, SMART, STYLISH **2** *Brit* **a :** full of tips **b** *of wool* **:** having an excessive or defective tip

²tippy \"\ *adj* -ER/-EST [⁴*tip* + *-y*] **:** given to tipping **:** liable to tip **:** UNSTEADY ⟨the ferry had a ~, untrustworthy feeling —Jean Stafford⟩ ⟨our canoe had . . . a certain ~ grace —*Outlook*⟩

tippy–toe \ˈtipēˌtō, -pi,-\ *n* [by alter.] **:** TIPTOE ⟨standing on my *tippy-toes*, I wedged it in the crotch of a limb —Helen Eustis⟩

tips *pl of* TIP, *pres 3d sing of* TIP

tip sheet *n* **:** a usu. folio publication containing special information or tips relating to a particular business or line of activity ⟨many mimeographed *tip sheets* are now on the market —Jo Ranson & R.M.Pack⟩; *esp* **:** a publication giving tips for gamblers (as on horse races or numbers games)

tip·si·fy \ˈtipsəˌfī\ *vt* -ED/-ING/-ES [*tipsy* + *-fy*] **:** to make tipsy **:** INTOXICATE

tip·si·ly \ˈtipsəlē, -li\ *adv* **:** in a tipsy manner **:** UNSTEADILY ⟨~ mutable, his mood changed . . . from hilarious to profoundly gloomy —Aldous Huxley⟩ ⟨the whole structure leaned ~ to the left —D.S.Mullen⟩

tip·si·ness \-sēnəs, -sin-\ *n* -ES **:** the quality or state of being tipsy

tip speed *n* **:** the velocity of the outer edge of a wheel or the tip of a propeller

tipstaff \ˈtipˌ=\ *n*, *pl* **tipstaves** *or* **tipstaffs** [contr. of ME *tipped staf*, fr. *tipped* having a tip (fr. *tip, tippe* tip + *-ed*) + *staf* staff — more at TIP, STAFF] **1 :** a staff tipped with metal used as a badge of office **2 :** an officer who bears a tipstaff **:** a court attendant **:** CONSTABLE, BAILIFF ⟨the judges and *tipstaves* parted the combatants —T.B.Macaulay⟩

tip stall *n* **:** a stalling of the wing tip of an airplane before the remainder of the wing is stalled that frequently results in the loss of lateral control

tip·ster \ˈtipstə(r)\ *n* -s [⁹*tip* + *-ster*] **:** one who gives or sells tips or private information esp. for gambling, stock speculation, or news writing ⟨many touts and ~*s* prepared to sell inside information —Dennis Craig⟩ ⟨is best known as a stock market ~ —Martin Gardner⟩ ⟨was the first editor to employ secret ~*s* —W.A.Swanberg⟩ ⟨police are often informed of crimes by ~*s*⟩

tipstock \ˈ=ˌ=\ *n* [¹*tip* + *stock*] **:** the detachable or movable forepart of a gunstock that lies beneath the barrel and forms a hold for the left hand — compare BUTTSTOCK

tip·sy \ˈtipsē, -si\ *adj* -ER/-EST [³*tip* + *-sy* (as in *tricksy*)] **1 a :** mildly affected by an intoxicating drink **:** BEFUDDLED, UNSTEADY ⟨before offering to intoxicate others . . . getting well ~ himself —Herman Melville⟩ ⟨was not ~, but she fell in in the dark —Rachel Henning⟩ **b :** showing, marked by, or producing mild intoxication ⟨her manner seemed almost ~, as if she were drunk —Kay Boyle⟩ **2 a :** emotionally affected as if mildly intoxicated ⟨as ~ on self-pity as they were on blood and glory 15 years ago —Anthony West⟩ **b :** TIPPY, ASKEW ⟨stump-scarred fields bounded by ~ fences —*Amer. Guide Series: Pa.*⟩ ⟨a piece of ~ printing that incurred . . . disapproval —Rosamond Lehmann⟩ **syn** see DRUNK

tipsy cake *n* **:** a sponge layer cake soaked in wine or brandy with custard or preserves between the layers, frosted with whipped cream, and decorated with toasted almonds

tipsy pudding *n* **:** stale sponge cake soaked in wine and esp. sherry and served with boiled custard

tipt *past part of* TIP

tip table *n* **:** TIP-TOP TABLE

tiptail \ˈ=ˌ=\ *n* [³*tip* + *tail*; fr. the bobbing of its tail when walking] **:** SPOTTED SANDPIPER

¹tip–tap \ˈ=ˌ=\ *n* -s [⁵*tip* + ⁵*tap*] **:** an alternating light knocking or tapping; *also* **:** the sound made by such tapping

²tip–tap \"\ *vi* **:** to make a tip-tap or its sound

tip–tilt \ˈ=ˌ=\ *vt* **:** to tilt or turn up at the tip — usu. used in past part. ⟨the scales *tip-tilted* with a slight excessive weight —J.G.Neihardt⟩ ⟨the mountain field *tip-tilted* by reason of its steepness —Willa Cather⟩ ⟨his nose was *tip-tilted* —Ethel Anderson⟩

¹tiptoe \ˈtip¦tō\ *n* [ME *tiptoo*, fr. *tip, tippe* tip + *too* toe — more at TOE] **:** the tip or end of a toe; *collectively* **:** the ends of the toes — usu. used with reference to motion or posture on the balls of the toes ⟨he paced over . . . and on ~*s* whispered into his ear —L.M.Uris⟩ ⟨standing on ~ to see over the crowd⟩ ⟨craves ideals high enough to give him the thrill of standing on ~ to reach them —J.H.Baker⟩ — **on tiptoe :** AROUSED, ALERT, ATIPTOE ⟨she was very animated, very much *on tiptoe* —L.C. Douglas⟩ ⟨the contest of skill that puts one *on tiptoe* to win —*Deerfield (Wis.) Independent*⟩

²tiptoe \"\ *adv* **:** on or as if on tiptoe ⟨using one hand to support himself . . . because he was standing ~ —Margaret Shedd⟩ ⟨suddenly find yourself standing ~ and full of new breath —E.G.Anderson⟩ ⟨day stands ~ on the misty mountaintops —Shak.⟩

³tiptoe \"\ *adj* **1 :** standing or walking on or as if on tiptoe ⟨approaching with ~ step⟩ ⟨~ touches of sportful elves —E.J. Banfield⟩ **2 :** SILENT, CAUTIOUS, STEALTHY ⟨a stillness suggesting motion, what might be called a ~ effect —G.W. Knight⟩ ⟨offered to guard me and was amusing with his modest ~ air —George Meredith⟩

⁴tiptoe \"\ *vi* **1 :** to stand or raise oneself on tiptoe ⟨great difficulty of seeing anything . . . even by ~*ing* and craning —Arnold Bennett⟩ **2 :** to walk or proceed quietly or cautiously on or as if on tiptoe ⟨~*ing* extremely carefully past his door, they heard how restlessly he slept —Glenway Wescott⟩ ⟨a cat *tiptoed* from the shadow of a fence —Glenn Scott⟩ ⟨~*ing* progressively deeper into the uncharted channels of educational TV —Delbert Clark⟩

tip·ton weed \ˈtiptən-\ *n* [*tipton* prob. fr. the name *Tipton*] **:** SAINT-JOHN'S-WORT

¹tip–top \ˈ=¦=\ *n* [¹*tip* + *top*] **1 :** the highest or utmost point **:** TOP, SUMMIT ⟨building a fire tower on the *tip-top* of the mountain⟩ **2 :** the highest degree or extent **:** CROWN, PINNACLE ⟨reaching the *tip-top* of happiness⟩ **3** *Eng* **:** the highest class or rank in society — usu. used in pl. ⟨hobnobbing with the *tip-tops*⟩ **4 :** ¹TIP 2c(2)

²tip–top \"\ *adj* **:** of or characteristic of the highest quality, rank, or class **:** EXCELLENT, FIRST-RATE ⟨a really *tip-top* man —H.J.Laski⟩ ⟨people from some *tip-top* West End house —Joseph Conrad⟩ ⟨kept the bridge in *tip-top* shape —Pearl Puckett⟩ ⟨horses . . . in *tip-top* shape, fit to run for the money —J.H.Winchester⟩

³tip–top \"\ *adv* **:** to the highest extent **:** very well **:** SURPASSINGLY ⟨colonel . . . uses me *tip-top* —Walt Whitman⟩ ⟨the mittens . . . fitted *tip-top* —J.C.Lincoln⟩

tip–top·per \ˈtip¦täpə(r)\ *n* **:** one of the first rank or class

tip–top table \ˈ=ˌ=-\ *n* **:** a table whose top is hinged to tip to a vertical position — called also *tilt-top table, tip table*

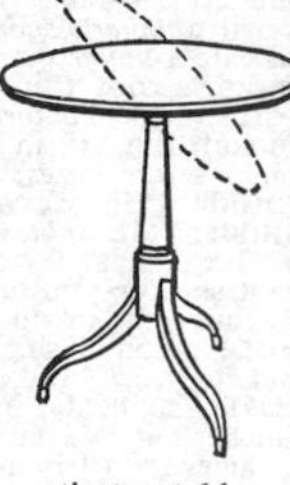

tip-top table

tip·u·la \ˈtipyələ\ *n* [NL, fr. L *tipula, tippula* water spider] **1** *cap* **:** the type genus of the family Tipulidae **2** -s **:** any fly of the genus *Tipula*

tip·u·lar·ia \ˌtipyəˈla(a)rēə\ *n*, *cap* [NL, fr. *Tipula* + *-aria*; fr. the supposed resemblance of the flower to the crane fly] **:** a genus of delicate terrestrial orchids with solid bulbs that produce in late summer a racemose scape of greenish purple flowers and in autumn a single ovate purple leaf which persists through winter — see CRANE-FLY ORCHID

ti·pu·li·dae \təˈpyüləˌdē\ *n pl*, *cap* [NL, fr. *Tipula*, type genus + *-idae*] **:** a large family of long-legged usu. slender two-winged flies comprising the crane flies and often resembling enormous mosquitoes

tip·u·loi·dea \ˌtipyəˈlȯidēə\ *n pl*, *cap* [NL, fr. *Tipula* + *-oidea*] **:** a superfamily of Nematocera including Tipulidae and various related families

¹tip–up \ˈ=ˌ=\ *n* -s [fr. *tip up*, v.] **1** [prob. so called fr. the bobbing of its tail when walking] **:** SPOTTED SANDPIPER **2 :** TILT 6

²tip–up \"\ *adj* **:** constructed so as to tip up or out of the way ⟨sat neatly on the little *tip-up* seat of the taxi —Elizabeth Taylor⟩

tip·u·ra \ˈtipəˌrä, -ˌrə\ *n*, *pl* **tipura** *or* **tipuras** *usu cap* **1 a :** a people of the Tripura state, Bengal **b :** a member of such people **2 :** the Tibeto-Burman language of the Tipura people

tip worm *n* **:** a worm that is the larva of a gallfly (*Contarinia vaccinii*) that infests the tips of cranberry vines

ti·queur \(ˈ)tē¦kər(·)\ *n* -s [F, fr. *tiquer* to have a tic, to twitch (fr. *tic*) + *-eur* -or] : one subject to a tic

¹ti·rade *in sense 1* (ˈ)tī¦rād *sometimes* təˈrād *or* təˈräd *or* təˈrad, *in sense 2* təˈräd *or* təˈrad\ *n* -s [F, pull, shot, tirade, fr. MF, fr. OIt *tirata*, fr. fem. of *tirato*, past part. of *tirare* to draw, pull, shoot; akin to OSp & OPg *tirar* to draw, pull, shoot, OF *tirer*] **1** : a protracted speech usu. marked by intemperate, vituperative, or harshly censorious language : a prolonged outpouring of invective : long-drawn-out harangue ⟨a tantrum of fire of invective : long-drawn-out harangue ⟨a tantrum of utmost frenzy, screaming a ~ of protest and rage —Marcia Davenport⟩ **2** : a baroque musical ornament consisting of a rapid run connecting two melody notes

²tirade \"\ *vi* -ED/-ING/-S : to make a tirade ⟨she might ~ at the moment —Rumer Godden⟩

ti·rak \təˈrak\ *n* -s [native name in India] : a physiological disease of Indian cotton prob. due to nutrient deficiency and characterized by premature yellowing and shedding of the leaves and cracking of the bolls before maturity

tir·a·lee \¦tirə¦lē\ *n* -s [imit.] : a succession of musical notes (as in a bugle call)

ti·ra·na \təˈränə\ *adj, usu cap* [fr. *Tirana*, Albania] : of or from Tirana, the capital of Albania : of the kind or style prevalent in Tirana

ti·rasse \təˈras, -räs\ *n* -s [F, drawnet, pedal coupler, fr. *tirasser* to catch with a drawnet, aug. of *tirer* to draw, pull, shoot — more at TIRADE] : a pedal coupler in an organ

¹tire \ˈtī(ə)r, -īə\ *vb* -ED/-ING/-S [ME *tyren, tyeren*, fr. OE *tȳrian, tēorian*] *vi* **1** : to become weary : have one's strength decrease or fail ⟨*tired* long before the race was over⟩ ⟨the pitcher seems to be *tiring* although it is only the seventh inning⟩ **2** : to have the patience, attention, interest, or liking reduced or exhausted ⟨never ~*s* of reading the Bible⟩ ⟨can describe it a thousand times before anyone ~*s* of it —Maxwell Mays⟩ ~ *vt* **1** : to exhaust or considerably decrease the physical strength of : FATIGUE, WEARY ⟨the long hike *tired* the younger scouts⟩ **2** : to wear out the patience of : satiate to the point of weariness or aversion : bore completely ⟨the endless chattering *tired* him and he left the room⟩ **3** : to use up : wear out : OVERWORK ⟨*tiring* the land by overcultivation⟩

syn WEARY, FATIGUE, EXHAUST, JADE, FAG, TUCKER: TIRE is a general term indicating draining or bringing about loss of energy, strength, endurance, or resolution ⟨very *tired* after the long day's work⟩ WEARY suggests the cumulative effect of tiring until one is unable or unwilling to continue ⟨I am *wearied* out — it is too much — I am but flesh and blood, and I must sleep —Edna S. V. Millay⟩ ⟨I am *wearied* of keeping up deceits —Louis Bromfield⟩ FATIGUE suggests a tiring out by undue or excessive effort or strain that brings lassitude and enervation ⟨the passengers drooped on the wooden benches, too *fatigued* even to get the cool drinks —Dan Jacobson⟩ ⟨I rested for the remainder of the daylight in a shrubbery, being, in my enfeebled condition, too *fatigued* to push on —H.G. Wells⟩ EXHAUST is the strongest of these words in indicating utter draining or consuming of energy until one is without strength and energy ⟨his bonus system would have speeded up labor in a way to *exhaust* men in a few years —M.R.Cohen⟩ ⟨capacity for abstract thinking was *exhausted* by this effort —A.M.Young⟩ JADE applies to causing loss of freshness, spirit, animation, or interest and becoming dull, languid, or listless through overexertion or overindulging ⟨next morning I awoke *jaded* with the sense of having dreamed awful things all through the night —Max Beerbohm⟩ ⟨to minds *jaded* with debauches of over-emphasis it does contrive to give a thrill —C.E.Montague⟩ FAG suggests work or exertion to the point of sagging or drooping with weakness and weariness ⟨with a gasp for breath said, "Lord, what a run. I'm *fagged* to death" —John Masefield⟩ ⟨the long march up the river had *fagged* them brutally; overtired, the rest periods did them little good and laboring on the trail was torture —Norman Mailer⟩ TUCKER is a colloquial expression meaning to fatigue and leave without strength, breath, or resolution ⟨all *tuckered* out from the long climb⟩

²tire \"\ *n* -s **1 tires** *pl but sing in constr* : MILK SICKNESS 1, TREMBLE 3 **2** : FATIGUE, WEARINESS

³tire \ˈtī(ə)r, -īə\ *n* -s [ME, short for ²*attire*] **1** *obs* : wearing apparel : often sumptuous dress : ATTIRE **2** : a woman's headband or hair ornamentation **3** : PINAFORE

⁴tire \"\ *vt* -ED/-ING/-S [ME *tiren*, short for *attiren* to *attire* — more at ATTIRE] ATTIRE : to dress (the hair) with a tire ⟨painted her face, and *tired* her head —2 Kings 9:30 (AV)⟩

⁵tire \"\ *n* -s [ME, prob. fr. ³*tire*] **1** : the aggregate of strakes of a wheel **2 a** : the metal hoop forming the tread of a wheel; *specif* : the steel band shrunk on the fellies of a wagon wheel — see WHEEL illustration **b** : a continuous solid, partly solid, or pneumatic rubber cushion encircling and fitting into the rim of a wheel, and usu. consisting when pneumatic of an external rubber-and-fabric covering containing and protecting from injury an air-filled inner tube — see BICYCLE illustration **c** : the external rubber-and-fabric covering of a pneumatic tire

⁶tire \"\ *vt* -ED/-ING/-S : to put a tire on : provide with tires ⟨the blacksmith . . . and his young helper were *tiring* a wagon wheel —Jackson Burgess⟩

⁷tire *archaic var of* ¹TIER

⁸tire \ˈtī(ə)r,-īə\ *n* -s [F, prob. back-formation fr. *tirant* tie beam, tie rod, fr. pres. part. of *tirer* to pull, draw — more at TIRADE] : the member of a flying buttress that takes the thrust

tire bagger *n* : a worker who shapes flat uncured drum-built tires in a vacuum box and inserts air bags in the tires

tire chain *n* : a chain designed to be fastened over the tread of a tire in order to give a firmer grip on a road and esp. to prevent skidding or slipping — called also *chain, skid chain*

tire chain

¹tired \ˈtī(ə)rd, -īəd\ *adj, often* -ER/-EST [ME *tyred*, fr. past part. of *tyren, tyeren* to tire — more at TIRE] **1** : drained of strength and energy : fatigued often to the point of exhaustion : WEARY ⟨when he was ~*est* he was least able to sleep —Robert Henderson⟩ **2** : obviously worn by hard use : DILAPIDATED, RUN-DOWN ⟨decided to rejuvenate four ~ chairs —*McCall's Needlework*⟩ ⟨a neighborhood of ~ houses⟩ **3** : completely out of patience : FED UP ⟨you make me ~ when you tell the same old story⟩ **4** : devoid of freshness or originality : HACKNEYED ⟨no one could remember how often the ~ joke had been repeated —*Newsweek*⟩ ⟨can best be described by that ~ adjective *quaint* —Richard Joseph⟩

²tired \"\ *adj* [⁵*tire* + *-ed*] : equipped or fitted out with tires

tired·ly \ˈtī(ə)rdlē, -īəd-, -li\ *adv* : in a tired manner ⟨sank ~ into a big red chair —*Time*⟩

tired·ness \-dnəs\ *n* -ES : the quality or state of being tired ⟨a team of helpers who . . . look ready to drop with ~ —Mollie Panter-Downes⟩

tire gage *n* : a gage for measuring the air pressure in a tire

tire·less \ˈtī(ə)rləs, -īəl-\ *adj* : seemingly incapable of tiring : INDEFATIGABLE ⟨a man of distinguished presence and ~ industry —H.U.Faulkner⟩ — **tire·less·ly** *adv* — **tire·less·ness** *n* -ES

tire·man \ˈ-, -,man, -,maa(ə)n\ *n, pl* **tiremen** [⁵*tire* + *man*] **1** : a manufacturer of or dealer in tires **2** : a worker who inspects and changes tires of buses

tire press *n* : a press for mounting or demounting solid tires

tires *pres 3d sing of* TIRE, *pl of* TIRE

tire·some \ˈtī(ə)rsəm, -īəs-\ *adj* : possessing a quality that tires, bores, or annoys : irritatingly tedious : WEARISOME ⟨the ~ chirping of a cricket —Mark Twain⟩ ⟨the endless flights of stone steps . . . were ~ —F. Tennyson Jesse⟩ ⟨there's some ~ engagement he wants to cut —John Buchan⟩ ⟨a nagging ~ woman —W.S.Maugham⟩ — **tire·some·ness** *n* -ES

tire·some·ly *adv* : in a tiresome manner ⟨tended to grow a little ~ facetious —A.C.Ward⟩

tiresomeweed \ˈ=ˌ=ˌ=\ *n* : EELGRASS 1

tirewoman \ˈ=ˌ=ˌ=\ *n, pl* **tirewomen** [³*tire* + *woman*] **1** : a lady's maid; *esp* : a wardrobe woman in a theater **2** : DRESSMAKER

tir·hu·tia \tirˈhüd·ēə\ *n* -s *usu cap* : MAITHILI

tiring *pres part of* TIRE

tiring-house \ˈ=ˌ=ˌ=\ *n* [*tiring* fr. gerund of ⁴*tire*] : a section of a theater reserved for the actors and used esp. for dressing and preparing for stage entrances

tiring irons *n pl but sing in constr* [*tiring* fr. pres. part. of ¹*tire*] : a puzzle game the object of which is to remove a series of rings from two or more metal loops which have but one opening and are intricately interlinked — called also *tarrying irons*

tiring-room \ˈ=ˌ=ˌ=\ *n* [*tiring* fr. gerund of ⁴*tire*] : a dressing room esp. in a theater

¹tirl \ˈtərl\ *vt* -ED/-ING/-S [prob. alter. (influenced by obs. E *tirve* to tirl, fr. ME *tirven*) of OE *tearflian* to turn, roll; akin to OHG *zerben* to turn over, OE *torfian* to throw, be tossed, ON *tyrfa* to cover with turf, *torf* turf — more at TURF] *chiefly Scot* : to strip the covering from : DIVEST, UNROOF

²tirl \"\ *vb* -ED/-ING/-S [alter. of ¹*trill*] *vi* **1** *chiefly Scot* : to make a rattling sound with a door latch or pin **2** *chiefly Scot* : to whirl esp. in moving or falling ~ *vt* **1** *chiefly Scot* : to cause to revolve : turn rapidly : TWIRL **2** *chiefly Scot* : to rattle (as a pin) by moving rapidly up and down

³tirl \"\ *n* -s **1** *chiefly Scot* : a bout or turn usu. at drinking or dancing **2** *chiefly Scot* : something that revolves (as a turnstile or wheel)

tirlie-wirlie *or* **tirly-whirly** \¦tərli¦(h)wərli\ *n* [dim. of ³*tirl* + *whirl*] *Scot* : an ornament consisting of a number of intervolved lines : an intricate contrivance

tir·ma \ˈtərmə\ *n* -s [native name in the Hebrides] *Scot* : OYSTER CATCHER

tiro *var of* TYRO

tir·o·dite \ˈtirə,dīt\ *n* -s [*Tirodi*, Central Provinces, India, its locality + E *-ite*] : a mineral $(Mg, Mn)_8Si_8O_{22}(O, OH)_2$ consisting of a basic silicate of magnesium and manganese of the amphibole group

tirolean *usu cap, var of* TYROLEAN

tirolese *usu cap, var of* TYROLESE

t iron *cap T, also* **tee iron** *n* **1** : a rod with a short crosspiece at the end used as a hook **2** : a T bar usu. of steel used in structures

ti·ro·ni·an \(ˈ)tī¦rōnēən\ *adj, usu cap* [L *tironianus*, fr. *tiron-* (fr. M. Tullius *Tiro fl* 1st cent. B.C. secretary of Cicero) + *-ianus* -ian] : of or relating to the learned freedman Tiro or the notae Tironianae

tirr \ˈtər\ *vb* -ED/-ING/-S [prob. short for obs. E *tirve* — more at TIRL (to strip)] *vt* **1** *chiefly Scot* : to tear off : STRIP, UNCOVER **2** *chiefly Scot* : to strip off the roof of **3** *chiefly Scot* : to remove the surface soil from esp. in quarrying ~ *vi*, *chiefly Scot* : to remove one's clothes : UNDRESS

tir·ra·lir·ra \,tirəˈlirə\ *n* -s [imit.] : the note of a lark or robin or a sound resembling it

tir·ri·vee *also* **tir·ra·vee** *or* **tir·ri·vie** \ˈtərə,vē\ *n* -s [origin unknown] **1** *Scot* : an outburst of temper **2** *Scot* : a general uproar : COMMOTION

tir·than·ka·ra \tirˈtəŋkərə\ *n* -s *often cap* [Skt *tīrthankara*, lit., ford-making, fr. *tīrtha* passage, ford + *karoti* he does, makes — more at KARMA] : one of the 24 founding jinas of Jain tradition venerated as breakers of the path across the stream of time to Nirvana who have shown the way to spiritual liberation in Jainism : a pioneer of faith

tir·u·chi·ra·pal·li \¦tirəchə¦räpəlē\ *adj, usu cap* [fr. *Tiruchirapalli* (Trichinopoly), India] : TRICHINOPOLY

tir·u·ray *also* **tir·u·rai** \¦tirə¦rī\ *n, pl* **tiruray** *or* **tirurays** *also* **tirurai** *or* **tirurais** *usu cap* **1 a** : a predominantly pagan people in the western part of Cotabato province, central Mindanao, Philippines **b** : a member of such people **2** : the Austronesian language of the Tiruray people

tis *pl of* TI

ti·sane \təˈzan\ *n* -s [F, fr. L *ptisana* peeled barley, barley water — more at PTISAN] : an infusion orig. of barley but now usu. of dried leaves or flowers (as linden blossoms or camomile or cherry stems) that is used as a beverage or for mildly medicinal effects : PTISAN

ti·se·li·us apparatus *also* **tiselius cell** \təˈsālēəs-, -¦zā\ *n, usu cap T* [after Arne *Tiselius* b1902 Swed. biochemist] : an apparatus characterized by a rectangular U-tube divided into two or three sections for carrying out electrophoresis esp. of proteins in a biological system (as blood plasma)

tish·ah b'ab *or* **tisha b'ab** *or* **tish·ah b'av** *or* **tisha b'av** \¦tishə¦bäv, -bōv\ *n, usu cap T & Ab or Av* [Heb *tish'āh bĕ'ābh* ninth of Ab] : a Jewish fast day that is observed on the 9th day of Ab in commemoration of the destruction of the First and Second Temples at Jerusalem — called also *Ninth of Ab*

tish·chen·ko reaction \təˈsheŋ(,)kō-, təshˈch\ *n, usu cap T* [after Vyacheslav E. *Tishchenko* †1941 Russian chemist] : the synthesis (as of ethyl acetate from acetaldehyde and aluminum ethoxide) of an ester from an aldehyde involving simultaneous oxidation and reduction of two molecules of the aldehyde in the presence of an aluminum alkoxide

tish·ri *or* **tiz·ri** \ˈtishrē\ *n* -s *usu cap* [Heb *tishrī*, fr. Assyr-Bab *tashritu* the seventh month] : the 1st month of the civil year or the 7th month of the ecclesiastical year in the Jewish calendar — see MONTH table

tis·su·al \ˈtish(y)əwəl, ˈti(,)shüəl, *chiefly Brit* ˈtisyəwəl *or* ˈti(,)syüəl\ *adj* : of or relating to tissue

¹tis·sue \ˈti(,)shü, ˈtish(,)yü, ˈti(,)shü, ˈtish(,)yü, *before a vowel often* -sh(y)əw; *chiefly South* -sh(y)ə *before a consonant or pause or before a vowel in a following word; chiefly Brit* ˈti(,)syü *or* ˈti(,)syü *or* ˈtisyəw; *chiefly dial* ˈtishē *or* -shi *in "tissue paper"*\ *n* -s [ME *tissu*, fr. OF, fr. past part. of *tistre* to weave, fr. L *texere* — more at TECHNICAL] **1 a** (1) *archaic* : a rich ornamented cloth usu. of silk interwoven with gold or silver threads (2) : a fine lightweight fabric often sheer or semitransparent; *esp* : a gauze of silk or wool **b** : something resembling a fabric of tissue : an intricate or interrelated number of things forming a web : a complicated mesh ⟨the testimony . . . is a ~ of lies —W.A.White⟩ ⟨most battlefield history of the past is a ~ of myths —S.L.A.Marshall⟩ **2 a** : TISSUE PAPER **b** : CARBON PAPER 2 **c** : CLEANSING TISSUE **3 a** : an aggregate of cells usu. of a particular kind or kinds together with their intercellular substance that form one of the structural materials out of which the body of a plant or an animal is built up — see COLLENCHYMA, PARENCHYMA, PROSENCHYMA, SCLERENCHYMA; CONNECTIVE TISSUE, EPITHELIUM, MUSCLE, NERVE **2 b** : something resembling the living tissue of a plant or animal ⟨give vitality and vigor to the ~*s* of our law —B.N. Cardozo⟩ ⟨collective bargaining . . . is part of the living ~ of society —*Current Biog.*⟩

²tissue \"\ *adj* [ME, fr. *tissu* tissue] : resembling a fabric of tissue in weight, texture, or appearance : characterized by unusual sheerness ⟨~ gingham⟩ ⟨~ faille⟩

³tissue \"\ *vt* -ED/-ING/-S [ME *tissuen*, fr. *tissu* tissue] : to weave into tissue : embroider by or as if by interweaving ⟨covered with cloth of gold *tissued* upon blue —Francis Bacon⟩

tissue culture *n* : the act, process, or technique of making body tissue grow in a culture medium outside of the organism; *also* : a culture of tissue (as fibrous tissue or epithelium)

tissued *adj* [fr. past part. of ³*tissue*] **1** : woven in the manner of tissue : having the splendor or delicacy of tissue **2** : wrapped in tissue paper ⟨a pair of brown shoes and a pair of black all ~ up —Richard Llewellyn⟩

tissue fluid *n* : fluid permeating the spaces between individual cells, being in osmotic contact with the blood and lymph, and serving in interstitial transport of nutrients and waste

tissue paper *n* -s : a thin gauzy paper weighing not over 12 to 15 pounds for a ream of 480 sheets cut 24x36 inches

tissue space *n* : an intercellular space

tis·suey \ˈtish(y)əw¦ē, ˈti(,)shül, |i, *chiefly Brit* ˈtisyəw| *or* ˈti(,)syül\ *adj* : resembling tissue

tis·wood \ˈti,swu̇d\ *n* [*tiss* of unknown origin + *wood*] **1 a** : SNOWDROP TREE 1 **b** : RED BAY **2** : the wood of a tisswood

tisty-tosty \¦tisti¦tästi\ *n* -ES [origin unknown] *dial Eng* : a ball made of flowers

tis·win *also* **tiz·win** \təzˈwēn\ *n* -s [MexSp *tesguino, tejuino, tecuin*, fr. Nahuatl *tecuini* heartbeat] : a fermented beverage made by Indians of the southwestern U.S.

¹tit \ˈtit, *usu* -id·+V\ *n* -s [ME *titte*, fr. OE *titt, tit, tite* — more at TEAT] **1 a** : TEAT 1 **b** : BREAST 1a — usu. considered vulgar **2** : something resembling or held to resemble a tit: **a** : a small metal part that ejects the finished nails from the bore in nail making **b** : TEAT 3

²tit \"\ *vb* **titted; titted; titting; tits** [ME *titten*] *chiefly Scot* : to pull forcibly : JERK, TUG, TWITCH

³tit \"\ *n* -s [ME *titte*, fr. *titten* to tit] *chiefly Scot* : a sharp or sudden pull : JERK, TUG, TWITCH

⁴tit \"\ *n* -s [*tit-* (as in *titmouse*)] **1 a** : a small horse **b** : an inferior or weedy horse **2** *archaic* : a girl or young woman: **a** : one of loose moral character : HUSSY **b** : one that is or is held to be admirable in some respect (as appearance)

⁵tit \"\ *n* -s [short for *titmouse*] : a small plump often long-tailed bird : TITMOUSE — often used with a qualifying term ⟨wren ~⟩ ⟨coal ~⟩

tit *abbr* **1** title **2** titular

¹ti·tan \ˈtītᵊn\ *n* -s [Gk] **1** *usu cap* : one of a family or race of earth giants in ancient Greek mythology whose power was destroyed by the Olympian gods and who are usu. held to have been characterized by gigantic size, immense brute strength, and primitive force and appetite rather than intelligence or morality **2** *sometimes cap* : one gigantic in size or power : a titanic being : one that stands out among others of a group esp. for greatness of stature or achievement ⟨one of the ~*s* of American higher education —*Saturday Rev.*⟩ ⟨five mountain ~*s* higher than the highest of the . . . Alps —*Geog. School Bull.*⟩ ⟨grand old ~ of American law —Fred Rodell⟩ **3** : TITAN CRANE

²titan \"\ *adj, usu cap* : TITANIC

titan- *or* **titano-** *comb form* [NL *titanium*] : titanium ⟨*titan*ate⟩ ⟨*titano*cyanide⟩ ⟨*titano*fluoride⟩

ti·ta·nate \ˈtītᵊn,āt, -ᵊnət\ *n* -s [*titan-* + *-ate*] **1** : any of various compounds (as barium titanate) that are multiple oxides or solid solutions of titanium dioxide with other metallic oxides **2** : an ester of the general formula $Ti(OR)_4$ obtainable by reaction of titanium tetrachloride with an alcohol or phenol in the presence of a base

ti·ta·nat·ed \-ād·əd\ *adj* [*titanate* + *-ed*] : blended with titanium dioxide ⟨~ lithopone⟩

ti·tan·augite \¦tītᵊn+\ *n* [G *titanaugit*, fr. *titan-* (fr. NL *titanium*) + *augit* augite (fr. L *augites*)] : a basaltic augite rich in titanium and usu. alkali

titan crane *n* : a massive crane with an overhanging counter-

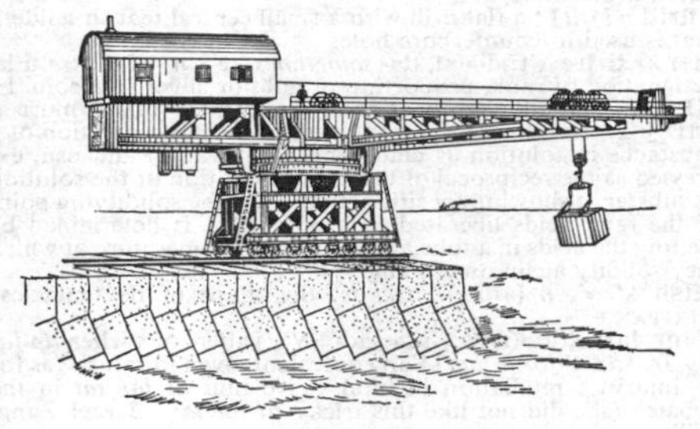

titan crane

balanced arm carrying a traveler and lifting crab supported by a carriage mounted on track rails and used esp. for lifting and setting in place heavy masonry blocks for piers and breakwaters — compare GOLIATH CRANE

ti·tan·ess \ˈtītᵊnəs\ *n* -ES *often cap* [*titan* + *-ess*] : a female titan

ti·ta·nia \tīˈtānēə, təˈt- *sometimes* -ˈtan- *or* -nyə\ *n* -s [NL, fr. *titanium*] **1** : TITANIUM DIOXIDE **2** : RUTILE 2

¹ti·ta·ni·an \(ˈ)tī¦tānēən, -¦tan-, -nyən *sometimes* təˈt-\ *adj, usu cap* [L *titanius* titanic (fr. Gk *titanios*, fr. *Titan* + *-ios* -y) + E *-an*] *archaic* : ¹TITANIC 1 ⟨begin with a *Titanian* revenge to shift mountains against heaven —John Florio⟩

²ti·ta·ni·an \(ˈ)tī¦tānēən, təˈt-, -nyən, *sometimes* -¦tan-\ *adj* [NL *titanium* + E *-an*] : of, relating to, or containing titanium

¹ti·tan·ic \(ˈ)tī¦tanik, -nēk *sometimes* təˈt-\ *adj* [Gk *titanikos*, fr. *Titan* + *-ikos* -ic] **1** *usu cap* : of, relating to, or held to have characteristics of the Titans of ancient Greek mythology **2** *sometimes cap* : resembling a titan (as in size or character): as **a** : marked by very great size : of enormous magnitude, power, scope, strength, or influence : COLOSSAL, GIGANTIC ⟨great factories hummed like one unanimous ~ loom —Donn Byrne⟩ ⟨a ~ archipelago —*Natural History*⟩ ⟨political change . . . on a ~ scale —H.J.Laski⟩ **b** (1) : manifesting superhuman power or force : exerting more than human strength : marked by tremendous brute force (2) : calling for the exertion of such strength or power ⟨the ~ labor of clearing away the debris after the air raid⟩ ⟨done a ~ job of streamlining and reorganizing the service —*Americas*⟩ **c** : EARTH-SHAKING ⟨a ~ civil war that all but destroyed the country —G.W.Johnson⟩ ⟨a ~ struggle⟩ **syn** see HUGE

²ti·tanic \(ˈ)tī¦tanik təˈt-, -ˈtān-, -nēk\ *adj* [NL *titanium* + E *-ic*] : of, relating to, or containing titanium — used esp. of compounds in which this element is tetravalent; compare TITANOUS

titanic acid *n* [²*titanic*] : any of various amorphous weakly acid substances that are hydrates of titanium dioxide obtainable from solutions of titanium tetrachloride or basic titanium sulfate: as **a** : a gelatinous highly hydrated substance that is the ortho acid **b** : a less highly hydrated substance

ti·tan·i·cal·ly \(ˈ)tī¦tanək(ə)lē, -nēk-, -li *sometimes* təˈt-\ *adv* [¹*titanic* + *-ally*] : in a titanic manner ⟨was ~ a failure at the job —Sinclair Lewis⟩ ⟨with ~ explosive results —*Atlantic*⟩

ti·tan·ich·thys \¦tītᵊnˈikthəs\ *n, cap* [NL, fr. Gk *Titan* + NL *-ichthys*] : a genus (the type of the family Titanichthyidae) of very large toothless arthrodiran fishes of the Upper Devonian of Ohio

titanic iron ore *or* **titaniferous iron ore** *n* [²*titanic*] : ILMENITE

titanic oxide *n* : TITANIUM DIOXIDE

ti·ta·nif·er·ous \¦tītᵊn¦if(ə)rəs\ *adj* [*titan-* + *-iferous*] : containing or yielding titanium

ti·tan·ism \ˈtītᵊn,izəm\ *n* -s *often cap* [*titan* + *-ism*] : the spirit characterizing or held to characterize a Titan: **a** : defiance of and headlong revolt against limits or restraints and esp. existing social or artistic conventions ⟨the *Titanism* of every kind that has marked our modern emancipation —Irving Babbitt⟩ **b** : a marked tendency to expansiveness in expression resulting in grandiosity and freedom from all restraint

ti·ta·nite \ˈtītᵊn,īt\ *n* -s [G *titanit*, fr. NL *titanium* + G *-it* -ite] : SPHENE

ti·ta·ni·um \tīˈtānēəm, təˈt- *sometimes* -ˈtan- *or* -nyəm\ *n* -s [NL, fr. Gk *Titan* + NL *-ium*] : a lustrous silvery gray light strong high-melting metallic element that is usu. hard and brittle in the cold but malleable when heated and ductile when pure, that has good corrosion resistance at ordinary temperatures and is tetravalent in most of its compounds, that is found combined in ilmenite, rutile, and other minerals, is widely distributed in small amounts esp. in igneous rocks, soils, and clays, and is the ninth most abundant element in the earth's crust, that is usu. produced in the form of sponge from titanium tetrachloride by reduction with magnesium or sodium and consolidated by melting, and that is used chiefly in the form of ferrotitanium in making steel and in other alloys as a structural material (as in aircraft, jet engines, missiles, and chemical equipment) — symbol *Ti*; see ELEMENT table

titanium carbide *n* : a very hard gray metallic substance approximating the composition TiC, made by heating titanium dioxide and carbon in the electric furnace, and used chiefly with tungsten carbide in cemented carbide compositions for cutting steel

titanium dioxide *n* : the compound TiO_2 that occurs naturally in three different crystal forms as rutile, anatase, and brookite, that is produced commercially from rutile or ilmenite as a white amorphous powder or in the rutile or anatase crystal forms, and that is used chiefly as a pigment or opacifier (as in paint, vitreous enamel, linoleum, rubber and plastics, printing ink, paper) because of its high covering power, brilliance and reflectivity, and resistance to light and fumes, and also in ceramic components for electronic equipment and in the form of large synthetic rutile crystals as gems

titanium oxide *n* **:** any of several oxides of titanium; *esp* **:** TITANIUM DIOXIDE
titanium tetrachloride *n* **:** a volatile liquid compound $TiCl_4$ that is made by the action of chlorine at high temperature on either titanium or titanium dioxide and so serves as a means of separating the titanium content of crude ores by distillation and that is used otherwise chiefly in skywriting and smoke screens because it fumes in moist air
titanium white *n* **:** titanium dioxide used as a pigment; *also* **:** a composite pigment containing titanium dioxide and an extender (as calcium sulfate)
titano- — see TITAN-
ti·tano·magnetite \ˌtīt³n(ˌ)ō, tīˌtanə, təˈt-, -ˌtānə+\ *n* [*titan-* + *magnetite*] **:** a titaniferous variety of magnetite
ti·tano·saur \tīˈtanəˌsȯ(ə)r, ˈtīt³n-\ *n* -S [NL *Titanosaurus*] **:** a reptile or fossil of the genus *Titanosaurus*
ti·tano·sau·rus \ˌtīˌtanəˈsȯrəs, ˌtīt³n-\ *n, cap* [NL, fr. Gk *Titan* + NL *-o-* + *-saurus*] **:** a genus of large Cretaceous sauropod dinosaurs chiefly of the southern hemisphere
ti·tano·silicate \ˌtīt³n(ˌ)ō, tīˌtanə, təˌt-, -ˌtānə+\ *n* [*titan-* + *silicate*] **:** SILICOTITANATE
ti·tano·there \tīˈtanəˌthi(ə)r, ˈtīt³n-\ *n* -S [NL *Titanotherium*] **:** a mammal or fossil of the family Brontotheriidae **:** BRONTOTHERE
ti·tano·the·ri·idae \(ˌ)tīˌtanəthəˈrīəˌdē, ˌtīt³n(ˌ)ōth-\ [NL *Titanotherium* + *-idae*] *syn of* BRONTOTHERIIDAE
ti·tano·the·ri·um \-nəˈthirēəm\ [NL, fr. Gk *Titan* + NL *-o-* + *-therium*] *syn of* MENODUS
ti·ta·nous \(ˈ)tīˌtanəs, təˈtan-, ˈtīt³n-\ *adj* [ISV *titan-* + *-ous*] **:** of, relating to, or derived from titanium — used esp. of compounds in which this element is trivalent; compare TITANIC
ti·ta·nyl \ˈtīt³nəl, -ənˌēl; tīˈtan³l, təˈt-\ *n* -S [*titan-* + *-yl*] **:** the group TiO consisting of titanium and oxygen that is a bivalent radical
ti·tar \ˈtēd·ə(r)\ *n* -S [Hindi *tītar*, fr. Skt *tittira* — more at TURTLE (turtledove)] **:** a francolin (*Francolinus pondicerianus*) of southern Asia
tit babbler *n* [⁵*tit*] **:** any of several small East Indian and Asiatic timaliine birds of *Macronus* and related genera
titbit *var of* TIDBIT
tit drill *n* [¹*tit*] **:** a flat drill with a small central teat to guide it that is used to counterbore holes
ti·ter *or* **ti·tre** \ˈtīd·ə(r), ˌtə- *sometimes* ˈtē\ *n* -S [F *titre* title, designation of rank, proportion of gold or silver in a coin, fr. MF *title, tiltre* title, designation of rank, fr. OF *title* — more at TITLE] **1 :** the strength of a solution or the concentration of a substance in solution as determined by titration and usu. expressed as the reciprocal of the highest dilution of the solution or substance showing specific activity **2 :** the solidifying point of the fatty acids liberated from a fat that is determined by melting the acids in a tube and noting the temperature at which they solidify again on cooling
titfish \ˈ=,=\ *n* [¹*tit* + *fish*; fr. the shape of its tentacles] **:** TREPANG
tit for tat \ˌtitfə(r)ˈtat, *usu* -ad·+V\ [alter. of earlier *tip for tap*, fr. ⁵*tip* + *for* + *tap*] **:** an equivalent given in return (as for an injury) **:** retaliation in kind ⟨gave him *tit for tat* in the debate⟩ ⟨she did not like this tricky *tit for tat* —Israel Zangwill⟩
¹**tith·able** \ˈtīthəbəl\ *adj* [ME, fr. *tithen* to tithe] **:** subject or liable to payment of tithes ⟨a tenth of his ~ property —F.M. Stenton⟩ ⟨a ~ person⟩
²**tithable** \ˈ"\ *n* -S **:** one that is tithable ⟨levied of each ~ in the parish —*Vestry Book of Bristol Parish (Va.)*⟩
¹**tithe** \ˈtīth\ *vb* -ED/-ING/-S [ME *tithen*, fr. OE *teogothian, tēothian*, fr. *teogotha, tēotha* tenth — more at ²TITHE] *vt* **1 :** to pay or give a tenth part of esp. for the support of the church **:** pay taxes in the form of tithes on ⟨~ an estate⟩ ⟨~ a crop⟩ ⟨~ one's income⟩ **2** *obs* **a :** to take a tenth part of or every tenth one from **:** divide into tenths ⟨divers of them were constrained to ~ themselves and eat the tenth man —Henry Spelman⟩ **b :** to reduce by one tenth of the original number (as by putting to death one man out of every ten) **:** DECIMATE **3 a :** to levy a tithe on **:** impose the payment of a tenth upon **:** tax to the amount of a tenth **:** exact tithe from **b :** to collect or exact one tenth from (as goods) as a tithe **:** take tithe of ⟨~ the product of the earth —Sydney Smith⟩ ~ *vi* **:** to pay tithe; *specif* **:** to give a tenth of one's income as a tithe esp. for the support of church or religious work ⟨church members are exhorted to ~⟩ ⟨a fundamentalist congregation . . . in which everyone ~*s* —Hugh Morrow⟩
²**tithe** \ˈ"\ *n* -S [ME *tigthe, tithe*, fr. OE *teogotha, tēotha* tenth; akin to OFris *tegotha* tenth, MLG *tegede*; all fr. a prehistoric WGmc alter. of the source of OHG *zehanto* tenth — more at TEIND] **1 :** a tenth part of something paid as a voluntary contribution or as a tax for religious purposes and esp. for the support of a priesthood or religious establishment: as **a :** a tenth part (as of a person's entire possessions or of the yearly increase thereof) paid in kind as a tax by the Hebrews and other ancient peoples **b :** an orig. voluntary but later legally required payment of one tenth of one's yearly income for the support usu. of the local parish church in medieval and later times **c :** a payment in kind or money consisting until the middle of the 19th century of one tenth of the yearly profits arising from land, stock, or personal industry and traditionally required of the inhabitants of a parish in the United Kingdom for the support of the parish church — see MIXED TITHE, PERSONAL TITHE, PRAEDIAL TITHE, TEIND **d :** a tenth of one's income given voluntarily for the support of church or religious work **2 :** the voluntary or required obligation represented by individual tithes — usu. used without article ⟨in the seventh century the payment of ~ was a religious duty —F.M.Stenton⟩ **3 a :** the tenth part of something **:** TENTH ⟨a hundred thousand a year . . . a cool ~ of a million a year to manipulate —G.A. Wagner⟩ **b :** a small part of something **:** an insignificant portion **:** one bit ⟨these are only a ~ of the treasures in the . . . museum —Elizabeth Montizambert⟩ ⟨passed over for men who have not a ~ of his ability —H.J.Laski⟩ ⟨no man . . . knows this country a ~ as well as the author —Louis Golding⟩ **4 :** a tax, levy, or tribute of usu. one tenth for a purpose other than a religious one ⟨forced to pay a fixed ~ that goes . . . into the private till of the Pasha —Joachim Joesten⟩
³**tithe** \ˈ"\ *adj* [ME, fr. ²*tithe*] **1 a :** due as or given in payment of tithe — see TITHE PIG **b :** of or relating to tithes ⟨~ gatherer⟩ ⟨~ payer⟩ **2 :** TENTH ⟨a ~ part⟩
tithe barn *n* [³*tithe*] **:** a barn orig. built to hold ecclesiastical tithes paid in kind and common in many parts of England
tithe man *n* **:** TITHINGMAN 3
tithe pig *n* **:** a pig set apart or given in payment of tithe
tithe proctor *n* **:** a collector of tithes
¹**tith·er** \ˈtīthə(r)\ *n* -S [ME, fr. *tithen* to tithe + *-er*] **1 :** one that pays tithes ⟨practically every member of the church is a ~ —*Emporia (Kans.) Gazette*⟩ **2 :** one that collects or advocates the payment of tithes
²**tith·er** \ˈtithə(r)\ *var of* TOTHER
¹**tithing** *n* -S [ME *tething, tithing*, fr. OE *tēothung*, fr. *tēothian* to tithe, take one tenth + *-ung* -ing — more at TITHE, -ING] **:** a small administrative division locally preserved in many parts of England apparently orig. consisting of ten men with their families or of the tenth part of the hundred — compare FRANKPLEDGE
²**tithing** *n* -S [ME, fr. gerund of *tithen* to tithe] **1 :** the act of one that tithes **:** a paying, levying, or taking of tithes **2 :** something that is taken or set apart as tithe **:** TITHE
tith·ing·man \ˈtīthiŋ,man\ *n, pl* **tithingmen** [ME, fr. OE *tēothingman*, fr. *tēothung* + *man*] **1 :** the chief man of an old English tithing **2 :** a British local peace officer **3** [²*tithing* + *man*] **:** a collector of tithes **4 a :** an elected local official having the functions of a peace officer in various American colonies (as Maryland and in New England) **b :** an annually elected official chosen in New England towns until well into the 19th century and charged primarily with preserving order in church during divine service and enforcing the observance of the Sabbath
tithing penny *n* [¹*tithing*] **:** a small customary duty traditionally paid under old English law: **a :** one paid by the tenants of a manor to the lord **b :** one paid by the lord of a manor at the hundred court **c :** one paid by each tithing to the sheriff to defray court expenses
tithing rod *n* [*tithing*man + *rod*] **:** a long rod used by tithingmen to keep order in church (as by tapping noisy or drowsy persons)
ti·tho·nia \təˈthōnēə, -nyə\ *n* [NL, prob. fr. L *Tithonis*, poetical name of Aurora, goddess of the dawn (fr. her marriage to *Tithonus*, son of Laomedon) + NL *-ia*] **1** *cap* **:** a genus of tall herbs (family Compositae) that are natives of Mexico and Central America but grown farther north as annual ornamentals and have alternate leaves and flower heads resembling sunflowers **2** -S **:** any plant of the genus *Tithonia* — called also *Mexican sunflower*
tithy·mal \ˈtithəməl, təˈthīm-\ *n* -S [L *tithymallus, tithymalus*, fr. Gk *tithymallos*] **:** SPURGE 1; *esp* **:** a spurge (*Tithymalus cyparissias*)
tith·y·ma·lop·sis \ˌtithəməˈläpsəs\ *n, cap* [NL, fr. *Tithymalus* + *-opsis*] *in some classifications* **:** a genus of chiefly perennial No. American spurges that is usu. included in *Euphorbia*
tith·y·ma·lus \ˌtithəˈmāləs, -mal-\ *n, cap* [NL, fr. L *tithymallus, tithymalus* tithymal] *in some classifications* **:** a genus of chiefly annual No. American spurges that is usu. included in *Euphorbia*
¹**ti·ti** \ˈtī,tī, ˈtīd·,ī\ *n* -S [prob. fr. Timucuan origin] **1 a :** a tree (*Cliftonia monophylla*) of the family Cyrillaceae that is found in the southern U.S. and has glossy leaves and racemes of fragrant white flowers succeeded by one-seeded drupes — called also *black titi, buckwheat tree* **b :** any of several trees of the genus *Cyrilla* — called also *white titi* **2 :** SOURWOOD **3** *Austral* **:** TI 1
²**ti·ti** \təˈtē\ *or* **tee·tee** \tēˈtē\ *n* -S [Sp *titi*, fr. Aymara *titi*, lit., little cat] **:** any of various small So. American monkeys of the genus *Callicebus* that resemble the squirrel monkeys of the genus *Saimiri* but have the head not so elongated posteriorly and the tail more thickly haired
³**ti·ti** \ˈtē,tē\ *n* -S [Maori] **1** *NewZeal* **:** a blue-footed petrel (*Pterodroma cookii*) **2** *NewZeal* **:** SOOTY SHEARWATER
¹**ti·tian** \ˈtishən\ *n* -S *often cap* [after *Titian* (Tiziano Vecelli) †1576 Ital. painter] **1 :** a brownish orange that is less strong, slightly yellower and lighter than spice, slightly yellower and lighter than prairie brown or Windsor tan, and slightly redder and darker than amber brown or gold pheasant **2 :** one having titian hair ⟨blondes, brunets, and ~*s*⟩
²**titian** \ˈ"\ *adj, often cap* **:** of the color titian ⟨~ hair⟩
ti·tian·esque \ˌtishəˈnesk\ *adj, usu cap* [*Titian* †1576 Ital. painter + E *-esque*] **:** after the manner of or suggesting the style of the Venetian painter Titian noted for his breadth of treatment, realism, and rich but subdued coloring
ti·til·la \tīˈtilə, təˈt-\ *n, pl* **titil·lae** \tīˈti(ˌ)lē; təˈti(ˌ)lē, -ˌlī\ [NL, fr. L *titillare* to tickle] **:** any of various processes on the external genitalia of male invertebrate animals believed to play a role in sexual activities
tit·il·late \ˈtid·ᵊlˌāt, -it³l-, *usu* -ād·+V\ *vt* -ED/-ING/-S [L *titillatus*, past part. of *titillare* to tickle, titillate] **1 :** to stimulate by or as if by tickling ⟨they . . . ~ the nymphs with their antennae —J.D.Hood⟩ ⟨the static machine, used . . . to ~ the skin —L.R.Harrison⟩ **2 :** to excite pleasurably or agreeably **:** arouse by stimulation ⟨*titillated* the prurient with the frankness of its carnal detail —S.H.Adams⟩ ⟨~ rather than satiate the reader's interest —Raymond Walters b. 1912⟩ **syn** see PLEASE
titillating *adj* [fr. pres. part. of *titillate*] **:** being a source of, marked by, or inducing a state of titillation **:** pleasantly stimulating or exciting ⟨~ thoughts⟩ ⟨a ~ feeling⟩ ⟨~ reading⟩ — **tit·il·lat·ing·ly** *adv*
tit·il·la·tion \ˌtid·³lˈāshən, ˌtit³l-\ *n* -S [ME *titillacione*, fr. L *titillation-, titillatio*, fr. *titillatus* (past part. of *titillare* to titillate) + *-ion-, -io* -ion] **1 :** the action of titillating or the state of being titillated; *esp* **:** a pleasurable excitement or stimulation (as of the mind or senses) **2 :** a sensation of being titillated **:** a transient reaction from or as if from being tickled **:** a slight thrill esp. of pleasure
tit·il·la·tive \ˈ==,ād·iv\ *adj* [*titillate* + *-ive*] **:** tending or serving to titillate ⟨a rowdy charmer with a ~ view of humanity —Charles Lee⟩
titius-bode law \ˌtētsēəsˈbōdə-\ *n, usu cap T&B* [after J.D. *Titius* †1796 Ger. mathematician, & Johann E. *Bode* †1826 Ger. astronomer] **:** BODE'S LAW
¹**tit·i·vate** *or* **tit·ti·vate** \ˈtid·ə,vāt, -itə-, *usu* -ād·+V\ *vb* -ED/-ING/-S [perh. fr. ¹*tidy* + *-vate* (as in *renovate*)] **:** to dress up (as by making small additions or alterations in attire) **:** spruce up **:** smarten up
²**titivate** \ˈ"\ *vt* -ED/-ING/-S [by alter.] **:** TITILLATE ⟨few . . . fans felt *titivated* with pleasurable anticipations —E.F.Carter⟩
tit·i·va·tion \ˌ==ˈvāshən\ *n* -S [*titivate* + *-ion*] **:** the action of dressing up or making small additions or improvements in one's dress ⟨she must be a perfect beauty . . . to look so well without any ~ —Alix King⟩
titlark \ˈtit,=\ *n* [*tit-* (as in *titmouse*) + *lark*] **:** PIPIT
¹**ti·tle** \ˈtīd·³l, -īt³l\ *n* -S [ME *titel, title*, fr. OF *titele, title*, fr. L *titulus* inscription, label, title] **1 a** *obs* **:** an inscription placed over, upon, or under something to describe, distinguish, explain, or entitle it **:** LEGEND **b :** an inscription placed on a cross usu. above a crucified person or on a crucifix ⟨Pilate wrote a ~, and put it on the cross —Jn 19:19 (AV)⟩ **c :** written material introduced into a motion picture or television program to give credits, explain an action, or represent dialogue — compare CREDIT, SUBTITLE **2 a :** the union of all the elements constituting legal ownership and being divided in common law into possession, right of possession, and right of property **b :** something that constitutes a legally just cause of exclusive possession **:** the body of facts or events that give rise to the ownership of real or personal property ⟨good ~ to an estate⟩ ⟨an imperfect ~⟩ **c :** the instrument (as a deed) that is evidence of a right **3 a :** something that justifies or substantiates a claim **:** sufficient proof or justification **:** a valid reason **:** a ground of right ⟨his services give him a ~ to our gratitude⟩ ⟨unable to establish his ~ of authorship⟩ **b :** an alleged or recognized right ⟨he has no ~ to anticipate our support⟩ **4 a :** a descriptive or general heading (as of a chapter in a book) **b :** the heading which names an act or statute, by which it is distinguished from others, and which at common law forms no part of the act but in case of ambiguity sometimes is referred to as an aid in interpretation **c :** the heading of a legal declaration setting forth the names of the parties and the court and the calendar or docket number of the case **5 a :** the distinguishing name of a written, printed, spoken, or filmed production (as a book, pamphlet, essay, or poem): as (1) **:** the principal name consisting of a word or phrase and sometimes appearing on the binding (as of a book) in the shortest form that will be distinctive — see HALF TITLE, SHORT TITLE, SUBTITLE (2) **:** all material on a title page preceding the author's name or its substitute and sometimes including a subtitle and various pieces of descriptive matter (3) **:** all the matter on a title page including punctuation marks esp. in an old or rare book **b :** a similar distinguishing name given to a picture, statue, musical composition, or other work **6 :** a sphere of work or a source of income or maintenance required by a bishop of a candidate for ordination **7 :** a descriptive name **:** a distinctive appellation or designation ⟨gallants, lads, boys, hearts of gold, all the ~*s* of good fellowship —Shak.⟩ ⟨earned for him the ~ of "father of the American psychological novel" —*Amer. Guide Series: N.J.*⟩ **8 :** a Roman Catholic parish church in or near Rome of which a cardinal is titular head **9 :** a division of an instrument or book; *esp* **:** one of a portion of a bill or act that usu. is larger than a section or article ⟨this act, divided into ~ and sections —*U.S.Code*⟩ **10** *obs* **:** an assertion of right **:** CLAIM ⟨an eagerness after employments in the state was looked upon . . . as the worst ~ a man could set up —Jonathan Swift⟩ **11 a :** an appellation of dignity, honor, distinction, or preeminence attached on a hereditary or acquired basis to a person or family by virtue of rank, office, precedent, privilege, or attainment, possession of or association with certain lands, or as a mark of respect ⟨no ~ of nobility shall be granted by the United States —*U.S.Constitution*⟩ — see COURTESY TITLE **b :** a person holding a title and esp. a title of nobility ⟨saw to it that their daughters married authentic foreign ~*s* —J.D.Hart⟩ **12 a :** TITLE PAGE **b :** the first book section containing the title page **c :** TITLE SPACE **d :** a gold-stamped leather label for a book backbone **e :** a specially printed title page for insertion in a deluxe book in place of or preceding a text title **13 :** a literary work or book as distinguished from a particular copy ⟨fifty ~*s* of fiction and ten copies of each in the library⟩ ⟨the press published 15 ~*s* last year —*Book Production*⟩ **14 :** CHAMPIONSHIP 1 ⟨won the boxing ~⟩ ⟨holder of the indoor tennis ~⟩
²**title** \ˈ"\ *vt* **titled; titled; titling** \-īd·³liŋ, -īt(³)liŋ\ **titles** [ME *titelen*, fr. *titel* title] **1 a :** to provide a title for (as a book) **:** furnish with a title **:** give a title to **b :** to stamp or otherwise print the title of (a book) on the front cover or backbone **2 a :** to designate or call by a title (as of relationship, rank, or office) **:** TERM, STYLE ⟨their sovereign *titled* himself King of the Franks —James Bryce⟩ **b :** to dignify with an appellation or designation of rank **:** endow with a title
³**title** \ˈ"\ *adj* [¹*title*] **:** of or relating to a title: as **a :** used for or in the production of a printed title (as on the backbone of a book) ⟨~ leather⟩ **b :** having the same name as the title of a production ⟨act the ~ role in *Hamlet*⟩ **c :** having the same title as or providing the title for the collection or production of which it forms a part ⟨~ essay⟩ ⟨~ poem⟩ ⟨~ song⟩ ⟨~ story⟩ **d :** of, relating to, or involving a championship (as in sports) ⟨~ match⟩ ⟨~ contest⟩ **e :** of, used in, or involved in the production of written material introduced into a motion picture or television program ⟨~ artist⟩ ⟨~ background⟩ ⟨~ music⟩ ⟨~ card⟩
title by occupancy 1 : a legal right of property acquired by taking the first possession of a thing or possession of a thing which belonged to nobody and appropriating it **2 :** sovereignty acquired in international law by a political state over territory not under the dominion of another state by effective exercise of control (as by settlement or by air patrol) and by public proclamation of the extent of the territory involved
title catalog *n* **:** a library catalog in which books and other works are listed only under their titles usu. arranged alphabetically — compare AUTHOR CATALOG
ti·tled \ˈtīd·³ld, -īt³ld\ *adj* [¹*title* + *-ed*] **:** having or bearing a title and esp. one of nobility **:** NOBLE ⟨a ~ family⟩
title deed *n* **:** the deed or one of the deeds constituting the muniments or evidences of a person's legal ownership
title entry *n* **:** a catalog entry of a writing under the title and usu. the first important or key word of the title — compare AUTHOR ENTRY
titleholder \ˈ==,==\ *n* **:** one that holds a title; *specif* **:** CHAMPION
title insurance *n* **:** insurance against loss due to an unknown defect in a title or interest in real estate
title page *n* **:** a usu. recto page of a book on which is given its full title and usu. the names of the author and the publisher and the place and sometimes the date of publication — compare HALF TITLE 1, IMPRINT
title piece *n* **1 :** a label usu. of leather adhered to the front cover or backbone of a book and impressed with the title **2 :** a literary work (as a poem) having the same title as the collection of which it forms a part ⟨a volume . . . with this poem as *title piece* —H.S.Canby⟩
ti·tler \ˈtīd·³lə(r), -īt(³)l-\ *n* -S [¹*title* + *-er*] **:** a device for holding a motion-picture camera and in front of it an easel or frame in which can be placed a card bearing a title
titles *pl of* TITLE, *pres 3d sing of* TITLE
title space *n* **:** a panel for the title between the bands of the backbone of a book
¹**tit·ling** \ˈtitlən, -liŋ\ *n* -S [ME, fr. *tit-* (as in *titmose* titmouse) + *-ling*] **1** *dial Brit* **:** PIPIT; *esp* **:** MEADOW PIPIT **2** *dial Brit* **:** HEDGE SPARROW
²**ti·tling** \ˈtīd·³liŋ, -īt(³)liŋ\ *n* -S [ME *titeling*, fr. gerund of *titelen* to title] **1 :** the action or occupation of one that titles; *specif* **:** a marking (as by stamping in gold) with a title **2 :** the title marked on something ⟨the ~ on a book cover⟩
titling letter *n* [²*titling*] **:** a letter of any all-capital font formerly in common use in title pages
ti·tlist \ˈtīd·³ləst, -īt(³)l-\ *n* -S [¹*title* + *-ist*] **:** TITLEHOLDER ⟨world auto-racing ~⟩
tit·man \ˈtitmən\ *n, pl* **titmen** [*tit-* (as in *titmouse*) + *man*] **1 :** the smallest in a litter of pigs **:** RUNT **2 :** a puny person **:** one stunted physically or mentally
tit·mouse \ˈtit,maus\ *n, pl* **tit·mice** \-ˌmīs\ [ME *titmose, titemose*, fr. (assumed) ME *tit, tite*, any small object or creature (perh. fr. OE *titt, tit* teat) + ME *mose* titmouse, fr. OE *māse*; akin to OHG *meisa* titmouse — more at TEAT] **:** any of numerous widely distributed small passerine birds of the family Paridae and esp. of the genus *Parus* that are related to the nuthatches but longer tailed, are arboreal and largely insectivorous although they do not creep up and down on tree trunks as do the nuthatches, have soft and fluffy plumage with gray, black, and white as the prevailing colors in most forms, and mostly nest in holes in trees although some build a pendulous nest — compare BLUE TIT, CHICKADEE, COAL TIT, CRESTED TITMOUSE, GREAT TIT, LONG-TAILED TIT, MARSH TIT, TUFTED TITMOUSE
titmouse blue *n* **:** MÉSANGE
ti·to·ism \ˈtēd·(ˌ)ō,izəm, -ē(ˌ)tō-\ *n* -S *usu cap* [*Tito* (Josip Broz) *b*1890? Yugoslav premier + E *-ism*] **:** the political, economic, and social policies associated with Tito; *specif* **:** nationalistically oriented policies and practices followed by a communist state or group independently of and often in opposition to the U.S.S.R. — compare BOLSHEVISM, LENINISM, MARXISM, MARXISM-LENINISM, STALINISM, TROTSKYISM
¹**ti·to·ist** \-ōəst\ *n* -S *usu cap* [*Tito* + E *-ist*] **:** a follower of Tito **:** an adherent of Titoism
²**titoist** \ˈ"\ *adj, usu cap* **:** of, relating to, or having the characteristics of Titoism or Titoists
ti·to·ki \təˈtōkē\ *n* -S [Maori] **:** a New Zealand tree (*Alectryon excelsum*) with large panicles of reddish flowers
ti·tra·ble \ˈtī·trəbəl\ *adj* [*titer* + *-able*] **:** TITRATABLE
ti·trant \ˈtī·trənt\ *n* -S [*titer* + *-ant*] **:** the substance (as a standard solution) that is added in a titration
ti·trat·able \ˈtī,trād·əbəl\ *adj* [*titrate* + *-able*] **:** capable of being titrated ⟨~ acidity⟩
ti·trate \ˈtī,trāt\ *vb* -ED/-ING/-S [*titer* + *-ate*] *vt* **:** to subject to titration **:** standardize, analyze, or determine by titration ~ *vi* **:** to perform titration
ti·tra·tion \tīˈtrāshən\ *n* -S [*titer* + *-ation*] **1 :** a determination of the reactive capacity usu. of a solution; *esp* **:** the analytical process of successively adding from a burette measured amounts of a reagent (as a standard solution) to a known volume of a sample in solution or a known weight of a sample until a desired end point (as a color change or a large change in potential of the solution) is reached ⟨acid-base ~⟩ ⟨oxidation-reduction ~⟩ ⟨electrometric ~*s*⟩ — see INDICATOR 2a **2 :** a process of making mixtures of decreasing amounts of one substance usu. in solution with unvarying amounts of another, until a mixture which contains the smallest amount of the substance still produces the desired effect (as precipitation, agglutination, or neutralization) or contains the two reagents in optimum proportions as determined by adding an indicator (as a hemolytic system in the Wassermann reaction or agglutinable cells in some virus titrations), or by animal or tissue culture inoculation (as in titration of toxins and viruses), or by observing the times of reaction (as in optimum proportions titrations)
titre *var of* TITER
ti tree *n* **1** *Austral* **:** ¹TI 1 **2** *Austral* **:** TEA TREE 2a
Ti·trim·e·ter \tīˈtrimèd·ə(r)\ *trademark* — used for a titrimetric instrument
ti·tri·met·ric \ˌtī·trəˈme·trik\ *adj* [*titration* + *-i-* + *-metric*] **:** of, relating to, or carried out by titrimetry — **ti·tri·met·ri·cal·ly** \-e·trək(ə)lē\ *adv*
ti·trim·e·try \tīˈtrimə·trē\ *n* -ES [*titration* + *-i-* + *-metry*] **:** measurement or analysis by titration
tits *pl of* TIT, *pres 3d sing of* TIT
tit-tat-toe *var of* TICKTACKTOE
titted *past of* TIT
¹**tit·ter** \ˈtid·ə(r), -itə-\ *vi* -ED/-ING/-S [imit.] **:** to give vent to laughter one is seeking to suppress **:** laugh lightly or in a subdued manner **:** laugh in a nervous, affected, or restrained manner esp. at a high pitch and with short catches of the voice
²**titter** \ˈ"\ *n* -S **:** an act or instance of tittering ⟨a ~ of feminine laughter —Willa Cather⟩
tit·ter·el \ˈtitərəl\ *n* -S [imit.] *dial Eng* **:** WHIMBREL
tittie *also* **titty** \ˈtitī\ *n, pl* **titties** [prob. baby talk alter. of ¹*sister*] *chiefly Scot* **:** SISTER; *also* **:** a young girl or woman
titting *pres part of* TIT
tittivate *var of* TITIVATE

tit·tle \ˈtid·ᵊl, -itᵊl\ *n* -s [ME *titel*, fr. ML *titulus* title, label, diacritical mark, fr. L, title, label] **1** : a point or small sign used as a diacritical, punctuation, or similar mark in writing or printing : as **a** *obs* : CEDILLA **b** : TILDE **c** : the dot over *i* or *j* **d** : a vowel point or accent (as in Hebrew or Arabic) **2** : a very small or minute part : the smallest particle : an extremely small or the least possible amount ⟨he meant not to lose one ~ of enjoyment —Winston Churchill⟩ — often used in the phrase *jot or tittle* ⟨burn books that depart one jot or ~ from the legends of the fathers —H.A.Overstreet⟩ ⟨better . . . that a million perish than that one jot or ~ of that unique value should be lost —Ruth Benedict⟩

tit·tle·bat \ˈtitᵊl,bat\ *n* -s [baby talk alter. of *stickleback*] *dial Eng* : STICKLEBACK

¹tittle-tattle \ˈ;tid·ᵊl;tad·ᵊl, ˈ;titᵊl;tatᵊl\ *n* [redupl. of ²*tattle*] : idle trifling talk esp. about trivial matters : petty gossip : empty prattle

²tittle-tattle \ˈ"\ *vi* : to talk idly : CHATTER, GOSSIP, PRATE

³tittle-tattle \ˈ"\ *adj* : characterized by or addicted to tittle-tattle : given to gossip : GOSSIPY

¹tit·tup *also* **tit·up** \ˈtid·əp\ *n* -s [imit. of the sound of a horse's hoofs] : the action of tittuping : as **a** : HAND GALLOP **b** : a lively movement (as a prance or caper)

²tittup *also* **titup** \ˈ"\ *vi* **tittupped** *or* **tittuped; tittupped** *or* **tittuped; tittupping** *or* **tittuping; tittups** : to move in a lively manner: as **a** : to walk with an up and down movement esp. in an affected manner designed to attract attention ⟨pretty girls *tittupped* along the sidewalk⟩ **b** : to gallop or canter easily although often with a false or exaggerated gait **c** : to hop here and there ⟨the cuckoo . . . *tittupped* about the shrubs —Haldane Macfall⟩

tit·tup·py \-əpē\ *adj* [²*tittup* + *-y*] : apt to tittup : RICKETY, SHAKY, UNSTEADY

tit·ty \ˈtid·ē, -itē, |iˈ\ *n* -ES [¹*tit* + *-y*] **1** : ¹TEAT 1 **2** *dial* : milk from the breast

tit·u·bant \ˈtichəbənt, ˈtit·əb-\ *adj* [L *titubant-, titubans*, pres. part. of *titubare* to titubate] : characterized by titubation : marked by wavering or vacillating : UNSTEADY

tit·u·bate \-,bāt\ *vi* -ED/-ING/-S [L *titubatus*, past part. of *titubare* to titubate] : to reel or stumble as if tipsy : STAGGER, TOTTER

tit·u·ba·tion \,==ˈbāshən\ *n* -s [L *titubation-, titubatio*, fr. *titubatus* + *-ion, -io* -ion] : the action of titubating; *specif* : a staggering gait observed in some nervous disturbances

¹tit·u·lar \ˈtichələ(r)\ *adj* [L *titulus* title + E *-ar*] **1 a** : existing in title or name only : NOMINAL ⟨held ~ sovereignty⟩ **b** : having the title and usu. the honors belonging to an office or dignity without exercising the associated duties, functions, or responsibilities ⟨the ~ head of the executive power was the president of the republic —D.W.S.Lidderdale⟩ **c** : having powers so limited and circumscribed or functions so few in number or restricted in scope as to resemble one having a title only ⟨~ leader of the Democratic party⟩ **2 a** : bearing a title : holding the title specified or involved ⟨whether our ~ officers are running this nation —Samuel Crowther⟩ **b** : bearing a title derived from a defunct ecclesiastical jurisdiction (as a monastery or an episcopal see) — see TITULAR ABBOT, TITULAR BISHOP **3** : of, associated with, or arising from a title ⟨~ rank⟩ ⟨~ honors⟩ **4** : of, relating to, of the nature of, or constituting a title ⟨the ~ theme of the book —N.M.Lawrence⟩ ⟨sponsors two national ~ events —W.F.Brown b. 1903⟩; *esp* : TITLE b ⟨performed well in the ~ role⟩ ⟨~ hero⟩ **5** : conferring a title or name; *specif* : constituting one of a group of Roman Catholic churches in or near Rome from which a cardinal derives his title

²titular \ˈ"\ *n* -s **1** *or* **titular of erection** *or* **titular of the teinds** *or* **titular of the tithes** : a layman having as a result of the Reformation title under Scots law to temporalities (as the title and revenues) but not the spiritualities of an ecclesiastical benefice : LORD OF ERECTION **2** : a person holding a title: as **a** (1) : one having the title and benefits of an office independently of the functions, duties, or other obligations attached to it (2) : a person entitled to enjoy an ecclesiastical benefice without performing its duties **b** : the incumbent (as a cardinal) of a Roman Catholic title in or near Rome **3** : the sacred person or thing (as Blessed Sacrament) from which a church derives its title or name — compare PATRON, PATRON SAINT

titular abbot *n* : one who holds the title of abbot derived from a destroyed or suppressed abbey

titular bishop *n* : a Roman Catholic bishop with the title of but without jurisdiction in a defunct see (as in former Christian lands now under Muslim control) — called also *bishop in partibus infidelium*

tit·u·lar·i·ty \,==ˈlarəd·ē\ *n* -ES [¹*titular* + *-ity*] : the quality or state of being titular ⟨the extreme ~ of titular party leadership —Blair Clark⟩

tit·u·lar·ly *adv* [¹*titular* + *-ly*] : in, by, or in respect of title ⟨England is ~ a kingdom —W.S.Landor⟩; *esp* : by title only : NOMINALLY ⟨~ an adviser, he is actually the director⟩

¹tit·u·lary \ˈtichə,lerē\ *adj* [L *titulus* + E *-ary*] *archaic* : TITULAR

²titulary \ˈ"\ *n* -ES *archaic* : one holding a title; *esp* : TITULAR 2a(2)

titup *var of* TITTUP

tityre-tu \ˈ;tid·ərē;t(y)ü\ *n* -s *usu cap 1st T* [fr. L *Tityre tu (patulae recubans sub tegmine fagi)* Tityrus, thou reclining beneath the shelter of the spreading beech tree, opening line of the 1st Eclogue of Vergil; fr. their being regarded as wealthy and idle] : one of a gang of roistering brawling young blades in 17th century London similar to the Mohocks

tity·us \ˈtid·ēəs, ˈtid-\ *n, cap* [NL, fr. L or Gk; L *Tityos*, name of a mythical giant, fr. Gk] : a genus of scorpions (family Buthidae) containing several whose venom is highly toxic to man

tiv \ˈtiv\ *n, pl* **tiv** *or* **tivs** *usu cap* **1 a** : a prominent peasant people of central Nigeria noted for brass casting, wood carving, and music — called also *Munchi* **b** : a member of the Tiv people **2** : the language of the Tiv people, belonging to the Central branch of the Niger-Congo language family

tiv·o·li \ˈtivəlē\ *n* -s [prob. fr. *Tivoli*, commune of central Italy, a pleasure resort near Rome] : a game resembling bagatelle and played on a special oblong board or table which has a curved upper end, a set of numbered compartments at the lower end, side alleys, and a surface studded with pins and sometimes furnished with numbered depressions or cups

25" 37" 9 7 5 3 1 10 2 4 6 8

board used in tivoli

ti·wa *also* **ti·gua** \ˈtēwə\ *n, pl* **tiwa** *or* **tiwas** *also* **tigua** *or* **tiguas** *usu cap* [Sp *tigua*, of AmerInd origin] **1 a** : any of several Tanoan peoples of north and south central New Mexico **b** : a member of any of such peoples **2** : the language of the Tiwa peoples

ti·wi \ˈtē(,)wē\ *n, pl* **tiwi** *or* **tiwis** *usu cap* **1** : an aboriginal people of Melville and Bathurst islands in northern Australia **2** : a member of the Tiwi people

ti·zeur \(ˈ)tē;zər(·), tə̇ˈz-; ˈtēzər\ *n* -s [modif. of F *tiseur* — more at TEASER] : ²TEASER

tizri *usu cap, var of* TISHRI

tizwin *var of* TISWIN

tiz·zick *dial var of* PHTHISIC

¹tiz·zy \ˈtizē\ *n* -ES [prob. alter. of ²*tester*] *Brit* : SIXPENCE

²tiz·zy \ˈtizē, -zi\ *n* -ES [origin unknown] : a highly excited and foolishly distracted or baffled state of mind esp. over a petty matter ⟨the story threw the town into a ~⟩

tjae·le \ˈchālē, -lə\ *n* -s [Sw; akin to ON *theli* frozen ground, OE *thel* board, plank, L *tellus* earth — more at THILL] : frozen ground; *esp* : permanently frozen ground ⟨the depth to which ~ formerly existed in central Montana —*Jour. of Geol.*⟩

tjan·ting \ˈchäntiŋ\ *n* -s [Jav] : a Javanese instrument for applying hot wax in batik work usu. consisting of a small thin copper cut with one or more capillary spouts and a handle of reed or bamboo

t joint *n, cap T* **1** : ¹TEE 2a **2** : TEE JOINT

tjurunga *or* **tjuringa** *var of* CHURINGA

tk *abbr* **1** tank **2** truck

TKO *abbr or n* -s technical knockout

tkof *abbr* take-off

tkr *abbr* tanker

tkt *abbr* ticket

tl *abbr* tael

TL *abbr* **1** thrust line **2** tie line **3** time loan **4** total loss **5** trade-last **6** truck load

Tl *symbol* thallium

tlach·tli \ˈtläcntlē\ *n* -s [Nahuatl] : a ball game played by Central American Indians (as the Aztecs and Mayas) in which the players endeavor by the use of only the leg, hip and elbow to send a solid rubber ball through two rings set vertically in the walls of an I-shaped court

tla·co \ˈtlä(,)kō\ *also* **tlac** \-äk\ *n* -s [Sp *tlaco*, fr. Nahuatl, half] : a small copper coin used in 19th century Mexico worth ⅛ of a real — called also *claco*

tla·co·pan \ˈtläkə,pän\ *n, pl* **tlacopan** *or* **tlacopans** *usu cap* **1** : a Nahuatl people of the Valley of Mexico belonging to the Aztec confederacy **2** : a member of the Tlacopan people

tla·pa·nec \ˈtläpə,nek, ,==ˈ=\ *n, pl* **tlapanec** *or* **tlapanecs** *usu cap* **1 a** : an Indian people of southeastern Guerrero, Mexico **b** : a member of such people **2** : the Supanecan language of the Tlapanec people

tlas·ca·la \tläˈskälə\ *also* **tlas·ca·lan** \-lən\ *n, pl* **tlascala** *or* **tlascalas** *also* **tlascalan** *or* **tlascalans** *usu cap* **1** : a Nahuatl people of the state of Tlaxcala, Mexico **2** : a member of the Tlascala people

TLC *abbr* tender loving care

tld *abbr* tooled

tlingit \ˈtliŋ(g)ət\ *also* **tlin·kit** \-ŋkət\ *n, pl* **tlingit** *or* **tlingits** *also* **tlinkit** *or* **tlinkits** *usu cap* **1 a** : a group of Indian peoples of the islands and coast of southern Alaska including chiefly the Auk, Chilkat, Sitka, Stikine, Tongass, and Yakutat **b** : a member of any of such peoples **2** : the language of the Tlingit peoples **3** : a language stock of the Na-dene phylum comprising only Tlingit — called also *Koluschan*

TLO *abbr* total loss only

tlr *abbr* **1** tailor **2** teller **3** trailer

TLZ *abbr* titanium-lead-zinc

TM *abbr* **1** technical manual; technical memorandum **2** tons per minute **3** trademark **4** traffic manager **5** training manual **6** trainmaster **7** trench mortar **8** true mean

Tm *symbol* thulium

t-man \ˈtē,man\ *n, pl* **t-men** *usu cap T* [*Treasury man*] : a special agent of the U. S. Treasury Department

t-maze \ˈ=,=\ *n, cap T* : a maze for the study of learning usu. consisting of a wood or metal structure shaped like the letter T in which the experimental subject must at a given point make a choice between a left or right turn with one choice usu. involving a reward

diagram of a partial T-maze

tmbr *abbr* timber

tme·sip·ter·is \məˈsiptərə̇s\ *n, cap* [NL, fr. Gk *tmēsis* act of cutting + NL *-pteris*] : a genus of epiphytic Australasian fern allies related to *Psilotum* and characterized by conspicuous vertical leaves and boat-shaped 2-celled synangia

tme·sis \(tə)ˈmēsə̇s\ *n, pl* **tme·ses** \-ē,sēz\ [LL, fr. Gk *tmēsis* act of cutting, fr. *temnein* to cut — more at TOME] : separation of parts of a compound word by the intervention of one or more words (as *what place soever* for *whatsoever place*)

TMG *abbr* track made good

TMH *abbr* tons per man hour

tmkpr *abbr* timekeeper

TML *abbr* three mile limit

TMO *abbr* telegraph money order

tmp *abbr* temperature

TMTD \,tē,em,tēˈdē\ *abbr or n* -s [*tetramethylthiuram disulfide*] tetramethylthiuram disulfide

tn *abbr* **1** ton **2** town **3** train

TN *abbr* **1** tariff number **2** telephone number **3** thermonuclear **4** true north

tnaim *var of* TENAIM

TNB \ˈ;tē,en;bē\ *abbr or n* -s [*trinitrobenzene*] trinitrobenzene

tnd *abbr* tinned

t network *n, cap T* : a network consisting of three impedance branches connected in star

tng *abbr* training

tnge *abbr* tonnage

tnoyim *var of* TENAIM

tnpk *abbr* turnpike

TNT \ˈ;tē,en;tē\ *abbr or n* -s [*trinitrotoluene*] trinitrotoluene

t-number \ˈ=,==\ *n, usu cap T* [*total light transmission + number*] : a number that is similar to the f-number but takes into account the amount of light actually transmitted by a lens after loss by absorption and reflection and that equals the f-number divided by the square root of the transmittance

t nut *n, cap T* **1** : a nut shaped like the head of a T bolt **2** : a nut which may be driven into a board to receive a bolt inserted from the opposite side

¹to \tə, *before a vowel following without pause often or regularly* tәw, *after a vowel usu* d·ə(w), *after a voiced consonant often* də(w; (ˈ)tü, (,)tü\ *prep* [ME *to, te*, fr. OE *tō* (prep. & adv.) & *te* (prep.); akin to OFris *tō* (to (adv.), *to, te, ti* (prep.), OS *tō* (adv.), *te* (prep.), OHG *zuo* (adv.), *za, zi, ze* (prep.) to, L *donicum, donec* as long as, while, until, *dum* while, until, Gk *-de* toward, OLith *do* to, and prob. to Goth *du* to] **1** — used as a function word to indicate spatial relationships or relationships that suggest motion: as **a** — used as a function word to indicate movement or an action or condition suggestive of movement toward (1) a place, person, or thing that is reached or is thought of as being reached ⟨drove ~ the city⟩ ⟨ran ~ his mother⟩ ⟨wore a new hat ~ the party⟩ ⟨a trip ~ the moon⟩ ⟨the boat is ~ the dock now⟩ ⟨went back ~ his original idea⟩ ⟨now ~ the matter at hand —A.J.Flynn⟩ ⟨on the telephone ~ central casting again —Lee Edson⟩ or (2) a place, person, or thing that is not reached or that is not fully reached ⟨turned his back ~ the door⟩ ⟨bowed ~ an acquaintance⟩ ⟨gazed philosophically ~ a burnished sea —R.W. Clark⟩ ⟨leaned ~ light verse and good humor —*Phoenix Flame*⟩ ⟨the great task . . . is now far along ~ completion —A.E.Stevenson b. 1900⟩ ⟨talks ~ the point⟩ or (3) a physical force ⟨bring the ship ~ the wind —C.S.Forester⟩ **b** — used as an intensive with *where* ⟨where will she go ~⟩ **c** — used as a function word to indicate a place or a thing to which one goes for a temporary stay ⟨has been ~ his uncle's house once⟩ ⟨went in and out ~ the sickroom —Seumas O'Kelly⟩ ⟨was ~ a show practically every night last week —Edward Newhouse⟩ **d** — used as a function word to indicate direction ⟨lived a few miles ~ the south⟩ ⟨a narrow paved road ~ the right just before the junction —Y.E.Soderberg⟩ ⟨a tendency ~ silliness⟩ **e** — used as a function word to indicate contact or proximity: as (1) : close against : ON, UPON ⟨his mother standing . . . with her hands ~ her eyes —Eve Langley⟩ ⟨applied polish ~ the table⟩ ⟨the houses had numbers painted ~ them —R.H.Newman⟩ (2) : in a state of attention or ready availability to ⟨stands ~ his post⟩ ⟨abundant slave labor was no longer ~ hand —Lancelot Hogben⟩ (3) : before and straight at esp. in defiance ⟨shall live and tell him ~ his teeth —Shak.⟩ **f** *archaic* : AT 2a — used with verbs of seeing and smelling ⟨a young girl's heart which he . . . smelled ~ like a rosebud —Nathaniel Hawthorne⟩ **g** (1) *chiefly substand* : AT 1 ⟨that time we was making hay ~ her dad's place —Richard Bissell⟩ (2) *chiefly Brit* : at the home of — usu. used with a personal name ⟨went also to dinner ~ Birrell —H.J.Laski⟩ **h** (1) — used as a function word to indicate the place or point that is the far limit (as of a measured distance) ⟨100 miles ~ the nearest town⟩ ⟨a short way ~ the store⟩ (2) — used as a function word to indicate the limit of extent (as in space) ⟨stripped ~ the waist⟩ ⟨wet ~ the skin⟩ ⟨saw through ~ the man's quality —Hallam Tennyson⟩ **i** — used as a function word to indicate relative position ⟨a beam perpendicular ~ the floor⟩ ⟨placed at right angles ~ the wall⟩ ⟨a line tangent ~ a circle⟩ ⟨stop the press if a sheet is not placed correctly ~ the guides —*Theory & Practice of Presswork*⟩ **2** — used as a function word to indicate purpose, intention, tendency, result, or end: as **a** (1) : for the purpose of : with a view to : aiming at : FOR ⟨came ~ our aid⟩ ⟨trained ~ a religious life⟩ ⟨living ~ ends outside ourselves —O.W.Holmes †1935⟩ ⟨tailored ~ your particular needs⟩ ⟨liked to sit down ~ a game of bridge⟩ (2) : in honor of : with all good wishes for ⟨built temples ~ their gods⟩ ⟨drink ~ his health⟩ (3) : for the making of : as a constituent part of ⟨tons of ore go ~ a few ounces of gold⟩ (4) : in support of ⟨calls witnesses to speak ~ his character⟩ ⟨gives abundant testimony ~ the . . . committee's ignorance and inefficiency —R.L.Roy⟩ (5) : for the cultivation of : WITH ⟨when the land was drained he planted it ~ cabbages and onions —Sherwood Anderson⟩ **b** (1) — used as a function word to indicate the result of an action or a process ⟨broken all ~ pieces⟩ ⟨sharpened ~ a point⟩ ⟨warehouse converted ~ a church —Alice Griffin⟩ ⟨tulips going ~ seed⟩ ⟨a brushy wilderness growing up ~ scrub oak —Clifton Johnson⟩ (2) : with the result of ⟨seems to argue ~ the same effect —Herbert Read⟩ ⟨~ their surprise, the train left on time⟩ **c** : in the capacity of : AS, FOR ⟨a sincere desire to have her ~ wife —J.E.Tilford⟩ **d** — used as a function word to indicate a determined condition or end ⟨born ~ riches⟩ ⟨sentenced ~ death⟩ **e** — used as a function word to indicate the object of a right or a claim ⟨a title ~ the property⟩ ⟨the pretender ~ the throne⟩ **3** — used as a function word to indicate a position or a relation in time: as **a** *chiefly dial* : AT 7 ⟨all ~ once —Helen Eustis⟩ ⟨ready ~ three o'clock —F.T.Elworthy⟩ **b** (1) : BEFORE ⟨arrived at five minutes ~ five⟩ ⟨a quarter ~ six⟩ (2) : TILL, UNTIL ⟨stayed on ~ the last minute⟩ ⟨from eight ~ five o'clock⟩ ⟨his edition . . . had the fullest and best apparatus ~ that time —I.M.Price⟩ (3) — used as a function word to indicate a limit in time ⟨a ceremony dating ~ the first century —*Springfield (Mass.) Union*⟩ **c** — used as a function word usu. in combination with *from* to indicate recurrence or continued succession ⟨a situation that changes from day ~ day⟩ **d** — used as a function word to indicate the precise time of an occurrence ⟨promised to pay ~ the day⟩ **e** *chiefly Brit* — used as a function word to indicate occurrence at a set time ⟨runs ~ schedule —*advt*⟩ ⟨a chance to get away ~ time —Noreen Routledge⟩ **4** — used as a function word to indicate addition, attachment, connection, belonging, possession, accompaniment, or response: as **a** *archaic* : in addition to : BESIDES ⟨foretell new storms ~ those already spent —Shak.⟩ **b** : attached to ⟨his fat pony that he drives ~ a basket phaeton —James Reynolds⟩ ⟨publishers would publish anything that had my name ~ it —G.B.Shaw⟩ ⟨a schooner riding ~ an anchor in the bay —Hall Caine⟩ **c** — used as a function word to indicate belonging or possession ⟨descendant of a great house with more than a dash of Italian blood ~ it —Eric Blom⟩ ⟨two rather obvious divisions ~ the investigation —*McGill News*⟩ ⟨there were green curtains ~ the bed —Virginia Woolf⟩ ⟨the key ~ the door⟩ ⟨had a severe sprain ~ her ankle —Lucien Price⟩ ⟨with a rasping bite ~ his voice —*Current Biog.*⟩ **d** — used as a function word to indicate a special often close relationship of a person to another person, a group, or an organization ⟨nephew ~ a powerful and wealthy man —Thomas Wolfe⟩ ⟨printer ~ the state —N.A.Crawford⟩ **e** (1) : to the accompaniment of ⟨sang ~ his guitar⟩ ⟨dancing ~ the radio —Louis Simpson⟩ ⟨rides ~ hounds⟩ ⟨nowadays you do it ~ cocktails —Arnold Bennett⟩ (2) : in complement to : OPPOSITE ⟨played Juliet ~ the Romeo of an unknown newcomer⟩ **f** : in response or reaction to ⟨comes ~ his call⟩ ⟨hardly knew what to say ~ it⟩ ⟨retaliate ~ mockery —Geoffrey Gorer⟩ ⟨flimsy houses that shake ~ the wind⟩ **g** : with respect to ⟨witnesses must speak only ~ facts of which they have direct knowledge —Edward Jenks⟩ ⟨liars they are ~ trade —J.M.Barrie⟩ **5 a** — used as a function word to indicate (1) the extent or degree (as of completeness or accuracy) ⟨assimilate penniless immigrants ~ a number which is truly astonishing —Samuel Van Valkenburg & Ellsworth Huntington⟩ ⟨died two and a half centuries ago ~ a month —*Times Lit. Supp.*⟩ ⟨loyal ~ a man⟩ ⟨would lose his billet ~ a certainty —Henry Lapham⟩ ⟨liked to run his day's program ~ the fraction of a second —Osbert Sitwell⟩ or (2) the extent and result (as of an action or a condition) ⟨beaten ~ death⟩ ⟨worn ~ a frazzle⟩ ⟨case sense is thus feeble ~ extinction in English —Weston La Barre⟩ ⟨limited his criticism ~ a few pleasantries⟩ ⟨increased the amount ~ $1000⟩ **b** (1) — used as a function word to indicate the last point or an intermediate point of a series ⟨the climate over the period was moderate ~ cool —W.E.Swinton⟩ ⟨prices are firm ~ rising —*U. S. News & World Report*⟩ ⟨the quality ranges all the way from very poor ~ good ~ excellent⟩ ⟨a noncommittal word that might be used of anything from babies ~ furnaces —J.C.Swaim⟩ (2) : INCLUDING ⟨six spades ~ the ace queen⟩ (3) : varying through the range between two similar colors or two slightly different magnitudes of a color characteristic ⟨a dark grayish olive ~ olive green⟩ ⟨a pale ~ grayish blue⟩ **6** — used as a function word to indicate a relation to one that serves as a standard: as **a** (1) — used as a function word to indicate similarity, correspondence, dissimilarity, or proportion ⟨compared him ~ a god⟩ ⟨a hat identical ~ the one she had on⟩ ⟨forms different ~ those in which they familiarly present themselves —John Dewey⟩ ⟨seemed to be of another race ~ them —A. Conan Doyle⟩ ⟨knee-high ~ a grasshopper⟩ (2) : in comparison with ⟨the present annoyances are nothing ~ the real dangers that might develop⟩ ⟨inferior ~ the earlier works⟩ **b** (1) — used as a function word to indicate agreement or conformity ⟨add salt ~ taste⟩ ⟨found nothing ~ his purpose —N.J.G.Pounds⟩ ⟨composed three operas, all ~ his own librettos —J.T.Howard⟩ ⟨made ~ certain conventional patterns —C.P.Fitzgerald⟩ ⟨drawings give sufficient detail for a fairly skilled man to work ~ them —*Brit. Bk. News*⟩ (2) : according to : within the range of ⟨~ the best of my knowledge, this book is still the standard work⟩ ⟨~ all appearances is really ill⟩ ⟨arguing ~ supposed general principles —*Times Lit. Supp.*⟩ **c** — used as a function word to indicate a proportion in terms of numbers or quantities: as (1) the proportion between two things in terms of a significant unit of measurement of one of the things; usu. used with *the* ⟨two monsoon seasons ~ the year —D.G.Bridson⟩ ⟨750 persons ~ the square mile —John McNulty⟩ or (2) the proportion between two things in terms of a common unit of measurement ⟨is only 28 years old ~ his brother's 45⟩ ⟨hold 60 seats ~ their opponents' 40⟩ ⟨offered odds of nine ~ one⟩ **7 a** (1) — used as a function word to indicate the application of an adjective ⟨agreeable ~ everyone⟩ ⟨blind ~ art⟩ ⟨unknown ~ us⟩ ⟨necessary ~ progress⟩ ⟨adequate ~ our needs⟩ ⟨feels cold ~ your teeth⟩ ⟨observable ~ our senses —W.L.Sullivan⟩ ⟨unattainable ~ ambition —Hugh Wray⟩ (2) — used as a function word to indicate the application of a noun ⟨our attitudes ~ our friends⟩ ⟨enemies ~ cultivation —James Stevenson-Hamilton⟩ ⟨disaster ~ the army⟩ ⟨without charge ~ the parents —James Britton⟩ ⟨similarity ~ others⟩ ⟨a stranger ~ the country⟩ ⟨an interested observer ~ the changeover —*Alaska Sportsman*⟩ ⟨competitors ~ the printed word —Joseph Trenaman⟩ (3) — used as a function word to indicate the relation of a verb to its complement or to a complementary element ⟨refers ~ the traditions⟩ ⟨refers him ~ the traditions⟩ ⟨must look ~ our postural tensions —A.T.Weaver⟩ ⟨started ~ kindergarten —*Newsweek*⟩ ⟨admits ~ disappointments —R.W.Steel⟩ ⟨democracy succumbed ~ dictatorship —C.E.Black & E.C. Helmreich⟩ ⟨~ parentage . . . he owed the sturdy nature that served him well —Thomas Woody⟩ **b** — used as a function word to indicate the object of address ⟨spoke ~ his father about it⟩ ⟨hail ~ thee, blithe Spirit —P.B.Shelley⟩ **c** (1) — used as a function word to indicate the receiver of an action or the one for which something is done or exists ⟨gives a dollar ~ the man⟩ ⟨make alterations ~ the text —H.G.G.Herklots⟩ ⟨the total effect was a gain ~ reading —Joseph Trenaman⟩ ⟨disputes certified ~ the board by the president —R.L. Putnam⟩ ⟨played the piano ~ royalty⟩ ⟨sat ~ a famous painter⟩ ⟨in the way of converts he died ~ something and had a moment of truth —W.J.Igoe⟩ ⟨~ their trained eyes and ears the fields are covered by red-hatted riders —W.B.Yeats⟩; often used with a reflexive pronoun to indicate exclusiveness (as of possession or use) or separateness ⟨the Dutch liner . . . which they had ~ themselves on the voyage —P.D.Whitney⟩

⟨medical school gets a chapter ~ itself —*Times Lit. Supp.*⟩ ⟨thought ~ himself⟩ ⟨kept himself ~ himself —F.W.Crofts⟩ (2) **:** in the opinion of **:** from the point of view of ⟨manifestly was somebody ~ them —Sidney Lovett⟩ ⟨~ him it seems unnecessary⟩ **d** (1) **:** at the hands of **:** through the agency of ⟨falls ~ the heavy blows of the enemy⟩ ⟨loses his closest friend ~ a violent death —Gene Baro⟩ ⟨captivities ~ thieving barons —R.B.Pearsall⟩ (2) **:** under the tutelage of ⟨went to school ~ the same teacher⟩ **8** — used as a function word to indicate that the following verb is an infinitive ⟨wants ~ go⟩ ⟨seems ~ evaporate⟩ ⟨something ~ do⟩ ⟨a happier place ~ be —Irving Kolodin⟩ ⟨overcame great opposition ~ launch modern sanitary legislation —David Spitz⟩ ⟨~ draw an analogy, we may be able —G.A.Miller⟩ ⟨sharpen their wits merely ~ survive —*Harper's*⟩ ⟨these people . . . whom it is our duty ~ properly represent —*Congressional Record*⟩; often used by itself at the end of a clause in place of an infinitive suggested by the preceding context ⟨knows more than he seems ~⟩ ⟨eats less than he ought ~⟩ ⟨maybe you'd like to go but I don't want ~⟩ ⟨I can't help it, I have ~⟩ ⟨Candy? I'd love ~⟩

²to \ˈtü\ *adv* [ME, fr. OE *tō* — more at ¹TO] **1 a** (1) — used as a function word to indicate direction toward ⟨birds with feathers wrong end ~⟩; used chiefly in the phrase *to and fro* ⟨children running ~ and fro⟩; used formerly in the phrase *to and again* ⟨work the boat ~ and again —Daniel Defoe⟩ (2) **:** close to the wind ⟨the gale having gone over, we came ~ —R.H.Dana⟩ **b** *obs* **:** in favor **:** PRO — used in the phrases *to and again* and *to and fro* ⟨all parties have been heard ~ and again —Thomas Burton⟩ **2 a :** into contact esp. with the frame of a door or a window ⟨the hall door snapped ~ —Nigel Dennis⟩ **b** (1) — used as a function word to indicate physical application or attachment ⟨set ~ his seal that it was true⟩ (2) **:** in or into harness ⟨put the horses ~⟩ **3** — used as a function word to indicate application or attention ⟨will stand ~ —Shak.⟩ **4 a :** to a state of consciousness or awareness ⟨brings her ~ with smelling salts⟩ **b** *archaic* **:** to a state of agreement or acquiescence ⟨forced to use a little fatherly authority to bring her ~ —Henry Fielding⟩ **5** *obs* **:** AGAIN — used in the phrase *to and again* **6 :** at hand **:** BY ⟨get to see 'em close ~ —Richard Llewellyn⟩

TO \(ˈ)tēˈō\ *abbr or n* -s **:** a table of organization ⟨this company is 30 over its *TO* already —A.J.Guerard⟩ ⟨our *TO* quota of noncoms is all filled up —James Jones⟩

TO *abbr* **1** technical order **2** telegraph office **3** telephone office **4** tincture of opium **5** transport officer **6** turn over

toa \ˈtōə\ *n* -s [Samoan] **1 :** a valiant Polynesian warrior **2 :** a tree of the genus *Casuarina; esp* **:** a tall usu. spreading tree (*C. equisetifolia*) of northern Australia and the Pacific islands having very hard tough wood used locally for implements and war clubs and being often cultivated in southeastern Asia esp. for fuel and for its value in erosion control

¹toad \ˈtōd\ *n* -s *often attrib* [ME *tade, tadde, tode,* fr. OE *tāde, tādie, tādige*] **1 a :** any of numerous tailless leaping amphibians that comprise *Bufo* and various other genera esp. of the family Bufonidae, feed chiefly on insects and other small invertebrates, produce an acrid and irritating but not seriously harmful secretion from skin glands which is their only means of defense, and as compared with the related frogs are generally more terrestrial in habit though returning to water to lay their eggs, squatter and shorter in build and with weaker hind limbs, and rough, dry, and warty rather than smooth and moist of skin — see AGUA, NATTERJACK; compare HORNED TOAD **b :** TOADFISH **2 :** a stupid contemptible person **:** a thing of no virtue or worth — sometimes used as a generalized term of abuse ⟨he's a perfect ~⟩ **3** *slang* **:** DERAIL

toad 1a

²toad \ˈ"\ *vb* -ED/-ING/-S **:** TOADY

toadback \ˈ=,=\ *adj* **:** having a section of 3-lobed shape with one of the lobes uppermost that gives a fancied resemblance to the back of a toad ⟨a ~ handrail⟩

toad bug *n* **:** any of several small predaceous bugs (family Gelastocoridae) having a broad flat body and projecting eyes

toad crab *n* **:** either of two relatively large rough spider crabs (*Hyas coarctatus* and *H. araneus*) living chiefly in deep water of arctic seas

toadeat \ˈ=,=\ *vb* [back formation fr. *toadeater*] **:** TOADY

toadeater \ˈ=,==\ *n* **1** *archaic* **:** a mountebank's assistant who eats or pretends to eat supposedly poisonous toads to permit his boss to show his skill in expelling the poison **2 a :** a fawning obsequious parasite **:** TOADY **b :** a servile dependent **:** a menial hanger-on

toadfish \ˈ=,=\ *n* **1 :** any of various marine fishes having jugular pelvic fins, a large thick head, a wide mouth, and scaleless slimy skin, constituting the family Batrachoididae, and including some (as members of a widespread genus *Thalassophryne*) that have venomous spines; *esp* **:** a common fish (*Opsanus tau*) of the American Atlantic coast — compare MIDSHIPMAN 2 **2 :** FROGFISH 1 **3 :** GLOBEFISH

toadflax \ˈ=,=\ *n* **1 :** a common European perennial herb (*Linaria vulgaris*) having showy yellow and orange flowers and being a naturalized weed in much of No. America; *broadly* **:** any of numerous plants of *Linaria* or the related genus *Kicksia* — see DEVIL'S FLAX **2 :** any of various plants not closely related to but usu. somewhat resembling the common European toadflax — see BASTARD TOADFLAX

toad–frog \ˈ=,=\ *n* **:** a tailless amphibian **:** TOAD, FROG

toadhead \ˈ=,=\ *n, NewEng* **:** GOLDEN PLOVER

toadied *past of* TOADY

toad·i·er \ˈtōdē(ə)r\ *n* -s **:** one that toadies

toadies *pl of* TOADY, *pres 3d sing of* TOADY

toad–in–the–hole \ˈ==ˈ=\ *n, pl* **toad–in–the–hole :** meat (as sausage) cooked in batter usu. by baking

toad·ish \ˈtōdish, -dēsh\ *adj* **:** suggestive of or suitable for toads ⟨a ~ hollow⟩ — **toad·ish·ness** *n* -ES

toad·less \ˈtōdləs\ *adj* **:** free from toads

toad·let \-lət\ *n* -s **:** a young or small toad

toad lily *n* **1 :** a showy Japanese herb (*Tricyrtis hirta*) of the family Melanthaceae that is often cultivated for its delicately spotted white flowers **2 :** a common white water lily (*Nymphaea odorata*) of No. America **3 :** a cultivated bulbous herb (*Fritillaria pyrenaica*) of southern Europe with ill-smelling usu. solitary wine-purple flowers **4 :** an Indian lettuce (*Montia chamissoi*) of moist areas at high elevations of western No. America with usu. decumbent stems and axillary or terminal racemes of small white or pink flowers

toad·ling \ˈtōdliŋ, -lēŋ\ *n* -s **:** TOADLET

toado \ˈtō(,)dō\ *n, pl* **toadoes** *or* **toados** [¹*toad* + *-o*] *Austral* **:** GLOBEFISH

toadpipe \ˈ=,=\ *n, dial chiefly Eng* **:** HORSETAIL 2 — often used in pl. but sing. in constr.

toadroot \ˈ=,=\ *n* **:** RED BANEBERRY

toad rush *n* **:** a low-growing nearly cosmopolitan annual rush (*Juncus bufonius*) of damp low-lying ground

toads *pl of* TOAD, *pres 3d sing of* TOAD

toad's–cheese \ˈ=,=\ *n, pl* **toad's–cheeses** *dial chiefly Eng* **:** a poisonous fungus

toad's–eye \ˈ=,=\ *or* **toad's–eye tin** *n, pl* **toad's–eyes :** a cassiterite with concentric structure and reddish color

toadshade \ˈ=,=\ *n* **:** a No. American trillium (*Trillium sessile*) with aromatic maroon sessile flowers

toad skin *n* **:** PHRYNODERMA

toad's–mouth \ˈ=,=\ *n, pl* **toad's–mouths :** a snapdragon (*Antirrhinum majus*)

toad snatcher *n, dial Brit* **:** REED BUNTING

toad sorrel *or* **toad's sorrel** *n* **:** SHEEP SORREL

toad spit *or* **toad spittle** *n* **:** CUCKOO SPIT 1a

toad spot *n* **:** one of the nonpigmented spots occurring on the genitals in dourine

toad–spotted \ˈ=,==\ *adj, obs* **:** foully blemished **:** most evil **:** INFAMOUS

toad–stabber \ˈ=,==\ *or* **toad–sticker** \ˈ=,==\ *n* **1 :** JACKKNIFE, POCKETKNIFE **2 :** SWORD

toadstone \ˈ=,=\ *n* **1 :** a bufonite or other petrifaction, stone, or similar object held to have formed in the head or body of a toad and formerly often worn esp. as a charm or antidote to poison **2 :** dark intrusive volcanic and usu. basaltic rock occurring in Carboniferous limestones of Derbyshire, England, often in broad sheets

toadstool \ˈ=,=\ *n* [ME *tadestool, todestool,* fr. *tade, tode* toad + *stool*] **1 :** a fungus having an umbrella-shaped pileus **2 :** a fleshy fungus that is poisonous or inedible as distinguished from an edible mushroom; *broadly* **:** a fleshy fungus with a conspicuous fruiting body usu. as distinguished from those (as bracket fungi or molds) with woody or inconspicuous fruiting structures

toadstool disease *n* **:** MUSHROOM ROOT ROT

¹toady \ˈtōdē, -di\ *adj* -ER/-EST [¹*toad* + *-y* (adj. suffix)] **1 :** resembling a toad esp. in lack of beauty or grace **:** HIDEOUS **2 :** full of toads ⟨a ~ path⟩

²toady \ˈ"\ *n* -ES [¹*toad* + *-y* (n. suffix)] **:** a truckler to the rich or powerful **:** SYCOPHANT, TOADEATER 2 **syn** see PARASITE

³toady \ˈ"\ *vb* -ED/-ING/-ES *vt* **:** to play the toady to **:** fawn upon with sycophancy **~** *vi* **:** to behave in the manner of a toady **:** engage in excessive deference and attention through motives of self-interest

toady·ish \ˈ-ish\ *adj* [²*toady* + *-ish*] **:** inclined to toady **:** marked by toadyism

toady·ism \-ē,izəm\ *n* -s **:** the behavior or attentions of a toady

to·a·la \təˈwälə\ *n, pl* **toala** *or* **toalas** *usu cap* **1 :** a Veddoid people of the interior of southwestern Celebes **2 :** a member of the Toala people

¹to–and–fro \ˌ==ˈ=\ *n* -s [fr. the adv. phrase *to and fro*] **1 a :** FLUCTUATION, VACILLATION **b :** a bandying of words or questions **:** an argumentative discussion **:** SQUABBLE **2 :** activity involving alternating movement in opposite directions ⟨the *to-and-fro* of the pendulum⟩ ⟨the noisy *to-and-fro* of a holiday crowd⟩

²to–and–fro \ˈ"\ *adj* [fr. the adv. phrase *to and fro*] **:** forward and backward **:** characterized by alternation (as in reciprocation or fluctuation) ⟨*to-and-fro* motion⟩ ⟨*to-and-fro* visiting between neighbors⟩

toa·ner *dial Eng var of* TONER

to–arrive \(ˌ)==ˈ=\ *adj* **:** of, relating to, sold by, or being a contract providing that goods shipped will arrive at a specified point or be shipped from a point of origin within a prescribed time ⟨a *to-arrive* contract⟩ ⟨*to-arrive* prices⟩ ⟨trading in *to-arrive* cotton⟩

toas *pl of* TOA

¹toast \ˈtōst\ *vb* -ED/-ING/-S [ME *tosten,* fr. MF *toster,* fr. LL *tostare* to roast, fr. L *tostus,* past part. of *torrēre* to dry, parch — more at THIRST] *vt* **1** *obs* **:** to make thoroughly hot and dry by or as if by the action of fire or the sun **2 a :** to make (as bread) crisp, hot, and brown by the action of heat ⟨a *~ed* cheese sandwich⟩ ⟨~ the bread very dark⟩ **b :** to warm thoroughly usu. before a fire ⟨*~ing* his toes on the fender⟩ **~** *vi* **:** to become toasted ⟨stale bread *~s* best⟩; *usu* **:** to warm thoroughly ⟨sitting *~ing* in the sun⟩

²toast \ˈ"\ *n* -s [ME *toste, toost,* fr. *tosten,* v.] **1 a :** a slice or piece of toasted bread — used in the phrase *as warm as a toast* **b :** sliced bread browned on both sides by a source of heat **c :** food prepared with toasted or other recooked bread — see FRENCH TOAST, MILK TOAST **d :** a light brown that is yellower and deeper than blush and stronger and slightly darker than cork — compare TOAST BROWN **2** [so called fr. the fact that pieces of spiced toast were used to flavor drinks] **a** *archaic* **:** a young woman in whose honor admirers drink **:** one such whose health is frequently proposed because of her beauty or charm **b :** a person whose health is drunk; *broadly* **:** something in honor of which persons drink **:** a sentiment that is drunk to **c :** a person who is the subject of public adulation ⟨as preacher at Notre Dame Cathedral, was the ~ of Paris —E.O.Hauser⟩ ⟨the unquestioned ~ of the season was the English soprano —*Information Please Almanac*⟩ **3** [³*toast*] **:** an act of proposing or of drinking in honor of a toast ⟨a dinner without *~s*⟩

³toast \ˈ"\ *vb* -ED/-ING/-S [²*toast*] *vt* **:** to propose or drink to as a toast **:** drink to the health or in honor of ⟨~ the flag⟩ ⟨the two antagonists were *~ing* each other's health —Mary K. Hammond⟩ **~** *vi* **:** to drink toasts **:** propose a toast

toast brown *n* **:** a moderate brown that is redder, lighter, and stronger than chestnut brown, coffee, auburn, or tobacco and lighter and slightly redder and stronger than bay — compare TOAST

toast·ee \(ˈ)tōˈstē\ *n* -s [³*toast* + *-ee*] **:** one whose health is drunk in a toast

¹toast·er \ˈtōstə(r)\ *n* -s [¹*toast* + *-er*] **1 :** one that toasts bread or other food: as **a :** a device (as a toasting fork or a double hinged grill) for toasting bread on a stove or over a flame **b :** an electrical appliance with one or more grills for similar use **2 :** a heated revolving inclined cylinder through which cut tobacco is passed to produce the effect of toasting

²toaster \ˈ"\ *n* -s [³*toast* + *-er*] **:** one that proposes toasts **:** TOASTMASTER

toasting fork *n* **1 :** a long-handled fork used to toast bread, marshmallows, or other foods usu. over an open fire or live coals **2 :** SWORD, RAPIER ⟨if I had given him time to get at his . . . pistol or his *toasting fork,* it was all up —Thomas Hughes⟩

¹toastmaster \ˈ=,==\ *n* [²*toast* + *master*] **:** one that presides (as at a banquet) and introduces the after-dinner speakers

²toastmaster \ˈ"\ *vt* **:** to serve as toastmaster at (a particular affair) ⟨~ a testimonial dinner⟩ **~** *vi* **:** to play the part or practice the art of a toastmaster

toastmaster's glass *n* **:** a drinking glass of apparently normal but actually minute capacity originally used by 18th century toastmasters

toastmistress \ˈ=,==\ *n* **:** a female toastmaster

toast rack *n* **:** a rack for holding several slices of toast on edge

toasts *pl of* TOAST, *pres 3d sing of* TOAST

toast tan *n* **:** a moderate brown that is lighter, stronger, and slightly yellower than chestnut brown, yellower, lighter, and slightly stronger than auburn, and yellower, lighter, and slightly less strong than bay

toasty \ˈtōstē, -ti\ *adj* -ER/-EST **1 :** having the appearance or taste of toast **2 :** pleasantly or comfortably warmed ⟨the room was snug and ~⟩

toa·toa \ˈtōəˌtōə\ *n* -s [Maori] **:** a New Zealand celery-topped pine (*Phyllocladus glaucus*) having strikingly whorled branches and often cultivated for ornament

to·at·tler \tōˈatlə(r)\ *n* -s [by alter.] *dial Eng* **:** TEETOTALER

tob *var of* TOBE

¹to·ba \ˈtōbə\ *n, pl* **toba** *or* **tobas** *usu cap* **:** a member of a Tatar people ruling northern China from the 4th to the 6th centuries

²toba \ˈ"\ *n, pl* **toba** *or* **tobas** *usu cap* [Sp, of AmerInd origin] **1 a :** a Guaicuru people of the Gran Chaco, Argentina **b :** a member of such people **2 :** the language of the Toba people

³toba \ˈ"\ *n* -s *usu cap* **:** a dialect of Batak (sense 2)

to·bac \təˈbak\ *n* -s [short for *tobacco*] **:** TOBACCO BROWN

to·bac·co \təˈba(ˌ)kō, -kə; -kəw, -kō+V\ *n, pl* **tobaccos** *also* **tobaccoes** *often attrib* [Sp *tabaco,* prob. fr. Taino, roll of tobacco leaves smoked by the Indians of the Antilles at the time of Columbus] **1 a :** a plant of the genus *Nicotiana* esp. when cultivated for its leaves; *usu* **:** a tall erect annual So. American herb (*N. tabacum*) with large ovate to lanceolate leaves and terminal clusters of tubular white or pink flowers **b :** a crop of tobacco ⟨~ is hard on land⟩ ⟨just got his ~ into the barns⟩ **2 a :** the leaves of cultivated tobacco prepared and processed for use in smoking or chewing or as snuff ⟨a plug of chewing ~⟩ **b :** manufactured products of tobacco (as cigars or cigarettes) for personal use ⟨users of ~⟩ **c :** the use of tobacco **:** the habit of smoking or chewing ⟨swore off ~⟩ **3 :** any of various plants felt to resemble or used like or as a substitute for tobacco — usu. used with a qualifying attributive — see INDIAN TOBACCO **4 :** a moderate brown that is redder and deeper than chestnut brown or coffee, darker and slightly redder than auburn, duller and very slightly yellower than bay, and duller and slightly yellower than toast brown — compare TOBACCO BROWN

tobacco 1a: *1* flowering stem and leaves, *2* detached flower

tobacco barn *or* **tobacco shed** *n* **:** a building in which tobacco is cured with or without supplemental heat

tobacco beetle *n* **:** CIGARETTE BEETLE

tobacco box *n* **1** *or* **tobacco–box skate :** LITTLE SKATE **2** *Austral* **:** FRIARBIRD

tobacco brown *n* **:** a moderate to strong yellowish brown that is darker than clay and darker and slightly yellower than Aztec — called also *tobac* — compare TOBACCO

tobacco brush *n* **:** a snowbrush (*Ceanothus velutina*)

tobacco budworm *n* **1 :** a small rusty often green-striped caterpillar that is the larva of a noctuid moth (*Heliothis virescens*) and that feeds on buds and young foliage esp. of various solanaceous plants **2 :** CORN EARWORM

tobacco bug *n* **:** a small black mirid bug (*Dicyphus minimus*) that has green legs and underside and that sucks the sap of tobacco leaves — called also *suck fly*

tobacco cloth *n* **:** a loose-weave cotton fabric used esp. to shade growing tobacco plants

tobacco dove *n* **:** a West Indian ground dove (*Columbigallina passerina*)

tobacco etch *n* **:** a virus disease of tobacco characterized by mild leaf mottling, chlorosis, and linear traces of necrosis

tobaccoey *var of* TOBACCOY

tobacco flea beetle *n* **:** a tiny reddish brown flea beetle (*Epitrix hirtipennis*) that is esp. destructive to solanaceous plants

tobacco hatchet *or* **tobacco spud** *n* **:** a hatchet made with a broad thin blade with a sharp edge beveled on one side only and used for cutting the butt of tobacco plants in harvesting

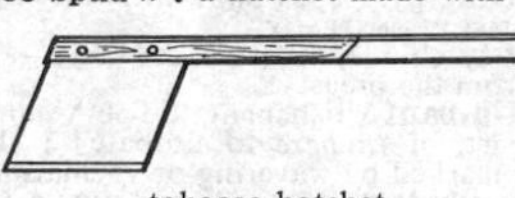
tobacco hatchet

tobacco hawkmoth *n* **:** the adult moth of a tobacco hornworm

tobacco heart *n* **:** a functional disorder of the heart characterized by irregularity of the heartbeat and caused by excessive use of tobacco

tobacco hornworm *n* **:** a large green obliquely white-striped caterpillar with a hornlike process near the posterior end that is the larva of a hawkmoth (*Manduca sexta*) and that feeds voraciously on tobacco and other solanaceous plants; *also* **:** the closely related and very similar tomato hornworm

tobacco indian *n, usu cap T&I* **:** a member of the Tionontati

tobacco juice *n* **1 :** saliva colored brown by the use of chewing tobacco or snuff **2 :** a dark brown oral discharge made by some grasshoppers when handled or disturbed

tobacco leaf miner *n* **:** POTATO TUBERWORM

tobacco mildew *n* **:** a disease of growing tobacco caused by a downy mildew (*Peronospora hyoscyami*); *also* **:** the fungus causing this disease

tobacco mosaic *n* **:** any of a complex of virus diseases of tobacco and other chiefly solanaceous plants that in their typical manifestation take the form of mosaics

tobacco moth *n* **:** a small brownish gray moth (*Ephestia elutella*) whose larva feeds in tobacco and other dried plant products — called also *cacao moth*

to·bac·co·nist \təˈbakənəst\ *n* -s [*tobacco* + connective *-n-* + *-ist*] **1** *obs* **:** a habitual user of tobacco **2 :** a dealer in tobacco esp. at retail

tobacco road *n, often cap T&R* [fr. *Tobacco Road,* novel (1932) by Erskine Caldwell *b*1903 Amer. writer, and play (1933) adapted by Jack Kirkland †1969 Amer. playwright, about poor whites in a depressed rural area of Georgia traversed by a run-down thoroughfare ("tobacco road") made in earlier days by rolling hogsheads of tobacco to market] **:** a squalid poverty-stricken area or community in which the life of the inhabitants is characterized as wretched, disorganized, and hopeless

tobacco–roader \=ˈ=(,)=ˈ==\ *n, often cap T&R* **:** one who dwells in or acts as if he dwelt in a tobacco road

tobacco–road·ish \-dish\ *adj, often cap T&R* **:** inclined to be like a tobacco road or its inhabitants

tobaccoroot \=ˈ=(,)=,=\ *n* **1 :** BITTERROOT 1 **2 :** a tall erect perennial No. American valerian (*Valeriana edulis*) with small white or yellowish flowers in a long panicle and a large edible root

tobaccos *pl of* TOBACCO

tobacco–sick \=ˈ=(,)=ˈ=\ *adj, of land* **:** depleted in fertility and often heavily infested with parasites after repeated use for tobacco cultivation

tobacco splitworm *n* **:** POTATO TUBERWORM

tobacco stick *also* **tobacco lath** *n* **:** one of the laths on which tobacco leaves or stalks are hung for curing

tobacco stopper *n* **:** a device for pressing down tobacco in a pipe

tobacco thrips *n* **1 :** a thrips (*Frankliniella fusca*) often injurious to growing tobacco and to peanuts in No. America **2 :** ONION THRIPS

tobacco tongs *n pl but sing or pl in constr* **:** metal tongs for taking a live coal from a fire to light a tobacco pipe

tobacco water *also* **tobacco liquor** *n* **:** an extract of tobacco used (as in gardening) as an insecticide

tobaccoweed \=ˈ=(,)=,=\ *n* **:** DEVIL'S-GRANDMOTHER

tobacco wilt *n* **:** a wilt disease of tobacco caused by a bacterium (*Pseudomonas solanacearum*) **:** BROWN ROT — compare GRANVILLE WILT

tobaccowood \=ˈ=(,)=,=\ *n* **:** WITCH HAZEL 2a(1)

tobacco worm *n* **:** TOBACCO HORNWORM

to·bac·coy *or* **to·bac·co·ey** \-akəwē, -wi\ *adj* **:** full of tobacco fumes; *also* **:** like or like that of tobacco or tobacco smoking ⟨a warm ~ hue⟩ ⟨a gurgling ~ noise —Mary McCarthy⟩

tobacs *pl of* TOBAC

to·ba·go·nian \ˌtōbəˈgōnēən, -nyən\ *n* -s *cap* [*Tobago,* island in the West Indies + E *-onian* (as in *Patagonian*)] **:** a native or inhabitant of the island of Tobago in the British West Indies

tobas *pl of* TOBA

¹to–be \=ˈ=\ *adj* [fr. the infinitive phrase *to be*] **:** that is to be **:** FUTURE — usu. used postpositively and often in combination ⟨mothers-*to-be*⟩ ⟨his victim *to-be* —Stuart Atkins⟩ ⟨a charming bride-*to-be*⟩

²to–be \ˈ"\ *n* -s [fr. the infinitive phrase *to be*] **:** what is to be **:** FUTURE ⟨I work and write for the *to-be* —Marie Corelli⟩

tobe *also* **tob** \ˈtōb\ *n* -s [Ar *thawb* garment] **:** a long shapeless sometimes draped and usu. cotton garment made like a shirt and worn by peoples of northern and central Africa

to·ber \ˈtōbə(r)\ *n* -s [Brit. slang *tober* road, highway, fr. Shelta *tobar* — more at TOBY] *dial Brit* **:** a circus lot

to·bi·ad \təˈbīəd\ *n* -s *usu cap* [*Tobias,* father of Joseph *fl ab* 210 B.C. founder of the Tobiads + E *-ad* (member of a group)] **:** a member of a Jewish party of the Maccabean period favoring the Hellenization of the Jews

to·bi·as acid \təˈbīəs-\ *n, usu cap T* [after Georg *Tobias,* 19th cent. Ger. chemist] **:** a crystalline naphthylaminesulfonic acid $H_2NC_{10}H_6SO_3H$ used as a dye intermediate; 2-amino-1-naphthalenesulfonic acid

to·bi·khar \ˌtōbəˈkär\ *n* -s *usu cap* [Gabrielino] **:** GABRIELINO

to·bi·ra \təˈbīrə\ *n* -s [Jap, lit., door] **:** a commonly cultivated shrub (*Pittosporum tobira*) of China and Japan with ornamental glossy leaves and white fragrant flowers in terminal umbels

tobira family *n* **:** PITTOSPORACEAE

¹to·bog·gan \təˈbägən\ *n* -s [CanF *tobogan, tabagan, tabagane,* of Algonquian origin; akin to Micmac *tobâgun* drag made of skin, Abnaki *udâbâgân,* Cree *otâbânâsk*] **1 :** a long flat-bottomed light sled made of thin boards curved up at one end with usu. low handrails at the

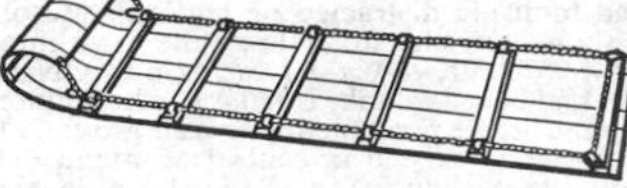
toboggan 1

sides and used for coasting, traveling, or transportation on snow or ice **2 a :** a slope or course of suitable steepness for use of a toboggan ⟨minutes are lost whenever we have to climb such a ~ —Michel Bouché⟩ **b :** a downward course (as of life or affairs) — used chiefly in the phrase *on the toboggan* ⟨on the ~ but still a long way from complete failure⟩ **c :** a sharp decline (as in value or price) ⟨prices hit the ~⟩ **3 :** a conveyor on which material moves down an incline under gravity **4** *or* **toboggan cap :** STOCKING CAP

²toboggan \"\ *vi* -ED/-ING/-S **1 :** to coast on a toboggan **:** slide rapidly on or as if on a toboggan **2 :** to decline suddenly and sharply (as in value) ⟨values ~*ed* on the market⟩ ⟨stocks may ~ in response to foreign tensions⟩

to·bog·gan·er \-gənə(r)\ *also* **to·bog·gan·ist** \-nə̇st\ *n* -S **:** one that toboggans

toboggan slide *or* **toboggan chute** *n* **:** a slide for coasting on toboggans usu. in the form of a steep wooden ice-covered chute

to·bo·sa grass \tə'bōsə-\ *n* [perh. after the *Toboso* Indians in northern Mexico, fr. Sp, of AmerInd origin] **:** a coarse range grass (*Hilaria mutica*) that is an important forage plant on semiarid plains and hills of the southwestern U. S. and adjacent Mexico

tobs *pl of* TOB

¹to·by \'tōbē, -bi\ *n* -ES [Shelta *tobar*, prob. modif. of IrGael *bōthar*] *Brit* **:** STREET, WAY, HIGHWAY; *also* **:** highway robbery — compare HIGHTOBY

²toby \"\ *n* -ES [fr. *Toby*, nickname for *Tobias*] **1** *or* **toby jug** *often cap T* **:** a small jug, pitcher, or mug that is generally used for ale and is shaped somewhat like a stout man with a cocked hat forming the brim; *also* **:** such a quantity (as of ale) as is served in a toby **2** *or* **to·bie** \"\ -S **:** a long slender cigar tapered at one end and made of strong inferior tobacco **3 :** *southern Africa* **:** GLOBEFISH

toby 1

toby fill·pot jug \-'fil,pät-\ *n, usu cap T&F* **:** TOBY 1

toby·man \'⸗⸗,mən\ *n, pl* **tobymen** [¹*toby* + *man*] *archaic* **:** HIGHWAYMAN

to·ca·lo·te \,tōkə'lōd·ē\ *n* -S [modif. of Sp *chicalote* — more at CHICALOTE] **:** a weedy European annual herb (*Centaurea melitensis*) widely naturalized in the New World and esp. in California of some importance as a honey plant

toc·ca·ta \tə'käd·ə, -kȧt, \tə\ *n* -S [It, fr. fem. of *toccato*, past part. of *toccare* to touch, play (a musical instrument) with the fingers, fr. (assumed) VL, to knock, strike a bell, touch — more at TOUCH] **:** a brilliant musical composition usu. for pipe organ or harpsichord, in free fantasia style, and usu. with many equal-timed notes in rapid movement

toc·ca·ti·na \,täkə'tēnə\ *n* -S [It, dim. of *toccata*] **:** a short toccata

to·cha·ri \tō'kärē\ *n pl, usu cap* [L, fr. Gk *Tocharoi*] **:** the Tocharian people

to·char·i·an *or* **to·khar·i·an** \tō'ka(a)rēən, -kär-\ *n* -S *cap* [L *Tochari* + E *-an*] **1 :** a member of a people of advanced culture and presumably European origin dwelling in central Asia during the first millennium of the Christian era until overrun by the Uighurs **2 a :** a language of central Asia known from documents from the seventh century A.D. and occurring in an eastern and a western dialect **b :** a branch of the Indo-European language family containing the Tocharian language — see INDO-EUROPEAN LANGUAGES table

tocharian A *n, cap T* **:** the eastern dialect of Tocharian

tocharian B *n, cap T* **:** the western dialect of Tocharian

to·cha·rish \tō'kärish\ *n, usu cap* [G *tocharisch*, fr. L *Tochari* + G *-isch* -ish] **:** TOCHARIAN 2

¹toch·er \'täkər\ *n* -S [IrGael *tochar*] *chiefly Scot* **:** marriage portion **:** DOT

²tocher \"\ *vt* -ED/-ING/-S *chiefly Scot* **:** to provide with a marriage portion **:** DOWER

tocher–good *n, Scot* **:** property given as a marriage portion

tock \'täk\ *n* -S [Pg *toco* toco, tock] **:** an African hornbill of the genus *Tockus*

¹to·co \'tō(,)kō\ *n* -S [Pg, fr. Tupi] **:** a large So. American toucan (*Ramphastos toco*) that is chiefly black with the rump and throat white, the latter tinged with yellow and bordered with red, and the under tail coverts crimson

²to·co *also* **to·ko** \"\ *n* -S [Hindi *ṭoko*, imper. of *ṭoknā* to blame] *Brit* **:** rigorous and usu. physical chastisement ⟨administer ~ to the wretched fags nearest at hand —Thomas Hughes⟩

toco- *or* **toko-** *comb form* [Gk *tokos*, fr. *tiktein* to bear, beget — more at THANE] **:** childbirth **:** offspring ⟨*toco*genetic⟩ ⟨*toco*logy⟩

toco·dynamometer *or* **toko·dynamometer** \¦tō(,)kō, ¦tä(-+\ *n* [ISV *toco-* + *dynamometer*] **:** an instrument by means of which the force of uterine puerperal contractions can be measured

to·col·o·gy *also* **to·kol·o·gy** \tō'käləjē\ *n* -ES [Gk *tokos* + E *-logy*] **:** the science of obstetrics

to–come \'⸗'⸗\ *n* -S [fr. the infinitive phrase *to come*] **:** what is to come **:** FUTURE ⟨tides of the long past and the infinite *to-come* —Nathaniel Hawthorne⟩

to·coph·er·ol \tə'käfə,rōl, -rōl\ *n* -S [ISV *toco-* + *-pher* + *-ol*] **:** any of several pale yellow fat-soluble oily liquid phenolic compounds that are derived from chroman and differ in the number and locations of methyl groups in the benzene ring, that have antioxidant properties and vitamin E activity in varying degrees, that are found in the dextrorotatory form esp. in oils from seeds (as wheat-germ oil and cottonseed oil), in leaves, and in fish-liver oils, that are made synthetically in the racemic form, and that are used in a mixture chiefly as antioxidants (as for stabilizing vitamin A in fats and oils) and in nutrition and veterinary medicine: as **a :** the compound $C_{29}H_{50}O_2$ obtained usu. from germ oils or by synthesis (as from trimethylhydroquinone and phytyl bromide) and often used in the form of its acetate or other esters — called also *alpha-tocopherol, vitamin E* **b :** a compound $C_{28}H_{48}O_2$ occurring usu. with alpha-tocopherol and gamma-tocopherol — called also *beta-tocopherol* **c :** a compound $C_{28}H_{48}O_2$ isomeric with beta-tocopherol and occurring with it and alpha-tocopherol and predominating in corn oil and with delta-tocopherol in soybean oil — called also *gamma-tocopherol* **d :** a compound $C_{27}H_{46}O_2$ said to have the highest antioxidant activity of the tocopherols and found with the others but esp. in soybean oil — called also *delta-tocopherol*

to·co·ro·ro \,tōkə'rōr(,)ō\ *n* -S [AmerSp, of imit. origin] **:** a Cuban trogon (*Priotelus temnurus*) having the bill serrated and the tail feathers concave at the end

toco·stome \'täkə,stōm, 'tōk-\ *n* -S [*toco-* + *-stome*] **:** a genital pore

toc·sin \'täksə̇n\ *n* -S [MF *toquassen, toquesin*, fr. OProv *tocasenh*, fr. *tocar* touch, ring a bell (fr. — assumed — VL *toccare* to ring a bell) + *senh* sign, bell, fr. ML & L *signum*; ML, bell, fr. LL, ringing of a bell, fr. L, mark, sign — more at TOUCH, SIGN] **1 :** an alarm bell or the ringing of a bell for the purpose of alarm **2 :** an urgent or warning thing or event ⟨these volumes . . . are both a ~ and an arsenal —S.K. Padover⟩ ⟨has so often thought of early summer as a time for ~*s* —*Economist*⟩ **3 :** something felt to resemble a warning bell (as in loudness, abruptness, or clarity) ⟨his ~ voice⟩

to·cus·so \tə'kü(,)sō\ *n* -S [Amharic *tokusso*] **:** a grass (*Eleusine tocussa*) cultivated in Ethiopia for its edible seeds which are used esp. in a dark heavy bread

¹tod \'täd\ *n* -S [ME] **1** *chiefly Scot* **:** FOX **2** *chiefly Scot* **:** a canny crafty person

²tod \"\ *n* -S [ME *todd, todde;* prob. akin to Fris *todde* rag, trash, D *tod, todde* rag, OHG *zotta* tuft of hair, ON *toddi* small piece, bit, and perh. to ON *tethja* to manure — more at TED] **1 :** any of various units of weight for wool; *esp* **:** a unit equal to 28 pounds **2** *chiefly dial* **:** a bundle, load, or mass (as of wool) often of a tod weight **3** *Brit* **:** a bushy clump or growth (as of ivy)

³tod \"\ *vi* **todded; todded; todding; tods** *archaic* **:** to produce or obtain a tod (as of wool)

⁴tod \"\ *n* -S [by shortening] **:** TODDY

to·da \'tōdə\ *n, pl* **todas** *also* **toda** *usu cap* **1 :** one of an aboriginal polyandrous people of light complexion and tall stature that reside in the Nilgiri hills of southern India and in Ceylon, that lead a peaceful pastoral life, and that practice a religion which is organized around the care and veneration of cattle and esp. the buffalo **2 :** the Dravidian language of the Todas

¹to·day \tə'dā\ *adv* [ME, fr. OE *tōdæge, tōdæg*, fr. *tō* to, at + *dæge*, dat. of *dæg* day — more at TO, DAY] **1 :** on or for this day **:** on the present day **2 :** at the present time **:** NOWADAYS

²today \"\ *n* -S **1 :** the day now present; *also* **:** any day contemporary with this day **2 :** the present time as currently existing ⟨the tasks of ~⟩ **2 :** the present time, epoch, or age

to·day·ish \-ish, -ēsh\ *adj* **:** of or characteristic of today **:** CURRENT, UP-TO-DATE

tod·dick \'tädik, -dēk\ *n* -S [²*tod* + *-ick* (alter. of *-ock*)] **1** *South* **a :** a measure used by a custom miller to take out his toll from the grist **b :** a portion of flour or meal taken by a miller as his toll **2** *South* **:** a small amount

¹tod·dle \'täd°l\ *vi* **toddled; toddled; toddling** \-d(°)liŋ\ **toddles** [origin unknown] **1 :** to walk with short tottering steps in the manner of a young child **:** progress slowly and usu. irregularly **2 a :** to take a stroll **:** SAUNTER **b :** to take one's departure and go

²toddle \"\ *n* -S **:** an act of toddling **:** a toddling gait or progress

tod·dler \-d(°)lə(r)\ *n* -S **:** one that toddles; *esp* **:** a young child

tod·dy \'tädē, -di\ *n* -ES [Hindi *tāṛī* juice of the palmyra palm, fr. *tāṛ* palmyra palm, fr. Skt *tāla*, perh. of Dravidian origin; akin to Kannada *taṛ* palmyra palm, Telegu *tāḍu*] **1 :** the fresh or fermented sap of various chiefly East Indian palms **2 :** a hot drink consisting of an alcoholic liquor, water, sugar, and spices (as cinnamon, cloves, and nutmeg) and often garnished with fruit ⟨whiskey ~⟩ ⟨applejack ~⟩

toddy bird *n* **:** any of several Indian birds (as various weaverbirds and wood swallows) that feed on palm juice

toddy cat *n, India* **:** PALM CIVET

toddy palm *also* **toddy tree** *n* **:** any of several wine palms; *esp* **:** JAGGERY PALM

toddy stick *n* **:** a stick knobbed or flattened at the end and used in making toddy

toddy stick

to·dea \'tōdēə, tə'dēə\ *n, cap* [NL, after H. J. *Tode* †1797 Ger. botanist] **:** a genus of delicate African and Australasian ferns (family Osmundaceae) distinguished from those of *Osmunda* by having the sporangia on the underside of the leaf — see CRAPE FERN

to·di·dae \'tōdə,dē\ *n pl, cap* [NL, fr. *Todus*, type genus + *-idae*] **:** a family of West Indian birds (order Coraciiformes) usu. comprising the single genus *Todus* — compare TODY

todlowrie \'(')⸗¦⸗⸗\ *n* -S [¹*tod* + *lowrie*] *Scot* **:** FOX, TOD

to–do \tə'dü\ *n* [fr. the infinitive phrase *to do*] **1 :** excited and usu. exaggerated stir **:** BUSTLE, COMMOTION ⟨the papers made a great *to-do* about his appointment⟩ ⟨a great flutter and *to-do* among the ladies of the church⟩ **2** *dial* **:** a formal or fancy party **:** a social affair of unusual style or show

tods *pl of* TOD, *pres 3d sing of* TOD

to·dus \'tōdəs\ *n, cap* [NL, fr. L, a small bird] **:** the type and usu. sole genus of the family Todidae — see TODY

to·dy \'tōdē, -di\ *n* -ES [modif. of F *todier*, fr. L *todus*, a small bird] **1 :** any of several tiny nonpasserine insectivorous West Indian birds constituting the genus *Todus*, being closely related to the kingfishers, having a long flattened bill with strong rictal bristles, and nesting in holes in banks — see GREEN TODY **2 :** any of various small brightly colored birds (as some American flycatchers) — compare ROYAL FLYCATCHER

¹toe \'tō\ *n* -S *often attrib* [ME *ta, to, too*, fr. OE *tā*; akin to OHG *zēha* toe, ON *tā* toe, L *digitus* finger, and prob. to Gk *deiknynai* to show — more at DICTION] **1 a** (1) **:** one of the terminal digits of a vertebrate's foot — distinguished from *finger* (2) **:** the fore end of a foot or hoof — opposed to *heel* **b** (1) **:** a terminal segment of a limb of an invertebrate (2) **:** either of the two processes in which the hinder part of the body of a rotifer usu. ends **c :** a part of something worn on or attached to a foot that covers or corresponds to its fore end ⟨the ~ of a boot⟩ ⟨the ~ of a horseshoe⟩ **2 :** a part that by its position, form or outline, or relation to other parts is felt to resemble a toe ⟨the ~ of Italy⟩: as **a** (1) **:** a prong or stub (as on a vinifera grape) from which vegetative growth arises (2) **:** one of the expanded extensions of a tree trunk where a root passes into the ground (3) **:** a single tuberous root of a dahlia **b** (1) **:** a journal or pivot supported in a step bearing (2) **:** a lateral projection at one end or between the ends of a piece (as a rod or bolt) by which it is moved; *often* **:** a projecting arm actuated by a cam on the valve-lifting rod in the beam type of steam engine (3) **:** a projection from the periphery of a revolving piece acting as a cam to lift another piece **c** (1) **:** the extreme bottom point of a seed trench prepared by a furrow opener (as of a grain drill) (2) **:** the lowest part of the slope of an earth embankment or a cliff (3) **:** the line of contact between the lower or downstream face and the base of a dam (4) **:** the bottom of a mine or quarry bench (5) **:** the lower edge of a mine dump (6) **:** the bottom of a drill hole for blasting **d :** a metal tip at the lower end of the foot of some wooden organ pipes; *also* **:** the lower end of a metal pipe foot or reed boot **e :** a board or other part of a structure occupying a low and forward position **f** (1) **:** the peen of a hammer (2) **:** the outer end of the hitting surface of a golf club or hockey stick — see GOLF illustration **g :** the corner of the butt of a gunstock that is lowermost when the gun is in firing position **h :** the front end of a railroad frog opposite the heel **3 :** TOE DANCE **4 :** a football player used solely or primarily for kicking — **on one's toes 1 :** full of life **:** ACTIVE, BUSY **2 :** alert and ready to seize any advantage or engage in any activity that comes one's way ⟨in working for real money you've got to be *on your toes* —W.L.Gresham⟩ — **toes up :** DEAD

²toe \"\ *vb* **toed; toed; toeing; toes** *vt* **1 :** to furnish with a toe; *esp* **:** to form the toe of (a knitted sock or stocking) by decreasing stitches — usu. used with *off* **2 :** to touch, reach, move, or crush with the forepart of the foot ⟨*toed* a chair into position⟩ ⟨~ your cigarette out⟩ ⟨simple homes *toeing* the sidewalk —P.J.Celliers⟩ ⟨~ a football⟩ **3 :** to drive (as a nail, spike, or rod) slantingly or aslant; *also* **:** to clinch or fasten by or with nails or rods so driven ⟨*toed* a brace between wall and floor⟩ ~ *vi* **:** to move the toes or move on the toes: as **a :** to move stealthily **:** TIPTOE ⟨~*ing* cautiously forward⟩ **b :** to stand, walk, or be placed so that the toes assume an indicated position or direction ⟨~ in⟩ ⟨~ along a straight line⟩ **c :** to tap with the toe in heel-and-toe dancing — **toe the line 1 :** to touch with the toes only in standing a line indicating a starting point (as in a race or match) **2 a** *or* **toe a line :** to act or conform rigorously to some rule or standard ⟨*toe a* party *line* without protest⟩ **b :** to accept one's responsibilities or stand to one's obligations — **toe the mark** *or* **toe a mark :** toe the line

¹toe–and–heel \¦⸗⸗¦⸗\ *adj* **:** HEEL-AND-TOE

²toe–and–heel \"\ *vi* **:** DANCE; *usu* **:** to do tap-dancing, jigging, or other vigorous dancing — often used with *it*

toe–and–heel click *n* **:** the striking of the toe of one foot against the heel of the other in tap-dancing

toe–biter \'⸗,⸗⸗\ *n* **1 :** TADPOLE 1 **2 :** any of several large aquatic insects that sometimes attack bathers: as **a :** a bug of the families Nepidae or Belostomatidae **b :** HELLGRAMMITE

toeboard \'⸗,⸗\ *n* **:** a support or reinforcement (as of board) for the toes or at the base of something ⟨the ~ of a swing⟩: as **a :** the sloping boards in the floor of an automotive vehicle in front of the forward seat **b :** a curved piece of wood fastened to the ground at the front of the circle used for shot putting, throwing the weight, or similar contests to prevent overstepping **c :** a low border (as about a staging) esp. to prevent dropping of tools or other objects

toe box *n* **1 :** a piece of leather or other material placed between the toecap and lining of a shoe and treated with a substance (as a gum) that hardens after the shoe is lasted permanently **2 :** BOXING 5

toe calk *n* **:** a calk on the toe of the shoe of a horse or ox

toe cap *n* **:** a separate piece of leather or other material covering the toe of a shoe and reinforcing or decorating it

toe clip *n* **1 :** a device that fits the toe of a shoe and is attached to a cycle pedal to receive the foot and keep it from slipping **2 :** ²CLIP c

toe crack *n* **:** a sand crack in the front wall of a horse's hoof

toed \¦tōd\ *adj* [¹*toe* + *-ed*] **1 :** having a toe or such or so many toes — used esp. in combination ⟨long-*toed*⟩ ⟨five-*toed*⟩ **2** [fr. past part. of ²*toe*] **:** driven obliquely ⟨a carefully ~ nail⟩; *also* **:** secured by diagonal or oblique nailing

toe dance *n* **:** a dance executed on the tips of the toes

toe–dance \'⸗,⸗\ *vi* [*toe dance*] **:** to dance a toe dance — **toe dancer** *n*

toe dog *n* **:** a short usu. two to four inch long piece of bar steel made with one end flattened and the other cupped to receive the end of the setscrew of a screw plug and used esp. for clamping thin work to a table

toedrop \'⸗,⸗\ *n* **:** FOOT DROP

toe hardie *n* **:** a half-round hardie

toehold \'⸗,⸗\ *n* **1 :** a hold or place of support for the toes (as in climbing): as **a :** a means of progressing (as in gaining entry or surmounting barriers) ⟨hoped his uncle could give him a ~ in the import business⟩ **b :** a slight footing **:** very little power, influence, or territory ⟨at this time the Turks had only a ~ in Europe⟩ **2 :** a wrestling hold in which the aggressor bends or twists his opponent's foot

toe–in \'⸗,⸗\ *n* -S [fr. *toe in*, v.] **1 :** CAMBER 2 **2 :** inclination of the wheels of an automotive vehicle so that either pair is closer together at the front than at the back — compare TOE-OUT

toeing *pres part of* TOE

toe–iron \'⸗,⸗(⸗)\ *n* **:** one of two upright projections of metal plate fitted to a ski between which the toe of the boot is held firm

toe–kissing \'⸗,⸗⸗\ *n* **:** an act of humble adoration **:** deeply obeisant conduct

toe·less \'tōlə̇s\ *adj* **:** lacking a toe ⟨a ~ shoe⟩

¹toenail \'⸗¦⸗\ *n* [¹*toe* + *nail*] **1 :** a nail of a toe **2 :** a nail that is toed (as in fitting a brace) **3 :** PARENTHESIS 3a

²toenail \"\ *vt* **:** to clinch or fasten by toed nails **:** TOE

toe–out \'⸗,⸗\ *n* -S [fr. *toe out*, v.] **:** inclination of the wheels of an automotive vehicle so that either pair is closer together at the back than at the front — compare TOE-IN

toepiece \'⸗,⸗\ *n* **:** a piece designed to form a toe (as of a shoe) or cover the toes of the foot

toe piling *n* **:** sharpened poles driven next to the upstream face of the mudsills of a dam to prevent water from getting under the foundations

toeplate \'⸗,⸗\ *n* **:** a metal tab attached to the toe of a shoe to prevent slipping or the wear due to heavy use

toep·ler pump \'teplə(r)-\ *n, usu cap T* [after August J. I. *Toepler* †1912 Ger. physicist, its inventor] **:** a gas pump that is used to produce vacuums or to transfer gases from one part of a system to another and that operates by the alternate lowering and raising of a column of mercury with the consequent alternate production of a vacuum in one tube and the exhausting of the gas through another

toe puff *n* **:** a piece of material (as fabric or metal) inserted as a stiffener in the toe of a shoe between the outside and the lining — compare BOXING 5, TOE BOX, TOE CAP

toe–punch \'⸗,⸗\ *also* **toe–mark** \'⸗,⸗\ *vt* **:** to mark (poultry) by punching holes through the membrane between the toes

toe ring *n* **1 :** a ring worn on the toe **2 :** a ferrule or a heavy ring on the end of a cant hook with a lipped lower surface that prevents slipping **3 :** a small paddock in which horses heated by exercise are walked to cool them off

toer·ne·bohm·ite *or* **tör·ne·bohm·ite** \'tərnə,bō,mīt, 'tər-, ,⸗⸗'⸗,⸗\ *n* -S [Alfred E. *Törnebohm* †1911 Swedish geologist + E *-ite*] **:** a mineral $Ce_3Si_2O_8OH$ that is a rare silicate of the cerium metals

toe rubber *n* **:** a rubber esp. for wear over a woman's high-heeled shoe that covers only the forepart of the shoe and is held in place by a strap extending around the back of the foot above the heel — compare FOOTHOLD 3, SANDAL 4

toe rubber

toes *pl of* TOE, *pres 3d sing of* TOE

toe shoe *also* **toe slipper** *n* **:** a ballet slipper with reinforced toe for toe dancing

toe strap *n* **:** any of various straps passing over or between the toes to give purchase (as on a deck) or hold something (as a ski) in position

toe–tap \'⸗,⸗\ *n* **:** tap-dancing done on the tips of the toes

toe·toe *also* **toi·toi** \¦tōē¦tōē, 'tōi,tōi\ *n* -S [Maori *toetoe*] **:** any of several coarse New Zealand sedges and grasses (as of the genera *Arundo* and *Cladium*); *specif* **:** a plant (*A. conspicua*) used by the Maoris for thatching

toe wall *n* **:** a low retaining wall; *esp* **:** an embankment wall in a railroad cut

toe weight *n* **:** a small metal weight attached to the toe of a horse's front hoof to regulate the gait

toey \'tōē\ *adj* [¹*toe* + *-y*, adj. suffix] *Austral* **:** NERVOUS, ANXIOUS, WORRIED

to–fall \'tü,fȯl\ *n* [ME *tofall*, fr. *to*, adv. + *fall*, n.] **1** *chiefly Scot* **:** a building built against another **:** LEAN-TO **2** *Scot* **:** the fall of night **:** NIGHTFALL

toff \'täf, 'tȯf\ *n* -S [prob. alter. of *tuft* (student at Oxford)] *chiefly Brit* **:** a person of superior social status and often notably stylish or fashionable — often used disparagingly

tof·fee *also* **tof·fy** \'tȯfē, -'täf-, -fi\ *n, pl* **toffees** *also* **toffies** [alter. of *taffy*] **1 a :** candy of brittle but tender texture made by boiling sugar and butter together to approximately 310° F or the hard crack stage **b :** BUTTERSCOTCH ⟨~ pie⟩ ⟨~ cookies⟩ **2** *chiefly Brit* **:** a piece of toffee

toffee–nosed \¦⸗⸗¦⸗\ *adj, Brit* **:** exhibiting undue airs of superiority **:** STUCK-UP

toff·ish \'täfish, 'tȯf-, -fēsh\ *adj, Brit* **:** resembling a toff esp. in smartness or style

to·fiel·dia \tə'fēldēə\ *n, cap* [NL, fr. Thomas *Tofield* †1779 Eng. botanist + NL *-ia*] **:** a genus of perennial herbs (family Liliaceae) growing in cool regions and having linear chiefly basal leaves and small spicate sessile flowers with 6 anthers and 3 styles — see FALSE ASPHODEL

tofore *adv* [ME *toforen, tofore*, fr. OE *tōforan*, fr. *tō* to + *foran* before, fr. *fore* — more at TO, FORE] *obs* **:** BEFORE ⟨would thou wert as thou ~ hast been —Shak.⟩

toft \'täft *also* 'tȯft\ *n* -S [ME, fr. OE, fr. ON *topt, tupt*] **1** *Brit* **a** (1) **:** a site for a dwelling and its outbuildings **:** HOMESTEAD (2) **:** a usu. enclosed garden plot attached to a homestead **b :** an entire holding comprising a homestead together with additional usu. arable land **2** *Brit* **:** an isolated hill or elevation **:** a knoll suitable for a building site

toft·man \'⸗,mən\ *n, pl* **toftmen** *Brit* **:** a holder of a toft; *usu* **:** SMALLHOLDER

toft ware *n, usu cap T* [after Thomas *Toft*, 17th cent. Eng. potter] **:** slip-decorated ceramic ware of a style made orig. by Thomas Toft

to·fu \'tō(,)fü\ *n* -S [Jap *tōfu*] **:** BEAN CURD

¹tog \'täg *also* 'tȯg\ *n* -S [short for obs. E cant *togeman, togemans, togman* cloak, prob. fr. E *toge* + obs. E cant *-mans* (n. suffix of unknown origin)] **1** *slang* **:** an outer garment; *esp* **:** COAT **2 togs** *pl* **:** CLOTHING ⟨the old ~*s* he sat around in —Theodore Dreiser⟩; *esp* **:** an outfit of clothes and accessories for a specified use ⟨riding ~*s*⟩ ⟨beach ~*s*⟩ ⟨getting into play ~*s* for golf or boating —Vance Packard⟩ **3 togs** *pl, Austral* **:** BATHING SUIT

²tog \"\ *vt* **togged; togged; togging; togs :** to put togs on **:** dress up — usu. used with *out* or *up* ⟨went to school *togged* out in their Sunday best —Frank Sullivan⟩ ⟨*togged* up as an ordinary seaman of a century ago —Charles Hamblett⟩

tog *abbr* together

to·ga \'tōgə\ *n* -S [L; akin to L *tegere* to cover — more at THATCH] **1 a :** the outer garment worn in public by citizens of ancient Rome consisting of a semicircular or long elliptical usu. undyed woolen cloth sometimes ornamented along the borders and so draped as to cover the left arm and leave the right arm free **b :** a similar loose wrap ⟨the colorful ~ of an African chieftain⟩ **c :** a professional, official, or academic gown ⟨don the ~ of a judge⟩ **2 :** OFFICE; *esp* **:** SENATORSHIP ⟨will seek a ~ next November —*Newsweek*⟩

to·gaed \'tōgəd\ *adj* **:** clad in or as if in a toga **:** TOGATED ⟨a ~ Roman senator⟩ ⟨parks, where ~ or equestrian Lincolns would look blandly down —*Nation*⟩

to·gat·ed \'tō,gād·əd\ *also* **to·gate** \-āt\ *adj* [*togated* fr. L *togatus* togated + E *-ed; togate* fr. L *togatus*, fr. *toga* + *-atus*

-ate] **1 :** wearing a toga **:** TOGAED ⟨a ~ senator⟩ **2 :** DIGNIFIED, STATELY ⟨~ language⟩

to·ga vi·ri·lis \ˌtōgəwə'rēləs\ *n, pl* **to·gae viri·les** \ˌtō-ˌgiwə'rē(ˌ)lās\ [L, men's toga] **:** the white toga of manhood assumed by boys of ancient Rome at the end of their fourteenth year

toge *n* -s [ME, fr. MF *togue, toge,* fr. L *toga*] *obs* **:** TOGA, CLOAK

to·ged \'tōgəd\ *adj, obs* **:** TOGATED ⟨the ~ consuls can propose —Shak.⟩

to·geth·er \tə'geth̲ə(r)\ *adv* [ME *togadere, togedere, togidere,* fr. OE *tōgadere, tōgædere, tōgædre,* fr. *tō* to + *gadere, gædere, gædre* together; akin to OFris *gader, gadur* together, MLG *tōgadere,* MHG *gater* together, *gatern* to unite — more at GATHER] **1 a :** in or into one place, mass, collection, or group (as body, company, or organization) ⟨sweep the rubbish ~⟩ ⟨call the members ~⟩ ⟨come ~ for discussion⟩ ⟨the girls got ~ by themselves⟩ ⟨gathered his scattered writings ~ for publication in one volume⟩ ⟨brought the two factions ~ in a new party⟩ **b :** in a body **:** as a group ⟨students and faculty ~ presented the petition⟩ ⟨~ our objective has been to hold tight to your attention —Richard Joseph⟩ **2 a :** in or into contact (as connection, collision, or union) ⟨fasten the parts ~⟩ ⟨mix these ingredients ~⟩ ⟨the opposing teams rushed ~⟩ ⟨held ~ by pins⟩ **b :** in or into a compacted or constricted mass or body ⟨folded and pressed the papers ~ into a small bundle⟩ ⟨sat all hunched ~⟩ **c :** in or into association or relationship (as of companionship, friendship, courtship, or cohabitation) ⟨colors that go well ~⟩ ⟨held ~ by ties of common interest⟩ ⟨circumstances threw them ~⟩ ⟨bringing industry and the liberal arts ~ —D.A.Shepard⟩ ⟨fought ~ in the war⟩ ⟨went ~ for years⟩ ⟨live ~ as man and wife⟩ **3 a :** at one time **:** SIMULTANEOUSLY, COINCIDENTALLY ⟨events that happened ~ —R.J.Goldwater⟩ ⟨what is learned through the most senses ~ will be most readily retained —I.A.Richards⟩ **b :** in succession **:** without intermission **:** on end **:** CONSECUTIVELY ⟨was moody for days ~ —Hugh Walpole⟩ ⟨sometimes lay hid for weeks ~ in cocklofts and cellars —T.B.Macaulay⟩ **4 a :** in or by combined action or effort **:** JOINTLY ⟨parents have ~ the responsibility for discipline⟩ ⟨~ we forced the door⟩ ⟨the family ~ earned one hundred dollars a week⟩ **b :** in or into agreement (as harmony, concert, or unison) **:** in unified action or interaction ⟨unable to get ~ on vacation plans⟩ ⟨the parts of the mechanism work ~ beautifully⟩ ⟨soloist and orchestra were not always quite ~⟩ **c :** in or into a unified or coherent structure or an integrated whole ⟨the play hangs ~⟩ ⟨the child who cannot put an easy sentence ~ —George Sampson⟩ ⟨have thrown ~ shacks of scrap lumber and tar paper —*Amer. Guide Series: Ark.*⟩ **5 a :** with each other **:** MUTUALLY, RECIPROCALLY ⟨were not on good terms ~⟩ ⟨consult ~ on possible . . . legislation —*New Republic*⟩ — used pleonastically and as an intensive after certain verbs ⟨join ~⟩ ⟨cooperate ~⟩ ⟨add a column of figures ~⟩ **b :** as a unit or sum **:** in the aggregate ⟨these arguments taken ~ make a convincing case⟩ ⟨the pair of meetings ~ seldom lasted more than three hours —J.K.Blake⟩ **c :** considered as a whole **:** counted or summed up ⟨richer than all his brothers ~⟩ ⟨all ~, there were 21 entries⟩ — compare ALTOGETHER 2 — **together with :** along with **:** in addition to **:** as well as ⟨the big island, *together with* its smaller neighbors⟩ ⟨these sums *together with* the previous balance⟩ ⟨arrested, *together with* a companion⟩

to·geth·er·ness *n* -ES **:** the quality or state of being or belonging together or of forming related parts of a unified whole: as **a :** ONENESS, UNITY ⟨a grasping of diverse entities into a value by reason of their real ~ in that pattern —A.N.Whitehead⟩ **b :** apprehension or sense of unity (as in the outer world or in the psyche) ⟨the psychology of ~⟩ **c :** ASSOCIATION ⟨the ~ of things, which impressed the artists of the North —G.C. Sillery⟩ **d :** physical closeness **:** PROPINQUITY ⟨the crowd . . . have nothing in common except ~ —Howard Griffin⟩ **e :** feeling of community **:** the emotional bond in a group (as a social organization or a family) **:** SOLIDARITY, COMMUNION ⟨a spontaneous . . . ~, as in invasions, floods, celebrations —Harold Rosenberg⟩ ⟨felt a deep flowing sense of ~ when we sang the Doxology —Lillian Smith⟩ ⟨that's what a home is made of — ~ —Edith Wharton⟩

tog·gen·burg \'tägənˌbərg\ *n* [fr. *Toggenburg,* district in northeastern Switzerland] **1** *usu cap* **:** a Swiss breed of brown hornless dairy goats with white stripes on the face **2** *often cap* -s **:** a goat of the Toggenburg breed

tog·gery \'täg(ə)rē, -ri\ *n* -ES *often attrib* [¹*tog* + *-ery*] **1 :** CLOTHING; *esp* **:** official or military dress ⟨the same ~ he first wore around the circuit —B.P.Thomas⟩ ⟨the campus ~ shop⟩ **2** *chiefly Brit* **:** a clothing shop ⟨opened a ~ on the town's main business street⟩

togging *pres part of* TOG

¹tog·gle \'tägəl\ *n* -s *often attrib* [origin unknown] **1 :** a piece or device for holding or securing: as **a :** a wood or metal pin inserted in a nautical knot to make it more secure or easier to slip **b** (1) **:** any crosspiece attached to the end of or to a loop in something (as a chain, rope, line, strap, belt) usu. to prevent slipping, to serve in twisting or tightening, or to hold something attached ⟨the ~ of a watch chain⟩ ⟨use a stick as a ~ in tightening a rope⟩ (2) **:** an object (as a chain or rope) with such a device **c :** a rod or screw with a T-head crosspiece or with a cone-shaped compressible nut that can pass through a hole in one direction but not in the opposite direction **d :** a button or frog capable of being engaged or disengaged for temporary purposes **e :** a short length of rope with a swivel and loop for tethering an animal **f :** a strap or cord fastened to the rear doorpost in an automobile as a handhold for passengers **g :** TOGGLE CHAIN **2 a :** TOGGLE JOINT **b :** a device having a toggle joint **c :** one of the bars of a toggle joint

²toggle \"\ *vt* **toggled; toggled; toggling** \-g(ə)liŋ\ **toggles** **1 :** to fasten with or as if with a toggle **:** hold fast with or as if with a toggle iron ⟨the sergeant would . . . ~ his holster —*Time*⟩ **2 a :** to furnish with a toggle **b :** to mend (as a harness) in makeshift or bungling fashion esp. with pieces of rope ⟨a *toggled* machine in danger of going to pieces at any moment —Hamlin Garland⟩ **c** *dial* **:** to add decoration to **:** make prettier **:** dress up ⟨put an ornament on a dress to ~ it up⟩ **3 :** to release (a bomb) from an airplane by a toggle switch instead of relying on the automatic release triggered by the bombsight ⟨all he had to do was ~ the bombs out —Bert Stiles⟩

toggle bolt *n* **:** a bolt that has a nut with pivoted flanged wings that close against a spring when passed through a constricted passage and open after emerging and that is used to fasten objects to thin or hollow walls

toggle bolt

toggle chain *n* **1 :** a device consisting of a short chain with a ring and toggle hook at one end and a ring at the other for regulating the effective length of a binding chain for a load of logs **2 :** a chain of any length with an end hook small enough to be inserted in a loose link that has been passed through a taut link

toggle clamp *n* **:** a clamp that locks by means of snap action across a dead center as in the toggle joint

toggle iron *or* **toggle harpoon** *n* **:** a harpoon with a pivoted crosspiece in a mortise near the point to prevent it from being drawn out when an animal is harpooned

toggle joint *n* **1 :** a device consisting of two bars jointed together end to end but not in line so that when a force is applied to the knee tending to straighten the arrangement the parts abutting or jointed to the ends of the bars will experience an endwise pressure which increases indefinitely as the bars approach a straight-line position ⟨*toggle joints* are used in stone crushers, in the double wagon brake, and in some kinds of presses⟩ **2 :** a joint consisting of a bar pivoted at its middle point to a supporting bar so that the former may be turned to any position and hence be used for lifting heavy objects (as tanks) by inserting the bar through a constricted opening and allowing it to assume a position normal to the supporting bar

toggle-joint press *or* **toggle press** *n* **:** a punch press operated by a toggle joint — called also *knuckle press*

toggle pin *n* **:** a pin with a shoulder and eye at one end and at the other a hinged locking device that prevents the pin from being withdrawn from a fitting until the locking device is in line with the pin

tog·gler \'täg(ə)lə(r)\ *n* -s **:** one that toggles

toggle riveter *n* **:** a riveter that upsets the stem and forms the rivet head by the action of a toggle mechanism

toggles *pl of* TOGGLE, *pres 3d sing of* TOGGLE

toggle switch *n* **:** an electric switch depending on a toggle-joint or knee-joint in conjunction with a spring to open or close the circuit quickly when the projecting lever is pushed through a small arc

to·ghuz·ghu \ˌtōˌgüz'gü, -ˌgu̇z-\ *n, pl* **toghuzghus** \-üz\ *usu cap* **1 :** a Uighur people of central Asia held to be the only Turkish group professing the Manichaean religion **2 :** a member of the Toghuzghu people

to·go \'tō(ˌ)gō\ *adj, usu cap* [fr. *Togo,* country in western Africa] **:** of or relating to Togo **:** of the kind or style prevalent in Togo

to·go·land·er \'⸗(ˌ)⸗ˌlandə(r), -la(a)nd-\ *n* -s *cap* [*Togoland,* territory in western Africa + E *-er*] **:** a native or inhabitant of Togoland in western Africa

¹to·go·lese \ˌtō(ˌ)gō'lēz, -lēs\ *adj, usu cap* [*Togo,* country in western Africa + E *-lese* (as in *Congolese*)] **1 :** of, relating to, or characteristic of the Republic of Togo in western Africa **2 :** of, relating to, or characteristic of the Togolese

²togolese \"\ *n, pl* **togolese** *cap* **:** a native or inhabitant of the Republic of Togo

togr *abbr* together

togs *pl of* TOG, *pres 3d sing of* TOG

togue \'tōg\ *n* -s [CanF] **:** LAKE TROUT

to·he·roa \ˌtōə'rōə\ *n, pl* **toheroa** *or* **toheroas** [Maori] **:** a large marine bivalve mollusk (*Amphidesma ventricosum*) of New Zealand used extensively for food

to·hi \'tōhē\ *n* -s [native name in eastern Africa] **:** a small tawny East African nagor (*Redunca redunca tohi*)

to·ho \tō'hō\ *v imper, chiefly Brit* [origin unknown] **:** STOP, HALT — used as a call to hunting dogs

TOHP *abbr, often not cap* takeoff horsepower

to·hu·bo·hu \ˌtōˌhü'bōˌhü\ *n* -s [Heb *tōhū wā-bhōhū* without form and void, fr. *tōhū* formlessness, confusion + *bōhū* emptiness] **:** CHAOS, CONFUSION ⟨bringing order out of the ~ of human relations —Walter Lippmann⟩

to·hun·ga \'tōˌhu̇ŋgə\ *n* -s [Maori] *NewZeal* **:** a Maori priest or performer of sacred rites **:** SAGE, MEDICINE MAN

toi \'tȯi\ *n* -s [Maori] **:** ¹TI 1

¹toil \'tȯil, *esp before pause or consonant* 'tȯiəl\ *n* -s [ME *toile* argument, dispute, battle, fr. AF *toyl,* fr. OF *tooil, toeil* battle, trouble, confusion, fr. *tooillier, toeillier* to stir, mix, soil, sully, disturb, dispute — more at ²TOIL] **1** *archaic* **a :** a hard struggle **:** BATTLE, BROIL ⟨returning from their famous Trojan ~s —P.B.Shelley⟩ **b :** a laborious effort to achieve (as a task) despite the difficulties **:** LABOR ⟨some books are a ~ to read —J.E.Gloag⟩ **2 :** strenuous fatiguing labor marked usu. by long duration, lack of relief, and physical or mental strain **:** WORK, DRUDGERY ⟨for years he led a life of unremitting physical ~ —John Buchan⟩ ⟨fifty years of intellectual ~ . . . produced the greatest of all medieval storehouses of knowledge —H.O.Taylor⟩ ⟨nothing to offer but blood, ~, tears, and sweat —Sir Winston Churchill⟩ **syn** see WORK

²toil \"\ *vb* -ED/-ING/-S [ME *toilen* to argue, struggle, fr. AF *toiller,* fr. OF *tooillier, toeillier* to stir, mix, soil, sully, disturb, dispute, fr. L *tudiculare* to crush, grind, fr. *tudicula* machine for crushing olives, dim. of *tudes* hammer; akin to L *tundere* to beat — more at STINT] *vi* **1 :** to work hard and long at tiring labor **:** DRUDGE, SLAVE ⟨bathed in sweat as they ~*ed* at their . . . digging —W.F.Hambly⟩ ⟨inventors ~*ing* over drafting boards —R.A.Billington⟩ **2 :** to proceed with laborious exertion **:** advance with much effort or strain **:** PLOD — usu. used with *along, up, on,* or *over* ⟨father's bowed figure ~*ing* along the path —Ellen Glasgow⟩ ⟨~*ed* up the steepest part of the hill —Willa Cather⟩ ⟨feel obliged to ~ on through 559 more pages —O.W.Holmes †1935⟩ ~ *vt* **1** *archaic* **:** to weary or harass (as a person or animal) with labor or exertion **:** OVERWORK ⟨vex and ~ themselves to get what they have no need of —Izaak Walton⟩ **2 :** to work on (as the soil) **:** TILL ⟨~*ed* and tilled the rocky land —E.W.Smith⟩ **3** *archaic* **:** to accomplish (as a task) with great effort **:** get or effect after much labor **:** WORK ⟨at last the thing is ~*ed* and hammered into fit shape —S.T.Coleridge⟩

³toil \"\ *n* -s [MF *toile* cloth, net, fr. L *tela* web, fr. *texere* to weave, construct — more at TECHNICAL] **1 :** a net or a series of nets spread so as to enclose and entrap game already in the area or driven into it as quarry — usu. used in pl. ⟨the practice of enclosing the land with ~s and stirring it with dogs —H.A.J. Munro⟩ **2 :** something by which one is held fast, entangled, or involved in seemingly inextricable difficulties **:** SNARE, TRAP ⟨would catch another Anthony in her strong ~ of grace —Shak.⟩ — usu. used in pl. ⟨in the ~s of the law⟩ ⟨the immense genius . . . caught in the ~s of the moral and aesthetic conventions of his day —Herbert Read⟩

⁴toil \"\ *vt* -ED/-ING/-S **:** to entangle in or as if in toils **:** ENSNARE, ENTRAP ⟨a ~*ed* bird⟩

¹toile \'twäl\ *n* -s [F — more at ³TOIL] **1 :** cloth of various fibers; *specif* **:** TOILE DE JOUY **2 :** a muslin model of a garment

²toi·lé \(')twä'lā\ *n* -s [F, fr. *toile* cloth, net + *-é* -ate (fr. L *-atus*)] **:** a closely worked solid pattern in lace making that is contrasted with a net ground

toile de jouy \ˌtwäldəzh'wē\ *n, pl* **toiles de jouy** \"\ *usu cap J* [F, lit., cloth of Jouy, fr. *Jouy*-en-Josar, Seine-et-Oise dept., France] **:** an upholstery and drapery fabric usu. made of cotton or linen and printed with characteristic designs (as of landscapes or florals) in one color on a cream or white background — called also *Jouy print*

toil·er \'tȯilə(r)\ *n* -s [²*toil* + *-er*] **:** one that toils **:** WORKER; *specif* **:** one that works for wages or hire ⟨~s in the fields⟩ ⟨no captain of industry, just a ~ in the ranks⟩

¹toi·let \'tȯilət, *usu* -lȯd.+V\ *n* -s *often attrib* [MF *toilette,* dim. of *toile* cloth — more at TOIL] **1 a** *obs* **:** a cloth or shawl put over the shoulders (as during shaving or hairdressing) **b** *archaic* **:** a cloth covering for a dressing table **:** TOILET CLOTH ⟨a ~ of blue velvet with a gold and silver fringe —*London Gazette*⟩ **2** *archaic* **a :** the equipment for a dressing room or dressing table **:** a toilet service or set **b :** DRESSING TABLE **3 a :** the act or process of dressing; *specif* **:** the process of washing, grooming, and arranging oneself for the day's activities or for a special occasion ⟨while making his ~ before dinner, he dropped his collar button⟩ ⟨hurried at her ~, which was soon made —Theodore Dreiser⟩ ⟨~ articles⟩ **b** *archaic* **:** the receiving of visitors by ladies while completing the final touches of their toilet **4** *archaic* **:** TOILETTE 3 **5 a :** TOILET ROOM, BATHROOM 1, LAVATORY 3a **b :** a fixture consisting typically of a water-flushed bowl with a toilet seat that is used for urination and defecation **:** WATER CLOSET **6 a :** local cleansing and application of aseptic dressings ⟨~ of an obstetrical patient⟩ ⟨~ of a surgical wound⟩ **b :** the removal of undesirable material (as mucus or dead tissue) from a passage or cavity ⟨tracheobronchial ~ after anesthesia⟩ ⟨~ of a tooth cavity before filling⟩

²toilet \"\ *vb* -ED/-ING/-S *vi* **1 :** to make one's toilet **:** DRESS **2 :** to go to the bathroom for washing or to the toilet for urinating or defecating — usu. used of a child ⟨learns all the accepted habits connected with eating, sleeping, and ~*ing* —J.D. Teicher⟩ ~ *vt* **1 :** GROOM **2 :** to see to the toileting of **:** set (as a child) on a toilet ⟨pick him up and ~ him —A.L. Gesell & Frances Ilg⟩

toilet cloth *or* **toilet cover** *n* **:** a covering of linen, silk, or tapestry spread over a dressing table

toilet glass *n* **:** a looking glass for a dressing table or dressing room

toilet glass

toilet paper *n* **:** a thin soft sanitary absorbent paper for use in toilet rooms

toilet powder *n* **:** a fine powder usu. with soothing or antiseptic ingredients for sprinkling or rubbing over the skin of the body (as after bathing) **:** DUSTING POWDER

toilet room *n* **1 :** a room for making the toilet **:** DRESSING ROOM **2 a :** a room or compartment equipped with one or more toilets **b :** a room (as in an office building or railroad station) equipped with one or more lavatories and toilets and if a men's room usu. with one or more urinals

toi·let·ry \'tȯilətrē, -ri\ *n* -ES *often attrib* [¹*toilet* + *-ry*] **:** an article or preparation used in making one's toilet (as a soap, lotion, cosmetic, toothpaste, shaving cream, cologne) ⟨~ manufacturers⟩ — usu. used in pl. ⟨a new line of *toiletries* for men⟩

toilet seat *n* **:** an oval or circular ring usu. of wood or plastic attached to the top of a toilet bowl at the back to support the buttocks and often covered with a hinged top

toilet set *n* **1 :** the vessels on a washstand (as a basin and ewer) **2 :** DRESSER SET

toilet soap *n* **:** a mild soap that is made from fatty materials of high quality usu. by milling and plodding to form cakes and that is often perfumed and colored and stabilized with preservatives

toilet table *n* **:** DRESSING TABLE

toi·lette \(')tȯi'let, (')twä'l-\ *n* -s [F — more at TOILET] **1** *archaic* **:** DRESSING TABLE **2 :** TOILET 3a **3 a :** formal or fashionable attire or style of dressing **b :** a particular costume or outfit ⟨noting each detail of her ~⟩ ⟨a ~ for each bridesmaid⟩

toilet training *n* **:** the process of training a child to control bladder and bowel movements and to use the toilet ⟨a great fuss about *toilet training* —Benjamin Spock⟩

toiletware \'⸗⸗ˌ⸗\ *n* **:** merchandise comprising articles (as combs, brushes, mirrors, manicure sets) for the equipment of dressing room, dresser, vanity, or bathroom

toilet water *n* **:** a perfumed liquid largely alcoholic in content for use in or after a bath or as a skin freshener — compare COLOGNE, FLORIDA WATER

toil·ful \'⸗fəl\ *adj* [¹*toil* + *-ful*] **:** marked by or demanding hard work or industry **:** LABORIOUS, TOILSOME ⟨~ care⟩ ⟨~ progress⟩ ⟨a ~ servant⟩

toil·ful·ly \-fəlē, -li\ *adv* **:** in a toilful manner **:** INDUSTRIOUSLY ⟨let them loiter in pleasure or ~ spin —Park Benjamin⟩

toi·li·net *or* **toi·li·nette** \ˌtȯilə'net\ *n* -s [prob. fr. F *toile* cloth, linen cloth + E *-inet, -inette* (as in *satinet, satinette*) — more at TOIL] **:** a fabric with silk or cotton warp and wool weft in use in the 19th century for fancy waistcoats

toiling *pres part of* TOIL

toils *pl of* TOIL, *pres 3d sing of* TOIL

toil·some \'⸗səm\ *adj* [¹*toil* + *-some*] **:** marked by or full of toil or effort **:** ARDUOUS, LABORIOUS, WEARISOME ⟨a ~ life⟩ ⟨a ~ journey⟩ ⟨a slow and ~ process⟩

toil·some·ly *adv* **:** in a toilsome manner **:** LABORIOUSLY ⟨delivered the loaves, making his rounds slowly and ~ —D.C. Jenkins⟩

toil·some·ness *n* -ES **:** the quality or state of being toilsome **:** LABORIOUSNESS

toilworn \'⸗ˌ⸗\ *adj* **:** showing the effects of or worn out with toil ⟨a ~ traveler⟩ ⟨a ~ farmer⟩ ⟨~ eyes⟩

to·ing and fro·ing \ˌtüiŋən'frōiŋ\ *n, pl* **toings and froings** [fr. the phrase *to and fro*] **:** a passing back and forth **:** a going hither and thither ⟨the clatter and bustle, the . . . *toing and froing* of the soldiery —Sheridan Le Fanu⟩

toise \'tȯiz\ *n* -s [MF, fr. (assumed) VL *tensa, tesa,* fr. L *tensa,* fem. of *tensus,* past part. of *tendere* to stretch — more at THIN] **:** an old French unit of length equal to 6 French feet, 6.396 U. S. feet, or 1.949 meters

toitoi *var of* TOETOE

to·jo·la·bal \ˌtōhōlə'bäl\ *n, pl* **tojolaba·les** \ˌ⸗⸗⸗'bä(ˌ)lās\ *usu cap* [Sp, of AmerInd origin] **1 a :** an Indian people of southeastern Chiapas in Mexico **b :** a member of such people **2 :** a Mayan language of the Tojolabal people

¹to·kay \(')tō'kā\ *n* -s *usu cap* [fr. *Tokay* (Tokaj), Hungary] **1 :** a sweet unfortified dessert wine usu. dark gold in color that is made near the town of Tokaj on the Tisza river in northeastern Hungary **2 :** a sweet dessert wine made by blending Angelica, port, and sherry wines — called also *California Tokay*

²tokay \"\ *n* -s [Malay *toke,* of imit. origin] **:** a Malaysian house lizard (*Gekko gecko*)

toke \'tōk\ *n* -s [origin unknown] *Brit* **:** FOOD; *esp* **:** a portion of bread

to·ke·lau·an \ˌtōkə'lau̇ən\ *n* -s *cap* [*Tokelau* islands, central Pacific ocean + E *-an*] **:** a native or inhabitant of the Tokelau islands of western Samoa

¹to·ken \'tōkən *sometimes* -kᵊŋ\ *n* -s [ME *taken, token,* fr. OE *tācen, tācn;* akin to OS *tēkan* sign, OHG *zeihhan,* ON *teikn,* Goth *taikn* sign, Gk *deiknynai* to show — more at DICTION] **1 :** an outward indication or expression (as a visible sign) **:** sensible evidence **:** PROOF ⟨~s of his profound grief⟩ ⟨saw the rainbow as . . . the ~ of a covenant between God and man —James Jeans⟩ ⟨from time to time said something . . . as a ~ of friendship —Douglas Stewart⟩ **2 :** a divine or miraculous sign **:** OMEN, PORTENT ⟨the most mighty gods by ~s send such dreadful heralds —Shak.⟩ ⟨the floor to the house where they stood up fell in and . . . folks said it was a bad ~ —Elizabeth M. Roberts⟩ **3 a :** something (as an act, gesture, or object) that serves as a sign or signification **:** MARK, EMBLEM ⟨a white flag is a ~ of surrender⟩ ⟨waved her handkerchief as a ~ of recognition⟩ ⟨gripped the clergyman's hand in ~ of his gratitude —Robert Grant †1940⟩ **b** (1) **:** a particular instance of an expression, symbol, or sentence ⟨if the word *man* is written twice and spoken once, there have arisen three ~s of the word *man*⟩ — contrasted with *type* (2) **:** the action of uttering, writing, or otherwise producing a token **4 :** a distinguishing mark **:** FEATURE, CHARACTERISTIC ⟨a boy of good make and mind, with the ~s on him of a refined nature —J.H.Newman⟩ **5** *archaic* **a :** usu. prearranged sign **:** SIGNAL ⟨he that betrayed him had given them a ~ —Mk 14:44 (AV)⟩ ⟨gave ~ that the host was closing for the night —E.A.Poe⟩ **6 a :** something given as a memento of regard or affection **:** SOUVENIR, KEEPSAKE ⟨an antique ~ my father gave my mother —Shak.⟩ ⟨give it to me as a going-away ~ —Lillian Hellman⟩ **b :** a vestige or reminder of something ⟨muse . . . over this ~ of bygone fashion —Virginia Woolf⟩ **c :** a small part or bit representing the whole **:** INDICATION ⟨only a ~ of what he hopes to accomplish⟩ ⟨this is the merest ~ of the subject —W.W.Howells⟩ **d :** something given or shown as a symbol or guarantee (as of authority, right, or identity) **:** PASSWORD ⟨say, by this ~, I desire his company —Shak.⟩ ⟨the book . . . was accompanied by no sign or ~ from him —William Black⟩ ⟨any member who reveals any ~ . . . is expelled —C.W.Ferguson⟩: as (1) **:** a small metal disk formerly given in the Church of Scotland as a warrant or voucher to members qualified to receive communion — called also *communion token* (2) *Brit* **:** a disk or strip of metal or leather having a peculiar mark designating a particular miner that is sent with each filled corf hewed or conveyed in a coal mine **7 :** a piece or disk (as of metal) certified as having a definite value for payment or exchange: as **a :** a piece (as of metal, cardboard, or hard rubber) fashioned in resemblance of a coin but not in imitation of any particular coin and issued for use as money by or on the authority of some person or body (as a bank or a business or commercial firm) other than a de jure government **b :** a piece resembling a coin issued on private or public authority for use by a particular group of people (as employees of a plantation or inmates of a prison) on specified terms **c :** a piece resembling a coin for use as a ticket on a public conveyance ⟨bus ~⟩ ⟨transportation ~⟩ ⟨a seven-and-a-half-cent ~⟩ **d :** TOKEN COIN **e :** a piece (as a coupon, certificate, label, or box top) redeemable for merchandise ⟨premium ~s⟩ ⟨a book ~⟩ **8 :** a piece resembling a medal issued as a souvenir or for advertising or political propaganda purposes **9 :** a game counter **10** *archaic* **a :** a quantity of paper sufficient for printing 250 impressions or for one hour's work for two men on a handpress **b :** a unit of presswork from one form varying from 250 to 500 impressions **syn** SEE PLEDGE, SIGN — **by the same token 1 :** for the same reason ⟨because his mind is flexible it responds quickly . . . to what is before it, and *by the same token* it can call up from within a host of appropriate ideas —J.M.Barzun⟩ **2 :** FURTHERMORE, ALSO — **more by token** *archaic* **:** the more so ⟨danger . . . from drug or pill; *more by token,* as there is a lot of apothecary's stuff aboard —Nathaniel Hawthorne⟩

²token \"\ *vb* **tokened; tokened; tokening** \-k(ə)niŋ\

tokens [ME *toknen, tokenen,* fr. OE *tācnian,* fr. *tācen, tācn,* n.] *vt* **:** to serve as a sign of **:** BETOKEN, SIGNIFY, SYMBOLIZE ⟨feeling remorse . . . ~*s* possible future pangs —F.B.Ebersole⟩ ~ *vi* **:** to occur as or provide with a token **:** INSTANCE

3**token** \"\ *adj* [1*token*] **:** done or given as a token esp. in partial fulfillment of an obligation or engagement **:** having semblance or serving as a sign or sample of the real thing **:** SIMULATED, MINIMAL, PERFUNCTORY ⟨sent a ~ force to join in the unpopular war⟩ ⟨~ damages of six cents⟩ ⟨a ~ bequest⟩

token book *n* **:** a book listing parishioners receiving communion tokens

token coin *n* **:** a coin having an intrinsic value less than its face value — compare STANDARD COIN

token money *n* **1 :** money (as paper currency or minor coins) of regular government issue having a greater face value than intrinsic value **2 :** a conventional medium of exchange consisting of tokens privately issued (as by a trader or a company) and circulating by consent among private persons esp. during the 17th, 18th, and early 19th centuries usu. to alleviate a scarcity of small coins

token payment *n* **:** a very small payment made upon a debt and intended by the payer merely to acknowledge the existence of the obligation

tokens *pl of* TOKEN

token sheet *n, archaic* **:** the last sheet of each token printed that is turned down to help in counting

tokes *pl of* TOKE

tokharian *cap, var of* TOCHARIAN

toko *var of* TOCO

toko- — see TOCO-

to·ko·no·ma \ˌtōkə'nōmə\ *n* -S [Jap] **:** a niche or recess opening from the living room of a Japanese house in which a kakemono may be hung

-to·kous \d·əkəs, tək-\ *adj comb form* [Gk *-tokos,* fr. *tiktein* to bear — more at THANE] **:** producing (such or so many) offspring ⟨deutero*tokous*⟩

tok-tok·kie *also* **tok·tok·je** \'täk,täkē\ *n* -S [Afrik *toktokkie* (formerly spelled *toktokje*), of imit. origin] **:** any of several African beetles of the genus *Psammodes* (family Tenebrionidae)

to·kus \'tōkəs\ *n* -ES [Yiddish *tokhes,* fr. Heb *taḥath* under, below] *slang* **:** BUTTOCKS

to·ku·shi·ma \ˌtōkə'shēmə\ *adj, usu cap* [fr. *Tokushima,* Japan] **:** of or from the city of Tokushima, Japan **:** of the kind or style prevalent in Tokushima

-to·ky \d·əkē, tə-\ *n comb form* -ES [Gk *-tokia,* fr. *-tokos* + *-ia* -y] **:** parturition **:** delivery ⟨deutero*toky*⟩

to·kyo *also* **to·kio** \'tōkē,ō\ *adj, usu cap* [fr. *Tokyo* or *Tokio,* Japan] **:** of or from Tokyo, the capital of Japan **:** of the kind or style prevalent in Tokyo

tol- *or* **tolu-** *comb form* [ISV, fr. *tolu*] **1 :** tolu ⟨*tol*uol⟩ **2 :** toluene ⟨*tolu*ic⟩ ⟨*tol*yl⟩ **:** toluic ⟨*tolu*ate⟩

tol *abbr* tolerance

1**to·la** \'tōlə\ *n* -S [Hindi *tolā,* fr. Skt *tulā* balance, scale, weight — more at TOLERATE] **:** a unit of weight of India equal to 180 grains troy or 0.4114 ounce

2**tola** \"\ *n* -S [AmerSp, fr. Aymara] **:** any of several So. American plants of the genera *Baccharis* and *Lepidophyllum*

3**tola** \"\ *n* -S [AmerSp] **:** a burial mound of Ecuador or Peru

tol·a·ble \'täləbəl\ *adj* [by alter.] *dial* **:** TOLERABLE

to·lan \'tō,lan\ *also* **to·lane** \-lān\ *n* -S [ISV *tol-* + *-an* or *-ane*] **:** a white crystalline unsaturated hydrocarbon $C_6H_5C{\equiv}CC_6H_5$ obtained synthetically from stilbene **:** diphenyl-acetylene

tolbooth *var of* TOLLBOOTH

tol·bu·ta·mide \täl'byüd·ə,mīd, -məd\ *n* [*tol-* + *but-* + *amide*] **:** a crystalline sulfonamide $CH_3C_6H_4SO_2NHCONHC_4H_9$ that lowers the blood sugar level and is administered orally in the treatment of mild to moderate adult diabetes; 1-*n*-butyl-3-(*para*-tolyl-sulfonyl)-urea

told [ME *tolde* (past), *told* (past part.), fr. OE (northern and Midland dial.) *talde* (past), *getald* (past part.) — more at TELL] *past of* TELL

tol-de-rol \ˌtäldə'räl\ *n* -S [origin unknown] — used as a nonsense refrain in some old songs

tol·do \'tōl(ˌ)dō, 'täl-\ *n* -S [AmerSp, fr. Sp, awning, canopy, cloth or canvas wagon covering, fr. OSp, fr. MF *taud* canopy on a ship, prob. of Gmc origin; akin to MLG & MD *telt* tent — more at TILT] **:** any of various Central or So. American shelters (as a covered dance platform or an Indian skin hut)

1**tole** *var of* TOLL

2**tole** \'tōl\ *n* -S [F *tôle* sheet metal (esp. iron), fr. F dial. (Bordeaux area), table, slab, fr. L *tabula* board, tablet — more at TABLE] **:** a decorative japanned or painted tin or other metal finished in various colors (as black with gilt designs) and used esp. for trays, lamps, and boxes

1**to·le·dan** \tə'lēdən\ *adj, usu cap* [Sp *toledano,* fr. *Toledo,* Spain + Sp *-ano* -an] **1 a :** of, relating to, or characteristic of Toledo, Spain **b :** of, relating to, or characteristic of the people of Toledo **2** *also* **to·le·do·an** \-dəwən\ [*Toledo,* Ohio + E *-an*] **a :** of, relating to, or characteristic of Toledo, Ohio **b :** of, relating to, or characteristic of the people of Toledo

2**toledan** \"\ *n* -S *cap* **1 :** a native or inhabitant of Toledo, Spain **2** *also* **toledoan** \"\ **:** a native or resident of Toledo, Ohio

1**to·le·do** \tə'lē(ˌ)dō\ *n* -S *usu cap* [fr. *Toledo,* Spain] **:** a finely tempered sword of a kind made in Toledo, Spain

2**toledo** \"\ *adj, usu cap* [fr. *Toledo,* Ohio] **:** of or from the city of Toledo, Ohio ⟨a *Toledo* factory⟩ **:** of the kind or style prevalent in Toledo

tol·er·a·bil·i·ty \ˌtäl(ə)rə'biləd·ē, ˌtälər'b-, -lətē, -i\ *n* **:** the quality or state of being tolerable

1**tol·er·a·ble** \'täl(ə)rəbəl, -älərb-, *dial* -äləb-\ *adj* [ME *tollerabill,* fr. L *tolerabilis,* fr. *tolerare* to endure, put up with + *-abilis* -able — more at TOLERATE] **1 :** capable of being borne or endured **:** physically or morally supportable **:** BEARABLE ⟨a ~ compromise can be worked out —P.E.James⟩ ⟨the task . . . of making life secure and ~ for every class in the empire —John Buchan⟩ **2 a :** meeting some minimum standard of acceptability **:** fit to be countenanced or permitted **:** ALLOWABLE, SUFFERABLE ⟨socially ~ conduct⟩ ⟨there could be no ~ apology for injustice —Oscar Handlin⟩ ⟨a ~ paragraph must have gone through six or seven versions —J.M.Barzun⟩ **b :** of moderate worth, excellence, or magnitude **:** fairly good **:** merely passable **:** MEDIOCRE, MIDDLING ⟨the advantages of a ~ income —William Black⟩ ⟨bring lunar and solar times into ~, though not exact, harmony —J.G.Frazer⟩

2**tolerable** \"\ *adv, dial* **:** TOLERABLY

tol·er·a·ble·ness *n* -ES **:** the quality or state of being tolerable

tol·er·a·bly \-əblē, -li\ *adv* **:** in a tolerable manner **:** ALLOWABLY, BEARABLY

tol·er·ance \'täl(ə)rən(t)s\ *n* -S [ME *tolleraunce,* fr. MF *tolerance,* fr. L *tolerantia,* fr. *tolerant-, tolerans* (pres. part. of *tolerare* to endure, put up with) + *-ia* -y — more at TOLERATE] **1 a :** capacity to endure pain or hardship **:** ENDURANCE, FORTITUDE, STAMINA **b (1) :** the ability to endure the effects of a drug or food or of physiologic insults whether on single or repeated intake or experience without showing unfavorable effects ⟨the degree of work ~ of a diseased heart⟩ ⟨a diabetic's ~ for sugar before glycosuria is produced⟩ ⟨an addict's increasing ~ for a drug, requiring increasing doses to produce a desired effect⟩ ⟨a ~ dose of radiation⟩ **(2) :** relative capacity of an organism to grow or thrive in the presence of one or more unfavorable environmental conditions ⟨many forest understory plants exhibit a high degree of shade ~⟩ ⟨varying heat ~*s* of different strains of rye⟩ **c :** the maximum amount of a pesticide residue that may lawfully remain on or in food expressed in parts per million by weight **2 a :** a permissive or liberal attitude toward beliefs or practices differing from or conflicting with one's own **:** sympathy or indulgence for diversity in thought or conduct **:** breadth of spirit or of viewpoint ⟨the basis of ~ is the knowledge that there may be a measure of truth in the other camp —*Times Lit. Supp.*⟩ — compare BIGOTRY **b :** the act of allowing something **:** TOLERATION ⟨those years represented a low in our standards of ethics and the peak in our ~ for corruption —Estes Kefauver⟩ **3 :** the allowable deviation from a standard: as **a :** the amount that coins either singly or in lots are legally allowed to vary above or below the standard of weight or fineness **b :** the range of variation permitted in maintaining a specified dimension in machining a piece **:** the difference between the upper and the lower limits between which a size must be held ⟨the blueprint called for a diameter of 0.255 inch plus or minus 0.0002, giving a manufacturing ~ of 0.0004 inch⟩ — compare ALLOWANCE **c :** a percentage difference allowed between a shipment's actual and its billed weight to compensate for variation between scales or between methods of weighing

tol·er·ant \-nt\ *adj* [F *tolérant,* fr. L *tolerant-, tolerans,* pres. part.] **1 :** showing understanding or leniency for conduct or ideas differing from or conflicting with one's own **:** bearing contrariety mildly **:** ENDURING, FORBEARING, INDULGENT ⟨he was stoical under pain, serene under annoyance, and ~ of everything save injustice —Agnes Repplier⟩ **2 a** *of an organism* **:** exhibiting environmental tolerance; *esp, of a plant* **:** capable of growth in shade **b :** capable of enduring or resisting the effect of a drug or a physiologic shock **syn** see FORBEARING

tol·er·ant·ly *adv* **:** in a tolerant manner

tol·er·ate \'tälə,rāt, *usu* -ād·+V\ *vt* -ED/-ING/-S [L *toleratus,* past part. of *tolerare* to endure, put up with; akin to OE *tholian* to endure, put up with, OHG *dolēn,* ON *thola,* Goth *thulan* to endure, put up with, L *tollere* to lift up, take away, *latus* carried (suppletive past part. of *ferre* to bear), Gk *tlēnai* to bear, Skt *tulā* balance, scale, weight; basic meaning: to lift, bear] **1 a :** to endure or resist the action of (a drug, food, or physiologic factor) without grave or lasting injury ⟨a premature baby . . . does not ~ fats very well —H.R.Litchfield & L.H.Dembo⟩ ⟨the average pilot cannot ~ an average of over 85 hours in the air per month without eventually showing evidence of deterioration —H.G.Armstrong⟩ **b :** to thrive despite (something unfavorable in the environment) **2 :** to permit the existence or practice of **:** allow without prohibition or hindrance **:** make no effort to prevent ⟨a legitimate government — that is, one that rests on consent — can ~ an opposition —Lindsay Rogers⟩ **3 :** to endure with forbearance or restraint **:** put up with **:** BEAR ⟨recommends that we should learn to ~ one another —A.J.Franck⟩ ⟨public opinion . . . will ~ almost anything —Christopher Hollis⟩ ⟨~ the offstage egotism and eccentricities of artists —John Mason Brown⟩ **syn** see BEAR

tol·er·a·tion \ˌ==ˈrāshən\ *n* -S [MF, fr. L *toleration-, toleratio,* fr. *toleratus* (past part. of *tolerare*) + *-ion-, -io* -ion] **1** *obs* **:** a legal permission or authorization **:** LICENSE **2 a :** the act or practice of tolerating something **b :** a government policy of permitting forms of religious belief and worship not officially favored, established, or approved **c :** TOLERANCE 2a **3 :** TOLERANCE 1b(1)

tol·er·a·tion·ist \-shənəst\ *n* -S **:** one that practices or promotes toleration

tol·er·a·tor \'==ˌrād·ə(r), -ātə-\ *n* -S **:** one that tolerates

tole·tan \tə'lētən, 'tälətən\ *adj, usu cap* [L *Toletanus,* fr. *Toletum* (Toledo), Spain + L *-anus* -an] **:** of or relating to Toledo, Spain **:** TOLEDAN

toleware \'=,=\ *n* [2*tole* + *ware*] **:** ware made of tole ⟨a ~ tea caddy⟩

tol·gua·cha \tōl'wächə\ *or* **to·loa·che** \tōl'wächē\ *n* -S [MexSp *toloache, toloachi,* fr. Nahuatl *toloatzin,* fr. *toloa* to nod + *-tzin,* honorific particle; fr. the reverence borne such plants by the Indians] **:** any of several plants of the genus *Datura; esp* **:** a narcotic annual herb (*D. meteloides*) used ceremonially by some California Indians

tol·i·dine \'tälə,dēn, -ˌdən\ *n* -S [ISV *tol-* + *-idine*] **:** any of several isomeric aromatic diamines $[-C_6H_3(CH_3)NH_2]_2$ that are homologues of benzidine and made from the nitrotoluenes by alkaline reduction: as **a :** a pearly crystalline compound made from *ortho*-nitrotoluene and used as a dye intermediate and in chemical analysis (as in testing for free chlorine after chlorination of water because of the intense blue color it gives with chlorine); 3,3′-dimethyl-benzidine — called also *ortho=tolidine* **b :** a crystalline compound made from *meta*-nitrotoluene and used as a dye intermediate; 2,2′-dimethyl-benzidine — called also *meta-tolidine*

tol·ite \'tä,līt\ *n* -S [ISV *tol-* + *-ite*] **:** TRINITROTOLUENE

1**toll** \'tōl\ *n* -S *often attrib* [ME *toll, tol,* fr. OE *toll;* akin to OFris *tolen, tolene* toll, OS *tolna,* OHG *zol,* ON *tollr;* all fr. a prehistoric WGmc-NGmc word borrowed fr. (assumed) VL *tolonium,* alter. of LL *telonium* customhouse, fr. Gk *telōnion,* fr. *telōnēs* collector of tolls or taxes, fr. *telos* tax, tribute; akin to Gk *tlēnai* to bear — more at TOLERATE] **1 :** a tax or fee paid for some liberty or privilege (as of passing over a highway or bridge or using a ferry, of keeping a booth or vending goods in a fair or market, or of importing or exporting goods) ⟨higher bridge and tunnel ~*s* —*Better Homes & Gardens*⟩ **2 a :** the right to take toll **b :** the former right of an English lord to levy a tallage or tax upon his villeins **3 :** a compensation taken for services rendered: as **a** *dial* **:** a portion of grain taken by a miller as his fee **b :** a charge for transportation, conveyance, or use of facilities (as of a port) **c :** a charge for a long-distance telephone call **4 :** the cost in loss or suffering at which something is achieved **:** damage done **:** EXACTION ⟨the flood took a heavy ~ —*Amer. Guide Series: Ind.*⟩ ⟨the large emotional ~ which expatriation usually exacts —Aline B. Saarinen⟩ ⟨defense takes an enormous ~ of money and manpower —Denis Healey⟩

2**toll** \"\ *vb* -ED/-ING/-S [ME *tollen,* fr. *tol, toll,* n.] *vi* **1 :** to take or levy toll **2** *obs* **:** to enter a horse in the tollbook of a market as for sale — used with *for* **~** *vt* **1 a :** to exact part of as a toll or duty ⟨~*ed* his tenant's crops⟩ **b :** to take (something) as toll **2 :** to exact a toll from (someone) **:** impose a levy on

3**toll** *or* **tole** \"\ *vb* -ED/-ING/-S [ME *tollen, tolen;* akin to ME *tullen, tillen* to attract, entice — more at TILL] *vt* **1 :** to lure along **:** ATTRACT, ENTICE ⟨I'll shoot the man that ~*s* her off . . . a girl what's been learned to work and mind —Emmett Gowen⟩ ⟨wild mares on the ranges . . . had ~*ed* off 300 head of horses and mules from his 1500 guarded animals —J.F. Dobie⟩ ⟨the coal-oil lantern . . . would surely ~ any murdering redskins within miles —Mari Sandoz⟩ **2 :** to lure (game) in any of various ways **:** DECOY ⟨they saw several loons and ~*ed* them by running towards them hallooing and waving a handkerchief, at which sight and cry the loon immediately swam towards them, until within 20 yards —J.J.Audubon⟩ **3 :** to scatter (bait) for attracting fish **:** CHUM **4 :** to lead or draw (domestic animals) in a desired direction (as by means of a bellwether or a lure) ⟨she had ~*ed* the young turkeys into the yard —Mary King⟩ ⟨~*ed* the sheep into the barn —E.B. White⟩ **~** *vi* **:** to respond to tolling **:** admit of being tolled ⟨these ducks ~ the most readily of all⟩

4**toll** \"\ *vb* -ED/-ING/-S [ME *tollen,* perh. fr. *tollen* to attract, entice] *vt* **1 a :** to give signal or announcement of **:** SOUND ⟨the clock ~*s* the hour⟩ ⟨the curfew ~*s* the knell of parting day —Thomas Gray⟩ **b :** to ring a toll for **:** announce by tolling ⟨~*ed* the president's death⟩ **c :** to call (someone) to or from a place or occasion ⟨forlorn! the very word is like a bell to ~ me back from thee to my sole self —John Keats⟩ **2 :** to cause the sounding of (a bell) in a controlled and regular manner by pulling a rope, striking with a hammer, or manipulating the clapper usu. to announce a church service or other public occasion or a death or funeral or to give an alarm — compare PEAL **~** *vi* **1 :** to sound with slow measured strokes ⟨never send to know for whom the bell ~*s;* it ~*s* for thee —John Donne⟩ **2 :** to cause a bell to toll

5**toll** \"\ *n* -S [ME, fr. *tollen,* v.] **1 a :** an act or instance of tolling **b :** a single stroke on a bell **2 :** the sound made by a toll

6**toll** \"\ *vt* -ED/-ING/-S [ME *tollen,* fr. AF *toller, touller,* fr. L *tollere* to lift up, take away — more at TOLERATE] **1 :** to take away **:** make null **:** REMOVE ⟨~ the statute of limitations⟩

toll·age \'tōlij, -lēj\ *n* -S [1*toll* + *-age*] **1 :** toll or payment or exaction of it **2** *obs* **:** TALLAGE

toll bait *n* [3*toll*] **:** chopped bait thrown out to attract fish

toll bar *n* [1*toll*] **:** a bar or gate used to stop passengers at a tollhouse

toll board *n* [1*toll*] **:** a telephone switchboard for making toll= call connections

tollbook *n* [1*toll* + *book*] **1** *obs* **:** a register of goods for sale at an old English market or fair **2** *obs* **:** a tax register

toll·booth *or* **tol·booth** \'tōl,=, *Scot* 'tō(l),= *or* 'täl,=\ *n* [ME *tolbothe, tollbothe,* fr. *tol, toll* toll + *bothe* booth — more at BOOTH] **1 :** a booth or other office where tolls are paid **:** CUSTOMHOUSE, TOLLHOUSE **2** *chiefly Scot* **:** a town or market hall **3** *Scot* **:** JAIL, PRISON

toll bridge *n* [1*toll*] **:** a bridge at which a toll is charged for crossing

toll call *n* [1*toll*] **:** a long-distance telephone call at charges above a local rate

toll collector *n* [1*toll*] **1 :** one who collects tolls or taxes of any kind **2 :** an indicator showing the number of persons paying toll at a tollhouse **3 :** a device automatically separating a miller's toll from his customer's grist

toll dish *n* [1*toll*] **:** a measure for the miller's share of the grain he grinds for a customer

1**toll·er** \'tōlə(r)\ *n* -S [ME, fr. OE *tollere,* fr. *toll* + *-ere* -er] **:** TOLL COLLECTOR 1, 3

2**toller** \"\ *n* -S [3*toll* + *-er*] **:** DECOY; *esp* **:** a dog trained to lure ducks

tollgate \'=,=\ *n* [1*toll* + *gate*] **:** a point usu. at a tollhouse where vehicles pause to pay toll for using a turnpike, tunnel, or bridge

tollgatherer \'=,===\ *n* [ME *tol gaderer,* fr. *tol, toll* toll + *gaderer* gatherer — more at GATHERER] **:** a collector of tolls or taxes **:** PUBLICAN

tollhouse \'=,=\ *n* [ME *tolhowse,* fr. *tol, toll* + *hous, howse* house — more at HOUSE] **:** a house or booth where tolls are taken (as on a highway or bridge)

toll in *vi* [4*toll*] **:** to call people to a church service by tolling

tolling *pres part of* TOLL

toll·man \'=,mən\ *n, pl* **tollmen** [1*toll* + *man*] **:** a collector of tolls (as on a highway or bridge) **:** a tollhouse keeper

tol-lol \(')täl'läl\ *adj* [alter. of *tolerable*] **:** PASSABLE, TOLERABLE

tollon *var of* TOYON

toll road *n* [1*toll*] **:** a road for the use of which a toll is collected

tolls *pl of* TOLL, *pres 3d sing of* TOLL

toll traverse *or* **toll travers** *n* **:** a toll paid in England for passage or traffic over the private property (as the ground, bridge, or ferry) of another

tollway \'=,=\ *n* [1*toll* + *way*] **:** TOLL ROAD

1**tol·ly** \'tälē, -li\ *n* -ES [alter. of *tallow*] **:** CANDLE

2**tolly** \"\ *n* -ES [native name in southern Africa] *southern Africa* **:** a young ox **:** STEER

tol·ly·gunge \'tälē,gənj\ *adj, usu cap* [fr. *Tollygunge,* India] **:** of or from the city of Tollygunge, India **:** of the kind or style prevalent in Tollygunge

toloache *var of* TOLGUACHA

tolonium chloride *n* [*tolonium,* NL, fr. *tol-* + *-onium*] **:** toluidine blue for medicinal use

tol·o·wa \'täləwə\ *n, pl* **tolowa** *or* **tolowas** *usu cap* **1 a :** an Athapaskan people of northwestern California **b :** a member of such people **2 :** a language of the Tolowa people

toloxy- *comb form* [*tol-* + *oxy-*] **:** any of three univalent radicals $CH_3C_6H_4O-$ composed of a tolyl radical united with oxygen **:** tolyl-oxy ⟨*toloxy*-propane-diol⟩ — compare PHENOXY-

tol·ses·ter \'tōl,sestə(r), ='==\ *n* -S [ME, fr. OE, fr. *tol* toll + *sester,* a measure, fr. OE, fr. L *sextarius,* fr. *sextus* sixth + *-arius* -ary — more at TOLL, SEXT] **:** a toll paid to the feudal lord by a tenant for liberty to brew and sell ale

tol·sey *or* **tol·zey** \'tōlzi\ *n* -S [ME *tolsell, tolsey,* fr. *tol, toll* toll + *-sell, -sey* (prob. fr. OE *sele* hall, house) — more at TOLL, SALOON] **1** *Brit* **:** TOWN HALL **2** *Brit* **:** a borough law court

1**tol·stoy·an** *also* **tol·stoi·an** \'tōlz,tōiən, 'täl-,'tōl-, -l,st-, ='==\ *adj, usu cap* [Count Lev (Leo) Nikolaevich *Tolstoy* (*Tolstoi*) †1910 Russ. novelist and religious philosopher + E *-an*] **:** of, relating to, or characteristic of Tolstoi or his writings

2**tolstoyan** *also* **tolstoian** \"\ *n* -S *usu cap* **:** a follower of Tolstoi, his philosophy of art, or his religious and moral doctrines

tol·stoy·ism \-ōi,izəm\ *n* -S *usu cap* [L. *Tolstoy* + E *-ism*] **:** the doctrines or practices of the Tolstoyans

tol·stoy·ist \-ōiəst\ *n* -S *usu cap* [L. *Tolstoy* + E *-ist*] **:** TOLSTOYAN

1**tolt** \'tōlt\ *n* -S [AF *tolte,* fr. ML *tolta* act of taking away, fr. L *tollere* to take away — more at TOLERATE] **:** a writ by which a cause pending in a court baron is removed into a county court

2**tolt** \"\ *n* -S [origin unknown] **:** an isolated peak rising abruptly from a plain in Newfoundland

tol·tec \'tōl,tek, 'täl-\ *also* **tol·teca** \=ˈtekə, -'tākə\ *n, pl* **toltec** *or* **toltecs** *usu cap* [Sp *tolteca,* of AmerInd origin] **1 :** a Nahuatlan people of central and southern Mexico **2 :** a member of the Toltec people — **tol·tecan** \(')=ˈtekən, -ˈtāk-\ *adj, usu cap*

to·lu \tə'lü, tō'-\ *or* **tolu balsam** *n* -S [Sp *tolú,* fr. Santiago de *Tolú,* Colombia] **:** BALSAM OF TOLU

tolu- — see TOL-

tolu·aldehyde \ˌtäl(ˌ)yü+\ *n* [*tol-* + *aldehyde*] **:** any of four aldehydes C_7H_7CHO that give the corresponding toluic acids on oxidation — compare PHENYLACETALDEHYDE

tol·u·ate \'tälyə,wāt\ *n* -S [ISV *tol-* + *-ate*] **:** a salt or ester of a toluic acid

tol·u·ene \-ə,wēn\ *n* -S [ISV *tol-* + *-ene*] **:** a light mobile liquid aromatic hydrocarbon $C_6H_5CH_3$ that resembles benzene but is less volatile, less flammable, and less toxic, that was obtained orig. by distilling balsam of tolu, that is produced commercially from light oils from coke-oven gas and coal tar and esp. since World War II from petroleum (as by dehydrogenation of methyl-cyclohexane or by the reforming of dimethylcyclopentane), and that is used chiefly as a solvent, as a raw material for trinitrotoluene, dyes, pharmaceuticals, and other organic compounds, and as a blending agent for gasoline esp. for use in aviation because of its high antiknock property — called also *methylbenzene*

toluene diisocyanate *n* **:** TOLYLENE DIISOCYANATE

toluenesulfonic acid \ˌ===;=;==-\ *n* [*toluene* + *sulfonic*] **:** any of three isomeric crystalline oily liquid strong acids $CH_3C_6H_4SO_3H$ of which the para and ortho isomers are obtained in a mixture by sulfonation of toluene and used in organic synthesis (as of dyes)

toluenesulfonyl \ˌ==;=;==\ *n* [*toluene* + *sulfonyl*] **:** any of three radicals $CH_3C_6H_4SO_2-$ derived from the toluenesulfonic acids; *esp* **:** the radical of *para*-toluenesulfonic acid — compare TOSYL

toluenesulfonyl chloride *n* **:** any of three solid or liquid acid chlorides $CH_3C_6H_4SO_2Cl$ made from the corresponding toluenesulfonic acids or from toluene and chlorosulfonic acid; *esp* **:** the crystalline para isomer used in making chloramine-T and *para*-toluenesulfonyl derivatives (as of amines and sugars)

tolu·ic acid \tə'lüik, 'tälyəwik-\ *n* [ISV *tol-* + *-ic*] **:** any of four isomeric crystalline carboxylic acids C_7H_7COOH derived from toluene and obtainable in the case of the ortho, meta, and para isomers $CH_3C_6H_4COOH$ by oxidation of the three corresponding xylenes — see PHENYLACETIC ACID

to·lu·i·dide \tə'lüə,dīd\ *n* -S [*toluidine* + *-ide*] **:** an amide analogous to an anilide in which hydrogen of the amido group is replaced by tolyl **:** an *N*-acyl derivative of toluidine

to·lu·i·dine \-,dēn, -ˌdən\ *n* -S [ISV *tol-* + *-idine*] **:** any of three isomeric amino derivatives $CH_3C_6H_4NH_2$ of toluene that are the ortho, meta, and para methyl homologues of aniline, that are usu. obtained by reducing the corresponding nitrotoluenes, and that are used chiefly as dye intermediates

toluidine blue *also* **toluidine blue O** *n, often cap T&B* **:** a basic dye or its chloride of the thiazine class that is closely related chemically to methylene blue and is used chiefly as a biological stain and in medicine to treat hemorrhage (as in functional uterine bleeding) because of its ability to inhibit the anticoagulant effect of heparin

toluidine red toner *or* **toluidine red** *also* **toluidine toner** *n, sometimes cap both Ts&R* **:** any of a group of red organic pigments that are related to the para reds but are more permanent — see DYE table I (under *Pigment Red 3*)

tol·u·if·era \ˌtälyə'wifərə\ [NL, fr. Sp *tolú* + L *-ifera* (neut. pl. of *-ifer* -iferous)] *syn of* MYROXYLON

tol·u·ol \'tälyə,wōl, -,wōl\ *n* -S [*tol-* + *-ol*] **:** TOLUENE — used esp. of commercial grades

tol·u·quinone \ˌtälyə+\ *n* [ISV *tol-* + *quinone*] **:** a methyl homologue $CH_3C_6H_3O_2$ of quinone; *esp* **:** a yellow crystalline compound made by oxidation of *ortho-* or *meta*-toluidine; 2-methyl-*para*-quinone

tolu tree *n* **:** a widely distributed usu. medium-sized tropical American tree (*Myroxylon balsamum*) that yields balsam of

Peru and balsam of Tolu and a fragrant durable rather hard showily figured yellowish to reddish or purplish wood which takes a fine polish and is used for high-grade furniture and cabinetwork

tol·u·yl·ene \'tälyə,wə,lēn\ *n* -S [ISV *tol-* + *-yl* + *-ene*] **1** : STILBENE **2** : TOLYLENE

toluylene blue *n, often cap T&B* : an indamine dye derived from tolylenediamine (sense a) and used as an oxidation-reduction indicator and biological stain

toluylene orange G *n, usu cap T&O* : a direct dye — see DYE table I (under *Direct Orange 6*)

tol·yl \'tä,lil, -lēl\ *n* -S [ISV *tol-* + *-yl*] **1** : any of three univalent radicals $CH_3C_6H_4$— derived from toluene by removal of one hydrogen atom from a carbon atom in the benzene ring in a position ortho, meta, or para to the methyl group — called also *cresyl;* used in the system adopted by the International Union of Pure and Applied Chemistry **2** : BENZYL — used with an initial Greek alpha ⟨α-tolyl⟩

tol·yl·ene \'tälə,lēn\ *n* -S [*tolyl* + *-ene*] : any of six bivalent radicals $CH_3C_6H_5$< derived from toluene by removal of two hydrogen atoms from carbon atoms in the benzene ring : methyl-phenylene

tolylene·diamine \"+\ *n* [*tolylene* + *diamine*] : any of six isomeric crystalline bases $CH_3C_6H_3(NH_2)_2$ derived from toluene of which some are used as dye intermediates: as **a** : an isomer obtained by reduction of dinitrotoluene (sense a); toluene-2,4-diamine — called also *meta-tolylenediamine* **b** : an isomer obtained by reduction of aminoazo-toluene; toluene-2,5-diamine — called also *para-tolylenediamine;* see SAFRANINE b

tolylene diisocyanate *n* : any of six isomeric esters $CH_3C_6H_3(NCO)_2$ of isocyanic acid or a mixture of them; *esp* : a liquid isomer made by reaction of tolylenediamine (sense a) and phosgene and used by itself or in a mixture with another meta isomer in making polyurethanes; 4-methyl-*meta*-phenylene diisocyanate

tol·y·peu·tes \,tälə'pyüd·(,)ēz\ *n, cap* [NL, fr. Gk *tolypeuein* to wind wool into a ball for spinning, fr. *tolypē* ball of wool; perh. akin to Gk *tylos* callus, knob — more at THOLE] : a genus of So. American armadillos containing the apar — **tol·y·peu·tine** \;==;pyü,tīn, -üd·ən\ *adj or n*

tol·y·po·sporium \,==,pō'spōrēəm\ *n, cap* [NL, fr. Gk *tolypē* + NL *-o-* + *-sporium*] : a genus of smut fungi that chiefly attack grasses — see LONG SMUT

tolzey *var of* TOLSEY

tom \'täm\ *n* -S [fr. *Tom,* nickname for *Thomas*] **1** *usu cap, obs* : TOM O'BEDLAM **2** : the male of various animals ⟨a ~ swan⟩: as **a** : a male cat : TOMCAT **b** : a male turkey : TURKEY-COCK **3** : a distance piece or small shore (as between frames in shipbuilding) **4** : a heavy lead weight by means of whose descent the bottom of a purse seine is puckered together **5** : LONG TOM 3

tom *abbr* tome

toma \'tōmə\ *n, pl* **toma** *or* **tomas** *usu cap* **1** : a people of adjacent parts of Liberia and Guinea **2** : a member of the Toma people

-to·ma \d·əmə, təmə\ *n comb form* -S [NL, fr. fem. of *-tomus* cutting, cut, segmented — more at -TOME] : animal having a (specified) type of segmentation — in generic names esp. of insects ⟨*Triatoma*⟩

¹tom·a·hawk \'tämə,hȯk *also* -mē,- *or* -mi,-\ *n* -S [fr. *tomahack* (in some Algonquian language of Virginia)] **1** : a light ax used both as a missile and as a hand weapon by the No. American Indians **2 a** : the stone hatchet of the Australian aborigines **b** : an ordinary hatchet

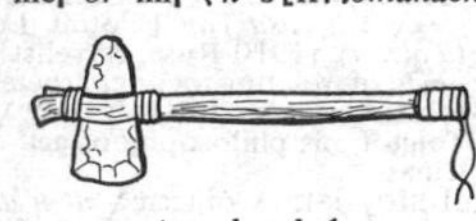
tomahawk 1

²tomahawk \"\ *vt* -ED/-ING/-S **1** : to cut, strike, or kill with a tomahawk **2** : to criticize or attack savagely : assail mercilessly ⟨battered, hacked, scalped, ~*ed* as I have been for three years —Hannah More⟩ **3** *Austral* : to cut (sheep) in unskillful shearing — **tom·a·hawk·er** \-kə(r)\ *n* -S

to·mal·ley \tə'mal·ē, 'täm,al·ē\ *n* -S [of Cariban origin; akin to Galibi *tumali* sauce of lobster or crab livers] : the liver of the lobster

¹to·man \tə'män\ *n* -S [Per *tōmān, tūmān,* of Mongol origin] **1** *also* **tu·man** \tə'm-\ **a** : an old Persian unit of monetary value equal at one time to 10,000 dinars **b** : a Persian gold coin issued up to 1927 **2** : a military division of 10,000 men among the Mongols and Tatars

²tom·an \'tämən\ *n* -S [ScGael, dim. of *tom* hill; akin to MIr *tomm* hill — more at TOMB] *Scot* : a mound or hillock

tom and jerry *n, pl* **tom and jerries** *usu cap T&J* [after Corinthian *Tom & Jerry* Hawthorne, chief characters of *Life in London* (1821) by Pierce Egan †1849 Eng. sportswriter] : a hot sweetened drink consisting of rum, water, and spices (as cinnamon and cloves) mixed with the yolk and white of an egg beaten separately and topped with nutmeg

to·mat·i·dine \tə'mad·ə,dēn\ *n* -S [*tomat*ine + *-idine*] : a crystalline steroid amine $C_{27}H_{45}NO_2$ obtained by hydrolysis of tomatine and isolated from the roots of the tomato plant

to·ma·ti·llo \,tōmə'tē(,)(y)ō, -ēl(,)yō\ *n, pl* **tomatilloes** *or* **tomatillos** [Sp, dim. of *tomate* tomato] : any of several solanaceous plants with fruits resembling small tomatoes: as **a** : a ground cherry (*Physalis ixocarpa*) of Mexico and the southern U. S. with an edible purplish viscid fruit **b** : JERUSALEM CHERRY

tom·a·tine \'tämə,tēn\ *n* -S [ISV *tomato* + *-ine*] : a crystalline antibiotic glycosidic alkaloid $C_{50}H_{83}NO_{21}$ that is active against fungi and is obtained esp. from the juice of the stems and leaves of tomato plants resistant to wilt

to·ma·to \tə'mā|d·(,)ō, |(,)tō, |d·ə, |tə *also* -mä| *or* -ma| *sometimes* -mal\ *n* -ES [alter. (prob. influenced by *potato*) of earlier *tomate,* fr. Sp, fr. Nahuatl *tomatl*] **1 a** : a plant of the genus *Lycopersicon; specif* : a So. American perennial herb (*L. esculentum*) widely cultivated usu. as an annual for its fruit and having interruptedly pinnate leaves and yellow flowers **b** : the large rounded or oblate pulpy berry of the tomato plant that is usu. red or yellow when ripe — see FRUIT illustration **2** *or* **tomato red** : a variable color averaging a deep reddish orange **3** *slang* **a** : WOMAN, GIRL **b** : PROSTITUTE

tomato black rot *n* : NAILHEAD SPOT

tomato blight *n* **1** : EARLY BLIGHT a **2** *or* **tomato yellows** : WESTERN TOMATO BLIGHT

tomato canker *n* : a bacterial canker of tomatoes caused by a spore-forming bacterium (*Corynebacterium michiganense*) and characterized by elongated brown cankers on the stems and sudden wilting of nearly mature plants and by spotting of the maturing fruits

tomato eggplant *n* : a tropical annual herb (*Solanum integrifolium*) sometimes grown for its white flowers and scarlet or yellow inedible fruit that resembles the fruit of the eggplant but is much smaller

tomato fruitworm *n* : CORN EARWORM — used esp. when the larva is infesting tomatoes

tomato gall *n* : a large irregular yellowish-green or reddish gall on the grapevine produced by a small two-winged fly (*Lasioptera vitis*)

tomato hornworm *n* : a caterpillar that is the larva of a hawkmoth (*Manduca quinquemaculata*), greatly resembles the tobacco hornworm, and feeds destructively on tomato, tobacco, and other solanaceous plants

tomato pinworm *n* : a pinworm that is the larva of a gelechiid moth (*Keiferia lycopersicella*) and that is an important pest of tomatoes esp. in parts of the western U. S.

tomato psyllid *n* : a psyllid bug (*Paratrioza cockerelli*) that is a pest on tomatoes and potatoes in parts of the western U. S.

tomato russet mite *or* **tomato mite** *n* : a widely distributed mite (*Vasates destructor*) that feeds on tomato leaves causing them to turn a russet color

tomato sphinx *n* : TOBACCO HAWKMOTH

tomato streak *n* : a virus disease of tomatoes, potatoes, peas, and a wide range of other plants believed to result from a mixed infection of potato mosaic and tomato mosaic and characterized by wilting and dark elongated streaks on stems and petioles and bronzing and necrosis of the leaves at first in spots but later in general — called also *spotted wilt*

tomato wilt *n* : either of two diseases of the tomato marked by wilting: **a** : a destructive disease caused by a fungus (*Fusarium lycopersici*) **b** : a disease caused by a bacterium (*Pseudomonas solanacearum*)

tomato worm *n* : TOBACCO HORNWORM — used esp. when the larva is feeding on tomato

¹tomb \'tüm\ *n* -S [ME *toumbe, tombe,* fr. AF *tumbe,* fr. LL *tumba* sepulchral mound, fr. Gk *tymbos;* akin to MIr *tomm* hill, L *tumēre* to be swollen — more at THUMB] **1 a** : a cavity in which a corpse is deposited : GRAVE **b** : any place of interment : the last resting place **2** : a house, chamber, or vault formed wholly or partly in the earth or entirely above ground for the reception of the dead ⟨was buried in a ~ in the institution he had founded —J.F.A.Jackson⟩ **3 a** : a monument (as in a church) erected to enclose the body and preserve the name and memory of the dead **b** : CENOTAPH **4** : a building or structure that resembles a tomb ⟨big, windowless stone buildings aptly known as ~*s* —*Christian Science Monitor*⟩

²tomb \"\ *vt* -ED/-ING/-S [ME *toumben,* fr. *toumbe* tomb] : to place or enclose in or as if in a tomb : BURY, ENTOMB

tom·bac *also* **tom·bak** \'täm,bak\ *or* **tam·bac** \'tam-\ *n* -S [*tombac* fr. F, fr. D *tombak; tombak* fr. D, fr. Malay *tĕmbaga* copper, prob. fr. Skt *tāmraka,* fr. *tāmra* dark red, copper; *tambac* fr. Siamese, fr. Malay *tĕmbaga*] : an alloy consisting essentially of copper and zinc and sometimes arsenic and used esp. for cheap jewelry and gilding

tomb·al \'tüməl\ *adj* [¹*tomb* + *-al*] : of, relating to, or serving as a tomb

tomb bat *n* : any of several Old World bats constituting the genus *Taphozous* of the family Emballonuridae and living in caves and tombs; *esp* : a common Egyptian bat (*T. perforatus*)

tom·bé \(')täm¦bā\ *adj* [F, fr. past part. of *tomber* to fall, fr. (assumed) VL *tumbare* to fall with a thump, tumble, of imit. origin] : fallen down — used of a ballet movement with accent on the descent

tomb·less \'tümləs\ *adj* : having no tomb

tom·bo·la \'tämbələ\ *n* -S [It, fr. *tombolare* to tumble, fr. *tombare* to fall, fr. (assumed) VL *tumbare* to tumble, fall with a thump, of imit. origin] *chiefly Brit* : HOUSE 15

tom·bo·lo \'tämbə,lō\ *n* -S [It, fr. L *tumulus* mound — more at TUMULUS] : a sand or gravel bar that connects an island with the mainland or with another island

tom·boy \'täm,bȯi\ *n* [*tom* + *boy*] **1** *obs* : STRUMPET, HARLOT **2** : a girl of boyish behavior : HOYDEN ⟨~ recalls the memory of a girl who could swim and fish, ride a bicycle, play tennis and baseball, shoot marbles, and win a snow fight as handily as any boy —Josephine Lawrence⟩

tom·boy·ful \-ōifəl\ *adj* : TOMBOYISH

tom·boy·ish \-ōi·ish\ *adj* : being or playing the tomboy : HOYDENISH ⟨even at her most ~, she had been dainty and fastidious —C.B.Kelland⟩ — **tom·boy·ish·ly** *adv* — **tom·boy·ish·ness** *n*

tombstone \'=,=\ *n* [*tomb* + *stone*] **1** : an inscribed stone placed horizontally over a grave : LEDGER **2** : GRAVESTONE, HEADSTONE

tombstone advertisement *n* [so called fr. its staid unexciting character] : a newspaper advertisement of the offering of a new issue of a security that does not give any specific information about it

¹tomcat \'=,=\ *n* [*tom* + *cat*] **1** : a male cat **2** *slang* : one who tomcats

²tomcat \"\ *vi, slang* : CAT 2 — often used with *around*

tomcat clover *n* : an annual clover (*Trifolium tridentatum*) of western No. America with usu. tridentate calyx lobes

tomcod \'=,=\ *n* [*tom* + *cod*] **1** : any of several small fishes of the genus *Microgadus* closely resembling the common codfish except in size: as **a** : a fish (*M. tomcod*) of the cold and temperate Atlantic coast that is olive to gray above and lighter below, has the ventral fins prolonged as filaments and a convex tail, and is sometimes taken by anglers **b** : a very similar fish (*M. proximus*) of the Pacific coast that is a minor sport fish and an excellent food fish though not fished commercially **2** : any of various croakers of the Pacific coast; *esp* : a kingfish (*Genyonemus lineatus*)

tom col·lins \-'kälənz\ *n, usu cap T&C* [fr. the name *Tom Collins*] : a collins with a base of gin

tom, dick, and harry *n, usu cap T&D&H* [fr. the names *Tom* (nickname for *Thomas*), *Dick* (nickname for *Richard*) & *Harry* (nickname for *Henry*)] : persons taken at random : the common run of humanity : EVERYBODY, EVERYONE — often used with *every* and disparagingly ⟨he hated the human race en masse, but truly loved *Tom, Dick, and Harry* —J.M. Barzun⟩ ⟨the government draws it all out and pays it to *Tom, Dick, and Harry* for relief —J.T.Flynn⟩ ⟨our columns thrown wide open for the views of every *Tom, Dick, and Harry* in the land —A.J.Russell⟩ ⟨an incessant helper of every *Tom, Dick, and Harry* who is in need —*Current Biog.*⟩

tome \'tōm\ *n* -S [MF or L; MF *tome,* fr. L *tomus,* fr. Gk *tomos* slice, section, roll of papyrus, tome, fr. *temnein* to cut; akin to Gk *tendein* to gnaw, L *tondēre* to shear, crop, MIr *tennaid* he splits] **1** : a volume forming part of a larger work ⟨a history in ten ~*s*⟩ **2** : BOOK ⟨over 259,000,000 copies of pocket-size ~*s* were printed —J.K.Hutchens⟩; *esp* : a large ponderous or a scholarly volume ⟨heavy books of reference or other large ~*s* that must stand much wear —Edith Diehl⟩ ⟨a huge twenty-seven-pound ~ as compared with the seven-and-a-half-pound volume —John Lawler⟩ ⟨adults often leave heavier ~*s* for cooler weather to dip into light summer fare —*N.Y. Times Bk. Rev.*⟩ ⟨two lines of poetry often tell us more, give us more, than the weightiest ~ of an erudite —Henry Miller⟩ ⟨waded conscientiously through many formidable ~*s* —W.S.Maugham⟩

-tome \,tōm\ *n comb form* -S [NL *-tomus,* fr. *-tomus* cutting, cut, segmented, fr. Gk *-tomos,* fr. *temnein* to cut] **1** : part : section ⟨angio*tome*⟩ ⟨gono*tome*⟩ **2** : cutting instrument ⟨micro*tome*⟩ ⟨pharyngo*tome*⟩

to·men·tel·la \,tōmən·'telə\ *n, cap* [NL, fr. L *tomentum* cushion stuffing + *-ella* — more at TOMENTUM] : a genus of fungi (family Thelephoraceae) having basidia borne on a cobwebby layer of hyphae

to·men·tose \tə'men,tōs, 'tōmən-\ *adj* [NL *tomentosus,* fr. L *tomentum* cushion stuffing + *-osus* -ose] : covered with densely matted hairs ⟨a ~ leaf⟩ — compare PUBESCENT

to·men·tous \tə'mentəs\ *adj* [NL *tomentosus*] : TOMENTOSE

to·men·tu·lose \-nchə,lōs\ *adj* [NL *tomentulosus,* dim. of *tomentosus* tomentose] : minutely or slightly tomentose

to·men·tum \tə'mentəm\ *n, pl* **tomen·ta** \-tə\ [NL, fr. L, cushion stuffing consisting of matted wool, hair, feathers, fr. earlier (assumed) L *tovimentum,* fr. L *tovi-* (akin to L *tumēre* to be swollen) + *-mentum* -ment — more at THUMB] **1** : pubescence composed of densely matted woolly hairs **2** : a flocculent investment of the deep surface of the pia mater made up of minute blood vessels

tomes's fiber *or* **tomes's fibril** \'tōmzəz-\ *n, usu cap T* [after Sir John *Tomes* †1895 Eng. dental surgeon] : one of the fibers extending from the odontoblasts into the dental canals : a dentinal fiber

¹tom·fool \'täm'fül\ *n* [ME *Thome Fole,* name given to half-wits, fr. *Thome* (nickname for *Thomas*) + *fol, fole* fool] **1** *usu cap* : a buffoon in a play or pageant : a professional clown **2** : one lacking in sense or good judgment : a great fool : BLOCKHEAD ⟨if any ~ points a gun at you —L.S.Marceau⟩ **3 a** : RAINBIRD b **b** : a West Indian flycatcher (*Myiarchus stolidus*)

²tomfool \'=;=\ *adj* : extremely foolish, stupid, or doltish; *also* : of, from, or characteristic of a tomfool ⟨don't know what ~ caper you're up to —C.B.Kelland⟩

³tomfool \'=;=\ *vi* : to act the tomfool ⟨this ~*ing* is no sort of use —G.B.Shaw⟩

tom·fool·ery \(')täm'fül(ə)rē, -ri\ *n* [¹*tomfool* + *-ery*] **1** : foolish or ridiculous trifling : nonsensical behavior or speech : NONSENSE ⟨indulge in ~⟩ **2** : an act, practice, speech, or thing that is nonsensical, foolish, or useless ⟨racehorses and football and *tomfooleries* of that sort —Sheila Kaye-Smith⟩ **3** : silly or trumpery trifles or ornaments ⟨among a lot of elegant ~ that makes it clear how the establishment got its name —*New Yorker*⟩

tom·fool·ish \-lish\ *adj* [¹*tomfool* + *-ish*] : given to tomfoolery : NONSENSICAL — **tom·fool·ish·ness** *n*

tom fool knot *or* **tom fool's knot** *n, often cap T&F* : a conjuror's knot consisting of two loops which disappear when the ends are pulled

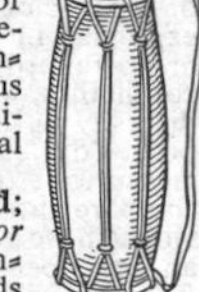
tom fool knot

to·mi·al \'tōmēəl\ *adj* [NL *tomium* + E *-al*] : relating to a tomium

-tomies *pl of* -TOMY

to·mis·to·ma \tə'mistəmə\ *n, cap* [NL, fr. Gk *tomos* cutting, sharp (fr. *temnein* to cut) + NL *-i-* + *-stoma;* more at TOME] : a genus of Malayan crocodilians resembling the gavials

to·mi·um \'tōmēəm\ *n, pl* **to·mia** \-ēə\ [NL, fr. Gk *tomos* cutting, sharp + NL *-ium*] : the cutting edge of the bill of a bird

tom·kin \'tämkən\ *n* -S : TAMPION

tom·my \'tämē, -mi\ *n* -ES [fr. *Tommy,* nickname for *Thomas*] **1** *dial Brit* **a** : a loaf or hunk of bread : a ration of bread; *also* : PROVISIONS **b** : the food carried by workmen as their daily allowance **2** : a short rod used as a key; *esp* : one for turning a capstan screw **3** *dial Eng* : SIMPLETON, FOOL **4** *usu cap* [*Tommy Atkins*] : a British soldier : TOMMY ATKINS **5 a** : TOMCOD 2 **b** : REQUIN

tommy at·kins \-'atkənz\ *n, pl* **tommy atkins** *usu cap T&A* [fr. *Thomas Atkins,* fictitious name used as model in official blank forms for private soldiers] : a white soldier of the British Army; *collectively* : such soldiers

tommy–ax \'==,=\ *n* [alter. (influenced by *ax*) of *tomahawk*] *Austral* : TOMAHAWK

tommy bar *n* : a bar used as a tommy to turn bolts and screws

tommycod \'==,=\ *n* [by alter.] : TOMCOD

tommy gun *n* [by shortening & alter.] : THOMPSON SUBMACHINE GUN; *broadly* : SUBMACHINE GUN

tommy–gun \'==,=\ *vt* [*tommy gun*] : to shoot with a tommy gun

tommy gunner *n* [*tommy gun* + *-er*] : an operator of a tommy gun

tom·my·hawk \'tämē,hȯk\ *vt* -ED/-ING/-S [alter. of ²*tomahawk*] *Austral* : TOMAHAWK 3

tommy hole *n* : a hole in a piece (as a collar) in which to insert the end of a tommy to turn it

tommy–knocker \'==,==\ *n, often cap T* [prob. fr. *Tommy* (nickname for *Thomas*) + *knocker;* fr. his being supposed to be responsible for the creaking of timbers in the mine] *West* : the ghost of a man killed in a mine

tommyrot \'==,=\ *n* [*tommy* + *rot*] : rank foolishness or nonsense ⟨such ~ has helped create a widespread and deep-rooted misunderstanding of science —John Pfeiffer⟩ ⟨how any sane and intelligent person can believe such ~ is inconceivable —A.H. & Ruth Verrill⟩

tommy rough *n, usu cap T* [*Tommy* (nickname for *Thomas*) + *rough;* fr. the roughness of the scales] : ROUGHY 1

tomnoddy \'=,==\ *n* [*Tom* (nickname for *Thomas*) + *noddy*] **1** *chiefly Scot* : ATLANTIC PUFFIN **2** : FOOL, DUNCE, NODDY

tom o'bed·lam \-ə'bedləm\ *n, pl* **tom o'bedlams** *usu cap T&B* [*Tom* (nickname for *Thomas*) + *o'* + *Bedlam,* popular name for the Hospital of St. Mary of Bethlehem, London, England, an insane asylum — more at BEDLAM] : a wandering mendicant either mad or feigning to be so : BEDLAMITE

to·mo·gram \'tōmə,gram\ *n* [ISV *tomo-* (fr. Gk *tomos* slice, section) + *-gram;* prob. orig. formed as G *tomogramm* — more at TOME] : a roentgenogram made by tomography

to·mo·graph \-raf, -räf\ *n* [ISV *tomo-* + *-graph*] : an X-ray machine used for tomography — **to·mo·graph·ic** \;==;grafik\ *adj*

to·mog·ra·phy \tə'mägrəfē\ *n* -ES [ISV *tomo-* (fr. Gk *tomos* slice, section) + *-graphy;* prob. orig. formed as G *tomographie*] : a technique of medical roentgenography by which details in one plane of body tissue appear clear and sharp while details of adjoining planes are blurred

¹to·mop·ter·id \tə'mäptərəd\ *adj* [NL *Tomopteridae,* family of polychaete worms, fr. *Tomopteris,* type genus + *-idae*] : of or relating to the genus *Tomopteris* or family Tomopteridae

²tomopterid \"\ *n* -S : a tomopterid worm

to·mop·ter·is \-rəs\ *n, cap* [NL, fr. Gk *tomos* slice, section + *pteris* fern; fr. its fernlike shape — more at TOME, PTERIS] : a genus (the type of the family Tomopteridae) of transparent free-swimming marine polychaete worms having long deeply divided or forked parapodia

to·morn \tə'mȯ(ə)rn\ *n or adv* [ME *to morne, to morn,* contr. of *to morgen, to morwen* — more at TOMORROW] *chiefly dial* : TOMORROW

¹to·mor·row \tə'mä|(,)rō, |rə *also* -'mȯ|; |rəw *or* |rō+V\ *adv* [ME *to morgen, to morwen,* fr. OE *tō morgenne, tō morgen,* fr. *tō* to + *morgenne,* dat. of *morgen* morning, morrow — more at MORN] : on or for the day after today : on or for the morrow

²tomorrow \"\ *n* -S [ME *to morwen,* fr. *to morwen* tomorrow (adv.)] **1** : the day after the present : MORROW ⟨the Senate took a recess until ~ —*Congressional Record*⟩ ⟨baffled as to how his ~*s* are to be spent —Florence Bullock⟩ **2** : FUTURE 1a

to·mor·row·er \|rəwə(r), |rōə(r)\ *n* -S [¹*tomorrow* + *-er*] : PROCRASTINATOR

to·mor·row·ness *n* -ES : the quality of being tomorrow

to·mo·sis \tə'mōsəs\ *n, pl* **tomoses** [NL, fr. Gk *tomos* slice, section + NL *-osis* — more at TOME] : a disease of cotton characterized by the fraying and perforation of the leaves

-to·mous \d·əməs, təməs\ *adj comb form* [NL *-tomus* — more at -TOME] **1** : cut : divided ⟨ortho*tomous*⟩ ⟨rhachi*tomous*⟩ **2** : cutting ⟨xylo*tomous*⟩

tompion *var of* TAMPION

toms *pl of* TOM

tom show *n, usu cap T* [after Uncle *Tom,* title character of *Uncle Tom's Cabin,* dramatization (1852) by George L. Aiken †1876 Am. actor & playwright of the novel *Uncle Tom's Cabin* (1852) by Harriet Beecher Stowe †1896 Am. author] : a traveling show performing *Uncle Tom's Cabin*

tomsk \'tämzk, 'tȯm-, -msk\ *adj, usu cap* [fr. *Tomsk,* city of western Siberia, U.S.S.R.] : of or from the city of Tomsk, U.S.S.R. : of the kind or style prevalent in Tomsk

tom·tate \'täm,tāt\ *n* -S [origin unknown] : a Florida and West Indian grunt (*Bathystoma rimator*); *also* : any of several related fishes

tom thumb *n, usu cap both Ts* [after *Tom Thumb,* legendary Eng. dwarf] : a dwarf type, race, or individual

tom tid·dler's ground \-'tidlə(r)z-\ *also* **tommy tiddler's ground** *n, usu cap both Ts* [fr. *Tom Tiddler, Tommy Tiddler,* name given to the player who is "it"] **1** : a game in which a player designated Tom Tiddler or Tommy Tiddler tries to catch the other players who invade the area designated as his property **2** : a place (as a no-man's-land) where pickings may be sought or had without effective interference ⟨this country was a *Tom Tiddler's ground* of raiding parties —T.E.Lawrence⟩ ⟨the border now became a sort of *Tom Tiddler's ground* filled with warring Kaffirs —Stuart Cloete⟩

tom·tit \(')täm'tit\ *n* [prob. short for *tomtitmouse*] : any of various small active birds: as **a** *dial Eng* : TITMOUSE; *esp* : BLUE TIT **b** *dial Eng* : WREN **c** *Irish* : TREE CREEPER **d** *South* : NUTHATCH **e** *Austral* : THORNBILL; *esp* : a common and widely distributed yellow-tailed thornbill (*Acanthiza chrysorrhoa*)

tomtitmouse \(')=¦=,=\ *n* [*Tom* (nickname for *Thomas*) + *titmouse*] *dial Eng* : BLUE TIT

¹tom-tom \'täm,täm\ *n* -S [Hindi *tamtam*] **1** : a small-headed drum of varying shape but typically long and narrow commonly beaten with the hands ⟨religious melodies chanted to the accompaniment of *tom-toms* —*Newsweek*⟩ **2** : TAM-TAM **3 a** : something used to make a noise suggestive of the tom-tom's beating **b** : an insistently monotonous beating, rhythm, or rhythmical sound ⟨the radiators beat an unending *tom-tom* like the Royal Watusi drums —S.J.Perelman⟩

tom-tom 1

²tom-tom \"\ *vb* **tom-tomed** *or* **tom-tommed; tom-tomed** *or* **tom-tommed; tom-toming** *or* **tom-tomming; tom-toms** *vi* : to sound a tom-tom esp. as a signal : make tom-tom sounds ⟨waving genial greetings to thousands of *tom-toming,* grass-skirted Africans —*Newsweek*⟩ ⟨she observed her feet *tom-toming* out the pattern of rhythm she was whistling —Jesse Lasky⟩ **~** *vt* **:** to sound on the tom-tom **:** play or execute on or as if on a tom-tom

³**tom-tom** \"\ *adj* **:** of or relating to the tom-tom ⟨traditional *tom-tom* beaters —*Time*⟩ **:** characteristic or suggestive of the tom-tom ⟨*tom-tom* muffs, with cords around the middle —Lois Long⟩

tom tram \-ˈtram\ *n, usu cap both Ts* [fr. *Tom Tram*, name of a legendary Eng. buffoon] *obs* **:** a professional fool **:** JESTER

tom walker *n, sometimes cap T&W* [*Tom* (nickname for Thomas) + *walker*] **1 tom walkers** *pl, dial* **:** STILTS **2** *slang* **:** a man on stilts

-to·my \d·əmē, təm-, -mi\ *n comb form* -ES [NL *-tomia*, fr. Gk, fr. *-tomos* cutting + *-ia* -y — more at -TOME] **:** incision **:** section ⟨cranio*tomy*⟩ ⟨laparo*tomy*⟩ ⟨sclero*tomy*⟩

¹**ton** *obs var of* TUN

²**ton** \ˈtən\ *n, pl* **tons** *also* **ton** [ME *tonne, toun* tun, unit of ship capacity or of weight — more at TUN] **1 :** any of various units of weight: **a :** a unit equal to 20 long hundredweight or 2240 pounds used chiefly in England — called also *long ton;* see MEASURE table **b :** a unit equal to 20 short hundredweight or 2000 pounds used chiefly in the U.S., Canada, and So. Africa — called also *short ton* **c :** METRIC TON **2 a :** a unit of internal capacity for ships equal to 100 cubic feet — called also *register ton;* see TONNAGE **b :** a unit approximately equal to the volume of a long ton weight of seawater used in reckoning the displacement of ships and equal to 35 cubic feet — called also *displacement ton* **c :** a unit of volume for cargo freight usu. reckoned at 40 cubic feet — called also *freight ton, measurement ton* **3 :** a European unit of quantity for timber equal to 480 board feet **4 :** a unit of cooling capacity equal to the cooling effect of a ton of ice melting in 24 hours **5 :** a great quantity **:** a large supply **:** LOT, HEAP — used chiefly in pl. ⟨~*s* of propaganda flooding the country⟩ ⟨he's got ~*s* of money, so they say⟩

³**ton** \"\ *n* -S [F *thon* — more at TUNNY] **:** TUNNY

⁴**ton** \ˈtōⁿ\ *n* -S [F, lit., tone, fr. L *tonus* — more at TONE] **1 a :** the prevailing fashion or mode **:** VOGUE **b :** SMARTNESS, STYLE ⟨conversation as the evidence of ~, and the attribute of rank —E.G.Bulwer-Lytton⟩ **2 :** the world of fashion **:** SMART SET ⟨the world of ~ which shook its head over a ruined friend —*Times Lit. Supp.*⟩

to·na·da \təˈnädə\ *n* -S [Sp, fr. *tono* tone (fr. L *tonus*) + *-ada* -ade, fr. LL *-ata*] **:** a Spanish folksong esp. of meditative character

to·na·di·lla \ˌtōnəˈdē(y)ə, -ēlyə\ *n* -S [Sp, dim. of *tonada*] **:** a short Spanish scenic intermezzo of the 18th century written for a few soloists for performance between the acts of a serious play and in the 19th century becoming a short comic opera with soloists, a chorus, and occas. instrumental movements

ton·al \ˈtōnᵊl\ *adj* [ML *tonalis*, fr. L *tonus* tone + *-alis* -al] **1 :** of or relating to tone, tonality, or tonicity **2 :** having tonality — compare ATONAL **3 :** having the intervals of a melodic subject that is repeated at a new pitch so modified as to remain in the same key ⟨~ fugue⟩ ⟨~ sequence⟩ ⟨~ imitation⟩ — compare REAL — **ton·al·ly** \-ᵊlē, -ᵊli\ *adv*

to·na·la·ma·tl \tōˈnälə,mäd·ᵊl\ *n* -S [Nahuatl, lit., book of days, fr. *tonalli* day + *amatl* paper, book] **1 :** an Aztec divinatory book based on the tonalpohualli **2 :** TONALPOHUALLI

ton·al·ism \ˈtōnᵊl,izəm\ *n* -S [*tonal* + *-ism*] **:** the practice of composing tonal music — opposed to *atonalism*

ton·al·ist \-ləst\ *n* -S [*tonal* + *-ist*] **:** one who adheres to tonality esp. in musical composition

to·nal·ite \ˈtōnᵊl,īt\ *n* -S [G *tonalit*, fr. *Tonale* (*Pass*) in the Lombard Alps + G *-it* -ite] **1 :** a granular igneous rock consisting of quartz, andesine, and small amounts of orthoclase **2 :** QUARTZ-DIORITE

to·nal·i·tive \tōˈnaləd·iv\ *adj* [*tonality* + *-ive*] **:** tending to tonality

to·nal·i·ty \tōˈnaləd·ē, -ətē, -i *sometimes* təˈ-\ *n* -ES [*tonal* + *-ity*] **1 :** tonal quality **2 :** the principle of organizing all the tones and chords of a piece of music in relation to one tone **:** the quality of having a keynote or tonic **:** the recognition or acceptance of key and key relationships — opposed to *atonality* **3 a :** the arrangement or interrelation of the colors or color nuances of a picture **:** color scheme **:** tone system **b :** the effect or quality resulting from closely related tones esp. in the darker values

to·nal·po·hual·li \tōˈnälpō,wälē\ *n* -S [Nahuatl] **:** an Aztec calendar period of 260 days like the tzolkin of the Maya calendar

tonal row *n* **:** TWELVE-TONE ROW

to-name \ˈ=,=\ *n* [ME, fr. OE *tōnama*, fr. *tō* to + *nama* name] **1** *obs* **:** SURNAME **2** *Scot* **:** NICKNAME

ton·a·wan·da pine \ˌtänəˈwändə-\ *n, usu cap T* [fr. *Tonawanda* Creek, northwestern N.Y.] **:** WHITE PINE 1a

tonca bean *var of* TONKA BEAN

ton·di·no \tänˈdē(ˌ)nō\ *n, pl* **tondi·ni** \-ēnē\ [It, dim. of *tondo* round] **1 :** a circular molding **2 :** a metal disk for striking a coin **3 :** a small tondo

ton·do \ˈtän(ˌ)dō\ *n, pl* **ton·di** \-ndē\ [It, plate, circular plaque, fr. *tondo* round, short for *rotondo*, fr. L *rotundus* — more at ROUND] **1 :** a circular painting **2 :** a sculptured medallion

¹**tone** \ˈtōn\ *pron* [ME *ton*, alter. (resulting from incorrect division of *thet on* the one, fr. OE *thæt ān*) of *on* — more at THAT, ONE] *chiefly dial* **:** ONE ⟨and by my faith . . . the ~ of us shall die —*Childe Maurice*⟩

²**tone** \"\ *n* -S *often attrib* [ME *ton, tone*, fr. L *tonus* tension, pitch, tone, fr. Gk *tonos* act of stretching, tension, pitch, tone, cord; akin to Skt *tāna* fibre, tone, Gk *teinein* to stretch — more at THIN] **1 :** vocal or musical sound; *esp* **:** sound quality of a specific character ⟨a voice with full, clear ~⟩ ⟨spoke in low ~*s*⟩ ⟨sweet ~ of a flute⟩ ⟨harsh ~⟩ **2 a :** a sound that has such regularity of vibration as to impress the ear with a definite pitch sensation and is further characterized musically by loudness and timbre **:** musical sound — compare NOISE **b :** WHOLE STEP **c :** TONE QUALITY **3 :** an ecclesiastical mode or a traditional tune or plain chant of the church ⟨the Gregorian ~⟩ **4 a :** accent or inflection of the voice as adapted to the emotion or passion expressed **:** vocal expressiveness **b :** vocal inflection characteristic of the speech of an individual, region, or nation **:** ACCENT **c :** artificial modulation in speaking or reading **:** singsong or affected intonation ⟨I never liked a man who spoke in a ~ of voice —O.Henry⟩ **5 a :** the musical pitch or intonation of a sound, word, or sentence often used to express differences of meaning or function — see TONE LANGUAGE **b :** one of the four notes or keys in which Chinese Mandarin sounds are pitched and which are often indicated beside the character or its romanized spelling by the figures 1, 2, 3, 4 **6 a :** a particular pitch or change of pitch constituting an element in the intonation of a phrase or sentence ⟨high ~⟩ ⟨mid ~⟩ ⟨low-rising ~⟩ ⟨falling ~⟩ **b :** WORD STRESS **7 :** style or manner of approach in speaking or writing **:** method of address ⟨began in a defiant ~⟩ ⟨seemed wise to adopt a conciliatory ~⟩ **8 a :** color quality or value **:** a tint or shade of color **:** a modification of a chromatic or achromatic color with respect to lightness or saturation **b :** the color that appreciably modifies a hue or white or black ⟨a bright, dark, or light ~ of blue⟩ ⟨the gray walls took on a greenish ~⟩ ⟨the soft ~*s* of the old marble⟩ **9 :** the general effect in painting of the harmonious combination of light and shade together with color **10 a :** the part of a print made from a photoengraving bearing the black or the color **b :** the relative darkness or color strength of different areas of a printed picture ⟨dark, middle, and light ~*s*⟩ **c :** the color of a photographic image ⟨sepia ~⟩ ⟨warm ~*s*⟩ **11 a** (1) **:** the state of a living body or of any of its organs or parts in which the functions are healthy and performed with due vigor (2) **:** overall vigor and well-balanced growth in a plant indicating satisfactory balance of environmental factors (as nutrients, moisture, light, heat) **b :** normal tension or responsiveness to stimuli **:** TONICITY; *specif* **:** TONUS **12 a :** healthy or normal elasticity **:** power to function or react under stress **:** RESILIENCY ⟨restore the ~ of the body politic⟩ ⟨fine ~ of a critical intelligence⟩ **b :** general or prevailing character, quality, or trend of moral or social behavior ⟨a city's low moral ~⟩ ⟨judge a school by its ~⟩ **c :** frame of mind **:** MOOD, TEMPER ⟨philosophical ~⟩ **d :** the character of a market as reflected in activity, supply and demand, and price trend ⟨the ~ of the stock market was steady⟩ **13 :** FEELING TONE **syn** see COLOR

³**tone** \"\ *vb* -ED/-ING/-S [ME *tonen*, fr. ²*tone*] *vt* **1 a** *obs* **:** to sound with a musical quality **b :** to utter with a particular or affected tone **:** INTONE **2 :** to give a particular intonation or inflection to ⟨fear *toned* his voice⟩ **3 a :** to impart tone to **:** improve or raise the quality of **:** STRENGTHEN ⟨exercise *toned* his muscles⟩ — used often with *up* ⟨prescribed a medicine to ~ up the system⟩ **b :** to reduce the emphatic or glaring quality of **:** make harmonious in color, appearance, or sound **:** SOFTEN, MELLOW — used usu. with *down* ⟨~ down clashing colors with brown tints⟩ ⟨advancing years had *toned* down his rash impulsiveness⟩ **c :** to change by treatment the tone or color of **:** modify in color; *specif* **:** to change the normal silver image of (a print, transparency, or lantern slide) into a colored image either by treatment with a solution containing some inorganic salt or by mordanting and dyeing **~** *vi* **1 a :** to assume a harmonious or pleasing color quality or tint ⟨the shingles will ~ with age and weathering⟩ — used often with *down* ⟨his clothes have *toned* down since his marriage⟩ **b** *of a photographic image* **:** to undergo a chemical reaction resulting in a change in color ⟨the average print will ~ in about 15 minutes —Jack Wright⟩ **2 :** to blend with respect to tone or color quality **:** harmonize in color ⟨the rug ~*s* with the woodwork⟩

tone accent *n* **:** PITCH ACCENT 2

tone arm *n* **:** the movable part of a phonograph that carries the pickup and permits the needle to follow the record groove spiral

tone cluster *n* **:** a combination of musical tones sounded together each of which is a scale degree apart from one or two neighboring tones in the group ⟨C-D-E struck simultaneously are a *tone cluster*⟩

tone color *n* [trans. of G *klangfarbe*] **1 :** TIMBRE 1b **2 :** COLOR 10b

tone control *n* **:** a usu. manual control by which a listener can adjust the relative amplitude of the high, low, and intermediate frequencies in a radio set

toned \ˈtōnd\ *adj* [²*tone* + *-ed*] **1 :** having or having been given tone or a specified tone **:** characterized or distinguished by a tone — often used in combination ⟨full-*toned*⟩ ⟨shrill-*toned*⟩ **2 :** having or characterized by linguistic tones — see TONE LANGUAGE **3 a** *of paper* **:** having a slight tint **:** of an off-white color **b** *of a coin or medal* **:** having a mellow tint as a result of age

tone-deaf \ˈ=ˌ=\ *adj* **:** relatively insensitive to differences in the pitch of musical tones

tone language *n* **:** a language (as Chinese, Sudanic, or Bantu) in which variations in tone are regularly used to distinguish words of different meaning that otherwise would sound alike

tone·less \ˈtōnləs\ *adj* **:** lacking in tone, modulation, or expression ⟨speaks her first complete sentence in that ~ bird-shrill voice —Lee Rogow⟩ ⟨theatrically ~ — lacking in any real quality or spirit —H.E.Clurman⟩ — **tone·less·ly** *adv* — **tone·less·ness** *n* -ES

tone long *n* **:** a vowel that is not long in Semitic or pre-Hebrew but becomes long in Hebrew by virtue of its position in relation to the accent of the word or phrase and may be shortened when that position is changed

to·neme \ˈtō,nēm\ *n* -S [²*tone* + *-eme*] **:** a phoneme consisting of a specific intonation in a tone language — **to·ne·mic** \tōˈnēmik\ *adj*

tone painting *n* **:** the use of varying timbres and sound symbolism in creating musical effects esp. in impressionistic composition or program music

tone picture *n* **:** a musical composition usu. for orchestra characterized by pictorial suggestion

tone poem *n* [²*tone* + *poem*] **:** an orchestral composition based on a literary subject or suggestive of poetic sentiments or images

tone poet *n* [trans. of G *tondichter*] **:** a composer of music; *esp* **:** a composer of program music

tone quality *n* **1 :** TIMBRE 1 **2 :** the character of musical tones with reference to their richness or perfection **3 :** the character of the effect produced by a harmonic combination of musical tones

ton·er \ˈtōnə(r)\ *n* -S **:** one that tones: as **a :** an organic pigment that contains no inorganic pigment or inorganic carrier **:** a full-strength organic pigment — see DYE table I (under *Organic pigments*); compare ⁴LAKE 1b **b :** one that tests the quality and color of paints **c :** a chemical solution capable of converting a silver photographic image to a colored image

tone-row \ˈ=ˌ=\ *n* [trans. of G *tonreihe*] **:** TWELVE-TONE ROW

tones *pl of* TONE, *pres 3d sing of* TONE

tone syllable *n* **:** an accented syllable

to·net·ic \tōˈned·ik\ *adj* [²*tone* + *-etic*] **:** relating to linguistic tones or to tone languages **:** dealing with or expressing intonation ⟨~ notation⟩ — **to·net·i·cal·ly** \-d·ək(ə)lē\ *adv*

to·ne·ti·cian \ˌtōnəˈtishən *sometimes* ˌtän-\ *n* -S [*tonetic* + *-ian*] **:** a student of tonetics

to·net·ics \tōˈned·iks\ *n pl but sing in constr* [fr. *tonetic*, after E *phonetic: phonetics*] **:** the use or study of linguistic tones **:** the science of intonation

to·nette \(ˈ)tōˈnet\ *n* -S [²*tone* + *-ette*] **:** a small simple end-blown flute typically of plastic with a range somewhat exceeding an octave often used in elementary music education

tonette

tone-up \ˈ=ˌ=\ *n* -S [fr. *tone up*, v.] **:** a toning-up exercise, treatment, or medicine

tone wheel *n* **:** a high-speed interrupter or commutator formerly used for producing a current of audio frequency in a radio receiver

toney *var of* TONY

ton-foot \ˈ=ˌ=\ *n* [²*ton* + *foot*] **:** FOOT-TON

¹**tong** \ˈtäŋ, ˈtȯŋ\ *n* -S [ME *tonge*, alter. of *tange* tang] **1** *dial* **:** TANG **2** *dial* **:** TINE

²**tong** \"\ *vb* -ED/-ING/-S [imit.] *vt, dial* **:** to cause (a bell) to give out a deep resonant tone **~** *vi, dial* **:** to give out a deep resonant tone

³**tong** \"\ *n* -S *dial* **:** a deep sound given out by a large bell

⁴**tong** \"\ *n* -S [fr. sing. of *tongs*] **:** TONGS

⁵**tong** \"\ *vb* -ED/-ING/-S [*tongs*] *vt* **:** to take, gather, hold, or handle with tongs ⟨~ oysters⟩ ⟨~ logs⟩ — often used with *up* **~** *vi* **:** to use tongs **:** take or gather something with tongs

⁶**tong** \"\ *n* -S [Chin (Cant) *t'ong* hall, meeting place] **:** a secret society or fraternal organization esp. among the Chinese in the U.S. formerly notorious for gang warfare and popularly associated with racketeering, gambling, and traffic in narcotics

⁷**tong** \"\ *n* -S [Afrik, tongue, flatfish, fr. MD *tonge, tong;* akin to OE *tunge* tongue — more at TONGUE] **:** a large commercially important southern African flatfish (*Austroglossus pectoralis*) much depleted by overfishing; *also* **:** a closely related fish (*A. microlepis*) distinguished by its minute scales

¹**ton·ga** \ˈtäŋgə\ *n* -S [Hindi *tāṅgā*] **:** a light 2-wheeled vehicle for two or four persons drawn by one horse and common in India

²**tonga** \ˈtäŋ(g)ə, ˈtȯŋ-\ *or* **ton·gan** \-)ən\ *n* -S [prob. fr. *Tonga* islands, southwest central Pacific ocean] **1** *also* **tongan creeper :** an epiphytic creeper (*Epipremnum mirabile*) of the family Araceae used in folk medicine in Malaysia **2 :** a drug formerly used in pharmacy consisting of equal parts of tonga bark and the root of a verbenaceous tree (*Premna arborea*)

³**tonga** \"\ *n, pl* **tonga** *usu cap* **1 a :** any of several Bantu-speaking peoples found respectively in southern Portuguese East Africa, west of Lake Nyasa, and on the upper Zambezi river **b :** a member of one of these peoples **2 :** any of the languages of the several Tonga peoples

⁴**ton·ga** \"\ *adj, usu cap* [fr. *Tonga* islands, southwest central Pacific ocean] **:** TONGAN

tonga bean *var of* TONKA BEAN

¹**ton·gan** \ˈtäŋ(g)ən, ˈtȯŋ-\ *n* -S *usu cap* [*Tonga* islands, southwest central Pacific ocean + E *-an*] **1 :** a member of a Polynesian people native to the Tonga islands of the southwest Pacific **2 :** the Polynesian language of the Tongans

²**tongan** \"\ *adj, usu cap* **:** of or relating to the Tonga islands or the Tongans or their language

ton·ga·re·van \ˌtäŋ(g)əˈrevən, ˌtȯŋ-, -ˈrāv-\ *adj, usu cap* [*Tongareva* island, central Pacific ocean + E *-an*] **:** of, relating to, or characteristic of the island, the people, or the language of Tongareva in the Manihiki islands in the central Pacific

ton·gass \ˈtäŋgəs\ *n, pl* **tongass** *or* **tongasses** *usu cap* **1 :** a Tlingit people at the mouth of Portland canal, Alaska **2 :** a member of the Tongass people

ton·ga·wal·la \ˌtäŋgəˈwälə\ *n* -S [Hindi *tāṅgāvālā*, fr. *tāṅgā* tonga + *-vālā* man — more at WALLAH] **:** a driver of a tonga

tong·er \ˈtäŋə(r), ˈtȯŋ-\ *n* -S [⁵*tong* + *-er*] **:** one that tongs

tong·kang \ˈtäŋˌkaŋ\ *n* -S [Malay] **:** a large native boat or junk used in the East Indies in fishing and in local trading

tongkingese *usu cap, var of* TONKINESE

tong·man \-mən\ *n, pl* **tongmen 1** [⁴*tong* + *man*] **:** one who handles tongs **:** TONGER **2** [⁶*tong* + *man*] **:** a member of a tong

tongs \ˈtäŋz, ˈtȯŋz\ *n pl but sometimes sing in constr* [ME *tanges, tonges*, pl. of *tange, tonge*, fr. OE *tang, tange;* akin to OHG *zanga* tongs, ON *tǫng*, Gk *daknein* to bite, Skt *daśati* he bites, *daṁśa* bite] **:** any of numerous devices or instruments for taking hold of objects (as hot coals, hot metal, rails, logs, pipes), for ease and convenience in handling, or for lifting, dragging, or carrying and consisting commonly of two legs that are joined at one end by a pivot or spring or of two pieces hinged that are like scissors or pincers — often used with *pair* ⟨a pair of ~⟩

tongs·man \-zmən\ *n, pl* **tongsmen** [*tongs* + *man*] **:** TONGER

¹**tongue** \ˈtəŋ\ *n* -S *often attrib* [ME *tunge*, fr. OE; akin to OHG *zunga* tongue, ON *tunga*, Goth *tuggo*, OL *dingua*, L *lingua*] **1 a :** a process of the floor of the mouths of most vertebrates that is attached basally to the hyoid bone, that consists essentially of a mass of extrinsic muscle attaching its base to other parts, intrinsic muscle by which parts of the structure move in relation to each other, and an epithelial covering rich in sensory end organs and small glands, and that serves esp. for taking and swallowing food, as the principal seat of the sense of taste, as an instrument for cleansing and grooming, as a tactile organ (as in a snake), and in some forms (as the toad) as a prehensile organ for the seizing of prey **b :** an analogous part of various invertebrate animals (as the radula of a mollusk or the lingula or proboscis of some insects) **2 :** the flesh of the tongue of an animal (as the ox or sheep) used as food **3 :** the agent of articulated speech **:** the power of communication or expression through speech ⟨though I speak with the ~*s* of men and of angels —1 Cor 13:1 (AV)⟩ ⟨wonders that no ~ can tell⟩ ⟨done to death by slanderous ~*s* —Shak.⟩ ⟨you had better hold your ~⟩ ⟨used the strongest words he could lay ~ to⟩ ⟨gave him the rough side of my ~⟩ **4 a :** a spoken language; *esp* **:** a speech used by a particular people or class or in a particular region **:** DIALECT **b :** a language other than one's own **:** a foreign or strange language **c tongues** *pl, archaic* **:** the learned languages (as Hebrew, Greek, and Latin) — used with *the* **d** *archaic* **:** a people having a distinct language ⟨gather all nations and ~*s* —Isa. 66:18 (AV)⟩ **e :** manner or quality of utterance with respect to tone or sound ⟨a soft ~⟩ or the sense of what is expressed ⟨a flattering ~⟩ ⟨a foolish ~⟩ or the intention of the speaker ⟨a flattering ~⟩ **f :** ecstatic usu. unintelligible utterance called forth in a moment of religious excitation ⟨any believer might offer a hymn, or a revelation, or a ~ —C.T.Craig⟩ — see GIFT OF TONGUES **g :** the cry of or as if of a hound pursuing or in sight of game — used esp. in the phrase *to give tongue* **5 :** TONGUEFISH **6 a :** a tapering cone of flame ⟨Pentecostal ~*s* of fire⟩ **b :** a tapering decorative element used in relief carvings esp. on moldings ⟨~ and dart molding⟩ — compare EGG AND DART **7 a :** a point or long narrow strip of land projecting from the mainland into a body of water **b :** a point of ice projecting nearly horizontally from the submerged part of an iceberg **c :** a current that runs rapidly between rocks **d :** the lower part of a valley glacier **e :** a minor subdivision or specifically developed part of a sedimentary formation that thins laterally to disappearance in one direction **f :** an offshoot from a body of intrusive igneous rock **g :** a narrow body of air projecting from a main air mass ⟨interlocking dry and moist ~*s* along a cold front⟩ **8 :** something resembling an animal's tongue in being elongated and fastened at one end only: as **a :** a movable pin in a buckle that passes through a hole in the strap to be secured; *also* **:** the corresponding pin of a brooch or clasp **b :** the index of a balance or scale **c :** a metal ball freely suspended inside a bell so as to strike against the sides as the bell is swung **d** (1) **:** the free vibrating end of the reed in an organ pipe or wind instrument (2) **:** the vibrating part of a Jew's harp **e :** the pole of a 2-horse vehicle ⟨wagon ~⟩ **f :** the flap of leather or other material under the lacing or buckles of a shoe at the throat of the vamp **g :** a switch piece consisting of a movable point with a suitable enclosing or supporting body structure and designed for use on one side of a railroad track esp. of a street railway **h :** TANG 2a **i :** the swiveling part of a carpenter's bevel **j :** the endpiece of a mainspring serving as its attachment to the inside of the enclosing barrel **k :** a short block of wood or iron so placed in the jaws of a gaff as to facilitate its sliding up and down the mast **9 a :** the projecting rib on one edge of a board that fits into a corresponding groove in an edge of another board to make a flush joint **b :** FEATHER 6 **syn** see LANGUAGE — **on the tip of one's tongue 1 :** about to be uttered or blurted out **2 :** just eluding recall ⟨had his name *on the tip of my tongue* but it's gone now⟩

²**tongue** \"\ *vb* -ED/-ING/-S *vt* **1 a** *archaic* **:** UTTER, SPEAK **b :** SCOLD, ABUSE **2 :** to touch or lick with or as if with the tongue ⟨cows *tonguing* the long grass⟩ ⟨~ a cigarette⟩ ⟨arms full of squirming, *tonguing* dog —Walter Karig⟩ **3 a :** to cut a tongue on ⟨~ a board⟩ **b :** to join (as boards) by means of a tongue and groove **4 :** to articulate (notes) by tonguing ⟨in vain did he lip and ~ the notes as instructed —Israel Zangwill⟩ ⟨a lightning-*tongued* cornet solo⟩ **~** *vi* **1 :** TALK, CHATTER — used often with *it* ⟨~ it all day long⟩ **2 a :** to project in a tongue **:** send out tongues ⟨forest belt of Siberia ~*s* southwards —C.D.Forde⟩ ⟨icebergs ~ out dangerously under the surface⟩ **b :** to thin to disappearance **:** taper off — used often with *out* ⟨the bed ~*s* out within 10 feet —*Jour. of Geol.*⟩ **3 :** to give tongue ⟨hounds *tonguing* frantically on the scent⟩ **4 :** to make a cut or slit in the stem of a plant before the operation of layering **5 :** to articulate notes on a wind instrument

tongue and groove *n* **:** a joint made by a tongue on one edge of a board fitting into a corresponding groove on the edge of another board

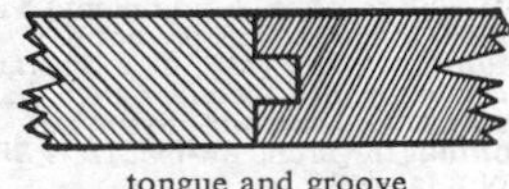

tongue and groove

tongue-and-lip joint \ˈ=ˌ=ˌ=-\ *n* **:** a tongue-and-groove joint for boards in which the board with the tongue has also a flush bead which serves to conceal the joint

tongue bit *n* **:** a horse's bit having a plate to keep the tongue under the mouthpiece

tongue-biter \ˈ=ˌ==\ *n* **:** a large parasitic isopod (*Codonophilus imbricatus*) of Australian waters that attaches itself to the tongue of marine fishes

tongue bone *n* **:** HYOID BONE

tongued \ˈtəŋd\ *adj* [ME *tunged*, fr. *tunge* tongue + *-ed*] **1 :** having a tongue or such a kind of tongue or so many tongues ⟨~ lightning⟩ — often used in combination ⟨double-*tongued*⟩ ⟨golden-*tongued*⟩ **2 :** provided with a tongue ⟨~ shoe⟩ ⟨~ lid of a paper box⟩ ⟨~ board⟩

tongue depressor *or* **tongue blade** *n* **:** a thin wooden blade rounded at both ends that is used by physicians chiefly for inspecting the throat

tongue fern *n* **:** any of several ferns (as *Cyclophorus lingua*) having fronds shaped like tongues

tonguefish \ˈ=ˌ=\ *n* **:** a small flatfish of the family Cynoglossidae

tongueflower \ˈ=ˌ=\ *n* [so called fr. its tongue-shaped lip] **1 :** an Australian orchid of the genus *Glossodia* **2 :** a plant or flower of the genus *Glossopetalon* (family Celastraceae)

tongue graft *n* **:** WHIP GRAFT 1

tongue grass *n* **1 :** PEPPERGRASS 1 **2 :** CHICKWEED

tongue in cheek *adv (or adj)* **:** with insincerity, irony, or whimsical exaggeration

tongue joint *n* **:** a joint usu. in metal with a tongue on one piece secured in a recess in the other

tongue-lash \'ₑ,ₑ\ *vb* [back-formation fr. *tongue-lashing*] **:** CHIDE, REPROVE **syn** see SCOLD

tongue-lashing \'ₑ,ₑₑ\ *n* [¹*tongue* + *lashing*] **:** a severe scolding

tongue·less \'təŋləs\ *adj* [ME *tungles*, fr. *tunge* tongue + *-les* -less] **1 :** having no tongue **2 :** lacking power of speech **:** SPEECHLESS, MUTE ⟨best grief is ~ —Emily Dickinson⟩

tongue·let \-lət\ *n* -s [¹*tongue* + *-let*] **:** a small part, process, or object resembling a tongue

tonguelike \'ₑ,ₑ\ *adj* [¹*tongue* + *like*] **:** resembling a tongue esp. in elongated form or in function

tongue of the trump [so called fr. the fact that the tongue is the essential part of a Jew's harp] *Scot* **:** the most important person

tongue-pad \'ₑ,ₑ\ *n, dial chiefly Brit* **:** a great or glib talker

tongue pipe *n* **:** REED PIPE

tongu·er \'təŋə(r)\ *n* -s [¹*tongue* + *-er*] **1 :** one that makes or inserts tongues (as on shoes, buckles, or boards) **2 :** a packing house worker who handles tongues

tongues *pl of* TONGUE, *pres 3d sing of* TONGUE

tongue-shaped \'ₑ;ₑ\ *adj* **:** having the form of a tongue **:** LINGULATE

tongue shell *n* **:** a brachiopod of *Lingula* or a related genus

tongue sole *n* **:** TONGUEFISH

tongue·ster \'təŋztə(r), -ŋ(k)st-\ *n* -s [¹*tongue* + *-ster*] **:** a glib or talkative person **:** a voluble speaker **:** BABBLER

tongue-tack·ed \'ₑ,takət\ *adj, Scot* **:** TONGUE-TIED

¹**tongue-tie** \'ₑ,ₑ\ *vt* [back-formation fr. *tongue-tied*] **:** to deprive of speech or the power of distinct articulation by or as if by a tongue-tie or a gag **:** make speechless, silent, or unable to speak freely

²**tongue-tie** \"\ *n* [back-formation fr. *tongue-tied*] **:** limited mobility of the tongue due to shortness of the frenum or to its adhesion to the gums

tongue-tied \'ₑ,ₑ\ *adj* [¹*tongue* + *tied*, past part. of *tie*] **1 :** suffering from tongue-tie **2 :** unable to speak freely from shyness or other cause ⟨he was *tongue-tied* by the sense that their minutes were numbered —Edith Wharton⟩

tongue tree *n* **:** the tongue of a vehicle

tongue twister *n* **:** a word, phrase, or sentence difficult to articulate readily because of a succession of similar chiefly consonantal sounds varied by small changes (as in "twin-screw steel cruiser", "shall he sell sea shells")

tongue-walk \'ₑ,ₑ\ *vt, Brit* **:** SCOLD

tongue worm *n* **:** a parasitic arthropod of the group Linguatulida

tonguey *or* **tonguy** \'təŋē, -ŋi\ *adj* [¹*tongue* + *-y*] **1 :** ready or voluble in speaking **:** GARRULOUS **2 :** of the nature of or affected by the tongue ⟨a ~ voice⟩

tongu·i·ness \-ŋēnəs\ *n* -ES **:** the quality of being tonguey

tonguing *n* -s [fr. gerund of ²*tongue*] **1 :** the act of one who tongues; *also* **:** the product of the act of making tongues ⟨~ of matched boards⟩ **2 a :** the act of using or applying the tongue; *esp* **:** TONGUE-LASHING, SCOLDING **b :** use of the tongue in attacking or articulating notes on a wind instrument ⟨~ rather than slurring is indicated for this passage⟩ — compare DOUBLE-TONGUE, SINGLE-TONGUE, TRIPLE-TONGUE

-to·nia \'tōnēə\ *n comb form* -s [NL, fr. *tonus* + *-ia* -y] **:** condition or degree of tonus ⟨hypo*tonia*⟩ ⟨somato*tonia*⟩

¹**ton·ic** \'tänik, -nēk\ *adj* [Gk *tonikos* of tension, of tone, fr. *tonos* tension, tone + *-ikos* -ic — more at TONE] **1 a :** relating to or characterized by tension **b :** producing or adapted to produce healthy muscular condition and reaction **c** *of muscular contraction* **:** maintained during prolonged periods **:** characterized by tonus — contrasted with *clonic* **d** *of bodily states* **:** marked or characterized by tonic muscular contraction ⟨~ convulsions⟩ **2 a :** increasing or restoring physical or mental tone **:** having the virtue or effect of a stimulant **:** INVIGORATING, REFRESHING, BRACING ⟨a ~ quality in her laughter —Agnes Repplier⟩ ⟨~ air of the upland morning put vigor into his blood —John Buchan⟩ ⟨~ therapy⟩ **b :** yielding a tonic substance **3 :** relating to or based on the first tone of the scale ⟨~ harmony⟩ **4 a :** VOICED 2 **b** *of a syllable* **:** bearing a principal stress or accent — compare POSTTONIC, PRETONIC **5 :** of or relating to speech tones or to languages using them **:** employing tones to distinguish words ⟨Chinese is a ~ language⟩

²**tonic** \"\ *n* -s **1 a :** a drug, medicine, or physical agent that increases body tone ⟨digitalis acts as a heart ~ by increasing cardiac tone⟩ ⟨sun baths are a ~ in some respiratory diseases⟩ **b :** something that invigorates, restores, refreshes, or stimulates ⟨his fear acted as a ~⟩ **c :** a liquid preparation for cleansing and toning the scalp **d** *chiefly NewEng* **:** a carbonated flavored beverage **:** SODA POP **2 :** the first degree of a major or minor scale constituting the tonal center of a musical composition which has an established tonality — called also *keynote* **3 :** a voiced sound

³**tonic** \"\ *vt* **tonicked; tonicked; tonicking; tonics** [²*tonic*] **:** to give a tonic to **:** strengthen by a tonic ⟨*tonicked* her children every winter with cod-liver oil⟩

tonic accent *n* **1 :** relative phonetic prominence (as from greater stress or higher pitch) of a spoken syllable or word **2 :** PITCH ACCENT

ton·i·cal \-nəkəl, -nēk-\ *adj* [Gk *tonikos* tonic + E *-al*] **:** TONIC 1,2

ton·i·cal·ly \-nək(ə)lē, -nēk-, -li\ *adv* [¹*tonic* + *-ally*] **:** in a tonic manner **:** BRACINGLY

to·nic·i·ty \tō'nisəd·ē, -ətē, -i\ *n* -ES [¹*tonic* + *-ity*] **1 :** the condition or property of possessing muscular, systemic, mental, or moral tone **:** VIGOR, HEALTH **2 :** muscular tonus **3 :** normal responsiveness of a plant to external stimuli

tonic sol-fa *n* **:** a system of solmization widely used in Great Britain and other countries to develop sightsinging that is based on tonality or key relationships and replaces the usual staff notation with the initial letters of the sol-fa syllables or the syllables themselves

tonier *comparative of* TONY

tonies *pl of* TONY

-tonies *pl of* -TONY

toniest *superlative of* TONY

ton·i·fy \'tänə,fī, 'tōn-\ *vt* -ED/-ING/-ES [⁴*ton* + *-ify*] **1 :** to give ton or style to **2** [¹*tone* + *-ify*] **:** to give tone to **:** tone up ⟨*tonifies* the system and rests the nerves⟩

¹**to·night** \tə'nīt, *usu* -īd·+V\ *adv* [ME *to night*, *to niht*, fr. OE *tō niht*, fr. *tō* to + *niht* night] **:** on this present night or the night following this present day

²**tonight** \"\ *n* [ME, fr. *to night*, adv.] **:** the present or the coming night **:** the night after the present day

tonikan *usu cap, var of* TUNICAN

toning [fr. gerund of ²*tone*] *n* -s *Brit* **:** a tint, shade, or tone (as of a fabric)

ton·ish *or* **ton·nish** \'tänish\ *adj* [⁴*ton* + *-ish*] **:** having ton **:** FASHIONABLE, STYLISH ⟨become a ~ poet and get into anthologies —Rose Macaulay⟩ — **ton·ish·ly** *adv* — **ton·ish·ness** *n* -ES

to·nite \'tō,nīt\ *n* -s [ISV *ton-* (fr. L *tonare* to thunder) + *-ite*] **:** a blasting explosive consisting of a mixture of guncotton with a nitrate and sometimes a nitro compound

ton·i·tro·cirrus \,tänə·(,)trō+\ *n* [NL, fr. L *tonitrus* thunder + NL *-o-* + *cirrus*] **:** FALSE CIRRUS

to·nit·ru·ous \tə'ni·trəwəs\ *also* **to·nit·ru·ant** \-wənt\ *adj* [*tonitruous* fr. L *tonitruum* thunder (fr. *tonitrus* thunder, fr. *tonare* to thunder) + E *-ous*; *tonitruant* fr. LL *tonitruant-*, *tonitruans*, fr. pres. part. of *tonitruare* to thunder, fr. L *tonitruum* thunder — more at THUNDER] **:** THUNDERING, FULMINATING

ton·jon \'tän,jän\ *n* -s [Hindi *tāmjhām*, *thāmjān*] **:** an open sedan chair used in India and Ceylon and carried by a single pole on men's shoulders

¹**tonk** \'täŋk\ *n* -s [imit.] **:** a heavy unmusical clang ⟨~ of a cowbell⟩

²**tonk** *var of* TUNK

³**tonk** \'täŋk\ *n* -s [by shortening] **:** HONKY-TONK

ton·ka bean *or* **ton·ca bean** \'täŋkə-\ *or* **ton·ga bean** \-ŋgə-\ *also* **ton·qua bean** \-ŋkə-\ *n* [prob. fr. Tupi *tonka*] **:** the seed of any of several plants of the genus *Dipteryx* (esp. *D. odorata* and *D. oppositifolia*) that has a pleasant odor due to the presence of coumarin and is used in the manufacture of coumarin, in perfumes, as a flavor for tobacco, and in making artificial vanilla extracts; *also* **:** a plant whose seed is a tonka bean

ton·ka·wa \'täŋkəwə\ *n, pl* **tonkawa** *or* **tonkawas** *usu cap* **1 a :** an Indian people of central Texas **b :** a member of such people **2 :** the language of the Tonkawa people **3 :** TONKAWAN

ton·ka·wan \-wən\ *n* -s *usu cap* [*tonkawa* + *-an*] **:** a language family perhaps related to Coahuiltecan and Karankawa of Texas that includes the Tonkawa language

ton-kilometer \'tən+\ *n* [²*ton* + *kilometer*] **:** a unit of freight carriage equal to the transportation of one metric ton of freight one kilometer

ton·kin \'tän'kin, -äŋ'-\ *also* **tonkin cane** *n* -s [fr. *Tonkin*, northern part of Vietnam] **:** a firm bamboo used for ski poles and fishing rods

¹**ton·kin·ese** \'täŋkə'nēz, -ēs\ *or* **tong·king·ese** \-kiŋ'ēz, -ēs\ *adj, usu cap* [*Tonkin*, *Tongking*, northern part of Vietnam + E *-ese*] **:** of or relating to Tonkin

²**tonkinese** \"\ *or* **tongkingese** \"\ *n, pl* **tonkinese** *or* **tongkingese** **1** *cap* **:** a native of Tonkin **2** *usu cap* **:** a dialect of Vietnamese spoken in Tonkin

ton·let \'tənlət\ *n* -s [F *tonnelet*, fr. MF, prob. fr. dim. of *tonnel*, *tonel* cask, barrel; fr. the resemblance of the bands to staves of a barrel — more at TUNNEL] **:** one of the horizontal overlapping bands forming a short skirt in late medieval armor

ton-mile \'ₑ;ₑ\ *n* [²*ton* + *mile*] **:** a statistical unit of freight transportation equivalent to a ton of freight moved one mile — compare CAR-MILE

ton-mileage \'ₑ;ₑₑ\ *n* [*ton-mile* + *-age*] **1 :** the total ton-miles performed by a carrier in a period of time **2 :** rate (as of fuel consumption) per ton-mile

ton·na \'tänə\ *n, cap* [NL, fr. ML *tunna*, *tonna* barrel, tun — more at TUNNEL] **:** a genus of large marine gastropods (family Tonnidae) lacking varix and operculum and having the body whorl greatly enlarged and the aperture very wide

ton·nage \'tənij, -nēj\ *n* -s [in sense 1, fr. ME, fr. MF, fr. OF *tonne* barrel, tun + *-age*; in other senses, fr. ²*ton* + *-age*] **1** *also* **tun·nage** \"\ **:** a duty formerly levied on every tun of wine imported and exported **2 a :** a duty or impost on vessels based on cargo capacity **b :** a duty, toll, or rate on goods per ton transported on canals **3 :** ships in terms of the total number of tons registered or carried or of the sum of their carrying capacity ⟨the ~ built in American shipyards is small⟩ ⟨the ~ devoted to Oriental trade⟩ **4 a :** the capacity of a merchant ship in units of 100 cubic feet of enclosed space — compare DEADWEIGHT CAPACITY, NET TONNAGE **b :** the displacement of a warship **5 :** total weight in tons **:** aggregate of tons shipped, carried, or mined ⟨this mine's daily ~ is large⟩ ⟨a railroad with the year's record for ~⟩ **6 :** the rating in tons of the pressure or thrust exerted by a machine or engine ⟨~ of a press⟩ ⟨~ of a rocket engine⟩

tonnage and poundage *n* [ME] **:** a duty on every tun of wine or pound of wool and other articles formerly granted as a subsidy to the crown on all goods exported or imported

tonnage coefficient *n* **:** the decimal by which the product of the length, breadth, and depth of a vessel must be multiplied to obtain the gross tonnage

tonnage deck *n* **:** the deck the space below which is included in estimating underdeck tonnage and which in vessels having more than one deck is the second from the keel

tonnage opening *n* **:** an opening left in a deck for bringing the space covered within the exemptions of a rule for calculating tonnage

tonnage train *n* **:** a freight train that is operated only when a definite tonnage of freight has accumulated

ton·neau \'tän,ō, tə'nō\ *n* -s [F, barrel, tun, kind of carriage with rear entrance & seats parallel to the wheels, fr. OF *tonel*, *tonnel* barrel, tun — more at TUNNEL] **1 :** the rear seating compartment of an automobile ⟨~ of a limousine⟩ ⟨sports car ~ with removable canvas cover⟩ **2 :** a shape of watch case or dial resembling a barrel in profile

ton·neaued \-ōd\ *adj* [*tonneau* + *-ed*] **:** having a tonneau

tonneau lamp *n* **:** a lamp mounted on the back of the front seat of a vehicle

tonneau windshield *n* **:** a windshield that is directly in front of the tonneau and is usu. attached to the back of the front seat

ton·ner \'tənə(r)\ *n* -s [²*ton* + *-er*] **:** an object (as a ship) having tonnage — usu. used in combination ⟨a thousand-*tonner*⟩

ton·ni·dae \'tänə,dē\ *n pl, cap* [NL, fr. *Tonna*, type genus + *-idae*] **:** a family of gastropod mollusks (suborder Taenioglossa) comprising the tun shells — see TONNA

tonnish *var of* TONISH

tono- *comb form* [Gk *tonos* tension, pitch, tone — more at TONE] **1 :** tone ⟨*tono*logy⟩ ⟨*tono*scope⟩ **2 :** pressure ⟨*tono*meter⟩ ⟨*tono*taxis⟩

tono·fibril *also* **tono·fibrilla** \¦tä(,)nō, ¦tō(,)nō+\ *n, pl* **tonofibrils** *also* **tonofibrillae** [NL *tonofibrilla*, fr. *tono-* + *fibrilla*] **:** any of a variety of intracellular or extracellular fibrils that are reinforcing or supporting elements

ton of refrigeration [²*ton*] **:** TON 4

ton·o·gram \'tänə,gram, 'tōn-\ *n* [*tono-* + *-gram*] **:** a curve recorded by a tonograph

ton·o·graph \-,raf, -räf\ *n* [ISV *tono-* + *-graph*] **:** a recording tonometer — **ton·o·graph·ic** \¦ₑₑ¦grafik\ *adj* — **to·nog·ra·phy** \tə'nägrəfē\ *n* -ES

ton·o·log·i·cal \¦tänᵊl¦äjəkəl, ¦tōn-\ *adj* **:** of or relating to tonology

to·nol·o·gy \tō'näləjē\ *n* -ES [*tono-* + *-logy*] **:** the comparative or historical science of tones or of speech intonation

to·nom·e·ter \tō'nämәd·ə(r)\ *n* [*tono-* + *-meter*] **1 :** an instrument or device for determining the exact pitch or the vibration rate of tones **2 :** an instrument for measuring tension (as of the eyeball) or pressure (as of blood or a gas) **3 :** a device for measuring vapor pressure

ton·o·met·ric \¦tänə¦me·trik, ¦tōn-\ *adj* [ISV *tono-* + *-metric*] **:** of or relating to tonometry or to the use of a tonometer

to·nom·e·try \tō'nämə·trē\ *n* -ES [ISV *tono-* + *-metry*] **:** the act or practice of measuring with a tonometer

ton·o·plast \'tänə,plast, 'tōn-\ *n* -s [ISV *tono-* + *-plast*; orig. formed in G] **:** the semipermeable protoplasmic membrane surrounding a plant-cell vacuole orig. regarded as a selfₑperpetuating structural membrane that actively secreted the vacuolar content but usu. held to be comparable to the plasma membrane

ton·oscope \-,skōp\ *n* [*tono-* + *-scope*] **:** an acoustical instrument for enabling a singer or player to see instantly any deviation from proper pitch of the tone being produced

tono·taxis \¦tä(,)nō, ¦tō(,)nō+\ *n* [NL, fr. *tono-* + *-taxis*] **:** responsiveness to a difference of osmotic pressure of the surrounding medium

tonqua bean *var of* TONKA BEAN

tons *pl of* TON

ton·sil \'tän(t)səl\ *n* -s [L *tonsillae* (pl.) tonsils] **1 a :** either of a pair of prominent masses of lymphoid tissue that lie one on each side of the throat between the anterior and posterior pillars of the fauces and are composed of lymph follicles grouped around one or more deep crypts and except for the exposed surface which is covered only by epithelium are surrounded by diffuse lymphoid tissue in a fibrous capsule **b :** any of various similar masses of lymphoid tissue — see PHARYNGEAL TONSIL **2 :** AMYGDALA 2

ton·sile \'tän(t)səl, -n,sil\ *adj* [L *tonsilis*, fr. *tonsus* (past part. of *tondēre* to shear, clip, crop) + *-ilis* -ile — more at TOME] *archaic* **:** suitable for being shorn or clipped

tonsill- *or* **tonsillo-** *comb form* [L *tonsillae* tonsils] **:** tonsil ⟨*tonsill*ectomy⟩ ⟨*tonsillo*tomy⟩

ton·sil·lar \'tän(t)sələ(r)\ *or* **ton·sil·lary** \-sə,lerē\ *adj* [NL *tonsillaris*, fr. L *tonsillae* tonsils + *-aris* -ar] **:** of, relating to, or affecting the tonsils

ton·sil·lec·tome \,tän(t)sə'lek,tōm\ *n* -s [*tonsill-* + *-ectome*] **:** an instrument for removing tonsils

ton·sil·lec·to·my \-ktəmē, -mi\ *n* -ES [*tonsill-* + *-ectomy*] **:** the surgical removal of the tonsils

ton·sil·lit·ic \¦ₑₑ¦lid·ik\ *adj* [NL *tonsillitis* + E *-ic*] **:** of, relating to, or affected with tonsillitis

ton·sil·li·tis \,ₑₑ'līd·əs, -ītəs\ *n* -ES [NL, fr. L *tonsillae* tonsils + NL *-itis*] **:** inflammation of the tonsils or a tonsil of varying degrees of severity and involving simple inflammation associated with acute pharyngitis, streptococcus infection (as in septic sore throat), or formation of an abscess (as in quinsy)

ton·sil·lo·tome \tän'silə,tōm\ *n* -s [ISV *tonsill-* + *-tome*] **:** a surgical instrument for cutting or removing tonsils

ton·sil·lot·o·my \,tän(t)sə'läd·əmē\ *n* -ES [*tonsill-* + *-tomy*] **:** incision of a tonsil

ton·sor \'tän(t)sə(r)\ *n* -s [L, fr. *tonsus* + *-or* — more at TONSURE] *archaic* **:** BARBER

ton·so·ri·al \(')tän¦sōrēəl, -¦sȯr-\ *adj* [L *tonsorius* tonsorial (fr. *tonsus* + *-orius* -ory) + E *-al*] **:** of or relating to a barber or his work ⟨~ parlor⟩

¹**ton·sure** \'tänchə(r)\ *n* -s [ME, fr. ML *tonsura*, fr. L, act of shearing, clipping, fr. *tonsus* (past part. of *tondēre* to shear, clip, crop) + *-ura* -ure — more at TOME] **1 :** the clipping or shaving of the head; *specif* **:** the shaving of a distinctive portion of the head as part of a rite accompanying admission to the clerical state **2 :** the shaven crown or patch worn by monks and various clerics **3 :** a bald spot that resembles a tonsure

²**tonsure** \"\ *vt* -ED/-ING/-S **:** to shave the head of **:** confer the tonsure upon

ton·sured \-(r)d\ *adj* [¹*tonsure* + *-ed*] **1 :** shaven or shorn in the manner of one having a tonsure **2 :** admitted by the rite of tonsure to the clerical state **3 :** having a bald spot

¹**ton·tine** \'tän·,tēn, ₑ'ₑ\ *n* -s [F, fr. Lorenzo *Tonti* †1695 Ital. banker in Paris who invented the scheme + F *-ine*, fr. *-ine*, fem. of *-in* -ine, adj. suffix] **:** a financial arrangement (as an insurance policy) whereby a group of participants share various benefits or advantages on such terms that upon the death or default of any member a part or all of his advantages are distributed among all the remaining members until on the death of all but one the whole goes to him or on the expiration of an agreed period the whole goes to those then remaining in the group; *collectively* **:** the share or right of each individual

²**tontine** \"\ *adj* **:** relating to or involving the principle or system upon which the tontine is based ⟨~ fund⟩ ⟨~ loan⟩

tontine insurance *n* **:** participating life insurance providing for distribution of surplus according to the tontine principle — compare DEFERRED DIVIDEND

ton·tin·er \-ēnə(r)\ *n* -s [¹*tontine* + *-er*] **:** a sharer in a tontine

ton·to \'tän(,)tō\ *n, pl* **tonto** *or* **tontos** *usu cap* [AmerSp, fr. Sp, fool, fr. *tonto* foolish] **1 :** one of various subgroups of the Apache people **2 :** an Indian of any one of several Apache subgroups

to·nus \'tōnəs\ *n* -ES [NL, fr. L, tension — more at TONE] **:** TONE 11a(1); *usu* **:** the state of partial contraction that is characteristic of normal muscle, is maintained at least in part by a continuous bombardment of motor impulses originating reflexly, and serves to maintain body posture and to hold the musculature in a state of readiness for specific demands — compare CLONUS

¹**tony** *n* -ES [fr. *Tony*, nickname for *Antony*] *obs* **:** FOOL, SIMPLETON

²**tony** *also* **toney** \'tōnē, -ni\ *adj* -ER/-EST [²*tone* + *-y*; influenced in meaning by ⁴*ton*] **:** HIGH-TONED, ARISTOCRATIC, STYLISH ⟨introduced me to all his ~ friends⟩ ⟨very expensive ~ restaurant⟩ **:** FASHIONABLE ⟨~ resort⟩ ⟨~ suburb⟩

³**tony** \"\ *n, pl* **tonys** *usu cap* [after *Tony*, nickname of *Antoinette* Perry †1946 Am. actress & producer] **:** any of several medallions awarded annually by a professional organization for notable performances in the theater

-to·ny \,tōnē, ,tᵊnē, -i\ *n comb form* -ES [NL *-tonia*] **:** -TONIA ⟨hyper*tony*⟩

too \(¦)tü\ *adv* [ME *to*, *too*, fr. OE *tō* to, too — more at TO] **1 :** in addition **:** ALSO, BESIDES, MOREOVER ⟨must sell the house and the furniture ~⟩ ⟨in this group are, ~, the many species of frogfishes —R.E.Coker⟩ ⟨~, the reader will become aware of the ingenuity —J.D.Vehling⟩ ⟨naturally they become weaker . . . and ultimately must perish miserably from starvation, while many ~ are killed by their stronger companions —James Stevenson-Hamilton⟩ **2 a :** to an excessive degree **:** EXCESSIVELY ⟨the economic interpretation is ~ simple —M.R. Cohen⟩ ⟨~ often leans the other way —M.S.Watson⟩ ⟨a ~ easy formula —Max Lerner⟩ ⟨~ large a house for us⟩ ⟨~ old to walk —R.W.Hatch⟩ **b :** to such a degree as to be regrettable, painful, or reprehensible ⟨that's ~ bad⟩ ⟨all ~ true⟩ ⟨these suspicions were only ~ justified —*New Republic*⟩ ⟨has gone ~ far⟩ — often doubled for emphasis ⟨the peasants are just ~, ~ quaint — William Newberry⟩ **c :** to a high degree **:** EXTREMELY, EXTRAVAGANTLY, VERY ⟨standing and looking ~ languishing down by the door —Elizabeth Bowen⟩ ⟨how ~ terrible —Martha Gellhorn⟩ ⟨the first slope wasn't ~ bad although it was steep —L.A.Viereck⟩ ⟨an episodic work without ~ consistent a texture —Irving Kolodin⟩ **3 :** SO 2d, INDEED ⟨I didn't. You did ~!⟩

toodle-oo \,tüdᵊl'ü\ *interj* [perh. imit. of an automobile horn] *chiefly Brit* **:** GOOD-BYE, SO LONG

took [ME (past), fr. OE *tōc* (past)] *past or dial past part of* TAKE

¹**tool** \'tül\ *n* -s *often attrib* [ME *tol*, *tool*, fr. OE *tōl*; akin to ON *tōl* tool, weapon, Goth *taujan* to do, make — more at TAW] **1 a :** an instrument (as a hammer or saw) used or worked by hand **:** an instrument used by a handicraftsman or laborer in his work **:** IMPLEMENT **b** (1) **:** the cutting or shaping part in a machine or machine tool (2) **:** a machine for shaping metal **:** MACHINE TOOL **c :** a particular kind of hand tool: as (1) **:** a bookbinder's instrument headed with a cut or engraved design with which impressions are made (as in finishing) (2) **:** a small brush used in painting window sashes **2 a :** an implement or object used in performing an operation or carrying on work of any kind **:** an instrument or apparatus necessary to a person in the practice of his vocation or profession ⟨a barber's chair, a photographer's camera, a scholar's books are all ~*s*⟩ **b :** something that serves as a means to an end **:** an instrument by which something is effected or accomplished ⟨words are the ~*s* with which men think —J.E.Gloag⟩ ⟨respected advertising as an indispensable ~ of business —*Newsweek*⟩ **c** *archaic* **:** SWORD, WEAPON **d** *slang* **:** PENIS **3 :** one who is or allows himself to be used or manipulated by another **:** DUPE, PUPPET ⟨believes the whole business of witchcraft . . . and thinks that the old women who were burned were the ~*s* of a great conspiracy against religion and society —O.W.Holmes †1935⟩ ⟨an easy ~, deferential, glad to be of use —T.S.Eliot⟩ **syn** see IMPLEMENT

²**tool** \"\ *vb* -ED/-ING/-S *vt* **1 a :** to cause (a vehicle) to move along **:** DRIVE ⟨~*ed* the car expertly through dark alleys and back streets —John Faulkner⟩ **b :** to convey in a vehicle ⟨~*ed* him everywhere in a jeep —Hugh Fosburgh⟩ ⟨~*ing* him out to the starboard boat circle off the bow —K.M.Dodson⟩ **2 :** to shape, form, or finish with a tool ⟨grotesque sandstone formations, ~*ed* by centuries of wind and weather into freak shapes —*Amer. Guide Series: Calif.*⟩ ⟨assumed that all aircraft parts are ~*ed* accurately —*Aero Digest*⟩: as **a :** to letter or ornament (a book cover) by means of heated hand tools **b :** to ornament the surface of (as a metal object) by means of hand tools **c :** to work on the surface of (a printing plate) with a hand tool (as to correct minor imperfections or engrave white lines) **3 :** to equip (as a plant or industry) with the necessary tools, machines, and instruments for volume production ⟨the engine would be abandoned before the plant could be ~*ed* to make it —W.W.Stout⟩ — often used with *up* ⟨showed how easy it is to accumulate stockpiles, ~ up war industries —J.P. Baxter b.1893⟩ ~ *vi* **1 a :** to drive or ride in a vehicle ⟨turned off the highway . . . and ~*ed* gently up the drive —R.P. Warren⟩ ⟨the usual crowd of space cadets ~*ing* along in a flying saucer —John McCarten⟩ **b :** to move along **:** PROCEED, TRAVEL ⟨my grandfather, in one race ~*ing* along at full gallop —Joyce Cary⟩ **2 :** to use tools **3 :** to equip a plant or industry for volume production by designing, building, and integrating the equipment (as machines, machine tools, precision instruments) required for making and assembling a product — often used with *up* ⟨~ up to make smaller cars⟩

too·lach \'tü,lach\ *n* -ES [native name in Australia] **:** a lightly built and heavily furred fawn gray wallaby (*Macropus greyi*) that is strikingly banded on face and rump and is nearly or wholly extinct due to excessive hunting

tool angle *n* **1 :** the angle included between the top and front faces of a cutting tool **2 :** an angle used to designate the form of the cutting edge of a tool — compare CLEARANCE 2e, CUTTING ANGLE, ⁶RAKE 3

tool apron *n* **:** APRON 3d(2)

toolbar \'ₑ,ₑ\ *n* **:** a frame mounted at the rear of a tractor to which various implements may be attached

tool bit *n* **:** cutting material of square cross section a few inches long that is shaped to perform a machining operation when clamped on a tool shank or holder

toolbox \'⸗,⸗\ *n* **1 :** a box or chest to hold tools — see BOX illustration **2 :** an adjustable mechanism containing the tool or cutter holder in a planing machine or other machine tool

tool crib *n* **:** CRIB 2g

tooled finish *n* **:** a finish on the face of a stone in which the corrugations made by the chisel or cutting tool extend in straight lines across the face of the stone

tooled joint *n* **:** a masonry joint in which the mortar is compressed and given a concave or V shape with a jointing tool while the mortar is still green — see JOINT illustration

tool engineer *n* **:** a specialist in tool engineering

tool engineering *n* **:** a division of industrial engineering whose function is to plan the processes of manufacture, develop the tools and machines, and integrate the facilities required for producing particular products with minimal expenditure of time, labor, and materials

tool·er \'tülə(r)\ *n* -s **:** one that tools ⟨a leather ~⟩

toolhead \'⸗,⸗\ *n* **:** a part of a machine (as of a lathe or planer) in which a tool or toolholder is clamped and which is provided with adjustments to bring the tool into the desired position

toolholder \'⸗,⸗⸗\ *n* **:** a short steel bar having a shank at one end to fit into the toolhead of a machine and a clamp at the other end to hold small interchangeable cutting bits

toolhouse \'⸗,⸗\ *or* **toolshed** \'⸗,⸗\ *n* **:** a house or shed (as in a garden) for storing tools

tooling *n* -s [fr. gerund of ²*tool*] **1 :** a mechanical operation performed with or an effect produced by a tool: as **a :** stone dressing having a tooled finish **b :** a gilt or blind impression stamped in intaglio on ornamental leatherwork **c :** special ornamental handwork (as with a chisel or gouge) in any of various materials (as wood, metal, or ivory) **2 :** a set or group of tools; *specif* **:** an assembly of tools in a factory or workshop

tool·less \'tülləs\ *adj* **:** having no tools

toolmaker \'⸗,⸗⸗\ *n* **:** one who makes and repairs tools; *specif* **:** a machinist who specializes in the construction, repair, maintenance, and calibration of the tools, jigs, fixtures, and instruments of a machine shop

toolmakers' button *n* **:** a small hardened steel jig for accurately locating holes to be drilled in a workpiece

toolmaking \'⸗,⸗⸗\ *n* **:** the act, process, or art of making tools

tool·man \'⸗mən\ *n, pl* **toolmen :** one who works with or makes tools; *specif* **:** a toolroom clerk

toolmark \'⸗,⸗\ *n* **:** a mark or impression made in tooling

toolmarking \'⸗,⸗⸗\ *n* **:** the marking of a steel tool with figures, letters, or symbols

toolplate \'⸗,⸗\ *n* **:** TOOLBOX 2

tool post *n* **:** a slotted or channeled post or analogous part in a lathe or other machine tool in which the cutting tool is clamped

tool pusher *n, slang* **:** a foreman who supervises drilling operations at an oil well or group of oil wells

tool rest *n* **:** a support for a tool; *specif* **:** an adjustable horizontal bar for supporting a hand tool when turning

toolroom \'⸗,⸗\ *n* **:** a room where tools are kept; *esp* **:** a room in a machine shop in which tools are made, stored, or loaned out to the workmen

toolroom lathe *n* **:** an engine lathe designed for extremely accurate machining

tools *pl of* TOOL, *pres 3d sing of* TOOL

toolslide \'⸗,⸗\ *n* **:** a part that supports a cutting tool (as in a tool post) and that contains or is mounted upon sliding members which may be moved in ways provided for the purpose

toolsmith \'⸗,⸗\ *n* **:** a smith who forges, dresses, hardens, and tempers tools **:** TOOLMAKER

tool steel *n* **1 :** hard usu. electric steel capable of being tempered so as to be especially suitable as a material for tools **2 :** a high-carbon or alloy steel used to make a cutting tool for machining metals **3 :** steel used to make tools and dies for various purposes (as press tools, die-casting dies, forging dies, or extrusion tools)

tool subject *n* **:** a subject studied to achieve competence in a skill for use in other subjects ⟨graduate students in sociology are required to take statistics as a *tool subject*⟩ — compare CONTENT SUBJECT

¹**toom** \'tüm\ *adj* [ME *tom, toom* empty, fr. OE *tōm* — more at TEEM] *chiefly Scot* **:** being without content or substance **:** EMPTY

²**toom** \"\ *vt* -ED/-ING/-S *chiefly Scot* **:** EMPTY, POUR

³**toom** \"\ *n* -s [²*toom*] *Scot* **:** a dumping ground

too-much·ness \tü'məchnəs\ *n* [fr. the phrase *too much* + *-ness*] **:** the quality or state of being excessive ⟨his prosodic devices, his lively games with adjectives and expletives, may weary us with a *too-muchness* today —*Times Lit. Supp.*⟩

¹**toon** \'tün\ *Scot var of* TOWN

²**toon** \"\ *n* -s [Hindi *tūn*, fr. Skt *tunna*] **1 :** an East Indian and Australian tree (*Cedrela toona*) with fragrant dark red wood and with flowers that yield a dye — called also *Moulmein cedar* **2 :** the wood of toon used esp. for furniture and general construction — called also *cedar, Indian mahogany, Moulmein cedar*

¹**too·na** \'tünə\ *n, cap* [NL, fr. E ²*toon*] **:** a small genus of Old World trees (family Meliaceae) closely related to *Cedrela* but having a short disk and completely winged seeds

²**toona** \"\ *n* -s [MexSp *tuna*] **:** a Mexican tree (*Castilloa elastica*) that is a minor source of rubber — compare CAUCHO

too·ner·ville \'tünə(r),vil, *esp south* -,vəl\ *adj, usu cap* [fr. the *Toonerville (trolley)*, a rickety trolley car in the comic strip *Toonerville Trolley* by Fontaine Fox *b*1884 Am. cartoonist] **:** of, relating to, or constituting a rickety or inefficient railroad line ⟨even the *Toonerville* locals are terribly overcrowded, so make your reservations now —T.H.Fielding⟩

toor·ie \'türi\ *n* -s [*toor* (Sc, alter. of E *tower*) + *-ie*] **:** a tassel on a Scotch bonnet

¹**toot** \'tüt\ *vi* -ED/-ING/-S [ME *toten, tooten*, fr. OE *tōtian* — more at TOUT] **1** *chiefly dial* **:** to stand out **:** show above ground **:** SPROUT **2** *chiefly dial* **a :** GAZE, PEEP, SPY **b :** to look searchingly **:** PRY

²**toot** \'tüt, *usu* -üd·+V\ *n* -s [ME *tote*, fr. *toten, tooten*, v.] *chiefly dial* **:** an elevation used or capable of being used as a lookout; *specif* **:** a rocky promontory

³**toot** \"\ *vb* -ED/-ING/-S [prob. of imit. origin like MLG & MD *tūten* to toot] *vi* **1 a** *of a wind instrument* **:** to sound a short blast ⟨a horn ~*ed* in the distance⟩ **b :** to sound a note or call suggesting the short blast of a wind instrument ⟨the ~*ing* of the heath hen could be heard each spring —A.A. Allen⟩ **2 :** to blow or sound a horn or other wind instrument esp. so as to produce short rapid blasts ⟨a trumpeter who has ~*ed* in many bands⟩ ⟨boarded a train a few miles out of town, and the entourage came puffing and ~*ing* up to the base of the platform —*Americas*⟩ **3 :** to drive, proceed, or move along esp. in a car ⟨agricultural-extension workers ~ around the . . . farmlands —Phil Gustafson⟩ **4** *slang* **:** to state the truth **:** assert something as a fact ⟨you're ~*ing*, you won't stop me —R.P.Warren⟩ ~ *vt* **1 :** to spread abroad **:** PROCLAIM, TRUMPET ⟨~*ed* his friend's praises wherever he went⟩ **2 a :** to sound (a note) on a horn or other wind instrument ⟨the bugle ~*ed* retreat⟩ **b :** to cause (a wind instrument) to produce a characteristic sound ⟨~ a horn⟩ ⟨~ a trumpet⟩ ⟨~ a whistle⟩ — **toot one's horn** *or* **toot one's own horn :** blow one's horn **:** BOAST ⟨goes around *tooting his horn* merely because he's charitable —Sinclair Lewis⟩

⁴**toot** \"\ *n* -s **:** a short blast sounded on a wind instrument (as a horn); *also* **:** a sound resembling or suggesting such a blast

⁵**toot** \'tüt\ *vb* -ED/-ING/-S [origin unknown] *vi, Scot* **:** to drink heavily ~ *vt, Scot* **:** to drink deeply of **:** QUAFF

⁶**toot** \'tüt, *usu* -üd·+V\ *n* -s **1** *Scot* **:** a drink of liquor **:** SNORT **2 a :** a drinking bout **:** SPREE ⟨used to go on a ~, and one night when he was drunk he told me —R.M.Dorson⟩ ⟨all hands went on a joyous ~ —James Dugan⟩ **b :** an act or period of unrestrained indulgence in some feeling or activity **:** BINGE, JAG ⟨any business taking off on an inflationary ~ —*Sacramento (Calif.) Bee*⟩ ⟨survived each of these emotional ~s —T.H.White b. 1915⟩

⁷**toot** \'tüt\ *interj* [prob. imit. of a tongue-clicking sound] *Scot* — used to express disapproval or disbelief

⁸**toot** \"\ *n* -s [origin unknown] *dial* **:** a worthless person **:** FOOL

⁹**toot** \'tüt\ *n* -s [PaG *dutt*, fr. MLG *tūte* horn, horn-shaped object; akin to Icel *tūta* sharp projection, Sw *tuta* fingerstall] *dial* **:** any of various conical containers: as **a :** a small paper bag **b :** a piece of paper twisted into the shape of a cone and used as a temporary container (as for mustard) **c :** ICE-CREAM CONE

toot·er \'tüd·ə(r), -ütə-\ *n* -s [³*toot* + *-er*] **:** one that toots

¹**tooth** \'tüth\ *n, pl* **teeth** \'tēth\ *often attrib* [ME *toth, tooth*, fr. OE *tōth*; akin to OHG *zand* tooth, ON *tönn*, Goth *tunthus*, L *dent-, dens*, Gk *odont-, odōn, odous*, Skt *danta* tooth, and prob. to OE *etan* to eat — more at EAT] **1 a :** one of the hard bony appendages that are borne on the jaws or in many of the lower vertebrates on other bones in the walls of the mouth or pharynx and serve esp. for the prehension and mastication of food and as weapons of offense and defense — see CANINE, FANG, INCISOR, MOLAR, PREMOLAR, TUSK; CROWN, ROOT; CEMENTUM, DENTIN, ENAMEL **b :** any of various usu. hard and sharp horny, chitinous, or calcareous processes about the mouth (as on the radula of a mollusk or the mastax of a rotifer) or about any part (as the forceps of an ear wig) of an invertebrate that functions like or resembles the vertebrate jaws **c :** a toothlike process on a bivalve shell — see HINGE TOOTH **2 :** a fondness or taste for something specified **:** LIKING ⟨an insatiable ~ for candy⟩ **3 :** an angular or rounded projection resembling or suggesting the tooth of an animal in shape, arrangement, or action ⟨a saw ~⟩ ⟨the *teeth* of a comb⟩ ⟨the *teeth* of a rake⟩: as **a :** one of the regular projections on the circumference or sometimes on the face of a wheel (as in a machine) that engage with the corresponding projections on another wheel esp. to transmit force and motion **:** COG **b :** a small sharp-pointed marginal lobe (as of a leaf) **c :** a sharp jagged point or projection ⟨their slopes loaded with packed snow and fanged with the brittle *teeth* of icicles —Victor Canning⟩ ⟨to the westward . . . a line of jagged *teeth* proclaim . . . our ultimate objective —Wynford Vaughan-Thomas⟩ **d :** any of the bricks or stones left projecting from a wall to provide for a subsequent extension **e :** a projection of paper between perforation holes on a severed perforated edge (as of a stamp) — called also *perforation tooth* **4 a :** something that injures, tortures, devours, or destroys as if by a biting, piercing, or gnawing action ⟨only the classic can endure the ~ of time —Elinor Wylie⟩ ⟨the *teeth* of the wind⟩ **b teeth** *pl* **:** effective means of compulsion, enforcement, or punishment ⟨started turning out the arms which would put *teeth* into neutrality —E.O.Hauser⟩ ⟨reluctant to pass legislation with *teeth* regarding this issue —T.L.Reller⟩ **5 :** a roughness of surface produced by mechanical or artificial means on a surface or thing: as **a :** a roughness of surface on a material (as paper or canvas) that enables it readily to take ink, crayon, paints, or water colors **b :** the roughness given an undercoat of paint to anchor the next coat **c :** a mat surface on a negative film; *specif* **:** a fine varnish coating that permits pencil marks in retouching — **from the teeth forward** *or* **from the teeth outward** *archaic* **:** not from the heart **:** in outward appearance only **:** on the surface — **in the teeth of 1 :** in or into direct contact or collision with **:** so as directly to confront or be confronted with ⟨headed north *in the teeth of* the steadily rising gale —N.R.Raine⟩ ⟨*in the teeth of* conditions to drive a normal actor crazy —Kenneth Tynan⟩ **2 :** in direct opposition to **:** in defiance of ⟨to express such views was to fly *in the teeth of* the age —Roy Lewis & Angus Maude⟩ — **set one's teeth on edge** *also* **put one's teeth on edge 1 :** to cause a disagreeable sensation in the teeth ⟨the fathers have eaten sour grapes, and *the children's teeth are set on edge* —Jer 31:29(RSV)⟩ **2 :** EXASPERATE ⟨the constant chattering of the children *set his teeth on edge*⟩ — **to one's teeth** *archaic* **:** to one's face **:** OPENLY ⟨that I shall live and tell him *to his teeth* —Shak.⟩ — **to the teeth** *adv* **:** COMPLETELY, FULLY ⟨armed *to the teeth*⟩ ⟨a theory in which my father upheld her *to the teeth* —Della Lutes⟩

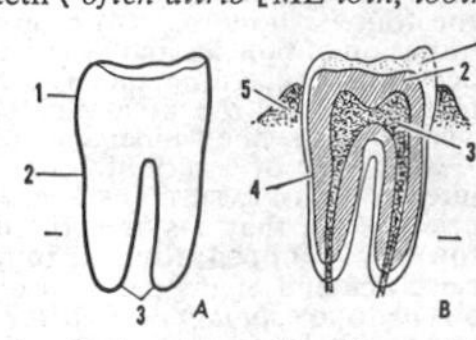

tooth 1a: *A*, outside of a molar: *1* crown, *2* neck, *3* roots; *B*, cross section of a molar: *1* enamel, *2* dentin, *3* pulp chamber, *4* cementum, *5* gum

²**tooth** \", 'tüth\ *vb* -ED/-ING/-S [ME *tothen, toothen*, fr. *toth, tooth*, n.] *vt* **1 :** to furnish with teeth; *specif* **:** INDENT, JAG ⟨~ a saw⟩ **2 :** to chew on **:** BITE **3 :** to lock into by means of teeth **4 :** to roughen the surface of (as with a toothing plane) ~ *vi* **:** to engage by means of teeth **:** GEAR, MESH

toothache \'⸗,⸗\ *n* [ME *tothache*, fr. *toth, tooth* + *ache*] **:** pain in or about a tooth

toothache bark *n* **:** the bark of the prickly ash

toothache grass *n* **:** a tall grass (*Ctenium aromaticum*) of southern U. S. that has dense one-sided spikes and a very pungent taste

toothache tree *n* **:** PRICKLY ASH 1

toothachy \'⸗,⸗⸗\ *adj* **:** suffering from or suggesting toothache

tooth and nail *adv* **:** with every available means of attack or defense **:** ALL OUT, FIERCELY ⟨swallowed their gallant words and fought the measure *tooth and nail* —C.G.Bowers⟩

toothbill \'⸗,⸗\ *n* **:** TOOTH-BILLED PIGEON

tooth-billed \'⸗,⸗\ *adj* **:** having a notched bill

tooth-billed pigeon *n* **:** a Samoan pigeon (*Didunculus strigirostris*) that has a bill superficially resembling that of the extinct dodo, a chiefly chestnut brown body with a greenish black head and neck, and a lower mandible with several notches near the end

toothbrush \'⸗,⸗\ *n* **:** a brush for cleaning the teeth

toothbrush mustache *n* **:** a small bristly mustache

toothbrush tree *n* **:** an Old World tree (*Salvadora persica*), whose twigs are sometimes bound in clusters and used as toothbrushes

tooth bud *or* **tooth germ** *n* **:** a mass of tissue having the potentiality of differentiating into a tooth

toothbrushes

toothcomb \'⸗,⸗\ *n, Brit* **:** a comb with fine teeth

tooth coral *n* **:** CACTUS CORAL

toothcup \'⸗,⸗\ *n* **1 :** a low-growing No. American herb (*Rotala ramosior*) found on sandy shores and having solitary flowers and regularly splitting capsules **2 :** a low herb (*Ammania coccinea*) of the family Lythraceae chiefly found in southern U. S. and having narrow leaves and flowers in clusters of two, three, or several in the leaf axils

toothed \'tütht *sometimes* -üthd\ *adj* [ME *tothed, toothed*, fr. *toth, tooth* tooth + *-ed*] **1 a :** provided with teeth ⟨a ~ animal⟩ **:** BITING ⟨a gray world, with ice and ~ winds —*N.Y. Times*⟩ **b :** having such or so many teeth — usu. used in combination ⟨buck-toothed⟩ **c :** COGGED ⟨a ~ wheel⟩ **2 :** having marginal projecting points **:** DENTATE

toothed bur clover *n* **:** a bur clover (*Medicago hispida*)

toothed herring *n* **:** MOONEYE 2a

toothed spurge *n* **:** an annual weed (*Euphorbia dentata*) of northeastern No. America with dentate leaves

toothed whale *n* **:** any of various whales comprising the suborder Odontoceti and having numerous simple conical teeth — compare WHALEBONE WHALE

tooth·er \'tüthə(r), -üthə-\ *n* -s [²*tooth* + *-er*] **:** one that cuts out the teeth of saws

tooth·ful \'tüth,fu̇l\ *n* -s **:** a small bite or mouthful; *esp* **:** a small drink of liquor

tooth fungus *n* **:** a fungus of the family Hydnaceae

toothier *comparative of* TOOTHY

toothiest *superlative of* TOOTHY

tooth·i·ly \'tüthəlē, -li\ *adv* **:** in a toothy manner ⟨bowing low and grinning ~ —E.J.Kahn⟩

tooth·ing \'tüthiŋ, -üth-, -ēŋ\ *n* -s [in sense 1, fr. ¹*tooth* + *-ing*; in sense 2, fr. gerund of ²*tooth*] **1 a :** an arrangement, formation, or projection consisting of or containing teeth or parts resembling teeth **:** INDENTATION, SERRATION **b :** an arrangement of bricks alternately projecting at the end of a wall to permit bonding into a later continuation of the wall **2 :** the act or process of furnishing with teeth or a tooth

tooth·less \'tüthləs\ *adj* [ME *tothles, toothles*, fr. *toth, tooth* + *-les* -less] **1 a :** not yet supplied with teeth **:** not having cut one's teeth ⟨a ~ baby⟩ **b :** not provided with teeth ⟨a ~ animal⟩ ⟨a ~ saw⟩ **c :** having lost one's teeth ⟨a ~ old woman⟩ **2 a :** lacking in sharpness or bite ⟨spoke in ~ generalities —Arthur Hepner⟩ **b :** lacking in means of enforcement or coercion **:** FUTILE, INEFFECTUAL ⟨a ~ piece of legislation —*Nature Mag.*⟩ — **tooth·less·ly** *adv* — **tooth·less·ness** *n* -ES

tooth·let \-lət\ *n* -s **:** a small tooth (as on a shell)

toothlike \'⸗,⸗\ *adj* **:** resembling or suggesting a tooth or teeth **:** SERRATE

tooth ornament *n* **:** DOGTOOTH 2

toothpaste \'⸗,⸗\ *n* **:** a paste dentifrice

toothpick \'⸗,⸗\ *n* [ME (Sc) *tuthpik*, fr. *toth, tooth, tuth* tooth + *pik* pick — more at TOOTH, PICK] **1 a :** a slender pointed piece of wood used after eating to remove bits of food lodged between the teeth **b :** a similar instrument of metal, bone, or plastic used for picking the teeth and cleaned for reuse **2 :** a wooden toothpick or a small flat tapering piece of wood or plastic used for spearing and holding together small portions of prepared food or for conveying one mouthful to the mouth **3 toothpicks** *pl* **:** FRAGMENTS, SPLINTERS ⟨the ship was smashed into ~*s* by the storm⟩ **4 :** a long thin object or person ⟨wearing heels that are ~*s*⟩ ⟨a ~ of a man⟩: as **a** (1) **:** ARKANSAS TOOTHPICK (2) *usu cap* **:** ARKANSAN — used as a nickname **b :** a slender pointed boat

tooth·pick·er \-kə(r)\ *n* **:** a worker who places glass beads on toothpicks for further processing in the manufacture of synthetic pearls

tooth powder *n* **:** a dentifrice in powder form

tooth rail *n* **:** COGRAIL

tooth rash *n* **:** STROPHULUS

tooths *pres 3d sing of* TOOTH

tooth sac *n* **:** DENTAL SAC

tooth shell *n* **1 :** a mollusk of the class Scaphopoda **2 :** the shell of a tooth shell having the shape of an elephant's tusk and formerly used as money by the Indians along the northwest coast of No. America

tooth·some \'tüthsəm\ *adj* [¹*tooth* + *-some*] **1 :** pleasing to the taste **:** DELICIOUS ⟨grandmother's ~ battercakes —S.H. Adams⟩ **2 :** AGREEABLE, PLEASANT ⟨the taste of power is ~ —Helen Howe⟩ **3 :** sexually attractive **:** DELECTABLE, LUSCIOUS ⟨a ~ blond baggage . . . standing there in an unbelievably tight emerald gown —*New Yorker*⟩ **syn** see PALATABLE

tooth·some·ly *adv* **:** in a toothsome manner

tooth·some·ness *n* -ES **:** the quality or state of being toothsome

toothwort \'⸗,⸗\ *n* **1 :** a European plant (*Lathraea squamaria*) parasitic on the hazel and beech and having a rootstock covered with toothlike scales **2 :** any of various hardy perennial creeping herbs comprising the genus *Dentaria* and including several that are cultivated for their showy usu. white, rose, or purple flowers — called also *pepperroot*; compare CORALWORT, CRINKLEROOT

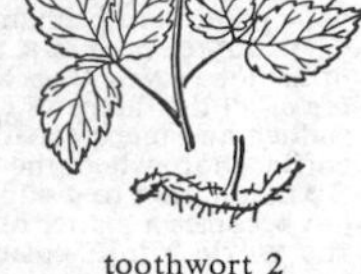
toothwort 2

toothy \'tüthē, -th̲, |i\ *adj* -ER/-EST [¹*tooth* + *-y*] **1 :** having or showing prominent teeth ⟨he smiled broad ~ smiles —Walter Goodman⟩ **2 a** *archaic* **:** BITING, SHARP ⟨~ critics —Robert Burns⟩ **b :** equipped with teeth **:** EFFECTUAL ⟨the pact is not as ~ as once intended —*Time*⟩ **3 :** TOOTHSOME ⟨the ~ morsel within —*Manufacturing Confectioner*⟩ **4** *of paper* **:** having a desirable roughness of surface

tooting *pres part of* TOOT

¹**too·tle** \'tüd·ᵊl, -ütᵊl\ *vb* **tootled; tootled; tootling** \-d·ᵊliŋ, -t(ᵊ)liŋ\ **tootles** [freq. of ³*toot*] *vi* **1 a :** to make a repeated tooting noise ⟨the birds *tootling* in the trees⟩ **b :** to toot gently, repeatedly, or continuously on a wind instrument ⟨the final chorus with three high trumpets *tootling* for dear life —Virgil Thomson⟩ **2 :** to write or talk nonsense **3 :** to drive or move along **:** make one's way ⟨cheerfully *tootling* around England in their cars last weekend —Mollie Panter-Downes⟩ ⟨think I'll ~ off to bed —Dorothy Sayers⟩ ~ *vt* **1 :** to toot continuously on ⟨musical instruments which are scraped, *tootled*, and banged by millions —*Newsweek*⟩ **2 :** to produce by a continued or prolonged tootling ⟨birds began to ~ their songs of joy —P.G.Wodehouse⟩

²**tootle** \"\ *n* -s **:** the act, action, or sound of tootling ⟨can make it give off ~*s* of varying lengths —*New Yorker*⟩ **2 :** feeble or verbose writing or speech **:** TWADDLE

too·tler \'tüd·ᵊlə(r), -üt(ᵊ)l-\ *n* -s **:** one that tootles

toot net *n* [¹*toot*] *Scot* **:** a large anchored fishing net

¹**too-too** \'tü'tü\ *adv* [redupl. of *too*] **:** to an unpleasantly or affectedly excessive degree ⟨openly sneered . . . at those who prefer the *too-too* refined type of whodunit —*Time*⟩

²**too-too** \"\ *adj* **:** going beyond the bounds of convention, good taste, or common sense **:** EXCESSIVE, EXTREME; *esp* **:** affected in manner or behavior **:** LA-DI-DA ⟨isn't he just *too-too* —Chet Straight⟩

³**too-too** \(')tü'tü\ *vi* -ED/-ING/-S [imit.] **:** to produce or utter a flat monotonous tootling sound

¹**toots** *pres 3d sing of* TOOT, *pl of* TOOT

²**toots** \'tüts\ *Scot var of* ⁷TOOT

³**toots** \'tüts\ *n* -ES [prob. short for *tootsie*] *slang* **:** WOMAN, GIRL ⟨hi, ~ . . . so you're out of jail again —H.T.Carter⟩

toot·sie \'tütsē, -si\ *n* -s [origin unknown] **1** *slang* **:** DEAR, SWEETHEART **2** *slang* **:** PARTY GIRL ⟨a ~ he picked up in the lobby of a hotel —Alfred Hayes⟩

toot·sy *also* **toot·sie** \'tu̇tsē, -si\ *n, pl* **tootsies** [alter. of *footsie*] **:** FOOT ⟨cover baby's *tootsies* —Joy Warren⟩

tootsy-wootsy \'tu̇tsē'wu̇tsē\ *n* -ES [by redupl.] **:** TOOTSIE 1

¹**top** \'täp\ *n* -s [ME *top, toppe*, fr. OE *top*; akin to OHG *zopf* end, tip, tuft of hair, ON *toppr* tuft of hair, crest, top and perh. to OE *tæppa* tap — more at TAP] **1 a** (1) **:** the highest point, level, or part of something **:** the upper end, edge, or extremity **:** SUMMIT, CROWN ⟨looked over the ~*s* of his half-spectacles —Marcia Davenport⟩ ⟨slopes leading toward the mesa-*top* —*Amer. Antiquity*⟩ ⟨the ~ of the beach —Sally Carrighar⟩ ⟨the ~ of the pass⟩ (2) **:** the highest part of the body **:** the head or top of the head — used esp. in the phrase *top to toe* (3) **:** the head of a plant; *esp* **:** the part of a plant with edible roots that is above ground ⟨beet ~*s*⟩ (4) **:** the part of a cut gem above the girdle **:** CROWN, BEZEL (5) **:** the upper part of a garment; *esp* **:** the jacket of pajamas (6) **:** a garment worn on the upper body (7) **:** TOP MILK **b** (1) **:** the highest or uppermost region or parts ⟨dive bombers . . . dive off the ~ of the sky —Ira Wolfert⟩; *esp* **:** the uppermost story (as the attic) of a building ⟨at the ~ of the house lived a medical student —W.B.Yeats⟩ — compare TREETOP (2) **:** the surface normally or at present facing upward as opposed to the undersurface **:** the side that overlies the whole ⟨cumulus clouds . . . with flat bases and rounded ~*s* —O.W.Perrie⟩ ⟨marked at several places to indicate where the ~ of the concrete should be —*Building, Estimating & Contracting*⟩ (3) **:** the part of a thing placed uppermost in use ⟨the ~ of the page⟩ (4) **:** the surface of the land or ocean ⟨the submarine came to the ~⟩; *also* **:** the point at which an underground shaft, tunnel, or well reaches the surface **2 a** *dial* **:** a crowning tuft: (1) **:** the hair on the head (2) **:** CREST 1a **b** *dial* **:** a tuft of textile fiber; *specif* **:** a bunch of flax tow placed on a distaff **c** (1) **:** a continuous strand of the longer wool fibers after straightening and separating from the short fibers by combing (2) **:** a similar strand of rayon staple fiber **3 :** a fitted, integral, or attached part or unit serving as an upper piece, endpiece, lid, or covering ⟨an ornamented steamboat smokestack ~ —Frederick Way⟩ ⟨saving box ~*s* for premiums⟩ ⟨a jar with a threaded ~⟩: as **a :** a metal, plastic, or fabric roof over the passenger compartment of a vehicle that is permanent or capable of being folded back, lowered, or removed **b :** the turndown part or band on a top boot **c** *Brit* **:** a ceiling esp. in a mine **d :** the upper of a shoe; *esp* **:** the parts above the vamp **e :** a circus or carnival tent **4 a :** a platform surround-

ing the head of a lower mast that serves to spread the topmast rigging, strengthen the mast, and furnish a standing place for men aloft **b** : a comparable part of the superstructure; *esp* : such a part on a warship used as a fire-control station or antiaircraft gun platform **5** : the part that is nearest in space or time to the source or beginning ⟨the ~ of the lake⟩ ⟨the ~ of the morning⟩; *specif* : the first half of an inning in the game of baseball **6** : TOPSAIL **7 a** (1) : the highest degree conceivable, attainable, or attained : ACME, PINNACLE ⟨singing at the ~ of a form that is unmatched anywhere —*Theatre Arts*⟩ ⟨the high temperature reading . . . compared with an 87.2 ~ on Friday —*N.Y. Times*⟩ (2) : the loudest or highest range of a sound ⟨shouted at the ~ of his lungs⟩ ⟨a soprano with a weak ~⟩ (3) *Brit* : ³HIGH 2b (4) : the price of the most expensive seats for a performance ⟨a show having a six-dollar ~⟩ **b** *archaic* : the highest realization or embodiment : the most perfect actualization or instance **c** : the height at which something that has been advancing recedes : culminating point : MAXIMUM ⟨sail with the ~ of the tide —Rachel Henning⟩ ⟨the all-time ~ for fishermen's earnings —*Pacific Fisherman*⟩ ⟨stocks bought at the ~ of the market⟩ **8 a** (1) : the highest position in rank, achievement, honor, success, or fame ⟨the ~ of his profession⟩ ⟨~ of the bill⟩ ⟨the ~ of his class⟩; *esp* : the position of a person or group wielding supreme authority ⟨bribery has reached from the ~ right down to the lowest clerical level —*Atlantic*⟩ ⟨access to someone very near the ~ —Thomas Barman⟩ (2) : a person or thing at the top ⟨the news of the rising situation got through . . . to the Congress . . . ~s —*Spark*⟩ **b** (1) : a playing card higher than any held in the same suit by an opponent (2) **tops** *pl* : aces and kings in a hand or the three highest honors in a suit (3) *or* **top score** : the highest match-point score made at duplicate bridge on a particular board or the highest total of match points scored during a session by one contestant or team **9 a** : the choicest part : the best or finest of its lot or kind : CREAM, PICK **b tops** *pl* : the choicest animals in a flock or herd **c tops** *pl, Brit* : ARISTOCRATS **10 a** : the part of a thing that is conventionally highest or occupies the most important position ⟨the arctic, the frozen ~ of the world —Carey Longmire⟩ ⟨our pilots rolled to the ~ of the runway —P.J.C. Friedlander⟩ ⟨the ~ of the room⟩ ⟨set her down at the ~ of the street —Maurice Hewlett⟩ **b** : the end of a billiard table opposite to that marked with the balkline in English billiards ⟨a *top*-of-the-table game⟩ **11** : TOP BOOT **12 a** : a button finished (as by plating) only on the face **13** : a forward spin given to a ball (as in golf, tennis, billiards, or cricket) by striking it on or near the top or above the center; *also* : the blow or stroke so given **14** : FIRST SERGEANT 1 **15** : the most volatile part that passes over first on distillation — often used in pl. ⟨refinery ~s⟩ **16** : a die marked with usu. only three different numbers rather than the usual six **17** : an outer ornamental or protective coating or layer ⟨a stainless steel watch band with a gold ~⟩ — compare BLACKTOP — **off one's top** : in a state of insanity or mental agitation — **on top** *adv* (*or adj*) **1 a** : in a state of accomplishment, success, or dominance ⟨extreme reactionary . . . elements have come out *on top* —*Nation*⟩ **b** : in the lead ⟨the horse went *on top* in the backstretch⟩ **2** *also* **on the top** *Brit* : in high gear **3** : above the clouds or bad weather ⟨when flying *on top*, your plane is in brilliant sunshine —*What Goes On Up There*⟩ — **on top of** *prep* **1 a** : in control of ⟨acted like a man *on top of* his job —*Newsweek*⟩ **b** : informed about ⟨readers right *on top of* all the news that's fit to print —*N.Y. Times*⟩ **2** : in sudden and unexpected proximity to ⟨I was right *on top of* the coffin shop when the door opened —Margery Allingham⟩ **3** : in addition to : superadded to ⟨writing *on top of* a regular job becomes a matter of stamina —N.M.Loomis⟩ — **on top of the world** : in a position of eminent success, happiness, or fame ⟨she was young, and prettier than the sea, and I was *on top of the world* —Barnaby Conrad⟩ — **over the top** *adv* (*or adj*) **1** : over the front of a trench in attacking **2** : over the assigned goal or limit ⟨the drive had gone *over the top* and considerably more than 200 dollars was collected —*Irish Digest*⟩ — **the top of one's head** *or* **the top of one's mind** : mental elements not directly involved in a present task or only partially directed or controlled ⟨with *the top of his mind* he listened to them —William Faulkner⟩ ⟨countless conferences at which everyone talked off *the top of their heads* —Goodman Ace⟩

²**top** \"\ *n* -s [ME *top, toppe*, fr. OE *top*; perh. akin to MD *dop* top, OHG *topf*] **1** : a child's toy that is commonly cylindrical, pear-shaped, or conoidal and has a tapering usu. steel-shod point on which it is made to spin by means of the fingers, a string, or a spring, or by whipping — see PEG TOP, WHIPPING TOP **2** : a conical block of wood with longitudinal grooves on its surface in which strands of rope slide in the process of twisting

top 1

³**top** \"\ *vb* **topped; topped; topping; tops** [ME *topen, toppen*, fr. *top, toppe* top — more at TOP (head)] *vt* **1** : to remove or cut the top of: as **a** : to prune the top or leaves of (a plant esp. of a root crop) ⟨~ carrots⟩ **b** : to execute by hanging **c** : to cut, break, or otherwise take off the top of (a steel ingot) to remove unsound metal **d** : to cut the top part from (a tree) in logging — compare CLIMBER 1a **e** : PINCH 1b (2) **f** : to remove the most volatile parts (as crude petroleum) from : STRIP 15a, SKIM **2 a** : to cover with a top or on the top : provide, form, or serve as a top for : complete by giving or serving as a covering, endpiece, crown, or cup for ⟨arches that ~ the windows —*Amer. Guide Series: N.H.*⟩ ⟨a black mop of curls *topping* a sleepy face —Winifred Bambrick⟩ ⟨the city's educational system is *topped* by four degree-granting colleges —*Amer. Guide Series: N.Y.*⟩ **b** (1) : to supply with a decorative or protective finish or a final touch — often used with *off* ⟨*topped* off the day with an hour's dancing —Bernard DeVoto⟩ (2) : to cover with another dye ⟨~ aniline black with methyl violet to prevent greening and crocking⟩ (3) : TIP 3 (4) : to resupply or esp. refuel (something partially exhausted) to capacity — usu. used with *off* ⟨log . . . showed she was *topped* off with fuel —Chesley Wilson⟩ (5) *West* : to finish breaking in (a horse) ⟨all these prospects had been *topped* and ridden several times —Jo Mora⟩ — usu. used with *off* or *out* ⟨the horse may still buck . . . but now the peeler can start *topping* it off —S.E.Fletcher⟩ **3 a** (1) : to be or become higher than : come to or over the top of : OVERTOP ⟨the water *topped* the boathouse⟩ ⟨*topped* by three other peaks in the state —*Amer. Guide Series: Vt.*⟩ (2) : to be in excess of ⟨ski crowds have *topped* 5000 in a single day —Jean Lunzer⟩ ⟨world wheat production has *topped* that of rice —Margaret K. Zieman⟩ ⟨the best year in its history . . . *topping* record 1953 —*Wall Street Jour.*⟩ **b** (1) : to be superior to : do better than : EXCEL, SURPASS, OUTDO ⟨intends to ~ herself in her next picture —Robert Trumbull⟩ ⟨~s everything of the kind in print —Alfred Frankenstein⟩ (2) : to perform (a part) better than before or better than someone else **c** : to gain ascendancy over : DOMINATE ⟨the base shall ~ the legitimate —Shak.⟩ **4 a** (1) : to rise to or reach the top of : ascend to the upper surface or esp. the summit of ⟨*topped* the backbone of the continent —A.B. Guthrie⟩ (2) : to go over the top of : CLEAR, SURMOUNT ⟨the horse *topped* the barrier⟩ (3) : to rise above the level of ⟨the plane was to ~ the storm —*Newsweek*⟩ **b** (1) : to be at the top of ⟨story that *topped* the nation's best-seller list —W.H.Whyte⟩ ⟨a great beech . . . *topped* a small knoll —Susan Ertz⟩ (2) : to be the highest card in (a suit) ⟨a suit *topped* by the ace⟩ (3) : to be in the most prominent or featured position of ⟨~ the bill⟩ **5** : COVER 10a **6** : to strike (a golf ball) above the center; *also* : to make (as a stroke) by hitting the ball in this way ~ *vi* : to make an end, finish, or conclusion — used with such prepositions as *off, out*, or *up*

⁴**top** \"\ *adj* [ME *top, toppe*, fr. *top, toppe*, n., top] **1 a** : of, relating to, or at the top : HIGHEST, TOPMOST, UPPERMOST ⟨~ floor⟩ ⟨in man the larynx sits at the ~ end of a windpipe —G. A.Miller⟩ **b** : serving as or constituting a top ⟨the ~ crust of a pie⟩ **2 a** (1) : foremost in order, rank, achievement, value, or precedence : CHIEF, HEAD, PREEMINENT ⟨the ~ painter of his time —Margaret Biddle⟩ ⟨two of the nation's ~ twenty-five banks —T.H.White b.1915⟩ ⟨ranked among the ~ six men of his class —*Current Biog.*⟩ ⟨~ priority⟩ (2) : of prime importance or interest ⟨it should have been . . . the ~ thought and concern of theater men —Bosley Crowther⟩ ⟨~ essential for stained-glass making is lead —H.L.Morrow⟩ ⟨the ~ news . . . has dealt with cases of flagrant corruption —Sidney Warren⟩ (3) : being the highest or a high card of a suit ⟨a suit headed by the four ~ honors⟩ (4) : responsible for the planning and initiation of policies and practices and for making the principal decisions concerning them — distinguished from *middle* ⟨~ management⟩ **b** : of a very high quality : extremely good : FIRST-CLASS ⟨the winner showed ~ form⟩ ⟨~ sports coverage —*advt*⟩ **3** : of a very high or the highest degree, amount, or intensity : GREATEST ⟨~ speed⟩ ⟨commodities selling at ~ prices⟩ **4** : that has or is fitted with a top ⟨~ buggy⟩

⁵**top** \"\ *vt* **topped; topped; topping; tops** [perh. fr. ¹*top*] : to raise one end of (as the yard of a sail) higher than the other

top- *or* **topo-** *comb form* [ME, fr. LL, fr. Gk, fr. *topos* — more at TOPIC] **1** : place : locality ⟨*topo*phobia⟩ **2** : local ⟨*topo*algia⟩ ⟨*top*ectomy⟩

top *abbr* topographic; topographical

TOP *abbr* temporarily out of print

top-and-butt \ˌ=ˈ=ˌ=\ *adj* : having the butt of one plank brought to the top of the other to make up a constant breadth in two layers ⟨*top-and-butt* planking⟩

toparch \ˈtōˌpärk, ˈtäˌp-\ *n* -s [LL *toparcha*, fr. Gk *toparchēs*, fr. *top-* + *-archēs* -arch] : a minor ruler or prince; *specif* : the governor of a toparchy

topar·chy \-kē\ *n* -ES [L *toparchia*, fr. Gk, fr. *toparchēs* toparch + *-ia* -y] : a small state or district consisting of a few cities or towns

top–armor \ˈ=ˌ==\ *n* : a railing of canvas or netting around a top on a ship

to·pa·to \təˈpād·(ˌ)ō\ *n* -ES [blend of *tomato* and *potato*] : POMATO

to·paz \ˈtōˌpaz\ *n* -ES [ME *topace*, fr. OF *topace, topaze*, fr. L *topazus, topazos*, fr. Gk *topazos, topazion*] **1 a** : a mineral $Al_2SiO_4(F,OH)$ consisting of a silicate of aluminum and usu. occurring in white orthorhombic translucent or transparent crystals or in white translucent masses **b** : a usu. yellow, reddish, or pink transparent mineral topaz used as a gem **c** : ORIENTAL TOPAZ **d** : a yellow quartz: as (1) : FALSE TOPAZ (2) : smoky quartz turned yellow by heating **2** : either of two large brilliantly colored So. American hummingbirds (*Topaza pella* and *T. pyra*) that have a metallic yellowish green throat with a tint like topaz in the center, a bright crimson belly and red back, and in the male the two tail feathers next to the central ones much longer than the rest, curved, and crossed **3** : a variable color averaging a dark orange yellow that is redder and duller than average amber (sense 3a)

to·paz·ine \ˈtōpəˌzēn, -əzən\ *adj* : resembling a topaz in color or luster

to·paz·o·lite \tōˈpazəˌlīt\ *n* -s [F, fr. *topaze* topaz + *-o-* + *-lite*] : a topaz-yellow or green garnet; *esp* : ANDRADITE

topaz quartz *n* : CITRINE

top banana *n* [so called fr. a burlesque routine involving three comedians in which the one that gets the punch line also gets a banana] : the leading comedian in a burlesque show

top billing *n* **1** : the position at the top of a theatrical bill usu. featuring the star's name ⟨she got *top billing*⟩ **2** : prominent emphasis, featuring, or advertising ⟨few of these incidents have received *top billing* in the U. S. press —Charles Abrams⟩

top block *n* : a block hung under the cap of a lower mast and used in lowering the topmast

top boot *n* : a high boot made often with light-colored leather bands around the upper part and worn esp. by riders (as in hunting or in livery)

top–bracket \ˈ=ˈ==\ *adj* : TOP-DRAWER ⟨the *top-bracket* group in capitalist society —D.J.Dallin⟩

top burton *n* : a burton having a fiddle block or double block and a single block used esp. for hoisting sails, yards, and rigging

topcap \ˈ=ˌ=\ *n* : the top part of a journal housing

top capping *n* : the application of a strip of camelback to the central area only of a worn tire tread — compare FULL CAPPING

top card *n* : TOP FLAT

topchrome \ˈ=ˌ=\ *vt or adj* [¹*top* + *chrome*] : AFTERCHROME

top cloth *n* : HAMMOCK CLOTH

topcoat \ˈ=ˌ=\ *n* [¹*top* + *coat*] : an outer coat: as **a** : a lightweight overcoat **b** : the long outer fur of an animal consisting of the part of the guard hairs that projects beyond the undercoat **c** : a final coating (as of paint) : OVERCOAT 2

top couple *n* : HEAD COUPLE

top cover *n* : combat airplanes flying at high altitude to protect from air attack a military force esp. of other airplanes flying at a lower altitude

top cow *n, dial* : BULL

top crop *n* : the harvest from the upper and younger portion of plants (as cotton)

topcross \ˈ=ˌ=\ *n* [¹*top* + *cross*] **1** : a cross in which usu. male superior or purebred individuals are mated with inferior stock to improve the average quality of the progeny; *also* : the product of such a cross — compare GRADE 5 **2** : a cross between an inbred line and a random-bred variety or strain of the same organism (as one between a strictly inbred line and a horticultural variety of maize); *also* : the first generation hybrid that is produced by such a cross — compare SINGLE CROSS

topcrossbred \ˈ=ˈ=ˌ=\ *n* : an individual produced by interbreeding an inbred sire of one breed or variety with a noninbred dam of another — compare TOPINCROSS

top dog *n* [so called in allusion to a dogfight] : a person or group in a position of authority or distinction esp. through victory in a hard-fought competition ⟨union leaders fight for power, try to prove that they should be *top dogs* —*Kiplinger Washington Letter*⟩

top–dog \ˈ=ˈ=\ *adj* [*top dog*] : of, relating to, or being a top dog ⟨they became *top-dog* in the government of the moment —T.R.Ybarra⟩

top–down \ˈ=ˈ=\ *adj* [fr. the phrase (*from the*) *top down*] : closely organized, controlled, and directed ⟨a *top-down* planned society —J.R.Chamberlain⟩

top drawer *n* : the highest level of society, authority, or excellence ⟨has a low social opinion of the . . . ruling class who do not come out of the *top drawer* —V.S.Pritchett⟩ ⟨the majority of critics currently place him in the *top drawer* —Granville Hicks⟩

top–drawer \ˈ=ˈ=(=)\ *adj* [*top drawer*] **1** : of the highest social level ⟨*top-drawer* socialites whom he has escorted —*Life*⟩ **2** : of the highest level of rank, excellence, or importance ⟨the *top-drawer* officials of the railroad —S.K.Farrington⟩ ⟨one of the *top-drawer* secrets of the war —*N. Y. Times*⟩

topdress \ˈ=ˌ=\ *vt* [¹*top* + *dress*, v.] : to scatter manure or fertilizer over (a growing crop, meadow, or lawn)

topdresser \ˈ=ˌ==\ *n* : one that applies topdressing

topdressing \ˈ=ˌ==\ *n* [fr. gerund of *topdress*] **1 a** : the act of one who topdresses soil **b** : the material used to topdress soil **2** : a surface layer of extraneous matter ⟨a sorry collection of old wheezes dressed out with a ~ of analytical jargon —Louis Untermeyer⟩

top–dye \ˈ=ˌ=\ *vt* : ³TOP 2b(2)

¹**tope** \ˈtōp\ *vb* -ED/-ING/-S [obs. *tope*, interj. used to wish good health before drinking, prob. fr. F, done! agreed!, fr. *tope*, 1st pers. sing. pres. indic. of *toper* to agree, consent, accept a bet, cover the opponent's stake, fr. Sp *topar* to take a bet, strike against, butt, bump, of imit. origin; prob. fr. the custom of drinking after a wager] *vt, archaic* : to drink (intoxicating liquor) frequently or to excess ~ *vi* : to drink intoxicating liquor to excess or in large drafts

²**tope** \"\ *n* -s [origin unknown] : any of several small sharks; *esp* : a cosmopolitan brownish or grayish bottom-dwelling shark (*Galeorhinus galeus*) having a liver extremely rich in vitamin A — called also *soupfin shark*

³**tope** \"\ *n* -s [Tamil *tōppu*] *India* : a grove, clump, or plantation of trees ⟨a mango ~⟩

⁴**tope** \"\ *n* -s [Hindi *top*, prob. fr. Skt *stūpa*] : a round cupola-topped building erected as a Buddhist shrine : STUPA

to·pec·to·my \təˈpektəmē, -mi\ *n* -ES [*top-* + *-ectomy*] : surgical removal of portions of the cortex of the frontal association area of the brain for the relief of mental disorders

to·pee *or* **to·pi** \tōˈpē, ˈ=ˌ=\ *n* -s [Hindi *topī*] : a lightweight helmetlike hat with a curved brim made orig. in India of sola pith that consists usu. of a cloth outer covering, an insulating layer of pith or cork, and a light inner framework to fit the head and is worn esp. for protection from the sun

topee

to·pe·ka \təˈpēkə\ *adj, usu cap* [fr. *Topeka*, Kansas] : of or from Topeka, the capital of Kansas ⟨*Topeka* flour mills⟩ : of the kind or style prevalent in Topeka

to·peng \ˈtōˌpeŋ\ *n* -s [Jav *topèng*] : a Javanese dramatic performance in which the actors wear grotesque masks and act in pantomime

to·pepo \təˈpe(ˌ)pō\ *n* -s [blend of *tomato* and *pepper*] : a reputed hybrid between the tomato and the sweet pepper

¹**top·er** \ˈtōpə(r)\ *n* -s [¹*tope* + *-er*] : one that topes : a heavy drinker; *esp* : DRUNKARD

²**toper** \"\ *n* -s [²*tope* + *-er*] : TOPE

top facing *n* : a finishing piece of leather or fabric appearing at the top of a shoe lining and frequently bearing the maker's trademark

top fermentation *n* : a violent alcoholic fermentation at a temperature of 14 to 30° C during which the yeast cells are carried to the top of the fermenting liquid used in the production of such liquors as ale, porter, and wines of high alcohol content and in distilling — compare BOTTOM FERMENTATION

top flat *n* : one of a series of flat cards in a carding machine arranged in an endless chain and guided by rollers over the main cylinder

top flight *n* : the highest level or degree of achievement, excellence, or eminence : TOP DRAWER ⟨leading families intermarry; practically everyone in the *top flight* is thus related —*Reader's Digest*⟩

topflight \ˈ=ˈ=\ *adj* [*top flight*] : of topmost rank or eminence : TOP-DRAWER

top·flight·er \ˈ=ˈflīd·ə(r)\ *n* -s : one that is topflight : TOP-NOTCHER ⟨a novice . . . not yet ready to challenge the ~s —Tom Siler⟩

top fruit *n, Brit* : TREE FRUIT

top·ful *or* **top·full** \ˈtäpˈfu̇l\ *adj* : full to the top : BRIMFUL

¹**top·gal·lant** \täpˈgalənt, ˈ=ˌ==, *usu. naut* təˈg-\ *adj* [¹*top* + *gallant*] **1 a** : of, relating to, or being a part next above the topmast and below the royal mast ⟨~ sail⟩ ⟨~ mast⟩ — see SAIL illustration, SHIP illustration **b** : raised above the adjoining portions — used of a rail, bulwark, or deck **c** : such that topgallant sails may be used : fresh but light ⟨~ breezes⟩ **2** : of the best or most excellent of its kind : very excellent : GRAND

²**topgallant** \"\ *n* -s **1** : a topgallant mast or sail **2 a** : something loftier or more elevated than others of its kind or other parts of the same structure **b** : the topmost point : PINNACLE, SUMMIT

topgallant bulwarks *n pl* : QUARTER BOARDS

topgallant forecastle *n* : an extra deck above the forecastle in the bow of a ship

top gear *n, Brit* : ³HIGH 2b

top–graft \ˈ=ˌ=\ *vt* : TOPWORK

top grain *n* : leather made from the grain side of a hide with nothing taken off the surface except the hair and associated epidermis

top grass *n* : a tall grass suitable for hay

to·pha·ceous \təˈfāshəs\ *adj* [L *tophaceus, tofaceus*, fr. *tophus, tofus* tufa + *-aceus* -aceous] **1** *archaic* : of the nature of tufa : GRITTY, SANDY **2** : having the characteristics of a tophus

top–hamper \ˈ=ˌ==\ *n* -s **1** : matter or weight (as spars, rigging, superstructure, or cargo) in the upper part of a ship ⟨*top-hamper* of guns, three hundred and forty tons of landing craft together with six sets of heavy davits —K.M.Dodson⟩ **2** : unnecessary cumbersome matter ⟨strip his long rambling paragraphs of their *top-hamper* of jargon —John Connell⟩

top hand *n* : a cowboy who is superior esp. as a rider or horsebreaker

top hat *n* **1** : BEAVER 3a **2** : SILK HAT **3** : OPERA HAT

top–hat \ˈ=ˈ=\ *adj* [*top hat*] : of or relating to the upper social classes : TOP-DRAWER

top–heavily \ˈ=ˈ===\ *adv* : in a top-heavy manner

top–heaviness \ˈ=ˈ===\ *n* : the quality or state of being top-heavy

top–heavy \ˈ=ˈ==\ *adj* **1** : having the top part too heavy for the lower part : lacking in stability or in danger of toppling over because of too much weight at the top ⟨high *top-heavy* wagons —*Amer. Guide Series: Mich.*⟩ ⟨the lyrics are often *top-heavy* with ideas —*New Republic*⟩ **2** : having a too high proportion of officers and esp. high-ranking officers ⟨a *top-heavy* bureaucracy⟩ **3 a** *of a financial structure* : OVERCAPITALIZED **b** *of a market* : technically weak with too many speculative holders likely to liquidate soon

to·phet \ˈtōfət\ *n* -s *usu cap* [ME *Tophet, Topheth*, shrine in the valley of Hinnom south of ancient Jerusalem where human sacrifices esp. those of children were performed to Moloch (Jer 7:31), Gehenna, hell, fr. Heb *tōpheth*] : GEHENNA, HELL ⟨what in *Tophet* is this —Cliff Farrell⟩

top–hole \ˈ=ˈ=\ *adj, chiefly Brit* : EXCELLENT, FIRST-CLASS

to·phus \ˈtōfəs\ *n, pl* **to·phi** \-ˌfī\ [L *tophus, tofus* — more at TUFA] **1** : TUFA **2** : a deposit of urates in cartilage and other tissues characteristic of gout

¹**topi** *var of* TOPEE

²**to·pi** \ˈtōpē\ *n, pl* **topi** [of Mande origin; akin to Mande *ndopa, ndope* antelope] : an antelope (*Damaliscus korrigum jimela*) of eastern Central Africa having a glossy purplish brown coat with a watered-silk appearance; *also* : any of various related antelopes native to districts south of the Sahara

to·pi·ar·i·an \ˌtōpēˈa(a)rēən, -ˈer-\ *adj* [L *topiarius* + E *-an*] : TOPIARY

to·pi·a·rist \ˈtōpēərəst\ *n* -s : one skilled in topiary gardening

¹**to·pi·ary** \ˈ==ˌerē\ *adj* [L *topiarius*, fr. *topia* ornamental gardening (irreg. fr. Gk *topos* place) + *-arius* -ary] : of, relating to, or being the practice or art of training, cutting, and trimming trees or shrubs into odd or ornamental shapes; *also* : characterized by such work

²**topiary** \"\ *n* -ES **1** : topiary art or gardening; *also* : a topiary garden **2 a** : a plant (as a box or yew) shaped by topiary art **b** : topiary plants

topiary 2b

topic \ˈtäpik, -pēk\ *n* -s [L *Topica* Topics, work by Aristotle in which the material is divided into topics, fr. Gk (*Ta*) *Topika*, fr. *topika*, neut. pl. of *topikos* of a place, of a commonplace, fr. *topos* place, commonplace + *-ikos* -ic; akin to Gk *topazein* to aim at, guess, Lith *tapti* to become, OE *thafian* to allow, agree, endure; basic meaning: to fall into place] **1 a** *obs* : a prepared form of argument applicable to a great variety of cases : a commonplace of argument or oratory **b** : one of the various general forms of argument employed in probable as distinguished from demonstrative reasoning **c** : ARGUMENT, REASON, CONSIDERATION **2 a** : a heading in an outlined argument or exposition : a phrase summarizing what is to be presented in a discourse or a section of it **b** (1) : the subject of a discourse or a section of it : THEME ⟨the ~ of his book⟩ (2) : a subject under discussion or consideration ⟨suggested inflation as the ~ for discussion⟩

¹**top·i·cal** \-pəkəl, -pēk-\ *adj* [Gk *topikos* of a place, of a commonplace + E *-al*] **1 a** : of or relating to a place **b** : designed for or involving local application or action (as on the body) ⟨a ~ remedy⟩ ⟨a ~ anesthetic⟩ **2** *obs* : not demonstrative : merely probable **3 a** : of, relating to, or arranged by topics ⟨a detailed record, on both a chronological and a ~ basis —Jacob Viner⟩ **b** : referring to the topics of the day or place : of local or temporary interest ⟨the ~, the contingent and therefore ephemeral stuff which all novels contain —Edward Sackville-West⟩ ⟨a ~, timely and useful study of civil liberty —J.B.Oakes⟩ — **top·i·cal·ly** \-k(ə)lē, -li\ *adv*

²topical \"\ *n* -s **:** a coin or postage stamp bearing a design relating to some general topic (as animals, flowers, or ships) that is often used as a theme for a collection

top·i·cal·i·ty \,==ˈkaləd·ē, -lətē, -i\ *n* -ES **1 :** the quality or state of being topical ⟨lectures and articles rather summarily thrown together . . . before they should lose ~ —*Times Lit. Supp.*⟩ **2 :** an item of merely topical interest ⟨the thriller . . . did reasonably well with its international *topicalities* —J.S. Sandoe⟩

top ice *n* **:** shaved ice blown into loaded refrigerator cars to complete icing

topic sentence *also* **topical sentence** *n* **:** a sentence that states the main or central thought of a paragraph or of a larger unit of discourse and is usu. placed at or near the beginning

-topies *pl of* -TOPY

top·i·nam·bour \,täpəˈnam,bu̇(ə)r, ,==,=ˈ=\ *also* **top·i·nam·bou** \-bü\ *or* **tob·i·nam·bur** \,täbəˈnam,bu̇(ə)r, ,==,=ˈ=\ *n* -S [*topinambour* fr. F, fr. Pg *tupinambor*, alter. of *tupinamba*, short for *batata tupinamba*, fr. *batata* potato (fr. Taino) + *Tupinambá* Tupinamba; *topinambou* fr. obs. F, fr. Pg *tupinambo, tupinamba; tobinambur* modif. of AmerSp *topinámbur*, fr. Pg *tupinambor*] **:** JERUSALEM ARTICHOKE

topincross \ˈ=ˈ=,=\ *n* [¹*top* + *incross*] **:** an individual produced by interbreeding an inbred sire with a noninbred dam of the same breed or variety — compare TOPCROSSBRED

toping *pres part of* TOPE

top·i·nish \ˈtäpənish\ *n, pl* **topinish** *or* **topinishes** *usu cap* **:** a subdivision of the Yakima

topkick \ˈ=,=\ *n* [¹*top* + *kick*, n.] **:** FIRST SERGEANT 1

topknot \ˈ=,=\ *n* **1 a :** an ornament (as a knot of ribbons, a bunch of flowers or feathers, or a pompon) forming a headdress or worn on a cap or as part of a hairdress **b** (1) **:** a crest of feathers (as on a cock) (2) **:** a tuft of hair on the top or forward part of a head **c :** an arrangement of hair high on the head and usu. in a knot **2 :** a small European flounder (*Zeugopterus punctatus*) having the anterior rays of the dorsal fin elongated; *also* **:** any closely related species

topknot pigeon *n* **:** a crested Australian wild pigeon (*Lopholaimus antarcticus*)

top·less \ˈtäpləs\ *adj* **1 a :** having no top ⟨~ bathing suit⟩ **b** *archaic* **:** so high as to reach up beyond sight **c :** nude above the waist ⟨~ waitress⟩ **d :** featuring topless waitresses or entertainers ⟨~ cabaret⟩ **2** *obs* **:** SUPREME

top-level \ˈ=ˈ==\ *adj* **:** very high or highest in level of authority, importance, or quality ⟨*top-level* management⟩ ⟨*top-level* news⟩ ⟨*top-level* scientists⟩

top lift *n* [¹*top*] **:** the bottom layer of a heel usu. made of leather, rubber, or composition — see SHOE illustration

top light *n* **1 :** a light at one of the tops of a ship sometimes indicating a flagship **2** *or* **toplighting** \ˈ=,==\ **:** light from above (as from a skylight)

topline \ˈ=,=\ *n* **:** the outline of the top of an animal's body

top-line \ˈ=ˈ=\ *adj* **1 :** named in or near the top line **:** most featured or prominently advertised **:** LEADING ⟨a *top-line* comedian⟩ ⟨*top-line* news⟩ **2 :** TOP-LEVEL

top·lin·er \-nə(r)\ *n, chiefly Brit* **:** a top-line person or thing; *specif* **:** HEADLINER

top lining *n* **:** a cloth on the after side of the lower cloths of a topsail to prevent chafing

top load *n* **:** a load of logs more than one tier high

top loader *n* **:** a worker who places logs at the top of a deck or load

top·loft·ical \ˈtäˈplȯftəkəl\ *adj* [prob. fr. *top loft* + *-ical*] **:** TOPLOFTY ⟨a pedantic . . . ~ jargon —Marguerite Wilkinson⟩

top·loft·i·ly \-tə̇lē, -li\ *adv* **:** in a toplofty manner ⟨looked down ~ on literary critics —Malcolm Cowley⟩

top·loft·i·ness \-tēnə̇s, -tin-\ *n* -ES **:** the quality or state of being toplofty

toplofty \ˈ=ˈ==\ *adj* [back-formation fr. *toploftical*] **:** very superior in air or in attitude **:** contemptuous of or elevated above the average or ordinary **:** DISDAINFUL, SUPERCILIOUS, HAUGHTY ⟨opinionated and ~ in its judgments —B.J.Stern⟩

topmaker \ˈ=,==\ *n* **:** one who deals in wool tops

topmaking \ˈ=,==\ *n* **:** the practice or trade of a topmaker

top·man \ˈ=mən\ *n, pl* **topmen 1 :** one whose work is done at or from the top: as **a :** TOP SAWYER 1 **b :** a miner who works at the surface **c :** a construction worker who works on the ground, shoveling dirt, loading, caring for equipment **d :** RACKMAN 2 **e :** a worker who attends to equipment and processing at the top of petroleum stills **2 :** a sailor or marine stationed in a top **3 :** a worker who assists in the operation of retort furnaces **4 :** a supervisor of brick-chimney builders

top·mast \ˈtäpməst *(usu naut)*, -p,mast, -,maa(ə)st, -,maist, -,mäst\ *n* [ME *toppe maste*, fr. *toppe* top + *maste*, *mast* mast — more at TOP, MAST] **:** the mast next above the lower mast that is topmost in a fore-and-aft rig and below the topgallant mast in a square-rigged ship — see SHIP illustration

top milk *n* **:** the upper layer of milk in a container enriched by whatever cream has risen

topminnow \ˈ=,(,)=\ *n* [¹*top* + *minnow*; fr. its swimming on the surface of the water] **1 :** any of numerous small viviparous surface-feeding fishes that constitute the family Poeciliidae and include many brilliantly colored freshwater fishes some of which are much used in mosquito control and others extensively kept in the tropical aquarium — compare GAMBUSIA, HELLERI, PLATY, SWORDTAIL **2 :** KILLIFISH 1

top·most \ˈtäp,mōst *also* -məst\ *adj* **:** that is at the very top **:** highest of all **:** UPPERMOST ⟨communication between the lowest classified worker and the ~ executive —H.F.Gracey⟩

top·most·ly *adv* **:** CHIEFLY

top-mounter \ˈ=ˈ==\ *n* **:** the member of a balance team whose position is atop the others

top necrosis *n* **:** a disease of potatoes caused by one or more of several viruses and characterized by death of the growing points and death of the plant progressively downward

topnotch \ˈ=,=\ *n* **:** the highest point possible or attainable ⟨a boat in the ~ of perfection —H.A.Calahan⟩

top-notch \ˈ=ˈ=\ *adj* [*top notch*] **:** of the highest or best attainable **:** TIP-TOP, FIRST-RATE, UNSURPASSED

top·notch·er \-chə(r)\ *n* -S **:** one that is top-notch

to·po *or* **top·po** \ˈtō(,)pō\ *n* -S [It] **:** a flat-bottomed and half-decked Venetian fishing boat powered by sails or oars

topo- — see TOP-

topo *abbr* topographic; topographical

topo·chemical \ˈtäpə, ˈtōpə+\ *adj* [*top-* + *chemical*] **1 :** of, relating to, or constituting a locally confined chemical reaction **2 :** of, relating to, or constituting a combined tactile and chemical sense (as that of the antennae of insects) that is fundamentally equivalent to olfaction

topo·cli·nal \ˈ=ˈklīnᵊl\ *adj* **:** of or relating to a topocline — **topo·cli·nal·ly** \-nᵊlē\ *adv*

topo·cline \ˈ==,klīn\ *n* [*top-* + *cline*] **:** a cline along a geographical axis and usu. without apparent ecological explanation

topo·deme \-,dēm\ *n* [*top-* + *deme*] **:** a population occupying a specified geographical range

top off *vt* **:** FINISH 2d

topog *abbr* topographer; topographic; topographical; topography

top·og·no·sia \,tä,pägˈnōzh(ē)ə, ,tō,p-\ *or* **top·og·no·sis** \-ōsə̇s\ *n, pl* **topognosias** *or* **topognosises** [NL, fr. *top-* + *-gnosia* or *-gnosis*] **:** recognition of the location of a stimulus on the skin or elsewhere in the body

to·pog·ra·pher \təˈpägrəfə(r), tōˈ-\ *n* -S [Gk *topographos* (fr. *topographein* to describe a place) + E *-er* — more at TOPOGRAPHY] **:** one who is skilled in or practices topography **:** one who describes, maps, or surveys the topography of a region

topo·graph·ic \ˈtäpəˈgrafik, ˈtōp-, -fēk\ *adj* [MGk *topographikos*, fr. Gk *topographia* topography + *-ikos* -ic] **:** TOPOGRAPHICAL 1a

topographic adolescence *or* **topographic youth** *n* **:** the condition of a district soon after the beginning of erosion by streams when main branches have well-developed narrow valleys and the areas between the streams are little modified

topo·graph·i·cal \ˈ==ˈgrafəkəl, -fēk-\ *adj* [MGk *topographikos* + E *-al*] **1 a** (1) **:** of, relating to, or concerned with topography ⟨~ engineer⟩ (2) **:** discovering, measuring, or exhibiting the topography of a region ⟨a ~ description⟩ ⟨a ~ survey⟩ **b :** of, relating to, or concerned with the artistic representation of a particular locality ⟨a ~ poem⟩ ⟨~ painting⟩ **2 :** of or relating to a mind made up of different strata and esp. of the conscious, preconscious, and unconscious **3 :** of, relating to, or concerned with the delineation of the structure and relations of the parts of a group or subject — **topo·graph·i·cal·ly** \-k(ə)lē, -li\ *adv*

topographical anatomy *n* **:** REGIONAL ANATOMY

topographic infancy *n* **:** the condition of a district freshly exposed to the action of surface waters when the original hollows are still occupied by lakes and ponds and the plains are imperfectly dissected by narrow stream gorges

topographic map *n* **:** a map intermediate between a general map and a plan on a scale large enough to show roads, plans of towns, and contour lines

topographic maturity *n* **:** the condition of a district in which the land is reduced to slopes, the original upland has been completely dissected, a new plain of erosion has just begun to appear, and many of the individual river valleys are mature but some of the headwaters of the tributaries may still be in the youthful stage

topographic old age *n* **:** the condition of a district reduced by erosion nearly to base level

to·pog·ra·phize \təˈpägrə,fīz, tōˈ-\ *vt* -ED/-ING/-S [*topography* + *-ize*] **:** to describe topographically

topo·grapho·met·ric \ˈtäpəˈgrafəˈme·trik, ˈtōp-\ *adj* [*topography* + *-o-* + *-metric*] **:** concerned with or devised for the measurement of heights, angles, and distances

to·pog·ra·phy \təˈpägrəfē, tōˈ-, -fi\ *n* -ES [ME *topographie*, fr. LL *topographia*, fr. Gk, fr. *topographein* to describe a place (fr. *topos* place + *graphein* to write) + *-ia* -y — more at TOPIC, CARVE] **1 a** (1) *obs* **:** the description of a particular place (as a city, town, manor, parish, or tract of land) (2) **:** the art or practice of graphic delineation in detail usu. on maps or charts of selected natural and man-made features of a place or region esp. in a way to show their relative positions and elevations (3) **:** topographical surveying **b** (1) **:** the configuration of a surface including its relief and the position of its natural and man-made features ⟨a map showing the ~ of the county⟩ (2) **:** the physical or natural features of an object or entity and their structural relationships ⟨statistics which reveal the economic ~ of our time —R.D.Mack⟩ **2 a :** REGIONAL ANATOMY **b :** a chart or illustration showing the location of body parts (as of a bird or mammal)

topo·log·i·cal \ˈtäpəˈläjəkəl, ˈtōp-\ *also* **topo·log·ic** \-jik\ *adj* **1 :** of or relating to topology **2 :** concerned with relations between objects abstracted from exact quantitative measurement ⟨~ dating involves nothing more than the notion of *before* and *after* —C.F.Hockett⟩ ⟨the ~ statement that this angle is smaller than that⟩ — **topo·log·i·cal·ly** \-jək(ə)lē\ *adv*

topological equivalence *n* **:** the relationship of two geometric figures capable of being transformed one into the other by a one-to-one transformation continuous in both directions

topological psychology *n* **:** a system or theory that describes individual or group behavior in terms of topological relations within a life space

to·pol·o·gist \təˈpäləjəst, tōˈ-\ *n* -S **:** a student of or specialist in topology

to·pol·o·gy \-jē, -ji\ *n* -ES [ISV *top-* + *-logy*] **1 :** topographical study of a particular place; *specif* **:** the history of a region as indicated by its topography **2 :** REGIONAL ANATOMY **3 :** a branch of mathematics that investigates the properties of a geometric configuration that are unaltered if the configuration is subjected to any one-to-one transformation continuous in both directions **4 :** TOPOLOGICAL PSYCHOLOGY

top onion *n* **1 :** one of the bulbils that often replace the flowers in the inflorescence of some onions and are used for propagation — called also *top set*; compare TREE ONION **2 :** TREE ONION

top·onym \ˈtäpə,nim, ˈtōp-\ *n* -S [ISV, back-formation fr. *toponymy*] **:** PLACE-NAME

top·onym·ic \ˈ==ˈnimik, -mēk\ *or* **top·onym·i·cal** \-mə̇kəl, -mēk-\ *adj* [*toponymy* + *-ic* or *-ical*] **:** of or relating to toponyms or toponymy

to·pon·y·my *also* **to·pon·o·my** \təˈpänəmē, tōˈ-, -mi\ *n* -ES [*toponymy* ISV *top-* + *-onymy*; *toponomy* fr. *top-* + Gk *onoma* name + E *-y* — more at NAME] **1 :** the place-names of a region or language or the esp. etymological study of them **2 :** the nomenclature of regional anatomy

topo·tax·is \ˈtäpəˈtaksə̇s, ˈtōp-\ *n* [NL, fr. *top-* + *-taxis*] **:** TROPISM

topo·type \ˈtäpə,tīp, ˈtōp-\ *n* [*top-* + *type*] **:** a specimen of a species collected at the locality at which the original type was obtained — **topo·typ·ic** \ˈ==ˈtipik\ *adj* — **topo·typ·i·cal** \-pəkəl\ *adj*

top out *vt* **1 :** to separate (the best animals) from a group ⟨*top out* hogs⟩ **2 :** to finish by putting on a cap or uppermost course ~ *vi* **:** to reach a summit or crest ⟨scraped through a wild-cherry thicket and *topped out* on the rock flat again —H.L. Davis⟩ ⟨investment boom . . . has *topped out* —*Newsweek*⟩

topped \ˈtäpt\ *adj* [ME, fr. ¹*top* + *-ed*] **:** having a top of a specified character — usu. used in combination ⟨flat-*topped*⟩

topped crude *n* [*topped* fr. past part. of ³*top*] **:** crude petroleum that has been treated (as by distillation) to remove some of its lighter components

top·per \ˈtäpə(r)\ *n* -S [¹*top* + *-er*] **1 :** one that puts tops on (as on containers) or removes tops (as from vegetables); *specif* **:** CLIMBER 1a **2 :** one that is at or on the top: as **a :** someone or something first-rate or surpassingly good **b :** a cover or a top layer or part **3 a :** SILK HAT **b :** OPERA HAT **4 :** something (as a joke) that surpasses or climaxes everything preceding **5 :** a woman's usu. short and boxy lightweight overcoat **6 :** one that transfers hose from leggers to footers

toppiece \ˈ=,=\ *n* **:** TOUPEE

¹**top·ping** \ˈtäpiŋ, -pēŋ\ *n* -S [ME, fr. gerund of *toppen* to top — more at TOP] **1 :** something that forms a top (as of a tuft of hair or feathers on the head or a forelock): as **a :** something (as a sauce, nuts, or whipped cream) used to garnish food and esp. dessert **b :** a finishing layer of mortar about ½ to 1 inch in thickness placed on concrete (as on a floor or sidewalk) **2 :** the action of one that tops: as **a :** the reduction of a tooth (as on a saw or gear) by filing **b :** the removal of volatile parts (as from crude oil) **3 :** something removed by topping: as **a :** the cut tops of plants **b :** refuse separated from hemp in hackling **c :** the finest bran **4 :** a feather from a golden pheasant's crest used in an artificial fly — see FLY illustration

²**topping** *adj* [fr. pres. part. of ³*top*] **1 :** highest in rank, degree, or eminence **2** *NewEng* **:** PROUD, PRETENTIOUS, ARROGANT **3** *chiefly Brit* **:** very fine **:** EXCELLENT

topping lift *n* **:** a strong tackle or rope running from the masthead and used to support, raise, or top the outer end of a boom or a yard — see SHIP illustration

topping plant *n* **:** an extraction plant for removing the lighter components of oil

top plate *n* **1 :** PLATE 5a(1) **2 :** the plate at the top of a partition

top·ple \ˈtäpəl\ *vb* **toppled; toppled; toppling** \-p(ə)liŋ\ **topples** [freq. of ³*top*] *vi* **1 :** to fall from or as if from top-heaviness **:** tumble down ⟨*toppled* backward to a sprawl on the pavement —Scott Fitzgerald⟩ **2 :** to be or appear on the verge of toppling **:** be or seem unsteady **:** TOTTER ⟨upon his head ~*s* a fantastic structure of bull's horns and feathers —H.V. Morton⟩ ~ *vt* **1 :** to cause to topple **:** push over **:** OVERTURN, UPSET ⟨the crowd outside *toppled* part of the churchyard wall in its crush —*Time*⟩ **2 :** to eject from a position of authority, power, or eminence **:** OVERTHROW ⟨two world wars . . . *toppled* six colonial empires —*Newsweek*⟩

toppo *var of* TOPO

top rake *n* **:** the angle between the face of a cutting tool that receives the chip and the normal to the surface being cut

toprope \ˈ=,=\ *n* **:** a rope for the hoisting or lowering of a topmast

top rot *n* **1 :** a rotting of the upper part of a plant symptomatic of various diseases of sugarcane **2 :** a rot starting in the upper part of the trunk (as in many trees)

top round *n* **:** the portion of a round steak situated on the inside of the round (sense 16a) — compare BOTTOM ROUND

tops \ˈtäps\ *adj* [fr. pl. of ¹*top*] **:** topmost in quality, ability, popularity, or eminence — used predicatively ⟨the opening essay . . . is ~ on the subject —*Commonweal*⟩ ⟨their personnel is ~ —Virgil Thomson⟩ — often used with *the* ⟨generally considered the ~ in the field —Fletcher Pratt⟩

top·sail \ˈtäpsəl *(usu naut)*, -p,sāl\ *also* **tops'l** \ˈtäpsəl\ *n* -S [*topsail* fr. ME *topseil*, *topsail*, fr. ¹*top* + *seil*, *sail* sail; *tops'l* contr. of *topsail* — more at SAIL] **1 :** the sail next above the lowermost sail on a mast in a square-rigged ship; *also* **:** one of two sails set one above the other next above the lowermost sail — see SAIL illustration, SHIP illustration **2 :** the sail set above and sometimes on the gaff in a fore-and-aft rigged ship

topsail schooner *n* **:** a two-masted schooner having square-rigged topsails on the foremast and rarely on the mainmast

top sawyer *n* **1 :** a worker at a sawpit who stands above the timber — compare BOTTOM SAWYER **2** *Brit* **:** a person in a position of advantage or eminence

top score *n* **:** TOP 8b(3)

top secret *adj* **:** demanding inviolate secrecy among top officials or a select few **:** classified as requiring the highest degree of concealment from a nation's enemies in a scale rating the value of information to a nation's security — compare CLASSIFICATION 1f

topsail schooner

top sergeant *n* **:** FIRST SERGEANT 1

top set *n* **:** TOP ONION

topset beds \ˈ=,=-\ *n pl* **:** the nearly level layers of sediment deposited on the top of a delta

topset onion *n* **:** TREE ONION

top-shelf \ˈ=ˈ=\ *adj* **:** TOP-DRAWER

top shell *n* **1 :** any of various marine snails constituting the family Trochidae and having a spiral and usu. regularly conical shell marked by a flat base and rhombic aperture and a multispiral operculum and sometimes used to make pearl buttons **2 :** TURBAN SHELL

top sickness *n* **:** a boron deficiency disease of tobacco marked esp. by a pale green color appearing first in the leaves of the terminal bud and by bases that are paler than the tips

¹**topside** \ˈ=,=\ *n, often attrib* [¹*top* + *side*] **1 a topsides** *pl* **:** the top portion of the outer surface of a ship on each side above the waterline **b :** the portion of a ship above the main deck and usu. below the top-hamper — distinguished from *side* **2 :** high ranking personnel **:** the highest level of authority ⟨the ~ of the . . . armies and navies know about them —*Newsweek*⟩ ⟨got straight from ~ the picture of the war as it unfolded —*Coast Artillery Jour.*⟩ ⟨a former ~ government information man —R.E.Jones⟩ **3 :** a place actually or figuratively above another (as the surface of the earth or sea) ⟨with a war surplus diving helmet, a painting machine air compressor and friends as a ~ crew, started diving —*N.Y.Times*⟩

²**topside** \ˈ=ˈ=\ *adv* **1** *also* **topsides :** on deck ⟨down in the engine room . . . quickly regretted ever having gone ~ —Joseph Whitehill⟩ **2 :** in or into a high position ⟨to transport visitors ~, a businessman built the first cog railroad —B.M. Bowie⟩ **:** on top ⟨slept ~ in the bunk⟩ **:** to or on the surface ⟨miners coming ~⟩ **3 :** in a position of authority **:** at a top level of rank ⟨charges of Communism ~ —*Newsweek*⟩

top side *n* **:** FELT SIDE

topside-turvy \ˈ=,=-\ˈtərvē\ *adv* [by alter.] **:** TOPSY-TURVY

top-size \ˈ=,=\ *vt* **:** SURFACE-SIZE

top slicing *n* **:** a method of mining large ore bodies from the top downward by consecutively removing a series of horizontal slices under a caved capping

tops·man \ˈtäpsmən\ *n, pl* **topsmen** [*tops* (poss. of ¹*top*) + *man*] *Brit* **:** HANGMAN

top smelt *n* **:** a common silversides (*Atherinops affinis*) of the Pacific coast of No. America that attains a length of one foot and is of some importance as a food fish

¹**topsoil** \ˈ=,=\ *n* **:** surface soil distinguished from subsoil and usu. including the average plow depth or the A-horizon — called also *loam*; distinguished from *solum*

²**topsoil** \"\ *vt* **:** to cover or dress with topsoil

top spin *n* [²*top*] **:** a rotary motion imparted to a ball which causes it to rotate forward in the direction of its flight

topstitch \ˈ=,=\ *vt* **:** to make a line of stitching on the outside of (a garment) close to a seam

topstone \ˈ=,=\ *n* **:** CAPSTONE

topswarm \ˈ=,=\ *n, dial Brit* **:** the first swarm of bees from a hive

top·sy·turn \ˈtäpsē,tərn\ *vt* [¹*topsy*-turvy + *turn*] **:** to turn upside down

top·sy-tur·vi·ly \ˈtäpsēˈtərvəlē, -siˈt-, -ˈtōv-, -ˈtəiv-, -li\ *adv* **:** in a topsy-turvy manner

top·sy-tur·vi·ness \-vēnə̇s, -vin-\ *n* -ES **:** the quality or state of being topsy-turvy

¹**top·sy-tur·vy** *also* **top·sy-tur·vey** \-vē, -vi\ *adv* [earlier *topsy-tirvy, topsy-tervy*, prob. fr. *tops* (pl. of ¹*top*) + *-y* (dim. suffix) + obs. E *tirve*, *terve* to turn, turn upside down (fr. ME *terven*, prob. fr. — assumed — OE *tierfan*) + E *-y* (dim. suffix); akin to OE *tearflian* to turn, roll — more at TIRL] **1 :** in an inverted posture **:** with the top or head downward **:** upside down ⟨fall *topsy-turvy*⟩ **2 :** in a state where proper or normal places, values, standards, objects, or facts are reversed ⟨the lives of two families are turned *topsy-turvy* —Evangeline Davis⟩

²**topsy-turvy** \"\ *adj, sometimes* -ER/-EST **:** turned topsy-turvy **:** totally disordered **:** REVERSED ⟨interprets the . . . licensing regulations to suit its own *topsy-turvy* hours of labor —Dorothy Sayers⟩

³**topsy-turvy** \"\ *vt* -ED/-ING/-ES **:** to turn or make topsy-turvy ⟨make in places the order of sedimentation a *topsy-turvied* sequence —W.E.Swinton⟩

⁴**topsy-turvy** \"\ *n* -ES **:** TOPSY-TURVINESS

top·sy-tur·vy·dom \-dəm\ *n* -S **1 :** TOPSY-TURVINESS **2 :** a state, existence, or world in which everything is turned topsy-turvy ⟨a quaint glimpse of *topsy-turvydom*; the laws of gravitation appear to be defied —F.A.A.Talbot⟩

top-timber \ˈ=,==\ *n* **:** one of the highest timbers on the side of a ship above the futtocks

top water *n* **:** the water lying above oil or gas in productive formations — compare BOTTOM WATER

top-water minnow \ˈ=ˈ==\ *n* **:** TOPMINNOW; *esp* **:** a common mosquito fish (*Gambusia affinis*)

top water plug *n* **:** an angling plug that floats on the surface of the water

topweight \ˈ=,=\ *n* **:** the heaviest weight carried by a horse in a race; *also* **:** a horse carrying it

topwork \ˈ=,=\ *vt* **:** to graft scions of another variety on the main branches of (as fruit trees) after removal of all smaller and some main and secondary branches usu. to obtain more desirable fruit — compare FRAMEWORK

-to·py \d·əpē, təp-, -pi\ *n comb form* -ES [NL *-topia*, fr. Gk, way, place, fr. *topos* place + *-ia* -y — more at TOPIC] **:** position **:** location ⟨hetero*topy*⟩

top yeast *n* **:** a yeast that produces carbon dioxide vigorously and has cells which tend to become clustered at the surface in brewing

toque \ˈtōk\ *n* -S [MF, fr. OSp *toca* woman's headdress, veil, toque] **1 a :** a soft hat with a very narrow brim and a full crown pleated into a snug headband, usu. ornamented with a plume, and worn esp. in the 16th century **b :** a woman's small brimless hat made in any of various soft close-fitting shapes **c :** TUQUE **2 a :** TOQUE MACAQUE **b :** BONNET MONKEY

toque macaque *or* **toque monkey** *n* [so called fr. the toquelike whorl of its scalp hair] **:** a small reddish or brown macaque (*Macaca sinica*) of southeastern Asia

toque 1a

to·qui·lla \tōˈkē(y)ə\ *n* -S [Sp, dim. of *toca* headband, toque] **1 :** JIPIJAPA **2 :** a very flexible and durable fiber derived from the leaves of the jipijapa from which panama hats and other wares are plaited

tor \ˈtȯ(ə)r\ *n* -S [ME *torre, tor*, fr. OE *torr*, prob. of Celt origin; akin to ScGael *torr* heap, mound, IrGael *torran* heap, hillock] **:** a high craggy hill **:** a rocky pinnacle or peak

tor *abbr* torpedo

to·ra \'tōrə\ *n* -s [Amharic *tōrā*] **:** a large reddish hartebeest (*Alcelaphus tora*) of eastern Africa

to·rad·ja *or* **to·ra·ja** \tə'räjə\ *n* -s *usu cap* [native name in central and south Celebes] **1 :** an Indonesian people of central Celebes **2 :** a member of the Toradja people

to·rah *or* **to·ra** \'tōrə, -ō(,)rä, tō'rä\ *n, pl* **to·roth** \tō'rōt(h), -rōs\ *or* **torahs** *or* **toras** *usu cap* [Heb *tōrāh*] **1 :** LAW, PRECEPT; *esp* **:** the body of divine knowledge and law found in the Jewish scriptures and tradition **2 a :** the first five books of the Old Testament **b :** SEPHER TORAH

to·ral \'tōrəl\ *adj* [NL *torus* + E *-al*] **:** of or relating to the torus of a flower

to·ran \'tōrən\ *or* **to·ra·na** \-nə\ *n* -s [Skt *torana*] **1 :** a gateway commonly of wood but sometimes of stone consisting of two upright pillars carrying one to three transverse lintels that is often minutely carved with symbolic sculpture and serves as a monumental approach to a Buddhist temple in India **2 :** a temporary arch or festoon erected in honor of a visiting dignitary in India — compare PAI-LOU, TORII

tor·bern·ite \'tȯrbər,nīt\ *n* -s [G *torbernit*, fr. *Torbern* O. Bergman †1784 Swed. chemist + G *-it* -ite] **:** a mineral $Cu(UO_2)_2(PO_4)_2.8\text{-}12H_2O$ consisting of a tetragonal hydrous uranium copper phosphate that is isomorphous with autunite, uranocircite, saléeite, zeunerite, and uranospinite, is of micaceous structure, and occurs in green tabular crystals or in foliated form — called also *chalcolite*

torc *n* -s [by alter.] **:** 1TORQUE

1**torch** \'tȯ(ə)rch, -ō(ə)ch\ *n* -ES *often attrib* [ME *torche*, fr. OF, bundle of twisted straw or tow, torch, fr. (assumed) VL *torca*; akin to L *torquēre* to twist — more at TORTURE] **1 :** a burning stick of resinous wood or twist of tow used to give light and usu. carried in the hand; *sometimes* **:** a chimneyless lamp mounted on a pole **:** FLAMBEAU **2 :** something (as wisdom or knowledge) likened to a torch as giving light or guidance ⟨the ~ of good reason was for the moment dimmed —Francis Hackett⟩ ⟨so that the ~ of his wisdom could be handed down the ages —H.J.Laski⟩ **3 :** any of various flowers that suggest a torch (as in being flame-colored, long-stemmed, and racemiform) or whose stalks are used for torches; *esp* **:** GREAT MULLEIN **4 :** any of various portable devices for emitting an unusually hot flame (as for vaporizing oil to start an oil engine, burning off old paint, or melting solder) ⟨an acetylene ~⟩ — compare BLOWTORCH **5** *chiefly Brit* **:** FLASHLIGHT **6 :** ARSONIST, INCENDIARY, PYROMANIAC ⟨the ~ . . . had touched off more fires than he could recollect —B.P.Battle & P.B.Weston⟩

2**torch** \"\ *vb* -ED/-ING/-ES *vt* **1 :** to set fire to, burn, sear, or illuminate with or as if with a torch **2 :** to catch (fish) with a jacklight ~ *vi* **:** to sing a torch song

3**torch** \"\ *vt* -ED/-ING/-ES [F *torcher* to daub or plaster with cob, to wipe, fr. OF, fr. *torche* bundle of twisted straw — more at 1TORCH] **:** to point (slating) with a mixture of lime and hair or mortar

torch azalea *n* **:** FLAME AZALEA

torchbearer \'ˌ=ˌ==\ *n* **1 :** one that carries a torch (as in an ancient relay race) **2 a :** one that adds to or transmits light (as of knowledge, civilization, or truth) ⟨~s of culture and inspired creators —Susanne K. Langer⟩ **b :** someone in the forefront of a campaign, crusade, or movement **:** LEADER ⟨~s of a revolt against the introspective novel —Henri Peyre⟩ **3** *usu* **torch bearer** *usu cap T&B* **:** the highest of the four ranks attainable by a camp fire girl — compare FIRE MAKER, TRAIL SEEKER, WOOD GATHERER

torch cactus *or* **torch thistle** *n* **:** any of several columnar cacti of the genus *Cereus* whose stems were used by No. American Indians for torches

torch dance *n* **:** a festival serpentine dance in which lighted torches are carried

1**torch·er** \'tȯrchər, 'tō(ə)chə(r\ *n* -s [1*torch* + *-er*] **1 :** one that gives light with or as if with a torch **2 :** a fish jacker **3 :** TORCH SINGER

2**torcher** \"\ *n* -s [3*torch* + *-er*] **:** one that torches slate roofs

tor·chère \(')tȯr¦she(ə)r\ *n* -s [F, fr. *torche* torch] **1 :** a tall ornamental stand for a candlestick or candelabrum used in the 18th century and usu. set on a tripod base **2 :** an electric floor lamp giving indirect light

torchère 2

torch flower *n* **1 :** PRAIRIE SMOKE 1 **2 :** POKER PLANT

torch ginger *n* **:** an East Indian rhizomatous perennial herb (*Phaeomeria magnifica*) of the family Zingiberaceae that is cultivated in warm regions for its showy foliage and red or pink flower heads which resemble cones and are borne on tall stems arising directly from the rhizome

1**torchlight** \'ˌ=ˌ=\ *n* [ME *torche lyghte*, fr. *torche* torch + *lyghte*, *light* light] **1 :** light given by torches ⟨a flood of ~ surged and swirled about them —J.B.Cabell⟩ **2 :** TORCH ⟨some 15,000 ~s were carried there to be used in the great celebration upon the completion of the canal —F.J. Haskin⟩

2**torchlight** \"\ *adj* **:** composed of torchbearers ⟨a ~ parade⟩ **:** lighted by torches ⟨a ~ rally⟩

torch lily *n* **1 :** KNIPHOFIA 2 **2 :** SPEAR LILY

torchlit \'ˌ=ˌ=\ *adj* [1*torch* + *lit*] **:** lighted by torches

torch·man \'ˌ=mən\ *n, pl* **torchmen 1 :** TORCHBEARER **2 :** one that uses a torch: as **a :** an acetylene welder **b :** a safecracker who uses a blowtorch

tor·chon \'tȯr,shän, ˌ=ˈ=\ *also* **torchon lace** *n* -s [F *torchon* dishcloth, duster, fr. OF, bundle of twisted straw, fr. *torche* — more at TORCH] **:** a coarse bobbin or machine-made lace made with fan-shaped designs forming a scalloped edge and used esp. for edgings and trimmings

torch pine *n* **1 :** LOBLOLLY PINE 1 **2 :** a pitch pine (*Pinus rigida*) of eastern No. America

torch singer *n* **:** a singer of torch songs

torch song *n* [fr. the phrase *carry a torch*] **:** a popular sentimental song of unrequited love

torch tree *n* **1 :** LOBLOLLY PINE 1 **2 :** an East Indian shrub (*Ixora parviflora*) with scarlet flowers **3 :** OCOTILLO 1

torch–tree family *n* **:** FOUQUIERIACEAE

torchweed \'ˌ=ˌ=\ *n* **:** MATCHWEED

torchwood \'ˌ=ˌ=\ *n* **1 :** a notably resinous or oily wood (as from the butt of some pines) suitable for burning as a torch **2 a :** any of several tropical American trees and shrubs constituting a genus (*Amyris*) that is usu. placed in the family Rutaceae and having fragrant resinous streaky yellowish brown wood that is very hard and heavy and is used locally for fuel and torches and to a limited extent in small cabinetwork; *esp* **:** either of two small trees (*A. elemifera* and *A. balsamifera*) chiefly of the West Indies and southern Florida with trifoliolate leaves, flowers in terminal panicles, and black oily aromatic drupes that ripen in the spring **b :** the wood of a torchwood

torchwood family *n* **:** BURSERACEAE

torchwort \'ˌ=ˌ=\ *n* **:** GREAT MULLEIN

torchy \'tȯrchē, -ō(ə)ch-, -chi\ *adj* -ER/-EST [*torch* (as in *torch song*) + *-y*] **:** of or relating to a torch song **:** characteristic of or appropriate to a torch song ⟨its leader's profound feeling for a ~ ballad —*Metronome*⟩ ⟨~ voice⟩

torcs *pl of* TORC

tor·cu·lar \'tȯ(r)kyələ(r)\ *also* **torcular he·ro·phi·li** \ˌ=ˌ==hə'räfə,lī\ *n, usu cap H* [NL *torcular Herophili*, lit., press of Herophilus, after *Herophilus fl* 300 B.C. Greek anatomist and surgeon] **:** the point at which the four great cranial venous sinuses meet

tor·dion \(')tȯrd¦yōⁿ\ *n, pl* **tordions** \-ōⁿ(z)\ [F, fr. MF, fr. *tordre* to twist, fr. (assumed) VL *torquere*, fr. L *torquēre* — more at TORTURE] **:** an early French dance similar to but slower than the galliard

1**tore** \'tō(ə)r\ *n* -s [prob. fr. L *torus* protuberance, bulge, cushion, torus] *Scot* **:** POMMEL

2**tore** [*tore* (past) alter. (influenced by *torn*) of archaic E *tare*, fr. ME *tar*, fr. OE *tær*; *tore* (past part.) fr. ME *tore*, *toren*, fr. OE *toren*] *past or dial past part of* TEAR

3**tore** \'tō(ə)r\ *n* -s [F, fr. L *torus*] **1 :** the torus of an architectural column **2 :** TORUS 4

4**tore** \"\ *n* -s [origin unknown] *dial Eng* **:** long pasture grass

to·re·ador \'tōrēə,dȯ(ə)r, 'tōr-,'tär-, -dō(ə)\ *n* -s [Sp, fr. *toreado* (past part. of *torear* to fight bulls, fr. *toro* bull, fr. L *taurus*) + *-or* — more at STEER] **1 :** BULLFIGHTER, TORERO **2 :** DUTCH VERMILION

tored *dial past part of* TEAR

to·re·do \tə'rē(,)dō\ *n* -s [by alter.] **:** TEREDO

to·re·nia \tə'rēnēə, -nyə\ *n* [NL, fr. Olaf *Toren* †1753 Swedish ship's chaplain + NL *-ia*] **1** *cap* **:** a genus of chiefly tropical Asiatic and African herbs (family Scrophulariaceae) having simple opposite leaves and tubular 2-lipped showy flowers with four perfect stamens **2** -s **:** any plant of the genus *Torenia*

to·re·ro \tə're(,)rō\ *n* -s [Sp, fr. LL *taurarius*, fr. L *taurus* bull + *-arius* -ary] **:** a matador or a member of his cuadrilla **:** BULLFIGHTER — compare BANDERILLERO, PICADOR

to·reu·tic \tə'rüd·ik\ *adj* [Gk *toreutikos*, fr. *toreutos* worked in relief (fr. *toreuein* to bore through, chase, fr. *toreus* boring tool) + *-ikos* -ic; akin to Gk *tetrainein* to pierce, bore — more at THROW] **:** of or relating to work wrought in metal by embossing or chasing or less commonly to similar work in other materials esp. when comparatively minute and highly finished — not used of the sculpturing of statuary

to·reu·tics \-ks\ *n pl but sing in constr* [fr. *toreutic*, after such pairs as E *economic: economics*] **:** the art or process of making toreutic work

tor·goch \'tȯr,gōk\ *n* -s [W, fr. *tor* belly + *coch* red, fr. L *coccum* kermes berry, scarlet, fr. Gk *kokkos*] *Wales* **:** SAIBLING 1

tor·gos \'tȯrgəs, -,gäs\ *n, cap* [NL, fr. Gk, vulture; prob. akin to OE *storc* stork — more at STORK] **:** a genus of Old World vultures having fleshy lappets on the head — see PONDICHERRY VULTURE

tor·gut *also* **tor·god** *or* **tor·got** \'tȯrgət, -əd\ *n, pl* **torgut** *or* **torguts** *usu cap* **:** a member of a division of the Eastern Mongols who migrated to the Volga in the reign of Genghis Khan but later returned to the valley of the Ili

tori *pl of* TORUS

to·ric \'tōrik, 'tȯr-,'tär-\ *adj* [ISV *tor-* (fr. NL *torus*) + *-ic*] **:** of, relating to, or shaped like a torus or segment of a torus

toric lens *n* **:** a simple lens having for one of its surfaces a segment of an equilateral zone of a torus and consequently having different refracting power in different meridians

tories *pl of* TORY

torify *usu cap, var of* TORYFY

to·rii \'tōrē,ē, 'tȯr-\ *n, pl* **torii** [Jap] **:** a Japanese gateway of light post-and-lintel construction designed usu. with delicately curved lines and commonly built at the approach to a Shinto shrine — compare PAI-LOU, TORAN

torii

to·ril \tə'rē(ə)l\ *n, pl* **tori·les** \-ē(,)lās\ *or* **torils** [Sp, fr. *toro* bull — more at TOREADOR] **:** a cell from which a bull enters the bullring

to·ri·lis \tə'rīləs, -rēl-\ *n, cap* [NL] **:** a genus of annual weedy herbs (family Umbelliferae) that are found in the northern hemisphere and have pinnately decompound leaves, compound umbels of white flowers, and fruits with five primary and four secondary ribs — see HEDGE PARSLEY

1**to·ri·nese** \¦tōrə¦nēz, -ēs\ *adj, usu cap* [It, fr. *Torino* Turin, commercial and manufacturing commune of northwest Italy + It *-ese*] **1 :** of, relating to, or characteristic of Turin, Italy **2 :** of, relating to, or characteristic of the people of Turin

2**torinese** \"\ *n, pl* **torinese** \"\ *cap* **:** a native or inhabitant of Turin

to·rin·gin \tə'rinjən\ *n* -s [NL *toringo* (specific epithet of *Pyrus toringo*, syn. of *Malus sieboldii*) (fr. Jap, a crab apple tree) + E *-in*] **:** a crystalline flavone glucoside $C_{21}H_{20}O_9$ that occurs in the bark of a shrubby Japanese crab apple (*Malus sieboldii*) and in the buds of several poplars and that yields chrysin and glucose on hydrolysis

tor·ma \'tȯrmə\ *n, pl* **tor·mae** \-,mē, -,mī\ [NL, fr. Gk, socket, joint; akin to Gk *tormos* hole, socket, pivot — more at TERM] **:** either of a pair of small sclerites lying between the clypeus and labrum of a higher dipteran

1**tor·ment** \'tȯr,ment, -ō(ə),m- *sometimes chiefly Brit* -,mənt\ *n* -s [ME, fr. OF, fr. L *tormentum* torture, instrument of torture, engine for hurling missiles, fr. *torquēre* to twist, turn — more at TORTURE] **1 a :** the infliction of torture (as by rack or wheel) to punish or coerce someone **b :** the pain suffered by a victim of torture **2 :** extreme pain or anguish of body or mind **:** severe distress **:** AGONY ⟨showed the bodily ~ she was suffering —George Meredith⟩ ⟨five minutes of her were ~ to the ear —John Buchan⟩ ⟨the ~ of the betrayed husband —T.S.Eliot⟩ **3 :** a raging storm **:** TEMPEST **4 a :** a source or cause of physical or mental suffering or vexation **:** something that agitates, troubles, or pains ⟨the task of editing her . . . is both a tease and a ~ —Mark Van Doren⟩ **b :** someone that causes vexation or pain **:** TORMENTOR ⟨burst out into violent rages, and was a ~ to his friends —Rumer Godden⟩

2**tor·ment** \(')¦ment\ *vt* -ED/-ING/-S [ME *tormenten*, fr. OF *tormenter*, fr. LL *tormentare*, fr. L *tormentum* torment] **1 a :** to cause (someone) severe suffering of body or mind **:** inflict pain or anguish on **:** AFFLICT, DISTRESS, RACK ⟨he was . . . ~*ed* with hunger and thirst —Nevil Shute⟩ ⟨she was . . . obviously ~*ed* by shyness —Compton Mackenzie⟩ ⟨problems that ~ men's hearts and warp men's lives —H.E.Fosdick⟩ **b :** to subject to extreme physical strain or agitation **:** stir up **:** DISTURB, TWIST ⟨the water is ~*ed* as if a hurricane had struck it —Alan Villiers⟩ ⟨lit another cigaret, or ~*ed* another pipe —Ellery Queen⟩ ⟨its atmosphere would be increasingly ~*ed* by aeroplanes —Eric Linklater⟩ **c :** to cause worry or vexation to **:** HARASS, PLAGUE, TROUBLE ⟨a last will and testament that was to ~ legal minds for a century to come —*Amer. Guide Series: Mass.*⟩ **2 :** to educe undue or unreal subtlety or complexity in **:** overrefine or complicate the interpretation of **:** read or explain deviously **:** DISTORT ⟨~*ed* the argument out of all honesty and directness⟩ ⟨~*s* the texts to yield readings more ingenious than probable⟩ **syn** see AFFLICT

tor·ment·ed·ly *adv* [*tormented* (past part. of 2*torment*) + *-ly*] **:** in a tormented, strained, or harassed manner **:** DISTRACTEDLY

tor·men·til \'tȯ(r)mən,til\ *n* -s [ME *turmentill*, fr. ML *tormentilla*, fr. L *tormentum* torment; fr. its use in allaying pain] **:** a yellow-flowered Eurasian herb (*Potentilla tormentilla*) with a root that contains an astringent and is used sometimes in tanning and dyeing; *broadly* **:** any of various plants of the genus *Potentilla*

1**tor·men·til·la** \ˌ=ˌ='tilə\ *n* -s [ML] **:** TORMENTIL

2**tormentilla** \"\ [NL, fr. ML, tormentil] *syn of* POTENTILLA

tor·ment·ing·ly *adv* [*tormenting* (pres. part. of 2*torment*) + *-ly*] **:** in a tormenting, straining, or trying manner

tor·ment·ing·ness *n* -ES **:** the quality or state of being tormenting **:** the disposition to give pain

tor·men·tor *also* **tor·ment·er** \(')=¦mentə(r)\ *n* -s [ME *tormentor*, fr. OF *tormenteor*, fr. *tormenter* to torment + *-eor* -or — more at TORMENT, -OR] **1 :** an officer who inflicts penal or coercive torture ⟨delivered him to the ~s, till he should pay all that was due —Mt 18:34 (AV)⟩ **2 :** one that causes extreme pain, annoyance, or vexation **:** an agent of harassment **:** PEST, PLAGUE, PERSECUTOR **3 :** a long iron meat fork used by sea cooks **4 :** a fixed curtain or flat joined to the forward end of each side scene wall on a theater stage, running offstage parallel to the stage front, and serving to prevent the audience from seeing into the wings **5 :** a screen covered to prevent echo during the taking of motion picture scenes **6** *or* **tormentor pole :** a pole used to raise or brace an aerial fire ladder

tor·men·tress \-n·trəs\ *n* -ES [ME, fr. *tormentor* + *-ess*] **:** a female tormentor

tor·mo·gen cell \'tȯ(r)məjən-, -,jen-\ *n* [Gk *tormos* socket, hole + E *-gen* — more at TERM] **:** a specialized epidermal cell in insects that forms a socket at the base of some hairs

torn [ME *torn*, *toren*, fr. OE *toren*] *past part of* TEAR

tor·na·da \tȯ(r)'nädə\ *n* -s [OProv, fr. fem. of *tornat*, past part. of *tornar* to turn, return, fr. L *tornare* to turn in a lathe, round off — more at TURN] **1 :** the refrain of a Provençal poem **2** [alter. of *tornata*] **:** the envoy of an Italian canzone

tor·nad·ic \(')tȯ(r)¦nādik, -nad-, -dēk *sometimes* tə(r)'n-\ *adj* [*tornado* + *-ic*] **:** relating to, characteristic of, or constituting a tornado

tor·na·do \tȯ(r)'nā(,)dō *sometimes* tə(r)'n-\ *n, pl* **tornadoes** *or* **tornados** [modif. (influenced by Sp *tornado*, past part. of *tornar* to turn, return, fr. L *tornare* to turn in a lathe) of Sp *tronada* thunderstorm, fr. fem. of *tronado*, past part. of *tronar* to thunder, fr. L *tonare* — more at THUNDER] **1 a** *archaic* **:** a tropical thunderstorm **b** *obs* **:** the season of such storms **2 a :** a squall accompanying a thunderstorm in Africa **b :** a violent destructive whirling wind accompanied by a funnel-shaped cloud that progresses in a narrow path often for many miles over the land, occurs in many parts of the world but most frequently in the central Mississippi valley, and is associated with a fall in barometric pressure so rapid that wooden structures are often lifted and burst open by the air confined within them — compare CYCLONE, HURRICANE **3 :** a violent or destructive windstorm **:** WHIRLWIND **4 :** something likened to a storm: as **a :** a spectacular display of energy or power **:** DYNAMO ⟨he was a ~ when in action —Stanley Walker⟩ ⟨the maid was no respecter of persons when the ~ of work was in her —Adrian Bell⟩ **b :** a surge of destruction or devastation ⟨seemed torn by a ~ of grief and rage —Rumer Godden⟩ **c :** a torrential volume **:** FRESHET, SPATE, RUSH ⟨a ~ of words: too many at once to get into my ears —Hugh McCrae⟩ ⟨a ~ of protest⟩ **d :** a riotous showing (as of color or sound) ⟨a ~ of applause⟩ **syn** see WIND

tornado lantern *or* **tornado lamp** *n* **:** HURRICANE LAMP

tor·nal \'tȯrnᵊl\ *adj* [NL *tornus* + E *-al*] **:** of or relating to the tornus

tor·nar·ia \tȯ(r)'na(a)rēə\ *n* [NL, fr. L *tornus* lathe, chisel + NL *-aria* — more at TURN] **1** *pl* **tornarias** *or* **tornari·ae** \-ē,ē\ **:** a free-swimming larva that resembles a bipinnaria and is the immature form of an acorn worm or a closely related enteropneust **2** *cap* **:** any of various larval enteropneusts of which the adult is unknown — used as if a generic name ⟨*Tornaria alba*⟩ — **tor·nar·i·an** \(')=¦rēən\ *adj*

tor·na·ta \tȯ(r)'nädə\ *n* -s [It, fr. fem. of *tornato*, past part. of *tornare* to turn, return, fr. L *tornare*] **:** TORNADA 2

1**torn–down** \'=¦=\ *adj* [fr. past part. of *tear down*] *dial* **:** RIOTOUS, ROUGH, UNRULY, VIOLENT

2**torn–down** \'=,=\ *n, dial* **:** an unruly person

törnebohmite *var of* TOERNEBOHMITE

tor·nillo \tȯ(r)'nē(,)(y)ō, -ni(,)lō\ *or* **tor·nilla** \-nē(y)ə, -nilə\ *n* -s [Sp *tornillo*, lit., small lathe, clamp, screw, dim. of *torno* lathe, vise, fr. L *tornus* lathe — more at TURN] **:** SCREW BEAN 1

torniquet *var of* TOURNIQUET

tor·note \'tȯr,nōt\ *n* -s [Gk *tornōtos* rounded with a lathe, fr. *tornousthai* to round with a lathe, fr. *tornos* lathe — more at TURN] **:** a monaxon sponge spicule having both ends abruptly pointed

torn size *n* **:** the size of a piece of household linen (as a bed sheet) before hemming

tor·nus \'tȯrnəs\ *n, pl* **tor·ni** \-,nī, -,nē\ *or* **tornuses** [NL, fr. L, lathe — more at TURN] **:** the inner or anal angle of the wing of an insect (as a moth)

1**to·ro** \'tō(,)ō, 'tȯ(,)rō\ *n* -s [Sp, fr. L *taurus* — more at STEER] **1** *chiefly Southwest* **:** BULL **2 a :** JACK CREVALLE **b :** a cowfish (*Lactophryes quadricornis*)

2**toro** \"\ *n* -s [Maori] **:** a New Zealand tree (*Myrsine salicina*) with reddish figured wood used for inlaying

toro bra·vo \ˌ=(,)=ˈbrä(,)vō\ *n* [Sp, lit., brave bull] **:** a fighting bull **:** a mettlesome animal in the bullring

to·roid \'tōr,ȯid\ *n* -s [NL *torus* + E *-oid*] **1 :** a surface generated by the rotation of a plane closed curve about an axis lying in its plane and not intersecting it **2 :** a body whose surface has the form of a toroid

to·roi·dal \(')tōr¦ȯidᵊl\ *adj* [NL *torus* + E *-oidal*] **:** of, relating to, or shaped like a torus or toroid **:** doughnut-shaped ⟨a ~ resistance coil⟩ ⟨the circulation in the atomic fireball develops a ~ form, with an updraft in the middle and a downdraft around the outside —W.W.Kellogg⟩ — **to·roi·dal·ly** \-ᵊlē\ *adv*

toroid coil *n* **:** a helical winding on a ring-shaped core

to·ron·to \tə'ränt·(,)ō, -n(,)tō, -ntə\ *adj, usu cap* [fr. *Toronto*, capital of Ontario, Canada] **:** of or from Toronto, the capital of Ontario **:** of the kind or style prevalent in Toronto

1**to·ron·to·nian** \tə¦rän·¦tōnēən, ¦tȯrən-·, ¦tärən-·, ¦rän-·, -ōnyən\ *adj, usu cap* [*Toronto*, capital of Ontario + E *-onian* (as in *Bostonian*)] **1 :** of, relating to, or characteristic of Toronto, Ontario **2 :** of, relating to, or characteristic of the people of Toronto

2**torontonian** \"\ *n* -s *cap* **:** a native or inhabitant of Toronto

to·ro·sau·rus \¦tōrō¦sȯrəs\ *n, cap* [NL, prob. fr. L *torus* protuberance, bulge + NL *-saurus*] **:** a genus of dinosaurs (suborder Ceratopsia) of the Laramie formation

to·rose \'tōr,ōs, 'tō,rōs, =ˈ=\ *adj* [L *torosus*, fr. *torus* protuberance, bulge + *-osus* -ose] **1 :** having the surface covered with rounded prominences **:** KNOBBED **2 :** cylindrical (as a plant member) with alternate swellings and contractions

toroth *pl of* TORAH

to·ro·to·ro \¦tōrō¦tōr(,)ō\ *n* -s [origin unknown] **:** a kingfisher (*Halcyon torotoro*) of New Guinea having an orange beak

torp *abbr* torpedo

tor·pe·din·i·dae \,tȯrpə'dinə,dē\ *n pl, cap* [NL, fr. *Torpedin-*, *Torpedo*, type genus + *-idae*] **:** a family of elasmobranchs (order Batoidei) consisting of the electric rays

1**tor·pe·do** \tȯ(r)'pē(,)dō\ *n* [L *torpedin-*, *torpedo* stiffness, numbness, crampfish, fr. *torpēre* to be stiff, numb — more at TORPID] **1** -ES **a** *or* **torpedo fish :** ELECTRIC RAY **b :** someone or something that paralyzes, benumbs, or stupefies **2** *cap* [NL *Torpedin-*, *Torpedo*, fr. L, crampfish] **:** the type genus of Torpedinidae **3** -ES **:** an engine or machine for destroying ships by blowing them up: as **a :** a metal case containing explosives that is anchored in a channel under water or at the surface or set adrift and so arranged that it will be exploded on contact by a vessel or electrically by an operator on shore — called also *submarine mine* **b :** a case containing high explosives carried on a long spar projecting from a war vessel or launch and exploded by contact or electrically — called also *spar torpedo* **c :** a dirigible self-propelling cigar-shaped submarine projectile filled with an explosive charge, projected from a ship often designed for that purpose against another at a distance, and controlled by compressed air and devices for keeping it on course and at a given depth **4** -ES **a :** a charge of explosive enclosed in a container or case and used for any of various military purposes — compare AERIAL TORPEDO **b :** an explosive cartridge or shell lowered or dropped into a bored oil well and there exploded to clear the well of obstructions or to open communication with a possible source of supply of oil **c :** a small firework that explodes when thrown against a hard object **d :** a detonating cartridge or shell placed on a rail to be exploded when crushed under the wheels of a railroad locomotive as a warning signal to the engineer **5** -ES **:** a professional gunman or assassin; *esp* **:** one employed by gangsters or racketeers

2**torpedo** \", *often* -dəw *in pres part*\ *vt* -ED/-ING/-ES **1 a :** to hit or sink (a ship) with a naval torpedo **:** strike (a military target) with a torpedo of any of various kinds **b :** to destroy or nullify altogether **:** EXPLODE, RUIN, SHATTER, WRECK ⟨this ~*es* the principal argument the union has relied on —A.H. Raskin⟩ ⟨the periodical which ~*ed* the great monthlies of the genteel age —H.S.Canby⟩ **2 :** to ignite or explode a charge in (an oil well or shaft) in order to clear away obstructions or increase output

torpedo boat *n* **:** a boat designed for firing torpedoes; *specif* **:** a small very fast thinly plated boat with one or more torpedo tubes carrying only light guns and relying on speed and inconspicuousness to get within torpedo range — compare MOTOR TORPEDO BOAT, SUBMARINE

torpedo–boat destroyer *n* [*torpedo boat*] **:** a large, swift, and powerful armed torpedo boat orig. intended principally for the destruction of torpedo boats but later used also as a formidable torpedo boat — compare DESTROYER

torpedo bomber *also* **torpedo plane** *n* **:** a military airplane designed to carry torpedoes

torpedo director *n* **:** a device for controlling the fire of torpedoes

torpedo grass *n* **:** a perennial grass (*Panicum repens*) that is native to the southeastern U. S., is used for pasture and forage, and has sharp-pointed rhizomes by which it spreads very aggressively

tor·pe·do·ist \tȯ(r)'pēdəwəst, -ēdōə-\ *n* -s **:** one that torpedoes; *esp* **:** TORPEDOMAN

torpedo juice *n* **:** a drink based on the fuel alcohol of naval torpedoes

¹torpedolike \=ˈ==,=\ *adj* [¹*torpedo* + *like*, adj.] **:** resembling a torpedo

²torpedolike \"\ *adv* [¹*torpedo* + *like*, adv.] **:** in the manner of a torpedo

tor·pe·do·man \-ēdō,man, -ēdə,m-, -mən\ *n, pl* **torpedomen :** a warrant officer (as in the U. S. Navy) whose specialty is supervision of underwater ordnance and related equipment

torpedo net *or* **torpedo netting** *n* **:** a netting made of steel links stretched by booms around a ship and extending beneath the surface of the water or extended across a harbor entrance as a protection against torpedoes

torpedo sand *n* **:** a coarse clean sand the particles of which all pass through a ⅜ inch mesh

torpedo tube *n* **:** a tube fixed near the waterline through which a torpedo is fired

tor·pex \ˈtȯr,peks\ *n* -ES *often cap* [*torpedo* + *explosive*] **:** a high explosive mixture consisting essentially of RDX, TNT, and aluminum and used for depth charges under water

¹tor·pid \ˈtȯrpəd, -ȯ(ə)p-\ *adj* [L *torpidus*, fr. *torpēre* to be stiff, numb, torpid; akin to Lith *tirpti* to become stiff, L *stirps* stem of a plant, trunk, stock, lineage, OE *starian* to stare — more at STARE] **1 a :** having lost motion or the power of exertion or feeling **:** DORMANT, NUMB **b :** sluggish in functioning or acting ⟨a ~ frog⟩ ⟨a ~ mind⟩ **2 :** lacking in energy or vigor **:** APATHETIC, DULL ⟨the bold and reckless young blood of ten years back was . . . turned into a ~, submissive, middle-aged, stout gentleman —W.M.Thackeray⟩ **syn** see LETHARGIC

²torpid \"\ *n* -S **:** a clinker-built eight-oared boat used for the Lent term races at Oxford university

tor·pid·i·ty \tȯ(r)ˈpidəd·ē, -idətē, -i\ *n* -ES [*torpid* + *-ity*] **:** the quality or state of being torpid **:** SLUGGISHNESS, TORPIDNESS

tor·pid·ly *adv* **:** in a torpid manner

tor·pid·ness *n* -ES [¹*torpid* + *-ness*] **:** TORPIDITY

tor·pi·fy *or* **tor·pe·fy** \ˈtȯ(r)pə,fī\ *vt* -ED/-ING/-ES [modif. (influenced by E *-ify*, *-fy*) of LL *torpefacere*, fr. *torpēre* to be torpid + *facere* to make — more at DO] **:** to make torpid **:** BENUMB, STUPEFY **syn** see DAZE

tor·pi·tude \-pə,tüd, -pə-,tyüd\ *n* -S [*torpid* + *-tude*] *archaic* **:** TORPIDITY

tor·por \ˈtȯrpər, ˈtȯ(ə)pə(r *sometimes* -,pȯ(ə)r *or* -,pȯ(ə)\ *n* -S [L, fr. *torpēre* to be torpid] **1 :** a state of mental and motor inactivity with partial or total insensibility **:** suspended animation **:** sluggishness or stagnation of function **:** DORMANCY ⟨a deathlike ~ has succeeded to her former intellectual activity —W.H.Prescott⟩ **2 :** mental or spiritual sluggishness **:** APATHY, LETHARGY ⟨tradition may result merely in ~ —Walter Moberly⟩

tor·por·if·ic \ˌtȯ(r)pəˈrifik, -fēk\ *adj* [L *torpor* + E *-i-* + *-fic*] **:** producing torpor **:** DULLING, STUPEFYING

tor·quate \ˈtȯr,kwāt\ *adj* [L *torquatus*, lit., wearing a torque, fr. *torquis*, *torques* + *-atus* -ate] **:** having a ring esp. of color around the neck **:** COLLARED, RING-NECKED

¹torque \ˈtȯ(ə)rk, -ȯ(ə)k\ *n* -S [F *torque*, fr. L *torquis*, *torques*, fr. *torquēre* to twist — more at TORTURE] **:** a usu. metal collar or neck chain worn by the ancient Gauls, Germans, and Britons ⟨these hands won many a ~ of gold —W.B.Yeats⟩

²torque *n* -S [L *torquēre* to twist] **:** something which produces or tends to produce rotation or torsion and whose effectiveness is measured by the product of the force and the perpendicular distance from the line of action of the force to the axis of rotation **:** a moment of force ⟨a pound-foot of ~ is the ~ produced by a force of one pound acting one foot from the center of rotation —*Consumer Reports*⟩ ⟨if the handle of the wrench were 1 foot long and a 10-pound force is put on its end, 10 pound-feet of ~ would be applied on the nut —*Principles of Automotive Vehicles*⟩ ⟨in addition to transforming fuel into heat, the engine converts heat into reciprocal motion, and it changes reciprocal motion into ~ —George Hafferkamp & J.H.Zich⟩; *broadly* **:** a turning or twisting force **:** rotary effort

torque arm *n* [²*torque*] **:** an arm to take the torque of the rear axle of an automotive vehicle that is connected at the rear with the differential case either rigidly or by a joint and at the front is always jointed to a cross member of the frame

torque converter *n* **:** a device for converting the speed and torque at the driving shaft of an automobile to that required by the driven shaft

tor·que·ma·da \ˌtȯ(r)k(w)əˈmä|də, -mä|, |thə\ *n* -S *usu cap* [after Tomas de *Torquemada* †1498, Spanish Dominican monk and first inquisitor general for all Spanish possessions] **:** PERSECUTOR ⟨the youthful and ubiquitous *Torquemadas* who serve as the subcommittee's chief counsel and chief consultant —R.H.Rovere⟩

torque·me·ter \ˈtȯ(r)k,mēd·ə(r)\ *n* [²*torque* + *-meter*] **:** an instrument to measure or record torque

torque tube *n* [²*torque*] **:** a tube surrounding the propeller shaft of an automotive vehicle to take the torque and being usu. a unit with the rear-axle housing at the rear but with a universal joint at the front where it is supported by a cross-frame member or by the rear end of the transmission case

torque wrench *n* **:** a wrench that measures and indicates the

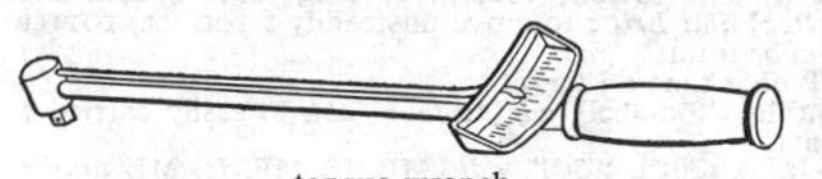

torque wrench

amount of turning and twisting force applied in tightening a nut or bolt

torr \ˈtȯ(ə)r\ *n, pl* **torr** [after Evangelista *Torricelli* †1647 Ital. mathematician and physicist and inventor of the barometer] **:** a unit of pressure equal to 1/760 of an atmosphere and very nearly equal to the pressure of a column of mercury 1 millimeter high at 0° C and standard gravity

tor·re·fac·tion \ˌtȯrəˈfakshən, ˌtär-\ *n* -S [L *torrefactus* (past part. of *torrefacere* to torrefy) + E *-ion*] **:** the act or process of torrefying or the state of being torrefied

tor·re·fy *also* **tor·ri·fy** \ˈ==,fī\ *vt* -ED/-ING/-ES [modif. (influenced by E *-fy*, *-ify*) of L *torrefacere*, fr. *torrēre* to dry, parch + *facere* to make — more at TORRENT, DO] **:** to dry or roast with fire **:** PARCH, SCORCH: as **a :** to subject (ores) to scorching heat so as to drive off volatile ingredients **:** ROAST **b :** to dry (drugs) on a hot metallic plate till they are friable or are reduced to the state desired

tor·rens system \ˈtȯ|rənz-, ˈtä|\ *n, usu cap T* [after Sir Robert *Torrens* †1884, Brit. pioneer in Australia] **:** a system of land title registration first introduced in Australia and widely used in England, Canada, the U. S., and elsewhere according to which the government guarantees properly registered titles, simplifying transfers and making title insurance unnecessary

¹tor·rent \ˈtȯrənt, ˈtär-\ *n* -S [F, fr. L *torrent-*, *torrens*, fr. *torrent-*, *torrens* burning, seething, rushing, fr. pres. part. of *torrēre* to dry, parch, burn; akin to OHG *derren* to dry, parch, ON *therra*, Skt *tarṣayati* he causes to thirst — more at THIRST] **1 :** a violent stream of a liquid (as water or lava); *esp* **:** a rushing stream of water (as a flooded river or one suddenly raised by a heavy rain or thaw and descending a steep incline) **2 a :** a mountain channel that is often dry though filled with rushing water at some times or seasons **b :** an intermittent branch **3 :** a raging flood **:** a tumultuous outpouring **:** FLUX, RUSH ⟨let loose a ~ of speculative buying —O.S.Nock⟩ ⟨engulfed in a ~ of enemy troops —H.L.Merillat⟩ ⟨philosophy . . . provided a foothold for man above the ~ of circumstance —John Buchan⟩

²torrent \"\ *adj* [L *torrent-*, *torrens*, adj.] **:** TORRENTIAL ⟨rich, grassy orchards and a ~ stream —M.C.A.Henniker⟩

torrent bow *n* [¹*torrent*] **:** a fragmentary rainbow formed in the spray of a torrent

torrent duck *n* **:** any of several ducks related to the mergansers and constituting the genus *Merganetta* that inhabit rushing streams of the Andes from Colombia to Chile

tor·ren·tial \tȯˈrenchəl, təˈr-, täˈr-\ *adj* [¹*torrent* + *-ial*] **1 a :** relating to or having the character of a torrent ⟨~ rains⟩ **b :** caused by or resulting from action of rapid streams ⟨~ gravel⟩ **c :** of, relating to, or being inhabitants of swiftly flowing waters ⟨~ adaptations⟩ **2 :** resembling a torrent in violence or rapidity of flow **:** COPIOUS, RUSHING, VIGOROUS ⟨it has all the ~ facility and fecundity characteristic of his style —Winthrop Sargeant⟩ ⟨because of his splendid costumes and his ~ speeches —Malcolm Cowley⟩

tor·ren·tial·ly \-chəlē, -li\ *adv* **:** in a torrential manner

tor·ren·ti·cole \təˈrentə,kōl\ *n* -S [¹*torrent* + *-i-* + *-cole*] **:** an organism that lives in swiftly flowing water

¹tor·re·ón *or* **torreon** \ˌtȯrēˈōn, -ēˈȯn, -ēˈän\ *adj, usu cap* [fr. *Torreón*, city of northeast Mexico] **:** of or from the city of Torreón, Mexico **:** of the kind or style prevalent in Torreón

²torreón \"\ *n, pl* **torreo·nes** \ˌ==ˈōnēz, -ˈō(,)nās\ [Sp, aug. of *torre* tower, fr. L *turris* — more at TOWER] **:** a prehistoric stone tower in the southwestern U.S.

tor·reya \ˈtȯrēə\ *n, cap* [NL, after John *Torrey* †1873 Am. botanist and chemist] **:** a genus of Asiatic and No. American trees (family Taxaceae) having two-ranked often ill-scented linear leaves and a large ovoid fruit resembling a drupe but being actually a large seed surrounded by a fleshy aril — see CALIFORNIA NUTMEG, STINKING CEDAR

tor·rey·ite \-ē,īt\ *n* -S [John *Torrey* †1873 + E *-ite*] **:** a mineral $(Mg,Mn,Zn)_7(SO_4)(OH)_{12}.4H_2O$ consisting of a basic hydrous sulfate of magnesium, manganese, and zinc

tor·rey pine \ˈtȯrē-\ *or* **torrey's pine** *n, usu cap T* [after John *Torrey* †1873] **:** a tall coniferous tree (*Pinus torreyana*) of California with dark green needles in fives and long cylindrical cones — called also *gray-leaf pine, Sabine pine, Soledad pine*

torrey tree *n, usu cap 1st T* [after John *Torrey* †1873] **:** STINKING CEDAR

tor·ri·cel·li·an \ˌtȯrəˈchelēən, ˌtär-, -rəˈsel-\ *adj, usu cap* [Evangelista *Torricelli* †1647 Ital. mathematician and physicist + E *-an*] **:** of or relating to the Italian physicist and mathematician Torricelli closely associated with Galileo and noted esp. for his researches in pneumatics

torricellian tube *n, usu cap 1st T* **:** a glass tube open at one end and hermetically sealed at the other and of such length that when filled with a liquid (as mercury) and immersed at the open end in a vessel of the same liquid allowing the enclosed liquid to descend till it is counterbalanced by the pressure of the atmosphere a vacuum will be produced at the upper end

torricellian vacuum *n, usu cap T* **:** the vacuum at the upper end of a Torricellian tube

tor·ri·cel·li's law *also* **torricelli's theorem** \-lēz-\ *n, usu cap Torricelli's* [after Evangelista *Torricelli* †1647] **:** a law in hydrodynamics: the speed of efflux of a liquid from an orifice is equal to that of a body falling freely through a distance equal to the total head of the liquid at the orifice

tor·rid \ˈtȯrəd, ˈtär-\ *adj, usu* -ER/-EST [L *torridus*, fr. *torrēre* to dry, parch — more at TORRENT] **1 a :** parched with heat esp. of the sun **:** HOT, DRY, SCORCHED ⟨the ~ June boulevard —Bruce Marshall⟩ **b :** giving off intense heat **:** SCORCHING ⟨the ~ heat of the desert —C.A. & Mary Beard⟩ **2 :** emotionally aroused or arousing **:** ARDENT, PASSIONATE, SULTRY ⟨~ talk of dynamiting managers' homes⟩ ⟨~ love letters⟩ ⟨a ~ beauty⟩ ⟨hot trumpets and ~ rhythms —Green Peyton⟩

tor·rid·i·ty \tȯˈridəd·ē, täˈr-, -idətē, -i\ *n* -ES [LL *torriditat-*, *torriditas*, fr. L *torridus* torrid + *-itat-*, *-itas* -ity] **:** TORRIDNESS

tor·rid·ly *adv* **:** in a torrid manner

tor·rid·ness *n* -ES **:** the quality or state of being torrid

tor·ri·do·ni·an \ˌtȯrəˈdōnēən\ *adj, usu cap* [Loch *Torridon*, inlet on northwest coast of Scotland + E *-ian*] **:** of, relating to, or constituting a division of the Precambrian — see GEOLOGIC TIME table

torrid zone *n* **:** the belt of the earth between the tropics over which the sun is vertical at some period of the year — see ZONE illustration

torrify *var of* TORREFY

tor·ro·ne \təˈrōnē\ *n* -S [It, fr. Sp. *turrón*, fr. *turrar* to roast, toast, fr. L *torrēre* to dry, parch — more at TORRENT] **:** a candy made of honey and almonds

torrs *pl of* TORR

tor·ru·bia \təˈrübēə\ *n, cap* [NL, after José *Torrubia* †1768 Span. naturalist] **:** a genus of tropical American shrubs and trees (family Nyctaginaceae) with fleshy leaves, greenish dioecious panicled flowers, and fleshy fruit — see BLOLLY

tors *pl of* TOR

tor·sade \(ˈ)tȯrˈsäd, -ˈsād\ *n* -S [F, fr. obs. F *tors* twisted (fr. LL *torsus*) + F *-ade*] **:** a twisted cord or ribbon used esp. as a hat ornament ⟨the crown decked with ~s of pearls —*Harper's*⟩

tor·sa·lo \ˈtȯ(r)sə,lō\ *n* -S [AmSp *tórsalo*] **:** a botfly (*Dermatobia hominis*) that attacks man and other mammals in warm parts of the Americas

¹torse \ˈtȯ(ə)rs\ *n* -S [MF *torse*, *torce*, fr. fem. of *tors* twisted] **:** a twisted band or wreath by which a heraldic crest is joined to the helmet

²torse \"\ *n* -S [F, fr. It. *torso*] **:** TORSO

tor·sel \ˈtȯrsəl\ *or* **tas·sel** \ˈtasəl\ *n* -S [*torsel* alter. of *tassel*, fr. F *tassel*, *tasseau*, fr. OF *tassel* clasp — more at TASSEL] **:** a piece of stone, iron, or wood to support the end of a beam or joist and distribute the weight

torsi *pl of* TORSO

tor·si·bil·i·ty \ˌtȯ(r)səˈbiləd·ē\ *n* -ES [LL *torsus* + E *-ibility*] **:** resistance to torsion; *also* **:** tendency (as of a twisted rope) to untwist

tor·si·gram \ˈtȯ(r)sə,gram\ *also* **tor·sio·gram** \-)shə,g-, -)sēə,g-\ *n* [*torsion* + *-gram*] **:** a torsion record made on a torsigraph

tor·si·graph *also* **tor·sio·graph** \-graf,-gräf\ *n* [ISV *torsion* + *-graph*] **:** a recording torsion meter

tor·sion \ˈtȯrshən, -ȯ(ə)sh-\ *n* -S [LL *torsus* (past part. of L *torquēre* to twist) + E *-ion* — more at TORTURE] **1 :** the act of turning or twisting **:** the state of being twisted **:** the twisting or wrenching of a body by the exertion of forces tending to turn one end or part about a longitudinal axis while the other is held fast or turned in the opposite direction **2 :** the limit of the ratio of the angle between the binormals at two points of a curve to the length of the arc joining the points as the length of the arc approaches zero — called also *second curvature* **3 :** the reactive torque that an elastic solid exerts by reason of being under torsion **4 :** the twisting of a body organ on its own axis ⟨the ~ of a loop of intestine around its own mesentery⟩ **syn** see STRESS

tor·sion·al *also* **tor·tion·al** \-shənᵊl,-shnəl\ *adj* **:** of, relating to, causing, or resulting from torsion — **tor·sion·al·ly** \-ᵊlē, -əl|, |i\ *adv*

torsion balance *n* **1 :** an instrument used to measure minute forces (as electrostatic or magnetic attraction and repulsion) by the torsion of a wire or filament, the angle of torsion being proportional to the amount of force exerted **2 :** a spring balance in which the weight is balanced by the torsion of a wire — compare EÖTVÖS BALANCE

torsion bar *n* **:** a device to minimize sideway and road jolts in automobiles

torsion electrometer *n* **:** a torsion balance used for measuring electric attraction or repulsion

torsion head *n* **:** the part of a torsion balance from which the wire or filament is suspended and which is usu. graduated with an angular scale for measuring the counterrotation required to neutralize the deflection

tor·sion·ing \-sh(ə)niŋ\ *n* -S [*torsion* + *-ing*] **:** the producing of torsion esp. to close an opening (as by twisting the free end of a cut artery)

torsion meter *n* **:** an instrument for determining the torque on a shaft — compare TORSIGRAPH

torsion modulus *n* **:** SHEAR MODULUS

torsion pendulum *n* **:** PENDULUM 1b

torsion scale *n* **:** a weighing scale in which the fulcrums of the levers or beams are wires or strips acting by torsion

torsk \ˈtȯ(ə)rsk\ *n, pl* **torsk** *or* **torsks** [of Scand origin; akin to Norw & Sw & Dan *torsk* codfish, ON *thorskr*; akin to MLG *dorsch* codfish, and prob. to ON *therra* to dry — more at TORRENT] **:** CODFISH

¹tor·so \ˈtȯr(,)sō, -ȯ(ə)(,)sō\ *n, pl* **torsos** \-sōz\ *or* **tor·si** \-sē\ *also* **torsoes** [It, stalk, stem, torso, fr. L *thyrsus* thyrsus, stalk, stem — more at THYRSUS] **1 :** the trunk of a sculptured representation of a human body; *esp* **:** the trunk of a statue whose head and limbs are mutilated **2 :** something (as a work of art or letters) that is mutilated or left unfinished ⟨three volumes and only a ~ completed —*Infantry Jour.*⟩ **3 a :** the human trunk ⟨she lifted his ~ with great strength and infinite solicitude —F.M.Ford⟩ **b :** something likened to the human torso (as the trunk of a tree) ⟨cypress trees, tough twisted ~es lashed by long winds —Carl Sandburg⟩ **c :** the part of a garment that covers the torso ⟨a black-and-white checked cotton with a long, graceful ~ has a button-on collar —*New Yorker*⟩

²torso \"\ *n* -S [modif. (influenced by ¹*torso*) of F (*colonne*) *torse* twisted column, fr. *colonne* column (fr. MF *colomne*) + *torse*, fem. of obs. *tors* twisted — more at COLUMN, TORSADE] **:** a twisted or spiral shaft or column

tort \ˈtȯ(ə)r|t, ˈȯ(ə)|, *usu* |d·+V\ *n* -S [ME, fr. MF, fr. ML *tortum*, fr. L, neut. of *tortus*, twisted, distorted, fr. past part. of *torquēre* to twist — more at TORTURE] **1** *obs* **:** injury or wrong done someone **2 :** a wrongful act for which a civil action will lie except one involving a breach of contract **:** a civil wrong independent of a contract — compare CRIME, DELICT, INJURY, TRESPASS

tor·ta \ˈtȯrd·ə\ *n* -S [Sp, cake, fr. LL, round loaf of bread] **1 :** a flat heap of moist crushed silver ore prepared for the patio process **2 :** an open pie with a base of bread or biscuit dough and a sweet or savory filling — called also *tourte*

tor·te \ˈtȯrd·ə, ÷ -rt\ *n, pl* **tor·ten** \-rtᵊn\ *or* **tortes** [G, prob. fr. It *torta*, fr. LL, round loaf of bread] **:** a cake or pastry made of many eggs, sugar, and often grated nuts or dry bread crumbs in place of flour and baked in a large flat form, being sometimes filled with jam and usu. covered with a rich frosting (as chocolate, mocha, or strawberry meringue) — compare LINZER TORTE, SACHER

tor·teau *also* **tor·teaux** \(ˈ)tȯrˈtō\ *n, pl* **torteaux** \-ōz\ [MF *torteau*, fr. OF *tortel* wafer, small round loaf of bread, dim. of *torte*, *tourte* round loaf of bread, fr. LL *torta*] **:** a heraldic roundel gules

tor·tel·li·ni \ˌtȯ(r)d·ᵊlˈēnē\ *n* -S [It (pl.), dim. of *tortelli* (pl.) a pasta, fr. LL *torta* round loaf of bread] **:** an alimentary paste of noodle dough cut in rounds, filled with savory fillings, and boiled

tort-feasor \ˈ=ˈfēzər, -,zȯ(ə)r\ *n* -S [F *tortfaiseur*, fr. MF, fr. *tort* wrong + *faiseur* doer, maker, fr. *fais-* (stem of *faire* to do, make, fr. L *facere*) + *-eur* -or — more at TORT, DO] **:** one that commits or is guilty of a tort

tor·ti·col·lis \ˌtȯrd·əˈkäləs\ *n* -ES [NL, fr. L *tortus* twisted + *-i-* + *collum* neck — more at TORT, COLLAR] **:** an abnormal and more-or-less fixed twisting of the neck associated in man with muscular contracture esp. of a sternocleidomastoid and in domestic and other lower mammals occurring esp. in conjunction with severe intestinal parasitism or ear disorders — called also *wryneck*

tor·ti·cone \ˈtȯrd·ə,kōn\ *n* [L *tortus* + E *-i-* + *cone*] **:** a turreted spiral cephalopod shell as distinguished from one with coils in one plane

tor·tie *also* **tor·ty** \ˈtȯrd·ē\ *n, pl* **torties** [by shortening & alter.] **:** TORTOISESHELL CAT

tor·tile \ˈtȯrd·ᵊl, -r,tīl, -r(,)til\ *adj* [L *tortilis*, fr. *tortus* (past part. of *torquēre* to twist) + *-ilis* -ile — more at TORTURE] **:** COILED, TWISTED, SINUOUS

tor·ti·lla \tȯ(r)ˈtē(y)ə\ *n* -S [AmSp, fr. dim. of Sp *torta* cake — more at TORTA] **:** a round thin cake of unleavened cornmeal bread usu. eaten hot with a topping or filling that may include ground meat, cheese, and any of various sauces — see ENCHILADA

tor·til·lé \ˌtȯ(r)tēˈ(y)ā\ *adj* [F, fr. past part. of *tortiller* to twist, wind, fr. (assumed) VL *tortiliare*, fr. L *tortilis* twisted — more at TORTILE] *heraldry* **:** wreathed with a spirally twisted band

tor·til·lon \ˌtȯ(r)d·ēˈ(y)än, -)ōn\ *n* -S [F, lit., twist, twisted object, fr. MF, fr. *tortiller* to twist] **:** a small rolled-paper stump used in charcoal drawing for rubbing or blending

tortional *var of* TORSIONAL

tor·tious \ˈtȯrshəs, -ȯ(ə)sh-\ *adj* [ME, fr. *tort* + *-ious*] **1** *obs* **a :** INJURIOUS, WRONGFUL **b :** IMPROPER, MISTAKEN **2 :** implying or involving tort for which the law gives damages ⟨~ conduct incurs liability⟩ — **tor·tious·ly** *adv*

tortious conveyance *n, old Eng law* **:** a wrongful conveyance of a greater estate than that of the conveyor

tor·tive \ˈtȯrd·iv\ *adv* [L *tortus* (past part. of *torquēre* to twist) + E *-ive* — more at TORTURE] **:** TWISTED, WREATHED

tor·tle \ˈtȯrd·ᵊl\ *dial var of* TURTLE

tor·toise \ˈtȯr|d·əs, -ȯ(ə)|, |təs *sometimes* |,tȯiz *or* |,tȯis\ *n, pl* **tortoises** *also* **tortoise** [ME *tortuce*, *tortous*, *tortuse*, prob. alter. (the gen. being taken as the n. attrib.) of *tortu*, fr. MF *tortue* — more at TURTLE] **1 :** a reptile of the order Testudinata **:** TURTLE — used esp. of terrestrial forms; see GIANT TORTOISE **2 :** someone or something regarded as slow, tardy, or laggard ⟨complacent about the ~. Reaction, plodding up from the rear —H.L.Smith b. 1906⟩ **3 :** TORTOISESHELL **4 :** a strong brown that is yellower, less strong, and slightly lighter than average russet, yellower and less strong than rust, and yellower and slightly duller than gold brown **5 :** TESTUDO 2

tortoise beetle *n* **1 :** any of numerous small tortoise-shaped beetles of the family Chrysomelidae many of whom have a brilliant metallic luster and whose larvae feed upon the leaves of various plants **2 :** any of several Australian tenebrionid beetles of *Helaeus* and related genera having broad margins to the elytra and prothorax

tortoise-core \ˈ=(,)=ˈ=\ *n* **:** a stone core shaped like the carapace of a tortoise and constituting the nodule from which prehistoric man flaked off material for tools

tortoise plant *n* **:** ELEPHANT'S-FOOT 1b

tortoise scale *n* **:** any of various thick-bodied to hemispherical soft scales; *esp* **:** LECANIUM 2

¹tor·toise·shell \ˈtȯ(r)d·ə|shel, -)t|, |əs(h),shel\ *n* **1 :** a substance that forms the horny plates covering the shell of some turtles and esp. the hawksbill turtle which provides almost all of the tortoiseshell of commerce and that is rich brown mottled with yellow, readily molded and welded when hot, and used in inlaying and in making ornamental articles **2** *or* **tortoiseshell butterfly :** any of several brilliantly colored butterflies of the genus *Nymphalis*; *esp* **:** either of two such butterflies (*N. milberti* and *N. j-album*) that in the larval state feed upon nettles

²tortoiseshell \"\ *adj* **:** made of tortoise shell or having a mottled coloration suggesting tortoise shell

tortoiseshell cat *or* **tortoiseshell** *n* **:** a usu. female domestic cat having a black, red, and cream or white blotched coat often with a white blaze on the face

tortoiseshell tiger *n* **:** CLOUDED LEOPARD

tortoiseshell turtle *n* **:** HAWKSBILL TURTLE

tor·to·ni \tȯ(r)ˈtōnē\ *n* -S [prob. after *Tortoni* 19th cent. Ital. restaurateur in Paris] **1 :** an ice cream made of heavy cream sometimes with minced almonds, chopped maraschino cherries, or other flavoring ingredients **2 :** BISCUIT TORTONI

¹tor·tri·cid \ˈtȯ(r)·trəsəd\ *adj* [NL *Tortricidae*] **:** of or relating to the Tortricidae

²tortricid \"\ *n* -S **:** a moth of the family Tortricidae

tor·tric·i·dae \tȯ(r)·ˈtrisə,dē\ *n pl, cap* [NL *Tortric-*, *Tortrix*, type genus + *-idae*] **:** a family of small moths usu. having a stout body, oblong lightly fringed wings, threadlike antennae, and a tuft of scales at the end of the abdomen, many of the larvae being leaf rollers and others living in various fruits and galls

tor·trix \ˈtȯr·triks, -ȯ(ə)·t-\ *n* [NL *Tortric-*, *Tortrix*, lit., female twister, fr. L *tortus* (past part. of *torquēre* to twist) + *-ric-*, *-rix*, fem. of *-or*; fr. its habit of twisting or rolling leaves to make a nest — more at TORTURE] **1** *cap* **:** a genus of moths that is the type of the family Tortricidae **2** -ES **:** any moth of the genus Tortrix or family Tortricidae — see ORANGE TORTRIX, TEA TORTRIX

torts *pl of* TORT

tor·tu·la·ce·ae \ˌtȯ(r)chəˈlāsē,ē\ [NL, fr. *Tortula*, genus of mosses (fr. L *tortus* twisted + *-ula*) + *-aceae*] *syn of* POTTIACEAE

tor·tu·os·i·ty \ˌtȯ(r)chəˈwäsəd·ē, -sətē, -i\ *n* -ES [LL *tortuositat-*, *tortuositas*, fr. L *tortuosus* tortuous + *-itat-*, *-itas* -ity] **1 a :** the quality or state of being tortuous **b :** something winding or twisted **:** a crooked place or part **:** BEND, SINUOSITY ⟨she began to indicate the *tortuosities* of the tree with tentative and hesitant strokes —*New Yorker*⟩ **2 :** an instance or trait of deviousness or crookedness **:** INDIRECTNESS ⟨had begun to bog down in the subtleties and *tortuosities* of his own thought —J.R.Ullman⟩ ⟨*tortuosities* of behavior that pride, thwarted passion and almost ghoulish severities and prohibitions had effected —*N. Y. Herald Tribune Bk. Rev.*⟩

tor·tu·ous \'tȯ(r)chəwəs\ *adj* [ME, fr. MF *tortueux*, fr. L *tortuosus*, fr. *tortus* twist (fr. *tortus*, past part. of *torquēre* to twist) + *-osus* -ous] **1 :** marked by repeated twists, bends, or turns **:** WINDING ⟨the channel is ~ and dangerous and constantly silting —L.F.Alexander⟩ ⟨we begin a ~ climb into the highlands —Tom Marvel⟩ ⟨a ~ length of water-cooled coils —D.W.Dresden⟩ ⟨products of a ~ hereditary line —Faubion Bowers⟩ **2 a :** marked by or resorting to devious or indirect tactics or strategy **:** crooked, treacherous, or sharp in device or method **:** lacking in straightforwardness, candor, or simplicity **:** TRICKY ⟨pursued a ~ policy in his testimony, disclosing this piece of evidence and withholding that —Rebecca West⟩ ⟨~ haggling over the price of comradeship —*Time*⟩ **b :** wandering from a direct or consecutive course in thought or action **:** deviating into irrelevant complexity or intricacy **:** CIRCUITOUS, INVOLVED ⟨the ~ workings of government by consent —*New Republic*⟩ ⟨the featureless hierophants of some ~ ceremony —V.S.Pritchett⟩ ⟨~ litigation⟩ **3 :** TORTIOUS 2 ⟨an agent who does a ~ act is not relieved from liability by the fact that he acted at the command . . . of his principal —J.D.Johnson⟩

tor·tu·ous·ly *adv* **:** in a tortuous manner

tor·tu·ous·ness *n* -ES **:** the quality or state of being tortuous

tor·tur·able \'tȯ(r)ch(ə)rəbəl\ *adj* [²*torture* + *-able*] **:** capable of being tortured

¹**tor·ture** \'tȯrchər, -ȯ(ə)chə(r\ *n* -S [F, fr. LL *tortura* act of twisting, torture, fr. L *tortus* (past part. of *torquēre* to twist, wind, torture) + *-ura* -ure; akin to OHG *drāhsil* turner, Gk *atraktos* spindle, Skt *tarku*] **1 a :** the infliction of intense pain (as from burning, crushing, wounding) to punish or coerce someone **:** torment or agony induced to penalize religious or political dissent or nonconformity, to extort a confession or a money contribution, or to give sadistic pleasure to the torturer ⟨no one shall be subjected to ~ or to cruel, inhuman or degrading treatment or punishment —*U. N. Declaration of Human Rights*⟩ **b** *obs* **:** an implement of torture **2 a :** anguish of body or mind **:** excruciating agony **:** extremity of suffering ⟨long ~ with Parkinson's disease —John Mason Brown⟩ ⟨she shrank in her convulsed, coiled ~ from the thought of such a thing —D.H.Lawrence⟩ **b :** an extreme annoyance or severe irritation **:** an intense strain **:** something pernicious or baneful **:** PLAGUE ⟨plays . . . would be torn line from line for the ~ of high school boys and girls —J.D.Adams⟩ ⟨many of their sidehill and downhill lies would have been ~ to a golfer with 20-20 vision —Tom Siler⟩ **3 :** distortion, overrefinement, or perversion of a meaning, an argument, or a line of thought or reasoning **:** STRAINING ⟨no ~ in interpretation would be required —E.W.Knight⟩ **4 :** the subjecting of material or equipment to extreme strain or abuse as a test of strength, endurance, or quality ⟨cars are put through thousands of miles of ~ —*Visit to the Proving Grounds*⟩

²**torture** \"\ *vb* **tortured; tortured; torturing** \-ch(ə)riŋ\ **tortures** *vt* **1 a :** to put to torture **:** punish or coerce by inflicting excruciating pain ⟨*tortured* my sister for three months . . . disfigured her face and broke her hands and legs —Ben Hecht⟩ **b :** to extract or obtain by torture ⟨*tortured* a confession from the prisoner⟩ **2 :** to cause intense suffering to **:** inflict anguish on **:** subject to severe pain **:** TORMENT ⟨set himself to ~ me as a schoolboy would devote a rapturous half hour to watching the agonies of an impaled beetle —Rudyard Kipling⟩ **3 :** to twist or wrench out of shape **:** DISTORT, WARP ⟨make it an easy matter to ~ wooden boards into uncouth shapes —*Amer. Guide Series: Conn.*⟩ ⟨language . . . strained and *tortured* —R.L.Cook⟩ ⟨unable to ~ her religious experience into the Calvinistic system —C.A.Dinsmore⟩ **~** *vi* **:** to cause excruciating pain or anguish **syn** see AFFLICT

tor·tured·ly \-chə(r)dlē\ *adv* [*tortured* (past part. of ²*torture*) + *-ly*] **:** in a tortured, strained, or anguished manner

tor·tur·er \-chərə(r)\ *n* -S **:** one that tortures

tor·ture·some \-chə(r)səm\ *adj* [¹*torture* + *-some*] **:** causing torture **:** intolerably painful ⟨slipped on their ~ pumps —William Maxwell⟩

tor·tur·ing·ly *adv* [*torturing* (pres. part. of ²*torture*) + *-ly*] **:** in a torturing manner **:** PAINFULLY

tor·tur·ous \'tȯrch(ə)rəs, -ȯ(ə)ch-\ *adj* [ME, fr. MF *tortureux*, fr. *torture* + *-eux* -ous] **1 :** causing, marked by, or accompanied by torture **:** cruelly painful ⟨the ~, far from finished battle —*Time*⟩ ⟨fell into ~ sleep —C.O.Gorham⟩ **2** [alter. of *tortuous*] **:** DISTORTED, TORTUOUS, TWISTING ⟨the dark-stained after rafter, that seasoned crossarm of ~ timber —Ralph Ellison⟩

tor·tur·ous·ly *adv* **:** in a torturous manner **:** PAINFULLY ⟨moved at a ~ slow pace —Norman Mailer⟩

torty *var of* TORTIE

to·ru \'tȯr(,)ü\ *n* -S [Maori] **:** a New Zealand tree (*Persoonia toru*) of the family Meliaceae with reddish wood that resembles toro

tor·u·la \'tȯr(y)ələ, 'tär-\ *n* [NL, fr. L *torus* protuberance, bulge, cushion + *-ula* — more at TORUS] **1** *pl* **toru·lae** \-,lē, -,lī\ *also* **torulas a :** any of various yeasts or yeastlike fungi that lack sexual spores, do not produce alcoholic fermentations, and are typically acid formers **b :** CRYPTOCOCCOSIS **2** *cap* **a :** a form genus of usu. dark colored chiefly saprophytic imperfect fungi (family Dematiaceae) with hyphae that develop numerous crosswalls and are converted into chains of conidia — see BLACK YEAST **b** *in some classifications* **:** a genus of yeasts including pathogens usu. placed in the genus *Cryptococcus* and various others (as the food yeast *T. utilis*) that are sometimes segregated in the genus *Torulopsis*

tor·u·lop·sis \,⸗⸗'läpsəs\ *n* [NL, fr. *torula* + *-opsis*] **1** *cap, in some classifications* **:** a genus of round, oval, or cylindrical yeasts that form no spores and no pellicle when growing in a liquid culture medium and that include forms which in other classifications are placed in *Torula* or *Cryptococcus* **2** *pl* **torulopsis :** TORULA 1a

tor·u·lose \'tȯr(y)ə,lōs, 'tär-\ *adj* [NL *torulosus*, dim. of L *torosus* torose] **:** somewhat torose

tor·u·lo·sis \,⸗⸗'lōsəs\ *n* -ES [NL, fr. *Torula* + *-osis*] **:** CRYPTOCOCCOSIS

tor·u·lous \'⸗⸗ləs\ *adj* [NL *torulosus*] **:** TORULOSE

tor·u·lus \-ləs\ *n, pl* **toru·li** \-,lī, -,lē\ [NL, dim. of L *torus* cushion, couch] **:** the socket in which the antenna of an insect articulates

to·rus \'tōrəs\ *n, pl* **to·ri** \-r(,)ī, -r(,)ē\ [NL, fr. L, protuberance, bulge, cushion, couch, torus molding] **1 :** a smooth rounded protuberance on a body part; *esp* **:** any of several bony ridges that may be present on the skull ⟨a supraocular ~⟩ **2 :** a large architectural molding of convex profile commonly occurring as the lowest molding in the base of a column or pilaster and next above the plinth — compare OVOLO; see BASE illustration, MOLDING illustration **3 a :** RECEPTACLE 3b **b :** the thickening of the membrane closing a bordered pit **4 :** a surface or solid shaped like a doughnut and formed by revolving a circle about a line in its plane without intersecting it **:** ANCHOR RING **5 :** a thickened vertical ridge bearing rows of uncini on the segments of many annelids **6 :** the driving member of a fluid coupling

¹**to·ry** \'tōrē, 'tȯrē, -ri\ *n* -ES [IrGael *tōraidhe* pursued man, robber, fr. MIr *tōir* pursuit] **1** *often cap* **a :** a dispossessed Irishman of the 17th century subsisting primarily by highway robbery and agrarian outrages perpetrated esp. upon the English settlers and soldiers **b :** any armed Irish papist or royalist of later times **2** *obs* **:** one in another country resembling an Irish tory **:** BANDIT, MARAUDER, OUTLAW, ROBBER, TERRORIST ⟨among the *tories* in the Highlands —James Kirkton⟩ **3** *usu cap* **:** one opposing the exclusion in 1679–80 of the Duke of York from the line of succession to the British throne principally because of his Roman Catholicism — usu. used disparagingly; opposed to *Whig* **4** *usu cap* **:** a member or supporter of the Tory party in British politics **5** *usu cap* **:** an American upholding the cause of the British Crown against the supporters of colonial independence during the American Revolution **:** LOYALIST — opposed to *Whig* **6** *sometimes cap* **:** one held to resemble a British Tory in politics esp. in allegiance to the established order **7 :** one who emphasizes order, tradition, stability, or accepted canons of taste, opinion, or conduct in any area of human interest or concern esp. at the expense of innovation **:** one who by temperament or sentiment is inclined to conservative principles

²**tory** \"\ *adj* **:** of, relating to, or characterized by Toryism: as **a** *usu cap* (1) **:** of, relating to, or constituting one of the two major British political groups of the 18th and early 19th centuries arising from the Cavaliers and associated chiefly with support at first of the Stuarts but later of the monarchy itself and also of the established Anglican Church and with the preservation of the traditional political structure esp. as represented by the unreformed House of Commons — compare LIBERAL, RADICAL, WHIG (2) **:** CONSERVATIVE 2b(1) (3) **:** favoring, belonging to, or composed of members of such a political group or party ⟨openly *Tory* in his sympathies⟩ ⟨formation of a *Tory* Government⟩ ⟨the tradition of authority is naturally a *Tory* tradition —H.R.H.Cecil⟩ **b** *often cap* **:** characterized by Toryism esp. in social and economic relationships ⟨Roosevelt Republicanism which is ~ in spirit but popular in its appeal —Walter Lippmann⟩ ⟨a slow-moving and ~ society —C.W. de Kiewiet⟩ **c :** tending toward extreme political and economic conservatism ⟨~ Democrats in the Senate —Henry Wallace⟩ **syn** see CONSERVATIVE

tory democracy *n, usu cap T&D* **:** a political philosophy advocating preservation of the established institutions and traditional principles characteristic of Toryism combined with political democracy and a social and economic program designed to benefit the common man ⟨the *Tory Democracy* of the British Conservative party⟩

tory democrat *n* -S *usu cap T&D* **:** an adherent or advocate of Tory Democracy

to·ry·fy *or* **to·ri·fy** \'⸗rə,fī, -rē,-\ *vt* -ED/-ING/-ES *usu cap* [²*tory* + *-fy*] **:** to make Tory **:** to influence by Tory principles or policies

to·ry·ish \-rēish, -ri·ish\ *adj, usu cap* [²*tory* + *-ish*] **:** inclined toward Toryism

to·ry·ism \-rē,izəm, -ri·iz-\ *n* -S *usu cap* [¹*tory* + *-ism*] **1 :** the principles, policies, and practices of or associated with Tories **2 :** the British Tory party or its members ⟨*Toryism* inflated its periphery to include . . . working-class elements —L.G.Noonan⟩

tory-rory *adj* [origin unknown] *obs* **:** UPROARIOUS, ROISTERING ⟨*tory-rory* rakes —P.A.Motteux⟩

toryweed \'⸗⸗,⸗\ *n* **:** HOUND'S-TONGUE 1

TOs *pl of* TO

to·sa·phist \'tōsəfəst\ *n* -S [*tosaphoth* + *-ist*] **:** a writer of tosaphoth

to·sa·photh \-ə,fōt\ *n pl* [MHeb *tōsāphōth*, lit., additions] **:** critical and explanatory glosses on the Talmud usu. in the margin

to·sca \'tōskə\ *n* -S [AmerSp, fr. Sp, fem. of *tosco* rough, unpolished, uncouth, prob. fr. L *tuscus* Tuscan; fr. the disreputable character of the inhabitants of the *Vicus Tuscus* Tuscan Street in ancient Rome] **1 :** a calcium carbonate deposit occurring in the loess of the pampas — compare CALICHE **2 :** a soft coral limestone deposit used for various purposes in Puerto Rico (as for masonry, road surfacing, ballast, and as fertilizer)

¹**tosh** \'täsh\ *dial Brit var of* TUSH

²**tosh** \"\ *or* **toshy** \-shi\ *adj* [origin unknown] *Scot* **:** tidily trim or comfortable **:** NEAT, SNUG — **tosh·ly** *adv*

³**tosh** \"\ *vt* -ED/-ING/-ES *Scot* **:** to make neat **:** TIDY — usu. used with *up*

⁴**tosh** \"\ *n* -ES [origin unknown] **:** sheer nonsense **:** BOSH, TWADDLE ⟨nobody . . . can possibly believe the sort of ~ that is contained in these latest Kremlin outpourings —*N. Y. Times*⟩ — often used interjectionally to express disapproval or disbelief

to-side \'⸗'⸗\ *n* [obs. *to* one (fr. ME, short for *ton*) + *side* — more at TONE, pron.] *archaic* **:** one side ⟨stepped a little a *to-side* to his fellow —John Bunyan⟩

tosk *also* **tosc** \'täsk\ *n* -S *usu cap* [Alb *tosk*] **1 :** one of the southern Albanians — compare GHEG **2** *also* **tosk·ish** \-kish\ **:** the dialect spoken by the Tosks of southern Albania

¹**toss** \'tȯs, 'täs\ *vb* **tossed** *or archaic* **tost** \-st\ **tossed** *or archaic* **tost; tossing; tosses** [prob. of Scand origin; akin to Sw dial. *tossa* to spread, scatter] *vt* **1 a :** to cause to rise and fall **:** throw around **:** HEAVE, TUMBLE ⟨storm-*tossed* sea⟩ ⟨waves from a passing steamer ~ the small boats⟩ ⟨~*ed* wildly on the rain came flocks of starlings —J.C.Powys⟩ **b :** to throw aloft **:** propel upward **:** CAST, FLIP ⟨~*ed* her up and caught her —Winifred Bambrick⟩ ⟨missed his footing and was ~*ed* by the bull⟩; *esp* **:** MATCH 5a ⟨I'll ~ you for it⟩ **c :** to drive involuntarily **:** BUFFET, SHUNT ⟨~*ed* to and fro and carried about with every wind of doctrine —Eph 4:14 (RSV)⟩ ⟨had begun life in poverty . . . ~*ed* about from one relative to another —Gamaliel Bradford⟩ **2 a :** to make uneasy **:** DISQUIET, DISTURB ⟨saintly aid to . . . the sin-*tossed* soul —H.O. Taylor⟩ **b :** to discuss or canvass exhaustively **:** BANDY, DEBATE ⟨various figures . . . were ~*ed* around in conversation with tribal leaders —*New Republic*⟩ ⟨her brain was a steam-wheel . . . everything that could be thought of was ~*ed*, nothing grasped —George Meredith⟩ **c :** to cause to shake **:** AGITATE, VIBRATE ⟨trees ~ their branches in the stiff breeze⟩ **d :** to stir up **:** CONCOCT, PREPARE ⟨got . . . a hot supper, ~*ing* it up herself —Clemence Dane⟩; *esp* **:** to mix lightly usu. with a fork and spoon until well coated with a dressing ⟨~ a salad⟩ ⟨~ carrots in butter⟩ **3 a :** to tilt suddenly or steeply so as to drain ⟨~*ed* his glass to his mouth, finished his drink —James Joyce⟩ **b :** to raise in a flourish or salute **:** BRANDISH, PEAK ⟨more fit . . . to lift a pitchfork than to ~ a pike —William Gouge⟩ — used chiefly in the phrase *toss oars* **c :** to elevate in a proud or spirited manner ⟨~*ed* her head angrily⟩ ⟨~ up your nose at obscure people —Christopher Smart⟩ **4 a :** to throw with force **:** FLING, HURL ⟨has been ~*ed* into jail and convicted of libel —J.A.Morris b. 1904⟩ ⟨the challenge is ~*ed* to the new president —Patrick McMahon⟩ ⟨Vesuvius . . . ~*es* out glowing bombs —Howel Williams⟩ **b** (1) **:** to throw gently often with an underhand motion **:** convey lightly **:** CHUCK, FLICK ⟨~ a ball to and fro⟩ ⟨~ peppermint sticks to . . . children —*Amer. Guide Series: La.*⟩ (2) **:** to utter or include in an offhand manner **:** introduce casually **:** INTERJECT ⟨the book has its . . . quota of gaily ~*ed* metaphors —Rex Lardner⟩ ⟨for what it may be worth, I ~ in . . . a very minor statistic —Agnes Rogers⟩ ⟨~*ing* off carefree farewells to shipboard friends —LaSelle Gilman⟩ ⟨criticism, ~*ed* off . . . in the most marginal way —F.R.Leavis⟩ **c :** to dispose of **:** CONSUME, SWALLOW ⟨~*es* down a lemonade —J.A.Michener⟩ ⟨raised her glass to her mouth and ~*ed* it off —*Encore*⟩ ⟨usually ~*ed* off half a dozen papers with his morning coffee —Edith Wharton⟩ **d :** to get rid of **:** DISCARD, JETTISON ⟨~ out the garbage⟩ ⟨the horse ~*ed* his rider⟩ ⟨~*ed* away $90,000 in film contracts to spend eighteen months on the novel —J.K. Hutchens⟩ ⟨would you rather ~ the evening and just go home now —Nicholas Monsarrat⟩ **e :** to put on carelessly or hurriedly ⟨~*ing* on my bathrobe, I would run to the kitchen —Marjorie Housepian⟩ **f :** to provide or turn out casually **:** execute in an apparently effortless manner ⟨~*es* off science fiction as a by-product of his rocket research⟩ ⟨she can ~ off roulades and staccati . . . and other vocal acrobatics —Irving Kolodin⟩ ⟨his mind ~*ed* up scheme after scheme —Lucien Price⟩ ⟨a monster cocktail party and buffet supper will be ~*ed* in honor of former employees —Bennett Cerf⟩ **~** *vi* **1 a :** to move restlessly **:** exhibit agitation or turbulence ⟨black water . . . swirled and ~*ed* over the ugly heads of jutting rocks —T.B.Costain⟩ ⟨his sentences pitched and ~*ed* on a surging sea of righteous indignation —*Horizon*⟩; *esp* **:** to twist and turn repeatedly ⟨~*ed* on their pillows worrying about their younger son —Josephine Pinckney⟩ **b :** to move jerkily or spasmodically **:** FLOUNCE, SWAY ⟨~*ed* out of the room . . . in one of her flighty humors —W.M.Thackeray⟩ ⟨the engine is ~*ing* a little as she takes one reverse curve after another —O.S. Nock⟩ **c :** to mix together with a dressing ⟨tomato wedges . . . and diced chicken go in a lettuce-lined salad bowl — ready to ~ —*Better Homes & Gardens*⟩ **2 :** to decide an issue by lot esp. by the toss of a coin ⟨the skippers ~*ed* and ours lost —Dal Stivens⟩ **3 :** to serve a handball **syn** see THROW

²**toss** \"\ *n* -ES **1** *archaic* **a :** an act or instance of heaving or shaking **:** TOSSING ⟨the little boat . . . pitches now with shorter ~ upon the narrower swell —Robert Southey⟩ **b :** a state of agitation **:** TURMOIL ⟨Boston is in a great ~ . . . about Dr. Channing and the abolitionists —H.W.Longfellow⟩ **2 a :** an act or instance of propelling through the air **:** PITCH, THROW ⟨after a few warm-up ~*es* . . . put the shot 63 feet 6 inches —*Newsweek*⟩ ⟨put the Indians in front with a 5-yard run after catching a 10-yard ~ —*N. Y. Times*⟩ **b :** an abrupt tilting or upward fling ⟨an almost disdainful ~ of the head —T.G. Henderson⟩ ⟨with a ~ of a hand . . . issues half a dozen birthday pronouncements —Barbara B. Jamison⟩ **3 :** an act or instance of deciding by lot and esp. by flipping a coin ⟨choice of sides . . . shall be decided by ~ —*Official Lawn Tennis Guide*⟩ — called also *toss-up* **4 :** an act or instance of being thrown or jettisoned **:** DEFEAT, TUMBLE ⟨took a ~ into a hole and . . . broke his leg —John Buchan⟩ ⟨diplomat . . . takes a professional ~ —Eric Keown⟩

³**toss** \'täs\ *n* -ES [by alter.] *Scot* **:** TOAST 1a

tos·sa \'täsə\ *or* **tossa jute** *n* -S [origin unknown] **:** a grayish or brown fiber obtained from a jute (*Corchorus olitorius*)

toss bombing *n* [¹*toss* + *bombing*, gerund of *bomb*] **:** bombing in which an airplane releases a bomb while pulling up in an Immelmann turn so that the bomb lobs forward as the plane flies away in an opposite direction

tossed salad [*tossed* (past part. of ¹*toss*) + *salad*] *n* **:** a salad made of greens often with added vegetables (as sliced tomato or cucumber) tossed in an oil dressing

toss·er \'tȯsə(r), 'täs-\ *n* -S **:** one that tosses

¹**tossing** [fr. gerund of ¹*toss*] *n* -S **1 :** an act or process of buffeting or shaking **:** AGITATION **2 :** an operation in tin refining in which the molten metal is lifted in a ladle and poured back in a fine stream to oxidize impurities

²**tossing** *adj* [in sense 1, fr. pres. part. of ¹*toss*; in sense 2 fr. ¹*tossing*] **1 :** being in a state of tumultuous agitation **:** HEAVING, RESTLESS ⟨~ skies⟩ ⟨a ~ insomniac⟩ **2 :** of or relating to an act of flipping or jettisoning ⟨~ pan⟩ ⟨~ process⟩ — **tossing·ly** *adv*

tosspot \'⸗,⸗\ *n* [¹*toss* + *pot*] **:** DRUNKARD, SOT ⟨assembled a group of ~*s* —John McCarten⟩

toss-up \'⸗,⸗\ *n* -S [fr. the phrase *toss up*] **1 :** TOSS 3 **2 :** a matter of luck **:** an even bet or choice ⟨regard the election results as a ~ —*N. Y. Times*⟩ ⟨it was a ~ whether to go right or left —Fred Majdalany⟩

tost *archaic past of* TOSS

tos·ta·da \tō'städə\ *also* **tos·ta·do** \-ä(,)dō\ *n* -S [MexSp *tostada*, fr. fem. of *tostado* fried, fr. Sp, toasted, roasted, browned, fr. past part. of *tostar* to toast, roast, fr. (assumed) VL *tostare* — more at TOAST] **:** a flat tortilla fried in deep fat and topped with a savory mixture (as of beans, meat, or vegetables)

tos·ta·men·te \,tōstə'mentē\ *adv* [It, fr. *tosto* quick, rapid] **:** RAPIDLY — used as a direction in music

tos·tão \tōs(h)'taùⁿ\ *n* -S [Pg, fr. It *testone* teston] **:** an old Portuguese silver coin equal to 100 reals **:** TESTON

tos·ti·cat·ed \'tästə,kātəd\ *adj* [by shortening & alter.] *dial Brit* **:** INTOXICATED

tos·to \'tō(,)stō\ *adv* (*or adj*) [It, fr. *tosto* quick, rapid, fr. (assumed) VL *tostus*, fr. L, past part. of *torrēre* to dry, parch, heat — more at TORRENT] **:** at a rapid tempo — used as a direction in music

tos·ton \tō'stōn\ *n* -S [Sp *tostón*, fr. Pg or It; Pg *tostão*, fr. It *testone*] **:** a silver coin formerly in use in various Latin American countries and equal to ½ peso or 4 reals

tos·yl \'täsəl\ *n* -S [*toluenesulfonyl*] **:** the para isomer of toluenesulfonyl or tolyl-sulfonyl

tos·yl·ate \-sə,lāt\ *vt* -ED/-ING/-S [*tosyl* + *-ate*] **:** to introduce a tosyl group into (a compound) — **tos·yl·a·tion** \,⸗⸗'lāshən\ *n* -S

¹**tot** \'tät, *usu* -äd.+V\ *vt* **totted; totted; totting; tots** [ME *totten*, fr. the L word *tot* (marked on the list)] *archaic* **:** to mark (an item on a list) with a tot

²**tot** \"\ *n* -S [L *tot* so much, so many; akin to Gk *tosos* so great, so many, Skt *tati* so many, L *istud*, neuter demonstrative pron. & adj. — more at THAT] **:** the word *tot* or letter *T* written against an item on a list to indicate receipt of a specified amount

³**tot** \"\ *n* -S [origin unknown] **1 :** a small child **:** TODDLER ⟨from tiny ~*s* in kindergarten to the oldest pupil —F.T. Williams⟩ **2 a :** a small glass or mug; *esp* **:** a British soldier's drinking cup **b :** a small quantity or allowance esp. of an alcoholic beverage **:** DRINK, SHOT ⟨ladles out generous ~*s* of . . . whiskey punch —J.S.Bradford⟩ ⟨poured his cup, smuggling in a good ~ of . . . rum —Willa Cather⟩ ⟨not all jack-tars take grog; many prefer money instead of their ~ —Luis Marden⟩

⁴**tot** \"\ *vb* **totted; totted; totting; tots** [*tot*, abbr.] *vt* **:** to add together **:** SUMMARIZE, TOTAL ⟨now your account is *totted* —John Masefield⟩ — usu. used with *up* ⟨the waiter . . . *totted* up the bill —Virginia Woolf⟩ ⟨Clubs began *totting* up attendance records for the 12 months —*Rotarian*⟩ ⟨*totted* up exactly how far he had gone since he first entered . . . journalism —*English Digest*⟩ **~** *vi* **:** to come to a total **:** indicate a result **:** ADD ⟨intelligence reports all *totted* up one way —*Scribner's*⟩

⁵**tot** \"\ *n* -S *chiefly Brit* **:** an exercise in addition **:** column of figures **:** SUM ⟨an oriental clerk, faced by a simple long ~ —Bryan Morgan⟩

⁶**tot** \'tät\ *Scot var of* ³TOTE

⁷**tot** \"\ *vi* **totted; totted; totting; tots** [prob. short for ¹*totter*] *dial Brit* **:** to move unsteadily **:** TODDLE, TOTTER

tot *abbr* total

TOT *abbr* time on target

tot·able \'tōd·əbəl\ *adj* [¹*tote* + *-able*] **:** easily carried **:** PORTABLE

¹**to·tal** \'tōd·ᵊl, 'tōtᵊl\ *adj* [ME, fr. MF, fr. ML *totalis*, fr. L *totus* whole, entire + *-alis* -al] **1 :** of or relating to something in its entirety ⟨the ~ effect of a room⟩ ⟨the writing is . . . unified by a simple ~ vision of the writer —William Barrett⟩ **2 a :** viewed as an entity **:** complete in all details **:** OVERALL, WHOLE ⟨culture . . . is the ~ spiritual product of any given time and place —*Modern Music*⟩ ⟨the ~ university, with its galaxy of graduate and professional schools —N.M.Pusey⟩ ⟨after the introduction of gunpowder . . . ~ armor had gradually fallen into disuse —*New Yorker*⟩ **b :** constituting an entire number or amount **:** AGGREGATE ⟨~ cost⟩ ⟨~ value⟩ ⟨~ extant manuscripts . . . are of considerable number —I.M. Price⟩ ⟨~ spending should be large enough to employ everyone who wants to work —George Soule⟩ **3 a :** unqualified in extent or degree **:** ABSOLUTE, UTTER ⟨~ darkness⟩ ⟨a ~ stranger⟩ ⟨the ~ abolition of poverty . . . is at the present moment technically possible —Bertrand Russell⟩ ⟨lines, characterized by ~ simplicity, are by far the hardest to put into another language —Wallace Fowlie⟩ **b :** having dictatorial powers **:** OMNIPOTENT, TOTALITARIAN ⟨the liberal state acknowledged many limitations in its demands upon men; the ~ state acknowledges none —A.M.Schlesinger b. 1917⟩ **c :** unlimited in character **:** concentrating all available personnel and resources on a single objective **:** ALL-OUT, THOROUGHGOING ⟨the nature of ~ war has erased the distinction between combatants and civilians —J.N.Moody⟩ ⟨urges a bold effort at making a ~ peace —*Atlantic*⟩ **syn** see WHOLE

²**total** \"\ *n* -S **1 a :** a result of addition **:** AGGREGATE, SUM ⟨column ~⟩ ⟨cumulative ~⟩ ⟨a ~ of 319 students registered for summer school⟩ ⟨when the final ~*s* were compiled they would show dollar volume close to . . . the all-time high —S.C.Pace⟩ **b :** a summation of factors **:** final result ⟨deviations from a ~ of zero cause the crane carriage to move forward or backward —T.W.Rodes⟩ **2 :** an entire quantity or configuration **:** AMOUNT, WHOLE ⟨a staggering ~ of devastation and destruction —T.F.Mueller⟩ ⟨word-complexes that cannot be reconstructed unit by unit, but only as ~*s* —John Ciardi⟩ **syn** see SUM — **in total** *adv* **:** as a whole ⟨little of the tie or shirt is visible, but the . . . coat is seen *in total* —S.D.Barney⟩

³**total** \"\ *adv* **:** TOTALLY ⟨now is he ~ gules, horridly tricked with blood —Shak.⟩

⁴**total** \"\ *vb* **totaled** *or* **totalled; totaled** *or* **totalled; totaling** *or* **totalling; totals** *vt* **1 :** to add up **:** COMPUTE ⟨these figures were arrived at by ~*ing* all entries —H.J. Hanham⟩ ⟨~ the sensuous possibilities latent in silk, linen, wool, leather, and furs —Hunter Mead⟩ **2 :** to come to a total of **:** amount to **:** NUMBER ⟨in July of this year consumer credit ~*ed* roughly $27 billion —*World*⟩ ⟨jute mills . . . ~ about a hundred —Walter Bally⟩ ⟨professing Christians ~*ed* less than one percent of the population —K.S.Latourette⟩ **~** *vi* **:** to compute a total **:** ADD ⟨this adding machine ~*s* to 999,999.99⟩

total abstinence *n* **:** ABSTINENCE 1c

total adhesion locomotive *n* **:** a locomotive with all wheels coupled to act as driving wheels

total and permanent disability insurance *n* **:** insurance against loss due to inability to follow a gainful occupation because of mental or physical impairment classified as permanent under the terms of a life insurance policy usu. after such disability has continued for a stated period (as six months)

total–annular eclipse *n* **:** an eclipse of the sun in which totality is observed in the middle part of the path of the moon's shadow but an annular eclipse at the ends of the path near the sunrise and sunset points

total cleavage *n* **:** holoblastic cleavage of an egg

total depravity *n* **:** the theological doctrine asserting that man in his every part is infected with a sinfulness due to original sin inherited from Adam and that by his own unaided action man cannot make any efficacious effort toward his salvation but can only remain in a corrupt state until regenerated by the Spirit of God — see CALVINISM

total disability *n* **:** incapacity to perform the duties of any substantially gainful occupation either permanently or temporarily due to accident or illness — compare PARTIAL DISABILITY, TEMPORARY TOTAL DISABILITY

total eclipse *n* **:** an eclipse in which one celestial body is completely obscured by the shadow or body of another

total heat *n* **:** the thermal equivalent of the energy required to convert unit mass of a liquid at one temperature (as the melting point of the substance) into saturated vapor at any other given temperature

to·tal·ism \-ᵊl,izəm\ *n* -s [¹*total* + *-ism*] **:** TOTALITARIANISM

to·tal·is·tic \¦tōd·ᵊl¦istik, -ōtᵊl-, -tēk\ *adj* [¹*total* + *-istic*] **:** TOTALITARIAN

¹**to·tal·i·tar·i·an** \(,)tō¦talə¦terēən, -¦ta(a)r-, -¦tär- *sometimes* ¦tōd·ᵊlə¦- *or* -ōtᵊl-\ *adj* [¹*total* + *-itarian* (as in *authoritarian*)] **1 a :** of or relating to centralized control by an autocratic leader or hierarchy **:** AUTHORITARIAN, DICTATORIAL ⟨~ theory and practice are solidly opposed to any institutional division of power —C.J.Friedrich⟩ ⟨fascism . . . is ~ by necessity —Carlo Sforza⟩; *esp* **:** DESPOTIC ⟨Sparta's militarist ~ dictatorship —Peter Viereck⟩ **b :** of or relating to a political regime based on subordination of the individual to the state and strict control of all aspects of the life and productive capacity of the nation esp. by coercive measures (as censorship and terrorism) ⟨the limited state, the agent of man, has been converted to the ~ state, the master of man —C.P.Patterson⟩ ⟨will Europe in the future be ~ and collectivist, or will it be democratic and individualist —C.J.Friedrich⟩ **2 a :** advocating or characteristic of totalitarianism ⟨~ liberal⟩ ⟨the ~ concept that the end justifies the means —J.W.Fulbright⟩ ⟨cracks down on free speech and free press with ~ ease —*Time*⟩ ⟨seize power . . . by force and make Greece Communist, with the ~ liquidation of all opponents —Sir Winston Churchill⟩ **b :** completely regulated by the state esp. as an aid to national mobilization in an emergency ⟨it accomplishes a ~ control of atomic energy for the time being —A.H.Vandenberg †1951⟩ ⟨almost all governments adopt ~ measures in time of war —John Gunther⟩ **c :** exercising autocratic powers **:** tending toward monopoly ⟨by its very nature . . . religion is ~ —J.S.Roucek⟩ ⟨antitrust legislation . . . to reverse the trend toward the ~ collectivism of big business —*Jour. of Politics*⟩ **3 :** TOTAL 3c ⟨a ~ war, striking at civilians more than at armies —*N.Y. Times*⟩

²**totalitarian** \"\ *n* -s **:** an advocate or practitioner of totalitarianism

to·tal·i·tar·i·an·ism \-ēə,nizəm\ *n* -s [¹*totalitarian* + *-ism*] **1 a :** centralized control by an autocratic ruler or hierarchy regarded as infallible ⟨in a democracy, forfeiture of sovereignty by the people means ~ —E.L.Klein⟩ ⟨ideally Christianity desires ~, too, but in the sense that men everywhere come to see the validity of its definition of man —*Times Lit. Supp.*⟩; *specif* **:** DESPOTISM ⟨the barbarism of the Turks and the ~ of the Spanish kings —*N. Y. Herald Tribune Bk. Rev.*⟩ **b :** the political concept of man as the servant of the state **:** COLLECTIVISM ⟨the essence of ~, in contrast with democracy, is that there is . . . no area where the citizen's initiative is supreme —Laurence Stapleton⟩ — compare INDIVIDUALISM **2 :** the quality or state of being totalitarian ⟨Pilgrim and Puritan women . . . functioned and reacted in the stern ~ of a male and theocratic civilization —*N. Y. Herald Tribune Bk. Rev.*⟩ ⟨~ is . . . not by accident the distinguishing characteristic of the Nazi state —H.J.Morgenthau⟩ **3 :** a totalitarian dogma, method, or regime ⟨championship of human values against all the insidious ~*s* —*New Yorker*⟩

to·tal·i·tar·i·an·ize \-,nīz\ *vt* -ED/-ING/-S **:** to make totalitarian

to·tal·i·ty \tō'taləd·ē, -ətē, -i\ *n* -ES [ML *totalitat-, totalitas,* fr. *totalis* total + L *-itat-, -itas* -ity] **1 :** an aggregate number or amount **:** SUM, WHOLE ⟨the ~ of universes —J.F.McComas⟩ ⟨a partial glimpse of the . . . ~ of truth —C.I.Glicksberg⟩ **2 a :** the quality or state of being complete or comprehensive **:** ENTIRETY, UNITY ⟨the port of New York, in its ~, includes all the navigable waterways within . . . twenty-five miles from the Statue of Liberty —*Amer. Guide Series: N. Y. City*⟩ ⟨your whole nature, in its physical and psychical ~ —J.C.Powys⟩ **b** (1) **:** the phase of an eclipse during which it is total **:** state of total eclipse (2) **:** the region from which the total phase of an eclipse may be observed **3 :** overall form or content **:** CONFIGURATION, ENTITY ⟨formal analysis . . . having to do with the ~ of a poem or a novel —C.W.Shumaker⟩ ⟨insists that the undivided ~ of the person must be the point of departure —Ruth Benedict⟩ **4 :** absolute or indiscriminate oppression ⟨weapons of ~ and terror —J.R.Oppenheimer⟩ ⟨the all-embracing ~ of the state —G.L.Dickinson⟩

to·tal·iza·tion \,tōd·ᵊlə'zāshən, -ōtᵊl-, -ᵊl,ī'-\ *n* -s [*totalize* + *-ation*] **:** an act or instance of totaling **:** SUMMATION

to·tal·i·za·tor *or* **to·tal·i·sa·tor** \'==(,)=,zād·ə(r), -ātə-\ *n* -s [*totalize* + *-ator*] **:** PARI-MUTUEL MACHINE

to·tal·ize \'tōd·ᵊl,īz, -ōtᵊl-\ *vt* -ED/-ING/-S [¹*total* + *-ize*] **1 :** to add up **:** TOTAL **2 :** to make totalitarian ⟨the drive of the Nazis . . . to ~ the people —MacKinley Helm⟩

to·tal·iz·er \-zə(r)\ *n* -s **:** one that totalizes; *specif* **:** PARI-MUTUEL MACHINE

totalled *past of* TOTAL

totalling *pres part of* TOTAL

total loss *n* **:** loss that makes property valueless to an insured

total lunar eclipse *n* **:** an eclipse in which the moon is completely immersed in the umbra of the earth's shadow

to·tal·ly \'tōd·ᵊlē, -ōtᵊl-, -ᵊli *sometimes* -ōtlē *or* -li\ *adv* **1 :** in a total manner **:** COMPLETELY, WHOLLY **2 :** as a whole **:** in toto

total–point scoring *n* **:** CUMULATIVE SCORING

total push *n* **:** a method of treating mental disorders by the employment of varied therapeutic techniques in a concerted and almost continuous series

total quantum number *n* **:** PRINCIPAL QUANTUM NUMBER

total recall *n* **:** the faculty of remembering with complete clarity and in complete detail

total reflection *n* **:** specular reflection in the more highly refractive of two media at their interface when the angle of incidence exceeds a certain critical value — compare CRITICAL ANGLE

totals *pl of* TOTAL, *pres 3d sing of* TOTAL

total score method *n* **:** a method of improving livestock by breeding animals selected for maximum excellence in as many desired traits as possible — compare TANDEM METHOD

total slip *n* **:** the part of a geologic fault displacement that is recorded by the maximum distance of separation of two originally contiguous points measured in the plane of the fault

total solar eclipse *n* **:** an eclipse of the sun in which the moon completely hides the solar surface or photosphere and thereby cuts off all direct rays of sunlight from the observer

total utility *n* **:** the degree of utility of an article, service, or other economic good considered as a whole — compare MARGINAL UTILITY

tot·a·nus \'tätᵊnəs\ *n, cap* [NL, fr. ML, moorhen] **:** a genus of shorebirds (family Scolopacidae) comprising various typical tattlers and being often included in the genus *Tringa*

to·ta·quine \'tōd·ə,k(w)ēn, -,k(w)ən\ *also* **to·ta·qui·na** \,==-'kēnə\ *n* -s [NL *totaquina,* fr. ML *totalis* total + Sp *quina* cinchona bark; fr. its containing the total alkaloids of cinchona bark — more at QUININE] **:** an antimalarial drug that is obtained as a yellowish brown powder by extraction of American cinchona bark and that contains quinine and other alkaloids but is less effective than quinine

to·ta·ra \'tōd·ə,rä, tō'tärə\ *n* -s [Maori] **:** a tall tree (*Podocarpus totara*) of New Zealand having hard reddish wood used for furniture and construction (as of bridges and wharves) and being the country's most valuable timber tree next to the kauri

¹**tote** \'tōt, *usu* -ōd·+V\ *vb* -ED/-ING/-S [origin unknown] *vt* **1 a :** to carry by hand **:** bear on the person **:** LUG, PACK ⟨longshoremen . . . ~ bananas on their shoulders —*Amer. Guide Series: La.*⟩ ⟨elegantly uniformed Army officers, *toting* briefcases —E.J.Kahn⟩ ⟨a-hollering for two of the little chaps to come and ~ the tub in for her —Frances Gaither⟩ **b :** to make a practice of carrying ⟨pistol-*toting* rangers patrol the sun-baked towns —H.B.Martin⟩ **2 :** to conduct or haul from one place to another **:** CONVEY, TRANSPORT ⟨*toted* her round to a few parties —B.C.L.Keelan⟩ ⟨horses . . . *toted* the ammunition —R.L.Neuberger⟩ ⟨carrier aircraft can ~ as many as 200 rockets —*Newsweek*⟩ ~ *vi* **1 a :** to carry a load ⟨you load and I'll ~⟩ **b** *South* **:** to take home leftover food ⟨cooks will sometimes demand the right to ~ . . . as part of their wages —*Amer. Guide Series: Mo.*⟩ **2** *South* **:** GO, TRAVEL

²**tote** \"\ *n* -s *often attrib* **1 :** something that is carried **:** BURDEN, LOAD **2 :** an act of carrying or hauling

³**tote** \'tōt\ *n* -s [short for ²*total*] *dial Brit* **:** an entire number or amount **:** TOTAL

⁴**tote** \'tōt, *usu* -ōd·+V\ *vb* -ED/-ING/-S **:** TOT, TOTAL

⁵**tote** \"\ *n* -s [short for *totalizator*] **:** PARI-MUTUEL MACHINE

tote bag *n* [¹*tote*] **:** a large 2-handled open-topped bag (as of canvas) used esp. for carrying small packages

tote board *n* [⁵*tote*] **:** a usu. electrically operated board (as in the infield of a racetrack) on which betting odds are posted

tote–box \'=,=\ *n* [¹*tote*] **:** a box or tray for storing, handling, and transporting materials in industrial operations

tote double *n* [⁵*tote*] **:** DAILY DOUBLE

to·tem \'tōd·əm, 'tōtəm\ *n* -s *often attrib* [Ojibwa *ototeman* his totem] **1 a :** an animal, plant, or other object serving as the emblem of a family or clan and often regarded as a reminder of its ancestry ⟨each clan has its ~ or ritualistic mascot —C.E. Wilson⟩ ⟨believes that . . . his own ancestors were birds like that which is now his ~ —Daisy Bates⟩ **b :** a usu. carved or painted emblem of a family or clan ⟨the aged and rotting raven ~ pictured at the right —*Alaska Sportsman*⟩ **c :** a family or clan identified by a common totemic object ⟨belonging to a ~ forbidden to marry either of the girls —Rex Ingamells⟩ **d :** a totemic object adopted by an individual ⟨the individual had his own ~, serving as familiar spirit in the case of shamans —C.S.Coon⟩ **2 :** something that serves as an emblem ⟨enamelled ~*s* of half the automobile clubs in Europe —*Times Lit. Supp.*⟩ esp. as a revered symbol ⟨his corpulent figure was the ~ of their belief —H.V.Gregory⟩ ⟨move uncritically among the ideological ~*s* of the modern world —W.F.Kerr⟩ **3 :** a dark reddish orange that is yellower, stronger, and slightly darker than average lacquer red, stronger and slightly lighter than ocher red, and redder and stronger than burnt sienna — called also *Mars red*

to·tem·ic \tō'temik, -mēk\ *adj* [*totem* + *-ic*] **1 a :** of, relating to, or characteristic of a totem or totemism ⟨~ animal⟩ ⟨~ ritual⟩ ⟨~ transfer of names and traits (especially brute strength, courage and cunning) from animals to men —B.A. Botkin⟩ **b :** resembling a totem ⟨ventilators in a roofscape become sculptured ~ figures —Howard Devree⟩ **2 :** based on or practicing totemism ⟨~ clan structure⟩ ⟨~ people⟩ — **to·tem·i·cal·ly** \-mək(ə)lē\ *adv*

to·tem·ism \'tōd·ə,mizəm, -ōtə,-\ *n* -s [*totem* + *-ism*] **1 a :** belief in kinship with or a mystical relationship between a group or an individual and a totem ⟨~ . . . derives whole tribes or families from an animal or plant —*Internat'l Encyc.*⟩ ⟨with the idea of the powerful animal ~ is closely connected —J.E. Turner⟩ **b :** the rites and practices (as food and word taboos) associated with a totemic relationship ⟨~, one element of which is that the human group generally respects all members of the totem class and refrains from eating them —A.C. Andrews⟩ **2 :** a system of social organization based on totemic affiliations ⟨the primary object of ~ was to implement the incest taboo —*African Abstracts*⟩

to·tem·ist \-məst\ *n* -s [*totem* + *-ist*] **1 :** a practitioner of totemism **2 :** a specialist in totemism

to·tem·is·tic \¦tōd·ə¦mistik, -ōtə¦-, -tēk\ *adj* **:** of or relating to totemists or totemism **:** TOTEMIC

to·tem·ite \'==,mīt\ *n* -s [*totem* + *-ite*] **:** TOTEMIST 1

totem pole *n* **1 a :** a pole or pillar carved and painted with a series of totemic symbols representing family lineage often interspersed with references to mythical or historical incidents and erected before the houses of Indian tribes of the northwest coast of No. America esp. of the Tlingit and Skittagetan language families ⟨the *totem pole* was . . . a symbol of family pride —L.H.Appleton⟩ **b :** something that resembles a totem pole ⟨made a big *totem pole* for the Scout jamboree⟩ **2 :** an order of rank **:** HIERARCHY ⟨entertain top men on the political *totem pole* —Mary Thayer⟩

totem pole 1a

tot·er \'tōd·ə(r)\ *n* -s **:** one that totes

tote road *n* [¹*tote*] **:** a road for hauling supplies esp. into a lumber camp ⟨the *tote road* to our clearing where we lived —Robert Frost⟩ ⟨sent a gang of swampers . . . into the woods to break a *tote road* and make camp —*Mich. Log Marks*⟩

totes *pres 3d sing of* TOTE, *pl of* TOTE

¹**toth·er** *or* **t'oth·er** \'təthə(r)\ *pron* [fr. earlier *the tother,* fr. ME, alter. (resulting from incorrect division) of *thet other,* fr. *thet* the (fr. OE *thæt*) + *other,* pron. — more at THAT, OTHER] *chiefly dial* **:** the other ⟨you cannot tell one from ~ —J.R. Lowell⟩

²**tother** *or* **t'other** \"\ *adj* [fr. earlier *the tother,* fr. ME, alter. (resulting from incorrect division) of *thet other,* fr. *thet* the (fr. OE *thæt*) + *other,* adj. — more at THAT, OTHER] *chiefly dial* **:** the other ⟨was obliged to go away . . . ~ night —W.M.Thackeray⟩

toti– *comb form* [L *totus* whole, entire] **:** whole **:** wholly ⟨*toti*palmate⟩

to·ti·es quo·ti·es \¦tōd·ē,ā'skwōd·ē,ās, 'tōshē,ēz-'kwōshē,ēz\ *adv* [L, as many times as] **:** REPEATEDLY — used of an indulgence in the Roman Catholic Church that may be gained or granted as often as the required works are performed ⟨an indulgence granted *toties quoties*⟩

toting *n* -s [fr. gerund of ¹*tote*] *South* **:** the practice of taking food home from an employer's kitchen or the food so taken ⟨servants . . . apt to regard a little ~ as a perquisite of the job —L.C.Stevens⟩ ⟨taking ~*s* from the icebox to her friends and family —David Riesman⟩

to·ti·pal·ma·tae \,tōd·əpal'mād·,ē\ [NL, fr. *toti-* + LL *palmatae,* fem. pl. of *palmatus* palmate] *syn of* PELECANIFORMES

to·ti·palmate \¦tōd·ə+\ *adj* [*toti-* + *palmate*] **:** having all four toes united by a web ⟨birds of the order Pelecaniformes are ~⟩ — **to·ti·pal·ma·tion** \,tōd·əpal'māshən, -pä'-\ *n*

to·tip·o·ten·cy \tō'tipəd·ənsē\ *n* -ES [*toti-* + *potency*] **:** ability to generate or regenerate a whole organism from a part ⟨~ of a begonia in producing a plant from a leaf cutting⟩

to·tip·o·tent \-nt\ *adj* [*toti-* + *potent*] **:** capable of development along any of the lines inherently possible to its kind ⟨a ~ homothallic fungus spore⟩ ⟨a mesenchyme cell is ~⟩ — **to·ti·potential** \¦tōd·ə+\ *adj* — **to·ti·potentiality** \"+\ *n*

to·to \'tō,tō\ *n* -s [of Bantu origin; akin to Swahili *mtoto* child] **:** a young one **:** BABY, CHILD ⟨asked the chief if there was a small boy, a ~, who would like to enter my service —R.S.B. Baker⟩; *esp* **:** the young of an animal ⟨saw two more rhinos . . . a mother and a half-grown ~ —*Natural History*⟩

to·to·aba *or* **to·tu·a·va** \tō'twävə\ *n* -s [MexSp *totuaba*] **:** a very large weakfish (*Cynoscion macdonaldi*) of the Gulf of California that reaches a weight of over 150 pounds and is highly prized as food

¹**to·to·nac** \,tōtə'näk\ *also* **to·to·na·co** \-ä(,)kō\ *or* **to·to·na·ca** \-ikə\ *n, pl* **totonac** *or* **totonacs** *also* **totonaco** *or* **totonacos** *or* **totonaca** *or* **totonacas** *usu cap* **1 a :** an Indian people of Puebla and Veracruz, Mexico, constituting with the Tepehua the Totonacan language family **b :** a member of such people **2 :** the language of the Totonac people

²**totonac** \¦==¦=\ *adj, usu cap* **:** TAJIN

to·to·na·can \¦==¦näkən\ *n* -s *usu cap* [*totonac* + *-an*] **:** a language family comprising Totonac and Tepehua

to·to·ra \tō'tōrə\ *n* -s [Quechua & Aymara *totora, tutura*] **:** a tule (*Scirpus californicus*) of No. and So. America and Easter Island having stems which are used in parts of Latin America for the construction of reed mats, rafts, and boats and the basal parts of which are used for food in the area of Lake Titicaca

totquot *n* -s [L *tot quot* as many as] *obs* **:** a dispensation permitting the holding of an unlimited number of benefices; *also* **:** a benefice held by such dispensation

tots *pres 3d sing of* TOT, *pl of* TOT

tot system *n* **:** a southern African system of paying colored agricultural workers part of their wages in tots of wine

totted *past of* TOT

tot·ten·ham \'tät(ᵊ)nəm\ *adj, usu cap* [fr. *Tottenham,* urban district of southeast England] **:** of or from the urban district of Tottenham, Middlesex, England **:** of the kind or style prevalent in Tottenham

tottenham pudding *n, usu cap T, Brit* **:** concentrated steam-sterilized swill for swine

¹**tot·ter** \'täd·ə(r), -ätə-\ *vb* -ED/-ING/-S [ME *toteren, totren;* perh. akin to OE *tealtrian* to waver, totter — more at TILT] *vi* **1** *obs* **:** to be indecisive **:** WAVER ⟨many likelihoods . . . which hung so ~*ing* in the balance —Shak.⟩ **2 a :** to oscillate or lean dizzily **:** SHIMMY, SWAY ⟨~*ed* and fell forward upon her bicycle —Maurice Hewlett⟩ ⟨buildings were still ~*ing* and flames were raging —D.D.S.Pool⟩ **b :** to become unstable **:** threaten to collapse ⟨so many thrones had ~*ed* to their fall —Robert Grant †1940⟩ ⟨virtue could seem momentarily to ~ —Louis Kronenberger⟩ **3 :** to move unsteadily **:** STAGGER, WOBBLE ⟨weak with fever, he ~*ed* to the window —Jean Stafford⟩ ~ *vt* **:** to cause to totter ⟨~*ed* walls, gates and circuses —P.E. Deutschman⟩

²**totter** \"\ *n* -s **1** *NewEng* **:** SEESAW **2 :** an unsteady gait **:** WOBBLE

tot·ter·er \-ərə(r)\ *n* -s **:** one that totters

tottering *adj* [fr. pres. part. of ¹*totter*] **1 a :** being in an unstable condition **:** oscillating or threatening to collapse **:** SWAYING, WOBBLY ⟨buildings dilapidated and ~ —Wilkie Collins⟩ ⟨a ~ wineglass in her hand —George Meredith⟩ **b :** walking unsteadily **:** REELING, WAVERING ⟨a ~ child just learning to walk⟩ ⟨a black pony, a ~ skeleton covered with dirt —*Punch*⟩ **2 :** lacking firmness or stability **:** INSECURE, SHAKY ⟨try to bolster a ~ regime by force of arms⟩ ⟨made a clutch at his ~ reason and steadied it —F.V.W.Mason⟩ — **tot·ter·ing·ly** *adv*

tot·tery \-ərē, -ri\ *adj* [¹*totter* + *-y*] **:** of an infirm or precarious nature **:** SHAKY, TOTTERING ⟨a ~ old man⟩ ⟨the first floor of a ~ ruin —Ion Braby⟩ ⟨may . . . owe his ~ throne to the Soviet Union —*Time*⟩

totting *pres part of* TOT

tot·tle \'täd·ᵊl\ *dial var of* TODDLE

tot·ty \'täd·ē\ *adj* [ME *toty,* prob. fr. *toteren, totren* to totter + *-y*] *archaic* **:** DAZED, FUDDLED

totuava *var of* TOTOABA

to·tum \'tōd·əm\ *n* -s [L *totum* all, the whole — more at TEETOTUM] *archaic* **:** TEETOTUM 1

tot–up \'=,=\ [fr. the phrase *tot up,* fr. ⁴*tot* + *up*] *chiefly Brit var of* ⁵TOT

touareg *usu cap, var of* TUAREG

touart *var of* TUART

tou·can \'tü,kan, -,kaa(ə)n, -,kän, (')tü¦kän *also* 'tükən\ *n* -s [F, fr. Pg *tucano,* fr. Tupi] **1 :** any of numerous fruit-eating birds of tropical America of the family Ramphastidae that have a very large but light and thin-walled beak often nearly as long as the body and are usu. brilliantly colored in beak as well as plumage with red, yellow, white, and black in striking contrast — see BILL illustration **2 :** HORNBILL

tou·can·et \¦tükə¦net\ *n* -s [*toucan* + *-et*] **:** any of several small So. and Central American toucans constituting the genus *Aulacorhynchus* and having both sexes predominantly green in color

¹**touch** \'təch, *dial* 'tech *or* 'tich\ *vb* -ED/-ING/-ES [ME *tochen, touchen,* fr. OF *tochier, tuchier,* fr. (assumed) VL *toccare* to knock, strike, strike a bell, touch, of imit. origin] *vt* **1 a :** to bring a bodily part briefly into contact with so as to feel ⟨~*ing* the delicate petals with gentle fingers⟩ **b :** to perceive or experience through the tactile sense ⟨afraid to ~ a hot iron⟩ ⟨~*ed* his face wonderingly with exploring fingertips⟩ **c :** to put one's fingers to (the hat or the forelock) as a salute or a sign of deference **2 :** to strike or push lightly **:** extend the hand or foot or an implement so as to reach, nudge, stir up, inspect, arouse ⟨if you ~ the snake he will strike⟩ ⟨turned as a hand ~*ed* his shoulder⟩ ⟨~*ed* the horse with the whip⟩ **3 a :** to examine by touching or feeling with the fingers **:** PALPATE **b :** to lay hands upon (one afflicted with scrofula) — compare KING'S EVIL **4 a** *archaic* **:** to play on (a stringed instrument) ⟨angels bending . . . to ~ their harps of gold —E.H. Sears⟩ **b** *archaic* **:** to perform (a melody) by playing or singing **5 a :** to take into the hands or mouth **:** make use of — used chiefly with expressed or implied negative ⟨never ~*es* alcohol in any form⟩ ⟨hardly ~*ed* his dinner⟩ ⟨had never ~*ed* a card before then⟩ ⟨hasn't ~*ed* the piano since his wife's death⟩ **b :** to put hands upon in any way or in any degree **:** disturb or affect by handling — used chiefly with expressed or implied negative ⟨your things haven't been ~*ed* while you were away⟩ ⟨don't ~ anything before the police come⟩ **c :** to have sexual intercourse with — used chiefly with real or implied negative ⟨doubt if he had ever ~*ed* a woman before his marriage⟩ **d :** to lay violent hands on **:** commit violence upon — used chiefly with expressed or implied negative ⟨swears he never ~*ed* the child⟩ **6 :** to have to do with **:** concern oneself with **:** meddle with — used chiefly with expressed or implied negative ⟨strictly his affair, I wouldn't ~ it for anything⟩ **7 a :** to gain the use of **:** get access to ⟨unable to ~ the capital of the estate⟩ **b** *slang* **:** pick up **:** STEAL **8 a** *obs* **:** to tamper with **:** BRIBE **b :** to rob by swindling **:** CHEAT **c :** pick the pocket of ⟨~*ed* him for his watch⟩ **d :** to induce to give or lend ⟨~*ed* him for ten dollars⟩ **9 a :** to cause to be briefly and lightly in contact or conjunction with something ⟨~*ed* his hand to his cap⟩ ⟨~*ed* his spurs to his horse⟩ ⟨solemnly raised and ~*ed* glasses⟩ ⟨~*ed* gloves with his opponent to start the last round⟩ **b :** to lay the scepter upon (an act of parliament) as a sign of royal assent **c :** to apply lightly to **:** spread thinly on ⟨~ a pimple with iodine⟩ **10 a** (1) **:** to meet without overlapping or penetrating **:** be or become contiguous or adjacent to **:** impinge upon **:** ADJOIN ⟨where the edges of the figure ~ the border⟩ (2) **:** to get to **:** REACH ⟨the speedometer needle ~*ed* 80⟩ **b :** to be tangent to **c :** to come up to in quality or value **:** compare with — used usu. with a negative ⟨nothing can ~ that cloth for durability⟩ ⟨not a fighter in his weight division to ~ him⟩ **d :** to sail as close to (the wind) as possible **11 a :** to deal with or treat of **:** HANDLE ⟨everything he ~*es* becomes clearer than before⟩ ⟨pamphlets ~*ing* nearly every aspect of rural life⟩ **b :** to make allusion or slight mention of **:** speak or tell of in passing ⟨~*ed* so many topics that only a confused impression remained at the end⟩ **12 :** to relate to **:** affect the interest of **:** CONCERN ⟨alert to anything that ~*ed* his personal honor⟩ ⟨their profession ~*es* our national defense very closely —Vannevar Bush⟩ **13 a :** to leave a mark or impression on **:** make signs of wear, use, or slight damage on — used chiefly with a negative ⟨so hard no ordinary cutter will ~ it⟩ ⟨his war experiences seem not to have ~*ed* him at all⟩ **b** *obs* **:** MAGNETIZE **c :** to harm slightly by or as if by contagion, contamination, or blight **:** taint, blemish, sour, spoil in a slight degree ⟨fruit ~*ed* by frost⟩ ⟨this horse is ~*ed* in the wind⟩ **d :** to give a delicate tint, line, or expression to ⟨a smile ~*ed* her lips⟩ ⟨admiration faintly ~*ed* with envy⟩ **14 a :** to test the purity of (as gold) with a touchstone **:** ASSAY, TRY **b :** to stamp or mark (as gold, silver) after an official assay **15 a :** to draw or delineate with light strokes ⟨the lines though ~*ed* but faintly are drawn right —Alexander Pope⟩ **b :** to improve or modify by or as if by light strokes **:** touch up **16 :** to reach the heart or secret of **:** guess at correctly **:** FATHOM ⟨there you ~*ed* the life of our design —Shak.⟩ **17 a :** to hurt the feelings of **:** WOUND, STING ⟨the insult ~*ed* him to the quick⟩ **b :** to shame or discomfit by hitting the truth ⟨his face hardened, the last remark had ~*ed* him on a sore spot⟩ **c :** to move to sympathetic feeling (as pity, gratitude, remorse,

tenderness) ⟨~*ed* by the loyalty of his friends⟩ ~ *vi* **1 a :** to feel something with a body part (as the hand or foot) **b :** to lay hand or finger on a person to cure disease (as scrofula) ⟨he ~*ed* for the king's evil⟩ **2 a :** to be in such a position that no space exists between **:** be in contact ⟨two spheres can ~ only at points⟩ ⟨sat with their heads nearly ~*ing*⟩ **b :** to be next to another suit in rank of playing cards ⟨diamonds ~ hearts⟩ ⟨diamonds and clubs are ~*ing* suits⟩ **3 a :** to come close **:** APPROACH **:** VERGE ⟨his actions ~ on treason⟩ **b** *of a sail* **:** to turn so close to the wind that the weather leech shakes ⟨keep the royals ~*ing*⟩ **4 :** to have a bearing **:** RELATE, PERTAIN — used with *on* or *upon* **5 a :** to make a brief or incidental stop on shore during a trip by water — used usu. with *at* ⟨~*ed* at several ports on the return voyage⟩ **b :** to treat a topic in a brief or casual manner — used with *on* or *upon* ⟨~*ed* upon many points without enlarging upon any of them⟩ **6 :** to improve or modify something with slight strokes or alterations **:** RETOUCH ⟨endlessly ~*ing* and retouching before he was satisfied with the picture⟩ **syn** see AFFECT, MATCH — **touch and go 1** *obs* **:** to pass quickly from point to point (as in a discourse) **2 a :** to touch bottom or an obstacle without sticking fast or foundering **b :** to succeed by a very narrow margin — **touch bottom 1 :** to scrape or settle upon the sea bottom **2 :** to reach the lowest possible point ⟨prices seemed to have *touched bottom* and a rise is expected⟩ ⟨that day our hopes *touched bottom*⟩ — **touch elbows :** to be in close contact in work, play, viewpoint **:** have close association ⟨place where you *touch elbows* with all sorts of people⟩ — **touch wood :** to touch or rap on something made of wood as a charm to ward off bad luck esp. after boasting of good luck

²**touch** \"\ *n* -ES [partly fr. ME *touche,* fr. OF, fr. *tochier, tuchier* to touch; partly fr. ¹*touch*] **1 a :** a light stroke, tap, or push ⟨ready to fall at a ~⟩ **b :** a light stroke of wit or satire **:** KNOCK, DIG **c :** the contact of a fencer's point or blade against the opponent's target that scores a point **2 a :** the act or fact of touching, feeling, striking lightly, or coming in contact ⟨saluted with a ~ to his cap⟩ **b :** PALPATION **3 :** the sense by which pressure or traction exerted on the skin or mucous membrane is perceived **:** the tactile sense as distinguished from the pain, temperature, and kinesthetic senses **4 :** mental or moral sensitiveness, responsiveness, or tact ⟨she has a wonderful ~ in dealing with children⟩ ⟨our high task to use our power with a sure hand and a steady ~ —A.E.Stevenson b. 1900⟩ ⟨a skilled writer but lacking the popular ~⟩ **5 :** a specified sensation conveyed through the tactile receptors **:** FEEL ⟨the velvety ~ of a fabric⟩ **6 a :** the act of rubbing gold or silver on a touchstone to test its quality **b :** the quality or degree of fineness of metal so tested **c :** the official stamp upon a tested metal of standard quality **d :** TOUCHMARK **e** *archaic* **:** tested or proven quality or character ⟨friends of noble ~ —Shak.⟩ **7 a** *obs* **:** TOUCHSTONE 1 **b :** TEST, TRIAL — used chiefly in the phrase *put to the touch* **8 a :** a visible effect **:** STAMP, MARK ⟨~ of the tropical sun⟩ ⟨woman with what we used to call the ~ of good breeding upon her —Morris Markey⟩ **b :** WEAKNESS, DEFECT ⟨a ~ in his wits⟩ ⟨one ~ of nature makes the whole world kin —Shak.⟩ **c** *obs* **:** injury to reputation **:** REPROACH, BLAME **9 :** something slight of its kind: as **a :** a light attack ⟨~ of fever⟩ **b :** a small quantity **:** TRACE, DASH ⟨~ of spring in the air⟩ ⟨~ of garlic in the salad⟩ ⟨a ~ of unreality about the whole affair⟩ **c :** a transient emotion **:** a flash of feeling ⟨momentary ~ of compunction⟩ **d** *archaic* **:** a brief mention, hint, or reminder **e :** a near approach **:** a close call ⟨beaten in the . . . backstroke championships by a mere ~ —Kate Kerry⟩ **f :** BIT, LITTLE — used adverbially with *a* ⟨as though she had said something ridiculous and a ~ discreditable —R.V.Cassill⟩ ⟨aimed a ~ too low and missed⟩ **10** *archaic* **:** AGREEMENT, COVENANT — used in the phrase *to keep touch* **11 a** *archaic* **:** the playing of an instrument (as a lute or piano) with the fingers; *also* **:** musical notes or strains so produced ⟨with sweetest ~*es* pierce your mistress' ears —Shak.⟩ **b :** a manner or method of touching or striking esp. the keys of a keyboard instrument ⟨requiring a staccato ~⟩; *also* **:** one's characteristic style in striking keys ⟨have a firm ~⟩ **c :** particular or characteristic action of a keyboard instrument with reference to the resistance of its keys to pressure ⟨a piano with a stiff ~⟩ ⟨typewriter with a light ~⟩ **12 :** a set of changes in change ringing less than the total number possible or less than a peal **13 :** a light or delicate stroke in creating or improving an artistic composition **:** an effective or touching-up detail ⟨that was a vivid ~ in his last story⟩ ⟨the work is complete except for the finishing ~*es*⟩ ⟨hotel service with a personal ~⟩ **14 :** distinctive manner or method ⟨this room needs a woman's ~⟩ **:** characteristic skill of a workman or artist in the manipulation of his instruments or materials ⟨the billiard player had lost his ~⟩ ⟨the painting shows the ~ of a master⟩ **15 :** a characteristic or distinguishing trait or quality **16 a** *slang* **:** an act of borrowing, swindling, or stealing ⟨beggar making his ~⟩ **:** THEFT **b :** a victim of borrowing or swindling ⟨recognized him early as a soft ~ for a loan —John Lardner⟩ **17** *slang* **a :** a method of inducing someone to buy or to accept a deal **b :** something that will sell at a named price **c :** a sale effected by dubious means **18 :** the state or fact of being in contact or communication ⟨lost ~ with the other boats in the fog⟩ ⟨keeping in ~ with distant relations⟩ ⟨kept in close ~ with headquarters by phone⟩ ⟨out of ~ with modern methods⟩ **19 :** ³TAG 1 **20 :** the broadest part of a plank worked top and butt **:** the angles of the stern timbers at the counters of a ship **21 :** the area outside of the sidelines in soccer or outside of and including the touchlines in rugby — used usu. with *in* or *into* ⟨kicked the ball into ~⟩ ⟨thrown in by a player standing in ~⟩

touch- *comb form* [obs. *touch-powder,* powder used for priming a gun, fr. ME *towchepoudre,* fr. MF *toucher* to touch, kindle (a fire) + ME *poudre* powder] **:** serving for quick ignition ⟨*touch*hole⟩ ⟨*touch*wood⟩

touch·able \ˈtəchəbəl\ *adj* **1 :** capable of being touched **:** TANGIBLE **2 :** EATABLE — **touch·able·ness** *n* -ES

touch and go *n* [fr. the v. phrase *touch and go*] **1 :** rapid movement from point to point **:** continuous flitting ⟨its swift *touch and go* of actual talk —J.L.Lowes⟩ **2 :** a highly uncertain or precarious situation or condition **:** a state of affairs so critical that the slightest turn may bring disaster or failure ⟨*touch and go* of guerrilla warfare⟩

touch-and-go \ˈ⸗⸗ˌ⸗\ *adj* [*touch and go*] **1 :** marked by restlessness or casualness of movement or execution ⟨*touch-and-go* dialogue⟩ **2 :** PRECARIOUS, HAIRBREADTH ⟨mule trains to haul your equipment the two *touch-and-go* miles —Horace Sutton⟩

touch-and-heal \ˈ⸗⸗ˌ⸗\ *n* -S [¹*touch*] **:** an herb (*Hypericum perforatum*)

touchback \ˈ⸗ˌ⸗\ *n* -S **:** an act or instance in football of being in possession of the ball behind one's own goal line when the ball is declared dead, the impetus putting the ball over the goal line having been given by an opponent — compare SAFETY 6b(2)

touchball \ˈ⸗ˌ⸗\ *n* **:** TOUCH FOOTBALL

touch body *or* **touch corpuscle** *n* **:** TACTILE CORPUSCLE

touch-box \ˈtəch,bäks\ *n* [*touch-* + *box*] **:** a box of lighted tinder formerly carried by soldiers for firing matchlocks

touch down *vt* **:** to place (the ball in rugby) by hand on the ground on or over an opponent's goal line in scoring a try or behind one's own goal line as a defensive measure ~ *vi* **:** to reach the ground **:** LAND ⟨the new bomber *touched down* just three hours later⟩

touchdown \ˈ⸗ˌ⸗\ *n* -S **1 a :** the act of touching a football down behind an opponent's goal; *specif* **:** the act of scoring six points by being lawfully in possession of the ball on, above, or behind an opponent's goal line when the ball is declared dead **b :** the act of a rugby player who first grounds the ball in his own in-goal **c :** the act of scoring two points in speedball by completion of a forward pass to a teammate in the opponent's end zone **2 :** the act or moment of making the landing gear of an airplane touch the surface with or without the intention of making a full landing

¹**tou·ché** \tüˈshā\ *interj* [F, past part. of *toucher* to touch] — used to acknowledge a hit in fencing or the success of an argument or the accuracy of an accusation

²**touché** \"\ *n* -S **1 :** a hit in fencing **:** TOUCH **2 :** a telling remark or home thrust in argument

touched *adj* [fr. past part. of ¹*touch*] **1 :** emotionally stirred ⟨she was both angry and in an odd way ~ —Sherwood Anderson⟩ **2 :** slightly unbalanced mentally **:** ECCENTRIC ⟨the ~ sea captain who remembers journeys to places that never were —Irving Howe⟩

touched bill *n* **:** a bill of health stating that a ship's company or a port is suspected of infectious disease

touch·eous \ˈtəchəs, ˈtech-\ *var of* TOUCHOUS

touch·er \ˈtəchə(r)\ *n* -S [ME, fr. *touchen* to touch + *-er*] **1 :** one that touches **2 :** a bowl which has touched the jack during its original course on a bowling green

touches *pres 3d sing of* TOUCH, *pl of* TOUCH

touch football *n* **:** football played informally and chiefly characterized by the substitution of touching for tackling

touch·hole \ˈtəch,hōl\ *n* [*touch-* + *hole*] **1 :** the vent in old-time cannons or firearms through which the charge was ignited **2 :** the hole in the cylinder of a gas engine with tube ignition in which the tube is inserted

touchier *comparative of* TOUCHY

touchiest *superlative of* TOUCHY

touch·i·ly \ˈtəchəlē, -li\ *adv* **:** in a touchy manner ⟨~ refusing offers of help⟩

touch in *vt* **:** to insert (detail) by light strokes of pencil or brush

touch·i·ness \-chēnəs, -chin-\ *n* -ES **:** the quality or state of being touchy **:** IRRITABILITY

¹**touching** *prep* [ME, fr. pres. part. of *touchen* to touch] **:** in reference to **:** as regards **:** CONCERNING ⟨good experimental verification of your hypothesis, ~ the cause of the abnormal phenomena —T.H.Huxley⟩ — often used with *as* ⟨now, as ~ things offered unto idols —1 Cor 8:1 (AV)⟩

²**touching** *adj* [fr. pres. part. of ¹*touch*] **:** capable of stirring emotions **:** AFFECTING, PATHETIC ⟨~ trust in her parents⟩ ⟨~ story⟩ **syn** see MOVING

touch·ing·ly *adv* [²*touching* + *-ly*] **:** in a touching manner **:** PATHETICALLY, MOVINGLY ⟨~ grateful⟩

touch·ing·ness *n* -ES **:** the quality or state of being touching ⟨~ of her devotion⟩

touch-in-goal \ˈ⸗⸗ˌ⸗\ *n* **:** any of the four areas of a rugby field back of the goal lines extended and outside of the touch-in-goal lines

touch-in-goal line *n* **:** a continuation of a touchline extending from a goal line to the nearest dead-ball line — see RUGBY illustration

touch judge *n* **:** either of two officials in rugby stationed one on each side of the field who assist the referee in determining when and where the ball goes into touch and when a goal has been kicked

touch·less \ˈtəchləs\ *adj* [²*touch* + *-less*] **:** not touchable **:** INTANGIBLE

touchline \ˈ⸗ˌ⸗\ *n* **1 :** either of the lines between and at right angles to the goal lines that bound the sides of the field of play in rugby and soccer — see RUGBY illustration **2** *Brit* **:** SIDELINE 3b ⟨does not like people who boo from the ~ and refuse to help the game on —*Times Lit. Supp.*⟩

touchmark \ˈ⸗ˌ⸗\ *n* **:** an identifying maker's mark impressed on pewter

touch-me-not \ˈ⸗⸗ˌ⸗\ *n* -S **1** [so called fr. the fact that the ripe pods burst open and scatter their seeds when touched] **a :** JEWELWEED **b :** SQUIRTING CUCUMBER **2** *obs* **:** LUPUS **3 :** a haughty, aloof, or prudish person; *esp* **:** a girl or woman inclined to be distant and cold

touch-me-not-ish \ˈtəchmē,nädish\ *adj* **:** not readily approachable **:** STANDOFFISH, PRUDISH — **touch-me-not-ish·ness** *n* -ES

touch needle *n* **:** a small bar of gold either pure or alloyed with silver in a known proportion for trying the fineness of a gold or silver article by comparing the streaks made by the article and the bar on a touchstone

touch off *vt* **1 :** to describe or characterize to a nicety **:** hit off ⟨a fine job of *touching off* the shallowness and confusion of his interloper role —*Newsweek*⟩ **2** [*touch* (as in *touchhole*)] **a :** to cause to explode by or as if by touching with fire **b :** to release or initiate with the sudden violence of an explosion ⟨the charges *touched off* a storm of protest —R.A. Billington⟩ **3 :** to start (a relay runner) by touching his extended hand

touch-off \ˈ⸗ˌ⸗\ *n* -S [*touch off*] **:** something that is touched off; *specif* **:** a fire of incendiary origin

touch·ous \ˈtəchəs, ˈtech-\ *adj* [²*touch* + *-ous*] *dial* **:** TOUCHY

touch-pan \ˈtəch,pan\ *n* [*touch-* + *pan*] **:** the pan of a flintlock

touch paper *n* [*touch-* + *paper*] **:** paper impregnated with potassium nitrate that burns steadily without flame and is used to aid the ignition of small fireworks

touchpiece \ˈ⸗ˌ⸗\ *n* **:** a coin (as an angel) or medal given by various English sovereigns as late as Queen Anne to persons touched by them for the cure of the king's evil

touch reader *n* **:** a blind person able to read braille or some other raised type with the fingers

touch spot *n* **:** PRESSURE SPOT

touchstone \ˈ⸗ˌ⸗\ *n* **1 :** a black siliceous stone related to flint and formerly used to test the purity of gold and silver by the streak left on the stone when rubbed by the metal ⟨holding out gold that's by the ~ tried —Shak.⟩ — called also *Basanite, Lydian stone* **2 :** a test or criterion for determining the quality or genuineness of a thing ⟨an original work is the ~ that exposes educated taste masquerading as sensibility —Clive Bell⟩ **syn** see STANDARD

touch system *n* **:** a method of typewriting that assigns a particular finger to each key and makes it possible to type without looking at the keyboard — compare HUNT AND PECK

touch-tackle \ˈ⸗ˌ⸗\ *n* **:** TOUCH FOOTBALL

touch-type \ˈ⸗ˌ⸗\ *vb* **:** to type by the touch system

touch up *vt* **1 :** to improve or perfect by small additional strokes or alterations ⟨*touch up* a picture by strengthening highlights and shadows⟩ ⟨the last act needs to be *touched up*⟩ **2 :** to stimulate by or as if by a flick of a whip ⟨*touch up* a team of horses⟩ ⟨his memory needs to be *touched up*⟩

touch-up \ˈ⸗ˌ⸗\ *n* -S [*touch up*] **1 :** an act or instance of touching up **:** RETOUCH **2 :** FLICK, HINT

touch watch *n* **:** a watch designed for reading in the dark or by the blind

touch·wood \ˈtəch,wu̇d\ *n* [*touch-* + *wood*] **:** ³PUNK 1, 2

touchy \ˈtəchē, -chi, *dial* ˈtech- *or* ˈtich-\ *adj* -ER/-EST [²*touch* + *-y*] **1 :** marked by an oversensitive irritable temperament, by general readiness to take offense on slight provocation, or by delicate easily wounded sensitivity about specific matters ⟨a ~, uneasy friend . . . his intensest friendships generally came to grief —David Cecil⟩ ⟨a little ~ about my spoon-feeding at first —Stephen Haggard⟩ ⟨a man who had grown too ~ to make judicious decisions —*Time*⟩ **2 :** responding quickly to a touch **:** extremely reactive: as **a** *of a body part* **:** acutely sensitive or irritable **b** *of a chemical* **:** highly explosive or inflammable **3 :** calling for tact, care, and caution in treatment **:** likely to cause offense, chagrin, or hurt pride **:** uncertain in issue **:** fraught with danger **:** PRECARIOUS ⟨the job of governorship, when all men seemed set against change, was a brittle, ~ business —Julian Dana⟩ ⟨military training is a ~ subject in the aftermath of war —M.W.Childs⟩ **4 :** composed of dots or short strokes ⟨~ pencil drawing⟩ **syn** see IRASCIBLE

toucouleur *usu cap, var of* TUKULÖR

¹**tough** \ˈtəf\ *adj* -ER/-EST [ME *tow, togh, tough,* fr. OE *tōh;* akin to OHG *zāhi* tough, ON *tā* ground trodden to hardness, OE *tengan* to press forward, *tenge* pressing, resting on] **1 a :** having the quality of being strong or firm in texture but flexible and not brittle **:** yielding to force without breaking **:** capable of resisting great strain without coming apart ⟨the ligaments of animals are ~⟩ **b :** not easily chewed or masticated ⟨steak so ~ we could hardly cut it⟩ **2 :** having great viscosity **:** GLUTINOUS, STICKY, TENACIOUS ⟨~ phlegm⟩ ⟨~ tar⟩ **3 a :** characterized by severity **:** STIFF, FORCEFUL ⟨when the law gets too ~, the courts don't convict —Gregor Felsen⟩ ⟨one change will be a ~*er* boycott ban —S.K.Galpin⟩ **b** (1) **:** characterized by uncompromising determination **:** ADAMANT, MILITANT ⟨had something with which to back a ~ and inflexible foreign policy —*New Statesman & Nation*⟩ (2) **:** AGGRESSIVE, THREATENING ⟨the thing to do is get ~ with that country —Harry Schwartz⟩ **4 :** capable of enduring strain, hardship, or severe labor **:** having or manifesting great physical resistance **:** unusually sturdy **:** HARDY ⟨the rigorous climate . . . creates a ~ people —Douglas Carruthers⟩ ⟨the Scots . . . were almost without exception very ~ fighting men —G.W.Johnson⟩ **5 :** very hard to influence or move **:** STUBBORN, UNYIELDING ⟨they view him . . . as a ~ antagonist —*N.Y. Times*⟩ ⟨insight into certain deep and persistent . . . traits and into the ~ fidelities —Clifton Fadiman⟩ ⟨the ~*est* judge . . . single-minded and implacable —M.S.Mayer⟩ **6 :** making unduly heavy or arduous demands **:** extremely difficult to cope with or comprehend ⟨had been a ~ winter —Heywood Broun⟩ ⟨found himself in a ~ spot —Barnaby Conrad⟩ ⟨one of the ~*est* languages in the world —Albert Hubbell⟩ ⟨the work that men do is not the ~ part of their lives —G.W.Brace⟩ **7 :** stubbornly fought **:** stoutly maintained ⟨had lost a ~ contest that went into extra innings —R.O.Boyer⟩ **8 a :** pertinaciously unruly **:** ROWDYISH, RUFFIANLY **:** tending toward viciousness ⟨problem children who were too ~ for the other schools —Green Peyton⟩ **b :** frequented by rowdy or criminal elements ⟨a patrolman on . . . the ~*est* waterfront beat —*Current Biog.*⟩ ⟨had a reputation as one of the ~*est* places in the state —*Amer. Guide Series: Nev.*⟩ **9 :** marked by a steely quality **:** without softness or sentimentality **:** harshly even brutally realistic ⟨his book is . . . unbelievably ~ —W.H.Auden⟩ ⟨a writer . . . who is ~ and blunt and calls a spade a spade —M. D.Geismar⟩ ⟨strongly influenced by American writing of the ~ school —*Brit. Bk. News*⟩ **syn** see STRONG

²**tough** \"\ *vt* -ED/-ING/-S **:** to bear unflinchingly **:** ENDURE — often used with *out* ⟨a friend with whom he was ~*ing* the winter out —A.B.Guthrie⟩ ⟨been ~*ing* out a dry spell —W.D. Overholser⟩ ⟨the boy wanted to ~ it out and be a cowboy —Ross Santee⟩

³**tough** \"\ *n* -S **:** a tough person; *esp* **:** ROWDY

⁴**tough** \"\ *adv* **:** in a tough manner ⟨tried to tell why he and his buddies talked ~ —*Time*⟩ ⟨talks ~ and insensitively but sends money —A.E.Stevenson b. 1900⟩

tough check *n* **:** a very strong cardboard used for shipping tags and tickets and made on a cylinder machine

tough·en \ˈtəfən\ *vb* **toughened; toughened; toughening** \-f(ə)niŋ\ **toughens** [¹*tough* + *-en*] *vt* **:** to make tough ⟨~*ed* by a rough-and-tumble environment where each man's revolver . . . made the law —R.A.Billington⟩ ~ *vi* **:** to become tough ⟨the language has suddenly ~*ed* and acquired a new menacing cadence —Edmund Stevens⟩

toughened glass *n* [*toughened* (past part. of *toughen*) + *glass*] **:** glass tempered by a control process of sudden cooling

toughhead \ˈ⸗ˌ⸗\ *n* [¹*tough* + *head*] *NewEng* **:** RUDDY DUCK

tough·ie *also* **toughy** \ˈtəfē, -fi\ *n, pl* **toughies** [¹*tough* + *-ie*] **:** one that is tough: as **a :** a loud rowdy person **:** tough character ⟨a square-jawed ~ who is not taking anything from anybody —Brand Blanshard⟩ **b :** a very intricate or difficult problem ⟨had worked on some real ~*s* . . . but this one topped them all —Franklin Sharpe⟩ **c :** a hard-boiled piece of writing ⟨the straight-out detective story as distinguished from . . . the ~ —Sergeant Cuff⟩

tough·ish \ˈtəfish\ *adj* **:** rather tough

tough·ly *adv* [ME, fr. ¹*tough* + *-ly*] **:** in a tough manner ⟨~ vigorous and humanly sympathetic storytelling —Anthony Boucher⟩

tough-minded \ˈ⸗ˈ⸗⸗\ *adj* [¹*tough* + *minded*] **:** tending toward or characterized by empiricism, materialism, or pessimism; *esp* **:** realistic or unsentimental in temper or habitual point of view **:** HARDHEADED, PRACTICAL — **tough-mind·ed·ly** *adv*

tough-mind·ed·ness *n* -ES **:** the quality or state of being tough-minded ⟨this educational process had the tendency to turn cynicism into *tough-mindedness* —C.G.Bolte⟩

tough·ness *n* -ES [ME *toughnes,* fr. ¹*tough* + *-nes* -ness] **1 :** the quality or state of being tough ⟨had a physical and moral ~ of fibre which enabled him . . . to endure misfortune —Sir Winston Churchill⟩ **2 :** the ability of a metal to absorb considerable energy before fracture **3 :** the quality of a paint or coating that causes it to resist chipping, abrasion, or cracking

tough pitch *n* **1 :** the exact state or quality of texture and consistency of refined and remelted copper containing about 0.02 to 0.05 percent oxygen **2** *also* **tough cake :** copper having the quality of tough pitch

tough-skinned \ˈ⸗ˈ⸗\ *adj* **1 :** having a tough skin **2 :** lacking sensitivity **:** not easily offended

touk *var of* TUCK

tou·lon \(ˈ)tüˈlän, tüˈlōⁿ\ *adj, usu cap* [fr. *Toulon,* seaport of southeast France] **:** of or from the city of Toulon, France **:** of the kind or style prevalent in Toulon

¹**tou·louse** \(ˈ)tüˈlüz\ *adj, usu cap* [fr. *Toulouse,* city of southern France] **:** of or from the city of Toulouse, France **:** of the kind or style prevalent in Toulouse

²**toulouse** \"\ *n, usu cap* **1 :** a French breed of large heavy geese having a large head, a short thick bill without a knob, and chiefly gray plumage **2** -S **:** a goose of this breed

tou·mey oak \ˈtümē-\ *n, usu cap T* [after James W. *Toumey* †1932 Am. forester] **:** an oak (*Quercus toumeyi*) of the southwestern U. S. having thin entire leaves and a thin shallow tomentose acorn cup

toun \ˈtün\ *Scot var of* TOWN

tou·pee \tüˈpā\ *n* -S [alter. of *toupet*] **1 :** a curl or lock of hair made into a topknot on a periwig or natural hairdress and worn esp. in the 18th century by men and women; *also* **:** a periwig with such a topknot **2 :** a small wig or section of false hair worn to cover a bald spot

tou·pet \"\ *n* -S [F, tuft of hair, forelock, fr. OF, dim. of *top, toup,* of Gmc origin; akin to OHG *zopf* end, tip, tuft of hair — more at TOP] **:** TOUPEE

¹**tour** \ˈtu̇(ə)r, ˈtu̇ə, *in sense 1 sometimes* ˈtau̇(ə)r *or* ˈtau̇ə\ *n* -S [ME, fr. MF, fr. OF *tor, tour, torn, tourn* lathe, circuit, turn — more at TURN] **1 a :** one's turn in an orderly arrangement or schedule **:** a shift usu. in a factory **b :** a period during which an individual or unit is on a specific duty or at one place ⟨assigned to short ~*s* of duty at a number of United States Army stations —*Current Biog.*⟩ ⟨my ~ of duty in Kenya lasted fourteen months —John Muggeridge⟩ **c :** a single circuit of a postal carrier around his route **2** *obs* **:** a circuitous movement **:** a revolution esp. of a heavenly body **3 a** (1) **:** a journey in which one returns to the starting point **:** a circular trip usu. for business, pleasure, or education during which various places are visited and for which an itinerary is often planned ⟨an inexpensive ~ of Europe —T.R.Ybarra⟩ ⟨a motor ~ of New England⟩ (2) **:** something resembling such a tour ⟨making a ~ of all the problems confronting the West —*N.Y. Times*⟩ **b** (1) **:** a brief turn **:** ROUND ⟨the very walks of the garden are so moist that . . . no person can make a ~ of it —Tobias Smollett⟩ (2) **:** a short drive or outing often representing a social occasion **c :** a circuit of an island **d :** a visit (as to a museum, factory, or historic site) for enjoyment or instruction usu. under the auspices of a guide ⟨a brief opening ceremony followed by a ~ of the new school⟩ ⟨the group made a conducted ~ of the battleground⟩ **e :** a series of professional engagements involving travel from one place to another ⟨after a successful nationwide ~, the play was made into a motion picture —*Current Biog.*⟩ ⟨took his small theatrical company on ~ in the provinces⟩ **4 :** a headdress of the 17th and 18th centuries usu. built high by adding false hair, pads, or trimmings **5** *obs* **:** the compass or range of something **:** sum and substance **6 :** one of the distinct portions of a more or less continuous song of a canary

²**tour** \ˈtu̇(ə)r, ˈtu̇ə\ *vb* -ED/-ING/-S *vi* **1 :** to direct one's steps **:** GO, PROCEED ⟨loves holding onto someone's hands and ~*ing* around the room —*Infant Care*⟩ **2 a :** to make a tour ⟨~*ed* through Central America and Mexico⟩ **b :** to go on tour esp. with or in a theatrical production ⟨the star headed an obedient company in the city or ~*ed* by himself —Margery Bailey⟩ ~ *vt* **1 a :** to make a tour of ⟨~*ed* the countryside instructing workers —*Americana Annual*⟩ **b :** to take on a tour ⟨the group was ~*ed* through the factory⟩ **2 :** to present (as a theatrical production) on a tour ⟨students . . . ~ a children's theater play for one week each spring —Alice Griffin⟩

tou·ra·co *or* **tu·ra·co** \ˈtu̇rəˌkō\ *or* **tu·ra·cou** *or* **tu·ra·koo** \-kü\ *n* -S [native name in western Africa] **:** any of various African birds that constitute the family Musophagidae, are mostly from one to two feet long, have a long tail, an erectile crest, a short stout often colored bill, lax and fluffy plumage, and red wing feathers which yield turacin — called also *plantain eater*

tour·bil·lion *or* **tour·bil·lon** \tu̇rˈbilyən, tu̇ə'-\ *n* -S [MF *tourbillon* whirl, vortex, whirlwind, fr. L *turbin-, turbo* — more at TURBINE] **1 :** something that whirls around or moves spirally: as **a :** WHIRLWIND **b :** a vortex esp. of a whirlwind or whirlpool **c :** a firework having a spiral flight **2 :** a watch in which the escapement is mounted on an epicyclic train and assumes all the vertical positions in one minute thereby neutralizing the position errors **3 :** the whirl of the hair near the vertex of the human head

tour de force \ˌtu̇rdə¦fō(ə)rs, -¦fȯ(ə)rs; ¦tu̇ədə¦fōəs, -¦fȯ(ə)s\ *n, pl* **tours de force** \"\ [F] **1 :** a feat of strength, skill, or artistic merit **2 :** a merely adroit or ingenious accomplishment or production

tou·relle \tu̇'rel\ *n* -s [F, fr. OF, dim. of *tor, tour* tower — more at TOWER] **1 :** a small tower (as one springing from corbeling or pier) **:** TURRET **2 :** something resembling a tourelle ⟨the pines' green ~s —Richard Llewellyn⟩

tour en l'air \ˌtu̇rän'ler\ *n, pl* **tours en l'air** \"\ [F] **:** a ballet turn in the air

tour·er \'tu̇rə(r)\ *n* -s [²*tour* + *-er*] **:** TOURING CAR

tou·rill \tu̇'ril\ *n* -s [G *tourill, tourille,* perh. modif. of F *tourie* carboy] **:** an absorption vessel in which a gas is passed over a liquid (as for removing moisture or a component of a gas mixture)

¹**touring** *n* -s [fr. gerund of ²*tour*] **1 :** the act of participating in a tour ⟨the ~ in quest of the picturesque —Anthony Trollope⟩ **2 :** TOURING CAR **3 :** cross-country skiing

²**touring** *adj* [in sense 1, fr. pres. part. of ²*tour;* in sense 2, fr. ¹*touring*] **1 :** traveling from place to place on a tour ⟨~ public⟩ **2 :** used in touring **:** suitable for use while touring **:** designed for the tourist trade

touring car *n* **:** an open automobile with two cross seats, usu. four doors, and a folding top — called also *phaeton, tourer*

tour·ism \'tu̇ˌrizəm\ *n* -s [¹*tour* + *-ism*] **1 :** the practice of touring **:** traveling for recreation **2 :** the guidance or management of tourists as a business or a governmental function **:** provision of itineraries, guidance, and accommodations for tourists **:** the economic activities associated with and dependent upon tourists

¹**tour·ist** \'tu̇rəst\ *n* -s [¹*tour* + *-ist*] **1 :** one that makes a tour **:** one that travels from place to place for pleasure or culture **:** one that stays overnight usu. at an inn or motel **2 :** TOURIST CLASS

²**tourist** \"\ *adj* **:** of, belonging to, suitable for, or serving tourists ⟨~ agency⟩ ⟨~ cottage⟩ ⟨~ rate⟩

³**tourist** \"\ *vb* -ED/-ING/-S *vi* **:** to make a tour ⟨would probably shudder at ~*ing* in his own country —Anne S. Mehdevi⟩ ~ *vt* **:** to visit while touring

tourist car *or* **tourist coach** *n* **:** a railway car equipped with less commodious and lower-priced sleeping accommodations than standard Pullman cars

tourist card *n* **:** a citizenship identity card issued to a tourist usu. for a stated period of time in lieu of a passport or a visa

tourist class *n* **:** a class of accommodations (as on a passenger ship) usu. less expensive and roomy than first or than second or cabin class

tourist court *n* **:** MOTEL

touristed *adj* [fr. past part. of ³*tourist*] **:** visited by throngs of tourists ⟨of the three islands, St. Thomas is the most ~ —Lawrence Martin⟩

tourist home *n* **:** a house in which rooms are available for rent to transients

tour·is·tic \(ˈ)tu̇¦ristik\ *also* **tour·is·ti·cal** \-təkəl\ *adj* [¹*tourist* + *-ic, -ical*] **:** of or relating to a tour or tourism **:** primarily catering or of interest to tourists ⟨traditional costumes are daily dress and not a holiday or ~ getup —Herbert Kubly⟩ ⟨one of two largest ~ hotels —Arnold Bennett⟩

tour·is·ti·cal·ly \-tək(ə)lē\ *adv* **:** in a touristic manner **:** with respect to tourists ⟨~ the country is probably twenty years behind —Horace Sutton⟩

tour·ist·ry \'tu̇rəstrē\ *n* -ES [¹*tourist* + *-ry*] **:** the fact or practice of touring; *also* **:** the whole body of tourists ⟨all the ruck and rabble of British ~ pour unhindered —R.L.Stevenson⟩

tour·isty \-tē\ *adj* [¹*tourist* + *-y*] **:** of, relating to, or characteristic of tourists **:** patronized by or popular with the tourist ⟨the shopfuls of ~ trinkets —*Mademoiselle*⟩ ⟨tourists descend . . . in busloads during summer, with the result the whole place is rather ~ —*N.Y.Times*⟩

tour je·té \ˌtu̇rzhə'tā\ *n, pl* **tour jetés** [F, lit., thrown turn] **:** a high turning leap in ballet starting with battement and finishing in arabesque — called also *jeté en tournant*

tour·lou·rou \¦tu̇rlü¦rü\ *n* -s [F] **:** GREAT LAND CRAB

tour·ma·line *also* **tur·ma·line** \'tu̇rmələn, 'tu̇əm-, -məˌlēn\ *n* -s [Sinhalese *toramalli* carnelian] **1 :** a mineral $(Na,Ca)(Li,Mg,Fe,Al)(Al,Fe)_6B_3Si_6O_{27}(O,OH,F)_4$ that consists of a complex borosilicate, fluoride, and hydroxide of aluminum, iron, magnesium, calcium, lithium, and sodium, that occurs usu. in 3-, 6-, or 9-sided prisms vertically striated but sometimes in compact or columnar masses, that is strongly dichroic, piezoelectric, and pyroelectric, that shows double refraction but absorbs one of the rays, and that makes a gem of great beauty when transparent and cut (hardness 7–7.5, sp. gr. 2.98–3.2) — compare SCHORL **2 :** a very pale green that is bluer and darker than emerald tint or microcline green and bluer and deeper than celadon tint

tourmaline pink *n* **:** a grayish purplish red that is redder, lighter, and stronger than average rose plum, bluer, lighter, and stronger than Aztec maroon, and bluer and paler than daphne pink

tourmaline tongs *n pl but sometimes sing in constr* **:** a simple form of polariscope consisting of two transparent plates of tourmaline cut parallel to the optic axis and mounted on a tongs-shaped support so that the object to be examined can be held between them and used esp. by jewelers for distinguishing glass from crystal

tour·ma·lin·ic \¦==¦linik\ *adj* **:** of the nature of or containing tourmaline

tour·ma·lin·iza·tion \ˌtu̇rmələnə'zāshən\ *n* -s [*tourmalinize* + *-ation*] **:** a process by which previously existing minerals are replaced wholly or in part by tourmaline

tour·ma·lin·ize \'tu̇rmələˌnīz\ *vt* -ED/-ING/-S [*tourmaline* + *-ize*] **:** to subject to tourmalinization

tourn \'tu̇(ə)rn\ *n* -s [AF, fr. OF *torn* circuit — more at TOUR] **1 :** the circuit or turn of an English sheriff to hold a court of record twice a year within a month after Easter and Michaelmas in every hundred in his county but abolished by the Sheriff's Act of 1887 **2 :** the court presided over by the sheriff

tour·na·ment \'tu̇rnəmənt, 'tər, 'tu̇ən, 'tə̄n-, 'təin- *sometimes* 'tō(r)n-\ *n* -s [ME *tornement, turnement,* fr. OF *torneiement,* fr. *torneier* to engage in mounted combat + *-ment* — more at TOURNEY] **1 a** (1) **:** a knightly sport originating in the middle ages in which mounted armored combatants armed usu. with blunted lances or swords and divided into two parties engaged one another to exhibit their skill, prowess, and courage and to win a prize or favor bestowed by the lady of the tournament chosen for the occasion (2) **:** the whole series of knightly sports, jousts, and tilts occurring at a particular time and place (3) **:** a modern contest in which mounted men tilt with lances at suspended rings **b :** something resembling a medieval tournament ⟨it is the ~ of open minds that settles things —William Alfred⟩ **2** *obs* **:** shock of battle **:** BATTLE, ENCOUNTER ⟨with cruel ~ the squadrons join —John Milton⟩ **3 a :** an athletic meeting comprising contests in a large number of sports **b :** an event by the military in which contests esp. adapted to military training (as artillery driving, wall scaling, wrestling) are held **c :** a trial of skill in which many contestants compete for championship in a series of elimination contests **d :** a fishing contest in which many anglers participate

tour·na·sin \'tu̇rnəsən\ *n* -s [F, fr. *tournaser* to shape pottery on the wheel, fr. *tourner* to turn, fr. OF *torner*] **:** a tool for smoothing and finishing roughly thrown pottery while it revolves on a wheel

tour·ne·dos *n, pl* **tour·ne·dos** \¦tu̇rnə¦dō\ [F, fr. *tourner* to turn (fr. OF *torner*) + *dos* back, fr. L *dorsum*] **:** a small fillet of beef usu. cut from the tip of the tenderloin and encircled by a strip of suet, salt pork, or bacon for quick cooking

tour·nee \tu̇r'nā\ *n* -s [G *tourné, tournee,* fr. F *tourné,* past part. of *tourner* to turn] **:** a game of skat in which the player turns a card from the skat as trump and can exchange two cards for the skat cards

tour·ne·for·tia \ˌtu̇rnə'fȯrshēə, -rd·ēə\ *n, cap* [NL, fr. Joseph Pitton de *Tournefort* †1708 Fr. botanist + NL *-ia*] **:** a large genus of tropical trees and shrubs (family Boraginaceae) having alternate leaves and terminal cymes of small flowers and a fruit that is a fleshy or spongy 4-celled drupe

tour·nette \(ˈ)tu̇r¦net\ *n* -s [F, fr. MF, fr. *tourner* to turn + *-ette*] **:** a horizontal revolving tablet similar to a potter's wheel on which a piece of pottery is placed for painting

tour·neur *R* tu̇r'nər, +V -'nər-; *-R* tu̇ə'nə̄, + *vowel in a word following without pause* -'nər- *or* -'nə̄ *also* -'nər\ *n* -s [F, lit., turner, fr. OF *torneeur,* fr. LL *tornator,* fr. L *tornatus* (past part. of *tornare* to turn) + *-or* — more at TURN] **:** the employee of a casino who is in charge of a roulette game and whose duties include turning the wheel

¹**tour·ney** \'tu̇rnē, 'tər-, 'tu̇ən-, 'tə̄n-, 'təin-, -ni\ *vi* **tourneyed; tourneyed; tourneying; tourneys** [ME *tourneyen,* fr. MF *tornoier, tourneier,* fr. OF, fr. *torn* lathe, circular movement — more at TOUR] **:** to perform in a tournament

²**tourney** \"\ *n* -s [ME, fr. MF *tournei,* fr. OF *tornei,* fr. *torneier* to engage in a tournament] **:** TOURNAMENT

tour·ney·er \-ēə(r)\ *n* -s [¹*tourney* + *-er*] **:** one that enters a tourney

¹**tour·ni·quet** \'tu̇rnəkət, 'tər-, 'tu̇ən-, 'tə̄n-, 'təin-, -nēk-\ *also* **tor·ni·quet** \'tō(r)n-\ *n* -s [F *tourniquet* instrument operated by turning, turnstile, tourniquet, fr. *tourner* to turn, fr. OF *torner* — more at TURN] **1 :** a device for arresting bleeding made of a bandage twisted tight usu. with a stick or of a piece of rubber tubing **2 :** TURNSTILE

²**tourniquet** \"\ *vt* -ED/-ING/-S **:** to apply a tourniquet or something resembling a tourniquet to

tour·nure \(ˈ)tu̇r¦nyu̇(ə)r\ *n* -s [F, manner in which a thing is fashioned, rounded form, bustle, fr. OF *torneüre* act of turning, rounded form, fr. ML *tornatura,* fr. L *tornatus* (past part. of *tornare* to turn) + *-ura* -ure — more at TURN] **:** BUSTLE; *sometimes* **:** the dress worn over this device

tours *pl of* TOUR, *pres 3d sing of* TOUR

tourte \'tu̇rt\ *n* -s [F, fr. OF *torte, tourte,* round loaf of bread, fr. LL *torta*] **:** TORTA 2

tourte bow \'tu̇rt-\ *n, usu cap T* [after François *Tourte* †1835 Fr. manufacturer of violin bows] **:** a violin bow made by François Tourte

¹**touse** *or* **towse** \'tau̇z\ *vb* -ED/-ING/-S [ME *-tusen, -tousen;* akin to Fris *tūsen* to pull, tear, OHG *zirzūsōn* to pull to pieces] *vt* **1 :** to pull or handle roughly **:** RACK, TEAR, WORRY **2 :** to tousle about **:** DISHEVEL ~ *vi* **:** to handle someone or something roughly **:** TUSSLE

²**touse** *or* **towse** \", 'tau̇s\ *n* -s **:** a noisy disturbance **:** ADO, FUSS

¹**tou·sle** *also* **tou·sel** *or* **tou·zle** *or* **tow·zle** *or* **tow·sle** \'tau̇zəl\ *vb* **tousled; tousled; tousling** \-z(ə)liŋ\ **tousles** [ME *touselen,* fr. *-tousen* to touse + *-len* -le] *vt* **1 :** to disorder by rough handling **:** DISHEVEL ⟨stood before the mirror arranging her hair which had been *tousled* by the wind —Thomas Wolfe⟩ **2 :** to indulge in tussling or horseplay with **:** pull or drag here and there ~ *vi* **:** to throw things into disorder **:** become disheveled ⟨full-cut hair ~*s* over his forehead and sideburns frame his . . . face —*Time*⟩

²**tousle** \", *in sense 1* 'tüzəl\ *n* -s **1** *Scot* **:** rough dalliance **:** TUSSLE **2 :** a tangled mass **:** disordered state ⟨~ of auburn curls —J.W.Vandercook⟩ ⟨the church . . . surrounded by a ~ of half-grown pines —Ruth Park⟩

tousled *adj* [fr. past part. of ¹*tousle*] **:** having a disheveled appearance **:** all tumbled together **:** extremely disordered ⟨his brown hair was ~, thick, and curly —Al Spiers⟩ ⟨a bed with the clothes ~ on it, a quilt . . . on the floor by the bed —Liam O'Flaherty⟩

tous-les-mois \ˌtülə'mwä\ *n* [F dial., by folk etymology (influence of F *tous les mois* all the months, every month) fr. F *tolomane,* fr. native name in West Indies] **:** starch from rootstocks of the edible canna often sold as arrowroot and used esp. in the preparation of foods for infants

tou·sly \'tau̇z(ə)lē\ *adj* -ER/-EST [¹*tousle* + *-y*] **:** TOUSLED

to usward *adv* [ME — more at USWARD] **:** USWARD ⟨the Lord . . . is long-suffering *to usward* —2 Pet 3:9 (ASV)⟩

tousy \'tüzi\ *adj* [¹*touse* + *-y*] **1** *chiefly Scot* **:** disheveled looking **:** TOUSLED **2** *chiefly Scot* **:** MAKESHIFT **:** ROUGH-AND-READY ⟨pretending you never took a ~ tea —Neil Munro⟩

¹**tout** \'tau̇t, *usu* -au̇d·+V\ *vb* -ED/-ING/-S [ME *tuten;* akin to OE *tōtian* to stick out, protrude, Norw *tyte* to stick out, ooze out, Fris *tūte* pipe, spout, snout] *vi* **1 :** to canvass for customers **:** solicit patronage **:** urge with annoying persistence ⟨peeled potatoes . . . and when otherwise unoccupied ~*ed* for custom from the passersby —E.M.Lustgarten⟩ **2 a** *chiefly Brit* **:** to spy out the movements of racehorses at their trials or to get by stealth or other improper means the secrets of the stable for betting purposes **b :** to give a tip on a racehorse ~ *vt* **1 :** to spy on **:** watch closely ⟨candidates are ~*ed* for possible political faux pas⟩ **2 a** *Brit* **:** to spy out information about (as a racing stable or horse) **b :** to give a tip on (a racehorse) to a bettor with the expectation of sharing in his winnings **3 :** to solicit importunately ⟨supplied the ideas and ~*ed* . . . businessmen for orders —Geoffrey Household⟩ **:** peddle in an annoyingly persistent manner ⟨the old woman of eighty who ~*ed Faris-Soir* . . . from café to café —Bruce Marshall⟩

²**tout** \"\ *n* -s **1 :** one that touts: as **a :** one who solicits custom ⟨tourists . . . besieged by ~*s* for tailoring and other establishments —H.R.Lieberman⟩ **b** *chiefly Brit* **:** one who secretly watches racehorses in training or gets racing information by improper means for betting purposes **c :** one who gives a tip on a racehorse for an expected compensation but esp. in hopes of a share in the winnings **2 :** the act of touting **:** LOOKOUT, WATCH ⟨a pickpocket on the ~ for a careless stroller⟩

³**tout** \'tau̇t, 'tüt\ *vt* -ED/-ING/-S [origin unknown] *Scot* **:** to tease in a vexing manner

⁴**tout** \'tau̇t\ *n* -s *chiefly Scot* **:** a slight illness

⁵**tout** \'tau̇t *also* 'tüt, *usu* -d·+V\ *vt* -ED/-ING/-S [alter. (perh. influenced by ¹*tout*) of ³*toot*] **:** to proclaim loudly **:** overly publicize **:** BALLYHOO ⟨~*ed* as the world's most elaborate suburban shopping development —*Wall Street Jour.*⟩ ⟨work is ~*ed* as the basic virtue —H.H.Mansfield⟩

tout·er \'tau̇d·ə(r)\ *n* -s [¹*tout* + *-er*] **:** ²TOUT

to·var·ia \tə'va(a)rēə\ *n, cap* [NL, fr. Simón *Tovario,* 18th cent. Span. physician + NL *-ia*] **:** a small genus (coextensive with the family Tovariaceae of the order Rhoeadales) of tropical American herbs having trifoliolate leaves and spicate flowers peculiar in having the sepals, petals, and stamens each eight while the gynoecium is composed of six carpels — **to·var·i·a·ceous** \tə¦va(a)rē¦āshəs\ *adj*

to·va·rich *or* **to·va·rish** \tə'värish, tō'-, -rēsh\ *n* -ES [Russ *tovarishch,* of Turkic origin] **1 :** COMRADE **2 :** an inhabitant of the Soviet Union

tove \'tōv\ *vi* -ED/-ING/-S [origin unknown] *Scot* **:** to smoke or emit a smoky smell

¹**tow** \'tō\ *vb* -ED/-ING/-S [ME *towen,* fr. OE *togian;* akin to OHG *zogōn* to tow, ON *toga;* akin to OE *tēon* to draw, pull, OHG *ziohan,* Goth *tiuhan* to draw, pull, L *ducere* to lead, draw, Gk *daidussesthai* to drag, Alb *nduk* to pull out, pluck] *vt* **1 :** to drag or pull along **:** HAUL, PROPEL ⟨tightening his hold on her wrist, he started through the . . . door, ~*ing* her along with him —Richard Burke⟩ ⟨men . . . ~*ed* and tugged by a perpetually retreating objective —Claud Cockburn⟩ **2 a :** to draw (as a ship or a disabled car) or pull along behind by a rope or chain ⟨~*ed* her into dry dock for repairs⟩ ⟨~*ed* the wrecked auto to the nearest garage⟩ ⟨a transport plane ~*ing* gliders⟩ ⟨more efficient for a tug to ~ the ship —*N. Y. Times*⟩ **b :** to push along (as a string of canal or river barges) — used of a powerboat behind a tow ~ *vi* **:** to move in tow ⟨piloting a ship that was ~*ing* into the river —Archie Binns⟩ ⟨riding out of town with a couple of pack ponies ~*ing* along behind him —H.L.Davis⟩ **syn** see PULL

²**tow** \"\ *n* -s *often attrib* **1 :** a rope or chain for towing ⟨coal barges . . . snapped their ~ in a storm —Joseph Mitchell⟩ **2 a :** the act or an instance of towing ⟨took a ~ for the last few miles —Alan Villiers⟩ **b :** the fact or state of being towed ⟨a damaged ship . . . in the ~ of a tug —E.L.Beach⟩ **3 :** something towed: as **a :** a boat or barge in tow or requiring towing **b :** a string of barges lashed together and pushed (as on the Mississippi river and tributaries) by a towboat ⟨watched the other ~ pass, the barges looming up in the night, and then the towboat —Richard Bissell⟩ ⟨puffing tugs with ~*s* of logs —*Amer. Guide Series: Wash.*⟩ ⟨flying the left glider in our ~ —J.W.Bellah⟩ **4 a :** something that tows (as a towboat or tugboat) ⟨two diesel-powered, screw-driven ~*s* —*Time*⟩ **b :** SKI TOW **5 :** the specimens taken in a townet ⟨sorting out the desired food from a plankton ~ —*Ecology*⟩ — **in tow** *adv* **1 :** in the state of being towed (as by a towline or towboat) ⟨passed a wrecker with a station wagon *in tow*⟩ **2 a :** under guidance or protection ⟨glad enough in such circumstances to be taken *in tow* by a friendly native⟩ **b :** in the character or position of a dependent, devoted, or subservient follower or admirer ⟨came round to see her with his latest protégé *in tow*⟩ ⟨kept him *in tow* . . . nearly six months —Dorothy Sayers⟩ ⟨a Navy officer passed with a good-looking girl *in tow* —Martin Dibner⟩

³**tow** \"\ *n* -s *often attrib* [ME, fr. OE *tow-* spinning; akin to ON *tō* tuft of wool for spinning, Goth *taui* work, doing, *taujan* to make, do — more at TAW] **1 :** short broken fiber removed from flax, hemp, or jute during scutching or hackling and used for yarn, twine, stuffing **2 :** HURDS **3 :** yarn or cloth made of tow — usu. used attributively ⟨~ trousers⟩ ⟨~ sack⟩ **4 :** a loose untwisted rope of textile filaments that is suitable for cutting into staple fiber ⟨rayon ~⟩

⁴**tow** \"\ *n* -s [ME (Sc), prob. fr. OE *toh-* (in *tohlīne* towline); akin to ON *tog, taug* rope, line, tow, OE *tēag* rope, cord, *togian* to tow — more at ¹TOW] **1** *archaic* **:** an attached iron chain or link for drawing a plow **2** *chiefly Scot & dial Eng* **:** ROPE: as **a :** a rope attached to a bell **b :** a ship's rope **c :** CABLE **d :** HANGMAN'S HALTER

towa \'tōə\ *n, pl* **towa** *or* **towas** *usu cap* **:** the language of the Jemez group of Pueblo Indians

tow·abil·i·ty \ˌtōə'biləd·ē\ *n* **:** the quality or state of being towable ⟨air transportability and ~ characteristics —*Aero Digest*⟩

tow·able \'tōəbəl\ *adj* **:** capable of being towed

tow·age \'tōij, -ōēj\ *n* -s *often attrib* [¹*tow* + *-age*] **1 :** the act or process of towing ⟨tugs available for deep-sea ~⟩ ⟨~ service⟩ ⟨~ fees⟩ **2 :** the price paid for towing

to·wai \'tōˌwī\ *n* -s [Maori] **:** KAMAHI

tow·an \'tau̇ən\ *n* -s [Corn] *dial Eng* **:** DUNE 1

¹**toward** \'t|ō(ə)rd, |ȯ(ə)rd, |ōəd, |ȯ(ə)d *also* 'tw| *or* tə'wȯ(ə)rd *or* tə'wȯ(ə)d\ *adj* [*toward* fr. ME, fr. OE *tōweard* facing, approaching, imminent, fr. *tō,* prep., to + *-weard* -ward; *towards* fr. ME *towardes,* alter. (influenced by *towardes,* prep., toward) of *toward* — more at TO] **1** *also* **towards a :** being about to take place **:** coming soon **:** being prepared ⟨could waddle fast enough if a meal was ~ —Kylie Tennant⟩ ⟨we have a trifling foolish banquet *towards* —Shak.⟩ **b** *obs* **:** threatening to happen **:** IMMINENT ⟨have you heard of no likely wars ~ —Shak.⟩ **c :** happening at the moment **:** AFOOT ⟨saw that there was a jest ~ and joined in —Charles Kingsley⟩ **d :** being planned or plotted — used predicatively ⟨the Governments . . . were privy to what was ~ —Hilaire Belloc⟩ **2 a** *obs* **:** quick to learn **:** APT, PROMISING ⟨spoken like a ~ prince —Shak.⟩ **b** *obs* **:** WELL-DISPOSED, AMIABLE, OBLIGING ⟨hath hitherto been very tractable and ~ —Richard Steele⟩ **c :** FAVORING, PROPITIOUS ⟨a ~ breeze⟩

²**toward** \"\ *or* **towards** \-dz\ *prep* [*toward* fr. ME, fr. OE *tōweard,* adv. & prep., fr. *tōweard,* adj.; *towards* fr. ME *towardes,* fr. OE *tōweardes,* alter. (influence of *-es* -s, gen. suffix) of *tōweard,* adj.] **1 a :** in the direction of **:** to a point approaching ⟨driving ~ town⟩ ⟨troops heading ~ the front⟩ ⟨comes ~ me —Willa Cather⟩ ⟨watch him lean over the dresser ~ the . . . mirror —R.P.Warren⟩ **b** *obs* **:** TO 1a(1) ⟨shall we ~ the Tower —Shak.⟩ **2 a :** along a course leading to **:** with a view to gaining **:** to the end or purpose of ⟨a long stride ~ disarmament⟩ ⟨a tendency ~ mischief⟩ ⟨the pressure ~ conformity⟩ ⟨looking ~ a mastery of the technique⟩ ⟨working ~ his doctorate⟩ ⟨beginnings ~ the formation of his own philosophy of life —H.F.West⟩ ⟨~ the goal of uniting all men of good will —*Harper's*⟩ **b :** in relation to **:** in the treatment or handling of ⟨an attitude ~ life⟩ ⟨measures taken ~ the colonies⟩ ⟨impartiality ~ the two —A.C.Sedgwick⟩ ⟨with malice ~ none —Abraham Lincoln⟩ ⟨the bias of many economists ~ government intervention —E.L.Dale⟩ ⟨an emotional block ~ mathematics —P.B.Sears⟩ **c** *usu* **towards :** in comparison with **:** with respect to ⟨how does it stand *towards* my past —Thomas Hardy⟩ **d :** in sympathy or affection for ⟨felt drawn ~ her without knowing why⟩ **e :** in tolerance for **:** in the presence of ⟨sensitized ~ tuberculin⟩ ⟨stable ~ . . . alkalies and solvents —H.J.Wolfe⟩ **3 a :** at a point in the direction of **:** NEAR ⟨took a cottage somewhere up ~ the Cape⟩ ⟨out ~ the blue-black ocean —William Beebe⟩ **b :** in such a position as to face **:** presented to **:** FACING ⟨pass the knife with the handle ~ the diner⟩ ⟨his back was ~ me⟩ ⟨lower left with face ~ camera —*N. Y. Times*⟩ ⟨with its northern outlook ~ the . . . Mountains —*Amer. Guide Series: N. H.*⟩ **4 :** at a time not long before **:** just prior to ⟨~ the end of the presidential campaign⟩ ⟨~ the dinner hour⟩ ⟨one afternoon ~ sundown —G.M. Smith⟩ **5 a :** in the way of help or assistance in **:** in furtherance of ⟨apply them ~ the solution of particular problems —W.L.Howard⟩ ⟨would do what he could ~ getting supper ready —W.D.Steele⟩ **b :** for the partial payment of **:** in defraying the costs of ⟨credited ~ the cost of your flight —Richard Joseph⟩ ⟨proceeds go ~ the provision of a scholarship⟩ **6** *obs* **:** in view or in store for ⟨something good was ~ me —Henry Fielding⟩ **7** *usu* **towards :** on the verge of **:** ABOUT, APPROXIMATELY ⟨there are *towards* six hundred persons —Edmund Burke⟩

toward·li·ness \-dlēnəs\ *n* -ES *archaic* **:** the quality or state of being toward or towardly: as **a :** APTNESS, PROMISE **b :** DOCILITY

¹**toward·ly** *adv* [ME, fr. ¹*toward* + *-ly* (adv. suffix)] *archaic* **:** in a towardly manner: as **a :** PROMISINGLY ⟨my scholars go ~ forward —Thomas Morley⟩ **b :** DOCILELY, OBLIGINGLY ⟨our friends will not behave ~ —William Penn⟩

²**towardly** *adj* [¹*toward* + *-ly,* adj. suffix] **1** *archaic* **:** likely to be favorable **:** ADVANTAGEOUS, PROPITIOUS ⟨choose a ~ hour —*Athenaeum*⟩ **2 :** developing favorably **:** PROMISING ⟨a child of ~ parts for her age —Jonathan Swift⟩ **3 a** *obs* **:** easily managed **:** DOCILE, OBLIGING **b :** favorably disposed **:** PLEASANT, AFFABLE ⟨she was very ~ and lenient in her behavior; she led him on to make pleasantries, and then applauded him —R.L.Stevenson⟩

towardness *n* -ES [ME *towardnesse,* fr. ¹*toward* + *-nesse* -ness] *obs* **:** the quality or state of being toward

towards \-dz\ *adv* [ME *towardes,* fr. *towardes,* adj., toward] *archaic* **:** FORWARD, ONWARD

towboat \'=,=\ *n* [¹*tow* + *boat*] **1 :** TUGBOAT **2 :** PUSH BOAT; *specif* **:** a compact usu. diesel-powered shallow-draft boat that is highly maneuverable by one-man controls and is equipped with squared bow and towing knees to enable it to push tows of barges on inland waterways

tow bug *n* [³*tow;* fr. its infestation of furniture upholstered in tow, flax, or straw] **:** CIGARETTE BEETLE

tow car *or* **tow truck** *n* **:** WRECKER 2b(3)

tow cloth *or* **tow linen** *n* **:** a coarse heavy linen in 18th century use for clothing — compare ³TOW 3

towed *past of* TOW

¹**towel** \'tau̇(ə)l\ *n* -s [ME *towele, towaille,* fr. OF *toaille,* of Gmc origin; akin to OS *thwahila, twahila* towel, MD *dwale, dwele,* OHG *dwahila, dwehila;* akin to OE *thwēal* washing, *thwēan* to wash, OHG *dwahan,* ON *thvā,* Goth *thwahan* to wash, OPruss *twaxtan* bath cloth] **1 :** a piece of absorbent cloth or paper often rectangular in shape for wiping or drying ⟨a bath ~⟩ ⟨a dish ~⟩ **2** *obs* **a :** NAPKIN 1 **b :** a piece of cloth used as a turban or sash **c :** VESPERAL 2 **d :** a cloth held by acolytes or spread over the rails before communicants during the celebration of the Eucharist

²**towel** \"\ *vb* **towelled** *also* **towelled; toweled** *also* **towelled; toweling** *also* **towelling** \-au̇(ə)liŋ\ **towels** *vt* **:** to rub or dry (as the body) with a towel ⟨~*ing* hard my hair, face, and the back of my neck —Joseph Conrad⟩ ⟨got out of the bath, ~*ed* herself dry —Aldous Huxley⟩ ~ *vi* **:** to use a towel

towel gourd *n* **:** DISHCLOTH GOURD

towel horse *n* **:** TOWEL RACK

toweling *also* **towelling** *n* -s **:** any of various absorbent fabrics used for making towels; *esp* **:** a fabric made of cotton or linen in any of various weaves and often woven in narrow widths with colored borders

towel rack *n* **:** a small rack with bars for hanging or drying towels (as in a kitchen or bathroom)

[1]**tow·er** \'tau̇(ə)r, 'tau̇ə, *esp in southern U.S.* 'tau̇wə(r\ *n* -s *often attrib* [ME *tour, tur, tor,* fr. OE *torr* & OF *tor, tur,* both fr. L *turris,* fr. Gk *tyrris, tyrsis*] **1 a :** a building or structure designed primarily for elevation that is higher than its diameter and high relative to its surroundings, that may stand apart (as a round tower, campanile, or pagoda), be attached (as a church belfry) to a larger structure, or project above or out from a wall, and that may be of skeleton framework (as an observation or transmission tower) **b :** such a structure used as a defense **:** CITADEL, FORTRESS **c :** a fortified prison **d :** a medieval engine of war for storming operations consisting of a tower on wheels having several platforms with the lowest sometimes occupied by a battering ram and the highest by soldiers (as archers and men with scaling ladders) **2 :** a structure or mass in the form of or resembling a tower: as **a :** a building for housing the mechanism (as levers) for operating the switches and signals of a railroad **:** SWITCH TOWER **b** (1) **:** FIRE TOWER 1 (2) **:** WATER TOWER 2 (3) **:** DRILL TOWER **c :** CONTROL TOWER **d :** a high office or apartment building **:** SKYSCRAPER ⟨the new owners of that uptown office ~ —*N. Y. Herald Tribune*⟩ **e :** a very high formation or pile (as of rock) **f :** a vertical structure of varying height through which gases or liquids are passed esp. to be purified, dried, fractionated, or absorbed — compare BUBBLE TOWER, COLUMN 3d, GLOVER TOWER, PLATE TOWER **g :** a structure on an elephant's back — compare HOWDAH **h :** a heraldic representation of a round tower closely resembling in form a modern rook in chess — compare CASTLE 6 **i :** [1]TOUR 4 **3 a :** one that provides support or protection **:** BULWARK, PILLAR ⟨thou hast been a shelter for me and a strong ~ from the enemy —Ps 61:3 (AV)⟩ — usu. used in the phrase *tower of strength* ⟨the king's name is a ~ of strength —Shak.⟩ ⟨has been a veritable ~ of strength in the affairs of this club —W.F.Brown b. 1903⟩ **b :** a place of refuge (as for contemplation or for avoidance of worldly problems) **:** RETREAT, SANCTUARY ⟨the only escape from this anguish of dissatisfaction was to ascend into those ~*s* of indifference —P.E. More⟩ ⟨content to stay within theology's safe academic ~ —*Newsweek*⟩ — compare IVORY TOWER **4 :** the high flight of a bird (as a hawk or eagle) **:** SOAR ⟨the peak of the ~⟩; *esp* **:** the steep flight upward of a wounded game bird

tower 1a

[2]**tower** \"\ *vb* -ED/-ING/-S [ME *towren, torren,* fr. *towr, tor* tower] *vi* **1 a :** to reach to a great height **:** RISE ⟨spires ~*ing* in the distance⟩ ⟨a great column of black smoke . . . ~*ing* up —Nevil Shute⟩ ⟨the powdered coiffures . . . ~*ed* as much as a yard high —Lois Long⟩ ⟨one moment he ~*ed* in imagination, the next he groveled in fear —G.D.Brown⟩ **b :** to rise above the surroundings **:** surpass others **:** OVERSHADOW — used with *above* or *over* ⟨the great forests ~*ed* above the toiling men and women —W.P.Webb⟩ ⟨~ above all the rest in vigor and height of intellect —Joshua Whatmough⟩ **2 a :** to fly high before swooping **:** SOAR ⟨the raven . . . ~*ed* steeply up from the rocks —Farley Mowat⟩ — used esp. of a hawk; compare STOOP **b :** to fly vertically upward before falling — used of a wounded game bird ⟨had another bird which ~*ed* —T.H.White b. 1906⟩ ~ *vt* **1** *archaic* **:** to raise aloft **:** lift up **:** ELEVATE ⟨gigantic trees . . . ~*ed* their lofty heads to the clouds —W.S.Mayo⟩ **2** *obs* **:** to soar into ⟨rising on stiff pennons ~ the mid aerial sky —John Milton⟩ **syn** see RISE

[3]**tow·er** \'tō(ə)r\ *n* -s [[3]*tow* + *-er*] **:** one that smooths ceramic ware with tow

tower bolt *n* **:** an esp. heavy sliding door bolt

tower clock *n* **1 :** a clock in a tower **2 :** TURRET CLOCK

tower cress *n* **:** a European cress (*Arabis turrita*) having stiff erect stems

towered *adj* [ME *toured,* fr. *tour* tower + *-ed* — more at TOWER] **:** having a tower **:** adorned or defended by towers ⟨a ~ church⟩ ⟨~ battlements⟩ ⟨~ cities please us then —John Milton⟩

tower house *n* **1 :** a medieval fortified castle (as in England and Scotland) **2 :** [1]TOWER 2a

[1]**towering** *adj* [fr. pres. part. of [2]*tower*] **1 a :** rising to a great height **:** IMPOSING ⟨the ~ pines⟩ ⟨the ~ structure of American prosperity —F.L.Allen⟩ **b :** impressively great **:** extremely high in relation to others **:** SURPASSING ⟨a figure of ~ prestige —R.H.Rovere⟩ **2 :** reaching a high point of intensity or violence **:** OVERWHELMING ⟨a ~ passion⟩ ⟨a ~ rage⟩ ⟨his superb and ~ contempt for his guilty stepfather —G.B.Shaw⟩ **3 :** going beyond proper bounds **:** EXCESSIVE, OVERWEENING ⟨~ ambitions⟩ ⟨a ~ poet's pride —William Cowper⟩

[2]**towering** *n* -s [fr. gerund of [2]*tower*] **:** a mirage in which objects some distance away appear to be stretched vertically to unnatural heights

tow·er·ing·ly *adv* **:** in a towering manner: as **a :** at a great height **:** LOFTILY ⟨elms standing ~ in the yard⟩ **b :** with great intensity **:** VIOLENTLY ⟨~ wrathful⟩

towerlike \'ˌ=ˌ=\ *adj* **:** resembling a tower

tow·er·man \'=mən\ *n, pl* **towermen :** one who attends to or works in a tower: as **a :** one employed in a railroad switch tower to control and direct the movement of cars and trains **b :** one who erects and maintains electric-power transmission towers **c :** FIRE LOOKOUT **d :** one who fills towers with limestone to be used in preparing acid for cooking wood chips in pulp making and papermaking

tower mustard *n* **1 :** a widely distributed cress (*Arabis glabra*) **2 :** TOWER CRESS

tower of babel *often cap T&B* **:** BABEL

tower of ivory : IVORY TOWER

tower of silence : a circular stone wall having a height of 20 to 30 feet and an outside circumference of 200 to 270 feet on which the Parsis expose their dead to vultures — called also *dakhma*

tower owl *n, Brit* **:** BARN OWL

tower pound *n, often cap T* [so called fr. the standard pound kept in the Tower of London] **:** a pound of 5400 grains or 349.91 grams **:** the legal mint pound of England before 1527

towers *pl of* TOWER, *pres 3d sing of* TOWER

tower shell *n* **:** SCREW SHELL

tower shooting *n* **:** shooting at targets that are thrown from a trap mounted on an elevated place (as a high tower) to appear from overhead at a height of at least 40 feet

tower silo *n* **:** a tall cylindrical silo built above ground of masonry, wood, or enameled steel

tower skull *also* **tower head** *n* **:** OXYCEPHALY

tower telescope *n* **:** a long-focus telescope designed for observation of the sun that is set vertically and fed by a coelostat and mirror

tower wagon *n* **:** a wagon or motor truck with a high adjustable platform on which workmen can stand (as when repairing overhead wires or cleaning and replacing streetlights)

tow·ery \'tau̇(ə)rē\ *adj, sometimes* -ER/-EST **1 :** having towers **:** TOWERED ⟨~ city⟩ **2 :** LOFTY, TOWERING ⟨~ trees⟩

towhead \'ˌ=ˌ=\ *n* [[3]*tow* + *head*] **1 a :** a head of hair resembling tow esp. in being flaxen or tousled **b :** a person having such a head of hair **2** *Midland & South* **:** a low alluvial island or shoal in a river **:** SANDBAR; *esp* **:** such a sandbar having clusters of cottonwoods on it ⟨paddled over to the ~ and hid in the cottonwoods —Mark Twain⟩ — **towheaded** \'ˌ=ˌ==\ *adj*

tow·hee \tə'(h)wē, -'hē, 'tō,hē\ *also* **towhee bunting** *n* -s [*towhee* imit.] **:** any of numerous American finches (genera *Pipilo* and *Chlorura*); *esp* **:** a common finch (*P. erythrophthalmus*) of eastern No. America having the male black, white, and rufous and the female with brown instead of black — called also *chewink;* see CALIFORNIA TOWHEE, GREEN-TAILED TOWHEE

tow·ie \'tōē\ *n* -s [origin unknown] **:** contract bridge for three or more and usu. up to six players in which three play at one time and are replaced in turn after each hand by one of the inactive players if any and in which the players bid for the dummy hand after six cards of it have been exposed and play each for himself with no permanent partnerships

towing *n* -s [fr. gerund of [1]*tow*] **1 :** TOWAGE 1 **2 :** [2]TOW 5

towing basin *or* **towing tank** *also* **tow tank** *n* **:** a long open tank filled with water through which models of ship or seaplane hulls or floats are towed to test their hydrodynamic characteristics

towing bridle *n* **1 :** a bridle with a hook in the center to which a towline is fastened when two boats are towed abreast **2 :** a length of wire hawser for passing around part of a ship's structure (as an after turret) to the ends of which the towing hawser may be connected by a set of shackles

towing light *n* **:** one of the two or more white lights depending on the number of craft being towed that are carried in a vertical line by a steamer towing other ships

towing net *var of* TOWNET

towing path *var of* TOWPATH

towing post *or* **towing timber** *n* **:** a heavy timber on deck for attaching a towline **:** BITT 1

towing sleeve *n* **:** SLEEVE TARGET

towing spar *n* **:** FOG BUOY 2

tow iron *n* **:** a harpoon with a towline attached

to wit *adv* [ME *to witen,* lit., to know — more at WIT] **:** that is to say **:** NAMELY, SCILICET, VIDELICET — often used to enumerate and call attention to particular matters embraced in more general preceding language ⟨the prime cause of dissatisfaction at all times and in all countries, *to wit,* poverty —G.W. Johnson⟩

to within *prep* **1** — used as a function word to indicate direction and movement to and somewhat past a point or to the outer limits of and some distance into a space ⟨jumped *to within* ½ inch of the record⟩ ⟨drove *to within* 50 yards of the green⟩ **2** — used as a function word to indicate duration up to and somewhat past a point in time ⟨worked hard *to within* five minutes of closing time⟩

towline \'ˌ=ˌ=\ *n* **:** a line (as a rope, cable, or hawser) used in towing (as a boat or automobile); *specif* **:** a line attached to an iron or harpoon by which a whaleboat is made fast to and often towed by a whale

tow linen *var of* TOW CLOTH

tow·man \'tōmən\ *n, pl* **towmen :** a garage worker who tows disabled vehicles

tow·mond \'tau̇mənd\ *or* **tow·mont** \-nt\ *n* -s [ME (Sc) *towlmonth,* fr. OE *twelf mōnath,* fr. *twelf* twelve + *mōnath* month — more at TWELVE, MONTH] *Scot* **:** TWELVEMONTH, YEAR

town \'tau̇n\ *n* -s *often attrib* [ME *town, toun,* fr. OE *tūn* enclosure, manor, village, town; akin to OHG *zūn* enclosure, fence, ON *tūn* hedge, enclosure, OIr *dūn* fortress] **1 a :** the usu. enclosed estate of a feudal lord including the chief dwelling (as a castle) and the community living in villenage around it **:** MANOR 2 **b** *Scot* **:** a farmhouse with its accompanying land and buildings **:** FARMSTEAD **2** *dial Eng* **:** a cluster or aggregation of houses recognized as a distinct place **:** a settlement with a place-name **:** VILLAGE, HAMLET **3 :** a place that is a population and business center and is so recognized geographically and politically: as **a :** a compactly settled area of any size as distinguished from surrounding rural territory **b :** a compactly settled area usu. larger than a village but smaller than a city in population and usu. incorporated and given definite boundaries and powers by law **:** a small municipality **c :** a large densely populated urban area; *specif* **:** CITY **d :** an English village without urban characteristics or the status of an episcopal see but having a periodic fair or market **:** MARKET TOWN **e :** an incorporated municipal unit in a Canadian province or an Australian state varying in population but usu. smaller than a city **4 a :** the particular town or city under consideration — usu. used without an article ⟨walked to the outskirts of ~⟩ ⟨new arrivals in ~⟩ ⟨was out of ~ all last week⟩ ⟨when the circus comes to ~⟩ ⟨left ~ in a hurry⟩ **b :** the capital city of a country (as London, England) ⟨aristocracy from every shire flocking to ~ for the coronation⟩ **c :** the neighboring large city **:** METROPOLIS ⟨commute daily to ~⟩ ⟨have an apartment in ~⟩ **d :** the business center of a city **:** DOWNTOWN ⟨parked on a residential street and walked the few blocks into ~⟩ ⟨a physician with an office at home and another in ~⟩ **e :** a section or district of a city characterized in some specified way (as by location, age, or inhabitants) ⟨the upper ~⟩ ⟨the old ~⟩ ⟨the French ~⟩ **5 :** the city as contrasted with the country **:** urban life — usu. used with *the* ⟨God made the country, and man made the ~ —William Cowper⟩ ⟨a poet not of nature but of the ~⟩ **6 a :** the citizens or inhabitants of a city or town **:** PUBLIC ⟨went to a number of plays that were drawing the ~ —W.S.Maugham⟩ **b :** the qualified voters of a town **:** ELECTORATE, CITIZENRY ⟨the ~ elects two representatives⟩ **c :** the governing officials of a town acting on behalf of the town as a corporation or of the whole body of inhabitants **d :** the townspeople of a college or university town that constitute a group distinct from and often antithetical to the academic community ⟨the usual battle between *Town* and Gown was developing, with clubs and quarterstaves as the weapons —T.B.Costain⟩ — compare GOWN 2b **e** *archaic* **:** the fashionable society of a city ⟨this vast universal Fool, the *Town* —John Dryden⟩ **7 :** a territorial area having the status of a unit of local government: as **a :** one of a number of territorial units into which the area of a New England state is divided usu. containing both rural and unincorporated urban areas under a single town government but sometimes containing or coterminous with an incorporated city or borough — called also *township* **b :** a territorial unit in a state (as New York) outside New England that usu. contains not only rural and unincorporated urban areas but also one or more incorporated villages or other municipal units **c :** TOWNSHIP 4b **8 :** a unit of local government found chiefly in the New England states constituting a municipal corporation or under broad grants from the state legislature exercising most of the powers of a municipal corporation and having a governmental structure in which the legislative power is exercised by the town meeting and administration is entrusted to a board of selectmen and other officials **9 :** something felt to resemble a town: as **a :** a collection of burrows of the prairie dog **b :** an aggregation of nests of penguins — **on the town** *adv (or adj)* **1** *also* **upon the town :** supported by poor relief provided by the town or parish **:** DESTITUTE ⟨a family *on the town* after the father's death⟩ **2 :** in carefree and often roving rollicking pursuit of the pleasures and diversions available (as in the night life of a big city) often in a spirit of welcome relief or abandon after a period of constraint or routine **:** out for a good time **:** footloose and fancy-free ⟨hired a baby-sitter and went out *on the town*⟩ ⟨a bunch of sailors *on the town* —Maxwell Griffith⟩ ⟨had decided to go out *on the town* . . . to all the dives —Dawn Powell⟩

town ball *n* [so called fr. the fact that it was played at the time of town meetings] **:** a ball game preceding and resembling baseball ⟨at recesses and at noon, we played . . . *town ball* and baseball —W.A.White⟩ — compare ROUNDER 3a

town car *n* **:** a 4-door automobile with a permanently enclosed passenger compartment in the rear separated from the driver's compartment by a sliding glass partition

town clerk *n* [ME *tounclerk,* fr. *toun* town + *clerk*] **1 :** a public officer charged with keeping the records (as marriage licenses and vital statistics) of a town and entering the official proceedings of its government **2 :** the secretary to the corporation, legal adviser, and chief administrative officer of a British local government (as of a town, borough, or city)

town crier *n* **:** a town officer who makes proclamations **:** CRIER b

town economy *n* **:** the stage or system in economic history in which the center of trade and commerce is a town (as a medieval walled town) with a distinct merchant class and considerable division of labor

town·ee \(')tau̇'nē\ *n* -s [*town* + *-ee*] **:** TOWNSMAN ⟨~*s* . . . who have had little more than an academic interest in agrarian questions —*Atlantic*⟩

town end *or* **town's end** *n* [ME] *dial* **:** one of the ends of a town or village street or road

town·er \'tau̇nə(r)\ *n* -s *slang* **:** a town or city dweller **:** TOWNSMAN ⟨the streets were crawling with people — ~*s* and visiting country cousins —Bill Ballantine⟩ — used esp. by circus troupes of the local citizenry ⟨the circus people, clannish and ever suspicious of ~*s* —Al Hine⟩

townet \'ˌ=ˌ=\ *or* **towing net** *n* **:** a fine-meshed net usu. much tapered and more or less conical in shape and kept open by a ring or hoop that is towed through water (as for the taking of plankton)

town·gate \'tün,gāt, 'tau̇n-\ *n* [*town* + *gate* (way, street)] **:** the main street of a town

town hall *n* [ME] **1 a :** the chief public building of a town used for public offices and for meetings (as of the town council and the courts) **b :** a large hall for public assemblies **2 :** GUILDHALL

town house *n* **1 :** a house in town as distinguished from a house in the country ⟨there was a smart *town house* and a rococo summer estate —Harriot B. Barbour⟩; *specif* **:** the city residence of one having a countryseat or having a chief residence elsewhere ⟨stayed at their *town house* for a few weeks during the social season⟩ **2** *usu* **townhouse** \'ˌ=ˌ=\ *chiefly Brit* **:** TOWN HALL 1

townier *comparative of* TOWNY

townies *pl of* TOWNY

towniest *superlative of* TOWNY

town·i·fy \'tau̇nə,fī\ *vt* -ED/-ING/-ES [*town* + *-ify*] **1 :** to cause to become urban ⟨a pleasant little village rapidly being *townified*⟩ **2 :** to stamp with the characteristics of the town or city or of urban life ⟨the long *townified* dress she'd put on —Christopher Isherwood⟩

town·i·ness \-nēnəs\ *n* -ES **:** the quality or state of being towny

town·ish \'tau̇nish\ *adj* [ME *townisch,* fr. *town* + *-isch* -ish] **1 :** of, relating to, or characteristic of a town or city or of the manners and style of urban life **:** appropriate for town or city **:** TOWNY ⟨the fabric . . . is definitely ~ —*N. Y. Times Mag.*⟩ **2 :** having the outlook or manners of a city-bred person ⟨always thought of myself as a ~ character⟩

town·ish·ly *adv* **:** in a townish manner

town·ish·ness *n* -ES **:** the quality or state of being townish

town·land \-nlənd\ *n, Irish* **:** a section of land constituted like a township as part of a parish ⟨looks after a ~ of 79 acres —J.M.Mogey⟩

town·let \-lət\ *n* -s **:** a small town ⟨this sleepy little ~ —Francis Ofner⟩

town library *n* **:** a public library serving a town and supported in whole or in part by public funds

town·ly *adj, archaic* **:** TOWNISH ⟨one of your ~ ladies —Henry Fielding⟩

town major *n* **:** an officer of a British garrison having the general supervision of good order (as in an occupied city during military operations)

town·man \-nmən\ *n, pl* **townmen** [ME *toun man,* fr. OE *tūnman* villager, fr. *tūn* town + *man* — more at TOWN] **:** TOWNSMAN 1

town manager *n* **:** an official appointed by the annual town meeting or by the selectmen to direct the administration of a town government

town mark *n* **:** a postmark showing the name of the town where mail has been stamped

town meeting *n* **:** a legal meeting of the inhabitants or taxpayers of a town entitled to vote on town matters for the transaction of public or governmental business

town order *n* **:** a nonnegotiable warrant approved by an auditor of a town (as in Maine) directing the treasurer to pay a specified sum of money to a designated person

town plan *n* **:** CITY PLAN

towns *pl of* TOWN

town·scape \'tau̇nz,kāp, -n,sk-\ *n* -s [*town* + *-scape*] **1 a :** a picture (as a painting) representing an urban scene ⟨spectacular ~*s* painted from rooftops —*Time*⟩ — compare CITYSCAPE **b :** the art of depicting such a scene (as by selection and composition of the man-made and natural elements that create a striking urban effect) **2 :** a portion of a town or city that the eye can comprehend in a single view ⟨viewed at twilight . . . a romantic ~, given a striking accent by the great arcs of viaduct —Lewis Mumford⟩ — compare LANDSCAPE 2b **3 :** the architectural art of achieving beauty in the design and spatial relationships created by the disposition and juxtaposition of structures (as civic buildings) in a town or city ⟨schools of architecture and planning . . . studying seriously the problems of ~ —H.M.Casson⟩

town·sen·dia \tau̇n'zendēə\ *n, cap* [NL, fr. David *Townsend* †1858 Am. botanist + NL *-ia*] **:** a genus of western American mostly low and tufted herbs (family Compositae) with large heads of purple-rayed or white-rayed flowers and achenes that are beset with bristly forked hairs — see EASTER DAISY

town·send's solitaire \'tau̇nzəndz-\ *n, usu cap T* [after John Kirk *Townsend* †1851 Am. ornithologist] **:** a solitaire (*Myadestes townsendi*) of western No. America

townsfolk \'ˌ=ˌ=, 'tau̇nz,fōk\ *n pl* **:** TOWNSPEOPLE

town·ship \'tau̇n,ship\ *n* [ME *township,* fr. OE *tūnscipe,* fr. *tūn* town + *-scipe* -ship] **1 a :** the inhabitants of a vill, manor, or medieval town; *esp* **:** such a community constituting a corporate body **b :** VILL, MANOR **c :** an imaginary social or tribal unit among the Anglo-Saxons **2 :** an ancient unit of administration in England identical in area with or a division of a parish **:** the area of a parish or chapelry with reference only to the inhabitants **3 :** an administrative unit (as a self-governing town) in a foreign country **4 a :** TOWN 7a **b :** a territorial area having the status of a unit of local government in some 16 northeastern and north central states lying between New York on the east and the Dakotas and Kansas on the west and usu. having a chief administrative officer or board although having fewer functions and powers than a New England town **c :** an unorganized subdivision of the county in Maine, New Hampshire, and Vermont in the form of a tract of land laid off by the state authorities **d :** an administrative district of the county used esp. for electoral purposes in some parts of the southern U. S. (as in North and South Carolina and Arkansas) **5 :** a geographical rather than a political division: **a :** a piece of land that is bounded on the east and west by meridians six miles apart at its south border, has a north-south length of six miles, and forms one of the chief divisions of a U. S. public-land survey — compare SECTION 7, RANGE 13 **b :** a subdivision of some provinces in Canada having certain specified powers of local government **c** *Austral* (1) **:** TOWNSITE (2) **:** the temporary settlement on such a site **6** *Scot* **:** a farm held jointly **7** *Philippines* **:** MUNICIPAL DISTRICT

township line *n* **:** one of the imaginary lines running east and west at 6-mile intervals and marking the relative north and south locations of townships in a U. S. public-land survey — compare [1]RANGE 13, TOWNSHIP 5a

township road *n* **:** a highway maintained by a town or township

town·site \'ˌ=ˌ=\ *n* **:** the site of a town ⟨each ~ must be selected with an eye to irrigation —R.A.Billington⟩; *specif* **:** a tract of land laid out with streets and subdivided into lots for the development of a town ⟨laid out a ~ on part of his extensive holdings —*Amer. Guide Series: La.*⟩

towns·man \'tau̇nzmən\ *n, pl* **townsmen** [ME *tounesman,* fr. OE *tūnesman,* fr. *tūnes* (gen. of *tūn* town) + *man* — more at TOWN] **1 a :** one born, residing, or holding citizenship in a town or city ⟨population . . . of whom one-third were *townsmen* and two-thirds countrymen —*Nineteenth Century & After*⟩ **b :** one marked by town or city ways ⟨designed for the . . . ~ spending a weekend in the country —*Brit. Bk. News*⟩ **2 :** a native, inhabitant, or citizen of a particular town ⟨a ~ . . . set up his blacksmith shop in front of his house —Allan Forbes & R.M.Eastman⟩ **3 :** one born, residing, or holding citizenship in the same town as another **:** fellow citizen ⟨earned the gratitude of his *townsmen*⟩ ⟨stopped to ask my fellow ~ —Dana Burnet⟩

townspeople \'ˌ=ˌ==\ *n pl* [*towns* (gen. of *town*) + *people*] **1 :** the inhabitants of a town or city **:** TOWNSMEN ⟨the villagers seem . . . less envious of the ~ than they used to be —S.P.B. Mais⟩ **2 :** the citizens or inhabitants of a particular town ⟨reporters interviewed the ~ —J.C.Lincoln⟩

townswoman \'ˌ=ˌ=ˌ=\ *n, pl* **townswomen 1 :** a woman native, inhabitant, or citizen of a particular town ⟨the *townswomen* brought soups and custards for the invalid —Willa Cather⟩ **2 :** a woman born, residing, or holding citizenship in the same town as another ⟨the flag presented him . . . by his *townswomen* —Caroline Ticknor⟩

town talk *n* **1 :** the common talk of a place (as a city or town) **:** public gossip ⟨disregarded the rumor as mere *town talk*⟩ ⟨the only real evidence is the *town talk* —J.A.Froude⟩ **2 :** the matter (as the subject or object) of public gossip ⟨was *town talk* for at least three days —W.M.Thackeray⟩

town way *n* **:** a road maintained by a town

townwear \'ˌ=ˌ=\ *n* **:** apparel (as of dark color or tailored style) that is suitable for wear in the city or to business

1towny \ˈtau̇nē, -ni\ *n* -ES [*town* + *-y*, dim. suffix] **:** TOWNSMAN ⟨don't want the *townies* here to get any more ideas than they've got already —W.L.Gresham⟩ ⟨the people described by the exurbanites as the *townies* —A.C.Spectorsky⟩

2towny \"\ *adj* -ER/-EST [*town* + *-y*, adj. suffix] **:** of, relating to, or having the characteristics of a town or city or of town or city life ⟨the competitive, ~ culture —W.H.Hudson †1922⟩ ⟨a trifle showy and ~ . . . in her delicate high-heeled shoes —Miles Franklin⟩

towpath \ˈ=,=\ *or* **towing path** *n* **:** a path (as along a canal) traveled by men or animals towing boats

towplane \ˈ=,=\ *n* **:** an airplane that tows gliders

towrope \ˈ=,=\ *n* **:** a line (as a rope, cable, or chain) used in towing (as a boat, car, or skier) ⟨a tug's ~⟩ ⟨hauling the car on a short ~⟩ ⟨nylon ~s for gliders⟩

1tow–row \ˈtau̇ˌrau̇\ *n* [redupl. & alter. of *6row*] **:** a noisy outburst **:** RACKET, RUMPUS ⟨a great *tow-row* of thunder —R.L.Stevenson⟩ ⟨a furious *tow-row* at once began between him and Madame —Christina Stead⟩

2tow–row \"\ *vi* **:** to make a tow-row

tows *pres 3d sing of* TOW, *pl of* TOW

tow sack *n* [*3tow*] *Midland & South* **:** GUNNYSACK

towse *var of* TOUSE

tow·ser \ˈtau̇zə(r)\ *n* -S [*1touse* + *-er*] **1 :** a large dog ⟨great, lionhearted ~ that he is —*Springfield (Mass.) Union*⟩ **2 :** a large rough person; *esp* **:** one full of energy — often used in the phrase *a towser for work*

towsle *var of* TOUSLE

towsy \ˈtau̇zē\ *var of* TOUSY

tow tank *var of* TOWING BASIN

tow target *n* **:** a practice target towed behind an airplane — compare SLEEVE TARGET

tow team *n* **:** an extra team of draft animals used to assist a regular team where the hauling is esp. difficult (as in towing logs up an incline)

tow truck *var of* TOW CAR

tow wheel *n* **:** a spinning wheel for making coarse tow yarn (as from flax fiber)

towz·ie \ˈtüzi\ *Scot var of* TOUSY

towzle *var of* TOUSLE

1tox- *or* **toxi-** *or* **toxo-** *comb form* [LL, fr. L *toxicum* poison — more at TOXIC] **1 :** toxic **:** poisonous ⟨*toxi*dermic⟩ ⟨*tox*in⟩ **2 :** toxin **:** poison ⟨*toxo*id⟩

2tox- *or* **toxi-** *or* **toxo-** *comb form* [Gk, fr. *toxon* bow, arrow — more at TOXIC] **1 :** bowed **:** arched ⟨*Toxo*donta⟩ **2 :** arrow **:** shaped like an arrow ⟨*Toxo*glossa⟩ ⟨*Toxi*fera⟩ **3 :** archery ⟨*toxo*phily⟩

tox *abbr* toxicology

toxa \ˈtäksə\ *n* -S [NL, fr. Gk *toxon* bow] **:** a sponge spicule curved like a bent bow

tox·al·bu·min \ˌtäksalˈbyümən\ *n* [ISV *1tox-* + *albumin*] **:** any of a class of toxic substances of protein nature **:** TOXIN

tox·a·phene \ˈtäksəˌfēn\ *n* -S [fr. *Toxaphene*, a trademark] **:** an insecticide obtained as a yellow waxy solid by chlorinating camphene

tox·as·ca·ris \täkˈsaskərə̇s\ *n*, *cap* [NL, fr. *2tox-* + *Ascaris*] **:** a cosmopolitan genus of ascarid roundworms that infest the small intestine of the dog and cat and related wild animals

tox·ca·tl \ˈtōˌskäd·əl\ *n* -S *usu cap* [Nahuatl *Toxcatl*, *Tozcatl*, lit., wet, slippery; fr. its occurring in the rainy season] **:** an Aztec new-year festival celebrated with a ceremonial including human sacrifice

tox·e·mia *also* **tox·ae·mia** \täkˈsēmēə\ *n* -S [NL, fr. *1tox-* + *-emia*] **1 :** an abnormal condition associated with the presence of toxic substances in the blood: as **a :** a generalized intoxication due to absorption and systemic dissemination of bacterial toxins from a focus of infection **b :** intoxication due to dissemination of toxic substances (as some by-products of protein metabolism) that cause functional or organic disturbances (as in the kidneys) **2 :** plant injury caused by insect or other toxin — **tox·e·mic** *also* **tox·ae·mic** \(ˈ)täkˈsēmik, -mek\ *adj*

toxemia of pregnancy **:** a disorder of unknown cause that is peculiar to pregnancy, is usu. of sudden onset, is marked by hypertension, albuminuria, edema, headache, and visual disturbances, and may or may not be accompanied by convulsions — compare ECLAMPSIA, PREECLAMPSIA

toxemic jaundice *n* **:** an enzootic hemolytic jaundice of Australian sheep that is associated with chronic copper poisoning and that results from feeding on pasture with a high copper and a low molybdenum content **:** YELLOWS

1tox·ic \ˈtäksik, -sēk\ *adj* [LL *toxicus*, fr. L *toxicum* poison, fr. Gk *toxikon* (*pharmakon*) arrow (poison), fr. *toxikon*, neut. of *toxikos* of a bow, fr. *toxon* bow, arrow (prob. fr. the source of L *taxus* yew) + *-ikos* -ic] **1 :** of, relating to, or caused by a poison or toxin ⟨~ drugs⟩ ⟨a ~ effect⟩ **2 :** affected by a poison or toxin ⟨a ~ patient⟩ **3 :** acting or likely to act as a poison **:** POISONOUS ⟨eggs are ~ to a hypersensitive or sensitized person⟩

2toxic \"\ *n* -S [F *toxique*, fr. L *toxicum* poison] **:** a toxic substance **:** something poisonous

toxic- *or* **toxico-** *comb form* [NL, fr. L *toxicum*] **:** poison ⟨*toxico*logy⟩ ⟨*toxico*phobia⟩ ⟨*toxic*emia⟩

tox·i·cal \-səkəl, -sēk-\ *adj* [LL *toxicus* + E *-al*] **:** TOXIC — **tox·i·cal·ly** \-sək(ə)lē, -sēk-, -li\ *adv*

1tox·i·cant \ˈtäksəkənt, -sēk-\ *n* -S [*1toxic* + *-ant*] **:** an agent or a substance that acts as a poison; *esp* **:** a preparation for insect control that kills rather than repels

2toxicant \"\ *adj* [ML *toxicant-*, *toxicans*, pres. part. of *toxicare* to poison, fr. L *toxicum* poison] **:** producing a toxic effect **:** POISONOUS

tox·ic·a·rol \täkˈsikəˌrōl, -rōl\ *n* -S [NL *toxicaria*, specific epithet of *Tephrosia toxicaria* (fr. *toxic-* + L *-aria* -ary) + E *-ol*] **:** a greenish yellow crystalline compound $C_{23}H_{22}O_7$ obtained from the roots of a tropical herb (*Tephrosia toxicaria*), derris, and cube **:** hydroxy deguelin

tox·ic·i·ty \täkˈsisəd·ē, -ətē, -i\ *n* -ES [ISV *1toxic* + *-ity*] **:** the quality, state, or relative degree of being toxic or poisonous ⟨the ~ of some antibiotics renders them clinically useless⟩

toxic jaundice *n* **:** hepatitis caused by toxic agents (as chemicals) and characterized by jaundice as a prominent symptom

tox·i·co·den·dron \-ndrən\ *n*, *cap* [NL, fr. *toxic-* + *-dendron*] *in some classifications* **:** a genus of trees, shrubs, or woody vines (family Anacardiaceae) comprising those members of the genus *Rhus* with fruits that are smooth and foliage that is poisonous to the touch

tox·i·co·der·ma \ˌtäksəkōˈdərmə\ *n* -S [NL, fr. *toxic-* + *-derma*] **:** a disease of the skin caused by a toxic agent

tox·i·co·dermatitis \ˌtäksə̇(ˌ)kō+\ *n* [NL, fr. *toxic-* + *dermatitis*] **:** an inflammation of the skin caused by a toxic substance

tox·i·co·gen·ic \ˌtäksəkōˈjenik\ *adj* [*toxic-* + *-genic*] **:** producing toxic products ⟨~ bacteria⟩

tox·i·cog·nath \ˈtäksəkəgˌnath\ *n* -S [*toxic-* + Gk *gnathos* jaw — more at -GNATHOUS] **:** either of a pair of poison fangs of a centipede that are structurally modified legs on the anterior segment of the body

tox·i·co·log·ic \ˌtäksəkəˈläjik, -sēk-, -jēk\ *also* **tox·i·co·log·i·cal** \-jə̇kəl, -jēk-\ *adj* **:** of or relating to toxicology or toxins

tox·i·col·o·gist \ˌtäksəˈkäləjə̇st\ *n* -S **:** a specialist in toxicology

tox·i·col·o·gy \-jē, -ji\ *n* -ES [*toxic-* + *-logy*] **:** a science that deals with poisons and their effect on living organisms, with substances otherwise harmless that prove toxic under particular conditions, and with the clinical, industrial, legal, or other problems involved

tox·i·co·mania \ˌtäksə̇(ˌ)kō+\ *n* [NL, fr. *toxic-* + *mania*] **:** addiction to a drug (as opium or cocaine)

tox·i·co·sis \ˌtäksəˈkōsə̇s\ *n*, *pl* **toxicoses** [NL, fr. *toxic-* + *-osis*] **:** a pathological condition caused by the action of a poison or toxin **:** TOXEMIA

toxic paralysis *n* **:** botulism of sheep

tox·i·der·mi·tis \ˌtäksəˌdə(r)ˈmīd·ə̇s\ *n* -ES [NL, fr. *1tox-* + *derm-* + *-itis*] **:** TOXICODERMATITIS

tox·if·era \täkˈsif(ə)rə\ [NL, fr. *2tox-* + *-fera* (fr. L, neut. pl. of *-fer* -ferous)] *syn of* TOXOGLOSSA

tox·if·er·ine \täkˈsifəˌrēn, -ˌrə̇n\ *n* -S [NL *toxifera* (specific epithet of the woody vine *Strychnos toxifera* that yields calabash curare) (fr. *1tox-* + *-fera*, fr. L, fem. of *-fer* -ferous) + E *-ine*] **:** any of several alkaloids obtained from calabash curare; *esp* **:** one $C_{40}H_{46}N_4O_2$ obtained usu. as its crystalline dichloride

tox·if·er·ous \(ˈ)täkˈsif(ə)rəs\ *adj* [ISV *1tox-* + *-ferous*] **:** producing or conveying poison ⟨a ~ gland⟩

tox·i·fy \ˈtäksəˌfī\ *vb* -ED/-ING/-ES [*1tox-* + *-fy*] **:** POISON

tox·i·gen·ic \ˌtäksəˈjenik\ *adj* [*1tox-* + *-genic*] **:** producing toxin — used chiefly of bacteria — **tox·i·ge·nic·i·ty** \ˌtäksəjə̇ˈnisəd·ē\ *n* -ES

tox·i·glos·sa \ˌtäksəˈgläsə\ [NL, fr. *2tox-* + *-glossa*] *syn of* TOXOGLOSSA

tox·in \ˈtäksən\ *n* -S [ISV *1tox-* + *-in*] **:** any of various poisonous substances that are specific products of the metabolic activities of living organisms, are colloidal substances related to proteins and usu. very unstable, are notably toxic when introduced into the tissues but are almost all destroyed by the digestive juices, and are typically capable of inducing antibody formation in suitable animals — see ANTITOXIN, ENDOTOXIN, EXOTOXIN; compare ABRIN, PTOMAINE, RICIN, VENOM **syn** see POISON

toxin–antitoxin \ˈ==ˈ==,==\ *n* **:** a mixture of toxin and antitoxin used esp. formerly in immunizing against the disease (as diphtheria) for which they are specific and characterized by engendering active immunity without the danger attendant upon use of a toxin alone

toxi·phobia \ˌtäksə+\ *n* [NL, fr. *1tox-* + *phobia*] **:** abnormal fear of poisons or of being poisoned

toxi·tabellae \"+\ *n pl* [NL, fr. *1tox-* + *tabellae* (pl. of *tabella*)] **:** tablets containing a poisonous ingredient (as mercuric chloride)

toxo- — see TOX-

tox·o·cara \ˌtäksəˈkarə\ *n*, *cap* [NL, fr. *2tox-* + Gk *kara* head — more at CEREBRAL] **:** a genus of nematode worms (family Ascaridae) including the common ascarids of the dog and cat — compare TOXASCARIS

1tox·o·dont \ˈtäksəˌdänt\ *or* **tox·o·don·tid** \ˌ==ˈdäntə̇d\ *adj* [*toxodont* fr. NL *Toxodontia*; *toxodontid* fr. NL *Toxodontia* + E *-id*] **:** of or relating to the Toxodontia

2toxodont \"\ *or* **toxodontid** \"\ *n* -S **:** a toxodont mammal or fossil

tox·o·don·ta \ˌ==ˈdäntə\ [NL, fr. *2tox-* + *-odonta*] *syn of* TOXODONTIA

1tox·o·don·tia \-nch(ē)ə\ *n pl*, *cap* [NL, fr. *2tox-* + *-odontia*] **:** a suborder of Notoungulata comprising generalized ungulates of the Paleocene to Pleistocene of So. America mostly of huge size equaling a large rhinoceros and having mostly persistent teeth that consist of large incisors, small lower canines, and high-crowned curved molars

2toxodontia \"\ [NL, fr. *2tox-* + *-odontia*] *syn of* NOTOUNGULATA

tox·o·glos·sa \ˌtäksəˈgläsə\ *n pl*, *cap* [NL, fr. *2tox-* + *-glossa*; fr. the usu. strongly barbed and arrowlike radula] **:** a group of marine carnivorous gastropods (suborder Stenoglossa) including the families Conidae and Terebridae and having the teeth of the radula reduced in number, large, and often perforated to serve as poison fangs with which a large poison gland in the esophagus communicates by slender ducts — **tox·o·glos·sate** \ˌ==ˈgläˌsāt\ *adj or n*

tox·oid \ˈtäkˌsȯid\ *n* -S [ISV *1tox-* + *-oid*; orig. formed in G] **:** a toxin (as of diphtheria or tetanus) treated so as to destroy its toxicity but leave it capable of inducing the formation of antibodies on injection

1tox·oph·i·lite \täkˈsäfəˌlīt\ *n* -S [*2tox-* + *-phil* + *-ite*] **:** one fond of or expert at archery

2toxophilite \"\ *also* **tox·oph·i·lit·ic** \=ˌ==ˈlid·ik\ *adj* **:** of or relating to archers or archery

tox·oph·i·ly \-lē\ *n* -ES [*2tox-* + *-phily*] **:** the study, practice, and love of archery **:** the sport or skill of archery

tox·oph·o·rous \(ˈ)täkˈsäf(ə)rəs\ *also* **tox·o·phor·ic** \ˌtäksəˈfȯrik, -ˈfär-\ *adj* [*1tox-* + *-phorous* or *-phoric*] **:** having actively poisonous properties

tox·o·plasm \ˈtäksəˌplazəm\ *n* -S [NL *Toxoplasma*] **:** a microorganism of the genus *Toxoplasma*

tox·o·plas·ma \ˌ==ˈplazmə\ *n* [NL, fr. *1tox-* + *-plasma*] **1** *cap* **:** a genus of parasitic microorganisms of uncertain systematic position usu. held to be protozoans related to the sporozoans but possibly belonging among the Fungi, prob. comprising a single species of very low host specificity, and being typically serious pathogens of vertebrates that invade the tissues and induce widespread miliary granulomatous lesions and ulceration **2** *pl* **toxoplasmas** \-məz\ *or* **toxoplasma·ta** \-məd·ə\ *also* **toxoplasma** **:** an organism of the genus *Toxoplasma* — see TOXOPLASMOSIS — **tox·o·plas·mic** \ˌ==ˈplazmik\ *adj*

tox·o·plas·mal \ˌ==ˈplazməl\ *adj* [NL *Toxoplasma* + E *-al*] **:** TOXOPLASMIC

tox·o·plas·mo·sis \ˌtäksəplazˈmōsə̇s\ *n*, *pl* **toxoplasmo·ses** \-ōˌsēz\ [NL, fr. *Toxoplasma* + *-osis*] **:** infection of man, dogs, or other mammals or of birds by toxoplasmas or disease caused by the presence of these organisms commonly involving extensive or fatal damage to the central nervous system and eyes esp. of infants, being apparently capable of transplacental transmission from mother to child, and in the adult being often subclinical in manifestation or resembling a mild influenza

tox·os·to·ma \täkˈsästəmə\ *n*, *cap* [NL, fr. *2tox-* + *-stoma*] **:** a genus of American songbirds closely related to the mockingbirds and containing most of the thrashers

tox·o·tae \ˈtäksəˌtē\ *n pl* [NL, fr. Gk *toxotai*, pl. of *toxotēs* archer, fr. *toxon* bow, arrow — more at TOXIC] **:** public slaves of ancient Athens often of Scythian origin, armed with bows, and serving as police

tox·o·tes \ˈtäksəˌtēz\ *n*, *cap* [NL, fr. Gk *toxotēs* archer] **:** a genus (the type of the family Toxotidae) of percoid fishes including solely the archerfish

1toy \ˈtȯi\ *n* -S [ME *toye* dalliance] **1** *obs* **a :** amorous dalliance **:** flirtatious or seductive behavior **b :** PASTIME, SPORT; *also* **:** a sportive or amusing act or acts **:** ANTIC **c :** a wild fancy **:** an odd conceit **:** WHIM, CAPRICE **d :** foolish dislike **:** AVERSION **2 a :** something (as a concern, preoccupation, interest) that is paltry or trifling **:** something without real or permanent value **b :** something uttered, written, or composed in jest or play or as a pure diversion **:** a light, gay, or diverting speech, play, or tune **:** a literary or musical trifle **c :** a small dainty, elegant, or showy article prized rather for its charm or interest than for utilitarian qualities **:** TRINKET, KNICKKNACK, BAUBLE **3 a :** something designed for amusement or diversion rather than practical use **b :** an article for the playtime use of a child either representational (as of persons, creatures, or implements) and intended esp. to stimulate imagination, mimetic activity, or manipulative skill or nonrepresentational (as balls, tops, jump ropes) and intended esp. to encourage manual and muscular dexterity and group integration **4 a :** something diminutive esp. in comparison with others of the same general class ⟨the tug was a ~ beside the ship that it guided⟩ **b :** a diminutive animal; *esp* **:** one of a breed or variety distinguished primarily by small size **5 :** something that can be toyed with: as **a :** a small or insignificant person **:** WEAKLING; *also* **:** one that is an object of derision or contempt **b :** WOMAN; *esp* **:** MISTRESS **6** *Scot* **:** a headdress of linen or woolen hanging down over the shoulders and formerly worn by old women of the lower classes

2toy \"\ *vb* -ED/-ING/-S *vi* **1 :** to dally amorously **:** indulge in a flirtation **2 :** to act as though unconcerned, indifferent, or not serious **:** deal lightly or without vigor or purpose **:** TRIFLE ⟨~ with great issues⟩ ⟨~s with his dinner⟩ **3 :** to while away the time in or as if in sport or play **:** amuse oneself as if with a plaything ~ *vt* **:** to spend or use up in toying; *also* **:** to bring (oneself) by toying into or out of a specified or implied condition

3toy \"\ *adj* **1 :** designed or made for use as a toy ⟨a ~ stove⟩ ⟨a set of ~ soldiers⟩ **2 :** resembling a toy esp. in diminutive size or in serving as a plaything for children ⟨a ~ house⟩

to·ya·ma \tōˈyämə\ *adj*, *usu cap* [fr. *Toyama*, Japan] **:** of or from the city of Toyama, Japan **:** of the kind or style prevalent in Toyama

toy dog *n* **:** a very small dog; *esp* **:** one of any of several breeds or varieties of tiny dogs kept purely as pets — compare ENGLISH TOY SPANIEL

to–year \təˈyi(ə)r\ *adv* [ME *to yeer*, fr. *to*, prep. + *yeer* year — more at YEAR] *dial Eng* **:** this year

toy·er \ˈtȯiə(r)\ *n* -S **:** one that toys

toy·ful \ˈtȯifəl\ *adj*, *archaic* **:** full of trifling play **:** SPORTIVE

toy·ish \ˈtȯi-ish\ *adj* **1 :** lacking in solid worth or import **:** FRIVOLOUS, TRIVIAL **2 :** resembling a toy esp. in diminutive or unsubstantial quality or in lack of real utility; *also* **:** fit for a plaything — **toy·ish·ly** *adv* — **toy·ish·ness** *n* -ES

toylike \ˈ=,=\ *adj* **:** resembling a toy esp. in small, dainty, or impractical quality ⟨~ masts⟩

toy·man \ˈtȯimən\ *n*, *pl* **toymen** **:** one who deals in toys: **a** *archaic* **:** a keeper of a trinket shop **b :** a maker of or dealer in children's toys

toy manchester *n* **1** *usu cap T&M* **:** an English breed of small long-legged black-and-tan terriers with erect ears **2** *or* **toy manchester terrier** *often cap both Ts & usu cap M* **:** a dog of the Toy Manchester breed

to·yo \ˈtō(ˌ)yō\ *n* -S [Jap] **:** a shiny smooth straw made chiefly in Japan from shellacked rice paper and used esp. for hats

to·yo·ha·shi \ˈtōyəˈhäshē\ *adj*, *usu cap* [fr. *Toyohashi*, Japan] **:** of or from the city of Toyohashi, Japan **:** of the kind or style prevalent in Toyohashi

toy·on *also* **to·llon** \ˈtōiˌän, ˈtōyən\ *n* -S [AmerSp *tollon*] **:** an ornamental evergreen shrub (*Photinia arbutifolia*) of the No. American Pacific coast having white flowers succeeded by persistent bright red berries — called also *California holly*, *Christmasberry*

toywort \ˈ=,=\ *n* [*1toy* + *wort*] **:** SHEPHERD'S PURSE

toze \ˈtōz\ *vt* -ED/-ING/-S [ME *tosen*, prob. fr. (assumed) OE *tǣsan*; akin to OE *tǣsan* to pull, tear — more at TEASE] *archaic* **:** to pull about esp. in disentangling **:** TEASE, COMB

to·zee \ˈtōzē\ *n* -S [perh. fr. D *toezien* to look on, take care, be careful, fr. MD *toesien*, fr. *toe* to + *sien* to see; akin to OE *tō* to and to OHG *sehan* to see — more at TO, SEE] **:** a curling tee

tp *abbr* **1** telephone **2** township **3** troop

TP *abbr* **1** target practice **2** teaching practice **3** technical paper **4** teleprinter **5** [L *tempore Paschale*] at Easter time **6** title page **7** total points **8** transport pilot **9** treaty port

TPD *abbr* tons per day

TPH *abbr* tons per hour

TPI *abbr*, *often not cap* **1** teeth per inch **2** threads per inch **3** tons per inch **4** turns per inch

tpk *abbr* turnpike

t plate *n*, *cap T* **:** a T-shaped plate used as a splice and for stiffening a joint where the end of one beam abuts against the side of another

TPM *abbr*, *often not cap* title page mutilated

TPN \ˌtēˌpēˈen\ *abbr or n* -S triphosphopyridine nucleotide

TPO *abbr* traveling post office

tpr *abbr* **1** taper **2** *often cap T&P&R* teleprinter **3** trooper

TPR *abbr* temperature, pulse, respiration

tps *abbr* **1** townships **2** troops

tpt *abbr* **1** transport **2** trumpet

tptr *abbr* trumpeter

TPW *abbr*, *often not cap* title page wanting

TQM *abbr* transport quartermaster

tr *abbr* **1** tare **2** tincture **3** trace; traced **4** track **5** train **6** transaction **7** transferred **8** transit **9** transitive **10** translated; translation; translator **11** transom **12** transport; transportation **13** transpose **14** travel **15** tray **16** tread **17** treasurer **18** treble **19** trill **20** troop **21** truss **22** trustee

TR *abbr* **1** tariff reform **2** technical regulation; technical report; technical representative **3** [L *tempore regis*] in the time of the king **4** tons registered **5** training regulation **6** transmit-receive **7** trust receipt

tra·ba·co·lo \trəˈbäkəˌlō\ *also* **tra·bas·co·lo** \-bäsk-\ *or* **trabaco·la** \-ələ\ *or* **trabaco·le** \-ə(ˌ)lā\ *n* -S [It *trabacolo*, *trabaccolo*] **:** a small coasting vessel of Italy

trabal \ˈtrābəl, -rab-\ *adj* [L *trabalis*, fr. *trabs*, *trabes* beam + *-alis* -al — more at THORP] **1 :** of or relating to a beam **:** large or diverging like a beam **2** [NL *trabalis*, fr. *trabs* (*cerebri*) corpus callosum, lit., cerebral beam + L *-alis* -al] **:** of or relating to the corpus callosum **:** CALLOSAL

tra·bant \trəˈbänt\ *n* -S [G *trabant*, *drabant*, fr. Czech *drabant*, fr. Per *darwān* porter, doorkeeper — more at DURWAN] **1 :** an armed attendant (as of a royal personage) **2 :** SATELLITE 4a(1)

trab·bel \ˈtrabəl\ *substand var of* TRAVEL

tra·bea \ˈtrābēə\ *n*, *pl* **trabe·ae** \-ē(ˌ)ē, -ēˌī\ [L; akin to *trabs*, *trabes* beam] **:** a toga with a border of colored stripes worn ceremonially by various men of rank in ancient Rome

tra·be·at·ed \ˈ==ˌād·ə̇d\ *also* **tra·be·ate** \-ēˌāt, -ēə̇t\ *adj* [*trabeated* fr. *trabeation* + *-ed*; *trabeate* back-formation fr. *trabeation*] *archit* **:** designed or constructed of horizontal beams or lintels **:** not arcuate

tra·be·a·tion \ˌ==ˈāshən\ *n* -S [L *trabes* beam + E *-ation*] **:** beamed as distinguished from arched construction; *also* **:** ENTABLATURE

trab·e·cle \ˈtrabə̇kəl\ *n* -S [NL *trabecula*] **:** TRABECULA

tra·bec·u·la \trəˈbekyələ\ *n*, *pl* **trabecu·lae** \-əˌlē, -ˌlī\ *also* **trabeculas** [NL, fr. L, little beam, dim. of *trabs*, *trabes* beam, timber, roof — more at THORP] **1 :** a small bar, rod, bundle of fibers, or septal membrane in the framework of a bodily organ or part (as the spleen) **2 a :** a row of cells bridging an intercellular space in a plant **b :** a fold, ridge, or bar projecting into or extending across a cell or into a sporangial cavity **c :** a row or plate of sterile cells extending in a moss across the cavity of a sporangium; *also* **:** one of the transverse thickenings on the peristome teeth of a moss **3 :** one of a pair of longitudinally directed more or less curved cartilaginous rods in the developing skull of a vertebrate that develop under the anterior part of the brain on each side of the pituitary body and subsequently fuse with each other and with the parachordal cartilages to form the base of the cartilaginous cranium

tra·bec·u·lar \-lə(r)\ *also* **tra·bec·u·late** \-lə̇t\ *or* **tra·bec·u·lat·ed** \-ˌlād·ə̇d\ *adj* [*trabecular*, *trabeculate* fr. NL *trabecula* + E *-ar* or *-ate*; *trabeculated* fr. NL *trabecula* + E *-ate* + *-ed*] **:** of, relating to, or constituting a trabecula ⟨~ tissue⟩ **:** having or consisting of trabeculae ⟨a ~ partition⟩

tra·bec·u·la·tion \ˌ==ˈlāshən\ *n* -S [NL *trabecula* + E *-ation*] **1 :** the formation of trabeculae in the lumen or on the walls of an organ (as the bladder) **2 :** trabecular condition ⟨the characteristic ~ of the spleen⟩

trab·e·cule \ˈtrabəˌkyül\ *n* -S [NL *trabecula*] **:** TRABECULA

tra·bes \ˈtrā(ˌ)bēz\ *n*, *pl* **trabes** [L] **:** BEAM

tra·bu·co \trəˈbü(ˌ)kō\ *n* -S [Sp, fr. Catal *trabuc* catapult, blunderbuss, fr. *tra-* across, through (fr. L *trans-*) + *buc* belly, bulk, hull, of Gmc origin; akin to OE *būc* belly — more at BUCKET] **1 :** BLUNDERBUSS **2 :** a strong Spanish cigar

trac \ˈtrak\ *abbr or n* -S tractor

tra·cau·lon \trəˈkȯˌlän, -lən\ *n*, *cap* [NL, prob. fr. *trachy-* + Gk *kaulos* stem, stalk — more at HOLE] *in some classifications* **:** a genus of herbaceous vines (family Polygonaceae) occurring in No. America and Asia, having prickly or bristly stems, prickly veined leaves mostly hastate or cordate at the base, racemose flowers, and angled fruits, and being commonly included in the genus *Polygonum*

1trace \ˈtrās\ *n* -S [ME, fr. MF, fr. *tracer*, *tracier* to trace — more at *2*TRACE] **1** *archaic* **:** a course or path that one follows **:** ROAD, ROUTE; *also* **:** a way of life or conduct **2 a traces** *pl* **:** the line of footprints left by an animal ⟨followed the ~s of the deer into the swamp⟩ **b :** the line or track left by something that has passed ⟨the ~ of a sleigh in the snow⟩ **c :** a path or trail beaten by or as if by the passage of feet ⟨a sheep ~ along the hill⟩; *also* **:** a marked or blazed trail through woods or over open lands **3 a** *obs* **:** FOOTPRINT **b :** a sign or evidence of something once present, influential, felt, or otherwise prominent **:** a mark left behind ⟨~s of an earlier civilization⟩ **c :** a neural or mental alteration produced by the learning process **:** ENGRAM **4 :** something traced or drawn (as a traced or lightly marked line): as **a :** the marking made by a recording instrument (as a seismograph or kymograph) **b :** the ground plan of a fortified work, defensive position, minefield, or other military installation either in reproduction (as on a map or photograph) or on the ground **c :** an unbroken line of hair (as on the back of some dogs) darker than or otherwise distinguished from the remainder of the coat **5 a :** the intersection of a line or plane with a plane or other surface and esp. with a plane of projection **b :** the line of intersection of a plane (as a fault or bedding plane) with the surface of the ground — compare STRIKE **c :** the usu. bright line or spot that moves across the screen of a cathode ray tube (as in a radar set or other electronic device); *also* **:** the path taken by such a line or spot **6 a :** a minute and often barely detectable amount or indication ⟨a mere ~ of a smile⟩ ⟨lost without a ~⟩ ⟨needs just a ~ more salt⟩ **b :** a very small quantity of a chemical constituent or component esp. when not quantitatively determined because of minuteness

²trace \"\ *vb* -ED/-ING/-S [ME *tracen*, fr. MF *tracer, tracier*, fr. (assumed) VL *tractiare* to drag, draw, fr. L *tractus*, past part. of *trahere* to draw, pull, drag — more at DRAW] *vt* **1 :** to make or record by drawing: as **a :** DELINEATE, SKETCH, OUTLINE ⟨~ a design for a fresco⟩ **b :** to form (as characters in writing) with care : write (as letters or figures) carefully or with nicety **c :** to copy (as a drawing, engraving, or manuscript) by following the lines or letters as seen through a transparent sheet superimposed on the original **d :** to impress or imprint (as a design or pattern) with or as if with a tracer; *also* **:** to make an imprint of such an item for (as a fabric, metal) **e :** to record (as the movements of a muscle) in the form of a curved, wavy, or broken line : make a tracing of ⟨the cardiograph ~*s* the heart action⟩ **f :** to make marks or lines on : adorn with tracery, chasing, or other linear ornamentation ⟨*traced* windows in Gothic churches⟩ **2** *archaic* **:** to walk or travel over : to pass through : TRAVERSE ⟨we do ~ this alley up and down —Shak.⟩ **3 a :** to follow the footprints of : pursue the trail of or course or route taken by : track down ⟨~ game to its lair⟩ **b :** to follow or study out in detail or step by step : outline or present the development, progress, or history of ⟨~ the history of a movement⟩ **c :** to discover or uncover by going backward over the evidence step by step : ascertain, establish, or attribute as a result of such retracing or reviewing ⟨~ the cause of an epidemic⟩ ⟨*traced* the failure of the project to indifference⟩ **d :** to discover traces or signs or evidence of : prove the existence or occurrence of ⟨could not ~ the hypothetical source of the Shakespearean play⟩ **e :** to make out by finding or examining traces or vestiges or remains : come to know, understand, or comprehend by such investigation ⟨~ the former course of a river⟩ ⟨~ him in his word, his works, his ways —William Cowper⟩ **f :** to find by following traces or the trail of; *esp* **:** to ascertain the whereabouts or disposition of (as something passing from hand to hand or place to place) ⟨unable to ~ a lost letter or one's relatives⟩ ⟨*traced* the missing man to Chicago⟩ **4 :** to lay out the trace of (a military installation) ~ *vi* **1 :** to make one's way : GO: as **a :** to follow a track, trail, or other indicated way **b** *dial Eng* **:** WALK, MARCH, TRUDGE; *also* **:** to ramble aimlessly **c** *archaic* **:** to perform dance steps : step a measure **d** *obs* **:** to tumble down : fall free **2 :** to be traceable historically : go back in time — usu. used with *to* ⟨a family that ~*s* to the Norman conquest⟩ **3 :** to record on the cataloguing card for a main entry the headings under which added entries have been made

³trace \"\ *n* -S [ME *trais*, pl., traces, fr. MF *trais, traiz*, pl. of *trait* pull, draft, strap for harnessing — more at TRAIT] **1 :** either of two straps, chains, or ropes of a harness extending from the collar or breast collar to a whiffletree attached to a vehicle or thing to be drawn : TUG — see HARNESS illustration **2 :** a short line usu. of wire or gut between a main fishing line and the hook or lure : LEADER **3 :** the vascular supply of a leaf or branch consisting of one or more vascular bundles that are extensions of the central vascular cylinder; *also* **:** one of the individual bundles of such a supply — see BRANCH TRACE, LEAF TRACE; compare GAP 6 **4 :** a connecting bar or rod pivoted at each end to the end of another piece and used for transmitting motion esp. from one plane to another; *specif* **:** such a piece in an organ-stop action to transmit motion from the trundle to the lever actuating the stop slider

⁴trace \"\ *vt* -ED/-ING/-S *archaic* **:** to fasten (as a horse) by traces : hitch up

⁵trace \"\ *vt* -ED/-ING/-S [ME *trasen, trassen*, prob. alter. of MF *tresser* to tress, fr. OF *trecier*] **:** PLAIT, BRAID; *specif* **:** to fasten (as onion bulbs or ears of corn) in bunches by braiding together the dry herbage (as of tops or shucks)

⁶trace \"\ *n* -S **:** a traced string (as of onions or ears of corn)

trace·abil·i·ty \ˌtrāsəˈbiləd·ē, -lətē, -i\ *n* **:** the quality or state of being traceable

trace·able \ˈtrāsəbəl\ *adj* [²*trace* + *-able*] **1 :** capable of being traced ⟨a ~ riverbed⟩ ⟨a barely ~ inscription⟩ **2 :** suitable or of a kind to be attributed : DUE, ASCRIBABLE — used with *to* ⟨a failure ~ to lack of energy⟩ — **trace·able·ness** \-bəlnəs\ *n* -ES — **trace·ably** \-blē, -li\ *adv*

trace–bearer \ˈ=,==\ *n* [³*trace*] **:** LAZY STRAP

trace bud *n* **:** a plant bud having a vascular trace and developing in the elongating portion of a stem — compare ADVENTITIOUS BUD

trace chain *n* **1 a :** a harness trace of chain **b :** a short chain by which a leathern trace is linked with a whiffletree **2 :** a long strong chain which is attached to a line and along which two or more pairs of draft animals are attached usu. by whiffletrees

trace element *n* [¹*trace*] **:** a chemical element (as zinc, boron, or iodine) found combined in minute quantities in plant or animal tissues and considered essential in the physiological processes of most plants and animals — called also *microelement, micronutrient, minor element;* compare MACRONUTRIENT

trace horse *n* [³*trace*] **:** an extra horse hitched beside a team to assist in drawing a load through a difficult spot (as up an incline); *also* **:** an outside horse of a team in which more than two are driven abreast

trace·less \ˈtrāsləs\ *adj* [¹*trace* + *-less*] **:** having or leaving no trace — **trace·less·ly** *adv*

trace of precipitation : a minute amount of precipitation (as of rain); *specif* **:** an amount measuring less than 0.01 inch

¹trac·er \ˈtrāsə(r)\ *n* -S [²*trace* + *-er*] **1 :** one that traces, tracks down, or searches out: as **a :** SEEKER **b :** a person professionally engaged in the tracing of missing persons or property and esp. of goods lost in transit **c :** a form or inquiry sent out to facilitate the tracing of an article or shipment lost in transit **2 :** one that makes tracings or traceries: as **a :** a draftsman, gilder, stainer, or other worker that traces designs, patterns, or markings **b :** one that traces (as drawings) on semitransparent paper or cloth esp. for blueprint reproduction — compare TRACING CLOTH, TRACING PAPER **3 :** a device (as a stylus) used in tracing a design or other matter: as **a :** TRACING WHEEL **b :** a tempered steel punch used in chasing or repoussé work on metal (as when cutting the outline of a design or when making and finishing corners or borders) **4 a** *or* **tracer ammunition :** ammunition containing a chemical composition to mark the flight of projectiles by a trail of smoke or fire **b :** a substance (as a fluorescent dye) used to trace the course of a process; *specif* **:** a labeled element or atom that can be traced throughout chemical, biological, or physical processes by its radioactivity or its unusual isotopic mass ⟨radioactive ~*s* administered to patients accumulate in tumors and other pathological tissue, where they can be detected⟩

²tracer \"\ *n* -S [³*trace* + *-er*] **:** TRACE HORSE

tracer bullet *n* **:** a bullet that contains a tracer and leaves a path of smoke or fire

trac·er·ied \ˈtrās(ə)rēd, -rid\ *adj* **:** decorated with or having tracery

trac·ery \-rē, -ri\ *n* -ES [²*trace* + *-ery*] **1 :** architectural ornamental work with ramified lines: as **a :** decorative openwork in the head of a Gothic window: (1) **:** BAR TRACERY (2) **:** PLATE TRACERY **b :** ornamentation resembling window tracery on other decorative objects (as panels of wood or metal) **c :** a similar decoration in some styles of vaulting in which the ribs of the vault give off the minor bars of which the tracery is composed **2 :** a decorative interlacing of lines suggestive of Gothic tracery : a pattern wrought by the interweaving or branching out of lines in ornamental or graceful figures ⟨the ~ of frost on a window pane⟩

tracery 1a(1)

traces *pl of* TRACE, *pres 3d sing of* TRACE

trache- *or* **tracheo-** *comb form* [NL, fr. ML *trachea*] **1 :** trachea ⟨*tracheo*scopy⟩ **2 :** tracheal and ⟨*tracheo*laryngeal⟩

tra·chea \ˈtrākēə, *chiefly Brit* trəˈkēə\ *n, pl* **trache·ae** \-ē,ē, -ē,ī\ *also* **tracheas** [ME, fr. ML, windpipe, trachea, fr. LL *trachia*, fr. Gk (*artēria*) *tracheia* rough (artery), fr. fem. of *trachys* rough, harsh; akin to Gk *thrassein, thrattein* to trouble, disturb — more at DARK] **1 :** the main trunk of the system of tubes by which air passes to and from the lungs in vertebrates that forms in man a tube about four inches long and somewhat less than an inch in diameter extending down the front of the neck from the larynx, bifurcating to form the bronchi, and having walls of fibrous and muscular tissue stiffened by incomplete cartilaginous rings which keep it from collapsing and lined with mucous membrane whose epithelium is composed of columnar ciliated mucus-secreting cells — compare SYRINX **2** [NL] **:** a xylem element or series of elements felt to resemble an animal trachea; *usu* **:** a xylem vessel **3** [NL] **:** one of the air-conveying tubules forming the respiratory system of most insects, millipedes, centipedes, many arachnids, and the onychophorans and in the insects constituting typically a system of ramifying and anastomosing tubules that are enlarged at various points into air sacs, penetrate to nearly all parts of the body, and have a cuticular lining which is stiffened by a spiral fiber or fibrous thickening — compare BOOK LUNG, SPIRACLE, STIGMA, TAENIDIUM

tra·che·al \-ēəl\ *adj* [NL *trachealis*, fr. ML *trachea* + L *-alis* -al] **1 :** of, relating to, or functioning in the manner of an animal trachea : resembling a trachea **2 :** TRACHEARY

tracheal commissure *n* **:** one of the large transverse tubes that unite the tracheal systems of the opposite sides of the body in an insect

tracheal gill *n* **:** one of the external filaments or leaflike plates connected with the tracheae of the inside of the body that form part of the respiratory system of some aquatic insect larvae and nymphs but rarely persist in the adult

tra·che·alis \ˌtrākēˈaləs, -ˈā-, -ˈä-\ *n, pl* **trache·ales** \-(ˌ)lēz\ [NL, lit., tracheal] **:** a muscle associated with the trachea and in man consisting of fibers that extend transversely between the ends of the cartilages and the intervals between them at the back of the trachea

tracheal sac *n* **:** an air sac of the tracheal system of an insect

tracheal tube *n* **:** a trachea of an insect or a branch of such a trachea

tracheal tug *or* **tracheal tugging** *n* **:** a downward pull of the trachea and larynx observed in aneurysm of the aorta

tracheal tympanum *n* **:** an enlarged and partially ossified segment of the trachea of some birds

tra·che·ar·ia \ˌtrākēˈa(a)rēə\ *n pl, cap* [NL, fr. *trache-* + *-aria*] *in former classifications* **:** a division of Arachnida comprising those that have no book lungs and including the mites, ticks, book scorpions, and harvestmen — **tra·che·ar·i·an** \ˌ==ˈa(a)rēən\ *adj or n*

¹tra·che·ary \ˈtrākē,erē\ *adj* [*trache-* + *-ary*] **1 :** breathing by means of tracheae **2 :** of, relating to, made up of, or being plant tracheae ⟨~ tissue⟩ ⟨a ~ element⟩

²tracheary \"\ *n* -ES [NL *Trachearia*] **:** a member of the division Trachearia : an arachnid that lacks book lungs

¹tra·che·ata \ˌ==ˈād·ə, -ād·ə\ *n pl, cap* [NL, fr. neut. pl. of *tracheatus* tracheate, fr. *trache-* + L *-atus* -ate] *in some esp former classifications* **:** a class or other group of Arthropoda comprising all or most of the arthropods with tracheal respiration

²tracheata \"\ [NL] *syn of* TRACHEOPHYTA

¹tra·che·ate \ˈtrākē,āt, -ēət; trəˈkēət\ *n* -S [NL *Tracheata*] **:** a tracheate arthropod

²tracheate \"\ *adj* [NL *tracheatus*] **:** having tracheae as breathing organs

tra·che·a·tion \ˌ==ˈāshən\ *n* -S [*trache-* + *-ation*] **:** the distribution and arrangement of the tracheae in a tracheate arthropod and esp. in the developing wing of an insect previous to the formation of the veins

tra·cheid \ˈtrākēəd, -ā,kēd\ *n, pl* **tracheids** *also* **tra·che·ides** \trāˈkēə,dēz, trəˈk-\ [ISV *trache-* + *-id;* prob. orig. formed in G] **:** a long tubular cell that is peculiar to xylem, functions in conduction and support, and is characterized by tapering closed ends which are not absorbed as in tracheae and by thickened strongly lignified walls which commonly have bordered pits — compare SIEVE CELL, TRACHEA 2, VESSEL; see XYLEM — **tra·che·idal** \trāˈkēəd³l, trəˈk-; ˌtrākēˈīd³l\ *adj*

tra·che·i·tis \ˌtrākēˈīd·əs\ *n* -ES [NL, fr. *trache-* + *-itis*] **:** inflammation of the trachea

trachel- *or* **trachelo-** *comb form* [NL, fr. Gk *trachēl-, trachēlo-*, fr. *trachēlos*] **1 a :** neck ⟨*trachelo*logy⟩ **b :** cervical and ⟨*trachelo*scapular⟩ **2 :** necklike anatomical structure : cervix 2a ⟨*trachelo*plasty⟩

trache·late \ˈtrakə,lāt, ˈtrāk-\ *adj* [NL *trachelatus*, fr. *trachel-* + L *-atus* -ate] **:** having the look of a neck ⟨an insect with a narrowed ~ prothorax⟩

tra·che·li·um \trəˈkēlēəm\ *or* **tra·che·li·on** \-lē,än, -ēən\ *n, pl* **trache·lia** \-lēə\ [NL, fr. Gk *trachēlos* neck + L *-ium* or Gk *-ion* (dim. suffixes)] **:** the part of the neck of a column above the gorgerin

trache·lo·mastoid \ˌtrakəlō, ˌtrākəlō, trəˈkēlō +\ *adj* [ISV *trachel-* + *mastoid*] **:** relating to or joining the neck and mastoid

trachelo–occipital \"+\ *adj* [ISV *trachel-* + *occipital*] **:** relating to or joining the neck and occiput

trachelo·plasty \ˈtrakəlō,plastē, ˈtrākəlō-, trəˈkēlō-\ *n* -ES [*trachel-* + *-plasty*] **:** a plastic operation on the neck of the uterus

trache·lor·rha·phy \ˌtrakəˈlȯrəfē, ˌtrāk-\ *n* -ES [ISV *trachel-* + *-rraphy*] **:** the operation of sewing up a laceration of the uterine cervix

trachelo·spermum \ˌtrakəlōˈspərməm ˌtrākəlō-, trəˌkēlō-\ *n, cap* [NL, fr. *trachel-* + *-spermum*] **:** a genus of Asiatic woody vines (family Apocynaceae) with opposite leaves, showy flowers in loose cymes, and elongated terete follicles — see STAR JASMINE

tracheo- — see TRACHE-

tra·cheo·bronchial \ˌtrākē(ˌ)ō, trəˌkēō+\ *adj* [*trache-* + *bronchial*] **:** of, relating to, affecting, or produced in the trachea and bronchi ⟨~ secretion⟩ ⟨~ lesions⟩

tracheo·bronchitis \"+\ *n* [NL, fr. *trache-* + *bronchitis*] **:** inflammation of the trachea and bronchi

tra·che·o·lar \trāˈkēələ(r)\ *adj* [*tracheole* + *-ar*] **:** of, relating to, or being a tracheole

tra·che·ole \ˈtrākē,ōl\ *n* -S [*trache-* + *-ole*] **:** one of the minute delicate endings of a branched trachea of an insect

tra·cheo·pho·nae \ˌtrākēəˈfō,nē, trəˌkē-\ *n pl, cap* [NL, fr. *trache-* + Gk *phōnē* sound, voice — more at BAN] *in former classifications* **:** a group comprising clamatorial birds with the syrinx thin-walled and tracheal, the syringeal muscles few, and the semirings few and thin and including the families Dendrocolaptidae, Formicariidae, and Conopophagidae — **tra·cheo·phone** \ˈtrākēə,fōn, trəˈk-\ *adj or n*

tra·cheo·pho·nine \ˌtrākēˈäfə,nīn, trəˌkē-, -,nən\ *or* **tra·che·oph·o·nous** \ˌtrākēˈäfənəs\ *adj* [NL *Tracheophonae* + E *-ine* or *-ous*] **:** of or relating to the Tracheophonae

tra·che·oph·y·ta \ˌtrākēˈäfəd·ə\ *n pl, cap* [NL, fr. *trache-* + *-phyta*] **:** a division of plants comprising green plants with a vascular system that contains tracheids or tracheary elements (as vessel elements or fibers) and including the subdivisions Psilopsida, Sphenopsida, Lycopsida, and Pteropsida — **tra·cheo·phyte** \ˈtrākēə,fīt\ *n* -S

tra·che·os·to·my \ˌtrākēˈästəmē\ *n* -ES [ISV *trache-* + *-stomy;* prob. orig. formed as F *trachéostomie*] **:** the surgical formation of an opening into the trachea through the skin

trache·ot·o·mize \ˌtrākēˈäd·ə,mīz\ *vt* -ED/-ING/-S [ISV *tracheotomy* + *-ize*] **:** to perform tracheotomy on

tra·che·ot·o·my \-ˈäd·əmē\ *n* -ES [*trache-* + *-tomy*] **:** the surgical operation of cutting into the trachea esp. through the skin

trach·ich·thy·i·dae \ˌtrā,kikˈthīə,dē, ˌtra,k-\ *n pl, cap* [NL, fr. *Trachichthys*, type genus (fr. Gk *trachys* rough + NL *-ichthys*) + *-idae*] **:** a family of reddish large-headed rough-bodied or spiny chiefly deep-sea fishes (order Berycomorphi) with numerous mucous channels about the head

trachin·i·dae \trəˈkinə,dē\ *n pl, cap* [NL, fr. *Trachinus*, type genus (fr. ML *trachina*, a fish, fr. Gk *trachys* rough) + *-idae*] **:** a family of percoid fishes that is constituted by the weevers and that sometimes with related elongated eellike fishes is placed in a separate suborder of Percomorphi or an independent order

¹trachi·noid \ˈtrakə,nȯid, ˈtrāk-\ *adj* [NL *Trachinus* + E *-oid*] **:** resembling or related to the Trachinidae

²trachinoid \"\ *n* -S **:** a trachinoid fish

tra·chip·ter·us [NL] *syn of* TRACHYPTERUS

¹tra·chle \ˈtrakəl, -räk-\ *vb* -ED/-ING/-S [perh. fr. Flem *tragelen, trakelen* to walk with difficulty, drag, trail; akin to MD *traech* slow, heavy, sluggish, OHG *trāgi* sluggish, slow, Lith *drižti* to become tired] *vt* **1** *Scot* **:** DISHEVEL, BEDRAGGLE, SOIL **2** *Scot* **:** to tire by overwork or overexertion; *also* **:** to put (as oneself) to inconvenience : BOTHER, TROUBLE ~ *vi, Scot* **:** to wear oneself out (as by work) : DRUDGE

²trachle \"\ *n* -S **1** *Scot* **a :** a source of fatigue (as a long and tiring walk or task) **b :** a cause of inconvenience, distress, or trouble **2** *Scot* **:** a listless sloven

trach·odon \ˈtrakə,dän, ˈtrāk-\ *n* [NL, fr. Gk *trachys* rough + NL *-odon*] **1** *cap* **:** a genus comprising large duck-billed dinosaurs of the Upper Cretaceous that resemble those of the *Iguanodon* but have a broad spatulate snout and commonly constituting a distinct family **2** -S **:** a dinosaur of the genus *Trachodon* — **trach·odont** \-nt\ *adj or n* — **trach·odon·tid** \ˌ==ˈdäntəd\ *adj or n*

tra·cho·ma \trəˈkōmə\ *n* -S [NL, fr. Gk *trachōma*, fr. *trachys* rough, harsh + *-ōma* -oma] **:** a chronic contagious conjunctivitis characterized by the presence on the conjunctival surfaces of inflammatory granulations that are eventually replaced by scar tissue and caused by a rickettsia (*Chlamydia trachomatis*) — **tra·choma·tous** \trəˈkäməd·əs, -ˈkōm-\ *adj*

tracho-medusae \ˌtrakō, ˈtrākō+\ *n pl, cap* [NL, alter. of *Trachymedusae*] **:** a suborder of Trachylina comprising medusae in which the tentacles arise from the edge of the umbrella and the gonads are developed in connection with the radial canals — **tracho·medusan** \"+\ *adj or n*

tra·chu·rus \trəˈkyürəs\ *n, cap* [NL, fr. Gk *trachouros* horse mackerel, fr. *trachys* rough + *oura* tail; akin to Gk *orrhos* buttocks — more at ASS] **:** a genus of marine carangid fishes including various important food fishes — compare COWANYOUNG, HORSE MACKEREL

trachy- *comb form* [in sense 1, fr. NL, fr. Gk, fr. *trachys* rough, harsh; in sense 2, fr. F, fr. *trachyte* — more at TRACHEA] **1 :** rough : strong ⟨*trachy*glossate⟩ ⟨*trachy*chromatic⟩ **2 :** trachytic ⟨*trachy*dolerite⟩ ⟨*trachy*andesite⟩

trachy·andesite \ˌtrakē, ˌtrākē+\ *n* [F *trachyandésite*, fr. *trachy-* + *andésite* andesite] **:** a lava intermediate in composition between trachyte and andesite — compare LATITE

trachy·basalt \"+\ *n* [G, fr. *trachy-* + *basalt*] **:** a rock that is intermediate in composition between trachyte and basalt and that contains both orthoclase and basic plagioclase

trachy·car·pous \ˌ==ˈkärpəs\ *adj* [ISV *trachy-* + *-carpous*] **:** rough-fruited

trachy·car·pus \ˌ==ˈkärpəs\ *n, cap* [NL, fr. *trachy-* + *-carpus*] **:** a small genus of low East Asiatic fan palms having leaf sheaths with a dense fibrous network which is made into ropes and netting — see HEMP PALM

trachy·chromatic \ˌ==+\ *adj* [ISV *trachy-* + *chromatic*] **:** deeply staining (as some marrow cells)

trachy·li·na \ˌ==ˈlīnə\ *n pl, cap* [NL, prob. fr. *trachy-* + L *linum* flax — more at LINEN] **:** an order of Hydrozoa comprising forms that lack a polyp stage and including the suborder Trachomedusae and Narcomedusae — **trachy·line** \ˈ==,līn, -,lən\ *adj*

trachy·li·nae \ˌ==ˈlī,nē\ [NL] *syn of* TRACHYLINA

trachy·medusae \ˌ==+\ [NL, fr. *trachy-* + *medusae*] *syn of* TRACHOMEDUSAE

tra·chyp·ter·us \trəˈkiptərəs\ *n, cap* [NL, fr. *trachy-* + *-pterus*] **:** a genus of large oceanic fishes (order Allotriognathi) comprising the dealfishes and usu. constituting a distinct family

trachy·sper·mous \ˌtrakēˈspərməs, ˌtrāk-\ *adj* [*trachy-* + *-spermous*] **:** rough-seeded

trachyte \ˈtra,kīt, ˈtrā,-\ *n* -S [F, fr. Gk *trachys* rough + F *-ite* — more at TRACHEA] **:** a usu. light-colored volcanic rock consisting of potash feldspar generally with more or less biotite, amphibole, or pyroxene, commonly exhibiting a subparallel texture, and being the effusive form of syenite

tra·chyt·ic \trəˈkid·ik\ *adj* [F *trachytique*, fr. *trachyte* + *-ique* -ic] **:** of or relating to a texture of igneous rocks in which lath-shaped feldspar microlites are arranged in subparallel lines that flow around the larger phenocrysts

trachy·toid \ˈtrakə,tȯid, ˈtrāk-\ *adj* [F *trachytoïde*, fr. *trachyte* + *-oïde* -oid] **:** resembling trachyte ⟨~ structure⟩

¹trac·ing \ˈtrāsiŋ, -sēŋ\ *n* -S [ME, gerund of *tracen* to trace — more at TRACE] **1 :** the act of one that traces **2 :** something that is traced or marked out: as **a :** a copy of a pattern or design made on a transparent sheet superimposed on an original or by use of transfer paper **b :** a record made by any of several instruments (as an ergogram or cardiogram) that register graphically some movement **c :** a mark left on the ice by a skate — called also *print* **3 :** a record of additional entries in respect to a particular item placed on its main entry card in a catalog

²tracing \"\ *adj* [ME, fr. pres. part. of *tracen* to trace] **:** used in or for making tracings ⟨~ board⟩ ⟨a ~ machine⟩

tracing cloth *also* **tracing linen** *n* **:** a fine transparent linen or cotton cloth sized on one side and used (as by architects or designers) for making tracings esp. in ink

tracing paper *n* **1 :** a tough semitransparent paper for tracing drawings **2 :** lithographic transfer paper

tracing wheel *n* **:** a needle-pointed or saw-toothed wheel with an attached handle that is used (as by tailors or patternmakers) with or without carbon paper to mark construction lines on patterns or fabric

¹track \ˈtrak\ *n* -S *often attrib* [ME *trak*, fr. MF *trac*, perh. of Gmc origin; akin to MD *tracken, trecken* to pull, haul, march, MLG *trecken* to pull — more at TREK] **1 a :** detectable evidence that something has passed (as the wake of a ship, a line of footprints, or a wheel rut) **b :** a rough path or way formed by or as if by repeated chance footfalls : TRAIL **c :** a way or road constructed and maintained for a specific purpose: as (1) **:** a path or course laid out esp. for racing or exercise ⟨a cinder ~⟩ ⟨a half-mile ~⟩; *esp* **:** a running track on which athletic races are contested — distinguished from *field* (2) **:** a metal way for wheeled vehicles; *specif* **:** one or more pairs of parallel lines of rails with the fastenings, ties, and sometimes ballast for a railroad, railway, or tramway **d :** a physical course by or on which something is recorded: as (1) **:** the portion of the dial of a timepiece on which minutes or seconds are marked off between concentric bands (2) **:** SOUND TRACK **2 a :** a footprint whether recent or fossil ⟨the huge ~ of an old bull elephant⟩ **b** *archaic* **:** a visible mark or sign : VESTIGE, TRACE **3 a :** the course along which something moves ⟨the ~ of a storm⟩ ⟨his ~ led him over mountains and through swamps⟩ ⟨the ~ of a bullet⟩ — used interjectionally by a skier to warn anyone ahead of him on a trail or run; see PACHISI illustration **b :** a way of life, conduct, or action : a course one adopts or follows : METHOD, PROCEDURE ⟨afraid the new administration would choose a different ~ in foreign affairs⟩ **c :** one of two or more courses of study covering the same general field usu. at different levels of intensity and offered by a school to meet the diverse needs of particular groups of students **d :** the projection on the earth's surface of the path along which an aircraft has actually flown **4 a :** a sequence of events or train of ideas : the order in which things happen or ideas come ⟨my pen goes in the ~ of my thoughts —Edmund Burke⟩ ⟨the recurrent ~ of the years⟩ **b :** the condition or fact of being aware of or in touch with something or some aspect (as the progress, count, extent, or worth) of something specified ⟨lost ~ of his friend's address⟩ ⟨keeping careful ~ of the costs⟩ **5 :** any of several things or parts that make or are associated with the making of a track: as **a :** the width of a wheeled vehicle as measured from wheel to wheel and usu. from the outside of the rims **b :** the tread of an automobile tire **c :** CATERPILLAR TREAD **6 :** the lower surface of the foot usu. of a bird **7** *Scot* **:** an odd spectacle : SIGHT **8 :** track-and-field sports; *esp* **:** those (as running or hurdling events) that are performed on the running track — distinguished from *field event* — **across the tracks** *adv* **:** in a run-down or unfashionable neighborhood — **in one's tracks :** where one stands or is at the moment : on the spot : INSTANTLY ⟨shot the thief *in his tracks*⟩

2track \"\ *vb* -ED/-ING/-S *vt* **1 a :** to follow the tracks or traces of **:** pursue by following marks made by (the pursued) **:** TRAIL ⟨~ a deer⟩ **b :** to follow until caught up with — used with adverbs of direction (as *down*) ⟨~ down a criminal⟩ **2 :** to mark out or beat down (a path or other course) **3 a :** to ascertain and follow up through vestiges **:** TRACE ⟨~ the course of an ancient wall⟩ **b :** to follow or plot the moving path of (a target) with an instrument (as a gun, telescope, or searchlight) for the purpose of determining point of aim, path of interception, or future position **4 :** to pass over **:** TRAVEL, TRAVERSE ⟨~ a desert⟩ **5 a :** to make tracks upon ⟨new snow ~*ed* by rabbits⟩; *esp* **:** to carry mud or other soiling agent on the feet and deposit it upon — often used with *up* ⟨don't ~ up my clean floor⟩ **b :** to carry (as mud) on the feet and deposit in stepping ⟨~*ed* mud all over the house⟩ **6 :** to furnish with tracks or rails — often used in compounds ⟨single-*track*⟩ ⟨double-*track*⟩ **~** *vi* **1 :** to make one's way **:** WALK, GO, TRAVEL — often used with *around, about,* or *up* ⟨got up late and ~*ed* about for a while⟩ **2 a :** to follow a track in searching ⟨takes a woodsman to really ~⟩ **b :** to move a camera toward, beside, or away from a subject on a smooth moving trolley or tricycle **c** *of a phonograph needle* **:** to follow the groove undulations of a recording **3 a** *of a pair of wheels* (1) **:** to maintain a constant distance apart on the straightaway (2) **:** to fit a track or rails **b** *of a rear wheel of a vehicle* **:** to accurately follow its corresponding fore wheel on a straightaway **c :** to be in perfect alignment with a corresponding part — used esp. of a gear or cutter **4 :** to leave tracks (as on a floor) ⟨~*ing* all over the house with his muddy boots⟩

3track \"\ *n* -S [by alter. of 3*tract*] *chiefly dial* **:** EXTENT; *esp* **:** an extent of land

4track \"\ *vb* -ED/-ING/-S [prob. modif. (influenced by 2*track*) of D *trekken* to pull, fr. MD *trecken* — more at TRACK (n.)] *vt* **1 :** to tow along; *esp* **:** to tow (as a ship) from the shore **2** *chiefly Scot* **:** to prepare (tea) by infusing **:** DRAW **~** *vi* **:** to become towed **:** travel in a towed boat

5track \"\ *n* -S *chiefly Scot* **:** TEAPOT

track·able \'trakəbəl\ *adj* **:** capable of being tracked **:** suitable for tracking

1track·age \-kij, -kēj\ *n* -S [4*track* + *-age*] **:** an act of towing **:** TOWAGE

2trackage \"\ *n* -S [1*track* + *-age*] **1 :** lines of railway track ⟨1000 miles of antiquated ~⟩ **2 a** *usu* **trackage right :** a right to use the tracks of another road **b** *usu* **trackage charge :** the charge for such right

track-and-field \ˌ≈ˌ≈'≈\ *adj* **:** of, relating to, or being a sport performed on a running track or on the field usu. encircled by it — see TRACK 8; compare FIELD EVENT

track and slide *n* [1*track*] **:** a combination on a mast for hoisting and lowering a sail

trackbarrow \'≈ˌ≈(ˌ)≈\ *n* [1*track* + *barrow*] **:** a wheelbarrow with a wheel grooved for use on railroad tracks

track boat *n* **:** a boat towed from the shore

track brake *n* **:** a brake (as on a streetcar) that presses the track instead of the wheels

track circuit *n* **:** an electrical circuit conducted partly through the rails of a track (as of a railway line)

tracked *past of* TRACK

1track·er \'trakə(r)\ *n* -S [2*track* + *-er*] **1 :** one that tracks (as by tracing): as **a :** one that tracks down game or criminals **b :** an instrument used to track a gunnery target; *also* **:** the operator of such an instrument **2 :** a maker of a track

2tracker \"\ *n* -S [4*track* + *-er*] **:** a tower of a boat or raft

tracker action *n* [1*tracker*] **:** a completely mechanical action in a pipe organ

track gage *n* **:** a tool by which the gage of a track (as of a railroad) is determined

track harness *n* **:** a light harness used in harness racing

trackhound \'≈ˌ≈\ *n* **:** a hound that tracks by scent

track indicator *n* **:** a device used to indicate the condition of a railroad track section

tracking *pres part of* TRACK

tracking shot *n* [*tracking* fr. pres. part. of 2*track*] **:** TRUCKING SHOT

track instrument *n* **:** a treadle device on a railroad track depressed by a passing train to operate an alarm (as near a crossing)

track jack *n* **:** a device for raising railway track during ballasting or other track operations

tracklayer \'≈ˌ≈(≈)\ *n* **1 a :** a workman engaged in work involved in putting railway tracks in place **b :** a machine used in track construction for advancing the rails and ties from supply cars in the rear to the point where they are to be placed in the track **2 :** a Caterpillar tractor

1tracklaying \'≈ˌ≈≈\ *adj* **1 :** used in the laying of tracks **2 :** of, relating to, or being a caterpillar tread vehicle

2tracklaying \"\ *n* [1*track* + *laying*, gerund of 1*lay*] **:** the laying of track on a railway line

track·less \'trakləs\ *adj* **1 :** having no track **:** UNTROD ⟨a ~ wilderness⟩ **2 :** making or leaving no tracks ⟨~ footsteps⟩ **3 :** not running on tracks or rails ⟨a ~ train⟩ — **track·less·ly** *adv* — **track·less·ness** *n* -ES

trackless trolley *n* **:** TROLLEYBUS

track·man \'trakmən\ *n, pl* **trackmen :** a worker engaged in the laying or maintenance of railway tracks or rails; *specif* **:** TRACKWALKER

track map *n* **:** a map showing existing physical plant including tracks, bridges, water service and mains, leases, station facilities, and all other physical property of a railway line

trackmaster \'≈ˌ≈≈\ *n* **:** ROADMASTER 1

track-mile \'≈'≈\ *n* **:** a mile of track (as of a railway line) ⟨costs per *track-mile*⟩

track oven *n* **:** a drying oven in which drying racks run on a track over a fire

track pan *n* **:** a very long shallow trough between the rails of a railroad track for holding water to be picked up by a moving steam locomotive

trackpot \'≈ˌ≈\ *n* [4*track* + *pot*] *chiefly Scot* **:** TEAPOT

track road *n* [4*track*] **:** TOWPATH

tracks *pl of* TRACK, *pres 3d sing of* TRACK

track scale *n* **:** a scale fitted with tracks for the weighing of loaded or empty railway cars

trackshifter \'≈ˌ≈≈\ *n* **:** an appliance used in shifting a railway track laterally

track shoe *n* **1 :** the shoe of a track brake **2 :** a heelless leather shoe having steel spikes on the sole to give traction to a runner

track shoe 2

1trackside \'≈ˌ≈\ *n* [1*track* + *side*] **:** the space beside a track

2trackside \'≈'≈\ *adj* **:** of, relating to, or situated in the area immediately adjacent to a track and esp. a railway track

track spike *n* **:** an appliance driven or screwed into a tie to hold a rail and tie plate

track storage *n* **:** storage in railroad cars on other than private or industrial tracks beyond the free time allowed for loading or unloading for which a charge in addition to demurrage is usu. made; *also* **:** the charge for such storage

trackwalker \'≈ˌ≈≈\ *n* **:** a worker employed to walk over and inspect a section of tracks

trackway \'≈ˌ≈\ *n* [1*track* + *way*] **1 :** a beaten or trodden path **:** ROADWAY **2 a :** one of two or more narrow paths of steel plates, smooth stone, or other suitable material laid in a public roadway otherwise formed of an inferior pavement (as of cobblestones) to provide an easy way for wheels **b :** a way (as a tramway or railway) with steel or other rails on which flange-wheeled vehicles travel **3 :** a usu. grooved or curved guide in which a door, drawer, or other movable part runs often on ball bearings

tracs *pl of* TRAC

1tract \'trakt\ *n* -S *often cap* [ME *tracte*, fr. ML *tractus*, fr. L, action of drawing, extension, length; fr. its being sung without a break by one voice] **:** the verses of Scripture sung or recited in the Roman liturgy of the mass after the gradual or instead of the alleluia on penitential days from Septuagesima to Holy Saturday, on ember days, and at most vigils and requiems

2tract \"\ *n* -S [ME *tracte*, modif. of L *tractatus* action of handling, discussion, treatise — more at TRACTATE] **1** *archaic* **:** a literary work dealing with a particular topic **:** TREATISE **2 :** a pamphlet, leaflet, or folder issued (as by a political or religious group) for propaganda; *esp* **:** one containing a religious exhortation, a doctrinal discussion, or a proselytizing appeal

3tract \'trakt\ *n* -S [L *tractus* action of drawing, trailing, extension, track, tract of land, space of time, fr. *tractus*, past part. of *trahere* to draw, pull, drag — more at DRAW] **1 a** *archaic* **:** extent or lapse of time **:** continued or protracted duration **:** COURSE **b :** a period in time **:** STRETCH ⟨hoping for a ~ of fair weather⟩ **c** *archaic* **:** a continuous course (as of action or events) **:** CONTINUITY **2 :** an area either large or small: as **a** (1) **:** a region or stretch (as of land) that is usu. indefinitely described or without precise boundaries ⟨a few large ~*s* for settlement⟩ ⟨the wooded ~ between the two rivers⟩ ⟨a great ~ of unexplored sea⟩ (2) **:** a precisely defined or definable area of land ⟨an 80 acre ~⟩ ⟨an urban census ~⟩ **b** (1) **:** a system of body parts or organs acting in concert to perform some function or serve some special purpose ⟨the digestive ~⟩ ⟨upper respiratory ~⟩ (2) **:** a bundle of nerve fibers having a common origin, termination, and function; *esp* **:** such a bundle within the spinal cord or brain — called also *fiber tract;* compare FASCICULUS (3) **:** PTERYLA **c :** a particular and usu. identifiable part of something ⟨large ~*s* of the job about which I know nothing —Robertson Davies⟩ ⟨psychological ~*s* that . . . lurk shapelessly outside the action of a novel —C.H. Rickword⟩ **3** *chiefly dial* **:** TRACK: as **a :** a footprint or other mark indicative of passage **b :** PATH, COURSE, WAY **c :** VESTIGE, TRACE

trac·ta·bil·i·ty \ˌtraktə'bilәd·ē, -lәtē, -i\ *n* [L *tractabilitas*, fr. *tractabilis* tractable + *-itas* -ity] **:** the quality or state of being tractable ⟨was only too delighted at this ~ —Thomas Hardy⟩

trac·ta·ble \'traktəbəl\ *adj* [L *tractabilis*, fr. *tractare* to handle, treat + *-abilis* -able] **1 a :** capable of being easily led, taught, or controlled **:** DOCILE, GOVERNABLE, PLIANT ⟨~ children⟩ ⟨a ~ horse⟩ **b :** ready to listen, yield, conform, or agree — used with *to* ⟨thou shalt find me ~ to any honest reason —Shak.⟩ **2 :** easily handled, managed, or wrought **:** MALLEABLE ⟨gold is ~⟩ **syn** see OBEDIENT

trac·ta·ble·ness *n* -ES **:** the quality or state of being tractable

trac·ta·bly \-blē, -li\ *adv* **:** in a tractable manner

1trac·tar·i·an \trak'terēən, -'ta(a)r-, -'tär-\ *n* -S [2*tract* + *-arian*] **1 :** one who writes, prints, or distributes tracts **2** *usu cap* [so called fr. the *Tracts for the Times*, series of pamphlets expounding Tractarianism] **a :** one of the authors of the *Tracts for the Times* **b :** a promoter or supporter of Tractarianism

2tractarian \(')≈'≈≈≈\ *adj* **1 :** of or relating to tractarians **2** *usu cap* **:** of or relating to Tractarianism

trac·tar·i·an·ism \≈'≈≈ə,nizəm\ *n* -S *usu cap* [1*tractarian* + *-ism*] **:** a system of principles set forth in a series of pamphlets issued at Oxford (1833–41) aimed at the Erastianism and liberalism of that day and urging a revival of the patristic sacramental piety and theology of the 17th century **:** the doctrines of the early leaders of the Oxford movement toward Catholicism in the Church of England — compare ANGLO-CATHOLICISM, LAUDIANISM

trac·tate \'trak,tāt, *usu* -ād·+V\ *n* -S [L *tractatus* action of handling, discussion, treatise, fr. *tractatus*, past part. of *tractare* to draw out, handle, discuss, treat — more at TREAT] **:** TREATISE, DISSERTATION, ESSAY ⟨an economic ~ of the first importance —*Manchester Guardian Weekly*⟩ **syn** see DISCOURSE

trac·ta·tor \-ād·ə(r), -ātə-\ *n* -S [LL, fr. L, handler, fr. *tractatus* (past part.) + *-or*] **1** *obs* **:** a writer of tracts or treatises **2** *usu cap* [so called fr. the *Tracts for the Times*, series of Tractarian pamphlets] **:** TRACTARIAN 2

trac·ta·tule \'traktə,tyül\ *n* -S [*tractate* + *-ule*] **:** a small or minor tractate

trac·tile \'trakt°l, -k,tīl, -k(,)til\ *adj* [L *tractus* (past part. of *trahere* to draw, pull) + E *-ile*] **:** capable of being drawn and esp. of being drawn out in length **:** DUCTILE — **trac·til·i·ty** \trak'tiləd·ē\ *n* -ES

tract index *n* [3*tract*] **:** a record kept by a register of deeds or other proper county official showing the location, size, and name of owner of each plot of land in a county

trac·tion \'trakshən\ *n* -S *often attrib* [ML *traction-, tractio*, fr. L *tractus* (past part. of *trahere* to draw, pull, drag) + *-ion-, -io* -ion — more at DRAW] **1 a :** the act of drawing or pulling **:** the state of being drawn; *also* **:** force exerted in drawing — opposed to *pulsion* **b :** the drawing of a body (as a vehicle) along a plane or gradient by motive power; *also* **:** the motive power employed in such drawing ⟨steam ~⟩ **2 :** power or influence that attracts **:** ATTRACTION **3 :** public utility transportation service (as electric railways and trolley lines) ⟨reviewing the interurban ~ charters⟩ ⟨sales of ~ bonds⟩ **4 a :** the adhesive friction of a body on a surface on which it moves (as of a wheel on a rail or a rope on a pulley) **b** (1) **:** the pulling of or tension established in one body part by another ⟨the gravitational ~ exerted by abdominal viscera on the diaphragm⟩ ⟨~ of skeletal muscle on the joints⟩ (2) **:** a pulling force exerted on a skeletal structure (as in fracture) by means of a special device or apparatus ⟨a ~ splint⟩; *also* **:** a state of tension created by such a pulling force ⟨a leg in ~⟩

trac·tion·al \-shən°l, -shnəl\ *adj* **:** of or relating to traction

traction engine *n* **1 :** a locomotive for drawing vehicles on highways or in the fields **2 :** a railway locomotive that moves by the friction of its driving wheels on rails — compare COG RAILWAY, RACK RAILWAY

traction fiber *n* **:** a spindle fiber that by its contraction is held to draw a mitotic chromosome to a pole of the spindle

traction sand *n* **:** sand carried by a locomotive or trolley car for spraying under the driving wheels to prevent slippage at starts or on grades — called also *engine sand*

traction sprayer *n* **:** an agricultural spray outfit on wheels that is operated by a power drive from the wheels and used esp. for spraying rows of truck crops

traction transport *n* **:** the rolling or sliding of particles along a stream bed by running water, over the ground surface by wind, or on a beach by waves and currents — compare SALTATION

traction wheel *n* **1 :** a locomotive driving wheel that acts by frictional adhesion to a smooth track **2 :** a smooth-rimmed friction wheel for giving motion (as to an endless link belt)

tract·ite \'trak,tīt\ *n* -S *usu cap* [2*tract* (in *Tract for the Times*, series of Tractarian pamphlets) + *-ite*] **:** TRACTARIAN

trac·tive \'traktiv, -tēv *also* -əv\ *adj* [L *tractus* (past part. of *trahere* to draw, pull) + E *-ive*] **:** that draws or is used or exerted in drawing or pulling; *also* **:** of or concerned with traction ⟨~ power⟩

tractive effort *n* **:** the force in pounds exerted by powered equipment (as a locomotive) as measured for statistical purposes at the rim of the driving wheels

trac·tor \'traktə(r)\ *n* -S *often attrib* [NL, fr. L *tractus* (past part. of *trahere* to draw, pull, drag) + *-or* — more at DRAW] **1 a** *archaic* **:** either of the pair of metal rods used in tractoration **b :** an instrument used to exert traction on a body part or tissue (as in surgical procedures) **2 :** an apparatus or device for the draft or sometimes propulsion of another body: as **a :** TRACTION ENGINE 1 **b** (1) **:** a 4-wheeled or caterpillar-tread rider-controlled automotive vehicle used esp. for drawing agricultural or other implements or for bearing and propelling such implements (2) **:** a smaller 2-wheeled apparatus controlled through handlebars by a walking operator and used similarly with gardening and lawn implements **c** *also* **tractor truck :** a motive power unit in the form of a truck with short chassis and no body used in a combination highway freight vehicle — see FULL TRAILER, SEMITRAILER **d :** a small harbor tug (as one designed to draw barges) — called also *marine tractor* **3** *also* **tractor airplane :** an airplane having the propeller forward of the main supporting surfaces — compare PUSHER

trac·to·ra·tion \ˌ≈tə'rāshən\ *n* -S *archaic* **:** a technique of therapy first used about 1796 by Elisha Perkins of Norwich, Conn., consisting in the operation of drawing over an affected part the points of two small rods of different metals, and held to be helpful in local inflammation or pains (as of rheumatism)

trac·tor·ist \'≈≈rəst\ *n* -S **:** a tractor operator

trac·tor·iza·tion \ˌ≈≈rə'zāshən, -ˌrī'z-\ *n* -S [obs. E *tractorize* to use tractors (fr. E *tractor* + *-ize*) + E *-ation*] **:** adoption of tractors as a source of draft power — compare MOTORIZATION

tractor-mounted \ˌ≈≈'≈≈\ *adj* **:** bolted or clamped to a tractor rather than drawn behind it ⟨*tractor-mounted* implements⟩

tractor propeller *n* **:** a propeller of an airplane that is placed at the forward end of its shaft and pulls on the shaft by rotating instead of pushing — compare PUSHER

trac·tot·o·my \trak'tad·əmē\ *n* -ES [ISV 3*tract* + *-o-* + *-tomy*] **:** CHORDOTOMY

trac·trix \'traktriks\ *n, pl* **tractri·ces** \trak'trī(,)sēz\ [NL, fr. L *tractus* (past part. of *trahere* to draw) + *-trix* — more at DRAW] **:** a curve in which the part of the tangent between the point of tangency and a given straight line is constant and which is an involute of a catenary

tracts *pl of* TRACT

tract society *n* **:** a society having as its aim the publication and distribution of religious tracts

trac·tus \'traktəs\ *n, pl* **tractus** [NL, fr. L, tract — more at TRACT] **:** TRACT 2b(2)

trad *abbr* tradition; traditional

trad·able *also* **trade·able** \'trādəbəl\ *adj* **:** that can be traded

trad·al \'trād°l\ *adj* **:** COMMERCIAL

1trade \'trād\ *n* -S [ME, path, track, course of conduct, fr. MLG, path, track; akin to OS *trada* tread, track, OHG *trata* tread, track, course, OE *tredan* to tread — more at TREAD] **1 a** *obs* **:** a path traversed or for traverse **:** COURSE, WAY **b** *archaic* **:** a track or trail left by a man or animal **:** TREAD 1 ⟨some savage beast's ~ —Edmund Spenser⟩ **2 a :** a course of action or conduct **:** mode of procedure or life **b :** a customary course of action **:** HABIT, PRACTICE ⟨thy sin's not accidental, but a ~ —Shak.⟩ **3 a :** the business one practices or the work in which one engages regularly **:** one's calling **:** gainful employment **:** means of livelihood **:** OCCUPATION ⟨wherever a . . . writer or any sort of artist is plying his ~ —C.E.Montague⟩ ⟨a doctor by ~ —*Times Lit. Supp.*⟩: as (1) **:** an occupation requiring manual or mechanical skill and training **:** a craft in which only skilled workers are employed ⟨the harness maker . . . had learned his ~ after five years' service as an apprentice —Sherwood Anderson⟩ ⟨worked at the printer's ~ while preparing for the teaching profession⟩ ⟨a carpenter carrying the tools of his ~⟩ (2) **:** the occupation of a merchant (as a retail merchant) ⟨had demeaned herself a little, as the daughter of a doctor, by marrying into ~ . . . when she married the matter-of-fact, industrious rising young cheese merchant —Florence Bullock⟩ ⟨English society . . . preserved intact the distinction between ~ and gentility —G.H.Sabine⟩ **b :** a workman engaged in a trade ⟨mechanical ~*s* can move in as soon as . . . sheets are placed —*Sweet's Catalog Service*⟩ **c** (1) **:** the group of persons engaged in a particular occupation, business, or industry ⟨as a member of the writing ~ —H.A. Smith⟩ ⟨the book and news ~ clearly oppose the adoption of a national censorship —*Publishers' Weekly*⟩ ⟨the word in the ~ is that May sales were not up to expectations —*Securities Outlook*⟩ (2) **:** a corporation, guild, union, or other organization of craftsmen in a Scottish burgh **4 a** (1) *archaic* **:** travel to and fro **:** coming and going (2) *obs* **:** dealings between persons or groups **:** INTERCOURSE ⟨have you any further ~ with us —Shak.⟩ (3) *dial* **:** FUSS, BOTHER **b** (1) **:** the business of buying and selling or bartering commodities **:** exchange of goods for convenience or profit **:** COMMERCE ⟨a materials shortage that affected first manufacturing, then ~⟩ **:** TRAFFIC ⟨a slump in the cotton ~⟩ ⟨laid off the new clerks when ~ was slack⟩ ⟨was doing a brisk ~ in umbrellas⟩ **:** MARKET ⟨souvenirs imported for the tourist ~⟩ ⟨children's books . . . issued annually for the Christmas ~ —*Bookman's Glossary*⟩; *specif* **:** exchange of merchandise between different places on a large scale ⟨maritime nations for whom world ~ is an important source of income⟩ ⟨carried on ~ in tea and spices with the Orient⟩ ⟨a ship engaged in the coastwise ~⟩ (2) **:** commodities for barter ⟨salt . . . which sold for 2 dollars cash per bushel, or 3 dollars in ~ —Andrew Ellicott⟩ (3) *archaic* **:** a trading expedition ⟨this new scheme of a ~ round the world —Daniel Defoe⟩ (4) **:** an act or instance of trading **:** TRANSACTION ⟨reported the ~ from the floor of the exchange⟩; *esp* **:** an exchange of property usu. without any use of money ⟨an even ~⟩ ⟨he's interested in making a ~ for another good pitcher —*N.Y.Times*⟩ ⟨repairing a car he had taken in ~⟩ (5) **:** a firm's customers **:** the clientele of a business ⟨a girl who waited on ~ in his father's shop —Sherwood Anderson⟩ ⟨sent notices to the ~ about the new location of the store⟩ ⟨a restaurant catering to the breakfast ~⟩ (6) **:** the group of firms or corporations engaged in a line of work **:** BUSINESS ⟨data reported for thirty-seven wholesale ~*s* —E.L.Smith⟩ **:** INDUSTRY ⟨in the rug and shawl ~*s* —C.M.Whittaker & C.C.Wilcock⟩ **5** *chiefly dial* **a :** STUFF; *specif* **:** FOODSTUFF ⟨all that ~ —Sir Walter Scott⟩ **b :** inferior matter or people **:** TRASH ⟨with beatings up . . . by sailors and rough ~ —Gershon Legman⟩ **6 :** TRADE WIND ⟨the steady drive of the ~*s* is changed to fitful inland airs —Marjory S. Douglas⟩

2trade \"\ *vb* -ED/-ING/-S *vt* **1** *obs* **:** to make one's way along or through **:** TREAD, TRAVERSE, LEAD **2** *obs* **a :** to pursue constantly as a course, end, or occupation **b :** to use regularly or habitually ⟨the Greek language which then was the most *traded* . . . through the whole universe —John Donne⟩ **c :** to bring to a state of practice, discipline, or familiarity **:** SCHOOL ⟨learned schoolmasters to ~ up the Christian youth in . . . liberal arts —Thomas Becon⟩ **3** *archaic* **:** to resort to for trade **:** engage in trade with ⟨captain of a ship *trading* the Indies —Amy Lowell⟩ **4 a** (1) **:** to give in exchange for another commodity **:** BARTER ⟨the white men who penetrated to the . . . wilds were always ready . . . to ~ rifles and watches —J.F.Cooper⟩ ⟨stolen horses, which would only be sold or *traded* off . . . hundreds of miles from home —J.F.Dobie⟩ (2) **:** to give in return **:** EXCHANGE ⟨reluctant to ~ the security and rewards of private life for the hazards . . . and the low pay of government office —*Time*⟩ ⟨~ off the right to navigate the lower Mississippi for a slice of the Newfoundland fisheries —E.S.Corwin⟩ ⟨~ a proven pitcher to another team for four rookies⟩; *also* **:** to make an exchange of ⟨when parties ~ votes on certain bills on purely party grounds —G.H. Benton⟩ ⟨~ places with someone who likes to sit by open windows⟩ **:** exchange in give-and-take ⟨we *traded* shots and I got winged —Harvey Fergusson⟩ **b :** to buy and sell (as stock) regularly ⟨~ holdings at a good profit⟩ **~** *vi* **1 a** (1) *chiefly dial* **:** to make one's way **:** WALK, PASS, GO ⟨where be ye *trading* today —Thomas Hardy⟩ (2) **:** to pass to and fro **:** come and go — used esp. of birds ⟨a place . . . over which the pigeons were *trading* between the stubbles and the wood —John Collier b. 1901⟩ **b** *obs* **:** to have dealings **:** NEGOTIATE ⟨would come and speak with him and ~ for a peace —Nicholas Lichefield⟩ **c** *archaic* **:** to occupy oneself **:** ENGAGE ⟨in private . . . she *traded* more deeply in the occult sciences —Sir Walter Scott⟩ **2 a :** to go for purposes of trade ⟨all the vessels that ~ to or from the Red sea —Samuel Johnson⟩ **b** (1) **:** to engage in the exchange, purchase, or sale of goods or other property **:** carry on trade **:** do business for profit ⟨prohibits American firms from *trading* with the enemy⟩ ⟨a company is formed to ~ in building materials —Edward Jenks⟩ (2) **:** to buy and sell securities, real estate, or goods for quick profits rather than for long-term investment ⟨he likes the stock . . . and he is accustomed to *trading* in and out of its shares —*A.B.C. of Puts & Calls*⟩ **c :** to deal in something not properly for sale **:** TRAFFIC — usu. used with *in* ⟨the chief justice . . . *traded* largely in pardons —T.B.Macaulay⟩ **d :** to deal regularly or frequently as a customer ⟨~*s* only with merchants she knows⟩ **:** make one's purchases **:** SHOP ⟨~*s* at his store when she is in town⟩ **e :** to have a specified price in securities trading **:** SELL ⟨the common ~*s* around 15 —*Investor's Reader*⟩ **3 :** to give one thing in return for another ⟨wanted to change his days off and got a friend to ~ with him⟩ **:** make an exchange ⟨wore each other's hat for a while and then *traded* back⟩ — **trade on** *also* **trade upon :** to take often unscrupulous advantage of **:** EXPLOIT ⟨*traded on* their influence . . . in securing special favors for contractors —T.C.Pease⟩ ⟨individuals who attempt to *trade on* . . . their social standing or their forebears —H.H.Arnold & I.C.Eaker⟩ ⟨the theater *trades on* a will to believe —Bernard DeVoto⟩ — **trade on the equity :** to use borrowed funds, bonds, or preferred stock in the operation of a company in order to augment profits for the common stockholder — compare LEVERAGE

3trade \"\ *adj* **1 :** of or relating to trade ⟨~ channels⟩ ⟨~ statistics⟩ ⟨~ problems⟩ **2 :** used in trade ⟨a ~ path⟩ ⟨a ~

ducat⟩ ⟨~ calendars⟩ ⟨~ catalogs of the mail-order houses⟩; *specif* : being merchandise for barter with primitive peoples usu. differing in material and form from the native product ⟨the relatively early displacement of native equipment by ~ goods —Eleanor Leacock⟩ ⟨~ tomahawks⟩ ⟨~ blankets⟩ **3 a** : intended for or limited to persons in business or industry rather than the general public ⟨a ~ fair⟩ ⟨a ~ show for film exhibitors⟩ ⟨a ~ price⟩ ⟨~ sales⟩ **b** : of, intended for, or used by people in a particular trade or occupation rather than the general public ⟨a ~ convention⟩ ⟨~ circles⟩ ⟨run ads in a ~ paper⟩ ⟨a ~ journal⟩ ⟨a ~ term not in most vocabularies⟩ **c** : that specializes in work for other craftsmen or concerns engaged in the same or a closely related business and that does not usu. deal directly with the ultimate user or consumer ⟨a ~ printing house⟩ ⟨a ~ compositor⟩ ⟨a ~ bindery⟩ **4 a** *also* **trades** : of, composed of, or representing the trades or trade unions ⟨a ~ club⟩ ⟨a ~ hall⟩ **b** : of, relating to, or training for a skilled manual or mechanical trade ⟨a ~ or professional work⟩ ⟨~ dictionaries⟩ ⟨~ students⟩ **5** : of or associated with a trade wind ⟨the ~ belts⟩ ⟨~ clouds⟩

[4]**trade** \"\ *adv* [[1]*trade* (sense 2)] *archaic* : in a regular course : regularly and steadily in the same direction; *specif* : in the manner and direction of a trade wind ⟨the winds . . . seemed to be more steadily against us, blowing almost ~ —Daniel Defoe⟩

tradeable *var of* TRADABLE

trade acceptance *n* : a time draft or bill of exchange for the amount of a specific purchase drawn by the seller on the buyer, bearing the buyer's acceptance and often his specification of the place of payment (as a bank in which he has funds), and being negotiable when executed according to statute — compare BANK ACCEPTANCE

trade agreement *n* **1** : an international agreement involving conditions of trade in goods and services **2** : COLLECTIVE AGREEMENT

trade area *or* **trading area** *n* : a geographic area within which a business enterprise or center of retail or wholesale distribution draws most of its business ⟨the wholesale *trading area* for groceries of the city⟩ ⟨a department store's *trading area*⟩ ⟨the *trading area* of a shopping center⟩

trade association *n* : an association of tradesmen, businessmen, or manufacturers in a particular trade or industry for the protection and advancement of their common interests

trade balance *n* : BALANCE OF TRADE

trade bill *n* : a time draft or bill of exchange becoming a trade acceptance when signed by an acceptor

trade binding *n* : EDITION BINDING

trade board *n* : one of the former British official boards consisting of representatives from the employers and workers of an industry and neutral appointed members and charged with setting minimum wages for the industry

trade book *n* **1** : a book intended for general readership ⟨a *trade book* . . . is not a juvenile, not a textbook, not a technical treatise, but the sort of thing that could (and the publisher hopes will) interest everybody —J.T.Winterich⟩ **2** : TRADE EDITION

trade card *n, Brit* : BUSINESS CARD ⟨the *trade card* of an 18th century English instrument maker engraved with illustrations on a large sheet of paper⟩

trade coin *n* : a coin intended for use in foreign trade

trade commissioner *n* : a government official stationed in a foreign country and usu. subordinate in rank to a commercial attaché but with similar duties

trade council *also* **trades council** *n* : a central organization of local trade unions : a central labor union

trade cumulus *n* : a peculiar small detached cumulus cloud characteristic of trade-wind regions

trade cycle *n, Brit* : BUSINESS CYCLE

trade discount *n* : a percentage deduction from the list price of goods allowed by a manufacturer or wholesaler to customers engaged in trade

trade dollar *n* : a dollar issued as a trade coin; *esp* : the U. S. silver dollar weighing 420 grains .900 fine issued 1873–85 for use in oriental trade

trade down *vi* : to stock or purchase lower priced merchandise or property ⟨start the season with better goods and then *trade down* —*Women's Wear Daily*⟩

trade edition *n* : an edition of a book in a standard format intended for general distribution; *esp* : such an edition as contrasted with a deluxe or library-bound or paperback edition or sometimes with an edition published by a book club — compare TEXT EDITION, TRADE BOOK

trade fixture *n* : FIXTURE 2c(3)

trade·ful \ˈtrādfəl\ *adj* : full of trade : COMMERCIAL

trade gap *n* : the extent to which a country's imports during a period have exceeded its exports and have been obtained through gold shipments, the sale of foreign assets, or credit : an unfavorable balance of trade — compare DOLLAR GAP

trade guild *n* **1** : a craft guild **2** *chiefly Brit* : TRADE UNION

trade in *vt* : to turn in as payment or part payment of a purchase or bill ⟨*trade* an old car *in* for a new one⟩

trade–in \ˈ=,=\ *n* -s [*trade in*] : an item of merchandise (as an automobile or refrigerator) taken as payment or part payment of a purchase

trade language *n* : a lingua franca (as a pidgin) used for trade

trade–last \ˈ=,=\ *n* -s : a complimentary remark by a third person that a hearer offers to repeat to the person complimented if the latter will first report a compliment made about the hearer — abbr. *T.L.*

trade·less \ˈtrādləs\ *adj* : having no trade

[1]**trademark** \ˈ=,=\ *n* **1** : a word, letter, device, sound, or symbol or some combination of these that is used in connection with merchandise, distinctly points inherently or by association to the not necessarily known origin or ownership of that to which it is applied, and is legally reserved to the exclusive use of the owner according to statutory provisions : a name or symbol used by a maker or seller to identify distinctively his products ⟨must display his ~ on his product for it to be legally valid⟩ ⟨a ~ can only be transferred in connection with the goodwill of the business —Edward Jenks⟩ — compare COPYRIGHT, SERVICE MARK **2** : a distinctive feature, characteristic, or eccentricity that becomes so associated with a person or thing as to be a sign or designation of that person or thing : an identifying mark or feature ⟨the derringers . . . became almost a ~ of gamblers —Elmer Keith⟩

[2]**trademark** \"\ *vt* **1** : to put or affix a trademark upon : label with a trademark **2** : to secure trademark rights for : to register the trademark of

trademark infringement *n* : an appropriation or imitation that is likely to deceive ordinary or unwary buyers into accepting the goods of one trader as those of another — compare UNFAIR COMPETITION

[1]**trade name** *n* **1 a** : the name by which an article is called among traders ⟨blue vitriol, a common *trade name* for copper sulfate⟩ **b** : an invented or arbitrarily adopted name that is given by a manufacturer or merchant to an article or service to distinguish it as one produced or sold by him or is generally so used by purchasers and that may be used and protected as a trademark **2** : the name or style under which a concern does business that will when it by association identifies a particular manufacturer or merchant be protected at common law against the use by others of a similar name which is calculated to deceive — compare UNFAIR COMPETITION

[2]**trade name** *vt* : to designate with a trade name

trade off *vi* : to exchange places with each other or with each other at intervals : ALTERNATE ⟨*traded off* with each other several years for first place in the bowling tournament⟩ ~ *vt* : to use alternately ⟨*trade off* large and small brushes for rough and fine work⟩

trade practice *n* : a method of competition, operating policy (as the use of standards of size, shape, and quality of materials), or business procedure common to members of a line of business or industry that may be formally adopted sometimes as a rule under government auspices

trade publisher *n* : a publisher of trade books

trad·er \ˈtrād·ə(r)\ *n* -s **1** : one that trades: **a** : a person whose business is buying and selling or barter : MERCHANT, DEALER ⟨a ~ to the East Indies⟩ **b** : a person who gets his livelihood by buying and selling for gain **c** (1) : one that buys and sells securities mainly for capital gains — often contrasted with *investor* (2) : an employee of a brokerage or investment house who actually executes orders either for customers or for the account of the house ⟨a government bond ~⟩ ⟨a bank stock ~⟩ **2** *obs* : PROSTITUTE **3** : a ship engaged in the coasting or foreign trade

trade rat *n* [so called fr. its habit of replacing with some other article any article it takes away] : PACK RAT

trade route *n* **1** : a route followed by traders (as in caravans) **2** : one of the sea lanes ordinarily used by merchant ships

trad·er·ship \ˈtrādə(r),ship\ *n* : the position of a trader

trades *pl of* TRADE, *pres 3d sing of* TRADE

trad·es·can·tia \,tradəˈskanch(ē)ə, -ntēə\ *n* [NL, fr. John *Tradescant* †1638 Eng. traveler and gardener + NL *-ia*] **1** *cap* : a genus of American herbs (family Commelinaceae) comprising the spiderworts and having mostly narrow elongated leaves and large white, pink, or violet ephemeral bracteate flowers **2** -s : any plant of the genus *Tradescantia* or of the related genus *Zebrina*

trade school *n* : a school usu. on the secondary level devoted esp. to teaching the practice and theory of skilled trades

trades council *var of* TRADE COUNCIL

trade secret *n* : a formula, pattern, process, or device that is used in one's business and that gives an advantage over competitors who do not know or use it

tradesfolk \ˈ=,=\ *n pl* : people in trade; *specif* : TRADESMEN

trades·man \ˈ=mən\ *n, pl* **tradesmen** [*trade's* (gen. of [1]*trade*) + *man*] **1 a** : one who trades : one who buys and sells things for a profit or means of living : SHOPKEEPER **b** : an employee of a shopkeeper **2** : a workman in one of the skilled trades : ARTISAN, CRAFTSMAN

tradespeople \ˈ=,==\ *n pl* : TRADESMEN

trade test *n* : a test of proficiency in a given trade (as plumbing) standardized by obtaining norms for novices, apprentices, journeymen, and experts in the trade

trade union *also* **trades union** *n* : LABOR UNION; *specif* : one limited in membership to workmen engaged in the same trade rather than the same craft, company, or industry

trade–union \ˈ=ˈ==\ *adj* [*trade union*] : of or relating to trade unions or trade unionism

trade unionism *also* **trades unionism** *n* : the system or the principles and theory of trade unions or adherence to these principles : UNIONISM

trade unionist *n* **1** : a member of a trade union **2** : an advocate of trade unionism

trade up *vi* : to stock, promote the sale of, or purchase higher priced merchandise or property ⟨a big opportunity to *trade up* into higher price lines . . . is seen by Buffalo housedress buyers —*Women's Wear Daily*⟩ ⟨a certain percentage of the customers who come into a store . . . to buy the leader end by *trading up* and purchasing a higher-priced product —J.G.Lippincott⟩ ⟨a homeowner who wants to move or *trade up* —*Time*⟩ ~ *vt* : to persuade (a customer) to purchase a higher-priced item ⟨showing her the better garment . . . helps *trade* a good many of them *up* and out of the price bracket they had intended to stay within —*Dry Goods Jour.*⟩

tra·dev·man \trəˈdevmən\ *n, pl* **tradevmen** [*tra*ining *dev*ices *man*] : a petty officer in the U. S. Navy who installs, operates, maintains, and repairs training devices used esp. in gunnery, aviation, and electronics instruction

trade warranty *or* **trading warranty** *n* : a warranty in a marine insurance policy restricting the use of an insured ship to the type of cargo, the service (as the lake trade), and sometimes the season for which it was designed

trade waste *n, Brit* : an industrial waste

trade wind *n* [[4]*trade*] : a wind blowing almost constantly in one direction; *esp* : a wind that blows almost continually toward the equator from the northeast in the belt between the northern horse latitudes and the doldrums and from the southeast in the belt between the southern horse latitudes and the doldrums and is produced as a result of the rotation of the earth and movement of the air toward the equatorial regions during circulation between the warmer and colder portions of the earth — called also *trade*; compare ANTITRADES, MONSOON

trading *adj* **1 a** : engaged or used in trade ⟨Britons have been largely a ~ and industrial people —*Lamp*⟩ ⟨a ~ boat⟩ **b** : frequented by traders or purchasers ⟨a ~ center⟩ **2** *of an officeholder* : JOBBING, VENAL, CORRUPT

trading area *var of* TRADE AREA

trading bank *n, Austral* : COMMERCIAL BANK

trading card *n* : one of a collection of cards (as playing cards of different back designs) collected and traded esp. by children

trading company *n* : a company organized to carry on commerce with foreign nations or in overseas territories ⟨*trading companies* played an important part in the early settlement of America —O.M.Dickerson⟩: **a** : REGULATED COMPANY **b** : a joint stock company for trade and usu. colonization legally incorporated (as by the British Crown) under a charter granting the company rights to a specific territory within an area claimed by the authority granting the charter including legal title, a monopoly of trade, and governmental and military jurisdiction **c** : an unincorporated company with limited liability for its associates organized principally to settle and develop a land grant obtained from a legally incorporated company

trading estate *n, Brit* : INDUSTRIAL PARK

trading limit *n* **1** : one of the prices above or below which trading on commodity exchanges is not allowed during any one day **2** : a maximum number of contracts an individual is allowed to hold at one time in commodities covered by regulation

trading market *n* : a securities market without a definite price trend and with few traders other than professionals

trading post *n* **1** : a station of a trader or trading company established in a sparsely settled region where trade in products of local origin is carried on with natives in exchange for goods they desire to purchase **2** : [7]POST 4b

trading stamp *n* : a printed stamp of value given as a premium by a retail dealer to a customer and when accumulated in numbers redeemable in merchandise to be selected from a list of articles of various values — compare COUPON

tra·di·tion \trəˈdishən\ *n* -s [ME *tradicion, tradicioun*, fr. MF & L; MF *tradition*, fr. L *tradition-, traditio* action of handing over, teaching, tradition — more at TREASON] **1** : an act of delivering or surrendering something to another: as **a** *Roman, civil, & Scots law* : transfer or acquisition of property by mere delivery with intent of both parties to transfer the title in cases permitted by law (as in a sale or donation) **b** : the ecclesiastical offense committed by a traditor **2** : the process of handing down information, opinions, beliefs, and customs by word of mouth or by example : transmission of knowledge and institutions through successive generations without written instruction ⟨a very different process from the ~ . . . which transmits culture from one generation of a society to another —A.L.Kroeber⟩ **3** : an inherited or established way of thinking, feeling, or doing : a cultural feature (as an attitude, belief, custom, institution) preserved or evolved from the past ⟨a rebellious break with the ~s of their forebears⟩ : usage or custom rooted in the past (as of a family or nation) ⟨older universities rich in ~⟩: as **a** (1) : a doctrine or practice or a body of doctrine and practice preserved by oral transmission (2) : a belief or practice or the totality of beliefs and practices not derived directly from the Bible but arising and handed down within the Christian community orig. by oral transmission (3) *often cap* : a teaching or of the body of an unwritten code of Jewish law believed to have been given by God to Moses on Sinai and later reduced to writing in the Mishnah (4) *often cap, Islam* : HADITH **b** : a belief or story or a body of beliefs and stories relating to the past and commonly accepted as historical but not verifiable ⟨a ~ has grown up that it was put there by mistake —*Amer. Guide Series: Va.*⟩ ⟨portray beautiful old Japanese ~s, like the legend of the fisher . . . beloved by the Sea God's daughter —Lafcadio Hearn⟩ ⟨biographical details purporting to be based on family ~ —W.J. Ghent⟩ **c** (1) : an inherited principle, standard, or practice or body of principles, standards, and practices serving as the established guide of an individual or group ⟨held always to the religious and doctrinal ~s of his Puritan ancestry —T.D. Bacon⟩ ⟨the American ~ of democracy⟩ ⟨the company's ~ of safety⟩ ⟨the isolationist ~ still dominated American thought —H.H.Sprout⟩ : CONVENTION ⟨an old German theatrical ~ which allows you to start a quarter of an hour later than advertised —Barry Carman⟩ (2) : a literary or artistic rule or standard (as of theme, style, symbolism) or a body of such conventions normative for a period or group (as the followers of a great artist) ⟨followed the Arabic ~ of using no representations of living objects in their art —Edith Diehl⟩ ⟨the title poem . . . represents a complete break with nineteenth-century ~ —F.R.Leavis⟩ (3) : a technique or set of habits used in making the artifacts characteristic of a period or culture ⟨the flaked-flint ~⟩; *also* : the cultural continuity associated with such a tradition in a given region ⟨the Acheulean ~⟩ **d** : a practice or pattern of events of long standing : CUSTOM ⟨summer camps . . . are located by ~ on lakes —E.W.Smith⟩ ⟨the old ~ of the absence of the men from the village . . . is continued in modern times by soldiers and labor migrants —Mary Tew⟩ **e** : the manner characteristic of an individual group, or system : customary method or style — usu. used with *in* ⟨the music . . . composed mainly in the British music hall ~ —Roger Manvell⟩ ⟨the member companies . . . whoop it up for Douglas fir plywood in the best trade association ~ —*Monsanto Mag.*⟩ **4** : a line of historical continuity or development marked by distinctive characteristics ⟨bred in the aristocratic ~⟩ ⟨psychiatry is an offshoot of the medical ~ —Edward Sapir⟩ ⟨the latter work . . . does not belong to the same manuscript ~ —Dorothy Robathan⟩ — often used with *in* ⟨in folk ~ singers almost invariably set new poems to tunes already in common use — S.P.Bayard⟩ **5 a** : cultural continuity embodied in a massive complex of evolving social attitudes, beliefs, conventions, and institutions rooted in the experience of the past and exerting an orienting and normative influence on the present ⟨a sense of ~⟩ **b** : the residual elements of past artistic styles or periods **6** : the force exerted by the past upon the present : cultural inertia ⟨bound by family ~ in his choice of career⟩ ⟨resist political ~⟩ **7** : something existing only in popular belief : inherited reputation or memory ⟨without social position save a ~ of gentility —Havelock Ellis⟩

tra·di·tion·al \-shənᵊl, -shnəl\ *adj* [ML *traditionalis*, fr. L *tradition-, traditis* tradition + *-alis* -al] **1** : of or relating to tradition : consisting of or derived from tradition : handed down from age to age without writing ⟨~ history⟩ **2** : following or conforming to tradition : based on an order, code, or practice accepted from the past : CONVENTIONAL ⟨~ morality⟩; *also* : observant of or holding to such traditions : TRADITIONALISTIC ⟨a ~ dramatist⟩ **3** : designed with conscious adherence to architectural styles of the past — compare CONTEMPORARY, MODERN

tra·di·tion·al·ism \-shənᵊl,izəm, -shnə,li-\ *n* -s [F *traditionalisme*, fr. ML *traditionalis* traditional + F *-isme* -ism] **1 a** : the doctrines, principles, or practices of those who follow or accept tradition **b** *often cap* : the beliefs of those opposed to modernism, liberalism, radicalism **c** : FUNDAMENTALISM **2** : orientation of a society toward old established values and institutions

tra·di·tion·al·ist \-shənᵊləst, -shnəl-\ *n* -s [F *traditionaliste*, fr. *traditionalisme*, after such pairs as MF *athéisme* atheism: *athéiste* atheist] : one who adheres to or advocates adherence to tradition : a believer in or proponent of traditionalism — **tra·di·tion·al·is·tic** \trəˌdishənᵊlˈistik, -shnəˈli-, -tēk\ *adj*

tra·di·tion·al·i·ty \trəˌdishəˈnaləd·ē\ *n* -ES : TRADITIONALISM, CONVENTIONALITY

tra·di·tion·al·ize \trəˈdishənᵊl,īz, -shnə,līz\ *vt* -ED/-ING/-S : to make traditional : imbue with traditions or traditionalism

traditional logic *n* **1** : a system of formal logic mainly concerned with the syllogistic forms of deduction that is based on Aristotle and includes some of the changes and elaborations made by the Stoics and the Scholastics : ARISTOTELIAN LOGIC — compare IMMEDIATE INFERENCE, OPPOSITION, SUBJECT-PREDICATE, SYLLOGISM, SYMBOLIC LOGIC **2** : inductive logic esp. as developed by Francis Bacon and J. S. Mill

tra·di·tion·al·ly \-nᵊlē, -nəlē, -i\ *adv* **1** : in a traditional manner ⟨a modernistic interior contrasting with a ~ designed exterior⟩ **2** : by tradition : CUSTOMARILY ⟨a district that ~ votes Republican⟩ **3** : according to traditional belief ⟨~ claimed to be the poet's birthplace⟩

[1]**tra·di·tion·ary** \-shə,nerē, -ri\ *adj* : of the nature of a tradition : founded on or derived from tradition : full of traditions : TRADITIONAL ⟨a ~ dignity⟩ ⟨a ~ legend⟩

[2]**traditionary** \"\ *n* -ES : TRADITIONALIST

tra·di·tion·ate \-shə,nāt, *usu* -ād·+V\ *vt* -ED/-ING/-S : to indoctrinate with tradition

tra·di·tion·er \-sh(ə)nə(r)\ *n* -s : TRADITIONIST

tra·di·tion·ism \-shə,nizəm\ *n* -s : TRADITIONALISM

tra·di·tion·ist \-ˌnəst\ *n* -s **1** : TRADITIONALIST **2** : one versed in traditions : one who transmits a tradition

tradition·less \=ˈ==ləs\ *adj* : having no traditions

traditions *pl of* TRADITION

trad·i·tive \ˈtradəd·iv, -ətiv\ *adj* [prob. fr. obs. F, fem. of *traditif*, fr. L *traditus* (past part. of *tradere* to hand over) + F *-if* -ive — more at TRAITOR] : TRADITIONAL

trad·i·tor \ˈtradəd·ə(r)\ *n, pl* **tradito·res** \ˌtradəˈtō(ˌ)ēz\ [ME *traditour* traitor, fr. L *traditor* — more at TRAITOR] **1** *obs* : TRAITOR **2** : one of the Christians giving up to the officers of the law the Scriptures, the sacred vessels, or the names of their brethren during the Roman persecutions

tra·duce \trəˈd(y)üs\ *vt* -ED/-ING/-S [L *traducere* to lead across, transfer, degrade, fr. *tra-, trans-* trans- + *ducere* to lead — more at TOW] **1 a** *obs* : to turn from one language or form into another **b** : to debase or pervert by translating **2 a** : to lower or disgrace the reputation of : expose to shame or blame by utterance of falsehood or misrepresentation ⟨feels that his country is being *traduced* and its war effort sneered at —Richard Watts⟩ **b** : to make mock of : VIOLATE, BETRAY ⟨is *traducing* our American principle of law that a man is presumed innocent until proven guilty —Agnes Meyer⟩ **syn** see MALIGN

tra·duce·ment *n* -s : an act of traducing

tra·duc·er \trəˈd(y)üsə(r)\ *n* -s : one that traduces; *esp* : CALUMNIATOR

[1]**tra·du·cian** \-üshən\ *n* -s [ML *traducianus*, fr. *traduc-, tradux* heredity (fr. L, layer, layerage, fr. *traducere* to lead across) + L *-ianus* -ian] : a believer in traducianism

[2]**traducian** \"\ *adj* : of or relating to traducianism or traducians

tra·du·cian·ism \-ə,nizəm\ *n* -s [NL *traducianismus*, fr. ML *traducianus* + L *-ismus* -ism] : a theological doctrine that the human souls of new infants are generated from the souls of their parents at the moment of conception much in the same manner as the generation of human bodies — compare CREATIONISM, INFUSIONISM

tra·du·cian·ist \-ənəst\ *n* -s [NL *traducianista*, fr. ML *traducianus* traducian + L *-ista* -ist] : a believer in traducianism — **tra·du·cian·is·tic** \=ˌ=shəˈnistik\ *adj*

tra·duc·tion \trəˈdəkshən\ *n* [LL *traduction-, traductio*, fr. L, act of transferring, fr. *traductus* (past part. of *traducere* to lead across, transfer) + *-ion-, -io* -ion] **1** : the act or an instance of traducing; *specif* : an act of defaming : DEFAMATION, SLANDER **2** : the repetition of a word or one of its derivatives or a term with a change in sense for rhetorical or argumentative effect **3** *obs* : something traduced; *esp* : TRADITION **4** : logical inference in which premises and conclusion are of the same order of generality

tra·duc·tive \-ktiv\ *adj* [LL *traductivus*, fr. L *traductus* (past part.) + *-ivus* -ive] *archaic* : capable of being deduced : DERIVATIVE

traf *abbr* traffic

[1]**traf·fic** \ˈtrafik, -fēk\ *n* -s *often attrib* [MF *trafique*, fr. OIt *traffico*, fr. *trafficare*] **1 a** : commercial activity usu. involving import and export trade ⟨nurtured by land and water ~, it grew into a commercial center —*Amer. Guide Series: Ark.*⟩ **b** : the activity of exchanging commodities by bartering or buying and selling ⟨~ with the Indians, exchanging jewelry for horses⟩ ⟨perishable and livestock ~ . . . consigned to other than morning markets —*Farmer's Weekly (So. Africa)*⟩ ⟨middle classes . . . conducting the ~ by which they live —Agnes Repplier⟩ ⟨proud of his snug ~ in rich men's bonds, mortgages and deeds —Leo Marx⟩ **c** : illegal or disreputable usu. commercial activity ⟨a few such experiences sent him back to the narcotics ~ —Frank O'Leary⟩ ⟨~ in honors . . . and pardons was incessant —T.B.Macaulay⟩ ⟨evidence of Red ~

in contraband arms —*Wall Street Jour.*⟩ ⟨prohibit transportation in interstate commerce for the white slave ~ —*Congressional Record*⟩ **2 a :** communication or dealings between individuals or groups **:** INTERCOURSE, BUSINESS ⟨held that there was no ~ between the human and the divine —John Buchan⟩ ⟨realized for us in the three-hours ~ of the stage —J.I.M. Stewart⟩ ⟨don't want any more ~ with his sort⟩ ⟨for through our lively ~ all the day —W.H.Auden⟩ **b :** reciprocal giving and receiving **:** EXCHANGE ⟨facilitate a lively ~ in ideas —F.L. Allen⟩ **3 a** *archaic* **:** GOODS ⟨you'll see a draggled damsel . . . her fishy ~ bear —John Gay⟩ **b traffics** *pl* **:** CARGO ⟨move bulk ~s over long distances at reasonable speeds —P.E. Garbutt⟩ **4 a** (1) **:** the circulation (as of vehicles or pedestrians) through an area **:** passage to and fro ⟨flooring . . . suitable for light ~ —*Nat'l Fire Codes*⟩ ⟨heavy lake ~ during the summer months⟩ (2) **:** the flow of vehicles, pedestrians, ships, or planes (as along a street or sidewalk or air or sea lane) ⟨will open a needed avenue . . . for passenger and freight ~ —M.M. Lilly & G.H.Kester⟩ ⟨the full flood of the Christmas ~ —Compton Mackenzie⟩ **b** (1) **:** the vehicles or pedestrians moving along a route ⟨air and sea ~ will be notified —*Science*⟩ ⟨construction of the building attracted the interest of sidewalk ~⟩ (2) **:** the volume of vehicles or pedestrians moving along a route ⟨engineers . . . who tabulate the ~ —A.W.Baum⟩ **c** (1) **:** the information or signals transmitted or received over a communications system **:** MESSAGES ⟨made arrangements for an interchange of ~ with other lines —H.W.Faulkner⟩ (2) **:** the flow of messages or signals through a communications system ⟨radio ~ has stepped up enormously —Pat Frank⟩ **d :** the volume of customers visiting a business establishment ⟨floor ~ in its showroom was up 60 percent —*Newsweek*⟩ **5 a :** the number of passengers or amount of cargo carried by a transportation system ⟨railroads handled more ~ than in the previous peak year —E.C.Helmreich⟩ ⟨oceangoing passenger ~ —*Current Biog.*⟩ **b :** the business of transporting passengers or freight ⟨proposals . . . to get a proper share of international air ~ —C.H.Grattan⟩ ⟨plans for a resurrected river ~ —*Amer. Guide Series: Minn.*⟩ **6 :** TRAFFIC DEPARTMENT — **the traffic will bear :** existing conditions will allow or permit ⟨their overhead is more than *the traffic will bear* —D.W.Brogan⟩ ⟨getting all *the traffic will bear* —C.E.Wright⟩ ⟨permitted to sell their surplus for whatever *the traffic will bear* —Joseph Wechsberg⟩

²**traffic** \", *esp in pres part* -fək\ *also* **traf·fick** \"\ *vb* **trafficked; trafficked; trafficking; traffics** *also* **trafficks** [MF *trafiquer*, fr. OIt *trafficare*] *vi* **1 a :** to engage in commercial activity **:** buy and sell regularly **:** TRADE ⟨got my living for a while by . . . *trafficking* in rabbit skins —Augusta Gregory⟩ ⟨last of the impresarios . . . who *trafficked* in art in the grand manner —Bernard Simon⟩ **b :** to engage in illegal or disreputable business or activity ⟨began to ~ in army promotions —Geoffrey Bruun⟩ **2 :** to carry on communication or negotiation **:** DEAL, BARGAIN ⟨will not ~ with the breakers of the peace —H.S.Truman⟩ ⟨convinced himself . . . the child was *trafficking* with bards, or druids, or witches —W.B.Yeats⟩ **3 :** to concentrate one's effort or interest **:** SPECIALIZE ⟨virtuoso soloists . . . continue to ~ in the well-worn favorites —Lawrence Morton⟩ ⟨characteristic of a medium which ~s in comedy extremes —*Newsweek*⟩ **4 :** to pass to and fro **:** WANDER ⟨spilled out of their houses to laugh and ~ along its . . . streets —Lucy Embury⟩ ~ *vt* **1 :** to journey over **:** TRAVEL ⟨most heavily *trafficked* highway in the state —*Amer. Guide Series: Vt.*⟩ ⟨venture to ~ them in the day, but few would risk such perilous thoroughfares by night —F.S.Merryweather⟩ **2 :** to make an exchange of **:** TRADE, BARTER ⟨pies and cakes being *trafficked* back and forth across the street —Arthur Miller⟩

traf·fic·abil·i·ty \ˌtrafikəˈbiləd·ē\ *n* **1 :** the quality of a terrain to permit passage (as of vehicles and troops) ⟨areas of low ~ and . . . beaches with steep gradients —J.F.Shaw⟩ **2 :** the ability of a military force to move over a terrain ⟨our failure to develop full cross-country ~ —*Combat Forces Jour.*⟩

traf·fic·able \ˈtrafikəbəl\ *adj* [²*traffic* + *-able*] **1 :** suitable for trading **:** used in trade **:** MARKETABLE ⟨required what may be called ~ material —Alexander Somerville⟩ **2 :** open to traffic **:** PASSABLE ⟨related . . . development to population and ~ roads —*Geog. Jour.*⟩

traf·fi·ca·tor \ˈtrafəˌkād·ə(r\ *n* -s [blend of ¹*traffic* and *indicator*] *Brit* **:** a movable directional signal on a vehicle

traffic block *n*, *Brit* **:** TRAFFIC JAM

traffic circle *n* **:** ROTARY 2

traffic cone *n* **:** a conical marker used on a road or highway (as for indicating an area under repair)

traffic cop *n* **:** a policeman who regulates the movement of traffic ⟨need a *traffic cop* at the intersection during rush hour⟩

traffic court *n* **:** a minor court for disposition of petty prosecutions for violations of statutes, ordinances, and local regulations governing the use of highways and motor vehicles

traffic density *n* **:** DENSITY OF FREIGHT TRAFFIC

traffic department *n* **:** a department in a company or agency that supervises any of various operations (as sales, transportation, public relations, or the maintaining of production schedules)

traffic divider *n* **:** a barrier (as a guardrail, fence, or concrete wall) placed between the lanes of a highway to divide the traffic moving in opposite directions

traffic engineer *n* **:** an engineer whose training or occupation is traffic engineering

traffic engineering *n* **:** a branch of highway engineering dealing with the planning and design of streets and highways and the safe, economical, and convenient control of traffic

traffic island *n* **:** a paved or planted island in a roadway designed to guide the flow of traffic; *also* **:** MEDIAN STRIP

traffic jam *n* **:** a jamming up (as of vehicular traffic) into a disorganized standstill ⟨the detour caused a *traffic jam* full of cursing honking drivers⟩

traf·fick·er \ˈtrafikə(r), -fēk-\ *n* -s **:** one that traffics: **a :** NEGOTIATOR, SCHEMER ⟨whole clan of . . . spies and ~s —R.L. Stevenson⟩ **b :** MERCHANT, DEALER ⟨groups of ~s who . . . made a market of their wares —Gilbert Parker⟩ ⟨a ~ in ideas —Ellery Sedgwick⟩

traffic lane *n* **:** LANE 3c

traffic management *n* **:** the management of the physical and cost-control phases of the receiving, handling, storing, and distributing of goods for industrial and commercial organizations

traffic manager *n* **1 :** an officer of the freight or passenger traffic department of a transport carrier who has charge of traffic solicitation, determination of rates and fares, and related traffic functions **2 :** a supervisor of the traffic functions of a commercial or industrial organization **3 :** the director of a large telegraph office

traffic pattern *n* **:** PATTERN 12

traffic sign *n* **:** a sign usu. on the side of a street or highway bearing symbols or words of warning or direction to motorists or pedestrians and often having a characteristic shape — compare STOP SIGN

traffic signal *or* **traffic light** *also* **traffic control signal** *n* **:** a usu. electrically operated signal (as a system of colored lights) for warning and controlling traffic ⟨a car racing its motor, waiting for the *traffic signal* to turn green⟩ — compare WIGWAG SIGNAL

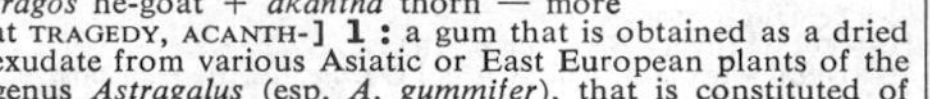
traffic signal

traffic unit *n* **:** a statistical unit combining ton-miles and passenger-miles and used by transportation agencies (as railroads, bus lines, airlines) in measuring the volume of passenger and freight traffic

trafficway \ˈ≈≈,≈\ *n* **1 :** RIGHT OF WAY 2b **2 a :** a roadway open to traffic **b :** HIGHWAY

trag *abbr* tragedian; tragedy; tragic

trag·a·canth \ˈtrajəˌkan(t)th, -ˌkaa(ə)n- *also* -ˌkən- *sometimes* -agə(ˌ)k- *or* -aigə *or* -gə(ˌ)s-\ *n* -s [MF *tragacanthe*, *tragacanth*, fr. L *tragacantha*, fr. Gk *tragakantha*, fr. *tragos* he-goat + *akantha* thorn — more at TRAGEDY, ACANTH-] **1 :** a gum that is obtained as a dried exudate from various Asiatic or East European plants of the genus *Astragalus* (esp. *A. gummifer*), that is constituted of bassorin and tragacanthin, that swells in water to a gel, and that is used chiefly as an emulsifying, suspending, and thickening agent and also as a demulcent and excipient for pills **2 :** a plant yielding tragacanth

trag·a·can·thin \ˌ≈≈ˈk|an(t)thən, ˌ≈≈ˈs|, |aan(-\ *n* -s **:** a substance obtained from tragacanth that is soluble in water forming a hydrosol — compare BASSORIN

tra·gal \ˈtrāgəl\ *adj* [NL *tragus* + E *-al*] **:** of or relating to the tragus

tra·ge·di·an \trəˈjēdēən\ *n* -s [ME *tragedien*, fr. MF, fr. *tragedie* + *-en* -an] **1 :** a writer of tragedies **2 :** an actor of tragedy; *esp* **:** one who specializes in tragic roles

tra·ge·di·enne \trəˌjēdēˈen\ *n* -s [F *tragédienne*, fr. MF *tragedienne*, fem. of *tragedien*] **:** an actress who specializes in tragic roles

trag·e·dize \ˈtrajəˌdīz\ *vt* -ED/-ING/-S [*tragedy* + *-ize*] *archaic* **:** to dramatize as a tragedy **:** make tragic

trag·e·dy \ˈtrajədē, -di\ *n* -ES [ME *tragedie*, fr. MF, fr. L *tragoedia*, fr. Gk *tragōidia*, fr. *tragos* he-goat + *-ōidia* (fr. *aeidein* to sing); prob. fr. the ancient Greek tragedy's having been influenced by the Peloponnesian satyr play, in which the satyrs were represented as goatlike rather than horselike creatures; akin to Gk *trōgein* to gnaw —more at ODE, TERSE] **1 a :** a medieval narrative poem or tale (as Chaucer's *Troilus and Criseyde*) typically describing the downfall of a great man **b** (1) **:** a drama in verse or prose and of serious and dignified character that typically describes the development of a conflict between the protagonist and a superior force (as destiny, circumstance, society) and reaches a sorrowful or disastrous conclusion that excites pity or terror ⟨in the classical ~ the solution was death —Domenico Vittorini⟩ — compare CATHARSIS, COMEDY (2) **:** a nondramatic work (as a novel) that resembles a tragic drama in character, development, and conclusion ⟨forcing the rhetoric of his ~ . . . in the final pages most painfully —Vernon Young⟩ **c :** an ancient Greek lyric poem sung by a chorus **d :** a literary genre consisting of tragic dramas ⟨relies upon the Aristotelian account of ~ —Cleanth Brooks & R.B.Heilman⟩ ⟨the study of ~ is the study of men at their best —G.K.Chalmers⟩ **2 a** (1) **:** a disastrous often fatal event or series of events **:** CALAMITY ⟨got back . . . to find myself in the midst of ~ —H.J.Laski⟩ ⟨the scene of some of our most sickening road *tragedies* —Priscilla Hughes⟩ ⟨revealed the evidence of a ~ of long ago —W.E.Swinton⟩ (2) **:** an unfortunate, sad, or discouraging occurrence or situation **:** bad luck **:** unhappy fate **:** MISFORTUNE ⟨the plight of these people is a human ~ which wrings the heart —H.G. Rickover⟩ ⟨a ~ that this rich . . . corner of the state has been so sadly neglected —*Sydney (Australia) Bull.*⟩ ⟨the ~ of plain women; to be valued, but not loved —Mary Austin⟩ **b :** an unqualified failure **:** FLOP, DISASTER ⟨the one architectural ~ on the university grounds —*Amer. Guide Series: Va.*⟩ ⟨last night's party was a ~⟩ **3** *obs* **:** LAMENTATION, JEREMIAD ⟨I wail, and make my woes a ~ —Edmund Spenser⟩ **4 :** the tragic quality or element ⟨comprehension of the ~ of life as well as of its warmth and humor —*Current Biog.*⟩

trag·e·laph \ˈtrajəˌlaf\ *n* -s [NL *Tragelaphus*] **:** an antelope of *Strepsiceros* or a related genus

tra·gel·a·phine \trəˈjeləˌfīn, -ˌfən\ *adj* [NL *Tragelaphus* + E *-ine*] **:** belonging or related to or typical of the genus *Strepsiceros* ⟨~ antelopes⟩ ⟨peculiarities of ~ anatomy⟩

tra·gel·a·phus \-ˌfəs\ [NL, fr. L, a kind of antelope, fr. Gk *tragelaphos*, fr. *tragos* he-goat + *elaphos* deer — more at TRAGEDY, ELK] *syn of* STREPSICEROS

tragi *pl of* TRAGUS

¹**trag·ic** \ˈtrajik, -jēk\ *adj* [L *tragicus*, fr. Gk *tragikos* of a he-goat, of tragedy, fr. *tragos* he-goat + *-ikos* -ic] **1 :** of, marked by, or expressive of tragedy **:** DISASTROUS, FEARFUL ⟨life will necessarily contain a ~ element —M.R.Cohen⟩ ⟨witnessed many uneasy, wakeful . . . even ~ nights —Walter de la Mare⟩ ⟨realize the ~ significance of the atomic bomb —H.S.Truman⟩ **2 a :** dealing with or treated in narrative or dramatic tragedy ⟨differentiates ~ fiction from the merely pathetic —Howard M. Jones⟩ ⟨conceptions of the ~ hero —W.H.Auden⟩ **b :** appropriate to or typical of dramatic tragedy ⟨to be truly ~ . . . a plot must do more than bring . . . emotions to a head —B.A.G.Fuller⟩ ⟨the ~ predicament of a mortal creature with immortal longings —Irwin Edman⟩ **c :** composing or acting in tragedies ⟨the Greek ~ poets⟩ ⟨a notable ~ actress⟩ **3 a :** saddeningly or regrettably serious or unpleasant **:** DEPLORABLE, LAMENTABLE ⟨passionate and ~ sense of life —H.M.McLuhan⟩ ⟨a . . . ~ symptom of our times that diplomats do punch nightclub girls —John Lardner⟩ **b** (1) **:** marked by a sense of tragedy or pessimism ⟨his account . . . is deeply ~ —Lionel Trilling⟩ ⟨a ~ reading of history —F.L.Baumer⟩ (2) **:** arousing feelings of melancholy **:** POIGNANT ⟨the ~ peace of the long evening —Ellen Glasgow⟩ ⟨a ~ little group of serious and gentle lads —W.E.Leonard⟩

²**tragic** \"\ *n* -s **1** *archaic* **:** a writer of tragedy **2 :** a tragic quality or element ⟨the ~ in life and art⟩; *specif* **:** the aesthetic quality in tragic drama that excites emotions of pity and terror in the beholder — compare CATHARSIS 2a

trag·i·cal \-jəkəl, -jēk-\ *adj* [L *tragicus* + E *-al*] **:** TRAGIC ⟨his subjects are frequently ~, sometimes shocking —Richard Garnett †1906⟩ ⟨raised a hand in ~ dismissal —Rafael Sabatini⟩ — **trag·i·cal·ness** *n* -ES

trag·i·cal·ly \-k(ə)lē, -li\ *adv* **1 :** in a tragic manner ⟨ridiculously and ~ identifies his passion for her —Edmund Wilson⟩ **2 :** to an unfortunate or disastrous degree **:** REGRETTABLY, WOEFULLY ⟨died at a ~ early age —*Times Lit. Supp.*⟩ ⟨was soon ~ evident that the cancer of totalitarianism was . . . spreading —Richard Hunt⟩

tragic flaw *n* **:** a flaw in the character of the hero of a tragedy that brings about his downfall ⟨the Oedipean *tragic flaw* is pride⟩

tragi·comedy \ˌtrajə+\ *n* [MF *tragicomedie*, fr. OIt *tragicomedia*, fr. OSp, fr. L *tragicocomoedia*, *tragicomoedia*, fr. *tragicus* tragic + *comoedia* comedy — more at COMEDY] **1 a** (1) **:** a literary genre consisting of dramas that combine tragic and comic elements with the tragic predominating ⟨Elizabethan ~ is . . . a subdivision of the larger classification, serious drama —P.W.Barber⟩ (2) **:** a drama of this genre **b :** the tragicomic quality or element ⟨some of the ~ remains and is the best thing in the film —*Time*⟩ **2 :** an event or situation having both serious and comic aspects ⟨the ~ of federal politics⟩

tragi·comic \"+\ *adj* [¹*tragic* + *comic*] **1 a :** of, relating to, or having the characteristics of tragicomedy ⟨a playwright specializing in ~ drama⟩ **b :** manifesting both tragic and comic aspects ⟨the ~ disparity . . . between man's aspirations and his accomplishments —B.R.Redman⟩ **2 :** marked by both pathetic and ludicrous characteristics ⟨a ~ character . . . an obscure and fatheaded young man —H.A.Smith⟩

tragi·comical \"+\ *adj* [*tragic* + *comical*] **:** TRAGICOMIC ⟨the girl's life . . . presented itself to me as a ~ adventure —Joseph Conrad⟩ — **tragi·comically** \"+\ *adv*

trag·i·on \ˈtrajēˌän\ *n* -s [NL, fr. *tragus* + Gk *-ion*, dim. suffix] **:** an anthropometric point in the notch of the tragus of the ear

trag·o·pan \ˈtragəˌpan\ *n* [NL, fr. L, a kind of vulture, fr. Gk *tragopan*, fr. *tragos* he-goat + *Pan*, ancient Greek god of woods and shepherds — more at TRAGEDY] **1** *cap* **:** a genus of brilliantly colored Asiatic pheasants having the back and breast covered usu. with white or buff ocelli and the head in the male ornamented with two bright-colored wattles and a pair of fleshy erectile horns — see CRIMSON TRAGOPAN **2** -s **:** any bird of the genus *Tragopan*

trago·po·gon \ˌtragəˈpōˌgän, -ōgən\ *n*, *cap* [NL, fr. L, salsify, fr. Gk *tragopōgōn*, fr. *tragos* he-goat + *pōgōn* beard; fr. the large pappus — more at -POGON] **:** a genus of Old World herbs (family Compositae) having entire linear leaves and long pedunculate heads of yellow or purple radiate flowers with a single series of involucral bracts — see SALSIFY, YELLOW GOATSBEARD

trag·ule \ˈtra(ˌ)gyül\ *n* -s [NL *Tragulus*] **:** CHEVROTAIN

¹**trag·u·lid** \ˈtragyələd\ *adj* [NL *Tragulidae*] **:** of or relating to the Tragulidae

²**tragulid** \"\ *n* -s **:** a mammal of the family Tragulidae **:** CHEVROTAIN

tra·gu·li·dae \trəˈgyüləˌdē\ *n pl*, *cap* [NL, fr. *Tragulus*, type genus + *-idae*] **:** a family of ruminant mammals (division Tragulina) comprising the chevrotains (as the kanchils, napus, and water chevrotain)

trag·u·li·na \ˌtragyəˈlīnə, -lēnə\ *n pl*, *cap* [NL, fr. *Tragulus* + *-ina*] **:** a division of Ruminantia comprising the chevrotains and extinct related forms — **trag·u·line** \ˈtragyəˌlīn, -ˌlēn, -ˌlən\ *adj*

trag·u·loid \ˈtragyəˌlȯid\ *adj* [NL *Traguloidea*] **:** of or relating to the Traguloidea

¹**trag·u·loi·dea** \ˌtragyəˈlȯidēə\ [NL, fr. *Tragulus* + *-oidea*] *syn of* TRAGULINA

²**traguloidea** \"\ *n pl*, *cap* [NL, fr. *Tragulus* + *-oidea*] *in some classifications* **:** a division of Tragulina comprising the chevrotains and a few related forms

trag·u·lus \ˈtragyələs\ *n*, *cap* [NL, fr. Gk *tragos* he-goat + L *-ulus*, dim. suffix] **:** a genus (the type of the family Tragulidae) comprising the typical chevrotains

tra·gus \ˈtrāgəs\ *n*, *pl* **tragi** [NL, fr. Gk *tragos*, a part of the ear, lit., he-goat — more at TRAGEDY] **1 :** the prominence in front of the external opening of the ear **2 :** one of the hairs of the external auditory meatus

traik \ˈtrāk\ *vi* [origin unknown] *Scot* **:** to fall ill **:** break down

¹**trail** \ˈtrāl, *esp before pause or consonant* -āəl\ *vb* -ED/-ING/-S [ME *trailen*, fr. MF *trailler* to tow, fr. (assumed) VL *tragulare*, fr. L *tragula* dragnet, sledge; prob. akin to L *trahere* to pull, draw, drag — more at DRAW] *vi* **1 a :** to hang down so as to drag along a surface **:** sweep the ground ⟨letting the flag ~ in the dust⟩ ⟨my silken outer garment ~*ed* over withered leaves —Amy Lowell⟩ ⟨his hand hit the wall and ~*ed* down it as he fell —Raymond Chandler⟩ **b :** to hang so as to touch or pile up on a surface ⟨the tablecloth ~s on the floor⟩ **c :** to hang or extend over a surface loosely or stragglingly ⟨no one looks right now with locks ~*ing* over one eye —*Country Life*⟩ **d :** to hang or extend so as to float freely or loosely ⟨would rather stroke faster with their arms and let their legs ~ —T.M. McDermott⟩ ⟨allowing one of the propellers to ~, thereby reducing the drag on that side of the ship —*Manual of Seamanship*⟩ **e :** to grow to such length as to droop over or rest upon the ground **:** spread and root extensively **:** CREEP 3c — used of a plant ⟨knew where the first arbutus ~*ed* in the spring —Grace Metalious⟩ **2 a :** to walk or proceed draggingly, heavily, or wearily **:** PLOD, TRUDGE ⟨~*ed* along at a snail's pace⟩ ⟨~*ed* dismally round his grounds praising the improvements —Virginia Woolf⟩ **b :** to follow unthinkingly as if led or pulled along ⟨his sister ~*ed* along after him —James Hensel⟩ **c** (1) **:** to lag behind **:** do poorly in relation to others (as in a contest) **:** LOSE ⟨bet on a horse that ~*ed* all the way and finished last⟩ ⟨~*ing* in the election with only 30 percent of the vote⟩ (2) *of a harness race driver* **:** to take a position behind the lead horse using him to set the pace and break the force of the wind **d** *archaic* **:** to fish by drawing the line along the water from a moving boat **:** TROLL **3 :** to move, flow, or extend slowly and esp. in thin or vaporous streams or spirals **:** DRIFT ⟨blood ~*ing* over the floor⟩ ⟨smoke ~*ing* from chimneys⟩ ⟨a thin veil of mist ~*ed* below —John Connell⟩ ⟨shadows o'er the landscape ~*ing* —H.W.Longfellow⟩ **4 a :** to extend in an erratic or uneven course or line **:** STRAGGLE ⟨stone walls ~ raggedly through the woods —*Amer. Guide Series: Vt.*⟩ ⟨ropes ~ in loops and tangles across the slanting deck —*Phoenix Flame*⟩ **b :** to wander (as from course, aim, or original character) so as to become weak, pointless, or ineffectual **:** DWINDLE — usu. used with *off* or *away* ⟨the discussion ~*ed* off into futilities⟩ ⟨voice ~*ing* off to a whisper —T.B.Costain⟩ ⟨this book rather ~s away at the close —Allan Nevins⟩ **5 :** to follow a trail **:** track game ⟨spent long days ~*ing* over the desert⟩ ⟨can . . . ~ like an Indian —W.P.Webb⟩ **6 :** to play a card in casino without building or taking **7 :** to tour with a trailer carrying camping supplies or providing living accommodations ⟨the art of ~*ing* lies in being away from the trailer as much as possible —*New Statesman & Nation*⟩ ~ *vt* **1 a :** to draw or drag (as a garment) along a surface **:** allow to sweep the ground **:** DRAGGLE ⟨when women ~*ed* long skirts through the dust —Justina Hill⟩ **b :** to hold or carry so as to draw an end or part along a surface **:** DRAG ⟨~ a log down a slope⟩ ⟨~ a line in fishing⟩ ⟨the winning crew ~*ed* their oars in salute⟩ ⟨passing the marble table, she ~*ed* her aging fingertips across its mute surface —Harriet La Barre⟩ **c :** to drag along by force **:** HALE ⟨they shall not ~ me through their streets —John Milton⟩ **d :** PULL, HAUL, TOW ⟨~ the wagons of an overland train⟩ **e :** to carry (as a firearm, pike, or lance) at the position of trail arms ⟨~ arms at a military funeral⟩ **2 a :** to drag heavily or wearily (as a limb or the body) ⟨moved slowly, ~*ing* his wounded foot⟩ **b :** to carry or bring along as an addition, burden, or encumbrance ⟨always ~s along two or three uninvited friends⟩ ⟨a dog ~*ing* a leash⟩ ⟨stepped off the train still ~*ing* a little sand —Sybille Bedford⟩ **c :** to draw along in one's wake ⟨~*ing* clouds of glory do we come —William Wordsworth⟩ ⟨~*ed* streamers of gray mist up the valley —Francis Ratcliffe⟩ **d :** to draw or stretch out (as an utterance, discussion, or affair) **:** PROTRACT ⟨no point in ~*ing* the business out any longer⟩ **3 :** to adorn (as pottery) with a trailing pattern or ornament (as of tracery) **4 a :** to follow upon the scent or trace of **:** TRACK, HUNT ⟨~*ed* the beast to its lair⟩ ⟨had to ~ the suspect halfway across the country⟩ **b :** to follow in the footsteps of **:** PURSUE, SHADOW ⟨reporters ~*ing* him constantly⟩ ⟨not daring to accost him . . . she had ~*ed* him to the railroad station —D.B.Chidsey⟩ **c :** to follow along behind (as a person) ⟨being careful always to ~ the queen at the prescribed distance⟩ **d :** to play a bowl in lawn bowling so as to strike and carry (the jack) backward **e :** to lag behind (as others in a competition) ⟨always ~s his classmates⟩ ⟨~*ing* the league-leading team by two and a half games⟩ ⟨~*ed* the other candidates on the ticket⟩ **5 :** to urge (livestock) along (as from a summer to a winter range) ⟨herders ~*ing* longhorns up from Texas —R.F.Adams⟩ **syn** see FOLLOW — **trail a pike :** to serve as a soldier ⟨*trailed a pike* in the Low Countries in the 1590s⟩ — **trail one's coat** *or* **trail one's coattails :** to invite a quarrel by provoking antagonism or dissent

²**trail** \"\ *n* -s [ME, fr. *trailen*, v.] **1 a :** something that trails or is trailed: as (1) **:** a trailing plant ⟨ivy had sent ~s down the steep banks —Flora Thompson⟩ (2) **:** a running ornament representing leaves or tendrils (as in Gothic moldings) (3) **:** a trailing arrangement (as of flowers) **:** SPRAY ⟨wore white roses on the shoulder — a ~, not a bunch —Clemence Dane⟩ (4) **:** the rear part of a gun carriage that rests on the ground when the piece is unlimbered (5) **:** a flattened anterior prolongation of the shell of various brachiopods **b :** TRAIL ARMS — used in the phrases *at the trail* and *at trail* **2 a :** something that follows or moves along in or as if in a path or wake or as if being drawn along **:** TRAIN ⟨the academic procession in a long ~⟩ ⟨a ~ of admirers⟩ ⟨rocket ~s⟩ ⟨smoke in thin blue ~s was coming from the brick chimneys —Calder Willingham⟩ **b** (1) **:** the transitory luminous streak in the sky produced by the passage of a meteor (2) **:** a continuous line produced photographically by permitting the image of a celestial body (as a star) to move over the plate **c :** a chain of consequences **:** AFTERMATH ⟨the . . . movement left a ~ of bitterness and prejudice behind it —Paul Blanshard⟩ **3 a :** a trace or mark left by something that has passed or been drawn or dragged along **:** SCENT, SPOOR, TRACK ⟨hounds picking up the ~⟩ ⟨a ~ of blood from the house to the barn⟩ ⟨got on the ~ of the killer⟩ ⟨discovered a rattlesnake ~ in the sand —Jack Kerouac⟩ **b :** SKIDDING TRAIL **c** (1) **:** a track made by passage (as through a wilderness or wild region) **:** a beaten path ⟨an Indian ~⟩ ⟨a deer ~⟩ ⟨tortuous mountain ~s⟩ ⟨wagon ~s⟩ ⟨the era of the cattle ~s⟩ ⟨stamping a ~ through the deep snow⟩ (2) **:** a blazed or otherwise marked path through a forest or mountainous region ⟨woodland ~s⟩ ⟨the state provides a 300-mile ~ for those enjoying walking trips⟩ (3) **:** a road or highway approximately following an historic trail or series of trails (as of Indians or pioneers) ⟨the Mohawk *Trail*⟩ **d :** SLOPE 1b **e :** a course followed or to be followed **:** ROUTE ⟨a milestone on his educational ~⟩ ⟨candidates hitting the campaign ~⟩ **4 :** the horizontal distance from the point of impact of a bomb dropped from a moving airplane to a vertical line from the airplane at the instant of impact — **in trail** *adv* **:** in single file **:** one behind the other ⟨planes flying *in trail*⟩ ⟨the party had marched *in trail* —Thomas Hardy⟩

³**trail** \"\ *n* -s [short for *entrail*] *archaic* **:** ENTRAIL 1; *esp* **:** the intestines of an animal (as a game bird or fish) served as food ⟨the thrush is presented with the ~ —Tobias Smollett⟩

t rail *n, cap T* **:** a rail having a head, a web, and a flat flange base so that a section resembles the letter T — called also *Vignoles rail*

cross section of T rail: *1* head, *2* web, *3* base

trail angle *n* **:** the angle between the trail sight and a vertical line from an airplane drawn at the instant of impact of a bomb dropped from the airplane

trail arms *n pl but sing in constr* [fr. the imperative phrase *trail arms*] **:** a position in military drill in which a rifle butt is raised a few inches from the ground and the muzzle inclined forward so that the barrel makes an angle of about 30 degrees with the vertical — often used as a command

trailblazer \ˈ=,==\ *n* **1 :** one that blazes a trail to guide others through a wilderness or unknown country **:** PATHFINDER ⟨the . . . valley began to echo with the thud of the ~'s ax —*Amer. Guide Series: Mich.*⟩ **2 :** one that discovers or tries out a new way (as of doing something) **:** PIONEER ⟨the ~s, the setters of new patterns in business —Frieda Curtis⟩

trailblazing \ˈ=,==\ *adj* **:** making or pointing a new way **:** PATHBREAKING ⟨a ~ experiment⟩ ⟨a unique and ~ effort in coordinated . . . techniques —Paul Fejos⟩

trail board *n* **:** one of the curved and carved boards on the sides of the cutwater near the figurehead of a ship

trail boss *n, West* **:** one in charge of a trail herd ⟨the *trail boss* put three hands in front to hold the leaders back —S.E. Fletcher⟩

trailbreaker \ˈ=,==\ *n* **:** TRAILBLAZER

trail bridge *or* **trail ferry** *n* **:** a boat or raft attached to a pulley running on a rope stretched across a stream and moved from side to side by the action of the current

trail car *n* **:** TRAILER 4a

trail cutter *n* **:** a cowboy who breaks through a moving herd of cattle to search for strays

trailed *past of* TRAIL

¹trail·er \ˈtrālə(r)\ *n* -s [¹*trail* + *-er*] **1 :** one that trails or follows a trail: as **a :** one that tracks **:** HUNTER ⟨a master shot, a ~ who was a match for any Apache —Stanley Walker⟩ **b :** one that travels over a trail ⟨here the ~s of yesterday . . . inscribed names and dates —A.B.Guthrie⟩ **2 :** something that trails or touches the ground in moving or hanging: as **a :** a trailing plant **:** CREEPER 3 **b :** TRAILING WHEEL **c :** a sprag to prevent a vehicle from running backward **3 :** one that trails, follows, or lags behind: as **a :** a hunting dog that yields the initiative to its bracemate **b :** a player in various goal games (as hockey, basketball, or soccer) that follows closely a teammate who is dribbling the puck or ball **c** (1) **:** a short motion-picture film made up of snatches from a feature picture and displayed in advance for advertising purposes (2) **:** a short film shown for the purpose of making an announcement to the theater audience (3) **:** a short length of blank film attached to the finish end of a reel so that the film will continue to feed through the projector mechanism after the light and sound are turned off — compare LEADER 1m **d :** music played for the close or fade-out of a performance (as of a theatrical skit or a film) ⟨for my last ~, I'll use *Only a Rose* —Gypsy Lee⟩ **4 :** a vehicle or one in a succession of vehicles hauled usu. by some other vehicle: as **a :** a car on a streetcar line pulled by another car **b :** a light 2-wheeled car pulled (as by a bicycle or motorcycle) **c :** a nonautomotive highway or industrial-plant vehicle designed to be hauled (as by a tractor, motortruck, or passenger automobile) ⟨flatbed ~⟩ ⟨truck ~⟩ ⟨goods ~⟩ **d :** one of several logging sleds that are hauled tandem by steam or gasoline power or by four to eight horses **e :** an automobile-drawn highway vehicle designed to serve wherever it is parked as a dwelling or as a place of business (as an office, laboratory, or field headquarters) **5 :** FROGGER 1 **6 :** PUSHER 1e

²trailer \"\ *vb* -ED/-ING/-S *vt* **:** to transport (a boat) by means of a trailer ⟨~*ing* an outboard cruiser from one body of water to another⟩ ~ *vi* **1 :** to live or travel in a trailer ⟨~*ing* about the country⟩ **2 :** to be transportable by trailer ⟨a light boat that ~s easily⟩

trailer camp *or* **trailer court** *or* **trailer park** *n* **:** an area where house trailers are congregated

trailer card *n* **:** a card that follows another card or group of cards in a computer and is provided to accommodate additional data or information

trailer coach *n* **:** HOUSE TRAILER

trail·er·ite \ˈtrālə,rīt\ *also* **trail·er·ist** \-rəst\ *n* -s [¹*trailer* + *-ite* or *-ist*] **:** a person living or accustomed to live in a trailer ⟨a six-acre camp occupied by about 400 ~s —Norma Browning⟩

trail·er·ship \-lə(r),ship\ *n* **:** a ship designed to carry trucks, trailers, and automobiles

trail·ery \ˈtrāl(ə)rē\ *n* -ES [²*trail* + *-ery*] **:** TRACERY, TRAIL 1a(2)

trail–eye \ˈ=,=\ *n* **:** LUNETTE 9

trail handspike *n* **:** a long stout handspike used in moving the trail of a gun carriage

trail herd *n, West* **:** a herd of cattle fit for trailing or being trailed esp. from the range to a railhead or market

¹trailing *n* -s [ME, fr. gerund of *trailen* to trail] **1 :** a trailing branch or shoot **:** RUNNER **2 :** the act or process of fusing bits of molten glass on glass articles to form decorative designs

²trailing *adj* [ME, fr. pres. part. of *trailen* to trail] **1 :** STRAGGLING, CREEPING ⟨a ~ plant⟩ **2 :** of, relating to, or borne by the trailing wheels ⟨a ~ truck⟩ ⟨~ weight⟩ — **trail·ing·ly** *adv*

trailing arbutus *n* **:** ARBUTUS 3

trailing edge *n* **:** the rearmost edge of an airfoil — compare LEADING EDGE

trailing fuchsia *n* **:** a New Zealand fuchsia (*Fuchsia procumbens*) that is often used in hanging baskets and has procumbent slender stems and purplish flowers without petals followed by persistent red fruits

trailing lantana *n* **:** a common So. American trailing perennial (*Lantana sellowiana*) with rosy lilac flowers that is used as an ornamental

trailing line *n* **:** a line having one end fastened to a rowlock on a boat and the other to an oar to prevent loss of the oar

trailing myrtle *n* **:** ¹PERIWINKLE 1a

trailing pea *n* **:** GROUNDNUT 2a

trailing phlox *n* **:** a tufted spring-blooming perennial phlox (*Phlox nivalis*) that is similar to moss pink but has larger flowers with shorter stamens and styles

trailing–point switch *n* **:** a switch so set that the points are directed away from a passing train — distinguished from *facing-point switch*

trailing pole tip *also* **trailing horn** *n* **:** the edge of the pole piece of a dynamo or motor which the wires on the armature pass as they enter the gap

trailing raspberry *n* **:** any of several prostrate plants of the genus *Rubus* (esp. *R. parvifolius*)

trailing sumac *n* **:** a poison ivy (*Rhus toxicodendron*)

trailing truck *n* **:** the wheel unit of a locomotive that is located behind the driving wheels and that serves to help support the weight

trailing wheel *n* **:** a rear wheel of a locomotive to which the motive force is not directly applied — compare DRIVING WHEEL

trailing wild bean *n* **:** a sprawling leguminous vine (*Strophostyles helvola*) of eastern No. America with trifoliolate leaves, purple flowers, and linear nearly terete pods

trail knee *n* **:** a knee to stiffen the stem of a boat

Traill's flycatcher \ˈtrā(ə)lz-\ *n, usu cap T* [after Thomas S. Traill †1862 Brit. encyclopedist] **:** ALDER FLYCATCHER

trail·man \ˈtrā(ə)lmən\ *n, pl* **trailmen 1 :** TRAILSMAN **2** *usu* **trail man :** one of a group of mounted cowboys driving a herd of cattle

trail net *n* **:** a net trailed or drawn behind a boat

trail plank *n* **:** a plank support for the trail of a gun carriage

trail plate *n* **:** the plate at the end of the trail of a gun carriage terminating in the lunette

trail rope *n* **:** DRAGROPE b

trails *pres 3d sing of* TRAIL, *pl of* TRAIL

trail seeker *n, usu cap T&S* **:** the first of four ranks attained by camp fire girls — compare FIRE MAKER, TORCH BEARER, WOOD GATHERER

trail sight *n* **:** the line of sight from a moving airplane to the point of impact of a bomb dropped by it taken at the instant of impact

trails·man \ˈtrā(ə)lzmən\ *n, pl* **trailsmen :** one that follows a trail

trail spade *n* **:** a metal spur, prong, or plate on the underside of the trail of a fieldpiece that is driven into the ground by the recoil and acts as a brake

trail teamster *n* **:** a logger that drives horses to tow logs over the flat part of a log chute

trail·way \ˈtrā(ə)l,wā\ *n* **:** a track or path esp. through a forest or mountainous region

¹train \ˈtrān\ *n* -s [ME *trayne, treyne*, fr. MF *traine*, fr. OF, fr. *trair* to betray, fr. L *tradere* to betray, deliver — more at TRAITOR] **1** *obs* **a :** a scheme to deceive or betray **:** ARTIFICE, TRICK **b :** GUILE, TREACHERY, TRICKERY **2** *obs* **:** a trap for an animal **:** SNARE

²train \"\ *vt* -ED/-ING/-S [ME *traynen, treynen*, fr. *trayne, treyne*, n.] **1 :** to draw by artifice or stratagem **:** DECOY, ENTICE, LURE **2 :** ATTRACT, PERSUADE, WIN

³train \"\ *n* -s [ME *trayn, trayne*, fr. MF *train* action of drawing, trail, train of a dress, procession of animals or vehicles, fr. OF, fr. *trainer* to draw, drag — more at ⁴TRAIN] **1 a :** the extended part of a skirt, gown, or state robe that lies on the floor and trails behind the wearer **b :** an animal's tail; *esp* **:** the trailing tail feathers of a peacock **c :** the moving length of something (as a serpent or a stream) **d :** the luminous trail or tail of a meteor or comet sometimes persisting in the sky for several seconds or minutes after the meteor or comet itself has passed **2 a :** the retinue or suite of a person of rank or consequence **:** FOLLOWING ⟨he is bringing a staff of 80 in his ~ —*Sydney (Australia) Bull.*⟩ **b :** a line or file of persons and often vehicles or animals proceeding together ⟨the little ~ of silent people carried her out . . . to the family burying ground —Margaret Deland⟩ **:** CARAVAN ⟨a camel ~⟩ **3 a :** an organization of military vehicles, men, and sometimes animals that furnishes supply, maintenance, and evacuation services to a combat unit — compare FIELD TRAIN **b :** the auxiliary ships assigned to supply and support a naval fleet or force **4 a :** proper arrangement or disposition **:** order designed or contrived to lead to some result ⟨was already in fair ~ to develop party out of faction —Learned Hand⟩ ⟨the mathematics set in ~ by these two pledges will force a reduction of the total armed forces —*New Statesman & Nation*⟩ **b :** a controlled or directed procedure **:** METHOD, PROCESS, WAY ⟨things proceeded in this ~ for several days —T.L.Peacock⟩ **c :** a line, course, or sequence of thoughts, actions, or events **:** an orderly succession **:** a connected series ⟨the ~ of years sped swiftly by —W.F.Brown b. 1903⟩ ⟨his mind still upon his own ~ of thought —Agnes S. Turnbull⟩ **d :** a set or progression of consequent or attendant events or conditions **:** a series of results or accompanying circumstances **:** AFTERMATH, SEQUEL ⟨in the ~ of peace came industry and all the arts of life —T.B.Macaulay⟩ **5 a :** a line of black powder or other explosive laid to lead fire to a charge **:** FUSE **b :** a line of carrion pieces laid as a lure for game **6** *obs* **a :** the path followed by a horse **b :** the kind of travel experienced by a horse **c :** MANEGE, CONTROL **d :** a horse's gait **7 :** a series of moving machine parts (as gears, links, cams, chain drives, or belt drives) for transmitting and modifying motion ⟨the ~ of a watch connects the barrel with the escapement⟩ ⟨gear ~⟩ ⟨the valve ~ of an automobile engine⟩ **8 a :** a connected line of railroad cars with or without a locomotive; *also* **:** an engine or motorcar with or without other engines or cars that displays markers **b :** an automotive tractor with one or more trailer units ⟨the number of truck-and-trailer ~s has multiplied six or seven times in recent years —R.L.Neuberger⟩ **9 :** a long narrow geological deposit (as of gravel); *esp* **:** one composed of glaciofluvial sand and gravel extending down a valley far beyond the terminus of a glacier — called also *valley train* **10 :** a succession of physical oscillations or disturbances ⟨earthquake waves run in . . . ~s —R.A. Daly⟩ ⟨the vibrations of a tuning fork cause a ~ of sound waves to pass through the atmosphere⟩ **11 a :** a series of connected pieces of chemical apparatus **b :** a series of vats or large bowls for scouring wool **12 :** ROLL TRAIN **13 :** a series of bombs dropped from an airplane one after another in close succession — sometimes used in the phrase *in train*

⁴train \"\ *vb* -ED/-ING/-S [ME *traynen*, fr. MF *trainer*, fr. (assumed) VL *traginare;* akin to L *trahere* to pull, draw, drag — more at DRAW] *vt* **1 a :** to draw along **:** DRAG, TRAIL ⟨when a whale is harpooned . . . he ~s with him the bold little creature who, greatly daring, has flung the fatal weapon —Francis Hackett⟩ **b :** to draw out **:** PROTRACT **2 :** to grow (a plant) in a manner designed to produce a desired form or effect usu. by bending, tying, and pruning; *esp* **:** to cause to grow symmetrically (as in an espalier or against a wall) by such means ⟨~*ing* fruit trees as espaliers against a sheltering wall⟩ **3 a :** to instruct or drill in habits of thought or action **:** shape or develop the character of by discipline or precept ⟨~ up a child in the way he should go, and when he is old he will not depart from it —Prov 22:6 (RSV)⟩ **b** (1) **:** to teach or exercise (someone) in an art, profession, trade, or occupation **:** direct in attaining a skill **:** give instruction to ⟨~*ed* several generations of field and track athletes⟩ ⟨~*ed* him in the law⟩ (2) **:** to cause (as judgment) to be disciplined **:** CULTIVATE ⟨perhaps we can ~ our taste —Virginia Woolf⟩ **:** develop skill or habits in ⟨~*ed* his hand to a patternmaker's delicate touch⟩ **c :** to teach (an animal) to obey commands **4 :** to aim or point at an object **:** bring to bear ⟨kept the shotgun ~*ed* on him —F.B. Gipson⟩ ⟨had ~*ed* his news camera on celebrities for 40 years⟩ ⟨~*ed* his spotlight on the creative artist —W.F.Kerr⟩ **5 :** to adapt (a microorganism) to utilize a nutrient or to grow in an environment not normally suitable (as by continued exposure to such nutrient or environment) ~ *vi* **1 :** DRAG, TRAIL ⟨her skirt ~*ed* on the ground⟩ **2 a :** to undergo instruction, discipline, or drill ⟨recruits were ~*ing* in army camps all over the nation⟩ ⟨~*ed* in a nearby hospital for a nursing career⟩ **b :** to undertake an athlete's conditioning regimen of exercise, practice, and diet ⟨many baseball teams ~ each spring in the South⟩ **3 :** to move in company **:** ASSOCIATE — used with *with* ⟨has always ~*ed* with the moderates⟩ **4 :** to travel by rail **:** go by train ⟨had planed, ~*ed*, and driven 1500 miles —Paul Gallico⟩ **syn** see TEACH

⁵train \"\ *n* -s [ME *trane*, fr. MD *traen, trane* fluid, drop, tear, train oil or MLG *trān;* akin to OS *trahni*, pl., tears, OHG *trahan* tear, *zahar* tear — more at TEAR] *archaic* **:** TRAIN OIL

train·able \ˈtrānəbəl\ *adj* [⁴*train* + *-able*] **:** capable of being trained ⟨labor supply is abundant, highly ~, well educated —*advt*⟩

train·asi·um \trāˈnāzēəm, -zhəm\ *n* -s [⁴*train* + *-asium* (as in *gymnasium*)] **:** an intricate steel framework of bars, ladders, and other devices about 30 feet high designed to provide a climber with a succession of 22 gymnastic exercises

train·band \ˈtrān,=\ *n* [alter. of *trained band*] **:** a 17th or 18th century company of citizen soldiery in England or America **:** a militia company

trainbearer \ˈ=,==\ *n* **1 :** an attendant who holds up the train of a robe or gown (as at a wedding or on a ceremonial occasion) **2 :** a long-tailed So. American hummingbird (*Lesbia victoriae*)

trainboy \ˈ=,=\ *n* **:** a boy who sells newspapers, candy, or other small merchandise on railroad trains

train case *or* **train box** *n* **:** a small piece of luggage used esp. for toilet articles and other necessaries of overnight travel

train dispatcher *n* **:** a railroad employee who directs the movement of trains within a division and coordinates their movement from one division to another with other dispatchers — compare TOWERMAN

train down *vi* [⁴*train*] **:** to reduce one's weight by exercise and diet

trai·neau \(ˈ)trāˈnō\ *n, pl* **trai·neaux** \-ō(z)\ [F *traîneau*, fr. OF *trainel*, fr. *trainer* to draw, drag — more at TRAIN] **:** SLEDGE, SLEIGH

train case

¹trained \ˈtrānd\ *adj* [fr. past part. of ⁴*train*] **1 :** having undergone a course of training ⟨we employ ~ personnel⟩ ⟨a government-*trained* physician⟩ **2 :** formed, shaped, or disciplined by training **:** qualified or conditioned by training ⟨a ~ mind⟩ ⟨a ~ nose⟩ ⟨readers ~ to be critical⟩

²trained \"\ *adj* [³*train* + *-ed*] **:** having a train ⟨a ~ gown⟩

trained nurse *n* **:** GRADUATE NURSE

trained seal *n* **:** an author, celebrity, or expert hired by a newspaper to lend color or authority to its coverage of a conspicuous news story ⟨the veteran newsmen, big byliners and *trained seals* who covered the royal wedding —*Time*⟩

train·ee \(ˈ)trāˈnē\ *n* -s [⁴*train* + *-ee*] **:** someone being trained for a job **:** APPRENTICE, LEARNER ⟨industrial management ~s⟩ ⟨job ~s⟩; *esp* **:** an enlisted person receiving basic training

train·er \ˈtrānə(r)\ *n* -s [⁴*train* + *-er*] **1 :** someone or something that trains: as **a :** one that educates or teaches **b :** one that coaches athletes **c :** one that trains animals for performances, shows, or competitions **d :** one that trains a gun; *esp* **:** one that controls the horizontal aiming of a naval gun — compare POINTER **e :** a member of a trainband **:** MILITIAMAN **f** (1) **:** an airplane used in training airmen; *esp* **:** one with duplicate controls used in training pilots (2) **:** a mechanical device for training pilots that simulates flight conditions **g :** any of numerous machines and devices used in various forms of training **h :** a tree whose top is below the general forest canopy and whose shading and abrasive action prevents sucker formation and hastens natural pruning on the crop trees **2 :** someone being trained **:** TRAINEE ⟨~s do practice teaching in connection with their teachers college courses⟩

train ferry *n* **:** a ferry equipped to carry railroad cars

train guard *n* **1 :** a force protecting a military train **2 :** a railroad guard

training *n* -s [fr. gerund of ⁴*train*] **1 a :** the teaching, drill, or discipline by which powers of mind or body are developed **:** EDUCATION ⟨many of us continue to believe in this ~ of the mind by language —Charlton Laird⟩ ⟨the ~ of statesmen is a large matter —Ernest Barker⟩ **b** (1) **:** the regimen of exercise, diet, and practice undergone by an athlete ⟨it was no light matter to break varsity football ~⟩ (2) **:** a pitch of proficiency developed by an athlete's regimen ⟨he was in perfect ~⟩ **c :** development of a particular skill or group of skills **:** instruction in an art, profession, or occupation **2 :** the control of plants, vines, or young trees so that they will grow in a desired shape or direction **3 :** the aiming or pointing of a gun, a camera, or a light

training aid *n* **:** a device (as a motion-picture film or a set of slides, charts, recordings, or models) to increase the effectiveness of training

training college *n, Brit* **:** TEACHERS COLLEGE

training day *n* **:** a day on which a volunteer military company is called out for drill or parade according to law

training school *n* **1 :** a school preparing students for a particular occupation or teaching a special skill **2 :** a correctional institution for the custody and reeducation of juvenile delinquents — compare INDUSTRIAL SCHOOL, REFORMATORY

training seat *n* **:** a small toilet seat fitted to a regular one and used for toilet training of children — compare POTTY-CHAIR

training ship *n* **1 :** a warship that carries naval-officer candidates on training cruises **2 :** a ship used to train men for the merchant marine

training table *n* **:** a table where men under an athletic training regimen eat meals planned to help in their conditioning ⟨a football *training table*⟩

training seat

training tackle *n* **:** TRAIN TACKLE

training wall *also* **training bank** *n* **:** a wall, bank, or jetty built to confine and direct the flow of a river or tide

train·less \ˈtrānləs\ *adj* **:** having no train

train line *n* **1 :** a continuous electric control circuit used on electric trains of two or more motor-driven cars for controlling the motors on the rear cars from the master controller in the cab of the first car **2** *or* **train pipe :** BRAKE PIPE

trainload \ˈ=;=\ *n* **:** the full freight or passenger cargo or capacity of a railroad train

train·man \ˈtrānmən, -,man\ *n, pl* **trainmen :** a member of a train crew supervised by a conductor

trainmaster \ˈ=,==\ *n* **1 :** an official in charge of the trains operating in a division or subdivision of a railroad **2 :** one in charge of the loading and unloading of a circus train

train–mile \ˈ=;=\ *n* **:** one mile traversed by one train used as a unit in railroad accounting

train off *vb* [⁴*train*] *vi* **1 :** to get out of training by relaxing a regimen or by going stale **2 :** SWERVE, VEER ~ *vt* **:** to eliminate (excess body weight) by exercise and diet

train of rolls : ROLL TRAIN

train oil *n* [⁵*train*] **:** WHALE OIL; *also* **:** oil from various other marine animals

train order *n* **:** a written message to an engineer or conductor giving instructions about the operation of a railroad train

trains *pl of* TRAIN, *pres 3d sing of* TRAIN

train shed *n* **1 :** a part of a railroad station that covers the tracks **2 :** a building to protect trains from the weather

train sheet *n* **:** a sheet used by a dispatcher to record the movement of railroad trains

trainsick \ˈ=,=\ *adj* **:** affected with train sickness

train sickness *n* **:** motion sickness induced by riding on a train

train signal *n* **:** a signal conveyed from the cars of a railroad train to the locomotive by a mechanical device

train stop *n* **:** a device for automatically applying the brakes to stop a railroad train if a signal goes unheeded

train tackle *n* **:** a tackle formerly used for training and running out guns esp. on shipboard

¹traipse *also* **trapes** \ˈtrāps\ *vb* **traipsed** *also* **trapesed; traipsed** *also* **trapesed; traipsing** *also* **trapesing; traipses** *also* **trapeses** [origin unknown] *vi* **1 :** to walk or tramp about **:** GAD, WANDER **2 :** to trail or hang down in disorderly fashion ~ *vt* **:** TRAMP, WALK

²traipse *also* **trapes** \"\ *n, pl* **traipses** *also* **trapeses 1 :** SLATTERN **2 :** a fatiguing walk

¹trait \ˈtrāt, *usu* -ād·+V; *Brit usu* ˈtrā\ *n* -s [MF, lit., pull, draft, fr. L *tractus* action of drawing, dragging, pulling, fr. *tractus*, past part. of *trahere* to draw, drag, pull — more at DRAW] **1 :** a stroke of or as of a pencil or brush **:** NOTE, TOUCH **2 :** a facial line or feature **:** LINEAMENT **3 :** a distinguishing quality (as of personal character) **:** FEATURE, MARK, PECULIARITY ⟨possessed what I think is the rarer ~, great physical bravery —Gretchen Finletter⟩ ⟨familiar ~s of church life —W.L.Sperry⟩ ⟨it is also a distinctly new medium with ~s and features of its own —Milton Klonsky⟩ **4 :** a characteristic of behavior or a typical artifact that distinguishes a human culture — called also *culture trait*

trait–complex \ˈ=;=,=\ *n* **:** ³COMPLEX 1a

trai·teur \(ˈ)trāˈtər(·)\ *n* -s [F, fr. *traiter* to treat, entertain, supply with food + *-eur* -or — more at TRATTORIA] **:** the keeper of a French or Italian eating house

trai·tor \ˈtrād·ə(r), -ātə-\ *n* -s [ME *traitre, traitour*, fr. OF *traitre, traitur*, fr. L *traditor*, fr. *traditus* (past part. of *tradere* to hand over, deliver, betray, fr. *trans-, tra-* trans- + *-dere* (fr. *dare* to give) + *-or* — more at DATE] **1 :** one that betrays another's trust or is false to an obligation or duty ⟨she sought to make me ~ to myself —John Milton⟩ ⟨valley boys who play golf are ~s to their class —M.S.Mayer⟩ **2 :** one that commits treason against his country (as by surrendering a fort or army unvanquished to an enemy) **:** one that violates his allegiance to his nation by levying war against it or by aiding its enemies

trai·tor·ism \-ə,rizəm\ *n* -s **:** BETRAYAL

trai·tor·ous \ˈtrād·ərəs, -ātər-,-ā·tr-\ *adj* [ME *traytrous*, fr. MF *traitreux*, fr. OF, fr. *traitre* traitor + *-eux* -ous — more at TRAITOR] **:** having the nature or quality of a traitor or of treason or betrayal **:** FALSE, PERFIDIOUS, TREACHEROUS, TREASONABLE **syn** see FAITHLESS

trai·tor·ous·ly *adv* [ME, fr. MF *traitreux* + ME *-ly*] **:** in a traitorous manner **:** FAITHLESSLY

trai·tor·ous·ness *n* -ES **:** the quality or state of being traitorous **:** PERFIDY

trai·tor·ship \-ād·ə(r),ship, -ātə-\ *n* **:** BETRAYAL, FALSITY

trai·tress *or* **trai·tor·ess** \ˈtrād·ərəs, -ātər-,-ā·tr-\ *n* -ES [ME *traitresse*, fr. *traitouresse*, fr. *traitre*, *traitour* traitor + *-esse* -ess] **:** a female traitor

trai·vel \ˈtrāvəl\ *Scot var of* TRAVEL

¹traj·ect \ˈtra,jekt, -jikt\ *n* -s [L *trajectus*, fr. *trajectus*, past part. of *trajicere, traicere* to throw across, cause to cross over, cross over, fr. *trans-, tra-* trans- + *-jicere, -icere* (fr. *jacere* to throw) — more at JET] **1 :** a place for passing across **:** a crossing route **:** FERRY **2 :** an act of crossing or traversing **:** PASSAGE

²tra·ject \trə'jekt\ *vt* -ED/-ING/-S [L *trajectus,* past part. of *trajicere, traicere*] **1 :** to cross over (as a river) **2 :** TRANSMIT ⟨~s sunlight through a prism⟩

tra·jec·tile \trə'jektᵊl, -k,tīl\ *adj* [*trajection* + *-ile*] **:** of, capable of, or marked by trajection

tra·jec·tion \trə'jekshən\ *n* -S [L *trajection-, trajectio,* fr. *trajectus* (past part. of *trajicere, traicere*) + *-ion-, -io* -ion] **1 :** transmission through space or some other medium **:** CROSSING **2 :** METATHESIS, TRANSPOSITION b(1)

¹tra·jec·to·ry \trə'jekt(ə)rē, -)ri\ *adj* [NL *trajectorius,* fr. L *trajectus* (past part. of *trajicere, traicere*) + *-orius* -ory] **:** of, relating to, or characteristic of a trajectory

²trajectory \"\ *n* -ES [NL *trajectoria,* fr. fem. of *trajectorius*] **1 a :** the curve that a body (as a planet or comet in its orbit, a projectile in passing from muzzle to first point of impact, or a rocket) describes in space **b :** a path, progression, or line of development likened to a physical trajectory ⟨the whole modern ~ from naturalism to symbolism —*New Republic*⟩ **2 :** a curve or surface that cuts all the curves or surfaces of a given system at the same angle

tra·jet \trázhā\ *n, pl* **trajets** \"\ [F, fr. L *trajectus* — more at TRAJECT] **:** TRAJECT, PASSAGE, COURSE, ROUTE, WAY

tra-la \trə'lä, (')trä¦lä\ *or* **tra-la-la** \¦trälə¦lä\ *also* **tra·li·ra** \¦trälə¦rä\ [origin unknown] — used to suggest gaiety, lightheartedness, or playful derision esp. in song

tral·a·ti·tious \¦tralə¦tishəs\ *adj* [L *tralatitius, tralaticius* (fr. *tralatus, translatus,* suppletive past part. of *transferre* to transfer) + *-itius, -icius* -itious — more at TRANSLATE] **1 :** having a character, force, or significance transferred or derived from something extraneous **:** METAPHORICAL, FIGURATIVE ⟨the primary and ~ meanings of a word⟩ **2 :** passed along as from hand to hand, mouth to mouth, or from generation to generation **:** handed down **:** TRADITIONAL ⟨among Biblical critics a ~ interpretation is one received by expositor from expositor —William Withington⟩ — **tral·a·ti·tious·ly** *adv*

tral·les alcoholometer *or* **tralles hydrometer** \'träləs-\ *n, usu cap T* [after Johann G. *Tralles* †1822 Ger. physicist] **:** an alcoholometer graduated so that its degrees indicate percentages by volume at 15.6°C

tra·lu·cent \trə'lüsᵊnt\ *adj* **:** TRANSLUCENT ⟨~ creatures as bright as rubies —Compton Mackenzie⟩

¹tram \'tram, -aa(ə)-\ *n* -S [F *trame* woof, weft, tram, fr. L *trama* woof, weft — more at TRAMA] **:** a loosely twisted silk yarn made by doubling and twisting two or more filaments together and usu. used for the weft of a fabric

²tram \"\ *n* -S [prob. fr. LG *traam* beam, handle of a barrow, fr. MLG *trāme;* akin to MD *traem, trame* beam, tooth of a rake, MLG *treme* crossbar] **1 a** *dial Brit* **:** a shaft of a vehicle (as a handbarrow or wheelbarrow) **b** *Scot* **:** LEG, LIMB **c** *dia Eng* **:** BENCH ⟨a ~ for dairy tubs⟩ **2 :** any of various vehicles: as **a :** a boxlike wagon often of steel running on a tramway or railway (as in a mine or logging camp) for conveying coal, ore, or logs **b** *chiefly Brit* **:** a passenger car of a street railway **:** STREETCAR ⟨that once characteristically British vehicle, the double-decked ~, is disappearing from one city after another —Paul Jennings⟩ **c :** a carrier that travels on an overhead cable or rails **3 a trams** *pl, chiefly Brit* **:** a streetcar line **b :** a tramway rail **c** (1) **:** TRAMWAY (2) **:** TRAMROAD

³tram \"\ *vb* **trammed; trammed; tramming; trams** *vi* **1** *Brit* **:** to travel in a tramcar **2** *Brit* **:** to operate a tram or a tramway system ~ *vt* **1 :** to haul (as coal) in a tram **2 :** to haul (lumber) over a tramway

⁴tram \"\ *n* -S [by shortening] **:** TRAMMEL 6c

⁵tram \"\ *n* -S [by shortening & alter.] *slang* **:** TROMBONE

tra·ma \'trāmə\ *n* -S [NL, fr. L, woof, weft, fr. *trahere* to pull, draw, drag — more at DRAW] **:** the loosely woven hyphal tissue in basidiomycetous fungi forming the central substance of the lamellae or other projections of the hymenophore — **tra·mal** \-məl\ *adj*

tramcar \'≈,≈\ *n* **1** *chiefly Brit* **:** ²TRAM 2b **2 :** ²TRAM 2a

tram crane *n* **:** a crane consisting of a short bridge without a trolley traveling on overhead rails

trame·tes \tramə,tēz, -rām-\ *n, cap* [NL, fr. *trama*] **:** a genus of pore fungi (family Polyporaceae) having leathery pileate sporophores with the meeting line between pores and context uneven

tram·less \'tramləs, -raam-\ *adj* **:** having no tram

tramline \'≈,≈\ *n, Brit* **:** a streetcar line

¹tram·mel \'traməl\ *n* -S [ME *tramayle, tramale,* fr. MF *tremail,* fr. LL *tremaculum,* fr. *tres* three + *macula* mesh, spot — more at THREE] **1 a :** a net for catching birds or fishes: as **a :** an anchored gill net **b :** TRAMMEL NET **2 a :** shackle used for regulating the motions of a horse and making him amble **3 :** something impeding activity, progress, or freedom as if by a net or shackle **:** RESTRAINT, CHECK — usu. used in pl. ⟨the poet's imagination must be free and has progressively thrown off the ~s of respectability, tradition, and more recently the established conventions of communication by language —N.E.Nelson⟩ ⟨bound by the ~s of human nature —Robert Graves⟩ ⟨the masses . . . sought to build an America free of the ~s of the Old World —H.J. Laski⟩ **4 :** an adjustable pothook for a fireplace crane **5 trammels** *pl, obs* **:** braids, plaitings, or tresses of a woman's hair **6 a** (1) **:** an instrument for drawing ellipses consisting of a cross with two grooves at right angles to each other and a beam carrying two pins which slide in those grooves and also a describing pencil (2) **:** any of various mechanical devices for drawing ellipses **:** ELLIPSOGRAPH **b** (1) **:** BEAM COMPASS — usu. used in pl. and often used with *pair* ⟨a pair of ~s⟩ (2) **:** either of the sliding parts on the beam of a beam compass **c :** any of various gages used for aligning or adjusting machine parts — called also *tram*

trammels 4

²trammel \"\ *vt* **trammeled** *or* **trammelled; trammeled** *or* **trammelled; trammeling** *or* **trammelling** \-m(ə)liŋ\ **trammels 1 a :** to catch (as fish) in a trammel **b** *obs* **:** to attach trammels to (a horse) **:** SHACKLE **2 :** to hold in or as if in a net **:** tie or fasten securely **:** ENMESH ⟨while suffering the almost irremediable homesickness of bereavement had now become ~ed in events —Ethel Wilson⟩ — sometimes used with *up* ⟨if the assassination could ~ up the consequence —Shak.⟩ **3 :** to impose restraints upon **:** prevent or impede the free play or exercise of **:** CONFINE ⟨writing about people whose speech and behavior were ~ed to a certain extent by the usages of polite society —Wolcott Gibbs⟩ ⟨their life was at once dangerously ~ed and dangerously free —John Buchan⟩ ⟨the classical models no longer ~, but assist him to be more effectively himself —H.O.Taylor⟩ ⟨these observations, by ~ing his every act, annihilate his freedom —J.G.Frazer⟩ **syn** see HAMPER

trammel net *n* **:** a rectangular net made of a middle layer that is slack and of fine mesh and two outer layers that are stretched and of coarse mesh so arranged that fish attempting to pass in either direction carry some of the fine net through the coarse and are thus pocketed

trammel point *n* **:** either of the metal points of a beam compass

tram·mer \'tramə(r), -raam-\ *n* -S [³*tram* + *-er*] **:** one that trams; *specif* **:** one that trams coal, ore, or waste rock **:** PUSHER

tra·mon·ta·na \¦trä(,)mōn'tänə\ *n* -S [It, fr. fem. of *tramontano*] **:** the north wind; *esp* **:** a dry cold strong northerly wind of the west coast of Italy

¹tramon·tane \trə'män,tān, 'tramən-\ *adj* [It *tramontano,* fr. L *transmontanus,* fr. *trans-* + *montanus* of a mountain — more at MOUNTAIN] **1 a :** TRANSALPINE — compare CISMONTANE **b :** of or characteristic of the countries north of the Alps **c :** coming from the north beyond the Alps ⟨a ~ wind⟩ **2 :** lying or being beyond any mountains **:** coming from the other side of the mountains ⟨sectionalism in Virginia had reared its head in a contest between a cismontane and a ~ people —*Amer. Guide Series: Va.*⟩ **3 :** FOREIGN, OUTLANDISH, BARBAROUS

²tramontane \"\ *n* -S [It *tramontano,* fr. *tramontano,* adj.] **1 :** one dwelling in a tramontane region: as **a :** an inhabitant of a country north of the Alps **b :** FOREIGNER, STRANGER **c :** BOOR **2** [It *tramontana*] **:** TRAMONTANA

¹tramp \'tramp, -aa(ə)-, -ai-, *in senses vi 1 & vt 1 chiefly dial* 'trämp *or* -rómp\ *vb* -ED/-ING/-S [ME *trampen;* akin to MLG *trampen* to stamp, tread, MD *tramperen* to stamp, Norw dial. *trumpa* to push, shove, Goth *anatrimpan* to crowd, MD *trappen* to stamp — more at TRAP] *vi* **1 a :** to walk or tread esp. with a heavy step ⟨a steady stream of visitors ~s every day through the magnificent exhibition —Mollie Panter-Downes⟩ ⟨man who was ~ing across the square in climbing boots —Willa Cather⟩ ⟨heard them ~ upstairs —Arnold Bennett⟩ ⟨~ on someone's toes⟩ **b :** to press one's foot ⟨~ed down on the gas pedal —Oakley Hall⟩ **2 a :** to travel about on foot **:** HIKE ⟨spent his holidays ~ing all over our native land —Joseph Conrad⟩ ⟨finds relaxation in . . . ~ing in the woods —*Current Biog.*⟩ ⟨~ed and climbed among the heights —H.N.Fowler⟩ **b :** to journey as a tramp **3 a :** to travel as a tramp ship ⟨three tiny steamers ~ing between Suez and Mukalla —Ladislas Farago⟩ **b :** to travel on a tramp ship ~ *vt* **1 :** to tread on forcibly and usu. repeatedly **:** trample so as to bruise or press down ⟨~ grapes for wine⟩ ⟨dig out the ground three feet deep, put in a foot of straw, leaves, or coarse litter, wet it thoroughly, and ~ it down one half —Emily Holt⟩ ⟨~ing the top of your silage 10 to 15 minutes a day for a week after filling will reduce top spoilage —*Deerfield (Wisc.) Independent*⟩ **2 a :** to travel or wander through on foot **:** hike or trudge through or along ⟨rode the subways and ~ed the streets —E.A.Weeks⟩ ⟨a naturalist ~ing the forests⟩ **b :** to make by trudging or hiking ⟨left home to ~ his way over the country —R.L.Taylor⟩

²tramp \'tramp, -aa(ə)-, -ai-, *in senses 3–5 chiefly dial* 'trämp *or* -rómp\ *n* -S **1 a :** a foot traveler **:** TRAMPER ⟨youthful ~s in search of work —Siegfried Kracauer⟩ **b :** a begging or thieving vagrant; *esp* **:** a lazy good-for-nothing beggar or sponger who travels about but will not work ⟨the ~ reappeared time and again as the hero of screen adventures —Lewis Jacobs⟩ **c :** a woman of loose morals; *specif* **:** PROSTITUTE ⟨the inflamed stateside demarcations between the nice girl and the ~ —*Christian Science Monitor*⟩ ⟨a girl who couldn't quite make up her mind whether she wants to be a wife or a kept woman or just a ~ off to try her luck in New York —Wolcott Gibbs⟩ **2 :** a journey on foot **:** a walking trip **:** HIKE ⟨forth for a long ~ —C.G.Bowers⟩ ⟨go for ~s on Saturday afternoons —Elizabeth Bowen⟩ **3 :** the act of tramping ⟨the dry ground was packed from the ~ of thousands of cattle and horses —J.F. Dobie⟩; *also* **:** a mark produced by this act **4 :** the succession of sounds made by the beating of feet of men or animals on a road, pavement, or floor ⟨the rhythmic ~ of marching armies —C.T.Lanham⟩ ⟨the ~s of so many horses —Walt Whitman⟩ **5 a :** a plate of iron worn to protect the sole of the foot or the shoe when digging with a spade; *also* **:** the part of the spade against which the foot is forced in digging **b :** a spiked piece of iron worn on the shoe in curling to prevent slipping **6** *or* **tramp ship** *or* **tramp steamer :** a ship not making regular trips between the same ports but taking a cargo when and where it offers and to any port **7 :** an unwanted up-and-down movement of an automobile on its front wheels ⟨tended to set up violent shimmy and ~ on the front end at high speeds —Roger Huntington⟩ **8 :** TRAMPOLINE **syn** see VAGABOND

³tramp \'tramp, -aa(ə)-, -ai-\ *adj* [²*tramp*] **1 :** having no fixed abode, connection, or destination ⟨a ~ dog⟩ ⟨a ~ printer⟩ ⟨a ~ and vagrant world, adrift in space —William James⟩ **2 :** UNWANTED, CONTAMINATING — used esp. of metallic particles ⟨whenever ~ iron threatens to contaminate a process or product, damage machinery, or give rise to sparking, magnets are the sentries that keep it out —*Steelways*⟩

tramp·dom \-dəm\ *n* -S **:** the realm of tramps; *also* **:** TRAMPS

tramp·er \-pə(r)\ *n* -S **1 :** one that tramps **:** VAGRANT: as **a :** a heavy walker **b :** one that takes long walks for pleasure or exercise **:** HIKER **2 :** an attachment for a cotton press for compacting the cotton during baling

tramp·ish \-pish\ *adj* **:** having the characteristics of a tramp esp. in appearance — **tramp·ish·ly** *adv* — **tramp·ish·ness** *n* -ES

¹tram·ple \'trampəl, -raam-,-raim-\ *vb* **trampled; trampled; trampling** \-p(ə)liŋ\ **tramples** [ME *tramplen,* freq. of *trampen* to tramp — more at TRAMP] *vi* **:** TRAMP ⟨the little boys lay down in the dust, heedless of the feet *trampling* everywhere about them —Pearl Buck⟩ ⟨*trampling* up and down the front porch, nervous as a cat —R.P.Warren⟩ ⟨if in addition to the year's four seasons the fifth of famine ~s through the land —Frederic Morton⟩: as **a :** to tread heavily so as to bruise, crush, or injure — usu. used with *on, upon,* or *over* ⟨a runaway horse had *trampled* on him and broken his hipbone —Vicki Baum⟩ ⟨the boy who has a garden will not ~ on other people's flower beds —Bertrand Russell⟩ **b :** to inflict injury or destruction **:** have a contemptuous or ruthless attitude **:** TYRANNIZE — usu. used with *on, over,* or *upon* ⟨he liked to ~ on his foes —M.R.Cohen⟩ ⟨pride and sensitiveness were his chief foes, and he would ~ on them —George Meredith⟩ ⟨his grim, repressive mother, who *trampled* on every innocent pleasure —Van Wyck Brooks⟩ ⟨*trampled* on conventions —Henry Adams⟩ ⟨if the great powers show themselves irresponsibly ready to ~ over any weak nation that seemed to be in their way —Vera M. Dean⟩ ~ *vt* **1 :** to press down in walking **:** crush or injure by or as if by treading **:** STAMP ⟨man was standing on a large push truck and *trampling* down a great pile of old newspapers and other trash —Thomas Whiteside⟩ ⟨shoes ~ his camera underfoot —Ray Duncan⟩ ⟨used to ~ the lumps of hard clay into powder —*Amer. Guide Series: Tenn.*⟩ ⟨will rediscover the morality their oppressors *trampled* into the dust —*Times Lit. Supp.*⟩ ⟨the utility combine is pressuring Congress to ~ down the law and the will of the people —*N. Y. Times*⟩ **2 :** to extinguish by stamping with the feet — usu. used with *out* ⟨a forbidden book is like a fire one tries to ~ out —*Encore*⟩

²trample \"\ *n* -S **:** the act or sound of trampling **:** a heavy and repeated tread of or as if of many feet

tram·po·line *also* **tram·po·lin** \¦trampə¦lēn, -raam-,-raim- *sometimes* '≈≈lən\ *n* -S [Sp *trampolin,* fr. It *trampolino,* fr. *trampoli* stilts, of Gmc origin; akin to MLG *trampen* to stamp, tread — more at TRAMP] **:** a resilient canvas sheet or web supported by springs in a metal frame used as a springboard in tumbling and exercising — **tram·po·lin·er** \¦≈≈¦lēnə(r)\ *or* **tram·po·lin·ist** \-nəst\ *n* -S

tramp's-trouble \'≈,≈≈\ *n, pl* **tramp's-troubles :** CHINA BRIER

tram rail *n* **:** a rail for a tram: as **a :** a rail of plates as distinguished from the later edge rail **b :** an overhead rail on which a trolley runs to convey a load (as in a shop)

tramroad \'≈,≈\ *n* **:** a roadway for trams consisting of parallel tracks made of usu. metal-faced wooden beams, stone blocks, metal plates, or rails; *specif* **:** a railway in a mine

trams *pl of* TRAM, *pres 3d sing of* TRAM

tramway \'≈,≈\ *n* **:** a way for trams: as **a :** TRAMROAD **b** *Brit* **:** a streetcar line; *also* **:** STREETCAR **c :** TRAM RAIL b **d :** ROPEWAY **e :** a light or temporary logging railroad often with wooden rails and operated by horsepower

tram·way·man \"mən\ *n, pl* **tramwaymen** *Brit* **:** an employee of a streetcar line

tran *abbr* transit

¹trance \'tran(t)s, -raa(ə)n-, -rain-, -rȧn-\ *vb* -ED/-ING/-S [ME *transen* to die, swoon, be in fear, fr. MF *transir* — more at ²TRANCE] *vi, obs* **:** to be in great suspense or extreme fear ~ *vt* [²*trance*] **1 :** to hold (as a person) benumbed, immobile, or unnaturally still ⟨her heart was clutched by a grip of ice, and she went as one *tranced* —C.G.D.Roberts⟩ ⟨a dead hot silence *tranced* sea, land, and sky —R.H.Horne⟩ **2 :** ENTRANCE, ENRAPTURE ⟨a romance . . . held me rapt through many a *tranced* hour —R.M.Bell⟩ ⟨ever the fiery Pentecost . . . ~s the heart through chanting hours and through the priest the mind inspires —R.W.Emerson⟩

²trance \"\ *n* -S [ME *traunce, trance,* fr. MF *transe,* fr. *transir* to pass, pass away, die, swoon, be in fear, fr. L *transire* to pass, pass away — more at TRANSIENT] **1 :** a state of partly suspended animation or of inability to function **:** DAZE, STUPOR ⟨in a calm ~, like a dead person, she crossed the street —Mary McCarthy⟩ ⟨lay stone-still in a ~ of terror and mournfulness —George Meredith⟩ ⟨the neigh of some horse . . . loud and sudden, that had burst the shell of my ~, causing thought to start to life again —Owen Wister⟩ **2 :** a somnolent state such as that of deep hypnosis appearing also in hysteria and in some spiritualistic mediums and characterized by limited sensory and motor contact with the surroundings and subsequent lack of recall ⟨fell into . . . a light kind of ~ that, he explains, is the first stage of hypnosis —Vance Packard⟩ ⟨in ~ they divine auspicious times for various tasks —*African Abstracts*⟩ **3 :** a state of profound abstraction or absorption accompanied by exaltation ⟨went into a ~ closely resembling religious rapture —R.G.Hubler⟩ ⟨would work himself into a condition of ecstasy which resembled a ~ . . . would fall down, and foam would break out on his lips —Maurice Samuel⟩

³trance \'trans\ *vi* -ED/-ING/-S [ME *trauncen*] *dial Brit* **:** to pass or travel over the ground **:** to move briskly **:** PRANCE

⁴trance \"\ *n* -S [perh. short for ¹*transit*] *chiefly Scot* **:** PASSAGE, PASSAGEWAY

tranced·ly \-nstlē, -nsədlē\ *adv* [*tranced* (past part. of ¹*trance*) + *-ly*] **:** in or as if in a trance

tranche \'träⁿsh\ *n* -S [F, fr. OF, fr. *trenchier, trancher* to cut — more at TRENCH] **:** SLICE, SECTION, PORTION; *specif* **:** a portion or series of a bond issue to be distributed in a foreign country

tran·chet \träⁿ'shā\ *n* -S [F, cutting tool, fr. MF, fr. *trancher* to cut] **1 :** a chisel-shaped flint implement peculiar to Neolithic times **2 :** CHOPPER 2c

tra·neen \trə'nēn\ *n* -S [IrGael *trāithnīn* blade of grass, herb bennet] *chiefly Irish* **:** something of little or no value **:** TRIFLE ⟨never cared a ~ for him —S.C.Hall⟩

tran·gam \'traŋgəm\ *n* -S [origin unknown] *archaic* **:** an odd device or puzzle **:** TRINKET, GIMCRACK

trank \'traŋk\ *n* -S [origin unknown] **1 :** a piece of leather large enough for one glove body **2 :** a cut glove body consisting of front and back without thumb, fourchettes, or gussets — see GLOVE illustration

tran·ky \'traŋkē\ *n* -ES [Per dial. *trānki*] **:** an undecked bark used in the Persian gulf

tran·quil \'traŋkwəl, -rank-, -raank-\ *adj, sometimes* **tranquiler** *or* **tranquiller;** *sometimes* **tranquilest** *or* **tranquillest** [L *tranquillus*] **1 a :** free from mental agitation **:** SERENE ⟨she became more ~, and was able to listen to his plans —Anthony Trollope⟩ ⟨the sort of heart that great men have, straightforward, undeviating, and ~ —Ruth Park⟩ **b :** free from disturbance or turmoil **:** QUIET, PEACEFUL ⟨~ as a rural church on a Sunday afternoon —Green Peyton⟩ ⟨a ~ twilight hour —Elinor Wylie⟩ ⟨has transformed a normally ~ agricultural region into one of factories —*Amer. Guide Series: Texas*⟩ ⟨celebrities . . . allowed to live and die in ~ privacy —E.M. Lustgarten⟩ ⟨peace can be made ~ and secure only by understanding and agreement —B.M.Baruch⟩ **2 :** unvarying in aspect **:** STEADY, STABLE ⟨when a few of the corpuscles have been fired across it, it becomes something very different from a ~ gas —K.K.Darrow⟩ ⟨her eyes and nostrils, usually so ~, were dilated —G.B.Shaw⟩ **syn** see CALM

tran·quil·iza·tion *or* **tran·quil·li·za·tion** \,traŋkwələ'zāshən, -rank-, -raank-, -wə,lī'-\ *n* -S **:** an act or process of tranquilizing

tran·quil·ize *or* **tran·quil·lize** \'traŋkwə,līz, -rank-, -raank-\ *vb* -ED/-ING/-S [*tranquil* + *-ize*] *vt* **:** to cause to be or become tranquil **:** PACIFY ⟨the perfect balance she had held . . . stirred and yet *tranquilized* him —Edith Wharton⟩; *specif* **:** to reduce or bring to a quiet or unagitated state by means of a chemical reaction ⟨nicotinamide . . . also *tranquilized* animals —D.W. Woolley⟩ ~ *vi* **:** to become tranquil **syn** see CALM

tran·quil·iz·er *or* **tran·quil·liz·er** \-zə(r)\ *n* -S **1 :** one that tranquilizes **2 :** a drug used to reduce anxiety and tension states or mental disturbances in people and animals

tran·quil·li·ty *or* **tran·quil·i·ty** \tran'kwiləd·ē, traan-, traŋ-, -ətē, -i\ *n* -ES [ME *tranquillite,* fr. MF *tranquillité,* fr. L *tranquillitat-, tranquillitas,* fr. *tranquillus* tranquil + *-itat-, -itas* -ity] **:** the quality or state of being tranquil ⟨emotion recollected in ~ —William Wordsworth⟩ ⟨the lasting peace which is the ~ of order —J.P.McGranery⟩ ⟨the ~ of the flowing stream is carefully measured⟩

tran·quil·lo \trän'kwē(,)lō\ *adv (or adj)* [It, fr. *tranquillo* tranquil, fr. L *tranquillus*] **:** in a quiet or calm manner — used as a direction in music

tran·quil·ly \'traŋkwəlē, -rank-, -raank-, -li\ *adv* **:** in a tranquil manner

tran·quil·ness *n* -ES [*tranquil* + *-ness*] **:** TRANQUILLITY

trans \'tran(t)s, -nz\ *adj* [*trans-*] **:** having or characterized by various atoms or groups on opposite sides of the molecule ⟨~ configuration around the double bonds⟩ — opposed to *cis*

trans- \(ˌ)tran(t)s, -raan-, -nz *sometimes chiefly Brit* -rȧn-\ *prefix* [L *trans-, tra-* across, beyond, to the other side, through, so as to change, fr. *trans* across, beyond, on or to the other side, through — more at THROUGH] **1 a :** across ⟨*trans*polar⟩ ⟨*trans*atlantic⟩ ⟨*trans*oceanic⟩ **b** (1) **:** beyond ⟨*trans*human⟩ ⟨*trans*mundane⟩ (2) **:** beyond (a specified chemical element) in the periodic table ⟨*trans*plutonium⟩ ⟨*trans*uranic⟩ **c :** through ⟨*trans*lucent⟩ ⟨*trans*cutaneous⟩ **d :** completeness of change ⟨*trans*shape⟩ **2 :** transverse ⟨*trans*frontal⟩ ⟨*trans*process⟩ **3 :** having certain atoms or groups on opposite sides of the molecule ⟨*trans*-dichloro-ethylene⟩ — opposed to *cis-* 3; compare ALL- 2b, ANTI- 7 **4 :** transfer **:** interchange — in names of chemical reactions and enzymes ⟨*trans*amination⟩

trans *abbr* **1** transaction **2** transfer; transferred **3** transformer **4** transit **5** transitional **6** transitive **7** translated; translation; translator **8** transmission **9** transmitter **10** transparent **11** transport; transportation **12** transpose **13** transverse

trans·abdominal \¦tran(t)s, -raan-, -nz+\ *adj* [*trans-* + *abdomin-* + *-al*] **:** passing, occurring, or cutting across the abdomen or through the abdominal wall

trans·ac·ci·den·ta·tion \,tran(t)saksəden·'tāshən\ *n* -S [ML *transaccidentation-, transaccidentatio,* fr. L *trans-* + ML *accident-, accidens* accident, after L *substantia* substance: ML *transubstantiation-, transubstantiatio* transubstantiation] **:** an orig. medieval theological doctrine that the accidents of the eucharistic bread and wine are changed into the body and blood of Jesus Christ at the moment of their consecration — compare TRANSUBSTANTIATION

trans·acetylase \¦tran(t)s, -raan-, -nz+\ *n* [*trans-* + *acetyl* + *-ase*] **:** any of several enzymes that catalyze the transfer of acetyl groups; *esp* **:** an enzyme that promotes the reversible conversion of acetyl coenzyme A to acetyl phosphate and is found in bacteria

¹trans·act \tran(t)'sakt, traan-, -n'za-\ *vb* -ED/-ING/-S [L *transactus,* past part. of *transigere* to drive through, complete, transact, fr. *trans-* + *-igere* (fr. *agere* to drive, act, do) — more at AGENT] *vi* **1 :** to prosecute negotiations **:** carry on business **:** NEGOTIATE ⟨desires to ~ only with honest men⟩ **2 :** to compromise esp. by compliance or concession in a matter of principle ~ *vt* **1** *archaic* **:** to turn over (as for settlement) **:** TRANSMIT, TRANSFER **2 :** to carry out **:** EFFECT, PERFORM ⟨on his father's farm, he ~ed the imperative residuum of chores —Irving Stone⟩; *esp* **:** to carry on **:** DO, CONDUCT ⟨hold a meeting . . . choose a moderator, ~ their business —R.W. Hatch⟩ ⟨that such business, because of its technical nature, be ~ed solely by . . . experts —F.A.Ogg & Harold Zink⟩ **3** *archaic* **:** to trade in or with **:** HANDLE, EXCHANGE **4 :** to make a transaction of; *esp* **:** to compound or compromise (as a dispute) by mutual agreement

²trans·act \tran'sakt\ *n* -S [LL *transactum,* fr. L, neut. of *transactus*] *dial Eng* **:** TRANSACTION

trans·ac·tion \tran(t)'sakshən, traan-, -n'za-\ *n* -S [ME, fr. LL *transaction-, transactio,* fr. L *transactus* + *-ion-, -io* -ion] **1 :** an act, process, or instance of transacting: as **a** (1) **:** an adjustment or compromise in Roman and civil law of a disputed claim effected by mutual agreement and resembling the accord and satisfaction of the common law (2) **:** COMPACT, COVENANT ⟨the atonement is to him no mere ~ . . . but the consequence of God's own nature and will —*Times Lit. Supp.*⟩ **b :** a communicative action or activity involving two parties or two things reciprocally affecting or influencing each other ⟨to intensify the ~ between the lay listener and the esthetic object —Arthur Berger⟩ ⟨thought transference implies that there is some ~ . . . between the agent and the subject —A.G.N. Flew⟩ ⟨men . . . get perspectives upon events as the spur of need drives them into interactions and ~s with events —H.L. Parsons⟩ **2 :** something that is transacted: as **a :** a business deal ⟨a profitable ~⟩ — often used in pl. ⟨service ~s were not sufficient to pay for necessary imports —W.M.W.Splawn⟩ **b transactions** *pl* **:** a publication usu. of a learned society or professional association in which are presented scholarly studies or research reports **:** PROCEEDING 3 ⟨besides many contributions to ~s and periodicals he edited the American edition —F.R.Packard⟩

trans·ac·tion·al \-shənᵊl, -shnəl\ *adj* **:** of, relating to, or involving a transaction ⟨the ~ nature of the atonement⟩; *specif* **:** realized in actuality ⟨the general trend of science, however, is directed toward ~ conceptions —Ludwig Von Bertalanffy⟩ — **trans·ac·tion·al·ly** \-shənᵊl\|ē, -shnəl\|, \|i\ *adv*

transaction tax *n* **:** TURNOVER TAX

trans·ac·tor \-ktə(r)\ *n* -s [L, fr. *transactus* + *-or*] **:** one that transacts

trans·admittance \¦tran(t)s, -raan-, -nz+\ *n* [*trans-* + *admittance*] **:** the ratio in an electron tube of the effective alternating-current component at one electrode to the corresponding effective voltage at another electrode with the potentials of the remaining elements being constant — compare TRANSCONDUCTANCE

[1]**trans·alpine** \(ˈ)tran(t)s, -raan-, -nz+\ *adj* [L *transalpinus*, fr. *trans-* + *Alpes* the Alps, mountains of south central Europe + L *-inus* -ine] **1 :** of, relating to, or situated on the farther side of the Alps ⟨~ Gaul . . . was the country included between the Rhine, the ocean, the Pyrenees, the Mediterranean, and the Alps —J.A.Froude⟩ ⟨Cracow, one of the best of the ~ universities —G.C.Sellery⟩ — opposed to *cisalpine* **2 :** of, relating to, or characteristic of the region or peoples beyond the Alps

[2]**transalpine** \"\ *n* [L *Transalpini* (pl.), fr. pl. of *transalpinus*, adj.] **:** a native or inhabitant of a transalpine country

trans·am·i·nase \tran(t)ˈsaməˌnās, traan-, -nˈza-\ *n* [*transamination* + *-ase*] **:** any of a group of enzymes that promote transamination usu. if pyridoxal phosphate is present as coenzyme and that are found in almost all animal tissues, in higher plants, and in many bacteria

trans·am·i·na·tion \(ˌ)=ˌ==ˈnāshən\ *n* [*trans-* + *amination*] **:** a reversible oxidation-reduction reaction in which an amino group is transferred typically from an alpha-amino acid to the carbonyl carbon atom of an alpha-keto acid and which is usu. promoted by a transaminase ⟨the ~ of glutamic acid in the presence of pyruvic acid yields alpha-ketoglutaric acid and alanine⟩

trans·an·i·ma·tion \(ˌ)tran(t)ˌsanəˈmāshən, -raan-, -nˌza-\ *n* [LL *transanimation-*, *transanimatio*, fr. L *trans-* + *anima* soul + *-ation-*, *-atio* -ation — more at ANIMATE] **:** METEMPSYCHOSIS

trans·an·nu·lar \(ˈ)tran(t)¦sanyələ(r), -raan-, -nˈza-\ *adj* [*trans-* + L *annulus* ring + E *-ar* — more at ANNULUS] **:** relating to or being tautomerism characterized by migration (as of a hydrogen atom) across a ring

[1]**trans·at·lan·tic** \¦tran(t)sət¦lantik, -raan-, -nzə-, -¦laan-, -tēk\ *adj* [*trans-* + *Atlantic (ocean)*] **1 :** crossing or extending across the Atlantic ocean ⟨~ voyage⟩ ⟨~ cable⟩ **2 a :** lying or situated beyond the Atlantic ocean ⟨travels to a ~ country⟩ **b :** of, relating to, or characteristic of a people, country, or region beyond the Atlantic ocean ⟨the tacit conflict and mutual yearning of two cultures, the old European and the new ~ —*Times Lit. Supp.*⟩ — **trans·at·lan·ti·cal·ly** \-tək(ə)lē\ *adv*

[2]**transatlantic** \"\ *n* -s **1 :** one that is or lives across the Atlantic or in a transatlantic country **2 :** a transatlantic ship

trans·border \(ˈ)tran(t)s, -raan-, -nz+\ *adj* [*trans-* + *border*] **:** situated or living beyond the border or frontier — often used of Asian regions or peoples

trans·ca·lent \tranzˈkālənt, -n(t)ˈsk-\ *adj* [*trans-* + L *calent-*, *calens*, pres. part. of *calēre* to be warm — more at LEE] **:** pervious to or permitting the passage of heat

trans·callosal \¦tranz, -raan-, -n(t)s+\ *adj* [*trans-* + NL (*corpus*) *callosum* + E *-al*] **:** passing through or by way of the corpus callosum ⟨a ~ section⟩ ⟨~ pathways⟩

[1]**trans·caucasian** \¦tranz, -raan-, -n(t)s+\ *adj, usu cap* [*Transcaucasia*, region south of the Caucasus mountains + E *-an*] **1 :** of, relating to, or characteristic of the region of Transcaucasia south of the Caucasus mountains **2 :** of, relating to, or characteristic of the people of Transcaucasia

[2]**transcaucasian** \"\ *n, cap* **:** a native or inhabitant of Transcaucasia

trans·ceiver \tranzˈsēvə(r), traan-, -n(t)(s)ˈ-\ *n* -s [*trans*mitter + re*ceiver*] **:** a radio transmitter-receiver that uses many of the same components for both transmission and reception

tran·scend \tranˈsend, traanˈ-\ *vb* -ED/-ING/-S [L *transcendere* to climb across, surmount, transcend, fr. *trans-* + *-scendere* (fr. *scandere* to climb) — more at SCAN] *vt* **1 a :** to rise above or go beyond the limits of **:** EXCEED ⟨servants whose loyalty and devotion ~ national and cultural boundaries —C.J. Friedrich⟩ ⟨instinctive courtesy which ~s mere good manners —Richard Joseph⟩ ⟨to possess by self-mastery the sources of love and hate is to ~ good and evil —Havelock Ellis⟩ **b :** to extend above or beyond (as the universe) ⟨~ material existence⟩ ⟨the Christian message ~s all temporal civilizations —Maria Sulzbach⟩ **2 :** to outstrip or outdo in some attribute, quality, or power **:** SURPASS ⟨some of the electrons . . . ~ this speed and take their leave —K.K.Darrow⟩ ⟨her compass ~*ed* that of her companions in the band —Thomas Hardy⟩ ⟨whose hatred, he says, ~s that of all other races —*Times Lit. Supp.*⟩ ⟨one who has infinitely ~*ed* him in reputation —Richard Garnett †1906⟩ **3** *obs* **:** to cross or climb over **:** MOUNT **4 :** to cause to rise or go upward **:** ELEVATE, RAISE ⟨man being ~*ed* toward the universal as worker and citizen —H.M. Parshley⟩ ~ *vi* **1** *obs* **:** to travel upward or onward **:** ASCEND **2 :** EXCEL, SURPASS ⟨it is the function of genius to ~⟩ **syn** see EXCEED

tran·scen·dence \-ndən(t)s\ *n* -s [LL *transcendentia*, fr. L *transcendent-*, *transcendens* + *-ia* -y] **:** the quality or state of being transcendent

tran·scen·den·cy \-nsē, -si\ *n* -ES [LL *transcendentia*] **:** TRANSCENDENCE

[1]**tran·scen·dent** *also* **tran·scen·dant** \-nt\ *adj* [*transcendent* fr. L *transcendent-*, *transcendens*, pres. part. of *transcendere* to transcend; *transcendant* fr. F, fr. pres. part. of obs. *transcendre* to transcend, fr. L *transcendere*] **1 a :** going beyond or exceeding usual limits **:** EXCELLING, SURPASSING ⟨his own detestation of the rigors of winter made the children's courage appear ~ —Elinor Wylie⟩ ⟨the ~ importance of news . . . in a democracy —F.L.Mott⟩ ⟨the poet . . . fuses the elements of a profound perception into a single ~ vision —George Whalley⟩ **b :** proceeding beyond or lying outside of what is perceived or presented in experience ⟨philosophers . . . often explicitly reject the notion of any ~ reality beyond thought . . . and claim to be concerned only with thought itself and its immanent necessities —W.P.Alston⟩ **c** *Kantianism* **:** being beyond the limits of all possible experience and knowledge — contrasted with *transcendental* 1b **2 :** being beyond comprehension **:** VAGUE, OBSCURE ⟨too ~, too difficult, and too unrelated to the human heart to satisfy other men —H.O.Taylor⟩ **3 :** being above material existence or apart from the universe ⟨the ideal of a ~ and holy being —M.R.Cohen⟩ ⟨the idea of a source and end of life, too ~ to the . . . powers of human life to be either simply comprehended by the human mind or easily manipulated —Reinhold Niebuhr⟩ — contrasted with *immanent*

[2]**transcendent** *also* **transcendant** \"\ *n* -s **:** one that transcends: as **a :** a person or thing that escapes classification in any accepted category; *specif* **:** a predicate that cannot be classed among the Aristotelian predicaments **b** *Kantianism* **:** something beyond the limits of experience and knowledge ⟨spirit . . . is a ~ over against that which can be perceived by the senses —R.K.Bultmann⟩

[1]**tran·scen·den·tal** \¦tranˌsen¦dentᵊl, ¦tran(t)sᵊn¦-, -raan-\ *adj* [ML *transcendentalis*, fr. L *transcendent-*, *transcendens* + *-alis* -al] **1 a** *Aristotelianism* **:** reaching or lying beyond the bounds of any category; *also* **:** METAPHYSICAL **b** *Kantianism* (1) **:** of or relating to the a priori and necessary conditions of human experience as determined by the constitution of the mind itself (2) **:** transcending what is determined by the contingent particularity of experience though not transcending all human knowledge — contrasted with *transcendent* 1b **2 :** TRANSCENDENT 1a ⟨few men have had his ~ capacity to stir the heart —J.H.Plumb⟩ ⟨the trout fisherman . . . with that ~ patience —Richard Jefferies⟩ ⟨an event of ~ importance —Rodrigo Miró⟩ **3 a :** incapable of being the root of an algebraic equation with rational integral coefficients ⟨π is a ~ number⟩ **b :** being, involving, or representing a function (as sin x, log x, e^x) that cannot be expressed by a finite number of algebraic operations **4 a :** extending or being beyond the limits of ordinary experience ⟨extreme ~ idealism which viewed the world as the visionary creation of the fallen soul of man —E.S.Bates⟩ ⟨a ~ world of concepts has therefore been envisaged by the philosophers —C.K.Ogden & I.A.Richards⟩ **b :** of or relating to the supernatural ⟨the vital ~ soul, belonging to the spiritual realm —Lewis Mumford⟩ ⟨find ~ motives for sublunary action —Aldous Huxley⟩ **c :** ABSTRUSE, ABSTRACT ⟨that ~ phraseology which defies exact translation —Herbert Read⟩ ⟨insensitive plodders . . . regrettably unable to follow the ~ speculations —C.W.Shumaker⟩ **d :** of or relating to transcendentalism ⟨the ~ belief . . . that every part of nature is an emblem, symbol, or analogue of a spiritual or intellectual truth —R.L. Cook⟩

[2]**transcendental** \"\ *n* -s **:** something that is transcendental: as **a :** a transcendental idea or doctrine **b** *Scholasticism* **:** any one of the broadest conceptions of being (as being, thing, one, truth) ⟨he appears to assume, in many places but particularly in his demonstrations of God, both that being (or some equivalent ~) is a genus, and that God is in it —H.T.Schwartz⟩

transcendental aesthetic *n, Kantianism* **:** a doctrine of the a priori forms of perception esp. of time and space

transcendental curve *n* **:** a curve whose equations contain transcendental functions

transcendental equation *n* **:** an equation containing transcendental functions of the unknowns

transcendental idealism *n, Kantianism* **:** a doctrine that the objects of perception are conditioned by the nature of the mind as to their form but not as to their content or particularity and that they have a kind of independence of the mind — called also *critical idealism*

tran·scen·den·tal·ism \-ᵊlˌizəm\ *n* -s [[1]*transcendental* + *-ism*] **1 a** (1) **:** a philosophic tendency or doctrine of Kantianism emphasizing a priori conditions of knowledge and experience or the unknowable character of ultimate reality (2) **:** a doctrine of post-Kantian idealism that emphasizes what transcends sense experience as being fundamental in reality **b :** a philosophy that asserts the primacy of the spiritual and the intuitive over the material and the empirical; *esp* **:** the 19th century New England movement stressing the presence of the divine within man as a source of truth and a guide to action **2 :** the quality or state of being transcendental; *esp* **:** visionary idealism of character or thought

[1]**tran·scen·den·tal·ist** \-ᵊləst\ *n* -s [[1]*transcendental* + *-ist*] **:** an advocate or adherent of transcendentalism

[2]**transcendentalist** \"\ *adj* **:** of or relating to transcendentalism ⟨the optimism inherent in the ~ vision of man's harmony with nature —L.T.Lemon⟩

tran·scen·den·tal·is·tic \¦=(ˌ)=¦dentᵊl¦istik\ *adj* [[1]*transcendentalist* + *-ic*] **1 :** TRANSCENDENTALIST **2 :** held or believed by a transcendentalist

tran·scen·den·tal·i·ty \ˌ=(ˌ)=den·ˈtaləd·ē\ *n* -ES [[1]*transcendental* + *-ity*] **:** the quality or state of being transcendental

tran·scen·den·tal·ize \ˌ=(ˌ)ˈdentᵊlˌīz\ *vt* -ED/-ING/-S [[1]*transcendental* + *-ize*] **1 :** to make transcendent **:** cause to transcend ⟨other Christian critics . . . ~ the values out of all significant contact with action —E.E.Aubrey⟩ **2 :** to make transcendental **:** IDEALIZE ⟨was so easy for him to ~ this emotion —H.S.Canby⟩

tran·scen·den·tal·ly \¦=(ˌ)=¦dentᵊlē, -ᵊli\ *adv* [[1]*transcendental* + *-ly*] **:** in a transcendental manner **:** to a transcendent extent

transcendental object *n, Kantianism* **:** a thing in itself or the mere form of an object representing in knowledge our reference of the content of experience to an independent object

transcendental philosophy *n* **:** TRANSCENDENTALISM

transcendental truth *n* **:** METAPHYSICAL TRUTH

tran·scen·dent·ly *adv* **:** in a transcendent manner **:** to a transcendent extent

tran·scen·dent·ness *n* -ES [[1]*transcendent* + *-ness*] **:** TRANSCENDENCE

transcending *pres part of* TRANSCEND

tran·scend·ing·ly *adv* [*transcending* (pres. part. of *transcend*) + *-ly*] **:** TRANSCENDENTLY

transcends *pres 3d sing of* TRANSCEND

tran·scen·sion \tranˈsenchən\ *n* -s [LL *transcension-*, *transcensio*, fr. L *transcensus* (past part. of *transcendere* to transcend) + *-ion-*, *-io* -ion] **:** an act, process, or instance of transcending

trans·conductance \¦tranz, -raan-, -n(t)s+\ *n* [*trans-* + *conductance*] **:** the ratio of a change in the current through one electrode in an electron tube to the change of voltage responsible for it in another electrode with the potentials of the remaining elements being constant — compare MUTUAL CONDUCTANCE

trans·con·ti·nen·tal \¦tranzˌkäntᵊn¦entᵊl, -raan-, -n(t)ˌsk-, -tə¦ne-\ *adj* [*trans-* + *continent* + *-al*] **1 :** extending or going across a continent ⟨a ~ railroad⟩ ⟨a ~ journey⟩ ⟨a ~ traveler⟩ **2 :** of, relating to, or situated on the farther side of a continent ⟨a ~ city⟩ ⟨a ~ product⟩ — **trans·con·ti·nen·tal·ly** \-ᵊlē\ *adv*

trans·cortical \(ˈ)tranz, -n(t)s+\ *adj* [*trans-* + NL *cortic-*, *cortex* cortex + E *-al*] **:** crossing the cortex of the brain; *esp* **:** passing from the cortex of one hemisphere to that of the other ⟨~ stimulation⟩

tran·scribe \tranzˈkrīb, traan-, -n(t)ˈsk-\ *vb* -ED/-ING/-S [L *transcribere*, fr. *trans-* + *scribere* to write — more at SCRIBE] *vt* **1 a :** to make a written copy of ⟨scrupulously *transcribed* from the surviving manuscripts of the war years —D.C.Mearns⟩ **b :** to make a copy of (dictated or recorded matter) in longhand or esp. on a typewriter ⟨taking dictation in the mornings, *transcribing* correspondence in the afternoons —Jean Holloway⟩ ⟨take letters down in shorthand or on the dictating machine and ~ them on the typewriter —E.M.Robinson⟩; *specif* **:** to read aloud (shorthand notes) ⟨lay aside this book and orally ~ your shorthand notes —*Law Stenographer*⟩ **c :** to reproduce in writing by more or less exact quotation **:** PARAPHRASE, SUMMARIZE ⟨I need not ~ any more of this part of the séance —Beverley Nichols⟩ ⟨what he expressed as a mere surmise was *transcribed* by others as a positive statement —Richard Semon⟩ **d :** to write down **:** RECORD ⟨a unique achievement in the amazing fidelity with which it ~s the life and mentality of an alien people —Amy Loveman⟩ ⟨if one looks the jungle straight in the face and ~s what is seen —William Beebe⟩ ⟨is endowed with . . . an unerring ear for *transcribing* speech —Angel Flores⟩ **2** *obs* **:** ASCRIBE, IMPUTE **3 a** (1) **:** TRANSLITERATE ⟨the larger part . . . would be unintelligible if *transcribed* in an alphabet or syllabary —K.S. Latourette⟩ ⟨*transcribed* into Cyrillic characters from the original Glagolitic —R.G.A.DeBray⟩ ⟨his hobby is *transcribing* books into braille —*N. Y. Herald Tribune*⟩ (2) **:** to represent (speech sounds) by means of phonetic symbols ⟨the letter *b* ~s Greek *beta*, which represented a phoneme with both stop and spirant allophones —W.G.Moulton⟩ (3) **:** to arrange (the letters of a cryptogram) by a prescribed route or system ⟨there are 39 routes by which the letters in the rectangle might have been *transcribed* to form the cryptogram —J.M.Wolfe⟩ **b :** TRANSLATE 2a ⟨*transcribed* English hymns into German —*Amer. Guide Series: Pa.*⟩ **c :** to transfer or convey (as information) from one recording form to another ⟨the account number could then be *transcribed* to the receiving ticket —H.D.McGuigan⟩ ⟨reproducers automatically ~ punching from one card to another —H.C.Zeisig & P.T.Martin⟩ **4** *obs* **:** COPY, IMITATE **5 :** to make a musical transcription of ⟨originally written for organ, the work was *transcribed* for symphony orchestra —*Current Biog.*⟩ **6 a :** to broadcast (a radio or television program) by electrical transcription **b :** to record (as on magnetic tape) for later broadcast ~ *vi* **1 a :** to make a copy of something in writing ⟨shall begin to ~ again and polish —T.B.Macaulay⟩ **b :** to reproduce in writing dictated or recorded matter ⟨ability to take dictation easily and ~ accurately on the typewriter —*Gregg Dictation Simplified*⟩ ⟨the belts are mailed to the . . . office for *transcribing* —*Dun's Rev.*⟩ **c :** to write down, set forth, or produce a factual or objective representation ⟨some ~ directly from nature —Thomas Munro⟩ ⟨no artist is content to ~ —*New Mexico Quarterly*⟩ **2 :** TRANSLATE 1a ⟨this question of whether they should . . . ~ into modern idiom —H.L.Savage⟩

tran·scrib·er \-bə(r)\ *n* -s **:** one that transcribes; *specif* **:** a person engaged in writing braille for the blind using either a slate and stylus or a braillewriter

transcribing machine *n* [*transcribing*, pres. part. of *transcribe*] **:** a business machine designed to play back electrically recorded dictation (as on a wax cylinder, plastic belt, disc, wire, or tape) for transcription

tran·script \ˈtranzˌkript, ˈtraan-, -n(t)ˌsk-\ *n* -s [ME, fr. ML *transcriptum*, fr. L, neut. of *transcriptus*, past part. of *transcribere* to transcribe] **1 a :** a written or printed copy ⟨a ~ of nine manuscript books —Gilbert Highet⟩ ⟨a volume . . . containing ~s from the papyrological collections —Jack Finegan⟩ **b :** a usu. typewritten copy of dictated or recorded matter ⟨the efficiency of shorthand instruction is to be judged entirely by . . . the ~s turned out by the pupils —C.G.Reigner⟩ **c :** an official or legal and often published copy or engrossment of a decree, testimony, or proceedings ⟨shall submit a ~ in duplicate of the ordinance⟩ ⟨courts have held that in a dispute as to what was said . . . the reporter's ~ must be accepted as final —*Law Stenographer*⟩ ⟨read the ~ of a round-table discussion appearing in the current issue —J.D.Adams⟩; *specif* **:** an official copy of a student's record at an educational institution **2 :** a copy, reproduction, or rendering (as of experience) set forth or expressed usu. in an art form ⟨inexperienced readers take literature more naïvely as ~ rather than interpretation of life —René Wellek & Austin Warren⟩ ⟨the book is a ~ from his own experience —*Brit. Bk. News*⟩ ⟨was an objective painter . . . returning always to his own type of studio-made ~s from life around him —Sheldon Cheney⟩ ⟨the formal content of the religion of the American Negro . . . is a ~, modified for his own uses, of the religion of his white masters in the days of slavery —W.L.Sperry⟩

tran·scrip·tion \tranzˈkripshən, traan-, -n(t)ˈsk-\ *n* -s [L *transcription-*, *transcriptio*, fr. *transcriptus* + *-ion-*, *-io* -ion] **1 :** an act, process, or instance of transcribing **2 :** something transcribed **:** COPY, TRANSCRIPT: as **a :** an arrangement of a musical composition often with some liberty in modification or embellishment for some instrument or voice other than that of the original composition **:** ARRANGEMENT ⟨his ripe scholarship is evidenced . . . in his ~s for organ of great symphonic works —E.C.Krohn⟩ **b :** a tape, disc, or other recording made for broadcast or rebroadcast of a radio or television program **:** ELECTRICAL TRANSCRIPTION ⟨continued on several hundred independent stations and . . . sent overseas by ~ —*Current Biog.*⟩

tran·scrip·tion·al \-shənᵊl, -shnəl\ *adj* **:** of, relating to, or produced by transcription — **tran·scrip·tion·al·ly** \-shənᵊlē, -shnəl-, -i\ *adv*

tran·scrip·tive \-ptiv, -tēv *also* -təv\ *adj* [L *transcriptus* (past part. of *transcribere* to transcribe) + E *-ive*] **:** that transcribes or is given to transcription **:** IMITATIVE; *also* **:** produced by transcribing ⟨~ art resulting from the Renaissance scientific search for natural truth —Sheldon Cheney⟩ — **tran·scrip·tive·ly** \-təvlē\ *adv*

trans·crystalline \(ˈ)tranz, -raanz, -n(t)s+\ *adj* [*trans-* + *crystal* + *-ine*] **:** across or through individual crystals as opposed to between or around them — used of fractures or cracks in metals

trans·cultural \"+\ *adj* [*trans-* + *culture* + *-al*] **:** extending through all human cultures or types of human beings ⟨a ~ ideal of freedom which would embrace all the peoples of the world —David Bidney⟩ ⟨~ psychotherapy seems to involve . . . concepts applicable to all human beings —Paula Brown⟩

trans·cul·tu·ra·tion \ˌtranzˌkəlchəˈrāshən, -n(t)ˌsk-\ *n* -s [ISV *trans-* + *culture* + *-ation*; prob. orig. formed in Sp] **:** a process of cultural transformation marked by the influx of new culture elements and the loss or alteration of existing ones — compare ACCULTURATION

trans·cur·rent \(ˈ)tranz, -raanz, -n(t)s+\ *adj* [L *transcurrent-*, *transcurrens*, pres. part. of *transcurrere* to run across, fr. *trans-* + *currere* to run — more at CURRENT] **:** running or extending transversely

trans·cutaneous *also* **trans·cutaneal** \¦tranz, -raanz, -n(t)s+\ *adj* [*trans-* + *cutaneous*, *cutaneal*] **:** passing or entering through the skin ⟨~ infection⟩ ⟨~ inoculation⟩

trans·dialect \(ˈ)tran(t)s, -raan-, -nz\ *vt* -ED/-ING/-S [*trans-* + *dialect*] **:** to translate from one dialect into another

trans·duc·er \tran(t)sˈd(y)üsə(r), traan-, -nzˈ-\ *n* -s [L *transducere* to lead across (fr. *trans-* + *ducere* to lead) + E *-er* — more at TOW] **:** a device actuated by power from one system and supplying power in the same or any other form to a second system (as a telephone receiver actuated by electric power and supplying acoustic power to the surrounding air or quartz crystals that produce electric power from mechanical power)

trans·duc·tion \-ˈdəkshən\ *n* -s [L *transductus* (past part. of *transducere*) + E *-ion*] **:** the act or process of leading or conveying over; *specif* **:** the transfer of genetic determinants from one microorganism to another or from one strain of microorganism to another by a viral agent (as a bacteriophage) — **trans·duc·tion·al** \-shnəl, -shənᵊl\ *adj*

trans·duc·tor \-ktə(r)\ *n* -s [L *transductus* + E *-or*] **:** a device for controlling or regulating alternating current consisting of two or more coils with a common magnetic core with one of the coils carrying a direct current and the others carrying the alternating current

[1]**tran·sect** \tranˈsekt, traan-\ *vt* -ED/-ING/-S [*trans-* + *-sect*] **:** to cut across or transversely ⟨dogs whose spinal cord had been ~*ed* —*Pharmacological Reviews*⟩ ⟨where a rock mass . . . is ~*ed* by natural cracks —W.J.Miller⟩ ⟨in ~*ing* these fields, the present study pursues . . . many patterns —*Books*⟩

[2]**transect** \ˈ=ˌ=\ *n* -s **:** a sample area of vegetation usu. in the form of a narrow continuous strip that is used esp. for the tabulation of data (as of frequency, size, or yield of different kinds of plants) likely to vary within a stand or area

tran·sec·tion \tranˈsekshən, traan-\ *n* [*trans-* + *section*] **:** CROSS SECTION 1a

trans·el·e·ment \tran(t)ˈseləmənt, -nˈze-\ *also* **trans·el·e·ment·ate** \-mən·ˌtāt\ *vt* -ED/-ING/-S [*transelement* fr. ML *transelementare*, fr. L *trans-* + *elementum* element; *transelementate* fr. ML *transelementatus*, past part. of *transelementare*] **:** to change or transpose the elements of **:** TRANSFORM — **trans·el·e·men·ta·tion** \=ˌ===ˈtāshən\ *n* -s

trans·empirical \¦tran(t)s, -raan-, -nz +\ *adj* [*trans-* + *empirical*] **:** being beyond experience **:** TRANSCENDENT ⟨positivism had as its basic motivation the elimination of ~ metaphysics —E.C.Moore⟩

tran·sen·na \tranˈsenə\ *n, pl* **transen·nae** \-eˌnē\ [L *trasenna*, *transenna* net, latticework, perh. of Etruscan origin] **:** a lattice or screen of stone or metal enclosing and protecting a shrine

tran·sept \ˈtranˌsept, ˈtraan-\ *n* -s [NL *transeptum*, fr. L *trans-* + *septum*, *saeptum* enclosure, wall — more at SEPTUM] **:** the transversal part of a cruciform church that crosses at right angles to the greatest length between the nave and the apse or choir; *also* **:** either of the projecting ends ⟨the north ~⟩ — see BASILICA illustration

transept aisle *n* **:** the aisle of a transept corresponding to the side aisle of a nave

tran·sep·tal \(ˈ)tran¦septəl, -raan-\ *adj* **:** of or relating to or like a transept ⟨~ style⟩ ⟨~ position⟩ ⟨~ towers⟩ — **tran·sep·tal·ly** \-lē\ *adv*

transept chapel *n* **:** a chapel opening off a transept

trans·esterification \¦tran(t)s, -raan-, -nz+\ *n* [*trans-* + *esterification*] **:** a reversible reaction in which one ester is converted into another (as by interchange of ester groups with an alcohol in the presence of a base)

trans·e·unt \ˈtran(t)sēənt\ *adj* [L *transeunt-*, *transiens*, pres. part. of *transire* to go across or beyond — more at TRANSIENT] **:** TRANSIENT 2

transeuntes *pl of* TRANSIENS

transf *abbr* **1** transfer; transferred **2** transformer

transfd *abbr* transferred

[1]**trans·fer** *R* tranzˈfər, traan-, -n(t)ˈsf-, ˈ=(ˌ)=, + *vowel* -fər·; -*R* -fə̄, + *suffixal vowel* -fər· *also* -fə̄r, + *vowel in a following word* -fər· *or* -fə̄ *also* -fə̄r\ *vb* **transferred; transferred; transferring; transfers** [ME *transferren*, fr. L *transferre*, fr. *trans-* + *ferre* to carry, bear — more at BEAR] *vt* **1 a :** to

carry or take from one person or place to another : TRANSPORT, REMOVE ⟨from underneath the litter he drew a packet . . . and *transferred* it deftly to the blue suit —D.M.Davin⟩ ⟨travelers were *transferred* to sloops to complete the journey —*Amer. Guide Series: N. J.*⟩ ⟨an effort was made to ~ a good share of the appointments from the president to congressmen —W.C. Ford⟩ **b** : to move or send to a different location esp. for business, vocational, or military purposes ⟨*transferred* her law practice to Greenville —*Current Biog.*⟩ ⟨the company plans to ~ him to its west coast plant⟩ ⟨was commandant at Fort Pitt . . . and in the latter year was *transferred* to the remote frontier —C.F.Cochran⟩ **c** : to cause to pass from one person or thing to another : TRANSMIT ⟨motion would be *transferred* from two cogged wheels to the big wheel through an endless chain —John Kobler⟩ ⟨no way in which he could ~ his own memories of European civilization into the Indian mind —Willa Cather⟩ **d** : to cause to transform : CHANGE — usu. used with *into* ⟨had *transferred* barren wastes . . . into fertile fields —Albert Hyma⟩ ⟨may upon occasion ~ himself into a tiger —Fay-Cooper Cole⟩ **2** : to make over or negotiate the possession or control of (a right, title, or property) by a legal process usu. for a consideration : CONVEY ⟨to preserve the farm intact he ~*s* it to one heir⟩ ⟨*transferred* a part of their holdings . . . for $25,000 worth of stock —Marquis James⟩ **3** : to print, impress, or otherwise copy (as a drawing or engraved design) from one surface to another ~ *vi* **1** : to go or move to a different place or region to carry on a business or vocation ⟨*transferred* from the bookshop to the concert agency and was . . . placed in charge of that division —*Current Biog.*⟩ ⟨the company is *transferring* to an eastern location⟩ ⟨will ~ to the armored division as soon as his papers can be cleared⟩; *specif* : to withdraw from one educational institution to enroll at another ⟨students can ~ to other leading colleges . . . without loss of credits —Ruth Wilson⟩ **2** : to change from one vehicle or transportation line to another ⟨took the streetcar and *transferred* to the bus —Robert Hazel⟩ **syn** see MOVE

²**transfer** \ˈ=,=\ *n* -s *often attrib* **1 a** : the conveyance of right, title, or interest in either real or personal property from one person to another by sale, gift, or other process **b** : the removal or acquisition of property by mere delivery with intent of the parties involved to transfer the title **c** : an order transferring shares of stock or money; *specif* : a telegraphic order to pay to one party money deposited by another at a distant office **2** : an act, process, or instance of transferring : TRANSFERENCE ⟨proposal for . . . a ~ of populations on a voluntary basis —*Current History*⟩ ⟨finds occasion for the ~ of his loyalty to a new cause⟩ **3** : one that is transferred: as **a** : a picture produced by affixing to a support an image orig. developed on a separate temporary support — compare BROMOIL TRANSFER, CARBON TRANSFER **b** : a drawing or writing printed in reverse from one surface on another; *specif* : a reverse pattern (as for embroidery or a trademark) waxed or inked on tissue paper for printing on a textile material with the heat and pressure of an iron **c** (1) : a drawing in lithographic crayon made or printed on paper and then impressed on stone or other material from which it is to be printed by lithography (2) : a specially prepared sheet of lithographic paper containing a design to be transferred from the original stone to a stone or metal printing surface **d** : TRANSFER PICTURE **e** : an individual shifted from one military unit to another ⟨orders the sergeant to check in the new ~*s*⟩ **f** : a student that changes from one school to another ⟨a limited number of ~*s* can be accepted by the college⟩ **4** : the distance a ship gains to the right or left from the time the helm is put over until it is on its new course — compare ADVANCE 8 **5 a** : a place where cars or trains are transferred to boats or ferries for water transportation; *also* : a boat or ferry used for this purpose **b** : TRANSFER HOUSE **c** : a point where a change is made from one form of power to another (as from electricity to steam) **d** (1) : a turnout connecting two tracks at a crossing with switches outside the end frogs of the crossing (2) : a track connecting roads that cross on separated grades **e** (1) : TRANSFER COMPANY (2) : a vehicle of such a company **f** : a ticket given with or without extra charge to a passenger on a public conveyance entitling him to continue his journey on another route or conveyance **6 a** : TRANSFERENCE 2 **b** : the carry-over or generalization of learned responses from one type of situation to another; *specif* : the application in one field of study or effort of knowledge, skill, power, or ability acquired in another ⟨there will be a certain degree of ~ from one skill to another if we direct our teaching to this end —Eliezer Rieger⟩ ⟨could not easily make the ~ from book to life —H.A.Overstreet⟩ **7** : the moving of knitted stitches from one machine (as a ribber) to another

trans·fer·abil·i·ty \tranz,fərəˈbilәd·ē, ,tranz(,)f-, traan-, -n(t)(,)sf-, -lətē, -i\ *n* : the quality or state of being transferable ⟨sterling ~ affords a means of multilateral settlement for . . . trade between nondollar countries outside the sterling area —R.F.Mikesell⟩

trans·fer·able *also* **trans·fer·ra·ble** \tranzˈfərəbəl, -n(t)ˈsf-, ˈtranz(,)f-, -n(t)(,)sf-, -raan-\ *adj* **1** : capable of being transferred or conveyed from one place or person to another ⟨good and bad are but names, very readily ~ to that or this —R.W. Emerson⟩ **2** : capable of being made over from one party to another so as to vest in the transferee all the transferor's legal rights, title, or interest in the property being transferred : NEGOTIABLE ⟨~ stock⟩ ⟨a ~ account⟩ ⟨some tickets are not ~⟩

transferable vote *n* : a vote that in balloting by proportional representation may be transferred to a candidate other than the one marked as first choice — compare HARE SYSTEM

transfer agent *n* : the officer, bank, or trust company that keeps the ownership records and makes the transfer of title of corporate stock or other registered securities

trans·fer·al *also* **trans·fer·ral** \tranzˈfərəl, traan-, -n(t)ˈsf-\ *n* -s [¹*transfer* + *-al*] : TRANSFERENCE, TRANSFER

trans·fer·ase \ˈtranzfə,rās, -n(t)sf-\ *n* -s [¹*transfer* + *-ase*] : any of various enzymes (as transaminases) that promote a transfer reaction

transfer book *n* : a register of transfers (as of shares of stock) from one party to another

transfer box *n* : a metal box in which one or more corresponding electric circuits are connected or branched

transfer caliper *n* : a caliper equipped with an adjustable or removable leg to permit use of the caliper in narrow or confined spaces — often used in pl.

transfer case *n* **1** : a filing unit for storage of inactive correspondence or records **2** : a housing containing gears used to distribute the driving power between the axles of vehicles equipped with more than one driving axle and usu. having a shifting lever for disengaging the front-wheel drive

transfer company *n* : a transportation company that transfers passengers or baggage usu. for a short distance between specified points or terminals

trans·fer·ee \,tranzfəˈrē, -raan-, -n(t)sf-\ *n* -s [¹*transfer* + *-ee*] **1** : a person to whom a transfer or conveyance is made — compare TRANSFERRER a **2** : one who is transferred (as from one position or place to another) ⟨reserve officer ~*s* —*All Hands*⟩ ⟨the various population shifts of ~*s*, refugees, displaced persons —E.M.Kulischer⟩

trans·fer·ence \tranzˈfərən(t)s, traan-, -n(t)ˈsf-; ˈtranzfər(ə)n(t)s, ˈtraan-, -n(t)sf-, -frən-\ *n* -s [NL *transferentia*, fr. L *transferent-, transferens* (pres. part. of *transferre* to transfer) + *-ia* -y] **1** : an act, process, or instance of transferring : CONVEYANCE, PASSAGE, TRANSFER **2** : the redirection toward a new object (as a psychoanalyst) of feelings and desires esp. as unconsciously retained from childhood

transference neurosis *n* : a neurosis developed in the course of psychoanalytic treatment and manifested by the reliving of infantile experiences in the presence of the analyst

transference number *n* : the fraction of the total current carried either by the anion or the cation in electrolysis — called also *transport number*

trans·fer·en·tial \,tranzfəˈrenchəl, -raan-, -n(t)sf-\ *adj* [NL *transferentia* + E *-al*] : of or relating to transference

transfer house *n* : a station where freight is rehandled before proceeding to final destination

transfer ink *n* : ink used in transferring designs (as from paper to stone) that often contains wax, soap, lampblack, and shellac

transfer molding *n* : a process of molding plastics in which the molding material is softened by preheating and then forced into a closed heated mold

transfer of fire : the shifting of artillery fire from one target to another with the application of corrections determined from the adjustment on the first target to the initial firing data for the second

transfer of training : TRANSFER 6b

trans·fer·o·type *also* **trans·fer·ro·type** \tranzˈfərə,tīp, -n(t)ˈsf-\ *n* [¹*transfer* + *-o-* + *type*] : a bromide print transferred from a paper backing to some other surface; *also* : the process by which this is done

transfer paper *n* : a paper coated with a special preparation for transferring a design or imprint to another surface by heat, pressure, or moisture — compare DECALCOMANIA

transfer payment *n* **1** : any of various public expenditures (as veterans benefits or unemployment compensation) made for purposes other than procuring goods or current services — usu. used in pl. **2** : money (as welfare payments or a pension) received by an individual or a family other than compensation (as wages or profits) for goods or services currently supplied or income (as interest or dividends) from investments

transfer picture *n* : a picture transferred or prepared for transference (as from specially prepared paper by means of the decalcomania process)

transfer printing *n* **1** : DECALCOMANIA **2** : a process of pottery decoration in which designs engraved on copper or drawn on stone are transferred to the ware by the use of tissue paper

transfer process *n* : any of several processes in which a pigmented or dyed image is transferred from one surface to another

transferrable *var of* TRANSFERABLE

transferral *var of* TRANSFERAL

transfer reaction *n* : a chemical reaction (as a transamination) in which a group is transferred from one molecule to another

transferred *past of* TRANSFER

transferred intent *n* : the intent to commit a specific wrong or crime that is imputed to a wrongdoer who in the execution of an intent to do some wrongful act commits an unintended wrong or crime

trans·fer·rer *also* **trans·fer·er** \tranzˈfərə(r), traan-, -n(t)ˈsf-\ *or* **trans·fer·or** *or* **trans·fer·ror** \ˈ;=(,)fər;ō(ə)r, -ō(ə)\ *n* -s [¹*transfer* + *-er* or *-or*] : one that transfers: as **a** *usu transferor* : one that makes or executes a conveyance of a title, right, or property ⟨the validity of a transfer, as between the *transferor* and the transferee, is governed by the law —J.F. Spindler⟩ **b** : one that transfers images from photographic negatives to zinc plates for printing by the lithographic process **c** : one that transfers designs from engraved lithographic stones directly to zinc plates or to cellophane sheets that will be photographed on zinc plates in preparation for printing by the lithographic process **d** : a worker who prints numerals, minute and second tracks, and the company name on watch dials with an engraved plate in a transfer machine

transferrible *archaic var of* TRANSFERABLE

trans·fer·rin \tranzˈferən, -n(t)ˈsf-\ *n* -s [*trans-* + L *ferrum* iron + E *-in* — more at FARRIER] : a beta globulin in blood plasma that is capable of combining with ferric ions and of transporting iron to various parts of the body — called also *siderophilin;* compare FERRITIN

transferring *pres part of* TRANSFER

transferring machine *n* : a press for impressing an engraved and hardened steel die on a soft steel roller that is afterward hardened and used to impress a plate (as for printing bank notes or stock certificates)

transfers *pres 3d sing of* TRANSFER, *pl of* TRANSFER

transfer stamp *n* : a sales transfer tax stamp

transfer table *n* : a platform with one or more tracks moving laterally on wheels for shifting railroad locomotives or cars from one track to another one parallel to it

transfer tax *n* **1** : INHERITANCE TAX 1 **2** : an excise tax levied upon the transfer of real or esp. intangible property among the living and often signified by revenue stamps affixed to the instrument effecting the transfer

transfer track *n* : a railroad station track for loading or unloading freight

trans·fig·u·ra·tion \(,)=,==ˈrāshən\ *n* -s [ME, fr. MF, fr. L *transfiguration-, transfiguratio*, fr. *transfiguratus* (past part. of *transfigurare* to transfigure) + *-ion-, -io* -ion] **1 a** : an act, process, or instance of changing or being changed in form or appearance : METAMORPHOSIS ⟨the autumnal ~ had just begun —*New Yorker*⟩ ⟨astonished people by becoming a society man . . . a ~ —Norman Douglas⟩ **b** : an act, process, or instance of undergoing an exalting, glorifying, or spiritual change ⟨in poetry and art may be seen the ~ of nature⟩ ⟨a new elevation of the mind of man . . . in this ~ the arts have a noble and vital part to play —Sir Winston Churchill⟩ **2** *usu cap* **a** : a church feast observed in some branches of the Christian church on August 6 in commemoration of the Transfiguration of Jesus recorded in the New Testament **b** : an artistic representation of the Transfiguration

trans·fig·ure \tranzˈfigyə(r), traan-, -n(t)ˈsf-, ÷ -gə(r)\ *vt* [ME *transfiguren*, fr. L *transfigurare*, fr. *trans-* + *figurare* to shape, fashion, form, fr. *figura* figure] **1** : to change the form or appearance of : TRANSFORM ⟨her face was *transfigured* by uncontrollable passion —Arnold Bennett⟩ ⟨his will has been *transfigured* by association with the wills of others —B.N. Cardozo⟩ — often used with *into* ⟨his . . . special gifts led him to ~ the wasteland into a circus —C.J.Rolo⟩ ⟨nationalism was *transfigured* into internationalism —C.B.Forcey⟩ **2** : EXALT, GLORIFY, SPIRITUALIZE ⟨the great cliffs and domes were *transfigured* in the hazy golden air —John Muir †1914⟩ ⟨music . . . will ~ plain meanings and clothe the verbal substance with a kind of incandescence —A.T.Davison⟩ ⟨the same sacrifice *transfigured* the communicants who shared the mystery —Oscar Handlin⟩ — often used with *into* ⟨her beautiful face was *transfigured* into the ravishingly angelic —Arnold Bennett⟩ ⟨the moment when good verse . . . is *transfigured* into a thing that takes the breath away —C.D.Lewis⟩ **syn** see TRANSFORM

¹**trans·finite** \(ˈ)tranz, -raanz, -n(t)s+\ *adj* [G *transfinit*, fr. *trans-* (fr. L) + *finit* finite, fr. L *finitus*, past part. of *finire* to limit, finish, end — more at FINISH] **1** : going beyond or surpassing any finite number, assemblage, or magnitude ⟨that world where pain and pleasure take on ~ values and all our arithmetic is dismayed —C.S.Lewis⟩ ⟨God . . . must be ~ beyond conception —C.O.Gorham⟩ **2 a** : being a power of a mathematical aggregate whose cardinal number is not finite ⟨aleph-null is the smallest ~ cardinal number⟩ **b** : being either an index of the ordered set of all natural numbers or generated from this index by purely algebraic means ⟨~ ordinal numbers⟩

²**transfinite** \"\ *n* -s : a transfinite number, assemblage, or magnitude

trans·fix \tranzˈfiks, traan-, -n(t)ˈsf-\ *vt* [L *transfixus*, past part. of *transfigere* to transfix, fr. *trans-* + *figere* to fix, fasten, pierce — more at DIKE] **1** : to pierce through with or as if with a pointed weapon or instrument : TRANSPIERCE, IMPALE ⟨he ~*es* the pig with his spear⟩ ⟨the knight must . . . ~ with his lance small rings suspended —*Amer. Guide Series: Md.*⟩ ⟨uses the hypodermic to puncture but not to ~ the vein⟩ ⟨he ~*ed* her with a piercing glance⟩ **2** : to affix, fasten, or hold motionless by or as if by piercing esp. with an absorbing emotion or interest — often used with *to* or *into* ⟨plunged their stout spears into his belly and ~*ed* him to the earth —A.A. Grace⟩ ⟨was ~*ed* to the spot with eyes that pierced —Zane Grey⟩ ⟨had seen the pain ~ his friend's face and . . . it was white —Owen Wister⟩ ⟨an idea occurred to him and ~*ed* him into a statue —Alvin Johnson⟩ ⟨poetry . . . ~*es* its subject in a form which has a life of its own forever —R.P.Blackmur⟩

trans·fix·ion \-kshən\ *n* -s [LL *transfixion-, transfixio*, fr. L *transfixus* + *-ion-, -io* -ion] **1** : an act, process, or instance of transfixing or of being transfixed ⟨there was only silence and ~ in the gray world above the forests —J.R.Ullman⟩ **2** : a piercing of a part of the body (as by a suture, nail, or other device) in order to fix it in position

¹**trans·form** \tranzˈfō(ə)rm, traan-, -n(t)ˈsf-, -ō(ə)m\ *vb* [ME *transformen*, fr. L *transformare*, fr. *trans-* + *formare* to form] *vt* **1 a** : to change completely or essentially in composition or structure : METAMORPHOSE — usu. used with *into* or *to* ⟨the sea king's daughter is ~*ed* into a river —Alfred Frankenstein⟩ ⟨life-giving water which ~*s* the dusty sagebrush lands into fertile fields —*Amer. Guide Series: Texas*⟩ ⟨the process which ~*ed* the lumber . . . into gunstocks —C.W.Mitman⟩ ⟨the processes by which policy is ~*ed* into law and administration —A.N.Holcombe⟩ **b** : to change the outward form or appearance of : ALTER ⟨for a moment the smile ~*ed* his face —J.C.Smith b.1924⟩ ⟨the drizzle that had so greatly ~*ed* the scene —Thomas Hardy⟩ ⟨science . . . has ~*ed* the world as the scene of the human drama —C.W.Eliot⟩ — often used with *into* or *to* ⟨an elaborate experiment in camouflage meant to ~ it into . . . farms and orange groves —J.G.Cozzens⟩ ⟨the setting sun suddenly ~*ed* the . . . peaks to furnace red —George Farwell⟩ **c** : to change in character or condition : CONVERT, TRANSFIGURE ⟨do not be conformed to this world but be ~*ed* by the renewal of your mind —Rom 12:2 (RSV)⟩ ⟨a change in the economic condition is not alone sufficient to ~ woman's situation —*Nation*⟩ — often used with *to* ⟨inventions and discoveries which quickly ~ the people . . . from barbarism to civilization —R.W.Murray⟩ **2** : to subject to a usu. mathematical or logical transformation **3 a** : to change (one form of energy) into another ⟨the engine ~*s* potential energy into motion⟩ **b** : to change (a current) in potential (as from high voltage to low voltage) or in type (as from alternating to continuous) ~ *vi* : to become transformed : CHANGE ⟨the growing Crepidula first becomes a male and later . . . ~*s* into a female —W.C.Allee⟩ ⟨a proton . . . can ~ into a neutron —R. E.Marshak⟩ ⟨sofas that ~ for use as a bed⟩

syn METAMORPHOSE, TRANSMUTE, CONVERT, TRANSMOGRIFY, TRANSFIGURE: these all signify in common to change one thing into another or different thing. TRANSFORM can mean a change in outward shape or form or in character, nature, or function ⟨the old rock quarry . . . has been *transformed* into a large baseball and football field and is used as a skating rink in the winter —*Amer. Guide Series: Minn.*⟩ ⟨water, in the shape of rain, will always *transform* that gray soil into a sort of sticky black glue —C.E.W.Bean⟩ ⟨*transform* the hunger and misery of the people into hatred —Stanley Ross⟩ METAMORPHOSE may add the idea of a supernaturally or magically induced change; it may be confined to a change in structure or habits marking a stage in the development of some form of animal life or a change induced by chemicals or powerful natural agencies, in general, however, suggesting an abrupt, striking, or violent alteration ⟨a plain girl *metamorphosed* into a dazzling beauty⟩ ⟨a caterpillar *metamorphosed* into a butterfly⟩ ⟨rocks *metamorphosed* by heat into hard crystals⟩ TRANSMUTE suggests an elemental change esp. involving a metamorphosis of a lower element or thing into a higher ⟨the alchemists had believed that base metals could be *transmuted* into gold by such a process —S.F.Mason⟩ ⟨modern atomic science can actually *transmute* metals — plutonium is a *transmuted* metal —*Time*⟩ ⟨art not only adds something new, but seems to *transmute* and enrich the old —Clive Bell⟩ CONVERT usu. stresses a change in detail that fits a thing to a given or esp. a new use or function rather than an overall change ⟨the stupendous task of *converting* virgin wilderness into farms and homes —*Amer. Guide Series: Texas*⟩ ⟨the business of *converting* novels into musicals —Lewis Funke⟩ TRANSMOGRIFY suggests a metamorphosis that is often grotesque or bewildering and sometimes preposterous ⟨the classical heroes and heroines were *transmogrified* into medieval knights and ladies —J.L.Lowes⟩ ⟨the monarch *transmogrified* into a horse, a beast, but still royal —Jean S. Untermeyer⟩ TRANSFIGURE suggests an exaltation or glorification in outward appearance ⟨in Bonnard's paintings, the colors of nature are marvelously heightened, enriched, *transfigured* —David Sylvester⟩ ⟨all the tenderness that had *transfigured* his face the day before shone there, as he bent over her —Clive Arden⟩

²**transform** \ˈ=,=\ *n* -s : TRANSFORMATION 6

trans·form·able \tranzˈfō(r)məbəl, traan-, -n(t)ˈsf-\ *adj* : capable of being transformed

trans·form·ance \-ōrmən(t)s\ *n* -s [¹*transform* + *-ance*] : TRANSFORMATION ⟨the ~ of any common event into a news story —Walter Rae⟩

trans·for·ma·tion \,tranzfə(r)ˈmāshən, ,traan-, -n(t)sf-\ *n* -s [ME, fr. LL *transformation-, transformatio*, fr. L *transformatus* (past part. of *transformare* to transform) + *-ion-, -io* -ion] **1** : an act, process, or instance of transforming or being transformed ⟨in the earliest time . . . ~*s* were common, and there was apparently no real line between animal and human —Frederica de Laguna⟩ ⟨~ of the farm lands into a magnificent estate —*Amer. Guide Series: Mich.*⟩ ⟨the ~ of policy into law —A.N.Holcombe⟩ ⟨the ~ of men's political thinking —Ellery Sedgwick⟩ ⟨the ~ of man's nature in Christ —Dietrich von Hildebrand⟩ **2 a** (1) : physiological change of one thing into another (as chemicals in assimilation and metabolism or larva into adult through metamorphosis (2) : SPERMIOGENESIS (3) : EVOLUTION 5b **b** : TRANSMUTATION d **c** : a change in the atomic arrangement of a metal or metal alloy **3** : TRANSFORMATION SCENE **4** : false hair esp. as worn by a woman to replace or supplement natural hair — compare TOUPEE 2 **5** : the changing of an expression, formula, or statement in logic into a different form without altering its substance or intent **6 a** : the substitution of one configuration (as by rotation or translation) for or the alteration of a mathematical expression (as by change of form or substitution of values) into another in accord with a mathematical rule **b** : a formula or rule governing such a substitution or alteration

trans·for·ma·tion·ist \-shənəst\ *n* -s [*transformation* + *-ist*] : TRANSFORMIST

transformation of coordinates : the introduction of a new set of mathematical coordinates that are stated distinct functions of the original coordinates

transformation range *n* : the range of temperature within which austenite forms or disappears when ferrous alloys are heated or cooled

transformation rule *n* : a principle in logic establishing the conditions under which one statement can be derived or validly deduced from one or more other statements esp. in a formalized language — called also *rule of deduction;* compare MODUS PONENS, MODUS TOLLENS

transformation scene *n* : a theatrical scene or setting that changes in sight of the audience; *specif* : a scene in the English pantomime in which the characters change to take part in the harlequinade proper

transformation temperature *n* : the temperature at which a change in phase occurs; *also* : the limiting temperature of a transformation range

trans·form·a·tive \tranzˈfō(r)məd·iv, traan-, -n(t)ˈsf-, -ətiv\ *adj* [ML *transformativus*, fr. L *transformatus* (past part. of *transformare* to transform) + *-ivus* -ive] : having the power or a tendency to transform : TRANSFORMING ⟨the ~ experience that individuals undergo as . . . they focus their minds upon a significant piece of writing —H.A.Overstreet⟩

transformed *past of* TRANSFORM

trans·form·er \-ōrmər, -ō(ə)mə(r\ *n* -s : one that transforms: as **a** : a device employing the principle of mutual induction to convert variations of current in a primary circuit into variations of voltage and current in a secondary circuit and typically consisting of two separate coils usu. with different numbers of turns wound on the same closed laminated iron core — see AUTOTRANSFORMER, CURRENT TRANSFORMER, PHASING TRANSFORMER **b** : a mythical figure (as a culture hero) in the legends of primitive cultures noted for bringing about the present order of the world by transforming its previous order

transformer oil *n* : an insulating oil (as a refined petroleum distillate) used esp. in transformers

transforming *pres part of* TRANSFORM

trans·form·ism \-ō(r),mizəm\ *n* -s [F *transformisme*, fr. *transformer* to transform (fr. L *transformare*) + *-isme* -ism] : EVOLUTION 5b ⟨regarded ~ as untenable . . . as no one had ever seen one species changing into another —R.H.Lowie⟩

trans·form·ist \-ōrməst, -ō(ə)m-\ *n* -s [F *transformiste*, fr. *transformer* + *-iste* -ist] : an adherent of transformism

transforms *pres 3d sing of* TRANSFORM, *pl of* TRANSFORM

trans·fus·able *or* **trans·fus·ible** \tranzˈfyüzəbəl, traan-, -n(t)ˈsf-\ *adj* : capable of being transfused ⟨~ blood⟩

trans·fuse \-üz\ *vt* -ED/-ING/-S [ME *transfusen*, fr. L *transfusus*, past part. of *transfundere* to transfuse, fr. *trans-* + *fundere* to pour — more at FOUND] **1 a** *archaic* : to transfer (a liquid) by or as if by pouring **b** (1) : to cause to flow or pass from one to another : TRANSMIT, INSTILL ⟨seeks to ~ his ideas throughout the land⟩ — often used with *into* or *to* ⟨~*s* his enthusiasm into others⟩ ⟨the animal spirits . . . are *transfused* from father to son —Laurence Sterne⟩ (2) : to flow or diffuse into or through

: PERMEATE ⟨the sunlight ~s the bay⟩ ⟨life is not merely an added property of matter but something that ~s and transforms it —H.J.Muller⟩ ⟨the wise men of the earth whose serenity ~s their style —H.S.Canby⟩ **2 a :** to transfer (as blood or saline) into a vein of a man or animal **b :** to subject (a patient) to transfusion ⟨the time to ~ patients is immediately after an injury occurs —*Commonweal*⟩

trans·fu·sion \-üzhən\ *n* -s [L *transfusion-, transfusio,* fr. *transfusus* + *-ion-, -io* -ion] **:** an act, process, or instance of transfusing; *esp* **:** the act or operation of transferring blood or other fluid into a vein or artery of a man or animal

transfusion cell *n* **:** PASSAGE CELL

trans·fu·sion·ist \-nəst\ *n* -s [*transfusion* + *-ist*] **:** one skilled in the transfusion of blood or other fluid

transfusion tissue *n* **:** tissue that is found characteristically around the vascular bundles of gymnosperm leaves and consists of both living cells like those of parenchyma with walls that are not lignified and thin-walled but lignified tracheids with bordered pits

trans·ge·na·tion \ˌtran(t)sjəˈnāshən, ˌtraan-, nzj-\ *n* -s [*trans-* + *gene* + *-ation*] **:** GENE MUTATION

trans·granular \(ˈ)tran(t)s, -raan-, -nz+\ *adj* [*trans-* + LL *granul*um little grain + E *-ar* — more at GRANULE] **:** TRANSCRYSTALLINE

1**trans·gress** \tran(t)sˈgres, traan-, -nzˈ-\ *vb* -ED/-ING/-ES [F *transgresser,* fr. L *transgressus,* past part. of *transgredi* to step beyond or across, cross, fr. *trans-* + *-gredi* (fr. *gradi* to step, go) — more at GRADE] *vt* **1 :** to go beyond limits set or prescribed by (law or command) **:** BREAK, VIOLATE ⟨had ~*ed* a solemn unwritten law and thereby fallen to the position of an enemy of society —Hamilton Basso⟩ ⟨~*ed* the divine law . . . is doomed to eternal punishment —A.C.McGiffert⟩ **2 :** to pass beyond or go over (a limit or boundary) **:** CROSS ⟨the adjacent seas ~*ed* almost all the coast . . . at the close of the last glaciation —J.B.Bird⟩ ⟨can migrate . . . and ~ their natural climatic barriers —S.A.Cain⟩ ⟨the power . . . to ~ economic and political boundaries —C.D.Forde⟩ **~** *vi* **1 :** to break or violate a command or law **:** TRESPASS, SIN ⟨we downrightly ~*ed* by . . . taking off our stockings to wade in the brook —Mary Austin⟩ **2 :** to go beyond a boundary or limit ⟨an Arctic sea ~*ed* southward through western Canada —E.B.Branson & W.A.Tarr⟩

2**transgress** \ˈ⸗,⸗\ *n* -ES **:** TRANSGRESSION b

trans·gres·sion \tran(t)sˈgreshən, traan-, -nzˈ-\ *n* -s [ME, fr. MF, fr. LL *transgression-, transgressio,* fr. L, act of crossing, passing over, fr. *transgressus* + *-ion-, -io* -ion] **:** an act, process, or instance of transgressing: as **a :** the infringement or violation of a law, command, or duty **:** SIN, TRESPASS ⟨God, what are my ~*s* that they brought me here —Henry Baerlein⟩ ⟨summoned me for . . . some ~ of college rules —A.D.White⟩ ⟨simple ingratitude to a benefactor was a pardonable ~ —George Meredith⟩ **b** (1) **:** UNCONFORMITY 3a (2) **:** the spread of the sea over land areas and the consequent unconformable deposition of sediments on older rocks **syn** see BREACH

1**trans·gres·sive** \-esiv, -sēv *also* -səv\ *adj* [L *transgress*us + E *-ive*] **1** *archaic* **:** disposed or tending to transgress, violate, or go beyond a limit **2 :** progressively overlapping or passing over or beyond ⟨a suite of ~ sediments⟩ ⟨the deposits of ~ seas⟩ **3 a :** going beyond the limits set by the ancestral condition usu. because of segregation and recombination of polygenic factors in the progeny of a hybrid ⟨~ variation⟩ ⟨~ inheritance⟩ **b** *of a plant* **:** being at different stages of the life history a part of more than one stratum of the community of which it is a member — **trans·gres·sive·ly** \-sə̇vlē, -li\ *adv*

2**transgressive** \"\ *n* -s **:** a transgressive element of an ecological community

trans·gres·sor \-esə(r)\ *n* -s [ME, fr. LL, fr. L *transgressus* + *-or*] **:** one that transgresses; *esp* **:** one who breaks a law or violates any known rule or principle of rectitude **:** SINNER ⟨the way of ~*s* is hard —Prov 13:15(AV)⟩

transhape *var of* TRANSSHAPE

tranship *var of* TRANSSHIP

trans·human \(ˈ)tranz, -raanz, -n(t)s+\ *adj* [*trans-* + *human*] **:** transcending human limits **:** SUPERHUMAN ⟨his profound intimation of ~ magnificence — the alien grandeur of nature —Robert Fitzgerald⟩

trans·hu·mance \tranzˈhyümən(t)s, traan-, -n(t)sˈ-\ *n* -s [F, fr. *transhumer* to practice transhumance (fr. Sp *trashumar,* fr. *tras-* trans- — fr. L *trans-* — + L *humus* earth, ground) + *-ance* — more at HUMBLE] **:** seasonal movement of livestock and esp. sheep between mountain and lowland pastures either under the care of herders or (as among various pastoral peoples) accompanied by the whole population of owners — compare NOMADISM

1**trans·hu·mant** \-nt\ *n* [F & Sp; F *transhumant* practicing transhumance, fr. Sp *trashumante,* fr. *trashumar* to practice transhumance] **1** *pl* **trans·hu·man·tes** \ˌtran(t)s(ˌ)hyüˈman·ˌtēz\ **:** a merino sheep of one of the great flocks kept in Spain by a system of transhumance esp. prior to the 19th century and esteemed for the quality and fineness of the wool **2** *pl* **transhumants :** a person who practices transhumance

2**transhumant** \"\ *adj* **:** of, relating to, or involving transhumance ⟨a ~ culture⟩ ⟨~ movements⟩

tran·sience \ˈtranchən(t)s, ˈtraan- *sometimes* -nzēən- *or* -n(t)sēən- *or* -nzhən- *or* -njən-\ *n* -s [fr. 1*transient,* after such pairs as E *permanent: permanence*] **:** the quality or state of being transient **:** PASSAGE, MOVEMENT ⟨the instability and ~ of all things in the stream of time —L.P.Smith⟩ ⟨the ~ of enthusiasms —O.S.J.Gogarty⟩ ⟨need for the canvass should be determined not by the size of the city but by . . . a high rate of ~ —Katharine T. Kinkead⟩

tran·sien·cy \-ənsē, -si\ *n* -ES [1*transient* + *-cy*] **:** TRANSIENCE ⟨a pervading sense of the ~ of all earthly things —Allan Nevins⟩ ⟨the lodging house . . . dates from the beginning of large-scale labor ~ —Nels Anderson⟩

tran·si·ens \ˈtran(t)sēˌenz, -nzē-\ *n, pl* **tran·se·un·tes** \ˌtran(t)sēˈün·ˌtēz, -nzēˈ-\ [NL *transeunt-, transiens,* fr. L, pres. part. of *transire*] **:** a phase in migratory locusts in which they exhibit characteristics in morphology and behavior intermediate between those typical of solitaria and gregaria

1**tran·sient** \ˈtranchənt, ˈtraan- *sometimes* -nzēənt *or* -n(t)sēənt *or* -nzhənt *or* -njənt\ *adj* [L *transeunt-, transiens,* pres. part. of *transire* to go across or beyond, cross over, pass, pass away, fr. *trans-* + *ire* to go — more at ISSUE] **1 a :** passing away in time or ceasing to exist **:** IMPERMANENT, TRANSITORY, SHORT-LIVED ⟨not even spring beauty . . . was so ~ — like music fading away —Ruth Suckow⟩ ⟨features of their culture were ~; they do not now exist —John Dewey⟩ ⟨the Leyden jar gave only ~ electrical current, but the voltaic cell . . . provided a continuous source of current —S.F.Mason⟩ ⟨if the patient is examined . . . when the circulatory impairment is ~ or rapidly compensated —Alfred Blalock⟩ **b :** passing through or by a place with only a brief stay or sojourn ⟨~ agricultural population with discouraged settlers constantly pulling up stakes and drifting on —*Amer. Guide Series: Ariz.*⟩ ⟨the hotel accommodates ~ guests⟩ ⟨the ~ butterfly —Edna S. V. Millay⟩ **c** *of a musical modulation* **:** introduced momentarily or in passing from one key to a third one **2 :** passing beyond itself **:** outwardly effective or efficient **:** EMANANT ⟨the creation of the universe considered as a ~ act⟩ — contrasted with *immanent* **3 :** passing from one person or thing to another ⟨dominant traits ~ through succeeding generations⟩

syn TRANSITORY, PASSING, EPHEMERAL, MOMENTARY, FLEETING, FUGITIVE, EVANESCENT, SHORT-LIVED: TRANSIENT often describes that which is short in its duration or stay and passes quickly ⟨after a *transient* seventh-century conquest by Assyria, Egypt experienced one more flourishing renascence (663–525) of its old patterns under native rulers —A.L.Kroeber⟩ ⟨guilt in Mrs. Clay's face as she listened . . . was *transient:* cleared away in an instant —Jane Austen⟩ ⟨the excitement of the examination may produce violent and rapid heart action, often associated with a *transient* systolic murmur —H.G.Armstrong⟩ TRANSITORY and PASSING may suggest the notion of the inevitability of changing, ending, or dying out ⟨their eyes were lifted from the earth . . . not concerned with its *transitory* things, soon to be consumed —H.O.Taylor⟩ ⟨the pleasures of taste, at best, are *transitory* —Virgil Thomson⟩ ⟨have omitted no important event and no incident of more than *passing* interest —Bernard De Voto⟩ ⟨men are given to the trick of having a *passing* fancy for somebody else in the midst of a permanent love, which reasserts itself afterwards just as before —Thomas Hardy⟩ EPHEMERAL may suggest the idea of living only for a day; it describes only that which endures for a similar brief period ⟨the life of the mayfly is *ephemeral*⟩ ⟨the very best of our experience is not as good as our dreams: our most exquisite moments are flawed and fragmentary . . . *ephemeral* —David Cecil⟩ MOMENTARY applies to that which endures only a moment or similar quite short period ⟨being a work of men's hands, it gave the child a *momentary* sense of comfort, of companionship in the dreadful wild —C.G.D.Roberts⟩ ⟨the *momentary* lulls between succeeding waves —C.B.Nordhoff & J.N.Hall⟩ FLEETING may suggest a flying transitoriness making it hard or impossible to arrest or apprehend the thing in question ⟨to take advantage of these *fleeting* opportunities, one must have a quick control over his own mind —S.M.Crothers⟩ ⟨how to seize the *fleeting* impressions of that dream —P.E. More⟩ FUGITIVE may suggest that whatever is described may be thought of as in flight and seeking to escape apprehension ⟨here is the last chance to feel young . . . but the days are *fugitive* and most of us are too busy —E.A.Weeks⟩ ⟨there were moments of *fugitive* sunshine, but of such brief duration that they but added to our misery —C.B.Nordhoff & J.N.Hall⟩ EVANESCENT describes that which is quite fleeting and likely to vanish away; it may apply to the delicate, fragile, unsubstantial, and airy ⟨the quality of her charm was *evanescent* . . . forever fleeing —Elinor Wylie⟩ ⟨of lusters with so *evanescent* a sheen their colours are felt, but never seen —Amy Lowell⟩ ⟨the scholar with perspective of his subject is aware . . . that part of his business is to distinguish the *evanescent* fad from permanent progress —A.L.Kroeber⟩ SHORT-LIVED stresses the fact of brevity of existence ⟨as *short-lived* as Wells' paper, lasting only from July 14 until October 15 —*Amer. Guide Series: Fla.*⟩

2**transient** \"\ *n* -s **1 :** one that is transient: as **a :** a transient guest or boarder ⟨motels cater chiefly to ~*s*⟩ **b :** an often homeless person traveling about usu. in search of work or a living ⟨a city of permanent ~*s* who shift . . . from one section to another — wherever they can find food and coal —Norman Cousins⟩ ⟨the great bulk of ~*s* are law-abiding individuals . . . in pursuit of employment —H.A.Bloch⟩ **2 a :** a temporary or rapidly changing state or condition of an electrical system; *specif* **:** a temporary electrical oscillation that occurs in a circuit because of a sudden change of voltage or of load **b :** a transient current or voltage

transient cause *n, Spinozism* **:** a cause originating or having its effects outside an entity — contrasted with *immanent cause*

transient current *n* **:** an oscillatory or aperiodic current that flows in a circuit for a short time following an electromagnetic disturbance (as a nearby stroke of lightning)

tran·sient·ly *adv* **:** in a transient manner **:** for a short time **:** BRIEFLY

transient second class *n* **:** a class of mail in the U.S. and Canada comprising newspapers and periodicals sent as separate issues by the public or as samples by the publisher

transient vendor *or* **transient dealer** *or* **transient merchant** *n* **:** any person who either as principal or agent engages in a temporary or transient business either in one locality or in traveling from place to place buying or selling goods, wares, or merchandise

tran·sil·ience \tranˈsilēən(t)s, traan-, -lyən-\ *n* -s [fr. *transilient,* after such pairs as E *resilient: resilience*] **:** an abrupt change or variation **:** TRANSITION; *specif* **:** such a change or variation in a geological formation

tran·sil·ient \-nt\ *adj* [L *transilient-, transiliens,* pres. part. of *transilire* to leap across, fr. *trans-* + *-silire* (fr. *salire* to leap) — more at SALLY] **:** passing abruptly from one thing to another; *specif* **:** marked by breaches of continuity or abrupt transitions or variations in geological structure ⟨~ rocks⟩

trans·illuminate \(ˈ)tran(t)s, -raan-, -nz+\ *vt* [*trans-* + *illuminate*] **:** to cause light to pass through; *specif* **:** to pass light through (a part of the body) to discover or examine a pathological condition

trans·illumination \"+\ *n* **:** an act, process, or instance of transilluminating

trans·illuminator \"+\ *n* **:** an instrument for effecting transillumination

trans·individual \"+\ *adj* [*trans-* + *individual* (n.)] **:** going between individuals **:** passing from one to another ⟨the question whether environmental influences . . . have a ~ action —*Human Embryology*⟩ ⟨the ~ processes of interaction and societal circumstances —P.A.Sorokin⟩

trans·i·re \tran(t)ˈsīˌrē\ *n* -s [L, to pass — more at TRANSIENT] *Eng* **:** a customs document describing the cargo, consignors, and consignees for clearance and entry of coasting vessels

trans·isthmian \(ˈ)tran(t)s, -raan-, -nz +\ *adj* [*trans-* + *isthm*us + *-ian*] **:** extending or going across an isthmus ⟨a ~ canal⟩ ⟨~ route⟩

tran·sis·tor \tranˈzistə(r), traan-, -n(t)ˈsi-\ *n* -s [1*tran*sfer + re*sistor;* fr. its transferring an electrical signal across a resistor] **:** an electronic device similar in use to the electron tube consisting of a small block of a semiconductor (as germanium) on which are placed three electrodes of which the emitter and the collector make contact at points very close together on one side of the block while a metal plate makes contact on the opposite side with the operation of the device depending upon the peculiar conducting properties of semiconductors in which electrons moving in one direction are considered as leaving holes that serve as carriers of positive electricity in the opposite direction

tran·sis·tor·ize \-təˌrīz\ *vt* -ED/-ING/-S **:** to equip (a device) with transistors

1**tran·sit** \ˈtran(t)sə̇t, ˈtraan-, -nzə̇t, *usu* -ə̇d·+V\ *n* -s [L *transitus,* fr. *transitus,* past part. of *transire* to go across, pass — more at TRANSIENT] **1 a :** an act, process, or instance of passing or journeying across, through, or over **:** JOURNEY, PASSAGE ⟨the ~ of so vast a body through Roman territory could not but be dangerous —J.A.Froude⟩ ⟨the ~ of radio signals from the earth to the moon and back —J.W.Townsend⟩ ⟨a fine case study of the ~ of ideas from Europe to America —R.E.Riegel⟩ ⟨our ~ across the little span of life —W.L.Sullivan⟩ **b :** passage across **:** CHANGE, TRANSITION ⟨to bolster morale . . . in the ~ from war to peace —Dixon Wecter⟩ ⟨the ~ from fall to winter, from this life to the next⟩ **c** (1) **:** the conveyance or carriage of persons or things from one place to another ⟨pigeons were used to provide the fastest ~ for written messages —W.G.East⟩ ⟨there were also commissions . . . on communications and ~ —C.E.Black & E.C.Helmreich⟩ ⟨uses all modes of ~ to ship his products⟩ (2) **:** the transportation esp. of people by means of bus, subway train, or other usu. local system of public conveyance ⟨the problems of urban ~ are complex⟩ — compare RAPID TRANSIT; *also* **:** the system, vehicles, or facilities engaged in such transportation ⟨within easy reach are . . . schools, shopping centers, and ~ —*advt*⟩ ⟨85 out of 100 shoppers . . . arrived there by ~, as against nine out of 100 by auto —Sam Stavisky⟩ **2 :** the passing of a planet across or through any special point or place on the zodiac **3 a :** the passage of a celestial body over the meridian of a place or through the field of a telescope — called also *culmination* **b :** the passage of a smaller body across the disk of a larger (as of Venus or Mercury across the sun's disk) **4** *or* **transit compass :** a variety of theodolite with the telescope mounted so that it can be transited — called also *transit theodolite* — **in transit** *adv* **:** in passage **:** in the process of transit ⟨billions of messages . . . are always *in transit* between individuals and group —Stuart Chase⟩ ⟨of those at sea half were in the combat zone and half *in transit* —J.P.Baxter b. 1893⟩ ⟨some are men who have never come to rest and are always *in transit* —Oscar Handlin⟩

2**transit** \"\ *vb* -ED/-ING/-S *vi* **1 :** to go over or through **:** PASS ⟨ships use the canal to ~ to the west⟩ ⟨to steer to a destination through which the line ~*ed* —David Beaty⟩ **2 :** to make a transit across a meridian, a celestial body, or the field of view of a telescope ⟨expects the planet to ~ shortly after midnight⟩ **~** *vt* **1 a :** to pass over or through **:** CROSS, TRAVERSE ⟨~*ed* La Perouse strait on the surface at night —E.L.Beach⟩ ⟨from San Juan to Guantánamo Bay you ~ the windward passage —Lee Rogow⟩ **b :** to cause to pass over or through **:** CONVEY ⟨the canal . . . can be operated around the clock to ~ a total of 36 ships daily —*Ships and the Sea*⟩ **2 :** to pass across (a meridian, a celestial body, or the field of view of a telescope) **3 :** to turn (a telescope) over about its horizontal transverse axis in surveying

tran·sit·able \-ə̇d·əbəl\ *adj* [2*transit* + *-able*] **:** capable of being crossed or passed over

transit charge *n* [1*transit*] **:** a charge provided in a carrier's transit tariff to cover costs incurred in serving a shipper with transit privileges

transit circle *n* **:** MERIDIAN CIRCLE

transit department *n* **:** the department of a bank that clears and collects checks or transit items drawn on out-of-town banks

transit duty *n* **:** a tax imposed on goods passing through a country

tran·sit·er \-d·ə(r)\ *n* -s [1*transit* + *-er*] **:** a transit attachment consisting of a wire that can be made to traverse the field of a transit at a rate that will keep it continuously bisecting an object (as a star) passing across the field of view and of a device for registering such passage across definite points in the field

transit floater *n* **:** a blanket insurance policy covering all types of shipments without requiring the insured to report all the numerous items to the underwriter in advance

transit instrument *n* **1 :** a telescope that is mounted at right angles to a horizontal east-west axis on which it revolves with its line of collimation in the plane of the meridian and that is used in connection with a clock and chronograph for observing the time of transit of a celestial body over the meridian of a place **2 :** TRANSIT 4

1**tran·si·tion** \tran(t)ˈsishən, traan-, -nˈzi-\ *n* -s [L *transition-, transitio,* fr. *transitus* (past part. of *transire* to go across, pass) + *-ion-, -io* -ion — more at TRANSIENT] **1 a :** a passage or movement from one state, condition, or place to another **:** CHANGE ⟨in what shadowy spot . . . does the ~ from the dead to the quick take place —*Treasury of Science*⟩ ⟨the ~ from childhood to adulthood⟩ ⟨the abrupt ~ of her features from assured pride to ludicrous astonishment and alarm —Arnold Bennett⟩ ⟨that evening at the time of ~ in the sky —Ethel Wilson⟩ ⟨here guided missiles can pass through a complete sea-land ~ —J.C.Waugh⟩ ⟨an age of ~ and flux⟩ **b :** a movement, development, or evolution from one stage, form, or style to another usu. of a later time or period ⟨the first phase of the movement was more in the nature of a ~ than a rebellion —Bernard Smith⟩ ⟨the ~ of American civilization from agricultural to urban —N.B.Fagin⟩ ⟨a ~ from native bronze to iron artifacts took place . . . under the influence of cultural borrowings —R.W.Murray⟩ ⟨the ~ of early English architecture⟩ ⟨a ~ . . . from the inorganic to the organic, from the inanimate to the living —W.R.Inge⟩ **2 a :** a passing from one subject to another esp. without abruptness ⟨having told all her griefs . . . was soon able to make a voluntary ~ to the oddities of her cousin —Jane Austen⟩; *specif* **:** a passage of discourse in which a shift of subject is gradually effected ⟨has a bleakly ungraceful habit of making his ~*s* in the form of a question as a topic sentence —B.H.Bronson⟩ **b** (1) **:** a musical modulation; *esp* **:** a transient modulation (2) **:** a sudden change of key (3) **:** a musical passage leading from one section of a piece to another **:** BRIDGE **c :** a change or moving from one dramatic scene to another usu. by a fade, sound effects, music, or narration ⟨uses an onstage narrator who streamlines the ~ between scenes —*Time*⟩ **3 :** an abrupt change in the energy state or energy level of an atomic electron, a nucleus, or a molecule accompanied in general by the loss or gain of a single quantum of energy — compare QUANTUM THEORY

2**transition** \"\ *adj, usu cap* **:** of, relating to, or being a biogeographic zone having plants and animals of the zones on each side ⟨the *Transition* zone between the Boreal and Austral zones of No. America⟩

tran·si·tion·al \-shənᵊl, -shnəl\ *adj* **1 :** of, relating to, or characterized by transition ⟨at this ~ point of its nightly roll into darkness —Thomas Hardy⟩ ⟨the Sudan is ~ between the hot desert . . . and the tropical rainy lands —D.D.Crary⟩ ⟨~ between gothic and roman —J.C.Tarr⟩ ⟨this ~ stage has become terminal in some races —Weston La Barre⟩ ⟨an effective ~ passage . . . which leads to the entry of the second subject —Dyneley Hussey⟩ **2** *usu cap* **a :** MESOLITHIC **b :** of or relating to Maya culture of the period A.D. 900–987 and overlapping and following the final stages of the Old Empire period — **tran·si·tion·al·ly** \-shənᵊlē, -shnəl-, -i\ *adv*

transitional cell *also* **transitional** *or* **transitional leukocyte** *n* **:** MONOCYTE

transitional epithelium *n* **:** epithelium consisting of two or three layers of cells that are usu. more or less flattened or cuboidal

transition area *n* **:** GRADED AREA

tran·si·tion·ary \-shəˌnerē\ *adj* [*transition* + *-ary*] **:** TRANSITIONAL

transition curve *or* **transition spiral** *n* **:** EASEMENT CURVE

transition element *or* **transition metal** *n* **:** any of the series of metals (as scandium, titanium, vanadium, chromium, manganese, iron, cobalt, nickel) that fall in the center of the long form of the periodic table, that include as inner series the lanthanide series and the actinide series, that have valence electrons in two shells instead of only one, and that are characterized in most cases by variable oxidation states and magnetic properties

transition fit *n* **:** a mechanical fit in which a clearance or interference fit may be obtained within the specified tolerance

transition point *n* **:** a single point at which different phases of matter are capable of existing together in equilibrium — called also *inversion point*

transition region *n* **:** the region of a plant axis within which the vascular arrangement characteristic of the stem changes to that of the root

transition temperature *n* **:** a transition point on a temperature scale

1**tran·si·tive** \ˈtran(t)səd·|iv, ˈtraan-, -nzə-, -ət|\ *adj* [LL *transitivus,* fr. L *transitus* (past part. of *transire* to cross over, pass) + *-ivus* -ive — more at TRANSIENT] **1 a** *of a verb form* **:** expressing an action that carries over from an agent or subject to an object **:** taking a direct object **b** *of a grammatical construction* **:** containing a transitive verb form **2 :** passing or leading successively on to members of a class or a series of developments **:** TRANSIENT 2 ⟨a moment connected with a wider complex of moments in a ~ chain that goes on indefinitely —Eliseo Vivas⟩ ⟨the main use of ~ parts is to lead us from one substantive conclusion to another —William James⟩; *specif* **:** of or relating to a logical relationship between x, y, and z such that if x has a specified relation to y and y to z then x has this relationship to z **3 :** of, relating to, or involving transition **:** TRANSITIONAL ⟨the ~ process of constructing a new philosophy out of the old⟩ **4 :** passing or descending to another in law ⟨a ~ covenant binds not only its original maker but also his representatives⟩ — **tran·si·tive·ly** \|ə̇vlē, -li\ *adv* — **tran·si·tive·ness** \|ivnə̇s\ *n* -ES

2**transitive** \"\ *n* -s **:** a verb form or grammatical construction expressive of transitive force

tran·si·tiv·i·ty \ˌtran(t)səˈtivəd·ē, -nzəˈ-\ *n* -ES [1*transitive* + *-ity*] **:** the quality or state of being transitive

trans·i·tiv·ize \ˈtran(t)səd·əˌvīz, -nzəd·-\ *vt* -ED/-ING/-S [1*transitive* + *-ize*] **:** to make (a verb form) transitive (as by adding a suffix)

tran·sit·man \ˈ⸗⸗mən\ *n, pl* **transitmen** [1*transit* + *man*] **:** one who uses the surveyor's or engineer's transit

transit mix *n* **:** concrete or mortar moistened and mixed in a truck mixer en route to or at the work site — compare READY-MIX

transit number *n* **:** a number assigned to a bank by an official organization (as the American Bankers Association) and printed on its checks for identification

tran·si·to·ri·ly \ˌtranzəˌtōrəlē, -raan-, -n(t)səˌ-, -tȯr-, -li\ *adv* **:** in a transitory manner **:** TRANSIENTLY, TEMPORARILY

tran·si·to·ri·ness \ˈ⸗⸗ˌtōrēnə̇s, -tȯr-, -rin-\ *n* -ES **:** the quality or state of being transitory ⟨the sense of the impermanence of things, the ~ of life —Laurence Binyon⟩

tran·si·to·ry \-rē, -ri\ *adj* [ME *transitorie, transitore,* fr. MF *transitoire,* fr. LL *transitorius,* fr. L, of or allowing passage, fr. *transitus* (past part. of *transire* to go across, pass, pass away) + *-orius* -ory — more at TRANSIENT] **1 a :** marked by the quality of passing away **:** EVANESCENT, TRANSIENT ⟨barter the ~ pleasures of the world for the heavenly hope —Nathaniel Hawthorne⟩ ⟨thoughts are illusive, ~, fleeting, thin shadows of reality —William Zukerman⟩ ⟨objects of sense . . . are ~ and ephemeral —Frank Thilby⟩ **b :** of brief duration : existing momentarily : TEMPORARY ⟨the depression of occipital activity may be ~, lasting only for minutes or seconds —Oscar Sugar⟩ ⟨those who spend a ~ period in the public service —O.G.Stahl⟩ ⟨a ~ and impermanent occurrence like a shriek —Samuel Alexander⟩ ⟨the postage stamp renders only one ~ service, which is wholly exhausted within one financial period —S.W.Rowland & Brian Magee⟩ **2 :** TRANSITIONAL **syn** see TRANSIENT

transitory action *n* **:** an action (as for debt) that may be brought in any county or district where jurisdiction can be secured over the person of the defendant — compare LOCAL ACTION

transit privileges *n pl* [*transit*] **:** a carrier service available to a shipper by which a through rate instead of two local rates is applied to a shipment that is stopped en route for storage or processing — compare MILLING-IN-TRANSIT

transit rate *or* **transit charge** *n* **:** a rate applied to a shipment that is milled, stored, or treated in transit

tran·si·tron \ˈtran(t)sə,trän, -nzə-\ *n* -s [perh. fr. *transition* + *-tron*] **:** a pentode operating under conditions where the transconductance of the tube is negative and permits the tube to be used in oscillator, trigger, or similar circuits

transits *pl of* TRANSIT, *pres 3d sing of* TRANSIT

transit theodolite *n* [¹*transit*] **:** TRANSIT 4

transit time *n* **1 :** the observed or predicted time of the transit of a celestial body across the meridian **2 :** the time required for a particle (as an electron) to traverse the distance between two specified points (as from cathode to plate in a vacuum tube)

tran·si·tus \ˈtran(t)sədəs, ˈtraan-, -nzə-, -ətəs\ *n* -ES [L, passage, transit — more at TRANSIT] **:** transit of a person or property en route from one place to another — compare STOPPAGE IN TRANSITU

¹**trans·jordanian** \¦tran(t)s, -raan-, -nz+\ *adj, usu cap* [fr. *Transjordania*, former name of Hashemite Kingdom of Jordan in northwest Arabia + E *-an*] **:** JORDANIAN

²**transjordanian** \"\ *n* -s *cap* **:** JORDANIAN

trans-jor·dan·ic \"+jȯ(r)¦danik\ *adj, usu cap J* [*trans-* + *Jordan*, river of eastern Palestine + *-ic*] **:** lying or situated beyond or across the Jordan river

transl *abbr* translated; translation

trans·lat·abil·i·ty \tran(t),slād·əˈbiləd·ē, -nz,lā-\ *n* **:** the quality or state of being translatable ⟨such a literary work is beyond ~ —Murray Krieger⟩

trans·lat·able \tran(t)ˈslād·əbəl, traan-, -nzˈl-, -ātəb-\ *adj* **:** capable of being translated ⟨sustenance readily ~ to the American home table —Lawton Mackall⟩ ⟨the social contacts . . . were all ~, sooner or later, into political manipulation —H.F.Graff⟩ ⟨languages . . . ~ into and from these symbolic characters —Caroline Yale⟩

trans·late \tran(t)ˈslāt, traan-, -nzˈ- *also* ˈ=,= *usu* -ād·+V\ *vb* -ED/-ING/-S [L *translatus, tralatus* (suppletive past part. of *transferre* to transfer, translate), fr. *trans-* + *latus*, suppletive past part. of *ferre* to bear, carry — more at BEAR, TOLERATE] *vt* **1 a :** to bear, remove, or change from one place or condition to another : TRANSPORT, TRANSFER, CONVEY — usu. used with *to* ⟨I was *translated* from the country to the city —Kenneth Mackenzie⟩ ⟨he *translated* the fight . . . to the public arena —L.M.Hughes⟩ ⟨a fine play has been superlatively *translated* to the screen —*Current Biog.*⟩ ⟨the saint's relics were *translated* from the crypt to the . . . shrine —Dorothy G. Spicer⟩ ⟨*translated* him to the War Department —N.W.Stephenson & H.W.H.Knott⟩ **b :** to remove or convey to heaven or to a nontemporal condition without death ⟨by faith Enoch was *translated* that he should not see death —Heb 11:5 (AV)⟩ ⟨those Muslims who hold that the Mahdi was *translated* in an earlier century⟩ **c :** to transfer (a bishop) from one see to another ⟨if a bishop be *translated* he must be introduced as the holder of the see —T.E.May⟩ **2 a :** to turn into one's own or another language : RENDER ⟨is learning to ~ Latin⟩ — usu. used with *into* ⟨Chinese ideograms are *translated* into Japanese —David Diringer⟩ ⟨had to ~ the characters into spoken Korean —Cornelius Osgood⟩ **b :** to transfer or turn from any special system of representation, set of symbols, or calculus into another such system, set, or calculus : TRANSCRIBE — usu. used with *into* ⟨imperative that the reporter ~ his notes into longhand —B.M.Metzger⟩ ⟨~ books into braille⟩ ⟨a linguistic code . . . can be *translated* into a binary code —R.W.Brown b. 1925⟩ ⟨~ mathematical truths into logical truths⟩ **c :** DECODE, ENCODE ⟨this solution will permit the cryptanalyst to ~ additional messages —W.W.R.Ball⟩ ⟨when he ~*s* his message into a coded one —Aaron Bakst⟩ **d :** to express in different words : PARAPHRASE — usu. used with *into* ⟨what remains of the poetry after we have *translated* it into prose⟩ ⟨the terminology used by technicians . . . is *translated* into the language of the layman —Lucile Bagwell⟩ **e :** to express in explanatory or more comprehensible terms : EXPLAIN, INTERPRET ⟨the element which is so difficult to ~ in the idea of fair play —Margaret Mead⟩ ⟨it ~*s* my childish impressions accurately enough —A.T.Quiller-Couch⟩ ⟨all such novels have their special language which you must ~ . . . to learn the real intention of the artist —M.D.Geismar⟩ — often used with *into* ⟨has *translated* Moloc's words into contemporary human terms —Wayne Burns⟩ **3 a :** to change the substance, form, or appearance of : TRANSFORM, TRANSMUTE, CONVERT — usu. used with *into* ⟨~*s* the girl into a witch⟩ ⟨the projection kinescope . . . ~*s* the video signal into a pattern of light and shadows on the tube face —C.L.Dawes⟩ ⟨cars are *translated* into scrap —*New Yorker*⟩ ⟨the time required to ~ new ideas into practical military weapons —H.S.Truman⟩ ⟨the prime mover which ~*s* energy into power —Roger Burlingame⟩ ⟨designers ~ the . . . styling of an import into a modified and wearable version for the American woman —Dorothy O'Neill⟩ **b** *Brit* **:** to transform (old garments or shoes) by repairing, renovating, or remaking from old materials ⟨for two of these the costumes were *translated* from old sets —E.K.Chambers⟩ ⟨a number of men were fixing up — *translating* — old boots —Robert Sandall⟩ **4 :** TRANSPORT, ENRAPTURE, ENTRANCE **5 :** to change the position of (a body or figure) in space without rotation **6 :** to repeat or forward (a message) by telegraphic translation ~ *vi* **1 a :** to practice rendering from one language or representational system into another ⟨he ~*s* for the patent attorney⟩; *also* **:** to make such a rendering or translation ⟨no one but a language learner needs to be told . . . that a word-for-word transposition does not ~ —Jackson Mathews⟩ ⟨in class the teacher asks him to ~⟩ **b :** to admit of or be adaptable to translation ⟨words that ~ into every language —D.D.Eisenhower⟩ ⟨a Portuguese word that does not ~ easily —David Dodge⟩ **2 :** to repeat or forward a message by telegraphic translation

trans·lat·er \-ād·ə(r), -ātə-\ *n* -s [¹*translate* + *-er*] **:** TRANSLATOR

trans·la·tion \tran(t)ˈslāshən, traan-, -nzˈl-\ *n* -s [ME *translacioun*, fr. MF or L; MF *translation*, fr. L *translation-, translatio*, fr. *translatus* (suppletive past part. of *transferre* to transfer, translate) + *-ion-, -io* -ion] **:** an act, process, or instance of translating: as **a :** a rendering from one language or representational system into another ⟨~ is an art that involves the re-creation of a work in another language for readers with a different background —Malcolm Cowley⟩; *also* **:** the product of such a rendering ⟨collaborated on a Chippewa grammar and on ~*s* of the Bible —*Amer. Guide Series: Minn.*⟩ ⟨is in possession of a single cipher message with its ~ —W.W.R.Ball⟩ **b :** the removal, transfer, or conveyance from one place or condition to another ⟨the bishop's ~ to a different see⟩ ⟨promotion and ~ to a higher . . . sphere of activity —Harold Stein⟩ ⟨his ~ to an unaccustomed office life —Manfred Nathan⟩ **c :** a change or alteration to a different substance, form, or appearance : TRANSFORMATION, TRANSMUTATION, CONVERSION ⟨a mechanical ~ of sound into light and color —Leon Becker⟩ ⟨the ~ of the scientific knowledge into practical instruments —Lewis Mumford⟩ ⟨the ~ of the common will into action —Clement Attlee⟩ ⟨the ~ of habits of life and modes of thought into wood and stone —*Amer. Guide Series: Conn.*⟩ ⟨an almost immediate ~ from reality to art —Marya Mannes⟩ **d** *Roman & Scots law* **:** a transfer of property; *esp* **:** an assignment by an assignee of a debt by deed to another **e** (1) **:** a shift in position without rotation (2) **:** translational or translatory motion **f :** the automatic repeating or forwarding of a message (as by a telegraphic relay) **g :** a moving of rectangular axes parallel to themselves

trans·la·tion·al \-shənᵊl, -shnəl\ *adj* **:** of, relating to, or involving translation: as **a :** of, consisting in, or resulting from translation from one language or system to another ⟨~ differences in connotation⟩ **b :** of, relating to, or characterized by uniform motion in one line or direction — **trans·la·tion·al·ly** \-shənᵊlē, -shnəl-, -li\ *adv*

trans·la·tive \-ād·iv\ *adj* [L *translativus*, fr. *translatus* + *-ivus* -ive] **1 :** of, relating to, or involving removal or transference from one person or place to another: as **a :** of, involving, or marked by translational motion **b :** operating to transfer a right from one person to another **2 :** of, relating to, or serving to translate or render from one language or system into another **3 :** FACTIVE 2a

trans·la·tor \tran(t)ˈslād·ə(r), traan-, -nzˈl-, -ātə- *also* ˈ=,==\ *n* -s [ME *translatour, translatore*, fr. MF or L; MF *translatour*, fr. L *translator*, fr. *translatus* + *-or*] **:** one that translates: as **a :** one that translates or renders from one language or system to another **b** *Brit* **:** a repairer of clothing, umbrellas, or old shoes **c :** the relay apparatus used in translation : REPEATER **d :** a part of a dial telephone system that controls the routing of the connection

trans·la·tor·ese \tran(t)¦slād·ə¦rēz, -nz¦l-, -ēs\ *n* -s [*translator* + *-ese*] **:** the jargon of a translator : poorly translated matter

trans·la·to·ry \ˈtran(t)slə,tōrē, ˈtraan-, -nzl-, -tȯr-, -ri\ *adj* [L *translatus* + E *-ory*] **:** TRANSLATIONAL b

translatory motion *n* **:** motion in which all points of a moving body move uniformly in the same line or direction

trans·lit·er·ate \tran(t)sˈlid·ə,rāt, traan-, -nzˈl-, -itə-, *usu* -ād·+V\ *vt* -ED/-ING/-S [*trans-* + L *litera* letter + E *-ate* — more at LETTER] **1 :** to represent or spell (words, letters, or characters of one language) in the letters or characters of another language or alphabet ⟨~ Sanskrit words with roman letters⟩ ⟨the New Testament was *transliterated* into rabbinic characters —B.M.Metzger⟩ **2 :** TRANSLATE 2a ⟨the ability of a restaurant waiter to ~ orders into a language understood only by himself and the cook —*Coronet*⟩

trans·lit·er·a·tion \(,)=,==ˈrāshən\ *n* -s [*transliterate* + *-ion*] **:** an act, process, or instance of transliterating ⟨a table of seven different systems of ~ of Russian —Gregory Razran⟩; *also* **:** the product of such transliterating ⟨Biblical Hebrew provides us with far stranger ~*s* from the cuneiform —S.L. Caiger⟩

trans·lit·er·a·tor \=ˈ==,rād·ə(r)\ *n* -s [*transliterate* + *-or*] **:** one that transliterates

trans·lo·cate \(ˈ)tran(t)¦slō,kāt, traan-, -nzˈl-, *usu* -ād·+V\ *vt* [prob. back-formation fr. *translocation*] **:** to change the location or position of : DISLOCATE, DISPLACE; *esp* **:** to transfer (as food materials or products of metabolism) from one location to another in the plant body

trans·location \¦tran(t)s, -raan-, -nz+\ *n* [*trans-* + *location*] **:** an act, process or instance of translocating ⟨water, wind, ice, and human agency are the chief factors in ~ and accumulation of dead shells in areas other than those in which they originate —H.J.Van Cleave⟩: as **a :** CONDUCTION 3; *esp* **:** the transfer of water from one part of a plant body to another **b :** the attachment of a broken-off segment of one chromosome to another; *esp* **:** the exchange of parts between nonhomologous chromosomes — compare CROSSING-OVER

trans·lu·cence \tran(t)ˈslüsᵊn(t)s, traan-, -nzˈl-\ *n* -s [fr. *translucent*, after such pairs as E *transparent: transparence*] **1 :** TRANSLUCENCY ⟨the soft ~ of the lighted globe⟩ **2 :** an act or instance of shining through or being outwardly apparent ⟨in his every act is the ~ of a noble character⟩

trans·lu·cen·cy \-nsē, -si\ *n* -ES [*translucent* + *-cy*] **:** the quality or state of being translucent : a partial transparency ⟨an X-ray picture . . . starting in the black, going up through the grays, and reaching a clear ~ —P.F.Titterington⟩ ⟨a ray of sunlight striking through the red or gold *translucencies* of wine in a glass —W.J.Locke⟩

trans·lu·cent \-nt\ *adj* [L *translucent-, translucens*, pres. part. of *translucēre* to shine through, fr. *trans-* + *lucēre* to shine — more at LIGHT] **1 :** shining or glowing through : PENETRATING, LUMINOUS ⟨the ~ rays of the sun⟩ **2 a :** TRANSPARENT ⟨materials used . . . for making windows or other ~ objects —*Notes & Queries on Anthropology*⟩ ⟨the water was ~, and I could readily watch from . . . the canoe what was going on —V.G. Heiser⟩ **b :** readily perceptible : CLEAR, LUCID ⟨his way of teaching, his ~ exposition —H.O.Taylor⟩ ⟨an interpretation . . . amazingly delicate and ~ —C.G.Poore⟩ ⟨the early piano is beautifully ~ throughout its compass —Robert Donington⟩ **3 :** admitting and diffusing light so that objects beyond cannot be clearly distinguished : partly transparent ⟨nothing could penetrate them except in the limited way that light penetrated ~ substances —Lewis Mumford⟩ ⟨the ~ skin showing the radiant rose beneath —W.H.Hudson †1922⟩ ⟨~ amber —Elinor Wylie⟩ **syn** see CLEAR

trans·lu·cent·ly *adv* **:** in a translucent manner

translucent reflector *n* **:** a partly transparent reflector used in semi-indirect lighting

trans·lu·cid \-üsəd\ *adj* [L *translucidus*, fr. *translucēre* to shine through] **:** TRANSLUCENT 3

trans·lu·nary \ˈtran(t)slü,nerē, -nzl-; (ˈ)tran(t)¦slünərē, -nz¦l-\ *adj* [*trans-* + L *luna* moon + E *-ary* — more at LUNAR] **:** located beyond the moon : ETHEREAL, VISIONARY — compare SUBLUNARY ⟨who can imagine a ~ visitor in Times Square —O.S.J.Gogarty⟩ ⟨his high ~ dreams —John Buchan⟩

Trans–Lux \ˈtran(t)sləks, -nzˈl-\ *trademark* — used for a device for projecting on a translucent screen the ticker tape of a market or exchange

trans·make \(ˈ)tran(t)s, -raan-, -nz+\ *vt* [*trans-* + *make*; trans. of Gk *metapoiein*] **:** to make over : REFASHION

trans·marine \¦tran(t)s, -raan-, -nz+\ *adj* [L *transmarinus*, fr. *trans-* + *mare* sea + *-inus* -ine — more at MARINE] **1 :** being or coming from beyond or across the sea ⟨a ~ people⟩ **2 :** passing over or extending across the sea : OVERSEAS ⟨the successive ~ thrusts of Britain, Japan, and the United States —*Foreign Policy Bull.*⟩

trans·medial *also* **trans·median** \(ˈ)tran(t)s, -raan-, -nz+\ *adj* [*trans-* + *median, medial*] **:** passing across or through the median plane

trans·methylation \¦tran(t)s, -raan-, -nz+\ *n* [*trans-* + *methylation*] **:** a chemical reaction in which a methyl group is transferred from one compound to another

trans·mi·grant \tran(t)ˈsmīgrənt, traan-, -nzˈm-\ *n* [L *transmigrant-, transmigrans*, pres. part. of *transmigrare*] **:** one who transmigrates; *esp* **:** an emigrant passing through a country en route to the one in which he will be an immigrant

trans·mi·grate \-ī,grāt, *usu* -ād·+V\ *vb* [L *transmigratus*, past part. of *transmigrare* to migrate to another place, fr. *trans-* + *migrare* to migrate] *vi* **1** *of the soul* **:** to pass at death from one body or being to another ⟨some believe that the soul may ~ into an animal as well as a person⟩ **2 :** to go or move from one place or country to another : MIGRATE ⟨*transmigrated* from the rocky mountain slopes to the fertile plains⟩ ~ *vt* **:** to cause to pass from one place or state of existence to another : subject to transmigration : TRANSFER ⟨the new Lama has the soul of the old one that has been *transmigrated* into him⟩ — compare REINCARNATE

trans·mi·gra·tion \,=,=ˈgrāshən\ *n* [LL *transmigration-, transmigratio*, fr. L *transmigratus* + *-ion-, -io* -ion] **:** an act, process, or instance of transmigrating: as **a** *also* **transmigration of souls :** the passing of the individual soul at death into a new body or new form of life usu. human or animal : METEMPSYCHOSIS — compare REINCARNATION **b :** the passage of cells through a membrane : DIAPEDESIS

trans·mi·gra·tor \tran(t)ˈsmī,grād·ə(r), traan-, -nzˈm-, -ātə-\ *n* [L *transmigratus* + E *-or*] **:** one that transmigrates — **trans·mi·gra·to·ry** \-īgrə,tōrē, -tȯr-, -ri\ *adj*

trans·mis·si·bil·i·ty \tran(t),smisəˈbiləd·ē, traan-, -nz,m-, -lətē, -i\ *n* -ES **:** the quality or state of being transmissible

trans·mis·si·ble \tran(t)ˈsmisəbəl, traan-, -nzˈm-\ *adj* [L *transmissus* + E *-ible*] **:** capable of being transmitted ⟨~ disease⟩ ⟨~ tradition⟩ ⟨~ characteristics⟩

trans·mis·sion \-ishən\ *n* -s *often attrib* [L *transmission-, transmissio*, fr. *transmissus* (past part. of *transmittere* to transmit) + *-ion-, -io* -ion] **1 :** an act, process, or instance of transmitting: as **a :** the overall proportion of radiant energy homogeneous with respect to wavelength that is transmitted perpendicularly through a substance bounded by plane nondiffusing parallel surfaces (as a plate of glass or other homogeneous isotropic nondiffusing medium or series of such media in contact with one another) and that is the ratio of the amount of energy emerging from the last surface to the amount incident upon the first with the difference between the two amounts resulting from losses of radiant energy due to reflection at the surfaces and absorptance and scattering within the medium — called also *attenuation factor* — compare TRANSMITTANCE 2 **b :** the passage of radio waves in the space between transmitting and receiving stations; *also* **:** the act or process of transmitting by radio or television **2 :** the gearing including the change gear and the propeller shaft or driving chain by which power is transmitted from the engine of an automobile to the live axle — called also *gearbox;* see SELECTIVE TRANSMISSION **3 :** the train of a watch **4 :** something that is transmitted : MESSAGE ⟨the machine records telegraphic ~*s*⟩

transmission bands *n pl* **:** the bands used in certain types of planetary transmission to clutch and stop the low and reverse speed drums

transmission case *n* **:** a jacket usu. of cast iron for the transmission of an automobile

transmission dynamometer *n* **:** a dynamometer in which power is measured without being absorbed or used up during transmission — compare ABSORPTION DYNAMOMETER

transmission efficiency *n* **:** the ratio of the power received over a transmission path to the power transmitted; *also* **:** the ratio of the output to the input power of a circuit or device

transmission grating *n* **:** a grating with opaque lines on a transparent background

transmission level *n* **1 :** the signaling-power amplitude at any point in a communication system **2 :** the radio field intensity at any point in a radio communication system

transmission line *n* **:** a metallic circuit of three or more conductors used to send energy usu. at high voltage over a considerable distance; *specif* **:** a usu. metallic line used for the transmission of signals or for the adjustment of circuit performance and often consisting of a pair of wires suitably separated, a coaxial cable, or a wave guide

transmission loss *n* **:** the loss of power or voltage of a transmitted wave or current in passing along a transmission line or path or through a circuit device — compare ABSORPTION 5, ATTENUATION 4

transmission rope *n* **:** a wire rope made of four or more strands of ordinary lay about a hemp center and used for the transmission of power on drive shafts and pulleys

transmission shaft *n* **:** a shaft in the transmission of an automotive vehicle that carries the sliding gears and makes the driving connection between the clutch and the propeller shaft

trans·mis·sive \tran(t)ˈsmisiv, traan-, -nzˈm-, -sēv *also* -səv\ *adj* [L *transmissus* (past part. of *transmittere* to transmit) + E *-ive*] **1 :** that transmits or serves to transmit ⟨the ~ function of the nerves⟩ ⟨the ~ powers of a legislature⟩ **2 :** that is or is capable of being transmitted or derived ⟨~ characteristics⟩

trans·mis·siv·i·ty \,tran(t)sməˈsivəd·ē, -nzm-\ *n* -ES [*transmissive* + *-ity*] **:** the quality or state of being transmissive; *specif* **:** the transmittance of a unit thickness of absorbing nondiffusing matter

trans·mis·som·e·ter \-ˈsäməd·ə(r)\ *n* [*transmission* + *-o-* + *-meter*] **:** a photometer or other instrument used for measuring transmission; *specif* **:** an instrument that measures the visibility or the capability of the air to transmit light

trans·mit \tran(t)ˈsmit, traan-, -nzˈm-, ˈ=,=, *usu* -id·+V\ *vb* **transmitted; transmitted; transmitting; transmits** [ME *transmitten*, fr. L *transmittere*, fr. *trans-* + *mittere* to send — more at SMITE] *vt* **1 a :** to cause to go or be conveyed to another person or place : SEND ⟨he secured soldiers' pay and *transmitted* it to their families —A.V.D.Honeyman⟩ ⟨prophets who are . . . a vehicle through which to ~ a revelation to the people —W.W.Howells⟩ ⟨said it sounded to him like common sense, and he would ~ it to his father —Upton Sinclair⟩ ⟨lists they shall sign and certify and ~ sealed to the seat of government —W.S.Sayre⟩ **b** (1) **:** to pass on or spread about : DISSEMINATE, COMMUNICATE ⟨the knowledge that objects of different weights fall at different speeds was *transmitted* in western society —Ralph Linton⟩ ⟨visual aids . . . are no better than the amount of information they ~ —J.K.Blake⟩ ⟨some of the original power of the master is *transmitted* to the disciple —C.D.Lewis⟩ (2) **:** to pass on by inheritance or heredity : HAND DOWN ⟨through the legacy of their art the great ages have *transmitted* to us a dim image of their glorious vitality —J.W.Krutch⟩ ⟨drew the inference that acquired habits cannot be *transmitted* —G.B.Shaw⟩ ⟨selective breeding aims to eliminate bad characteristics and ~ the good⟩ **c :** to give or convey (a disease or infection) to another person or organism ⟨attempts to ~ colds artificially . . . are successful —C.H. Andrews⟩ ⟨human beings who are apparently well can ~ infectious disease —Morris Fishbein⟩ ⟨mosquitos ~ malaria⟩ **2 a** (1) **:** to cause (as light or force) to pass or be conveyed through space or a medium ⟨the telephone ~*s* sound⟩ ⟨the power which an engine develops is *transmitted* to the wheels . . . by certain essential parts —Joseph Heitner⟩ ⟨objects of higher temperature than the skin . . . ~ heat to it —F.A. Geldard⟩ ⟨arches . . . ~ their loads to the walls of the river gorge —*Amer. Guide Series: Minn.*⟩ (2) **:** to admit the passage of : CONDUCT ⟨glass ~*s* light⟩ ⟨metals ~ electricity⟩ **b :** to send out (a signal) either by radio waves or over a wire line ~ *vi* **1 :** to pass by transmission an obligation entailing either a right or a duty **2 :** to send out a signal either by radio waves or over a wire line **syn** see CARRY, SEND

trans·mit·ta·ble \tran(t)ˈsmid·əbəl, traan-, -nzˈm-, -itəb-\ *adj* **:** capable of being transmitted ⟨infections easily ~ to children —Morris Fishbein⟩ ⟨~ power⟩

trans·mit·tal \-id·ᵊl, -itᵊl\ *n* -s [*transmit* + *-al*] **:** TRANSMISSION ⟨report its findings and recommendations . . . for ~ to Congress —*New Republic*⟩ ⟨the ~ of evil from one generation to another —*Time*⟩ ⟨its values permeate the culture through the same process of ~ —J.K.Feibleman⟩

trans·mit·tance \-itᵊn(t)s\ *n* -s [*transmit* + *-ance*] **1 :** TRANSMISSION **2 :** the fraction of radiant energy that having entered a layer of absorbing matter reaches its further boundary — compare TRANSMISSION 1a

trans·mit·tan·cy \-ᵊnsē, -si\ *n* -ES [*transmit* + *-ancy*] **:** the capacity for transmission: **a :** the ratio of the transmittance of a solution of a material to that of an equal thickness of the solvent **b :** TRANSMITTANCE 2

trans·mit·ter \tran(t)ˈsmid·ə(r), traan-, -nzˈm-, -itə-\ *n* -s [*transmit* + *-er*] **:** one that transmits: as **a** (1) **:** a part on a telephone into which one speaks and which contains a mechanism for converting sound waves into equivalent electric waves (2) **:** the portion of a telegraph instrument by which the message is sent **b** (1) **:** a radio or television transmitting set (2) **:** TRANSMITTING STATION

transmitting set *n* [*transmitting* (gerund of *transmit*) + *set*] **:** an apparatus for transmitting radio waves; *specif* **:** the portion of a complete transmitting station that produces and modulates radio-frequency current and delivers it to the broadcasting antenna

transmitting station *n* **:** an assemblage of equipment to send out or transmit radio waves including an antenna transmitting set and telephone transmitter or key

trans·mog·ri·fi·ca·tion \tran(t),smägrəfəˈkāshən, traan-, -nz-,m-\ *n* -s [fr. *transmogrify*, after such pairs as E *identify: identification*] **:** an act, process, or instance of transmogrifying ⟨~ into a porcupine —Florence B. Lennon⟩ ⟨in one of her more extensive ~*s*, imagined herself as a carpenter planing a board —R.S.Hillyer⟩

trans·mog·ri·fy \tran(t)ˈsmägrə,fī, traan-, -nzˈm-\ *vt* -ED/-ING/-ES [origin unknown] **:** to change or alter in form, appearance, or structure often with grotesque or humorous effect ⟨educational philosophy has been *transmogrified* since 1890 —*Amer. Council of Learned Soc. Newsletter*⟩ — usu. used with *into* ⟨wondering how the caricatured capitalism of his forbears can be *transmogrified* into a harmonious . . . way of life —*Current Biog.*⟩ ⟨plausibly *transmogrified* the sons of grocers . . . into haughty young bloods —H.M.McLuhan⟩ ⟨training which permits them to understand that an actress can be *transmogrified* into a rivet boy —C.J.Hitch⟩ **syn** see TRANSFORM

trans·mon·tane \tran(t)¦smän ¦tān, traan-, -nz¦m-\ *adj* [L *transmontanus* — more at TRAMONTANE] **:** TRAMONTANE ⟨~ country⟩ ⟨the ~ section of the state —J.H.Peeling⟩

trans·mun·dane \-mən¦dān\ *adj* [*trans-* + L *mund*us world + E *-ane* (as in *mundane*)] **:** extending or lying beyond the world ⟨whatever of ~ metaphysical insight . . . we may carry —William James⟩

trans·mu·ral \-myůrəl\ *adj* [*trans-* + L *mur*us wall + E *-al* — more at MUNITION] **:** extending or lying across a wall; *esp* **:** involving the whole thickness of a wall ⟨~ myocardial infarction⟩

trans·mut·abil·i·ty \tran(t)ˌsmyüd·əˈbiləd·ē, -nzˌm-\ *n* **:** the quality or state of being transmutable

trans·mut·able \tran(t)ˈsmyüd·əbəl, -nzˈm-\ *adj* [ME, fr. ML *transmutabilis*, fr. L *transmutare* to transmute + *-abilis* -able] **:** capable of being transmuted

trans·mu·ta·tion \ˌtran(t)smyüˈtāshən, ˌtraan-, -nzm-\ *n* [ME *transmutacioun*, fr. MF or L; MF *transmutation*, fr. L *transmutation-*, *transmutatio*, fr. *transmutatus* (past part. of *transmutare* to transmute) + *-ion-*, *-io* -ion] **:** an act, process, or instance of transmuting or being transmuted: as **a** *or* **transmutation of metals :** the conversion of base metals into gold or silver **b :** TRANSFER 1 — used esp. in the phrase *transmutation of possession* **c :** the change of one species into another — compare LAMARCKISM **d** (1) **:** the conversion of one element into another by a nuclear reaction (2) **:** the conversion of one nuclide into another

trans·mu·ta·tion·ist \-sh(ə)nəst\ *n* -s [*transmutation* + *-ist*] **:** one who believes in or advocates a theory of transmutation esp. of species

trans·mut·ative \tran(t)ˈsmyüd·əd·iv, traan-, -nzˈm-, -ütətiv\ *adj* [ML *transmutativus*, fr. L *transmutatus* + *-ivus* -ive] **:** of, relating to, or involving transmutation **:** serving or tending to transmute ⟨a ~ effect⟩ ⟨a ~ force⟩

trans·mute \-üt, *usu* -üd·+V\ *vb* -ED/-ING/-S [ME *transmuten*, fr. L *transmutare* to change, shift, fr. *trans-* + *mutare* to change — more at MISS] *vt* **1 :** to change or alter in form, appearance, or nature **:** CONVERT ⟨a pronounced stabilization that will ~ the economic and social life of the African —Peter Scott⟩ ⟨the interaction of . . . forces ~*s* custom and produces a new tradition —B.N.Cardozo⟩ — often used with *into* ⟨how does the chlorophyll . . . ~ the dross of earth into living tissue —D.C.Peattie⟩ ⟨~ the abundant raw materials . . . into finished products —A.W.Long⟩ ⟨~ their national integrity into a decisive weapon of national defense —W.O.Douglas⟩ **2 :** to change into another substance or element esp. gold or silver ⟨made it possible to smash atoms and ~ elements —*Current Biog.*⟩ — often used with *into* ⟨the alchemists . . . cared little for answers that did not lead them to the philosopher's stone, which would ~ base metals into gold —*Lamp*⟩ **~** *vi* **:** to undergo a change or transformation in form, nature, or substance ⟨the music gradually ~*s* and builds to a shattering climax —*Time*⟩ — often used with *into* ⟨energy converts into matter as naturally as matter ~*s* into energy —Gerard Piel⟩ **syn** see TRANSFORM

trans·national \(ˈ)tran(t)s, -raan-, -nz+\ *adj* [*trans-* + *national*] **:** extending or going beyond national boundaries ⟨an abatement of nationalism and the creation of ~ institutions which will render boundaries of minor importance —*New Republic*⟩ ⟨by the diffusion of culturally important words . . . ~ vocabularies have grown up —Edward Sapir⟩

transnatural \"+\ *adj* [*trans-* + *natural*] **:** being above or beyond nature **:** SUPERNATURAL ⟨credited many confusions in human knowledge to one's seeking natural causes . . . when the true reasons or causes were ~ —J.W.Yolton⟩

transnature \"+\ *vt* [*trans-* + *nature*] *archaic* **:** to change the nature of **:** TRANSELEMENT

trans-neptunian \¦tran(t)s, -raan-, -nz+\ *adj*, *usu cap N* [*trans-* + *Neptune*, formerly most distant known planet + E *-ian*] **:** lying beyond the orbit of the planet Neptune

trans·ocean \(ˈ)tran(t)s, -raan-, -nz+\ *adj* [*trans-* + *ocean*] **:** TRANSOCEANIC

trans·oceanic \(¦)tran(t)s, -raan-, -nz+\ *adj* [*trans-* + L *ocean*us ocean + E *-ic*] **1 :** lying or dwelling beyond the ocean ⟨a ~ country⟩ **2 :** crossing or extending across the ocean ⟨~ telephone⟩ ⟨the first to make a ~ crossing by air —H.G. Armstrong⟩

tran·som *also* **tran·some** \ˈtran(t)səm, ˈtraan-\ *n* -s *often attrib* [ME *traunsum*, *traunsom*, prob. fr. L *transtrum* crossbeam, transom, rowers' thwart, fr. *trans* across + *-trum*, suffix denoting an instrument — more at TRANS-, -TRON] **1 :** a transverse piece in a structure **:** CROSSPIECE: as **a :** LINTEL **b** *or* **transom bar :** a horizontal crossbar in a window, over a door, or between a door and a window or fanlight above it — distinguished from *mullion* **c :** the horizontal bar or member of a cross or gallows **d** (1) **:** any of several transverse timbers or beams secured to the sternpost of a boat (2) *or* **transom frame :** the aftermost frame of the square body secured to the sternpost and supporting the overhanging stern **e :** a usu. broad and flat metal piece connecting the cheeks, the sidepieces of the trail, or similar parts of a gun carriage **f :** the vane of a cross-staff **g :** the board or planking forming the stern of a square-ended boat **h :** a transverse horizontal strut between parallel or nearly parallel members (as in a frame) **i :** a crossbeam joining the side frames of a truck of a railway car **2** *or* **transom window :** a window above a door or other window built on and commonly hinged to a transom **3 :** a seat or couch built at the side of a cabin or stateroom of a boat usu. with lockers or drawers underneath

tran·somed \-md\ *adj* [*transom* + *-ed*] **:** having a transom — used of doors or windows

transom knee *n* **:** a knee bolted to a transom or after timber of a ship

transom stern *n* **:** a stern of a boat formed by or shaped from a transom frame

tran·son·ic \(ˈ)tran¦sänik, -raan-, -nēk\ *also* **trans-son·ic** \-nz¦s-, -n(t)s¦s-\ *adj* [*trans-* + *-sonic* (as in *supersonic*); fr. the fact that such speeds are transitional between subsonic and supersonic speeds] **1 :** of, being, or relating to a speed approximating the speed of sound in air **:** relating to a speed in air of about 1087 feet per second or about 741 miles per hour at sea level — often used of aeronautical speeds between 600 and 900 miles per hour; compare SONIC, SUBSONIC, SUPERSONIC **2 :** moving, capable of moving, or utilizing air currents moving at a transonic speed

trans·orbital \(ˈ)tran(t)s, -raan-, -nz+\ *adj* [*trans-* + *orbit* + *-al*] **:** passing through or occurring by way of the eye socket ⟨a ~ lobotomy⟩

trans·ovar·i·al \¦tran(t)sō¦va(a)rēəl, -nzō-\ *or* **trans·ovar·i·an** \-ēən\ *adj* [*trans-* + *ovary* + *-al* or *-an*] **:** passing through or occurring by way of the ovary ⟨~ passage⟩ ⟨wood ticks have been shown to be infectable . . . and capable of ~ transmission to their offspring —K.F.Maxcy⟩ — **trans·ovar·i·al·ly** \-lē\ *or* **trans·ovar·i·an·ly** *adv*

transp *abbr* **1** transparent **2** transportation

trans·pacific \¦tranz, -raan-, -n(t)s+\ *adj* [*trans-* + *Pacific (ocean)*] **1 :** crossing or extending across the Pacific ocean ⟨~ flight⟩ ⟨steamships on the ~ run⟩ ⟨~ service⟩ **2 :** lying, dwelling, or situated across or beyond the Pacific ⟨~ peoples⟩ ⟨~ regions⟩

trans·pa·dane \¦tranzpə¦dān, -n(t)sp-; (ˈ)tranz¦pāˌdān, -n(t)¦sp-\ *adj* [L *transpadanus*, fr. *trans-* + *Padus* the Po, river in northern Italy + L *-anus* -an] **:** lying or situated on the farther or usu. north side of the river Po — opposed to *cispadane*

trans·palatine \(ˈ)tranz, -raan-, -n(t)s+\ *adj* [*trans-* + L *palat*um palate + E *-ine*] **:** of, relating to, or being the transverse bone of the skull of a reptile

trans·par·ence \tranzˈpa(a)rən(t)s, traan-, -n(t)ˈsp-, -per-\ *n* -s [ML *transparentia*] **:** TRANSPARENCY ⟨the ~ of water —George Copeland⟩ ⟨the sky above its domes . . . is of sheer ~ —E.O.Hauser⟩

trans·par·en·cy \-nsē, -si\ *n* -ES [ML *transparentia*, fr. *transparent-*, *transparens* transparent + L *-ia* -y] **1 :** the quality or state of being transparent ⟨many marine invertebrates tend towards ~ —W.H.Dowdeswell⟩ ⟨the absolute ~ of the air on this gracious day —Walter Pater⟩ ⟨the marvelous fluidity, ~, and curiosity of his nature —V.S.Pritchett⟩ **2 :** something that is transparent: as **a :** a picture or other matter for exhibition made upon glass, thin cloth, paper, or film and intended to be viewed by the aid of light shining through it or by projection — compare SLIDE 6b(1), LANTERN SLIDE **b :** a framework covered with thin cloth or paper bearing a device for public display and lighted from within

trans·par·ent \-nt\ *adj* [ME, fr. ML *transparent-*, *transparens*, pres. part. of *transparēre* to show through, fr. L *trans-* + *parēre* to be visible, appear, show — more at APPEAR] **1 a :** having the property of transmitting light without appreciable scattering so that bodies lying beyond are entirely visible **:** PELLUCID ⟨this plastic is more ~ than even high-quality plate glass —Harland Manchester⟩ ⟨the ~ or hazy air —Mary Webb⟩ — opposed to *opaque* and usu. distinguished from *translucent* **b :** so loose or open in texture as to admit the passage of light **:** SHEER, DIAPHANOUS ⟨~ velvet⟩ ⟨a ~ yoke⟩ **c :** TRANSLUCENT ⟨~ soap⟩ ⟨his ~ womanly hands —J.R.Green⟩ **2 a :** free from pretense or deceit **:** OPEN, FRANK, GUILELESS ⟨a man of such ~ sincerity that he is incapable of presenting a ghost-written speech —*N. Y. Times*⟩ ⟨the most important quality in a teacher . . . is genuine and ~ truthfulness —C.W.Eliot⟩ ⟨the child's ~ countenance⟩ **b :** easily detected or seen through **:** OBVIOUS ⟨embarked on an elaborate fraud ~ to the world —Otis Ferguson⟩ ⟨his writings . . . are so flat, so ~, so palpably taken from the nearest authorities —H.O.Taylor⟩ ⟨the man's ~ fear of discovery —Luke Short⟩ **c :** readily understood **:** PERSPICUOUS, CLEAR ⟨a style of ~ clarity that needs no artifices to make it vivid —C.H.Dreier⟩ ⟨that part of the chamber music which becomes ~ only after study or explication —Robert Evett⟩ ⟨the art . . . so ~ in all of its effects that the need is seldom felt to analyze —Philip Rahv⟩ **3 :** pervious to any specified form of radiation (as X rays or ultraviolet light) **syn** see CLEAR

transparent chromium oxide *n* **:** a moderate to strong green that is bluer and darker than Hooker's green

trans·par·ent·ize \-n·ˌtīz\ *vt* -ED/-ING/-S **:** to make transparent ⟨a process developed to ~ tracing paper⟩

trans·par·ent·ly *adv* **:** in a transparent manner ⟨red brilliance of the wines shines ~ in the glasses —*Time*⟩ ⟨the concise and yet ~ lucid exposition —Ernest Nagel⟩ ⟨he was . . . ~ truthful —A.P.Davies⟩ ⟨sulked, faltered, and prevaricated ~ —Arthur Morrison⟩

trans·par·ent·ness *n* -ES [*transparent* + *-ness*] **:** TRANSPARENCY 1

trans·pep·ti·da·tion \(ˌ)tranzˌpeptəˈdāshən, -n(t)ˌspe-\ *n* -s [*trans-* + *peptide* + *-ation*] **:** a chemical reaction (as the reversible conversion of one peptide to another by a proteinase) in which an amino acid residue or a peptide residue is transferred from one amino compound to another

trans·personal \(ˈ)tranz, -raan-, -n(t)s+\ *adj* [*trans-* + *personal*] **:** extending or going beyond the personal or individual ⟨to transcend the immediacy of desire and to live for ends which are ~ —Walter Lippmann⟩ ⟨suggestions that he had enlisted ~ powers —Vernon Young⟩

trans·phenomenal \¦tranz, -raan-, -n(t)s+\ *adj* [*trans-* + *phenomenal*] **:** existing or lying beyond the phenomenal or apparent: **a :** of or relating to a reality that is beyond or above that which is apparent to human senses **b :** of or relating to what exists in itself and is the ground of what appears to our senses — compare THING-IN-ITSELF

trans·phosphorylase \(ˈ)tranz, -raanz, -n(t)s+\ *n* [*transphosphoryl*ation + *-ase*] **:** any of a group of enzymes that promote transphosphorylation processes — compare KINASE 2, PHOSPHATASE, PHOSPHOGLUCOMUTASE, PHOSPHORYLASE

trans·phosphorylation \¦tranz, -raanz, -n(t)s+\ *n* [*trans-* + *phosphorylation*] **:** phosphorylation in which an organic phosphate group is transferred from one molecule to another and which is usu. promoted by a transphosphorylase

tran·spic·u·ous \tranzˈpikyəwəs, -n(t)ˈsp-\ *adj* [NL *transpicuus*, fr. L *transpicere* to look through, see through, fr. *trans-* + *-spicere* (fr. *specere* to look, see) — more at SPY] **:** clearly seen through or understood **:** TRANSPARENT

trans·pierce \tranzˈpi(ə)rs, -n(t)ˈsp-\ *vt* [MF *transpercer*, fr. OF, fr. *trans-* (fr. L) + *percer* to pierce — more at PIERCE] **1 :** to penetrate sharply or painfully ⟨my spear . . . *transpierced* his back, and fixed him to the ground —Alexander Pope⟩ **2 :** to pass or extend through ⟨a metal rod . . . ~*s* the box —*Athenaeum*⟩

tran·spir·able \tranzˈpīrəbəl, -n(t)ˈsp-\ *adj* [MF, fr. *transpirer* to transpire + *-able*] **:** capable of being transpired ⟨~ fluids⟩ **:** permitting transpiration ⟨a ~ membrane⟩

tran·spi·ra·tion \ˌtranzpəˈrāshən, ˌtraan-, -n(t)sp-\ *n* -s [MF fr. *transpirer* + *-ation*] **:** an act, process, or instance of transpiring: as **a :** the passage of fluid (as water) through skin or animal membrane in the form of a vapor; *also* **:** something that is transpired **:** PERSPIRATION **b :** the emission or exhalation of watery vapor from the surfaces of leaves or other parts of plants **c :** the passing of gases through fine tubes or porous substances because of differences of pressure or temperature — compare THERMAL TRANSPIRATION

transpiration ratio *n* **:** the amount of water used to produce one pound of dry matter in a plant

transpiration stream *or* **transpiration current** *n* **:** the current of water usu. containing many substances in solution that rises through the xylem of plants

tran·spire \tranzˈpī(ə)r, traan-, -n(t)ˈsp-, -īə\ *vb* -ED/-ING/-S [MF *transpirer*, fr. L *trans-* + *spirare* to breathe — more at SPIRIT] *vt* **1 :** to cause (as a gas or liquid) to pass through a tissue or substance or its pores or interstices **2 :** to excrete or give off (as moisture or vapor) through the skin, a membrane, or living cells **:** PERSPIRE, EXUDE, EXHALE **~** *vi* **1 :** to emit moisture, vapor, or perfume; *specif* **:** to give off or exude watery vapor from the surfaces of leaves or other parts ⟨a plant ~*s* more freely on a hot dry day⟩ **2 :** to pass out or escape in the form of a vapor from a living body ⟨moisture ~*s* through the skin⟩ **3 a :** to become known or apparent **:** DEVELOP ⟨it *transpired* that he had still been sitting . . . when the bomb struck —C.D.Lewis⟩ ⟨it soon *transpired* that there were two . . . conceptions of this problem —C.H.Malik⟩ ⟨only good faculties, it *transpired*, were inherited —Walter Lippmann⟩ **b :** to be revealed **:** leak out **:** come to light ⟨had to wait until 1934 for the secret to ~ —E.C.Wagenknecht⟩ ⟨it had just *transpired* that he had left gaming debts behind him —Jane Austen⟩ **4 :** to come to pass **:** HAPPEN, OCCUR ⟨a course of events which ~ with unbelievable rapidity —H.G.Moseley⟩ ⟨I gave an honest account of what *transpired* —J.A.Michener⟩ ⟨more things ~ on a racetrack than are chronicled in the newspapers —Gerald Beaumont⟩ **syn** see HAPPEN

tran·spi·rom·e·ter \ˌtranzpəˈrämәd·ə(r), -n(t)sp-\ *n* [*transpire* + *-o-* + *-meter*] **:** an instrument or apparatus for measuring plant transpiration

trans·place \tranzˈplās, -n(t)ˈsp-\ *vt* [*trans-* + *place*] **1 :** to put in another place **:** TRANSPOSE **2 :** to interchange the places of

trans·placental \¦tranz, -raan-, -n(t)s+\ *adj* [ISV *trans-* + NL *placenta* + ISV *-al*] **:** passing through or occurring by way of the placenta ⟨~ passage of nutrients⟩ ⟨~ immunization⟩

[1]**trans·plant** \tranzˈplant, traan-, -n(t)ˈsp-, -laa(ə)nt, -laint, -lånt\ *vb* [ME *transplaunten*, fr. LL *transplantare*, fr. L *trans-* + *plantare* to plant] *vt* **1 a :** to remove and plant in another place; *specif* **:** to lift and reset in another soil or situation ⟨~*ed* mulberry trees from his . . . nursery —*Amer. Guide Series: Conn.*⟩ **b :** to remove from one location and introduce in another ⟨traps and ~*s* beaver to other sections of the state⟩ ⟨~ ladybirds⟩ **2 :** to remove from a place or country and settle elsewhere **:** TRANSPORT — usu. used with *to* or *from* ⟨wished to ~ his family to America⟩ ⟨many institutions were ~*ed* from Europe⟩ ⟨his office staff is ~*ed* to his vacation spot —*U. S. News & World Report*⟩ **3 :** to transfer (an organ or tissue) from one body or part of a body to another ⟨~*ed* one twin's kidney to the other⟩ ⟨reported that cancer tissues can be ~*ed* from man to other animals⟩ **~** *vi* **1** *obs* **:** to go elsewhere to settle **:** EMIGRATE **2 :** to admit of being removed from one place or soil to another ⟨some plants do not ~ as well as others⟩

[2]**transplant** \ˈ=,=\ *n* **1 :** the act or process of transplanting ⟨the operation called corneal grafting, or ~, can restore sight —Eleanor Early⟩ ⟨as long as six hours after death . . . successful ~*s* could be carried out —E.A.Graham⟩ **2 :** a person or thing that is transplanted ⟨a tall Montanan, a Texas ~, pitched the grounds from his cup into the fire —Luke Short⟩ ⟨these tiny ~*s* . . . provide a kind of fishing that has no exact parallel —J.O.Cartier⟩ ⟨$2 a thousand for seedlings and $5 a thousand for ~*s* —*Amer. Guide Series: Pa.*⟩ ⟨never since doctors discovered how to replace fogged corneas . . . have there been eye ~*s* to go round —*Time*⟩

trans·plant·able *pronunc at* [1]TRANSPLANT + əbəl\ *adj* **:** capable of being transplanted

trans·plan·ta·tion \ˌtranzˌplan·ˈtāshən, ˌtraan-, -n(t)ˌsp-laan-, -lån-\ *n* [[1]*transplant* + *-ation*] **:** an act, process, or instance of transplanting or being transplanted: as **a :** a magical cure of a disease by causing it to pass from the afflicted person to another **b :** the removal of tissue from one part of the body or from one individual and its implantation or insertion in another esp. by surgery ⟨corneal ~⟩ ⟨the ~ of lung tissue⟩

trans·plant·er *pronunc at* [1]TRANSPLANT + ə(r)\ *n* **:** one that transplants; *esp* **:** a machine for transplanting plants by making furrows or holes and watering each transplant as it is dropped

trans·polar \(ˈ)tranz, -raan-, -n(t)s+\ *adj* [*trans-* + *polar*] **:** going or extending across either of the polar regions ⟨~ passage⟩ ⟨~ air route⟩ ⟨~ warfare⟩

tran·spon·der *also* **tran·spon·dor** \tranzˈpändə(r), traan-, -n(t)ˈsp-\ *n* -s [*transponder*, fr. *trans*mitter + *res**ponder*; *transpondor*, alter. (influenced by *responsor*) of *transponder*] **:** a radio or radar set that upon receiving a designated signal usu. in the form of a coded series of pulses emits a radio signal of its own that may also be coded — compare INTERROGATOR

trans·pon·tine \(ˈ)tranz¦pän·ˌtīn, -n(t)¦sp-\ *adj* [*trans-* + L *pont-*, *pons* bridge + E *-ine* — more at FIND] **1 :** lying or situated on the other side of a bridge ⟨~ night life⟩ ⟨~ newspaper⟩ — opposed to *cispontine* **2 :** resembling or characteristic of a class of melodramas once popular in theaters of the part of London south of the Thames

[1]**trans·port** \tranzˈpō(ə)rt, traan-, -n(t)ˈsp-, -pȯ(ə)rt, -ōət, -ȯ(ə)t, ˈ=,=, *usu* -d·+V\ *vt* -ED/-ING/-S [ME *transporten*, fr. MF or L; MF *transporter*, fr. L *transportare*, fr. *trans-* + *portare* to carry — more at FARE] **1 :** to transfer or convey from one person or place to another **:** CARRY, MOVE ⟨on this vessel he ~*ed* a heavy load of ammunition —L.H.Bolander⟩ ⟨in the early days copper ore was ~*ed* in wagons —*Amer. Guide Series: Tenn.*⟩ ⟨will ~ the industry to a better competitive level —T.D. Rice⟩ ⟨endeavor to ~ ourselves into the position of a contemporary spectator —Roger Fry⟩ **2 :** to carry away with strong or intensely pleasurable emotion **:** INFLAME, ENRAPTURE ⟨his anger ~*s* him⟩ ⟨the test of greatness in a work of art is . . . that it ~*s* us —Herbert Read⟩ ⟨didn't realize that just a man and a red cloth and a bull could . . . ~ a person —Barnaby Conrad⟩ **3 :** to convey or cause to be conveyed into banishment usu. to a penal colony ⟨was eventually ~*ed* for stealing a gentleman's gold watch —Osbert Sitwell⟩ **4** *Scot* **a :** to transfer (a minister) to another charge **b :** to remove (a parish church) to another part of the parish **syn** see BANISH, CARRY

[2]**transport** \ˈ=,=\ *n* -s *often attrib* [ME, fr. *transporten* to transport] **1** *obs* **:** the conveyance of property **:** TRANSFER **2 a :** TRANSPORTATION 1a ⟨the arduous ~ . . . of three and a half tons of stores —*Brit. Bk. News*⟩ ⟨then came the ~ of the huge disk to California —David England⟩ ⟨it is maintained that ~ in large tanks affects the wine quality —G.G.Weigend⟩ **b :** TRANSPORTATION 1b **3 a :** the state of being moved by strong or intensely pleasurable emotion **:** FRENZY, ECSTASY, RAPTURE ⟨in a ~ at possessing . . . a fortune —G.B.Shaw⟩ ⟨each expressed . . . an authentic ~ of personal joy —C.E. Montague⟩ **b :** an instance or fit of such transport ⟨~*s* of delight —T.B.Macaulay⟩ ⟨~*s* of rage —Jane Austen⟩ ⟨a bitter cynicism has succeeded to ~*s* of pugnacious hatred —G.B. Shaw⟩ **4 a :** a ship used for carrying soldiers or military equipment and stores ⟨a fleet of warships sailed with accompanying ~*s* filled with troops⟩ ⟨served as a seaman on ~*s* in the Pacific —*Current Biog.*⟩ — compare FREIGHTER **b :** a truck, plane, or other vehicle used to carry persons or goods from one place to another ⟨impatient drivers will . . . try to get around long, slow-moving trucks or ~*s* —T.S.Smith⟩ ⟨jet prototype that could be used as a bomber or a ~ —Horace Sutton⟩ **c :** TRANSPORTATION 4b ⟨the economics of ~ will . . . dictate the kind of vehicle to be used —John Kemp⟩ ⟨one must understand the whole picture of ~ —N.J.Curry⟩; *also* **:** a system or organized means of public conveyance or travel **:** TRANSIT ⟨they work in factories and offices, use ~, and live in residential suburbs —Sybille Bedford⟩ ⟨this shortage of efficient ~ —John Kobler⟩ **5 :** a person who is transported or banished as a convict ⟨many early American settlers were ~*s*⟩ **6 :** an exchange of molecules or other particles together with their kinetic energy and momentum across the boundary between adjacent layers of a fluid **syn** see ECSTASY

trans·port·abil·i·ty \tranzˌpōr|d·əˈbiləd·ē, traan-, -n(t)ˌsp-, -pōə|, -pȯ(r)|, |təˈ- -lətē, -i\ *n* **:** the quality or state of being transportable

trans·port·able \tranzˈpōr|d·əbəl, traan-, -n(t)ˈsp-, -pōə|, -pȯ(r)|, |təb-\ *adj* **1 :** capable of being transported ⟨a tiny ~ organ —S.E.White⟩ **2** *chiefly Brit* **:** of, relating to, or incurring transportation or banishment ⟨committed a ~ crime⟩

trans·port·al \|d·ᵊl\ *n* -s [[1]*transport* + *-al*] **:** TRANSPORTATION

trans·por·ta·tion \ˌtranzpə(r)ˈtashən, ˌtraan-, -n(t)sp-\ *n* -s [L *transportat*us (past part. of *transportare* to transport) + E *-ion*] **1 a :** an act, process, or instance of transporting or being transported ⟨arranging for the ~ of his luggage⟩ ⟨~ of the troops overseas is accomplished by ships and planes⟩ **b :** the conveyance or movement of sediment or rock materials either as solid particles or in solution from one place to another on or near the earth's surface by water, ice, air, or gravity **2** *obs* **:** TRANSPORT 3 **3 :** banishment usu. to a penal colony — compare DEPORTATION ⟨was convicted and sentenced to ~ for life —Joseph Chiari⟩ **4 a :** means of conveyance or travel from one place to another ⟨his ~ is a battered coupé —*Phoenix Flame*⟩ ⟨cluttering up the road with ~ —G.S.Patton⟩; *also* **:** the cost of such means of conveyance or travel ⟨the state providing ~ for each child . . . to the extent of 70 cents per day —*Amer. Guide Series: Minn.*⟩ **b :** public conveyance of passengers, goods, or materials esp. as a commercial enterprise ⟨a single railroad . . . monopolizes all the railroad ~ through that valley —O.W.Holmes †1935⟩ ⟨nation whose very existence . . . depends on ~ —*Motor Transportation in the West*⟩

trans·por·ta·tion·al \¦==¦tāshənᵊl, -shnəl\ *adj* **:** of, relating to, or characteristic of transportation ⟨~ routes⟩ ⟨~ organization⟩ ⟨~ effect of eroding streams⟩

transportation insurance *n* **:** MARINE INSURANCE

trans·port·ed \(ˈ)tranz¦pōr|d·əd, -raan-, -n(t)¦sp-, -pȯr|, -ōə|, -ȯ(ə)|, |təd\ *adj* [fr. past part. of [1]*transport*] **1 :** carried or moved from one person or place to another: as **a :** condemned or sent into banishment usu. to a penal colony ⟨first seeing Australia as a ~ felon⟩ **b :** carried or moved along on or near the earth's surface by a natural force (as a river, ocean current, or glacier) ⟨~ clays⟩ ⟨~ soils⟩ **2 :** impassioned or enraptured by strong and usu. pleasurable emotion ⟨instantly he felt ~ from the sphere of his work —R.L.Cook⟩ — **trans·port·ed·ly** *adv*

trans·port·ee \¦tranzpōr¦tē, -n(t)sp-, -pȯr-\ *n* -s [[1]*transport* + *-ee*] **:** one who has been transported or banished as a convict

trans·port·er *pronunc at* [1]TRANSPORT + ə(r)\ *n* -s **:** one that transports or serves as a means of transportation; *specif* **:** any of various apparatus for moving loose material with dispatch esp. in loading or unloading ships

transporter bridge *n* **:** a bridge designed to span a navigable

transporter bridge

waterway between low shores and made of a high framework from which is suspended a car for carrying traffic back and forth

transporting *pres part of* TRANSPORT

trans·port·ive *pronunc at* ¹TRANSPORT + iv\ *adj* [¹*transport* + *-ive*] **:** tending to transport or to cause transports ⟨~ and triumphant thought —Nathaniel Hawthorne⟩

transport number *n* **:** TRANSFERENCE NUMBER

transport pilot *n* **:** a pilot licensed by the federal government to operate a transport plane

transports *pres 3d sing of* TRANSPORT, *pl of* TRANSPORT

trans·pos·abil·i·ty \tranz,pōzəˈbiləd·ē, -n(t),sp-\ *n* **:** the quality or state of being transposable

trans·pos·able \tranzˈpōzəbəl, traan-, -n(t)ˈsp-\ *adj* **:** capable of being transposed or interchanged

trans·pos·al \-ōzəl\ *n* -s [¹*transpose* + *-al*] **:** TRANSPOSITION

¹**trans·pose** \-ōz\ *vb* -ED/-ING/-s [ME *transposen*, fr. MF *transposer*, modif. (influenced by *poser* to put, place) of L *transponere* to change the position of, transfer (perfect stem *transpos-*), fr. *trans-* + *ponere* to put, place — more at POSITION, POSE] *vt* **1 :** to change in form or nature **:** TRANSFORM, TRANSMUTE — usu. used with *into* or *to* ⟨Jesus the revealer is *transposed* into a figurine in a manger —I.G.Whitchurch⟩ ⟨~*s* himself completely from the role of systematic philosopher into that of biblical theologian —Joyce Hertzler⟩ ⟨what command has conceived . . . these groups now ~ to action —*Target Germany*⟩ **2 :** to render into another language, style, or manner of expression **:** TRANSLATE — usu. used with *into* ⟨~*s* the Latin into English⟩ ⟨~*s* the verse into prose⟩ ⟨actual figures . . . are *transposed* into simple records which are kept by the client —*Jour. of Accountancy*⟩ **3** *obs* **:** to alter in use, significance, or intent **:** MISAPPLY, CORRUPT **4 :** to transfer from one place or period to another **:** SHIFT, REMOVE — usu. used with *to* or *into* ⟨with the advance of astronomy, the domicile of the Deity had been *transposed* to the unknown center of the universe —S.F.Mason⟩ ⟨items which had no place . . . were not *transposed* into the new situation —D.J. Lehmer⟩ **5 :** to change the relative place or normal order of **:** INTERCHANGE ⟨~*s* the letters to change the spelling⟩ ⟨had *transposed* economy and security in his table of priorities —*Atlantic*⟩ **6 :** to write or perform (a musical composition) in a different key with consequent raising or lowering of pitch **7 :** to bring (as a term of an algebraic equation) from one side to the other with the corresponding change of its sign **8 :** to cause (the wires of a telegraph or telephone circuit) to cross at intervals to eliminate the effect of induction from neighboring wires or noise-making disturbances (as lightning) ~ *vi* **:** to transpose something, esp. a musical composition ⟨is learning to ~ with ease and skill⟩

²**transpose** \"\ *n* -s **:** TRANSPOSITION

transposing instrument *n* [*transposing* (pres. part. of ¹*transpose*) + *instrument*] **1 :** a musical instrument that sounds pitches different from those indicated by the notation **2 :** an instrument with a shifting keyboard for mechanically causing the music to sound in a different key

trans·po·si·tion \,tranzpəˈzishən, ,traan-, -n(t)sp-\ *n* -s [ML *transposition-*, *transpositio*, fr. L *transpositus* (past part. of *transponere* to transpose) + *-ion-*, *-io* -ion] **:** an act, process, or instance of transposing or being transposed: as **a :** transfer or removal from one place or time to another — usu. used with *into* or *to* ⟨the . . . ~ of the sentiments of the novel and its age into a different setting and a different period —Martin Turnell⟩ **b** (1) **:** a change or interchange in order or place esp. of letters or words **:** METATHESIS ⟨Latin admits the ~ of words more readily than English⟩ (2) **:** the rearrangement of the letters of a message in cryptography **c** (1) **:** a change of a musical composition or passage into another key (2) **:** a composition or passage so transposed **d** (1) **:** the transfer of any term of an equation from one side over to the other side with a corresponding change of the sign (2) **:** a mathematical permutation or interchange of two letters or symbols **e :** the displacement of a viscus to a side opposite from that which it normally occupies ⟨~ of the heart⟩ **f :** CONTRAPOSITION 2 **g :** the process of reversing the tonal or density values of a photographic image **h :** REARRANGEMENT 2

trans·po·si·tion·al \¦==¦zishənᵊl, -shnəl\ *adj* **:** of, relating to, or involving transposition

transposition cipher *n* **:** CIPHER 2a(2)

trans·prose \tranz, traanz, -n(t)s+\ *vt* [*trans-* + *prose*] *archaic* **:** to change from verse into prose

trans·rational \(ˈ)tran(t)s, -raan-, -nz+\ *adj* [*trans-* + *rational*] **:** going beyond or surpassing human reason or the rational ⟨an ultramundane and ~ Creator —J.A.Martin⟩

trans·rectification \¦tran(t)s, -raan-, -nz+\ *n* [*trans-* + *rectification*] **:** the rectification taking place in the circuit of one electrode of a vacuum tube when an alternating voltage is applied to another electrode

trans·rhe·nane \¦tran(t)srēˌnān, -nzr-; tran(t)sˈrēˌnān, -nz'-, -reˌ-\ *adj* [L *transrhenanus*, fr. *trans-* + *Rhenus* the Rhine, river of western Europe + *-anus* -an] **:** situated or lying on the other side of the Rhine; *specif* **:** GERMAN — opposed to *cisrhenane*

trans·seg·men·tal \¦tranzseg¦mentᵊl, -n(t)sseg-, -nseg-\ *adj* [*trans-* + *segment* + *-al*] **:** extending across or beyond the limits of a body segment or segmental part

trans·shape \tranz, traanz, -n(t)s-, -nch+\ *also* **tran·shape** \tran, traan+\ *vt* [*trans-* + *shape*] **:** to change into another shape or form **:** TRANSFORM

trans·ship \"+\ *also* **tran·ship** \"+\ *vb* [*trans-* + *ship*] *vt* **:** to transfer for further transportation from one ship or conveyance to another ⟨sailed . . . in the *Speedwell* for Plymouth, England, where they *transshipped* to the larger *Mayflower* —Ralph Hammond-Innes⟩ ⟨the river steamer into which the . . . cargo had been *transshipped* —F.V.W.Mason⟩ ⟨about half this tonnage is *transshipped* by boat, truck, rail, and plane ~ *vi* **:** to change from one ship or conveyance to another ⟨men were *transshipping* from the . . . trucks to lorries and wagons —F.W.Crofts⟩

trans·ship·ment \"+mənt\ *also* **tran·ship·ment** \"+mənt\ *n* [*transship* + *-ment*] **:** the act or process of transshipping

trans–sonic *var of* TRANSONIC

trans·subjective \¦tranz, -raanz, -n(t)s+\ *adj* [*trans-* + *subjective*] **:** of, relating to, or being in a state of existence independent of an individual mind or mode of thinking though not necessarily independent of the modes of thought common to all men **:** objective in universal rather than individual experience ⟨concepts are necessarily ~, for they are of universal validity —Alfred Stern⟩

trans·temporal \(ˈ)tranz, -raanz, -n(t)s+\ *adj* [*trans-* + *temporal*] **:** crossing the temporal lobe of the cerebrum

trans·tracheal \"+\ *adj* [*trans-* + *trachea* + *-al*] **:** extending or effected through the trachea ⟨~ anesthesia⟩

tran·sub·stan·tial \¦transəb¦stanchəl, -raan-, -bˈst-, -taan-, -tain-\ *adj* [ML *transubstantiare* to transubstantiate + E *-al*] **:** changed or capable of being changed from one substance to another — **tran·sub·stan·tial·ly** \-chəlē\ *adv*

tran·sub·stan·ti·ate \,==ˈtanchē,āt, -bˈst-, -taan-, -tain-, *usu* -ād·+V\ *vb* -ED/-ING/-s [ML *transubstantiatus*, past part. of *transubstantiare*, fr. L *trans-* + *substantia* substance] *vt* **1 :** to change into another substance **:** TRANSFORM, TRANSMUTE — usu. used with *into* or *to* ⟨the ancient alchemists hoped to ~ base metals into gold⟩ ⟨the content of experience is not merely shuffled by the poet but is . . . *transubstantiated* —Eliseo Vivas⟩ **2 :** to change (the eucharistic elements of bread and wine) into the body and blood of Christ according to the doctrine esp. of the Roman Catholic Church ⟨after the consecration . . . the bread is transmuted, *transubstantiated*, converted, and transformed into the true body itself of the Lord —R.M. French⟩ ~ *vi* **:** to undergo transubstantiation ⟨at what words and moment do the bread and wine ~ —Valentine Ughet & Eleanor Davis⟩

tran·sub·stan·ti·a·tion \,==,==ˈāshən\ *also* **trans·sub·stan·ti·a·tion** \-nzsəb-, -n(t)ssəb-\ *n* [ME, fr. ML *transubstantiation-*, *transubstantiatio*; fr. *transubstantiatus* + L *-ion-*, *-io*, -ion] **:** an act, process, or instance of transubstantiating or being transubstantiated; *specif* **:** the change in the eucharistic elements at their consecration in the Roman Catholic mass from the substance of bread and wine to the substance of the body and blood of Christ with only the accidents (as taste, color, shape, and smell) of the bread and wine remaining — distinguished from *consubstantiation*; compare TRANSACCIDENTATION

tran·su·date \ˈtran(t)sə,dāt\ *n* -s [NL *transudatus*, past part. of *transudare* to transude] **:** a product of transudation

tran·su·da·tion \,==ˈdāshən\ *n* -s [NL *transudation-*, *transudatio*, fr. *transudatus* + L *-ion-*, *-io* -ion] **1 :** the act or process of transuding or being transuded **2 :** TRANSUDATE

tran·su·da·tive \tranˈsüdəd·iv\ *adj* [NL *transudatus* + E *-ive*] **:** of, relating to, or constituting transudation or a transudate

tran·sude \tranˈsüd, traan-\ *vb* -ED/-ING/-s [NL *transudare*, fr. L *trans-* + *sudare* to sweat, perspire — more at SWEAT] *vi* **:** to pass through a membrane or permeable substance **:** EXUDE ⟨the serum of the blood has not *transuded* into the lung tissue proper —Robert Chawner⟩ ⟨a hand . . . squeezed and unsqueezed a blob of mud which *transuded* from the cracks of his fist —J.R.Guss⟩ ~ *vt* **:** to cause to pass through **:** permit passage of **:** EXUDE ⟨the capillary wall ~*s* fluids and dissolved matter into the tissue spaces⟩

tran·sumpt \-səm(p)t\ *n* -s [ME, fr. ML *transumptum*, fr. neut. of *transumptus*, past part. of *transumere* to transcribe, fr. L, to take from one to another] *Scot* **:** a copy of a writing or legal document; *esp* **:** an exemplified copy

tran·sump·tion \-(p)shən\ *n* -s [ML *transumption-*, *transumptio* transcription, fr. L, transferal of terms, fr. *transumptus* (past part. of *transumere* to take from one to another, fr. *trans-* + *sumere* to take, fr. *sub-* up + *emere* to take) + *-ion-*, *-io* -ion — more at SUB-, REDEEM] **:** an act, process, or instance of making a copy ⟨only experts could read the original, a ~ in the ordinary hand —H.W.Smith⟩

tran·sump·tive \-(p)tiv\ *adj* [L *transumptivus*, fr. *transumptus* + *-ivus* -ive] **:** of, relating to, or characterized by the transfer or substitution of terms **:** METAPHORICAL ⟨the ~ power of poetry —R.P.Blackmur⟩

trans–uranian \¦tran(t)s, -raan-, -nz+\ *adj, usu cap U* [*trans-* + *Uranus*, planet between Saturn and Neptune + E *-ian*] **:** extending or lying beyond the orbit of the planet Uranus

trans·u·ra·ni·um \¦tran(t)syə¦rānēəm, ¦raan-, -nz-\ *or* **trans·u·ran·ic** \-¦ranik\ *also* **trans·u·ra·ni·an** \-¦rānēən\ *adj* [*transuranium* fr. *trans-* + *uranium*; *transuranic*, ISV *trans-* + *uranium* + *-ic*; *transuranian*, ISV *trans-* + *uranium* + *-an*] **:** having an atomic number greater than that of uranium ⟨the known ~ elements belong to the actinide series⟩

trans·urethral \"+\ *adj* [ISV *trans-* + *urethra* + *-al*] **:** extending or effected through the urethra ⟨~ prostatectomy⟩ ⟨~ manipulation⟩

transv *abbr* transverse

trans·vaal daisy \(ˈ)tran(t)s¦väl-, -raan-, -nz¦-\ *n, usu cap T* [fr. *Transvaal*, province of northeast Union of So. Africa] **:** a widely cultivated southern African perennial herb (*Gerbera jamesoni*) having flower heads with orange to flame-colored strap-shaped rays — called also *Barberton daisy*

trans·val·u·ate \tran(t)sˈvalyə,wāt, traan-, -nzˈ-\ *vt* [back-formation fr. *transvaluation*] **:** TRANSVALUE

trans·val·u·a·tion \(,)==,==ˈwāshən\ *n* [*trans-* + *valuation*] **:** the act or process of transvaluing or altering the value or worth placed on something ⟨in his ~ of values, sought to do away with this Christian ethic and return to pagan standards —Grace Foster⟩ ⟨rebellion . . . involves a genuine ~ where the direct or vicarious experience of frustration leads to full denunciation of previously prized values —R.K.Merton⟩

trans·value \=ˈval,yü\ *vt* [*trans-* + *value*] **:** to value on a different basis and esp. one that repudiates conventional or accepted standards **:** REEVALUATE ⟨war ~*s* all values —Curtis Bradford⟩ ⟨psychoanalysis . . . has not only permeated and *transvalued* the mental sciences, but indirectly also belles lettres —A.A.Brill⟩

trans·vase \tran(t)sˈvās, -nzˈ-\ *vt* -ED/-ING/-s [F *transvaser*, fr. OF, fr. L *trans-* + *vas* vessel, vase] **:** to pour out of one vessel into another ⟨~*s* the water⟩

¹**trans·ver·sal** \(ˈ)tran(t)s¦vərsəl, -raan-, -nz¦-, -vōs-, -vəis-\ *adj* [ME, fr. ML *transversalis*, fr. L *transversus* transverse + *-alis* -al] **:** extending or lying across **:** TRANSVERSE ⟨a ~ line⟩ ⟨~ vibrations⟩ — **trans·ver·sal·ly** \-səlē, -li\ *adv*

²**transversal** \"\ *n* -s **:** a line that traverses or intersects a system of lines (as the sides of a triangle) or the sides produced

trans·ver·sale \¦träⁿsver¦säl\ *adj* [F, fem. of *transversal*, fr. ML *transversalis*] **:** placed so as to include three numbers in a row horizontally — used of a bet in roulette

trans·ver·sa·lis \,tran(t)svə(r)ˈsaləs, -raan-, -nzv-, -ˈsāl-, -ˈsäl-\ *n* -ES [NL, fr. ML, transversal] **:** any of several transverse bodily parts (as muscles or arteries) — usu. used with an orienting term ⟨~ abdominis⟩

trans·ver·sa·ry \tran(t)sˈvərsərē, -nzˈ-\ *n* -ES [L *transversarium* crossbeam, fr. neut. of *transversarius* situated transversely, fr. L *transversus* transverse + *-arius* -ary] **:** a crosspiece on a nautical cross-staff

¹**trans·verse** \tran(t)sˈvərs, traan-, -nzˈ-, -ˈvōs, -ˈvəis\ *vt* -ED/-ING/-s [ME *transversen*, fr. MF *transverser*, fr. LL *transversare* to cross, fr. L *transversus* transverse] **1 :** to lie or pass across **:** CROSS ⟨the artery ~*s* the bone⟩ **2** *archaic* **:** to go counter to **:** OPPOSE, TRAVERSE **3 :** OVERTURN, REVERSE ⟨~ the saying⟩ **4** *obs* **:** ALTER, TRANSFORM

²**transverse** \(ˈ)=¦=\ *adj* [L *transversus*, fr. past part. of *transvertere* to turn or direct across, fr. *trans-* + *vertere* to turn — more at WORTH] **:** extended or lying across or in a crosswise direction ⟨from the ~ hall, the stairway ascends gracefully —*Amer. Guide Series: Va.*⟩ ⟨uses ~ leaf springs set perpendicular to the axle⟩ ⟨the ~ strokes in the letter K⟩ — opposed to *longitudinal*

³**transverse** \"\ *n* -s **:** something (as a piece, muscle, or part) that is transverse or athwart; *specif* **:** TRANSEPT

⁴**transverse** \"\ *adv, archaic* **:** TRANSVERSELY

⁵**transverse** \=¦=\ *vt* [*trans-* + *verse*] **:** to turn or render into verse **:** VERSIFY

transverse artery *n* [²*transverse*] **:** one of the small branches of the basilar artery supplying the pons and adjacent parts

transverse axis *n* **:** the axis through the foci of a conic and esp. of a hyperbola

transverse bone *n* **:** a bone connecting the pterygoid and maxilla in some reptiles and forming part of the apparatus for erecting the fangs in various snakes

transverse carpal ligament *n* **:** a dense transverse band of fibers passing over flexor tendons at the wrist

transverse colon *n* **:** the middle portion of the colon that extends across the abdominal cavity — see DIGESTION illustration

transverse crevasse *n* **:** a crevasse that commonly opens across a glacier where the slope of its floor abruptly steepens

transverse crural ligament *n* **:** a transverse band of fibers passing over the extensor tendons above the ankle

transverse dihedral *n* **:** DIHEDRAL 2

transverse facial artery *n* **:** a branch of the superficial temporal artery that supplies the parotid gland, masseter muscle, and adjacent parts

transverse facial vein *n* **:** a vein of the side of the face tributary to the temporal vein

transverse fault *n* **:** an extended dip fault

transverse fissure *n* **1 :** the cleft below the hemispheres of the brain through which the pia mater extends to form the choroid plexuses **2 :** a cleft of the liver **3 :** a fracture that starts at a crystalline center inside a railhead and spreads outward

transverse flute *n* **:** the modern flute — compare RECORDER 3a

transverse framing *n* **:** a system of ship construction in which the frames are closely spaced to furnish most of the strength to the ship's structure — opposed to *Isherwood system*

transverse joint *n* **:** the metatarsal joint

transverse ligament *n* **:** any of various ligaments: as **a :** one that crosses between the greater and lesser tubercles of the humerus **b :** the transverse part of the cruciate ligament of the atlas **c :** one crossing the notch in the lower border of the acetabulum **d :** one connecting the digital ends of the metatarsal bones in the sole of the foot **e :** CORACOID LIGAMENT

trans·verse·ly *adv* [²*transverse* + *-ly*] **:** in a transverse direction or line **:** CROSSWISE, ATHWART

transverse mass *n* **:** the ratio of the accelerating force to the acceleration when the acceleration is perpendicular to the line of motion

trans·verse·ness *n* -ES **:** the quality or state of being transverse

transverse process *n* **:** a lateral process of a vertebra: **a :** DIAPOPHYSIS **b :** PARAPOPHYSIS

trans·vers·er \-sə(r)\ *n* -s [¹*transverse* + *-er*] **1 :** one that transverses **2 :** PLANE TABLE

transverse rib *n* [²*transverse*] **:** a rib in a vaulting that crosses a nave or aisle at right angles to the long axis of the building

transverse sinus *n* **:** either of two large venous sinuses of the cranium that begin at the internal occipital protuberance and terminate at the jugular foramen on either side to become the internal jugular vein — called also *lateral sinus*

transverse suture *n* **:** the suture between the frontal and facial bones

transverse table *n* **:** TRANSFER TABLE

transverse vein *n* **:** CROSSVEIN 2

transverse vibration *n* **:** a vibration in which the element moves to and fro in a direction perpendicular to the direction of the advance of the wave

transverse wave *n* **:** a wave in which the vibrating element (as the electric field in light waves or the particles of a vibrating medium) moves in a direction perpendicular to the direction in which the wave advances

trans·ver·sion \tran(t)sˈvərzhən, -nzˈ-\ *n* -s [L *transversus* (past part. of *transvertere* to turn or direct across) + E *-ion* — more at TRANSVERSE] **:** an act, process, or instance of transversing

trans·ver·sum \tran(t)sˈvərsəm, -nzˈ-\ *n* -s [NL, fr. L, neut. of *transversus* transverse] **:** the transverse bone of a reptile's skull

trans·ver·sus \-rsəs\ *n, pl* **transver·si** \-r,sī\ [NL, fr. L, transverse] **:** a transversalis muscle — often used in combination

transversus ab·dom·i·nis \-əbˈdämənəs\ *n* [NL, lit., transversus of the abdomen] **:** a flat muscle with transverse fibers that forms the innermost layer of the anterolateral wall of the abdomen and ends in a broad aponeurosis which joins that of the opposite side at the linea alba with its upper three fourths passing behind the rectus abdominis muscle and the lower fourth in front of it

trans·vert·er \tran(t)sˈvərd·ə(r), -nzˈ-\ *n* -s [L *transvertere* + E *-er*] **:** a machine that consists of a fixed transformer, commutator, and brushes which revolve at synchronous speed and by which a three-phase alternating current can be converted into a direct current at one end of the line and reconverted into a three-phase alternating current at the terminal point

trans·ves·tic \tran(t)sˈvestik, traan-, -nzˈ-, -tēk\ *adj* [*transvestism* + *-ic*] **:** of, relating to, or characterized by transvestism ⟨patients with ~ tendencies —*Jour. Amer. Med. Assoc.*⟩

trans·ves·tism \-e,stizəm\ *also* **trans·ves·ti·tism** \-estə,tizəm\ *n* -s [*transvestism* fr. G *transvestismus*, fr. L *trans-* + *vestire* to clothe + G *-ismus* -ism, fr. L; *transvestitism* fr. G *transvestitismus*, fr. *transvestit* transvestite + *-ismus* — more at VEST] **:** the practice of adopting the dress, the manner, and frequently the sexual role of the opposite sex

¹**trans·ves·tite** \-e,stīt, *usu* -īd·+V\ *n* -s [G *transvestit*, fr. L *trans-* + *vestitus*, past part. of *vestire* to clothe] **:** one who practices transvestism

²**transvestite** \"\ *adj* **:** addicted to wearing garments of the other sex

¹**tran·syl·va·nian** \¦tran(t)səl¦vānyən, -raan-, -nēən\ *adj, usu cap* [*Transylvania*, region of northwest & central Romania + E *-an*] **1 :** of, relating to, or characteristic of Transylvania **2 :** of, relating to, or characteristic of the people of Transylvania

²**transylvanian** \"\ *n* -s *cap* **:** a native or inhabitant of Transylvania

trant \ˈtrant, ˈtränt\ *vi* [back-formation fr. *tranter*] *dial Eng* **:** to work as a tranter

trant·er \-tə(r)\ *n* -s [alter. of earlier *trauenter*, *traunter*, fr. ML *travetarius*, perh. fr. L *transvectus* (past part. of *transvehere* to carry across, transport, fr. *trans-* + *vehere* to carry) + *-arius* -ary — more at WAY] *dial Eng* **:** one that does odd jobs of transporting or peddling usu. with a horse and cart

trant·lum \ˈtrantləm\ *n* [origin unknown] *dial Brit* **:** TRIFLE, TRINKET — usu. used in pl.

tranz·sche·lia \tran(z)ˈshēlēə\ *n, cap* [NL, fr. *Tranzschel*, prob. a surname + NL *-ia*] **:** a genus of rusts (family Pucciniaceae) with 2-celled teliospores resembling those of the genus *Puccinia* but with two or more attached to a common stalk

¹**trap** \ˈtrap\ *n* -s [ME *trap*, *trappe*, fr. OE *treppe*, *træppe* & OF *trape* (of Gmc origin); akin to MD *trappe* trap, step, stairs, MHG *trappe*, *treppe* step, stairs, MLG & MD *trappen* to stamp, OE *treppan* to tread, Lith *drebėti* to shake, quiver, Skt *dravati* he runs, melts; basic meaning: running, tripping] **1 a :** a device (as a pitfall, snare, or clamp that springs shut suddenly) for taking game or destructive animals **:** GIN ⟨sets his ~*s* along the river⟩ ⟨caught like a rat in a ~⟩ **b** (1) **:** FISH TRAP (2) **:** LOBSTER POT **c :** TRAP CROP **2 :** something by which one is unsuspectingly or deceptively caught or stopped in an action or progress ⟨the Indians could be superb fighters . . . adepts at ~*s* and ambushes —Seth Agnew⟩ ⟨prepared defensive ~*s* for his opponent's attacks —G.A.Craig⟩ ⟨with ~*s* and obstacles . . . confronting us on every hand —B.N.Cardozo⟩ ⟨expensive ~*s* for ignorant tourists —Ann Leighton⟩ **3 a** (1) **:** a hinged or collapsible door or cover of an enclosed space or pit designed to give way when walked on (2) **:** DROP 3c **b :** any of various covered openings constructed in the floor of a stage for the passage of persons or scenery; *also* **:** a device or machinery used to effect such a passage **4 a** (1) **:** a wooden instrument used in playing trapball and consisting of a pivoted arm on one end of which is placed the ball to be thrown into the air by striking the other end (2) **:** a similar device used in knur and spell **b :** a device for hurling clay pigeons into the air **c :** SAND TRAP 2 **d :** the act or an instance of stopping or catching a ball close to or against the ground **e :** MOUSETRAP 2a **f :** ²TILT 6 **g :** a piece of leather webbing laced between the thumb and forefinger of a baseball glove to form a pocket for receiving the ball **5 a** *Brit* **:** DECEIT, TRICKERY ⟨a clever, ready-witted fellow, up to all sorts of ~ —Samuel Lover⟩ **b** *Brit* **:** POLICEMAN, DETECTIVE **c** *slang* **:** MOUTH ⟨shut your ~ and listen —Richard Llewellyn⟩ **6 :** a light often sporty 2- or 4-wheeled horse-drawn carriage accommodating usu. 2 to 4 persons in various seating arrangements (as face-to-face or back-to-back) **7 :** any of various devices for preventing the passage of something often while allowing other matter to proceed: as **a :** a device for drains or sewers consisting of a bend or partitioned chamber in which the liquid forms a seal to prevent the passage of sewer gas **b :** STEAM TRAP **c :** a device to separate sand and silt from flowing water **d :** a place in a water pipe or pump where something (as an air pocket) is held or retained **e :** a device to catch mercury or amalgam escaping from amalgamation plates **f :** a usu. sharply tuned circuit consisting of either conventional coils and condensers or transmission lines to eliminate an unwanted signal **g :** a site of imperfection in the crystal structure of a solid at which otherwise mobile electrons and holes can be confined or trapped often more or less temporarily **8 :** SMASH 2b **9 a :** a percussion instrument — usu. used in pl. ⟨likes to play the ~*s*⟩ ⟨has a set of ~*s*⟩ **b traps** *pl* **:** the group of percussion instruments esp. in a dance or theater orchestra **10 :** the degree to which printing ink will trap ⟨the sample definitely indicates poor ~ . . . due to improper tackiness of the inks, one printing over the other —*Graphic Arts Monthly*⟩

²**trap** \"\ *vb* **trapped** *or archaic* **trapt**; **trapped** *or archaic* **trapt**; **trapping**; **traps** [ME *trappen*, fr. *trap*, *trappe* trap] *vt* **1 a :** to catch or take in or as if in a trap or snare by skill, craft, or trickery **:** ENTRAP, ENSNARE ⟨~*s* muskrats in the fall of the year⟩ ⟨~ wasps in a jar containing beer and treacle —F.D. Smith & Barbara Wilcox⟩ ⟨*trapped* him . . . by forcing him to follow her into her home —Harrison Smith⟩ ⟨avoids the danger of being *trapped* upon cross-examination —Paul Wilson⟩ **b :** to place (as a person) in a restricted or difficult position **:** CONFINE, ENTANGLE ⟨the crash tools . . . useful in freeing persons *trapped* or imprisoned in a wrecked airplane —H.G.Armstrong⟩ ⟨those with food . . . share with the utterly *trapped* —Wallace Stegner⟩ ⟨*trapped* in a series of events over which he has no control —William Murray⟩ ⟨a story of people *trapped* in a criminal situation through their weakness rather than sin —David Dempsey⟩ — sometimes used with *into* ⟨his reliance on feeling . . . frequently *trapped* him into absurdities and muddleheadedness —F.B.Millett⟩ **c :** to induce (an opponent) usu. by passing to bid or bet unwisely in a card game **2 :** to provide or set (a place) with traps: as **a :** to set (a place or area) with traps to catch an animal or a person ⟨had a permit from the mortgage company to ~ its lands —H.L.

Davis⟩ ⟨has the place *trapped* with all sorts of burglar alarms —Erle Stanley Gardner⟩ **b :** to install a trap in (as a drain) ⟨the law usually requires that drains be *trapped*⟩ **c :** to construct traps on (as a golf course) ⟨the greens are heavily *trapped* —*New Yorker*⟩ **3 :** to separate out : STOP, HOLD ⟨these mountains ~ rains and fogs generated over the ocean —*Amer. Guide Series: Calif.*⟩ ⟨a scheme which ~*s* sunlight and turns it into motive power —*English Digest*⟩ **4 a :** to stop or catch (as a soccer ball or baseball) immediately after a bounce **b :** to catch (as a base runner) off base ⟨~*s* many runners with his quick pick-off throw⟩ **c :** MOUSETRAP ⟨one of the big problems we had on offense was *trapping* the guards — Bob Hicks⟩ **5 :** to accept (superimposed ink often of another color) during a subsequent printing **6 :** TRAPNEST ~ *vi* **1 :** to set traps for game; *also* **:** to make a business of trapping animals ⟨began to ~ for a living —R.L.Neuberger⟩ **2 :** to become trapped (as steam in a radiator) **3 :** to employ tactics in a card game designed to trap another player **syn** see CATCH

3trap \"\ *n* -S [ME *trappe*, modif. (prob. influenced by OSp *trapo* cloth, modif. of LL *drappus*) of MF *drap* cloth — more at DRAB] **1** *obs* **:** an ornamented cloth covering esp. for a horse **:** TRAPPING — usu. used in pl. **2 traps** *pl* **:** personal belongings **:** GOODS, LUGGAGE ⟨put our little household ~*s* into a freight car and went back —W.A.White⟩

4trap *vt* **trapped; trapped; trapping; traps** [ME *trappen*, fr. *trappe* cloth, trap] **:** to clothe or provide with or as if with traps or trappings **:** CAPARISON ⟨horse *trapped* for battle — P.H.Davis⟩ ⟨wrapped and *trapped* in their accouterments — Bruce Marshall⟩ ⟨feathers in which she has *trapped* out that idea —*Irish Digest*⟩

5trap \"\ *also* **traprock** \ˈ=,=\ *n* -S [*trap* fr. Sw *trapp*, fr. *trappa* stair, fr. MLG *trappe*; akin to MD *trappe* step, stair; *traprock* fr. *5trap* + *rock*; fr. its occurring in sheetlike masses that rise above one another like steps — more at TRAP (snare)] **1 :** any of various dark-colored fine-grained igneous rocks (as basalt or amygdaloid) used esp. in road making **2 :** an arrangement of rock strata involving their structural relations or varied lithology and texture that favors the accumulation of oil and gas

6trap \"\ *n* -S [D, fr. MD *trappe*] *Scot* **:** a movable flight of steps **:** STEPLADDER

trapa \ˈtrāpə, -rapə\ *n, cap* [NL, prob. short for (assumed) ML *calcitrappa* caltrop — more at CALTROP] **:** a small Old World genus of aquatic herbaceous plants with finely dissected submerged leaves, rhombic floating leaves that have inflated spongy petioles, and solitary white flowers followed by horned or spiny fruits — see TRAPACEAE, WATER CHESTNUT

tra·pa·ce·ae \trəˈpāsē,ē\ *n pl, cap* [NL, fr. *Trapa*, type genus + *-aceae*] *in some classifications* **:** a family of dicotyledonous plants (order Myrtales) that contains solely the genus *Trapa* and that is commonly treated as a subfamily or tribe of Onagraceae

trapball \ˈ=,=\ *n* **:** an old game of ball played with a trap; *also* **:** the ball used in the game

trap brilliant \ˈtrap-\ *n* [*trap* prob. fr. D, step, fr. MD — more at TRAP (snare)] **:** DOUBLE BRILLIANT

trap car *n* [*1trap*] **:** a railroad car used for less-than-carload shipments usu. within terminal or city limits **:** FERRY CAR

trap crop *n* **:** a crop planted to attract noxious insects or other pests so that they may be destroyed to prevent damage to nearby or later crops

trap cut *n* [*trap* prob. fr. D, step] **:** STEP CUT

trapdoor \ˈ=ˈ=\ *n* [ME *trappe dor*, fr. *trappe* trap + *dor* door — more at TRAP (snare), DOOR] **1 :** a lifting or sliding door covering an opening in a roof, ceiling, or floor **2 :** a ventilating door in a level of a mine — called also *weather door*

trap-door spider \ˈ=,=-\ *n* **:** any of various often large burrowing spiders esp. of the family Ctenizidae that construct a tubular subterranean silk-lined nest topped with a hinged lid

trap drum *n* **:** the bass drum in a set of traps to which are attached the various rhythm devices (as cymbal and block)

trap drummer *n* **:** a performer on traps

trapes *var of* TRAIPSE

1tra·peze \(ˈ)traˈpēz *sometimes* trəˈp-\ *n* -S [F *trapèze*, fr. NL *trapezium*] **:** a gymnastic or acrobatic apparatus consisting of a short horizontal bar suspended by two parallel ropes

2trapeze \"\ *vi* -ED/-ING/-S **:** to perform or act on or as if on a trapeze ⟨hedges intertwined with crimson flowers, among which . . . birds were *trapezing* —Malcolm Lowry⟩ ⟨legal scholars *trapezing* around in cycles . . . without coming to rest on the floor of fact —F.S.Cohen⟩

trapeze artist *n* **:** a usu. professional performer on the trapeze

tra·pe·zi·al \traˈpēzēəl *sometimes* trəˈp-\ *adj* **:** of or relating to a trapezium or trapezius

tra·pe·zi·form \-zə,fȯrm\ *adj* [prob. fr. (assumed) NL *trapeziformis*, fr. *trapezium* + L *-iformis* -iform] **:** having the form of a trapezium

tra·pez·ist \-zəst\ *n* -S **:** TRAPEZE ARTIST

tra·pe·zi·um \-zēəm\ *n, pl* **trapeziums** \-ēəmz\ *or* **trape·zia** \-ēə\ [NL, fr. Gk *trapezion* small table, trapezium, dim. of *trapeza* table, fr. *tra-* four (akin to Gk *tettares* four) + *peza* foot; akin to Gk *pod-, pous* foot — more at FOUR, FOOT] **1 a :** a quadrilateral having no two sides parallel **b** *Brit* **:** TRAPEZOID 1b **2 :** the greater multangulum of the carpus

trapezium 1

tra·pe·zi·us \-zēəs\ *n* -ES [NL, fr. *trapezium*; fr. the pair on the back forming together the figure of a trapezium] **:** a large flat triangular superficial muscle of each side of the back that arises from the occipital bone, ligamentum nuchae, and the spinous processes of the last cervical and all the thoracic vertebrae, is inserted into the outer part of the clavicle, the acromion, and the spine of the scapula, and serves chiefly to rotate the scapula so as to present the glenoid cavity upward

trape·zo·he·dral \traˌpēzōˈhēdrəl, trəˌpēz-, ˌtrapəz- *sometimes chiefly Brit* -hed-\ *adj* [NL *trapezohedron* + E *-al*] **:** of, relating to, or resembling a trapezohedron

trape·zo·he·dron \-drən, -rōn\ *n, pl* **trapezohedrons** \-nz\ *or* **trapezohe·dra** \-drə\ [NL, fr. *trapezium* + *-o-* + *-hedron*] **:** a crystalline form whose faces are trapeziums: **a :** a tetragonal trisoctahedron **b :** an 8-faced hemihedral form of the tetragonal system **c :** a 12-faced hemihedral form of the hexagonal system **d :** a 6-faced tetartohedral form of the hexagonal system — called also *trigonal trapezohedron*

trapezohedron a

1trap·e·zoid \ˈtrapə,zȯid\ *n* -S [NL *trapezoides*, fr. Gk *trapezoeidēs* trapezium-shaped, fr. *trapeza* table + *-oeidēs* -oid] **1 a** *Brit* **:** TRAPEZIUM 1a **b :** a quadrilateral having only two sides parallel **2 :** the lesser multangulum of the carpus

2trapezoid \"\ *adj* **:** of, relating to, or having the form of a trapezoid; *sometimes* **:** TRAPEZIAL

trap·e·zoi·dal \ˌ=ˈzȯid³l\ *adj* [*1trapezoid* + *-al*] **1 :** TRAPEZOID **2 :** TRAPEZOHEDRAL

trapezoidal projection *n* **:** a projection in which straight parallels and straight converging meridians divide the field into trapezoids

trapezoidal rule *n* **:** an approximate rule for determining the area under a curve

trapezoidal thread *n* **:** BUTTRESS THREAD

trapezoid body *n* **:** a bundle of transverse fibers in the dorsal part of the pons

trapfall \ˈ=,=\ *n* [*1trap* + *fall*] **:** TRAP, PITFALL

trap gun *n* **:** a shotgun designed for trapshooting

trap house *n* **:** the enclosure from which clay targets are released in trapshooting and skeet shooting — see HIGH-HOUSE, LOW-HOUSE

tra·pi·che \trəˈpēchē\ *n* -S [Sp, fr. L *trapetes* oil mill, olive mill, fr. Gk *trapētēs* wine presser, fr. *trapein* to press grapes — more at TREPIDATION] **1 :** a sugar mill; *also* **:** a sugar plantation **2 :** a rude mill for grinding ores or minerals

traplight \ˈ=,=\ *n* **:** any of several devices using a light to trap or collect insects

trapline \ˈ=,=\ *n* **:** a line or series of traps; *also* **:** the route along which such a line of traps is set

trap load *n* **:** the charge of powder and shot best adapted for trapshooting; *also* **:** a shotshell loaded for trapshooting

1trapnest \ˈ=,=\ *n* **:** a nest equipped with a hinged door designed to trap and confine a hen so that individual egg production may be determined

2trapnest \"\ *vt* **:** to determine the productivity of (individual domestic fowls) by means of a trapnest

trap net *n* **:** FISH TRAP, POUND NET

trapped *past of* TRAP

trapper \ˈtrapə(r)\ *n* -S [*2trap* + *-er*] **1 :** one that traps: as **a :** one whose business is trapping animals for furs or food or for sale alive **b :** one that traps fish **2 :** a boy who attends to the opening and closing of ventilation doors in a mine **3 :** one that manages a trap for trapshooting **4 :** a horse that draws a trap **5** *Brit* **:** a pointsman who points or switches trucks or cars into a siding

1trap·ping \ˈtrapiŋ, -pēŋ\ *n* -S [ME, fr. gerund of *trappen* to trap — more at TRAP (to catch)] **:** the act of catching something or someone in a trap; *specif* **:** the occupation of a trapper

2trapping \"\ *n* -S [ME, fr. gerund of *trappen* to clothe — more at TRAP (to clothe)] **1 :** CAPARISON 1 — usu. used in pl. ⟨the heavy cart horses slipped and stamped . . . shaking their bells and ~*s* —Oscar Wilde⟩ **2 trappings** *pl* **:** articles of decoration or dress ⟨Christmas ~*s* such as lacy gilt butterflies, silver paper harps . . . paper angels —*New Yorker*⟩ ⟨the usual ~*s* of rather shabby but gallant old age, which included . . . a cross gleaming gold on her breast —Virginia Woolf⟩; *also* **:** outward signs ⟨the visible ~*s* of success, the automobiles, the applause . . . the consciousness of opulence and distinction —F.A.Swinnerton⟩ ⟨little oligarchies masquerading in the ~*s* of democracy —F.A.Ogg & P.O.Ray⟩

3trapping \"\ *n* -S [*trap* (*cut*) + *-ing*] **1 :** the cutting of a gem in a step cut **2** [*trap* (*brilliant*) + *-ing*] **:** the cutting of a trap brilliant

1trap·pist \ˈtrapəst\ *n* -S *usu cap* [F *trappiste*, fr. La Trappe, Normandy + *-iste* -ist] **:** a member of a reformed branch of the Roman Catholic Cistercian Order established in 1664 at the monastery of La Trappe in Normandy and united with the Cistercians since 1892

2trappist \"\ *adj, usu cap* **:** of or relating to the Trappist life, spirit, or system

trappist cheese *n, usu cap T* [so called fr. its having originated in the Trappist monastery of Mariastern in Bosnia] **:** a semisoft pale yellow cheese of mild flavor usu. made of fresh whole cow's milk — called also *Port du Salut, Port Salut*

trap·pist·ine \-pə,stēn, -tīn\ *n* -S *usu cap* **:** a Roman Catholic nun of a group affiliated with the Cistercians of the Strict Observance

trap play *n* **:** MOUSETRAP 2a

trap·poid \ˈtra,pȯid\ *adj* [*5trap* + *-oid*] **:** of, relating to, or resembling trap or traprock

trap·py \ˈtrapē, -pi\ *adj* -ER/-EST **1 :** of, relating to, or containing traps or snares **:** TRICKY, DIFFICULT ⟨riding them through thickly timbered country over breakneck fences and ~ ground —W.A.Kerr⟩ ⟨the snow lies deep and soft over the ~ holes and crevices —F.G.Jackson⟩ **2 :** having a short quick rather high gait — used of a horse

traprock *var of* TRAP

traps *pl of* TRAP, *pres 3d sing of* TRAP

trapse *var of* TRAIPSE

trap seal *n* **:** the sealing value of a trap as measured vertically from the mean liquid surface level down to the dip of the trap

trap shoot *n* **:** a match at trapshooting

trapshooter \ˈ=,==\ *n* **:** one who engages in trapshooting

trapshooting \ˈ=,==\ *n* **:** shooting at clay pigeons sprung into the air from a trap

trap shot *n* **1 :** TRAPSHOOTER **2 :** a half volley (as in tennis) made by hitting the ball immediately after it hits the ground

trapstick \ˈ=,=\ *n* **:** a stick used in playing the game of trapball

trap strip *n* **:** a planted area in which the plants serve as a trap crop

trapt *archaic past of* TRAP

trap tree *n* **:** a tree deadened or felled for the purpose of luring insect pests where they can easily be destroyed

tra·pun·to \trəˈpün(,)tō\ *n* -S [It, fr. past part. of *trapungere* to embroider, fr. *tra-* across, through (fr. L *trans*) + *pungere* to prick, fr. L — more at TRANS-, PUNGENT] **:** a decorative quilted design in high relief worked through at least two layers of cloth by outlining the design in running stitch and then padding it from the underside by the insertion of yarn or cotton

trap weir *n* **:** a weir built in the form of a fish trap

1trash \ˈtrash, -aa(ə)-, -ai-\ *n* -ES [of Scand origin; akin to Norw *trask* lumber, trash, *trase* rag; akin to OE *teran* to tear — more at TEAR] **1 :** something worth relatively little or nothing: as **a :** JUNK, RUBBISH ⟨trampling down a great pile of old newspapers and other ~ —Thomas Whiteside⟩ ⟨was sweeping the ~ in their backyard —Erskine Caldwell⟩ **b :** TRASH FISH ⟨none . . . attains any great size, and they are considered as ~ by fishermen —*Copeia*⟩ **c** (1) **:** empty talk or discourse **:** NONSENSE ⟨what ~ are you talkin' anyway —Owen Wister⟩ ⟨this book is utter ~ . . . pure quackery and without scientific standing —Conway Zirkle⟩ (2) **:** inferior or worthless writing or artistic matter ⟨a corner of fiction in which sadistic and poorly written ~ is becoming the norm —Geoffrey Moore⟩ ⟨one of the most lugubrious bits of sentimental ~ . . . ever released —C.F.Wittke⟩ ⟨music that is only ~⟩ **d :** MONEY ⟨drudge, sweat . . . for every gain, for vile contaminating ~ — Edward Young⟩ **2 :** something in a crumbled or broken condition or mass: as **a :** woody or vegetable matter fallen or strewn on the ground ⟨a big drift of logs and ~ —F.B.Gipson⟩ **b :** CANE TRASH **3 :** a worthless person **:** NO-GOOD, POOR WHITE ⟨put a bullet past his ear, just to let the ~ know the sound of it —Winston Churchill⟩; *collectively* **:** such persons as a group or class **:** RIFFRAFF ⟨the loudmouth ~ . . . from the slums of cities —T.H.Fielding⟩ ⟨I am a poor man . . . but I ain't ~ —R.P.Warren⟩ **4 :** the lower leaves of the burley tobacco plant **syn** see REFUSE

2trash \"\ *vt* -ED/-ING/-ES **:** to free from trash or refuse **:** LOP, CROP; *specif* **:** to strip outer leaves from (immature sugarcane)

3trash \"\ *vb* -ED/-ING/-ES [of Scand origin; akin to Sw *traska* to jog, trudge, tramp] *vi, dial Brit* **:** to plod about tiringly esp. in the wet **:** TRUDGE, TRAMP ~ *vt, dial Brit* **:** to wear out (as a person) with exertion **:** JADE, FATIGUE

4trash \"\ *vt* -ED/-ING/-ES [prob. fr. obs. F *trachier, tracier* to trace, track, fr. MF — more at TRACE] **1** *obs* **:** to hold back (as a hunting dog) by a trash **2** *archaic* **:** RESTRAIN, HINDER

5trash \"\ *n* -ES *dial Eng* **:** a long light cord used to slow or check a hunting dog in the field **:** LEASH

trash bug *n* **:** an aphis lion that is the larva of a lacewing of the family Chrysopidae and that piles debris on its back

trash can *n* **:** a metal receptacle for dry refuse

trash·ery \-shərē\ *n* -ES [*1trash* + *-ery*] **:** TRASH, RUBBISH

trash farming *n* **:** a method of cultivation in which the soil is loosened by subsurface tillage or other methods that leave stubble and other vegetational residues on or near the surface to check erosion and serve as a mulch — called also *stubble mulch farming*

trash fish *n* **1 :** ROUGH FISH **2 :** any of various sea fishes that have no market value as human food but are sometimes used for reduction (as to oil or meal for domestic animals)

trash fishery *n* **:** the business or practice of catching and marketing trash fish

trash ice *n* **:** broken or crumbled ice mixed with water

trash·i·ness \ˈtrashēnəs, -raash-,-raish-\ *n* -ES **:** the quality or state of being trashy

trashrack \ˈ=,=\ *n* **:** 3RACK 6

trash·trie \ˈtrashtri\ *n* -S [alter. of *trashery*] *Scot* **:** TRASH, RUBBISH — used esp. of food and drink

trashy \ˈtrashē, -raash-,-raish-, -shi\ *adj* -ER/-EST **1 :** resembling or containing trash **:** of inferior quality **:** WORTHLESS ⟨the cheap and ~ brandy . . . put into so many light wines — O.S.J.Gogarty⟩ ⟨crude in writing, ~ in feeling, implausible — Edmund Wilson⟩ ⟨its score contains some of the *trashiest* pages ever written —Winthrop Sargeant⟩ **2 :** covered or strewn with dried or withered vegetable matter usu. from a previous crop ⟨the seedbed was rough and ~ —Louis Bromfield⟩

trask·ite \ˈtra,skīt\ *n* -S *usu cap* [John Trask *fl* 1617 Eng. religious leader + E *-ite*] **:** SEVENTH-DAY BAPTIST

trass \ˈtras\ *also* **ter·race** *or* **tar·ras** \təˈras\ *n, pl* **trasses** *also* **terraces** *or* **tarrases** [D *trass, terras*, fr. F *terrasse* pile of earth, terrace, fr. MF — more at TERRACE] **:** a light-colored volcanic tuff resembling pozzolana in composition and occurring esp. on the lower Rhine where it is ground for use in a hydraulic cement

1tras·tev·er·ine \(ˈ)traˈstevə,rēn, -,rən\ *adj, usu cap* [It *trasteverino*, fr. L *transtiberinus*, fr. *trans-* + *tiberinus* of the Tiber, fr. *Tiberis* Tiber river + *-inus* -ine] **1 :** of, relating to, or characteristic of the Trastevere region across the Tiber river from Rome **2 :** of, relating to, or characteristic of the people of the Trastevere

2trasteverine \"\ *n, pl* **trasteverines** \-nz\ *or* **trasteveri·ni** \,=,==ˈrē(,)nē\ *cap* [It *trasteverino*, fr. L *transtiberini*, pl., trasteverines] **:** a native or inhabitant of the Trastevere

1trat·tle \ˈtrat³l\ *vi* -ED/-ING/-S [ME (Sc) *tratlen*] *Scot* **:** PRATTLE, CHATTER, GOSSIP

2trattle \"\ *n* -S [earlier *tretle*, prob. alter. of obs. E dial. *treddle*, fr. ME *tredel, tyrdyl*, fr. OE *tyrdel*, dim. of *tord* turd — more at TURD] *dial Eng* **:** a pellet or dropping of any of various animals (as sheep or rabbits) — usu. used in pl.

trat·to·ria \,trätəˈrēə\ *n* -S [It, fr. *trattore* innkeeper, restaurant owner (fr. F *traiteur*, fr. *traiter* to treat, settle, entertain — fr. OF *tretier, traitier* — + *-eur* -or) + *-ia* -y — more at TREAT] **:** an eating house **:** RESTAURANT

trau·chle \ˈträkəl\ *var of* TRACHLE

trau·lism \ˈtrȯ,lizəm, -raů,l-\ *n* -S [Gk *traulismos*, fr. *traulizein* to mispronounce, lisp, stammer, fr. *traulos*, adj., mispronouncing letters, lisping, stammering + *-izein* -ize] **:** STAMMERING, STUTTERING

trau·ma \ˈtraůmə *also* -rȯmə\ *n, pl* **trauma·ta** \-məd·ə,-mətə\ *or* **traumas** [Gk, wound — more at THROE] **1 :** an injury or wound to a living body caused by the application of external force or violence ⟨injuries . . . such as sprains, bruises, fractures, dislocation, concussion — indeed *traumata* of all kinds —*Lancet*⟩ **2 a :** a psychological or emotional stress or blow that may produce disordered feelings or behavior ⟨separation from its mother was the greatest ~ to the young child —Carl Binger⟩ ⟨the moral energies of America were exhausted by the ~ of the Civil War —*New Republic*⟩ **b :** the state or condition of mental or emotional shock produced by such a stress or by a physical injury **:** TRAUMATISM ⟨effects of the ~ induced by the wound —J.W.Aldridge⟩ ⟨what was the nature of this ~, following as it did an acute anxiety state — Elizabeth Rosenberg⟩ ⟨the war left a lasting ~ —Edmund Wilson⟩ **syn** see WOUND

traumat- *or* **traumato-** *comb form* [LL, fr. Gk, fr. *traumat-, trauma*] **:** wound **:** trauma ⟨*traumatism*⟩

trau·mat·ic \(ˈ)trȯ¦mad·|ik, trəˈm-, -at|, |ēk *also* (ˈ)traů¦m-\ *adj* [LL *traumaticus*, fr. Gk *traumatikos*, fr. *traumat-, trauma* wound + *-ikos* -ic] **:** of, relating to, or resulting from a trauma ⟨cases of ~ rupture —*Jour. Amer. Med. Assoc.*⟩ ⟨bringing up the details of a ~ experience . . . so as to banish the effects of the experience and make it possible for them to live in the present —Malcolm Cowley⟩ — **trau·mat·i·cal·ly** \|ək(ə)lē, |ēk-, -li\ *adv*

traumatic acid *n* **:** a crystalline unsaturated dicarboxylic acid $HOOC(CH_2)_8CH{=}CHCOOH$ that is obtained esp. from the pods of green beans or by synthesis and that promotes healing of plant wounds; 2-dodec-ene-dioic acid — see WOUND HORMONE

trau·ma·tism \ˈtrȯmə,tizəm, ˈtraům-\ *n* -S [ISV *traumat-* + *-ism*] **:** the development of a state of mental or physical shock from a blow, injury, or stress ⟨~ of the pancreas can cause changes in the amount of insulin secreted⟩ ⟨repressions and ~*s* which may have catastrophic results for whole nations —*Times Lit. Supp.*⟩; *also* **:** the condition produced by such a development ⟨fractures, sprains . . . burns, and similar ~*s* —*Jour. Amer. Med. Assoc.*⟩ **syn** see WOUND

trau·ma·ti·za·tion \,trȯməd·əˈzāshən, ,traům-, |təˈz-, |d·,ī'z-, |,tī'z-\ *n* -S **:** the act or process of traumatizing

trau·ma·tize \ˈ=mə,tīz\ *vt* -ED/-ING/-S [*traumat-* + *-ize*] **:** to inflict a trauma upon (the body or mind) ⟨if the nerve is crushed so that the sheath is torn or *traumatized* —R.G. Grenell & H.S.Burr⟩ ⟨response to trauma is governed by . . . type of injury inflicted and region *traumatized* —*Yrbk. of Dentistry*⟩ ⟨case history of a young man who . . . was *traumatized* by an uncommonly hideous childhood, with which he took refuge in a violent fantasy —J.B.Martin⟩

trau·ma·to·pho·bia \,=mad·əˈfōbēə\ *n* [NL, fr. *traumat-* + *phobia*] **:** excessive or disabling fear of war or physical injury usu. resulting from experiences in combat

trau·ma·trop·ic \¦=mə¦träpik\ *adj* [*trauma* + *-tropic*] **:** of, relating to, or characterized by traumatropism

trau·mat·ro·pism \=ˈma·trə,pizəm\ *n* [*trauma* + *tropism*] **:** a modification of the orientation of an organ (as a plant root) as a result of wounding

trav *abbr* **1** travel **2** traveler **3** travels

1travail \trəˈvā(ə)l, ˈtra,väl *sometimes* traˈvā(ə)l *or* ˈtravəl\ *n* -S [ME, fr. OF, fr. *travaillier, traveillier* to labor, travail] **1 a :** physical or mental work or exertion esp. of a painful or laborious nature **:** LABOR, TOIL, DRUDGERY ⟨tackles his outdoor ~ with the furious drive of a bulldozer —R.L.Taylor⟩ ⟨sat glum and thoughtful, his mind in unproductive ~ —Rafael Sabatini⟩ ⟨periods of high intellectual achievement and ~, of critical analysis and doubt —*Times Lit. Supp.*⟩ **b :** a physical or mental exertion or piece of work **:** TASK, EFFORT ⟨manfully undertakes his assigned ~⟩ ⟨my literary ~ —G.B.Shaw⟩ — often used in pl. ⟨reminisced on the ~*s* of campaigning —*N.Y. Times*⟩ **c :** pain or suffering resulting from physical struggle or mental conflict **:** AGONY, TORMENT ⟨chose . . . to share France's ~ as earlier he had shared her happier days —Paul Farmer⟩ ⟨rises joyously superior to the outward calamities . . . and celebrates the greatness of the human spirit whose ~ he describes —J.W.Krutch⟩ ⟨the ~ of an artist in a society of so many material conveniences —M.D.Geismar⟩ — sometimes used in pl. ⟨takes up some of the special ~*s* of the upper classes —Rex Lardner⟩ **2 :** LABOR, PARTURITION ⟨woman must marry because the race must perish without her ~ —G.B. Shaw⟩ ⟨suggested that the nation had been long in ~, and had at last produced a man —John Buchan⟩ **3** *obs* **:** TRAVEL 2 **syn** see WORK

2travail \"\ *vb* -ED/-ING/-S [ME *travailen, traveilen*, fr. OF *travaillier* to labor, toil, trouble, torture, fr. (assumed) VL *tripaliare* to torture, fr. (assumed) VL *tripalium* instrument of torture, fr. L *tripalis* having three stakes, fr. *tri-* + *palus* stake — more at POLE] *vi* **1 :** to labor hard **:** DRUDGE, TOIL ⟨~*s* hard for his daily wage⟩ **2 :** LABOR 3 **3** *obs* **:** TRAVEL 2 ~ *vt* **1** *archaic* **:** TROUBLE, TORMENT, HARASS **2** *obs* **:** to put to laborious mental or physical work **:** DRIVE

3tra·vail \trəˈvī\ *n, pl* **travails** \-vīz\ *also* **tra·vaux** \-vō\ [F, fr. MF, fr. (assumed) VL *tripalium* instrument of torture] **:** TRAVOIS 1

tra·vat·ed \ˈtrā,vād·əd\ *adj* [It *travato* (fr. *trave* beam — fr. L *trabs, trabes* — + *-ato* -ate) + E *-ed*] *of a ceiling* **:** divided into traves

trave \ˈtrāv\ *n* -S [ME, fr. MF, beam, fr. L *trabs, trabes* — more at THORP] **1 :** a frame to confine an unruly horse or ox for shoeing **2 :** CROSSBEAM **3 :** a division or bay (as in a ceiling) made by or as if by crossbeams

1travel \ˈtravəl\ *vb* **traveled** *or* **travelled; traveled** *or* **travelled; traveling** *or* **travelling** \-v(ə)liŋ\ **travels** [ME *travellen, travailen* — more at TRAVAIL] *vi* **1** *obs* **:** TRAVAIL **2 a :** to go or proceed on or as if on a trip or tour **:** JOURNEY ⟨the country through which we have been ~*ing* —Louis Bromfield⟩ ⟨many young birds ~ north during June —*Amer. Guide Series: La.*⟩ ⟨the surge . . . ~*ed* southwards along the coast —J.A.Steers⟩ ⟨even ideas and emotions ~*ed* slowly in those days —Clive Bell⟩ **b** (1) **:** to move or go as if by traveling **:** PASS ⟨my mind ~*ed* back to a hot sultry day in the little . . . town —Rex Keating⟩ ⟨her eyes ~*ed* about the room — Mary R. Rinehart⟩ ⟨US 190 ~*s* through a wide stretch . . . of virgin pine —*Amer. Guide Series: La.*⟩ ⟨most parts of the world are ~*ing* toward a tighter system —Bertrand Russell⟩ ⟨the path . . . for the inspired genius to ~ —H.J.Laski⟩ (2) **:** to move or join in a company or group **:** ASSOCIATE ⟨~*ed* in left wing circles —Oden & Olivia Meeker⟩ — usu. used with *with* ⟨no harder a drinker than most of the crowd he ~*ed* with —Robert Sylvester⟩ ⟨the liberal intellectuals who . . . ~*ed* with the party —Margaret Marshall⟩ **c** *dial* **:** to go on foot **:** WALK ⟨did you ~ or come by boat —*Amer. Guide Series: N.C.*⟩ **d :** to go on a specified circuit or route ⟨in the frontier towns most ministers ~*ed*⟩ ⟨offering premiums for stallions to ~ —Robert Jarvis⟩ **e :** to go from place to place as a salesman or business agent ⟨salesman . . . was ~*ing* out of St. Louis —E.A.Duddy⟩ — often used with *in* ⟨man who ~*ed* in ladies' undies, wholesale —O.S.J.Gogarty⟩ **3 a :** to move, advance, or undergo transmission from one place to another ⟨the bayonet entered the right rib cage . . . and ~*ed* upward —Raymond Boyle⟩ ⟨the pain . . . ~*ed* all the way into his head —Ira Wolfert⟩ ⟨the sound ~*ed* onto the stage —Warwick Braithwaite⟩ **b :** to undergo transportation or dissemination ⟨loup, like weakfish, ~*s* poorly and should be eaten within a few hours after being caught —A.J.Liebling⟩ ⟨cases . . . which ~ in freight cars must be securely packed —Edwin Sutermeister⟩ ⟨the whole concept of impressionism . . . didn't ~ well —R.M.Coates⟩ ⟨that typical regionalism which ~*s* so poorly in literature —V.S.Pritchett⟩ **c :** to move in a given direction or path or through a given distance ⟨the needles . . . ~ down the face of the cam —W.E.Shinn⟩ ⟨the crankpin ~*s* in a circular path⟩ ⟨the stylus ~*s* in a groove⟩ **d :** to move briskly ⟨the souped-up car can really ~⟩ **4 :** to walk or run with the ball illegally (as in basketball) ~ *vt* **1** *obs* **:** TRAVAIL **2 a :** to journey through or over **:** TRAVERSE ⟨everyone should ~ at least part of its beautiful valley —Bernard DeVoto⟩ ⟨~*ed* the twenty feet of green carpet with his eyes fixed straight ahead —Scott Fitzgerald⟩ ⟨certain roads can be ~*ed* only on horseback —W.E.Rudolph⟩ **b :** to follow (a course or path) as if by traveling **:** PURSUE ⟨no other social right has ~*ed* so arduous a road —V.L.Parrington⟩ ⟨readers . . . often voyaged into the world celebrated by the romantic novelist, but few ~*ed* the other way —J.D.Hart⟩ **c :** to pass over or along (a specified distance) ⟨individual cells often have to ~ great distances —*New Biology*⟩ ⟨the modern travel book has itself ~*ed* a long way from the formal diary —*Geog. Jour.*⟩ **d :** to cover or visit (a place or region) as a commercial traveler ⟨~*ed* the Midwest for a soft drink firm —Tom Siler⟩ **3 :** to cause to travel **:** DRIVE, SHIP ⟨the beast . . . could scarcely be ~*ed* upon a caravel —Galbraith Welch⟩ ⟨choose the best time of year to ~ cattle⟩ ⟨~*ing* the stallion to different farms —*Producing Farm Livestock*⟩ — **travel light :** to travel with a minimum of equipment or baggage ⟨the Australian *travels light:* a spear, a boomerang club, and perhaps a spear-thrower for a man —A.L.Kroeber⟩

²travel \"\ *n* -s [ME *travel, travail* — more at TRAVAIL] **1** *obs* **:** TRAVAIL **2 a :** the act of traveling, going, or journeying **:** PASSAGE ⟨dislikes the discomforts of ~ —Agnes Repplier⟩ ⟨outlined the probable steps leading to ~ in outer space —*Current Biog.*⟩ ⟨~ on the plateau is comparatively rapid —E.E.Shipton⟩ **b :** a journey esp. to a distant or unfamiliar place **:** TOUR, TRIP ⟨set out on another ~, this time to the Pacific —*Current Biog.*⟩ ⟨longest ~ for a cake to make without a bruise —*Postal Service News*⟩ ⟨to town and back is a long day's ~⟩ — often used in pl. ⟨extended our ~*s* to parts of the rugged mountains totally unknown —C.B.Hitchcock⟩ **3 travels** *pl* **:** an account or narration of one's travels esp. in book form ⟨enjoys reading ~*s*⟩ **4 :** power or speed of movement ⟨the most necessary qualifications of a dog are ~ . . . and nose —Eric Parker⟩ ⟨the new racing shell has tremendous ~⟩ **5 :** the number of persons or things traveling **:** TRAFFIC ⟨~ on the turnpike is heavy on holidays⟩ **6 a :** the movement or progression of something along a route or course ⟨the farther the film tray is from the workplace, the more reach or ~ is required —E.M.Harwell⟩ ⟨during combustion the ~ of the flame . . . should progress at a fairly uniform rate —Ernest Venk⟩ ⟨a device to time the ~ of satellites around the earth⟩ **b :** the motion of a piece of machinery esp. to and fro in a prescribed line or direction ⟨a timing device to make the high-voltage source perform at the set position of piston ~ —*Aircraft Power Plants*⟩

trav·el·able *or* **trav·el·la·ble** \ˈtrav(ə)ləbəl\ *adj* **:** capable of being traveled **:** PASSABLE ⟨highway crews soon had the roads ~ after the storm⟩

travel agency *or* **travel bureau** *n* **:** an office or enterprise engaged in selling, arranging, or furnishing information about personal transportation or travel

travel agent *n* **:** a person engaged in selling or arranging personal transportation, tours, or trips

traveled *or* **travelled** *adj* [fr. past part. of ¹*travel*] **1 :** that has traveled or is experienced in travel **2 :** ERRATIC 2 ⟨the ~ stones are of all dimensions —J.D.Dana⟩

trav·el·er *or* **trav·el·ler** \-v(ə)lə(r)\ *n* -s [ME *travellour, travaillour,* fr. *travellen, travailen* to travel + *-our* -or] **1 :** one that travels: as **a :** one that goes on a trip or journey ⟨the worst of ~*s*, detesting all modes of transportation —Agnes Repplier⟩; *specif* **:** one that travels to distant or unfamiliar places **b** *dial Brit* **:** TRAMP **c :** TRAVELING SALESMAN **2 :** something that travels fast or well (as a vehicle or draft animal) **3 a :** an iron ring (as on the inboard block of the sheet of a fore-and-aft sail) that travels on a line, bar, or spar of a ship and slides thereon **b** *or* **traveler iron :** a bar or rod running transversely on the deck on which a ring in one end of the sheet or the block of a sheet tackle of a fore-and-aft sail travels back and forth — called also *horse* **4 :** any of various devices (as a traveling crane) for carrying or suspending something being transported laterally; *esp* **:** a crab or winch moved on an elevated track and used in erecting steel bridges or other large work **5 :** a small metal clip that slides on the ring of a ring spinner and guides the yarn to the bobbin **6 :** a stage curtain that is drawn across the proscenium — contrasted with *drop curtain*

traveler's check *n* **:** a draft issued by a bank or express company payable on presentation by any correspondent of the issuer — called also *banker's check*

traveler's–delight \ˈ=(=)=ˌ=ˈ=\ *n, pl* **traveler's–delights :** GROUNDNUT 2a

traveler's–grass \ˈ=(=)=ˈ=\ *n, pl* **traveler's–grasses :** SETTLER'S TWINE

traveler's–joy \ˈ=(=)=ˈ=\ *n, pl* **traveler's–joys :** any of several climbing plants of the genus *Clematis; esp* **:** a vigorous woody climber (*C. vitalba*) of Europe and the Mediterranean region with fragrant greenish white flowers borne in axillary panicles in summer and autumn — compare OLD-MAN'S BEARD, VIRGIN'S BOWER

traveler's letter of credit : LETTER OF CREDIT 1

traveler's palm *n* **:** TRAVELER'S-TREE

traveler's–tree \ˈ=(=)=ˈ=\ *n, pl* **traveler's–trees :** a tree (*Ravenala madagascariensis*) of Madagascar having distichous leaves whose petioles contain large quantities of clear watery sap and yield a refreshing drink

traveling *or* **travelling** *adj* [ME *traveling,* fr. pres. part. of *travellen, travailen* to travel, travail — more at TRAVAIL] **1 :** that travels **2 :** that is carried, used by, or accompanies a traveler ⟨~ companion⟩

traveling apron *n* **:** APRON 3a(1)

traveling backstay *n* **:** a backstay attached to a mast by a traveler sliding up and down with the yard

traveling bag *n* **:** a bag carried by hand and designed to hold a traveler's clothing and other personal articles

traveling card *n* **:** a card issued by a local union that enables a worker to take a job outside the jurisdiction in which the card is issued

traveling carriage *n* **:** a carriage designed for long-distance travel

traveling case *n* **:** a usu. stiff and box-shaped traveling bag

traveling clock *n* **:** a small clock or large watch mounted in a folding case that serves as an easel when opened

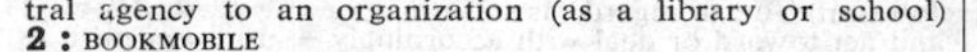

traveling clock

traveling crane *n* **:** CRANE 3a

traveling fellow *n* **:** the holder of a traveling fellowship

traveling fellowship *n* **:** a fellowship whose terms permit or direct the holder to travel or go abroad for study or research

traveling–head shaper *n* **:** a shaper whose reciprocating toolhead is mounted on a bed in such a way that the head may be fed laterally on ways provided on the bed prior to each cutting stroke — called also *traverse shaper*

traveling library *n* **1 :** a collection of books loaned by a central agency to an organization (as a library or school) **2 :** BOOKMOBILE

traveling microscope *n* **:** a microscope provided with cross hairs and mounted in such a way that it can be moved along a base with a screw for the purpose of making accurate measurements of distance

traveling nut *n* **:** a nut that travels on a revolving screw

traveling platform *or* **traveling sidewalk** *n* **:** a contrivance on the principle of the flat horizontal endless belt or conveyer designed for transporting objects or persons through a limited distance

traveling post office *n* **:** RAILWAY MAIL CAR

traveling rings *n pl* **:** swinging gymnastic rings arranged in a row — compare FLYING RINGS

traveling salesman *or* **traveling man** *n* **:** a traveling representative of a business concern who solicits orders usu. in an assigned territory by showing samples or catalogs or by demonstration of his company's products or services — called also *commercial traveler, drummer*

traveling staircase *or* **traveling stairs** *n* **:** MOVING STAIRCASE

traveling steady *n* **:** FOLLOW REST

traveling table *n* **:** a table or platform arranged to move on rollers or wheels

traveling wave *n* **:** a wave in which the particles of the medium move progressively in the direction of the wave propagation with such a gradation of speeds that the faster overtake the slower and are themselves in turn overtaken — compare STANDING WAVE

traveling–wave tube *n* **:** an electron tube used for the generation of microwave frequency radiation or for amplification at ultrahigh frequencies whose operation depends on the interaction of a beam of electrons with an electromagnetic wave

travellable *var of* TRAVELABLE

travelled *var of* TRAVELED

traveller *var of* TRAVELER

travel line *n, usu cap T* **:** LINE OF TRAVEL

travelling *var of* TRAVELING

travelling matt *or* **travelling matte** *n* **:** a film containing silhouettes of subjects or figures used to mask off selected areas during printing of motion-picture film

trav·el·ogue *also* **trav·el·og** \ˈtravəˌlȯg *also* -läg\ *n* -s [²*travel* + *-logue, -log*] **:** a talk, lecture, or discourse on travel usu. with illustrations (as slides or motion pictures) — **trav·el·ogu·er** \-gə(r)\ *n* -s

travel shot *n* **:** a motion-picture shot made with the camera on a dolly accompanying the actors as they move from one set or place to another

travel sickness *n* **:** sickness (as nausea or vertigo) due to the motion of travel in a vehicle

travel time *n* **:** a usu. specified period of time spent in traveling at work or from the entrance of a business establishment to the place where work is actually done (as in portal-to-portal travel or deadheading) for which compensation may be demanded or paid

tra·vers·able *pronunc at* ²TRAVERSE + əbəl\ *adj* **1 :** capable of being traversed or passed over **:** PASSABLE ⟨much of this . . . country is ~ only by four-wheel-drive vehicle or pack train —Joyce R. Muench⟩ **2 :** proper to be traversed in pleading **:** DENIABLE ⟨a ~ presentment⟩ ⟨a ~ issue⟩

tra·vers·al *pronunc at* ²TRAVERSE + əl\ *n* -s **:** the act or an instance of traversing

¹traverse \ˈ=(ˌ)= *or* =ˈ= — *see* ²TRAVERSE\ *n* -s [ME *travers;* partly fr. MF *traverse* crosspiece, fr. *traverser* to cross, traverse & L *transversa,* fem. of *transversus* lying across, past part. of *transvertere* to turn across; partly fr. MF *travers* way across, passage, fr. L *transversum,* fr. neut. of *transversus* — more at *transverse*] **1 :** something that crosses or lies or is laid across: as **a :** CROSSPIECE, TRANSOM **b :** BAR, BARRIER **c :** a screen, curtain, or sliding partition placed or drawn crosswise in a room, hall, or theater **d :** a collapsible fire screen with leaves usu. of pierced brass opening out like a fan from an upright standard **2 :** something that opposes or impedes **:** OBSTACLE, ADVERSITY ⟨~*s*, toils, and trouble⟩ **3 a :** a formal denial of some particular matter of fact alleged by the opposite party in a stage of legal pleadings ⟨matter was heard . . . on the petition, the returns, the ~*s* thereto —J.R.Martin⟩ **b** *obs* **:** DISPUTE, CONTROVERSY **4 a :** a compartment or recess formed by a partition, curtain, or screen **b :** a screened stall in a church or chapel **c :** a gallery or loft of communication extending from side to side in a church or other large building **5 :** a route or way across or over: as **a :** a zigzag course made by a sailing ship with contrary winds **b :** a zigzag road or course up a steep grade **c :** the course followed in a traverse (as on skis); *also* **:** a zigzag in such a course **6 a :** PASSAGE, TOLL TRAVERSE **b :** the act or an instance of traversing **:** CROSSING ⟨the only practicable route for human ~ —J.H.Bretz⟩ ⟨the ~ of a gorge might . . . take many weeks —E.E.Shipton⟩ ⟨their longest expeditions . . . have been mere ~*s* leaving great unexplored areas in between —Ralph Linton⟩ **c :** a horizontal or diagonal crossing of a mountainside or slope **d :** the crossing of a gap or pass from one side to the other **e :** a zigzag ascent or descent of a slope esp. on skis **f :** the act or position of traversing in fencing **7 :** a projecting wall or bank of earth in a trench constructed to protect the occupants from enfilading fire or to localize shell bursts **8 a :** a traversing or lateral movement (as of the saddle of a lathe carriage); *also* **:** a device for imparting such movement **b :** the lateral movement of a gun about a pivot or on a carriage to change the direction of fire; *also* **:** the total possible lateral movement of a gun on its carriage **9 :** a forward oblique movement of a horse with tail turned to one side and head to the other **10 a :** TRAVERSE SURVEY **b :** a line surveyed across a plot of ground **11** *New Eng* **:** BOBSLED 2 **12 :** the distance through which the yarn or roving laying device travels when winding the yarn

²tra·verse \trəˈvərs, -ˈvə̄s, -ˈvəis *sometimes* traˈv- *or* ˈtra,v- *or* ˈtra,və(r)s\ *vb* -ED/-ING/-S [ME *traversen,* fr. MF *traverser,* fr. LL *transversare* to cross, fr. L *transversus* lying across, transverse] *vt* **1 a :** to go against or act in opposition to **:** OPPOSE ⟨I accept nobody's precepts *traversing* my moral freedom —George Santayana⟩ ⟨since demands ~ each other we have to make a choice —H.J.Laski⟩ **b** (1) **:** to deny (an allegation of fact) formally at law (2) **:** to deny or take issue upon (an indictment) (3) **:** to deny or impeach the validity of (an inquest of office) **c** *obs* **:** DISCUSS, DEBATE **2 a :** to pass through (something) **:** PENETRATE ⟨gladness ~*s* his being⟩ **b** *archaic* **:** to cross or mark with a line, bar, or stripe **3 a :** to go or travel across or over ⟨walking through the streets they had *traversed* two nights before —Floyd Dell⟩ ⟨they drew close to the shore, having *traversed* a range of lofty hills —Elinor Wylie⟩ ⟨little water ~*s* the steep rocky course of the river bed —N.R.Heiden⟩ ⟨the old community is *traversed* by heavy traffic —*Amer. Guide Series: Conn.*⟩ **b :** to move along or through (something) ⟨the current *traversing* the lamp is simply a migration of electrons —K.K.Darrow⟩ **c :** to advance or go through (as a time or an area of activity) ⟨the revolutionary period the world is *traversing* —André Mesnard⟩ ⟨the journeying of the individual scientist if he chooses to ~ the scientific circle —F.A.Geldard⟩ ⟨*traversing* new paths in the area of city planning —C.H.Sawyer⟩ **d :** to go over, consider, or make a study of **:** EXAMINE, SURVEY ⟨~*s* . . . the now century-old arguments against the well-known traditional dogmas —Irwin Edman⟩ ⟨a period . . . more thoroughly *traversed* by historians —R.B.Morris⟩ ⟨a wide area of investigation, only partially *traversed* in recent decades —René Wellek & Austin Warren⟩ **e :** to lie or extend across (something) **:** CROSS ⟨a small bridge which ~*s* a rivulet —George Borrow⟩ ⟨a well-kept lawn *traversed* by concrete walks —*Amer. Guide Series: N.J.*⟩ ⟨the principal islands are *traversed* by large rivers —W.C. Forbes⟩ ⟨a career which . . . ~*s* the whole scope of business opportunities —A.W.McCain⟩ **f :** to draw or construct (a geometrical figure) with one continuous stroke **4 :** to go or move to and fro over or along ⟨continued a long time *traversing* my bedchamber —Mary W. Shelley⟩; *specif* **:** to ascend, descend, or cross (a slope or gap) by means of a traverse ⟨the climber *traversing* the face of the cliff⟩ **5 :** to move or turn (something) laterally or crosswise; *specif* **:** to move (as a gun) to right or left on a pivot or mount ⟨so jammed . . . that it was impossible to ~ the gun turrets —E.J.Kohn⟩ **6 :** to plane (wood) across the grain esp. as a preliminary to trying up a board or floor **7 :** to make or carry out a traverse survey of ~ *vi* **1 a :** to move or go across or along ⟨deep in thought he ~*s* to and fro⟩ ⟨watching cars *traversing* along the highway⟩ ⟨a glass tube which ~*s* up and down the depth of the pot —H.R. Mauersberger⟩ **b** *archaic* **:** to move or shift from one topic or viewpoint to another **c :** to move or dodge from side to side ⟨the boxer ~*s* cunningly⟩ **2 :** to move or turn laterally **:** SWIVEL, PIVOT ⟨the gun ~*s* smoothly on its bearings⟩ **3 :** to execute a traverse on horseback **4 :** to slide one's blade in fencing toward the opponent's hilt while exerting prolonged pressure on his blade **5 :** to make a traverse in climbing or skiing ⟨one can zigzag or ~ up any length of slope with the least effort —Hans Georg⟩ **6 :** to make a traverse survey **syn** see DENY

³traverse \ˈ=ˈ= *or* ˈ=(ˌ)= — *see* ²TRAVERSE\ *adj* [ME *travers,* fr. MF, fr. L *transversus* — more at TRAVERSE, n.] **:** lying or being in a direction across something else **:** TRANSVERSE

⁴traverse *adv* [ME *travers,* fr. *travers,* adj.] *obs* **:** TRAVERSELY

traverse board *n* **:** a navigation device consisting of a small board marked with the four points of the compass with eight holes bored at each point to represent each half hour in a watch and used to peg the courses made by a ship in each half hour

traverse circle *n* **:** a circular track usu. of iron on which the wheels of a heavy gun carriage move when the gun is traversed

traverse drill *n* **1 :** a machine tool for drilling slots in which the work or tool has a lateral motion back and forth **2 :** a drilling machine in which the spindle holder can be adjusted laterally

traverse feed *n* **:** a feed on a machine operating in a lateral direction

traverse flute *n* **:** TRANSVERSE FLUTE

traverse jury *n* **:** a jury impaneled to try a civil or criminal case **:** TRIAL JURY — distinguished from *grand jury*

traverse·ly *pronunc at* ³TRAVERSE + lē *or* li\ *adv* **:** CROSSWISE, TRANSVERSELY

tra·vers·er *pronunc at* ²TRAVERSE + ə(r)\ *n* -s **:** one that traverses: **a :** a form of conveyor (as for moving fuel to furnaces) **b :** a turner who works with a traverse shaper **c :** one that traverses or denies at law **d :** TRANSFER TABLE

traverse rod *or* **traverse track** *n* **:** a metal rod or track with a pulley mechanism for drawing a curtain

traverse rod

traverses *pl of* TRAVERSE, *pres 3d sing of* TRAVERSE

traverse sailing *n* **:** plane sailing in which a ship follows two or more courses in succession with the difference in latitude and departure being added algebraically to find a single resultant course and distance

traverse shaper *n* **:** TRAVELING-HEAD SHAPER

traverse survey *n* **:** a survey used esp. for long narrow strips of country in which a series of lines joined end to end are completely determined as to length and azimuth and are often used as a basis for triangulation

traverse table *n* **1 :** a navigation or surveying table giving the difference of latitude and departure corresponding to any given course and distance and containing the lengths of the two sides of a right-angled triangle usu. for every degree of angle and for all lengths of the hypotenuse from 1 to 100 **2 :** TRANSFER TABLE

traversing *pres part of* TRAVERSE

traversing bridge *n* **:** a movable bridge consisting of a structure like a girder that can be drawn backward

traversing circle *n* **:** TRAVERSE CIRCLE

traversing crane *n* **:** CRANE 3a

traversing gear *n* **:** the gear used in traversing a gun or other piece of machinery

traversing mandrel *n* **:** a mandrel that traverses or moves longitudinally; *specif* **:** a mandrel in a suitable support usu. driven by a separate belt for securing to a lathe carriage (as in order to carry a reamer)

traversing screw jack *or* **traversing jack** *n* **:** a screw jack that besides the raising and lowering device has a base piece with a slideway along which the jack proper can be traversed — called also *swing jack*

trav·er·tine *also* **trav·er·tin** \ˈtravə(r)ˌtēn, -ˌtᵊn, -tən\ *n* -s [F, fr. It *travertino, tivertino,* fr. L (*lapis*) *tiburtinus* tiburtine (stone), fr. *lapis* stone + *tiburtinus* tiburtine — more at TIBURTINE] **:** a mineral consisting of a massive usu. layered calcium carbonate (as aragonite or calcite) formed by deposition from spring waters or esp. from hot springs — called also *calcareous sinter*

traves *pl of* TRAVE

¹travesty \ˈtravəstē, -sti\ *n* -ES [F *travesti,* past part. of *travestir* to disguise, fr. It *travestire,* fr. *tra-* across, through (fr. L *trans*) + *vestire* to dress, fr. L, fr. *vestis* garment — more at TRANS-, WEAR] **1 a :** a burlesque translation or literary or artistic imitation usu. grotesquely incongruous in style, treatment, or subject matter **:** PARODY ⟨achieves a ludicrous effect in his ~ of the epic as a melodramatic farce⟩ ⟨the image I saw there . . . but a ~, cunningly made of enameled clay or some other material, and put there by some malicious enemy to mock me —W.H.Hudson †1922⟩ **b :** a literary or artistic work that because of various inadequacies is only an inferior or grotesque imitation of its prototype ⟨some of them deliberately distort to achieve a primitive effect and the result is a ~ —Esther Warner⟩ **c :** a debased or distorted imitation or representation **:** SHAM, MOCKERY ⟨such a ~ of a horse . . . that if it had been galloped it would have fallen down and broken its neck —David Masters⟩ ⟨dismembered so much and misinterpreted so much else as to leave . . . a ~ rather than a document —Irving Kolodin⟩ ⟨had been arrested and tried and four of them executed . . . a shocking ~ on justice —R.M.Lovett⟩ ⟨a ~ of democracy . . . votes were openly sold and openly quoted on the market —C.P.Fitzgerald⟩ **2 :** a change in dress or appearance usu. for dramatic purposes and often to represent the opposite sex **:** MAKEUP, DISGUISE ⟨the falling of the masks occasions a living change . . . when they continue dancing, unmasked, still in their *travesties* —Sacheverell Sitwell⟩ ⟨the male principle . . . evaporated into ~, girls assuming the dress of boys —Lincoln Kirstein⟩ **syn** see CARICATURE

²travesty \"\ *vt* -ED/-ING/-ES **1 :** to change in dress or appearance **:** DISGUISE ⟨the great medieval style was . . . *travestied* in materials and design —*Amer. Guide Series: Mich.*⟩ **2 :** to make a travesty of **:** PARODY, BURLESQUE ⟨to ~ human nature without . . . cruelty is a great and wonderful art —J.S.Clarke⟩ ⟨later examples . . . *travestied* the classic style rather than copied it —*Amer. Guide Series: Mass.*⟩

travis \ˈtrāvəs, -rav-\ *n* -ES [alter. of ¹*traverse*] *dial Brit* **:** a partition between stable stalls; *also* **:** STALL

travois \ˈtraˌvȯi, trəˈvȯi, (ˈ)travˈwä\ *also* **travoise** \ˈtraˌvȯiz, trəˈvȯiz\ *or* **travoy** \ˈtraˌvȯi, trəˈvȯi\ *n, pl* **travois** \-ȯiz, -äz\ *also* **travoises** \-ȯizəz\ *or* **travoys** \-ȯiz\ [CanF *travois,* alter. of F *travail* — more at TRAVAIL] **1 :** a primitive vehicle used by the Plains Indians of No. America consisting of two trailing poles serving as shafts for dog or horse and bearing a platform or net for the load **2** *usu* **travoy :** ALLIGATOR 6b

travoy \ˈtraˌvȯi, trəˈvȯi\ *vb* -ED/-ING/-S *vt* **:** to haul (a log) in or by a travois ~ *vi* **:** to transport a log or lumber by a travois

¹trawl \ˈtrȯl\ *vb* -ED/-ING/-S [prob. fr. obs. D *tragelen,* fr. MD, fr. *tragel* dragnet] *vi* **1 :** to fish or catch fish with a trawl **2 :** TROLL 2 ~ *vt* **:** to catch or gather (fish) with a trawl

²trawl \"\ *n* -s [prob. fr. obs. D *tragel* dragnet, fr. MD, prob. fr. L *tragula* — more at TRAIL] **1 :** a large conical net with a device for keeping its mouth open that is dragged along the sea bottom in gathering fish or other marine life **2 :** SETLINE

trawl·abil·i·ty \ˌtrȯləˈbiləd·ē\ *n* **:** suitability for trawling ⟨~ of the area —*Commercial Fisheries Rev.*⟩

trawl·able \ˈtrȯləbəl\ *adj* **:** capable of being trawled **:** suitable for trawling ⟨the inshore waters . . . prolific in good ~ fish —W.J.Dakin⟩

trawl board *n* **:** OTTER BOARD

trawl·er \ˈtrȯlə(r)\ *n* -s **:** a person or craft that fishes by trawling

trawl·er·man \-mən\ *n, pl* **trawlermen :** a fisherman who uses a trawl or mans a trawler

trawl line *n* **:** SETLINE

trawlnet \ˈ=ˌ=\ *n* [¹*trawl* + *net*] **:** TRAWL

1tray \'trā\ *n* -s [ME *tray, trey,* fr. OE *trēg, trīg;* akin to OSw *trö* wooden grain measure, OE *trēow* tree, wood — more at TREE] **1 :** an open variously shaped receptacle of wood, metal, or other material with a flat bottom and a low rim for holding, carrying, or exhibiting articles ⟨a ~ of sandwiches⟩ ⟨a jeweler's ~⟩ ⟨a silver card ~⟩ **2** *dial Eng* **:** HURDLE 1a **3 :** a flat or curved piece of metal used to hold ammunition or any part of the mechanism of a gun; *specif* **:** a brass or steel part of the breech mechanism of a heavy cannon — called also *plugtray* **4 :** BOARD 5f(1) **5 :** an appliance consisting of a flanged body and a handle for use in holding plastic material against the gums or teeth in making negative impressions for dentures **6 :** PLATE 1a(3)

2tray \"\ *vt* -ED/-ING/-S **:** to arrange (as fruits for dehydration) on trays

3tray \"\ *n* -s [alter. of *trey*] **:** ROYAL ANTLER

tray agriculture *n* **:** HYDROPONICS

tray ceiling *n* **:** a ceiling under a gabled roof at a height part way up toward the ridge having the appearance of an inverted tray

tray·ful \'trā,fu̇l\ *n* -s **:** as much as a tray will hold

tray-top table *also* **tray table** *n* **1 :** a tea table with a raised edge, rim, or gallery (as on a tray) **2** *usu tray table* **:** a low table formed by a serving tray supported by a stand

tray table

t-r box *n, often cap T&R* [transmit-receive *box*] **:** DUPLEXER

trc *abbr* tierce

treach·er·ous \'trech(ə)rəs\ *adj* [ME *trecherous, tricherous,* fr. MF *trechereus, trichereus,* fr. OF, fr. *trecherie, tricherie* + *-eus* -ous] **1 :** characterized by or manifesting treachery **:** marked by a ready disposition to betray confidence or faith pledged **:** violating or capable of violating allegiance **:** DISLOYAL, FALSE, PERFIDIOUS, TRAITOROUS ⟨the fiercest and most ~ of foes —H.O.Taylor⟩ ⟨his life, among these ~ demons, depended on a hair —R.L.Stevenson⟩ ⟨~ intrigues⟩ **2 a :** likely to betray confidence or trust **:** UNRELIABLE, UNTRUSTWORTHY ⟨a ~ memory⟩ **b :** providing insecure footing or support ⟨~ quicksands⟩ **c :** characterized by usu. hidden dangers, hazards, or perils ⟨found the inlets . . . too ~ and shallow to admit large vessels —*Amer. Guide Series: N.C.*⟩ ⟨the climbing was . . . exacting and ~ —D.L.Busk⟩ **syn** see FAITHLESS

treach·er·ous·ly *adv* [ME *tricherously,* fr. *trecherous, tricherous* + *-ly*] **:** in a treacherous manner **:** by or with treachery ⟨~ wounded by one of the enemy generals who had invited him to a parley —Robert Graves⟩ ⟨doomed . . . to a wife unworthy of him, just because of . . . a moon ~ sentimental —Donn Byrne⟩

treach·er·ous·ness *n* -ES **:** the quality or state of being treacherous ⟨his ~ was . . . concealed under an appearance of honest and awkward dullness —John Fiske⟩

treach·ery \-rē, -ri\ *n* -ES [ME *trecherie, tricherie,* fr. OF, fr. *trechier, trichier* to trick, cheat, deceive + *-erie* -ery] **1 a :** violation of allegiance or of faith and confidence **:** betrayal of trust **:** TREASON ⟨to oppose . . . the party organization would be regarded by most members as little short of ~ —R.M. Dawson⟩ **b :** an instance of treachery **:** an act of perfidy or treason ⟨blackmail the colonel into one of the greatest *treacheries* of history —Fletcher Pratt⟩ **2 :** something treacherous; *specif* **:** something that is or is likely to be unstable or unreliable

1trea·cle \'trēkəl\ *n* -s *often attrib* [ME *triacle,* fr. MF *triacle, tiriacle,* fr. L *theriaca,* fr. Gk *thēriakē* antidote against a poisonous bite, fr. fem. of *thēriakos* of a wild animal, fr. *thērion* wild animal, poisonous animal, dim. of *thēr* wild animal — more at FIERCE] **1 a :** a medicinal compound formerly in wide use as a remedy against poison — compare THERIACA 1 **b** *archaic* **:** something resembling treacle in being a remedy **2** *chiefly Brit* **a :** MOLASSES **b :** a blend of molasses, invert sugar, and corn syrup used as a table syrup — called also *golden syrup* **3 :** something (as a tone of voice, manner, or compliment) resembling treacle in being heavily sweet and cloying ⟨collapsing at the close in a ~ of hideous sentimentality —*Dial*⟩

2treacle \"\ *vt* **treacled; treacled; treacling** \-k(ə)liŋ\ **treacles :** to smear, spread, or sweeten with treacle ⟨*treacled* the paper and attached it to the window —P.G.Wodehouse⟩

treacle mold *or* **treacle mould** *n* [prob. so called from its fancied resemblance to dripping treacle] **:** a rounded mold or nosing somewhat deeply undercut

treacle mustard *n* **1 :** a wallflower of the genus *Erysimum; esp* **:** WORMSEED MUSTARD **2 :** HARE'S-EAR 2

treaclewort \'=,=\ *n* -s **:** a pennycress (*Thlaspi arvense*)

trea·cly \-k(ə)lē, -li\ *adj* [*treacle* + *-y*] **:** resembling or held to resemble treacle (as in quality or appearance) **:** composed of treacle **:** as cloying or sticky as treacle ⟨saturated with black ~ oil —Audrey Barker⟩ ⟨purveyors of ~ Pollyannaish fiction —*Nashville Tennessean*⟩ ⟨~ sentimentalities⟩

1tread \'tred\ *vb* **trod** \'träd\ *also* **treaded; trodden** \'träd°n\ *or* **trod** *also* **tread; treading; treads** [ME *treden,* fr. OE *tredan;* akin to OHG *tretan* to step, tread, ON *trotha,* Goth *trudan* to tread, and perh. to Gk *dramein* to run, OE *treppan* to step — more at TRAP] *vt* **1 a :** to step or walk on **:** move about over esp. by walking ⟨went on to ~ the great smooth dome of the . . . summit —G.W.Murray⟩ ⟨the south pole, never before *trodden* by the foot of human beings —A.L.Kroeber⟩ **b :** to step or walk along **:** FOLLOW, PURSUE ⟨the avenue . . . she had *trodden* —Kathleen Freeman⟩ ⟨the safest road to ~ —H.J. Laski⟩ ⟨has *trod* the thin line between abstraction and strict realism —R.M.Coates⟩ **2 a** (1) **:** to step firmly or walk with pressure on (as a person) in an effort to crush, beat down, injure, or destroy — usu. used in phrases ⟨~ to dirt the rest of mankind —John Milton⟩ ⟨being *trod* to death like a frog —Jonathan Swift⟩ ⟨they were *trodden* under foot⟩ (2) **:** to thresh (as grain) usu. by trampling on a threshing floor — sometimes used with *out* (3) **:** to press out the juice of (grapes) by trampling usu. in a vat (4) **:** to wash (as clothes) by trampling usu. in a washtub **b :** to subdue or repress as if by trampling **:** conquer by crushing or oppressing **:** treat with contemptuous cruelty — usu. used with an adv. ⟨the masses were a good deal *trodden* down —F.E.Gretton⟩ **3 :** to copulate with (a hen) **:** COVER — used of a male bird **4 :** to form or make by the action of the feet in walking **:** BEAT ⟨countless footsteps have *trodden* a path to his door⟩ — sometimes used with *out* ⟨herds . . . *trod* out great lanes of habitual migration —C.D.Forde⟩ **5 :** to press down by walking or stamping upon ⟨~ soil⟩ **6 :** to execute by stepping or dancing ⟨~ a measure⟩ **7 :** to get, bring, or put into or out of some condition by walking or trampling — used with an adv. ⟨~ a grass fire out⟩ ⟨slippers *trodden* down at the heel⟩ **8 :** to step upon (as a treadle or pedal) in order to impart motion **:** press downward with the foot or feet (as in treadling or pedaling) ⟨this wheel . . . was *trodden* by a donkey —John Higgs⟩ **9 :** to brace (an archer's bow) by pressing the foot against the center **10 :** to apply the tread to (an automotive tire) **~** *vi* **1 a :** to move on foot **:** set down the feet in walking **:** PACE, STEP, WALK ⟨they *trod* cautiously, drawing closer and closer —O.E.Rölvaag⟩ ⟨where . . . the foot of a white man had rarely *trod* —Leslie Gardiner⟩ **b :** to proceed as if by walking ⟨in 18th century English history the author ~*s* with his accustomed ease and mastery —*Times Lit. Supp.*⟩ **2 :** to step or set foot on something ⟨fools rush in where angels fear to ~ —Alexander Pope⟩: as **a :** to set foot so as to press, crush, or injure **:** TRAMPLE — used with *on* or *upon* ⟨~ upon the grapes⟩ **b :** to put one's foot down upon something esp. in an accidental or unintentional manner **c :** to press firmly on something with a foot ⟨resolutely *trod* on the accelerator —James Lord⟩ **3 :** COPULATE — usu. used of a male bird **4** *chiefly dial* **:** to yield to treading or being trodden upon **:** become affected by tramping or trampling — used esp. of soil — **tread on one's toes :** to give offense (as by wounding in a tender spot or encroaching on one's rights, privileges, or feelings) — **tread the boards** *or* **tread the stage :** to act as a stage player **:** perform a part in a drama — **tread the steps of** *obs* **:** to walk in the steps of **:** follow the example of ⟨*tread the steps of* their parents merely by instinct —Thomas Brown⟩ — **tread water :** to keep the body nearly upright in the water and the head above water by a treading motion of the feet usu. aided by the hands ⟨trying to regain his breath while he *treaded water* —Nathaniel Benchley⟩ ⟨rose under the stern and *trod water* —Leslie Charteris⟩

2tread \"\ *n* -s *often attrib* [ME *trede, tred,* fr. *treden,* v.] **1 :** a mark (as a footprint, a rut of a wheel, or the imprint of a tire) made by or as if by treading **2 a** (1) **:** the action of treading ⟨that incessant ~ of feet wearing the rough stones smooth —Charles Dickens⟩ (2) **:** an act or an instance of treading **:** STEP **b :** manner of stepping **:** style of walking ⟨walked with a springy, catlike ~ —Tom Marvel⟩ ⟨the careful ~ of one conscious of his alcoholic load —Thomas Hardy⟩ **c :** the sound of treading ⟨I hear the ~ of hateful steps —John Milton⟩ ⟨the corner echoed . . . with the ~ of feet —Charles Dickens⟩ **3** *Scot* **a :** habitual course or manner of action **:** CUSTOM, PRACTICE **b :** customary occupation **:** regular business **:** EMPLOYMENT, LABOR, TRADE **4 a** *archaic* **:** the action of a male bird in copulation **b :** CHALAZA 1 **5 :** an injury of one foot by another foot of a horse (as in overreaching) **6 a** (1) **:** the part of the bottom surface of a shoe including or excluding the heel that touches level ground (2) **:** the part of a wheel that bears on a road or rail; *esp* **:** the thickened face of an automobile tire (3) **:** CATERPILLAR TREAD **b :** the design (as a raised or inset pattern of corrugations) on a tread ⟨a recognizable hobnail ~ —Frank Cameron⟩ **7 :** the distance in inches between the central points of contact with the ground of the two front wheels or the two rear wheels of a vehicle — compare WHEELBASE **8 a :** the upper horizontal part of a step (as in a stair) on which the foot is placed **b :** the width of such a part of a step **:** the horizontal distance between consecutive risers ⟨a stair with a 12-inch ~⟩ **c :** the flat or gently sloping surface of one of a series of steplike geologic landforms ⟨the ~ of a terrace⟩ **9 :** the length of the keel of a ship **10 :** the part of a rail on which the wheels of a railroad car bear

tread·er \-də(r)\ *n* -s [ME *treder,* fr. *treden* to tread + *-er* — more at TREAD] **:** one that treads ⟨automobile tire ~*s*⟩ ⟨the use of ~*s* in wine making⟩

1trea·dle \'tred°l\ *n* -s *often attrib* [ME *tredel* step of a stair, treadle, fr. OE, step of a stair, fr. *tredan* to step, tread + *-el,* suffix used to denote a means or an instrument] **1 a :** a swiveling or lever device pressed by the foot to drive a machine actuated by foot power and usu. operating a crank by means of a connecting rod **b :** one attached directly to the end of a crank (as in a bicycle) **:** PEDAL **c :** a device resembling such a treadle; *specif* **:** a lever actuated by a passing train to operate an alarm at a crossing or by a motor vehicle to operate a highway traffic control mechanism **2 :** CHALAZA 1

2treadle \"\ *vb* **treadled; treadled; treadling** \-d(°)liŋ\ **treadles** *vi* **:** to operate a treadle; *specif* **:** to proceed by pedaling a bicycle **~** *vt* **1 :** to operate (as a machine) by a treadle **2 :** to tread over (clay) ⟨a brickmaker, with boards or wooden shoes on his feet, ~*s* clay to pick out stones⟩

1treadmill \'=,=\ *n* [*1tread* + *mill*] **1 a :** a mill worked by persons treading on steps on the periphery of a wide wheel having a horizontal axis and used formerly in prison discipline **b :** a mill worked by an animal (as a horse or dog) treading an endless belt and used also on a stock farm or ranch to exercise a bull difficult to control as well as to utilize his power for belt operations **c :** a similar device used in studies of physiological functions **2 :** a wearisome routine resembling continued activity on a treadmill

2treadmill \"\ *vi* **:** to labor on or as if on a treadmill

tread plate *n* **:** a metal plate attached to a stair tread to prevent slipping

tread-softly \'=;==\ *n* -ES [fr. the imper. phrase *tread softly*] **:** SPURGE NETTLE

treadway bridge \'=,=-\ *n* [*treadway* fr. *2tread* + *way*] **:** a floating bridge having two tracks as a roadway

treadwheel \'=,=\ *n* [*1tread* + *wheel*] **:** a wheel turned by a person or animal by treading, climbing, or pushing with the feet upon its periphery or face — compare TREADMILL 1

treas *abbr* treasurer; treasury

trea·son \'trēz°n\ *n* -s [ME *tresoun,* fr. OF *traison,* fr. ML *tradition-, traditio,* fr. L, action of handing over, teaching, tradition, fr. *traditus* (past part. of *tradere* to hand over, betray) + *-ion-, -io* -ion — more at TRAITOR] **1 :** the betrayal of a trust or confidence **:** breach of faith **:** PERFIDY, TREACHERY ⟨corruption in public office is ~ —A.E.Stevenson b.1900⟩ **2 a :** the offense of attempting by overt acts to overthrow the government of the state to which the offender owes allegiance or to kill or personally injure the sovereign or his family — see HIGH TREASON 1 **b** (1) **:** the betrayal in early English law of a lord by his vassal (2) **:** the violation in early feudal law by a vassal of his allegiance to his superior by one or more undefined acts of a serious nature (as betrayal to an enemy, adultery with the superior's wife, or forgery of his seal) — see PETIT TREASON **3** *obs* **:** an act or an instance of treason ⟨rebellions and ~*s* against their princes —Matthew Sutcliffe⟩

trea·son·able \-°nəbəl\ *adj* [ME *tresounable,* fr. *tresoun* treason + *-able*] **:** relating to, consisting of, or involving treason **:** having the characteristics of or partaking of the guilt of treason **:** PERFIDIOUS, TREACHEROUS ⟨a ~ betrayal of American interests —Elmer Davis⟩ ⟨participation in a ~ conspiracy —Henry Hallam⟩

trea·son·ably \-blē\ *adv* [ME *tresounably,* fr. *tresounable* + *-ly*] **:** in a treasonable manner

treason felony *n* **:** an offense under English law partaking of the nature of treason (as devising by overt act to depose or levy war against the sovereign to compel changes of policy or to intimidate or overawe Parliament) and usu. involving life imprisonment rather than the death penalty

trea·son·ous \-°nəs\ *adj* [ME *tresounous,* fr. *tresoun* + *-ous*] **:** full of, abounding in, or characterized by treason **:** TREASONABLE ⟨tried for ~ crimes —John Dryden⟩

treasr *abbr* treasurer

trea·sur·able \'trezh(ə)rəbəl, 'trāzh-\ *adj* [*2treasure* + *-able*] **:** worthy of being treasured **:** PRECIOUS ⟨~ additions to the record library —C.M.Smith⟩ ⟨the ~ stuff of English poetry —Robert Fitzgerald⟩

1trea·sure \-zhə(r)\ *n* -s *often attrib* [ME *tresor, tresour,* fr. OF *tresor,* fr. L *thesaurus* hoard, treasure, fr. Gk *thēsauros*] **1 a** (1) **:** wealth (as money, plate, jewels, or precious metals) accumulated, stored, or hoarded up ⟨the pirate's ~⟩ ⟨digging for buried ~⟩ (2) **:** wealth of any kind or in any form **:** RICHES ⟨if the ~ of the men who run the railroad is elsewhere committed —*Value Line*⟩ ⟨a military victory won at unparalleled cost of blood and ~ —Henry Hazlitt⟩ **b :** a stock or store of money in reserve **2 a :** something of great worth or value **:** something valued and preserved as precious ⟨some of the richest ~*s* of sculpture and painting —Wilmot Harrison⟩ ⟨regions richest in these archeological ~*s* —*Amer. Guide Series: Ind.*⟩ **b :** a person esteemed as rare or precious **:** GEM 2b, JEWEL 2b(1) ⟨my maid is a ~⟩ **3 :** a valuable store, accumulation, or reserve supply **:** a collection of precious things ⟨this immense ~ of accumulated human thought and experience —Charlton Laird⟩ ⟨the illustrations are a ~ of charming Georgian houses —Anne Douglas⟩

2treasure \"\ *vt* **treasured; treasured; treasuring** \-zh(ə)riŋ\ **treasures** [ME *tresoren, tresouren,* fr. *tresor, tresour,* n.] **1 :** to collect and store up (something of value) for preservation, security, or future use **:** HOARD ⟨~ gold⟩ **2 :** to store away and preserve in or as if in the memory **:** retain and guard from being diminished, injured, forgotten, or lost ⟨not only did he ~ the lines of his favorite poets —Clark Wissler⟩ ⟨he ~*s* every least indication that she may be softer than her sister —E.K.Brown⟩ — sometimes used with *up* ⟨*treasured* up those pithy bits of local speech —Willa Cather⟩ **3 :** to hold or keep as precious **:** regard as dear and worthy of careful preservation **:** CHERISH, PRIZE ⟨those who *treasured* the New England tradition of local self-government —*Amer. Guide Series: N.H.*⟩ ⟨a book which will always be *treasured* —Herbert Read⟩ **syn** see APPRECIATE

treasure-house \'==,=\ *n* [ME *tresorhous, tresourhous,* fr. *tresor, tresour* treasure + *hous* house] **1 :** a building where treasure is kept **:** TREASURY **2 :** a place or source (as a collection) where many things of value can be found ⟨cities that are among Europe's finest *treasure-houses* of art and history —*Geog. Jour.*⟩ ⟨this book is a *treasure-house* of marvelous reading —Hal Lehrman⟩

treasure hunt *n* **1 :** an instance of searching for something that has real or imagined value **2 :** a game in which each player or team tries to be first to find whatever has been hidden

trea·sur·er \-zh(ə)rə(r)\ *n* -s [ME *tresorer, tresourer,* fr. OF *tresorier,* fr. *tresor* + *-ier*] **1 :** one having official charge of treasure; *esp* **:** a guardian of a collection of treasures (as in a cathedral church) **:** CURATOR **2 :** an officer entrusted with the receipt, care, and disbursal of funds: as **a :** one performing such functions for a king, noble, or other dignitary — see TREASURER OF THE HOUSEHOLD **b :** a governmental officer charged with receiving, keeping, and disbursing public revenues — compare CHANCELLOR OF THE EXCHEQUER, COMPTROLLER, FIRST LORD OF THE TREASURY, LORD HIGH TREASURER OF ENGLAND, TREASURER OF THE UNITED STATES **c :** the executive financial officer of a nongovernmental organization (as a club, society, or business corporation) **3 :** one having charge of keeping something valuable or precious ⟨the secrets of which thou seemest to be a too faithful ~ —Sir Walter Scott⟩ **4** *obs* **:** one that treasures something **:** a keeper, hoarder, or preserver of something precious

treasurer of the household *often cap T&H* **:** an officer of the English royal household who has only nominal duties and whose office is filled by a member of the House of Commons, usu. one of the principal Government whips

treasurer of the united states *often cap T & cap U&S* **:** an officer of the U.S. Treasury Department having charge of the receipt and keeping of all government moneys and their disbursal upon warrants properly drawn and countersigned

trea·sur·er·ship \-(r),ship\ *n* [ME *tresorership,* fr. *tresorer* + *-ship*] **:** the office of treasurer

treasure ship *n* **:** a ship with a cargo of gold, silver, jewels, or other valuables; *esp* **:** one returning from the New World to Spain in the 16th century

trea·sur·ess \-zhərəs\ *n* -ES [ME *tresouresse,* irreg. fr. *tresourer* + *-esse* -ess] **:** a female treasurer

treasure trove *n, pl* **treasure troves** [AF *tresor trové,* lit., found treasure, fr. OF *tresor* treasure + *trové,* past part. of *trover* to find, fr. (assumed) VL *tropare* — more at TREASURE, TROUVÈRE] **1 :** something in the nature of treasure that anyone finds; *specif* **:** gold or silver in the form of money, plate, or bullion which is found in the earth or otherwise hidden and the owner of which is not known **2 :** a discovery or something discovered that is full of treasures **:** a valuable and productive source ⟨natural gas and petroleum are veritable *treasure troves* of paraffin . . . and aromatic hydrocarbons —*Science*⟩ ⟨the diary . . . is a *treasure trove* to the abnormal psychologist —V.L.Parrington⟩

trea·sury \'trezh(ə)rē, 'trāzh-, -ri\ *n* -ES *often attrib* [ME *tresorie, tresourie,* fr. OF *tresorie,* fr. *tresor* treasure + *-ie* -y — more at TREASURE] **1 a :** a place (as a room or building) in which stores of wealth or valuable objects are kept ⟨in the ~ of the cathedral . . . there is a fine, whole, uncut chasuble —Daniel Rock⟩ **b :** the place of deposit and disbursement of collected funds; *esp* **:** one where public revenues are deposited, kept, and disbursed **c :** the funds (as of a government, business corporation, or individual) kept or held to be kept in such a depository **2** *obs* **:** TREASURE ⟨thy sumptuous buildings . . . have cost a mass of public ~ —Shak.⟩ **3** *usu cap* **a :** a governmental department having charge of finances (as the collection, management, and expenditure of public revenues) **b :** the building in which the business of such a government department is transacted **4 :** TREASURE-HOUSE 2 ⟨the old house, a ~ of beams and paneling —Thomas Wood †1950⟩ ⟨edited another collection and called it *Treasury* of Science —G.I. Schwartz⟩ **5 :** the weekly payment of a theatrical company **6** *usu cap* **:** a government security (as a note or bill) issued by or under the authority of the Treasury ⟨a decline in *Treasuries* and . . . corporate bonds —*Mag. of Wall Street*⟩ **7** *often cap* **a :** an ancient Greek building for archives and treasures located near a sanctuary **b :** BEEHIVE TOMB

treasury bench *n, usu cap T&B* [so called fr. its being occupied by the First Lord of the Treasury] **:** the first row of seats on the right of the speaker in the British House of Commons and other Commonwealth parliamentary chambers that is occupied by cabinet ministers and other members of the Government — compare FRONT BENCH

treasury bill *n* **:** a short-term obligation issued by a government at a discount, bearing no interest, and payable at par at maturity

treasury bond *n* **:** a government bond issued by or under the authority of the Treasury

treasury certificate *n* **:** an interest-bearing obligation of the U.S. Treasury with a maturity up to one year

treasury currency *n* **:** currency (as coins, United States notes, or Federal Reserve notes) other than gold coin or gold certificates for which the U.S. Treasury is directly responsible

treasury note *n* **:** a currency note issued directly by a governmental treasury; *esp* **:** one issued by the U.S. Treasury in payment for silver bullion purchased under the Sherman Silver Purchase Act of 1890 — compare FEDERAL RESERVE NOTE, GREENBACK, SILVER CERTIFICATE

treasury of merits *or* **treasury of the church** *or* **treasury of the saints** *usu cap C* **:** the superabundant satisfaction of Christ for men's sins and the excess of merit of the Virgin Mary and the saints forming a store held in Roman Catholic theology to be effective to the salvation of others and to be available for dispensation through indulgences

treasury savings certificate *n* **:** a registered nontransferable certificate of the U.S. government issued between 1921 and 1924 in denominations of $25, $100, and $1000 maturity value five years from date of issue with the interest rate being about 4½ percent per annum compounded semiannually if held to maturity

trea·sury·ship \-rē,ship\ *n* **:** TREASURERSHIP ⟨took the ~ of the navy —George Bancroft⟩

treasury stock *n* **:** issued stock reacquired by a corporation and held as an asset — compare UNISSUED STOCK

treasury warrant *n* **:** a warrant for the payment of money into or from a public treasury

1treat \'trēt, *usu* -ēd.+V\ *vb* -ED/-ING/-S [ME *treten,* fr. OF *traitier* to treat, manage, fr. L *tractare* to pull violently, handle, manage, fr. *tractus,* past part. of *trahere* to draw, pull, drag — more at DRAW] *vi* **1 :** to carry on negotiations with another with the object of a settlement **:** discuss terms of accommodation or settlement **:** NEGOTIATE ⟨the commander-in-chief . . . was to ~ for an armistice —Bernard Pares⟩ ⟨willing to ~ with you but . . . afraid that your terms may be too high —W.M.Thackeray⟩ **2 :** to deal with a matter or subject esp. in writing or speaking **:** give an exposition **:** DISCOURSE — usu. used with *of* but sometimes with *with* ⟨the fifth essay ~*s* of the problems of map engraving —Jean Mitchell⟩ ⟨~*s* in detail of the origin of the council —R.A.Hall b.1911⟩ ⟨his article . . . ~*s* with an important conservation subject —*Nature Mag.*⟩ **3 :** to pay another's expenses (as for a meal or drink) usu. at a public place **:** bear the expense of another's entertainment **:** give or bear the expenses of a treat esp. as a compliment, an expression of regard or friendship, or as a bribe **~** *vt* **1 a :** to deal with (as a subject or theme) in speech or writing **:** ARGUE, DISCUSS, EXPOUND ⟨lectured enthusiastically about each of the poets . . . whom he ~*ed* —D.M.Allen⟩ ⟨literary history . . . has constantly to ~ problems of intellectual history —René Wellek & Austin Warren⟩ ⟨monthly programs ~ different aspects of astronomy —*Amer. Guide. Series: N.Y.City*⟩ **b :** to give artistic or literary treatment to **:** deal with in an artistic way **:** present or represent artistically esp. in a specified manner or style ⟨a romantically ~*ed* bronze group —*Amer. Guide Series: Minn.*⟩ ⟨the hall, ~*ed* in the Corinthian order —*Amer. Guide Series: Vt.*⟩ **c :** to handle, manage, or otherwise deal with ⟨food is plentiful and ~*ed* with imagination —Cecil Beaton⟩ **2** *obs* **:** to negotiate with a view to settling or arranging **:** discuss the terms of **:** ARRANGE **3 a :** to deal with or bear oneself toward in some specified way **:** behave or act towards **:** assume an attitude or form of behavior to **:** USE ⟨the worker's stay on the job depends on whether he is ~*ed* right or wrong —Carl Sandburg⟩ ⟨note with what scant respect the generals . . . were ~*ed* —C.H.Dewhurst⟩ ⟨the tones of nature require . . . to be ~*ed* relatively by the painter —C.W.H. Johnson⟩ **b :** to regard (as something or in a particular way) and act toward or deal with accordingly — usu. used with *as* ⟨asking me to ~ the news . . . as strictly confidential —O.S.

Nock⟩ ⟨adopted into the tribe and ~*ed* as an Indian squaw — *Amer. Guide Series: Md.*⟩ ⟨regional laws . . . ~*ed* defamation as a private delict —T.F.T.Plucknett⟩ **4 a :** to show hospitality to : ENTERTAIN, FEAST ⟨a host who ~*s* all the great persons in princely lodgings —John Evelyn⟩ **b** (1) **:** to provide (as another person) gratuitously with food, drink, entertainment, or some other source of enjoyment or gratification esp. as a compliment, gesture of kindness, or bribe — usu. used with *to* ⟨he ~*ed* her to a strawberry soda⟩ (2) **:** to provide (oneself) with a similar source of enjoyment or gratification — usu. used with *to* ⟨~*ed* herself to a new mink coat⟩ **c :** to provide with something that is or is held (as in irony or for amusement) to be a source of pleasure or gratification ⟨the Americans were ~*ed* to a remarkable display as the Tripolitan ship blew up —C.S.Forester⟩ ⟨when he punished he ~*ed* the culprit to ten minutes of biting irony first —Storm Jameson⟩ **5 a :** to care for (as a patient or part of the body) medically or surgically **:** deal with by medical or surgical means **:** give a medical treatment to ⟨during his hospital stay, he was ~*ed* with . . . transfusions of blood —*Jour. Amer. Med. Assoc.*⟩ ⟨120 persons were ~*ed* for miscellaneous . . . injuries — *Pasadena (Calif.) Independent*⟩ **b :** to seek cure or relief of (as a disease) ⟨~ a bruise with hot applications⟩ **6 a :** to subject to some action (as of a chemical reagent) **:** act upon with some agent ⟨~ a substance with sulfuric acid⟩ ⟨metals . . . ~*ed* to make maintenance a simple thing —Betty Pepis⟩ **b :** to subject (as a natural or manufactured article) to some process to improve the appearance, taste, usefulness, or some other quality **:** PROCESS ⟨~ rugs by washing⟩ ⟨port is a wine that is ~*ed*⟩ **syn** DEAL (*with*), HANDLE: TREAT in the sense of doing about, serving, or coping with is usu. accompanied by context indicating an attitude, temperament, point of view determining behavior or a manner of approach or execution ⟨*treat* all controversial questions impartially⟩ ⟨*treat* a subject realistically⟩ ⟨*treat* with care⟩ ⟨*treating* her guests cavalierly by *treating* with scorn nearly all the ancient virtues —A.W.Hummel⟩ ⟨before Massasoit died he made his sons promise to *treat* the Brown family kindly —J.R.Clift⟩ DEAL (*with*) may suggest managing, controlling, authoritative disposing ⟨she *dealt with* moral problems as a cleaver *deals with* meat —James Joyce⟩ ⟨the dean *dealt with* the matter promptly⟩ ⟨the only previous meeting . . . had *dealt* essentially *with* the immediate problems of military cooperation —F.W.D.Deakin⟩ and sometimes it suggests a relationship between persons or parties on a more or less even basis ⟨we're *dealing with* a ruthless foe that knows exactly what he wants —L.B.Salomon⟩ HANDLE is often interchangeable with TREAT and DEAL (*with*); it may suggest a placing, directing, disposing, or manipulating with or as if with the hand ⟨*handle* an ax skillfully⟩ ⟨*handle* the distribution of tickets⟩ ⟨*handling* the arrangement of flowers⟩ ⟨the federal government picked up a group of unfilled functions that the states could not *handle* —A.A.Berle⟩

²**treat** \"\ *n* -s **1** *obs* **:** ENTREATY 2 **2 a** *archaic* **:** an entertainment of food and drink freely provided **:** FEAST ⟨when the tired glutton labors through a ~ —Alexander Pope⟩ **b :** an entertainment (as a picnic) given without expense to those invited **:** a pleasure party gratuitously arranged ⟨~*s* for young people are being organized —Frank Frost⟩ **3** *obs* **a :** the way in which one is treated **:** TREATMENT **b :** the treatment accorded to guests or visitors **:** RECEPTION, WELCOME **4 :** something that affords gratification or pleasure **:** a great satisfaction **:** a cause of joy, delight, or sometimes amusement **:** something highly enjoyable often by being unexpected ⟨there may be pineapple chunks . . . as a ~ for tea —A.D.Rees⟩ ⟨the London theatrical season is providing some distinguished ~*s* for Coronation visitors —Mollie Panter-Downes⟩ ⟨enjoy the ~ of hearing him talk —*Christian Science Monitor*⟩

³**treat** \ˈtrēt\ *n* -s [ME *trait, tret,* fr. AF *trait*] *dial Eng* **:** bran of medium coarseness — compare CHISEL

treat·able \ˈtrēd·əbəl, -ētəb-\ *adj* [ME *tretable,* fr. MF *traitable,* fr. L *tractabilis* — more at TRACTABLE] **1 a** *archaic* **:** easily managed, handled, or dealt with **:** open to appeal or argument **:** DOCILE, TRACTABLE ⟨those arts by which the people were rendered more ~ —A.A.Cooper⟩ **b** *obs* **:** gentle and moderate rather than violent in nature ⟨in France . . . changes of seasons are less ~ than they are with us —William Temple⟩ **2 :** capable of being treated **:** yielding or responsive to treatment ⟨~ aluminum alloys⟩ ⟨a ~ disease⟩

treat·er \ˈtrēd·ə(r), -ētə-\ *n* -s [ME *treyter,* fr. MF *traiteur,* fr. *traitier* to treat, negotiate + *-eur* -or — more at TREAT] **1 :** one that negotiates terms of a settlement **:** NEGOTIATOR **2** [¹*treat* + *-er*] **:** one that treats: as **a :** one that treats materials (as timber, oil, or beer) with chemicals **b :** an apparatus (as an agitator) for treating materials

treating *n* -s [ME *treting,* fr. gerund of *treten* to treat — more at TREAT] **:** the action of one that treats; *specif* **:** the gratuitous provision of food, drink, or entertainment to a person in order to influence one or more votes at an election ⟨~ is a statutory offense in the United Kingdom⟩

trea·tise \ˈtrēd·əs, -ētəs, *chiefly Brit* -əz\ *n* -s [ME *tretis,* fr. AF *tretiz,* prob. fr. OF *traitier* to treat — more at TREAT] **1 :** a writing (as a book or article) that treats a subject; *specif* **:** one that provides in a systematic manner and for an expository or argumentive purpose a methodical discussion of the facts and principles involved and conclusions reached ⟨the great source book and ~ on canon law —G.C.Sellery⟩ ⟨preparation of this ~ on the natural resources of Louisiana —J.B. Robson⟩ **2** *obs* **:** a spoken or written narrative **:** ACCOUNT, STORY, TALE ⟨my bell of hair would at a dismal ~ rouse and stir —Shak.⟩ **syn** see DISCOURSE

treat·ment \ˈtrētmənt\ *n* -s [¹*treat* + *-ment*] **1 :** the action or manner of treating: as **a :** conduct or behavior towards another party (as a person, thing, or group) ⟨regulations . . . for the ~ of all interned civilians —J.S.Pictet⟩ **b :** the action or manner of treating a patient medically or surgically ⟨diagnosis and ~ of tuberculosis⟩ ⟨required immediate medical ~⟩ **c :** subjection of something to the action of an agent or process ⟨the ~ of water supplies to make them safely potable —A.C. Morrison⟩ ⟨sewage ~⟩ **d :** the action or manner of dealing with something often in a specified way ⟨get capital gains ~ on income from a patent sale —J.T.Norman⟩ ⟨views . . . on the proper ~ of the conquered southern states —Carol L. Thompson⟩ ⟨a passage remarkable for its ~ of the age-old problem of freedom and authority —R.M.Weaver⟩ **e :** literary or artistic handling (as of a subject) esp. in terms of style ⟨two figures of sufficient importance to warrant ~ in separate chapters—R.A.Hall b.1911⟩ ⟨the architectural ~ is based . . . on the domestic style of northern Italy —*Amer. Guide Series: La.*⟩ **f :** preventive guidance and corrective training esp. of juvenile delinquents and youthful criminal offenders **2 :** an instance of treating ⟨the best ~*s* to date of several . . . bits of American history —John Bakeless⟩ ⟨a series of upper sidewall ~*s* in the architectural orders —*Amer. Guide Series: N.Y.*⟩ ⟨charges . . . $1 per ~ for occupational therapy —*Jour. Amer. Med. Assoc.*⟩ **3** *obs* **:** ENTERTAINMENT, FEAST ⟨accept such ~ as a swain affords —Alexander Pope⟩ **4 :** something (as a fertilizer or preserver) used in treating ⟨a seed disinfectant ~⟩ **5 :** an outline of the action of a proposed screenplay or television script that is considerably more detailed than a synopsis — compare SCENARIO, SCRIPT **6 :** the techniques or actions customarily applied in a specified situation: as **a :** a pattern of actions (as insults, annoyances, or physical punishment) designed to punish or persuade ⟨the new recruit got the ~ from a brutal sergeant⟩ **b :** a pattern of actions (as the bestowal of gifts and favors) designed to reward, encourage, or convince ⟨getting the standard ~ of cocktail parties, press interviews and deals with advertisers —*Time*⟩ **c :** the provision (as by a shop or restaurant) of the goods and services associated with a usu. specified fee or order ⟨the full ~ is $250 and up —Lois Long⟩

treats *pl of* TREAT, *pres 3d sing of* TREAT

trea·ty \ˈtrēd·|ē, -ēt|, |i\ *n* -ES *often attrib* [ME *tretee,* fr. MF *traité,* fr. ML & L; ML *tractatus* treaty, fr. L, handling, treatment, treatise, fr. *tractatus,* past part. of *tractare* to handle, manage, discuss, treat — more at TREAT] **1** *obs* **:** TREATISE ⟨in his excellent ~ of bodies —Sir Thomas Browne⟩ **2 :** the action of treating and esp. of negotiating **:** discussion aimed at an adjustment of differences or the reaching of an agreement — usu. used in the phrase *in treaty* ⟨unable to endure his loneliness, he was in ~ for a new wife —*Times Lit. Supp.*⟩ **3 a :** an agreement or arrangement made by negotiation: (1) **:** PRIVATE TREATY (2) **:** a contract in writing between two or more political authorities (as states or sovereigns) formally signed by representatives duly authorized and usu. ratified by the lawmaking authority of the state ⟨the president . . . shall have power, by and with the advice and consent of the Senate, to make *treaties* —*U.S. Constitution*⟩ — see PERSONAL TREATY, REAL TREATY; compare BILATERAL, CONVENTION, EXECUTIVE AGREEMENT, MULTILATERAL, PROTOCOL **b :** a document in which such a contract is set down **4 :** a formal meeting between representatives of the U. S. government and of one or more Indian tribes designed to produce a settlement (as of issues in dispute) ⟨Congress had promised them a ~, which was to have been holden about this time —Rufus Putnam⟩ **5 :** an agreement or contract (as between companies) providing for treaty reinsurance

treaty indian *n, usu cap I* **:** a No. American Indian belonging to a tribe that has signed a treaty with the U. S. or Canada

trea·ty·ite \|ē,īt\ *n* -s *usu cap* [*treaty* + *-ite*] **:** a supporter of the treaty of 1921 establishing the Irish Free State

treaty port *n* **:** one of a number of seaports, river ports, and inland cities in China, Japan, and Korea formerly open by treaty to commerce with other nations orig. as exceptions to a general policy of nonintercourse

treaty reinsurance *n* **:** reinsurance under a general agreement that automatically reinsures in accordance with its terms all risks of a given class to a predetermined extent as soon as they are insured by the direct underwriter

treb·bia·no \trebˈyä(,)nō\ *n* -s *usu cap* [It, perh. fr. L *Trebulanus* of Trebula, fr. *Trebula,* an ancient town in Campania, Italy + *-anus* -an] **:** UGNI BLANC

¹**tre·ble** \ˈtrebəl\ *n* -s [ME *treble, trible,* fr. MF *treble,* fr. *treble,* adj.] **1 a :** the highest of the four voice parts in vocal music **:** SOPRANO **b** (1) **:** a singer taking this part (2) *chiefly Brit* **:** a boy singer taking this part **c :** a musical instrument taking this part **d :** a high-pitched or shrill voice, tone, or sound ⟨a child's ~⟩ **e :** the highest bell of a ring in change ringing **f :** the upper half of the musical pitch range — contrasted with *bass* **g :** the higher portion of the audio frequency range in sound recording and broadcasting involving frequencies above 1000 cycles per second **2 :** something that is treble in construction, uses, amount, number, value, or other characteristic: **a :** a rack on which new sheets of handmade paper or sheets of newly printed paper are dried **b :** a win of three races by one horse

²**treble** \"\ *vb* **trebled; trebled; trebling** \-b(ə)liŋ\ **trebles** [ME *treblen,* fr. MF *trebler,* fr. *treble,* adj.] *vt* **:** to make three times as much or as many or as great **:** increase threefold **:** multiply by three ⟨the first daily penny paper . . . *trebled* its circulation —Alistair Cooke⟩ ⟨the commercial value of the looms was doubled or *trebled* overnight —*Irish Digest*⟩ ~ *vi* **1 :** to speak or sing in a treble tone **2 :** to become threefold **:** grow to three times the size, amount, or number ⟨its population has *trebled* since 1900 —*Amer. Guide Series: Pa.*⟩

³**treble** \"\ *adj* [ME *treble, trible,* fr. MF *treble,* fr. L *triplus* — more at TRIPLE] **1 a :** having three parts, elements, things, or uses **:** consisting of three members, sets, or layers **:** THREEFOLD ⟨a ~ row of bright red coral beads —R.M.Fox⟩ ⟨twenty-five strokes from the ~ whips —Lord Dunsany⟩ ⟨a lofty tower . . . with ~ walls —John Dryden⟩ **b :** having a threefold character **:** occurring in three kinds or existing in three ways ⟨every episode has its double and ~ meaning —Frederic Harrison⟩ **2 :** three times repeated **:** triple in number or amount **:** three times as much or as many ⟨~ salaries were paid —W.O.Douglas⟩ ⟨a newspaper with a circulation ~ that of its competitor⟩ ⟨sold for ~ the price⟩ ⟨a claim for ~ damages⟩ **3 a :** relating to or having the range of a musical treble ⟨~ violin⟩ ⟨~ voice⟩ **b :** high or sharp in tone **:** ACUTE, HIGH-PITCHED, SHRILL ⟨with her constant ~ cry —Ethel Wilson⟩ **c :** of, relating to, or having the range of treble in sound recording and broadcasting ⟨~ frequencies⟩ **4 :** of, relating to, or constituting a fishhook consisting of 3 single hooks fastened back to back usu. with an angle of 120 degrees between adjacent hooks — compare GANG HOOK

⁴**treble** *adv* [ME, fr. *treble,* adj.] *obs* **:** TREBLY

treble bob *n* **:** one of the chief methods of change ringing in which the treble has a uniform but zigzag course and all the bells dodge — see CHANGE RINGING illustration

treble clef *n* **1 :** G CLEF **2 :** TREBLE STAFF

treble staff *n* **:** the musical staff carrying the G clef

treblet *var of* TRIBLET

treble viol *n* **:** a 6-stringed viol made an octave higher than the bass viol and used chiefly in ensemble playing — called also *descant viol*

treble staff

tre·bly \-blē\ *adv* [³*treble* + *-ly*] **1 :** in a treble manner or degree **:** TRIPLY ⟨they have been ~ fortunate —Ernest Barker⟩ **2 :** in a treble tone ⟨listening to children ~ chant —*Brit. Books of the Month*⟩

treb·u·chet \ˈtrebyə,shet\ *n* -s [ME *trebochet,* fr. MF *trebachet,* fr. OF, fr. *trebuchier* to stumble, trip, fall, fr. *tre-* (fr. L *trans-, tra-*) + *-buchier* (fr. *buc, bu* trunk of the body, of Gmc origin; akin to OHG *būh* belly — more at BUCKET] **1** *or* **tre·buck·et** \ˈtrē,bəkət\ **:** a medieval military engine designed to hurl stones and similar missiles with great force by means of a heavy weight fastened to the short arm of a lever which falls and raises the end of the long throwing arm with great velocity **2 :** a small delicately poised balance or scale made with a pan that tilts and used esp. in assaying and by chemists

tre·cen·tist \trāˈchentəst\ *n* -s *sometimes cap* [It *trecentista,* fr. *trecento* + *-ista* -ist] **:** a poet or artist of the trecento

tre·cen·to \-n·(,)tō\ *n* -s *sometimes cap* [It, lit., three hundred (abbr. of thirteen hundred), fr. *tre* three (fr. L *tres*) + *cento* hundred, fr. L *centum* — more at THREE, HUNDRED] **:** the 14th century; *specif* **:** the 14th century period in Italian literature and art

trech·mann·ite \ˈtrekmə,nīt\ *n* -s [Charles O. *Trechmann* †1917 Eng. mineralogist + E *-ite*] **:** a silver arsenic sulfide prob. $AgAsS_2$ occurring in small red rhombohedral crystals

tre cor·de \ˈtrāˈkȯrdā\ *adv (or adj)* [It, lit., three strings] **:** with soft pedal released — used as a direction in piano music at the close of a passage una corda

tre·cu·lia \trəˈkyülēə\ *n, cap* [NL, fr. Auguste A. L. *Trécul* †1896 Fr. botanist + NL *-ia*] **:** a small genus of African trees and shrubs (family Moraceae) having undivided coriaceous leaves, dioecious flowers, and large edible fruits — see BREADFRUIT

tre·dec·ile \trəˈdesəl\ *n* -s [L *tres* three + *decem* ten + E *-ile* — more at THREE, TEN] **:** the astrological aspect including 108 degrees

tre·decillion \ˌtrē+\ *n, often attrib* [L *tres* three + E *decillion*] — see NUMBER table

tre·drille \trəˈdril\ *or* **tre·dille** \-ˈdil\ *n* -s [alter. (influenced by L *tres* three) of *quadrille*] **:** a 3-handed card game similar to ombre popular in the 17th and 18th centuries

¹**tree** \ˈtrē\ *n* -s *often attrib* [ME *tre, tree,* fr. OE *trēow;* akin to OFris & ON *trē* tree, OS *trio, treo* tree, OHG *apholtra* apple tree, Goth *triu* tree, wood, Gk *drys* tree, *dory* spear, Skt *dāru* wood, *dru* tree, branch, wood] **1 a :** a woody perennial plant having a single main stem that may be short but is usu. considerably elongated, has generally few or no branches on its lower part, and is crowned with a head of branches and foliage or (as in palms) of foliage only — compare HERB, SHRUB **b :** a shrub or herb that grows naturally in or is trained into an arborescent form ⟨old rose ~*s*⟩ ⟨a sturdy banana ~⟩ ⟨some plants that are tall ~*s* under favorable conditions are mere shrubs at the extremes of their range⟩ **2 a** *archaic* **:** the substance of trees esp. as a source of structural material **b :** a piece of wood (as a stick, stave, post, or pole) either dressed or undressed and usu. adapted to a particular use: as (1) **:** a piece (as a bar, lever, brace, or support) forming a part of a structure or implement — usu. used in combination — see AXLETREE, CHESSTREE, CROSSTREE, DOUBLETREE, SINGLETREE, WHIFFLETREE (2) *obs* **:** the shaft of a spear or lance (as of a spade) **c :** a structure or fabrication of or typically or originally of wood: as (1) *obs* **:** SHIP (2) *archaic* **:** GALLOWS (3) *chiefly Scot* **:** a wooden container (as a cask for ale) (4) **:** SADDLETREE (5) **:** SHOE TREE **d** *sometimes cap* **:** CHRISTMAS TREE ⟨gifts clustered under the ~⟩ **3 :** something having the typical form of or felt to resemble a tree: as **a :** a design, diagram, or diagrammatic representation that depicts a branching from an original stem ⟨a genealogical ~⟩ **b :** an arborescent aggregation of crystals — see LEAD TREE **c :** a much-branched system of channels esp. in an animal body ⟨the vascular ~⟩; *also* **:** a cast of such a tree ⟨a bronchial ~ prepared by corrosion techniques⟩ — **as trees walking :** without clear definition or outlines **:** INDISTINCTLY, OBSCURELY — **up a tree** *adv (or adj)* **:** at a disadvantage or in an embarrassing position **:** CORNERED, TRAPPED

²**tree** \"\ *vb* **treed; treed; treeing; trees** *vt* **1 a :** to drive to or up a tree **:** cause to take refuge in a tree ⟨*treed* by a bull⟩ ⟨dogs ~*ing* small game⟩ **b :** to put into a position of extreme disadvantage **:** CORNER; *esp* **:** to bring (an evasive individual) to bay **2 a :** to furnish or construct with a tree ⟨~ an axle⟩ **b :** to plant or cover with trees **c** (1) **:** to fit (as a shoe) with a tree (2) **:** to shape and stretch (as a saddle) over a tree ~ *vi* **1 a :** to take refuge in a tree ⟨the coon soon *treed*⟩ **b :** to cause an animal to take refuge esp. in a tree ⟨the dogs *treed* early that night⟩ **2 :** to take the form of a tree ⟨crystals ~*ing* in a saturated solution⟩

tree agate *n* **:** moss agate when the dendritic markings resemble trees

tree aloe *n* **:** QUIVER TREE

tree ant *n* **:** any of several chiefly tropical ants (genus *Oecophylla*) that build their nests in trees of leaves sewn together by a secretion of the web-spinning larvae which the adults handle like shuttles

tree azalea *n* **:** a tall shrub (*Azalea arborescens*) of the southeastern U.S. often cultivated for its very fragrant white or pink flowers from which showy purple stamens protrude

tree bear *n* **:** RACCOON

tree belt *n* **:** a strip of ground lying between the sidewalk line and the curb line, usu. turfed, and commonly planted with shade trees — called also *tree lawn*

treebine \ˈ=,=\ *n* -s **:** any of various cultivated vines of the genus *Cissus*

tree boa *n* **:** an arboreal boa; *esp* **:** a member of either of two tropical American genera (*Boa* and *Epicrates*) of moderate-sized bird-eating boas

tree bracket *n* **:** a bracket-shaped fungus (as of the genus *Polyporus*)

tree burst *n* **:** the explosion of a projectile on contact with some part of a tree showering fragments down on the surrounding area

tree cactus *n* **:** any of several arborescent cacti; *esp* **:** SAGUARO

tree calf *n* **:** calfskin leather chemically treated so as to change its color and produce on it a treelike design ⟨a book bound in *tree calf*⟩

tree cat *n* **:** PALM CIVET

tree cat's-claw *n* **:** TEXAS CATCLAW

tree celandine *n* **:** PLUME POPPY

tree civet *n* **:** PALM CIVET b

tree class *n* **:** one of the size or age groups into which forest trees are commonly divided ⟨seedling, sapling, pole, standard are generally recognized *tree classes*⟩

tree clover *n* **1 :** WHITE SWEET CLOVER **2 :** an annual clover (*Trifolium ciliatum*) of the western U. S. having pink flowers with ciliate or bristle-margined calyx teeth

tree clubmoss *n* **:** a common and widely distributed clubmoss (*Lycopodium obscurum*) with underground creeping stems and erect aerial branches suggesting little trees

tree cobra *n* **:** MAMBA

tree cony *n* **:** TREE HYRAX

tree coral *n* **:** an arborescent coral; *usu* **:** a large branching ivory coral found esp. off the coast of Bermuda

tree cotton *n* **1 a :** an East Indian cotton plant (*Gossypium arboreum*) cultivated esp. for ornament **b :** the fiber obtained from tree cotton **c :** SEA ISLAND COTTON **2 a :** SILK COTTON TREE **b :** KAPOK

tree crab *n* **1 :** PURSE CRAB **2 :** MANGROVE CRAB

tree cranberry *n* **:** CRANBERRY BUSH

tree creeper *n* **1 :** a creeper of the family Certhiidae: as **a** (1) **:** a common European creeper (*Certhia familiaris*) that is brown streaked with buff above and silvery below and that has a slender curved bill (2) **:** the No. American brown creeper **b :** any of various Australian birds of the genus *Climacteris* **2 :** WOODHEWER 1

tree cricket *n* **:** any of several arboreal usu. pale or whitish American crickets (genus *Oecanthus*) noted for their loud stridulation — see SNOWY TREE CRICKET

tree cypress *n* **:** STANDING CYPRESS

treed *adj* [in sense 1, fr. ¹*tree* + *-ed;* in sense 2, fr. past part. of ²*tree*] **1 :** planted or grown with trees **:** WOODED **2 :** subjected to treeing: as **a :** driven up a tree ⟨a ~ animal⟩ **b :** fitted on a tree ⟨~ shoes⟩ ⟨no mark of stirrup iron across the instep of his freshly ~ boots —*Century Mag.*⟩

tree daisy *or* **tree aster** *n* **:** DAISYBUSH

tree digger *n* **:** a horse-drawn or tractor-drawn implement that consists essentially of a U-shaped blade which is passed under young trees in the nursery row to cut back roots and loosen the plant in the soil so that it may be lifted readily by hand (as for transplanting)

tree dog *n* **:** a dog (as a coonhound) used for treeing game

tree-dozer \ˈ=,==\ *n* **:** a device with heavy teeth mounted on the front of a track-laying tractor and used to clear land of brush, small trees, and roots

tree duck *n* **:** any of several long-legged and long-necked arboreal ducks (genus *Dendrocygna*) mostly of warm regions that are related to the sheldrakes and somewhat to the geese and have a complete bony orbit and the plumage usu. chestnut varied with black and white

tree farm *n* **:** an area of forest land managed in such a way as to ensure continuous commercial production under a systematic program of conservation and reforestation

tree farmer *n* **:** one engaged in tree farming

tree farming *n* **:** a systematic program of conservation and reforestation designed to ensure continuous commercial production of timber

tree fern *n* **1 :** any of various ferns exhibiting an arborescent habit with a caudex that is woody and elongated, belonging chiefly to the families Cyatheaceae and Marattiaceae but including some members of the Polypodiaceae, and being chiefly tropical and esp. abundant in Australia and New Zealand **2 :** any of several ferns that usu. grow on or about trees: as **a :** GRAY POLYPODY **b :** ROYAL FERN

treefish \ˈ=,=\ *n* **:** a California rockfish (*Sebastodes serriceps*) that is olive to blackish above, shades to yellow below, and is marked with transverse black bands

tree frog *n* **:** any of various Old World arboreal frogs (family Polypedatidae) related to those of the family Ranidae but distinguished by adhesive suckers on the toes; *broadly* **:** a tailless arboreal amphibian (as the New World spring peeper)

tree fruit *n* **:** a tree that produces table fruit; *also* **:** a fruit (as an apple, peach, or cherry) produced by such a tree — compare SMALL FRUIT

tree fuchsia *n* **:** KONINI

tree goose *n* [fr. the belief that the barnacle (shellfish) from which the goose was believed to stem is produced by trees] **:** BARNACLE GOOSE

tree guard *n* **:** any of various devices for protecting the trunk of a tree from animal and mechanical injury

tree heath *n* **1 :** a shrubby heath (*Erica arborea*) of the Mediterranean and Caucasian region cultivated for its nearly globular white flowers **2 :** a plant of the genus *Dracaena* **3 :** a New Zealand heathlike shrub or small tree (*Dracophyllum scoparium*) of the family Epacridaceae with tiny white flowers in dense racemes

tree hoopoe *n* **:** WOOD HOOPOE

treehopper \ˈ=,==\ *n* **:** any of numerous small leaping homopterous insects constituting the family Membracidae, living chiefly on branches and twigs, and injuring them by sucking sap — see BUFFALO TREEHOPPER

tree house *n* **:** a dwelling or playhouse built among the branches of a tree

tree huckleberry *n* **:** FARKLEBERRY

tree hyrax *or* **tree dassie** *n* **:** any of several largely arboreal African hyraxes that constitute the genus *Dendrohyrax* — called also *tree cony, tree dassie*

Representative Trees

Maximum Ht. 70 ft.
ARBORVITAE or WHITE CEDAR
Maximum Ht. 130 ft.
ASH (White Ash)
Ht. 50-60 ft. Maximum Ht. 100 ft.
BALSAM FIR
Ht. Usually 60-70 ft. Sometimes 130 ft.
BASSWOOD or LINDEN
Ht. Usually 70-80 ft.
Maximum Ht. 130 ft.
BEECH
Ht. Rarely over 60-80 ft.
PAPER BIRCH
Ht. Usually 60-70 ft.
Maximum Ht. 100 ft.
BUTTERNUT
Ht. 40-50 ft. Maximum Ht. 100 ft.
RED CEDAR or JUNIPER
Sometimes over 100 ft.
COTTONWOOD or POPLAR
Ht. Usually not over 25-30 ft.
DOGWOOD (Blue Dogwood)
Maximum Ht. 130 ft.
ELM
(see also Tupelo) Maximum Ht. 140 ft.
GUM TREE or SWEET GUM
Maximum Ht. 100 ft.
HEMLOCK
Maximum Ht. 130 ft.
HICKORY (Shagbark)
Maximum Ht. 100 ft.
HORSE CHESTNUT
Ht. 70-80 ft.
LOCUST
Maximum Ht. 130 ft.
MAPLE (Sugar Maple)
Maximum Ht. 150 ft.
OAK (White Oak)
Ht. Sometimes over 200 ft.
WHITE PINE
Ht. Sometimes 80-90 ft.
SASSAFRAS
Maximum Ht. 100 ft.
BLACK SPRUCE
Maximum Ht. 180 ft.
SYCAMORE or BUTTONWOOD
Maximum Ht. 200 ft.
TULIP TREE
Occasionally over 100 ft.
TUPELO or SOUR GUM
Ht. Sometimes 130 ft.
WALNUT (Black Walnut)

treeing *pres part of* TREE

tree ipomoea *n* **:** any of various shrubby ipomoeas; *esp* **:** a plant (*Ipomoea crassicaulis*) native to tropical America and the southern U.S.

tree kangaroo *n* **:** TREE WALLABY

tree lark *n, Brit* **:** TREE PIPIT

tree lawn *n* **:** TREE BELT

tree·less \'trēləs\ *adj* **:** lacking trees — **tree·less·ness** *n* -ES

tree·let \-lət\ *n* **:** a small or young tree (as a seedling or sapling)

treelike \'=,=\ *adj* **:** resembling a tree esp. in form or size **:** ARBORESCENT

tree lilac *n* **:** a lilac of treelike form; *esp* **:** a broad-spreading white-flowered Japanese tree (*Syringa amurensis japonica* or *S. japonica*) that may exceed 35 feet in height

tree line *n* **:** TIMBERLINE

treelined \'=,=\ *adj* **:** having a row of trees usu. on each side ⟨a ~ street⟩

treeling \'trēliŋ\ *n* -S **:** a small or young tree **:** TREELET

tree lucerne *n, chiefly Austral* **:** TAGASASTE

tree lungwort *n* **1 :** a lichen (*Sticta pulmonacea*) growing on trees and rocks, having a lacunary thallus that suggests lung tissue, and used formerly in folk medicine in the treatment of pulmonary diseases **2 :** a bluebell (*Mertensia virginica*)

tree lupine *n* **:** an evergreen shrub (*Lupinus arboreus*) of the Pacific coast of the U.S. that has showy yellow or blue to violet flowers and is naturalized in New Zealand where it is used as a sand binder

tree mallow *n* **:** an arborescent mallow of the genus *Lavatera*

tree marten *n* **:** PINE MARTEN

tree martin *n* **:** TREE SWALLOW

tree medic *n* **:** a shrubby yellow-flowered medic (*Medicago arborea*) of southern Europe that is sometimes used as an ornamental

tree mildew *n* **:** a powdery mildew (*Phyllactinia corylea*) common on many trees and shrubs

tree milk *n* **1 :** the milky juice of an East Indian climbing plant (*Gymnema lactiferum*) of the family Asclepiadaceae that is used locally for food **2 :** the juice of a cow tree (*Brosimum galactodendron*)

tree molasses *n, chiefly dial* **:** MAPLE SYRUP

tree moss *n* **1 :** a moss or lichen growing on trees **2 :** a moss or club moss resembling a miniature tree; *esp* **:** a moss of the genus *Climacium*

tree mouse *n* **1 :** any of numerous small arboreal myomorph rodents: as **a :** any African long-clawed murid of *Dendromus* or related genera **b :** either of two cricetids of western No. America that are congeneric with the lemming mice **c :** any of a genus (*Vandeleuria*) of tropical eastern Asian climbing murids with very long tails and the great toe of the hind foot opposable and resembling a thumb **2 :** WHITE-BREASTED NUTHATCH

tree myrtle *n* **1 :** any of various shrubs of the genus *Ceanothus* (esp. *C. arboreus*) **2 :** any of various plants of the genus *Myrtus*

[1]**tre·en** \'trēən\ *adj* [ME, fr. OE *trēowen*, fr. *trēow* tree, wood + *-en* — more at TREE] **1 :** made of wood **:** WOODEN **2** *obs* **:** of, relating to, or derived from trees

[2]**treen** \'trēn\ *chiefly dial pl of* TREE

[3]**treen** \"\ *n, pl* **treen** [[1]*treen*] **1 :** small woodenware **2 :** an article (as a bowl or other utensil) made from wood — usu. used in pl.

[1]**tree·nail** *also* **tre·nail** *or* **trun·nel** \'trē,nāl, 'tren[ə]l, 'trən[ə]l\ *n* -S [ME *trenayle*, fr. *tre, tree* tree, wood + *nayle, nail* nail — more at NAIL] **1 :** a wooden pin or peg made ordinarily of dry compressed timber so as to swell in its hole (as in a wooden ship) when moistened and used chiefly for fastening planking and ceiling to frames **2 :** GUTTA

[2]**treenail** \"\ *vt* **:** to fasten with treenails

treenware \'=,=\ *n* [[1]*treen* + *ware*] **:** TREEN

tree nymph *n* **:** a nymph (as a dryad or hamadryad) who is associated with a tree

tree of heaven *also* **tree of the gods :** an Asiatic tree (*Ailanthus altissima*) having foliage similar to that of the sumacs and ill-scented staminate flowers, being widely grown as a shade and ornamental tree esp. because of its resistance to smoke injury, and naturalized in many parts of the U.S.

tree of jesse *usu cap J* [after *Jesse*, father of David in the Bible] **:** JESSE TREE

tree of life 1 a [trans. of NL *arbor vitae*] **:** ARBORVITAE 1 **b :** BHUTAN CYPRESS **c :** [1]DATE 2 **2 :** a highly conventionalized and often ornate representation of a tree or vine used as a decorative motif and prob. of ultimately Assyrian origin

tree of porphyry *usu cap P* [after *Porphyry*, 3d cent. A.D. Greek philosopher] **:** a diagrammatic representation of the logical division of the highest genus, being, or substance into successive dichotomies

tree of Porphyry

tree onion *n* **:** any of several perennial garden onions that constitute a variety (*Allium cepa* var. *viviparum*) of the common onion, are grown chiefly as a curiosity or for early salad onions, and are propagated by bulbils that replace the flowers in the inflorescence — called also *Egyptian onion, top onion;* compare MULTIPLIER ONION

tree orchid *n* **:** an orchid of the genus *Epidendrum*

tree oyster *n* **:** MANGROVE OYSTER

tree partridge *n* **1 :** a Central American partridge of the genus *Dendrortyx* **2 :** HILL PARTRIDGE 1

tree peony *n* **:** a shrubby Chinese peony (*Paeonia suffruticosa*) having biternate leaves and large showy flowers and being the only woody cultivated peony and the source of many horticultural varieties

tree pie *n* **:** an Asiatic bird of the genus *Crypsirina* that is related to the common magpies and has a long graduated tail and plumage which is black or varied with orange-brown, buff, black, and white

tree pipit *n* **:** a European pipit (*Anthus trivialis*) of somewhat arboreal habits

tree planting *n* **:** the transplanting of a seedling or sapling tree to a permanent position; *also* **:** an exercise or ceremony attending such an act

tree poppy *n* **:** any of several shrubby to arborescent California plants of the family Papaveraceae: as **a :** MATILIJA POPPY **b :** BUSH POPPY

tree porcupine *n* **:** an American porcupine of the family Erethizontidae; *esp* **:** a So. or Central American prehensile-tailed porcupine of the genus *Coendou*

tree primrose *n* **:** an evening primrose (*Oenothera biennis*)

treer \'trē(ə)r\ *n* -S [[1]*tree* (boot tree) + *-er*] **:** a worker who cleans and dresses completed shoe uppers and irons out wrinkles

tree rat *n* **1** *Austral* **:** ROOF RAT **2 :** a member of an African murid genus (*Thallomys*) of arboreal rodents

tree ring *n* **:** ANNUAL RING

tree-ripe \'=¦=\ *also* **tree-ripened** \'=¦==\ *adj* **:** ripening or allowed to ripen on the tree to the stage of maximum palatability ⟨*tree-ripe* peaches⟩ — compare MARKET-RIPE

tree root rot *n* **:** MUSHROOM ROOT ROT

tree rose *n* **:** a rose that is budded at the apex of the stout trunk of the understock to produce a head of growth resembling the crown of a dwarf tree — called also *standard rose*

tree-run \'=¦=\ *adj* **:** as taken from the tree without grading or sorting — used of fruits

tree runner *n* **:** NUTHATCH; *esp* **:** an Australian nuthatch of the genus *Neositta*

trees *pl of* TREE, *pres 3d sing of* TREE

tree·scape \'trē,skāp\ *n* -S [[1]*tree* + *-scape*] **:** a landscape including many trees or groups of trees

tree shrew *n* **:** any of various small arboreal mammals (family Tupaiidae) of southeastern Asia that in appearance greatly resemble squirrels but may be distinguished by the very long pointed snout and sometimes by a distichous tail — compare PENTAIL

tree sparrow *n* **1 :** a European sparrow (*Passer montanus*) that is smaller than the house sparrow and has a black spot on the ear coverts **2 :** an American sparrow (*Spizella arborea*) that is larger than the chipping sparrow, breeds in northern No. America, and winters in the U.S.

tree·speel·er \'trē,spēlə(r)\ *n* -S [[1]*tree* + [2]*speel* + *-er*] *Brit* **:** TREE CREEPER 1a(1)

tree spirit *n* **:** a supernatural being (as a deity or nymph) associated with a tree

tree squirrel *n* **:** an arboreal squirrel; *esp* **:** a typical squirrel of the genus *Sciurus* as distinguished from a ground squirrel or a flying squirrel

tree steppe *n* **:** land predominantly covered with grass but bearing scattered and usu. isolated trees ⟨much of the African veld is typical *tree steppe*⟩

tree stool *n* **:** the stump of a tree

tree sugar *n, chiefly dial* **:** MAPLE SUGAR

tree surgeon *n* **:** a specialist in tree surgery

tree surgery *n* **:** operative treatment of diseased trees esp. for the control of decay; *broadly* **:** practices (as pruning, spraying, fertilizing, repair of damage, protection from lightning injury, or moving) that form part of the professional care of specimen or shade trees

tree swallow *n* **1 :** WHITE-BELLIED SWALLOW **2 :** an Australian and Polynesian swallow (*Hirundo nigricans*) that nests in holes in trees — called also *tree martin*

tree swift *n* **:** any of several atypical swifts of the genus *Hemiprocne* of India and the East Indies which are often isolated in a distinct family, which have unusually soft plumage and are mostly crested, and in which the sexes are dissimilar and the young differ markedly from adults

tree toad *n* **:** any of numerous tailless amphibians of arboreal habits esp. of the family Hylidae **:** TREE FROG — see HYLA; compare SPRING PEEPER

tree tobacco *n* **:** an evergreen arborescent So. American tobacco (*Nicotiana glauca*) that has glaucous and glabrous foliage and yellow flowers, is naturalized in parts of the southwestern U.S. and in Australia and southern Africa, and is occas. responsible for poisoning of livestock **:** WILD TOBACCO

tree tomato *n* **1 :** a So. American arborescent shrub (*Cyphomandra betacea*) of the family Solanaceae **2 :** the egg-shaped reddish brown edible fruit of the tree tomato in flavor somewhat resembling a tomato

treetop \'=,=\ *n* **1 :** the topmost branches or tuft of a tree **2 treetops** *pl* **:** the height or line marked by the tops of a row or clump of trees

tree trimmer *n* **:** OAK PRUNER

tree veld *n* **:** African tree steppe

tree viper *n* **:** any of several arboreal prehensile-tailed green and yellow vipers of equatorial Africa constituting a genus (*Atheris*) of the family Viperidae

tree wallaby *n* **:** any of several shapely arboreal wallabies (genus *Dendrolagus*) of tropical Australia and New Guinea having the tail long, slender, and furred, and the hind legs but slightly longer than the forelegs — called also *tree kangaroo*

tree warden *n* **:** a local officer charged in some jurisdictions with the care of trees — compare FIRE WARDEN

tree wax *n* **:** any of various fats, waxes, or waxy secretions produced by or found on trees or shrubs; *specif* **:** JAPAN WAX

treey \'trē·ē\ *adj* [[1]*tree* + *-y*] **:** full of trees **:** WOODED

tree yucca *n* **:** JOSHUA TREE

[1]**tref** \'trāv\ *n, pl* **tre·fi** \-vē\ [W, town, home, dwelling place, tref; akin to Corn *tref, tre* dwelling place, town, Bret *trev* division of a parish, OE *thorp* village — more at THORP] **:** a homestead or hamlet under old Cymric law; *usu* **:** a group or area acting as a single community as regards cattle and plowing, constituting a taxable unit, and consisting typically of nine houses, one plow, one oven, one churn, one cat, one cock, and one herdsman

[2]**tref** \'trāf\ *or* **te·re·fah** *or* **te·re·fa** \tə'rāfə\ *or* **tre·fah** *or* **tre·fa** \'trāfə\ *adj* [Yiddish & Heb; Yiddish *treyf, treyfe*, fr. Heb *ṭĕrēphāh* animal torn by wild beasts, torn flesh — more at TEREFAH] **:** ritually unclean or unfit according to Jewish law — opposed to *kosher*

trefah *or* **trefa** *var of* TEREFAH

tre·flée *also* **tre·flé** \trā'flā\ *or* **tref·ly** \'treflē\ *adj* [F *treflé* (fem. *treflée*), fr. *trefle* trefoil (fr. L *trifolium*) + *-é* -ate (fr. L *-atus*)] **1 :** BOTONÉE **2 :** ornamented with trefoils along the edge ⟨a bend ~⟩

[1]**tre·foil** \'trē,fȯil, 'tre,-\ *n* -S [ME, fr. MF *trefeuil, trefeul*, fr. L *trifolium*, fr. *tri-* + *folium* leaf — more at BLADE] **1 a** (1) **:** a clover of the genus *Trifolium* (2) **:** any of several similar trifoliolate leguminous herbs; *esp* **:** BLACK MEDIC — see BIRD'S-FOOT TREFOIL **b** *archaic* **:** WOOD SORREL **c :** a trifoliolate leaf (as of a clover) **2 :** an ornament or symbol in the form of a stylized trifoliolate leaf **:** a figure enclosed by three joined foils: as **a :** a 3-lobed foliation in Gothic tracery **b :** a heraldic bearing or figure depicted as a cloverleaf with stem usu. pointing down **c :** an emblem having a 3-lobed outline ⟨the Girl Scout ~⟩ **3 :** a cluster of three linked or closely related or associated items **4 :** a triangular area of a molar tooth with protocone, paracone, and metacone forming the angles

trefoils 2a

[2]**trefoil** \"\ *adj* **:** of, relating to, or having the shape of a trefoil: **a :** having three leaves or three lobes **b** *of an arch* **:** having an intrados with a 3-lobed outline — see ARCH illustration

tre·foiled \-ld\ *adj* **:** made like a trefoil or with trefoils

trefoth *or* **trefot** *pl of* TREFAH

trega- *or* **treg-** *comb form* [trillion + *-ega-, -eg-* (as in *mega-, meg-*)] **:** one million millions **:** trillion **:** 10^{12} ⟨*tregerg*⟩ ⟨*tregadyne*⟩

trega·dyne \'tregə,dīn\ *n* [*trega-* + *dyne*] **:** one trillion dynes

treg·erg \'tre,gərg\ *n* [*trega-* + *erg*] **:** one trillion ergs

treg·et·our \'trejəd·ə(r)\ *n* -S [ME, fr. OF *tresgeteor*, fr. *tresgeter* to throw across, juggle (fr. *tres-* across — fr. L *trans-* — + *geter, jeter* to throw, fr. L *jactare*) + *-eor* -or — more at JET] *archaic* **:** JUGGLER, MAGICIAN

tre·ha·la \trə'hälə\ *n* -S [prob. fr. F *tréhala*, fr. Turk *tıgala*, fr. Per *tīghāl*] **:** a sweet edible substance constituting the pupal covering of an Asiatic beetle (prob. *Larinus maculatus*)

tre·ha·lase \'trēhə,lās, trə'hä,-\ *n* -S [ISV *trehala* + *-ase*] **:** an enzyme that accelerates the hydrolysis of trehalose and is found in yeasts and molds

tre·ha·lose \-,lōs\ *n* -S [ISV *trehala* + *-ose*] **:** a crystalline nonreducing disaccharide sugar $C_{12}H_{22}O_{11}$ that yields only glucose on hydrolysis and that is obtained from trehala, ergot of rye, and many fungi in which it is stored instead of starch; α-D-glucosyl α-D-glucoside

treil·lage \'trālij\ *n* -S [F, fr. MF, fr. *treille* vine arbor (fr. L *trichila* arbor, summerhouse) + *-age*] **:** latticework for supporting vines or other growth **:** an espalier trellis; *also* **:** GRILL, LATTICE ⟨a room divided by ~⟩

treitz's muscle \'trītsəz-\ *n, usu cap T* [after Wenzel *Treitz* †1872 Austrian physician] **1** *or* **treitz's ligament :** a band of smooth muscle extending from the junction of the duodenum and jejunum to the left crus of the diaphragm **2 :** RECTOCOCCYGEUS

[1]**trek** \'trek\ *n* -S [Afrik, fr. MD *treck* pull, haul, fr. *trecken* to haul, migrate] **1** *chiefly southern Africa* **a :** a journey by ox wagon; *esp* **:** an organized expedition or migrational movement by a group of settlers to a new home **b :** a day's travel on such a journey or expedition **:** STAGE **2 :** a trip or movement esp. when involving difficulties or complex organization ⟨shortage of housing with the consequent ~ into apartments —*Yale Rev.*⟩ ⟨his ~ up from slavery —J.H.Johnson⟩ ⟨made a ~ to town⟩

[2]**trek** \"\ *vb* **trekked; trekked; trekking; treks** [Afrik, fr. MD *trecken* to pull, haul, march, migrate; akin to MLG *trecken* to pull, OHG *trechan*] *vi* **1** *chiefly southern Africa* **a :** to travel by ox wagon **b :** to migrate usu. by ox-wagon train to a new home **2 :** to make one's way slowly or arduously; *broadly* **:** to make a journey **:** GO — usu. used with *to* ~ *vt, chiefly southern Africa* **:** to provide draft for (as a vehicle) **:** PULL, DRAW

trekboer \'=,=\ *n, pl* **trekboers** *or* **trekboere** [Afrik, fr. *trek* + *boer*] **:** a migratory grazier of southern Africa

trek·ker \'trekə(r)\ *n* -S [Afrik, fr. *trek* to trek + *-er*] **:** one that treks

trek ox *n, southern Africa* **:** a draft ox

trek wagon *n* **:** a large 6-wheeled covered wagon used esp. in southern Africa in trekking and designed to provide lodging and storage space as well as seating for trekkers

trel·lage \'trelij\ *n* -S [by alter.] **:** TREILLAGE

[1]**trel·lis** \'treləs\ *n* -ES [ME *trelis*, fr. MF *treliz* fabric of coarse weave, trellis, fr. (assumed) VL *trilicius* woven with triple thread, fr. L *trilic-, trilix* — more at DRILLING] **1 a :** a structure or frame of latticework used as a screen or as a support for climbing plants **b :** a construction (as a bower or summerhouse) chiefly or wholly of latticework **c :** an arrangement that forms or gives the effect of a lattice ⟨a ~ of interlacing streams⟩ **2 :** a modification of the lattice in heraldic depiction in which the pieces are shown as nailed at the joints without interlacing

trellis 1a

[2]**trellis** \"\ *vt* -ED/-ING/-ES [ME *trelesen*, fr. *trelis* trellis] **1 :** to provide with a trellis; *esp* **:** to train (as a vine) on a trellis **2 :** to cross or interlace on or through **:** INTERWEAVE ⟨an ornate design ~*ed* the wall⟩

[3]**trellis** \"\ *adj* [ME *trelis*, fr. *trelis*, n.] **:** having a latticed arrangement ⟨a ~ drainage pattern⟩

trellis cipher *n* **:** a cipher that uses a grille to place the words of a hidden message in a cover text

trel·lised \-st\ *adj* [ME *trelest*, fr. past part. of *trelesen* to trellis] **:** having or furnished with a trellis or a latticed arrangement **:** trained upon a trellis ⟨~ roses⟩ ⟨a ~ cretonne⟩

trellised armor *n* **:** a medieval armor having bands crossing at right angles with a large rivethead or boss in each intervening square

trelliswork \'==,=\ *n* **:** LATTICEWORK, MESHWORK

trem *abbr* tremolo

tre·ma \'trēmə\ *n, cap* [NL *Tremat-, Trema*, fr. Gk *trēmat-, trēma* hole — more at THROW] **:** a genus of tropical shrubs and trees (family Ulmaceae) having alternate distichous leaves and cymose polygamous flowers succeeded by small drupes

-tre·ma \·'trēmə\ *n comb form* [NL *-tremat-, -trema*, fr. Gk *trēmat-, trēma* hole — more at THROW] **1** *pl* **-tremas** \-məz\ *or* **-trema·ta** \-məd·ə, -mətə\ **:** hole **:** orifice **:** opening ⟨*helicotrema*⟩ **2 :** creature having (such) an opening — in generic names ⟨*Eurytrema*⟩

tre·mad·oc \trə'madək\ *adj, usu cap* [fr. *Tremadoc*, village of northwest Wales] **:** of or relating to a subdivision of the European Cambrian — see GEOLOGIC TIME table

trem·a·lith \'tremə,lith, 'trēm-\ *n* -S [Gk *trēma* hole + E *-lith* — more at THROW] **:** a minutely punctate coccolith — compare DISCOLITH

tre·man·do \trā'män(,)dō\ *adj* [It, trembling, fr. verbal of *tremare* to tremble, modif. of L *tremere* — more at TREMBLE] **:** TREMOLANDO

tre·man·dra \trə'mandrə\ *n, cap* [NL, fr. L *tremere* to tremble + NL *-andra*] **:** a small genus of Australian low shrubs that is the type of the family Tremandraceae

tre·man·dra·ce·ae \,trēmən'drāsē,ē\ *n pl, cap* [NL, fr. *Tremandra*, type genus + *-aceae*] **:** a family of exclusively Australian shrubs or undershrubs (order Geraniales) with solitary pink or purple regular flowers succeeded by 2-celled capsules — **tre·man·dra·ceous** \¦==¦drāshəs\ *adj*

-tre·ma·ta \'trēməd·ə, -mətə\ *n pl comb form* [NL, pl. of *-trema*] **:** creatures having (such) an opening — in names of orders and other higher taxa ⟨*Derotremata*⟩

trem·a·to·da \,tremə'tōdə, ,trēm-\ *n pl, cap* [NL, fr. Gk *trēmatōdēs* pierced with holes, fr. *trēmat-, trēma* hole + *-ōdēs* -ode — more at THROW] **:** a class of Platyhelminthes including the flukes and related parasitic flatworms that usu. have no cellular epidermis or cilia but have a chitinous cuticle covering the body, suckers for adhesion, and a well-developed alimentary canal, and being commonly divided into three subclasses Monogenea, Aspidogastrea, and Digenea that differ significantly in reproductive behavior, in parasitic relations, and in structure — **trem·a·to·dan** \¦==¦tōd[ə]n\ *or* **trem·a·to·de·an** \-dēən\ *adj*

[1]**trem·a·tode** \'==,tōd\ *adj* [NL *Trematoda*] **1 :** of or relating to the Trematoda **2 :** caused by a trematode worm

[2]**trematode** \"\ *n* -S **:** a flatworm (as a liver fluke) of the class Trematoda

trem·a·to·sau·rus \,treməd·ə'sȯrəs\ *n, cap* [NL, fr. Gk *trēmat-, trēma* hole + NL *-saurus*] **:** a genus of large labyrinthodont amphibians (order Stereospondyli) from the Triassic rocks of Germany having an elongated triangular roughly sculptured skull

[1]**trem·ble** \'trembəl\ *vb* **trembled; trembled; trembling** \-b(ə)liŋ\ **trembles** [ME *tremblen*, fr. MF *trembler*, fr. ML *tremulare*, fr. L *tremulus* tremulous, fr. *tremere* to tremble; akin to Gk *tremein* to tremble, Lith *trimti*, Toch A *träm-*] *vi* **1 :** to shake involuntarily (as with fear, cold, excitement, fatigue) **:** SHIVER, SHUDDER, QUIVER **2 :** to move, sound, pass, or come to pass as if shaken or tremulous ⟨the building *trembled* but did not fall⟩ ⟨dusk was *trembling* on the verges of the hills —Nancy Hale⟩ **3 :** to become affected with tremulousness **:** fear greatly **:** become strongly affected ⟨I ~ for you⟩ ⟨*trembling* to think of what might have happened⟩ ~ *vt* **1** *obs* **:** to fear exceedingly **:** shudder at **2 :** to make tremble **:** cause to tremble **3 :** to speak or say tremulously ⟨*trembled* out a few words of appreciation⟩

[2]**tremble** \"\ *n* -S **1 :** an act of trembling **:** a fit or spell of involuntary shaking or quivering **:** a tremor or series of tremors **:** vibratory movement **2 :** AMERICAN ASPEN **3 trembles** *pl but sing in constr* **:** poisoning of livestock and esp. cattle caused by a toxic alcohol present in white snakeroot and rayless goldenrod which are common in parts of the western and central U.S., marked by muscular tremors, weakness, and constipation, and often progressing to coma and death — compare MILK SICKNESS, TREMETOL

trem·ble·ment \'trembəlmənt\ *n* -S [F, fr. OF, fr. *trembler* to tremble + *-ment*] **1 :** a condition or instance of trembling or quivering **:** TREMOR **2 :** a terrifying thing **:** a cause of trembling **3 a :** TREMOLO **b :** a musical trill

[1]**trem·bler** \'tremb(ə)lə(r)\ *n* -S **1 :** one that trembles or causes or records trembling **2 :** any of various West Indian birds of the genera *Cinclocerthia* and *Rhamphocinclus* of the family Mimidae **3 :** the vibrating hammer or spring contact piece of an electrical hammer break (as of the electric ignition apparatus for an internal-combustion engine)

[2]**trembler** *or* **tremblor** *var of* TEMBLOR

trem·bleuse cup \trä[n]'blœz\ *n* [F *trembleuse* trembleuse cup, fr. fem. of *trembleur* trembler, fr. *trembler* to tremble + *-eur* -er — more at -OR] **:** an old cup that fits into an elevated rim in the center of a saucer

[1]**trembling** *n* -S [ME, fr. gerund of *tremblen* to tremble] **:** the action or condition of one that trembles: as **a :** [2]TREMBLE 3 **b :** LOUPING ILL

[2]**trembling** *adj* [fr. pres. part. of [1]*tremble*] **:** that trembles **:** shaking with or as if with fear or other emotion **:** FEARFUL, VIBRATING, QUAKING — **trem·bling·ly** *adv* — **trem·bling·ness** *n* -ES

trembling hammer *n* [[2]*trembling*] **:** TREMBLER 3

trembling poplar *or* **trembling tree** *n* **1 :** EUROPEAN ASPEN **2** *or* **trembling aspen :** AMERICAN ASPEN

trembling prairie *n* **:** SHAKING PRAIRIE

trem·bly \'tremb(ə)lē, -li\ *adj* -ER/-EST [[1]*tremble* + *-y*] **:** marked by trembling **:** TREMULOUS; *also* **:** SHY, TIMID

tre·mel·la \trə'melə\ *n, cap* [NL, fr. L *tremere* to tremble + *-ella*] **:** a genus of fungi (family Tremellaceae) with yellowish and gelatinous sporophores having convolutions like those of the brain — **trem·el·line** \'tremə,līn, -,lən\ *adj*

trem·el·la·ce·ae \,tremə'lāsē,ē\ *n pl, cap* [NL, fr. *Tremella*, type genus + *-aceae*] **:** a family of basidiomycetous fungi (order Tremellales) having the basidium longitudinally or obliquely septate or divided

trem·el·la·les \-ā(,)lēz\ *n pl, cap* [NL, fr. *Tremella* + *-ales*] **:** an order of basidiomycetous fungi (subclass Heterobasidiomycetes) having the basidiocarp well developed and varying from gelatinous to waxy or even horny in texture esp. when dry and being mostly saprophytes but including some parasites of mosses, other fungi, insects, or vascular plants — see AURICULARIACEAE, TREMELLACEAE

trem·el·loid \ˈtreməˌlȯid\ *adj* [NL *Tremella* + E *-oid*] **1 :** resembling or related to fungi of the genus *Tremella* **2 :** GELATINOUS

trem·el·lose \-ˌlōs\ *adj* [NL *Tremella* + E *-ose*] **:** GELATINOUS

tre·men·dous \trəˈmendəs, trēˈ- *sometimes* -njəs\ *adj* [L *tremendus*, fr. gerundive of *tremere* to tremble, tremble at, dread — more at TREMBLE] **1 :** such as may excite trembling **:** such as may arouse dread, awe, or terror **:** TERRIFYING, DREADFUL ⟨a ~ fact in human experience; that a whole civilization should be dependent on technology —Walter Lippmann⟩ **2 a :** astonishing by reason of extreme size, power, greatness, or excellence ⟨a countryside of ~ sweeping plains —Alan Moorehead⟩ **b :** unusually large or great **:** HUGE, VAST ⟨a ~ sensitivity to the slightest hint of criticism —Peggy Durdin⟩ ⟨an advertising man with ~ talents —M.E.Bennett⟩ **syn** see MONSTROUS

tre·men·dous·ly *adv* **:** to a tremendous degree or extent **:** EXTREMELY, GREATLY ⟨the ~ destructive powers of the new weapon —Raphael Demos⟩ ⟨the experience has been ~ educational —Sherwood Anderson⟩ ⟨~ preoccupied with his prestige and reputation —Margaret Mead⟩ ⟨~ bad films about the lives of celebrated musicians —*London Times*⟩

tre·men·dous·ness *n* -ES **:** the quality or state of being tremendous

trem·e·tol \ˈtreməˌtȯl, -tōl\ *n* -S [irreg. fr. L *tremere* to tremble + *-ol* — more at TREMBLE] **:** an unsaturated alcohol obtained as an oil of aromatic odor from the white snakeroot and rayless goldenrod that causes trembles in animals

tre·mex \ˈtrēˌmeks\ *n* [NL, prob. fr. Gk *trēma* hole + *-ex* (as in *Sirex*)] **1** *cap* **:** a genus of wood wasps (family Siricidae) with larvae that bore in weakened or dead wood of trees **2** -ES **:** any wood wasp of the genus *Tremex*

trem·ie \ˈtremē\ *n* -S [F *trémie* hopper, fr. L *trimodia* measure or vessel containing three modii, fr. *tri-* + *modius*] **:** an apparatus for depositing and consolidating concrete under water consisting essentially of a tube of wood or sheet metal with a top in the form of a hopper and being usu. handled by a crane

tre·mis·sis \trəˈmisəs\ *n, pl* **tremis·ses** \-ˈmiˌsēz\ [LL *tremis, tremissis*, fr. L *tres* three + *-mis, -missis* (as in *semis, semissis*) — more at THREE, SEMIS] **:** a Byzantine triens or a similar gold coin of early western Europe

¹trem·o·lan·do *also* **trem·u·lan·do** \ˌtreməˈlän(ˌ)dō\ *adv* (*or adj*) [It, lit., trembling, fr. ML *tremulandum*, gerund of *tremulare* to tremble — more at TREMBLE] **:** TREMULOUS — used as a direction in music to perform in a tremolo

²tremolando *also* **tremulando** \"\ *n, pl* **tremolandos** \-ōz\ *or* **tremolan·di** \-ndē\ **:** a tremolo effect esp. by the strings of an orchestra

¹trem·o·lant \ˈtreməlant\ *also* **trem·u·lant** \-myəl-\ *n* -S [It *tremolante* tremolo stop, fr. *tremolante* tremulous, fr. ML *tremulant-, tremulans*, pres. part. of *tremulare* to tremble] **1 :** an organ pipe having a tremolant note **2 :** a device to impart a vibration causing a tremolant sound in a musical instrument

²tremolant \"\ *adj* **:** having a vibrant tremolo note

trem·o·lite \ˈtreməˌlīt\ *n* -S [F *trémolite*, fr. *Tremola* valley in the Alps, southern Switzerland + F *-ite*] **:** a mineral $Ca_2Mg_5Si_8O_{22}(OH)_2$ of the amphibole group that is a white or gray calcium magnesium silicate and occurs in long blade-shaped or short stout crystals and also in columnar, fibrous, or granular masses (sp.gr. 2.9–3.1) — **trem·o·lit·ic** \ˌ==ˈlid·ik\ *adj*

trem·o·lo \ˈtreməˌlō\ *n* -S *often attrib* [It, fr. *tremolo* tremulous, fr. L *tremulus*] **1 a :** the rapid reiteration of a musical tone or of alternating tones of a chord so as to produce a tremulous effect **b :** a perceptible rapid variation of pitch in the voice esp. in singing similar to the vibrato of a stringed instrument **2** *or* **tremolo stop :** a mechanical contrivance in an organ for periodically interrupting the flow of tone and causing a tremulous effect

trem·o·lo·so \ˌ==ˈlō(ˌ)sō\ *adv* (*or adj*) [It, fr. *tremolo* + *-oso* -ous (fr. L *-osus*)] **:** with tremolo — used as a direction in music

¹trem·or \ˈtremə(r) *sometimes* ˈtrēm-\ *n* -S [ME *tremour*, fr. MF, fr. L *tremor*, fr. *tremere* to tremble — more at TREMBLE] **1 a** (1) **:** a trembling or shaking of the body or one of its parts usu. associated with physical weakness or emotional stress ⟨the ~ of age⟩ (2) **:** a state of quivering excitement **:** tremulous agitation ⟨in a ~ of anticipatory delight⟩ (3) **:** an involuntary quivering of voluntary muscle involving an entire muscle, a muscle group, or some of the fibers of a muscle, varying in intensity and duration and occurring in conjunction with debilitated states or as a specific sign of organic disorders ⟨a coarse ~ of the hands⟩ ⟨the fine ~ associated with central nervous lesions⟩ **b :** a single shaking or quivering movement characteristic of a state of tremor ⟨cold ~s shook her from time to time⟩ **c :** a quaver in the voice esp. in speaking **2 a :** a quivering or vibratory motion ⟨the ~ of a leaf in a breeze⟩ **3 :** a feeling of uncertainty or insecurity ⟨not without ~s did we agree to the new plan⟩ ⟨all the ~s of arriving and departing —F.A.Swinnerton⟩ ⟨a child that . . . flies to its mother to . . . forget its ~s —W.H.Hudson †1922⟩

²tremor \"\ *vi* -ED/-ING/-S **:** to experience tremor

tremor disk *n* **:** the enlarged image of a star as registered on a photographic plate that results from the tremors of the atmosphere during the exposure

trem·or·less \-(r)ləs\ *adj* **:** free from tremor — **trem·or·less·ly** *adv*

trem·or·ous \-mərəs\ *adj* [*tremor* + *-ous*] **:** characterized by tremor **:** full of tremors ⟨a ~ state⟩ ⟨~ voices⟩

trem·our \ˈtremə(r)\ *archaic var of* TREMOR

¹trem·u·lant \ˈtremyələnt\ *adj* [ML *tremulant-, tremulans*, pres. part. of *tremulare* to tremble — more at TREMBLE] **:** TREMULOUS, TREMBLING

²tremulant \"\ *n* -S [G, fr. It *tremolante* — more at TREMOLANT] **:** TREMOLO 2b

trem·u·late \ˈtremyəˌlāt\ *vi* -ED/-ING/-S [back-formation fr. *tremulation*] **:** TREMBLE, QUIVER

trem·u·la·tion \ˌ==ˈlāshən\ *n* -S [ML *tremulatus* (past part. of *tremulare* to tremble) + E *-ion*] **:** an act or the condition of trembling (as from fear or uncertainty)

trem·u·lous \ˈtremyələs\ *adj* [L *tremulus* — more at TREMBLE] **1 :** characterized by or affected with trembling or tremors **:** QUIVERING, PALPITATING, SHAKING, VIBRATING ⟨~ hands⟩ ⟨leaves ~ in the breeze⟩ **2 :** affected with fear or timidity **:** TIMOROUS, WAVERING ⟨a shy ~ girl⟩ **3 :** such as is caused by a tremulous state or characteristic of a tremulous individual or thing ⟨a ~ handwriting⟩ ⟨a ~ reply⟩ ⟨night with no cloud to sully its ~ radiance —E.J.Banfield⟩ **4 :** exceedingly sensitive **:** easily shaken or disordered ⟨a ~ and bitter joy —C.A.Lejeune⟩ — often used with *to* ⟨~ to criticism⟩ — **trem·u·lous·ly** *adv* — **trem·u·lous·ness** *n* -ES

trenail *var of* TREENAIL

¹trench \ˈtrench\ *n* -ES *often attrib* [ME *trenche* track cut through a wood, fr. MF, act of cutting, cut, fr. *trenchier* to cut] **1 a :** a long narrow cut in the ground **:** DITCH, FOSSE ⟨dig a ~ for sewer pipe⟩ **b :** a long narrow excavation used for military defense and often having the excavated dirt mounded up in front of it as an earthwork — compare APPROACH TRENCH, BUNKER, DUGOUT, FIRE TRENCH, PARALLEL 1c, SLIT TRENCH **c** *obs* **:** a protective earthwork ⟨resolved that the ditches . . . should be deepened, and the ~es heightened —Fynes Moryson⟩ **2 :** something that resembles a trench: as **a** *archaic* **:** FURROW, GROOVE ⟨these ~es made by grief and care —Shak.⟩ **b :** FIRING LINE 2 ⟨in the cultural struggle . . . schools are the frontline ~es —Paul Blanshard⟩ **3 a :** a narrow steep-sided depression eroded by a stream **:** CANYON, GULLY **b :** a long straight comparatively narrow intermontane depression often occupied by parts of two or more drainage systems **:** TROUGH **c :** a long narrow steep-sided depression in an ocean floor **:** OCEAN DEEP — compare CANYON

²trench \"\ *vb* -ED/-ING/-ES [in sense 1, fr. MF *trenchier* to cut, cut across, trench, prob. modif. of L *truncare* to cut off; in other senses, partly fr. ME *trenche*, n. and partly fr. MF *trenchier* — more at TRUNCATE] *vt* **1 a :** to make a cut in **:** CARVE, INCISE ⟨inscriptions . . . ~ed in one of the stones —John Webb⟩ ⟨surface ~ing at numerous points on the . . . outcrop —W.H.A.Lawrence⟩ **b** *obs* **:** to make a gash in **:** SLASH ⟨the wide wound, that the boar had ~ed in his soft flank —Shak.⟩ **2 a** (1) **:** to dig a protective trench in ⟨~ a hill⟩ (2) **:** to protect with or as if with a trench ⟨~ an outpost⟩ **b :** to turn over (soil) two or more times the depth of a spade **c** (1) **:** to cut a drainage trench in **:** DITCH ⟨~ land to drain it⟩ (2) **:** to drain by trenches **d :** to bury in or confine by means of a trench ⟨~ing logs to prevent rolling —*Glossary of Terms Used in Forest Fire Control*⟩ ⟨stopping more than 3000 small fires and ~ing in nearly 100 big ones —W.B.Greeley⟩ **e :** ENTRENCH 2 ~ *vi* **1 a** *obs* **:** to approach a military objective by a series of trenches ⟨like powerful armies ~ing at a town —Edward Young⟩ **b** *archaic* **:** to extend out **:** STRETCH ⟨the land ~ed away west for fifteen hundred miles —Daniel Defoe⟩ **2 a :** ENTRENCH 2 ⟨~ing on other domains which were more vital —Sir Winston Churchill⟩ **b :** to come close **:** VERGE ⟨catches himself . . . ~ing upon presumption —T.V.Smith⟩ **3 :** to dig a trench ⟨~ around the spot right down to the clay —*Sydney (Australia) Bull.*⟩

trench·an·cy \ˈtrenchənsē, -si\ *n* -ES **:** the quality or state of being trenchant

trench·ant \-chənt\ *adj* [ME *trenchaunt*, fr. MF *trenchant*, pres. part. of *trenchier* to trench] **1 a** *archaic* **:** having a cutting edge **:** KEEN, SHARP ⟨a second less and the ~ blade had shorn through his heart —Bram Stoker⟩ **b :** adapted for cutting **:** SECTORIAL ⟨a ~ tooth⟩ **2 :** vigorously effective **:** keenly articulate **:** BRISK ⟨a most ~ defender of civil rights —Zechariah Chafee⟩ ⟨discussed with a fearless and ~ pen the religious issues of the day —H.K.Rowe⟩; *specif* **:** CAUSTIC ⟨disillusioned satirist, ~, arrogant, and absolute master of a mordant pen —J.L.Lowes⟩ **3 a :** sharply perceptive **:** COGENT, PENETRATING ⟨a ~, plotless, constantly unfolding view of . . . conditions brought by the war to our cities —Leslie Rees⟩ ⟨the author's ~ imagination —*New Yorker*⟩ **b :** well-defined **:** CLEAR-CUT, DISTINCT ⟨the ~ divisions between right and wrong, honest and dishonest —Edith Wharton⟩ **syn** see INCISIVE

trench·ant·ly *adv* **:** in a trenchant manner

trench artillery *n* **:** artillery emplaced in trenches for firing at high angles against targets at close range

trenchboard \ˈ=ˌ=\ *n* **:** duckboards running lengthwise of the bottom of a trench to keep the occupants out of accumulated mud and water

trench cart *n* **:** a low-wheeled narrow handcart for conveying ammunition through trenches

trench coat *n* **1 :** a waterproof military overcoat with a removable woolen lining designed for wear in trenches **2 :** a loose double-breasted raincoat or sport coat with a convertible collar, deep pockets, wide belt, tabs on the sleeves, and straps on the shoulders, usu. made of tan waterproofed gabardine or cotton twill

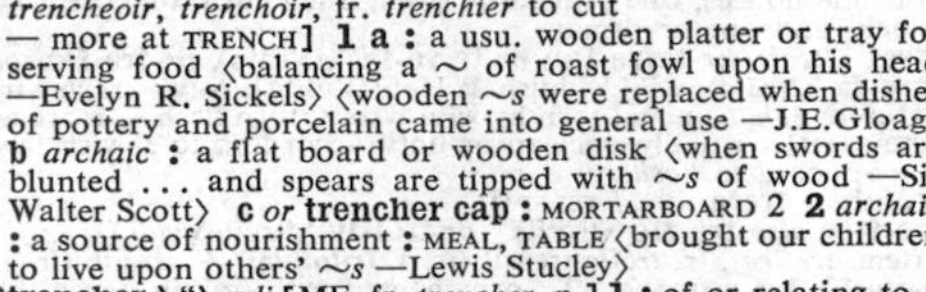

trench coat 2

trench digger *n* **:** a machine for excavating trenches

trenched *adj* [fr. past part. of ²*trench*] **1 :** furrowed or drained by trenches **:** GROOVED, INCISED ⟨tributaries ran due north . . . in deeply ~ valleys —W.G.East⟩ **2** [¹*trench* + *-ed*] **:** provided with protective trenches ⟨stared at the ~ and fortified hill —Kenneth Roberts⟩

¹tren·cher \ˈtrenchə(r)\ *n* -S [ME *trencher, trenchour* knife, wooden platter on which meat was cut up, trencher, fr. MF *trencheoir, trenchoir*, fr. *trenchier* to cut — more at TRENCH] **1 a :** a usu. wooden platter or tray for serving food ⟨balancing a ~ of roast fowl upon his head —Evelyn R. Sickels⟩ ⟨wooden ~s were replaced when dishes of pottery and porcelain came into general use —J.E.Gloag⟩ **b** *archaic* **:** a flat board or wooden disk ⟨when swords are blunted . . . and spears are tipped with ~s of wood —Sir Walter Scott⟩ **c** *or* **trencher cap :** MORTARBOARD 2 **2** *archaic* **:** a source of nourishment **:** MEAL, TABLE ⟨brought our children to live upon others' ~s —Lewis Stucley⟩

²trencher \"\ *adj* [ME, fr. *trencher*, n.] **1 :** of or relating to a trencher or to the eating of meals ⟨~ knife⟩ ⟨~ companion⟩ **2** *archaic* **:** PARASITIC, SYCOPHANTIC ⟨some ~ knight —Shak.⟩

³trench·er \"\ *n* -S [²*trench* + *-er*] **:** one that digs trenches

trencher-fed \ˈ==ˌ=\ *adj, Brit* **:** boarded around at various places instead of in hunt kennels — used of foxhounds

trenchering *n* -S [¹*trencher* + *-ing*] *obs* **:** eating utensils

tren·cher·man \ˈ==mən\ *n, pl* **trenchermen** [¹*trencher* + *man*] **1 :** a hearty eater **:** GOURMAND ⟨soldier's rations . . . so generous as to be improbable even in those days of hearty *trenchermen* —G.E.Fussell⟩ **2** *archaic* **:** HANGER-ON, SPONGER

trencher salt *n* **:** an individual salt dish or squat open salt-cellar placed near a trencher

trencherwoman \ˈ==ˌ==\ *n, pl* **trencherwomen :** a female gourmand

trenches *pl of* TRENCH, *pres 3d sing of* TRENCH

trench fever *n* **:** an infectious disease characterized by fever and pain in muscles, bones, and joints, believed to be caused by a rickettsia transmitted by the body louse, and constituting a major medical problem during World War I

trench foot *n* [so called fr. its prevalence among soldiers serving in the trenches during World War I] **:** a painful condition of the feet resembling frostbite and marked by inflammation, swelling, mottled discoloration, burning pain, blisters, and in severe cases gangrene due to the combined effect of cold and wet upon the feet — compare IMMERSION FOOT

trenching *pres part of* TRENCH

trench knife *n* **:** a knife with a strong double-edged blade about eight inches long suited for use in hand-to-hand fighting

trench·more \ˈtrenchˌmō(ə)r\ *n* -S [perh. fr. the name *Trenchmore*] **:** a boisterous English folk dance of the 16th and 17th centuries or its music in triple time and dotted rhythm

trench mouth *n* [so called fr. its prevalence among soldiers in the trenches] **1 :** VINCENT'S ANGINA **2 :** VINCENT'S INFECTION

trench-plow \ˈ=ˌ=\ *vb* [*trench* + *plow*, v.] *vi* **:** to bring lower soil to the surface by plowing a furrow a second time with a plow set much deeper ~ *vt* **:** to plow (a field) to double depth

trench plow *n* **:** a plow adapted for deep plowing

trench silo *n* **:** a trench often dug into a bank or slope, sometimes lined with concrete, and used mostly in regions of low rainfall for making and storing silage

trench warfare *n* **:** warfare in which the opposing forces attack and counterattack from a relatively permanent system of trenches protected by barbed-wire entanglements

¹trend \ˈtrend\ *vb* -ED/-ING/-S [ME *trenden* to turn, revolve, fr. OE *trendan*; akin to OFris *trind, trund* round, OE *trinda, trinde* round lump, ball, *trendel* circle, ring, MLG *trent* ring, boundary, MHG *trendel* disk, spinning top, *trinnen* to run forth, tear away from, *trennen* to break off, sever, OE *teran* to tear — more at TEAR] *vi* **1 a :** to extend in a general direction **:** follow a general course ⟨jagged ranges of mountains . . . ~ north and south —G.R.Stewart⟩ ⟨the track led into caverns that ~ed upwards into the rock —John Masefield⟩ **b :** to veer in a new direction **:** take a turn **:** BEND, CURVE ⟨Penobscot Bay . . . ~s deeply into Maine —Bernard De Voto⟩ **2 a :** to show an inherent tendency or general drift **:** INCLINE, MOVE ⟨selling costs have ~ed upward —*Printers' Ink*⟩ ⟨the direction Italian thought is ~ing —Fletcher Pratt⟩ ⟨people have a right to know how affairs of such great moment are ~ing —Arthur Krock⟩ **b :** to become deflected **:** SHIFT ⟨the flow of population may ~ his way —Alfred Marshall⟩ ~ *vt* **:** to cause to follow or conform to a trend ⟨laying the several courses . . . and ~ing them to the abutments —*Civil Engineer & Architect's Jour.*⟩ ⟨~ed costs⟩

²trend \"\ *n* -S **1 a :** the line of direction or movement **:** ORIENTATION, FLOW ⟨the long northeastern ~ of the coast —Samuel Van Valkenburg & Ellsworth Huntington⟩ **b :** the directional line of a rock bed or petroleum deposit **:** STRIKE ⟨postulation of possible mineral ~s —*Economic Geology*⟩ ⟨the ~s of all the oil-bearing belts are known with considerable accuracy —John Pain⟩ **c :** the lower end of the shank of an anchor from about the length of one of the arms to the throat **2 a :** a prevailing tendency or inclination **:** DRIFT, LEANING ⟨the ~ of opinion was distinctively conservative —C.L.Becker⟩ ⟨contemporary ~s in education⟩ ⟨the ~ toward government participation in economic affairs —Louis Wasserman⟩ **b :** a general movement **:** SWING ⟨the ~ away from the land —Frank Hamilton⟩ ⟨the ~ toward shorter work periods —H.M. Diamond⟩ **c :** a current style or preference **:** VOGUE ⟨the longer waistline ~ —Dorothy O'Neill⟩ ⟨the ~ of yellow in kitchens —*Dun's Rev.*⟩ **d :** a line of development **:** APPROACH ⟨important new ~s in cancer have appeared in the clinical literature —D.A.Karnofsky⟩ **3 a :** the general movement over a sufficiently long period of time of some statistical progressive change ⟨~ of the stock market⟩ ⟨population ~⟩ ⟨upward ~ of the cost of living⟩ **b :** a straight line or other statistical curve showing the tendency of some function to grow or decline over a period of time ⟨a sensitive barometer of giving ~s through mass mailings —Jerome Ellison⟩ ⟨~s in parasitization —*Jour. of Economic Entomology*⟩ **syn** see TENDENCY

tren·del \ˈtrendᵊl\ *n, pl* **trendels** *or* **trendel** [Yiddish *trendl*, fr. MHG *trendel* disk, spinning top] **:** DREIDEL

tren·de·len·burg position \ˈtrendᵊlənˌbərg-\ *n, usu cap T* [after Friedrich *Trendelenburg* †1924 Ger. surgeon] **:** a position of the body for medical examination or operation in which the patient is placed head down on a table inclined at about 45 degrees from the floor with the knees uppermost and the legs hanging over the end of the table

tren·dle \ˈtrendᵊl\ *n* -S [ME, circle, ring, wheel, trendle, fr. OE *trendel* circle, ring; akin to MHG *trendel* disk — more at TREND] *dial Brit* **:** a large shallow round or oval usu. wooden tub or trough

trend line *n* **:** a line on a graph showing a statistical trend

tren·tal \ˈtrentᵊl\ *n* -S [ME, fr. ML *trentale*, fr. (assumed) VL *trenta, trinta* thirty, fr. L *triginta* — more at TRICENARY] **:** a series of 30 Roman Catholic masses for the dead usu. celebrated 30 consecutive days

trente-et-qua·rante \ˌträ͞ⁿtākəˈrä͞ⁿt\ *or* **trente-qua·rante** \ˌträⁿk-\ *n* [F *trente et quarante*, lit., thirty and forty; fr. the fact that the number dealt must never exceed 40 and the color nearest 31 wins] **:** ROUGE ET NOIR

tren·te·pohl·ia \ˌtrentəˈpōlēə\ *n, cap* [NL, fr. Johann F. *Trentepohl* †1806 Ger. botanist + NL *-ia*] **:** a genus (the type of the family Trentepohliaceae) of terrestrial usu. reddish or orange-tinted green algae growing partly prostrate on rocks and tree trunks and found as the algal components of various lichens — see ROCK VIOLET

tren·te·pohl·i·a·ce·ae \ˌ==ˌpōlēˈāsēˌē\ *n pl, cap* [NL, fr. *Trentepohlia*, type genus + *-aceae*] **:** a family of aquatic or terrestrial green algae (order Ulotrichales) characterized by branching filaments without hairs and both prostrate and upright systems of growth and by isogamous sexual reproduction — see RED RUST 3a — **tren·te·pohl·i·a·ceous** \ˌ==ˌ==ˈāshəs\ *adj*

tren·tine \ˈtrenˌtēn, -ˌtīn\ *adj, usu cap* [Council of *Trent* (1545–63), nineteenth ecumenical council of the Roman Catholic Church held in the town of Trent, & *Trent*, town in northeastern Italy + E *-ine*] **:** TRIDENTINE

¹tren·ton \ˈtrentᵊn\ *adj, usu cap* [fr. *Trenton*, New Jersey] **:** of or from Trenton, the capital of New Jersey ⟨*Trenton* potteries⟩ **:** of the kind or style prevalent in Trenton

²trenton \"\ *n* -S *usu cap* [fr. *Trenton* Falls, New York] **:** a subdivision of the American Ordovician sometimes considered as the equivalent of the whole Middle Ordovician and sometimes restricted to a portion of this series

tren·to·ni·an \tren·ˈtōnēən\ *n* -S *cap* [*Trenton*, New Jersey + *-an*] **:** a native or resident of Trenton, New Jersey

tre·pak \trəˈpäk, ˈtrā-,\ *n* -S [Russ, fr. *trepat'* to brake, beat, tap; akin to Lith *trepsti* to stamp with the feet, trample — more at TREPIDATION] **:** a fiery Ukrainian folk dance performed by men and featuring the leg-flinging prisiadka

¹tre·pan \trəˈpan, trēˈ-, -ˈpaa(ə)n\ *n* -S [ME *trepane*, fr. ML *trepanum*, fr. Gk *trypanon* auger, trepan — more at TRYPAN-] **1 :** TREPHINE **2 a :** a heavy tool consisting of vertical chisels fixed to a horizontal bar and used in boring mine shafts **b :** a machine tool for trepanning metals

²trepan \"\ *vt* **trepanned; trepanned; trepanning; trepans** [ME *trepanen*, fr. *trepane* trepan] **1 :** to use a trephine on (the skull) **2 a :** to bore (as a mine shaft) with a trepan **b** (1) **:** to remove a disk or cylindrical core from (a metal plate, ingot, or forging) with a trepan (2) **:** to turn annular grooves or recesses in (as a metal block held in a lathe)

³trepan \"\ *n* -S [origin unknown] **1** *archaic* **:** DECOY, TRICKSTER **2** *archaic* **:** a deceptive device or maneuver **:** SNARE

⁴trepan \"\ *vt* **trepanned; trepanned; trepanning; trepans** **1** *archaic* **:** ENTRAP, LURE **2** *archaic* **:** SWINDLE

trep·a·na·tion \ˌtrepəˈnāshən\ *n* -S [ME *trepanacioun*, fr. MF *trepanation*, fr. *trepan* (fr. ML *trepanum*) + *-ation*] **1 :** the act or process of perforating a skull with a surgical instrument **2 :** a hole in the skull produced surgically ⟨hundreds of crania showing ~s . . . have received close scrutiny by prehistorians —W.T.Corlett⟩

tre·pang \trəˈpaŋ, trēˈ-, -ˈpaiŋ\ *n* -S [Malay *tĕripang*] **:** any of several large holothurians mostly of the genera *Actinopyga* and *Holothuria* that are taken in vast quantities in northern Australia and the East Indies and to some extent along other warm coasts, boiled, dried, smoked, and used esp. by the Chinese for making soup — called also *bêche-de-mer*

trepanning *n* -S [ME, fr. gerund of *trepanen* to trepan] **1 :** TREPANATION **2 :** the act or process of removing a disk or core of metal ⟨~ is a preliminary step in defusing an unexploded bomb⟩

treph·i·na·tion \ˌtrefəˈnāshən\ *n* -S [²*trephine* + *-ation*] **:** an act or instance of trephining; *esp* **:** TREPANATION

¹tre·phine \ˈtrēˌfīn; trəˈfīn, -ˈfēn\ *n* -S [F *tréphine*, fr. obs. E *trefine, trafine*, fr. L *tres fines* three ends, fr. *tres* three + *fines*, pl. of *finis* end — more at THREE, FINAL] **1 :** a surgical instrument for cutting out circular sections (as of bone or corneal tissue) **2 :** TREPHINATION

²trephine \"\ *vb* -ED/-ING/-S *vi* **:** to perform a trephination ~ *vt* **:** to operate on with or extract by means of a trephine ⟨two young men whose skulls had been *trephined* because of head injury —R.S.Woodworth⟩ ⟨a graft *trephined* from a fresh cadaver eye —*Yrbk. of the Eye, Ear, Nose & Throat*⟩

treph·o·cyte \ˈtrefəˌsīt\ *n* -S [ISV *treph-* (fr. Gk *trephein* to nourish) + *-o-* + *-cyte* — more at ATROPHY] **:** a blood cell found in many invertebrates and concerned primarily with the transport of substances between the body cells

treph·one \ˈtreˌfōn\ *n* -S [ISV, modif. of Gk *trephein* to nourish] **:** any of various substances in the blood serum and body fluids that promote the growth of cells

trep·id \ˈtrepəd\ *adj* [L *trepidus*] **:** TIMOROUS, TREMBLING — **trep·id·ly** *adv*

trep·i·dant \ˈtrepədənt\ *adj* [L *trepidant-, trepidans*, pres. part. of *trepidare* to trepidate] **:** TIMID, TREMBLING

trep·i·date \ˈtrepəˌdāt\ *vi* -ED/-ING/-S [L *trepidatus*, past part. of *trepidare* to trepidate] *archaic* **:** to feel trepidation ⟨causes our mind to ~ with quaking fear —*Fraser's Mag.*⟩

trep·i·da·tion \ˌ==ˈdāshən\ *n* -S [L *trepidation-, trepidatio*, fr. *trepidatus* (past part. of *trepidare* to tremble, trepidate, fr. *trepidus* trembling, agitated) + *-ion-, -io* -ion; akin to OE *thrafian* to urge, push, press, OS *thrabōn* to trot, high-step, MLG *draven*, Sw *trava* to trot, Gk *trapein* to press grapes, Lith *trepsti, trepseti* to stamp, trample, Skt *trpra* unsteady, hasty, anxious] **1 a** *archaic* **:** a tremulous motion **:** QUIVERING, TREMOR **b :** the quality or state of being trepid **:** nervous agitation **:** APPREHENSION ⟨the high quality . . . should make readers turn with eagerness and without too much ~ to the 200-page anthology —*Times Lit. Supp.*⟩ ⟨shocked safe and sane businessmen into a state of indignant ~ —Thorstein Veblen⟩ **2 a :** a libration of one of the celestial spheres adduced under the Ptolemaic system to explain small changes in position of the ecliptic and the stars **b :** a small fluctuation in the longitude of the sun or moon **syn** see FEAR

tre·pid·i·ty \trəˈpidədē\ *n* -ES [L *trepidus* trembling + E *-ity*] **:** TREPIDATION 1b

trep·o·ne·ma \ˌtrepəˈnēmə\ *n* [NL, fr. Gk *trepein* to turn + NL *-o-* + *-nema* — more at TROPE] **1** *cap* **:** the type genus of Treponemataceae comprising anaerobic spirochetes that are parasitic in warm-blooded animals and man, have an undulating or rigid body without a columella, and sometimes terminate in tapering ends resembling flagella — see SYPHILIS, YAWS **2** *pl* **treponema·ta** \-məd·ə\ *or* **treponemas :** any spirochete of the genus *Treponema* — **trep·o·nem·a·tous** \ˌ==ˈnemad·əs, -ˈnēm-\ *adj*

trep·o·ne·mal \¦==¦nēməl\ *adj* [NL *Treponema* + E *-al*] **1 :** caused by treponemata **2 :** acting on or affecting treponemata

trep·o·ne·ma·ta·ce·ae \ˌtrepəˌnēmə'tāsēˌē\ *n pl, cap* [NL, fr. *Treponemat-*, *Treponema*, type genus + *-aceae*] **:** a family of Spirochaetales comprising small variable spirochetes without obvious structural differentiation and including a number of parasites of vertebrates, some of which are important pathogens — see BORRELIA, LEPTOSPIRA, TREPONEMA

trep·o·ne·ma·to·sis \-'tōsə̇s\ *n, pl* **treponemato·ses** \-ōˌsēz\ [NL, fr. *Treponemat-*, *Treponema* + *-osis*] **:** infection with or disease caused by spirochetes of the genus *Treponema* — compare BEJEL, PINTA, SYPHILIS, YAWS

trep·o·neme \'trepəˌnēm\ *n* -S [NL *Treponema*] **:** TREPONEMA 2

trep·o·ne·mi·ci·dal \¦==¦nēmə¦sīdᵊl\ *adj* **:** destroying treponemata

trep·o·ne·mi·cide \ˌ==ˈ==ˌsīd\ *n* -S [ISV *treponem-* (fr. NL *Treponemata*) + *-i-* + *-cide*] **:** an agent that kills treponemata

trep·o·sto·ma·ta \ˌtrepə'stōməd·ə\ *n pl, cap* [NL, fr. Gk *trepein* to turn + NL *-o-* + *-stomata*] **:** an order of Bryozoa (class Gymnolaemata) comprising Paleozoic forms resembling corals and having conical or prismatic zooecial tubes with flat or curved partitions — **trep·o·stome** \'==ˌstōm\ *adj or n*

trep·pe \'trepə\ *n* -S [G, lit., step, stairs, fr. MHG *treppe*, *trappe* — more at TRAP] **:** the graduated series of increasingly vigorous contractions that results when a corresponding series of identical stimuli is applied to a rested muscle

tre·ron \'trēˌrän\ *n, cap* [NL, fr. Gk *trērōn* timid, shy, dove; akin to Gk *trein* to flee, be afraid — more at TERROR] **:** a genus comprising fruit-eating pigeons of southern Asia, the East Indies, and other warm parts of the Old World that have the plumage largely green shading into purple or maroon and being the type of a subfamily of Columbidae or sometimes of a distinct family

tres *abbr* trestle

tre·set·te \trā'set·ē, trə-\ *n* -S [It, lit., three-seven; fr. the fact that 3 or 7 points are scored at one time] **:** an Italian card game in which players may score by melding and by winning counting cards in tricks

-tre·sia \-'trēzh(ē)ə\ *n comb form* -S [NL, fr. Gk *trēsis* (akin to Gk *tetrainein* to pierce) + NL *-ia* — more at THROW] **:** perforation ⟨procto*tresia*⟩ ⟨spheno*tresia*⟩

¹tres·pass \'trespəs, -eˌspas, -eˌspaa(ə)s, -eˌspas, -eˌspȧs\ *n* -ES [ME *trespas*, fr. OF, passage, crossing, trespass, fr. *trespasser* to go across, pass through] **1 a :** a violation of moral or social ethics **:** OFFENSE, TRANSGRESSION ⟨forgive us our ~*es* —*Bk. of Com. Prayer*⟩; *esp* **:** SIN ⟨the fatal ~ done by Eve —John Milton⟩ **b :** an unwarranted infringement ⟨never worried about their . . . ~ on generosity —Audrey Barker⟩ **2 a** (1) **:** an unlawful invasion of the person, property, or rights of another that is committed with actual violence or violence implied by law **:** a tort involving actual or implied violence (2) **:** the action for injuries done by such an act **b :** TRESPASS QUARE CLAUSUM FREGIT **syn** see BREACH

²trespass \"\ *vb* -ED/-ING/-ES [ME *trespassen*, fr. MF *trespasser*, fr. OF, to go across, pass through, trespass, fr. *tres* across, through (fr. L *trans*) + *passer* to pass — more at TRANS-, PASS] *vi* **1 a :** to commit an offense **:** ERR, SIN ⟨his errors of taste, when he ~*es* . . . have consist in taking a subject too seriously or too lightly —T.S.Eliot⟩ ⟨scrupulous fairness even to those who ~ against him —S.L.A.Marshall⟩ **b :** to make an unwarranted or uninvited incursion **:** cross an established boundary line ⟨~ on an angler's casting area⟩ ⟨~ on a busy executive's time⟩ ⟨not their duty to train the infants . . . but merely to see that they do not ~ upon adult attention by outraging the rules of etiquette —Margaret Mead⟩ ⟨felt the ambassador had ~*ed* on domestic affairs —*Time*⟩ **2 :** to commit a trespass; *esp* **:** to enter unlawfully upon the land of another ~ *vt* **:** VIOLATE ⟨~ the bounds of good taste⟩ ⟨~*ed* a doctor's office —W.G.Eliasberg⟩

syn ENCROACH, ENTRENCH, INFRINGE, INVADE: TRESPASS applies to a usu. unwarranted, unlawful, or offensive intrusion ⟨farmers bothered by hunters *trespassing* on their fields⟩ ⟨have *trespassed* on your hospitality too long —Dorothy Sayers⟩ ENCROACH may apply to an invasion of another's territory or usurpation of his privileges, rights, or possessions, often accomplished gradually or stealthily ⟨leading his tribesmen in defense of their homes against *encroaching* white settlers —*Current Biog.*⟩ ⟨that the Argentine militarists would seek to *encroach* on the territories of neighboring states —Vera M. Dean⟩ ⟨their work is closely related but it is not synonymous; neither should ever *encroach* on the field of prerogatives of the other —H.H.Arnold & I.C.Eaker⟩ ENTRENCH may suggest an aggressive position and determination to maintain control ⟨the ultimate result was that the railroad *entrenched* itself so strongly in the state's political field —*Amer. Guide Series: N.J.*⟩ ⟨spokesmen for the coal industry have expressed concern that the unregulated producers may cut their prices sharply in strategic areas to *entrench* themselves at the expense of coal —Walter Goodman⟩ INFRINGE applies to any degree of encroachment that can be considered a clear breach of law, ethics, equity, or rights ⟨a well-regulated militia being necessary to the security of a free state, the right of the people to keep and bear arms shall not be *infringed* —*U.S.Constitution*⟩ ⟨was very critical whenever the military power seemed to *infringe* on civil rights —W.K.Boyd⟩ INVADE may indicate entrance into another's sphere or territory with hostile intent and injurious effect ⟨in the years after the Civil War, it was not only the carpetbaggers who had *invaded* the South —Oscar Handlin⟩ ⟨no good comes from attempts to *invade* authority and responsibility —Dean Acheson⟩ ⟨she'll probably insult you for *invading* what she calls their privacy —Hamilton Basso⟩

trespass board *or* **trespass notice** *or* **trespass sign** *n* **:** a notice on private property legally prohibiting trespass

tres·pass·er \-sə(r)\ *n* -S [ME *trespassour*, fr. MF *trespasseor*, fr. OF *trespasser* to trespass + *-or*] **:** one that trespasses; *specif* **:** one that commits a trespass against another or his property — compare INVITEE, LICENSEE

trespass offering *n* **:** GUILT OFFERING

trespass on the case : a form of action or a writ formerly employed to redress various wrongs or injuries to person or property which were not the immediate result of alleged violence and for which no adequate remedy was provided by the common-law action of trespass — called also *action on the case*

trespass quare clausum fregit : the tort of wrongful entry on real property

trespass to try title : an action of trespass quare clausum fregit or its equivalent under codes and practice acts brought as a means of determining the title to land

¹tress \'tres\ *n* -ES [ME *tresse*, fr. OF *trece*] **1 a** *archaic* **:** a plait of hair **:** BRAID ⟨her yellow golden hair was trimly woven and in ~*es* wrought —Edmund Spenser⟩ **b :** a long lock of hair; *esp* **:** the long unbound hair of a woman — usu. used in pl. ⟨a wealth of long and lustrous-dusky ~*es* tangled on the snow-white pillow —R.P.Warren⟩ **2 :** a flexible shoot or frond ⟨branches weaved like the ~*es* of marine weeds —William Sansom⟩

²tress \"\ *vt* -ED/-ING/-ES [ME *tressen*, fr. MF *tresser*, fr. OF *trecier*] **:** to form into tresses **:** BRAID, PLAIT ⟨~ hair⟩ ⟨beautiful liquid braids ~*ed* by the streamlet —Julian Green⟩

tressed \-st\ *adj* [ME, fr. past part. of *tressen* to tress] **1 :** BRAIDED, PLAITED ⟨beds of ~ gazelle hide —Ida Treat⟩ **2 :** having tresses — usu. used in combination ⟨a red-*tressed* ex-waitress —*Newsweek*⟩

tres·sure \'treshə(r)\ *n* -S [ME *tressour*, fr. *tressour*, *tressure* band for the hair, headdress, fr. MF *tresseor*, *tressure*, fr. *tresser* to tress + *-or*, *-ure*] **1 :** a narrow orle usu. enriched with fleurs-de-lis **2 :** an inner encircling ornamentation on a coin or medal bordering the device — **tres·sured** \-(r)d\ *adj*

tressy \'tresē\ *adj* -ER/-EST *archaic* **:** abounding in or resembling tresses

tres·tine \'treˌstīn\ *also* **trez·tine** \-ez,t-\ *n* -S [prob. fr. L *tres* three + E *tine* (of an antler) — more at THREE] **:** ROYAL ANTLER

¹tres·tle *or* **tres·sel** \'tresəl\ *n* -S *often attrib* [ME *trestel*, fr. MF, modif. (influenced by OF *treste*, *trestre* trestle, var. of *traste*, *trastre*, fr. L *transtrum* crossbeam) of (assumed) VL *transtellum* trestle, fr. L *transtillum*, dim. of *transtrum* crossbeam, transom — more at TRANSOM] **1 a :** a movable support or scaffolding usu. having diagonally spreading legs **:** HORSE 2c ⟨put boards on a ~ to saw them⟩ ⟨painters at work on a ~⟩ **b** (1) **:** TRESTLE TABLE (2) **:** a divided foot on a piece of furniture (3) **:** a braced frame serving as a support (as for a table top or drawing board) **c :** a braced framework of timbers, piles, or steelwork usu. of considerable height for carrying a road or railroad over a depression — compare VIADUCT **2 a** *archaic* **:** a three-legged stool or support **:** TRIPOD **b :** a low usu. three-legged stool or bench used as a heraldic bearing

²trestle \"\ *vt* **trestled; trestled; trestling** \-s(ə)liŋ\ **trestles :** to set on or support by means of trestles

trestle bent *n* **:** a transverse frame supporting the ends of the stringers in adjacent spans of a trestle

trestle bridge *n* **:** a bridge supported by trestlework

tres·tle·man \'==mən\ *n, pl* **trestlemen :** a worker who unloads loose cargo (as sand or ore) from freight cars and puts it on conveyors or into boats

trestle table *n* **:** a table supported on trestles ⟨set up *trestle tables* for a church supper⟩ ⟨a large . . . *trestle table* rather like a drafting board —Carl Jonas⟩; *specif* **:** a table having two or three trestle supports connected by a longitudinal bar instead of legs

trestle table

trestletree \'==ˌ=\ *n* **:** one of a pair of timber cross-pieces fixed fore and aft on the masthead to support the crosstrees, top, and fid of the mast — usu. used in pl.

trestlework \'==ˌ=\ *n* **1 :** a system of connected trestles supporting a structure (as a bridge, pier, or scaffold) **2 :** a structure composed of trestlework

trestling *n* -S **:** TRESTLEWORK 1

tret \'tret\ *n* -S [MF *trait* pull, draft, turn of the scale, pull of the scale — more at TRAIT] **:** an allowance of 4 pounds for every 104 pounds of suttle weight formerly added to various commodities (as spices) to offset deterioration in transit or chaff removed in cleaning

tre·ta yuga \'trād·ə-\ *n* [Skt *tretāyuga*, fr. *tretā* third throw of the dice, triad (fr. *traya* triple, threefold, fr. *tri* three) + *yuga* yoke, age of the world — more at THREE, YOKE] *Hinduism* **:** the second age of a world cycle

tre·val·ly \trə'valē\ *n* -ES [origin unknown] **1 :** an Australian carangid food fish (*Caranx georgianus*); *broadly* **:** any of several carangid fishes **2 :** BLACK TREVALLY; *broadly* **:** any of several related fishes chiefly of tropical and subtropical seas

tre·vis *or* **tre·viss** \'trāvə̇s, 'trev-\ *Scot var of* TRAVERSE

trev·or·ite \'trevəˌrīt\ *n* -S [T. G. *Trevor*, 20th cent. Brit. mine inspector + E *-ite*] **:** a black or brown-black mineral $NiFe_2O_4$ consisting of an oxide of nickel and iron and constituting a member of the magnetite series

trew \'trü\ *vi* -ED/-ING/-S [ME (Sc) *trewen*, fr. OE *trēowan*, *trēowian* — more at TROW] *Scot* **:** BELIEVE, TRUST

trews \'trüz\ *n pl* [ScGael *triubhas* — more at TROUSERS] **1 :** tight-fitting full-length trousers of tartan worn by some Scottish regiments **2 :** close-cut tartan short drawers sometimes worn under the kilt in Highland dress

trey \'trā\ *n* -S [ME *treye*, *treis*, fr. MF *treie* (fr. L *tria*, neut., three) & *treis*, fr. L *tres*, masc. & fem., three — more at THREE] **1 :** the side of a die or domino that has three spots **2 :** a card numbered three or having three main pips

trey–trip *n* -S [prob. fr. *trey* + *trip*, v.] *obs* **:** an old dicing game

trf *abbr* **1** tariff **2** transfer

TRF *abbr, often not cap* tuned radio frequency

trfd *abbr* transferred

trfr *abbr* transfer

TRH *abbr* Their Royal Highnesses

¹tri \'trī\ *adj* [by shortening] **:** TRICOLOR 1b ⟨a ~ dog⟩

²tri \"\ *n* -S **:** a tri dog

tri- *comb form* [ME, fr. L; akin to Gk *tri-*, L *tria* three — more at THREE] **1 :** three ⟨*tri*arch⟩ ⟨*tri*act⟩ **:** characterized by or having three or three parts ⟨*tri*crotic⟩ ⟨*tri*cycle⟩ ⟨*tri*pod⟩ **2 :** three times or in three ways ⟨*tri*farious⟩ ⟨*tri*sonant⟩; *also* **:** into three ⟨*tri*sect⟩ **3 :** thrice **:** every third ⟨*tri*weekly⟩ ⟨*tri*ennial⟩ **4 :** containing three atoms, radicals, or groups (of a specified kind) ⟨*tri*bromide⟩

tri·able \'trīəbəl\ *adj* [ME, fr. AF, fr. *trien* to try + *-able* — more at TRY] **1 :** liable or subject to undergo a judicial or quasi-judicial examination or trial ⟨a case ~ without a jury⟩ ⟨a case ~ by a national labor relations board examiner⟩ **2** *obs* **:** that may or can be tried **:** capable of being attempted or put to a test

tri·a·can·thi·dae \ˌtrīə'kan(t)thəˌdē\ *n pl, cap* [NL, fr. *Triacantha*, type genus (fr. *tri-* + *acantha*) + *-idae*] **:** a family of marine fish (suborder Balistoidea) that have a protractile upper jaw, live chiefly on sandy bottoms where they feed on mollusks, and comprise the hornfishes

triacetate \(')trī+\ *n* [ISV *tri-* + *acetate*] **:** an acetate containing three acetate groups ⟨cellulose ~ fiber⟩

triacetin \"+\ *n* [ISV *tri-* + *acet-* + *-in*] **:** ACETIN

¹tri·acid \"+\ *adj* [ISV *tri-* + *acid*, adj.] **1 :** able to react with three molecules of a monobasic acid or one of a tribasic acid to form a salt or ester — used esp. of bases **2 :** containing three hydrogen atoms replaceable by basic atoms or radicals — used esp. of acid salts

²triacid \"\ *n* **:** an acid (as phosphoric acid or citric acid) having three acid hydrogen atoms

tri·a·con·tane \ˌtrīə'känˌtān, ˌtrēə-\ *n* -S [ISV *triacont-* (fr. Gk *triakonta* thirty) + *-ane* — more at TRICENARY] **:** a solid paraffin hydrocarbon $C_{30}H_{62}$; *esp* **:** the normal crystalline hydrocarbon $CH_3(CH_2)_{28}CH_3$ occurring in many mineral oils and in the wax coatings of apple skins and various flowers

tri·a·con·ta·no·ic acid \¦==¦käntə¦nōik-\ *n* [*triacontane* + *-oic*] **:** MELISSIC ACID

tri·a·con·ter \ˌ=='käntə(r)\ *n* -S [Gk *triakontērēs*, fr. *triakonta* thirty] **:** a Hellenic galley carrying 30 banks of oars

tri·act \'trīˌakt\ *n* -S [*tri-* + *-act*] **:** a triactinal sponge spicule

tri·actinal \(')trī¦aktənəl, ¦trīˌak¦tīnᵊl\ *also* **tri·ac·tine** \(')trīˌakˌtīn, -ˌtən\ *adj* [*tri-* + *-actinal* or *-actine*] **:** having three rays ⟨a ~ sponge spicule⟩

¹tri·ad \'trīˌad, -īəd\ *n* -S [L *triad-*, *trias*, fr. Gk; akin to Gk *treis* three — more at THREE] **:** a union or group of three esp. of three closely related persons, beings, or things **:** TRINITY ⟨a ~ of deities⟩ ⟨a ~ of symptoms⟩: as **a :** a gnomic literature in medieval Wales and Ireland consisting of short aphorisms grouped in threes and in prose marked by rhythm and assonance and applying to various subjects (as history, laws, or morals) **b :** a trivalent element, atom, or radical **c :** a chord of three tones consisting of a root with its third and fifth and constituting the harmonic basis of tonal music — called also *common chord*; see MAJOR TRIAD, MINOR TRIAD; compare FIRST INVERSION, SECOND INVERSION **d :** a group of three individuals maintaining a sociologically significant relationship — compare DYAD **e :** a group of three strophes in a classical ode consisting of strophe, antistrophe, and epode

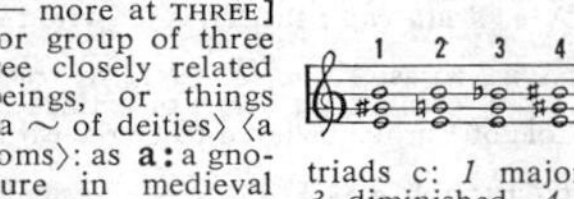

triads c: *1* major, *2* minor, *3* diminished, *4* augmented, *5* first inversion, *6* second inversion

²triad \"\ *adj* **:** having symmetry that results in repetition after every 120-degree rotation ⟨a ~ crystal axis⟩

tri·adel·phous \ˌtrīə¦delfəs\ *adj* [ISV *tri-* + *-adelphous*] **:** being or having stamens joined by filaments into three fascicles ⟨a ~ flower⟩

tri·a·de·num \ˌtrīə'dēnəm\ *n, cap* [NL, fr. *tri-* + Gk *adēn* gland — more at ADEN-] *in some classifications* **:** a genus of No. American herbs (family Guttiferae) comprising two forms usu. included in the genus *Hypericum* but distinguished when separated chiefly by the pink or purple flowers and the three large glands alternating with three sets of stamens

tri·ad·ic \(')trī¦adik, -dēk\ *adj* **:** having the characteristics of or constituting a triad **:** consisting of or involving a triad ⟨a ~ poem⟩ ⟨the ~ nature of color vision —*Medical Physics*⟩ ⟨an erudite ~ biography of Lenin, Trotsky, and Stalin —R.A. Bauer⟩ ⟨suggested the use of ~ definitions in which the verbal symbol is made responsible both to an object or field of objects and to a detailed description of the objects —C.W. Shumaker⟩ ⟨thus language involves what logicians call a ~ relation. There is the speaker, the thing said, and the one spoken to —John Dewey⟩ — **tri·ad·i·cal·ly** \-dək(ə)lē, -dēk-, -li\ *adv*

tri·ad·ism \'trīəˌdizəm, -īˌaˌd-\ *n* -S **1 :** state of being a triad **:** consisting of triads **:** threefold division or constitution ⟨the acceptance of ~ as the natural tonality —*ETC.*⟩ **2 :** a system based on a triad

tri·aene \'trīˌēn\ *n* -S [Gk *triaina* trident; akin to Gk *treis* three] **:** an elongated sponge spicule with three divergent rays at one end — **tri·ae·nose** \trī'ēˌnōs\ *adj*

¹tri·ae·noph·o·rid \¦trīˌē¦näf(ə)rəd\ *adj* [NL *Triaenophoridae*, family of tapeworms, fr. *Triaenophorus*, type genus + *-idae*] **:** of or relating to the genus *Triaenophorus* or the family Triaenophoridae

²triaenophorid \"\ *n* -S **:** a triaenophorid tapeworm

tri·ae·noph·o·rus \ˌ=='näf(ə)rəs\ *n, cap* [NL, fr. Gk *triaina* trident + NL *-phorus*] **:** a genus (the type of the family Triaenophoridae) of pseudophyllidean tapeworms that includes a form (*T. crassus*) parasitic as adults in pike and having larvae which form large cysts in the flesh of whitefish and make it unfit for human consumption

tri·age \trē'äzh, *in sense 1 also* 'trīij\ *n* -S [F, sorting, sifting, selecting, fr. *trier* to pick out, sift + *-age*] **1** *Brit* **a :** the process of grading marketable produce **b :** the lowest grade of coffee berries consisting of broken material **2 :** the sorting of and allocation of treatment to patients and esp. battle and disaster victims according to a system of priorities designed to maximize the number of survivors

¹tri·a·kid \'trīəkəd, trī'ak-\ *adj* [NL *Triakidae*] **:** of or relating to the Triakidae

²triakid \"\ *n* -S **:** SMOOTH DOGFISH

tri·ak·i·dae \trī'akəˌdē\ *n pl, cap* [NL, fr. *Triakis*, type genus (fr. Gk *triakis* three times) + *-idae*; fr. the three-pointed teeth] *in some classifications* **:** a family of elasmobranch fishes comprising the common smooth dogfishes

tri·a·kis·octahedron \¦trīəkə̇s, trī'ak- + \ *n* [ISV *triakis-* (fr. Gk *triakis* three times) + *octahedron*; akin to Gk *treis* three — more at THREE] **:** a trigonal trisoctahedron

tri·a·kis·tetrahedron \"+\ *n* [ISV *triakis-* + *tetrahedron*] **:** a trigonal tristetrahedron

¹tri·al \'trī(ə)l\ *n* -S [AF, fr. *trier* to try + E *-al* — more at TRY] **1 a :** the action or process of trying or putting to the proof **:** subjection of a person or thing to a test, examination, or participation in a contest or competition to determine something in question or to settle a controversy ⟨when several candidates are proposed for the chieftainship the choice is sometimes determined by a ~ of skill among the candidates —J.G.Frazer⟩ **b :** a trial match: as (1) **:** PRELIMINARY b (2) **:** HEAT 5a(2),5b **2 :** the formal examination of the matter in issue in a cause before a competent tribunal for the purpose of determining such issue **:** the mode of determining a question of fact in a court of law: as **a :** such an examination of an issue of law when it is before a judge alone or of fact when it is usu. before a judge and jury **b :** all proceedings from the time when the parties are called to try their cases in court or from the time when issue is joined to the time of its final determination **c :** such proceedings subsequent to swearing in a jury **3 a :** the state or fact of being tried by suffering; *esp* **:** a test (as of one's virtue, faith, patience, or stamina) by being subjected to affliction or temptation ⟨the 20th century . . . has been a time of recurring ~ —D.D.Eisenhower⟩ ⟨hotels are a ~ of both spirit and flesh —Nathaniel Peffer⟩ ⟨purified by ~⟩ ⟨the clock's greatest ~ occurred . . . when a bomb fell on the roof —Roy MacNab⟩ **b :** something that brings about such a trial ⟨despite all setbacks and hard ~*s* —*N.Y.Times*⟩ ⟨through the ~*s* of an epidemic —Martha T. Stephenson⟩ ⟨the ~*s* and tribulations of traveling over desert, across rocky divide, and floundering in the snowbanks —T.D.Clark⟩ ⟨the relinquishment of this work on account of illness was to her a great ~ —Elizabeth Hanscom⟩ ⟨I must have been a ~ to the secretary, for all my ideas were of the most precise and British order —Georgina Grahame⟩; *broadly* **:** a source of vexation or annoyance **4 :** a trying out as an experiment to test practicability, workability, or efficacy **:** a temporary and experimental use or application ⟨made his first ~ on the Delaware with a queer-looking boat having a row of paddles on each side —*Amer. Guide Series: N.J.*⟩ ⟨all sorts of sleeping bags have been developed and many have been given extensive ~*s* under various conditions —Morris Fishbein⟩ ⟨after many pauses and many ~*s* of other subjects —Jane Austen⟩ ⟨a conductor's duty to give all well-written works a ~ —Warwick Braithwaite⟩ ⟨a brief ~ of the plan would convince the people of its futility —F.A.Ogg & P.O.Ray⟩ **5** *obs* **:** direct personal knowledge **:** EXPERIENCE **6 :** an act of making an attempt **:** ENDEAVOR, EFFORT **7 a :** a sample or test piece used in proving the quality of a product or material or the progress and effectiveness of a mechanical operation **b** (1) **:** COLOR TRIAL (2) **:** an essay of a stamp **8 :** EXAMINATION: as **a :** the examination of a candidate for the Presbyterian ministry **b :** the final examination of the term in some English public schools

syn TRIBULATION, AFFLICTION, VISITATION, CROSS: TRIAL implies a test of one's patience, self-control, courage, or resistance to temptation ⟨the unfinished dresses . . . so saturated with smoke that he knew she found it a *trial* to work on them next morning —Willa Cather⟩ ⟨the child's disobedience in public was quite a *trial* to his mother⟩ TRIBULATION, when it is not completely interchangeable with TRIAL, stresses the suffering of a trial, sometimes connoting a suffering divinely imposed as a test of virtue ⟨the conquest of transatlantic trade by steam navigation softened the incredible *tribulations* of the old sailing ship voyage —Oscar Handlin⟩ ⟨a simple record of people trying to contend with the gigantic *tribulations* of poverty —*New Yorker*⟩ ⟨out of this time of trial and *tribulation* will be born a new freedom and glory for all mankind —Sir Winston Churchill⟩ AFFLICTION stresses the imposition of trouble or suffering ⟨the dark and senseless *afflictions* of a nightmare —Kenneth Roberts⟩ ⟨death and taxes . . . these twin *afflictions* —T.E.Ennis⟩ ⟨from early boyhood the sacrilegious and belligerent Simon had been a growing *affliction* to his parents —L.C. Douglas⟩ VISITATION heightens the idea of affliction, stressing the severity of suffering in suggesting an ordeal ⟨a maiming accident or some other *visitation* of blind fate —Joseph Conrad⟩ ⟨*visitations*, attacks, pestilences—Vicki Baum⟩ ⟨his inborn fatalism leads him to regard famines as inevitable *visitations* —Tom Marvel⟩ CROSS can suggest an undeserved suffering or a suffering borne for the sake of a larger unselfish or professedly unselfish good ⟨an ungrateful child was the *cross* she bore⟩ ⟨endure the *cross* of poverty and neglect⟩

— **on trial** *adv (or adj)* **:** in the state of being examined, tested, or tried out for a period ⟨became an itinerant preacher *on trial* —Marie A. Kasten⟩; *specif* **:** on approval for test or use for a specified period ⟨have goods sent out *on trial*⟩ ⟨coeducation was still *on trial* in the East —Hannah C. Hull⟩

²trial \"\ *adj* **1 :** of, relating to, or employed in a trial **2 :** made, done, or entered into by way of trial, experiment, or test **:** not intended to be permanent or final unless successful **3 :** used in trying, testing, fitting, or experimenting **4 :** serving as a sample, specimen, proof, or test piece ⟨a ~ subscription to a magazine⟩

³trial \"\ *adj* [ISV *tri-* + *-al*] **:** being or relating to forms of pronouns or nouns denoting three (as in the Polynesian and Melanesian languages) — compare DUAL, QUADRUAL

⁴trial \"\ *n* -S **:** the trial number, a form denoting it, or a word in that form

trial and error *n* **:** a finding out of the best way to reach a desired result or a correct solution by trying out one or more ways or means and by noting and eliminating errors or causes of failure; *also* **:** the trying of this and that until something succeeds

trial at bar 1 : a trial before three or more judges of the court in which the proceeding is brought used chiefly in causes célèbres or to consider novel points of law **2 :** trial before a judicial or quasi-judicial tribunal and esp. before a court of justice **:** trial by a court and by a jury

tri·alate \(')trī+\ *adj* [*tri-* + *alate*] **:** having three wings

trial at nisi prius 1 : a trial conducted as a result of the issuance of a writ of nisi prius **2 :** the original trial of the facts in issue before a judge or jury as distinguished from the hearing of the case before an appellate court or on review

trial balance *n* **:** a list of the debit and credit balances of accounts in a double-entry ledger at a given date prepared primarily for the purpose of testing their equality or in the case of a subsidiary ledger of testing its accuracy against the control account

trial balloon *n* **1 :** a balloon sent up to test air currents and wind velocity **2 :** a project or scheme tentatively announced in order to test public opinion ⟨*trial balloons* . . . leaked to the press —Don Pryor⟩ — compare KITEFLYING

trial brief *n* **:** BRIEF 2d

trial by battle *or* **trial by combat :** a trial of a dispute formerly determined by the outcome of a personal battle or combat between the parties or in an issue joined upon a writ of right between their champions — called also *judicial combat, wager of battle*

trial by certificate : a trial of an issue formerly determined exclusively by the testimony of a person (as a military officer) certifying to what is peculiarly within his knowledge (as that a soldier is absent)

trial by inspection : a trial of a case formerly settled by the individual observation and decision of the judge upon the testimony of his own senses without the intervention of a jury

trial by jury : a trial in which the issue is determined by a judge and a jury usu. of 12 members whose province is to determine facts in issue

trial by ordeal : a trial formerly determined by the manner in which an accused sustains some form of ordeal

trial by record : a trial in which a matter of record is pleaded and in which the opposite party pleads that there is no such record and which involves inspection of the record itself and no other evidence — compare NUL TIEL RECORD

trial by the country : trial by a jury chosen from the country or vicinity

trial color proof *n* **:** COLOR TRIAL

trial court *n* **:** the court before which issues of fact and law are first determined as distinguished from an appellate court

trial docket *n* **:** DOCKET 2a(3)

trial examiner *n* **:** a person appointed to hold hearings on various matters and to investigate and report facts sometimes with recommendations to an administrative or quasi-judicial agency or tribunal

trial horse *n* **:** one set up as an opponent for a champion in trial competitions or workouts ⟨he offered his 12-meter yacht . . . and her crew to the syndicate as a *trial horse* —*Life*⟩

tri·al·ism \ˈtrīə,lizəm\ *n* -s [*tri-* + *-alism* (as in *dualism*)] **1 :** TRIADISM **2** [G *trialismus*, fr. *tri-* + *-alismus* (as in *dualismus* dualism)] **:** a federation or union of three states

tri·al·ist \-ləst\ *n* -s **1 :** an adherent or advocate of trialism **2 :** one that has an entry in or competes in a trial contest

trial judge *n* **:** a judge of a trial court

trial judge advocate *n* **:** a judge advocate detailed to act as a prosecutor of an accused before a court-martial

trial jury *n* **:** a jury impaneled to try a cause **:** PETIT JURY

tri·alkyl \(ˈ)trī +\ *adj* [*tri-* + *alkyl*] **:** containing three alkyl groups esp. in place of hydrogen

trial lawyer *n* **:** a lawyer who engages chiefly in the trial of cases before courts of original jurisdiction as distinguished from one whose functions are carried out mainly in his office or who is concerned with argument before appellate courts

trial marriage *n* **:** a proposed form of marriage in which a man and woman are married but for only a stated period — compare COMPANIONATE MARRIAGE

trial of the pyx : the annual assay of the coins in the British mint that have been placed in the pyx

tri·a·logue \ˈtrīə,lȯg *also* -läg\ *n* -s [*tri-* + *-alogue* (as in *dialogue*)] **:** a scene, discourse, or colloquy in which three persons share

trial piece *n* **:** something made as a specimen: as **a :** a coin struck for testing a die often in a different metal and on a different size planchet from that used for the actual coin **b :** a carving done to test an artist's skill or conception found esp. in ancient art

trial run *n* **:** a testing exercise **:** EXPERIMENT, TEST ⟨a *trial run* of the seaworthiness of a new ship⟩ ⟨one great advantage of prose fiction is that it permits a kind of *trial run* for ideas under conditions approximating those of real life —H.O.Brogan⟩

trials *pl of* TRIAL

tri·amine \(ˌ)trī+\ *n* [*tri-* + *amine*] **:** a compound containing three amino groups

tri·amino \"+\ *adj* [*triamino-*] **:** relating to or containing three amino or substituted amino groups

triamino- *comb form* [*tri-* + *amin-*] **:** containing three amino groups — in names of organic compounds ⟨1,2,4-*triamino*benzene⟩

tri·an·drous \(ˈ)trī¦andrəs\ *adj* [NL *triandrus*, fr. *tri-* + *-andrus* -androus] **:** having three stamens

tri·an·gle \ˈtrī,aŋgəl, -aiŋ-\ *n* -s [ME, fr. L *triangulum*, fr.

triangles: *1* equilateral, *2* isosceles, *3* right-angled, *4* obtuse, *5* scalene

neut. of *triangulus* having three angles, triangular, fr. *tri-* three (akin to L *tria, tres* three) + *angulus* angle — more at THREE, ANGLE] **1 :** a usu. plane polygon having three sides — compare SPHERICAL TRIANGLE; see AREA table **2 :** a symbol (as of the Trinity in Christian art or as of life in primitive art), design, or decorative motif shaped like a triangle **3 :** a triangular object, marking, area, or arrangement **:** a triangle-shaped thing: as **a :** a hoisting or weighing device consisting of a tripod of poles or spars from the apex of which is suspended a pulley or balance **b :** a frame formed of three halberds or poles stuck in the ground and united at the top and used formerly to bind British soldiers undergoing corporal punishment — often used in pl. ⟨men were frequently sent to the ~s —*Time*⟩ **c :** a musical percussion instrument of indefinite pitch usu. made of a rod of steel bent into the form of a triangle open at one angle and sounded by striking with a small metal rod; *also* **:** a similar piece of metal used in the same way as an instrument of call ⟨a mess cook was beating the commissary ~ —K.M.Dodson⟩ **d :** a triangular area near the base of the wing in dragonflies **e :** a thin flat right-angled triangular instrument of wood or plastic usu. cut with acute angles of 45 degrees or of 30 degrees and 60 degrees and used in drafting **f :** a triangular postage stamp **4 a :** a group of three **:** TRIAD ⟨France's three-party coalition was described . . . as a type of ~ hard to break and impossible to maintain —P.S.Mowrer⟩ ⟨~ in an economic enterprise, composed of management, party leadership and labor-union organization —S.N.Harper & R.B.Thompson⟩ **b :** a situation involving three persons; *esp* **:** one involving the love of two men for one woman or of two women for one man and the resulting complications ⟨a comedy of the eternal ~, where the lover is a man . . . and the husband is a fat, lazy, hungry, cowardly, protesting cuckold —Leslie Rees⟩

triangle crab *n* **:** a small delicate triangular Australian crab (*Trigonoplax unguiformis longirostris*) living among weeds below the tide line

tri·an·gled \-gəld\ *adj* **:** having three angles **:** TRIANGULAR

triangle of forces : a vector diagram whose sides represent three forces in equilibrium — compare FORCE POLYGON

triangle of hes·sel·bach \-ˈhesəl,bäk\ *usu cap H* [after Franz K. *Hesselbach* †1816 Ger. surgeon] **:** an area of the abdominal wall bounded laterally by the deep epigastric artery, medially by the margin of the rectus muscle, and below by Poupart's ligament

triangle of mars \-ˈmärz, ˈmäz\ *usu cap T&M* [after *Mars*, Roman god of war and agriculture] **:** GREAT TRIANGLE

triangle of scarpa *usu cap S* **:** SCARPA'S TRIANGLE

triangle spider *n* **:** a small American spider (*Hyptiotes cavatus*) that lives among the dead branches of evergreen trees, constructs a triangular web usu. composed of four radii crossed by a double elastic fiber, holds the thread at the apex of the web, and stretches it tight but lets go and springs the net when an insect comes in contact with it

¹tri·an·gu·lar \(ˈ)trī¦aŋgyələ(r), -aiŋ-\ *adj* [LL *triangularis*, fr. L *triangulum* triangle + *-aris* -ar] **1 a :** of, relating to, or consisting of a triangle **:** having three angles, corners, or sides **:** having the form of a triangle ⟨a ~ plot of land⟩ ⟨a ~ ruler⟩ ⟨he had a ~ face with high and broad forehead —J.M. Phalen⟩ **b :** having a principal surface of triangular shape ⟨a ~ chair⟩ ⟨a ~ table⟩ **2 a :** having a base that is a triangle ⟨a ~ prism⟩ ⟨a ~ pyramid⟩ **b :** shaped or edged like a triangular prism or pyramid **3 a** (1) **:** of, relating to, or involving three elements, factions, parts, persons, or states ⟨before the child enters the ~ mother-father-child relationship —Edmund Bergler⟩ ⟨a ~ trade between Peru, Europe, and the United States —H.T.Brundidge⟩ ⟨a ~ agreement⟩ (2) *of a military group* **:** based primarily on three units ⟨a ~ army division⟩ — compare SQUARE **b :** of or relating to a love triangle ⟨~ plot of a novel⟩ ⟨a ~ love affair⟩ — **tri·an·gu·lar·i·ty** \(ˈ)trī¦aŋgyəˈlarəd·ē, -aiŋ-, -lətē, -i *also* -ler-\ *n* -ES — **tri·an·gu·lar·ly** *adv*

²triangular \"\ *n* -s **:** TRIANGLE 3f

triangular compass *n* **:** a compass having three legs of which one is attached by a double joint used for transferring three points (as the vertices of a triangle) from one drawing to another

triangular crab *n* [so called fr. the shape of the carapace] **:** OXYRHYNCH 1

tri·an·gu·la·ris \(,)trī,aŋgyəˈla(a)rəs\ *n, pl* **triangulares** [NL, fr. LL *triangularis*, adj., triangular] **:** a triangular body part (as a muscle); *specif* **:** a flat triangular muscle extending from the base of the mandible to the angle of the mouth and upper lip

triangular numbers *n pl* **:** the successive sums $\frac{n(n+1)}{2}$ of the first *n* natural numbers 1, 3, 6, 10, 15, . . . representable by dots arranged in triangles

triangular trade *n* **:** multilateral trade in which country A's purchases from country B are paid for by earnings from country A's sales to country C

¹tri·an·gu·late \(ˈ)trī¦aŋgyələt, -aiŋ-, -ə,lāt, *usu* -d·+V\ *adj* [ML *triangulatus*, past part. of *triangulare* to make triangles, fr. L *triangulum* triangle] **:** consisting of or marked with triangles **:** having triangular markings — **tri·an·gu·late·ly** *adv*

²tri·an·gu·late \-,lāt, *usu* -ād·+V\ *vb* -ED/-ING/-S [L *triangulum* triangle + E *-ate*] *vt* **1 :** to divide into triangles **:** give triangular form to **2** [back-formation fr. *triangulation*] **:** to survey, map, or determine by triangulation ⟨every culture is a moral geometry . . . a contingent means of *triangulating* one's course through reality —Weston La Barre⟩ ~ *vi* **:** to use triangulation **:** make a determination by triangulation

tri·an·gu·la·tion \(,)‚‚‚ˈlāshən\ *n* -s [ML *triangulation-, triangulatio* action of making triangles, fr. *triangulatus* (past part. of *triangulare* to make triangles, fr. L *triangulum* triangle) + L *-ion-, -io* -ion — more at TRIANGLE] **1 :** the operation of measuring the elements necessary to determine the network of triangles into which any part of the earth's surface is divided in surveying and to fix the positions and distances apart of their vertices ⟨a surveyor who wants to measure the distance across a lake cannot use a tape measure or surveyor's chain so he must resort to a method called ~ —J.S.Allen⟩ ⟨as ~s cover only a small part of the continents and fail completely over the oceans, many geodetic systems exist —W.A. Heiskanen⟩; *broadly* **:** any similar trigonometric operation performed for finding a position or location by means of bearings from two fixed points a known distance apart ⟨~ on radio signals from the satellite will offer a supplemental means of location —*Science*⟩ **2 :** a calculation or prediction based on known facts ⟨a new isolationist formulation was bound to come — a new ~ by which the old emotions would try to make terms with the new realities —A.M.Schlesinger b.1917⟩

tri·an·gu·la·tor \‚ˈ‚‚,lād·ə(r)\ *n* -s **:** one that triangulates

tri·annual \(ˈ)trī+\ *adj* [*tri-* + *annual*] **1** *obs* **:** TRIENNIAL **2 :** made, appearing, or occurring three times a year ⟨a ~ estimate of value⟩ ⟨a ~ advertisement⟩

tri·annulate \"+\ *adj* [*tri-* + *annulate*] **:** provided with or composed of three rings

tri·a·non \ˈtrēə,nän\ *n* -s [fr. *Trianon*, one of two small villas in the royal park at Versailles, France] **:** a small elegant villa; *esp* **:** one in the grounds of a larger establishment

tri·ap·sal \(ˈ)trī¦apsəl\ *also* **tri·ap·si·dal** \-səd³l\ *adj* [*triapsal* fr. *tri-* + *apse* + *-al*; *triapsidal* fr. *tri-* + *apsidal*] **:** having three apses — used of a building ⟨the apses in a ~ church may be side by side at the east end or they may be projected from a central tower⟩

tri·arch \ˈtrī,ärk, -ȧk\ *adj* [*tri-* + *-arch*] **:** having three xylem strands or groups ⟨a ~ root⟩

tri·ar·chy \-kē, -ki\ *n* -ES [Gk *triarchia*, fr. *tri-* three + *-archia* -archy — more at TRI-] **1 :** government by three persons **:** TRIUMVIRATE **2 :** a country under three rulers **3 :** one of three districts in a triarchy each under a ruler

tri·ar·thrus \trīˈärthrəs\ *n, cap* [NL, fr. *tri-* + Gk *arthron* joint — more at ARTHR-] **:** a genus of small Ordovician trilobites of which one form (*T. eatoni*) is often found with antennae and appendages in a good state of preservation

tri·articulate \¦trī+\ *adj* [*tri-* + *articulate*] **:** having three joints

tri·aryl \(ˈ)trī+\ *adj* [*tri-* + *aryl*] **:** containing three aryl groups in the molecule

triarylmethane dye \(ˈ)‚¦‚‚¦‚,‚-\ *n* [*triaryl* + *methane*] **:** any of a class of basic, acid, mordant acid, and direct dyes derived from triphenylmethane or diphenyl-naphthyl-methane usu. by introduction of one or more auxochromic groups (as amino, methylamino, dimethylamino, or hydroxyl groups) and characterized in general by brilliance but not by fastness — see TRIPHENYLMETHANE DYE

tri·as \ˈtrīəs\ *adj or n, usu cap* [ISV, fr. L, triad] **:** TRIASSIC

¹tri·as·sic \(ˈ)trī¦asik\ *adj, usu cap* [ISV *triass-* (fr. L *trias* three, triad) + *-ic*; fr. the European Triassic being subdivided into the triad of Bunter, Muschelkalk, and Keuper] **:** of or relating to a division of the Mesozoic in which gymnosperms (as the cycads) are the most distinctive plants, the amphibians decline but the reptiles and ammonites develop rapidly, mammals prob. exist but are few, small, and primitive — see GEOLOGIC TIME table

²triassic \"\ *n* -s *usu cap* **:** the Triassic period or system of rocks

tri·as·so·chelys \trī¦asō+\ *n, cap* [NL, fr. *triasso-* (fr. ISV *triassic* + *-o-*) + *Chelys*] **:** a genus of extinct turtles of the lower Mesozoic of Europe believed to be the earliest true turtles

tri·as·ter \trīˈastə(r)\ *n* -s [ISV *tri-* + *-aster*] **:** a mitotic figure resulting from tripolar usu. abnormal division of a nucleus

tri·at·ic stay \(ˈ)trī¦ad·ik-\ *n* [*triatic* prob. fr. *tri-* + *-ate* + *-ic*] **:** JUMPER STAY

tri·at·o·ma \trīˈad·əmə\ *n* [NL, fr. L *tria* three + NL *-toma* — more at TRI-] **1** *cap* **:** a genus of large blood-sucking bugs that are usu. placed in the family Reduviidae but sometimes assigned to a separate family and that feed on mammals and sometimes transmit Chagas' disease to their hosts — see CONENOSE **2** -s **:** any bug of the genus *Triatoma*

tri·a·tome \ˈtrīə,tōm\ *n* -s [NL *Triatoma*] **:** TRIATOMID, CONENOSE

tri·atomic \¦trī+\ *adj* [ISV *tri-* + *atomic*] **1 :** consisting of three atoms **:** having three atoms in the molecule **2 :** having three replaceable atoms or radicals

¹tri·at·o·mid \(ˈ)trī¦ad·əməd\ *also* **tri·atom·ic** \¦trīə¦tämik\ *adj* [NL *Triatoma* + E *-id* or *-ic*] **:** of or relating to *Triatoma* or various closely related genera

²triatomid \"\ *n* -s **:** a triatomid bug **:** CONENOSE

tri·axial \(ˈ)trī+\ *adj* [ISV *tri-* + *axial*] **:** having three axes **:** having three components ⟨~ ware composed of flint, clay, and feldspar⟩; *specif* **:** being a diagram with three axes for representing graphically three variables — **tri·axiality** \(ˌ)trī+\ *n*

tri·ax·on \(ˈ)trī¦ak,sän\ *n* -s [NL, fr. *tri-* + Gk *axōn* axis — more at AXIS] **:** a sponge spicule having three axes crossing at right angles to form six rays

tri·ax·o·nia \,trī,akˈsōnēə\ *or* **tri·ax·on·i·da** \-ˈsänədə\ [NL, fr. *triaxon* + *-ia* or *-ida*] *syn of* HYALOSPONGIAE

tri·a·zine \ˈtrīə,zēn, trīˈa,z-, -,zən\ *n* [ISV *tri-* + *azine*; orig. formed as Sw *triazin*] **1 :** any of three parent compounds $C_3H_3N_3$ containing a ring composed of three carbon and three nitrogen atoms that are distinguished by indication of the relative positions of the atoms in the ring or of only the nitrogen atoms; *esp* **:** the symmetrical or 1,3,5-isomer from which cyanuric compounds are derived — compare STRUCTURAL FORMULA **2 :** any of various derivatives of the three parent triazines

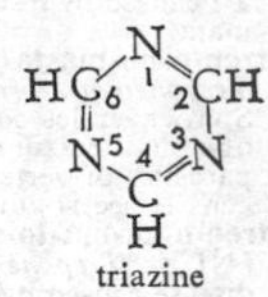

triazine

tri·az·i·nyl \trīˈaz³n,il\ *n* -s [*triazine* + *-yl*] **:** a univalent radical $C_3H_2N_3$ derived from one of the parent triazines

tri·azo \(ˈ)trīˈa(,)zō, -ˈā-\ *adj* [ISV *triazo-*] **1 :** AZIDO **2 :** TRISAZO — not used systematically

triazo- *comb form* [ISV *tri-* + *az-*] **:** AZIDO- — esp. in names of organic compounds

tri·a·zole \ˈtrīə,zōl, trīˈa,z-\ *n* [ISV *tri-* + *azole*] **1 :** any of four parent compounds $C_2H_3N_3$ containing a ring composed of two carbon atoms and three nitrogen atoms that are distinguished by indication of the relative positions of the four atoms in the ring or of only the nitrogen atoms ⟨vicinal or 1,2,3-*triazole*⟩ **2 :** any of various derivatives of the four parent triazoles — see OSOTRIAZOLE — **tri·a·zol·ic** \¦trīə¦zälik\ *adj*

tri·az·o·lyl \trīˈazə,lil\ *n* -s [ISV *triazole* + *-yl*] **:** a univalent radical $C_2H_2N_3$ derived from one of the parent triazoles

trib *abbr* **1** tribal **2** tribunal; tribune **3** tributary

tribade \ˈtribəd; trəˈbäd, -ˈbad\ *n* -s [F, fr. L *tribad-, tribas*, fr. Gk, fr. *tribein* to rub; akin to L *terere* to rub — more at THROW] **:** a woman who practices tribadism — **tri·bad·ic** \trəˈbadik\ *adj*

trib·a·dism \ˈtribə,dizəm\ *n* -s [ISV *tribade* + *-ism*] **:** a homosexual practice among women which attempts to simulate heterosexual intercourse

trib·a·dy \-,dē\ *n* -ES [ISV *tribade* + *-y*] **:** TRIBADISM

trib·al \ˈtrībəl\ *adj* **1 :** of, relating to, or characteristic of a tribe ⟨~ customs⟩ **2 :** resembling a tribe in possessing a sense of identification with and loyalty to the habits, traits, and values characteristic of a close-knit familistic, sociocultural, occupational, or political group or in ceremonial or ritualistic activity ⟨the ~ rites of rushing and initiation in a college fraternity⟩ — **trib·al·ly** \-bəlē, -li\ *adv*

trib·al·ism \-bə,lizəm\ *n* -s **1 a :** tribal life, organization, or society **b :** tribal feeling, peculiarities, or characteristics **2 :** strong ingroup loyalty and sentimental attachment to one's own group and its traits ⟨legislative ~⟩ ⟨a reversion to religious ~⟩

trib·al·ist \-ələst\ *n* -s **:** an advocate of tribalism

trib·al·is·tic \¦‚‚¦listik\ *adj* **:** TRIBAL ⟨may leave the reader with the feeling that prejudices are ~ —E.R.Clinchy⟩

tri·basic \(ˈ)trī+\ *adj* [*tri-* + *basic*] **1 :** having three hydrogen atoms capable of replacement by basic atoms or radicals — used of acids (as phosphoric acid) **2 :** containing three atoms of a univalent metal or their equivalent ⟨~ sodium phosphate Na_3PO_4⟩ **3 :** having three basic hydroxyl groups **:** able to react with three molecules of a monobasic acid — used of bases and basic salts — **tri·basicity** \¦trī+\ *n*

tribe \ˈtrīb\ *n* -s [ME *tribu, tribe*, fr. OF & L; OF *tribu*, fr. L *tribus* one third of the Roman people, division of the people, tribe; perh. akin to L *tria, tres* three — more at THREE] **1 a** (1) **:** a social group comprising numerous families, clans, or generations together with slaves, dependents, or adopted strangers ⟨the twelve ~s of Israel⟩ ⟨although the idea of consanguinity persists, the ~, as it expands, depends more and more on common social and political institutions, and less on actual kinship —A.H.Keane⟩ (2) **:** an endogamous social group held to be descended from a common ancestor and composed of numerous families, exogamous clans, bands, or villages that occupies a specific geographic territory, possesses cultural, religious, and linguistic homogeneity, and is commonly united politically under one head or chief — see CLAN; compare NATION (3) **:** a primitive group acting under a chief ⟨nomadic ~s⟩ **b** (1) **:** a large family group distinguished by close-knit ties, unusually well-marked family traits, or a number of eminent, talented, or successful members ⟨feeding and lodging . . . the whole ~ of near and distant cousins —Oliver La Farge⟩ (2) **:** a large family of offspring ⟨devotion . . . to children is graphically illustrated by the Christmas cards which . . . feature the smiling faces of the ~ —*Amer. Fabrics*⟩ **c** (1) **:** a political division of the Roman people orig. constituting one of the three voting units of the assembly of centuries and representing one of the three primitive tribes of ancient Rome and later being set up on a territorial basis, with the number of tribes increased — compare CURIA 1a (2) **:** PHYLE 1 **2 :** a group of persons having a common character, occupation, avocation, or interest ⟨of a ~ that accepts the failure of the large interests in life —Donn Byrne⟩ ⟨the whole ~ of American literary critics —C.I.Glicksberg⟩ ⟨as fishermen . . . we are beginners, and the humblest and greenest of the ~ —John Mason Brown⟩ **3 a :** a category of taxonomic classification to which various names have been assigned sometimes equivalent to or ranking just below a suborder but more commonly ranking below a subfamily; *also* **:** a natural group irrespective of taxonomic rank ⟨the cat ~⟩ ⟨rose ~⟩ **b :** a group of closely related animals or strains within a breed **4 :** a group of animals, birds, or sometimes inanimate objects having a common characteristic or being together in a flock or group ⟨this highly unbeloved feathered ~ —Morris Gilbert⟩ ⟨a ~ of sparrows⟩ ⟨a ~ of tray-shaped baskets —Elizabeth Bowen⟩

-tribe \,trīb\ *n comb form* -s [Gk *tribein* to rub — more at TRIBADE] **1 :** one that rubs against — used esp. of flowers during cross-fertilization ⟨pleuro*tribe*⟩ ⟨sterno*tribe*⟩ **2 :** instrument for crushing, compressing, or rubbing ⟨angio*tribe*⟩ ⟨osteo*tribe*⟩

tribe·less \ˈtrībləs\ *adj* **:** being without tribal affiliation

tribe·let \-lət\ *n* -s **:** a small tribe

tribes·man \ˈtrībzmən\ *n, pl* **tribes·men** \"\ **:** a member of a tribe

tribespeople \ˈ‚,‚‚\ *n pl* **:** the people of a tribe

tribeswoman \ˈ‚,‚‚\ *n, pl* **tribeswomen :** a female member of a tribe

tri·blas·tic \(ˈ)trī¦blastik\ *adj* [*tri-* + *-blastic*] **:** TRIPLOBLASTIC

trib·let \ˈtriblət\ *or* **treb·let** \ˈtreb-\ *n* -s [F *triboulet*, prob. fr. MF *tribouler, triboler* to press, oppress, trouble, afflict (fr. LL *tribulare* to oppress, afflict) + *-et* — more at TRIBULATION] **:** any of various mandrels used in making rings or nuts or in drawing tubes

tribo- *comb form* [F, fr. Gk *tribein* to rub — more at TRIBADE] **:** friction ⟨*tribo*fluorescence⟩ ⟨*tribo*phosphorescent⟩

tribo·electric \¦trībō, ¦tribō+\ *adj* [*tribo-* + *electric*] **:** of, relating to, or marked by triboelectricity

tribo·electricity \"+\ *n* -ES [*tribo-* + *electricity*] **:** a positive charge of electricity generated by friction (as by rubbing glass with silk) or a negative charge generated by friction (as by rubbing hard rubber with fur) — compare TRIBOELECTRIC SERIES

triboelectric series *n* **:** a sequence of substances so arranged that any one of them is positively electrified by rubbing it with any other substance farther on in the list — compare TRIBOELECTRICITY

tri·bo·li·um \trīˈbōlēəm\ *n, cap* [NL, fr. Gk *tribolos*, any of various prickly plants + NL *-ium* — more at TRIBULUS] **:** a genus of small brown beetles (family Tenebrionidae) whose larvae feed on dry cereal products — see FLOUR BEETLE

tribo·luminescence \¦trībō, ¦tribō+\ *n* -ES [ISV *tribo-* + *luminescence*] **:** the emission of light from various substances usu. in flashes due to grinding, crushing, or tearing apart thought to be due to piezoelectric discharges — called also *piezoluminescence* — **tribo·luminescent** \"+\ *adj*

tri·bom·e·ter \trīˈbäməd·ə(r)\ *n* [F *tribomètre*, fr. Gk *tribein* to rub + F *-mètre* -meter] **:** an instrument for measuring sliding friction

tribon \ˈtri,bōn, ˈtrī,bän\ *n* -s [LL, fr. Gk *tribōn*; akin to Gk *tribein* to rub — more at TRIBADE] **:** a garment made of coarse cloth worn the year round as the only garment by Spartan men — compare CHITON, CHLAMYS, HIMATION

tri·bo·ne·ma \,trībəˈnēmə, ,trib-\ *n, cap* [NL, fr. Gk *tribos* action of rubbing (fr. *tribein* to rub) + NL *-nema*] **:** a genus (the type of the family Tribonemaceae of the order Heterotrichales) of simple filamentous freshwater yellow-green algae having asexual spores formed within the cells and freed by the breaking of the filaments into H-shaped pieces — see CONFERVA

tri·bo·physics \ˌtrībō, ˌtribō+\ *n pl but usu sing in constr* [*tribo-* + *physics*] **:** the physics of friction

tri·bo·rine triamine \(ˈ)trī+-\ *n* [*triborine* fr. *tri-* + *borine*] **:** BORAZOLE

¹tribrach \ˈtrīˌbrak, ˈtri,-\ *n* -s [L *tribrachys*, fr. Gk, having three short syllables, fr. *tri-* three (akin to Gk *treis* three) + *brachys* short — more at THREE, BRIEF] **:** a metrical foot of three short syllables of which two belong to the thesis and one to the arsis; *also* **:** a foot of three light syllables none of which carries a speech accent — **tri·brach·ic** \(ˈ)trīˌbrakik, trəˈb-\ *adj*

²tri·brach \ˈtrīˌbrak\ *n* -s [*tri-* + Gk *brachiōn* arm — more at BRACE] **:** a three-branched object, figure, or implement — **tri·brachi·al** \(ˈ)trīˌbrakēəl, -brāk-\ *adj*

tribrom- *or* **tribromo-** *comb form* [ISV *tri-* + *brom-*] **:** containing three atoms of bromine — in names of chemical compounds ⟨*tribromo*acetic acid⟩; compare BROM-

tri·bromide \(ˈ)trī+\ *n* [*tribrom-* + *-ide*] **:** a binary compound containing three atoms of bromine combined with an element or radical

tri·bro·mo·ethanol \(ˈ)trīˌbrōmō+\ *n* [*tribrom-* + *ethanol*] **:** a crystalline bromine derivative CBr_3CH_2OH of ethyl alcohol used as a basal anesthetic — called also *tribromoethyl alcohol*

tri·bro·mo·ethyl alcohol \"+-\ *n* [*tribromoethyl* fr. *tribrom-* + *ethyl*] **:** TRIBROMOETHANOL

trib·u·late \ˈtribyəˌlāt, *usu* -ād.+V\ *vt* -ED/-ING/-S [LL *tribulatus*, past part. of *tribulare* to oppress, afflict] **:** to cause to endure tribulation

trib·u·la·tion \ˌ==ˈlāshən\ *n* -s [ME *tribulacioun*, fr. OF *tribulacion*, fr. LL *tribulation-, tribulatio*, fr. *tribulatus* (past part. of *tribulare* to oppress, afflict, fr. L, to press, fr. *tribulum* threshing board) + L *-ion-, -io* -ion; akin to L *terere* to rub — more at THROW] **:** distress or suffering resulting from oppression, persecution, affliction, or sometimes contact with the physical environment ⟨found it nothing but a burden and a ~ —Jean Stafford⟩; *also* **:** an instance of such suffering **:** a trying experience ⟨explorers describing their hardships and ~s —*Report: Chapin Library*⟩ **syn** see TRIAL

trib·u·lus \ˈtribyələs\ *n, cap* [NL, fr. L, caltrop, fr. Gk *tribolos*, any of various prickly plants, threshing board studded with spikes; akin to L *tribulum* threshing board] **:** a genus of chiefly tropical or subtropical herbs (family Zygophyllaceae) introduced into No. America with pinnate leaves and yellow or white flowers succeeded by a spiny or prickly fruit of five indehiscent tuberculate carpels — see BURNUT, CALTROP 1b

tri·bu·na \trəˈb(y)ünə\ *n* -s [It — more at TRIBUNE] **:** ²TRIBUNE

tribu·nal \trīˈbyünᵊl, trəˈb- *sometimes* ˈtribyən-\ *n* -s [L, fr. *tribunus* Roman official, judge] **1 :** ²TRIBUNE: as **a :** the seat of a judge or one acting as a judge **:** the bench on which a judge and his associates sit for administering justice **b :** JUDGMENT SEAT ⟨appear before the august and holy ~ of God —J. N.Davies⟩ **2 :** a court or forum of justice **:** a person or body of persons having authority to hear and decide disputes so as to bind the disputants ⟨the Supreme Court is the highest ~ of the United States⟩ **3 :** something that decides or judges **:** something that determines or directs a judgment or course of action ⟨the ~ of events —George Santayana⟩ ⟨answerable to no ~ but that of their own judgment —Edith Wharton⟩

trib·u·nate \ˈtribyənət, -ˌnāt\ *n* -s [L *tribunatus*, fr. *tribunus* Roman official + *-atus* -ate] **:** TRIBUNESHIP

¹tribune \ˈtriˌbyün, trəˈb-\ *n* -s [ME, fr. L *tribunus* head of the tribe, chieftain, commander, tribune, fr. *tribus* tribe — more at TRIBE] **1 :** a Roman official under the monarchy and the republic: **a :** a commander of troops furnished the Roman army by the tribes **b :** a military commander chosen from the plebeians **c :** an officer elected from the plebeians with the specific function of protecting the individual citizen and esp. the plebeian from the arbitrary action of the patrician magistrates **2 a :** an officer or body in any country whose function is like that of a Roman tribune esp. in defending the common people ⟨Congress as the ~ of the people —Max Lerner⟩ **b :** a person other than a member of an official legislative, executive, or judicial body who defends the rights of the individual ⟨suggested that trade-union leaders serve as ~s in management with a veto power over management decisions —H.M. Magid⟩ ⟨the writer . . . is still the ~ of the person, the critic of institutions —Rex Warner⟩

²tribune \"\ *n* -s [F, fr. It *tribuna*, fr. ML, fr. L *tribunal*] **1 :** the raised platform in one end of a Roman basilica used esp. as the official station of the praetor and commonly placed in a semicircular apse **2 a :** the bishop's throne in a basilican church or the apsidal structure containing it **b :** an apsidal structure in a public building (as an Italian church) **3 :** a dais or platform from which an assembly is addressed

tribune·ship \-ˌship\ *n* **:** the office, function, or term of office of a tribune

trib·u·ni·cial *or* **trib·u·ni·tial** \ˌtribyəˈnishəl\ *adj* [LL *tribunicialis, tribunitialis*, fr. L *tribunicius, tribunitius* tribunician + *-alis* -al] **:** TRIBUNICIAN

trib·u·ni·cian *or* **trib·u·ni·tian** \-shən\ *adj* [L *tribunicius, tribunitius* (fr. *tribunus* Roman official + *-icius, -itius* -itious) + E *-an*] **:** of, relating to, characteristic of, or resembling a Roman tribune or his office

¹trib·u·tary \ˈtribyəˌterē, -ri\ *adj* [ME *tributarie*, fr. L *tributarius*, fr. *tributum* tribute + *-arius* -ary] **1 a :** paying tribute to another to acknowledge submission, to obtain protection, or to purchase peace ⟨bringing one territory under the domination of the other, making it ~, or capturing its wealth —*Notes & Queries on Anthropology*⟩ **b :** SUBJECT, DEPENDENT, SUBORDINATE ⟨no conquering race ever lived . . . among a ~ one without begetting children on it —A.T.Quiller-Couch⟩ ⟨the freight rates and the tariffs which were to keep the South a ~ section —*Current Biog.*⟩ ⟨the elimination of poverty and the furtherance of social justice would in themselves cure all the ~ maladjustments —Oscar Handlin⟩ **2 :** paid or owed as tribute **:** of the nature of tribute **3 :** providing with or serving as a channel for supplies or additional matter ⟨receiving two ~ lanes from who should say what remote hamlets —Compton Mackenzie⟩ ⟨a ~ stream⟩ ⟨~ to the city are approximately 30,000,000,000 feet of pine timber —*Amer. Guide Series: Oregon*⟩

²tributary \"\ *n* -ES [ME *tributarie*, fr. LL *tributarius*, fr. L, adj., tributary] **1 :** a person (as a ruler) or state that pays tribute to a conquering power ⟨all the people that is found therein shall be *tributaries* unto thee —Deut 20:11 (AV)⟩ **2 :** one that is tributary to another: as **a :** a stream feeding a larger stream or a lake — compare BRANCH **b :** a vein that empties into a larger vein

¹trib·ute \ˈtri(ˌ)byü|t *also* -byə| *sometimes* -(ˌ)byü|; *usu* |d.+V\ *n* -s [ME *tribut*, fr. L *tributum*, fr. neut. of *tributus*, past part. of *tribuere* to bestow, grant, pay, allot, fr. *tribus* one third of the Roman people, tribe — more at TRIBE] **1 a :** an annual or stated sum of money or other valuable thing paid by one ruler or nation to another as an acknowledgment of submission, as the price of peace and protection, or by virtue of some treaty ⟨foreseen that foreigners would pay ~ to the country for the right to carry away a wealth of liquid gold —P.E.James⟩; *also* **:** the tax levied for such a payment **b** (1) **:** an esp. large or excessive tax, impost, duty, rental, or tariff imposed by a government, sovereign, lord, or landlord (2) **:** an exorbitant or extralegal impost levied by a person or group having the power of coercion ⟨the monopolistic combinations of war industries levied a ~ on the . . . consumer so wasteful that it led to proposals to draft capital —T.W.Arnold⟩ ⟨compelled to join unions and pay ~ against their wills —M.K.Hart⟩ **c :** the liability to pay tribute ⟨no English king had been more successful . . . in bringing British tribes under ~ —F.M.Stenton⟩ **2 a :** something given or contributed voluntarily as due or deserved **:** an offering, gift, a service rendered, or token manifesting respect, allegiance, gratitude, or affection ⟨floral ~s were placed at the community honor roll —*Springfield (Mass.) Union*⟩ ⟨a surprise cocktail party — a ~ they had paid to no other person —*Current Biog.*⟩ ⟨build a shrine and offer ~ —Agnes Repplier⟩ ⟨the work had been selected as a ~ in honor of the Coronation —*London Calling*⟩; *specif* **:** PRAISE, ENCOMIUM ⟨will receive so many ~s that it may seem unnecessary to add to the general paean —Harold Nicolson⟩ **b :** something usu. admirable or praiseworthy resulting from and attributable to something specified — usu. used in the phrase *a tribute to* ⟨this first semblance of law in the gold country is a ~ to the common sense of the majority —Julian Dana⟩ ⟨the sarcastic and bitter opposition must be taken as a ~ to the power of the art —Arnold Bennett⟩ **3 :** a proportion of the ore raised or of its value given to the miner or the owner of the land as his recompense in one system of payment

²tribute \"\ *vb* -ED/-ING/-S [ME *tributen*, fr. *tribut* tribute] *vt* **:** to pay as tribute ⟨deserve praise for the intention, and I ~ it the more willingly as it is the only praise I can give them —Bernhard Berenson⟩ ~ *vi* **:** to mine on the tribute system

tribute money *n* **:** money paid as tribute; *specif* **:** the annual tax of a didrachm or half shekel paid by each Jew for the support of the temple

trib·ut·er *or* **trib·u·tor** \|d.ə(r), |tə-\ *n* -s **:** one that mines on the tribute system

tri·butyl phosphate \(ˈ)trī+-\ *n* [*tributyl* fr. *tri-* + *butyl*] **:** a liquid inorganic ester $(C_4H_9)_3PO_4$ made from normal butyl alcohol and phosphorus oxychloride and used chiefly as a solvent and plasticizer (as for nitrocellulose lacquers and cellulose plastics)

tri·butyrin \"+\ *n* [ISV *tri-* + *butyrin*] **:** the bitter oily liquid triglyceride $C_3H_5(OOCC_3H_7)_3$ of butyric acid used as a plasticizer **:** glycerol tri-butyrate — called also *butyrin*

tri·calcium \(ˈ)trī+\ *also* **tri·calcic** \"+\ *adj* [*tricalcium* fr. NL, fr. *tri-* + *calcium*; *tricalcic* ISV *tri-* + *calcic*] **:** containing three atoms or equivalents of calcium in the molecule

tricalcium phosphate *n* **:** CALCIUM PHOSPHATE 1a(3)

tri·car \ˈtrī,=\ *n* [*tri-* + *car*] *Brit* **:** a 3-wheeled vehicle

tri·car·bal·lyl·ic acid \(ˌ)trīˌkärbəˈlilik-\ *n* [*tri-* + ISV *carballylic*, former name of tricarballylic acid, fr. *carb-* + *allyl* + *-ic*] **:** a crystalline tricarboxylic acid $C_3H_5(COOH)_3$ found in immature beets and obtainable from citric acid by dehydration followed by hydrogenation; 1,2,3,-propane-tricarboxylic acid

tri·carbocyanine \"+\ *or* **tricarbocyanine dye** *n* [*tri-* + *carbocyanine*] **:** any of a class of cyanine dyes in whose structure the two heterocyclic rings are joined by a seven-carbon chain (as $=CH-CH=CH-CH=CH-CH=CH-$); *esp* **:** any such dye containing two quinoline rings

tri·carboxylic \"+\ *adj* [*tri-* + *carboxylic*] **:** containing three carboxyl groups in the molecule

tricarboxylic acid cycle *n* **:** KREBS CYCLE

tri·carinate \(ˈ)trī+\ *adj* [*tri-* + *carinate*] **:** having three ridged keels

tri·carpellary \"+\ *also* **tri·carpellate** \"+\ *adj* [*tri-* + *carpellary* or *carpellate*] **:** having or made up of three usu. fused carpels

¹trice \ˈtrīs\ *vt* -ED/-ING/-S [ME *tricen, trisen*, fr. MD *trisen* to hoist by block and tackle, fr. *trise* windlass, capstan, pulley; akin to MLG *trīsse* windlass, pulley] **1 :** to haul up or in and lash or secure with a small rope — usu. used with *up* ⟨prisoners are *triced* up by the wrists or hands —S.J.Barrows⟩ **2 :** to raise with or as if with a line — often used with *up* ⟨~ up a window shade⟩

²trice \"\ *n* -s [ME *trise*, fr. *trisen* to trice] **:** a brief space of time **:** INSTANT, MOMENT — used chiefly in the phrase *in a trice* ⟨in a ~ she was asleep —*Irish Digest*⟩

tri·ce·nar·i·um \ˌtrīsᵊnˈa(a)rēəm\ *n* -s [ML, fr. L, neut. of *tricenarius* of thirty] **:** TRENTAL

¹tri·ce·nary \ˈtrīsᵊnˌerē, ˈtris-; trīˈsenərē, -ˈsēn-\ *n* -ES [ML *tricenarium*] **:** TRENTAL

²tricenary \"\ *adj* [L *tricenarius* of thirty, fr. *triceni* thirty each + *-arius* -ary; akin to L *triginta* thirty, Gk *triakonta*, Skt *trimśat* thirty, L *tres* three — more at THREE] **1 :** having or lasting 30 days ⟨a ~ month⟩ **2 :** based on the number 30 ⟨a ~ scale⟩

tri·cephalous \(ˈ)trī+\ *adj* [ISV *tri-* + *-cephalous*] **:** having or depicted with three heads

tri·ceps \ˈtrīˌseps\ *n, pl* **triceps·es** \-psəz\ *also* **triceps** [NL *tricipit-, triceps*, fr. L, three-headed, fr. *tri-* + *-cipit, -ceps* (fr. *capit-, caput* head) — more at HEAD] **:** a muscle that arises from three heads: **a :** the great extensor muscle situated along the back of the upper arm, arising by three heads, and inserted into the olecranon at the elbow **b :** the gastrocnemius and soleus muscles viewed as constituting together one muscle

tri·cer·a·tops \trīˈserəˌtäps\ *n* [NL, fr. *tri-* + *cerat-* + *-ops*] **1** *cap* **:** a genus of huge herbivorous ornithischian dinosaurs (suborder Ceratopsia) from the Cretaceous of Montana, Wyoming, and Colorado having a skull with two large horns above the eyes, a median horn on the nose, a horny beak, and a great bony hood or transverse crest over the neck, hoofed toes five in front and three behind, and a large strong tail **2** -ES **:** any animal or fossil of the genus *Triceratops*

tricerion *var of* TRIKERION

-trices *pl of* -TRIX

tricesimo–secundo *var of* TRIGESIMO-SECUNDO

trich- *or* **tricho-** *comb form* [NL, fr. Gk, fr. *trich-, thrix* hair; akin to MIr *gairbdriuch* bristle, Lith *drỹkti* to hang down in long threads, *driẽkti* to stretch] **:** hair **:** filament ⟨*tricho*pathy⟩ ⟨*trich*atrophic⟩

-tri·cha \trəkə\ *n comb form, pl* **-tricha** [NL, fr. Gk *-trichos* -trichous] **:** one or ones having (such) ciliation — in names of taxa ⟨Gastro*tricha*⟩ ⟨Oxy*tricha*⟩

tri·chal·cite \trīˈkalˌsīt\ *n* -s [G *trichalcit*, fr. *tri-* + *chalc-* + *-it* -ite] **:** a mineral $Cu_3(AsO_4)_2.5H_2O$(?) that is a hydrous arsenate of copper

¹trich·ech·i·dae \trəˈkekəˌdē\ *n pl, cap* [NL, fr. *Trichechus*, type genus + *-idae*] **:** a family of aquatic mammals consisting of the manatees

²trichechidae \"\ [NL, fr. *Trichechus* + *-idae*] *syn of* ODOBENIDAE

¹trich·ech·odont \-kəˌdänt\ *adj* [NL *Trichechus* + E *-odont*] **:** having or being molar teeth with rows of tubercles confluent into transverse crests ⟨some sirenians, mastodons, and related animals have ~ molars⟩

²trichechodont \"\ *n* -s **:** a trichechodont mammal

trich·e·chus \ˈtrikəkəs, trəˈkekəs\ *n, cap* [NL, fr. *trich-* + Gk *echein* to have, hold — more at SCHEME] **:** a genus of mammals (family Trichechidae) comprising the manatees

-triches *pl of* -THRIX

trichi \ˈtrikē, -ki\ *n* -ES [by shortening] **:** TRICHINOPOLY

-tri·chi \trəˌkī\ *n pl comb form* [NL, fr. Gk *trich-, thrix* hair] **:** persons having (such) hair ⟨leio*trichi*⟩

-trich·ia \ˈtrikēə\ *n comb form* -s [NL, fr. *trich-* + *-ia*] **1 :** condition of having (such) hair ⟨oligo*trichia*⟩ ⟨hypo*trichia*⟩ **2 :** hairiness ⟨glosso*trichia*⟩

tri·chi·a·sis \trəˈkīəsəs\ *n* -ES [LL, fr. Gk, fr. *trich-* + *-iasis*] **:** a turning inward of the eyelashes often causing irritation of the eyeball

-trichies *pl of* -TRICHY

tri·chil·ia \trīˈkilēə\ *n, cap* [NL, fr. Gk *tricheilos* three-lipped, fr. *tri-* three (akin to Gk *treis* three) + *cheilos* lip — more at THREE, GILL] **:** a genus of tropical African and American trees and shrubs (family Meliaceae) having odd-pinnate leaves and panicles of rather large flowers with four or five petals — see MAFURA

¹tri·chi·na \trəˈkīnə\ *n, pl* **trichi·nae** \-ī(ˌ)nē\ *also* **trichinas** [NL, fr. Gk *trichinos* of hair, fr. *trich-, thrix* hair + *-inos* -ine; akin to Lith *driẽkti* to stretch — more at TRICH-] **1 :** a small slender nematode worm (*Trichinella spiralis*) that as an adult is a short-lived parasite of the intestines of a flesh-eating mammal (as man, rat, or hog) where it pairs and produces immense numbers of larvae which migrate to the muscles either directly or through the blood, establish themselves in or between the muscle fibers where they become encysted and may persist for years, and if consumed by a new host in raw or insufficiently cooked meat are liberated by the digestive processes and rapidly become adult to initiate a new parasitic cycle — see TRICHINOSIS **2 :** TRICHINOSIS — **tri·chi·nal** \-ˈnᵊl\ *adj*

²trichina \"\ [NL] *syn of* TRICHINELLA

trich·i·nat·ed \ˈtrikəˌnād.əd\ *adj* [NL *trichina* + E *-ate* + *-ed*] **:** parasitized by trichinae **:** TRICHINIZED

trich·i·nel·la \ˌtrikəˈnelə\ *n* [NL, fr. *trichina* + L *-ella*] **1** *cap* **:** a genus (coextensive with the family Trichinellidae of the order Enoplida) of nematode worms comprising the trichinae and being often isolated in a distinct superfamily **2** *pl* **trich·i·nel·lae** \-eˌlē, -lī\ **:** TRICHINA 1

trich·i·nel·li·a·sis \ˌtrikənəˈlīəsəs\ *n, pl* **trichinellia·ses** \-əˌsēz\ [NL, fr. *Trichinella* + *-iasis*] **:** TRICHINOSIS

trich·i·ni·a·sis \ˌ==ˈnīəsəs\ *n, pl* **trichinia·ses** \-əˌsēz\ [NL, fr. *trichina* + *-iasis*] **:** TRICHINOSIS

trich·i·niza·tion \ˌ==nəˈzāshən, -ˌnīˈz-\ *n* -s **:** the quality or state of being trichinized

trich·i·nize \ˈ==ˌnīz\ *vt* -ED/-ING/-S [NL *trichina* + E *-ize*] **:** to cause to become trichinous **:** affect with trichinae ⟨was estimated that at least 139 prisoners were *trichinized* —F.H. Hathaway⟩

¹trich·i·nop·o·ly \ˌ==ˈnäpəlē, -li\ *n* -ES [fr. *Trichinopoly*, city in southern India] **:** a cheroot made in India

²trichinopoly \"\ *adj, usu cap* [fr. *Trichinopoly*, India] **:** of or from the city of Trichinopoly, India **:** of the kind or style prevalent in Trichinopoly

tri·chi·no·scope \trəˈkīnəˌskōp\ *n* [ISV *trichina* + *-o-* + *-scope*] **:** a device for detecting larval trichinae in meat microscopically

trich·i·nosed \ˈtrikəˌnōst, -ōzd\ *adj* [NL *trichinosis* + E *-ed*] **:** TRICHINOUS

trich·i·no·sis \ˌ==ˈnōsəs\ *n, pl* **trichino·ses** \-ōˌsēz\ [NL, fr. *trichina* + *-osis*] **:** infestation with or disease caused by trichinae contracted by eating raw or undercooked infested food and esp. pork and marked initially by colicky pains, nausea, and diarrhea and later by muscular pain, dyspnea, fever, and edema

tri·chi·nous \ˈtrikənəs, trəˈkīn-\ *adj* ISV *trichin-* (fr. NL *trichina*) + *-ous*] **1 :** infested with trichinae ⟨~ meat⟩ **2 :** of, relating to, or involving trichinae or trichinosis ⟨~ infection⟩ ⟨~ manifestations⟩

trich·i·on \ˈtrikēˌän\ *n* -s [NL, fr. Gk, dim. of *trich-, thrix* hair — more at TRICH-] **:** the point where the normal hairline and middle line of the forehead intersect

trich·ite \ˈtriˌkīt\ *n* -s [in sense a, fr. G *trichit*, fr. *trich-* + *-it* -ite; in sense b, fr. NL *trichites*, fr. *trich-* + *-ites* -ite; in sense c, prob. fr. *trich-* + *-ite*] **:** a minute acicular body: as **a :** a hairlike crystallite occurring singly or in clusters **b :** a hairlike siliceous spicule occurring in some sponges in fascicles **c :** one of the slender rods supporting the cytopharynx of some ciliated protozoans

tri·chit·ic \trəˈkid.ik\ *adj* **:** containing, relating to, or having the characteristics of a trichite

trich·i·u·ri·dae \ˌtrikēˈyürəˌdē\ *n pl, cap* [NL, fr. *Trichiurus* type genus (fr. *trich-* + *-i-* + *-urus*) + *-idae*] **:** a family of deep-sea fishes including cutlass fishes and a few related forms and with the snake eels constituting a distinct suborder of Percomorphi

trichlor- *or* **trichloro-** *comb form* [ISV *tri-* + *chlor-*] **:** containing three atoms of chlorine — in names of chemical compounds ⟨*sym-trichloro*benzene⟩; compare CHLOR-

tri·chloride \(ˈ)trī+\ *n* [*trichlor-* + *-ide*] **:** a binary compound containing three atoms of chlorine combined with an element or radical

tri·chloroacetic acid \(ˈ)trī+-\ *also* **tri·chloracetic acid** \"+-\ *n* [ISV *trichlor-* + *acetic*] **:** a strong vesicant pungent deliquescent crystalline acid CCl_3COOH made usu. by chlorinating acetic acid or by oxidizing chloral and used in medicine as a caustic and astringent and esp. in the form of salts in weed control — abbr. *TCA*

tri·chlo·ro·ethane \(ˈ)trīˌklōr(ˌ)ō, -ō(ˌ)rō+\ *n* [*trichlor-* + *ethane*] **:** either of two nonflammable irritating liquid isomeric compounds $C_2H_3Cl_3$: **a :** the isomer CH_3CCl_3 that is made usu. by heating acetyl chloride with phosphorus pentachloride and is the parent compound of DDT and other insecticides — called also *1,1,1-trichloroethane* **b :** the isomer $CH_2ClCHCl_2$ that is made usu. by the action of chlorine on vinyl chloride or ethylene dichloride and is used chiefly as a solvent — called also *1,1,2-trichloroethane*

tri·chlo·ro·ethylene \"+\ *also* **tri·chlor·ethylene** \ˌtrīˌklōr+\ *n* [ISV *trichlor-* + *ethylene*] **:** a mobile nonflammable liquid $CHClCCl_2$ obtained usu. by heating symmetrical tetrachloroethane with hydrated lime and used chiefly as a solvent, a degreasing agent for metals, and in medicine as an inhalation analgesic and anesthetic

tri·chlo·ro·methane \(ˈ)trīˌklōr(ˌ)ō, -ō(ˌ)rō+\ *n* [ISV *trichlor-* + *methane*] **:** CHLOROFORM

tri·chlo·ro·nitrophenol \"+\ *n* [*trichlor-* + *nitrophenol*] **:** a pale yellow crystalline compound $O_2NC_6HCl_3OH$ derived from *ortho*-nitrophenol and used in streams for killing the sea lamprey — called also *3,4,6-trichloro-2-nitrophenol*

tri·chlo·ro·phenoxyacetic acid \"+-\ *n* [*trichlor-* + *phenoxy-* + *acetic*] **:** a crystalline irritating compound $Cl_3C_6H_2OCH_2COOH$ resembling dichlorophenoxyacetic acid, made from the corresponding trichloro-phenol and chloroacetic acid, and used chiefly in the form of esters as a weed killer esp. for woody plants — usu. used with initial numbers ⟨*2,4,5-trichlorophenoxyacetic acid*⟩; called also *2,4,5-T*

tri·chlo·ro·silane \"+\ *n* [*trichlor-* + *silane*] **:** a fuming flammable mobile liquid $SiHCl_3$ made usu. by heating silicon in hydrogen chloride and used in making organosilicon compounds — called also *silicochloroform*

tricho- — see TRICH-

trich·o·bacteria \ˌtrikə+\ *n pl* [NL, fr. *trich-* + *bacteria*] **1 :** filamentous bacteria **2 :** flagellated bacteria

tricho·bezoar \"+\ *n* [ISV *trich-* + *bezoar*] **:** HAIR BALL

tricho·bilharzia \"+\ *n, cap* [NL, fr. *trich-* + *Bilharzia*] **:** a genus of digenetic trematode worms (family Schistosomatidae) including forms that normally parasitize aquatic birds and are leading causers of swimmer's itch in man

trich·o·blast \ˈtrikəˌblast\ *n* [ISV *trich-* + *-blast*; orig. formed in G] **:** IDIOBLAST

trich·o·bothrium \ˌtrikə+\ *n, pl* **trichobothria** [NL, fr. *trich-* + *bothrium*] **:** a sensory hair on an arthropod or other invertebrate; *also* **:** a sensory organ consisting of one or more such hairs together with its supporting structures

trich·o·branchia \"+\ *n* [NL, fr. *trich-* + *-branchia*] **:** a gill of a decapod crustacean with filamentous branches arranged in series around an axis — **trich·o·branchiate** \"+\ *adj*

trich·o·ceph·a·li·a·sis \-ˌsefəˈlīəsəs\ *n, pl* **trichocephalia·ses** \-əˌsēz\ [NL, fr. *Trichocephalus* + *-iasis*] **:** TRICHURIASIS

trich·o·ceph·a·lus \ˈsefələs\ [NL, fr. *trich-* + *-cephalus*] *syn of* TRICHURIS

trich·o·ce·rat·i·dae \-səˈrad.əˌdē\ *n pl, cap* [NL, fr. *Tricho-cerat-, Trichoceras*, type genus (fr. *trich-* + *-cerat-, -ceras*) + *-idae*] **:** a small family of two-winged flies related to the Tipulidae and comprising the winter crane flies

trich·o·cer·cous \ˌ==ˈsərkəs\ *adj* [*trich-* + *cerc-* + *-ous*] *of a cercaria* **:** having a spiny tail

trich·o·cyst \ˈtrikəˌsist\ *n* [*trich-* + *-cyst*] **:** one of the minute projectile structures that release adhesive threads when discharged, are common in the ectoderm of protozoans, and are comparable to but less complex than nematocysts — **trich·o·cys·tic** \ˌ==ˈsistik\ *adj*

trichode \ˈtriˌkōd, -rī,k-\ *n* -s [Gk *trichōdēs* like hair, fr. *trich-* + *-ōdēs* -ode] **:** TRICHOME

trich·o·dec·tes \ˌtrikəˈdekˌtēz\ *n, cap* [NL, fr. *trich-* + *-dectes*] **:** the type genus of Trichodectidae including various biting lice of domesticated mammals

trich·o·dec·ti·dae \-ktəˌdē\ *n pl, cap* [NL, fr. *Trichodectes*, type genus + *-idae*] **:** a widespread family of biting lice that have a single simple tarsal claw and include economically important parasites of mammals — see CAT LOUSE

trich·o·der·ma \ˌ==ˈdərmə\ *n, cap* [NL, fr. *trich-* + *-derma*] **:** a form genus of imperfect fungi (family Moniliaceae) having nonseptate conidia borne in heads on 2-branched or 3-branched conidiophores

trich·o·des·mi·um \-ˈdezmēəm\ *n, cap* [NL, fr. *trich-* + *desm-* + *-ium*] **:** a small genus of filamentous blue-green algae of the family Oscillatoriaceae — see SEA BLOOM

trich·odon·ti·dae \ˌ==ˈdäntəˌdē\ *n pl, cap* [NL, fr. *Trichodont-, Trichodon*, type genus (fr. *trich-* + *-odont-, -odon*) + *-idae*] **:** a family of elongate compressed scaleless large-eyed percoid fishes comprising the sandfishes

trich·o·gen \ˈtrikəjən\ *n* -s [ISV *trich-* + *-gen*; orig. formed in G] **:** a trichogenous cell

tri·chog·e·nous \trəˈkäjənəs\ *also* **trich·o·gen·ic** \ˌtrikəˈjenik\ *adj* [*trich-* + *-genous* or *-genic*] **:** producing hair; *esp* **:** being one of the hypodermal cells of insects and other arthropods that produce the chitinous hairs or spinules on the surface of the body and limbs

trich·o·gram·ma \ˌtrikə'gramə\ *n, cap* [NL, fr. *trich-* + Gk *gramma* letter, small weight — more at GRAM] **:** a genus of minute hairy-winged chalcid flies that are parasitic as larvae in the eggs of other insects

trich·o·gyne \'trikəˌjīn\ *n* -s [ISV *trich-* + *-gyne*] **:** a prolonged terminal receptive portion of a procarp or an archicarp — compare CARPOGONIUM — **trich·o·gyn·i·al** \ˌtrikə'jinēəl\ *or* **trich·o·gyn·ic** \-nik\ *adj*

trich·oid \'triˌkȯid\ *adj* [Gk *trichoeidēs*, fr. *trich-* + *-oeidēs* -oid] **:** HAIRLIKE, CAPILLARY

trich·o·lae·na \ˌtrikə'lēnə\ *n, cap* [NL, fr. *trich-* + L *laena* cloak] **:** a genus of African grasses with one-flowered silky spikelets in small open panicles — see NATAL GRASS

tri·chol·o·gist \trə'käləjəst\ *n* -s **:** an expert in trichology

tri·chol·o·gy \-jē, -ji\ *n* -ES [ISV *trich-* + *-logy*] **:** scientific study of hair ⟨comparative ~⟩

trich·o·lo·ma \ˌtrikə'lōmə\ *n, cap* [NL, fr. *trich-* + Gk *lōma* hem, fringe — more at LOMATINE] **:** a genus of white-spored agarics having a pileus with thin commonly sinuate lamellae and no volva or annulus and including both edible and inedible forms of various colors

tri·cho·ma \trə'kōmə\ *n* -s [NL, fr. Gk *trichōma* growth of hair] **:** TRICHOME 1

tri·chom·a·nes \trə'kämə,nēz\ *n, cap* [NL, fr. L, a plant, fr. Gk, waterwort, fr. *trich-* + *-manes* (prob. fr. stem of *mainesthai* to rave, be mad about) — more at MIND] **:** a genus of chiefly tropical often epiphytic ferns (family Hymenophyllaceae) that have delicate usu. much-divided fronds with flattened sporangia within a transverse ring — see BRISTLE FERN

tri·cho·ma·to·sis \trəˌkōmə'tōsəs\ *n* -ES [NL, fr. *trichomat-*, *trichoma* + *-osis*] **:** PLICA 1

tri·chom·a·tous \trə'kämədəs\ *adj* [ISV *trichomat-* (fr. NL *trichomat-*, *trichoma* trichome) + *-ous*] **:** bearing trichomes

trichome \'triˌkōm, -rī,k-\ *n* -s [G *trichom*, fr. Gk *trichōma* growth of hair, fr. *trichoun* to cover with hair, fr. *trich-*, *thrix* hair — more at TRICH-] **1 a :** an epidermal hair structure on a plant — compare EMERGENCE 3 **b :** a strand or chain of cells (as in a filamentous colony of bacteria or algae) **2 :** one of the tufts of brightly colored and often orange hairs on the bodies of myrmecophilous insects that releases an aromatic secretion attractive to ants; *also* **:** one of the constituent hairs — **tri·cho·mic** \trə'kōmik\ *adj*

trich·o·mo·na·ci·dal \ˌtrikəˌmänə'sīdᵊl, -ˌmōn-; trəˌkämənə-\ *adj* [*trichomonad* + *-cidal*] **:** tending or used to destroy trichomonads ⟨~ action⟩ ⟨~ agent⟩

trich·o·mon·ad \ˌtrikə'mäˌnad, -'mō,n-, -nəd; trə'kämə,nad\ *n* -s [NL *Trichomonad-*, *Trichomonas*] **:** a flagellated protozoan of *Trichomonas* or a closely related genus

trich·o·mona·dal \ˌtrikə'mänədᵊl, -ˌmōn-\ *or* **trich·o·mon·al** \ˌtrikə'mänᵊl, -ˌmōn-; trə'kämənᵊl\ *adj* [*trichomonal* fr. *trichomonad* + *-al*] **:** of, relating to, or caused by trichomonads ⟨~ vaginitis⟩

trich·o·mon·as \ˌtrikə'mänəs, -'mōn-; trə'kämənəs\ *n, cap* [NL, fr. *trich-* + *-monas*] **:** a genus (the type of the family Trichomonadidae) of polymastigote parasitic flagellated protozoans that have four anterior flagella and another at the margin of an undulating membrane or in some classifications also include forms with three or five anterior flagella and that are parasites of the alimentary or genitourinary systems of numerous vertebrate and invertebrate hosts including man — see TRICHOMONIASIS

trich·o·mo·ni·a·sis \ˌtrikəmə'nīəsəs, trəˌkäm-\ *n, pl* **trichomonia·ses** \-əˌsēz\ [NL, fr. *Trichomonas* + *-iasis*] **:** infection with or disease caused by trichomonads: as **a :** a human vaginitis characterized by a persistent discharge and caused by a trichomonad (*Trichomonas vaginalis*) that sometimes also invades the male urethra and bladder **b :** a venereal disease of domestic cattle marked by abortion, sterility, and pyometra and caused by a trichomonad (*T. foetus*) **c :** one or more diseases of various birds apparently caused by trichomonads (as *T. diversa* or *T. gallinorum*) and characterized by ulceration and necrosis of the upper digestive tract or by inflammatory changes of the ceca accompanied by severe diarrhea

trich·o·mycosis \ˌtrikə+\ *n* [NL, fr. *trich-* + *mycosis*] **:** a disease of the hair caused by fungi

trich·o·phyl·lous \-'filəs\ *adj* [ISV *trich-* + *-phyllous*] **:** of, relating to, or having hairlike leaves or hairlike divisions of the leaf ⟨some xerophytes have the leaves reduced to ~ processes⟩

trich·o·phyte \'trikəˌfīt\ *n* -s [NL *Trichophyton*] **:** a fungus of the genus *Trichophyton*

tricho·phy·tia \ˌ≈≈'fidēə\ *n* -s [NL, fr. *Trichophyton* + *-ia*] **:** TRICHOPHYTOSIS

trich·o·phy·tid \ˌtrikə'fīdəd, trə'käfəd-\ *n* -s [ISV *trichophyte* + *-id*] **:** a skin eruption accompanying infection by trichophytes

trich·o·phy·ton \ˌtrikə'fīˌtän, trə'käfə,t-\ *n* [NL, fr. *trich-* + Gk *phyton* plant — more at PHYT-] **1** *cap* **:** a genus of ringworm fungi (family Moniliaceae) having hyaline single-celled spores and being parasitic in the skin and hair follicles of man and lower mammals — compare EPIDERMOPHYTON **2** *pl* **trichophy·ta** \-ədə\ *also* **trichophytons :** any fungus of the genus *Trichophyton*

trich·o·phyt·o·sis \ˌtrikəˌfīd'ōsəs, trəˌkäfə'tō-\ *n* -ES [NL, fr. *Trichophyton* + *-osis*] **:** disease of the skin, nails, or hair caused by fungi of the genus *Trichophyton*

tricho·plax \'trikəˌplaks\ *n, cap* [NL, fr. *trich-* + Gk *plax* flat surface — more at PLEASE] **:** a genus of minute marine animals that are sometimes classed among the Mesozoa but are prob. larval hydrozoans and that have a completely ciliated discoid body composed of three layers of cells but not otherwise differentiated

tricho·pore \-ˌpō(ə)r, -ō(ə)r, -ōə, -ȯ(ə)\ *n* [*trich-* + *-pore*] **:** a pore in the cuticle of an insect through which a sensory hair or bristle protrudes

trich·op·ter \trə'käptə(r)\ *n* -s [NL *Trichoptera*] **:** CADDIS FLY

trich·op·tera \-tərə\ *n pl, cap* [NL, fr. *trich-* + *-ptera*] **:** an order of insects consisting of the caddis flies and formerly treated as a suborder of Neuroptera — **tri·chop·ter·an** \-rən\ *adj or n* — **tri·chop·ter·ous** \-rəs\ *adj*

tri·chop·ter·on \-əˌrän\ *n, pl* **trichop·tera** \-ərə\ [NL, sing. of *Trichoptera*] **:** one of the Trichoptera

tri·chop·ter·yg·i·dae \≈ˌ≈≈'rijəˌdē\ *n pl, cap* [NL, fr. *Trichopteryg-*, *Trichopteryx*, type genus (fr. *trich-* + *-pteryx*) + *-idae*] **:** a family of clavicorn beetles having 3-jointed tarsi and the wings fringed with long hairs and including the smallest beetles known

tri·chord \(')trī¦kȯrd, -ȯ(ə)d\ *adj* [Gk *trichordos* three-stringed, fr. *tri-* three + *-chordos* stringed, fr. *chordē* string — more at TRI-, YARN] **:** of, relating to, or being a piano having three strings tuned in unison to each digital throughout most of its compass

trich·o·san·thes \ˌtrikə'sanˌthēz\ *n, cap* [NL, irreg. fr. *trich-* + *-anthes*; fr. the fringed corolla lobes] **:** a large genus of Asiatic and Australian herbs (family Cucurbitaceae) having entire or lobed leaves and white flowers succeeded by fleshy fruits of various forms — see SNAKE GOURD

trich·o·sclereid \¦≈≈+\ *n* [*trich-* + *sclereid*] **:** a long slender hairlike sclereid — compare BRACHYSCLEREID

tri·cho·sis \trə'kōsəs\ *n, pl* **tricho·ses** \-ōˌsēz\ [NL, fr. Gk *trichōsis* growth of hair, fr. *trichoun* to cover with hair, fr. *trich-*, *thrix* hair — more at TRICH-] **:** HAIRINESS

trich·o·spo·ron \ˌtrikə'spōrˌän, trə'käspəˌrän\ *n, cap* [NL, fr. *trich-* + *spora* seed, spore — more at SPORE] **:** a genus of parasitic imperfect fungi (order Moniliales) some of which are reputed skin or hair parasites of man

trich·o·spo·rum \ˌtrikə'spōrəm, trə'käspərəm\ [NL, fr. *trich-* + *spora* seed] *syn of* AESCHYNANTHUS

tricho·stasis \ˌtrikə'stāsəs, -'stas-; trə'kästəsəs\ *n* -ES [NL, fr. *trich-* + *-stasis*] **:** persistence commonly with excessive development of the lanugo of a fetus

trich·o·ste·ma \ˌtrikə'stēmə, trə'kästəmə\ *n, cap* [NL, fr. *trich-* + Gk *stēma* stamen, fr. *stēmōn* thread — more at STAMEN] **:** a genus of No. American herbs or undershrubs (family Labiatae) having axillary whorls of small blue flowers with four exserted stamens and a deeply lobed ovary — see BLACK SAGE, BLUE CURLS

trich·o·stron·gyle \ˌtrikə'sträṅ,jīl\ *n* -s [NL *Trichostrongylus*] **:** a worm of the genus *Trichostrongylus*

¹trich·o·stron·gy·lid \¦≈≈'stränjələd\ *adj* [NL *Trichostrongylidae*] **:** of or relating to the Trichostrongylidae

²trichostrongylid \"\ *n* -s **:** a nematode worm of the family Trichostrongylidae

trich·o·stron·gyl·i·dae \ˌ≈≈ˌsträn'jiləˌdē\ *n pl, cap* [NL, fr. *Trichostrongylus*, type genus + *-idae*] **:** a family of nematode worms (suborder Strongylina) that have a reduced buccal capsule with three or fewer basal teeth and parasitize the alimentary tract of vertebrates — see HYOSTRONGYLUS, TRICHOSTRONGYLUS

trich·o·stron·gy·lo·sis \ˌ≈≈ˌ≈jə'lōsəs\ *n* -ES [NL *Trichostrongylus* + *-osis*] **:** infestation with or disease caused by roundworms of the genus *Trichostrongylus* chiefly in young sheep and cattle where it is commonly marked by diarrhea, inappetence, and loss of condition — compare BLACK SCOUR

trich·o·strongylus \¦≈≈+\ *n, cap* [NL, fr. *trich-* + *Strongylus*] **:** a genus (the type of the family Trichostrongylidae) containing nematode worms that are parasites of birds and of mammals including man and comprising forms formerly placed in the genus *Strongylus* — see BLACK SCOUR WORM

trich·o·su·rus \ˌtrikə's(y)u̇rəs\ *n, cap* [NL, fr. Gk *trichōsis* growth of hair + NL *-urus* — more at TRICHOSIS] **:** a genus of marsupials comprising the common Australian opossums from which the opossum fur of commerce is obtained

trich·o·thal·lic \¦≈≈¦thalik\ *adj* [*trich-* + *thall-* + *-ic*] **:** having a filamentous thallus or one ending in hairs or hairlike branches — used esp. of an alga that grows by the action of an intercalary meristem

trich·o·the·ci·um \ˌ≈≈'thēsh(ē)əm\ *n, cap* [NL, fr. *trich-* + *-thecium*] **:** a genus of imperfect fungi (family Moniliaceae) having erect unbranched septate conidiophores and 2-celled hyaline or bright-colored spores — see PINK ROT

trich·o·til·lo·ma·nia \ˌ≈≈ˌtilə'mānēə\ *n* [NL, fr. *trich-* + Gk *tillein* to pull, pluck + *mania*] **:** abnormal desire to pull out one's hair — **trich·o·til·lo·man·ic** \¦≈≈¦≈≈¦manik\ *adj*

trich·o·tom·ic \¦≈≈¦tämik\ *adj* [ISV *trichotomy* + *-ic*] **:** belonging to, characterized by, or based upon a trichotomy **:** TRICHOTOMOUS

tri·chot·o·mize \trī'kädəˌmīz\ *vt* -ED/-ING/-S [*trichotomy* + *-ize*] **:** to make a trichotomy of

tri·chot·o·mous \-əməs\ *adj* [*trichotomy* + *-ous*] **:** divided or dividing into three parts or into threes **:** three-forked **:** THREEFOLD ⟨~ branching⟩ — **tri·chot·o·mous·ly** *adv*

tri·chot·o·my \-mē\ *n* -ES [prob. fr. (assumed) NL *trichotomia*, fr. Gk *trichotomein* to trisect (fr. *tricha* threefold — akin to Gk *treis* three — + *temnein* to cut) + L *-ia* -y — more at THREE, TOME] **1 :** a dividing into three parts, elements, or classes ⟨the ~ of speech-sciences into phonetics, phonemics, and historical phonetics —R.S.Wells⟩ — compare POLYTOMY **2 :** a system divided or divisible into three constituents or elements ⟨to speak of man as a ~, . . . having a division into three parts —Gottfried de Purucker⟩

-tri·chous \trəkəs\ *adj comb form* [Gk *-trichos*, fr. *trich-*, *thrix* hair — more at TRICH-] **:** having (such) hair **:** haired ⟨peri*trichous*⟩

tri·chro·ic \(')trī¦krōik\ *adj* [Gk *trichroos* three-colored (fr. *tri-* three + *-chroos* -chroous) + E *-ic* — more at TRI-] **:** exhibiting trichroism

tri·chro·ism \'trīˌkrōˌizəm\ *n* -s [ISV *trichro-* (fr. Gk *trichroos* three-colored) + *-ism*] **1 :** pleochroism in which the colors are unlike when a crystal is viewed in the direction of three different axes **2 :** polychromasia with three colors occurring in different individuals of a group or in different parts of one individual

tri·chro·mat \'trīkrōˌmat\ *n* -s [back-formation fr. *trichromatic*] **:** one that requires that three primary colors be mixed in order to match the spectrum as he sees it **:** one having normal or nearly normal color vision — compare DICHROMAT, MONOCHROMAT; DEUTERANOMALY, PROTANOMALY

tri·chromatic \¦trī+\ *adj* [*tri-* + *chromatic*] **1 a :** of, relating to, consisting of, or employing three colors **b :** relating to, done by, or constituting three-color photography — compare PROCESS PRINTING **2 a :** relating to or exhibiting trichromatism **b :** characteristic of a trichromat

tri·chro·ma·tism \trī'krōməˌtizəm\ *n* [*trichromatic* + *-ism*] **1 :** the quality or state of being trichromatic **:** the use of three colors (as in photography) **2** *also* **tri·chro·ma·cy** \-əsē\ -ES **:** vision in which all of the fundamental colors are perceived though not necessarily with equal facility — compare DICHROMATISM, MONOCHROMATISM

tri·chrome \(')trī¦krōm\ *adj* [ISV *tri-* + *-chrome*] **:** TRICHROMATIC: as **a :** of or relating to apparatus for printing three colors ⟨a ~ typewriter⟩ **b :** coloring tissue elements differentially in three colors ⟨a ~ biological stain⟩

tri·chromic \"+\ *adj* [*tri-* + *chromic*] **:** TRICHROMATIC

tri·chro·nous \'trīkrənəs\ *adj* [Gk *trichronos*, fr. *tri-* three + *-chronos* -chronous — more at TRI-] **:** TRISEMIC

trich·u·ra·ta \ˌtrikyə'rādə, -rād·ə\ [NL, fr. *Trichuris* + *-ata*] *syn of* DORYLAIMINA

trich·u·ri·a·sis \ˌ≈≈'rīəsəs\ *n, pl* **trichuria·ses** \-əˌsēz\ [NL, fr. *Trichuris* + *-iasis*] **:** infestation with or disease caused by worms of the genus *Trichuris*

¹trich·u·rid \trə'kyu̇rəd\ *adj* [NL *Trichuridae*] **:** of or relating to the Trichuridae

²trichurid \"\ *n* -s **:** a nematode worm of the family Trichuridae

trich·u·ri·dae \trə'kyu̇rəˌdē\ *n pl, cap* [NL, fr. *Trichurus* + *-idae*] **:** a family of nematode worms (order Enoplida) that are parasitic in the intestines of vertebrates and have a slender body sometimes with a thickened posterior end and a tubular capillary esophagus — see CAPILLARIA, TRICHURUS

trich·u·ris \-rəs\ *n, cap* [NL, fr. *trich-* + *-uris* (fr. Gk *oura* tail); fr. the lashlike anterior part that is often mistaken for a tail] **:** a genus (the type of the family Trichuridae) of nematode worms comprising the whipworms

trichy \'trikē, -ki\ *n* -ES [alter. of *trichi*] **:** TRICHINOPOLY

-tri·chy \trəkē, -ki\ *n comb form* -ES [NL *-trichia*] **:** the condition of having (such) hair ⟨lisso*trichy*⟩

tricing *pres part of* TRICE

tri·cin·i·um \trī'sinēəm\ *n* -s [LL, song by three voices, trio, fr. *tri-* + *-cinium* (fr. *canere* to sing) — more at CHANT] **:** a 16th century 3-part vocal composition

tri·cip·i·tal \(')trī¦sipədᵊl, -ətᵊl\ *adj* [NL *tricipit-*, *triceps* + E *-al* — more at TRICEPS] **1** *of a muscle* **:** having three heads **2 :** of, relating to, or being a triceps muscle ⟨the ~ pull on the humerus⟩

tri·city \'≈¦≈≈\ *n* **:** a group of three adjacent and usu. economically interacting cities; *also* **:** one of the cities of such a group

¹trick \'trik\ *n* -s [ME *trik*, fr. ONF *trique*, fr. *trikier* to trick, cheat, deceive] **1 a :** a mean crafty procedure or practice **:** an artifice or stratagem designed to deceive, delude, or defraud ⟨scrupled at no ~ however unfair that would get her her own way⟩ **b :** a mischievous or roguish act **:** a piece of tomfoolery (as a prank or practical joke) ⟨playing harmless ~*s* on one another⟩ **c :** an unwise, indiscreet, or childish action **:** a stupid procedure ⟨it's a fool's ~ to trust a stranger too far⟩ **d :** a deceptive, dexterous, or ingenious feat or procedure designed to puzzle or amuse ⟨a juggler's ~*s*⟩ ⟨learned to do card ~*s*⟩ ⟨taught his dog several ~*s*⟩ **2 a** *archaic* **:** a small article (as a toy, trifle, or knickknack) **b tricks** *pl* **:** the small miscellaneous articles that supplement an arrangement ⟨the ~*s* and bits that give a room personality⟩; *also* **:** PERSONAL EFFECTS, TRAPS ⟨left his ~*s* at the camp⟩ **c** *dial* **:** an amulet or charm against misfortune **3 a :** an habitual peculiarity of behavior or manner **:** HABIT, CUSTOM ⟨a horse with the ~ of shying at dead leaves⟩ ⟨a small stream that had the unfortunate ~ of overflowing every spring⟩ ⟨had a ~ of appearing to drowse while he listened⟩ **b :** a characteristic and identifying feature (as of fashion or expression) ⟨a ~ of speech⟩ ⟨the ~ of that voice, I do well remember —Shak.⟩ **c :** a delusive appearance esp. when caused by art or legerdemain **:** an optical illusion ⟨a mere ~ of vision⟩; *also* **:** something causing such an effect ⟨some ~ of lighting made her appear gaunt and haggard⟩ **4 :** a rough or preliminary outline sketch of a heraldic representation **5 :** KNACK: as **a :** a quick or effective way of getting a result or attaining an end ⟨knows the ~ to make my lady laugh —Shak.⟩ **b (1) :** an artful or artificial expedient or contrivance **:** a technical device or formality (as of an art or craft) ⟨the ~*s* of stage technique⟩ ⟨the ~ of depicting perspective on a flat surface⟩ **(2) tricks** *pl* **:** the special skills and deft laborsaving methods that characterize an expert ⟨learning the ~*s* of the trade⟩ **c (1) :** an act involving or requiring skillful dexterity or ingenuity ⟨the ~ is to make everything appear natural⟩ **(2) :** a precise, skillful, and usu. rapid effecting of an aim or result often by the use of a substitute or an alternate means ⟨shaving a bit from the edge will do the ~ and make the door fit⟩ **6 a :** the cards played in one round of a card game **b :** a scoring unit in a card game: as **(1) :** one consisting of the cards won in one round of play **(2) :** ODD TRICK **(3) :** HONOR-TRICK **c :** a card as a potential score winner ⟨an ace of trumps is a sure ~ in bridge⟩ **7 :** a continuous stretch of some activity: as **a :** a sailor's turn of duty at the helm usu. lasting for two hours **b :** SHIFT 2b(2) **c :** a trip taken as part of one's employment ⟨returned from a long ~ in the rural areas⟩ **d** *slang* **:** a professional engagement of a prostitute **8 a :** a small creature (as a pony): as **(1) :** CHILD **(2) :** a neat trim pretty young woman ⟨the cutest ~ you ever want to see⟩ **b** *slang* **:** the customer of a prostitute **9 :** a cut in a needlebar of a knitting machine to receive a needle

syn RUSE, STRATAGEM, MANEUVER, ARTIFICE, WILE, FEINT, DODGE: TRICK may indicate cheating or fraud, clever device or contrivance that pleases, deludes, or surprises, or a playful prank or practical joke ⟨such *tricks* as the substitution of goat's milk for cow's milk —Claire Sterling⟩ ⟨*tricks* and devices to conceal evasions and violations of ethical principles —H.A. Wagner⟩ ⟨a competent and resourceful musician who always knew what he was doing, was familiar with the *tricks* of the trade —P.H.Lang⟩ ⟨the *trick* is always to tag the other fellow as Red —T.H.White b.1915⟩ ⟨ringing doorbells and extracting treats under threat of *tricks* has made Halloween a profitable grab bag for most kids —*Springfield (Mass.) Union*⟩ RUSE may imply an intention at false impression, as to divert attention from the truth or from what one intends ⟨used the old *ruse* of oxen dragging trees to create a dust that would give the English the impression of a large force moving —Stuart Cloete⟩ ⟨threw his cap and a large stone into the river and this *ruse* succeeded in convincing his pursuers that he was drowned —S.P.B.Mais⟩ STRATAGEM may apply to a single ruse that outwits or entraps; it is applicable to a more or less carefully laid plan involving deception ⟨driven to every possible trick and *stratagem* to entrap some man into marriage —G.B.Shaw⟩ ⟨a dazzling sea-fighter who by downright courage, *stratagem* and audacity succeeded in frightening the British people —C.B Palmer b. 1910⟩ MANEUVER may suggest an instance of tactics or manipulation, often adroit and astute ⟨the last of all the company to depart, and, by a *maneuver* of Mrs. Bennet, had to wait for their carriage a quarter of an hour —Jane Austen⟩ ⟨thanks to Italy's mysterious *maneuvers* by way of keeping valuable information well hidden —Claudia Cassidy⟩ ARTIFICE may suggest ingenious contrivance or invention, with or without deception ⟨the *artifices* by which friends endeavor to spare one another's feelings —G.B.Shaw⟩ ⟨the forthright story of a man's life told in a style of transparent clarity that needs no *artifices* to make it vivid —C.H.Driver⟩ WILE may imply an attempt to ensnare or beguile by deceptive allurement ⟨were I to lure him here with cunning *wile* —W.S.Gilbert & A.S. Sullivan⟩ FEINT indicates a diversion or distraction of attention away from one's genuine intent ⟨tricked the enemy commander by a *feint* off Tinian Town and sent Marines ashore at the opposite end of the island —*Current Biog.*⟩ DODGE refers to any artful expedient ⟨largely disfranchised by various police measures and legislative *dodges* which prevent his getting to the polls —W.L.Sperry⟩ ⟨a special *dodge* to get electric light for his father's house without paying for it —J.B.S.Haldane⟩

²trick \"\ *adj* **1 :** of or relating to or involving tricks or trickery ⟨~ photography⟩ **:** skilled in or used for tricks ⟨~ dice⟩ ⟨a ~ horse⟩ **2 :** conspicuously smart, attractive, effective, or able; *esp* **:** trickily or intriguingly fashioned or devised **3 a :** somewhat defective and inclined to function abnormally on occasion ⟨a ~ lock that doesn't always catch⟩ **b** *of a bodily joint* **:** inclined to lock or give way unexpectedly ⟨a ~ knee resulting from a football injury⟩

³trick \"\ *vb* -ED/-ING/-S *vt* **1 :** to deceive by cunning or artifice **:** impose on, defraud, or cheat usu. by specious means **:** affect or induce by deceit or trickery ⟨~ another in a sale⟩ ⟨~ him into consent⟩ **2 :** to obtain or bring about by trickery ⟨advertising designed to ~ your purse⟩ **3 a :** to dress or adorn esp. fancifully or ornately **:** ORNAMENT, DECORATE ⟨a request ~*ed* with expressions of devotion⟩ — usu. used with *up*, *out*, *off* ⟨~*ed* out in a gaudy lodge uniform⟩ ⟨planned to ~ ourselves up for the party⟩ **b :** to put in order **:** ARRANGE, PREEN ⟨horses with manes and tails ~*ed* and beribboned⟩ **4 :** to draw in outline (as with a pen); *specif* **:** to delineate (as a coat of arms) by outline sketches in which the tinctures are indicated by abbreviations and the repetition of a charge by numbers ~ *vi* **1 :** to practice trickery or fraud **2 :** to practice or play tricks or pranks **:** TRIFLE — usu. used with *with* **syn** see DUPE

¹trick·er \-kə(r)\ *n* -s **:** one that tricks **:** TRICKSTER

²tricker \"\ *dial var of* TRIGGER

trick·ery \-k(ə)rē, -ri\ *n* -ES **1 :** deception by tricks and stratagems **:** the practice of crafty underhand ingenuity to deceive or cheat ⟨swindled by the sharper's ~⟩ **2 :** tricks used or intended to deceive or harm **syn** see DECEPTION

trickier *comparative of* TRICKY

trickiest *superlative of* TRICKY

trick·i·ly \'trikəlē, -li\ *adv* **:** in a tricky manner

trick·i·ness \-kēnəs, -kin-\ *n* -ES **:** the quality or state of being tricky

tricking *pres part of* TRICK

trick·ing·ly *adv* **:** in a tricking manner **:** so as to cheat or deceive **:** ARTFULLY

trick·ish \'trikish\ *adj* **:** given to or characterized by tricks or trickery **:** somewhat tricky — **trick·ish·ly** \-kəshlē\ *adv* — **trick·ish·ness** \-kishnəs\ *n* -ES

¹trick·le \'trikəl\ *vb* **trickled; trickled; trickling** \-k(ə)liṅ\ **trickles** [ME *triklen*] *vi* **1 a :** to run or fall in drops **:** flow in a thin gentle stream ⟨water *trickled* down the walls⟩ ⟨tears *trickling* from her eyes⟩ **b :** to drip with some liquid **:** emit a liquid in fine streams or drops ⟨onions made her eyes ~⟩ **2 a :** to move (as in going or departing) one by one ⟨summer visitors are now *trickling* home⟩ ⟨his audience *trickled* out⟩ **b :** to dissipate slowly ⟨his enthusiasm *trickled* away⟩ ~ *vt* **1 :** to pour forth or cause to flow in drops or in a thin stream **2 :** to let pass or go one by one

²trickle \"\ *n* -s **:** something that trickles or seems to trickle **:** a thin slow stream **:** DRIP ⟨a mere ~ of water left in the river⟩

trickle charge *n* **:** a slow continuous charge for an electric storage battery

trickle charger *n* **:** a device for providing a storage battery with a trickle charge

trick·less \'≈ləs\ *adj* **:** free from tricks or trickery **:** having no trick

trick·let \-lət\ *n* -s [²*trickle* + *-et*] **:** a thin stream **:** RILL

trickling filter *n* **:** an artificial bed of broken rock or other coarse material through which sewage or industrial wastes trickle after being sprayed on intermittently so that organic matter present is oxidized and removed by biological growths formed on the surfaces of the rock

trick·ling·ly *adv* **:** in a trickling manner

trick·ly \'trik(ə)lē\ *adj* -ER/-EST [¹*trickle* + *-y*] **:** marked by trickling

trick or treat *n* **:** a Halloween pastime in which children go from door to door asking for goodies supposedly with the idea of playing tricks on people who do not comply; *also* **:** the spoils so won

trick-or-treat \¦≈≈¦≈\ *vi* [*trick or treat*] **:** to engage in trick or treat — **trick-or-treater** \¦≈≈¦≈≈\ *n*

trick-o-the-loop \¦≈≈¦≈\ *n, Irish* **:** STRAP GAME

trick points *n pl* **:** TRICK SCORE 1

tricks *pl of* TRICK, *pres 3d sing of* TRICK

trick score *n* **1 :** a bridge score for odd tricks won or in contract bridge bid and won by the declarer's side **2 :** the section of a bridge score sheet reserved for recording the trick score

tricks·i·ness \'triksēnəs, -sin-\ *n* -ES **:** the quality or state of being tricksy

trick·some \-səm\ *adj* **:** full of tricks **:** addicted to playing tricks **:** TRICKSY

trick·ster \-stə(r)\ *n* -s [¹*trick* + *-ster*] **:** one that tricks: as **a :** a dishonest person who defrauds others by trickery **:** a confidence man **b :** a person (as a stage magician) skilled in the use of tricks and illusion **c** : a mischievous supernatural being found in the folklore of various primitive peoples, often functioning as a culture hero, and much given to capricious acts of sly deception

trick·ster·ing \-ərïŋ, -rēŋ\ *n* -s : the acts or practices of a trickster

tricksy \'triksē, -si\ *adj* -ER/-EST [*tricks* (pl. of ¹*trick*) + -*y*] **1** *archaic* : tricked out : artfully embellished; *esp* : smartly attired ⟨the ~ pomp of fairy pride —J.R.Drake⟩ **2** : full of tricks or pranks : given to roguish mischief : PRANKISH ⟨~ sprites of woods and fields⟩ **3 a** *archaic* : having or manifesting the cunning or craftiness of a trickster : UNCERTAIN, EVASIVE, DECEIVING, DECEPTIVE **b** : difficult to cope with or handle : TRYING ⟨a ~ job⟩

trick valve *n* : a slide valve (as of a steam engine) having a supplementary steam passage connecting the forward and back parts of its face and thus reducing the valve travel

trick work *n* : work involving a trick or knack or the use of tricks and esp. artificial devices; *specif* : literary or artistic work characterized solely by technical dexterity

tricky \'trikē, -ki\ *adj* -ER/-EST [¹*trick* + -*y*] **1** : of or characteristic of a trickster : given to or manifesting trickery ⟨a ~ diplomat⟩ ⟨this ~ policy⟩ **2 a** : deceptively safe, easy, manageable, or orderly : TICKLISH ⟨a ~ situation⟩ ⟨a ~ passage in the final movement⟩ **b** : manifesting or requiring skill or aptitude in doing, making, or handling : INTRICATE ⟨a ~ set of controls⟩; *broadly* : INGENIOUS ⟨~ gadgets⟩ ⟨~ rhymes⟩ **3** : TRICK 3 **syn** see SLY

¹**tri·clad** \'trī,klad\ *adj* [NL *Tricladida*] : of or relating to the Tricladida

²**triclad** \"\ *n* -s : a turbellarian worm of the order Tricladida : PLANARIAN

tri·clad·i·da \ˌ=ˈkladədə\ *n pl, cap* [NL, fr. *tri-* + *clad-* + -*ida*] : an order of Turbellaria comprising chiefly free-living flatworms with the intestine composed of a median anterior division and two lateral posterior divisions with side branches and including marine, freshwater, and terrestrial forms — see PLANARIAN

tricli·nate \(ˈ)trīˈklīnət, 'triklə,nāt\ *adj* [*tri-* + L *clinatus*, past part. of *clinare* to bend — more at LEAN] : TRICLINIC

tri·clin·ic \(ˈ)trīˈklinik\ *adj* [ISV *tri-* + -*clinic*] : having or characterized by three unequal axes intersecting at oblique angles — used esp. of a crystal

triclinic system *n* : a crystal system characterized by three unequal axes intersecting at oblique angles — see CRYSTAL SYSTEM illustration

tri·clin·i·um \trīˈklinēəm\ *n, pl* **triclin·ia** \-ēə\ [L, fr. Gk *triklinion*, fr. *tri-* three + *klinion*, dim. of *klinē* couch — more at TRI-, CLIN-] **1** : a couch used by ancient Romans for reclining at meals, extending round three sides of a table, and usu. divided into three parts **2** : a dining room furnished with a triclinium

tri·cli·no·he·dric \(ˌ)trīˌklīnəˈhēdrik, -hed-\ *adj* [ISV *tri-* + *clin-* + *hedr-* (fr. Gk *hedra* seat) + -*ic* — more at SIT] : TRICLINIC

tric·o·lette \ˌtrikəˈlet, *usu* -ed·+V\ *n* -s [*tricot* + -*lette* (as in *flannelette*)] : a usu. silk or rayon knitted fabric used esp. for women's clothing

tri·colon \(ˈ)trī+\ *n* [Gk *trikōlon*, neut. of *trikōlos* 3-limbed, fr. *tri-* three + *kōlon* limb, part of a strophe — more at TRI-, CALK] : a period in classical prosody composed of three cola

¹**tri·col·or** \'trī,kələ(r) *sometimes* 'trē,k-, *chiefly Brit* 'tri,k-\ *n* [F *tricolore*, fr. *tricolore*, adj., three-colored, fr. LL *tricolor*, fr. L *tri-* + *color* — more at COLOR] : a flag of three colors ⟨the French ~⟩

²**tricolor** \"\ *adj* [F *tricolore* three-colored] **1 a** *or* **tri·col·ored** \'trī,kələ(r)d\ [*tricolored* fr. F *tricolore*, adj. + E -*ed*] : having three colors : marked with or employing three colors ⟨~ plumage⟩ ⟨a ~ process in photography⟩ **b** *of a dog* : having a coat of black, tan, and white **2** : of, relating to, or characteristic of a tricolor or a nation whose flag is a tricolor; *often* : FRENCH ⟨the intricacies of ~ politics⟩

tri·conch \'trī,käŋk *also* -kȯŋk\ *adj* [Gk *trikonchos*, fr. *tri-* three + *konchē* conch, apse — more at TRI-, CONCH] : having apses on three sides of a square central mass ⟨many Syrian churches are built on a ~ plan⟩

tri·con·odon \trīˈkänə,dän\ *n* [NL, fr. *tri-* + *con-* + -*odon*] **1** *cap* : a genus of small generalized Jurassic mammals that have teeth with three simple cones and are associated with Marsupialia or Multituberculata or more usu. placed with a few related forms in the order Triconodonta **2** -s : any mammal or fossil of the genus *Triconodon* — **tri·con·odon·tine** \ˌ==ˌ==ˈdän,tīn, -n,tēn, -nt°n\ *n* -s

¹**tri·con·odont** \trīˈkänə,dänt\ *adj* [NL *Triconodont-*, *Triconodon*] **1** : having or being teeth with three simple cones — compare TRITUBERCULY **2** [NL *Triconodonta*] : of or relating to the Triconodonta

²**triconodont** \"\ *n* -s [NL *Triconodonta*] : a triconodont mammal

tri·con·odon·ta \(ˌ)=ˌ==ˈdäntə\ *n pl, cap* [NL *Triconodont-*, *Triconodon*] : an order of Jurassic primitive mammals that are of uncertain relationships and prob. not on the direct ancestral line of higher mammals — see TRICONODON

tri·consonantal \(ˌ)trī +\ *adj* [*tri-* + *consonantal*] : containing or consisting of three consonants

¹**tri·corn** \'trī,kȯrn\ *n* -s [L *tricornis* 3-horned, fr. *tri-* + -*cornis* -horned (fr. *cornu* horn) — more at HORN] **1** : an imaginary 3-horned beast **2** *usu* **tri·corne** \"\ [*tricorne* fr. F, fr. *tricorne*, adj., having three corners] : COCKED HAT 1a **3** : a lateral cerebral ventricle

²**tricorn** *also* **tricorne** \"\ *adj* [*tricorn* fr. L *tricornis*; *tricorne* fr. F, fr. L *tricornis*] : having three horns or corners

tri·cornered \(ˈ)trī+\ *adj* [*tri-* + *cornered*] : THREE-CORNERED, TRICORN

tri·cornute \(ˌ)=+\ *adj* [*tri-* + *cornute*] : having three horns or horn-shaped processes

tri·corporal \(ˈ)trī+\ *or* **tri·corporate** \"+\ *or* **tri·corporated** \"+\ *adj* [L *tricorpor* (fr. *tri-* + *corpor-*, *corpus* body) + E -*al* or -*ate* or -*ate* + -*ed* — more at MIDRIFF] : having or represented with three bodies conjoined to one head

trico·sane \'trīkə,sān, 'trik-\ *n* -s [ISV *tri-* + *eicosane*] : a paraffin hydrocarbon $C_{23}H_{48}$; *esp* : the low-melting crystalline normal hydrocarbon $CH_3(CH_2)_{21}CH_3$

tri·costate \(ˈ)trī+\ *adj* [ISV *tri-* + *costate*] : having three costae

tri·cot \'trē(,)kō *also* 'trikət\ *n* -s [F, fr. *tricoter* to knit, fr. MF, to agitate, skip, hop, dance, fr. OF *estriquier* to move vivaciously, of Gmc origin; akin to OE *strican* to move, glide over — more at STRIKE] **1** : a plain warp-knitted fabric in flat form that is more resistant to runs than jersey and is made of nylon, wool, rayon, silk, or cotton in sheer to opaque qualities esp. for use in clothing (as underwear) **2** : a twilled clothing fabric of wool with fine warp ribs or of wool and cotton with fine weft ribs

tric·o·tine \ˌtrikəˈtēn\ *n* -s [F, fr. *tricot* + -*ine*] : CAVALRY TWILL

tri·cotyledonous \(ˌ)trī+\ *adj* [*tri-* + *cotyledon* + -*ous*] : having three cotyledons ⟨a ~ seedling⟩

tri·cou·ni \trīˈkōnē\ *trademark* — used for a nail or iron fastened to the sole of a boot for mountain climbing

tri·cresol \(ˈ)trī + \ *n* [ISV *tri-* + *cresol*] : CRESOL 2

tri·cresyl \"+\ *n* [ISV *tri-* + *cresyl*] : TRITOLYL

tricresyl phosphate *n* : an oily flame-resistant mixture of isomeric inorganic esters $(CH_3C_6H_4)_3PO_4$ made from cresols or cresylic acid and usu. phosphorus oxychloride and used chiefly as a plasticizer and solvent, as a fire retardant, and as a lead scavenger in gasoline : tritolyl phosphate — not used systematically

tri·crot·ic \(ˈ)trīˈkräd·ik\ *adj* [Gk *trikrotos* having a triple beat (fr. *tri-* three + -*krotos*, fr. *krotein* to beat, clap) + E -*ic* — more at TRI-, CROTAL] : of, relating to, or characterized by tricrotism

tricro·tism \'trīkrə,tizəm, 'trik-\ *n* -s [*tricrotic* + -*ism*] : a condition of the arterial pulse in which there is a triple beat

tric·trac *also* **trick·track** \'trik,trak\ *n* -s [F *trictrac*, of imit. origin; fr. the clicking sound made by the pegs] : a variety of backgammon formerly played with pegs; *broadly* : BACKGAMMON 1

¹**tri·cuspid** \(ˈ)trī+\ *adj* [NL *tricuspid-*, *tricuspis*, fr. L, having three points, fr. *tri-* + *cuspid-*, *cuspis* point] **1** : having three cusps **2** : of, relating to, or involving the tricuspid valve of the heart ⟨~ disease⟩

²**tricuspid** \"\ *n* : a tricuspid anatomical structure; *esp* : a tooth having three cusps

tri·cuspidate \"+\ *also* **tri·cuspidated** \"+\ *adj* [*tri-* + *cuspidate*, *cuspidated*] : cuspidate with three points : TRICUSPID ⟨a ~ leaf⟩

tricuspid valve *n* : a valve situated at the opening of the right auricle of the heart into the right ventricle and resembling in structure the mitral valve but consisting of three triangular membranous flaps

¹**tri·cy·cle** \'trī,sikəl, -,sək-, -,sēk- *sometimes* -,sīk-\ *n* [F, fr. *tri-* + Gk *kyklos* wheel — more at WHEEL] : a 3-wheeled vehicle propelled by pedals, hand levers, or a motor: as **a** (1) : a 3-wheeled velocipede used orig. by women or girls instead of a bicycle (2) : a child's vehicle with a pair of small rear wheels and a larger front wheel to which are attached the pedals and the handles for steering **b** : a 3-wheeled velocipede with two large wheels in the rear and one small wheel in front attached to a steering handle, propelled by pedals, and formerly used by girls **c** : a 3-wheeled velocipede equipped with a box or case for light haulage **d** : a 3-wheeled and often motorized invalid chair **e** : any of various power-driven 3-wheeled vehicles (as a motorcycle) — compare TRICAR

tricycle a(2)

²**tricycle** \"\ *vi* **tricycled**; **tricycled**; **tricycling** \-k(ə)liŋ\ **tricycles** : to ride a tricycle — **tri·cy·cler** \-k(ə)lə(r)\ *n*

tricycle landing gear *n* : landing gear for an airplane having two laterally-spaced wheels aft and a single wheel forward of the center of gravity

tri·cyclene \(ˈ)trī+\ *n* [ISV *tricyclic* + -*ene*] : a crystalline saturated tricyclic terpene hydrocarbon $C_{10}H_{16}$ found in crude alpha-pinene and also made synthetically — called also *cyclene*; not used systematically

tri·cyclic \(ˈ)trī+\ *adj* [*tri-* + *cyclic*] : containing three usu. fused rings in the molecular structure (as in anthracene)

tri·cy·clist \'trī,siklәst, -,sək-, -,sēk-, -,sīk-\ *n* : one that rides a tricycle

tricyclo- *comb form* [ISV *tri-* + *cycl-*] : tricyclic ⟨*tricyclo*alkanes⟩

tri·dac·na \trəˈdaknə\ *n* [NL, fr. L, an oyster, fr. Gk *tridaknos* eaten at three bites, fr. *tri-* three + -*daknos* (fr. *daknein* to bite) — more at TONGS] **1** *cap* : a genus of marine bivalves (family Tridacnidae) having no anterior adductor muscle and an equivalve shell the valves of which are very thick and heavy and strongly plicated at the margin — see GIANT CLAM **2** -s : any mollusk of the genus *Tridacna* : GIANT CLAM

tri·dac·ni·dae \-nə,dē\ *n pl, cap* [NL, fr. *Tridacna*, type genus + -*idae*] : a small family of chiefly tropical thick-shelled marine bivalve mollusks (suborder Cardiacea) — see TRIDACNA

tri·dactyl \(ˈ)trī+\ *or* **tri·dactylous** \"+\ *also* **tri·dac·tyle** \-ˈdakt°l\ *adj* [*tridactyl*, *tridactylous* fr. Gk *tridaktylos*, fr. *tri-* three + *daktylos* finger; *tridactyle* fr. F, fr. Gk *tridaktylos* — more at TRI-] : having three fingers or toes ⟨the ~ foot of some reptiles⟩

tri·daily \(ˈ)trī+\ *adj* [*tri-* + *daily*] : occurring, appearing, or being made, done, or acted upon three times a day or every three days

trid·dler \'trid(°)lə(r)\ *n* -s [prob. alter. of obs. E *treadler* one who pedals, fr. E ²*treadle* + -*er*] *dial* : PECTORAL SANDPIPER

tri·decane \(ˈ)trī+\ *n* [ISV *tri-* + *decane*; fr. the number of carbon atoms] : a paraffin hydrocarbon $C_{13}H_{28}$; *esp* : the liquid normal hydrocarbon $CH_3(CH_2)_{11}CH_3$ obtained from petroleum

tri·decanoic acid \(ˌ)trī+-\ *n* [*tridecane* + -*oic*] : a crystalline fatty acid $C_{12}H_{25}COOH$ made synthetically

tri·dec·ene \trīˈde,sēn\ *n* -s [*tridecane* + -*ene*] : any of six straight-chain isomeric olefin hydrocarbons $C_{13}H_{26}$

tri·dec·yl \trīˈdesəl\ *n* -s [ISV *tridecane* + -*yl*] : an alkyl radical $C_{13}H_{27}$ derived from a tridecane; *esp* : the normal radical $CH_3(CH_2)_{11}CH_2$—

tri·dec·yl·ene \-sə,lēn\ *n* -s [ISV *tridecyl* + -*ene*] : any of numerous isomeric olefin hydrocarbons $C_{13}H_{26}$ including the tridecenes

¹**tri·dent** \'trīd°nt\ *n* -s [L *trident-*, *tridens*, fr. *tri-* + *dent-*, *dens* tooth — more at TOOTH] **1 a** (1) : a 3-pronged scepter or spear serving in classical mythology as the attribute or symbol of a sea god (2) : a representation of such a trident serving as a symbol of naval power or supremacy and as such often borne by Britannia or appearing on coins **b** : a 3-pronged spear used by ancient Roman retiarii **c** : a 3-pronged fish spear **2** : something felt to resemble a trident (as in shape, use, or emblematic significance)

²**trident** \"\ *adj* : having three teeth, processes, or points

tri·den·tal \(ˈ)trīˈdent°l\ *adj* **1** : of or relating to a trident : having the form of a trident **2** : divided into three points or prongs

tri·den·tate \-n,tāt\ *adj* [NL *tridentatus*, fr. *tri-* + -*dentatus* -dentate] : having three teeth, processes, or points ⟨a ~ leaf⟩

trident bat *n* : any of numerous African and Asiatic leaf-nosed bats of *Asellia* and related genera distinguished by a tripartite frontal expansion of the nose leaf

¹**tri·den·tine** \(ˈ)trīˈdent°n, -en,tēn, -en,tīn\ *adj, usu cap* [NL *tridentinus*, fr. *Tridentum* Trent, town in northeastern Italy + L -*inus* -ine] **1** : of or relating to Trent, Italy **2** : of or relating to or based on the Council of Trent

²**tridentine** \"\ *n* -s *usu cap* : a Roman Catholic who conforms to the Tridentine profession of faith resulting from the Council of Trent and issued in 1564

tri·dermic \(ˈ)trī+\ *adj* [ISV *tri-* + *dermic*] : derived from all three germ layers

tri·digitate \"+\ *adj* [ISV *tri-* + *digitate*] : TRIDACTYL; *often* : having three slender elongated lobes, processes, or leaflets

tri·dimensional \ˌtrī+\ *adj* [ISV *tri-* + *dimensional*] : of, relating to, or concerned with three dimensions ⟨~ space⟩ ⟨a ~ motion-picture technique⟩ — **tri·dimensionality** \"+\ *n*

Tri·di·one \trīˈdī,ōn\ *trademark* — used for trimethadione

tri·drachm \'trī,dram\ *n* [Gk *tridrachmon* three drachmas, fr. neut. of *tridrachmos* worth three drachmas, fr. *tri-* three + -*drachmos* (fr. *drachmē* drachma) — more at TRI-, DRAM] : an ancient Greek silver coin worth three drachmas

tri·duo \'tredə,wō\ *n* -s [It or Sp, fr. L *triduum*] : TRIDUUM

trid·u·um \'trijəwəm, -idyəw-\ *n* -s [L, space of three days, irreg. fr. *tri-* + *dies* day — more at DEITY] **1** : a term of three days; *specif* : three days of prayer that in the Roman Catholic Church usu. precedes a feast or some religiously important occasion (as first communion)

trid·y·mite \'tridə,mīt\ *n* -s [G *tridymit*, fr. Gk *tridymos* threefold (irreg. fr. *tri-* three + *didymos* twin) + G -*it* -ite; fr. its common occurrence in trillings — more at TRI-, DIDYM-] : a mineral SiO_2 that is a silica, differs from quartz in its usu. minute thin tabular orthorhombic forms of crystallization, and is found in cavities in trachyte and similar rocks (hardness 7, sp. gr. 2.28–2.33)

triecious *var of* TRIOECIOUS

tried \ˈtrīd\ *adj* [ME, fr. past part. of *trien* to try, test — more at TRY] **1** : found good, faithful, or trustworthy through experience or testing ⟨a ~ friend⟩ ⟨a ~ recipe⟩ ⟨did not forget that which was old and ~ —Edison Marshall⟩ **2** : subjected to trials or distress ⟨a kind but much-*tried* father⟩ **syn** see RELIABLE

tried and true *adj* : proved good, desirable, or feasible in actual practice : shown or known to be worthy ⟨a *tried and true* sales technique⟩ ⟨*tried and true* friends⟩

tri·ene \'trī,ēn, =ˈ=\ *n* -s [-*triene*] : a chemical compound containing three double bonds; *esp* : TRIOLEFIN

-tri·ene \ˌtrī,ēn, ˌ=ˈ=\ *n suffix* -s [*tri-* + -*ene*] : chemical compound containing three double bonds ⟨octa*triene*⟩

¹**tri·en·nial** \(ˈ)trīˈenēəl, -nyəl\ *adj* [L *triennium* period of three years (fr. *tri-* + -*ennium*, fr. *annus* year) + E -*al* — more at ANNUAL] **1** : continuing or having a term of three years ⟨a ~ reign⟩ ⟨a ~ parliament⟩ **2** : occurring, appearing, or being made, done, or acted upon every three years ⟨a ~ election⟩

²**triennial** \"\ *n* -s [L *triennium* + E -*al*, n. suffix] : a triennial event, appearance, or occasion: as **a** : a triennial episcopal visitation in the Church of England **b** : a third anniversary **c** : something (as a serial publication) that appears every three years

tri·en·nial·ly \-əlē, -li\ *adv* : every three years

tri·en·ni·um \-ēəm\ *n, pl* **trienniums** \-ēəmz\ *or* **trien·nia** \-ēə\ [L] : a period of three years

tri·ens \'trī,enz, 'trē,än(t)s\ *n, pl* **trien·tes** \trīˈen·,tēz, trēˈen·,täs\ [L, third part, triens; akin to L *tres* three — more at THREE] **1** : a bronze coin of ancient Rome equal to ⅓ as **2** : an ancient Byzantine gold coin equal to ⅓ solidus; *also* : any of several similar ancient coins (as of Spain)

tri·en·ta·lis \ˌtrī,en·ˈtaləs, -äl-,-äl-\ *n, cap* [NL, prob. fr. L *triantalis* vessel, receptacle, fr. *trientalis* having a third of a foot, fr. *trient-*, *triens* third part + -*alis* -al] : a genus of delicate Eurasian and No. American herbs (family Primulaceae) having a whorl of entire leaves and several white stellate flowers on slender peduncles followed by 5-valved capsules — see STARFLOWER

tri·er \'trī(ə)r, -īə\ *n* -s [ME *triour*, fr. *trien* to try + -*our* -or] **1** : a person who examines or studies a situation or problem and makes public a valid decision thereon: as **a** : one that tries judicially : JUDGE, JURY **b** *or* **tri·or** \"\ : a person appointed by an English court to try challenges of jurors **c** : a member of an English royal commission formerly allocating or referring petitions to the proper authority **d** : LORD TRIER **e** *usu cap* : one of a body of commissioners in the Church of England appointed in 1654 to examine those presented to benefices **f** *chiefly dial* : UMPIRE **2** : one that tests or is used in testing something: as **a** : INVESTIGATOR, EXAMINER **b** : a worker that tests some product (as pipe or milk) **c** : an implement usu. in the form of a sharpened tapering tube or probe for sampling material (as flour, seeds, or processed meats) for inspection or testing **d** : something that constitutes a test of the individual and esp. of his character or mettle ⟨a ~ of men's spirit⟩ **3** : one that tries: as **a** : one that separates a desired product from impurities : REFINER; *esp* : a renderer of fats **b** : one that makes an effort

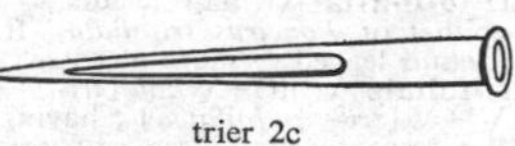
trier 2c

tri·er·ar·chy \'trīə,rärkē, -,räk-, -ki\ *n* -ES [Gk *triērarchia*, fr. *triērarchos* one who furnishes a trireme, commander of a trireme (fr. *triērēs* trireme — akin to Gk *treis* three — + -*archos* -arch) + -*ia* -y — more at THREE] : the ancient Athenian plan whereby individual citizens furnished and maintained triremes or other naval equipment as part of their civic duty

tries *pres 3d sing of* TRY, *pl of* TRY

tri·este \(ˈ)trēˈest *sometimes* trēˈestē *or* -,stā *or* -,stə\ *adj, usu cap* [fr. *Trieste*, Italy] : of or from the city of Trieste, Italy : of the kind or style prevalent in Trieste

tri-ester \(ˈ)trī+\ *n* [ISV *tri-* + *ester*] : a compound containing three ester groups

¹**tri·es·tine** \trēˈestən, -,stēn, -,stīn\ *or* **tri·es·tene** \-,stēn\ *adj, usu cap* [*Trieste*, seaport in northeastern Italy + E -*ine*] : TRIESTE

²**triestine** \"\ *or* **triestene** \"\ *n* -s *cap* : TRIESTINO

tri·es·ti·no \ˌtrē,eˈstē(,)nō\ *n, pl* **triestinos** \-nōz\ *or* **triesti·ni** \-nē\ *cap* [It, fr. *Trieste*, Italy + It -*ino* (fr. L -*inus* -ine)] : a native or resident of Trieste, Italy

¹**tri·e·ter·ic** \ˌtrīəˈterik\ *n* -s [L *trieterica*, fr. fem. of *trietericus* occurring every third year] : a trieteric festival esp. in honor of Bacchus

²**trieteric** \"\ *adj* [L *trietericus*, fr. Gk *trietērikos*, fr. *trietēris* triennial festival (fr. *tri-* three + *etos* year) + -*ikos* -ic — more at TRI-, WETHER] : occurring in alternate years — used of an ancient Greek rite

tri·ethanolamine \(ˌ)trī+\ *n* [ISV *tri-* + *ethanolamine*] : a high-boiling viscous soluble hygroscopic basic amino alcohol $(HOCH_2CH_2)_3N$ that is usu. made from ammonia and ethylene oxide, often contains considerable amounts of diethanolamine and ethanolamine, and is used chiefly as a corrosion inhibitor in aqueous solution and in making fatty acid soaps; tris-(2-hydroxyethyl)-amine — not used systematically

tri·ethiodide \"+\ *n* [*tri-* + *ethiodide*] : a compound with three units of ethyl iodide

tri·ethyl \(ˈ)trī+\ *adj* [ISV *tri-* + *ethyl*] : containing three ethyl groups in the molecule

tri·ethylamine \(ˌ)trī+\ *n* [ISV *triethyl* + *amine*] : a water-soluble flammable liquid tertiary amine $(C_2H_5)_3N$ that has a strong ammoniacal odor, is usu. made by reaction of ethyl chloride with ammonia, and is used chiefly in synthesis (as of quaternary ammonium compounds)

tri·ethylene glycol \(ˈ)trī+ . . . -\ *n* [ISV *tri-* + *ethylene*] : a high-boiling soluble hygroscopic liquid ether glycol $(-CH_2OCH_2CH_2OH)_2$ that resembles diethylene glycol, is made similarly, and is used chiefly as a solvent, as an air disinfectant, in the dehydration of gases, and in the form of esters as a plasticizer

triethylenemelamine \"+\ *n* [ISV *triethylene* + *melamine*] : a cytotoxic crystalline compound $C_3N_3(NC_2H_4)_3$ made from ethylenimine and cyanuric chloride and used chiefly as a textile finishing agent and in medicine like nitrogen mustard

tri·facial \(ˈ)trī+\ *adj or n* [ISV *tri-* + *facial*] : TRIGEMINAL

trifacial nerve *n* : TRIGEMINAL NERVE

tri·far·i·ous \(ˈ)trīˈfa(a)rēəs\ *adj* [L *trifarius* of three ways, fr. *trifariam* in three ways, fr. *tri-* + -*fariam* (akin to Skt -*dhā* in *dvidhā* in two ways) — more at BIFARIOUS] : facing three ways; *esp* : occurring in whorls of three ⟨~ leaves⟩

tri·fid \'trī,fid, -,fəd\ *adj* [L *trifidus* split into three, fr. *tri-* + -*fidus* (fr. stem of *findere* to split) — more at BITE] **1** : divided partway to the base into three lobes with narrow sinuses : TRIDENT **2** *of a cipher alphabet* : constructed by matching the letters of the alphabet with 3-unit equivalents of such a nature that exactly as many of them can be constructed as there are letters of the alphabet (as by using the twenty-seven 3-digit numbers made up of one or more of the numerals 1, 2, and 3 for a 27-letter alphabet) — compare FRACTIONAL SUBSTITUTION

tri·flagellate \(ˈ)trī+\ *adj* [*tri-* + *flagellate*] : having three flagella ⟨a ~ protozoan⟩

¹**tri·fle** \'trīfəl\ *n* -s [ME *trifle*, *trufle*, fr. OF *trufle*, *trufe* mockery, trickery] **1** *obs* : an idle, nonsensical, or fictitious tale **2** : something of very little value or importance: as **a** : a paltry trinket or knickknack : BAUBLE **b** : a creative work of no great or enduring value and often of purely topical interest **c** *obs* : a person of no account **d** : an insignificant or relatively small amount (as of money) ⟨cost only a ~⟩ **3 a** *chiefly Brit* : a dessert of sponge cake spread with jam or jelly, sprinkled with crumbled macaroons, soaked in wine, and served with custard and whipped cream **b** *chiefly Brit* : a dessert (as of soft fruit) served with custard and whipped cream **4 a** : a pewter of moderate hardness (as of 83 parts tin and 17 antimony) used esp. for small utensils **b trifles** *pl* : utensils made of trifle — **a trifle** *adv* : to some small degree : SLIGHTLY ⟨*a trifle* annoyed at the delay⟩

²**trifle** \"\ *vb* **trifled**; **trifled**; **trifling** \-f(ə)liŋ\ **trifles** [ME *triflen*, *truflen*, fr. OF *trufler*, *trufer* to mock, trick] *vi* **1 a** : to talk jestingly or mockingly with intent to delude : indulge in beguiling or misleading talk ⟨I fear he did but ~ and meant to wreck thee —Shak.⟩ **b** : to act without seriousness of purpose or mood or due respect : speak, write, carry on an affair, or act with levity or flippancy : be heedless, indifferent, or frivolous where concern or respect are desirable : PLAY, FLIRT — often followed by *with* ⟨~ with your health⟩ ⟨*trifled* with the boy's affections⟩ **2** : to waste time (as in idleness or foolish pastimes) : LOITER, DALLY ⟨*trifling* through the summer vacation⟩ **3** : to handle something idly : TOY, FIDGET — usu. followed by *with* ⟨*trifling* with the silverware at his place⟩ ~ *vt* **1** : to spend or waste in trifling or on trifles — usu. used with *away* ⟨~ away money⟩ **2** *obs* : to make or treat as trivial — **to be trifled with** : to be treated lightly or disrespectfully with impunity ⟨no man *to be trifled with*⟩ ⟨the text is not *to be trifled with*⟩ ⟨like a king not *to be trifled with* —Alfred Tennyson⟩

tri·fler \-f(ə)lə(r)\ *n* -s [ME, fr. *triflen* to trifle + -*er*] : one that trifles; *usu* : a shallow frivolous person : IDLER

1**tri·fling** \-f(ə)liŋ, -lēŋ\ *n* -s [ME, fr. gerund of *triflen* to trifle] : trifling conduct: as **a** : light talk : BADINAGE **b** : a wasting or waste of time : effort or activity without value

2**trifling** \"\ *adj* [fr. pres. part. of 2*trifle*] : lacking in significance or solid worth: as **a** : FRIVOLOUS ⟨~ talk⟩ **b** : TRIVIAL ⟨a ~ gift⟩ ⟨these ~ quarrels⟩ **c** *chiefly dial* : LAZY, SHIFTLESS ⟨a ~ fellow who never amounted to much⟩ **syn** see PETTY

tri·fling·ly *adv* : in a trifling manner

tri·fling·ness *n* -ES : the quality or state of being trifling

trifluor- or **trifluoro-** *comb form* [ISV *tri-* + *fluor-*] : containing three atoms of fluorine ⟨*trifluoro*acetic⟩ — in names of chemical compounds; compare FLUOR-

tri·fluoride \(ˈ)trī+\ *n* [*trifluor-* + *-ide*] : a binary compound containing three atoms of fluorine combined with an element or radical

1**tri·focal** \"+\ *adj* [*tri-* + *focal*] **1** : having three focal lengths **2** *of an eyeglass lens* : having one part that corrects for near vision, one for intermediate vision (as at arm's length), and one for distant vision

2**trifocal** \"\ *n* -s **1** : a trifocal glass or lens **2 trifocals** *pl* : eyeglasses with trifocal lenses — compare BIFOCAL 2

tri·fold \ˈtrīˌfōld\ *adj* [*tri-* + *-fold*] : THREEFOLD, TRIPLE

tri·fo·li·a·ta \(ˌ)trīˌfōlēˈädə, -ˈādə\ *n* -s [NL (specific epithet of *Poncirus trifoliata*), fr. *tri-* + L *foliata*, fem. of *foliatus* leaved — more at FOLIATE] : TRIFOLIATE ORANGE

tri·foliate \(ˈ)trī+\ *adj* [*tri-* + *foliate*] **1** or **tri·foliated** \"+\ [*tri-* + *foliated*] : having three leaves ⟨a ~ plant⟩ **2** : TRIFOLIOLATE — see TRIFOLIATE ORANGE

trifoliate orange *n* : a hardy deciduous Chinese orange (*Poncirus trifoliata*) that has trifoliolate leaves and small fragrant very acid fruits and is widely cultivated for ornament or hedging and esp. as a stock for budding various table oranges

tri·foliolate \(ˈ)trī+\ *adj* [ISV *tri-* + *foliolate*] : having three leaflets ⟨a ~ leaf⟩ — compare TRIFOLIATE; see LEAF illustration

tri·fo·li·o·sis \(ˌ)trīˌfōlēˈōsəs\ *n*, *pl* **trifolioses** [NL, fr. *Trifolium* + *-osis*] : CLOVER DISEASE

tri·fo·li·um \trīˈfōlēəm\ *n* [NL, fr. L, three-leaved grass, trefoil, fr. *tri-* + *folium* leaf — more at BLADE] **1** *cap* : a very large genus of herbs (family Leguminosae) comprising the common clovers, being widely distributed in temperate regions, and having digitately or pinnately trifoliolate leaves and red, purple, pink, or white chiefly globose heads of flowers with a persistent corolla followed by a membranous and indehiscent pod **2** -s : any plant of the genus *Trifolium*

tri·fo·ri·al \(ˈ)trīˈfōrēəl\ *adj* [ML *triforium* + E *-al*] : of or relating to a triforium

tri·fo·ri·um \trīˈfōrēəm\ *n*, *pl* **trifo·ria** \-ēə\ [ML, prob. fr. L *tri-* + *fores* door; fr. its often having three openings to each bay — more at DOOR] : a gallery or open space forming an upper story to the aisle of a church and typically constituting an arcaded story between the nave arches and clerestory

tri·form \(ˈ)trī+\ *also* **tri·formed** \"+\ *adj* [*triform* fr. L *triformis*, fr. *tri-* + *forma* form; *triformed* fr. L *triformis* + E *-ed* — more at FORM] : having a triple form, constitution, or character : having three manifestations

1**tri·fur·cate** \ˈtrīfərˌkāt, -kət; (ˈ)trīˈfərkət\ *also* **tri·fur·cat·ed** \-ˌkād·əd\ *adj* [L *trifurcus* (fr. *tri-* + *furca* fork) + E *-ate* or *-ate* + *-ed* — more at FORK] : having or divided into three branches or forks : TRICHOTOMOUS

2**tri·fur·cate** \ˈtrīfərˌkāt\ *vi* : to fork or divide into three branches — **tri·fur·ca·tion** \ˌtrī(ˌ)fərˈkāshən\ *n*

1**trig** \ˈtrig\ *adj*, *sometimes* **trigger**; *sometimes* **triggest** [ME, of Scand origin; akin to ON *tryggr* faithful, trustworthy, Norw & Dan *tryg* easy, confident, safe — more at TRUE] **1** *dial Brit* : TRUSTY, FAITHFUL **2** *chiefly Scot* : ACTIVE, BRISK, LIVELY **3 a** *chiefly Scot* : pleasingly neat, trim, and orderly; *sometimes* : CONCISE ⟨a ~ summary⟩ **b** : pleasingly trim and stylish in dress : SPRUCE, SMART ⟨a ~ secretary in tailored black⟩; *also* : marked by trimness and style ⟨a ~ little hat⟩ **4** : extremely or excessively precise : STIFF, PRIM, FORMAL **5** *dial chiefly Brit* : marked by sound strong condition : FIRM, VIGOROUS **6** *dial Brit* : fully filled : STUFFED, CRAMMED **syn** see NEAT

2**trig** \"\ *vt* **trigged; trigged; trigging; trigs 1 a** *dial chiefly Brit* : to put in order : TIDY — usu. used with *up* **b** : to dress in a trig manner : make smart or noticeable in costume — usu. used with *out* or *up* ⟨*trigged* out in her best for the meeting⟩ **2** *dial chiefly Brit* : to fill completely : STUFF, CRAM

3**trig** \"\ *vt* **trigged; trigged; trigging; trigs** [perh. of Scand origin; akin to ON *tryggja* to make firm, make trusty, *tryggr* faithful, trustworthy] *chiefly dial* : to make secure or firm : restrain from moving or shifting: as **a** : to stop or slow the motion of (a wheel) usu. with a wedge or other block **b** : to support with props or wedges

4**trig** \"\ *n* -s **1 a** *chiefly dial* : something (as a stone or block) used as a support in trigging **b** : a brick bedded to the proper height to hold a mason's line level in the center of a course **2** : a manually operated eccentric cam mounted near the end of a scale beam by means of which the beam can be held stationary at the lower limit of its motion

5**trig** \"\ *vi* **trigged; trigged; trigging; trigs** [origin unknown] *dial Eng* : TROT, RUN

6**trig** \"\ *n* -s [perh. modif. (influenced by 1*trigger*) of D *trek* pull, draft, tug, haul, fr. MD *treck* — more at TREK] **1** *dial Eng* : a line from which to start in a race or game **2** *dial Brit* : a small or shallow ditch or trench esp. when used to mark a boundary

7**trig** \"\ *vt* **trigged; trigged; trigging; trigs** *dial Brit* : to mark or bound with a trig ⟨*trigged* the ground with his heel⟩

8**trig** \"\ *n* -s [by shortening] : TRIGONOMETRY

trig *abbr* trigonometric; trigonometrical

tri·ga \ˈtrēgə, -rīgə\ *n*, *pl* **tri·gae** \-rēˌgī, -rīˌjē\ [LL, contr. of L *trijuga*, fem. of *trijugus* of a team of three, threefold, fr. *tri-* + *jugum* yoke, team — more at YOKE] **1** : an ancient Roman 3-horse chariot **2** : a 3-horse team (as for a triga)

trig·a·mist \ˈtrigəməst\ *n* -s : one who practices trigamy

trig·a·mous \-məs\ *adj* [Gk *trigamos* thrice married] **1** : being or relating to a trigamist or trigamy : living in trigamy **2** : having staminate, pistillate, and hermaphrodite flowers in the same head

trig·a·my \-mē\ *n* -ES [LL *trigamia*, fr. LGk, fr. Gk *trigamos* thrice married (fr. *tri-* three + *gamos* marriage) + *-ia* -y — more at BIGAMY] : the act of marrying or condition of being married three times; *esp* : the condition of having three spouses at one time

tri·gem·i·nal \(ˈ)trīˈjemənəl\ *adj* [NL *trigeminus* + E *-al*] **1** : of, relating to, or being the trigeminal nerve — see TRIGEMINAL NEURALGIA **2** [L *trigeminus* threefold, triple + E *-al*] : exhibiting or involving a pause after every third beat ⟨a ~ pulse⟩

trigeminal nerve *also* **tri·gem·i·nal** \"\ *n* -s : either of the fifth pair of cranial nerves that are mixed nerves and in man are the largest of the cranial nerves and that arise by a small motor and a larger sensory root which both emerge from the side of the pons with the sensory root bearing the Gasserian ganglion and dividing into ophthalmic, maxillary, and mandibular nerves and the motor root supplying fibers to the mandibular nerve and through this to the muscles of mastication

trigeminal neuralgia *n* : neuralgia involving one or more branches of the trigeminal nerve, being often extremely severe, and occurring in paroxysms

tri·gem·i·nus nerve \(ˈ)trīˈjemənəs-\ *or* **trigeminus** \⸗ˈ⸗⸗⸗\ *n*, *pl* **trigemini** [NL *trigeminus*, fr. L, threefold, triple, fr. *tri-* + *geminus* twofold, twin — more at GEMINATE] : TRIGEMINAL NERVE

tri·generic \ˌtrī+\ *adj* [*tri-* + *generic*] : of or relating to three types or kinds; *esp* : showing characteristics of or resulting from interbreeding members of three genera ⟨a ~ hybrid⟩

tri·ger process \trēˈzhā-\ *n*, *usu cap T* [after M. Triger, 19th cent. Fr. engineer] : a method of sinking through water-bearing ground in which a shaft is lined with tubbing and provided with an air lock so that work proceeds under air pressure

trigesimo-secundo \trīˈjesə(ˌ)mōsəˈkən(ˌ)dō\ *or* **tricesimo-secundo** \trīˈses-\ *n* -s [L *trigesimo secundo*, *tricesimo secundo*, abl. of *trigesimus secundus*, *tricesimus secundus* thirty-second, fr. *trigesimus*, *tricesimus* thirtieth (akin to L *triginta* thirty) + *secundus* second — more at TRICENARY, SECOND] : THIRTY-TWOMO — see BOOK tables

trigged *past of* TRIG

1**trig·ger** \ˈtrigə(r)\ *n* -s [3*trig* + *-er*] **1** *chiefly dial* : a catch or block used to hold the wheel of a carriage on a declivity **2** : a block used in shipbuilding to hold a boat on the ways — compare 2TRIGGER 1b

2**trigger** \"\ *n* -s [alter. (prob. influenced by 1*trigger*) of earlier *tricker*, fr. D *trekker*, fr. MD *trecker* something that pulls, fr. *trecken* to pull, haul — more at TREK] **1** : a piece (as a lever) connected with a catch or detent as a means of releasing it: as **a** (1) : the part of the action of a firearm moved by the finger to release the hammer or firing pin in firing (2) : a device that fires an explosive ⟨using an A-bomb as ~ for an H-bomb⟩ **b** : a lever pivoted on the ground ways with the upper end forced against the sliding ways by a hydraulic ram against the lower end in such a manner that the releasing of the trigger allows a ship to be launched by sliding down the ground ways **2** : something that acts like or is felt to resemble a mechanical trigger esp. in being a sensitive means of initiating a process or reaction that produces a relatively large effect; *esp* : something (as an external stimulus) that initiates a physiological or pathological process ⟨the odor of food may be a ~ for salivation⟩ **3** [by shortening] : TRIGGERFISH

3**trigger** \"\ *adj* **1** : of, relating to, or associated with a trigger ⟨~ covers⟩ **2** : functioning as or in a manner analogous to a trigger — see TRIGGER MECHANISM

4**trigger** \"\ *vb* -ED/-ING/-S *vt* **1** : to release by pulling a mechanical trigger ⟨~ a rifle⟩; *broadly* : to cause the explosion of ⟨~ a missile with a proximity fuse⟩ **2** : to initiate, actuate, or set off esp. by means of a comparatively weak impulse ⟨a single neutron may ~ an extensive chain reaction⟩ ⟨an indiscreet remark that ~*ed* off a long and costly strike⟩ ⟨the complex mechanism that ~*s* blood clotting⟩ ~ *vi* : to release a mechanical trigger

trigger area *or* **trigger zone** *n* : a sensitive area of the body stimulation of which gives rise to reaction elsewhere in the body; *esp* : a hypersensitive area that evokes referred pain elsewhere when stimulated ⟨an attack of trifacial neuralgia initiated by a chance brushing of the *trigger area* of the upper lip⟩ — compare TRIGGER MECHANISM

triggered *adj* : having a trigger — usu. used in combination ⟨a feather-*triggered* trap —*Report: Smithsonian Institution*⟩

trigger finger *n* **1** : a finger used in pressing the trigger of a firearm; *also* : the forefinger of the dominant hand **2** : a finger in which flexion or extension may be momentarily obstructed by spasm followed by a snapping into place

triggerfish \ˈ⸗⸗ˌ⸗\ *n* [2*trigger* + *fish*] : any of numerous deep-bodied fishes constituting *Balistes* and related genera of the family Balistidae, having an anterior dorsal fin with two or three stout erectile spines of which the second locks the larger first in position when both are erect, inhabiting chiefly warm seas, being often fantastically colored, and including edible forms and others that are distinctly poisonous — see QUEEN TRIGGERFISH

trigger guard *n* : a semicircular band of metal that encloses vertically the trigger of a firearm

trigger hair *n* : CNIDOCIL

trigger-happy \ˈ⸗⸗ˌ⸗⸗\ *adj* **1** : urgently desirous of shooting usu. to the point of overlooking or ignoring other factors involved : irresponsible in the use of firearms ⟨*trigger-happy* hunters determined to bag their limit⟩; *esp* : inclined to shoot before clearly identifying the target ⟨restraining *trigger-happy* sentries⟩ **2** : inclined to be irresponsible in matters that might lead to or precipitate war ⟨nations are not so *trigger-happy* as they once were —*New Republic*⟩; *broadly* : aggressively belligerent in attitude ⟨*trigger-happy* critics⟩

trig·ger·less \ˈtrigə(r)ləs\ *adj* : lacking a trigger

trig·ger·man \-mən, -ˌman, -ˌmaa(ə)n\ *n*, *pl* **triggermen 1** : a gunman who shoots the victim in a murder by a gang; *also* : a gangster's personal bodyguard **2** : a man who operates the trigger at the launching of a ship

trigger mechanism *n* : something (as a specific act or stimulus) that in interaction with the body constitutes a physiological trigger; *esp* : such a trigger by which an attack (as of disease or referred pain) is precipitated ⟨certain climatic and meteorological factors are required before the *trigger mechanism* setting off acute rheumatic fever can act —H.M.Margolis⟩ — compare TRIGGER AREA

trigger plant *n* : HAIR-TRIGGER FLOWER

trigger point *n* : a small trigger area

trigger pull *n* **1 a** *or* **trigger squeeze** : the pressure applied to a trigger to fire a firearm **b** : the weight in pounds that will cause complete movement of the trigger of a cocked firearm **2** : the mechanical linkage of trigger and other parts that directly fire the cartridge in a firearm; *also* : the movement of these parts

triggest *superlative of* TRIG

trigging *pres part of* TRIG

tri·gin·tal \trīˈjintᵊl\ *n* -s [ME *trigental*, fr. ML *trigentale*, *trigintale*, fr. L *triginta* thirty — more at TRICENARY] : TRENTAL

1**trig·lid** \ˈtrigləd\ *adj* [NL *Triglidae*] : of or relating to the Triglidae

2**triglid** \"\ *n* -s : a fish of the family Triglidae : GURNARD

trig·li·dae \-ləˌdē\ *n pl*, *cap* [NL, fr. *Trigla*, type genus (fr. LL, red mullet, fr. Gk *trigla*, *triglē*) + *-idae*; akin to Gk *strix* owl — more at STRIDENT] : a family of scorpaenid fishes comprising the gurnards

tri·glo·chin \trīˈglōkən\ *n*, *cap* [NL, fr. *tri-* + Gk *glōchin-*, *glōchis* projecting point; fr. the pronged look of the fruit — more at GLOSS] : a widely distributed genus of marsh herbs (family Juncaginaceae) having basal ligulate leaves, small spicate flowers, and tricarpellary fruits — see ARROW GRASS

trig loop *n* [4*trig*] : a steel loop in which the end of the weigh beam of a hand-operated grain scale moves up and down

1**tri·glot** \ˈtrīˌglät, *usu* -äd.+V\ *n* -s [ISV *tri-* + Gk *glōtta* language — more at -GLOT] : a book or edition in three languages

2**triglot** \"\ *adj* [ISV *tri-* + *-glot*] : containing, printed in, or treating three languages

trig·ly *adv* [1*trig* + *-ly*] : in a trig manner ⟨a ~ dressed woman⟩

tri·glyceride \(ˈ)trī+\ *n* [ISV *tri-* + *glycer-* + *-ide*] : a triester of glycerol with one, two, or three different acids ⟨the ~*s* in natural fats —T.P.Hilditch⟩

tri·glyph \ˈtrīˌglif\ *n* [L *triglyphus*, fr. Gk *triglyphos*, fr. *tri-* three + *glyphē* carved work — more at TRI-, GLYPH] : an architectural ornament in the frieze of the Doric order consisting of a slightly projecting rectangular tablet, having two vertical channels of V section and two corresponding chamfers or half channels on the vertical sides, and being repeated alternately with the metopes — see GLYPH

tri·glyphed \-ft\ *adj* : provided or decorated with triglyphs

tri·glyph·ic \(ˈ)trīˈglifik\ *adj* : consisting of, relating to, or adorned with triglyphs

trig·ness *n* -ES [1*trig* + *-ness*] : the quality or state of being trig ⟨the ~ of his quarters⟩

tri·gon \ˈtrīˌgän\ *n* -s [L *trigonum*, fr. Gk *trigōnon*, fr. neut. of *trigōnos* three-cornered, triangular, fr. *tri-* three + *-gōnos* -cornered, -angled (fr. *gōnia* corner, angle) — more at TRI-, -GON] **1** : TRIANGLE **2 a** : TRIPLICITY 1 **b** : TRINE 2 **3** : an ancient triangular harp of oriental and perhaps Assyrian origin having four strings and a shrill tone and often used for banquet music — called also *sabbeka*, *sackbut*, *sambuca* **4** : the cutting region of the crown of an upper molar that usu. comprises the anterior part and includes the protocone, paracone, and metacone

trigon- *or* **trigono-** *comb form* [L, fr. Gk *trigōn-*, *trigōno-*, fr. *trigōnos*] : triangular ⟨*Trigon*ella⟩ ⟨*trigono*type⟩

trigon *abbr* trigonometric; trigonometrical; trigonometry

1**trigona** *pl of* TRIGONUM

2**tri·go·na** \trīˈgōnə\ *n*, *cap* [NL, prob. fr. fem. of L *trigonus* triangular, fr. Gk *trigōnos*] : a genus of stingless honeybees of the Old and New World tropics

trig·o·nal \ˈtrigənᵊl\ *adj* [L *trigonalis*, fr. *trigonum* triangle] **1** : of, relating to, or characteristic of triangles : having three angles : TRIANGULAR **2** : of or relating to a trigon or the trigone **3** : of, relating to, or being the division of the hexagonal crystal system or the forms belonging to it characterized by a vertical axis of threefold symmetry — see TRIGONAL SYSTEM — **trig·o·nal·ly** \-nəlē\ *adv*

trigonal system *n* : a crystal system that is characterized by three equal and equally inclined axes and that is commonly held to be a division of the hexagonal system

trigonal trapezohedron *n* : TRAPEZOHEDRON d

trigonal trisoctahedron *n* : a trisoctahedron whose faces are triangles

trigonal tristetrahedron *n* : a tristetrahedron whose faces are triangles

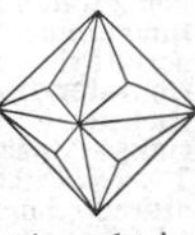

trigonal trisoctahedron

tri·gone \ˈtrīˌgōn\ *n* -s [F, lit., triangle, fr. L *trigonum*] **1** *also* **tri·gon** \-ˌgän\ : a triangular body part; *specif* : a smooth triangular area on the inner surface of the bladder limited by the apertures of the ureters and urethra **2** : a thickening of plant cell walls that occurs when three or more cells adjoin

trig·o·nel·la \ˌtrigəˈnelə\ *n*, *cap* [NL, fr. L *trigonum* triangle + *-ella* — more at TRIGON] : a genus of widely distributed herbs (family Leguminosae) having pinnately trifoliolate leaves, capitate or racemose flowers, and linear pods — see FENUGREEK

trig·o·nel·line \-eˌlēn, -elən\ *n* -s [ISV *trigonell-* (fr. NL *Trigonella*) + *-ine*] : a crystalline alkaloid $CH_3N^+C_5H_4COO^-$ obtained esp. from the seeds of fenugreek, from coffee beans and other seeds, and from sea urchins and jellyfish and found in the urine (as after ingestion of nicotinic acid) : the *N*-methyl-betaine of nicotinic acid

tri·go·neu·tic \ˌtrīgəˈn(y)üd·ik\ *adj* [*tri-* + Gk *goneuein* to beget (akin to Gk *gonos* offspring) + E *-tic* (as in *genetic*) — more at GON-] : having three broods annually

tri·go·nia \trīˈgōnēə\ *n*, *cap* [NL, fr. L *trigonus* triangular (fr. Gk *trigōnos*) + NL *-ia*; fr. the shells suggesting the form of a triangle — more at TRIGON] **1** : a genus of pearly-shelled bivalve mollusks (suborder Arcacea) including many extinct forms which characterize the Mesozoic rocks and a few living forms which survive on the coast of Australia **2** [NL; fr. the often triangular shape of the fruit] : a genus (the type of the family Trigoniaceae) of chiefly climbing tropical American shrubs

tri·go·ni·a·ce·ae \⸗ˌ⸗⸗ˈāsēˌē\ *n pl*, *cap* [NL, fr. *Trigonia*, type genus + *-aceae*] : a family of tropical American shrubs or woody vines (order Geraniales) with irregular often spurred flowers and 2-celled capsular fruit — **tri·go·ni·a·ceous** \⸗ˌ⸗⸗ˈāshəs\ *adj*

tri·go·nid \ˈtrīgəˌnid\ *n* -s [1*trigon* + *-id*] : the part of a lower molar corresponding to the trigon of an upper molar

trigo·nite \ˈtrīgəˌnīt, ˈtrig-\ *n* -s [G *trigonit*, fr. *trigon-* + *-it* -ite] : a mineral $MnPb_3H(AsO_3)_3$ consisting of an acid lead manganese arsenite and occurring in yellow to brown triangular wedge-shaped crystals (hardness 2–3)

tri·go·ni·tis \ˌtrīgəˈnīd·əs\ *n* -ES [NL, fr. *trigonum* trigone + *-itis*] : inflammation of the trigone of the bladder

trigono- — see TRIGON-

trigo·no·ceph·a·lous \ˌtrigənōˈsefələs, (ˌ)trīˌgōnə's-\ *or* **trigo·no·ce·phal·ic** \-ˌsəˈfalik\ *adj* [ISV *trigon-* + *-cephalous* or *-cephalic*] : having a somewhat triangular flat head — **trigo·no·ceph·a·ly** \ˌtrigənōˈsefəlē, (ˌ)trīˌgōnə's-\ *n* -ES

trig·o·noc·er·ous \ˌtrigəˈnäsərəs\ *adj* [*trigon-* + *cer-* (fr. Gk *keras* horn) + *-ous* — more at CEREBRAL] : having horns of triangular cross section ⟨some goats are ~⟩

trigono·dodecahedron \ˌtrigənō, (ˌ)trīˌgōnə+\ *n* [ISV *trigon-* + *dodecahedron*] : a trigonal tristetrahedron : the hemihedral form of the isometric trapezohedron

trig·o·nom·e·ter \ˌtrigəˈnämәd·ə(r)\ *n* -s [prob. fr. (assumed) NL *trigonometres*, fr. NL *trigonometria*, after such pairs as L *geometria* geometry: *geometres* geometer] : one skilled in trigonometry or trigonometric surveying

trig·o·no·met·ric \ˌtrigənəˈme·trik, -rēk\ *also* **trig·o·no·met·ri·cal** \-trəkəl, -rēk-\ *adj* [*trigonometric* prob. fr. (assumed) NL *trigonometricus*, fr. NL *trigonometria* trigonometry + L *-icus* -ic; *trigonometrical* prob. fr. (assumed) NL *trigonometricus* + E *-al*] : of, relating to, or involving trigonometry : performed by the rules of trigonometry — **trig·o·no·met·ri·cal·ly** \-rək(ə)lē, -rēk-, -li\ *adv*

trigonometric curve *n* : a curve whose equation involves trigonometric functions

trigonometric equation *n* : an equation that involves trigonometric functions

trigonometric function *also* **trigonometric ratio** *n* **1** : a function (as the sine, cosine, tangent, cotangent, secant, or cosecant) of an arc or angle most simply expressed in terms of the ratios of pairs of sides of a right-angled triangle — called also *circular function* **2** : the inverse (as the arc sine, arc cosine, arc tangent, arc cotangent, arc secant, or arc cosecant) of a trigonometric function

trigonometric identity *n* : an identity involving or based on trigonometric functions

trigonometric parallax *n* : the direct measurement of the parallax or distance of a celestial body from a base line of known length (as the earth's radius or the radius of its orbit) and the angles at the ends of the base line giving reliable results for stars up to distances of about 100 light-years

trigonometric series *n* : a mathematical series whose terms proceed by sines and cosines of integral multiples of a variable angle

trigonometric solution *n* : solution (as of a cubic equation) in terms of or by means of trigonometric functions

trig·o·nom·e·try \ˌtrigəˈnämə·trē, -ri\ *n* -ES *often attrib* [NL *trigonometria*, fr. *trigon-* + *-metria* -metry] : a branch of mathematics dealing with the relations holding among the sides and angles of triangles and among closely related magnitudes and esp. with methods of deducing from given parts other required parts

tri·go·non \trīˈgōˌnän\ *n* -s [Gk *trigōnon* triangle — more at TRIGON] : TRIGON 3

trigo·no·type \ˈtrigənəˌtīp, trīˈgōnə-\ *n* [ISV *trigon-* + *type*] : TRAPEZOHEDRON d

trig·o·nous \ˈtrigənəs\ *adj* [L *trigonus*, fr. Gk *trigōnos* — more at TRIGON] : having three angles or corners : triangular in cross section

trigons *pl of* TRIGON

tri·go·num \trīˈgōnəm\ *n*, *pl* **trigonums** \-nəmz\ *or* **trigo·na** \-nə\ [NL, fr. L, triangle — more at TRIGON] : TRIGONE: as **a** *or* **trigonum men·ta·le** \-ˌmenˈtā(ˌ)lē, -tā-, -ˈtä-\ [NL, trigone of the chin] : a somewhat triangular enlargement of the anteromedian part of the human mandible forming the bony support of the chin **b** *or* **trigonum ha·ben·u·lae** \-həˈbenyə(ˌ)lē, -ˌlī\ : a triangular area in the optic thalamus

tri·gram \ˈtrīˌgram, -aa(ə)m\ *n* [*tri-* + *-gram*] **1 a** : a three-letter inscription **b** : TRIGRAPH 2 **2 a** : a figure made by three lines or elements **b** : one of the eight possible combinations of three whole or broken lines used in Chinese and Japanese divination and symbolism

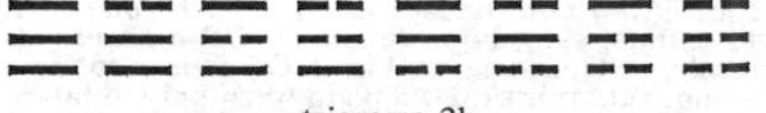

trigrams 2b

tri·gram·mat·ic \ˌtrīgrəˈmad·ik\ *adj* [Gk *trigrammatos* of three letters (fr. *tri-* three + *grammat-*, *gramma* letter) + E *-ic* — more at TRI-, GRAM] : of, relating to, or consisting of a trigram

tri·graph \ˈtrīˌgraf, -aa(ə)f, -aif, -áf\ *n* [*tri-* + *-graph*] **1** : three letters spelling a single consonant, vowel, or diphthong ⟨*sch* of *schism*, *cch* of *bacchic*, *pph* of *sapphic*, *tth* of *Matthew*, and *eau* of *beau* are ~*s*⟩ **2** : a cluster of three successive letters ⟨THE is a high frequency ~⟩

tri·graph·ic \(ˈ)trīˈgrafik\ *adj* **1** : of, relating to, or consisting of a trigraph ⟨a ~ unit⟩ **2** : proceeding (as in encipherment) by groups of three letters at a time ⟨~ substitution⟩

trigs *pres 3d sing of* TRIG, *pl of* TRIG

tri·gyn·ia \trīˈjinēə, -ˈgi-\ *n pl*, *cap* [NL, fr. *tri-* + *-gynia*] *in former classifications* : an order of plants having flowers with three pistils — **tri·gyn·ian** \(ˈ)⸗ˈ⸗⸗ən\ *adj*

tri·halide \(ˈ)trī+\ *n* [*tri-* + *hal-* + *-ide*] : a binary compound containing three atoms of halogen combined with an element or radical

tri·he·dral \(ˈ)trīˈhēdrəl\ *adj* [*tri-* + *-hedral*] **1** : having three faces **2** : of or relating to a trihedral angle — **trihedral** *n*

trihedral angle *n* : a polyhedral angle with three faces

tri·he·dron \trīˈhēdrən\ *n*, *pl* **trihedrons** \-drənz\ *or* **trihedra** \-drə\ [NL, fr. *tri-* + *-hedron*] : a figure formed by three planes meeting in a point

tri·hybrid \(ˈ)trī+\ *n* [*tri-* + *hybrid*] **1 :** an individual or strain heterozygous for three factors and esp. for three recessive genes **2 :** an individual or strain resulting from the interbreeding of three distinct kinds of individuals ⟨held the Australian aborigines to be ~*s* formed by admixture of Negrito and two distinct Australoid elements⟩ — **tri·hybrid·ism** \ˈ"+\ *n*

tri·hydrate \ˈ"+\ *n* [*tri-* + *hydrate*] **:** a chemical compound with three molecules of water

tri·hydrated \ˈ"+\ *adj* [*tri-* + *hydrated*] **:** combined with three molecules of water

tri·hy·dric \(ˈ)trī¦hīdrik\ *adj* [ISV *tri-* + *-hydric;* prob. orig. formed as F *trihydrique*] **1** *archaic* **:** containing three atoms of acid hydrogen **2 :** TRIHYDROXY — used esp. of alcohols and phenols

tri·hy·droxy \ˌtrī¸hī¦dräksē\ *adj* [ISV *trihydroxy-*] **:** containing three hydroxyl groups in the molecule

trihydroxy- *comb form* [ISV *tri-* + *hydroxy-*] **:** containing three hydroxyl groups — in names of chemical compounds ⟨*trihydroxy*benzoic acid⟩

tri·iodide \(ˈ)trī+\ *n* [ISV *tri-* + *iod-* + *-ide*] **:** a binary compound containing three atoms of iodine combined with an element or radical

tri·iodothyronine \ˈ"+\ *n* [*tri-* + *iod-* + *thyronine*] **:** a crystalline iodine-containing phenolic amino acid $C_{15}H_{12}I_3NO_4$ that occurs in the levorotatory L-form in small amounts with thyroxine but is usu. made synthetically, is believed to be formed from thyroxine by loss of one iodine atom per molecule, has a more rapid and potent but briefer physiological action than thyroxine, and is used esp. in the form of its soluble sodium salt in the treatment of hypothyroidism and metabolic insufficiency

tri·ju·gate \ˈtrījəˌgāt; (ˈ)trī¦jüg·ət, -ˌgāt\ *adj* [ISV *trijug-* (fr. L *trijugus* threefold) + *-ate* — more at TRIGA] **:** having three pairs of leaflets ⟨a ~ leaf⟩

tri·kaya \trəˈkī(y)ə, -kāyə\ *n* -s [Skt *trikāya* three bodies, fr. *tri* three + *kāya* body, mass (akin to Skt *cinoti* he heaps up) — more at THREE, POET] **:** a Mahayana Buddhist doctrine of the three bodies of the Buddha — see DHARMAKAYA, NIRMANAKAYA, SAMBHOGAKAYA

¹trike \ˈtrīk\ *n* -s [by shortening & alter.] **:** TRICYCLE

²trike \ˈ"\ *vi* -ED/-ING/-S **:** TRICYCLE

tri·ke·rion \trēˈkēryȯn\ *or* **tri·ce·ri·on** \trīˈsirēˌän\ *n, pl* **trike·ria** \-yä\ *or* **trice·ria** \-ēä\ [MGk *trikērion*, fr. Gk *tri-* three + MGk *kērion* wax candle, fr. Gk, honeycomb, fr. *kēros* wax — more at TRI-, CEREUS] **:** a three-branched candlestick symbolizing the Trinity and used in the Eastern Orthodox Church by bishops (as in pronouncing a benediction)

triketo- *comb form* [ISV *tri-* + *ket-*] **:** containing three ketone groups — in names of chemical compounds ⟨*triketo*cholanic acid⟩; compare KET-

tri·ketone \(ˈ)trī+\ *n* [*tri-* + *ketone*] **:** a chemical compound containing three ketonic carbonyl groups

tri·labiate \ˈ"+\ *adj* [*tri-* + *labiate*] **:** having three lips ⟨a ~ corolla on a flower⟩

tri·lacunar \¦trī +\ *adj* [*tri-* + *lacunar*] **:** having three leaf gaps — compare MULTILACUNAR, UNILACUNAR

tri·laminar \(ˈ)trī+\ *also* **tri·laminate** \ˈ"+\ *adj* [*tri-* + *laminar* or *laminate*] **:** having or built up of three layers

¹tri·lateral \ˈ"+\ *adj* [L *trilaterus* (fr. *tri-* + *later-, latus* side) + E *-al* — more at LATERAL] **1 :** having three physical or material sides ⟨a ~ figure⟩ **2 :** involving three interests often to the disadvantage of other interested parties ⟨a ~ agreement⟩ ⟨~ oligopoly in the market place —G.L.Bach⟩ — **tri·laterality** \(¦)trī+\ *n* — **tri·laterally** \(ˈ)trī+\ *adv*

²trilateral \ˈ"\ *n* **:** a figure having three sides **:** TRIANGLE

tri·lat·er·a·tion \(ˌ)=ˌlad·əˈrāshən\ *n* -s [*trilateral* + *-ation*] **:** the measurement of the lengths of the three sides of a series of touching or overlapping triangles on the earth's surface for the determination of the relative position of points by geometrical means (as in geodesy, map making, and surveying) — compare TRIANGULATION

tri·laurin \(ˈ)trī+\ *n* [ISV *tri-* + *laurin*] **:** the crystalline triglyceride $C_3H_5(OOCC_{11}H_{23})_3$ of lauric acid reported in laurel leaves and the fats of various seeds **:** glycerol tri-laurate

tril·by \ˈtrilbē, -bi\ *n* -ES [fr. *Trilby*, heroine who is an artist's model whose feet are objects of admiration in the novel *Trilby* (1894) by George du Maurier †1896 Brit. artist and novelist] **1 :** FOOT — usu. used in pl. **2** *also* **trilby hat** [so called fr. the fact that it was worn in the original London stage version (1895) of the novel *Trilby*] *chiefly Brit* **:** a soft felt hat with indented crown

tri·lem·ma \trīˈlemə\ *n* -s [*tri-* + *-lemma* (as in *dilemma*)] **1 :** an argument analogous to a dilemma but presenting three instead of two alternatives in the premises **2 :** a state of things in which it is difficult to determine which one of three courses to pursue

tri·lete \ˈtrīˌlēt\ *adj* [NL *Triletes*, genus of spores with trigonous apertures, perh. irreg. fr. *tri-* + L *latus* side] **:** TRIGONOUS

tri·linear \(ˈ)trī+\ *adj* [*tri-* + *linear*] **:** of, relating to, or included by three lines ⟨a ~ chart⟩

tri·lineate \ˈ"+\ *also* **tri·lineated** \ˈ"+\ *adj* [*tri-* + *lineate, lineated*] **:** marked with three usu. longitudinal streaks (as of color)

tri·lingual \ˈ"+\ *adj* [*tri-* + *lingual*] **:** consisting of, having, or expressed in three languages ⟨a ~ dictionary⟩; *also* **:** familiar with or able to use three languages ⟨~ students⟩ — **tri·lin·gual·ly** \-əlē, -li\ *adv*

trili·sa \ˈtriləsə, ˈtrīl-\ *n, cap* [NL, anagram of *Liatris*] **:** a genus of herbs (family Compositae) of the southern U.S. distinguished from *Liatris* by the corymbose panicles of flower heads and involucral bracts of two or three series only — see WILD VANILLA

¹tri·literal \(ˈ)trī+\ *adj* [*tri-* + *literal*] **:** consisting of three letters and esp. of three consonants ⟨~ roots in Semitic languages⟩ — **tri·literalism** \ˈ"+\ *n* — **tri·literally** \ˈ"+\ *adv*

²triliteral \ˈ"\ *n* **:** a root or word that is triliteral

tri·literality \(¦)trī+\ *also* **tri·literalness** \(ˈ)trī+\ *n* **:** the quality or state of being triliteral

tri·lithon \(ˈ)trī¦liˌthän, ˈtriləˌth-\ *also* **tri·lith** \ˈtrīˌlith\ *n* -s [NL *trilithon*, fr. Gk, neut. of *trilithos* of three stones, fr. *tri-* three + *lithos* stone — more at TRI-] **:** an ancient stone monument consisting of two upright megaliths carrying a third as a lintel

¹trill \ˈtril\ *vb* -ED/-ING/-S [ME *trillen*, prob. of Scand origin; akin to Sw & Norw *trilla* to roll, Dan *trille;* akin to MD *trillen* to tremble, vibrate, MLG *triseln* to roll, reel, MHG *trollen* to run with short steps, OE *treppan* to tread — more at TRAP] *vi* **1 :** TURN, TWIRL, ROLL, REVOLVE **2 :** to flow in a small stream or in drops rapidly succeeding each other **:** TRICKLE **~** *vt* **:** to cause to flow in a small stream

²trill \ˈ"\ *also* **thrill** \ˈthril\ *n* -s [*trill* fr. It *trillo*, fr. *trillare; thrill* alter. (influenced by ²*thrill*) of *trill*] **1 a :** the alternation of two musical tones a scale degree apart — called also *shake* **b :** VIBRATO **c :** a rapid reiteration of the same tone esp. on a percussion instrument **2 :** a sound felt to resemble a musical trill **:** WARBLE ⟨the liquid ~ of a thrush⟩ **3 a :** the rapid vibration of one speech organ against another (as of the tip of the tongue against the teethridge, the uvula against the back of the tongue, or the lips against each other) **b :** a speech sound so made **c :** a letter or word pronounced with a trill

³trill \ˈ"\ *vb* -ED/-ING/-S [It *trillare*, prob. fr. D *trillen* to tremble, vibrate, fr. MD] *vt* **:** to impart the quality of a trill to **:** utter as or with a trill ⟨~ the *r*⟩; *also* **:** to vibrate, shake, or move to and fro so as to cause a trill **~** *vi* **:** to utter a trill **:** play or sing with a trill **:** have a trembling sound **:** QUAVER

tril·la·do \trəˈyä(ˌ)dō, -ä(ˌ)thō\ *n* -s [AmerSp, fr. Sp, past part. of *trillar* to thresh, prob. fr. *trillo* threshing machine, fr. L *tribulum* threshing board — more at TRIBULATION] **:** market coffee prepared by drying the beans in the sun

trill·er \ˈtrilə(r)\ *n* -s [³*trill* + *-er*] **:** one that trills; *esp* **:** any of several cuckoo shrikes (genus *Lalage*) of Australia and the Pacific islands that are commonly largely black and white and are noted for their trilling calls — called also *caterpillar-eater*

tril·li·a·ce·ae \ˌtrilēˈāsēˌē\ *n pl, cap* [NL, fr. *Trillium*, type genus + *-aceae*] *in some classifications* **:** a small family of herbs (order Liliales) that have perennial rootstocks, entire leaves variously arranged, and often showy flowers of 3 petals and 3 sepals with 6 stamens followed by a globose or 3-lobed berry, comprise the trilliums and closely related plants, and are usu. included in the family Liliaceae

tril·ling \ˈtriliŋ, -lēŋ\ *n* -s [prob. fr. *tri-* + *-ling*] **:** a compound crystal consisting of three individuals — compare TWIN

¹tril·lion \ˈtrilyən, ˈtriy-\ *n* -s [F, fr. *tri-* + *-illion* (as in *million*) — more at MILLION] **1** — see NUMBER table **2 :** a very large number

²trillion \ˈ"\ *adj* **:** being a trillion in number

¹tril·lionth \-n(t)th\ *adj* **1 :** being number one trillion in a countable series — see NUMBER table **2 :** being one of a trillion equal parts into which anything is divisible

²trillionth \ˈ"\ *n, pl* **trillionths** \-yən(t)s, -yən(t)ths\ **1 :** number one trillion in a countable series **2 :** the quotient of a unit divided by one trillion **:** one of a trillion equal parts of anything **3 :** a minute part

tril·li·um \ˈtrilēəm\ *n* [NL, fr. *tri-* + *-illium* (as in *cillium, verticillium*)] **1 a** *cap* **:** a genus of chiefly No. American herbs (family Liliaceae) having short rootstocks and an erect stem bearing a whorl of three leaves and a large solitary flower at the summit with a corolla that is white, pink, purple, yellow, or greenish and is followed by a many-seeded berry — see WAKE-ROBIN **b** -s **:** any plant of the genus *Trillium* **2** -s **:** the dried rhizome of purple trillium formerly used as an astringent and tonic

trillium 1b

trillium family *n* **:** LILIACEAE, TRILLIACEAE

tril·lo \ˈtri(ˌ)lō, ˈtrē(-\ *n, pl* **trilli** \-lē\ *or* **trilloes** [It] **1 :** TRILL 1a **2 :** TREMOLO

trills *pl of* TRILL, *pres 3d sing of* TRILL

tri·lobate \(ˌ)trī-+\ *or* **tri·lobated** \ˈ"+\ *or* **tri·lobed** \ˈ"+\ *adj* [*tri-* + *lobate, lobated*, or *lobed*] **:** having or divided into three lobes ⟨a ~ leaf⟩

tri·lo·ba·tion \ˌtrīləˈbāshən\ *n* **:** the condition of being trilobate

tri·lobe \ˈtrī+ˌ-\ *n* [*tri-* + *lobe*] **:** something having or distinguished by three lobes; *esp* **:** a trilobate gear wheel

tri·lo·bi·ta \ˌtrīləˈbīd·ə\ *n pl, cap* [NL, fr. *Trilobites*] **:** a division of Arthropoda that is treated as a subclass of Crustacea or made a separate class and comprises the trilobites

tri·lo·bite \ˈtrīləˌbīt\ *n* -s [NL *Trilobites* division of Arthropoda comprising the trilobites, fr. Gk *trilobos* three-lobed (fr. *tri-* three + *lobos* lobe) + L *-ites* -ite — more at TRI-, SLEEP] **:** any of numerous extinct Paleozoic marine arthropods that constitute the group Trilobita, have delicate biramous appendages and the segments of the body divided by furrows on the dorsal surface into a median axis and two lateral pleura, are usu. of a flattened oval form, and besides the longitudinal lobes present the three transverse body regions of head, thorax, and pygidium of which the first is covered by a continuous shield, the second consists of a variable number of free segments, and the last of a number of coalescent segments — **tri·lo·bit·ic** \¦=¦bid·ik\ *adj*

trilobite larva *n* **:** a 3-lobed larva that is a developmental form of limulus and resembles a trilobite

tri·locular \(ˈ)trī+\ *or* **tri·loculate** \ˈ"+\ *adj* [ISV *tri-* + *locular*] **:** having three cells or cavities

tril·o·gy \ˈtriləjē, -ji\ *n* -ES [Gk *trilogia*, fr. *tri-* + *-logia* -logy] **1 :** a series of three dramas or sometimes three literary or musical compositions that although each is in one sense complete have a close mutual relation and form one theme or develop aspects of one basic concept **2 :** a group of three connected classical Greek tragedies played serially (as at the festival of Dionysus) **3 :** a group of three related things, topics, or sayings **:** TRIAD

tri·loph·odon \trīˈläfəˌdän\ [NL, fr. *tri-* + *loph-* + *-odon*] *syn of* GOMPHOTHERIUM

tri·loph·odont \-nt\ *adj* [ISV *tri-* + *loph-* + *-odont*] **:** having or being teeth with three crests

¹trim \ˈtrim\ *vb* **trimmed; trimmed; trimming; trims** [fr. (assumed) ME *trimen, trymen*, fr. OE *trymian, trymman* to strengthen, confirm, arrange, fr. *trum* strong, firm, secure; akin to Gk *drymos* forest, Skt *druma* tree, *dāruṇa* hard, *dāru* wood — more at TREE] *vt* **1 a** (1) *archaic* **:** to build or repair (a ship) and provide with fittings and supplies for sailing (2) *obs* **:** to furnish or prepare for use ⟨he had not so *trimm'd* and dressed his land as we this garden —Shak.⟩; *also* **:** to restore to a usable condition **b :** to prepare (as a lamp) for most efficient burning **2 a :** to embellish with or as if with ribbons, lace, or ornaments **:** DECORATE, ADORN ⟨these rich fabrics are often extravagantly *trimmed* with flowers —*Women's Wear Daily*⟩ ⟨a handsome edifice of . . . colonial sand-mold brick, *trimmed* with marble —*Amer. Guide Series: Minn.*⟩ **b :** to arrange a display of goods in (a shop window) **3 a** (1) **:** to administer a beating to **:** CHASTISE, THRASH (2) **:** to defeat esp. resoundingly ⟨*trimmed* him at chess⟩ **b :** DEFRAUD, CHEAT, SWINDLE **4 a** (1) **:** to make trim, neat, regular, or less bulky by or as if by cutting, shortening, or clipping ⟨has his hair *trimmed* before it needs cutting —H.W. Hayes⟩ ⟨~ a page of a book⟩ (2) **:** to prepare (an animal) for exhibition esp. by ordering and styling the coat **b :** to reduce by removing excess or extraneous matter **:** cut away matter to lessen the size of ⟨~s his 190 pounds down to a sinewy 170 by race time —Bill Wolf⟩ ⟨~ the hides of those parts which cannot be made into usable leather —*advt*⟩ ⟨*trimmed* of its branches, a ramrod-backed tree whisks out of the logging camp by rail —*Monsanto Mag.*⟩ ⟨~ the budget⟩ **c :** to take off or away by or as if by cutting, clipping, or lopping ⟨*trimmed* thousands from federal payrolls —*Grit*⟩ ⟨~ excess fat from meat —*Better Homes & Gardens*⟩ ⟨*trimmed* out description that intervenes between two consecutive actions —K.A.Spaulding⟩ **5 a** (1) **:** to cause (as a ship) to assume a desirable position in the water by the arrangement of ballast, cargo, or passengers ⟨the captain made us ~ the boat, and we got her to lie a little more evenly —R.L.Stevenson⟩ (2) **:** to adjust for horizontal movement or for motion upward or downward ⟨*trimming* the blimp satisfactorily⟩ ⟨*trimmed* to fly at a lift coefficient corresponding to a minimum glide angle —*Aero Digest*⟩ ⟨if the boat is properly *trimmed*, she submerges on a practically even keel —Kendall Banning⟩ **b :** to adjust (as a sail) to a desired position ⟨~ cargo⟩ **~** *vi* **1 a :** to maintain a middle position between opposing parties so as to appear to be neutral or to favor each equally **b :** to change one's views so as to correspond to the momentarily popular or winning opinion ⟨if . . . he begins to ~ or equivocate, then he won't be for us and we won't be for him —*Amer. Mercury*⟩ **2 :** to assume or cause a boat or ship to assume a desired position in the water ⟨the art of navigation lies in *trimming* to the storm —J.A.Froude⟩ **syn** see STABILIZE — **trim one's sails :** to adjust oneself or one's actions or expenditures to prevailing conditions ⟨had to *trim his sails* in accordance with the prevalent faith —C.H.Sykes⟩

²trim \ˈ"\ *adj* **trimmer; trimmest 1** *obs* **:** EXCELLENT, FINE; *also* **:** PLEASANT, GAY **2** *archaic* **:** suitably adjusted, equipped, or prepared for service or use **:** in good order **:** well trimmed **3 :** exhibiting neatness, good order, or compactness of line or structure **:** free from anything unkempt, disordered, or extraneous **:** having clean lines or proper proportion **:** being in good order or repair ⟨~, new bungalows —*Amer. Guide Series: Ark.*⟩ ⟨the gravel paths are squared and ~ —Emily Hahn⟩ ⟨not fat, like grass-fed cattle, but ~ and supple, like deer —John Burroughs⟩ **syn** see NEAT

³trim \ˈ"\ *adv* **:** TRIMLY — used chiefly in combination ⟨the *trim*-cut forest vistas —W.M.Thackeray⟩

⁴trim \ˈ"\ *n* -s **1 a :** the state of readiness to sail of a ship or its cargo, ballast, engines, or rigging **b** (1) **:** the condition or state of readiness for action or use of a person or thing **:** FITNESS ⟨weighing 160 pounds, the writer is in fine physical ~ —*Current Biog.*⟩; *esp* **:** a suitable or excellent condition for a particular task or for general action ⟨working himself into physical ~ to stand the strain —S.H.Adams⟩ ⟨get a strange system called democracy into working ~ —Elspeth Huxley⟩ ⟨cars in full road ~ —R.F.Baxter⟩ (2) **:** the condition of a person with respect to personal qualities **:** CHARACTER, DISPOSITION **2 a :** clothing, dress, or appearance esp. when rich or ornate **b :** material used as adornment, ornament, or trimming or fully or partly ornamental fixtures ⟨sentences full of rich ~ . . . that a lesser man might forbear to use —Rex Lardner⟩: as (1) **:** TRIMMING 2 (2) **:** the lighter woodwork or metal in the finish of a building (as a molded architrave around an opening to protect the plastering); *also* **:** an ornamental or protective framing (as of wood, metal, or stone) around an opening or at a corner or eave ⟨a double-winged massive building of light brown brick with red stone ~ —*Amer. Guide Series: Minn.*⟩ ⟨serve as architectural ~ and have no structural value at all —G.E.Strehan⟩ (3) **:** the hardware of a building and esp. of its doors (4) **:** the interior furnishings of an automobile body including seat, floor, and sidewall coverings, hardware, lights, armrests, and other accessories; *also* **:** ornamental metalwork on the outside of an automotive vehicle ⟨chrome ~⟩ (5) **:** WINDOW DRESSING **3 a :** the position of a ship, boat, seaplane, or float in water esp. with reference to the horizontal ⟨could feel the altered ~ of the boat as her bows sank and her stern rose on the slope —C.S.Forester⟩; *also* **:** the measure of the difference between the draft of a ship forward and that aft ⟨designed . . . to float at a draft of 12 feet forward and 15 feet aft, giving a ~ of 3 feet by the stern —E.L.Aftwood⟩ **b :** the relation between the plane of a sail and the direction of motion of the ship **c :** the buoyancy status of a submarine ⟨using the ballast pumps to alter the ~ of the submarine —David Masters⟩ ⟨submarine custom for the diving officer to control the speed until he is satisfied with the submerged ~ —E.L.Beach⟩ **d :** the attitude of a lighter-than-air craft relative to a fore-and-aft horizontal plane **e :** the attitude with respect to wind axes at which an airplane will continue in level flight with free controls **4 :** something that is trimmed off or cut out ⟨a man making axle shafts . . . picked up a piece of discarded ~ —B.M.Bowie⟩ **5 a :** the portion of the outside edges of printed sheets or pages esp. of a book that is to be trimmed off **b :** the maximum width of finished paper with deckle edges removed that can be made on a paper machine **6 :** a haircut that neatens up the lines of a previous haircut without changing the style **7 :** the small strings at the top and throat of a racket which bind the main strings — **trim by the bow** *of watercraft or aircraft* **:** lower at the bow than at the stern — **trim by the stern** *of watercraft or aircraft* **:** lower at the stern than at the bow

tri·mas·ti·gote \(ˈ)trī¦mastəˌgōt\ *adj* [alter. of earlier *trimastigate*, fr. *tri-* + *mastig-* + *-ate*] **:** TRIFLAGELLATE

trime \ˈtrīm\ *n* -s *usu cap* [prob. fr. *tri-* + *-ime* (as in *dime*)] **:** the U.S. silver three-cent piece issued 1851–1873

tri·mellitic acid \¦trī+. . .-\ *n* [ISV *tri-* + *mellitic*] **:** a crystalline tricarboxylic acid $C_6H_3(COOH)_3$ obtained indirectly from mellitic acid, by oxidation of coal, and in other ways; 1,2,4-benzene-tricarboxylic acid

tri·mer \ˈtrīmə(r)\ *n* -s [ISV *tri-* + *-mer*] **:** a compound formed by the union of three molecules of a simpler compound or of a radical **:** a polymer formed from three molecules of a monomer — **tri·mer·ic** \(ˈ)trī¦merik\ *adj*

trim·era \ˈtrimərə\ [NL, fr. neut. pl. of *trimerus* trimerous] *syn of* PSEUDOTRIMERA

trim·ere·su·rus \ˌtrimərəˈsu̇rəs\ *n, cap* [NL, fr. Gk *trimerēs* of three parts + NL *-urus*] **:** a genus of usu. green prehensile-tailed arboreal Asiatic pit vipers closely related to the bushmaster — see HABU

tri·mer·ide \ˈtrīməˌrīd, -ˌrəd\ *n* -s [*trimer* + *-ide*] **:** TRIMER

trim·er·ite \ˈtriməˌrīt\ *n* -s [G *trimerit*, fr. Gk *trimerēs* of three parts + G *-it* -ite] **:** a mineral $Be(Mn,Ca)(SiO_4)$ consisting of a silicate of manganese, calcium, and beryllium and occurring in salmon-colored tabular crystals (hardness 6–7, sp. gr. 3.5)

tri·mer·iza·tion \ˌtrīmərəˈzāshən, -ˌrīˈz-\ *n* -s [*trimer* + *-ization*] **:** polymerization resulting in a trimer

trim·ero·rhi·nus \ˌtrimərōˈrīnəs\ *n, cap* [NL, fr. *tri-* + *mer-* + *-rhinus*] **:** a genus of African back-fanged snakes (family Boigidae) — see SCHAAPSTECKER

trim·er·ous \ˈtrimərəs\ *adj* [NL *trimerus*, fr. Gk *trimerēs* of three parts, fr. *tri-* three + *meros* part — more at TRI-, MERIT] **1 :** having the parts in threes — used of a flower and often written *3-merous* **2** *of an insect* **a :** having three or apparently three segments in each tarsus **b :** belonging to the Pseudotrimera

tri·mes·ic acid \(ˈ)trī¦mesik-\ *n* [ISV *tri-* + *mes-* (in *mesitylene*) + *-ic*] **:** a crystalline tricarboxylic acid $C_6H_3(COOH)_3$ formed by the oxidation of mesitylene and in other ways; 1,3,5-benzene-tricarboxylic acid

tri·mes·ter \(ˈ)trī¦mestə(r)\ *n* -s [F *trimestre*, fr. L *trimestris* of three months, fr. *tri-* + *mensis* month — more at MOON] **1 :** a period of three or about three months **2 :** one of three terms into which the academic year is divided at some educational institutions — **tri·mes·tral** \-strəl\ *adj* — **tri·mes·tri·al** \-rēəl\ *adj*

tri·metaphosphate \¦trī+\ *n* [*tri-* + *metaphosphate*] **:** a cyclic trimeric metaphosphate — compare SODIUM PHOSPHATE

¹trim·e·ter \ˈtriməd·ə(r)\ *n* [L *trimetrus*, fr. Gk *trimetros*, fr. *tri-* three + *metron* measure — more at TRI-, MEASURE] **:** a line of three measures consisting of three dipodies (as in classical iambic, trochaic, and anapestic verse) or three feet (as in modern English verse)

²trimeter \ˈ"\ *adj* **:** having three measures in a foot

tri·metha·di·one \(¦)trī¦methəˈdīˌōn\ *n* -s [*trimethyl* + connective *-a-* + *-dione*] **:** a crystalline anticonvulsant $C_6H_9NO_3$ used chiefly in the treatment of petit mal epilepsy; 3,5,5-trimethyl-2,4-oxazolidine-dione

tri·methine \(ˈ)trī+\ *n* [*tri-* + *methine*] **:** CARBOCYANINE

trimethoxy- *comb form* [*tri-* + *methoxy-*] **:** containing three methoxyl groups — in names of chemical compounds ⟨*trimethoxy*coumarin⟩

tri·methyl \(ˈ)trī+\ *adj* [ISV *tri-* + *methyl*] **:** containing three methyl groups in the molecule

tri·meth·yl·amine \(¦)trī¦methəl+\ *n* [ISV *trimethyl* + *amine*] **:** an irritating gaseous or volatile liquid tertiary amine $(CH_3)_3N$ that has a fishy odor, that is only slightly more basic than ammonia, that is flammable and forms explosive mixtures with air, that is formed as a degradation product of many nitrogenous animal and plant substances (as in herring brine and the distillate of sugar-beet residues), that is made commercially by catalytic reaction of methanol and ammonia at high temperature, and that is used chiefly in making choline and other quaternary ammonium compounds

tri·meth·yl·benzene \(¦)trī¦methəl+\ *n* [ISV *trimethyl* + *benzene*] **:** any of three trimethyl derivatives of benzene: **a :** HEMIMELLITENE **b :** MESITYLENE **c :** PSEUDOCUMENE

tri·meth·yl·carbinol \ˈ"+\ *n* [ISV *trimethyl* + *carbinol*] **:** BUTYL ALCOHOL c

tri·methylene \(ˈ)trī+\ *n* [ISV *tri-* + *methylene*] **1 :** CYCLOPROPANE **2 :** a bivalent radical $-CH_2CH_2CH_2-$ containing three methylene groups and isomeric with propylene

tri·meth·yl·ene·tri·ni·tra·mine \(ˌ)=¸=¸=¸trīˈnīˈtrəmən, -ˌmēn\ *n* [*trimethylene* + *trinitr-* + *amine*] **:** CYCLONITE

tri·meth·yl·ethylene \(¦)=¦=¦=+\ *n* [*trimethyl* + *ethylene*] **:** AMYLENE a

trimethyl·pyridine \(¦)trī¦methəl+\ *n* [*trimethyl* + *pyridine*] **:** COLLIDINE a

tri·metric \(ˈ)trī+\ *adj* [*tri-* + Gk *metron* measure + E *-ic*] **:** ORTHORHOMBIC

trimetric projection *n* **:** axonometric projection in which the three spatial axes are represented as unequally inclined to the drawing surface and equal distances along the axes are drawn unequal

tri·met·ro·gon \trīˈmeˑtrəˌgän\ *n* -s [*tri-* + Gk *metron* measure + E *-gon*] **:** a system of aerial mapping involving the use of a single assembly containing three cameras with which one vertical and two oblique right and left aerial photographs are taken simultaneously at regular intervals over the area being mapped

trimline \ˈ=ˌ=\ *n* [⁴*trim* + *line*] **:** the boundary of an area from which a glacier has receded that is often indicated by changes in vegetation

trim·ly *adv* **:** in a trim manner **:** with trimness ⟨~ attired⟩

trimmed *past of* TRIM

trim·mer \ˈtrimə(r)\ *n* -s [¹*trim* + *-er*] **1 a :** one that by hand or by machine trims articles in manufacturing or industrial processes: as (1) **:** one that puts the finishing touches or parts to a product (2) **:** one that cuts or smooths articles to the proper shape or size (3) **:** one that stows coal or freight on a ship so as to distribute the weight properly **b :** an instrument or machine with which trimming is done: as (1) **:** any of various circular-saw machines for trimming lumber (2) **:** a machine for cutting stacks of books or paper (3) **:** an apparatus for trimming a pile of coal into a regular form (as a cone or prism) (4) **:** a flat board or metal surface having a movable cutting blade attached to one edge for trimming the edges of prints and films — called also *trimming board* (5) **:** a small adjustable circuit element and esp. a condenser used to tune a circuit to a desired frequency **2 :** a beam that receives the end of a header in floor framing (as about a hole left for stairs or to avoid bringing joists near chimneys) **3 :** one that does not adhere to one set of opinions esp. in politics **:** one that fluctuates or holds a middle position between parties so as to appear to favor each **:** one that for the sake of expediency will modify his policy, position or opinions ⟨a ~ who in the interests of his personal safety evaded the responsibility of joining the one or the other side —M.R.Cohen⟩ **4 :** one that inflicts chastisement by words or blows **5 :** a night line used in pike fishing **6 :** one that arranges displays (as in a store) **7 :** an engine in a hump classification yard assigned to retrieve misdirected cars

trimmer arch *n* **:** an arch built between trimmers in the thickness of an upper floor to support a hearth

trimmer condenser *n* **:** a small variable condenser used as a trimmer

trimmer joist *n* **:** TRIMMING JOIST

trimmer signal *n* **:** a signal near the summit in a hump yard to convey information about movements from the classification tracks toward the summit

trimmest *superlative of* TRIM

trimming *n* -s [fr. gerund of 1*trim*] **1 a :** the act of one who trims **b :** the act or process of retrieving misdirected freight cars in a hump classification yard **2 a :** a decorative accessory or additional item which serves to finish, decorate, or complete ⟨~*s* for a hat⟩ **b :** an additional garnishing that is not essential but adds to the interest or attractiveness of a main item ⟨roast beef, Yorkshire pudding and all the ~*s* —Vera Caspary⟩ ⟨a factual report of what occurred, without adding the ~*s* of the public relations people —R.S.Low⟩ **c :** an extra figure, fill-in, or chorus in a square dance — usu. used in pl.

trimming board *n* **:** TRIMMER 1b(4)

trimming hatch *or* **trimming hole** *n* **:** a hatchway at a distance from a main hatch through which to load grain or similar cargo to bring it uniformly close up to the deck

trimming house *n* **:** the part of a railway shop in which the final stages of car rebuilding (as assembly, painting, and stenciling) are completed

trimming joist *n* **:** a joist into which timber trimmers are framed

trimming machine *n* **:** a woodworking machine consisting of a lever-operated knife and adjustable guides for shearing surfaces true to any required angle

trimming tab *n* **:** TAB 1h

trimming tank *n* **:** a tank either forward or aft and usu. in the extreme ends utilized for changing the trim of a ship by admitting or discharging water ballast

trim·ness *n* -ES **:** the quality or state of being trim

tri·modal \(')trī+\ *adj* [*tri-* + *modal*] **:** having three statistical modes — **tri·modality** \¦trī+\ *n*

tri·mo·da ne·ces·si·tas \¦trīmədənə'sesə,tas, ¦trimə,dä-,ne'kesə,täs\ *n* [ML, lit., necessity of three kinds] **:** the threefold burden or charge on Anglo-Saxon landholders of army service, repair of strongholds, and repair of bridges

tri·molecular \¦trī+\ *adj* [*tri-* + *molecular*] **:** relating to or formed from three molecules

tri·monthly \(')trī+\ *adj* [*tri-* + *monthly*] **:** occurring, appearing, or being made, done, or acted upon every three months

tri·morph \'trī,mȯrf\ *n* [ISV, back-formation fr. *trimorphism*] **:** any of the three crystalline forms of a trimorphous substance ⟨rutile, brookite, and anatase are ~*s* of titanium dioxide⟩

tri·mor·phic \(')trī¦mȯrfik\ *adj* [*trimorph*ism + *-ic*] **:** exhibiting trimorphism

tri·mor·phism \(')trī¦mȯr,fizəm\ *n* -s [ISV *trimorph-* (fr. Gk *trimorphos* having three forms) + *-ism*] **1 :** polymorphism in which there are three distinct forms of a species or of a particular caste — compare DIMORPHISM a **2 :** occurrence of three distinct forms of organs (as leaves or flowers) on individuals of the same species **:** HETEROGONY **3 :** the property of crystallizing in three different forms

tri·mor·phous \-ˌfəs\ *adj* [Gk *trimorphos*, fr. *tri-* three + *-morphos* -morphous — more at TRI-] **:** of, relating to, or characterized by trimorphism

tri·motor \'trī,==\ *n* [*tri-* + *motor*] **:** an airplane powered with three motors

trims *pres 3d sing of* TRIM, *pl of* TRIM

trim size *n* **:** the actual size of something (as a magazine or book page) after excess material required in production has been cut off

trimstone \'=,=\ *n* **:** stone used to trim a wall of brick or stone masonry or for copings, cornices, and other ornament

trim tab *n* **:** TAB 1h

tri·myristin \¦trī+\ *n* [ISV *tri-* + *myristin*] **:** the solid triglyceride $C_3H_5(OOCC_{13}H_{27})_3$ of myristic acid found esp. in nutmegs **:** glycerol tri-myristate

trin \'trin\ *n* -s [prob. fr. *tri-* + tw*in*] **:** TRIPLET 3

trin *abbr* trinity

tri·nacri·an \(')trī¦nakrēən, trə'n- *also* -nāk-\ *adj, usu cap* [*Trinacria*, ancient name of Sicily (fr. L, fr. Gk *Trinakria*) + E *-an*] **:** SICILIAN

1**tri·nal** \'trīnᵊl\ *adj* [LL *trinalis* threefold, three, fr. L *trini* three each + *-alis* -al; akin to L *tres* three — more at THREE] **1 :** THREEFOLD **2 :** 3TRIAL

2**trinal** \"\ *n* -s **:** 4TRIAL

1**tri·na·ry** \'trīnərē\ *adj* [LL *trinarius*, fr. L *trini* three each + *-arius* -ary] **:** TERNARY, THREEFOLD

2**trinary** \"\ *n* -ES **:** a ternary group or set **:** TRIAD

tri·nate \'trī,nāt\ *vi* -ED/-ING/-S [NL *trinatus*, past part. of *trinare*, prob. fr. L *trini* three each] **:** to celebrate three masses on the same day (as Christmas)

trin·co·ma·li wood *or* **trin·co·ma·lee wood** \¦triŋkōmə¦lē-\ *n, often cap T* [fr. *Trincomali*, *Trincomalee*, seaport in Ceylon] **1 :** a tropical Asiatic timber tree (*Berrya ammonilla*) of the family Tiliaceae with hard dark wood **2 :** the wood of the trincomali wood tree

1**trin·dle** \'trindᵊl, *dial* -n(d)ᵊl\ *n* -s [ME *trindel*, fr. OE *tryndel*, *trendel* circle, ring — more at TRENDLE] **1** *dial Eng* **:** a round or circular object; *specif* **:** the wheel of a wheelbarrow **2 :** either of a pair of metal plates that are inserted between the backbone and boards of a rounded and backed book to force the backbone temporarily into a flat shape while the fore edge is being trimmed

trindles 2

2**trin·dle** \-n(d)ᵊl\ *vi* [ME *trindelen*, prob. fr. *trindel* trindle] *dial* **:** ROLL, TRUNDLE

1**trine** \'trīn\ *vi* -ED/-ING/-S [ME *trinen*, of Scand origin; akin to Dan *trine* to step, go, Sw dial. *trina* to go, march, OSw *trin* step, tread] **1** *archaic* **:** MARCH, GO **2** *archaic* **:** HANG

2**trine** \"\ *adj* [ME, fr. MF *trin*, *trine*, fr. L *trinus*, fr. *trini* three each — more at TRINAL] **1 :** THREEFOLD, TRIPLE **2 :** of, relating to, or being the favorable astrological aspect of two heavenly bodies 120 degrees apart

3**trine** \"\ *n* -s **1 a :** a group of three **:** TRIAD **b** *cap* **:** TRINITY **2 :** the trine astrological aspect of two heavenly bodies **3 trines** *pl* **:** TRIPLETS

4**trine** \"\ *vt* -ED/-ING/-S **:** to put in the aspect of a trine

trine immersion *n* **:** the practice of immersing a candidate for baptism three times in the names in turn of the Trinity

tri·neural fasciculus \(')trī+ . . . -\ *n* [*trineural* fr. *tri-* + *neural*] **:** a bundle of fibers in the upper part of the spinal cord joined with the 9th, 10th, and 11th cranial nerves

t ring *n, cap T* **:** a ring such that T sections are formed by passing normal radial planes through the ring; *specif* **:** a piston ring having a T-shaped cross section

trin·ga \'triŋgə\ *n, cap* [NL, fr. Gk *tryngas*, a bird] **:** a genus of sandpipers including the solitary sandpipers and sometimes the tattlers

trin·gine \'triŋ,gīn, -rin,jīn\ *or* **trin·goid** \-riŋ,gȯid\ *adj* [NL *Tringa* + E *-ine* or *-oid*] **:** of or relating to the genus *Tringa*

trin·gle \'triŋgəl\ *n* -s [F, rod, tringle, alter. of MF *tingle*, fr. MD *tingel*, *tengel* lath] **:** a narrow straight molding usu. of square section **:** FILLET

trin·i·dad \'trinə,dad, -daa(ə)d, ,=='=\ *adj, usu cap* [fr. *Trinidad*, island in the West Indies] **:** of or from the West-Indian island of Trinidad **:** of the kind or style prevalent in Trinidad **:** TRINIDADIAN

trinidad asphalt *also* **trinidad pitch** *n, usu cap T* **:** a natural asphalt found in a pitch lake in the island of Trinidad, widely used in the U. S. for sheet asphalt pavements, and containing when refined about 44 percent colloidal clay and 56 percent bitumen

1**trin·i·dadian** \¦==¦dadēən, -dād-,-daad-\ *adj, usu cap* [*Trinidad* + E *-an*] **1 :** of, relating to, or characteristic of the island of Trinidad **2 :** of, relating to, or characteristic of the people of Trinidad

2**trinidadian** \"\ *n* -s *cap* [*Trinidad* + E *-an*, n. suffix] **:** a native or inhabitant of the island of Trinidad

tri·nil man \'trē,nil-\ *n, usu cap T* [fr. *Trinil*, village in Java where parts of the Java man were found] **:** JAVA MAN

1**trin·i·tar·i·an** \¦trinə¦terēən, -nə¦ta(a)r-, -nə¦tār-\ *adj* [NL *trinitarius* (fr. LL *trinitas* trinity + L *-arius* -ary) + E *-an* — more at TRINITY] **1** *usu cap* **:** of or relating to the order of Trinitarians **2** *usu cap* **:** of or relating to the Trinity, the doctrine of the Trinity, or adherents to that doctrine **3 :** having three parts or aspects **:** THREEFOLD, TRIPLE

2**trinitarian** \"\ *n* -s *usu cap* [NL *trinitarius* + E *-an*, n. suffix] **1 :** a member of the Roman Catholic Order of the Holy Trinity founded at Rome in 1198 for the ransoming of Christian captives from the Muslims but devoted today mainly to teaching and nursing — called also *Mathurin*, *Redemptionist* **2 :** one who subscribes to the doctrine of the Trinity

trin·i·tar·i·an·ism \,=='==ə,nizəm\ *n* -s *usu cap* **1 :** the doctrine of the Trinity **2 :** belief in or adherence to the doctrine of the Trinity

trinitr- *or* **trinitro-** *comb form* [ISV *tri-* + *nitr-*] **:** containing three nitro groups — in names of chemical compounds ⟨*trinitro*cellulose⟩

tri·nitramine \(')trī+\ *n* [*tri-* + *nitramine*] **:** a compound containing three nitramine groups in the molecule

tri·nitrate \"+\ *n* [*tri-* + *nitrate*] **:** a nitrate containing three nitrate groups in the molecule

tri·nitride \(')trī¦nī·,trīd, -nī·trəd\ *n* [ISV *trinitr-* + *-ide*] **:** a binary compound containing three atoms of nitrogen combined with an element or radical; *esp* **:** AZIDE

tri·ni·trin \(')trī¦nī·trən\ *n* -s [ISV *trinitr-* + *-in*] **:** NITROGLYCERIN

tri·ni·tro \(')trī¦nī·(,)trō\ *adj* [*trinitro-*] **:** containing three nitro groups in the molecule

tri·ni·tro·benzene \(¦)trī¦nī·trō+\ *n* [ISV *trinitr-* + *benzene*] **:** a light yellow crystalline compound $C_6H_3(NO_2)_3$ that is a more powerful yet more stable explosive than trinitrotoluene but is little used because of the difficulties of its preparation usu. indirectly from toluene — called also *TNB*, *1,3,5-trinitrobenzene*

tri·ni·tro·cresol \"+\ *n* [ISV *trinitr-* + *cresol*] **:** any of several trinitro derivatives $(NO_2)_3C_6H(CH_3)OH$ of the three cresols; *esp* **:** a high explosive similar to picric acid made by nitrating *meta*-cresol — see CRESYLITE

tri·ni·tro·glycerin \"+\ *n* [*trinitr-* + *glycerin*] **:** NITROGLYCERIN

tri·ni·tro·phenol \"+\ *n* [ISV *trinitr-* + *phenol*] **:** any of six trinitro derivatives $(NO_2)_3C_6H_2OH$ of phenol; *esp* **:** PICRIC ACID

tri·ni·tro·phenylmethylnitramine \"+ *pronunciations at* PHENYL, METHYL, & NITRAMINE\ *n* [*trinitr-* + *phenyl* + *methyl* + *nitramine*] **:** TETRYL

tri·ni·tro·toluene \(¦)trī¦nī·trō+\ *n* [ISV *trinitr-* + *toluene*] **:** the flammable toxic symmetrical trinitro derivative $CH_3C_6H_2(NO_2)_3$ of toluene that is obtained by nitrating toluene as the light yellow crystalline alpha form darkening to reddish brown on exposure to light, that is stable at temperatures up to 100° C and even higher and is insensitive to friction or ordinary shock but is a high explosive, and that is used either alone as bursting charge for shells, bombs, and grenades or as an ingredient of various explosives and is also used as an intermediate in chemical synthesis (as of phloroglucinol) — called also *TNT*, *2,4,6-trinitrotoluene*

tri·ni·tro·toluol \"+\ *n* [ISV *trinitr-* + *toluol*] **:** TRINITROTOLUENE — not used systematically

tri·ni·tro·xylene \"+\ *n* [ISV *trinitr-* + *xylene*] **:** any of several trinitro derivatives $(CH_3)_2C_6H(NO_2)_3$ of the three xylenes or a mixture of such derivatives used as an explosive

1**trin·i·ty** \'trinəd·ē, -nətē, -i\ *n* -ES [ME *Trinite*, *trinite*, fr. OF *trinité*, fr. LL *trinitat-*, *trinitas* (trans. of Gk *trias*), fr. L, triad, fr. *trini* three each (akin to L *tria*, *tres* three) + *-itat-*, *-itas* -ity — more at THREE] **1 a** (1) *cap* **:** the union of three persons or hypostases (as the Father, the Son, and the Holy Spirit) in one godhead so that all the three are one God as to substance but three persons or hypostases as to individuality **:** the triune God (2) *usu cap* **:** the Christian doctrine of the Trinity **b** *often cap* **:** a union or group of three deities **:** TRIAD **2** *usu cap* **:** TRINITY SUNDAY **3** [ME *trinite*, fr. L *trinitas*] **:** the state of being threefold **4 a :** something having three parts or aspects **b :** a group of three ⟨its ~ of churches standing in stately dignity —*Amer. Guide Series: Conn.*⟩ **5 a :** HERB TRINITY **b :** a common No. American spiderwort (*Tradescantia virginiana*)

2**trinity** \"\ *adj, usu cap* **1 :** of, dedicated to, or bearing a symbol of the Trinity **2 :** associated with or occurring on or about Trinity Sunday ⟨*Trinity* Monday⟩ **3** [fr. *Trinity* House, established in 1514 in Deptford, England] **:** of or associated with a semigovernmental association of English mariners authorized by Parliament to erect and maintain English coastal lighthouses and other navigational aids and to license pilots ⟨*Trinity* pilots⟩ ⟨*Trinity* dues⟩ ⟨a *Trinity* buoy keeper⟩ **4** [fr. *Trinity* river, Texas] **:** of or relating to a subdivision of the Comanchean — see GEOLOGIC TIME table

trinity column *n* **:** a column of triangular plan for all or part of its height built as a religious memorial

trinity lily *n* **:** a large-flowered white trillium (*Trillium grandiflorum*)

trinity mixture *n* **:** a livestock concentrate that is made up of one quarter alfalfa meal, one quarter linseed oil meal, and one half tankage or meat scrap and is used esp. for feeding growing hogs

trinity sunday *n, usu cap T&S* [ME *trinite sonday*] **:** the Sunday next after Whitsunday observed as a feast in honor of the Holy Trinity

trinity term *n, usu cap 1st T* **1 a :** the term from May 22 to June 12 during which the superior courts of England were formerly open — compare EASTER TERM, HILARY TERM, MICHAELMAS TERM **b** *also* **trinity sitting :** the sitting of the High Court of Justice of England between June 9 and July 31 **2 :** the third academic term in an English university from about mid April to about the end of June — compare HILARY TERM, MICHAELMAS TERM

trinitytide \'===,=\ *n, usu cap* **:** the season of the church year between Trinity Sunday and Advent

1**trin·ket** \'triŋkət, *usu* -əd·+V\ *n* -s [perh. fr. ME *trenket*, *trynket* shoemaker's knife, small knife, fr. ONF *trenquet*, fr. *trenquer* to cut, prob. modif. of L *truncare* to cut off — more at TRUNCATE] **1 :** a small article of equipment ⟨put up his ~*s* in his duffel bag⟩ **2 a :** a small ornament (as a jewel or ring) **b :** a vain ornament **:** GAUD **3 :** a thing of little value **:** TRIFLE

2**trinket** \"\ *vi* -ED/-ING/-S [perh. fr. 1*trinket*] **:** to deal clandestinely **:** INTRIGUE — **trin·ket·er** \-əd·ə(r), -ətə-\ *n* -s

trin·ket·ry \-ətrē, -ri\ *n* -ES **:** small items of personal ornament ⟨the finish . . . makes a big change in your costume ~ —*Harper's Bazaar*⟩

trin·kle \'triŋkəl\ *vi* -ED/-ING/-S [ME *trinkelen*, prob. alter. of *triklen* to trickle] *dial* **:** to flow down by drops **:** TRICKLE

trink·lied \'triŋ,klēt\ *n, pl* **trinklie·der** \-ēdə(r)\ [G, fr. *trinken* to drink (fr. OHG *trinkan*) + *lied* song, fr. OHG *liod* — more at DRINK, LAUD] **:** DRINKING SONG

trin·kums \'triŋkəmz\ *also* **trinkum-trankums** \¦=kəm-¦traŋkəmz\ *n pl* [*trinkums* alter. (influenced by L nouns ending in *-um*) of *trinkets*; *trinkum-trankums* redupl. of *trinkums*] **:** TRINKETS, FRIPPERY

tri·nodal \(')trī+\ *or* **tri·no·dine** \(')trī¦nōdᵊn, trī'nō,dīn, 'trīnə,dīn\ *adj* [L *trinodis* three-knotted (fr. *tri-* + *nodus* knot) + E *-al* or *-ine* — more at NODE] **:** having three nodes

tri·no·da necessitas \(¦)trī|¦nōdə-, (¦)trē|-\ *n* [NL, by alter. (influence of L *trinodis*)] **:** TRIMODA NECESSITAS

tri·no·men \(')trī¦nōmən\ *n* [*tri-* + L *nomen* name — more at NAME] **:** TRINOMIAL 2

1**tri·no·mi·al** \trī'nōmēəl\ *n* -s [*tri-* + *-nomial* (as in *binomial*, n.)] **1 :** a polynomial of three terms **2 :** a trinomial name

2**trinomial** \(')=¦===\ *adj* [*tri-* + *-nomial* (as in *binomial*, adj.)] **1 :** consisting of three mathematical terms **2 :** being a name belonging to botanical or zoological nomenclature composed of a first term designating the genus, a second term designating the species, and a third term designating the subspecies or variety to which an organism belongs **3 :** of or relating to trinomials ⟨~ nomenclature⟩

tri·no·mi·al·ism \='==ə,lizəm\ *n* -s **:** a system of nomenclature (as in biological classification) involving the use of trinomial terms

tri·no·mi·al·ist \-ˌləst\ *n* -s **:** an adherent of trinomialism

tri·no·mi·al·ly \(')=¦===lē, -li\ *adv* **:** in a trinomial manner

trins *pl of* TRIN

tri·nuclear \(')trī+\ *adj* [*tri-* + *nuclear*] **:** having three nuclei ⟨~ cyanine dyes⟩ — compare TRICYCLIC

tri·nucleate \"+\ *adj* [*tri-* + *nucleate*] **:** having three nuclei

tri·nucleotide \"+\ *n* [*tri-* + *nucleotide*] **:** a nucleotide consisting of three mononucleotides in combination

tri·nucleus \"+\ *n, cap* [NL, fr. *tri-* + *nucleus*] **:** a widely distributed genus (the type of the family Trinucleidae) of Ordovician trilobites in which the glabella and cheeks form three rounded elevations on the head

1**trio** \'trē(,)ō\ *n* -s [F, fr. It, modif. (influenced by *duo*) of L *tria* three — more at THREE] **1 a :** a musical composition for three voice parts or three instruments **b :** the secondary or episodic division of a minuet or scherzo (as in a sonata or symphony) or of a march or of various dance forms usu. contrasted in key and in a quieter style than the primary division **c :** a performance of such a composition **d :** a dance by three people **2 :** a group or set of three: as **a :** the performers of a musical or dance trio **b :** three playing cards of the same rank **c :** a male and two female domestic animals (as poultry) forming a breeding or exhibition group

2**trio** \"\ *n, pl* **trio** *or* **trios** *usu cap* **1 a :** a Cariban people of the boundary between Brazil and British and Dutch Guiana **b :** a member of such people **2 :** the language of the Trio people

tri·obol \(')trī+\ *n* [L *triobolus*, fr. Gk *triōbolon*, fr. *tri-* three + *obolos* obol — more at TRI-, OBOL] **:** an ancient Greek coin worth 3 obols or ½ drachma

tri·octahedral \(¦)trī+\ *adj* [*tri-* + *octahedral*] **:** having all three of the available octahedrally coordinated positions occupied ⟨a ~ mica⟩

tri·ode \'trī,ōd\ *n* -s [*tri-* + *-ode*] **:** an electron tube with an anode, a cathode, and a control grid

tri·o·dia \trī'ōdēə\ *n* [NL, prob. fr. Gk, meeting of three roads, fr. *triodos* point where three roads meet (fr. *tri-* three + *hodos* way, road) + *-ia* -y — more at CEDE] **1** *cap* **:** a genus of Australian and in some classifications American perennial grasses having long narrow leaves and florets with prominently 3-nerved lemmas **2** -s **:** any grass of the genus *Triodia* **:** SPINIFEX 2

tri·odion \trē'ȯthyȯn\ *n, pl* **tri·odia** \-yȧ\ [MGk *triōidion*, fr. Gk *tri-* three + *ōidē* ode — more at ODE] **:** a liturgical book of the Eastern church containing the offices from the fourth Sunday before Lent to Easter including canons having usu. only three odes instead of the regular nine

tri·odon \'trīə,dän\ *n, cap* [NL, fr. *tri-* + *-odon*] **:** a small genus (coextensive with the family Triodontidae) of Indo-Pacific puffers having the fused teeth of the lower jaw forming a single plate and those of the upper jaw two plates one on each side

1**tri·odon·toid** \¦trīə¦dän·,tȯid\ *adj* [NL *Triodont-*, *Triodon* + E *-oid*] **:** resembling or related to the genus *Triodon* or the family Triodontidae

2**triodontoid** \"\ *n* -s **:** a triodontoid fish

tri·odon·toph·o·rus \,trīə,dän·'täfərəs\ *n, cap* [NL, fr. *tri-* + *odont-* + *-phorus*] **:** a genus of nematode worms (family Strongylidae) parasitic in the intestine of horses

tri·oe·cious *or* **tri·ecious** \(')trī¦ēshəs\ *adj* [NL *Trioecia*, order of plants in former classifications (fr. *tri-* + *-oecia*) + E *-ous*] **:** having staminate, pistillate, and hermaphrodite flowers on different plants ⟨a ~ species⟩ — **tri·oe·cious·ly** *adv*

tri·ol \'trī,ȯl, -,ōl\ *n* -s [*-triol*] **:** a chemical compound (as phloroglucinol) containing three hydroxyl groups

-tri·ol \"\ *n suffix* -s [*tri-* + *-ol*] **:** chemical compound containing three hydroxyl groups ⟨1,2,4-benzene*triol*⟩

tri·ole \'trē,ōl, -rī,-\ *n* -s [prob. fr. *tri-* + *-ole*] **:** TRIPLET 4

tri·olefin \(')trī+\ *n* [*tri-* + *olefin*] **:** any of a series of hydrocarbons having the general formula C_nH_{2n-4} and containing three double bonds

tri·olein \"+\ *n* [ISV *tri-* + *olein*] **:** the oily liquid triglyceride $C_3H_5(OOC_{17}H_{33})_3$ of oleic acid found in olive oil and other nondrying oils **:** glycerol tri-oleate

tri·o·let \¦treə¦lā\ *n* -s [F, prob. dim. of It *trio* — more at TRIO] **1 :** a poem or stanza of eight lines in which the first is repeated as the fourth and seventh and the second as the eighth and the rhyme scheme is *ABaAabAB* **2 a :** TRIPLET 4 **b :** a short trio

tri·ol·o·gy \trī'äləjē\ *n* -ES [by alter. (influence of *trio*)] **:** TRILOGY

Tri·o·nal \'trīə,nal\ *trademark* — used for sulfonethylmethane

-tri·one \'trī,ōn\ *n suffix* -s [*tri-* + *-one*] **:** chemical compound containing three carbonyl groups — in names of triketones or tri-oxo compounds that are not true triketones ⟨imidazole*trione*⟩

1**tri·on·y·chid** \(')trī¦änə(,)kid, ¦trīə¦nikəd\ *adj* [NL *Trionychidae*] **:** of or relating to the Trionychidae

2**trionychid** \"\ *n* -s **:** a turtle of the family Trionychidae

tri·onych·i·dae \,trīə'nikə,dē\ *n pl, cap* [NL *Trionych-*, *Trionyx*, type genus + *-idae*] **:** a family of soft-shelled freshwater turtles containing both fossil Tertiary and living forms in which the horny plates of carapace and plastron are replaced by leathery skin and constituting a distinct superfamily of Cryptodira

tri·on·y·choid \(')trī¦änə,kȯid\ *or* **try·on·y·choi·de·an** \(¦)trī,änə¦kȯidēən\ *adj* [*trionychoid* fr. NL *Trionychoidea*, order of soft-shelled turtles, fr. *Trionych-*, *Trionyx* + *-oidea*; *trionychoidean* fr. NL *Trionychoidea* + E *-an*] **:** resembling or related to the Trionychidae

tri·onyx \'trīə,niks, trī'än-\ *n, cap* [NL, fr. *tri-* + *-onyx*] **:** a genus (the type of the family Trionychidae) of soft-shelled turtles that usu. includes both Old World and New World turtles but is sometimes restricted to Old World forms

tri·op·i·dae \trī'äpə,dē\ *n pl, cap* [NL *Triop-*, *Triops*, type genus + *-idae*] **:** a family of small active sessile-eyed aquatic crustaceans (order Notostraca) — see LEPIDURUS, TRIOPS

tri·ops \'trī,äps\ *n, cap* [NL, fr. *tri-* + *-ops*] **:** a genus of fresh-water crustaceans (family Triopidae) having the head and thorax covered with an oval shield-shaped shell and a small third median eye

trior *var of* TRIER

trios *pl of* TRIO

tri·ose \'trī,ōs *also* -ōz\ *n* -s [ISV *tri-* + *-ose*] **:** either of two simple sugars $C_3H_6O_3$ containing three carbon atoms: **a :** GLYCERALDEHYDE **b :** a sweet crystalline compound $HOCH_2COCH_2OH$ that is formed usu. in an equilibrium mixture with glyceraldehyde by oxidation of glycerol and is the simplest ketose **:** dihydroxy-acetone

triose phosphate *n* **:** a phosphoric ester or acylal of a triose; *esp* **:** either of two monophosphates $C_3H_5O_2(OPO_3H_2)$ or an equilibrium mixture of them formed as intermediates in carbohydrate metabolism — compare ALDOLASE

trio sonata *n* **:** a sonata of the Baroque period having two upper parts for like instruments (as violins or trumpets) and a figured bass part played by a bass instrument (as bass viol or cello) with the indicated harmony realized by a keyboard instrument

tri·os·te·um \trī'ästēəm\ *n, cap* [NL, short for *Triosteospermum*, fr. *tri-* + *oste-* + *-spermum*; fr. the usu. three bony nutlets of the fruit] **:** a genus of Asiatic and No. American herbs (family Caprifoliaceae) having connate or perfoliate entire leaves and purple or yellowish tubular flowers usu. sessile in the axils — see FEVERROOT

tri·ox·an \trī'äk,san, -sən\ *n, chiefly Brit var of* TRIOXANE

tri·ox·ane \-,sān\ *n* [ISV *tri-* + *oxa-* + cyclohexa*ne*] **:** a crystalline combustible heterocyclic trimer $(CH_2O)_3$ of formaldehyde with an odor resembling chloroform that is depolymerized into formaldehyde by traces of mineral acids — called also *symmetrical trioxane;* compare PARAFORMALDEHYDE

tri·ox·ide \-,sīd, -səd\ *n* [ISV *tri-* + *ox-* + *-ide*] **:** an oxide containing three atoms of oxygen

trioxy- *comb form* [ISV *tri-* + *oxy-*] **:** containing three oxy groups

tri·oxy·methylene \(¦)trī¦äksē+\ *n* [ISV *trioxy-* + *methylene*] **:** TRIOXANE — usu. used with initial Greek alpha ⟨α-*trioxymethylene*⟩

[1]**trip** \'trip\ *n* -s [ME] *dial Eng* **:** a small flock (as of birds or mammals)

[2]**trip** \"\ *vb* **tripped** *also* **tript; tripped** *also* **tript; tripping; trips** [ME *trippen*, fr. MF *triper, treper* to dance, hop, trample, of Gmc origin; akin to LG *trippen, trippeln* to stamp, trample, MD *trepelen, trappelen* to stamp, trample, OE *treppan* to tread — more at TRAP] *vi* **1 a :** to dance, skip, or caper with light quick steps ⟨nymphs and shepherds . . . ~ no more in twilight ranks —John Milton⟩ **b :** to move with light quick steps **:** walk or move lightly **:** move the feet nimbly ⟨she . . . *tripped* lightly with him into the church —T.L.Peacock⟩ **2 :** to catch the foot against something so as to stagger, hop, or fall **:** stumble over something (as an obstacle in one's path) **:** make a false step ⟨the child . . . got up only to ~ on her skirt and tumble headlong again —O.E.Rölvaag⟩ ⟨*tripped* over his own feet⟩ **3 :** to fall into an error **:** make a mistake or false step **:** offend against morality, propriety, or accuracy **:** ERR, SLIP ⟨his careful reasoning which never ~*s* —H.O.Taylor⟩ ⟨nor do we ever find him *tripping* even in a matter of detail —Virginia Woolf⟩ **4 :** to stumble in articulation **:** falter in speaking ⟨drinking . . . till his tongue ~*s* —John Locke⟩ ⟨he shall stammer, cluck and ~ —Robert Graves⟩ **5 :** to make a journey or excursion ⟨*tripped* frequently to France to . . . visit troops —S.L.A.Marshall⟩ **6 :** to run past the pallet of the escapement without previously locking — used of a tooth of the escape wheel of a watch **7 :** to become strained or twisted out of the perpendicular — used of the floor of a ship between the keel and keelson **8 a :** to actuate a mechanism by the operation of some device **b :** to become operative or actuated as the result of the operation of some mechanical device ~ *vt* **1 a :** to cause to stumble or lose one's footing (as by suddenly checking the motion of a foot or leg) **:** cause to take a false step **:** throw off balance ⟨someone must have *tripped* him⟩ — often used with *up* **b :** to cause to fail or be checked by putting an obstacle in the way **:** HALT, OBSTRUCT **2 :** to detect in a misstep, error, or inconsistency **:** catch in a fault or blunder — usu. used with *up* ⟨any military man familiar with firearms could ~ you up —Kenneth Roberts⟩ ⟨wrongdoing inevitably ~*s* up itself —*Irish Digest*⟩ ⟨questions designed to ~ him up⟩ **3 a** *archaic* **:** to perform (as a dance) lightly or nimbly ⟨come and ~ it as you go, on the light fantastic toe —John Milton⟩ ⟨the young folks *tripped* it away on the grass —Harriet Martineau⟩ **b :** to dance upon (a surface) with a light and nimble step **4 :** to raise (an anchor) from the bottom by its cable or buoy rope so that it hangs free **5 a :** to pull (a yard) into a perpendicular position for lowering **b :** to hoist (a topmast) far enough to enable the fid to be withdrawn preparatory to housing or sending down **6 :** to release, let fall, set free, or otherwise operate (as a weight, compressed spring, switch, or other mechanism) esp. by removing a catch or detent **:** actuate (as a connecting, disconnecting, or controlling mechanism) by some device **7 :** to separate the petals of (a legume flower) in search of nectar causing vigorous springing apart of style and stamens and discharge of pollen that dusts over an insect (as a bee) and resulting in cross-pollination **8 :** WEDGE 5 **9 :** to raise (the bottom) even with the top of a scenery drop by an auxiliary set of lines in order to fold the drop in half and usu. out of audience view — **trip the light fantastic** [fr. the phrase *to trip on the light fantastic toe*] **:** DANCE

[3]**trip** \"\ *n* -s *often attrib* [ME, fr. *trippen* to trip] **1 :** a stroke, catch, or other movement by which one (as a wrestler) causes his antagonist to lose footing **:** the action of tripping someone **2 a :** a relatively short run of a vehicle usu. between two points or to a point and return ⟨extra ~*s* were scheduled by bus, railroad, and plane companies in anticipation of heavy holiday traffic⟩ **b :** VOYAGE, JOURNEY ⟨left China for a four-year . . . ~ abroad —Arthur Mathers⟩ ⟨my ~ around the world —Wendell Willkie⟩ ⟨a ~ to the moon⟩ ⟨missile on a ~ down the Atlantic range⟩; *esp* **:** one that is short or is undertaken for some usu. specified purpose ⟨a ~ to the dentist⟩ ⟨a day ~⟩ ⟨vacation ~*s*⟩ **c :** a single tour of travel in the course of a business operation ⟨a delivery ~⟩ ⟨a postal carrier's two ~*s* a day⟩ **d :** the distance involved in a trip ⟨the only other village was one day's mule ~ farther into the interior —C.B.Hitchcock⟩ **e :** something held to resemble physical passage from one place to another ⟨their marriage and their ~ through life —J.P.Marquand⟩ ⟨the idea started on a long ~ around . . . conference tables —Laura Fermi⟩ **3 :** an error, failure, mistake, blunder, or similar misstep ⟨a ~ in one point would have spoiled all —John Berridge⟩ **4 :** a light lively movement of the feet **:** a quick light step ⟨the ~ of children's feet⟩ **5 :** a false step caused by stumbling over something or otherwise losing one's balance **:** STUMBLE **6 :** a single board in beating to windward **:** the distance covered by a sailing ship on a single tack **7 :** the action in coursing by a dog of throwing the hare off its feet or of seizing it but losing hold in an unsuccessful effort to kill **8 :** the catch of fish made or brought in on a single voyage to a fishing ground (as by a commercial fishing vessel) **9 a :** the action of tripping mechanically (as a valve held open against a spring) **b** (1) **:** a usu. automatic device for tripping a mechanism (as a catch or detent) (2) **:** TUP 2 **10 :** a number of cars coupled together and hauled as a train in mining operations

trip *abbr* triple; triplicate

tri·pack \'trī+,-\ *n* [*tri-* + *pack*] **:** a combination of three superposed but separable films each sensitive to a different primary color for simultaneous exposure in one camera in color photography — compare BIPACK, INTEGRAL TRIPACK

tri·palmitin \(')trī+\ *n* [ISV *tri-* + *palmitin*] **:** the crystalline triglyceride $C_3H_5(OOCC_{15}H_{31})_3$ of palmitic acid found in small amounts in palm oils and various fats: glycerol tripalmitate

trip·a·ra \'tripərə\ *n* -s [NL, fr. *tri-* + *-para*] **:** a woman who has borne three children

tri·part \'trī+,-\ *adj* [*tri-* + *part*] **:** having or divided into three parts **:** THREEFOLD ⟨the conventional ~ balance of power system —Carleton Beals⟩

[1]**tri·par·tite** \(')trī¦pär,tīt, -pȧl *also* ¦d·,īt; *usu* -īd·+V\ *adj* [ME, fr. L *tripartitus*, fr. *tri-* + *partitus* — more at PARTITE] **1 a :** divided into or being in three parts **:** composed of three parts or kinds ⟨a ~ seismograph⟩ ⟨Plato's doctrine of the ~ soul —Helen North⟩ **b :** involving or of the nature of division into three parts ⟨a ~ division⟩ **2 :** having three corresponding parts or copies ⟨make indentures ~⟩ **3 a :** made between or involving three parties ⟨a ~ bloc⟩ ⟨a ~ treaty⟩ ⟨a ~ alliance⟩ ⟨~ discussions⟩ **b :** composed of or involving representatives of labor, management, and the public with each group having equal status with the other two ⟨a ~ pension board⟩ ⟨~ arbitration⟩ **4 a :** consisting of three parts or divisions ⟨these larvae had a . . . typically ~ gut —J.W.Jenkinson⟩ **b :** divided into three parts nearly to the base ⟨a ~ leaf⟩

[2]**tripartite** \"\ *n* -s [ME, fr. L *tripartitus*] **:** something (as a document, agreement, or book) divided into or made in three parts

tri·par·ti·tion \¦trī(,)pär'tishən, ,tripər-\ *n* [LL *tripartition-*, *tripartitio* threefold partition, fr. L *tripartitus* + *-ion-, -io* -ion] **:** the act of dividing or the state of being divided into three parts **:** partition into or among three ⟨~ of a uranium nucleus⟩

tri·par·tit·ism \·'pär¦,tīd·,izəm, -'pȧl, -ī,tiz- *also* ¦d·,ī-\ *also* **tri·par·tism** \·'pär¦,tizəm, -,pȧl, ¦d·,iz-\ *n* -s **:** the organization on a tripartite basis of a usu. governmental board concerned with labor relations ⟨~ . . . is designed to foster compromise —Clark Kerr⟩

tri·paschal \(')trī+\ *adj* [*tri-* + *paschal*] **:** including three passover feasts

trip coil *var of* TRIPPING COIL

tripe \'trīp\ *n* -s *often attrib* [ME, fr. OF] **1 a :** a wall of the stomach of a ruminant and esp. of the ox used as an article of food: (1) **:** the walls of the paunch or rumen — called also *plain tripe* (2) **:** the walls of the reticulum resembling honeycomb in form — called also *honeycomb tripe* **b :** an individual piece or portion of such a part of the stomach ⟨eaten . . . sheep ~*s* dipped in honey —Stephen Longstreet⟩ ⟨ox ~*s* are selected for good color and condition from ox stomachs —*New Zealand Jour. of Agric.*⟩ **2** *archaic* **:** BELLY 1a ⟨he hath his ~ full —James Howell⟩ **3 :** ENTRAIL 2 — usu. used in pl. ⟨shooting a man or cutting his ~*s* out —Joyce Cary⟩ ⟨felt a seasick rising of his ~*s* —Eric Linklater⟩ **4** *archaic* **:** a worthless or inferior and usu. disgusting person **5 :** something that is poor, worthless, and often offensive **:** inferior stuff **:** second-rate material **:** nonsensical rubbish **:** TRASH ⟨calling the report a mess of ~ —C.E.Montague⟩ ⟨the mass of popular-science ~ dished out to the American public —J.R.Newman⟩ ⟨get a little easy money by writing ~ —Bennett Cerf⟩

tripe-de-roche \trēpdə'rōsh\ *n* [F] **:** ROCK TRIPE

tripehound \'≈,≈\ *n, Austral* **:** DOG

tri·pel·en·na·mine \,trī,pe'lenə,mēn, -mən\ *n* -s [*tri-* + *pyridine* + *ethylenediamine*] **:** an antihistamine drug $C_{16}H_{21}N_3$ derived from pyridine and ethylenediamine and used in the form of its crystalline citrate or hydrochloride

trip engine *n* **:** an engine with valves worked by a trip gear

tri·peptide \(')trī+\ *n* [ISV *tri-* + *peptide;* prob. orig. formed as G *tripeptid*] **:** a peptide that yields three molecules of amino acid on hydrolysis

tri·personal \"+\ *adj, sometimes cap* [*tri-* + *personal*] **:** consisting of or existing in three persons — used of the Godhead

tri·personality \(')trī+\ *n, often cap* [*tripersonal* + *-ity*] **:** the state of being tripersonal **:** existence as three persons in one Godhead **:** TRINITY ⟨the *Tripersonality* of the Deity is the very cornerstone of our religion —Clement Carlyon⟩

trip·ery \'trīp(ə)rē\ *n* -ES [F *triperie*, fr. OF, fr. *tripe* + *-erie* -ery] **:** a place where tripe is prepared or sold

tripe stone *n* **:** a variety of the mineral anhydrite composed of contorted plates suggesting pieces of tripe

tri·petaloid \(')trī+\ *adj* [*tri-* + *petaloid*] **:** having the appearance or form of three petals ⟨~ flowers⟩

tri·petalous \"+\ *adj* [*tri-* + *-petalous*] **:** having three petals

trip-free \'≈,≈\ *adj* **:** free to trip on the occurrence of any condition (as an overload) for which provision is made even if the normal operating lever or the control-switch closing contact is held in the closed position ⟨a *trip-free* circuit breaker⟩

trip gear *n* **:** a gear for tripping; *specif* **:** a rapid cutoff gear worked by a trip

[1]**trip-hammer** \'≈,≈\ *n* **:** a massive power hammer having a helve that is tripped and allowed to fall by cam or lever action

[2]**trip-hammer** \"\ *adj* **:** resembling or held to resemble the action of a trip-hammer esp. in being characterized by repeated pounding or involving great pressure ⟨*trip-hammer* motion⟩ ⟨under *trip-hammer* questioning⟩

tri·phane \'trī,fān\ *n* -s [F, fr. LGk *triphanēs* appearing threefold, fr. Gk *tri-* three + *-phanēs* appearing, shining (fr. *phainein* to show) — more at TRI-, FANCY] **:** SPODUMENE

tri·phase \'trī+,-\ *adj* [ISV *tri-* + *phase*] **:** THREE-PHASE

tri·pha·sic \(')trī¦fāzik\ *adj* [ISV *triphase* + *-ic*] **1 :** having or occurring in three phases **2 :** THREE-PHASE

tri·phenol \(')trī+\ *n* [*tri-* + *phenol*] **:** a chemical compound containing three phenolic hydroxyl groups

tri·phenyl \"+\ *adj* [*triphenyl-*] **:** containing three phenyl groups in the molecule ⟨a ~ salt⟩

triphenyl- *comb form* [ISV *tri-* + *phenyl*] **:** three phenyl groups in the molecule

tri·phenyl·amine \(¦)trī¦fenᵊl, -fēn- +\ *n* [ISV *triphenyl-* + *amine*] **:** a crystalline tertiary amine $(C_6H_5)_3N$ that is practically neutral and that is made from diphenylamine, iodobenzene, and copper powder and in other ways

tri·phenyl·carbinol \"+\ *n* [ISV *triphenyl-* + *carbinol*] **:** a crystalline alcohol $(C_6H_5)_3COH$ made by reaction of methyl benzoate or benzophenone with phenyl-magnesium bromide and converted by acetyl chloride or hydrogen chloride into triphenylmethyl chloride — compare TRIPHENYLMETHYL

tri·phenyl·ene \trī'fenᵊl,ēn, -fēn-\ *n* [ISV *triphenyl-* + *-ene*] **:** a crystalline, tetracyclic aromatic hydrocarbon $C_{18}H_{12}$ present in coal tar and structurally constituted as though three *ortho*-phenylene radicals were joined to form a central hexagonal ring

tri·phenyl·formazan \(¦)trī¦fenᵊl, -fēn- +\ *n* [*triphenyl-* + *formazan*] **:** a red insoluble compound $C_6H_5N{=}NC(C_6H_5){=}NNHC_6H_5$ obtained by reaction of benzaldehyde phenylhydrazone with benzenediazonium chloride or by reduction of triphenyltetrazolium chloride

tri·phenyl·methane \"+\ *n* [ISV *triphenyl-* + *methane*] **:** a crystalline hydrocarbon $CH(C_6H_5)_3$ that is the parent compound of many dyes and that is made by the reaction of chloroform with benzene in the presence of aluminum chloride and in other ways

triphenylmethane dye *also* **triphenylmethane color** *n* **:** any of a group of triarylmethane dyes (as pararosaniline, crystal violet, or aurin) derived from triphenylmethane and used as mothproofing agents in the case of some colorless derivatives as well as dyes, organic pigments, and biological stains in the case of colored derivatives — compare LEUCO BASE, XANTHENE DYE

tri·phenyl·methyl \"+\ *n* [ISV *triphenyl-* + *methyl*] **:** the univalent radical $C(C_6H_5)_3$ derived from triphenylmethane by removal of the nonaromatic hydrogen atom and isolated as the first organic free radical in the form of very active yellow solutions by treating triphenylmethyl chloride $C(C_6H_5)_3Cl$ in solution usu. with finely divided silver or zinc — compare TRIPHENYLCARBINOL

triphenyl phosphate *n* **:** a crystalline nonflammable inorganic ester $(C_6H_5)_3PO_4$ used chiefly as a plasticizer and fire retardant (as for cellulose plastics)

tri·phenyl·tetrazolium chloride \(¦)trī¦fenᵊl, -fēn- + . . .-\ *n* [*triphenyl-* + *tetrazolium*] **:** a colorless crystalline salt $C(C_6H_5)_3N_4Cl$ that is obtained by oxidative ring closure of triphenylformazan and that gives back triphenylformazan on reduction (as by enzymes or reducing sugars) so that the red color formed can serve as a stain for tissues, as a test for viability (as of seeds), and as an analytical reagent — called also *tetrazolium chloride, 2,3,5-triphenyltetrazolium chloride, TTC*

[1]**tri·phib·i·an** \(')trī¦fibēən\ *n* -s [*tri-* + *-phibian* (as in *amphibian*, n.)] **1 :** a person and esp. a military commander who is triphibian **2 :** a triphibian airplane

[2]**triphibian** \"\ *adj* [*tri-* + *-phibian* (as in *amphibian*, adj.)] **1 a :** adept at war alike on land, at sea, and in the air **b :** designed for or equipped to operate from land, water, snow, or ice as well as in the air ⟨a ~ airplane⟩ **2 :** TRIPHIBIOUS 1 ⟨a ~ military operation⟩

tri·phib·i·ous \(')trī¦fibēəs\ *adj* [*tri-* + *-phibious* (as in *amphibious*)] **1 :** employing, involving, or constituted by land, naval, and air forces and often including airborne troops in coordinated attack ⟨~ operations⟩ ⟨~ forces⟩ ⟨~ strategy⟩ ⟨~ warfare⟩ ⟨~ landing exercises⟩ **2 :** TRIPHIBIAN 1 ⟨~ marines⟩ ⟨~ airplanes⟩

trip hook *n* **:** SLIP HOOK

tripho·ra \'trifərə, -rīf-\ *n, cap* [NL, fr. *tri-* + *-phora;* fr. the fact that it usu. bears three flowers] **:** a genus of American terrestrial orchids having fleshy tubers, ovate usu. clasping leaves, axillary flowers that have an erect lip but are crestless and spurless, and fruit that is a drooping capsule — see NODDING CAP

tri·phosphate \(')trī+\ *n* [*tri-* + *phosphate*] **1 :** a salt or ester of triphosphoric acid — compare ADENOSINE TRIPHOSPHATE, SODIUM TRIPOLYPHOSPHATE **2 :** a salt containing three phosphate radicals

tri·phos·pho·pyridine nucleotide \(¦)trī¦fäsfō+. . .-\ *n* [*tri-* + *phosph-* + *pyridine*] **:** a coenzyme $C_{21}H_{28}N_7O_{17}P_3$ of numerous dehydrogenases (as that acting on glucose 6-phosphate) that occurs esp. in red blood cells and plays a role in intermediate metabolism similar to that of diphosphopyridine nucleotide but acting often on different metabolites — called also *codehydrogenase II, coenzyme II, TPN*

tri·phosphoric acid \¦trī+. . .-\ *n* [*tri-* + *phosphoric*] **:** a polyphosphoric acid $H_5P_3O_{10}$ that is a partial anhydride of three molecules of orthophosphoric acid, is capable of hydrolysis into orthophosphoric acid and pyrophosphoric acid, and is known chiefly in the form of salts and esters

triph·thong \'trif,thȯŋ, ÷ 'trip,- *also* -thäŋ\ *n* -s [*tri-* + *-phthong* (as in *diphthong*)] **1 :** a speech item consisting of three successive sounds (as in the first word following the consonant in *r*-droppers' pronunciation of *fire house* or *powerhouse* or of the word *wow* or for the letters preceding the *pe* of *yipe*) made with the tongue in vowel articulatory positions and serving or capable of serving metrically as a monosyllable — compare [2]CENTERING, DIPHTHONG **2 :** TRIGRAPH

triph·thong·al \(')≈¦≈(g)əl\ *adj* **:** of, relating to, or having the character of a triphthong

triph·y·lite \'trifə,līt\ *also* **triph·y·line** \-lēn, -lən\ *n* -s [*triphylite* alter. (influenced by *-ite*) of *triphyline*, fr. G *triphylin*, fr. *tri-* + *phyl-* + *-in* *-ine;* fr. its three bases] **:** a grayish green or bluish orthorhombic phosphate of lithium, iron, and manganese isomorphous with lithiophilite and commonly massive

tri·pinnate *also* **tri·pinnated** \(')trī+\ *adj* [*tri-* + *pinnate* or *pinnated*] **:** thrice pinnate **:** bipinnate with each division pinnate (as the leaves of an aralia or various ferns) — **tri·pinnately** \"+\ *adv*

tri·pinnatifid \¦trī+\ *adj* [*tri-* + *pinnatifid*] **:** thrice pinnately cleft **:** bipinnatifid with segments again pinnatifid

tri·pinnatisect \"+\ *adj* [*tri-* + *pinnatisect*] **:** tripinnatifid with the divisions extending nearly to the base or midrib

tripl- *or* **triplo-** *comb form* [Gk *triploos*, fr. *tri-* three + *-ploos* (as in *diploos* double) — more at TRI-, DOUBLE] **:** triple ⟨*triplo*pia⟩ ⟨*triplo*blastic⟩

tripl *abbr* triplicate

tri·plane \'trī+,-\ *n* [*tri-* + *plane*] **:** an airplane with three main supporting surfaces superposed

trip·lar·is \tri'pla(a)rəs\ *n, cap* [NL, fr. LL, threefold, fr. L *triplus* triple + *-aris* -ar] **:** a genus of tropical American shrubs and trees (family Polygonaceae) mostly with ant-infested hollow stems, dioecious flowers, and prominently winged fruit — see ANT TREE

[1]**tri·ple** \'tripəl\ *vb* **tripled; tripled; tripling** \-p(ə)liŋ\ **triples** [ME *triplen*, fr. LL *triplare*, fr. L *triplus* triple] *vt* **1 :** to make three times as great or as much or as many **:** make threefold **:** multiply by three **:** TREBLE ⟨~ the possible 3 percent to 9 —Gabriel Kolko⟩ ⟨recreation facilities for children were *tripled* —*Current Biog.*⟩ **2 a :** to advance (a base runner in baseball) by a three-base hit **b :** to bring about the scoring of (a run in baseball) by a three-base hit ~ *vi* **1 :** to become three times as great **:** grow to three times the former number, size, or amount **:** increase threefold **:** TREBLE ⟨the population has almost *tripled* since 1930 —*Amer. Guide Series: Mich.*⟩ **2 :** to make a three-base hit in baseball

[2]**triple** \"\ *n* -s [ME, fr. L *triplus*] **1 a :** a triple sum, quantity, or number **:** a threefold amount **:** the product of a number multiplied by three ⟨add more than ~ to his income —H.C.W. Angelo⟩ ⟨increased to ~ its original size⟩ **b :** a combination of three usu. of related character and united **:** a group, set, or series of three **2 triples** *pl but sing or pl in constr* **:** a system for ringing changes on seven bells consisting of three pairs plus tenor **3 :** TRIPLET 2 **4 :** THREE-BASE HIT **5 :** TRIPLE VALVE **6 :** TURKEY 6

[3]**triple** \"\ *adj* [MF or L; MF, fr. L *triplus*, fr. *tri-* + *-plus* (as in *duplus* double) — more at DOUBLE] **1 :** being three times as much or as great or as many **:** multiplied by three **:** of three times the amount or quantity **:** THREEFOLD **2 :** consisting of three usu. combined members, things, or sets **:** having three parts joined together ⟨overcrowding produced ~ sessions in some schools⟩ **3 :** having a threefold relation or character **:** having three applications **:** combining three often dissimilar things or qualities **:** existing or occurring in three ways ⟨worked as a double or even ~ agent —*Time*⟩ **4 :** taken by threes or in groups of three **5 :** three times repeated **:** TREBLE **6 :** having three beats per measure ⟨~ time⟩ ⟨~ rhythm⟩ **7 a** *of meter* **:** having units of three components (as syllables) ⟨~ feet⟩ **b** *of rhyme* **:** involving correspondence of three syllables (as in *unfortunate-importunate*)

[4]**triple** \"\ *var of* TRIPPLE

triple-a \¦≈≈¦≈\ *adj, usu cap A* **:** A1 ⟨a *triple-A* priority⟩ ⟨*triple-A* rating⟩ ⟨*triple-A* investments⟩

triple-awned grass *or* **triple-awn grass** \¦≈≈¦≈-\ *n* **:** NEEDLEGRASS 2

tripleback \'≈≈,≈\ *adj* **:** constituting a sofa or settee (as in the Chippendale or Sheraton style) having a back in three parts like chair backs

triple block *n* **:** a pulley block with three sheaves

triple bond *n* **:** a chemical bond consisting of three covalent bonds between two atoms in a molecule and usu. represented in structural formulas by three lines, three dots, or six dots that denote three pairs of electrons (as in the formulas for acetylene HC≡CH, HC⋮CH, or HC:::CH) — compare DOUBLE BOND, UNSATURATED b

triple counterpoint *n* **:** three-part musical counterpoint so written that any part is transposable above or below any other

triple crown *n, usu cap T&C* **1 :** an unofficial title in horse racing representing the championship achieved by a horse that wins the three classic races for three year olds: **a :** one in English racing representing the winning of the Two Thousand Guineas, the Derby, and the St. Leger **b :** one in American racing representing the winning of the Kentucky Derby, the Belmont Stakes, and the Preakness Stakes **2 :** the unofficial title representing the championship attained by a baseball player who at the end of a single season leads his league in batting average, home runs, and runs batted in

triple-expansion engine *n* **:** a compound engine using three cylinders successively

triple first *n* **1 :** first-class honors in three different major courses of study esp. at Cambridge and Oxford universities **2 :** a student who takes a triple first

triple fugue *n* **:** a musical fugue with three subjects

triple fusion *n* **:** the fusion involving two polar nuclei and a sperm nucleus that occurs in double fertilization in a seed plant and results in the formation of the endosperm

tri·ple·gia \(')trī¦plēj(ē)ə\ *n* -s [NL, fr. *tri-* + *-plegia*] **:** hemiplegia plus paralysis of a limb on the opposite side

triple-header \,≈≈'hedə(r)\ *n* **:** a sports program consisting of three consecutive contests ⟨a basketball *triple-header*⟩ — compare DOUBLEHEADER

triple-nerved \¦≈≈¦≈\ *adj* **:** having three nerves; *usu* **:** having a prominent vein on each side of the midrib above the base ⟨the *triple-nerved* leaf of a sunflower⟩

triple play *n* **:** a play or a continuous sequence of plays in baseball by which three outs are made during a single at bat

triple point *n* **1 :** a point of a plane curve such that every straight line through the point meets the curve in three coincident points there **2 :** a point on a phase diagram representing a set of conditions under which the gaseous, liquid, and solid phases of a substance (as water) can exist in equilibrium — compare ICE POINT

tri·pler \'trip(ə)lə(r)\ *n* -s **:** a circuit usu. associated with a vacuum tube in an electronic device that accepts a signal of one frequency and delivers a signal three times that at the input

triple-rivet \¦≈≈¦≈≈\ *vt* **:** to rivet (a joint) in such manner that all the rivets used are arranged in three rows

triple root *n* **:** a root x_0 of an algebraic equation $f(x)=0$ such that $(x-x_0)^3$ is a factor of $f(x)$ while $(x-x_0)^4$ is not

triples *pres 3d sing of* TRIPLE, *pl of* TRIPLE

triple salt *n* **1 :** a salt (as microcosmic salt) yielding on hydrolysis three different cations or anions **2 :** a salt regarded as a molecular combination of three distinct salts rather than as a coordination complex — compare DOUBLE SALT

triple scalar product *n* **:** the scalar product of a vector with the vector product of two other vectors

triple screw *n* **:** a screw with three parallel threads

Triple Sec *trademark* — used for a sweet colorless orange-flavored liqueur higher in alcoholic content than curaçao but distilled from spirit in which peel from the curaçao orange as well as neroli and orrisroot have been macerated
triple sheer *n* : a dress fabric of rayon or rayon and silk similar to sheer but made opaque instead of transparent
triple-space \ˈ≈-ˈ≈\ *vt* : to type (copy) leaving two blank line spaces between lines of copy ~ *vi* : to type on every third line space
triple star *n* : a system of three stars apparently in close proximity
trip·let \ˈtriplət, *usu* -əd.+V\ *n* -s [²*triple* + -*et*] **1** : a unit of three lines of verse **2** : a collection of three of a kind : a combination of three united : a set or group of three ⟨fraction ~*s*⟩ **3 a** : one of three children or offspring born at one birth **b triplets** *pl* : a group of three offspring born at one birth **4** : a group of three musical notes or tones performed in the time of two of the same value **5** : a combination of three lenses (as in a camera or microscope) **6 triplets** *pl* : three cards of a kind esp. in poker **7** : a composite gemstone made by cementing together three parts of which the top and bottom are usu. genuine and the middle a colored substitute **8 a** : a spectrum line or an energy level of an atom, molecule, or nucleus having three components associated with the three possible orientations of one quantum unit of spin **b triplets** *pl* : three lines in a spectrum closely adjacent or in sets of three (as in the spectrum of iron)
tripletail \ˈ≈,≈\ *n* **1 a** : a large edible marine percoid fish (*Lobotes surinamensis*) which occurs in the warm seas along the American Atlantic coast from Cape Cod to northern So. America and in which the long dorsal and anal fins extend backward and with the caudal fin appear like a three-lobed tail **b** : either of two fishes (*L. pacificus* and *L. erate*) of the Pacific and Indian oceans closely related to the Atlantic tripletail **2** : a spadefish (*Chaetodipterus faber*)
triple thread *n* : one of three equal parallel threads on the same screw with each thread being 120 degrees ahead of the next succeeding — compare DOUBLE THREAD
triple threat *n* : a football player (as a back) adept at running, kicking, and forward passing
triple-threat \ˈ≈-ˈ≈\ *adj* [*triple threat*] : adept in three different fields of activity or in three different phases of the same activity ⟨an international *triple-threat* man of the arts: he can draw, he can write, and he is an excellent photographer —*N.Y. Herald Tribune*⟩
triple-throw switch *n* : a switch that by a single throw makes a triple adjustment (as of circuits in an electrical connection, of organ stops on a console, or of tracks in a railroad switchyard)
triplet lily *n* : any plant of the genus *Brodiaea*
triple-tongue \ˈ≈-ˈ≈\ *vi* : to articulate the notes of triplets in fast tempo on a wind instrument by using the tip and the back of the tongue alternately to interrupt the breath stream beginning each successive triplet with the tip — compare DOUBLE-TONGUE, SINGLE-TONGUE
triple tree *n, archaic* : GALLOWS
triple valve *n* : the automatic valve under a railroad car that controls the automatic air brake by regulating by three openings the intake, exhaust, and equalization of compressed air in the brake piston
¹**triplex** \ˈtri,pleks, -rī,p-\ *n* -ES [L, triple] : something (as a building or apartment) that is triplex
²**triplex** \"\ *adj* [L, fr. *tri-* + *-plex* -fold — more at SIMPLE] **1** : having three parts or elements : THREEFOLD, TRIPLE ⟨~ windows⟩ ⟨~ cable⟩ **2** : having three principal operative parts or motions : producing a threefold effect ⟨~ chain block⟩ ⟨~ pump⟩ — compare DUPLEX **3 a** : containing three apartments or dwelling units ⟨~ buildings⟩ **b** : having three floors or levels ⟨a ~ apartment⟩ **4 a** : consisting of a middle lined with paper on both sides ⟨~ paperboard⟩ **b** : consisting of three webs of paper laminated with an adhesive (as glue, wax, or asphalt) ⟨a ~ bag⟩ **5** : having three doses of a given dominant gene — used of a tetraploid cell or individual
triplex process *n* : a process for making steel in which the material is partially treated in a Bessemer, transferred without interruption to an open-hearth furnace for the second stage of the treatment, and then finished in an electric furnace
¹**trip·li·cate** \ˈtripləkət, -lēk- *sometimes* -lə,kāt; *usu* \d.+V\ *adj* [ME, fr. L *triplicatus*, past part. of *triplicare* to triple, fr. *triplic-, triplex* triple, threefold] **1** : made in three identical copies : THREEFOLD ⟨a ~ agreement⟩ **2** : THIRD — used of one of a set of copies ⟨the ~ copy shall be delivered directly to the collector of customs —*U.S.Code*⟩
²**trip·li·cate** \-lə,kāt, *usu* -ād.+V\ *vt* -ED/-ING/-S **1** : to multiply by three : increase threefold : TRIPLE **2** : to reproduce twice; *specif* : to make an original and two carbon copies of
³**triplicate** *like* ¹TRIPLICATE\ *n* -s : a third thing like two others of the same kind; *specif* : one of three identical copies of something (as a document or letter) ⟨the ~ . . . is forwarded to the administrative agency —*Jour. of Accountancy*⟩ — **in triplicate** *adv* : in an original and two identical copies ⟨prepared the manuscript *in triplicate* —W.A.White⟩
trip·li·ca·tion \,triplə'kāshən\ *n* -s [MF, fr. LL *triplication-, triplicatio* action of tripling, fr. L *triplicatus* + *-ion-, -io* -ion] **1 a** : a legal pleading showing why the last pleading of the opposing party should not be given legal effect : an equitable rebutter **b** : the plaintiff's reply to the defendant's rejoinder in Roman and civil law resembling the surrejoinder in common law **c** : the defendant's answer to the plaintiff's replication in early English law **2** : the action of tripling or making threefold or adding three together **3** : something that is triplicated or threefold
tri·plic·i·ty \triˈplisəd.ē, trīˈp-\ *n* -ES [ME *triplicite*, fr. LL *triplicitas* threefold quality, fr. L *triplic-, triplex* triple + *-itas* -ity — more at TRIPLEX] **1** : one of the groups of three signs each distant 120 degrees from the other into which the signs of the zodiac are divided — called also *trigon* **2** : the quality or state of being triple or threefold ⟨~ of stars⟩ **3** : a group or combination of three : TRINITY, TRIO **4** : an extreme form of duplicity or double-dealing
trip line *n* **1** : a line or light rope used to operate a trip (as to free a dog hook in logging) **2** : HAULBACK 1
tripling *pres part of* TRIPLE
trip·lite \ˈtri,plīt\ *n* -s [G *triplit*, fr. *tripl-* + *-it* -ite; fr. its threefold cleavage] : a dark brown monoclinic basic phosphate of manganese, iron, magnesium, and calcium $(Mn,Fe,Mg,Ca)_2(PO_4)(F,OH)$ generally with a fibrous massive structure
triplo- — see TRIPL-
trip·lo·blas·tic \ˌtriplō'blastik\ *adj* [*tripl-* + *-blastic*] : having three primary germ layers
trip·lo·blas·ti·ca \,≈≈'≈stəkə\ *n pl, often cap* [NL, fr. *tripl-* + Gk *blastika*, pl. of *blastikos* budding, fr. *blast-* + *-ikos* -ic] : animals having three germ layers — used when these are held to form a natural group comprising the worms and all higher forms
trip·lo·caulescent \ˌtri(,)plō+\ *adj* [*tripl-* + *caulescent*] : lacking the capacity of reproduction until an axis of the third order is attained — used of plants (as the common plantain) in which the primary axis produces foliage leaves, the secondary axis bracteal leaves, and the tertiary axis the flowers; compare DIPLOCAULESCENT, HAPLOCAULESCENT
trip·lo·chiton \,triplō+\ *n, cap* [NL, fr. *tripl-* + *chiton*] : a small genus comprising tall tropical African trees with palmately lobed alternate leaves like those of the maple and being included in Sterculiaceae or made the type of a separate family — see OBECHE
¹**trip·loid** \ˈtri,plȯid\ *adj* [ISV *tripl-* + *-oid*] : threefold in appearance or arrangement; *specif* : having or being a chromosome number that is three times the monoploid number ⟨a ~ cell⟩ — compare POLYPLOID
²**triploid** \"\ *n* -s : a triploid individual
trip·loid·ite \ˈtri,plȯi,dīt\ *n* -s [*triplite* + *-oid* + *-ite*] : a mineral $(Mn,Fe)_2(PO_4)(OH)$ consisting of a yellowish or reddish brown basic phosphate of manganese and iron isomorphous with wolfeite and probably with sarkinite
trip·loi·dy \ˈtri,plȯidē\ *n* -ES [*triploid* + *-y*] : the state of being triploid ⟨~ in higher animals is not common —H.P. Riley⟩
trip·lum \ˈtripləm\ *n* -s [ML, fr. neut. of L *triplus* triple — more at TRIPLE] **1** : the third voice part in medieval polyphony counting upward from the tenor inclusive **2** : a musical composition for three voice parts
tri·ply \ˈtriplē, -li\ *adv* : to a triple degree : in three times the amount or sum : in a threefold manner ⟨mystery seems to be ~ and darkly compounded —B.R.Redman⟩ ⟨the ~ divine principle, Love —Mary B. Eddy⟩
¹**tri·pod** \ˈtrī,päd\ *n* -s [L *tripod-, tripus*, fr. Gk *tripod-, tripous* three-footed, fr. *tri-* three + *pod-, pous* foot — more at TRI-, FOOT] **1 a** : a vessel (as a pot or caldron) resting on three legs or feet **b** (1) : the seat of the priestess of Apollo at Delphi in ancient Greece when delivering oracles ⟨a tone . . . less reminiscent of the priestess on the ~ —B.N.Cardozo⟩ (2) : an oracular seat held to resemble the one at ancient Delphi ⟨after the inauguration . . . the editor returned to his ~ —Arthur Krock⟩ **2** : a structure or piece of apparatus (as a stool, table, or altar) supported on three legs **3 a** : a three-legged support; *esp* : a three-legged stand used to support a portable instrument (as a camera) and usu. consisting of a small table or head jointed to each of the three legs which are often telescopic **b** : a frame set in a field on which hay is piled for curing **4 a** : a tripodal bone **b** : a sponge spicule having three equal rays

tripod 3a

²**tripod** \"\ *adj* : having or supported on three feet or legs ⟨a ~ vase⟩
trip·o·dal \ˈtripəd³l, ˈtrī,päd³l\ *adj* **1** : having three feet or legs : forming a tripod **2** : having three processes — used of a bone
tri·pod·ic walk \(ˈ)trī'pädik-\ *n* : a mode of walking in which two feet on one side and one median foot on the other are used simultaneously (as in many insects)
tripod puller *n* : a stump puller that lifts the stump vertically out of the ground by means of chains passing over pulleys attached to a tripod
tripod table *n* : a table supported by a shaft from whose lower end radiate three curved or slanting legs
trip·o·dy \ˈtripədē\ *n* -ES [LL *tripodia*, fr. Gk, fr. *tripod-, tripous* three-footed + *-ia* -y] : a unit or group of three feet in prosody
tri·point·ed \ˈtrī+,-\ *adj* [*tri-* + *pointed*] : having three points ⟨a ~ vase⟩
tri·polar \(ˈ)trī+\ *adj* [*tri-* + *polar*] : having three poles ⟨~ mitoses⟩
¹**trip·o·li** \ˈtripəlē, -li\ *n* -s [F, fr. *Tripoli*, region in northern Africa, its locality] **1** : an earth consisting of very friable soft schistose deposits of silica regardless of their mode of origin and including diatomite and kieselguhr **2** : an earth consisting of deposits of friable and dustlike silica not of diatomaceous material and possibly derived from the decomposition of siliceous limestone
²**tripoli** \"\ *adj, usu cap* [fr. *Tripoli*, Libya] **1** : of or from Tripoli, a capital of Libya : of the kind or style prevalent in Tripoli **2** [fr. *Tripoli*, Lebanon] : of or from the city of Tripoli, Lebanon : of the kind or style prevalent in Tripoli
¹**tri·pol·i·tan** \trəˈpälət³n\ *adj, usu cap* [*tripolitan* back-formation fr. *Tripolitania; tripolitanian* fr. *Tripolitania* + E *-an*] **1** *or* **tri·pol·i·ta·nian** \trəˌpälə'tānyən, ˌtri,päl-, ˌtripəl-, -ānēən\ : of or belonging to Tripolitania, No. Africa **2** [*Tripoli*, former Barbary state in northern Africa + *-itan* (as in *metropolitan*)] : of or belonging to the Barbary state of Tripoli
²**tripolitan** \"\ *or* **tripolitanian** \"\ *n* -s *cap* [*tripolitan* back-formation fr. *Tripolitania; tripolitanian* fr. *Tripolitania* + E *-an*, n. suffix] : one of the people of Tripolitania, Libya, chiefly inhabited by Berbers and Arabs with some European, Turkish, and Negro elements
trip·o·lite \ˈtripə,līt\ *n* -s [*Tripoli*, northern Africa + E *-ite*] : TRIPOLI; *specif* : TRIPOLI 1
tri·polyphosphate \(ˌ)trī+\ *n* [*tri-* + *polyphosphate*] : TRIPHOSPHATE — not used systematically
tri·pos \ˈtrī,päs\ *n* -ES [modif. (influenced by Gk nouns ending in *-os*) of L *tripus* tripod — more at TRIPOD] **1** *archaic* : TRIPOD **2** [so called fr. the three-legged stool on which he sat at the disputation] **a** (1) *usu cap* : a Bachelor of Arts (as at Cambridge University) formerly appointed to dispute humorously or satirically at commencement with candidates for degrees (2) *or* **tripos verses** : a set of humorous verses originally composed by this official but following the abolition of his office published independently at each commencement until 1894 (3) : the list of successful candidates for honors printed on the back of a paper containing tripos verses **b** (1) : the final examination instituted in the first half of the 18th century for honors in mathematical science (as at Cambridge university) — compare OPTIME, WRANGLER (2) : the final honors examination in classics to which formerly only those were admitted who had previously obtained honors in mathematics (3) : a final honors examination (as at Cambridge university) in a subject (as theology) other than mathematics and classics **c** : an honors course or school (as at Cambridge university)
trip·pant \ˈtripənt\ *adj* [²*trip* + *-ant*] : PASSANT 1 ⟨three goats ~ argent —Edward Almack⟩
tripped *past of* TRIP
trip·per \ˈtripə(r)\ *n* -s [ME *trippere*, fr. *trippen* to trip + *-ere* -er — more at TRIP] **1** : a person that trips: as **a** *chiefly Brit* : one that takes a trip : EXCURSIONIST, TOURIST ⟨a kind of traveller's companion for the literary-minded ~ —*New Yorker*⟩ ⟨like a day ~ who has missed the last train home —Elizabeth Bowen⟩ **b** : one (as an extra employee on a street railway) employed by the trip **c** : DECKMAN 2c **2** : a device or mechanism that trips: as **a** : a contrivance operated by a passing train to work a signal, switch, or alarm **b** : a projecting piece on a railroad track for operating a catch on a passing train to apply the brakes or sound a warning **c** : a mechanism for releasing the prop of a wicket in a movable dam **d** : a device for causing the load on a conveyor to be discharged into a hopper or other receptacle
trip·pery \ˈtripəri\ *adj* [*tripper* + *-y*] *chiefly Brit* : TOURISTY
¹**trip·pet** \ˈtripət\ *n* -s [ME *tripet*, fr. *trippen* to trip + *-et*] **1** *dial* : the pointed piece of wood used in the game of tipcat **2** : a cam, wiper, or projecting piece that strikes another piece at definite times
²**trippet** \"\ *dial Eng var of* TRIVET
tripping *adj* [fr. past part. of ²*trip*] **1** : PASSANT 1 ⟨three hinds ~ proper —H.S.London⟩ **2** : moving lightly and quickly : LIGHT-FOOTED, NIMBLE, QUICK ⟨bursts out into a ~ singing measure —H.S.Bennett⟩ ⟨~ lines⟩ **3** *archaic* : stumbling, erring, or sinning in moral behavior **4** : used to trip a mechanism ⟨a ~ device⟩
tripping bracket *n* : a plate or bar attached to a ship's beam or structural member to prevent free flanges from bending
tripping coil *also* **trip coil** *n* : a coil forming part of an automatic circuit breaker
tripping line *n* **1** : a small rope attached to a yard or upper mast and used to trip it and guide it to the deck **2** : a line used in tripping or capsizing a sea anchor
trip·ping·ly *adv* : in a light, nimble, quick manner : with agility, dexterity, or smoothness of execution ⟨speak the speech . . . ~ on the tongue —Shak.⟩
tripping relay *n* : a trip-free relay
tripp·ke·ite \ˈtripkē,īt\ *n* -s [G *trippkeit*, fr. Paul *Trippke* †1880 Polish mineralogist + G *-it* -ite] : a tetragonal arsenite of copper of unknown formula characterized by short often bent prismatic crystals which can be broken into flexible fibers because of the excellent prismatic cleavages
¹**trip·ple** \ˈtripəl\ *n* -s [Afrik *trippel*, fr. *trippel* to tripple] *chiefly southern Africa* : a gait in which the horse moves both near and both off legs alternately and which somewhat resembles the amble
²**tripple** \"\ *or* **tri·ple** \"\ *vi* -ED/-ING/-S [Afrik *trippel*, fr. D *trippelen*, to trip along, amble; akin to LG *trippeln* to stamp, trample — more at TRIP] *chiefly southern Africa* : to go at a tripple
trips *pl of* TRIP, *pres 3d sing of* TRIP
trip·sa·coid \ˈtripsə,kȯid\ *adj, often cap* [NL *Tripsacum* + E *-oid*] : resembling or related to the genus *Tripsacum*
trip·sa·cum \ˈtripsəkəm\ *n, cap* [NL, fr. Gk *tripsis* rubbing, friction, resistance to rubbing; akin to Gk *tribein* to rub — more at THROW] : a genus of coarse perennial grasses of the southern U. S. and So. America having androgynous spikes with the 2-flowered staminate spikelets above and the pistillate below with the latter embedded in the joints of the rachis — see GAMA
trip scale *n* : an equal-arm balance having pans which are flat platforms or shallow trays elevated above the beam — compare PLATFORM SCALE
tripsill \ˈ≈,≈\ *n* [³*trip* + *sill*] : a timber placed across the bottom of the sluiceway in a splash dam against which rest the planks closing the dam

trip scale

tript *past of* TRIP
trip·tane \ˈtrip,tān\ *n* -s [*tri-* methyl + *p* (alter. of *b* in *butane*) + *butane*] : a liquid hydrocarbon $(CH_3)_3CCH(CH_3)_2$ that is one of the highest antiknock motor fuels known and hence is a valuable blending agent esp. for aviation gasolines to increase their power; 2,2,3-trimethyl-butane
trip·ter·al \ˈtriptərəl\ *adj* [Gk *tripteros* having three wings (fr. *tri-* three + *-pteros* -pterous) + E *-al*] : having three rows of columns ⟨the later temple . . . ~ at the ends —D.S.Robertson⟩ — compare DIPTERAL
trip-toe \ˈ≈,≈\ *n* -s : HOBBLEBUSH
trip·ton \ˈtrip,tän, -ptən\ *n* -s [G, fr. Gk, neut. of *triptos* rubbed, ground, verbal of *tribein* to rub — more at THROW] : suspended nonliving debris (as bits of mineral matter or humus or organic remains) in a body of water — compare PLANKTON, SESTON
trip·tote \ˈtrip,tōt\ *n* -s [LL *triptoton*, fr. LGk *triptōton*, neut. of *triptōtos* having only three cases, fr. Gk *tri-* three + *-ptōtos* (fr. *piptein* to fall, influenced in meaning by Gk *ptōsis* case, fall) — more at TRI-, PTOSIS, FEATHER] : a noun having three cases only — compare DIPTOTE
trip·tych *also* **trip·tich** \ˈtrip(,)tik, -,tēk\ *n* -s [Gk *triptychos* threefold, fr. *tri-* three + *-ptychos* (fr. *ptychē* fold, layer)] **1** : a writing tablet with three waxed leaves hinged for folding together and used by the ancient Romans for everyday writing **2 a** : a picture or carving in three compartments side by side; *esp* : a picture serving as an altarpiece and consisting of a central panel and two flanking panels of half its size that fold over it — compare DIPTYCH 3, POLYPTYCH **b** : something resembling or held to resemble such a 3-part picture; *esp* : a work (as in art, literature, or music) made up of three matching or contrasting parts
trip·tyque *also* **tryp·tique** *or* **tryp·tyque** \(ˈ)trip'tēk\ *n* -s [F *triptyque*, lit., triptych, fr. Gk *triptychos*] : a customs pass for the temporary importation of an automobile into a specified country
trip·u·hy·ite \,tripə'wē,īt\ *n* -s [*Tripuhy*, locality in eastern Brazil + E *-ite*] : a mineral $Fe_2Sb_2O_7$ (?) consisting of an oxide of antimony and iron in greenish yellow to dark brown fine-grained aggregates
trip wire *n* **1** : a low-placed wire used to discourage trespassing on lawns or grass **2** : a wire concealed close to the ground and used esp. in military operations to actuate a warning signal or set off an explosive device usu. when pulled or moved
tripy·laea \,tripə'lēə, ,tri,pī'l-\ *or* **tripy·lar·ia** \-la(a)rēə\ [NL *Tripylaea* fr. *tri-* + Gk *pylē* opening; NL *Tripylaria* fr. *tri-* + Gk *pylē* + NL *-aria*] *syn of* TRIPYLEA
tripy·lea \-lēə\ *n pl, cap* [NL, fr. *tri-* + Gk *pylē* opening, orifice — more at PYLON] : a suborder of Radiolaria comprising protozoans with or without spiculate skeletons and with the central capsule pierced by three openings
¹**tripy·le·an** *or* **tripy·lae·an** \ˈ≈(,)≈'lēən\ *also* **tripy·lar·i·an** \-ˈla(a)rēən\ *adj* : of or relating to the Tripylea
²**tripylean** *or* **tripylaean** \"\ *also* **tripylarian** \"\ *n* -s : a tripylean protozoan
tri·que \ˈtrē(,)kā\ *n, pl* **trique** *or* **triques** *usu cap* **1 a** : an Indian people of the western part of the state of Oaxaca, Mexico **b** : a member of such people **2** : the language of the Trique people
tri·que·an \(ˈ)trē'kāən\ *n* -s *usu cap* : a language family comprising Trique
tri·quetra \trīˈkwē·trə, -we·t-\ *n* -s [L, fem. of *triquetrus* three-cornered] : a triangle-shaped figure or decoration; *esp* : one formed of three interlaced arcs or loops
tri·quet·ric \(ˈ)trīˈkwe·trik\ *adj* [L *triquetra* + E *-ic*] : of, relating to, or like triquetra
tri·quetrous \-wē·trəs, -we·t-\ *adj* [L *triquetrus*, fr. *tri-* + *-quetrus* -pointed, -cornered — more at WHET] : having three corners or salient angles or edges; *specif* : having three acute angles ⟨the ~ stems of many sedges⟩

triquetra

tri·quetrum \≈'≈·trəm\ *n, pl* **tri·quetra** \-rə\ [NL, fr. L, neut. of *triquetrus*] **1 a** : PYRAMIDAL BONE **b** : WORMIAN BONE **2** : TRISKELION
tri·quinate \(ˈ)trī+\ *adj* [*tri-* + *quinate*] : ternate with the divisions quinate
tri·racial \"+\ *adj* [*tri-* + *racial*] : of, relating to, or descended from three divisions or stocks of mankind; *specif* : of Negro, white, and Indian ancestry ⟨the ~ group of Cajuns⟩
tri·radial \"+\ *adj* [*tri-* + *radial*] : TRIRADIATE — **tri·radially** \"+\ *adv*
¹**tri·radiate** \"+\ *adj* [*tri-* + *radiate*] : having three radiating branches ⟨~ sponge spicules⟩ — **tri·radiately** \"+\ *adv*
²**triradiate** \"\ *n* -s : something (as a sponge spicule) having three radiating branches
tri·radiated \(ˈ)trī+\ *adj* [*tri-* + *radiated*] : TRIRADIATE
tri·radius \"+\ *n* [*tri-* + *radius*] : a group of ridges forming a Y at the base of each finger on the palm of the hand
tri·rat·na \triˈrətnə\ *n* -s *usu cap* [Skt, three gems, fr. *tri* three + *ratna* gift, treasure, gem; akin to Skt *rāti* he gives, *rai* wealth, property — more at THREE, REAL] **1** *Buddhism* : the triad of the Buddha, the dharma, and the sangha **2** *Jainism* : the three conditions necessary for the attainment of nirvana: right knowledge, right faith, and right conduct
tri·rectangular \ˌtrī+\ *adj* [*tri-* + *rectangular*] *of a spherical triangle* : having three right angles
tri·reg·num \trīˈregnəm\ *n* [NL, lit., triple reign, fr. L *tri-* + *regnum* reign — more at REIGN] : TIARA 1b
tri·reme \ˈtrī,rēm\ *n* -s [L *triremis*, fr. *tri-* + *remus* oar — more at ROW] : an ancient galley having three banks of oars
tri·rhombohedral \(ˌ)trī+\ *adj* [*tri-* + *rhombohedral*] : of or relating to a group of the hexagonal system characterized by three different types of rhombohedrons
tris *pl of* TRI
tris- \(ˌ)tris\ *prefix* [Gk, fr. *tris*, fr. *treis* three — more at THREE] : thrice : tripled ⟨tristetrahedron⟩ — esp. in complex chemical expressions ⟨*tris*-(2-chloroethyl)-amine⟩
tri·saccharide \(ˈ)trī+\ *n* [ISV *tri-* + *saccharide*] : any of a class of sugars (as raffinose) that yield on complete hydrolysis three monosaccharide molecules
tris·agion \trēˈsäyȯn\ *n, pl* **tris·agia** \-yä\ *usu cap* [MGk, fr. neut. of LGk *trisagios* thrice holy, fr. Gk *tris-* + *hagios* holy] **1** : a hymn to or invocation of God as the thrice holy ⟨the ~ of Isa 6:3⟩ **2** : a requiem service of the Eastern Church
trisail *var of* TRYSAIL
tris·azo \(ˈ)tris+\ *adj* [ISV *tris-* + *azo*] : containing three azo groups in the molecule ⟨~ dyes⟩
tri·sect \(ˈ)trīˈsekt\ *vt* -ED/-ING/-S [*tri-* + *-sect*] : to divide into three usu. equal parts
tri·sec·tion \(ˈ)trīˈsekshən\ *n* : the operation or result of trisecting
tri·sec·tor \-ktə(r)\ *n* -s : one that trisects
tri·sec·trix \-,triks\ *n, pl* **trisectri·ces** \,≈≈'≈trə,sēz\ [*trisec-* (fr. *trisector*) + *-trix*] : a curve that trisects an arbitrary angle
tri·seme \ˈtrī,sēm\ *n* -s [Gk *trisēmos*] : a syllable or foot of three morae
tri·se·mic \(ˈ)trīˈsēmik\ *or* **tri·seme** \ˈtrī,sēm\ *adj* [*trisemic* fr. Gk *trisēmos* of three time units (fr. *tri-* three + *-sēmos*, fr.

sēmeion unit of time, mark, sign, fr. sēma sign) + E -ic; triseme fr. Gk trisēmos — more at TRI-, SEMANTICS] : consisting of or equal in duration to three morae ⟨a ~ syllable⟩
tri·septate \(ˈ)trī+\ adj [tri- + septate] : having three septa
tri·se·tum \trīˈsēd·əm\ n, cap [NL, fr. tri- + seta] : a widely distributed genus of perennial tufted forage grasses having spikelets with several bisexual flowers and a lemma bearing a dorsal awn
tri·shaw also **tri·sha** \ˈtrī,shȯ\ n -s [tri- + rickshaw, ricksha] : a light 3-wheeled vehicle propelled by pedaling and used in the Far East esp. for transporting passengers — compare PEDICAB
tri·silicate \(ˈ)trī+\ n [ISV tri- + silicate] : a silicate containing three atoms of silicon in the molecule
tris·kai·deka·pho·bia \,tri,skī,dekəˈfōbēə\ n [NL, fr. Gk triskaideka, treiskaideka thirteen (fr. treis three + kai and + deka ten) + NL phobia — more at THREE, TEN] : fear of the number 13
triskele \ˈtri,skēl, ˈtrī,s-\ or **triske·lis** \ˈtriskələs\ n, pl **triskeles** \-kēlz, -kə,lēz\ [Gk triskelēs three-legged, fr. tri- three + -skelēs (fr. skelos leg) — more at CYLINDER] : TRISKELION
tri·skel·i·on \trīˈskelēən, trə'-, -ē,än\ n, pl **triskelions** \-nz\ also **triskel·ia** \-ēə\ [NL, fr. Gk triskelēs] : a figure composed of three usu. curved or bent branches radiating from a center — compare TETRASKELION

triskelion

tris·mus \ˈtrizməs\ n -ES [NL, fr. Gk trismos grating, grinding; akin to Gk trizein to screech, creak — more at STRIDENT] : spasm of the muscles of mastication characterized by difficulty in opening the mouth and resulting from any of various abnormal conditions or diseases : LOCKJAW
tris·octahedron \(ˈ)tris, trəs+\ n [tris- + octahedron] : a solid (as a crystal) having 24 congruent faces meeting on the edges of a regular octahedron — compare TRAPEZOHEDRON
tri·sodium \(ˈ)trī+\ adj [tri- + sodium] : containing three atoms of sodium in the molecule
trisodium phosphate n : SODIUM PHOSPHATE 1c
tri·some \ˈtrī,sōm\ n -s [tri- + -some] : TRISOMIC
[1]**tri·so·mic** \(ˈ)trīˈsōmik\ adj [tri- + -somic] : having one or a few chromosomes triploid in otherwise diploid nuclei usu. because of nondisjunction
[2]**trisomic** \"\ n -s : a trisomic individual
tri·so·my \ˈtrī,sōmē\ n -ES [[1]trisomic + -y] : the condition of being trisomic
tri·splanchnic \(ˈ)trī+\ adj [ISV tri- + splanchnic] **1** : of or relating to the three splanchnic cavities of the head, chest, and abdomen **2** : of or relating to the sympathetic nervous system
tri·stachy·ous \(ˈ)trīˈstākēəs, -ˈstak-\ adj [tri- + Gk stachys ear of grain + E -ous — more at STING] : having three spikes
tris·tania \trəˈstānēə, -stan-\ n [NL, fr. Jules M. C. Tristan †1861 Fr. botanist + NL -ia] **1** cap : a genus of Australasian trees and shrubs (family Myrtaceae) having small yellow or white flowers with numerous stamens united in five columns — see RED BOX 2, WATER GUM **2** -s : any plant of the genus Tristania
tri-state \ˈtrī+,-\ adj : of or relating to a region including three adjoining states or parts of three such states usu. centering around a point where the three states join ⟨the tri-state area of Arkansas, Mississippi, and Tennessee⟩ ⟨a tri-state commission⟩
triste \ˈtrēst\ adj [ME trist, triste, fr. MF triste, fr. L tristis; perh. akin to OE thrist, thriste bold, brazen, shameless, OHG drīsti] : SAD, DISMAL, DULL, DEPRESSING ⟨a ~ quartet could be heard —Donald Heiney⟩ ⟨the whole ~ thin landscape —May Sarton⟩
tri·stearate \(ˈ)trī+\ n [tri- + stearate] : a stearate derived from three molecules of stearic acid
tri·stearin \"+\ n [ISV tri- + stearin] : the crystallizable triglyceride $C_3H_5(OOCC_{17}H_{35})_3$ of stearic acid reported esp. in hard fats, formed by the hydrogenation of various unsaturated fats or triglycerides (as triolein), and used chiefly in textile sizes, polishing materials, and leather stuffing : glycerol tristearate
tris·tetrahedron \(ˈ)tris, trəs+\ n [tris- + tetrahedron] : a solid (as a crystal) of the tetrahedral class of the isometric system having 12 triangular faces and related to the trapezohedron of the holohedral class — compare DELTOHEDRON

tristetrahedron

tris·te·za \trəˈstāzə, -stezə\ n -s [Pg, lit., sadness, sorrow, fr. L tristitia, fr. tristis sad] **1** : a highly infectious disease of grafted citrus trees with bitter orange rootstocks attributed to a virus and characterized by rotting of the rootlets and consequent wilting and death of the trees — compare QUICK DECLINE **2** : TEXAS FEVER
trist·ful \ˈtristfəl\ adj [ME trist sad + -ful] : SAD, MELANCHOLY — **trist·ful·ly** \-fəlē\ adv — **trist·ful·ness** n -ES
tris·tich \ˈtri(,)stik, -,stēk\ n -s [tri- + -stich] : a strophic unit or stanza of three lines : TERCET, TRIPLET — **tristich·ic** \(ˈ)triˈstikik, -rīˈs-, -kēk\ adj
tris·ti·chous \ˈtristəkəs\ adj [LGk tristichos in three rows, fr. Gk tri- three + stichos row — more at DISTICH] : arranged in three esp. vertical rows ⟨a ~ leaf⟩
tri·stimulus \(ˈ)trī+\ adj [tri- + stimulus] : of or relating to values giving the amounts of three stimuli (as of the colors red, green, and blue) that when combined additively produce a match for the color being considered ⟨~ colorimetry⟩
tri·sty·lous \(ˈ)trīˈstīləs\ adj [tri- + -stylous] : having three styles ⟨~ flowers⟩ — **tri·sty·ly** \ˈ≈,≈lē\ n -ES
tri·substituted \(ˈ)trī+\ adj [tri- + substituted] : having three substituent atoms or groups in the molecule
tri·sul \trəˈshül\ or **tri·su·la** \-lə\ n -s [Skt triśūla, lit., having three points, fr. tri three + śūla spit, spear, point — more at THREE, CULEX] : a trident or 3-pointed emblem or ornament associated esp. with the god Siva
tri·sulfide \(ˈ)trī+\ n [tri- + sulfide] : a binary compound containing three atoms of sulfur combined with an element or radical
tri·sulfonic acid \(ˌ)trī+...-\ n [tri- + sulfonic] : an acid containing three sulfonic acid groups
tri·syllabic \ˌtrī, ˌtri+\ adj [prob. fr. (assumed) NL trisyllabicus, fr. L trisyllabus of three syllables, trisyllabic (fr. Gk trisyllabos, fr. tri- three + syllabē syllable) + -icus -ic — more at TRI-, SYLLABLE] : of or relating to a trisyllable : having three syllables ⟨a ~ word⟩ — **tri·syllabically** \"+\ adv
tri·syl·la·bism \trīˈsilə,bizəm, triˈ-\ n [trisyllabic + -ism] : the state of being trisyllabic
tri·syllable \(ˈ)trī, (ˈ)tri+\ n [modif. (influenced by syllable) of MF trisyllabe, fr. LL trisyllaba (pl.), fr. L, neut. pl. of trisyllabus trisyllabic] : a word of three syllables
trit- or **trito-** comb form [Gk, fr. tritos; akin to Gk treis three — more at THREE] : third : tertiary ⟨tritonymph⟩ ⟨tritovum⟩
trit abbr triturate
tri·tag·o·nist \(ˈ)trīˈtagənəst, -ˈtaig-\ n -s [Gk tritagōnistēs, fr. trit- + agōnistēs actor — more at PROTAGONIST] : the actor taking the part of third importance in a play (as in the ancient Greek theater) — compare DEUTERAGONIST, PROTAGONIST
trit·an·ope \ˈtrītᵊn,ōp, -rit-\ n -s [ISV, fr. NL tritanopia] : one affected with tritanopia
trit·an·opia \,≈ˈōpēə\ n -s [NL, fr. trit- + anopia blindness, fr. [2]a- + -opia; fr. the fact that only ⅓ of the colors of the spectrum can be perceived by a tritanope] : dichromatism in which the spectrum is seen in tones of red and green — called also blue-yellow blindness
trit·an·opic \,≈ˈäpik, -ˈōp-\ adj : characterized by or affected by tritanopia ⟨~ vision⟩ ⟨a ~ person⟩
tri·taph \ˈtrī,taf\ n -s [tri- + Gk taphos tomb — more at EPITAPH] : a tomb containing three small chambers or cists
trite \ˈtrīt, usu -īd·+V\ adj -ER/-EST [L tritus, past part. of terere to rub, wear out by use, make trite — more at THROW] **1 a** : used or occurring so often as to have lost interest, freshness, or force : STALE, VAPID ⟨~ diction⟩ ⟨a ~ and commonplace observation —Earl of Chesterfield⟩ ⟨a subject which will seem ~ to some —J.M.Moore⟩ ⟨a ~ plot⟩ **b** : characterized by commonplace expression, treatment, or point of view : composed of or employing clichés or platitudes ⟨a ~ speech⟩ ⟨poet . . . can be not only ~, he can be pompous, inflated —Times Lit. Supp.⟩ ⟨too many ~ objects in shiny yellow brass or dull black iron —New Yorker⟩ **2 a** : worn by much rubbing ⟨~ coins⟩ **b** : much-traveled : BEATEN ⟨a ~ path⟩ ⟨all these regions are ~ and familiar —Norman Douglas⟩

syn TRITE, HACKNEYED, STEREOTYPED, THREADBARE, and SHOPWORN all apply to something, esp. a once effective idea or expression in writing or art or a dramatic plot, lacking the power to evoke attention or interest because it lacks freshness. TRITE applies to something spoiled by too long familiarity with it, suggesting commonplaceness or total lack of power to impress ⟨the foregoing remarks doubtless sound trite and commonplace —M.R.Cohen⟩ ⟨it is as true as it is trite to liken the desert to a sea and the camel to a ship —C.S.Coon⟩ ⟨one could wish however that he had found a less trite and commonplace way of ending his chapters —Geog. Jour.⟩ HACKNEYED, often interchangeable with TRITE, stresses the idea of such constant use that all significance or force is dulled or destroyed ⟨the hackneyed pictures we have seen again and again —C.M. Smith⟩ ⟨used the hackneyed old theme of the vanity of earthly power for one of his best poems —Susanne K. Langer⟩ ⟨a hackneyed and cheap melodrama⟩ STEREOTYPED stresses an imitative quality, a usu. total lack of originality or creativity ⟨most advertising today is stereotyped — using the same words, the same ideas that we have had for more than 50 years —Printers' Ink⟩ ⟨a stereotyped novel about a young girl growing to womanhood⟩ THREADBARE applies to what has been used or exploited so much that its possibilities of interest have been totally exhausted ⟨when one writer hit upon a good phrase the others took it up and used it until it became threadbare —Stanley Walker⟩ ⟨this charge is becoming threadbare with repetition —J.H.Pollack⟩ ⟨our self-deceptive pretence of jollity at a threadbare joke —Nathaniel Hawthorne⟩ SHOPWORN suggests a loss, from constant use, of some or most of the qualities that appeal or arouse interest ⟨there hardly exists a more shopworn plot than the one about the show that during its preparation has to battle against all sorts of obstacles to emerge in the end a sensational success —Vicki Baum⟩ ⟨when a book as unusual as this appears the old adjectives seem too shopworn to do it justice —Graham Bates⟩ ⟨he has devoted his very considerable talents to a shopworn theme: the building of the first space platform —J.F.McComas⟩

tri·te·leia \,trīd·ᵊlˈīə, -ˈē(y)ə\ n [NL, fr. tri- + Gk teleios complete; akin to Gk telos end; fr. the trimerous flowers — more at WHEEL] **1** cap : a genus of American bulbous herbs (family Liliaceae) that have grasslike leaves and umbels of white, blue, or violet flowers with the stamens borne on the tube of the perianth in two series and are sometimes included in Brodiaea **2** -s : any plant of the genus Triteleia
trite·ly adv : in a trite manner ⟨~ expressed sentiments⟩
trit·encephalon \,trīd·, ˌtrid· +\ n [NL, fr. trit- + encephalon] **1** : the third and hindmost of the primary brain vesicles **2** : TRITOCEREBRUM
trite·ness n -ES : the quality of being trite ⟨there was a certain ~ in these reflections —Edith Wharton⟩ ⟨camera work of almost unbelievable ~ and stodginess —Newsweek⟩
triter comparative of TRITE
tri·ternate \(ˈ)trī+\ adj [tri- + ternate] of leaves : thrice ternate : ternately decompound — **tri·ternately** \"+\ adv
tri·terpene \"+\ n [ISV tri- + terpene] : any of a class of terpenes $C_{30}H_{48}$ (as squalene) containing three times as many atoms in the molecule as monoterpenes; also : a derivative of such a terpene
[1]**tri·ter·pe·noid** \(ˈ)trīˈtərpə,nȯid\ adj [triterpene + -oid] : relating to a triterpene in molecular structure ⟨~ sapogenins⟩
[2]**triterpenoid** \"\ n -s : a triterpene or triterpene derivative (as lanosterol or oleanolic acid)
tritest superlative of TRITE
tri·the·ism \ˈtrīthē,izəm, (ˈ)trīˈth-\ n, sometimes cap [tri- + -theism] : a belief in three gods; specif : the doctrine that the Father, Son, and Holy Spirit of Christianity are three distinct Gods
tri·the·ist \ˈtrī(,)thēəst, (ˈ)trīˈth-\ n [LGk tritheos believing in three gods + E -ist] : a believer in tritheism
tri·the·is·tic \ˌtrīthēˈistik\ also **tri·the·is·ti·cal** \-təkəl\ adj : of, relating to, or adhering to tritheism
tri·the·ite \ˈtrī(,)thē,īt, (ˈ)trīˈth-\ n -s [LGk tritheitēs, fr. tritheos believing in three gods (fr. Gk tri- three + theos god) + Gk -itēs -ite — more at TRI-, THE-] : TRITHEIST
trith·e·mim·er \,trithəˈmimə(r)\ n -s [modif. (influenced by trit-) of NL trihemimeris, fr. tri- + hemi- + -meris (fr. Gk meris part) — more at MERIT] : a group of three half feet in classical prosody : a catalectic colon of a foot and a half
trith·e·mim·er·al caesura \,≈≈ˈmimərəl-\ n : a caesura in classical verse occurring after the third half foot
tri·thing \ˈtrīthiŋ\ n -s [ME, fr. OE thrithing — more at RIDING] archaic : RIDING
trithio- comb form [ISV tri- + thi-] : containing three atoms of sulfur usu. in place of three oxygen atoms — in names of chemical compounds ⟨trithiocarbonic⟩
tri·thio·carbonate \(ˌ)trīˌthīō+\ n [trithiocarbonic + -ate] : a salt or ester of trithiocarbonic acid
tri·thio·carbonic acid \"+. . -\ n [trithio- + carbonic] : an unstable acid H_2CS_3 obtained by reaction of carbon disulfide with alkali sulfides in the form of its alkali salts from which it can be precipitated as a reddish ill-smelling oil
tri·thi·o·nate \trīˈthīənət, -,nāt\ n [ISV trithionic + -ate] : a salt of trithionic acid
tri·thi·on·ic acid \ˌtrī,thīˈänik-\ n [ISV tri- + thionic] : the thionic acid $H_2S_3O_6$ containing three atoms of sulfur in the molecule
trithri·nax \ˈtrīˈthrī,naks, ˈtrithrə,n-\ n, cap [NL, fr. tri- + Gk thrinax three-pronged fork, perh. fr. thrin- (akin to L terni three each) + akmē point, edge; fr. the form of the leaves — more at TERN, EDGE] : a genus of So. American fan palms having tough leaves with fibrous spiny sheaths, biconvex petiole, and prominent ligule
trit·i·at·ed \ˈtrid·ē,ād·əd also -ishē-\ adj [NL tritium + E -ate + -ed] : containing tritium esp. as a constituent of a chemical compound
trit·i·cal \ˈtrid·əkəl\ adj [trite + -ical (as in critical)] archaic : TRITE
trit·i·ca·le \,trid·əˈkā(,)lē\ n -s [NL, blend of Triticum and Secale] : an amphidiploid hybrid between wheat and rye — sometimes used as if a generic name
tri·ti·ceous \trəˈtishəs\ adj [NL triticeus, fr. L, of or resembling wheat, fr. triticum wheat + -eus -eous] : of, relating to, or being a small nodule of cartilage within the lateral thyrohyoid ligament
tri·ti·ceum \trəˈtish(ē)əm\ n, pl **triti·cei** \-shē,ī\ [NL, fr. neut. of triticeus] : a triticeous cartilage
trit·i·cum \ˈtrid·əkəm\ n [NL, fr. L, wheat; akin to L terere to rub, thresh — more at THROW] **1** cap : a genus of cereal grasses including the wheats and distinguished by the 2- to 5-flowered flattened spikelets in a terminal cylindrical spike with a flexuous rachis **2** -s : the dried rhizome of a couch grass (Agropyron repens)
trit·ide \ˈtrid,īd\ n -s [NL tritium + E -ide] : a binary compound of tritium analogous to a hydride
trit·ish \ˈtrīd·ish\ adj : somewhat trite ⟨~ expressions⟩
trit·i·um \ˈtrid·ēəm, -itē- also -ishē-\ n -s [NL, fr. trit- + -ium] : the radioactive isotope of hydrogen that has atoms of three times the mass of ordinary light hydrogen atoms, that has a half-life of about 12.5 years and emits beta rays to form helium of mass number 3, and that can be produced by bombardment of lithium with neutrons — symbol H^3, ^3H, T
trito- — see TRIT-
tri·to·cerebral \ˌtrid·ō+\ adj [NL tritocerebrum + E -al] : of or relating to the tritocerebrum
tri·to·cerebrum \"+\ n [NL, fr. trit- + cerebrum] : the third segment of the brain of an insect innervating the labrum — compare HINDBRAIN
tri·to·cone \ˈtrid·ə+,-\ n [trit- + cone] : the cusp of a mammalian premolar corresponding in position to the metacone of a true molar
tri·to·co·nid \,≈ˈkōnəd\ n -s [tritocone + -id] : the cusp of a lower molar corresponding to a metaconid
tri·tolyl \(ˈ)trī+\ adj [tri- + tolyl] : containing three tolyl radicals in the molecule
tritolyl phosphate n : TRICRESYL PHOSPHATE
[1]**trit·o·ma** \ˈtrid·əmə\ [NL, fr. Gk tritomos thrice cut, fr. tri- three + -tomos (fr. temnein to cut); fr. the trimerous flowers — more at TOME] syn of KNIPHOFIA
[2]**tritoma** \"\ n -s [NL] : KNIPHOFIA 2
trit·o·mite \ˈtrid·ə,mīt\ n -s [G tritomit, fr. Gk tritomos thrice cut + G -it -ite; fr. the fact that the crystals leave trihedral cavities in the gangue] : a complex fluosilicate chiefly of calcium, thorium, cerium, yttrium, and containing boron
[1]**tri·ton** \ˈtrītᵊn\ n -s [L Triton, Greco-Roman demigod of the sea, fr. Gk Tritōn] **1** often cap **a** : one of a class of minor sea divinities or partly human monsters usu. represented as having the upper body like that of a human and the lower body like that of a fish — compare MERMAID **b** : a representation of a triton in art or heraldry **2** or **triton shell** [NL, fr. L Triton; fr. the sea god Triton being often represented holding a trumpet made of a conch shell] **a** : any of various large marine gastropod mollusks esp. of the family Cymatiidae having a heavy elongated conical shell with the surface wrinkled and roughened or covered with a hairy periostracum and the lip usu. toothed or ridged **b** : a shell of one of these mollusks **3** : any of various aquatic salamanders : NEWT, EFT
[2]**triton** \"\ [NL] syn of TRITURUS
[3]**tri·ton** \ˈtrī,tän\ n -s [trinitrotoluene] : TRINITROTOLUENE
[4]**triton** \"\ n -s [Gk, neut. of tritos third — more at TRIT-] : the nucleus of the tritium atom consisting of one proton and two neutrons — symbol t; compare DEUTERON
tri·tone \ˈtrī,tōn\ n [Gk tritonos of three tones, fr. tri- three + tonos tone — more at TRI-, TONE] **1** : a musical interval of three whole steps **2** : an augmented fourth — called also mi contra fa
tri·to·nia \trīˈtōnēə\ n [NL, fr. L Triton + NL -ia] **1** cap : a genus of So. African bulbous plants (family Iridaceae) much cultivated for ornament and having ensiform leaves and yellow, red, or orange flowers with a tubular perianth that bears three stamens on the throat **2** -s : any plant of the genus Tritonia — see MONTBRETIA
tri·ton·ic \(ˈ)trīˈtänik\ adj **1** usu cap : of, relating to, or characteristic of the demigod Triton **2** sometimes cap : of, relating to, or characteristic of tritons
tri·ton·i·dae \trīˈtänə,dē\ [NL, fr. [1]triton + -idae] syn of CYMATIIDAE
tri·ton·oid \ˈtrītᵊn,ȯid\ adj [[1]triton + -oid] : resembling a triton mollusk
tri·ton's horn or **triton's trumpet** n, usu cap Triton's : TRITON 2b
tri·to·nymph \ˈtrid·ō+,-\ n [trit- + nymph] : any of various acarids in their third developmental stage — compare DEUTONYMPH — **tri·to·nymphal** \ˌ≈≈+\ adj
tri·tor \ˈtrīd·ə(r)\ n -s [L, grinder, fr. tritus (past part. of terere to rub, grind) + -or — more at THROW] : a grinding surface developed on a tooth — **tri·tor·al** \-d·ərəl\ adj
tri·triacontane \ˌtrī+\ n [ISV tri- + triacontane] : a paraffin hydrocarbon $C_{33}H_{68}$; esp : the normal hydrocarbon $CH_3(CH_2)_{31}CH_3$
tri·trichomonas \"+\ n, cap [NL, fr. tri- + Trichomonas] : a genus of flagellates that is related to Trichomonas but distinguished by three anterior flagella and is often held to be indistinguishable from or a subgenus of Trichomonas
tri·tubercular or **tri·tuberculate** \ˌtrī+\ adj [tri- + tubercular, tuberculate] **1** of a tooth : having three cusps : TRICUSPID **2** : of or relating to trituberculy
tri·tu·ber·cu·la·ta \,trītə,bərkyəˈlād·ə, -ˈlād·ə\ [NL, fr. neut. pl. of trituberculatus trituberculate, fr. tri- + tuberculatus tuberculate — more at TUBERCULATE] syn of PANTOTHERIA
tri·tu·ber·cu·lism \,trītəˈbərkyə,lizəm\ n -s [trituberculate + -ism] : TRITUBERCULY
tri·tu·ber·cu·ly \-,lē\ n -ES [trituberculate + -y] : the state of being tritubercular or showing evidence of having developed from a tritubercular ancestral type — used esp. in reference to a theory of the origin of mammalian molar teeth supposing them to have developed through tritubercular forms; compare MULTITUBERCULY
trit·u·ra·ble \ˈtrichərəbəl\ adj [LL triturare to thresh + E -able] : capable of being triturated
trit·u·ral \ˈtrichərəl\ adj [L tritura act of rubbing or threshing + E -al] : adapted for grinding ⟨the ~ border of a tooth⟩
[1]**trit·u·rate** \ˈtrichə,rāt\ vt -ED/-ING/-S [LL trituratus, past part. of triturare to thresh, fr. L tritura act of rubbing or threshing, fr. tritus (past part. of terere to rub, grind) + -ura -ure — more at THROW] **1** : RUB, GRIND, BRUISE, MASTICATE ⟨~ one's food⟩ **2** : to rub or grind to a very fine or impalpable powder : pulverize and comminute thoroughly ⟨~ a drug with a diluent⟩
[2]**trit·u·rate** \-rət\ n -s : a triturated substance : TRITURATION 2
trit·u·ra·tion \,trichəˈrāshən\ n -s [LL trituration-, trituratio act or process of threshing, fr. trituratus (past part.) + L -ion-, -io -ion] **1** : the act or process of triturating or state of being triturated : COMMINUTION ⟨~ of food in the gizzard⟩ **2 a** : a triturated powder; esp : a powder made by triturating a substance with lactose as a diluent
trit·u·ra·tor \ˈtrichə,rād·ə(r)\ n -s [LL, thresher, fr. trituratus (past part.) + L -or] : one that triturates; specif : an apparatus that triturates drugs
tri·tu·rus \trīˈtürəs, -īˈtyü-\ n, cap [NL, prob. fr. Triton the sea god + NL -urus — more at TRITON] : a genus of chiefly aquatic salamanders comprising the typical newts and having a small tongue free along the sides, four to five toes, and a compressed tail
tri·tyl \ˈtrīd·ᵊl\ n -s [ISV triphenylmethyl] : TRIPHENYLMETHYL
tri·tyl·odon \trīˈtilə,dän\ n, cap [NL, fr. tri- + tyl- + -odon] : a genus of extinct vertebrates from the lower Mesozoic of Africa and Europe in many respects intermediate between reptiles and mammals and formerly classed as primitive mammals but now usu. placed among the reptiles forming with a few related forms the family Tritylodontidae
[1]**tri·tyl·odont** \-nt\ adj [NL Tritylodont-, Tritylodon] : of or relating to the genus Tritylodon
[2]**tritylodont** \"\ n -s : an animal or fossil of the genus Tritylodon
tri·tyl·odon·ti·dae \(,)trī,tiləˈdäntə,dē\ n pl, cap [NL, fr. Tritylodont-, Tritylodon, type genus + -idae] : a family of extinct vertebrates of the order Ictidosauria — see TRITYLODON
tri·um·fet·ta \,trīəmˈfed·ə\ n, cap [NL, irreg. fr. Giovanni Battista Trionfetti †1708 Ital. botanist] : a large genus of tropical herbs and shrubs (family Tiliaceae) clothed with stellate hairs and bearing yellow flowers followed by bristly capsules — see BURBARK
[1]**tri·umph** \ˈtrīəm(p)f also -ī,əm-; before a consonant following without pause (as in "triumphs") often -m(p), before a pause or vowel sometimes -mp; also ÷ -m(p)th\ n -s [ME triumphe, fr. MF, fr. L triumphus, alter. of OL triumpus, fr. triumpe! shout repeated at the ceremonial departure of the Roman priests during the Arval fertility festival, prob. of non-IE origin; akin to the source of Gk thriambos, hymn sung in processions honoring the god of fruits Dionysus] **1 a** : an ancient Roman ceremonial in honor of a general after his decisive victory over a foreign enemy beginning with his entrance into the city preceded by the senate and magistrates, the spoils, and the captives in chains and followed by his army in marching order and ending with sacrificial offerings and a public feast **b** : a triumphal procession or stately esp. public show or pageant ⟨fishing and hunting expeditions had a sacred character. Their successes were celebrated with festivals and ~s —H.M.Parshley⟩ **2 a** : an occasion of victory esp. such as to elicit satisfaction, exultation, or acclaim : a decisive victory ⟨another great oratorical ~ —A.C.Cole⟩ ⟨wartime scientific and technical ~s —Gerard Piel⟩ ⟨the ~ of industrialism —C.I.Glicksberg⟩ **b** : satisfaction resulting from a victory : EXULTATION ⟨evil expression of ~ on the man's face —Georgina Grahame⟩ ⟨eyes were full of a wild hilarity and a wilder ~ —Elinor Wylie⟩ **c** : something resulting from or signifying a noteworthy victory or success ⟨conference room — that ~ of fretwork and frenchified interior decoration —R.H.Rovere⟩ ⟨concedes in a ~ of understatement —M.W.Straight⟩ **3** : a state of joy or exultation for success ⟨great ~ and rejoicing was in heaven —John Milton⟩ **4 a** : a card game of medieval France or any of several games (as loo) derived from it **b** : a precursor of whist played

in England in the 16th century **c** *archaic* : TRUMP CARD **syn** see VICTORY

²triumph \", *sometimes in pres part* trīˈəm-\ *vb* -ED/-ING/-S [L *triumphare*, fr. *triumphus* triumph] *vi* **1 a** : to receive the honor of a triumph **b** : to celebrate victory or success with exaltation : exult boastfully ⟨sorrow on thee and all the pack of you that ~ thus upon my misery —Shak.⟩ **2** : to obtain victory : be successful : PREVAIL ⟨~*ing* over death, and chance —John Milton⟩ ⟨proponents of the income tax ~*ed* eventually —W.B.Lockling⟩ ⟨originality constantly ~*ed* over convention —G.G.Coulton⟩ **3** : to be prosperous : FLOURISH ⟨where commerce ~*ed* on the favoring gales —John Trumbull⟩ ~ *vt* : CONQUER

tri·um·phal \trīˈəm(p)fəl *also* ˈtrī,əm-\ *adj* [ME, fr. L *triumphalis*, fr. *triumphus* triumph + *-alis* -al] **1** : of, relating to, or used in a triumph : in honor of a triumph ⟨a ~ crown⟩ ⟨a ~ feast⟩ ⟨tricolored banners and ~ emblems —W.M. Thackeray⟩ ⟨paraded our prizes in a ~ procession through the streets —R.H.Davis⟩ **2** : TRIUMPHANT 4 ⟨~ success —Virgil Thomson⟩

triumphal arch *n* **1** : a monumental structure pierced by at least one lofty and typically arched passageway and usu. commemorating a notable victory, person, or event **2** : the great arch in an early esp. basilican church leading into the choir or sanctuary

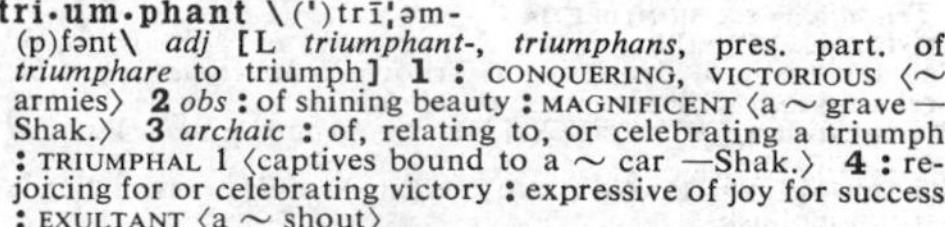
triumphal arch 1

triumphal arch motive *n* : a triple bay having an arch in the central and widest compartment

triumphal column *n* : a monumental column commemorating a victor or a victory

tri·um·phant \(ˈ)trīˈəm(p)fənt\ *adj* [L *triumphant-, triumphans*, pres. part. of *triumphare* to triumph] **1** : CONQUERING, VICTORIOUS ⟨~ armies⟩ **2** *obs* : of shining beauty : MAGNIFICENT ⟨a ~ grave —Shak.⟩ **3** *archaic* : of, relating to, or celebrating a triumph : TRIUMPHAL 1 ⟨captives bound to a ~ car —Shak.⟩ **4** : rejoicing for or celebrating victory : expressive of joy for success : EXULTANT ⟨a ~ shout⟩

tri·um·phant·ly *adv* : in a triumphant manner : VICTORIOUSLY

tri·um·pha·tor \ˈtrīəm,fād·ə(r)\ *n* -S [L, fr. *triumphatus* (past part. of *triumphare*) + *-or*] **1** : one granted a triumph in ancient Rome **2** : one to whom an ovation is given

triumphing *see* ²TRIUMPH\ *adj* : having or celebrating a triumph : TRIUMPHANT ⟨letting out a kind of ~ cry —Mary Deasy⟩ ⟨its abundance of telling detail and its dramatic solidity give it a crude and ~ power —Charles Lee⟩

tri·um·vir \trīˈəmvə(r) *sometimes* ˈtrī,əm-\ *n, pl* **triumvirs** \-)z\ *also* **triumvi·ri** \-ˈ-və,rī, -və,rē\ [L, back-formation fr. *triumviri*, pl., fr. *trium* of three (gen. of *tres* three) + *viri*, pl. of *vir* man — more at THREE, VIRILE] : one of a commission or ruling body of three : a member of a triumvirate

tri·um·vir·al \(ˈ)trīˈəmvərəl\ *adj* [L *triumviralis*, fr. *triumvir* + *-alis* -al] : of or relating to triumvirs or a triumvirate

tri·um·vi·rate \trīˈəmvərə̇t, -və,rāt, *usu* |d.+V\ *n* -S [L *triumviratus*, fr. *triumvir* + *-atus* -ate] **1** : the office or government of triumvirs **2** : a body of triumvirs **3** : a group, party, or association of three ⟨a world-famed ~ of painters —*Time*⟩ ⟨a ~ of little burros —William Beebe⟩ ⟨coalesce the ~ of foreign aid programs —*Foreign Policy Bull.*⟩

¹tri·une \ˈtrī,yün *also* -ī(,)ün\ *n* -S [*tri-* + L *unus* one — more at ONE] : TRINITY

²triune \"\ *adj, sometimes cap* : being three in one — used esp. of unity of the Trinity in the Godhead ⟨professed faith in the ~ God —J.C.Brauer⟩

tri·un·gu·lin \trīˈəŋgyələn\ *n* -S [ISV *tri-* + *ungul-* (fr. L *ungula* claw, fr. *unguis* nail) + *-in* — more at NAIL] **1** : a larva that is the first larval stage of various hypermetamorphic beetles (as oil beetles and blister beetles), is active and of the campodeiform type but during later development becomes legless and parasitic, and in the best-known forms feeds on eggs of bees, wasps, or locusts **2** *or* **triungulid** : the active spiny campodeiform primary larva of a strepsipteral insect that seeks out and attacks the hymenopteran or sometimes homopteran host in which further development takes place

tri·uni·ty \(ˈ)trīˈyünəd·ē *also* -ī,ü-\ *n* [*tri-* + *unity*] : the quality or state of being triune : TRINITY

tri·u·ret \,trīyüˈret, ˌ==ˈ=\ *n* -S [*tri-* + *-uret*] : a crystalline compound $CO(NHCONH_2)_2$ related to urea and biuret; 1,3-di-carbamoyl-urea

tri·u·rid \trīˈyürə̇d\ *n* -S [NL *Triurid-, Triuris*] : a plant of the family Triuridaceae

tri·u·ri·da·ce·ae \(,)trī,yüraˈdāsē,ē\ *n pl, cap* [NL, fr. *Triurid-, Triuris*, type genus + *-aceae*] : a small family of saprophytic leafless herbs (order Triuridales) living in the tropics of both hemispheres and having star-shaped flowers with the perianth segments often fringed or tailed

tri·u·ri·da·les \-ā(,)lēz\ *n pl, cap* [NL, fr. *Triurid-, Triuris* + *-ales*] : an order of monocotyledonous plants coextensive with the family Triuridaceae

tri·u·ris \trīˈyürə̇s\ *n, cap* [NL, fr. *tri-* + *-uris* (fr. Gk *oura* tail) — more at -UROUS] : a genus (the type of the family Triuridaceae) of saprophytic herbs

tri·valence *or* **tri·valency** \(ˈ)trī+\ *n, pl* **trivalences** *or* **trivalencies** [*trivalence* ISV, fr. *trivalent*, after such pairs as E *present: presence; trivalency* fr. *trivalent*, after such pairs as E *regent: regency*; trans. of G *dreiwertigkeit*] : the quality or state of being trivalent

¹tri·valent \"+\ *adj* [ISV *tri-* + *valent*; trans. of G *dreiwertig*] **1** : having a valence of three **2** : TRIPLE — used of homologous chromosomes when three are present and associate in synapsis

²trivalent \"\ *n* -S : a trivalent chromosome group

tri·valve \ˈtrī+,-\ *adj* [*tri-* + *valve*] : having three valves

tri·valvular \(ˈ)trī+\ *adj* [*tri-* + NL *valvula* valve + E *-ar*] : TRIVALVE

tri·van·drum \trə̇ˈvandrəm\ *adj, usu cap* [fr. *Trivandrum*, India] : of or from the city of Trivandrum, India : of the kind or style prevalent in Trivandrum

tri·variant \(ˈ)trī+\ *adj* [ISV *tri-* + *variant*] : capable of threefold variation : having three degrees of freedom — used of a physical-chemical system; compare PHASE RULE

tri·ver·bi·al \(ˈ)trīˌvərbēəl\ *adj* [*tri-* + L *verbum* word + E *-ial*; fr. the three words *do* (I grant), *dico* (I deliver), *addico* (I adjudge) used by praetors in court on the dies fasti — more at WORD] : of or relating to the dies fasti

¹triv·et \ˈtrivə̇t, *usu* -əd·+V\ *n* -S [ME *trevet*, fr. OE *trefet*, prob. modif. (influenced by OE *thrifēte* three-footed, fr. *thrie*, *thrēo* three + *fēt* feet) of LL *tripes* tripod & L *triped-, tripes* three-footed, fr. *tri-* + *ped-, pes* foot — more at THREE, FOOT] **1** : a usu. three-legged stand (as to hold a kettle near a fire) : a tripod with short legs **2** : a usu. ornamental metal stand with short feet esp. for use under a hot dish at table and often electrified **3** : a metal rack for holding meat roasting in a pan

trivet 2

²trivet \"\ *n* -S [origin unknown] : a knife for cutting pile loops in fabrics or carpets

trivet table *n* : a three-legged table

triv·ia \ˈtrivēə\ *n pl but sometimes sing in constr* [NL, fr. pl. of L *trivium* crossroads, influenced in meaning by L *trivialis* trivial] : unimportant matters : TRIFLES ⟨much of our research is wasted on ~ —P.G.Hoffman⟩ ⟨the undifferentiated ~ that impinge on consciousness —Robert Humphrey⟩ ⟨caught up in the ~ of everyday things —Honor Tracy⟩

triv·i·al \ˈtrivēəl\ *adj* [in sense 1, fr. ME, fr. ML *trivialis*, fr. *trivium* + L *-alis* -al; in other senses, fr. L *trivialis* that may be found everywhere, common, ordinary, trivial, fr. *trivium* crossroads, place where three roads meet, fr. *tri-* + *via* way, road — more at VIA] **1** : of or belonging to the trivium **2** : COMMON, ORDINARY, COMMONPLACE ⟨the ~ round, the common task —John Keble⟩ ⟨~ pyrite —A.M.Bateman⟩ — see TRIVIAL NAME 2,3 **3 a** : of little worth or importance : INSIGNIFICANT, FLIMSY, MINOR, SLIGHT ⟨~ objections⟩ ⟨~ inconveniences⟩ ⟨where a painter discards many ~ points of exactness —C.E. Montague⟩ ⟨a ~ act of will —Allen Tate⟩ ⟨the capital as well as the ~ sins —Henry Miller⟩ ⟨wages from both jobs were ~, but he also got tips —Leonard Berry⟩ **b** : concerned with trivialities ⟨a ~ young woman —Sinclair Lewis⟩ ⟨dissertation need not be dull or ~ —J.M.England⟩ ⟨a ~ and badly ordered mind —John Dewey⟩ **4** : SPECIFIC ⟨the species of *Quercus* are notoriously variable in ~ characters —C.H.Muller⟩ — see TRIVIAL NAME 1 **syn** see PETTY

triv·i·al·i·ty \,trivēˈaləd·ē, -lətē, -i\ *n* -ES **1** : the quality or state of being trivial ⟨no one would wish to banish ~ from the theater —*New Republic*⟩ **2** : something trivial : TRIFLE ⟨tend to waste time on *trivialities* —Stewart Cockburn⟩ ⟨made such a fuss over a ~ —Elizabeth Taylor⟩ **3** : concern with or inclination to trivial matters ⟨forests . . . ground into pulp to minister to our ~ —Irving Babbitt⟩

triv·i·al·iza·tion \,trivēələˈzāshən, -,līˈz-\ *n* -S : the act, process, or result of trivializing ⟨take for granted the ~ of our lives —W.W.Phelps⟩ ⟨the ~ of education⟩

triv·i·al·ize \ˈ===,līz\ *vt* -ED/-ING/-S : to make trivial : reduce to triviality ⟨a *trivialized* curriculum —Norman Foerster⟩

triv·i·al·ly \ˈtrivēəlē, -li\ *adv* : in a trivial manner or by trivial means ⟨~ motivated demands —R.W.Firth⟩

trivial name *n* **1** : SPECIFIC EPITHET **2** : the vernacular name of an organism as distinguished from the scientific name **3** : the common name for a chemical substance (as camphor or quinoline) ⟨a *trivial name* . . . differs from a systematic name in that it tells little or nothing about structure —A.M.Patterson⟩

triv·i·al·ness *n* -ES : the quality or state of being trivial

triv·i·um \ˈtrivēəm\ *n, pl* **triv·ia** \-ēə\ [ML, fr. L, place where three roads meet] **1** : the three liberal arts of grammar, rhetoric, and logic forming the elementary division of the seven liberal arts in medieval schools and required of all who would obtain bachelor's status — compare QUADRIVIUM **2** [NL, fr. L] : the three anterior rays in an echinoderm — opposed to *bivium*

tri·vol·tine \trīˈvōl,tēn, (ˈ)=ˌ=ˈ tᵊn\ *adj* [prob. fr. *tri-* + It *volta* turn (fr. — assumed — VL *volvita*, fr. *volvitare*, freq. of L *volvere* to roll) + E *-ine* — more at VOLT] : producing three broods a season ⟨~ races⟩ — used esp. of silkworms

triv·vet \ˈtrivə̇t\ *n* -S [prob. alter. of E dial. *trivant* truant, alter. of E *truant*] *dial* : a flighty frivolous person

¹tri·weekly \(ˈ)trī+\ *adj* [*tri-* + *weekly*] **1** : occurring, appearing, or being made, done, or acted upon three times a week ⟨a ~ publication⟩ ⟨~ train service⟩ **2** : occurring, appearing, or being made, done, or acted upon every three weeks

²triweekly \"\ *n* : a triweekly publication

³triweekly \"\ *adv* : three times a week ⟨a newspaper published ~⟩

-trix \(·)(,)triks, (·)_trēks\ *n suffix, pl* **-tri·ces** \(·)_trə,sēz, (·)ˈtrī(,)sēz\ *or* **-trixes** [ME, fr. L, fem. of *-tor*, ending of agent nouns, fr. *-tus*, past part. ending + *-or* — more at -ED] **1** : female that does or is associated with a (specified) thing ⟨avia*trix*⟩ ⟨narra*trix*⟩ ⟨inheri*trix*⟩ — compare -TRESS **2** : straight line — in geometry ⟨trisec*trix*⟩ ⟨direc*trix*⟩ ⟨trac*trix*⟩

tri·zo·ic \(ˈ)trīˈzōik\ *adj* [*tri-* + *-zoic*] : containing three sporozoites ⟨a ~ spore⟩

tri·zonal \(ˈ)trī+\ *adj, sometimes cap* [*tri-* + *zonal*] : of, relating to, or concerned with the combined affairs of three administrative areas

tri·zygotic \,trī+\ *adj* [*tri-* + *zygotic*] : produced from three zygotes ⟨~ triplets⟩ — compare FRATERNAL 2

trk *abbr* **1** track **2** truck **3** trunk

trm *abbr* terminal

trml *abbr* terminal

trng *abbr* turning

tro·ad·ic \trōˈadik\ *adj, usu cap* [*Troad*, territory surrounding the ancient city of Troy in northwestern Mysia in Asia Minor (fr. L *Troad-, Troas*, fr. Gk *Trōad-, Trōas*) + E *-ic*] : of or relating to ancient Troy ⟨a *Troadic* ornament⟩

troat \ˈtrōt\ *vi* -ED/-ING/-S [obs. F *trout, trut*, interj., sound made to incite animals, fr. MF] : to cry in rutting time — used esp. of a buck

tro·bri·and·er \ˈtrōbrēəndə(r), -ē,an-\ *n* -S *cap* [*Trobriand* Islands, group of small islands in the Solomon Sea + E *-er*] : a native or inhabitant of the Trobriand Islands

tro·bri·and islander \ˈtrōbrēənd-, -ē,and-\ *n, cap T&I* [*Trobriand Islands* + E *-er*] : TROBRIANDER

tro·car *also* **tro·char** \ˈtrō,kär, -,kȧ, ˈtrōkə(r)\ *n* -S [F *trocart*, fr. *trois* three (fr. L *tres*) + *carre* side of a sword blade, fr. *carrer* to square, make square, fr. L *quadrare*; fr. its triangular point — more at THREE, QUADRATE] : a sharp-pointed instrument fitted with a cannula and used to pierce a body cavity and be withdrawn leaving the hollow cannula in place to serve as a drainage outlet

tro·cas \ˈtrōkəs\ *also* **tro·ca** \-kə\ *or* **trocas shell** *n, pl* **trocas** [NL *Trochus*] : a top shell that is fished commercially (as for making pearl buttons)

troch \ˈträk\ *chiefly Scot var of* TROUGH

troch *abbr* troche

troch- *or* **trocho-** *comb form* [NL, fr. Gk, fr. *trochos* wheel, fr. *trechein* to run — more at TROCHEE] : wheel : resembling a wheel : round ⟨*Trocho*dendron⟩ ⟨*Trochel*minthes⟩ ⟨*trocho*phora⟩

-troch \·,träk\ *n comb form* -S [NL *-trocha*] : ciliated band ⟨meso*troch*⟩ ⟨proto*troch*⟩

tro·cha \ˈtrōkə\ *or* **tro·chas** \-kəs\ *n, pl* **trochas** [NL *Trochus*] : TROCAS

-tro·cha \·trəkə\ *n comb form, pl* **-trochas** \-kəz\ *also* **-tro·chae** \-rə,kē\ [NL, fr. fem. sing. of *-trochus* having (such) a ciliated band, fr. Gk *trochos* wheel] : creature or larva having (such) a ciliated band ⟨actino*trocha*⟩

¹tro·cha·ic \trōˈkāik, -āēk\ *adj* [MF *trochaïque*, fr. L *trochaicus*, fr. Gk *trochaikos*, fr. *trochaios (pous)* trochee + *-ikos* -ic — more at TROCHEE] : of, relating to, or consisting of trochees ⟨~ verse⟩ — **tro·cha·i·cal·ly** \-ā̇k(ə)lē\ *adv*

²trochaic \"\ *n* -S : a trochaic foot or verse

trochaic dactyl *n* **1** : a foot in classical prosody having the time value of a trochee but containing two short syllables instead of the usual one **2** : a cyclic dactyl

tro·cha·ize \ˈtrōkə,īz\ *or* **tro·chee·ize** \-kē,-\ *vt* -ED/-ING/-S [*trochaize* fr. *trochaic* + *-ize*; *trocheize*, fr. *trochee* fr. *trochee* + *-ize*] : to change into a trochee : make trochaic

tro·chal \ˈtrōkəl\ *adj* [*troch-* + *-al*] : resembling a wheel

trochal disc *n* : the expanded flat to somewhat funnel-shaped disc at the anterior end of a rotifer's body that serves to draw in food or to propel the animal

tro·cha·lop·o·da \,trōkəˈläpədə, ,träk-\ *n pl, cap* [NL, fr. Gk *trochalos* round (fr. *trochos* wheel) + NL *-poda*] *in some classifications* : a group of Hemiptera comprising terrestrial bugs with the coxae articulated by a ball-and-socket joint

tro·cha·lop·o·dous \ˌ==ˈläpədəs\ *adj* [NL *Trochalopoda* + E *-ous*] **1** : having the coxae articulated by a ball-and-socket joint — used of an insect **2** : of or relating to the Trochalopoda

tro·chan·ter \trōˈkantə(r), -ˈkaan-\ *n* -S [NL, fr. Gk *trochantēr*, fr. *trechein* to run] **1** : a rough prominence or process at the upper part of the femur of many vertebrates serving for the attachment of muscles and in birds for articulation with the ilium, being usu. two on each femur in mammals though occasionally one or (as in horses and rhinoceroses) three, and in man constituting a larger prominence situated at the outer part of the upper end of the shaft at its junction with the neck and a smaller at the lower back part of the junction of the shaft and neck — called also respectively *great trochanter* or *greater trochanter, lesser trochanter* **2** : the second segment counting from the base of the leg of an insect that is usu. small and short and in some insects consists of two or rarely of several distinct parts — see TROCHANTIN 1

tro·chan·ter·al \-tərəl\ *adj* : of, relating to, or constituting a trochanter

tro·chan·ter·ic \ˌtrōkənˈterik\ *adj* : of or relating to a trochanter

trochanteric fossa *n* : a depression at the base of the internal surface of the greater trochanter of the femur for the attachment of the tendon of the external obturator muscle

tro·chan·te·ri·on \ˌ==ˈtirē,än\ *n* -S [NL, dim. of *trochanter*] : TROCHANTER POINT

trochanter point *n* : the highest point upon the greater trochanter — called also *trochanterion*

tro·chan·tin *also* **tro·chan·tine** \trōˈkantᵊn\ *n* -S [F *trochantin*, dim. of *trochanter*, fr. Gk *trochantēr*] **1** : the proximal of the two segments into which the trochanter of the leg of an insect may be divided and which is often united with the coxa **2** : the lesser trochanter of the femur — **tro·chan·ti·nal** \-tᵊnᵊl\ *adj* — **tro·chan·tin·i·an** \ˌtrōkənˈtinēən\ *adj*

trochar *var of* TROCAR

tro·che \ˈtrōkē, -kī\ *n* -S [short for *trochisk*, fr. ME *trocis*, fr. LL *trochiscus*, fr. Gk *trochiskos* small wheel, troche, dim. of *trochos* wheel — more at TROCH-] : a medicinal tablet or lozenge usu. of circular or oval form; *esp* : one used as a demulcent (as for soreness or irritation in the throat)

troch·e·am·e·ter \,träkēˈaməd·ə(r)\ *n* [prob. fr. Gk *trochia* wheel track (fr. *trochos* wheel + *-ia* -y) + E *-meter*] : an instrument used to count the revolutions of a wheel

tro·chee \ˈtrō(,)kē\ *n* -S [F *trochée*, fr. L *trochaeus*, fr. Gk *trochaios (pous)* running (foot), trochee, fr. *trochaios* running, fr. *trochos* running race, racecourse, fr. *trechein* to run; akin to OIr *droch* wheel, Lith *drožti* to run quickly, Arm *durgn* potter's wheel] : a prosodic foot of two syllables of which the first is long and the second short (as in Latin *ante*) or the first stressed and the second unstressed (as in English *motion*) — symbol —◡; compare IAMB

troch·el·minth \ˈträkəl,minth\ *n* -S [NL *Trochelminthes*] : an animal of the phylum Trochelminthes

troch·el·min·thes \ˌ==ˈmin(t)thēz\ *n pl, cap* [NL, fr. *troch-* + *helminthes*] *in some classifications* : a phylum of invertebrates including the Rotifera, the Gastrotricha, and a few obscure forms

trochi *pl of* TROCHUS

¹tro·chid \ˈtrōkə̇d\ *adj* [NL *Trochidae*] : of or relating to the Trochidae

²trochid \"\ *n* -S : a mollusk of the family Trochidae

troch·i·dae \ˈträkə,dē\ *n pl, cap* [NL, fr. *Trochus*, type genus + *-idae*] : a family of marine gastropod mollusks (suborder Rhipidoglossa) with a conical operculate shell flattened at the base and having an oblique aperture and a very lustrous nacreous lining — see TOP SHELL, TROCHUS

tro·chi·form \ˈtrōkə,fȯrm, ˈträk-\ *adj* [NL *trochus* + E *-iform*] : shaped like a top or a top shell

troch·i·li \ˈträkə,lī\ *n pl, cap* [NL, fr. pl. of *trochilus*] : a suborder of Apodiformes consisting of the hummingbirds

tro·chil·i·dae \trōˈkilə,dē\ *n pl, cap* [NL, fr. *trochilus* + *-idae*] : a family of small often brilliantly colored birds (order Apodiformes) consisting of the hummingbirds — **tro·chil·i·dine** \-,dīn, -,dən\ *adj*

troch·i·line \ˈträkə,līn, -lən\ *adj* [NL *trochilus* + E *-ine*] : of or relating to the hummingbirds

troch·i·lus \-kələs\ *n* [NL, fr. L, a small bird, perh. the golden-crested kinglet, fr. Gk *trochilos* crocodile bird, wren; akin to Gk *trechein* to run — more at TROCHEE] **1** *pl* **troch·i·li** \-kə,lī\ **a** : CROCODILE BIRD **b** : any of several Old World warblers (as the goldcrest or the willow warbler) **c** : HUMMINGBIRD **2** *cap* : a formerly extensive genus of hummingbirds that is usu. restricted to a long-tailed Jamaican hummingbird (*T. polytmus*) **3** *pl* **trochili** : SCOTIA

tro·ching \ˈtrōkiŋ\ *n* -S [ME, fr. *troche* cluster of tines on an antler (fr. MF, cluster) + *-ing*] : a small point of a stag's antler

tro·chis·ca·tion \,trōkə̇ˈskāshən\ *n* -S [ISV *trochisc-* (fr. LL *trochiscus*) + *-ation*] : the process of forming or forming into troches

tro·chis·cus \trōˈkiskəs\ *n, pl* **trochis·ci** \-i,s(k)ī\ [LL — more at TROCHE] : TROCHE

tro·chite \ˈtrō,kīt\ *n* -S [NL *trochites*, fr. Gk *trochos* wheel + L *-ites* -ite — more at TROCH-] : a joint of the stem of a fossil crinoid that suggests a wheel — **tro·chit·ic** \trōˈkid·ik\ *adj*

troch·lea \ˈträklēə\ *n* -S [NL, fr. L, sheaf of pulleys, fr. Gk *trochileia, trochilea*; akin to Gk *trochos* wheel, *trechein* to run — more at TROCHEE] : an anatomical structure felt to resemble a pulley: as **a** : the articular surface on the medial condyle of the humerus that articulates with the ulna **b** : the fibrous ring in the inner upper part of the orbit through which the tendon of the trochlear muscle of the eye passes **c** : the smooth depression on the front of the femur between the condyles

troch·le·ar \-ēə(r)\ *adj* [NL *trochlearis*, fr. *trochlea* + L *-aris* -ar] **1 a** : of, relating to, or being a trochlea **b** : of, relating to, or being a trochlear nerve or trochlear muscle **2** : rounded and narrow in the middle like the wheel of a pulley ⟨a ~ plant embryo⟩

trochlear fossa *n* : a depression in the antero-medial aspect of each orbital plate of the frontal bone that forms a point of attachment for the corresponding superior oblique muscle

troch·le·ar·i·form \,träklēˈa(a)rə,fȯrm\ *adj* [NL *trochlearis* + E *-iform*] : TROCHLEAR 2

troch·le·ar·is \ˌ==ˈa(a)rə̇s\ *n* -ES [NL] **1** : SUPERIOR OBLIQUE MUSCLE **2** : TROCHLEAR NERVE

trochlear muscle *n* : SUPERIOR OBLIQUE MUSCLE

trochlear nerve *also* **trochlear** *n* -S : either of the 4th pair of cranial nerves arising from the dorsal aspect of the brainstem on either side of the anterior medullary velum and supplying the superior oblique muscle of the eye with motor fibers

trocho- — see TROCH-

troch·o·blast \ˈträkə,blast\ *n* [*troch-* + *-blast*] : a ciliate cell on a trochophore

troch·o·ce·pha·lia \,träkōsəˈfālēə\ *n* -S [NL, fr. *troch-* + *-cephalia* -cephaly] : an abnormal roundness of the skull caused by premature union of the frontal and parietal bones — **troch·o·ce·phal·ic** \ˌ===ˈfalik\ *adj*

troch·o·den·dra·ce·ae \,träkōden'drāsē,ē\ *n pl, cap* [NL, fr. *Trochodendron*, type genus + *-aceae*] : a family of eastern Asiatic trees (order Ranales) having apetalous flowers that are not aromatic — see EUPTELEA, TROCHODENDRON — **troch·o·den·dra·ceous** \ˌ===ˈdrāshəs\ *adj*

tro·cho·den·dron \,träkōˈdendrən\ *n, cap* [NL, fr. *troch-* + *-dendron*] : a genus (the type of the family Trochodendraceae) of evergreen trees growing in Japan and Korea and having bright green flowers in racemes and brown fruit

¹tro·choid \ˈtrō,kȯid\ *n* -S [Gk *trochoeidēs* round like a wheel, circular, fr. *troch-* + *-oeidēs* -oid] **1** : the curve generated by a point on the radius of a circle as the circle rolls on a fixed straight line — compare CYCLOID **2** *or* **trochoid joint** : PIVOT JOINT

²trochoid \"\ *adj* [in sense 1, fr. NL *Trochus* + E *-oid*; in sense 2, fr. ¹*trochoid*] **1 a** : TROCHIFORM **b** : of or relating to a top shell **2** : admitting of rotation on a longitudinal axis

tro·choi·dal \trōˈkȯidᵊl\ *adj* [¹*trochoid* + *-al*] **1** : of, relating to, or having the properties of a trochoid **2** [obs. E *trochoid* mollusk of the family Trochidae, trochid (fr. NL *Trochus* + E *-oid*) + E *-al*] : TROCHOID — **tro·choi·dal·ly** \-ᵊlē\ *adv*

tro·choi·des \trōˈkȯi,dēz\ *n, pl* **trochoides** [NL, fr. Gk *trochoeidēs* round like a wheel] : PIVOT JOINT

tro·chom·e·ter \trōˈkäməd·ə(r)\ *n* [*troch-* + *-meter*] : an odometer for vehicles

tro·choph·o·ra \trōˈkäf(ə)rə\ *n* -S [NL, fr. *troch-* + *-phora*] : TROCHOPHORE

troch·o·phore \ˈträkə,fō(ə)r, -fȯ(ə)r\ *n* -S [NL *trochophora*] : a free-swimming larva characteristic of various aquatic invertebrates (as many worms, rotifers, mollusks) in typical cases having a bilaterally symmetrical ovoid or pyriform body with an equatorial preoral circlet of cilia, a mouth, an intestine, an anal opening, an apical sensory plate, and sometimes nephridial tubes and a second ciliated band behind the mouth — compare MÜLLER'S LARVA

troch·o·sphere \-,sfi(ə)r\ *n* [*troch-* + *sphere*] : TROCHOPHORE

troch·o·tron \ˈträkə,trän\ *n* -S [*troch-* + *-tron*] : a high-vacuum tube or a mass spectrograph in which the ion paths controlled by magnetic and electric fields are trochoids

troch·o·zoa \,träkəˈzōə\ *n pl, cap* [NL, fr. *troch-* + *-zoa*] *in some esp former classifications* : a group of Invertebrata including all those (as the annelids and mollusks) whose early larval stage is normally a trochophore — **troch·o·zo·ic** \ˌ==ˈzōik\ *adj*

troch·o·zo·on \ˌ==ˈzō,än\ *n, pl* **trocho·zoa** \-ōə\ [NL] **1** : an organism of the group Trochozoa **2** : a hypothetical ancestral organism having essentially the organization of a trochophore

-trochs *pl of* -TROCH

tro·chus \ˈtrōkəs\ *n* [NL, fr. L, wheel, iron hoop, fr. Gk *trochos* wheel — more at TROCH-] **1 a** *cap* : a genus of chiefly Old World tropical marine gastropods (family Trochidae) with beautifully nacreous bluntly conical shells including a large Indo-Pacific species (*T. niloticus*) extensively used in making buttons and ornamental objects **b** -ES : TOP SHELL **2** *pl* **tro·chi** \-ō,kī\ *or* **trochuses** : the inner preoral band of cilia of a trochal disc; *broadly* : TROCHAL DISC

trock \'träk\ *chiefly Scot var of* TRUCK

tro·co \'trō(,)kō\ *n* -S [prob. modif. of It *trucco* trucks (game) — more at TRUCKS] : an old English game played on a lawn with wooden balls and cues with spoon-shaped iron tips and having as its object the sending of a ball through an iron ring on a pivot in the center of the field — called also *lawn billiards*

troc·to·lite \'träktə,līt\ *n* -S [G *troktolit*, fr. Gk *trōktēs*, a sea fish (in LL *trocta*, a trout) + G *-lit* -lite; fr. the resemblance to the speckled skin of a trout — more at TROUT] : gabbro that is chiefly labradorite and olivine with little or no pyroxene

¹trod \'träd\ *n* -S [ME, fr. OE *trod* (neut.), *trodu* (fem.) track, trace; akin to ON *troth* act of treading, *trotha* to tread — more at TREAD] **1** *chiefly dial* : a footprint or other trace of passage **2** *chiefly dial* : FOOTPATH, TRAIL **3** *dial Eng* : a wheel's tread

²trod \"\ *vb*, *pres part* **trodding**; *pres 3d sing* **trods** [ME *trodden*, fr. *trod*, n.] *vt* **1** *chiefly Scot* : to follow the course of : TRACE, TRACK **2** : to follow as a chosen course or path ⟨the eccentric is forced . . . to ~ a lonely way —Martin Gardner⟩ ~ *vi*, *chiefly dial* : to progress by walking; *usu* : STROLL, RAMBLE

³trod [ME *troden* (past pl.), alter. of *treden* (past pl.), fr. OE *trǣdon* (past pl.)] *past of* TREAD

trodden [ME *troden* (past part.), alter. (prob. influenced by *trod*, n.) of *treden* (past part.), fr. OE *getreden*] *past part. of* TREAD

toe·ger·ite \'trōgə,rīt\ *n* -S [G *trögerit*, fr. R. *Tröger*, 19th cent. Ger. mining official + G *-it* -ite] : a mineral $(UO_2)_3(AsO_4)_2.12H_2O$ that is a hydrous arsenate of uranium and occurs in lemon-yellow crystals

trof·fer \'träfə(r), 'trōf-\ *n* -S [*troff* (alter. of *trough*) + *-er*] : an inverted trough serving as a support and reflector for a usu. fluorescent lighting unit

troft \'trōft, 'träft\ *n* -S [by alter.] *dial* : TROUGH

trog·gin \'trägən\ *n* -S [fr. obs. E dial. (Sc) *trog* to barter, bargain, prob. fr. F *troquer*] *Scot* : peddlers' wares

troglo- *comb form* [NL, fr. Gk *trōglo-*, fr. *trōglē* hole, cave] : cave-dwelling : troglodytic ⟨*troglo*biont⟩

trog·lo·bi·ont \'träglō'bī,änt, trä'glōbē,-\ *n* -S [*troglo-* + *-biont*] : an animal living in or restricted to caves; *esp* : one occurring in the lightless waters of caves

trog·lo·dyte \'träglə,dīt\ *n* -S [L *Troglodytae*, pl., a cave-dwelling people of Ethiopia, fr. Gk *trōglodytai* cave dwellers, fr. *trōglodytēs* one who enters caves, fr. *trōglē* hole, cave + *-dytēs* one who enters (fr. *dyein* to enter) — more at TERSE, ADYTUM] **1 a** : a member of a primitive people dwelling in caves or pits : CAVE DWELLER **b** : an animal (as an ant) that lives under the surface of the ground **2 a** : a person felt to resemble (as in appearance, ways of living, or degradation or brutality of nature) a troglodyte; *esp* : an unsocial seclusive person **b** : an anthropoid ape (as a chimpanzee or gorilla)

trog·lo·dy·tes \,träglə'dī,tēz, trä'glädə,-\ *n*, *cap* [NL, fr. Gk *trōglodytēs*] **1** : a genus of typical wrens including the common wren of the Old World, the American house wren, and related birds **2** *in former classifications* : a genus comprising the gorilla and chimpanzee and being an invalid homonym of the wren genus

trog·lo·dyt·ic \;träglə;did·ik\ *adj* [L *troglodyticus* of or relating to the cave dwellers of Ethiopia, fr. Gk *trōglodytikos* of or relating to cave dwellers, fr. *trōglodytēs* troglodyte + *-ikos* -ic] **1 a** : of or relating to cave dwellers or their ways **b** : dwelling in or involving residence in caves ⟨a ~ life⟩ **2** : coarse, brutal, or degraded in appearance, ways of living, or nature ⟨two ~ types . . . locked in unfraternal conflict —A.J.Liebling⟩ **3** : primitive or outmoded in character ⟨a ~ organization⟩ ⟨his ~ political ideas —G.W.Johnson⟩

trog·lo·dyt·i·dae \,==ˈdid·ə,dē\ *n pl*, *cap* [NL, fr. *Troglodytes*, type genus + *-idae*] : a family of passerine birds consisting of the wrens, formerly including also the thrashers, mockingbirds, and related forms and sometimes being made a subfamily of Timaliidae

trog·lo·dyt·ism \'==,dī,tizəm\ *n* -S : a condition or style of conduct typical of or suitable to a troglodyte

trog·lo·tre·ma \,träglə·'trēmə\ *n*, *cap* [NL, fr. *troglo-* + *-trema*] : a genus (the type of the family Troglotrematidae) of small spiny egg-shaped digenetic trematodes including a worm (*T. salmincola*) responsible for salmon poisoning of dogs and other canines in the northwestern U.S.

trog·lo·tre·mat·i·dae \,träglətrə'mad·ə,dē\ *n pl*, *cap* [NL, fr. *Troglotrema*, type genus + *-idae*] : a small family of trematode worms that are parasitic for the most part in mammals — see PARAGONIMUS, TROGLOTREMA

tro·go·der·ma \,trōgə'dərmə\ *n*, *cap* [NL, fr. *trogo-* (fr. Gk *trōgein* to gnaw) + *-derma*] : a genus of dermestid beetles including several that are destructive to stored food — see KHAPRA BEETLE

tro·gon \'trō,gän\ *n* [NL, fr. Gk *trōgōn*, pres. part. of *trōgein* to gnaw — more at TERSE] **1** *cap* : the type genus of Trogonidae comprising tropical American birds with brilliant lustrous plumage **2** -S : any bird of the genus *Trogon*; *broadly* : a bird of the family Trogonidae — see QUETZAL

tro·gon·i·dae \trō'gänə,dē\ *n pl*, *cap* [NL, fr. *Trogon*, type genus + *-idae*] : a family (coextensive with the order Trogoniformes) of showy tropical nonpasserine forest birds that have a short stout dentate bill and heterodactylous feet — see TROGON

tro·gon·oid \'trōgə,nȯid\ *adj* [*trogon* + *-oid*] : resembling or related to the trogons

trogs *also* **troggs** \'trägz\ *n pl* [alter. of ME (Sc) *troughth* troth, fr. OE *trēowth* fidelity — more at TRUTH] *chiefly Scot* : TROTH

trogue \'trōg\ *n* -S [alter. of *trough*] *Brit* : a wooden trough forming a mine drain

tro·ic \'trōik\ *adj*, *usu cap* [L *troicus*, fr. Gk *trōikos*, fr. *Trōs*, *Trōos* Tros, legendary founder of Troy + *-ikos* -ic] : TROJAN

troi·ka \'trȯikə\ *n* -S [Russ *troika*, fr. *troe* three; akin to Lith *treji* three, Skt *tri* — more at THREE] : a Russian vehicle drawn by three horses abreast; *also* : a team for such a vehicle

tro·i·lite \'trōə,līt, 'trȯi,-\ *n* -S [G *troilit*, fr. Dominico *Troili*, 18th cent. Ital. scientist who described a meteorite in which it occurs + G *-it* -ite] : a mineral FeS that is a native ferrous sulfide, is a variety of pyrrhotite with almost no iron deficiency, and occurs in meteorites

troi·lus butterfly \'trȯiləs-, 'trōələs-\ *also* **troilus** *n* -ES [fr. *Troilus*, son of Priam, king of Troy, fr. L, fr. Gk *Trōilos*] : a large American swallowtail (*Papilio troilus*) that is black with yellow marginal spots on the front wings and blue on the rear

troilus verse *or* **troilus stanza** *n*, *usu cap T* [fr. *Troilus and Criseyde*, narrative poem in rhyme royal (*ab*1385) by Geoffrey Chaucer †1400 Eng. poet] : RHYME ROYAL

¹tro·jan \'trōjən\ *n* -S [ME, fr. L *Trojani*, pl., Trojans, fr. *Troja*, *Troia* Troy] **1** *cap* : a native or inhabitant of Troy **2** *usu cap* : one who shows qualities (as pluck, endurance, determined energy) attributed to the defenders of ancient Troy — used chiefly in the phrase *like a Trojan* **3** *usu cap* : a gay and often somewhat irresponsible or disreputable companion

²trojan \"\ *adj*, *usu cap* [ME, fr. L *trojanus*, fr. *Troja*, *Troia* Troy, ancient city in Asia Minor that according to Greek legend was besieged, captured, and destroyed by the Greek armies during the ten-year Trojan War about 1200 B.C. (fr. *Tros*, legendary king of Phrygia and founder of Troy, fr. Gk *Trōs*, *Trōos*) + L *-anus* -an] **1** : of, relating to, or resembling that of ancient Troy or its inhabitants ⟨a *Trojan* spirit⟩ **2** : of, relating to, or constituting a Trojan horse ⟨a *Trojan* threat to our economy⟩

trojan asteroid *or* **trojan** *n* -S *usu cap T* [so called fr. its being one of the group whose members bear the names of Trojan heroes] : an asteroid whose average position is at one corner of an equilateral triangle formed with the sun and the planet Jupiter either eastward or westward of the planet

trojan group *n*, *usu cap T* : TROJAN ASTEROIDS

trojan horse *n*, *usu cap T* [so called fr. the gigantic and hollow wooden horse filled with soldiers by means of which the Greeks gained entrance into Troy during the Trojan War and insured the conquest of the city] **1** : a device of placing espionage and propaganda agents inside the country of an intended victim for purposes of sabotage and direction of native subversive groups — compare FIFTH COLUMN **2** : a person, organization, or factor that is intended or likely to undermine an established institution

¹troke \'trōk\ *vb* -ED/-ING/-S [F *troquer*] *Scot* : BARTER, TRAFFIC, EXCHANGE, DEAL, NEGOTIATE — **trok·er** \-kər\ *n* -S *Scot*

²troke \"\ *n* -S *Scot* : ²TRUCK

tro·land \'trōlənd\ *n* -S [after Leonard T. *Troland* †1932 Am. psychologist and physicist] : PHOTON 2

¹troll \'trōl\ *vb* -ED/-ING/-S [ME *trollen* to ramble, roll, prob. fr. MF *troller* to ramble, of Gmc origin; akin to MHG *trollen* to run with short steps — more at ³TROLL] *vt* **1** : to cause to move round and round : BOWL, ROLL ⟨~*ed* it . . . as a child does a hoop —R.S.B.Baker⟩ **2 a** : to sing the parts of (as a round or catch) in succession **b** : to sing loudly or freely **c** : to celebrate in song ⟨that all tongues shall ~ you —Francis Beaumont & John Fletcher⟩ **3** : to speak or recite in a rolling voice or very rapidly **4** *obs* : to move very rapidly : WAG ⟨to dress and ~ the tongue and roll the eye —John Milton⟩ **5 a** : to angle for with a hook and line drawn through the water from a moving boat **b** : to angle in ⟨~ the lakes —Jackson Rivers⟩ **c** : to pull through or as if through the water behind a boat ⟨two or three surface lures were ~*ed* continuously during daylight hours —*Commercial Fisheries Rev.*⟩ ~ *vi* **1** : to move around : CIRCULATE, ROLL **2** : to fish esp. by drawing a hook along or through the water with a line behind a moving boat ⟨~*ed* for bass —Walt Sibley⟩ **3 a** : to take part in a troll : sing or play in a jovial manner : sound with a rolling tone **b** : to be constantly in mind (as a melody) **4** : to speak rapidly : wag the tongue **5** *archaic* : to pass from hand to hand ⟨the wassail round in good brown bowls . . . blithely ~*s* —Sir Walter Scott⟩

²troll \"\ *n* -S **1** *Eng* : a hawker's cart : TROLLEY **2 a** : the process of trolling **b** (1) : the lure (as a spoon) used in trolling (2) : the line with its lure and hook used in trolling **3** : a song sung in parts successively : CATCH, ROUND **4** : a slovenly or loose woman : TROLLOP

³troll \"\ *n* -S [Norw *troll* & Dan *trold*, fr. ON *troll* giant, fiend, demon; akin to MHG *trolle* ghostly monster, boor, lout, *trollen* to run with short steps, ON *tramr* demon, monster, MHG *tremen* to totter, stagger, MLG *trampen* to stamp, tread, OE *treppan* to tread — more at TRAP] : a supernatural being in Germanic and Scandinavian folklore and mythology having sometimes the form of a dwarf and sometimes of a giant and inhabiting caves or hills

troll–drum \'=,=\ *n* [³*troll*] : a drum employed for shamanistic or magical purposes by the Lapps

troll·er \-lə(r)\ *n* -S : one that trolls: as **a** : one who fishes with a troll **b** : a singer of catches or rounds **c** : a boat used in trolling for fish

¹trol·ley *or* **trol·ly** \'trälē, -li\ *n*, *pl* **trolleys** *or* **trollies** [prob. fr. ¹*troll* + *-y* (dim. suffix)] **1 a** *dial Eng* : a low wheeled cart **b** *Brit* : a railroad dump car **c** *Brit* : a small truck used in mines **d** : a small wheeled car used usu. on a wooden track to move lumber from a portable sawmill to a yard **2 a** : a current collector operating in connection with a trolley wire — see BOW TROLLEY, PANTOGRAPH 2, WHEEL TROLLEY **b** : an electric car : TROLLEY CAR, STREETCAR **3** : a wheeled carriage running on an overhead rail or track (as of a parcel railway in a shop or store) : the wheeled truck of a traveling crane or of a ropeway from which a load is suspended **4** : a movable block used on a cable in skidding logs **5** *Brit* : a four-wheel stretcher used to transport patients in a hospital **6** *chiefly Brit* : a table or shelved stand on wheels usu. equipped with a handle and used for conveying something (as food or books) **7** *Brit* : a hand-propelled cart: as **a** : CADDIE CART **b** : PUSHCART — **off one's trolley** : mentally disorganized : unable for the time being to follow a reasonable and sensible course

²trolley *or* **trolly** \"\ *vb* **trolleyed** *or* **trollied**; **trolleyed** *or* **trollied**; **trolleying** *or* **trollying**; **trolleys** *or* **trollies** *vt* : to convey by a trolley ⟨was ~*ing* a packing case aboard a lift —Richard Church⟩ ~ *vi* : to ride on a trolley ⟨so ~ to your hotel for freshening up —James Cerruti⟩

³trolley *var of* TROLLY

trolleybus \'==,=\ *n* : a street-railway vehicle electrically propelled by power from two overhead wires and similar in appearance to a motor bus — called also *trolley coach*

trolley car *n* : a public conveyance for carrying passengers that runs on tracks with motive power derived through a trolley

trolley harp *n* : HARP 3a

trolley line *or* **trolley road** *n* : a system of transportation by means of trolley cars or trolleybuses

trolley locomotive *n* : an electrically operated locomotive that obtains power through a trolley

trol·ley·man *or* **trol·ly·man** \'==mən\ *n*, *pl* **trolleymen** *or* **trollymen** : a man who works on a trolley or electric car; *esp* : a motorman or conductor of an electric car

trolley pole *n* : the pole on various types of trolley cars and trolleybuses by which electrical contact is made with the power line

trolley retriever *n* : a trolley catcher with a supplementary movement to pull down the pole

trolley shoe *n* : a metal current-collecting device for an electrically propelled vehicle receiving power from overhead wires

trollflower \'=,=\ *n* [part trans. of G *trollblume*, prob. fr. *trollen* to trot, roll (fr. MHG, to run with short steps) + *blume* flower; prob. fr. the round shape — more at TROLL] : GLOBEFLOWER a

trolling *n* -S [fr. gerund of ¹*troll*] : the act of one that trolls; *specif* : fishing with a troll

trol·li·us \'träləs\ *n*, *cap* [NL, fr. G *troll*blume trollflower] : a genus of herbs (family Ranunculaceae) that are native to the north temperate regions, have palmately lobed leaves and fruit consisting of a head of follicles, and are often cultivated as ornamentals for their large yellow or lilac flowers with sepals and petals colored alike — see GLOBEFLOWER a

troll–madam \'=,==\ *n* [modif. (influenced by ¹*troll*) of MF *trou-madame*] : TROU MADAME

¹trol·lop \'träləp\ *n* -S [prob. irreg. fr. G dial. *trolle* trollop, prostitute, fr. MHG *trulle* prostitute, mistress — more at TRULL] **1 a** : an unkempt slovenly woman : SLATTERN **b** : a woman of loose morals : WANTON **c** *Midland* : a dissatisfied restless woman **2** : something that dangles or drags untidily : a straggly mass ⟨a ~ of soldiery . . . out-of-step, blurred and miserable —Bruce Marshall⟩

²trollop \"\ *vi* -ED/-ING/-S **1** : to work, walk, or act in a sluggish or slovenly manner : slouch along : SLUMP **2** *chiefly Scot* : to dangle or hang soggily : become bedraggled **3** : to behave like a trollop : display a wanton manner

trol·lope \'träləp\ *interj*, *usu cap* [fr. Frances *Trollope* †1863 Eng. novelist known for her criticism of bad manners in her book *Domestic Manners of the Americans* (1832)] — used as a cry of protest against bad manners or boorish behavior esp. in a theater

¹trol·lop·i·an *also* **trol·lop·e·an** \trə'läpēən, -'lōp-, 'trälə,pēən\ *adj*, *usu cap* [Anthony *Trollope* †1882 Eng. novelist + E *-an*, adj. suffix] : of, relating to, or characteristic of the works or the style of the English novelist Anthony Trollope

²trollopian \"\ *n* -S *usu cap* [Anthony *Trollope* †1882 + E *-an*, n. suffix] : an admirer of the writings of the English novelist Anthony Trollope

trol·lopy \'träləpē\ *adj* : resembling or characteristic of a trollop

troll plate *n* : a rotative disk with spiral ribs or grooves by which several pieces (as the jaws of a chuck) can be moved radially in or out

trolls *pres 3d sing of* TROLL, *pl of* TROLL

¹trol·ly *or* **trol·ley** \'trälē, -li\ *n*, *pl* **trollies** *or* **trolleys** [prob. fr. Flem *tralie* trellis, lattice, mesh, network, lace, fr. MD *tralie*, *trallie* latticework, prob. fr. L *trichila*, *tricla* bower, arbor] : an English bobbin lace with a heavy thread outlining the designs on a net ground

²trolly *var of* TROLLEY

trom·ba \'trämbə, 'trōm-\ *n*, *pl* **trom·be** \-bā\ [It — more at TROMBONE] **1** : TRUMPET **2** : an organ stop imitating the tone quality of a trumpet

tromba da ti·rar·si \-dətə'rärsē\ *n*, *pl* **trombe da tirarsi** [It] : a slide trumpet

trom·bic·u·la \träm'bikyələ\ *n*, *cap* [NL, fr. *Trombidium* + *-cula* -cle] : a genus of mites that is the type of the family Trombiculidae and that contains some mites that in the Orient transmit tsutsugamushi disease

¹trom·bic·u·lid \-yələd\ *adj* [NL *Trombiculidae*] : of or relating to the Trombiculidae

²trombiculid \"\ *n* -S : a mite of the family Trombiculidae

trom·bi·cu·li·dae \,trämbə'kyülə,dē\ *n pl*, *cap* [NL, fr. *Trombicula*, type genus + *-idae*] : a large and widely distributed family of mites whose nymphs and adults feed on early stages of small arthropods but whose larvae are parasites on terrestrial vertebrates including man — compare TROMBIDIIDAE; see CHIGGER, TROMBICULA

trom·bi·di·a·sis \,trämbə'dīəsəs\ *also* **trom·bi·di·o·sis** \,==,dī'ōsəs\ *n*, *pl* **trombidia·ses** \,==ˈdīə,sēz\ [NL, fr. *Trombidium* + *-iasis* or *-osis*] : infestation with chiggers

¹trom·bid·i·id \träm'bidēəd\ *adj* [NL *Trombidiidae*] : of or relating to the Trombidiidae

²trombidiid \"\ *n* -S : a mite of the family Trombidiidae

trom·bi·di·idae \,trämbə'dīə,dē\ *n pl*, *cap* [NL, fr. *Trombidium* + *-idae*] : a large and widely distributed family of mites that feed in all stages on other arthropods — compare TROMBICULIDAE

trom·bid·i·um \träm'bidēəm\ *n*, *cap* [NL] : a genus of mites that is the type of the family Trombidiidae

trom·bi·doi·dea \,trämbə'dȯidēə\ *n pl*, *cap* [NL, fr. *Trombidium* + *-oidea*] *in some esp former classifications* : a superfamily of mites that includes the harvest mites, the red spiders, and others of minor importance

trom·bone \(')träm'bōn, (,)trəm'bōn\ *n* -S [It, aug. of *tromba*

trombone

trumpet, of Gmc origin; akin to OHG *trumpa*, *trumba* trumpet — more at TRUMP (trumpet)] **1 a** (1) : a brass wind instrument that has a cupped mouthpiece, that consists of a long cylindrical metal tube bent twice upon itself and ending in a bell and that has its first crook as a movable slide thereby permitting the player to control the length of the vibrating column and produce any pitch within its compass of E to b♭′ — compare VALVE TROMBONE (2) : a player on this instrument **b** : a large-scale pipe-organ stop of a quality similar to that of the trombone **2** : an early blunderbuss having a large trumpet-shaped muzzle **3** : a U-shaped section that resembles the slide of a trombone and that adjusts tuning in a wave-guide or coaxial-line circuit

trombone–action *adj* : PUMP-ACTION

trombone coil *n* : a continuous steam or hot-water coil in which each intermediate section of pipe is connected at its ends by return bends to the parallel section on either side

trom·bon·ist \-nəst\ *n* -S : a player on the trombone

trom·mel \'träməl\ *n* -S [G, drum, fr. MHG *trummel*, fr. *trumme* — more at DRUM] : a screen usu. of cylindrical or conical shape that is mounted on a revolving and slightly inclined longitudinal shaft and is used esp. for screening or sizing rock, ore, or coal

tro·mom·e·ter \trō'mäməd·ə(r)\ *n* [Gk *tromos* trembling (akin to Gk *tremein* to tremble) + E *-meter* — more at TREMBLE] : an instrument for measuring or detecting minute earth tremors — **trom·o·met·ric** \;trämə;me·trik\ *or* **trom·o·met·ri·cal** \-rəkəl\ *adj* — **tro·mom·e·try** \trō'mämə·trē\ *n* -ES

trompe *also* **tromp** \'trämp\ *n* -S [F *trompe*, lit., trumpet, fr. OF — more at TRUMP] : an apparatus (as for a Catalan forge) in which air is sucked through sloping holes in the upper end of a large vertical wooden tube and led to a furnace by a stream of falling water that is discharged below

trompe l'oeil \trōⁿ'plər, -lā\ *n*, *pl* **trompe l'oeils** \"\ [F] : deception of the eye esp. by a painting: as **a** : the intensification of the reality of component objects in an unnaturally arranged still life through the use of minute detail and the careful rendition of tactile and tonal values **b** : the use in mural and ceiling decoration of painted detail suggestive of architectural or other three-dimensional elements but often characterized by exaggerated perspective, abrupt contrast of light and shade, or general stylization which stresses artificiality

trom·pil \'trämpəl\ *n* -S [F *trompille*, fr. *trompe*] : an aperture in a trompe

trom·pi·llo \träm'pē(,)(y)ō\ *n* -S [Sp, prob. dim. of *trompa* horn, trumpet, nozzle, prob. of Gmc origin like It *tromba* trumpet — more at TROMBONE] : a weedy nightshade (*Solanum elaeagnifolium*) ranging from the central U.S. to So. America with silvery foliage, violet, blue, or white flowers, and a roundish berry widely used by the natives to curdle milk — called also *prairie berry*, *purple nightshade*, *silverleaf nightshade*

-tron \,trän\ *n suffix* -S [Gk, suffix denoting an instrument (as Gk *arotron* plow, fr. stem of *aroun* to plow); akin to OE *-thor*, suffix denoting an instrument, ON *-thr*, L *-trum*, MIr *-thar*, Skt *-tra*] **1** : vacuum tube ⟨magne*tron*⟩ **2** : device for the manipulation of subatomic particles ⟨cyclo*tron*⟩ ⟨iso*tron*⟩

tro·na \'trōnə\ *n* -S [Sw, prob. fr. Ar *naṭrūn* natron — more at NATRON] : a gray-white or yellowish white monoclinic mineral $Na_3H(CO_3)_2.2H_2O$ consisting of a hydrous acid sodium carbonate in crystals or fibrous or columnar masses as a deposit from various soda-brine springs and lakes (hardness 2.5–3, sp. gr. 2.11–2.14)

tro·na·dor \;trōnə;dō(ə)r\ *n* -S [AmerSp, lit., thunderer, fr. Sp, fr. *tronar* to thunder, modif. of L *tonare*; fr. its noisy dehiscence — more at THUNDER] **1** : a Central American, Mexican, and West Indian woody herb (*Abutilon trisulcatum*) **2** : the bast fiber of the tronador used esp. for ropes and nets

tron·age \'trōnij\ *n* -S [AF, fr. *trone* + OF *-age*] **1 a** : a medieval toll or duty for compulsory weighing of coarse goods (as wool) at the public trone **b** : the act of weighing such goods **2** : the right of demanding tronage

trone \'trōn\ *also* **tron** \'trän\ *n* -S [AF *trone*, fr. OF, fr. L *trutina* balance, scales, fr. Gk *trytanē*; akin to Gk *tryma* hole, *tetrainein* to pierce; fr. the opening in which the tongue of the scale moves — more at THROW] *chiefly Scot* : one of various weighing machines; *specif* : one for heavy wares having two horizontal bars crossing each other and beaked at the extremities

trone weight *n* : an old standard of weight used in Scotland before 1618 based on a pound containing 21 to 28 ounces avoirdupois

tro·nom·e·ter \trō'näməd·ə(r)\ *n* [alter. of *tromometer*] : a device for measuring finger tremor used to diagnose nervous disturbances

tro·ö·don \'trōə,dän\ *n*, *cap* [NL, fr. *tro-* (prob. fr. Gk *trōgein* to gnaw) + *-odon* — more at TERSE] : a genus (the type of the family Troödontidae) of aberrant Upper Cretaceous No. American ornithopod dinosaurs with the skull expanded above into an enormous rugose bony dome ornamented with prongs and spikes

¹tro·ö·dont \-nt\ *adj* [NL *Troödont-*, *Troödon*] : of or relating to the *Troödon*

²troödont \"\ *n* -S : a dinosaur of the genus *Troödon*

troo·lie \'trülē\ *n* -S [Galibi *turluri*] **1** : one of the immense leaves of the bussu used for thatching **2** *also* **troolie palm** : BUSSU

¹troop \'trüp\ *n* -S [MF *troupe*, fr. *troupeau* herd, crowd, fr. OF, of Gmc origin; akin to OE *throp*, *thorp* group, village — more at THORP] **1 a** : a group of soldiers : a body of armed men ⟨the small ~ . . . that guarded the settlement was drawn up on parade —Leslie Thomas⟩ **b** (1) : a cavalry unit corresponding to an infantry company (2) : a company of horse artillery **c** : armed forces : SOLDIERS — usu. used in pl. ⟨victorious ~*s*⟩ **2 a** : a collection of people or things : COMPANY ⟨a mobile and dynamic ~ whose major aims are the improvement of the mind —E.O.Hauser⟩ **b** : a considerable number : a large quantity ⟨she had . . . ~*s* of friends —Havelock Ellis⟩ ⟨~*s* of servants and endless leisure —Letitia Fairfield⟩ **3** : a flock of animals or birds ⟨suddenly started a ~ of tall giraffes —H.R.Haggard⟩ ⟨~*s* of finches and linnets up here —Richard Jefferies⟩ **4 a** : a unit of at least five boy scouts of the Boy Scouts of America under the leadership of a scoutmaster **b** : a unit of the Girl Scouts comprising a group of usu. 8 to 32 girls and 1 or 2 adult leaders who meet regularly to carry on Girl Scout activities

²troop \"\ *vb* -ED/-ING/-S *vi* **1 :** to gather in crowds **:** come together **:** ASSEMBLE ⟨armies at the call of trumpet . . . ~ to the standard —John Milton⟩ **2 :** to go one's way **:** WALK ⟨~*ed* off to market —Bessie Hackett⟩ ⟨~*ed* away to the ball game⟩ **3 :** to consort in company **:** ASSOCIATE — usu. used with *with* ⟨a snowy dove ~*ing* with crows —Shak.⟩ **4 :** to move in an orderly manner **:** march in or as if in file ⟨the fourth grade ~*ed* in —Frances G. Patton⟩ ⟨pushed back their chairs and ~*ed* into the kitchen —Kenneth Roberts⟩ **5 :** to move in large numbers **:** go as a big group **:** THRONG ⟨the miners ~ home . . . trailing slowly in gangs across the white field —D.H.Lawrence⟩ ⟨hordes of hysterical revelers ~*ing* through their rooms —Green Peyton⟩ ~ *vt, obs* **:** to unite with or form into a troop — **troop the colors** *Brit* **:** to perform a ceremony consisting essentially in carrying the colors slowly before elements of the Brigade of Guards (as on the sovereign's birthday)

troop carrier *n* **1 :** an armored cross-country vehicle designed esp. to carry infantry troops **2 :** a transport airplane used to carry troops and their supplies esp. in a tactical situation or area

troop committee *n* **:** a group of parents and other interested adults organized as a committee for advising and assisting a Girl Scout troop

troop duck *n* **:** GREATER SCAUP

troop·er \-pə(r)\ *n* -S **1 a** (1) **:** an enlisted cavalryman (2) **:** the horse of a cavalryman **b :** PARATROOPER **2 a :** a mounted policeman **b :** one of a body of state police usu. using motorized vehicles **3 :** TROOPSHIP

troopfowl \'⸗,⸗\ *n* [¹*troop* + *fowl*; fr. its living in flocks] *dial* **:** SCAUP DUCK

troopial *var of* TROUPIAL

troop school *n* **:** a part of the system of military education in the U.S. armed forces in which both officers and enlisted men receive instruction within their own unit

troopship \'⸗,⸗\ *n* **:** a ship built or fitted for the conveyance of troops **:** TRANSPORT

¹troost·ite \'trü,stīt\ *n* -S [Gerard *Troost* †1850 Am. geologist + E *-ite*] **:** a variety of willemite occurring in large reddish crystals in which the zinc is partly replaced by manganese

²troostite \"\ *n* -S [F, fr. Louis J. *Troost* †1911 Fr. chemist + F *-ite*] **:** slightly tempered martensite that etches dark and cannot be resolved by the optical microscope — **troost·it·ic** \trü'stid·ik\ *adj*

¹trop- *or* **tropo-** *comb form* [ISV, fr. Gk, fr. *tropos* — more at TROPE] **1 :** turn **:** turning **:** change ⟨*tropo*meter⟩ ⟨*tropo*sphere⟩ **2 :** affinity for **:** tendency to turn toward **:** tropism ⟨*tropic*⟩ ⟨*tropo*taxis⟩

²trop- *also* **tropa-** *comb form* [ISV, fr. *tropine*] **1 :** tropine ⟨*trop*ate⟩ ⟨*tropa*cocaine⟩ **2 :** atropine ⟨*trop*oyl⟩

trop *abbr* tropic; tropical

tro·pa·cocaine \'trōpə+\ *n* [ISV ²*trop-* + *cocaine*] **:** a crystalline alkaloid $C_{15}H_{19}NO_2$ that is obtained from coca leaves grown esp. in Java or is made synthetically and that acts like cocaine but is about one half as toxic **:** the ester of pseudotropine and benzoic acid

tro·pae·o·la·ce·ae \,trōpēō'lāsē,ē\ *n pl, cap* [NL, fr. *Tropaeolum*, type genus + *-aceae*] **:** a family of plants (order Geraniales) coextensive with the genus *Tropaeolum* — **tro·pae·o·la·ceous** \¦⸗⸗⸗¦lāshəs\ *adj*

tro·pae·o·lin *or* **tro·pe·o·lin** \trō'pēələn\ *n* -S *often cap* [ISV *tropaeol-* (fr. NL *Tropaeolum*) + *-in*] **:** any of several orange or orange-yellow azo dyes some of which (as methyl orange) are used as acid-base indicators or as biological stains

tro·pae·o·lum \-ləm\ *n* [NL, dim. of L *tropaeum* trophy — more at TROPHY] **1** *cap* **:** a genus of tropical American diffuse or climbing pungent herbs constituting the family Tropaeolaceae and having lobed or dissected peltate leaves and showy variously colored spurred flowers succeeded by a fruit composed of three distinct rugose carpels — see CANARYBIRD FLOWER, NASTURTIUM 2 **2** -S **:** any plant or flower of the genus *Tropaeolum*

tro·pa·ion \trō'pā,(y)än, -'pī,än\ *n* -S [Gk — more at TROPHY] **:** TROPHAEUM

tro·pane \'trō,pān\ *n* -S [²*trop-* + *-ane*] **:** a bicyclic tertiary amine $C_8H_{15}N$ that is the parent compound of atropine, cocaine, and related alkaloids and that may be regarded as cycloheptane with a methyl-imino bridge **:** dihydro-tropidine

tro·par·ion \trō'par(,)yōn\ *n, pl* **tropa·ria** \-yä\ [LGk, dim. of Gk *tropos* trope] **:** a short hymn in rhythmic prose sung or chanted liturgically in the Eastern Orthodox Church; *specif* **:** a stanza of an ode (sense 2)

tro·pate \'trō,pāt\ *n* -S [ISV ²*trop-* + *-ate*] **:** a salt or ester of tropic acid

trope \'trōp\ *n* -S [L *tropus*, fr. Gk *tropos* turn, way, manner, style; akin to Gk *trepein* to turn, L *trepit* he turns, and perh. to Skt *trapate* he is ashamed] **1 :** the use of a word or expression in a different sense from that which properly belongs to it for giving life or emphasis to an idea; *also* **:** an instance of such use **:** FIGURE OF SPEECH **2 a** (1) **:** any one of certain melodic decorations gradually developed in Gregorian music and employed at the close of psalms and responses (2) **:** a phrase or verse added as an embellishment or interpolation to the sung parts of the mass (as introit or kyrie) esp. during the medieval period **b :** any of the 44 groups or arrangements of the twelve-tone scales into two 6-note chords as developed by Josef Hauer and used by him as a basis of musical composition

¹-trope \‚trōp\ *n comb form* -S [F, fr. Gk *tropos* turn, direction, way] **1 :** turn **:** change **:** affinity for ⟨chromo*trope*⟩ ⟨neuro*trope*⟩ **2 :** body characterized by (such) an inversion ⟨hemi*trope*⟩ **3 :** instrument and esp. optical instrument that functions by rotating, reversing, or reflecting ⟨rheo*trope*⟩ ⟨thauma*trope*⟩

²-trope \"\ *adj comb form* [F, fr. Gk *-tropos*, fr. *trepein* to turn] **:** turning **:** being reverted ⟨aniso*trope*⟩ ⟨hemi*trope*⟩

tro·pe·ine \'trōpē,ēn, -‚ən\ *n* -S [alter. of *tropine*] **:** any of a series of crystalline basic esters of tropine; *esp* **:** such an ester made synthetically

tro·per \'trōpə(r)\ *n* -S [ME *tropere*, fr. OE, fr. ML *troparium*, *troperium*, fr. L *tropus* trope] **:** a medieval book containing tropes or sequences for farsing the sung parts of the mass

tro·pe·sis \trō'pēsəs\ *n* -ES [NL, fr. Gk *tropē* action of turning (akin to Gk *tropos* turn) + NL *-sis*] *Haeckelism* **:** the rudimentary will or tendency to action possessed by all substance

troph- *or* **tropho-** *comb form* [F, fr. Gk, fr. *trephein* to nourish — more at ATROPHY] **:** nutrition ⟨*tropho*pathy⟩ ⟨*troph*allaxis⟩ ⟨*tropho*spore⟩

tro·phae·um \trō'fēəm\ *n, pl* **tro·phaea** \-ēə\ [L — more at TROPHY] **:** an ancient Greek or Roman monument commemorating a military victory

tro·phal \'trōfəl\ *adj* [NL *trophi* + E *-al*] **:** of, relating to, or constituting trophi

troph·al·lac·tic \¦träfə¦laktik\ *adj* [fr. NL *trophallaxis*, after such pairs as NL *prophylaxis*: E *prophylactic*] **:** of, relating to, constituting, or involving trophallaxis

troph·al·lax·is \‚⸗⸗'laksəs\ *n, pl* **trophallax·es** \-k‚sēz\ [NL, fr. *troph-* + Gk *allaxis* barter, fr. *allassein* to change, fr. *allos* other — more at ELSE] **:** exchange of food (as from salivary or other glands) between organisms **:** the association of different organisms and esp. social insects on the basis of such a unilateral or mutual exchange

troph·amnion \'träf+\ *n* [NL, fr. *troph-* + *amnion*] **:** a nutritive sheath that sometimes invests the embryonic portion of the insect egg esp. in polyembryonic insects — see PARANUCLEUS

troph·ectoderm \"+\ *n* [*troph-* + *ectoderm*] **:** TROPHOBLAST

tro·phe·ma \trō'fēmə\ *n* -S [NL, fr. *troph-* + Gk *haima* blood — more at HEM-] **:** the blood of the uterine mucous membrane that nourishes the embryo

tro·phi \'trō,fī\ *n pl* [NL, pl. of *trophus* mouth, fr. Gk *trophos* feeder, fr. *trephein* to nourish] **1 :** the mouthparts of an arthropod (as an insect) including the labrum, labium, maxillae, mandibles, and hypopharynx with their appendages **2 :** the masticating organs of a rotifer including the incus and the two mallei; *broadly* **:** MASTAX

troph·ic \'träfik, -fēk\ *adj* [F *trophique*, fr. Gk *trophikos*, fr. *trophē* food (fr. *trephein* to nourish) + *-ikos* -ic] **1 :** relating to or functioning in nutrition **:** NUTRITIONAL ⟨~ disorders⟩ ⟨~ hormones⟩ **2 :** ³TROPIC — **troph·i·cal·ly** \-fək(ə)lē, -fēk-, -li\ *adv*

-troph·ic \‚'träfik, -rōf-, -fēk, *sometimes* ‚trə(‚)fik\ *also* **-tro·phous** \‚trəfəs\ *adj comb form* [NL *-trophia* -trophy + E *-ic* or *-ous*] **1 a** *also* **-trophous :** of or relating to a (specified) type of nutrition ⟨hyper*trophic*⟩ ⟨hyper*trophous*⟩ **b :** having a (specified) nutritional requirement ⟨mono*trophic*⟩ **2 :** -TROPIC 1,2 ⟨glyco*trophic*⟩ ⟨lipo*trophic*⟩

tro·phied \'trōfēd\ *adj* [*trophy* + *-ed*] **:** adorned with trophies ⟨the long ~ banquet hall⟩

trophies *pl of* TROPHY, *pres 3d sing of* TROPHY

-trophies *pl of* -TROPHY

tro·phis \'trōfəs\ *n, cap* [NL, fr. Gk, well-fed, nursling, fr. *trephein* to nourish] **:** a small genus of tropical American trees (family Moraceae) having alternate leaves, small dioecious green flowers in usu. spicate or racemose clusters, and a nearly round thin-fleshed fruit with a single rather large seed

troph·ism \'trä,fizəm\ *n* -S [ISV *troph-* + *-ism*] **:** fundamental nutrition involving the actual metabolic exchanges of the tissues

troph·o·bi·ont \¦träfō¦bī,änt\ *n* -S [*troph-* + *-biont*] **:** a participant in trophobiosis

troph·o·bi·o·sis \‚⸗⸗bī'ōsəs\ *n, pl* **trophobio·ses** \-'ō‚sēz\ [NL, fr. *troph-* + *-biosis*] **1 :** a relation in which an organism of one kind aids and protects an organism of another kind in return for some food product — compare CLEPTOBIOSIS **2 :** TROPHALLAXIS

troph·o·bi·ot·ic \¦⸗⸗¦äd·ik\ *adj* [*troph-* + *-biotic*] **:** of, relating to, or engaging in trophobiosis ⟨~ insects⟩ ⟨the ~ relation between some ants and the aphids from which they obtain sweet secretions⟩

troph·o·blast \'träfə‚blast\ *n* [ISV *troph-* + *-blast*] **:** a special layer of ectodermal tissue that forms the outer surface of the blastodermic vesicle of many mammals, destroys the tissues of the uterus with which it comes in contact, is held to supply nutrition to the embryo and to secure the attachment of the egg to the wall of the uterus, and becomes differentiated into an outer syncytial or plasmodial syntrophoblast and an inner cellular cytotrophoblast which enter into the formation of the placenta — **troph·o·blas·tic** \¦⸗⸗¦blastik\ *adj*

tropho·chromatin \¦träfō+\ *n* [ISV *troph-* + *chromatin*; orig. formed in G] **:** chromatin that is held to be concerned with vegetative functions only — compare IDIOCHROMATIN

troph·o·cyte \'träfə‚sīt\ *n* -S [ISV *troph-* + *-cyte*] **1 :** a cell esp. of the insect fat body that has a trophic function **2 :** a nutritive cell of the insect ovary or testis

troph·o·derm \-‚dərm\ *n* -S [*troph-* + *-derm*] **:** TROPHOBLAST

tropho·dynamic \¦träfō+\ *adj* [*troph-* + *dynamic*] **:** of or relating to trophodynamics

tropho·dynamics \"+\ *n pl but sing or pl in constr* [*troph-* + *dynamics*] **:** the dynamics of nutrition

troph·o·gen·ic \¦träfə¦jenik\ *adj* [*troph-* + *-genic*] **1 :** brought about by or resulting from differences in food or feeding rather than genetically determined ⟨the various castes of social insects are usu. held to be ~ in origin⟩ — compare BLASTOGENIC **2** *also* **tro·phog·e·nous** \trō'fäjənəs\ [*troph-* + *-genous*] **:** of, relating to, or being the upper level in a lake in which inorganic matter is converted to organic through photosynthetic activity — compare TROPHOLYTIC

tro·phog·e·nist \⸗'⸗⸗nəst\ *n* -S [*trophogenic* + *-ist*] **:** an advocate of the trophogenic theory of caste determination in insects

tro·phol·o·gy \trō'fäləjē\ *n* -ES [ISV *troph-* + *-logy*] **:** a branch of science dealing with nutrition

troph·o·lyt·ic \¦träfə¦lid·ik\ *adj* [*troph-* + *-lytic*] **:** of, relating to, or being the deeper part of a lake in which dissimilation of organic matter tends to predominate — compare TROPHOGENIC

tro·phon \'trō‚fän\ *n* -S [NL, perh. fr. LGk *trophos* plaster, fr. *trophos* feeder — more at ATROPHY] **:** any of numerous small gastropod mollusks (family Muricidae) having the shell heavily sculptured and broadened by winglike varices

troph·o·ne·ma \‚träfə'nēmə\ *n, pl* **trophonema·ta** \-'nēməd·ə -'nem-\ [NL, fr. *troph-* + *-nema*] **:** one of the glandular filaments that develop from the inner uterine surface in viviparous elasmobranchs and secrete a nutritive fluid for the embryo

tropho·neurosis \¦träfō+\ *n* [NL, fr. *troph-* + *neurosis*] **:** a functional disease of a part due to failure of nutrition from defective nerve action in the parts involved

tropho·neurotic \"+\ *adj* [ISV, fr. NL *trophoneurosis*, after such pairs as NL *narcosis*: ISV *narcotic*] **:** of, relating to, constituting, or affected by a trophoneurosis

tropho·nucleus \"+\ *n* [NL, fr. *troph-* + *nucleus*] **1 :** MACRONUCLEUS **2 :** the nucleus of a trypanosome or related flagellate as distinguished from the kinetoplast esp. when held to be a metabolic control center — compare KINETONUCLEUS

troph·o·phore \'träfə‚fō(ə)r\ *n* -S [*troph-* + *-phore*] **:** one of the amoeboid cells that give rise to gemmules in a sponge — **tro·phoph·o·rous** \trō'fäf(ə)rəs\ *adj*

troph·o·plasm \'träfə‚plazəm\ *n* [ISV *troph-* + *-plasm*] **:** relatively unspecialized protoplasm held to be nutritive as distinguished from highly active differentiated protoplasm (as idioplasm, kinoplasm, archoplasm) — **troph·o·plas·mat·ic** \¦⸗⸗plaz¦mad·ik\ *adj* — **troph·o·plas·mic** \¦⸗⸗¦plazmik\ *adj*

troph·o·plast \'träfə‚plast\ *n* -S [ISV *troph-* + *-plast*, orig. formed in G] **:** a plant plastid

troph·o·some \-‚sōm\ *n* -S [*troph-* + *-some*] **1 :** the nutritive zooids of a hydroid — compare GONOSOME **2 :** a storage organ in an adult mermithid worm consisting of the fat-filled syncytial remains of the intestine

troph·o·sphere \-‚sfi(ə)r\ *n* [*troph-* + *sphere*] **:** the trophoblast of the hedgehog

troph·o·spon·gia \‚⸗⸗'spənjēə, -pän-\ *n* -S [NL, fr. *troph-* + *-spongia*] **:** the vascular spongy mucous membrane between the wall of the uterus and the trophoblast — **troph·o·spon·gi·al** \¦⸗⸗¦spənjēəl, -pän-\ *adj*

troph·o·spon·gium \‚⸗⸗'spənjēəm, -pän-\ *n* -S [NL, fr. *troph-* + *-spongium*] **:** an intracellular canal system variously held to be the Golgi apparatus, ingrowths of surrounding cells, or an observational artifact

troph·o·tax·is \-'taksəs\ *n, pl* **trophotax·es** \-k‚sēz\ [NL, fr. *troph-* + *-taxis*] **:** a chemotaxis in which the stimulating agent may serve as food to the organism

troph·o·thy·lax \-'thī‚laks\ *n* -ES [NL, fr. *troph-* + Gk *thylax* pouch, sack] **:** a depression or pocket on the underside of the body behind the mouth in various ant larvae in which food is placed by the attendant worker ants

troph·o·trop·ic \¦⸗⸗¦träpik\ *adj* [*trophotropism* + *-ic*] **:** of, relating to, or characterized by trophotropism

tro·phot·ro·pism \trō'fä·trə‚pizəm\ *n* [ISV *troph-* + *-tropism*] **:** a chemotropism in which food or a nutritive substance constitutes the orienting factor

-trophous — see -TROPHIC

troph·o·zo·ite \‚träfə'zō‚īt\ *n* -S [*troph-* + *zo-* + *-ite*] **:** a vegetative protozoan as distinguished from a reproductive or resting form — used esp. of a parasite (as a sporozoan)

troph·o·zo·oid \-ō‚ōid\ *n* [*troph-* + *zooid*] **1 :** an imperfect zooid or individual of the sexual generation of some free-swimming tunicates that never becomes sexually mature or detached from its parent **2 :** a nutritive zooid of a scyphozoan colony

¹tro·phy \'trōfē, -fi\ *n* -ES *often attrib* [MF *trophee*, fr. L *trophaeum*, *tropaeum*, fr. Gk *tropaion*, fr. neut. of *tropaios* of turning, of defeat, fr. *tropē* action of turning, enemy's retreat; akin to Gk *trepein* to turn — more at TROPE] **1 a :** a memorial of an ancient Greek or Roman victory raised on the field of battle or in case of a naval victory on the nearest land or sometimes in the chief city either of the victorious or the conquered people and consisting originally of spoils (as armor or weapons) of the defeated enemy fixed to the trunk of a tree or to a post on an elevated site with an inscription and a dedication to a divinity **b :** a representation of such a memorial (as on a medal); *also* **:** an architectural ornament representing a group of arms and military weapons offensive and defensive **2 :** an evidence or memorial of victory or conquest: as **a :** something (as arms, flags, standards) taken from an enemy by force of arms and preserved as a memorial **b :** spoils of the hunting field esp. when suitable for mounting **c :** something (as a laurel wreath, a medal, or a piece of plate) given or received as an award for victory in a contest ⟨a mantel covered with tennis *trophies*⟩ **3 :** something kept or cherished usu. as a memento and gained by personal effort ⟨*trophies* of her social success⟩ ⟨gathered *trophies* of an earlier civilization⟩ ⟨less a wife than a ~⟩

²trophy \"\ *vt* -ED/-ING/-ES **:** to place trophies on or in **:** honor or adorn with a trophy

-tro·phy \‚trəfē, -fi\ *n comb form* -ES [NL *-trophia*, fr. Gk, fr. *troph-* + *-ia* -y] **:** nutrition **:** nourishment **:** nurture **:** growth ⟨eu*trophy*⟩ ⟨noso*trophy*⟩ ⟨pedo*trophy*⟩

trophy cress *n* **:** NASTURTIUM 2

tro·phy·less \'trōfēləs\ *adj* **:** having or meriting no trophies

trophy money *or* **trophy tax** *n* **:** an annual English tax for militia equipment by housekeepers levied in the City of London

trophy room *n* **:** a room for the keeping and exhibition of trophies

trophywort \'⸗⸗‚⸗\ *n* [*trophy* + *wort*] **:** NASTURTIUM 2

tro·pia \'trōpēə\ *n* -S [NL, fr. Gk *tropē* action of turning + NL *-ia*] **:** deviation of an eye from the normal position with respect to the line of vision when the eyes are open **:** STRABISMUS

-tro·pia \‚'trōpēə\ *n comb form* -S [NL, fr. Gk, turn, deviation, fr. *-tropos* -trope + *-ia* -y] **:** condition of (such) a deviation in the line of vision ⟨eso*tropia*⟩ ⟨hyper*tropia*⟩

¹trop·ic \'träpik, -pēk\ *n* -S [ME *tropik*, fr. L *tropicus* of a turn, of a turning of the sun, fr. Gk *tropikos* of the solstice, fr. *tropē* action of turning (akin to Gk *trepein* to turn) + *-ikos* -ic — more at TROPE] **1** *obs* **:** either of the solstitial points; *also* **:** BOUNDARY, LIMIT **2 :** either of the two small circles of the celestial sphere on each side of and parallel to the equator at a distance of 23½ degrees which the sun reaches at its greatest declination north or south **3 a :** either of the two parallels of terrestrial latitude corresponding to the celestial tropics — see TROPIC OF CANCER, TROPIC OF CAPRICORN **b tropics** *pl, often cap* **:** the region lying between these parallels of latitude or near them on either side — usu. used with *the* ⟨life in the ~*s*⟩

²tropic \"\ *adj* **1 :** of, relating to, or occurring in the tropics **:** TROPICAL ⟨~ breezes⟩ ⟨~ fruits⟩ ⟨gorgeous ~ butterflies —William Beebe⟩ **2 :** associated with or occurring during the greatest north or south declination of the moon ⟨a ~ tide⟩

³tropic \"\ *adj* [¹*trop-* + *-ic*] **1 :** of, relating to, or characteristic of tropism or of a tropism **2** *of a hormone* **:** influencing the activity of a specified gland

-trop·ic \‚'träpik, -pēk, *in some words* -rōp-\ *adj comb form* [F *-tropique*, fr. ¹*-trope* + *-ique* -ic] **1 :** turning, changing, or tending to turn or change esp. in a (specified) manner or in response to a (specified) stimulus ⟨bacterio*tropic*⟩ ⟨enantio*tropic*⟩ ⟨geo*tropic*⟩ ⟨helio*tropic*⟩ ⟨iso*tropic*⟩ ⟨chemo*tropic*⟩ **2 :** attracted specif. to (such) a tissue, organ, or system ⟨neuro*tropic*⟩ ⟨viscero*tropic*⟩ **3 :** -TROPHIC 1 ⟨ecto*tropic*⟩ ⟨endo*tropic*⟩

trop·ic acid \'träpik-\ *n* [*tropic* ISV, fr. *atropic* of or relating to atropine, fr. *atrop-* (in *atropine*) + *-ic*] **:** a crystalline acid $HOCH_2CH(C_6H_5)COOH$ known in dextrorotatory, levorotatory, and racemic forms of which the last is obtained by hydrolysis of atropine and various other alkaloids or by synthesis **:** α-phenyl-hydracrylic acid

¹trop·i·cal \'träpəkəl, -pēk-, *in sense 2* 'trōp-\ *adj* [¹*tropic* + *-al*] **1 a** (1) **:** of, relating to, characteristic of, or incident to the tropics ⟨~ fruits⟩ ⟨~ agriculture⟩ (2) **:** being within the tropics ⟨~ latitudes⟩ (3) **:** suitable for use in the tropics ⟨~ worsteds⟩ **b** *of a sign of the zodiac* **:** beginning at one of the tropics **c** *usu cap* **:** of, relating to, being, or native to an American biogeographic zone that lies next below the Austral, is bounded to the north by a line marking a minimum accumulation in growth season temperature above 43 degrees Fahrenheit of 26,000 degrees, is nearly or wholly frost-free, and includes most of the region between the tropics of Cancer and Capricorn **2** [L *tropicus* (fr. Gk *tropikos*, fr. *tropos* turn, style + *-ikos* -ic) + E *-al* — more at TROPE] **:** rhetorically changed from its exact original sense **:** having the nature of a trope **:** FIGURATIVE, METAPHORICAL

²trop·i·cal \'träpəkəl, -pēk-\ *n* -S **1 :** TROPICAL FISH **2 a :** a lightweight suiting of various fibers (as worsted) made in plain open weave with a clear finish and used esp. for hot-weather wear **b :** a garment (as a man's suit) of such a fabric

tropical air *n* **:** air of a mass originating in the tropics and characterized by high temperature and humidity

tropical almond *n* **:** MALABAR ALMOND

tropical apricot *n* **:** MAMMEE 1b

tropical aquarium *n* **:** an aquarium maintained at a uniform warmth by artificial heating and used for the keeping and breeding of tropical fish

tropical bleach *n* **:** a bleach for use under tropical conditions that is made by adding enough lime to a fairly dry bleaching powder to react with most of the water present

tropical cyclone *n* **:** a cyclone in the tropics characterized by winds rotating at the rate of 75 miles an hour or more — see HURRICANE, TYPHOON

tropical disease *n* **:** a disease that is indigenous to and may be endemic in a tropical area but may also occur in sporadic or epidemic form in a nontropical area

tropical duckweed *n* **:** WATER LETTUCE

tropical dysentery *n* **:** AMEBIASIS

tropical fish *n* **:** any of numerous exotic aquarium fishes requiring controlled water temperatures for satisfactory growth — compare BETTA, DANIO, MOLLIENISIA, PLATY, SWORDTAIL, TETRA

tropical fowl mite *n* **:** a poultry mite (*Bdellonyssus bursa*) that infests chickens and turkeys in warm regions of the New World including parts of southern U. S.

tropical hen flea *n* **:** STICKTIGHT FLEA

trop·i·ca·li·an \¦träpə¦kālēən\ *adj, usu cap* [NL *Tropicalia*, marine realm including all tropical coral-reef seas (fr. L *tropicus* + Gk *hals* sea + NL *-ia*) + E *-an* — more at TROPIC, SALT] **:** of, relating to, being, or native to the marine biogeographic realm that includes all seas within the isocryme of 68° F and is characterized by the presence of reef-building corals

trop·i·cal·i·ty \‚träpə'kaləd·ē\ *n* -ES [¹*tropical* + *-ity*] **:** a thing or quality characteristic of the tropics

trop·i·cal·iza·tion \‚träpəkələ'zāshən\ *n* -S **1 :** the quality or state of being tropicalized **2 :** an act of tropicalizing

trop·i·cal·ize \'träpəkə‚līz\ *vt* -ED/-ING/-S *see -ize in Explan Notes* [¹*tropical* + *-ize*] **1 :** to make tropical (as in character, conditions, or appearance) **2 :** to fit or adapt for use in a tropical climate esp. by measures designed to combat the effects of fungi and moisture

tropical kudzu *n* **:** a tropical vine (*Pueraria phaseoloides*) grown esp. in the East Indies as a cover crop and for erosion control

tropical lake *n* **:** a lake with surface temperature constantly above 4°C

trop·i·cal·ly \-pək(ə)lē, -pēk-, -li\ *adv* **1 :** in a way typical of the tropics **2 :** by the use of tropes

tropical maritime air *n* **:** air of a mass originating over tropical oceans and characterized by high temperature and humidity

tropical medicine *n* **:** a branch of medicine dealing with tropical diseases and other special medical problems of tropical regions

tropical month *n* **:** a period that equals the mean time of the moon's revolution from any point of the ecliptic back to the same point and amounts to 27 days, 7 hours, 43 minutes, and 4.7 seconds of mean solar time

tropical rain forest *n* **:** RAIN FOREST 1

tropical rat mite *n* **:** a widely distributed mite (*Bdellomyssus bacoti* or a closely related species) that is primarily a parasite of rodents but sometimes bites humans causing painful itching and irritation and that has been implicated as a vector or potential vector of rodent and other diseases

tropical seal *n* **:** WEST INDIA SEAL

tropical storm *n* **:** a tropical cyclone with strong winds that are of less intensity than hurricane winds

tropical ulcer *n* **1 :** leishmaniasis of the skin — compare ORIENTAL SORE **2 :** a chronic sloughing sore of unknown cause occurring usu. on the legs and prevalent in wet tropical regions

tropical year *n* **:** the period occupied by the sun's center in passing from one equinox to the same again and having a mean length of 365 days, 5 hours, 48 minutes, 45.5 seconds : SOLAR YEAR

tropic bird *n* : any of several totipalmate birds constituting the genus *Phaëthon* found chiefly in tropical seas often far from land, somewhat resembling terns but being more nearly related to the frigate bird and the gannets, and having plumage of a satiny texture and mostly white with a few black markings, a greatly elongated central pair of tail feathers, and a bright-colored bill

tropic of cancer *often cap T & usu cap C* [so called fr. the sign of the zodiac at which it touches the ecliptic] : the parallel of latitude that is approximately 23½ degrees north of the equator and is the northernmost latitude reached by the overhead sun — see ZONE illustration

tropic of capricorn *often cap T & usu cap C* [so called fr. the sign of the zodiac at which it touches the ecliptic] : the parallel of latitude that is approximately 23½ degrees south of the equator and is the southernmost latitude reached by the overhead sun — see ZONE illustration

trop·i·co·pol·i·tan \ˌträpəkōˈpälətᵊn\ *adj* [[1]*tropic* + *-opolitan* (as in *cosmopolitan*)] : inhabiting all tropical countries : occurring throughout the tropics

trop·i·cor·bis \ˌträpəˈkȯrbəs\ *n, cap* [NL, fr. *tropicus* tropical (fr. L, of a turning of the sun) + L *orbis* ring, circle — more at TROPIC, ORB] : a genus of New World freshwater snails (family Planorbidae) of medical importance as hosts of the schistosome (*Schistosoma mansoni*) in endemic focuses in No. and So. America

tropics *pl of* TROPIC

trop·i·dine \ˈträpəˌdēn, -dən\ *n* -s [ISV [2]*trop-* + *-idine*] : an oily alkaloid $C_8H_{13}N$ obtained by the chemical dehydration of tropine

trop·i·do·lep·tus \ˌträpədōˈleptəs\ *n, cap* [NL, fr. *tropido-* (fr. Gk *tropid-, tropis* ship's keel) + Gk *leptos* small; akin to Gk *tropos* turn — more at TROPE, LEPT-] : a genus of articulate brachiopods widely distributed in Devonian formations where they are important index fossils and characterized by a concavo-convex shell wide at the hinge and with broad rounded ribs

-tropies *pl of* -TROPY

tro·pine \ˈtrōˌpēn, -pən\ *n* -s [ISV, fr. *atropine*] : a poisonous hygroscopic crystalline heterocyclic amino alcohol $C_8H_{15}NO$ derived from tropane and obtained by hydrolysis of atropine and other solanaceous alkaloids or by synthesis — see ECGONINE, TROPEINE

tro·pism \ˈtrōˌpizəm\ *n* -s [ISV *-tropism*] **1 a** : involuntary orientation by an organism or one of its parts that involves turning or curving accomplished by active movement or more often by structural alteration (as through turgor changes or differential growth), that constitutes a positive or negative response to a source of stimulation (as a light or a temperature or chemical gradient), and that in motile organisms may be indistinguishable from a taxis — compare NASTIC MOVEMENT, REFLEX 4 **b** : a reflex reaction involving such movement **2** : an innate tendency to react in a definite manner to stimuli : a natural inborn inclination

-tro·pism \-trəˌpizəm, *in some words* ·ˌtrōˌpizəm\ *n comb form* -s [ISV, fr. [1]*-trope* + *-ism*] : tendency to turn toward : affinity for : tropism ⟨helio*tropism*⟩ ⟨neuro*tropism*⟩

tro·pis·mat·ic \ˌtrōpizˈmad·ik\ *adj* [*tropism* + *-atic* (as in *automatic*)] : constituting a tropism esp. in being innate and essentially automatic

tro·pis·tic \trōˈpistik, -tēk\ *adj* [fr. *tropism*, after such pairs as E *optimism: optimistic*] : of, relating to, or characteristic of tropism ⟨~ responses⟩

tropo- — see TROP-

trop·o·log·i·cal \ˌträpəˈläjəkəl\ *also* **trop·o·log·ic** \-jik\ *adj* [*tropological* fr. LL *tropologicus* + E *-al*; *tropologic* fr. ME *tropologik*, fr. LL *tropologicus*, fr. LGk *tropologikos*, fr. *tropologia* tropology + Gk *-ikos* -ic] **1** : characterized or varied by tropes : TROPICAL, FIGURATIVE **2** : of, relating to, or involving tropology; *often* : MORAL — **trop·o·log·i·cal·ly** \-jək(ə)lē\ *adv*

tro·pol·o·gy \trōˈpäləjē\ *n* -ES [LL *tropologia*, fr. LGk, fr. *tropos* trope (fr. Gk, turn, manner, style) + Gk *-logia* -logy — more at TROPE] **1 a** : a figurative mode of speech or writing **b** : a mode of biblical interpretation stressing a moral meaning inhering in the metaphorical character of language **2** : a treatise on or compilation of tropes

trop·o·lone \ˈträpəˌlōn\ *n* -s [[2]*trop-* + *-ol* + *-one*] : a crystalline unsaturated enolic ketone $C_7H_6O_2$ containing the seven-membered ring of tropane and tropine — see STIPITATIC ACID, THUJAPLICIN

tro·pom·e·ter \trōˈpämədə(r)\ *n* [ISV [1]*trop-* + *meter*] : a device to measure rotation (as of the eyeball) or amount of torsion of a long bone

tropo·myosin \ˌträpō+\ *n* [[2]*trop-* + *myosin*] : a crystallizable protein of relatively low molecular weight found in muscle and resembling myosin

tro·po·pause \ˈtrōpəˌpȯz, ˈträp-\ *n* [ISV *tropo*sphere + *pause*] : the region at the top of the troposphere

tro·poph·i·lous \trōˈpäfələs\ *also* **trop·o·phil** \ˈträpəˌfil\ *adj* [[1]*trop-* + *-philous* or *-phil*] : physiologically adjusted to or thriving in an environment that undergoes marked periodic changes (as in temperature, soil moisture, or available light)

trop·o·phyte \ˈträpəˌfīt\ *n* -s [[1]*trop-* + *-phyte*] : a tropophilous plant ⟨trees of the northern deciduous forests are typical ~s adapted to a mesophytic summer and a xerophytic winter⟩

tro·po·sphere \ˈtrōpəˌsfi(ə)r, ˈträp-, -iə\ *n* [ISV [1]*trop-* + *sphere*] : the portion of the atmosphere that is below the stratosphere, extends outward about 7 to 10 miles from the earth's surface, and is the portion in which temperature generally rapidly decreases with altitude, clouds form, and convection is active

tro·po·spher·ic \ˌ==ˈsfirik, -fer-\ *adj* : of, relating to, or occurring in the troposphere

tropo·stereoscope \ˌträpō+\ *n* [[1]*trop-* + *stereoscope*] : a stereoscope consisting essentially of two adjustable tubes side by side provided with caps to hold the images observed

trop·o·tac·tic \ˌträpəˈtaktik\ *adj* [[1]*trop-* + *-tactic*] : of, relating to, or constituting a tropotaxis

trop·o·tax·is \ˌ==ˈtaksəs\ *n* [NL, fr. [1]*trop-* + *-taxis*] : a taxis in which an organism orients itself through a process of simultaneous comparison of stimuli of different intensity acting on separate end organs

-tro·pous \-trəpəs\ *adj comb form* [Gk *-tropos*, fr. *trepein* to turn — more at TROPE] : turning or curving in (such) a way : exhibiting (such) a tropism ⟨ana*tropous*⟩

trop·o·yl \ˈträpəˌwil\ *n* -s [[2]*trop-* + *-oyl* (as in *benzoyl*)] : the radical $HOCH_2CH(C_6H_5)CO—$ of tropic acid

trop·po *also* **tropo** \ˈträ(ˌ)pō\ *n* -s [[1]*tropic* + *-o*, n. suffix] *slang* : a condition of mental disorder or tension occurring in troops on tropical service

trop·tom·e·ter \träpˈtämədə(r)\ *n* [irreg. fr. [1]*trop-* + *-meter*] : an instrument for measuring the angular distortion of a bar or piece undergoing a torsion test

-tro·py \·trəpē, -pi\ *n comb form* -ES [F *-tropie*, fr. Gk *-tropia* turn, fr. *-tropos* [2]-trope + *-ia* -y] **1** : condition of turning or curving in (such) a way or of exhibiting (such) a tropism ⟨hemi*tropy*⟩ **2** : change in a (specified) way or in response to a (specified) stimulus

tro·pyl \ˈtrōpəl\ *n* -s [[2]*trop-* + *-yl*] **1** : TROPOYL **2** : the univalent radical $C_8H_{14}N$ derived from tropine

[1]trot \ˈträt, *usu* -ăd·+V\ *n* -s [ME, fr. MF, fr. *troter* to trot] **1 a** (1) : a moderately fast gait of a horse or other quadruped in which the legs move in diagonal pairs — compare PACE 5b (2) : a gait of a man or other biped that falls between a walk and a run in speed and action : a jogging pace (as of one hurrying); *also* : brisk movement or activity ⟨tasks that kept him on the ~ all day⟩ (3) : an elastic running dance step in moderate tempo; *also* : a dance featuring such a step **b** : a journey or ride on horseback ⟨pleasant to go for a ~ on a fresh summer morning⟩ **c** : TROTTING RACE ⟨a mile ~ for three-year-olds⟩ **d** : the sound of a trotting animal **2 a** : a small child **b** : an old woman ⟨one of the sourest ~s in the village⟩ **3** : PONY 4 **4 trots** *pl but sing or pl in constr* : DIARRHEA — not often in polite use

[2]trot \"\ *vb* **trotted; trotted; trotting; trots** [ME *trotten*, fr. MF *troter*, fr. OF, of Gmc origin; akin to OHG *trottōn* to tread, MHG *trotten* to run, OE *tredan* to tread — more at TREAD] *vi* **1** : to ride, drive, or proceed at a trot ⟨the fox *trotted* over the knoll⟩ ⟨*trotting* behind a pair of matched bays⟩ **2** : to move or proceed briskly : JOG, HURRY ⟨keep him *trotting*⟩ ⟨the toddler *trotted* after his father⟩ ~ *vt* **1 a** : to ride, drive, or cause to go at a trot ⟨*trotting* the filly toward home⟩ **b** : to traverse at a trot ⟨loved to ~ the hills and valleys⟩ **2** : to draw (one) out so as to make sport of : subject to ridicule — **trot in double harness** : to get along smoothly; *esp* : to live contentedly in wedlock

[3]trot \"\ *n* -s [short for *trotline*] : TROTLINE; *also* : one of the short lines with hooks that are attached at intervals to the main line of a trotline

[4]trot \"\ *vi* : to use a trotline in fishing

trotcozy \ˈ=,==\ *n* [[2]*trot* + *cozy*] *Scot* : a covering for the head and shoulders worn esp. when riding

[1]troth \ˈtrō\|th, ˈtrȯ\|, ˈträ\|\ *n, pl* **troths** \|ths, \|t͟hz\ [ME *trouth*, fr. OE *trēowth* — more at TRUTH] **1** : loyal or pledged faithfulness : FIDELITY ⟨the evidence bespoke his *troth*⟩ **2 a** : one's pledged word ⟨insisted on his ~ that such a thing could not be so⟩ **b** : one's faith as pledged in a solemn undertaking and esp. in an agreement to marry; *also* : the act of making such a pledge : BETROTHAL

[2]troth \", -ōt͟h\ *vt* -ED/-ING/-s [ME *trouthen*, fr. *trouth*, n., troth] : PLEDGE, BETROTH

troth·less *pronunc at* [1]TROTH +ləs\ *adj* : lacking in loyalty : FAITHLESS

[1]trothplight \ˈ=,=\ *n* [ME *trouth plight*, fr. *trouth* troth + *plight*] *archaic* : a solemn pledge usu. to enter into the married estate

[2]trothplight \"\ *vt* [ME *trouth plighten*, fr. *trouth* troth + *plighten* to pledge — more at PLIGHT] *archaic* : BETROTH

trotline \ˈ=,=\ *n* [prob. fr. [2]*trot* + *line*] : SETLINE 1; *esp* : a comparatively short setline used (as for catching catfish or crabs) near shore or along streams

trot out *vt* **1** : to lead out and show the paces of (as a horse) **2** : to bring forward and put on display ⟨always able to *trot out* some new excuse⟩

trot·sky·ism \ˈträtskēˌizəm\ *n* -s *usu cap* [Leon *Trotsky* †1940 Russ. Communist leader + E *-ism*] : the political, economic, and social principles advocated by Trotsky; *esp* : the theory and practice of communism developed by or associated with Trotsky and usu. including adherence to the concept of worldwide revolution as opposed to socialism in one country — compare STALINISM, TITOISM

[1]trot·sky·ist \-ēəst\ *n* -s *usu cap* [Leon *Trotsky* + E *-ist*] : a follower of Trotsky : an adherent of Trotskyism

[2]trotskyist \"\ *adj, usu cap* : of, relating to, or having the characteristics of Trotskyism or Trotskyists

[1]trot·sky·ite \-ēˌīt\ *n* -s *usu cap* [Leon *Trotsky* + E *-ite*] : TROTSKYIST

[2]trotskyite \"\ *adj, usu cap* : TROTSKYIST

trot·ter \ˈträd·ə(r), -ätə-\ *n* -s [ME *trotter*, fr. *trotten* to trot + *-er* — more at TROT] **1** : one that trots: as **a** : a horse that trots; *usu* : a standardbred trained for or used in harness racing **b** *Brit* : a person who runs errands : an errand boy : MESSENGER **2 a** : the foot of a quadruped esp. when prepared for use as food **b** : the human foot ⟨go in and wash your dirty little ~s⟩

[2]trotter \"\ *n* -s [[4]*trot* + *-er*] : a fisherman who uses a trotline

trotter oil *n* : NEAT'S-FOOT OIL

trot·teur *R* trăˈtœr, +V -ˈtər·; *-R* -ˈtō, + *vowel in a word following without pause* -ˈtər· *or* -ˈtō *also* -ˈtōr\ *n* -s [F, fr. *trotter* to trot (fr. MF *troter*) + *-eur* -or — more at TROT] : a woman's tailored garment (as a suit, coat, dress, or hat) suitable for walking or outdoor wear

trotteur tan *n, often cap 1st T* : [2]BAY 2

trot·tie \ˈträd·ē\ *n* -s [[1]*trot* + *-ie*] : a small child : TODDLER

trotting *n* -s [fr. gerund of [2]*trot*] : harness racing for trotters

trotting race *n* : a harness race for trotters

trot·toir \trăˈtwär\ *n* -s [F, fr. *trotter* to trot + *-oir* (fr. L *-orium* -ory)] : FOOTPATH, SIDEWALK

trot·ty \ˈträd·ē\ *adj* [[1]*trot* + *-y*] : going at a trot; *broadly* : LIVELY, BRISK

tro·tyl \ˈtrōd·ᵊl\ *n* -s [*trot-* (fr. *trinitrotoluene*) + *-yl*] : TRINITROTOLUENE

[1]trou·ba·dour *also* **trou·ba·dor** \ˈtrübəˌdō(ə)r, -dȯ(ə)r, -du̇(ə)r, -ōə, -ō(ə), -ùə\ *n* -s *often attrib* [F *troubadour*, fr. MF, fr. OProv *trobador*, fr. *trobar* to compose in verse, prob. fr. (assumed) VL *tropare* to compose, fr. L *tropus* trope — more at TROPE] **1** : one of a class of lyric poets and poet-musicians often of knightly rank flourishing from the 11th to the end of the 13th century chiefly in Provence, the south of France, and the north of Italy and cultivating a lyric poetry intricate in meter and rhyme and usu. of a romantic amatory strain — compare TROUVÈRE **2** : a strolling minstrel; *also* : anyone who in music, verse, or rhetorical prose promotes some cause

[2]troubadour \"\ *vi* -ED/-ING/-s : to act the part of a troubadour

trou·ba·dour·ish \-rish\ *adj* : suited to or like that of a troubadour

[1]trou·ble \ˈtrəbəl\ *vb* **troubled; troubled; troubling** \-b(ə)liŋ\ **troubles** [ME *troublen, troblen*, fr. OF *troubler, tourbler*, fr. (assumed) VL *turbulare*, fr. L *turbidare* to trouble, make turbid, fr. *turbidus* disordered, troubled, turbid — more at TURBID] *vt* **1 a** : to agitate mentally or spiritually : bring distress or uncertainty of mind to : WORRY, BOTHER ⟨sorrows that ~ the strongest spirit⟩ ⟨her failure to remember the address *troubled* her⟩ **b** (1) *archaic* : to do harm to : MISTREAT, OPPRESS (2) : to produce physical disorder in : cause physical distress or suffering to ⟨*troubled* with increasing deafness⟩ ⟨severe pain continued to ~ her⟩ **c** : to put to exertion or inconvenience usu. by asking some service ⟨did not want to ~ her sister with the care of the children⟩ ⟨~ you to pass the butter⟩ **2 a** : to put into confused motion : cause to become turbulent or turbid through moving ⟨a strong wind *troubled* and ruffled the sea⟩ **b** *archaic* : to interfere with or bring into disorder : CHECK, DISARRANGE ~ *vi* **1 a** : to become mentally agitated : WORRY, BOTHER ⟨a man who refuses to ~ over trifles⟩ **b** : to make an effort : be at pains ⟨the will to ~ infinitely with the problems of his position⟩ **2** *obs* : to become physically agitated (as of water) : become obscured or dark (as of the sky)

[2]trouble \"\ *n* -s [ME, fr. OF *trouble, tourble*, fr. *troubler, tourbler* to trouble] **1** : the quality or state of being troubled : UNEASINESS, ANNOYANCE; *also* : an instance of distress, annoyance, or perturbation **2** : a cause of disturbance, annoyance, or distress (as an annoying or injurious event or experience): as **a** : civil disorder : public unrest or demonstrations of dissatisfaction ⟨watched with concern the ~ in the neighboring state⟩ ⟨labor ~⟩ **b** : an effort made : EXERTION, PAINS ⟨took the ~ to call and inquire after his aunt⟩ **c** (1) : a condition of physical distress, debility, or ill health (2) : DISEASE, AILMENT (3) *dial Eng* : labor in childbirth **d** : pregnancy out of wedlock ⟨get a girl in ~⟩ **e** : a personal characteristic that is a handicap or a source of distress ⟨his greatest ~ was a too-trusting nature⟩ **3** : one (as a person) that is a source of distress, disturbance, and esp. inconvenience ⟨never meant to be such a ~ to her sister⟩ **syn** see EFFORT

troubled *adj* [ME, fr. past part. of *troublen* to trouble] : characterized by or indicative of trouble ⟨these ~ areas⟩ ⟨a ~ expression⟩

trou·bled·ly *adv* : in a troubled manner

trou·bled·ness *n* -ES : the quality or state of being troubled

troubled waters *n pl* : a situation or condition of disorder or confusion ⟨a mischievous rogue ready to make the most of *troubled waters*⟩

trouble light *n* : any of various lighting devices designed to provide emergency illumination or to provide light in places not normally illuminated

trouble light

troublemaker \ˈ==,==\ *n* : one that is a source of trouble; *esp* : a person that consciously or unconsciously foments strife and disagreement often from ulterior motives

troublemaking \ˈ==,==\ *n* : the behavior of a troublemaker

trouble man *n* : TROUBLESHOOTER 1

trou·ble·ment \ˈtrəbəlmənt\ *n* -s [MF, fr. *trouble* + *-ment*] *chiefly dial* : a condition or source of trouble

troubleproof \ˈ==,=\ *adj* : free from or not subject to trouble; *esp* : not readily put out of order

trou·bler \ˈtrəb(ə)lə(r)\ *n* -s [ME *trublere*, fr. OF *troubleur*, fr. *troubler* to trouble + *-eur* -or — more at TROUBLE] : one that troubles

troubleshoot \ˈ==,=\ *vb* [back-formation fr. *troubleshooter*] *vi* : to operate or serve as a troubleshooter ~ *vt* : to investigate or deal with in the role of troubleshooter

troubleshooter \ˈ==,==\ *n* **1** : a skilled workman employed to locate causes of trouble in machinery and technical equipment and to make needed repairs — called also *trouble man* **2** : an expert at clearing or bridging an obstruction at a critical point or restoring flow past a bottleneck in political, military, or business affairs or industrial relations : a mediator of disputes come to an impasse

trou·ble·some \ˈtrəbəlsəm\ *adj* **1** : giving trouble or anxiety : DISTURBING, VEXATIOUS ⟨a ~ infection⟩ ⟨these ~ activities of our enemies⟩ **2** *archaic* : characterized by disturbance : TURBULENT **3** *archaic* : AFFLICTED, DISTRESSED **4** : requiring or involving sustained or tiring effort, attention, study, or application : DIFFICULT, BURDENSOME, WEARISOME — **trou·ble·some·ly** *adv* — **trou·ble·some·ness** *n* -ES

trouble spot *n* : a spot at which trouble is esp. likely to occur or break out ⟨a *trouble spot* in a mechanism⟩ ⟨Asiatic *trouble spots*⟩

trou·bling·ly *adv* : in a troubling manner : so as to produce trouble

trou·blous \ˈtrəbləs\ *adj* [ME *troublous*, fr. OF *troubleus*, fr. *trouble* + *-eus* -ous] **1** : full of trouble : TROUBLED, AFFLICTED; *also* : AGITATED, STORMY **2** : causing trouble : TURBULENT, DISTURBING — **trou·blous·ly** *adv* — **trou·blous·ness** *n* -ES

trou-de-loup \ˌtrüdəˈlü\ *n, pl* **trous-de-loup** \"\ [F, lit., wolf's hole] : a pit in the form of an inverted cone or pyramid having a pointed stake in the middle and forming one of a group constructed as an obstacle to the movements of an enemy — usu. used in pl.

[1]trough \ˈtrȯ\|f *sometimes* ˈträ\|, *chiefly by bakers* ˈtrō, *chiefly by Brit bakers* ˈtraů, *dial* \|th *or* \|ft\ *n, pl* **troughs** \|ts, \|vz, \|ths, \|t͟hz\ *n* -s *often attrib* [ME, fr. OE *trog, troh*; akin to OHG & ON *trog* trough, OE *trēow* tree, wood — more at TREE] **1 a** : a large long and usu. comparatively shallow open vessel that is often V-shaped in cross section and used esp. to hold water or feed for domestic animals **b** : any of various containers used for some domestic or industrial purpose: as (1) : a bowl, tank, or basin in which something is prepared or processed (as by kneading, washing, brewing, or tanning) (2) : the vessel under a grindstone that holds water for cooling in grinding; *also* : the place where a grindstone stands (3) : PNEUMATIC TROUGH (4) : a buddle or other vessel in which mining slimes are sorted in water (5) : the vessel used for the plating bath in the electroplating process **c** *chiefly dial* : TOMB, COFFIN **d** *chiefly dial* : any of various small boats (as a dugout) that somewhat resemble a trough for cattle **2 a** : a conduit for water: as (1) *chiefly dial* : a walled drain (2) *chiefly dial* : a wooden channel forming the headrace of a mill (3) : EAVES TROUGH **b** (1) : a long and narrow or shallow channel or depression (as between waves or hills) (2) : an elongated structural depression of the earth (as a graben, a geosyncline, a trench, or an ocean deep) **c** : a usu. recessed channel enclosing and concealing utilitarian structural elements (as piping or wiring) **3 a** : the part of a gravity wave or ripple on a liquid that is the lowest part of the oscillating surface at any given instant — contrasted with *crest* **b** : the minimum attained by a wave variable during the passage of a complete cycle: as (1) : an elongated area of low barometric pressure usu. with a minimum pressure at each end and between two anticyclones — opposed to *ridge* (2) : the low point in a business cycle (3) : a low part of a statistical curve that is between higher parts and is usu. concave upward

[2]trough \"\ *vt* -ED/-ING/-s : to make into or treat in a trough

trough conveyor *n* : a band conveyor with the sides of the band turned up to form a trough

trough gutter *n* : an eaves trough of rectangular or V-shaped section usu. hung below the eaves of a house

troughing *n* -s **1** : an arrangement or system of troughs : TROUGHS **2** : material for a trough

trough keel *n* : a keel in a yacht having the form of a trough into which molten lead is poured as ballast — compare BAR KEEL

trough roof *n* **1** : M ROOF **2** : a roof of hollowed-out split logs laid from ridge to eaves

trough shell *n* : a bivalve mollusk of the family Mactridae

trough·ton level \ˈtraůtᵊn-\ *n, usu cap T* [after Edward *Troughton* †1835 Eng. instrument maker] : DUMPY LEVEL

troughway \ˈ=,=\ *n* : the channel of a trough

troughy *pronunc at* [1]TROUGH +ē *or* i\ *adj* : having deep troughs

trou ma·dame \ˌtrüməˈdam\ *n* [F *trou-madame*, lit., hole madam, fr. MF; fr. the exclamation of the women players when one of them fails to score] : a variety of bagatelle in which the arches are scored to the player and the holes against him

[1]trounce \ˈtraůn(t)s\ *vt* -ED/-ING/-s [origin unknown] : to thrash or punish severely: as **a** : FLOG, CUDGEL **b** : to defeat decisively **c** : to censure sternly : castigate verbally **d** *dial chiefly Eng* : INDICT, SUE

[2]trounce \ˈtraůns\ *vi* [prob. alter. of [3]*trance*] *Scot & dial Eng* : to make a tiresome or rambling journey : TRAMP

[3]trounce \"\ *n* -s *dial Eng* : a long tiring ramble or journey

trounc·er \ˈtraůn(t)sə(r)\ *n* -s [[1]*trounce* + *-er*] : one that trounces: as **a** : WAISTER **b** *Brit* : a helper on a truck or delivery wagon

trou·pand \ˈtrüˌpand\ *n* -s [Afrik, lit., wedding pledge, fr. *trou* to wed (fr. MD *trouwen*, fr. *trouw* faithful) + D *pand* pledge, pawn, fr. MF *pan*; akin to OE *trēowe* faithful — more at TRUE, PAWN] : a southern African bird that is a variety of the European roller (*Coracias garrulus*)

[1]troupe \ˈtrüp\ *n* -s [F, fr. MF — more at TROOP] : COMPANY, TROOP; *esp* : a group of performers on the stage

[2]troupe \"\ *vi* -ED/-ING/-s : to travel in a troupe; *also* : to perform as a member of a theatrical troupe

troup·er \-pə(r)\ *n* -s : a member of a troupe; *esp* : ACTOR

troup·i·al *also* **troop·i·al** \ˈtrüpēəl\ *n* -s [F *troupiale*, fr. *troupe* flock, troop; fr. its living in flocks] : a bird of the family Icteridae; *esp* : one of the larger brilliant yellow-and-black or orange-and-black orioles of Central and So. America

trous-de-loup *pl of* TROU-DE-LOUP

trouse \ˈtrüz, ˈtraůz\ *n* -s [ScGael *triubhas*] **1** *obs* : TREWS, DRAWERS **2** *archaic* : TROUSERS, BREECHES

trou·ser \ˈtraůzə(r)\ *adj* [back-formation fr. *trousers*] : of, relating to, or designed for use with trousers ⟨~ pockets⟩

trou·sered \-(r)d\ *adj* : wearing or accustomed to wear trousers

trou·ser·ing \-z(ə)riŋ\ *n* -s : a fabric used or suitable for trousers

trou·sers \-zə(r)z\ *n pl* [alter. (influenced by *-ers* as in *drawers*) of *trouse*, fr. ScGael *triubhas*, prob. fr. OF *trebus* breeches] **1** *archaic* : TREWS **2 a** *also* **trouser** : an outer garment extending from the waist to the ankle or sometimes only to or just below the knee, covering each leg separately, made close-fitting or loose-fitting in accord with the fashion of different periods, and worn typically by men and boys **b trouser** *n sing* : half or one leg of a pair of trousers ⟨snagged his left ~ on the wire⟩ **3** : baggy pantaloons worn by both sexes in the Near East **4** : PANTALETS **5** *also* **trouserings** : the hair on the hindquarters of a dog esp. when profuse and full

trous·seau \ˈtrü(ˌ)sō, trüˈsō\ *n, pl* **trous·seaux** \-ō(z)\ *or* **trousseaus** \-ōz\ [F, fr. OF, little bundle, dim. of *trousse* bundle — more at TRUSS] : the personal possessions of a bride usu. including clothes, accessories, and household linens and wares

[1]trout \ˈtraůt, *usu* -aůd·+V\ *n, pl* **trout** *also* **trouts** [ME *troute, trute*, fr. OE *trūht*, fr. LL *tructa, troctа*, a trout, a shark, fr. Gk *trōktēs* sea fish with sharp teeth, fr. *trōgein* to gnaw — more at TERSE] **1** : any of various fishes of the family Salmonidae that are on the average much smaller than the typical salmons, are mostly restricted to cool clear freshwaters though some are anadromous, and are highly regarded for their attractive colorations, rich well-flavored flesh, and gameness as an angling fish: **a** : any of various Old or New World fishes of the genus *Salmo* — see BROWN TROUT, CUTTHROAT TROUT, RAINBOW TROUT, SEA TROUT 1, STEELHEAD 1 **b :** any of various No. American fishes of the genera *Salvelinus* or *Cristivomer* — see BROOK TROUT, CHAR, DOLLY VARDEN, LAKE TROUT **2 :** any of various fishes felt to resemble the salmonid trouts: as **a** *Austral* **:** a fish of the family Galaxiidae **b** *South* **:** LARGEMOUTH BLACK BASS **c :** a large cyprinid fish (*Gila elegans*) of the drainage of the Colorado and Gila rivers **d :** WEAKFISH

²trout \"\ *vi* -ED/-ING/-S **:** to fish for trout

troutbird \ˈ=,=\ *n* [so called fr. its speckled plumage] **:** GOLDEN PLOVER

trout-colored \ˈ=,==\ *adj* **:** white with spots of black, bay, or sorrel ⟨a *trout-colored* horse⟩

trout·er \ˈtrau̇d·ə(r)\ *n* -S **:** one that fishes for trout

trout·less \ˈtrau̇tləs\ *adj* **:** having or producing no trout ⟨~ waters⟩

trout·let \-lət\ *also* **trout·ling** \-liŋ\ *n* -S [¹*trout* + *-let* or *-ling*] **:** a fingerling trout

trout lily *also* **trout flower** *n* [prob. so called fr. the speckled leaves] **:** DOGTOOTH VIOLET

trou·ton's rule \ˈtrau̇tᵊnz-\ *n, usu cap T* [after Frederick T. *Trouton* †1922 Eng. physicist] **:** a statement in physical chemistry: the molar heats of vaporization of pure liquids are proportional to the absolute temperatures of their boiling points

trout-perch \ˈ=ˈ=\ *n* **:** a small freshwater fish (*Percopsis omiscomaycus*) of the central and eastern U.S.

¹trouty \ˈtrau̇d·ē\ *n* -ES [¹*trout* + *-y* (dim. suffix)] **:** a little trout

²trouty \"\ *adj* -ER/-EST [¹*trout* + *-y* (adj. suffix)] **:** containing or likely to contain abundant trout ⟨a ~ stream with deep pools and fast water⟩

trou·vaille \trüˈvī\ *n* -S [F, fr. OF *trouver* to compose, find] **:** a lucky find **:** WINDFALL

trou·vère \trüˈva(a)(ə)r\ *n* -S [F, fr. OF *troverre, troveor,* fr. *trover, trouver* to compose, find, fr. (assumed) VL *tropare* — more at TROUBADOUR] **:** one of a school of poets flourishing in northern France from the 11th to the 14th centuries and producing works that are typically the chansons de geste and are of a prevailingly narrative character — compare TROUBADOUR

trou·veur *R* trüˈvœr, + V -ˈvər-; -*R* -ˈvə̄, + *vowel in a word following without pause* -ˈvər- *or* -ˈvə̄ *also* -ˈvə̄r\ *n* -S [MF, fr. OF *troveor* to compose] **:** TROUVÈRE

trove \ˈtrōv\ *n* -S [short for *treasure trove*] **1 :** a thing found ⟨I was pleased by one of my ~*s* —Christopher Morley⟩ — compare TREASURE TROVE **2 :** a collection of objects ⟨a modest ~ of earrings —*New Yorker*⟩; *usu* **:** one deliberately concealed, previously lost sight of or not appreciated at its real value, or consciously assembled ⟨assembled a rich ~ of Chinese porcelain⟩ ⟨a ~ of new family letters . . . were made available to the biographer —*N.Y. Herald Tribune Bk. Rev.*⟩

tro·ver \ˈtrōvə(r)\ *n* -S [MF, to compose, find (taken as a n.), fr. OF] **1 :** a coming into possession **2 :** an action to recover the value of personal chattels or goods wrongfully converted by another to his own use

¹trow \ˈtrō\ *vb* -ED/-ING/-S [ME *trowen, trewen,* fr. OE *trēowan, trēowian;* akin to OS *triuwian* to believe, trust, ON *trūa* to believe, have faith in, Goth *trauan* to confide in, OE *trēowe* faithful — more at TRUE] **1** *obs* **a :** BELIEVE, TRUST **b :** HOPE, EXPECT **2** *archaic* **:** THINK, SUPPOSE **3** — formerly appended to questions to express contempt or indignant surprise ⟨what is the matter, ~ —Shak.⟩

²trow \"\ *n* -S [ME, fr. *trowen* to trow] **:** BELIEF, FAITH, COVENANT

³trow \"\ *Scot var of* TROLL

⁴trow \"\ *n* -S [ME, fr. OE *trog, troh* trough, canoe, boat — more at TROUGH] **:** any of several boats: as **a** *chiefly dial* **:** a catamaran or other double boat used in spearing salmon **b** *Brit* **:** a small fishing boat **c :** a bluff low flat-bottomed sailing barge used esp. in England for river and coastal haulage

⁵trow \"\ *dial chiefly Brit var of* TROUGH

¹trow·el \ˈtrau̇(ə)l\ *n* -S [ME *trowell, truel,* fr. MF *truelle,* fr. LL *truella, trulla* vessel for liquids, mason's trowel, fr. L *trulla* small ladle, dim. of *trua* ladle; akin to OE *thwiril* stick for stirring, OHG *dwiril,* Icel *thyrill,* Gk *torynē* stick for stirring, OHG *dweran* to stir — more at TURBID] **:** any of various hand tools or implements consisting of a flat or less commonly curved blade with a handle and used (as by bricklayers, plasterers, molders) to apply, spread, shape, and smooth loose or plastic material; *also* **:** a scoop-shaped or flat-bladed gardening implement used esp. for taking up and setting small plants

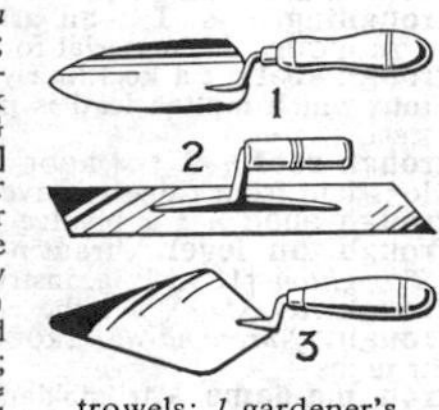

trowels: *1* gardener's, *2* plasterer's, *3* bricklayer's

²trowel \"\ *vt* **troweled** *or* **trowelled; troweled** *or* **trowelled; troweling** *or* **trowelling; trowels :** to smooth, dress, shape, mix, or apply with or as if with a trowel — **trow·el·er** \-lə(r)\ *n* -S

trow·el·man \-lmən\ *n, pl* **trowelmen :** a workman who uses a trowel

trow·ie \ˈtrōi\ *adj* [³*trow* + *-ie*] *Scot* **:** belonging to or influenced by a troll

trow·ing \ˈtrōiŋ\ *n* -S [ME, fr. gerund of *trowen* to believe, trust — more at TROW] **:** BELIEF, CREED, OPINION

trowl \ˈtrōl\ *chiefly dial var of* TROLL

trowman \ˈ=mən\ *n, pl* **trowmen** [ME, fr. ⁴*trow* + *man*] **:** an owner or operator of a fishing trow

trows·ers \ˈtrau̇zə(r)z\ *n pl* [by alter.] **:** TROUSERS 2

trowth \ˈtrōth\ *n* -S [ME(Sc) *trowth, trewth,* fr. OE *trēowth* — more at TRUTH] *chiefly Scot* **:** TROTH, TRUTH

trox \ˈträks\ *n, cap* [NL, fr. Gk *trōx* gnawer, fr. Gk *trōgein* to gnaw — more at TERSE] **:** a genus of medium-sized brownish beetles with large vertical mandibles including several typical skin beetles and others that feed on carrion or dung

troy \ˈtrȯi\ *adj* [ME *troye, troie,* fr. *Troyes,* city in France where it was prob. introduced] **:** expressed in troy weight — abbr. *t*

troy pound *n* [ME] **:** POUND 1a

troy weight *n* [ME] **:** a series of units of weight based on a pound of 12 ounces and the ounce of 20 pennyweights or 480 grains — see MEASURE table

trp *abbr* **1** troop **2** tropical

trs *abbr* **1** transfer **2** transpose **3** troops

trsd *abbr* **1** transferred **2** transposed

tru *abbr* trustee

tru·an·cy \ˈtrüənsē, -si\ *n* -ES **:** an act or instance of playing truant **:** the state of being truant

¹tru·ant \ˈtrüənt\ *n* -S [ME, fr. OF, vagrant, beggar, of Celt origin; akin to W *tru, truan* miserable, wretched, *truan* wretch, OIr *trōg* miserable, ScGael *truaghan* miserable person, *truagh* wretched] **1** *obs* **:** an idle vagrant **:** VAGABOND **2 :** one who stays away from business or shirks duty; *esp* **:** one who stays out of school without permission **syn** see VAGABOND

²truant \"\ *adj* **1 :** wandering from business or duty **:** shirking responsibility **:** IDLE; *esp* **:** absent from school without permission **2 :** resembling or characteristic of a truant ⟨try to govern this ~ pen —C.B.Fairbanks⟩ — **tru·ant·ly** *adv*

³truant *vb* -ED/-ING/-S [ME *truanten,* fr. *truant* vagrant] *vi* **:** to idle away time esp. while shirking some duty **:** willfully neglect a required task **:** absent oneself without permission ⟨have ~*ed* so much that . . . many can't do more than second-grade reading —Marjorie Rittwagen⟩ **~** *vt* **:** to waste or fritter away **:** play truant from

truant officer *n* **:** ATTENDANCE OFFICER

tru·ant·ry \-ntrē,-ntri\ *n* -ES **:** TRUANCY ⟨thought I had had enough of ~ —R.L.Stevenson⟩

¹trub \ˈtrəb\ *n* -S [origin unknown] **:** TRUFFLE 1

²trub \ˈtrüb, ˈtrəb\ *n* -S [G *trub, trüb;* akin to OHG *truobi* dim, murky, turbid, OE *drōf* dirty, muddy, turbid, ME *draf* dregs, draff — more at DRAFF] **:** a haze formed either during boiling or cooling of wort and removed as a step of the brewing process

tru·betz·koy·an \ˌtrübətˈskȯiən\ *adj, usu cap* [Nikolai *Trubetzkoi* †1938 Russ. linguist + E *-an*] **:** relating to or characteristic of the linguistic methods or terminology of Nikolai Trubetzkoi

¹truce \ˈtrüs\ *n* -S [ME *trewes, triwes,* pl. of *trewe, triewe* agreement, treaty, truce, fr. OE *trēow* fidelity, allegiance, agreement, pledge; akin to OHG *triuwa* fidelity, ON *trū* trust, faith, Goth *triggwa* alliance, pact, OE *trēowe* faithful — more at TRUE] **1 :** a suspension of fighting esp. of considerable duration by agreement of the commanders of opposing forces **:** a temporary cessation of hostilities **:** ARMISTICE, CEASE-FIRE **2 :** a respite esp. from a disagreeable or painful state or action **:** an intermission of rest and quiet **:** a brief interruption ⟨the parts of his complex and tortured spirit come together in a ~ —Virginia Woolf⟩ ⟨a reconciliation with his critics might have been effected . . . or, at least, a ~ —Harold Rosenberg⟩

²truce \"\ *vb* -ED/-ING/-S *vi* **:** to make a truce ⟨has *truced* with the party's younger strong man —*Springfield (Mass.) Union*⟩ **~** *vt, obs* **:** to bring to an end with a truce

truce·less \-ləs\ *adj* **:** marked by unending hostilities **:** having no hope of a truce

truce of god *usu cap T & cap G* [trans. of ML *Treuga Dei*] **:** the cessation of hostilities between armies or individuals during part of the week (as from Wednesday evening to Monday morning) and during various holy seasons enjoined and imperfectly enforced in western Europe by the church from 1027 to as late as the 13th century — compare PEACE OF GOD 2

tru·cha \ˈtrü(ˌ)chä\ *n* -S [Sp, fr. LL *tructa,* a trout — more at TROUT] *chiefly Southwest* **:** TROUT

tru·cial \ˈtrüshəl, -üsēəl\ *adj, often cap* [¹*truce* + *-ial;* fr. the maritime truce made in 1835 between the British government and several Arab states of the Oman peninsula] **:** of, relating to, or involving several territorial areas in the vicinity of the Persian Gulf for which the government of Great Britain assumes responsibility nominally in an advisory capacity ⟨nearly 400 miles of coast belongs to the *Trucial* sheikhs —*Americana Annual*⟩

¹truck \ˈtrək\ *vb* -ED/-ING/-S [ME *trukken, trukien,* fr. OF *troquer*] *vt* **1 :** to give in exchange **:** SWAP ⟨I would not ~ this brilliant day to rule —John Keats⟩ **2 a :** to exchange with an expectation of gain **:** BARTER ⟨maintain a trade with their neighbors and ~ their work with them for any necessaries —W.E.Roth⟩ **b :** to dispose of by bartering ⟨some of our kings have . . . ~*ed* away for foreign gold the interests and glory of their crown —Edmund Burke⟩ **3 :** to deal with or pay on the truck system **~** *vi* **1 :** to exchange commodities **:** BARTER ⟨the disposition peculiar to mankind to ~ —A.C. Pigou⟩ **2 a :** to negotiate or traffic esp. in an underhanded way **b :** to establish a familiar basis **:** have intercourse **3** *Scot* **:** to go about on insignificant affairs **:** PUTTER

²truck \"\ *n* -S **1 a :** the practice of trading by exchanging goods **:** BARTER **b :** a shrewd trade **:** DEAL **2 :** commodities appropriate for barter or for small trade ⟨accepted these simple gifts but ordered them all paid for out of the trading ~ —S.E. Morison⟩ **3 :** close association **:** CONTACT, DEALINGS ⟨with all such nonsense I have never had any ~ —Daniel George⟩ ⟨never at any time did he have the slightest ~ with . . . vulgarity —Clinton Rossiter⟩ ⟨wouldn't want you to have ~ with the family —Clemence Dane⟩ **4 :** payment of wages in goods instead of cash ⟨the worst conditions, long hours, irregular payment of wages, ~ . . . were to be found —J.H.Plumb⟩ — see TRUCK SYSTEM **5 :** vegetables that are grown for the market ⟨a good piece of land . . . by the springs to raise ~ on —J.F.Dobie⟩ **6 :** heterogeneous small articles often of little value **:** HODGE-PODGE; *also* **:** RUBBISH ⟨any such mess of ~ —Kenneth Roberts⟩ ⟨drawstring bags . . . hold almost enough ~ to be classified as luggage —*New Yorker*⟩

³truck \"\ *adj* **1 :** of or relating to the truck system **2 :** consisting of or dealing in garden stuff

⁴truck \"\ *n* -S [prob. fr. L *trochus* iron hoop, fr. Gk *trochos* wheel, fr. *trechein* to run — more at TROCHEE] **1 :** a small wheel; *specif* **:** a small strong wheel usu. of wood or iron for a gun carriage **2 :** a small wooden cap at the top of a flagstaff or a masthead usu. having holes in it for reeving flag or signal halyards — see SHIP illustration **3 :** a wheeled vehicle used for moving heavy articles: as **a :** a strong cart or wagon used for hauling ⟨the horses died of starvation and the men harnessed themselves to ~*s* —H.E. Scudder⟩ **b :** HAND TRUCK **c :** a small heavy rectangular frame supported on four wheels used instead of rollers for moving heavy objects **d :** a small flat-topped car sometimes with stakes or vertical ends to prevent the load from falling that is usu. pushed or pulled by hand **e :** a shelved stand mounted on casters **4 a** *Brit* **:** an open railroad freight car **b :** a swiveling carriage consisting of a frame with one or more pairs of wheels and the necessary boxes and springs esp. to carry and guide one end of a locomotive or a railroad car in turning sharp curves **5 a :** an automotive vehicle built for the transportation of goods on its own chassis **b :** a motorized vehicle equipped with a swivel for hauling a trailer

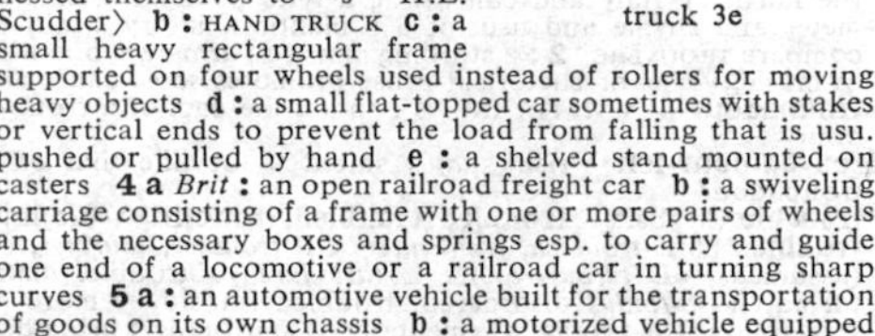
truck 3e

⁵truck \"\ *vb* -ED/-ING/-S *vt* **:** to load or transport on a truck **~** *vi* **1 :** to transport goods by truck **:** be employed in driving a truck **2 :** to execute a trucking step — usu. used with *down* ⟨singing at the top of his lungs . . . ~*ing* down the trail —Margaret Hastings⟩ **3 :** TRACK 2b

⁶truck \"\ *adj* **:** of, relating to, used by, or made for a truck ⟨a ~ tire⟩ ⟨~ route⟩

truck·age \ˈtrəkij\ *n* -S [⁴*truck* + *-age*] **1 :** money paid for the conveyance of goods on a truck **:** FREIGHT **2 :** conveyance by trucks

truckaway \ˈ=,=,=\ *n* -S [¹*truck* + *away*] **:** the delivery of one or more vehicles or tractors mounted on special trailers usu. from an assembly plant to a dealer — compare DRIVEAWAY

truck box *n* **:** an open body on a motortruck

truck company *n* **:** LADDER COMPANY

truck crop *n* **:** a vegetable crop that is grown in truck farming ⟨lettuce is a *truck crop* in California⟩

truck·ee pine \ˈtrəkē-\ *n, usu cap T* [fr. *Truckee* river, western Nevada] **:** JEFFREY PINE

truckee trout *n, usu cap 1st T* **:** TAHOE TROUT

¹truck·er \ˈtrəkə(r)\ *n* -S [¹*truck* + *-er*] **1 a :** one that barters **b** *Scot* **:** an itinerant huckster **:** PEDDLER **2 :** TRUCK FARMER

²trucker \"\ *n* -S [⁵*truck* + *-er*] **1 a :** one whose business is transporting goods by truck **b :** a truck driver **2 :** a laborer who conveys materials from place to place within an industrial establishment usu. doing related jobs (as weighing, sorting, or loading)

truck farm *n* **:** a farm devoted to the production of vegetables for the market

truck farmer *n* **:** one that operates a truck farm

truck farming *n* **:** the production of crops of some vegetables on an extensive scale in regions esp. suited to their culture primarily for shipment to distant markets — compare MARKET GARDENING

truck garden *n* **:** a garden where vegetables are raised for market

truck gardener *n* **:** one that operates a truck garden

truck gardening *n* **:** the raising of vegetables for market

truckhead \ˈ=,=\ *n* [⁴*truck* + *head*] **:** a military installation where supplies that have been brought forward by truck are unloaded and distributed

truck horse *n* **:** DRAFT HORSE

truck house *n* **:** a storehouse for goods used for or received in barter esp. in the early trading with Indians

¹trucking *n* -S [fr. gerund of ¹*truck*] **1 :** BARTERING **2 :** TRUCK FARMING

²trucking *n* -S [fr. gerund of ⁵*truck*] **1 :** the process or business of transporting goods on trucks **2 :** a swaying shuffling jitterbug step in which the feet are moved forward alternately with the toes turned in and then turned out and which is performed with one upraised hand beating time

trucking shot *or* **truck shot** *n* **:** a scene photographed from a moving dolly — called also *tracking shot*

¹truck·le \ˈtrəkəl\ *n* -S [ME *trookel, trocle,* fr. L *trochlea* sheaf of pulleys — more at TROCHLEA] **1 a :** a small wheel; *esp* **:** PULLEY **b :** a small roller used to move a heavy object **:** CASTER **2 :** TRUCKLE BED **3** *dial Eng* **:** a small barrel-shaped cheese

²truckle \"\ *vi* **truckled; truckled; truckling** \-k(ə)liŋ\ **truckles** [fr. *truckle* (in *truckle bed*)] **1** *obs* **:** to sleep in a truckle bed **2** [so called fr. the fact that the truckle bed was usu. pushed under the larger standard bed] **:** to act in a subservient manner **:** yield to the wishes or the will of another **:** bend obsequiously **:** SUBMIT ⟨he would ~ to no man —V.L. Parrington⟩ ⟨people who will always ~ to those who have money —Archibald Marshall⟩

truckle bed *n* [ME *trookel bed,* fr. *trookel* truckle + *bed*] **:** TRUNDLE BED

truck·ler \ˈtrək(ə)lə(r)\ *n* -S **:** one that truckles

truck light *n* **:** a light at the truck of a mast

truckline \ˈ=,=\ *n* **:** a carrier using trucks and related freight vehicles to provide service to shippers

truckload \ˈ=ˈ=\ *n* **1 :** a load that fills a truck **2 :** the minimum weight specified by the tariff for shipping at truckload rates

truckload rate *n* **:** a rate quoted for shipping a truckload

truck·man \ˈtrəkmən\ *n, pl* **truckmen 1 :** one who conveys goods by truck **:** a truck driver **:** TRUCKER **2 :** a member of a ladder company

truckmaster \ˈ=,==\ *n* [²*truck* + *master*] **1** *archaic* **:** an officer in charge of trade with Indians esp. among the early settlers **2 :** a noncommissioned officer who supervises the operation and maintenance of military vehicles

truck mixer *n* **:** a concrete mixer mounted on the chassis of a truck used for mixing and delivering concrete

truck patch *n* **:** a small area devoted to the production of vegetables usu. for domestic use

¹trucks *pres 3d sing of* TRUCK, *pl of* TRUCK

²trucks \ˈtrəks\ *n, pl* **trucks** [It *trucco* (fr. *truccare* to push, hit a ball, play at billiards, prob. fr. — assumed — VL *trudicare,* fr. L *trudere* to thrust, push) + E *-s,* pl. suffix — more at THREAT] **:** a table game resembling billiards played with little balls

truck system *n* **:** the system of paying wages in goods instead of cash

truck tractor *n* **:** TRACTOR 2c

truck trailer \ˈ=ˈ==\ *n* **1 :** a nonautomotive freight vehicle to be drawn by a motortruck **2** *usu* **truck-trailer :** a combination of a truck trailer and its motortruck

truckway \ˈ=,=\ *n* **:** a roadway for trucks

truck wholesaler *n* **:** WAGON JOBBER

tru·cu·lence \ˈtrəkyələn(t)s\ *sometimes* ˈtrük-\ *also* **tru·cu·len·cy** *n, pl* **truculences** *also* **truculencies** [*truculence* fr. *truculent; truculency* fr. L *truculentia* wildness, fierceness, fr. *truculentus* wild, cruel, fierce + *-ia* -y] **:** the quality or state of being truculent ⟨made up for his lack of stature by a great show of ~ —Carol Bache⟩ ⟨as sure a sign of ~ as the closed fist of a man —Edison Marshall⟩

tru·cu·lent \-nt\ *adj* [L *truculentus,* fr. *truc-, trux* wild, fierce; perh. akin to MIr *tru* given to death] **1 :** feeling or evincing savage ferocity **:** CRUEL, FIERCE ⟨the fangs of these powerful ~ brutes —W.H.Hudson †1922⟩ ⟨the swordfish . . . ~ and fearless —F.C.Lane⟩ **2 :** possessing an inherent capacity for destruction **:** DEADLY ⟨the sleek ~ ships steamed along blackly behind their guns —Ira Wolfert⟩ ⟨go out and inspect the ~ bomb —*Christian Science Monitor*⟩ **3 :** scathingly harsh **:** VITRIOLIC, VITUPERATIVE ⟨a ~ document devoted mostly to vilifying —*Time*⟩ ⟨when every English traveler . . . published a volume of ~ disparagement —V.L.Parrington⟩ **4 :** aggressively self-assertive **:** antagonistic to compromise **:** BELLIGERENT, PUGNACIOUS ⟨as ~ as a small boy who thinks his big brother can lick anybody —*Time*⟩ ⟨tribute is paid to . . . his rather ~ skill as a negotiator —Norman MacKenzie⟩

tru·cu·lent·ly *adv* **:** in a truculent manner ⟨he looked up ~ —L.C.Douglas⟩ ⟨strive for security by ~ asserting their vested interests —J.S.Schapiro⟩

tru·dell·ite \trüˈdeˌlīt\ *n* -S [Harry W. *Trudell* *b*1884 Am. mineralogist + E *-ite*] **:** a mineral $Al_{10}Cl_{12}(OH)_{12}(SO_4)_3 \cdot 3OH_2O$(?) consisting of a hydrous basic aluminum chloride and sulfate and occurring in amber-yellow masses

¹trudge \ˈtrəj\ *vb* -ED/-ING/-S [origin unknown] *vi* **:** to walk or march on foot steadily and esp. toilsomely or wearily ⟨we *trudged* a hundred yards or so through deep, untrodden snow —John Connell⟩ **~** *vt* **:** to trudge along or over

²trudge \"\ *n* -S **:** a long tiring walk **:** TRAMP ⟨a strenuous ~ of twenty-three miles —R.L.Newberger⟩

trud·gen crawl \ˈtrəjən-\ *n* [after John *Trudgen,* 19th cent. Eng. amateur swimmer] **:** a crawl stroke in which a scissors kick is combined with the flutter kick

trudgen stroke *or* **trudgen** *also* **trud·geon** \ˈtrəjən\ *n* -S **:** a swimming stroke in which a double overarm motion is used and the legs execute a scissors kick

trudg·er \ˈtrejə(r)\ *n* -S **:** one that trudges

¹true \ˈtrü\ *adj, usu* **truer** \-üə(r); -ü(ə)r, -ùə\ *usu* **truest** \-üəst\ [ME *trew, trewe,* fr. OE *trēowe* faithful, trustworthy; akin to OHG *gitriuwi* faithful, trustworthy, ON *tryggr,* Goth *triggws* faithful, trustworthy, OIr *dreb* certain, OPruss *druwis* faith, Lith *drūtas* strong, thick, Skt *dāruṇa* hard, *dāru* wood — more at TREE] **1 a :** steady, firm, and dependable in allegiance or devotion to a loved one, friend, leader, group, or cause **:** not false or perfidious ⟨his musical idiom was unique, and by remaining ~ to it, he expressed himself with the utmost clarity —J.D.Cook⟩ ⟨all ~ men were needed to save the country —Shelby Foote⟩; *specif* **:** steadfast in observing marriage or other vows ⟨a lover absolutely ~ in act and word and thought —H.O.Taylor⟩ **b :** HONEST, JUST, UPRIGHT ⟨he was absolutely ~, genuinely square in his relations to those about him —W.A.White⟩ **c** *archaic* **:** TRUTHFUL, VERACIOUS ⟨dare to be ~; nothing can need a lie —George Herbert⟩ **2 a** (1) **:** conformable to fact **:** in accordance with the actual state of affairs **:** not false or erroneous **:** not inaccurate ⟨mathematics, I thought, had a better chance of being ~ than anything else that passed as general knowledge —Bertrand Russell⟩ ⟨it is ~ that there is an underlying intention to keep patronage alive —Herbert Read⟩ (2) **:** conformable to nature, reality, or an original **:** accurate in delineating or expressing the essential elements ⟨fiction is *truer* than history, because it goes beyond the evidence —E.M.Forster⟩; *specif* **:** describing actual events that happened ⟨a ~ story⟩ **b** (1) **:** being on a level transcending phenomenal or everyday existence **:** IDEAL ⟨nobler ideas — *truer* because they are more in harmony with man's situation in the universe —Liston Pope⟩ ⟨the same event can be said to be ~ for faith but untrue for science —W.R.Inge⟩ ⟨appropriate to the inward search and responsive to ~ values —Pietro Belluschi⟩ (2) **:** being more genuinely characteristic of or operative in than manifest motives or appearances **:** ESSENTIAL ⟨the party's principles and policies, rather than its actual social composition, should be the criterion of its ~ nature —N.D.Palmer & S. C. Leng⟩ ⟨a better understanding of the ~ motives in human behavior —*Printers' Ink*⟩ **c :** being that which is the case rather than what is believed, assumed, or claimed ⟨the ~ dimension of the world refugee problem is clearly being ignored or sidestepped —Gertrude Samuels⟩ ⟨sent her back to bed without telling her the president's ~ condition —*Time*⟩ **d** (1) **:** consistent with expectation or previous performance ⟨remains ~ to its background of cattle barons —*Amer. Guide Series: Texas*⟩ (2) **:** confirmed by later experience or investigation ⟨the lawyer's premonition was ~ —Leo Marx⟩ **3 a :** properly so called: as (1) **:** void of deceit **:** SINCERE, UNFEIGNED ⟨~ love⟩ (2) **:** not sham, counterfeit, or adulterated **:** GENUINE ⟨returned to the ~ faith⟩ ⟨expect to make ~ and rapid progress in civil rights —D.D.Eisenhower⟩ (3) **:** being essentially what it is called ⟨the ~ coastline was . . . 140 kilometers from the apparent coastline —Valter Schytt⟩ ⟨the ~ stomach, the abomasum, forms only about one seventh to one tenth of the total capacity of the ruminant stomach —S.J.Watson⟩ (4) **:** designed or functioning in a manner regarded as essential to meeting a standard ⟨none of these institutions could be regarded as a ~ university because none had a faculty capable of examining for the higher degrees —J.B.Conant⟩ ⟨a ~ textbook is one especially prepared for the use of pupil and teacher —*Textbooks in Education*⟩ **b** (1) **:** possessing all the fundamental characters of and belonging to the same natural group as ⟨a lizard is a ~ reptile⟩ ⟨a whale is a ~ but not a typical mammal⟩ (2) **:** TYPICAL ⟨the ~ cats may be distinguished from fossil allies by characters of the dentition⟩ **4 a :** such as it should be **:** PROPER, FITTING ⟨facts presented in their ~ order and bearing⟩ **b** (1) **:** LEGITIMATE, RIGHTFUL ⟨the ~ and legal successors of the old régime —*Geog. Jour.*⟩ (2) **:** related by blood ⟨would a ~ child always take precedence of an adopted child —*Notes & Queries on Anthropology*⟩ **5 :** that can be relied on **:** TRUSTWORTHY ⟨heard by ~ telling that you have money and means —Augusta Gregory⟩ ⟨claim that his polls are a ~ representation of the opinions of the whole nation —*Current Biog.*⟩; *specif* **:** determined with respect to a statistical population rather than a sample ⟨prefer the narrow range with bias to a *truer* average with wider dispersed values —*Photogrammetric Engineering*⟩ **6 a :** placed, fitted, or formed accurately ⟨the blocks of granite were so ~ that practically no mortar was used —*Amer. Guide Series: Nev.*⟩ **b :** comformable to a standard, rule, or pattern **:** EXACT, ACCURATE, CORRECT ⟨supply the disposal agency with the originals or ~ copies of all documents —*U. S. Code*⟩ ⟨singing on ~ pitch⟩ **c :** molded by environment, family, or culture and marked by similar attitudes and characteristics ⟨a ~ product of his age, being neither more skeptical nor more credulous than any other —J.A.Rushing⟩ ⟨a ~ child of the rising West —H.E.Starr⟩ **d :** best fitting one's aptitudes or interests ⟨found his ~ vocation after many false starts⟩ **7 a :** reliable or accurate in function **:** EXACT ⟨the machine is *truer* than the hand —Edward Bellamy⟩ **b :** accurate, quick, or complete in measuring, grasping, or comprehending fact ⟨a ~ understanding of our heritage —W.R.Steckel⟩ ⟨whose turns and rhythms of speech have been caught by a ~ ear —B.R.Redman⟩ ⟨imagination is *truer* than reason is —O.S.J.Gogarty⟩ **8 :** related to a fixed point; *specif* **:** determined with reference to the earth's axis rather than the magnetic poles ⟨~ north⟩ ⟨~ west⟩ **9 :** logically necessary **:** universally valid **10 :** NARROW, RESTRICTED, STRICT ⟨a how-to-do-it booklet in the *truest* sense of the word —Mary S. Switzer⟩ **11 :** corrected for error — compare TRUE ALTITUDE **syn** see FAITHFUL, REAL

²true \"\ *n* -s **1 :** something that is true **:** ultimate truth **:** REALITY — usu. used with *the* **2 :** the quality or state of being accurate (as in alignment or adjustment) — used in the phrases *in true* and *out of true* ⟨the rail level may sag out of ~ —O.S.Nock⟩

³true \"\ *vt* **trued; trued; trueing** *also* **truing; trues :** to make level, square, balanced, or concentric **:** bring or restore to a desired mechanical accuracy or form ⟨*trued* an engine cylinder that had got out of round by boring it oversize⟩ ⟨*trued* an unbalanced grinding wheel with a dressing diamond⟩ ⟨repaired a worn housing by mounting it on centers in a lathe and taking a light *trueing* cut⟩ ⟨~s up a fixture with the machine spindle by using a dial indicator⟩

⁴true \"\ *adv, usu* -ER/-EST [ME *trewe*, fr. *trewe*, adj., true] **1 :** in accordance with fact or reality **:** TRUTHFULLY, HONESTLY ⟨your childish lips spoke *truer* than you suspected —Rosa Luxemburg⟩ **2 a :** without variation from path or position **:** in true **:** EXACTLY, ACCURATELY ⟨the bullet flew straight and ~⟩ ⟨the doors . . . still hang perfectly ~ —*Amer. Guide Series: Md.*⟩ — often used as an interjection for emphasis or as a signal of confirmation, admission, or endorsement of a fact ⟨~, there was a blot on the escutcheon of that lady —W.S. Gilbert⟩ **b :** without change ⟨a variety that comes ~ from seed⟩ **:** without variation from or of type ⟨genuine mutations usu. breed ~⟩

true airspeed *n* **:** the velocity of an airplane in its flight path relative to the air through which it is moving

true altitude *n* **:** the pressure altitude corrected for temperature

true balsam *n* **:** BALSAM 1b(2)

true bearing *n* **:** bearing relative to true north

true bill *n* **:** a bill of indictment returned by the grand jury endorsed as warranting prosecution of the accused under the indictment

true blue *n* **1 :** the blue color adopted from old association of blue with constancy and fidelity by the Covenanters; *also* **:** PRESBYTERIANISM **2 a :** thoroughgoing or uncompromising loyalty, fidelity, or orthodoxy **b :** a true-blue person ⟨a staunch Conservative himself, a *true blue*, and they knew his color when they went to vote —Flora Thompson⟩

true-blue \'=¦=\ *adj* [*true blue*] **:** of unswerving loyalty esp. to a party or group using blue as its special color ⟨*true-blue* Presbyterians⟩ ⟨a *true-blue* Tory⟩

trueborn \'=¦=\ *adj* **:** genuinely such by birthright ⟨though banish'd, yet a ~ Englishman —Shak.⟩

true branching *n* **:** a branched arrangement of filaments of bacteria or algae due to protoplasmic bifurcation or cell growth and fission along more than one axis — compare FALSE BRANCHING

truebred \'=¦=\ *adj* **:** PUREBRED; *also* **:** THOROUGHGOING

true bug *n* **:** an insect of the order Hemiptera; *esp* **:** a typical winged insect of the suborder Heteroptera as distinguished from the highly varied members of the suborder Homoptera

true course *n* **:** the course of a ship or airplane measured with respect to true north

true discount *n* **:** ARITHMETICAL DISCOUNT

true dolphin *n* [so called to distinguish it from other cetaceans commonly called dolphins] **:** a dolphin of the genus *Delphinus*

true-false test \(')=¦=-\ *n* **:** an objective test consisting of a series of statements each of which is to be marked as either true or false

true fly *n* **:** ⁵FLY 2a

true fruit *n* **:** a fruit produced from only carpellary tissue — compare ACCESSORY FRUIT

true guest *n* **:** SYMPHILE

true heading *n* **:** the heading measured clockwise from true north

truehearted \'=¦==\ *adj* [ME, fr. ¹*true* + *hearted*] **:** FAITHFUL, STEADFAST, LOYAL — **true·heart·ed·ness** *n*

truehedge columnberry \¦=,=¦==- — *see* BERRY\ *n* [*true* + *hedge* + *column* + *berry*] **:** an upright barberry that is a variety (*Berberis thunbergii erecta*) of the Japanese barberry

true horizon *n* **:** HORIZON 1b(1); *also* **:** the horizon at sea

true leveller *n, usu cap T&L* **:** DIGGER 2

true-life \'=¦=\ *adj* **:** true to life ⟨a *true-life* story⟩

truelove \'=¦=\ *n* [ME *trewe love*, fr. OE *trēowe lufu* faithful love, fr. *trēowe* faithful + *lufu* love — more at TRUE, LOVE] **1 a :** faithful love **b :** one truly beloved or loving **:** SWEETHEART ⟨a lady young in beauty waiting until my ~ comes —J.C.Ransom⟩ **2 a :** HERB PARIS **b :** a trillium (*Trillium erectum*)

true lover's knot *also* **truelove knot** *n* [ME *trewe love knot*] **1 :** FISHERMAN'S KNOT **2 :** LOVE KNOT

true middle lamella *n* **:** the intercellular cementing layer of the middle lamella

true·ness *n* -ES [ME *trewenesse*, fr. OE *trēownes* object of trust, fr. *trēowe* faithful, trustworthy + *-nes* -ness] **:** the quality or state of being true: as **a :** correspondence with reality **b :** exactness of adjustment

true pelvis *n* **:** the lower more contracted part of the pelvic cavity

truepenny \'=,==\ *n* [¹*true* + *penny*] **:** an honest or trustworthy person

true plane *n* **:** a plane surface of metal made by repeated scraping with a scraper and testing with a surface plate

¹truer *comparative of* TRUE

²tru·er \'trüə(r); -ü(ə)r, -üə\ *n* -s [³*true* + *-er*] **:** one that trues: as **a :** a device for trueing abrasive wheels **b :** one that trues objects (as optical lenses, green clay blocks, or springs) to bring them into correct condition, size, or alignment

true rib *n* **:** one of the ribs whose costal cartilages connect directly with the sternum and that in man constitute the first seven pairs

trues *pl of* TRUE, *pres 3d sing of* TRUE

true seal *n* **:** a seal of the family Phocidae as distinguished from sea lions and eared seals of the family Otariidae

true skin *n* **:** DERMIS

true soil *n* **:** SOLUM 2

truest *superlative of* TRUE

true sun *n* **:** the sun that is observed in the sky — distinguished from *mean sun*

true time *n* **1 :** APPARENT TIME **2 :** MEAN SOLAR TIME

true-to-scale process *n* **:** a photomechanical process based on the insolubilizing action of iron salts on gelatin wherein a lithographic image is obtained by contact exposing a line original to blueprint paper that is squeegeed without development to the surface of a moist gelatin printing pad

true vocal cord *n* **:** either of the lower pair of vocal cords that enclose the lower part of the elastic membrane of the larynx, that extend from the inner surface of the thyroid cartilage near the median line to a process of the corresponding arytenoid cartilage on the same side of the larynx, and that when drawn taut, approximated, and subjected to the flow of breath produce voice

true wind *n* **:** the wind relative to a fixed point the observation of which is not affected by the motion of the observer — compare APPARENT WIND

truewood \'=,=\ *n* [¹*true* + *wood*] *Austral* **:** sound heartwood

truff \'trəf\ *n* -s [origin unknown] **:** BULL TROUT 1

truf·fle \'trəfəl, -rüf-,-rúf-\ *n* -s [modif. of MF *truffe*, fr. OProv *trufa*, fr. (assumed) VL *tufera*, *tufer*, alter. of L *tuber* hump, tumor, truffle — more at TUBER] **1 a :** the edible subterranean fruiting body of various European fungi of the genus *Tuber* usu. dark-colored, warty or rugose, resembling a rounded or ovoid tuber, and filled with ascospores; *broadly* **:** any similar fruiting body of a fungus of the family Tuberaceae **b :** a fungus that produces truffles **2 :** FALSE TRUFFLE **3 :** a candy made of chocolate, butter, and sugar shaped into balls and coated with cocoa, macaroon crumbs, or chopped nuts

truf·fled \-ld\ *adj* **:** cooked, stuffed, or garnished with truffles

trug \'trəg, -rüg\ *n* -s [origin unknown] **1** *Brit* **:** an old unit of measure for wheat equal to 0.67 bushel **2** *Brit* **:** a coarse basket made of strips of wood and used esp. for carrying fruit, vegetables, or flowers

truing *pres part of* TRUE

tru·ism \'trü,izəm\ *n* -s [¹*true* + *-ism*] **:** an undoubted or self-evident truth; *esp* **:** one too obvious or unimportant for mention

tru·is·tic \(')trü¦istik\ *also* **tru·is·ti·cal** \-stəkəl\ *adj* [fr. *truism*, after such pairs as E *theism: theistic, theistical*] **:** of, relating to, or being a truism ⟨it is a ~ statement that a blind child can do everything but see —*Proceedings: Annual Education Congress*⟩

Truk·ese \(')trü¦kēz, (')trü¦k-, ¦trə¦k-\ *n, pl* **trukese** *cap* [*Truk* islands (fr. Trukese *Cuuk* Truk islands, fr. *cuuk* mountains, heights) + E *-ese*] **1 :** a Micronesian native or inhabitant of the Truk islands in the Caroline islands **2 :** the Austronesian language spoken in the Truk islands

trull \'trəl\ *n* -s [obs. G *trulle* prostitute (now *trulle* lass, wench, hussy), fr. MHG, prostitute, mistress; akin to MHG *trolle* ghostly monster, boor, lout, blockhead, ON *troll* giant, fiend, demon — more at TROLL] **:** PROSTITUTE, STRUMPET

trul·lo \'trü(,)lō\ *n, pl* **trul·li** \-lē\ [It] **:** a round stone building made with conical roof and without mortar found in southern Italy and esp. in Apulia

¹tru·ly \'trülē, -li\ *adv* [ME *trewely*, fr. OE *trēowlīce*, fr. *trēowe* faithful + *-līce* -ly — more at TRUE] **1 a** *archaic* **:** with constancy **:** FAITHFULLY **b :** SINCERELY — often used as a complimentary close after *yours* **2 a :** in agreement with fact **:** TRUTHFULLY ⟨a passion to see and to report ~ —Gladys Wrigley⟩ **b :** conformably with nature **:** REALISTICALLY ⟨the characters are all quietly funny; they are all ~ drawn —Coulton Waugh⟩ **3 :** with exactness of construction or operation **:** ACCURATELY ⟨the early engineers, who built so well, and so ~ —O.S.Nock⟩ **4 a :** INDEED — often used as an intensive ⟨~, she is fair⟩ or interjectionally to express astonishment or doubt **b :** without feigning, falsity, or inaccuracy in truth or fact **:** GENUINELY ⟨~ noble expressions of human feeling —M.R.Cohen⟩ ⟨whether you merely exist or ~ live —Dana Burnet⟩ **5 :** PROPERLY, RIGHTLY, RIGHTFULLY

²truly \"\ *n* -ES *Brit* **:** TRUTH, VERACITY, TRUSTWORTHINESS — used in such phrases as *by my truly*

tru·meau \(')trü¦mō\ *n, pl* **tru·meaux** \-ōz\ [F] **1 :** a central pillar supporting the tympanum of a large doorway esp in a medieval building **2 :** an overmantel treatment of 18th century France consisting of a pier glass surmounted by an oil painting or decorative often carved panel

¹trump \'trəmp\ *n* -s [ME *trumpe*, *trompe*, fr. OF *trompe*, prob. of Gmc origin; akin to OHG *trumpa*, *trumba* trumpet, ON *trumba*; prob. of imit. origin like MHG *trumme* drum — more at DRUM] **1 a :** TRUMPET **b** *chiefly Scot* **:** JEW'S HARP **2 :** a sound of or as if of trumpeting ⟨would pick up this same shell . . . and wind a ~ that was heard in the far corner of the field —S.H.Holbrook⟩ ⟨roaring like the ~ of judgment —H.L. Davis⟩

²trump \"\ *n* -s [alter. of ¹*triumph*] **1 a :** any of various cards and usu. all the cards of a suit designated by chance or by an auction or declaration that if legally played will win over a card that is not of this suit **b** *or* **trump suit :** the suit whose cards are all trumps — often used in pl. **c :** a card (as a heart or tarot) with a special function or value in a game (as hearts or tarok) **d :** TRUMP CARD **2 :** an old English card game that is a precursor of whist **3 a :** an influential factor or final resource ⟨kept a political ~ up his sleeve —*Economist*⟩ ⟨you put me to my ~s by asking me for additional matter . . . for I considered myself exhausted on that score long ago —*Harper's*⟩ **b :** a dependable and exemplary individual **:** CRACKERJACK, PEACH ⟨my father came out a ~ . . . he offered to pay for the furniture —H.J.Laski⟩

³trump \"\ *vb* -ED/-ING/-S *vt* **1 :** to take with a trump ⟨~ a trick⟩ **2 :** to get the better of **:** OUTDO, TOP ⟨giving the young men spades in years and effortlessly ~*ing* them with Old World charm —R.L.Shayon⟩ ~*vi* **1 :** to play a trump **2 :** to take a trick with a trump

trump card *n* **1 a :** the last card that is dealt in a whist hand and is turned up to determine trump but if not played is restored to the dealer's hand after the first trick **b :** a card of a trump suit **2 :** a telling argument or decisive factor **:** CLINCHER ⟨justice . . . is the *trump card* of the western world —*Times Lit. Supp.*⟩ ⟨its real *trump card* . . . is its humane price —*New Yorker*⟩

trumped-up \'=¦=\ *adj* [fr. past part. of *trump up*] **:** fraudulently concocted **:** MADE-UP, SPURIOUS ⟨*trumped-up* charges⟩ ⟨a *trumped-up* excuse⟩ ⟨an elaborately *trumped-up* trial —T.C. Chubb⟩

¹trum·pery \'trəmp(ə)rē, -ri\ *n* -ES [ME *trompery*, fr. MF *tromperie*, fr. *tromper* to deceive + *-ie* -y] **1** *obs* **:** DECEIT, FRAUD — often used in pl. ⟨left none of his *trumperies* and double-dealings unrevealed —Robert Dallington⟩ **2 a :** trivial or useless articles of equipment **:** BRIC-A-BRAC, PARAPHERNALIA ⟨a wagon loaded with household ~ —Washington Irving⟩ ⟨farm families loaded down with balloons, dolls, and other ~ of the pitchman —*Amer. Guide Series: Pa.*⟩ **b :** worthless nonsense **:** MUMBO JUMBO, TWADDLE ⟨a piece of propaganda ~ —*Time*⟩ ⟨the *trumperies* of a forced symbolism —Robert Pick⟩ **c** *archaic* **:** tawdry finery ⟨the ~ in my house —Shak.⟩ **d** *dial Brit* **:** garden refuse **:** WEEDS

²trumpery \"\ *adj* **1 :** of small worth or poor quality **:** tastelessly superficial **:** CHEAP, TAWDRY ⟨charm primitive peoples with mirrors, glass beads, and other ~ baubles⟩ ⟨the demands mankind makes of fiction may be slight, ~, ridiculous, or meretricious —Bernard De Voto⟩ **2 a :** FRAUDULENT, TRUMPED-UP ⟨the ~ pathos of a tenth-rate novel —Hugh Walpole⟩ ⟨encourages the bringing of ~ actions . . . even though no damage has been suffered —*Manchester Guardian Weekly*⟩ **b :** worthy of contempt **:** DESPICABLE ⟨seemed in her own eyes both deluded and . . . ~ —Elizabeth Taylor⟩ ⟨encouraged two or three ~ fellows . . . to cut scurvy jokes at my expense —George Borrow⟩

¹trum·pet \'trəmpət, *usu* -əd·+V\ *n* -s *often attrib* [ME *trumpette*, *trompette*, fr. MF *trompette*, fr. OF *trompe* trumpet + *-ette* — more at TRUMP (trumpet)] **1 a** (1) **:** a wind instrument consisting of a long cylindrical metal tube commonly once or twice curved and ending in a bell, producing its tones by the vibration of the player's lips against a cup-shaped mouthpiece, having valves that enable the use of all scale tones in its normal compass of written F sharp below middle C as indicated on the treble staff to the C two octaves above middle C, and usu. constructed in B flat thereby sounding a whole step lower than the notation indicates — compare BUGLE, CORNET (2) **:** a metal wind instrument (as the cornet) similar in shape and method of tone production to the trumpet **b :** a clarion call or one that utters it ⟨sounded forth the first tidings and ~ of Reformation —John Milton⟩ ⟨a powerful ~ who stirred the pulse of mankind —M.R.Cohen⟩ **2 a :** a trumpet player ⟨persuaded the ~s, who were satisfied with playing high notes, to play *good* notes —Cy Feuer⟩ **b** *obs* **:** MESSENGER, SPOKESMAN ⟨be thou the ~ of our wrath —Shak.⟩ **3 :** something that resembles a trumpet or its tonal quality: as **a :** an 8-foot pipe-organ reed stop with a penetrating tone **b :** TRITON 2 **c :** a funnel-shaped instrument (as a megaphone or a diaphragm horn) for collecting, directing, or intensifying sound — see EAR TRUMPET, SPEAKING TRUMPET **d** (1) **:** a trumpet-shaped flower esp. of a plant of the genera *Datura*, *Campsis*, *or Bignonia* (2) **trumpets** *South* **:** any of several pitcher plants having long trumpet-shaped leaves; *esp* **:** a swamp plant (*Sarracenia flava*) **e** (1) **:** a stentorian voice (2) **:** a penetrating cry (as of an elephant) (3) **:** a shrill hum (as of a mosquito) **f :** a funnel-shaped guide for material (as the fiber web leaving a carding machine)

modern trumpet

²trumpet \"\ *vb* -ED/-ING/-S *vi* **1 :** to blow a trumpet ⟨practicing soldiers ~*ed* and bugled —Charles Dickens⟩ **2 a :** to make a shrill trumpetlike sound ⟨~ like . . . a wounded cow elephant —Charles Beadle⟩ **b :** to make a vociferous proclamation ⟨~s from his editorials on war and politics —H.S. Canby⟩ ~ *vt* **1 :** to give vociferous utterance to **:** proclaim loudly ⟨orders ~*ed* to us that morning —Kenneth Roberts⟩ ⟨was not going to ~ his criticisms while on foreign soil —Blair Clark⟩ **2 :** to bring to public notice by or as if by the sounding of trumpets ⟨a triumph which must be ~*ed* —Sophie Kerr⟩ ⟨Italy's most ~*ed* living writer —*Time*⟩; *also* **:** to summon or denounce by or as if by blowing a trumpet

trumpet animalcule *n* **:** a trumpet-shaped infusorian of *Stentor* or a related genus

trumpet arch *n* **:** a conical squinch

trumpetbush \'==,=\ *n* [so called fr. the shape of the flowers] **:** YELLOW ELDER

trumpet call *n* **1 :** a call sounded on a trumpet; *specif* **:** FANFARE **2 :** an urgent or rousing summons ⟨*trumpet calls* to the European crusade against Bolshevism —*Manchester Guardian Weekly*⟩ ⟨a *trumpet call* to faith —H.E.Fey⟩

trumpet creeper *n* **:** a No. American woody vine (*Campsis radicans*) having pinnate leaves and large red trumpet-shaped flowers — called also *trumpet vine*

trumpet-creeper family *n* **:** BIGNONIACEAE

trum·pet·er \'trəmpəd·ə(r), -ətə-\ *n* -s *except sense 3c(1)* [ME *trumpatour*, fr. *trumpete* trumpet + *-our* -or — more at TRUMPET] **1 a :** a trumpet player; *specif* **:** an agent (as a herald) who gives signals with a trumpet **b :** one that praises or advocates **:** EULOGIST, SPOKESMAN ⟨became his toady and ~ —Robertson Davies⟩ ⟨~ for democratic support of the League of Nations —*Saturday Rev.*⟩ **2** *or* **trumpeter muscle :** BUCCINATOR **3 a :** any of several large highly gregarious easily domesticated forest-dwelling So. American birds (genus *Psophia*) that are related to the cranes, have long legs, a long neck, a head and beak very similar to those of domestic fowl, soft plumage which is mostly blackish with yellowish green or purplish iridescence on neck and breast, and a loud clear prolonged cry, and are often kept in Brazil to protect poultry; *esp* **:** a bird (*P. crepitans*) of Guiana and Brazil **b :** TRUMPETER SWAN **c** (1) *usu cap* **:** an Asiatic breed of pigeons that have a shell crest, heavily feathered feet, and a prolonged melodious call and that are best known from a strain developed in Germany (2) **:** a bird of the Trumpeter breed **4 a :** any of several Australian and New Zealand marine spiny-finned fishes (family Latrididae); *esp* **:** a choice food fish (*Latris lineata*) that is silvery with olive longitudinal stripes and reaches a weight of 60 to 80 pounds **b :** any of several other fishes that make a trumpeting or grunting noise when caught: as (1) **:** an Australian striped perch (*Heliotes sexlineatus*) (2) *or* **trumpeter perch :** a related fish (*Pelates quadrilineatus*)

trumpeter bullfinch *n* **:** a thick-billed Afro-Asian terrestrial finch (*Erythrospiza githaginea*) that is predominantly pink-tinged brown with a pale gray crown

trumpeter swan *n* **:** a No. American wild swan (*Olor buccinator*) that is found chiefly from the Mississippi valley westward but is becoming rare, is pure white with no yellow on the lores, and is noted for its sonorous voice

trumpet fish *n* **1 :** BELLOWS FISH 1 **2 :** CORNETFISH

trumpet flower *n* **1 :** a plant having trumpet-shaped flowers: as **a :** TRUMPET CREEPER **b :** TRUMPET HONEYSUCKLE **c :** CROSS VINE 1 **d :** DATURA 2 **e :** YELLOW ELDER **f :** YELLOW OLEANDER **2 :** a trumpet-shaped flower

trumpet fly *n* **:** BOTFLY

trumpet honeysuckle *n* **:** a No. American honeysuckle (*Lonicera sempervirens*) having coral-red or orange flowers with a slenderly trumpet-shaped corolla — called also *trumpet flower*, *trumpet vine*

trumpet hypha *n* **:** one of the conducting cells in the tissues of the stems of brown algae of the family Laminariaceae that resemble sieve tubes and are long with swollen ends

trumpeting *n* -s [fr. gerund of ²*trumpet*] **1 :** the act or process of blowing a trumpet or producing a similarly penetrating sound ⟨startled awake by martial ~⟩ **2 :** an act or instance of heralding or proclaiming by or as if by the blowing of trumpets ⟨the ~ of Red peace banners —Han Suyin⟩

trumpet-leaf \'==,=\ *n* **:** TRUMPET 3d(2)

trumpet leg *n* **:** a furniture leg turned in the shape of a horn with the flared end up and the small end joining the foot

trumpetlike \'==,=\ *adj* **:** resembling a trumpet in shape or sound

trumpet lily *n* **1 a :** a lily (*Lilium longiflorum*) that is native to Formosa and the Ryukyu islands and is widely cultivated for its large fragrant pure white funnelform flowers which are borne singly or in pairs **b :** CALLA 2 **c :** DATURA 2 **2 :** the flower of a trumpet lily

trumpet marine *n* [prob. so called fr. its resemblance to large speaking trumpets used formerly on Italian and other European ships] **:** a triangular medieval bowed musical instrument about six feet long having one long catgut string that produces powerful and coarse-toned natural harmonics when played — called also *monochord*

trumpet leg

trumpet milkweed *n* **:** WILD LETTUCE 1b(3)

trumpet narcissus *or* **trumpet daffodil** *n* **:** a plant of the genus *Narcissus* with the corona elongated into a trumpet **:** a typical daffodil

trum·pet·ry \'trəmpətrē, -ri\ *n* -ES **:** the sound of trumpets ⟨amidst fanfare and ~ —J.C.Moloney⟩

trumpet-shaped \'==,=\ *adj* **1 :** conical but flaring at the broad end **2** *bot* **:** tubular with the limb spreading

trumpet shell *n* **:** TRITON 2

trumpet tree *n* **:** TRUMPETWOOD

trumpet vine *n* **1 :** TRUMPET CREEPER **2 :** TRUMPET HONEYSUCKLE

trumpetweed \'==,=\ *n* **:** any of several herbs: as **a :** TRUMPET MILKWEED **b** (1) **:** a boneset (*Eupatorium perfoliatum*) (2) **:** a joe-pye weed (*E. maculatum*)

trumpetwood \'==,=\ *n* **:** a tropical American tree (*Cecropia peltata*) with large peltate leaves and hollow stems — called also *imbauba*

trumping *pres part of* TRUMP

trump-poor \'=¦=\ *adj* [²*trump*] **:** lacking general strength but strong in trumps — used of a hand at cards

trumps *pl of* TRUMP, *pres 3d sing of* TRUMP

trump signal *n* **:** the high-low used in a card game as a request to a partner to lead a trump

trump suit *n* **:** TRUMP 1b

trump up *vt* [³*trump*] **1 :** to concoct esp. with intent to deceive **:** FABRICATE, INVENT ⟨*trump up* extra tasks to keep the children busy —Gertrude H. Hildreth⟩ ⟨*trump up* false charges of treason —R.A.Billington⟩ **2** *archaic* **:** to cite as support for an action or claim **:** ALLEGE ⟨necessity is *trumped up* for a plea —Samuel Palmer⟩ **3 :** to call forth by an act of will **:** EVOKE, SUMMON ⟨never able to *trump up* the courage to have a showdown —Mary B. Miller⟩

trun *dial past of* THROW

trun·cal \'trəŋkəl\ *adj* [L *truncus* trunk + E *-al*] **:** of or relating to the trunk of the body

[1]**trun·cate** \'trəŋ,kāt, *usu* -ād·+V\ *vt* -ED/-ING/-S [L *truncatus*, past part. of *truncare* to cut off, mutilate, fr. *truncus* trunk, torso; prob. akin to W *trwch* broken, truncated, Lith *trenkti* to push violently, jolt and perh. to OE *thringan* to crowd, throng — more at THRONG] **1 :** to abbreviate by or as if by cutting off : LOP ⟨lower ends of the ridges . . . are *truncated* by glacial erosion —W.J.Miller⟩ ⟨~ the value of pi from eight decimal places to 3.14⟩ ⟨~ a news item to fit available space⟩ ⟨games . . . abruptly *truncated* by the arrival of the evening papers —H.G.Wells⟩ **2 :** to replace (as an edge or corner of a crystal) by a plane and esp. by a plane that is equally inclined to the adjoining faces

[2]**truncate** \"\ *adj* [L *truncatus*, past part. of *truncare*] **1 :** having the end square or even as if cut off ⟨a ~ leaf⟩ ⟨a ~ feather⟩ **2 :** lacking an apex — used of a spiral (as of a gastropod mollusk) shell in which the apex of the young shell breaks off naturally

trun·cat·ed \-ād·əd,-ātəd\ *adj* [ME, fr. L *truncatus* (past part. of *truncare* to cut off) + E *-ed*] **1 a :** having the apex replaced by a plane section and esp. by one parallel to the base ⟨volcanic mountains . . . bluntly ~, owing to the whole top of the original cone having been blown away —C.A.Cotton⟩ **b :** having the edges or corners cut off by a line or plane — compare BEVELED ⟨transformed into ~ spheres —D.W Van Krevelen & Johannes Schuyer⟩ **2 a :** abbreviated by or as if by lopping : cut short : CURTAILED ⟨~ headlands . . . are products of wave erosion —C.L.White & G.T.Renner⟩ ⟨the present disc . . . includes the whole of the usually ~ orchestral introduction —Edward Sackville-West & Desmond Shawe-Taylor⟩ ⟨words ~ by his impatience —Frances Winwar⟩ **b :** marred by mutilation : MAIMED, MANGLED ⟨a ~ body⟩ ⟨the ~ economy . . . must be made to grow new industrial limbs —*Time*⟩ ⟨such a ~ quotation does not do justice to the . . . argument —*Nation*⟩ **c :** lacking an expected or normal element (as a syllable) at beginning or end : ACEPHALOUS, CATALECTIC ⟨a ~ line of verse⟩ **3 :** squared off at the end; *specif* : TRUNCATE

truncated cone *or* **truncated pyramid** *n* **:** a cone section or pyramid lacking an apex and terminating in a plane usu. parallel to the base

truncated pyramid

truncated cube *n* **:** a solid bounded by six equal regular octagons and eight equal regular triangles formed by cutting off the corners of a cube

trun·ca·tel·la \,trəŋkə'telə\ *n, cap* [NL, fr. L *truncatus* (past part.) + *-ella*] **:** a genus (the type of the family Truncatellidae) of snails that are usu. terrestrial near the sea but occas. occur in either salt water or freshwater and that have a small somewhat cylindrical shell which is truncate in the adult and the ctenidium replaced by a pulmonary sac

trun·cate·ly *adv* **:** in a truncated form or manner

trun·ca·tion \,trəŋ'kāshən\ *n* -S [LL *truncation-, truncatio*, fr. L *truncatus* (past part. of *truncare* to cut off) + *-ion-, -io* -ion] **1 a :** an act or instance of truncating ⟨loss of section . . . by ~ following uplift —*Jour. of Geol.*⟩ ⟨~ of street corners should be aimed at . . . to increase visibility —John Kemp⟩ **b :** omission at the beginning or end of an element (as an unstressed syllable) normally present or expected in a line or other unit of verse — compare CATALEXIS, BROKEN-BACKED LINE **c :** a truncated point or area ⟨the ~ on the edge of a crystal⟩ **2 :** the replacement of an edge or solid angle (as of a crystal) by a plane and esp. by one equally inclined to the adjoining faces **3 :** the quality or state of being truncated ⟨after revising his work . . . gave it an effect of ~ and bareness —Van Wyck Brooks⟩

trun·ca·ture \'trəŋkə,chu̇(ə)r\ *n* -S **:** TRUNCATION

[1]**trun·cheon** \'trənchən\ *n* -S [ME *tronchoun*, fr. MF *tronchon*, fr. (assumed) VL *truncion-, truncio*, fr. L *truncus* trunk, torso + *-ion-, -io* -ion — more at TRUNCATE] **1 :** a broken remnant esp. of a shattered spear or lance ⟨an arm embowed in armor . . . holding a ~ of a broken lance —*Burke's Peerage*⟩ **2 a** *obs* **:** a heavy club : BLUDGEON ⟨thy leg a stick compared with this ~ —Shak.⟩ **b :** a staff carried as a symbol of authority; *esp* : BATON ⟨a king at arms, whose hand the armorial ~ held —Sir Walter Scott⟩ **c :** a policeman's billy : NIGHTSTICK ⟨constables kept the crowd off with ~*s* —Arnold Bennett⟩ **3 :** a relatively thick stem cutting or long branch (as of a willow) used for propagating a plant

[2]**truncheon** \"\ *vt* -ED/-ING/-S *archaic* **:** to beat with a truncheon

trun·cheoned \-chənd\ *adj* **:** having a truncheon

trun·cus \'trəŋkəs\ *n* -ES [L] **:** TRUNK 1a, 1b, 6a

truncus ar·te·ri·o·sus \,==(,)är,tirē'ōsəs\ *n* [NL, arterial trunk] **:** the part of the arterial system within the pericardium connecting the ventricle and ventral aorta in anamniotes and early developmental stages of amniotes; *specif* : the part of the truncus arteriosus between the bulbus arteriosus and the ventral aorta

[1]**trun·dle** \'trənd°l, ÷ -n°l\ *n* -S [alter. of *trendle*] **1 a :** a small wheel or roller ⟨the tip end of the nozzle rolls along on a freewheeling little ~ —*New Yorker*⟩ **b :** CIRCLET, HOOP ⟨the circular rampart being like a hoop or ~ —Jacquetta & Christopher Hawkes⟩ **c :** a small vertical pin in the action of an organ stop for transmitting motion from the stop knob to the trace **2 a :** LANTERN PINION **b :** any of the bars of such a trundle **3 :** a low-wheeled cart or truck

[2]**trundle** \"\ *vb* **trundled; trundled; trundling** \-n(d)(°)liŋ\ **trundles** *vt* **1 a :** to propel by causing to rotate : BOWL, ROLL ⟨*trundled* a new tire through the sand —Vicki Baum⟩ **b** *archaic* **:** to cause to revolve : SPIN ⟨attains the same result by *trundling* the glass during reheating —H.J.Powell⟩; *esp* : to remove water from (a mop) by twirling **2 a :** to transport in a wheeled vehicle : HAUL, WHEEL ⟨the local bus . . . *trundling* its load —Adrian Bell⟩ ⟨was put into a wheelchair and *trundled* down to the hospital library —Ben Benson⟩ ⟨*trundled* wheelbarrows of dirt —R.A.Billington⟩ **b :** to cause to move on trundles : CONVEY, PUSH ⟨machines . . . are *trundled* around on ball-bearing turntables —Bryan Morgan⟩ ~ *vi* **1 a :** to progress by revolving ⟨start a barrel *trundling* down a chute⟩ **b :** BOWL 4 **2 a :** to move on or as if on wheels : ROLL ⟨rickety old vehicles . . . ~ from city to city with loads of chickens —*N.Y.Times*⟩ ⟨the tram *trundled* away from them —Richard Blaker⟩ ⟨heaped-up cloud towers were *trundling* across the heavens —Eugene Walter⟩ **b :** to ride in a wheeled vehicle : TRAVEL ⟨called a taxi and *trundled* down to the offices —Dorothy Sayers⟩ ⟨*trundling* off aboard a suburban bus —Bennett Cerf⟩ **c :** to move ponderously : CHURN, LUMBER ⟨a battery had *trundled* into position . . . and was thoughtfully shelling the distance —Stephen Crane⟩ **3 :** to move or go at a constant rate esp. with a rolling gait ⟨a moving bundle of brush, he *trundled* away into the thicket —Margaret Peattie⟩

trundle bed *n* **1 :** a low bed usu. on casters that can be pushed under a higher bed — called also *truckle bed* **2 :** a two-bed unit designed to allow one bed to be slid under the other

trundle bed

trundlehead \'==,=\ *n* **1 :** one of the disks forming the ends of a lantern pinion **2 :** the drumhead of a capstan

trun·dler \-n(d)(°)lə(r)\ *n* -S **:** one that trundles; *esp* : the bowler in cricket

trundle–tail \'==,=\ *n, archaic* **:** a curly-tailed dog : MONGREL ⟨bobtail tyke or *trundle-tail* —Shak.⟩

trung cha \'tru̇ŋ¦chä\ *n, pl* **trung cha** *or* **trung chas** *usu cap T&C* **1 :** a mountain people of Tonkin in Vietnam **2 :** a member of the Trung Cha people

[1]**trunk** \'trəŋk\ *n* -S [ME *trunke, tronke* chest, box, trunk, fr. MF *tronc*, fr. L *truncus* trunk of a tree, torso, shaft of a column] **1 a :** the main stem of a tree apart from its limbs and roots **b** (1) **:** the human body apart from the head and appendages (2) *obs* **:** BODY **c** (1) **:** the thorax of an insect (2) **:** the body of a fish from the operculum to the anus **d :** the central part of anything; *specif* : the shaft of a column or pilaster **2 a** (1) **:** a box or tank for keeping fish alive after they are caught (2) *dial Brit* **:** HOOP NET **b** *obs* **:** an ornamental chest (as a jewel casket) or a box (as a packing case) used for storage **c** (1) **:** a piece of luggage that has a rigid frame, that is too large to be carried by hand, and that is used usu. for transporting a traveler's clothing and other personal effects (2) **:** the luggage compartment of an automobile **d** (1) **:** a superstructure over a ship's hatches usu. level with the poop deck, extending from one half to three quarters of the length of the ship, and having the main deck carried around it (2) **:** the roof and upper part of the sides of the cabin of a boat projecting above the deck (3) **:** the housing for a centerboard or rudder — see CENTERBOARD illustration **3 a :** PIPE, TUBE — compare TRUNK ENGINE **b :** PROBOSCIS; *esp* : the long muscular tubular extension of the nose of the elephant having the nostrils at its tip, serving as a prehensile organ either by coiling about an object to be seized or by the use of a small movable grasping process at its extremity, and used esp. to convey food or drink to the mouth and as a weapon **c** *or* **trunk glass** *obs* **:** TELESCOPE **4 trunks** *pl* **a** *obs* **:** TRUNK HOSE **b** *archaic* **:** BREECHES, KNICKERBOCKERS **c :** men's shorts worn chiefly for sports **5 a :** a passage or duct (as a wooden box conduit for carrying air to mine workings) **b :** LAUNDER **c :** WIND-TRUNK **d** (1) **:** a vertical shaft between decks (as a casing for access or ventilation) (2) **:** a chute for loading or coaling a ship **6 a :** the principal channel of a tributary system ⟨nerve ~⟩ ⟨~ of a river⟩ ⟨~ of an artery⟩ **b :** a circuit between two telephone exchanges or telephone switching devices for making connections between subscribers **c :** TRUNK LINE

[2]**trunk** \"\ *adj* **1 a :** of, relating to, or resembling a box or trunk ⟨~ lid⟩ ⟨~ load⟩ ⟨~ buoy⟩ **b :** used for storing luggage ⟨~ compartment⟩ **2 a :** of or relating to the torso ⟨determining ~ height . . . of these pygmies —*Amer. Anthropologist*⟩ **b :** of or relating to a tree trunk ⟨~ borer⟩ **3 :** having or consisting of a tube ⟨~ piston⟩ **4 :** having, using, or controlling the flow in a duct or chute ⟨~ machine⟩ **5 :** of, relating to, or constituting a primary segment or principal channel ⟨~ road⟩ ⟨~ stream⟩ ⟨~ pipeline⟩ ⟨~ wire of a teletype service⟩ ⟨~ airline⟩

[3]**trunk** \"\ *vt* -ED/-ING/-S **:** to enclose in a trunk or casing

trunkback \'=,=\ *n* **:** LEATHERBACK 1

trunk cabin *n* **:** a cabin on a boat (as a yacht) with the upper portion projecting above the deck

trunk call *n* **:** a long-distance telephone call

trunk deck *n* **:** the top of a ship's trunk usu. containing the hatchways, ventilators, and deck openings

trunk dial *n* **:** a spring-driven clock having an elongated case below the large dial to accommodate a pendulum

[1]**trunked** *adj* [fr. past part. of obs. E *trunk* to cut off, truncate, fr. ME *trunken*, fr. L *truncare* — more at TRUNCATE] **:** having the head or top cut off : TRUNCATED

[2]**trunked** \¦trəŋkt\ *adj* [[1]*trunk* + *-ed*] **1 :** having a trunk — often used in combination ⟨straight-*trunked*⟩ ⟨single-*trunked*⟩ ⟨gray-*trunked* beeches —E.W.Smith⟩ **2 :** having a proboscis ⟨~ mammal⟩

trunk engine *n* **1 :** a steam engine having a piston rod that is a pipe of sufficient diameter to enable one end of the connecting rod to be attached to the crank and the other end to pass within the pipe and be pivoted to the piston **2 :** an engine (as most internal-combustion engines) having a trunk piston

trunkfish \'=,=\ *n* **:** BOXFISH

trunk·ful \'trəŋk,fu̇l\ *n, pl* **trunk·fuls** *also* **trunks·ful** \-k,fu̇lz, -k,sfu̇l\ **1 :** as much or as many as a trunk will hold ⟨twenty ~*s* of memorabilia —R.L.Taylor⟩ ⟨*trunksful* of letters —*Time*⟩ ⟨elephants blowing ~*s* of the cooling water over parched . . . backs —Tom Marvel⟩ **2 :** a great many ⟨a ~ of ancient jokes —*Newsweek*⟩

trunk glacier *n* **:** a valley glacier formed by the flowing together of tributary glaciers

trunk hose *or* **trunk breeches** *n pl* [*trunk* prob. fr. obs. E *trunk* to cut off, truncate; fr. the fact that it was a truncated hose] **:** short full breeches reaching about halfway down the thigh and sometimes attached to the hose, usu. padded and slashed, and worn chiefly in the late 16th and early 17th centuries — see NETHERSTOCK illustration

trunking *n* -S [fr. gerund of [3]*trunk*] **1 :** an act or instance of employing a trunk **2 a :** a casing to protect electrical conductors **b :** TRUNK 5d(1) **3 a :** the provision of adequate trunks and switching facilities in either a manual or automatic communications system **b :** the interconnections provided

trunk·less \'trəŋkləs\ *adj* **:** lacking a body; *esp* : severed from the trunk ⟨~ head⟩ ⟨~ brushwood⟩

trunk line *n* **1 :** a system (as for transportation) handling long-distance through traffic : MAIN LINE ⟨like any highway system, the federal airways have their main *trunk lines* as well as feeder routes —*Monsanto Mag.*⟩; *specif* : one of the railway systems whose main lines run from Chicago to New York **2 a :** a main supply channel (as a natural-gas main) **b :** a direct link (as a telephone circuit between two switchboards)

trunkmaker \'=,==\ *n* [so called fr. the fact that in making trunks the pages were used as lining] *archaic* **:** a depository for unsalable books

trunknose \'=,=\ *n* **:** ELEPHANT SEAL

trunk piston *or* **trunk plunger** *n* **:** an elongated hollow piston in a single-acting engine or pump which is open at the end and in which the end of the connecting rod is pivoted

trunk room *n* **:** a storage room esp. for storing luggage

trunk scald *n* **:** winter sunscald affecting the trunk of a tree

trunk sleeve *n* [*trunk* prob. fr. obs. E *trunk* to cut off, truncate; fr. its being a truncated sleeve — more at TRUNKED] **:** a large usu. slashed and padded sleeve resembling trunk hose

trunk turtle *n* **:** LEATHERBACK 1

trunkway \'=,=\ *n* [[2]*trunk* + *way*] **:** TRUNK 5d(1)

trunk whale *n* **:** SPERM WHALE

trun·nel \'trən°l\ *var of* TREENAIL

trun·nion \'trənyən\ *n* -S [F *trognon* core, stalk, stump] **1 :** either of two opposite gudgeons on which a cannon is swiveled — see CANNON illustration **2 :** a pin or pivot usu. mounted on bearings for rotating or tilting something — **trun·nioned** \-yənd\ *adj*

[1]**truss** \'trəs\ *vt* -ED/-ING/-ES [ME *trussen*, fr. OF *trousser, tourser*, prob. fr. (assumed) VL *torciare*, fr. *torca* bundle, torch — more at TORCH] **1 a :** to secure closely or tightly : BIND, TIE ⟨attacked and ~*ed* a guard —*Springfield (Mass.) Union*⟩ — often used with *up* ⟨the victim, a middle-aged woman, had been expertly ~*ed up* —E.D.Radin⟩ **b :** to arrange for cooking by binding the wings or legs of (as fowl) close to the body **c :** to bind together the staves of (a barrel) with hoops to force into the desired shape and assure tightness of joints **2** *archaic* **:** to pack into a bundle **3 a :** to put clothes on (the body) so as to confine tightly ⟨gentlemen ~*ed* in broadcloth to the Adam's apple —*Amer. Guide Series: N. Y. City*⟩ **b** *archaic* **:** to fasten or arrange the clothing of; *specif* : to draw tight and tie firmly (as laces or strings) **c** *archaic* **:** to arrange (the hair) in a neat fashion : DRESS **4** *archaic* **:** HANG — often used with *up* **5 :** to take fast hold of; *esp* : to seize and bear off — used of a hawk or other bird of prey **6 :** to support by a truss : strengthen or stiffen (as a beam or girder) by a brace or braces esp. so as to constitute a truss

[2]**truss** \"\ *n* -ES [ME *trusse*, fr. OF *trousse, tourse*, fr. *trousser, tourser* to truss] **1 a :** something bound or packed together : BUNDLE, PACK ⟨bearing a ~ of trifles at his back —Edmund Spenser⟩ **b** *Brit* **:** any of various units of quantity for hay or straw: as (1) **:** a bundle of old hay weighing 56 pounds (2) **:** a bundle of new hay weighing 60 pounds (3) **:** a bundle of straw weighing 36 pounds **2 :** a connection to secure a yard to a mast; *specif* : an iron band around a lower mast with a pivoted attachment to a lower yard at the center to keep the yard in position and allow it to be braced around **3 a :** BRACKET 1 **b :** an assemblage of members (as beams, bars, rods) typically arranged in a triangle or combination of triangles to form a rigid framework (as for supporting a load over a wide area) that cannot be deformed by the application of exterior force without deformation of one or more of its members **c :** a tripod of logs or timbers on which hay is piled for curing in the field **4 :** a device worn to hold a hernia in place **5 :** a compact flower cluster (as in the lilac) or fruit cluster (as in the tomato)

[3]**truss** \"\ *adj, archaic* **:** compactly framed

truss beam *n* **:** a beam reinforced by a truss rod or formed of straight or cambered pieces joined by trussing

truss bow *n* **:** a semicircular jointed portion of a truss holding the center of a lower yard to the mast

truss bridge *n* **:** a bridge supported mainly by trusses — see BRIDGE illustration

trus·sell \'trəsəl\ *n* -S [ME, bundle, trussell, fr. MF *troussel, trousel*, dim. of OF *trousse* truss] **:** the upper die of an old English apparatus for striking coins by hand with a hammer — compare PILE 3a

truss·er \'trəsə(r)\ *n* -S **:** one that trusses ⟨a ~ of hay⟩ ⟨a ~ of poultry⟩: as **a :** a machine for trussing barrels **b :** the operator of a trussing machine

truss hoop *n* **1 a :** the band of a truss encircling the mast **b :** one of the truss bands that encircle a yard **2 :** a hoop placed around the staves of a barrel (as by a trusser) to force them into shape and position

trussing *n* -S [fr. gerund of [1]*truss*] **1 :** the members forming a truss **2 :** the trusses and framework of a structure

truss leg *n* **:** a leg having the form of a prolonged corbel or console — see LEG illustration

truss rod *n* **1 :** a tensioned rod for trussing a wooden beam **2 :** a diagonal tie rod in a truss

trusswork \'=,=\ *n* **:** work consisting of trusses

[1]**trust** \'trəst\ *n* -S [ME *trust, trost*, prob. of Scand origin; akin to ON *traust* trust; akin to OHG *trōst* trust, Goth *trausti* agreement, pact, ON *trūa* trust, faith, OE *trūwian* to trust, inspire with trust, *trēowe* faithful, trustworthy — more at TRUE] **1 a :** assured reliance on some person or thing : a confident dependence on the character, ability, strength, or truth of someone or something : BELIEF ⟨nor should a physician do anything to diminish the ~ reposed by the patient in his own physician —W.T. & Barbara Fitts⟩ ⟨the ~ that farmer places in the fertilizer operator —*Monsanto Mag.*⟩ ⟨being ignorant of these matters, I take it all on ~ —H.J.Laski⟩ **b :** a person or thing in which confidence is placed : a basis of reliance, faith, or hope ⟨God, thou art my ~ from my youth —Ps 71:5 (AV)⟩ ⟨if I have made gold my ~ —Job 31:24 (RSV)⟩ **2 a :** dependence on something future or contingent : confident anticipation : HOPE ⟨hurried down to those who were waiting in joyful ~ —George Meredith⟩ **b :** reliance on future payment for merchandise or other property delivered : CREDIT ⟨sell on ~⟩ **3 a :** an equitable right or interest in property distinct from the legal ownership of it : a property interest held by one person for the benefit of another — see LIVING TRUST, MASSACHUSETTS TRUST, PASSIVE TRUST, SPENDTHRIFT TRUST, TESTAMENTARY TRUST **b** (1) **:** a combination of firms or corporations formed by an agreement legally establishing a trust whereby stockholders in the separate corporations exchange their shares for shares representing proportionate interest in the principal and income of the combination and surrender to the trustees the management and operation of the combined firms or corporations (2) **:** a combination or aggregation of business entities formed by any of various means; *esp* : one that reduces competition or is thought to present a threat of reducing competition **4** *archaic* **:** TRUSTWORTHINESS ⟨there's no ~, no faith, no honesty in men —Shak.⟩ **5 a** (1) **:** a charge or duty imposed in faith or confidence or as a condition of some relationship ⟨accept, as a sacred ~, the obligation to promote to the largest possible extent the welfare of such peoples —B.A.G.Cohen⟩ (2) **:** something committed or entrusted to one to be used or cared for in the interest of another ⟨no religious test shall ever be required as a qualification to any office or public ~ under the United States —*U. S. Constitution*⟩ **b :** the condition, obligation, or right of one to whom something is confided : responsible charge or office ⟨feel that my ~ as chairman of the board of this bank requires me to exert every effort —W.W.Aldrich⟩ ⟨sometimes people fail in their ~, but they live up to it far more often —*Boy Scout Handbk.*⟩ **c :** CARE, CUSTODY ⟨a child committed to his ~⟩

syn CONFIDENCE, RELIANCE, DEPENDENCE, FAITH: TRUST implies an assured attitude toward another which may rest on blended evidence of experience and more subjective grounds such as knowledge, affection, admiration, respect, or reverence ⟨to Miss Biddums he confided with equal *trust* his tattered garments and his more serious griefs —Rudyard Kipling⟩ ⟨his youthful optimism and his cheerful *trust* in men —Katherine McNamara⟩ CONFIDENCE may indicate a feeling of sureness about another that is based on experience and evidence without strong effect of the subjective ⟨both of whom had profound *confidence* in him —T.M.Spaulding⟩ ⟨he apparently has won the *confidence* of farm workers, merchants and others, who continue to elect him —Harold Callender⟩ RELIANCE may be used readily in contexts in which assuredness in another has formed the basis for some choice or decision ⟨his diffidence had prevented his depending on his own judgment in so anxious a case, but his *reliance* on mine made everything easy —Jane Austen⟩ ⟨had written out his Christmas sermon with a good deal of care and an excessive *reliance* on what other preachers had said before him —Compton Mackenzie⟩ DEPENDENCE is likely to suggest lack of independence and inability to act for one's self while relying on another ⟨the drastic effect on a girl's life of the mother's *dependence* on her —Leslie Rees⟩ ⟨a woman who did not regard the change from economic independence on an employer to economic *dependence* on a man, as an honorable promotion —Virginia Woolf⟩ FAITH may indicate a confidence that transcends, waives, or violates factual evidence ⟨although I already had great *faith* in the mental capacity of the Polynesians, even I was astounded at the facility with which the students forged ahead —V.G.Heiser⟩ ⟨a lasting *faith* that not everything in the dreams I dreamed as an undergraduate can possibly have been false —T.R.Ybarra⟩

— **in trust** *adv* **:** in the care or possession of a trustee ⟨the property of the State to be forever held *in trust* for the people —*Amer. Guide Series: Mich.*⟩

[2]**trust** \"\ *adj* **:** held in trust

[3]**trust** \"\ *vb* -ED/-ING/-S [ME *trusten, trosten*, prob. of Scand origin; akin to ON *treysta* to trust, *traust* trust] *vi* **1 a :** to place confidence : DEPEND — often used with *in* or *to* ⟨hope for the best, and ~ in God —Sydney Smith⟩ ⟨flung together a jumble of material, and ~*ed* to its timeliness to sell —V.L.Parrington⟩ ⟨~ to luck⟩ **b :** to be confident : HOPE ⟨need not succumb to panic, however, if we will ~ and not be afraid —J.W.McKelvey⟩ ⟨will see you soon, I ~⟩ **2 :** to sell or deliver on credit ~ *vt* **1 a :** to commit or place with confidence : confer as a trust : ENTRUST ⟨~ my precious flowers to a mere man —Margaret Deland⟩ ⟨such trees must be cared for . . . almost no owner would, or does, ~ them to a tenant —B.H.Hibbard⟩ **b :** to permit to stay or go somewhere or to do something without fear or misgiving : venture confidently ⟨sealed my letter, and not ~*ing* it out of my own hands, delivered it myself —Charles Dickens⟩ **c :** to confer a trust on : give something into the care or possession of ⟨~*ed* his son with the family car⟩ ⟨~*ed* him with her story⟩ **2 a :** to rely on the truthfulness or accuracy of : BELIEVE, CREDIT ⟨if we may ~ him as a witness⟩ ⟨if rumor may be ~*ed*⟩ **b :** to place confidence in : have faith in : rely on ⟨~ the storekeeper from whom you buy your baseball mitt to sell you a good one —*Boy Scout Handbk.*⟩ ⟨was widely ~*ed* and loved by the community as a whole —K.S.Latourette⟩ ⟨~ him to know when to keep quiet⟩ **c :** to hope or expect confidently ⟨~*ed* the sight of that barren mountainside would compensate us for all the discomforts —W.H.Hudson †1922⟩ ⟨~*ed* to find oil on the land⟩ **3 :** to extend credit to ⟨do you suppose he'd mind ~*ing* me for the other dollar-ninety —MacKinlay Kantor⟩ **syn** see RELY

trust·abil·i·ty \,trəstə'bilədē\ *n* **:** the quality or state of being trustable

trust·able \'trəstəbəl\ *adj* **:** capable of being trusted

trust account *n* **:** an account opened with a trust company under which a living or testamentary trust is set up

trust agreement *n* **:** an agreement establishing and setting forth the material terms of a trust

trustbuster \'=,==\ *n* [[1]*trust* + *buster*] **:** one who seeks to break up business trusts; *specif* : a federal official (as a district attorney) who prosecutes trusts under the antitrust laws

trust–busting \'=,==\ *n* **:** a legal action or political campaign to break up trusts

trust certificate *n* **:** a certificate issued and sold as one of a series by the trustee of designated trust property (as an investment trust, railroad equipment, or business trust) legally held evidencing a specified fractional equitable or beneficial interest in the trust property existing in the holder or registered owner of the certificate, incorporating the particular trust agreement, setting forth the principal rights of the certificate owner to share in the income, profits, or gains realized from the trust property and in any current or future distributions of it, and prescribing the mode of transfer of the certificate

trust company *n* **:** a corporation organized to perform the fiduciary functions of trusts and agencies; *esp* **:** COMMERCIAL BANK

trust deed *n* **:** a deed conveying property in trust and often used as a mortgage to secure an obligation

[1]**trust·ee** \ˌtrəˈstē\ *n* -s [[3]*trust* + *-ee*] **1 :** one to whom something is entrusted **:** one trusted to keep or administer something ⟨custodians of very glorious traditions, and the ~*s* of a spiritual wealth —W.R.Inge⟩: as **a :** a member of a board entrusted with administering the funds and directing the policy of an institution or organization (as a school, hospital, philanthropic foundation) **b :** a country charged with the supervision of a trust territory **2 a :** a person whether real or juristic to whom property is legally committed in trust **:** one holding legal title to property which he must administer for the benefit of a beneficiary or for a purpose recognized as legally charitable or as lawful by statute **b :** one in whose hands the effects of another are attached by the trustee process **c :** one held to a fiduciary duty similar in some respects to that of a trustee ⟨the directors of a bank may be ~*s* for the depositors⟩ ⟨directors of a corporation are ~*s* for the stockholders⟩ ⟨a guardian is ~ of his ward's property⟩

[2]**trustee** \"\ *vb* **trusteed; trusteed; trusteeing; trustees** *vt* **:** to commit to the care of a trustee ⟨required to either sell or ~ their holdings in one or the other end of the business —*Springfield (Mass.) Union*⟩ ⟨whose scheme of social organization is to be adopted in the *trusteed* areas of the world —Isaiah Bowman⟩ ~ *vi* **:** to serve as trustee

[3]**trustee** *var of* TRUSTY

trusteed plan *n* [*trusteed* fr. past part. of [2]*trustee*] **:** a pension or retirement plan under which contributions are paid to a trustee who invests the funds and pays benefits to eligible employees — compare UNFUNDED PLAN

trustee ex ma·le·fi·cio \-ˌek,smaləˈfikē,ō, -mäl-\ *or* **trustee ex de·lic·to** \-,eksdəˈlik(,)tō\ *n* **:** a person treated as a trustee because guilty of wrongdoing and compelled to account as though he were a trustee for property to which he has legal title for the benefit of those injured and equitably entitled to it

trustee in bankruptcy : a person in whom the property of a bankrupt is vested by a court for the benefit of the creditors and who administers the property under the direction of the court for the purpose of distributing the net proceeds therefrom pro rata among his creditors according to the priority of their established claims

trustee in in·vi·tum \-,inənˈwē,tùm, -ˈvīd·əm\ *n* **:** a person treated as a trustee of property because he has acted without authority or in excess of his authority in respect to that property

trustee process *n* **:** the process of attachment by garnishment or in the New England states by foreign attachment — compare EQUITABLE GARNISHMENT

trustee security *n* **:** a security in which a trustee may properly invest and which is often described in the trust instrument or in an approved list established in accordance with law

trust·ee·ship \,trəˈstē,ship\ *n* **1 :** the office or function of a trustee **2 :** authorized supervisory control by one or more countries as trustee of the administration of a trust territory under the international system of the United Nations

trust·en \ˈtrəsᵊn\ *vi* -ED/-ING/-S [ME *trustnen*, fr. [1]*trust* + *-nen* -en] *dial Eng* **:** TRUST

trust·er \ˈtrəstə(r)\ *n* -s **1 :** one that relies, credits, or believes **2** *Scots law* **:** one that creates a trust

trust estate *n* **:** an estate subject to a trust or held in trust

trust·ful \-stfəl\ *adj* **:** full of trust **:** being without suspicion **:** CONFIDING ⟨great brown eyes, clear and ~ —C.B.Nordhoff & J.N.Hall⟩ — **trust·ful·ly** \-fəlē, -li\ *adv* — **trust·ful·ness** *n* -ES

trust fund *n* **1 :** TRUST ESTATE; *esp* **:** money, securities, or similar property settled or held in trust **2 :** a property for which the holder or manager is held accountable as if he were a trustee

trustier *comparative of* TRUSTY

trusties *pl of* TRUSTY

trustiest *superlative of* TRUSTY

trust·ifi·ca·tion \,trəstəfəˈkāshən\ *n* -s [fr. *trustify*, after such pairs as E *ramify: ramification*] **:** the process of forming a trust or of organizing into a system of trusts ⟨~ went on at a rapid pace; the size of American business expanded greatly —Isaac Lippincott⟩

trust·ify \ˈ⸗⸗,fī\ *vb* -ED/-ING/-ES [[1]*trust* + *-ify*] *vt* **:** to form into a trust ⟨a *trustified* industry⟩ ~ *vi* **:** to form a trust ⟨put a damper on the urge to ~ —J.R.Chamberlain⟩

trust·i·ly \ˈtrəstəlē, -li\ *adv* [ME *trustily, trostily*, fr. *trusty, trosty* trusty + *-ly*] **:** in a trusty manner

trust indenture *n* **:** a document under which a trust (as a mutual investment fund) is conducted

trust·i·ness \ˈtrəstēnəs, -tin-\ *n* -ES **:** the quality or state of being trusty

trusting *pres part of* TRUST

trust·ing·ly *adv* **:** in a trusting manner

trust·ing·ness *n* -ES **:** the quality or state of being trusting

trust institution *n* **:** a corporation engaged in the business of administering estates and trusts; *also* **:** the trust department of a trust company or other banking institution

trust instrument *n* **:** the legal document (as a will, deed, agreement, or a declaration of trust) by which a trust is created

trus·tle \ˈtrəsəl\ *dial var of* TRESTLE

trust·less \ˈtrəstləs\ *adj* **1 :** not deserving of trust **:** FAITHLESS, FALSE, UNTRUSTWORTHY ⟨keep your heart for men like me and safe from ~ chaps —A.E.Housman⟩ **2 :** DISTRUSTFUL ⟨winning the trust of a ~ mind —Constance Woolson⟩ — **trust·less·ly** *adv* — **trust·less·ness** *n* -ES

trust·man \ˈtrəst,man, -,mən\ *n, pl* **trustmen :** one whose occupation is handling trusts either in the service of a trust institution or privately

trust mortgage *n* **1 :** a mortgage made to a trustee generally to secure an issue of bonds or a series of obligations wherein the rights of the parties are declared in a trust agreement set forth or referred to in the mortgage **2 :** a mortgage given by a debtor in distress to a trustee of all his business assets with authority to the trustee to operate the business until the debts are paid and then return the assets to the debtor or with authority to foreclose if the business cannot be operated profitably

trust officer *n* **:** an officer of a trust institution

trus·tor \ˈtrəstə(r), ˌtrəˈstȯ(ə)r\ *n* -s [[3]*trust* + *-or*] **:** the donor, settlor, grantor, or other person creating a trust by transferring his property to a trustee

trust property *n* **:** property held in or subject to a trust

trust receipt *n* **:** a trust agreement between a bank and its debtor by which the bank gives up possession of collateral security to the debtor without abandoning its title to the security and the debtor agrees to hold the security in trust for the bank and if the security is sold to hold the proceeds in trust for the bank and to pay them to the bank in settlement of the indebtedness

trusts *pl of* TRUST, *pres 3d sing of* TRUST

trust territory *n* **:** a non-self-governing territory placed under an administrative authority by the Trusteeship Council of the United Nations as being a former mandate under the League of Nations, a territory taken from a former enemy state as a result of World War II, or a territory voluntarily placed under the international system by the state responsible for its administration

trustwoman \ˈ⸗,⸗⸗\ *n, pl* **trustwomen :** a woman whose occupation is handling trusts either in the service of a trust institution or privately

trust·wor·thi·ly \ˈtrəs,twərt͟həlē, -wət͟h-,-wəit͟h-, -li\ *adv* **:** in a trustworthy manner

trust·wor·thi·ness \-t͟hēnəs, -t͟hin-\ *n* **:** the quality or state of being trustworthy

trust·wor·thy \-t͟hē,-t͟hi\ *adj* **:** worthy of confidence **:** DEPENDABLE ⟨an obedient and ~ officer —Stanley Pargellis⟩ ⟨no ~ story can be put together from the myth, tradition, and conscious fiction —H.O.Taylor⟩ **syn** see RELIABLE

[1]**trusty** \ˈtrəstē, -sti\ *adj* -ER/-EST [ME *trusty, trosty*, fr. *trust, trost* trust + *-y* — more at TRUST] **1** *archaic* **:** having trust **:** CONFIDING, TRUSTFUL **2 :** fit to be trusted **:** deserving confidence **:** TRUSTWORTHY ⟨his ~, battered camera —Tom Marvel⟩ **3** *obs* **:** involving trust ⟨might at some great and ~ business in a main danger fail you —Shak.⟩ **syn** see RELIABLE

[2]**trusty** \"\ *also* **trust·ee** \ˌtrəˈstē *or like* TRUSTY\ *n, pl* **trusties** *also* **trustees** [*trustee* alter. (influenced by [1]*trustee*) of *trusty*] **:** a trusty or trusted person; *specif* **:** a convict considered trustworthy and allowed special privileges

truth \ˈtrüth\ *n, pl* **truths** \-üt͟hz *also* -üths\ [ME *trewthe, treuthe*, fr. OE *trēowth, trīewth*; akin to OHG *getriuwida* fidelity, ON *tryggth* faith, trustiness; derivative fr. the root of E [1]*true*] **1 a** *archaic* **:** the quality or state of being faithful **:** FIDELITY, CONSTANCY ⟨whispering tongues can poison ~ —S.T.Coleridge⟩ **b :** sincerity in character, action, and speech **:** genuineness in expressing feeling or belief **:** TRUTHFULNESS, HONESTY ⟨gives a man a clear conscious view of his own opinions and judgments, a ~ in developing them —J.H. Newman⟩ ⟨the absolute ~ of his speech, and the rectitude of his behavior —R.W.Emerson⟩ **2 :** something that is true or held to be true: as **a** (1) **:** the real state of affairs **:** something that is the case **:** FACT ⟨the hard ~ was that few of America's allies believed that the . . . islands were worth fighting for —*Newsweek*⟩ ⟨the present definition of insanity has little relation to the ~*s* of mental life —B.N.Cardozo⟩ (2) **:** the body of things, events, and facts that make up the universe **:** actual existence **:** ACTUALITY ⟨the facets of reality . . . together comprising what the human spirit can call ~ —*General Education in a Free Society*⟩ (3) *often cap* **:** a fundamental or spiritual reality conceived of as being partly or wholly transcendent of perceived actuality and experience ⟨modern man . . . was capable of the relative and changing ~*s* of science, incapable and afraid of any supratemporal ~ reached by Reason's metaphysical effort or of the divine —Jacques Maritain⟩ ⟨got only the facts and not the ~ —W.A.White⟩ (4) **:** the world of a particular person or in a particular manner ⟨a psychotic's ~ is what "I" make it —Weston La Barre⟩ ⟨the ~ of speculative inquiry had been replaced by the ~ of empirical investigation —R.M.Weaver⟩ **b** (1) **:** a true relation or account ⟨to say ~, it can only be regarded as a kind of literary curiosity —Daniel George⟩ ⟨~ is stranger than fiction⟩ (2) **:** a judgment, proposition, statement, or idea that accords with fact or reality, is logically or intuitively necessary, or follows by sound reasoning from established or necessary truths ⟨two plus two equals four . . . that is a ~ anywhere —W.J.Reilly⟩ ⟨there are ~*s* which cannot be verified, yet we cannot help accepting them as true —Rubin Gotesky⟩; *specif* **:** a proposition or statement taken as an axiom, postulate, or principle in a field of study or inquiry ⟨questioned the basic ~*s* of thermodynamics⟩ (3) **:** TRUISM, PLATITUDE ⟨a ~ we are in danger of forgetting —Marie Hildegarde⟩ (4) **:** a notion having wide and uncritical acceptance among a group or in a field and liable to be proved false ⟨worshipped their flimsy hypotheses into ~*s* —Weston La Barre⟩ **c :** the body of true statements and propositions; *also* **:** the body of statements and propositions accepted, studied, or proved in a field ⟨seems to suggest that these are different and unrelated ~*s* — theological truth, psychotherapeutic truth, political truth —R.L.Howe⟩ ⟨every way of abstracting produces its own kind of ~ —S.I.Hayakawa⟩ **3 a :** relationship, conformity, or agreement with fact or reality or among true facts or propositions **:** the property in a conception, judgment, statement, proposition, belief, or opinion of being in accord with what is in fact or in necessity ⟨~ (or falsity) is a property of declarative sentences —Philip Hallie⟩ ⟨the test for ~ is objective and is not concerned with ministering to subjective feelings, needs, or desires —Jim Cork⟩ — see COHERENCE THEORY, CORRESPONDENCE THEORY, EMPIRICAL TRUTH, FORMAL TRUTH, METAPHYSICAL TRUTH, NORMATIVE TRUTH, PRAGMATISM, SEMANTIC CONCEPTION **b** *chiefly Brit* **:** TRUE 2 ⟨these squares must be tested for ~ —Laurence Town⟩ ⟨her propeller shaft was a trifle out of ~ —C.S. Forester⟩ **c** (1) **:** fidelity to an original or a possible original ⟨an ignorant, uneducated man may be a competent judge of the ~ of the representation of a sandal —Joshua Reynolds⟩ ⟨ability to build up the ~ of his characters through spare, pungent dialogue —Arthur Knight⟩ (2) **:** the conformity of a work of art to the essential significance of the subject, to the artist's conception or intent, or to some standard **:** the coherence of form and content in an apparently necessary whole ⟨what the imagination seizes as Beauty must be *Truth* — whether it existed before or not —John Keats⟩ ⟨a sturdy example of functional ~ in architecture —*Amer. Guide Series: Vt.*⟩ **4 a** *often cap* **:** abstract truth personified as a goddess **b** *cap, Christian Science* **:** GOD

syn VERACITY, VERITY, VERISIMILITUDE: TRUTH is a general term ranging in meaning from a transcendent idea to an indication of conformity with fact and of avoidance of error, misrepresentation, or falsehood ⟨the *truths* of religion are more like the *truths* of poetry than like the *truths* of science; that is, they are vision and insight, apprehended by the whole man, and not merely by the analysing mind —*Times Lit. Supp.*⟩ ⟨*truth* as the opposite of error and of falsehood —C.W.Eliot⟩ VERACITY commonly indicates rigid and unfailing adherence to, observance of, or respect for truth ⟨question an opponent's *veracity*⟩ ⟨his passion for *veracity* always kept him from taking any unfair rhetorical advantages of an opponent —Aldous Huxley⟩ ⟨I cannot, indeed, guarantee the absolute *veracity* of any of my apparently authentic law reports —J.R.Sutherland⟩ VERITY usu. designates the quality of a state or thing in being true or entirely in accordance with factual reality or with what should be so regarded; sometimes the word designates that which is marked by lasting, ultimate, transcendent value ⟨most primitive and national religions have also started out, naturally enough, with the assumption of their own *verity* and importance —A.L.Kroeber⟩ ⟨the old *verities* and truths of the heart, the old universal truths lacking which any story is ephemeral and doomed — love and honor and pity and pride and compassion and sacrifice —William Faulkner⟩ VERISIMILITUDE usu. indicates the quality of a representation that causes one to accept it as true ⟨to convey human nature in fiction requires the highest degree of *verisimilitude*: events that seem just like those of life as the reader's experience has led him to conceive of life must happen to people who seem just like human beings in a succession which seems just like the course of human affairs —E.K.Brown⟩

— in truth *adv* **:** in accordance with fact **:** ACTUALLY, REALLY

truth·ful \ˈtrüthfəl\ *adj* **:** telling or disposed to tell the truth **:** accurate and sincere in describing reality — **truth·ful·ly** \-fəlē, -li\ *adv* — **truth·ful·ness** *n* -ES

truth-function \ˈ⸗,⸗⸗\ *n* [trans. of G *wahrheitsfunktion*] **:** a sentential or propositional function whose truth-value depends only on the truth-values of its arguments — **truth-functional** \(ˈ)⸗ˈ⸗(⸗)⸗⸗\ *adj* — **truth-functionally** \(ˈ)⸗ˈ⸗(⸗)⸗⸗⸗\ *adv*

truth·less \ˈtrüthləs\ *adj* **1 :** UNTRUTHFUL **2 :** UNTRUE — **truth·less·ness** *n* -ES

truth or consequences *n* **:** a game in which each participant in turn is asked a question by a leader and if he refuses to answer or answers falsely is punished by a penalty suggested by the leader or the group

truths *pl of* TRUTH

truth serum *also* **truth drug** *n* **:** any of several hypnotics or anesthetics said to be useful in inducing a subject under questioning to talk freely

truth table *n* [trans. of G *wahrheitstafel*] **:** a table that lists underneath one or more truth-functions the various truth-values of the truth-functions for given truth-values of their arguments (*see table at right*)

truth-value \ˈ⸗,⸗(,)⸗\ *n* [trans. of G *wahrheitswert*] **:** either the truth or the falsehood of a proposition or statement; *sometimes* **:** one of the interpreted or uninterpreted values attached to a formula in a many-valued logic

truthy \ˈtrüthē, -t͟hē\ *adj* **:** TRUTHFUL

trut·ta \ˈtrəd·ə, -rüd·ə\ *n, cap* [NL, fr. ML *trutta, tructa* trout, fr. LL *tructa, troctа*, a trout, a shark — more at TROUT] *in some classifications* **:** a subgenus of *Salmo* or sometimes a separate genus comprising trouts that differ from the typical trouts in being marked with small black spots and in having smaller scales and fewer vertebrae and including the brown trout of Europe and the rainbow and cutthroat trouts of America

trut·ta·ceous \ˌtrəˈtāshəs\ *adj* [NL *truttaceus*, fr. ML *trutta* trout + L *-aceus* -aceous] **:** of, relating to, or resembling a trout

tru·xi·llic acid \(ˈ)trüˈhē(y)ik-, -hilik-; ˌtrəkˈsilik-\ *n* [ISV *truxilline* + *-ic*] **1 :** any of several crystalline stereoisomeric cyclic dicarboxylic acids $(C_6H_5)_2C_4H_4(COOH)_2$ that yield cinnamic acid on distillation; 2,4-diphenyl-cyclobutane-1,3-dicarboxylic acid: as **a :** an acid obtained from alpha-truxilline by hydrolysis or from cinnamic acid by irradiation — called also *alpha-truxillic acid* **b :** an acid obtained from alpha-truxillic acid by heating with acetic anhydride and sodium acetate and convertible again into the alpha isomer by stronger heating — called also *gamma-truxillic acid* **c :** an acid obtained from the potassium salt of alpha-truxillic acid by fusion with potassium hydroxide — called also *epsilon-truxillic acid* **2 :** TRUXINIC ACID

tru·xi·lline \trüˈhē(y)ən, -hilən; ˌtrəkˈsilən\ *n* -s [ISV *truxill-* (in *Truxillo coca*) + *-ine*] **:** either of two isomeric amorphous alkaloids $C_{38}H_{46}N_2O_8$ that are obtained from Truxillo coca and that yield on hydrolysis methanol, levorotatory ecgonine, and an acid: **a :** the isomer that yields alpha-truxillic acid — called also *alpha-truxilline* **b :** the isomer that yields beta-truxinic acid — called also *beta-truxilline*

tru·xi·llo coca \trüˈhē(,)(y)ō-\ *n, usu cap T* [fr. *Truxillo* (Trujillo), city in northwestern Peru] **:** COCA 2b

trux·in·ic acid \ˌtrəkˈsinik-\ *n* [ISV *truxilline* + *-ic*] **:** any of several crystalline stereoisomeric cyclic dicarboxylic acids $(C_6H_5)_2C_4H_4(COOH)_2$ that are isomeric with the truxillic acids and that also yield cinnamic acid on distillation; 3,4-diphenyl-cyclobutane-1,2-dicarboxylic acid: as **a :** an acid obtained from beta-truxilline by hydrolysis — called also *beta-truxillic acid, beta-truxinic acid* **b :** an acid obtained from the potassium salt of beta-truxinic acid by fusion with potassium hydroxide — called also *delta-truxillic acid, delta-truxinic acid*

trv *abbr* traverse

[1]**try** \ˈtrī\ *vb* **tried; tried; trying; tries** [ME *trien*, fr. AF *trier*, fr. OF, to pick out, sift] *vt* **1 a :** to examine or investigate judicially **:** examine by witnesses or other judicial evidence and the principle of law ⟨no fact *tried* by a jury shall be otherwise reexamined in any court of the United States, than according to the rules of the common law —*U.S.Constitution*⟩ ⟨the paucity of women on the superior bench is a serious shortcoming in ~*ing* these cases —*Current Biog.*⟩ **b** (1) **:** to conduct the trial of ⟨they arrested him and he was *tried* before a Federal jury —*Amer. Guide Series: Md.*⟩ (2) **:** to participate as lawyer or counsel in the judicial examination of ⟨any lawyer who has ever *tried* a real case —A.T.Vanderbilt⟩ **2 a :** to put to test by experiment, investigation, or trial (as for determining strength, endurance, worth, accuracy, truth, or utility) ⟨taught school, practiced law, *tried* mining —*Amer. Guide Series: Oregon*⟩ ⟨put his shoulder to the door, then he *tried* the shutters —Elsie Singmaster⟩ ⟨some other apparently inaccessible peak on which to ~ their ardor and endurance — S.P.B.Mais⟩ ⟨~*ing* their luck casting plugs into the surf — R.M.Hodesh⟩ — often used with *out* ⟨*tried* out several occupations —Bernard Kalb⟩ ⟨*tried* out various hypotheses as to the nature of heat —S.F.Mason⟩ ⟨~ out a play on the road⟩ **b :** to test to the limit or breaking point **:** subject to extreme trial (as of severe or continuous strain or extreme or undue hardship, provocation, or affliction) ⟨don't work too hard, darling, or ~ your eyes —Elizabeth Taylor⟩ ⟨here is a tale that will ~ your credulity —O.S.J.Gogarty⟩ ⟨enough to ~ the patience of a saint —Alban Baer⟩ **c :** to demonstrate, discover, or settle by a test or trial ⟨hath still been *tried* a holy man —Shak.⟩ ⟨ready to ~ the question with his fists —George Meredith⟩ **3 a** *obs* **:** PURIFY, REFINE ⟨silver *tried* in a furnace of earth, purified seven times —Ps 12:6 (AV)⟩ **b :** to melt down (as oil, tallow, or lard) and procure in a pure state **:** RENDER — often used with *out* ⟨~ out whale oil from the blubber⟩ ⟨~ out chicken fat for cracklings⟩ **4** *obs* **:** to know by experience **:** EXPERIENCE **5 :** to fit or finish with accuracy — usu. used with *up* ⟨the steel square . . . is used . . . for laying out and ~*ing* up right angles —G.A.McGarvey & H.H.Sherman⟩ **6 :** to attempt through the exertion of effort, labor, or thought ⟨*tries* to stop short at irony —A.M.Mizener⟩ ⟨*tried* to demonstrate the existence of a real language of science —T.H.Savory⟩ ⟨~ to swim a mile⟩ **:** make an effort for the purpose of ⟨*tried* walking without a crutch⟩ **7 :** TEASE 5 ~ *vi* **1** *of a ship* **:** to lie in a gale head to the wind under very little canvas **2 :** to make an attempt to achieve something or to carry out some action ⟨the girls will always be ~*ing* harder —*Management Behavior & Foreman Attitude*⟩ ⟨an adolescent urge to ~ for a good-night kiss —Lane Kauffmann⟩ — often used with *and* and a following verb ⟨a sad mistake to ~ and swim against the stream —George Santayana⟩ ⟨must therefore ~ and carry them with us on policy —Hugh Gaitskell⟩

syn ATTEMPT, ESSAY, ENDEAVOR, STRIVE, STRUGGLE: TRY is a simple word without much suggestive power; it may be used in reference to an attempt undertaken experimentally, tentatively, or uncertainly, or to an attempt ending in failure ⟨freedom in thought, the liberty to *try* and err —H.L.Mencken⟩ ⟨*tried* to have me assassinated three times —W.M. Thackeray⟩ ATTEMPT is almost always synonymous with TRY but may occas. be preferred in references to ventures of greater magnitude ⟨Father . . . do Thou finish above what I on earth have *attempted* —Thomas De Quincey⟩ ⟨here Shakespeare tackled a problem which proved too much for him. Why he *attempted* it at all is an insoluble puzzle —T.S.Eliot⟩ ESSAY, a rather formal term, may connote a preliminary canvassing or first beginning of a venture or its large and comprehensive nature ⟨the sculpture which attempted to unite repose and action . . . in a way which Phidias and Donatello were too prudent to *essay* —W.C.Brownell⟩ ⟨it is that continuity of evolution . . . that I have *essayed* to describe —J.L. Lowes⟩ ENDEAVOR may accentuate greater exertion, repeated effort, or continued search for expedients ⟨no art *endeavors* to express the emotions of the artist —Samuel Alexander⟩ ⟨the first step for every aspirant to culture is to *endeavor* to see things as they are —C.W.Eliot⟩ ⟨the wretch whom with such infinite pains and care I had *endeavored* to form —Mary W. Shelley⟩ STRIVE heightens notions of persistent, vigorous exertion to overcome opposition or hindrance ⟨her visitor, who held herself rigidly erect, and *strived* to mask her nervousness —G.B.Shaw⟩ ⟨was *striving* to come out of the filth, the flies, the poverty, the fishy smells —Sherwood Anderson⟩ ⟨loved his country deeply, and *strove* to serve her by lifting contemporary disputes into a larger air —John Buchan⟩ STRUGGLE implies continuing violent or strenuous exertion ⟨heroes fallen or *struggling* to advance —William Wordsworth⟩ **syn** see in addition AFFLICT, PROVE

— try conclusions : to test one's skill or strength against another person, an obstacle, or a challenging test — usu. used

TRUTH TABLE

a statement	a statement	*p* and *q* conjunction	*p* or *q* (inclusive) alternation	*p* if and only if *q* biconditional	if *p* then *q* conditional	not both *p* and *q* alternative denial	neither *p* nor *q* joint denial	*p* or *q* (exclusive) incompatibility	not *p* denial
p	q	$p \cdot q$	$p \vee q$	$p \equiv q$	$p \supset q$	$p \mid q$	$p \downarrow q$	$p + q$	$\sim p$
T	T	T	T	T	T	F	F	F	F
T	F	F	T	F	F	T	F	T	
F	T	F	T	F	T	T	F	T	T
F	F	F	F	T	T	T	T	F	

This table presents truth-values of the most important truth-functional connectives (conjunction ·, alternation ᵛ, biconditional ≡, conditional Ↄ, alternative denial |, joint denial ↓, incompatibility +, and denial ~). Examples: A conjunction $p \cdot q$ is true only if both of its arguments are true; a biconditional $p \equiv q$ is true only if its arguments are either both true or both false.

with *with* ⟨the fascination of the mountains is only fully known to . . . hardy bush-walkers who . . . *try conclusions* with them —*Walkabout*⟩ — **try one's hand :** to attempt something for the first time as an experiment or out of curiosity — usu. used with *at* ⟨*trying his hand* at an adventurous romance for boys —J.D. Hart⟩

²try \"\ *n* -ES **1** *obs* **:** TRIAL, TEST **2 :** an attempt esp. when undertaken with little hope of success, as one of a series, or when ending in failure ⟨an agreement . . . is not impossible, and they at least want to make a good ~ at it —Mark Gayn⟩ ⟨would go down in history as a nice ~ —R.M.Yoder⟩ ⟨hurled the cannonball farthest on the thirteenth through fifteenth *tries* —*Current Biog.*⟩ **3 a :** a play in rugby in which a player grounds the ball on or behind the opponent's goal line and which scores usu. four points and entitles the scoring side to try for a place-kick at the goal **b :** TRY FOR POINT

try back *vi* **:** to go back over something that has already been covered or attempted

try cock *n* **1 :** one of two or more cocks arranged one above the other to ascertain the water level in a steam boiler **:** GAUGE COCK **2 :** a cock for withdrawing a small quantity of liquid (as for testing)

try for point : an attempt made after scoring a touchdown in the game of football to kick a goal so as to score an additional point or to again carry the ball across the opponents' goal line or complete a forward pass in the opponents' end zone so as to score two additional points

try·gon \ˈtrīˌgän\ *n* -S [L, fr. Gk *trygōn*, of imit. origin] **:** STINGRAY

try·gon·i·dae \trīˈgänəˌdē\ [NL, fr. *Trygon*, genus of stingrays (fr. L *trygon* stingray) + *-idae*] *syn of* DASYATIDAE

try gun *n* **:** a gun having an adjustable stock to allow the user to determine the size and shape of stock best suited to him

trying *adj* [fr. pres. part. of ¹*try*] **:** causing severe hardship, annoyance, or irritation **:** severely straining the powers of endurance ⟨exposed their bodies to dangers greater than those of battle in long and ~ journeys —R.W.Southern⟩ ⟨no work on earth is more ~ than creative writing —Arnold Bennett⟩ ⟨his sorely tried and infuriatingly ~ wife —Charles Lee⟩ — **try·ing·ly** *adv* — **try·ing·ness** *n* -ES

try·ma \ˈtrīmə\ *n* -S [NL, fr. Gk, hole; fr. the inside of the drupe being hollow — more at TRONE] **:** a nutlike drupe (as the fruit of the walnut or hickory) in which the epicarp and mesocarp separate as a somewhat fleshy or leathery rind from the hard 2-valved endocarp

try on *vt* **1 :** to put on (a garment) in order to ascertain the fit **2 :** to use or test experimentally esp. to determine convenience or simplicity of operation **3** *Brit* **:** to attempt to impose upon a person **:** try to outwit a person by means of ⟨if you'd *tried on* anything funny, he'd have said so —Robert Westerby⟩ ⟨I am not the right woman to *try* this *on* with —Elizabeth Bowen⟩

try-on \ˈ=ˌ=\ *n* -S [*try on*] **1 :** the action or an instance of trying on ⟨in a fitting room for a *try-on* —*Architect & Building News*⟩ **2** *Brit* **:** an attempt at deceit ⟨this letter's a *try-on*, doesn't mean what it says —Henry Green⟩

try out *vi* **:** to participate in competition for a position esp. on an athletic team or in a play ⟨*try out* for the basketball team⟩ ⟨*try out* for the male lead⟩

tryout \ˈ=ˌ=\ *n* -S [*try out*] **:** an experimental performance or demonstration ⟨advisable to give actual classroom ~ to books under consideration before final adoption commitments —V.M.Rogers⟩ ⟨the first real ~ of collective security —T.J. Hamilton⟩: as **a :** a test of the performance of an athlete, actor, or other person to determine his ability to fill a part or position or meet the standards of a class ⟨scoring 590 points during ~s for U.S. shooting team —*Sports Illustrated*⟩ ⟨a card describing his radio ~ —*Current Biog.*⟩ **b :** a public performance or series of performances of a play prior to its official opening to determine public response and discover faults and make improvements ⟨the ~ period when he has to feed new lines to actors or to extract old lines from them fast enough for the changes to be incorporated by the next evening's performance —John Gassner⟩

try·pa \ˈtrīpə\ *n* -S [NL, fr. Gk *trypa*, *trypē* hole — more at TRYPAN-] **:** a pore in the front wall of the zooecium of a bryozoan — **tryp·i·ate** \ˈtripēət, -ēˌāt\ *adj*

trypa·flavine \ˌtripə, ˈtrīpə+\ *n* [ISV *trypa* (fr. Gk, hole) + *flavine*; fr. its use in disinfecting wounds] **:** the hydrochloride of acriflavine **:** ACRIFLAVINE

trypan- *or* **trypano-** *comb form* [NL, fr. Gk, fr. *trypanon* auger, borer, trepan, fr. *trypan* to bore, pierce through, fr. *trypa* hole; akin to OSlav *truplŭ* hollow, Gk *tetrainein* to pierce — more at THROW] **1 :** borer **:** auger ⟨*trypanosome*⟩ **2 :** trypanosome ⟨*trypanocidal*⟩

trypan blue \ˈtripən-, ˈtriˌpan-, trəˈpan-\ *n* [*trypan* ISV *trypan-*; fr. its being trypanocidal] **:** a disazo dye derived from tolidine and H acid that has limited use as an intravitam stain and esp. formerly in medicine

tryp·a·ne·id \ˌtripəˈnēəd\ *adj or n* [NL *Trypaneidae*] **:** TRYPETID

tryp·a·ne·idae \ˌtripəˈnēəˌdē\ [NL, fr. *Trypanea*, genus of trypetids (fr. Gk *trypanon* borer) + *-idae*] *syn of* TRYPETIDAE

trypano·ci·dal \trəˌpanəˈsīdᵊl, ˌtripənōˈs-\ *adj* [*trypan-* + *-cidal*] **:** tending or used to destroy trypanosomes

trypano·cide \trəˈpanəˌsīd, ˈtripənōˌs-\ *n* -S [ISV *trypan-* + *-cide*] **:** a trypanocidal agent

trypano·rhyn·cha \trəˌpanəˈriŋkə, ˌtripənōˈr-\ *n pl*, *cap* [NL, fr. *trypan-* + Gk *rhynchos* snout — more at RHYNCH-] **:** an order of Cestoda comprising tapeworms parasitic in elasmobranch fishes and distinguished by a scolex with two or four bothridia and four spiny retractile tentacles for attachment to the host — **trypano·rhyn·chan** \ˌ=ˌ==ˈriŋkən, ˌ===-\ *adj or n*

trypano·so·ma \trəˌpanəˈsōmə, ˌtripənōˈs-\ *n* [NL, fr. *trypan-* (fr. Gk, fr. *trypanon* auger, borer) + *-soma*] **1** *cap* **:** a genus (the type of the family Trypanosomatidae) comprising flagellates that as adults are elongated and somewhat spindle-shaped, have a posteriorly arising flagellum which passes forward at the margin of an undulating membrane and emerges near the anterior end of the body as a short free flagellum, and are parasitic in the blood or rarely the tissues of vertebrates, that in the development phase which occurs in the digestive tract of a blood-sucking invertebrate and usu. an insect pass through a series of changes comparable to the typical forms of members of the genera *Leishmania*, *Leptomonas*, and *Crithidia*, multiply freely, and pass ultimately to the mouthparts or salivary structures whence they may be inoculated into a new vertebrate host bitten by the invertebrate host, and that are responsible for various serious diseases of man and domestic animals — compare CHAGAS' DISEASE, DOURINE, NAGANA, SLEEPING SICKNESS, SURRA **2** *pl* **trypanosomas** \-məz\ *or* **trypanosoma·ta** \-mədə\ **:** any flagellate of the genus *Trypanosoma*; *often* **:** any member of the family Trypanosomatidae that has the typical form of a mature blood trypanosome ⟨some leptomonads become typical ~s under culture in special media⟩

trypano·so·mat·i·dae \-ˌsōˈmadəˌdē\ *n pl*, *cap* [NL, fr. *Trypanosomat-*, *Trypanosoma*, type genus + *-idae*] **:** a family of strictly parasitic more or less slender and elongated uniflagellate protozoans (order Protomonadina) having a single nucleus and a kinetoplast that includes serious pathogens of man and domestic animals usu. having complex host relations — see CRITHIDIA, HERPETOMONAS, LEISHMANIA, LEPTOMONAS, PHYTOMONAS, TRYPANOSOMA

trypano·some \trəˈpanəˌsōm, ˈtripənōˌs-\ *n* -S [NL *Trypanosoma*] **:** a protozoan of the genus *Trypanosoma*

trypano·so·mi·a·sis \ˌ=ˌ==ˌsōˈmīəsəs, ˌ===-\ *n*, *pl* **trypanosomia·ses** \-əˌsēz\ [NL, fr. *Trypanosoma* + *-iasis*] **:** infection with or disease caused by trypanosomes — compare CHAGAS' DISEASE, ENCEPHALITIS, SLEEPING SICKNESS, SURRA

trypan red \TRYPAN *as in* TRYPAN BLUE\ *n* [*trypan* ISV *trypan-*] **:** a disazo dye derived from benzidine and beta-naphthylamine and formerly used as a remedy in trypanosomiasis

tryp·ar·sa·mide \trəˈpärsəˌmīd, -məd\ *n* [fr. *Tryparsamide*, a trademark] **:** a crystalline organic arsenical $H_2NCOCH_2NHC_6H_4AsO_3HNa.½H_2O$ used in the treatment of African sleeping sickness and syphilis of the central nervous system

¹try·petid \trəˈpedəd, -pēd-\ *adj* [NL *Trypetidae*] **:** of or relating to the Trypetidae

²trypetid \"\ *n* -S **:** a fly of the family Trypetidae

try·pet·i·dae \-pedəˌdē\ *n pl*, *cap* [NL, fr. *Trypeta*, type genus (fr. Gk *trypētēs* borer, fr. *trypan* to bore) + *-idae* — more at TRYPAN-] **:** a family of acalyptrate muscoid flies having a piercing ovipositor and having the wings usu. banded or spotted that includes a number of important pests of various fruits (as the Mediterranean fruit fly)

tryp·o·graph \ˈtripəˌgraf, -räf\ *n* [Gk *trypan* to bore, pierce through + E *-o-* + *-graph*] **:** a mimeograph using a stencil made by placing treated paper over a metal plate having sharp corrugations and writing with a stylus whose pressure causes the corrugations to pierce the paper and form the design — **tryp·o·graph·ic** \ˌ=ˌ=ˈgrafik\ *adj*

try-pot \ˈ=ˌ=\ *n* **:** a metallic pot used on a whaler or on shore to render blubber

tryp·sin \ˈtripsən\ *n* -S [ISV *try-* (fr. Gk *tryein* to wear out (i.e., digest) + *-psin* (as in *pepsin*) — more at THROE] **1 :** a crystallizable proteinase that differs from pepsin in several ways (as in being most active in a slightly alkaline medium and in hydrolyzing esters as well as amides) and that is produced and secreted in the pancreatic juice in the form of inactive trypsinogen and activated in the intestine — compare CHYMOTRYPSIN **2 :** a preparation from the pancreatic juice differing from pancreatin in containing principally proteolytic enzymes and used chiefly as a digestive and lytic agent

tryp·sin·ize \-sə,nīz\ *vt* -ED/-ING/-S **:** to subject to the action of trypsin

tryp·sin·o·gen \tripˈsinəjən, -ˌjen\ *n* -S [ISV *trypsin* + *-o-* + *-gen*] **:** the crystallizable precursor of trypsin present in the acinar cells of the pancreas and converted into trypsin by the action of trypsin itself, enterokinase, or other proteolytic enzyme

trypt·amine \ˈtriptəˌmēn, tripˈtaˌm-, -mən\ *n* [*trypt-* (in *tryptophan*) + *amine*] **:** a crystalline amine $C_8H_6NCH_2CH_2NH_2$ formed by decomposition of tryptophan or made synthetically; 3-(2-amino-ethyl)-indole — compare SEROTONIN

tryp·tic \ˈtriptik\ *adj* [ISV *trypsin* + *-tic* (as in *peptic*)] **1 :** of or relating to trypsin or to its action **2 :** produced by trypsin ⟨~ digestion⟩

tryptique *also* **tryptyque** *var of* TRIPTYQUE

tryp·tone \ˈtripˌtōn\ *n* -S [ISV *trypsin* + *-tone* (as in *peptone*)] **:** a peptone produced by the action of trypsin

tryp·to·phan \ˈtriptəˌfan\ *also* **tryp·to·phane** \-fān\ *n* -S [ISV *tryptic* + *-o-* + *-phane*] **:** a crystalline amino acid $(C_8H_6N)CH_2CH(NH_2)COOH$ that is obtained in the levorotatory L form from casein, fibrin, and other proteins (as by tryptic digestion) and in the racemic form by synthesis, that differs from most other naturally occurring amino acids in its instability toward mineral acids, and that is essential in the nutrition of animals and man; β-3-indolyl-alanine

tryp·topha·nase \ˈtriptəfəˌnās, tripˈtäf-, -āz\ *n* -S [*tryptophan* + *-ase*] **:** an enzyme that catalyzes the decomposition of tryptophan into indole, pyruvic acid, and ammonia and that is present esp. in the colon bacillus

try·sail *also* **tri·sail** \ˈtrīsəl (*usual nautical pronunc*), -ˌsāl\ *n* [²*try* + *sail*] **1 :** a fore-and-aft sail bent to a gaff, hoisted on a lower mast or a small mast close abaft and usu. connected to a lower mast, and used chiefly as a storm sail — see SHIP illustration **2 :** a small and strongly made sail either triangular or with a very short gaff set in place of the mainsail of a yacht in heavy weather

try square *n* **:** an instrument consisting of two straightedges secured at right angles to each other and used for laying off right angles and testing whether work is square — called also *right-angle gauge*

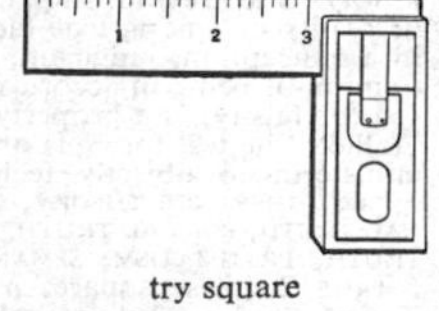
try square

¹tryst \ˈtrist, -rīst\ *n* -S [ME *tryst*, *trist*, *triste* agreement, tryst, appointed station in hunting, fr. OF *triste* appointed station in hunting, watch post, ambush, prob. of Scand origin; akin to ON *treysta* to make strong and safe, make firm, trust, *traust* trust — more at TRUST] **1** *Scot* **:** a mutual agreement **2 a :** an agreement esp. between lovers to meet at a specified time and place ⟨the merciless sea keeps ~ with the fury of the winds —Lilian S. Taylor⟩ **b :** an agreed upon meeting; *also* **:** a place specified for a tryst ⟨suburban ~s that offered real cover —Rebecca West⟩ **3** *Scot* **:** MARKET, FAIR; *esp* **:** a fixed annual cattle market **syn** see ENGAGEMENT

²tryst \"\ *vb* -ED/-ING/-S [ME *trysten*, *tristen*, fr. *tryst*, *trist* tryst] *vi* **1** *chiefly Scot* **:** to agree upon a meeting **:** make a tryst; *also* **:** to keep a tryst **:** MEET **2** *obs Scot* **:** to come to terms **:** NEGOTIATE **3** *obs* **:** to happen at the same time ~ *vt* **1** *Scot* **:** to agree to meet at a certain time or place **:** make tryst with **2** *Scot* **:** to affect with good or evil **:** VISIT

tryst·er \-stə(r)\ *n* -S **:** one that trysts

tryworks \ˈ=ˌ=\ *n pl* [¹*try* + *works*] **:** a brick furnace in which try-pots are placed; *also* **:** the furnace with the pots

ts *abbr* teaspoon; teaspoonful

TS *abbr* **1** *often not cap* tensile strength **2** test solution **3** tool steel **4** tough situation **5** transport and supply **6** transverse section **7** tub-sized **8** typescript

t's *or* **ts** *pl of* T

tsaddik *also* **tsadik** *var of* ZADDIK

tsa·de \ˈtsä-(ˌ)de, -)dē\ *n* -S [Heb *ṣādhē*] **:** SADHE

tsa·ko·ni·an \tsəˈkōnēən\ *n* -S *usu cap* [*Tsakon*, region in the eastern Peloponnesus, Greece + E *-an*] **:** a modern dialect of Greek spoken in a restricted area in the Peloponnesus and preserving some features of ancient non-Koine dialect

tsa·ma \ˈtsämə\ *n* -S [Afrik, fr. Hottentot (Nama dial.) *tsamas*] *Africa* **:** WATERMELON

tsam·ba \ˈtsämbə\ *also* **tsam·pa** \-mpə\ *n* -S [Tibetan *tsampa*] **:** flour made from parched ground barley or wheat that is the chief cereal food in and near Tibet

tsan·tsa \ˈtsäntsə\ *n* -S [Jivaro] **:** a shrunken head; *specif* **:** one prepared by a Jivaro Indian

tsao \ˈtsau̇\ *n* -S [Chin (Pek) *tsao³*] **:** JUJUBE

tsar *var of* CZAR

tsat·lee \ˈtsatˌlē\ *n* -S [modif. of Chin (Pek) *Ch'i¹-li³*, lit., seven li] **:** rough irregular raw silk from China

t scale *n*, *usu cap T* [*t* (as in *t-test*)] **:** a scale for expressing the results of all tests in comparable form as standard scores orig. based upon the performance of a representative group of twelve-year-old children having a mean of 50 and a standard deviation of 10

tscheff·kin·ite \ˈchefkəˌnīt\ *n* -S [G *tschewkinit* — more at CHEVKINITE] **:** CHEVKINITE

tscher·mig·ite \ˈchərmiˌgīt, ˈcher-\ *n* -S [G *tschermigit*, fr. *Tschermig*, Bohemia, its locality + G *-it* -ite] **:** ALUM 1b

tsedakah *var of* TZEDAKAH

tsessebe *or* **tesseby** *var of* SASSABY

tset·saut \ˈtsetˌsau̇t\ *n*, *pl* **tsetsaut** *or* **tsetsauts** *usu cap* **1 a :** an Athapaskan people of west central British Columbia **b :** a member of the Tsetsaut people **2 :** the language of the Tsetsaut people

tset·se \ˈsˌetsē, ˈtˌ, ˈtsˌ, ˌēt-, -tsi *sometimes* -tsə *or* ˈsēsē *or* ˈsēsi\ *or* **tsetse fly** *n*, *pl* **tsetse** *or* **tsetses** *or* **tsetse flies** [Afrik, fr. Tswana *tsêtsê*] **:** any of several muscoid flies of the genus *Glossina* that occur in Africa south of the Sahara desert — see NAGANA, SLEEPING SICKNESS

tsetse disease *or* **tsetse fly disease** *n* **:** NAGANA

TSH *abbr* **1** Their Serene Highnesses **2** thyroid stimulating hormone

t-shaped \ˈ=ˌ=\ *adj*, *cap T* **:** having the shape of a capital T

tshi *usu cap*, *var of* TWI

tshi·lu·ba \chəˈlübə\ *n*, *usu cap* **:** one of the four major trade languages of Congo used most widely in the southern part of the country — called also *Luba*; compare KINGWANA, KONGO, LINGALA

t-shirt *cap T*, *also* **tee shirt** \ˈtē,=\ *n* [so called fr. its being T-shaped] **:** a slip-on collarless short-sleeved undershirt of cotton jersey for men; *also* **:** a cotton or wool jersey outer shirt of similar design for men and women made with short or long sleeves and sometimes a collar

T-shirt 1

tshon \ˈchōn\ *usu cap*, *var of* CHON

tshwr *abbr* thundershower

tsim·shi·an \ˈchimshēən, ˈtsi-\ *or* **chimme·sy·an** \-mzēən, -msē-\ *n*, *pl* **tsimshian** *or* **tsimshians** *or* **chimmesyan** *or* **chimmesyans** *usu cap* **1 a :** an Indian people of the lower Skeena and Nass valleys and the adjacent coast of British Columbia **b :** a member of such people **2 :** a language of the Tsimshian people **3 :** a language family of the Penutian stock comprising only the Tsimshian language

tsi·nan \ˈjēˈnän, ˈtsē-\ *adj*, *usu cap* [fr. *Tsinan* (Chinan), China] **:** of or from the city of Tsinan, China **:** of the kind or style prevalent in Tsinan

tsine *n*, *pl* **tsine** \ˈ(t)sīn\ [Burmese *tsaiṅ*] **:** BANTENG

tsing·tao \ˈchiŋˈdau̇, ˈtsiŋˈtau̇\ *adj*, *usu cap* [fr. *Tsingtao*, China] **:** of or from the city of Tsingtao, China **:** of the kind or style prevalent in Tsingtao

tsi·tsi·har \ˈtsētsēˌhär, ˈchēchē-\ *adj*, *usu cap* [fr. *Tsitsihar*, Manchuria] **:** of or from the city of Tsitsihar, Manchuria **:** of the kind or style prevalent in Tsitsihar

tsitsith *var of* ZIZITH

t slot *cap T*, *also* **tee slot** *n* **:** a T-shaped slot

t-slot cutter *n*, *cap T* **:** a small side-milling cutter with a necked-down shank for completing the bottoms of T slots

TSO *abbr* town suboffice

tsotsil *usu cap*, *var of* TZOTZIL

tsp *abbr* teaspoon; teaspoonful

TSP *abbr* trisodium phosphate

tspn *abbr* teaspoon; teaspoonful

tspt *abbr* transport

t square *cap T*, *also* **tee square** *n* [so called fr. its shape] **:** a

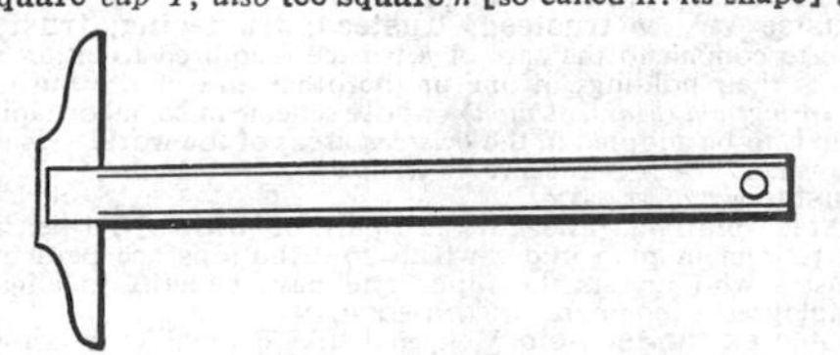
T square

ruler with a crosspiece or head at one end used in making parallel lines or as a support for triangles used in drawing lines at different angles to the ruler

TSR *abbr* traveling stock reserve

TSS *abbr* twin-screw steamer

tstm *abbr* thunderstorm

t-stop system *n*, *usu cap T* [*t* (symbol for *total light transmission*)] **:** a system for indicating camera apertures by means of T-numbers

t-strap \ˈ=ˌ=\ *n*, *cap T* **1 :** a T-shaped part of an open shoe formed by a strap rising from the throat over the instep and either fastening to an ankle strap or dividing at the top to form an ankle strap **2 :** a shoe and esp. a sandal having a T-strap

TSU *abbr* this side up

tsu·bo \ˈ(t)sü(ˌ)bō\ *n*, *pl* **tsubo** [Jap] **:** a Japanese unit of area equal to 35.58 square feet

tsu·ga \ˈ(t)sügə\ *n*, *cap* [NL, fr. Jap, larch] **:** a genus of Asiatic and No. American evergreen trees (family Pinaceae) comprising the hemlocks and being distinguished by drooping branches, linear leaves with persistent petiole bases, and reflexed cones

tsugaresinol \ˌ==ˈ=ˌ=\ *n* [NL *Tsuga* + E *resinol*] **:** CONIDENDRIN

tsu·ku·pin \ˈ(t)sükəpən\ *n* -S [native name in the Yap islands] **:** a large sailing canoe of the Yap islands having a triangular sail and a single outrigger

tsu·meb·ite \ˈ(t)süməˌbīt\ *n* -S [*Tsumeb*, region in southwestern Africa + E *-ite*] **:** a mineral $Pb_2Cu(PO_4)(OH)_3.3H_2O$ consisting of a hydrous basic lead copper phosphate and occurring in small emerald-green monoclinic crystals (hardness 3.5, sp. gr. 6.1)

tsu·nami \(t)süˈnämē, -namē\ *n*, *pl* **tsunamis** *also* **tsunami** [Jap, fr. *tsu* port, harbor + *nami* wave, sea] **:** a seismic disturbance of the ocean **:** a great sea wave produced by submarine earth movement or volcanic eruption **:** TIDAL WAVE — **tsu·namic** \-mik\ *adj*

tsu·tsu·ga·mu·shi disease \ˌ(t)sütsəgəˈmüshē-\ *n* [Jap *tsutsugamushi* scrub typhus mite, fr. *tsutsuga* sickness + *mushi* insect] **:** an acute febrile disease resembling louse-borne typhus orig. known from Japan but widely distributed in the western Pacific area and caused by a rickettsia (*Rickettsia tsutsugamushi* or *R. orientalis*) transmitted by larval mites (esp. *Trombicula akamushi*) that also occur on several voles which act as reservoir hosts of the infection —called also *scrub typhus*

tsutsugamushi mite *n* **:** any of several mites of the genus *Trombicula* that are vectors of the rickettsia causing tsutsugamushi disease

tswa \ˈ(t)swä, ˈchwä, chəˈwä\ *n*, *pl* **tswa** *or* **tswas** *usu cap* **1 a :** a southeastern African people chiefly of northern Transvaal and southern Mozambique **b :** a member of such people **2 :** a Bantu language of the Tswa people

tswa·na *or* **chua·na** \ˈ(t)swänə, ˈchwä-, chəˈwä-\ *n*, *pl* **tswana** *or* **tswanas** *or* **chuana** *or* **chuanas** *usu cap* **1 a :** any of the various Bantu-speaking Negro peoples dwelling between the Orange and Zambezi rivers, particularly in Bechuanaland, southern Africa **b :** a member of any of such peoples **2 :** a Bantu language of the Tswana people — compare SOTHO

tswett column \ˈswet-\ *n*, *usu cap T* [after Mikhail *Tswett* †1920 Russ. botanist] **:** a tubular glass device with a stopcock at the bottom used for the chromatographic separation of related compounds and esp. of plant pigments (as in chlorophyll) — compare CHROMATOGRAPHY

TT *abbr* **1** teetotaller **2** telegraphic transfer **3** teletype; teletypewriter **4** torpedo tube **5** Trinity term **6** tuberculin tested

Tt *symbol* trigesimo-secundo

TTC \ˌtēˌtēˈsē\ *abbr or n* -S triphenyltetrazolium chloride

t-test \ˈ=ˌ=\ *n* [*t* (prob. abbr. of *true*)] **:** a statistical test involving means of normal populations with unknown standard deviations and using small samples based on a variable t equal to the difference between the mean of the sample and the mean of the population divided by a quotient formed by dividing the standard deviation of the sample by the square root of the number in the sample

TTL *abbr* to take leave

t-tube \ˈ=ˌ=\ *n*, *cap 1st T* **:** a rubber tube in the form of a T used to drain the common bile duct

TU *abbr* **1** thermal unit **2** toxic unit **3** trade union **4** traffic unit **5** transmission unit

tu·a·mo·tu \ˌtüəˈmō(ˌ)tü\ *n* -S *usu cap* [Tuamotu *tua* back + *motu* islet] **:** the Polynesian language of the Tuamotuan people

¹tu·a·mo·tu·an \ˌ==ˈmōtüən\ *adj*, *usu cap* [*Tuamotu* islands, So. Pacific Ocean + E *-an*, adj. suffix] **:** of or relating to the Tuamotu archipelago or its inhabitants

²tuamotuan \"\ *n* -S *usu cap* [*Tuamotu* islands + E *-an*, n. suffix] **1 :** a native of the Tuamotu islands **2 :** TUAMOTU

tuan \tüˈän\ *n* -S [Malay] **:** SIR, MASTER, LORD — used as a form of respectful address to a male by Malay-speaking persons

tuan be·sar \-bāˈsär\ *n* [Malay, great master] **:** a European boss in colonial Malaysia

tua·reg *also* **toua·reg** \ˈtwäˌreg\ *n*, *pl* **tuareg** *or* **tuaregs** *also* **touareg** *or* **touaregs** *usu cap* [Ar *Tawāriq*] **1 :** one of the dominant nomads of the central and western Sahara and along the Middle Niger from Timbuktu to Nigeria who are perhaps descendants of the ancient Gaetulians, have preserved their Hamitic speech in great purity and also their alphabet derived prob. from the Punic but have adopted the Muslim religion, are tall, of Mediterranean features, and occas. light-haired, and whose men wear a cloth about the face but whose women go unveiled — compare TIFINAGH **2 :** TAMASHEK

tu·art *also* **tou·art** \ˈtüə(r)t\ *n* -S [native name in Western Australia] **:** an Australian white gum (*Eucalyptus gomphocephala*) yielding hard durable timber used esp. for ships

tu·a·ta·ra \ˌtüəˈtärə\ *also* **tu·a·te·ra** \-ˈterə\ *n* -S [Maori *tuatàra*, fr. *tua* back + *tara* spine] **:** a large reptile (*Sphenodon punctatum*) formerly common in New Zealand but now confined to certain islets near the coast that is the only surviving rhynchocephalian, has a pineal body which shows distinct traces of having functioned as an eye in past ages, reaches a length of two and a half feet, is dark olive-green with small white or yellowish specks on the sides, has yellow spines along the back except on the neck, and in general resembles an iguana

tu·ath \ˈtüə\ *n* -s [IrGael, state, country, tribe, people, fr. OIr — more at DUTCH] **:** STATE 5a; *also* **:** the territory occupied by a tuath

¹tub \ˈtəb\ *n* -s [ME *tubbe, tobbe,* fr. MD; akin to MLG *tubbe, tobbe* tub] **1 :** a wide low vessel usu. about the size of a half barrel and orig. formed with wooden staves, round bottom, and hoops but now often of metal or plastic ⟨a galvanized wash ~⟩ ⟨a ~ for lard⟩ **2** *Brit* **:** SAPPHIRINE GURNARD **3 :** something shaped like or felt to resemble a tub: as **a :** an old, inferior, or slow-moving boat **b :** an old-fashioned pulpit **c** (1) **:** a box or bucket in which coal or ore is sent up a shaft (2) **:** KEEVE (3) **:** a tram used underground (4) **:** a puddling tub **d :** an old-fashioned hand-drawn fire engine **e** *slang* **:** an excessively corpulent person **f :** a container in which a unit of commercial fishing gear is coiled down; *sometimes* **:** ¹SKATE 2b **g :** a mail hamper **4 :** a vessel to contain water for bathing **:** BATHTUB; *also* **:** a bath or the act of taking a bath ⟨nothing like a hot ~ to relax tired muscles⟩ **5 a :** the amount that a tub will hold **:** the contents of a tub ⟨a ~ of butter was consumed⟩ **b** *Brit* **:** a keg holding about four gallons and formerly used to smuggle spirits **6 a :** a pair-oared gig with a place for a coach in the stern used esp. in training oarsmen **b :** a rack for topsail halyards **c :** a lookout enclosure on a mast **7 :** a synchronized swimming stunt in which from a back layout position the knees are brought to the chest and the body is rotated at least once in a horizontal position

tub 1

²tub \"\ *adj* **1 :** of, relating to, or like a tub **:** using or kept in a tub ⟨~ butter⟩ **2 :** WASH ⟨~ silk⟩

³tub \"\ *vb* **tubbed; tubbed; tubbing; tubs** *vt* **1 :** to wash or bathe in a tub ⟨*tubbing* clothes bright and early on Monday⟩ **2 :** to line (as a mine shaft) with tubbing **:** keep back water with tubbing — sometimes used with *off* **3 a :** to put or store in a tub ⟨always *tubbed* his pork in sweetened brine⟩ **b :** to plant in a tub ⟨*tubbed* azalias⟩ **4 :** to coach (a rower) in a tub ~ *vi* **1 :** to use a bathtub **:** take a bath **:** BATHE **2 :** to undergo washing ⟨synthetics that ~ well⟩ **3 :** to practice rowing in a tub

¹tu·ba \ˈtübə\ *n* -s [Ar *ṭūbā* blessed (found in Koran 13:28 and interpreted by various commentators as meaning a tree), fr. Aram, goodness] **:** a mythical tree believed to grow in the Muslim paradise

²tu·ba \ˈt(y)übə\ *n* -s *see sense 2* [It, fr. L, trumpet — more at TUBE] **1 :** a large low-pitched member of the bugle or saxhorn family of brass wind instruments having a conical bore and a cup-shaped mouthpiece and typically made to be held upright but in the largest sizes often made to encircle the player's body for easier carrying in marching bands — compare HELICON, SOUSAPHONE **2** *pl usu* **tu·bae** \-ü,bē\ **:** a straight bronze trumpet of the ancient Romans **3 :** a powerful organ reed stop of 8-foot pitch **4 :** a high-powered radar transmitter used to jam enemy radar

tuba 1

³tu·ba \ˈtübə\ *n* -s [Tag *tubâ*] **1 a :** any of various plants (as a derris or the physic nut) whose sap, bark, or seeds yield toxic substances used esp. in Malaysia and the Philippines as fish poisons; *also* **:** one of these toxic substances **2 a :** the usu. fermented sap of a palm (as a nipa or coconut palm) that is used esp. in the Philippines in the distillation of alcohol and is the source of beno **:** TODDY 1 **b :** BENO

⁴tuba \"\ *n, pl* **tuba** *or* **tubas** *usu cap* **:** one of the tatarized Samoyed

tuba clarion *n* **:** a 4-foot pipe-organ tuba

tub·age \ˈt(y)übij\ *n* -s [¹*tube* + *-age*] **1 :** TUBING **2 :** the act or process of inserting in a usu. smoothbore gun of large caliber a tube of wrought iron or steel that increases the strength but decreases the caliber of the gun

tu·ba·ic acid \tüˈbāik-\ *n* [ISV ³*tuba* + *-ic*] **:** a crystalline phenolic acid $C_3H_5C_8H_5O(OH)COOH$ derived from coumaran and formed from rotenone by cleavage with strong alkali

tub·al \-bəl\ *adj* **:** of, relating to, or involving a tube and esp. a fallopian tube

tubal pregnancy *n* **:** ectopic pregnancy in a fallopian tube

tuba major *n* [NL, major tuba] **1 :** a 16-foot pipe-organ tuba **2 :** an 8-foot tuba mirabilis

tuba mi·rab·i·lis \-məˈrabələs\ *n* [NL, wonderful tuba] **:** a very loud high-pressure solo pipe-organ stop of the trumpet class

tu·bate \ˈt(y)ü,bāt\ *adj* [¹*tube* + *-ate*] **:** having or forming a tube **:** TUBIFORM, TUBULAR ⟨a ~ gland⟩

tü·ba·tu·la·bal \,tübətüˈläbəl\ *n, pl* **tübatulabal** *or* **tübatulabals** *usu cap* [Shoshoni, pine-nut eaters] **1 a :** a Shoshonean people of the upper Kern river valley, south central California **b :** a member of such people **2 :** the language of the Tübatulabal

tub·ba·ble \ˈtəbəbəl\ *adj* **:** suitable for tubbing **:** capable of being washed without damage

tub·bal \ˈtəbəl\ *n* -s [prob. alter. of *twibil*] *dial Eng* **:** MATTOCK

tub basket *n* **:** a round basket having a wooden bottom and straight sides of veneer staves

tubbed *past of* TUB

¹tub·ber \ˈtəbə(r)\ *n* -s [prob. alter. (influenced by *-er*) of *twibil*] **:** a Cornish mining pickax

²tubber \"\ *n* [¹*tub* + *-er*] **:** one that makes or works with tubs: as **a :** COOPER **b :** a worker who cleans jewelry in a tumbling machine **c :** a user of a tub (as a washer or bather)

tub·bie \ˈtəbi\ *n* -s [¹*tub* + *-ie*] *dial Brit* **:** COOPER; *also* **:** a cooper's helper

tub·bi·ness \ˈtəbēnəs\ *n* -ES **:** the quality or state of being tubby **:** CORPULENCE

tub·bing \ˈtəbiŋ, -bēŋ\ *n* -s [¹*tub* + *-ing*] **1 :** the making of tubs; *also* **:** materials for making tubs **:** tub stock **2 :** a lining of timber or metal for a shaft (as in a mine); *esp* **:** a watertight shaft lining consisting of a series of cast-iron cylinders bolted together and used to sink through water-bearing strata

tub·bish \-bish\ *adj* **:** resembling a tub **:** rather tubby

tub·by \-bē, -bi\ *adj* -ER/-EST **:** resembling or suggesting a tub: as **a :** resembling a tub in round thick clumsy outline; *esp* **:** pudgily fat **b :** sounding dull and without proper resonance or freedom of sound ⟨a ~ violin⟩

tub–cart \ˈ=,=\ *n* **:** GOVERNESS CART

tub chair *n* **:** a large rounded upholstered easy chair usu. with semicircular back and no separate arms — compare BARREL CHAIR

tub desk *n* **:** a desk with an open top having divisions for filing cards

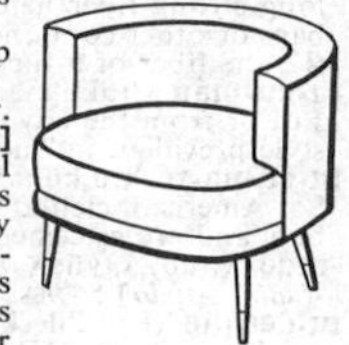
tub chair

¹tube \ˈt(y)üb\ *n* -s *often attrib* [F, fr. L *tubus;* akin to L *tuba* trumpet] **1 a :** a hollow elongated usu. cylindrical body that is used esp. to convey fluids and is mechanically nearly or precisely the same as a pipe but in use is arbitrarily associated with particular items and devices ⟨a mélange of iron pipes and glass ~*s*⟩ ⟨pipes leading to a boiler and continuous through valves with the ~*s* of the boiler proper⟩ **b** (1) **:** a slender channel within a plant or animal body **:** DUCT — see BRONCHIAL TUBE, FALLOPIAN TUBE, POLLEN TUBE (2) **:** the narrow basal portion of a gamopetalous corolla or a gamosepalous calyx **:** the united part of a monadelphous androecium (3) **:** a more or less cylindrical sometimes crooked or spirally twisted case secreted or constructed by many annelids, a few larval insects, and some other animals for protection or concealment (4) **:** one of the siphons of a bivalve mollusk **2 a** *archaic* **:** something (as a telescope) with a tube or tubular part as its chief feature **b** *archaic* **:** a cannon or other firearm **c :** TUBULAR SKATE **3 :** any of various usu. cylindrical structures or devices felt to resemble or functioning in the manner of a tube: as **a :** the inner cylinder of a built-up gun usu. extending from the inner face of the breechblock to the muzzle, carrying the rifling on its inner surface, and surrounded by the jacket and hoops if any are used; *also* **:** the whole cylindrical piece of metal surrounding the bore **b** (1) **:** an often complex piece of laboratory or technical apparatus usu. of glass and commonly serving to isolate or convey a product of reaction ⟨a distillation ~⟩ — see FERMENTATION TUBE (2) **:** TEST TUBE **c :** a collapsible cylindrical metal container from which a paste is dispensed by squeezing ⟨a toothpaste ~⟩ **d** (1) **:** a tunnel for vehicular or rail traffic (2) **:** a tunnel housing an aqueduct or other underground duct (3) *Brit* **:** SUBWAY 1b **e :** a hollow cylindrical device (as a cannula) used for insertion into bodily passages or hollow organs for removal or injection of materials **f** (1) *archaic* **:** PIPE 6a (2) **:** the basically cylindrical part connecting the mouthpiece and bell of a wind instrument **g :** a cylindrical core without flange or head on which yarn or thread may be wound **h :** a woman's narrow fitted garment (as a skirt or dress) **4 :** INNER TUBE **5 :** ELECTRON TUBE **6 :** VACUUM TUBE

²tube \"\ *vb* -ED/-ING/-S *vt* **:** to furnish with, enclose in, or pass through a tube ⟨~ a well⟩ ⟨~ media in bacteriology⟩; *also* **:** to form into or wind on a tube ⟨~ yarn⟩ ~ *vi, chiefly Brit* **:** to go by subway

tube cell *n* **1 :** one of the two cells that is produced by division of the microspore nucleus in the development of the male gametophyte in higher plants and that functions in development of the pollen tube **2 :** any of the cells in a wheat grain having long axes parallel to those of the epicarp cells, appearing as rings in transection, and forming the inner epidermis of the grain

tube coral *n* **:** an organ-pipe coral or a related fossil coral

tu·bec·to·my \t(y)üˈbektəmē\ *n* -ES [¹*tube* + *-ectomy*] **:** surgical excision of a fallopian tube

tube culture *n* **:** a culture of microorganisms in a test tube

tube curare *n* **:** CURARE 3

tubed *adj, of a horse* **:** tracheotomized and fitted with a metal breathing tube (as for the relief of broken wind)

tube door *n* **:** a door in the smoke chamber of some boilers to permit access to the fire tubes

tube–feed \ˈ=,=\ *vt* **:** to feed through or by means of a tube — compare GAVAGE

tubeflower \ˈ=,==\ *n* **:** an East Indian shrub (*Clerodendron siphonanthus*) having white flowers with a long slender corolla tube

tube foot *n* **:** one of numerous small tentacular flexible tubular processes of starfishes, sea urchins, and most holothurians bearing at the end an adhesive sucker, being extensions of the water-vascular system, employed in crawling or in holding on to objects, and serving also in respiration and as tactile organs

tube generator *n* **:** a generator of alternating current in which electron tubes are used to convert the applied electric power into audio or radio-frequency power

tubehearted \ˈ=,==\ *adj* **:** having pulsating sinuses functioning as a heart

tube·less \ˈt(y)übləs\ *adj* **:** lacking a tube; *specif* **:** being a pneumatic tire that does not depend on an inner tube for airtightness

tube·let \-lət\ *n* -s **:** a small tube **:** TUBULE

tubelike \ˈ=,=\ *adj* **:** resembling or having the form of a tube

tubemaker \ˈ=,==\ *n* **:** one that makes tubes; *esp* **:** an animal or larva that lives in a tubular case of its own fabrication

tube·man \ˈ=mən\ *n, pl* **tubemen** *Brit* **:** a subway worker

tube mill *n* **:** a grinding mill that consists of a long revolving tube containing flint pebbles or steel balls or slugs and is used for pulverizing (as in cement manufacturing) — compare BALL MILL

tube–nosed \ˈ=,=\ *adj* **:** having the nostrils prolonged in the form of horny tubes ⟨petrels are *tube-nosed* birds⟩

tube–nosed bat *n* **:** any of several fruit bats (genus *Nyctimene*) of Australia and the southwest Pacific distinguished by nostrils drawn out into diverging tubes

tube nucleus *n* **:** the one of the two nuclei formed by mitotic division of a microspore during the formation of a pollen grain that is held to control subsequent growth of the pollen tube and that does not divide again — compare GENERATIVE NUCLEUS

tube of bel·li·ni \-bəˈlēnē\ *usu cap B* [after Lorenzo *Bellini* †1704 Ital. anatomist] **:** any of the large excretory ducts of the uriniferous tubules of the kidney that open on the free surface of the papillae

tube pan *n* **:** a deep round pan used for baking large cakes and having a hollow tube in the center that permits heat to reach the center of the batter

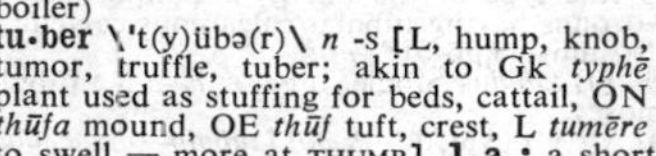
tube pan

tube plate *n* **:** a plate or sheet perforated with holes for the reception of tubes (as in a boiler)

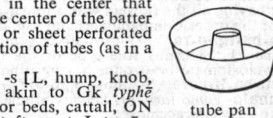

¹tu·ber \ˈt(y)übə(r)\ *n* -s [L, hump, knob, tumor, truffle, tuber; akin to Gk *typhē* plant used as stuffing for beds, cattail, ON *thūfa* mound, OE *thūf* tuft, crest, L *tumēre* to swell — more at THUMB] **1 a :** a short thickened fleshy stem or terminal portion of a stem or rhizome that is usu. formed underground, bears minute scale leaves each with a bud capable under suitable conditions of developing into a new plant, and constitutes the resting stage of various plants (as the potato or the Jerusalem artichoke) — compare BULB, CORM, TUBEROUS ROOT **b :** a fleshy root, rhizome, or other plant structure resembling a tuber in appearance ⟨a dahlia ~⟩ — not used technically **c tubers** *pl* **:** a tuberous crop; *specif* **:** a crop of potatoes ⟨soon be time to harvest ~*s*⟩ **2** [NL, fr. L] **:** the type genus of Tuberaceae comprising fungi whose fruiting bodies are typical truffles **3 :** an anatomical prominence **:** TUBEROSITY, TUBERCLE, PROTUBERANCE

²tub·er \"\ *n* -s [¹*tube* + *-er*] **:** one that makes or works with tubes: as **a :** a worker who installs or fits tubes or tubing (as in a boiler assembly) **b :** an operator of a machine who forms material (as rubber or plastic) into a continuous strip or tube; *also* **:** such a machine ⟨a ~ that coats wire with insulation⟩ **c :** ⁴COPPER **d :** a textile worker who rewinds cloth from large rolls into smaller rolls to inspect it and cut out imperfections — called also *winder* **e :** a worker who makes round belting from strips of leather

tu·ber·a·ce·ae \,t(y)übəˈrāsē,ē\ *n pl, cap* [NL, fr. *Tuber,* type genus + *-aceae*] **:** a family of ascomycetous fungi (order Tuberales) having ascocarps that resemble tubers and vary in size from that of an acorn to that of a large apple and bearing asci in a wholly enclosed hymenial layer — see TRUFFLE, TUBER 2 — **tu·ber·a·ceous** \ˈ;==ˈrāshəs\ *adj*

tuber railway *n, chiefly Brit* **:** an underground railway **:** SUBWAY

tu·ber·a·les \,t(y)übəˈrā(,)lēz\ *n pl, cap* [NL, fr. *Tuber* + *-ales*] **:** a small order of fungi (subclass Euascomycetes) with a closed hypogeal ascocarp — see TUBERACEAE

tuber ci·ne·re·um \səˈnirēəm\ *n* [NL, ashy hump] **:** an eminence of gray matter which lies on the lower surface of the brain between the optic tracts and in front of the mammillary bodies and of which the upper surface forms part of the floor of the third ventricle and the lower surface bears the infundibulum to which the pituitary gland is attached

tu·ber·cle \ˈt(y)übə(r)kəl\ *n* -s [L *tuberculum,* dim. of *tuber*] **1 :** a small knobby prominence or excrescence: as **a** (1) **:** a prominence on the crown of a molar tooth (2) **:** a small rough prominence (as on the front of the head of the tibia for the patellar ligament or on the femur at the upper part of the junction of the neck and great trochanter or on the ulna at the base of the coronoid process) on a bone usu. being smaller than a tuberosity and serving for the attachment of one or more muscles or ligaments (3) **:** an eminence near the head of a rib that articulates with the transverse process of a vertebra **b :** any of several prominences in the central nervous system that mark the nuclei of various nerves ⟨the acoustic ~⟩ **c :** NODULE 2b(3) **d** (1) **:** a small tuber (2) **:** a tuberous root (as of a dahlia) that bears adventitious buds and functions like a true tuber **e :** TUBERCULE 2 **2 a :** a small discrete lump in the substance of an organ or in the skin: (1) **:** the specific lesion of tuberculosis consisting of a packed mass of epithelioid cells, giant cells, disintegration products of leukocytes and bacilli, and usu. a necrotic center (2) **:** a similar mass occurring as a local tissue reaction in diseases other than tuberculosis **b :** TUBERCULOSIS — not used technically

tubercle bacillus *n* **:** a bacterium (*Mycobacterium tuberculosis*) that is the cause of tuberculosis

tu·ber·cled \-ld\ *adj* **:** TUBERCULATE

tubercled orchid *also* **tubercled orchis** *n* **:** GREEN REIN ORCHIS

tubercle of darwin *usu cap D* **:** DARWIN'S TUBERCLE

tubercle of ro·lan·do \-rōˈlan(,)dō\ *usu cap R* [after Luigi *Rolando* †1831 Ital. anatomist] **:** TUBERCULUM CINEREUM

tubercul- *or* **tuberculo-** *comb form* [NL, fr. L *tuberculum,* dim. of *tuber* — more at TUBER] **1 a :** tubercle ⟨*tubercular*⟩ **b :** tuberculous ⟨*tuberculid*⟩ **2 :** tubercle bacillus ⟨*tuberculin*⟩ **3 :** tuberculosis ⟨*tuberculo*therapy⟩

tubercula *pl of* TUBERCULUM

¹tu·ber·cu·lar \təˈbərkyələr, t(y)üˈ-, -ˈbə̄k-, -ˈbəik-, -lə(r)\ *adj* [NL *tubercularis,* fr. *tubercul-* + L *-aris* -ar] **1 :** of, relating to, resembling, or constituting a tubercle **:** TUBERCULATE ⟨a ~ process⟩ ⟨identification by ~ analysis⟩ **2 :** characterized by the presence of tubercular lesions ⟨~ leprosy⟩ — often distinguished from *tuberculous* **3 a :** of, relating to, or affected with tuberculosis **:** TUBERCULOUS ⟨a ~ child⟩ **b :** intended for tuberculars ⟨a ~ hospital⟩ **c :** caused by the tubercle bacillus ⟨~ meningitis⟩ **4 :** characterized by a weak or sickly state that requires cure or amendment ⟨~ finances⟩ — **tu·ber·cu·lar·ly** *adv*

²tubercular \"\ *n* -s **:** a person having tuberculosis

tu·ber·cu·lare \tə,bərkyəˈla(a)rē\ *n* -s [NL, fr. neut. sing of *tubercularis* tubercular] **:** DARWIN'S TUBERCLE

tu·ber·cu·lar·ia \-a(a)rēə\ *n, cap* [NL, fr. *tubercularis* + *-ia*] **:** a genus (the type of the family Tuberculariaceae) comprising fungi with often red or pink sporodochia and including some that cause diebacks of woody plants

tu·ber·cu·lar·i·a·ce·ae \=,==,la(a)rēˈāsē,ē\ *n pl, cap* [NL, fr. *Tubercularia,* type genus + *-aceae*] **:** a large family of mainly saprophytic imperfect fungi (order Moniliales) having the conidia formed typically in sporodochia — see FUSARIUM, SPORODOCHIUM, TUBERCULARIA — **tu·ber·cu·lar·i·a·ceous** \=;==;==;āshəs\ *adj*

¹tu·ber·cu·late \təˈbərkyələt, t(y)üˈ-, -ˈbə̄k-, -ˈbəik-, -yə,lāt, *usu* -d·+V\ *or* **tu·ber·cu·lat·ed** \-yə,lād·əd, -ātəd\ *adj* [*tuberculate* fr. NL *tuberculatus,* fr. *tubercul-* + L *-atus* -ate; *tuberculated* fr. NL *tuberculatus* + E *-ed*] **1 :** having a tubercle **:** characterized by tubercles **2 :** TUBERCULAR — **tu·ber·cu·late·ly** *adv*

²tuberculate \"\ *n* -s [*tubercule* + *-ate*] **:** the aggregate of tubercules in an iron pipe

tu·ber·cu·la·tion \=,==ˈlāshən\ *n* -s [*tubercule* + *-ation*] **1 a :** formation of or affection with tubercles **b :** a growth or arrangement of tubercles **2 :** the collection of tubercules in or on iron pipe **:** TUBERCULATE

tu·ber·cule \ˈt(y)übə(r),kyül\ *n* -s [F, fr. L *tuberculum*] **1 :** TUBERCLE **2 :** a small knob or button of rust formed on the inside of an iron pipe

tu·ber·cu·led \-ld\ *adj* **:** TUBERCULATE

tu·ber·cu·lid \təˈbərkyələd\ *or* **tu·ber·cu·lide** \-yə,līd\ *n* -s [ISV *tubercul-* + *-id, -ide*] **:** a tuberculous lesion of the skin; *esp* **:** one that is an id

tu·ber·cu·li·form \-yələ,fȯrm\ *adj* [NL *tuberculiformis,* fr. *tubercul-* + L *-iformis* -iform] **:** sufficiently short and blunt as to resemble a tubercle ⟨a ~ process on the head of an insect⟩

tu·ber·cu·lin \təˈbərkyələn, t(y)üˈ-, -ˈbə̄k-, -ˈbəik-\ *n* -s [ISV *tubercul-* + *-in*] **:** a sterile liquid containing the growth products of or specific substances extracted from the tubercle bacillus and used in the diagnosis of tuberculosis esp. in children and cattle — see OLD TUBERCULIN, TUBERCULIN TEST

tuberculin test *also* **tuberculin reaction** *n* **:** a test for hypersensitivity to tuberculin in which tuberculin is injected usu. into the skin of the individual tested and the appearance of inflammation at the site of injection is construed as indicating past or present tubercular infection — compare MANTOUX TEST

tuberculo- — see TUBERCUL-

tu·ber·cu·lo·cid·al \tə;bərkyəlōˈsīdᵊl\ *adj* [*tubercul-* + *-cidal*] **:** destroying tubercle bacilli

tu·ber·cu·lo·derm \=ˈ===,dərm\ *also* **tu·ber·cu·lo·der·ma** \=,===ˈdərmə\ *n* -s [NL *tuberculoderma,* fr. *tubercul-* + *-derma*] **:** a tuberculous lesion of the skin **:** TUBERCULID

tu·ber·cu·loid \təˈbərkyə,lȯid\ *adj* [ISV *tubercul-* + *-oid*] **:** resembling tuberculosis esp. in being marked by the presence of tubercles **:** TUBERCULAR 2 ⟨~ leprosy⟩

tu·ber·cu·lo·ma \=,==ˈlōmə\ *n, pl* **tuberculomas** \-məz\ *also* **tuberculoma·ta** \-məd·ə\ [NL, fr. *tubercul-* + *-oma*] **:** a large solitary caseous tubercle of tuberculous character occurring esp. in the brain

tu·ber·cu·lose \təˈbərkyə,lōs\ *adj* [NL *tuberculosus* tuberculous] **:** TUBERCULATE

tu·ber·cu·lo·sectorial \tə;bərkyə(,)lō+\ *adj* [*tubercul-* + *sectorial*] **:** of, relating to, or being a lower molar occurring in many carnivorous mammals (as the dog) and being laterally compressed with sharp anterior cusps and a heel composed of low blunt cusps

tu·ber·cu·lo·sis \tə,bərkyəˈlōsəs, t(y)ü-, -,bə̄k-, -,bəik- *sometimes* ÷ -kəˈ- *or* ,t(y)übə(r)k-\ *n* -ES [NL, fr. *tubercul-* + *-osis*] **1 :** an acute or chronic highly variable communicable disease of man and some other vertebrates caused by the tubercle bacillus (*Mycobacterium tuberculosis*), found in any tissue in the body but esp. those of the respiratory tract whence it spreads from local lesions or by way of the lymph or blood vessels, and characterized by toxic symptoms (as fever, night sweats, or loss of weight) from absorption of toxic products of tissue destruction or by allergic manifestations that involve inflammatory infiltrations, formation of tubercles, caseation, and fibrosis — see MILIARY TUBERCULOSIS **2 :** any of several bacterial diseases of plants (as the olive or sugar beet) in which enlargements or pockets are formed

tu·ber·cu·lo·stat \təˈbərkyəlō,stat\ *n* -s [*tubercul-* + *-stat*] **:** an agent that inhibits the growth of the tubercle bacillus — **tu·ber·cu·lo·stat·ic** \=;===ˈstad·ik\ *adj*

tu·ber·cu·lo·stearic acid \tə;bərkyə(,)lō+...-\ *n* [*tubercul-* + *stearic*] **:** a fatty acid $C_{18}H_{37}COOH$ obtained from the wax of tubercle bacilli and differing from most naturally occurring fatty acids in that it contains an odd number of carbon atoms and its structure is branched; 10-methyl-stearic acid

tu·ber·cu·lo·toxin \"+\ *n* [*tubercul-* + *toxin*] **:** a toxic substance from the tubercle bacillus

tu·ber·cu·lous \təˈbərkyələs, t(y)üˈ-, -ˈbə̄k-, -ˈbəik-\ *adj* [NL *tuberculosus,* fr. L *tuberculum* tubercle (dim. of *tuber*) + *-osus* -ose — more at TUBER] **1 :** of, relating to, or characterized by tubercles **:** TUBERCULAR, TUBERCULATE ⟨a ~ chitinized wing case⟩ **2 a :** constituting or affected with tuberculosis ⟨a ~ patient⟩ ⟨a ~ process⟩ **b :** caused by or resulting from the presence or products of the tubercle bacillus ⟨~ peritonitis⟩ ⟨~ meningitis⟩ — **tu·ber·cu·lous·ly** *adv*

tu·ber·cu·lum \-ləm\ *n, pl* **tubercu·la** \-lə\ [L] **:** TUBERCLE

tuberculum ci·ne·re·um \-səˈnirēəm\ *n* [NL, ashy tubercle] **:** an elevation on the lateral aspect of the medulla oblongata produced by the spinal trigeminal tract and its nucleus

tuber fern *n* **:** a common tropical fern (*Nephrolepis cordifolia*) with bright green leaves on shaggy stipes and small fleshy edible tubers along the prostrate stolons

tuber flea beetle *n* **:** a chrysomelid beetle (*Epitrix tuberis*) that is destructive to potatoes and some other plants in parts of western Canada and U. S.

tu·ber·in \ˈt(y)übərən\ *n* -s [*tuber* + *-in*] **:** a globulin constituting the principal protein of the potato tuber

tuber indexing *n* **:** EYE INDEXING

tu·ber·iza·tion \,t(y)übərəˈzāshən\ *n* -s [*tuber* + *-ization*] **:** the process of forming tubers

tu·ber·less \ˈt(y)übə(r)ləs\ *adj* **:** lacking or deficient in tubers

tuber line *n* **:** a clonal population resulting from the continued propagation from one original tuber (as of the potato)

tuber moth *n* **:** POTATO MOTH

tu·ber·oid \ˈt(y)übə,rȯid\ *adj* [ISV *tuber* + *-oid*] **:** resembling a tuber ⟨a ~ root⟩

tuber roll *n* **:** TABLE ROLL

tube·rose \ˈt(y)ü,brōz *sometimes* -übə,rōz *or* -ōs\ *n* -s [NL *tuberosa* (specific epithet of *Polianthes tuberosa*), fr. fem. of L *tuberosus* tuberous] **:** a Mexican bulbous herb (*Polianthes tuberosa*) commonly cultivated for its spike of fragrant white single or double flowers that resemble small lilies

tu·ber·os·i·ty \ˌt(y)übəˈräsəd·ē, -ətē, -i\ *n* -ES [MF *tuberosité*, fr. L *tuberosus* + MF *-ité* -ity] **:** an obtuse prominence: as **a** *archaic* **:** a swollen mass **b :** any of various large prominences on bones (as the lateral eminences of the head of the tibia, the rough eminence on the ischium on which the body rests when sitting, that on the inner front aspect of the radius for the attachment of the biceps tendon or on the cuboid and navicular bones of the foot) usu. serving for the attachment of muscles or ligaments **c :** TUBERCLE 1a(3)

tu·ber·ous \ˈt(y)übərəs\ *also* **tu·ber·ose** \-bəˌrōs\ *adj* [L *tuberosus*, fr. *tuber* + *-osus* -ose — more at TUBER] **1** *archaic* **:** covered with or divided into knobby prominences **:** KNOBBED **2 a :** consisting of, bearing, or resembling a tuber **b :** of, relating to, or being a tuber or tuberous root of a plant **:** having or reproducing by such structures — **tu·ber·ous·ly** *adv*

tuberous begonia *n* **:** any of various begonias that have tuberous roots and usu. large showy and often double flowers and that are complex hybrids commonly treated as a horticultural species (*Begonia tuberhybrida*) — compare FIBROUS-ROOTED BEGONIA, RHIZOMATOUS BEGONIA

tuberous root *n* **:** a thick fleshy root resembling a tuber but lacking buds or scale leaves, functioning esp. in storage in biennial or perennial plants in which new growth is from a crown, and being simple and solitary (as in the beet or turnip) or variously fascicled (as in the dahlia) — compare FIBROUS ROOT; see ROOT illustration — **tuberous–rooted** \ˈ⸗⸗⸗ˈ⸗⸗\ *adj*

tuberous water lily *n* **:** a water lily (*Nymphaea tuberosa*) of the northeastern U. S. with large white or pale rose odorless flowers and tuberous creeping rhizomes

tuber root *n* **:** BUTTERFLY WEED 1

tubers *pl of* TUBER

tubes *pl of* TUBE, *pres 3d sing of* TUBE

tube saw *n* **:** TUBULAR SAW

tube set *n* **:** a radio receiving set containing electron tubes

tube shell *n* **:** BLIND SHELL 2

tube snout *n* **:** a slender marine fish (*Aulorhyndus flavidus*) having the head prolonged as a tubular snout with the small mouth at its end, related to the pipefishes, and sometimes occurring in dense schools off the Pacific coast of No. America

tube spinner *or* **tube weaver** *n* **:** any of various spiders (as of the genera *Tegenaria* and *Agelena*) that construct a flat web connected with a tubular nest in which the spider hides

tube transmitter *n* **:** a radio transmitting set using a tube generator

tube well *n* **:** a driven well

tube worm *n* **:** an annelid worm (as a serpulid) building and living in a tube

tube wrench *n* **:** PIPE WRENCH

tubfast \ˈ⸗ˌ⸗\ *adj* [¹*tub* + *fast*] **:** able to resist ordinary domestic laundry procedures ⟨~ cottons⟩

tub file *n* **:** a file of cards or papers so housed that all or a large part of it may be uncovered at one time

tubfish \ˈ⸗ˌ⸗\ *Brit var of* TUB 2

tub front *n, chiefly Brit* **:** BLOCKFRONT

tubi- *comb form* [NL, fr. L *tubus* — more at TUBE] **:** tube ⟨*tubi*valve⟩ ⟨*Tubi*pora⟩

tu·bic·o·la \t(y)üˈbikələ\ *n pl, cap* [NL, fr. *tubi-* + *-cola* (fr. L *-cola* inhabitant) — more at -COLOUS] *in some esp former classifications* **:** an order of Annelida comprising the tube worms and being nearly equivalent to Sedentaria

tu·bic·o·lae \-kəˌlē\ *n pl, cap* [NL, fr. *tubi-* + *-colae* (pl. of *-cola*)] *in former classifications* **:** a group of animals distinguished by the tubes they construct: **a :** SEDENTARIA **b :** a small group of spiders that build tubular nests

tu·bic·o·lous \-kələs\ *adj* [*tubi-* + *-colous*] **1** *also* **tu·bi·cole** \ˈt(y)übəˌkōl\ [*tubi-* + *-colous* or *-cole*] **:** living in a self-constructed tube ⟨a ~ annelid⟩ **2** [NL *Tubicolae* + E *-ous*] **:** spinning a tubular web ⟨~ spiders⟩ **3** *or* **tu·bic·o·lar** \t(y)üˈbikələ(r)\ [NL *Tubicola* + E *-ous* or *-ar*] **:** of or relating to the Tubicola or Tubicolae

tu·bi·fa·cient \ˌt(y)übəˈfāshənt\ *adj* [*tubi-* + *-facient*] **:** secreting or constructing a tube

tu·bi·fex \ˈt(y)übəˌfeks\ *n* [NL *Tubific-, Tubifex*, fr. *tubi-* + L *-fic-, -fex* (fr. *facere* to make, do) — more at DO] **1** *cap* **:** a genus (the type of the family Tubificidae) of slender red or brown oligochaete worms having four bundles of setae on each segment and living in tubes in fresh or brackish water and being widely used as food for aquarium fish **2** *pl* **tubifex** *or* **tubifexes :** any worm of the genus *Tubifex*

¹**tu·bif·i·cid** \t(y)üˈbifəsəd\ *adj* [NL *Tubificidae*] **:** of or relating to the Tubificidae

²**tubificid** \ˈ"\ *n* -S **:** a worm of the family Tubificidae

tu·bi·fic·i·dae \ˌt(y)übəˈfisəˌdē\ *n pl, cap* [NL, fr. *Tubific-, Tubifex*, type genus + *-idae*] **:** a nearly cosmopolitan family of aquatic oligochaete worms that do not reproduce asexually (as by budding or division) — see TUBIFEX

tu·bi·flo·rae \ˌt(y)übəˈflōrˌē\ [NL, fr. *tubi-* + *florae*] *syn of* POLEMONIALES

tu·bi·flo·ra·les \ˌt(y)übəflōˈrā(ˌ)lēz\ [NL, fr. *tubi-* + *flora* + *-ales*] *syn of* CAMPANULALES

tu·bi·flo·rous \ˈt(y)übəˈflōrəs\ *adj* [*tubi-* + *-florous*] **:** TUBULIFLOROUS

tu·bi·form \ˈt(y)übəˌfȯrm\ *adj* [*tubi-* + *-form*] **:** having the form of a tube **:** tubular in form

tu·bi·nar·es \ˌt(y)übəˈna(a)(ˌ)rēz\ [NL, fr. *tubi-* + L *nares*, pl. of *naris* nostril — more at NARIS] *syn of* PROCELLARIIFORMES

tu·bi·nar·i·al \ˈ⸗⸗ˈna(a)rēəl\ *also* **tu·bi·nar·ine** \-)rən, -)ˌrīn\ *adj* [NL *Tubinares* + E *-ial* or *-ine*] **1 :** having the nostrils tubular **2 :** of or relating to the Procellariiformes

tub·ing \ˈt(y)übiŋ, -bēŋ\ *n* -S [¹*tube* + *-ing*] **1 a :** material in the form of a tube **:** a length or piece of tube ⟨rubber ~⟩ ⟨a roll of copper ~⟩: as (1) **:** TUBULAR FABRIC (2) **:** a special grade of high-test pipe fitted with threads and couplings of special design **b :** a series of tubes **:** the tubes of a particular system or apparatus ⟨renewed the ~ of the boiler⟩ **2** [fr. gerund of ²*tube*] **:** the act or an instance of making or installing tubes

tu·bip·o·ra \t(y)üˈbipərə\ *n, cap* [NL, fr. *tubi-* + *-pora*] **:** a genus (the type of the family Tubiporidae of the order Alcyonacea) of corals comprising the organ-pipe corals — **tu·bi·pore** \ˈt(y)übəˌpō(ə)r\ *adj or n*

tub·man \ˈtəbmən\ *n, pl* **tubmen** [¹*tub* + *man*] **1** [so called fr. the fact that his place in the Court was beside the tub used as a measure of capacity in excise cases] **:** a junior barrister in the former English Court of Exchequer having except in crown business precedence in motion over all juniors except the postman **2 :** one whose work involves the use of tubs or vats: as **a :** a tender of the tubs in which hog carcasses are scalded preparatory to dehairing **b :** a worker who dyes hosiery or knit goods in a vat or dyeing machine

tu·bo·cu·ra·rine \ˌt(y)übōk(y)üˈräˌrēn, -ärən\ *n* [ISV *tubo-* (fr. L *tubus* tube) + *curare* + *-ine*; fr. its being shipped in sections of hollow bamboo] **:** a toxic alkaloid of the isoquinoline group or its crystalline quaternary ammonium chloride $C_{38}H_{44}Cl_2N_2O_6.5H_2O$ that is obtained chiefly from the bark and stems of the So. American pareira brava vine and in its dextrorotatory form constitutes the chief active constituent of curare (sense 3) and that is used similarly

tu·boid \ˈt(y)üˌbȯid\ *adj* [¹*tube* + *-oid*] **:** resembling a tube **:** approaching the tubular in form

tub orchard *n* **:** a group of fruit trees cultivated in tubs so that they may be brought indoors for storage (as for subsequent forcing into bloom in greenhouses or for culture beyond their normal limits of hardiness)

tub preacher *n* [¹*tub* (sense 3c)] **:** a ranting dissenting preacher

tubs *pl of* TUB, *pres 3d sing of* TUB

tub–size \ˈ⸗ˌ⸗\ *vt* **:** to pass (paper) through a tub or vat containing a sizing solution (as of gelatin or starch) — compare BEATER-SIZE, SURFACE-SIZE

tub sugar *n* **:** soft maple sugar that is run into wooden or tin tubs for storage

tub–thumper \ˈ⸗ˌ⸗⸗\ *n* **:** one who engages in impassioned or ranting utterance ⟨at least one *tub-thumper* for every known variety of panacea —Earl Brown⟩

¹**tub–thumping** \ˈ⸗ˌ⸗⸗\ *n* **:** an act or instance of engaging in impassioned or ranting utterance ⟨a terrific job of *tub-thumping* for a novel —Bennett Cerf⟩

²**tub–thumping** \ˈ"\ *adj* **:** marked by tub-thumping ⟨a *tub-thumping* socialist —Anthony West⟩

tu·bu·lar \ˈt(y)übyələ(r)\ *adj* [L *tubus* tube + E *-ular* — more at TUBE] **1 a :** having the form of a tube ⟨a ~ process⟩ **b :** having or consisting of a tube ⟨a ~ calyx⟩ **:** made up of tubes **:** FISTULOUS ⟨a ~ hymenium⟩ **c :** provided with tubes ⟨a ~ boiler⟩ **:** involving the use of tubes or made of tubular stock ⟨a ~ chair⟩ ⟨a radiator of ~ construction⟩ **2 :** relating to or sounding as if produced through tubes ⟨a ~ respiratory sound⟩

tubular bridge *n* **1 :** a bridge supported chiefly by steel tubes **2 :** a plate-girder bridge in the form of a rectangular tube

tubular chimes *or* **tubular bells** *n pl* **:** GLOCKENSPIEL 2

tubular fabric *n* **:** a woven, knitted, or braided fabric made in circular seamless form ⟨jersey is usually knit as a *tubular fabric*⟩ ⟨*tubular fabric* for pillowcases⟩

tubular floret *n* **:** DISK FLOWER

tubular girder *n* **:** a plate girder having two or more vertical webs with a space between them and solid members joining them top and bottom to form a tube of rectangular cross section with one or more cells

tu·bu·lar·ia \ˌt(y)übyəˈla(a)rēə\ *n* [NL, fr. L *tubulus* tubule, tube + NL *-aria*] **1** *cap* **:** a genus (the type of the family Tubulariidae) of anthomedusan hydroids having hydranths with two circles of tentacles at the summits of long, slender usu. simple stems and small adelocodonic gonophores that cluster at the bases of the outer tentacles **2** -S **:** any hydroid of the genus *Tubularia* or sometimes of the family Tubulariidae — **tu·bu·lar·i·an** \ˈ⸗⸗ˈla(a)rēən\ *adj or n*

tu·bu·lar·i·ae \ˈ⸗⸗ˈla(a)rēˌē\ *or* **tu·bu·lar·i·da** \-ˈlarədə\ [NL *Tubulariae* fr. *Tubularia*; NL *Tubularida* fr. *Tubularia* + *-ida*] *syn of* ANTHOMEDUSAE

tu·bu·lar·i·ty \ˌt(y)übyəˈlarəd·ē, -ətē, -i *also* -ˈler-\ *n* -ES **:** the quality or state of being tubular

tubular lock *n* **:** a rim lock with the tumblers contained in a fixed tube that usu. projects through the door

tu·bu·lar·ly *adv* **:** in a tubular manner or form

tubular pile *n* **:** a pile consisting of a steel tube driven into the ground and filled with concrete after the enclosed earth has been removed

tubular–pneumatic action *n* **:** an action in a pipe organ in which the opening and closing of the mouth of the pipe is controlled by air pressure regulated by the depressing and releasing of the key

tubular rivet *n* **:** a rivet with a tubular shank

tubular saw *n* **:** a crown saw esp. when having considerable length compared to its diameter

tubular skate *n* **:** an ice skate having the frame composed of tubing

tu·bu·lary \ˈt(y)übyəˌlerē\ *adj* [L *tubulus* tubule, tube + E *-ary*] **:** being, made up of, or involving tubes ⟨~ ducts⟩

tu·bu·late \ˈt(y)übyələt, -yəˌlāt\ *also* **tu·bu·lat·ed** \-yəˌlād·əd\ *adj* [*tubulate* fr. L *tubulatus*, fr. L *tubulus* tubule, tube + *-atus* -ate; *tubulated* fr. L *tubulatus* + E *-ed*] **1 :** provided with a tube **2 :** having the form of a tube

tu·bu·la·tion \ˌ⸗⸗ˈlāshən\ *n* -S [L *tubulation-, tubulatio*, fr. *tubulus* + *-ation-, -atio* -ation] **1 :** the act of shaping or making a tube or of providing with a tube **2 a :** arrangement or an array of tubes **b :** a tubular piece (as a juncture, connection, or orifice)

tu·bu·la·ture \ˈt(y)übyələˌchü(ə)r, -ˌchər\ *n* -S [*tubulate* + *-ure*] **:** TUBULATION 2

tu·bule \ˈt(y)üˌbyül\ *n* -S [L *tubulus* tubule, tube, dim. of *tubus* tube — more at TUBE] **:** a small tube; *esp* **:** a very slender elongated channel in an anatomical structure

tubuli- *comb form* [NL, fr. L *tubulus* tubule, tube] **1 :** tubule **:** tubulus ⟨*tubuli*ferous⟩ **2 :** tubular ⟨*tubuli*florous⟩

tu·bu·li·bran·chi·a·ta \ˌt(y)übyələˌbraŋkēˈäd·ə, -ˈād·ə\ *n pl* [NL, fr. *tubuli-* + *Branchiata*] *in former classifications* **:** an artificial group of gastropod mollusks including those (as of the genus *Vermetus*) having a tubular shell — **tu·bu·li·bran·chi·ate** \ˈ⸗⸗⸗ˈbraŋkēət, -ēˌāt\ *adj or n*

tu·bu·li·den·ta·ta \ˌt(y)übyələˌdenˈtäd·ə, -ˈtād·ə\ *n pl, cap* [NL, fr. neut. pl. of *tubulidentatus* having tubelike teeth, fr. *tubuli-* + *-dentatus* -dentate] **:** an obscure order of Mammalia of protungulate or possibly creodont ancestry comprising the aardvark and extinct related forms that are distinguished by teeth composed of a cluster of upright parallel vasodentin columns with individual pulp canals — **tu·bu·li·den·tate** \ˈ⸗⸗⸗ˈden·ˌtāt\ *adj or n*

tu·bu·lif·era \ˌt(y)übyəˈlif(ə)rə\ *n pl, cap* [NL, fr. *tubulifer* tubuliferous] **1** *in some classifications* **:** a group of Hymenoptera comprising the families Serphidae and Chrysididae or the Chrysididae alone and being distinguished by a tubular ovipositor **2 :** a suborder of Thysanoptera including those that have the last segment of the abdomen tubular — **tu·bu·lif·er·an** \-rən\ *n* -S

tu·bu·lif·er·ous \ˈ⸗⸗ˈlif(ə)rəs\ *adj* [NL *tubulifer*, fr. *tubuli-* + L *-fer* -ferous] **:** having or made up of tubules

tu·bu·li·floral \ˈt(y)übyələ+\ *adj* [ISV *tubuli-* + *floral*] **:** having tubular flowers

tu·bu·li·flo·rous \ˈ"+ˈflōrəs\ *adj* [ISV *tubuli-* + *-florous*] **:** having all the flowers with tubular corollas — used of plants of the order Campanulales and esp. of the family Compositae

tu·bu·lip·o·ra \ˌt(y)übyəˈlipərə\ *n, cap* [NL, fr. *tubuli-* + *-pora*] **:** a genus (the type of the family Tubuliporidae) of cyclostomate bryozoans having tubular calcareous calyculi — **tu·bu·li·pore** \ˈt(y)übyələˌpō(ə)r\ *n* -S

tubulo- *comb form* [L *tubulus* tubule, tube + E *-o-*] **:** tubular and ⟨*tubulo*racemose⟩

tu·bu·lo·saccular \ˈt(y)übyə(ˌ)lō+\ *adj* [*tubolo-* + *saccular*] **:** consisting of tubular and saccular elements

tu·bu·lous \ˈt(y)übyələs\ *also* **tu·bu·lose** \-yəˌlōs\ *adj* [NL *tubulosus*, fr. L *tubulus* + *-osus* -ose] **1 :** resembling or having the form of a tube **2 :** made up of or containing tubes or a tubular element (as florets) ⟨a ~ boiler⟩ — **tu·bu·lous·ly** *adv*

tu·bu·lure \ˈt(y)übyəˌlu̇(ə)r\ *n* -S [F, fr. *tubule* (fr. L *tubulus*) + *-ure*] **:** a short tubular opening (as at the top of a retort)

tu·bu·lus \ˈt(y)übyələs\ *n, pl* **tubu·li** \-yəˌlī\ [L — more at TUBULE] **1 :** TUBULE **2** [NL, fr. L] **:** a slender tubular extensile ovipositor of some flies

tub wheel *n* **:** a drum used like a tumbling barrel esp. for washing skins

tu·can·de·ra *also* **tu·con·de·ra** \ˌtükənˈderə\ *n* -S [Pg *tocandera*, fr. Tupi *tocandira, tucanguira*, fr. *tucan* toucan + *guira* bird; fr. its size] **:** any of various large ponerine ants (esp. *Paraponera clavata*) of Central and So. America

tu·ca·no \tüˈkä(ˌ)nō\ *n, pl* **tucano** *or* **tucanos** *usu cap* **1 a :** a group of peoples of Colombia and northern Ecuador **b :** a member of any people of such group **2 :** the language of the Tucano people

tu·ca·no·an \ˌtükəˈnōən\ *adj, usu cap* **:** of or relating to the Tucano or their language

tu·chun \ˈdüˈjüen\ *n, pl* **tuchuns** *also* **tuchun** *often cap* [Chin (Pek) *tu*¹-*chün*¹, lit., overseer of troops] **1 :** a Chinese military governor (as of a province) **2 :** a Chinese warlord

tu–chung \ˈdüˈju̇ŋ\ *n* -S [Chin (Pek) *tu*⁴ *chung*⁴] **:** a very hardy Chinese tree (*Eucommia ulmoides*) that resembles an elm in appearance and is a potential source of rubber

¹**tuck** \ˈtək\ *vb* -ED/-ING/-S [ME *tuken, touken, tucken*, fr. OE *tūcian* to ill-treat, punish; akin to MD *tucken* to tug, OHG *zucken* to jerk, OE *togian* to pull — more at TOW] *vt* **1** *obs* **:** SCOLD, UPBRAID **2 a :** to pull up or gather into a fold — usu. used with *up* or *in* ⟨a geisha ~s her robe well up to her knees —Lafcadio Hearn⟩ **b :** to make a tuck in; *esp* **:** to shorten or ornament with a tuck ⟨the bodice was minutely ~*ed* —Kay Boyle⟩ **c :** to knit in tuck stitch **3** *archaic* **:** to draw up and gird the clothes of **4 :** to put into a snug place ⟨~*ed* her notebook under her arm —Dorothy Sayers⟩; *specif* **:** to put into a snug place that affords concealment or isolation ⟨philosophically ~*ed* his handful of medals into an old cigar box —*Time*⟩ ⟨beaches lie ~*ed* in between its rocky cliffs —*Amer. Guide Series: Maine*⟩ — often used with *away* ⟨a modern colonial brick structure . . . has been ~*ed* away in a corner —*Amer. Guide Series: Conn.*⟩ ⟨many of his bitterest attacks were ~*ed* away in footnotes —J.S.Schapiro⟩ **5 a :** to push in the loose end or edge of so as to hold tightly ⟨~*ed* in the sheets⟩ ⟨forgot to ~ in your shirttail —John Steinbeck⟩ ⟨~*ed* a blanket around the child⟩ **b :** to cover (as a person) by tucking in the bedclothes ⟨is ~*ing* him in now⟩ ⟨~*ed* him up at last in his crib —Marcia Davenport⟩ **6** *archaic* **:** HANG 1b(1) — usu. used with *up* **7 :** EAT — usu. used with *away* or *in* ⟨~*ed* away both steak and chicken —W.T.Musgrove⟩ ⟨~ in as much as they desire —*Scand Mag.*⟩ **8 :** to take (fish) from a large seine with a tuck seine **9 :** to put into a tuck position ⟨~ the legs to the chest —N.C.Loken⟩ ~ *vi* **1 :** to draw together into tucks or folds **2 :** to eat heartily — usu. used with *into* or *in* ⟨the careless abandon of a vegetarian ~*ing* into his beans —*Science*⟩ **3 a :** to fit in snugly ⟨the helicopter . . . ~s away into a hangar at the open end of the ship —Douglas Willis⟩ **b :** to fit in under something that binds ⟨tailored shirts which ~ in —*Women's Wear Daily*⟩ — **tuck one's tail :** to be reduced to shame or confusion ⟨hated to *tuck his tail* and back down now —F.B.Gipson⟩

²**tuck** \ˈ"\ *n* -S [ME *tucke*, fr. *tuken, tucken* to tuck] **1 a** (1) **:** a fold stitched or woven into cloth for the purpose of shortening, decorating, or controlling fullness (2) **:** a gusset in the side of a paper bag **b :** something that shortens or diminishes **:** CUT ⟨the opera lasts five hours if you take no ~s in score —Claudia Cassidy⟩ **2 :** TUCK SEINE **3 :** the part of a vessel where the ends of the lower planks meet under the stern **4** *Brit* **a :** a large meal **:** SPREAD **b :** FOOD; *esp* **:** sweet foods (as pastry, jam, and candy) **5 a :** an act or instance of pushing in a loose end or edge so as to secure ⟨gave the blankets a few more ~s⟩ **b** (1) **:** the act of tucking a strand of rope between or under other strands (2) **:** the joint so made **6 a :** a flap on a book cover that folds over and fits into a slot or a band on the opposite cover so as to keep the book closed — called also *tuck-in* **b :** the part of the end flap of a paperboard box that is inserted into the body to secure the end **7 :** the end of a cigar that is to be lighted **8 :** a body position used in diving, gymnastics, and dancing in which the knees are bent, the thighs drawn tightly to the chest, and the hands clasped around the shins — compare LAYOUT 5, ¹¹PIKE **9 :** a fabric or leather covering for the steel shank of a shoe

1 2

tuck 1a(1): *1* plain tucks, *2* cross tucks

³**tuck** \ˈtək\ *also* **touk** \ˈtu̇k\ *n* -S [obs. E *tuk, touk* to beat the drum, sound the trumpet, fr. ME *tukken*, fr. ONF *toquer* to touch, strike, fr. (assumed) VL *toccare* — more at TOUCH] **:** a sound of or as if of a drumbeat ⟨danced silently to the ~ of drum —J.G.Frazer⟩

⁴**tuck** \ˈtək\ *n* -S [MF *estoc* thrusting sword, fr. OF, tree trunk, sword point — more at ESTOC] *archaic* **:** RAPIER

⁵**tuck** \ˈ"\ *n* -S [prob. fr. ²*tuck*] **:** VIGOR, ENERGY, TOUGHNESS ⟨seemed to kind of take the ~ all out of me —Mark Twain⟩

⁶**tuck** \ˈ"\ *n* -S [by shortening & alter.] **:** TUXEDO

tuck·a·hoe \ˈtəkəˌhō\ *n* -S [*tockawhoughe*, lit., it is round (in some Algonquian language of Virginia)] **1 a :** either of two American plants having rootstocks used as food by the Indians: (1) **:** ARROW ARUM (2) **:** GOLDEN CLUB **b :** the edible rootstock of a tuckahoe **2 :** the large edible sclerotium of a subterranean fungus (*Poria cocos*) that is firm and white inside with a hard brown exterior — called also *Indian bread* **3** *usu cap* **:** VIRGINIAN; *esp* **:** a Virginian living east of the Blue Ridge mountains — used as a nickname

tuckaway \ˈ⸗⸗ˌ⸗\ *adj* [fr. the phrase *tuck away*] **:** capable of being folded and put out of the way ⟨~ table⟩

tuck box *n, Brit* **:** a box of delicacies from home

tuck comb *n* **:** a comb for holding the hair or a hat in place

tucked *past of* TUCK

tucked up *adj* [fr. past part. of *tuck up*, v.] **1 :** drawn in or up **:** CONTRACTED; *esp* **:** having the flanks drawn in and the abdomen small either as a normal feature (as in greyhounds and some rabbits) or as an indication of ill health or poor condition (as in most domestic mammals) **2** *Brit* **a :** CRAMPED, HAMPERED **b :** EXHAUSTED

¹**tuck·er** \ˈtəkə(r)\ *n* -S [ME *touker*, fr. *tuken, touken* to tuck + *-er* — more at TUCK] **1 :** one that tucks: as **a** (1) **:** an attachment on a sewing machine for making tucks (2) **:** an operator of a tucker attachment — called also *corder, pleater* **b :** the mechanism of a hay press or baler that folds in the hay to make the outside of the bales neat and square **2 :** a piece of lace or cloth used to fill in the low neckline of a dress **:** CHEMISETTE — compare BIB AND TUCKER **3** *chiefly Austral* **:** FOOD **4 :** SQUARE DANCE; *esp* **:** a square dance in which there is a dancer without a partner

²**tucker** \ˈ"\ *vt* -ED/-ING/-S [¹*tuck* + *-er* (freq. suffix as in *batter*)] **:** EXHAUST ⟨it ~*ed* me, that act —A.B.Guthrie⟩ — often used with *out* ⟨plain ~*ed* out —Laura Krey⟩ **syn** see TIRE

tucker–bag \ˈ⸗⸗ˌ⸗\ *n, chiefly Austral* **:** a bag used esp. by travelers in the bush to hold food

¹**tuck·et** \ˈtəkət\ *n* -S [prob. fr. ³*tuck* (influenced in meaning by obs. E *tuk* to beat the drum, sound the trumpet) + *-et*] **:** a fanfare on a trumpet

²**tucket** \ˈ"\ *n* -S [prob. of Algonquian origin; akin to *tockawhoughe* tuckahoe (in some Algonquian language of Virginia), Delaware *p'tuckqueu* it is round] **:** a green ear of corn

¹**tuck–in** \ˈ⸗ˌ⸗\ *n* -S [fr. *tuck in*, v.] **1** *chiefly Brit* **:** a large meal **:** SPREAD **2 :** ²TUCK 6a **3 :** material (as cloth) that is to be tucked in

²**tuck–in** \ˈ"\ *adj* **:** designed to be held in place by being tucked in ⟨a *tuck-in* blouse⟩

tuck·ing \ˈtəkiŋ\ *n* -S [²*tuck* + *-ing*] **:** a fabric that has tucks woven or sewn into it

tucking–comb \ˈ⸗⸗ˌ⸗\ *n* **:** BACK COMB

tuck–out \ˈ⸗ˌ⸗\ *n* -S [²*tuck*] *chiefly Brit* **:** a large meal **:** SPREAD

tuck plate *n* **:** OXTER PLATE

tuck–point \ˈ⸗ˌ⸗\ *vt* [²*tuck*] **:** to finish (the mortar joints between bricks or stones) with a narrow ridge of putty or fine lime mortar — **tuck–pointer** \ˈ⸗ˌ⸗⸗\ *n*

tucks *pres 3d sing of* TUCK, *pl of* TUCK

tuck seine *also* **tuck net** *n* **:** a seine about 70 fathoms long and very deep in the middle that is used to take fish from a larger seine

tuck–shop \ˈ⸗ˌ⸗\ *n, Brit* **:** a confectioner's shop **:** CONFECTIONERY

tuck stitch *n* **:** a pattern stitch for circular-knit garments that is made by taking on more than one loop in a stitch

tuck–up \ˈ⸗ˌ⸗\ *n* -S [fr. *tuck up*, v.] **:** the sharp upward curve of the underline behind the ribs (as of a greyhound or other dog of racy build)

tucky \ˈtəkē\ *or* **tucky lily** *n* -ES [perh. fr. ²*tuck* + *-y*] **:** SPATTERDOCK

tucondera *var of* TUCANDERA

tu·co–tu·co \ˈtü(ˌ)kōˈtü(ˌ)kō\ *also* **tu·cu–tu·cu** \-kü . . . kü\ *n* -S [AmerSp *tucutuco*, imit. of its cry] **:** any of various So. American hystricomorph burrowing rodents comprising the genus *Ctenomys* and resembling the No. American pocket gophers but lacking cheek pouches

tu·cum \tüˈküm\ *also* **tu·cu·ma** \-mə\ *n* -S [Pg *tucumã*, fr. Tupi *tucumã*] **1** *also* **tucum palm a :** any of several chiefly Brazilian palms of the genus *Astrocaryum* (esp. *A. tucuma*) with leaf bases that yield a coarse fiber used esp. for cordage and hats and with seeds that yield an edible oil **b :** a low spiny Brazilian palm (*Bactris setosa*) with leaves that yield a long strong fiber held to resemble wool and used locally for bags or other containers, fishing nets, and shoemakers' twines **2 :** the fiber of a tucum

tu·cu·mán \ˌtükü'män\ *adj, usu cap* [fr. *Tucumán*, Argentina] **:** of or from the city of Tucumán, Argentina **:** of the kind or style prevalent in Tucumán

tu·cu·na·ré \ˌtü,künəˈrā\ *n* -S [Pg, fr. Tupi] **:** any of several So. American cichlid river fishes (genus *Cichla*) that resemble bass and are esteemed for sport and food

-tude \ˌtüd, ·ˌtyüd\ *n suffix* -S [MF or L; MF *-tude*, fr. L *-tudin-, -tudo*] **:** -NESS ⟨omni*tude*⟩ ⟨parvi*tude*⟩

tu·desque \t(y)üˈdesk\ *adj, usu cap* [F, fr. Sp *tudesco*, of Gmc origin; akin to OHG *thiutisc, diutisc* German — more at DUTCH] **:** GERMAN

tu·dor \ˈt(y)üdə(r)\ *adj, usu cap* [fr. *Tudor*, English royal house] **1 :** of or relating to the English royal family reigning from 1485 to 1603 **2 a :** of or relating to the Tudor period or its culture ⟨*Tudor* drama⟩ **b :** marked by Tudor arches, shallow moldings, and an abundance of paneling on the walls ⟨a *Tudor* manor house⟩

tudor arch *n, usu cap T* **:** a low elliptical or pointed arch drawn from three, four, or five centers; *esp* **:** a pointed arch drawn from four centers — SEE ARCH illustration

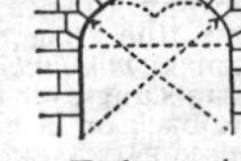
Tudor arch

tu·dor·esque \ˌt(y)üdəˈresk\ *adj, usu cap* [*Tudor*, royal house + E *-esque*] **:** of, relating to, or resembling the style of the Tudor period

tudor flower *n, usu cap T* **:** a trefoil flower used in the decorations of the late English Gothic art

tue iron \ˈtyü-\ *n* [alter. of earlier *tew iron*, by folk etymology fr. MF *tuyere* — more at TUYERE] **:** TUYERE

tues·day \ˈt(y)üzdē, -di *also* -z(ˌ)dā\ *n* -S *usu cap* [ME *tiwesday, tewisday*, fr. OE *tīwesdæg*; akin to OFris *tiesdei* Tuesday, OHG *zīostag*, ON *tȳsdagr, tȳrsdagr*; all fr. a prehistoric WGmc-NGmc compound formed from the components represented by OE *Tīw*, god of war, and *dæg* day; trans. of L *Martis dies*, lit., day of Mars (Roman god of war); trans. of Gk *hēmera Areios*, lit., day of Ares (Greek god of war) — more at DEITY, DAY] **:** the third day of the week **:** the day following Monday

tues·days \"+z\ *adv, usu cap* **:** on Tuesday repeatedly **:** on any Tuesday

tu·fa \ˈt(y)üfə\ *n* -S [It *tufo*, fr. OIt, fr. L *tophus, tofus*, prob. fr. Osco-Umbrian] **1 :** TUFF **2 :** a porous rock formed as a deposit from springs or streams — usu. used of calcareous deposits ⟨calcareous ~⟩

tu·fa·ceous \t(y)üˈfāshəs\ *adj* [It *tufaceo*, fr. L *tofaceus*, fr. *tofus* tufa + *-aceus* -aceous] **:** of, relating to, or resembling tufa

tu·fan \tüˈfän\ *n* -S [Ar *ṭūfān* deluge, fr. Gk *typhōn* typhoon — more at TYPHOON] *India* **:** a violent storm

tuff \ˈtəf\ *n* -S [MF *tuf*, fr. OIt *tufo* tufa] **:** a rock composed of the finer kinds of volcanic detritus usu. more or less stratified and in various states of consolidation — called also *tufa*

tuff·a·ceous \ˌtəˈfāshəs\ *adj* [*tuff* + *-aceous*] **:** of, relating to, or resembling tuff

tuf·fet \ˈtəfət\ *n* -S [alter. (influenced by *-et*) of [1]*tuft*] **1 :** TUFT 1b **2 :** a low seat (as a hassock or a stool)

tuf·foon \(ˌ)təˈfün\ *archaic var of* TYPHOON

[1]**tuft** \ˈtəft\ *n* -S [ME, modif. of MF *tufe, tofe, toffe*, prob. of Gmc origin; akin to ON *toppr* tuft, OHG *zopf* — more at TOP] **1 :** a small cluster of elongated flexible outgrowths or parts attached or close together at the base and free at the opposite ends: as **a** (1) **:** a small bunch of hairs on the body (2) **:** a small beard on the chin **:** IMPERIAL **b :** a growing bunch of grass, leaves, flowers, or small plants **c :** a bunch of feathers; *specif* **:** the crest of a bird **d :** a bunch of soft fluffy threads cut off short and used to ornament cloth (as in a bedspread) **2 :** a small group (as of trees) **:** CLUMP, CLUSTER ⟨a ~ of pines —*U.S. Geographic Board*⟩ **3 :** MOUND ⟨the house . . . was set high on a ~ of land —*Yankee*⟩ **4 a :** a gold tassel formerly worn by titled undergraduates at Cambridge or Oxford Universities **b** *Brit* **:** a titled undergraduate at Cambridge or Oxford **5 a :** a cluster of loops or cut threads used as a finish for the tying threads of quilts, mattresses, or upholstery **b :** a covered button or leather disk for similar use **6 :** a coil of capillaries **7 :** one of the projections of extra warp or filling yarns drawn through a fabric or a carpet so as to produce a surface of raised loops or cut pile

[2]**tuft** \"\ *vb* -ED/-ING/-S *vt* **1 a :** to provide with a tuft **b :** to weave (a fabric) with tufts **2 a :** to beat (as a covert) for deer **b :** to rouse (game) by beating **3 :** to make (as a mattress or cushioned seat) firm by drawing stitches tightly through the padding at regular intervals and covering each depression on the surface with a tuft **~** *vi* **:** to form into tufts **:** grow into tufts

[1]**tuft·taf·fe·ta** \ˌtəft+\ *n* -S [blend of [1]*tuft* + *taffeta*] **:** a taffeta having a pile that is arranged in tufts

[2]**tuftaffeta** \"\ *adj* **1 :** made of tuftaffeta **2** *obs* **:** clothed in tuftaffeta

tufted coquette *n* **:** a Central American hummingbird (*Lophornis ornatus*) having a large crest and cervical tufts; *broadly* **:** any of several related birds

tufted deer *n* **:** a deer of the genus *Elaphodus* related to the muntjacs but having minute antlers that are largely concealed by a frontal tuft of long coarse hair

tufted duck *or* **tufted pochard** *n* **1 :** an Old World duck (*Aythya fuligula*) having a tufted head but in most characteristics similar to the typical scaup ducks **2 :** RING-NECKED DUCK

tufted hair grass *n* **1 :** TUSSOCK GRASS a **2 :** a slender wiry grass (*Deschampsia caespitosa*) of the north temperate zone

tufted loosestrife *n* **:** a primulaceous bog or marsh herb (*Naumburgia thyrsiflora*) of the north temperate zone that has small yellow flowers in heads on close racemes

tufted pansy *n* **:** a European violet (*Viola cornuta*) that has the spur of the corolla unusually prolonged — called also *horned violet*

tufted puffin *n* **:** a puffin (*Lunda cirrhata*) of the northern Pacific that is chiefly blackish brown above and below and has white cheeks and a large yellow plume over each eye

tufted titmouse *n* **:** an ashy gray titmouse (*Parus bicolor*) with a pointed crest that is found in the eastern U.S. chiefly south of New England and in the Midwest

tufted vetch *n* **:** a common perennial vetch (*Vicia cracca*) of temperate regions that has dense elongate clusters of flowers

tuft·er \ˈtəftə(r)\ *n* -S **:** one that tufts: as **a :** a hound used to drive deer out of cover **b :** a worker who tufts mattresses, cushions, quilts, or pads

tuft–hunted \ˈ=ˌ==\ *adj* **:** sought out by tuft-hunters

tuft–hunter \ˈ=ˌ==\ *n* [[1]*tuft* (sense 4)] **:** one that seeks association with persons of title or high social status **:** SNOB

[1]**tuft–hunting** \ˈ=ˌ==\ *n* **:** the practice of tuft-hunters

[2]**tuft–hunting** \"\ *adj* **:** of or relating to tuft-hunters **:** SNOBBISH

tuft·i·ly \ˈtəftəlē\ *adv* **:** in a tufty manner

tufting *n* -S [fr. gerund of [2]*tuft*] **1 :** the act of one that tufts **:** a process of making tufts **2 :** TUFTS; *esp* **:** tufts used for decoration

tuft·let \ˈtəftlət\ *n* -S **:** a small tuft

tufts *pl of* TUFT, *pres 3d sing of* TUFT

tufty \-ftē\ *adj* -ER/-EST **1 :** growing in tufts **:** forming tufts ⟨little ~ plants —Katherine Mansfield⟩ **2 :** having many tufts ⟨a ~ stretch of marshland —Helen Eustis⟩

[1]**tug** \ˈtəg\ *vb* **tugged; tugged; tugging; tugs** [ME *tuggen, toggen*; akin to OE *tēon* to pull, draw — more at TOW] *vi* **1 :** to pull hard ⟨*tugged* at the chains with the aid of two husky comrades —T.B.Costain⟩ ⟨jerked the shade and let it ~ halfway up —Barnaby Conrad⟩ ⟨insistent memories that *tugged* . . . from every cranny —Timothy Wharton⟩ **2 :** to struggle in opposition **:** CONTEND ⟨a person . . . *tugging* and wrestling with doubts and conflicts —*Omnibook*⟩ **3 :** to exert oneself laboriously **:** STRUGGLE, LABOR ⟨*tugged* all his life to make a living⟩ **~** *vt* **1 :** to pull at hard **:** strain at ⟨each oar was *tugged* by five or six slaves —T.B.Macaulay⟩ **2 a :** to move by pulling hard **:** pull with effort **:** DRAG, HAUL ⟨stuck fast until a team of cattle could . . . ~ them out of the slough —T.B.Macaulay⟩ ⟨the five year development plan now being *tugged* into shape —*Economist*⟩ **b :** to carry with difficulty **:** LUG ⟨~ about a mental burden of protest —J.G.Gilkey⟩ **3** *obs* **:** to handle roughly **:** MAUL **4 :** to tow with a tugboat **syn** see PULL

[2]**tug** \"\ *n* -S [ME *tugge*, fr. *tuggen* to tug] **1 :** something that is used as a connection for pulling: as **a :** a trace of a harness **b :** a short leather strap or loop **c :** a rope or chain used for pulling **d :** the iron hook of a hoisting tub to which a tackle is fastened to pull the tub up a mine shaft **2 a :** an act or instance of tugging **:** a hard pull ⟨making his own bed with a few careless ~*s* —Marcia Davenport⟩ **b :** a strong pulling force ⟨enables him to defy the awful ~ of gravity —G.E.Fox⟩ ⟨knows . . . why the ~ of the past has so much power —Norman Cousins⟩ **3 a :** a hard struggle **:** a big effort ⟨the stream was easy on the eastern side, but I saw that the ~ was to come, for the main torrent swept . . . near the western bank —A.W. Kinglake⟩ **b :** a struggle between two people or forces ⟨the ~ within him between conservative and liberal —John Mason Brown⟩ **4 a :** TUGBOAT **b :** an airplane used to pull a glider

[3]**tug** \"\ *n* -S [prob. alter. (influenced by [2]*tug*) of [1]*tog* & *toge*] **1** *Brit* **a :** COLLEGER 1 **b :** KING'S SCHOLAR **2** *chiefly Brit* **:** an uncouth, dirty, or unscrupulous person

tugboat \ˈ=ˌ=\ *n* **:** a strongly built powerful boat used for towing and pushing esp. in harbors and on inland waterways — called also *towboat, tug*

tugboat

tug chain *n* **1 :** a short chain at the end of a harness tug to attach it to the whiffletree **2 :** a harness tug made of chain

tug·ger \ˈtəgə(r)\ *n* -S **:** one that tugs: *specif* **:** a small portable hoist used in a mine and usu. mounted on a column and driven by air or electricity

tug·less \ˈtəgləs\ *adj* **:** not having a tug ⟨a ~ harness⟩

tug·man \-gmən\ *n, pl* **tugmen :** one who works on a tugboat

tug–of–war \ˈ==ˈ=\ *n, pl* **tugs–of–war 1 :** a struggle for supremacy ⟨a continual *tug-of-war* between the authorities and the masses —Alexander Dallin⟩ **2 :** an athletic contest in which two teams pull against each other at opposite ends of a rope

tu·grik *or* **tu·ghrik** \ˈtüˌgrēk\ *n* -S [Mongol *dughurik*, lit., round thing, wheel] **1 :** the basic unit of monetary value of the Mongolian People's Republic — see MONEY table **2 :** a note or coin representing one tugrik

tugurium *var of* TEGURIUM

tui \ˈtüē\ *n* -S [Maori] **:** a predominantly glossy iridescent black New Zealand honey eater (*Prosthemadera novaeseelandiae*) with white markings on throat, neck, and wings that is a notable mimic and often kept as a cage bird — called also *parson bird*

tuille \ˈtwē(ə)l\ *n* -S [ME *toile*, fr. MF *tuille, teuille* tile, fr. L *tegula* — more at THATCH] **:** one of the hinged plates before the thigh in plate armor — see ARMOR illustration

tuil·lette \twēˈlet\ *n* -S [F *tuilette*, dim. of *tuile* tile, fr. MF *tuille, teuille*] **:** a small tuille for protecting the hip

tuil·yie *or* **tuil·zie** \ˈtülyi\ *n or vb* [ME (Sc) *tulȝe*, fr. MF *tooil, toeil* battle, trouble, fr. OF — more at TOIL] *chiefly Scot* **:** QUARREL, STRUGGLE

tu·in·ga \tüˈiŋgə\ *n* -S [Samoan] **:** a headdress of bleached human hair worn by Samoan men or women of very high rank in important ceremonies and dances

tu·ism \ˈt(y)üˌizəm\ *n* -S [L *tu* thou + E *-ism* — more at THOU] **:** the use of the second person (as in apostrophe or in rhetorical evasion of the first person); *also* **:** an instance of such use

tu·i·tion \t(y)üˈishən\ *n* -S [ME *tuicioun*, fr. OF *tuicion*, fr. L *tuition-, tuitio*, fr. *tuitus* (past part. of *tuērī* to look at, watch over, protect) + *-ion-, -io* -ion; perh. akin to OIr *tūath* left, northerly, lucky, favorable, Goth *thiuth* good, beneficial, ON *thȳdr* kind, meek] **1** *archaic* **:** protection, care, or custody esp. as exercised by a parent or guardian over a child or ward **:** GUARDIANSHIP ⟨powers which the father hath, in the right of ~ during minority —John Locke⟩ **2 :** the act of teaching **:** the services or guidance of a teacher **:** INSTRUCTION ⟨pursued his studies under private ~⟩ ⟨the high costs of ~⟩ ⟨received careful ~ from his mother⟩ **3 :** the price of or payment for instruction ⟨~ has risen sharply⟩

tu·i·tion·al \-shənᵊl\ *adj* **:** of or relating to tuition **:** designed to teach ⟨~ films⟩

t'u–jen \ˈtüˈrən\ *n, pl* **t'u–jen** *usu cap* [Chin(Pek) *t'u³-jen²*] **:** T'U-LAO

tu·kra \ˈtükrə\ *n* -S [Hindi *ṭukrā* piece, bit, scrap] **:** a disorder of the leaves and shoots of the mulberry tree in India caused by the feeding of a mealybug (*Phenacoccus hirsutus*) and characterized by curling of the leaves

tu·ku·lör \ˌtükü'lər\ *or* **tu·ku·ler** \-ˈle(ə)r\ *also* **tou·cou·leur** \-ˈlər\ *n* -S *usu cap* [F *Toucouleurs*, pl., Tukulörs, fr. Wolof *Tokoror*, fr. *Tekrur*, locality in Senegal] **:** any of a group of mixed negroid peoples of eastern Senegal who are tall and black and chiefly Muslim

tu·ku·tu·ku \ˈtü(ˌ)küˈtü(ˌ)kü\ *n* -S [Maori] **:** decorative Maori latticework usu. of flax or kiekie stems and in the form of panels that are used esp. between the carved posts of communal buildings (as a meetinghouse)

[1]**tu·la** \ˈtülə\ *also* **tula metal** *n* -S [fr. *Tula*, city in central U.S.S.R.] **:** NIELLO 1

[2]**tula** \"\ *or* **tula istle** *n* -S [MexSp *tula*] **:** a coarse nearly white Mexican istle fiber that is sometimes used locally for cord or fabric and commercially esp. for brushes and that is obtained from an agave (*Agave lecheguilla*)

[3]**tula** \"\ *adj, usu cap* [fr. *Tula*, U.S.S.R.] **:** of or from the city of Tula, U.S.S.R. **:** of the kind or style prevalent in Tula

tu·la·di \ˈtülədē\ *n* -S [CanF *touladi*, fr. Montagnais] **:** LAKE TROUT b

tu·la·fa·le \ˌtüləˈfälā\ *n, pl* **tulafale** [Samoan *tūlāfale*] **:** a Samoan native chief functioning as an adviser and debater on matters of public policy and expected to be thoroughly informed on matters of traditional lore

t'u–lao \ˈtüˈlaů\ *n, pl* **t'u–lao** *usu cap T* [Chin(Pek) *t'u³-lao³*] **:** any of various Tai groups of southern China

tu·la·pai \ˌtüˈläˌpī\ *n* -S [Apache] **:** a fermented beverage made by Apache Indians of sprouted fermented corn often with various roots or herbs

tu·la·re \tüˈlärā\ *n* -S [AmerSp *tulares*, pl., tule fields, fr. Sp *tule*] **:** TULE LAND

tu·la·re·mia \ˌtüləˈrēmēə\ *n* -S [NL, fr. *Tulare* county, Calif. where it was first discovered + NL *-emia*] **:** an infectious disease of rodents, man, and some domestic animals caused by a bacterium (*Pasteurella tularensis*) that is transmitted by the bites of insects or is occas. acquired by man through handling infected animals and in man marked by headache, chills, fever, and other constitutional symptoms of toxemia — **tu·la·re·mic** \ˌ==ˈrēmik\ *adj*

tu·la·si \ˈtüləsē\ *n* -S [Skt *tulasī* — more at TULSI] *India* **:** HOLY BASIL

[1]**tul·bagh·ia** \ˌtəlˈbagēə\ [NL, fr. Ryk *Tulbagh* †1771 Dutch governor of Cape Colony + NL *-ia*] *syn of* AGAPANTHUS

[2]**tulbaghia** \"\ *n* -S [NL] **:** a plant of the genus *Agapanthus*

tul·chan \ˈtəlkən\ *also* **tul·chin** \-kən\ *n* -S [ScGael *tulchan*] **1 :** a stuffed calfskin used esp. formerly to induce a cow to let down her milk **2** *or* **tulchan bishop :** one of the bishops appointed in the Reformed Presbyterian Church of Scotland in 1572 who consented to hand over the larger part of the revenues of their dioceses to the lay patrons who had obtained their appointment

tu·le \ˈtülē, -li\ *n* -S [Sp, fr. Nahuatl *tollin, tullin*] **1 :** any of several large New World bulrushes (*Scirpus californicus, S. acutus*, and *S. lacustris*) or cattails that grow abundantly on overflowed land and are sometimes used for making native reed products (as mats or rafts) **2** *or* **tule land :** land on which tules are the dominant or characteristic native plant — usu. used in pl. and with *the* ⟨plans for draining and cultivating the ~*s*⟩ **3** *usu cap* **:** SAN BLAS

tule beetle *n* **:** a carabid beetle (*Agonum maculicolle*) of marshy areas of California that produces a strong nauseous odor

tule fog *n* **:** a dense low-flying mobile fog occurring esp. in the San Francisco area

tule goose *n* **:** a goose that winters in the Sacramento valley of California and prob. breeds in the arctic and that is a variety (*Anser albifrons gambelli*) of the white-fronted goose distinguished chiefly by its large size

tule mint *n, West* **:** CANADA MINT

tule potato *also* **tule root** *n, West* **:** WAPATOO

tule wren *n* **:** a long-billed marsh wren (*Telmatodytes palustris paludicola*) of the western U. S.

tu·li·ac \ˈt(y)üləˌak\ *n* -S [origin unknown] *dial Eng* **:** SKUA

tu·lip \ˈt(y)üləp\ *n* -S *often attrib* [NL *tulipa*, fr. Turk *tülbend* turban; fr. the flower's resemblance to a turban — more at TURBAN] **1 a** (1) **:** any of various plants constituting the genus *Tulipa* and including many that have been so long cultivated for their showy flowers as to make it impossible to identify them surely with existing tulip species though the dwarf early types commonly are assigned to a species (*T. suaveolens*) while later taller forms are assigned to a species (*T. gesneriana*) — see COTTAGE TULIP, DARWIN TULIP, LADY TULIP (2) **:** a flower or bulb of a tulip **b :** any of various southern African plants of the genus *Homeria* (family Iridaceae) having flowers that resemble tulips and including several forms that are poisonous to cattle **2 :** something felt to resemble a tulip: as **a :** a swelling of the metal of the muzzle of an old-fashioned gun **b** (1) **:** a wineglass that in silhouette suggests the flower of a tulip (2) **:** a style in women's dress in which a close waist and full tapered skirt suggests an inverted tulip

tu·li·pa \ˈt(y)üləpə\ *n, cap* [NL] **:** a large genus of Eurasian bulbous herbs (family Liliaceae) having coated bulbs, linear or broadly lanceolate leaves, and commonly a single showy flower with six equal perianth segments and six hypogynous stamens — see TULIP

tulip ear *n* **:** an erect pointed ear (as of a dog) often with the tip drooping — **tulip–eared** \ˈ==ˌ=\ *adj*

tulip fire *or* **tulip blight** *n* **:** a destructive disease of tulips caused by a mold (*Botrytis tulipae*) and marked by gray to brown lesions on leaves, petals, scapes, and bulb that often result in extensive necrosis

tulipflower \ˈ==ˌ=\ *n* **:** WHEEL TREE 2

tulip lancewood *n, Austral* **:** TULIPWOOD 2a(2)

tulip mold *n* **:** TULIP FIRE; *also* **:** the fungus causing the disease

tulip mosaic *n* **:** a virus disease of tulips marked esp. by the striking color break in the flower which takes the form of irregular striping or marginal feathering

tulip oak *n* **:** an Australian tree of the genus *Tarrietia* (family Sterculiaceae) characterized by pink or reddish strong wood used for furniture and interior finish work

tu·lip·o·ma·nia \ˌt(y)üləpəˈmānēə\ *n* [*tulip* + *-o-* + *mania*] **:** an excessive fad or passion for acquiring or growing tulips; *specif* **:** such a mania prevailing in Holland about 1634 and accompanied by wild speculation in bulbs ultimately ended by governmental interference — **tu·lip·o·ma·ni·ac** \-ēˌak\ *n*

tulip orchid *n* **:** a Mexican epiphytic orchid (*Cattleya citrina*) much grown for its usu. solitary pendent very showy fragrant yellow flower with a white-bordered lip

tulip poppy *n* **1 :** a commonly cultivated glaucous annual poppy (*Papaver glaucum*) of Asia Minor with cup-shaped scarlet flowers on tall erect stems **2 :** a perennial Mexican herb (*Hunnemannia fumariaefolia*) of the family Papaveraceae that closely resembles the California poppy but has bright orange-colored stamens and two separate sepals

tulip root *n* **:** a disease of various grasses and esp. cereal grasses caused by a strain of the bulb eelworm and characterized esp. by bulbous swellings in the stem and distortions of leaves

tulip shell *n* **:** BAND SHELL; *esp* **:** a variable predominantly gray and brown mollusk (*Fasciolaria tulipa*) occurring on the coast of the southern U. S.

tulip tree *n* **1** *or* **tulip poplar :** a tall No. American timber tree (*Liriodendron tulipifera*) having truncate somewhat lobed leaves, large greenish yellow flowers that resemble tulips, and soft white wood that is much used esp. for cabinetwork and woodenware — see TREE illustration **2 :** any of various trees with tulip-shaped flowers: as **a :** MAJAGUA a **b :** PORTIA TREE **c :** BANANA SHRUB **d** *Austral* (1) **:** WARATAH (2) **:** an evergreen tree (*Lagunaria pattersonii*) of the family Malvaceae with large solitary axillary rosy pink flowers

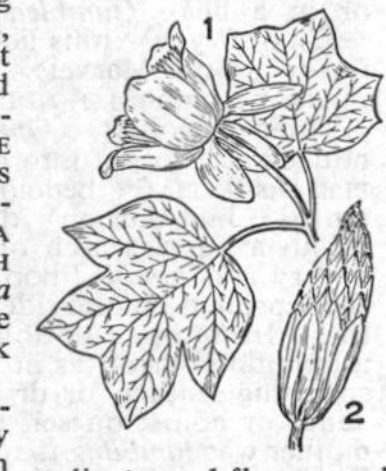

tulip tree; *1* flower and leaves, *2* fruit

tulip tree scale *n* **:** a scale (*Toumeyella liriodendri*) that occurs mainly in the eastern half of the U. S. on magnolia, poplar, and a few other trees

tulip valve *n* **:** an intake valve (as on an engine) with a cup-shaped to trumpet-shaped head

tulipwood \ˈ==ˌ=\ *n* **1 :** wood of the No. American tulip tree **:** WHITEWOOD **2 a :** any of several showily striped or variegated woods: as (1) **:** the rose-colored wood of a Brazilian tree (*Physocalymma scabberimum* of the family Lythraceae) much used by cabinetmakers for inlaying (2) *Austral* **:** the wood of a tree (*Harpullia pendula*) — called also *Moreton Bay tulipwood* (3) *Austral* **:** the wood of the emu apple **b :** any tree that yields such a tulipwood **3 :** AUBURN

tu·li·san \ˌtüləˈsän\ *n, pl* **tulisa·nes** \-äˌnās\ [Tag *tulisán*] **:** a Philippine bandit **:** LADRONE

tulle \ˈtül *sometimes* ˈtůl *or* ˈtəl\ *n* -S [F, fr. *Tulle*, city in central France where it was orig. made] **:** a sheer and often stiffened machine-made net made with a usu. hexagonal mesh and of silk, rayon, or nylon and used chiefly for veils, evening dresses, or ballet costumes — compare ILLUSION

tulle gras *n* **:** fine-meshed gauze impregnated with a fatty substance (as vegetable oil or soft paraffin) and used in medicine as an application to raw surfaces

tul·li·bee \ˈtələˌbē\ *n* -S [CanF *toulibi*, prob. fr. Cree *otonabi*, lit., water-mouth] **:** any of several whitefishes of central and northern No. America; *esp* **:** a common cisco (*Leucichthys artedi*) that is a commercially important food fish

tul·ly's powder \ˈtəlēz-\ *n, usu cap T* [after William *Tully* †1859 Am. physician] **:** a powder composed of a mixture of morphine sulfate, camphor, powdered glycyrrhiza, and precipitated calcium carbonate and formerly used as an anodyne and antispasmodic

tul·nic \ˈtülnēk\ *n* -S [Romanian] **:** a very long wooden trumpet formerly used to convey warnings (as of invasion) between Romanian communities

tu·los·to·ma·ce·ae \t(y)üˌlästəˈmāsēˌē\ *n pl, cap* [NL, fr. *Tulostoma*, type genus (prob. fr. *tyl-* + *stoma*) + *-aceae*] **:** a family of fungi (order Sclerodermatales) comprising the stalked puffballs and distinguished by having sporocarps similar to the Lycoperdaceae but with the unchambered gleba raised on a stalk

tul·sa \ˈtəlsə\ *adj, usu cap* [fr. *Tulsa*, Okla.] **:** of or from the city of Tulsa, Okla. ⟨a *Tulsa* oil company⟩ **:** of the kind or style prevalent in Tulsa

tul·san \-sən\ *n* -S *cap* [*Tulsa*, Okla. + E *-an*] **:** a native or resident of Tulsa, Okla.

tul·si \ˈtülsē\ *n* -S [Hindi *tulsī*, fr. Skt *tulasī*, prob. of Dravidian origin; akin to Tamil *tuḷay*, Kanarese *toḷaci*] *India* **:** HOLY BASIL

tul–tul \ˈtülˈtül\ *n* -S [native name in New Guinea] **:** an assistant or deputy of a Polynesian native headman

tu·lu \ˈtü(ˌ)lü\ *n, pl* **tulu** *or* **tulus** *usu cap* **1 :** one of a Dravidian people in India on the coast near Mangalore **2 :** a Dravidian language of the west coast of Mysore in southern India

tul·war *also* **tul·waur** \ˌtəlˈwär\ *n* -S [Hindi *talwār, tarwār*, fr. Skt *taravāri*] **:** a curved saber or scimitar used in the Orient and esp. in northern India

[1]**tum** \ˈtəm\ *vt* **tummed; tummed; tumming; tums** [origin unknown] **1 :** to card (wool) as a preliminary to finer carding **2 :** to open or tease out (wool) before carding

[2]**tum** \"\ *n* -S [imit.] **1 :** the sound of a plucked string (as of a banjo) **2 :** the sound of a drum

[3]**tum** \"\ *vi* **tummed; tummed; tumming; tums :** to make a tum or tum-tum

tuman *var of* TOMAN

tu·ma·ta·ku·ru *also* **tu·ma·tu·ku·ru** \ˌtüˌmädəˈkü(ˌ)rü, -mad-\ *n* -S [Maori *tumatakuru*] **:** a New Zealand shrub or tree (*Discaria toumatou*) of the family Rhamnaceae having stout sharp spines used by the Maoris for tattooing — called also *Irishman, matagory, wild Irishman*

tum·bak \(ˌ)təmˈbak, tům-\ *or* **tum·ba·ki** \-ˈbäkē\ *or* **tum·bek** \-bek\ *or* **tumbeki** \-ˈbekē\ *n* -S [Ar *tunbak* & Turk *tumbeki*, both fr. Per *tambākū*, fr. Sp *tabaco* — more at TOBACCO] **:** a coarse Persian tobacco prob. derived from a tropical American plant (*Nicotiana tabacum*)

[1]**tum·ble** \ˈtəmbəl\ *vb* **tumbled; tumbled; tumbling** \-b(ə)liŋ\ **tumbles** [ME *tumblen*, freq. of *tumben, tomben* to dance, jump, fr. OE *tumbian*; akin to MHG *tūmeln* to turn, reel, OHG *tūmōn* to turn, reel, ON *tumba* to tumble] *vi* **1 a :** to perform gymnastic feats of rolling and turning ⟨a man . . . paid for *tumbling* upon his hands —Samuel Johnson⟩ ⟨to keep in shape, the . . . general ~*s* —*Time*⟩ **b :** to turn end over end in falling or in flight ⟨rooks *tumbling* and cawing above the high elm tops —Flora Thompson⟩ ⟨a projectile ~*s* when the twist of the rifling is too slow for the bullet⟩ ⟨machine-gun

bullets, badly *tumbling*, fell in among the ridges —S.L.A. Marshall⟩ **2 a :** to fall suddenly and helplessly **:** pitch headlong **:** fall to the ground ⟨~ from a scaffold⟩ ⟨tripped over a stone and *tumbled*⟩ ⟨one . . . whose horse has *tumbled* —G.B. Shaw⟩ **b :** to suffer a usu. sudden downfall, overthrow, or defeat ⟨once again a government ~*s*⟩ ⟨the small ~ with the great —Arnold Bennett⟩ **c :** to decline suddenly and sharply (as in price or value) **:** DROP ⟨the stock market *tumbled* —*N.Y. Times*⟩ **d :** to fall into ruin or decay **:** break down **:** COLLAPSE ⟨the wall finally *tumbled*⟩ ⟨deserted buildings . . . *tumbling* into ruins —*Amer. Guide Series: Nev.*⟩ — often used with *down* ⟨old houses *tumbling* down⟩ ⟨the structure of society does not ~ down when we probe its framework —Zechariah Chafee⟩ **3 :** to roll over and over, back and forth, or around **:** thrash about **:** twist and turn **:** TOSS ⟨*tumbled* in her sleep⟩ ⟨his children *tumbled* like brown puppies about his threshold —Pearl Buck⟩ ⟨laughed all day together *tumbling* in the hay —George Meredith⟩ ⟨thoughts were *tumbling* about in her brain like cargo loose in a rolling ship —Arnold Bennett⟩ **4 a :** to fall or issue forth hurriedly, confusedly, and all in a heap **:** pour out pell-mell ⟨books *tumbling* from the presses⟩ ⟨gold coins *tumbled* out on the counterpane —T.B.Costain⟩ ⟨words *tumbling* eagerly from his lips⟩ **b :** to move in a stumblingly hurried, confused, or disorderly way **:** rush helter-skelter ⟨*tumbled* into his clothes⟩ ⟨customers *tumbling* out of the tavern as the fire trucks arrived⟩ **5 :** to come by chance or unexpectedly **:** STUMBLE, HAPPEN ⟨treated his wife and children as the most delightful accidents against whom he had, most happily, *tumbled* —Hugh Walpole⟩ — usu. used with *in*, *into*, or *upon* ⟨the individuality you always *tumbled* upon in an English . . . village —H.J.Laski⟩ **6 :** to have a receding upward slope — compare TUMBLE HOME **7 :** to come to understand the point or implication (as of something obscure or devious that is being said or done) **:** catch on **:** wise up ⟨nobody ~*s* till we're dragging the damned aristocrats out of their cursed beds —W.G.Hardy⟩ — usu. used with *to* ⟨suspicious for some time . . . and all of a sudden I *tumbled* to it —W.S. Maugham⟩ ⟨advertisers . . . had not *tumbled* to the extensive possibilities for fakery in photography —Andy Logan⟩ **~** *vt* **1 a :** to cause to tumble or roll head over heels **:** make fall **:** throw down or over **:** PITCH, TOSS ⟨*tumbled* him on the bed⟩ **b :** to bring down (as in hunting) **:** DROP ⟨~ a rabbit with a shotgun⟩ **c :** to cause to fall from high place or power **:** TOPPLE ⟨had reached a pinnacle . . . and now he was *tumbled* from it —Winifred Bambrick⟩ **d :** to cause to fall to the ground **:** knock down **:** FELL ⟨*tumbled* a policeman —Richard Free⟩ ⟨*tumbled* the trees —V. W. Von Hagen⟩ **2 :** to cause to fall into ruins **:** DEMOLISH ⟨~*s* down steeples —Shak.⟩ ⟨*tumbling* the majestic house of worship —Claudia Cassidy⟩ **3 a :** to throw together in a confused and disorderly way **:** fling about or in a heap ⟨*tumbled* them helter-skelter into the boxes —Elinor Wylie⟩ ⟨hills lie *tumbled* about in a sort of mad confusion —Tom Marvel⟩ **b :** to push or roll about **:** cause to pitch or stumble **:** BUNDLE, TOSS ⟨*tumbled* about like a football —Tobias Smollett⟩ ⟨*tumbling* him into the position at short notice⟩ **c :** to put into a state of disorder or disarray **:** RUMPLE, DISHEVEL ⟨~ bedclothes⟩ ⟨one gets so *tumbled* in such a crowd —Jane Austen⟩ **d** *archaic* **:** to turn over or throw about (as in a hasty search or examination) ⟨walked through the library and *tumbled* books —Lord Byron⟩ **e :** to turn (as a sheet printed on one side that is to be backed up by the same form) from top to bottom **4 :** to whirl (objects or material) in a tumbling barrel (as in polishing or coating metallic objects, softening leather, or drying clothes) — **tumble to** *Brit* **:** to adapt or adjust oneself to **:** fall in with **:** fit into ⟨really his mother was *tumbling to* things wonderfully well —Sheila Kaye-Smith⟩ — **tumble up 1 :** to go or come quickly on deck ⟨men are still *tumbling up* from below, racing to their battle stations —E.L.Beach⟩ **2** *dial* **:** to roll hay into bundles for pitching

[2]**tumble** \"\ *n* -s **1 a :** a random and disorderly collection **:** a mass of objects or material piled up or thrown together in confusion **:** HEAP ⟨a ~ of books and papers on the floor⟩ ⟨could look out . . . at the ~ of lesser hills and valleys, dotted here and there with towns and settlements —R.M.Coates⟩ **b** *NewEng* **:** a small pile of hay in a field **c :** a confused, disorderly state or condition **:** DISARRAY, MESS ⟨viewed the ~ of the bed⟩ ⟨cut through the ~ of wordy, circular arguments⟩ **2 :** an act of tumbling or falling: as **a :** a gymnastic or acrobatic feat of tumbling (as a somersault) ⟨practice a ~⟩ **b :** an accidental fall ⟨take a ~⟩ ⟨injured in a ~ from a horse⟩ ⟨no ability to pick herself up after a ~ —F.A.Swinnerton⟩ — compare ROUGH-AND-TUMBLE **c :** a usu. sudden descent from a higher level or position **:** DOWNFALL, DROP ⟨the premier's ~ from office⟩ ⟨a ~ in stock market prices⟩ ⟨a ~ from high estate⟩ **d :** a rolling, tossing, and falling movement (as of a watercourse) ⟨the ~ of the waves⟩ ⟨the . . . river does a series of ~*s* over rocky ledges —Y.E.Soderberg⟩ **3 :** TUMBLING BARREL **4 :** a sign of recognition or interest; *esp* **:** an indication of responsive social or amatory interest ⟨you wouldn't even give me a ~ —Dorothy Parker⟩

tumblebug \'==,=\ *n* [[1]*tumble* + *bug*] **:** any of various scarabaeid beetles (as members of the genera *Scarabaeus*, *Canthon*, *Copris*, or *Phanaeus*) that form globular masses of dung which they roll and bury in holes excavated in the ground, in which they lay their eggs, and which serve as food for the larvae

tumble cart *also* **tumble car** *n* **:** a rough dumpcart having its wheels solid and made fast to the axle

tumbled *past of* TUMBLE

tumbledown \'==,=\ *adj* [fr. the phrase *tumble down*] **:** ready to fall **:** falling into decay **:** DILAPIDATED, RAMSHACKLE ⟨a ~ shack⟩ ⟨a ~ clapboard house, now serving as a junk shop —*Amer. Guide Series: N.Y. City*⟩ ⟨~ temples —Glenway Wescott⟩

tumbledung \'==,=\ *n* [[1]*tumble* + *dung*] **:** TUMBLEBUG

tumble grass *n* **:** WITCHGRASS 2

[1]**tumble home** *vi* **:** to incline inward above the waterline or greatest breadth **:** FALL HOME — compare [3]BATTER; used chiefly of the sides of a ship

[2]**tumble home** *n* **:** a receding upward slope (as of a ship's sides) **:** an inclination inward from the greatest breadth ⟨as in all ships of the period, her sides have considerable *tumble home* —H.G. Smith⟩ ⟨the *tumble home* of a building toward the top⟩

tumble mustard *n* **:** a tall European biennial herb (*Sisymbrium altissimum*) that has pinnatifid leaves and long slender seed pods and is often a troublesome weed in No. America

tum·bler \'təmb(ə)lə(r)\ *n* -s [ME, fr. *tumblen* to tumble + *-er* — more at TUMBLE] **1 :** one that tumbles: as **a :** one that performs gymnastic or acrobatic feats (as somersaults or handsprings) **:** ACROBAT **b :** a dog formerly bred for taking rabbits by suddenly seizing animals attracted or distracted by its circuitous tumbling progress **c** *or* **tumbler pigeon :** any of various domestic pigeons that tumble or somersault backward in flight or on the ground **d** (1) **:** the pupa of a mosquito (2) **:** TUMBLEBUG **e** *chiefly dial* **:** TUMBLE CART, TUMBREL **f :** ROLY-POLY 4b **2 :** a drinking glass made usu. without a foot or stem and orig. with a pointed or convex base so that it could not be set down until empty **3 a :** a movable obstruction in a lock (as a lever, latch, wheel, slide, pin) that must be adjusted to a particular position (as by a key) before the bolt can be thrown **b :** a piece that is attached to or forms part of the hammer of a gunlock, that is acted on by the mainspring, and that bears the notches for the sear point to enter **c** (1) **:** a projecting piece on a revolving shaft or rockshaft for actuating another piece; *specif* **:** the click that moves the rack in a striking mechanism one tooth for each blow struck (2) **:** the movable part of a tumbler gear **d :** a pin or one of a pair of pins engaging the ends of a ring stopper and shank painter **e :** one of the levers suspending the harness in a loom **f :** NEEDLE 8d **4 :** a device or mechanism for tumbling or revolving: as **a :** a clothes-drying device consisting of a revolving cage in which hot air is agitated by fan action **b :** TUMBLING BARREL **c :** a drum in which hides are treated (as washed and softened) in leather manufacturing **5 a :** a worker that operates a tumbling device (as a tumbling barrel) **b :** one that deburrs and cleans parts (as of watches or guns) by tumbling them with abrasives

tumbler bearing *n* **:** any of the intermediate swiveling or pivoted bearings for a square shaft (as in a gantry) that can be knocked aside (as by a traveling crab moving along the shaft and gearing with it)

tumbler cart *n* **:** a horse-drawn 2-wheeled farm cart with a tank for handling liquid or semiliquid materials

tumbler cup *n* **:** a drinking cup with a pointed or convex bottom — compare TUMBLER 2

tumbler gear *n* **:** any of various reversing or speed-changing gears used esp. in modern machine tools that have one or more idle wheels journaled in a swinging frame moved and clamped in position by the operator

tumbler switch *n* **:** a snap switch in which the blades are actuated by a lever being pushed up or pulled down

tumbles *pres 3d sing of* TUMBLE, *pl of* TUMBLE

tumbleweed \'==,=\ *n* [[1]*tumble* + *weed*] **:** any plant that habitually breaks away from its roots in the autumn and is driven by the wind as a light, rolling mass over the fields and prairies: as **a :** WINGED PIGWEED **b :** RUSSIAN THISTLE **c :** any of several amaranths (as *Amaranthus graecizans*)

[1]**tumbling** *n* -s [ME, fr. gerund of *tumblen* to tumble — more at TUMBLE] **1 :** the act or process of tumbling **2 :** the skill, practice, or sport of executing gymnastic tumbles **3 :** a continuous violent pitching rotation of an aerodynamic body

[2]**tumbling** *adj* [ME, fr. pres. part. of *tumblen* to tumble] **:** tipped or slanted to the right or left of vertical position — used esp. of a cattle brand ⟨the *Tumbling* T brand⟩ — see BRAND illustration

tumbling barrel *n* **:** a revolving barrel, cask, or box in which objects or materials (as small metal parts, castings, plastics, leather, or clothing) undergo a process (as finishing, polishing, coating, softening, or drying) by being whirled about and so brought into vigorous frictional contact — called also *rattler*, *rumble*, *rumbler*, *scouring barrel*

tumbling bay *n* **:** an overfall in a canal **:** WEIR

tumbling box *n* **:** a tumbling barrel for small objects

tumbling mustard *n* **:** TUMBLE MUSTARD

tumbling pigweed *n* **:** PIGWEED a

tumbling rod *n* **:** a rod having a cam or lever rigidly attached to transmit an intermittent motion

tumbling shaft *n* **1 :** CAMSHAFT **2 :** COUNTERSHAFT 2

tumbling verse *n* **:** an early modern English verse form having four stresses but no prevailing type of foot and no regular number of syllables

tum·boa \,təm'bōə\ [NL, fr. native name in Mossamedes, southwestern Africa] *syn of* WELWITSCHIA

tum·brel *or* **tum·bril** \'təmbrəl\ *n* -s [ME *tombrel*, *tumrel*, fr. ML & OF; ML *tumbrellum*, *tumberellum* cucking stool, fr. OF *tumberel*, *tomberel* dumpcart, tumble cart, fr. *tomber*, *tumer* to dance, leap, turn, tumble, of Gmc origin; akin to MLG *tummelen* to turn, leap, dance, OHG *tūmōn* to turn, reel — more at TUMBLE] **1** *obs* **:** an instrument of punishment **:** *specif* **:** CUCKING STOOL **2 a :** a farmer's dumpcart or wagon; *esp* **:** one for manure **b :** a vehicle carrying condemned persons (as political prisoners during the French Revolution) to a place of execution ⟨gaping crowds . . . watch Shanghai's ~*s* rumble past —*Time*⟩ **c** *archaic* **:** a two-wheeled cart accompanying troops to convey supplies (as tools or ammunition) **3** *dial Eng* **:** an osier or willow cage for fodder

tum·bu fly \'tüm,bü-\ *n* [*tumbu* of Bantu origin; akin to Kongo *timuka* fly, *mbu* mosquito, Swahili *imbu*] **:** an African fly (*Cordylobia anthropophaga*) of the family Muscidae whose larva lives as a subcutaneous parasite in various mammals and sometimes in man

tu·me·fa·cient \,t(y)ümə'fāshənt\ *adj* [L *tumefacient-*, *tumefaciens*, pres. part. of *tumefacere* to swell, cause to swell, fr. *tumēre* to swell + *facere* to make, do — more at THUMB, DO] **1 :** SWOLLEN **2 :** producing swelling

tu·me·fac·tion \,=='fakshən\ *n* -s [MF, fr. L *tumefactus* (past part. of *tumefacere* to swell, cause to swell) + MF *-ion*] **1 :** the act or process of tumefying **:** state of being tumefied ⟨incite previously normal tissue to ~ —*Amer. Jour. of Veterinary Research*⟩ **2 :** SWELLING ⟨~*s* on the chest wall or sinus tracts —J.B.Barnwell⟩

tu·me·fac·tive \,==,faktiv, -tēv *also* -təv\ *adj* [L *tumefactus* (past part.) + E *-ive*] **:** TUMEFACIENT 2

tu·me·fy \'==,fī\ *vb* -ED/-ING/-ES [MF *tumefier*, fr. L *tumēre* to swell + MF *-fier* -fy] *vi* **1 :** to rise in a tumor **:** SWELL **2 :** to become puffed up (as with pride) **~** *vt* **:** to cause to swell **:** produce a tumor in

tumeric *var of* TURMERIC

tu·mes·cence \t(y)ü'mesᵊn(t)s\ *n* -s [L *tumēre* to swell + E *-escence*] **1 :** the quality or state of being tumescent **:** DISTENTION, INFLATION: as **a :** swelling or teeming fullness ⟨the lush ~ of equatorial vegetation⟩ ⟨the ~ of the life force within him —Sidney Monas⟩ ⟨lyrics . . . distinguished by a kind of ~ —Cyril Connolly⟩ **b :** INFLATION ⟨a current critical ~ —J.L. Lievsay⟩ **c :** readiness for sexual activity marked by rising emotional excitement and physical tension with vascular congestion of the sex organs ⟨~ . . . is the really essential part of the process —Havelock Ellis⟩ **2 :** swollen part **:** SWELLING ⟨prairie relieved only by . . . ~*s* —Clifton Fadiman⟩

tu·mes·cent \-sᵊnt\ *adj* [L *tumescent-*, *tumescens*, pres. part. of *tumescere* to swell up, incho. of *tumēre* to swell] **1 :** somewhat tumid, swollen, or inflated ⟨~ tissue⟩ **2 :** BOMBASTIC, TUMID 3 **3 :** swelling with fullness of thought or emotion **:** TEEMING, PREGNANT ⟨a ~ flow of thought —H.G.Wells⟩

tum·fie \'təm(f)fi\ *n* -s [origin unknown] *Scot* **:** a stupid or awkward person

tu·mid \'t(y)üməd\ *adj* [L *tumidus*, fr. *tumēre* to swell — more at THUMB] **1 :** marked by swelling **:** SWOLLEN, DISTENDED ⟨puffy, ~ flesh⟩ ⟨a badly infected, ~ leg⟩ **2 :** formed as if by swelling or inflation **:** BULGING, PNEUMATIC, PROTUBERANT ⟨so high as heaved the ~ hills —John Milton⟩ ⟨a ~ membrane⟩ ⟨sails ~ in the spanking breeze⟩ ⟨the ~ whorls of a shell⟩ **3 :** overblown and pretentious (as in language or style) **:** BOMBASTIC, TURGID ⟨the ~ . . . structure of our sentences —Thomas De Quincey⟩ **syn** see INFLATED

tu·mid·i·ty \t(y)ü'midəd·ē, -dətē, -i\ *n* -ES **:** the quality or state of being tumid **:** INFLATION; *specif* **:** inflation of language or style ⟨speeches ridiculed for their ~ and bombast⟩

tu·mid·ly *adv* **:** in a tumid manner

[1]**tu·mi·on** \'t(y)ümē,än\ [NL, prob. fr. Gk *thumion*, a yew] *syn of* TORREYA

[2]**tumion** \"\ *n* -s **:** STINKING CEDAR

tummed *past of* TUM

tum·mer \'təmə(r)\ *n* -s [[1]*tum* + *-er*] **:** a small drum similar to the doffer for transferring the cotton from the first to the second cylinder in the double carding process of cotton manufacture

tumming *pres part of* TUM

tum·mock \'təmək\ *n* -s [ScGael *tom* hillock (akin to MIr *tomm* hill) + E *-ock* — more at TOMB] *chiefly Scot* **:** HILLOCK

tum·my \'təmē, -mi\ *n* -ES [baby-talk for *stomach*] **:** ABDOMEN, BELLY, STOMACH 1c ⟨makes that sweet . . . little baby cuddle down on his ~ —*Parents' Mag.*⟩ ⟨sit square with their *tummies* in —*Irish Digest*⟩ ⟨*tummies* are flattened by . . . foundations and girdles —*Corset & Underwear Rev.*⟩

tu·mor \'t(y)ümə(r)\ *n* -s *see -or in Explan Notes* [L, fr. *tumēre* to swell — more at THUMB] **1** *obs* **:** TUMIDITY **2 a :** a swollen or distended part **:** SWELLING, PROTUBERANCE ⟨houses that bulged with the ~*s* and warts of . . . ornamental architecture —W.A.White⟩ **b :** a mass of abnormal tissue growing in or on the plant or animal body; *specif* **:** such a mass of noninflammatory and independent tissue arising without obvious cause from cells of preexistent tissue, possessing no physiologic function, and characteristically unrestrained in growth and structure — compare CANCER, NEOPLASM, SARCOMA **3** *archaic* **a :** swelling conceit **:** ARROGANCE ⟨the ~ of insolence —Samuel Johnson⟩ **b :** turgidity of style **:** BOMBAST ⟨style . . . so far from ~ that it rather wanted a little elevation —Henry Wotton⟩

tu·mor·al \-mərəl\ *adj* **:** of, relating to, or constituting a tumor ⟨a ~ mass⟩ ⟨a ~ syndrome⟩

tumorlike \'==,=\ *adj* **:** resembling a tumor

tu·mor·ous \'t(y)ümərəs\ *adj* [LL *tumorosus*, fr. L *tumor* + *-osus* -ose] **1** *obs* **a :** SWOLLEN **b :** ARROGANT, VAINGLORIOUS **c :** BOMBASTIC **2 :** of, relating to, or resembling a tumor ⟨a ~ condition⟩ ⟨~ porches and bays —Lewis Mumford⟩

tumor virus *n* **:** a cell-free filtrate or an agent contained in such that is associated with or held to be a specific virus responsible for a neoplastic disease — compare MYXOMATOSIS 1, SHOPE PAPILLOMA

tump \'təmp, 'tümp\ *n* -s [origin unknown] **1** *chiefly dial Eng* **:** a small rise of ground: as **a :** MOUND, HUMMOCK **b :** MOLEHILL **c :** ANTHILL **d :** [1]BARROW 2, TUMULUS **2 :** a clump of vegetation (as trees, shrubs, or grass); *esp* **:** one making a dry spot in a swamp

tum·phy \'təm(p)fi\ *var of* TUMFIE

tump·line \'təm,plīn\ *n* [*tump* of Algonquian origin (akin to Abnaki *mádûmbi* pack strap) + *line*] **:** a sling formed by a strap slung over the forehead or chest for carrying a pack on the back or in hauling loads (as household goods or game) — see PACKSACK illustration

tums *pres 3d sing of* TUM, *pl of* TUM

[1]**tum–tum** \'təm,təm\ *also* **tum–ti–tum** \,təm(p)tē'təm\ *n* -s [imit.] **:** a reiterated tum or strumming

[2]**tum–tum** \"\ *vi* **:** to make a tum-tum **:** STRUM

tum·tum \'təm,təm\ *n* -s [perh. alter. of [1]*tandem*] *India* **:** DOGCART

tu·mu·lar \'t(y)ümyələ(r)\ *adj* [L *tumulus* mound, hillock + E *-ar* — more at TUMULUS] **:** of, relating to, or characterized by tumuli ⟨a ~ cemetery⟩ ⟨~ epoch⟩

tu·mu·lary \-ə,lerē\ *adj* [L *tumulus* + E *-ary*] **1 :** of, relating to, or placed over a tomb **:** SEPULCHRAL ⟨a ~ stone⟩ ⟨a ~ style⟩ **2 :** TUMULAR

tu·mu·lose \-ə,lōs\ *or* **tu·mu·lous** \-ələs\ *adj* [L *tumulosus*, fr. *tumulus* + *-osus* -ose] **:** full of small hills or mounds **:** TUMULAR ⟨out there on those plains, in that ~ landscape —Malcolm Lowry⟩

[1]**tu·mult** \'t(y)ü,məlt *sometimes* -ü̦məlt *or* 'tə̦m-\ *n* -s [ME *tumulte*, fr. MF, fr. L *tumultus*; akin to Skt *tumula* noisy, L *tumēre* to swell — more at THUMB] **1 a :** disorderly and violent movement, agitation or milling about, of a crowd accompanied usu. with great uproar and confusion of voices **:** COMMOTION, TURMOIL ⟨~ in the city⟩ ⟨mob was in ~ over the death of its idol —Anthony Benis⟩ **b :** a noisy and turbulent popular uprising **:** DISTURBANCE, RIOT ⟨the ~*s* and disorders of the Great Rebellion —T.S.Eliot⟩ ⟨during a hundred years . . . no ~ of sufficient importance to be called an insurrection —T.B. Macaulay⟩ **2 a :** a confusion of loud noise and usu. turbulent or agitated movement **:** HUBBUB, DIN ⟨the ~ of the elements⟩ ⟨talking loudly enough to make himself heard above the ~ —John Bainbridge⟩ ⟨the bells . . . made a jangling ~ —H.G. Wells⟩ ⟨the sound of the lava, a ~ of rock in molten pressure under moving earth —Richard Llewellyn⟩ **b :** a random or disorderly medley or profusion (as of objects or colors) **:** JUMBLE, RIOT 4 ⟨in the palace itself, what a ~ of statuary —*Horizon*⟩ **3 a :** violent agitation of mind or feelings **:** highly disturbing mental or emotional excitement or stress **:** FERMENT, TURBULENCE ⟨stood bewildered, her soul in a ~ —Hilaire Belloc⟩ ⟨seek refuge in religion from the ~*s* of a strong emotional temperament —T.S.Eliot⟩ **b :** a violent outburst of unrestrained emotion **:** PAROXYSM ⟨a ~ of weeping —W.G. Hardy⟩ ⟨a ~ of rejoicing in camp —H.E.Scudder⟩ **syn** see COMMOTION

[2]**tumult** \"\ *vi* -ED/-ING/-S **:** to make a tumult **:** RIOT ⟨a whole people . . . ~*ing* even to the fear of a revolt —John Milton⟩

tu·mul·tu·ary \t(y)ü'məlchə,werē, tə'm-\ *adj* [L *tumultuarius*, fr. *tumultus* tumult + *-arius* -ary] **1 a :** composed of hastily levied and unorganized troops **:** UNDISCIPLINED, IRREGULAR ⟨a ~ army⟩ ⟨their ~ array is incapable of contending with the order and weapons of modern tactics —Edward Gibbon⟩ **b :** carried on or brought about (as by a tumultuous mob) in a confused, wildly irregular, or sporadic manner ⟨~ wars⟩ ⟨~ violence⟩ ⟨a ~ attack of the . . . peasantry —T.B.Macaulay⟩ ⟨dread all rude and ~ innovation —V.L.Parrington⟩ **2 :** marked by haste and confusion **:** done precipitately and without plan **:** huddled up **:** HAPHAZARD, AIMLESS ⟨a ~ and giddy choice —Edmund Burke⟩ ⟨rushed into a ~ discussion of chances and possibilities —Sir Walter Scott⟩ **3 :** marked by or tending toward tumult **:** TUMULTUOUS ⟨~ reception —J.G.Lockhart⟩ ⟨the ~ . . . tide of life —R.L.Stevenson⟩

tu·mul·tu·ate \-chə,wāt\ *vb* -ED/-ING/-S [L *tumultuatus*, past part. of *tumultuari* to make a tumult, fr. *tumultus*] *vi* **:** to raise a disturbance **:** TUMULT, RIOT ⟨an oppressive action likely to make the people ~⟩ **~** *vt* **:** to make tumultuous **:** cause to riot

tu·mul·tu·a·tion \=,=='wāshən\ *n* -s [ME *tumultuacion*, fr. L *tumultuation-*, *tumultuatio*, fr. *tumultuatus* (past part.) + *-ion-*, *-io* -ion] **:** the act or process of making a tumult **:** DISTURBANCE

tu·mul·tu·ous \t(y)ü'məlch(ə)wəs, tə'm-, -chəs\ *adj* [L *tumultuosus*, fr. *tumultus* tumult + *-osus* -ose] **1 :** marked by tumult **:** full of commotion and uproar **:** RIOTOUS, STORMY, BOISTEROUS ⟨a ~ reception⟩ ⟨~ applause⟩ ⟨the ~ years of his administrations —F.L.Mott⟩ ⟨a fierce, ~ battle —J.L.Motley⟩ **2 :** tending or disposed to cause or incite a tumult ⟨a ~ and irresponsible group⟩ ⟨an unlawful and ~ design —Thomas Hobben⟩ ⟨a factious and ~ person —*Amer. Guide Series: Md.*⟩ **3 :** marked by violent or overwhelming turbulence or upheaval ⟨~ passions⟩ ⟨~ sensations⟩ ⟨his blazing power . . . and his ~ creative imagination —Orville Prescott⟩ ⟨a ~ river . . . overflowing its banks —W.S.Maugham⟩

tu·mul·tu·ous·ly *adv* **:** in a tumultuous manner **:** STORMILY, BOISTEROUSLY, RIOTOUSLY ⟨a crowd demonstrating ~⟩

tu·mul·tu·ous·ness *n* -ES **:** the quality or state of being tumultuous **:** STORMINESS, BOISTEROUSNESS ⟨the ~ of the sea⟩

tu·mu·lus \'t(y)ümyələs\ *n*, *pl* **tumu·li** \-ə,lī\ [L; akin to L *tumēre* to swell — more at THUMB] **1 :** an artificial hillock or mound (as over a grave); *esp* **:** one over the grave of a person buried in ancient times **:** BARROW **2 :** a small domal mound of lava

[1]**tun** \'tən\ *n* -s [ME *tonne*, *tunne*, *toun*, fr. OE *tunne* cask, barrel, tun, prob. of Celt origin; akin to MIr *tonn* skin, hide — more at TUNNEL] **1 a :** a large cask esp. for holding wine or beer **b :** a large receptacle (as a tub or chest) ⟨sends you . . . this ~ of treasure —Shak.⟩ ⟨the wash was made up freshly in a deep washing ~ —*Veterinary Record*⟩ **c :** a brewer's fermenting vat **:** MASH TUN **2 :** any of various units of liquid capacity; *esp* **:** a unit equal to 252 wine gallons **3 a :** something that resembles a large barrel ⟨that ~ of man —Leslie Hotson⟩ **b** (1) *dial Eng* **:** CHIMNEY, CHIMNEY POT ⟨the crooked smoke . . . from our cottage ~*s* —Llewelyn Powys⟩ (2) **:** CHIMNEY STACK

[2]**tun** \"\ *vt* **tunned**; **tunned**; **tunning**; **tuns** [ME *tonnen*, *tunnen*, fr. *tonne*, *tunne* tun] **1** *archaic* **:** to put into or store in a tun **:** CASK **2** *archaic* **:** to cause to flow into or as if into a tun **:** POUR, SWILL ⟨used to ~ down beer . . . during dinner —*Fraser's Mag.*⟩

[3]**tun** \'tün\ *n* -s [Mayan] **:** a period of 360 days composed of 18 months of 20 days each and used as the basis of the Maya long count to which is added the uayeb to make the 365-day year of the Maya calendar — see UINAL; compare TZOLKIN

[1]**tu·na** \'t(y)ünə\ *n* -s [Sp, fr. Taino] **1 :** any of various flat-jointed prickly pears of the genus *Opuntia*; *esp* **:** a tropical American plant (*O. tuna*) **2 :** the edible fruit of a tuna plant

[2]**tuna** \"\ *n*, *pl* **tuna** *or* **tunas** [AmerSp, alter. of Sp *atún* tunny, modif. of Ar *tūn*, fr. L *thunnus*, *thynnus* — more at TUNNY] **1 a :** any of numerous large vigorous scombroid fishes including forms highly esteemed for sport and as food — see ALBACORE, BLUEFIN 2, DOGTOOTH TUNA, YELLOWFIN TUNA **b :** any of various related but usu. smaller fishes — see BONITO, LITTLE TUNA **2** *or* **tuna fish :** the flesh of a tuna esp. when canned for use as food

[3]**tu·na** \'tünə\ *n* -s [Maori] **:** an eel (*Anguilla sucklandii*) of New Zealand waters

tun·able *also* **tune·able** \'t(y)ünəbəl\ *adj* **1** *archaic* **a :** full of melody **:** TUNEFUL **b :** sounding in harmony **:** ATTUNED **c :** free from discord **:** CONCORDANT **2 :** capable of being tuned or made harmonious ⟨new receivers are ~ to an alternative station —E.B.Bishop⟩ ⟨seemed to say that men were of ~ metal —Van Wyck Brooks⟩ — **tun·ably** *also* **tune·ably** \-nəblē, -li\ *adv*

tun·able·ness *also* **tune·able·ness** *n* -ES *archaic* **:** the quality or state of being tunable

tuna clipper *n* **:** a diesel-powered boat used on the Pacific coast for tuna fishing and made with the deckhouse forward, bait tanks aft, and iron racks around the stem from which men fish with heavy bamboo poles

tunbellied \'=,==\ *adj* [[1]*tun* + *bellied*] *archaic* **:** POTBELLIED

tunbelly \'=,==\ *n* -ES [back-formation fr. *tunbellied*] *archaic* **:** POTBELLY 1, 2

tundish \'=,=\ *n* [ME, fr. [1]*tun* + *dish*] **:** FUNNEL, POURING BASIN

tun·dra \'təndrə, 'tün-\ *n* -s *often attrib* [Russ, of Finno-Ugric origin; akin to Finn *tunturi* arctic hill, Lapp *tundar* hill] **:** a level or undulating treeless plain that is characteristic of arctic and subarctic regions, marks the limit of arborescent vegetation, consists of black mucky soil with a permanently frozen subsoil, and supports a dense growth of mosses and lichens (as the reindeer moss) and of dwarf caespitose herbs and shrubs often with showy flowers

tundra vole *n* : a vole (*Microtus operarius*) that constitutes an important part of the food supply of the smaller fur-bearing carnivores of far northern No. America

¹tune \'t(y)ün\ *n* -s [ME, alter. of *ton, tone* — more at TONE] **1 a** *archaic* : quality of sound : TONE ⟨thou hast a tongue: come, let us hear its ~ —Horace Smith⟩ **b** : manner of utterance : INTONATION ⟨the straightforward ~ . . . of early English poetry —Louis Untermeyer⟩; *specif* : phonetic modulation ⟨differences . . . are probably more in language ~ than in actual pronunciation —A.J. Tresidder⟩ **c** : a general attitude or bearing : APPROACH ⟨when the tables are turned . . . changes his ~ —A.J.Toynbee⟩ ⟨so struck by facts he was . . . collecting that he altered his ~ —C.L.Boltz⟩ **d** *archaic* : a frame of mind : MOOD ⟨being in . . . bad ~ for a fête —Thomas Moore⟩ **2 a** : a musical composition ⟨play a ~ on the piano⟩ **b** : an easily remembered musical air, often being the uppermost part esp. of a short or simple construction (as of a ballad or psalm or of some operatic arias) : MELODY ⟨dance ~⟩ ⟨to the ~ of "America"⟩ **c** : a dominant course or theme ⟨stand the expense and not insist upon calling the ~ —I.I.Rabi⟩ ⟨the alluring ~ of the new Pied Piper —*Sydney (Australia) Bull.*⟩ **d** : a contrapuntal activity : ACCOMPANIMENT ⟨glowing speeches, delivered to the ~ of more cheers —*Phoenix Flame*⟩ **3 a** : correct musical pitch or consonance ⟨a competent musician knows with certainty when an instrument is out of ~ —Clive Bell⟩ **b** : a harmonious relationship : AGREEMENT, CONCORD ⟨drawings more in ~ with the text —*N.Y. Times Bk. Rev.*⟩ ⟨a portfolio of stocks . . . out of ~ with present market conditions —*Outlook*⟩ ⟨I was out of ~ with everything and everyone about me —Anne S. Mehdevi⟩ **c** : RESONANCE 1b(2) **4** : a scale of magnitude : AMOUNT, EXTENT ⟨technical difficulties . . . dehumanize us to such a ~ as to make us indifferent —J.C.Powys⟩ — usu. used in the phrase *to the tune of* ⟨subsidized Japan to the ~ of two billion dollars in five years —*Atlantic*⟩ ⟨custom-made to the ~ of $40 or $50 apiece —*Amer. Fabrics*⟩ ⟨turns out electricity from coal to the ~ of 150,000 kilowatts —*Newsweek*⟩

²tune \"\ *vb* -ED/-ING/-S *vi* **1** : to produce musical tones : SING, HUM ⟨a breeze *tuning* through the frigid silence —John Galsworthy⟩ ⟨my children could ~ before they could speak —A.B.Evans⟩ **2** : to become attuned or receptive ⟨develop new attitudes to their tasks as they sensitively ~ to the requirements of their responsibilities —C.C.Brown⟩ ⟨that other part of his mind *tuning* in and clocking up the platitude —James Jones⟩ **3** : to adjust a receiver with respect to resonance ⟨~ in to a program⟩ ⟨~ about for good music —E. C.Aldrich⟩ ⟨by *tuning* in on just one station of known location, the direction from the direction finder to the station can be determined —*Introduction to Electronics*⟩ ~ *vt* **1 a** : to adjust in musical pitch or cause to be in tune ⟨~ a violin⟩ ⟨~ it up a minor or a major third —Deems Taylor⟩ **b** *archaic* (1) : to express in song ⟨little birds that ~ their morning's joy —Shak.⟩ (2) : to lead off (as a hymn) **c** : to give a musical intonation to ⟨he *tuned* a marvellous prose —Edmund Wilson⟩ **2** *archaic* : to influence in a desired direction ⟨the most effective way . . . of *tuning* public opinion —J.H.Blunt⟩ **3 a** : to bring into harmony : ATTUNE ⟨the colors . . . are not perfectly *tuned* to each other —Mildred J. O'Brien⟩ ⟨she was not *tuned* to a mood of self-reproach —Herman Wouk⟩ ⟨the stallion's sense is very keen . . . he knows instantly whether his man is *tuned* in to him —Henry Wynmalen⟩ **b** : to make responsive : ADAPT ⟨whether the touch is firm or light it can be *tuned* to the operator's rhythm —*Print*⟩ **c** (1) : to adjust for precise functioning : put in first-class working order ⟨has good plugs and points and has just recently been *tuned* —Phil Gresho⟩ — often used with *up* ⟨~ up a plane on the flight line⟩ (2) : to put in readiness : KEY ⟨we were tautly *tuned* for it —F.A.Perry⟩ — often used with *up* ⟨was pretty well *tuned* up for the challenge —Norman Cousins⟩ **4 a** : to adjust with respect to resonance ⟨a means of *tuning* the electrodes is usu. provided . . . to facilitate voltage adjustment —F.W.Curtis⟩ ⟨~ a television set to the local channel⟩ ⟨~ in a program⟩ ⟨~ out static⟩ ⟨a hearing aid . . . that automatically ~*s* down loud and harsh noises —*Newsweek*⟩ **b** : to establish radio contact with ⟨~ in a directional beacon⟩

tuneable *var of* TUNABLE

tuned *adj* [fr. past part. of ²*tune*] **1 a** : put in tune : HARMONIZED, MELODIOUS ⟨a carillon of ~ bells⟩ **b** : furnished with a tune ⟨musical comedy well ~ —*New Yorker*⟩ **2** : adjusted for resonance ⟨~ amplifier⟩ ⟨~ circuit⟩

tuned-in \¦⸗¦⸗\ *adj* : ALERT, RECEPTIVE ⟨grow attached to a teacher they think of as properly *tuned-in* —R.A.Arthur⟩

tune·ful \'t(y)ünfəl\ *adj* **1 a** : having a musical sound : MELODIOUS ⟨a ~ song⟩ ⟨a ~ bell⟩ **b** *archaic* : producing melody; *esp* : fond of singing ⟨free as the birds of the air, and like them . . . ~ —William Bartram⟩ **2** *archaic* : of or relating to music ⟨members of the ~ trade —John Dryden⟩ — **tune·ful·ly** \-fəlē, -li\ *adv*

tune·ful·ness *n* -ES : the quality or state of being tuneful

tune·less \'t(y)ünləs\ *adj* **1** : lacking musical quality : UNMELODIOUS **2** : making no music : SOUNDLESS

tun·er \-nə(r)\ *n* -s : one that tunes or is used for tuning: as **a** : a specialist in tuning musical instruments ⟨piano ~⟩ **b** : a workman who adjusts a mechanism for peak performance ⟨power-loom ~⟩ ⟨typewriter ~⟩ ⟨a ~ of old cars⟩ **c** (1) : TUNING FORK (2) : PITCH PIPE (3) : a device for tuning an organ flue pipe consisting of an adjustable flap or opening near its top by which the vibrating length of the air chamber may be changed (4) : a device attached to the tailpiece of a bowed stringed musical instrument to facilitate the tuning of the upper strings **d** (1) : an instrument (as a tuning capacitor) for tuning an electric circuit (2) : the part of a receiving set consisting of the circuit used to adjust resonance

tunes *pl of* TUNE, *pres 3d sing of* TUNE

tunesmith \'⸗,⸗\ *n* [¹*tune* + *smith*] : a composer esp. of popular songs

tune up *vi* **1** : to limber up the vocal chords : sing out ⟨the company *tuned up* and sang with goodwill —B.L.K.Henderson⟩ **2 a** : to bring the instruments of a musical ensemble to a common pitch ⟨the orchestra is *tuning up* and the concert is about to begin⟩ **b** : to make a tentative effort or a trial run ⟨a few soapbox orators are *tuning up* near the bandstand —Winston Brebner⟩

tune-up \'⸗,⸗\ *n* -s [*tune up*] **1** : a general adjustment to insure operation at peak efficiency ⟨periodic oil changes . . . and motor *tune-ups* in the spring and fall are essential —*Automobilist*⟩ **2** : a preliminary trial : WARM-UP ⟨takes a practice jump with her mount . . . in a *tune-up* for the rugged international competition —*N.Y.Times*⟩

tung \'təŋ\ *var of* TUNG TREE

tun·ga \'təŋgə\ *n, cap* [NL, fr. Pg, fr. Tupi] : a genus of fleas having conspicuous mouthparts, the setae on the head very small or missing entirely, and no ctenidia on the head or pronotum — see CHIGOE

tun·gan \(')təŋ¦gän, (')tu̇ŋ-\ *also* **dun·gan** \(')də-, (')du̇-\ *n, pl* **tungan** *or* **tungans** *also* **dungan** *or* **dungans** *usu cap* [G *Tunganen, Dunganen*, fr. Jagatai *Döngan*, prob. fr. *dönmek* to convert] **1 a** : a Mongolized Turkish people of Turkestan found also in large numbers in Kansu Province and the Sining region of Chinghai Province in northwest China **b** : a member of such people **2** : the language of the Tungan people

tung–hu \'du̇ŋ'hü\ *n pl, usu cap* : the eastern Tatars of ancient Chinese history

tun·go \'təŋ(,)gō\ *n* -s [native name in So. Australia] *Austral* : RAT KANGAROO

tung oil *n* [part trans. of Chin (Pek) *yu²-t'ung²* tung tree oil, fr. *yu²* oil + *t'ung²* tung tree] **1** : a pale yellow pungent drying oil obtained chiefly from the seeds of the tung tree and composed of glycerides esp. of eleostearic acid and other unsaturated acids, that polymerizes to a hard gel on long standing or on heating, and that is used chiefly in quick-drying varnishes and paints and as a waterproofing agent — called also *China wood oil, wood oil* **2** : JAPANESE TUNG OIL

tung oil tree *n* : TUNG TREE

tungst- *or* **tungsto-** *comb form* [ISV, fr. *tungsten*] **1** : tungsten ⟨*tungsto*boric⟩ **2** : tungstic acid ⟨*tungst*ate⟩

tung·state \'təŋ,stāt, -,stət, *usu* -d·+V\ *n* -s [ISV *tungst-* + *-ate*] : a salt of tungstic acid; *esp* : a normal salt (as sodium tungstate Na_2WO_4) derived from the acid H_2WO_4 or its monohydrate — called also *wolframate;* compare METATUNGSTATE, PARATUNGSTATE

tung·sten \-stən\ *n* -s [Sw, fr. *tung* heavy + *sten* stone; akin to ON *thungr* heavy, *thisl* pole, OE *thīsl, thixl* pole, shaft, OHG *dīhsala*, L *temo* pole, shaft, OSlav *tęgnǫti* to drag, pull, Skt *tanoti* he stretches, and to ON *steinn* stone — more at THIN, STONE] **1** : a gray-white heavy high-melting ductile hard polyvalent metallic element that resembles chromium and molybdenum in many of its properties, that is found combined in scheelite, wolframite, and other minerals and is extracted by the successive formation of an alkali metal tungstate, tungstic acid, and tungsten trioxide, reduction of the trioxide with hydrogen to a gray-black metal powder, and compaction by powder metallurgy to massive metal, and that is used in the pure form chiefly for electrical purposes (as for filaments for incandescent lamps and contact points) and with other substances in hardening steel and other alloys and in making carbides — called also *wolfram;* symbol *W;* see ELEMENT table **2** *obs* **a** : SCHEELITE **b** : WOLFRAMITE

tungsten bronze *n* : any of a series of highly colored lustrous crystalline compounds of variable composition that are mixed oxides of tungsten and usu. sodium or other alkali metal, that are good conductors of electricity, and that can be made by reduction of a normal tungstate (as sodium tungstate Na_2WO_4 with tungsten) or of tungsten trioxide with sodium

tungsten carbide *n* : a compound of tungsten and carbon; *esp* : a fine very hard crystalline gray powder WC made by heating tungsten or tungsten trioxide with carbon at a high temperature and usu. bonded with cobalt or nickel in cemented carbide compositions esp. for cutting tools, abrasives, and dies

tung·sten·ite \-stə,nīt\ *n* -s [*tungsten* + *-ite*] : a mineral WS_2 consisting of a tungsten sulfide and occurring in small lead-gray folia (hardness 2.5)

tungsten lamp *n* : an incandescent lamp with a filament of metallic tungsten — compare OSMIUM LAMP

tungsten trioxide *n* : a compound WO_3 found naturally as tungstite, obtained by chemical treatment as a heavy yellow crystalline powder (as in the extraction of tungsten), and used chiefly in the production of tungsten powder

tung·stic \-stik, -tēk\ *adj* [ISV *tungsten* + *-ic*] : of, relating to, or containing tungsten : WOLFRAMIC — used esp. of compounds in which this element is hexavalent

tungstic acid *n* **1** : TUNGSTEN TRIOXIDE **2** : any of various acids derived from tungsten trioxide; *esp* : the simplest acid H_2WO_4 analogous in composition to chromic acid and obtained as a yellow powder or as the white monohydrate $H_2WO_4.H_2O$ but known chiefly in the form of salts — compare HETEROPOLY ACID, METATUNGSTIC ACID, PHOSPHOTUNGSTIC ACID

tungstic ocher *n* : TUNGSTITE

tungstic oxide *n* : TUNGSTEN TRIOXIDE

tung·stite \'təŋz,tīt, -ŋ(k),stīt\ *n* -s [*tungst-* + *-ite*] : a mineral $WO_3.H_2O(?)$ consisting of a hydrous tungsten trioxide and occurring in yellow or yellowish green pulverulent masses

tung·sto·boric acid \¦təŋ(,)stō+-\ *n* [*tungst-* + *boric*] : BOROTUNGSTIC ACID

tung·sto·phosphate \"+\ *n* [*tungst-* + *phosphate*] : PHOSPHOTUNGSTATE

tung·sto·phosphoric acid \"+-\ *n* [*tungst-* + *phosphoric*] : PHOSPHOTUNGSTIC ACID

tung·sto·silicate \"+\ *n* [ISV *tungst-* + *silicate*] : SILICOTUNGSTATE

tung·sto·silicic acid \"+-\ *n* [ISV *tungst-* + *silicic*] : SILICOTUNGSTIC ACID

tung tree \'təŋ-\ *also* **tung** *n* -s [Chin (Pek) *t'ung²*] : any of several plants of the genus *Aleurites; esp* : a Chinese tree (*A. fordii*) grown for its seeds which yield tung oil

tun·gus *also* **tun·guz** \(')tu̇ŋ¦güz\ *n, pl* **tungus** *or* **tunguses** *also* **tunguz** *or* **tunguzes** *usu cap* [Russ, one of the Tungus, prob. fr. Turko-Tatar *toŋguz* hog; fr. the fact that they are often hog breeders] **1 a** : a Mongoloid people related to the Manchu that are widely spread over Eastern Siberia and including many still nomadic groups — called also *Evenk;* see GOLDI, LAMUT; compare OLCHA **b** : a member of such people **2** *also* **tun·guse** \-z\ : the Tungusic languages of the Tungus peoples

¹tun·gu·sic \-zik\ *n* -s *usu cap* : a subfamily of Altaic languages spoken in Manchuria and northward and including Tungus, Lamut, Manchu, and Goldi

²tungusic \"\ *adj, usu cap* **1** *also* **tun·guse** \-z\ *or* **tun·gu·sian** \-zēən, -zhən\ : of or relating to the Tungus people or their language **2** : of or relating to Tungusic

tu·nic \'t(y)ünik, -nēk\ *n* -s [L *tunica* tunic, integument, membrane, of Sem origin; akin to Heb *kuttōneth* coat — more at CHITON] **1 a** : a simple slip-on garment made with or without sleeves and usu. knee-length or longer, belted at the waist, and worn as an under or outer garment by men and women of ancient Greece and Rome **b** : SURCOAT **2 a** (1) : MANTLE 2b(2) (2) : TUNICA **b** : a natural integument ⟨the ~ of a seed⟩ **3 a** : a long usu. plain close-fitting jacket made with a high collar and worn (as by a soldier or policeman) esp. as part of a uniform **b** : an undress coat worn by British soldiers **4** : TUNICLE 1b, 1c **5 a** : a short overskirt usu. cut in one piece with the bodice and either belted or fitted at the waist **b** : a usu. belted overblouse or jacket that is hip length or longer **c** : a short loose garment resembling a Grecian tunic worn by women for active sports (as for dance practice)

¹tu·ni·ca \'t(y)ünəkə\ *n, pl* **tuni·cae** \-nə,kē, -,kī, -,sē\ [L] **1** : an enveloping or covering membrane or layer of body tissue **2** [NL, fr. L] : the outer of the two growth regions into which the apical meristem is held to be divisible in the tunica-corpus theory

²tunica \"\ *n* -s [NL (genus name of the coat flower *Tunica saxifraga*), fr. L, tunic] : COAT FLOWER

³tu·ni·ca \'t(y)ünəkə, ⸗'nēkə\ *n, pl* **tunica** *or* **tunicas** *usu cap* [Tunica, the people] **1 a** : an Indian people of the lower Yazoo river valley in Mississippi **b** : a member of such people **2** : the language of the Tunica people

tunica al·bu·gi·nea \-,albyə'jinēə, -bə'gi-\ *n, pl* **tunicae albugine·ae** \-'jinē,ē, -'ginē,ī\ [NL, white-spotted coat] : a white fibrous capsule esp. of the testis, ovary, eye, or spleen

tunica–corpus theory \'⸗⸗⸗'⸗⸗-\ *n* : a theory in plant morphology: each apical meristem consists of an outer tunica and an inner corpus

¹tu·ni·can \'t(y)ünəkən, ⸗'nēkən\ *also* **to·ni·kan** \'tōnəkən, tə'nēk-\ *adj, usu cap* **1** : of or relating to the Tunica or their language **2** : of or relating to Tunican

²tunican \"\ *also* **tonikan** \"\ *n* -s *usu cap* **1** : a language family of the Gulf phylum comprising the Tunica language **2** *in former classifications* : a language stock comprising Tunican, Atakapan, and Chitimachan

¹tu·ni·cary \'t(y)ünə,kerē\ *n* -ES [L *tunica* + E *-ary*, n. suffix] : TUNICATE

²tunicary \"\ *adj* [L *tunica* + E *-ary*, adj. suffix] : of or relating to a covering membrane

tu·ni·ca·ta \,t(y)ünə'kād·ə, -kād·ə\ [NL, fr. neut. pl. of L *tunicatus* tunicate] *syn of* UROCHORDA

¹tu·ni·cate \'t(y)ünəkə̇t, -nēk- *sometimes* -nə,kāt; *usu* \|d·+V\ *also* **tu·ni·cat·ed** \-nə,kād·əd, -ātəd\ *adj* [*tunicate* fr. L *tunicatus*, past part. of *tunicare* to clothe with a tunic, fr. *tunica* tunic; *tunicated* fr. L *tunicatus* + E *-ed* — more at TUNIC] **1 a** : covered with a tunic **b** : coated with layers; *specif* : having numerous concentric coats or layers (as an onion) **2 a** (1) : having a tunic or mantle (2) : of or relating to the Urochorda **b** : having each joint buried in the preceding funnel-shaped one ⟨the ~ antennae of an insect⟩

²tunicate \"\ *n* -s [NL *Tunicata*] : an animal of the subphylum Urochorda

tunica va·gi·na·lis \-,vajə'naləs, -nā-\ *n, pl* **tunicae vaginales** \-a(,)lēz, -ā(,)lēz\ [NL, vaginal coat] : a pouch of serous membrane covering the testis and derived from the peritoneum

tunic flower *n* : COAT FLOWER

tu·ni·cin \'t(y)ünəsən\ *n* -s [²*tunicate* + *-in*] : a substance in the test of many tunicates that resembles the cellulose of plants

tu·nicked *also* **tu·niced** \'t(y)ünikt, -nēkt\ *adj* : having or wearing a tunic ⟨wearing ~ bathing suits —Elizabeth Enright⟩

tu·ni·cle \'t(y)ünəkəl, -nēk-\ *n* -s [ME, fr. L *tunicula* little tunic, little membrane, dim. of *tunica* tunic, membrane] **1 a** *obs* : a small tunic **b** : a short dalmatic worn by a subdeacon over the alb during mass **c** : a short close-fitting vestment worn by a bishop under the dalmatic at pontifical ceremonies **2** : a covering membrane or integument : MANTLE 2b(2), ¹TUNICA

tunics *pl of* TUNIC

tuning *n* -s [fr. gerund of ²*tune*] **1 a** (1) : the act or process of putting in tune ⟨final assembly, regulating, ~ and voicing of . . . pianos —*Baldwin Piano Co. Catalog*⟩ (2) : the quality or state of being tuned ⟨a small violoncello of standard ~ —Robert Donington⟩ **b** : an adaptive influence or state of adaptation ⟨gave him the right ~ for feeling like a piece of God's creation —Eric Manners⟩ **2** *obs* : the production of musical sounds ⟨sentimental and rapturous ~*s* —Henry Brooke⟩ **3** : an act or process of adjusting with respect to resonance; *specif* : adjustment of the frequency response of receiving equipment (as of a radio) to resonate with the received signal — compare FLAT TUNING, SHARP TUNING

tuning bar *n* : a tuning instrument used esp. by bands and orchestras and made of a steel bar set on a resonance box that gives the pitch when struck

tuning capacitor *or* **tuning condenser** *n* : a variable capacitor used to vary the resonant frequency of an oscillatory circuit (as in tuning a radio receiver)

tuning coil *n* : a tuner consisting of a coil of variable inductance

tuning cone *n* : a hollow metal cone used in tuning open organ pipes

tuning eye *n* : a cathode ray tube designed to aid in precise tuning of a radio circuit

tuning fork *n* : a two-pronged metal implement not affected by moderate differences of temperature that gives a persistent fixed tone nearly free from harmonics when struck and is useful for tuning musical instruments and ascertaining standard pitch

tuning fork

tuning hammer *or* **tuning wrench** *n* : a hammer-shaped wrench used in tuning pianos and made with heads hollowed to fit over the tuning pegs

tuning peg *or* **tuning pin** *n* : an adjustable pin to which the strings (as of a piano or a violin) are fastened and by means of which the pitch may be varied ⟨the creak of *tuning pegs* in their sockets —Mark Harris⟩

tuning pipe *n* : PITCH PIPE; *specif* : one of a set of pitch pipes used esp. for tuning stringed musical instruments

tuning slide *n* : an adjustable crook or slide in a metal wind musical instrument used for tuning to another instrument

¹tu·nis \'t(y)ünəs\ *n* [fr. *Tunis* (Tunisia), country in No. Africa where the breed originated] **1** *usu cap* : an old Asiatic breed of hornless medium-wooled fat-tailed sheep valued esp. for their ability to produce and develop rapidly a good quality meat lamb **2** *pl* **tunis** *often cap* : a sheep of the Tunis breed

²tunis \"\ *adj, usu cap* [fr. *Tunis*, Tunisia] : of or from Tunis, the capital of Tunisia : of the kind or style prevalent in Tunis : TUNISIAN

tunis grass *n, usu cap T* [fr. *Tunis* (Tunisia), No. Africa] : a No. African grass (*Sorghum virgatum*) used for forage

tu·ni·sia \t(y)ü'nēzh(ē)ə, -nizh-\ *adj, usu cap* [fr. *Tunisia*, country in No. Africa] : of or from Tunisia : of the kind or style prevalent in Tunisia : TUNISIAN

¹tu·ni·sian \-zh(ē)ən\ *n* -s *cap* [*Tunisia*, No. Africa + E *-an*, n. suffix] : a native or inhabitant of Tunis or Tunisia

²tunisian \"\ *adj* [*Tunisia* + E *-an*, adj. suffix] : TUNISIA

¹tunk \'təŋk\ *also* **tonk** \'täŋk, 'təŋk\ *n* -s [imit.] : TAP, RAP, THUMP ⟨got a bad ~ on her head, and a few scratches —Marguerite Tate⟩

²tunk \"\ *also* **tonk** \"\ *vb* -ED/-ING/-S *vt* : to strike lightly or sharply : RAP, TAP ⟨~*ed* their heads together⟩; *esp* : to tap (as car wheels) with a hammer to test for flaws ~ *vi* : to give a tunk : TAP ⟨~*ing* on a drum⟩

³tunk \"\ *or* **tonk** \"\ *n* -s [prob. fr. ¹*tunk*] : a game of rummy for two to five players with deuces wild

tunker *usu cap, var of* DUNKER

tun·ket \'təŋkə̇t, *usu* -əd·+V\ *n* -s [prob. euphemism for *tophet*] : HELL — used interjectionally to express curiosity, puzzlement, or exasperation ⟨what in ~ did he mean, upside-down eyes —Helen Eustis⟩ ⟨why in ~ didn't you tell me so —Della Lutes⟩

tunnage *var of* TONNAGE

tunned *past of* TUN

¹tun·nel \'tən³l\ *n* -s *often attrib* [ME *tonel*, fr. MF *tonel, tonnel* cask, tun, fr. OF, fr. *tonne* tun, fr. ML *tunna, tonna* barrel, tun, of Celt origin; akin to MIr *tonn* skin, hide, W *ton;* akin to L *tondēre* to shear, crop — more at TOME] **1** : TUNNEL NET 1 **2 a** *archaic* : a chimney flue **b** *dial* : FUNNEL **c** : a hollow conduit or recess : TUBE, WELL ⟨drive shaft ~⟩ ⟨drying ~⟩; *specif* : SHAFT TUNNEL **d** : a bodily channel ⟨a more or less circular ~, the neural canal —W.E.Swinton⟩ **e** : WIND TUNNEL **3 a** : a covered passageway ⟨the ~ of a long nave —George Santayana⟩; *specif* : a nearly horizontal passageway through or under an obstruction ⟨railroad ~ through a mountain⟩ ⟨take the midtown ~ from Long Island to New York⟩ **b** (1) : a subterranean gallery (as in a cave or mine) (2) : ADIT **c** : a narrow enclosed pressurized corridor connecting two pressurized personnel compartments of an airplane **d** : the burrow of an insect or other animal ⟨mole's ~⟩ ⟨termite ~*s* in beams⟩ **e** : something that resembles a corridor ⟨a ~ of trees⟩ ⟨headlights created their own ~ of light —Paul Scott⟩ ⟨trapped in the ~ of their own logic —Douglas Stewart⟩; *specif* : an arch formed by partners' joined hands in a square dance

²tunnel \"\ *vb* **tunneled** *or* **tunnelled; tunneled** *or* **tunnelled; tunneling** *or* **tunnelling** \-n(³)liŋ\ **tunnels** *vt* **1** *archaic* : to catch in a tunnel net **2 a** : to pass through a covered channel : advance by or as if by excavating a tunnel ⟨belt ~*ed* through wide black patent girdle —*Women's Wear Daily*⟩ ⟨larvae . . . ~*ing* their way through the cappings —*Gleanings in Bee Culture*⟩ **b** : to penetrate with or as if with a tunnel : make a passage through or under ⟨the acid water . . . ~*ed* it, so that it is honeycombed —Marjory S. Douglas⟩ ⟨lights ~ the darkness⟩ ~ *vi* **1 a** : to make or use a tunnel ⟨with a view to keeping the gradient down . . . proposed to ~ under the ridge —O.S.Nock⟩ ⟨a creaking train . . . ~*ed* through the hill —J.A. Michener⟩ **b** : UNDERMINE ⟨appeared to be ~*ing* under all the established values —Sherwood Anderson⟩ **2** *physics* : to pass through a potential barrier ⟨electrons . . . ~ back to the vacant sites —Frederick Seitz⟩

tunnel effect *n* : the quantum mechanical phenomenon sometimes exhibited by moving particles that succeed in passing from one side of a potential barrier to the other although of insufficient energy to pass over the top

tun·nel·er *or* **tun·nel·ler** \-n(³)lə(r)\ *n* -s : one that tunnels: as **a** : a workman employed in excavating a tunnel **b** : a machine used in tunneling (as in mining to cut a drift)

tunneling *or* **tunnelling** *n* -s [fr. gerund of ²*tunnel*] **1** : a tunnel or series of tunnels **2** : the act or process of making a tunnel

tunnel kiln *n* : CONTINUOUS KILN

tunnellike \'⸗⸗,⸗\ *adj* : resembling a tunnel

tunnel net *n* **1** : a long conical net for game or fish : FYKE **2** : the narrow part of a pound net connecting the heart with the pot

tunnel of cor·ti \-'kȯrd·ē, -r,tē\ *usu cap C* [after Alfonso *Corti* †1876 Ital. anatomist] : a spiral passage in the organ of Corti

tunnel of love : a dark tunnel in an amusement park through which passengers are conveyed usu. by boat

tunnel right *n* : the mineral right to all previously undiscovered veins and lodes within 3,000 feet of the portal of an exploratory tunnel and 300 feet on each side of its center line and to a claim 1500 feet in length on any vein that crosses it at right angles

tunnel vault *n* : BARREL VAULT

tunnel vision *n* : a field of vision of 70 percent or less from the straight-ahead position resulting in elimination of the peripheral field

tunnel weaver *n* : TUBE SPINNER

tun·ner \'tənə(r)\ *n* -s *Brit* **:** a brewer's workman in charge of a tun

tunning *pres part of* TUN

tun·ny \'tənē, -ni\ *also* **tunnyfish** \'==,=\ *n, pl* **tunnies** *also* **tunny** [earlier *tonny, tony*, modif. (prob. influenced by *-y*, dim. suffix) of MF *thon* or OIt *tonno*, both fr. OProv *ton*, fr. L *thunnus, thynnus*, fr. Gk *thynnos*, of non-IE origin; akin to the source of Heb *tannīn* serpent, sea monster] **:** TUNA; *esp* **:** BLUEFIN 2

tu·no \'tü(,)nō\ *or* **tu·nu** \-nü\ *n* -s [AmerSp, prob. fr. Miskito *túno*] **1 :** a Central American tree (*Castilloa fallax*) closely related to the Central American rubber tree but producing a nonelastic rubber **2** *also* **tuno gum :** the resinous gum of the tuno tree

tun of gold [¹*tun*] *obs* **:** 100,000 gold coins (as guilders or florins)

tuns *pl of* TUN, *pres 3d sing of* TUN

tun shell *n* [¹*tun*] **1 :** a gastropod mollusk of the family Tonnidae **2 :** a shell of one of the Tonnidae

¹**tup** \'təp\ *n* -s [ME *tupe, tuppe*] **1 a :** *chiefly Brit* **:** RAM 1a **b** *archaic* **:** one who is likened to a ram; *specif* **:** CUCKOLD **2 :** a heavy metal body (as the hammer head of a steam hammer or the weight of a pendulum)

²**tup** \"\ *vb* **tupped; tupped; tupping; tups** *vi, chiefly Brit* **:** to come in heat **:** be ready to accept a ram ~ *vt, chiefly Brit* **:** to copulate with (a ewe) **:** COVER

tu·paia \t(y)ü'pīə\ *n* [NL, fr. Malay *tupai* squirrel] **1** *cap* **:** a genus (the type of the family Tupaiidae) that is the chief genus of tree shrews **2** *also* **tu·paya** \"\ *n* -s **:** TREE SHREW

¹**tu·pai·id** \-īəd\ *adj* [NL *Tupaiidae*] **:** of or relating to the Tupaiidae

²**tupaiid** \"\ *n* -s **:** a member of the Tupaiidae **:** TREE SHREW

tu·pai·idae \t(y)ü'pīə,dē\ *n pl, cap* [NL, fr. *Tupaia*, type genus + *-idae*] **:** a family of small arboreal mammals of southeastern Asia and the Pacific islands that comprise the tree shrews and are held to be insectivores or treated as primates of lowly organization and then placed with the lemurs and tarsiers in the suborder Prosimii

tu·pe·lo \'t(y)üpə,lō\ *n* -s [Creek *ito opilwa*, lit., swamp tree] **1 :** a tree of the genus *Nyssa*: as **a :** BLACK GUM 1a — see TREE illustration **b :** TUPELO GUM **2 :** the wood of a tupelo

tupelo gum *n* **:** a swamp tree (*Nyssa aquatica*) occurring esp. in the southeastern U. S. and having brilliant glossy foliage and softer wood than the related black gums

tu·pi \'tü,pē, =\'=\ *n, pl* **tupi** *or* **tupis** *usu cap* **1 a :** a group of Tupi-Guaranian peoples of Brazil esp. living in the valleys of the Amazon, Tapajoz, Araguaia, and Xingu **b :** a member of any of such peoples **2 :** the language of the Tupi people serving as a lingua franca in the valley of the Amazon

tu·pi·an \-ēən\ *adj, usu cap* **:** of, relating to, or designating the Tupi or other Tupi-Guaranian peoples or their languages

tupi-guarani \'=;=;==;=\ *n, usu cap T&G* **1 a :** a So. American people spread over an area from far eastern Brazil to the Peruvian Andes and from the Guianas to Uruguay **b :** a member of such people **2 a :** TUPI-GUARANIAN **b :** GUARANI 2

¹**tupi-guaranian** \'=;=;==;==\ *adj, usu cap T&G* **:** of or relating to Tupi-Guarani

²**tupi-guaranian** \"\ *n, usu cap T&G* **:** a language stock widely distributed in tropical So. America including Tupi, Guarani, and many other languages

tu·pik *also* **tu·pek** \'tüpik\ *n* -s [Esk] **:** an Eskimo summer dwelling; *specif* **:** a sealskin tent

tu·pi·nam·ba \,tüpə'nambə, -,nam'bä\ *n, pl* **tupinamba** *or* **tupinambas** *usu cap* **1 a :** a group of extinct Tupian peoples of the Brazilian coast from the mouth of the Amazon to the southern part of the State of São Paulo **b :** a member of any of such peoples **2 :** the language of the Tupinamba people

tuppence *var of* TWOPENCE

tuppenny *var of* TWOPENNY

tupping *n* -s [fr. gerund of ²*tup*] *chiefly Brit* **:** BREEDING — used of sheep

tups *pl of* TUP, *pres 3d sing of* TUP

tuque \'t(y)ük\ *n* -s [CanF, fr. F *toque*, fr. MF — more at TOQUE] **:** a warm knitted stocking cap; *esp* **:** a close-fitting pointed cap of double thickness made by folding one of the closed ends of a tapered tubular knitted piece up into the other

tu quo·que \'t(y)ü'kwōkwē\ *n, pl* **tu quoques** [L, you also] **:** a retort charging an adversary with being or doing what he criticizes in others ⟨has always the same childlike defence, a *tu quoque* —*Times Lit. Supp.*⟩

¹**tur** \'tü(ə)r\ *n* -s [Russ, urus, Caucasian goat; akin to L *taurus* bull — more at STEER] **:** any of several Caucasian wild goats (as *Capra cylindricornis* of the eastern, *C. severtzowi* of the western, and *C. caucasica* of the central Caucasus)

²**tur** \"\ *n* -s [Hindi *tuar*, fr. Skt *tubarī*, of Dravidian origin; akin to Tamil *tuvarai* tur, Kanarese *togari*] *India* **:** PIGEON PEA

tu·ra·cin \'t(y)ürəsən\ *n* -s [NL *Turacus* + E *-in*] **:** an amorphous red porphyrin pigment containing copper obtained from feathers of the touraco — compare UROPORPHYRIN

turaco *or* **turacou** *or* **turakoo** *var of* TOURACO

tu·ra·cus \'t(y)ürəkəs\ *n, cap* [NL, fr. F *touraco*] **:** a genus of birds (family Musophagidae) comprising various typical touracos

¹**tu·ra·ni·an** \t(y)ə'rānēən, t(y)ü'-, t(y)u'-\ *n* -s *usu cap* [Per *Tūrān* Turkistan, the region north of the Oxus + E *-ian*] **1 a** (1) **:** a member of any of the peoples of Ural-Altaic stock (2) **:** a member of any division of a nomadic people held to have preceded the Aryans in Europe and Asia **b :** a member of any tribe or nationality of Turkic or Tataric stock **2 :** the total body of Turanian languages

²**turanian** \"\ *adj, usu cap* **1 :** of, relating to, or constituting various language families of Asia (as Altaic and Uralic) **2 a :** of, relating to, or constituting peoples speaking the Turanian languages **b :** of, relating to, or constituted by Turanians

tu·ran·ite \'t(y)ürə,nīt, t(y)u'ra,-\ *n* -s [Russ *turanit*', fr. Per *Tūrān* Turkistan + Russ *-it*' -ite (fr. L *-ita, -ites*)] **:** a basic vanadate of copper prob. $Cu_5(VO_4)_2(OH)_4$

tu·ra·nose \-,nōs\ *n* -s [G *turanos*, fr. Per *Tūrān* Turkistan + G *-os* -ose; fr. its being obtained from a manna found in Turkistan] **:** a crystalline reducing disaccharide sugar $C_{12}H_{22}O_{11}$ obtained by the partial hydrolysis of melezitose; 3-α-glucosyl-fructose

turb \'tərb\ *n* -s [ME *turbe*, fr. MF, fr. L *turba* crowd — more at TURBID] *archaic* **:** a number of individuals or units gathered together (as a crowd, swarm, heap, troop, or clump)

¹**tur·ban** \'tərbən, 'təb-, 'təib-\ *n* -s *often attrib* [MF *turbant*, fr. It *turbante*, modif. of Turk *dülbend, tülbend*, fr. Per *dulband*] **1 :** a headdress worn chiefly in countries of the eastern Mediterranean and southern Asia esp. by Muslims and made of a cap around which is wound a long cloth **2** *archaic* **:** MUSLIM **3 :** an emblematic representation of a turban (as on a Muslim funeral monument or in a heraldic device) **4 :** a symbolic representation of Islam in the form of a turban ⟨I was better fitted for the ~ than the cowl —Linda Villari⟩ **5 :** a headdress resembling a Muslim turban: as **a :** a fashionable headdress for women esp. in the 19th century **b :** a cloth, bandanna, or towel wrapped or tied about the head ⟨their black skins and snow-white linen being set off by colored ~*s* —C.R.Darwin⟩ **c :** a woman's brimless close-fitting hat usu. of draped fabric **6 :** TURBAN SHELL **7 :** a dish (as a fillet of fish) formed in the shape of a turban to permit the center to be filled with a suitable accompanying mixture ⟨~ of filet of sole with quenelles of shrimp and caviar Moscovite —*Newsweek*⟩

turban 5c

²**turban** \"\ *vt* -ED/-ING/-S **:** to envelop with or as if with a turban ⟨the wreaths, like mist, that ~ thy dusk brow —H.H. Milman⟩ ⟨~*ed* in a wet huck towel —Peter De Vries⟩

turban buttercup *n* **:** any of several commonly cultivated double-flowered buttercups derived from a Eurasian tuberous-rooted buttercup (*Ranunculus asiaticus*) and characterized by bright yellow flowers often two inches across

tur·baned *or* **tur·banned** \-nd\ *adj* [¹*turban* + *-ed*] **:** wearing a turban ⟨~ police —*Nat'l Geographic*⟩ ⟨~, long-robed Moslems —Jill Donisthorpe⟩ ⟨~ Indian generals —*Newsweek*⟩

turban lily *n* **:** a European lily (*Lilium pomponium*) cultivated for its deep-red spotted flowers shaped like turbans

turban shell *n* [modif. (influenced by ¹*turban*) of NL *turbin-, turbo*] **1 :** any of numerous marine snails (family Turbinidae) with a thick spiral nacreous operculate shell — see CAT'S-EYE, GREEN SNAIL, STARSHELL **2 :** the shell of a turban shell

turban squash *n* **:** any of various winter squashes constituting a distinct variety (*Cucurbita maxima turbaniformis*) and having hard-shelled fruit shaped somewhat like a turban and usu. with an evident rounded central portion protruding from the end farthest from the stem

¹**tur·ba·ry** \'tərbərē\ *n* -ES [ME, fr. ML *turbaria*, fr. *turba* turf, peat (of Gmc origin; akin to OE *turf*) + L *-aria* -ary — more at TURF] **1 :** the ground where turf or peat may be dug esp. for fuel **:** PEAT BOG **2 :** an easement under English law to dig turf or peat on a common or on another's land

²**turbary** \"\ *adj* [¹*turbary*; fr. the fact that the remains of such sheep are found in turbaries of the period] **:** of, relating to, or constituting hogs or sheep domesticated in prehistoric times

tur·ba·trix \,tər'bā·triks\ *n, cap* [NL *Turbatric-, Turbatrix*, fr. L, female disturber, fem. of *turbator* one that disturbs, fr. *turbatus* (past part. of *turbare* to disturb) + *-or* — more at TURBID, -TRIX] **:** a genus of small slender nematode worms (family Cephalobidae) including the vinegar eel

tur·beh *or* **tur·be** \'tər,be\ *n* -s [Turk *türbe*, fr. Ar *turbah*] **:** a Muslim tomb or mausoleum

tur·bel·lar·ia \,tərbə'la(a)rēə\ *n pl, cap* [NL, fr. L *turbellae* (pl.) bustle, stir (dim. of *turba* crowd, confusion, tumult) + NL *-aria*; fr. the tiny eddies created in water by their cilia — more at TURBID] **:** a class of Platyhelminthes comprising mostly free-living comparatively small soft-bodied more-or-less leaf-shaped externally ciliated flatworms widely distributed in salt or fresh water but occas. living on land or as parasites — see ACOELA, ALLOIOCOELA, POLYCLADIDA, RHABDOCOELA, TRICLADIDA

¹**tur·bel·lar·i·an** \'==;la(a)rēən\ *adj* [NL *Turbellaria* + E *-an*] **:** of or relating to the Turbellaria

²**turbellarian** \"\ *n* -s **:** a turbellarian worm

tur·bid \'tərbəd, 'təb-, 'təib-\ *adj* [L *turbidus* confused, disordered, turbid, fr. *turba* confusion, tumult, crowd; akin to L *turbare* to throw into disorder, disturb, make turbid, Gk *tyrbē* confusion, tumult, ON *thorp* crowd, *thyrpask* to crowd, OHG *dweran* to stir, Skt *tvarati* he hurries] **1 a :** having the lees or sediment disturbed **:** thick or opaque with matter in suspension **:** cloudy or muddy in physical appearance ⟨near the banks the waters become ~ —Mark Van Doren⟩ ⟨grossly ~ urine need not necessarily mean pyuria —*Jour. Amer. Med. Assoc.*⟩ ⟨many of the feldspars . . . are ~ owing either to minute inclusions or to partial kaolinization —*Jour. of Geol.*⟩ **b :** heavy with smoke or mist **:** DARK, DENSE, THICK ⟨the air without had the ~ yellow light of sandstorms —Willa Cather⟩ **2 a :** having an appearance held to resemble physical turbidity **:** characterized by being cloudy, muddy, dull, impure, or polluted **:** lacking in clarity or translucence ⟨whirled onward . . . in that ~ stream of wrong-belief and lust —L.P.Smith⟩ ⟨~ depths of degradation and misery —C.I.Glicksberg⟩ **b :** confused in thought or feeling **:** characterized by or producing obscurity (as of thought or feeling) **:** mentally confused, muddled, perplexed, disturbed, or troubled **:** lacking in lucidity ⟨making the imagination ~ with monstrous fancies and misshapen dreams —Oscar Wilde⟩ ⟨~ longings and passionate regrets —Curtis Dahl⟩

syn MUDDY, ROILY: TURBID modifies whatever is literally or figuratively stirred up and disturbed by or as if by sediment so that it is made opaque, obscured, or confused ⟨similar treatments, generally applied to *turbid* water and frequently to clear water suspected of pollution —A.C.Morrison⟩ ⟨*turbid* feelings, arising from ideas not fully mastered, had to clarify and adjust themselves —H.O.Taylor⟩ ⟨the *turbid* ebb and flow of human misery —Matthew Arnold⟩ MUDDY suggests turbidness resulting from mixture with or suspension of mud, dross, or impurity that muddles and makes unclear or impure ⟨the pond was *muddy* after the storm⟩ ⟨the *muddy* and slow-moving plot has something to do with spying and counterspying —Anthony Boucher⟩ ROILY describes what is turbid and agitated and swirling ⟨where the *roily* Monongahela meets the clear Allegheny —J.M.Weed⟩

tur·bi·dim·e·ter \,tərbə'dimədə·ər\ *n* [ISV *turbidity* + *-meter*] **:** an instrument for measuring and comparing the turbidity of liquids by viewing light through them and determining how much light is cut off by them **2 :** NEPHELOMETER

tur·bi·di·met·ric \'tərbədə'me·trik\ *adj* [*turbidimetry* + *-ic*] **:** of, relating to, or using turbidimetry or a turbidimeter ⟨~ methods⟩ ⟨~ control tests⟩

tur·bi·di·met·ri·cal·ly \-rək(ə)lē\ *adv* [*turbidimetric* + *-ally*] **:** by the use of turbidimetry or a turbidimeter ⟨the rate of coagulation is followed ~ —*Eastman Kodak Monthly Abstract Bull.*⟩

tur·bi·dim·e·try \,tərbə'dimə·trē\ *n* -ES [ISV *turbidity* + *-metry*] **:** the determination and measurement of the concentration of suspended matter in a liquid by use of a turbidimeter

tur·bid·i·ty \,tər'bidəd·ē\ *n* -ES [ML *turbiditat-, turbiditas*, fr. L *turbidus* turbid + *-itat-, -itas* -ity] **:** the quality or state of being turbid **:** CONFUSION, MUDDINESS, OBSCURITY

tur·bid·ly *adv* **:** in a turbid manner **:** with muddiness, confusion, or obscurity

tur·bid·ness *n* -ES [*turbid* + *-ness*] **:** TURBIDITY ⟨lime water produces a ~ when added to the fresh water —William Saunders⟩

tur·bi·na·do \,tərbə'nä(,)dō\ *also* **turbinado sugar** *n* -s [AmerSp, prob. fr. Sp *turbina* turbine (fr. F *turbine*) + *-ado* -ate; fr. its being sprayed with water while spinning in a centrifuge — more at TURBINE] **:** partially refined cane sugar that has been washed and dried, is off-white, yellowish, or grayish in color, and is used in industry and food processing

¹**tur·bi·nal** \'tərbən³l, 'təb-, 'təib-\ *adj* [L *turbin-, turbo* top, whirlwind, whirl + E *-al* — more at TURBINE] **1 :** TURBINATE 1, 2 **2 :** of, relating to, or being one of the usu. several thin plicated bony or cartilaginous plates covered with olfactory and mucous membrane and borne on the walls of the nasal chambers

²**turbinal** \"\ *n* -s **:** a turbinal bone or cartilage

¹**tur·bi·nate** \-bənət, bə,nāt, *usu* -d·+V\ *adj* [L *turbinatus* shaped like a top, fr. *turbin-, turbo* top, whirlwind, whirl + *-atus* -ate — more at TURBINE] **1 :** spiral with whorls decreasing rapidly from base to apex — used of a gastropod shell **2 :** shaped like a top or an inverted cone **:** narrow at the base and broad at or near the apex ⟨a ~ seed capsule⟩ **3 :** TURBINAL

²**turbinate** \"\ *n* -s **1 :** a turbinate shell **2 :** TURBINATE BONE

turbinate bone *n* **:** a turbinal bone or process; *esp* **:** one of three such bones or processes which in man are borne on the lateral wall of the nasal fossa on each side and of which the middle and superior are processes of the ethmoid and the inferior and largest is a separate curved bony plate horizontally placed and separating the inferior and middle meatuses in the nose — called also *nasal concha*

tur·bi·nat·ed \-bə,nād·əd\ *adj* [L *turbinatus* turbinate + E *-ed*] **:** TURBINATE

turbinato- *comb form* [L *turbinatus* turbinate] **:** conically ⟨*turbinato*concave⟩ ⟨*turbinato*cylindrical⟩ ⟨*turbinato*globose⟩

tur·bine \'tər|bən, 'tə|, 'təi|, |,bīn\ *n* -s *often attrib* [F, fr. L *turbin-, turbo* spinning object, whirlwind, top, whirl; akin to L *turbare* to throw into disorder, disturb, make turbid — more at TURBID] **:** a rotary engine actuated by the reaction or impulse or both of a current of fluid (as water, steam, gas, or mercury vapor) subject to pressure and usu. made with a series of curved vanes on a central spindle arranged to rotate with the whole being enclosed by a casing provided with redirecting vanes and passageways which permit the inlet and outlet of the fluid in a desired manner — compare AXIAL-FLOW, RADIAL-FLOW

tur·bi·nec·to·my \,tərbə'nektəmē\ *n* -ES [ISV *turbin*al + *-ectomy*] **:** surgical removal of one or more turbinate bones

turbine-electric locomotive *n* **:** an electric locomotive having generators powered by turbine engines for the production of its own electric power

turbine generator *n* **:** an electric generator driven by a steam, gas, or hydraulic turbine

tur·bi·nel·la \,tərbə'nelə\ *n* [NL, fr. L *turbin-, turbo*- top, whirl + *-ella* — more at TURBINE] *syn of* XANCUS

turbinella oak *n* [NL *turbinella* (specific epithet of *Quercus dumosa turbinella*), fr. L *turbin-, turbo* + *-ella*] **:** a scrub oak (*Quercus dumosa turbinella*) of No. America having acorn cups shaped like tops

turbine locomotive *n* **:** a locomotive powered by a steam or gas turbine engine that transmits motion directly to the driving wheels through gearing or that drives generators for producing electricity for the electric motors that move the driving wheels

turbine-propeller engine *n* **:** an airplane propulsion system in which a turbine drives a compressor and a propeller with thrust being derived from the propeller and also from the exhaust jet of the turbine

tur·bin·er \'tərbənər, -r,bīn-\ *n* -s [*turbine* + *-er*] **:** a turbine-propelled ship

tur·bin·i·dae \,tər'binə,dē\ *n pl, cap* [NL, fr. *Turbin-, Turbo*, type genus + *-idae*] **:** a family of gastropod mollusks (suborder Rhipidoglossa) of which *Turbo* is the type genus

tur·bit \'tərbət\ *n* [origin unknown] **1** *usu cap* **:** a breed of fancy pigeons having a short head and beak, a frilled breast, a peak or a shell crest, variously colored wings except the quills, and a white body **2** -s *often cap* **:** a bird of the Turbit breed

¹**tur·bo** \'tər(,)bō\ *n* [NL *Turbin-, Turbo*, fr. L, top, whirl — more at TURBINE] **1** *cap* **:** a genus (the type of the family Turbinidae) of marine snails that usu. have a heavy turbinate shell with a pearly lining, a rounded aperture, and a calcareous operculum **2** *pl* **turbi·nes** \-rbə,nēz\ *or* **turbos :** TURBAN SHELL

²**turbo** \"\ *n* -s [*turbo-*] **1 :** TURBINE **2** [by shortening] **:** TURBOSUPERCHARGER

turbo- *comb form* [*turbine*] **1 :** coupled directly to a driving turbine ⟨*turbo*alternator⟩ ⟨*turbo*blower⟩ ⟨*turbo*compressor⟩ ⟨*turbo*dynamo⟩ ⟨*turbo*exciter⟩ ⟨*turbo*fan⟩ ⟨*turbo*generator⟩ ⟨*turbo*pump⟩ **2 :** consisting of or incorporating a turbine ⟨*turbo*machine⟩ ⟨*turbo*motor⟩ ⟨*turbo*ventilator⟩

tur·bo·car \'tərbō+,-\ *n* [*turbo-* + *car*] **:** an automotive vehicle propelled by a gas turbine

tur·bo·charge \"+,-\ *vt* [*turbo-* + *charge*] **:** to supercharge (an engine) by means of a turbine-driven compressor

tur·bo·charger \"+,-\ *n* [*turbo-* + *charger*] **:** a centrifugal blower driven by exhaust gas turbines and used to supercharge an engine

tur·bo·compound engine \"+. . .-\ *n* [*turbo-* + *compound*] **:** an engine compounded by using the exhaust jet of the principal component to drive smaller auxiliary turbines

tur·bo·jet \'tərbō,jet, 'təb-, 'təib-, *usu* -ed·+V\ *n* [*turbojet engine*] **1 :** TURBOJET ENGINE **2 :** an airplane powered by turbojet engines

turbojet engine *n* [*turbo-* + *jet* + *engine*] **:** an airplane propulsion system in which the power developed by a turbine is used to drive a compressor that supplies air to a burner and hot gases from the burner pass through the turbine and thence to a rearward-directed thrust-producing exhaust nozzle

tur·bo·prop \-,präp\ *n* [by shortening] **1 :** TURBO-PROPELLER ENGINE **2 :** an airplane powered by turbo-propeller engines

tur·bo-propeller engine \'tər(,)bō+. . . -\ *n* [*turbo-* + *propeller* + *engine*] **:** a jet engine having a turbine-driven propeller and designed to produce thrust principally by means of a propeller although additional thrust is usu. obtained from the hot exhaust gases which issue in a jet

turboprop engine *n* [*turbo-propeller engine*] **:** TURBO-PROPELLER ENGINE

turboprop-jet engine *n* [*turbo-propeller* (*engine*) + *jet engine*] **:** TURBO-PROPELLER ENGINE

tur·bo·ram·jet engine \'tərbō'ram,jet-\ *n* [*turbo-* + *ramjet engine*] **:** a jet engine consisting essentially of a turbojet engine with provisions for burning additional fuel in the tail pipe or the portion of the engine to the rear of the turbine and thus making it possible to obtain higher gas temperatures in the exhaust jet than can be tolerated by the turbine blades

tur·bo·supercharged \'tər(,)bō+\ *adj* [*turbosupercharger* + *-ed*] **:** equipped with a turbosupercharger

tur·bo·supercharger \"+\ *n* [*turbo-* + *supercharger*] **:** a turbine compressor driven by hot exhaust gases of an airplane engine for feeding rarefied air at high altitudes into the carburetor of the engine at sea-level pressure so as to increase engine efficiency and the plane's rate of climb

tur·bot \'tərbət\ *n, pl* **turbot** *also* **turbots** [ME, fr. OF *turbut, tourbot*] **1 a :** a large European flatfish (*Psetta maxima*) that is highly esteemed as a food fish, may reach a weight of 30 to 40 pounds, and has a brownish upper surface marked with scattered tubercles and a white undersurface **b :** any of various other flatfishes (as of the families Pleuronectidae and Bothidae) that are felt to resemble the European turbot: as (1) **:** HALIBUT (2) **:** DIAMOND FLOUNDER (3) **:** a New Zealand flatfish (*Ammotretis guntheri*) **2 :** any of several triggerfishes or filefishes esp. of the Caribbean area

turbt *abbr* turbulent

tur·bu·la·tion \,tərbyə'lāshən\ *n* -s [*turbul*ent + *-ation*] **:** the enforced movement of photographic bath to overcome stagnation at the surface of film or paper during processing

tur·bu·la·tor \'==,lād·ə(r)\ *n* -s [*turbulent* + *-ator*] **:** a device to cause turbulence of fluids (as for mixing or scrubbing)

tur·bu·lence \'tərbyələn(t)s, 'təb-, 'təib-, ÷ -bəl-\ *n* -s [LL *turbulentia*, fr. L *turbulentus* turbulent + *-ia* -y] **1 :** the quality or state of being turbulent: as **a :** wild unruly disorderly commotion **:** disposition to stormy unruliness **:** violent agitation or disturbance **:** great perturbation **:** disorderly or tumultuous conduct ⟨the landmark of order in the midst of ~ and crime —S.H.Holbrook⟩ ⟨the ~ of the Scottish border in the early seventeenth century —Henry Cavendish⟩ ⟨the political changes accomplished this day do not imply ~, upheaval, or disorder —D.D.Eisenhower⟩ **b :** highly irregular atmospheric motion characterized by rapid changes in wind speed and direction and the presence of up and down currents **c :** departure in a fluid from a smooth or streamline flow with accompanying sinuosity and eddies due to an obstruction or to exceeding a critical speed **2 :** an instance or case of turbulence ⟨gigantic ~*s* set up in this vast poisonous atmosphere by the planet's . . . rapid rotation —*Springfield (Mass.) Daily News*⟩

syn see COMMOTION

tur·bu·len·cy \-nsē\ *n* -ES [LL *turbulentia*] *archaic* **:** TURBULENCE ⟨what a tale of terror . . . its ~ tells —E.A.Poe⟩ ⟨like *turbulencies* in the affairs of men —John Milton⟩

tur·bu·lent \-nt\ *adj* [L *turbulentus* tumultuous, stormy, turbulent, fr. *turba* confusion, tumult, crowd + *-ulentus* -ulent] **1 :** disposed or given to insubordination and disorder **:** causing great unrest **:** inciting violence or disturbance ⟨their physical courage and prowess . . . were the talk of the less ~ settlers —*Amer. Guide Series: Minn.*⟩ ⟨the hot and ~ feelings which boiled and surged in her —Virginia Woolf⟩ **2 :** being in a state of violent commotion **:** characterized by great agitation or tumult **:** violently disturbed or agitated **:** STORMY, TEMPESTUOUS ⟨a ~ childhood filled with frustration and fears —*Diseases of the Nervous System*⟩ ⟨the ~ waters of party politics —Victor Lewis⟩ ⟨the ~ years of the revolutionary period⟩ **3** *obs* **:** causing or tending to cause turbulence **:** having a disturbing or exciting effect ⟨whose heads that ~ liquor fills with fumes —John Milton⟩ **4 :** characterized by random fluctuations of velocity — see TURBULENT FLOW; compare CRITICAL VELOCITY

turbulent flow *n* **:** a fluid flow in which the velocity at a given point varies erratically in magnitude and direction with time and is thus essentially variable in pattern — contrasted with LAMINAR FLOW; compare STREAMLINE FLOW

tur·bu·lent·ly *adv* **:** in a turbulent manner ⟨the river rolls ~ boiling —W.C.Baldwin⟩

turcism *n* -s *usu cap* [ML *turcus* Turk + E *-ism*] *obs* **:** TURKISM

türck's column \'tirks-\ *n, usu cap T* [after Ludwig *Türck* †1868 Austrian neurologist] **:** DIRECT PYRAMIDAL TRACT

tur·co \'tür(,)kō\ *n* -s [AmerSp, fr. Araucanian *thurcu*] **:** a tapacolo (*Pteroptochos megapodius*) of Chile

turco- *or* **turko-** *comb form, usu cap* [*turco-* fr. ML *Turcus* Turk; *turko-* fr. ¹*turk*] **1 :** Turkic ⟨*Turko*-Tatar⟩ **2 :** Turkish ⟨*Turko*man⟩ **3 :** Turkish and ⟨*Turco*-Greek⟩

tur·col·o·gist \,tər'käləjəst\ *n, usu cap* [*turco-* + *-logist* (as in *geologist*)] **:** a specialist in Turkic languages and literature

turcoman *usu cap, var of* TURKOMAN

tur·co·phil \'tərkə,fil\ *n* -s *usu cap* [*turco-* + *-phil*] **:** one who admires or is partial to Turkey or Turkish ways

tur·co·pole \'tərkə,pōl\ *n* -s [ML *turcopulus, turcopolus*, fr. MGk *tourkopoulos*, lit., son of a Turk, fr. LGk *Tourkoi* (pl.) Turks (fr. Turk *Türk* Turk) + MGk *-poulos* child of, alter.

(prob. influenced by L *pullus* young of an animal) of Gk *pōlos* young animal, young man or woman — more at FOAL] **:** a light-armed soldier of the Order of St. John of Jerusalem

tur·co·po·lier \ˈ==pō,li(ə)r\ *n* -s [alter. (influenced by F *turcopolier*, fr. ML *turcopolarius*) of ME *turkepler*, fr. ML *turcopolarius*, fr. *turcopolus* turcopole + L *-arius* -ary] **:** a high official of the Order of St. John of Jerusalem who is ex officio the commander of the turcopoles

turd \ˈtərd\ *n* -s [ME *tord, turd*, fr. OE *tord*; akin to MD *tort* dung, ON *tordyfill* dung beetle, OE *teran* to tear — more at TEAR (divide)] **1 a :** a piece of dung — sometimes considered vulgar **b** *archaic* **:** EXCREMENT, FILTH **2 :** one that is esp. vile and contemptible — usu. considered vulgar

tur·di·dae \ˈtərdə,dē\ *n pl, cap* [NL, fr. *Turdus* + *-idae*] **:** a widely distributed family of singing birds (suborder Passeres) containing the true thrushes and a greater or lesser number of related birds (as often the bluebirds, wheatears, stonechats, Old World warblers, Old World redstarts, solitaires, and water ouzels, and the mockingbirds and thrashers)

tur·di·form \-,fȯrm\ *adj* [L *turdus* thrush + E *-iform*] **:** having the form or structure of a thrush

tur·doid \ˈtər,dȯid\ *adj* [L *turdus* + E *-oid*] **:** THRUSHLIKE

tur·dus \ˈtərdəs\ *n, cap* [NL, fr. L, thrush — more at THRUSH] **:** a genus of thrushes that is the type of the family Turdidae and includes the European blackbird, the mistle thrush, fieldfare, ring ouzel, and the American robin

tu·reen \t(y)əˈrēn, t(y)u̇ˈ-, t(y)üˈ-\ *n* -s [alter. of earlier *terrene, terene*, fr. F *terrine*, fr. MF, fr. fem. of *terrin* of earth, fr. (assumed) VL *terrinus*, fr. L *terra* earth + *-inus* -ine — more at TERRACE] **1 :** a deep footed vessel with a cover from which cooked foods (as soup, sauce, or eggs) are served at table **2 :** CASSEROLE 2

tureen 1

¹turf \ˈtər\|f, ˈtə̄\|, ˈtəi\|\ *n, pl* **turfs** \|fs\ *or* **turves** \|vz\ [ME, fr. OE; akin to OHG *zurba* turf, ON *torf*, Skt *darbha* tuft of grass] **1 :** a piece cut or pared off from the upper stratum of earth with its green growth preserved ⟨*turves* of native grasses are placed on the fronts of terraces —*New Zealand Jour. of Agric.*⟩ **2 :** the upper stratum of earth and vegetable mold that is filled with the roots of grass and other small plants forming a thick mat ⟨a glade of ~ at the end of which he could see the beginning of a formal garden —John Buchan⟩ **3 a :** a slab of peat esp. when used or ready for fuel ⟨lit his pipe from a red ~ —Padraic Fallon⟩ **b :** PEAT ⟨an Irish bog . . . from which ~ has been or can be cut —John Godley⟩ **4 a :** a track or course for horse racing **b :** the sport or business of horse racing **5** *slang* **:** a territory held by a gang to be under its control

²turf \ˈ"\ *adj* [ME, fr. ¹*turf*] **1 :** of or relating to turf **:** made of turf **2 :** of or relating to the sport of horse racing

³turf \ˈ"\ *vb* -ED/-ING/-S [ME *turven*, fr. ¹*turf*] *vt* **1 a :** to cover with turf **b :** to lay under the turf **:** BURY **2 :** to dig for turf **:** take turf from **3** *chiefly Brit* **:** to eject forcefully **:** KICK, THROW — usu. used with *out* ⟨going to ~ out those corny souvenirs of yours —Earle Birney⟩ ⟨a dog must be ~*ed* out of the chair —Joanna Cannan⟩ ~ *vi* **:** to gather turfs

turf accountant *n, Brit* **:** BOOKMAKER 2

turf ant *n* **:** PAVEMENT ANT

turf·dom \|fdəm\ *n* -s [¹*turf* + *-dom*] **:** the horse-racing world

turf·en \|fən\ *adj* [¹*turf* + *-en*] **:** made of turf **:** covered with turf

turfing daisy *n* [fr. gerund of ³*turf*] **:** a low densely tufted perennial herb (*Matricaria tchihatchewii*) of Asia Minor that has small white flower heads and is used as a ground cover in dry places

turf·ite \|,fīt\ *n* -s [¹*turf* + *-ite*] **:** TURFMAN

turf·man \|fmən\ *n, pl* **turfmen** [²*turf* + *man*] **1 :** a devotee of horse racing **:** one who owns and races horses **2 :** one who specializes in the study of fine grasses, their care, and uses

turf tan *n* **:** a light brown that is yellower and deeper than blush and redder and deeper than cork

turf webworm *n* **:** GRASS WEBWORM

turfy \|fē, |fi\ *adj, sometimes* -ER/-EST [¹*turf* + *-y*] **1 :** abounding with turf **:** made of or covered with turf ⟨green ~ knolls —William Bartram⟩ **2 :** having the nature or appearance of peat **3 :** of, relating to, or smacking of horse racing

tur·gen·cy \ˈtərjənsē, ˈtə̄j-, ˈtəij-, -si\ *n* -ES [*turgent* + *-cy*] *archaic* **:** the quality or state of being swollen

tur·gent \-nt\ *adj* [ME, fr. L *turgent-, turgens*, pres. part. of *turgēre* to be swollen — more at TURGID] *obs* **:** noticeably swelling **:** SWOLLEN

tur·ges·cence \,tərˈjesᵊn(t)s, ,tə̄ˈ-, ,təiˈ-\ *n* -s [L *turgescere* to swell, begin to swell (inchoative of *turgēre* to be swollen) + E *-ence* — more at TURGID] **1 :** the act of swelling **:** the quality or state of being turgescent **2 :** the quality or state of being pompous **:** BOMBAST ⟨somewhat out of the . . . romantic mode to give this book a ~ it does not need —N.L.Rothman⟩ **3 :** a turgid state **:** TURGOR

tur·ges·cen·cy \-nsē, -si\ *n* -ES [L *turgescere* + E *-ency*] *archaic* **:** TURGESCENCE

tur·ges·cent \-nt\ *adj* [L *turgescent-, turgescens*, pres. part. of *turgescere* to swell, become swollen] **:** becoming turgid, distended, or inflated **:** SWELLING

tur·gid \ˈtərjəd, ˈtə̄j-, ˈtəij-\ *adj* [L *turgidus*, fr. *turgēre* to be swollen; perh. akin to L *tumēre* to swell, be swollen — more at THUMB] **1 :** distended by or as if by some internal agent or expansive force **:** being in a normal or abnormal state of distention **:** SWOLLEN, TUMID ⟨~ limbs⟩ ⟨healthy living cells are ~⟩ **2 :** excessively embellished esp. in style or language **:** vainly ostentatious **:** BOMBASTIC, POMPOUS ⟨an effete classical tradition long ago . . . given over to ~ rhetorical display —Roger Fry⟩ **syn** see INFLATED

tur·gid·i·ty \,(ə)rˈjidədē, ,tə̄ˈ-, ,təiˈ-, -ətē, -i\ *n* -ES [L *turgidus* + E *-ity*] **:** the quality or state of being turgid **:** condition of being swollen ⟨plants . . . placed in a moist chamber to determine if they would regain ~ —*Jour. of Forestry*⟩ ⟨an unrelieved ~ settles over the movie —Hollis Alpert⟩

tur·gid·ly *adv* **:** in a turgid manner ⟨incidents, unpleasant fragments of . . . life churned ~ in his brain —Norman Mailer⟩

tur·gid·ness *n* -ES [*turgid* + *-ness*] **:** TURGIDITY

tur·gor \ˈtərgər; ˈtə̄gə(r, ˈtəig-\ *n* -s [LL, turgidity, swelling, fr. L *turgēre* to be swollen] **:** the normal state of turgidity and tension in living cells; *esp* **:** the distention of the protoplasmic layer and wall of a plant cell by the fluid contents that is an essential feature of growth and movements in many parts of plants — compare TURGOR PRESSURE, WILT

turgor deficit *n* **:** DIFFUSION PRESSURE DEFICIT

turgor movement *n* **:** a reversible change in position of a plant part due to a change in turgor pressure of various cells (as in sleep movements) — compare NYCTITROPISM

turgor pressure *n* **:** the actual pressure developed by the fluid in a turgid plant cell as a result of endosmosis as contrasted with the potential maximum pressure that fluid of the same concentration could theoretically develop

tu·ri \ˈtürē\ *n, pl* **turi** *or* **turis** *usu cap* **1 :** a Pathan people inhabiting northern West Pakistan **2 :** a member of the Turi

tu·ri·ca·ta \,türəˈkäd·ə\ *n* -s [MexSp] **:** an argasid tick (*Ornithodoros turicata*) of Mexico and the southwestern U. S. that is a pest on hogs and cattle and sometimes transmits relapsing fever to man

tu·rin \ˈt(y)u̇rən, t(y)u̇ˈrin\ *adj, usu cap* [fr. *Turin*, commune & manufacturing commune of northwest Italy] **:** of or from the city of Turin, Italy **:** of the kind or style prevalent in Turin

tu·ri·on \ˈt(y)u̇rē,än\ *n* -s [NL *turion-, turio*, fr. L, sprout, tendril, young branch; prob. akin to L *tumēre* to swell, be swollen — more at THUMB] **:** a scaly shoot (as of asparagus and some duckweeds) developed from a bud on a subterranean or submerged rootstock — **tu·ri·on·if·er·ous** \ˌt(y)u̇rēəˈnif(ə)rəs\ *adj*

¹turk \ˈtərk, ˈtə̄k, ˈtəik\ *n* -s [ME, fr. MF or Turk; MF *Turc*, fr. ML or Turk; ML *Turcus* fr. Turk *Türk*] **1** *usu cap* **a :** a member of any of numerous Asiatic peoples speaking Turkic languages who live in the region ranging from the Adriatic to the Okhotsk and who are racially mixed but are held to have risen in the Altai mountains and western Siberia **b :** a member of the dominant race of the Ottoman Empire **2** *cap* **:** a native or inhabitant of Turkey **3** *usu cap, archaic* **:** one who is cruel, hardhearted, or tyrannical ⟨a terrible *Turk* at keeping his wife up to her social duties —W.W.Hunter⟩ **4** *usu cap* **:** MUSLIM; *specif* **:** a Muslim subject of the Turkish sultan **5** *usu cap* **:** a Turkish horse; *specif* **:** a Turkish strain of Arab and crossbred horses **6** *usu cap* **:** one of a group of people of mixed white, Indian, and Negro ancestry esp. in So. Carolina — often used disparagingly

²turk \ˈ"\ *n* -s [F *turc*; prob. fr. *Turc* Turk] **:** PLUM CURCULIO; *also* **:** the larva of various destructive beetles

tur·ka·na \tu̇rˈkänə\ *n, pl* **turkana** *or* **turkanas** *usu cap* **1 :** a people resembling the Masai and living between Lake Rudolf and the Nile in East Africa **2 :** a member of the Turkana people

türk cell \ˈtirk-\ *or* **türk's cell** *n, usu cap T* [after Wilhelm *Türk* †1916 Austrian physician] **:** a large cell resembling a lymphocyte, having densely basophilic cytoplasm and eccentric nucleus with peripheral chromatin and central clear area, and being rare in normal blood but commonly present in diseases of lymphoid tissues

turk·dom \ˈtərkdəm\ *n* -s *usu cap* [¹*turk* + *-dom*] **:** the realm controlled by the Turks

tur·ken \ˈtərkən\ *also* **turk·hen** \-k,hen\ *n* -s [*turken* blend of *turkey* and *chicken*; *turkhen* fr. *turkey* + *hen*] **:** a type of chicken sometimes held to constitute a separate breed and distinguished by a rough red unfeathered neck; *also* **:** one of these birds often erroneously reported to be a hybrid between turkey and chicken

¹turkey *n* -s *usu cap* [ME, fr. *Turkey*, country of southeast Europe and southwest Asia] *obs* **:** TURQUOISE 1

²tur·key \ˈtərkē, ˈtə̄k-, ˈtəik-, -ki\ *adj, usu cap* [fr. *Turkey*, country of southeast Europe and southwest Asia] **1 :** of or from Turkey **:** of the kind or style prevalent in Turkey **:** TURKISH **2 :** believed to be of Turkish origin

³turkey \ˈ"\ *n* -s *often attrib* [short for *turkey-cock*] **1 :** a bird of the family Meleagrididae: as **a** (1) **:** a large American bird (*Meleagris gallopavo*) orig. distributed from southern Mexico throughout much of the eastern and central U. S. and northward into Canada but extinct over much of the northern and western part of its range though reintroduced as a game bird in some regions and successfully reestablished as far north as Pennsylvania, occurring in several subspecies in various parts of its range, and having typically a bronzy lustrous plumage, a naked carunculate head, and a tail that in the male is spread fanlike in display (2) **:** any of various domesticated birds derived primarily from a Mexican variety of the wild turkey and raised chiefly for their flesh — see BELTSVILLE SMALL WHITE, BOURBON RED, BRONZE, NARRAGANSETT **b :** OCELLATED TURKEY **2** *Austral* **a :** a bustard (*Choriotis australis*) **b :** BRUSH TURKEY **3 :** a lumberman's kit or itinerant worker's pack ⟨carrying a long-handled double-bitted ax and a ~ of clothes across his shoulder —J.H.Stuart⟩ **4 a :** a theatrical production that is a failure **:** FLOP ⟨a ~ about a rich actor who financed a play to star himself —Stanley Frank⟩ **b :** something that has a conspicuous lack of success ⟨the idea was a complete ~ —Mac Davis⟩ **5 :** practical action without delay or evasion **:** straight facts leading to a realistic solution **:** BUSINESS — usu. used in the phrase *talk turkey* ⟨will be willing to talk ~ . . . and to end the war —*Kiplinger Washington Letter*⟩ **6 :** three successive strikes in bowling — called also *triple*

domestic turkey-cock

⁴turkey \ˈ"\ *n* -s *usu cap* **:** TURKEY LEATHER

turkeyback \ˈ==,=\ *n* [³*turkey*] *NewEng* **:** GREATER YELLOWLEGS; *esp* **:** one of large size

turkey beard *n* **:** an American plant of the genus *Xerophyllum* (esp. *X. asphodeloides*)

tur·key·berry \ˈ==- — see BERRY\ *n* **1 a :** either of two nightshades (*Solanum mammosum* and *S. torvum*) of the West Indies **b :** the fruit of either of these plants **2 a** *also* **turkeyberry tree :** a West Indian tree (*Cordia collococca*) **b :** the berry of the turkeyberry **3 :** CORALBERRY 1 **4 :** PARTRIDGEBERRY 1

turkey berry *n, usu cap T* [²*turkey*] **:** PERSIAN BERRY

turkey bird *n* [³*turkey*] *dial Eng* **:** WRYNECK

turkey blue *n, often cap T* [²*turkey*] **:** TURKISH BLUE

turkeybush \ˈ==,=\ *n* [³*turkey*] **:** a tropical African spiny shrub (*Caesalpinia oligophylla*) introduced into Australia where it forms dense weedy scrub

turkey buzzard *n* **1 :** an American vulture (*Cathartes aura*) that is common in So. and Central America and in the southern U. S. but rare north of Pennsylvania, that is blackish brown with the nearly naked wrinkled skin of the head and foreneck red, that is about five feet in spread of wings and very graceful in flight, and that feeds on carrion only — called also *turkey vulture* **2** *Africa* **:** BROMVOEL

turkey call *n* **1 :** the gobbling sound made by a turkey-cock **2 :** an instrument imitating a gobbling sound and used as a decoy by hunters of wild turkey

turkey carpet *n, usu cap T* [²*turkey*] **1 :** TURKISH CARPET **2 :** ORIENTAL RUG

turkey-cock \ˈ==,=\ *n* [²*turkey* + *cock*; fr. confusion with the guinea fowl, supposed to be imported from Turkish territory] **1 :** a male turkey **2 :** a strutting pompous person

turkey corn *n* [³*turkey*] **:** SQUIRREL CORN

turkey cup sponge *or* **turkey cup** *n, usu cap T* [²*turkey*] **:** a Turkey sponge (*Spongia officinalis mollissima*) with fine elastic durable fibers

turkey dance *n* [³*turkey*] **:** a mimetic social dance of American Indians with a jigging step, erratic course, and often realistic head jerking

turkey fig *n, usu cap T* [²*turkey*] **1 :** a common cultivated fig (*Ficus carica*) **2** *Austral* **:** INDIAN FIG 2a(2)

turkey fish *n* [³*turkey*] **:** LION-FISH 1

turkeyfoot \ˈ==,=\ *n, pl* **turkeyfoots** [³*turkey* + *foot*; fr. the shape of the spike] **:** any of several No. American grasses of the genus *Andropogon*

turkey gnat *n* **:** a small black fly (*Simulium meridionale*) that injures poultry esp. in the southern and western U. S. and has been reported as a vector of leucocytozoan diseases of turkeys; *broadly* **:** any of various simuliid flies

turkey-gobbler \ˈ==,==\ *n* **:** TURKEY-COCK 1

turkey grape *n* **:** POST-OAK GRAPE

turkey grass *n, dial Eng* **:** CLEAVERS

turkey gum *n, usu cap T* [²*turkey*] **:** GUM ARABIC

turkey leather *n, usu cap T, Brit* **:** an oil-tawed leather used esp. for bookbindings

turkey louse *n* [³*turkey*] **:** a biting louse (*Lipeurus gallipavonis*) that infests turkeys and eats their feathers

turkey morocco *n, usu cap T* [²*turkey*] **:** morocco made in Turkey or as if in Turkey

turkey mullein *n* [³*turkey*] **:** a prostrate soft-leaved annual weed (*Eremocarpus setigerus*) of the family Euphorbiaceae of the Pacific coast of the U. S. whose small black seeds are said to be eaten by turkeys and whose herbage is used by Indians to stupefy fish — called also *doveweed*

¹turkey oak *n, usu cap T* [²*turkey*] **:** a brittle-branched oak (*Quercus cerris*) that is a native of the Balkans but widely planted — called also *Adriatic oak, cerris*

²turkey oak *n* [³*turkey*] **:** any of several oaks of the southern U. S.: as **a :** RED OAK 1b **b :** an oak (*Quercus laevis*) of dry sandy barrens having shining leaves with bristle-tipped lobes suggesting a turkey's toes **c :** an oak (*Quercus incana*) of the southeastern U. S. with heavily tomentose young branchlets

turkey pea *n* [³*turkey*] **1 a :** SQUIRREL CORN **b :** HOARY PEA **c :** HARBINGER-OF-SPRING **2 :** DEVIL'S SHOESTRINGS

turkey pod *n* **:** MOUSE-EAR CRESS

turkey red *n* [²*turkey*] **1** *usu cap T* **a :** a brilliant durable red produced upon cotton by means of alizarin or formerly madder in connection with an aluminum mordant and oil or other fatty matter — called also *alizarine red* **b :** cotton cloth dyed with this red **2** *often cap T* **:** a moderate red that is yellower and very slightly darker than cerise, yellower and darker than claret (sense 3a), yellower and very slightly lighter than Harvard crimson (sense 1), and yellower, slightly darker, and very slightly less strong than average strawberry (sense 2a) — called also *Adrianople red, Levant red, Turkish red* **3** *usu cap T* **:** an iron oxide pigment similar to Indian red

turkey-red oil *n* **1 :** an inferior grade of olive oil used in producing Turkey red **2 :** a sulfonated oil used in dyeing (as with alizarin dyes) and as a wetting and emulsifying agent; *esp* **:** sulfated castor oil or its sodium salt

turkey rhubarb *n, usu cap T* **:** Chinese rhubarb formerly imported through Turkey

turkeys *pl of* TURKEY

turkey shoot *n* [³*turkey*] **1 a :** a contest of marksmanship with a gun using live turkeys as targets **b :** a similar contest for prizes usu. using moving targets **2 :** something resembling a turkey shoot

turkey sponge *n, usu cap T* [²*turkey*] **:** any of various superior commercial sponges of the Adriatic and Mediterranean seas

turkey stone *also* **turkey slate** *n, usu cap T* [²*turkey*] **1 :** TURQUOISE **2** *or* **turkey oilstone a :** a whetstone or oilstone from Turkey **b :** NOVACULITE

turkey toilet sponge *also* **turkey toilet** *n, usu cap 1st T* **:** a Turkey sponge (*Spongia officinalis adriatica*) of fine quality but less valuable than the Turkey cup sponge

turkey trot *n* [³*turkey*] **:** a ragtime dance of the period of World War I danced with the feet well apart and with a characteristic rise on the ball of the foot followed by a drop upon the heel

turkey-trot \ˈ==,=\ *vi* [*turkey trot*] **:** to dance the turkey trot

turkey umber *n* [²*turkey*] **1** *usu cap T* **:** raw umber from the island of Cyprus **2** *often cap T* **:** RAW UMBER 2

turkey vulture *n* [³*turkey*] **:** TURKEY BUZZARD

turkey wheat *n, usu cap T* [²*turkey*] **1 :** INDIAN CORN **2 :** CRIMEAN WHEAT

turkey wing *n* [³*turkey*] **:** an ark shell (*Arca occidentalis*)

turkey work *n, often cap T* [²*turkey*] **:** needlework imitating the designs and texture of Oriental rugs made by knotting worsted yarn on canvas or coarse cloth and used formerly for upholstery and carpets

turkhen *var of* TURKEN

¹tur·ki \ˈtərkē, ˈtürkē, ˈtə̄k-, ˈtəik-, ˈtu̇(ə)k-, -ki\ *adj, usu cap* [Per *turkī*, fr. *Turk* Turk, fr. Turk *Türk*] **1 :** of or relating to the peoples of Turkic speech **2 :** of or relating to any central Asian Turkic language particularly of the eastern group

²turki \ˈ"\ *n* -s *usu cap* **1 :** one of the Turki peoples **2 :** any central Asian Turkic language particularly of the eastern group

¹turk·ic \ˈtərkik, ˈtə̄k-, ˈtəik-, -kēk\ *adj, usu cap* [¹*turk* + *-ic*] **1 a :** of or relating to a subfamily of Altaic languages **b :** of or relating to the peoples speaking these languages **2 :** TURKISH

²turkic \ˈ"\ *n* -s *usu cap* **:** a subfamily of Altaic languages including Azerbaijani, Kazak, Kirghiz, Turkish, Turkoman, Uighur, Uzbek, and Yakut

turk·i·cize \-kə,sīz\ *vt* -ED/-ING/-S *often cap* [¹*turkic* + *-ize*] **:** TURKIZE

¹tur·kis \ˈtərkə̇s\ *n pl but sometimes sing in constr* [ME *turkas*, fr. MF *turquoises, turquaises* (pl.), prob. fr. fem. pl. of *turquoys, turqueis* Turkish — more at TURQUOISE] *Scot* **:** a pair of pincers

²turkis \ˈ"\ *n* -ES [ME *turkeis* — more at TURQUOISE] **:** TURQUOISE ⟨that all the turf was rich in plots that looked each like a garnet or a ~ in it —Alfred Tennyson⟩

¹turk·ish \ˈtərkish, ˈtə̄k-, ˈtəik-, -kēsh\ *adj, usu cap* [¹*turk* + *-ish*] **1 :** of, relating to, or characteristic of Turkey **b :** of, relating to, or characteristic of the Turkish people **2 :** of, relating to, or characteristic of the Turkic subfamily of Ural-Altaic languages; *specif* **:** of, relating to, or characteristic of the Turkish language

²turkish \ˈ"\ *n* -ES *usu cap* **1 :** the Turkic language of the Republic of Turkey **2 :** TURKIC

turkish bath *n, usu cap T* **:** a bath in which the bather passes through a succession of steam rooms of increasing temperature followed by a rubdown, massage, and cold shower

turkish bean *n, usu cap T* **:** SCARLET RUNNER

turkish blue *n, often cap T* **:** a grayish purplish blue that is redder than average delft and redder, lighter, and stronger than average navy blue — called also *Turkey blue*

turkish boxwood *n, usu cap T* **:** the wood of a box (*Buxus sempervirens*)

turkish carpet *n, usu cap T* **1 :** a handmade one-piece carpet made in Turkey having a deep generally woolen pile with a weft of different material **2 :** an English carpet woven in the Turkish manner

turkish checkers *n pl but usu sing in constr, usu cap T* **:** checkers in which each player has 16 men and all 64 squares of the checkerboard are used, single men move forward, sideward, or diagonally forward, and kings move any distance in any direction

turkish coffee *n, usu cap T* **:** a decoction of pulverized coffee in thin sugar syrup

turkish crescent *n, usu cap T* **:** PAVILLON CHINOIS

turkish-crescent red *n, often cap T* **:** CHRYSANTHEMUM 4

turkish delight *or* **turkish paste** *n, usu cap T* **:** a confection of jellylike or gummy consistency usu. cut in cubes and dusted with sugar

turkish geranium oil *n, usu cap T* **:** PALMAROSA OIL

turkish knot *n, usu cap T* **:** GHIORDES KNOT

turk·ish·ly *adv, usu cap* **:** in a characteristically Turkish manner ⟨his defense was *Turkishly* impregnable —T.E.Lawrence⟩

turkish music *n, usu cap T* **:** JANISSARY MUSIC 1b

turk·ish·ness *n* -ES *usu cap T* **:** the quality or state of being Turkish

turkish oak *n, usu cap T* **:** VALONIA OAK

turkish pepper *n, usu cap T* **:** PIMIENTO; *also* **:** a paprika made from it

turkish red *n, often cap T* **:** TURKEY RED

turkish saddle *n, usu cap T* [trans. of NL *sella turcica*] **:** SELLA TURCICA

turkish tobacco *n, usu cap 1st T* **:** a very aromatic tobacco of small leaf size grown chiefly in Turkey and Greece and adjoining territories and used esp. in blended cigarettes

turkish towel *n, usu cap 1st T* **:** a towel made of Turkish toweling

turkish toweling *n, usu cap 1st T* **:** a cotton terry cloth used esp. for towels

turkish walnut *n, usu cap T* **:** ENGLISH WALNUT

turk·ism \ˈtər,kizəm\ *n* -s *usu cap* [¹*turk* + *-ism*] **:** the customs, beliefs, institutions, and principles of the Turks

turk·ize \-,kīz\ *vt* -ED/-ING/-S *often cap* [¹*turk* + *-ize*] **:** to make Turkish

tur·kle \ˈtərkəl\ *n* -s [by alter.] *dial* **:** TURTLE

turk·man \ˈtərkmən, ˈtə̄k-, ˈtəik-\ *n, pl* **turkmen** *usu cap* [alter. (influenced by ¹*turk* & *man*) of *turkoman*] **:** TURKOMAN 1

¹turk·men \-kmən, -k,men\ *adj, usu cap* [Per *Turkmēn* Turkoman] **:** TURKMENIAN

²turkmen \ˈ"\ *n* -s *usu cap* **:** TURKOMAN 2

turk·me·ni·an \,tərkˈmēnēən\ *adj, usu cap* [Per *Turkmēn* Turkoman + E *-ian*] **:** of or relating to the Turkomans or the Republic of Turkmen, U. S. S. R.

turko- — see TURCO-

tur·ko·man *or* **tur·co·man** \ˈtərkəmən, ˈtə̄k-, ˈtəik-\ *n, pl* **turkomans** *or* **turcomans** *usu cap* [ML *Turcomannus*, fr. Per *Turkmān, Turkmēn*, fr. *turkmān, turkmēn* resembling a Turk, fr. *Turk* Turk — more at TURKI] **1 :** a member of a group of peoples of East Turkic stock living chiefly in the Turkmen, Uzbek, Kazak, and Karakalpak republics of the U. S. S. R. **2 :** the Turkic language of the Turkoman people

turkoman carpet *or* **turkoman rug** *n, usu cap T* **:** any of a number of oriental rugs made by various Turkoman peoples

tur·ko-tatar \ˌtər(,)kō+\ *n, cap both Ts* [*turco-* + *tatar*] **:** TURKIC

turks *pl of* TURK

turk's-cap lily \ˈ=,=-\ *also* **turk's cap** *n, usu cap T* **:** either of two lilies having nodding flowers with strongly revolute perianth segments: **a :** a widely cultivated lily (*Lilium martagon*) with rather small dull purple flowers **b :** an American native lily (*Lilium superbum*) with flowers resembling those of the tiger lily

turk's-cap moss *n, usu cap T* **:** an urn moss (*Physcomitrium turbinatum*)

türk's cell *usu cap T, var of* TÜRK CELL

turk's head *n, usu cap T* **1** *or* **turk's-head cactus** \'⸗,⸗-\ *or* **turk's cap** *or* **turk's-cap cactus** \'⸗,⸗-\ **:** a globular West Indian cactus (*Cactus intortus*) deeply furrowed and spiny with a cap of whitish hairs resembling a fez from which the red flowers and fruit arise **2 :** a knot that is ornamental as well as practical and is considered to resemble a small turban

Turk's head 2

turk's-turban \'⸗¦⸗⸗\ *n, pl* **turk's-turbans** *usu cap 1st T* **:** TUBEFLOWER

tur·ku \'tu̇r(,)ku̇\ *adj, usu cap* [fr. *Turku*, seaport city of southwest Finland] **:** of or from the city of Turku, Finland **:** of the kind or style prevalent in Turku

turle knot \'tərl-\ *n* [after Major W. G. *Turle*, 19th cent. Eng. fisherman] **:** a knot made with a variety of slip noose and used in angling to tie a gut or nylon leader to a hook or fly — called also *turtle knot*

turle knot

tur·lough \'tər,läk\ *n* -s [IrGael *turloch*, fr. *tur* dry + *loch* lake, fr. OIr — more at LAKE] *Irish* **:** a winter lake that is dry or marshy in summer

turmaline *var of* TOURMALINE

1**tur·mer·ic** \'tərmərik, 'tə̄m-, 'təim-, -rēk\ *or* **tu·mer·ic** \'t(y)üm-\ *n* -s [modif. of MF *terre merite* saffron, fr. ML *terra merita*, lit., deserving or deserved earth] **1 a** (1) **:** an East Indian perennial herb (*Curcuma longa*) with a large aromatic deep yellow rhizome (2) **:** the cleaned, boiled, sun-dried, and usu. pulverized rhizome of the turmeric plant used as a coloring agent, a condiment (as in pickling and in curry powder), or a stimulant (3) **:** a yellow to reddish brown dyestuff obtained from turmeric **b :** any of several closely related plants yielding a similar product **2 :** any of several plants (as the bloodroot or goldenseal) yielding colored juices or otherwise felt to resemble the East Indian turmeric **3 :** MIMOSA 3

2**turmeric** \"\ *adj* **:** of, relating to, or obtained from turmeric

turmeric paper *n* **:** paper impregnated with an extract of turmeric and used as a test for alkaline substances which turn it from yellow to reddish brown and for boric acid which turns it red brown

turmeric root *n* **1 :** BLOODROOT **2 :** GOLDENSEAL 2

turmeric yellow *n* **:** CURCUMIN

tur·mit \'tərmət\ *or* **tur·mut** \-mət\ *dial Brit var of* TURNIP

1**tur·moil** \'tər,mȯil, 'tə̄,-, 'təi,-\ *n* -s [origin unknown] **:** an utterly confused, extremely agitated, or tumultuous state or condition: as **a :** the inner confusion of a disturbed or distressed mind or spirit ⟨the child's inner life is often a ~ of terrors and anxieties —W.R.Inge⟩ ⟨an odd ~ of shame and triumph in her heart —Louis Bromfield⟩ **b :** disruptive commotion **:** disordered activity ⟨the mad ~ of governmental investigation —W.S.Lynch⟩ ⟨keep executives in a constant ~ making decisions —R.E.Cross⟩ **c :** active strife ⟨rose to his greatest heights in the excitement and ~ of battle —Robert Bruce⟩ **syn** see COMMOTION

2**turmoil** \"\ *vb* -ED/-ING/-S *vt* **1 :** to produce a state of harassment in **:** DISQUIET, WORRY **2 :** TOSS, UPSET ~ *vi* **:** LABOR, TOIL

tur·moil·er \-lə(r)\ *n* -s [2*turmoil* + *-er*] **:** one that makes or causes turmoil

1**turn** \'tərn, 'tə̄n, 'təin\ *vb* -ED/-ING/-S [ME *turnen;* partly fr. OE *tyrnan & turnian* to turn, fr. ML *tornare*, fr L, to turn on a lathe, round off, fr. *tornus* lathe, chisel, fr. Gk *tornos* dividers, lathe; partly fr. OF *torner*, *tourner*, fr. ML *tornare;* akin to L *terere* to rub — more at THROW] *vt* **1 a :** to cause to move in a curved esp. circular path around or as if around an axis or a center **:** make rotate or revolve ⟨~ a wheel⟩ ⟨~ a crank⟩ ⟨great wheel ~*s* its axle when it can —Theodore Roethke⟩ ⟨shaft . . . can be ~*ed* . . . at higher than 50,000 revolutions per minute —*Ford Times*⟩ ⟨how that little scrapper could hold and ~ a miner's drill —N.C.Wilson⟩ **b** (1) **:** to cause to move around in such a path far enough or enough times to effect a desired end (as of locking, opening, or shutting) ⟨~ a key in a lock⟩ ⟨~*ed* the knob till the door opened⟩ ⟨~ a screw tight⟩ ⟨shut the door and ~*ed* the bolt —Paul Horgan⟩ ⟨~ the cap to release it⟩ ⟨~*ed* the handle to the shut position⟩ (2) **:** to affect or alter the functioning of (as a mechanical device) by or as if by operation of a control moving in this way ⟨~*ed* the lamp as low as it would go⟩ ⟨~*ed* the heating pad too high⟩ ⟨~*ed* the steam iron to *rayon*⟩ **c :** to execute or perform by rotating or revolving like a rolling wheel ⟨~ a double somersault⟩ ⟨~ handsprings⟩ or like a spinning top ⟨~*s* a clumsy pirouette —G.C.Menotti⟩ **d :** to twist to one side or out of line or shape **:** WRENCH ⟨so easy . . . to plant a swift blow, to ~ a fragile wrist —H.A.Overstreet⟩ ⟨stumbled along, ~*ing* his ankle at frequent intervals —Peggy Bennett⟩ **2 a** (1) **:** to cause to change position, posture, or part exposed by moving through an arc of a circle ⟨nurse could easily ~ a patient twice her size⟩ ⟨leaned out, and ~*ed* his heavy shoulders . . . around to gaze up into the dark night —Glenway Wescott⟩ ⟨kept ~*ing* his hat in his hands⟩ ⟨~*ed* his chair to the fire⟩ (2) **:** to cause to move around a center so as to see or to show another side or angle ⟨~*ing* the pages of the book⟩; *specif* **:** to turn the leaves of (a book) **:** read or search through (3) **:** to cause (as the beam or platform of a scale) to move up or down **:** cause to register weight ⟨~*ed* the scale at 160 pounds⟩ (4) **:** to cause to move or stir in any way ⟨a fate she did not ~ a finger to escape —V.L.Parrington⟩ **b :** to revolve mentally **:** consider and reconsider in various aspects or from several points of view **:** think over **:** PONDER ⟨~*ed* the question every which way but could find no answer⟩ ⟨was still ~*ing* the idea about when he fell asleep⟩ — usu. used with *over* ⟨~*ing* the scenes and characters over in his mind —Ernest Newman⟩ ⟨appeared to be ~*ing* something over in his mind —Douglas Stewart⟩ ⟨disturbing thought . . . persisted. He ~*ed* it over continuously as he rode —T.B.Costain⟩ **3 a :** to reverse the position of (as by making the uppermost side or part the undermost, or the outermost side or part the innermost, or the front the back) **:** reverse the sides or surfaces of **:** INVERT ⟨~ an hourglass⟩ ⟨~ pancakes⟩ ⟨~ a phonograph record⟩ ⟨coat can be ~*ed* and worn either side out⟩ ⟨~ 4 thin veal fillets in 1 oz. seasoned flour —*Modern Woman*⟩ ⟨~*ed* the rug frequently to equalize wear⟩: (1) **:** to dig or plow so as to invert the turf or bring the lower soil to the surface ⟨soil should be ~*ed* after the harvest⟩ ⟨was eager to get home and begin ~*ing* his ground —G.S.Perry⟩ ⟨sod . . . almost had to be ~*ed* by main strength, piece by piece —O.E. Rölvaag⟩ (2) **:** to make (as a garment) over by unpicking the stitching, reversing the material, and resewing ⟨~ a dress⟩ ⟨~ a collar⟩ (3) **:** to invert feet up and face down (as a character, rule, or slug) in setting type (as in place of a letter or matter temporarily unavailable or to draw attention to a change to be made) **b :** to reverse or upset the order or disposition of **:** change drastically the arrangement of things in ⟨found everything ~*ed* topsy-turvy⟩ ⟨robbers had ~*ed* the room upside down⟩ ⟨in adapting the novel . . . have ~*ed* the story on its head —Arthur Knight⟩ **c** (1) **:** to disturb or upset the mental balance of **:** DERANGE, UNSETTLE ⟨thwarted affections had ~*ed* her brain —Kathleen Freeman⟩ ⟨a mind ~*ed* by grief⟩ (2) **:** to affect the power of judgment of (as by causing to become infatuated or to harbor extravagant notions of pride or conceit) — used chiefly in the phrase *turn one's head* ⟨success had not ~*ed* his head⟩ ⟨silly girl's head had been ~*ed* by a handful of compliments⟩ **d :** to cause (the stomach) to revolt (as at something swallowed) **:** UPSET ⟨very thought of food ~*ed* his stomach⟩ **e :** to set in another esp. contrary direction ⟨~*ed* his horse and rode away⟩ ⟨hard car to ~ in a narrow street⟩ **4 a :** to cause to have or take another path or direction **:** bend or change the course of ⟨~ the channel of a stream⟩ ⟨saddle stock spooked and I had to run them two miles to ~ them —Bruce Siberts & W.D.Wyman⟩ ⟨~ a car into a stream of traffic⟩: as (1) **:** to reverse the course or direction of **:** make go back ⟨captured cart was ~*ed* and rumbled past —F.V.W.Mason⟩ ⟨series of revolts which was definitely to ~ the tide against reaction —C.L.Jones⟩ (2) **:** to cause to retreat ⟨police used fire hoses and tear gas to ~ the mob⟩ (3) **:** to check the course of (as by interposing an obstacle) **:** make go back or go aside **:** keep out or off ⟨wires are close enough together . . . to ~ hogs and sheep —*Fence*⟩ ⟨struck like a club in the dark . . . not to be ~*ed* by any plea —R.O.Bowen⟩ (4) **:** to cause (a ball) to break — used of a cricket bowler ⟨flights the ball well, ~*s* it markedly any way —*Sunday Express* (*Johannesburg*) *So. Africa*⟩ **b** (1) **:** to alter the drift, tendency, or natural or expected result of (as a course of thought, action, or progress) ⟨alliance . . . led directly to war, and ~*ed* the course of history —L.L.Snyder⟩ ⟨is not facts . . . but what people think about the facts that ~*s* elections —*Times Lit. Supp.*⟩ ⟨~*ed* the talk to baseball⟩ (2) **:** to divert esp. from a course of action, an intention, an attitude ⟨would not be ~*ed* from his life of senseless pleasure⟩ ⟨a plea that would have ~*ed* a heart of stone⟩ **c** (1) **:** to change direction by bending a course around or about **:** take a usu. circular or elliptical path around **:** ROUND ⟨~*ed* the corner at full speed⟩ ⟨watched the leading boat ~ the first marker⟩ (2) **:** to get around in this way **:** get to the other side of ⟨ship had ~*ed* the cape and was now homeward bound⟩ ⟨a play designed to ~ the end of the defensive line⟩ ⟨was so intent on surprising the enemy . . . that his right flank was ~*ed*, and he suffered . . . a crushing defeat —R.L.Conolly⟩ **d :** to pass or go beyond (as an amount) ⟨was waiting for the clock to ~ ten⟩ ⟨~*ed* seventeen the day he graduated⟩ ⟨this robust man, just ~*ed* fifty, died of cerebral hemorrhage —Padraic Colum⟩ ⟨~*ed* of seventy years, he had withdrawn from active business —F.L. Paxson⟩ **5 a** (1) **:** to direct or point (as a glance) in a specified way ⟨had ~*ed* his face from the curious onlookers⟩ ⟨~*ed* a pair of stricken eyes on his mother —T.B.Costain⟩ ⟨~*ing* more and more hostile looks in her direction —Charles Lee⟩ ⟨will find anxious eyes all over the town ~*ed* toward the dropping mercury —Judson Philips⟩ (2) **:** to present by or as if by a change in direction or position ⟨~ the cheek even to the smiter's hand —P.B.Shelley⟩ ⟨apologized for ~*ing* his back to his guests⟩ ⟨face she ~*ed* to the world was always serene⟩ ⟨cattle had ~*ed* tail to the storm —F.B.Gipson⟩ ⟨the novel, a powerful modern agency for civilization . . . must ~ to the light many ugly realities —Carl Van Doren⟩ ⟨always ~*ed* his left profile to the cameras⟩ (3) **:** to change the direction of (as the face) **:** direct another way or various ways ⟨stood alone in the open doorway ~*ing* his eyes speculatively⟩; *often* **:** to cause to be directed away or aside ⟨~*ed* her face and wept⟩ ⟨staring match to see who would first ~ his eyes⟩ (4) *archaic* **:** to cause (as oneself) to face or go another way or a specified way **b :** to bring to bear by moving, aiming, pointing, or focusing esp. from a point of rest **:** TRAIN ⟨~*ed* his light into the dark doorway⟩ — usu. used with *on* or *upon* ⟨~*ed* the binoculars on those retreating backs —Maurice Duggan⟩ ⟨cannon were ~*ed* on the city and street fighting broke out —C.L.Jones⟩ ⟨had been vaguely ~*ing* his torch on the number plates of a short line of cars —Elizabeth Bowen⟩ ⟨~*ed* his cameras directly upon the violence and brutality of life —Arthur Knight⟩ ⟨bring them into his study and ~ upon them the light of his critical analysis —V.L.Parrington⟩ **c** (1) **:** to direct (as the mind) toward or away from something ⟨~ his thoughts to home⟩ ⟨recording companies must ~ their attention . . . to other kinds of music —P.H.Lang⟩ ⟨was free to ~ his whole mind and will to work —Carl Van Doren⟩ ⟨urging him to ~ his thoughts towards religion —R.A.Hall b. 1911⟩ ⟨sought to ~ man's curious mind from this world to the next —Marjory S. Douglas⟩ ⟨~ public attention to the fascinating underworld of the unconscious —C.I.Glicksberg⟩ ⟨cool evenings and heavy dews that ~ the mind toward sweaters —Virgil Thomson⟩ (2) *archaic* **:** to direct (oneself) toward or away from a concern with someone or something **d** (1) *obs* **:** to lead or bring (a person) to or into some state or situation by influencing or causing to become involved ⟨all the trouble thou hast ~*ed* me to —Shak.⟩ (2) **:** to induce or influence (a person) to change his way of life (as from ungodly to godly or from one religious faith to another) ⟨a popish place like that! They'll ~ her . . . sure as death and taxes —Angus Mowat⟩ (3) *archaic* **:** to direct the course of (as a series of events) ⟨Apollo ~ all to the best —Shak.⟩ **e** (1) **:** to direct the employment of (as to some use or purpose) **:** make use of **:** APPLY, DEVOTE — used with *to* ⟨~ anthropological knowledge to practical uses —Ralph Linton⟩ ⟨studying how they could best ~ to their own benefit the doctrines they found —F.L. Paxson⟩ ⟨~*ed* misfortune to good account —Sir Winston Churchill⟩ ⟨~*s* her compassion to finding ways in which she and her staff can help —*Lamp*⟩ ⟨sawmill and gristmill were erected . . . and a soda spring nearby ~*ed* to the use of the Saints —R.A.Billington⟩ (2) **:** to make use of (as a person) for or in the accomplishment of a purpose ⟨~*ed* every available workman on the unexpected order⟩ ⟨~*ed* all hands onto the job of cleaning up⟩ **f** (1) **:** to direct or bring to bear in opposition esp. by reversing the use or application of something **:** cause to rebound or recoil ⟨tests the Communists' underlying contention . . . and ~*s* their argument against them —Arthur Knight⟩ ⟨secured or collected Japanese swords, then ~*ed* them upon their former owners —R.W.Thorp⟩ (2) **:** to lead or cause to dislike **:** make antagonistic **:** PREJUDICE — used with *against* ⟨~ a child against its mother⟩ ⟨campaign to ~ the people against their leaders⟩ ⟨had an arrogant manner that ~*ed* many against him⟩ **g** (1) **:** to cause to go or move in a particular direction ⟨~*ed* his steps homeward⟩ (2) **:** to make go or move elsewhere **:** DRIVE, SEND ⟨~ cows to pasture⟩ ⟨farmers round about ~ into these woods their young cattle —John Burroughs⟩ ⟨~*ed* the cat into the cellar for the night⟩; *esp* **:** to send or order away ⟨officers were ~*ed* adrift by the mutineers⟩ — usu. used with *away, from, off, out of* ⟨kind of man who would ~ a homeless child from his door⟩ ⟨~*ed* his wayward son out of his house⟩ ⟨no deserving person is ever ~*ed* away from that mission⟩ ⟨kept busy ~*ing* hunters off his land⟩ (3) **:** to convey or direct into or out of a receptacle by turning (as by inverting a container or operating a cock or faucet) ⟨don't need a recipe — just ~ the meat into a pot, heat, and serve⟩ ⟨mixture was ~*ed* into a baking tin and popped into a preheated oven⟩ ⟨asked by the police to ~ the contents of her handbag out onto the table⟩ **6 a** (1) *archaic* **:** to change the nature or appearance of **:** METAMORPHOSE, TRANSMUTE (2) **:** to make acid or sour **:** CURDLE, FERMENT ⟨hot weather may ~ milk⟩ (3) **:** to change the color of (as foliage) **b** (1) **:** to cause to become something specified **:** CONVERT, TRANSFORM — used with *into* or *to* ⟨giant elms that ~ those streets into great cathedrals in summer —Maxwell Mays⟩ ⟨~*ed* an almost impossible challenge into a remarkable personal triumph —C.H. Driver⟩ ⟨had ~*ed* disappointment into contentment and failure into success —Ellen Glasgow⟩ ⟨would ~ their ancient town into just another dormitory-suburb —Sam Pollock⟩ ⟨device that ~*s* the sun's light directly into electricity —E.C.Bullard⟩ ⟨tries to ~ every contact into a vote —R.L.Duffus⟩ ⟨gadget that was going to ~ us all into a nation of gawking illiterates —R.M. Yoder⟩ ⟨claim the desert can be ~*ed* to farmland —*Newsweek*⟩ ⟨cannot leave his comedy ~*ed* to sadness by the sentencing of the youths —K.F.Thompson⟩ (2) **:** to render in another language or another form of expression **:** TRANSLATE, PARAPHRASE — usu. used with *into* ⟨beautifully sculptured French has been ~*ed* into equally impressive English —*Times Lit. Supp.*⟩ ⟨selected a group of translators . . . to ~ into Latin a considerable number of important Greek books —G.C. Sellery⟩ ⟨struggled to ~ Indian legends and colonial tales into verse —Howard M. Jones⟩; *also* **:** to phrase differently **:** give a different cast or form to **c :** to cause to become of a specified nature or appearance — used with *into* or *to* ⟨~*s* the marble pillars above into a dusky silver⟩ ⟨salt air of the Cape is said to ~ the shingles on roofs and walls to a distinctive gray —Jackson Rivers⟩ ⟨wondered if the contortionist would be able to ~ himself into his right shape again⟩ **d :** to exchange for something else **:** dispose of by exchanging for an equivalent ⟨~*ed* his stocks and bonds into cash⟩ ⟨~ a pocketful of coins into paper money⟩ **e :** to change (as a person) so as to make different in a specified way **:** affect so as to cause a specified reaction ⟨starvation, thirst, heat and chills ~ them mad or sullen —Charles Lee⟩ ⟨~*s* your tongue black if you drink too much of it —R.H.Newman⟩ ⟨last year's drought ~*ed* things worse —*Christian Science Monitor*⟩ ⟨improvements ~*ed* them obsolete —Roger Burlingame⟩ ⟨if the resulting bungles . . . do not ~ the cold war hot —*Times Lit. Supp.*⟩ **f :** to cause to be regarded in a particular way **:** make the subject (as of ridicule) — used esp. in the phrase *turn to ridicule* ⟨humiliates him by patronizing him and ~*s* to ridicule his abilities and ambitions —Edmund Wilson⟩ **7 a :** to shape or fashion esp. in a rounded form by applying a cutting tool while revolving in a lathe **:** form in a lathe ⟨~ a set of table legs⟩ ⟨craftsmen ~*ing* small ivory figurines⟩ ⟨most effective cutting rate in relation to the material being ~*ed* —*Industrial Improvement*⟩ **b :** to give a rounded form to by any means (as carving or molding) ⟨showed him how to ~ the volute of a capital —Van Wyck Brooks⟩: as (1) *archaic* **:** to cause (as an arch) to be built **:** CONSTRUCT (2) **:** to cut off the rind or skin of (as an orange) in a narrow spiral strip **:** remove the stone from (as an olive) by paring off the flesh in such a strip (3) **:** to make a curved section in (a piece of needlework); *specif* **:** to perform the operations necessary to make the curved form of (a heel of a stocking) ⟨looking down at her as she sat ~*ing* a heel —J.M.Barrie⟩ **c** (1) **:** to shape or mold artistically, gracefully, or neatly esp. in curved or rounded form as if on a lathe ⟨girl with magnificently ~*ed* ankles —*New Yorker*⟩ ⟨a long nyloned leg, a trifle thin but well ~*ed* —Earle Birney⟩ (2) **:** to fashion skillfully (as a piece of literary work) ⟨really knows how to ~ a sentence⟩ ⟨has a knack for ~*ing* a phrase —W.O.Douglas⟩ ⟨man's obviously literate, can ~ neat and precise phrases —Rex Ingamells⟩ ⟨slick, quick, well ~*ed* plays —H.A.L.Craig⟩ ⟨speaks rather elegant and carefully ~*ed* English —Winthrop Sargent⟩ ⟨a gentle squib of beautifully ~*ed* parody —*Britain Today*⟩; *sometimes* **:** to execute skillfully ⟨performances are . . . well ~*ed* —Edward Sackville-West & Desmond Shawe-Taylor⟩ **d** *obs* **:** to equip specially by nature **:** ADAPT, FIT ⟨by nature ~*ed* to play the rake —Jonathan Swift⟩ **8 :** to make a fold, crook, bend, or curve in by or as if by pressure: as **a** *obs* **:** FOLD **b** *obs* **:** PLAIT **c :** to bend or twist so as to encircle ⟨creepers ~*ed* their tendrils about a picket fence⟩ ⟨had a snake ~*ed* round his arm⟩ **d :** to form by bending ⟨~ a lead pipe⟩ ⟨tubing had been ~*ed* in a U-shaped curve⟩ **e** (1) **:** to cause (the edge of a blade) to bend back or over **:** cause to give by meeting resistance (as from a hard surface) ⟨even ordinary slicing tends to ~ a fine edge —L.D.Bement⟩ **:** BLUNT, DULL ⟨if skins are too thick, they are reduced . . . with a moon knife with a ~*ed* edge —H.R.Procter⟩ ⟨thinks the edge of this objection can be ~*ed* —R.J.Spilsbury⟩ (2) **:** to dull or soften (as the power to cut or penetrate) in something that is done or expressed — used chiefly in the phrase *turn the edge of* or sometimes *turn the point of* ⟨spoke slowly and softly with a smile that did little to ~ the edge of his attack⟩ ⟨this . . . approach . . . ~*s* the edge of certain hostile criticisms —*Jour. of Philosophy*⟩ **9 a :** to keep (as money) moving, circulating, or passing in trade; *specif* **:** to dispose of (a stock) so as to make room for another ⟨pushcart vendor of oranges may ~ his stock every day —J.W.Wingate⟩ **b :** to make or gain chiefly by buying or selling or performing work or services) ⟨were not able to ~ a penny in the present market⟩ ⟨scheme to sell tea cheaply to the colonies and ~ a quick penny at the same time —James Street⟩ ⟨known to be ~*ing* a profit this year —Doyle Smee⟩ ⟨doing odd jobs to ~ an honest penny —John Dos Passos⟩ ⟨tricks . . . by which a more or less dishonest dollar can be ~*ed* —V.O.Key⟩ ~ *vi* **1 a :** to move around on an axis or about a center **:** move in circles or through an arc of a circle **:** revolve or rotate as a wheel does **:** wheel or whirl around ⟨wheel ~*ed* rapidly⟩ ⟨gate creaked as it ~*ed* on its hinges⟩ ⟨heavens . . . ~ in silence round the pole —A.E. Housman⟩ ⟨key would not ~ in the lock⟩ ⟨meat was ~*ing* on the spit⟩ **b :** *of the head or brain* **:** to have a sensation of whirling **:** become giddy or dizzy **:** REEL ⟨I'll look no more lest my brain ~ —Shak.⟩ ⟨hated heights; they always made his head ~⟩ **c** (1) **:** to have as a decisive factor **:** HINGE — usu. used with *on* or *upon* ⟨problems will rarely ~ on simple questions of right or wrong —H.G.Rickover⟩ ⟨the second act . . . the one upon which the whole work ~*s* —Virgil Thomson⟩ ⟨the trouble ~*ed* substantially on the failure . . . to consult and inform our allies —*New Republic*⟩ ⟨guilt or innocence . . . ~*s* on the identification of the weapon —*Irish Digest*⟩ ⟨argument ~*s* upon a point not of ethics but logic —Gail Kennedy⟩ (2) **:** to have a center (as of interest) in something specified **:** concentrate attention **:** relate principally — used with *around* or *about* ⟨social activity ~*ed* largely around official and church activities —C.L.Jones⟩ ⟨story ~*s* about a tormented passion felt by a dying young girl —Charles Lee⟩ or with *on* or *upon* ⟨discussion ~*ed* solely upon the feasibility of the scheme⟩ ⟨differences of opinion have ~*ed* mainly upon . . . how the success in Vienna can be turned to advantage here —J.E. Williams⟩ **2 a :** to shift one's position as if by moving on an axis or through the arc of a circle ⟨suffer with cramps in the muscles . . . when they ~ or stretch —Morris Fishbein⟩ ⟨had lain twisting and ~*ing* as he bemoaned their fate —O.E. Rölvaag⟩ ⟨~*ed* on his side⟩ ⟨tossed and ~*ed*, sighing and groaning —Kenneth Roberts⟩ ⟨enough to make a person ~ in his grave⟩ **b :** to move in a circular course or as if on an axis so as to face in various directions or in the opposite direction ⟨cabin was so small that a dog could hardly ~ in it —Tobias Smollett⟩ ⟨can ~ on a dime for repeated depth-charge attacks —J.C.Furnas⟩ ⟨~*ed* on his heel and walked away⟩ ⟨boat could ~ in its own length⟩ **c :** to incline from a horizontal position (as up or down from a point of rest) — used of a scale or balance **d :** to come by turning the leaves of a book ⟨~ ahead to the third chapter⟩ ⟨one can only leaf through the pictures or ~ to a list at the end of the book —Jane G. Mahler⟩ **3 a :** to direct one's course ⟨was completely lost, hadn't the faintest idea which way to ~⟩ ⟨was content to go whichever way his feet ~*ed*⟩ ⟨they ~*ed* into a street in which there was considerable activity —Irwin Shaw⟩ **b** (1) **:** to reverse a course or direction **:** go backward or in the opposite direction **:** become reversed ⟨market ~*ed* sharply in the afternoon⟩ ⟨nervous footpad ~*ed* and fled⟩ ⟨luck ~*ed* and he went broke⟩; *specif* **:** to change from ebb to flow or flow to ebb ⟨you should start half an hour to an hour before the tide ~*s* —Peter Heaton⟩ (2) **:** to have a reactive usu. adverse effect **:** RECOIL ⟨the . . . advantage — the buoyancy and liveliness of their lightly loaded craft — abruptly ~*ed* against them —Walter O'Meara⟩ **c :** to change one's course **:** take a different course or direction ⟨~*ed* toward home⟩ ⟨~ to the left at the foot of the hill⟩ ⟨~*ed* from the road into a tree-shaded lane⟩ ⟨rabbit ran out and ~*ed* along the hedge —Adrian Bell⟩ ⟨surge which had traveled southwards along our east coast later ~*ed* and moved northwards —J.A.Steers⟩ ⟨economy has begun to ~ downward —L.H.Keyserling⟩ ⟨corporate profits are ~*ing* upward —*Newsweek*⟩: as (1) **:** to execute or perform any of various maneuvers or procedures for changing course or direction (as of a ship or a fleet, a body of troops, a swimmer, skater, skier, or dancer); *specif* **:** to change direction by tacking (2) **:** to walk here and there **:** take a turn — used with *about* ⟨was at home in the country . . . ~*ing* about his grounds, sauntering by a brookside —Van Wyck Brooks⟩ (3) *of the wind* **:** to blow from a different quarter **:** SHIFT ⟨in the afternoon the wind ~*ed* into the east —Kenneth Roberts⟩ ⟨the wind ~*ed* and the sky cleared⟩ (4) **:** BREAK 5b(1) **d :** to change direction at, along, or by means of a bend or curve ⟨main road ~*s* sharp right at the fork⟩ ⟨highway ~*s* gradually away from the river⟩ ⟨river did indeed finally ~ to the left —Tom Marvel⟩ ⟨long hall runs the length of the building without ~*ing*⟩ **4 a :** to change position so as to face or be directed another way ⟨everywhere the eye ~*s* . . . it encounters propaganda —*N. Y. Times Mag.*⟩; *often* **:** to move one's head or body so as to face in another direction or to see something behind or to one side **:** face about ⟨heard his name called but did not ~⟩ ⟨astonished dignitaries were ~*ing* to stare at him —Al Hine & J.P.O'Neill⟩ **b :** to change position so as to face toward or away from someone or something ⟨however one ~*s*, one cannot evade the truth —R.M.Weaver⟩ ⟨~ from a gruesome sight⟩ ⟨~*ed* expectantly toward the door⟩ ⟨had taken fright at our behavior and ~*ed* to the captain pitifully —Joseph Conrad⟩ **c :** to change one's position or attitude or reverse one's course of action to one of opposition or hostility: (1) **:** to change from submission or friendliness to resistance or opposition ⟨even a worm will ~⟩ — usu. used with *against* ⟨felt that the whole world had suddenly ~*ed* against him⟩ ⟨even the younger men had ~*ed* against me —W.B.Yeats⟩ (2) **:** to vent anger or resentment — used with *on* or *upon* ⟨~*ed* upon them with a ferocity which made a savage of him on the spot —Virginia Woolf⟩ ⟨must come up with solutions or his party will be quick to ~ on him —*New Republic*⟩ (3) **:** make a sudden violent assault ⟨bulls often ~*ed* on the wounded, and the hunter could thus induce a fight —C.D.Forde⟩ ⟨dog had suddenly and for no apparent reason ~*ed* on his master⟩ **5 a :** to direct one's attention or thoughts to or away from someone or something ⟨men have

~ed from the discussion of universals —H.O.Taylor⟩ ⟨~s away in this book from his previous shock-treatment style of writing —Henry Cavendish⟩ ⟨played for society dances before ~ing to the blues —Hubert Creekmore⟩ ⟨former has ~ed to religion while the latter is still trying to live with uncertainty —Granville Hicks⟩; *also* **:** to find itself directed in this way ⟨riding to Canterbury, his mind naturally ~ed to church history —S.M.Crothers⟩ ⟨the thoughts of pioneers ~ed to self-government —R.A.Billington⟩ ⟨English prose ~ed to the sea in the early eighteenth century —W.P.Webb⟩ **b** (1) **:** to change one's way of life or thought by being converted to religion or a godly life ⟨~ to God⟩ ⟨disciples must ~, i.e. change their dispositions and habits —*Interpreter's Bible*⟩; *specif* **:** to change one's religion esp. as between Roman Catholic or Protestant ⟨he's a Catholic and I'm going to ~ —Victoria Lincoln⟩ ⟨feeling . . . that you've been praying for me to ~ —Ruth Park⟩ (2) **:** to go over to another side or party esp. by deserting or revolting **:** DEFECT **c :** to address oneself or direct one's attention to another subject **:** concern oneself with something different ⟨let us ~ now from mechanics to medicine —Benjamin Farrington⟩ ⟨now let us ~ to the United States and its theater —Marc Connelly⟩ ⟨kept wishing the speaker would ~ to something less gloomy⟩; *also* **:** to come in its course **:** move on ⟨talk, by some odd chance, had ~ed to the value of reticence in art —Thomas Wood †1950⟩ ⟨one evening over a cocktail the conversation ~ed to trout —Alexander MacDonald⟩ **d :** to betake oneself (as for information, help, or support) **:** have recourse — used with *to* ⟨for the historical presentation of contemporary literature one must ~ to . . . foreign critics —F.B.Millett⟩ **:** REFER ⟨the book to which one ~s inevitably for information on whaling —Hal Nielson⟩ ⟨book . . . that can be ~ed to again and again —Arthur Knight⟩ **:** RESORT ⟨government is not likely to ~ to private sources for dollars at higher rates of interest —J.C.Harsch⟩ ⟨for relaxation he ~s to tennis —*Current Biog.*⟩ ⟨painful illness led him to ~ to drugs⟩ ⟨employers ~ed to the regions where cheap labor was to be found —Oscar Handlin⟩ ⟨few experts . . . to whom it could ~ for knowledge and counsel —C.W.de Kiewiet⟩ ⟨a man to ~ to in time of need⟩ **e :** to direct one's efforts or interests **:** devote or apply oneself ⟨fewer studying medicine and more ~ing to agriculture and dairy science —*Irish Digest*⟩ ⟨came out of the army with nothing in mind to ~ to⟩ ⟨~ed to the study of the law with enthusiasm⟩ **6 a :** to become changed, altered, or transformed (as in nature, character, or appearance): as (1) *archaic* **:** to become different (2) **:** to change color — used esp. of leaves ⟨by the first of October most of the leaves have ~ed —W.H.Upson⟩ ⟨hickories were ~ing slowly and here and there the boughs were brushed with wine-color —Ellen Glasgow⟩ (3) **:** to become sour, rancid, or tainted ⟨found that the milk had ~ed⟩ (4) **:** to be variable or inconstant (5) **:** to become mentally unbalanced **:** become deranged **b** (1) **:** to become transformed or converted into something else (as by receiving a new character or new properties) **:** pass from one state to another **:** CHANGE — used with *into* or *to* ⟨water had ~ed to ice⟩ ⟨passive neglect ~ed into active antagonism —G.G.Coulton⟩ ⟨went away a fledgling and he has ~ed into a man —Louis Bromfield⟩ ⟨friendship . . . ~s into conflict, and in the end a formal duel is held —R.A.Hall b. 1911⟩ ⟨puzzled look . . . ~ed quickly to one of understanding —T.B.Costain⟩ ⟨no clear dividing line between fluids and jellies . . . one may ~ readily into the other —*New Biology*⟩ (2) **:** to become changed so as to be of a specified nature **:** change to **:** GROW ⟨hair had ~ed gray⟩ ⟨face ~ed white⟩ ⟨milk ~ed sour⟩ ⟨animal ~ed nasty⟩ ⟨weather ~ed bad⟩ ⟨voice ~ed shrill⟩ ⟨cautious ones ~ed moderately optimistic —*Biddle Survey*⟩ ⟨country ~ed thin and poor, with great patches of naked ground —H.L.Davis⟩ (3) **:** to become someone or something specified by change from another state **:** come to be ⟨~ state's evidence⟩ ⟨both poets in the end ~ed men of action —Osbert Sitwell⟩ ⟨dancing-school teacher who ~s call girl —Anthony Boucher⟩ ⟨in Latin America physicians frequently ~ author and statesman —*Americas*⟩ ⟨wartime diary of a journalist ~ed lieutenant commander —A.A. Ageton⟩ ⟨walls rise sheer around the courtyard ~ed theater —Claudia Cassidy⟩ ⟨picture themselves ~ing explorer and going home down the Amazon —*Geog. Jour.*⟩ **7 :** to become curved or bent (as from pressure); *esp* **:** to become blunted by bending ⟨the knife's edge had ~ed⟩ **8 :** to become upset **:** become nauseated — used of the stomach **9 a :** to operate a lathe **b :** to admit of fashioning on a lathe ⟨beech is largely used . . . since it ~s easily in the lathe —F.D.Smith & Barbara Wilcox⟩ ⟨ivory ~s well⟩ **10** *of merchandise* **:** to become stocked and disposed of **:** turn over **:** change hands **11** *of a goat* **:** to come in heat again after service by a buck

syn REVOLVE, ROTATE, GYRATE, CIRCLE, SPIN, TWIRL, WHIRL, WHEEL, EDDY, SWIRL, PIROUETTE: TURN is a general rather colorless word interchangeable with most of the others in their less specific uses. REVOLVE may suggest regular circular motion on an orbit around something exterior to the item in question; it may refer to the dependence of the less important, the secondary, on something cardinal or pivotal which resolves or determines ⟨though local questions, such as the State Bank and state aid to railroads, gave rise to sharp contests, politics usually *revolved* around national questions —A.B.Moore⟩ ⟨everything in that house *revolved* upon Aunt Mary —Margaret Deland⟩ ROTATE is likely to suggest a circular motion on an interior axis within the thing under consideration which may be not moving otherwise ⟨the earth *rotates* on its axis while it revolves on its orbit⟩ GYRATE may suggest the regularity of REVOLVE but it is likely to be used to indicate a fluctuating or swinging back and forth which describes circular or spiral patterns ⟨stocks *gyrated* dizzily on uncertainty over the foreign situation —*Wall Street Jour.*⟩ ⟨a low cloud of dust raised by the dog *gyrating* madly about —Joseph Conrad⟩ CIRCLE may simply indicate a movement around in a more or less circular pattern, or it may indicate any lack of straight directness in a winding course ⟨a flock of black ibises *circled* high overhead wheeling endlessly on the ascending air currents —Dillon Ripley⟩ ⟨the essayist's licence to *circle* and meander —Virginia Woolf⟩ SPIN indicates rapid sustained rotation on an inner axis or fast circling around an exterior point ⟨he who but ventures into the outer circle of the whirlpool is *spinning*, ere he has time for thought in its dizzy vortex —Bayard Taylor⟩ TWIRL adds to the ideas of SPIN those of dexterity, lightness, or easy grace ⟨this . . . book . . . I toss i' the air, and catch again, and *twirl* about —Robert Browning⟩ WHIRL stresses force, power, speed, and impetus of rotary or circular motion ⟨and collections of opaque particles *whirled* to shore by the eddies —William Bartram⟩ ⟨the withered leaves had gathered violence in pursuit, and were *whirling* after her like a bevy of witches —Ellen Glasgow⟩ WHEEL may suggest either going in a circular or twisted course or turning on an arc or curve to a new course ⟨a familiar sight is the turkey vulture *wheeling* against the skies to the north —*Amer. Guide Series: Ariz.*⟩ ⟨she had crossed the threshold to the porch, when, *wheeling* abruptly, she went back into the hall —Ellen Glasgow⟩ EDDY suggests the circular movement, sometimes fast, sometimes slow, of an eddy; it may be used in situations involving indirection, futility, or isolation from main currents ⟨as the smoke slowly *eddied* away —Stephen Crane⟩ ⟨the dead leaves which *eddied* slowly down through the windless calm —Rebecca West⟩ ⟨waves of friends and reporters *eddied* through the apartment —*Time*⟩ SWIRL suggests more rapidity, flow, or graceful attractiveness than EDDY ⟨further than ever comet flared or vagrant star-dust *swirled* —Rudyard Kipling⟩ ⟨the black water was running like a millrace and raising a turbulent coil as it *swirled* and tossed over the ugly heads of jutting rocks —T.B.Costain⟩ ⟨her dark hair *swirled* about her face —Helen Howe⟩ PIROUETTE suggests the light graceful turning of a ballet dancer ⟨ashes *pirouetted* down, coquetting with young beeches —Alfred Tennyson⟩

syn see in addition DEPEND

syn DIVERT, DEFLECT, AVERT, SHEER: TURN is comprehensive in its scope and devoid of specific connotation; it could be used in any of the citations in the following, although with some loss of force and distinctness. DIVERT stresses the idea of turning a thing or a person from a natural, expected course, way, or pattern into another ⟨vast quantities of water can be *diverted* from one to the other watershed with very little engineering work —B.K.Sandwell⟩ ⟨the machinery of our economic life has been *diverted* from peace to war —Clement Attlee⟩ DEFLECT is more likely to be used in reference to bouncing, refraction, or ricochet from a straight course or fixed direction ⟨when they were fired at a thin film of metal, the majority passed through without being substantially *deflected* from their courses —James Jeans⟩ In more figurative uses, it implies a turning, refracting, or deviating from a clearly evident course, direction, or pattern ⟨he underwent all those things — but none of them *deflected* his purpose —Hilaire Belloc⟩ ⟨after all, she had perhaps purposely *deflected* the conversation from her own affairs —Edith Wharton⟩ ⟨the spirit . . . of the Romance tongues *deflecting* it from classical constructions —H.O. Taylor⟩ AVERT implies no particular previously set course or pattern but usu. indicates either a turning away of one's eyes, attention, or the like from the unpleasant or a turning of the course of exterior developments to avoid the dangerous or unpleasant ⟨tried unsuccessfully to *avert* her horrified eyes from the sight⟩ ⟨Athenian statesmen *averted* a social revolution by successfully carrying through an economic and political revolution —A.J.Toynbee⟩ SHEER, orig. nautical, is likely to involve a sharp turning or veering, as of a ship, or, in more figurative use, a sharply sudden divergence from a path or course previously followed ⟨a griffon, wheeling here and there about, kept reconnoitring us . . . till he *sheered* off —John Keats⟩

— **turn a blind eye :** to refuse to see **:** be oblivious ⟨might *turn a blind eye* to the use of violence —Arthur Krock⟩ — **turn a cold shoulder to :** to treat with neglect or indifference **:** SNUB — **turn a deaf ear :** to refuse to listen — **turn a flange :** to form a flange on (as around a metal sheet or boiler plate) by stretching, bending, and hammering or rolling the metal — **turn a hair :** to give a sign of discomposure or disturbance — used in negative constructions ⟨came through the ordeal without *turning a hair*⟩ ⟨never *turned a hair*⟩ — **turn around one's finger** *or* **turn around one's little finger :** to do what one likes with **:** manage easily — **turn color 1 :** to become of a different color ⟨leaves are *turning color*⟩ ⟨dyes are fast and cloth will not *turn color*⟩ **2 a :** BLUSH, FLUSH **b :** to grow pale — **turn edge** *archaic, of a blade* **:** to have the edge turned over **:** become blunt — **turn flukes** *of a whale* **:** to raise the tail and dive — **turn loose 1 a :** to set free (as a tied horse) so as to have the run of a pasture **b :** to free from all restraints **:** permit to go one's own way ⟨is going to *turn* the savages *loose* on us —Dorothy C. Fisher⟩ ⟨poetry is not a *turning loose* of emotion —T.S.Eliot⟩ **2 :** to fire off (as a gun or a bullet) **:** DISCHARGE **3 :** to open fire ⟨everything aboard *turned loose* on him —Bill Alcine⟩ **4 :** to speak esp. at length and without restraint ⟨after the director spoke the workers *turned loose* on him —A.R.Williams⟩ — **turn one's back on** *or* **turn one's back upon 1 :** to put behind one **:** depart from ⟨with this month of March we *turn our backs on* winter —Faith Baldwin⟩ ⟨Eskimo *turn their backs* abruptly *on* the sea . . . up a valley from the shore —C.D.Forde⟩ **2 :** REJECT, DENY ⟨my conscience will not let me *turn my back upon* a call to service —F.D.Roosevelt⟩ ⟨would be *turning one's back on* history —Pius Walsh⟩; *often* **:** to reject unceremoniously or treat with contempt **3 :** ABANDON, FORSAKE, DESERT ⟨*turning our backs upon* the rest of mankind and refusing to enter the cooperative scheme —Stephen Duggan⟩ ⟨*turned his back on* his own people⟩ — **turn one's coat :** to change one's uniform or colors **:** go over to the opposite party — **turn one's hand 1** *archaic* **:** to lay one's hand esp. to kill — used with *upon* **2** *or* **turn a hand a :** to engage in manual work ⟨plans must be drawn before *a hand* can be *turned* to building⟩ **b :** set to work **:** be employed **:** apply oneself — used with *to* ⟨had begun *turning his hand* to occasional literary journalism —Cecil Sprigge⟩ ⟨could *turn their hand* to almost anything in the line of pantomime —Winthrop Palmer⟩ — **turn one's stomach :** to disgust completely **:** NAUSEATE, SICKEN ⟨wanted to change the public mind . . . succeeded mainly in *turning its stomach* —J. D.Hart⟩ — **turn over a new leaf :** to make a radical change esp. for the better in one's way of living or doing ⟨*turned over a new leaf* at forty and became a pillar of the church⟩; *also* **:** to promise or attempt such a change ⟨forever involved in scandals . . . and forever *turning over a new leaf* —Jean Stafford⟩ — **turn tail 1 :** to run away (as from danger or opposition) ⟨might have to carry him out on a stretcher, but he wouldn't *turn tail* again —Hamilton Basso⟩ **:** retreat from a position ⟨administration *turned tail* and ran —Elmer Davis⟩ **2 :** to turn one's back **:** ABANDON, FORSAKE, REJECT — used with *on* or *upon* ⟨fellows who *turned* their *tails* on the land —John Galsworthy⟩ — **turn the other cheek :** to respond to injury or unkindness with patience **:** forgo retaliation — **turn the scale** *also* **turn the balance 1 :** to register weight — used with *at* ⟨hand baggage *turned the scale* at 60 pounds⟩ **2 :** to decide or determine something doubtful **:** prove decisive ⟨sharper claw or oilier feather might *turn the balance* —W.C.Allee⟩ ⟨air support can make much difference, but can it . . . *turn the scales* —B.H.Liddell Hart⟩ — **turn the tables** [fr. *turn the tables* to reverse the relative positions as in a board game] **1 :** to bring about a reversal of the relative conditions or fortunes of two contending persons or parties **2 :** to show that an argument advanced for or against a thesis actually favors the other side — **turn the trick :** to bring about the desired result or effect — **turn thumbs down :** to express disapproval, condemnation, or rejection ⟨at least one legislative body has *turned thumbs down* on a proposal to investigate the schools —*Nation*⟩ — **turn to windward :** to beat to windward — **turn turtle 1 :** to capsize bottom upward — used of a boat **2 :** OVERTURN ⟨automobile *turned turtle*⟩

²turn \"\ *n* -s [ME; partly fr. OF *tor, tour, torn, tourn* lathe, circuit, turn (partly fr. L *tornus* lathe; partly fr. OF *torner, tourner* to turn); partly fr. ME *turnen*, v.] **1 a :** the action or an act of turning or moving about or as if about a center or axis **:** REVOLUTION, ROTATION ⟨~ is the motion employed to turn the hand either empty or loaded by movement that rotates the hand, wrist, and forearm about the long axis of the forearm —*Methods-Time Measurement*⟩ ⟨knowledge and entertainment are brought with the ~ of a dial —*Girl Scout Handbk.*⟩ ⟨almost any ~ of the kaleidoscope of nature may set up in the artist this . . . vision —Roger Fry⟩ **b :** a single revolution or turning motion ⟨twists and ~s of the head⟩ ⟨each ~ of the wheels brought them nearer home⟩ ⟨only three ~s of the moon —Virginia Woolf⟩ ⟨grand old leaps and ~s of the imperial ballet discipline —*Time*⟩: as (1) **:** any of various rotating or pivoting movements in dancing whether executed singly or in couples — see CIRCLE TURN, OPEN TURN, REVERSE TURN, ROCK TURN (2) **:** a revolution by a gymnast of less than a circle around a bar **2 a :** the action or an act of giving or taking a direction or a different direction **:** change of course or posture ⟨forgot to make the usual ~ at the corner⟩ ⟨illegal left ~⟩ ⟨gentle ~s may be performed by rudder alone —R.P.Holland⟩ ⟨controls had jammed in a ~ —Phil Gustafson⟩: as (1) **:** a drill maneuver in which troops in mass formation change direction without preserving alignment and which is executed by the pivot file facing in the new direction and marching at the half step until the others move up and place themselves in succession on the new line — compare WHEEL (2) **:** a change of course by a ship in formation or a simultaneous change of course by the ships of a unit (3) **:** any of various shifts of direction in skiing — see CHRISTIANIA, JUMP TURN, KICK TURN, SNOWPLOW TURN, STEM CHRISTIANIA, STEM TURN, STEP TURN, TELEMARK (4) **:** an interruption of a curve in figure skating **b :** the action or an act of turning aside (as from a straight course, a normal development, or a manifest trend) **:** DEFLECTION, DEVIATION ⟨gave the story so many twists and ~s the reader becomes lost⟩: as (1) **:** a sudden change of not less than a right angle in direction made by the quarry in coursing when hotly pursued ⟨hound gave the hare a ~⟩ (2) **:** BREAK 4c(6) (3) **:** a forward stroke in cricket made with the face of the bat at an angle that sends the ball to the on side ⟨would open his account with a ~ to the on side, generally forward of square leg —*Calling All Cricketers*⟩ **c :** the action or an act of turning so as to face or move in the opposite direction **:** reversal of posture or course ⟨an about ~⟩ ⟨wait for the ~ of the tide⟩ ⟨sales have never been higher at this season — and there are few signs of a ~ —*Nation's Business*⟩: as (1) **:** a complete reversal of direction in a swimming race (2) **:** a complete reversal of a skate in figure skating **d :** a change effected by turning over to another side or face about ⟨lost a fortune on one ~ of the cards⟩ **e :** a place at which something turns, turns off, or turns back **:** point or part at or along which a change of course or direction takes place **:** ANGLE, BEND, CURVE ⟨stopped at a ~ in the road⟩ ⟨river has many ~s⟩ ⟨couldn't get the piano around the ~ in the hallway⟩ ⟨swept around a ~ of the trees, down the nearest avenue toward us —B.T.Cleeve⟩: as (1) *dial Eng* **:** a pit sunk in some part of a drift in lead mining (2) **:** a curved part of a running track or racetrack ⟨took the lead on the run to the clubhouse ~ —*N.Y.Times*⟩ ⟨too big to move easily around the ~s —Albion Hughes⟩ (3) **:** the point on a golf course at which the return journey is begun **:** end of the first nine holes or start of the last nine holes ⟨was three up at the ~⟩ ⟨made the ~ in 35 —*N.Y.Times*⟩ (4) **:** a point of junction between two curves in figure skating **3 a** (1) *obs* **:** JOURNEY, TOUR, TRIP (2) **:** TOURN **b** (1) **:** the action or an act of walking esp. briefly around or out and back ⟨usually took a ~ around the block before going to bed⟩ ⟨going to have a ~ under the stars before I follow you —Agnes S. Turnbull⟩ ⟨took a short ~ through the garden — to the row of tamarisk trees and back —Willa Cather⟩ ⟨so incurably soft as not to be able to face a gentle ~ round an ordinary suburban garden —Osbert Lancaster⟩ (2) **:** a short trip (as a walk, ride, drive) out and back or round about ⟨had enough gas for a half hour's ~ in the park⟩ ⟨studied navigation — why, if I had taken one ~ down the harbor I should have known more about it —H.D.Thoreau⟩ **c** *chiefly dial* **:** a single trip and return (as by a team in hauling logs) **4 a :** a movement by a wrestler intended to throw his opponent **b** *archaic* **:** ARTIFICE, STRATAGEM, TRICK, WILE ⟨beheld in either field a farmer at work and proposed to play the two a ~ —Joseph Campbell⟩ **5 a :** an act or deed affecting another esp. when performed out of the usual course **:** a usu. incidental or unexpected act of service or disservice ⟨one good ~ deserves another⟩ ⟨when you turned me out you did me the best ~ you ever did me —W.S.Maugham⟩ ⟨actually the worms do the cattle farmers a good ~ —B.C.Cronwright⟩ ⟨you've had a rotten deal . . . The man . . . has done you a bad ~ —Dorothy Sayers⟩ **b** *chiefly Scot* **:** a stroke of work **:** piece of work **:** JOB, TASK — compare HAND'S TURN **6 :** something that comes in its own due order or at often regular intervals: as **a :** a period of action or activity **:** GO, SPELL ⟨went on deck and took a ~ at the wheel⟩ ⟨a ~ at the lathe in his cellar workshop —Otis Fellows⟩ ⟨catch their breath between ~s on the ice —H.W. Wind⟩ ⟨enjoys spectator sports, bridge, and a ~ on the dance floor —*Current Biog.*⟩; *specif* **:** a bout of wrestling **b :** a place, time, or opportunity accorded an individual or unit of a series in simple succession or in or as if in a scheduled order ⟨rooms were thoroughly cleaned each in its ~⟩ ⟨was waiting his ~ in a doctor's office⟩ ⟨is pointed out to him that his ~ will come —Richard Joseph⟩ ⟨took our ~ and did our bit —G.B.Shaw⟩ ⟨class took ~s expressing opinions —Eleanor S. Lowman⟩ ⟨~ of the surrealists for market appreciation is probably next —J.T.Soby⟩; *often* **:** a recurring chance or opportunity coming to each in alternation or succession (as in a game) **c :** a period during which one of a number of persons or groups successively employed is on duty **:** SHIFT, TOUR ⟨increases . . . to 6 cents from 4 cents on the afternoon ~ —*Wall Street Jour.*⟩ ⟨will add a second ~ employing another 1000 —*Wall Street Jour.*⟩ **d :** a short act or piece of any kind esp. in or for a variety show ⟨announced each act and said a few words between ~s —Pete Martin⟩ ⟨can recall virtually every routine and ~ he ever learned —R.B.Gehman⟩ ⟨a song-and-dance ~⟩ ⟨cabaret ~s⟩ ⟨chief ~ consisted of four performing elephants —Osbert Sitwell⟩; *also* **:** the performer of such an act ⟨commended only one of the ~s, a young man . . . who sang *Danny Boy* —Patrick Campbell⟩ **e** (1) **:** an event in any gambling game after which bets are settled — called also *coup* (2) **:** the order of the last three cards in faro — used in the phrase *call the turn* **7 :** something that revolves or that turns or moves around or as if around a center: as **a** (1) LATHE; *esp* **:** a watchmaker's lathe (2) *chiefly dial* **:** SPINNING WHEEL (3) **:** a catch or latch for a cupboard or cabinet door that is operated by turning a knob or handle **b** (1) **:** a musical ornament consisting of a group of four or more notes that wind about the principal or written note by including the notes next above and next below beginning either on the upper note or (as often in 19th century music) on the principal note ⟨executes the ~s with beautiful ease —Irving Kolodin⟩ (2) **:** a sign indicating this musical ornament **8 :** a special purpose, need, or requirement **:** CONVENIENCE, EXIGENCY — used chiefly in the phrase *serve one's turn* ⟨the philosophy that serves one's ~ best —J.C.Powys⟩ ⟨hoping . . . to exploit and then disown him after he had served their ~ —*Times Lit. Supp.*⟩ **9** *obs* **:** an event or course or series of events **10 a :** the action or an act of changing **:** ALTERATION, MODIFICATION ⟨a nasty ~ in the weather⟩ ⟨tea too weak and not hot enough, and the milk verging to the ~ —E.O.Schlunke⟩ **b :** a change in tendency, trend, or drift or in conditions, circumstances, or affairs ⟨hoped for a ~ in his luck⟩ ⟨credit situation probably won't cause an adverse ~ in the economy —M.S.Rukeyser⟩ ⟨~ of fortune which made him a prisoner of war —G.F.Hudson⟩ ⟨fairly sharp ~s characterize British history —*Current History*⟩ ⟨a ~ for the better in the bitter labor-management feud —Mary K. Hammond⟩ ⟨market for used cars took a definite ~ for the worse —Leo Wolman⟩ ⟨laughing up their sleeves at the ~ of affairs —Edward Bok⟩ **c :** the time when something changes its direction or its course (as of development) or when a change in trend or circumstances takes place ⟨the ~ of the seasons — the low point between the end of the winter season and the pickup of the spring-summer boom —*N.Y.Times*⟩ ⟨decided to wait until the ~ of the year⟩ ⟨our literary taste at the ~ of the century —M.D.Geismar⟩ ⟨born just after the ~ of the century⟩ ⟨years at the ~ of the twentieth century were vintage years —W.A.White⟩ **d** *Brit* **:** the middle price between a stock jobber's buying and selling prices **:** change in price **11 a :** distinctive quality or character ⟨peculiar ~ of the Greek genius —H.J.J.Winter⟩ ⟨the ~ and genius of our language —Thomas Gray⟩ **b** (1) **:** a turning or fashioning of language esp. skillfully or for a special effect **:** arrangement of words ⟨saw in the ~ of her phrase an opportunity to exhibit a small verbal neatness —Dorothy C. Fisher⟩ ⟨stylist . . . will appreciate the ~ of the phrase —Gilbert Seldes⟩ ⟨never at a loss for a ~ of a phrase to illustrate a point —Harvey Graham⟩ ⟨shocks us . . . by its Machiavellian ~ of phrase —Béla Menczer⟩ (2) **:** a particular form of expression or detail of style of discourse; *esp* **:** a peculiarity of phrasing ⟨some of the most felicitous ~s of thought and phrase in poetry —J.L.Lowes⟩ ⟨Scandinavian strain . . . is shown more clearly by ~s of expression than by the forms of individual words —F.M. Steuton⟩ ⟨altered his dress, his mannerisms, and his ~s of speech —Geoffrey Gorer⟩ ⟨studded with his special capering marks and ~s of style —Richard Eberhart⟩ ⟨uses many dialect ~s —H.H.Reichard⟩ ⟨even an advanced student misses idiomatic ~s —Geoffrey Bullough⟩ **c :** the shape or mold in which something is fashioned ⟨gown showed off the ~ of her neck and shoulder⟩ **:** CAST ⟨an unbelievably evil ~ of countenance⟩ **12 a :** the state or manner of being coiled or twisted ⟨spinning yarns . . . in various grades, sizes, and degrees of twist or ~ —*Whitlock Cordage*⟩; *specif* **:** the distance along the axis of a rope in which a strand makes one spiral **b :** a single round (as of rope passed about an object or laid in a coil or of wire wound on the core of an induction coil), twist (as of the strands of a rope), or whorl (as of a convoluted form) ⟨snail shell with seven ~s⟩ ⟨stove was cracked and held together with many ~s of heavy wire —Brian Harwin⟩ ⟨~s around the drum of the windlass began to slip —H.A.Chippendale⟩ ⟨one ~ of wire when carrying one ampere of current is known as one ampere turn —Irving Frazee⟩ ⟨give a yarn ten ~s of twist per inch of length —Werner Von Bergen & H.R.Mauersberger⟩ ⟨the axial length of one complete turn or helix of a wire in a cable —L.F.Hickernell & A.A.Jones⟩ **c :** a coiling, twisting, or winding of one thing (as a cord, rope, or wire) about another ⟨a ~ is taken round the most convenient article

(a) (b) (c)

turn 7b(1): *1* as written, *2* as performed: *a* with sign over the note, *b* with sign following, *c* with chromatic that will take the strain —*Fire Service Drill Bk.*⟩ **13 :** any of several measures of quantity (as for some commodities): as **a :** a varying measure for selling fish **b :** a load of wood; *esp* **:** a number of logs hauled on one trip **c :** a bundle of 60 skins in the fur trade **d** *chiefly dial* **:** a quantity of corn (as a sackful) taken to a mill at one time for grinding **14 a :** natural or special ability or aptitude **:** BENT, INCLINATION ⟨renown . . . rests not on his geometry or his ~ for affairs —Benjamin Farrington⟩ ⟨a fellow with a real practical ~ —O.W.Holmes †1894⟩ ⟨a ~ for logical presentation —Jane Addams⟩ ⟨a pretty ~ for anecdote —W.S.Gilbert⟩ ⟨must possess . . . artistic sensibility and a ~ for clear thinking —Clive Bell⟩ — used esp. in the phrase *turn of mind* ⟨am of an optimistic ~ of mind —G.P.Brockway⟩ ⟨had a philosophic ~ of mind —John Mason Brown⟩ ⟨help to stimulate an inquiring ~ of mind —Warwick Braithwaite⟩ ⟨men of a speculative ~ of mind —M.R.Cohen⟩ **b** (1) *obs* **:** a particular characteristic (as of a person) or a characteristic act (2) *dial* **:** DISPOSITION, PERSONALITY **15 a :** direction of movement **:** DRIFT, TENDENCY, TREND ⟨the individuals who took a decisive part in them — who gave a ~ to the events —Herbert Read⟩ ⟨the oriental ~ of seeking nirvana —Warren Weaver⟩ ⟨provide a clue as to the ~ of events a few seconds before they happen —Princess Indira⟩ **b :** a special twist, construction, or interpretation ⟨gave the hoary old yarn a new ~⟩ ⟨gave a native ~ to the designs which they imitated —O. Elfrida Saunders⟩ **16 a :** a disordering spell or attack (as of illness, faintness, dizziness) ⟨some ~ of disease had begun to parade erotic images before his eyes —W.B.Yeats⟩ ⟨a delicate man, who had survived, mother alone knows how many bad ~*s* —Blanche E. Baughan⟩ ⟨isn't a real snake on the carpet, it is only one of my ~*s* —Margaret Macdonald⟩ **b :** a nervous start or shock (as from alarm, fright, or surprise) ⟨gives one quite a ~ to discover that one's husband is a murderer —Denis Johnston⟩ ⟨had given me a ~ . . . she was so close to the edge —Joseph Conrad⟩ ⟨gave him a nasty ~, but he put on a bold front —W.S.Maugham⟩ **c : turns** *pl* **:** MENSES **17 a :** a complete transaction involving a purchase and sale of securities or vice versa; *also* **:** a profit from such a transaction **b :** TURNOVER 8c ⟨wash goods department may find that three ~*s* a year are feasible —J.W. Wingate⟩ **18 :** something turned or to be turned: as **a** (1) **:** a character or slug inverted in setting type (2) **:** a piece of type placed bottom up or a character temporarily keyed (as by a Monotype operator) in place of another of the same width to be inserted later by hand; *also* **:** the replacement of a turn by the proper character ⟨~*s* have been made in most of the galleys⟩ **b :** TURN SHOE — **at every turn** *adv* **:** on every occasion **:** in every instance **:** CONSTANTLY, CONTINUALLY ⟨commission would find itself hampered *at every turn* —T.W. Arnold⟩ ⟨fights public housing *at every turn* —*New Republic*⟩ — **by turns** *adv* **:** one after another in regular succession **:** ALTERNATELY, SUCCESSIVELY ⟨was praised and blamed *by turns*⟩ ⟨washed the dishes *by turns*⟩ ⟨stores that are *by turns* curious, tragic, ennobling, disturbing, and heartening —C.R. Hewitt & Jenifer Wayne⟩ — **in turn** *adv* **:** in due order of succession **:** SUCCESSIVELY ⟨new waves of hope arise to shatter themselves *in turn* against the sands of despair —M.R.Cohen⟩ ⟨revision of estimated sales . . . and this, *in turn*, will mean revision in production schedules —J.K.Blake⟩ **:** ALTERNATELY ⟨*in turn* caustic and idyllic —Mark Gayn⟩ ⟨each *in turn* comes into the ascendant at the other's expense —A.J.Toynbee⟩ — **on the turn** *adv (or adj)* **:** in the act or course of turning **:** at the point of turning ⟨tide is *on the turn*⟩ — **out of turn** *adv* **1 :** not in turn **:** not in due order of succession ⟨play *out of turn*⟩ **2 :** imprudently, unadvisedly, or at a wrong time or place ⟨throwing their weight around . . . and talking *out of turn* —Joseph Mitchell⟩ ⟨might be condemned for heresy if he spoke *out of turn* —Peter Wiles⟩ — **to a turn** *adv* **:** to perfection **:** precisely right **:** EXACTLY, PERFECTLY ⟨food was superb, the roast done *to a turn*⟩ ⟨sung and danced *to a turn* by the comedy team —*Theatre Arts*⟩

³turn \ˈtərn, ˈtu̇rn\ *vi* -ED/-ING/-S [G *turnen*, fr. OHG *turnēn* to turn (in general), fr. ML *tornare* — more at ¹TURN] **:** to practice or perform gymnastic exercises

turn·able \ˈtərnəbəl\ *adj* [ME *turneabylle*, fr. *turnen* to turn + *-able*] **:** capable of being turned

¹turn about *vb* [¹*turn* + *about*, adv.] *vi* **:** to face about **:** reverse one's position, direction, course, or policy ~ *vt* **:** to cause to face in the opposite direction ⟨*turn* a car *about*⟩

²turn about *or* **turn and turn about** *adv* [²*turn* + *about*, adv.] **:** by turns

turnabout \ˈ=,=,=\ *n* -S [¹*turn about*] **1 a :** an act or instance of turning about **:** a change or reversal of direction ⟨boat capable of a quick ~⟩ or trend ⟨sharp ~ in farm prices⟩ or policy or of relative position or role ⟨~ humor of husbands who bake cookies and send them to wives —Walter Karig⟩ **b :** a changing from one side or allegiance to another ⟨~ witness⟩ **c :** TURNCOAT, RENEGADE **2 a** *obs* **:** TURNSTILE **b :** MERRY-GO-ROUND **3 :** a reversible garment

turn and bank indicator *n* **:** an instrument combining the functions of a turn indicator and a lateral inclinometer

turn around *or* **turn round** *vb* **:** to turn about

turnaround \ˈ=,=,=\ *n* -S [*turn around*] **1 :** a space (as a widened section of a driveway) designed to permit the turning around of a vehicle **2 :** a reversal of one's course, attitude, position, or policy **:** TURNABOUT **3 :** the time required for a round trip (as of a ship, airplane, or other vehicle) including loading and unloading at both points and necessary maintenance; *also* **:** the overhauling of a vehicle

turn away *vt* **1 :** DEFLECT, AVERT ⟨proper clothing and genteel speech would *turn away* the adverse criticisms —Oscar Handlin⟩ ⟨a soft answer *turneth away* wrath —Prov 15:1 (AV)⟩ **2 a :** to send away **:** REJECT, DISMISS **b :** REPEL **c :** to refuse admittance or acceptance to ⟨hundreds were *turned away* from the theater⟩ ~ *vi* **:** to start to go away **:** LEAVE, DEPART, ABANDON ⟨when the audience *turns away* there is something wrong with the writer's communication line —Stuart Chase⟩

turnaway \ˈ=,=,=\ *n* -S [*turn away*] **1 :** a turning away **:** DESERTION **2 :** the act of refusing admittance

turn back *vi* **1 a :** to stop going forward **:** refuse to go ahead **b :** to go in the reverse direction **:** RETURN ⟨it was getting late, time to *turn back*⟩ **2 :** to refer to an earlier time or place ⟨*turn back* to the first page⟩ ~ *vt* **1 :** to drive back or away **:** cause to return or to reverse direction ⟨refugees were *turned back* at the frontier⟩ **2 :** to stop the advance of **:** CHECK **3 :** to fold back

¹turnback \ˈ=,=\ *n* -S [*turn back*] **1 :** COWARD, QUITTER **2 :** a part (as of a garment) that is turned back ⟨~ of a hat brim⟩

²turnback \ˈ"\ *or* **turned-back** \ˈ=,=\ *adj* [*turn back* or *turned back*, past part. of *turn back*] **:** folded back on itself ⟨~ sleeve⟩

turn bench *n* **:** a watchmaker's lathe

turn bolt *n* **:** a latch bolt that operates by turning a knob or handle

turn bridge *n* **:** PIVOT BRIDGE

turnbuckle \ˈ=,==\ *n* **1 :** a link with a screw thread at one end and a swivel at the other or a right-and-left screw link used for tightening a rod or stay **2 :** a gravitating catch for fastening a shutter, the end of a chain, or a hasp

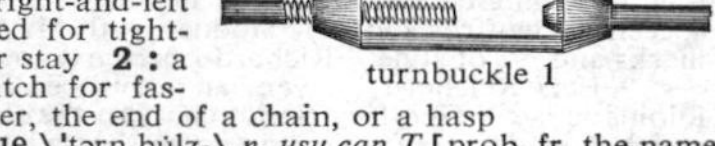
turnbuckle 1

turn·bull's blue \ˈtərn,bu̇lz-\ *n, usu cap T* [prob. fr. the name *Turnbull*] **:** an iron blue pigment having a coppery luster formed as a precipitate when an alkali metal ferricyanide and a ferrous salt are brought together in solution and formerly regarded as ferrous ferricyanide — compare PRUSSIAN BLUE

turn button *n* **:** BUTTON 5a

turncap \ˈ=,=\ *n* **:** a chimney cap that turns with the wind so as to present its opening to leeward

turncoat \ˈ=,=\ *n* [¹*turn* + *coat*, n.] **:** one who forsakes his party or his principles **:** RENEGADE, APOSTATE

turncock \ˈ=,=\ *n* **1 :** a stopcock with a plug that is turned in opening or closing **2 :** a person employed to turn on or off water supplied intermittently (as to dwellings or street flushing operations)

turn down *vi* **1 :** to take a downward course or direction ⟨corners of his mouth began to *turn down*⟩ **2 :** to be capable of being folded or doubled down ⟨collar *turns down*⟩ ~ *vt* **1 :** to fold or double down ⟨corner of the page has been *turned down*⟩ **2 :** to turn upside down **:** INVERT ⟨*turn down* the first card dealt⟩ **3 :** to reduce in height or intensity by turning a valve or stopcock or control ⟨*turn down* the lights⟩ ⟨*turn down* the thermostat for the night⟩ ⟨*turn* the radio *down*⟩ **4 :** to refuse to accept **:** DECLINE, REJECT ⟨reasons . . . for *turning down* two such eligible suitors —Leon Edel⟩ **5** *chiefly Brit* **:** to liberate or release for stocking purposes ⟨*turn down* foxes⟩

¹turndown \ˈ=,=\ *adj* [*turn down*] **:** capable of being turned down; *esp* **:** made to wear with the upper part turned down ⟨blouse with a ~ collar⟩

²turndown \ˈ"\ *n* -S [*turn down*] **1 :** the act of turning down **:** REJECTION **2 :** something turned down ⟨the ~ of the sheet covered the frayed edge of the blanket⟩ **3 :** DOWNTURN

turn·dun \ˈtərn,dən\ *n* -S [native name in Australia] **:** BULL-ROARER

turned \ˈtərnd, ˈtənd, ˈtəind\ *adj* [ME, fr. past part. of *turnen* to turn — more at TURN] **1 :** shaped in or as if in a lathe ⟨chair made entirely of ~ members⟩ ⟨well-*turned* phrases⟩ — see LEG illustration **2 :** REVERSED, INVERTED ⟨~ letters⟩

turned shoe *var of* TURN SHOE

turned trump *n* **:** TRUMP CARD 1a

tur·nel \ˈtərnᵊl\ *n* -S [origin unknown] *dial Eng* **:** TUB

¹turn·er \ˈtərnər, ˈtənə(r, ˈtəinə(r\ *n* -S [ME, fr. *turnen* to turn + *-er*] **1 :** one that turns or is used for turning ⟨cake ~⟩ ⟨log ~ in a sawmill⟩; *specif* **:** a tool used for shaping material in a lathe **2 :** one whose work is turning: as **a :** one that shapes pottery, stone, or wooden articles on a lathe **b :** an operator of a machine for cutting out jewelry stock or watch parts **c :** a garment worker who turns finished parts or articles of clothing to the right side

food turner

²tur·ner \ˈ"\ *n* -S [prob. alter. of *tournois*] **:** a 17th century copper coin of Scotland worth two Scots pennies

³turn·er \ˈtərnər, ˈtu̇rn-\ *n* -S [G, fr. *turnen* to perform gymnastic exercises + *-er* — more at TURN] **:** a member of a turnverein **:** GYMNAST

tur·nera \ˈtərnərə\ *n, cap* [NL, after William *Turner* †1568 Eng. physician and botanist] **:** a large genus (the type of the family Turneraceae) of tropical American dicotyledonous plants having alternate leaves and solitary axillary yellow flowers often with the peduncle and petiole coherent — see DAMIANA, YELLOW ALDER

tur·ner·a·ce·ae \,tərnəˈrāsē,ē\ *n pl, cap* [NL, fr. *Turnera*, type genus + *-aceae*] **:** a family of mostly tropical American herbs or shrubs (order Parietales) having flowers with five stamens, three styles, and a free ovary — **tur·ner·a·ceous** \¦==¦rāshəs\ *adj*

tur·ner·esque \¦tərnə¦resk\ *adj, usu cap* [Joseph M. W. *Turner* †1851 Eng. landscape painter + E *-esque*] **:** resembling or suggesting the work of the painter Turner **:** having brilliant color effects in the manner of Turner's paintings of landscapes and seascapes ⟨*Turneresque* sunset⟩

turner harp *n* [¹*turner*; fr. its being between the immature and mature stages of development] **:** a harp seal three years old

turner hood *n* [¹*turner*] **:** a hooded seal three years old

turner's yellow *n* [after J. M. W. *Turner*] **1** *often cap T* **:** ORPIMENT **2** *usu cap T* **:** CASSEL YELLOW 1

tur·nery \ˈtərnərē, ˈtən-, ˈtəin-, -nəri\ *n* -ES [¹*turner* + *-y*] **1 :** the process of fashioning material into cylindrical or other forms by means of a lathe **2 :** things or forms made by a turner or in the lathe; *esp* **:** turned ornamentation ⟨chairs of wood, the seats triangular, the backs, arms, and legs loaded with ~ —Horace Walpole⟩ **3 :** MACHINE SHOP

turn–furrow \ˈ=,(,)=\ *n* [¹*turn* + *furrow*] **:** MOLDBOARD 1a

turngate \ˈ=,=\ *n* **:** TURNSTILE

turn·halle \ˈtu̇rn,hälə\ *also* **turn·hall** \ˈtərn,hȯl\ *n* -S [G *turnhalle*, fr. *turnen* to perform gymnastic exercises + *halle* hall, fr. OHG *halla* — more at TURN, HALL] **:** a building used as a school of gymnastics

tur·ni·ces \ˈtərnə,sēz\ *n pl, cap* [NL, pl. of *Turnic-, Turnix*] **:** a small suborder of Gruiformes comprising the button quails and the plain wanderer

tur·nic·i·dae \,tərˈnisə,dē\ *n pl, cap* [NL, fr. *Turnic-, Turnix*, type genus + *-idae*] **:** a usu. monotypic family of Old World chiefly terrestrial birds (suborder Turnices) comprising the button quails — see TURNIX — **tur·ni·cine** \ˈtərnə,sīn, -sən\ *adj*

tur·ni·co·mor·phae \,tərnəkōˈmȯr,fē\ *n pl, cap* [NL, fr. *Turnic-, Turnix* + *-o-* + *-morphae*] *in former classifications* **:** superfamily equivalent to Turnices

turn in *vt* **1 a :** to deliver up **:** hand over ⟨*turn in* an expense account⟩ ⟨*turned in* his badge and quit⟩ **b :** to inform on **:** BETRAY ⟨*turn in* a wanted man to police⟩ **c :** to give an account of oneself respecting **:** acquit oneself of ⟨*turns in* a fine performance as the hero's father⟩ ⟨*turned in* a piece of good reporting —Ellen Smith⟩ **2 :** to turn under ⟨*turn in* a fodder crop as green manure⟩ ~ *vi* **1 :** to turn from a road or path so as to enter ⟨their neighbors were *turning in* at their own gate —Dorothy C. Fisher⟩ **2 :** to go to bed ⟨must have known how late he had *turned in* —Edward Newhouse⟩

turn in upon oneself : to be or become absorbed in one's own thoughts and feelings **:** INTROVERT ⟨are Americans *turning in upon themselves* . . . allowing an almost neurotic concern with internal subversion to do duty for a genuine policy —Barbara Ward⟩

turn–in \ˈ=,=\ *n* -S [*turn in*] **:** something that turns in or is turned in; *specif* **:** the portion of a book covering that overlaps the three edges of both boards and is secured smoothly to them

turn indicator *n* **:** an instrument for indicating either the amount or the rate of turn of an airplane about its vertical axis — compare RELATIVE INCLINOMETER

turning *n* -S [ME, fr. gerund of *turnen* to turn — more at TURN] **1 :** the act or course of one that turns: as **a :** rotation about an axis ⟨the slow ~ of the earth⟩ **b :** BEND, FLEXURE ⟨count the ~*s* of a coil of wire⟩ **c :** deviation from the way or proper course ⟨straighten out the ~*s* of the old road⟩ ⟨a kind act that was to lead, after many ~*s*, to his own undoing —*Time*⟩ **d :** the act of reversing direction **:** ABOUT-FACE **2 :** the place or point of a change in direction ⟨when we come to the ~ I shall run right past it —Margaret Kennedy⟩ ⟨let only the few wrong ~*s* be retraced —Oscar Handlin⟩ ⟨one of the major ~*s* in the cultural history of the West —Irving Horne⟩ **3 a :** the act or process of forming by use of the lathe **:** TURNERY **b :** the shape of a turned member ⟨staircase with balusters of three different ~*s* on each tread —*Amer. Guide Series: Conn.*⟩ ⟨a trumpet-shaped ~⟩ **c turnings** *pl* **:** the chips or curls detached in the process of turning from the material turned ⟨cleaning pads made from metal ~*s*⟩ **4 :** the amount of cloth (as the width of a seam) folded under along a raw edge for a seam or narrow hem

turning bar *n* **:** HORIZONTAL BAR

turning basin *n* **:** an enlarged space at the end of a canal or narrow channel to permit boats to turn around

turning bridge *n* **:** PIVOT BRIDGE

turning chisel *n* **:** a chisel used for shaping or finishing work in a lathe — see CHISEL illustration

turning engine *n* **1 :** LATHE 1 **2 :** a small engine for turning over a larger engine or turbine (as for inspection or adjustment)

turning gouge *n* **:** a tool used in woodworking for roughing down surfaces in a lathe

turning movement *n* **:** an attack in which a command is separated into two parts operating out of mutual supporting distance one of which is to hold the enemy while the other is to make a wide detour and strike at a vital point deep in the enemy's rear — compare ENVELOPMENT

turning plow *n* **:** MOLDBOARD PLOW

turning point *n* **1 :** a point at which a course of events or a situation undergoes a significant change of direction or character **:** CLIMAX, CRISIS ⟨1858 marked the *turning point* in the resistance of science to the new ideas concerning man's antiquity —R.W.Murray⟩ ⟨*turning point* in a disease⟩ ⟨*turning point* in a tragedy⟩ **2 :** a high or low point on a graph or plotted curve **3 :** a point the height of which is determined before a differential leveling instrument is moved and which is used to determine the height of the instrument after the resetting

turning rest *n* **:** a rest (as a T-shaped rest) serving as a fulcrum for a turning tool

turning saw *n* **:** COMPASS SAW

turning sickness *n* **:** an African cattle disease marked by circling movements, incoordination of the hind legs, loss of orientation, and frequently death and believed to be related to East Coast fever

turning spur *n* **:** a spur track with a curved branch returning to the main line for reversing the direction of a locomotive or train

turning square *n* **:** a square piece of lumber suitable for turning into a roller

tur·nip \ˈtərnəp, ˈtōn-, ˈtəin-\ *n* -S *often attrib* [alter. of earlier *turnepe*, prob. fr. ¹*turn* + *neep*; fr. the well-rounded root] **1 :** either of two biennial herbs having thick edible roots eaten as a vegetable or used for feeding stock: **a :** a plant (*Brassica rapa*) having hairy leaves and typically flattened roots much broader than long **b :** RUTABAGA **2 :** a large or thick pocket watch ⟨after consulting a large ~ watch of florid gold and enamel —Ann Bridge⟩ **3 a :** a stupid person **:** BLOCKHEAD **b :** a dull or unexciting work

turnip aphid *or* **turnip louse** *n* **1 :** CABBAGE APHID **2 :** a greenish plant louse (*Rhopalosiphum pseudobrassicae*) destructive to turnips and other brassicas

turnip bean *n* **:** YAM BEAN

turnip beetle *n* **:** a chrysomelid beetle (*Entomoscelis americana*) that injures turnip plants in parts of Canada

turnip cabbage *n* **1 :** KOHLRABI **2 :** RUTABAGA

turnip flea *or* **turnip flea beetle** *or* **turnip jack** *n* **:** STRIPED FLEA BEETLE

turnip fly *n* **1** TURNIP FLEA **2 :** the adult of the cabbage maggot **3 :** TURNIP SAWFLY

turnip foot *n* **:** a ball foot with a long curved neck

turnip ghost *n, Brit* **:** a jack-o'-lantern made from a turnip rind; *broadly* **:** BUGABOO

turnip grass *n* **:** a grass (*Panicum bulbosum*) of the southwestern U. S. and adjacent Mexico used for hay

turnip leaf miner *n* **:** the maggot of a small fly (*Scaptomyza flaveola*) related to the drosophilas and introduced into America from Europe that is destructive to turnips and related vegetables

turnip maggot *n* **:** the larva of the turnip fly

turnip radish *or* **turnip-rooted radish** *n* **:** any of various radishes with somewhat spherical roots

turnip foot

turnip–rooted \¦==¦==\ *adj* **:** having a round flattened root

turnip–rooted celery \ˈ==,==-\ *also* **turnip celery** *n* **:** CELERIAC

turnip–rooted chervil *n* **:** the edible spindle-shaped tuber of a European biennial (*Chaerophyllum bulbosum*); *also* **:** the plant itself

turnip–rooted parsley *n* **:** HAMBURG PARSLEY

turnip sawfly *n* **:** a European sawfly (*Athalia spinarum*) that cuts slits on the margins of turnip leaves in which to lay its eggs

turnip shell *n* **:** any of several large thick shelled marine gastropod mollusks of *Rapa* and related genera of the group Rachiglossa; *also* **:** the shell of such a mollusk

turnip tops *or* **turnip greens** *n pl* **:** the fresh young leaves of the turnip used as a green vegetable

turnipweed \ˈ==,=\ *n* **:** JOE-PYE WEED

turnipwood \ˈ==,=\ *n* **1 :** BASTARD ROSEWOOD **2 :** an Australian rosewood (*Dysoxylum fraserianum*) with bark that when fresh smells like a rutabaga

tur·nipy \ˈtərnəpē\ *adj* **1 :** resembling a turnip in shape or taste **2 :** lacking vitality **:** BLOODLESS, SOULLESS

tur·nix \ˈtərniks\ *n* [NL, short for L *coturnix* quail] **1** *cap* **:** a genus comprising small 3-toed birds that live on grassy plains of southern Europe, Asia, and northern Africa and are related to the plovers and sand grouse and constituting with the genus *Pedionomus* the family Turnicidae **2** -ES **:** any bird of the genus *Turnix* **:** BUTTON QUAIL

turnkey \ˈ=,=\ *n* -S [¹*turn* + *key*] **:** one who has charge of the keys of a prison **:** JAILER, WARDER

turn–key job \ˈ=,=-\ *n* **:** a job or contract in which the contractor agrees to complete the work of building and installation to the point of readiness for operation or occupancy

turn meter *n* **:** an instrument that measures the angular velocity of an airplane about a predetermined axis

turn of a hair : the narrowest possible chance or closest approach without contact ⟨missed the approaching car by a *turn of a hair*⟩

turn off *vt* **1 a :** DISMISS, DISCHARGE ⟨at Jamaica he *turned off* the troublesome crew —W.P.Webb⟩ **b :** to dispose of **:** get rid of **:** SELL; *esp* **:** to consign (fat stock) to market **2 :** to turn aside **:** DEFLECT, EVADE ⟨*turn off* an importunate question with a laugh —H.G.Dwight⟩ **3 :** to turn out **:** PRODUCE, ACCOMPLISH, EXECUTE ⟨so versatile an artist . . . who can . . . *turn off* half a dozen Viennese songs —Irving Kolodin⟩ **4 :** to shut off or stop the flow of by or as if by turning a valve or stopcock or switch ⟨*turn off* the water⟩ ⟨*turn off* the ignition of a motor⟩ ⟨*turn off* a gas burner⟩ **5 a :** HANG 1b(1) ⟨when he was caught at last and *turned off* —Richard Hallet⟩ **b** *Brit* **:** to join in marriage **6 a :** to remove (material) by the process of turning **b :** to shape or produce by turning ~ *vi* **1 :** to deviate from a straight course or from a main road or route ⟨*turn off* into a side road⟩ ⟨*turned off* when he ought to have gone straight on⟩ **2 a** *Brit* **:** to go off **:** turn bad **:** SPOIL **b :** to change to a specified state **:** BECOME ⟨the evening had *turned off* cool —Hamilton Basso⟩

turnoff \ˈ=,=\ *n* -S [*turn off*] **1 a :** a turning off **b :** a place where one turns off ⟨a wrong ~⟩ **c :** a side road **:** BRANCH **d :** a ramp leading from an express highway or turnpike **2 a :** completed product (as from a loom) **b :** number or weight of marketed livestock ⟨average annual ~ of fat bullocks —R.M.Bowman⟩

turn of speed : ability to go fast **:** capacity for speed ⟨develop great hardiness, courage, and a *turn of speed* —Richard Pollock⟩ ⟨showed a remarkable *turn of speed* —John Buchan⟩

turn of the bilge : the part of the hull between the keel and vertical sides

turn of the market *Brit* **:** ²TURN 10d

turn of the scale : the slight excess in weight that turns a scalepan downward and that usu. constitutes an advantage to a buyer

turn on *vt* **1 :** to cause to flow by or as if by opening a valve or tap ⟨*turn* the water *on* full⟩ ⟨her charm could be *turned on* and off at will⟩ **2 :** to cause to operate ⟨*turn* the radio *on*⟩

turn out *vt* **1 a :** to drive out **:** EXPEL, EVICT ⟨voters have never *turned* a party *out* of power during a period of prosperity —*Newsweek*⟩ ⟨if you can't behave decently I'll have you *turned out* —Margaret Kennedy⟩ **b :** to put (as a horse) to pasture **2 a :** to turn inside out ⟨*turning out* his pockets to show they were empty⟩ **b :** to empty the contents of esp. for cleaning or rearranging; *also* **:** CLEAN ⟨three maids who were *turning out* the drawing room —Ethel Anderson⟩ **3 :** to cause to point outward ⟨*turns* his toes *out* like a dancer⟩ **4 :** to produce by or as if by machine **:** make with rapidity or regularity ⟨*turned out* literally thousands of airplanes and trained pilots —W.L.Davidson⟩ ⟨*turns out* books faster than most men write letters —Arthur Knight⟩ **5 :** to equip, dress, or finish in a careful or elaborate way ⟨*turned out* in a cutaway, striped trousers, a careful collar-and-tie effect, white carnation —C. W.Morton⟩ ⟨many of them are married, with wives who insist on *turning* them *out* well groomed —S.P.B.Mais⟩ **6 :** to put out (a light) by turning a valve or a switch **7 :** to call (as a company) out from rest or from shelter and into formation ~ *vi* **1 a :** to come or go out from home in answer to a summons or invitation ⟨students and faculty *turn out* to aid in shoveling the streets clear —Corey Ford⟩ ⟨*turn out* for football practice⟩ **b :** to get out of bed ⟨*turned out* about two in the morning to make our final preparations for landing —H. L.Merillat⟩ **2 :** to prove to be in the result or end ⟨if what he envisages *turned out* to be really a frontier —W.P.Webb⟩ **:** END ⟨stories that *turn out* happily⟩ ⟨waiting to see how the game *turned out*⟩ **:** become in maturity or eventually ⟨the oldest boy . . . *turned out* ornery as a bobcat —Jean Stafford⟩

turnout \ˈ=,=\ *n* -S [*turn out*] **1 :** an act of turning out ⟨fireman ready for a sudden ~⟩ ⟨drank beer . . . for the few minutes until ~ time —Nigel Balchin⟩ ⟨party work did stimulate ~ —R.M.Goldman⟩ **2** *chiefly Brit* **a :** STRIKE 7a **b :** STRIKER 8 **3 :** a gathering of people for a special purpose ⟨largest ~ ever to appear at a board meeting —David Clinton⟩ ⟨the opening game brought only a small ~⟩ **4 a** : a place where something turns out or branches off ⟨on the highway just beyond the ~ to the white church⟩ **b** : a widened space in a highway for vehicles to pass each other or for parking **c** : a track arrangement enabling locomotives and cars to pass from one track to another and consisting of a switch and frog with all connecting and operating parts **d** : a device or structure (as a joint of pipe) through which material (as water from an irrigation canal) is released **5 a** : a clearing or emptying out **b** : an act of cleaning and setting in order ⟨gave all the rooms a good ~ twice a year⟩ **6 a** : a coach or carriage together with the horses, harness, and attendants : EQUIPAGE ⟨smart ~ with two men on the box and a crest on the door —Frances P. Keyes⟩ **b** : manner of furnishing or outfitting : EQUIPMENT, RIG **c** : manner of dress : clothes or costume esp. for a particular occasion : GETUP ⟨belief that smart ~ on parade was the be-all and end-all of the military life —Al Newman⟩ **7** : net quantity of produce yielded : OUTPUT, PRODUCT **8 turnouts** *or* **turnout clothes** *pl* : BUNKER SUIT **9** : a position of the feet in ballet with the heels back to back

turn over *vt* **1 a** : to turn or roll from one side to the other : INVERT ⟨*turn* a stone *over*⟩ **b** : to turn from an upright position : OVERTURN, UPSET ⟨a big wave *turned* the boat *over*⟩ **2** : to reverse the layers of (as soil) **3** : to search (as papers) by lifting or moving one by one ⟨*turn over* clothes⟩ ⟨*turning over* old letters⟩ **4** : to think over : meditate on ⟨*turning* the advice *over* in his mind⟩ **5** : to read or examine (as a book) while turning the pages ⟨idly *turning over* a magazine⟩ **6** : to hand over : DELIVER, TRANSFER ⟨funds thus collected are *turned over* to union officials —H.M.Diamond⟩ ⟨*turn over* a regiment to a new commander⟩ **7 a** : to receive and dispose of (a stock of merchandise) ⟨*turn over* its inventory 18 times a year —*Time*⟩ **b** : to handle in business : do business to the amount of ⟨wrote home . . . that he was *turning over* a hundred pounds a week —H.V.Morton⟩ **8** : to transfer (as a word) from the end of one line to the beginning of the next line or from the foot of one column or page to the head of the next ~ *vi* **1** : to tip or roll over : UPSET, CAPSIZE, OVERTURN **2** : ROTATE ⟨engine *turning over* at 6000 revolutions per minute⟩ **3 a** *of one's stomach* : to heave with nausea **b** *of one's heart* : to seem to leap or lurch convulsively

[1]**turnover** \ˈ=,=\ *n* -s [*turn over*] **1** : an act or result of turning over ⟨~ on a horizontal bar⟩ : UPSET ⟨collision and ~ of a bus⟩ **2** : a turning from one side, place, or direction to its opposite : SHIFT, REVERSAL; *esp* : a marked shift of votes from one party to another **3** : a reorganization with a view to a shift in personnel : SHAKE-UP **4** : something that is turned over : a part (as the leaf of a book, the flap of an envelope, or a welt in a shoe) turned or folded over **5** : a triangular or semicircular pocket of filled pastry made by turning half of a square or circle of pastry over the other and enclosing a filling ⟨apple ~⟩ ⟨chicken ~⟩ **6** *or* **turnover apprentice** *archaic* : one whose indentures are transferred from one master (as a master printer) to another to enable him to complete his apprenticeship **7 a** : the amount of business done : degree of business activity ⟨gilt-edged securities were firm but the ~ small⟩ **b** : the amount of material on which some process has been performed ⟨the ~ of a mine⟩ or the rate at which material is processed ⟨~ of a machine⟩ **8 a** : movement (as of goods, animals, or people) into, through, and out of a place considered all as a single process ⟨a rapid ~ of patients in a well-organized hospital⟩ ⟨daily ~ of hogs in the stockyards⟩ **b** : the receipt, placing on sale, and disposal of a stock of merchandise; *also* : the rate at which goods are sold **c** : a cycle of purchase, sale, and replacement of a stock of goods, ⟨a ~ four times a year⟩; *also* : the ratio of sales for a stated period to average inventory **d** : the number of persons hired within a period to replace those leaving or dropped from a working force; *also* : the ratio of this number to the number in the average force maintained **9** *Brit* : a light essay on a matter of current interest beginning in the last column of page one of a newspaper and continuing onto page two **10** : TURNOVER FREQUENCY

[2]**turnover** \"\ *adj* [*turn over*] : capable of being turned over : made with a part folded over ⟨~ collar⟩

turnover frequency *n* : the frequency (as 500 cycles per second) at which the transition is made from constant velocity recording to constant amplitude recording in making phonograph records

turnover hinge *n* : a hinge designed so that the door to which it is attached can be swung open flat against the wall

turnover tax *n, Brit* : a tax on total transactions or gross sales usu. applicable to all sales of commodities by manufacturers, wholesalers, and retailers

[1]**turnpike** \ˈ=,=\ *n* [ME *turnepike*, fr. *turnen* to turn + *pike* (point)] **1** *obs* : a revolving frame bearing spikes and used as a barrier in medieval warfare **2** : TOLL BAR, TOLLGATE **3** *or* **turnpike road a** : a toll road; *esp* : a toll expressway **b** : a free road orig. maintained as a toll road **c** : a main road : a paved highway having a crowned surface **4** *Scot* : a winding spiral stairway

[2]**turnpike** \"\ *vt* -ED/-ING/-S **1** : to make into or like a turnpike road **2** : CROWN 5c

turnpike geranium *n* : JERUSALEM OAK 1

turnpike man *n* : a man who collects tolls at a turnpike

turn·pik·er \-kə(r)\ *n* [*turnpike* + *-er*] : one that travels on a turnpike

turnpin \ˈ=,=\ *n* : a tapered hardwood pin used to enlarge the ends of lead pipe

turnplate \ˈ=,=\ *n* **1** : TURNTABLE **2** : TURNSHEET

turnplow \ˈ=,=\ *n* : MOLDBOARD PLOW

turn ratio *or* **turns ratio** *n* : the ratio of the number of turns in one of two inductively coupled circuits to the number in the other

turn round *var of* TURN AROUND

turn–round \ˈ=,=\ *n* -s [*turn round*] **1** : a place for turning around **2** : TURNABOUT 3

turnrow \ˈ=,=\ *n* : a strip of usu. uncropped land at the side or end of a field upon which a plow may be turned at the end of the furrow

turns \ˈtərnz\ *n pl* [fr. pl. of [2]*turn*] : a watchmaker's lathe — often used with *pair*

turnscrew \ˈ=,=\ *n* [[1]*turn* + *screw*] : a device for turning screws : SCREWDRIVER, WRENCH

turnsheet \ˈ=,=\ *n* : a heavy, flat, iron or steel plate used in place of rails at track intersections for turning cars from one line to another — called also *turnplate*

turn shoe *also* **turned shoe** *n* : a light flexible single-soled shoe or slipper usu. worn by women and made by sewing upper and sole together both wrong side out, removing the last, turning right side out, attaching the heel, and finishing

turn–sick \ˈ=,=\ *n* [obs. E *turn-sick* vertigo, fr. ME *turnseke*, fr. *turnseke*, adj., dizzy, fr. *turn* + *seke* sick] : GID

turn·sole \ˈtərn,sōl\ *n* -s [ME *turnesole*, fr. MF *tournesol*, fr. OIt *tornasole*, fr. *tornare* to turn (fr. ML) + *sole* sun, fr. L *sol* (acc. *solem*) — more at TURN, SOLAR] **1** : any of several plants whose flowers or stems are supposed to follow the movement of the sun: **a** : HELIOTROPE 1b **b** : SUNFLOWER **c** : SUN SPURGE **d** : a double-flowered tulip (*Tulipa suaveolens*) of southern Russia **2** : a European annual herb (*Chrozophora tinctoria*) of the family Euphorbiaceae the juice of which is turned blue by ammonia **3 a** : a purple dye obtained from the turnsole (sense 2) **b** : LITMUS

turnspit \ˈ=,=\ *n* [[1]*turn* + *spit*] **1 a** : one who turns a spit **b** : a small dog with long body and short crooked legs formerly used in a treadmill to turn a spit **c** : ROASTING JACK **2** : a spit that may be rotated

turnstile \ˈ=,=\ *n* **1 a** : a post with four arms pivoted on the top set in a gateway or passageway so that persons can pass through but cattle cannot **b** : a similar device set in an entrance for controlling or counting the persons entering ⟨~s at the ball park were clicking busily⟩ **2** : a device resembling in appearance a turnstile and turned by hand to traverse the turret slide of a lathe **3** *or* **turnstile antenna** : a television transmitting antenna consisting of two horizontal dipoles at right angles to each other usu. used in the VHF-UHF frequency range and when it is desired to have signals transmitted in all directions equally well

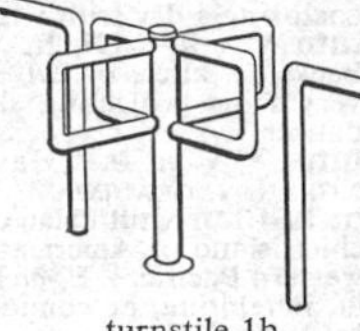

turnstile 1b

turnstone \ˈ=,=\ *n* [[1]*turn* + *stone*; fr. its habit of turning over stones to find food] : any of various widely distributed migratory shorebirds (genus *Arenaria*) of the family Charadriidae that typically resemble the related plovers and sandpipers in form and habits; *esp* : a widely distributed New and Old World bird (*A. interpres*) having the upperparts variegated with black and chestnut, the breast black, and the abdomen white — see BLACK TURNSTONE, RUDDY TURNSTONE

turntable \ˈ=,==\ *n* **1** : a revolvable platform: as **a** : a pivoted structure that supports a platform or track and revolves in a horizontal plane for turning wheeled vehicles ⟨locomotive ~⟩ **b** : LAZY SUSAN **c** : a support with horizontal bearings for holding a reel for winding or unwinding rope **d** : a rotating platform that carries a phonograph record **2** : a machine that reproduces speech or music from records and transcriptions for radiobroadcasting **3** : a stunt performed on the trampoline consisting of a front drop followed by a horizontal rotation of the body in the air into a second front drop

turntable ladder *n* : AERIAL LADDER

turntail \ˈ=,=\ *n* [fr. the phrase *turn tail*] : one who turns tail and runs away : DESERTER, COWARD

turn the trencher *n* : SPIN THE PLATE

turn to *vi* : to apply oneself to work : act vigorously ⟨all hands *turn to* and help the cook with the dishwashing —H.A. Calahan⟩ ⟨must sometimes *turn to* and earn a living like other persons —Jacob Epstein⟩

turn–to \ˈ=,=\ *n* -s [*turn to*] **1** : FIGHT, BOUT **2** : a turning of one's attention and efforts to the business at hand : a setting to work

turn–tree \ˈ=,=\ *n, Brit* : the drum of a windlass

turn under *vt* **1** : to bend or fold downward or underneath ⟨pull the end of the sheet down and *turn* it *under*⟩ **2** : to put (as soil) underneath from the surface by plowing or digging ~ *vi* : to bend or curve toward the underside

turn–under \ˈ=,==\ *n* -s [*turn under*] **1** : the act of turning under **2** : a curving at or toward the underside or the amount of such curvature

turn up *vt* **1 a** : to turn or fold so as to bring the bottom side on top or on the outside ⟨*turn up* a coat collar⟩ ⟨*turned up* his shirt cuffs⟩ **b** : to shorten (as a skirt) esp. by making a hem or increasing the width of a hem **c** : to make (a cuff) by folding over the bottom of a sleeve or pant leg **2 a** : to bring from underneath to the surface (as by digging or plowing) **b** : FIND, DISCOVER ⟨readily have *turned up* additional examples of the term —C.J.Lovell⟩ ⟨the papers soon *turned up* evidence of skullduggery —*Newsweek*⟩ **3** : to raise or increase by turning a valve or stopcock ⟨*turn up* the flame of a burner⟩ ⟨*turn* the lights *up*⟩ **4** *Brit* **a** : to look up (as a word) in a book ⟨assuming again that the interested reader will *turn up* the poem —F. R.Leavis⟩ **b** : to refer to (a book) : CONSULT **5 a** : to bring to a supine position **b** : KILL **6** : to call (a crew) on deck **7** : to turn (a card) face upward **8** *Brit* **a** : to give up : RELINQUISH **b** : to turn loose : set free **9** : to reach a rotational speed of : develop power to the extent of ⟨engine *turns up* 101 horsepower⟩ ~ *vi* **1** : to appear or come to light unexpectedly or after being lost ⟨number of new species will *turn up* —C.H. Curran⟩ **2 a** : to turn out to be ⟨*turned up* missing at roll call⟩ : become visible or evident ⟨name is always *turning up* in the newspapers⟩ **b** : to arrive or show up at an appointed or expected time or place ⟨*turned up* half an hour late for work⟩ **3** : to happen or occur unexpectedly ⟨something always *turned up* to prevent their meeting⟩ **4** *of a ship* : TACK — **turn up one's nose** : to show scorn or disdain — **turn up one's toes** *slang* : DIE

[1]**turnup** \ˈ=,=\ *n* -s [*turn up*] **1** *chiefly Brit* : DISTURBANCE, FUSS, ROW; *esp* : FISTFIGHT, SET-TO **2 a** : the turned-up part of an article of clothing **b** *chiefly Brit* : a cuff on a trouser leg ⟨the black mud closed over his shoes and the ~s of his trousers —Graham Greene⟩ **3 a** : a card turned faceup to fix or propose the trump **b** : UPCARD 1a

[2]**turnup** \"\ *adj* [*turn up*] **1** : turned up ⟨~ nose⟩ **2** : made or fitted to be turned up ⟨~ collar⟩

turn·ver·ein \ˈtərnvə,rīn, ˈtu̇rn-, -nfə,-\ *n* [G, fr. *turnen* to perform gymnastic exercises + *verein* society, club — more at TURN, VEREIN] : an association of gymnasts and athletes : an athletic club

[1]**turn·wrest** \ˈ=,rest\ *or* **turn·wrist** \-rist\ *adj* [[1]*turn* + *wrest* or *wrist* (dial. var. of *wrest*)] *Brit* : having a reversible moldboard ⟨~ plow⟩

[2]**turnwrest** \"\ *or* **turnwrist** \"\ *n, Brit* : SWIVEL PLOW

tu·ro·ni·an \t(y)u̇ˈrōnēən\ *adj, usu cap* [F *turonien* of Tours, fr. LL *Turoni* Tours, France (fr. L *Turones, Turoni*, a people of ancient Gaul) + F *-en* -an] : of, relating to, or constituting a subdivision of the European Cretaceous — see GEOLOGIC TIME table

tu·ro·phile \ˈt(y)u̇rə,fīl\ *n* -s [irreg. fr. Gk *tyros* cheese + E *-phile* — more at TYR-] : a gourmet of cheese : a cheese fancier

turp \ˈtərp\ *vb* -ED/-ING/-S [by shortening] : TURPENTINE

[1]**tur·pen·tine** \ˈtərpən,tīn, ˈtəp-, ˈtəip-, -pᵊm,-\ *n* -s [ME *terebentyne, terbentyne, turpentyne*, fr. MF & ML; MF *terebentine, terbentine, tourbentine*, fr. ML *terbentina* (fr. L *terebinthina*) & L *terebinthina*, fem. of *terebinthinus* of terebinth, fr. *terebinthus* terebinth (fr. Gk *terebinthos*) + *-inus* -ine] **1 a** : a yellow to brown semifluid oleoresin that exudes from the terebinth tree — called also *Chian turpentine* **b** : any of various oleoresins that are derived from coniferous trees and are obtained in crude form as yellowish viscous exudates of characteristic odor and taste from incisions in the tree trunks and that usu. thicken and solidify in the air: as (1) : CANADA BALSAM (2) : VENICE TURPENTINE 1 (3) : STRASBOURG TURPENTINE (4) : GALIPOT (5) : RUSSIAN TURPENTINE **2** *or* **turpentine oil a** : the colorless or slightly yellowish mobile flammable pungent biting essential oil that is obtained by distillation from turpentine oleoresins esp. from longleaf, slash, and other pines, that is a mixture of terpenes with alpha-pinene usu. as the principal component, that oxidizes in air to a solid, and that is used chiefly as a solvent and thinner (as in paints and varnishes), as a raw material for synthetic camphor and other chemicals, and in medicine — called also *gum spirits, gum turpentine, spirits of turpentine* **b** : a similar oil obtained by steam distillation of chipped pine stumpwood and butt logs or of extracts of the chips — called also *steam-distilled wood turpentine, wood turpentine*; compare PINE OIL **a c** : a similar oil obtained by the carbonization of pinewood — called also *destructively distilled wood turpentine* **d** : a similar oil obtained as a by-product of the sulfate process — called also *sulfate turpentine* **3 a** : TURPENTINE TREE c **b** : TURPENTINE WEED

[2]**turpentine** \"\ *vb* -ED/-ING/-S *vt* **1** : to saturate or rub with turpentine : apply turpentine to **2** : to extract turpentine from (pine trees) by scarifying or wounding the surface to make resin exude ~ *vi* : to collect or make turpentine

turpentine beetle *n* : any of several bark beetles of the genus *Dendroctonus* (esp. *D. valens*) whose larvae live under the bark of pine stumps or trees

turpentine borer *n* : a borer that is the larva of a buprestid beetle (*Buprestis apricans*) and that bores in pines in the southeastern U.S.

turpentine moth *n* : any of several small moths (family Tortricidae) whose larvae eat the tender shoots of pine and fir trees causing an exudation of pitch or resin

turpentine orchard *n* : a stand of pine bled for turpentine

turpentine pine *n* : LONGLEAF PINE

tur·pen·tin·er \-īnə(r)\ *n* -s : a worker who gathers turpentine

turpentine substitute *n* : a petroleum distillate intermediate between gasoline and kerosine

turpentine tree *n* : a tree that yields a turpentine or turpentinic product: as **a** : TEREBINTH **b** : a pine or other turpentine-producing conifer — compare VENICE TURPENTINE **c** : any of several Australian trees (as various eucalypts) that yield a resinous fluid; *esp* : a tree (*Syncarpia laurifolia*) of the family Myrtaceae that is often grown for shelterbelts and hedging

turpentine weed *n* : any of several No. American herbs with an odor resembling that of turpentine: as **a** (1) : PRAIRIE DOCK 1 (2) : COMPASS PLANT **a b** : a California blue curls (*Trichostema laxum*) with purple or deep blue flowers

tur·pen·tin·ic \ˌtərpən·ˈtinik\ *also* **tur·pen·tin·ous** \ˈ==-,tīnəs\ *or* **tur·pen·tiny** \-nē\ *adj* **1** : of or relating to turpentine **2** : resembling turpentine

tur·peth \ˈtərpəth\ *n* -s [alter. (influenced by NL *turpethum* turpeth, fr. Ar *turbid*) of earlier *turbith*, fr. ME *turbit*, fr. MF *turbit*, fr. Ar *turbid*] **1** : the root of a tropical Asiatic and Australian vine (*Operculina turpethum*) formerly used in medicine as a purgative; *also* : the plant itself — called also *Indian jalap, vegetable turpeth* **2** *also* **turpeth mineral** : CALOMEL

tur·pis cau·sa \ˈtərpə̇sˈkōzə\ *n* [L, base cause] : a cause or consideration that is base or immoral and therefore not sufficient to support a contractual obligation

turpis con·trac·tus \-kən·ˈtraktəs\ *n* [L, base contract] : an immoral and therefore unenforceable contract

tur·pi·tude \ˈtərpə,tüd, ˈtəp-, ˈtəip-, -ə-,tyüd\ *n* -s [MF, fr. L *turpitudo*, fr. *turpis* vile, foul, base + *-tudo* -tude; prob. akin to L *trepit* he turns — more at TROPE] : inherent baseness or vileness of principle, words, or actions : DEPRAVITY ⟨moral ~⟩; *also* : a base act or action ⟨the various ~s of modern society⟩

turps \ˈtərps\ *n pl but usu sing in constr* [by shortening & alter.] : TURPENTINE

[1]**tur·quoise** *also* **tur·quois** \ˈtər,k(w)ȯiz, ˈtə̄,-, ˈtəi,-\ *n, pl* **turquoises** [ME *turkeis, torcas, turcas*, fr. MF *turquoyse, turquaise*, fr. fem. of *turquoys, turqueis* Turkish, fr. OF, fr. *Turc* Turk] **1** : a mineral $CuAl_6(PO_4)_4(OH)_8.5H_2O$ consisting of a blue, bluish green, or greenish gray hydrous basic copper aluminum phosphate isomorphous with chalcosiderite, occurring usu. in reniform masses with a botryoidal surface, taking a high polish, and changing sometimes to a green tint but when sky blue valued as a gem and mined in Persia and Arizona and New Mexico **2 a** : a variable color averaging a light greenish blue that is deeper and slightly greener than average turquoise blue and greener and deeper than average aqua or average robin's-egg blue (sense 1) **b** : a light bluish green that is bluer and paler than average turquoise green, slightly deeper and very slightly bluer than average aqua green (sense 1), and bluer, lighter, and stronger than robin's-egg blue (sense 2)

[2]**turquoise** *also* **turquois** \"\ *adj* **1 a** : consisting of turquoise ⟨a ~ carving⟩ **b** : set or set off with turquoise or turquoises ⟨a ~ brooch⟩ **2** : of either of the colors turquoise or turquoise blue

tur·quoise·berry \ˈ==,- — *see* BERRY\ *n* **1** : a Tasmanian herb (*Drymophila cyanocarpa*) of the family Liliaceae with white flowers and blue fruits **2** : ASIATIC SWEETLEAF

turquoise blue *n* : a variable color averaging a light greenish blue that is paler and slightly bluer than average turquoise (sense 2a), deeper and very slightly greener than average aqua, and greener and deeper than average robin's-egg blue (sense 1)

turquoise green *n* : a variable color averaging a light bluish green that is greener and deeper than turquoise (sense 2b) or average aqua green (sense 1) and bluer and deeper than robin's-egg blue (sense 2)

tur·ret \ˈtər·ət, ˈtə·rət, ˈtu̇rət usu -əd.+V\ *n* -s *often attrib* [ME *turet, touret*, fr. MF *torete, turete, tourete*, fr. OF, dim. of *tor, tur* tower — more at TOWER] **1** : a little tower; *specif* : an ornamental structure at one of the angles of a larger structure **2** *heraldry* : a small tower on top of a larger tower **3** : a holder for several tools or devices: as **a** : a pivoted toolholder in a machine tool by which each of various tools can be rapidly moved to the work — called also *turrethead* **b** : a device for supplying steam from the boiler of a locomotive to auxiliary devices (as a whistle or injector) **c** (1) : a manifold on a fire apparatus supplying heavy streams of water directly from pumps (2) *also* **turret nozzle** *or* **turret pipe** : a monitor mounted on the bed of a fire truck or on the deck of a fireboat **d** : a television device holding usu. four lenses and used in association with the camera tube : LENS TURRET **4 a** : a military siege device consisting of a building often square in form, sometimes having as many as 20 stories, usu. moved on wheels, and carrying soldiers, rams, ladders, and bridges for breaching or scaling a wall **b** : an enclosed, cylindrical, or dome-shaped armored structure usu. revolving, containing one or more guns, and forming part of a military vehicle, airplane, or ship: as (1) : a gunner's fixed or movable enclosure in an airplane usu. capable of being rotated on one or more axes and often of being raised or lowered so as to protrude a maximal distance only when manned for action (2) : a revolving structure on a warship protecting the breech portion of the one or more guns mounted within it — compare BARBETTE (3) : the upper structure of a tank rotatable for swinging the gun mounted within it

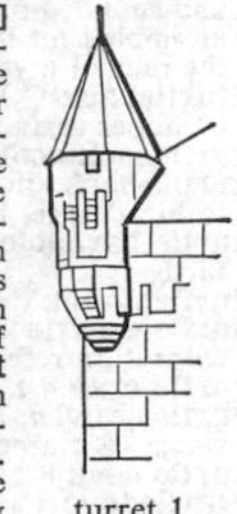

turret 1

turret angle-rack tool *n* : a tool for turning short tapers in a turret lathe

turret captain *n* : a petty officer (as in the U.S. Navy) appointed to the command of a turret crew and ranking next to the officer while in a turret

turret clock *n* : a clock for a turret or tower having one or more dials separate from the movement

turret cutter *n* : a coal cutter adjustable to various heights of coal cutting and mounted on a pivoted frame — called also *overcutter*

turret deck *n* : a narrow superstructure running from stem to stern on the upper deck of a steam cargo ship having a rounded gunwale and sides curved inward convexly

turret drier *n* : a wooden building of usu. five stories with ventilating and heating devices used for drying leather

turret drill *n* : a single-spindle or gang drill in which the spindle supports a head carrying a number of tools and so designed that each tool may in turn be brought to a position suitable for performing its function

tur·ret·ed \-əd·əd\ *adj* [*turret* + *-ed*] **1** : furnished with or as if with turrets ⟨a ~ fortress⟩ ⟨a ~ cloud⟩ **2** *of a seashell* : having whorls forming a high conical spiral

turrethead \ˈ==,=\ *n* : TURRET 3a

turret lathe *n* : a lathe having a turret for holding various different cutting tools

turret slide tool *n* : a vertically or horizontally adjustable slide that supports one or more cutting tools for use with a turret lathe

turret spider *n* : a Californian spider (*Atypoides riversi*) that forms burrows with external turrets

turret steamer *n* : a whaleback steamer with hatch coamings extending almost continuously fore and aft

turret taper tool *n* : a tool held in the turret of a turret lathe and used for turning tapers

turret tuner *n* : a radio tuner having a number of complete circuits mounted in a drum by whose rotation switching to different stations is done

tur·ri·cal \ˈtərə̇kəl\ *adj* [L *turris* tower + E *-ical* — more at TOWER] : of, relating to, or resembling a turret

tur·ric·u·la \(ˌ)təˈrikyələ\ *n, pl* **turricu·lae** \-yə,lē\ [NL, fr. L, small tower, dim. of *turris* tower] : a utensil or ornament (as a candlestick) shaped like a tower

tur·ric·u·lar \-lə(r)\ *adj* [L *turricula* small tower + E *-ar*] : shaped like or resembling a tower

tur·ric·u·late \-yələt, -yə,lāt\ *or* **tur·ric·u·lat·ed** \-ād·əd\ *adj* [L *turricula* + E *-ate* or *-ated* (fr. *-ate* + *-ed*)] : having a small turret : formed like a small turret : TURRETED

Tur·ri·dae \ˈtərə,dē\ [NL, fr. *Turris*, type genus + *-idae*] *syn of* TURRITIDAE

tur·rif·er·ous \(ˌ)təˈrif(ə)rəs\ *adj* [L *turrifer* turriferous (fr. *turris* tower + *-fer* -ferous) + E *-ous*] : bearing towers

tur·ri·lite \ˈtərə,līt\ *n* -s [NL *Turrilites*] : an ammonoid or fossil of the genus *Turrilites*

Tur·ri·li·tes \ˌ==ˈlīd·(ˌ)ēz\ *n, cap* [NL, fr. L *turris* tower + Gk *lithos* stone] : a genus of Cretaceous ammonoid cephalopods having a spiral sinistral turreted shell with the later whorls more or less separate

tur·ri·lit·i·cone \ˌtərəˈlid·ə,kōn\ *n* -s [*turrilite* + *-i-* + *cone*] : an ammonite asymmetrically coiled like a gastropod with a high spire

Tur·ris \ˈtərə̇s\ *n, cap* [NL, fr. L, tower — more at TOWER] : a genus of small marine snails having a graceful shell shaped like a spindle and being the type of the family Turritidae

tur·ri·tel·la \ˌtərəˈtelə\ *n* [NL, irreg. fr. L *turris* + NL *-ella*] **1** *cap* : a genus (the type of the family Turritellidae) of marine gastropod mollusks having an elongated turreted shell composed of many whorls with a rounded aperture and a horny multispiral operculum **2** *also* **tur·ri·tel·lid** \-lə̇d\ -s **:** any mollusk or shell of the genus *Turritella* or family Turritellidae — see SCREW SHELL

¹tur·ri·tid \'tərəd·ə̇d\ *also* **tur·rid** \'tərə̇d\ *adj* [NL *Turridae* & *Turritidae*] **:** of or relating to the Turritidae

²turritid \"\ *also* **turrid** \"\ *n* -s **:** a mollusk of the family Turritidae

tur·rit·i·dae \(,)tə'rid·ə,dē\ *n pl, cap* [NL, irreg. fr. *Turris*, type genus + *-idae*] **:** a large and widely distributed family of marine gastropod mollusks (suborder Stenoglossa) — see TURRIS

tur·rum \'tərəm\ *n* -s [native name in Australia] **:** a large Australian trevally prob. of the genus *Caranx*

turs *pl of* TUR

turse \'tərs\ *n* -s [ME(Sc) *turs* bundle, truss, fr. MF *tourse* — more at TRUSS] *chiefly Scot* **:** BUNDLE, LOAD

tur·si·ops \'tərsē,äps\ *n, cap* [NL, fr. *Tursio*, genus of dolphins (fr. L, a kind of dolphin, fr. Gk *thyrsiōn*, fr. *thyrsos* thyrsus) + *-ops*] **:** a genus of rather large heavy-bodied dolphins having a truncate beak and a dorsal fin shaped like a sickle

¹tur·tle \'tər|d·ᵊl, 'tə̄|, 'təi|, |tᵊl\ *n* -s [ME *turtil*, *turtle*, fr. OE *turtla*, fr. L *turtur*, of imit. origin like Gk *tetraōn* heath cock, *tetrix*, a bird (perh. the pipit), Skt *tittira* francolin] *archaic* **:** TURTLEDOVE ⟨the voice of the ~ is heard in our land —Song of Sol 2:12 (AV)⟩

²turtle \"\ *n, pl* **turtles** *also* **turtle** *often attrib* [prob. by folk etymology (influence of ¹*turtle*) fr. F *tortue*, prob. fr. (assumed) VL *tartaruca*, fr. LL *tartarucha*, fem. of *tartaruchus* of Tartarus, fr. Gk *tartarouchos*, fr. *Tartaros* Tartarus, the infernal regions; fr. the turtle's having been regarded in ancient times as an infernal creature] **1 :** a reptile of the order Testudinata — used esp. of the more aquatic and esp. marine members of the order; compare TERRAPIN, TORTOISE; see GREEN TURTLE **2 :** SIENNA BROWN **3 a :** the curved section of the plate cylinder of a type-revolving press to which the type matter is locked **b :** a 2-wheeled form truck for making up and transporting a newspaper page prior to stereotyping **4 :** TURTLENECK

turtle 1a

³turtle \"\ *vi* **turtled**; **turtled**; **turtling** \|d·ᵊliŋ, |t(ᵊ)l-\ **turtles :** to catch turtles esp. as an occupation

¹turtleback \'==,=\ *n* [²*turtle* + *back*] **:** a raised convex surface: as **a :** an oval boss esp. on furniture **b :** a raised obstruction sometimes illuminated and placed in the pavement at a street intersection for the guidance of traffic **c :** a convex deck at the bow or stern and sometimes extending from bow to stern of a boat so made to shed the seas quickly — called also *turtle deck* **d :** a roughly shaped artifact of stone chipped flat on one side and rounded on the other and prob. a blank form from which an implement might be chipped **e :** a rounded projection on the rear of a vehicle

²turtleback \"\ *or* **turtle-backed** \'==,=\ *adj* **:** having a back or upper surface shaped like the back of a turtle

turtleback scale *n* **:** a soft scale (*Lecanium hesperidium*)

turtle-back shooting *n* **:** archery shooting with high trajectory to hit a target laid flat on the ground

turtle barnacle *n* **:** a barnacle living on the shell of a marine turtle

turtlebloom \'==,=\ *n* **:** TURTLEHEAD

turtle cowrie *n* **:** a large cowrie (*Cypraea testudinaria*) in coloration resembling the shell of a tortoise

turtle crab *n* **:** GULF-WEED CRAB

turtle crawl *n* **1 :** the trail of a tortoise between its nest and the water **2 :** a pen in which turtles are kept

turtle deck *n* **:** TURTLEBACK c

¹turtledove \'==,=\ *n* [ME *turtildove*, fr. *turtil*, *turtle* turtledove + *dove* — more at TURTLE] **1 a :** an Old World wild dove of *Streptopelia* or related genera; *esp* **:** a common European bird (*S. turtur*) noted for its plaintive cooing and being mostly cinnamon brown with a white-bordered black patch on each side of the neck and white-tipped outer tail feathers **b :** MOURNING DOVE **c :** a small Australian dove (*Stictopeleia cuneata*) of terrestrial habits **2 :** BELOVED, SWEETHEART **3 :** a dark gray to reddish gray

²turtledove \"\ *vi* -ED/-ING/-S **:** to be affectionately demonstrative

turtle grass *n* **1 :** EELGRASS 1 **2 :** a submerged marine plant (*Thalassia testudinum*) of the family Hydrocharitaceae of the coasts of Florida and the West Indies with elongated linear leaves and dioecious flowers

turtle green *n* **:** a moderate yellow green that is greener and paler than average moss green and yellower and paler than average pea green or apple green (sense 1)

turtlehead \'==,=\ *n* [²*turtle* + *head*; so called fr. the shape of the flower] **:** CHELONE; *esp* **:** a showy perennial herb (*Chelone glabra*) of marshy lands of eastern and central No. America with waxy lanceolate to ovate leaves and flowers with the lower parts creamy white and the upper parts pale pink to deep purple

turtle knot *n* **:** TURLE KNOT

turtleneck \'==,=\ *n* **:** a high close-fitting turnover collar used esp. for sweaters; *also* **:** a sweater with a turtleneck

turtle peg *n* **:** a detachable sharp steel spearhead attached to a cord for use in harpooning sea turtles

tur·tler \|d·ᵊlə(r), |t(ᵊ)l-\ *n* -s [²*turtle* + *-er*] **1 :** one that hunts turtles or their eggs **2 :** one that deals in turtles

turtleneck

turtles *pl of* TURTLE, *pres 3d sing of* TURTLE

turtle shell *n* **1 :** TORTOISE SHELL **2 :** TURTLE COWRIE

turtle stone *n* **:** a calcareous concretion divided in the interior by cracks partly or wholly filled by crystallized minerals **:** SEPTARIUM

turt·let \-lə̇t\ *n* -s [²*turtle* + *-et*] **:** a young or small-sized turtle

turtling *pres part of* TURTLE

tur·to·sa \,tər'tōsə\ *n* -s [origin unknown] **:** AFRICAN OAK

turves *pl of* TURF

¹tus·can \'təskən\ *n* -s [ME, fr. L *tuscanus*, adj., Etruscan, fr. *Tusci* Etruscans + *-anus* -an] **1** *cap* **a** *archaic* **:** ETRUSCAN **b :** a native or inhabitant of Tuscany in Italy **2** *cap* **a :** the Italian language spoken in Tuscany **b :** the standard literary dialect of Italian **3** *usu cap* **:** a fine wheat straw of Italian origin used for hats

²tuscan \"\ *adj, usu cap* [L *tuscanus*] **1 a** *archaic* **:** ETRUSCAN **b :** relating to, situated in, inhabiting, or coming from Tuscany in Italy **2 a :** of or relating to one of the classical orders of architecture that is of Roman origin and is rudely plain in style **b :** of or relating to the art of Tuscany principally from the 14th through the 16th centuries and comprising the Florentine and Sienese schools

tuscan brown *n, often cap T* **:** a moderate brown to reddish brown that is darker than pencil-wood — called also *Etruscan*, *Mecca*, *Mohawk*

tuscan red *n, often cap T* **1 :** a moderate reddish brown that is yellower and deeper than roan, redder, slightly darker, and much stronger than mahogany, and redder, stronger, and slightly darker than oxblood — called also *madder Indian red*, *mascara* **2 :** a purplish red pigment that is an iron red made by treating ferric oxide with a lake (as an alizarin lake)

tuscan tan *n, often cap 1st T* **:** SAUTERNE 2

tus·ca·ny \-nē, -ni\ *n* -ES *often cap* [fr. *Tuscany*, region in west-central Italy] **:** COLCOTHAR 2

tus·ca·ro·ra \,təskə'rōrə, -'rȯrə\ *n, pl* **tuscarora** *or* **tuscaroras** *usu cap* [Tuscarora *Skä-rū-rĕⁿ*, lit., Indian hemp gatherers] **1 a :** an Iroquoian people of No. Carolina and later of New York and Ontario **b :** a member of such people **2 :** the language of the Tuscarora people

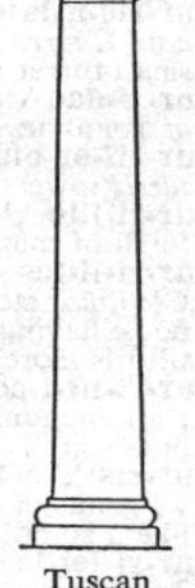
Tuscan order

tusch \'tu̇sh\ *n* -ES [G] **:** a flourish or fanfare of brass wind musical instruments and drums

tusche \'tu̇shə\ *n* -s [G, back-formation fr. *tuschen* to ink up, lay on color, fr. F *toucher*, lit., to touch — more at TOUCH] **:** a substance constituted like lithographic ink and used in lithography for drawing and painting and in etching and silk-screen process as a resist

tusch·er \-shə(r)\ *n* -s [*tusche* + *-er*] **:** one that prepares drawings on lithographic stones or plates using tusche and a steel pen

tus·cu·lan \'təskyələn\ *adj, usu cap* [L *Tusculanus*, fr. *Tusculum*, ancient town of Latium + L *-anus* -an] **:** of or relating to ancient Tusculum

¹tush \'təsh\ *n* -ES [ME *tusch*, fr. OE *tūsc*; akin to OFris *tusk* tooth, Goth *tunthus* — more at TOOTH] **:** a long pointed tooth **:** TUSK: as **a :** a horse's canine **b :** a small or dwarfed tusk in an Indian elephant

²tush \"\ *interj* [ME *tussch*] — used to express disdain, contempt or reproach ⟨~; these are trifles, and mere old wives' tales —Christopher Marlowe⟩

³tush \'tu̇sh\ *or* **tush·in** \-shə̇n\ *n, pl* **tush** *or* **tushes** *or* **tushin** *or* **tushins** *usu cap* **:** a member of a Georgian people north of Tiflis

tushed \'təsht\ *adj* **:** having tushes **:** TUSKED

tush·ery \'təshərē\ *n* -ES [²*tush* + *-ery*] **:** writing of poor quality distinguished esp. by the presence of affectedly archaic diction

tu·si *also* **tus·si** \'tüsē, -si\ *or* **tut·si** \'tüts-\ *n, pl* **tusi** *or* **tusis** *also* **tussi** *or* **tussis** *or* **tutsi** *or* **tutsis** *usu cap* **:** the ruling and cattle-owning class of the Rundi in Urundi in East Africa who presumably are cognate with the Hima people northward and whose extreme average height suggests an affinity with the Nilotes — called also *Watusi*

¹tusk \'təsk\ *n* -s [ME, alter. of *tux*, fr. OE *tūx*; akin to OE *tūsc* tush — more at TUSH] **1 a :** an elongated greatly enlarged tooth that projects when the mouth is closed, serves to dig up food or as a weapon, and is usu. a canine tooth but on an elephant an incisor **b :** a long protruding tooth **2 :** one of the small projections on a tusk tenon

²tusk \"\ *vb* -ED/-ING/-S *vt* **1 :** to dig or turn up with a tusk; *also* **:** to gash or gore with a tusk in the manner of an elephant **2 :** to equip or adorn with or as if with tusks ~ *vi* **1 :** to thrust or dig up the ground with a tusk **2 :** to bare or gnash the teeth

³tusk \"\ *n* -s [Shetland Norse; akin to Norw, Dan, & Sw *torsk* codfish — more at TORSK] **:** CUSK 1

tusked \-kt\ *adj* [ME, fr. *tusk* + *-ed*] **1 :** furnished with or having tusks **2** *heraldry* **:** having teeth or tusks

tus·ke·gee \,tə'skēgē\ *n, pl* **tuskegee** *or* **tuskegees** *usu cap* **1 :** a Muskogean people of east central Alabama **2 :** a member of the Tuskegee people — compare CRUK

tusk·er \'təskə(r)\ *n* -s [¹*tusk* + *-er*] **:** an animal having tusks; *specif* **:** a male elephant with two normally developed tusks — compare HINE

tusk·less \-klə̇s\ *adj* **:** devoid of a tusk

tusklike \'=,=\ *adj* **:** resembling a tusk esp. in exceptional size or in form ⟨a ~ canine tooth⟩

tusk shell *n* **:** TOOTH SHELL

tusk tenon *n* **:** a tenon strengthened by one or more smaller tenons underneath forming a steplike outline

tusk tenon

tusky \'təskē\ *adj* -ER/-EST **:** having tusks

tus·sah \'təsə\ *or* **tus·sore** \'təsō(ə)r, -sȯ(ə)r\ *also* **tus·ser** *or* **tus·sur** \'təsə(r)\ *n* -s [Hindi *tasar*] **1 :** an Oriental silkworm that is the larva of a moth (*Antheraea paphia* syn. *A. mylitta*) and that produces a brownish silk; *also* **:** a sometimes cultivated Chinese silkworm (*A. pernyi*) producing a similar silk **2 a :** the uneven tan filament produced by the wild silkworms of China and India that is coarser, stronger, and shorter than cultivated silk **b :** any of various fabrics (as pongee and shantung) made of this silk and used in its natural tan color or dyed

tus·sal \'təsəl\ *adj* [L *tussis* cough + E *-al*; perh. akin to L *tundere* to strike — more at STUTTER] **:** relating to or manifested by a cough

tus·sic \'təsik\ *adj* [LL *tussicus*, fr. L *tussis* + *-icus* -ic] **:** relating to or manifested by cough

tussie-mussie *var of* TUZZY-MUZZY

tus·si·la·go \,təsə'lā(,)gō\ *n, cap* [NL, fr. L, coltsfoot, irreg. fr. *tussis* cough; prob. fr. the use of the coltsfoot in folk medicine as a cough remedy] **:** a monotypic genus of low creeping yellow-flowered perennial composite herbs comprising the coltsfoots

tus·sis \'təsə̇s\ *n* -ES [L] **:** COUGH

tus·sive \'təsiv, -sēv *also* -səv\ *adj* [L *tussis* + E *-ive*] **:** relating to, of the nature of, or caused by a cough

¹tus·sle \'təsəl\ *vb* **tussled**; **tussled**; **tussling** \-s(ə)liŋ\ **tussles** [ME *tussillen*, freq. of *-tusen*, *-tousen* to touse — more at TOUSE] *vi* **:** to struggle esp. roughly or violently **:** SCUFFLE — usu. used with *with* ⟨likes to ~ with a large tuna⟩ ⟨will ~ with the university's postwar development budget —*Newsweek*⟩ ⟨a strong man who could ~ with evil and conquer —Vera Caspary⟩ ~ *vt, archaic* **:** to struggle or scuffle with **syn** see WRESTLE

²tussle \"\ *n* -s **1 :** a physical contest or struggle **:** SCUFFLE ⟨a ~ to get through the door first⟩ ⟨a hard ~ with the nasty sea —*Appalachia*⟩ **2 :** a rough argument, controversy, or struggle against difficult odds for success ⟨a constant ~ with insomnia —Lucien Price⟩ ⟨a sharp ~ with temptation —Samuel Butler †1902⟩ ⟨a constant ~ to find the money to pay our bills —Eileen McCarthy⟩ ⟨his lifelong ~ . . . with the intricacies of the language —B.D.Wolfe⟩

tus·sock \'təsək, -sēk\ *n* -s [origin unknown] **1 a :** a dense tuft (as of grass or hair) **b :** a small hummock of more solid ground in marsh or bog usu. covered with and bound together by the roots of low vegetation (as grasses or sedges) ⟨raised ~s of blueberries⟩ ⟨crossed the marsh by jumping from ~ to ~⟩ **c** *also* **tussock land** *chiefly NewZeal* **:** land covered with tussock grasses **d :** TUSSOCK SEDGE **2 :** TUSSOCK MOTH

tussock bellflower *n* **:** a perennial bellflower (*Campanula carpatica*) that grows in clumps with stems decumbent and spreading and has solitary flowers with an open bell-shaped corolla

tussock caterpillar *n* **:** a caterpillar that is the larva of a tussock moth, is covered with long tufts or bushes of hair, and includes several which eat the leaves of various shade and fruit trees and often become destructive pests

tus·socked \-kt\ *adj* **:** having or characterized by the presence of tussocks; *also* **:** covered with tussock grass

tus·sock·er \-kə(r)\ *n* -s *NewZeal* **:** TRAMP

tussock grass *n* **:** any of various grasses or sedges that typically grow in tussocks: as **a :** a tall stout cespitose grass (*Poa flabellata*) valuable for fodder introduced into Scotland from the Falkland islands **b :** an Australian grass (*Poa caespitosa*) **c :** SMUT GRASS **d :** GREAT BULRUSH **e :** a sedge that forms dense tufts in wet meadows or boglands; *esp* **:** TUSSOCK SEDGE

tussock moth *n* **:** any of numerous dull-colored moths esp. of the family Lymantriidae which in most of the common forms have wingless females

tussock sedge *n* **:** a common No. American sedge (*Carex stricta*) growing in dense tufted clumps and having wiry stems and leaves that are much used in making matting

tus·socky \-kē\ *adj* **:** having the form of tussocks **:** full of or covered with tussocks or tufts ⟨a cliff covered with ~ bents —H.S.Tegner⟩

¹tussore *var of* TUSSAH

²tus·sore \'təsō(ə)r, -sȯ(ə)r\ *n* -s **:** SEASHELL PINK

tussur *var of* TUSSAH

¹tut \'tu̇t, 'tət\ *n* -s [origin unknown] **:** a game of ball (as rounders); *also* **:** a base in rounders

²tut *the actual sound represented by the spelling "tut" is made by placing the tip of the tongue against the alveolar ridge and suddenly sucking in air; often read as* 'tət, *usu* -əd·+V\ *or* **tut–tut** *interj* [origin unknown] — used to express disapproval or disbelief ⟨~, ~, you shouldn't listen in on such conversations —Erle Stanley Gardner⟩

³tut \'tət\ *n* -s [origin unknown] *dial Eng* **:** PIECE — used esp. in the phrases *by tut*, *by the tut*, and *upon tut*; compare TUTWORK

tu·ta·nia \t(y)ü'tānēə\ *n* -s [William *Tut*in, 18th cent. Eng. manufacturer + Brit*annia* (metal)] **:** a silver-white alloy of tin with other metals (as antimony and copper) that is used for tableware

tutball \'=,=\ *n* [¹*tut* + *ball*] *dial Eng* **:** STOOLBALL, ROUNDERS

tu·tcho·ne \tü'chōnē\ *n, pl* **tutchone** *or* **tutchones** *usu cap* **1 :** an Athapaskan people of southwestern Yukon, Alaska **2 :** a member of the Tutchone people

tu·tee \(')t(y)ü;tē\ *n* -s [²*tutor* + *-ee*] **:** one who is being tutored **:** PUPIL ⟨each advisee or ~ was working . . . in a different corner of a very wide field —Mary McCarthy⟩

tu·te·la \t(y)ü'tēlə\ *n, pl* **tute·lae** \-ē,lē\ [L, protection, guardianship, guardian] **1** *Roman, civil, & Scots law* **:** the right or power of a tutor over his ward **:** the relation of a tutor to his ward or pupil **2** *Roman law* **:** a guardianship over a woman regardless of age who is not under marital or paternal power exercised by certain of her relatives by law

tu·te·lage \'t(y)üd·ᵊlij, -üt²l-, -ᵊlēj\ *n* -s [L *tutela* protection, guardianship, guardian (fr. *tutus*, past part. of *tuērī* to look at, protect, guard) + E *-age* — more at TUITION] **1 :** an act or action of guarding or protecting **:** GUARDIANSHIP, PROTECTION **2 :** the state of being under a guardian or tutor; *also* **:** the right or power of a tutor over his pupil **:** DEPENDENCE **3 a :** INSTRUCTION; *esp* **:** individual instruction accompanied by close personal attention and a conscious attempt at guidance ⟨were held together by the firm solicitude of the publisher's widow —Willa Cather⟩ ⟨under his ~ she trained for a contest —*Current Biog.*⟩ **b :** a determining influence exerted over an individual by a person, school, or movement ⟨began his intellectual career under the ~ of the neo-Kantians —J.G.Gray⟩

¹tu·te·lar \-ᵊlə(r)\ *adj* [LL *tutelaris*, fr. L *tutela* + *-aris* -ar] **:** TUTELARY ⟨a ~ deity⟩

²tutelar \"\ *n* -s **:** one that is tutelary

¹tu·te·lary \'t(y)üd·ᵊl,erē, -üt²l-, -ri\ *adj* [L *tutelarius*, n., guardian, fr. *tutela* + *-arius* -ary] **1 :** having the guardianship or charge of protecting a person or a thing **:** GUARDIAN, PROTECTING ⟨~ goddesses⟩ **2 :** of or relating to a guardian or to the protection afforded by a guardian ⟨~ authority⟩

²tutelary \"\ *n* -ES **:** a tutelary power (as a deity)

tu·te·lo \tü'tā(,)lō\ *n, pl* **tutelo** *or* **tutelos** *usu cap* **1 a :** a Siouan people of Virginia and No. Carolina **b :** a member of such people **2 :** the language of the Tutelo people

tu·tin \'tütə̇n\ *n* -s [¹*tutu* + *-in*] **:** a poisonous crystalline glucoside $C_{15}H_{18}O_6$ obtained from the tutu and other plants of the genus *Coriaria*

tu·ti·or·ism \'t(y)üshēə,rizəm, -üd·ē-\ *n* -s [L *tutior* safer (comp. of *tutus* safe, fr. past part. of *tuērī* to look at, protect, guard) + E *-ism* — more at TUITION] **:** a viewpoint in the probabilistic controversy that the argument favoring liberty as distinguished from law must be either certain or the most probable of all possible opinions to furnish a basis for action — compare PROBABILISM 2

tu·ti·or·ist \-,rə̇st\ *n* -s [L *tutior* + E *-ist*] **:** an adherent or advocate of tutiorism

tut money *n, dial Eng* **:** pay for tutwork

¹tu·tor \'t(y)üd·ə(r), -ütə-\ *n* -s [ME *tutour*, *tutor*, fr. MF & L; MF *tuteur*, fr. L *tutor*, fr. *tutus* (past part. of *tuērī* to look at, protect, guard) + *-or* — more at TUITION] **1 :** a person charged with the instruction and guidance of another: as **a :** a private teacher or instructor **:** MENTOR **b :** a college teacher esp. in a British university who guides the individual studies of undergraduates working in his special field **c :** a college teacher ranking below an instructor **d :** a college officer having administrative or counseling functions **2 :** a person in Roman and civil law who has the charge of the person and estate of a pupil or child under the age of puberty — see TUTOR DATIVE; compare CURATOR 1, GUARDIAN 3

²tutor \"\ *vb* -ED/-ING/-S *vt* **1 :** to have the guardianship, tutelage, or care of **2 :** to teach, guide, or instruct usu. on an individual basis and in a special subject or for a particular occasion or purpose **:** COACH ⟨~*ed* in Latin⟩ ⟨has never been ~*ed* in patience⟩ **3 :** to inform or instruct secretly or underhandedly ⟨~ a witness⟩ ⟨~*ed* in the art of deceit⟩ ~ *vi* **1 :** to do the work of a tutor; *specif* **:** to give private instruction **2 :** to receive instruction esp. privately ⟨had to ~ in Latin in order to pass⟩ **syn** see TEACH

tu·tor·age \-ərij\ *n* -s [¹*tutor* + *-age*] **:** the office, function, or work of a tutor **:** TUTORSHIP, TUITION

tutor dative *n* [part trans. of L *tutor dativus*] **:** a guardian appointed by a Roman magistrate in the absence of a testamentary guardian or a statutory guardian from among the close relatives who is entitled to act without confirmation by any magistrate in accordance with a certain order of preference; *sometimes* **:** a testamentary guardian

tu·tor·ess \-ərə̇s\ *n* -ES **:** a female tutor

tu·tor·hood \-ə(r),hu̇d\ *n* -s [¹*tutor* + *-hood*] **1 :** TUTORSHIP, TUTORAGE **2 :** TUTORS

¹tu·to·ri·al \t(y)ü'tōrēəl, -'tȯr-\ *adj* [L *tutorius* of a tutor (fr. *tutor*) + E *-al*] **:** of, relating to, or involving a tutor ⟨a ~ position⟩ ⟨the ~ staff⟩ ⟨a ~ manner⟩ ⟨the ~ method⟩

²tutorial \"\ *n* -s **:** a class or seminar that is conducted by a tutor for a single student or for a small number of students and that consists mainly of discussion and individual instruction

tu·tor·less \'t(y)üd·ə(r)lə̇s\ *adj* **:** being without a tutor

tu·tor·ly *adj* **:** of, relating to, or befitting a tutor

tu·tor·ship \-(r),ship\ *n* -s [¹*tutor* + *-ship*] **1 :** the office, function, or practice of a tutor ⟨the ~ may be held for a year⟩ **2 :** TUTELAGE 3 ⟨under the ~ of her parents⟩

tu·toy·er \,tütwə'yā\ *vt* -ED/-ING/-S [F, to address with the pronoun *tu* ("thou"), fr. MF, fr. *tu* thou, fr. L — more at THOU] **:** to address familiarly

tu·trix \'t(y)ü·triks\ *n, pl* **tutri·ces** \t(y)ü·'trī(,)sēz, 't(y)ü·trə,sēz\ *or* **tutrixes** [LL, fem. of L *tutor*] **:** TUTORESS

tuts *pl of* TUT

tut·san \'tətsən\ *n* -s [ME *totsane*, *toutsayne*, fr. (assumed) MF *toute-saine* (whence F), fr. *toute* (fem. of *tout* all, fr. — assumed — VL *tottus*, alter. of L *totus*) + *saine*, fem. of *sain* healthy, fr. L *sanus* healthy, sane] **:** a Eurasian St.-John's-wort (*Hypericum androsaemum*) from which a healing salve is made in Spain

tutsi *usu cap, var of* TUSI

tut·te le cor·de \'tüd·ālā'kȯrdā\ *adv* (*or adj*) [It, lit., all the strings] **:** TRE CORDE

¹tut·ti \'tüd·|ē, 'tu̇|, |t|, |i\ *adj* (*or adv*) [It, masc. pl. of *tutto* all, fr. (assumed) VL *tottus*, alter. of L *totus*] **:** ALL — used as a direction in music for voices or instruments to sing or play together; compare SOLO

²tutti \"\ *n* -s **1 :** a passage performed by all the players or singers **2 :** the total tonal effect produced by an orchestra or chorus performing together

tut·ti-frut·ti \'tüd·|ē'früd·|ē, 'tu̇t|...üt|, |i...|i\ *n* -s [It *tutti frutti*, lit., all fruits] **:** a confection or ice cream containing chopped usu. candied fruits

tut-tut *var of* TUT

¹tut·ty \'təd·ē\ *n* -ES [ME *tutie*, fr. MF, fr. Ar *tūtiyā'*, fr. Per, fr. Skt *tuttha*, *tūtaka*] **:** a yellow or brown amorphous substance that is obtained as a sublimation product in the flues of furnaces smelting zinc and that consists of a crude zinc oxide

²tut·ty \'təti\ *n* -ES [origin unknown] *dial Eng* **:** FLOWER, NOSEGAY

¹tu·tu \'tü,tü\ *n* -s [Maori] **:** any of several New Zealand shrubs or small trees of the genus *Coriaria*; *esp* **:** a shrubby tree (*C. ruscifolia*) with a juicy black edible receptacle consisting of the enlarged fleshy petals and enclosing a dry fruit with a poisonous seed

²tutu \"\ *n* -s [F, fr. (baby talk) *cucu*, *tutu* backside, alter. of *cul* — more at CULET] **:** a very short projecting skirt worn by a ballet dancer

³tutu \"\ *n* -s [Hawaiian *tūtū*] *Hawaii* **:** GRANNY, GRANDPA

tutu

¹tu·tu·i·lan \,tütü'ēlən\ *adj, usu cap* [*Tutuila*, chief island of American Samoa in the southwestern Pacific + E *-an*] **:** relating to, situated in, inhabiting, or coming from Tutuila

²tutuilan \"\ *n* -s *cap* **:** a native or inhabitant of Tutuila

tutu ta·glio·ni \-täl'yōnē\ *n, usu cap 2d T* [after Maria *Taglioni* †1884 Ital. ballet dancer] **:** an ankle-length tutu

tu·tut·ni \tü'tətnē\ *n, pl* **tututni** *or* **tututnis** *usu cap* **1 :** an Athapaskan people or group of peoples of the lower Rogue river valley and adjacent Pacific coast in Oregon **2 :** a member of the Tututni people or group of peoples

tutwork \'⸗,⸗\ *n* [[3]*tut* + *work*] *dial Eng* **:** PIECEWORK; *specif* **:** excavation in Cornwall paid for by measure or by weight

tu·vin·i·an \tü'vinēən\ *n* -S *cap* [*Tuva*, autonomous region in U. S. S. R. + E *-inian* (as in *Abyssinian*)] **:** TANNU-TUVAN

tu-whit tu-whoo \tü'(h)wit·tü'(h)wü\ *n* [imit.] **:** the cry of an owl

tux \'təks\ *n* -ES [by shortening] **:** TUXEDO

tux·e·do \,tək'sē(,)dō, -ēdə\ *n* -ES [fr. *Tuxedo* Park, resort near *Tuxedo* Lake, N. Y.] **1 a** *also* **tuxedo jacket :** a single-breasted or double-breasted jacket usu. black or midnight blue made with notched silk lapels **b :** semiformal evening dress for men — compare EVENING DRESS b(2) **2** *also* **tuxedo coat :** a woman's unbelted straight-hanging coat characterized by a single band forming the collar and the wide full-length lapels

tuxedo sofa *n* **:** an upholstered sofa with slightly curved arms that are the same height as the back

tuxedo sofa

tu·yere \tü'ye(ə)r, twē'-, 'twi(ə)r\ *n* -S [F *tuyère*, fr. MF *tuyere*, fr. *tuyau* pipe, fr. OF *tuel*, *tuyau* — more at TEWEL] **:** a nozzle through which an air blast is delivered to a forge or blast furnace; *also* **:** a port or vent between tiered grate sections of a boiler furnace

tuyere box *n* **:** an air belt or air chamber from which air is supplied to the tuyeres in a Bessemer converter

tuyere notch *also* **tuyere arch** *n* **:** an opening in the wall of a furnace hearth or crucible for a tuyere

tuz·la \'tüzlə\ *n* -S *usu cap* [Turk, fr. Lake *Tuz*, Turkey] **:** a central Anatolian rug very similar to a Konia

tuz·zy-muz·zy \'təzē'məzē\ *also* **tus·sie-mus·sie** \'təsē-'məsē\ *n, pl* **tuzzy-muzzies** *also* **tussie-mussies** [ME *tusmose*, *tussemose*] *archaic* **:** a garland of flowers **:** NOSEGAY

TV \(')tē¦vē *sometimes* 'tē‚vē *or* -vi\ *abbr or n* -S television

TV *abbr* terminal velocity

TVI *abbr* television interference

tw *abbr* **1** *cap* Twaddell (hydrometer) **2** twisted

[1]**twa** \'twȧ, 'twȯ\ *or* **twae** \'twā, 'twē\ *Scot var of* TWO

[2]**twa** \'twä\ *n, pl* **twa** *or* **twas** *usu cap* **1 :** any of several diverse peoples of central and southern Africa **2 :** a member of one of the Twa peoples

twad·dell \(')twä¦del *also* (')twȯ¦del *or* '⸗‚dᵊl\ *adj, usu cap* [*Twaddell* (*hydrometer*)] **:** according to the reading of a Twaddell hydrometer ⟨degrees ~⟩

twaddell hydrometer *n, usu cap T* [after William *Twaddell* †1840? Scot. inventor] **:** a hydrometer for liquids heavier than water graduated with an arbitrary scale to give specific gravity when a reading is multiplied by 0.005 and added to unity

[1]**twad·dle** \'twädᵊl *also* -wȯd-\ *n* -S [prob. alter. of [2]*twattle*] **1 :** empty silly talk **:** idle chatter **:** GABBLE ⟨~ about the poet's amorous intrigues —*Times Lit. Supp.*⟩ ⟨that reasoning was unadulterated ~ —F.D.Roosevelt⟩ **2 :** TWADDLER

[2]**twaddle** \"\ *vb* **twaddled; twaddled; twaddling** \-d(ᵊ)liŋ\ **twaddles** [prob. alter. of [1]*twattle*] **:** PRATE, BABBLE

twad·dler \-d(ᵊ)lə(r)\ *n* -S **:** one that writes or talks twaddle

twaddling *adj* **1 :** EMPTY, TRIVIAL **2 :** given to talking twaddle ⟨boot out that ~ doctor —Marcia Davenport⟩

twad·dly \-d(ᵊ)lē, -li\ *adj* **:** talking twaddle **:** composed of twaddle

[1]**twain** \'twān\ *adj* [ME *tweyen*, *twein*, *twain*, adj. & pron., fr. OE *twēgen*, nom. & accus. masc. — more at TWO] *archaic* **:** TWO ⟨Nature's ~ circumscriptions of man's station —H.B.Alexander⟩

[2]**twain** \"\ *pron* [ME *tweyen*, *twein*, *twain*] **:** TWO ⟨mark ~⟩

[3]**twain** \"\ *n* -S [ME *tweyen*, *twein*, *twain*, fr. *tweyen*, *twein*, *twain*, adj. & pron.] **1 :** TWO **2 :** COUPLE, PAIR ⟨the doings of this talented ~ —Osbert Sitwell⟩ — **in twain** *adv* **:** in halves **:** into two parts **:** APART, ASUNDER ⟨one mountain at the base of which we passed was literally split *in twain* —Francis Kingdon-Ward⟩

[4]**twain** \"\ *vb* -ED/-ING/-S [ME *twaynen*, fr. *tweyen*, *twein*, *twain*, adj.] **:** DIVIDE, PART, SUNDER

twain cloud *n* **:** CUMULOSTRATUS

twaite \'twāt\ *or* **twaite shad** *also* **thwaite** *or* **thwaite shad** \'t(h)wāt-\ *n* -S [origin unknown] **:** a European shad (*Alosa finta*)

twal *or* **twall** \'twal\ *Scot var of* TWELVE

twa·na \'twänə\ *n, pl* **twana** *or* **twanas** *usu cap* **1 a :** a Salishan people of the Hood canal region in Washington **b :** a member of such people **2 :** a language of the Twana people

[1]**twang** \'twaŋ, -aiŋ\ *n* -S [imit.] **1 :** a harsh quick ringing sound like that of a plucked bowstring ⟨could hear the ~ and slam of a screen door —Laurence Critchell⟩ **2 a :** nasal speech or resonance — called also *nasal twang* ⟨the ~ of the backwoods journalist —Ben Crisler⟩ **b :** the characteristic speech of a region, locality, or group of people ⟨a cockney ~⟩ ⟨the ~ of native speech —Hersteinn Palsson⟩ ⟨a good clean American ~ —D.C.Peattie⟩ **3 a :** an act of plucking or twitching **:** a sharp picking or pulling **b :** PANG, TWINGE ⟨feel ~*s* of conscience —R.L.Neuberger⟩

[2]**twang** \"\ *vb* -ED/-ING/-S *vi* **1 a :** to give forth the quick harsh ringing sound of or as if of the plucked string of a bow or a musical instrument ⟨the bow ~*ed* and the arrow shot across —T.B.Costain⟩ ⟨the fence gate ~*ed* —Elizabeth Bowen⟩ **b :** to produce a twanging sound by or as if by plucking a stringed musical instrument ⟨~*ed* away at his guitar⟩ **2 :** to speak or sound with a nasal intonation ⟨the voices of the card players came ~*ing* up the stairwell —Jean Stafford⟩ **3 :** to vibrate, throb, or twitch with or as if with pain or tension ⟨a blistered heel, a ~*ing* tendon —D.R.Brower⟩ ⟨their eyeballs danced and their muscles ~*ed* —*English Digest*⟩ ~ *vt* **1 a :** to cause to sound with a twang **:** pluck the strings of ⟨encouraged them to ~ lutes, scrape fiddles and burst into humorous song —John Blofeld⟩ **b :** to play (music) by plucking a stringed instrument **:** pick or beat out (a tune) ⟨banjo players ~*ed* music for a breakdown —*Amer. Guide Series: Fla.*⟩ **2 :** to utter or pronounce with a nasal twang ⟨the high timbre with which he ~*ed* out his cynicisms —Josephine Pinckney⟩ **3 a :** to pluck the string of (a bow) ⟨~*ed* his bow⟩ **b :** to discharge (an arrow) from a bow ⟨~*ed* off an arrow that missed the deer⟩

[3]**twang** \"\ *n* -S [alter. (influenced by [1]*twang*) of *tang*] **1 :** a persisting flavor, taste, or odor **:** TAINT, TANG ⟨butter left uncovered in a refrigerator readily takes on a ~ from other foods⟩ **2 :** NOTE, SUGGESTION, TRACE ⟨likes a sporty ~ about his apparel —*advt*⟩

twang·i·ness \'twaŋēnə̇s, -aiŋ-, -ŋinə̇s\ *n* -ES **:** the quality or state of being twangy **:** the resonance of a plucked string or of nasal intonation

[1]**twan·gle** \'twaŋgəl, -aiŋ-\ *vb* **twangled; twangled; twangling** \-g(ə)liŋ\ **twangles** [freq. of [2]*twang*] **:** TWANG ⟨held the strands on either side so that the snapped ends could not ~ as they broke loose —John Brophy⟩

[2]**twangle** \"\ *n* -S **:** a twanging sound ⟨the spinet player . . . was playing ~*s* on his keyboard —Christopher Morley⟩

twangy \-gē, -gi\ *adj* -ER/-EST **1 :** having the resonance of a plucked string ⟨heard the parlor clock strike twelve with its old ~ chime —Helen Eustis⟩ **2 :** having the resonance of nasal intonation ⟨his voice was a high, ~, unmusical New England drawl —Irving Stone⟩

twank \'twaŋk, -aiŋk\ *vb* -ED/-ING/-S [imit.] *vi, dial chiefly Eng* **:** to sound with an abrupt twang ~ *vt, dial chiefly Eng* **:** to cause to sound with an abrupt twang

twan·kay tea *or* **twan·key tea** \'twaŋ,kā-, -(,)kē-\ *n, usu cap 1st T* [fr. Chin (Pek) *T'un*[2]*-ch'i*[1] (Tunki), town in Anhwei prov., China] **:** a green tea of inferior quality and of open leaves

twa·some \'twȧsəm, -wȯs-\ *Scot var of* TWOSOME

twat \'twä|t *also* 'twȯ|; *usu* |d·+V\ *n* -S [origin unknown] **1 :** VULVA — usu. considered vulgar **2** *slang* **:** BUTTOCKS **3** *slang* **:** WOMAN

twatch·el \'twachəl\ *n* -S [ME angel*twacche* earthworm + *-el* — more at ANGLETWITCH] **:** an earthworm used as bait by a fisherman

[1]**twat·tle** \'twätᵊl\ *vi* -ED/-ING/-S [perh. alter. of [1]*tattle*] *dial Eng* **:** to talk idly **:** CHATTER, PRATE, TWADDLE

[2]**twattle** \"\ *n* -S *dial* **:** the act of prating **:** idle talk **:** TWADDLE

t wave \'tē,wāv\ *n, usu cap T* **:** the deflection of the electrocardiogram produced during the retreat of the excitation wave from the ventricle — compare P WAVE, QRS COMPLEX

tway \'twā\ *dial Brit var of* TWO

tway·blade \'twā,blād\ *n* **:** any of several orchids having a pair of leaves; *esp* **:** a plant of either of two genera (*Listera* and *Liparis*)

tweag \'twēg\ *dial var of* TWEAK

[1]**tweak** \'twēk\ *vb* -ED/-ING/-S [alter. of earlier *twick*, fr. ME *twikken*, fr. OE *twiccian* to pluck, catch hold of — more at TWITCH] *vt* **1 :** to pinch and pull with a sudden jerk and twist **:** JERK, JOG, SNATCH, TWITCH ⟨elevated the gun barrel . . . and ~*ed* the lanyard —Arthur Mayse⟩ ⟨~*ed* his memory —Olive H. Prouty⟩ ⟨figures long standard . . . are ~*ed* across a minuscule stage —H.M.Robinson⟩ ⟨~*ed* the bulbous end of his nose —Francis King⟩ **2 :** to pull the nose of **:** pull by the nose ⟨political techniques of ~*ing* babies and shaking hands —*Springfield* (*Mass.*) *Union*⟩ ~ *vi* **:** TWITCH ⟨he sat . . . ~*ing* feebly and blinking his eyes —Richard Church⟩ ⟨has been ~*ing* at my conscience ever since —K.I.Brown⟩

[2]**tweak** \"\ *n* -S **1 :** an act of tweaking **:** a sharp pinch or jerk **:** TWIST, TWITCH ⟨a ~ of the nose⟩ **2 :** AGITATION, DISTRESS

tweaky \'twēkē, -ki\ *adj* -ER/-EST **1 :** THIN, NERVOUS, TWITCHY **2 :** ACID, BITING, SHARP

twee \'twē\ *n* -S [imit.] **:** a thin or shrill piping note (as of a horn or small bird)

tweed \'twēd\ *n* -S [alter. (influenced by *Tweed* river, Scotland) of [1]*tweel*] **1 a :** a woolen coating and suiting fabric of Scottish origin having a rough appearance and made usu. in twill weaves **b :** an imitation of this fabric **2 tweeds** *pl* **:** tweed clothing **:** a tweed suit ⟨the man in the gray ~*s* —P.B.Kyne⟩

tweed·dale \'twēd,dāl\ *adj, usu cap* [fr. *Tweeddale* (Peeblesshire) County, Scotland] **:** PEEBLESSHIRE

tweed·ed \'twēdə̇d\ *adj* **:** wearing tweeds **:** clothed in tweeds ⟨a sprucely ~ man in his fifties —*New Yorker*⟩

tweed·i·ness \'twēdēnə̇s, -din-\ *n* -ES **:** the quality or state of being tweedy **:** a homely, informal, or outdoor look or character seen in one wearing tweeds

[1]**twee·dle** \'twēdᵊl\ *vb* **tweedled; tweedled; tweedling** \-d(ᵊ)liŋ\ **tweedles** [prob. of imit. origin] *vi* **1 :** to sing or whistle in modulation **:** PIPE, CHIRP **2 :** to play negligently on a musical instrument ~ *vt* **:** to cajole or entice by music

[2]**tweedle** \"\ *n* -S **:** a sound of tweedling ⟨the squeal and the blare and the ~ of bagpipes —W.C.Williams⟩

[3]**tweedle** \"\ *dial var of* TWIDDLE

twee·dle·dum and twee·dle·dee \,twēdᵊl'dəmən,twēdᵊl'dē\ *n, usu cap both Ts* [[1]*tweedle* + *dum* (imit. of a low musical note) & *dee* (imit. of a high musical note)] **:** two objects, persons, or groups differing superficially or insignificantly **:** a practically indistinguishable pair

tweedy \'twēdē, -di\ *adj, usu* -ER/-EST **1 :** of tweed **:** resembling or suggesting tweed in texture, color, or appearance ⟨~ attire⟩ **2 a :** given to or fond of wearing tweeds **:** dressed in tweeds **b :** homely, informal, or outdoorsy in taste, inclination, or habits

tweeg \'twēg\ *n* -S [Delaware *twi'kw*] **:** HELLBENDER 1a

[1]**tweel** \'twēl, *esp before pause or consonant* -ēəl\ *Scot var of* TWILL

[2]**tweel** \"\ *n* -S [F *tuile*, lit., tile, alter. of OF *teule*, *tiule*, fr. L *tegula* — more at THATCH] **:** the closure of a glass furnace: **a :** a clay covering for the furnace mouth **b :** a counterweighted furnace door

tween \'twēn\ *prep* [ME *twene*, short for *betwene* — more at BETWEEN] **:** BETWEEN

tween-brain \'⸗,⸗\ *n* **:** DIENCEPHALON

tween-deck \'⸗¦⸗\ *adj* **:** located or carried between decks

tween deck *n* **:** any deck of a ship but the upper or the lowest

tweeny *or* **tween·ie** \'twēnē, -ni\ *n, pl* **tweenies** [*tween* + *-y*, *-ie*] **:** BETWEENMAID

tweer *var of* TWIRE

[1]**tweet** \'twēt, *usu* -ēd·+V\ *n* -S [imit.] **1 :** a chirping note ⟨the sharp ~*s* of the referee's whistle —Nathaniel Benchley⟩ **2 :** a high note emitted by sound-reproducing equipment — contrasted with *woof*

[2]**tweet** \"\ *vb* -ED/-ING/-S **:** CHIRP ⟨songbirds are ~*ing* —Richard Bissell⟩

tweet·er \'twēd·ə(r), -ētə-\ *n* -S **:** a small loudspeaker responsive only to the higher acoustic frequencies and reproducing sounds of high pitch — compare WOOFER

twee·tle \'twēd·ᵊl, -ētᵊl\ *vb* **tweetled; tweetled; tweetling** \-d·ᵊliŋ, -t(ᵊ)liŋ\ **tweetles** [by alter.] **:** TWEEDLE ⟨the flutes *tweetling* high —Mary Deasy⟩

[1]**tweeze** *or* **tweese** \'twēz\ *n* -S [short for *etweese*, fr. pl. of *etwee*, fr. F *étui*, fr. OF *estui* container, fr. *estuier* to keep, preserve, retain, perh. fr. (assumed) VL *studiare* to take care of, fr. L *studium* zeal, application, study — more at STUDY] *obs* **:** a case of small instruments (as of a surgeon or barber) **:** ETUI

[2]**tweeze** \'twēz\ *vt* -ED/-ING/-S [back-formation fr. *tweezers*] **:** to extract, pluck, or remove with tweezers ⟨~*s* the hairs out of his ears —*Newsweek*⟩ ⟨*tweezed* out the little triangular stitches of black thread —Robert Hazel⟩

[1]**tweez·er** \-zə(r)\ *n* -S [[1]*tweeze* + *-er*] **1** *obs* **:** TWEEZE **2 :** TWEEZERS

[2]**tweezer** \"\ *vb* -ED/-ING/-S [back-formation fr. *tweezers*] *vt* **:** to draw, place, or hold with or as if with tweezers ⟨coaxing smoke from a cigarette stub which . . . he had ~*ed* between two pieces of wire —A.M.Robinson⟩ ~ *vi* **:** to use tweezers

[3]**tweezer** \"\ *n* -S [origin unknown] *dial* **:** AMERICAN MERGANSER

tweez·ers \-ə(r)z\ *n pl but sometimes sing in constr* [[1]*tweeze* + *-er* + *-s*] **1 :** any of various small pincer-shaped tools used for plucking, holding, or manipulating (as for removing superfluous hair or handling watch parts) **2** *obs* **:** ETUI, TWEEZE

tweezers

[1]**twelfth** \'twel|f(t)th, |ft, -eu̇|, *rapid or substand* |th; *the sound transcribed* f *may be bilabial instead of labiodental — the voiceless cognate of* b̲\ *adj* [ME *twelfte*, *twelfthe*, adj. & n., fr. OE, fr. OE *twelfta* (akin to OHG *zwelifto* twelfth, ON *tolfti*), fr. *twelf* twelve + *-ta* (fr. *-otha*, *-tha* -th) — more at TWELVE] **1 :** being number 12 in a countable series ⟨the ~ day⟩ — see NUMBER table **2 :** being one of 12 equal parts into which something is divisible ⟨a ~ share of the money⟩

[2]**twelfth** \"\ *n, pl* **twelfths** \|f(t)ths, |f(t)s\ [ME *twelfte*, *twelfthe*] **1 :** number 12 in a countable series ⟨the ~ of the month⟩ **2 :** the quotient of a unit divided by 12 **:** one of 12 equal parts of something ⟨one ~ of the total⟩ **3** *usu cap* **a** [ME *twelthe*, short for *twelfte day*, *twelthe day*] **:** EPIPHANY **b** [by shortening] **:** TWELFTHTIDE **4 a :** a musical interval comprising an octave and a fifth **b :** a note or tone at this interval **c :** an organ stop that produces tones at this interval above the pitch indicated by the notation

twelfth-cake \'⸗,⸗\ *also* **twelfth-night cake** \'⸗¦⸗-\ *n, sometimes cap T* **:** a cake made for a Twelfth Night celebration that contains a bean or a coin for determining the ruler of the feast

twelfth cranial nerve *or* **twelfth nerve** *n* **:** HYPOGLOSSAL NERVE

twelfth day *n, usu cap T* [ME *twelfte day*] **:** EPIPHANY

twelfth night *n, usu cap T&N* [ME *twelfte night*, fr. OE *twelfte niht*] **1 :** the eve preceding Epiphany marking the end of medieval Christmas festivities **2 :** the evening of Epiphany

twelfthtide *n, usu cap, obs* **:** the 12-day season after Christmas ending with Epiphany

twell \twəl, (,)twel\ *dial var of* [1]TILL

[1]**twelve** \'twelv, -eu̇v, *chiefly South* -e(ə)v\ *adj* [ME *twelf*, *twelve*, adj. & pron., fr. OE *twelf;* akin to OHG *zwelif* twelve, ON *tolf*, Goth *twalif;* all fr. a prehistoric Gmc compound whose first constituent is represented by OE *twēgen*, *twā*, *tū* two, and whose second constituent is prob. akin to Lith *-lika* (as in *dvylika* twelve, *vënůlika* eleven) — more at TWO, ELEVEN] **:** being one more than 11 in number ⟨~ years⟩ — see NUMBER table

[2]**twelve** \"\ *pron, pl in constr* [ME *twelf*, *twelve*] **:** 12 countable persons or things not specified but under consideration and being enumerated ⟨~ are here⟩ ⟨~ were found⟩

[3]**twelve** \"\ *n* -S [ME *twelf*, *twelve*, fr. *twelf*, *twelve*, adj. & pron.] **1 :** 10 and two **:** twice six **:** six times two **:** three times four **2 a :** 12 units or objects ⟨a total of ~⟩ **b :** a group or set of 12 ⟨arranged by ~*s*⟩ **3 :** the numerable quantity symbolized by the arabic numerals 12 **4 :** 12 o'clock — compare BELL table, TIME illustration **5 :** the 12th in a set or series; *esp* **:** an article of clothing of the 12th size ⟨wears ~*s*⟩ **6 twelves** *pl* **:** TWELVEMO

[1]**twelve·fold** \'⸗¦fōld\ *adj* [[1]*twelve* + *-fold*] **1 :** having 12 parts or aspects **2 :** being 12 times as large, as great, or as many as some understood size, degree, or amount ⟨a ~ increase⟩

[2]**twelvefold** \"\ *adv* **:** to 12 times as much or as many **:** by 12 times ⟨increased ~⟩

twelve hours *n pl* **1** *Scot* **a :** NOON **b** MIDNIGHT **2** *Scot* **:** a noon lunch

twelve-men's morris \'⸗,⸗-\ *n* **:** morris played with 12 counters

twelve-mile limit \'⸗¦⸗-\ *n* **:** a limit of the marginal sea of 12 miles included in the territorial waters of a state

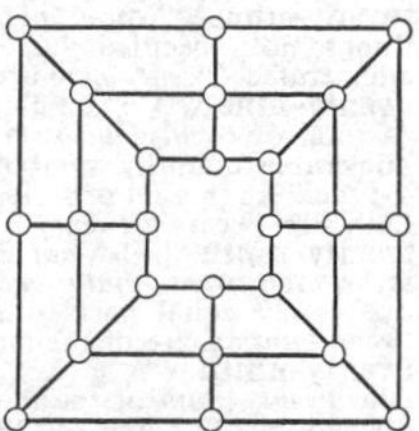
twelve-men's morris board

twelve·mo \'⸗,mō\ *n* -S [[1]*twelve* + *-mo* (as in *duodecimo*)] **:** the size of a piece of paper cut 12 from a sheet; *also* **:** paper or a page of this size — called also *duodecimo;* abbr. *12 mo;* symbol *12°;* see BOOK tables

twelvemonth \'⸗,⸗\ *n* [ME *twelfmoneth*, fr. *twelf* twelve + *moneth* month] **:** YEAR ⟨kept out of the police courts for a whole ~ —*Punch*⟩

twelve-note \'⸗¦⸗\ *adj* **:** TWELVE-TONE

twelve·pen·ny \'⸗pəni *or* -nē *or* -,pen- *Brit* '⸗pəni\ *adj* **:** sold for, worth, or costing a shilling

twelv·er \-və(r)\ *n* -S *usu cap* **:** a member of a major Shi'ite sect which acknowledges 12 imams and holds that the 12th will reappear as the Mahdi before the Last Day and of which the tenets and organization have been the state religion of Persia since the 16th century — called also *imami;* compare SEVENER

twelve-spotted asparagus beetle \'⸗¦⸗⸗-\ *n* **:** a European asparagus beetle (*Crioceris duodecimpunctata*) that is naturalized in eastern No. America

twelve-tone \'⸗¦⸗\ *adj* **:** of or relating to music based on the 12 chromatic tones of the octave used in any chosen order without regard for the major-minor system ⟨*twelve-tone* technique of composition⟩

twelve-tone row *n* **:** the 12 chromatic tones of the octave placed in a chosen fixed order and constituting with some permitted permutations and derivations the melodic and harmonic material of a movement or work — called also *tone-row*

twelve-wired bird of paradise \'⸗¦⸗-\ **:** a bird of paradise (*Seleucides ignotus*)

[1]**twen·ti·eth** \'twentēə̇th, -ntiə̇th, *in rapid speech sometimes* -wənē- *or* -ni-\ *adj* [ME *twentithe*, fr. OE *twentigotha*, fr. *twentig* twenty + *-otha* -th] **1 :** being number 20 in a countable series ⟨the ~ day⟩ — see NUMBER table **2 :** being one of 20 equal parts into which something is divisible ⟨a ~ share of the money⟩

[2]**twentieth** \"\ *n* -S **1 :** number 20 in a countable series ⟨the ~ of the month⟩ **2 :** the quotient of a unit divided by 20 **:** one of 20 equal parts of something ⟨one ~ of the total⟩

twentieth-century cut \¦⸗⸗⸗¦⸗⸗⸗-\ *n* **:** a gem cut with 80 or 88 facets with the table replaced by a low pyramidal range of facets carried to a central point — compare BRILLIANT

[1]**twen·ty** \'twentē, -nti, *in rapid speech sometimes* -wənē *or* -ni\ *adj* [ME, fr. OE *twēntig*, *twentig*, n., group of 20, fr. *twēn-*, *twen-* (akin to OE *twēgen*, *twā*, *tū* two) + *-tig* group of 10 — more at TWO, EIGHTY] **:** being one more than 19 in number ⟨~ years⟩ — see NUMBER table

[2]**twenty** \"\ *pron, pl in constr* [ME, fr. *twenty*, adj.] **:** 20 countable persons or things not specified but under consideration and being enumerated ⟨~ are here⟩ ⟨~ were found⟩

[3]**twenty** \"\ *n* -ES [ME, fr. *twenty*, pron.] **1 :** two tens **:** twice 10 **:** 10 times two **:** four times five **2 a :** 20 units or objects ⟨a total of ~⟩ **b :** a group or set of 20 ⟨arranged by *twenties*⟩ **3 :** the numerable quantity symbolized by the arabic numerals 20 **4 twenties** *pl* **a :** the numbers 20 to 29 inclusive ⟨a score in the *twenties*⟩ ⟨low grades in the *twenties*⟩ **b :** the members of a series or set of successive numbers that end in 20 to 29 inclusive ⟨the *twenties* of the preceding century⟩ ⟨lives in the *twenties* in the next block⟩ **c :** the portion of a continuum lying between 20 and 30 on a scale of measurement or segmentation ⟨temperatures in the *twenties* tomorrow⟩ ⟨a man in his *twenties*⟩ ⟨dresses selling in the *twenties*⟩ ⟨in the latitude of the *twenties*⟩ **5 :** the 20th in a set or series; *esp* **:** an article of clothing of the 20th size ⟨wears a ~⟩ **6 a :** a twenty-pound note **b :** a twenty-dollar bill

[1]**twenty-eight** \¦⸗⸗¦⸗\ *adj* **:** being one more than 27 in number ⟨*twenty-eight* years⟩ — see NUMBER table

[2]**twenty-eight** \"\ *pron, pl in constr* **:** 28 countable persons or things not specified but under consideration and being enumerated ⟨*twenty-eight* are here⟩ ⟨*twenty-eight* were found⟩

[3]**twenty-eight** \"\ *n* **1 :** eight and 20 **:** four times seven **2 a :** 28 units or objects ⟨a total of *twenty-eight*⟩ **b :** a group or set of 28 **3 :** the numerable quantity symbolized by the arabic numerals 28 **4 :** the 28th in a set or series; *esp* **:** an article of clothing of the 28th size ⟨wears a *twenty-eight*⟩

[4]**twenty-eight** \"\ *n* **:** a West Australian yellow-collared parakeet (*Platycercus zonarius semitorquatus*)

[1]**twenty-eighth** \¦⸗⸗¦⸗\ *adj* **1 :** being number 28 in a countable series ⟨the *twenty-eighth* day⟩ — see NUMBER table **2 :** being one of 28 equal parts into which something is divisible ⟨a *twenty-eighth* share of the money⟩

[2]**twenty-eighth** \"\ *n* **1 :** number 28 in a countable series ⟨the *twenty-eighth* of the month⟩ **2 :** the quotient of a unit divided by 28 **:** one of 28 equal parts of something ⟨one *twenty-eighth* of the total⟩

[1]**twenty-fifth** \¦⸗⸗¦⸗\ *adj* **1 :** being number 25 in a countable series ⟨the *twenty-fifth* day⟩ — see NUMBER table **2 :** being one of 25 equal parts into which something is divisible ⟨a *twenty-fifth* share of the money⟩

[2]**twenty-fifth** \"\ *n* **1 :** number 25 in a countable series ⟨the *twenty-fifth* day of the month⟩ **2 :** the quotient of a unit divided by 25 **:** one of 25 equal parts of something ⟨one *twenty-fifth* of the total⟩

[1]**twenty-first** \¦⸗⸗¦⸗\ *adj* **1 :** being number 21 in a countable series ⟨the *twenty-first* day⟩ — see NUMBER table **2 :** being one of 21 equal parts into which something is divisible ⟨a *twenty-first* share of the money⟩

[2]**twenty-first** \"\ *n* **1 :** number 21 in a countable series ⟨the *twenty-first* of the month⟩ **2 :** the quotient of a unit divided by 21 **:** one of 21 equal parts of something ⟨one *twenty-first* of the total⟩

twenty-first·er \,⸗⸗'⸗ə(r)\ *n* -S [*twenty-first* + *-er*] **:** the celebration of a 21st birthday

[1]**twenty-five** \¦⸗⸗¦⸗\ *adj* **:** being one more than 24 in number ⟨*twenty-five* years⟩ — see NUMBER table

[2]**twenty-five** \"\ *pron, pl in constr* **:** 25 countable persons or things not specified but under consideration and being enumerated ⟨*twenty-five* are here⟩ ⟨*twenty-five* were found⟩

[3]**twenty-five** \"\ *n* **1 :** five and 20 **:** five fives **:** the square of five **2 a :** 25 units or objects ⟨a total of *twenty-five*⟩ **b :** a group or set of 25 ⟨arranged by *twenty-fives*⟩ **3 :** the numerable quantity symbolized by the arabic numerals 25 **4 :** the 25th in a set or series; *esp* **:** an article of clothing of the 25th size ⟨wears a *twenty-five*⟩ **5 :** a 25-caliber pistol — usu. written .25

[1]**twenty-four** \¦⸗⸗¦⸗\ *adj* **:** being one more than 23 in number ⟨*twenty-four* years⟩ — see NUMBER table

[2]**twenty-four** \"\ *pron, pl in constr* **:** 24 countable persons or things not specified but under consideration and being enumerated ⟨*twenty-four* are here⟩ ⟨*twenty-four* were found⟩

³**twenty-four** \"\ *n* **1 :** four and 20 : twice 12 : 12 times two : three times eight : four times six : two dozen **2 a :** 24 units or objects ⟨a total of *twenty-four*⟩ **b :** a group or set of 24 **3 :** the numerable quantity symbolized by the arabic numerals 24 **4 :** the 24th in a set or series; *esp* : an article of clothing of the 24th size ⟨wears a *twenty-four*⟩ **5 twenty-fours** *pl, archaic* : TWENTY-FOURMO

twenty-four·mo \ˌ==ˈ=ˌmō\ *n* -s [*twenty-four* + *-mo*] : the size of a piece of paper cut 24 from a sheet; *also* : paper or a page of this size — abbr. *24mo;* symbol *24°;* see BOOK tables

¹**twenty-fourth** \ˌ==ˈ=\ *adj* **1 :** being number 24 in a countable series ⟨the *twenty-fourth* day⟩ — see NUMBER table **2 :** being one of 24 equal parts into which something is divisible ⟨a *twenty-fourth* share of the money⟩

²**twenty-fourth** \"\ *n* **1 :** number 24 in a countable series ⟨the *twenty-fourth* of the month⟩ **2 :** the quotient of a unit divided by 24 : one of 24 equal parts of something ⟨one *twenty-fourth* of the total⟩

¹**twenty-nine** \ˌ==ˈ=\ *adj* : being one more than 28 in number ⟨*twenty-nine* years⟩ — see NUMBER table

²**twenty-nine** \"\ *pron, pl in constr* : 29 countable persons or things not specified but under consideration and being enumerated ⟨*twenty-nine* are here⟩ ⟨*twenty-nine* were found⟩

³**twenty-nine** \"\ *n* **1 :** nine and 20 **2 a :** 29 units or objects ⟨a total of *twenty-nine*⟩ **b :** a group or set of 29 **3 :** the numerable quantity symbolized by the arabic numerals 29 **4 :** the 29th in a set or series; *esp* : an article of clothing of the 29th size ⟨wears a *twenty-nine*⟩

¹**twenty-ninth** \ˌ==ˈ=\ *adj* **1 :** being number 29 in a countable series ⟨the *twenty-ninth* day⟩ — see NUMBER table **2 :** being one of 29 equal parts into which something is divisible ⟨a *twenty-ninth* share of the money⟩

²**twenty-ninth** \"\ *n* **1 :** number 29 in a countable series ⟨the *twenty-ninth* of the month⟩ **2 :** the quotient of a unit divided by 29 : one of 29 equal parts of something ⟨one *twenty-ninth* of the total⟩

¹**twenty-one** \ˌ==ˈ=\ *adj* : being one more than 20 in number ⟨*twenty-one* years⟩ — see NUMBER table

²**twenty-one** \"\ *pron, pl in constr* : 21 countable persons or things not specified but under consideration and being enumerated ⟨*twenty-one* are here⟩ ⟨*twenty-one* were found⟩

³**twenty-one** \"\ *n* **1 :** one and 20 : three times seven **2 a :** 21 units or objects ⟨a total of *twenty-one*⟩ **b :** a group or set of 21 **3 :** the numerable quantity symbolized by the arabic numerals 21 **4 :** the 21st in a set or series; *esp* : an article of clothing of the 21st size ⟨wear a *twenty-one*⟩ **5** *or* **21** [trans. of F *vingt-et-un*] : a card game the object of which is to be dealt cards having a higher count than those of the dealer up to but not exceeding 21 — called also *blackjack, vingt-et-un*

twenty-penny nail \ˌ==ˈ==-\ *n* : a 4-inch nail

twenty questions *n pl but sing in constr, often cap T&Q* : a game in which one player or team tries to determine from yes and no answers to not more than 20 questions what word or object the others have chosen to be guessed

¹**twenty-second** \ˌ==ˈ==\ *adj* **1 :** being number 22 in a countable series ⟨the *twenty-second* day⟩ — see NUMBER table **2 :** being one of 22 equal parts into which something is divisible ⟨a *twenty-second* share of the money⟩

²**twenty-second** \"\ *n* **1 :** number 22 in a countable series ⟨the *twenty-second* of the month⟩ **2 :** the quotient of a unit divided by 22 : one of 22 equal parts of something ⟨one *twenty-second* of the total⟩ **3 :** a pipe-organ stop of 1-foot pitch

¹**twenty-seven** \ˌ==ˈ==\ *adj* : being one more than 26 in number ⟨*twenty-seven* years⟩ — see NUMBER table

²**twenty-seven** \"\ *pron, pl in constr* : 27 countable persons or things not specified but under consideration and being enumerated ⟨*twenty-seven* are here⟩ ⟨*twenty-seven* were found⟩

³**twenty-seven** \"\ *n* **1 :** seven and 20 : three times nine : the cube of three **2 a :** 27 units or objects ⟨a total of *twenty-seven*⟩ **b :** a group or set of 27 **3 :** the numerable quantity symbolized by the arabic numerals 27 **4 :** the 27th in a set or series; *esp* : an article of clothing of the 27th size ⟨wears a *twenty-seven*⟩

¹**twenty-seventh** \ˌ==ˈ==\ *adj* **1 :** being number 27 in a countable series ⟨the *twenty-seventh* day⟩ — see NUMBER table **2 :** being one of 27 equal parts into which something is divisible ⟨a *twenty-seventh* share of the money⟩

²**twenty-seventh** \"\ *n* **1 :** number 27 in a countable series ⟨the *twenty-seventh* day of the month⟩ **2 :** the quotient of a unit divided by 27 : one of 27 equal parts of something ⟨one *twenty-seventh* of the total⟩

¹**twenty-six** \ˌ==ˈ=\ *adj* : being one more than 25 in number ⟨*twenty-six* years⟩ — see NUMBER table

²**twenty-six** \"\ *pron, pl in constr* : 26 countable persons or things not specified but under consideration and being enumerated ⟨*twenty-six* are here⟩ ⟨*twenty-six* were found⟩

³**twenty-six** \"\ *n* **1 :** six and 20 : two times 13 **2 a :** 26 units or objects ⟨a total of *twenty-six*⟩ **b :** a group or set of 26 **3 :** the numerable quantity symbolized by the arabic numerals 26 **4 :** the 26th in a set or series; *esp* : an article of clothing of the 26th size ⟨wears a *twenty-six*⟩

⁴**twenty-six** \"\ *n* : a gambling game in which one wins if he rolls his chosen number 26 or more times in 13 rolls of 10 dice

¹**twenty-sixth** \ˌ==ˈ=\ *adj* **1 :** being number 26 in a countable series ⟨the *twenty-sixth* day⟩ — see NUMBER table **2 :** being one of 26 equal parts into which something is divisible ⟨a *twenty-sixth* share of the money⟩

²**twenty-sixth** \"\ *n* **1 :** number 26 in a countable series ⟨the *twenty-sixth* of the month⟩ **2 :** the quotient of a unit divided by 26 : one of 26 equal parts of something ⟨one *twenty-sixth* of the total⟩

¹**twenty-third** \ˌ==ˈ=\ *adj* **1 :** being number 23 in a countable series ⟨the *twenty-third* day⟩ — see NUMBER table **2 :** being one of 23 equal parts into which something is divisible ⟨a *twenty-third* share of the money⟩

²**twenty-third** \"\ *n* **1 :** number 23 in a countable series ⟨the *twenty-third* of the month⟩ **2 :** the quotient of a unit divided by 23 : one of 23 equal parts of something ⟨one *twenty-third* of the total⟩

¹**twenty-three** \ˌ==ˈ=\ *adj* : being one more than 22 in number ⟨*twenty-three* years⟩ — see NUMBER table

²**twenty-three** \"\ *pron, pl in constr* : 23 countable persons or things not specified but under consideration and being enumerated ⟨*twenty-three* are here⟩ ⟨*twenty-three* were found⟩

³**twenty-three** \"\ *n* **1 :** three and 20 **2 a :** 23 units or objects ⟨a total of *twenty-three*⟩ **b :** a group or set of 23 **3 :** the numerable quantity symbolized by the arabic numerals 23 **4 :** the 23d in a set or series; *esp* : an article of clothing of the 23d size ⟨wears a *twenty-three*⟩ **5 :** a railway telegraph signal for a message of greatest urgency **6 :** the end : that's all — compare TWENTY-THREE SKIDDOO

twenty-three skiddoo *v imper* : SCRAM ⟨*twenty-three skiddoo* to anyone who says different —H.A.Smith⟩

twenty-twenty \ˌ==ˈ==\ *or* **20/20** \"\ *adj* : having the normal visual acuity of the human eye that according to one common scale can distinguish at a distance of 20 feet characters one-third inch in diameter

¹**twenty-two** \ˌ==ˈ=\ *adj* : being one more than 21 in number ⟨*twenty-two* years⟩ — see NUMBER table

²**twenty-two** \"\ *pron, pl in constr* : 22 countable persons or things not specified but under consideration and being enumerated ⟨*twenty-two* are here⟩ ⟨*twenty-two* were found⟩

³**twenty-two** \"\ *n* **1 :** two and 20 : twice 11 : 11 times two **2 a :** 22 units or objects ⟨a total of *twenty-two*⟩ **b :** a group or set of 22 **3 :** the numerable quantity symbolized by the arabic numerals 22 **4 :** the 22d in a set or series; *esp* : an article of clothing of the 22d size ⟨wears a *twenty-two*⟩ **5 :** a 22-caliber rifle or pistol — usu. written .22

twerp *also* **twirp** \ˈtwərp, -wəp\ *n* -s [origin unknown] : an insignificant or contemptible fellow ⟨don't mind the silly ~ —Earle Birney⟩

twi *or* **tshi** *also* **tchi** \ˈchwē, ˈtwē, ˈchē\ *n* -s *usu cap* **1 :** a dialect of Akan spoken by the Akwapim people **2 :** a literary language based on the Twi dialect and used by the Akim, Akwapim, Ashanti, and other Akan-speaking peoples

twi- *prefix* [ME, fr. OE; akin to OFris & OS *twi-*, OHG *zwi-*, ON *tvi-, tvē-*, L *bi-* (fr. OL *dui-*), Gk *di-*, Lith *dvi-* twi-, OE *twēgen, twā, tū* two — more at TWO] : two : double : doubly : twice ⟨*twi*-circle⟩ ⟨*twi*-faced⟩

twi *abbr* twilight

twi·bil *or* **twi·bill** \ˈtwī,bil, -bəl\ *n* -s [ME, a kind of two-bladed ax, mattock, fr. OE *twibill*, fr. *twi-* + *bill* two-edged sword — more at BILL] **1 :** a double-headed battle-ax **2** *dial Eng* : a reaping hook esp. for cutting beans

¹**twice** \ˈtwīs\ *adv* [ME *twies, twys*, fr. OE *twiges*, fr. *twiga, twiwa* twice + *-es* -s; akin to OE *twi-* —more at TWI-] **1 :** for a first and second time : on two occasions ⟨~ absent without leave⟩ **2 :** two times : as multiplied by two : in doubled quantity, amount, or degree ⟨~ two is four⟩ ⟨would be guaranteed ~ over —*Newsweek*⟩ — **at twice** *adv* **1 :** at two different times or operations ⟨pay a debt *at twice*⟩ **2 :** at the second time or operation ⟨succeeded *at twice*⟩

²**twice** \"\ *adj, archaic* : TWOFOLD

twice-accented octave \ˌ=ˈ===-\ *n* : TWO-LINE OCTAVE

twice-born \ˈ=ˌ=\ *adj* [ME *twys borne*] **1 :** born a second time : REINCARNATED **2 :** having undergone a definite experience of fundamental moral and spiritual renewal : having experienced a religious conversion : REGENERATE ⟨the Anabaptist view that the church should consist exclusively of *twice-born* individuals⟩ **3 :** of or being one of the three upper Hindu varnas of ancient Aryan origin in which boys undergo an initiation ceremony symbolizing spiritual birth and are invested with the sacred thread

twice-laid \ˈ=ˌ=\ *adj* : made from the ends of rope and strands of used rope ⟨*twice-laid* rope⟩

twic·er \ˈtwīsə(r)\ *n* -s [¹*twice* + *-er*] **1 :** one that does something twice or does two things: as **a :** one that attends two Sunday church services **b** *Brit* : a printer who works as both compositor and pressman — usu. used disparagingly **2** *chiefly Brit* **a :** CHEAT, CROOK **b :** a two-time loser ⟨he's already a ~. Any time he's picked up carrying a gun he's liable to get life —Hartley Howard⟩

twice-stabbed ladybird \ˈ=ˌ=-\ *n* : a small black predatory beetle (*Chilocoris stigma*) of the family Coccinellidae marked with a bright orange dot on each wing cover and important as a predator on citrus scale insects in Florida

twicet \ˈtwīst\ *substand var of* TWICE

twice-told \ˈ=ˌ=\ *adj* [ME *twies told*] **1** *obs* : counted twice : reckoned or added up two times **2 a :** narrated twice **b :** HACKNEYED, OLD, TRITE — used chiefly in the phrase *a twice-told tale*

twi·child \ˈtwīchəl(d)\ *n* [*twi-* + *child*] **1 :** one who is in his dotage **2 :** DOTAGE

twick·en·ham \ˈtwik(ə)nəm\ *adj, usu cap* [fr. *Twickenham*, England] : of or from the municipal borough of Twickenham, England : of the kind or style prevalent in Twickenham

¹**twid·dle** \ˈtwid°l\ *vb* **twiddled; twiddled; twiddling** \-d(°)liŋ\ **twiddles** [origin unknown] *vi* **1 :** to be busy with trifles : act or play negligently with something : FIDDLE ⟨*twiddled* with his moustaches⟩ **2 :** to turn or jounce lightly : JIGGLE, QUIVER, TWIRL ⟨the log . . . ~s round and round in the water —J.B.S.Haldane⟩ ~ *vt* : to rotate (something) lightly or idly : play with : TURN, TWIRL ⟨vaguely *twiddled* his cigar —James Lord⟩ ⟨I closed the safe door and *twiddled* the knob —C.B.Kelland⟩ — **twiddle one's thumbs :** to spend time vacantly : do nothing ⟨kept the manager busy and left me *twiddling my thumbs*⟩

²**twiddle** \"\ *n* -s : an act of twiddling or twirling something : TURN, TWIST ⟨gave the wheel a ~ to avoid a casual dog —P.G.Wodehouse⟩

³**twiddle** \"\ *vi* **twiddled; twiddled; twiddling** \-d(°)liŋ\ **twiddles** [imit.] **1 :** to chatter or gabble idly **2 :** to play negligently on a musical instrument

twiddle-twaddle \ˈ==ˌ==\ *n* [redupl. of *twaddle*] : empty chatter : TWADDLE

twiddling line *n* **1** *obs* : a line fastened to a ship's steering wheel to steady or secure it **2 :** a line holding the rudder of an open boat in a desired position

twid·dly \ˈtwid(°)lē, -li\ *adj* -ER/-EST : TWIDDLING, TWISTING, TRIVIAL ⟨they would walk through the ~ lanes —Aldous Huxley⟩ ⟨~ food⟩

twifallow *vt* [*twi-* + *fallow*] *obs* : to plow for the second time

twi·fold \ˈtwī,fōld\ *adj* [ME, fr. OE *twifeald*, fr. *twi-* + *-feald* -fold] : TWOFOLD

twi-formed \ˈ=ˌ=\ *also* **twi-form** \ˈ=ˌ=\ *adj* [*twi-* + *formed or -form*] : having two shapes or bodies : combining incongruous constituents

¹**twig** \ˈtwig\ *n* -s [ME *twigge*, fr. OE; akin to OE *twig*, MLG *twich*, OHG *zwīg* twig, OE *twēgen, twā, tū* two — more at TWO] **1 :** a small shoot or branch usu. without its leaves : a portion of stem of no definite length or size **2 :** a minute branch of a nerve or artery ⟨auricular ~s of the coronary arteries —C.H.Best & N.B.Taylor⟩ **3 :** a divining rod ⟨with the twirl of a hazel ~ has found water on dozens of small holdings —*Irish Digest*⟩

²**twig** \"\ *vt* **twigged; twigged; twigging; twigs :** to beat with or as if with a twig : SWITCH

³**twig** \"\ *vt* **twigged; twigged; twigging; twigs** [prob. alter. of E dial. *twick* to twist, twitch, tweak, fr. ME *twikken* — more at TWEAK] : PULL, TWITCH

⁴**twig** \"\ *n* -s : PULL, TUG

⁵**twig** \"\ *vb* **twigged; twigged; twigging; twigs** [perh. fr. ScGael *tuig* I understand, perceive] *vt* **1 :** NOTICE, OBSERVE, PERCEIVE, WATCH ⟨reflected that the paratrooper might not have *twigged* him —Earle Birney⟩ **2 :** to understand the meaning of : COMPREHEND ⟨by their use of words you can ~ what is wrong with them —Christopher Morley⟩ ~ *vi* : NOTICE, UNDERSTAND ⟨she probably *twigged* instinctively about things being a bit rough for him —H.E.Bates⟩

⁶**twig** \"\ *n* -s [origin unknown] *Brit* : FASHION, MODE, STYLE ⟨a plan she formed for going to the ball in proper ~ —Samuel Lover⟩

twig beetle *n* : any of various small beetles that bore in twigs; *esp* : BARK BEETLE

twig blight *n* : a dying back (as in fire blight or brown rot) of the terminal branches or twigs of woody plants — compare DIEBACK, WITHERTIP

twig borer *n* : any of various small beetles or their larvae or the larvae of small moths that bore in twigs of trees or shrubs — compare APPLE TWIG BORER, PEACH TWIG BORER

twig budding *n* : a modified shield budding (as in budding dormant English walnuts in California) in which the scion consists of a prong, spur, or twig

twig caterpillar *n* : any of several slender loopers (family Geometridae) that assume a resting and protective position on the side of a twig to which they attach by the anal prolegs

twig drop *n* : the shedding of twigs or small branches because of nutritional disturbances

twig gall *n* : any of numerous galls that develop on the twigs of trees or shrubs

twigged \ˈtwigd\ *adj* [¹*twig* + *-ed*] : having twigs esp. of a specified kind or color

twig·gen \ˈtwigən\ *adj* [¹*twig* + *-en*] *archaic* : made of twigs : covered with wickerwork

twig·gery \ˈtwigərē, -ri\ *n* -ES [¹*twig* + *-ery*] : all the twigs of a shrub or tree ⟨this ailing tree was the only survivor . . . and so its ~ had to accommodate the sparrows —C.D.Stewart⟩

twig girdler *n* : a cerambycid beetle (*Oncideres cingulata*) that lays its eggs in twigs of various hardwood trees in the eastern U.S. and girdles the twigs so that they fall off

twig·gy \ˈtwigē, -gi\ *adj* -ER/-EST [¹*twig* + *-y*] : of, relating to, or suggesting twigs: as **a :** DELICATE, SLIGHT, THIN ⟨the sandpipers staggered on ~ legs —Christopher Morley⟩ **b :** abounding in twigs ⟨~ trees —John Evelyn⟩

twig insect *n* : STICK INSECT

twig·let \ˈtwiglət\ *n* -s : a small twig

twiglike \ˈ=ˌ=\ *adj* : resembling a twig

twig pruner *n* : an American longicorn beetle (*Elaphidionoides villosum*) whose larvae bore in the twigs of various hardwood trees and cut them off as if pruned

twig rush *n* : any of the rushlike sedges of the genus *Cladium* (esp. *C. mariscoides*) most of which have harsh-edged leaves

twigwithy \ˈ=ˌ==\ *n* [¹*twig* + *withy*] : OSIER 1a

twi·light \ˈtwī,līt, usu -īd-+V\ *n, often attrib* [ME, fr. OE *twi-* + *light*] **1 :** the light from the sky between full night and sunrise or between sunset and full night produced by diffusion of sunlight through the atmosphere and its dust — compare ASTRONOMICAL TWILIGHT, CIVIL TWILIGHT, NAUTICAL TWILIGHT **2 a :** a state of imperfect clarity, of dubiety, indefiniteness, indistinctness, or transition ⟨the cynical, truculent democratic ~ to which they are expected to be loyal —R.S.Lynd⟩ ⟨he created a ~ which dimmed the brightness of Mother's success —Dorothy C. Fisher⟩ ⟨a ~ between belief and disbelief —Walter Moberly⟩ **b :** a period of decline ⟨approaching the inglorious ~ of his career —Oscar Handlin⟩ **3** *or* **twilight blue a :** a variable color averaging a pale purplish blue to pale violet that is lighter than dusk blue **b :** a grayish blue that is redder and paler than electric, greener and paler than copenhagen, and redder, lighter, and stronger than Gobelin

twilight arch *n* : the shadow of the earth on the atmosphere seen rising in the eastern sky during evening twilight and setting in the western sky during morning twilight as an arched pinkish band with a dark bluish area beneath

twilight band *n* : a narrow zone in which a pilot flying at the edge of the on-course radio beam can detect both the on-course and off-course signals

twi·light·ed \-,līd·əd, -līt·əd\ *adj* [*twilight* + *-ed*] : TWILIT

twilight effect *n* : a serious error in radio bearings that may arise from upheavals in the Heaviside layer at about sunset

twilight sleep *n* : a state in which awareness of pain is dulled and memory of pain is dimmed or effaced and which is produced by hypodermic injection of morphine and scopolamine and used chiefly in childbirth

twilight state *n* : a dreamy state lacking touch with present reality, occurring in epilepsy, hysteria, and schizophrenia, and sometimes induced with narcotics

twilight vision *n* : rod vision by the dark-adapted eye in dim light : SCOTOPIA — compare DUPLICITY THEORY, PURKINJE PHENOMENON

twi·lighty \ˈtwī,līd·ē, -līt·ē, -i\ *adj* : having the color or brightness of twilight

twilight zone *n* **1 :** the lowest part of the photic region of the ocean **2 :** a zone lying on the border between two distinguishable fields, situations, subjects, or groups and exhibiting a blend of the characteristics of both without the distinctness of either ⟨a kind of *twilight zone* between East and West, an area which declines to be dominated by either —J.C.Harsch⟩ ⟨this *twilight zone* of what is implied but not actually stated —*Jour. of the Patent Office Society*⟩ ⟨increasing the area and the obscurity of the *twilight zone* which lies between state and federal functions —*New Republic*⟩ **3 :** TWILIGHT BAND

twi·lit \ˈtwī,lit\ *adj* [*twi-* + *lit*] : lighted by or as if by twilight : DIM ⟨a boat on a ~ river —Anthony West⟩

¹**twill** \ˈtwil\ *n* -s [ME *twyll, twylle*, fr. OE *twilic* having a double thread, modif. (influenced by *twi-*) of L *bilic-, bilix*, fr. *bi-* + *-lic-, -lix* (akin to L *licium* thread)] **1 :** a fabric with a twill weave ⟨gabardine and serge are ~s⟩ **2** *or* **twill weave :** a basic textile weave producing an allover surface pattern of fine diagonal lines or ribs usu. all running to the left or right and made by floating weft or warp threads over groups of two or more threads and staggering these floats regularly or irregularly to form a slanting line ⟨herringbone is a reversed or pointed ~⟩ ⟨gabardine has a steep ~⟩ **3 :** a basketry pattern made by passing one or more wefts over two or more warps

twill 2

²**twill** \"\ *vt* -ED/-ING/-S : to make (cloth) with a twill weave

³**twill** \"\ *n* -s [by alter.] *dial Eng* : QUILL

twilled \ˈtwild\ *adj* : made with a twill weave

twill·ing \ˈtwiliŋ, -lēŋ\ *n* -s : a twilled weave or part or the act or process by which it is produced

twil·ly \ˈtwilē, -li\ *n* -ES [by alter.] : WILLOW 3a

twilt \ˈtwilt\ *dial var of* QUILT

TWIMC *abbr* to whom it may concern

¹**twin** \ˈtwin\ *adj* [ME, fr. OE *twinn* twofold, double, two by two; akin to OHG *zwinal* born a twin, *zwiniling* twin, ON *tvinnr, tvennr* two by two, in pairs, OE *twēgen, twā, tū* two — more at TWO] **1 a :** born with one other at the same birth ⟨a ~ brother⟩ ⟨a ~ lamb⟩ **b :** born as a pair at one birth ⟨~ girls⟩ **2 a :** made up of two similar, related, or connected members or parts : DOUBLE ⟨meet this ~ (not alternative) responsibility —H.M.Wriston⟩ ⟨this is the first half of the Crisis Question, this time a ~ question —Hazel Sullivan⟩ **b :** paired in a close or necessary relationship : MATCHING ⟨the ~ threats of war and inflation —*New Republic*⟩ **c :** having or consisting of two identical units **d** (1) : constituting two similar, closely associated, or otherwise paired persons, topics, or objects ⟨~ waiting rooms —*Amer. Guide Series: N. Y. City*⟩ ⟨two girls in ~ yellow dresses —Scott Fitzgerald⟩ ⟨the ~ realms of tactics and strategy —S.L.A.Marshall⟩ (2) : being one of a pair of similar or associated persons or things ⟨across the bay lies its ~ city⟩ **3 :** formed by twinning of crystals

²**twin** \"\ *n* -s [ME, fr. OE *getwinn*; akin to OE *twinn* twofold — more at ¹TWIN] **1 a :** either of two offspring produced at a birth esp. in a species that ordinarily brings forth but one at a birth — see IDENTICAL TWIN **b twins** *pl, usu cap* : GEMINI 1 **2 :** one of two persons or things closely related to or resembling each other ⟨a powder compact that was the ~ of the one the old guy had found —Hartley Howard⟩ **3 :** a pair of offspring that are twins ⟨he was one of a ~⟩ **4** *or* **twin crystal :** a compound crystal composed of two or more crystals or parts of crystals of the same kind that are grown together in a specific manner so that there is at least one plane and the direction perpendicular thereto that are related in the same way to the crystallographic axes of both parts of the twin **5 :** a well drilled on the same location as an existing oil well or gas well to tap a different producing formation ⟨an oil well may have four or five ~s⟩

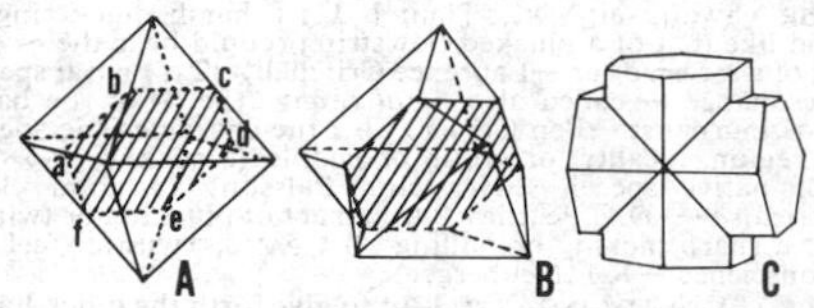

twin 4: *A* octahedron showing twinning plane *a b c d e f*; *B* contact twin; *C* penetration twin

³**twin** \"\ *vb* **twinned; twinned; twinning; twins** [ME *twinnen*, fr. *twin*, adj. & n.] *vt* **1** *Scot* : to put asunder : cause to be separated: PART, DIVIDE, SUNDER **2 :** to bear as twins **3 a :** to bring together in close association : LINK, COUPLE, JOIN ⟨whose name will always remain *twinned* with that of the . . . institute —B.R.Redman⟩ **b :** DUPLICATE, MATCH, PARALLEL ⟨sat at a spacious desk whose highly polished surface *twinned* his upper half in reverse —V.V.Nabokov⟩ ~ *vi* **1** *Scot* : to go apart : SEPARATE **2 :** to bring forth twins **3** *archaic* : to be born at the same birth with another **4** *obs* : to become coupled or combined : JOIN **5 :** to grow as a twin crystal

twin-axis \(ˈ)=ˈ==\ *n* : the axis common to both individuals of a twin crystal

twin band mill *n* : a sawmill with both a right-hand and a left-hand saw that are adjustable and may be mounted on separate frames

twin bed *n* : one of a pair of matching single beds

twin·berry \ˈ=- — *see* BERRY\ *n* **1 :** a shrubby No. American honeysuckle (*Lonicera involucrata*) with purple involucrate flowers **2 :** PARTRIDGEBERRY

twin bill *n* : DOUBLEHEADER

twinborn \ˈ=ˌ=\ *adj* : born at the same birth

twin city *adj, usu cap T&C* [fr. the *Twin Cities*, nickname for Minneapolis and St. Paul, Minn.] : of or relating to the adjoining cities of Minneapolis and St. Paul, Minn. ⟨*Twin City* newspapers⟩

t winding *n, cap T* : an electrical T connection

twin disease *var of* TWIN-LAMB DISEASE

twin·dle \ˈtwin°l\ *n* -s [²*twin* + *-le*] *dial* : TWIN

¹**twine** \ˈtwīn\ *n* -s [ME *twin, twyne*, fr. OE *twīn*; akin to MD

twijn & twern twine, MHG *zwirn,* ON *tvinni* twine, OE *twēgen, twā, tū* two — more at TWO] **1 :** a strong string composed of two or more plies or strands twisted together and used for various purposes (as binding small parcels and making nets) **2 :** a twined or interlaced part or object: as **a :** the stem of a plant or vine **b :** a coil, twist, or convolution formed or seeming to be formed by winding **c :** something snarled or knotted **:** TANGLE **3 :** an act of twining, interlacing, or embracing **4** *dial Brit* **:** a peculiar ocean ripple preceding a southeast gale on the coast of Great Britain **5 :** a light grayish olive color that is greener and paler than hemp, darker than Quaker gray, and redder and darker than average citron gray — called also *anamite, dune*

2twine \"\ *vb* -ED/-ING/-S [ME *twinen,* fr. *twin, twyne,* n.] *vt* **1 :** to twist together **:** form by twisting or winding of threads **:** BRAID, WEAVE ⟨~ a wreath of flowers⟩ **2 a :** INTERLACE ⟨remembered . . . the way she had *twined* and untwined her fingers —John Buchan⟩ **b :** to cause to encircle or enfold another **:** clasp (something) about another **:** WRAP ⟨*twined* her arms around him⟩ **c :** to cause to be encircled with something else ⟨*twined* the porch pillars with wreathed flowers⟩ **3** *dial* **:** TWIST, WRENCH, WREST ~ *vi* **1 :** to coil about something **:** twist in spirals ⟨a vine that ~*s* about the tree trunk⟩ **:** WIND **2 :** to stretch or move in a winding or sinuous manner **:** MEANDER, UNDULATE ⟨a snake *twined* over the ground⟩ ⟨a river ~*s* through the valley⟩ **3** *dial Brit* **:** SQUIRM **syn** see WIND

twin–engine \ˈ=ˌ=\ *or* **twin–engined** \ˈ=ˌ==\ *adj* **1 :** having two cylinders or two rows of cylinders **2 :** having two engines — used of an airplane

twin·er \ˈtwīnə(r)\ *n* -S **:** one that twines: as **a :** a plant (as a morning glory) that climbs by twining about a support **b :** TWINE REELER

twine reeler *n* **:** a machine similar to the spinning mule for twisting twine and ply yarns

twinflower \ˈ=,=\ *n* **:** LINNAEA 2: **a :** a low prostrate subshrub (*Linnaea borealis*) of northern parts of Europe and Asia with opposite leaves and fragrant usu. pink flowers borne in pairs **b :** a similar plant (*L. borealis americana* or *L. americana*) of northern No. America

1twinge \ˈtwinj\ *vb* -ED/-ING/-S [ME *twengen,* fr. OE *twengan;* prob. akin to OHG *dwengen* to compel, apply force to, *dwingan* to oppress, overcome, compel — more at THONG] *vt* **1** *dial* **:** PLUCK, TWEAK, TWITCH **2 :** to cause (one) a sharp or smarting pain **:** PRICK ~ *vi* **:** to feel a sudden sharp local pain **:** suffer a stabbing or smarting sensation

2twinge \"\ *n* -S **1** *obs* **:** TWEAK, TWITCH **2 a :** a sudden sharp stab of pain ⟨would have shrugged off ~*s* and creakings like mine as something quite to be expected in their early fifties —Edith M. Stern⟩ **b :** a moral or emotional pang **:** PRICKING ⟨a ~ of fear⟩ ⟨a ~ of conscience⟩ ⟨a ~ of envy⟩ **syn** see PAIN

twin·gle \ˈtwiŋ(g)əl\ *vb* -ED/-ING/-S [origin unknown] *dial Brit* **:** TWIST, WRIGGLE

twingle–twangle \ˈ=ˌ=ˈ=ˌ=\ *also* **twing–twang** \ˈtwiŋˈ=\ *n* [*twingle-twangle* redupl. of *²twangle; twing-twang* redupl. of *twang*] **:** the twang of a musical instrument

twinier *comparative of* TWINY

twiniest *superlative of* TWINY

twi–night \ˈtwī,=\ *adj* [*twi*light + *night*] **:** of or relating to a baseball doubleheader in which the first game is played in the late afternoon and the second continues into the evening under lights

1twink \ˈtwiŋk\ *vi* -ED/-ING/-S [ME *twinken* — more at TWINKLE] **:** WINK, TWINKLE

2twink \"\ *n* -S [ME, fr. *twinken,* v.] **:** WINK, TWINKLING — used esp. in the phrase *in a twink*

3twink \"\ *vt* -ED/-ING/-S [origin unknown] *dial Eng* **:** PUNISH, THRASH

4twink \"\ *n* -S [imit.] *dial Brit* **:** CHAFFINCH

1twin·kle \ˈtwiŋkəl\ *vb* **twinkled; twinkled; twinkling** \-k(ə)liŋ\ **twinkles** [ME *twinklen,* fr. OE *twinclian;* akin to ME *twinken* to wink, twinkle, MD *twinc* wink of an eye, MHG *zwinken* to blink] *vi* **1 :** to shine with a flickering, sparkling, or intermittent light **:** give off a fluctuating radiance **:** SCINTILLATE ⟨stars *twinkled* in the night sky⟩ ⟨street lamps *twinkled* dully —Wilson Collison⟩ ⟨tiny wavelets *twinkling* among the black boulders —William Beebe⟩ **2 a :** to flutter the eyelids **:** blink the eyes open and shut **b :** to emit gleams of joy, merriment, or other vivid usu. happy feeling **:** FLASH, GLITTER, SPARKLE ⟨his eyes *twinkled* in a friendly way —T.B.Costain⟩ **c :** to beam with gay or lively feeling ⟨~*s* happily through gold-rimmed spectacles —*Irish Digest*⟩ **3 :** to move in flashing or evanescent manner **:** flutter or flit rapidly ⟨the buggy *twinkled* away in the sunlight —Katherine Mansfield⟩ ⟨her little feet *twinkled* on the pavement —A.R.Foff⟩ ~ *vt* **1 :** to cause to shine with fluctuating or intermittent light **:** give off radiance from ⟨*twinkled* her blue eyes⟩ ⟨in the dark coverts the . . . beetle ~*s* its tiny lamp —Haldane MacFall⟩ **2 :** to transmit or communicate by a gleam of the eyes ⟨stopped *twinkling* mischief at him —Richard Blaker⟩ ⟨not one bright star to ~ hope and light to him —Meg Dyan⟩ **3 :** to flicker or flirt rapidly **:** twitch with flashing motions ⟨deer feeding, *twinkling* their scuts as they moved —Maurice Hewlett⟩

2twinkle \"\ *n* -S **1 :** a winking or blinking of the eyes **:** a flutter or quiver of the eyelids **2 :** the instant's duration of a flicker of the eyelids **:** TWINKLING, WINK — used esp. in the phrase *in a twinkle* ⟨and in a ~ it is gone —D.G.Campbell⟩ **3 :** an intermittent radiance **:** FLICKER, GLEAM, SPARKLE ⟨a laughing ~ in his bright eye —Charles Dickens⟩ **4 :** a rapid flashing motion **:** FLIRT ⟨a ~ of long, black-stockinged legs —Flora Thompson⟩ **5 :** a ballroom dance step in which one foot is brought forward, then to the side of the other, and finally to the rear or these movements executed in reverse order

twin·kler \-k(ə)lə(r)\ *n* -S **:** one that twinkles ⟨some very new, very young stars who proved to be rather ineffectual ~*s* —A.H.Dent⟩

twin·kling \-k(ə)liŋ, -lēŋ\ *n* -S [ME, fr. gerund of *twinklen* to twinkle — more at TWINKLE] **1 a :** a winking of the eye **b :** the time required for a wink **:** INSTANT ⟨the kettle will boil in a ~ —*Punch*⟩ ⟨his patient would be carried off by meningitis in the ~ of an eye —Jean Stafford⟩ **2 a :** a momentary repetitive variation in brightness of a star due to the varying density of the air which produces constantly changing refractive and interference effects **:** SCINTILLATION **b :** a radiance likened to the twinkling of a star (as the gleam of an eye or the glimmering of city lights) **3 :** a rapid flashing motion ⟨the ~ of their wings was as in sweet rhythm to the ~ of their hues —Jack McLaren⟩

twin·kly \-k(ə)lē, -li\ *adj* [*²twinkle* + *-y*] **:** TWINKLING, BEAMING, SMILING ⟨a tall, ~ Scotsman —Philip Hamburger⟩

twin–lamb disease \ˈ=ˈ=-\ *or* **twin disease** *n* **:** PREGNANCY DISEASE

twinleaf \ˈ=,=\ *n* **:** an American perennial herb (*Jeffersonia diphylla*) with leaves of two leaflets and simple naked one-flowered scapes

twin–lens camera \ˈ=ˈ=-\ *n* **:** a camera fitted with two lenses optically corrected to make them identical in their application

twin·ly *adj* [*²twin* + *-ly*] **:** of, relating to, or appropriate to a twin

twinned \ˈtwind\ *adj* [*²twin* + *-ed*] **1 :** born two at one birth **2 :** closely linked or associated **:** COUPLED **3 :** formed by twinning ⟨~ crystal⟩

twin·ner \ˈtwinə(r)\ *n* -S **:** one that bears twins

twinning *n* -S [fr. gerund of *³twin*] **1 :** the bearing of twins **:** production of a pair instead of one **2 :** the coupling, association, or comparison of two persons or things ⟨the usual ~ of Homer and Vergil —George Saintsbury⟩ **3 :** the assemblage of two or more crystals or parts of crystals in nonparallel but rational position with reference to each other — compare TWIN 4, SECONDARY TWINNING

twins *pl of* TWIN, *pres 3d sing of* TWIN

twin–screw \ˈ=ˈ=\ *adj* **:** having a right-handed screw propeller and a left-handed screw propeller parallel to each other one on each side of the plane of the keel — compare SINGLE-SCREW

twin–screw pump *n* **:** a displacement pump consisting of a casing containing two parallel screws with intermeshing threads fitted to prevent backward movement of fluid

twin·ship \ˈtwin,ship\ *n* [*¹twin* + *-ship*] **:** the quality or state of being twin **:** close similarity or association ⟨regimes . . . that hide their ~ to communism —*N. Y. Times Mag.*⟩

twin sister *n* **1 :** a girl born as one of twins **2 :** TWINFLOWER

twinspur \ˈ=,=\ *n* **:** an erect annual herb (*Diascia barberae*) with flowers colored rosy pink with a yellow spot in the throat and growing in terminal racemes

1twin·ter \ˈtwintə(r)\ *n* -S [ME, fr. OE *twiwintre* two years old, fr. *twi-* + *winter*] *dial Brit* **:** a sheep, ox, or horse that has lived through two winters

2twinter \"\ *adj* [fr. (assumed) ME, fr. OE *twiwintre*] *dial Brit* **:** two years old — used esp. of sheep and cattle ⟨a ~ ewe⟩

twin valve *n* **:** a valve with one supply and two discharge openings

twiny \ˈtwīnē, -ni\ *adj* -ER/-EST [in sense 1, fr. *¹twine* + *-y;* in sense 2, fr. *²twine* + *-y*] **1 :** of, relating to, or resembling twine **2 :** TWINING, INTERLACING

twire \ˈtwī(ə)r\ *or* **tweer** \ˈtwi(ə)r\ *vi* -ED/-ING/-S [perh. akin to MHG *zwieren* to wink] **1** *archaic* **:** to peep out **:** PEER **2** *obs* **:** TWINKLE

1twirl *R* ˈtwərl, *esp before pause or consonant* ˈtwər·əl; *–R* ˈtwəl *or* ˈtwəil\ *vb* -ED/-ING/-S [perh. of Scand origin; akin to Norw dial. *tvirla, tvilla* to spin, twirl; akin to Fris *dwerlje, dwirlje* to whirl, MD *dwerelen* to whirl, OHG *dweran* to stir — more at TURBID] *vi* **1 :** to revolve rapidly **:** become whirled round **:** SPIN ⟨~*ing* about the floor⟩ **2 :** to writhe like a snake **:** move with sinuous twisting motion **:** UNDULATE **3 :** to pitch in a baseball game ~ *vt* **1 a :** to rotate rapidly **:** cause to take a circular, curving, or spiral course **:** SPIN, TWIST, WHIRL ⟨~*ed* his moustaches⟩ ⟨she ~*ed* the beater furiously —Christopher Bloom⟩ ⟨~*ed* an auburn curl about her finger⟩ ⟨spied two policemen ~*ing* their billies —W.A.Swanberg⟩ **b :** to flourish (a drum major's baton) in more or less elaborate whirling figures **2 :** PITCH 3b(2) **syn** see TURN

2twirl \"\ *n* -S **1 :** an act of rotating or spinning something or of revolving **:** a rapid circling or turning **:** WHIRL ⟨stood watching a skater's ~*s* and figure eights⟩ ⟨the flash and ~ of batons to strident martial music⟩ **2 :** something that turns or is turned or has a round or spiral form **:** COIL, CONVOLUTION, TWIST, WHORL ⟨distinctive loops and ~*s* of individual handwriting⟩ ⟨the spiral ~ of a seashell⟩

twirl·er \ˈtwərlər; ˈtwəlǝ(r, ˈtwəil-\ *n* -S **:** someone or something that twirls: as **a :** a baseball pitcher **b :** BATON TWIRLER **c :** any of various whirling toys

twirl·i·gig \-lē,gig, -lə,g-\ *n* -S [alter. of *whirligig*] **:** WHIRLIGIG BEETLE

twirling *n* -S **:** the act or practice of one that twirls; *esp* **:** the act or technique of a baseball pitcher or a baton twirler

twirly \ˈtwərlē, -wəl-,-wəil-, -li\ *adj* -ER/-EST **:** CURLED, CURVED, TWISTED, SPIRAL ⟨exercise books with a ~ wire binder —Christopher Morley⟩

twirp *var of* TWERP

twis *pl of* TWI

1twist \ˈtwist\ *vb* -ED/-ING/-S [ME *twisten,* fr. OE *-twist* (in compounds) rope; akin to OFris & MLG *twist* quarrel, MD, quarrel, twine, OE *twēgen, twā, tū* two — more at TWO] *vt* **1 a :** to unite by winding a thread, strand, or wire around another **:** join by or as if by winding threads or strands together ⟨not less than two yarns are . . . ~*ed* together to form a strand —*Manual of Firemanship* (*Gt. Brit.*)⟩ **b :** PLAIT, WREATHE **c :** ENTWINE, INTERLACE **2 :** to coil around something **:** TWINE ⟨~*ed* her hair in ringlets around her finger⟩ **3 :** to associate intimately (as by a Luddite initiation) **4 a :** to wring, wrench, or wrest so as to dislocate or distort; *esp* **:** SPRAIN ⟨~*ed* my ankle⟩ **b :** to wrest the meaning or sense of **:** PERVERT, TORTURE ⟨one of those political phrases which can be ~*ed* to mean whatever the user wants it to mean —Arthur Krock⟩ ⟨tends to exaggerate and ~ many facts out of proportion —H.E.Salisbury⟩ **c :** to tighten up (facial muscles) **:** CONTORT ⟨~*ed* his face into a grin⟩ **d :** to pull off, turn, or break by means of a turning strain **:** force by torsion ⟨kept on tightening the nut until he ~*ed* it right off the bolt⟩ **e :** to cause to move with any of various turning motions (as by pivoting, revolving, or spiraling) ⟨~*ed* her rocking chair toward the table —Arnold Bennett⟩ **f :** to form into a spiral shape ⟨a pig's tail ~*ed* into a corkscrew⟩ **g :** to cause to take on moral, mental, or emotional deformity **:** WARP ⟨their lives and minds have been warped, ~*ed* and soured by the boom-boom, big-hit policy that now governs the game —John Lardner⟩ **h :** to wrest into an alien or unnatural form **:** force into a desired shape **:** DEFLECT, DISTORT, DIVERT ⟨~*ed* as many things as I could into laughing matters —J.B.Benefield⟩ ⟨~*ed* the authority of the church to the side of wealthy pewholders —V.L.Parrington⟩ **i :** to take (a winding, indirect, or devious course) to a destination or objective ⟨excitement one gets from watching a good broken-field runner ~*ing* his way to a long touchdown —Jerome Stone⟩ **5 :** to turn (a sheet of paper) for printing on the reverse by the work-and-twist method **6 :** to use misrepresentation or trickery to induce someone to drop (a life insurance policy) and buy (another) usu. in a different company **:** switch (life insurance) unscrupulously for someone ~ *vi* **1 :** to coil or wind with sinuous or tortuous motion **:** follow a winding course ⟨a narrow stream that ~*s* through green valleys —*Amer. Guide Series: N. C.*⟩ **2 a :** to turn or change shape under torsion ⟨the blade ~*ed* in the vise⟩ **b :** to bend into or assume a spiral shape **c :** SQUIRM, WRITHE ⟨he ~*ed* uneasily in his chair —T.B.Costain⟩ **3** *of a ball* **:** to rotate while taking a curving path or direction **4 :** to turn around **:** face about ⟨~*ed* around to see the approaching procession⟩ **5 :** to move forward while turning on an axis **:** advance while spinning ⟨if you travel fast . . . you might easily ~ over the edge into one of the steep ravines —Rose Macaulay⟩ ⟨the ball ~*ed* slowly from the pitcher's hand⟩ **syn** see CURVE, WIND — **twist one's arm :** to subject to overmastering pressure **:** COMPEL ⟨*twisted my arm* until I consented to drink —Hyman Goldberg⟩ — **twist around one's finger :** to influence (another) at will **:** dominate wholly (as by wiles or cajolery) — **twist the lion's tail** *often cap L* **:** to vex or anger Britain

2twist \"\ *n* -S [ME, fr. *twisten,* v.] **1 :** something formed by twisting or winding: as **a :** a thread, yarn, cord, or rope formed by twisting two or more strands together **b :** a strong tightly twisted sewing silk used esp. for buttonholes **c :** a complete turn of a fiber, yarn, roving, or cord about its axis: (1) **:** the hardness of a cord expressed as the number of such turns per inch (2) **:** the state of being so twisted **d :** a baked piece of twisted dough ⟨a bread ~⟩ ⟨cinnamon ~*s*⟩ **e :** tobacco leaves twisted into a thick compact roll **f :** a strip of citrus peel twisted above a drink in order to flavor it with the expressed oils and sometimes dropped into the drink itself **2 a :** the fleshing between an animal's hind legs; *esp* **:** the juncture of the thighs of cattle or sheep **b :** the curved tail of an animal (as a pug) **3** *obs* **:** the continuing thread of life **4 a :** the act of turning something or the state of being turned on or as if on its axis ⟨rounded a sharp corner with deft ~*s* of a file⟩ **b :** the spin given the ball in any of various games (as baseball) — compare CURVE, ENGLISH **c :** a spiral turn or curve (as that of an animal's horn) **d :** the spiral rifling of a gun barrel; *esp* **:** the distance in which rifling makes one complete turn of the barrel ⟨a 12-inch ~⟩ **e** (1) **:** torque or torsional stress applied to a body (as a rod or shaft) (2) **:** torsional strain (3) **:** the angle through which a thing is twisted **f :** a warp in lumber that bends one or more of the four corners of a board out of the plane of the others **5** *Brit* **:** a vigorous appetite **6 a :** a turning aside **:** BEND, DEFLECTION, DEVIATION ⟨the road wound through the hills with many a ~ and turn⟩ **b :** a local or individual peculiarity of pronunciation or inflection ⟨his outlandish ~ of tongue —Harriot B. Barbour⟩ **c :** a strong individual tendency or bent **:** a marked inclination or bias **:** ECCENTRICITY, IDIOSYNCRASY ⟨all sorts of strange characters, of every race and mind, poets, philosophers, cranks of every ~, were in our class —John Reed⟩ **d :** a wresting or distortion of meaning or sense **:** PERVERSION ⟨gave the facts an imperceptible ~ here and there to make the prisoner seem guilty⟩ **e :** a kinked or tangled confusion **:** an involved or intricate mess **7** *Brit* **:** a screw of paper used as a container **:** CORNET ⟨eats his sour olives out of a ~ of paper —Elizabeth Monroe⟩ **8 a :** an unexpected turn or development **:** a movement of action, plot, or policy in an unpredictable or astonishing direction ⟨~*s* of history which give piquancy to the past —G.P. Musselman⟩ ⟨provides a fictional account with an unusual ~ —T.C.Chubb⟩ **b :** DEVICE, TRICK ⟨all the old ~*s* of oratory were tried, but where there had been cheers before, there were now embarrassed silences —*Atlantic*⟩ ⟨acquainted with all the ~*s* that make for efficient cooking —Jane Nickerson⟩ **c :** a novel approach, procedure, or method **:** GIMMICK ⟨a teacher uses a new ~ for an assignment —W.D.Baker⟩ ⟨a new ~ in spending and saving habits —Sylvia F. Porter⟩ ⟨a ~ on the chain-letter idea —Saul Carson⟩ **9** *also* **twist disease :** a disease of wheat and rye that is caused by a fungus (*Dilophospora alopecuri*) often in association with an eelworm (*Anguina tritici*) and that causes earcockle of wheat **10 :** a front or back dive in which the diver beginning usu. at the highest point of the dive executes in corkscrew fashion but without bending the body a half turn or a complete turn by twisting the shoulders sideways so that the body follows the movement — compare FULL TWIST, HALF TWIST **11** *slang* **:** GIRL, WOMAN; *esp* **:** FLOOZY ⟨the blonde . . . looked like a two-bit ~ —Mickey Spillane⟩ **12** *Brit* **:** a warp thread **13 :** a spiral often colored line in the stem of a glass — compare AIR TWIST

twist bit *n* **:** a boring bit resembling a twist drill — compare SPUR BIT

twist disease *n* **1 :** a destructive disease of young salmonoid fishes due to injury of cartilage and perichondrium resulting from invasion of these tissues by a myxosporidian protozoan (*Myxosoma cerebralis*) **2 :** TWIST 9

twist dive *n* **:** a competitive diving category including those dives in which the body from a standing or running approach rotates around both a transverse and a longitudinal axis — compare *back dive, front dive, inward dive, reverse dive*

twist drill *n* **:** a drill having one or usu. two deep helical grooves extending from the point to the smooth portion of the shank

twisted *past of* TWIST

twisted cubic *n* **:** a cubic space curve cut by an arbitrary plane in three points

twisted curve *n* **:** SPACE CURVE

twisted flower *n* **:** a plant of the genus *Strophanthus*

twisted gear wheel *n* **:** SCREW WHEEL; *esp* **:** one having its axis parallel to that of another wheel that meshes with it

twisted heath *n* **:** a low evergreen shrub (*Erica cinerea*) of southern Europe naturalized at Nantucket in the U. S. with small bell-shaped rosy purple flowers — called also *Scotch heath*

twist·ed·ly *adv* **:** in a twisted manner

twisted pair *n* **:** an electric cable consisting of two insulated conductors twisted together for minimized induction and having no common wrap

twisted pine *n* **:** LODGEPOLE PINE a

twisted shovel *n* **:** a shovel cultivator with curved and twisted blades for throwing soil toward the roots of cultivated crops

twisted–stalk \ˈ=ˌ=,=\ *n* **:** a plant of the genus *Streptopus* of the family Liliaceae with slightly twisted stem, nodding usu. greenish or purplish flowers, and red berries — called also *liverberry;* see ROSE MANDARIN

twisted stomach worm *or* **twisted wireworm** *n* **:** a stomach worm (*Haemonchus contortus*)

twist·er \ˈtwistə(r)\ *n* -S [*¹twist* + *-er,* n. suffix] **1 :** one that twists: as **a :** TWISTER-IN **b :** THROWSTER **c :** one that twists (as dough or yarn) or shapes (as pretzels or tobacco) into twists **d :** a ball with a combined onward and spinning motion ⟨a curve in baseball, a break ball in cricket, and a ball with English in billiards are all called ~*s*⟩ **e :** a textile machine or device for twisting single yarns into plied yarns or for adding twist to yarns without plying **f :** SPANISH WINDLASS **g :** SWIVEL PLOW **h :** a device for twisting small stumps out of the ground **i :** a device by which an arm or hand may be painfully twisted (as to subdue a prisoner) **2 :** a tornado, waterspout, sand column, or dust whirl in which the rotatory ascending movement of a column of air is esp. apparent ⟨a ~ may change from a tornado to a waterspout and back again many times as it crosses bays and rivers —S.D.Flora⟩ **3 :** a somersault in which an acrobat performs a difficult twist of his body in air **4 :** a twisted roll, doughnut, or cruller **5 a :** a shifty, tricky, or unprincipled person **:** someone evasive, devious, or unreliable ⟨he's a ~, but I'll be able to make him see that it'll pay him to be straight with me —Dorothy Sayers⟩ **b :** an insurance agent who unscrupulously induces someone to drop one policy and buy another usu. in a different company **6 a :** something difficult, overwhelming, confusing, or dumbfounding **:** POSER ⟨I might believe it tomorrow, but it's a bit of a ~ now, this minute —A.E.Coppard⟩ **b :** TONGUE TWISTER **7** *dial* **:** MALLARD **syn** see WIND

twister–in \ˌ==ˈ=\ *n, pl* **twisters–in** [*twist in,* v. + *-er*] **:** a textile worker who twists or ties new warp threads onto ends left in the harness

twisthand \ˈ=,=\ *n* [*¹twist* + *hand*] **:** a lace maker

twist·i·cal \ˈtwistəkəl\ *adj* [*²twist* + *-ical*] **:** CROOKED, DEVIOUS, TORTUOUS

twist·i·fi·ca·tion \ˌtwistəfəˈkāshən\ *n* -S [*¹twist* + *-i-* + *-fication*] **1 :** an act of twisting **:** something twisting or twisted **:** TORTUOSITY ⟨his reporting articles are nearly totally free from ~ of fact into doctrine —W.R.Cross⟩ **2** *South & Midland* **:** a dancing game in which each couple in turn weaves in and out among others who stand in two lines

twist·i·fy \ˈ==,fī\ *vt* -ED/-ING/-ES [back-formation fr. *twistification*] **:** to make twisting

twist·i·ness \-tēnəs, -tin-\ *n* -ES **:** the quality or state of being twisty **:** SINUOSITY, TORTUOSITY

twisting *n* -S [fr. gerund of *¹twist*] **:** the use of misrepresentation or trickery to get someone to lapse a life insurance policy and buy another usu. in another company

twisting–in \ˌ==ˈ=\ *n, pl* **twistings–in** [fr. gerund of *twist in,* v.] **:** the attaching of the ends of a new warp to those of the old by twisting them together — compare TYING-IN

twisting paper *n* **:** a paper with high tensile strength in the machine direction that is cut into narrow strips and twisted into yarn or in lighter weights used for wrapping small pieces of candy

twis·tle \ˈtwisəl\ *n* -S [*²twist* + *-le* (alter. of *-el*)] *Scot* **:** TWIST, WRENCH

twists *pres 3d sing of* TWIST, *pl of* TWIST

twist serve *n* **:** an overhand tennis serve that imparts spin to the ball and causes it to bounce high and to the left of the receiver

twist–set \ˈ=ˌ=\ *vt* **:** to fix the twist in (yarns) by a steam treatment in order to prevent kinking or snarling during weaving or knitting

twisty \ˈtwistē, -ti\ *adj* -ER/-EST [*²twist* + *-y*] **1 :** full of twists, bends, or sinuosities **:** WINDING ⟨~ roads are a pleasure to drive on —J. Eason Gibson⟩ **2 :** DEVIOUS, EVASIVE, TRICKY ⟨she begged him for love of her to beware of all that ~ sex —James Stephens⟩

1twit \ˈtwit, *usu* -id·+V\ *vt* **twitted; twitted; twitting; twits** [alter. of earlier *twite,* short for *atwite,* fr. ME *atwiten,* fr. OE *ætwītan* fr. *æt* at + *wītan* to guard, look after, reproach, blame; akin to OHG *wīzan* to punish, reproach, ON *vīta* to punish, blame, Goth *fraweitan* to avenge, *witan* to observe — more at AT, WIT] **1 :** to subject to ridicule or reproach **:** TAUNT ⟨nearly every day finds him . . . *twitting* reporters on their personal and professional weaknesses —*New Republic*⟩ ⟨some seamen were *twitting* him about dressing so formally —Joseph Whitehill⟩ **2 :** to impute or make game of as a fault ⟨*twitted* him his laziness⟩ **syn** see RIDICULE

2twit \"\ *n* -S **1 :** an act of twitting **:** TAUNT **2** *Brit* **:** a silly peevish person **:** FOOL ⟨making a silly ~ of yourself —Noel Coward⟩ **3 :** a nervous or jumpy state **:** JITTERS ⟨what a ~ she had been in —Martha Gellhorn⟩ ⟨giving everybody the ~*s* —Richard Llewellyn⟩

3twit \"\ *n* -S [imit.] **:** TWITTER, CHIRP

4twit \"\ *n* -S [origin unknown] **:** a defect in yarn or roving; *usu* **:** a thin and weak place caused by too much twist

1twitch \ˈtwich\ *vb* -ED/-ING/-ES [ME *twicchen;* akin to OE *twiccian* to pluck, catch hold of, LG *twicken* to pinch, tweak, OHG *gizwickan*] *vt* **1 :** to pull with a sudden motion **:** JERK, PLUCK ⟨be sure he does not ~ his handwheel back and forth —*Coast Artillery Jour.*⟩ ⟨~*ed* him by the sleeve⟩ **2 :** to nip or pinch with or as if with pincers **:** inflict a pinching sting or smart on ⟨misgivings ~*ed* him at the prospect⟩ **3 :** to move (a body part) with a sudden jerky motion ⟨cows ~*ed* their flanks to drive off flies⟩ **4 :** to snatch as a thief or pickpocket ⟨~*ed* a purse from his pocket⟩ **5** *dial Brit* **a :** to draw tight with a cord **b :** draw (a cord) tight **6 :** to close on (a mineral lode) **:** NARROW — used of the surrounding rock **7** *NewEng* **:** SKID

— used of logs ~ *vi* **1 :** PULL, PLUCK ⟨~*ed* at my sleeve⟩ ⟨~*ed* at her skirt⟩ **2 a :** to move jerkily **:** JUMP, QUIVER ⟨her lips began to ~ —Marcia Davenport⟩ ⟨chestnuts ~*ed* on hot tin drums —Horace Sutton⟩ **b :** to ache with a sudden stabbing pain or twinge ⟨his corn ~*ed* like a bad tooth⟩ ⟨her conscience ~*ed* at the memory⟩ **3 :** PINCH 4 **syn** see JERK

²twitch \"\ *n* -ES **1 :** an act of twitching **:** a short sudden pull or jerk ⟨by a dexterous ~ got possession of the cuttings —John Buchan⟩ **2 :** a sudden sharp pain **:** PANG, TWINGE ⟨felt again the ~ of an old wound⟩ ⟨ignored a passing feeble ~ of conscience⟩ **3 :** a loop of rope or strap that is tightened over a horse's upper lip as a restraining device by twisting an attached stick **4 :** PINCH 4 **5 a :** a short spastic contraction of the muscle fibers **:** a simple muscular contraction **:** an involuntary muscular jerk ⟨the nerve was electrically stimulated and the muscle ~ was recorded —C.H.Thienes⟩ **b :** a slight jerk or motion of a body part ⟨saw by an icy ~ of her eyebrows that this would be presuming —Marcia Davenport⟩

³twitch \"\ *or* **twitch grass** *n* -ES [alter. of *quitch (grass)*] **1 :** COUCH GRASS 1a **2 :** SLENDER FOXTAIL

⁴twitch \"\ *vi* -ED/-ING/-ES **:** to clear land of twitch grass **:** gather and burn twitch grass

¹twitch·el \ˈtwichəl\ *n* -S [ME *twychel*, alter. of *twychen*, fr. OE *twicen* fork in a road; akin to OE *twi-* — more at TWI-] *dial Eng* **:** a path between hedges

²twitchel \"\ *n* -S [¹*twitch* + *-el* (suffix used to denote an instrument)] *dial Eng* **:** NOOSE, TWITCH

³twitchel \"\ *vt* **twitchelled; twitchelled; twitchelling; twitchels** *dial Eng* **:** to tie up with a twitchel

twitch·ell process \ˈtwichəl-\ *n*, *usu cap T* [after Ernst *Twitchell* †1929 Am. chemist] **:** a process for the acid hydrolysis of fats into fatty acids and glycerol that employs live steam and a Twitchell reagent as catalyst

twitchell reagent *n*, *usu cap T* [after E. *Twitchell*] **:** any of various sulfonated products used as catalysts in the Twitchell process: as **a :** a sulfonic acid made by condensing oleic acid with naphthalene in the presence of sulfuric acid **b :** a sulfonated petroleum product

twitch·er \-chə(r)\ *n* -S [¹*twitch* + *-er*] **:** one that twitches

twitchfire \ˈ=ˌ=\ *n* [³*twitch* + *fire*] **:** a fire for burning twitch grass from land ⟨like the drift of ~*s* blown in June —John Drinkwater⟩

twitch road *n* **:** a logging road

twitchy \ˈtwichē, -chi\ *adj* -ER/-EST [¹*twitch* + *-y*] **:** FIDGETY, IRRITABLE

twite \ˈtwīt\ *or* **twite finch** *n* -S [*twite* of imit. origin] **:** a linnet (*Carduelis flavirostris*) of northern Europe and Great Britain

twitlark \ˈ=ˌ=\ *n* [³*twit* + *lark*] *dial Eng* **:** MEADOW PIPIT

twits *pres 3d sing of* TWIT, *pl of* TWIT

twitted *past of* TWIT

twit·ten \ˈtwitᵊn\ *n* -S [perh. alter. of ME *twichen* — more at TWITCHEL] *dial Eng* **:** a narrow lane

¹twit·ter \ˈtwid·ə(r), -itə-\ *vb* **twittered; twittered; twittering** \-id·əriŋ, -itər-, -i·tr-\ **twitters** [ME *twiteren*; akin to OHG *zwizzirōn* to twitter, chirp; both of imit. origin] *vi* **1 :** to utter the successive chirping notes of a bird **:** make a bird's continuing small noises ⟨birds ~*ed* in the trees⟩ **2 a :** to chatter in light inconsequential fashion **:** talk busily of small or negligible things ⟨a home filled with ~*ing* gentlewomen —*Times Lit. Supp.*⟩ **b :** to laugh a light or silly laugh **:** GIGGLE, TITTER **3 :** to tremble with agitation **:** FLUTTER, QUIVER ⟨held up the amulet in a hand that ~*ed* —*Strand Mag.*⟩ ~ *vt* **1 :** to chirp out (as a bird's small noises) **2 :** to shake rapidly back and forth **:** FLUTTER ⟨raised his right hand above his head and ~*ed* his fingers —*Literary Review*⟩

²twitter \"\ *n* -S **1 :** a trembling agitation **:** a pitch of wild excitement **:** QUIVER ⟨your father's being so bent on it sets me all in a ~ —W.D.Howells⟩ **2 :** the chirping sounds of birds **3 :** a light chattering **:** GABBLE ⟨the ~ of the sportscasters and sports reporters —*Harper's*⟩

³twitter \"\ *n* -S [prob. fr. E dial. *twitter* pus, quittor, alter. of ¹*quitter* & *quittor*] **1 :** the refuse of the case of a sperm whale after the oil is pressed out **2 :** the thick tough tissue lining the case of a sperm whale

twit·ter·a·tion \ˌtwid·əˈrāshən\ *n* -S [¹*twitter* + *-ation*] **:** FLUTTER, TWITTER, TIZZY

twitterboned \ˈ==ˌ=\ *adj* [E dial. *twitter* pus, quittor + *boned*] *dial Brit, of a horse* **:** having an excrescence on the hoof

twit·ter·er \ˈtwid·ərə(r), -itə-\ *n* -S **:** one that twitters

twit·tery \-ərē, -ri\ *adj* [¹*twitter* + *-y*] **:** nervously agitated or infirm ⟨women for our mates who have great constitutional strength and are not ~ —James Thurber⟩

twitting *pres part of* TWIT

twit-twat \ˈtwi·ˌtwät, -it·ˌw-\ *n* -S [imit.] **:** HOUSE SPARROW

¹twit·ty \ˈtwid·ē, -itē, -i\ *adj* -ER/-EST [²*twit* + *-y*] **1** *dial Brit* **:** ILL-TEMPERED, PEEVISH **2 :** CHIRPING, TWITTERING ⟨a little ~ bird —Kenneth Roberts⟩

²twitty \"\ *adj* -ER/-EST [⁴*twit* + *-y*] *of yarn* **:** varying in diameter **:** full of twits **:** UNEVEN

twixt \ˈtwikst\ *prep* [ME *twix*, short for *betwix* — more at BETWIXT] **:** BETWEEN ⟨~ the charge and the conviction there is frequently great difference —Philip Wittenberg⟩

twiz·zle \ˈtwizəl\ *vb* -ED/-ING/-S [prob. alter. of ²*twistle*] *Brit* **:** SPIN, TWIRL

twizzle-twig \ˈ==ˌ=\ *n*, *dial Eng* **:** a common rush (*Juncus articulatus*) of the north temperate zone

¹two \ˈtü\ *adj* [ME *twa*, *two*, adj. & pron., fr. OE *twā* (fem. & neut.); akin to OE *twēgen* two (masc.), *tū* (neut.), OHG *zwēne* (masc.), *zwā*, *zwō* (fem.), *zwei* (neut.), ON *tveir* (masc.) *tvær* (fem.), *tvau* (neut.), Goth *twai* (masc.), *twos* (fem.), *twa* (neut.), L *duo*, Gk *dyo*, Skt *dva*] **:** being one more than one in number ⟨~ years⟩ — see NUMBER table

²two \"\ *pron, pl in constr* [ME *twa*, *two*] **1 :** two countable persons or things not specified but under consideration and being enumerated ⟨~ are here⟩ ⟨~ were found⟩ **2 :** a small approximate number of indicated things **:** so — used with a unitary noun and *or* ⟨fire a shot or ~⟩ ⟨come in a minute or ~⟩

³two \"\ *n* -S **1 :** twice one **2 a :** two units or objects ⟨a total of ~⟩ **b :** a group or set of two ⟨arranged by ~*s*⟩ **3 a :** the numerable quantity symbolized by the arabic numeral 2 **b :** the figure 2 **4 :** two o'clock — compare BELL table, TIME illustration **5 :** the second in a set or series: as **a :** a playing card marked to show that it is second in a suit **b :** a domino with two spots on one of its halves **c :** a die with two spots on the side uppermost **d :** an article of clothing of the second size ⟨wears a ~⟩ **6 :** a two-dollar bill **7 :** something having as an essential feature two units or members; *specif* **:** an opening bid in contract bridge of two in a suit when treated as a forcing bid and essential to a system of bidding — used chiefly in the phrases *forcing two* and *two demand* ⟨two-demand system⟩ — **in two** *adv* **:** into two more or less equal parts ⟨cut it *in two*⟩ — **in two twos** *adv, Brit* **:** in a very short time ⟨if she isn't here *in two twos* —James Stephens⟩

¹two-a-day \ˈ=ˌ=ˈ=\ *adj* **1 :** used or presented twice a day ⟨a *two-a-day* theatrical attraction⟩ **2 :** presenting an entire vaudeville bill twice daily ⟨a *two-a-day* house⟩

²two-a-day \"\ *n* [¹*two-a-day*] **:** something used or presented twice daily; *esp* **:** a vaudeville show with two performances daily

two-along \ˌ==ˈ=\ *or* **two-on** \ˈ=ˈ=\ *adv* **:** with hand-sewn threads fastened on alternate ends of the sections ⟨a book sewed *two-along*⟩

two-and-one-half striper \ˌ==(ˌ)=ˈ=-\ *n* **:** LIEUTENANT COMMANDER

two-arched \ˈ=ˈ=\ *adj* **:** having two temporal openings separated by a bony bar consisting of the fused prolongations of the postorbital and squamosal bones — used of a diapsid reptile

two-base hit \ˈ=ˈ=-\ *or* **two-bagger** \ˈ=ˈ==\ *n* **:** a base hit that enables a batter to reach second base safely **:** DOUBLE

two-beat \ˈ=ˈ=\ *adj* **1** *of jazz* **:** characterized by the accentuation of alternate beats in four-four time **2 :** playing or devoted to two-beat jazz (as Dixieland) ⟨a *two-beat* jazzman⟩ ⟨*two-beat* fans⟩

two-bid \ˈ=ˌ=\ *n* **:** an opening bid in contract bridge of two in a suit; *esp* **:** one treated as a forcing bid

two-bit \ˈ=ˈ=\ *adj* [*two bits*] **1 :** of the value of two bits ⟨a *two-bit* cigar⟩ **2 :** of small worth or importance **:** TRIFLING, PETTY, SMALL-TIME ⟨the attitude of a lot of the big cattlemen was that the *two-bit* ranchers were a nuisance —Bruce Siberts & W.D.Wyman⟩

two bits *n pl but sing or pl in constr* **1 :** the value of a quarter of a dollar ⟨shot craps for *two bits* a throw —C.G.Norris⟩ **2 :** something of small worth or importance ⟨an era that would make the achievements of the past look like *two bits* —W.S. Maugham⟩

two-block \ˈ=ˌ=\ *vt* [fr. the n. phrase *two blocks*] **1 :** to haul upon (tackle) so that the two blocks are chockablock ⟨*two-blocked* the tackle and snapped the cable⟩ **2 :** to hoist (as a signal flag or anchor) to the full extent

two-blocks \ˈ=ˌ=\ *adv* [fr. the n. phrase *two blocks*] **:** CHOCKABLOCK

two-body problem \ˈ=ˈ==-\ *n* **:** the problem of determining the previous or subsequent motion and the data for computing the places at any time of two bodies when given the Newtonian law of gravitation and the masses of two bodies with their positions and motions at any moment

two-bottom plow \ˈ=ˈ==-\ *n* **:** a plow having two moldboards or disks for plowing two furrows at a time

¹two-by-four \ˌ=bəˈ=\ *adj* **1 :** measuring two units (as inches) by four **2 :** SMALL ⟨from *two-by-four* enterprises set up in barns and kitchens . . . to the big industrial plants —*N.Y. Herald Tribune Bk. Rev.*⟩ **:** PETTY, CRAMPED ⟨narrow, tight, *two-by-four* lives —Manuel Komroff⟩

²two-by-four \"\ *n* [¹*two-by-four*] **:** a piece of lumber having finished dimensions of 1⅝ by 3⅝ inches

two-by-twice \ˈ=ˌbəˈ=\ *adj* **:** limited in size **:** SMALL, CRAMPED ⟨a *two-by-twice* sandwich shop⟩

two-card poker \ˈ=ˈ=-\ *n* **:** poker in which each player's hand contains only two cards, a pair is the highest-ranking hand, and unpaired hands are ranked by the rank of their cards with no counting of straights or flushes

two-centered arch \ˈ=ˈ==-\ *n* **:** an arch whose intrados curve is described from two centers

A B C

two-centered arches: blunt, *A;* equilateral, *B;* acute, *C*

two cents *n pl* **1 :** a sum or object of very small value **:** practically nothing ⟨said angrily that for *two cents* he'd punch your nose⟩ ⟨realized it was my mistake and felt like *two cents*⟩ **2** *or* **two cents worth :** an opinion offered on a topic under discussion ⟨giving each speaker the feeling that he is getting in his *two cents worth* —Dwight MacDonald⟩

two-charge rate \ˈ=ˈ=-\ *n* **:** a rate based upon the amount (as of electricity) used by a customer and upon his maximum demand

two-club system \ˈ=ˈ=-\ *n* **:** a system of bidding in contract bridge in which an opening bid of two clubs is artificial and forcing to game and the bidder's partner responds two diamonds to show a hand with less strength than one ace and one king

two-color \ˈ=ˈ==\ *adj* **1 :** having two colors **2** *of a photomechanical process* **:** printing in two colors

two-control airplane \ˌ==ˈ=-\ *n* **:** an airplane with no rudder in which control is achieved by means of ailerons and elevators only

two-course \ˈ=ˈ=\ *adj* **:** TWO-FIELD

two-cycle \ˈ=ˈ==\ *adj, of an internal combustion engine* **:** having a two-stroke cycle

2-D \ˈ=ˈ=\ *adj* **:** TWO-DIMENSIONAL 3

¹two-decker \ˈ=ˈ==\ *n* -S **1 a :** a ship with two decks **b :** an old-time warship with guns on two decks **2 :** something (as a bus) having two levels or layers

²two-decker \"\ *adj* **:** having two decks, levels, layers, or classifications ⟨a *two-decker* bus⟩ ⟨a *two-decker* tariff⟩ **:** DOUBLE-DECK

two-demand bid \ˌ==ˈ=-\ *n* **:** DEMAND BID

two-demand system *n* **:** CULBERTSON SYSTEM

two-dimensional \ˌ==ˈ=(=)=\ *adj* **1 :** having two dimensions; *specif* **:** having the coordinates of its points depending on two independent variables **2 a :** designed or effective primarily as a flat or surface composition ⟨*two-dimensional* painting or sculpture in the round⟩ **b :** lacking depth of literary characterization **:** MECHANICAL, WOODEN **3 :** not specially designed to give an illusion of depth or varying distances — used esp. of a motion picture; compare THREE-DIMENSIONAL — **two-dimensionally** \ˌ==ˈ=(=)=ē\ *adv*

two-dimensionality \ˌ==ˌ=ˈ===\ *n* [*two-dimensional* + *-ity*] **:** the aspect or quality of being two-dimensional

two-dimensional motion *n* **:** UNIPLANAR MOTION

two-dimensional ramjet engine *n* **:** an airplane propulsion system of the ramjet type in which the flow passage of rectangular cross section has two sides parallel

two-dollar broker \ˈ=ˈ==-\ *n* **:** a broker who executes orders for other exchange members on the floor for a commission formerly of two dollars per 100 shares

two-double \ˈ=ˈ==\ *adj* **:** DOUBLE; *specif* **:** bent over in posture ⟨ran back to their bench *two-double* with laughter —Mary Webb⟩

two-edged \ˈ=ˈ=\ *adj* **:** DOUBLE-EDGED

two-egg \ˈ=ˈ=\ *adj* **:** DIZYGOTIC

two-em dash \ˈ=ˈ=-\ *n* **:** a printing dash that is two ems wide

two-eye berry \ˈ=ˈ=-\ *n* **1** *also* **two-eyes** \ˈ=ˌ=\ *pl but sing or pl in constr* **:** PARTRIDGEBERRY 1 **2 :** TWINFLOWER

two-faced \ˈ=ˈfāst\ *adj* **1 :** having two faces **2 :** DOUBLE-DEALING **:** FALSE **3 :** AMBIGUOUS — **two-fac·ed·ly** \ˈ=ˈfāsədlē, -āstlē, -li\ *adv* — **two-fac·ed·ness** \-sədnəs, -stnəs\ *n*

two-family house \ˈ=ˈ=(=)=-\ *n* **:** a house divided either vertically and designed for two families living side by side but separated by a party wall or horizontally and designed for two families occupying separate apartments one above the other — called also *duplex house*

two-fer \ˈtüfə(r)\ *n* -S [alter. of *two for* (as in such phrases as *two for a nickel*)] **1 :** a cheap item of merchandise; *specif* **:** a cigar selling at two for a nickel **2 :** a free coupon entitling the bearer to purchase two tickets to a specified theatrical production for the price of one at the box office

two-field \ˈ=ˈ=\ *adj* **:** of, using, or being a system of crop rotation in which the land is divided into two parts alternately left fallow

two-fisted \ˈ=ˈ==\ *adj* **:** VIRILE, VIGOROUS ⟨a red-blooded, go-getting, *two-fisted* American he-man —Weston La Barre⟩ ⟨a real *two-fisted* battle training —Carl Mann⟩

¹twofold \ˈ=ˈ=\ *adj* [ME *twafald*, *twofold*, fr. *twa*, *two* two + *-fald*, *-fold* -fold] **1 :** having two parts or aspects ⟨the office of a clergyman is ~: public preaching and private influence —R.W.Emerson⟩ **:** DOUBLE, DUAL, BINARY **2 :** being twice as large, as great, or as many as some understood size, degree, or amount ⟨a ~ increase⟩ **3 :** DIAD ⟨~ symmetry⟩

²twofold \"\ *adv* [ME *twafald*, *twofold*, fr. *twafald*, *twofold*, adj.] **1 :** to twice as much or as many **:** by two times ⟨increased ~⟩ **2** *Scot* **:** so as to be doubled up or bent over (as with age)

two-fold \ˈ=ˌ=\ *n* [¹*two* + *fold*] **:** two stage flats hinged together so that they fold face to face

two·fold·ness *n* -ES **:** the quality or state of being twofold

twofold purchase *or* **twofold tackle** *n* **:** a tackle of two double blocks with the standing part of the rope fast to the block from which the hauling part comes ⟨the *twofold purchase* . . . is commonly used for hoisting boats —*Manual of Seamanship*⟩

twofold truth *n* **:** a theory that truth is not necessarily unitary but may have a theological side and a philosophic side each governing in its own realm even though it may contradict the other

two-foot octave \ˈ=ˈ=-\ *n* **:** ONE-LINE OCTAVE

two-foot pitch *n* **:** the pitch of a two-foot stop on a pipe organ

two-foot stop *n* **:** a pipe-organ stop sounding pitches two octaves higher than the notes indicate — compare EIGHT-FOOT STOP

two-forked \ˈ=ˈ=\ *adj* **:** divided into two parts somewhat after the manner of a fork **:** DICHOTOMOUS, BIFURCATE

two-forty \ˈ=ˈ==\ *n* [so called fr. its having once been a trotting record] **1 :** a speed of a mile in two minutes and forty seconds ⟨ran like *two-forty*⟩ **2 :** high speed

two-four \ˈ=ˈ=\ *or* **two-four time** *n* **:** the time of a musical composition having two quarter notes or tones or their equivalent to a measure and indicated by the time signature 2/4 ⟨a quick dance in *two-four*⟩

2, 4-D \ˈ=ˌ=ˈ=\ *abbr or n* -S dichlorophenoxyacetic acid

2, 4, 5-T \ˈ=ˌ=ˌ=ˈ=\ *abbr or n* -S trichlorophenoxyacetic acid

two-gun \ˈ=ˈ=\ *adj* **:** carrying two guns **:** adept at the use of two guns ⟨a fighting *two-gun* marshal —*Popular Western*⟩

two-handed \ˈ=ˈ==\ *adj* [ME *too-honded*, fr. *too*, *two* two + *honded*, *handed* handed] **1** *or* **two-hand** \ˈ=ˈ=\ **:** designed for or requiring the use of both hands ⟨a *two-hand* manual alphabet⟩ **2 :** requiring two persons for operation ⟨a *two-handed* saw⟩ **3 :** STOUT, STRONG **4 :** having or efficient with two hands — **two-hand·ed·ly** *adv* — **two-hand·ed·ness** *n*

two-headed snake \ˈ=ˈ==-\ *n* **1 :** a snake (as some small boas and the cylinder snakes) with a blunt tail that resembles a head **2 :** a limbless lizard of the family Amphisbaenidae

two-high \ˈ=ˈ=\ *adj* **:** of or being a rolling mill with two rolls one over the other — compare THREE-HIGH

two-hole \ˈ=ˌ=\ *n* **:** the favored position at the rail behind the lead horse in harness racing

two-holer \ˈ=ˈ==\ *n* **:** a privy with two openings

two kettle *n, pl* **two kettle** *or* **two kettles** *usu cap T&K* **:** a Dakota people constituting a division of the Tetons

two-leaved solomon's-seal \ˈ=ˈ=-\ *n*, *usu cap 1st S* **:** FALSE LILY OF THE VALLEY

two leg *n* **:** MIDDLE AND LEG

two-line \ˈ=ˈ=\ *adj* **:** of twice the depth or point size of the type or letter named or understood ⟨a *two-line* initial⟩ ⟨a *two-line* letter⟩ — distinguished from *double*

two-lined chestnut borer \ˈ=ˈ=-\ *n* **:** a chestnut borer (*Agrilus bilineatus*)

two-line octave \ˈ=ˈ=-\ *n* [so called fr. the two accent marks of the symbol C″ representing the first C above middle C] **:** the musical octave that begins on the first C above middle C — see PITCH illustration

two·ling \ˈtüliŋ, -lēŋ\ *n* -S [¹*two* + *-ling*] **:** a twin crystal

two-man \ˈ=ˈ=\ *adj* **:** of or relating to two individuals: as **a :** consisting of two individuals ⟨a *two-man* committee⟩ **b** (1) **:** done, presented, or produced by two individuals ⟨a *two-man* comedy act⟩ (2) **:** that features the work of two artists ⟨a *two-man* exhibition⟩ **c** (1) **:** designed for or limited to two individuals ⟨a *two-man* bobsled⟩ or requiring two individuals to operate or handle ⟨a *two-man* saw⟩ (2) **:** managed or controlled by only two individuals ⟨a *two-man* shop⟩

two-mast·er \ˈ=ˈ=ə(r)\ *n* -S [¹*two* + *mast* + *-er*] **:** a ship having two masts

two-minded \ˈ=ˈ==\ *adj* **:** having two inconsistent attitudes toward something

two-name paper \ˈ=ˈ=-\ *n* **:** negotiable paper on which two signatures appear with both parties liable for payment

two-nerved \ˈ=ˈ=\ *adj* **:** having two nerves; *specif* **:** having two main veins ⟨a *two-nerved* leaf⟩

two·ness \ˈtünəs\ *n* -ES **:** the quality or state of being two **:** DUALITY

two old cat \ˌtüˈōlˌkat, ˌtüˌōlˈk-\ *also* **two o' cat** \ˌtüəˈk-\ *n* **:** one old cat played with two batters

two-on *var of* TWO-ALONG

two pair *n* **1** *Brit* **:** a lodging situated on the third floor **2** *or* **two pairs :** a pair of one denomination and another of different denomination held in the same hand in poker and ranking between one pair and triplets — see POKER illustration

two-pair \ˈ=ˈ=\ *adj* [*two pair*] **1** *Brit* **:** situated on the third story above two flights of stairs ⟨a *two-pair* front room⟩ **2 :** containing two pairs ⟨a *two-pair* poker hand⟩

two-part \ˈ=ˈ=\ *n*, *Scot* **:** two thirds

two-part code *n* **:** a code book having an encoding part listing the plaintext segments in alphabetical and logical order each with its code group or groups assigned at random and a decoding part listing in alphabetical or numerical order the code groups with their plaintext equivalents — compare ONE-PART CODE

two-part form *n* **:** a song form composed of two repeated parts or sections of which the first often modulates to a related key and the second returns to the original key

two-part time *or* **two-part measure** *n* **:** DUPLE TIME

two-party \ˈ=ˈ==\ *adj* **:** consisting of two major political parties having almost equal voting strength with little or no opposition from other parties ⟨the *two-party* system in U.S. politics⟩

two·pence *Brit* ˈtəpən(t)s *or* -pᵊm(-, *US* " *or* ˈtü,pen-\ *also* **tup·pence** \ˈtəpən(t)s, -pᵊm(-\ *n, pl* **twopence** *or* **twopences** [ME *two pens*] **1 :** the sum of two usu. British pennies **2 :** a coin worth two pennies now in Britain issued only for maundy money

¹two·pen·ny *Brit* ˈtəp(ə)ni, *US* " *or* -nē *or* ˈtü,pen-\ *adj* [¹*two* + *penny*] **1 :** of the value of or costing twopence **2 :** CHEAP, MEAN

²twopenny \"\ *also* **tup·pen·ny** \ˈtəp(ə)n-\ *n* **1 :** weak ale orig. sold at twopence for a quart or more **2 :** TWOPENCE 2 **3 :** BIT, WHIT — usu. used in the phrase *don't care a tuppenny*

twopenny grass *n* **:** MONEYWORT

twopenny-halfpenny \ˌtəp(ə)niˈhāp(ə)ni\ *adj* **1 :** of the value of or costing twopence halfpenny **2 :** PETTY

two-phase \ˈ=ˈ=\ *adj* **:** supplying or supplied with two alternating currents in separate circuits differing in phase usu. by a quarter cycle ⟨a *two-phase* generator⟩ ⟨a *two-phase* motor⟩

¹two-piece \ˈ=ˈ=\ *adj* [¹*two* + *piece*] **:** consisting of two separate pieces; *esp* **:** forming a clothing ensemble with matching but separate top and bottom parts (as jacket and skirt, halter and shorts) ⟨a *two-piece* dress⟩ ⟨a *two-piece* playsuit⟩

²two-piece \"\ *or* **two-piec·er** \ˈ=ˈpēsə(r)\ *n* **:** a garment or ensemble consisting of a matching but separate top and bottom

two pipe *adj* **:** of or being a steam or water heating system in which there are separate supply and return pipes so that each radiator receives a direct supply of the hot water or steam

two-platoon system \ˌ==ˈ=-\ *n* **:** a practice in football of training and playing separate offensive and defensive units

¹two-ply \ˈ=ˈ=\ *adj* [¹*two* + *ply*] **1 :** woven as a double cloth ⟨*two-ply* carpet⟩ **2 :** consisting of two strands ⟨*two-ply* yarn⟩

²two-ply \"\ *n* **:** a board consisting of two layers of wood

two-point \ˈ=ˈ=\ *adj* **1 :** having or concerned with two points ⟨a *two-point* equidistant map projection⟩ **2 :** being in contact or supported at two points

two-point landing *n* **:** a landing of an airplane in which the initial contact with the landing surface is made with the two main wheels

two-point perspective *n* **:** linear perspective in which parallel lines along the width and depth of an object are represented as meeting at two separate points on the horizon that are 90 degrees apart as measured from the common intersection of the lines of projection

two-point problem *n* **:** a problem in plane-tabling in which two points are mapped on the paper and a third is occupied on the ground to do which a fourth point is occupied temporarily

two-point threshold *or* **two-point limen** *n* **:** the smallest separation at which two points applied simultaneously to the skin can be distinguished from one

two-price \ˈ=ˈ=\ *adj* **:** of or being a system of government regulation of farm commodity prices providing fixed supports for domestic sales and none for export sales

two-revolution press \(ˌ)=ˌ==ˈ==-\ *n* **:** a cylinder press in which the cylinder revolves continuously during the forward and return strokes of the bed — compare STOP-CYLINDER PRESS

two-rowed barley \ˈ=ˈ=-\ *n* **:** a barley having only the central spikelet of each cluster fertile so that the spike appears to have two rows — compare FOUR-ROWED BARLEY

twos \ˈtüz\ *vi* -ED/-ING/-ES [fr. pl. of ³*two*] **:** to go around in the company of a member of the opposite sex ⟨you don't have to be always *twosing* with a person if you feel that way about them —S.V.Benét⟩

twoscore \ˈ=ˈ=\ *adj* **:** being 40 in number

two-seat·er \ˈ=ˈsēd·ə(r)\ *n* [¹*two* + *seat* + *-er*] **1 :** something seating two persons: as **a :** an automobile with one seat accommodating a driver and one passenger **b :** an airplane with two open cockpits in tandem **2 :** something having two seats; *specif* **:** an automobile having front and back seats

two-seed-in-the-spirit predestinarian baptist *n, usu cap 1st T & both Ss & P & B* **:** a member of a strongly Calvinistic Baptist sect resembling the Primitive Baptists but believing that mankind is divided into the offspring of God who will be saved and the offspring of the Devil who will be lost

two-shear \ˈ=ˌ=\ *adj, Brit, of a sheep* **:** that has been shorn twice ⟨a *two-shear* ram⟩
two-shot \ˈ=ˌ=\ *n* **:** a camera shot of two persons
two-sided \ˈ=ˈ==\ *adj* **1 a :** having two sides **:** BILATERAL **b** *of a sheet of paper* **:** having opposite surfaces that are different in color or texture **2 :** DOUBLE-FACED, HYPOCRITICAL — **two-sid·ed·ness** *n*
two·some \ˈtüsəm\ *n* -S [ME (Sc) *twasum*, fr. *twa* two + *-sum* -some] **1 :** a group of two persons or things **:** COUPLE, DUO ⟨the dancer and her husband have been a popular ~ —*Springfield (Mass.) Daily News*⟩ **2 :** a golf single
two-speed \ˈ=ˌ=\ *adj* **:** adapted for producing or for receiving either of two speeds ⟨a *two-speed* motor⟩ ⟨a *two-speed* axle⟩
two-spined stickleback \ˈ=ˌ=-\ *n* **:** a stickleback that is a variety of the three-spined stickleback and is distinguished from the typical form by the presence of two rather than three dorsal spines
two-spot \ˈ=ˌ=\ *n* **1 :** an unimportant person or thing; *esp* **:** a two of any card suit **2 :** a two-dollar bill
two-spotted ladybird \ˈ=ˌ==-\ *n* **:** a European predaceous ladybird (*Adalia bipunctata*) that is now common in the northern U.S., feeds on aphids on hardwoods, and often hibernates in houses
two-spotted spider mite *also* **two-spotted mite** *n* **:** a widely distributed plant-feeding mite (*Tetranychus bimaculatus*) that feeds on various usu. herbaceous plants but is sometimes a serious pest in orchards
two-star \ˈ=ˌ=\ *adj* **1 :** of a moderate degree of excellence ⟨a *two-star* restaurant⟩ **2 :** being or having the military rank of major general or rear admiral ⟨a *two-star* general⟩
1**two-step** \ˈ=ˌ=\ *n* [¹*two* + *step*] **1 :** a ballroom dance executed with a sliding step-close-step in march or polka time **2 :** a piece of music for the two-step **3 :** a walking step used in skiing in which a forward swing of both poles and a walking step with one ski is followed by a strong push of the poles and a gliding step with the other ski
2**two-step** \"\ *vi* **:** to dance the two-step
two-story \ˈ=ˌ==\ *or* **two-storied** \ˈ=ˌ==\ *adj* **:** having two floors or levels ⟨a *two-story* house⟩
two-striped grasshopper \ˈ=ˌ=-\ *n* **:** a short-horned grasshopper (*Melanoplus bivittatus*) with two yellow stripes along its back that is sometimes a destructive pest of field crops (as alfalfa) in many parts of the U.S.
two-strip·er \ˈ=ˈstrīpə(r)\ *n* **:** LIEUTENANT 2b
two-stroke cycle \ˈ=ˌ=-\ *n* **:** a working cycle of a piston in an internal combustion engine consisting of two strokes in which the piston during the first stroke compresses the fuel mixture on one side while receiving the expansive thrust of previously compressed gases on the other side and during the second draws in a fresh charge on one side while expelling burnt gases on the other — compare FOUR-STROKE CYCLE
two-suit·er \ˈ=ˈsüd·ə(r)\ *n* -S **1** *or* **two-suit hand** \ˈ=ˌ=-\ **:** a bridge hand containing two suits each of five or more cards **2 :** a man's wardrobe case designed to hold two suits and accessories
two-third·er \ˈ=ˈ=ə(r)\ *n* -S [*two thirds* + *-er*] **:** an apprentice printer who has served most of his apprenticeship
two-thirds rule \ˈ=ˌ=-\ *n* **:** a political principle requiring that two thirds rather than a simple majority of the members of a politically organized group must concur in order to exercise the power to make decisions binding upon the whole group — compare MAJORITY RULE
two-thirds vote *n* **:** a vote requiring the concurrence of two-thirds of the members of a politically organized group
two-three \ˈtü;ˈ, ˈtü;=\ *adj* **:** ²FEW 2, SEVERAL
two-throw \ˈ=ˌ=\ *adj* **1 :** capable of being thrown or cranked in two directions usu. opposite to one another ⟨a *two-throw* crank⟩ ⟨a *two-throw* switch⟩ **2 :** having two cranks set near together and opposite to one another ⟨a *two-throw* crankshaft⟩
1**two-time** \ˈ=ˌ=\ *vt* **1 :** to betray (a spouse or lover) by secret lovemaking with another **2 :** DOUBLE-CROSS — **two-tim·er** \ˈ=ˌtīmə(r)\ *n*
2**two-time** \ˈ=ˌ=\ *adj* **:** that has done, suffered, or received something twice ⟨a *two-time* medal winner⟩
two-toed \ˈ=ˌ=\ *adj* **:** having two toes on each foot
two-toed anteater *n* **:** SILKY ANTEATER
two-toed sloth *n* **:** a sloth of the genus *Choloepus* having two functional claws on each front foot and three on each back foot; *specif* **:** a Central American sloth (*C. hoffmanni*)

two-toed sloth of Central America

two-tone \ˈ=ˌ=\ *or* **two-toned** \ˈ=ˌ=\ *adj* **:** having some parts of one color and others of another color or of a different shade of the same color
two-to-one \ˌtüd·əˈwən\ *adj* **:** of or being a gear for reducing or increasing a velocity ratio two to one
two-tooth \ˈ=ˌ=\ *n, pl* **two-tooths** *Brit* **:** a sheep having two permanent teeth erupted and being usu. between one and two years old ⟨buy more *two-tooths* to build up the ewe flock⟩
two-toothed longhorn \ˈ=ˌ=-\ *n* **:** a cerambycid beetle (*Ambeodontus tristis*) the larva of which is a destructive wood borer in New Zealand
1**two-track** \ˈ=ˌ=\ *vi* [¹*two* + *track*] *of a horse* **:** to move forward and to one side simultaneously without turning the neck or body
2**two-track** \ˈ=ˌ=\ *n* **:** an act of two-tracking **:** a two-tracking movement
two-twenty \ˈ=ˌ==\ *n* **:** a 220-yard race common in running, skating, and swimming
two-up \ˈ=ˌ=\ *n* **:** a gambling game in which players bet that two coins tossed from a small wooden kip will fall both heads or both tails
two-valued \ˈ=ˌ==\ *adj* **:** possessing only the truth-values of truth and falsehood ⟨*two-valued* logic⟩ — compare MANY-VALUED
two-way \ˈ=ˌ=\ *adj* **1 :** being a cock or valve that will connect a pipe or channel with either of two others at will **2 a :** moving or allowing movement in opposite directions at the same time ⟨*two-way* traffic⟩ ⟨a *two-way* street⟩ **b :** moving or allowing movement in either of two directions ⟨*two-way* adjustment⟩ **3 a :** involving or allowing an exchange between two individuals or groups ⟨*two-way* communication by radiotelephone⟩ ⟨a *two-way* scholarship program for U.S. and foreign universities⟩ ⟨*two-way* trade⟩; *specif* **:** of or being equipment designed for both sending and receiving messages by wire or radio ⟨a mobile *two-way* radio for his taxi⟩ **b :** involving mutual responsibility or reciprocal relationships **:** affecting, entered into by, or binding on both parties ⟨a *two-way* guarantee⟩ ⟨political alliance is a *two-way* thing —T.H.White b. 1915⟩ **4 :** involving two participants **:** TWO-SIDED ⟨lost to his opponent in the *two-way* race for the governorship⟩ **5 a :** that may be used in either of two manners ⟨a shirt with a *two-way* collar⟩ ⟨*two-way* cattle fat enough to sell to either slaughterers or feeders⟩ **b** *of a bid in contract bridge* **:** made sometimes on a strong and sometimes on a weak hand for the purpose of withholding information from the opponents ⟨a *two-way* three-bid⟩ ⟨a *two-way* no-trump bid⟩
two-way plow *n* **:** SWIVEL PLOW
two-way plug *n* **:** CURRENT TAP
two-way stretch *n* **1 :** a characteristic of some materials of being stretchable in two directions **2 :** a woman's girdle of two-way stretch material
two-way switch *n* **:** one of two electrical switches (as at the top and bottom of a stair) controlling a single outlet
two-wheel·er \ˈ=ˈ(h)wēlə(r)\ *n* **:** a 2-wheeled vehicle: as **a :** a 2-wheeled cab or hansom **b :** BICYCLE ⟨a child learning to ride his new *two-wheeler*⟩
two-winged \ˈ=ˌ=\ *adj* **:** having one pair of wings **:** DIPTEROUS
two-winged fly *n* **:** an imaginal insect of the order Diptera having typically a single pair of wings and halteres instead of a second pair

two-worlds theory \ˈ=ˌ=-\ *n* **:** philosophic dualism; *specif* **:** interactionist dualism
twp *abbr* township
twr *abbr* tower
t wrench *n, cap T* **:** a T-shaped wrench that consists of a handle or lever with a fixed or removable socket to fit over a nut or bolt head
twy·er \ˈtwīə(r), -ēə\ *n* -S [by alter.] **:** TUYERE
tx *abbr* tax
txn *abbr* taxation
-ty \d·ē, tē, |ī\ *n suffix* -ES [ME *-te, -tee, -tie*, fr. OF *-té*, fr. L *-tat-, -tas*; akin to Gk *-tēt-, -tēs* -ty, Skt *-tāt, -tāti*] **:** quality **:** condition **:** degree ⟨apriori*ty*⟩
ty *abbr* **1** territory **2** truly **3** type
ty·chism \ˈtīˌkizəm\ *n* -S [Gk *tychē* chance, fortune + E *-ism*; akin to Gk *tynchanein* to happen, happen on, attain, *teuchein* to make, build — more at DOUGHTY] **1 :** a theory that chance is an objective reality; *esp* **:** a theory in evolution that variation may be purely fortuitous — contrasted with *uniformitarianism* **2 :** a proposition that absolute chance is operative in the cosmos
tychite \ˈtīˌkīt, ˈtiˌk-\ *n* -S [Gk *tychē* + E *-ite*; fr. its chance discovery among other crystals] **:** a rare mineral $Na_6Mg_2(SO_4)(CO_3)_4$ that is an octahedral sulfate and carbonate of sodium and magnesium (hardness 3.5–4, sp. gr. 2.59)
tychi·us \ˈtikēəs, ˈtik-\ *n, cap* [NL, fr. Gk *Tychios*, name of a maker of shields in Homer's *Iliad*] **:** a genus of weevils containing some that feed destructively esp. on clovers
ty·chon·ic \(ˈ)tīˈkänik, (ˈ)tē¦-\ *or* **ty·cho·ni·an** \-kōnēən\ *adj, usu cap* [NL *Tychon-, Tycho* (Latinized form of *Tycho* Brahe †1601 Dan. astronomer) + E *-ic* or *-ian*] **:** of or relating to Tycho Brahe or his system of astronomy
ty·cho·parthenogenesis \ˈtīkō+\ *n* [NL, fr. Gk *tychē* chance + NL *-o-* + *parthenogenesis* — more at TYCHISM] **:** parthenogenesis occurring in a species in which it is not the usual method of reproduction
ty·cho·potamic \ˌtī(ˌ)kō+\ *adj* [ISV *tych-* (fr. Gk *tychē*) + *-o-* + *potamic*] *of an aquatic organism* **:** thriving chiefly in still waters (as of ponds) and occurring only incidentally in flowing waters — compare AUTOPOTAMIC, EUPOTAMIC
ty·coon \(ˈ)tīˈkün\ *n* -S [Jap *taikun*, fr. Chin (Pek) *ta*[4] great + *chün*[1] ruler] **1 :** SHOGUN **2 a :** a businessman of exceptional wealth, power, and influence **b :** a masterful and potent leader (as in politics)
tyd·den *or* **tyd·dyn** \ˈtithən, ˈtəth-\ *n* -S [W *tyddyn*, fr. MW, fr. *tŷ* house + *dyn* hill; akin to L *tegere* to cover and to OIr *dūn* fortress — more at THATCH, TOWN] *Wales* **:** a small farm **:** HOMESTEAD
tyd·ie \ˈtidē\ *n* -S [prob. fr. ME *tydife*] **:** a small bird variously identified as a wren or the blue titmouse — compare TIDLEY
1**tye** \ˈtī\ *n* -S [ME, casket, fr. OE *tēag*, of unknown origin] **1** *obs* **:** a small box (as for the storage of valuables) **2** *Brit* **:** a launder for washing ores
2**tye** \"\ *vt* -ED/-ING/-S *Brit* **:** to wash (ores) in a tye
3**tye** \"\ *n* -S [ME, fr. OE *tēag*, of unknown origin] **1** *obs* **:** a piece of enclosed land **2** *dial Eng* **:** a large pasture or common
4**tye** \"\ *n* -S [ME, tie — more at TIE] **:** a chain or rope one end of which passes through the mast or through a block and is made fast to the center of a yard, the other end being attached to a tackle by means of which a yard is hoisted or lowered — see SAIL illustration
ty·ee \ˈtīˌē\ *n* -S [Chinook jargon, fr. Nootka *ta·yi·* elder brother, senior] **1 :** CHIEF, BOSS, LEADER **2** *also* **tyee salmon :** a king or chinook salmon esp. when of large size
tyer *var of* TIER
Ty·fon \ˈtīˌfän\ *trademark* — used for a diaphragm horn used esp. in signaling during a fog at sea
tyg \ˈtig\ *n* -S [origin unknown] **:** a large usu. slip-decorated ceramic drinking cup with two or more handles
tygh \ˈtī\ *n, pl* **tygh** *or* **tyghs** *usu cap* **1 :** a Shahaptian people of west central Oregon **2 :** a member of the Tygh people
tying *adj* [fr. *tying*, pres. part. of ²*tie*] **:** relating to, constituting, or putting into effect a tying agreement ⟨~ contract⟩ ⟨~ clause⟩ ⟨~ arrangement⟩
tying agreement \ˈ==-\ *n* **:** an often illegal agreement by one party to sell a product or service only on condition that the buyer will also purchase another and different product or service or will not purchase the product or service from any other supplier or will adhere to some other restriction; *esp* **:** one that compels a buyer to purchase an undesired product or service in order to purchase a desired product or service
tying-in \ˈ==ˈ=\ *n* -S **:** the attaching of the ends of a new warp to those of the old by tying them together — compare TWISTING-IN
tyke *also* **tike** \ˈtīk\ *n* -S [ME *tyke*, fr. ON *tīk* bitch; akin to MLG *tīke* bitch] **1 :** DOG; *esp* **:** an inferior or mongrel dog **2 a :** an unpleasing and usu. clumsy, churlish, or eccentric person **b :** a small child esp. when an object of pity or commiseration ⟨poor little ~⟩ **c :** YORKSHIREMAN
tyl- *or* **tylo-** *comb form* [Gk, fr. *tylos, tylē* knob, lump, callus, pad — more at THOLE] **:** knob **:** knobbed ⟨*tyl*aster⟩ ⟨*Tylo*saurus⟩ **:** pad ⟨*Tylo*poda⟩
tyl·a·rus \ˈtīlərəs, təˈla(a)rəs\ *n, pl* **tyla·ri** \ˈ==ˌrī, -ˌrē; =ˈ=ˌrī, -ˌrē\ [NL, modif. of Gk *tylēros* callous, fr. *tylos, tylē* callus] **:** a pad on the undersurface of a bird's toe
tyl·as·ter \ˈtīˌlastə(r), ˈtiˌl-\ *n* [NL, fr. *tyl-* + *-aster*] **:** a small sponge spicule with the ends of the rays knobbed
tyle *var of* TILE
ty·lench \ˈtīˌleŋk, təˈl-\ *n* -S [NL *Tylenchus*] **:** ²TYLENCHID
1**ty·len·chid** \tīˈleŋkəd, təˈl-\ *adj* [NL *Tylenchidae*] **:** of or relating to the Tylenchidae
2**tylenchid** \"\ *n* -S **:** a worm of the family Tylenchidae
ty·len·chi·dae \-kəˌdē\ *n pl, cap* [NL, fr. *Tylenchus*, type genus + *-idae*] **:** a family of soil-dwelling or plant-parasitic phasmid nematode worms (superfamily Tylenchoidea) related to the Heteroderidae but usu. having a bursa in the male — see TYLENCHULUS, TYLENCHUS; compare HETERODERA
ty·len·choid \-ŋˌkȯid\ *adj* [NL *Tylenchoidea*] **:** of or relating to the Tylenchoidea
tylen·choi·dea \ˌtīˌleŋˈkȯidēə, ˌtiˌl-, -enˈk-\ *n pl, cap* [NL, fr. *Tylenchus* + *-oidea*] **:** a superfamily of soil-dwelling or plant-parasitic nematodes (order Rhabditida) with a dorsal esophageal gland opening near the base of the buccal spear — see HETERODERA, TYLENCHIDAE
ty·len·chu·lus \tīˈleŋkyələs, təˈl-\ *n, cap* [NL, fr. *Tylenchus* + *-ulus*] **:** a genus of nematode worms (family Tylenchidae) that includes the destructive citrus nematode
ty·len·chus \-kəs\ *n, cap* [NL, fr. *tyl-* + Gk *enchos* spear] **:** a genus of nematode worms (family Tylenchidae) usu. restricted to soil-dwelling forms that are saprophagous or feed on roots but formerly including numerous serious plant parasites (as the bulb eelworm) that are mostly placed in the genus *Anguina*
tyler *var of* TILER
tyl·i·on \ˈtilēˌän\ *n, pl* **tyl·ia** \-ēə\ [NL, fr. *tyl-* + *-ion* (as in *rhinion*)] **:** a craniometric point on the anterior edge of the optic groove at the median line of the skull
tylo- — see TYL-
ty·lo·pod \ˈtīləˌpäd\ *n* -S [NL *Tylopoda*] **:** a mammal or fossil of the suborder Tylopoda — **ty·lop·o·dous** \(ˈ)tīˈläpədəs\ *adj*
ty·lop·o·da \tīˈläpədə\ *n pl, cap* [NL, fr. *tyl-* + *-poda*] **:** a suborder of Artiodactyla or in some classifications a division of Ruminantia comprising the camels and extinct related forms
ty·lo·ri·an \(ˈ)tīˈlōrēən\ *adj, usu cap* [Sir Edward B. *Tylor* †1917 Eng. anthropologist + E *-an*] **:** of, relating to, or constituting the anthropological writings or theories of Sir Edward Burnett Tylor
ty·lo·sau·rus \ˌtīləˈsȯrəs\ *n, cap* [NL, fr. *tyl-* + *-saurus*] **:** a genus of large pythonomorph reptiles from the Upper Cretaceous of Kansas, New Mexico, and Texas having a short body, long tail, and pentadactyl limbs functioning as paddles
ty·lose \ˈtiˌlōs, təˈl-\ *n* -S [F, fr. Gk *tylōsis*] **:** TYLOSIS
ty·lo·sis \tīˈlōsəs\ *n, pl* **tylo·ses** \-ōˌsēz\ [NL, fr. Gk *tylōsis* act of making or becoming callous, fr. *tyloun* to make callous, make knobby, fr. *tylos* callus, knob — more at THOLE] **1 :** one of the protrusions from plant parenchyma cells into adjacent tracheary elements usu. through a pit-pair and often numerous enough to completely fill the lumen **2 :** a thickening and hardening of an organ or body part **:** CALLOSITY
ty·lo·soid \tīˈlōˌsȯid\ *n* -S [NL *tylosis* + E *-oid*] **:** a protrusion into a resin canal of a conifer resembling a tylosis but produced by proliferation of epithelial cells
ty·lo·style \ˈtīləˌstīl\ *n* [*tyl-* + *style*] **:** a uniradiate pointed sponge spicule with a knob at the blunt end
ty·lo·stylus \¦tīlō+\ *n, pl* **tylostyli** [NL, fr. *tyl-* + *stylus*] **:** TYLOSTYLE
ty·los·urus \ˌtīləˈsürəs\ *n, cap* [NL, irreg. fr. Gk *tylos* callus, pad, knob + NL *-urus*; fr. the structure of the caudal keel — more at THOLE] **:** a genus of needlefishes (family Belonidae) including commercially important food fishes
ty·lo·tate \ˈtīlōˌtāt\ *adj* [NL *tylotus* tylote + E *-ate*] **:** knobbed at both ends ⟨a ~ sponge spicule⟩
ty·lote \ˈtīˌlōt\ *n* -S [NL *tylotus*, fr. Gk *tylōtos* knobbed, fr. *tyloun* to make knobby — more at TYLOSIS] **:** a slender elongate sponge spicule with a knob at both ends
ty·lot·ic \(ˈ)tī¦läd·ik\ *adj* [fr. NL *tylosis*, after such pairs as NL *narcosis*: E *narcotic*] **:** of, relating to, or marked by tylosis
ty·lot·ox·ea \ˌtīlōˈtäksēə, -ˌtäkˈsēə\ *n, pl* **tylotox·e·ae** \-ēˌē\ [NL, fr. *tylotus* tylote + *oxea*] **:** a rodlike sponge spicule tapering toward the ends one of which is sharp and one knobbed — **ty·lot·ox·e·ate** \sēət\ *adj*
ty·lus \ˈtīləs\ *n, pl* **tyli** [NL, fr. Gk *tylos* knob — more at THOLE] **:** a central prominence on the upper front side of the head of some hemipterons
ty·lwyth teg \ˌtəˈlüithˈteg\ *n* [W *tylwyth* family (fr. *tŷ* house + *llwyth* tribe) + *teg* fair, beautiful; akin to L *tegere* to cover and to OHG *loh* enclosure — more at THATCH, LOCK, THIG] **:** the fairies of Welsh folklore
tymbal *var of* TIMBAL
tym·ba·lon \ˈtimbəˌlän\ *n* -S [by alter.] **:** TIMBAL
tymp \ˈtimp\ *n* -S [short for *tympan*] **:** the stone or the water-cooled iron casting protecting the top of the opening through which molten slag and iron continually pass into the forehearth in an old type open-front iron blast furnace
tym·pan *also* **tim·pan** \ˈtimpən\ *n* -S [in sense 1a, fr. ME *tympan, timpan*, fr. OE *timpana*, fr. L *tympanum*; in sense 1b, fr. IrGael *tiompan*, fr. L *tympanum* drum; in other senses fr. ML *tympanum* eardrum & L *tympanum* drum, architectural panel — more at TYMPANUM] **1 a :** DRUM **b :** a Celtic bowed stringed musical instrument **2 a** *obs* **:** TYMPANUM 1a(1) **b :** any of various membranous plates functioning basically like the membranous tympanum of the ear **3 a** *or* **tympan sheet :** a sheet of material (as paper or cloth) in a printing press that is placed between the impression surface (as the platen or impression cylinder) and the paper to be printed **:** DRAWSHEET **b** *or* **tympan frame :** either of two frames that hold the tympan sheet of a handpress: (1) **:** an inner frame over which the tympan sheet is drawn (2) **:** an outer frame that holds the tympan sheet in place **4 :** an architectural panel **:** TYMPANUM
tympan- *or* **tympano-** *comb form* [NL *tympanum*] **1 :** tympanum **:** tympanic membrane ⟨*tympan*itis⟩ ⟨*tympano*tomy⟩ **2 :** tympanic and ⟨*tympano*eustachian⟩
tym·pa·nal \ˈtimpənᵊl\ *adj or n* [NL *tympanum* + E *-al*] **:** TYMPANIC
tym·pa·ni *n pl but sometimes sing in constr* [modif. (influenced by *tympanum*) of It *timpani*] **:** TIMPANI
1**tym·pan·ic** \(ˈ)timˈpanik, -nēk\ *adj* [L & NL *tympanum* + E *-ic*] **1 :** of, relating to, associated with, or constituting an anatomical tympanum and esp. the eardrum — see TYMPANIC ANTRUM, TYMPANIC BONE, TYMPANIC CANAL, TYMPANIC MEMBRANE, TYMPANIC NERVE **2 :** of or relating to an architectural tympanum **3 :** resembling or resembling that of a drum ⟨a ~ roll of steady artillery —P.S.Wolff⟩
2**tympanic** \"\ *n* -S **:** a tympanic body part (as a bone or nerve)
tympanic antrum *n* **:** a large air-containing cavity in the mastoid process communicating with the tympanum and often being the seat of dangerous inflammation
tympanic bone *n* **:** a bone of the skull of a mammal that encloses a part of the middle ear, supports the tympanic membrane, and is often fused with the temporal bone
tympanic canal *n* **:** a minute canal leading into the middle ear and transmitting the tympanic nerve (sense 1)
tympanic cavity *n* **:** the cavity of the middle ear
tympanic membrane *n* **:** a thin membrane closing externally the cavity of the middle ear like the head of a drum and in mammals being deeply located at the bottom of the external auditory meatus, in birds and reptiles more superficially, and in frogs and toads on the surface — see EAR illustration
tympanic nerve *n* **1 :** a branch of the glossopharyngeal nerve arising from the petrosal ganglion and distributed to the walls of the tympanum of the ear where it takes part in forming a plexus — called also *Jacobson's nerve* **2 :** a branch of the facial nerve to the stapedius muscle
tympanic notch *n* **:** a notch in the tympanic plate filled by Shrapnell's membrane
tympanic plate *n* **:** the tympanic bone of man having in the adult the form of a plate fused with the petrous part of the temporal bone
tym·pani·form \ˈtimpənəˌfȯrm, (ˈ)timˈpan-\ *adj* [*tympan-* + *-iform*] **:** resembling a tympanum
tym·pan·ing \ˈtimpəniŋ\ *n* -S [*tympan* + *-ing*] **:** material used in making a tympan for a printing press
tym·pa·nism \ˈtimpəˌnizəm\ *n* -S [ISV *tympany* + *-ism*] **:** TYMPANITES
tym·pa·nist \ˈtimpənəst\ *n* -S [L *tympanista*, fr. Gk *tympanistēs*, fr. *tympanizein* to beat a drum, fr. *tympanon* drum + *-izein* -ize — more at TYMPANUM] **:** one that beats a drum; *specif* **:** a member of an orchestra who plays the kettledrums
tym·pa·ni·tes \ˌtimpəˈnīd·(ˌ)ēz\ *also* **tym·pa·ni·tis** \-d·əs\ *n* -ES [ME *tympanites*, fr. LL, fr. Gk *tympanitēs*, fr. *tympanon*] **:** a distension of the abdomen caused by accumulation of air or gas in the intestinal tract or peritoneal cavity — compare BLOAT
tym·pa·nit·ic \¦==¦nid·ik\ *adj* [LL *tympaniticus*, fr. *tympanites* + L *-icus* -ic] **1 :** of, relating to, or affected with tympanites **2 :** resonant on percussion **:** hollow-sounding
tym·pa·ni·tis \ˌtimpəˈnīd·əs\ *n* -ES [NL, fr. *tympan-* + *-itis*] **:** OTITIS MEDIA
tym·pa·no·hy·al \¦timpənō¦hīəl\ *n* -S [*tympan-* + *hy-* + *-al*] **:** the proximal segment in the hyoid arch becoming a part of the styloid process of the temporal bone in adult man
tym·pa·non \ˈtimpəˌnän\ *n, pl* **tympa·na** \-pənə\ *also* **tympanons** [Gk — more at TYMPANUM] **:** TYMPAN 1a
tympan paper *n* **:** a hard paper treated with oil or glycerin and used as a tympan on printing presses
tym·pa·nu·chus \ˌtimpəˈn(y)ükəs\ *n, cap* [NL, fr. Gk *tympanon* drum + *-ochos* (fr. *echein* to have, hold) — more at SCHEME] **:** a genus of American grouse consisting of the prairie chickens
tym·pa·num \ˈtimpənəm\ *n, pl* **tympa·na** \-nə\ *also* **tympanums** [ML & L; ML *tympanum* eardrum, fr. L, drum, architectural panel, fr. Gk *tympanon* drum, kettledrum; akin to Gk *typtein* to strike, beat — more at TYPE] **1 a** (1) **:** the tense double membrane separating the outer and middle ear **:** TYMPANIC MEMBRANE — called also *eardrum* (2) **:** MIDDLE EAR **b :** a thin tense membrane covering an organ of hearing (as in the leg) of an insect — see INSECT illustration **c** (1) **:** a membrane in a sound-producing organ that acts as a resonator (2) **:** TRACHEAL TYMPANUM **d :** one of the naked areas on the neck of the prairie chicken and other grouse that are expanded when the esophagus is inflated in display **2 a :** the recessed face of a pediment situated within the frame made by the upper and lower cornices and usu. shaped like a triangle or panel **b :** the space within an arch and above a lintel or a subordinate arch spanning the opening below the arch **3 :** TYMPAN 1a **4 :** a water-raising wheel resembling a Persian wheel **5 :** EPIPHRAGM 2a **6 :** the diaphragm of a telephone
tym·pa·ny \ˈtimpənē\ *n* -ES [ML *tympanias*, fr. Gk, fr. *tympanon* drum] **1 a :** TYMPANITES **b :** resonance on percussion **2** *archaic* **a :** a condition of being swollen out or inflated (as with pride, arrogance, or self-satisfaction) **b :** bombastic or turgid style (as of expression) **3 :** TYMPAN
tymps *pl of* TYMP
tymp stick \ˈtimpˌ=\ *n* [*tymp*, short for *tympani*] **:** a timpani drumstick
tyn·dall beam *or* **tyndall cone** \¦tindᵊl-\ *n, usu cap T* [after John *Tyndall* †1893 Brit. physicist] **:** the luminous path formed in the Tyndall effect by the breaking up of the entering light by the suspended particles

tyndall blue *n, usu cap T* **:** bluish plane-polarized light (as in the sky) scattered in the Tyndall effect

tyndall effect *also* **tyndall phenomenon** *n, usu cap T* [after John *Tyndall* †1893] **:** the scattering of a beam of light when passed through a medium containing small suspended particles (as smoky or mist-laden air or colloidal solutions) — compare RAYLEIGH SCATTERING

tyn·dall·om·e·ter \ˌtindᵊlˈämәd·ә(r)\ *n* [*tyndall (beam)* + *-o-* + *-meter*] **:** an apparatus for measuring the brightness of the Tyndall beam — called also *Tyndall meter;* compare NEPHELOMETER

tyne *var of* TINE

typ- *or* **typo-** *comb form* [Gk, fr. *typos* — more at TYPE] **:** type **:** image **:** model ⟨*typ*onym⟩ ⟨*typo*logy⟩

typ *abbr* **1** typewriter; typewritten **2** typical **3** typographer; typographic; typographical

typ·able *or* **type·able** \ˈtīpәbәl\ *adj* **:** that may be typed

typ·age \ˈtīpij\ *n* -S [²*type* + *-age*] **:** TYPECASTING

typ·al \ˈtīpәl\ *adj* [¹*type* + *-al*] **1 :** of or relating to a type **2 :** serving as a type **:** TYPICAL

¹**type** \ˈtīp\ *n* -S *often attrib* [LL *typus,* fr. L & Gk; L *typus* image, fr. Gk *typos* blow, impression, image, model, type, fr. *typtein* to strike, beat; akin to L *stuprum* defilement, dishonor, Skt *tupati, tumpati* he hurts] **1 a :** something that serves as a symbolic representation usu. of a thing yet to come into being **:** PREFIGURATION, TOKEN ⟨concludes that the whole of the Old Testament is one great prophecy, one great ~ of what was to come —A.J.Maas⟩ ⟨a ~ of the one who was to come —Rom 5:14 (RSV)⟩ ⟨a Christian ~ differs from an allegory in that the historical reference is not lost sight of —*Oxford Dict. of the Christian Church*⟩ **b :** one (as an object, a person, or a kind of entity) that possesses or exemplifies qualities of a higher category **:** MODEL, EXEMPLAR: as (1) **:** a lower taxonomic category selected as a standard of reference for a higher category and usu. chosen as the subgroup most perfectly exemplifying the higher category; *also* **:** the specimen or series of specimens on which a taxonomic species or subspecies is actually based — see TYPE SPECIMEN (2) **:** a simple chemical compound used as a model or pattern to which other compounds are conveniently regarded as being related and from which they may be actually or theoretically derived **2 a** *obs* **:** a figurative representation **:** IMAGE **b :** a distinctive mark or sign ⟨the banked foundations that are such a ~ of old-time rural winter life⟩ **c :** the central figure on either side of a coin, medal, or piece of paper money **d** (1) **:** a postage stamp design esp. when differing from another only in small details ⟨~ one has thin, ~ two thick letters and numerals⟩ or when appearing on stamps of more than one denomination or on stamps differing in other details (as paper, perforation, or watermark) ⟨the 1 cent and 3 cent stamps were of the same ~⟩ (2) **:** the arrangement of a particular overprint or surcharge on a stamp **3 a :** a usu. metal, wood, or plastic rectangular block having on its face a relief character of which an inked impression will produce a printed character ⟨a piece of ~⟩ **b :** a collection of such blocks ⟨a case of ~⟩ ⟨a font of ~⟩; *also* **:** a composed assembly of such single blocks from which something is to be printed or of comparable units cast in the form of a solid slug ⟨a ~ page⟩ ⟨a galley of ~⟩ **c :** characters forming the faces of typebars (as in a typewriter) **d :** characters functioning as type in photocomposition **e :** TYPEFACE ⟨a very condensed ~⟩ **f :** a printed impression from type **:** printed matter ⟨very small ~ can be hard to read⟩ **4 a :** qualities common to a number of individuals that serve to distinguish them as an identifiable class or kind: as (1) **:** a set of determinable and usu. physically measurable qualities that on the average is held in common by the members of a relatively homogeneous human group (as a family, a tribe, or a race) (2) **:** the combination of characters that fits an individual or kind of individual to a particular use or function ⟨meat ~ poultry⟩ ⟨a strong horse of draft ~⟩ (3) **:** the morphological, physiological, or ecological characters by which relationship between organisms may be recognized (4) **:** qualities (as of bodily contour and carriage) that are felt to indicate excellence in members of a group ⟨won the show with a beagle of superior ~⟩ (5) **:** a form of structure or symmetry common to a group of crystals (6) **:** the general form of a word as contrasted with its particular instances in speech or writing — called also *type-word;* contrasted with *token* ⟨if a man twice says "it's raining," he utters two tokens of one ~ —D.C.Williams⟩ **b :** an individual exhibiting distinguishable qualities of its kind **:** a typical and often superior specimen ⟨a dog that is a ~ beagle⟩ **c :** a group or category exhibiting such type **:** a particular kind, class, or group ⟨infections of the most deadly ~⟩ ⟨oranges of a seedless ~⟩ ⟨a physique of the pyknic ~⟩: as (1) **:** a large taxonomic category characterized by basic rather than detailed similarities among its members and being essentially equivalent to division or phylum of other taxonomic systems (2) **:** any of various closely related minor categories usu. distinguishable on physiologic or serological bases — compare BLOOD GROUP, PHYSIOLOGIC RACE, SEROTYPE (3) **:** a group of soils developed from like parent material and having similar horizons, texture, and profile arrangement (4) **:** a class of objects or a style peculiar to a particular archaeological site or period (5) **:** one of a hierarchy of mutually exclusive classifications of arguments in a logical calculus suggested as a means of resolving the logical paradoxes ⟨individuals, classes of individuals, and classes of classes of individuals are entities of progressively higher ~s⟩ ⟨a class cannot be of the same ~ as its members⟩ — compare RUSSELL'S PARADOX **d :** something felt to be distinguishable as a variety or kind **:** SORT ⟨a new ~ submarine⟩ ⟨won't stand for that ~ of behavior⟩ **5** [origin unknown] **:** a canopy sounding board for a pulpit

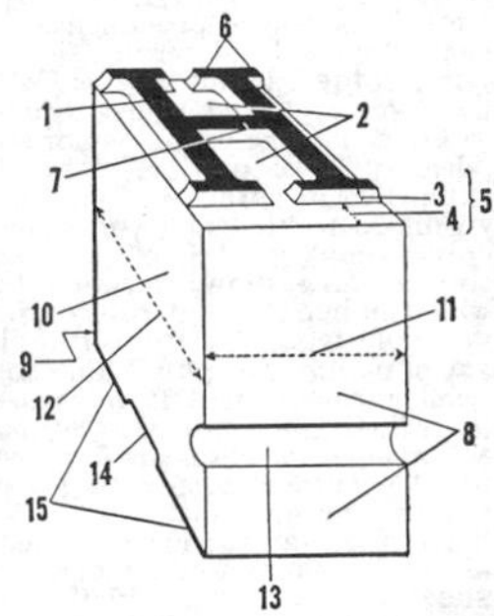

type 3: *1* face, *2* counters, *3* bevel, *4* shoulder, *5* beard, *6* serifs, *7* crossbar, *8* belly, *9* back, *10* body, shank, or stem, *11* set size, *12* point size, *13* nick, *14* groove, *15* feet

syn KIND, SORT, STRIPE, KIDNEY, ILK, DESCRIPTION, NATURE, CHARACTER: TYPE may suggest strong and clearly marked similarities throughout the items included, so that each is typical of the group ⟨the landforms are related to these rock *types* —A.E.Trueman⟩ ⟨that most dangerous *type* of critic: the critic with a mind which is naturally of the creative order —T.S.Eliot⟩ KIND in most uses is likely to be very indefinite and involve any criterion of classification whatever ⟨each *kind* of mental or bodily activity —Herbert Spencer⟩ ⟨their soil yields treasures of every *kind* —H.T.Buckle⟩ ⟨the *kind* of fear here treated of is purely spiritual —Charles Lamb⟩ It may suggest criteria of grouping dependent on natural, intrinsic characteristics ⟨Sinic philosophers conceived yin and yang as two different *kinds* of matter . . . yin symbolized water and yang fire —A.J.Toynbee⟩ SORT is often a close synonym of KIND ⟨the *sort* of culture I am trying to define —J.C.Powys⟩ and may be used in situations having a suggestion of disparagement ⟨the *sort* of journals put out by the learned societies —*New Republic*⟩ ⟨Victorianism of a meaner and baser *sort* —F.B.Millett⟩ ⟨what *sort* of idiots have you got around here —A.W.Long⟩ TYPE, KIND, and SORT are usu. interchangeable and are used most of the time without attention to special connotations. STRIPE and KIDNEY are used mostly of people rather than things; the first may suggest political attitude or affiliation, the second persuasion, disposition, or social level ⟨all Fascists are not of one mind, one *stripe* —Lillian Hellman⟩ ⟨economic dogmatists of whatever *stripe* —*Atlantic*⟩ ⟨the crown representative and comptroller were political appointees, and like many men of that *kidney* had never done a fair share of the work —S.E.Morison⟩ ILK, orig. indicating clan or family, may suggest grouping on the basis of status, attitude, or temperament ⟨no matter if . . . your ancestors spoke only to Cabots and their *ilk* —Stanley Walker⟩ ⟨one great composer is worth twenty of your *ilk* —Bella & Samuel Spewack⟩ DESCRIPTION, NATURE, and CHARACTER are close synonyms of TYPE and KIND mostly in phrases beginning with *of.* DESCRIPTION may suggest a grouping in which all salient details of description or definition are involved; NATURE may suggest inherent, essential characteristics rather than superficial, ostensible, or tentative ones; and CHARACTER may stress distinctive or individualizing criteria ⟨all embargoes are not of this *description.* They are sometimes resorted to . . . with a single view to commerce —John Marshall⟩ ⟨the few hitherto known phenomena of a similar *nature* —*Amer. Jour. of Science*⟩ ⟨until the invention of printing advertising was necessarily of this primitive *character* —Charles Presbrey⟩ **syn** see in addition SYMBOL

²**type** \"\ *vb* -ED/-ING/-S *vt* **1 :** to represent beforehand as a type **:** PREFIGURE **2 :** to produce a copy of; *also* **:** REPRESENT, TYPIFY **3** [by shortening] **:** TYPEWRITE **4 :** to subsume under, classify as a member of, or identify as belonging to a type: as **a :** to determine the natural type of (as a sample of blood or a culture of bacteria) **b :** TYPECAST **c :** to cast (an actor) repeatedly in the same sort of role ⟨~ an actor as a butler or a gangster⟩ ~ *vi* [by shortening] **:** TYPEWRITE

typeable *var of* TYPABLE

typebar \ˈ=,=\ *n* **1 :** one of the bars on a typewriter that bears type for printing **2 :** ³SLUG 2c

typecase \ˈ=,=\ *n* **:** CASE 1d(1)

typecast \ˈ=,=\ *vt* [in sense 1, prob. back-formation fr. *typecasting;* in sense 2, fr. ¹*type* + *cast*] **1 :** to produce by typecasting ⟨~ ornament⟩ ⟨~ sorts⟩ **2 :** to cast (a theatrical performer) in a part calling for the same type of physique, personal quality, and temperament as that characterizing the actor in real life

typecasting *n* [¹*type* + *casting*] **:** the casting of printing type (as letters, rules, slugs, or borders) by pouring or forcing material (as type metal) in a molten or plastic state into a mold or matrix

type culture *n* **:** a viable culture of an organism that is directly descended from the strain or isolation on which the original description of the organism is based

type cutter *n* **:** an engraver of punches for making type

typeface \ˈ=,=\ *n* **1 :** the face of printing type; *also* **:** its printed impression **2 :** all type of a single design regardless of size ⟨our wide latin ~ comes in ten sizes, from 6 to 48 point⟩ — called also *face*

type family *n* **:** FAMILY 4c

typeform \ˈ=,=\ *n* **:** FORM 8a

typefounder \ˈ=,==\ *n* [¹*type* + *founder*] **:** one that is engaged in the design and production of metal printing type for hand composition

typefounding \ˈ=,==\ *n* [¹*type* + *founding*] **:** the business or occupation of a typefounder **:** the manufacture of metal printing type

typefoundry \ˈ=,==\ *n* [¹*type* + *foundry*] **:** the manufacturing establishment of a typefounder

type gauge *n* **:** LINE GAUGE

type genus *n* **:** the genus of a taxonomic family or subfamily from which the name of the family or subfamily is formed and which in practice is more often selected because it is the largest, best-known, or earliest-described genus or the one first used as the basis of a family or subfamily name than because its structure is most representative of the larger group as a whole

type height *n* **:** HEIGHT TO PAPER

type-high \ˈ=ˈ=\ *adj (or adv)* **:** having the same foot-to-face height as printing type and being 0.9186 inch in English-speaking countries ⟨plates must be mounted *type-high*⟩

type-high gage *n* **:** a fixed gage for measuring height to paper

typeholder \ˈ=,==\ *n* **:** a bookbinder's tool consisting of a head for holding set type and a handle and used for hand-stamping lettering (as on a book cover) — called also *pallet*

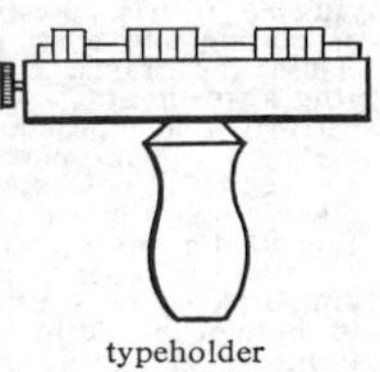
typeholder

type lice *n pl* **1 :** imaginary lice that the victim of a printer's joke is invited to observe by close scrutiny of set type previously soaked with water and squeezed together by the jokester at the moment of the victim's inspection thereby squirting dirty water in his face **2 :** the joke involving the scrutiny for type lice

type locality *n* **1 :** the source of an original type specimen **2 a :** the place whence a geological item (as a formation or series) derives its name and where it is typically displayed **b :** the first or original source of a geologic feature (as a fossil or particular kind of igneous rock)

type material *n* **:** a group of equivalent specimens collected at the type locality at one time and used wholly or partially in the identification and description of a new taxonomic entity

typ·embryo \(ˈ)tī¦p+\ *n* [*typ-* + *embryo*] **:** an embryo at the stage of development in which it first exhibits specific characteristics of the major natural group to which it belongs

type metal *n* **:** an alloy used in making type or stereotype or other plates and in backing up electrotype plates and consisting essentially of lead, antimony, and tin often with a little copper

type method *n* **:** the practice of basing the name of a taxon upon a type and accepting as validly published only those names so based

type o *n, usu cap O* **:** a blood group characterized by a serum that does not agglutinate the cells of any other member of the ABO system — called also *universal donor*

type object *n* **:** an object on which the original scientific description of a given class of objects is based

type page *n* **:** the printed area of a page (as of a book)

typ·er \ˈtīpә(r)\ *n* -S [²*type* + *-er*] **:** TYPIST

type-revolving press \ˈ==,==-\ *n* **:** an early rotary press printing from special tapered type fastened around the circumference of a cylinder

type rule *or* **type scale** *n* **:** LINE GAUGE

types *pl of* TYPE, *pres 3d sing of* TYPE

typescript \ˈtīp,skript\ *n* [²*type* + *manuscript*] **:** typewritten matter esp. when used as printer's copy

type section *n* **:** the original sequence of strata as described for a given locality

type series *n* **1 :** a group of representatives of a taxon (as a subspecies or species) selected to demonstrate the extent of variation of that unit ⟨a syntypic *type series*⟩ **2 :** SERIES 10

typeset \ˈ=,=\ *vt* **:** to set in type **:** COMPOSE ⟨~ a magazine article⟩ ⟨surcharges and overprints are usually ~ and printed in black —*Scott's Standard Postage Stamp Catalogue*⟩

typesetter \ˈ=,==\ *n* **:** one that sets type: **a :** COMPOSITOR, KEYBOARDER **b :** TYPESETTING MACHINE

typesetting machine *n* [fr. gerund of *typeset*] **:** any of various keyboard machines for automatically composing printing type either by assembling and sometimes distributing ordinary foundry type or a modification of it or more often by producing keyboarded matter through forcing hot metal into matrices

type species *n* **:** the species of a genus with which the generic name is permanently associated and upon which the original generic description is largely or wholly based **:** the type of a genus **:** GENOTYPE

type specimen *n* **:** a specimen or individual designated as type of a species or lesser group and serving as the final criterion of the characteristics of that group — compare HOLOTYPE, ISOTYPE, PARATYPE, TOPOTYPE

type station *or* **type site** *n* **:** the place of discovery of prehistoric remains that have been agreed upon as the standard for a specified culture

type theory *n* **:** the theory that chemical compounds are derived by substitution from a limited number of type compounds (as hydrogen, water, ammonia, and methane) and that developed into the modern unitary theory

type wash *n* **:** an ink solvent for cleaning type or printing plates

type wheel *n* **:** a wheel made with raised characters on its periphery and used in some typewriters, printing telegraphs, and other printing devices

type-word \ˈ=,=\ *n* **:** TYPE 4a(6) ⟨twenty tokens of the *type-word* "the" may occur on a single page⟩

type·write \ˈtī,prīt, *usu* -īd·+V\ *vb* [back-formation fr. *typewriter*] *vt* **:** to write (as a letter) with a typewriter ~ *vi* **:** to use a typewriter

type·writ·er \-īd·ә(r), -ītә-\ *n* [¹*type* + *writer*] **1 :** any of various instruments or machines for writing in characters similar to those produced by printers' types; *esp* **:** one in which the characters are produced by steel types striking the paper through an inked ribbon with the types being actuated by corresponding keys on a keyboard and the paper being held by a platen that is automatically moved along with a carriage when a key is struck **2** [*typewrite* + *-er*] **:** TYPIST **3 :** a printing typeface that is designed to imitate typewriting and that usu. has all characters of the same set

SPACE BAR

typewriter keyboard

typewriting *n* [fr. gerund of *typewrite*] **1 :** the act, study, or art of using a typewriter **2 :** the printing done with a typewriter **3 :** a typewritten paper

typewriting telegraph *n* **:** a telegraph system using apparatus similar to a typewriter as transmitter or receiver or both

typey *var of* TYPY

typh- *or* **typho-** *comb form* [NL *typhus*] **:** typhus **:** typhoid ⟨*typho*sepsis⟩

ty·pha \ˈtīfә\ *n, cap* [NL, fr. Gk *typhē* cattail — more at TUBER] **:** a genus of tall erect herbs (family Typhaceae) that occur in fresh and salt marshes and have sword-shaped leaves and monoecious flowers in dense spikes with the staminate uppermost — see CATTAIL

ty·pha·ce·ae \tīˈfāsē,ē\ *n pl, cap* [NL, fr. *Typha,* type genus + *-aceae*] **:** a family of perennial marsh plants (order Pandanales) with creeping rootstocks, long linear leaves, and cylindrical spikes of flowers — **ty·pha·ceous** \(ˈ)tī¦fāshәs\ *adj*

ty·phic \ˈtifik\ *adj* [ISV *typh-* + *-ic*] **1 :** of or relating to typhus **2 :** TYPHOID

typhl- *or* **typhlo-** *comb form* [in sense 1, fr. Gk, blind, fr. *typhlos;* in sense 2, fr. Gk *typhlon,* fr. neut. of *typhlos* blind — more at DEAF] **1 :** blind ⟨*typhlo*sole⟩ **:** blindness ⟨*typhlo*logy⟩ **2 :** cecum ⟨*typhl*itis⟩ ⟨*typhlo*tomy⟩

typh·li·tis \tiˈflīd·әs\ *n* -ES [NL, fr. *typhl-* + *-itis*] **:** inflammation of the cecum

typh·lo·cy·ba \ˌtiflәˈsībә\ *n, cap* [NL, prob. fr. *typhl-* + Gk *kybistan* to turn somersaults, tumble] **:** a widely distributed genus of leafhoppers that includes several destructive pests of various cultivated trees and crop plants

typh·lol·o·gy \tiˈflälәjē\ *n* -ES [*typhl-* + *-logy*] **:** the scientific study of blindness, its causes, effects, and control **:** a branch of science that deals with blindness

typh·lo·molge \ˌtiflō+\ *n, cap* [NL, fr. *typhl-* + *Molge*] **:** a genus of neotenic salamanders (family Plethodontidae) of underground waters that are known from a single species (*T. rathbuni*) of Texas and that lack functional eyes

typh·lop·i·dae \tiˈfläpә,dē\ *n pl, cap* [NL, fr. *Typhlop-, Typhlops,* type genus (fr. Gk *typhlōp-, typhlōps* blind-eyed, fr. *typhl-* + *-ōp-, ōps* eye) + *-idae* — more at EYE] **:** a widely distributed family of small burrowing snakes having the whole body covered with uniform cycloid scales, the mouth not distensible, and the teeth restricted to the upper jaw — see BLIND SNAKE

typh·lo·so·lar \ˌtiflә¦sōlә(r)\ *adj* **:** of, relating to, or constituting a typhlosole

typh·lo·sole \ˈ==,sōl\ *n* -S [*typhl-* + Gk *sōlēn* channel, pipe — more at SYRINGE] **:** a longitudinal fold of the wall projecting into the cavity of the intestine esp. in bivalve mollusks, some annelids, and starfishes

ty·phoe·an \(ˈ)tī¦fēәn\ *adj, usu cap* [L *Typhoeus,* giant of Greek mythology buried under Mt. Etna (fr. Gk *Typhōeus*) + E *-an*] **:** of, relating to, or resembling the mythical monstrous giant Typhoeus

¹**ty·phoid** \ˈtī,fȯid *also* (ˈ)tīˈf-\ *adj* [in sense 1, fr. NL *typhus* + E *-oid;* in sense 2, fr. ²*typhoid*] **1 :** of, relating to, or typical of typhus **:** of the kind occurring in typhus ⟨in tuberculous meningitis . . . the patient sinks into the ~ state —R.M. Goepp †1950 & H.F.Flippin⟩ **2 :** of, relating to, or constituting typhoid fever ⟨the ~ bacillus⟩

²**typhoid** \"\ *or* **typhoid fever** *n* -S [*typhoid* fr. *typhoid fever,* trans. of F *fièvre typhoïde*] **1 :** a communicable disease characterized by fever, diarrhea, prostration, apathy, headache, splenomegaly, eruption of rose spots, leukopenia, and inflammation of the intestinal mucosa and caused by a bacterium (*Salmonella typhosa*) **2 :** any of several diseases of domestic animals in some respects felt to resemble human typhus or typhoid: as **a :** FOWL TYPHOID **b :** HOG CHOLERA **c :** INFECTIOUS ANEMIA **d :** shipping fever of horses

ty·phoi·dal \(ˈ)tī¦fȯidᵊl\ *adj* [²*typhoid* + *-al*] **:** of, relating to, or resembling typhoid fever

typhoid fly *n* **:** HOUSEFLY

typhoid mary *n, usu cap T&M* [after *Typhoid Mary,* name given to Mary Mallon †1938 Irish cook in U.S. who was found to be a typhoid carrier] **:** one that is by force of circumstances a center or focus from which something undesirable spreads ⟨authoritarianism . . . is carried by *Typhoid Marys,* unwitting sources of infection —S.P.Hayes b. 1910⟩

ty·pho·ni·an \(ˈ)tī¦fōnēәn\ *also* **ty·phon·ic** \-ˈfänik\ *adj, often cap* [L *Typhon,* monster of Greek mythology identified with the Egyptian god Set (fr. Gk *Typhōn*) + E *-ian, -ic*] **:** of, relating to, or resembling the monster Typhon of ancient mythology or the Egyptian god Set ⟨the gazelle is a ~ symbol in Egyptian art⟩

typhonic \"\ *adj* [Gk *typhōnikos,* fr. *typhōn* whirlwind + *-ikos* -ic] **:** of, relating to, resembling, or suggestive of a typhoon

ty·phoon \(ˈ)tī¦fün\ *n* -S [alter. (influenced by Gk *typhōn* whirlwind and Chin — Cant — *taai fung* typhoon, fr. *taai* great + *fung* wind) of earlier *touffon, tufan,* fr. Ar *ṭūfān* hurricane, deluge, fr. Gk *typhōn* whirlwind; akin to Gk *typhein* to smoke — more at DEAF] **:** a tropical cyclone occurring in the region of the Philippines or the China sea **syn** see WIND

ty·phous \ˈtīfәs\ *adj* [NL *typhus* + E *-ous*] **:** of or relating to typhus **:** resembling or characteristic of typhus

typh·u·la \ˈtifyәlә\ *n, cap* [NL, fr. Gk *typhē* cattail + NL *-ula* — more at TUBER] **:** a genus of club fungi (family Clavariaceae) with simple or slightly branched filamentous sporophores

ty·phus \ˈtīfәs\ *also* **typhus fever** *n* -ES [NL *typhus,* fr. Gk *typhos* fever, delusion, pride; akin to Gk *typhein* to smoke — more at DEAF] **1 :** any of three human rickettsial diseases: **a :** a severe febrile disease characterized by high fever, stupor alternating with delirium, intense headache, and a dark red rash and caused by a rickettsia (*Rickettsia prowazekii*) that is transmitted esp. by body lice **b :** MURINE TYPHUS **c :** TSUTSUGAMUSHI DISEASE **2 :** CANICOLA FEVER

typ·ic \ˈtipik, -pēk\ *adj* [F *typique,* fr. LL *typicus,* fr. Gk *typikos,* fr. *typos* type + *-ikos* -ic] **:** TYPICAL; *esp* **:** conforming to type

typ·i·cal \ˈtipәkәl, -pēk-\ *adj* [LL *typicalis,* fr. *typicus* typical + L *-alis* -al] **1 :** constituting or having the nature of a type **:** representing something by a form, model, or resemblance **:** EMBLEMATIC, PREFIGURATIVE **2 a :** combining or exhibiting the essential characteristics of a group sharing the nature of a type ⟨a ~ Victorian Sunday dinner⟩ ⟨the ~ modern girl⟩ **b :** conforming to a type ⟨a ~ species⟩ **syn** see REGULAR

typical bathyal zone *n* **:** the upper half of the bathyal zone

typ·i·cal·i·ty \ˌtipәˈkaləd·ē, -lәtē, -i\ *n* -ES [*typical* + *-ity*] **:** TYPICALNESS

typ·i·cal·ly \ˈtipәk(ә)lē, -pēk-, -li\ *adv* **:** in a typical manner

typ·i·cal·ness \-kәlnәs\ *n* -ES **:** the quality or state of being typical

ty·pi·con *or* **ty·pi·kon** \ˈtēpēˌkȯn\ *n, pl* **typi·ca** \-kä\ *or* **typicons** \-kȯnz\ *or* **typi·ka** \-kä\ [MGk *typikon*, fr. neut. of *typikos* prescribed, regular, fr. Gk, typical] **:** a book containing rules and rubrics for the religious services of the church year in the Eastern Church

typier *comparative of* TYPY

-typies *pl of* -TYPY

typiest *superlative of* TYPY

typ·i·fi·ca·tion \ˌtipəfəˈkāshən\ *n* -s [fr. *typify*, after such pairs as E *purify*: *purification*] **1 :** the act of typifying **2 :** something that constitutes a type

typ·i·fy \ˈtipəˌfī\ *vt* -ED/-ING/-ES [LL *typus* type + E *-ify* — more at TYPE] **1 :** to represent by an image, form, model, or resemblance **:** PREFIGURE **2 :** to embody the essential or salient characteristics of **:** be the type of ⟨the genus *Rosa typifies* the family Rosaceae⟩

typ·i·ness \ˈtīpēnəs\ *n* -ES **:** the quality or state of being typy ⟨a difficult class to judge because all the animals showed marked ~ and finish⟩

typing *n* -s [fr. gerund of ²*type*] **:** TYPEWRITING

typ·ist \ˈtīpəst\ *n* -s [²*type* + *-ist*] **:** one who typewrites; *specif* **:** one employed to type letters, records, memoranda, and other business papers and often to do office clerical work

typ·iste \ˈtīpəst\ *chiefly Austral var of* TYPIST

ty·po \ˈtī(ˌ)pō\ *n* -s **1** [short for *typographer*] **:** PRINTER; *esp* **:** COMPOSITOR **2** [short for *typographical (error)*] **:** a typographical error

typo- — see TYP-

¹**ty·po·graph** \ˈtīpəˌgraf, -rȧf *sometimes* ˈtip-\ *n* [*typ-* + *-graph*] **1 :** a keyboard-operated slugcasting machine that uses circulating matrices and functions on principles basically similar to those of the linotype **2 :** LUDLOW

²**typograph** \"\ *vt* -ED/-ING/-S [back-formation fr. *typography*] **:** to produce (stamps) by letterpress ⟨the stamp will be ~*ed* instead of engraved —Edwin Mueller⟩ ⟨made excellent lithographed forgeries of two of the ~*ed* German stamps for the use of agents —John Easton⟩

ty·pog·ra·pher \tīˈpägrəfə(r) *sometimes* təˈp-\ *n* -s [ML *typographus* printer (fr. Gk *typos* impression, cast + *-graphos* writer) + E *-er* — more at TYPE, -GRAPHER] **1 :** COMPOSITOR, TYPESETTER ⟨newspaper ~*s*⟩ **2 :** PRINTER ⟨printed in foreign countries by foreign ~*s* —André Morize⟩ **3 :** a designer who specializes in the choice and arrangement of type matter

ty·po·graph·ic \ˌtīpəˈgrafik, -fēk *sometimes* ˌtip-\ *or* **ty·po·graph·i·cal** \-fəkəl, -fēk-\ *adj* [*typographic* fr. NL *typographicus*, fr. ML *typographia* typography + L *-icus* -ic; *typographical* fr. NL *typographicus* + E *-al*] **1 a :** of, relating to, or used in typography ⟨the ~ art⟩ **b :** occurring in typesetting or typewriting ⟨a ~ error⟩ **c :** of typographers ⟨~ union⟩ **d :** of or relating to letterpress or relief printing as distinct from other forms of printing (as lithography, intaglio, or stencil) **2 :** of or relating to representation by types or symbols **:** EMBLEMATIC, FIGURATIVE — **ty·po·graph·i·cal·ly** \-fək(ə)lē, -fēk-, -li\ *adv*

typographical printing *n* **:** LETTERPRESS 1a

ty·pog·ra·phy \tīˈpägrəfē *sometimes* təˈp-\ *n* -ES [ML *typographia*, fr. Gk *typos* impression, cast + L *-graphia* -graphy — more at TYPE] **1 :** LETTERPRESS ⟨in ~ the ink is deposited only on the raised parts of the plate —Andries Voet⟩ **2 :** the art of letterpress printing esp. with regard to design or execution ⟨books of fine format and ~ —*Amer. Guide Series: Oregon*⟩ **3 a :** the style, arrangement, or appearance of matter printed by letterpress ⟨this advertisement has good ~, is easily seen and read —W.M.Krieger⟩ ⟨the ~ seems curiously fitted to the personality of the poems —*Commonweal*⟩ **b :** matter and esp. lettering that resembles letterpress but is produced by some other means ⟨photocomposed ~⟩ ⟨an offset printing job with excellent ~⟩

ty·po·lithography \ˌtī(ˌ)pō+\ *n* [ISV *typ-* + *lithography*] **:** a branch of lithography in which impressions from printers' types are transferred to stone for reproduction

ty·po·log·i·cal \ˌtīpəˈläjəkəl *sometimes* ˌtip-\ *also* **ty·po·log·ic** \-jik\ *adj* [*typology* + *-ical* or *-ic*] **1 :** of or relating to typology **2 :** of or relating to types — **ty·po·log·i·cal·ly** \-jək(ə)lē\ *adv*

ty·pol·o·gist \tīˈpäləjəst *sometimes* təˈp-\ *n* -s [*typology* + *-ist*] **:** a student of or expert in typology; *broadly* **:** one that is preoccupied with types

ty·pol·o·gize \-ˌjīz\ *vt* -ED/-ING/-S [*typology* + *-ize*] **:** to deal with in a typological manner **:** interpret through use of types or make a type of

ty·pol·o·gy \-jē\ *n* -ES [*typ-* + *-logy*] **1 :** a doctrine or theory of types; *specif* **:** a doctrine that things in the Christian dispensation are symbolized or prefigured by things in the Old Testament (as the sacrifice of Christ and the Eucharist by the sacrifice of the Paschal Lamb) **2 :** study of or study based on types ⟨the ~ of the idealistic morphology —Franz Schwanitz⟩: as **a :** classification (as of archeological remains or bacterial strains) based on comparative study of types **b :** comparative study of languages or aspects of languages as to their structures rather than their historical relations **c :** the distinction in the study of prose rhythm of types of internal structure of rhythmic systems or series in terms of combination of word units, juncture, and pause **d :** study and esp. analysis or division of humanity in terms of social types ⟨the ~ of union management relations⟩ ⟨the ~ of religious groups⟩

ty·po·mor·phic \ˌtīpəˈmȯrfik *sometimes* ˌtip-\ *adj* [*typ-* + *-morphic*] **:** characteristically occurring under particular conditions (as of temperature and pressure) or in particular processes of formation ⟨~ texture due to formation from a gel⟩ ⟨a ~ mineral⟩

ty·po·nym \ˈtīpəˌnim *sometimes* ˈtip-\ *n* -s [*typ-* + *-onym*] **1 :** a taxonomic name based on an indication of a type specimen or type species rather than on a description or diagnosis **2 :** a rejected isogenotypic name — **ty·pon·y·mal** \(ˈ)tīˈpänəməl *sometimes* təˈp- *or* **ty·po·nym·ic** \ˌtīpəˈnimik *sometimes* ˌtip-\ *or* **ty·pon·y·mous** \(ˈ)tīˈpänəməs *sometimes* təˈp-\ *adj*

ty·po·phile \ˈtīpəˌfīl *sometimes* ˈtip-\ *n* -s [*typ-* + *-phil*] **:** a lover of printed matter or typography — **ty·po·phil·ic** \ˌ==ˈfilik\ *adj*

typos *pl of* TYPO

ty·po·script \ˈtīpəˌskript\ *n* [*typ-* + manu*script*] **:** typewritten matter **:** TYPESCRIPT

ty·po·telegraph \ˌtī(ˌ)pō+\ *n* [*typ-* + *telegraph*] **:** a printing telegraph — **ty·po·telegraphy** \"+\ *n*

ty·po·there \ˈtīpəˌthi(ə)r *sometimes* ˈtip-\ *n* -s [NL *Typotheria*] **:** a mammal or fossil of the suborder Typotheria

ty·po·the·ria \ˌ==ˈthirēə\ *n pl, cap* [NL, fr. pl. of *Typotherium*, genus of herbivorous mammals, fr. *typ-* (prob. influenced in meaning by F slang *type* peculiar individual, fr. F *type* type, fr. Gk *typos*) + *-therium*] **:** a suborder of Notoungulata or sometimes a separate order comprising small So. American Tertiary and Pleistocene mammals somewhat similar to the rodents and having clavicles, usu. five toes, and simple persistently growing teeth

ty·poth·e·tae \tīˈpäthəˌtē *sometimes* təˈp-\ *n pl but sing in constr* [NL, lit., typesetters, fr. *typ-* + Gk *-thetai*, pl. of *-thetēs* (fr. *tithenai* to place, set) — more at DO] **:** an association of master printers (as in the U.S. and Canada)

typp \ˈtip\ *n* -s [*thousand yards per pound*] **:** a unit of yarn size representing the number of thousands of yards of a yarn that weigh one pound

typw *abbr* typewriter

typy *or* **typ·ey** \ˈtīpē\ *adj* **typier**; **typiest** [¹*type* + *-y*] **:** characterized by strict conformance to type **:** exhibiting superior bodily conformation ⟨a sound ~ heifer⟩ ⟨one of the *typiest* litters we have seen⟩

-ty·py \ˌtīpē, ˌd·əpē, -pi\ *n comb form* -ES [¹*type* + *-y*] **:** condition, process, or art related to or involving the use of (such) a type ⟨helio*typy*⟩

tyr- *or* **tyro-** *comb form* [Gk, fr. *tyros* cheese — more at BUTTER] **:** cheese ⟨*tyr*amine⟩ ⟨*tyro*toxin⟩

ty·ra·mine \ˈtīrəˌmēn, ˈtir-; tīˈramən, təˈr-\ *n* [ISV *tyrosine* + *amine*] **:** a crystalline phenolic amine $HOC_6H_4CH_2CH_2NH_2$ obtained from tyrosine by strong heating or by bacterial action and found also in the secretions of cephalopods and in various plants (as mistletoe and ergot)

ty·ran·ni \təˈraˌnī, -a(ˌ)nē; tīˈraˌnī\ *n pl, cap* [NL, fr. L, pl. of *tyrannus* tyrant] **:** a suborder of Passeriformes that comprises birds possessing little power of song and having the tendon of the hind toe separate and the intrinsic muscles of the syrinx reduced to usu. one pair the ends of which are inserted on the sides instead of the tips of its cartilaginous semirings and that includes the So. American antbirds, oven birds, and woodhewers together with the tyrant flycatchers and related birds of both hemispheres

ty·ran·ni·cal \təˈranəkəl, -nēk- *also* (ˈ)tīˈr-\ *also* **ty·ran·nic** \-nik, -nēk\ *adj* [*tyrannic* fr. L *tyrannicus*, fr. Gk *tyrannikos*, fr. *tyrannos* tyrant + *-ikos* -ic; *tyrannical* fr. L *tyrannicus* + E *-al*] **1 a** *archaic* **:** of, relating to, or associated with an absolute rule or ruler **b :** behaving as if an absolute ruler esp. in unjust severity in government **:** DESPOTIC ⟨a ~ administration⟩ **c :** given to oppressive, harsh, unjust, or arbitrary behavior or exercise of power ⟨a ~ parent⟩ ⟨some men become ~ when raised to a position of authority⟩ **2 a :** typical of a tyrannical individual **:** of the kind associated with tyranny ⟨~ abuse⟩ ⟨a ~ suppression of liberty⟩ **b :** tending to dominate in a stultifying or repressive manner usu. by reason of inexorability or omnipresence ⟨~ tasks⟩ ⟨tradition . . . more powerful, continuous, and even ~ —Laurence Binyon⟩ **syn** see ABSOLUTE

ty·ran·ni·cal·ly \-nək(ə)lē, -nēk-, -li\ *adv* **:** in a tyrannical manner

ty·ran·ni·ci·dal \təˌranəˈsīdᵊl, (ˌ)tīˌr-\ *adj* **:** of, relating to, or dealing with tyrannicide ⟨~ schemes⟩

ty·ran·ni·cide \=ˈranəˌsīd\ *n* -s [in sense 1, fr. F, fr. L *tyrannicidium*, fr. *tyrannus* tyrant + *-i-* + *-cidium* -cide (killing); in sense 2, fr. F, fr. L *tyrannicida*, fr. *tyrannus* + *-i-* + *-cida* -cide (killer)] **1 :** the act of killing a tyrant **2 :** the killer of a tyrant

tyran·nid \=ˈranəd, ˈtiran-\ *n* -s [NL *Tyrannidae*] **:** a bird of the family Tyrannidae

ty·ran·ni·dae \təˈranəˌdē, tīˈr-\ *n pl, cap* [NL, fr. *Tyrannus*, type genus + *-idae*] **:** a large exclusively American family of birds that are most numerous in So. and Central America but well represented in the U.S. and Canada, comprise the tyrant flycatchers, are mostly strictly insectivorous and take their prey on the wing, have a flattened bill often hooked at the tip and usu. bristly at the gape, and with the pittas, cotingas, and related birds constitute a superfamily of the suborder Tyranni

tyran·nis \=ˈranəs, ˈtiran-\ *n* -ES [L, fr. Gk, fr. *tyrannos* tyrant] **:** absolute rule (as by a local dictator in ancient Greece or medieval Italy)

tyr·an·nize \ˈtirəˌnīz\ *vb* -ED/-ING/-S *see -ize in Explan Notes* [MF *tyranniser*, fr. LL *tyrannizare*, fr. *tyrannus* tyrant + *-izare* -ize] *vi* **:** to act the tyrant **:** exercise arbitrary power **:** rule or act with unjust and oppressive severity — often used with *over* ⟨no habit could ~ over him⟩ ~ *vt* **:** to treat tyrannically **:** OPPRESS

tyr·an·niz·er \-zə(r)\ *n* -s **:** one that tyrannizes

ty·ran·no·saur \təˈranəˌsȯ(ə)r, tīˈr-\ *n* -s [NL *Tyrannosaurus*] **:** a very large bipedal carnivorous dinosaur (*Tyrannosaurus rex*) of the Upper Cretaceous of No. America

ty·ran·no·sau·rus \təˌranəˈsȯrəs, (ˌ)tīˌr-\ *n* [NL, fr. Gk *tyrannos* tyrant + NL *-saurus*] **1** *cap* **:** a genus of theropod dinosaurs from the Upper Cretaceous of Montana and Wyoming closely related to *Ceratosaurus* and including a single species (*T. rex*) — see TYRANNOSAUR **2** -ES **:** TYRANNOSAUR

tyr·an·nous \ˈtirənəs\ *adj* [ME, fr. L *tyrannus* + ME *-ous*] **:** marked by tyranny and esp. by unjust severity **:** OPPRESSIVE ⟨~ disregard of human rights⟩ ⟨a proper protest against all ~ demands . . . that insist upon everybody's using a word in a particular sense —R.G.F.Robinson⟩ ⟨escaping the ~ heat of the sun by the custom of siesta⟩ **syn** see ABSOLUTE

tyr·an·nous·ly *adv* **:** in a tyrannous manner **:** so as to be tyrannous

tyr·an·nous·ness *n* -ES **:** the quality or state of being tyrannous

tyr·an·nus \təˈranəs, tīˈr-\ *n, cap* [NL, fr. L, tyrant] **:** the type genus of Tyrannidae comprising the kingbird and closely related birds or in former classifications the greater part of the family

tyr·an·ny \ˈtirənē, -ni\ *n* -ES [ME *tyrannie*, fr. MF, fr. ML *tyrannia*, fr. L *tyrannus* tyrant + *-ia* -y] **1 a :** absolute government (as of an ancient Greek city-state) in which power is vested in a single ruler — compare AUTOCRACY **b :** the power, authority, office, and administration of such a ruler **c :** a city or other administrative unit under such government **2 :** rigorous, cruel, oppressive, and unjustly severe government whether by a single absolute ruler or other controlling power **3 a :** oppressive, severe, and unjust domination ⟨the ~ of a harsh overseer⟩ ⟨subject to the ~ of fanaticism⟩ **b :** a severe and rigorous condition or effect ⟨the ~ of the open night's too rough for Nature to endure —Shak.⟩ **c :** an oppressive effect that derives from the inexorable, relentless, or omnipresent quality of something in question ⟨the useful ~ of the word name —Edward Sapir⟩ ⟨two travelers escaped from the ~ of ham and eggs —John Buchan⟩ **4 a :** a tyrannical act **:** an instance of tyranny ⟨all the petty *tyrannies* of domestic life⟩ **b** *obs* **:** lawless and violent activity

¹**ty·rant** \ˈtīrənt\ *n* -s [ME *tyran, tirant, tirand*, fr. OF *tyran, tyrant*, fr. L *tyrannus*, fr. Gk *tyrannos*] **1 a :** an absolute ruler unrestrained by law or constitution; *often* **:** a usurper of sovereignty **b** *obs* **:** a ruling personage (as a prince or governor) **c :** a ruler who exercises absolute power oppressively or brutally **:** DESPOT **2 a :** a person in a position of control who exercises unlawful or improper authority or lawful or proper authority in an arbitrary or oppressive manner **:** one who by unfair or unreasonable demands or rigorous exploitation imposes burdens and hardships on those under his control ⟨our Latin teacher was a bitter ~⟩ **b :** something that imposes burdens and hardships like a human tyrant ⟨that ~, time⟩ **3 :** TYRANT FLYCATCHER

²**tyrant** \"\ *vi* -ED/-ING/-S **:** to act the tyrant **:** TYRANNIZE

tyrant flycatcher *also* **tyrant bird** *n* **:** a flycatcher of the family Tyrannidae

tyrant wren *n* **:** a small yellow-crested So. American tyrant flycatcher (*Tyrannulus elatus*)

tyre *chiefly Brit var of* TIRE

¹**tyr·i·an** \ˈtirēən\ *adj* [L *tyrius* Tyrian (fr. Gk *tyrios*, fr. *Tyros* Tyre, famous maritime city of ancient Phoenicia) + E *-an*] **1** *usu cap* **:** of or relating to ancient Tyre or its people **2** *often cap* **:** of the color Tyrian purple

²**tyrian** \"\ *n* -s *cap* **:** a native or inhabitant of ancient Tyre

tyrian alphabet *n, usu cap T* **:** a Moabite alphabet prevailing in Phoenicia during the ascendancy of Tyre

tyrian blue *n, often cap T* **:** a grayish blue to grayish purplish blue

tyrian pink *n, often cap T* **:** a strong to vivid purplish red that is bluer and slightly darker than spring beauty

tyrian purple *n, often cap T* [so called fr. its chief source in ancient times, the city of Tyre] **1 :** a crimson or purple dye $C_{16}H_8Br_2N_2O_2$ of the indigo class used by the ancient Greeks and Romans and prepared from the adrectal glands of gastropod mollusks (as of the genus *Thais*) or made synthetically; 6,6′-dibromo-indigo — see DYE table I (under *Vat Blue*); compare MUREX 1b **2 :** a strong to vivid purplish red that is redder and darker than Tyrian pink

tyrian rose *n, often cap T* **:** a vivid purplish red that is redder and less strong than Indiana, redder and lighter than rubellite, and redder and darker than Persian rose

tyro- — see TYR-

ty·ro *also* **ti·ro** \ˈtī(ˌ)rō\ *n* -s [ML *tyron-, tyro, tiron-, tiro*, fr. L *tiron-, tiro* young soldier, new recruit, tyro] **:** a beginner in any field **:** one familiar with the rudiments of a subject but lacking in practical experience **:** NOVICE ⟨advice from the expert to the ~⟩

ty·ro·ci·dine \ˌtīrəˈsīdᵊn, -ī,dēn\ *or* **ty·ro·ci·din** \-īdᵊn\ *n* -s [*tyrosine* + *-cide* + *-ine*] **:** a crystalline antibiotic of a basic polypeptide nature produced by a soil bacillus (*Bacillus brevis*) and constituting the major component of tyrothricin

ty·rode solution \ˈtīˌrōd-\ *or* **tyrode's solution** *n, usu cap T* [after Maurice V. *Tyrode* †1930 Am. pharmacologist] **:** physiological saline containing sodium chloride 0.8, potassium chloride 0.02, calcium chloride 0.02, magnesium chloride 0.01, sodium bicarbonate 0.1, and sodium dihydrogen phosphate 0.005 percent

¹**ty·rog·ly·phid** \tīˈrägləfəd, ˌtīrəˈglifəd\ *adj* [NL *Tyroglyphidae*] **:** ACARID 2

²**tyroglyphid** \"\ *also* **ty·ro·glyph** \ˈtīrəˌglif\ *n* -s [*tyroglyphid* fr. ¹*tyroglyphid*; *tyroglyph* fr. NL *Tyroglyphus*] **:** ACARID 2

ty·ro·glyph·i·dae \ˌtīrəˈglifəˌdē\ [NL, fr. *Tyroglyphus* + *-idae*] *syn of* ACARIDAE

ty·rog·ly·phus \tīˈrägləfəs, ˌtīrəˈglif-\ [NL, fr. Gk *tyr-* + *-glyphos* (fr. *glyphein* to carve) — more at CLEAVE] *syn of* ACARUS

¹**tyro·le·an** *also* **tiro·le·an** \təˈrōlēən *also* (ˈ)tīˌrōl- *or* ˌtirəˈl-\ *adj, usu cap* [*Tyrol, Tirol*, province in western Austria + E *-ean*] **:** of, relating to, or characteristic of the Tirol or its inhabitants **:** of the kind or style used or made in the Tirol

²**tyrolean** *also* **tirolean** \"\ *n* -s *cap* **:** a native or inhabitant of the Tirol

tyro·lese *also* **tiro·lese** \ˌtirəˈlēz, -ēs *also* ˌtīr-\ *adj or n, usu cap* [*Tyrol, Tirol*, Austria + E *-ese*] **:** TYROLEAN

tyrolese green *n, often cap T* **:** MALACHITE GREEN 3

tyrol green \təˈrōl-, ˈtīˌrōl-, ˈtiˌrōl- *also* ˈtiˌräl- *or* ˈtirəl-\ *n, often cap T* [fr. *Tyrol* (Tirol), Austria] **:** TERRE VERTE 2

ty·ro·li·an \təˈrōlēən *also* (ˈ)tīˈr-\ *adj or n, usu cap* [*Tyrol* (Tirol), Austria + E *-ian*] **:** TYROLEAN

ty·ro·li·enne \təˌrōlēˈen, ˌti,r-, (ˌ)tīˌr-\ *n* -s *sometimes cap* [F, fr. fem. of *tyrolien* Tyrolean, fr. *Tyrol* + F *-ien* -ian, fr. L *-ianus*] **:** a Tyrolean peasants' song or melody characterized by the yodel

tyr·o·lite \ˈtirəˌlīt\ *n* -s [G *tirolit*, fr. *Tirol*, Austria + G *-it* -ite] **:** a mineral $Cu_5Ca(AsO_4)_2(CO_3)(OH)_4.6H_2O$(?) that is a hydrous hydroxide, arsenate, and carbonate of copper and calcium

tyrolite green *n, often cap T* **:** APHRODITE 3

ty·rone \təˈrōn, *by outsiders* (ˈ)tīˈr-\ *adj, usu cap* [fr. *Tyrone*, county of west central Northern Ireland] **:** of or from County Tyrone, Northern Ireland **:** of the kind or style prevalent in County Tyrone

ty·ron·ic \(ˈ)tīˈränik\ *adj* [L *tiron-, tiro* tyro + E *-ic*] **:** of, relating to, or characteristic of a tyro **:** AMATEURISH

tyro·sin·ase \ˈtirəsəˌnās, ˈtir-, -āz\ *n* -s [ISV *tyrosine* + *-ase*] **:** a copper-containing enzyme that promotes the reaction of oxygen and tyrosine or other phenols (as *para*-cresol) giving rise to a series of oxidation products including an ortho diphenol, an orthoquinone, and a melanin and that is widely distributed in plants and animals — compare POLYPHENOL OXIDASE

tyro·sine \-ˌsēn, -sən\ *n* -s [irreg. fr. Gk *tyros* cheese + ISV *-ine* — more at BUTTER] **1 :** a crystalline phenolic alpha-amino acid $HOC_6H_4CH_2CH(NH_2)COOH$ obtained in its levorotatory L form by the hydrolysis of proteins (as casein or fibroin) and also made synthetically in the racemic form; *para*-hydroxyphenylalanine **2 :** either of two crystalline acids that are ortho and meta isomers of tyrosine — compare DIIODOTYROSINE, DOPA, THYRONINE

tyro·sin·osis \ˌ===səˈnōsəs\ *n* -ES [NL, fr. ISV *tyrosine* + NL *-osis*] **:** a condition of faulty metabolism of tyrosine marked by the excretion of unusual amounts of tyrosine in the urine

tyro·sin·uria \-səˈn(y)u̇rēə\ *n* -s [NL, fr. ISV *tyrosine* + NL *-uria*] **:** the excretion of unusual amounts of tyrosine in the urine

tyro·syl \ˈ==ˌsil\ *n* -s [ISV *tyrosine* + *-yl*] **:** the acyl radical $HOC_6H_4CH_2CH(NH_2)CO-$ of tyrosine

ty·ro·thri·cin \ˌtīrəˈthrīsᵊn, -risᵊn\ *n* -s [NL *Tyrothric-, Tyrothrix*, generic name formerly applied to various spore-forming bacteria (fr. *tyr-* + *-thrix*) + E *-in*] **:** an antibiotic mixture consisting chiefly of tyrocidine and gramicidin usu. extracted from a soil bacillus (*Bacillus brevis*) as a gray to brown powder and used for local applications esp. for infections caused by gram-positive bacteria

tyr·rhe·ni \təˈrēˌnī\ *n pl, usu cap* [L, fr. pl. of *tyrrhenus* Etruscan] **:** the Etruscan people; *also* **:** the supposed immigrant ancestors of the historic Etruscans

tyr·rhe·ni·an \təˈrēnēən\ *also* **tyr·rhene** \ˈtiˌrēn, təˈr-\ *adj, usu cap* [*tyrrhene* fr. L *tyrrhenus*, fr. Gk *tyrrhēnos*; *tyrrhenian* fr. L *tyrrhenus* + E *-ian*] **:** of or relating to the Tyrrheni

tyr·tae·an \(ˌ)tarˈtēən\ *adj, usu cap* [*Tyrtaeus* 7th cent. B.C. Greek elegiac poet + E *-an*] **:** of, relating to, or styled in the manner of the Spartan poet Tyrtaeus noted as a writer of spirited martial and patriotic songs in the 7th century B.C.

ty·son·ite \ˈtīsᵊnˌīt\ *n* -s [S. T. *Tyson* 19th cent. Am. naturalist + E *-ite*] **:** FLUOCERITE

ty·son's gland \ˈtīsᵊnz-\ *n, usu cap T* [after Edward *Tyson* †1708 Eng. anatomist] **:** GLAND OF TYSON

tys·tie \ˈtistē, ˈtēs-\ *n* -s [of Scand origin; akin to ON *theist, theisti* black guillemot] *Brit* **:** BLACK GUILLEMOT

tythe *chiefly Brit var of* TITHE

ty·to \ˈtī(ˌ)dō, (ˌ)tō\ *n, cap* [NL *Tyton-, Tyto*, fr. Gk *tytō* owl, of imit. origin] **:** a cosmopolitan genus of owls coextensive with the family Tytonidae

ty·ton·i·dae \tīˈtänəˌdē\ *n pl, cap* [NL, fr. *Tyton-, Tyto*, type genus + *-idae*] **:** a monotypic family of owls comprising the barn owls and being distinguished by an unnotched sternum and large clavicles fused with it — compare BUBONIDAE, STRIGIDAE

tyu·ya·mu·nite \ˌtyü(y)əˈmüˌnīt, ˌchü-\ *n* -s [*Tyuya Muyun*, name of a hill in Fergana, Turkistan, U.S.S.R. + E *-ite*] **:** a mineral $Ca(UO_2)_2(VO_4)_2.nH_2O$ that is a hydrous vanadate of calcium and uranium and that is important as an ore of uranium

tzaddik *also* **tzadik** *var of* ZADDIK

tzar *var of* CZAR

tze·da·kah *or* **tse·da·kah** *or* **ze·da·kah** \tsəˈdō(ˌ)kō\ *n, pl* **tzeda·koth** *or* **tzeda·kot** *or* **tseda·koth** *or* **tseda·kot** \tsəˈdōkəs, tsəˌdäˈkōt(h)\ [Heb *ṣĕdāqāh*, lit., righteousness] **:** right behavior as traditionally manifested among Jews by acts of charity; *broadly* **:** CHARITY

tzel·tal \(ˈ)(t)selˈtäl\ *or* **tzen·tal** \-enˈtäl\ *n, pl* **tzeltal** *or* **tzelta·les** \=ˈtä(ˌ)läs\ *or* **tzental** *or* **tzenta·les** *usu cap* **1 a :** an Indian people of central Chiapas, Mexico **b :** a member of such people **2 :** a Mayan language of the Tzeltal people

¹**tzi·gane** \(t)sēˈgän\ *n* -s *sometimes cap* [F *tzigane, tsigane*, fr. Hung *cigány, czigány*] **:** GYPSY

²**tzigane** \"\ *adj, sometimes cap* **:** of or relating to gypsies **:** of the kind or style used or made by gypsies ⟨~ music⟩

tzim·mes *also* **tzim·es** \ˈtsiməs\ *n, pl* **tzimmes** *also* **tzimes** [Yiddish *tsimes*] **:** a sweetened combination of vegetables (as carrots and potatoes) or of meat and carrots often with dried fruits (as prunes) that is stewed or baked in a casserole

tzitzith *also* **tzitzis** *var of* ZIZITH

tzol·kin \ˈ(t)sōlˌkēn\ *n* -s [Mayan *tzol* to set in order + *kin* day] **:** a period of 260 days constituting a complete cycle of all the permutations of 20 day names with the numbers 1 to 13 that constitutes the Maya sacred year — compare TUN

tzo·tzil *also* **tso·tsil** \(ˈ)(t)sōtˈsē(ə)l, -)sōt-\ *or* **zo·tzil** \(ˈ)sō-, (ˈ)sō-\ *n, pl* **tzotzil** *or* **tzo·tzi·les** \ˌ==ˈsē(ˌ)läs\ *usu cap* **1 a :** an Indian people of central Chiapas, Mexico **b :** a member of such people **2 :** a Mayan language of the Tzotzil people

tz'u-chou \(ˈ)(t)süˈjō\ *n* -s *usu cap T* [fr. *Tz'u-chou*, district in southern Hopeh province, northeast China] **:** a Chinese pottery made in Honan province during the Sung period and having usu. a cream-colored glaze over a buff or gray body

tzut \ˈ(t)süt\ *or* **tzu·te** \-ü(ˌ)tā\ *n* -s [of AmerInd origin] **:** a brightly patterned square of cotton used by Guatemalans esp. as a head cover

tzu·tu·hil *also* **zu·tu·hil** *or* **zu·tu·gil** \ˌ(t)süd·əˈwē(ə)l, -ˈhē-\ *n, pl* **tzutuhil** *or* **tzu·tuhi·les** \ˌ==ˈwē(ˌ)läs, -ˈhē-\ *usu cap* **1 a :** an Indian people of the south shore of Lake Atitlan, Guatemala **b :** a member of such people **2 :** a Mayan language of the Tzutuhil people

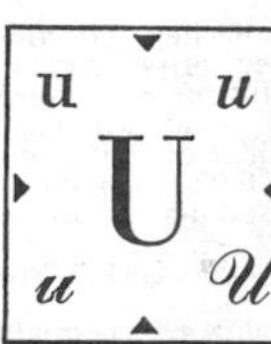

¹u \'yü\ *n, pl* **u's** *or* **us** \'yüz\ *often cap, often attrib* **1 a :** the 21st letter of the English alphabet **b :** an instance of this letter printed, written, or otherwise represented **c :** a speech counterpart of orthographic *u* (as long *u* in *mute*, short *u* in *cut*, or *u* in *rule*) **2 :** a printer's type, a stamp, or some other instrument for reproducing the letter *u* **3 :** someone or something arbitrarily or conveniently designated *u* esp. as the 20th or when j is used for the 10th the 21st in order or class **4 :** something having the shape of the letter U
²u *abbr, often cap* **1** uncirculated **2** uncle **3** [G *und*] and **4** under **5** unified **6** uniform **7** union; unionist **8** unit; united **9** universal **10** university **11** unpleasant **12** upper
³u *symbol, cap* **1** *ital* intrinsic energy **2** uranium
UA *abbr* **1** ultra-audible **2** underwriting account
uakari *var of* OUAKARI
U and O *abbr* use and occupancy
uang \'wäŋ\ *n* -s [Atjehnese *uĕng*] **:** a rhinoceros beetle (*Oryctes rhinoceros*)
ua·yeb \'wī,eb\ *n* -s *sometimes cap* [Mayan] **:** a period consisting of five nameless days added to a tun to make the 365-day year of the Maya calendar
ubaid \ü'bād, -bīd\ *or* **al 'ubaid** \,alə¦b-\ *adj, usu cap U* [fr. *al 'Ubaid* (Tell el-Obeid), locality in southern Iraq] **:** of or relating to an early Bronze Age culture in Mesopotamia prior to 3000 B.C.
uban·gi \yü'baŋ(g)ē, -aaŋ-, -aiŋ- *sometimes* ü'bäŋ-\ *n* -s *usu cap* [fr. *Ubangi-Shari*, territory in French Equatorial Africa] **:** a Sara woman of the district of Kyabé village in Africa with lips pierced and distended to unusual dimensions with wooden disks
ube \'übē, 'ü,bā\ *adj, usu cap* [fr. *Ube*, seaport city of southwest Honshu, Japan] **:** of or from the city of Ube, Japan **:** of the kind or style prevalent in Ube
uber·ri·ma fi·des \yü'berəmə'fī(,)dēz\ *n* [L, lit., most abundant faith] **:** GOOD FAITH ⟨the rights of the parties . . . should be interpreted in a spirit of *uberrima fides* —H.B.Brown⟩
ubi·e·ty \yü'bīəd·ē\ *n* -ES [L *ubi* where + E *-ety* (as in *society*) — more at UBIQUITY] *archaic* **:** the quality or state of being in a place: as **a :** the state of being placed in a definite local relation **:** POSITION, LOCATION **b :** the abstract quality of being in position **:** WHERENESS ⟨no woozy timelessness or lack of ~ in the drama —R.B.Heilman⟩
ubi·quar·i·an \,yübə'kwa(a)rēən\ *n* -s *usu cap* [L *ubique* everywhere + E *-arian*] **:** UBIQUITARIAN
ubi·quist \'yübəkwəst\ *n* -s [L *ubique* everywhere + E *-ist*] **1** *usu cap* **:** UBIQUITARIAN **2 :** an organism that is distributed more or less uniformly through a region
¹ubiq·ui·tar·i·an \(,)yü¦bikwə¦ta(a)rēən\ *adj, often cap* [*ubiquity* + *-arian*] **:** of or relating to the doctrine of the Ubiquitarians
²ubiquitarian \"\ *n* -s *usu cap* **:** one of a school of Lutheran clergymen holding that as Christ is omnipresent his body is everywhere (as in the Eucharist)
ubiq·ui·tism \yü'bikwə,tizəm\ *n* -s *usu cap* [*ubiquity* + *-ism*] **:** the doctrine that Christ's body is omnipresent
ubiq·ui·tous \-wəd·əs, -wətəs\ *adj* [*ubiquity* + *-ous*] **:** existing or being everywhere at the same time **:** occurring or capable of appearing everywhere or in many places throughout a particular area, sphere, or production **:** OMNIPRESENT ⟨the ~ little wolf of the high country —*Amer. Guide Series: Oregon*⟩ ⟨bricks . . . made from a ~ gray mud —Christopher Rand⟩ ⟨the ~ functionalism of modern society —Hannah Arendt⟩ ⟨nothing . . . escapes the ~ eyes of our Treasury Department —Harvey Breit⟩ ⟨the ~ paperback⟩ ⟨a ~, active salesman —J.S.Redding⟩ — **ubiq·ui·tous·ly** *adv* — **ubiq·ui·tous·ness** *n* -ES
ubiq·ui·ty \-wəd·ē, -wətē, -i\ *n* -ES [L *ubique* everywhere (fr. *ubi* where + *-que*, enclitic generalizing particle) + E *-ity*; akin to Oscan *puf* where, L *quis* who and to L *-que* and — more at WHO, SESQUI-] **1 :** the theological doctrine formulated by Luther that Christ's glorified body is omnipresent **2 :** presence everywhere or in many places esp. simultaneously **:** OMNIPRESENCE ⟨the ~ of the printed word —Reinhold Niebuhr⟩ ⟨the ~ of unreliable editions —Abram Chasins⟩ ⟨achieved a certain ~ by shuttling back and forth in hot and dusty trains —Agnes & W.E.Hocking⟩
ubi sunt \'übē¦sunt, 'üb-\ *adj* [L, where are] **:** of or relating to a type of esp. medieval verse in which the poem or its stanzas begin with the Latin words *ubi sunt* or their equivalent in another language and which has as a principal theme the transitory nature of all things
ubi su·pra \,=='süprə\ *adv* [L, where above] **:** where above mentioned
u-boat \'=,=\ *n, usu cap U* [trans. of G *u-boot*, short for *unterseeboot*, lit., undersea boat] **:** a German or an Austrian submarine
u-bolt \'=,=\ *n, cap U* **:** a U-shaped bolt having both arms threaded to receive nuts and used as a fastening device

U-bolt

ubus·su \,übə'sü\ *or* **ubussu palm** *n* [Pg *ubussú, bussú, ubuçu, buçu* — more at BUSSU] **:** BUSSU
UC *abbr* **1** undercarriage **2** under charge **3** under construction **4** *often not cap* uppercase **5** utility cargo
uca \'yükə\ *n, cap* [NL, fr. Tupi *uça, usa*] **:** a genus consisting of the typical fiddler crabs
ucha·ti·us bronze *or* **uchatius metal** \ü'kätsēəs-\ *n, usu cap U* [after Franz, Baron *Uchatius* †1881 Austrian general & inventor] **:** STEEL BRONZE
uche·an *also* **yu·chi·an** \'yüchēən, ='==\ *n, usu cap* [*uchee* or *yuchi* + *-an*] **:** a language family of the southeastern U.S. comprising the Yuchi language and possibly related to Siouan and Muskogean
uchee *usu cap, var of* YUCHI
uck·ers \'əkərz\ *n pl but sing in constr* [origin unknown] *Brit* **:** LUDO
ucs *abbr* unconscious
ucu·uba \,ükə'(w)übə\ *also* **ucu·hu·ba** \-'hübə\ *n* -s [Pg, fr. Tupi *ucu-uva*] **:** BANAK; *esp* **:** a Brazilian tree (*Virola sebifera*) having seeds that yield a hard yellowish edible fat used chiefly in candles and soap
ucuuba butter *or* **ucuuba tallow** *or* **ucuuba oil** *n* **:** a yellowish white fat obtained from the seeds of banaks (esp. *Virola sebifera*) and used in soap and candles
UD *abbr* **1** upper deck **2** urban district **3** [L *ut dictum*] as directed
¹udal \'yüdᵊl\ *adj* [ON *ōthal* inherited property — more at ATHELING] **:** of, relating to, or constituting udal
²udal \"\ *n* -s **:** an alodial system of land tenure extant only in Shetland and Orkney — compare ODAL
UDC *abbr* urban district council
ud·der \'ədə(r)\ *n* -s [ME, fr. OE *ūder*; akin to OHG *ūtar* udder, ON *jūgr*, L *uber*, Gk *outhar*, Skt *ūdhar*] **1 :** a large pendulous organ consisting of two or more mammary glands enclosed in a common envelope and each provided with a single nipple ⟨a cow's ~⟩ **2 :** MAMMARY GLAND, BREAST ⟨the ~s of a sow⟩ ⟨a lioness, with ~s all drawn dry —Shak.⟩
ud·der·less \'==ləs\ *adj* **:** destitute or deprived of an udder
udi \'üdē\ *also* **udic** \-dik\ *or* **udin** \-dᵊn\ *n* -s *usu cap* **:** a north Caucasic language
udish \'üdish\ *n* -ES *usu cap* **:** UDI
ud·murt \(')üd¦mü(ə)rt\ *n* -s *usu cap* [Votyak, Votyak man] **:** VOTYAK
udo \'ü(,)dō\ *n* -s [Jap] **:** a stout Japanese herb (*Aralia cordata*) the blanched young shoots of which are used esp. as a vegetable and in salads
udom·e·ter \yü'däməd·ə(r)\ *n* [L *uvidus, udus* damp, moist, wet + E *-o-* + *-meter* — more at HUMOR] **:** RAIN GAGE — **udo·me·tric** \,yüdə¦me·trik\ *adj*
udom·o·graph \yü'dämə,graf\ *n* [*udometer* + *-o-* + *-graph*] **:** a self-registering rain gage
UDT *abbr* **1** underdeck tonnage **2** underwater demolition team
UE *abbr* university extension
ufa \(')ü¦fä\ *adj, usu cap* [fr. *Ufa*, capital of Bashkir Republic, U.S.S.R.] **:** of or from the city of Ufa, U.S.S.R. **:** of the kind or style prevalent in Ufa
ufer \'yüfə(r)\ *n* -s [D *juffer* miss, lady, pole, beam, euphroe — more at EUPHROE] **:** a fir pole from 4 to 7 inches in diameter and from 20 to 40 feet in length
UFO \,yü,ef¦ō\ *abbr or n* -s **:** an unidentified flying object — compare FLYING SAUCER
ufra disease \'üfrə-\ *n* [prob. fr. Ar *'ufrah* dust color] **:** a disease of rice (as in India) caused by an eelworm (*Ditylenchus angustus*) and characterized by first whitish and then brownish leaf tips, stem distortion above the last node, and arrested development of the ear and in heavily attacked plants by decay
ugan·da \(y)ü'gandə, ü'gän-\ *adj, usu cap* [fr. *Uganda*, country in eastern Africa] **:** of, relating to, or characteristic of Uganda **:** UGANDAN
¹ugan·dan \-dən\ *adj, usu cap* [*Uganda*, country in eastern Africa + E *-an*] **:** of, relating to, or characteristic of Uganda
²ugandan \"\ *n* -s *cap* **:** a native or inhabitant of Uganda
uga·ra·ño \,ügə'rän(,)yō\ *n* -s *usu cap* [Sp, of AmerInd origin] **:** a dialect of the Zamuco people
uga·ri·tian \,ügə'rishən, -rēsh-\ *n* -s *usu cap* [*Ugarit*, ancient city + E *-ic*] **:** UGARITIC
¹uga·rit·ic \¦==¦rid·ik\ *adj, usu cap* [*Ugarit*, ancient city in northwest Syria + E *-ic*] **1 :** of, relating to, or characteristic of the ancient city of Ugarit or its inhabitants **2 :** of, relating to, or characteristic of the Ugaritic language
²ugaritic \"\ *n* -s *usu cap* **:** the Semitic language of ancient Ugarit closely related to Phoenician and Hebrew
ug·gle·some \'əgəlsəm\ *adj* [obs. E *uggle* horrible (fr. ME *uggen* to inspire horror or disgust, to fear, fr. ON *ugga* to fear) + E *-some*; akin to ON *uggr* fear — more at UGLY] *archaic* **:** HORRIBLE
ugh *often read as* 'əg *or* 'ək *or* 'ə\ *interj* — used to indicate the sound of a cough or grunt or to express disgust or horror
ug·li \'əglī\ *n, pl* **uglis** *or* **uglies** [prob. alter. of ³*ugly*; fr. the unattractive appearance of its wrinkled skin] **:** TANGELO
uglies *pl of* UGLY
ug·li·fi·ca·tion \,əgləfə'kāshən\ *n* -s [fr. *uglify*, after such pairs as E *purify*: *purification*] **:** the action of making ugly
ug·li·fi·er \'əglə,fī(ə)r, -īə\ *n* -s [*uglify* + *-er*] **:** one that uglifies ⟨~s of the landscape⟩
ug·li·fy \-,fī\ *vt* -ED/-ING/-ES [¹*ugly* + *-fy*] **:** to make ugly ⟨beautifying our environment instead of ~*ing* it —Matthew Lipman⟩
ug·li·ly \-lə̇lē, -li\ *adv* [ME, fr. ¹*ugly* + *-ly*] **:** in an ugly manner ⟨the yellow box . . . ~ lettered in black —Hortense Calisher⟩
ug·li·ness \-lēnəs, -lin-\ *n* -ES [ME *uglines*, fr. ¹*ugly* + *-nes* -ness] **1 :** the quality or state of being ugly ⟨observe the ~ of poverty —John Reed⟩ ⟨moral ~ trespasses into the aesthetic —E.M.Forster⟩ **2 :** an ugly thing or characteristic
¹ug·ly \'əglē, -li\ *adj* -ER/-EST [ME *uglike, ugly* frightful, unpleasing in appearance, fr. ON *uggligr* frightful, fr. *uggr* fear + *-ligr* -ly — more at -LY] **1 :** FRIGHTFUL, TERRIBLE, HORRIBLE, DIRE ⟨inflicting a very ~ though not necessarily fatal wound —D.D.Martin⟩ **2 a** (1) **:** offensive to the sight **:** of unpleasing, disagreeable, or loathsome appearance **:** not beautiful **:** UNSIGHTLY, HIDEOUS ⟨~ people⟩ ⟨an ~ color⟩ ⟨houses were cheaply constructed and ~ —Sherwood Anderson⟩ (2) **:** INAESTHETIC ⟨an ~ line⟩ **b :** offensive or unpleasing to any sense ⟨~ sounds⟩ ⟨~ smells⟩ **3 :** morally offensive or objectionable **:** REPULSIVE, VILE, BASE ⟨~ crimes⟩ ⟨~ habits⟩ **4 a :** causing or likely to cause inconvenience, embarrassment, or discomfort **:** TROUBLESOME ⟨an ~ situation⟩ ⟨told him the ~ truth about himself —Eden Phillpotts⟩ **b** (1) **:** THREATENING ⟨~ weather⟩ ⟨an ~ cloud⟩ (2) **:** HEAVY, VIOLENT ⟨an ~ sea⟩ **c :** ILL-NATURED, SURLY, QUARRELSOME ⟨an ~ temper⟩
syn HIDEOUS, ILL-FAVORED, UNSIGHTLY: UGLY may apply to whatever is strongly displeasing to view or contemplate or to whatever calls forth repulsion, repugnance, loathing, or dread ⟨an *ugly* sight he was, thin, stooping, bald, stiff-jointed, with an ulcered face patched with plasters —Robert Graves⟩ ⟨acres of *ugly* wooden tenement houses line the drab streets —*Amer. Guide Series: Mass.*⟩ ⟨an *ugly* story of low passion, delusion, and waking from delusion —George Eliot⟩ HIDEOUS applies to what is extremely ugly and revolting, horrible, or odious ⟨false eyebrows and false moustaches were stuck upon them, and their *hideous* countenances were all bloody and sweaty —Charles Dickens⟩ ⟨a yell of agony so appalling and *hideous* —Sheridan Le Fanu⟩ ⟨a *hideous* business, in which nearly all the humane alleviations of brutal violence, introduced and practiced in the days when professional armies fought for a dynasty or for a point of honor, were disregarded —W.R. Inge⟩ ILL-FAVORED describes one with unpleasing, disagreeable, or unpleasant features but does not in general have more dire connotation ⟨*ill-favored* and lean-fleshed —Gen 41:3 (AV)⟩ UNSIGHTLY, close to UGLY, may apply to something unattractive that blemishes what might have been pleasing ⟨*unsightly* hovels⟩ ⟨*unsightly* areas of houses quickly built and poorly kept —*Amer. Guide Series: Va.*⟩ ⟨an *unsightly* scar⟩
²ugly \"\ *adv* [ME, fr. ¹*ugly*] *chiefly dial* **:** UGLILY
³ugly \"\ *n* -ES [¹*ugly*] **:** one that is ugly
ugly duckling *n* [fr. *The Ugly Duckling* (1835?), story by Hans Christian Andersen †1875 Dan. author] **:** an immature or dependent person or thing that is despised or neglected because of unprepossessing appearance or unpromising qualities but that develops or is capable of developing into a person or thing worthy of attention or respect ⟨from the beginning Alaska was treated pretty much as our *ugly duckling* —W.O.Douglas⟩ ⟨bacteriology is still too often taught as the *ugly duckling* of botany —Justina Hill⟩
ugly-nest caterpillar *n* **:** a gregarious caterpillar that is the larva of a tortricid moth (*Archips cerasivorana*) and that feeds chiefly on black cherry and chokecherry in northern U.S. and Canada and webs the leaves together into an irregular nest
ugni blanc \¦ünyē¦blä\ⁿ, ¦ünyē-\ *n* [F, fr. *Ugni*, name of a type of grape + *blanc* white, fr. MF — more at BLANK] **:** a white table wine of Chablis type made in California — called also *Trebbiano*
¹ugri·an \'(y)ügrēən\ *adj, usu cap* [Old Russian *Ugre* (pl.) Hungarians + E *-ian*] **1 :** of, relating to, or characteristic of the Ugrians **2 :** UGRIC
²ugrian \"\ *n* -s *usu cap* **:** a member of the eastern division of the Finno-Ugrian peoples including the Magyars, Voguls, and Ostyaks — compare FINNO-UGRIAN
ugric \-grik\ *adj, usu cap* [*ugrian* + *-ic*] **:** of, relating to, or characteristic of the languages of the Ugrians — see URALIC LANGUAGES table
ugro- *comb form, usu cap* [*ugrian*] **:** Ugrian and ⟨*Ugro*-Aryan⟩ ⟨*Ugro*-Finnic⟩
ug·rug \'ə,grəg\ *n* -s [Esk] *Alaska* **:** BEARDED SEAL
ug·some \'əgsəm\ *adj* [ME, fr. *uggen* to fear, inspire dread or loathing + *-some* — more at UGGLESOME] *archaic* **:** FRIGHTFUL, HORRID, LOATHSOME ⟨the depth of the wood beyond was so ~ —John Masefield⟩
ugt *abbr* urgent
UH *abbr* upper half
UHF *abbr, often not cap* ultrahigh frequency
uh-huh *a disyllabic utterance with* m- *or* n-*sounds at beginning & end, an h-like interval of voicelessness between, & heavier stress on the first member; in the registering of gratification the voiced members are more prolonged, about equal in stress, & the sound is higher in pitch*, 'əⁿ¦həⁿ\ *interj* — used to indicate affirmation, agreement, or gratification
uh·lan \'(')ü¦län, '(y)ülən\ *n* -s [G *ulan, uhlan*, fr. Pol *ulan*, fr. Turk *oğlan* boy, servant] **:** a lancer of a class of Tatarian origin introduced into European armies in Poland and esp. prominent in the Prussian armies (as in the Franco-Prussian war of 1870) who were armed with lances, pistols, sabers, and later with carbines and were employed chiefly as skirmishers and scouts
ui *abbr* [L *ut infra*] as below
UI *abbr* unemployment insurance
¹ui·ghur *or* **ui·gur** \'wē,gü(ə)r, -,gər\ *n, pl* **uighur** *or* **uighurs** *or* **uigur** *or* **uigurs** *usu cap* [Uighur *Uighur*] **1 :** a member of a Turkic people who developed a powerful kingdom and a considerable culture in Mongolia and eastern Turkestan between the 8th and 12th centuries A.D. and who now form a majority of the population of Chinese Turkestan and are found chiefly in the oasis towns of the Tarim basin — compare YARKANDI **2 a :** the Turkic language of the Uighur people **b :** an alphabet based on Sogdian and employed for Turkic languages from the 6th to the 12th centuries — called also *neo-Sogdian*
²uighur *or* **uigur** \"\ *adj, usu cap* **1 :** of, relating to, or characteristic of the Uighurs **2 a :** of, relating to, or characteristic of the Uighur language **b :** of, relating to, or characteristic of the Uighur alphabet
ui·ghu·ri·an *or* **ui·gu·ri·an** \(')wē¦gürēən\ *adj or n, usu cap* [¹*uighur* + *-ian*] **:** UIGHUR
ui·ghu·ric *or* **ui·gu·ric** \-rik\ *adj, usu cap* [¹*uighur* + *-ic*] **:** UIGHUR
ui·nal \wē'näl\ *n* -s [Mayan] **:** one of the eighteen 20-day periods into which a tun is divided in the Maya calendar **:** a Maya month
uin·ta *also* **uin·tah** \yü'(w)intə, yə'wi-\ *n, pl* **uinta** *or* **uintas** *or* **uintah** *or* **uintahs** *usu cap* **1 :** a division of the Ute in northeastern Utah **2 :** a member of the Uinta division of the Ute
uin·ta·ite *also* **uin·tah·ite** \-tə,īt\ *n* -s [*Uinta* or *Uintah* mountains of northeast Utah + E *-ite*] **:** a black lustrous asphalt occurring esp. in Utah that is useful in the arts (as in the manufacture of paints, varnishes, and inks) and for waterproofing
uin·ta·there \-tə,thi(ə)r\ *n* -s [NL *uintatherium*] **:** UINTATHERIUM 2
uin·ta·the·ri·um \=,=='thirēəm\ *n* [NL, fr. *Uinta* co., southwest Wyo. + NL *-therium*] **1** *cap* **:** a genus (the type of the family Uintatheriidae) of large herbivorous ungulate mammals of the order Dinocerata from the Eocene of Wyoming resembling elephants in size and in the conformation of their limbs and having three pairs of bony protuberances respectively on the parietal, maxillary, and nasal bones of the skull, a pair of canine tusks guarded by downwardly directed processes of the lower jaw but no upper incisors, and a proportionately very small brain **2** *pl* **uin·ta·the·ria** \-rēə\ **:** a mammal of the genus *Uintatherium*
uin·tjie \'änchē\ *n* -s [Afrik *euntjie, uintjie*, a species of *Moraea*, dim. of MD *enioen, eyuun* onion, fr. L *union-, unio* — more at ONION] *southern Africa* **:** the edible corm of various plants esp. of the family Iridaceae that when boiled tastes like a chestnut
uit·land·er \'āt,landə(r)\ *n* -s *often cap* [Afrik, fr. MD *utelander*, fr. *utelant* foreign territory (fr. *ute* out + *land, lant* land) + *-er*, fr. L *-arius*; akin to OE *ūt* out & to OE *land* — more at OUT, LAND, -ER] **:** FOREIGNER, OUTLANDER; *esp* **:** a British resident in the former So. African republics of the Transvaal and Orange Free State
uitotan *usu cap, var of* WITOTOAN
uitoto *usu cap, var of* WITOTO
uit·span \(')āt¦span\ *vb* [Afrik, fr. MD *utespannen*, fr. *ute* out (akin to OE *ūt* out) + *spannen* to bind, hitch up — more at OUT, SPAN] *southern Africa* **:** OUTSPAN
uji \'ü(,)jē\ *n* -s [Jap, maggot] **:** a silkworm disease in Japan caused by the parasitic larva of the uji fly
uji fly *n* **:** a tachinid fly (*Sturmia sericaria*) of Japan
ukase \yü'kās *sometimes* yü'käz *or* (y)ü'käz *or* (y)ü'káz; '=,=\ *n* -s [F & Russ; F *ukase*, fr. Russ *ukaz*, fr. *ukazat'* to show, direct, order; akin to OSlav *u-* away, thoroughly, L *au-* away, Skt *ava-* away, and to OSlav *kazati* to show; prob. akin to Gk *teknōr, tekmar* sign, token, Skt *kāśate* he appears, shines] **1** *also* **ukaz** \ü'käz, -káz\ -ES **:** a proclamation or order by a Russian emperor or government having the force of law **2 :** EDICT, DECREE ⟨the ~ of a board of trustees, a legislature, a political party —A.M.Schlesinger b. 1917⟩ ⟨government by ~⟩
uke \'yük\ *n* -s [by shortening & alter.] **:** UKULELE
uki-yo-e \ü'kēyō,yā\ *also* **uki·yo·ye** \-ēyō,yā\ *n* -s [Jap *ukiyoe* genre picture, fr. *ukiyo* world, life + *e* picture] **:** a Japanese artistic movement from the 17th through the 19th centuries characterized by paintings and color prints depicting contemporary life and pleasures
¹ukrain·ian \(')yü¦krānēən, -ānyən *sometimes* (')(y)ü¦krīn-\ *adj, usu cap* [fr. *Ukraine*, constituent republic of the U.S.S.R. in east central Europe + E *-ian*] **1 a :** of, relating to, or characteristic of the Ukraine **b :** of, relating to, or characteristic of the people of the Ukraine **2 :** of, relating to, or characteristic of the Ukrainian language
²ukrainian \"\ *n* -s *cap* **1 :** a native or inhabitant of the Ukraine **2 :** the Slavic language of the Ukrainian people **3 :** RUTHENIAN 2
uku \'ü,kü\ *n* -s [Hawaiian] **:** a grayish blue-tinged snapper (*Aprion virescens*) of Hawaiian seas that is common in the markets and highly esteemed as food
uku·le·le *also* **uke·le·le** \,yükə'lālē, -āli, *sometimes* ,ük-\ *n* -s [Hawaiian *'ukulele*, fr. *'uku* small person, flea + *lele* jumping; prob. fr. the Hawaiian nickname of Edward Purvis 19th cent. Brit. army officer who was small and quick and who popularized the instrument] **:** a small guitar of Portuguese origin popularized in Hawaii in the 1880s, strung typically with four strings that are plucked or strummed with the fingers, and used esp. in accompanying songs or dances

ukulele

UL *abbr* upper left
ula \'yülə\ *n pl* [NL, fr. Gk *oula*, pl. of *oulon*; prob. akin to Gk *eilein* to roll, *eilyein* to roll, wrap — more at VOLUBLE] **:** the buccal gums
¹-u·la \(y)ələ\ *n suffix, pl* **-ulas** \-ləz\ *or* **-ulae** \-,lē, -,lī\ [L — more at -ULE] **:** small one ⟨Clan*gula*⟩ ⟨siphon*ula*⟩ ⟨plac*ula*⟩
²-ula *pl of* -ULUM
ulae \(')ü¦lī\ *n* -s [Hawaiian *'ulae*] *Hawaii* **:** LIZARD FISH
ula·ma *or* **ule·ma** \¦ülə¦mä\ *n, pl* **ulama** *or* **ulamas** *or* **ulema** *or* **ulemas** [Ar, Turk & Per; Turk & Per *'ulemā*, fr. Ar *'ulamā*, fr. pl. of *'ālim* knowing, learned, fr. *'alama* to know] **1 :** a group of Muslim theologians and scholars who are professionally occupied with the elaboration and interpretation of the Muslim legal system from a study of its sources in the Koran and hadith, are usu. found gathered in groups at various urban centers where they function individually as teachers, jurisconsults, and theologians, and constitute the highest body of religious authorities in Islam — compare ALIM, SHARI'A **2 :** a member of an ulama
ulan ba·tor \¦ü,län¦bä,tō(ə)r\ *adj, usu cap U&B* [fr. *Ulan Bator* (Urga), capital of Mongolian People's Republic] **:** URGA
ulan ude \¦ü,län¦ü(,)dā, -nü¦dā\ *adj, usu cap both Us* [fr. *Ulan Ude*, capital of Buryat-Mongol Republic, U.S.S.R.] **:** of or from the city of Ulan Ude, U.S.S.R. **:** of the kind or style prevalent in Ulan Ude
-u·lar \yələ(r)\ *adj suffix* [L *-ularis*, fr. *-ulus, -ula, -ulum* -ule + *-aris* -ar] **:** of, relating to, or resembling ⟨crevic*ular*⟩ — chiefly in words where the base word is derived from a Latin word having a diminutive in *-ulus, -ula*, or *-ulum* ⟨tub*ular*⟩ ⟨valv*ular*⟩
ula·ula \¦ülə¦ülə\ *n* -s [Hawaiian *'ula'ula*] *Hawaii* **:** any of several brightly colored snappers commonly used as food
ULC *abbr* upper left center
¹ul·cer \'əlsə(r)\ *n* -s [ME, fr. L *ulcer-, ulcus* sore, ulcer; akin to Gk *helkos* wound, ulcer, Skt *arśas* hemorrhoids] **1 :** a break in skin or mucous membrane that is characterized by loss of surface tissue on an inflammatory base and by disintegration and necrosis of epithelial tissue and that is associated with slow healing and with pus if infected ⟨a stomach ~⟩ ⟨a varicose ~⟩ — compare ABSCESS **2 :** something that festers and corrupts like an open sore
²ulcer \"\ *vb* -ED/-ING/-S **:** ULCERATE
ul·cer·ate \-ə,rāt, *usu* -ād·+V\ *vb* -ED/-ING/-S [ME *ulceraten*, fr. L *ulceratus*, past part. of *ulcerare* to ulcerate, fr. *ulcer-, ulcus* ulcer] *vt* **:** to affect with or as if with an ulcer ⟨an *ulcerated* stomach⟩ ~ *vi* **:** to undergo ulceration
ul·cer·a·tion \,==='rāshən\ *n* -s [L *ulceration-, ulceratio*, fr. *ulceratus* + *-ion-, -io* -ion] **1 :** the process of forming an ulcer or of becoming ulcerated **2 :** the state of being ulcerated **3 :** ULCER
ul·cer·a·tive \'əlsə,rād·|iv, -s(ə)rə|, |t|, |ēv *also* |əv\ *adj* [L *ulceratus* + E *-ive*] **:** of, relating to, or characterized by an ulcer or by ulceration
ulcerative colitis *n* **:** a nonspecific inflammatory disease of

the colon of unknown cause characterized by diarrhea with discharge of mucus and blood, cramping abdominal pain, and inflammation and edema of the mucous membrane with patches of ulceration

ulcerative lymphangitis *n* **:** pseudoglanders or a related condition in cattle

ulcer disease *n* **:** a common and destructive bacterial disease of young trout esp. in hatcheries that is characterized by extensive skin lesions and sloughing ulcerations and is distinguished with difficulty from furunculosis

ul·cered \'əlsə(r)d\ *adj* [*ulcer* + *-ed*] **:** ULCEROUS, ULCERATED

ulcero- *comb form* [L *ulcer-, ulcus*] **1 :** ulcer ⟨*ulcero*genic⟩ **2 :** ulcerous and ⟨*ulcero*glandular⟩

ul·cero·membranous \¦əlsərō+\ *adj* [ISV *ulcero-* + *membranous*] **:** characterized by ulceration and the formation of a membrane or esp. a false membrane

ul·cer·ous \'əls(ə)rəs\ *adj* [L *ulcerosus* affected with sores or ulcers, fr. *ulcer-, ulcus* ulcer + *-osus* -ous] **1 :** having the nature or character of an ulcer ⟨~ lesions⟩ **2 :** affected with an ulcer **:** ULCERATED ⟨an ~ person⟩

ul·cus \'əlkəs\ *n, pl* **ul·cera** \-lsərə\ [L *ulcer-, ulcus*] **:** ULCER

ule *or* **hu·le** \'ül(,)ā\ *n* -s [AmerSp *ule, hule,* fr. Nahuatl *ulli*] **1** *also* **ule tree :** a tree of the genus *Castilloa* that yields caucho **2 :** CAUCHO

-ule \,yül\ *n suffix* -s [F&L; F *-ule,* fr. L *-ulus,* masc. dim. suffix, *-ula,* fem. dim. suffix, *-ulum* neut. dim. suffix] **:** small one ⟨*cymule*⟩ ⟨*veinule*⟩

ulema *var of* ULAMA

-u·lent \(y)ələnt\ *adj suffix* [L *-ulentus, -olentus;* prob. akin to L *olēre* to smell — more at ODOR] **:** that abounds in (a specified thing) **:** that has (a specified thing) in marked amount or degree ⟨*nidorulent*⟩

ulet·ic \yü'led·ik\ *adj* [NL *ula* + E *-etic*] **:** of or relating to the gums

ulex \'yü,leks\ *n* [NL *Ulic-, Ulex,* fr. L, a shrub resembling rosemary] **1** *cap* **:** a genus of Eurasian spiny shrubs (family Leguminosae) including the common furze that are usu. destitute of true leaves and have solitary or racemose yellow flowers with a 2-lipped colored calyx **2** -ES **:** any plant of the genus *Ulex*

ulex·ine \yü'lek,sēn, -ksən\ *n* -s [NL *Ulex* + E *-ine*] **:** cytisine from the seeds of a furze (*Ulex europaeus*)

ulex·ite \'(y)ü,lek,sīt\ *n* -s [George L. *Ulex* †1883 Ger. chemist + E *-ite*] **:** a mineral $NaCaB_5O_9.8H_2O$ consisting of a hydrous sodium calcium borate and occurring in white rounded crystalline masses rather common in borate deposits (hardness 1, sp. gr. 1.65)

-uli *pl of* -ULUS

ulig·i·nous \yü'lijənəs\ *adj* [L *uliginosus,* fr. *uligin-, uligo* moisture, marshiness, fr. *udus, uvidus* damp, moist — more at HUMOR] **:** growing in wet or swampy ground

ul·lage \'əlij, -lēj\ *n* -s [ME *ulage, oylage,* fr. MF *eullage, oillage* act of filling a cask, filling to replace leakage, fr. *eullier, ouiller* to fill a cask (fr. OF *ouil* eye, bunghole, fr. L *oculus* eye) + *-age* — more at EYE] **:** the amount that a container (as a cask or tank) lacks of being full **:** OUTAGE

ul·laged \-jd\ *adj* [*ullage* + *-ed*] **:** short of the full measure of its contents ⟨an ~ cask⟩

ul·la·gone \,ələ'gōn\ *also* **ul·i·can** \,ələ'kän\ *n* -s [IrGael *olagón, olagán,* of imit. origin] *Irish* **:** a cry of sorrow **:** DIRGE

ul·la grass \'ülə-\ *n* [Bengali *ulu*] **:** a coarse East Indian and Australian grass (*Themeda gigantea*) that is used as a source of paper pulp — called also *kangaroo grass, oat grass*

ull·mann·ite \'əlmə,nīt\ *n* -s [G *ullmannit,* fr. Johann C. *Ullmann* †1821 Ger. mineralogist + G *-it* -ite] **:** a mineral NiSbS consisting of nickel antimonide and sulfide, usu. containing a little arsenic, and occurring massive with steel-gray color and metallic luster

ul·lo·a's ring *or* **ulloa's bow** *or* **ulloa's circle** \ü(l)'yōəz-\ *n, usu cap U* [after Antonio de Ulloa †1795 Span. naval officer and scientist] **:** FOGBOW

ullu·cu \ü'yü(,)kü\ *or* **ollu·co** \ō'yü(,)kō\ *n* -s [AmerSp & Quechua; AmerSp *ulluco, alluco, olluca,* fr. Quechua *ullucu*] **:** an Andean plant (*Ullucus tuberosus*) of the family Basellaceae having a creeping stem that roots wherever it touches the ground and tuberous roots which are used in place of potatoes

ul·ma·ce·ae \,əl'māsē,ē\ *n pl, cap* [NL, fr. *Ulmus,* type genus + *-aceae*] **:** a family of trees and shrubs (order Urticales) distinguished by the alternate stipulate pinnately veined simple leaves and small apetalous perfect or unisexual flowers — see CELTIS, PLANERA, TREMA, ULMUS

ul·ma·ceous \-shəs\ *adj* [NL *Ulmaceae* + E *-ous*] **:** of or relating to the Ulmaceae

ul·mar·ia \,əl'ma(a)rēə\ [NL, fr. L *ulmus* elm + NL *-aria;* fr. the resemblance of its leaves to those of the elm — more at ELM] *syn of* FILIPENDULA

ul·mic \'əlmik\ *or* **ul·mous** \-məs\ *adj* [*ulmin* + *-ic* or *-ous*] **:** of or relating to ulmin

ul·min \-mən\ *n* -s [L *ulmus* elm + E *-in*] **:** any of a group of brown to black organic substances found esp. in soil, peat, or coal and obtained artificially by the action of various reagents on sugars

ul·min·ic \,əl¦minik\ *adj* [*ulmin* + *-ic*] **:** ULMIC

ul·mo \'ül(,)mō\ *n* -s [Sp, fr. Araucanian] **:** MUERMO

ul·mus \'əlməs\ *n, cap* [NL, fr. L, elm — more at ELM] **:** a genus of trees (the type of the family Ulmaceae) comprising the elms that are widely distributed in temperate regions and have simple serrate oblique leaves, often drooping branches, and fascicled perfect flowers unfolding before the leaves and succeeded by orbicular samaras

ul·na \'əlnə\ *n, pl* **ul·nae** \-,nē, -,nī\ *or* **ulnas** [NL, fr. L, elbow, arm, ell — more at ELL] **1 :** the postaxial or inner one of the two bones of the forearm or corresponding part of the forelimb of vertebrates above fishes that in man forms with the humerus the elbow joint and serves as a pivot in rotation of the hand and that in many animals is fused with the radius and then often much reduced in size — see CORONOID PROCESS, OLECRANON, SEMILUNAR NOTCH, SIGMOID CAVITY **2 :** the hypercoracoid bone of a fish

ul·nad \'əl,nad\ *adv* [NL *ulna* + E *-ad*] **:** toward the ulna

ul·nar \'əlnə(r)\ *adj* [NL *ulnaris,* fr. *ulna* + L *-aris* -ar] **1 :** of or relating to the ulna **2 :** located on the same side of the forearm as the ulna

ulnar artery *n* **:** an artery that is the larger of the two terminal branches of the brachial artery, runs along the ulnar side of the forearm, and gives off near its origin the anterior and posterior ulnar recurrent arteries

ul·nare \,əl'na(a)rē, -'närē\ *or* **ul·nar** \'əlnə(r)\ *n, pl* **ulnar·ia** \-a(a)rēə, -ärēə\ *or* **ulnars** [NL *ulnare,* fr. neut. of *ulnaris* ulnar] **1 :** the third carpal bone or element of the proximal row counting from the radial side; *specif* **:** CUNEIFORM 1b **2** *or* **ulnar carpal :** a bone of a bird prob. representing the ulnare and centrale and sometimes also the fifth metacarpal

ulnar nerve *n* **:** a large nerve arising from the medial part of the brachial plexus, passing down the inner side of the arm and forearm, and resting upon the medial epicondyle of the humerus at the elbow

ulnar recurrent artery *n* **:** either of the two small terminal branches of the ulnar artery that supply the upper forearm and elbow region

ulnar vein *n* **:** any of several veins of the forearm; *esp* **:** either of the two veins running up the anterior and posterior aspects of the inner side of the forearm and opening into the median basilic vein either separately or uniting to form a short single trunk and constituting with it the basilic vein

ulno- *comb form* [NL *ulna*] **:** ulnar and ⟨*ulno*carpal⟩ ⟨*ulno*radial⟩

ul·no·condylar \¦əlnō+\ *adj* [*ulno-* + *condylar*] **:** of, relating to, or constituting the medial epicondyle of the humerus

ulo *var of* ULU

ulo- *comb form* [NL *ula*] **:** connection with or relation to the gums ⟨*ulo*rrhagia⟩

¹ulob·o·rid \yü'läbərəd\ *adj* [NL *Uloboridae*] **:** of or relating to the Uloboridae

²uloborid \"\ *n* -s **:** a spider of the family Uloboridae

ulo·bor·i·dae \,yülə'bōrə,dē\ *n pl, cap* [NL *Uloborus,* type genus + *-idae*] **:** a family of spiders having a cribellum and calamistrum and spinning an orb web

ulob·o·rus \yü'läbərəs\ *n, cap* [NL, fr. Gk *ouloboros* having a deadly bite, fr. *oulos* deadly, destructive (akin to Gk *ollynai* to destroy) + *-boros* (fr. *bibrōskein* to eat, devour) — more at VORACIOUS] **:** a genus (the type of the family Uloboridae) of orb-spinning spiders

-u·lose \(y)ə,lōs *also* -ōz\ *n suffix* -s [*levulose*] **:** ketose sugar — esp. in names of 2-keto sugars ⟨*heptulose*⟩ ⟨*xylulose*⟩

ulo·thrix \'yülə,thriks\ *n, cap* [NL *Ulotrich-, Ulothrix,* fr. Gk *oulotrich-, oulothrix* having curly hair — more at ULOTRICHOUS] **:** a genus (the type of the family Ulotrichaceae) of green algae that are common in ponds and consist of simple filaments with band-shaped green chloroplasts

ulot·ri·cha·ce·ae \yü,lä·trə'kāsē,ē\ *n pl, cap* [NL, fr. *Ulotrich-, Ulothrix,* type genus + *-aceae*] **:** a family of green algae (order Ulotrichales) — see ULOTHRIX — **ulot·ri·cha·ceous** \¦≈¦≈≈'kāshəs\ *adj*

ulot·ri·cha·les \≈,≈≈'kā(,)lēz\ *n pl, cap* [NL *Ulotrich-, Ulothrix* + *-ales*] **:** an order of green algae that includes the family Ulotrichaceae and in some classifications also Ulvaceae and that comprises freshwater or marine forms having a multicellular thallus with usu. simple or branched filaments sometimes aggregated to form pseudoparenchymatous masses or sheets, asexual reproduction effected by zoospores, and sexual reproduction by fusion of isogametes or of differentiated egg and sperm cells

ulot·ri·chan \≈'lä·trəkən\ *adj* [NL *Ulotrichi* + E *-an*] **:** ULOTRICHOUS

ulot·ri·choid \-rə,kȯid\ *adj* [NL *Ulotrich*ales + E *-oid*] **:** resembling or related to the order Ulotrichales

ulot·ri·chous \-rəkəs\ *adj* [NL *Ulotrichi* (pl.) division of mankind having crisp or woolly hair (fr. Gk *oulotrich-, oulothrix* having curly or woolly hair, fr. *oulos* curly, woolly + *trich-, thrix* hair) + E *-ous;* akin to Gk *eilein* to roll, *eilyein* to roll, wrap — more at TRICH-, VOLUBLE] **:** exhibiting ulotrichy **:** having woolly or crisp hair

ulot·ri·chy \-kē\ *n* -ES [NL *Ulotrichi* + E *-y*] **:** the condition of having woolly or crisp hair

-u·lous \yələs\ *adj suffix* [L *-ulus,* dim. suffix] **:** being slightly or minutely ⟨*hirsutulous*⟩ ⟨*viscidulous*⟩

ul·pan \'ül,pän\ *n, pl* **ulpa·nim** \¦ülpä¦nēm\ [NHeb *ūlpān,* fr. Mishnaic Aram (*bēth*) *ūlpānā* (house) of study, fr. Aram *alaph* to teach, train] **:** an Israeli study center for newcomers in which intensive training in Hebrew and cultural subjects is given

¹ul·ster \'əlztə(r), -lst-\ *adj, usu cap* [fr. *Ulster,* former province of northern Ireland (now partly in the Republic of Ireland)] **1 :** of or from the former province or the present region of Ulster, Ireland **:** of the kind or style prevalent in Ulster **2 :** NORTHERN IRELAND **3 :** of or from the province of Ulster, Republic of Ireland **:** of the kind or style prevalent in Ulster province

²ulster \"\ *n* -s **:** a long loose overcoat of Irish origin made of frieze or other heavy overcoating

ul·ster·ette \¦≈≈¦ret\ *n* -s [²*ulster* + *-ette*] **:** a light ulster

ul·ste·ri·an \,əlz'tirēən, ,əl'st-\ *adj, usu cap* [*Ulster,* former province of northern Ireland + E *-ian*] **:** of or relating to a subdivision of the American Devonian — see GEOLOGIC TIME table

ul·ster·ite \'əlztə,rīt, -lst-\ *n* -s *cap* [*Ulster,* former province of northern Ireland + E *-ite*] **:** ULSTERMAN

ulster king of arms *also* **ulster** *usu cap U&K&A* **:** the chief officer of arms for Ireland from 1552 to 1943 — compare IRELAND KING OF ARMS, NORROY AND ULSTER KING OF ARMS

ul·ster·man \'≈≈mən\ *n, pl* **ulstermen** *cap* **:** a native or inhabitant of Ulster or of Northern Ireland

ulster office *n, usu cap U&O* **:** the office of arms of which Ulster King of Arms was head **:** OFFICE OF ARMS 2

ulsterwoman \¦≈¦≈≈\ *n, pl* **ulsterwomen** *cap* **:** a woman born in Ulster or of Ulster descent

ult *abbr* **1** ultimate; ultimately **2** ultimo

ul·te·ri·or \,əl¦tirē(r), -tēr-\ *adj* [L, situated beyond, farther, further, compar. of (assumed) *ulter* situated beyond (whence *ultra* beyond, adv. & prep.), fr. *uls* beyond (prep.) — more at ALL] **1 a :** occurring at a subsequent time **:** FURTHER, FUTURE ⟨~ actions⟩ ⟨without ~ argument⟩ **b :** more distant **:** REMOTER ⟨without . . . any purpose, immediate or ~ —G.B. Shaw⟩ ⟨~ reasons⟩ **c :** situated on the further side **:** THITHER ⟨~ regions⟩ **2 :** going beyond what is avowed, manifest, or proper **:** not apparent **:** HIDDEN, LATENT ⟨eyes . . . with no ~ thought behind —Gilbert Parker⟩ ⟨look too closely for an ~ purpose in all knowledge —Bertrand Russell⟩ ⟨not a line in the book without an ~ motive —A.J.A.Waldock⟩ — **ul·te·ri·or·ly** *adv*

ul·ti·ma \'əltəmə\ *n* -s [L, fem. of *ultimus* last] **:** the last syllable of a word ⟨antepenult, penult, and ~⟩ ⟨"Mama," she said, accenting the ~ —Jean Stafford⟩

ul·ti·ma·cy \-məsē, -si\ *n* -ES [*ultimate* + *-cy*] **1 :** the quality or state of being ultimate ⟨denied the ~ of these social values —F.I.Carpenter⟩ **2 :** ULTIMATE, FUNDAMENTAL ⟨not to pry into the *ultimacies* of metaphysics —C.H.Whiteley⟩

ul·ti·ma ra·tio \¦əltəmə'räd·ē,ō; ¦əltəmə'rāshē,ō, -ā,shō\ *n* [NL] **:** the last or final argument **:** the last resort (as force) ⟨impaired by methods in which violence is the *ultima ratio* —*New Republic*⟩ ⟨the strike is the *ultima ratio* of Trade Unionism —Hewlett Johnson⟩

¹ul·ti·mate \'əltəmət, *usu* -ād·+V\ *adj* [ML *ultimatus* completed, last, final, fr. LL, past part. of *ultimare* to come to an end, be last, fr. L *ultimus* farthest, furthest, last, final, superl. of (assumed) *ulter* situated beyond — more at ULTERIOR] **1 a :** most remote in space or time **:** FARTHEST, EARLIEST ⟨man's ~ destiny⟩ ⟨~ origins⟩ ⟨faded farther and farther away into ~ distance —Hugh Walpole⟩ **b :** last in a progression **:** FINAL ⟨swallowing the ~ crumb of gingerbread —Elinor Wylie⟩ ⟨this ~ book of my autobiography —Osbert Sitwell⟩ **c :** EVENTUAL ⟨saw no hope of any ~ escape —R.L. Stevenson⟩ ⟨endurance based on a serene faith in ~ rescue —W.J.Ghent⟩ **d :** EXTREME, UTMOST ⟨at the ~ rakish angle, she wore a black . . . beret —Raymond Chandler⟩ ⟨certainty of an ~ act — murder —Frederic Morton⟩ ⟨not averse to immense sacrifice — even to the ~ sacrifice — if it will win the war —*Jour. Amer. Med. Assoc.*⟩ **2 a :** tended toward by all that precedes **:** arrived at as the last result ⟨~ truths⟩ ⟨consideration of the ~ questions of religion —*McCormick Theological Seminary Cat.*⟩ ⟨the fugue was considered the ~ vehicle for profound musical expression —A.E.Wier⟩ **b :** finally reckoned ⟨the ~ damage of that hurricane was not known for weeks —Marjory S. Douglas⟩ **c :** using an economic good in a way that diminishes or destroys its utility ⟨~ buyer⟩ ⟨~ consumer⟩ ⟨~ purchaser⟩ **3 a :** BASIC, FUNDAMENTAL, ORIGINAL, PRIMITIVE ⟨the English alphabet . . . owes its ~ origin to the Phoenician —Norbert Wiener⟩ ⟨~ title to the soil —D.E.Clark⟩ ⟨the ~ control of education —*General Education in a Free Society*⟩ ⟨the ~ nature of things —A.N. Whitehead⟩ **b :** incapable of further analysis, division, or separation ⟨the ~ ingredients of matter —James Jeans⟩ **c :** ELEMENTAL 2a(2) ⟨~ analysis⟩ ⟨~ composition⟩ **4 :** MAXIMUM ⟨~ speeds which may be attained by airplanes in the future —H.G.Armstrong⟩ — used esp. of strain, strength, or stress at the instant of breaking or rupture ⟨the ~ strength of any concrete structure —*Building, Estimating & Contracting*⟩ **syn** see LAST

²ultimate \"\ *n* -s **1 :** something that is ultimate **:** something final or fundamental ⟨search for ~*s* and grand generalizations ends in a universality devoid of all content —E.H.Eby⟩ ⟨an absurdity . . . carried to its ~ —W.H.Camp⟩ **2 :** ACME, PEAK, LAST WORD ⟨an automobile that is the ~ in luxurious transportation⟩

³ul·ti·mate \-,māt, *usu* -ād·+V\ *vb* -ED/-ING/-S *vi* **:** to come to an end or issue **:** EVENTUATE, END ~ *vt* **:** to bring to an end or issue

ultimate analysis *n* **:** the determination of the percentage of constituent elements of a chemical substance

ultimate destination *n* **:** the final destination in the territory of an enemy or under its control making goods contraband under the doctrine of continuous voyage

ultimate fact *n* **:** a basic fact essential to maintain a cause of action or to establish a defense thereto as distinguished from the subsidiary individual facts that are offered in evidence as tending to prove a basic fact

ultimate line *n* **:** RAIE ULTIME

ul·ti·mate·ly *adv* [¹*ultimate* + *-ly*] **:** in the ultimate stage **:** in the end **:** at last **:** FINALLY, BASICALLY, FUNDAMENTALLY ⟨doubted not that I should ~ succeed —Mary W. Shelley⟩ ⟨~ the towns were able to establish themselves as centers of freedom —R.A.Hall b. 1911⟩ ⟨were estranged; but ~ they became friends again —E.E.Hume⟩

ultimate mortality table *n* **:** a mortality table based on experience from which the effect of medical selection has been eliminated by the passage of a stated period (as five years)

ul·ti·mate·ness *n* -ES **:** the state or degree of being ultimate

ultimate reality *n, often cap U&R* **:** something that is the supreme, final, and fundamental power in all reality ⟨*ultimate reality* in Judaism, Christianity, and Islam is God⟩

ultimate tensile strength *n* **:** TENSILE STRENGTH

ul·ti·ma thule \,əltəmə-\ *n, usu cap U&T* [L, farthest Thule] **:** THULE

ul·ti·ma·tion \,əltə'māshən\ *n* -s [LL *ultimatus* (past part. of *ultimare* to come to an end) + E *-ion* — more at ULTIMATE] **:** the act or result of ultimating **:** the state of being ultimate

ul·ti·ma·tum \,əltə'mā|d·əm, |təm *also* -mä| *or* -ma|\ *n, pl* **ultimatums** \-mz\ *or* **ultima·ta** \|d·ə, |tə\ [NL, fr. ML, neut. of *ultimatus* final — more at ULTIMATE] **1 :** a final proposition, condition, or demand; *esp* **:** one whose rejection will end negotiations and cause a resort to force or other direct action **2 :** the farthest point or stage to be reached **:** a final objective or end **:** ULTIMATE

ul·ti·mo \'əltə,mō\ *adj* [L *ultimo* (*mense*) in the last month, fr. abl. sing. masc. of *ultimus* last — more at ULTIMATE] **:** of or occurring in the month preceding the present — abbr. *ult.* ⟨your letter received on the 25th *ult.*); compare INSTANT, PROXIMO

ul·ti·mo·branchial \¦əltəmō+\ *adj* [L *ultimus* last + E *-o-* + *branchia* + *-al*] **:** relating to or derived from the last gill pouch

ultimobranchial body *n* **:** a hollow vesicle of the embryo believed to be derived from the fifth pharyngeal pouch

ul·ti·mo·gen·i·tary \-¦jenəd·,erē\ *adj* [fr. *ultimogeniture,* after E *primogeniture: primogenitary*] **:** of or relating to ultimogeniture

ul·ti·mo·geniture \¦≈≈≈+\ *n* -s [L *ultimus* last + E *-o-* + *-geniture* (as in *primogeniture*)] **:** a system of inheritance by which the youngest son or sometimes daughter or collateral heir succeeds to the estate — called also *postremogeniture;* opposed to *primogeniture;* compare BOROUGH-ENGLISH

ul·ti·mus he·res \¦ültəməs'hā,rās\ *or* **ultimus hae·res** \-'hī,-\ *n* [ML] **:** the last heir — in feudal law often applied to the sovereign as taking property when other capable heirs fail

¹ul·to·ni·an \,əl¦tōnēən\ *adj, usu cap* [ML *Ultonia* Ulster, former province of northern Ireland + E *-an*] **1 :** of, relating to, or characteristic of Ulster **2 :** of, relating to, or characteristic of the people of Ulster

²ultonian \"\ *n* -s *cap* **:** ULSTERMAN

¹ul·tra \'əltrə\ *adj* [*ultra-*] **:** going beyond others or beyond due limit **:** EXTREME, FANATICAL, UNCOMPROMISING, SUPERLATIVE ⟨~ political individualism taught by liberal political leaders —*Metropolitan Mag.*⟩ ⟨treat yourself to . . . ~ dinners —Michael Frome⟩

²ultra \"\ *n* -s [*ultra-*] **1 :** ULTRAIST, EXTREMIST, RADICAL **2** *usu cap* [F, short for *ultraroyaliste,* fr. *ultra-* (fr. L) + *royaliste* royalist, fr. *royal* + *-iste* -ist] **:** a member of a political group active in 19th century France following the Bourbon restoration composed largely of returned emigrés and associated principally with a desire to restore the political and social order prevailing before the Revolution of 1789

ultra- *prefix* [L, fr. *ultra* beyond (adv. & prep.), fr. abl. sing. fem. of (assumed) *ulter* situated beyond — more at ULTERIOR] **1 :** beyond in space **:** on the other side **:** TRANS- ⟨*ultra*tropical⟩ ⟨*ultra*median⟩ **2 :** beyond the range or limits of **:** transcending **:** SUPER- ⟨*ultra*microscopic⟩ ⟨*ultra*sonic⟩ **3 :** beyond what is common, ordinary, natural, right, proper, or moderate **:** excessively **:** exceedingly **:** HYPER- ⟨*ultra*complex⟩ ⟨*ultra*critical⟩ ⟨*ultra*formal⟩ ⟨*ultra*modern⟩

ul·tra·atomic \¦əltrə+\ *adj* [*ultra-* + *atomic*] **:** of, relating to, or constituting particles smaller than atoms

ul·tra·basic \"+\ *adj* [ISV *ultra-* + *basic*] **:** extremely basic **:** very low in silica and rich in ferromagnesian minerals ⟨~ igneous rocks⟩ ⟨peridotite is ~⟩

ul·tra·centrifugal \"+\ *adj* [¹*ultracentrifuge* + *-al*] **:** of, relating to, or obtained by means of an ultracentrifuge — **ul·tra·centrifugally** \"+\ *adv*

ul·tra·centrifugation \"+\ *n* [²*ultracentrifuge* + *-ation*] **:** processing in an ultracentrifuge ⟨purified by repeated ~*s* —*Jour. of General Microbiology*⟩

¹ul·tra·centrifuge \"+\ *n* [*ultra-* + *centrifuge*] **:** a very high-speed centrifuge that effects the sedimentation of colloidal and other small particles and is useful esp. in determining mean size and size distribution of such particles and molecular weights of proteins and other high polymers

²ultracentrifuge \"\ *vt* **:** to subject to the action of an ultracentrifuge

ul·tra·condenser \"+\ *n* [ISV *ultra-* + *condenser*] **:** the condenser of an ultramicroscope

ul·tra·conservatism \"+\ *n* [*ultra-* + *conservatism*] **:** extreme conservatism ⟨~ is the chief characteristic of their cult —H.H.Shenk⟩

ul·tra·conservative \"+\ *adj* [*ultra-* + *conservative*] **:** extremely conservative ⟨a few ~ newspapers —E.A.Peers⟩ ⟨there exists a large ~ religious group —R.W.Murray⟩

ul·tra·dolichocephalic \"+\ *adj* [*ultra-* + *dolichocephalic*] **:** having a very long or narrow head or both and a cephalic index of 64 or less

ul·tra·dolichocephaly \"+\ *n* [*ultra-* + *dolichocephaly*] **:** the quality or state of being ultradolichocephalic

ul·tra·dolichocranial \"+\ *adj* [*ultra-* + *dolichocranial*] **:** having a very long or narrow skull or both and a cranial index of 60 to 65

ul·tra·dolichocrany \"+\ *n* [*ultra-* + *dolichocrany*] **:** the quality or state of being ultradolichocranial

ul·tra·fashionable \"+\ *adj* [*ultra-* + *fashionable*] **:** extremely fashionable

Ul·tra·fax \'əltrə,faks\ *trademark* — used for a very high-speed facsimile transmission that uses television techniques for scanning, transmission, and reproduction

¹ul·tra·filter \¦əltrə+\ *n* [ISV *ultra-* + *filter*] **:** a dense filter used for the filtration of a colloidal solution that holds back the dispersed particles but not the liquid

²ultrafilter \"\ *vt* **:** to cause to pass through an ultrafilter

ul·tra·filtrate \"+\ *n* [²*ultrafilter* + *-ate*] **:** the liquid that has passed through an ultrafilter

ul·tra·filtration \"+\ *n* [ISV *ultra-* + *filtration*] **:** the process of passing through an ultrafilter

ul·tra·gaseous \"+\ *adj* [*ultra-* + *gaseous*] **:** having the properties exhibited by gases under pressures of one millionth of an atmosphere or less

ul·tra·high frequency \"+-\ *n* [*ultra-* + *high*] **:** a radio frequency in the second from the highest range of the radio spectrum — see RADIO FREQUENCY table

ultrahigh-frequency *adj* [*ultrahigh frequency*] **:** of or relating to ultrahigh frequency or a radio wave having such a frequency

ul·tra·ism \'əltrə,izəm\ *n* -s [¹*ultra* + *-ism*] **1 :** the principles of those who advocate extreme measures (as radicalism) **2 :** an instance or example of radicalism ⟨he pleaded for freedom of speech and of the press, denounced sectionalism and ~ on either side —W.E.Smith⟩

¹ul·tra·ist \-əəst\ *n* -s [¹*ultra* + *-ist*] **:** an adherent of ultraism **:** EXTREMIST, RADICAL ⟨the organ of the Argentine ~*s* . . . roundly rejected Madrid's claim to chieftainship —*Times Lit. Supp.*⟩

²ultraist \"\ *or* **ul·tra·is·tic** \¦≈≈¦istik\ *adj* **:** of, relating to, or characteristic of ultraism

ul·tra·mafic \¦əltrə+\ *adj* [*ultra-* + *mafic*] **:** ULTRABASIC

¹ul·tra·marine \"+\ *or* **ultramarine blue** *n* [ML *ultramarinus* coming from beyond the sea; fr. the fact that lapis lazuli came originally from Asia] **1 a :** a costly pure blue pigment formerly prepared by powdering lapis lazuli **b :** a brilliant blue pigment of similar composition but having commonly a reddish or greenish cast that is usu. prepared by powdering the product from calcining essentially a mixture of kaolin, soda ash, sulfur, and charcoal or other reducing agent and that is used chiefly in paints, printing inks, paper, and laundry bluing — called also *French blue, new blue* **c :** any of various pigments that are usu. produced by modifications of the

U
V

above process or by replacing the sodium or the sulfur in ordinary ultramarine by other elements ⟨silver ~⟩ **2 :** a vivid blue that is redder, lighter, and stronger than Ch'ing and redder than Cleopatra — called also *Armenian blue*

²ultramarine \"\ *adj* [ML *ultramarinus*, fr. L *ultra-* + *mare* sea + *-inus* -ine — more at MARINE] **:** situated beyond the sea ⟨~ provinces⟩ **:** coming from beyond the sea

ultramarine ash *n* [*¹ultramarine*] **1 :** a delicate bluish gray pigment obtained as a residuum from lapis lazuli after the extraction of ultramarine and used by the old masters as a middle or neutral tint for flesh, skies, and draperies **2 :** a variable color averaging from blue ultramarine ash to gray ultramarine ash

ultramarine green *n* **1 :** an ultramarine pigment of strong green cast **2 :** a blackish green that is bluer and paler than cannon

ultramarine yellow *n* **1 :** YELLOW ULTRAMARINE **2 :** LIGHT CHROME YELLOW

ul·tra·metamorphic \¦əltrə+\ *adj* [*ultrametamorphism* + *-ic*] **:** of or relating to ultrametamorphism

ul·tra·metamorphism \"+\ *n* [*ultra-* + *metamorphism*] **:** metamorphism at temperatures and pressures just below the fusion temperature of rock

ul·tra·micro \"+\ *adj* [ultramicro-] **:** smaller in size than micro **:** being on a scale smaller than micro

ultramicro- *comb form* [*ultra-* + *micr-*] **:** of, involving, or being for quantities of material smaller than micro quantities **:** on a scale smaller than micro

ul·tra·microanalysis \"+\ *n* [*ultramicro-* + *analysis*] **:** chemical analysis (as of quantities of the order of a few micrograms) on a scale smaller than microanalysis

ul·tra·microbe \"+\ *n* [ISV *ultra-* + *microbe*] **:** ULTRAVIRUS

ul·tra·microchemical \"+\ *adj* [fr. *ultramicrochemistry*, after E *chemistry: chemical*] **:** of, relating to, or using the methods of ultramicrochemistry

ul·tra·microchemistry \"+\ *n* [*ultramicro-* + *chemistry*] **:** chemistry dealing with very minute quantities of substances (as a microgram or less) — compare MICROCHEMISTRY

ul·tra·micrometer \"+\ *n* [*ultra-* + *micrometer*] **:** an extremely sensitive micrometer (as one capable of measuring to one millionth of an inch or less) frequently utilizing a variable capacitance that controls the frequency of an oscillator

ul·tra·micron \"+\ *n* [*ultra-* + *micron*] **:** SUBMICRON

ul·tra·microorganism \"+\ *n* [*ultra-* + *microorganism*] **:** ULTRAVIRUS

ul·tra·microscope \"+\ *n* [back-formation fr. *ultramicroscopic*] **:** an apparatus for making ultramicroscopic particles visible consisting of a compound microscope with a condenser that projects intense light from one side so that what is actually seen against an otherwise dark field is the light scattered by the particles rather than the particles themselves — called also *dark-field microscope* — **ul·tra·microscopy** \"+\ *n*

ul·tra·microscopic \"+\ *adj* [ISV *ultra-* + *microscopic*] **1 :** too small to be seen with an ordinary microscope **:** SUBMICROSCOPIC **2** [*ultramicroscope* + *-ic*] **:** of or relating to an ultramicroscope or to ultramicroscopy

¹ul·tra·modern \"+\ *adj* [*ultra-* + *modern*] **:** being beyond the norm of the modern **:** extreme in typically modern ideas or tendencies ⟨~ ideas⟩ ⟨~ equipment⟩ ⟨~ artists⟩

²ul·tra·modern \"+\ *n* **:** one that is ultramodern

ul·tra·modernist \"+\ *n* **:** ULTRAMODERN

¹ul·tra·montane \"+\ *n* -s [in sense 1, fr. ML *ultramontanus*, fr. *ultramontanus* situated beyond the mountains; in other senses fr. *²ultramontane*] **1** *usu cap* **:** a Roman Catholic ecclesiastic in a country north of the Alps **2 :** one who lives beyond the mountains: as **a** *archaic* **:** one who lives north of the Alps — compare TRAMONTANE **b :** one who lives south of the Alps **3** *sometimes cap* **:** a supporter of ultramontanism

²ultramontane \"\ *adj* [ML *ultramontanus*, fr. L *ultra-* + *mont-*, *mons* mountain + *-anus* -an — more at MOUNT] **1 :** situated beyond the mountains **:** of or relating to countries or peoples beyond the mountains: as **a :** of or relating to countries or peoples to the north of the Alps **b :** of or relating to Italy **2** *sometimes cap* [fr. the fact that the papal seat was located the other side of the Alps from the French] **:** of, relating to, or supporting ultramontanism ⟨~ party⟩ **3 :** claiming an absolute supremacy or a privileged superiority

ul·tra·montanism \"+\ *n* -s *sometimes cap* [F *ultramontanisme*, fr. *ultramontain* ultramontane (fr. ML *ultramontanus*) + *-isme* -ism] **:** the policy of advocating the greatest possible enhancement of papal power and authority — compare GALLICANISM

ul·tra·montanist \"+\ *n* [*²ultramontane* + *-ist*] **:** a supporter of ultramontanism

ul·tra·mundane \"+\ *adj* [L *ultramundanus*, fr. *ultra* beyond + *mundus* world + *-anus* -an — more at ULTERIOR] **:** situated beyond the world or beyond the limits of the solar system

ul·tra·nationalism \"+\ *n* [*ultra-* + *nationalism*] **:** great or excessive devotion to or advocacy of national interests and rights esp. as opposed to international considerations

¹ul·tra·nationalist \"+\ *or* **ul·tra·nationalistic** \"+\ *adj* [*ultra-* + *nationalist* or *nationalistic*] **:** of, relating to, or characterized by ultranationalism

²ul·tra·nationalist \"+\ *n* **:** a supporter of ultranationalism

ul·tra·profound \"+\ *adj* [*ultra-* + *profound*] **:** extremely profound

ul·tra·rapid picture \"+-\ *n* [*ultra-* + *rapid*] **:** a slow-motion picture

ul·tra·red \"+\ *adj* [*ultra-* + *red*] **:** INFRARED

ul·tra·short \"+\ *adj* [*ultra-* + *short*] **:** having a wavelength below 10 meters and frequencies above 30 megacycles per second ⟨~ radiations⟩

¹ul·tra·sonic \"+\ *adj* [*ultra-* + *sonic*] **:** SUPERSONIC — **ul·tra·sonically** \"+\ *adv*

²ultrasonic \"\ *n* **:** an ultrasonic wave or frequency

ul·tra·son·ics \,əltrə'säniks, -nēks\ *n pl but usu sing in constr* [fr. *¹ultrasonic*, after such pairs as E *economic: economics*] **:** the science of ultrasonic phenomena **:** SUPERSONICS

ul·tra·sound \¦əltrə+\ *n* [*ultra-* + *sound*] **:** a wave phenomenon of the same physical nature as sound but with frequencies above the range of human hearing — called also *supersound*

ul·tra·structure \"+\ *n* [*ultra-* + *structure*] **:** the invisible ultimate physicochemical organization of protoplasm

¹ul·tra·violet \"+\ *adj* [*ultra-* + *violet*] **1** *of radiation* **:** beyond the visible spectrum at its violet end **:** having a wavelength shorter than those of visible light and longer than those of X rays — compare INFRARED **2 :** relating to, producing, or employing ultraviolet radiation ⟨~ lamp⟩ ⟨~ filter⟩

²ultraviolet \"\ *n* **:** ultraviolet radiation

ultraviolet light *n* **:** ultraviolet radiation

ultraviolet microscope *n* **:** FLUORESCENCE MICROSCOPE

ultraviolet spectrum *n* **:** a spectrum of ultraviolet radiation characterized by short wavelengths and high quantum energies as compared to visible light

ul·tra vi·res \¦əltrə¦vī(,)rēz\ *adv (or adj)* [NL] **:** beyond the scope or in excess of legal power or authority (as vested in a corporation, an official, or a legislative body) ⟨an *ultra vires* contract⟩ ⟨the official acted *ultra vires*⟩

ul·tra·virus \¦əltrə+\ *n* [ISV *ultra-* + *virus*; prob. formed in F] **:** an ultramicroscopic or filterable virus

ul·tro·ne·ous \,əl'trōnēəs\ *adj* [L *ultroneus* voluntary, spontaneous, fr. *ultro* beyond, beyond expectation, spontaneously, fr. abl. sing. masc. or neut. of (assumed) *ulter* situated beyond — more at ULTERIOR] *Scots law* **:** that voluntarily offers testimony without being cited ⟨an ~ witness⟩

¹ulu \'ü,lü\ *also* **ulo** \-,lō\ *n* -s [Inupik] **:** an Eskimo woman's knife resembling a food chopper with a crescent-shaped blade

²ulu \'ü,lü\ *n* -s [prob. fr. Bengali, ulla grass] **:** an Indian grass (*Imperata arundinacea*) used for forage and pasture

ulua \ü'lüwə\ *n* -s [Hawaiian] **:** any of several large cavallas (genus *Caranx*) of Hawaiian waters highly prized as food and sport fishes

ulu-juz \¦ülə¦jüz\ *n, pl* **ulu-juz** *or* **ulu-juzes** *usu cap U* **1 :** one of the major divisions of the Kazak **2 :** a member of the Ulu-juz people

ulu·lant \'əlyələnt, 'yül-\ *adj* [L *ululant-, ululans*, pres. part. of *ululare*] **:** HOWLING, WAILING ⟨dark wasteland . . . ~ with bitter wind —Rudi Blesh⟩ ⟨yell . . . had a keening, ~ quality —C.B.Goolrick⟩

ulu·late \-ə,lāt, *usu* -ād·+V\ *vi* -ED/-ING/-S [L *ululatus*, past part. of *ululare* to howl, wail, of imit. origin] **:** to utter a loud mournful usu. protracted and rhythmical sound **:** cry out **:** HOWL, WAIL ⟨the *ululating* air raid danger signal —J.D. Mabbott⟩ ⟨*ululating* wolves⟩ ⟨crowds on the stands *ululated* with joy —Robert Lynd⟩ **syn** see ROAR

ulu·la·tion \,══'lāshən\ *n* -s [L *ululation-, ululatio*, fr. *ululatus* + *-ion-, -io* -ion] **1 :** a loud mournful usu. protracted and rhythmical sound **:** HOWL **2 :** the action of ululating **:** HOWLING ⟨the ~ of the ambulance —Christopher Morley⟩ ⟨the ~ of our despair —Sidney Alexander⟩

-u·lum \yələm\ *n suffix, pl* **-ulums** \-ləmz\ *or* **-u·la** \-lə\ [L — more at -ULE] **:** small one ⟨septulum⟩ ⟨frenulum⟩

-u·lus \yələs\ *n suffix, pl* **-u·lus·es** \-ləsəz\ *or* **-u·li** \-,lī\ [L — more at -ULE] **:** a small one ⟨phoeniculus⟩

¹ul·va \'əlvə\ *n, cap* [NL, fr. L, sedge] **:** a genus of green seaweeds (the type of the family Ulvaceae) having a thin flat edible thallus that resembles a lettuce leaf and is two cells thick — see SEA LETTUCE

²ul·va \'ülwə, 'ül(,)vä\ *or* **ul·ua** \'ülwə\ *n, pl* **ulva** *or* **ulvas** *or* **ulua** *or* **uluas** *usu cap* **1 a :** a people of Nicaragua and Honduras **b :** a member of such people **2 :** a language of the Ulva people

ul·va·ce·ae \,əl'vāsē,ē\ *n pl, cap* [NL, fr. *¹Ulva*, type genus + *-aceae*] **:** a widely distributed family of thin green algae having either a flat or a hollow tubular thallus, reproducing by the conjugation of planogametes or of zoospores, and being classed among the Ulotrichales or now more commonly placed in the order Ulvales — **ul·va·ceous** \¦══'vāshəs\ *adj*

ul·va·les \,══'vā(,)lēz\ *n pl, cap* [NL, fr. *¹Ulva* + *-ales*] **:** an order of green algae (class Chlorophyceae) that is coextensive with the family Ulvaceae

ul·ya·novsk \ül'yänəfsk, -əvsk\ *adj, usu cap* [fr. *Ulyanovsk*, city of eastern Soviet Russia] **:** of or from the city of Ulyanovsk, U.S.S.R. **:** of the kind or style prevalent in Ulyanovsk

ulys·se·an \yü'lisēən\ *adj, usu cap* [*Ulysses*, hero of Homer's *Odyssey* + E *-an*] **:** of, relating to, or resembling Ulysses

um *a prolonged* m *sound*\ *interj* [imit.] — used to express hesitation or doubt or to indicate inarticulateness

um *abbr* unmarried

'um *like* 'EM\ *pron* [alter. of *'em*] *chiefly dial* **:** THEM

uma \'(y)ümə\ *n* [NL, perh. fr. Aymara, head, helmet] **1** *cap* **:** a genus of American lizards (family Iguanidae) comprising the fringefoots **2** -s **:** FRINGEFOOT

uman·gite \(y)ü'maŋ,gīt\ *n* -s [G *umangit*, fr. Sierra de *Umango*, province in northwestern Argentina + G *-it* -ite] **:** a mineral Cu_3Se_2 consisting of a copper selenide and occurring in dark red masses (hardness 3, sp. gr. 5.62)

uma·til·la \,yümə'tilə\ *n, pl* **umatilla** *or* **umatillas** *usu cap* **1 :** a Shahaptian people of northeastern Oregon **2 :** a member of the Umatilla people

umay·yad \ü'mī(y)əd, ə'm-\ *or* **omay·yad** \ō'mī(y)əd, ə'm-\ *also* **om·mi·ad** \ō'mīəd, ə'm-\ *n* -s *usu cap* [*Umayyah* (*Ommiah*), ancestor of Muawiyah I †A.D.680 founder of the dynasty + E *-ad*] **1 :** a member of a dynasty of caliphs ruling the Muslim empire from A.D. 661 to 750 **2 :** a member of a dynasty of caliphs established in Spain from A.D. 756 to 1031

umb *abbr* umbilicus

um·bel \'əmbəl\ *n* -s [L *umbella* parasol, umbrella — more at UMBRELLA] **1 :** a racemose inflorescence that is characteristic esp. of the family Umbelliferae and has the flower stalks in a cluster arising from a common point at the apex of the main stalk and reaching approximately the same height and sometimes branching again to form similar secondary clusters — see INFLORESCENCE illustration **2 :** an arrangement of parts resembling an umbel

um·beled *or* **um·belled** \-ld\ *adj* **:** bearing or producing umbels **:** UMBELLATE

umbell- *or* **umbelli-** *comb form* [NL, fr. L *umbella* parasol, umbrella] **:** umbel **:** umbellate ⟨*umbell*oid⟩ ⟨*umbelli*form⟩

um·bel·la \,əm'belə\ *n, pl* **umbel·lae** \-e,lē, -lī\ *or* **umbellas** [NL, fr. L, parasol, umbrella] **:** UMBEL

um·bel·la·les \,əmbə'lā(,)lēz\ *n pl, cap* [NL, fr. *umbell-* + *-ales*] **:** a large order of chiefly herbaceous dicotyledonous plants that have umbels or corymbs of small uniovulate flowers with epigynous stamens and 1 to 5 carpels followed by fruits which are drupes or cremocarps and that include several economically important plants (as the carrot and parsnip) — see CORNACEAE, UMBELLIFERAE

um·bel·lar \'əmbələ(r), ,əm'bel-\ *adj* [*umbell-* + *-ar*] **:** of or relating to an umbel **:** UMBELLATE

um·bel·late \'əmbə,lāt, ,əm'belət\ *also* **um·bel·lat·ed** \'əmbə,lād·əd\ *adj* [*umbellate* fr. NL *umbellatus*, fr. *umbell-* + L *-atus* -ate; *umbellated* fr. NL *umbellatus* + E *-ed*] **1 :** bearing, consisting of, or arranged in umbels **2 :** resembling an umbel in form — **um·bel·late·ly** *adv*

um·bel·let \'əmbələt\ *n* -s [*umbell-* + *-et*] **:** UMBELLULE

umbellic acid *n* [*umbellic* fr. *umbell-* (in *umbelliferone*) + *-ic*] **:** an acid $C_6H_3(OH)_2CH{=}CHCO_2H$ formed as a yellow powder by hydrolysis of umbelliferone; 2,4-dihydroxy-cinnamic acid

um·bel·li·fer \,əm'beləfə(r)\ *n* -s [NL *Umbelliferae*] **:** a plant of the family Umbelliferae

um·bel·lif·er·ae \,əmbə'lifə,rē\ *n pl, cap* [NL, fr. fem. pl. of *umbellifer* umbelliferous] **:** a large and economically important family of often fragrant or aromatic plants (order Umbellales) with alternate mostly compound leaves, small flowers in simple or compound involucrate umbels, and dry 2-carpellary ribbed fruits that split at maturity and are borne from the apex of a common axis — compare ANISE, CARAWAY, CARROT, CELERY, DILL, PARSLEY

um·bel·lif·er·one \-ə,rōn\ *n* -s [ISV *umbellifer* + *-one*, orig. formed as G *umbelliferon*] **:** a crystalline phenolic lactone $C_9H_6O_3$ found in many plants, obtained by the distillation of resins (as galbanum or asafetida) from various umbellifers, and also made synthetically; 7-hydroxy-coumarin — compare HERNIARIN

um·bel·lif·er·ous \¦══¦lif(ə)rəs\ *adj* [NL *umbellifer* umbelliferous (fr. *umbella* umbel — fr. L, parasol, umbrella — + L *-ifer* -iferous) + E *-ous* — more at UMBRELLA] **1 :** producing umbels **2** [NL *Umbelliferae* + E *-ous*] **:** of or relating to the Umbelliferae

um·bel·li·florae \,əm¦belē+\ [NL, fr. *umbell-* + *florae*] *syn of* UMBELLALES

um·bel·lu·la \,əm'belyələ\ *n, cap* [NL, dim. of *umbella* umbel] **:** a genus (the type of the family Umbellulidae) of deep-sea alcyonarians consisting of a cluster of large flowerlike polyps at the summit of a long slender stem that stands upright in the mud and is supported by a bulbous base

um·bel·lu·late \-ə,lāt\ *adj* [NL *umbellula* umbellule + E *-ate*] **:** arranged in umbellules

um·bel·lule \'əmbə,lül, -əl,yül; ,əm'bel(,)yül\ *n* -s [NL *umbellula*, dim. of *umbella*] **:** a secondary umbel in a compound umbel

um·bel·lu·lif·er·ous \¦əm,belyə¦lif(ə)rəs\ *adj* [*umbellule* + *-iferous*] **:** bearing umbellules

um·bel·lu·lone \,əm'belyə,lōn\ *n* -s [ISV *umbellul-* (fr. NL *Umbellularia*, genus of dicotyledonous trees, fr. *umbellula* — dim. of *umbella* umbel — + *-aria*) + *-one*] **:** an unsaturated oily compound $C_{10}H_{14}O$ that is derived from the leaves of California laurel and is a ketonic derivative of thujene

¹um·ber \'əmbə(r)\ *n* -s [ME *umbre*, fr. MF, fr. L *umbra* shade, shadow, grayling] **1 :** a grayling (*Thymallus thymallus*) **2** *also* **umber bird :** HAMMERKOP

²umber \"\ *n* -s [prob. fr. obs. E, shade, shadow, color, fr. ME *umber, umbre* shade, shadow, fr. MF *umbre*, fr. L *umbra* — more at UMBRAGE] **1 :** a brown earth that is darker in color than ocher and sienna because of its content of manganese oxides as well as iron oxides, that is highly valued by artists as a permanent pigment, and that is used either in the greenish brown raw state or dark brown burnt state — see BURNT UMBER **2 a :** RAW UMBER 2 **b :** BURNT UMBER 2

³umber \"\ *adj* **:** of, relating to, or having the characteristics of umber; *specif* **:** of the color of raw umber or burnt umber

⁴umber \"\ *vt* **umbered; umbered; umbering** \-b(ə)riŋ\ **umbers :** to stain umber **:** DARKEN ⟨each battle sees the other's ~*ed* face —Shak.⟩

⁵umber \"\ *vt* [L *umbrare*, fr. *umbra* shade, shadow] *chiefly dial* **:** ²SHADE 1

umbilic *n* -s [L *umbilicus* navel, middle, center] *obs* **:** a middle point **:** CENTER

um·bil·i·cal \,əm'biləkəl, -¦bilēk- *sometimes* ¦əmbə¦līk-\ *adj* [NL *umbilicalis*, fr. L *umbilicus* navel, center + *-alis* -al — more at NAVEL] **1 a :** of, relating to, or used at the navel ⟨~ infection⟩ ⟨~ discharge⟩ ⟨~ surgery⟩ ⟨~ tape⟩ **b :** of or relating to the central region of the abdomen — see ABDOMINAL REGION illustration **2** *archaic* **:** relating to or occupying the center **:** CENTRAL ⟨supported, as to its arched roof, by one ~ pillar —Daniel Defoe⟩ **3 :** attached by or as if by an umbilical cord **:** intimately related ⟨the connection between the hard-core . . . supporters and the know-nothings . . . seems at times almost ~ —R.H.Rovere⟩

umbilical artery *n* **:** either of a pair of arteries that arise from the hypogastric arteries of the mammalian fetus and pass through the umbilical cord to the placenta to which they carry the impure blood from the fetus

umbilical cord *n* **1 a :** a cord arising from the navel that connects the fetus with the placenta and contains the two umbilical arteries and the umbilical vein **b :** YOLK STALK **2 :** a cable conveying power to a rocket or spacecraft before takeoff; *also* **:** a tethering or supply line (as for an astronaut outside a spacecraft or an aquanaut underwater)

umbilical fissure *n* **:** the anterior part of the longitudinal fissure on the undersurface of the liver that lodges the umbilical vein in the fetus

umbilical hernia *n* **:** a hernia of abdominal viscera at the umbilicus

um·bil·i·cal·ly \-k(ə)lē, -li\ *adv* **:** by means of or as if by means of an umbilical cord **:** INTIMATELY ⟨embryos nourished ~⟩ ⟨~ tied to . . . complex, tentative liberalism —H.J.Bresler⟩

umbilical vein *n* **:** a vein that passes through the umbilical cord to the fetus and returns the purified and nutrient blood from the placenta to the fetus

umbilical vesicle *n* **:** the yolk sac of a mammalian embryo usu. having the form of a fluid-filled pouch, corresponding to the yolk sac of an oviparous vertebrate, and having a transitory connection with the alimentary canal by way of the vitelline duct

um·bil·i·car·ia \,əm,bilə'ka(a)rēə\ *n, cap* [NL, fr. LL *umbilicaris* umbilical (fr. L *umbilicus* navel + *-aris* -ar) + NL *-ia*] **:** a small genus related to *Lecanora* and composed of foliose umbilicate lichens that are used esp. in folk medicine as a purgative — see ROCK TRIPE

um·bil·i·cate \,əm¦biləkət, -lə,kāt, *usu* -d·+V\ *or* **um·bil·i·cat·ed** \-lə¦kād·əd\ *adj* [*umbilicate* fr. L *umbilicatus*, fr. *umbilicus* navel + *-atus* -ate; *umbilicated* fr. L *umbilicatus* + E *-ed*] **1 :** resembling a navel; *specif* **:** depressed like a navel **2** *of a mollusk shell* **:** PERFORATE

um·bil·i·ca·tion \,əm,bilə'kāshən\ *n* -s [L *umbilicus* + E *-ation*] **1 :** a depression resembling a navel ⟨an ~ in the center of a nodule⟩ **2 :** the condition of having umbilications ⟨vesicles . . . with a greater tendency to ~ —Joseph Stokes⟩

um·bil·i·cus \,əm'biləkəs, -'bilēk- *also* ,əmbə'līkəs\ *n, pl* **umbili·ci** \,═'══,kī, -,sī, -,kē; ,══'═,kī, -,sī\ *or* **umbilicuses** [L — more at NAVEL] **1 a :** a small depression in the middle of the abdomen where the umbilical cord is attached in the embryo **b :** the place where the extraembryonic structures are continuous with those of the body proper of the embryo **2 :** a cavity in the center of the base of a spiral shell that is surrounded by the whorls **3 a :** HILUM **b :** a rootlike attachment of the thallus in a lichen **4 :** a central point **:** CORE, HEART ⟨the key to control, the ~ of this . . . sea —J.P.O'Donnell⟩

um·bil·root \'əmbəl,═\ *n* [prob. fr. ME *umble* humble, lowly growing + *root* — more at HUMBLE] **:** SHOWY LADY'S-SLIPPER

um·ble pie \'əmbəl-\ *n* [*umbles*] *archaic* **:** HUMBLE PIE 1

um·bles \'əmbəlz\ *n pl* [ME, alter. (prob. influenced by *umble* humble) of *noumbles, nombles* numbles — more at NUMBLES] **:** the entrails of an animal (as a deer, hog, or sheep) used as food **:** NUMBLES, HUMBLES ⟨sat beside the hearth with the menials and ate ~ —Robert Graves⟩

um·bo \'əm(,)bō\ *n, pl* **umbo·nes** \,əm'bō(,)nēz\ *or* **umbos** [L — more at NAVEL] **1 :** the boss of a shield sometimes having a sharp spike **2 :** a rounded elevation often accompanied by a corresponding depression on the opposite surface: as **a :** an elevation in the tympanic membrane of the ear **b :** an elevation in a cone scale of a pine tree **3 :** one of the lateral prominences just above the hinge of a bivalve shell **:** BEAK 1d(1)

um·bo·lateral \¦əmbō+\ *adj* [*umbo* + *lateral*] **:** of, relating to, or located at the sides of the umbo of a bivalve shell

um·bo·nal \'əmbənᵊl, ¦əm¦bōn-\ *adj* [L *umbon-, umbo* + E *-al*] **:** of, relating to, or having the characteristics of an umbo ⟨long ~ projections frequently contain hollow spaces between . . . calcareous layers —K.H.Barnard⟩

um·bo·nate \-,nət, -,nāt\ *or* **um·bo·nat·ed** \-══¦nād·əd\ *adj* [*umbonate* fr. L *umbon-, umbo* + E *-ate, umbonated* fr. L *umbon-, umbo* + E *-ate* + *-ed*] **:** having or forming an umbo

um·bone \'əm,bōn\ *n* -s [L *umbon-, umbo* boss of a shield, projection, knob] **1** *obs* **:** PISTIL, STYLE **2 :** UMBO 3

um·bon·ic \¦əm¦bänik\ *also* **um·bo·ni·al** \-bōnēəl\ *adj* [L *umbon-, umbo* + E *-ic* or *-ial*] **:** UMBONAL

um·bon·u·late \¦əm¦bänyələt, -,lāt\ *adj* [dim. of *umbonate*] **:** slightly umbonate

um·bra \'əmbrə\ *n, pl* **umbras** \-brəz\ *or* **um·brae** \-,brē, -rī\ *except sense 5* [L] **1 a :** GHOST, PHANTOM ⟨a spectral ~ pointing heavenward —Walter Besant & James Rice⟩ **b :** one that tags along with another **:** SHADOW 10a ⟨the dependable ~ of the guest of honor⟩ **2 :** a shaded area **:** DARKNESS ⟨sealed off in the ~ beyond the flame tips —Robert Hazel⟩ **3 a :** a shadow excluding all light from a given source; *specif* **:** the part of the shadow of a celestial body having all the light from the primary source geometrically excluded and having a conical shape in bodies of the solar system — compare PENUMBRA 1 **b** (1) **:** PENUMBRA 2 (2) **:** the central dark part of a sunspot **4 :** any of several food fishes of the genus *Umbrina*; *esp* **:** a Mediterranean food fish (*U. cirrhosa*) that is much esteemed as a market fish **5** *cap* [NL, fr. L, shade, shadow, grayling, umbra] **:** a genus (the type of the family Umbridae) of small bottom-dwelling freshwater fishes containing the mudminnows of northern No. America and southeastern Europe

um·brac·u·la \,əm'brakyələ\ *n, cap* [NL, fr. L *umbraculum* parasol, umbrella, fr. *umbrare* to shade] **:** a genus (the type of the family Umbraculidae) of gastropod mollusks comprising the typical umbrella shells

um·bra·cu·li·dae \,əmbrə'kyülə,dē\ *n pl, cap* [NL, fr. *Umbracula*, type genus + *-idae*] **:** a family of gastropod mollusks (suborder Tectibranchia) that includes the umbrella shells

¹um·brage \'əmbrij, -rēj\ *n* -s [ME, fr. MF, fr. L *umbraticum*, neut. of *umbraticus* of the shade, fr. *umbratus* (past part. of *umbrare* to shade, fr. *umbra* shade, shadow) + *-icus* -ic; akin to Lith *unksna* shadow] **1 a :** an area of comparative darkness **:** SHADE ⟨lying . . . at the foot of some tree of friendly ~ —Charlotte Brontë⟩ **b :** an overshadowing influence or power **:** SHADOW ⟨compete in the ~ of big city printing wages and other costs —J.R.Malone⟩ **2 :** the thick shady branches of a tree or bush **:** FOLIAGE ⟨the thrush sings in that ~ —L.P. Smith⟩ ⟨chimney pots veiled under blossomy ~ —Thomas Carlyle⟩ **3** *archaic* **:** something providing protection **:** SHELTER, REFUGE **4 a :** an indistinct indication **:** vague suggestion **:** SUSPICION, HINT ⟨the least ~ of a reflection upon this accident —Roger North⟩ **b :** a reason for doubt **:** SUSPICION ⟨the man toward whom our . . . State Department has never felt ~, let alone taken exception —H.L.Ickes⟩ **5 :** DISPLEASURE, RESENTMENT, ANNOYANCE ⟨persons who feel most ~ from the overshadowing aristocracy —Sir Walter Scott⟩ — usu. used in the phrases *give umbrage* or *take umbrage* ⟨would give ~ to them by not sending an invitation⟩ ⟨never take ~ unless you can lick the guy —Jackie Gleason⟩ **6** *obs* **:** an alleged purpose or motive **:** PRETEXT, PRETENSE ⟨veiling the murder with the ~ of devotion and justice —Edmund Hickeringill⟩ **7** *obs* **:** the state of being in disfavor **:** DISESTEEM **syn** see OFFENSE

²umbrage \"\ *vt* -ED/-ING/-S **1 :** to cast into shadow **:** SHADE **2 :** to cause to become insulted or angry ⟨*umbraged* . . . by finding no crumbs —Sylvia T. Warner⟩

um·bra·geous \,əm¦brājəs\ *adj* **1 a :** providing protection from heat and light **:** SHADY ⟨~ willow trees⟩ ⟨his winged cloak and ~ fedora —*Times Lit. Supp.*⟩ **b :** protected by shade **:** filled with shade or shadows **:** SHADOWY ⟨making a glowworm halo in the ~ alleys —R.L.Stevenson⟩ ⟨cool ~ woodlands⟩ **2 :** inclined to take offense easily **:** BELLIGERENT, RESENTFUL ⟨have not been as ~ . . . in demanding their territory back —John Gunther⟩ ⟨~ students⟩ — **um·bra·geous·ly** *adv* — **um·bra·geous·ness** *n* -ES

um·bral \ˈəmbrəl\ *adj* [*umbra* + *-al*] **:** of or relating to an umbra **:** SHADED, DARKENED ⟨the moon's ~ cone⟩ ⟨whispering somewhere in the ~ reaches of the room —*Omnibook*⟩

umbral symbol *n* **:** a symbol indicating substitution in turn of each of *n* given values followed by addition of the results obtained ⟨the *umbral symbol a* in the expression $x^a y_a$ which stands for $x^1y_1+x^2y_2+\ldots+x^ny_n$⟩

um·brat·ed \ˌəmˈbrād·əd\ *adj* [L *umbratus* (past part. of *umbrare* to shade) + E *-ed*] **:** drawn indistinctly or in outline on a heraldic field ⟨many an ~ charge is . . . displayed upon a parti-colored field —M.R.Holmes⟩

um·brat·ic \ˌəmˈbrad·ik\ *or* **um·brat·i·cal** \-d·əkəl\ *adj* [*umbratic* fr. L *umbraticus* of the shade, secluded, fr. *umbratus* (past part. of *umbrare*) + *-icus* -ic; *umbratical* fr. L *umbraticus* + E *-al*] **1** *archaic* **:** SECLUDED, RETIRING **2** *obs* **:** SHADOWY, INDISTINCT

um·bra·tile \ˈəmbrəˌtīl\ *adj* [L *umbratilis*, fr. *umbratus* (past part. of *umbrare*) + *-ilis* -ile] **1 :** carried on in seclusion **:** RECONDITE **2** *archaic* **:** of an insubstantial nature **:** SHADOWY

umbra tree *n* [*umbra* modif. (influenced by L *umbra* shade) of Tupi *umbu*] **:** a So. American tree (*Phytolacca dioica*) that has large dark leaves and is cultivated in southern Europe

um·bre \ˈəmbə(r)\ *n* -S [prob. fr. NL *umbra*, fr. L, shade] **:** HAMMERKOP

¹um·brel·la \ˌəmˈbrelə *also* ˈ=ˌ==\ *n* -S [It *ombrella*, modif. (influenced by *ombra* shade, shadow, fr. L *umbra*) of L *umbella* parasol, umbrella, dim. of *umbra* — more at UMBRAGE] **1 a :** a small portable usu. cloth canopy that is fastened to a frame with hinged ribs radiating from a center pole, has a circular convex shape when open, can be opened or closed by means of a sliding catch, and provides protection against the weather — see PARASOL **b :** a large canopy of similar design whose center pole may be placed firmly in the ground or attached esp. to a table ⟨garden furniture with colored ~s —Christopher Morley⟩ — see BEACH UMBRELLA **2 :** something resembling an umbrella in shape or function: as **a :** a metal cover secured over a ship's smokestack to keep out precipitation **b :** a bell-shaped structure composed chiefly of jellylike mesoglea that forms the main part of the body of a jellyfish, has muscular ectodermal cells lining the lower concave surface, and serves as a swimming organ by means of contractions **c** (1) **:** the arched overhanging foliage of a tree ⟨the creamy ~s of the hemlock —C.G.Glover⟩ (2) **:** the canopy formed by leaves and branches in a wooded area ⟨see the pine wood spread its broad ~ —Cyril Connolly⟩ **d :** the open canopy of a parachute **e :** a formation of planes maintained over surface operations or a landmass for defense against attack ⟨throwing up an air ~ over Europe —*Springfield (Mass.) Union*⟩ **f :** a heavy barrage of shell fire ⟨the main battery guns were laying an ~ over the carrier —F.J.Bell⟩ **3 :** a unifying, conditioning, stabilizing, or controlling factor, agency, category, or authoritative influence ⟨both parties are ~s for diverse groups —J.E.McLean⟩ ⟨organization cost, an ~ which covers the publisher's expenses —H.M.Silver⟩ ⟨maintain a price ~ over the industry —A.D.H.Kaplan⟩ ⟨combined under the ~ of Fascism —T.E.M.McKitterick⟩

umbrella 1a

²umbrella \"\ *adj* **1 :** of, relating to, or having the characteristics of an umbrella **2 :** taking in many individuals or groups **:** ALL-EMBRACING ⟨an ~ organization sheltering a host of subdivided activities —O.O.Trullinger⟩ **3 :** having a roof supported on a single post ⟨a series of ~ sheds on a train platform⟩

³umbrella \"\ *vt* -ED/-ING/-S **1 :** to protect or cover with or as if with an umbrella ⟨each man ~*ed* from the downpour —*Manchester Guardian Weekly*⟩ **2 :** to provide with or as if with an umbrella ⟨the new job . . . : to ~ the invasion —*Time*⟩

umbrella ant *n* [so called fr. the fact that it sometimes carries bits of leaves on its back] **:** LEAF-CUTTING ANT

umbrella bird *n* **:** any of several So. and Central American birds of the genus *Cephalopterus* (as *C. ornatus*) that are about the size of a jackdaw and in the male are entirely black with a radiating crest curving forward over the head and a long feathered lappet depending from the breast

umbrella bush *n* **:** a small Australian acacia (*Acacia oswaldi*) used in hedges

umbrella catalpa *n* **:** a horticultural catalpa that is obtained by grafting a scion or scions of a dwarf variety (*C. bignonioides* var. *nana*) on a tall straight bole of the common catalpa (*C. bignonioides*) and that is characterized by a dense umbrella-shaped head formed of numerous leaf-bearing branches

umbrella fern *n* **:** an Australasian fern of the genus *Gleichenia*

umbrella grass *n* **:** any of several plants having outspread inflorescence: as **a :** AUSTRALIAN MILLET **b :** an Australian grass (*Aristida ramosa*) **c :** a sedge of the genus *Fuirena*

umbrella leaf *n* **:** a No. American herb (*Diphylleia cymosa*) with two large peltate stem leaves or a solitary lobed basal one

umbrellalike \ˌ=ˈ==ˌ=, ˈ=ˌ==ˌ=\ *adj* **:** resembling an umbrella ⟨an ~ dome fourteen feet in diameter —S.M.Spencer⟩

umbrella palm *n* **1 :** a widely cultivated pinnate-leaved palm (*Hedyscepe canterburyana*) native to Lord Howe Island and having a crown of recurved leaves **2 :** UMBRELLA PLANT 1

umbrella patent *n* **:** a patent in which claims are made all-embracing in order to give some color of right for litigating against those alleged to infringe it

umbrella pine *n* **1 :** a tall Japanese evergreen tree (*Sciadopitys verticillata*) of the family Pinaceae that has a symmetrical crown and needle-shaped leaves borne in umbrellalike whorls at the ends of the twigs **2 a :** STONE PINE 2 **b :** TANYOSHO PINE

umbrella plant *n* **1** *or* **umbrella sedge :** an African sedge (*Cyperus alternifolius*) that bears large terminal whorls of slender leaves and is often cultivated as an ornamental aquatic **2 :** any of several plants of the genus *Eriogonum* of the western U.S. **3 :** MAYAPPLE 1

umbrella pulley *n* **:** a pulley having a semispherical projecting skeleton boss

umbrella shell *n* **:** a marine gastropod of *Umbracula* or a related genus having a large thick foot, small head, and small external shell resembling that of a limpet and only partly covering the body

umbrella tent *n* **:** a tent resembling an umbrella and having a center pole with a framework of metal ribs

umbrella thorn *n* **:** an acacia (*Acacia heteracantha* or *A. litakunensis*) of the Africa bushveld having a flat-topped crown, straight thorns, and curved prickles — called also *haak-en-steek*

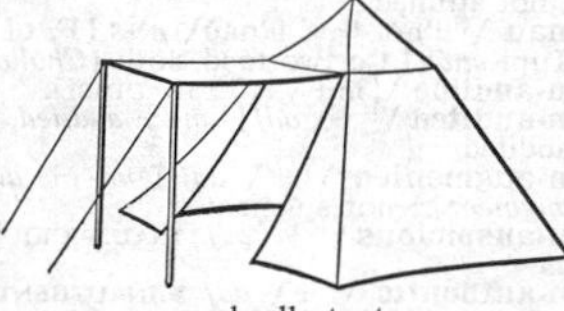
umbrella tent

umbrella tree *n* **1** *or* **umbrella magnolia :** an American magnolia (*Magnolia tripetala*) having large leaves clustered at the ends of the branches **2 a :** an Australian tree (*Brassaia actinophylla*) of the family Araliaceae having digitate leaves arranged like the ribs of an umbrella **b :** UMBRELLA BUSH **3 :** any of various other trees or shrubs resembling an umbrella esp. in the arrangement of leaves or the shape of the crown of foliage: as **a :** BLUE DOGWOOD **b :** PORTIA TREE **c :** MALABAR ALMOND 1 **d :** a cultivated tree of the southern U.S. that forms a variety (*Melia azedarach umbraculiformis*) of the chinaberry and is characterized by branches arising at a common level and radiating from the trunk like the ribs of an umbrella

umbrellawort \ˌ=ˈ==ˌ=, ˈ=ˌ==ˌ=\ *n* [¹*umbrella* + *wort*] **:** a plant of the genus *Mirabilis*

um·brette \ˌəmˈbret\ *or* **om·brette** \(ˈ)äm-\ *n* -S [NL *umbretta*, fr. F *ombrette*, fr. *ombre* shade, shadow (fr. L *umbra*) + *-ette* — more at UMBRAGE] **:** HAMMERKOP

¹um·bri·an \ˈəmbrēən\ *adj, usu cap* [L *Umbria*, province in central Italy + E *-an* (adj. suffix)] **1 a :** of, relating to, or characteristic of the Italian province of Umbria **b :** of, relating to, or characteristic of the people inhabiting Umbria **2 :** of, relating to, or characteristic of the Italic language of ancient Umbria

²umbrian \"\ *n* -S *cap* [L *Umbria* + E *-an* (n. suffix)] **1 a :** a member of a people of ancient Italy occupying Umbria **b :** a native or inhabitant of the Italian province of Umbria **2 :** the Italic language of ancient Umbria

um·bri·dae \ˈəmbrəˌdē\ *n pl, cap* [NL, fr. *Umbra*, type genus + *-idae*] **:** a family of small bottom-dwelling freshwater fishes (order Haplomi) including the genus *Umbra*

um·brif·er·ous \ˌəmˈbrif(ə)rəs\ *adj* [L *umbrifer*, fr. *umbra* shade, shadow + *-ifer* -iferous] *archaic* **:** UMBRAGEOUS 1a

um·bri·na \ˌəmˈbrīnə\ *n, cap* [NL, fr. L *umbra* + NL *-ina*] **:** a common widely distributed genus of croakers (family Sciaenidae) including a European umbra (*U. cirrhosa*) and the yellowfin croaker of the Pacific coast of No. America

um·brine \ˈəmˌbrīn, -ˌbrən\ *n* -S [NL *Umbrina*] **:** UMBRA 4

um·brous \ˈəmbrəs\ *adj* [L *umbrosus*, fr. *umbra* shade, shadow + *-osus* -ose — more at UMBRAGE] **:** SHADY, SHADOWED

um·bun·du \əmˈbün(ˌ)dü\ *n* -S *usu cap* **:** a Bantu language of central Angola — called also *Mbundu*

umbu-rana \ˌümbəˈränə\ *n* -S [Tupi, fr. *umbu* umbra tree + *rana* false] **:** a So. American timber tree (*Torresia cearensis*) of the family Leguminosae that yields a yellow wood used for furniture — called also *roble*

ume \ˈōˈmā, mˈmā\ *n* -S [Jap] **:** JAPANESE APRICOT

um·faan \ˈəmˌfän\ *n* -S [Afrik, fr. Zulu *umfana* boy, dim. of *umfo* man, person] **:** a boy employed in southern Africa to care for small children or perform general work

um-hum *a sound made with the organs of speech in position for* m, *a voiced beginning which usu. has the heaviest stress, and a voiced ending separated by an* h-*like period of voicelessness*\ *interj* [origin unknown] — used to express affirmation, agreement, comprehension, or interest

umi·ak *also* **oo·mi·ak** *or* **oo·mi·ack** \ˈüməˌak\ *n* -S [Esk] **:** an open Eskimo boat that consists of a wooden frame covered with hide and is usu. propelled with broad paddles — compare KAYAK

umiak

umi·ri *or* **umi·ry** \ˌüməˈrē\ *n, pl* **umiris** *or* **umiries** [Pg *umiri*, fr. Tupi *umiri*] **1 :** a fragrant balsam derived from So. American trees of the genus *Humiria* (esp. *H. floribunda* and *H. balsamifera*) **2 :** a tree of the genus *Humiria*

um·land \ˈümˌland\ *n* -S [G, fr. *um-* around + *land*, fr. OHG *lant* — more at LAND] **:** the environs of a city, town, or village that is part of the main community through common economic and cultural activities — compare HINTERLAND 2

¹um·laut \ˈümˌlau̇t\ *n* -S [G, fr. *um-* around, about (fr. MHG *um-*, *umb-*, fr. *umbe*, prep., around, about, fr. OHG *umbi*) + *laut* sound, fr. MHG *lūt*, akin to OE *hlūd* loud — more at EMBER DAY, LOUD] **1 a :** the change of a vowel caused by partial assimilation to a succeeding sound; *esp* **:** the fronting or raising of a back or low vowel (as *a*, *o*, or *u*) caused by an *i* or *j* orig. standing in the following syllable but now usu. lost or altered ⟨~ is a striking characteristic of the Germanic languages⟩ **b :** a vowel resulting from such partial assimilation **2 :** a diacritical mark ¨ placed esp. over a German vowel to indicate umlaut

²umlaut \"\ *vt* -ED/-ING/-S **1 :** to produce by umlaut **2 :** to write or print an umlaut over

umlaut vowel *n* **:** a reflex of a vowel produced by umlaut; *broadly* **:** a front-rounded vowel

umo·ho·ite \ˈyüməˌhōˌīt\ *n* -S [*U* (symbol for *uranium*) + *Mo* (symbol for *molybdenum*) + *H* (symbol for *hydrogen*) + *O* (symbol for *oxygen*) + *-ite*] **:** a mineral $(UO_2)MoO_4.4H_2O$ consisting of hydrous uranium molybdate

ump \ˈəmp\ *n* -S [by shortening] **:** UMPIRE 1b ⟨calling the ~s . . . dirty names in close decisions —L.M.Uris⟩

¹umph *like* ¹HUMPH\ *interj* [origin unknown] — usu. used to express skepticism or disgust

²umph \ˈüm(p)f, ˈəm-\ *n* -S [by alter.] **:** OOMPH ⟨needs that ~, even if he is just 30 —*Springfield (Mass.) Daily News*⟩

um·pir·age \ˈəmˌpīrij, -rēj\ *n* -S [¹*umpire* + *-age*] **1 :** the office or authority of an umpire ⟨hoped the ~ of the war would fall into their hands —Gilbert Burnet⟩ **2 a :** an act or instance of umpiring ⟨cemented by the mild ~ of the federal union —Edward Everett⟩ **b :** a decision of an umpire **:** ARBITRAMENT ⟨the time for making the ~ was further extended —E.H.East⟩

¹um·pire \ˈəmˌpī(ə)r, -pīə\ *n* -S [ME *umpere*, *oumpere*, alter. (resulting from incorrect division of *a noumpere*) of *noumpere*, fr. MF *nomper*, *nonper* not equal, not paired (i.e., a third person), fr. *non-* + *per* equal, even, fr. L *par* — more at PAIR] **1 :** one having authority to arbitrate and make a final decision: as **a** (1) **:** an attorney at law appointed to judge a legal matter disputed by arbitrators (2) **:** an impartial third party chosen by labor and management to arbitrate disputes arising under the terms of a labor agreement **b :** an official in a sport (as baseball or cricket) who rules on the plays **2 :** a military officer who observes and evaluates training maneuvers ⟨~s rushed about to decide how this battle of blank ammunition was going —O.N.Bradley⟩

²umpire \"\ *vb* -ED/-ING/-S *vt* **:** to supervise and decide in the capacity of umpire ⟨differences have to be . . . *umpired* by the president —Anthony Leviero⟩ ⟨can see . . . policemen *umpiring* the roughest games —Margaret Mead⟩ ~ *vi* **:** to act in the capacity of umpire **:** ARBITRATE ⟨appointed to ~ in the labor disputes⟩ ⟨*umpired* for the California league —Darrell Berrigan⟩

umpire assay *n* **:** an assay to decide the value of a shipment (as of ore, concentrate, bullion) when previous assays made by the buyer and seller are not in agreement

umpire-in-chief \ˈ=ˌ==ˈ=\ *n, pl* **umpires-in-chief :** an umpire stationed behind the catcher in baseball or softball who calls balls and strikes

umpire·ship \ˈ=ˌ=ˌship\ *n* **:** UMPIRAGE

ump·qua \ˈəm(p)kwə\ *n, pl* **umpqua** *or* **umpquas** *usu cap* [Umpqua *ākwa*] **1 a :** an Athapaskan people of western Oregon **b :** a member of such people **2 :** a language of the Umpqua people

ump·teen *also* **um·teen** \ˌəm(p)ˈtēn\ *adj* [blend of *umpty* and *-teen* (as in *thirteen*)] **:** very many **:** indefinitely numerous ⟨tonight, like ~ other nights —W.H.Auden⟩ ⟨an . . . audience estimated in the ~ millions —R.B.Considine⟩

ump·teenth *also* **um·teenth** \-ēn(t)th\ *adj* **:** being the latest or last in an indefinitely numerous series ⟨postponed for the ~ time —*Time*⟩ ⟨made the ~ mistake that day⟩

ump·ti·eth \ˈəm(p)tēəth\ *adj* **:** UMPTEENTH

ump·ty \ˈəm(p)tē, -ti\ *adj* [prob. alter. of *-enty* (as in *twenty*, *seventy*)] **:** such and such ⟨~ percent of all new houses —*Kansas City Star, Mo.*⟩ — often used in combination ⟨the *umpty*-fifth regiment —Bill Mauldin⟩

um·quhile *also* **um·while** \ˈəmˌ(h)wīl\ *adj* [ME, fr. OE *ymbhwīle*, adv., at times, sometimes, fr. *ymb*, *ymbe* around, about, at + *hwīle* while — more at EMBER DAY, WHILE] *chiefly Scot* **:** of old **:** FORMER, LATE, DECEASED

UMS *abbr* universal military service

um suff \ˈümˈsüf\ *n* -S [Ar *umm sūf* sudd, lit., mother (i.e., source) of wool, fr. *ṣūf-al-baḥr*, a maritime plant, lit., wool of the sea] **:** a wiry grass (*Vossia procera*) that is found in the Nile and often makes up a considerable part of the river's sudd

UMT *abbr* universal military training

¹un \ˌən, ᵊn\ *pron* [alter. of ¹*hin*] *dial* **:** HIM

²un \"\ *pron* [by alter.] *dial* **:** ONE ⟨that ~ got away clean —Frank Yerby⟩ ⟨some of them were bad ~s —A.L.Burt⟩ — often used in combination ⟨we will but you-*uns* won't —J.M. Allen⟩

¹un- *prefix* [ME, fr. OE; akin to OHG *un-* un-, ON *ō*, *ū-*, Goth *un-*, L *in-*, Gk *a-*, *an-*, Skt *a-*, *an-* un-, OE *ne* not — more at NO] **1 :** not **:** IN-, NON- — in adjectives formed from adjectives ⟨*un*capacious⟩ ⟨*un*gratifiable⟩ ⟨*un*neighborlike⟩ ⟨*un*strenuous⟩ including adjectivally used past and present participles ⟨*un*camouflaged⟩ ⟨*un*chosen⟩ ⟨*un*dressed⟩ ⟨*un*soothing⟩ and adjectives formed by adding *-ed* to nouns ⟨*un*bearded⟩, in nouns formed from nouns ⟨*un*ostentation⟩, and rarely in verbs formed from verbs ⟨*un*be⟩; sometimes in words that have a meaning that merely negates that of the base word and are thereby distinguished from words that prefix *in-* or a variant of it (as *im-*) to the same base word and have a meaning positively opposite to that of the base word ⟨*un*artistic⟩ ⟨*un*moral⟩ **2 :** opposite of **:** contrary to — in adjectives formed from adjectives ⟨*un*constitutional⟩ ⟨*un*graceful⟩ ⟨*un*palatable⟩ ⟨*un*warlike⟩ including adjectivally used past and present participles ⟨*un*affected⟩ ⟨*un*stinting⟩ and adjectives formed by adding *-ed* to nouns ⟨*un*principled⟩, and in nouns formed from nouns ⟨*un*rest⟩

²un- *prefix* [ME, fr. OE *un-*, *on-*, alter. of *and-* against — more at ANTE-] **1 a :** do the opposite of **:** reverse (a specified action) **:** DE- 1a, ¹DIS- 1a — in verbs formed from verbs ⟨*un*bend⟩ ⟨*un*dress⟩ ⟨*un*fold⟩ **b :** cause to cease to — in verbs formed from verbs ⟨*un*be⟩ **2 a :** deprive of **:** remove (a specified thing) from **:** remove — in verbs formed from nouns ⟨*un*flesh⟩ ⟨*un*frock⟩ ⟨*un*sex⟩; compare DE-, ¹DIS- **b :** release from **:** free from — in verbs formed from nouns ⟨*un*hand⟩ **c :** remove from **:** extract from **:** bring out of — in verbs formed from nouns ⟨*un*bosom⟩ ⟨*un*heaven⟩; compare DE-, ¹DIS- **d :** cause to cease to be — in verbs formed from nouns ⟨*un*king⟩; compare ¹DIS- **3 :** completely ⟨*un*loose⟩ — compare ¹DIS-

un *abbr* **1** unified; unifying **2** union **3** unit **4** united **5** university

un·abashed \ˌənəˈbasht, -aa(ə)sh, -aish-\ *adj* [¹*un-* + *abashed*, past part. of *abash*] **:** not abashed ⟨a tinseled charm and ~ sentimentality —Jerome Stone⟩ — **un·abashed·ly** \-shədlē, -shtl-, -li\ *adv*

un·abated \ˌən+\ *adj* [¹*un-* + *abated*, past part. of ¹*abate*] **:** not abated **:** at full strength or force ⟨the popularity of his books among young people has continued almost ~ —Sarah G. Bowerman⟩ — **un·abat·ed·ly** *adv*

un·abbreviated \"+\ *adj* **:** not abbreviated

unability *n* [ME *unabilite*, fr. ¹*un-* + *abilite* ability] *obs* **:** INABILITY

¹un·able \ˌən+\ *adj* [ME, fr. ¹*un-* + *able*, adj.] **1 :** not able **:** INCAPABLE ⟨the sun is ~ to melt the snow down to this underlying part —*Amer. Guide Series: N.H.*⟩ **2 a :** UNQUALIFIED, INCOMPETENT, INEFFICIENT **b :** IMPOTENT, HELPLESS ⟨like an ~ phoenix in hot ashes —*Time*⟩

²un·a·ble \ˌəˈnābəl\ *vt* [ME *unablen*, prob. fr. ²*un-* + *ablen* to enable — more at ABLE] **:** DISABLE, INCAPACITATE ⟨so *unabled* by the gout that she cannot dress herself —Samuel Johnson⟩

una boat \ˈyünə-\ *n, usu cap U* [fr. *Una*, the first boat of this kind taken to England (1853)] *Brit* **:** CATBOAT

¹un·abridged \ˌən+\ *adj* [¹*un-* + *abridged*, past part. of *abridge*] **1 :** not abridged **:** COMPLETE ⟨presented an ~ version of the play⟩ ⟨an ~ reprint of a novel⟩ **2 :** being the most complete of its class ⟨an ~ dictionary⟩

²unabridged \"\ *n* -S **:** an unabridged dictionary

un·absolved \"+\ *adj* [¹*un-* + *absolved*, past part. of *absolve*] **:** not absolved

un·absorbable \"+\ *adj* **:** not capable of being absorbed

un·absorbed \"+\ *adj* [¹*un-* + *absorbed*, past part. of *absorb*] **:** not absorbed

un·abused \"+\ *adj* [¹*un-* + *abused*, past part. of *abuse*] **:** not abused **:** used or treated properly

un·academic *also* **un·academical** \"+\ *adj* **:** not academic or scholarly **:** not formal or conventional **:** belonging to or arising from the realities of common life rather than the rules or theories of the schoolroom

un·accented *also* **un·accentuated** \"+\ *adj* [¹*un-* + *accented* (past part. of *accent*) or *accentuated* (past part. of *accentuate*)] **:** not accented **:** UNSTRESSED

un·acceptable \"+\ *adj* [ME *unacceptabylle*, fr. ¹*un-* + *acceptabylle*, *acceptable* acceptable] **:** not acceptable **:** not pleasing or welcome ⟨a slang word ~ in polite society —Scott Seegers⟩ — **un·ac·cept·able·ness** *n* -ES

un·acceptance \"+\ *n* **:** lack of acceptance

un·accepted \ˌən+\ *adj* [¹*un-* + *accepted*, past part. of *accept*] **:** not accepted; *specif* **:** not having had responsibility for its maintenance accepted by a government ⟨a street ~ by the city⟩

un·accessible \"+\ *adj* **:** INACCESSIBLE

un·acclimated *or* **un·acclimatized** \"+\ *adj* [¹*un-* + *acclimated* (past part. of *acclimate*) or *acclimatized* (past part. of *acclimatize*)] **:** not acclimatized

un·accommodated \"+\ *adj* [¹*un-* + *accommodated*, past part. of *accommodate*] **:** not accommodated **:** UNPROVIDED

un·accommodating \"+\ *adj* **:** not accommodating — **un·ac·com·mo·dat·ing·ly** *adv*

un·accompanied \"+\ *adj* [¹*un-* + *accompanied*, past part. of *accompany*] **:** not accompanied ⟨dramatic energy was ~ by a sufficiently developed sense of dramatic form —Leslie Rees⟩; *specif* **:** being without instrumental accompaniment ⟨the soloist sang ~⟩

un·accomplishable \"+\ *adj* [¹*un-* + *accomplish* + *-able*] **:** not capable of being accomplished

un·accomplished \"+\ *adj* [¹*un-* + *accomplished*, past part. of *accomplish*] **1 :** not accomplished **:** INCOMPLETE, UNFINISHED **2 :** lacking talent, poise, grace, or achievement

un·accountability \"+\ *n* **:** the quality or state of being unaccountable

¹un·accountable \"+\ *adj* **1 :** not to be accounted for **:** INEXPLICABLE ⟨perceptible only as ~ influences that distort and hinder progress —C.H.Rickword⟩ ⟨gave her an ~ thrill of pleasure —G.B.Shaw⟩; *esp* **:** not consonant with reason or rule **:** STRANGE, MYSTERIOUS **2 :** not accountable or responsible **:** free from control ⟨the power of management has been aggrandized and left largely exempt and ~ —G.B.Hurff⟩ — **un·ac·count·able·ness** *n* -ES — **un·accountably** \"+\ *adv*

²unaccountable \"+\ *n* **:** a person or thing that is unaccountable

un·accounted \"+\ *adj* [¹*un-* + *accounted*, past part. of *account*] **:** not accounted — often used with *for* ⟨the balance remained ~ for⟩

un·accredited \"+\ *adj* **:** not accredited

un·accusable \ˌən+\ *adj* [¹*un-* + *accuse* + *-able*] **:** not accusable — **un·accusably** \"+\ *adv*

un·accused \"+\ *adj* [¹*un-* + *accused*, past part. of *accuse*] **:** not accused

un·accustomed \"+\ *adj* **1 :** not customary **:** UNUSUAL, UNCOMMON, STRANGE, NEW ⟨in contact with many varieties of ~ foods —*Current Biog.*⟩ **2 :** not habituated **:** UNFAMILIAR — usu. used with *to* ⟨toxic substances to which it is ~ in its native habitat —W.H.Dowdeswell⟩

un·achievable \"+\ *adj* **:** not capable of being achieved

un·achieved \"+\ *adj* [¹*un-* + *achieved*, past part. of *achieve*] **:** not achieved

un·aching \"+\ *adj* **:** not aching

un·acknowledged \"+\ *adj* [¹*un-* + *acknowledged*, past part. of *acknowledge*] **:** not acknowledged

unacknowledging *adj* [¹*un-* + *acknowledging*, pres. part. of *acknowledge*] **:** not acknowledging

una cor·da \ˈünəˈkȯrdə\ *adv (or adj)* [It, lit., one string; fr. the fact that the soft pedal shifts the hammers so that they do not strike all the strings available for each note] **:** with soft pedal depressed — used as a direction in piano music; compare TRE CORDE

una corda pedal *n* **:** SOFT PEDAL

un·acquaintance \"+\ *n* **:** the quality or state of being unacquainted **:** lack of acquaintance **:** IGNORANCE ⟨displays a brilliant ~ with the thought, manners, and beliefs of the period —R.E.Roberts⟩

un·acquainted \"+\ *adj* **1 :** not having experience or knowledge **:** IGNORANT **2 :** not acquainted — **un·ac·quaint·ed·ness** *n* -ES

un·acquired \"+\ *adj* **:** not acquired; *esp* **:** INNATE

un·actable \"+\ *adj* **:** not actable ⟨an ~ play⟩

un·acted \"+\ *adj* [¹*un-* + *acted*, past part. of *act*] **:** not performed ⟨the fault unknown, is as a thought ~ —Shak.⟩ ⟨an ~ play⟩ ⟨is not fermentable and so is ~ on by yeast —William Jago⟩

un·active \"+\ *adj* **:** INACTIVE

un·actuated \"+\ *adj* [¹*un-* + *actuated*, past part. of *actuate*] **:** not actuated

un·adaptable \"+\ *adj* **:** not adaptable

un·adapted \"+\ *adj* **:** not adapted

un·addicted \"+\ *adj* **:** not addicted

un·addressed \"+\ *adj* [¹*un-* + *addressed*, past part. of *address*] **:** not addressed ⟨an ~ envelope⟩

uña de ga·to \ˈünyədəˈgä(ˌ)tō\ *n* [AmerSp, lit., cat's claw] **:** any of various shrubs or trees of the southwestern U.S. and Spanish America having sharp recurved prickles or thorns; *esp* **:** CAT'S-CLAW
un·adept \ˌən+\ *n* **:** one who is not an adept **:** LAYMAN
un·adjusted \ˌən+\ *adj* **:** not adjusted ⟨~ children⟩
un·administered \"+\ *adj* [ˡ*un-* + *administered*, past part. of *administer*] **:** not administered
un·admirable \"+\ *adj* **:** not worthy of admiration
un·admiring \"+\ *adj* **:** not admiring
un·admonished \"+\ *adj* [ˡ*un-* + *admonished*, past part. of *admonish*] **:** not admonished
un·adopted \"+\ *adj* [ˡ*un-* + *adopted*, past part. of adopt] **:** not adopted ⟨an heroic manner of a kind hitherto ~ in symphonic works —H.J.Foss⟩
un·adored \"+\ *adj* [ˡ*un-* + *adored*, past part. of *adore*] *archaic* **:** not adored **:** UNWORSHIPED
un·adorned \ˌənəˈdȯ(ə)rnd, -ȯ(ə)nd\ *adj* [ˡ*un-* + *adorned*, past part. of *adorn*] **:** not adorned **:** lacking adornment, embellishment, or decoration ⟨a simple ~ account of the coronation —Elinor Wylie⟩ — **un·adorn·ed·ness** \-nədnəs\ *n* -ES
un·adulterated *also* **un·adulterate** \ˌən+\ *adj* [ˡ*un-* + *adulterated* (past part. of *adulterate*) or *adulterate*, adj.] **:** not adulterated **:** PURE, UNMIXED, UNCORRUPTED ⟨here is genius ~, superb, enormous —Amy Loveman⟩ — **un·adul·ter·at·ed·ly** *adv*
un·advanced \"+\ *adj* [alter. (influenced by ˡ*advance*) of ME *unavanced*, fr. ˡ*un-* + *avanced*, *avaunced*, past part. of *avancen*, *avauncen* to advance] **:** not advanced ⟨the relatively ~ state of descriptive theory —*Psycholinguistics*⟩
un·advantageous \"+\ *adj* **:** not advantageous — **un·ad·van·ta·geous·ly** *adv*
un·adventurous \"+\ *adj* **:** not adventurous **:** lacking in boldness ⟨our clothes were for the most part ~ like our conversation —W.B.Yeats⟩ — **un·ad·ven·tur·ous·ly** *adv* — **un·ad·ven·tur·ous·ness** *n*
un·advertised \"+\ *adj* [ˡ*un-* + *advertised*, past part. of *advertise*] **:** not advertised **:** UNANNOUNCED
un·advisable \"+\ *adj* **1 :** not capable of being advised **2 :** INADVISABLE — **un·ad·vis·able·ness** *n* — **un·advisably** \"+\ *adv*
un·ad·vised \ˌənədˈvīzd\ *adj* [alter. (influenced by *advised*) of ME *unavised*, fr. ˡ*un-* + *avised* advised] **1 :** done without due consideration **:** RASH, INCONSIDERATE **2 :** not prudent **:** INDISCREET — **un·ad·vis·ed·ly** \-zədlē, -li\ *adv* — **un·ad·vis·ed·ness** \-dnəs\ *n* -ES
un·aerated \ˌən+\ *adj* [ˡ*un-* + *aerated*, past part. of *aerate*] **:** not aerated
un·aesthetic \"+\ *adj* **:** INAESTHETIC
un·affable \"+\ *adj* **:** not affable
un·affected \"+\ *adj* [ˡ*un-* + *affected*, past part. of *affect* (to act upon)] **1 a :** not influenced mentally or emotionally **:** UNMOVED ⟨remained almost entirely ~ by each other's writings —Richard Garnett †1906⟩ **b :** undergoing no change when acted upon ⟨fibers remain apparently ~ when subjected to quite severe hydrolytic treatments —H.R.Mauersberger⟩ **2** [ˡ*un-* + *affected*, adj.] **a :** GENUINE, SINCERE ⟨stared at me in ~ astonishment —Allen Upward⟩ **b :** free from affectation **:** PLAIN, SIMPLE, NATURAL ⟨consciously elaborate fashion which began to supplant the ~ early American style —*Amer. Guide Series: N.C.*⟩ ⟨spoke with the confidence of the ~ —Marguerite Steen⟩ **syn** see NATURAL
un·af·fect·ed·ly *adv* **:** in an unaffected manner
un·af·fect·ed·ness *n* **:** the quality or state of being unaffected
un·affecting \"+\ *adj* **1** *archaic* **:** being without affectation **2 :** not affecting **:** creating no effect on the feelings **:** UNMOVING
un·affectionate \"+\ *adj* **:** lacking affection **:** not affectionate — **un·af·fec·tion·ate·ly** *adv*
un·affianced \"+\ *adj* [ˡ*un-* + *affianced*, past part. of *affiance*] **:** not affianced
un·affiliated \ˌən+\ *adj* [ˡ*un-* + *affiliated*, past part. of *affiliate*] **:** not affiliated
un·afflicted \"+\ *adj* **:** not afflicted
un·affrighted \"+\ *adj* **:** UNAFRAID — **un·af·fright·ed·ly** *adv*
un·affronted \"+\ *adj* [ˡ*un-* + *affronted*, past part. of *affront*] **1 :** not insulted **2 :** not met face to face **:** not confronted
unaflow *var of* UNIFLOW
un·afraid \ˌən+\ *adj* [ME *unaffraid*, fr. ˡ*un-* + *affraid*, *affraied* afraid] **:** not afraid or frightened **:** not fearful **:** oblivious of dangers or perils or calmly resolute in braving them **syn** see BRAVE
un·aggravated \"+\ *adj* [ˡ*un-* + *aggravated*, past part. of *aggravate*] **:** not aggravated
un·aggressive \"+\ *adj* **:** not aggressive **:** not given to fighting or assertiveness — **un·ag·gres·sive·ly** *adv* — **un·ag·gres·sive·ness** *n*
un·agitated \"+\ *adj* **:** not mentally or physically disturbed — **un·ag·i·tat·ed·ly** *adv*
un·aided \"+\ *adj* [ˡ*un-* + *aided*, past part. of *aid*] **:** not aided **:** being without help — **un·aid·ed·ly** *adv*
un·aimed \"+\ *adj* [ˡ*un-* + *aimed*, past part. of *aim*] **:** being without a fixed target **:** not aimed **:** RANDOM
un·aired \"+\ *adj* [ˡ*un-* + *aired*, past part. of *air*] **:** not ventilated
un·akin \"+\ *adj* **:** not akin **:** UNRELATED
una·lach·ti·go \ˌünəˈlächtəˌgō\ *n, pl* **unalachtigo** *or* **unalachtigos** *usu cap* [Delaware, lit., tidewater people] **1 :** a Delaware Indian people of northern Delaware, southeastern Pennsylvania, and southern New Jersey **2 :** a member of the Unalachtigo people
un·alarmed \ˌən+\ *adj* [ˡ*un-* + *alarmed*, past part. of *alarm*] **:** not alarmed
un·alarming \"+\ *adj* [ˡ*un-* + *alarming*, pres. part. of *alarm*] **:** not alarming
un·alert \"+\ *adj* **:** not alert
un·alienable \"+\ *adj* **:** INALIENABLE — **un·alienably** \"+\ *adv*
un·alienated \"+\ *adj* [ˡ*un-* + *alienated*, past part. of *alienate*] **:** not alienated ⟨good and accessible land . . . left ~ from the Crown —B.K.Sandwell⟩
un·alike \"+\ *adj* **:** not alike **:** DISSIMILAR ⟨as ~ as any two people could be —Edita Morris⟩
unal·ist \ˈyünᵊləst\ *n* -S [L *unus* one + E *-alist* (as in *pluralist*) — more at ONE] **:** a holder of one benefice
un·alive \ˌən+\ *adj* **:** slow of perception or feeling **:** not alive **:** UNALERT ⟨~ to the beauties of the music⟩
un·allayed \"+\ *adj* [ˡ*un-* + *allayed*, past part. of *allay* (to alloy)] **:** UNALLOYED
un·alleviated \"+\ *adj* [ˡ*un-* + *alleviated*, past part. of *alleviate*] **:** not alleviated **:** acting at full strength ⟨~ pain⟩
un·allied \"+\ *adj* **:** not allied **:** having no connection or relation ⟨~ species⟩
un·allowable \"+\ *adj* **:** not allowable **:** IMPERMISSIBLE
un·allowed \"+\ *adj* [ˡ*un-* + *allowed*, past part. of *allow*] **:** not allowed **:** UNPERMITTED
un·alloyed \"+\ *adj* [ˡ*un-* + *alloyed*, past part. of *alloy*] **:** not alloyed **:** UNMIXED, UNQUALIFIED, PURE ⟨~ metals⟩ ⟨~ happiness⟩
un·alluring \"+\ *adj* **:** not alluring **:** UNATTRACTIVE, PLAIN
un·alterability \"+\ *n* **:** INALTERABILITY
un·alterable \"+\ *adj* **:** not capable of being altered **:** INALTERABLE, UNCHANGEABLE ⟨an ~ ground rule to be followed —C.F.Robinson⟩ — **un·al·ter·able·ness** *n* -ES — **un·alterably** \"+\ *adv*
un·altered \ˌən+\ *adj* [ˡ*un-* + *altered*, past part. of *alter*] **:** not altered **:** remaining in an original state **:** UNCHANGED ⟨persisting ~ through time —Arthur Pap⟩
un·amalgamated \"+\ *adj* [ˡ*un-* + *amalgamated*, past part. of *amalgamate*] **:** not amalgamated
un·amazed \"+\ *adj* **:** not amazed **:** being without astonishment or surprise
un·ambiguity \"+\ *n* **:** lack of ambiguity **:** possession of one clear meaning
un·ambiguous \"+\ *adj* **:** not ambiguous **:** having or being a single clearly defined or stated meaning **:** CLEAR, PRECISE ⟨~ evidence⟩ — **un·am·big·u·ous·ly** *adv*
un·ambition \"+\ *n* **:** lack of ambition
un·ambitious \"+\ *adj* **:** not ambitious **:** lacking ambition ⟨happy ~ irresponsibility —*Partisan Rev.*⟩ — **un·am·bi·tious·ly** *adv* — **un·am·bi·tious·ness** *n* -ES
un·amenable \"+\ *adj* **:** not amenable ⟨~ to persuasion⟩ — **un·amenably** \"+\ *adv*
un·amendable \"+\ *adj* [ME, fr. ˡ*un-* + *amenden* to amend + *-able*] **:** not amendable
un·amended \"+\ *adj* [ME, fr. ˡ*un-* + *amended*, past part. of *amenden* to amend] **:** not amended
un–american \"+\ *adj, usu cap A* **:** not American **:** not characteristic of or consistent with American customs, principles, or traditions
un–americanism \"+\ *n, usu cap A* **:** the quality or state of being un-American **:** lack of or contrariety to Americanism
una·mi \üˈnämē\ *n, pl* **unami** *or* **unamis** *usu cap* **1 :** a Delaware Indian people chiefly of central New Jersey and southeastern Pennsylvania **2 :** a member of the Unami people
un·amiability \ˌən+\ *n* **:** lack of amiability
un·amiable \"+\ *adj* [ME, fr. ˡ*un-* + *amiable*] **:** not amiable — **un·ami·a·ble·ness** *n* — **un·amiably** \"+\ *adv*
una·mo \üˈnä(ˌ)mō\ *n* -S [AmerSp] **:** a So. American palm (*Jessenia polycarpa*) the seeds of which yield an oil
un·amortized \ˌən+\ *adj* [ˡ*un-* + *amortized*, past part. of *amortize*] **:** not amortized
un·amused \"+\ *adj* **:** not amused
un·amusing \"+\ *adj* **:** not amusing — **un·amus·ing·ly** *adv*
unan *abbr* unanimous
un·analogous \ˌən+\ *adj* **:** not analogous
un·analyzable \"+\ *adj* **:** not analyzable ⟨this weight of evidence is something mystical and ~ —M.R.Cohen⟩
un·analyzed \"+\ *adj* [ˡ*un-* + *analyzed*, past part. of *analyze*] **:** not analyzed ⟨an ~ compound⟩
un·anchor \"+\ *vt* [²*un-* + *anchor*, v.] **:** to loosen from or as if from an anchor ⟨any marked disturbance of the society . . . ~s him —Paul Radin⟩
un·aneled \"+\ *adj* [ˡ*un-* + *aneled*, past part. of *anele*] *archaic* **:** not having received extreme unction
un·angelic \"+\ *adj* **:** not angelic **:** HUMAN, DEMONIC
un·animated \"+\ *adj* [ˡ*un-* + *animated*, past part. of *animate*] **1 :** INANIMATE **2 :** not enlivened **:** DULL
unan·i·mism \yüˈnanəˌmizəm\ *n* -S [F *unanimisme*, fr. *unanime* unanimous (fr. L *unanimus*) + *-isme* -ism] **:** a doctrine that the unifying principles in human groups are more significant (as for representation in literature) than personal individualities
una·nim·i·ty \ˌyünəˈniməd-ē, -mətē, -i\ *n* -ES [ME *unanimite*, fr. MF *unanimité*, fr. L *unanimitat-*, *unanimitas*, fr. *unanimus* unanimous + *-itat-*, *-itas* -ity] **:** the quality or state of being unanimous
unan·i·mous \yüˈnanəməs\ *adj* [L *unanimus*, fr. *unus* one + *animus* soul, mind — more at ONE, ANIMATE] **1 :** being of one mind **:** agreeing in opinion, design, or determination **:** CONSENTIENT ⟨the assembly was ~⟩ ⟨the members of the council were ~ in their approval of the report⟩ **2 :** formed with or indicating unanimity **:** having the agreement and consent of all without dissent ⟨a ~ vote⟩ — **unan·i·mous·ly** *adv*
unanimous consent *n* **:** the silent consent of an assembly to a routine or minor matter proposed by the chairman
un·annealed \ˌən+\ *adj* [ˡ*un-* + *annealed*, past part. of *anneal*] **:** not annealed
un·annotated \"+\ *adj* [ˡ*un-* + *annotated*, past part. of *annotate*] **:** not annotated
un·announced \"+\ *adj* [ˡ*un-* + *announced*, past part. of *announce*] **:** not announced **:** being without announcement
un·anointed \"+\ *adj* [ˡ*un-* + *anointed*, past part. of *anoint*] **:** not anointed
un·answerable \"+\ *adj* **:** not answerable ⟨an ~ question⟩; *specif* **:** IRREFUTABLE, CONCLUSIVE, DECISIVE ⟨an ~ argument⟩ — **un·an·swer·able·ness** *n* -ES — **un·answerably** \"+\ *adv*
un·answered \"+\ *adj* [ME, fr. ˡ*un-* + *answered*, past part. of *answeren* to answer] **1 :** not replied to ⟨an ~ letter⟩ **2 :** not refuted ⟨an ~ argument⟩ **3 :** not responded to in kind **:** UNREQUITED ⟨~ love⟩
un·anticipated \"+\ *adj* [ˡ*un-* + *anticipated*, past part. of *anticipate*] **:** not anticipated **:** UNEXPECTED, UNFORESEEN ⟨~ and disconcerting lines of development —H.W.Glidden⟩
un·anxious \"+\ *adj* **:** not anxious **:** being without worries, fears, or doubts — **un·anx·ious·ly** *adv*
un·apologetic \"+\ *adj* **:** not apologetic **:** offering or being put forward with no apology ⟨an ~ believer⟩
un·apostolic \"+\ *adj* **:** not in accordance with apostolic belief, doctrine, or practice — **un·apostolically** \"+\ *adv*
un·appalled \ˌən+\ *adj* [ˡ*un-* + *appalled*, past part. of *appall*] **:** not appalled **:** UNFRIGHTENED
un·apparent \"+\ *adj* **:** not apparent ⟨the answer was at first ~⟩
un·appealable \"+\ *adj* **:** not appealable **:** not subject to appeal — **un·appealably** \"+\ *adv*
un·appealing \"+\ *adj* **:** not appealing **:** UNATTRACTIVE
un·appeasable \"+\ *adj* **:** not appeasable **:** IMPLACABLE — **un·appeasably** \"+\ *adv*
un·appeased \"+\ *adj* [ˡ*un-* + *appeased*, past part. of *appease*] **:** not appeased
un·appetizing \"+\ *adj* **:** not appetizing **:** INSIPID, UNINTERESTING, UNATTRACTIVE ⟨durably bound and ~ volumes on zoological and chemical subjects —Edmund Wilson⟩ — **un·ap·pe·tiz·ing·ly** *adv*
un·applauded \"+\ *adj* [ˡ*un-* + *applauded*, past part. of *applaud*] **:** not applauded **:** UNPRAISED
un·applicable \"+\ *adj* **:** INAPPLICABLE
un·applied \"+\ *adj* [ˡ*un-* + *applied*, past part. of *apply*] **:** not applied
un·appreciable \"+\ *adj* **:** INAPPRECIABLE
un·appreciated \"+\ *adj* [ˡ*un-* + *appreciated*, past part. of *appreciate*] **:** not appreciated **:** without recognition or thanks
un·appreciative \"+\ *adj* **:** not appreciative
un·apprehensive \"+\ *adj* **1 :** slow to comprehend **:** DULL, UNINTELLIGENT **2 :** slow to recognize danger; *also* **:** not recognizing danger **:** UNAFRAID — **un·ap·pre·hen·sive·ness** *n*
un·apprised \"+\ *adj* [ˡ*un-* + *apprised*, past part. of *apprise*] **:** not apprised **:** UNINFORMED
un·approachable \"+\ *adj* **1 :** not approachable **:** physically inaccessible ⟨the scholastic notion of a material substance ~ by us —William James⟩ **2 :** discouraging intimacies **:** RESERVED — **un·ap·proach·able·ness** *n* -ES — **un·approachably** \"+\ *adv*
un·approached \"+\ *adj* [ˡ*un-* + *approached*, past part. of *approach*] **:** not approached; *specif* **:** of a standard unattained by any other in its class ⟨as a description of manners . . . the book is ~ by any others —Carl Van Doren⟩
un·appropriated \"+\ *adj* [ˡ*un-* + *appropriated*, past part. of *appropriate*] **1 :** not granted to any one to the exclusion of others ⟨~ public domain⟩ **2 :** not granted for or applied to a specific purpose ⟨~ taxes⟩
un·approved \"+\ *adj* [ˡ*un-* + *approved*, past part. of *approve* (to sanction)] **:** not approved **:** UNSANCTIONED
un·apt \"+\ *adj* [ME, fr. ˡ*un-* + *apt*] **1** *obs* **:** UNADAPTED, UNFIT **2 :** UNSUITABLE, INAPPROPRIATE ⟨an ~ citation⟩ **3 :** not accustomed and not likely **:** not disposed ⟨I am a soldier and ~ to weep —Shak.⟩ **4 :** INAPT, SLOW, DULL, BACKWARD — **un·apt·ly** *adv* — **un·apt·ness** *n*
un·architectural \"+\ *adj* **:** not consonant with architectural principles
un·arguable \"+\ *adj* **:** INARGUABLE — **un·arguably** \"+\ *adv*
un·argued \"+\ *adj* [ˡ*un-* + *argued*, past part. of *argue*] **1 :** being without debate **2 :** not argued against **:** UNDISPUTED
un·argumentative \"+\ *adj* **:** not argumentative — **un·ar·gu·men·ta·tive·ly** *adv*
un·arm \"+\ *vt* [ME *unarmen*, fr. ²*un-* + *armen* to arm] **:** DISARM
un·armed \"+\ *adj* [ME, fr. ˡ*un-* + *armed*] **1 :** not armed or armored **:** having or being no weapons **2 :** having no hard and sharp projections (as spines, prickles, spurs, or claws)
un·armored \"+\ *adj* **:** not armored; *also* **:** lightly armored
unarmored scale *n* **:** any of various scales (as a soft scale) belonging to families other than Diaspididae and usu. lacking a substantial waxy covering; *esp* **:** COCCID
un·arrested \"+\ *adj* [ME *unarested*, fr. ˡ*un-* + *arested*, past part. of *aresten* to arrest] **:** not arrested
un·artful \"+\ *adj* **1 :** lacking craft **:** ARTLESS **2 :** lacking skill — **un·artfully** \"+\ *adv*
un·articulate \"+\ *adj* **:** INARTICULATE
un·articulated \"+\ *adj* [ˡ*un-* + *articulated*, past part. of *articulate*] **:** not articulated
un·artificial \"+\ *adj* **:** INARTIFICIAL — **un·artificially** \"+\ *adv*
un·artistic \"+\ *adj* **:** not artistic
una·ry \ˈyünərē\ *adj* [L *unus* one + E *-ary*, adj. suffix — more at ONE] **1 :** occurring as molecules of only one kind **2 :** containing only one component — used of a physical-chemical system
un·ascertainable \ˌən+\ *adj* **:** not ascertainable
un·ascertained \"+\ *adj* [ˡ*un-* + *ascertained*, past part. of *ascertain*] **:** not ascertained
unasgd *abbr* unassigned
un·ashamed \ˌən+\ *adj* **:** not ashamed **:** being without guilt, self-consciousness, or doubt **:** PROUD, UNABASHED ⟨~ individualism⟩ — **un·ashamedly** \"+\ *adv* — **un·ashamedness** \"+\ *n*
un·asked \"+\ *adj* [ME, fr. ˡ*un-* + *asked*, past part. of *asken* to ask] **1 :** not being asked **:** UNINVITED **2 :** not requested ⟨~ advice⟩
un·asking \"+\ *adj* [ˡ*un-* + *asking*, pres. part. of *ask*] **:** not asking **:** not expressing a desire
un·aspirated \"+\ *adj* [ˡ*un-* + *aspirated*, past part. of *aspirate*] **:** not aspirated
un·aspiring \"+\ *adj* [ˡ*un-* + *aspiring*, pres. part. of *aspire*] **:** not aspiring **:** satisfied with one's possessions or position — **un·as·pir·ing·ness** *n* -ES
un·assailable \"+\ *adj* **:** not assailable **:** not liable to doubt, attack, or question ⟨an ~ argument⟩ ⟨an ~ alibi⟩ — **un·as·sail·able·ness** *n* -ES — **un·assailably** \"+\ *adv*
un·assailed \"+\ *adj* [ˡ*un-* + *assailed*, past part. of *assail*] **:** not assailed **:** free from attack
un·assayed \ˌən+\ *adj* [ME, fr. ˡ*un-* + *assayed*, past part. of *assayen* to assay] **:** not assayed **:** UNATTEMPTED
un·assented \"+\ *adj* **:** not assented — used of a stock or bond the holder of which refuses to deposit it by way of assent to an agreement altering its status (as in a readjustment)
un·assertive \"+\ *adj* **:** not assertive **:** MODEST, SHY, RETIRING
un·assignable \"+\ *adj* **:** not assignable
un·assigned \"+\ *adj* [ME, fr. ˡ*un-* + *assigned*, past part. of *assignen* to assign] **:** not assigned ⟨~ personnel⟩
un·assimilable \"+\ *adj* **:** not assimilable ⟨eccentrics who are ~ in a civilized society —Bernard Frechtman⟩
un·assimilated \"+\ *adj* [ˡ*un-* + *assimilated*, past part. of *assimilate*] **:** not assimilated ⟨a disturbing ~ element in the whole society —Oscar Handlin⟩
un·assisted \"+\ *adj* [ˡ*un-* + *assisted*, past part. of *assist*] **:** not assisted **:** lacking help
un·associated \"+\ *adj* [ˡ*un-* + *associated*, past part. of *associate*] **:** not associated
un·assorted \"+\ *adj* **:** UNSORTED, MIXED
un·as·suage·able \ˌənəˈswājəbəl\ *adj* [ˡ*un-* + *assuage* + *-able*] **:** not capable of being assuaged
un·assuaged \ˌən+\ *adj* [ˡ*un-* + *assuaged*, past part. of *assuage*] **:** not assuaged ⟨an ~ desire⟩
un·assuming \"+\ *adj* **:** not assuming **:** not bold or forward **:** not arrogant or presuming **:** MODEST, RETIRING ⟨~ to a fault, skeptical about the value of his work —*Man*⟩ — **un·as·sum·ing·ness** *n* -ES
un·assured \"+\ *adj* [ME, fr. ˡ*un-* + *assured* safe, assured] **1 :** UNSAFE **2 :** not assured **:** lacking boldness or confidence
un·astonished \"+\ *adj* [ˡ*un-* + *astonished*, past part. of *astonish*] **:** not astonished
un·aton·able \ˌənəˈtōnəbəl\ *adj* [ˡ*un-* + *atone* + *-able*] **:** IRRECONCILABLE
un·atoned \ˌən+\ *adj* [ˡ*un-* + *atoned*, past part. of *atone*] **:** not atoned **:** UNEXPIATED
un·attached \"+\ *adj* [ˡ*un-* + *attached*, past part. of *attach*] **1 a :** not assigned or committed to a particular task, organization, or person; *specif* **:** not committed by engagement, marriage, date, or other promise to a particular person of the opposite sex ⟨an unhappily married man whose passion for his acres is interrupted by his meeting an ~ girl —James Stern⟩ **b :** not seized, taken, or arrested as security for any legal judgment or decree that may later be obtained **2 :** not joined or united ⟨~ polyps⟩
un·attack·able \ˌənəˈtakəbəl\ *adj* **:** not attackable — **un·at·tack·ably** \-blē\ *adv*
un·attacked \ˌən+\ *adj* [ˡ*un-* + *attacked*, past part. of *attack*] **:** not attacked **:** free from attack
un·at·tain·able \ˌənəˈtānəbəl\ *adj* **:** not attainable ⟨an ~ ideal⟩ — **un·at·tain·able·ness** *n* — **un·at·tain·ably** \-blē\ *adv*
un·attained \ˌən+\ *adj* [ˡ*un-* + *attained*, past part. of *attain*] **:** not attained **:** UNREACHED
un·attainted \"+\ *adj* [ˡ*un-* + *attainted*, past part. of *attaint*] **1** *obs* **:** IMPARTIAL ⟨with ~ eye, compare her face with some that I shall show —Shak.⟩ **2** *archaic* **:** UNINFECTED, UNTAINTED **3 :** not attainted
un·attempted \"+\ *adj* [ˡ*un-* + *attempted*, past part. of *attempt*] **1 :** not attempted **:** UNTRIED **2** *obs* **:** UNATTACKED
un·attended \"+\ *adj* [ˡ*un-* + *attended*, past part. of *attend*] **1 :** not attended: **a :** lacking a guard, escort, caretaker, or other watcher ⟨~ women⟩ ⟨an ~ lighthouse⟩ ⟨a fire left ~⟩ **b :** lacking people in attendance ⟨an ~ meeting⟩ **2 :** UNACCOMPANIED ⟨problems . . . ~ with dangers —G.F.Eliot⟩ **3 a :** not cared for **:** UNTENDED ⟨if left ~ the road would quickly lose its alignment —O.S.Nock⟩ **b :** not watched with care, attentiveness, or accuracy ⟨sudden August storms that burst ~ —Oscar Handlin⟩ ⟨do not live out our lives ~ by divinity —*Amer. Scholar*⟩
un·attentive \"+\ *adj* **:** not attentive
un·attenuated \"+\ *adj* [ˡ*un-* + *attenuated*, past part. of *attenuate*] **:** not attenuated
un·attested \"+\ *adj* [ˡ*un-* + *attested*, past part. of *attest*] **:** not attested
un·attired \"+\ *adj* [ME *unatired*, fr. ˡ*un-* + *atired*, *attired*, past part. of *atiren*, *attiren* to attire] **:** UNCLOTHED
un·attractive \"+\ *adj* **:** not attractive **:** lacking beauty, interest, or charm **:** PLAIN, DULL, DREARY ⟨the ~ appearance and slovenly habits of his third wife —Alan Hynd⟩ ⟨as ~ as are most mining regions —Samuel Van Valkenburg & Ellsworth Huntington⟩ — **un·attractively** \"+\ *adv* — **un·attractiveness** \"+\ *n*
un·attuned \"+\ *adj* [ˡ*un-* + *attuned*, past part. of *attune*] **:** not attuned
unau \yüˈnȯ, ˈ=,=, üˈnau̇\ *n* -S [F, of Tupian origin; akin to Tupi *unáu*] **:** a two-toed sloth (*Choloepus didactylus*)
un·audible \ˌən+\ *adj* **:** INAUDIBLE
un·audited \"+\ *adj* [ˡ*un-* + *audited*, past part. of *audit*] **:** not audited
un·augmented \"+\ *adj* [ˡ*un-* + *augmented*, past part. of *augment*] **:** not augmented
un·auspicious \"+\ *adj* **:** INAUSPICIOUS — **un·aus·pi·cious·ly** *adv*
un·authentic \"+\ *adj* **:** INAUTHENTIC — **un·authenticity** \"+\ *n*
un·authenticated \"+\ *adj* [ˡ*un-* + *authenticated*, past part. of *authenticate*] **:** not authenticated
un·authoritative \"+\ *adj* **:** not authoritative — **un·authoritatively** \"+\ *adv*
un·au·tho·rized \ˌəˈnȯthəˌrīzd\ *adj* **:** not authorized ⟨an ~ use of government airplanes⟩ ⟨~ speeches⟩ — **un·au·tho·riz·ed·ly** \-zədlē\ *adv*
un·availability \ˌən+\ *n* **:** lack of availability ⟨the ~ of medical supplies endangered the wounded⟩
un·avail·able \ˌənəˈvāləbəl\ *adj* **1 :** UNAVAILING **2 :** not available — **un·avail·able·ness** *n* — **un·avail·ably** \-blē\ *adv*
unavailable energy *n* **:** energy that is incapable of doing work under existing conditions — compare AVAILABLE ENERGY, DEGRADATION OF ENERGY, ENTROPY
un·availing \ˌən+\ *adj* [ˡ*un-* + *availing*, pres. part. of *avail*] **:** not availing **:** FUTILE, USELESS — **un·avail·ing·ly** *adv*
un·avenged \"+\ *adj* [ˡ*un-* + *avenged*, past part. of *avenge*] **:** not avenged
un·averted \"+\ *adj* [ˡ*un-* + *averted*, past part. of *avert*] **:** not turned aside

una vo·ce \ˈünəˈvōkā, ˈyünəˈvōsē\ *adv* [L, with one voice] : with one voice : UNANIMOUSLY

un·avoid·abil·i·ty \ˌənə,vȯidəˈbiləd·ē\ *n* : the quality or state of being unavoidable

un·avoidable \ˌən+\ *adj* [¹*un-* + *avoid* + *-able*] : not avoidable : incapable of being shunned or prevented : INEVITABLE ⟨~ mistakes⟩ ⟨natural and ~ material of verse —H.O.Taylor⟩ — **un·avoid·able·ness** *n* -ES — **un·avoidably** \"+\ *adv*

unavoidable casualty *or* **unavoidable accident** *n* : an unintended occurrence that cannot be avoided by the degree of care required of a person under all the circumstances : a casualty or accident happening without fault of any person involved — compare ACT OF GOD

un·avowed \"+\ *adj* : not avowed : not affirmed, mentioned, or declared — **un·avowedly** \"+\ *adv*

un·awakened \"+\ *adj* [¹*un-* + *awakened*, past part. of *awaken*] : not awakened; *specif* : not enlivened or activated ⟨~ taste buds⟩ ⟨~ emotions⟩

¹un·aware \ˌənəˈwa(a)(ə)r, -we|, |ə\ *adv* [back-formation fr. *unawares*] : UNAWARES ⟨may involve himself ~ —W.G.Perry & C.P.Whitlock⟩

²unaware \"\ *adj* [¹*un-* + *aware*] : not aware : lacking knowledge or acquaintance : UNCONSCIOUS ⟨~ of the seriousness of the situation —H.W.Van Loon⟩ — **un·aware·ly** *adv* — **un·aware·ness** *n*

un·awar·ed·ly \-wa(a)rədlē, -wer-\ *adv* [obs. E *unawared*, adj., not forewarned (fr. E ¹*un-* + assumed obs. E *awared*, past part. of assumed obs. E *aware*, v., to alert, fr. E *aware*, adj.) + E *-ly*] : without warning : UNEXPECTEDLY ⟨his voice became ~ loud —H.D.Skidmore⟩

un·awares \-wa(a)(ə)rz, -we|, |əz\ *adv* [¹*un-* + *aware* + *-s*, adv. suffix (fr. ME *-s*, *-es*, gen. sing. ending of nouns) — more at -'S] **1** : without design, attention, preparation, or premeditation ⟨as to my pronunciation, it improved rapidly and ~ —George Santayana⟩ **2** : without warning : SUDDENLY, UNEXPECTEDLY ⟨a malicious gust of wind caught them ~ —Aldous Huxley⟩ — **at unawares** *or* **at unaware** *adv, archaic* : UNAWARES ⟨let destruction come upon him *at unawares* —Ps 35:8 (AV)⟩

un·awed \ˌən+\ *adj* : not awed

unb *abbr* unbound

un·backed \ˌən+\ *adj* [¹*un-* + *backed*, past part. of *back*] **1** : never mounted by a rider : UNBROKEN **2** : not supported or encouraged : UNAIDED **3** : having no back ⟨an ~ stool⟩

un·baffled \"+\ *adj* [¹*un-* + *baffled*, past part. of *baffle*] : not baffled: as **a** : UNPERPLEXED **b** : UNHINDERED **c** : having no baffles ⟨an ~ boiler⟩

un·bag \"+\ *vt* [²*un-* + *bag*] : to pour, take, or let go out of a bag

un·bailable \"+\ *adj* : not bailable ⟨an ~ offense⟩

un·baked \"+\ *adj* [¹*un-* + *baked*, past part. of *bake*] **1** : not baked ⟨~ tile⟩ **2** *obs* : IMMATURE

¹un·balance \"+\ *vt* [²*un-* + *balance*, v.] : to put out of balance ⟨raise taxes and ~ the budget —Reinhold Niebuhr⟩ ⟨everybody's face has a feature or features that ~ it —Wally Westmore⟩; *specif* : to derange mentally ⟨ardor in the cause . . . threatened to ~ his mind —J.F.Fulton⟩

²unbalance \"\ *n* [¹*un-* + *balance*, n.] : lack of balance : IMBALANCE; *specif* : mental derangement ⟨the ~ of even the full-fledged paranoiac is sometimes hard to detect —H.A.Overstreet⟩

un·balanced \"+\ *adj* **1 a** : not in equipoise : having no counterpoise or having insufficient counterpoise **b** : being or being thrown out of equilibrium **c** : mentally disordered or deranged **2** : not brought to an equality of debit and credit ⟨an ~ account⟩ **3** : of, relating to, or being an offensive line or backfield formation in football with more players on one side of the center **4** : containing a singleton or void with reciprocally greater length in another suit or suits — used of a hand in bridge or its distribution

un·ballast \ˌən+\ *vt* [²*un-* + *ballast*] : to remove ballast from

un·ballasted \"+\ *adj* [¹*un-* + *ballasted*, past part. of *ballast*] **1** : not furnished with or steadied by ballast : UNSTEADY **2** : lightly provided with reason or sense

un·bandage \"+\ *vt* [²*un-* + *bandage*] : to remove a bandage from

un·banded \"+\ *adj* **1** : not provided with a band ⟨an ~ bird⟩ **2** *obs* : UNFASTENED

un·banked \"+\ *adj* [¹*un-* + *banked*, past part. of *bank* (to deposit in a bank)] : not deposited in a bank

un·baptize \"+\ *vt* [²*un-* + *baptize*] : to remove the effect of baptism from

un·baptized \"+\ *adj* [ME, fr. ¹*un-* + *baptized*, past part. of *baptizen* to baptize] : not baptized; *also* : HEATHENISH, PROFANE

un·bar \"+\ *vt* [ME *unbarren*, fr. ²*un-* + *barren* to bar] : to remove a bar from : UNBOLT, OPEN

un·barbarize \"+\ *vt* [²*un-* + *barbarize*] : to make less barbarous : CIVILIZE

un·barbed \ˌən+\ *adj* [¹*un-* + *barbed*, past part. of *barb*] : not provided with a barb ⟨an ~ fishhook⟩

un·barbered \"+\ *adj* [¹*un-* + *barbered*, past part. of *barber*] : not barbered : UNCUT, UNSHAVEN

un·bare \"+\ *vt* [²*un-* + *bare*] : STRIP, UNCOVER, BARE

un·barred \"+\ *adj* [¹*un-* + *barred*, past part. of *bar*] **1** : not secured by a bar : UNLOCKED **2** [¹*un-* + *barred*] : not marked with bars ⟨~ plumage⟩

un·bashful \"+\ *adj* : not bashful — **un·bashfully** \"+\ *adv*

un·bated \"+\ *adj* [¹*un-* + *bated*, past part. of *bate* (to moderate)] **1** : UNABATED **2** *archaic* : not blunted

un·bathed \"+\ *adj* [¹*un-* + *bathed*, past part. of *bathe*] : not bathed

un·battered \"+\ *adj* [¹*un-* + *battered*, past part. of *batter* (to beat)] : not battered : free from blows

unbd *abbr* unbound

¹un·be \ˌənˈbē\ *vi* [ME *unbeen*, fr. ¹*un-* + *been* to be] *archaic* : to lack or cease to have being

²unbe *vt* [²*un-* + *be*] *obs* : to cause to cease to be

un·bearable \ˌən+\ *adj* [ME *unberable*, fr. ¹*un-* + *beren* to bear + *-able*] : not bearable : UNENDURABLE — **un·bear·able·ness** *n* -ES — **un·bearably** \"+\ *adv*

un·bearded \"+\ *adj* : having no beard

un·bearing \"+\ *adj* : not bearing : BARREN, INFERTILE

un·beat·able \ˌənˈbēd·əbəl, -ētəb-\ *adj* [¹*un-* + *beat* + *-able*] : not capable of being defeated : possessing unsurpassable qualities

un·beaten \ˌən+\ *adj* **1** : not ground into small bits by beating **2** : UNTROD **3** : UNDEFEATED

un·beauteous \"+\ *adj* : not beauteous : PLAIN, UNATTRACTIVE — **un·beau·te·ous·ness** *n*

un·beautified \"+\ *adj* [¹*un-* + *beautified*, past part. of *beautify*] : not beautified : not provided with beautiful features

un·beautiful \"+\ *adj* : not beautiful : UNATTRACTIVE; *esp* : UGLY — **un·beautifully** \"+\ *adv*

un·beautify \"+\ *vt* [²*un-* + *beautify*] : to deprive of beauty

un·beclouded \"+\ *adj* [¹*un-* + *beclouded*, past part. of *becloud*] : UNCLOUDED

un·become \"+\ *vt* [¹*un-* + *become*] : not to become : MISBECOME

un·becoming \"+\ *adj* : not becoming : UNSUITABLE, INDECOROUS, IMPROPER ⟨charged with conduct ~ to a soldier —James Jones⟩ — **un·be·com·ing·ly** *adv* — **un·be·com·ing·ness** *n*

un·bed \"+\ *vt* [²*un-* + *bed*] : to stir or remove from a bed

un·befitting \"+\ *adj* : not befitting : UNSUITABLE — **un·be·fit·ting·ly** *adv* — **un·be·fit·ting·ness** *n*

un·befriended \"+\ *adj* [¹*un-* + *befriended*, past part. of *befriend*] : having no friend

un·beginning \"+\ *adj* [¹*un-* + *beginning*, pres. part. of *begin*] : having no beginning

un·begot \"+\ *adj* [¹*un-* + *begot*, past part. of *beget*] *archaic* : UNBEGOTTEN

un·begotten \"+\ *adj* [¹*un-* + *begotten*, past part. of *beget*] **1** : not begotten **2** : having never been generated : SELF-EXISTENT, ETERNAL

un·be·gun \ˌənbəˈgən, -bē|-\ *adj* [ME *unbegunnen*, fr. OE, fr. ¹*un-* + *begunnen*, past part. of *beginnan* to begin] **1** : existing from all eternity without beginning **2** : not yet begun

un·beheld \ˌən+\ *adj* [¹*un-* + *beheld*, past part. of *behold*] : UNSEEN

un·beholden \"+\ *adj* [¹*un-* + *beholden*, adj.] **1** : not beholden **2** [¹*un-* + *beholden*, archaic past part. of *behold*] : UNBEHELD

un·be·known \ˌənbə|nōn, -bē|-\ *or* **un·be·knownst** \-ōnzt, -ōn(t)st\ *adj* [*unbeknown* fr. ¹*un-* + obs. E *beknown* known, familiar, fr. ME *beknowen*, past part. of *beknowen* to become acquainted with, fr. OE *becnāwan*, fr. *be-* + *cnāwan* to know; *unbeknownst* irreg. fr. *unbeknown* — more at KNOW] : happening without one's knowledge : UNKNOWN — usu. used with *to* ⟨two elderly women ~ to anybody —J.H.Holmes⟩

un·belief \ˌən+\ *n* [ME *unbeleve*, fr. ¹*un-* + *beleve* belief] : withholding of belief : incredulity or skepticism esp. in matters of religious faith ⟨a reaction . . . against rationalism and ~ —A.C.McGiffert⟩

un·believable \"+\ *adj* [¹*un-* + *believable*] : not believable : INCREDIBLE — **un·believably** \"+\ *adv*

¹un·believe \"+\ *vb* [¹*un-* + *believe*] : DISBELIEVE

²unbelieve \"\ *vt* [²*un-* + *believe*] : to reject from belief

un·believer \"+\ *n* [¹*un-* + *believer*] **1** : one that does not believe : an incredulous person : DOUBTER, SKEPTIC **2** : DISBELIEVER, INFIDEL

un·believing \"+\ *adj* [ME *unbylefynge*, fr. ¹*un-* + *bylefynge*, *bilevinge*, pres. part. of *bileven* to believe] **1** : not believing : INCREDULOUS, DOUBTING, DISTRUSTING, SKEPTICAL **2** : disbelieving esp. a particular divine revelation — **un·be·liev·ing·ly** *adv* — **un·be·liev·ing·ness** *n* -ES

un·belonging \"+\ *adj* [¹*un-* + *belonging*, pres. part. of *belong*] : not belonging ⟨never taking a thing ~ to them —James Still⟩

un·be·loved \ˌənbəˈləvd\ *adj* : UNLOVED

un·belt \ˌən+\ *vt* [ME *unbelten* to ungird, fr. ²*un-* + *belten* to belt] : to remove one's belt; *also* : to remove (as a sword) by removing a belt

un·belted \"+\ *adj* : not furnished with a belt

un·bend \"+\ *vb* [ME *unbenden*, fr. ²*un-* + *benden* to bend] *vt* **1** : to free from flexure : make or allow to become straight ⟨~ a bow⟩ **2** : to remit from strain or exertion : set at ease for a time : cause to relax ⟨~ the mind from study⟩ **3** *obs* : SLACKEN **4 a** : to unfasten (as a sail) from a spar or stay **b** : to cast loose or untie (as a rope) ~ *vi* **1 a** : to relax one's severity, stiffness, or austerity ⟨she *unbent* a little, losing something of her marble acquiescence —A.J.Cronin⟩ **b** : to give oneself wholeheartedly to affability, mirth, or amusement ⟨an office party where everyone ~*s* and regrets it —Frederick Laws⟩ **2** : to cease to be bent : become straight or relaxed

un·bendable \"+\ *adj* : not bendable; *esp* : not capable of being turned from a goal : of set purpose : SINGLE-MINDED, FIRM ⟨a man of ~ perseverance —*Times Lit. Supp.*⟩

un·bending \"+\ *adj* [¹*un-* + *bending*, pres. part. of *bend*] **1** : not bending : UNYIELDING ⟨the ~, wind-swept ruggedness of that tree —H.A.Overstreet⟩ **2 a** : not given to altering a purpose or opinion : RESOLUTE, INFLEXIBLE ⟨a man of violent temper, stern and ~ in the performance of what he considers to be his duty —C.B.Nordhoff & J.N.Hall⟩ **b** : that does not unbend : cool, aloof, or unsocial in manner or mien : RESERVED — **un·bend·ing·ly** *adv* — **un·bend·ing·ness** *n* -ES

²unbending *adj* [fr. pres. part. of *unbend*] : that unbends : given to relaxation

un·beneficed \ˌən+\ *adj* [¹*un-* + *beneficed*, past part. of *benefice*] : not beneficed

un·beneficial \"+\ *adj* : not beneficial : HARMFUL

un·benefited \"+\ *adj* [¹*un-* + *benefited*, past part. of *benefit*] : not benefited : UNHELPED

un·benevolent \"+\ *adj* : not benevolent : desiring or causing harm

un·benight \"+\ *vt* [²*un-* + *benight*] *archaic* : to free from night or darkness

un·benign \"+\ *adj, archaic* : UNBENIGNANT

un·benignant \"+\ *adj* : not benignant : MALIGNANT — **un·be·nig·nant·ly** *adv*

un·bent \"+\ *adj* [ME, fr. ¹*un-* + *bent*] **1** : not bent : UNBOWED **2** *obs* : UNWRINKLED **3** : UNSUBDUED

un·bequeathed \"+\ *adj* [¹*un-* + *bequeathed*, past part. of *bequeath*] : not bequeathed

un·bereft \"+\ *adj* [¹*un-* + *bereft*, past part. of *bereave*] *archaic* : not bereft

un·beseem \"+\ *vt* [¹*un-* + *beseem*] : to be unbecoming or unbefitting to

un·besought \"+\ *adj* [¹*un-* + *besought*, past part. of *beseech*] : not requested : not asked for

un·bespoken \ˌən+\ *adj* [¹*un-* + *bespoken*, past part. of *bespeak*] : not bespoken

un·be·think \ˌənbiˈthiŋk\ *vt* [ME *unbethinken*, *umbethinken*, *umbethenken* to bethink, consider, fr. OE *ymbthencan*, *ymbethencan* to consider, fr. *ymb*, *ymbe* around + *thencan* to think — more at EMBER DAY, THINK] *dial Brit* : BETHINK

un·beveled \"+\ *adj* [¹*un-* + *beveled*, past part. of *bevel*] : not beveled

un·bewailed \"+\ *adj* [¹*un-* + *bewailed*, past part. of *bewail*] *archaic* : UNMOURNED

unbewitch *vt* [²*un-* + *bewitch*] *obs* : DISENCHANT

un·biased \ˌən+\ *adj* **1** : free from bias **2** : characterized by complete absence of prejudice, favoritism, undue or unwarranted preference, or personal interest : resolute in evenness and equality ⟨~ by self-profit —Alfred Tennyson⟩ ⟨a daughter's story of her father, startlingly honest and ~ —*English Jour.*⟩ **3** *of a statistic* : having an expected value equal to a population parameter being estimated **syn** see FAIR

un·bi·ased·ly *adv* : in an unbiased manner

un·bib·li·cal \ˌənˈbibləkəl\ *adj* : contrary to, not conforming with, or unsanctioned by the Bible : UNSCRIPTURAL — **un·bib·li·cal·ly** \-lək(ə)lē\ *adv*

un·bid \ˌənˈbid\ *adj* [ME *unbedde*, fr. ¹*un-* + *bedde*, *biden*, past part. of *bidden* to entreat, invite — more at BID] : UNBIDDEN

un·bid·da·ble \-dəbəl\ *adj, Brit* : INTRACTABLE

un·bid·den \ˌənˈbidᵊn\ *adj* [ME *unbiden*, *unbeden*, fr. OE *unbeden*, fr. ¹*un-* + *beden*, past part. of *biddan* to entreat — more at BID] : not bidden : UNASKED, UNINVITED

un·bigoted \ˌən+\ *adj* : not bigoted : UNBIASED

un·bind \ˌənˈbīnd\ *vt* [ME *unbinden*, fr. OE *unbindan*, *onbindan*, fr. *un-*, *on-* un- + *bindan* to bind] **1 a** : to remove a band from : free from shackles or fastenings : UNTIE, UNFASTEN, LOOSE **b** : to set free : give or restore liberty to : RELEASE **2 a** : to free (as a cord) by or as if by untying a knot or releasing a catch; *also* : to untangle or loose (a knot) by separating the parts **b** : to make less binding, controlling, or restrictive ⟨~*s* the strictures which restrain the full joy in marriage —J.A.Pike⟩

un·binding \ˌən+\ *adj* : not binding; *esp* : not imposing a duty or obligation : without restrictive force ⟨the contract was ~⟩

un·bitt \ˌən+\ *vt* [²*un-* + *bitt*] : to remove the turns of (a rope or cable) from a bitt

un·bitted \"+\ *adj* [¹*un-* + *bitted*, past part. of *bit*] : UNBRIDLED, UNCONTROLLED

un·bitter \"+\ *adj* : not bitter : having or exhibiting no feelings of malice, resentment, or revenge ⟨remarkably ~ toward . . . her captors —J.K.Hutchens⟩

un·blacked \"+\ *adj* [¹*un-* + *blacked*, past part. of *black*] : not blacked ⟨~ shoes⟩

un·blackened \"+\ *adj* [¹*un-* + *blackened*, past part. of *blacken*] : not blackened

un·blamable \"+\ *adj* : BLAMELESS — **un·blamably** \"+\ *adv*

un·blamed \"+\ *adj* [ME, fr. ¹*un-* + *blamed*, past part. of *blamen* to blame] : not blamed

un·blanched \"+\ *adj* [ME, fr. ¹*un-* + *blanched*, *blaunched*, past part. of *blanchen*, *blaunchen* to blanch] : not whitened : UNBLEACHED

un·blasted \"+\ *adj* : UNBLIGHTED

un·bleached \"+\ *adj* [¹*un-* + *bleached*, past part. of *bleach*] : not bleached

un·blemished \ˌən+\ *adj* [ME *unblemisshed*, fr. ¹*un-* + *blemisshed*, past part. of *blemisshen* to blemish] : not blemished : free from physical or moral spots or stains : PURE

un·blenched \"+\ *adj* [¹*un-* + *blenched*, past part. of *blench* (to flinch)] : not disconcerted : UNDAUNTED

un·blenching \"+\ *adj* [¹*un-* + *blenching*, pres. part. of *blench* (to flinch)] : UNBLENCHED, UNFLINCHING — **un·blench·ing·ly** *adv*

un·blended \"+\ *adj* [ME, fr. ¹*un-* + *blended*, past part. of *blenden* to blend, mix] : not blended : UNMIXED

un·blent \"+\ *adj* [¹*un-* + *blent*, past part. of *blend*] : UNBLENDED

un·blessed *also* **un·blest** \ˌənˈblest\ *adj* [ME, fr. ¹*un-* + *blessed*, *blest*] **1 a** : UNCONSECRATED **b** : UNHOLY, EVIL, ACCURSED **c** : excluded from or not having received blessing and esp. religious blessing **2** : not provided with a good : UNFORTUNATE, LACKING ⟨his hut which was ~ with electricity —L.K.Liang⟩ — **un·bless·ed·ness** \-sədnəs\ *n*

un·blighted \ˌən+\ *adj* : not blighted : FRESH, PURE — **un·blight·ed·ly** *adv*

un·blind \"+\ *vt* [²*un-* + *blind*] : to free from blindness or illusion

un·blinded \"+\ *adj* : not blinded; *also* : being without illusion : UNDECEIVED

un·blinking \"+\ *adj* [¹*un-* + *blinking*, pres. part. of *blink*] **1** : not blinking **2** : not exhibiting signs of emotion, doubt, or confusion ⟨stood ~ in District Court and accepted a sentence of a year —*Springfield (Mass.) Daily News*⟩ **3** : honest, accurate, and fearless in examination ⟨~ sincerity is the first requisite in writing amateur plays —*Harper's*⟩ — **un·blink·ing·ly** *adv*

un·block \"+\ *vt* [²*un* + *block*] : to free from being blocked ⟨~ an alien's assets⟩; *specif* : to play the cards of (a suit) so that the last trick on which a hand can follow suit will be taken by a higher card in the hand of the partner who has the remaining cards of a combined holding

un·blocked \"+\ *adj* [¹*un-* + *blocked*, past part. of *block*] : not shaped by a block ⟨an ~ hat⟩

un·blooded \"+\ *adj* [¹*un-* + *blooded*, past part. of *blood*] **1** : UNBLOODIED **2** [¹*un-* + *blooded*, adj.] : not purebred

un·bloodied \"+\ *adj* [¹*un-* + *bloodied*, past part. of *bloody*] : not bloodied

unbloodily *adv* : in an unbloody manner

un·bloody \ˌən+\ *adj* : not bloody ⟨pagan emperors who fought easy and ~ wars —Albert Solomon⟩; *specif* : BLOODLESS

unbloody sacrifice *n* : EUCHARIST

un·blotted \ˌən+\ *adj* [¹*un-* + *blotted*, past part. of *blot*] : not blotted; *esp* : PURE, UNDEFILED

¹un·blown \"+\ *adj* [¹*un-* + *blown* (open, having bloomed)] : not blown; *esp* : not yet in blossom

²unblown \"\ *adj* [¹*un-* + *blown* (moved or acted upon by moving air)] : not blown by the wind

un·blunted \"+\ *adj* [¹*un-* + *blunted*, past part. of *blunt*] : not blunted : SHARP, KEEN

un·blurred \"+\ *adj* : not blurred : sharply delineated : CLEAR

un·blushing \"+\ *adj* **1** : not blushing **2** : SHAMELESS, UNABASHED ⟨two ~ of self-portrayals —P.R.Levin⟩ — **un·blush·ing·ly** *adv* — **un·blush·ing·ness** *n* -ES

un·boastful \"+\ *adj* : not boastful : MODEST — **un·boast·fully** \"+\ *adv*

un·bodied \"+\ *adj* [partly fr. ¹*un-* + *bodied* (having a body); partly fr. past part. of *unbody*] **1** : having no body : INCORPOREAL; *also* : DISEMBODIED **2** : FORMLESS

un·bodily \"+\ *adj* [ME, fr. ¹*un-* + *bodily*] : INCORPOREAL

un·body \"+\ *vt* [²*un-* + *body*] : DISEMBODY

un·boiled \"+\ *adj* : not boiled

un·bolt \"+\ *vt* [²*un-* + *bolt* (to fasten)] : to open, loosen, or unfasten by or as if by withdrawing a bolt

¹un·bolted \"\ *adj* [¹*un-* + *bolted*, past part. of *bolt* (to sift)] : not bolted : UNSIFTED ⟨~ flour⟩; *also* : COARSE, GROSS

²unbolted \"\ *adj* [¹*un-* + *bolted*, past part. of *bolt* (to fasten)] : not fastened by bolts

un·bonnet \"+\ *vb* [²*un-* + *bonnet*, n.] *vi* : to remove one's bonnet esp. as a mark of respect ~ *vt* : to take a bonnet from

un·bon·net·ed \ˌənˈbanəd·əd\ *adj* [¹*un-* + *bonnet*, n. + *-ed*] : having no bonnet or other headgear on : UNCOVERED, BAREHEADED

un·bookish \ˌən+\ *adj* : not bookish : not given to reading; *also* : UNLEARNED

un·bored \"+\ *adj* [¹*un-* + *bored*, past part. of *bore* (to pierce)] : not bored : UNPIERCED; *also* : not provided with a bore

un·born \"+\ *adj* [ME, fr. OE *unboren*, fr. ¹*un-* + *boren* born] **1** : not born : not brought into life ⟨his male descendant, as yet ~ —Joseph Hitrec⟩; *broadly* : still to appear : FUTURE ⟨projected figures are ~ statistics, statistics of the future —*New Yorker*⟩ **2** : existing without birth

un·borrowed \"+\ *adj* [¹*un-* + *borrowed*, past part. of *borrow*] : not borrowed; *esp* : NATURAL, NATIVE, INHERENT

un·bosom \"+\ *vt* [²*un-* + *bosom*, n.] **1 a** : to give expression to : DISCLOSE, REVEAL ⟨freely ~*ing* his perplexities and his anguish —J.S.C.Abbott⟩ **b** : to express the thoughts or feelings of (oneself) ⟨~*s* herself in conversations, in letters, in intimate diaries —H.M.Parshley⟩ **2** *archaic* : to spread out : DISPLAY ~ *vi* : to unbosom oneself

un·bottomed \"+\ *adj* [¹*un-* + *bottomed*, past part. of *bottom*] : BOTTOMLESS

un·bought \"+\ *adj* [ME, fr. OE *unboht*, fr. ¹*un-* + *boht* bought, past part. of *bycgan* to buy — more at BUY] : not bought

¹un·bound \"+\ *adj* [ME *unbounden*, fr. OE *unbunden*, fr. ¹*un-* + *bunden* bound, past part. of *bindan* to bind — more at BIND] : not bound: as **a** (1) : UNFASTENED (2) : UNCONFINED **b** : not having the leaves fastened or sewn together ⟨an ~ book⟩ **c** : not held in chemical or physical combination

²unbound *adj* [prob. fr. ¹*un-* + (assumed) obs. E *bound*, past part. of E *bound* (to set limits to)] *obs* : UNBOUNDED

un·bounded \ˌən+\ *adj* [¹*un-* + *bounded*, past part. of *bound* (to set limits to)] **1** : having no bound : unlimited in extent, degree, or quantity ⟨wealth poured in . . . and luxury grew more ~ —J.S.Froude⟩ ⟨~ space⟩ ⟨the work was received with ~ enthusiasm —*Amer. Guide Series: Ind.*⟩ **2** : UNCHECKED, UNCONTROLLED, UNRESTRAINED ⟨the ~ freedom of pure mathematics —Samuel Alexander⟩ — **un·bound·ed·ly** *adv* — **un·bound·ed·ness** *n*

un·bowdlerized \"+\ *adj* [¹*un-* + *bowdlerized*, past part. of *bowdlerize*] : not bowdlerized : UNEXPURGATED

un·bowed \"+\ *adj* [ME, fr. ¹*un-* + *bowed* (bent down)] **1** : not bowed down **2** : UNSUBDUED

un·box \"+\ *vt* [²*un-* + *box*] : to remove from a box

un·boyish \"+\ *adj* : not boyish : uncharacteristic of a boy

un·brace \ˌənˈbrās\ *vt* [ME *unbracen* to carve, remove clothing or armor from, fr. ²*un-* + *bracen* to fasten tightly — more at BRACE] **1** *archaic* : CARVE, DISJOINT **2 a** : to remove the holding power of by or as if by untying a bond **b** : to free or detach by or as if by untying a brace; *specif* : to untie the string from (a bow) **3** : ENFEEBLE, WEAKEN

un·braced \ˌən+\ *adj* [partly fr. ¹*un-* + *braced*, past part. of *brace*; partly fr. past part. of obs. E *unbrace* to unfasten, remove clothing or armor from, fr. ME *unbracen*] **1 a** *obs* : not tied by braces ⟨his doublet all ~ —*Shak.*⟩ **b** : wearing unfastened or loosened clothing **2 a** *obs, of a drum* : not taut : free from tension **b** : UNFLEXED, RELAXED

un·bracketed \"+\ *adj* [¹*un-* + *bracketed*, past part. of *bracket*] : not bracketed : not enclosed in brackets

un·braid \"+\ *vt* [²*un-* + *braid*] : to separate the strands of (as a braid) : UNRAVEL

un·braided \"+\ *adj* [¹*un-* + obs. E *braided* tarnished, fr. E *braided*, adj.] **1** *obs* : UNTARNISHED **2** [¹*un-* + *braided*, adj.] : not braided

un·branched \"+\ *adj* [¹*un-* + *branched*, past part. of *branch*] **1** : having no branch ⟨an ~ trunk⟩ **2** : not branched ⟨a leaf with ~ veins⟩ **3** : having a straight chain of atoms in the molecule : NORMAL 10e

un·branching \"+\ *adj* [¹*un-* + *branching*, pres. part. of *branch*] : not branching

un·branded \"+\ *adj* [¹*un-* + *branded*, past part. of *brand*] : not branded; *specif* : not marked with the owner's name or mark ⟨~ cattle⟩

un·breakable \"+\ *adj* [ME *unbrekable*, fr. ¹*un-* + *breken* to break + *-able*] : not breakable; *also* : not breakable under ordinary usage

un·breakfasted \"+\ *adj* [¹*un-* + *breakfasted*, past part. of *breakfast*] **1** : not having eaten breakfast **2** : not supplied with breakfast

un·breaking \"+\ *adj* [¹*un-* + *breaking*, pres. part. of *break*] : not breaking

un·breathable \ˌən+\ *adj* : not breathable ⟨sufficient carbon dioxide gas to render the atmosphere absolutely ~ —Valentine Williams⟩
un·breathed \"+\ *adj* [¹*un-* + *breathed*, past part. of *breathe*] : not breathed
un·breathing \"+\ *adj* [¹*un-* + *breathing*, pres. part. of *breathe*] **1** : not breathing; *esp* : holding one's breath **2** *archaic* : not stirred by a breeze or wind : CALM, STILL
un·bred \"+\ *adj* [¹*un-* + *bred*, past part. of *breed*] **1** *obs* : UNBORN **2** *obs* : not well-bred : ILL-BRED **3** : UNTAUGHT, UNTRAINED **4** : not now bred and usu. never having been bred ⟨an ~ heifer⟩
un·breech \"+\ *vt* [²*un-* + *breech*] : to remove the breeches of
un·breeched \"+\ *adj* [¹*un-* + *breeched*] : not wearing breeches
un·bribable \"+\ *adj* [¹*un-* + *bribe*, v. + *-able*] : not bribable : INCORRUPTIBLE
un·bribed \"+\ *adj* [¹*un-* + *bribed*, past part. of *bribe*] **1** : uncorrupted by bribery **2** : not obtained by bribery
un·bridgeable \"+\ *adj* [¹*un-* + *bridge*, v. + *-able*] : not bridgeable ⟨an ~ stream⟩ ⟨the ~ gap between the experiences and attitudes of frontline soldiers and of the civilians back home —R.G.Davis⟩
un·bridged \"+\ *adj* [¹*un-* + *bridged*, past part. of *bridge*] : not crossed by a bridge
un·bridle \"+\ *vt* [ME *unbridlen*, fr. ²*un-* + *bridlen* to bridle] : to free or loose from a bridle; *broadly* : to set loose : FREE ⟨his annoyance had *unbridled* his tongue —J.H.Wheelwright⟩
un·bridled \"+\ *adj* [ME, fr. ¹*un-* + *bridled*, past part. of *bridlen* to bridle] **1** : not confined by a bridle **2** : completely at liberty : UNRESTRAINED, UNGOVERNED, UNCHECKED ⟨extolled the benevolence of ~ competition in human affairs —Joseph Schiffman⟩ ⟨fantastic charges and ~ insults —William Ridsdale⟩ ⟨~ enthusiasm⟩
un–british \"+\ *adj, usu cap B* : not characteristic of or consistent with British customs, habits, or traditions
un·broached \"+\ *adj* [¹*un-* + *broached*, past part. of *broach* (to tap)] : not broached
un·broke \"+\ *adj* [ME, fr. ¹*un-* + *broke*] **1** : UNBROKEN **2** : not broke ⟨a few raw ~ horses —Bruce Siberts & W.D. Wyman⟩
un·broken \"+\ *adj* [ME, fr. ¹*un-* + *broken*] : not broken: as **a** : UNVIOLATED **b** : WHOLE, INTACT, COMPLETE ⟨~ control of the economic, social and political life —G.M.McBride⟩ **c** : UNSUBDUED, UNTAMED ⟨half-educated and totally ~ to society —*Punch*⟩; *esp* : not trained for service or use ⟨~ range horses⟩ **d** : not interrupted ⟨magnificent gleaming cars in an ~ procession —Winifred Bambrick⟩ ⟨an ~ series of evolving organisms —Waldemar Kaempffert⟩ ⟨100 miles of ~ forest —*Amer. Guide Series: Maine*⟩ **e** : UNPLOWED **f** : not disorganized — **un·bro·ken·ly** *adv* — **un·bro·ken·ness** *n*
un·brook·able \ˌən¦bru̇kəbəl\ *adj* [¹*un-* + *brook*, v. + *-able*] : UNENDURABLE
un·brother \ˌən+\ *vt* [²*un-* + *brother*] : to deprive of the status of brother
un·broth·er·ly *adj* : not characteristic of or befitting a brother
un·bruised \ˌən+\ *adj* [ME *unbrused*, fr. ¹*un-* + *brused*, past part. of *brusen* to bruise, crush] : not bruised : UNINJURED, SOUND
un·brushed \"+\ *adj* [¹*un-* + *brushed*, past part. of *brush* (to use a brush on)] : not brushed
un·buckle \"+\ *vb* [ME *unboclen*, fr. ²*un-* + *boclen* to buckle] *vt* : to loose the buckle of : UNFASTEN ⟨~ a shoe⟩ ~ *vi* : to loosen a buckle
un·budded \"+\ *adj* [¹*un-* + *budded*, past part. of *bud*] : not budded
un·budge·abil·i·ty \ˌən,bəjə'biləd·ē\ *n* : the quality or state of being unbudgeable
un·budge·able \ˌən¦bəjəbəl\ *adj* [¹*un-* + *budge*, v. + *-able*] : that cannot be budged ⟨smile blandly with ~ composure —G.N.Kates⟩ — **un·budge·ably** \-blē\ *adv*
un·budging \ˌən+\ *adj* [¹*un-* + *budging*, pres. part. of *budge*] : not budging : resisting movement or change — **un·budg·ing·ly** *adv*
un·build \"+\ *vb* [²*un-* + *build*] : DEMOLISH, RAZE
un·built \"+\ *adj* [ME *unbylyt*, fr. ¹*un-* + *bylyt*, *bilt*, past part. of *bilden* to build — more at BUILD] **1** : not built : not yet constructed **2** : not occupied with a building ⟨an ~ plot⟩ — often used with *on* ⟨ground as yet ~ on⟩
un·bulky \"+\ *adj* : not bulky
un·bung \"+\ *vt* [²*un-* + *bung*] : to remove the bung from
un·burden \"+\ *vt* [²*un-* + *burden*] **1** : to free or relieve from a burden and esp. from something oppressing or depressing the mind or spirit ⟨~*s* himself . . . of all the accumulated resentment and dislike of years —S.M.Fitzgerald⟩ **2** : to relieve oneself from esp. by expression ⟨~ the worries he can't confess in the office —W.H.Whyte⟩ **syn** see RID
un·burdened \"+\ *adj* [¹*un-* + *burdened*, past part. of *burden*] : not burdened : having no weight or load ⟨~ by an overarching theory —Alex Inkeles⟩
un·buried \"+\ *adj* [ME, fr. OE *unbyrged*, fr. ¹*un-* + *byrged*, past part. of *byrgan* to bury] : not buried
un·burned \"+\ *adj* [ME *unbirned*, fr. ¹*un-* + *birned*, past part. of *birnen* to burn] : not burned ⟨built of ~ bricks⟩
un·burnished \"+\ *adj* : not burnished : UNPOLISHED, DULL
un·burnt \ˌən+\ *adj* [¹*un-* + *burnt*, past part. of *burn*] : UNBURNED
un·burst \"+\ *adj* : not burst
un·bury \"+\ *vt* [ME *unberien*, fr. ²*un-* + *berien* to bury] : DISINTER, EXHUME
un·busy \"+\ *adj* : not busy : UNOCCUPIED
un·buttered \"+\ *adj* [¹*un-* + *buttered*, past part. of *butter*] : not buttered : lacking butter ⟨water and ~ bread⟩
un·button \"+\ *vb* [ME *unbotonen*, fr. ²*un-* + *botonen* to button] *vt* **1** : to loose the buttons of : unfasten by loosing buttons ⟨~*ed* his coat⟩; *also* : to remove (a button) from a buttonhole **2** : to open as if by unbuttoning ⟨~*ed* my heart to him —*Omnibook*⟩ ⟨a team of experts in the code room has ~*ed* it —E.O.Hauser⟩; *specif* : to open the hatches or apertures of (an armored vehicle) ~ *vi* : to undo a button
un·buttoned \"+\ *adj* [¹*un-* + *buttoned*, adj.] **1 a** : not buttoned **b** : not provided with buttons **2** : not under constraint : free and unrestricted in action or expression ⟨this ~ and disrespectful age —Curtis Bok⟩ ⟨outburst of ~ rhetoric —F.L. Allen⟩ **3** : deprived of strength or stability ⟨her moral fiber had suddenly become ~ —Ellen Glasgow⟩
un·buttressed \"+\ *adj* [¹*un-* + *buttressed*, past part. of *buttress*] : not buttressed : UNSUPPORTED ⟨one of the few really ~ statements in the book —Priscilla Robertson⟩
unc *abbr* **1** uncertain **2** uncirculated **3** uncut
un·cage \ˌən+\ *vt* [²*un-* + *cage*] : to release from or as if from a cage
un·cal \'əŋkəl\ *adj* [*uncus* + *-al*] : of or relating to an uncus
un·calcified \ˌən+\ *adj* [¹*un-* + *calcified*, past part. of *calcify*] : not calcified
un·calculated \"+\ *adj* : not planned or thought out beforehand : IMPROVISED ⟨a rough and ~ style —Winthrop Sargeant⟩
un·calculating \"+\ *adj* : not based on or marked by calculation : not self-interested ⟨flung his defiance at the entrenched enemy with the courage of ~ youth —V.L.Parrington⟩ — **un·cal·cu·lat·ing·ly** *adv*
un·called \"+\ *adj* [ME, fr. ¹*un-* + *called*, past part. of *callen* to call] : not asked for or invited; *specif* : not called for payment ⟨protected by paid-up and ~ capital —*Economist*⟩
un·called–for \ˌən¦kōld,fō(ə)r, -ō(ə)\ *adj* [¹*un-* + *called for*, past part. form of the phrase *call for*] **1** : not called for or needed : UNNECESSARY ⟨in those areas rationing has on the surface seemed *uncalled-for* —*Harper's*⟩ **2 a** : not warranted : being without cause or occasion : GRATUITOUS ⟨much of his bitterness is *uncalled-for* —Thomas Halton⟩ **b** : RUDE, IMPERTINENT ⟨an *uncalled-for* comment⟩ ⟨his display of temper was *uncalled-for*⟩
¹**un·cal·low** \,ən'kalə\ *vb* -ED/-ING/-S [²*un-* + *callow*, n.] *vt*, *dial Eng* : to remove the layer of soil above the subsoil from ~ *vi*, *dial Eng* : to clear off the layer of soil above the subsoil
²**uncallow** \"\ *n*, *dial Eng* : the layer of soil above the subsoil
un·candid \ˌən+\ *adj* : not frank or aboveboard : DISINGENUOUS ⟨was sometimes ~, to put no harsher name to his conduct —Broadus Mitchell⟩ — **un·can·did·ly** *adv* — **un·can·did·ness** *n*
un·candor \"+\ *n* : lack of candor
un·cannily \"+\ *adv* : in an uncanny manner : to an uncanny degree ⟨the present crop of ~ human robots —H.W.Baldwin⟩
un·canniness \"+\ *n* : the quality or state of being uncanny ⟨a curlew added to the ~ of the quiet solitude as its wail swept across the night —Myrtle R. White⟩
un·canny \"+\ *adj* **1 a** : arousing feelings of dread or of inexplicable strangeness : seeming to have a supernatural character, cause, or origin : EERIE, MYSTERIOUS, WEIRD ⟨it was that saddest, most ~ thing — a deserted house —Clara Morris⟩ ⟨~ as the shadows of unfamiliar furniture on the walls of an inn —A.T.Quiller-Couch⟩ **b** : extending to a degree beyond what is normal or expected : suggesting superhuman or supernatural powers or qualities ⟨showed an ~ ability to gauge the public's taste —A.E.Peterson⟩ ⟨his ~ skill with firearms —S.H.Holbrook⟩ **2** *chiefly Scot* : PUNISHING, SEVERE **3** *chiefly Scot* : DANGEROUS **syn** see WEIRD
un·canonical \"+\ *adj* **1** : not being in accord with church canons ⟨an ~ marriage⟩ **2** : not belonging to the canon of biblical books ⟨an ~ work⟩ **3** : UNSANCTIONED, UNORTHODOX ⟨his ~ religious ideas⟩ — **un·canonically** \"+\ *adv*
un·canonize \"+\ *vt* [²*un-* + *canonize*] : to deprive of canonical authority or status
un·cap \"+\ *vt* [²*un-* + *cap*] : to remove a cap or covering from; *specif* : to remove the caps from (a honeycomb) preparatory to extracting honey
un·capable \"+\ *adj* : INCAPABLE
un·capitalized \"+\ *adj* [¹*un-* + *capitalized*, past part. of *capitalize*] : not capitalized
un·cared–for \ˌən¦ka(a)rd,fō(ə)r, -ke\ |əd,fō(ə)\ *adj* [¹*un-* + *cared for*, past part. form of the phrase *care for*] **1** : not cared for : UNHEEDED ⟨the *uncared-for* and undisciplined life of the medieval student —G.M.Trevelyan⟩ **2** : RUN-DOWN ⟨an *uncared-for* look has begun to pervade the residential areas —Faubion Bowers⟩
un·careful \ˌən+\ *adj* **1** : not taking care : CARELESS **2** : having no care : CAREFREE
un·car·ia \,əŋ'ka(a)rēə\ *n, cap* [NL, fr. L *uncus* hook + NL *-aria* — more at ANGLE] : a large genus of chiefly tropical Asiatic woody vines (family Rubiaceae) having axillary heads of yellow flowers with valvate corollas succeeded by large septicidal many-seeded capsules — see GAMBIER
un·caring \ˌən+\ *adj* [¹*un-* + *caring*, pres. part. of *care*] : HEEDLESS, OBLIVIOUS ⟨sat around as bored and ~ as castaways on a Pacific atoll —Truman Capote⟩
un·carpeted \"+\ *adj* [¹*un-* + *carpeted*, past part. of *carpet*] : not covered or provided with a carpet
un·cart \"+\ *vt* [²*un-* + *cart*, n.] : to take or discharge from a cart
un·case \"+\ *vb* [²*un-* + *case*] *vt* **1** *archaic* : to take off the clothes of ⟨at once ~ thee —Shak.⟩ **2** : to take out of or free from a case or covering : DISCLOSE, UNCOVER; *specif* : to spread to view : DISPLAY ⟨~ the colors⟩ ~ *vi*, *archaic* : STRIP, UNDRESS ⟨I proceeded to ~, entrenching myself behind a chair —*Spirit of the Times*⟩
un·castrated \"+\ *adj* [¹*un-* + *castrated*, past part. of *castrate*] **1** : not castrated : ENTIRE, INTACT **2** : not expurgated ⟨has printed the ~ text for the first time⟩
un·cataloged \"+\ *adj* [¹*un-* + *cataloged*, past part. of *catalog*] : not cataloged
un·catch·able \ˌən¦kachəbəl, -kech-\ *adj* : not able to be caught ⟨the ~ quality of a shooting star —*View*⟩
un·catholic \ˌən+\ *adj* : not catholic; *specif* : not adhering to, favoring, accepted by, or suitable to a universal Christian church
un·catholicize \"+\ *vt* [²*un-* + *catholicize*] : to make uncatholic
un·caught \"+\ *adj* [ME, fr. ¹*un-* + *caught*, past part. of *cacchen* to catch — more at CATCH] : being at large : FREE ⟨was a bonny girl and could not in the nature of things be long ~ —Israel Zangwill⟩
un·caused \"+\ *adj* [¹*un-* + *caused*, past part. of *cause*] : having no antecedent cause : SELF-EXISTENT ⟨argues backward to a first great cause, which is itself ~ —G.W.Knox⟩
un·ceasing \"+\ *adj* [ME *uncesinge*, fr. ¹*un-* + *cesinge*, pres. part. of *cesen* to cease] : not ceasing : CONTINUOUS, INCESSANT ⟨high hills whose owners wage ~ warfare with drought and isolation —*Amer. Guide Series: Texas*⟩ — **un·ceas·ing·ly** *adv* — **un·ceas·ing·ness** *n* -ES
un·celebrated \"+\ *adj* [¹*un-* + *celebrated*, past part. of *celebrate*] **1** : not formally honored or commemorated ⟨baseball is . . . new to song and story and ~ in the fine arts —M.R. Cohen⟩ **2** : not famous : OBSCURE ⟨untried or ~ author —*Manchester Guardian Weekly*⟩
un·celestial \"+\ *adj* : EARTHY, WORLDLY ⟨a gift from heaven, designed to serve his own rather ~ purpose —R.D.Altick⟩
un·cemented \"+\ *adj* [¹*un-* + *cemented*, past part. of *cement*] : not held together by cement or other substance
un·censored \"+\ *adj* **1** : not subjected to censorship ⟨~ news reports⟩ **2** : not inhibited or restrained in expression ⟨the presentation of ~ observations by the characters of each other —Robert Humphrey⟩
un·censured \"+\ *adj* [¹*un-* + *censured*, past part. of *censure*] : not subjected to blame or criticism
un·center \"+\ *vt* [²*un-* + *center*] : to remove from a center
un·ceremonious \ˌən+\ *adj* **1** : not ceremonious : INFORMAL **2** : ABRUPT, RUDE ⟨his ~ dismissal from office⟩ — **un·cer·e·mo·ni·ous·ly** *adv* — **un·cer·e·mo·ni·ous·ness** *n*
¹**un·certain** \"+\ *adj* [ME, fr. ¹*un-* + *certain*] **1 a** : not fixed in time : being of indefinite date ⟨the exact moment of departure is ~⟩ **b** : indeterminate in number, amount, or extent ⟨engagements being irregular, the income is ~ —*Official Register of Harvard Univ.*⟩ ⟨a tract of ~ acreage —*Amer. Guide Series: Md.*⟩ **2** : not certain to occur : PROBLEMATICAL ⟨her success in new parts was very ~ —G.B.Shaw⟩ **3 a** : not known, demonstrated, or apparent beyond doubt : open to doubt : QUESTIONABLE ⟨unless further evidence is found, his story must remain ~⟩ **b** : AMBIGUOUS ⟨told him, in no ~ terms, what he thought of his behavior⟩ **c** : not clearly identified, defined, or located ⟨a fire of ~ origin destroyed the capitol —*Amer. Guide Series: Pa.*⟩ ⟨a play of ~ authorship⟩ ⟨the two bartenders, sallow women of ~ age —William Sansom⟩ **4 a** : not fixed in place, direction, or course : WANDERING ⟨the silver thread of water tracing its ~ course along the valley floor —E.A.McCourt⟩ **b** : not assured, consistent, or dependable in action, behavior, or effect : ERRATIC, UNRELIABLE ⟨ramshackle buildings lean over the water on their ~ stilts —*Amer. Guide Series: N.Y.City*⟩ ⟨a gun with a rather ~ trigger —D.M.MacKay⟩ **c** : not settled or fixed in character, quality, or state : subject to accident, chance, or change : UNPREDICTABLE ⟨everything is ~ about the army —Walt Whitman⟩ ⟨leading a somewhat ~ existence —*Fortnight*⟩ ⟨~ health⟩ **5 a** : not having certain knowledge or conviction : not assured : DOUBTFUL ⟨tolerant but never ~ of his convictions —W.A. White⟩ **b** : not definitely directed : UNDECIDED ⟨of great ambition, but ~ aim⟩ **c** : HESITANT, TENTATIVE ⟨touching the flowers, the ornaments, the books with ~ fingers —Edith Sitwell⟩ ⟨an ~ gentleness in his tone —Marguerite Steen⟩ **6** : CHANGEABLE, FICKLE, VARIABLE ⟨an ~ breeze⟩ ⟨an ~ friend⟩ ⟨a beautiful and ~ time, cold and wet and dry and warm —Josephine Johnson⟩ — **un·cer·tain·ly** *adv* — **un·cer·tain·ness** *n*
²**uncertain** \"\ *adv* : UNCERTAINLY
un·cer·tain·ty \"+tē *or* ti\ *n* [ME *uncertainte*, fr. ¹*uncertain* + *-te* -ty] **1** : the quality or state of being uncertain : lack of certainty **2** : something that is uncertain : something doubtful or unknown
syn UNCERTAINTY, DOUBT, DUBIETY, DUBIOSITY, SKEPTICISM, SUSPICION, and MISTRUST can all indicate a lack of sureness about something or someone. UNCERTAINTY stresses a lack of certitude ranging from a small falling short of definite knowledge to an almost complete lack of it or even any conviction, esp. about an outcome or result ⟨drove without any *uncertainty* or hesitation as to her route —Margaret Deland⟩ ⟨renewed *uncertainty* about the business outlook —Leo Wolman⟩ ⟨convince others without having experienced either *uncertainty* or conviction himself —C.D.Lewis⟩ ⟨the long *uncertainty* and bloody confusion that attended the breakdown of the Roman Empire —Lewis Mumford⟩ DOUBT can imply uncertainty about the truth or reality of something or an inability to make a decision in respect to it or arrive at conviction even after study, esp. about religious belief ⟨no man likes to have his intelligence or good faith questioned, especially if he has *doubts* about it himself —Henry Adams⟩ ⟨after a very few days more of *doubt* and indecision, the great question of whither he should go was settled —Jane Austen⟩ ⟨a *doubt* about the existence of evil⟩ ⟨the strong religious *doubt* of the nineteenth century⟩ DUBIETY is close to UNCERTAINTY in stressing a questionableness, a lack of sureness, commonly implying also a wavering between conclusions ⟨it threw a kind of *dubiety* upon Susan's moral conduct —Charles Lamb⟩ ⟨no matter how small the technical probable error of the measurements might be, the *dubiety* of the result cannot be less than 3 in 105 —N.E.Dorsey & Churchill Eisenhart⟩ ⟨with presumable Scotch *dubiety* he would be inclined to distrust such items on the table as potatoes and ice cream and coffee — completely unknown in his day in Scotland —Alan Gregg⟩ DUBIOSITY is interchangeable with DUBIETY but may be distinguished from it in often suggesting vagueness, indistinctness, or mental confusion ⟨she pronounced distinctly and without a shadow of *dubiosity* —George Meredith⟩ SKEPTICISM suggests an unwillingness to believe without definitive demonstration, often applying to an habitual or temperamental frame of mind that tends to oppose belief not based on rational or scientific demonstration ⟨*skepticism* about all facile answers to basic questions of conduct⟩ ⟨created *skepticism* about the wisdom of foreign aid —Henry Wallace⟩ ⟨has found that *skepticism* rather than dogmatism is the key to human freedom —*New Republic*⟩ ⟨a religious *skepticism*⟩ SUSPICION stresses a conjectural belief that something is not true, real, or right, generally carrying also the idea of an accompanying uncertainty, doubt, or skepticism ⟨a strong *suspicion* that the new instrument with which Einstein has presented the mathematicians is being put to uses for which it was never intended —W.R.Inge⟩ ⟨public *suspicion* of the colleges —J.B.Conant⟩ ⟨the basic and healthy *suspicion* of power that is not strictly circumscribed by the rule of the law —Max Lerner⟩ MISTRUST, in this context, implies a doubt based on suspicion or an anticipation of wrong, falsehood, or evil, in action or result, and precluding faith, confidence, or trust ⟨most physicists have a traditional *mistrust* of philosophy —W.V.Houston⟩ ⟨intracommunity bickering, conflict and *mistrust* obscure the steady vision of extracommunity danger —A.E.Stevenson b. 1900⟩ ⟨his general *mistrust* of the human race —L.P.Stryker⟩
uncertainty principle *n* : a principle in quantum mechanics: it is impossible to assert in terms of the ordinary conventions of geometrical position and of motion that a particle (as an electron) is at the same time at a specified point and moving with a specified velocity for the more accurately either factor can be measured the less accurately the other can be ascertained
un·certitude \ˌən+\ *n* : INCERTITUDE
un·ces·sant \ˌən¦sesᵊnt\ *adj* [ME, alter. (influenced by ¹*un-*) of *incessant*, *incessant* incessant] *archaic* : INCESSANT
un·chain \ˌən+\ *vt* [²*un-* + *chain*] : to free by or as if by removing a chain : set loose : RELEASE ⟨reflexes ~*ed* by localized mechanical stimuli —Piero Leonardi⟩
un·chal·lenge·able \ˌən¦chalənjəbəl, -alēn-\ *adj* : not able to be challenged or disputed ⟨a position of ~ supremacy —*Harper's*⟩ — **un·chal·lenge·ably** \-blē\ *adv*
un·challenged \ˌən+\ *adj* [¹*un-* + *challenged*, past part. of *challenge*] : not challenged : UNDISPUTED ⟨emerged the ~ political head —A.L.Funk⟩
un·chambered \"+\ *adj* [¹*un-* + *chambered*, past part. of *chamber*] : not having a chamber
un·chancy \"+\ *adj* **1** *chiefly Scot* : ILL-FATED, ILL-OMENED, UNLUCKY **2** *chiefly Scot* : unsafe to meddle with : DANGEROUS
un·changeability \"+\ *n* [ME *unchangeabilite*, fr. *unchangeable*, *unchangeabil* unchangeable + *-ite* -ity] : the quality or state of being unchangeable
un·changeable \"+\ *adj* [ME, fr. ¹*un-* + *changeable*] : not changeable : IMMUTABLE ⟨a fixed and ~ part of the germ plasm —M.F.A.Montagu⟩ — **un·change·able·ness** *n* — **un·change·ably** \"+\ *adv*
un·changed \ˌən¦chānjd\ *adj* [ME *unchaunged*, fr. ¹*un-* + *chaunged*, *changed*, past part. of *chaungen*, *changen* to change] : not changed : UNALTERED ⟨the causes which produced them have remained ~ —*World's Work*⟩ — **un·chang·ed·ness** \-jədnəs\ *n* -ES
un·changing \ˌən+\ *adj* [ME *unchaunginge*, fr. ¹*un-* + *chaunginge*, *changinge*, pres. part. of *chaungen*, *changen* to change] : CHANGELESS, CONSTANT ⟨a country of immovable and ~ traditions —Laurence Binyon⟩ — **un·chang·ing·ly** *adv* — **un·chang·ing·ness** *n* -ES
un·chaperoned \"+\ *adj* [¹*un-* + *chaperoned*, past part. of *chaperon*] : not accompanied by a chaperon
un·characteristic \"+\ *adj* : not characteristic : not typical or distinctive ⟨a book ~ of its author⟩ — **un·characteristic·ally** \"+\ *adv*
uncharge *vt* [ME *uncharge* to remove a load or burden from, fr. ²*un-* + *chargen* to load, put a load on — more at CHARGE] *obs* : ACQUIT ⟨even his mother shall ~ the practice and call it accident —Shak.⟩
un·charged \ˌən+\ *adj* [ME, not burdened, fr. ¹*un-* + *charged*, past part. of *chargen*] : not charged; *specif* : having no electric charge
un·charitable \"+\ *adj* [ME, fr. ¹*un-* + *charitable*] : not charitable : HARSH, SEVERE ⟨a thing all pious words and ~ deeds —Charles Reade⟩ ⟨criticism . . . which he now feels to have been unjust and ~ —Richard Garnett †1906⟩ — **un·char·i·ta·ble·ness** *n* — **un·charitably** \"+\ *adv*
un·charity \"+\ *n* : lack of charity ⟨a double sin, that of ~ and that of pride —Ruth Park⟩
un·charm \"+\ *vt* [²*un-* + *charm*] **1** : to divest of power to charm **2** : to free from or as if from a charm
un·charming \"+\ *adj* [¹*un-* + *charming*, adj.] : lacking charm ⟨writes an ugly ~ style —O.W.Holmes †1935⟩
un·charnel \"+\ *vt* -ED/-ING/-S [²*un-* + *charnel*, n.] : to remove from a charnel house or the grave : EXHUME
un·charred \"+\ *adj* [¹*un-* + *charred*, past part. of *char* (to burn)] : not charred
un·charted \"+\ *adj* [¹*un-* + *charted*, past part. of *chart*] : not charted : not recorded or plotted on a map, chart, or plan : UNKNOWN ⟨headed westward into the ~ wilderness —*Amer. Guide Series: Texas*⟩ ⟨assigned to explore previously ~ areas of space —*Springfield (Mass.) Republican*⟩ ⟨the great ~ region in the realm of letters —J.L.Lowes⟩
un·chartered \"+\ *adj* [¹*un-* + *chartered*, past part. of *charter*] : not chartered : IRREGULAR
un·chary \"+\ *adj* : not chary : not cautious or reserved ⟨have said too much unto a heart of stone and laid mine honor too ~ out —Shak.⟩
un·chaste \ˌən+\ *adj* [ME, fr. ¹*un-* + *chaste*] : not chaste : lacking in chastity ⟨an ~ woman⟩ ⟨~ conduct⟩ — **un·chaste·ly** *adv* — **un·chaste·ness** *n*
un·chastened \"+\ *adj* [¹*un-* + *chastened*, past part. of *chasten*] : not chastened
un·chastity \"+\ *n* [ME *unchastite*, fr. ¹*un-* + *chastite*, *chastete* chastity] : the quality or state of being unchaste : lack of chastity
un·check \"+\ *vt* [¹*un-* + *check*] : to impose no check on
un·checked \"+\ *adj* [ME *unchekked*, fr. ¹*un-* + *chekked*, *cheked*, past part. of *chekken*, *cheken* to check] **1** : not checked : not curbed or hindered : UNRESTRAINED ⟨a harmonious development that continued ~ for more than fifty years —*Amer. Guide Series: Maine*⟩ ⟨~ extravagance⟩ **2** *obs* : not contradicted ⟨it lives there ~ that Antonio hath a ship of rich lading wrecked —Shak.⟩
un·cheerful \"+\ *adj* [ME *uncherefull*, fr. ¹*un-* + *chereful*, *cherefull* cheerful] : not cheerful or cheering : GLOOMY ⟨a moody and ~ person⟩ ⟨an ~ place⟩ — **un·cheerfully** \"+\ *adv* — **un·cheer·ful·ness** *n*
un·child \"+\ *vt* [²*un-* + *child*, n.] **1** *archaic* : to bereave of children **2** : to divest of childhood or childlike characteristics
un·chivalrous \"+\ *adj* : not chivalrous : lacking in chivalry ⟨~ scorners of its old maids —G.D.Brown⟩ — **un·chiv·al·rous·ly** *adv*
un·choke \"+\ *vt* [²*un-* + *choke*] : to clear of obstruction ⟨~ the clogged channels of international trade —E.S.Griffith⟩
un·christen \"+\ *vt* [²*un-* + *christen*] : to annul the christening or baptism of

un·christened \"+\ *adj* [ME *uncristned,* fr. ¹*un-* + *cristned,* past part. of *cristnen* to christianize, christen] **:** not made Christian **:** not christened **:** UNNAMED

un·christian \"+\ *adj* **1 :** not of the Christian faith ⟨love for the ~ neighbor —John Dillenberger & Claude Welch⟩ **2 a :** contrary to Christianity or the Christian spirit or character **:** not becoming to or like a Christian ⟨ashamed to have to recognize how fundamentally ~ his actual assumptions, motives, and attitudes are —F.R.Leavis⟩ **b :** BARBAROUS, UNCIVILIZED ⟨sitting up to ~ hours —Arnold Bennett⟩

un·christianize \"+\ *vt* [²*un-* + *christianize*] **:** to make unchristian **:** turn from Christianity

un·chris·tian·ly *adv* **:** in an unchristian manner

un·church \ˌən+\ *vt* [²*un-* + *church,* n.] **1 :** to expel from or cause to be separated from a church **:** EXCOMMUNICATE **2 :** to deprive of a church or of status as a church

un·churched \"+t\ *adj* [¹*un-* + *church,* n. + *-ed*] **:** not belonging to or connected with a church ⟨the vast masses of ~ peoples —J.C.Brauer⟩

unci *pl of* UNCUS

un·cia \ˈənchēə\ *n, pl* **unci·ae** \-ē,ē\ [L — more at OUNCE] **:** a twelfth part: as **a :** INCH **b :** a bronze coin of the ancient Roman republic worth 1/12 as **c :** a bronze coin of ancient Sicily worth 1/12 litra

¹**un·cial** \ˈənchəl\ *adj* [L *uncialis,* fr. *uncia* twelfth part, ounce, inch + *-alis* -al] **1 :** of or relating to an inch or ounce **2** [LL *uncialis,* fr. L] **:** written or in the style or size of uncials ⟨~ script⟩ — **un·cial·ly** \-chəlē\ *adv*

²**uncial** \"\ *n* -s **1 :** a book hand used esp. in Greek and Latin manuscripts of the 4th to the 8th centuries A.D. and consisting of somewhat rounded separated majuscules but having cursive forms for some letters **2 :** an uncial letter **3 :** a manuscript written in uncial

ROMAN UNCIAL

uncials 1

un·cif·er·ous \ˌənˈsif(ə)rəs\ *adj* [*uncus* + *-iferous*] **:** bearing a hook or hooklike structure

¹**un·ci·form** \ˈən(t)səˌfȯrm\ *adj* [NL *unciformis,* fr. LL *unci-* (fr. L *uncus* hook) + L *-formis* -form — more at ANGLE] **:** UNCINATE, HOOKLIKE

²**unciform** \"\ *n* -s [NL *unciforme,* fr. neut. of *unciformis*] **:** HAMATUM

unciform process *n* **1 :** the hamulus of the hamatum **2 :** the uncinate process of the ethmoid bone

un·ciliated \ˌən+\ *adj* **:** not ciliate

un·ci·nal \ˈən(t)sənᵊl\ *adj* [L *uncin*us hook (fr. *uncus* hook) + E *-al*] **:** UNCINATE

un·ci·nar·ia \ˌən(t)səˈna(a)rēə\ *n* [NL, fr. L *uncinus* hook + NL *-aria*] **1** *cap* **:** a genus of hookworms (family Ancylostomatidae) usu. restricted to a few parasites of carnivorous mammals but formerly often including most of the common hookworms **2** -s **:** HOOKWORM

un·ci·na·ri·a·sis \ˌən(t)sənəˈrīəsə̇s\ *n, pl* **uncinaria·ses** \-īəˌsēz\ [NL, fr. *Uncinaria* + *-iasis*] **:** ANCYLOSTOMIASIS

un·ci·nate \ˈən(t)sənə̇t, -səˌnāt\ *adj* [L *uncinatus,* fr. *uncinus* hook + *-atus* -ate] **1 :** bent at the tip like a hook **:** HOOKED **2 a :** of, relating to, or constituting an uncus **b :** affecting or involving the uncinate gyrus; *also* **:** marked by hallucinatory sensations of taste and smell ⟨an ~ fit⟩

un·ci·nat·ed \-səˌnād·əd\ *adj* [L *uncinatus* + E *-ed*] **:** UNCINATE

uncinate gyrus *or* **uncinate convolution** *n* **:** a subdivision of the hippocampal convolution containing olfactory association centers and marked by a thick layer of myelinated fibers upon its surface

uncinate process *n* **1 :** a backwardly directed and often somewhat curved process on many ribs of birds that is in such a position that it crosses or overlaps one or more other ribs and serves to stiffen the walls of the thorax **2 :** an irregular downwardly and backwardly directed process of each lateral mass of the ethmoid bone that articulates with the inferior turbinate bones

un·ci·na·tum \ˌən(t)səˈnād·əm\ *n, pl* **uncina·ta** \-d·ə\ *or* **uncinatums** [NL, fr. L, neut. of *uncinatus*] **:** HAMATUM

un·cin·u·la \ˌənˈsinyələ\ *n, cap* [NL, fr. L *uncinus* hook + *-ula*] **:** a genus of powdery mildews (family Erysiphaceae) having perithecia with several asci and simple or rarely forked appendages hooked or coiled at the apex

un·ci·nus \ˌənˈsīnəs\ *n, pl* **unci·ni** \-īˌnī\ [NL, fr. L, hook] **:** a small hooklike structure or process: as **a :** one of the minute chitinous hooks found in large numbers in the tori of some tubicolous annelids **b :** one of the hooklike lateral teeth of the radula of a gastropod **c :** a hooked cilium of various infusorians

un·circulated \ˌən+\ *adj* [¹*un-* + *circulated,* past part. of *circulate*] *of a coin* **:** issued for use as money but kept out of circulation (as for preservation in a collection) — compare PROOF

un·circumcised \"+\ *adj* [ME, fr. ¹*un-* + *circumcised,* past part. of *circumcisen* to circumcise] **1 :** not circumcised ⟨this ~ Philistine —1 Sam 17:26 (RSV)⟩ **2 :** spiritually impure **:** HEATHEN ⟨it fell into . . . ~ hands —F.H.Ellis⟩

un·circumcision \"+\ *n* **1 a :** the state or condition of being uncircumcised ⟨neither circumcision counts for anything nor ~, but keeping the commandments of God —1 Cor 7:19 (RSV)⟩ **b :** repudiation of one's circumcision **2 :** those not circumcised **:** GENTILES

un·circumscribed \"+\ *adj* [¹*un-* + *circumscribed,* past part. of *circumscribe*] **:** not circumscribed **:** UNBOUNDED

un·circumstantial \"+\ *adj* **:** not circumstantial **:** not entering into minute particulars

un·civil \"+\ *adj* **1 :** not civilized **:** BARBAROUS, SAVAGE ⟨keep them from ~ outrages —Shak.⟩ **2 :** lacking in courtesy **:** ILL-MANNERED, IMPOLITE ⟨want nothing from you but to get away from your ~ tongue —Willa Cather⟩ **3 :** not conducive to civic harmony and welfare ⟨civilization is ~ because human beings are divided into . . . sects, races, nations, classes and cliques —John Dewey⟩ **syn** see RUDE

un·civilized \"+\ *adj* **1 :** not civilized **:** BARBAROUS, RUDE, SAVAGE ⟨fighting is crude and ~, especially if the weapons are efficient —Margaret Mead⟩ ⟨shuddered at the responsibility for getting them up at that ~ hour —Jean & Franc Shor⟩ **2 :** remote from civilization **:** WILD ⟨a hidden river, entirely ~ with no roads or trails touching it —Patricia Spring⟩

un·civilly \"+\ *adv* **:** in an uncivil manner

un·claimed \"+\ *adj* [¹*un-* + *claimed,* past part. of *claim*] **:** not claimed; *specif* **:** not called for by an owner or consignee ⟨~ goods⟩

un·clamp \"+\ *vt* [²*un-* + *clamp*] **:** to loosen the clamp of **:** free from a clamp

un·clarity \"+\ *n* **:** lack of clarity **:** AMBIGUITY, OBSCURITY ⟨the *unclarities* in the theory of instincts —Abram Kardiner⟩

un·clasp \"+\ *vb* [²*un-* + *clasp*] *vt* **1 a :** to open the clasp of ⟨~*ed* his briefcase and took out his notes⟩ **b :** to open or cause to be opened (as a clenched hand) **2** *obs* **:** to open up **:** REVEAL ⟨in her bosom I'll ~ my heart —Shak.⟩ ~ *vi* **:** to loosen a hold or grip

un·classifiable \"+\ *adj* **:** not capable of being classified ⟨this ~ zoological freak —R.K.Buehrle⟩

un·classified \"+\ *adj* **1 :** not placed in or belonging in a class ⟨an ~ specimen⟩ ⟨an ~ student⟩ **2 :** not subject to a security classification ⟨~ documents⟩

¹**un·cle** \ˈəŋkəl\ *n* -s [ME, fr. OF *uncle, oncle,* fr. L *avunculus* mother's brother; akin to OE *ēam* uncle, mother's brother, OHG *ōheim* mother's brother, ON *afi* grandfather, Goth *awo* grandmother, L *avus* grandfather, OIr *aue* grandson, Lith *avynas* mother's brother] **1 a :** the brother of one's father or mother **b :** the husband of one's aunt — often used as a term of affectionate respect for an older man (as a close friend of the family) **2 :** one who helps, advises, or encourages ⟨he played ~ to so many movements —H.G.Wells⟩ **3** *slang* **:** PAWNBROKER ⟨~ gave little for them but you got the money readily —Albert Szent-Györgyi⟩ **4** — used as a cry of surrender ⟨you want me to holler ~, you want me to crawl for you —Maritta Wolff⟩

²**uncle** \"\ *vt* -ED/-ING/-S **:** to refer to as uncle **:** address as uncle ⟨grace me no grace nor ~ me no uncle —Shak.⟩

³**uncle** \"\ *usu cap* — a communications code word for the letter *u*

un·clean \ˌənˈklēn\ *adj* [ME *unclene,* fr. OE *unclǣne,* fr. ¹*un-* + *clǣne* clean] **1 a :** morally impure ⟨something sneaking and ~ about secret code messages —Fletcher Pratt⟩ ⟨feels ~ when he discovers he has been used for an experiment —A.P. Davis⟩ **b :** WICKED ⟨commands even the ~ spirits, and they obey him —Mk 1:27 (RSV)⟩ **2 a :** ritually prohibited as food ⟨an ~ animal⟩ ⟨~ meat⟩ **b :** ceremonially unfit or defiled ⟨people who were ~ in the eyes of the law —C.T.Craig⟩ **3 a :** DIRTY, FILTHY ⟨an ~ shirt⟩ ⟨an ~ glass⟩ **b :** not desirable or wholesome as food — used of fish that have just spawned **4 :** lacking in clarity and precision of conception or execution **:** IMPURE, MUDDLED ⟨a compromised and ~ design —N.W. Sharpe⟩ ⟨had some trouble with her intonation, and much of her double-stopping was ~ —*Musical Digest*⟩ — **un·clean·ness** \-ēnnə̇s\ *n*

unclean hands *n pl* **:** the condition of being guilty of unfair, inequitable, fraudulent, oppressive, or other unconscionable or illegal misconduct constituting grounds for refusing an application for relief in a court of equity

un·clean·li·ness \ˌənˈklenlēnə̇s, -enlin-\ *n* [¹*uncleanly* + *-ness*] **:** the quality or state of being uncleanly

¹**un·clean·ly** \-enlē, -li\ *adj* [ME *unclenly,* fr. OE *unclǣnlic,* fr. ¹*un-* + *clǣnlic* pure — more at CLEANLY] **1 :** morally unclean **:** IMPURE ⟨~ thoughts⟩ **2 :** physically unclean **:** FILTHY ⟨his ~ habits of spitting —Hamlin Garland⟩

²**un·clean·ly** \ˌənˈklēnlē\ *adv* [*unclean* + *-ly*] **:** in an unclean manner

un·clear \ˌən+\ *adj* [ME *unclere,* fr. ¹*un-* + *clere* clear] **1 :** difficult to grasp or understand **:** INDISTINCT, OBSCURE ⟨their descriptions of human behavior become vague, dull, and ~ —P.A.Sorokin⟩ **2 :** confused or uncertain in statement or understanding ⟨are very ~ in their religious thinking —Vilhjalmur Stefansson⟩ ⟨the law itself was ~ as to the distinction —*World's Work*⟩ — **un·clear·ly** *adv* — **un·clear·ness** *n*

un·cleared \"+\ *adj* [¹*un-* + *cleared,* past part. of *clear*] **:** not cleared; *specif* **:** not cleared of trees or brush ⟨~ land⟩

un·cleave \"+\ *vi* [²*un-* + *cleave* (to adhere)] **:** to become detached

un·cleft \"+\ *adj* **:** not cleft

un·cle·hood \ˈəŋkəlˌhu̇d\ *n* **:** the state of being an uncle

uncle–in–law \ˈ⸗⸗,⸗\ *n, pl* **uncles–in–law 1 :** the husband of one's aunt **2 :** the uncle of one's spouse

un·clench \ˌən+\ *vb* [²*un-* + *clench*] *vt* **1 :** to open or force open from a clenched position **:** RELAX ⟨~*ed* his hands⟩ ⟨with a determined effort he ~*ed* her grasp⟩ **2 :** to release from a grip ~ *vi* **:** to become unclasped or relaxed ⟨his hands continued to clench and ~⟩

uncle sam *n, usu cap U&S* [fr. *U. S.,* abbr. of *United States;* prob. fr. an originally jocular interpretation of the letters U. S. stamped on casks of meat supplied to the U.S. Army during the War of 1812 as standing for *Uncle Sam,* nickname of Samuel Wilson †1854 Am. meat packer] **1 :** the U.S. government personified ⟨doesn't like people who work for *Uncle Sam* —Merle Miller⟩ **2 :** the American nation or people ⟨a distorted picture of *Uncle Sam*⟩

un·cle·ship \ˈəŋkəlˌship\ *n* **:** the quality or state of being an uncle

uncle tom *n, usu cap U&T* [after *Uncle Tom,* hero of the novel *Uncle Tom's Cabin* (1851–52) by Harriet Beecher Stowe †1896 Am. author] **:** a Negro having a humble and submissive attitude or philosophy

un·clinch \"+\ *vt* [²*un-* + *clinch*] **:** UNCLENCH

un·clipped *or* **un·clipt** \"+\ *adj* [ME *unclipped,* fr. ¹*un-* + *clipped,* past part. of *clippen* to clip, cut] **:** not clipped ⟨~ hair⟩ ⟨~ wings⟩ ⟨an ~ coin⟩

un·cloak \"+\ *vb* [²*un-* + *cloak*] *vt* **1 :** to remove a cloak or cover from **2 :** REVEAL, UNMASK ~ *vi* **:** to take off a cloak

un·clog \"+\ *vt* [²*un-* + *clog*] **:** to free from a difficulty or obstruction

un·cloister \"+\ *vt* [²*un-* + *cloister*] **:** to release from a cloister or confinement **:** set free

un·close \"+\ *vb* [ME *unclosen,* fr. ²*un-* + *closen* to close] *vt* **1 :** OPEN ⟨~ the window⟩ **2 :** DISCLOSE, REVEAL ~ *vi* **:** to become opened ⟨her eyes *unclosed*⟩

un·closed \"+\ *adj* [ME, fr. ¹*un-* + *closed*] **:** not closed or settled **:** not concluded

un·clothe \"+\ *vt* [ME *unclothen,* fr. ²*un-* + *clothen* to clothe] **1 a :** to strip of clothes **:** UNDRESS **b :** to take cloths from ⟨~ the sails of a windmill⟩ **2 a :** DIVEST ⟨*unclothed* his heart of bitterness⟩ **b :** UNCOVER ⟨*unclothed* his secret thoughts⟩

un·clothed \"+\ *adj* [ME, fr. ¹*un-* + *clothed,* past part. of *clothen* to clothe] **:** not clothed **:** NAKED

un·cloud \ˌən+\ *vb* [²*un-* + *cloud*] *vt* **:** to free from or as if from clouds **:** clear from obscurity or gloom ~ *vi* **:** to become free from clouds

un·clouded \"+\ *adj* [¹*un-* + *clouded,* past part. of *cloud*] **:** not covered by clouds **:** not darkened **:** CLEAR ⟨ideas given to the ~ mind by intuition —S.F.Mason⟩ — **un·cloud·ed·ly** *adv* — **un·cloud·ed·ness** *n* -ES

un·clubbable *also* **un·clubable** \"+\ *adj* **:** not clubbable **:** UNSOCIABLE ⟨an ~ man⟩

un·clutch \"+\ *vt* [²*un-* + *clutch*] **:** UNCLENCH

un·clutter \"+\ *vt* [²*un-* + *clutter*] **:** to make neat and orderly **:** straighten out ⟨instead of trying to clean out or ~ the old one, he would simply build a new shack —G.S.Perry⟩

un·cluttered \"+\ *adj* [¹*un-* + *cluttered,* past part. of *clutter*] **:** not cluttered **:** having nothing extraneous or unnecessary **:** NEAT ⟨his prose is ~, pungent, witty —Nona B. Brown⟩

¹**un·co** \ˈəŋ(ˌ)kō\ *adj* [ME (Sc) *unkow,* alter. of ME *uncouth* strange, unaccustomed — more at UNCOUTH] **1** *chiefly Scot* **a :** STRANGE, UNKNOWN **b :** UNCANNY, WEIRD **2** *chiefly Scot* **:** out of the ordinary **:** REMARKABLE

²**unco** \"\ *adv* **:** EXTREMELY, REMARKABLY ⟨the ~ refined and the queasy had best give it a wide berth —Orville Prescott⟩

³**unco** \"\ *n* -s **1 uncos** *pl, chiefly Scot* **:** NEWS, TIDINGS **2** *chiefly Scot* **:** STRANGER

un·coach \ˌən+\ *vt* [²*un-* + *coach*] **:** to remove from a coach or car

un·coagulable \"+\ *adj* **:** INCOAGULABLE

un·coagulated \"+\ *adj* **:** not coagulated; *specif, of blood* **:** kept from coagulating esp. by additives (as oxalate ion)

un·coated \"+\ *adj* **:** not having a coating ⟨~ paper⟩

un·cock \"+\ *vt* [²*un-* + *cock*] **1 :** to remove the hammer of (a firearm) from a cocked position ⟨~ my gun and went sneaking back on my tiptoes —Mark Twain⟩ **2 :** to let down the brim of (a cocked hat) ⟨his three-cornered hat with one side ~*ed* so that it flapped —Kenneth Roberts⟩

un·codified \"+\ *adj* [¹*un-* + *codified,* past part. of *codify*] **:** not codified ⟨their ~ theology —D.S.Taylor⟩

un·coffin \"+\ *vt* [²*un-* + *coffin*] **:** to remove from or as if from a coffin ⟨~ warfare from the winding sheets of the past —Tom Wintringham⟩

un·coffined \"+\ *adj* [¹*un-* + *coffined,* past part. of *coffin*] **:** not coffined **:** not placed in a coffin

unco guid *n, pl in constr* **:** those who profess a strict morality — used with *the* ⟨the *unco guid* magnified the scandal . . . in order piously to deplore it —R.D.Altick⟩

un·coil \ˌən+\ *vb* [²*un-* + *coil*] *vt* **:** to release or pay out from a coiled state or position **:** UNWIND ⟨~*ing* the scarf from his throat —Eve Langley⟩ ⟨we all ~*ed* ourselves — it had been a tight fit —Thomas Wood †1950⟩ ~ *vi* **:** to become released from a coiled state or position ⟨~*ed* to his full height and glared down on the bewildered bartender —Edna Ferber⟩

un·coiled \"+\ *adj* [¹*un-* + *coiled,* past part. of *coil* (to wind)] **:** not coiled

un·coined \"+\ *adj* [ME *unkoyned,* fr. ¹*un-* + *koyned, coyned,* past part. of *koynen, coynen* to coin] **1 :** not minted ⟨~ metal⟩ **2 :** not fabricated **:** not artificial or counterfeit **:** NATURAL ⟨a fellow of plain and ~ constancy —Shak.⟩

uncolike \ˈ⸗⸗,⸗\ *adj, Scot* **:** STRANGE

un·collected \ˌən+\ *adj* **1 :** not self-composed **:** DISCONCERTED ⟨was in a very ~ and nervous state⟩ **2 :** not gathered into one place or body ⟨his poems are as yet ~ —W.B.Cairns⟩ **3 :** not yet paid ⟨an ~ debt⟩

¹**un·collectible** \"+\ *adj* **:** not capable of being collected ⟨an ~ debt⟩

²**uncollectible** \"\ *n* -s **:** an uncollectible account **:** a bad debt

un·colored \"+\ *adj* **1 :** having no color ⟨~ cloth⟩ ⟨~ paper⟩ **2 :** not distorted by an irrelevant, prejudiced, or deceptive quality or addition ⟨gave a plain ~ account of the accident⟩ **syn** see FAIR

un·colt \"+\ *vt* [²*un-* + *colt,* n.] **:** UNHORSE

un·combed \"+\ *adj* [¹*un-* + *combed,* past part. of *comb*] **:** not combed **:** UNKEMPT ⟨unwashed, ~, with his clothes half buttoned —Hall Caine⟩

un·com·bine \ˌənkəmˈbīn\ *vt* [²*un-* + *combine*] **:** to break apart **:** SEPARATE

un·com·bined \-nd\ *adj* [¹*un-* + *combined,* adj.] **:** not combined **:** FREE

un·come–at–able \ˌən+\ *adj* [¹*un-* + *come-at-able*] **:** INACCESSIBLE, UNATTAINABLE

un·comeliness \"+\ *n* **:** the quality or state of being uncomely

¹**un·comely** \"+\ *adj* [ME *uncomly,* fr. ¹*un-* + *comly* comely] **1 :** not fitting **:** IMPROPER ⟨clumsy, ~ methods of management and care —Brooks Atkinson⟩ **2 :** not pleasing to the sight **:** UNATTRACTIVE ⟨she had always been ~ in his eyes —Agnes Repplier⟩

²**uncomely** *adv* [ME *uncomly,* fr. *uncomly,* adj.] *obs* **:** in an uncomely manner **:** IMPROPERLY ⟨behaveth himself ~ toward his virgin —1 Cor 7:36 (AV)⟩

un·comfortable \ˌən+\ *adj* **1 a :** causing annoyance, embarrassment, or uneasiness **:** DISCONCERTING ⟨has an ~ way of surprising me just when I feel surest —J.O.Hannay⟩ ⟨was at once a valuable and an ~ contributor —M.A.D.Howe⟩ **b :** causing physical discomfort ⟨an ~ chair⟩ ⟨an ~ day⟩ **2 :** feeling discomfort **:** physically or mentally ill at ease **:** UNEASY ⟨even when the heat is not extreme, a sudden rise may make us ~ —Ellsworth Huntington⟩ ⟨grew ~ beneath his sideward, estimating eye —G.D.Brown⟩ — **un·com·fort·a·ble·ness** *n* — **un·comfortably** \"+\ *adv*

un·comforted \"+\ *adj* [¹*un-* + *comforted,* past part. of *comfort*] **:** not comforted

un·comforting \"+\ *adj* **1 :** not giving comfort ⟨a foreign country in wartime . . . is an ~ place to be —Max Beerbohm⟩ **2 :** causing discomfort ⟨vital and sometimes ~ truths —William Plomer⟩

un·comfy \"+\ *adj* **:** UNCOMFORTABLE

un·commercial \"+\ *adj* **1 :** not engaged in or related to commerce **2 :** not based on commercial principles **:** not conducive to financial success ⟨might prove arty and hence ~ —H.E.Clurman⟩

un·commissioned \"+\ *adj* [¹*un-* + *commissioned,* past part. of *commission*] **:** not commissioned

un·committed \"+\ *adj* [¹*un-* + *committed,* past part. of *commit*] **:** not committed; *specif* **:** not obligated or pledged to a particular belief, allegiance, or program ⟨have stayed ~ in the great controversy that divides the world —Patrick O'Donovan⟩

¹**un·common** \ˌən+\ *adj* **1 :** not ordinarily encountered **:** INFREQUENT, RARE ⟨during the worst of the blitz, it was no ~ experience for him to hear a nearby building collapse —*Current Biog.*⟩ **2 :** more than ordinary **:** unusually large or great ⟨has been doing an ~ amount of business —*N. Y. Times*⟩ **3 :** remarkable in character, quality, or kind **:** EXCEPTIONAL, OUTSTANDING ⟨it was to the ~ character and ability of his mother that . . . he owed the greatest debt —C.A.Dinsmore⟩ — **un·com·mon·ly** *adv* — **un·com·mon·ness** *n*

²**uncommon** \"\ *adv, chiefly dial* **:** UNCOMMONLY ⟨the route back . . . was ~ hard —Bernard DeVoto⟩

un·communicable \"+\ *adj* **:** INCOMMUNICABLE

un·communicated \"+\ *adj* [¹*un-* + *communicated,* past part. of *communicate*] **1 :** not communicated **:** not told or imparted **2 :** not having partaken of Communion

un·communicative \"+\ *adj* **1 :** unwilling to talk or impart information ⟨when he works . . . is quiet, withdrawn, ~ —Barbara B. Jamison⟩ ⟨~ regarding plans —*Current Biog.*⟩ **2 :** not disposed to associate with others **:** RESERVED **syn** see SILENT

un·com·mu·ni·ca·tive·ly *adv* **:** in an uncommunicative manner

un·com·mu·ni·ca·tive·ness *n* **:** the quality or state of being uncommunicative

un·compacted \ˌən+\ *adj* [¹*un-* + *compacted,* past part. of *compact* (to compress)] **:** not packed together; *specif* **:** not compressed ⟨~ soil⟩

un·com·pah·gre \ˌənkəmˈpägrē\ *n, pl* **uncompahgre** *or* **uncompahgres** *usu cap* [*Uncompahgre* valley, southwestern Colorado, site of the reservation to which this people was assigned] **1 :** a Ute people of southwestern Colorado **2 :** a member of the Uncompahgre people

un·companied \ˌən+\ *adj* [¹*un-* + *companied,* past part. of *company*] **:** UNACCOMPANIED

un·companionable \"+\ *adj* **:** UNSOCIABLE ⟨thought her morose and ~ —Elmer Davis⟩

un·companioned \"+\ *adj* [¹*un-* + *companioned,* past part. of *companion*] **1 :** having no companion ⟨the ~ boy beyond them working away in almost total darkness —Daniel Corkery⟩ **2 :** marked by a lack of companionship **:** LONELY, SOLITARY ⟨one of those contemplative ~ walks which it was his habit to take —G.W.Cable⟩

un·compassionate \"+\ *adj* **:** HARDHEARTED, UNFEELING ⟨nor silver-shedding tears could penetrate her ~ sire —Shak.⟩

un·compelled \"+\ *adj* [ME, fr. ¹*un-* + *compelled,* past part. of *compellen* to compel] **:** not compelled

un·compensated \"+\ *adj* [¹*un-* + *compensated,* past part. of *compensate*] **:** not compensated or compensated for ⟨this last ~ federal post —*Current Biog.*⟩ ⟨~ differences in polarization at glass surfaces —D.L.Drabkin⟩

un·complaining \"+\ *adj* [¹*un-* + *complaining,* pres. part. of *complain*] **:** not complaining **:** PATIENT ⟨~ courage⟩ — **un·com·plain·ing·ly** *adv* — **un·com·plain·ing·ness** *n*

un·complete \"+\ *adj* [ME *uncomplet,* fr. ¹*un-* + *complet* complete] **:** INCOMPLETE

un·completed \"+\ *adj* [¹*un-* + *completed,* past part. of *complete*] **:** not completed **:** UNFINISHED ⟨an ~ building⟩ ⟨an ~ play⟩

un·complex \"+\ *adj* **:** not complex ⟨an ~, uniform culture —Margaret Mead⟩

un·compliant \ˌən+\ *adj* **:** not compliant **:** INFLEXIBLE

un·complicated \"+\ *adj* [¹*un-* + *complicated,* past part. of *complicate*] **1 :** not complicated by something outside itself ⟨~ adrenal insufficiency —*Jour. Amer. Med. Assoc.*⟩ ⟨men whose understanding is obviously ~ by any personal acquaintance with the classics —Albert Lynd⟩ **2** [¹*un-* + *complicated,* adj.] **:** not complex **:** easy to understand or manage **:** SIMPLE ⟨a big, bouncy, ~ girl —Frances G. Patton⟩ ⟨small and ~ cars for those who are really interested in motoring —*Country Life*⟩

un·complimentary \"+\ *adj* **:** not complimentary **:** DEROGATORY ⟨an ~ remark⟩

un·complying \"+\ *adj* [¹*un-* + *complying,* pres. part. of *comply* (to accord)] **:** not complying **:** RIGID, STIFF ⟨an ~ attitude⟩

un·composed \"+\ *adj* **:** not composed **:** not properly organized **:** SHAPELESS, UNFORMED ⟨the fitness of publishing so ~ a thing —John Howe⟩

un·compounded \"+\ *adj* [¹*un-* + *compounded,* past part. of *compound*] **1 :** not constituting a compound **:** UNMIXED ⟨an ~ substance⟩ **2 :** not involved **:** SIMPLE, UNCOMPLICATED ⟨a simple and ~ idea —Virginia Woolf⟩

un·comprehended \"+\ *adj* [¹*un-* + *comprehended,* past part. of *comprehend*] **:** not understood ⟨an ~ mystery⟩

un·comprehending \"+\ *adj* [¹*un-* + *comprehending,* pres. part. of *comprehend*] **:** not comprehending **:** lacking understanding ⟨her able and ~ father —Harry Levin⟩ ⟨a kind woman and magnificently ~ —Sinclair Lewis⟩ — **un·com·pre·hend·ing·ly** *adv*

un·comprehensible \"+\ *adj* [ME, alter. (influenced by ¹*un-*) of *incomprehensible*] **:** INCOMPREHENSIBLE

un·comprehensive \"+\ *adj* **1** *obs* **:** INCOMPREHENSIBLE **2 :** not comprehensive

un·compressed \"+\ *adj* **:** not compressed

un·compromising \ˌən+\ *adj* [¹*un-* + *compromising,* pres. part. of *compromise*] **1 :** not making or accepting a compromise **:** making no concessions **:** INFLEXIBLE, UNYIELDING ⟨was as conciliatory in the moment of triumph as he had been ~ while the conflict lasted —A.L.Kennedy⟩ **2 :** marked by an absence or avoidance of compromise or concession : being without reservation : WHOLEHEARTED ⟨the same deep sense of duty and ~ honesty which characterized his whole life —J.T. Sellin⟩ — **un·com·pro·mis·ing·ly** *adv* — **un·com·pro·mis·ing·ness** *n* -ES

un·concealed \"+\ *adj* : not concealed : OPEN ⟨regarded him with ~ hatred⟩

un·conceivable \"+\ *adj* [¹*un-* + *conceive* + *-able*] : INCONCEIVABLE — **un·con·ceiv·able·ness** *n* — **un·conceivably** \"+\ *adv*

un·concern \"+\ *n* **1** : lack of care or interest : INDIFFERENCE ⟨~ for the great problems of our day —H.G.Rickover⟩ ⟨a tone of casual ~ —E.T.Thurston⟩ **2** : lack of anxiety ⟨flinging itself with confidence and ~ over wide spaces in the trees —Weston LaBarre⟩

un·concerned \"+\ *adj* [¹*un-* + *concerned*] **1** : lacking care, interest, or feeling ⟨convincing the ~, the apathetic, and the downright hostile —Benjamin Fine⟩ ⟨~ if his girl deserts him —K.E.Read⟩ **2** : not occupied or engaged ⟨readers ~ with style and philosophical illumination —R.A.Cordell⟩ **3** : not anxious or solicitous : easy in mind : not worried ⟨the prisoner seems entirely ~ as to the outcome of the examination —D.D. Martin⟩ **syn** see INDIFFERENT

un·concernedly \"+\ *adv* : in an unconcerned manner

un·concernedness \"+\ *n* : the quality or state of being unconcerned

un·concernment \"+\ *n* [¹*un-* + *concernment*] : UNCONCERN

un·conditional \"+\ *adj* : not limited in any way : not bound or restricted by conditions or qualifications : ABSOLUTE, UNRESERVED ⟨~ surrender⟩ ⟨an ~ offer⟩ ⟨an ~ admirer⟩ — **un·conditionally** \"+\ *adv* — **un·con·di·tion·al·ness** *n* -ES

un·conditionality \"+\ *n* [*unconditional* + *-ity*] : the quality or state of being unconditional

un·conditioned \ˌən+\ *adj* **1 a** : not subject to limitations or conditions : ABSOLUTE, INFINITE ⟨it is a consciousness of the ~ and universal that makes people religious —Clive Bell⟩ **b** : INCONCEIVABLE, UNKNOWABLE **2** : not dependent on conditioning or learning : NATURAL ⟨an ~ response⟩ — **un·con·di·tioned·ness** *n* -ES

unconditioned reflex *n* : a reflex that is inborn or dependent on physiological maturation rather than on learning

un·condoned \ˌən+\ *adj* [¹*un-* + *condoned*, past part. of *condone*] : not condoned

un·confessed \"+\ *adj* [¹*un-* + *confessed*, past part. of *confess*] : not confessed

un·confident \"+\ *adj* : lacking in confidence : UNSURE — **un·con·fi·dent·ly** *adv*

un·confiding \"+\ *adj* : not confiding : UNCOMMUNICATIVE ⟨had been singularly glum and ~ during the last week of preparation —Gerald Beaumont⟩

un·confine \"+\ *vt* [back-formation fr. *unconfined*] : to release from confinement or restraint

un·confined \"+\ *adj* [¹*un-* + *confined*] **1** : not kept within limits : UNBOUNDED, UNCONTROLLED ⟨on with the dance! let joy be ~ —Lord Byron⟩ **2** : not secured or kept confined ⟨her ~ hair fell to her shoulders⟩

un·confirmed \"+\ *adj* **1** *obs* : not instructed : IGNORANT **2** : not finally established or authorized : not settled : TENTATIVE ⟨an ~ letter of credit⟩ **3** : not corroborated or supported by evidence ⟨~ rumors⟩

un·conformability \"+\ *n* : the quality or state of being unconformable

un·conformable \"+\ *adj* **1** : not correspondent ⟨a description ~ to previous accounts⟩ **2** : not conforming; *specif* : not conforming to the practices and teachings of the Church of England esp. as prescribed by the Acts of Uniformity **3** : exhibiting geological unconformity — **un·conformably** \"+\ *adv*

un·conformist \"+\ *n* : NONCONFORMIST

un·conformity \ˌən+\ *n* **1** *archaic* : lack of conformity **2 a** : lack of continuity in deposition between rock strata in contact corresponding to a period of nondeposition, weathering, or erosion either subaerial or subaqueous prior to the deposition of the younger beds and consequently to a gap in the stratigraphic record **b** : the surface of contact between unconformable strata — compare DISCONFORMITY, NONCONFORMITY

un·congeal \"+\ *vi* [²*un-* + *congeal*] : THAW

un·congenial \"+\ *adj* **1 a** : not sympathetic ⟨the ~ roommates were always fighting⟩ **b** : not compatible — used of a plant stock or scions **2 a** : not fitted : UNSUITABLE ⟨their work had been ~ to the social structure and traditions of the land —G.M.Trevelyan⟩ ⟨an ~ soil⟩ **b** : not to one's taste : DISAGREEABLE ⟨the task was ~ to one sensitive to rebuffs —H.K. Rowe⟩ ⟨found the pursuit ~ and resolved to abandon it —U.B.Phillips⟩ — **un·congenially** \"+\ *adv*

un·congeniality \"+\ *n* : the quality or state of being uncongenial

un·connected \"+\ *adj* **1 a** : not joined or grouped together : SEPARATE ⟨the supreme agent by which disparate and hitherto ~ things are brought together in poetry —I.A.Richards⟩ **b** : not coherent : DISJOINTED ⟨spoke in ~ phrases⟩ ⟨an ~ argument⟩ **2** : having no family or other personal ties ⟨a lonely ~ person⟩ — **un·con·nect·ed·ly** *adv* — **un·con·nect·ed·ness** *n*

un·con·quer·able \ˌənˈkäŋk(ə)rəbəl *sometimes* -ˈkōŋ-\ *adj* [¹*un-* + *conquer* + *-able*] **1** : incapable of being conquered : INDOMITABLE ⟨a tribute to his courage, his sagacity, and his ~ will —R.E.Danielson⟩ **2** : incapable of being surmounted : INSUPERABLE ⟨seems to create ~ difficulties in man's life —H.E.Salisbury⟩ — **un·con·quer·able·ness** *n* -ES — **un·con·quer·ably** \-blē\ *adv*

un·conquered \ˌən+\ *adj* [¹*un-* + *conquered*, past part. of *conquer*] : not conquered ⟨this stark, ~ land —Guy Priest⟩

un·conscient \"+\ *adj* : lacking consciousness

un·conscientious \"+\ *adj* : not conscientious — **un·con·sci·en·tious·ly** *adv* — **un·con·sci·en·tious·ness** *n*

¹un·con·scio·na·ble \ˌənˈkänch(ə)nəbəl\ *adj* **1** : not guided or controlled by conscience : UNSCRUPULOUS ⟨an ~ villain⟩ **2 a** : EXCESSIVE, EXORBITANT ⟨advertising and promotion costs an ~ amount —G.P.Brockway⟩ ⟨was staying up there an ~ time —Joseph Conrad⟩ **b** : lying outside the limits of what is reasonable or acceptable : shockingly unfair, harsh, or unjust : OUTRAGEOUS ⟨the grinding poverty, the ~ death rate, and the appalling illiteracy —*Commonweal*⟩

²unconscionable \"\ *adv* : UNCONSCIONABLY

un·con·scio·na·bly \-blē, -li\ *adv* : in an unconscionable manner or to an unconscionable extent

¹un·conscious \ˌən+\ *adj* **1 a** : not knowing or perceiving : not aware ⟨seemed quite ~ of her scrutiny —A.T.Quiller-Couch⟩ ⟨happily ~ of the new calamity at home —Charles Dickens⟩ **b** : free from self-awareness ⟨would never again be quite the same ~ creature —John Galsworthy⟩ **2 a** : not possessing mind or consciousness : NONCONSCIOUS ⟨~ matter⟩ **b** (1) : not marked by conscious thought, sensation, or feeling ⟨~ processes behind conscious mental states⟩ (2) : of or relating to the unconscious **c** : having no consciousness for the time being ⟨he lay inert, breathing heavily and ~ —Dorothy Sayers⟩ **3** : not consciously held, exercised, or displayed : not realized ⟨found in the countryside the profound, ~ content that animals find —Rose Macaulay⟩ ⟨~ bias⟩ **4** : not deliberately planned, organized, or carried out : not consciously directed ⟨is language an ~ collective growth, with a life of its own, beyond individual control —A.L.Guérard⟩ ⟨the ~ choice of words —W.F.Mackey⟩ — **un·con·scious·ly** *adv* — **un·con·scious·ness** *n*

²unconscious \"\ *n* **1** : the absolute principle of the universe according to the doctrine of panpneumatism **2** : the greater part of the psychic apparatus accumulated through life experience that is not ordinarily integrated or available to consciousness yet is manifested as a powerful motive force in overt behavior esp. in neurosis and is often revealed (as through dreams, slips of the tongue, or dissociated acts) **3** : COLLECTIVE UNCONSCIOUS — compare SUBCONSCIOUS

un·consecrated \"+\ *adj* [¹*un-* + *consecrated*, past part. of *consecrate*] : not consecrated

un·consequential \"+\ *adj* : INCONSEQUENTIAL

un·considered \"+\ *adj* [¹*un-* + *considered*, past part. of *consider*] **1** : not considered or worth consideration : INCONSIDERABLE ⟨a snapper-up of ~ trifles —Shak.⟩ ⟨too humble and ~, himself, to view with alarm the discomfiture of his superiors —Katharine F. Gerould⟩ **2** : not resulting from consideration ⟨what he should avoid is prejudice — the holding of ~ opinions —R.B.West⟩

un·consolable \"+\ *adj* [by alter.] : INCONSOLABLE — **un·consolably** \"+\ *adv*

un·consolidated \"+\ *adj* : loosely arranged : not stratified ⟨~ soil⟩

un·consonant \"+\ *adj* : INCONSONANT

un·conspicuous \"+\ *adj* : INCONSPICUOUS

unconstancy *n* [*unconstant* + *-cy*] *obs* : INCONSTANCY

un·constant \ˌən+\ *adj* [ME, fr. ¹*un-* + *constant*] *archaic* : INCONSTANT

un·constellated \"+\ *adj* [¹*un-* + *constellated*, past part. of *constellate*] : not forming part of a constellation ⟨a star in exile, ~ at the south —Hugh McCrae⟩

un·constitutional \"+\ *adj* : not according to or consistent with the constitution of a state or society; *specif* : contrary to the U. S. Constitution — **un·constitutionality** \"+\ *n* — **un·constitutionally** \"+\ *adv*

un·constrained \"+\ *adj* [ME *unconstreynd*, fr. ¹*un-* + *constreynd*, past part. of *constreynen*, *constrainen* to constrain] : not constrained : not acting or done under constraint — **un·constrainedly** \"+\ *adv*

un·constraint \"+\ *n* : freedom from constraint : EASE ⟨there was a perfect ~, and they all seemed to feel like one enormous family —Bernard Pares⟩

un·consumed \"+\ *adj* [¹*un-* + *consumed*, past part. of *consume*] : not consumed

un·con·tain·able \ˌənkən·ˈtānəbəl\ *adj* [¹*un-* + *contain* + *-able*] : not containable : IRREPRESSIBLE ⟨felt ~ indignation —N.M.Pusey⟩

un·contaminated \ˌən+\ *adj* [¹*un-* + *contaminated*, past part. of *contaminate*] : not contaminated ⟨~ primitive societies still going their own way —A.L.Kroeber⟩

un·content \"+\ *adj* [¹*un-* + *content*, adj.] : UNCONTENTED

un·contented \"+\ *adj* : not contented : DISCONTENTED

un·contestable \"+\ *adj* [by alter.] : INCONTESTABLE — **un·contestably** \"+\ *adv*

un·contested \"+\ *adj* [¹*un-* + *contested*, past part. of *contest*] : not contested : UNCHALLENGED ⟨~ superiority⟩

un·continuous \"+\ *adj* : DISCONTINUOUS

un·contradicted \"+\ *adj* [¹*un-* + *contradicted*, past part. of *contradict*] : not contradicted

un·control \"+\ *n* : lack of control ⟨the keen, grey eyes, with their dash of wildness and ~ —H.W.Nevinson⟩

un·controllability \"+\ *n* : the quality or state of being uncontrollable ⟨the ~ of a forest fire whipped by a dry south wind —A.R.Mead⟩

un·controllable \"+\ *adj* [¹*un-* + *controllable*] **1** *obs* : INDISPUTABLE **2** *archaic* : free from the control of a superior power : ABSOLUTE **3** : incapable of being controlled : UNMANAGEABLE ⟨rumor, irresponsible and ~, is dangerous to public morale —F.L.Mott⟩ — **un·con·trol·la·ble·ness** *n* -ES — **un·controllably** \"+\ *adv*

un·con·trolled \ˌənkən·ˈtrōld\ *adj* : not being under control : UNRESTRAINED ⟨the greatest ~ public health problem —G.T. Harrell⟩ — **un·con·trolled·ly** \-l(ə)dlē\ *adv*

un·controvertible \ˌən+\ *adj* : INCONTROVERTIBLE — **un·controvertibly** \"+\ *adv*

un·conventional \"+\ *adj* : not conventional : not bound by or in accordance with convention : being out of the ordinary ⟨~ behavior⟩ ⟨~ weapons⟩ — **un·conventionally** \"+\ *adv*

un·conventionalism \"+\ *n* : UNCONVENTIONALITY

un·conventionality \"+\ *n* : the quality or state of being unconventional

un·conversable \"+\ *adj*, *archaic* : not inclined or suited to conversation or sociability

un·convert \"+\ *vt* [²*un-* + *convert*] : to reverse the conversion of : restore to a state before conversion

un·converted \"+\ *adj* [¹*un-* + *converted*, past part. of *convert*] **1** : not changed in opinion or action; *specif* : not induced to accept a religious faith : UNREGENERATE ⟨the minds of men as yet ~ —H.O.Taylor⟩ **2** : not changed in form or function ⟨~ wood⟩ ⟨a plant that has stood idle, ~ to war use —*Christian Science Monitor*⟩

un·convertibility \"+\ *n* [*unconvertible* + *-ity*] : INCONVERTIBILITY

un·convertible \"+\ *adj* : INCONVERTIBLE — **un·convertibly** \"+\ *adv*

un·convince \ˌən+\ *vt* [²*un-* + *convince*] : to cause to abandon a conviction ⟨a man thus steeled to his beliefs . . . is not easily *unconvinced* —John Dollard⟩

un·convinced \"+\ *adj* [¹*un-* + *convinced*, past part. of *convince*] : not convinced : DUBIOUS ⟨admitted the force of the argument but remained ~⟩

un·convincing \"+\ *adj* : not convincing : IMPLAUSIBLE ⟨as ~ as a forced smile —Jan Struther⟩ — **un·con·vinc·ing·ly** *adv* — **un·con·vinc·ing·ness** *n* -ES

un·convoluted \"+\ *adj* : not convoluted

un·cooked \"+\ *adj* [¹*un-* + *cooked*, past part. of *cook*] : not cooked : RAW ⟨an ~ dish⟩ ⟨an ~ and slapdash theory of human nature —W.L.Sullivan⟩

un·cooled \"+\ *adj* [¹*un-* + *cooled*, past part. of *cool*] : not cooled

un·cooperative \"+\ *adj* : not cooperative : REFRACTORY ⟨an ~ attitude⟩ ⟨an ~ witness⟩

un·coordinated \"+\ *adj* : not coordinated : lacking proper or effective coordination ⟨~ scheduling often resulted in conflicting games in the same neighborhood —*Current Biog.*⟩ ⟨~, scattered agencies —*Scientific American*⟩

un·coquettish \"+\ *adj* : not coquettish : not trifling or insincere ⟨~ behavior⟩ — **un·co·quet·tish·ly** *adv*

uncor *abbr* uncorrected

un·cord \ˌən+\ *vt* [ME *uncorden*, fr. ²*un-* + *cord*, n.] : to release from cords : loosen the cords of

un·cordial \"+\ *adj* : not cordial : lacking in friendly warmth ⟨looked ~ and standoffish as they drove past —H.L.Davis⟩ — **un·cordially** \"+\ *adv*

un·core prist \ˈəŋ,kō(ə)rˈprist\ *n* [AF, still ready] : an old plea at law that payment of a debt was and still is tendered

un·cork \ˌən+\ *vt* [²*un-* + *cork*] **1** : to draw a cork from ⟨~*ed* the bottle of wine⟩ **2 a** : to release from a sealed or pent-up state ⟨~*ed* another surprise last week —*Springfield (Mass.) Union*⟩ **b** : to let go or propel with sudden force ⟨~*ed* a wild pitch that got past the catcher⟩

un·corporal \"+\ *adj*, *archaic* : INCORPOREAL ⟨~ as the light —S.V.Benét⟩

un·corrected \"+\ *adj* [ME, fr. ¹*un-* + *corrected*, past part. of *correcten* to correct] **1** : not made correct : left faulty or wrong ⟨an ~ error⟩ **2** : not subjected to correction or improvement by discipline or guidance ⟨let her children grow up ~⟩ **3 a** : not neutralized ⟨~ astigmatism⟩ **b** : not adjusted ⟨an ~ score⟩

un·corrupt \"+\ *adj* [ME, fr. ¹*un-* + *corrupt*] : INCORRUPT

un·corrupted \"+\ *adj* [ME, fr. ¹*un-* + *corrupted*, past part. of *corrupten* to corrupt] **1** : not subjected to corruption : not decomposed **2** : free from moral corruption : not debased or made corrupt ⟨though his associates were dishonest, he remained ~⟩ ⟨~ values⟩ — **un·cor·rupt·ed·ly** *adv* — **un·cor·rupt·ed·ness** *n*

un·corruptible \"+\ *adj* [ME, fr. ¹*un-* + *corruptible*] *archaic* : INCORRUPTIBLE ⟨the glory of the ~ God —Rom 1:23 (AV)⟩

un·cor·rupt·ness *n* [*uncorrupt* + *-ness*] *archaic* : the quality or state of being incorrupt

un·corseted \ˌən+\ *adj* [¹*un-* + *corset* + *-ed*] **1** : not wearing a corset **2** : not controlled, inhibited, or restricted ⟨their language is as ~ and as robust as English —Harrison Smith⟩

uncos *pl of* UNCO

un·costly \"+\ *adj* : INEXPENSIVE

¹un·countable \"+\ *adj* **1 a** : INNUMERABLE ⟨~ shingles devastated by white ants —William Beebe⟩ **b** : impossible to count ⟨uncounted and ~ sums paid out by various individuals for electioneering activities of their own —*Nation*⟩ **2** : INESTIMABLE ⟨a source of ~ joy⟩

²uncountable \"\ *n* : MASS NOUN

un·counted \"+\ *adj* [ME *uncountit*, fr. ¹*un-* + *countit*, past part. of *counten* to count] **1** : not counted ⟨a stack of ~ bills⟩ **2** : INNUMERABLE ⟨~ millions of people —W.J.Reilly⟩

un·couple \"+\ *vb* [ME *uncouplen*, fr. ²*un-* + *couplen* to couple] *vt* **1** : to loose (dogs) from a couple : RELEASE ⟨*uncoupled* the hounds⟩ **2** : DETACH, DISCONNECT ⟨~*s* the 20-foot lengths of aluminum pipe —W.C.Fournier⟩ ⟨~ railroad cars⟩ ⟨~ their minds from all their usual interests —Susanne K. Langer⟩ **3** : to throw off or release a coupler of (a pipe organ) ~ *vi* **1** : to unleash hounds for the chase ⟨~ in the western valley; let them go —Shak.⟩ **2** : to detach a connection ⟨don't ~ until she drains —Wirt Williams⟩

un·coursed \"+\ *adj* [¹*un-* + *course*, n. + *-ed*] : not laid or placed in courses — used of masonry

un·courteous \"+\ *adj* [ME *uncurteis*, fr. ¹*un-* + *curteis* courteous] : lacking in courtesy ⟨the idea of being ~ to any man in my own house is particularly grievous to me —Anthony Trollope⟩ — **un·cour·te·ous·ly** *adv* — **un·cour·te·ous·ness** *n*

un·courtly \"+\ *adj* **1** : not suitable for a court : lacking in courtliness ⟨a little squat, ~ figure —Laurence Sterne⟩ **2** : not favoring a court ⟨an ~ faction⟩

un·couth \ˌənˈküth\ *adj* [ME, fr. OE *uncūth*, fr. ¹*un-* + *cūth* known, familiar — more at COUTH] **1 a** *archaic* : not known or familiar to one : UNACCUSTOMED ⟨toiled out my ~ passage —John Milton⟩ **b** *archaic* : seldom experienced : WONDERFUL, UNCOMMON, RARE **c** *obs* : MYSTERIOUS, UNCANNY ⟨surprised with an ~ fear —Shak.⟩ **d** : not usually or normally encountered or used : ODD, UNFAMILIAR ⟨the air was full of the sounds of ~ instruments —Arnold Bennett⟩ ⟨whipped the crutch out of his armpit, and sent that ~ missile hurtling through the air —R.L.Stevenson⟩ **2 a** : seldom visited or frequented : DESOLATE, SOLITARY ⟨if this ~ forest yield anything savage —Shak.⟩ **b** : UNCOMFORTABLE, UNPLEASANT ⟨found conditions rough and ~ —E.M.Coulter⟩ **3 a** : strange or clumsy in shape or appearance : OUTLANDISH ⟨crouching down behind the bulwarks, ~ in his equipment —Nevil Shute⟩ ⟨made his own glass, thick and ~ but homemade —O.S.J. Gogarty⟩ **b** : lacking in polish and grace : RUGGED ⟨a composer with a bold, ~ quality —Aaron Copland⟩ ⟨the essential jargon is necessarily ~ —*Times Lit. Supp.*⟩ **c** : awkward and uncultivated in appearance, manner, or behavior : RUDE ⟨the inherent courtesy and tenderness of the untutored and ~ human being —Harrison Smith⟩ **d** : marked by or revealing a lack of cultivation and refinement : BOORISH ⟨their laughter was often ~, often boastful —Bergen Evans⟩ ⟨~ to converse while at meals —Nora Waln⟩ ⟨embarrassed by the ~ stare —Liam O'Flaherty⟩ — **un·couth·ly** *adv* — **un·couth·ness** *n* -ES

un·covenanted \ˌən+\ *adj* [¹*un-* + *covenanted*, past part. of *covenant*] **1 a** : not granted or entered into under a covenant; *specif* : not assured by divine promises or conditions ⟨the ~ mercies of God⟩ **b** : not having entered into relationship with God through the appointed means **2 a** : not having joined in a league or assented to a covenant or agreement; *specif* : not having signed or adhered to the Scottish National Covenant of 1638 or the Solemn League and Covenant of 1643 **b** : not employed under a covenant ⟨served for many years as an ~ official of the Indian Civil Service⟩ — compare COVENANTED 1a

un·cover \"+\ *vb* [ME *uncoveren*, fr. ²*un-* + *coveren* to cover] *vt* **1** : to make known : bring to light : DISCLOSE, REVEAL ⟨~*ing* political scandals —*Phoenix Flame*⟩ ⟨acquaintance with her ~*s* the reason for this success —S.J.Beck⟩ **2 a** : to expose to view by removing some covering object or material ⟨fragments ~*ed* by excavating parties —*Amer. Guide Series: Pa.*⟩ ⟨~*ed* seventy villages in the valley —*Current Biog.*⟩ **b** : to lay bare by removing clothes from ⟨opened his shirt to ~ his chest⟩ **c** : to drive (as a fox) from cover **3 a** : to take the cover from : divest of covering ⟨~ the box⟩ **b** : to take off the hat from ⟨~*ed* his head⟩ **4 a** : to expose (a line of soldiers) by the moving of forward units to right or left **b** : to deprive of protection : leave open to enemy fire or attack ~ *vi* **1** : to remove a cover or covering ⟨~, dogs, and lap —Shak.⟩ **2** : to take off the hat as a token of respect : bare one's head ⟨the crowd stood and the men ~*ed* —Tom Lea⟩

un·covered \"+\ *adj* [ME *uncovert*, fr. ¹*un-* + *covert*, *covered*, past part. of *coveren* to cover] **1** : not supplied with a cover or covering ⟨an ~ pit⟩: as **a** : having no roof ⟨an ~ shed⟩ **b** : BARE ⟨~ legs⟩ **c** : BAREHEADED ⟨was caught ~ by the downpour⟩ **2** : not protected: as **a** : not covered by insurance or included in a social insurance or welfare program **b** : not covered by collateral ⟨an ~ note⟩ **3** : not taken care of; *specif* : not provided with a teacher ⟨an ~ class⟩

un·cowl \"+\ *vt* [²*un-* + *cowl*] : to remove a cowl or similar covering from ⟨think us friends — ~ your face —S.T.Coleridge⟩

un·creased \"+\ *adj* [¹*un-* + *creased*, past part. of *crease*] : lacking a crease ⟨~ trousers⟩

¹un·create \"+\ *adj* [¹*un-* + *create*, adj.] : UNCREATED

²un·create \"+\ *vt* [²*un-* + *create*, v.] : to deprive of existence : ANNIHILATE

un·created \"+\ *adj* [¹*un-* + *created*, past part. of *create*] **1** : not existing by creation : ETERNAL, SELF-EXISTENT **2** : not yet created ⟨misery ~ till the crime of thy rebellion —John Milton⟩ — **un·cre·at·ed·ness** *n*

un·creation \"+\ *n* [²*uncreate* + *-ion*] : the act of uncreating

un·creative \"+\ *adj* : not creative : STERILE ⟨an ~ imagination⟩ — **un·cre·a·tive·ness** *n*

un·creditable \ˌən+\ *adj* : DISCREDITABLE

un·credited \"+\ *adj* [¹*un-* + *credited*, past part. of *credit*] : not credited : not believed or trusted ⟨what the light of your mind . . . pronounces incredible . . . leave ~ —Thomas Carlyle⟩

un·crippled \"+\ *adj* [¹*un-* + *crippled*, past part. of *cripple*] : not crippled or deformed ⟨grow up emotionally ~ —Alfred Werner⟩

un·critical \"+\ *adj* **1** : not critical : lacking in discrimination : not evaluating or judging ⟨she was absolutely ~, she believed everything —Audrey Barker⟩ ⟨a devoted, almost ~ admirer —D.W.Brogan⟩ **2** : marked by a disregard for or improper use of critical standards or procedures ⟨news sources reflected ~ estimates of the number of juvenile addicts —D.W. Maurer & V.H.Vogel⟩ — **un·critically** \"+\ *adv*

un·criticized \"+\ *adj* [¹*un-* + *criticized*, past part. of *criticize*] : not subjected to criticism ⟨many of the most ~ concepts of science and philosophy are . . . human constructions —J.W. Krutch⟩

un·cropped \"+\ *adj* [¹*un-* + *cropped*, past part. of *crop*] **1** : not cut or picked : not browsed ⟨~ flowers⟩ **2** : not subjected to cutting or trimming ⟨~ hair⟩ ⟨an ~ dog⟩ ⟨the dog's ~ ears⟩ **3** : not used for a crop : not cultivated ⟨~ soil⟩ ⟨~ land⟩

un·cross \"+\ *vt* [²*un-* + *cross*] : to change the position of so as no longer to be crossed ⟨~*ed* her legs and smoothed her skirt —J.P.Marquand⟩

un·crowded \"+\ *adj* : not crowded : having or allowing sufficient room ⟨an ~ train⟩ ⟨an ~ view⟩

un·crown \"+\ *vt* [ME *uncrounen*, fr. ²*un-* + *crounen* to crown] **1** : to deprive of a crown : DEPOSE, DETHRONE **2** : to reveal as if by taking off a crown : DISPLAY

un·crowned \"+\ *adj* [¹*un-* + *crowned*] **1** : not having or wearing a crown ⟨the coin shows an ~ head⟩ **2** : having royal power or status without formal royal rank or title ⟨an almost mythical figure, one of the ~ rulers of Europe and Asia —*Manchester Guardian Weekly*⟩

un·crumple \"+\ *vb* [²*un-* + *crumple*] *vt* : to smooth the creases and wrinkles from ⟨*uncrumpled* the letter . . . laid it on his knee, and ironed it with the palm of his hand —J.F. Powers⟩ ~ *vi* : to become free from creases or wrinkles

un·crystallized \"+\ *adj* : not crystallized; *specif* : not finally or definitely formed ⟨~ ideas⟩

unct *abbr* uncut

unc·tion \ˈəŋ(k)shən\ *n* -S [ME *unctioun*, *unccioun*, fr. L *unction-*, *unctio* act of anointing, fr. *unctus* (past part. of *unguere* to anoint, smear) + *-ion-*, *-io* -ion — more at OINTMENT] **1 a** : the act of anointing that is a symbol of consecration ⟨this act of ~, not the act of crowning, which is the essential feature of a coronation —H.V.Morton⟩ **b** (1) : the anointing of the sick with oil that is a religious rite of healing (2) *often cap* : the seventh and last sacrament of the Eastern Orthodox Church — compare EXTREME UNCTION, HOLY UNCTION **2** : a benign spiritual influence ⟨all human systems based on material premises are minus the ~ of divine Science —Mary B. Eddy⟩ **3 a** : the application of a soothing or lubricating oil or ointment **b :** something that is used for anointing **:** OINTMENT, UNGUENT ⟨bought an ~ of a mountebank —Shak.⟩ **c :** something that soothes or eases ⟨lay not that flattering ~ to your soul —Shak.⟩ **4 a :** religious or spiritual fervor or the expression (as in language or manner) of such fervor ⟨was always a powerful preacher; but oh, the ~ of the discourse this morning —George Borrow⟩ **b :** exaggerated, assumed, or superficial earnestness of language or manner **:** UNCTUOUSNESS ⟨students like polemics, but they detest preachment and they loathe ~ —H.N.Fairchild⟩ **c :** an earnest and sympathetic absorption in something one is acting, doing, or speaking ⟨an intelligent, not very original man — but doing his work with pleasant ~ —O.W.Holmes †1935⟩

unc·tion·al \-shənᵊl, -shnəl\ *adj* [*unction* + *-al*] **:** full of or characterized by spiritual or devotional fervor

unc·tion·less \-shənləs\ *adj* **:** lacking in unction

unc·tious \ˈəŋ(k)shəs\ *adj* [ME *unctius*, alter. (influenced by *unctioun* unction) of *unctuous*] **:** UNCTUOUS — **unc·tious·ness** *n* -ES

unc·tu·os·i·ty \ˌəŋ(k)chəˈwäsəd·ē, -sətē, -i\ *n* -ES [ME *unctuosite*, fr. MF or ML; MF *unctuosité*, fr. ML *unctuositat-*, *unctuositas*, fr. *unctuosus* unctuous + L *-itat-*, *-itas* -ity] **:** the quality or state of being unctuous

unc·tu·ous \ˈəŋ(k)chəwəs, -)chəs, -)sh-\ *adj* [ME, fr. MF or ML; MF *unctueux*, fr. ML *unctuosus*, irreg. fr. L *unctum* ointment (fr. neut. of *unctus*, past part. of *unguere* to anoint) + *-osus* -ous — more at OINTMENT] **1 a :** having the nature or qualities of an unguent or ointment **:** FATTY, GREASY, OILY ⟨rubbed on an ~ preparation⟩ **b :** rich in oil or fat **:** containing a great deal of grease ⟨it took floods of drink to wash down these ~ and heavily flavored courses —Silas Spitzer⟩ **c :** having some of the nature or qualities of grease ⟨an ~ vapor⟩ **d :** smooth and greasy in texture or appearance ⟨~ with kitchen smoke —Nathaniel Hawthorne⟩ **:** suggestive of fat or grease ⟨~ feel⟩ **2 a :** rich in organic matter and easily workable ⟨~ soil⟩ **b :** PLASTIC ⟨a layer of fine ~ clay —C.O.Dunbar⟩ **3 :** full of unction; *esp* **:** revealing or marked by a smug, ingratiating, and false earnestness or spirituality **:** OILY ⟨the devastating portrait of the ~ literary opportunist —R.A Cordell⟩ ⟨his ~ morality, which sickens later ages —Roy Lewis & Angus Maude⟩ — **unc·tu·ous·ly** *adv* — **unc·tu·ous·ness** *n* -ES

un·culled \ˈ¦ən+\ *adj* [1*un-* + *culled*, past part. of *cull*] **:** not subjected to culling

un·cultivable \"+\ *adj* **:** not able to be cultivated ⟨thickets of indigenous trees are preserved on ~ land —C.B.Palmer⟩

un·cultivatable \"+\ *adj* **:** UNCULTIVABLE

un·cultivated \"+\ *adj* **1 a :** lacking in education or refinement **:** UNCULTURED ⟨the people are ignorant and ~ —Edmund Wilson⟩ **b :** BARBAROUS, UNCIVILIZED ⟨an ~ age⟩ **2 a :** not put under cultivation **:** not tilled ⟨~ land⟩ **b :** growing or developing without care ⟨an ~ plant⟩ **3 :** not developed by training or education ⟨an ~ genius⟩

un·cultivation \"+\ *n* **:** lack of cultivation

un·culture \"+\ *n* **:** lack of culture ⟨ignorance, ~ or, at the best, mediocrity has triumphed —Malcolm Cowley⟩

un·cultured \"+\ *adj* [1*un-* + *cultured*, past part. of *culture*] **1 :** not subjected to cultivation ⟨a wild ~ scene —T.L.Peacock⟩ **2 :** not improved or refined by education **:** BACKWARD ⟨its dreary, unjust, and ~ society —Edward Shils⟩

un·cumbered \"+\ *adj* [1*un-* + *cumbered*, past part. of *cumber*] **:** UNENCUMBERED

un·curable \"+\ *adj* [by alter.] **:** INCURABLE

uncurbable *adj* [1*un-* + *curb* + *-able*] *obs* **:** not capable of being curbed

un·curbed \ˈ¦ən+\ *adj* [1*un-* + *curbed*, past part. of *curb*] **:** not curbed **:** not restrained or held back ⟨sat erect in his saddle with the innate confidence of the ~ —Francis Hackett⟩

un·cured \"+\ *adj* [1*un-* + *cured*, past part. of *cure*] **1 :** not made healthy ⟨an ~ wound⟩ ⟨an ~ patient⟩ **2 :** not subjected to a preservative process ⟨~ hides⟩ ⟨~ meat⟩

un·curious \"+\ *adj* **:** INCURIOUS

un·curl \"+\ *vb* [2*un-* + *curl*] *vi* **:** to become straightened out from a curled or coiled position ~ *vt* **:** to straighten the curls of **:** UNROLL

un·curled \"+\ *adj* [1*un-* + *curled*, past part. of *curl*] **:** not having curls ⟨~ hair⟩ **:** not having a curled shape or position ⟨lay ~ on the bed⟩

un·current \"+\ *adj* **:** not current; *specif* **:** not passing in common payment **:** not receivable at par or full value ⟨~ coins⟩

un·curse \"+\ *vt* [2*un-* + *curse*] **:** to free from a curse ⟨somebody discovered that it was a moral book, and so a good many people *uncursed* him —*Manchester Guardian Weekly*⟩

un·cursed \"+\ *adj* [1*un-* + *cursed*, adj.] **:** not cursed or afflicted ⟨his dialogue is ~ with flabbiness —John Mason Brown⟩

un·curtain \"+\ *vt* [2*un-* + *curtain*] **:** to remove a curtain from **:** REVEAL, UNVEIL

un·curtained \"+\ *adj* [1*un-* + *curtained*, past part. of *curtain*] **:** not having a curtain ⟨the ~ windows⟩

un·cus \ˈəŋkəs\ *n, pl* **un·ci** \ˈənˌsī\ [NL, fr. L, hook, barb — more at ANGLE] **:** HOOK, CLAW: as **a :** the anterior curved end of the hippocampal convolution **b :** the head of the malleus of the mastax in a rotifer that is often hooked or bears one or more teeth **c** (1) **:** a median beaked plate or process dorsal to the copulatory apparatus of a male insect (2) **:** an appendix of the copulatory bulb in a male spider

un·customary \"+\ *adj* **:** not customary **:** RARE, UNCOMMON ⟨an ~ access of rage shook my body —L.A.Fiedler⟩

un·customed \"+\ *adj* [in sense 1, fr. ME, fr. 1*un-* + *custom*, *customs* + *-ed;* in other senses, fr. 1*un-* + *customed*, past part. of *custom*] **1 :** not having passed through the customs ⟨was charged with being in possession of ~ goods —*Auckland* (*New Zealand*) *Weekly News*⟩ **2** *archaic* **:** UNACCUSTOMED **3** *archaic* **:** UNUSUAL

un·cut \"+\ *adj* [ME *unkitt*, fr. 1*un-* + *kitt* cut] **1 a :** not subjected to a cut or incision (as with a knife) ⟨glad to get out of the house with my throat ~ —Tobias Smollett⟩ **b :** not subjected to cutting ⟨~ grass⟩ ⟨~ trees⟩ **2 :** not reduced or shaped by cutting ⟨an ~ diamond⟩ **3** *of a book or periodical* **:** having leaves whose edges have not been trimmed subsequent to the printing of the sheets; *broadly* **:** not having the folds of the leaves slit — compare UNOPENED **4 :** not abridged or curtailed ⟨an ~ text⟩ ⟨an ~ performance of the opera⟩

uncut velvet *n* **:** a velvet with a looped pile

un·dam \ˈ¦ən+\ *vt* [2*un-* + *dam*] **:** to release from or as if from a dam

un·damaged \"+\ *adj* [1*un-* + *damaged*, past part. of *damage*] **:** not damaged or injured **:** UNHURT, SOUND

un·da mar·is \ˈəndəˈma(a)rəs\ *n* [NL, lit., wave of the sea] **:** an 8-foot pipe organ stop producing undulations from two ranks of pipes tuned slightly apart or from one rank tuned slightly flat and used in connection with other stops — compare VOIX CELESTE

un·damped \ˈ¦ən+\ *adj* [1*un-* + *damped*, past part. of *damp*] **1 :** not stifled or checked **:** not depressed ⟨proceed with ~ ardor⟩ **2 :** not checked or retarded by a damper ⟨~ vibrations⟩ ⟨~ musical strings⟩ **3 :** not dampened by moisture **4** *of an electrical or mechanical oscillation* **:** not damped **:** maintained with undiminished amplitude

undamped waves *n pl* **:** CONTINUOUS WAVES

un·dangerous \"+\ *adj* **:** not dangerous

un·daring \"+\ *adj* **:** not daring **:** afraid or unwilling to venture or take risks **:** TIMID

un·darkened \"+\ *adj* [1*un-* + *darkened*, past part. of *darken*] **:** not darkened **:** CLEAR

un·dashed \"+\ *adj* [1*un-* + *dashed*, past part. of *dash*] **1 :** not dashed **:** not qualified or diluted ⟨belief ~ with doubt⟩ **:** UNDAUNTED **2 :** provided with no dash

un·datable \"+\ *adj* **:** not capable of being given a date

un·dated \"+\ *adj* [1*un-* + *dated*, past part. of *date*] **1 :** not dated **:** bearing no date ⟨an ~ letter⟩ **2 :** having no specified date of termination **:** having no limit or no end ⟨~ securities⟩

un·daughterliness \"+\ *n* **:** attitude or behavior unbecoming a daughter

un·daughterly \"+\ *adj* [1*un-* + *daughterly*] **:** unbecoming a daughter

un·daunt·able \ˈ¦ən¦dȯntəbəl, -dän-, -dȧn-\ *adj* [1*un-* + *daunt*, v. + *-able*] **:** incapable of being daunted **:** INTREPID, FEARLESS, INDOMITABLE

un·daunted \ˈ¦ən+\ *adj* [1*un-* + *daunted*, past part. of *daunt*] **:** not daunted **:** courageous with an undiminished resolution or boldness **:** UNDISMAYED, UNDASHED ⟨~ by repeated failure⟩ ⟨~ in the face of death⟩ **syn** see BRAVE

un·daunt·ed·ly *adv* **:** in an undaunted manner **:** with undiminished spirit or courage

un·daunt·ed·ness *n* -ES **:** unshaken courage or resolution

un·dazzled \ˈ¦ən+\ *adj* [1*un-* + *dazzled*, past part. of *dazzle*] **:** not dazzled

un·dé *or* **un·dée** \ˈəndā\ *or* **on·dé** \ōⁿˈdā\ *or* **on·dy** \ˈändē\ *or* **un·dy** \ˈəndē\ *adj* [AF *undé* & *undee* (fem. of *undé*), fr. OF *unde, onde* wave (fr. L *unda*) + *-é* (fr. L *-atus* -ate) — more at WATER] **:** WAVING, WAVY — used of division lines

un·dead \ˈ¦ən+\ *n, pl* **undead :** VAMPIRE 1 — used with *the*

un·dealt \"+\ *adj* [1*un-* + *dealt*, past part. of *deal*] **:** not dealt ⟨~ cards⟩ ⟨problems still ~ with⟩

un·dear \"+\ *adj* **:** not dear **:** DISESTEEMED, CHEAP

un·debatable \"+\ *adj* **:** not subject to debate **:** INDISPUTABLE ⟨~ facts⟩

un·debauched \"+\ *adj* **:** INNOCENT, UNCORRUPTED

undec- *comb form* [L *undecim*, prob. fr. *unus* one + *decem* ten — more at ONE, TEN] **:** eleven ⟨*undec*ane⟩ ⟨*undec*ennial⟩ ⟨*undec*illion⟩

un·dec·a·gon \ˌənˈdekəˌgän\ *n* -S [*undec-* + *-agon* (as in *decagon*)] **:** a plane figure having eleven angles and eleven sides

un·de·cane \ˈəndəˌkān, ˌənˈdeˌ-\ *n* -S [*undec-* + *-ane*] **:** any of several liquid isomeric paraffin hydrocarbons $C_{11}H_{24}$; *esp* **:** the normal hydrocarbon $CH_3(CH_2)_9CH_3$ — called also *hendecane*

un·dec·a·no·ic acid \ˈ¦ən¦dekə¦nōik-\ *n* [*undecane* + *-oic*] **:** a crystalline acid $CH_3(CH_2)_9COOH$ usu. made by hydrogenation of undecylenic acid — called also *undecylic acid*

un·deceivable \ˈ¦ən+\ *adj* **1** *obs* **:** not deceiving **:** not deceitful **2 :** not capable of being deceived ⟨~ common sense⟩

un·deceive \"+\ *vt* [2*un-* + *deceive*] **:** to free from deception, fraud, fallacy, or mistaken ideas **:** set straight **:** DISABUSE — **un·deceiver** \"+\ *n*

un·dec·e·no·ic acid \ˈ¦ən¦desə¦nōik-\ *n* [*undec-* + *-ene* + *-oic*] **:** any of several isomeric straight-chain unsaturated acids $C_{10}H_{19}COOH$ (as undecylenic acid)

un·decent \ˈ¦ən+\ *adj, archaic* **:** INDECENT

un·de·cep·tion \ˌəndəˈsepshən\ *n* **:** the act of undeceiving **:** a being undeceived

un·decidable \ˈ¦ən+\ *adj* **:** not capable of being decided

un·decided \"+\ *adj* [1*un-* + *decided*, past part. of *decide*] **1 :** not yet determined **:** UNSETTLED **2 :** WAVERING, INCONSTANT, IRRESOLUTE ⟨fitful, ~ rain on the face of the land —Rudyard Kipling⟩ — **un·de·cid·ed·ly** *adv* — **un·de·cid·ed·ness** *n*

un·de·cil·lion \ˌəndəˈsilyən\ *n, often attrib* [*undec-* + *-illion* (as in *million*)] — see NUMBER table

un·decimal \ˈ¦ən¦desəməl\ *adj* [*undec-* + *-imal* (as in *decimal*)] **:** numbered or proceeding by elevens **:** based on the number 11

un·de·ci·pher·abil·i·ty \ˈ¦əndəˌsīfərə¦biləd·ē\ *n* **:** the quality or state of being undecipherable

un·decipherable \ˈ¦ən+\ *adj* **:** not capable of being deciphered ⟨scratched with marks which were long ~ —Charlton Laird⟩ ⟨looked at him with a face which was quite ~ —G.K.Chesterton⟩ — **un·decipherably** \"+\ *adv*

un·deciphered \"+\ *adj* [1*un-* + *deciphered*, past part. of *decipher*] **:** not deciphered

un·decisive \"+\ *adj* **:** INDECISIVE — **un·decisively** \"+\ *adv* — **un·decisiveness** \"+\ *n*

un·deck \"+\ *vt* [2*un-* + *deck*] **:** to divest of ornament

un·decked \"+\ *adj* [in sense 1, fr. 1*un-* + *decked*, past part. of *deck*, v.; in sense 2, fr. 1*un-* + *deck*, n. + *-ed*] **1 :** not decked **:** UNADORNED **2 :** not having a deck ⟨~ rowboat⟩

un·declared \"+\ *adj* [1*un-* + *declared*, past part. of *declare*] **:** not declared **:** not announced or openly acknowledged ⟨~ war⟩ ⟨~ emergency⟩

un·declinable \"+\ *adj* [1*un-* + *decline*, v. + *-able*] **1 :** INDECLINABLE **2 :** that cannot be refused or rejected ⟨~ offer⟩ **3** *obs* **:** UNAVOIDABLE — **un·de·clin·able·ness** *n* -ES — **un·de·clin·ably** \-blē\ *adv*

un·declined \ˈ¦ən+\ *adj* [1*un-* + *declined*, past part. of *decline*] **:** having no inflected forms ⟨~ noun⟩

un·de·co·ic acid \ˈ¦əndə¦kōik-\ *n* [*undecane* + *-oic*] **:** any of the monocarboxylic acids $C_{10}H_{21}COOH$ derived from the undecanes

un·decomposable \ˈ¦ən+\ *adj* **:** not subject to decomposing or division ⟨a soul postulated as ~ and immortal activity —M.T. Keeton⟩ ⟨a feeling is a simple and ~ mental state —G.S. Brett⟩

un·decomposed \"+\ *adj* **:** not decomposed

un·decorated \"+\ *adj* **:** not decorated **:** left without ornament or embellishment **:** PLAIN ⟨~ arch⟩ ⟨~ facts⟩

un·decorative \"+\ *adj* [1*un-* + *decorate* + *-ive*] **:** not decorative ⟨~ use of adjectives —Josephine Miles⟩; *sometimes* **:** UNSIGHTLY, UGLY

un·decorous \"+\ *adj* **:** INDECOROUS

un·decorticated \"+\ *adj* [1*un-* + *decorticated*, past part. of *decorticate*] **:** not decorticated **:** WHOLE ⟨~ cottonseed⟩

un·decyl \ˈ¦ən¦desəl, -dēs-\ *n* [ISV *undec-* + *-yl*] **:** an alkyl radical $C_{11}H_{23}$ derived from an undecane; *esp* **:** the normal radical $CH_3(CH_2)_9CH_2$ — called also *hendecyl*

un·dec·y·len·ate \ˌənˌdesəˈleˌnāt, -ˈlēˌ-\ *n* -S [*undecylenic* + *-ate*] **:** a salt or ester of undecylenic acid

un·dec·y·len·ic acid \ˈ¦=¦==¦lenik-, -lēnik-\ *n* [*undecylene* $C_{11}H_{22}$ (fr. *undecyl* + *-ene*) + *-ic*] **:** a liquid or crystalline acid $CH_2{=}CH(CH_2)_8COOH$ that is a component of perspiration, that is formed from ricinoleic acid in the vacuum distillation of castor oil, and that is used sometimes in the form of a salt in the treatment of fungous infections esp. of the skin; 10-undecenoic acid

un·de·cyl·ic acid \ˈ¦əndə¦silik-\ *n* [*undecyl* + *-ic*] **:** UNDECOIC ACID; *esp* **:** UNDECANOIC ACID

un·dedicated \ˈ¦ən+\ *adj* **:** not dedicated

undée *var of* UNDÉ

undeeded *adj* [1*un-* + *deed*, n. + *-ed*] *obs* **:** not exploited in deeds ⟨my sword . . . I sheathe again ~ —Shak.⟩

un·defaced \ˈ¦ən+\ *adj* [ME, fr. 1*un-* + *defaced*, past part. of *defacen* to deface — more at DEFACE] **:** not defaced or obliterated

un·de·feat·able \ˈ¦əndə¦fēd·əbəl\ *adj* [1*un-* + *defeat*, v. + *-able*] **:** incapable of being defeated or of accepting defeat **:** UNCONQUERABLE, INVINCIBLE

un·defeated \ˈ¦ən+\ *adj* [1*un-* + *defeated*, past part. of *defeat*] **:** not defeated **:** not having suffered a defeat ⟨the team was ~ and untied all season⟩

un·defendable \"+\ *adj* **:** not capable of being defended esp. by military action ⟨~ islands⟩ — **un·de·fend·able·ness** *n* -ES

un·defended \"+\ *adj* [1*un-* + *defended*, past part. of *defend*] **1 :** not guarded or protected ⟨left the goal ~⟩ ⟨~ frontier⟩ **2 :** not provided with legal assistance

un·defiled \"+\ *adj* [ME, fr. 1*un-* + *defiled*, past part. of *defilen* to defile — more at DEFILE] **:** UNTAINTED, UNCORRUPTED, PURE ⟨learn to speak pure English ~ —Van Wyck Brooks⟩

un·definable \ˈ¦ən+\ *adj* **:** INDEFINABLE — **un·de·fin·able·ness** *n* -ES — **un·definably** \"+\ *adv*

un·defined \"+\ *adj* [1*un-* + *defined*, past part. of *define*] **1 :** not defined **:** not precisely limited, determined, or distinguished **:** VAGUE ⟨some ~ sense of excitement —W.H. Wright⟩ **2 :** not capable of being described or limited in words **:** PRIMITIVE ⟨~ term⟩ ⟨~ concept⟩ — **un·de·fined·ly** \-nədlē, -nd-\ *adv* — **un·de·fined·ness** \-nədnəs, -n(d)nəs\ *n* -ES

un·deflected \ˈ¦ən+\ *adj* [1*un-* + *deflected*, past part. of *deflect*] **:** not deflected ⟨~ ray⟩

un·deflowered \"+\ *adj* [1*un-* + *deflowered*, past part. of *deflower*] **:** VIRGIN, INNOCENT, UNTOUCHED

un·deformed \"+\ *adj* **:** not deformed **:** free of deformity or deformation

un·degenerate \"+\ *adj* **:** not degenerate **:** showing no loss of vigor

un·deify \"+\ *vt* [2*un-* + *deify*] **:** to degrade from the state of deity

un·delayed \"+\ *adj* [ME, fr. 1*un-* + *delayed*, past part. of *delayen* to delay — more at DELAY] **:** not delayed **:** IMMEDIATE

un·deliberate \ˈ¦ən+\ *adj* **:** not intended **:** not calculated — **un·de·lib·er·ate·ness** *n*

un·delight \ˈ¦ən+\ *n* **:** want of delight **:** UNHAPPINESS

un·delightful \"+\ *adj* **:** not delightful **:** UNPLEASANT — **un·delightfully** \"+\ *adv*

un·deliverable \"+\ *adj* **:** not capable of being delivered to an addressee ⟨~ mail⟩ ⟨~ parcel⟩

un·delivered \"+\ *adj* [ME, fr. 1*un-* + *delivered*, past part. of *deliveren* to deliver — more at DELIVER] **:** not delivered

un·delude \"+\ *vt* [2*un-* + *delude*] **:** UNDECEIVE

un·demanding \"+\ *adj* **:** not demanding **:** not exacting ⟨simple, ~ affection⟩

un·democratic \"+\ *adj* **:** not democratic **:** not agreeing with democratic doctrine or practice or ideals ⟨objected to volunteering on the ground that it was ~ —*World's Work*⟩ — **un·democratically** \"+\ *adv*

un·democratize \"+\ *vt* [2*un-* + *democratize*] **:** to cause to cease to be democratic

un·demonstrable \"+\ *adj* **:** INDEMONSTRABLE — **un·demonstrably** \"+\ *adv*

un·demonstrated \"+\ *adj* [1*un-* + *demonstrated*, past part. of *demonstrate*] **:** not supported by proof or logical demonstration ⟨~ faith⟩

un·demonstrative \ˈ¦ən+\ *adj* **:** restrained or reserved in expression of feeling **:** not effusive — **un·demonstratively** \"+\ *adv* — **un·demonstrativeness** \"+\ *n*

un·deniable \"+\ *adj* [1*un-* + *deny* + *-able*] **1 :** plainly true **:** readily conceded **:** INCONTESTABLE, INDISPUTABLE ⟨~ evidence of a witness⟩ ⟨~ guilt⟩ **2 :** unquestionably excellent or genuine ⟨~ literary classic⟩ ⟨applicant would have to produce ~ references —*Country Life*⟩ — **un·de·ni·able·ness** *n* -ES — **un·de·ni·ably** \-blē, -li\ *adv*

un·denied \ˈ¦ən+\ *adj* [1*un-* + *denied*, past part. of *deny*] **:** not denied **:** not contested or disputed

un·denominational \ˈ¦ən+\ *adj* **:** not restricted or belonging to a denomination **:** UNSECTARIAN ⟨~ religious instruction⟩ — **un·denominationally** \"+\ *adv*

un·dependable \"+\ *adj* **:** not dependable **:** UNRELIABLE — **un·de·pend·able·ness** *n* — **un·dependably** \"+\ *adv*

un·depressed \ˈ¦ən+\ *adj* **1 :** not dejected **2 :** not pressed down or sunken

un·deprivable \"+\ *adj* **1 :** that cannot be deprived **:** not deposable **2 :** that one cannot be deprived of ⟨~ possession of property⟩

1un·der \ˈ¦əndə(r)\ *adv* [ME, adv. & prep., fr. OE; akin to OHG *untar*, adv. & prep., under, ON *undir*, adv. & prep., Goth *undar*, prep., under, L *infra* below, underneath, *inferus* low, situated beneath, Skt *adha* below] **1 :** further down or along in a writing ⟨see ~ for further discussion⟩ **2 a :** in or into a position below or beneath something ⟨wears a girdle ~⟩ **:** down below ⟨get ~ quick⟩ **b :** below the surface of the water ⟨a gust put the lee deck ~ —Nelson Hayes⟩ **c :** below the horizon ⟨sun went ~ an hour ago⟩ **3 :** below some quantity or limit ⟨ten dollars or ~⟩ — often used in combination ⟨*under*bid⟩ ⟨*under*ripe⟩ ⟨*under*staffed⟩ **4 :** in or into a condition of subjection, regulation, or subordination ⟨kept his disappointment ~⟩ ⟨I keep my body ~ —1 Cor 9:27 (AV)⟩ **5 a :** down to defeat, ruin, or death ⟨weaker competitors will be forced ~⟩ **b :** into unconsciousness ⟨enough ether to put him ~⟩ **c :** so as to be overwhelmed **:** out of sight ⟨buried ~ by the avalanche⟩ ⟨snowed ~ in the election⟩ **6 :** through a range downward ⟨children of eight and ~⟩

2under \"\ *prep* [ME — more at 1UNDER] **1 a :** during the ascendancy of ⟨born ~ a lucky star⟩ **b :** lower than and overhung by **:** having directly overhead ⟨every place ~ the sun⟩ ⟨~ tropical skies⟩ **2 :** in the shelter of ⟨living ~ the same roof⟩ ⟨huddled ~ the tree⟩ ⟨at anchor close ~ the island⟩ ⟨crawled out from ~ the bed⟩ ⟨~ the lee of the bank⟩ **3 :** using for concealment ⟨fled ~ cover of darkness⟩ ⟨entered the house ~ the pretext of asking for directions⟩ **4 :** at the foot of ⟨cottage nestling ~ the hill⟩ ⟨encamped ~ the town walls⟩ ⟨in this little combe ~ the Downs —T.W.Sharp⟩ **5 a :** below or beneath so as to be covered or enveloped or concealed ⟨sleeping ~ blankets⟩ ⟨wore a sweater ~ his jacket⟩ ⟨a kind heart ~ a gruff manner⟩ ⟨mailed ~ separate cover⟩ **b :** below the surface of ⟨diving ~ water⟩ ⟨burrowing ~ the earth⟩ **6 a :** below so as to support or carry ⟨with a good horse ~ him⟩ ⟨put runners ~ a sleigh⟩ ⟨put jacks ~ a beam⟩ **b :** topped or crowned with ⟨~ a huge periwig⟩ **:** surmounted by ⟨sailing ~ full canvas⟩ ⟨marching ~ a foreign flag⟩ **7 :** at a point below and close to ⟨hit him just ~ the ear⟩ ⟨drew a line ~ the last word⟩ ⟨put one number ~ the other and add them⟩ **8 a :** required by **:** in accordance with **:** bound by ⟨~ contract to deliver⟩ ⟨statement ~ oath⟩ ⟨~ the necessity of selling⟩ ⟨rights ~ the law⟩ **b :** suffering restriction, restraint, or control by ⟨sent home ~ guard⟩ ⟨ship placed ~ quarantine⟩ ⟨living ~ strict disciplinary rules⟩ ⟨~ a system of collective security —A.O.Walfers⟩ **c :** in conditions or circumstances of ⟨shocks and strains any language undergoes ~ rapid diffusion —I.A.Richards⟩ **9 a :** weighed upon or oppressed by ⟨travel ~ a heavy load⟩ ⟨laid ~ heavy obligation⟩ ⟨prohibited ~ severe penalties⟩ ⟨laboring ~ a misapprehension⟩ ⟨collapsed ~ the intolerable strain of waiting⟩ ⟨lawmakers are ~ conflicting pressures —*Wall Street Jour.*⟩ **b :** receiving or undergoing the action or application of **:** exposed to the effect of ⟨land ~ irrigation⟩ ⟨go ~ the surgeon's knife⟩ ⟨~ the influence of a strong emotion⟩ ⟨bravery ~ fire⟩ ⟨came ~ suspicion of theft⟩ ⟨stand up ~ punishment⟩ ⟨in London ~ the bombing —A.N.Whitehead⟩ **c :** in process of ⟨~ repair⟩ ⟨~ discussion⟩ ⟨~ construction⟩ **d :** devoted to the cultivation of **:** planted to ⟨most of the acreage ~ corn⟩ **e :** contained or enclosed by ⟨thousands of acres ~ fence —*Amer. Guide Series: Texas*⟩ **10 a :** subject to the bidding or authority of **:** led by ⟨served ~ three colonels⟩ **b :** during the reign or administration of ⟨extended the empire ~ the next king⟩ **c :** subject to the guidance and instruction of ⟨studied piano ~ a famous virtuoso⟩ **11 a :** within the grouping or designation of ⟨matters that come ~ this head⟩ ⟨classified ~ Diptera⟩ **b :** having as name or title ⟨traveling ~ an assumed name⟩ **:** in the section designated as ⟨looked for it ~ Minerals⟩ ⟨listed ~ Occupations⟩ **c :** attested or warranted by ⟨issued ~ the royal seal⟩ **d :** bearing as signature or indication of authorship ⟨published several works ~ a pen name⟩ **12 a :** inferior to **:** falling short of **:** exceeded by **:** of, for, or in less than ⟨exempting incomes ~ four thousand⟩ ⟨boys ~ fifteen⟩ ⟨sold ~ the list price⟩ ⟨a mile ~ four minutes⟩ **b :** lower in rank or quality than ⟨hardly speak to anyone ~ a colonel⟩ **c :** lower than or less than the standard or required degree of ⟨while his children are still ~ age⟩ ⟨company was so fearfully ~ strength —F.V.W.Mason⟩ — often used in combination ⟨this whiskey is considerably *under*proof⟩ **d :** one thirty-second less than ⟨~ ½ means 15/32⟩ — used on the London stock exchange **13 :** next after in a card game ⟨betting ~ the opener⟩ — **under ditch :** below the water level of a ditch or canal and therefore capable of irrigation — **under night** *Scot* **:** during the night **:** concealed by the darkness — **under one** *obs* **:** at the same time **:** TOGETHER — **under one's hat 1 :** in one's head **2 :** to oneself **:** SECRET ⟨keep the news *under your hat*⟩

3under \"\ *adj* [ME, fr. 1*under*] **1 a :** lying below or beneath ⟨gnawed his ~ lip⟩ — often used in combination ⟨sea's *under*current⟩ ⟨*under*surfaces of furniture⟩ **b :** placed on the ventral side of an animal's body — often used in combination ⟨*under*parts of fish⟩ **c :** facing or protruding downward — often used in combination ⟨*under*surface of a leaf⟩ **2 :** enclosed beneath a covering — often used in combination ⟨*under*layer of a bud⟩ **3 :** lower in rank or authority **:** SUBORDINATE ⟨~ bookkeepers⟩ — often used in combination ⟨*under*servants of a household⟩ **4 :** lower than usual, proper, or desired in amount, quality, or degree ⟨~ dose of medicine⟩ ⟨ready to fill in if the program proves to be ~⟩ **5 :** SUBDUED ⟨keep the musical accompaniment ~ during the scene⟩

4under \"\ *n* -S [1*under*] **:** something that falls short in amount, quality, length, or duration; *specif* **:** a broadcast program lasting less than the time allotted for it

underact \ˈ¦==¦=\ *vb* [1*under* + *act*] *vt* **1 :** to perform (a dramatic part) with less than the requisite skill or vigor **2 :** to perform with restraint for greater dramatic impact or personal force ~ *vi* **:** to perform feebly or with restraint ⟨the rest of the cast knew how to ~ for the greatest small-screen effectiveness —Saul Carson⟩

underaction \ˈ¦==¦==\ *n* [3*under* + *action*] **1 :** subordinate action **:** a minor action incidental or subsidiary to the main story **:** EPISODE **2 :** subnormal or insufficient action ⟨~ of focusing muscles of the eye⟩

underactivity \ˈ¦==ˌ=¦===\ *n* [3*under* + *activity*] **:** an abnormally low degree of activity ⟨~ of thyroid gland⟩

underactor \ˈ=ˌ=\ *n* [3*under* + *actor*] **:** a subordinate actor

1**un·der·age** \ˌ=ˈ=\ *adj* [2*under* + *age*, n.] **:** of less than mature or legal age

2**un·der·age** \ˈəndərij\ *n* -s [1*under* + *-age*] **:** SHORTAGE, DEFICIT

underair \ˈ=ˌ=\ *n* [3*under* + *air*] **:** the lowest strata of the atmosphere

1**underarm** \ˈ=ˌ=\ *adj* [in sense 1, fr. 2*under* + *arm*, n.; in sense 2, fr. 3*under* + *arm*, n.] **1 :** placed under or on the underside of the arm ⟨~ seams⟩ ⟨~ handbag⟩ **2 :** UNDERHAND ⟨~ bowling⟩ ⟨~ pitching delivery⟩ ⟨~ pass in basketball⟩

2**underarm** \ˌ=ˈ=\ *adv* [1*under* + *arm*] **:** UNDERHAND ⟨learning to throw ~⟩

underback \ˈ=ˌ=\ *n* [2*under* + *back*] **:** a vessel used in brewing that receives the wort as it flows from the mash tun

underbake \ˌ=ˈ=\ *vt* [1*under* + *bake*] **:** to bake less than fully

underbarring \ˈ=ˌ=\ *n* [3*under* + *barring*] **:** barring on the part of the feathers not visible on the surface

underbear \ˌ=ˈ=\ *vt* [ME *underberen*, fr. OE *underberan*, fr. *under*, adv. + *beran* to bear — more at BEAR] **1** *archaic* **:** SUPPORT, ENDURE **2** *obs* **:** to line or trim at the bottom

underbearer \ˈ=ˌ=\ *n* [3*under* + *bearer*] **:** one who assists in bearing the coffin at a funeral — compare PALLBEARER

underbed \ˈ=ˌ=\ *n* [3*under* + *bed*] **:** a mass or layer underlying or supporting something laid over it; *specif* **:** a mattress laid under a feather bed

underbelly \ˈ=ˌ=\ *n* [3*under* + *belly*] **:** the lower surface of a body or mass ⟨see a vast ruddy brilliance flash on the *underbellies* of clouds —Marjory S. Douglas⟩ ⟨~ of a bomber⟩; *esp* **:** a vulnerable area ⟨Sicilian and Italian campaigns . . . could now be launched across the sea against the ~ of Hitler's Europe —Sir Winston Churchill⟩

under bevel *n* **:** a bevel whose angle is acute

1**underbid** \ˌ=ˈ=\ *vb* [1*under* + *bid*] *vt* **1** *obs* **:** UNDERVALUE **2 :** to bid less than (a competing bidder) **3 :** to bid (a hand of cards) at less than the strength of the hand warrants ~ *vi* **:** to offer too little in bidding; *specif* **:** to bid less than should be bid or than can reasonably be made on a hand of cards — **underbidder** \ˌ=ˈ=\ *n*

2**underbid** \"\ *n* **1 :** an act of underbidding **2 :** a contract in bridge that is lower than can be made

underbill \ˌ=ˈ=\ *vt* [1*under* + *bill*] **:** to bill (goods) at less than the real amount

underbit \ˈ=ˌ=\ *n* [3*under* + *bit*] **:** an earmark for cattle corresponding to the overbit but on the lower side of the ear — see EARMARK illustration

underbite \ˌ=ˈ=\ *vt* [1*under* + *bite*] **:** to etch insufficiently

underblow \ˌ=ˈ=\ *vt* [1*under* + *blow*] **:** to blow (as a pipe or other wind instrument) with insufficient energy to sound the fundamental tone so that only a set of feeble high overtones is heard — compare OVERBLOW

underbodice \ˈ=ˌ=\ *n* [3*under* + *bodice*] **:** a bodice worn under an open blouse or jacket

underbody \ˈ=ˌ=\ *n* [3*under* + *body*] **1 a** *obs* **:** the lower part of a woman's dress **b** *dial* **:** a garment (as a petticoat, corset cover, slip) worn under an outer garment **2 a :** the lower part of an animal's body **:** UNDERPARTS **b :** the underwater part of a ship's hull **c :** the lower parts of the body of a vehicle or airplane; *esp* **:** the undersurfaces of an automotive vehicle

underbowed \ˌ=ˈ=\ *adj* [1*under* + *bowed* (furnished with a bow)] **:** using a bow that is too weak or beneath one's strength

underbraced \ˌ=ˈ=\ *adj* [1*under* + *braced*, past part. of *brace*] **1 :** strengthened underneath by stretchers ⟨~ table legs⟩ **2 :** not sufficiently braced; *specif* **:** depending upon some of its joints for its rigidity ⟨~ truss⟩

underbranch \ˈ=ˌ=\ *n* [3*under* + *branch*] **:** a lower branch

underbreath \ˈ=ˌ=\ *n* [3*under* + *breath*] **:** WHISPER, UNDERTONE ⟨spoke in an ~ —George Meredith⟩

1**underbred** \ˌ=ˈ=\ *adj* [1*under* + *bred*] **1 :** marked by lack of good manners or social poise **:** not well-bred **:** ILL-BRED **2 :** of inferior or mixed breed ⟨~ dog⟩

2**underbred** \ˈ=ˌ=\ *n* -s **:** an underbred animal

underbreeding \ˌ=ˈ=\ *n* [3*under* + *breeding*] **:** the condition or quality of being underbred

underbright \ˈ=ˌ=\ *n* -s [3*under* + *bright* (brightness)] **:** a streak of very bright light occasionally seen below clouds near the horizon

underbrim \ˈ=ˌ=\ *n* [3*under* + *brim*] **:** a facing on the underside of a hat brim

1**underbrush** \ˈ=ˌ=\ *n* [3*under* + *brush*] **1 :** shrubs, bushes, or small trees growing beneath large trees in a wood or forest **:** BRUSH **2 :** a tangled, obstructing, or impeding mass ⟨heavy ~ of footnotes to impede the general reader —Owen Lattimore⟩

2**underbrush** \"\ *vt* **:** to clear of underbrush ~ *vi* **:** to cut or clear away underbrush

underbuild \ˌ=ˈ=\ *vt* [1*under* + *build*] **1 :** to build a supporting structure underneath **:** build beneath **2 :** to build below the standard of (one's position) **3 :** to fall short of standards of construction in the building of

underburn \ˌ=ˈ=\ *vt* [1*under* + *burn*] **:** to burn (as clay) at a less than normal temperature

underbush \ˈ=ˌ=\ *n* [3*under* + *bush*] **:** UNDERBRUSH

underbutler \ˈ=ˌ=\ *n* [3*under* + *butler*] **:** a butler's assistant

underbuy \ˌ=ˈ=\ *vi* [1*under* + *buy*] **:** to buy insufficient quantities

undercanopy \ˈ=ˌ==\ *n* [3*under* + *canopy*] **:** UNDERSTORY

un·der·capitalize \ˌəndə(r)+\ *vt* [1*under* + *capitalize*] **1 :** to supply with insufficient capital for efficient operation **2 :** to issue a relatively small amount of securities in relation to the earnings and assets of (a business)

undercard \ˈ=ˌ=\ *n* [3*under* + *card*] **:** a program (as of boxing matches) supporting the featured match

undercarriage \ˈ=ˌ=\ *n* [3*under* + *carriage*] **1 :** a supporting framework ⟨~ of a field gun⟩ ⟨~ of a wagon⟩ ⟨~ of an automobile⟩ **2 :** the landing gear of an airplane

undercart \ˈ=ˌ=\ *n* [3*under* + *cart*] *Brit* **:** LANDING GEAR

undercast \ˈ=ˌ=\ *n* [3*under* + *cast*] **1 :** a passage for air carried under a road or floor of a mine **2 :** a cloud layer beneath a flying aircraft

1**undercharge** \ˌ=ˈ=\ *vt* [1*under* + *charge*] **1 :** to charge less than is usual or suitable for; *also* **:** to charge (a person) too little for something ⟨~ an oil company for shipments⟩ **2 a :** to load (a gun) with too small an explosive charge **b :** to give (a storage battery) an insufficient charging

2**undercharge** \ˈ=ˌ=\ *n* **:** a charge that is less than is usual or suitable; *specif* **:** a rate assessed a shipper or consignee that is less than the rate prescribed by the tariff

underchurched \ˌ=ˈchərcht\ *adj* [1*under* + *-churched* (fr. *church*, n. + *-ed*)] **:** not having sufficient churches to meet existing needs ⟨an ~ suburb⟩

underclass \ˌ=ˈ=\ *adj* [back-formation fr. *underclassman*] **:** being or belonging to an underclassman

underclassman \ˌ=ˈ=mən\ *n*, *pl* **underclassmen** [3*under* + *class*, n. + *man*] **:** a member of the freshman or sophomore class in a college or secondary school

underclay \ˈ=ˌ=\ *n* [3*under* + *clay*] **:** a layer of clay beneath a coal bed often containing fossil roots of coal plants and constituting fireclay

undercliff \ˈ=ˌ=\ *n* [3*under* + *cliff*] **:** a terrace or subordinate cliff on a shore consisting of material fallen from the cliff above

un·der·clothe \ˈ=ˌklōth\ *vt* [back-formation fr. *underclothing*] **:** to supply with underclothes

underclothed \ˌ=ˈ=\ *adj* [1*under* + *clothed*, past part. of *clothe*] **:** inadequately clothed

underclothes \ˈ=ˌ=\ *n pl* [3*under* + *clothes*] **:** clothes worn under others; *esp* **:** UNDERWEAR

underclothing \ˈ=ˌ=\ *n* [3*under* + *clothing*] **:** UNDERWEAR

underclub \ˌ=ˈ=\ *vi* [1*under* + *club*, n.] **:** to use a golf club not designed to yield the distance needed to be covered ⟨failed to reach the green through *underclubbing*⟩

1**undercoat** \ˈ=ˌ=\ *n* [3*under* + *coat*] **1 :** a coat or jacket formerly worn under another **2 :** a growth of short hair or fur partly concealed by a longer growth ⟨a dog's ~⟩ **3 a :** a coat of paint under another **b :** a paint prepared for use under a finishing coat ⟨red lead ~⟩ **c :** GROUND COAT 2b **4** *Brit* **:** the course of crushed stone that is immediately under the wearing surface of a bituminous pavement **5** *dial* **:** PETTICOAT

2**undercoat** \"\ *vt* **1 :** to apply an undercoat to ⟨~ steelwork with a primer⟩ **2 :** to apply a special waterproof coating to the undersurfaces of a vehicle

undercoater \ˈ=ˌ=\ *n* **:** UNDERCOAT 3b

undercoating \ˈ=ˌ=\ *n* [fr. gerund of 2*undercoat*] **:** UNDERCOAT 3

under-color \ˈ=ˌ=\ *n* [3*under* + *color*] **:** the color of the undercoat of an animal

undercolored \ˌ=ˈ=\ *adj* [1*under* + *colored*] **1 :** having less color than needed or proper **2 :** having or relating to undercolor

un·der·compounded \ˌəndə(r)+\ *adj* [1*under* + *compounded*] *of a dynamo or motor* **:** having the shunt and series field coils so related that voltage decreases with increasing load

underconsciousness \ˌ=ˈ=\ *n* [3*under* + *consciousness*] **:** SUBCONSCIOUS

underconsumption \ˌ==ˈ=\ *n* [3*under* + *consumption*] **:** consumption of less than is produced that is caused by insufficient purchasing power and is a cause of business depression

undercook \ˌ=ˈ=\ *vt* [1*under* + *cook*] **:** to cook insufficiently or less than thoroughly

undercool \ˌ=ˈ=\ *vt* [1*under* + *cool*] **1 :** to cool less than required for some specified or understood purpose **2 :** SUPERCOOL ⟨glass is an ~*ed* liquid which does not form crystals upon solidification —*Electrical Manufacturing*⟩

undercourse \ˈ=ˌ=\ *n* [3*under* + *course*] **:** a layer (as of flooring) immediately under a course of tiles **:** a course (as of shingles) laid beneath a covering course

undercover \ˌ=ˈ=\ *adj* [2*under* + *cover*] **:** acting or executed in secret **:** SURREPTITIOUS ⟨~ scheme⟩; *specif* **:** employed or engaged in spying or secret investigation ⟨~ agent⟩

undercover man *n* **:** one who undertakes to secure evidence of criminal or illegal actions by working with or among those who are under suspicion; *also* **:** one who secures a position (as in a business or factory) for the purpose of illicitly obtaining confidential information

undercovert \ˈ=ˌ=\ *n* [3*under* + *covert*] **1 :** a covert of underbrush **2 :** one of the small basal feathers of the underside of a bird's wing or tail

undercroft \ˈ=ˌ=\ *n* [ME *under croft*, fr. 3*under* + *croft*, *crofte* vault, crypt — more at CROFT] **:** a subterranean room; *esp* **:** a vaulted chamber under a church **:** CRYPT

undercrossing \ˈ=ˌ=\ *n* [3*under* + *crossing*] **:** UNDERPASS

undercrowded \ˌ=ˈ=\ *adj* [1*under* + *crowded*] **:** having fewer than the usual or desirable number of members ⟨~ insect population⟩ ⟨~ profession⟩

undercrowding \ˌ=ˈ=\ *n* [3*under* + *crowding*, gerund of *crowd*] **:** the condition or fact of being undercrowded

1**undercurrent** \ˈ=ˌ=\ *n* [3*under* + *current*] **1 :** a current below the upper currents or surface of a fluid body (as water or air) **2 :** a tendency of opinion or feeling not openly displayed and often contrary to the one publicly shown ⟨an ~ in favor of the accused had set in⟩ **3 undercurrents** *pl* **:** broad branch sluices in placer mining set at small inclination into which water carrying fine gold is diverted from the main sluice to lessen the velocity of flow in order to promote the settling **4 :** an electric current whose intensity is lower than a specified amount

2**undercurrent** \"\ *adj* **:** running under the surface **:** passing in secret **:** HIDDEN ⟨~ protest⟩

1**undercut** \ˌ=ˈ=\ *vb* [1*under* + *cut*, v.] *vt* **1 :** to cut away the underpart of ⟨~ a vein of ore⟩ **2 :** to cut away material from the underside of (an object) so as to leave an overhanging portion in relief ⟨~ the leaves of a wood carving⟩ **:** cut free from beneath ⟨~ the skin of the cheek in plastic surgery⟩ **3 a :** to offer to sell at lower prices than or to work for lower wages or serve for lower fees than (a competitor) **b :** to accept or offer to accept a lower scale of (prices or wages) than is standard or general **c :** to have in gin rummy a count as low as or lower than the count of (the knocker) **4 a :** to cut (a book cover) in stamping with an improperly prepared die **b :** to hollow out or trim off a part of (a stamping die) to reduce impression pressure **5 :** to eat under laterally so as to leave without proper support — used of the action of etching acid on the lines of a printing surface **6 :** to cut obliquely into (a tree) below the main cut and on the side toward which the tree will fall **7 :** to strike (the ball) in golf, tennis, or hockey obliquely downward so as to give a backspin or elevation to the shot **8 :** to cut from (a forest) less timber than the growth warrants or less than the estimated annual cut ~ *vi* **1 :** to perform the action of cutting away beneath **2 :** to cut one foot into the place occupied by the other in dancing

2**undercut** \ˈ=ˌ=\ *n* [partly fr. 1*undercut*; partly fr. 3*under* + *cut*, n.] **1 :** the action or result of cutting away from the underside of anything ⟨~ of a vehicle⟩ ⟨~ of a tooth cavity for anchoring a filling⟩ **2** *Brit* **:** TENDERLOIN 1 **3 a :** a notch cut before felling in the base of a tree to determine the direction of falling and to prevent splitting **b :** KERF 2 **c :** part of a founding mold cut away so as to require special measures in removing the pattern from the mold **4 a :** a cut (as in tennis) made with an underhand stroke **b :** BACKSPIN **5 :** a replacement of one foot by the other in dancing **:** COUPÉ

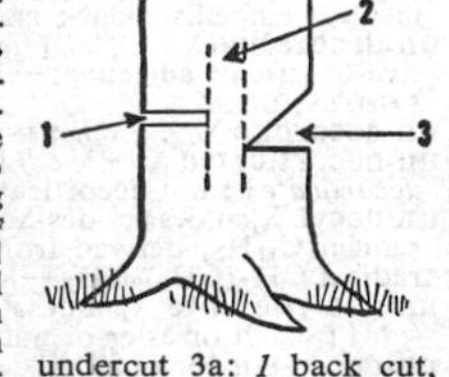

undercut 3a: *1* back cut, *2* holding wood, *3* undercut

3**undercut** \ˌ=ˈ=\ *adj* [fr. past part. of 1*undercut*] **:** cut away below or on the underside **:** having under material cut or carved away so as to be left standing out in relief ⟨~ rims and figures on pottery⟩

undercutter \ˌ=ˈ=\ *n* **:** one that undercuts or makes undercuts: as **a :** a logger who chops the undercut in a tree that is to be felled **b :** a mine worker who operates a machine for cutting the bottom or side of the working face of coal so that it will not shatter when blasted

1**underdeck** \ˈ=ˌ=\ *n* [3*under* + *deck*] **:** a lower deck of a ship

2**underdeck** \"\ *adj* [2*under* + *deck*, n.] **:** belonging to or carried in a space below the main deck or the tonnage deck

underdeck tonnage *n* **:** the gross cubical capacity of a ship less the spaces above the tonnage deck

underdeveloped \ˌ===ˈ=\ *adj* [1*under* + *developed*, past part. of *develop*] **1 :** not normally or adequately developed ⟨~ muscles⟩ ⟨~ sense of responsibility⟩ ⟨~ chin⟩ **2 :** insufficiently developed to give a satisfactory photographic image ⟨~ negative⟩ **3 :** failing to realize a potential economic level of industrial production and standard of living because of lack of capital for exploitation of natural resources, shortage of technically trained personnel, low medical standards, or because of culture traits resistant to change ⟨a program of technical assistance for ~ areas⟩

underdevelopment \ˌ===ˈ=\ *n* **:** lack of adequate development ⟨~ of film⟩ ⟨~ of industrial resources⟩

underditch \ˌ=ˈ=\ *vt* [1*under* + *ditch*] **:** to dig an underground ditch in (a field or farm) so as to drain the surface

underdo \ˌ=ˈ=\ *vb* [1*under* + *do*] *vi* **:** to do less than one can or than is requisite or proper ~ *vt* **1 :** to do less thoroughly than one can or should; *esp* **:** to cook (as meat) rare **2** *obs* **:** UNDERACT

underdog \ˈ=ˌ= *also* ˈ=ˈ=\ *n* [3*under* + *dog*] **1 :** a loser in a struggle **2 :** a victim of social injustice or of ruthless persecution **3 :** the predicted loser of a game or match **:** one not favored in the odds

underdone \ˌ=ˈ=\ *adj* [1*under* + *done*] **:** not thoroughly done; *esp* **:** cooked for a comparatively short or an insufficient time **:** RARE ⟨~ steak⟩ ⟨~ cabbage⟩

1**underdrag** \ˌ=ˈ=\ *vb* [1*under* + *drag*] *vt* **:** to exert pull on the underside of (an overlying mass of rock) ~ *vi* **:** to undergo a pull from the underside

2**underdrag** \ˈ=ˌ=\ *n* **:** the combined tensile stresses exerted by an overthrust rock mass upon rocks which overlie it but are not themselves under compressive thrusting stresses and therefore tend to be stretched and broken by normal faulting

1**underdrain** \ˈ=ˌ=\ *n* [3*under* + *drain*] **:** a concealed drain with openings through which the water enters when the water table reaches the level of the drain ⟨an ~ below a filter bed⟩

2**underdrain** \ˌ=ˈ=\ *vt* **:** to drain by forming an underdrain ⟨~ a meadow⟩

underdrainage \ˈ=ˌ=\ *n* **:** the drainage of soil by means of drains placed beneath the surface

underdraw \ˌ=ˈ=\ *vt* [1*under* + *draw*] **1 :** to draw a line under **:** UNDERSCORE **2 :** to draw or depict inadequately **3 :** to overlay or line (a roof or ceiling) with thin boards or lath and plaster **4 :** to draw from (an account) less than the amount credited

underdrawers \ˈ=ˌ=\ *n pl* [3*under* + *drawers*] **:** an article of underwear covering the lower body and the legs ⟨calf-length ~⟩

1**underdress** \ˈ=ˌ=\ *n* [3*under* + *dress*, n.] **:** clothing worn under outer clothing; *esp* **:** a decorative petticoat showing where the overskirt is draped back

2**underdress** \ˌ=ˈ=\ *vi* [1*under* + *dress*, v.] **:** to dress more simply or less formally than is customary ⟨after three winters of wartime ~*ing* —*Time*⟩

underdrift \ˈ=ˌ=\ *n* [3*under* + *drift*] **:** UNDERCURRENT

underdrive \ˈ=ˌ=\ *n* [3*under* + *drive*] **:** a transmission gear which transmits to the driven shaft a speed less than engine speed or less than the speed provided by the normal gear set

underdriven \ˌ=ˈ=\ *adj* [1*under* + *driven*, past part. of *drive*] **:** driven from below ⟨~ millstone⟩

1**underearth** \ˈ=ˌ=\ *adj* [2*under* + *earth*, n.] **:** SUBTERRANEAN

2**underearth** \"\ *n* [3*under* + *earth*] **1 :** the soil beneath the earth's surface **:** an underlying layer (as of clay) **2 :** the depths of the earth

undereaten \ˌ=ˈ=\ *adj* [1*under* + *eaten*, past part. of *eat*] **:** eaten or worn away from beneath ⟨~ cliffs⟩

underemployed \ˌ==ˈ=\ *adj* [1*under* + *employed*, past part. of *employ*] **:** having less than full-time employment

underemployment \ˌ===ˈ=\ *n* [3*under* + *employment*] **1 :** a state of less than full employment of the labor force in an economy **:** the existence of numbers of workers without jobs **2 :** the partial employment of a worker **3 :** the utilization of workers at more menial or less skilled tasks than their training or abilities permit

1**underestimate** \ˌ=ˈ=(ˌ)=\ *vt* [1*under* + *estimate*, v.] **1 :** to estimate as being less than the actual size, quantity, or number ⟨~ the cost of new building⟩ **2 :** to place too low a value on **:** take too lightly ⟨~ an opponent⟩ ⟨~ the seriousness of a threat of suicide⟩

2**underestimate** \"\ *or* **underestimation** \ˌ=ˌ==ˈ=\ *n* [3*under* + *estimate*, n., or *estimation*] **1 :** the act of underestimating **2 :** an estimate that falls below the truth or actuality

underexcited \ˌ==ˈ=\ *adj* [1*under* + *excited*] **:** operated with field excitation below normal ⟨~ dynamo⟩

1**underexercise** \ˌ=ˈ=ˌ=\ *vi* [1*under* + *exercise*, v.] **:** to exercise too little ⟨overeating and *underexercising*⟩

2**underexercise** \"\ *n* [3*under* + *exercise*, n.] **:** inadequate amount or frequency of exercise

underexpose \ˌ==ˈ=\ *vt* [1*under* + *expose*] **:** to expose (a photographic plate or film) for less time than is needed ⟨an *underexposed* negative is lacking in density and in shadow detail —C.B.Neblette⟩

underexposure \ˌ==ˈ=\ *n* **:** the act or result of underexposing

underfall \ˈ=ˌ=\ *n* [3*under* + *fall*] **:** a lower mountain slope — usu. used in pl.

1**underfeed** \ˌ=ˈ=\ *vt* [1*under* + *feed*] **1 :** to feed with too little food **2 :** to feed with fuel from the underside

2**underfeed** \ˈ=ˌ=\ *adj* **:** being fed or feeding from beneath ⟨~ stoking of a furnace⟩ — opposed to *overfeed*

underfill \ˈ=ˌ=\ *n* -s [3*under* + *fill*] **1 :** a rolled or forged member (as of steel) that is imperfect because of insufficient material **2 :** an incompletely filled can or container

underfire \ˌ=ˈ=\ *vt* [1*under* + *fire*] **1 :** to fire (as brick) insufficiently **2 :** to fire from beneath ⟨~ a coke oven⟩

underfit \ˌ=ˈ=\ *adj* [1*under* + *fit*, past part. of *fit*] **:** greatly reduced in volume and therefore in ability to erode or transport as a consequence of stream piracy ⟨an ~ stream⟩

underflow \ˈ=ˌ=\ *n* [3*under* + *flow*] **:** a flowing under **:** movement of water through subsurface material

1**underfold** \ˌ=ˈ=\ *vt* [1*under* + *fold*, v.] **:** to fold within so as to hide

2**underfold** \ˈ=ˌ=\ *n* [3*under* + *fold*, n.] **:** a fold lying under or beneath a surface or beneath another fold

1**underfoot** \ˌ=ˈ=\ *adv* [ME *underfot*, *underfoot*, fr. 2*under* + *fot*, *foot* foot] **1 a :** under the foot esp. against the ground ⟨hated emblem torn down and trampled ~⟩ **b :** on the bottom of the foot **:** between the foot and the ground ⟨soles with no inside seams or nails ~⟩ ⟨felt the soft turf ~⟩ **2 a :** below, at, or before one's feet ⟨violets growing ~⟩ **b :** UNDERGROUND ⟨felt a tremor ~⟩ **3 a :** under the bottom (as of a ship) ⟨a strong current ~⟩ **b** *of an anchor* **:** under the forefoot **4 :** in the way ⟨the children are always getting ~⟩

2**underfoot** \"\ *adj* **1 :** being under or obstructing the foot ⟨clear a factory floor of ~ hazards⟩ **2 :** ABJECT, DOWNTRODDEN, DESPISED ⟨the city's most famous ~ characters, the cats of New York —*Park East*⟩

3**underfoot** \"\ *vt* -ED/-ING/-S [1*under* + *foot*, n.] **1 :** to support beneath **:** PROP, UNDERPIN **2 :** to replace the footings beneath

underfooting \ˈ=ˌ=\ *n* [1*underfoot* + *-ing*] **:** FOOTING 1 ⟨treacherous ~ resulted in scores of injuries —*N. Y. Times*⟩

underframe \ˈ=ˌ=\ *n* [3*under* + *frame*] **:** the lower or lowermost of two or more superimposed frames **:** a frame supporting a superstructure (as of a railroad car) **:** CHASSIS

underframing \ˈ=ˌ=\ *n* [3*under* + *framing*] **:** the material or structural members of an underframe

underfrequency relay \ˈ=ˌ==-\ *n* [3*under* + *frequency*] **:** a relay actuated by a fall in electrical frequency

underfur \ˈ=ˌ=\ *n* [3*under* + *fur*] **:** the thick soft sometimes curly and barbed fur lying beneath the longer and coarser hair of a mammal — compare UNDERCOAT 2

undergage \ˈ=ˌ=\ *n* [3*under* + *gage*] **:** a no-go gage of the limit-gage type used for metal sheets or plates

undergarment \ˈ=ˌ=\ *n* [3*under* + *garment*] **:** a garment to be worn under another

undergear \ˈ=ˌ=\ *n* [3*under* + *gear*] **:** gear placed below or under something else **:** running gear and chassis of a vehicle

undergird \ˌ=ˈ=\ *vt* [1*under* + *gird*] **1 :** to gird below **:** make secure underneath ⟨took measures to ~ the ship —Acts 27:17 (RSV)⟩ **2 :** to brace up **:** STRENGTHEN, SUPPORT ⟨faith ~*s* moral principles —I.G.Whitchurch⟩

undergirth \ˈ=ˌ=\ *n* [3*under* + *girth*] **:** a band or rope used in undergirding

underglaze \ˈ=ˌ=\ *adj* [2*under* + *glaze*] **1 :** applied before the glaze is put on ⟨~ painting on porcelain⟩ **2 :** suitable for applying under the glaze ⟨~ color⟩ ⟨~ pigment⟩ — compare OVERGLAZE

undergo \ˌ=ˈ=\ *vb* [ME *undergon*, *undergoon*, fr. 1*under* + *gon*, *goon* to go — more at GO] *vt* **1** *obs* **:** to move or pass under or underneath **2** *obs* **:** UNDERTAKE **3** *obs* **:** to partake of **4 :** to submit to **:** ENDURE, SUFFER, SUSTAIN ⟨tragic hero rises above . . . the world man ~*es* —W.E.Allen⟩ **5 :** to go through **:** be the subject of (as a process) **:** receive the effect of ⟨~ martyrdom⟩ ⟨~ surgery⟩ ⟨~ examination⟩ ⟨~ a moral conversion⟩ ⟨words which had *undergone* certain derivational processes —Stanley Newman⟩ ⟨~ complete metamorphosis⟩ ~ *vi* **:** ENDURE ⟨the self acts as well as ~*es* —John Dewey⟩ ⟨the inarticulate merely ~ —S.V.Benét⟩ **syn** see EXPERIENCE

undergoer \ˌ=ˈ=\ *n* **:** one that undergoes

undergown \ˈ=ˌ=\ *n* [3*under* + *gown*] **:** a gown worn under another gown or other garment usu. so that the neckline, sleeves, or skirt shows for contrast

undergrad \ˌ=ˈ=\ *n* -s [by shortening] *slang* **:** UNDERGRADUATE

undergrade \ˌ=ˈ=\ *adj* [2*under* + *grade*, n.] **1 :** below or inferior to standard grade **:** not of first grade ⟨~ fruit⟩ ⟨~ lumber⟩ **2 :** below the grade of the track or roadway ⟨~ crossing⟩

1**un·der·graduate** \ˌəndə(r)+\ *n* [2*under* + *graduate*] **1 :** a student at a college or university who has not taken a first degree **:** a candidate for a bachelor's degree or a first degree in a school or profession (as medicine) **:** a member of one of the four traditional collegiate classes **2 :** one whose training is not yet perfect **:** NOVICE

2**undergraduate** \"\ *adj* **1 :** of, relating to, or engaged in college or university studies prior to the first degree ⟨~ course⟩ ⟨~ student⟩ ⟨~ medical studies⟩ **2 :** of, relating to, or charac-

teristic of undergraduates ⟨retain the ~ fervor —H.M. McLuhan⟩
undergraduate·ship \"+ˌship\ *n* **:** the condition or status of an undergraduate
un·der·grad·u·ette \ˌəndə(r)ˌgrajəˈwet\ *n* [blend of [1]*undergraduate* and *-ette*] *Brit* **:** CO-ED
undergreen \ˈ⸗ˌ⸗\ *adj* [[1]*under* + *green*] **:** green on the underside ⟨~ willow⟩
undergroom \ˈ⸗ˌ⸗\ *n* [[3]*under* + *groom*] **:** a groom's helper **:** STABLEBOY
[1]**underground** \ˌ⸗ˈ⸗\ *adv* [[2]*under* + *ground*, n.] **1 :** beneath the surface of the earth ⟨water flowing ~⟩ ⟨burrowing ~⟩ **2 :** in or into hiding or secret operation ⟨an ideology driven ~ develops into a more virulent form —W.O.Douglas⟩ ⟨the association soon became subversive and went ~ —Harold Ingrams⟩
[2]**underground** \ˈ⸗ˌ⸗\ *adj* **1 :** being, growing, or situated below the surface of the ground ⟨~ cave⟩ ⟨~ cellar⟩ ⟨~ stream⟩ ⟨~ rhizomes⟩ **2 :** dwelling in an underworld ⟨mythical ~ people⟩ **3 :** used or adapted for use or wear underground **:** employed or performing duties underground ⟨~ foreman⟩ ⟨~ shovel⟩ **4 :** done or occurring underground esp. away from public knowledge **:** conducted or conveyed by secret or stealthy means ⟨~ revolutionary activity⟩ ⟨the ~ life of civilized societies —Edward Sapir⟩
[3]**underground** \"\ *n* [[2]*underground*] **1 :** the place or space beneath the surface of the ground **:** a subterranean space or channel **2 :** ground or soil lying beneath the surface or beneath something else **3 :** an underground city railway system ⟨the London *Underground*⟩ **4 a :** a movement or group organized in strict secrecy among citizens in an occupied or totalitarian country for maintaining communications, popular solidarity, and concerted resistive action pending liberation ⟨the ~ in Occupied France⟩ **b :** a clandestine conspiratorial cell or organization set up for revolutionary or other disruptive purposes esp. against a civil order — used with *the* ⟨the Communist ~ in wartime Germany⟩
underground·er \"+ə(r)\ *n* -s [[3]*underground* + *-er*] **1 a :** one that works underground **b :** one that rides on an underground railway **2 :** a member of the underground
underground railroad *n* **1 :** UNDERGROUND RAILWAY **2** *usu cap U&R* **:** a system of cooperation among active antislavery people in the U.S. before 1863 by which fugitive slaves were secretly helped to reach the North or Canada
underground railway *n* **:** a railway running in a subway usu. beneath the street level of a city
undergrove \ˈ⸗ˌ⸗\ *n* [[3]*under* + *grove*] **:** a grove of shrubs or low trees under taller ones
undergrow \ˌ⸗ˈ⸗\ *vi* [[1]*under* + *grow*] **:** to grow beneath something or up from beneath
undergrown \ˌ⸗ˈ⸗\ *adj* [[1]*under* + *grown*] **1 :** of small stature **:** not grown to full height or size **2 :** grown over with an undergrowth
undergrowth \ˈ⸗ˌ⸗\ *n* [[3]*under* + *growth*] **:** low growth more or less completely covering the floor of a forest and including seedlings and saplings and shrubs and herbs **2 :** a condition of incomplete or imperfect growth
underhair \ˈ⸗ˌ⸗\ *n* [[3]*under* + *hair*] **:** a growth of fine hair underneath the coarser outer hair of some mammals
[1]**underhand** \ˌ⸗ˈ⸗\ *adv* [[2]*under* + *hand*] **1 a :** by secret means **:** in a clandestine manner **:** not openly **:** not fairly ⟨mean revenge, committed ~ —John Dryden⟩ **b** *archaic* **:** QUIETLY, UNOBTRUSIVELY **2 :** with the target seen below the bow hand **3** [[1]*under* + *hand*] **:** with an underhand motion ⟨toss a ball ~⟩
[2]**underhand** \ˈ⸗ˌ⸗\ *adj* **1 :** aimed so that the target is seen below the bow hand ⟨~ shooting at long range⟩ **2 :** marked by or treated with secrecy, chicanery, and deception or by hidden craft and deceit **:** not honest, open, and aboveboard **:** SLY ⟨a coward with an ~ streak of cruelty —G.J.Becker⟩ ⟨stooping to ~ methods to gain his end⟩ **3 :** done so as to evade notice **:** marked by quiet unobtrusiveness or subtlety ⟨from his intellectual superiority he is deemed to exert an ~ influence against the officers —Herman Melville⟩ **4 :** performed with the hand kept below the level of the shoulder ⟨flip an ~ pass in football⟩ ⟨~ shot for the basket⟩; *also* **:** using such a manner of throwing ⟨~ bowler⟩ ⟨~ pitcher⟩ **5 :** working from above downward ⟨~ surface mining⟩ **syn** see SECRET
[3]**underhand** \"\ *n* [[2]*underhand*] **:** a ball delivered underhand **:** an underhand delivery
[4]**underhand** \ˌ⸗ˈ⸗\ *vt* [[1]*underhand*] **:** to throw, pass, or pitch (a ball) in an underhand manner
[1]**underhanded** \ˌ⸗ˈ⸗⸗\ *adj* **1 :** UNDERHAND 2 ⟨did not look quite like a professional gambler, but something . . . in his countenance suggested an ~ mode of life —Willa Cather⟩ **2 :** insufficiently provided with hands or workers **:** SHORT-HANDED, UNDERMANNED **syn** see SECRET
[2]**underhanded** \"\ *adv* **:** UNDERHAND ⟨the ball must be delivered ~, not thrown or jerked —*Quarterly Rev.*⟩
un·der·hand·ed·ly *adv* **:** in a secret or deceitful manner ⟨old line aristocratic diplomats ~ undermined the attempt . . . to align Germany with the Western democracies —C.G.Bowers⟩
un·der·hand·ed·ness *n* -ES **:** DECEITFULNESS, TRICKERY
underhanging \ˌ⸗ˈ⸗⸗\ *adj* [[1]*under* + *hanging*, pres. part. of *hang*] **:** UNDERHUNG 1 ⟨~ jaw⟩
underharvest \ˌ⸗ˈ⸗⸗\ *vt* [[1]*under* + *harvest*] **:** to take less of the crop of (as fishes) than is desirable to maintain a satisfactory balance of nature
underhew \ˌ⸗ˈ⸗\ *vt* [[1]*under* + *hew*] **:** to hew (timber) to scant dimensions
underhive \ˌ⸗ˈ⸗\ *vt* [[1]*under* + *hive*] **:** to hive (bees) in insufficient space
underhold \ˈ⸗ˌ⸗\ *n* [[3]*under* + *hold*] **1 :** an encircling grip secured advantageously by a wrestler under his opponent's arms **2 :** a handhold with which a climber maintains balance by pulling against the pressure of his feet — see LAYBACK
underhole \ˌ⸗ˈ⸗\ *vt* [[1]*under* + *hole*] **:** to cut away the lower portion of or to cut under (a coal seam)
underhook \ˌ⸗ˈ⸗\ *vt* [[1]*under* + *hook*] **:** to pass an arm under so as to hook in wrestling
un·der·housed \ˌəndə(r)ˈhau̇zd\ *adj* [[1]*under* + *-housed* (fr. *house*, n. + *-ed*)] **1 :** having too few houses **2 :** inadequately housed
underhousemaid \ˈ⸗⸗ˈ⸗ˌ⸗\ *n* [[3]*under* + *housemaid*] **:** an assistant housemaid
underhung \ˌ⸗ˈ⸗\ *adj* [[1]*under* + *hung*, past part. of *hang*] **1** *of a lower jaw* **:** projecting beyond the upper jaw **:** UNDERSHOT **2 :** having an underhung jaw ⟨this poor creature, heavy-bodied, bowlegged and ~ —J.A.Thomson⟩ **3 :** suspended so that the point of support is beneath the load; *specif* **:** resting on a track at the bottom instead of being suspended from above ⟨~ sliding door⟩
underinsurance \ˌ⸗⸗ˈ⸗⸗\ *n* [[3]*under* + *insurance*] **:** insurance in an amount insufficient to cover the possible loss or to satisfy the requirements of a coinsurance clause
un·derivative \ˌən+\ *adj* **:** not derivative or imitative **:** ORIGINAL ⟨a natural and ~ poet —Florence B. Lennon⟩
un·derived \"+\ *adj* **:** not derived or secondary **:** PRIMARY, SIMPLE
underjaw \ˈ⸗ˌ⸗\ *n* [[3]*under* + *jaw*] **:** lower jaw
underjawed \ˌ⸗ˈ⸗\ *adj* **:** having the underjaw prominent
underkeeper \ˈ⸗ˌ⸗⸗\ *n* [[3]*under* + *keeper*] **:** a subordinate keeper ⟨~ of a game forest⟩
underlaid \ˌ⸗ˈ⸗\ *adj* [fr. past part. of *underlay*] **1 :** laid or placed underneath **2 :** having something laid or lying underneath often by way of support or strengthening ⟨bed of sand ~ with shale⟩ ⟨the theology of India is ~ with pantheism —J.W. Draper⟩
underlain *past part of* UNDERLIE
[1]**underlap** \ˌ⸗ˈ⸗\ *vt* [[1]*under* + *lap*] **:** to project under the edge or end of ⟨the forward end of each plank ~s the overlapping rear end of the next⟩
[2]**underlap** \ˈ⸗ˌ⸗\ *n* **:** a section of a garment extending beneath another; *esp* **:** the front edge of a coat or dress that is closed by placing one side of the front under the other
[1]**underlay** *past of* UNDERLIE
[2]**underlay** \ˌ⸗ˈ⸗\ *vt* [ME *underleyen, underleggen*, fr. OE *underlecgan*, fr. [1]*under* + *lecgan* to lay — more at LAY] **1 :** to cover, line, or traverse the bottom of ⟨~ the Atlantic with a cable⟩ **:** give support to on the underside or below **:** place a line or layer beneath or inside of — used with *with* ⟨slates *underlaid* with roofing paper⟩ ⟨~ the pavement with traprock⟩ **2 a :** to raise or support by something laid under ⟨~ a cut to bring it up to the right height for printing⟩ **b** *obs* **:** to put a tap on (a shoe)
[3]**underlay** \ˈ⸗ˌ⸗\ *n* **1 :** something that is laid under: as **a :** a piece of leather or other material placed between the outside and the lining of a shoe upper beneath a cutout or perforation **b :** a thickness of paper placed under type or a cut to bring it up to the proper height for printing — compare OVERLAY **c :** a contrasting facing or lining used esp. with sheer fabrics **d :** material placed under flooring or carpeting for insulation or reducing noise and wear **2 :** a basic trend not evident upon the surface **:** UNDERCURRENT ⟨beneath all the wild rumors there was an ~ of fact⟩
underlayer \ˈ⸗ˌ⸗⸗\ *n* [[3]*under* + *layer*] **:** a layer that underlies another **:** SUBSTRATUM
un·der·lay·ment \ˌəndə(r)ˈlāmənt\ *n* -s **:** UNDERLAY 1d ⟨plywood ~ for flooring tile⟩
underleaf \ˈ⸗ˌ⸗\ *n* [[3]*under* + *leaf*] **1 :** the underside of a leaf **2 :** AMPHIGASTRIUM
[1]**underlease** \ˈ⸗ˌ⸗\ *n* [[3]*under* + *lease*] **:** SUBLEASE
[2]**underlease** \ˌ⸗ˈ⸗\ *vb* **:** SUBLET
un·der·les·see \ˌəndə(r)ˌleˈsē\ *n* [[3]*under* + *lessee*] **:** one to whom an underlease is granted **:** SUBTENANT
[1]**underlet** \ˌ⸗ˈ⸗\ *vt* [[1]*under* + *let*, v.] **1 :** to let below the real value **2 :** SUBLET
[2]**underlet** \"\ *adj* [[1]*under* + *let*, past part. of *let*] **:** let in or introduced from below or from the bottom
[3]**underlet** \ˈ⸗ˌ⸗\ *n* -s **:** the water introduced into the mash tun from beneath the false bottom in brewing
[1]**underlie** \ˌ⸗ˈ⸗\ *vb* [ME *underliggen, underligen, underlien*, fr. OE *underlicgan*, fr. [1]*under* + *licgan* to lie — more at LIE] *vt* **1 a** *obs* **:** to submit to the will or direction of **b** *obs* **:** to undergo the infliction of (a penalty or judgment) **c** *Scot* **:** to surrender oneself to (law) **d** *obs* **:** to assume the expense of or responsibility for **2 :** to lie or be situated under ⟨shale ~s the coal⟩ ⟨delta *underlain* by a clay bed⟩ ⟨granite on the outside *underlain* with basalt —*Science*⟩ **3 :** to be at the basis of **:** form the foundation of **:** SUPPORT ⟨political ideas *underlying* the revolution⟩ ⟨law of gravitation and his equations of motion apply to and ~ immense realms of physical experience —Julian Huxley⟩ **4 :** to lie concealed beneath the obvious exterior of ⟨the human and personal actualities that ~ the impersonality of justice —F.R.Leavis⟩ ⟨probe the mysterious causality that may ~ chance —H.C.Webster⟩ **5 :** to exist as a claim or security superior and prior to (another) ⟨a first mortgage ~s a second⟩ **~** *vi* **1** *obs* **:** to lie in the grave **2** *Brit* **:** to incline from the vertical **:** HADE
[2]**underlie** \ˈ⸗ˌ⸗\ *n* **1** *Brit* **:** SLOPE **2 :** the angle made by the center line of a stull with a line normal to the hanging wall at their point of incidence — called also *underset*
un·der·li·er *pronunc at* [1]UNDERLIE + ə(r)\ *n* **:** something that lies under; *specif* **:** UNDERLYING COMPANY
underlife \ˈ⸗ˌ⸗\ *n* [[3]*under* + *life*] **:** life beneath the surface or concealed from common knowledge
[1]**underline** \ˌ⸗ˈ⸗\ *vt* [[1]*under* + *line* (to cover inner surface of)] **:** to provide with an underlining ⟨collar *underlined* with black —*advt*⟩
[2]**underline** \"\ *vt* [[1]*under* + *line* (to mark with a line)] **1 a :** to mark (a word) with a line underneath **:** UNDERSCORE **b :** to put emphasis upon **:** stress in or as if in utterance ⟨~s the unity of knowledge and the consequent unity which should be aimed at in education —R.M.Hutchins⟩ **2 :** to make evident the significant character or importance of ⟨British weakness was *underlined* when the French fleet escaped from Toulon —J.H.Plumb⟩ ⟨hydrogen bomb explosions *underlined* in a horrifying fashion the likely consequences of atomic attack —Barbara Ward⟩ **3 :** to announce in advance by or as if by an underline ⟨his book is *underlined* for publication next month⟩
[3]**underline** \ˈ⸗ˌ⸗\ *n* **1 a :** a horizontal line placed underneath something ⟨words with a single ~ are to be set in italics⟩ **b underlines** *pl* **:** a set of guiding lines placed underneath a sheet to be written on **2 a :** explanatory or descriptive wording underneath an illustration **:** LEGEND **b :** a line placed below the notice of a current performance announcing a performance shortly to follow **3 :** the outline of the lower part of an animal's body between the front and rear legs ⟨~ well tucked up⟩; *also* **:** the ventral surface of a quadruped's body ⟨brown above, with the ~ lighter⟩
underlineation \ˌ⸗⸗ˌ⸗⸗ˈ⸗⸗\ *n* [[3]*under* + *lineation*] **:** the action of underlining or the markings so made
underlinen \ˈ⸗ˌ⸗⸗\ *n* [[3]*under* + *linen*] **:** underwear usu. of lightweight material
[1]**un·der·ling** \ˈəndə(r)liŋ, -lēŋ\ *n* -s [ME, fr. [1]*under* + *-ling*] **1 a :** one who is under the orders of another **:** SUBORDINATE, INFERIOR ⟨the fault . . . is . . . in ourselves, that we are ~s —Shak.⟩ **b :** a person of small importance ⟨scientists need to be used not as lackeys or ~s —Vannevar Bush⟩ **2** *dial* **:** an underdeveloped, imperfect, or weakly offshoot or offspring
[2]**underling** \"\ *adj* [ME, fr. *underling*, n.] **1 :** subordinate or inferior in authority or prestige to another **:** serving under another ⟨fearful of ~ aggression —V.L.Parrington⟩ **2** *dial* **:** underdeveloped, imperfect, or weakly in growth
[1]**underlining** \ˈ⸗ˌ⸗⸗\ *n* [[3]*under* + *lining*] **:** lining placed on the under or the inner side of something
[2]**underlining** \"\ *n* [fr. gerund of [2]*underline*] **:** the action of drawing lines underneath in writing or printing or lines so drawn **:** UNDERSCORING ⟨letters . . . with their ~s and broken sentences and postscripts —G.H.Genzmer⟩
underlip \ˌ⸗ˈ⸗\ *n* [[3]*under* + *lip*] **1 :** the lower lip **2 :** the lower edge of the mouth in an organ flue pipe
underlit \ˌ⸗ˈ⸗\ *adj* [[1]*under* + *lit*, past part. of *light*] **:** insufficiently lighted ⟨working in dingy ~ rooms⟩
underload \ˈ⸗ˌ⸗\ *n* [[3]*under* + *load*] **:** a load markedly below full capacity **:** an inadequate or insufficient load
underload starter *n* **:** a motor starter provided with an underload switch
underload switch *n* **:** a switch that opens a circuit when the current falls below a predetermined value and that is used to protect a motor from racing upon decrease of load
[1]**underlook** \ˌ⸗ˈ⸗\ *vt* [[1]*under* + *look*, v.] **1 :** to look or glance at from underneath or from lowered eyes **:** look covertly at **2 :** to miss or omit because one has looked too low
[2]**underlook** \ˈ⸗ˌ⸗\ *n* [[3]*under* + *look*, n.] **:** a covert glance
underlooker \ˈ⸗ˌ⸗⸗\ *n* [[3]*under* + *looker*] **:** an assistant to a manager (as of a mine) usu. engaged in superintendence and overseeing
un·der·ly \ˈəndə(r)lē\ *adj* [[1]*under* + *-ly*] **1** *archaic* **:** below average **2** *archaic* **:** being in poor health
underlying \ˌ⸗ˈ⸗⸗\ *adj* [fr. pres. part. of *underlie*] **1 a :** lying under or beneath ⟨the ~ strata⟩ **b :** IMPLICIT, FUNDAMENTAL ⟨~ principles⟩ **2 :** innate or organic but evident only on close inspection ⟨~ identity about the motley immigrants⟩ **3 :** anterior and prior in claim ⟨~ mortgage⟩
underlying bond *n* **:** a bond secured by a mortgage on corporate property prior to other claims
underlying company *n* **:** a company that is part of a larger consolidated organization and is kept in existence only because of nontransferable rights or franchises that it possesses
underman \ˈ⸗ˌ⸗\ *n, pl* **undermen** [[3]*under* + *man*] **1 :** a man who is subordinate to, inferior to, or in some way disadvantageously placed with respect to others ⟨unreasoning revolt of the ~ —A.E.Wiggam⟩ **2 :** a member of an acrobatic team who supports the others in his act
undermanned \ˌ⸗ˈ⸗\ *adj* [[1]*under* + *manned*, past part. of *man*] **:** furnished with an inadequate force of men **:** SHORT-HANDED, UNDERSTAFFED ⟨attract labor to ~ industries —*Economist*⟩
undermatched \ˌ⸗ˈ⸗\ *adj* [[1]*under* + *matched*, past part. of *match*] **:** married to a social inferior
undermeaning \ˈ⸗ˌ⸗⸗\ *n* [[3]*under* + *meaning*] **:** a meaning implied or discoverable but not directly expressed ⟨saw in the Old Testament stories an allegorical ~ which explained . . . the relation of matter and spirit —*New Statesman*⟩
undermentioned \ˌ⸗ˈ⸗⸗\ *adj* [[1]*under* + *mentioned*, past part. of *mention*] *Brit* **:** mentioned below **:** included in the list that follows **:** FOLLOWING
undermill \ˌ⸗ˈ⸗\ *vt* [[1]*under* + *mill*] **:** to mill (grain) without loss of all the bran and other particles eliminated by full milling
undermine \ˌ⸗ˈ⸗\ *vt* [ME *underminen*, fr. [1]*under* + *minen* to mine — more at MINE] **1 :** to excavate the earth beneath esp. for the purpose of causing to fall **:** form a mine under **:** SAP ⟨~ a wall⟩ **2 a :** to wash away supporting material from under ⟨flood water *undermined* the building's foundation⟩ ⟨stream ~s the glacier⟩ **b :** to make a passage under ⟨fence *undermined* by dogs⟩ **c :** to erode underneath or the underlayer of ⟨an ulcer may ~ the adjacent mucous membrane⟩ **3 :** to remove the foundation or support of subtly or by underhand means **:** subvert or weaken insidiously or secretly ⟨the way a writer handles the social situation either supports or ~s it —Peter Crowcroft⟩ ⟨selling below cost . . . to ~ competition —*Time*⟩ ⟨~ public confidence in its judicial system⟩ **4 :** to weaken or ruin by degrees ⟨prolonged overwork had *undermined* his health⟩ **syn** see WEAKEN
underminer \ˌ⸗ˈ⸗⸗\ *n* -s **:** one that undermines
un·der·min·ing·ly *adv* **:** so as to undermine
[1]**undermost** \ˈ⸗ˌ⸗\ *adj* [[1]*under* + *-most*] **:** lowest in relative position ⟨~ layer⟩
[2]**undermost** \"\ *adv* **:** in the lowest or lower position **:** on the underside ⟨with the dark layer ~⟩ ⟨put the rubber sheet ~⟩
un·dern \ˈəndə(r)n, ˈun-\ *n* -s [ME, third hour of the morning (9:00 a.m.), noon, fr. OE; akin to OHG *untarn, untorn* noon, ON *undorn* midafternoon, midmorning, Goth *undaurni*mats noon meal, and prob. to OHG *untar* between, among — more at INTER-] **1** *dial* **:** the time from noon to sundown **:** AFTERNOON **2** *dial* **:** a light meal in the forenoon or in the afternoon
[1]**un·der·neath** \ˌəndə(r)ˈnēth\ *prep* [ME *undernethe, undernethen*, prep. & adv., fr. OE *underneothan*, fr. [2]*under* + *neothan* below — more at BENEATH] **1 :** directly beneath ⟨put the date ~ the address⟩ **:** close under esp. so as to be covered or hidden ⟨beetles found ~ stones and logs⟩ ⟨stowed away ~ the flooring⟩ **2 :** below an upper layer of or inside an outer surface or covering of ⟨wore his swim suit ~ his slacks⟩ ⟨blood vessels just ~ the skin⟩ **3 :** under subjection or submission to ⟨living ~ a crushing tyranny⟩ **4 :** under the outward appearance or obvious aspect of ⟨~ the discursive chat of his letters is the firm fabric of economic fact —V.L.Parrington⟩ ⟨treachery lying ~ a mask of friendliness⟩
[2]**underneath** \"\ *adv* [ME *undernethe, undernethen*] **1 :** under or below an object or a surface often with the implication of being covered or concealed ⟨scrape off the paint to show the grain of the wood ~⟩ ⟨soaked through his jacket to the shirt ~⟩ **2 :** beneath by way of support ⟨house with a solid foundation ~⟩ **3 :** farther or lower down on the page ⟨column of figures with the totals given ~⟩ **4 :** on the lower or downward side ⟨pot blackened ~⟩
[3]**underneath** \ˌ⸗ˈ⸗\ *adj* **1** *dial* **:** SECRET, SURREPTITIOUS **2 :** not evident on the surface ⟨~ meanings⟩ **3 :** lying or working underneath ⟨~ wrestler⟩ ⟨~ man of an acrobatic team⟩
[4]**underneath** \ˌ⸗ˈ⸗\ *n* -s **:** the bottom surface **:** UNDERSIDE ⟨wipe the ~ of the glass⟩ ⟨looking at the ~s of the china for makers' names⟩
undernote \ˈ⸗ˌ⸗\ *n* [[3]*under* + *note*] **:** a subdued note **:** UNDERTONE ⟨spoke abruptly, low and cold, but with that same ~ of excitement —J.H.Wheelwright⟩
undernoted \ˌ⸗ˈ⸗⸗\ *adj* [[1]*under* + *noted*, past part. of *note*] *chiefly Brit* **:** mentioned or listed below or in what follows ⟨applications are invited for the ~ posts —*advt*⟩
undernourished \ˌ⸗ˈ⸗⸗\ *adj* [[1]*under* + *nourished*, past part. of *nourish*] **:** supplied with insufficient nourishment or less than the minimum quantity of foods essential for sound health and growth
undernourishment \ˌ⸗ˈ⸗⸗⸗\ *n* **:** lack of sufficient nourishment
undernutrition \ˌ⸗⸗ˌ⸗ˈ⸗⸗\ *n* [[3]*under* + *nutrition*] **:** a condition of deficient body nutrition from an inadequate intake of food or from failure to assimilate or utilize food elements
underpaid \ˌ⸗ˈ⸗\ *adj* [[1]*under* + *paid*, past part. of *pay*] **:** receiving less than adequate pay
underpaint \ˌ⸗ˈ⸗\ *vt* [[1]*under* + *paint*] **:** to apply preliminary layers of paint to
underpainting \ˈ⸗ˌ⸗⸗\ *n* **:** preliminary painting; *specif* **:** such painting done on a canvas or panel and covered completely or partially by the final layers of paint
underpan \ˈ⸗ˌ⸗\ *n* [[3]*under* + *pan*] **:** a protective metal covering fitting under the engine, clutch, and transmission case of an automobile
underpants \ˈ⸗ˌ⸗\ *n pl* [[3]*under* + *pants*] **:** short or long pants worn under an outer garment **:** DRAWERS
underpart \ˈ⸗ˌ⸗\ *n* [[3]*under* + *part*] **1 :** a part lying on the lower side or underneath; *specif* **:** one of the parts on the ventral side of a bird or animal's body ⟨a rodent with ~s approaching pure white⟩ **2 :** a subordinate or auxiliary part or role
[1]**underpass** \ˈ⸗ˌ⸗\ *n* [[3]*under* + *pass*] **:** a passage beneath: **a :** a grade separation where clearance to traffic on the upper level is obtained by depressing partially or completely (as with a tunnel) the grade of the lower level — compare OVERPASS **b :** the lower level of a grade separation — called also *undercrossing*
[2]**underpass** \"\ *vt* **:** to provide (a crossing) with an underpass
underpay \ˌ⸗ˈ⸗\ *vt* [[1]*under* + *pay*] **:** to pay inadequately
underpayment \ˌ⸗ˈ⸗⸗\ *n* [[3]*under* + *payment*] **1 :** insufficient payment ⟨~ of a tax obligation⟩ **2 :** payment of inadequate salary or wages
underpeopled \ˌ⸗ˈ⸗⸗\ *adj* [[1]*under* + *peopled*] **:** sparsely populated
[1]**underpick** \ˈ⸗ˌ⸗\ *adj* [[3]*under* + *pick*, n. (throw of the shuttle)] *of a loom* **:** having the picking arm or shuttle-driving device under the shuttle boxes — compare OVERPICK
[2]**underpick** \"\ *n* **:** an underpick loom
underpin \ˌ⸗ˈ⸗\ *vt* [[1]*under* + *pin*] **1 :** to replace or strengthen the foundation of ⟨~ a sagging building⟩ **2 :** to form part of the foundation of ⟨*underpinning* wall⟩ ⟨principles which should ~ a free society —Barbara Ward⟩ **3 :** SUPPORT, SUBSTANTIATE ⟨~ his thesis that American democracy is not an exportable commodity —V.O.Key⟩ ⟨*underpinned* with thick footnotes —*Newsweek*⟩ ⟨is this section of the play the acting is strongly *underpinned* by a script —E.R.Bentley⟩
underpinner \ˈ⸗ˌ⸗⸗\ *n* **:** a supporting brace **:** PROP
underpinning \ˈ⸗ˌ⸗⸗\ *n* [[3]*under* + *pinning*] **1 a :** the material and construction used for support and introduced beneath a wall already constructed **b :** the foundation of a frame house **2 :** a method of lining a mine shaft by supporting the upper section of brickwork on a curb by shores or props, excavating below, and building up to this curb from another curb inserted lower down **3 :** SUPPORT, PROP ⟨military security depends upon a strong economic ~ —H.S.Truman⟩ **4 :** UNDERWEAR — used usu. in pl. **5 :** a person's legs — used usu. in pl. ⟨still unsteady on his ~s when he came out for the seventh —*Ring*⟩
underpitch \ˈ⸗ˌ⸗\ *adj* [[1]*under* + *pitch*, v.] **:** formed by the incomplete intersection of unequal usu. cylindrical vaults springing from the same level ⟨~ groining⟩
underplant \ˌ⸗ˈ⸗\ *vt* [[1]*under* + *plant*] **1 :** to plant or sow among or under other taller growing plants or trees **2 :** to plant a crop or trees under (an existing stand or plantation)
[1]**underplay** \ˌ⸗ˈ⸗\ *vb* [[1]*under* + *play*] *vt* **1 :** to play a card lower than (a held high card) ⟨~ed his ace⟩ **2 :** to act or present (as a role or a scene) with restraint or subdued force **:** refrain from emphasizing or exaggerating **:** play down ⟨~ the comic elements of an opera⟩ ⟨continued briskly ~*ing* the drama of his news —Louis Auchincloss⟩ **~** *vi* **:** to play a role or scene with restraint or subdued force
[2]**underplay** \ˈ⸗ˌ⸗\ *n* **1 :** an act or instance of underplaying **2 :** hidden or underlying action ⟨a subtle ~ of antagonism beneath the polite conversation⟩
underplot \ˈ⸗ˌ⸗\ *n* [[3]*under* + *plot*] **1 :** a dramatic plot that is subordinate to the main action **2 :** a hidden scheme or trick
underpole \ˌ⸗ˈ⸗\ *vt* [[1]*under* + *pole*] **:** to pole (as copper) insufficiently
underpopulated \ˌ⸗ˈ⸗⸗⸗\ *adj* [[1]*under* + *populated*, past part. of *populate*] **:** having a lower density of population than is normal or desirable
underpowered \ˌ⸗ˈ⸗⸗\ *adj* [[1]*under* + *powered*] **:** driven by an engine of insufficient power ⟨~ truck⟩
underpower relay \ˈ⸗⸗ˌ⸗\ *n* **:** a relay actuated by a fall in wattage below a set level

underpraise \ˌ=ˈ=\ *vt* [¹*under* + *praise*] **:** to withhold due praise from

underpresence \ˈ=ˌ=ˌ=\ *n* [³*under* + *presence*] **:** a force or personality felt as present in inanimate nature

underprice \ˌ=ˈ=\ *vt* [¹*under* + *price*] **1 :** to set a price on that is below the current price or below the real value **2 :** to undercut (a competitor) in prices

¹underprint \ˌ=ˈ=\ *vt* [¹*under* + *print*] **1 :** to print or impress on the under side of **2 :** to print with less density or firmness of outline than is needed

²underprint \ˈ=ˌ=\ *n* **1 :** a light-colored overall pattern printed on a stamp underneath the design **2 :** printing on the back of a stamp

underprivilege \ˈ=ˌ=ˌ(=)=\ *n* [³*under* + *privilege*] **:** condition of being deprived of or barred from enjoyment of an average or accepted standard of living **:** relative poverty ⟨right of labor to speak their protests against economic ~ —R. M. La Follette †1953⟩

underprivileged \ˌ=ˈ=ˌ(=)=\ *adj* [¹*under* + *privileged*] **:** deprived through social or economic oppression of some of the fundamental rights theoretically belonging to all members of a civilized society ⟨children from ~ homes⟩ **:** socially and economically depressed **:** POOR ⟨epidemics in ~ areas of the city⟩

underprize \ˌ=ˈ=\ *vt* [¹*under* + *prize*] **:** UNDERVALUE

underproduction \ˌ=ˌ=ˈ=\ *n* [³*under* + *production*] **:** the production of less than is demanded or of less than the usual supply

underproductive \ˌ=ˌ=ˈ=\ *adj* [¹*under* + *productive*] **:** not capable of adequate production ⟨~ agricultural system⟩

underpromotion \ˌ=ˌ=ˈ=\ *n* [³*under* + *promotion*] **:** the promotion of a pawn to bishop, knight, or rook in chess

underproof \ˌ=ˈ=\ *adj* [²*under* + *proof*, n.] **:** containing less alcohol than proof spirit

¹underprop \ˌ=ˈ=\ *vt* [¹*under* + *prop*] **1 :** to prop up from below **:** UNDERPIN **2 :** UPHOLD, SUPPORT ⟨~ a reputation⟩ **3 :** to serve as a prop or support underneath

²underprop \ˈ=ˌ=\ *n* **:** a prop placed underneath or supporting something

underpropping \ˈ=ˌ=ˌ=\ *n* -s **:** FOUNDATION, SUPPORT

underquote \ˌ=ˈ=\ *vt* [¹*under* + *quote*] **:** to quote a lower price than ⟨~ competitors⟩

underrate \ˌ=ˈ=\ *vt* [¹*under* + *rate*] **:** to rate too low **:** set too low an estimate upon **:** UNDERVALUE ⟨human nature is consistently *underrated* in business —John Galsworthy⟩ ⟨overpraised by some critics, who have thus naturally provoked others to ~ it —A.T.Quiller-Couch⟩

¹underreach \ˌ=ˈ=\ *vt* [¹*under* + *reach*] **:** to reach under or below **:** clear under (as a log) so as to pass a chain

²underreach \ˈ=ˌ=\ *n* **:** a pole used to lever up a bogged log

underread \ˌ=ˈ=\ *vt* [¹*under* + *read*] **1 :** to take a reading below the correct reading of (a test) **:** to read (as a temperature, measurement, or weight) as lower than that actually registered **2 :** to read with less than full or due understanding, appreciation, or alertness ⟨~ the poets whose reputations they wish to demolish —F.A.Pottle⟩

underreader \ˈ=ˌ=ˌ=\ *n* [³*under* + *reader*] **:** an assistant reader

underream \ˌ=ˈ=\ *vt* [¹*under* + *ream*] **:** to enlarge (an oil= well hole) below the casing

underreamer \ˈ=ˌ=ˌ=\ *n* **:** a reamer for operating below the casing of a borehole to enlarge the hole for the reception of the pipe

underreport \ˌ=ˌ=ˈ=\ *vt* [¹*under* + *report*] **:** to report an amount for (as income) less than the actual one

underrepresented \ˌ=ˌ=ˌ=ˈ=ˌ=\ *adj* [¹*under* + *represented*, past part. of *represent*] **:** inadequately represented ⟨in pollen statistics . . . species producing small quantities will tend to be ~ —S.A.Cain⟩ ⟨farm laborers . . . are also ~ in unemployment figures —*Harper's*⟩

underripe \ˌ=ˈ=\ *adj* [¹*under* + *ripe*] **:** not fully ripe ⟨~ berries⟩

underround \ˌ=ˈ=\ *vt* [¹*under* + *round*] **:** to round (the lips or a vowel) less than usual in relation to the height of the tongue

¹underruff \ˌ=ˈ=\ *vi* [¹*under* + *ruff*] **:** to ruff with a trump smaller than one already played so as to avoid discarding from another suit

²underruff \ˈ=ˌ=\ *n* **:** the act of underruffing

¹underrun \ˌ=ˈ=\ *vb* [¹*under* + *run*] *vt* **1 :** to pass or extend under ⟨~ and uplifted by advancing masses of colder air⟩ **2 a :** to pass along under in order to examine (a cable) **b :** to separate and put in order the parts of (a tackle) **c :** to take in (a net or trawl line) for emptying and resetting **d :** to lift and empty out (a hose) by walking along and shifting the hold successively along the length **~** *vi* **:** to flow or persist in a suppressed or underlying stream

²underrun \ˈ=ˌ=\ *n* **1 :** UNDERCURRENT **2 :** a run (as of goods or printed copies) short of the quantity ordered by a customer **3 :** the amount by which the actual cut of merchantable lumber falls below a log scale estimate **4 :** the lower contact surface of a third rail or trolley wire

unders *pl of* UNDER

undersailed \ˌ=ˈ=\ *adj* [¹*under* + *-sailed* (fr. *sail*, n. + *-ed*)] **:** equipped with too small or too few sails

undersanded \ˌ=ˈ=\ *adj* [¹*under-* + *-sanded* (fr. *sand*, n. + *-ed*)] *of concrete* **:** not containing enough sand for normal use and working conditions

undersaturated \ˌ=ˈ=ˌ=ˌ=\ *adj* [¹*under* + *saturated*] **:** UNSATURATED ⟨~ rocks⟩

undersaturation \ˌ=ˌ=ˌ=ˈ=\ *n* **:** the quality or state of being undersaturated

¹underscore \ˌ=ˈ=\ *vt* [¹*under* + *score*] **1 :** to draw a line under **:** UNDERLINE ⟨twenty lines of it were heavily *underscored* in red ink —L.C.Douglas⟩ **2 :** EMPHASIZE ⟨the conference also *underscored* the very great importance of isotopes to industry, biology, and medicine —R.J.Bunche⟩ **3 :** to provide (action on film) with accompanying music

²underscore \ˈ=ˌ=\ *n* **1 :** a line drawn under a word or line esp. for indicating emphasis or italic letters **:** UNDERSCORING **2 :** music accompanying the action and dialogue of a film

underscrub \ˈ=ˌ=\ *n* [³*under* + *scrub*] **:** scrubby growth under trees **:** UNDERBRUSH

¹undersea \ˌ=ˈ=\ *adj* [²*under* + *sea*, n.] **1 :** being or carried on under the sea or under the surface of the sea ⟨~ oil deposits⟩ ⟨~ fighting⟩ **2 :** designed for use under the surface of the sea ⟨~ fleet⟩ ⟨~ cable⟩

²undersea \"\ *or* **underseas** \ˌ=ˈ=\ *adv* [²*under* + *sea*, n. or *seas*, pl. of *sea*, n.] **:** under the sea **:** beneath the surface of the sea ⟨photographs taken ~⟩

undersecretariat \ˌ=ˌ=ˌ=ˈ(ˌ)=\ *n* [³*under* + *secretariat*] **:** the office and staff of an undersecretary **:** a subdivision of a ministry

un·der·secretary \ˌəndə(r)+\ *n* [³*under* + *secretary*] **:** a subordinate or assistant secretary; *specif* **:** a secretary immediately subordinate to a principal secretary ⟨~ of the Treasury⟩ ⟨the British ~ for India⟩

undersecretary·ship \"+ˌship\ *n* **:** the position of undersecretary

undersell \ˌ=ˈ=\ *vt* [¹*under* + *sell*] **1 :** to sell articles at a lower price than **:** to sell cheaper than (the same article offered elsewhere) **:** UNDERCUT **2 :** to appeal to or persuade inadequately or with restraint ⟨discovered that ~*ing* actually boosted its business —*Time*⟩

undersense \ˈ=ˌ=\ *n* [³*under* + *sense*] **1 :** an inner awareness **:** SUBCONSCIOUSNESS **2 :** an underlying sense or meaning ⟨the mind has to make no effort to get the ~ of what is happening —J.C.Powys⟩

underservant \ˈ=ˌ=ˌ=\ *n* [³*under* + *servant*] **:** a subordinate servant

¹underset \ˌ=ˈ=\ *vt* [ME *undersetten*, fr. ¹*under* + *setten* to set — more at SET] **1 :** UNDERPIN **2 :** to place underneath something else

²underset \ˈ=ˌ=\ *n* **1 :** UNDERCURRENT **2 a :** an underlying vein of ore **b :** UNDERLIE

³underset \"\ *adj* [fr. past part. of ¹*underset*] **:** insufficiently filled (as with printed matter) so as to be partly blank ⟨~ page⟩ ⟨~ column⟩

undersetting \ˈ=ˌ=ˌ=\ *n* [ME, fr. ³*under* + *setting*, gerund of *setten* to set] **:** something set or built under as a support **:** UNDERPINNING

un·der·set·tle \ˈəndə(r)ˌsed·ᵊl\ *n* [ME *undersetle*, fr. ³*under* + *-setle* dweller, fr. OE *-setla*, akin to OE *sittan* to sit — more at SIT] **:** one of a class of subtenants formerly under the peasant proprietors in England

undersexed \ˌ=ˈ=\ *adj* [¹*under* + *sexed*] **:** characterized by a subnormal or inadequate degree of sexual desire or interest ⟨the American woman has become cold and ~ —William Faulkner⟩

undersheriff \ˈ=ˌ=ˌ=\ *n* [³*under* + *sheriff*] **:** a sheriff's deputy; *specif* **:** one on whom the sheriff's powers devolve by the sheriff's direction or in case of his incapacity or a vacancy in the office

undershirt \ˈ=ˌ=\ *n* [³*under* + *shirt*] **:** a collarless undergarment with or without sleeves and usu. of cotton jersey

¹undershoot \ˌ=ˈ=\ *vt* [¹*under* + *shoot*, v.] **1 :** to shoot short of or below (a target) **2 :** to fall short of (a runway) in landing an airplane **~** *vi* **:** to shoot so as to strike below or short of the mark

²undershoot \ˈ=ˌ=\ *n* **:** an act or an instance of undershooting

³undershoot \"\ *n* [³*under* + *shoot*, n. (branch)] **:** a shoot (as of a plant) that springs out below a higher or more important shoot

undershore \ˌ=ˈ=\ *vt* [ME *undershoren*, fr. ¹*under* + *shoren* to shore — more at SHORE (to support)] **1 :** to shore up **2 :** to furnish support or justification for **:** UPHOLD ⟨~ an argument⟩

undershorts \ˈ=ˌ=\ *n pl* [³*under* + *shorts*] **:** short loose-fitting underpants

undershot \ˈ=ˌ=\ *adj* [¹*under* + *shot*, past part. of *shoot*] **1 :** having the lower incisor teeth or lower jaw projecting beyond the upper when the mouth is closed ⟨~ bulldog⟩ **2 :** moved by water passing beneath

undershot wheel *n* **:** a vertical waterwheel into the circumference of which are set blades that are pushed by water passing underneath

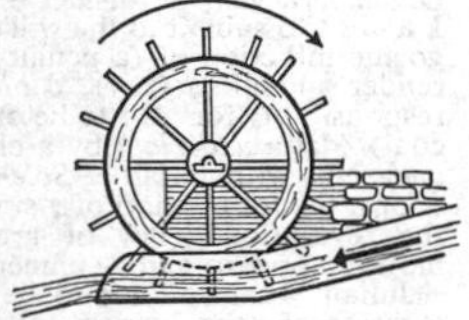

undershot wheel

undershrub \ˈ=ˌ=\ *n* [³*under* + *shrub*] **1 :** SUBSHRUB 1 **2 :** a small low-growing shrub; *esp* **:** a woody chamaephyte

undershrubby \ˈ=ˌ=ˌ=\ *adj* **:** tending to be a low shrub or subshrub

underside \ˈ=ˌ=, ˌ=ˈ=\ *n* [³*under* + *side*] **1 :** the side or surface lying underneath ⟨~ of a leaf⟩ **2 :** the side usu. hidden from sight **:** the worse side ⟨with the ~ of civilization revealing itself in slum and brothel —R.M.Kain⟩

undersign \ˌ=ˈ=\ *vt* [¹*under* + *sign*] **:** to write one's name at the foot or end of (as a letter or legal instrument)

undersigned \ˌ=ˈ=\ *n, pl* **undersigned** [fr. past part. of *undersign*] **:** one who signs his name at the end of a document — used with *the* ⟨the ~ testifies⟩ ⟨the ~ all agree⟩

undersigner \ˌ=ˈ=\ *n* **:** one that undersigns **:** UNDERSIGNED, SUBSCRIBER

undersize \ˈ=ˌ=\ *n* [³*under* + *size*] **1 :** size below the normal or average **2 :** the portion of ground material (as ore or coal) that passes through a specific size of screen

¹undersized *also* **undersize** \ˌ=ˈ=\ *adj* [*undersized* fr. ¹*under* + *sized; undersize* fr. ²*under* + *size*, n.] **:** of a size less than is common, proper, normal, or average ⟨~ trout⟩

²undersized *adj* [¹*under* + *sized*, past part. of *size* (to treat with size)] **:** not sufficiently sized ⟨~ paper⟩

underskirt \ˈ=ˌ=\ *n* [³*under* + *skirt*] **:** a skirt worn under an outer skirt; *esp* **:** PETTICOAT

underslip \ˈ=ˌ=\ *n* [³*under* + *slip*] **:** SLIP 6a

underslope \ˈ=ˌ=\ *n* [³*under* + *slope*] **:** an earmark for cattle corresponding to the overslope but on the lower side of the ear — see EARMARK illustration

undersluice \ˈ=ˌ=\ *n* [³*under* + *sluice*] **:** a sluice covered from view or lying beneath another structure; *specif* **:** a wasteway for sluicing out canals in which the waste escapes beneath other structures

underslung \ˈ=ˌ=\ *adj* [¹*under* + *slung*, past part. of *sling*] **1 a** (1) **:** having the point of support above rather than underneath ⟨~ desk drawer⟩ **:** having the principal bulk below the point of support ⟨~ bowl of a pipe⟩ (2) *of a vehicle frame* **:** suspended so as to extend below the axles **b :** having a low center of gravity **:** built low to the ground **:** having short legs **:** SQUAT **2 :** UNDERSHOT 1 ⟨bullet head and ~ jaw⟩

undersold *past of* UNDERSELL

undersong \ˈ=ˌ=\ *n* [³*under* + *song*] **1 a :** a subordinate melody or part; *esp* **:** a droning accompaniment **b :** UNDERTONE **2** *archaic* **:** REFRAIN

undersow \ˌ=ˈ=\ *vt* [¹*under* + *sow*] **:** to sow (a crop) with or after a main crop to grow on after the main crop has been harvested ⟨barley was *undersown* with lespedeza⟩

underspend \ˌ=ˈ=\ *vb* [¹*under* + *spend*] *vt* **:** to spend less than or less than the whole of **~** *vi* **:** to spend at less than the normal rate

underspin \ˈ=ˌ=\ *n* [³*under* + *spin*] **:** BACKSPIN

undersquare \ˈ=ˌ=\ *n* [³*under* + *square*] **:** an earmark for cattle made on the lower side of the ear **:** UNDERCROP — see EARMARK illustration

understaffed \ˌ=ˈ=\ *adj* [¹*under* + *staffed*, past part. of *staff*] **:** having an inadequate staff ⟨overcrowded and ~ hospitals⟩

un·der·stand \ˌəndə(r)ˈstand, -aa(ə)nd\ *vb* **un·der·stood** \-ˈtu̇d\ **understood** *or archaic* **understanded**; **understanding**; **understands** [ME *understanden, understonden*, fr. OE *understandan, understondan*, fr. ¹*under* + *standan, stondan* to stand — more at STAND] *vt* **1 :** to grasp the meaning of **:** COMPREHEND: as **a :** to apprehend the meaning or idea of by knowing what is conveyed by the words or signs used ⟨~ Russian⟩ ⟨~ a message in code⟩ ⟨~ a wink⟩ ⟨a tongue not ~*ed* of the people —*Bk. of Com. Prayer*⟩ **b :** to grasp the reasonable or logical character of **:** interpret or explain successfully to oneself ⟨I can ~ why he was disappointed⟩ ⟨his behavior is hard to ~⟩ ⟨must be made to ~ the importance of this step⟩ **c :** to make out clearly the speech of ⟨spoke in such a thick accent no one could ~ him⟩ **d :** to have thorough or technical acquaintance with or expertness in the practice of ⟨being well informed about science is not the same thing as ~*ing* science —J.B.Conant⟩ ⟨~ finance⟩ ⟨master builders had to ~ both carpentry and stonework —G.B.Saul⟩ **e :** to be thoroughly familiar with the character or essential nature and propensities of ⟨need someone who ~*s* children⟩ ⟨liked him better when he came to ~ him better⟩ **2 a :** to know, consider, or accept as a fact, truth, or principle without further mention or explanation or without utter certainty ⟨*understood* that customary procedures obtained⟩ **b :** to consider as a possible fact **:** infer or come to regard as plausible or probable without certain knowledge or proof **:** know through rumor or hearsay ⟨we ~ that he is returning from abroad next week⟩ ⟨was *understood* to be in favor of the plan⟩ **c :** to accept as established or laid down as a condition whether or not explicitly stated ⟨am I to ~ that your refusal is final⟩ **3 :** to regard in a particular way or with a particular meaning in mind **:** interpret in a single one of a number of possible ways ⟨by the money price of goods . . . I ~ always the quantity of pure gold or silver for which they are sold —Adam Smith⟩ ⟨by poetical colors the neoclassicist ~*s* words, elegant phrases, figures of speech —Irving Babbitt⟩ **4 :** to supply in thought as if present **:** take as meant though not expressed ⟨the phrase "to be married" is commonly *understood* after the word *engaged*⟩ ⟨~ the subject of an imperative⟩ **5** *archaic* **:** to be familiar with **:** recognize from previous knowledge ⟨abundance of kinds of creatures that we did not ~ —Daniel Defoe⟩ **6** *obs* **:** to know how to conduct (oneself) properly **7** *obs* **:** to prop up **:** SUPPORT **~** *vi* **1 :** to have the use of the intellectual faculties **:** have the power of comprehension **2 :** to achieve a mental grasp of the nature, significance, or causal explanation of something ⟨the more he was educated, the less he *understood* —Henry Adams⟩ ⟨doubt if they really can ~ about politics —Christopher Hollis⟩ **3 :** to show a sympathetic or tolerant or indulgent attitude toward something ⟨she relied on him to ~ and sympathize —John Galsworthy⟩

syn COMPREHEND, APPRECIATE: UNDERSTAND and COMPREHEND are very often interchangeable. For very wide and general concepts UNDERSTAND is more likely to be used than COMPREHEND ⟨*understand* Shakespeare's preeminence⟩ ⟨*comprehend* the dramatic action of Macbeth⟩ ⟨to *understand* the present institutions, we must therefore *comprehend* something of their history —J.B.Conant⟩ UNDERSTAND is wider in its use, ranging from the mere physical act of sensory perception or very casual consideration to a full and profound realization of inner nature, rationale, or significance ⟨the racket prevented my *understanding* the telephone operator⟩ ⟨when you throw an apple upward and let it fall . . . the mechanics of the thing . . . seem natural; you *understand* them without even using your intellect —Wolfgang Langewiesche⟩ ⟨those enlightened ones who in the clear beam of their purified vision beheld and *understood* the sorrows, the struggles, the vain angers and hatreds of imperfect mortality —Laurence Binyon⟩ COMPREHEND may focus attention on thought processes rather than their conclusions ⟨with what terrible earnestness Woodrow Wilson was trying to *comprehend* the problem —W.A.White⟩ COMPREHEND may stand between *sense* or *feel* and *understand* in suggesting less reflection and analysis than the latter ⟨dissimilar as her parents had appeared to be, there was a bond between them which Dorinda felt without *comprehending* —Ellen Glasgow⟩ APPRECIATE stresses full and just perception, esp. of value, arrived at with insight and discrimination ⟨I could not *appreciate* its excellence, having no background of previous displays to use for purposes of comparison —Robert Graves⟩ ⟨fully to *appreciate* the American experience . . . would require a rehearsal of the whole of American history —H.S.Commager⟩

— give one to understand 1 : to intimate or convey to one without direct or positive assertion ⟨it is reported that the Democrats have been quietly *given to understand* that the White House approves of their action —*New Republic*⟩ **2 :** to make one understand **:** tell plainly and forcibly **— understand each other :** to be in agreement esp. without having exchanged explicit declarations or assurances; *often* **:** to be in collusion

un·der·stand·abil·i·ty \ˌəndə(r)ˌstandəˈbiləd·ē, -aan-, -lətē, -i\ *n* **:** the quality or state of being understandable

un·der·stand·able \ˌəndə(r)ˈstandəbəl, -aan-\ *adj* [ME, fr. *understanden* + *-able*] **1 :** capable of being readily understood **:** INTELLIGIBLE **2** *obs* **:** able to understand or comprehend **— un·der·stand·able·ness** *n* -ES **— un·der·stand·ably** \-blē, -li\ *adv*

understanded *archaic past part of* UNDERSTAND

un·der·stand·er \ˌəndə(r)ˈstandə(r), -aan-\ *n* -s [ME *understander, understonder*, fr. *understanden, understonden* + *-er*] **1 :** one that understands **2 :** one that stands under or supports; *specif* **:** UNDERMAN 2 **3** *obs* **a :** FOOT **b :** BOOT **4** *obs* **:** a spectator in the pit of a theater

¹understanding *n* -s [ME, fr. OE, fr. *understandan* to understand + *-ing*] **1 :** the act of grasping mentally **:** COMPREHENSION, DISCERNMENT, INTERPRETATION ⟨a clear ~ of the reasons for his failure⟩ **2 a :** the ability to understand **:** the power of comprehending, analyzing, distinguishing, and judging ⟨an argument aimed at the ~ rather than the emotions⟩ **b :** the condition of having attained to full comprehension ⟨the book deals with matters beyond a child's ~⟩ **3 a :** the faculty or ability of subsuming the particular under the general or of apprehending general relations of particulars; *also* **:** JUDGMENT 10b **b :** the power to make experience intelligible by bringing perceived particulars under appropriate concepts **c :** the capacity to formulate and apply to experience concepts and categories, to judge, and to draw logical inferences — distinguished from *reason;* compare DIANOIA, RATIO 1b, TECHNE **4 a :** friendly or harmonious relationship ⟨working for better ~ between nations⟩ ⟨had never been much ~ between the brothers⟩ **b :** an agreement of opinion or feeling **:** adjustment of differences ⟨reached an ~ with the children about television programs⟩ **c :** a mutual agreement not formally entered into but in some degree binding on each side ⟨a monetary ~ between two countries⟩; *esp* **:** an informal engagement to marry **d :** an understood or acknowledged condition, limitation, or provision ⟨allowed to plow up the footpaths during the war on the ~ that they restored them afterward —S.P.B.Mais⟩ **5 :** SIGNIFICATION, MEANING ⟨according to the usual ~ of the word⟩ **syn** see REASON

²understanding *adj* [ME, fr. pres. part. of *understanden* to understand] **1** *archaic* **:** KNOWING, INTELLIGENT, SKILLFUL **2 :** endowed with or displaying understanding ⟨~ heart⟩ **3 :** possessed of a tolerant, kindly, humane, or sympathetic attitude ⟨~ parents⟩ **— un·der·stand·ing·ly** *adv* **— un·der·stand·ing·ness** *n* -ES

understands *pres 3d sing of* UNDERSTAND

understate \ˌ=ˈ=\ *vt* [¹*under* + *state*] **1 :** to represent as being less than the true number, size, intensity **:** state inadequately or less strongly than may be done truthfully ⟨~ taxable income⟩ ⟨~ the logical difficulties of a proposed scheme⟩ **2 :** to state or describe with deliberate restraint esp. so as to achieve an effective contrast **:** withhold obvious emphasis from ⟨story is told with . . . *understated* force —*Time*⟩

understated \ˌ=ˈ=\ *adj* [fr. past part. of *understate*] **:** simply effective **:** avoiding obvious emphasis or embellishment ⟨handsome, ~ suit with simple details —Dorothy Hawkins⟩

understatement \ˌ=ˈ=ˌ=\ *n* [³*under* + *statement*] **1 :** the act of understating **:** a statement below the truth ⟨~ of population growth⟩ **2 :** restrained statement in ironic contrast to what might be said **:** studied avoidance of emphasis or exaggeration ⟨we have been taught to value terseness and ~ —Irving Howe⟩

understeer \ˈ=ˌ=\ *n* **:** the tendency of an automobile to go straight ahead and turn less sharply than the driver intends **— understeer** \ˌ=ˈ=\ *vi*

¹understock \ˌ=ˈ=\ *vt* [¹*under* + *stock*] **:** to stock (as a farm or store) with less than the usual or desirable number or quantity

²understock \ˈ=ˌ=\ *n* **1 :** an inadequate supply **2 :** STOCK 5b(1)

understocking \ˈ=ˌ=ˌ=\ *n* [³*under* + *stocking*] **1** *archaic* **:** a stocking for the lower leg **2 :** a stocking worn for support or warmth under another stocking

un·der·stood \ˌəndə(r)ˈstu̇d\ *adj* [fr. past part. of *understand*] **1 :** fully apprehended as to meaning or causal relations or essential nature **2 :** settled or settled upon by common often tacit agreement **:** IMPLICIT ⟨our breakfasts together had become habitual, the invitation ~ —R.C.Peace⟩

understory \ˈ=ˌ=ˌ=\ *n* [³*under* + *story*] **1 :** a foliage layer lying beneath and shaded by the main canopy of a forest **2 a :** the plants (as seedlings, shrubs, and herbs) that form the foliage understory of a forest — sometimes distinguished from *ground cover* **b :** a layer of low vegetation underlying a layer of taller (as of grama grass beneath wheatgrass)

understrapper \ˈ=ˌ=ˌ=\ *n* [³*under* + *strapper*] **:** an inferior agent or official **:** a petty subordinate **:** UNDERLING ⟨country being run into the ground by a bunch of big-headed ~*s* who went around lording it over the taxpayers —H.L.Davis⟩

understratum \ˈ=ˌ=ˌ=\ *n* [³*under* + *stratum*] **:** SUBSTRATUM

understrength \ˌ=ˈ=\ *adj* [²*under* + *strength*, n.] **:** deficient in strength ⟨~ solution of disinfectant⟩; *specif* **:** having fewer personnel than prescribed by a table of organization

understress \ˌ=ˈ=\ *vt* [¹*under* + *stress*] **:** to stress insufficiently **:** fail to give due emphasis to

understring \ˌ=ˈ=\ *vt* [¹*under* + *string*] **:** to string (a bow) with too long a cord

¹understroke \ˌ=ˈ=\ *vb* [¹*under* + *stroke*] *vt* **:** UNDERLINE, UNDERSCORE **~** *vi* **:** to execute an understroke

²understroke \ˈ=ˌ=\ *n* **:** a stroke executed underneath or with a downward sweep

understructure \ˈ=ˌ=ˌ=\ *n* [³*under* + *structure*] **:** a structure for supporting something above **:** FOUNDATION, BASIS

understrung \ˌ=ˈ=\ *adj* [¹*under* + *strung*, past part. of *string*] **:** LOW-STRUNG

¹understudy \ˈ=ˌ=ˌ=\ *vb* [¹*under* + *study*] *vi* **:** to study another actor's part in order to be his substitute in an emergency **~** *vt* **1 :** to study (a part or character) as understudy **:** prepare as understudy to (an actor) **2 :** to learn (as a job or procedure) thoroughly by observation or apprenticeship ⟨~ a banking operation⟩

²understudy \"\ *n* **:** one who stands prepared to act another's part or take over the work or duties of another

undersupply \ˌ=ˌ=ˈ=\ *n* [³*under* + *supply*] **:** an inadequate supply or amount

¹undersurface \ˈ=ˌ=ˌ=\ *n* [³*under* + *surface*] **:** the surface that lies underneath **:** UNDERSIDE

2undersurface \"\ *adj* [2*under* + *surface*, n.] : existing or moving below the surface ⟨~ craft⟩

undertail \ˈ==ˌ=\ *adj* [2*under* + *tail*, n.] : lying or extending under the tail ⟨~ wing coverts⟩

undertake \¦==¦=\ *vb* [ME *undertaken*, fr. 1*under* + *taken* to take — more at TAKE] *vt* **1** : to take in hand : enter upon : set about : ATTEMPT ⟨~ a task⟩ ⟨~ a journey⟩ ⟨~ to campaign for office⟩ ⟨when armed uprisings have been *undertaken* by single oppressed classes —M.R.Cohen⟩ **2** : to take upon oneself solemnly or expressly : put oneself under obligation to perform : CONTRACT, COVENANT ⟨a player ~*s* to win nine tricks provided he may declare his own trumps —J.B.Pick⟩ **3** : GUARANTEE, PROMISE ⟨the magician who ~*s* to make or stop rain —J.G.Frazer⟩ **4** : to accept as a charge : engage to look after or attend to : accept the responsibility for the care of ⟨~ a patient⟩ ⟨lawyer may refuse to ~ a case which appears to him unsound —H.S.Drinker⟩ **5** *archaic* **a** : to engage with in combat **b** : to engage with in argument or competition : take on **6** *obs* : REPROVE, CHIDE **7** *obs* : to take in or receive by hearing or interpreting ~ *vi* **1** *archaic* : to enter into an engagement or contract : PLEDGE — used with *for* **2** *archaic* : to give surety or assume responsibility — used with *for* **3** *obs* : to engage in a venture or enterprise

un·der·tak·er \¦əndə(r)¦tākə(r), *in sense 4* ˈ==ˌ==\ *n* [ME, fr. *undertaken* + *-er*] **1** : one that undertakes : one that launches an enterprise : one that engages in any project or business : one that takes the risk and management of business : ENTREPRENEUR **2** *obs* **a** : one engaged in scholarly and scientific exploration of a subject **b** : one engaged upon the compiling or composition of a work for publication **c** : a book publisher **d** : an organizer of a stage production **3** : one that stipulates or covenants to perform work for another : CONTRACTOR, SUBCONTRACTOR **4** : one whose business is to prepare the dead for burial and to arrange and manage funerals **5 a** : an Englishman taking over ownership of forfeited lands in Ireland in the 16th and 17th centuries **b** : a political leader undertaking to influence members of Parliament esp. in securing supplies for the sovereign in 17th century England

un·der·tak·er·ly *adj* : having the manner or tone of an undertaker ⟨sees my grief, and assumes an ~ air —George Meredith⟩

1undertaking *n* [ME, fr. gerund of *undertaken* to undertake] **1** : the act of one who undertakes or engages in a project or business; *specif* : the business of an undertaker **2** : something undertaken : a business, work, or project which one engages in or attempts : ENTERPRISE ⟨large-scale ~*s* involving large expenditures of money —E.L.Bernays⟩ **3** : PLEDGE, PROMISE, GUARANTEE; *specif* : a promise or security required by law

2undertaking *adj* [ME, fr. pres. part. of *undertaken* to undertake] *archaic* : willing to undertake an enterprise assuming the risks as organizer or manager; *esp* : ready to engage in literary production or act as publisher

undertenancy \ˈ==ˌ===\ *n* [3*under* + *tenancy*] : a tenancy held from a tenant

undertenant \ˈ==ˌ==\ *n* [3*under* + *tenant*] : the tenant of a tenant : one who holds lands or tenements by an underlease

under-the-counter \¦===¦==\ *adj, of a sale* : made from concealed stocks of scarce or rare goods or goods priced below the legal fixed price; *broadly* : UNLAWFUL, ILLICIT

under-the-table \¦===¦==\ *adj* [fr. the phrase *under the table*] : carried out in a secret or confidential manner : SUB-ROSA ⟨has the *under-the-table* backing of the remnants of the discredited political faction —*New Orleans* (*La.*) *Times-Picayune*⟩

underthings \ˈ==ˌ=\ *n pl* [3*under* + *things*, pl. of *thing*] : women's underwear

underthought \ˈ==ˌ=\ *n* [3*under* + *thought*] : a suppressed or concealed thought

1underthrust \¦==¦=\ *vt* [1*under* + *thrust*] **1** : to thrust underneath or out from underneath ⟨sulky ~ lower lip⟩ **2** : to insert or move (a rock mass) into position by underthrust faulting

2underthrust \ˈ==ˌ=\ *n* **1** : the insertion by compressive stresses and faulting of one mass of rock under another — compare THRUST FAULT **2** : the stress that produces an underthrust

undertide \ˈ==ˌ=\ *n* [3*under* + *tide*] : UNDERCURRENT

1undertime \ˈ==ˌ=\ *n* [3*under* + *time*, n.] **1** : a time less than the time allotted for the performance of some task or the completion of a program or speech **2** : working time that is less than full time or a required minimum

2undertime \¦==¦=\ *vt* [1*under* + *time*, v.] : to allow too short a time for ⟨~ a photographic exposure⟩

undertint \ˈ==ˌ=\ *n* [3*under* + *tint*] : a subdued tint

1undertone \ˈ==ˌ=\ *n* [3*under* + *tone*] **1 a** : a low or subdued utterance ⟨gossiping in a corner in ~*s*⟩ **b** : an underlying or accompanying sound ⟨~ of droning insects⟩ **c** : COMBINATION TONE **2 a** : a subdued or implicit emotional quality underlying the surface of an utterance or action ⟨sneering and malicious ~ on nearly every page —John Morris⟩ ⟨uneasiness in Paris had deeper ~*s* of fear —*Atlantic*⟩ **b** : the underlying tendency of a market as distinguished from its behavior at any one time ⟨despite a weak start, utilities displayed a strong ~ in today's session⟩ **3** : a subdued color: as **a** : the color of a pigment thinly laid on a white or light-colored ground **b** : a color seen through and modifying another or other colors **c** : the color of the light transmitted (as by a paint or varnish film) — compare OVERTONE 2

2undertone \"\ *vt* : to express in an undertone

undertook *past of* UNDERTAKE

undertow \ˈ==ˌ=\ *n* [3*under* + *tow*] : the current beneath the surface that sets seaward or along the beach when waves are breaking upon the shore — compare OFFSET, 5RIP 2, SEA PUSS

undertread \¦==¦=\ *vt* [1*under* + *tread*] *archaic* : to tread beneath the feet : SUBJUGATE, OPPRESS

undertrick \ˈ==ˌ=\ *n* [3*under* + *trick*] : a trick by which a declarer in bridge falls short of making his contract

undertrimmer \ˈ==ˌ==\ *n* [3*under* + *trimmer*] : one that fits and sews linings to shoe uppers

undertrump \¦==¦=\ *vb* [1*under* + *trump*] : UNDERRUFF

underturner \ˈ==ˌ==\ *n* [3*under* + *turner* (after *turn under*, v.)] : a worker that removes burrs from clock pinions

underutilization \¦==ˌ==(ˌ)=¦==\ *n* [3*under* + *utilization*] : insufficient utilization : wasteful failure to utilize fully

undervaluation \¦==ˌ==¦==\ *n* [3*under* + *valuation*] **1** : the act of undervaluing **2** : a rate or value not equal to the real worth

1undervalue \¦==¦=(ˌ)=\ *vt* [1*under* + *value*, v.] **1** : to value, rate, or estimate below the real worth : set too low a value upon ⟨*undervalued* the things he did not know —Agnes Repplier⟩ **2** : to esteem lightly : treat as of little worth **3** : to cause to decrease in value or estimation : DEPRECIATE ⟨the dollar was *undervalued* in terms of foreign currencies —E.W.Kemmerer⟩

2undervalue \"\ *n* [3*under* + *value*] : a rate or price less than the real worth

undervest \ˈ==ˌ=\ *n* [3*under* + *vest*] : UNDERSHIRT

undervitalized \¦==¦==ˌ=\ *adj* [1*under* + *vitalized*, past part. of *vitalize*] : lacking normal vitality or energy ⟨pallid, ~, shy, sensitive creatures —O.W.Holmes †1894⟩

undervoltage \ˈ==ˌ==\ *adj* [2*under* + *voltage*] : devised so as to become operative when the voltage in a line drops below a definite value ⟨~ relay⟩

undervoltage protection *n* : the protection of a circuit by an automatic device against operation on reduced voltage

undervoltage release *n* : the automatic release of connections to the main circuit during an interval of reduced or no voltage

underwaist \ˈ==ˌ=\ *n* [3*under* + *waist*] : a waist for wear under another garment; *specif* : WAIST 4a(3)

1underwater \¦==¦==\ *adj* [2*under* + *water*, n.] **1** : lying, growing, performed, worn, or operating below the surface of the water ⟨~ caverns⟩ ⟨~ operation of a submarine⟩ ⟨~ signaling⟩ **2** : being below the waterline of a ship ⟨~ body⟩ ⟨~ valve⟩ **3** *of a security* : not backed by assets : having no equity if all liabilities were paid

2underwater \"\ *adv* [2*under* + *water*, n.] : under the water : under the surface of the water ⟨once stayed ~ for twenty-four hours —*New Yorker*⟩ ⟨could move more quickly ~ —Sir Winston Churchill⟩

3underwater \ˈ==ˌ==\ *n* [3*under* + *water*] : the water under the surface (as of the ocean) ⟨fired from ~⟩ ⟨the ~*s* were infested by submarines —*Irish Statesman*⟩ ⟨knows the ~ of the bay . . . like the back of her hand —George Bradshaw⟩

under way *adv* [prob. fr. D *onderweg*, *onderwege*, fr. MD *onderwegen*, *onderwege*, fr. *onder* between, among + *wegen*, *wege*, dat. & acc. pl. of *wech* way; akin to OHG *untar* between, among and to OHG *wec* way — more at INTER-, WAY] **1** : in motion : not at rest : not moored : not at anchor **2** : into motion from a standstill ⟨an electric train gets *under way* rapidly⟩ **3** : in process of development : in progress toward completion : AFOOT ⟨preparations for a big celebration were *under way*⟩ ⟨before the discussion was well *under way*⟩

underway \¦==¦=\ *adj* [*under way*] : occurring, performed, or used while traveling or in motion ⟨~ training unit⟩ ⟨~ refueling⟩ ⟨~ clothing⟩

underwear \ˈ==ˌ=\ *n* [3*under* + *wear*] : a garment worn next to the skin and under other clothing ⟨stripped down to his ~⟩ ⟨filmy silk ~⟩ ⟨heavy woollen ~⟩

under weigh *adv* [by folk etymology] : under way

1underweight \¦==¦=\ *n* [3*under* + *weight*] **1** : weight below normal, average, or requisite weight : want of weight : the amount of the deficiency; *specif* : the amount by which the actual shipping weight of lumber differs from the standard weight upon which freight charges are computed **2** : the condition of weighing less than the weight normal for an age or height **3** : a person or article whose weight is less than normal or standard

2underweight \"\ *adj* [2*under* + *weight*, n.] : weighing less than the normal amount; *esp* : below the normal weight for the age

underwent *past of* UNDERGO

1underwing \ˈ==ˌ=\ *n* [3*under* + *wing*] **1** : one of the posterior wings of an insect ⟨~ of a moth⟩ **2** : any of numerous noctuid moths belonging to *Catocala* and related genera and having the hind wings banded with red and black or other contrasting colors **3** : the surfaces underneath a bird's wing

2underwing \"\ *adj* [2*under* + *wing*, n.] : placed or growing underneath the wing ⟨~ coverts⟩

underwit \ˈ==ˌ=\ *n* [3*under* + *wit*] : an underwitted person : HALF-WIT

underwitted \¦==¦==\ *adj* [1*under* + *witted*] : weak in intellect : HALF-WITTED

underwood \ˈ==ˌ=\ *n* [ME *underwode*, fr. 3*under* + *wode* wood — more at WOOD] **1** : UNDERGROWTH, UNDERBRUSH **2** : the sprout growth in a cutover forest which is reproducing itself

underwooded \ˈ==ˌ==\ *adj* : covered with undergrowth

underwool \ˈ==ˌ=\ *n* [3*under* + *wool*] : short woolly underfur or underhair (as of a rabbit)

1underwork \¦==¦=\ *vb* [1*under* + *work*, v.] *vi* **1** : to do less work than is proper or suitable **2** : to do work for less than current rates ~ *vt* **1** *obs* : to work against secretly : UNDERMINE **2 a** : to expend too little work upon ⟨~ a painting⟩ **b** : to exact too little work from ⟨~ a horse⟩ ⟨~*ed* committee⟩ **3** : to do like work at a less price than

2underwork \ˈ==ˌ=\ *n* [3*under* + *work*, n.] : a supporting structure built underneath

underworker \ˈ==ˌ==\ *n* [3*under* + *worker*] **1** : one that underworks **2** : an assistant workman

underworld \ˈ==ˌ=\ *n* [3*under* + *world*] **1** *archaic* : the world lying below the heavens : EARTH **2** : the place of departed souls : HADES **3 a** : a region underground or in the ocean depths **b** : the side of the earth opposite to one **4 a** : the world of activity among the lower forms of life **b** : a social sphere or level of society regarded as lying below the level of ordinary life and experience; *esp* : the world of organized crime

underwrite \¦==¦=\ *vb* [ME *underwriten*, fr. 1*under* + *writen* to write — more at WRITE] *vt* **1** : to write under or at the end of something else **2** : to write one's name under or set one's name to (an insurance policy) for the purpose of thereby becoming answerable for a designated loss or damage on consideration of receiving a premium percent : insure on life or property; *also* : to assume (a sum or risk) by way of insurance **3** : to subscribe to : agree to : CONFIRM ⟨U.S. might tolerate, accept, permit a compromise in Indochina without fully *underwriting* it —Frank Gorrell⟩ **4 a** : to agree to purchase (a security issue) on a fixed date at a fixed price with a view to public distribution **b** : to contract for the purchase of (securities) under an agreement to buy any portion of shares offered to a corporation's existing shareholders that remain unsold ⟨~ a stock issue on a standby basis⟩ **c** : to put up funds for or guarantee financial support of ⟨corporations have undertaken to ~ a sizable proportion of the orchestras' deficits —Howard Taubman⟩ **5 a** : to write in a manner inadequate to represent the real worth or importance of ⟨~ his parts, lightly sketching the characters and counting on the actors to fill them in —W.S.Maugham⟩ **b** : to drop below (as a person or a standard) in quality of writing ~ *vi* **1** *obs* : to give a guarantee or become surety **2** : to carry on the business of an underwriter

underwriter \ˈ==ˌ==\ *n* **1** : one that underwrites : GUARANTOR, SUPPORTER ⟨the citizen taxpayer has succeeded . . . as the principal ~ of the costs of science —*Scientific American Reader*⟩ **2** : one that underwrites a policy of insurance : an individual or company that insures : INSURER **3** : one that underwrites or shares in underwriting a security issue **4** : one who selects risks to be solicited ⟨life ~⟩ or classifies and rates the acceptability of risks solicited ⟨fire ~⟩ ⟨home-office ~⟩

underwriting \ˈ==ˌ==\ *n* [3*under* + *writing*] : the earlier writing in a palimpsest

un·descended \¦ən+\ *adj* [1*un-* + *descended*, past part. of *descend*] : not having descended; *specif* : retained in the inguinal canal instead of descending normally into the scrotum ⟨~ testicle⟩

un·describable \"+\ *adj* [1*un-* + *describe* + *-able*] : INDESCRIBABLE

un·described \"+\ *adj* [1*un-* + *described*, past part. of *describe*] : not described

un·descried \"+\ *adj* [1*un-* + *descried*, past part. of *descry*] : not descried : UNSEEN

un·descriptive \"+\ *adj* : not effective in describing

un·deserve \"+\ *vt* [back-formation fr. *undeserved*] : to fail to deserve

un·deserved \"+\ *adj* [ME, fr. 1*un-* + *deserved*, past part. of *deserven* to deserve — more at DESERVE] : not deserved : not merited : not justified ⟨~ reputation as a coward⟩ ⟨~ praise⟩ — **un·deservedly** \"+\ *adv* — **un·deservedness** \"+\ *n*

un·deserving \"+\ *adj* [1*un-* + *deserving*, pres. part. of *deserve*] : not deserving ⟨~ of forgiveness⟩

un·de·serv·ing·ly *adv* **1** : UNWORTHILY ⟨~ honored⟩ **2** : UNJUSTLY ⟨~ punished⟩

un·designated \"+\ *adj* [1*un-* + *designated*, past part. of *designate*] : not designated

un·designed \"+\ *adj* [1*un-* + *designed*, past part. of *design*] : not designed : UNINTENTIONAL — **un·designedly** \"+\ *adv*

un·designing \"+\ *adj* : having no artful, ulterior, or fraudulent purpose : SINCERE, ARTLESS — **un·de·sign·ing·ly** *adv* — **un·de·sign·ing·ness** *n* -ES

un·desirability \"+\ *n* : the quality or state of being undesirable ⟨~ of concentrating all authority in a single individual —N.R.Collins⟩

1un·desirable \"+\ *adj* [1*un-* + *desirable*] : not desirable : UNWANTED, OBJECTIONABLE ⟨~ impurities in steel⟩ ⟨led astray by ~ companions⟩ ⟨legislation excluding ~ aliens⟩ — **un·de·sir·able·ness** *n* — **un·desirably** \"+\ *adv*

2undesirable \"\ *n* : one that is undesirable ⟨rounding up vagrants, drunks, ~*s*⟩

undesirable discharge *n* : a formal release from military service under conditions other than honorable

un·desire \¦ən+\ *n* : absence of desire

un·desired \"+\ *adj* [ME, fr. 1*un-* + *desired*, past part. of *desiren* to desire — more at DESIRE] : not desired : UNSOUGHT, UNWANTED ⟨~ result⟩ ⟨~ unemployment⟩ — **un·de·sired·ly** \-ī(ə)rdlē, -īəd-, -īrəd-, -li\ *adv*

un·desiring \"+\ *adj* [1*un-* + *desiring*, pres. part. of *desire*] : not desiring : UNDESIROUS

un·desirous \"+\ *adj* : lacking desire : feeling no desire

un·despairing \"+\ *adj* [1*un-* + *despairing*, pres. part. of *despair*] : not despairing : UNDAUNTED

un·despoiled \"+\ *adj* [1*un-* + *despoiled*, pres. part. of *despoil*] : not despoiled ⟨~ wilderness⟩

un·destroyable \"+\ *adj* [ME *undistriable*, fr. 1*un-* + *destroyen*, *distrien* to destroy + *-able* — more at DESTROY] : INDESTRUCTIBLE

un·detachable \"+\ *adj* : not detachable ⟨~ part of a property⟩

un·detached \"+\ *adj* : not detached : INTEGRAL 1

undetd *abbr* undetermined

un·detectable \¦ən+\ *adj* : not detectable : escaping observation ⟨~ traces of poison⟩

un·detected \"+\ *adj* [1*un-* + *detected*, past part. of *detect*] : not detected : UNOBSERVED

un·determinable \"+\ *adj* : INDETERMINABLE

un·determinate \"+\ *adj* : INDETERMINATE

un·determined \"+\ *adj* [ME, fr. 1*un-* + *determined*, past part. of *determinen* to determine — more at DETERMINE] **1** : not yet definitely or authoritatively decided, settled, or fixed ⟨~ boundary⟩ : not yet positively identified or ascertained ⟨~ species⟩ **2** : not bounded by definite limits or restrictions : not fixed or precise in signification or use : VAGUE **3** : not determinate in form or character **4** : undecided in purpose — **un·determinedness** \"+\ *n*

un·deterred \"+\ *adj* [1*un-* + *deterred*, past part. of *deter*] : not deterred ⟨pursued his own path . . . ~ by lack of popular appreciation and understanding —Osbert Sitwell⟩

un·developable \"+\ *adj* : not capable of being developed ⟨~ surface⟩

un·developed \"+\ *adj* [1*un-* + *developed*, past part. of *develop*] : not developed ⟨~ natural resources⟩ : lacking in development : IMMATURE ⟨~ social awareness⟩

un·deviable \"+\ *adj* : UNDEVIATING

un·deviating \"+\ *adj* [1*un-* + *deviating*, pres. part. of *deviate*] : keeping a true course : UNSWERVING ⟨evolution as an ~ upward march from the level of very simple organisms to much more complex ones —L.C.Eiseley⟩ ⟨~ loyalty⟩ — **un·de·vi·at·ing·ly** *adv*

un·devil \"+\ *vt* [2*un-* + *devil*, n.] **1** *archaic* : to free from diabolical possession **2** *archaic* : to divest of the character of a devil

un·devised \¦ən+\ *adj* [1*un-* + *devised*, past part. of *devise*] **1** : not devised by will ⟨~ portion of an estate⟩ **2** : not intended : UNPLANNED

un·devout \"+\ *adj* [ME, fr. 1*un-* + *devout*] : lacking in devoutness — **un·de·vout·ly** *adv*

un·diagnosable \"+\ *adj* [1*un-* + *diagnose* + *-able*] : not capable of being diagnosed ⟨~ complaint⟩

un·diagnosed \"+\ *adj* [1*un-* + *diagnosed*, past part. of *diagnose*] : not diagnosed : eluding diagnosis ⟨~ disease⟩

undid *past of* UNDO

un·didactic \¦ən+\ *adj* : not didactic : simply informative or descriptive

un·dies \ˈəndēz, -diz\ *n pl* [by shortening & alter. fr. *underwear*] : UNDERWEAR; *esp* : women's underwear

un·differenced \¦ən+\ *adj* [1*un-* + *differenced*, past part. of *difference*] : UNDIFFERENTIATED

un·differentiated \"+\ *adj* [1*un-* + *differentiated*, past part. of *differentiate*] : not differentiated : UNIFORM

un·digested \"+\ *adj* [1*un-* + *digested*, past part. of *digest*] **1** : not digested : UNASSIMILATED ⟨~ food⟩ ⟨~ mass of facts gathered at random⟩ **2** *of securities* : not absorbed by the market : not sold to permanent investors

un·dignified \"+\ *adj* : not dignified : lacking in dignity or injurious to dignity ⟨felt it to be ~ to accept a tip⟩ ⟨scrambling on all fours in an ~ manner⟩ — **un·dignifiedly** \"+\ *adv*

un·dignify \"+\ *vt* [2*un-* + *dignify*] : to take dignity from

un·diluted \"+\ *adj* : not diluted : PURE, UNQUALIFIED, UNMITIGATED ⟨~ racial strain⟩ ⟨~ pleasure⟩ ⟨~ nonsense⟩

un·diminishable \"+\ *adj* [1*un-* + *diminish* + *-able*] : not capable of being diminished ⟨~ greatness⟩

un·diminished \"+\ *adj* [1*un-* + *diminished*, past part. of *diminish*] : not lessened or weakened ⟨zeal ~ through the years⟩

un·dimmed \"+\ *adj* [1*un-* + *dimmed*, past part. of *dim*] : not dimmed : CLEAR, BRIGHT

1un·dine \¦ən¦dēn\ *n* -S [NL *undina*, fr. L *unda* wave + *-ina*, fr. fem. of *-inus* -ine (adj. suffix) — more at WATER] : a water nymph : an elemental spirit of the water : NIX — compare GNOME, SALAMANDER, SYLPH

2un·dine \", ˈənˌdīn\ *or* **undine dropper** *n* -S [*undine*, ISV, fr. *und-* (fr. L *undare* to wave, overflow, inundate, fr. *unda* wave) + *-ine*] : a glass vessel used by physicians for irrigating the eye or a nasal passage

undine

un·diocesed \¦ən+\ *adj* [1*un-* + *diocese* + *-ed*] : unprovided with a diocese : having no diocese

un·diplomatic \"+\ *adj* : TACTLESS, IMPOLITIC

un·dipped \"+\ *adj* [1*un-* + *dipped*, past part. of *dip*] **1** : not dipped **2** : UNBAPTIZED

un·directed \"+\ *adj* [1*un-* + *directed*, past part. of *direct*] **1** : not directed : not guided : left without direction ⟨earnest but ~ efforts⟩ **2** : not addressed : not superscribed ⟨~ letter⟩

un·disbanded \"+\ *adj* [1*un-* + *disbanded*, past part. of *disband*] : not disbanded

un·discerned \"+\ *adj* [1*un-* + *discerned*, past part. of *discern*] : not discerned : UNSEEN

un·discernible \"+\ *adj* : INDISCERNIBLE — **un·dis·cern·ible·ness** *n* — **un·discernibly** \"+\ *adv*

un·discerning \"+\ *adj* [1*un-* + *discerning*, pres. part. of *discern*] : lacking discernment — **un·dis·cern·ing·ly** *adv*

un·discharged \"+\ *adj* [1*un-* + *discharged*, past part. of *discharge*] : not discharged ⟨~ ammunition⟩ ⟨~ debts⟩

un·disciplinable \"+\ *adj* : resisting discipline : UNRULY

un·discipline \¦ən+\ *n* : want of discipline

un·disciplined \"+\ *adj* [ME, fr. 1*un-* + *disciplined*] **1** : lacking in discipline : UNRULY, WILD ⟨~ behavior⟩ **2** : not subjected to discipline : UNTRAINED ⟨~ talent⟩ — **un·dis·ci·plined·ness** *n* -ES

un·disclosed \"+\ *adj* [1*un-* + *disclosed*, past part. of *disclose*] : not made known ⟨sold for an ~ sum⟩ : not named or identified ⟨acting on information from an ~ source⟩ ⟨acting in behalf of an ~ principal⟩

un·dis·cour·age·able \¦əndə̇¦skər·ijəbəl, -kə·ri-\ *adj* [1*un-* + *discourage* + *-able*] : not capable of being discouraged

un·discouraged \¦ən+\ *adj* [1*un-* + *discouraged*, past part. of *discourage*] : not discouraged

un·discoverable \"+\ *adj* : not discoverable : resisting or escaping discovery — **un·dis·cov·er·ably** \-blē\ *adv*

un·discovered \"+\ *adj* [1*un-* + *discovered*, past part. of *discover*] : not discovered : HIDDEN, UNEXPLORED

un·discriminated \"+\ *adj* [1*un-* + *discriminated*, past part. of *discriminate*] : not discriminated : INDISCRIMINATE

un·discriminating \"+\ *adj* : not discriminating : failing to make or to recognize distinctions ⟨~ condemnation of a class⟩ ⟨sweeping, ~ generalization⟩ — **un·dis·crim·i·nat·ing·ly** *adv*

un·discussed \"+\ *adj* [ME, fr. 1*un-* + *discussed*, past part. of *discussen* to discuss — more at DISCUSS] : not discussed ⟨leaving the main question still ~⟩

un·disgraced \"+\ *adj* [1*un-* + *disgraced*, past part. of *disgrace*] : not disgraced

un·disguisable \"+\ *adj* [1*un-* + *disguise*, v. + *-able*] : not disguisable ⟨~ voice⟩

un·disguise \"+\ *n* [1*un-* + *disguise*, n.] : absence of disguise or pretense

un·disguised \"+\ *adj* [ME, fr. 1*un-* + *disguised*, *disgised* disguised — more at DISGUISED] : not disguised or concealed : PLAIN, FRANK, OPEN ⟨~ admiration⟩ ⟨~ hatred⟩ — **un·disguisedly** \"+\ *adv*

un·dismayed \¦ən+\ *adj* [1*un-* + *dismayed*, past part. of *dismay*] : not dismayed : not discouraged : unshaken in purpose ⟨wholly ~ by the commercial failure of the three movies he had made —R.L.Taylor⟩

un·dispensed \"+\ *adj* [1*un-* + *dispensed*, past part. of *dispense*] : not freed by dispensation

un·display \"+\ *n* : advertising run usu. in the classified columns of a newspaper and set solid without illustration or surrounding white space

un·disposed \"+\ *adj* [ME, fr. 1*un-* + *disposed*] : not disposed: as **a** : INDISPOSED, DISINCLINED **b** : not distributed : not placed : not sold : not assigned to a use

un·disputable \"+\ *adj* : INDISPUTABLE — **un·dis·put·able·ness** *n* — **un·disputably** \"+\ *adv*

un·disputed \"+\ *adj* [¹*un-* + *disputed*, past part. of *dispute*] : not disputed : UNCHALLENGED, UNQUESTIONED ⟨~ leader of his party⟩ ⟨~ claims to excellence⟩ ⟨man of ~ competence⟩ ⟨~ possession of a region⟩ — **un·dis·put·ed·ly** *adv*

un·dissected \"+\ *adj* : not dissected ⟨~ coastal plain⟩

un·dissembled \"+\ *adj* [¹*un-* + *dissembled*, past part. of *dissemble*] **1** : not pretended : GENUINE ⟨~ cordiality⟩ **2** : UNDISGUISED ⟨expression of ~ hatred⟩

un·dissembling \"+\ *adj* [¹*un-* + *dissembling*, pres. part. of *dissemble*] : lacking guile or pretense : FRANK, OPEN ⟨~ friendliness⟩

un·dissociated \"+\ *adj* : not electrolytically dissociated ⟨~ molecules of a salt solution⟩

un·dissolved \ˌən+\ *adj* [¹*un-* + *dissolved*, past part. of *dissolve*] : not dissolved

un·distinct \"+\ *adj* [ME, fr. ¹*un-* + *distinct*] : INDISTINCT — **un·dis·tinct·ly** *adv* — **un·dis·tinct·ness** *n*

un·distinctive \"+\ *adj* **1** : not distinctive **2** : making no distinctions : not discriminating : IMPARTIAL

un·distinguishable \"+\ *adj* [¹*un-* + *distinguish* + *-able*] : INDISTINGUISHABLE — **un·dis·tin·guish·able·ness** *n* — **un·distinguishably** \"+\ *adv*

un·distinguished \"+\ *adj* [¹*un-* + *distinguished*, past part. of *distinguish*] : not distinguished: as **a** : not to be distinguished or set off as separate from others or each other : not recognized as distinct **b** : confusedly mingled with something else ⟨an ~ shriek in the general uproar⟩ **c** : indistinctly heard or seen **d** : incapable of resolution into constituent parts or forms by the perceptive powers **e** : unmarked by any distinction or elevation above the rest : receiving no special respect : having no special fame, honor, or notoriety ⟨~ record of service⟩

un·distinguishing \"+\ *adj* [¹*un-* + *distinguishing*, pres. part. of *distinguish*] : INDISCRIMINATE — **un·dis·tin·guish·ing·ly** *adv*

un·distorted \"+\ *adj* **1** : not distorted : FAITHFUL ⟨~ image⟩ ⟨~ reproduction of sound⟩ **2** : not extreme : NORMAL ⟨~ point of view⟩

un·distracted \"+\ *adj* : not distracted : not drawn aside ⟨~ pursuit of a goal⟩

un·distributed \"+\ *adj* [¹*un-* + *distributed*, past part. of *distribute*] : not distributed

undistributed middle *n* : a syllogistic fallacy in which neither premise conveys information about all members of the class designated by the middle term ⟨the argument "All men are sinners, and all weaklings are sinners, therefore all men are weaklings" says nothing about all sinners and has an *undistributed middle*⟩

un·disturbed \ˌən+\ *adj* [¹*un-* + *disturbed*, past part. of *disturb*] : not disturbed

un·disturbedly \"+\ *adv* : in an undisturbed manner

un·dis·turbed·ness *n* : the quality or state of being undisturbed

un·disturbing \ˌən+\ *adj* [¹*un-* + *disturbing*, pres. part. of *disturb*] : not disturbing

un·diversified \"+\ *adj* : not diversified

un·diverted \"+\ *adj* [¹*un-* + *diverted*, past part. of *divert*] **1** : not diverted : UNDEFLECTED **2** : not amused

un·diverting \"+\ *adj* : not diverting

un·dividable \"+\ *adj* [¹*un-* + *divide*, v. + *-able*] : INDIVISIBLE

un·divided \"+\ *adj* [ME, fr. ¹*un-* + *divided*, past part. of *dividen* to divide — more at DIVIDE] **1** : not divided: as **a** : not parted by conflict of opinion ⟨presented an ~ front⟩ **b** : not separated out into parts or shares ⟨an ~ interest in a hardware store⟩ **c** : not directed or given to more than one object ⟨~ attention⟩ ⟨~ affection⟩ **d** : not shared by or among others ⟨~ responsibility⟩ **2** : not lobed or cleft : not branched : ENTIRE **3** : held under the same common title by joint tenants or tenants in common whose shares may be equal or unequal in value or quantity and who often are entitled to share joint possession before partition and assignment of a separate title to each owner in severalty

un·di·vid·ed·ly *adv* : in an undivided manner

un·di·vid·ed·ness *n* : the quality or state of being undivided

undivided profits *n pl* : earnings of a business enterprise which have been retained instead of being distributed to stockholders or owners; *esp* : a net worth account often appearing in bank statements and showing accumulated profits which have not been transferred to surplus

un·divine \ˌən+\ *adj* : not divine

un·divined \"+\ *adj* [¹*un-* + *divined*, past part. of *divine*] : not divined : UNFORESEEN, UNIMAGINED, UNPERCEIVED

un·di·vine·ly *adv* **1** *obs* : in a manner unworthy of a clergyman **2** : in a manner unlike God

un·divulged \ˌən+\ *adj* [¹*un-* + *divulged*, past part. of *divulge*] : not divulged

un·do \ˌən'dü\ *vb* [ME *undon*, fr. OE *undōn*, fr. ²*un-* + *dōn* to do — more at DO] *vt* **1 a** : to open or loose by releasing a lock or other fastening ⟨*undid* the door⟩ ⟨*undid* the package⟩ **b** : to fix (any of various closures) in an open or free position ⟨*undid* the bolt⟩ ⟨*undid* a button⟩ **c** (1) : to loosen or remove the clothing of : UNDRESS (2) : to unbutton or untie the fastenings of (as a garment) : OPEN **2** : to make of no effect or as if not done : make null : bring to naught : CANCEL ⟨a hostility to science, to a wish that its work could be *undone* —D.W.Brogan⟩ ⟨*undid* the spell by an incantation —Ben Riker⟩ **3 a** : to destroy the worldly means or standing of : ruin the reputation or hopes of ⟨held to an intransigence that *undid* him⟩ ⟨technological advances had taken away his market and *undone* him⟩ **b** : to upset the composure of : UNMAN ⟨mention of the boy would still ~ her sometimes⟩ **c** : to entice or betray into unchastity : SEDUCE ⟨*undid* a neighbor's young daughter⟩ **4** : to unravel the secret of : EXPLAIN, INTERPRET ~ *vi* : to come open ⟨the newspaper . . . *undid* with the suddenness of a pocket map —Elizabeth Bowen⟩ **syn** see DESTROY

un·do·able \-üəbəl\ *adj* : impossible to do : not feasible ⟨seems to me to have done the almost ~ —*Saturday Rev.*⟩

un·dock \ˌən+\ *vb* [²*un-* + *dock* (to take a ship to a dock)] *vt* **1** : to take (a ship) away from a dock or wharf **2** : to take (a ship) out of dry dock ~ *vi* : to move away from a dock (as at sailing time) ⟨some luggage in new trunks came on board in the afternoon. We ~*ed* at midnight —Joseph Conrad⟩

un·docked \"+\ *adj* [¹*un-* + *docked*, past part. of *dock* (to cut off)] : not docked : UNABRIDGED

un·doctored \"+\ *adj* [¹*un-* + *doctored*, past part. of *doctor*] : not doctored

un·doctrinaire \"+\ *adj* : not doctrinaire : not rigidly theoretical or devoted to preconceived notions : not committed to a party program : not dogmatic ⟨knowledgeable, clearheaded, ~, civilized . . .; his independent intelligence kept free of all labels and fashions —*Manchester Guardian Weekly*⟩

un·documented \"+\ *adj* [¹*un-* + *documented*, past part. of *document*] **1** : lacking documents : unsupported by the evidence of documents or the conclusions of scholarship **2** : not registered or enrolled : not licensed — used of a boat

un·doer \"+\ *n* [ME, fr. *undon* to undo + *-er* — more at UNDO] : one that undoes : DESTROYER; *esp* : one that ruins a woman : SEDUCER

un·dog \"+\ *vt* [²*un-* + *dog* (to fasten with a dog)] : to loose from a fastening dog or catch ⟨the quartermaster . . . *undogged* the ports —Gordon Webber⟩

un·dogmatic *also* **un·dogmatical** \"+\ *adj* : not dogmatic : not committed to dogma ⟨spoke of my ~ state, no longer influenced by or dependent on any formal religious observance —*Atlantic*⟩

undoing *n* [ME, fr. gerund of *undon* to undo — more at UNDO] **1** : LOOSING, UNFASTENING **2 a** : a bringing to naught : DESTRUCTION, RUIN ⟨cocaine . . . leads to his complete ~ by destroying his mental equipment —A.C.Morrison⟩ **b** : a cause of ruin ⟨a redhead who was to prove my ~ —C.C.Wertenbaker⟩ **3** : the reversal, cancellation, or annulment of something done : reinstatement of a condition existing previous to some act or accomplishment ⟨would settle for nothing less than the complete ~ of his country's calamitous defeat and humiliation⟩

un·domestic \ˌən+\ *adj* : not domestic: as **a** : unrelated to home **b** : not home-loving **c** : not homelike

un·domesticate \"+\ *vt* [²*un-* + *domesticate*] : to make undomestic : undo the taming of

un·domesticated \"+\ *adj* [¹*un-* + *domesticated*, past part. of *domesticate*] : not domesticated ⟨a few ~ horses left⟩

¹**un·done** \ˌən'dən\ *adj* [ME *undon, undoon*, fr. ¹*un-* + *don, doon* done — more at DONE] : not done ⟨a task ~⟩

²**undone** \"\ *adj* [ME *undon, undoon*, fr. past part. of *undon*, *undoon* to undo — more at UNDO] **1** : DESTROYED, RUINED ⟨a mind ~⟩ **2** : UNFASTENED ⟨his package came ~ while passing through the New York post office —Jane Shellhase⟩

un·double \ˌən+\ *vb* [²*un-* + *double*] : UNFOLD

un·doubled \"+\ *adj* [¹*un-* + *doubled*, past part. of *double*] : not doubled

un·doubtable \"+\ *adj* [ME *undoutable*, fr. ¹*un-* + *doutable* doubtable — more at DOUBTABLE] : not open to doubt or challenge : SURE, UNQUESTIONABLE

un·doubted \"+\ *adj* [ME *undouted*, fr. ¹*un-* + *douted*, past part. of *douten* to doubt — more at DOUBT] : not doubted : ASSURED, CERTAIN, GENUINE, UNDISPUTED ⟨produced several ~ masterpieces —K.S.Davis⟩

un·doubt·ed·ly *adv* [ME *undoutedly*, fr. *undouted* + *-ly*] : in an undoubted manner : ASSUREDLY ⟨mounds that ~ contain human bones —*Amer. Guide Series: Minn.*⟩

un·doubtful \ˌən+\ *adj* [ME *undouteful*, fr. ¹*un-* + *douteful* doubtful — more at DOUBTFUL] **1** : not open to doubt : firmly established ⟨an ~ pedigree⟩ **2** : feeling no doubt : CONFIDENT ⟨a child ~ of the stork —W.J.Locke⟩

un·doubting \"+\ *adj* [¹*un-* + *doubting*, pres. part. of *doubt*] : not doubting : CONFIDENT

un·doubt·ing·ly *adv* : in an undoubting manner : without hesitation : CONFIDENTLY

un·dowered \ˌən+\ *adj* [¹*un-* + *dowered*, past part. of *dower*] : given no dowry

un·drain·able \ˌən'drānəbəl\ *adj* **1** : INEXHAUSTIBLE **2** : incapable of being drained ⟨an ~ swamp⟩

un·drained \ˌən+\ *adj* : not drained

un·dramatic \"+\ *adj* : lacking dramatic force or quality : UNSPECTACULAR ⟨moved with quiet assurance and ~ bearing⟩

un·dramatically \"+\ *adv* : in an undramatic or unshowy manner : QUIETLY

un·drape \"+\ *vt* [²*un-* + *drape*] : to strip of drapery : UNCOVER, UNVEIL

un·draw \"+\ *vb* [²*un-* + *draw*] *vt* : to draw aside (as a curtain) : OPEN ~ *vi* : to become drawn back or aside

un·drawn \"+\ *adj* [¹*un-* + *drawn*, past part. of *draw*] : not drawn: as **a** : not milked or tapped : not eviscerated **b** : not extended or dragged : not pulled or stretched **c** : not represented in a drawing

un·dreaded \"+\ *adj* [¹*un-* + *dreaded*, past part. of *dread*] : not dreaded

un·dreading \"+\ *adj* [¹*un-* + *dreading*, pres. part. of *dread*] : not dreading

un·dreamed *also* **un·dreamt** \"+\ *adj* [¹*un-* + *dreamed, dreamt*, past part. of *dream*] : not dreamed : not thought of : UNIMAGINED — usu. used with *of* ⟨*undreamed-of* capacity for cooperation with their fellows —J.H.Robinson †1936⟩ ⟨impersonal forces have been set in motion on a scale ~ of in the early days of the republic —John Dewey⟩ ⟨the printing press was probably ~ of a half century before its invention⟩

un·dreaming \"+\ *adj* [¹*un-* + *dreaming*, pres. part. of *dream*] : not dreaming

¹**un·dress** \ˌən+\ *vb* [²*un-* + *dress*, v.] *vt* **1** : to remove the clothes or covering of : DIVEST, STRIP ⟨~*ed* himself and went to bed⟩ **2** *obs* : to undo the dressing of (the hair) : take down : UNBIND **3** : to free or deprive of concealment or privacy : EXPOSE ⟨asked to ~ his past —Eugene Gressman⟩ ~ *vi* : to take off one's clothes : DISROBE

²**undress** \"\ *n* [¹*un-* + *dress*, n.] **1** : informal dress: as **a** : a loose robe or dressing gown for lounging or informal wear **b** : ordinary dress — distinguished from *full dress* **c** : UNDRESS UNIFORM **2** : NAKEDNESS, NUDITY ⟨the usual models in differing degrees of ~ —*New Orleans States*⟩

³**undress** \"\ *adj* **1** : of, relating to, or worn as informal attire ⟨made the engine-room staff change from dungarees to ~ blues before going to chow —Fletcher Pratt⟩ **2** : marked by relaxed informality or unpretentiousness ⟨the ~ style which a man keeps for his intimates —John Buchan⟩ ⟨look at the ~ side of things —*New Yorker*⟩

un·dressed \"+\ *adj* [ME, fr. ¹*un-* + *dressed*, past part. of *dressen* to dress — more at DRESS] **1** : not dressed: as **a** : DISARRANGED, UNGROOMED ⟨with hair ~ and clothing in disarray she bore down like an avenging fury⟩ **b** : ROUGH, UNFINISHED ⟨~ granite⟩ ⟨~ hides⟩ **c** : left without medication, bandage, or dressing ⟨an ~ wound⟩ **d** : UNTENDED, UNTRIMMED ⟨~ grounds⟩ ⟨an ~ vine⟩ **e** : left without sauce, garnish, or condiment — used of foods **f** : prepared so as not to deteriorate but not fully processed or ready for use — used of game fish, game animals, or hides **2 a** : not clothed or not fully clothed : nearly or altogether naked **b** : not ordered or prepared for public presentation or appearance : not arranged to be seemly, persuasive, or attractive ⟨man's ~ thoughts —C.T. Ryan⟩ **3 a** : wearing informal or ordinary dress **b** : not properly dressed

undressed kid *n* : kid leather finished with a nap surface usu. on the flesh side of the skin

undress uniform *n* : a military or naval uniform for use on other than formal occasions

un·dried \ˌən+\ *adj* [ME, fr. ¹*un-* + *dried*, past part. of *drien* to dry — more at DRY] : not dried

un·drinkable \"+\ *adj* : not drinkable

un·driven \"+\ *adj* [¹*un-* + *driven*, past part. of *drive*] **1** : not driven **2** : DRIVEN — used of snow ⟨pure as ~ snow —*Times Lit. Supp.*⟩

un·drooping \"+\ *adj* : not drooping

un·drowned \"+\ *adj* [¹*un-* + *drowned*, past part. of *drown*] : not drowned

un·drugged \"+\ *adj* [¹*un-* + *drugged*, past part. of *drug*] **1** : not drugged **2** : freed of the effects of a drug

un·drunk \"+\ *adj* [¹*un-* + *drunk*, past part. of *drink*] **1** : UNSWALLOWED **2** [¹*un-* + *drunk* (intoxicated)] : not intoxicated

undsgd *abbr* undersigned

undtkr *abbr* undertaker

un·dubbed \ˌən+\ *adj* [¹*un-* + *dubbed*, past part. of *dub*] : not dubbed

un·dubitable \"+\ *adj* : INDUBITABLE ⟨~ piety —*Nation*⟩ — **un·du·bi·ta·bly** \-blē\ *adv*

un·due \"+\ *adj* [ME *undewe, undue*, fr. ¹*un-* + *dewe, due* due — more at DUE] **1** : not due : not yet payable ⟨an ~ debt⟩ ⟨an ~ bond⟩ **2 a** : unsuited to the time, place, or occasion : IMPROPER, INAPPROPRIATE, INOPPORTUNE ⟨~ behavior⟩ **b** : exceeding or violating propriety or fitness : EXCESSIVE, IMMODERATE, UNWARRANTED ⟨desire for ~ private profit —T.W.Arnold⟩ ⟨his sartorial equipment stops just short of ~ elegance —Philip Hamburger⟩ **3** *archaic* : contrary to justice, right, or law : UNLAWFUL

undue influence *n* : such influence over another often presumed from the existence of very close relationships as destroys his free agency in the eye of the law : such influence as prevents a person from exercising his own will and substitutes in its place the will of another (as by constraint, machination, or urgency of persuasion)

un·dug \ˌən+\ *adj* [¹*un-* + *dug*, past part. of *dig*] : not dug

un·duke \"+\ *vt* [²*un-* + *duke*] : to deprive of dukedom

un·du·lance \'ənjələn(t)s, 'ənd(y)əl-\ *n* -S [fr. undulant, after such pairs as E *abundant: abundance*] : the quality or state of being undulant ⟨his prose has some of the ~ of the sea —*New Yorker*⟩

un·du·lant \-lənt\ *adj* [²*undul*ate + *-ant*] **1** : moving with the rise and fall of waves : FLUCTUATING, HEAVING, RIPPLING ⟨~ waters away —Amy Lowell⟩ ⟨a ripe and ~ figure, which she covered no more than sufficiently to meet the police requirements —R.L.Taylor⟩ **2** : having a form or outline like that of waves : ROLLING ⟨well-kept farms and ~ meadows —*Amer. Guide Series: Vt.*⟩

undulant fever *n* : BRUCELLOSIS a

un·du·lar \-lə(r)\ *adj* [LL *undula* + E *-ar*] : having the form or movement of waves

¹**un·du·late** \'ənjələt, 'ənd(y)əl-, -ˌlāt, *usu* -d·+V\ *adj* [L *undulatus*, fr. (assumed) *undula* small wave (dim. of *unda* wave) + *-atus* -ate — more at WATER] **1** : bending in gradual curves ⟨the ~ margin of a leaf⟩ : WAVY — compare REPAND, SINUATE **2** : UNDULATING ⟨slumber in ~ rhythms —Amy Lowell⟩

²**un·du·late** \-ˌlāt, *usu* -ād·+V\ *vb* -ED/-ING/-S [LL *undula* small wave (fr. — assumed — L) + E *-ate*, v. suffix] *vi* **1** : to form or move in waves : rise and fall with the movement or appearance of the ocean surface : FLUCTUATE, SURGE ⟨the water seemed bound down with a dark, oily skin that stirred and *undulated* —Victor Canning⟩ ⟨veiled women *undulating* to the sound of gongs —Anthony Carson⟩ ⟨the orange candle flame . . . made the jades ~ like green pools —Amy Lowell⟩ **2** : to rise and fall in volume, pitch, or cadence ⟨the rooftop siren's wail *undulated* for minutes⟩ ⟨his prose flows and ~*s* in beguiling patterns of rhythm⟩ **3** : to exhibit a form or outline like that of waves : present a wavy appearance ⟨a sandy waste ~*s* southward —Rex Keating⟩ ~ *vt* **1** : to move or cause to move in wavy, sinuous, or flowing manner ⟨danced . . . with their entire bodies, moving slowly, *undulating* their abdomens —Richard Wright⟩ **2** : to give (something) a wavy form **syn** see SWING

un·du·lat·ed \-ād·əd, -ātəd\ *adj* [L *undulatus* + E *-ed*] **1** : having wavy markings or a wavy form or outline **2** : UNDULATE 1

undulating *adj* [fr. pres. part. of *undulate*] **1** : rising and falling in waves : FLUCTUATING ⟨I often gaze on that waste of ~ water —L.P.Smith⟩ **2** : resembling waves in form : having a wavy outline : ROLLING, SCALLOPED ⟨broad, ~ prairie land —*Amer. Guide Series: Minn.*⟩ ⟨her small white straw hat had an ~ brim —*Sydney (Australia) Bull.*⟩ **3** : rising and falling in volume, pitch, or metrical stress or quantity ⟨~ string arpeggios —Julian Herbage⟩

undulating cadence *n* : a metrical cadence in which the foot is an amphibrach or an amphimacer — called also *rocking rhythm;* compare FALLING RHYTHM, RISING RHYTHM

undulating membrane *n* : a vibratile cytoplasmic membrane: **a** : a lateral expansion of the periplast in some flagellates that is usu. bordered by a flagellum **b** : a row of laterally fused long cilia associated in many ciliates with the oral structures

un·du·la·tion \ˌ==ˈlāshən\ *n* -S [fr. (assumed) NL *undulation-, undulatio*, fr. LL *undula* small wave + L *-ation-, -atio* -ation] **1 a** : a rising and falling in waves : HEAVING, PULSING, SURGING, SWELLING ⟨the bay broke up into long oily ~*s* —Edith Wharton⟩ **b** : a wavelike motion to and fro, up and down, or from side to side in a fluid or elastic medium propagated continuously among its particles but with little or no permanent translation of the particles in the direction of the propagation : VIBRATION **2 a** : TREMOLO 1a **b** : the pulsation caused by the vibrating together of two tones not quite in unison **c** : VIBRATO **3** : a wavy appearance, outline, or form : a wavelike curve or series of curves : a rippling, rolling, or corrugated surface : WAVINESS ⟨the country spread all about us . . . rolling in gentle swells and ~*s* like a summer sea —Blanche E. Baughan⟩ ⟨the ~*s* of his dark, old-fashioned locks of hair —Kay Boyle⟩

un·du·la·tor \'==ˌlād·ə(r), -ātə-\ *n* -S : one that undulates ⟨a lovely blonde lady ~ —*Wall Street Jour.*⟩

un·du·la·to·ry \'ənjələˌtōrē, 'ənd(y)əl-, -tȯr-, -ri\ *adj* : of or relating to undulation : moving in or resembling waves : UNDULATING

undulatory theory *n* : a theory in physics: light is transmitted from luminous bodies to the eye and other objects by an undulatory movement — called also *wave theory*

un·dulled \ˌən+\ *adj* [¹*un-* + *dulled*, past part. of *dull*] : not dulled ⟨~ by time, he was worn smoother by it —Stuart Cloete⟩

un·du·lous \'ənjələs, 'ənd(y)əl-\ *adj* [*undul*ate + *-ous*] : UNDULATING, UNDULATORY

un·du·ly \ˌən'd(y)ülē, -li\ *adv* [ME *undewely, unduely*, fr. *undewe, undue* undue + *-ly* — more at UNDUE] : in an undue manner; *esp* : EXCESSIVELY ⟨~ pessimistic about the chance for the reward of merit —J.M.England⟩

un·dunged \ˌən+\ *adj* [¹*un-* + *dunged*, past part. of *dung*] : not dunged : not manured ⟨~ and untilled land —Fred Bradbury⟩

un·duplicated \"+\ *adj* [¹*un-* + *duplicated*, past part. of *duplicate*] : not duplicated

un·durable \"+\ *adj* : not durable

un·duteous \"+\ *adj* : UNDUTIFUL

un·dutiful \"+\ *adj* : not dutiful

un·dutifully \"+\ *adv* : in an undutiful manner

un·du·ti·ful·ness *n* : the quality or state of being undutiful

undutiful will *or* **unduteous will** *n* : a will that does not make the minimum provision required by law for some heir of the testator who may then claim his legitimate share unless the testator had a lawful reason for disinheriting him : an inofficious will subject to being declared entirely void

undy *var of* UNDÉ

un·dyed \ˌən+\ *adj* [¹*un-* + *dyed*, past part. of *dye*] : not dyed

un·dying \"+\ *adj* [ME, fr. ¹*un-* + *dying*] : not dying : IMMORTAL, PERPETUAL ⟨~ fame⟩ — **un·dy·ing·ly** *adv* — **un·dy·ing·ness** *n* -ES

un·dynamic \"+\ *adj* : not dynamic : STATIC ⟨a static village community and a completely ~ type of agriculture —Barbara Ward⟩

un·eager \ˌən+\ *adj* **1** : lacking spirit or animation : IMPASSIVE, UNEXPRESSIVE ⟨decrepit, colorless, ~ things —Arthur Symons⟩ **2** : showing no eagerness : RELUCTANT ⟨foreigners stubbornly ~ to accept our way of life —Joseph Barnes⟩ ⟨fresh from college and ~ for the moment to marry the boy back home —P.E.Deutschman⟩ — **un·eagerly** \"+\ *adv* — **un·eagerness** \"+\ *n*

un·earned \"+\ *adj* [¹*un-* + *earned*, past part. of *earn*] : not earned: **a** : not due to worth or merit : UNMERITED ⟨felt he was enjoying an ~ importance⟩ ⟨~ luck —Shak.⟩ **b** : not gained by labor or service ⟨~ revenue⟩ ⟨accepted the ~ rewards that came his way⟩ **c** : received in advance of delivery (as of goods) or of service performed ⟨~ collections amounting to several thousand dollars⟩ **d** : scored as a result of an error by the opposing team — used of a run in baseball

unearned income *n* **1** : income (as dividends) that is not derived from personal labor or service but usu. merely from ownership of property and that is sometimes taxed at a higher rate than earned income **2** : income resulting from transfer payments

unearned increment *n* : an increase in the value of property (as land) that is due to no labor or expenditure on the part of the owner but to natural causes (as the increase of population or the general progress of society) creating an increased demand for it and that is sometimes specially taxed

unearned premium *n* : the share of a total insurance premium applicable to the unexpired portion of a policy term

unearned premium reserve *n* : a reserve established at the end of any accounting period in insurance to represent premiums paid in advance for which protection is to be given in the future

un·earth \ˌən+\ *vt* [ME *unerthen*, fr. ²*un-* + *erthen* to earth] **1 a** : to dig up out of the earth : bring up, uncover, or recover from underground : EXHUME, DISINTER ⟨~ a hidden treasure⟩ ⟨~*ed* a cache of . . . whiskey —Georg Meyers⟩ ⟨archaeologists . . . have ~*ed* many valuable Indian relics —*Amer. Guide Series: Conn.*⟩ **b** : to drive out of the ground (as from a hole or burrow) ⟨~ a badger⟩ **2** : to bring from concealment, obscurity, or oblivion : bring to light : UNCOVER, DISCOVER ⟨~ carefully hidden evidence⟩ ⟨~ a plot⟩ ⟨the facts ~*ed* by patient research⟩ ⟨~*ed* proof that the accused was innocent —Robert Brennan⟩ ⟨~*ed* a sheaf of yellowing catalogs —David Anderson⟩ **syn** see DISCOVER

un·earthed \"+\ *adj* [¹*un-* + *earthed*, past part. of *earth*] *chiefly Brit* : not grounded electrically ⟨the death of a man at an ~ pasteurizing plant —*Farmers Weekly (London)*⟩

un·earthliness \"+\ *n* : the quality or state of being unearthly: as **a** : SPIRITUALITY, UNWORLDLINESS ⟨the impressive ~ of the preacher's expression⟩ **b** : EERINESS, PRETERNATURALNESS ⟨amid its amazing thrill, a strange ~ —Gilbert Murray⟩

un·earthly \"+\ *adj* : not earthly: as **a** : not belonging to or characteristic of this earth : not terrestrial ⟨the ~ beauty of the fish and plant life . . . were probably comparable to a trip to the moon —John Tassos⟩ ⟨the most ~ region within reach of man —Walter Sullivan⟩ **b** : passing beyond natural limits : PRETERNATURAL, SUPERNATURAL, CELESTIAL ⟨beings of ~ splendor —W.M.Thackeray⟩ ⟨an ~ melody⟩ ⟨an ~ light⟩

c : WEIRD, EERIE ⟨a moonlit . . . landscape ~ with expectancy —Ann F. Wolfe⟩ ⟨an ~ soaring wail —D.C.Peattie⟩ **d** : not worldly or mundane : SPIRITUAL, IDEAL ⟨~ love⟩ ⟨revelation granted to us of what is ~ —Algernon Blackwood⟩ **e** : not conforming to the usual experience, observation, or custom of everyday life : FANTASTIC, PREPOSTEROUS ⟨his picture of the ~ leisureliness of English journalism —*New Yorker*⟩ ⟨have to get up at ~ hours —George Meredith⟩

un·ease \ˌən+\ *n* [ME *unese*, fr. [1]*un-* + *ese* ease] **1** : mental or spiritual discomfort: **a** : vague dissatisfaction : MISGIVING ⟨my ~ over the lack of stylistic assurance —R.D.Darrell⟩ **b** : anxiety and foreboding : DISQUIET ⟨worry and ~ harried her for the next weeks —Adria Langley⟩ **c** : emotional strain : TENSION ⟨a sense of menace, of ~ runs through their conversation —T.H.White b. 1915⟩ **d** : lack of ease (as in social relations) : EMBARRASSMENT ⟨~ in the presence of . . . the great man —H.S.Canby⟩ **2** *obs* : physical discomfort ⟨such ~ as in a coach . . . in passing over a furrow —Thomas Hobbes⟩ **3** : AWKWARDNESS, UNCOMFORTABLENESS ⟨the ~ of their garments —William Faulkner⟩ ⟨the ~ of this divorce of tradition from environment —*Times Lit. Supp.*⟩

un·easily \"+\ *adv* [ME *unesily*, fr. *unesy* uneasy + *-ly*] : in an uneasy manner: **a** *obs* : not easily : with difficulty **b** : with troubled feelings (as of discomfort, worry, or foreboding) : APPREHENSIVELY, DISTURBEDLY ⟨strange fish . . . sought ~ for an outlet to the ocean —William Beebe⟩ ⟨astronomers ~ ignoring irregularities in the movements of the heavenly bodies —Benjamin Farrington⟩ **c** : with embarrassment : UNCOMFORTABLY ⟨coloring ~ under his gaze —Israel Zangwill⟩ **d** : RESTLESSLY, FIDGETINGLY ⟨kept shifting his position ~⟩ **e** : AWKWARDLY ⟨his body . . . is punily, ~ built —Osbert Sitwell⟩ ⟨a little self-consciously and ~ aggressive —M.P. O'Connor⟩ **f** : not firmly : PRECARIOUSLY ⟨held the chairmanship ~ against mounting opposition⟩

un·easiness \"+\ *n* **1** : the quality or state of being uneasy: **a** : mental or spiritual discomfort : DISTRESS, PERTURBATION ⟨the ~ that our most generous . . . ideals have their roots in childhood guilts —Irwin Edman⟩ **b** : a feeling of worry, apprehension, or foreboding : ANXIETY, DISQUIET ⟨reluctant to be awake . . . her ~ amounted almost to alarm —Jean Stafford⟩ **c** : RESTLESSNESS, INSTABILITY ⟨the misery and ~ of the incompletely assimilated —Edward Shils⟩ **d** : physical discomfort : MALAISE, QUEASINESS ⟨conscious of a certain ~ in the organs —Arnold Bennett⟩ **e** : AWKWARDNESS ⟨~ of diction —R.W.Southern⟩ **f** : EMBARRASSMENT, DISCOMPOSURE ⟨conscious of her ~ among these sophisticated women⟩ **2** *archaic* : HARDSHIP, VICISSITUDE ⟨without these ~*es* to mingle with these benefits, I might be too much puffed up —Samuel Richardson⟩

[1]**un·easy** \"+\ *adj* [ME *unesy*, fr. [1]*un-* + *esy* easy] **1 a** *archaic* : causing physical discomfort : UNCOMFORTABLE ⟨why rather, sleep, liest thou . . . upon ~ pallets —Shak.⟩ **b** *archaic* : causing mental discomfort : DISTRESSING ⟨a great and ~ disappointment —Samuel Johnson⟩ **c** *obs* : disagreeable in behavior : ANNOYING ⟨a sour . . . nature makes him ~ to those who approach him —Joseph Addison⟩ **2** *archaic* **a** : not easy : DIFFICULT ⟨the road will be ~ to find —Sir Walter Scott⟩ ⟨I think it not ~ to get the cause —Shak.⟩ **b** : hard to traverse — used esp. of a road or watercourse ⟨the flood . . . roars horrible along the ~ race —John Dryden⟩ **3** : marked by lack of ease : AWKWARD, EMBARRASSED ⟨gave an ~ laugh⟩ ⟨an ~ . . . silence fell on the group —John Steinbeck⟩ **4** : mentally upset : WORRIED, APPREHENSIVE ⟨~ about his health⟩ ⟨~ at the threat of expulsion —*Amer. Guide Series: Calif.*⟩ **5 a** : RESTLESS, UNQUIET ⟨the first ~ stir of the sleeper —Lewis Mumford⟩ ⟨the ~ atmosphere of the city —Winifred Bambrick⟩ **b** : CHOPPY, TROUBLED ⟨~ waters⟩ **6** : PRECARIOUS, UNSTABLE ⟨an ~ coalition government⟩ ⟨an ~ peace⟩

[2]**un·easy** \"\ *adv* : UNEASILY ⟨~ lies the head that wears a crown —Shak.⟩

un·eatable \ˌən+\ *adj* : not fit to be eaten : INEDIBLE ⟨so undercooked as to be ~ —Sylvia T. Warner⟩ ⟨food atrocious and ~ —*Harper's*⟩

un·eaten \"+\ *adj* [ME *unete, uneten*, fr. [1]*un-* + *ete, eten*, past part. of *eten* to eat] : not eaten : UNCONSUMED ⟨gave the dog the ~ remnants of the roast⟩

[1]**un·eath** \"+\ *adj* [ME *uneathe*, fr. OE *unēathe*, fr. [1]*un-* + *ēathe* easy — more at EATH] *archaic* : not easy : DIFFICULT, HARD ⟨who he was, ~ was to descry —Edmund Spenser⟩

[2]**uneath** \"\ *adv* [ME *uneathe*, fr. OE *unēathe*, fr. *unēathe* uneasy] *archaic* : not easily : with difficulty : SCARCELY ⟨I ~ the fancy might control —S.T.Coleridge⟩

un·economic *also* **un·economical** \ˌən+\ *adj* : not economic : COSTLY, WASTEFUL ⟨~ ebb and flow of manpower —Welles Hangen⟩ — **un·economically** \"+\ *adv* — **un·economicalness** \"+\ *n* -ES

un·edified \"+\ *adj* [[1]*un-* + *edified*, past part. of *edify*] : not edified : UNINSTRUCTED, UNENLIGHTENED ⟨the ~ heathen —Charles Lamb⟩

un·edifying \"+\ *adj* [[1]*un-* + *edifying*, pres. part. of *edify*] : not edifying: as **a** : not instructive : UNENLIGHTENING, UNILLUMINATING ⟨that rare and useful but ~ variation —G.B. Shaw⟩ **b** : not inspiring or uplifting : IMMORAL, UNSAVORY ⟨~ conduct⟩ ⟨an ~ story⟩ ⟨~ episodes . . . enliven the histories of travellers —T.H.Savory⟩

un·edited \"+\ *adj* [[1]*un-* + *edited*, past part. of *edit*] : not edited: as **a** : left unrevised ⟨this first novel . . . bravely ~ —E.B.Garside⟩ **b** : UNCENSORED, UNCUT ⟨an ~ record⟩ ⟨~ film not yet reviewed by the censors⟩ **c** : not yet edited : still unpublished ⟨found an ~ manuscript of a famous medieval mystic⟩

un·educable \ˌən+\ *adj* : INEDUCABLE

un·educated \"+\ *adj* [[1]*un-* + *educated*, past part. of *educate*] : not educated: as **a** : lacking in education : UNTAUGHT **b** : ILLITERATE **syn** see IGNORANT

un·effectual \"+\ *adj* : INEFFECTUAL

un·elaborate \"+\ *adj* : INELABORATE

un·elastic \"+\ *adj* : INELASTIC

un·elected \"+\ *adj* : not counted among the elect ⟨died ~⟩ ⟨the ~ multitude⟩

un·elegant \ˌən+\ *adj* : INELEGANT

un·elevated \"+\ *adj* : not elevated : EARTHBOUND

un·eligible \"+\ *adj* : INELIGIBLE

un·eloquent \"+\ *adj* : lacking in eloquence : INELOQUENT ⟨an earnest but ~ speaker⟩ — **un·eloquently** \"+\ *adv*

un·emancipated \"+\ *adj* : not emancipated : not freed: **a** : held in the power of another; *specif* : held in slavery or bondage ⟨~ serfs⟩ **b** : subject to the paternal power ⟨an ~ minor child —E.B.Denny⟩ **c** : bound by or adhering to accepted mores implying or entailing subservience or restraints ⟨the ~ woman⟩

un·embarrassed \"+\ *adj* [[1]*un-* + *embarrassed*, past part. of *embarrass*] **1** : free from embarrassment : UNASHAMED, UNABASHED ⟨an ~ greeting as if nothing untoward had happened⟩ **2** : not constrained : NATURAL ⟨their ~ good breeding —Earl of Chesterfield⟩ **3** : free of encumbrance : UNENCUMBERED ⟨dream of punctual tenants and ~ properties —Anthony Trollope⟩ — **un·embarrassedly** \"+\ *adv*

un·embellished \ˌən+\ *adj* [[1]*un-* + *embellished*, past part. of *embellish*] : lacking embellishment : UNADORNED, PLAIN ⟨~ walls⟩ ⟨a forthright, ~ style⟩

un·embittered \"+\ *adj* [[1]*un-* + *embittered*, past part. of *embitter*] : not embittered : UNRESENTFUL ⟨take their stings with gay ~ lips —Sara Teasdale⟩

un·embodied \"+\ *adj* [[1]*un-* + *embodied*, past part. of *embody*] **1** : DISEMBODIED, INCORPOREAL ⟨~ spirits⟩ **2** : not collected into a body : not yet organized ⟨~ militia⟩

un·embroidered \"+\ *adj* [[1]*un-* + *embroidered*, past part. of *embroider*] : lacking adornment or elaboration : PLAIN, SIMPLE ⟨the author's ~ . . . approach will appeal to readers looking for a concise account —*Jour. of Accountancy*⟩

un·emendable \"+\ *adj* : not emendable

un·emotional \"+\ *adj* : not emotional: as **a** : not easily aroused or excited : IMPASSIVE, COLD, STOLID ⟨in the little church he had seemed most ~, and had been most moved —John Galsworthy⟩ **b** : little influenced by emotion or sentiment : UNFEELING, HARD-BOILED ⟨could be cruel in a completely ~ way⟩ **c** : marked by less than usual emotion : UNIMPASSIONED ⟨made an ~ appeal to the audience⟩ **d** : involving a minimum of emotion : INTELLECTUAL ⟨put disagreements on an intelligent and ~ basis —K.D.Miller⟩ — **un·emotionally** \"+\ *adv*

un·emotionality \"+\ *n* : the quality or state of being unemotional : IMPASSIVITY, OBJECTIVITY ⟨handled the delicate matter with complete ~⟩ ⟨the scientific virtue of ~⟩

un·emphatic \"+\ *adj* : not emphatic: **a** : lacking emphasis or force of expression ⟨~ student writing⟩ **b** : commanding little attention : INCONSPICUOUS ⟨cruel at first only in an ~ and spasmodic way —E.K.Brown⟩ **c** : marked by a lack of stress or insistence ⟨was ~ in his refusal⟩ ⟨an ~ affirmation⟩ **d** : not sharply delineated : not salient ⟨an ~ detail in a painting⟩ **e** : carrying no stress in pronunciation ⟨an ~ syllable⟩ — **un·emphatically** \"+\ *adv*

un·employability \"+\ *n* : the quality or state of being unemployable

[1]**un·employable** \"+\ *adj* : not acceptable for employment as a worker

[2]**unemployable** \"\ *n* -s : an unemployable person

un·employed \ˌən+\ *adj* [[1]*un-* + *employed*, past part. of *employ*] : not employed: **a** : not being used ⟨~ time⟩ ⟨~ tools⟩ ⟨a method as yet ~⟩ **b** : not engaged in a gainful occupation : out of work ⟨~ workers⟩ **c** : not invested ⟨~ capital⟩ **d** : FREE 5g

un·employment \"+\ *n* : lack of employment : IDLENESS; *specif* : involuntary idleness of a worker seeking work at prevailing wages

unemployment benefit *n* : payment (as by a union or an employer or according to the provisions of a governmental social security program) to an unemployed worker of a sum of money per week — compare DOLE

unemployment compensation *n* : the system of unemployment benefits provided in the U. S. by state laws adopted pursuant to the Federal Social Security Act

unemployment insurance *n* : insurance (as provided by state laws adopted pursuant to the Federal Social Security Act) against loss of earnings by payments for a limited period during which a worker is involuntarily unemployed

un·encapsulated \ˌən+\ *adj* : not encapsulated ⟨an ~ tumor⟩

un·enciphered \"+\ *adj* [[1]*un-* + *enciphered*, past part. of *encipher*] : not converted to cipher ⟨~ messages⟩

un·enclosed \"+\ *adj* [[1]*un-* + *enclosed*, past part. of *enclose*] : not enclosed: **a** : not fenced in : COMMON ⟨~ land⟩ **b** : not kept within convent walls ⟨~ nuns⟩

un·encrypted \"+\ *adj* [[1]*un-* + *encrypted*, past part. of *encrypt*] : not encoded : not cryptic : CLEAR ⟨~ language⟩

un·encumbered \"+\ *adj* [[1]*un-* + *encumbered*, past part. of *encumber*] **1** : free of encumbrance : UNBURDENED, UNHAMPERED ⟨a lucid, ~ book, sparing of footnotes⟩ ⟨planning to live an ~ life⟩; *specif* : free from a temporary estate or interest (as a mortgage, lien, or dower right) ⟨pass it on to their heirs . . . intact and ~ —H.P.Becker⟩ **2** : having no dependents (as spouse or children) ⟨reliable, ~ woman . . . would like position as housekeeper —*Vancouver (Canada) Sun*⟩

un·encysted \"+\ *adj* [[1]*un-* + *encysted*, past part. of *encyst*] : not encysted

un·ended \"+\ *adj* [ME, fr. [1]*un-* + *ended*, past part. of *enden* to end] : not ended : UNFINISHED ⟨that contest was still ~ —C.L.Jones⟩

un·ending \"+\ *adj* [[1]*un-* + *ending*, pres. part. of *end*] : never ending : ENDLESS: **a** : not coming to an end : continuing indefinitely into the future : CONTINUOUS, EVERLASTING ⟨the . . . dream of ~ progress —W.R.Inge⟩ **b** : going on from time immemorial : TIMELESS, AGELONG ⟨the reef's ~ creation —P.A. Zahl⟩ **c** : UNDYING, ETERNAL ⟨~ love⟩ **d** : going on continually : INCESSANT, PERPETUAL ⟨an ~ struggle carried on at every club meeting⟩ **e** : extending with no apparent end : INTERMINABLE ⟨the ~ levee, covered with scraggy grass —*Amer. Guide Series: La.*⟩ **f** : passing all limits : EXTRAVAGANT, EGREGIOUS ⟨the most ~ ass in Christendom —Thomas Carlyle⟩

un·end·ing·ly \ˌə'nendiŋlē, -dēŋ-, -li\ *adv* : in an unending manner : EVERLASTINGLY ⟨a good housekeeper who is ~ mopping out dark corners —Dwight MacDonald⟩

un·end·ing·ness \-ŋnə̇s\ *n* -ES : the quality or state of being unending

un·endorsed \ˌən+\ *adj* [[1]*un-* + *endorsed*, past part. of *endorse*] **1** : bearing no endorsement ⟨an ~ check⟩ **2** : not approved ⟨a proposal as yet ~ by the governor⟩

un·endowed \"+\ *adj* [[1]*un-* + *endowed*, past part. of *endow*] **1** *archaic* : having no dowry : DOWERLESS **2** : not equipped or provided ⟨~ with . . . genius —J.L.Lowes⟩ ⟨~ with the finer graces⟩

un·endued \"+\ *adj* [[1]*un-* + *endued*, past part. of *endue*] : not supplied : UNENDOWED ⟨~ with foresight⟩

un·endurable \"+\ *adj* : not endurable : UNBEARABLE ⟨~ agony⟩ ⟨he is under ~ domestic . . . pressure —Nicolas Monjo⟩

un·endurably \"+\ *adv* : in an unendurable manner : INTOLERABLY

un·enduring \"+\ *adj* : not lasting : SHORT-LIVED

un·energetic \ˌən+\ *adj* : lacking energy or enterprise : SLOW-GOING ⟨~ incompetents —S.P.Sherman⟩

un·enforceable \"+\ *adj* : not enforceable ⟨an ~ law⟩ : not capable of being brought about by compulsion ⟨~ reforms⟩

un·enforced \"+\ *adj* : not enforced : UNFORCED, UNCOMPELLED; *specif* : not enforced by legal or police action : DORMANT ⟨an ~ speed limit⟩

un·enfranchised \"+\ *adj* : not free; *specif* : not granted or not allowed to exercise political rights (as suffrage) ⟨he and his still ~ fellow citizens are restless —*Manchester Guardian Weekly*⟩

un·engaged \"+\ *adj* : not engaged: **a** : not pledged or promised; *specif* : not promised in marriage ⟨agreed to continue seeing him but on an ~ basis⟩ **b** : not occupied or employed : not busy : FREE ⟨left her ~ a good part of the afternoon⟩

un·engaging \"+\ *adj* : not engaging : lacking in charm : UNATTRACTIVE ⟨an ~ manner⟩

un-english \ˌən+\ *adj, usu cap E* **1** : not characteristically English ⟨what could be more *un-English* than a languid female in a turban —George Santayana⟩ **2** : not agreeing with standard or generally accepted usage of the English language ⟨*un-English* pronunciation⟩ ⟨an *un-English* sentence⟩

un·englished \"+\ *adj, usu cap E* [[1]*un-* + *englished*, past part. of *english*] : not translated into English ⟨left certain passages of the Latin *un-Englished*⟩

un·enjoyable \"+\ *adj* : not capable of being enjoyed : producing no pleasure : JOYLESS ⟨had a thoroughly ~ time⟩

un·enjoyed \"+\ *adj* [[1]*un-* + *enjoyed*, past part. of *enjoy*] : not enjoyed: as **a** : not partaken of : UNUSED ⟨pleasures passed by ~⟩ **b** : giving no joy : DREARY, JOYLESS ⟨a disconsolate and ~ matrimony —John Milton⟩

un·enjoying \"+\ *adj* [[1]*un-* + *enjoying*, pres. part. of *enjoy*] : not able to experience or express enjoyment : SAD, MELANCHOLY ⟨an ~ miser⟩

un·enlarged \ˌən+\ *adj* **1** : not enlarged upon : kept brief ⟨leave the notice ~ —Elizabeth B. Browning⟩ **2** : NARROW, ILLIBERAL ⟨a man of ~ views⟩ **3** : not enlarged : not larger or greater than formerly, normally, or usu. present ⟨the ~ first pair of legs of a lobster⟩

un·enlightened \"+\ *adj* **1** *archaic* : not lighted : not illuminated ⟨a place ~ by the cheery rays of the sun⟩ **2 a** : not enlightened : IGNORANT, UNINSTRUCTED, UNINFORMED ⟨lamentably ~ as to the laws —Helen Martin⟩ **b** : BACKWARD, BENIGHTED ⟨the devices by which ~ men . . . preserved the unjust social order —C.C.Walcutt⟩

un·enlightening \"+\ *adj* : not enlightening : not tending to inform or clarify ⟨an ~ comment⟩

un·enlivened \"+\ *adj* [[1]*un-* + *enlivened*, past part. of *enliven*] : not enlivened : not brightened or made lively — often used postpositively ⟨a life ~ by romance⟩

un·ennobled \"+\ *adj* : not ennobled : LOWLY, SIMPLE ⟨the ~ soldier in the ranks⟩

un·enquiring \"+\ *adj* [[1]*un-* + *enquiring*, pres. part. of *enquire*] : marked by unquestioning, uncritical, or unconsidered acceptance or action : ACQUIESCENT, UNTHINKING ⟨deplored a too trustful, ~ repetition of the teacher's opinions⟩

un·enriched \"+\ *adj* [[1]*un-* + *enriched*, past part. of *enrich*] **1** : not made wealthy — often used postpositively ⟨a politician ~ by graft⟩ **2** : not improved by addition of new content; *specif* : not improved in nutritive value by addition of vitamins and minerals in processing ⟨~ bread⟩

un·enrolled \"+\ *adj* [[1]*un-* + *enrolled*, past part. of *enroll*] : not enrolled : not holding membership in a group or organization

un·enslaved \"+\ *adj* [[1]*un-* + *enslaved*, past part. of *enslave*] **1** : not enslaved : EMANCIPATED, FREE ⟨happy ~ citizenry⟩ **2** : not disposed to be servile ⟨an ~ spirit⟩

un·entailed \"+\ *adj* [[1]*un-* + *entailed*, past part. of *entail*] : not restricted as to course of descent upon the owner's death ⟨an ~ estate⟩

un·entangle \"+\ *vt* [[2]*un-* + *entangle*] : DISENTANGLE

un·entangled \"+\ *adj* [[1]*un-* + *entangled*] : not entangled: **a** : not trapped or caught **b** : not complicated : UNINVOLVED ⟨dream-consciousness, blessedly ~ with all one's own problems —*Publ's Mod. Lang. Assoc. of Amer.*⟩

un·entered \ˌən+\ *adj* [ME, fr. [1]*un-* + *entered*, past part. of *enteren, entren* to enter] : not entered: **a** : not recorded or registered **b** : not penetrated ⟨an ~ cave⟩

un·enterprising \"+\ *adj* : lacking in enterprise : not bold or venturesome : LETHARGIC, CONSERVATIVE ⟨has become ~ and sluggish because . . . so prosperous and comfortable —H.G.Wells⟩

un·entertained \"+\ *adj* [[1]*un-* + *entertained*, past part. of *entertain*] : not entertained : not amused ⟨a play that left the audience completely ~⟩

un·entertaining \"+\ *adj* : not entertaining : UNAMUSING ⟨a quite ~ letter⟩

un·entertainingly \"+\ *adv* : in an unentertaining manner

un·enthralled \"+\ *adj* [[1]*un-* + *enthralled*, past part. of *enthrall*] : not enslaved : free of the domination of others ⟨judgment ~ —John Milton⟩

un·enthusiasm \"+\ *n* : lack of enthusiasm : PERFUNCTORINESS ⟨said . . . with polite ~ —Edna Ferber⟩

un·enthusiastic \"+\ *adj* **1** : lacking ardor or excitement : SPIRITLESS ⟨an ~ performance by an orchestra⟩ **2** : marked by a lack of sympathy or disinclination to praise : LUKEWARM ⟨an ~ review⟩ ⟨was . . . ~ about most of her relatives —Margaret Mead⟩ **3** : not buoyant : not optimistic ⟨~ about the prospects of success⟩

un·enthusiastically \"+\ *adv* [*unenthusiastic* + *-ally*] : in an unenthusiastic manner : with no great warmth or interest ⟨agreeing to the proposal ~⟩

un·entitled \ˌən+\ *adj* [[1]*un-* + *entitled*, past part. of *entitle*] : not entitled : having no title or right : UNWORTHY ⟨a distinction to which he was ~⟩

un·entombed \"+\ *adj* [[1]*un-* + *entombed*, past part. of *entomb*] : not entombed : UNBURIED

un·entreated \"+\ *adj* [[1]*un-* + *entreated*, past part. of *entreat*] : not entreated : not asked or requested

un·enviable \"+\ *adj* **1** : not so desirable as to attract envy ⟨a very low, altogether ~ standard of living⟩ ⟨what an ~ problem has the writer of a classic in his next work —Leslie Rees⟩ **2** : so undesirable as to be incapable of arousing envy ⟨~ notoriety⟩ ⟨an ~ reputation for bad dealing⟩ **3** : AWKWARD, EMBARRASSING ⟨placed in the ~ position of resorting to an act which he planned to make a major campaign issue —Mary K. Hammond⟩

un·envied \"+\ *adj* [[1]*un-* + *envied*, past part. of *envy*] **1** : not envied : inspiring no envious feelings ⟨lived in an unostentatious and so ~ way⟩ **2** : not coveted ⟨the submerged fifth of the present population . . . forgotten because it lives upon ~ land —*Harper's*⟩

un·envious \"+\ *adj* : marked by an absence of envy : not malicious : UNGRUDGING ⟨an amiable, ~ person⟩ ⟨in friendly and thoroughly ~ correspondence with them all —J.G. Lockhart⟩ ⟨~ irony —R.P.Warren⟩

un·enviously \"+\ *adv* : in an unenvious manner ⟨had gone his own way ~ —Meredith Nicholson⟩

un·envying \"+\ *adj* [[1]*un-* + *envying*, pres. part. of *envy*] : free of envy ⟨strains . . . which charm to silence the ~ nightingales —P.B.Shelley⟩

un·episcopal \ˌən+\ *adj* **1** : having no bishops **2** : not episcopalian **3** : not befitting a bishop — **un·episcopally** \"+\ *adv*

un·epitaphed \"+\ *adj* [[1]*un-* + *epitaphed*, past part. of *epitaph*] : not provided or honored with an epitaph ⟨lived a niggardly patron and died ~⟩

un·equable \"+\ *adj* **1** : not equable or temperate ⟨an ~ climate⟩ **2** : IRREGULAR, UNSTABLE ⟨~ movement⟩

un·equably \"+\ *adv* : in an unequable manner : IRREGULARLY

[1]**un·equal** \"+\ *adj* **1 a** : not of the same measurement, quantity, amount, or number as another : UNLIKE ⟨cutting planks of ~ length⟩ ⟨~ amounts of butter⟩ ⟨classes of ~ size⟩ ⟨~ costs⟩ **b** : not like or not the same as another in degree, worth, quality, ability, or status ⟨two machines operating at ~ speeds⟩ ⟨several pieces of ~ workmanship⟩ ⟨men of ~ capacity⟩ ⟨statistics . . . ~ in value —*Geog. Jour.*⟩ ⟨poems . . . of widely ~ merit —*College English*⟩ **c** *archaic* : ODD — used of numbers **2 a** : not like or not the same for each member of a group or class ⟨~ chances for success⟩ **b** : not uniform in quantity or quality, measure or degree : VARIABLE, IRREGULAR, UNEVEN ⟨~ pulsations⟩ ⟨~ and different movements of the heavenly bodies —Benjamin Farrington⟩ ⟨a most ~ writer —*Times Lit. Supp.*⟩ **c** : showing variation in appearance, structure, or proportion ⟨the tips of the ~ towers —Janet Flanner⟩ **d** : not level : RUGGED ⟨an ~ surface⟩ **3 a** : badly balanced or matched : UNEVEN ⟨~ odds⟩ ⟨an ~ fight⟩ ⟨farmers were ready to abandon their ~ struggle with a stubborn soil —*Amer. Guide Series: Mass.*⟩ **b** : contracted between unequals ⟨~ marriages⟩ ⟨~ treaties⟩ ⟨an ~ match⟩ **c** *archaic* : not equable : INTEMPERATE ⟨her spirits . . . were more disturbed, more ~, than she had often seen them —Jane Austen⟩ **4 a** *archaic* : not equitable : UNJUST, UNFAIR ⟨to punish me for what you made me do seems much ~ —Shak.⟩ **b** *obs* : acting unfairly : PARTIAL ⟨an ~ parent —Matthew Prior⟩ **5** : incapable of meeting the requirements of a situation or task : INADEQUATE, INSUFFICIENT — usu. used with *to* ⟨~ to the pace⟩ ⟨a mere politician will prove ~ to the position⟩ ⟨timber ~ to the strain⟩ ⟨felt ~ to the coming interview⟩ ⟨they were ~ to the wild country —Emil Lengyel⟩

[2]**unequal** \"\ *n* **1** : one that is not equal to or not on a basis of equality with another — usu. used in pl. ⟨a comparison of ~*s*⟩ ⟨a society of ~*s* —Walter Moberly⟩ **2** : a mathematical quantity that is either less or greater than another ⟨if ~*s* are added to ~*s* in the same order, the sums are unequal in the same order⟩

[3]**unequal** \"\ *adv, archaic* : UNEQUALLY ⟨~ match'd —Shak.⟩

un·equal·able \ˌə'nēkwələbəl\ *adj* [[1]*un-* + *equal*, v. + *-able*] : incapable of being equaled : UNSURPASSABLE, INCOMPARABLE ⟨two ~ men —Robert Lonthey⟩

unequal counterpoint *n* : counterpoint in which the musical parts move in unequal notes

un·equaled \ˌən+\ *adj* [[1]*un-* + *equaled*, past part. of *equal*] : not equaled : UNPARALLELED ⟨~ cruelty⟩ ⟨~ success⟩ ⟨an ~ job of shirking —S.E.Hyman⟩ ⟨an ~ degree of resistance —*Steinway Cat.*⟩ : UNRIVALED, MATCHLESS ⟨flowers ~ for size and beauty⟩ ⟨craftsmen whose skill is ~ —*Quarterly Rev.*⟩ : UNPRECEDENTED ⟨for killing two . . . bulls he would receive the ~ sum of thirty thousand dollars —Barnaby Conrad⟩

unequal hour *n* : HOUR 5

un·equality \ˌən+\ *n* [by alter.] : INEQUALITY

un·equal·ize \ˌə'nēkwəˌlīz\ *vt* [[1]*unequal* + *-ize*] : to cause to be unequal ⟨the more you ~ opportunity, the more you ~ men —A.E.Wiggam⟩

un·equally \ˌən+\ *adv* : in an unequal manner: **a** : in unequal amounts or shares ⟨profits divided ~⟩ **b** : with unequal treatment for each : with partiality : UNJUSTLY ⟨angry that they had been dealt with so ~⟩ **c** : not uniformly : UNEVENLY, IRREGULARLY ⟨snow scattered ~ over the mountainside⟩

un·equalness \"+\ *n* [[1]*un-* + *equalness*] *archaic* : INEQUALITY

unequal temperament *n* : a temperament that keeps pure or nearly pure intonation in some keys and accumulates the dissonances in the little-used keys

unequal voices *n pl* : mixed voices in singing

un·equipped \ˌən+\ *adj* [[1]*un-* + *equipped*, past part. of *equip*] : not provided with what is needed : UNPREPARED ⟨~ with the necessary outfit for the sport⟩ ⟨his gentle background left him ~ to face today's realities —Gordon Merrick⟩

un·equitable \"+\ *adj* : INEQUITABLE

un·equivocal \"+\ *adj* **:** not equivocal **:** leaving no doubt: **a :** expressing only one meaning **:** leading to only one conclusion **:** CLEAR, UNAMBIGUOUS ⟨~ evidence⟩ ⟨take an ~ position on an issue⟩ **b :** expressed in full and definite terms **:** EXPLICIT, CERTAIN ⟨the plain and ~ language of the laws —R.B.Taney⟩ **c :** expressing finality **:** carrying no implication of later change or revision **:** CONCLUSIVE, ABSOLUTE ⟨her dangerous inability to make an ~ refusal⟩ ⟨an ~ promise⟩ ⟨an ~ guarantee to respect the nation's sovereignty in the future⟩ ⟨the ~ diagnosis . . . is at present difficult —*Jour. Amer. Med. Assoc.*⟩ **d :** not open to challenge **:** UNQUESTIONABLE, UNMISTAKABLE ⟨had an ~ success in the role⟩ ⟨an ~ loss of prestige⟩ ⟨these people enjoy . . . an ~ social position —W.H.Auden⟩

un·equivocally \"+\ *adv* **:** in an unequivocal manner: **a :** CLEARLY, UNAMBIGUOUSLY ⟨come out ~ with their own position —K.S.Latourette⟩ **b :** EXPLICITLY ⟨little . . . can be said ~ about the theoretical work —G.E.K.Branch & Melvin Calvin⟩ **c :** CONCLUSIVELY, ABSOLUTELY ⟨clinical experience ~ demonstrates —*Therapeutic Notes*⟩ **d :** UNMISTAKABLY ⟨speaks . . . ~ with the voice of his literary age —T.S.Eliot⟩

un·equivocalness \"+\ *n* **:** the quality or state of being unequivocal

un·eradicable \"+\ *adj* [1*un-* + *eradicate* + *-able*] **:** INERADICABLE

un·erasable \"+\ *adj* [1*un-* + *erase* + *-able*] **:** incapable of being erased

un·erect \"+\ *adj* **:** not erect **:** bowing down **:** SUBMISSIVE ⟨no merit but a love, slavish and ~ —R.L.Stevenson⟩

un·erected \"+\ *adj* [1*un-* + *erected*, past part. of *erect*] **:** not erected **:** not uplifted or inspired ⟨an ~ spirit⟩

un·erring \"+\ *adj* **1 :** committing no error **:** FAULTLESS ⟨people of ~ taste in clothes and furniture —Albert Dasnoy⟩ **2 :** matching a standard with the greatest exactness or accuracy ⟨perform with ~ exactness⟩ ⟨aped his mannerisms in ~ fashion⟩ ⟨the youngsters noted his weakness with . . . ~ precision —G.D.Brown⟩ **3 :** not wandering from the intended course or purpose **:** going right to the mark **:** UNDEVIATING, SURE ⟨~ marksmanship⟩ ⟨~ as a shaft of light —J.L.Lowes⟩ ⟨the ~ and merciless power of retribution in Nature —E.T. Thurston⟩ **syn** see INFALLIBLE

un·erringly \"+\ *adv* **:** in an unerring manner: **a :** INFALLIBLY ⟨believed capable of interpreting the Bible ~⟩ **b :** with precision **:** ACCURATELY, NEATLY ⟨a play ~ performed⟩ ⟨caught the traits of his rustic characters ~⟩

un·err·ing·ness \ˌ='==nə̇s\ *n* -ES **:** the quality or state of being unerring **:** INFALLIBILITY

un·erupted \¦ən+\ *adj* [1*un-* + *erupted*, past part. of *erupt*] *of a tooth* **:** not yet emerged through the gum

un·escapable \"+\ *adj* [1*un-* + *escape*, v. + *-able*] **1 :** incapable of being escaped or ignored **:** INESCAPABLE, UNAVOIDABLE ⟨every Tube station . . . is papered with ~ assertions —C.E.Montague⟩ **2 :** necessarily to be considered and dealt with ⟨an ~ crisis⟩ ⟨the ~ expansion of the nation's foreign policy —D.S.Freeman⟩ **3 :** following logically or from the evidence **:** INEVITABLE ⟨an ~ conclusion⟩

un·escapably \"+\ *adv* **:** in an unescapable manner **:** UNAVOIDABLY, INEVITABLY ⟨no other writer . . . is more ~ national in his every gesture and trick of mind —H.L.Mencken⟩

un·escaped \"+\ *adj* [1*un-* + *escaped*, past part. of *escape*] **:** not escaped **:** RETAINED ⟨~ vapors⟩

un·escorted \¦ən+\ *adj* [1*un-* + *escorted*, past part. of *escort*] **:** not escorted **:** lacking an escort **:** UNATTENDED, UNACCOMPANIED ⟨~ ladies not admitted⟩

un·espied \"+\ *adj* [ME, fr. 1*un-* + *espied*, past part. of *espien* to espy] **:** passing unseen **:** escaping notice or detection ⟨got into the forbidden area ~⟩

un·essayed \"+\ *adj* [1*un-* + *essayed*, past part. of *essay*] **:** not essayed **:** UNATTEMPTED ⟨leaves no tyrannical evasion ~ —John Milton⟩

1un·essential \"+\ *adj* **1 :** not essential **:** DISPENSABLE, UNIMPORTANT ⟨~ illustrations⟩ ⟨other freedoms . . . seem vague and ~ —E.H.Erikson⟩ **2** *archaic* **:** void of essence **:** having no real being **:** INSUBSTANTIAL ⟨the void profound of ~ night —John Milton⟩

2unessential \"\ *n* **:** something that is unessential or that can be dispensed with as unimportant or unneeded ⟨not . . . waste time in attacking ~*s* —F. Tennyson Jesse⟩

un·established \"+\ *adj* [1*un-* + *established*, past part. of *establish*] **:** not firmly based ⟨a reputation as yet ~⟩: **a :** having little or no previous success; *specif* **:** not yet published ⟨short stories by ~ writers —*Atlantic*⟩ **b** *of a church* **:** not made a national or state institution **c** *Brit* **:** outside the permanent or regular staff of a business or institution ⟨an ~ post⟩ ⟨an ~ appointment⟩

un·esteemed \"+\ *adj* [1*un-* + *esteemed*, past part. of *esteem*] **:** not esteemed **:** UNHONORED, UNRESPECTED ⟨~ worth⟩

un·esthetic \"+\ *adj* **:** not esthetic ⟨something ~ about the word —Edward Sapir⟩

un·estimable \"+\ *adj* [by alter.] **:** INESTIMABLE

un·ethical \"+\ *adj* **:** not conforming to approved standards of behavior, a socially accepted code, or professionally endorsed principles and practices ⟨~ practices in the handling of public funds⟩ ⟨considered such advertising by physicians ~⟩ — **un·ethically** \"+\ *adv*

un·etymological *also* **un·etymologic** \"+\ *adj* **:** not based on or in accordance with etymology ⟨the *unetymologic* doubling of consonants —R.C.Clark⟩

un·evadable \"+\ *adj* [1*un-* + *evade* + *-able*] **:** not evadable ⟨the . . . downright ~ pressures of realities —Thomas De-Quincey⟩

un·evad·ably \¦==¦==blē\ *adv* **:** in an unevadable manner **:** INESCAPABLY ⟨the images are . . . ~ concrete —F.R.Leavis⟩

un·evaluated \¦ən+\ *adj* [1*un-* + *evaluated*, past part. of *evaluate*] **:** not examined and appraised as to worth or significance ⟨~ data⟩

un·evangelical \"+\ *adj* **:** not conforming to or agreeing with the Christian gospels **:** not according with the doctrines or practices of Protestant Christianity ⟨~ rites⟩

un·evaporated \"+\ *also* **un·evap·o·rate** \¦==¦==ˌrə̇t\ *adj* [*unevaporated* fr. 1*un-* + *evaporated* past part. of *evaporate*; *unevaporate* fr. 1*un-* + obs. *evaporate* evaporated, fr. L *evaporatus*, past part. of *evaporare* to evaporate] **1 :** not dissipated **:** EXTANT ⟨an ~ remnant⟩ **2 :** not passed off in the form of vapor ⟨the ~ residue⟩

un·even \¦ən+\ *adj* [ME, fr. OE *unefen*, fr. 1*un-* + *efen* even] **1 a** *archaic* **:** not equal in size, number, or quantity **:** UNEQUAL 1a ⟨two pipes of glass very ~ in length —Robert Boyle⟩ **b :** not divisible by two without a remainder **:** ODD 3 **2 a :** not even **:** not level or flat **:** RUGGED ⟨proceeding slowly over the ~ ground⟩ ⟨miles of ~ country —*Amer. Guide Series: Pa.*⟩ **:** having irregularities of surface (as breaks, indentations, or roughnesses) **:** RAGGED ⟨large, ~ teeth⟩ ⟨~ ranks⟩ ⟨~ handwriting⟩ **b :** varying from the straight or parallel ⟨a building with ~ vertical lines⟩ **c :** varying or inconsistent **:** not uniform **:** SPOTTY, IRREGULAR ⟨~ earnings⟩ ⟨~ combustion⟩ ⟨~ subway traffic —*N.Y.Times*⟩ ⟨a stove at one end . . . gave very ~ heat —*Amer. Guide Series: Calif.*⟩ ⟨germination may be ~ or poor —*Farmer's Weekly (So. Africa)*⟩ **d :** varying markedly in quality ⟨an ~ performance⟩ ⟨an ~ achievement . . . its writing ranges from the human and impassioned to the dully academic —David Hall⟩ **3** *obs* **:** UNJUST, INEQUITABLE ⟨complains of the bishops' ~ hand over these pamphlets —John Milton⟩ **4 :** UNEQUAL 3a ⟨vaudeville troupes . . . waged an ~ battle against the church —*Amer. Guide Series: N.J.*⟩ **syn** see ROUGH

uneven–aged \¦=¦==¦=\ *adj* [*uneven* + *aged*] *of a forest* **:** consisting of trees of three or more age classes

un·evenly \¦ən+\ *adv* [ME, fr. *uneven* + *-ly*] **:** in an uneven manner or degree: **a :** in unequal parts ⟨time ~ divided between play and study⟩ **b :** not uniformly or consistently **:** IRREGULARLY ⟨mowed the lawn very ~⟩ ⟨~ fitted boards —*Amer. Guide Series: Oregon*⟩ ⟨when biographical facts are scanty, they are also apt to be ~ distributed —*Times Lit. Supp.*⟩ **c :** without proper balance **:** on unequal terms **:** UNFAIRLY ⟨teams ~ matched⟩

un·evenness \"+\ *n* [ME *unevennesse*, fr. *uneven* + *-nesse* -ness] **1 :** the quality or state of being uneven: **a :** INEQUALITY ⟨~ of height⟩ **b :** ROUGHNESS ⟨the ~ of land surfaces⟩ ⟨the ~ of the path⟩ **c :** lack of uniform quality **:** IRREGULARITY, INCONSISTENCY ⟨the ~ of the essays detracts from the book's overall effect —F.R.Dulles⟩ **d :** temperamental instability ⟨the ~ of his moods and behavior⟩ **2 :** an uneven place ⟨file down the ~*es*⟩

un·eventful \"+\ *adj* **1 :** marked by no noteworthy incidents **:** PLACID, COMMONPLACE ⟨an ~ life⟩ ⟨the voyage . . . was throughout pleasant and ~ —Havelock Ellis⟩ **2 :** passing without untoward incident **:** NORMAL ⟨made an ~ landing⟩ ⟨recovery was ~ —*Lancet*⟩ **3 :** unworthy of particular notice **:** ORDINARY

un·eventfully \"+\ *adv* **:** in an uneventful manner

un·eventfulness \"+\ *n* **:** the quality or state of being uneventful

un·evoked \¦ən+\ *adj* [1*un-* + *evoked*, past part. of *evoke*] **:** not enforced **:** DORMANT ⟨a law that has gone ~ since its passage⟩

un·evolved \"+\ *adj* [1*un-* + *evolved*, past part. of *evolve*] **:** not evolved **:** not unfolded **:** UNDEVELOPED, PRIMITIVE

un·exact \"+\ *adj* **:** INEXACT

un·exacting \¦ən+\ *adj* **:** not demanding **:** UNCRITICAL

un·exaggerated \"+\ *adj* [1*un-* + *exaggerated*, past part. of *exaggerate*] **:** not magnified or colored **:** UNVARNISHED ⟨an ~ report of the event⟩ ⟨the ~ truth of the matter⟩

un·exalted \"+\ *adj* **:** UNELEVATED, UNINSPIRED ⟨not ~ by religious faith —William Wordsworth⟩

un·examinable \"+\ *adj* **1 :** not susceptible to inquiry **:** INSCRUTABLE ⟨~ intention —John Milton⟩ **2 :** not determinable by examination ⟨what a student most needs to get from literature is intangible and . . . ~ —*Quarterly Jour. of Speech*⟩

un·examined \"+\ *adj* [ME, fr. 1*un-* + *examined*, past part. of *examinen* to examine] **:** not subjected to examination (as critical scrutiny, analysis, or comparison) **:** not carefully weighed **:** not collated ⟨an ~ premise⟩ ⟨several ~ copies of the manuscript are being made available for study⟩

un·examining \"+\ *adj* [1*un-* + *examining*, pres. part. of *examine*] **:** not weighing or considering **:** UNCRITICAL, UNTHINKING ⟨an ~ and undiscriminating public⟩

un·ex·am·pled \¦==¦=pəld\ *adj* [1*un-* + *example* + *-ed*] **:** having no example, precedent, or parallel **:** UNIQUE ⟨a time of ~ prosperity⟩ — often used postpositively ⟨its system of public parks ~ to my knowledge —A.B.Guthrie⟩

un·excelled \¦ən+\ *adj* [1*un-* + *excelled*, past part. of *excel*] **:** not capable of being bettered or improved upon **:** UNSURPASSED, SUPERB ⟨an ~ view of the mountains⟩ ⟨an ~ academic record⟩

un·excepted \"+\ *adj* [1*un-* + *excepted*, past part. of *except*] **1** *obs* **:** not objected to **:** UNQUESTIONED, UNCRITICIZED **2 :** having no exception **:** UNALTERABLE ⟨nature's ~ law —P.J.Bailey⟩

un·ex·cep·tion·abil·i·ty \ˌənikˌsepsh(ə)nə'biləd·ē\ *n* [*unexceptionable* + *-ity*] **:** UNEXCEPTIONABLENESS

un·ex·cep·tion·able \¦==¦sepsh(ə)nəbəl\ *adj* [1*un-* + obs. *exception* to take exception (fr. *exception*, n.) + *-able*] **:** not open or liable to objection, criticism, or reproach **:** ACCEPTABLE, UNIMPEACHABLE ⟨starts from an ~ premise⟩ ⟨two ~ witnesses —G.G.Coulton⟩ ⟨had always maintained an ~ character —Sheridan Le Fanu⟩ ⟨his work was ~ —S.F. Mason⟩ ⟨this part of the . . . plan is perhaps ~ —*New Republic*⟩

un·ex·cep·tion·able·ness \ˌ=='=(=)==nə̇s\ *n* -ES **:** the quality or state of being unexceptionable **:** ACCEPTABILITY, IRREPROACHABILITY

un·ex·cep·tion·ably \¦==¦sepsh(ə)nəblē, -li\ *adv* **1 :** in an unexceptionable manner **:** UNIMPEACHABLY, IRREPROACHABLY ⟨behaving ~⟩ **2** *archaic* **:** without exception **:** UNEXCEPTIONALLY, UNIVERSALLY

un·ex·cep·tion·al \-shənᵊl,-shnəl\ *adj* [1*un-* + *exception* + *-al*] **1 :** open to no objection **:** UNEXCEPTIONABLE ⟨only the ~ work of the aircraft and engine manufacturers . . . enabled the expedition to take place —*World Today*⟩ **2 :** allowing no exception **:** UNALTERABLE ⟨an ideal language, with ~ rules —E.W.Hall⟩ **3 :** constituting no exception to the general rule **:** ORDINARY, COMMONPLACE ⟨as ~ an incident as this must be in a doctor's career —*New Republic*⟩

un·ex·cep·tion·al·ly \-ᵊl¦ē, -əl|, |i\ *adv* [*unexceptional* + *-ly*] **:** without exception **:** in every case **:** UNIVERSALLY ⟨have ~ taken for granted the one thing which they were attempting to prove —M.F.A.Montagu⟩

un·exchangeable \¦ən+\ *adj* **:** not capable of being substituted one for another **:** INCOMMUTABLE

un·excitable \"+\ *adj* **:** incapable of being stirred or energized **:** not responsive to stimuli ⟨an ~ temperament⟩

un·excited \"+\ *adj* [1*un-* + *excited*, past part. of *excite*] **1 :** marked by a lack of excitement **:** CALM ⟨make an ~ appraisal of the situation⟩ **2 :** not affected by outward stimuli

un·exciting \"+\ *adj* **:** not exciting **:** PROSAIC, COMMONPLACE ⟨an ~ life⟩ ⟨an ~ novel⟩

un·excluding \"+\ *adj* [1*un-* + *excluding*, pres. part. of *exclude*] **:** not excluding **:** COMPREHENSIVE ⟨a taste so catholic, so ~ —Charles Lamb⟩

un·exclusive \"+\ *adj* **:** not exclusive **:** INCLUSIVE, COMPREHENSIVE

un·exclusively \"+\ *adv* **:** in an unexclusive manner **:** COMPREHENSIVELY, UNIVERSALLY

un·excogitable \¦əˌnek¦skäjəd·əbəl\ *adj* [modif. of LL *inexcogitabilis*, fr. L *in-* 1in- + *excogitare* to excogitate + *-abilis* -able] **:** not capable of being thought out or contrived

un·excusable \¦ən +\ *adj* [1*un-* + *excusable*] **:** INEXCUSABLE

un·excused \¦ən+\ *adj* [1*un-* + *excused*, past part. of *excuse*] **:** not excused; *specif* **:** not officially excused or permitted ⟨~ absences⟩

un·executed \"+\ *adj* [1*un-* + *executed*, past part. of *execute*] **:** not carried out **:** UNPERFORMED ⟨an ~ plan⟩; *specif* **:** not carried out legally according to its terms ⟨an ~ agreement⟩

un·exemplary \"+\ *adj* [1*un-* + L *exemplum* example + E *-ary*] **1** *obs* **:** having no precedent **:** UNEXAMPLED **2 :** not exemplary **:** not fit to be taken as a model ⟨an ~ husband⟩

un·exemplified \"+\ *adj* [1*un-* + *exemplified*, past part. of *exemplify*] **1** *obs* **:** UNEXAMPLED **2 :** not provided with an illustrative example **:** not exemplified ⟨titles of odd form and ~ significance —E.A.Robinson⟩

un·exercised \"+\ *adj* [ME, fr. 1*un-* + *exercised*, past part. of *exercisen* to exercise] **:** not exercised: **a :** not put to use or trial **:** UNTRIED, UNPRACTICED ⟨a faculty left ~⟩ ⟨I cannot praise a fugitive and cloistered virtue, ~ and unbreathed —John Milton⟩ **b :** not made effective in action **:** not exerted **:** UNCLAIMED ⟨an ~ right⟩ ⟨a privilege ~ for years⟩ **c :** not accustomed to physical exercise **:** SEDENTARY, INACTIVE ⟨skiing . . . within the reach of the most ~ —*Times Lit. Supp.*⟩ **d** *archaic* **:** not fitted or prepared by exercise **:** UNTRAINED

un·exhausted \¦ən+\ *adj* [1*un-* + *exhausted*, past part. of *exhaust*] **1 :** not emptied or drawn off completely ⟨an ~ well⟩ **2 :** not completely expended **:** not used up ⟨an ~ fund⟩

un·exhaustible \"+\ *adj* [by alter.] **:** INEXHAUSTIBLE

un·existence \"+\ *n* **:** absence of existence **:** NONEXISTENCE

un·existing \¦ən+\ *adj* [1*un-* + *existing*, pres. part. of *exist*] **:** NONEXISTENT

un·ex·or·cis·able \¦=¦=(ˌ)=¦sīzəbəl\ *adj* [1*un-* + *exorcise* + *-able*] **:** incapable of being exorcised

un·ex·or·cis·ably \-blē\ *adv* **:** in an unexorcisable manner ⟨image ~ haunting him —Aldous Huxley⟩

un·exorcised \¦ən+\ *adj* [1*un-* + *exorcised*, past part. of *exorcise*] **:** not exorcised **:** not driven off or expelled ⟨an ~ specter⟩

un·expanded \"+\ *adj* [1*un-* + *expanded*, past part. of *expand*] **1 :** not enlarged upon **:** not expounded or developed fully ⟨an ~ comparison⟩ ⟨left the idea ~⟩ **2 :** not unfolded **:** not spread open ⟨~ leaves⟩

un·expansive \"+\ *adj* **:** not expansive: **a :** showing no tendency or inclination to expand ⟨~ bodies⟩ **b :** not given to high spirits or effusiveness **:** RESTRAINED ⟨an ~ man⟩

un·expectable \"+\ *adj* [1*un-* + *expect* + *-able*] **:** incapable of being expected **:** UNPREDICTABLE ⟨kept bringing out one unexpected and wholly ~ thing after another —Nathaniel Hawthorne⟩ ⟨who could have been more ~ —Christopher Morley⟩

un·expected \"+\ *adj* [1*un-* + *expected*, past part. of *expect*] **:** not expected **:** UNLOOKED-FOR, UNFORESEEN, SURPRISING ⟨~ news⟩ ⟨an ~ guest⟩ ⟨the ~ always happens⟩

un·ex·pect·ed·ly \"lē, -li\ *adv* **:** in an unexpected manner **:** SURPRISINGLY ⟨arrived ~ early⟩ ⟨was ~ successful⟩

un·ex·pect·ed·ness \ˌ=='==nə̇s\ *n* -ES **:** the quality or state of being unexpected ⟨the ~ of the warm welcome⟩

un·expedient \¦ən+\ *adj* [ME, fr. 1*un-* + *expedient*] *archaic* **:** INEXPEDIENT

un·expended \"+\ *adj* [1*un-* + *expended*, past part. of *expend*] **:** not expended **:** not consumed **:** not used up ⟨~ provisions⟩ **:** not spent ⟨an ~ portion of a fund⟩ ⟨an ~ balance⟩

un·expensive \"+\ *adj* **:** INEXPENSIVE — **un·expensively** \"+\ *adv* — **un·expensiveness** \"+\ *n*

un·experienced \"+\ *adj* [partly fr. 1*un-* + *experience*, n. + *-ed*; partly fr. 1*un-* + *experienced*, past part. of *experience*] **:** not experienced: **a :** having no experience **:** INEXPERIENCED ⟨an ~ practitioner⟩ **b :** UNTRIED ⟨quite unknown and ~ by most —R.C.McCall⟩

unexpert *adj* [ME, fr. 1*un-* + *expert*] *obs* **:** lacking practical knowledge or experience **:** UNEXPERIENCED ⟨a pure celibate and altogether ~ of women —Aphra Behn⟩

un·expiated \"+\ *adj* [1*un-* + *expiated*, past part. of *expiate*] **:** not expiated **:** not atoned for ⟨~ crimes⟩

un·expired \¦ən+\ *adj* [1*un-* + *expired*, past part. of *expire*] **:** not yet run out **:** not terminated ⟨elected to fill the senator's ~ term⟩ ⟨an ~ lease⟩

un·explainable \"+\ *adj* **:** not capable of being explained **:** UNACCOUNTABLE, INEXPLICABLE ⟨an ~ fear⟩ ⟨an ~ custom of changing the ship's name —*N. Y. Herald Tribune*⟩

un·ex·plain·ably \¦==¦==blē, -bli\ *adv* **:** in an unexplainable manner **:** INEXPLICABLY

un·explained \¦ən+\ *adj* [1*un-* + *explained*, past part. of *explain*] **:** not explained or accounted for ⟨an ~ error⟩

un·explicit \"+\ *adj* **:** not explicit **:** lacking full and clear expression **:** VAGUE, AMBIGUOUS ⟨the more basic the premise the more likely it is to remain ~ —L.A.White⟩

un·explicitly \"+\ *adv* **:** in an unexplicit manner **:** UNCLEARLY, VAGUELY

un·exploded \"+\ *adj* [1*un-* + *exploded*, past part. of *explode*] **:** not exploded **:** charged with explosive **:** UNDISCHARGED, LIVE 3c ⟨~ ammunition⟩ ⟨an ~ shell⟩

un·exploited \"+\ *adj* [1*un-* + *exploited*, past part. of *exploit*] **:** not exploited **:** not taken advantage of **:** UNUSED ⟨left a blunder of the opposition completely ~⟩; *specif* **:** not turned to economic account **:** UNDEVELOPED ⟨vast ~ natural resources —*Amer. Guide Series: Oregon*⟩

un·explored \"+\ *adj* [1*un-* + *explored*, past part. of *explore*] **:** not explored **:** not looked into or investigated ⟨minor writings still ~ by scholars⟩ ⟨~ areas of the subconscious mind⟩; *specif* **:** not penetrated or ranged over for purposes of geographical discovery ⟨~ wilderness⟩

un·exposed \"+\ *adj* **:** not exposed: **a :** not laid open to view **:** not brought to light ⟨many ~ cases of official corruption⟩ **b :** not made subject to an action or influence; *specif* **:** not subjected (as sensitive photographic film) to the action of radiant energy

un·expressed \"+\ *adj* [1*un-* + *expressed*, past part. of *express*] **:** not expressed: **a :** not uttered in words **:** UNSPOKEN ⟨~ emotion⟩ ⟨vague ~ ideas⟩ **b :** not conveyed **:** TACIT ⟨the ~ terms of the agreement⟩

un·expressible *also* **un·expressable** \"+\ *adj* [1*un-* + *express* + *-ible*, *-able*] **:** INEXPRESSIBLE

un·expressive \"+\ *adj* [1*un-* + *express* + *-ive*] **1** *obs* **:** incapable of being expressed in words **:** transcending expression or description **:** INEFFABLE, INEXPRESSIBLE ⟨the fair, the chaste, and ~ she —Shak.⟩ **2 :** not expressive **:** lacking expression **:** failing to convey the meaning or feeling intended ⟨an ~ face⟩ ⟨~ voices chanting the correct service —L.P.Smith⟩

un·expugnable \"+\ *adj* [ME, modif. of L *inexpugnabilis* inexpugnable] **:** INEXPUGNABLE 1

un·expurgated \"+\ *adj* [1*un-* + *expurgated*, past part. of *expurgate*] **:** not expurgated **:** UNCENSORED ⟨volumes of the best plays, ~ —Havelock Ellis⟩

un·extended \"+\ *adj* **1 :** not extended **:** not stretched out ⟨an ~ arm⟩ **2 :** not having the property of extension ⟨an ~ substance⟩

un·extenuated \¦ən+\ *adj* [1*un-* + *extenuated*, past part. of *extenuate*] **:** having no extenuation **:** UNMITIGATED

un·extinct \"+\ *adj* **1 :** still burning **:** UNEXTINGUISHED ⟨one spark of fire . . . ~ —John Fletcher⟩ **2 :** still in use **:** not superseded **:** ACTIVE, EXTANT

un·extinguishable \"+\ *adj* **1 :** incapable of being stopped from burning **:** UNQUENCHABLE **2 :** incapable of being ended or suppressed ⟨~ laughter⟩

un·extinguished \"+\ *adj* [1*un-* + *extinguished*, past part. of *extinguish*] **:** not extinguished: **a :** not put out **:** UNQUENCHED ⟨an ~ fire⟩ **b :** not ended **:** still living ⟨observed . . . tokens of ~ or returning passion —T.L.Peacock⟩

un·extirpated \"+\ *adj* [1*un-* + *extirpated*, past. part. of *extirpate*] **:** not rooted out **:** not wholly destroyed ⟨vicious habits still ~⟩

un·extorted \"+\ *adj* [1*un-* + *extorted*, past part. of *extort*] **:** not extorted **:** freely given ⟨~ affection⟩

un·extricable \"+\ *adj* **:** INEXTRICABLE

un·eyed \"+\ *adj* [1*un-* + *eyed*, past part. of *eye*] **:** UNOBSERVED, UNSEEN

un·fabled \"+\ *adj* **:** not fictitious **:** REAL, ACTUAL

un·fabricated \"+\ *adj* [1*un-* + *fabricated*, past part. of *fabricate*] **:** not worked, shaped, or processed into final form **:** not manufactured ⟨~ material⟩

un·face·able \ˌən'fāsəbəl\ *adj* [1*un-* + *face*, v. + *-able*] **:** not capable of being faced **:** REVOLTING ⟨an unknown and ~ horror —John Strachey⟩

un·faced \¦ən+\ *adj* **:** not provided with a facing ⟨~ surface⟩ ⟨~ brick⟩

un·fact \"+\ *n* **:** a deliberate falsehood made to pass as fact (as for partisan or propagandistic purpose)

un·fad·able \¦ən¦fādəbəl\ *adj* [1*un-* + *fade* + *-able*] **1 :** not subject to fading **:** FAST, EVERLASTING ⟨a fabric of ~ color⟩ **2 :** incapable of being forgotten **:** MEMORABLE, DEATHLESS ⟨an ~ act of political courage —*Manchester Guardian Weekly*⟩

un·faded \¦ən+\ *adj* [1*un-* + *faded*, past part. of *fade*] **:** not faded **:** FRESH ⟨moments that live again in remembrance ~ —W.W.Gibson⟩

un·fading \"+\ *adj* [1*un-* + *fading*, pres. part. of *fade*] **1 :** not losing color or freshness ⟨~ flowers⟩ **2 :** not losing value, importance, effectiveness, or appeal ⟨an ~ honor⟩

un·fail·ing \¦ən¦fāliŋ, -lēŋ\ *adj* [ME, fr. 1*un-* + *failing*, pres. part. of *failen* to fail] **:** not failing or liable to fail: **a :** not desisting **:** CONSTANT, UNFLAGGING ⟨~ good spirits⟩ ⟨~ courtesy⟩ **b :** EVERLASTING, INEXHAUSTIBLE ⟨a subject of ~ interest⟩ ⟨~ pleasure⟩ **c :** INFALLIBLE, SURE ⟨an ~ test⟩ ⟨the ~ mark of an amateur⟩

un·fail·ing·ly *adv* [ME, fr. *unfailing* + *-ly*] **:** in an unfailing manner **:** without fail **:** INVARIABLY, UNFLAGGINGLY ⟨prolific and ~ bad writers —Whitney Balliett⟩ ⟨no other living conductor so ~ attentive . . . to the music —Virgil Thomson⟩

un·fail·ing·ness *n* -ES **:** the quality or state of being unfailing

un·fainting \"+\ *adj* [1*un-* + *fainting*, pres. part. of *faint*] **:** not losing courage or vigor **:** PERSISTING ⟨~ diligence⟩

un·fair \"+\ *adj* **:** not fair: **a :** marked by injustice, partiality, or deception **:** UNJUST, DISHONEST ⟨~ methods⟩ ⟨an ~ trial⟩ ⟨an ~ critic⟩ ⟨an ~ judgment⟩ ⟨taking an ~ advantage of another person⟩ **b :** providing an insufficient or inequitable basis for judgment or evaluation **:** not representative ⟨an ~ instance to cite⟩ **c :** not according with merit or importance **:** DISPROPORTIONATE, EXCESSIVE ⟨an ~ share⟩ **d** *of the wind* **:** UNFAVORABLE 2a **e** (1) **:** not straight or smoothly curving ⟨~ lines⟩ (2) **:** not properly aligned or fitted together ⟨drilled ~ holes⟩ **f :** not equitable in business dealings (as in competition, wage scales, or attitude toward a labor union) ⟨~ to organized labor⟩

unfair competition *n* **1 a :** business competition effected by an act that is deceptive and in effect a fraud on the public or that otherwise violates the legal or equitable rights of a competitor or the public **b :** an improper or inequitable obtaining by one competitor of the benefits belonging to another ⟨passing off on the public the goods of one person as those of another is a form of *unfair competition*⟩ **2 :** a competitive practice contrary to the ethical standards of business or in violation of existing law as interpreted by a federal trade commission or a state agency

unfair labor practice *n* **:** a practice on the part of an employer or of an employee declared unfair under a national or state labor relations act that provides civil remedies to employer or employee administered by a labor relations board

unfair list *n* **:** a list of employers declared by the union compiling and publishing it to be unfair to organized labor

un·fairly \"+\ *adv* **:** in an unfair manner: **a :** UNJUSTLY, INEQUITABLY ⟨raised his prices ~⟩ **b :** with partiality ⟨decided the case ~⟩ **c :** UNREASONABLY ⟨it might, therefore, not ~ be assumed —T.H.Huxley⟩ **d :** not in accordance with the rules governing a competition ⟨played so ~ no one enjoyed playing with him⟩

unfair method of competition : UNFAIR TRADE PRACTICE

un·fairness \"+\ *n* **:** the quality or state of being unfair: **a :** INJUSTICE ⟨recognized the ~ of the decision⟩ **b :** improper alignment or fit ⟨noticed the ~ of the rivet holes⟩

unfair practice *n* **1 :** a trade practice with respect to the public or a competitor that is forbidden by statute and that is therefore subject to control by a federal trade commission **2 :** UNFAIR COMPETITION

unfair trade practice *n* **:** a trade practice declared by a federal trade commission to be an unfair method of competition pursuant to power given it by a legislative act designed to curb dishonesty, misrepresentation, and unethical and monopolistic business practices contrary to public policy and good morals in the business community

un·faith \ˌən+\ *n* [ME *unfeith*, fr. ¹*un-* + *feith* faith] **1 :** absence of faith **:** DISBELIEF ⟨a silent manifesto of ~ in the future of our body politic —Max Beerbohm⟩ **2 :** a nonreligious faith; *esp* **:** a faith actively opposed to religion

un·faithful \"+\ *adj* [ME *unfeithful*, fr. ¹*un-* + *feithful* faithful] **:** not faithful: **a :** having no religious faith **:** INFIDEL **b** (1) **:** not observing or adhering to vows, allegiance, or duty **:** DISLOYAL ⟨an ~ servant⟩ (2) **:** failing to perform a function or duty ⟨defects . . . make him ~ to his work —Samuel Alexander⟩ **c :** not faithful to marriage vows ⟨his ~ wife had eloped with her latest lover —Harrison Smith⟩ **d** *archaic* **:** wanting in good faith **:** DISHONEST ⟨this ~ dealing with your brother —Thomas Otway⟩ **e :** INACCURATE, UNTRUSTWORTHY ⟨an ~ copy of a document⟩

un·faithfully \"+\ *adv* [ME *unfeithfully*, fr. *unfeithful* + *-ly*] **:** in an unfaithful manner

un·faithfulness \"+\ *n* [ME *unfeithfulnesse*, fr. *unfeithful* + *-nesse* -ness] **:** the quality or state of being unfaithful

un·fallen \"+\ *adj* [¹*un-* + *fallen*, past part. of *fall*] **:** not morally fallen **:** marked by a state of prelapsarian innocence ⟨~ man⟩ ⟨an atmosphere as ~ as the original Garden —L.A. Fiedler⟩

un·fallible \"+\ *adj* **:** INFALLIBLE

un·faltering \"+\ *adj* [¹*un-* + *faltering*, pres. part. of *falter*] **:** not wavering or weakening **:** UNHESITATING, STEADY, FIRM ⟨a leader who demanded ~ belief from his followers⟩

un·falteringly \"+\ *adv* **:** in an unfaltering manner **:** UNHESITATINGLY, FIRMLY ⟨has ~ held to the old idea of liberal democracy —M.R.Cohen⟩

un·famed \ˌən+\ *adj* **:** unknown to fame **:** not famous ⟨passed his life ~⟩

un·familiar \"+\ *adj* **:** not familiar: **a :** not well known **:** STRANGE, UNACCUSTOMED ⟨new and ~ tasks⟩ ⟨an ~ place⟩ ⟨an industrial aspect ~ in this section of the state —*Amer. Guide Series: Ark.*⟩ **b :** UNKNOWN ⟨an artist ~ to all of us⟩ **c :** not well acquainted ⟨technical students . . . ~ with the study of the humanities —G.W.Chapman⟩

un·familiarity \"+\ *n* [*unfamiliar* + *-ity*] **:** the quality or state of being unfamiliar **:** STRANGENESS, NOVELTY ⟨his ~ with this quarter of the city⟩ ⟨an ~ with the new rules slowed down his play⟩ ⟨the ~ of the scene⟩

un·familiarized \"+\ *adj* [¹*un-* + *familiarized*, past part. of *familiarize*] **:** not made familiar or accustomed ⟨the plan itself would . . . startle an ~ conscience —S.T.Coleridge⟩

un·fancied \"+\ *adj* **:** UNIMAGINED ⟨some growth ~ yet —Robert Browning⟩

un·fanned \"+\ *adj* [¹*un-* + *fanned*, past part. of *fan*] **:** not fanned **:** not excited **:** not aroused ⟨~ by any enthusiasm⟩

un·fantastic \"+\ *adj* **:** not fantastic **:** EVERYDAY, REALISTIC ⟨a completely rational, ~ plan⟩

un·fashionable \ˌən+\ *adj* [¹*un-* + *fashion*, n. + *-able*] **1** *obs* **:** poorly fashioned **:** UNSHAPELY, DISTORTED **2 :** not in accord with or not following current fashion **:** not favored socially **:** OUT-OF-DATE, OUTMODED ⟨~ clothes⟩ ⟨melodrama of the now ~ kind —Daniel George⟩ ⟨it is ~ and indiscreet to profess admiration —Saul Maloff⟩

un·fashionableness \"+\ *n* **:** the quality or state of being unfashionable

un·fashionably \"+\ *adv* **:** in an unfashionable manner

un·fashioned \"+\ *adj* [¹*un-* + *fashioned*, past part. of *fashion*] **:** not fashioned: **a :** not shaped **:** UNWROUGHT ⟨an ~ jewel⟩ **b** *archaic* **:** not polished **:** UNREFINED, INELEGANT ⟨a precise ~ fellow —Richard Steele⟩

un·fasten \"+\ *vt* [ME *unfastnen*, fr. ²*un-* + *fastnen* to fasten] **:** to make loose: **a** *obs* **:** make less firm **:** WEAKEN ⟨~ his resolutions —Thomas Carte⟩ **b :** UNPIN, UNBUCKLE ⟨~ the bolt of a door⟩ ⟨~ a belt⟩ **c :** UNDO ⟨~ the buttons of a dress⟩ **d :** DETACH ⟨~ a boat from its moorings⟩ **e :** UNTIE ⟨~*ed* the string and opened the package⟩

un·fastened \"+\ *adj* [¹*un-* + *fastened*, past part. of *fasten*] **:** not fastened: **a :** UNBOUND, LOOSE ⟨~ hair⟩ **b :** UNLOCKED ⟨an ~ door⟩

un·fastidious \ˌən+\ *adj* **:** not fastidious: **a :** UNTIDY, CARELESS ⟨~ in her dress⟩ **b :** lacking in refinement **:** COARSE

un·fathered \"+\ *adj* [¹*un-* + *father*, n. + *-ed*] **1 :** having no father **:** FATHERLESS, ILLEGITIMATE, BASTARD ⟨~ offspring⟩ **2 :** having no known origin ⟨~ slanders⟩

un·fatherly \"+\ *adj* **:** not befitting a father ⟨an ~ attitude⟩

un·fathomable \"+\ *adj* [¹*un-* + *fathom* + *-able*] **:** not capable of being fathomed ⟨~ depths⟩: **a :** INCOMPREHENSIBLE, INSCRUTABLE ⟨the ~ mentality of a child⟩ ⟨all that is cryptic and ~ in humanity —J.L.Lowes⟩ **b :** IMMEASURABLE, IMPENETRABLE ⟨the ~ darkness of empty space —H.G.Wells⟩ — **un·fath·om·able·ness** *n* -ES

un·fath·om·ably \ˌ;=ˈ==blē, -bli\ *adv* **:** to an unfathomable degree: **a :** IMMEASURABLY ⟨~ deep⟩ **b :** INCOMPREHENSIBLY ⟨continued to ~ to eat —A.J.Cronin⟩

un·fathomed \ˌən+\ *adj* [¹*un-* + *fathomed*, past part. of *fathom*] **1 :** not fathomed **:** UNSOUNDED ⟨the dark ~ caves of ocean —Thomas Gray⟩ **2 :** UNDETERMINED, IMMENSE ⟨the thought of the ~ might of man —J.J.Chapman⟩

un·fatigued \"+\ *adj* [¹*un-* + *fatigued*, past part. of *fatigue*] **:** not fatigued **:** UNWEARIED

un·fatiguing \"+\ *adj* [¹*un-* + *fatiguing*, pres. part. of *fatigue*] **:** not fatiguing **:** UNTIRING ⟨~ work⟩

un·faulty \"+\ *adj, archaic* **:** free of fault **:** BLAMELESS, INNOCENT ⟨the poor ~ baby —Samuel Richardson⟩

un·favorable \"+\ *adj* [ME, fr. ¹*un-* + *favorable*] **1 a :** not disposed to favor **:** OPPOSED, CONTRARY ⟨~ comment⟩ ⟨reasons for being ~ to the proposal⟩ **b :** expressing disapproval **:** NEGATIVE ⟨an ~ response⟩ **2 a :** tending to retard, discourage, or make more difficult **:** DISADVANTAGEOUS ⟨an atmosphere ~ to calm discussion⟩ ⟨an ~ business climate⟩ ⟨an ~ wind⟩ **b :** indicative of an unsuccessful outcome **:** boding ill ⟨~ weather for a camping trip⟩ ⟨conditions ~ for a new enterprise⟩ **3 a :** not pleasing **:** DISAGREEABLE, UNDESIRABLE ⟨an ~ feature of the plan⟩ **b :** having the value of imports exceed that of exports ⟨an ~ balance of trade⟩ **4** *archaic* **:** repulsive in looks **:** ILL-FAVORED, UGLY

un·favorableness \"+\ *n* **:** the quality or state of being unfavorable

un·favorably \"+\ *adv* [ME, fr. *unfavorable* + *-ly*] **:** in an unfavorable manner

un·feared \ˌən+\ *adj* [in sense 1, fr. ME *unferd*, fr. ¹*un-* + *ferd*, *ferd*, past part. of *feren* to frighten; in sense 2, fr. ¹*un-* + *feared*, past part. of *fear* — more at FEAR] **1** *obs* **:** not frightened **:** UNAFRAID ⟨stand upright and ~ —Ben Jonson⟩ **2 :** not feared ⟨an ~ adversary⟩

un·fearful \"+\ *adj* **:** free of fear **:** FEARLESS

un·fearing \"+\ *adj* [¹*un-* + *fearing*, pres. part. of *fear*] **:** having no fear **:** DAUNTLESS ⟨~ minds —Sir Walter Scott⟩

un·feasibility \"+\ *n* **:** the quality or state of being unfeasible **:** IMPRACTICABILITY

un·feasible \"+\ *adj* **:** not feasible **:** IMPRACTICABLE ⟨a suggested reform that was ~ in the prevailing circumstances⟩

un·feather \"+\ *vt* [ME *unfetheren*, fr. ²*un-* + *fetheren* to feather] **:** to deprive (as a bird) of feathers **:** PLUCK, DEPLUME, STRIP

un·feathered \"+\ *adj* [¹*un-* + *feathered*, past part. of *feather*] **1 a :** having no plumage ⟨~ legs of the Orpington⟩ **:** UNFLEDGED ⟨the ~ brood⟩ **b :** PLUCKED ⟨an ~ goose⟩ **2 :** not fully developed **:** CALLOW ⟨that ~, two-legg'd thing, a son —John Dryden⟩ **3 :** not equipped with feathers ⟨~ arrows⟩

un·featured \"+\ *adj* **1** *obs* **:** having ill-formed features **:** DEFORMED **2 :** lacking features **:** UNVARIED ⟨an ~ wilderness⟩ ⟨my highway is ~ air —W.E.Channing⟩ **3 :** not displayed or advertised as a feature attraction ⟨an ~ performer⟩

un·fed \ˌən+\ *adj* [ME *unfedd*, fr. ¹*un-* + *fedd*, past part. of *feden* to feed] **1 :** not provided with food ⟨worrying over her ~ pets⟩ **2 :** not given support or sustenance ⟨a grudge that remained ~⟩

un·feed \"+\ *adj* [¹*un-* + *feed*, past part. of *fee*] **:** not rewarded with a fee or gratuity **:** UNPAID, UNTIPPED ⟨the breath of an ~ lawyer —Shak.⟩ ⟨cork crumbs in wine opened by an ~ waiter —O.Henry⟩

un·feeling \"+\ *adj* [ME *unfeling*, fr. ¹*un-* + *feling* feeling] **1 a :** devoid of feeling or sensation **:** INSENSATE ⟨an ~ tree⟩ ⟨an ~ corpse⟩ **b** *archaic* **:** INSENSITIVE, COLD ⟨should to fame your hearts ~ be —James Thomson †1748⟩ **2 :** devoid of kindness or sympathy **:** HARDHEARTED, CRUEL ⟨an ~ wretch⟩ ⟨~ enough to laugh at her predicament⟩ ⟨the ~ governor sought to terrify her into compliance with his demands —Herman Melville⟩ — **un·feel·ing·ly** *adv* — **un·feel·ing·ness** *n*

un·feigned \"+\ *adj* [ME *unfeined*, fr. ¹*un-* + *feined* feigned] **:** not feigned or pretended ⟨an ~ interest in people —Geoffrey Bruun⟩ ⟨with ~ curiosity —Louis Auchincloss⟩ **syn** see SINCERE

un·feignedly \"+\ *adv* **:** in an unfeigned manner **:** SINCERELY ⟨~ glad to see his old teacher⟩

un·felicitous \"+\ *adj* **:** INFELICITOUS

un·fel·lowed \ˌən¦fe(ˌ)lōd, -ləd\ *adj* [in sense 1, fr. ¹*un-* + *fellowed*, past part. of *fellow*, in sense 2, fr. ¹*un-* + *fellow*, n. + *-ed*] **1** *obs* **:** having no equal **:** PEERLESS, MATCHLESS **2 :** having no companion **:** UNMATED, ALONE

un·felted \"+\ *adj* **:** not felted ⟨~ material⟩

un·feminine \"+\ *adj* **:** not suitable to or appropriate for a woman **:** not characteristic of a woman **:** unexpected in a woman ⟨an ~ depth of voice⟩ ⟨a quite ~ insight into the mystique of fly-fishing —Stuart Keate⟩

un·fenced \"+\ *adj* [¹*un-* + *fenced*, past part. of *fence*] **1 :** not protected **:** UNGUARDED ⟨the ~ shore⟩ **2 :** not enclosed; *esp* **:** not closed in with a fence ⟨an ~ pasture⟩

un·fermentable \"+\ *adj* **:** incapable of undergoing fermentation ⟨~ sugar⟩

un·fermented \"+\ *adj* [¹*un-* + *fermented*, past part. of *ferment*] **:** not fermented ⟨~ grape juice⟩

un·fertile \"+\ *adj* **:** not fertile **:** INFERTILE

un·fertilized \"+\ *adj* [¹*un-* + *fertilized*, past part. of *fertilize*] **:** not fertilized ⟨an ~ egg⟩

un·festive \"+\ *adj* **:** not festive **:** lacking holiday atmosphere or spirit ⟨~ streets⟩ ⟨unpopular domestic measures . . . hinted at in his ~ Christmas broadcast —Mollie Panter-Downes⟩

un·fetter \"+\ *vt* [ME *unfeteren*, fr. ²*un-* + *feteren* to fetter] **1 :** to free from fetters **:** UNSHACKLE ⟨~ a prisoner⟩ **2 :** to loose from restraint **:** EMANCIPATE, LIBERATE ⟨~ the mind from prejudice⟩

un·fettered \"+\ *adj* [¹*un-* + *fettered*, past part. of *fetter*] **:** not fettered or bound **:** not restrained or limited **:** UNTRAMMELED, FREE ⟨~ competition⟩ ⟨believe in freedom of opinion and the ~ pursuit of knowledge —*advt*⟩

un·feued \ˌən+\ *adj* [¹*un-* + *feued*, past part. of *feu*] *Scots law* **:** not in feu **:** free or freed from feu-duties

un·figured \"+\ *adj* **1 :** not marked by figurative language ⟨an ~ style⟩ **2 a :** containing no artistic patterns or figures ⟨an ~ pattern⟩ **b :** not including human figures ⟨~ paintings⟩

un·filed \"+\ *adj* [in sense 1, fr. ¹*un-* + *filed*, past part. of *file* (to rub); in sense 2, fr. ¹*un-* + *filed*, past part. of *file* (to arrange)] **1** *archaic* **:** not smoothed **:** UNPOLISHED ⟨my rude ~ apology —George Wither⟩ **2 :** not placed on file or in a file ⟨several ~ documents⟩

un·filial \"+\ *adj* **:** not observing the obligations of a child to a parent **:** not befitting a son or daughter **:** UNDUTIFUL ⟨an ~ child⟩ ⟨~ behavior⟩ ⟨gave his father an ~ answer⟩

un·fillable \"+\ *adj* [ME, fr. ¹*un-* + *fillable* capable of being filled, fr. *fillen* to fill + *-able*] **:** incapable of being filled **:** INSATIABLE ⟨an ~ hole⟩ ⟨an ~ maw⟩

un·filled \"+\ *adj* [¹*un-* + *filled*, past part. of *fill*] **1 :** not filled **:** EMPTY, BLANK ⟨an ~ bottle⟩ ⟨~ spaces⟩ **2 :** not containing a filler

un·filtered \"+\ *adj* [¹*un-* + *filtered*, past part. of *filter*] **:** not filtered

un·financial \"+\ *adj* **:** not current in payment of dues **:** not in good financial standing — used esp. of a member of a fraternal organization

un·findable \"+\ *adj* [¹*un-* + *find* + *-able*] **:** not capable of being found — used esp. of a person sought by law enforcement authorities ⟨he was ~, and finally . . . we all gave up looking for him —Edmond Taylor⟩

un·fine \"+\ *adj* [ME, fr. ¹*un-* + *fine*] **1** *obs, of a wine* **:** poor in flavor **:** ROUGH **2** *of the weather* **:** INCLEMENT, STORMY

un·finish \"+\ *n* **:** lack of finish **:** unfinished state ⟨canvases in various stages of ~ —*Time*⟩

un·finishable \"+\ *adj* [¹*un-* + *finish*, v. + *-able*] **:** incapable of being finished ⟨an ~ tale⟩

un·finished \"+\ *adj* [¹*un-* + *finished*, past part. of *finish*] **:** not finished: **a :** not brought to an end or to completion ⟨an ~ poem⟩ ⟨an ~ house⟩ ⟨~ work⟩ **b :** left in the rough state **:** UNPOLISHED, CRUDE ⟨~ wood⟩ ⟨~ steel⟩ **c** (1) **:** subjected to no other processes (as bleaching or dyeing) after coming from the loom **:** UNBLEACHED, UNDYED — used of a wool fabric ⟨~ cloth⟩ (2) *of a worsted fabric* **:** finished with a slight nap in contrast to the usual hard napless finish **d** (1) *of a market animal* **:** inadequately fattened (2) *of a feeder* **:** not yet fattened

unfinished business *n* **:** matters postponed from a previous meeting **:** matters pending at adjournment

un·fin·ished·ness \ˌ=ˈ==nəs\ *n* -ES **:** the quality or state of being unfinished **:** CRUDENESS

un·fired \ˌən+\ *adj* [¹*un-* + *fired*, past part. of *fire*] **1 :** not set on fire **:** not ignited ⟨~ coals⟩ **2 :** not subjected to or treated by fire; *esp* **:** not yet baked in a kiln **:** GREEN 7a(8) ⟨the ~ clay⟩ **3 :** not exploded **:** UNDISCHARGED ⟨an ~ shell⟩ **4 :** not animated **:** not aroused **:** UNINSPIRED ⟨so grave and ~ a countenance —*McClure's*⟩

un·firm \"+\ *adj* **:** not firm: **a :** not compact **:** LOOSE ⟨~ earth⟩ **b :** not firmly set **:** UNSTEADY, INSECURE ⟨an ~ stance⟩ — **un·firmly** \"+\ *adv* — **un·firmness** \"+\ *n*

un·fir·ma·ment·ed *adj* \ˌən¦fərmə¸mentəd *sometimes* -¸man-\ [¹*un-* + *firmament* + *-ed*] **:** having no bounding firmament **:** UNBOUNDED ⟨~ space⟩

un·fishable \ˌən+\ *adj* **:** unsuitable for fishing ⟨an ~ stream⟩ ⟨turbulent, ~ water —Edward Grey⟩

un·fished \"+\ *adj* [¹*un-* + *fished*, past part. of *fish*] **:** not used for fishing ⟨~ waters⟩

¹unfit \"+\ *adj* **:** not fit: **a :** not adapted to an end, object, or design **:** UNSUITABLE, INAPPROPRIATE ⟨land ~ for farming⟩ ⟨food ~ for human consumption⟩ **b :** not fitted **:** not qualified **:** INCAPABLE, INCOMPETENT ⟨clearly ~ by temperament to assume such a responsibility⟩ ⟨eliminated ~ candidates by examination⟩ **c** (1) **:** physically or mentally unsound ⟨certified as ~ for army service⟩ (2) **:** not qualified by reason of poor physical condition ⟨reported drunk and ~ for duty⟩

²unfit \"\ *n* **:** one that is unfit ⟨many are moral failures . . . or physical ~*s* —D.D.Lescohier⟩

³unfit \"\ *vt* [²*un-* + *fit*] **:** to make unfit **:** DISABLE, DISQUALIFY ⟨has a record that ~*s* him for the presidency⟩ ⟨an education that *unfitted* him for the life of a farmer⟩ ⟨doing one's duty . . . apparently *unfitted* one for doing anything else —Edith Wharton⟩

un·fit·ly *adv* **:** in an unfit manner **:** UNSUITABLY, INAPPROPRIATELY

un·fit·ness *n* **:** the quality or state of being unfit: **a :** UNSUITABILITY, INAPPROPRIATENESS ⟨the ~ of the gesture⟩ **b :** poor physical condition ⟨the ~ of many factory workers⟩ **c :** INCOMPETENCE ⟨could not conceal his ~ for the work⟩

un·fitted \ˌən+\ *adj* [¹*un-* + *fitted*, past part. of *fit*] **:** not adapted **:** not qualified ⟨felt himself temperamentally ~ for the ministry⟩

un·fitting \"+\ *adj* **:** not fitting **:** UNSUITABLE, IMPROPER ⟨an ~ atmosphere⟩

un·fit·ting·ly *adv* **:** in an unfitting manner **:** UNSUITABLY

un·fix \ˌən+\ *vt* [²*un-* + *fix*] **1 :** to loosen from a fastening **:** detach from something that holds ⟨~ the flagpole⟩ **:** DISENGAGE ⟨~ bayonets⟩ **2 :** to make unstable **:** UNSETTLE, UNHINGE ⟨~ the mind⟩ ⟨a new discovery that ~*ed* all established notions⟩ **3 :** to make (a chemical compound) soluble **:** DISSOLVE

un·fixable \"+\ *adj* **1 :** incapable of being held in a fixed state **:** UNSTABLE, INDETERMINATE **2 :** incapable of breeding true **:** manifest only in the heterozygous state — used of a genetic character

un·fixed \"+\ *adj* **1 :** not set in a definite place **:** DETACHED, FREE **2 :** not settled upon definitely **:** UNDETERMINED ⟨a date as yet ~⟩ **3 :** UNSTABLE, VAGUE ⟨~ as were her general notions of what men ought to be —Jane Austen⟩

un·fixedness \"+\ *n* **:** the quality or state of being unfixed **:** INSTABILITY

un·flagging \"+\ *adj* **:** not flagging **:** continuing with vigor **:** SUSTAINED, TIRELESS ⟨~ energy⟩ ⟨~ enthusiasm⟩ ⟨~ courtesy⟩

un·flaggingly \"+\ *adv* **:** in an unflagging manner **:** STEADILY, PERSEVERINGLY ⟨waved and smiled ~ —R.H.Rovere⟩

un·flattering \"+\ *adj* **:** not flattering **:** revealing or displaying truly or in a starkly realistic way **:** CANDID, ACCURATE ⟨an ~ mirror⟩ ⟨an ~ portait⟩; *esp* **:** tending to show or represent unfavorably ⟨an ~ remark⟩ ⟨the full ~ light of morning —Walter de la Mare⟩ ⟨an ~ illustration of the tone of our civilization —*Popular Science Jour.*⟩

un·flatteringly \"+\ *adv* **:** in an unflattering manner

un·flavored \"+\ *adj* **:** not flavored

un·flawed \"+\ *adj* **:** free of flaws **:** FLAWLESS, PERFECT ⟨an ~ gem⟩ ⟨flowers and shrubs glowing under a blazing sun and an ~ sky —Sean O'Faolain⟩

un·flecked \"+\ *adj* [¹*un-* + *flecked*, past part. of *fleck*] **:** not flecked **:** stainlessly pure **:** SPOTLESS ⟨the pure heart, by thoughts of ill ~ —Gilbert Murray⟩

un·fledged \"+\ *adj* [¹*un-* + *fledged*, past part. of *fledge*] **1 a :** not fledged **:** not feathered **:** not ready for flight ⟨found a small, ~ English sparrow on the doorstep —*advt*⟩ **b** *of an arrow* **:** not equipped with vanes ⟨shot an ~ arrow⟩ **2 a :** not fully developed **:** IMMATURE, CALLOW ⟨an ~ writer⟩ ⟨~ judgment⟩ **b :** of, relating to, or characteristic of youth and inexperience ⟨in those ~ days was my wife a girl —Shak.⟩

un·flesh \"+\ *vt* [²*un-* + *flesh*, n.] **:** to deprive of flesh

¹unfleshed \"+\ *adj* [¹*un-* + *fleshed*, past part. of *flesh*] **:** not fleshed: **a :** not incited to the hunt by the taste of flesh ⟨an ~ hound⟩ **b :** not initiated **:** INEXPERIENCED ⟨an ~ novice⟩

²unfleshed \"\ *adj* [²*un-* + *flesh*, n. + *-ed*] **:** deprived of flesh ⟨an ~ skull⟩

un·fleshliness \ˌən+\ *n* **:** the quality or state of being unfleshly **:** SPIRITUALITY

un·fleshly \"+\ *adj* **:** not carnal **:** SPIRITUAL

un·flexed \ˌən+\ *adj* [¹*un-* + *flexed*, past part. of *flex*] **:** not flexed **:** UNBENT ⟨performing the movement with an ~ position of the knees⟩

un·flexible \"+\ *adj* **:** INFLEXIBLE

un·flickering \"+\ *adj* **:** not flickering **:** STEADY ⟨an ~ light⟩ — **un·flick·er·ing·ly** *adv*

un·flinching \"+\ *adj* [¹*un-* + *flinching*, pres. part. of *flinch*] **:** not flinching or shrinking **:** UNWAVERING, STEADFAST ⟨remain ~ when a gun roars out —*Amer. Guide Series: Maine*⟩ ⟨lived a life of ~ probity —R.G.Swing⟩ ⟨an ~ determination to take the whole evidence into account —A.N.Whitehead⟩

un·flinch·ing·ly *adv* **:** in an unflinching manner **:** without shrinking or wincing **:** STEADFASTLY, RESOLUTELY ⟨bear pain ~ and . . . without complaint —D.C.Buchanan⟩ ⟨took ~ the severe blow of the defeat —W.H.Chamberlin⟩

un·flower \ˌən+\ *vt* [²*un-* + *flower*, n.] **:** to strip (as a plant) or empty (as a basket) of flowers

un·fluctuating \"+\ *adj* [¹*un-* + *fluctuating*, pres. part. of *fluctuate*] **:** not fluctuating **:** UNWAVERING ⟨an ~ guide⟩ **:** UNVARYING, STEADY ⟨~ in his principles⟩ **:** CONSTANT ⟨~ health⟩ ⟨an ~ amount⟩ **:** STABLE ⟨an ~ currency⟩

un·flurried \"+\ *adj* **:** not flurried **:** free of agitation or nervous tension **:** CALM ⟨~ service⟩ ⟨~ and good-natured as they pass your baggage through —E.A.Weeks⟩

un·flustered \"+\ *adj* [¹*un-* + *flustered*, past part. of *fluster*] **:** not flustered **:** SERENE

un·focused *also* **un·focussed** \"+\ *adj* [¹*un-* + *focused*, past part. of *focus*] **1 :** not adjusted to a focus ⟨her eyes . . . stared blankly, ~ —Raymond Chandler⟩ **2 :** not concentrated at one point or upon one objective ⟨an uncertain, ~ young man⟩ ⟨diversity . . . in our huge ~ country —Owen Wister⟩

un·fold \"+\ *vb* [ME *unfolden*, fr. OE *unfealdan*, fr. ²*un-* + *fealdan* to fold — more at FOLD] *vt* **1 a :** to open the folds of **:** spread or straighten out **:** EXPAND ⟨~ a tablecloth⟩ ⟨~*ed* the map⟩ ⟨~ the arms⟩ **b :** to open wide (as a gate) ⟨hell shall ~ . . . her widest gates —John Milton⟩ **c :** to remove (as a package) from the folds **:** UNWRAP ⟨began ~*ing* a brown paper parcel —W.B.Yeats⟩ **2 :** to open to the view or understanding **:** make known **:** REVEAL ⟨stand and ~ yourself —Shak.⟩; *esp* **:** to make clear by gradual disclosure and often by recital or explanation ⟨~*ed* his story through dialogue —W.K.Ferguson⟩ ⟨~*ed* to me his desires for the university —A.C.Benson⟩ ~ *vi* **1 a :** to open from a folded state **:** open out **:** EXPAND ⟨plane . . . wheels began to ~ —Howard Hunt⟩ **b :** BLOSSOM ⟨buds beginning to ~⟩ **c :** to move toward full development ⟨if the . . . child were permitted to ~ amid rich and stimulating surroundings —Margaret Mead⟩ **2 :** to open out gradually to the view **:** become visible or known ⟨a panorama of carefully tilled farm lands . . . ~*s* before the visitor's eyes —*Amer. Guide Series: Mich.*⟩ ⟨suppressed his comment and let the narrative ~ simply and objectively —R.A.Cordell⟩ **3 :** to develop a parasitic vowel by anaptyxis

syn UNFOLD, EVOLVE, DEVELOP, ELABORATE, and PERFECT can mean in common to cause something to emerge from a state in which its potentialities are not apparent, are unrealized, or are incompletely realized, into a state where they are apparent or partly or fully realized. UNFOLD usu. suggests a natural process by which the true or complete character of something is unveiled or disclosed ⟨a bud *unfolds* itself into a flower⟩ ⟨hitherto chemistry has not succeeded in *unfolding* the principles by which metals are formed —*Encyc. Americana*⟩ ⟨the creative spirit gains sustenance and vigor for its own *unfolding* —Edward Sapir⟩ ⟨the episodes of this life began to *unfold* themselves in his mind —Fred Majdalany⟩ EVOLVE implies an unfolding gradually and in an orderly way, often suggesting a slowness and complexity of process, sometimes carrying strongly the idea of natural development by an inner process ⟨slowly, through ages and centuries, we have *evolved* a picture of the world we live in —*Fortune*⟩ ⟨the program we have *evolved* as a result of a year of deliberation is now complete in general outline —J.B.Conant⟩ ⟨the new order which seemed to be *evolving* —E.M.Forster⟩ ⟨the germinal situation out of which this book *evolves* —N.L.Rothman⟩ DEVELOP, in this connection, implies a passing through several stages, stressing the unfolding, usu. slow, of latent possibilities ⟨the scientific writer must also have a broad point of view, *developed* by experience, reading, and reflection —C.E.Kellogg⟩ ⟨the viscose process was *developed* from the inventions of three Englishmen —*Amer. Guide Series: Va.*⟩ ⟨the quarrel grew hot, and finally *developed* into a lawsuit —Gilbert Highet⟩ ELABORATE implies labor or effort to develop or realize the clear possibilities of something that is only in the germ or only partly formulated ⟨only a system with order and progress in the heart of it could *elaborate* itself so perfectly and so intricately —J.A.Thomson⟩ ⟨escapes death from surgical infection because a Frenchman, Pasteur, and a German, Koch, *elaborated* a new technique —R.B.Fosdick⟩ ⟨did the tubercle bacillus *elaborate* some strange substance which tended to stimulate the mind —Harry Sylvester⟩ PERFECT implies an unfolding or developing of something so that it stands as a complete or finished product ⟨a series of complementary inventions, the phonograph, the moving picture, the gasoline engine, the steam turbine, the airplane, were all sketched in, if not *perfected*, by 1900 —Lewis Mumford⟩ ⟨conditions required of both Japanese and Americans a relentless *perfecting* of such cooperative efforts —T.C.Mendenhall b. 1910) **syn** see in addition SOLVE

¹un·fold·ed \ˌən¦fōldəd\ *adj* [*un-* + *folded*, past part. of *fold* (to pen)] : not confined in a sheepfold

²unfolded \"\ *adj* [in sense 1, fr. past part. of *unfold;* in sense 2, fr. ¹*un-* + *folded*, past part. of *fold* (to double over)] **1** : opened out : DISCLOSED, DISPLAYED ⟨~ flowers⟩ ⟨littering with ~ silks the polished counter —William Cowper⟩ **2** : not folded

un·fold·ing \-ldiŋ, -ldēŋ\ *n* -s [fr. gerund of *unfold*] : the act or process of unfolding : **a** : expansion or opening out from or as if from folds ⟨the ~ of a bud⟩ **b** : DEVELOPMENT, EVOLUTION ⟨profoundly influenced the ~ of her childish mind —Norman Douglas⟩ **c** : EXPLICATION, EXPOSITION ⟨a lengthy and patient ~ only possible in a book —H.N.Southern⟩

un·fold·ment \-l(d)mənt\ *n* -s [*unfold* + *-ment*] **1** : the act or process of unfolding : DEVELOPMENT, EVOLUTION ⟨during the story's ~ the character grows —*Sat. Eve. Post*⟩ ⟨help those who are seeking spiritual ~ —*Amer. Mercury*⟩ **2** : full manifestation or realization ⟨the journey of the soul to its final ~ —M.L.Bach⟩

un·foliaged \ˌən+\ *adj* : lacking foliage ⟨trees still ~⟩

un·followed \"+\ *adj* [¹*un-* + *followed*, past part. of *follow*] : having no followers or retainers ⟨come back . . . alone, ~ —Sir Walter Scott⟩

unfooled \"+\ *adj* [²*un-* + *fooled*, past part. of *fool*] : not fooled : not taken in ⟨remaining ~ high-flown idealism —Max Lerner⟩

un·footed \ˌən+\ *adj* [¹*un-* + *footed*, past part. of *foot*] : UNTROD ⟨the ~ woods —Owen Wister⟩

un·forced \"+\ *adj* : not forced: **a** : not compelled : VOLUNTARY, WILLING ⟨gained the ~ attention of the group⟩ **b** : achieved without strain : marked by ease and naturalness ⟨a voice with a pleasingly ~ quality⟩ : apparently effortless ⟨one of the most ~ humorous sagas of our time —G.F. Whicher⟩ ⟨so sure and ~ is its pathos —*Manchester Guardian Weekly*⟩

un·fordable \"+\ *adj* : incapable of being forded : IMPASSABLE ⟨an ~ river⟩

un·foreknowable \"+\ *adj* : not capable of being foreknown ⟨the ~ future⟩

un·forensic \"+\ *adj* : not forensic : unsuitable for courts or in public debate ⟨~ rhetoric⟩

un·foreseeable \"+\ *adj* [¹*un-* + *foresee* + *-able*] : incapable of being foreseen, foretold, or anticipated : UNPREDICTABLE ⟨the ~ future⟩ ⟨~ events⟩ ⟨an ~ effect⟩ ⟨~ consequences⟩ ⟨if no ~ disabilities or restraints are put upon us —*Economist*⟩

un·foreseen \"+\ *adj* [¹*un-* + *foreseen*, past part. of *foresee*] : not foreseen : UNEXPECTED ⟨~ circumstances⟩ ⟨~ developments⟩ ⟨an ~ contingency⟩

un·forest \"+\ *vt* [²*un-* + *forest*, n.] : deprive of woods : DEFOREST

un·forested \"+\ *adj* [¹*un-* + *forested*] : not wooded ⟨~ land⟩

un·forethoughtful \ˌən+\ *adj* : not forethoughtful : IMPROVIDENT, CAREFREE

un·forewarned \"+\ *adj* [¹*un-* + *forewarned*, past part. of *forewarn*] : not forewarned : taken by surprise

un·forfeitable \"+\ *adj* : not subject to forfeiture : INALIENABLE ⟨an ~ right⟩

un·forgettable \"+\ *adj* [¹*un-* + *forget* + *-able*] : incapable of being forgotten : MEMORABLE ⟨an ~ occasion⟩ ⟨an ~ face⟩ ⟨that exciting and ~ night —Arnold Bennett⟩ ⟨a poignant and ~ expression of one of the deepest truths of human life —J.L. Lowes⟩

un·for·get·ta·bly \¦==¦==blē, -bli\ *adv* : in an unforgettable manner : to an unforgettable degree ⟨the thought takes hold and clings ~ —J.A.Macy⟩

un·forgivable \"+\ *adj* [¹*un-* + *forgive* + *-able*] : incapable of being forgiven : UNPARDONABLE ⟨the ~ sin⟩ ⟨an ~ crime⟩

un·forgivably \"+\ *adv* : in an unforgivable manner : to an unforgivable extent : UNPARDONABLY, INTOLERABLY ⟨careful not to offend ~⟩ ⟨was ~ impartial in his arrests —Morley Callaghan⟩

un·forgiveness \"+\ *n* : UNFORGIVINGNESS

un·forgiving \"+\ *adj* : marked by an inability or unwillingness to forgive : RELENTLESS

un·forgivingness \"+\ *n* [*unforgiving* + *-ness*] : the quality or state of being unforgiving : IMPLACABILITY, VINDICTIVENESS ⟨the ~ of passionate hearts —John Galsworthy⟩

un·fork \"+\ *vt* [²*un-* + *fork*] : to dismount from (a horse) ⟨~*ed* his horse and walked along with him —A.B.Guthrie⟩

un·forked \"+\ *adj* [¹*un-* + *forked*] : not forked ⟨the ~ tail of a bird⟩

un·form \ˌən+\ *vt* [²*un-* + *form*] : to undo the form of : make formless

un·formal \"+\ *adj* : INFORMAL

un·formalized \"+\ *adj* [¹*un-* + *formalized*, past part. of *formalize*] **1** *archaic* : not made rigid or unbending : FLEXIBLE **2** : not put into definite shape or arrangement

un·formed \"+\ *adj* [ME *unfourmed*, fr. ¹*un-* + *fourmed*, past part. of *fourmen* to form] : not formed ⟨an as yet ~ government⟩ : not arranged in regular shape, order, or relations: **a** : UNDEVELOPED, IMMATURE ⟨an ~ character⟩ ⟨~ still in body and mind —Kathleen Freeman⟩ **b** : marked by crudity or lack of finish : UNPOLISHED **c** : INCHOATE, AMORPHOUS ⟨this ~ government is the "legitimate" one —Frank Gorrell⟩

un·formidable \"+\ *adj* : not formidable : UNIMPOSING

un·formulable \"+\ *adj* : not reducible to formula : incapable of being formulated ⟨~ presuppositions —*New Republic*⟩

un·formulated \"+\ *adj* [¹*un-* + *formulated*, past part. of *formulate*] : not formulated : not expressed by formula or in systematic form ⟨~ desires⟩ ⟨~ plans⟩

un·fortified \"+\ *adj* [¹*un-* + *fortified*, past part. of *fortify*] : not fortified: **a** : not protected by fortification ⟨an ~ frontier⟩ **b** : lacking moral strength or stamina : UNSTABLE, WEAK ⟨shows . . . a heart ~, a mind impatient —Shak.⟩ **c** : not strengthened : UNSUPPORTED ⟨~ premises⟩; *esp* : not strengthened or enriched (as a food or drink) ⟨~ wine⟩ ⟨~ margarine⟩

¹un·fortunate \"+\ *adj* : not fortunate: **a** : not favored by fortune : UNSUCCESSFUL, UNLUCKY ⟨sending the ~ naval commander into exile —A.J.Toynbee⟩ **b** : marked or accompanied by or resulting in misfortune ⟨an ~ decision⟩ ⟨~ investments⟩ ⟨an ~ night for all concerned⟩ ⟨had an ~ experience with a neighborhood cleaner —Richard Joseph⟩ **c** : UNTOWARD, UNPROMISING ⟨an ~ location for the business⟩ ⟨~ social consequences —Willy Richardson⟩ **d** : UNSUITABLE, INEPT ⟨rather an ~ choice in the circumstances —Denis Johnston⟩ ⟨his ~ personality —P.I.Wellman⟩ **e** : lacking felicity of expression : INFELICITOUS ⟨an ~ term⟩ ⟨his phrasing was rather ~ —*Nation*⟩ **f** : DEPLORABLE, REGRETTABLE ⟨an ~ lapse of taste —Saul Maloff⟩ **g** *of a sign of the zodiac* : having an unfortunate influence : UNPROPITIOUS **syn** see UNLUCKY

²unfortunate \"\ *n* : an unfortunate person ⟨leave off tormenting that ~ —Ellen Glasgow⟩ ⟨one of those ~*s* without influence or money —Kenneth Roberts⟩ : a social outcast (as a prisoner or prostitute) ⟨one more ~ . . . gone to her death —Thomas Hood †1845⟩

un·fortunately \ˌən+\ *adv* : in an unfortunate manner : UNLUCKILY

un·fortunateness \"+\ *n* : the quality or state of being unfortunate

un·fossiliferous \"+\ *adj* : not fossiliferous ⟨~ sandstone⟩

un·fought \"+\ *adj* [¹*un-* + *fought*, past part. of *fight*] : not fought : UNCONTESTED ⟨an ~ field⟩

un·foul \"+\ *vt* [²*un-* + *foul*] : to cause to become disentangled ⟨dived into the river, ~*ed* the lines, and made them fast —*N.Y.Times*⟩

un·found \"+\ *adj* [¹*un-* + *found*, past part. of *find*] : not found : remaining unknown : UNDISCOVERED ⟨a path that links our shores with a shore ~ —S.R.Lysaght⟩

un·founded \"+\ *adj* [¹*un-* + *founded*, past part. of *found*] **1** *obs* : BOTTOMLESS, UNSTABLE ⟨the ~ deep —John Milton⟩ **2** : lacking a sound basis in reason or fact : BASELESS, GROUNDLESS, ILLUSIVE ⟨an ~ accusation⟩ ⟨~ suspicions⟩ ⟨his . . . rash and most ~ assertion —J.M.Kemble⟩ ⟨that hope proved to be ~ —Edith Sitwell⟩

un·found·ed·ly \¦=¦===lē\ *adv* [*unfounded* + *-ly*] : without foundation or reasonable cause : UNWARRANTABLY

un·frame \"+\ *vt* [²*un-* + *frame*] **1** : to take apart : break down : DESTROY ⟨the women's exuberance will . . . the houses ~ —Robinson Jeffers⟩ **2** *obs* : to throw into confusion : DISRUPT

un·framed \"+\ *adj* [¹*un-* + *framed*, past part. of *frame*] : not provided with a frame ⟨an ~ picture⟩

un·frank \"+\ *adj* : not candid : DISINGENUOUS, SLY ⟨men with . . . that glistening ~ expression that wives know —Sinclair Lewis⟩

un·fraternal \"+\ *adj* : not fraternal : UNBROTHERLY

un·fraught \"+\ *adj* : not fraught : not burdened ⟨minds empty and ~ with matter —Francis Bacon⟩

un·free \ˌən+\ *adj* [ME, fr. ¹*un-* + *free*] : not free : lacking freedom: **a** : bound to the land ⟨a primarily agrarian society of . . . landlords and their ~ tenants —R.H.Hilton⟩ **b** *obs* : not holding the status or privileges of membership (as in a civic body or guild) **c** : marked by a lack of political freedom ⟨colonies do not have to remain ~ —Wendell Willkie⟩ **d** : marked by a lack of personal liberty ⟨we are all to some degree oppressed, ~ —William James⟩ **e** : brought about by coercion ⟨a unity which is artificial because it is ~ —*Atlantic*⟩

un·freedom \"+\ *n* : lack of freedom ⟨these newcomers — black and white — toiled under some degree of ~ . . . were bound servants for greater or lesser terms —Oscar Handlin⟩ ⟨gains his sense of security by this very ~ of conforming —H.A.Overstreet⟩

un·freeman \"+\ *n* [ME *unfreman*, fr. *unfree* + *man*] *archaic* : one that is not a freeman

un·freeze \"+\ *vb* [²*un-* + *freeze*] *vt* **1** : to cause to thaw ⟨unseasonably warm temperatures *unfroze* the ground early⟩ **2** : to free (as prices or raw materials) from regulation or control ⟨the liberals wanted land rents *unfrozen* immediately —Arnaldo Cortesi⟩ **3** : to release (as funds) for expenditure, withdrawal, or exchange ⟨the Fund must ~ the vast resources it now has cached away in various central banks —*New Republic*⟩ ~ *vi* : THAW

un·french \"+\ *adj, usu cap F* : not characteristically French ⟨the work of these Odéon actors seemed strangely *un-French* —*New Republic*⟩

un·frequency \"+\ *n* [*unfrequent* + *-cy*] *archaic* : INFREQUENCY

un·frequent \"+\ *adj* : INFREQUENT

un·frequented \"+\ *adj* [¹*un-* + *frequented*, past part. of *frequent*] : not often visited or traveled over ⟨trails . . . lead to ~ lakes —*Amer. Guide Series: Mich.*⟩ ⟨the car . . . soon turned into an ~ street —Alexander Forbes⟩

un·frequently \ˌən+\ *adv* : not frequently : INFREQUENTLY, RARELY, SELDOM ⟨in these conflicts, the animals were by no means ~ the conquerors —C.W.Webber⟩

un·friend \"+\ *n* [ME *unfrend*, fr. ¹*un-* + *frend* friend] *chiefly Scot* : one that is not a friend : ENEMY ⟨I am no ~ to plainness —R.L.Stevenson⟩

un·friended \"+\ *adj* [¹*un-* + *friended*, past part. of *friend*] : having no friends : not befriended : FRIENDLESS ⟨leave me to go through the remainder of my life ~ —W.S.Gilbert⟩

un·friendliness \"+\ *n* : the quality or state of being unfriendly : ill feeling : HOSTILITY, ANTAGONISM ⟨greeted each other with obvious ~⟩ ⟨a miserable business to have any ~ on the raft —Mark Twain⟩

un·friendly \"+\ *adj* [ME *unfrendly*, fr. ¹*un-* + *frendly* friendly] : not friendly: **a** : not showing or marked by the disposition or attitude of one that is or wishes to be a friend ⟨an ~ action for him to take after years of close association⟩ **b** : not well disposed : UNSYMPATHETIC, HOSTILE ⟨an ~ reviewer⟩ ⟨an ~ nation⟩ **c** : marked by lack of warmth : COLD ⟨received an ~ reception⟩ **d** : INHOSPITABLE, UNFAVORABLE ⟨a place ~ to meditation⟩ ⟨the ~ and lonesome environment at high altitude —H.G.Armstrong⟩ **e** *of a fire* : spreading beyond intended limits : out of control

un·friendship \"+\ *n* [ME *unfrendship*, fr. *unfrend* unfriend + *-ship*] *chiefly Scot* : ill will : ENMITY

un·frightened \"+\ *adj* : not frightened : FEARLESS

un·frock \"+\ *vt* [²*un-* + *frock*, n.] **1** : to deprive or divest of a frock; *specif* : to deprive of priestly function or privilege : DEGRADE 1b, DEPOSE ⟨trained for the . . . ministry but was ~*ed* 27 years ago on charges of modernism and heresy —*Time*⟩ **2** : to remove from a position of honor or privilege : DISCHARGE ⟨a physician ~*ed* by the medical association⟩

un·frozen \"+\ *adj* [¹*un-* + *frozen*] : not frozen: **a** : not congealed ⟨~ ground⟩ **b** : not chilled ⟨an ~ dessert⟩

un·fructify \"+\ *vt* [²*un-* + *fructify*] : to make unfruitful

un·frugal \"+\ *adj* : EXTRAVAGANT, LAVISH

un·fruitful \"+\ *adj* [ME, fr. ¹*un-* + *fruitful*] : not fruitful: **a** : not producing offspring : INFERTILE, STERILE ⟨an ~ marriage⟩ **b** : yielding no valuable result : FRUITLESS, UNPROFITABLE ⟨an ~ effort⟩ ⟨this unsavory and ~ piece of research —Douglass Cater⟩ **c** (1) : not bearing fruit ⟨an ~ tree⟩ (2) : not producing crops : BARREN ⟨~ soil⟩ **syn** see STERILE

un·fruitfully \"+\ *adv* [ME, fr. *unfruitful* + *-ly*] : in an unfruitful manner : UNPRODUCTIVELY, UNPROFITABLY ⟨negotiations proceeded ~⟩

un·fruitfulness \"+\ *n* : the quality or state of being unfruitful : UNPRODUCTIVENESS, STERILITY

un·fueled \ˌən+\ *adj* [¹*un-* + *fueled*, past part. of *fuel*] : not provided with fuel : UNFED, SELF-SUSTAINED

un·fulfill \"+\ *vt* [back-formation fr. *unfulfilled*] : to fail to fulfill (as an obligation) : NEGLECT

un·fulfillable \"+\ *adj* [¹*un-* + *fulfill* + *-able*] : incapable of being fulfilled : UNREALIZABLE ⟨an ~ offer⟩ ⟨~ wishes⟩

un·fulfilled \"+\ *adj* [ME, fr. ¹*un-* + *fulfilled*, past part. of *fulfillen* to fulfill] : not fulfilled: **a** : not filled : UNSUPPLIED, UNSATISFIED ⟨vital ~ needs of the nation —H.S.Truman⟩ **b** : not carried out : not accomplished ⟨a great mission ~ —*Quarterly Rev.*⟩ **c** : not converted into reality : not completely achieved ⟨a still ~ desire⟩ ⟨the inheritors of ~ renown —P.B.Shelley⟩ **d** : marked by failure to realize or attain to full potentialities of experience or development ⟨~ and uneasy men —Sinclair Lewis⟩ ⟨~ as a woman —H.M.Parshley⟩

un·fulfillment \"+\ *n* **1** : failure to fulfill : lack of execution ⟨~ of an obligation⟩ **2** : failure to achieve fulfillment : lack of consummation : DISSATISFACTION ⟨had arrived at this . . . final ~ —Fred Majdalany⟩ ⟨consume themselves in ~ —*Yale Rev.*⟩

un·fumed \"+\ *adj* [¹*un-* + *fumed*, past part. of *fume*] **1** *obs* : not distilled **2** : not exposed to fumes : not fumigated

un·functional \"+\ *adj* : not functional: **a** : not related directly to or fitted for everyday needs or activities : IMPRACTICAL, INEFFICIENT **b** : not conforming to functionalist theory

un·funded \"+\ *adj* [¹*un-* + *funded*, past part. of *fund*] : not funded : FLOATING ⟨an ~ debt⟩

unfunded life insurance trust *n* : a life insurance trust under which the insured agrees to pay the premiums on the subject policies during his lifetime

unfunded plan *n* : a pension or retirement plan under which the employer is free to finance payments to retired workers on a pay-as-you-go basis — compare INSURED PLAN, TRUSTEED PLAN

un·funny \ˌən+\ *adj* : not funny : failing to achieve the humor intended : UNAMUSING ⟨an ~ joke⟩ ⟨a feverish and ~ comedy —Robert Hatch⟩

un·furl \"+\ *vb* [²*un-* + *furl*] *vt* **1** : to release or open out (as a sail or flag) from a furled state : cast loose ⟨~ the sails and get under way⟩ : spread out for display ⟨the flag which the legation ~*ed* on state occasions —Jenny G. Walker⟩ **2** : to open out (as a scene) to the view : UNFOLD, UNROLL ⟨with nature's wonders all ~*ed* to our delighted vision —W.S. Gilbert⟩ ~ *vi* : to open wide : UNFOLD ⟨strange plants ~*ed* —D.D.Randall⟩

un·furnish \"+\ *vt* [²*un-* + *furnish*] **1** *archaic* : to strip (as a place or a man) of means of defense **2** *obs* : DIVEST ⟨that which may ~ me of reason —Shak.⟩ **3** : to clear (as a house or apartment) of furniture : DISMANTLE

un·furnished \"+\ *adj* [¹*un-* + *furnished*, past part. of *furnish*] : not furnished: **a** : not provided or equipped : UNPREPARED ⟨~ with money or skill⟩ ⟨valleys . . . ~ with tracks —E.E.Shipton⟩ **b** : not provided with furniture; *specif* : not so provided by the landlord ⟨an ~ apartment⟩

un·furrowed \"+\ *adj* [¹*un-* + *furrowed*, past part. of *furrow*] : having no furrows: **a** : UNPLOWED, UNTRENCHED ⟨an ~ field⟩ **b** : UNWRINKLED ⟨an ~ throat⟩ ⟨~ fruit⟩

un·fused \"+\ *adj* : not fused: **a** : not blended by or as if by melting ⟨~ material in a blast furnace⟩ **b** : not joined ⟨~ lower leg bones⟩

un·fussing \"+\ *adj* [¹*un-* + *fussing*, pres. part. of *fuss*] : UNFUSSY

un·fussy \"+\ *adj* : not fussy: **a** : not easily flustered : EASYGOING ⟨managed the motel in an efficient, ~ way⟩ **b** : not greatly concerned with ways and means : not particular ⟨was quite ~ about the choice of a restaurant⟩ **c** : not cluttered with pretentious or nonessential matters : SIMPLE, UNCOMPLICATED ⟨keep the affair as ~ as possible⟩ ⟨the color pictures are just right, plain and realistic and ~ —Harvey Breit⟩

ung *abbr* [L *unguentum*] ointment

un·gag \ˌən+\ *vt* [²*un-* + *gag*] : to remove a gag from; *esp* : to release from censorship

un·gain \ˌən¦gān\ *adj* [ME *ungeyn*, fr. ¹*un-* + *geyn* gain — more at GAIN (direct)] **1** *dial Brit* **a** : hard to reach or do **b** : INACCESSIBLE, INCONVENIENT **b** : INTRACTABLE **2** *dial* : UNGAINLY

un·gained \ˌən+\ *adj* [¹*un-* + *gained*] : not gained ⟨men prize the thing ~ more than it is —Shak.⟩

un·gainful \"+\ *adj* : not gainful

un·gain·li·ness \ˌən'gānlēnəs, -lin-\ *n* -ES : the quality or state of being ungainly

¹un·gain·ly \ˌən¦gānlē, -li\ *adj, sometimes* -ER/-EST **1 a** : lacking in smoothness or dexterity : CLUMSY ⟨a very tall ~ gentleman . . . made her one of the clumsiest bows that was ever performed —W.M.Thackeray⟩ ⟨~ and eloquent, monstrous and exquisite . . . by turns —Virginia Woolf⟩ **b** : hard to handle : UNWIELDY ⟨the cello, some thought . . . was rather an ~ instrument for a girl —Osbert Lancaster⟩ **2** : lacking in grace or refinement : COARSE, UGLY ⟨an ~ grey homespun coat —Robert Lynd⟩ ⟨~ frame houses with scrollwork —*Amer. Guide Series: Calif.*⟩ **syn** see AWKWARD

²ungainly \"\ *adv, archaic* : in an ungainly manner ⟨waddles ~ by —*Westminster Gazette*⟩

un·gain·say·able \ˌən¦gān¦sāəbəl\ *adj* [¹*un-* + *gainsay* + *-able*] : incapable of being contradicted — **un·gain·say·ably** \-blē\ *adv*

un·gallant \ˌən+\ *adj* : not gallant; *esp* : DISCOURTEOUS — **un·gallantly** \"+\ *adv*

un·garbled \"+\ *adj* [ME *ungarbeled*, fr. ¹*un-* + *garbeled*, past part. of *garbelen* to garble] **1** *archaic* : not sorted or sifted **2** : not distorted : CLEAR

un·garmented \"+\ *adj* [¹*un-* + *garmented*, past part. of *garment*] : not garmented

un·garnish \"+\ *vt* [²*un-* + *garnish*] *archaic* : to divest of decoration or equipment

un·garnished \"+\ *adj* [ME, fr. ¹*un-* + *garnished*] : free of embellishment : PLAIN, SIMPLE ⟨the village church's ~, stone facade —Kay Boyle⟩

un·gartered \"+\ *adj, archaic* : not gartered ⟨chid . . . for going ~ —Shak.⟩

un·gathered \"+\ *adj* [ME *ungadered*, fr. ¹*un-* + *gadered*, past part. of *gaderen* to gather] **1** : not collected or drawn together; *esp* : not assembled in book sequence ⟨~ signatures⟩ **2** : not harvested ⟨~ crops⟩

un·gear \"+\ *vt* [²*un-* + *gear*] **1** *archaic* : to remove the harness from (a draft animal) : UNHITCH ⟨~*ed* the mules, and crawled under the wagon for shade —J.H.Beadle⟩ **2** : to disconnect by or as if by throwing out of gear ⟨~ the pinion of a machine⟩ ⟨jangle your nerves . . . ~ you for the life you might have selected —Isa Glenn⟩

un·ge·mach·ite \'əngə,mä,kīt\ *n* -s [Henri-Léon *Ungemach* †1936 Belgian crystallographer + E *-ite*] : a mineral $K_3Na_9Fe(SO_4)_6(OH)_3.9H_2O$ consisting of a hydrous basic sulfate of potassium, sodium, and iron

un·generosity \ˌən+\ *n* [*ungenerous* + *-ity*] : lack of magnanimity : MEANNESS, SPITE ⟨the ill-tempered *ungenerosities* of a nerve-wracked woman —W.J.Locke⟩

un·generous \"+\ *adj* **1** : lacking in courtesy or magnanimity : PETTY, SMALL ⟨it seems ~ to end this review of a splendid work of scholarship on a critical note —*Times Lit. Supp.*⟩ **2** : lacking in largess : NIGGARDLY, PARSIMONIOUS ⟨~ response to an appeal for funds⟩ — **un·generously** \"+\ *adv*

un·genial \"+\ *adj* : DISAGREEABLE; *esp* : not arousing a sympathetic response ⟨considered the most ~ theory with scrupulous faith —Elinor Wylie⟩

un·genteel \ˌən+\ *adj* : lacking in courtesy or refinement : IMPOLITE, INELEGANT — **un·genteelly** \"+\ *adv*

un·gentle \"+\ *adj* [ME *ungentil*, fr. ¹*un-* + *gentil* gentle] **1 a** : not of the nobility : LOWBORN **b** *archaic* : UNGENTEEL **2** : lacking in softness or congeniality : HARSH, ROUGH — **un·gently** \"+\ *adv*

ungentleman *vt* [²*un-* + *gentleman*, n.] *obs* : to disqualify as a gentleman

un·gentlemanlike \ˌən+\ *adj* [¹*un-* + *gentlemanlike*] *archaic* : UNGENTLEMANLY

un·gentlemanliness \"+\ *n* [*ungentlemanly* + *-ness*] : the quality or state of being ungentlemanly

un·gentlemanly \"+\ *adj* : unworthy of a gentleman : ILL-BRED, IGNOBLE

un·gentleness \"+\ *n* [ME *ungentilnesse*, fr. *ungentil* ungentle + *-nesse* -ness] **1** *obs* : lack of civility : DISCOURTESY, RUDENESS **2** : lack of kindness or consideration : INHUMANITY

un·genuine \"+\ *adj* : not genuine — **un·genuinely** \"+\ *adv*

un·getatable \"+\ *adj* [¹*un-* + *getatable*] : hard to reach : INACCESSIBLE

un·ghosted \ˌən+\ *adj* [¹*un-* + *ghosted*, past part. of *ghost*] : not ghostwritten : FIRSTHAND ⟨asked the maestro himself to write an ~ introduction —Lionel Trilling⟩

un·ghostly \"+\ *adj, archaic* : not spiritual

un·gifted \"+\ *adj* **1** : lacking talent **2** *archaic* : EMPTY-HANDED

un·gild \"+\ *vt* [²*un-* + *gild*] : to remove gilding from

un·gilded *or* **un·gilt** \"+\ *adj* [*ungilded* fr. ¹*un-* + *gilded; ungilt* fr. ME, fr. ¹*un-* + *gilt*] *archaic* : not overlaid with gilding ⟨frames gilded and ~ —*London Gazette*⟩

un·ginned \"+\ *adj* [¹*un-* + *ginned*, past part. of *gin*] : not ginned ⟨~ cotton⟩

un·gird \"+\ *vt* [ME *ungyrden*, fr. OE *ongyrdan*, fr. *on-* ²*un-* + *gyrdan* to gird] **1** : to divest of a restraining band or girdle : free from constriction ⟨~*ed* his camels —Gen 24:32 (RSV)⟩ **2** *archaic* : to loosen or lay aside by or as if by undoing a belt ⟨*ungirt* and cast off that cloak —John Jackson⟩ ⟨~ thy strangeness, and tell me —Shak.⟩

un·girdled \"+\ *adj* [¹*un-* + *girdled*, past part. of *girdle*] : not girdled

un·girt \"+\ *adj* [ME *ungyrt;* partly fr. past part. of *ungyrden* to ungird; partly fr. ¹*un-* + *gyrt*, past part. of *gyrden*, *girden* to gird] **1** : wearing no belt or girdle or wearing one that is not snugly fastened ⟨wandering through the woods . . . ~, unsandaled —P.B.Shelley⟩ **2** : lacking in discipline or compactness : LOOSE, SLACK ⟨did not run on in ~ dithyrambs . . . but worked quietly with her finely chosen materials —Carl Van Doren⟩

un·girth \"+\ *vt* [²*un-* + *girth*] *archaic* : to release by undoing a girth ⟨~*ing* his saddle —Henry Brooke⟩

un·give \"+\ *vi* [²*un-* + *give*] *dial Brit* : to lose rigidity : become pliable : MELT

un·given \"+\ *adj* : not given ⟨a person not ~ to words —John Mason Brown⟩

un·giving \"+\ *adj* [¹*un-* + *giving*, pres. part. of *give*] **1** : exhibiting parsimony : FRUGAL, STINGY ⟨stingy, ~ people —Vance Packard⟩ **2** : characterized by rigidity : ADAMANT, INFLEXIBLE ⟨if the mother is a cold, ~, stern and disciplinary one —Carl Binger⟩

un·glaciated \ˌən+\ *adj* [¹*un-* + *glaciated*, past part. of *glaciate*] : not glaciated

un·glad \"+\ *adj* [ME, fr. OE *unglæd*, fr. ¹*un-* + *glæd* glad] : not glad

un·glamorous \"+\ *adj* : lacking romantic appeal : COMMONPLACE, HUMDRUM ⟨~ jobs . . . greasing engines, operating turntables, wielding a shovel —*advt*⟩ ⟨a relatively small and ~ settlement —R.L.Beals⟩ — **un·glamorously** \"+\ *adv*

un·glazed \"+\ *adj* : not glazed: as **a** : lacking a vitreous finish ⟨~ pottery⟩ **b** *of paper* : having a smooth machine finish : not calendered **c** : not furnished with glass ⟨~ openings . . . to admit as much light and air as possible —*Materials Handling in the Wool Industry*⟩

un·glorified \"+\ *adj* [ME, fr. ¹*un-* + *glorified*, past part. of *glorifien* to glorify] : not glorified

un·glorious \"+\ *adj* [ME, fr. ¹*un-* + *glorious*] *archaic* : INGLORIOUS

un·glossed \"+\ *adj* [¹*un-* + *glossed*, past part. of *gloss*] : not glossed

un·glove \ˌən+\ *vt* [ME *ungloven*, fr. ²*un-* + *glove*, n.] : to uncover by or as if by removing a glove ⟨her hand . . . when *ungloved*, glitters with heavy rings —Israel Zangwill⟩ ⟨Soviet Russia *ungloved* its winged fist —*Time*⟩

un·glue \"+\ *vt* [²*un-* + *glue*] : to disjoin by or as if by dissolving an adhesive ⟨~ a stamp from an envelope by steaming⟩ ⟨~ children from a TV set⟩

un·gna·dia \ˌənˈnādēə, ˌəngəˈnā-\ *n, cap* [NL, fr. Baron David von *Ungnad* 16th cent. Austrian diplomat + NL *-ia*] : a monotypic genus of shrubs or small trees (family Sapindaceae) comprising the buckeyes of southwestern No. America and distinguished by shining dark green leaves, rose-colored flowers, and poisonous black seeds

un·god \ˌən+\ *vt* [²*un-* + *god*] *archaic* : to strip of divinity ⟨men cannot come to pull God out of his throne, and ~ him —William Gurnall⟩

un·goddess \"+\ *vt* [²*un-* + *goddess*, n.] *archaic* : to deprive of the status of a goddess

un·godlike \"+\ *adj* : not godlike

un·godlily \"+\ *adv* [*ungodly* + *-ly*] : in an ungodly manner

un·godliness \"+\ *n* [*ungodly* + *-ness*] : the quality or state of being ungodly : WICKEDNESS

¹**un·godly** \"+\ *adj* **1 a** : denying God or disobedient to him : IMPIOUS, IRRELIGIOUS **b** : contrary to moral law or Christian precepts : SINFUL, WICKED **2 a** : offensive to civilized taste : INDECENT **b** : OUTRAGEOUS ⟨do you expect me to get up at that ~ hour —Zane Grey⟩ ⟨stir up an ~ scandal —W.H. Wright⟩

²**ungodly** \"\ *adv, dial* : EXTREMELY ⟨I was ~ proud —Saul Bellow⟩

ungored *adj* [¹*un-* + *gored*, past part. of *gore*] *obs* : unwounded by or as if by stabbing ⟨keep my name *ungor'd* —Shak.⟩

un·gotten *or* **un·got** \ˌən+\ *adj* [ME, fr. ¹*un-* + *gotten* or *got*, past part. of *getten* to get] **1** *obs* : not begotten **2** : not gathered or obtained

un·governable \"+\ *adj* : not capable of being governed, ruled, or restrained : UNBRIDLED ⟨make France nearly ~ —D.W.Brogan⟩ ⟨a harsh and ~ temper⟩ **syn** see UNRULY

un·governableness \ˌən+\ *n* : the quality or state of being ungovernable ⟨the ~ of youth⟩

un·gov·er·na·bly \ˌ≈¦≈≈≈blē, -bli\ *adv* : in an ungovernable manner ⟨made him ~ ferocious —T.B.Macaulay⟩

un·governed \"+\ *adj* [¹*un-* + *governed*, past part. of *govern*] : not subjected to regulation or control : UNRESTRAINED, WILD ⟨~ trade⟩ ⟨~ youth⟩ ⟨~ rage⟩

un·gowned \"+\ *adj* [¹*un-* + *gowned*, past part. of *gown*] : not gowned

un·grace \"+\ *n* [ME, fr. ¹*un-* + *grace*] : lack of grace

un·graced \"+\ *adj* [¹*un-* + *grace*, n. + *-ed*] : lacking in beauty or distinction : GRACELESS ⟨thatched cottages overrun by ~ building —*Manchester Guardian Weekly*⟩

un·graceful \ˌən+\ *adj* : lacking in charm or felicity : AWKWARD, INELEGANT ⟨his stature low . . . his bearing ~ —Sir Walter Scott⟩ ⟨his concessions were ~ —S.E.Morison & H.S. Commager⟩ — **un·gracefully** \"+\ *adv*

un·gracefulness \"+\ *n* : the quality or state of being ungraceful

un·gracious \"+\ *adj* [ME, fr. ¹*un-* + *gracious*] **1** *archaic* : lacking in spiritual grace : PROFANE, WICKED ⟨take heed of . . . converse with lewd, profane and ~ company —Joseph Mede⟩ **2 a** *obs* : exhibiting bad breeding : BOORISH, CRUDE ⟨~ wretch, fit for the mountains . . . where manners ne'er were preached —Shak.⟩ **b** : showing bad taste or lack of courtesy : SURLY ⟨it seems ~ to insist upon the futility of so much earnest . . . effort, prompted by motives which are so splendid —Norman Angell⟩ ⟨this curt summary is not meant to be ~ —B.R. Redman⟩ **3 a** : lacking in attraction : UNCONGENIAL ⟨urban life tends to put an ~ stamp upon the human face —Irwin Shaw⟩ **b** : DISAGREEABLE, THANKLESS ⟨it would be an ~ task to catalog them —M.R.Cohen⟩ **syn** see RUDE

un·graciously \"+\ *adv* [ME, fr. *ungracious* + *-ly*] : in an ungracious manner

un·graciousness \"+\ *n* : the quality or state of being ungracious

un·graded \"+\ *adj* [¹*un-* + *graded*, past part. of *grade*] **1** : not leveled or reduced to a gradual slope or gradient ⟨~ road⟩ **2 a** : not classified according to grades ⟨~ material⟩ ⟨~ jobs⟩ **b** : not assigned to a specific grade ⟨~ teacher⟩

ungraded school *n* : a usu. rural one-room elementary school with one teacher in which pupils are not classified by grades

un·graduated \ˌən+\ *adj* : not graduated

un·grafted \"+\ *adj* [¹*un-* + *grafted*, past part. of *graft*] : not grafted

un·grammatical *also* **un·grammatic** \"+\ *adj* **1** : not following rules of grammar ⟨the colloquial and ~ Latin he spoke —Gilbert Highet⟩ **2 a** : INCORRECT 5 **b** : SUBSTANDARD b **3** : varying from established practice ⟨~ oppositions of tonality —W.H.Mellers⟩ — **un·grammatically** \"+\ *adv*

un·granted \"\ *adj* [¹*un-* + *granted*, past part. of *grant*] : not granted

ungranted land *n* : PUBLIC LAND

un·graspable \"+\ *adj* [¹*un-* + *grasp*, v. + *-able*] : incapable of being seized or comprehended ⟨of all the eluding and ~ objects that ever I tried to get mind or hands on —Mark Twain⟩

un·grasped \"+\ *adj* [¹*un-* + *grasped*, past part. of *grasp*] : not fully apprehended ⟨the ~ infinite ground of all being —Philip Wheelwright⟩

un·grateful \ˌən+\ *adj* [¹*un-* + *grateful*] **1 a** : showing no gratitude : THANKLESS ⟨an ~ child refusing help to his aging parents⟩ **b** : appearing to lack appreciation ⟨few composers being professional conductors, the unfortunate guest is likely to give a pretty ~ . . . performance —Deems Taylor⟩ **c** *archaic* : failing to respond to cultivation : LISTLESS ⟨where vegetation is found at all, it is more ~ than . . . blankness —Herman Melville⟩ **2 a** : of a disagreeable nature : DISTASTEFUL ⟨the work of security boards is an ~ task at best —Sidney Hook⟩ **b** : offensive to the senses : HARSH, REPELLENT ⟨unidiomatic instrumental writing and ~ chord dispositions —Virgil Thomson⟩ ⟨the reeds . . . sent forth an ~ stench —Jonas Hanway⟩ — **un·gratefully** \"+\ *adv*

un·gratefulness \"+\ *n* : the quality or state of being ungrateful

un·gratified \"+\ *adj* [¹*un-* + *gratified*, past part. of *gratify*] : not satisfied : DISCONTENTED, RESTLESS

un·grave \"+\ *vt* [²*un-* + *grave*, n.] : to dig up : DISINTER

un·graven \ˌən+\ *adj* [ME, fr. ¹*un-* + *graven*, past part. of *graven* to grave, engrave] *archaic* : not engraved

un·greased \"+\ *adj* [ME *ungrecyd*, fr. ¹*un-* + *grecyd*, past part. of *grecen*, *gresen* to grease] : not greased

un·greeted \"+\ *adj* [¹*un-* + *greeted*, past part. of *greet*] : not greeted

un·gregarious \"+\ *adj* : not gregarious

un·groomed \"+\ *adj* [¹*un-* + *groomed*, past part. of *groom*] : not groomed

un·ground \"+\ *adj* [ME *ungrond*, fr. ¹*un-* + *grond*, past part. of *grinden* to grind] : not ground

un·grounded \"+\ *adj* [ME, fr. ¹*un-* + *grounded*, past part. of *grounden* to ground] **1 a** : lacking a solid foundation : BASELESS **b** : lacking basic information : UNINSTRUCTED **2** : not connected electrically with the ground

un·grown \"+\ *adj* : not grown

un·grudged \"+\ *adj* [¹*un-* + *grudged*, past part. of *grudge*] : not grudged

un·grudging \"+\ *adj* : being without envy or reluctance : GENEROUS, WHOLEHEARTED ⟨~ admiration⟩ ⟨~ hospitality⟩ — **un·grudgingly** \"+\ *adv*

¹**un·gual** \ˈəŋgwəl, ˈəŋg-\ *also* **un·gui·nal** \-wənᵊl\ *adj* [*ungual* fr. L *unguis* nail, claw, hoof + E *-al*; *unguinal*, irreg. (influenced by L *unguin-*, *unguen* ointment, fr. *unguere* to anoint) fr. L *unguis* + E *-al* — more at NAIL, OINTMENT] : of, relating to, or resembling a nail, claw, or hoof

²**ungual** \"\ *n* -s : NAIL, HOOF, CLAW

un·guaranteed \ˌən+\ *adj* [¹*un-* + *guaranteed*, past part. of *guarantee*] : not guaranteed

un·guard \"+\ *vt* [back-formation fr. *unguarded*] : to expose to attack : leave unprotected

un·guarded \"+\ *adj* [¹*un-* + *guarded*] **1 a** : unprotected by a guard : vulnerable to attack ⟨an ~ gate⟩; *specif* : not protected by another piece or card ⟨an ~ queen⟩ **b** : not having a protective shield or barrier ⟨an ~ precipice⟩ **2 a** : free from guile or wariness : DIRECT, INCAUTIOUS ⟨their ~, childish gaze —*New Yorker*⟩ **b** : marked by lack of caution : having the guard down ⟨in an ~ moment spilled the beans⟩ **c** : not disguised : OPEN, REVEALING ⟨every indiscreet and ~ expression of yours —Earl of Chesterfield⟩ — **un·guardedly** \"+\ *adv*

un·guent \ˈəŋgwənt, ˈəngwə-, ÷ˈənjə- *sometimes* ÷ˈəŋgənt *or* ÷ˈəŋgə-\ *n* -s [ME, fr. L *unguentum* — more at OINTMENT] : a lubricant or salve (as for sores or burns) : CERATE, OINTMENT

un·guen·tar·i·um \ˌəŋgwənˈta(a)rēəm, ˌəngwə-, ÷ˌənjə- *sometimes* ÷ˌəŋgə- *or* ÷ˌəngə-\ *n, pl* **unguentaria** [L *unguentarium (vas)*, fr. neut. of *unguentarius* of or relating to ointment, fr. *unguentum* ointment + *-arius* -ary] : an ancient Greek or Roman glass jar to hold unguents

un·guerdoned \ˌən+\ *adj* [ME *unguerdonned*, fr. ¹*un-* + *guerdonned*, past part. of *guerdonnen*, *gerdonen* to guerdon] : not guerdoned

un·guessable \"+\ *adj* [¹*un-* + *guess*, v. + *-able*] : incapable of being guessed ⟨the angler forever bets . . . against unknowable odds for ~ returns —Philip Wylie⟩

un·guessed \"+\ *adj* [ME *ungessid*, fr. ¹*un-* + *gessid*, past part. of *gessen* to guess] **1** : lying beyond conjecture : MYSTERIOUS, UNIMAGINABLE **2** : not taken into consideration : UNFORESEEN, UNSUSPECTED

ungui- *comb form* [L *unguis* nail, claw, hoof — more at NAIL] : nail : claw

un·guic·u·la·ta \ˌəŋˌgwikyəˈlād·ə, ˌənˌg-, -ˈlad·ə\ *n pl, cap* [NL, fr. neut. pl. of *unguiculatus* unguiculate] *in former classifications* : a major division of Mammalia comprising mammals with nails or claws as distinguished from hoofed mammals and cetaceans — compare UNGULATA

¹**un·guic·u·late** \ˌ≈¦kyələt, -ˌlāt\ *also* **un·guic·u·lat·ed** \-ˌlād·əd\ *adj* [*unguiculate* fr. NL *unguiculatus*, fr. L *unguiculus* fingernail (fr. L *unguis* + *-culus* -cle) + *-atus* -ate; *unguiculated* fr. NL *unguiculatus* + E *-ed*] **1 a** : having nails or claws **b** : of or relating to the Unguiculata **2** : tapering below into a claw or a stalklike base ⟨an ~ petal⟩

²**unguiculate** \"\ *n* -s [NL *Unguiculata*] : a mammal of the division Unguiculata

un·guided \ˌən+\ *adj* : not guided: as **a** : lacking one to show the way ⟨~ tour⟩ **b** : lacking leadership or control ⟨~ days and rotten times —Shak.⟩ **c** : not subject to guidance after launching ⟨~ missile⟩

un·guif·er·ate \ˌənˈgwifərət, ˌənˈg-\ *adj* [*ungui-* + *-fer* + *-ate*] : having nails, claws, or hooklike processes

un·guiltily \ˌən+\ *adv* [*unguilty* + *-ly*] : INNOCENTLY

un·guilty \"+\ *adj* [ME *ungilty*, fr. OE *ungyltig*, fr. ¹*un-* + *gyltig* guilty — more at GUILTY] : not guilty : INNOCENT

un·gui·rostral \ˌəŋgwə, ˌəng-+\ *adj* [*ungui-* + *rostral*] : having a hard horny nail at the end of the bill ⟨~ duck⟩

un·guis \ˈəŋgwəs, ˈəng-\ *n, pl* **ungues** [L — more at NAIL] **1 a** : a nail, claw, or hoof on a digit of a vertebrate **b** : one of the tarsal claws or terminal chitinous hooks on the foot of an insect **c** : the hard chitinous hook through which the poison gland opens on the chelicera of a spider **2** : a narrow pointed base of a petal

un·gui·trac·tor \-wəˌtraktə(r)\ *n* -s [*ungui-* + *retractor*] : a sclerite of the insect pretarsus that is partially invaginated within the tarsus

un·gu·la \ˈəŋgyələ\ *n, pl* **ungu·lae** \-ˌlē\ [L, dim. of *unguis*] : UNGUAL — **un·gu·lar** \-lə(r)\ *adj*

un·gu·la·ta \ˌ≈≈ˈlād·ə, -ˈlad·ə\ *n pl, cap* [NL, fr. neut. pl. of LL *ungulatus* ungulate] *in former classifications* : a major division of Mammalia comprising hoofed mammals as distinguished from cetaceans and those with nails or claws — compare UNGUICULATA

¹**un·gu·late** \ˈəŋgyələt, -ˌlāt\ *also* **un·gu·lat·ed** \-ˌlād·əd\ *adj* [*ungulate* fr. LL *ungulatus*, fr. L *ungula* + *-atus* -ate; *ungulated* fr. LL *ungulatus* + E *-ed*] **1** : having hoofs **2** : of or relating to the Ungulata

²**ungulate** \"\ *n* -s [NL *Ungulata*] : a mammal of the division Ungulata

un·guled \ˈəŋ,g(y)üld, -ˌg(y)əld\ *adj* [L *ungula* + E *-ed*] : having hoofs or claws of a heraldic tincture different from that of the body

un·gu·li·grade \ˈəŋgyələˌgrād, ˈəng-\ *adj* [L *ungula* + E *-i-* + *-grade*] : walking on hoofs

un·gum \ˌənˈgəm\ *vt* [²*un-* + *gum*] **1** : UNGLUE **2** : DEGUM

un·gummed \-md\ *adj* [¹*un-* + *gummed*, past part. of *gum*] : devoid of adhesive

un·gutted \ˌən+\ *adj* [¹*un-* + *gutted*, past part. of *gut*] : not gutted

un·gyved \"+\ *adj* [¹*un-* + *gyved*, past part. of *gyve*] : not gyved : UNFETTERED

un·habitable \"+\ *adj* [ME, fr. ¹*un-* + *habitable*] : not habitable

un·habitual \ˌən(h)ə-\ *adj* : not habitual

un·habituated \ˌən(h)ə-\ *adj* [¹*un-* + *habituated*, past part. of *habituate*] : UNACCUSTOMED

un·hackneyed \ˌən+\ *adj* [¹*un-* + *hackneyed*] **1** *archaic* : lacking knowledge or proficiency : GREEN, INEXPERIENCED ⟨a man ~ and unpracticed in the world —Laurence Sterne⟩ **2** : being out of the ordinary : FRESH, ORIGINAL ⟨children have such an ~ way of looking at their world —Alice Dalgliesh⟩

un·hailed \"+\ *adj* [¹*un-* + *hailed*, past part. of *hail*] : not hailed

un·hair \"+\ *vb* [ME *unheeren*, fr. ²*un-* + *heer* hair] *vt* **1** *archaic* : to deprive of hair : make bald ⟨I'll ~ thy head —Shak.⟩ **2** : DEHAIR; *specif* : to remove (guard hairs) from pelts used for garments by hand or machine to improve appearance of the fur ~ *vi* : to become dehaired

un·hair·er \ˌənˈha(a)rə(r), -he|\ *n* -s [*unhair* + *-er*] : a workman who unhairs hides or skins

un·hair·ing \|riŋ, |rēŋ\ *n* -s [fr. gerund of *unhair*] : an act or process of removing hair; *esp* : depilation of skins or hides

unhairing machine *n* : a machine for removing hair from hides and skins preparatory to tanning

un·hallow \ˌən+\ *vt* [²*un-* + *hallow*] *archaic* : to make profane ⟨nothing more ~s a man . . . than a habit of wrath —John Milton⟩

un·hallowed \"+\ *adj* [ME *unhalewed*, fr. OE *unhālgod*, fr. ¹*un-* + *halgod*, past part. of *hālgian* to hallow — more at HALLOW] **1** : not blessed : UNCONSECRATED ⟨buried in ~ ground⟩ **2 a** : unsanctioned by or showing lack of reverence for religion : IMPIOUS, PROFANE ⟨bow before the idol, and taste the ~ ecstasy —L.P.Smith⟩ **b** : suited for or inhabited by devils : FIENDISH **3 a** : contrary to law or accepted social standards : ILLEGITIMATE ⟨~ relations between men and women—Anne D. Sedgwick⟩ **b** : used for immoral purposes ⟨wrecked health and ~ hotel rooms —Chad Walsh⟩

un·halted \"+\ *adj* [¹*un-* + *halted*, past part. of *halt*] : not halted

un·halved \"+\ *adj* [¹*un-* + *halved*, past part. of *halve*] : not played in the same number of strokes as one's opponent at golf ⟨~ holes⟩

un·hammered \"+\ *adj* : not hammered

un·hampered \"+\ *adj* [¹*un-* + *hampered*, past part. of *hamper*] **1 a** : not held in check : LIBERATED, LOOSED ⟨outlet for healthy and ~ action —B.N.Cardozo⟩ **b** : not impeded by external influences ⟨~ by tradition⟩ ⟨the priest was ~ by scruple —V.L.Parrington⟩ ⟨bridle paths, ~ by thoroughfares —*Amer. Guide Series: Texas*⟩ **2** : not subjected to control and esp. to government control : FREE, UNRESTRICTED ⟨~ dissemination of any news a reporter can smell out —Alistair Cooke⟩ **3** : not obstructed : CLEAR ⟨had an ~ view over the whole town —A.V.Borosini⟩

un·hand \ˌən+\ *vt* [²*un-* + *hand*, n.] : to remove the hand from : let go

un·handily \"+\ *adv* : in an unhandy manner

un·handiness \"+\ *n* : the quality or state of being unhandy

un·handled \"+\ *adj* [¹*un-* + *handled*, past part. of *handle*] : not tamed or disciplined : WILD ⟨youthful and ~ colts —Shak.⟩

un·handsome \"+\ *adj* **1 a** : lacking in external beauty or refinement : HOMELY, INELEGANT ⟨her portrait . . . is very pretty or at least not ~ —Robert Lynd⟩ **b** *obs* : AWKWARD, CLUMSY **2** : not gratifying : DISAGREEABLE, UNPLEASANT ⟨the ~ business of losing money —*U.S.Investor*⟩ **3** : deficient in courtesy or taste : IMPOLITE, RUDE ⟨~ language or behavior⟩ — **un·handsomely** \"+\ *adv*

un·handsomeness \"+\ *n* : the quality or state of being unhandsome

un·handy \ˌən+\ *adj* **1** : hard to handle : UNWIELDY ⟨an ~, sprit-rigged, shallow-draft sloop —Vincent McHugh⟩ **2** : lacking in skill or dexterity : AWKWARD, INCOMPETENT ⟨a clumsy dissector . . . and ~ at most of the practical work —H.G. Wells⟩ ⟨have not shown themselves ~ in foreseeing trouble, and checking it —*Contemporary Rev.*⟩

un·hang \"+\ *vt* [ME *unhangen*, fr. ²*un-* + *hangen* to hang] : to detach from a hanging support ⟨~ a mirror from the wall⟩

un·hanged \"+\ *adj* [ME, fr. ¹*un-* + *hanged*, past part. of *hangen* to hang] : not executed by hanging ⟨there lives not three good men ~ in England —Shak.⟩

un·happily \"+\ *adv* [ME, fr. *unhappy* + *-ly*] : in an unhappy manner : LAMENTABLY, UNFORTUNATELY

un·happiness \"+\ *n* [ME *unhappynes*, fr. *unhappy* + *-nes* -ness] : the quality or state of being unhappy : MISERY, SADNESS

un·happy \"+\ *adj* [ME, fr. *unhap* misfortune, trouble (fr. ¹*un-* + *hap*) + *-y*] **1** *archaic* : OBSTREPEROUS, TROUBLESOME ⟨these ~ Highland clans are again breaking into general commotion —Sir Walter Scott⟩ **2 a** : being out of luck : MISERABLE, UNFORTUNATE ⟨~ caravans, straggling afoot through swamps and canebrakes —*Amer. Guide Series: Ark.*⟩ **b** : causing or subject to disaster : INAUSPICIOUS, ILL-STARRED ⟨a particularly ~ moment for a scandal to blow up —Green Peyton⟩ ⟨in a few ~ regions the people swim to work in . . . record precipitation —T.H.Fielding⟩ **c** : full of misery : WRETCHED ⟨people may play with impunity at any game in this ~ world except . . . Life, Love, and Death —Lafcadio Hearn⟩ **3** : lacking in skill or felicity : AWKWARD, INEPT ⟨~ references to "unsystematic systems" —S.E.Martin⟩ ⟨two fine singers a little ~ in the French language —Edward Sackville-West & Desmond Shawe-Taylor⟩ **4 a** : dejected in spirit : MELANCHOLY, SAD ⟨was ~ when alone, always craved a public —M.R.Cohen⟩ **b** : mentally disquieted : DISTURBED, DISSATISFIED ⟨~ . . . with the outcome of our China policy —W.W.Kaufmann⟩ ⟨if you're ~ without statistics —Richard Joseph⟩ **c** : causing dejection or discontent : DISCOURAGING ⟨the ~ history of eleven months of truce talks shows that every difficulty solved begets a difficulty to be solved —*Time*⟩ **5 a** : of an unpleasant nature : DISAGREEABLE, DISTRESSING ⟨nagging has been defined as the constant reiteration of the ~ truth —*English Digest*⟩ ⟨the whole ~ problem of school integration —*Newsweek*⟩ **b** : of a depressing character : CHEERLESS, DREARY ⟨an ~ view of twisted antennae and grimy rooftops⟩

un·harbor \ˌən+\ *vt* [²*un-* + *harbor*] *Brit* : to drive (an animal) from cover

un·harden \"+\ *vt* [²*un-* + *harden*] : to make soft : DISARM, MELT ⟨sang in a manner . . . to ~ the most critical heart —*Musical Digest*⟩

un·hardened \"+\ *adj* [¹*un-* + *hardened*] : not hardened

un·hardy \"+\ *adj* [ME, fr. ¹*un-* + *hardy*] : not hardy

un·harmed \"+\ *adj* [ME, fr. ¹*un-* + *harmed*, past part. of *harmen* to harm] : not harmed : SAFE, UNSCATHED

un·harmful \"+\ *adj* : not harmful — **un·harmfully** \"+\ *adv*

un·harming \"+\ *adj* [¹*un-* + *harming*, pres. part. of *harm*] : doing no injury

un·harmonious \"+\ *adj* : INHARMONIOUS — **un·harmoniously** \"+\ *adv*

un·harness \ˌən+\ *vt* [ME *onharnesen*, fr. *on-* ²*un-* + *harnesen*, *harneisen* to harness] : to divest of harness ⟨~ a horse⟩

un·harnessed \"+\ *adj* : not harnessed; *esp* : not utilized ⟨seething with ~ energy —Henry Miller⟩

un·harried \"+\ *adj* : not harried

un·harrowed \"+\ *adj* [¹*un-* + *harrowed*, past part. of *harrow*] : not harrowed

un·harvested \"+\ *adj* [¹*un-* + *harvested*, past part. of *harvest*] : not harvested

un·hasp \"+\ *vt* [ME *unhaspen*, fr. ²*un-* + *haspen* to hasp] *archaic* : to unfasten the hasp of : OPEN ⟨endeavored to ~ the casement —Emily Brontë⟩

un·hasting \"+\ *adj* [¹*un-* + *hasting*, pres. part. of *haste*] : DELIBERATE, UNHURRIED

un·hasty \"+\ *adj* : LEISURELY, SLOW

un·hat \"+\ *vi* [²*un-* + *hat*, n.] *archaic* : to doff the hat as a mark of respect

un·hatched \"+\ *adj* [¹*un-* + *hatched*, past part. of *hatch*] **1** : not hatched from or as if from the egg ⟨an ~ chick⟩ ⟨an ~ plot⟩ **2** : not fully incubated ⟨an ~ egg⟩

un·hatted \"+\ *adj* : not wearing a hat

un·haunted \ˌən+\ *adj* [¹*un-* + *haunted*, past part. of *haunt*] **1** : not inhabited : UNFREQUENTED ⟨a region . . . ~ by birds —Alfred Sutro⟩ **2** : not disturbed : UNTROUBLED ⟨~ by any pang —W.D.Howells⟩

un·hazarded \"+\ *adj* [¹*un-* + *hazarded*, past part. of *hazard*] *archaic* : not hazarded : UNTRIED

un·hazardous \"+\ *adj* : not dangerous

un·head \"+\ *vt* [ME *unhevden*, fr. ²*un-* + *heved* head, n. — more at HEAD] *archaic* : to separate the head or top from

un·healable \ˌən+\ *adj* [ME *unheleable*, fr. ¹*un-* + *helen* to heal + *-able*] : incapable of being healed

un·healed \"+\ *adj* [ME *unheled* fr. ¹*un-* + *heled*, past part. of *helen* to heal] : not healed

un·health \"+\ *n* [ME *unhelthe*, fr. OE *unhǣlth*, fr. ¹*un-* + *hǣlth* health] : lack of health or vigor : ILLNESS, INFIRMITY

un·healthful \"+\ *adj* [¹*un-* + *healthful*] **1** *obs* : UNHEALTHY **2** : detrimental to good health : UNWHOLESOME

un·healthfulness \"+\ *n* : the quality or state of being unhealthful

un·healthily \"+\ *adv* : in an unhealthy manner

un·healthiness \"+\ *n* : the quality or state of being unhealthy

un·healthy \"+\ *adj* [¹*un-* + *healthy*] **1** : UNHEALTHFUL 2 ⟨an ~ climate⟩ **2 a** : not in good health : SICKLY, WEAK **b** : evincing abnormality : DISEASED, MORBID ⟨~ wounds and ulcers —Robert Chawner⟩ ⟨register . . . unhappiness, the boy with nightmares, the girl with ~ greed —Caroline H. Tunstall⟩ **3 a** : of a dangerous nature : RISKY, UNSOUND ⟨dropping depth charges at six knots is ~ for the boat that does it —Alexander Forbes⟩ ⟨it would be ~ . . . to criticize the regime —*Atlantic*⟩ ⟨on the lookout for ~ speculative developments —C.E.Egan⟩ **b** : of a harmful nature : BAD, INJURIOUS ⟨had an ~ habit . . . of borrowing money —R.W.Thorp⟩ ⟨produce inflation, or other ~ results —*Internat'l Bank for Reconstruction & Development Report*⟩ **c** : morally contaminated : CORRUPT, DEPRAVED ⟨an ~ alliance between thugs and politicians⟩

un·heard \ˌən+\ *adj* [ME *unherd*, fr. ¹*un-* + *herd*, past part. of *heren* to hear] **1 a** : not perceived by the ear **b** : not given a hearing **2** *archaic* : UNHEARD-OF

un·heard-of \ˌ≈ˈ≈ˌ≈\ *adj* [¹*un-* + *heard of*, past part. form of the phrase *hear of*, fr. ¹*hear* + *of*] : previously unknown : NEW, UNPRECEDENTED ⟨a first novel by an *unheard-of* writer⟩ ⟨amphibious operations . . . would soon be necessary on an *unheard-of* scale —J.P.Baxter b. 1893⟩

un·hearing \ˌən+\ *adj* [¹*un-* + *hearing*, pres. part. of *hear*] : not hearing

un·heartsome \"+\ *adj, chiefly Scot* : CHEERLESS, SAD

un·heated \"+\ *adj* : not heated

un·heaven \"+\ *vt* [²*un-* + *heaven*, n.] *archaic* : to separate from heaven

un·heavenly \"+\ *adj* : not heavenly : GROSS, SINFUL

un·hedged \"+\ *adj* [¹*un-* + *hedged*, past part. of *hedge*] : not hedged : UNPROTECTED, UNQUALIFIED

un·heeded \"+\ *adj* [¹*un-* + *heeded*, past part. of *heed*] : not heeded : DISREGARDED, IGNORED — **un·heed·ed·ly** *adv*

un·heedful \"+\ *adj, archaic* : not attentive : CARELESS, NEGLIGENT

un·heeding \ˌən+\ *adv (or adj)* [¹*un-* + *heeding*, pres. part. of *heed*] : in an inattentive manner : ABSENTLY, UNOBSERVANTLY ⟨so sunk was he in . . . abstraction that he walked ~ by a large circle of people —Herman Wouk⟩ — **un·heed·ing·ly** *adv*

unheedy *adj* [¹*un-* + obs. E *heedy* attentive, careful, fr. E *heed* + *-y*] *obs* : HEEDLESS

un·hele \ˌən¦hē(ə)l\ *vt* [ME *unhelen*, fr. OE *unhelian*, fr. ²*un-* + *helian* to conceal — more at HELL] **1** *obs* : UNCOVER, REVEAL **2** *dial* : to strip of thatch

un·helm \ˌən+\ *vt* [ME *unhelmen*, fr. ²*un-* + *helmen* to helm] *archaic* : to divest of a helmet ⟨~*ed* themselves to quench their thirst —G.A.Lawrence⟩

un·helped \"+\ *adj* [ME, fr. ¹*un-* + *helped*, past part. of *helpen* to help] : not helped : UNAIDED

un·helpful \"+\ *adj* : not helpful : offering no assistance : USELESS, UNCOOPERATIVE ⟨a curiously ~ manual —Robertson Davies⟩ ⟨icily neutral, disagreeably ~ —H.H.Johnston⟩ — **un·helpfully** \"+\ *adv*

un·helping \"+\ *adj*, *archaic* : UNHELPFUL

un·hemmed \"+\ *adj* [ME, fr. ¹*un-* + *hemmed*, past part. of *hemmen* to hem] : not hemmed

un·heralded \ˌən+\ *adj* [¹*un-* + *heralded*, past part. of *herald*] **1** : not publicly acclaimed : ANONYMOUS, UNRECOGNIZED ⟨~ in his large charities —D.S.Muzzey⟩ ⟨a new and ~ talent —Eric Newton⟩ **2** : UNEXPECTED, UNFORESEEN ⟨a totally ~ telegram that his daughter . . . died last night —M.A. D.Howe⟩

un·heroic *also* **un·heroical** \"+\ *adj* : not heroic : TIMID, UNIMPRESSIVE ⟨~ policy of nonintervention —H.S.Commager⟩ ⟨the gasoline drums were heavy, ~, yet dangerous to handle —K.M.Dodson⟩ — **un·heroically** \"+\ *adv*

un·hesitant \"+\ *adj* : not hesitant : IMMEDIATE, FORTHRIGHT

un·hesitating \"+\ *adj* [¹*un-* + *hesitating*, pres. part. of *hesitate*] : not curbed or qualified : FREE, WHOLEHEARTED — **un·hesitatingly** \"+\ *adv*

un·hewn \ˌən+\ *adj* : not given a finished form by or as if by hewing : ROUGH, UNPOLISHED ⟨houses . . . of ~ gray stone roughly cemented together —Martha Kean⟩ ⟨a rough, ~ soldier —Susanna Centlivre⟩

un·hidden \"+\ *adj* : not hidden

un·highlighted \"+\ *adj* [¹*un-* + *highlighted*, past part. of *highlight*] : not highlighted

un·hindered \"+\ *adj* [¹*un-* + *hindered*, past part. of *hinder*] : not hindered or restrained

un·hinge \"+\ *vt* [²*un-* + *hinge*] **1 a** : to remove (as a door) from the hinges **b** : to swing open on or as if on hinges ⟨will not . . . ~ my jaws to speak again —A.J.Munby⟩ **2 a** : to interrupt the normal functioning of : DISRUPT, DISORDER ⟨dislocates a shoulder, ~*s* a joint —Lafcadio Hearn⟩; *specif* : DERANGE ⟨a shock so great as almost to ~ the mind —Bernard DeVoto⟩ **b** : to stir up or throw into turmoil : DISCOMPOSE, UPSET ⟨the obvious sarcasm *unhinged* his temper⟩ ⟨sudden excitement *unhinged* all precision —R.L.Shayon⟩ **c** : to make precarious or cause to waver : SWAY, UNSETTLE ⟨neither oratory, anticlericalism, nor last-minute attempts to capitalize on the threat of "Fascism" . . . could ~ the Italian voter —*Newsweek*⟩ ⟨supplies are coming in very irregularly and ~ the trade —*London Daily News*⟩ **3** : to split or break apart : CRACK, DISMEMBER ⟨smashed . . . where they threatened to ~ the entire Allied line —Milton Lehman⟩

un·hinged \ˌən¦hinjd\ *adj* [in sense 1, fr. past part. of *unhinge*; in sense 2, fr. ¹*un-* + *hinged*, past part. of *hinge*] **1 a** : no longer joined by or as if by a hinge **b** : DERANGED, DISORGANIZED ⟨a belief . . . that the United Nations could keep the world from becoming *unhinged* in another war —Norman Cousins⟩ **2** *of a stamp* : never mounted or hinged

un·hinge·ment \ˌ=ˈ=mənt\ *n* -s [*unhinge* + *-ment*] : an act or instance of unhinging or state of being unhinged

un·hired \ˌən+\ *adj* [¹*un-* + *hired*, past part. of *hire*] : not hired

un·historical *also* **un·historic** \"+\ *adj* : not historical — **un·historically** \"+\ *adv*

un·hit \"+\ *adj* [¹*un-* + *hit*, past part. of *hit*] : not hit ⟨the bear lumbered off, ~, up the canyon to safety —*Time*⟩

un·hitch \"+\ *vt* [²*un-* + *hitch*] : to free from or as if from being hitched : UNFASTEN

un·hive \"+\ *vt* [²*un-* + *hive*] : to drive from or as if from a hive

un·holily \ˌən+\ *adv* : in an unholy manner

un·holiness \"+\ *n* : the quality or state of being unholy

un·hollowed \"+\ *adj* [¹*un-* + *hollowed*, past part. of *hollow*] : not hollowed

un·holpen \"+\ *adj* [ME, fr. ¹*un-* + *holpen*] *archaic* : UNHELPED

¹**un·holy** \"+\ *adj* [ME, fr. OE *unhālig*, fr. ¹*un-* + *hālig* holy — more at HOLY] **1** : irreligious or showing disregard for what is holy : PROFANE, WICKED ⟨souls ~ and unclean —John Wesley⟩ ⟨may excommunicate the heretical as well as the ~ —A.C. McGiffert⟩ **2 a** : violating accepted civil or social standards : CORRUPT, IMMORAL ⟨an ~ reputation for branding everything they could, regardless of ownership —*Amer. Guide Series: Ariz.*⟩ **b** : deserving of censure : DAMNING, REPREHENSIBLE ⟨add condescension to bad manners in a singularly ~ combination —*Geog. Jour.*⟩ ⟨an ~ alliance between public utility companies⟩ **3 a** : of a sinister character : FIENDISH, MALICIOUS ⟨delirium of grandeur is more dangerous still if the man is ready to live and to die . . . for his ~ dream —A.L.Guérard⟩ ⟨takes ~ joy . . . in telling off brutally his family of three —Parker Tyler⟩ **b** : shockingly big or barbarous : GOD-AWFUL, RAUCOUS ⟨rarely . . . has society been in such an ~ mess —*Nation*⟩ ⟨an ~ clatter as of ash and refuse cans being dragged across sidewalks —Charles Breasted⟩ ⟨next morning, at an ~ hour, I heard . . . an air-raid siren —*Sydney (Australia) Bull.*⟩

²**unholy** \"\ *n* : an impious or disreputable person

un·home \ˌən+\ *vt* [²*un-* + *home*] : to make homeless

un·homelike \"+\ *adj* : not homelike

un·homeliness \"+\ *n* [*unhomely* + *-ness*] : lack of intimacy or warmth : ALOOFNESS, FORMALITY

un·homely \"+\ *adj* : UNINVITING

un·homogeneity \"+\ *n* [*unhomogeneous* + *-ity*] : the quality or state of being inhomogeneous

un·homogeneous \"+\ *adj* : INHOMOGENEOUS

un·honest \"+\ *adj* [ME, fr. ¹*un-* + *honest*] : DISHONEST — **un·honestly** \"+\ *adv*

un·honesty \"+\ *n* [ME *unhoneste*, fr. ¹*un-* + *honeste* honesty] *archaic* : DISHONESTY

un·honored \"+\ *adj* : not honored

un·hood \"+\ *vt* [²*un-* + *hood*] : to remove a hood or covering from : EXPOSE

un·hooded \"+\ *adj* [in sense 1, fr. past part. of *unhood*; in sense 2, fr. ¹*un-* + *hooded*] **1** : divested of a hood **2** : not having a hood

un·hoodwinked \ˌən+\ *adj* [¹*un-* + *hoodwinked*, past part. of *hoodwink*] : not deceived

un·hook \"+\ *vt* [²*un-* + *hook*] **1** : to remove from a hook ⟨~*ing* a mug from the rack —Richard Llewellyn⟩ **2** : to unfasten by disengaging a hook ⟨~*ed* the collar of his uniform —*Irish Digest*⟩

un·hooked \"+\ *adj* [in sense 1, fr. ¹*un-* + *hooked*; in sense 2, fr. past part. of *unhook*] **1** : not hooked **2** : having the hooks unfastened

un·hoped \ˌən+\ *adj* [ME, fr. ¹*un-* + *hoped*, past part. of *hopen* to hope] *archaic* : UNHOPED-FOR

un·hoped-for \ˌ=ˈ=ˌ=\ *adj* [¹*un-* + *hoped-for*, past part. form of the phrase *hope for*, fr. *hope* + *for*] : not anticipated : UNEXPECTED ⟨an *unhoped-for* piece of luck⟩

un·hopeful \ˌən+\ *adj* [ME, fr. ¹*un-* + *hope*, n. + *-ful*] : not hopeful — **un·hopefully** \"+\ *adv*

un·hoping \"+\ *adj* [¹*un-* + *hoping*, pres. part. of *hope*] : DESPAIRING, HOPELESS

un·hopped \"+\ *adj* : made without hops ⟨~ beer worts⟩

un·horned \"+\ *adj* : not horned

un·horse \"+\ *vt* [ME *unhorsen*, fr. ²*un-* + *horsen* to horse] : to dislodge from or as if from a horse : put out of action : OVERTHROW, UNSEAT ⟨~ a rider⟩ ⟨Republicans are in a scramble . . . to try to ~ the state's Democratic senator —*N.Y. Times*⟩ ⟨reports of the maltreatment of the sick and wounded nearly *unhorsed* the . . . general staff —James Dugan⟩

unhorsing *n* -s [fr. gerund of *unhorse*] : an act or instance of overthrowing ⟨the definitive ~ of the militarists —*Commonweal*⟩

un·hospitable \ˌən+\ *adj* : INHOSPITABLE — **un·hospitably** \"+\ *adv*

un·hostile \"+\ *adj* : not hostile : AMICABLE, BENIGN

un·house \ˌən¦haüz\ *vt* [ME *unhousen*, fr. ²*un-* + *housen* to house] : to eject from or deprive of a protective shelter ⟨thousands of refugees are still *unhoused*⟩ ⟨*unhoused* his bleating flock —Phineas Fletcher⟩

un·housed \-zd\ *adj* [¹*un-* + *housed*, past part. of *house*] : not housed

un·houseled \ˌən+\ *adj* [¹*un-* + *houseled*, past part. of *housel*] *archaic* : not having received the sacrament ⟨cut off even in the blossoms of my sin, ~, disappointed —Shak.⟩

un·hulled \"+\ *adj* [in sense 1, fr. ¹*un-* + *hull*, n. + *-ed*; in sense 2, fr. ¹*un-* + *hulled*, past part. of *hull*] **1** : not having a hull **2** : not having been hulled

un·human \"+\ *adj* : INHUMAN — **un·humanly** \"+\ *adv*

un·humanize \"+\ *vt* [²*un-* + *humanize*] : DEHUMANIZE

un·humble \"+\ *adj* : not humble

un·humbled \"+\ *adj* [¹*un-* + *humbled*, past part. of *humble*] : not humbled

un·humorous \"+\ *adj* : not funny or jocular : SERIOUS, SOBER — **un·humorously** \"+\ *adv*

un·hung \ˌən+\ *adj* [¹*un-* + *hung*, past part. of *hang*] : not hung; *esp* : not executed by hanging

un·hunted \"+\ *adj* : not hunted

un·hurried \"+\ *adj* : not hurried : LEISURELY — **un·hurriedly** \"+\ *adv*

un·hurriedness \"+\ *n* : the quality or state of being unhurried : CALMNESS, PLACIDITY

un·hurt \"+\ *adj* [ME, fr. ¹*un-* + *hurt*] : not hurt or damaged : INTACT, UNINJURED

un·hurtful \"+\ *adj* [¹*un-* + *hurtful*] *archaic* : HARMLESS

un·hurting \"\ *adj* [¹*un-* + *hurting*] : not causing hurt : BENIGN, GENTLE ⟨smiled . . . in her ~ way —N.H.Matson⟩

un·hus·band·ed \ˌən¦həzbəndəd\ *adj* [in sense 1, fr. ¹*un-* + *husbanded*, past part. of *husband*; in sense 2, fr. ¹*un-* + *husband*, n. + *-ed*] **1** : not tilled : UNCULTIVATED ⟨~ land⟩ **2** : not having a husband ⟨the ~ young lady . . . lives with her married sister —John Gould⟩

un·husk \ˌən+\ *vt* [²*un-* + *husk*] : to strip of or as if of a husk : EXPOSE, SHUCK

un·husked \ˌən¦həskt\ *adj* [in sense 1, fr. past part. of *unhusk*; in sense 2, fr. ¹*un-* + *husked*] **1** *obs* : stripped of the husk **2** : still in the husk : not shucked

un·hygienic \ˌən+\ *adj* : not healthful or sanitary — **un·hygienically** \"+\ *adv*

un·hymned \"+\ *adj* [¹*un-* + *hymned*, past part. of *hymn*] : not hymned : UNSUNG

un·hyphenated \"+\ *adj* : not hyphenated

un·hysterical \"+\ *adj* : not hysterical — **un·hysterically** \"+\ *adv*

uni- *prefix* [ME, fr. MF, fr. L, fr. *unus* — more at ONE] : one : single ⟨*uni*axial⟩ ⟨*uni*cellular⟩ ⟨*uni*lateral⟩

uni·algal \ˌyünē+\ *adj* [*uni-* + *algal*] : of, relating to, or derived from a single algal individual or cell ⟨a ~ culture⟩

uni·ate \ˈyünēˌāt, -ēˌat *also* -ēˌāt\ *or* **uni·at** \-ēˌat, -ēət\ *n* -s *usu cap* [Russ *uniyat*, fr. Pol *uniat*, fr. *unja* union (of the Greek and Roman Catholic churches), fr. LL *unio* — more at UNION] : a Christian of an Eastern rite not belonging to the Latin patriarchate but in union with and submitting to the authority of the Roman papacy : one who belongs to an ecclesiastical body that accepts Roman Catholic doctrines in matters of faith but utilizes different forms of liturgy and discipline and is directly governed by a patriarch of its own

uni·at·ism \-əˌtizəm\ *n* -s *often cap* : the system of faith, practice, and ecclesiastical government of the Uniates or Uniate bodies

uni·axial \ˌyünē+\ *adj* [*uni-* + *axial*] **1** : having but one axis: as **a** : having but one optic axis or line of no double refraction ⟨~ crystals of calcite or quartz⟩ **b** : MONAXIAL **2** : of, relating to, or affecting but one axis ⟨~ stress⟩ — **uni·axially** \"+\ *adv*

uni·bi·va·lent \ˌyünə+, ˌyünə¦bīvələnt\ *adj* [*uni-* + *bivalent*] : of, relating to, or being an electrolyte (as sodium carbonate Na_2CO_3) that dissociates into two univalent ions and one bivalent ion

unica *pl of* UNICUM

uni·cameral \ˌyünə+\ *adj* [*uni-* + *camera* + *-al*] : having a single chamber: as **a** : consisting of a single legislative chamber ⟨a ~ government⟩ **b** : UNILOCULAR ⟨a ~ fruiting body of a fungus⟩ — **uni·camerally** \"+\ *adv*

uni·cameralism \"+\ *n* : use or advocacy of a unicameral system in government

uni·capsula \ˌyünə+\ *n*, *cap* [NL, fr. *uni-* + *capsula*] : a genus of myxosporidian parasites — see WORMY HALIBUT

un·iced \ˌən+\ *adj* : not containing or chilled with ice : not specially cooled

uni·cell \ˈyünəˌsel\ *n* [*uni-* + *cell*] : a unicellular organism

¹**uni·cellular** \ˌyünə+\ *adj* [*uni-* + *cellular*] : having or consisting of a single cell — **uni·cellularity** \"+\ *n*

²**unicellular** \"\ *n* -s : a unicellular organism

unicellular animal *n* : PROTOZOAN

uni·cen·tric \ˌyünə¦sen·trik, -rēk\ *adj* [*uni-* + *-centric*] : having a single center (as of origin or dispersal) ⟨a ~ genus of plants⟩

uni·cist \ˈyünəsəst\ *n* -s [*unicity* + *-ist*] : an advocate or adherent of a theory of unicity

uni·ci·ty \yüˈnisədē, -sətē, -i\ *n* -ES [L *unicus* sole, single, unique + E *-ity* — more at UNIQUE] : the quality or state of being unique of its kind : ONENESS ⟨the question of the ~ of the distemper virus⟩ ⟨the ~ of each angelic form within its species —W.N.Clarke⟩

uni·color \ˌyünə+\ *or* **uni·colored** \"+\ *adj* [*uni-* + *color* or *colored*] : of a uniform color

uni·col·or·ous \ˌ=ˈ=kələrəs\ *adj* [*uni-* + *color* + *-ous*] : of one color throughout ⟨a ~ insect⟩

uni·consonantal \ˌyünə+\ *also* **uni·consonantic** \"+\ *adj* [*uni-* + *consonantal* or *consonantic*] : of or containing one consonant

uni·constant \"+\ *adj* [*uni-* + *constant*] : having, characterized by, or based on one constant ⟨a ~ theory of isotropy⟩

¹**uni·corn** \ˈyünəˌkȯrn\ *n* -s [ME *unicorne*, fr. OF, fr. LL *unicornis* (trans. of Gk *monokeros*), fr. L, adj., having one horn, fr. *uni-* + *cornu* horn — more at HORN] **1 a** (1) : a fabulous animal possibly based on faulty old descriptions of the rhinoceros and generally depicted (as in heraldry) with the body and head of a horse, the hind legs of a stag, the tail of a lion, and in the middle of the forehead a single long straight horn held to be a sovereign remedy against poisoning (2) : a representation of a unicorn **b** (1) *obs* : the one-horned rhinoceros (2) *or* **unicorn whale** : NARWHAL (3) : a normally bicorn mammal (as an ox) having the horn buds surgically altered to produce a single median horn **2** : a Scottish gold coin of the 15th and 16th centuries weighing 59 grains and having the figure of a unicorn on the obverse **3** *or* **unicorn horn** : material reputed to be the horn of the fabulous unicorn and formerly used for ornament, as an antidote, or as a talisman **4** : a team of three horses harnessed with one as leader to a pair; *also* : an equipage with such a team **5** *obs* : HOWITZER **6** : any of several plants (as a colicroot or blazing star) felt to resemble unicorn horn (as in form of root or reputed medical worth)

unicorn 1a(1)

²**unicorn** \"\ *adj* [L *unicornis*] : having a single horn or hornlike process ⟨a ~ uterus⟩

unicorn antelope *n* : TAKIN

unicorn beetle *n* : any of various large beetles (as some scarabaeids) having a hornlike prominence on the head or prothorax

unicorn bird *n* : HORNED SCREAMER

unicorn caterpillar *n* : a caterpillar that is the larva of a unicorn moth

unicorn fish *n* **1** : NARWHAL **2 a** : any of several surgeonfishes (genus *Teuthis*) of the Pacific ocean having a long bony hornlike projection extending forward from the skull above the eye **b** : any of various filefishes having a long dorsal spine

unicorn moth *n* : a moth (*Schizura unicornis*) of the family Notodontidae whose caterpillar has a horn on its back

unicorn plant *n* : a No. American annual herb (*Martynia louisianica*) having large whitish or yellowish flowers mottled with purple or yellow within and a capsule with a long curving beak

unicorn-plant family *n* : MARTYNIACEAE

unicorn root *n* **1** : COLICROOT 1 **2** : GRUBROOT **3** : SWAMP PINK 3

unicorn shell *n* : any of several marine snails of the division Rachiglossa (as members of the genus *Latirus*) having a prominent spine on the lip of the shell

unicorn's horn *n* **1** : UNICORN 3 **2** : UNICORN ROOT

uni·cum \ˈyünəkəm, -nēk-\ *n*, *pl* **uni·ca** \-kə\ [L, fr. neut. of *unicus* sole, single, unique — more at UNIQUE] : a thing unique in its kind; *esp* : a sole existing exemplar (as of a writing)

uni·cur·sal \ˌyünə¦kərsəl\ *adj* [*uni-* + L *cursus* course + E *-al* — more at COURSE] *of an irreducible curve* : having coordinates expressible rationally through a single parameter — opposed to *bicursal*

uni·cuspid \ˌyünə+\ *also* **uni·cuspidate** \"+\ *adj* [*uni-* + *cuspid* or *cuspidate*] : having a single cusp ⟨canines and other ~ teeth⟩

uni·cy·cle \ˈyünəˌsīkəl\ *n* [*uni-* + *-cycle* (as in *tricycle*)] : any of various vehicles that have a single wheel, are used for personal transport, exercise, or haulage, and are propelled usu. by pedals or applied draft — **uni·cy·clist** \-k(ə)ləst\ *n*

unicycle

un·ideaed \ˌən+\ *adj* [¹*un-* + *idea* + *-ed*] : lacking in originality of thought : deficient in ideas

un·ideal \"+\ *adj* : lacking ideals or ideal qualities : deficient in idealism

un·identifiable \"+\ *adj* : impossible to identify : so defective, damaged, or altered as to defy recognition

un·identified \"+\ *adj* [¹*un-* + *identified*, past part. of *identify*] : not identified though not necessarily unidentifiable

uni·dextral \ˌyünə+\ *adj* [*uni-* + *dextral*] : using one hand preferentially : exhibiting handedness either right or left — **uni·dextrality** \"+\ *n*

uni·dimensional \"+\ *adj* [*uni-* + *dimensional*] **1** : having a single dimension that is usu. construed as length **2** : having or dealing with a single aspect ⟨a prose statement of fact is ~, its value being measured wholly in terms of its truth —Mary Sheehan⟩ — **uni·dimensionality** \"+\ *n*

un·idiomatic \ˌən+\ *adj* : not conforming to established or accepted idiom — **un·idiomatically** \"+\ *adv*

uni·direct \ˌyünə+\ *vt* [back-formation fr. *unidirectional*] : to cause to go in a single direction : RECTIFY

uni·directional \"+\ *adj* [*uni-* + *directional*] : having, involving, moving, or responsive (as to sound) in a single direction : not subject to change or reversal of direction ⟨a ~ antenna⟩ ⟨a ~ approach to a problem⟩

unidirectional current *n* : DIRECT CURRENT

uni·directivity \"+\ *n* [*uni-* + *directivity*] : a property (as of a microphone, loudspeaker, or antenna) of operating more effectively in one direction than another

uni·face \"+\ *also* **uni·faced** \"+\ *adj* [*uni-* + *face*, n. or *faced*] : having a design on only one side ⟨~ coin⟩ ⟨~ medal⟩ ⟨~ bank note⟩

uni·facial \ˌyünə+\ *adj* [*uni-* + *facial*] : having but one principal or in some way specialized surface ⟨~ corals in which all the polyps are on one surface⟩ ⟨a primitive ~ flint tool flaked only on one face⟩ — **uni·facially** \"+\ *adv*

uni·factorial \"+\ *adj* [*uni-* + *factorial*] : relating to or controlled by a single gene

uni·fi·able \ˈyünəˌfīəbəl\ *adj* [*unify* + *-able*] : capable of being unified

unif·ic \yüˈnifik\ *adj* [*uni-* + *-fic*] : tending to produce unity

uni·fi·ca·tion \ˌyünəfəˈkāshən\ *n* -s [fr. *unify*, after such pairs as E *identify: identification*] **1** : the act, process, or result of unifying : state of being unified **2** : the use of the same set of pipes for securing on the same organ manual two or more stops at different pitches

uni·fi·ca·tion·ist \-sh(ə)nəst\ *n* -s : an advocate or adherent of a scheme of unification and esp. one of political unification (as of separate or divided states)

unified *past of* UNIFY

unified command *n* : an armed force (as a task force containing army, navy, and air force units) of two or more services operating under a single commander

unified field theory *n* : a mathematical theory of fields developed by Einstein and involving Maxwell's electromagnetic theory and Einstein's mathematical theory of gravitation as special cases

uni·fi·er \ˈyünəˌfī(ə)r, -fīə\ *n* -s : one that unifies

unifies *pres 3d sing of* UNIFY

uni·filar \ˌyünə+\ *adj* [*uni-* + *filar*] : having or involving use of only one thread, wire, or fiber

uni·flagellate \"+\ *adj* [*uni-* + *flagellate*] : having a single flagellum

uni·flo·rous \ˌyünə¦flōrəs\ *also* **uni·floral** \"+\ *adj* [*uni-* + *-florous* or *floral*] : bearing a solitary flower

uni·flow *also* **una·flow** \ˌyünə+\ *adj* [*uni-* or *una-* (alter. of *uni-*) + *flow*, n.] : flowing in one direction without reversal ⟨~ traffic⟩

uniflow engine *n* : an engine in which the steam or gas enters through admission valves at the ends of the cylinder and escapes through exhaust ports uncovered by the piston as it nears the end of its stroke

uni·foliate \ˌyünə+\ *also* **uni·foliar** \"+\ *adj* [*uni-* + *foliate* or *foliar*] **1** : having only one leaf **2** : UNIFOLIOLATE

un·i·foliolate \"+\ *adj* [*uni-* + *foliolate*] *of a leaf* : compound but having only a single leaflet and distinguishable from a simple leaf by the basal joint

¹**uni·form** \ˈyünəˌfȯrm\ *adj*, *sometimes* -ER/-EST [MF *uniforme*, fr. L *uniformis*, fr. *uni-* + *-formis* -form] **1** : marked by lack of variation, diversity, change in form, manner, worth, or degree : showing a single form, degree, or character in all occurrences or manifestations ⟨the Shasta dam . . . will keep the flow of the Sacramento relatively ~ throughout the year —*Amer. Guide Series: Calif.*⟩ ⟨Great Russian itself has dialects, though generally speaking for so widespread a language it is remarkably ~ —W.J.Entwistle & W.A.Morison⟩ **2** : marked by complete conformity to a rule or pattern or by similarity in salient detail or practice : CONSONANT, ALIKE ⟨how far churches are bound to be ~ in their ceremonies —Richard Hooker⟩ **3** : marked by unvaried and changeless appearance (as of surface, color, or pattern) ⟨so many ~ red hills —Willa Cather⟩ **4** : consistent in conduct, character, or effect : lacking in variation, deviation, or unequal or dissimilar operation ⟨the constitution has conferred on Congress the right to establish a ~ rule of naturalization —R.B.Taney⟩ **syn** see LIKE, STEADY

²**uniform** \"\ *vt* -ED/-ING/-S **1** : to bring into uniformity **2** : to clothe with a uniform ⟨~ soldiers in khaki⟩

³**uniform** \"\ *n* -s [F *uniforme*, fr. *uniforme*, adj.] **1** : dress of a distinctive design or fashion adopted by or prescribed for members of a particular group (as an armed service, an order, or a social or work group) and serving as a means of identification ⟨the blue ~ of the navy⟩ ⟨a school ~⟩ ⟨the gang's ~ of blue jeans and red caps⟩ **2** : a garment or outfit of a widely copied style or prescribed design ⟨her usual ~ of white gloves with a tailored suit⟩ — **out of uniform** : wearing a military uniform that is not according to regulations

⁴**uniform** \"\ *usu cap* — a communications code word for the letter *u*

uni·for·mal \ˌ=ˈ=fȯrməl, -fō(ə)m-\ *adj* [L *uniformis* + E *-al*] *archaic* : UNIFORM

uniform flow *n* : flow of a fluid in which each particle moves along its line of flow with constant speed and in which the cross section of each stream tube remains unchanged — compare STEADY FLOW

uni·form·ist \ˈ=ˌ=ˌfȯrməst\ *n* -s : an advocate of uniformity

¹**uni·form·i·tar·i·an** \ˌyünəˌfȯrməˈterēən, -ta(a)r-, -tār-\ *n* -s [*uniformity* + *-arian*] : a believer in uniformitarianism : an advocate of uniformity

²**uniformitarian** \"\ *adj* : of, relating to, or adhering to a doctrine of uniformitarianism

uni·form·i·tar·i·an·ism \-əˌnizəm\ *n* -s **1** : a geological doctrine that existing processes acting in the same manner and with essentially the same intensity as at present are sufficient to account for all geological changes — compare CATASTROPHISM **2** : a philosophic doctrine that the world is subject to law — contrasted with *tychism*

uni·form·i·ty \ˌ══'fȯ(r)məd·ē, -ətē, -i\ *n* -ES [ME *uniformite*, fr. MF *uniformité*, fr. LL *uniformitat-*, *uniformitas*, fr. L *uniformis* uniform + *-itat-*, *-itas* -ity — more at UNIFORM] **1 :** the quality or state or an instance of being uniform (as by conformance to one pattern or adherence to one standard) ⟨the insistence on ~ in religion⟩ ⟨a rule of ~ that all duties, imposts, and excises shall be uniform throughout the U.S.⟩ **2 :** the condition of having the constituent elements lacking in individuality or variability or so arranged as to give a uniform effect to the whole to which they belong; *often* **:** SAMENESS, MONOTONY

uniformity of nature : a doctrine or principle of the invariability or regularity of nature; *specif* **:** one that holds identical antecedent states or causes to be uniformly followed by identical effects — called also *principle of the uniformity of nature*

uni·form·ize \'══ˌfȯrˌmīz\ *vt* -ED/-ING/-S [F *uniformiser*, fr. *uniforme* uniform + *-iser* -ize] **:** to make uniform

uni·form·less \-mləs\ *adj* **:** having no uniform **:** not wearing a uniform

uni·form·ly \ˌ══'══lē\ *adv* **:** in a uniform manner **:** so as to be uniform

uni·form·ness *n* -ES **:** the quality or state of being uniform

uniform system *n* **:** a system of photographic diaphragm or stop marking in which the numbers are proportional to the intensities of the light permitted to pass and hence to the times required for exposure

uni·fy \'yünəˌfī\ *vb* -ED/-ING/-ES [LL *unificare*, fr. L *uni-* + *-ficare* -fy] *vt* **1 a :** to cause to be one **:** make into a coherent group or whole **:** give unity to **:** HARMONIZE ⟨war *unifies* a people torn by rivalries⟩ ⟨a *unified* design⟩ ⟨would also be technically possible to ~ the world and abolish war —Bertrand Russell⟩ **b :** to issue (as bonds) in order to combine several issues into one ⟨a *unified* bond⟩ **2 :** to secure (a stop in a pipe organ) by unification ~ *vi* **:** to become one **:** CONSOLIDATE

syn INTEGRATE, CONSOLIDATE, COMPACT, CONCENTRATE agree with UNIFY in meaning to gather or combine parts or elements so as to form a close mass or coherent structure. UNIFY, the most general term, emphasizes unity in action or harmony in effect; the elements involved may be similar or diverse; they may be physically close or far apart; things may be *unified* deliberately or as a result of evolution, but rarely by imposition from without ⟨making only slow progress in *unifying* the economy of the world —W.S.Thompson⟩ ⟨frequently a minority group is *unified* by persecution⟩ ⟨the room, despite its clutter of furniture, was *unified* by the use of blue in the drapes and the rug⟩ INTEGRATE implies a close and harmonious relation both between individual parts and between each part and the whole and has favorable connotation; more than any of the other terms here discussed, it implies a beneficial effect for the components as well as for the whole ⟨an *integrated* personality⟩ ⟨a well-adjusted child is one that is *integrated* into his group⟩ ⟨narrative and background are *integrated* in their proper proportions —John Barkham⟩ ⟨its culture is more stable and better *integrated* —A.L.Kroeber⟩ CONSOLIDATE, usu. used of things that are alike or homogeneous, orig. points to a drawing together or thickening; likewise, in its transferred uses, it implies strengthening through solidarity ⟨organize state leagues for political action in order to *consolidate* the labor vote —G.S.Watkins⟩ ⟨two marriages with the Dutch Vandergraves had *consolidated* these qualities of thrift and handsome living —Edith Wharton⟩; when used of organizations, corporations, or the like, *consolidate* suggests close union not only in purpose or effect, but in administration ⟨several agencies were *consolidated* in one department⟩ ⟨the two companies were *consolidated* under one management⟩ COMPACT, when used of physical objects, means to stick or cake together, reducing the size of the whole by reducing the space between parts ⟨rain *compacts* the soil⟩ ⟨dry, powdered snow is better for skiing than wet snow which is soon *compacted*⟩ COMPACT in its transferred uses means to shape (a whole) from various parts, joined closely enough to hold together, without any implication as to the balance or harmony of the whole ⟨the loosely *compacted* hosts of thegns and peasants —F.M.Stenton⟩ COMPACT may, however, imply density, leaving no room for any but the parts mentioned ⟨it is based on solid facts, nay, is *compacted* of solid facts from the first sentence to the last —*Times Lit. Supp.*⟩ CONCENTRATE usu. carries the implication of bringing together things or parts that were scattered or diffused and of massing them around a point or center; the emphasis is not so much on unity or integrity of a whole as on accumulation of like elements ⟨people of Scandinavian and German origin are *concentrated* in the Middle West⟩ ⟨the control of the major part of the country's wealth is *concentrated* in a few hands⟩; figuratively, CONCENTRATE means to fix one's mental powers on one thing, so that all distracting thoughts or objects are eliminated ⟨the ability to *concentrate* on the task at hand is essential to all achievement⟩; a similar implication of eliminating that which weakens, dilutes, or adulterates is found in scientific and technical use ⟨evaporated milk is more *concentrated* than fresh milk⟩ ⟨a miner *concentrates* ore by separating the base from the precious materials⟩

uni·grav·i·da \ˌyünə'gravədə\ *n* [NL, fr. *uni-* + L *gravida*] **:** a woman in her first pregnancy

uni·ju·gate \yü'nijəˌgāt, ˈyünəˈjüˌ, ǀgət\ *adj* [*uni-* + *jugate*] **:** having one pair of leaflets — used of a pinnate leaf

uni·lacunar \ˌyünə+\ *adj* [*uni-* + *lacunar*] **:** having a single leaf gap — compare MULTILACUNAR, TRILACUNAR

uni·lateral \"+\ *adj* [*uni-* + *lateral*] **1 a :** of, relating to, or involving one side **:** done, made, undertaken, or shared by one of two or more persons or parties **:** dealing with or affecting one side of a subject **:** ONE-SIDED ⟨urged a ~ halting of nuclear bomb tests —T.A.Bailey⟩ **b :** constituting or relating to a contract or engagement by which an express obligation to do or forbear is imposed on but one party (as in a deed poll) ⟨in a ~ simple contract, a promise is exchanged for an act or forbearance⟩ **2 a :** produced or arranged on or directed toward one side **:** having dependent parts so oriented ⟨a ~ raceme⟩ ⟨~ flowers⟩ **b :** affecting or occurring in but one side of the body or a body part or organ **c :** pronounced with the oral passage open on one side of the tongue only — compare LATERAL 4 **3 :** tracing descent through either the maternal or paternal line only ⟨a ~ clan⟩ — contrasted with *bilateral* **4 :** having only one side; *specif* **:** being a surface on which a continuous path may be drawn from any point to any other point even to the exactly opposite point through the surface without piercing the surface or crossing its border — compare MÖBIUS BAND **5** *of a machined part* **:** having for a nominal diameter the smallest or largest size that the specified tolerances permit — **uni·laterally** \"+\ *adv*

unilateral compound pitting *n* **:** pitting in plant cell walls in which one large pit occurs opposite two or more small pits in an adjacent cell

uni·lateralism \ˌyünə+\ *n* -S **:** the state of being unilateral

uni·lateralist \"+\ *adj* **:** UNILATERAL

uni·laterality \"+\ *n* **:** UNILATERALISM

unilateral system *n* **:** a system of tolerances and allowances as applied to cylindrical mating surfaces having for its basis unilateral holes and involving measurement of the high and low limits of tolerance in one direction from the basic size

uni·lineal \ˌyünə+\ *adj* [*uni-* + *lineal*] **:** UNILATERAL 3

uni·linear \"+\ *adj* [*uni-* + *linear*] **:** progressing or unfolding in a linear manner **:** developing in or involving a series of stages usu. from the primitive to the more advanced ⟨~ social evolution⟩ **:** involving such a trend ⟨a ~ cultural sequence⟩

unilinear evolution *n* **:** EVOLUTION 6a

uni·lingual \ˌyünə+\ *adj* [*uni-* + *lingual*] **:** composed in or using one language only

uni·literal \"+\ *adj* [*uni-* + *literal*] **:** consisting of or involving one letter only

un·illuminated \ˌən+\ *adj* [ˡ*un-* + *illuminated*, past part. of *illuminate*] **1 :** deficient in mental or spiritual enlightenment **2 :** not lighted **:** LIGHTLESS, DARK ⟨the ~ side of Mars —R.S. Richardson⟩

un·illuminating \"+\ *adj* **:** not providing light; *esp* **:** failing to enlighten or clarify ⟨an ~ report⟩ — **un·illuminatingly** \"+\ *adv*

un·illusioned \"+\ *adj* **:** free from illusion — compare DISILLUSION

uni·locular \ˌyünə+\ *adj* [*uni-* + *locular*] **:** containing a single cavity

un·imaginable \ˌən+\ *adj* **:** not imaginable or comprehensible usu. because of the extreme degree at which some cogent factor exists ⟨~ privations⟩ ⟨intergalactic distances that are ~ to the lay mind⟩ — **un·imaginableness** \"+\ *n* — **un·imaginably** \"+\ *adv*

un·imaginative \"+\ *adj* **:** not imaginative: as **a :** deficient in creative or imaginative quality **:** PROSAIC ⟨~ development of a musical theme⟩ **b :** dealing or adapted to deal only with concrete facts **:** PRACTICAL ⟨the ~ calculating machine⟩ — **un·imaginatively** \"+\ *adv* — **un·imaginativeness** \"+\ *n*

un·imagined \"+\ *adj* [ˡ*un-* + *imagined*, past part. of *imagine*] **:** not imagined **:** not yet thought of **:** UNIMAGINABLE

un·imitable \ˌən+\ *adj* [alter. (influenced by ˡ*un-*) of *inimitable*] *archaic* **:** INIMITABLE

uni·manual \ˌyünə+\ *adj* [*uni-* + *manual*] **:** of or relating to one hand **:** executed with one hand

uni·modal \ˌyünə+\ *adj* [*uni-* + *modal*] **:** having a single mode ⟨a ~ statistical distribution⟩ — **uni·modality** \"+\ *n*

uni·molecular \"+\ *adj* [*uni-* + *molecular*] **:** relating to or involving a single molecule or single molecular species **:** MONOMOLECULAR ⟨~ reactions⟩

un·impaired \ˌən+\ *adj* [ˡ*un-* + *impaired*, past part. of *impair*] **:** not damaged or made less ⟨an argument ~ by logic⟩ ⟨his speech remained ~⟩ ⟨emerged from the trial with ~ prestige⟩

un·impassioned \"+\ *adj* **:** not impassioned; *esp* **:** marked by calm reasonableness and free from purely emotional appeal ⟨an ~ discussion of the problem⟩ **syn** see SOBER

un·impassionedly \"+\ *adv* **:** in an unimpassioned manner

un·im·peach·abil·i·ty \ˌənəmˌpēchə'bilǝd·ē\ *n* **:** the quality or state of being unimpeachable

un·impeachable \ˌən+\ *adj* **:** not impeachable **:** not to be called in question **:** exempt from liability to accusation **:** IRREPROACHABLE, BLAMELESS ⟨an ~ reputation⟩ ⟨information from an ~ source⟩ ⟨an easy and ~ literary style⟩ — **un·im·peach·able·ness** \-əbəlnəs\ *n* -ES — **un·im·peach·ably** \-əblē\ *adv*

un·impeached \"+\ *adj* [ˡ*un-* + *impeached*, past part. of *impeach*] **:** not impeached; *also* **:** UNIMPEACHABLE

un·impeded \"+\ *adj* [ˡ*un-* + *impeded*, past part. of *impede*] **:** free from anything that impedes or hampers ⟨an ~ sweep of meadows and hills formed a peaceful setting⟩ ⟨~ demands⟩ — **un·im·ped·ed·ly** *adv*

un·implemented \"+\ *adj* [ˡ*un-* + *implemented*, past part. of *implement*] **:** not yet brought into effect ⟨an ~ trade agreement⟩

un·importance \"+\ *n* **:** the quality or state of being unimportant

un·important \"+\ *adj* **:** lacking in importance **:** TRIVIAL, MINOR, UNIMPRESSIVE — **un·importantly** \"+\ *adv*

un·imposing \"+\ *adj* **:** not imposing ⟨~ kindness⟩; *esp* **:** lacking in impressiveness

un·impregnated \ˌən+\ *adj* **:** not impregnated; *esp* **:** not inseminated

un·impressed \"+\ *adj* **:** not impressed: as **a :** bearing no impress **b :** not moved to serious regard

un·impressible \"+\ *adj* **:** not impressible; *esp* **:** lacking in mental sensibility or responsiveness

un·impressionable \"+\ *adj* **:** not sensitive or susceptible to impression **:** INSENSITIVE, UNYIELDING ⟨an ~ mind⟩ ⟨the ~ stones⟩

un·impressive \"+\ *adj* **:** not impressive — **un·impressively** \"+\ *adv* — **un·impressiveness** \"+\ *n*

un·improvable \"+\ *adj* **:** not improvable

ˡunimproved *adj* [ˡ*un-* + *improved*, past part. of *improve* (to reprove)] *obs* **:** not subjected to censure **:** UNREPROVED

²un·improved \ˌən+\ *adj* [ˡ*un-* + *improved*, past part. of *improve* (to better)] **:** not improved: as **a** *of land* **:** not tilled, built upon, or otherwise improved for use **:** retained in the wild or natural state ⟨a farm with 50 acres of improved and 68 acres of ~ land⟩ ⟨~ woodlands⟩ **b :** not used or employed advantageously or for a valuable purpose ⟨opportunity ~ may become a source of repining⟩ **c :** not selectively bred for better quality or productiveness **:** of the kind occurring in nature or as a result of chance interbreeding; *often* **:** being a scrub ⟨~ native cattle yielding little meat and less milk⟩ **d** *of a road* **:** lacking a hardened surface and usu. unsuitable for all year travel

un·incisive \"+\ *adj* **:** deficient in incisiveness

un·incorporate \"+\ *adj* **1 :** UNEMBODIED **2 :** UNINCORPORATED

un·incorporated \"+\ *adj* **:** not incorporated **:** lacking corporate status ⟨an ~ village⟩

un·indifferent \"+\ *adj* **:** not indifferent; *esp* **:** lacking in impartiality **:** PREJUDICED — **un·indifferently** \"+\ *adv*

un·indorsed \"+\ *adj* [ˡ*un-* + *indorsed*, past part. of *indorse*, var. of *endorse*] **:** not indorsed; *esp* **:** lacking a formal written endorsement ⟨an ~ check⟩

un·industrialized \ˌən+\ *adj* [ˡ*un-* + *industrialized*, past part. of *industrialize*] **:** not industrialized

un·industrious \"+\ *adj* **:** not industrious **:** LAZY — **un·industriously** \"+\ *adv*

un·infected \"+\ *adj* **:** free from infection

un·infectious \"+\ *adj* **:** incapable of causing infection

un·inflammable \ˌən+\ *adj* **:** not flammable **:** incapable of combustion — not used technically

un·inflected \"+\ *adj* **:** not inflected ⟨an ~ voice⟩ ⟨~ words⟩

un·influenced \"+\ *adj* [ˡ*un-* + *influenced*, past part. of *influence*] **:** not influenced

un·informed \"+\ *adj* **:** not informed; *esp* **:** lacking in knowledge, awareness, or information ⟨the ~ public⟩

un·inhabitable \"+\ *adj* [ME, fr. ˡ*un-* + *inhabitable*] **:** not inhabitable **:** unfit for habitation

un·inhabited \"+\ *adj* [ˡ*un-* + *inhabited*, past part. of *inhabit*] **:** not inhabited **:** UNOCCUPIED, VOID ⟨a barren nearly ~ country⟩; *esp* **:** not used as a regular dwelling place by human beings ⟨gaping doors of ~ houses⟩

un·in·hab·it·ed·ness *n* -ES **:** the quality or state of being uninhabited

un·inhibited \ˌən+\ *adj* **:** free from inhibition; *often* **:** boisterously informal ⟨a thoroughly ~ party⟩ — **un·in·hib·it·ed·ly** *adv*

ˡun·initiate \"+\ *adj* [ˡ*un-* + *initiate*, adj.] **:** UNINITIATED

²uninitiate \"\ *n* **:** one that is not initiated or that lacks relevant knowledge and experience **:** TYRO

un·initiated \ˌən+\ *adj* [ˡ*un-* + *initiated*, past part. of *initiate*] **:** not initiated **:** deficient in relevant experience **:** INEXPERIENCED, GREEN

un·injured \"+\ *adj* [ˡ*un-* + *injured*, past part. of *injure*] **:** not injured

un·injurious \"+\ *adj* **:** doing no harm **:** incapable of causing injury (as to health) ⟨toys with ~ paints⟩

un·inked \"+\ *adj* [ˡ*un-* + *inked*, past part. of *ink*] **:** not inked **:** free from ink

uni·nodal \ˌyünə+\ *adj* [*uni-* + *nodal*] **:** having a single node

uni·nominal \"+\ *adj* [F, fr. *uni-* + *nominal*, fr. ML *nominalis* — more at NOMINAL] **1 :** based on the principle of having only one member (as of a legislature) selected from each electoral district ⟨a ~ electoral system⟩ ⟨a ~ ballot⟩ — compare LIST SYSTEM, PROPORTIONAL REPRESENTATION, SINGLE-MEMBER DISTRICT **2 a :** having, relating to, or consisting of a single name or identifying term **b :** of, relating to, or constituting a system of nomenclature in which items have single names

un·inquiring \ˌən+\ *adj* **:** not inquiring; *esp* **:** deficient in curiosity

un·inspected \"+\ *adj* [ˡ*un-* + *inspected*, past part. of *inspect*] **:** not inspected

un·inspired \"+\ *adj* **:** not inspired; *esp* **:** deficient in originality of thought and development ⟨~ writing⟩ ⟨a perfunctory and ~ treatment⟩

un·inspiring \"+\ *adj* **:** not inspiring; *often* **:** unattractive and depressing to the spirit

un·instructed \"+\ *adj* **:** not instructed: as **a :** deficient in knowledge or enlightenment **:** IGNORANT ⟨the ~ masses⟩ **b :** not provided with instructions; *esp* **:** not directed how to vote ⟨an ~ delegation⟩

un·insulated \"+\ *adj* [ˡ*un* + *insulated*, past part. of *insulate*] **:** not insulated

un·insurable \"+\ *adj* **:** not insurable; *esp* **:** too risky to be coverable by insurance

un·insured \"+\ *adj* [ˡ*un-* + *insured*, past part. of *insure*] **:** not insured

uninsured plan *n* **:** a usu. funded pension or retirement plan not providing for the guarantee of benefits by an insurance company — compare INSURED PLAN

un·integrated \"+\ *adj* **:** not integrated; *esp* **:** deficient in personality integration

un·integration \"+\ *n* **:** the quality or state of being unintegrated

un·intelligence \"+\ *n* **:** the quality or state of being unintelligent

un·intelligent \"+\ *adj* **:** lacking intelligence **:** DULL, SLOW, STUPID — **un·intelligently** \"+\ *adv*

un·intelligibility \"+\ *n* **1 :** the quality or state of being unintelligible **2 :** something that is unintelligible ⟨depending too much on jargon and other *unintelligibilities* for effect⟩

un·intelligible \"+\ *adj* [ˡ*un-* + *intelligible*] **:** not intelligible **:** difficult to comprehend **:** OBSCURE — **un·intelligibleness** \"+\ *n* — **un·intelligibly** \"+\ *adv*

un·intended \ˌən+\ *adj* **:** not intended; *esp* **:** not deliberate

un·intentional \"+\ *adj* **:** not intentional — **un·intentionally** \"+\ *adv*

un·interest \"+\ *n* **:** a lack of means to stir interest ⟨the drab ~ of the town—T.H.Jones⟩

un·interested \"+\ *adj* [ˡ*un-* + *interested*, past part. of *interest*] **:** not interested: as **a :** having no interest and esp. no property interest in **:** not personally concerned **b :** not having the mind or feelings engaged **:** INATTENTIVE, APATHETIC **syn** see INDIFFERENT

un·interestedly \"+\ *adv* **:** in an uninterested manner

un·interestedness \"+\ *n* **:** the quality or state of being uninterested

un·interesting \"+\ *adj* **:** not attracting interest or attention **:** DULL, BORING ⟨a very ~ account of her trip⟩ — **un·interestingly** \"+\ *adv* — **un·interestingness** \"+\ *n*

un·intermitted \"+\ *adj* [ˡ*un-* + *intermitted*, past part. of *intermit*] **:** not intermitted **:** CONTINUOUS — **un·in·ter·mit·ted·ly** *adv*

un·intermittent \"+\ *adj* **:** not intermittent

un·interpreted \"+\ *adj* [ˡ*un-* + *interpreted*, past part. of *interpret*] **:** not interpreted

un·interrupted \"+\ *adj* **:** not interrupted **:** CONTINUOUS — **un·interruptedly** \"+\ *adv* — **un·interruptedness** \"+\ *n*

un·intimate \"+\ *adj* **:** not intimate; *often* **:** distant or shy in social relationships

uni·nucleate \ˌyünə+\ *also* **uni·nuclear** \"+\ *adj* [*uni-* + *nucleate* or *nuclear*] **:** having a single nucleus

un·inventive \ˌən+\ *adj* **:** not inventive **:** lacking powers of invention — **un·inventively** \"+\ *adv* — **un·inventiveness** \"+\ *n*

un·invested \"+\ *adj* **:** not invested ⟨~ funds⟩

un·invited \"+\ *adj* [ˡ*un-* + *invited*, past part. of *invite*] **:** not invited

un·inviting \"+\ *adj* **:** not inviting; *esp* **:** not appealing to the senses

un·involved \"+\ *adj* **:** not involved

unio \'yünēˌō\ *n* [NL, fr. L, a large pearl — more at ³UNION] **1** *cap* **:** the type genus of the family Unionidae comprising freshwater mussels that have an oblong shell pearly within and covered without by a greenish or blackish epidermis **2** *pl* **unios** \-ōz\ *or* **uni·on·i·des** \ˌ══'änəˌdēz\ **:** any mussel of *Unio* or a related genus — **uni·oid** \'══ˌȯid\ *adj*

un·ocular \ˌyünē+\ *adj* [*uni-* + *ocular*] **:** MONOCULAR

uni·o·la \yü'nīələ, ˌyünē'ōlə\ *n*, *cap* [NL, fr. LL, a kind of plant, prob. fr. *unio* oneness, unity, union] **:** a small genus of showy No. American perennial grasses having ample panicles of 2-edged spikelets of which the lowermost glumes are empty and including several that are valued as sand stabilizers — see SEA OAT

ˡun·ion \'yünyən\ *n* -S [ME, fr. MF, fr. LL *union-*, *unio* oneness, unity, union, fr. L *unus* one + *-ion-*, *-io* -ion — more at ONE] **1 a :** an act or instance of uniting or joining two or more things into one **:** a bringing into intimate and usu. fixed association: as (1) **:** an associating of nonmaterial or abstract items ⟨a ~ of Latin and Nordic elements⟩ ⟨a gracious ~ of elegance and strength⟩ (2) **:** a uniting (as of groups, factions, people) into a coherent and usu. harmonious whole ⟨bring about the ~ of the troubled household⟩ ⟨arranged a ~ of the opposing factions in the church⟩; *esp* **:** the formation of a single political unit from two or more separate and independent units usu. through a surrender to the whole of the principal governmental powers of the parts or by the incorporation of separate entities into an already existing unit ⟨the ~ of Scotland and England took place on May 1, 1707⟩ (3) **:** a consolidation of benefices or churches (4) **:** a uniting in marriage; *also* **:** SEXUAL INTERCOURSE, COPULATION (5) **:** the growing together of severed parts ⟨the ~ of a fractured bone⟩ (6) **:** the conscious identification of one's will with that of divinity which constitutes the third and highest stage in mystical striving and in which the soul is held to have experimental knowledge of God — called also *unitive way* **b :** the state or result of being subjected to union **:** a unified condition **:** COMBINATION, JUNCTION ⟨exhibiting an excellent ~ of beef and milk qualities⟩ **2** *obs* **:** ONENESS **3 :** something that is made one **:** something formed by a combining or coalition of parts or members **:** a consolidated body or group: as **a :** a confederation or league of independent individuals (as nations or persons) for some common end or purpose — see CUSTOMS UNION, LABOR UNION, POSTAL UNION **b :** a political unit constituting an organic whole formed usu. from previously independent units which have surrendered their principal powers to the government of the whole that may be the government of one of the units (as in the case of England and Scotland in 1707) or a newly created government (as of the U. S. in 1789) ⟨we, the people of the United States, in order to form a more perfect ~ —*U. S. Constitution*⟩ — compare CONFEDERATION, FEDERATION, LEAGUE **c :** a 19th century British governmental unit primarily for the administration of poor relief formed by uniting two or more parishes under a board of guardians — called also *poor-law union*; compare RURAL DISTRICT **d** *usu cap* **:** an organization on a college or university campus providing facilities for recreational, social, and cultural activities and sometimes dining facilities; *also* **:** the building in which such an organization is housed **e :** a union cloth **f :** a chemical combination **:** BOND 3e **g :** a plant society esp. when consisting of plants linked by common habit ⟨an herbaceous perennial ~ within the greasewood-shad-scale association⟩ **h :** the point of joining or state of being joined of stock and scion in a plant graft ⟨weak ~s may need to be bridged by mutually compatible intermediates⟩ **4 a :** a device emblematic of the union of two or more sovereignties borne on a national flag typically in the upper inner corner or constituting the whole design of the flag **b :** the upper inner corner of a flag **:** CANTON **5 :** any of various devices for connecting machine or other parts: as **a :** the elastic pipe connecting a tender with the locomotive feed pipe **b :** a coupling for pipes or pipes and fittings designed to facilitate connection or disconnection — compare FLANGE UNION

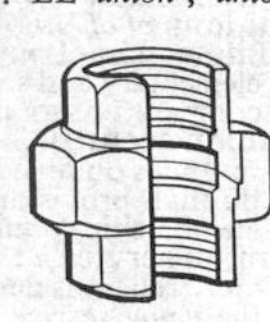

pipe union, partly cut away

²union \"\ *adj* **1 a :** of, relating to, dealing with, or constituting a union (as a labor union) ⟨~ affairs⟩ ⟨a ~ contract⟩ **b** *usu cap* **:** of, relating to, or being the side favoring the federal union in the U. S. Civil War ⟨*Union* troops⟩ ⟨a *Union* cavalry officer⟩ **c** (1) *of yarn* **:** spun from a mixture of two or more fibers (2) *of cloth* **:** having warp and weft threads of different fibers **d** *of a literary language* **:** artificially created by a selection of vocabulary and usages from related dialects or languages with the intent of serving all equally **2 :** formed by union usu. of diverse elements ⟨a ~ ticket in politics⟩

³union \"\ *n* -S [L *union-*, *unio*, fr. *unus* one — more at ONE] *archaic* **:** a large pearl of exceptional quality and worth

⁴union \"\ *usu cap* — a communications code word for the letter *u*

union calendar *n*, *usu cap U* **:** a legislative calendar of the U.S. House of Representatives listing all public bills for raising

revenue or involving a governmental expenditure or government property — compare PRIVATE CALENDAR
union card *n* **1 :** a card certifying personal membership in good standing in a labor union **2 :** something felt to resemble a union card esp. in being a prerequisite to employment or in providing evidence of ingroup status ⟨the Ph.D. . . . a *union card* for the teaching profession —Douglas Bush⟩
union catalog *n* **:** a library catalog combining in one series and usu. alphabetically by authors a number of catalogs or the contents of more than one library
union day *n, usu cap U&D* **:** the anniversary of the founding of the Union of South Africa on May 31, 1910 observed in the Union as a legal holiday
union depot *n* **:** UNION STATION
union district *n* **:** a school district made by uniting two or more elementary or secondary school districts
union down *adv* **:** with the flag reversed so that its union is downward ⟨a flag flown *union down* is a signal of distress at sea⟩
un·ion·eer \ˌyünyəˈni(ə)r, -iə\ *n* -S **:** a member or advocate of a union; *esp* **:** a labor union executive
union elbow *n* **:** an elbow pipe union
¹uni·o·nid \ˈyünēəˌnid\ *adj* [NL *Unionidae*] **:** of or relating to the Unionidae
²unionid \"\ *n* -S **:** a mollusk of the family Unionidae
uni·on·i·dae \ˌ==ˈänəˌdē\ *n pl, cap* [NL, fr. *Union-, Unio,* type genus + *-idae*] **:** a very large family of freshwater mussels (suborder Submytilacea) having a pearly often roughly sculptured shell with a thick epidermis and larvae that pass through a glochidium stage and being represented in nearly all parts of the world but chiefly in No. America where the nacreous shells of many of them are used for button making
unionides *pl of* UNIO
un·ion·ism \ˈyünyəˌnizəm\ *n* -S **:** the principle or policy of forming or adhering to a union **:** an advocacy or movement in favor of union: as **a** *usu cap* **:** adherence to the policy of a firm federal union between the states of the United States esp. during the Civil War period **b :** the principles, theory, or system of combination of workers in the same occupation, trade, or industry ⟨horizontal ~⟩; *also* **:** the labor union movement ⟨the advance of ~⟩ **c :** advocacy of the principles of the British Unionists
un·ion·ist \-nəst\ *n* -S **:** an advocate or promoter of union and esp. of some form of unionism: as **a** *usu cap* **:** one loyal to the federal union of the U. S. during the Civil War **b** *usu cap* **:** a member of a former British political party advocating legislative union between Great Britain and Ireland **c :** an adherent or supporter of the labor union movement; *esp* **:** an active member of a labor union **d :** an advocate of religious union and esp. of the amalgamation of related Protestant sects
un·ion·is·tic \ˌ==ˈnistik, -tēk\ *adj* **:** of, relating to, characteristic of, or favoring union or unionists
un·ion·ization \ˌyünyənəˈzāshən, -əˌnīz-\ *n* -S **1 :** the quality or state of being unionized **2 :** the act of unionizing
un·ion·ize \ˈ==ˌnīz\ *vt* -ED/-ING/-S *see -ize in Explan Notes* [¹*union* + *-ize*] **:** to cause to become a member of or subject to the rules of a labor union ⟨planned to ~ the shop⟩ **:** form into a labor union ⟨*unionizing* previously unorganized groups⟩
union jack *n, often cap U&J* **:** a jack consisting of the union of a national ensign
union jet burner *n* **:** a gas burner in which two jets unite to produce a single flat flame
union joint *n* **:** a joint (as between pipes) formed by means of a union
union label *n* **:** an identifying mark attached to goods indicating that they have been produced by union labor or that particular goods or services have been sold or done by that labor
union list *n* **:** a usu. alphabetical catalog of periodicals or other serials that provides bibliographical information and locates files in libraries
union–made \ˌ==ˈ=\ *adj* **:** made by union labor
unions *pl of* UNION
union school *n* **:** an elementary, secondary, or combined elementary and secondary school that serves a union district — compare CONSOLIDATED SCHOOL
union security *n* **:** guaranteed preservation of union status or revenues obtained through clauses in a labor contract and esp. through provisions for closed or union shop, maintenance of membership, preferential hiring, or the checkoff
union service *n* **:** a worship service sponsored jointly by two or more religious denominations or communions ⟨urged to attend the *union service* in the Congregational or Baptist Churches⟩
union shona *n, usu cap U&S* **:** SHONA 3
union shop *n* **:** an establishment in which the employer by agreement is free to hire nonmembers as well as members of the union but retains nonmembers on the payroll only on condition of their becoming members of the union within a specified time ⟨a *union shop* clause in a collective agreement⟩ — compare CLOSED SHOP
union station *n* **:** a station used jointly by two or more railroad or other transport companies (as bus or truck lines)
union suit *n* **:** an undergarment with shirt and drawers in one piece
union tannage *n* **:** tannage by means of a mixture of vegetable tanning materials
union tee *n* **:** a T pipe fitting with a male or female union on one end of the main run
unios *pl of* UNIO
uni·oval \ˌyünē+\ *or* **uni·ovular** \"+\ *adj* [*uni-* + *oval* or *ovular*] **:** MONOVULAR
uni·ovulate \"+\ *adj* [*uni-* + *ovulate*] **:** having a single ovule or ovum
unip·a·ra \yüˈnipərə\ *n* -S [NL, fr. *uni-* + *-para*] **:** a woman who has borne one child
uni·parental \ˌyünə+\ *adj* [*uni-* + *parental*] **:** having or involving a single parent; *esp* **:** PARTHENOGENETIC — **uni·parentally** \"+\ *adv*
unip·a·rous \yüˈnipərəs\ *adj* [*uni-* + *-parous*] **1 a :** producing but one egg or offspring at a time **b :** having produced but one offspring **:** once heretofore pregnant **2 :** producing but one axis at each branching ⟨a ~ cyme⟩
uni·partite \ˌyünə+\ *adj* [*uni-* + *partite*] **:** not divided or divisible into parts

union suit

uni·ped \ˈyünəˌped\ *n* -S [*uni-* + *-ped*] **:** one having only one foot or leg
uni·personal \ˌyünə+\ *adj* [*uni-* + *personal*] **:** existing as one person
uni·personalist \"+\ *n* **:** one who believes that the deity is unipersonal
uni·personality \"+\ *n* **:** the quality or state of being unipersonal
uni·phase \"+\ *adj* [*uni-* + *phase*] **:** having but one phase ⟨a ~ conflict⟩; *esp* **:** SINGLE-PHASE
uni·planar \"+\ *adj* [*uni-* + *planar*] **:** lying or occurring in one plane **:** PLANAR 1
uniplanar motion *n* **:** motion of a rigid body or fluid such that each point or particle moves in a plane parallel to a given plane — called also *two-dimensional motion*
uni·pod \ˈyünəˌpäd\ *n* -S [*uni-* + *-pod* (as in *tripod*)] **:** a one-legged support (as for a camera)
uni·polar \ˌyünə+\ *adj* [*uni-* + *polar*] **:** having or oriented in respect to a single pole: as **a :** having, produced by, or acting by a single magnetic or electrical pole **b** *of a nerve cell* **:** having but one process ⟨~ ganglion cells⟩ **c :** based on or controlled by a single compelling factor ⟨a ~ coalition in politics⟩ — **uni·polarity** \"+\ *n*
unipolar induction *n* **:** induction (as in a conducting circuit) by only one pole of a magnet
unip·o·rous \yüˈnipərəs\ *adj* [*uni-* + *porous*] **:** having one pore; *specif* **:** having wood cells with a single row of bordered pores or disk-shaped markings
unip·o·tent \yüˈnipədˌənt\ *adj* [*uni-* + *potent*] **:** having power in one way only; *esp* **:** capable of developing only in one direction or to one end product ⟨~ cells⟩
uni·potential \ˌyünə+\ *adj* [*uni-* + *potential*] **1 :** UNIPOTENT **2 :** having the same electrical potential as something else ⟨a ~ lens⟩
uni·pulse \ˈ==ˌ=\ *n* [*uni-* + *pulse*] **:** a single wave **:** PULSE
uni·quantic \ˌyünə+\ *adj* [*uni-* + *quantic*] **:** of, relating to, or giving rise to a single quantum of energy
¹unique \yüˈnēk, ˈ=ˌ=\ *adj, sometimes* -ER/-EST [F, fr. L *unicus* sole, single, unique, fr. *unus* one + *-icus* -ic — more at ONE] **1 a :** being the only one **:** SOLE ⟨earning money whose ~ object could be nothing but Cyril's welfare —Arnold Bennett⟩ ⟨has thus preserved the original and often ~ records —G.B. Parks⟩ ⟨you are a miracle, a wonder, a mystery . . . one single ~ and inimitable living thing —J.C.Powys⟩ **b** *of a book* **:** known to exist in no other copy **2 :** being without a like or equal **:** single in kind or excellence **:** UNEQUALED ⟨they stand alone, ~, objects of supreme interest —A.B.Osborne⟩ ⟨as historian he knows that events, like persons, are ~ —J.M. Barzun⟩ ⟨remains singularly himself, a ~ lyrist of the first water —I.L.Salomon⟩ ⟨an almost ~ experience —Havelock Ellis⟩ ⟨tendencies present in our contemporary world which make our own times somewhat ~ —M.B.Smith⟩ ⟨story of his life is considerably more ~ than most autobiographies —Dorothy C. Fisher⟩ — sometimes used with *to* ⟨the problem of what to do with surplus women is by no means ~ to our own society — Ralph Linton⟩ or *with* ⟨by no means ~ with the song sparrow —*Nature Mag.*⟩ **3 :** UNUSUAL, NOTABLE ⟨possessed ~ ability in the raising of funds —C.F.Thwing⟩ ⟨the wife of a career diplomat has a ~ opportunity to observe the world political scene —Ray Pierre⟩ ⟨a frankness ~ in literature —David Daiches⟩ ⟨~ peace and privacy —R.W.Hatch⟩ ⟨cheap, nourishing, and a ~ dining experience —T.H.Fielding⟩ ⟨the most ~ characteristic of that environment —R.A.Billington⟩ ⟨she's the most ~ person I ever met —Arthur Miller⟩ ⟨the most ~ theater in town —*advt*⟩ **4 :** capable of being performed in only one way ⟨the factorization of a number into its prime factors is ~⟩ **syn** see SINGLE, STRANGE
²unique \"\ *n* -S **:** something (as a specimen, thing, circumstance, or person) that is unique **:** the only one of its kind ⟨mistaking the ~ for the typical —W.J.Reilly⟩ ⟨the zest of the collector for possession of a ~ —Roy Bedichek⟩ ⟨a display of glass, including undercoated ~*s* —*Danish Foreign Office Jour.*⟩ ⟨the phoenix, the ~ of birds —Thomas De Quincey⟩
unique·ly *adv* **:** in a unique manner **:** so as to be unique
unique·ness *n* -ES **:** the quality or state of being unique
uniqueness theorem *n* **:** a theorem in mathematics: a given problem has at most one solution
uniq·ui·ty \yüˈnikwədˌē, -wətē, -i\ *n* -ES [*unique* + *-ity*] **1 :** UNIQUENESS **2 :** a unique item
uni·radiate \ˌyünə+\ *adj* [*uni-* + *radiate*] **:** having a single ray or radius; *esp* **:** MONAXON
uni·ramous \"+\ *or* **uni·ramose** \"+\ *adj* [*uni-* + *ramous* or *ramose*] **:** consisting of a single process **:** UNBRANCHED ⟨the appendages of crustaceans may be ~ or biramose⟩
uni·reme \ˈyünəˌrēm\ *n* -S [*uni-* + *-reme* (as in *trireme*)] **:** a galley having but one tier of oars
un·ironed \ˌən+\ *adj* [*un-* + *ironed*, past part. of *iron*] **1 :** not restrained or confined with fetters **2 :** not pressed with a flatiron
unis *abbr* unison
uni·serial \ˌyünə+\ *or* **uni·seriate** \"+\ *adj* [*uni-* + *serial* or *seriate*] **:** forming or arranged in a single series **:** having parts in a single row or on one side only of an axis
uni·sexual \"+\ *adj* [*uni-* + *sexual*] **:** of, relating to, or restricted to one sex: **a :** male or female but not hermaphroditic **b :** DICLINOUS ⟨a ~ flower⟩ — **uni·sexuality** \"+\ *n* — **uni·sexually** \"+\ *adv*
¹uni·son \ˈyünəsən, -əzən\ *n* -S [MF, fr. ML *unisonus*, adj., having the same sound, fr. L *uni-* + *sonus* sound — more at SOUND] **1** *archaic* **:** a tone identical in pitch with another; *also* **:** a tone from which intervals are reckoned **2 a :** identity in musical pitch; *specif* **:** the interval of a perfect prime represented by the vibration ratio of 1:1 **b :** the state of being so tuned or sounded **c :** the writing, playing, or singing of parts in a musical passage at the same pitch or in octaves — compare HARMONY 2b **3 a :** a harmonious agreement or union **:** CONCORD **b :** an instance or means of such agreement **:** a sympathetic response **:** ASSENT ⟨~*s* of overmastering thoughts⟩ — **in unison** *adv* **:** in precise and perfect agreement **:** so as to harmonize exactly ⟨speaking *in unison*⟩
²unison \"\ *adj* **1** *archaic* **a :** CONCORDANT, CONSONANT **b :** EQUIVALENT **2 a :** identical in musical pitch **:** UNISONOUS ⟨~ singing⟩ ⟨a ~ passage⟩ **b :** tuned to the same pitch — used of a string and esp. of any one of two or three piano strings that are struck by one hammer ⟨~ strings⟩ **c :** having a pitch that corresponds with the notation (as of a pipe-organ stop)
unis·o·nal \yüˈnisᵊnəl\ *adj* [¹*unison* + *-al*] **:** UNISONOUS 1
unis·o·nance \-nən(t)s\ *n* -S [²*unison* + *-ance*] **:** a blending of sound into unison ⟨the first two sounds reach the ear as a ~ —*Newsweek*⟩
unis·o·nant \-nt\ *adj* [¹*unison* + *-ant*] **:** UNISONOUS 1
uni·so·no \ˌünēˈsō(ˌ)nō\ *adv (or adj)* [It, fr. ML *unisonus*] **:** in unison — used as a direction esp. in ensemble instrumental music
unis·o·nous \yüˈnisᵊnəs\ *adj* [ML *unisonus*] **1 :** being in unison **:** having the same degree of gravity or acuteness **:** sounded alike in pitch **2 :** alike in nature **:** CONCORDANT
un·issued stock \ˌən+-\ *n* [¹*un-* + *issued*, past part. of *issue*] **:** stock authorized (as under the charter of a corporation) but not yet issued — compare TREASURY STOCK
¹unit \ˈyünət, *usu* -əd.+V\ *n* -S [back-formation fr. *unity*] **1 a** (1) **:** the first natural number **:** a number that is the least whole number and is expressed by the numeral 1 (2) **:** a single thing (as a magnitude or number) that constitutes an undivided whole **b :** a number that divides every element of a set of numbers **c :** a determinate quantity (as of length, time, heat, value, or housing) adopted as a standard of measurement for other quantities of the same kind: as (1) **:** a fractional part of the width of a printing character (as ¹⁄₁₈ of ordinary roman capital M) used in measuring the set of a piece of type and being of the same width for all type of the same point size and proportionally wider or narrower for larger or smaller point sizes (2) **:** an amount of work (as 120 hours of classroom work in a completed course of a secondary school) used in education in calculating student credits (as for graduation or college entrance) (3) **:** an amount of a biologically active agent (as a drug, serum, vitamin, or antigen) required to produce a specific result under strictly controlled conditions — compare BIOASSAY, RAT UNIT (4) **:** one percent per ton of a fertilizing ingredient ⟨a fertilizer containing 5 percent of nitrogen, 10 percent of phosphoric acid, and 10 percent of potash includes 25 fertilizer ~*s*⟩ **2 a :** a single thing or person or group that is a constituent and isolable member of some more inclusive whole **:** a member of an aggregate that is the least part to have clearly definable separate existence and that normally forms a basic element of organization within the aggregate ⟨the township in the usual ~ of government⟩ ⟨the family as a basic ~ of society⟩ **b :** one of the commonly more or less repetitive sections combined in assembling a manufactured article (as a bookcase or kitchen cabinet) **c :** a part of a military establishment that has a prescribed organization (as of personnel and materiel) ⟨in the army ~*s* vary in size and complexity from the squad to the army⟩ **d :** a piece or complex of apparatus serving to perform one particular function ⟨a train drawn by two diesel ~*s*⟩ ⟨a power station with one ~ out of order⟩ **e :** a combination of two or more securities offered at a single price ⟨a ~ of one share of preferred stock and two shares of common offered at $110⟩ **f :** a course or part of a course in an elementary or secondary school focusing on a central theme and making use of resources from numerous subject areas and the pupils' own experience **g :** BARGAINING UNIT **h :** a fraction of an annual pension or a retirement income benefit earned as a result of each year's service prior to retirement **i :** a subdivision of a Girl Scout camp comprised of girls and counselors who live together and plan their own activities in a manner comparable to a Girl Scout troop **j :** a molecule or portion of a molecule esp. as combined in a larger molecule **:** RESIDUE ⟨repeating ~*s* in a polymer⟩
²unit \"\ *adj* **1 a :** of, relating to, forming, or involving some unit ⟨~ sales⟩ ⟨studies of ~ distribution⟩ **b :** existing or occurring per unit ⟨the ~ weight of cement⟩ ⟨a ~ increment⟩ ⟨calculating the ~ rise or vertical change per running foot⟩ **2 :** having independent existence **:** INDIVIDUAL
unit·able *also* **unite·able** \yüˈnīd·əbəl, -ītə-\ *adj* [*unite* + *-able*] **:** capable of union by growth or otherwise **:** that can be joined together
unit·age \ˈyünəd·ij\ *n* -S [¹*unit* + *-age*] **1 :** specification of the amount constituting a unit (as of a vitamin) **2 :** amount in units ⟨a ~ of 50,000 per capsule⟩
unit·al \-nəd·ᵊl\ *adj* [¹*unit* + *-al*] **:** UNITARY
¹uni·tar·i·an \ˌyünəˈterēən, -ta(a)r-, -tār-\ *n* -S [NL *unitarius* unitarian (fr. L *unitus* — past part. of *unire* to unite — + *-arius* -ary) + E *-an*] **1** *usu cap* **a :** a Christian who believes that the deity exists only in one person **:** a unipersonalist who denies the doctrine of the Trinity **:** a member of a Christian denomination who in general affirms the principles of individual freedom of belief, the free use of reason in religion, commitment to advancing truth, religious tolerance, universal brotherhood of man, a creedless church, a united world community, and support of a vigorous program of liberal social action **b :** a non-Christian monotheist (as a Muhammadan) **2 a :** an advocate of a theory or doctrine founded upon unity; *specif* **:** MONIST **b :** an advocate of unity or a unitary system; *specif* **:** one who advocates centralization in government **c :** an observer of the dramatic unities
²unitarian \"\ *adj* **1** *usu cap* **:** of, relating to, or involving Unitarians or their doctrines **2 :** UNITARY 1: as **a :** MONISTIC **b :** of, relating to, or advocating centralization in government or administration
unitarian hypothesis *also* **unitarian view** *n* **:** a theory in immunology: a single pure antigen will produce only one variety of antibody which when brought into contact with the antigen in appropriate form can react in various ways (as by agglutinating, precipitating, fixing complement, or opsonizing)
uni·tar·i·an·ism \-əˌnizəm\ *n* -S **1** *cap* **:** the principles and practices of Unitarians **2** *sometimes cap* **:** a unitarian or unitary system (as of government)
uni·tar·i·ness \ˈyünəˌterēnəs, -rin-\ *n* -ES **:** the quality or state of being unitary
uni·tary \-ˌterē, -ri\ *adj* [¹*unit* & *unity* + *-ary*] **1 :** of, relating to, based upon, or characterized by unity ⟨a ~ movement in politics⟩ **:** MONISTIC **2 a :** having the character of a unit **:** not divided or discontinuous ⟨a ~ process⟩ **b :** functioning as a unit esp. of measurement ⟨established a ~ distance on which to base subsequent calculations⟩ ⟨a ~ university⟩ **c :** of, relating to, or constituting a system of government in which power is held by a central authority and may be delegated to but is not derived from constituent subdivisions — distinguished from *federal* **3 a :** of, relating to, or involving the use of units ⟨a ~ approach to a problem⟩ ⟨the ~ method in arithmetic⟩ **b :** made up of discrete units ⟨a ~ loudspeaker with four speaker units associated in a single assembly⟩
unitary color *n* **:** PSYCHOLOGICAL PRIMARY
unitary theory *n* **:** a theory in chemistry: molecules are units whose parts are bound together in definite structure with mutual and reciprocal influence on each other — compare DUALISM 4
unit banking *n* **:** banking carried on by individual banks without branches or corporate relationships with other banks
unit card *n* **:** a library catalog card containing full information about a book or other printed item and reproduced in quantity so that it may be not only used for a main entry but adapted for all secondary entries
unit cell *n* **:** the simplest polyhedron that by indefinite repetition makes up the lattice of a crystal and embodies all the characteristics of its structure
unit character *n* **1 :** a natural character that is inherited on an all or none basis **2 :** a natural character dependent on the presence or absence of a single gene **:** a typical Mendelian or qualitative character
unit class *n* **:** a class with a single member
unit construction *n* **:** a system of building in which large sections (as of a ship) can be fabricated independently and subsequently assembled
unit cost *n* **:** the cost allocated to a selected unit and commonly calculated as the cost over a period of time divided by the number of items produced
¹unite \yüˈnīt, *usu* -īd.+V\ *vb* -ED/-ING/-S [ME *uniten*, fr. LL *unitus*, past part. of *unire*, fr. L *unus* one — more at ONE] *vt* **1 a :** to put together to form a single unit ⟨~ the fighting forces of the friendly nations⟩ **b :** to cause to adhere ⟨~ bricks with mortar⟩ **c :** CONNECT ⟨a dirt road ~*s* the farm road with the main highway⟩ **d :** to relate integrally ⟨often the ideas are yoked, but not *united* —T.S.Eliot⟩; *esp* **:** to link by a legal or moral bond ⟨a purpose that *united* all factions⟩ ⟨a treaty to ~ all the independent nations⟩ **2 :** to possess (as qualities) in combination ⟨the bride *united* beauty and intelligence⟩ ~ *vi* **1 a :** to become one or as if one ⟨particles which can ~ to form a new compound —T.S.Eliot⟩ ⟨mutterings of the crowd *united* in a thunderous cheer —Darrell Berrigan⟩ **b :** to become combined by or as if by adhesion or mixture ⟨the broken bones of a child ~ rapidly⟩ ⟨clouds of devastating smoke that ~ with the river fog . . . to form smog —*Amer. Guide Series: Pa.*⟩ **2 :** to act in concert ⟨all parties *united* in signing the petition⟩ **3 :** to enter into association for or as if for a common purpose ⟨the group *united* to improve the city's schools⟩
syn COMBINE, CONJOIN, CONCUR, COOPERATE: UNITE often indicates joining, merging, coalescing, adhering together to form a new unit, permanent or temporary ⟨the North West Company *united* with the Hudson's Bay Company —*Amer. Guide Series: Wash.*⟩ ⟨in France the whole people saw at once what was upon them; the single word *patrie* was enough to *unite* them in a common enthusiasm and stern determination — W.R.Inge⟩ COMBINE may apply to a temporary uniting or joining or to one which leaves the components distinct ⟨a gift for *combining*, for fusing into a single phrase, two or more diverse impressions —T.S.Eliot⟩ ⟨wealth and sophistication *combine* with breezy western characteristics in this town —*Amer. Guide Series: Texas*⟩ ⟨innumerable factors *combine* in the inextricable complexity of our general story —Hilaire Belloc⟩ CONJOIN is likely to stress the notion of jointure, often of more or less equal things or forces, at a specific point ⟨nature had lavished gifts and aspirations upon him, but they were so mixed and contradictory that only by a fortunate miracle did some of them *conjoin* to produce the rich poetry by which he is remembered —R.D.Altick⟩ CONCUR is likely to be used of things that happen to merge, work together, or coincide when another course of action is probable or plausible ⟨two opposite forces *concurred* in bringing about the Council of Nicaea — A.P.Stanley⟩ COOPERATE indicates a joining of strength or force in some specific situation with no fusion or loss of identity ⟨sent a joint expedition, under British command, to *cooperate* with the White Russians at Murmansk and Archangel against the Bolshevist forces —J.M.Hanson⟩ **syn** see in addition JOIN
²unite \ˈyüˌnīt, =ˈ=\ *n* -S [fr. obs. *unite* joint, united, fr. ME *unit*, fr. LL *unitus*] **:** an old British gold 20-shilling piece issued first by James I in 1604 for England and Scotland and bearing in the design and inscription reference to the uniting of the two crowns — called also *jacobus*
uniteable *var of* UNITABLE
united *adj* [fr. past part. of ¹*unite*] **1 :** made one **:** COMBINED, JOINED **2 :** relating to or produced by joint action **:** CONJOINT ⟨their ~ consent⟩ **3 :** formed by or resulting from union **4 :** being or living in agreement **:** HARMONIOUS ⟨a ~ family⟩ — **unit·ed·ly** *adv* — **unit·ed·ness** *n* -ES
united baptist *n, usu cap U&B* **:** a member of a Baptist sect formed in the late 18th century by a union of some Separate Baptist and Regular Baptist churches of the South
united brethren *n pl, usu cap U&B* **1 :** MORAVIANS **2 :** Christians of several denominations descending from the United Brethren in Christ originating among Germans in the U.S. during the religious awakening of the late 18th century, formally organized in 1800, and resembling Methodism in doctrine and polity
united front *n* **1 :** a state or appearance of unity, common purpose, or general agreement usu. presented by a heterogeneous group in the face of opposition or danger from an outside source ⟨that Western Europe will continue to present a *united front* against the threat of Communist aggression — *Springfield (Mass.) Union*⟩ **2 :** POPULAR FRONT ⟨the appearance of a *united front* in each country controlled by the Russians after World War II⟩

united kingdom *adj, usu cap U&K* [fr. the *United Kingdom* (Great Britain and Northern Ireland)] **:** of or from the United Kingdom **:** of the kind or style prevalent in the United Kingdom

united nations *adj, usu cap U&N* **1 :** of or relating to the United Nations organization or community **2 :** of or relating to the United Nations territory which is an enclave of New York, N.Y.

united presbyterian *n, usu cap U&P* **:** a Presbyterian of the United Presbyterian Church of North America formed by merger in 1858 or of the United Presbyterian Church in the U.S.A. formed by a merger including the former in 1958

¹united states *n pl but usu sing in constr* [fr. the *United States* of America] **1** *usu cap* **:** a federation of states esp. when forming a nation in a usu. specified territory ⟨advocating a *United States* of Europe⟩ **2 :** United States English **:** written or spoken English exhibiting peculiarities typical of the United States of No. America

²united states *adj, usu cap U&S* [fr. the *United States* of America] **:** of or from the United States of No. America ⟨a *United States* ship⟩ **:** of the kind or style prevalent in the United States

united states court of appeals *usu cap U&S* **:** a court in each of the 11 federal judicial districts of the U. S. that functions as a court of record, exercises appellate jurisdiction, is presided over by three or sometimes two judges, and may be overruled only by the Supreme Court of the U. S.

united statesian \\ˌ⁼ˌ⁼ˈstātsēən\\ *n* -S *usu cap U&S* [*United States* of America + *-ian*] **:** a native or resident of the United States of No. America

united-statesian \\"\\ *adj, usu cap U&S* **:** UNITED STATES

united states note *n, usu cap U&S* **:** a piece of United States paper money

united states standard thread *n, usu cap U&S* **:** an American screw thread that has a thread angle of 60 degrees and varies from 3½ to 64 threads per inch

united states value *n, usu cap U&S* **:** a value of imported merchandise that is obtained by deducting from its value in U. S. wholesale markets specified enumerated expenses of importation and that is used esp. as a basis for assessing customs duties

unit·er \\yü'nīd·ə(r), -ītə-\\ *n* -S **:** one that unites

uni·terminal \\ˌyünə+\\ *adj* [*uni-* + *terminal*] **:** POLAR 2b

unites *pres 3d sing of* UNITE, *pl of* UNITE

unit factor *n* **:** a gene that controls the inheritance of a unit character — compare POLYGENE

unit fraction *n* **:** a fraction whose numerator is unity and whose denominator is an integer

unit heater *n* **:** a heater consisting essentially of a fan or blower and an indirect radiator enclosed in a common casing and designed to circulate and warm the air of a continuous enclosed space (as a room)

unities *pl of* UNITY

uniting *pres part of* UNITE

uni·tion \\yü'nishən\\ *n* -S [LL *unition-, unitio,* fr. *unitus* (past part. of *unire* to unite) + L *-ion-, -io* -ion — more at UNITE] **:** an act of uniting or the state of being united **:** JUNCTION

unit·ism \\'yünə,tizəm\\ *n* -S [*¹unit* + *-ism*] **:** MONISM

uni·tive \\'yünəd·iv, -ətiv\\ *adj* [LL *unitivus,* fr. *unitus* (past part. of *unire* to unite) + L *-ivus* -ive] **:** characterized by or tending to produce union — **uni·tive·ly** *adv* — **uni·tive·ness** *n* -ES

unitive way *n* **:** UNION 1a(6)

unit·ization \\ˌyünəd·ə'zāshən, -nətə'z-, -nə,tī'z-\\ *n* -S **1 :** the quality or state of being unitized **2 :** the act of unitizing: as **a :** the uniting of diverse properties into a single operational unit **b :** the assembling and securing of goods or packages into a unit of use or sale

unit·ize \\'yünə,tīz\\ *vt* -ED/-ING/-S *see -ize in Explan Notes* [*¹unit* + *-ize*] **:** to convert into a unit: as **a :** to aggregate discrete elements into (a functional whole) ⟨~ an oil field⟩ ⟨a car with a *unitized* body⟩ **b :** to divide and package or otherwise finish (an aggregate of material) into units designed for the ultimate buyer or user ⟨~ bulk merchandise⟩

unit·iz·er \\-zə(r)\\ *n* -S **:** an auto factory stock clerk who packs parts or accessories in matched sets

unit line *n* **:** a field line (as in a magnetic field) representing one unit of flux

unit lock *n* **:** a lock set whose parts are permanently combined and which can be applied to a door as a single unit

unit magnetic pole *n* **:** a unit of magnetic pole strength equal to the strength of a magnetic pole that repels an identical pole at a distance of one centimeter with a force of one dyne

unit marker *n* **:** a device (as a guidon) that serves to identify a unit (as of a military force)

unit modifier *n* **:** a compound adherent adjective or a phrase or sentence used as an adherent modifier

unit of account : a monetary unit or measure of value (as a coin) in terms of which accounts are kept and values stated

unit of fire : a prescribed quantity of ammunition for a given organization or weapon based on the number of rounds that on the average are expected to be used in one day

unit of value 1 : the amount of some one thing taken as a standard by comparison with which to reckon the value of other things **2** *or* **unit of assessment :** the unit of length, surface, capacity, or weight that an assessor uses in calculations of or values for the assessment of taxes

unit operation *n* **:** a physical change to which material is subjected esp. in coordination with a unit process (as filtration, distillation, or extraction)

unit organ *n* **:** an organ with comparatively few sets of pipes that by the use of duplexing and unification are made available by means of different stop names on all manuals and at various pitches

unit price *n* **:** a price quoted in terms of so much per agreed or standard unit of product or service ⟨agreed to take the gravel at a *unit price* of 50 cents a yard⟩; *often* **:** an inclusive price quoted to cover all incidentals (as transportation or installation) as well as the basic unit of product or service ⟨purchasing on a *unit price* relieves the buyer of inconvenience but may be more expensive⟩ ⟨quoted a *unit price* for the funeral⟩

unit process *n* **:** a chemical change (as nitration, diazotization, or esterification) to which material is subjected as a step in manufacture

unit pulse *n* **:** the shortest telegraphic signaling pulse **:** BAND

uni·trivalent \\ˌyünə+\\ *adj* [*uni-* + *trivalent*] **:** of, relating to, or designating an electrolyte that dissociates into three univalent ions and one trivalent ion

unit rule *n* **:** a rule that may be adopted optionally by a delegation to a Democratic national convention under which the entire vote of the delegation shall be cast as a unit as determined by a majority vote

units *pl of* UNIT

unit-set \\ˌ⁼ˌ⁼\\ *adj, of printing type* **:** cast with a set expressible in units — compare POINT-SET

unit solid angle *n* **:** STERADIAN

unit switch *n* **:** a switch designed to establish or interrupt an electric-power circuit repeatedly under normal operating conditions

unit value *n* **:** the set of a printing character measured in units

unit vector *n* **:** a vector of unit magnitude used to specify a particular spatial direction

unit vote *n* **:** a vote cast by a political subdivision as a single unit regardless of the number of persons voting or eligible to vote

unit watermark *n* **:** a watermark on a stamp that is a single entire design — called also *simple watermark*

uni·ty \\'yünəd·ē, -ətē, -i\\ *n* -ES [ME *unite,* fr. OF *unité,* fr. L *unitat-, unitas,* fr. *unus* one + *-itat-, -itas* -ity — more at ONE] **1 a :** the quality or state of being or consisting of one **:** ONENESS, SINGLENESS **b** (1) **:** a definite quantity or aggregate of quantities or magnitudes taken as one or for which 1 is made to stand in calculation ⟨in a table of natural sines the radius of the circle is regarded as ~⟩ (2) **:** the singular multiplier in any system multiplication by which leaves the multiplicand unchanged and which is distinguished from a unit in not entering into addition ⟨in any system there may be many units (as 1 and *i* in complex numbers) yet only one if any ~⟩ (3) *archaic* **:** UNIT 1a(1) **2 a :** a condition of concordant harmony **:** the state of those that are in full agreement **:** ACCORD ⟨attaining ~ of purpose through thorough discussion⟩ ⟨living in contented ~⟩ **b :** continuity without deviation or change (as in purpose or action) **:** absence of diversity **3 a :** the quality or state of being made one **:** a uniting into one **:** UNIFICATION ⟨the strength that lies in ~⟩ ⟨seeking ~ with the several groups in order that they might become a more effective competitor in world markets⟩ **b :** a combination or ordering of parts in a literary or artistic production such as to constitute a whole or promote an undivided total effect **:** the reference of the elements of a composition to a single main idea or point of view; *also* **:** conformity to this principle or the singleness of effect or symmetry and consistency of style and character secured **4 a :** the quality or state of constituting a whole and esp. one organized from distinguishable parts or elements **b :** a totality of related parts **:** an entity that is a complex or systematic whole — compare ORGANIC 5b **5 :** any of four peculiar characteristics of an estate held by several in joint tenancy according to which joint tenants have one and the same interest accruing by one and the same conveyance, commencing at the same time, and held by one and the same undivided possession **6 :** any of three principles governing the structure of drama, derived by writers of the French classical school from the Aristotelian canon, and as rigidly formulated requiring the action of a play to be represented as occurring in one place, within one day, and with nothing irrelevant to the plot — called also respectively *unity of place, unity of time, unity of action* **7** *usu cap* **:** a 20th century American religious movement that utilizes for the most part a conservative Protestant Christian theology in its teachings but adds the two distinctive doctrines of reincarnation and the regeneration of the body, and emphasizes health, successful living, and prosperity

unity in variety : a principle that aesthetic value or beauty in art depends on the fusion of various elements into an organic whole which produces a single impression

unity of science movement : SCIENTIFIC EMPIRICISM 1

unity stress *n* **:** accent (as of *up* and *on* in *upon*) that unites the meanings of words

uni·univalent \\ˌyünə, -nē+\\ *adj* [*uni-* + *univalent*] **:** of, relating to, or designating an electrolyte that dissociates into two univalent ions

univ *abbr* universal; universally; university

¹uni·va·lent \\ˌyünəˈvālənt, yü'nivələnt\\ *adj* [ISV *uni-* + *valent*] **:** having a valence of one: as **a :** capable usu. of combining with only one atom of another element ⟨the hydrogen atom . . . is taken to be ~ —N.N.Greenwood⟩ **b** *of a chromosome* **:** lacking a synaptic mate **:** SINGLE **c** *of an antibody* **:** capable of agglutinating or precipitating but not both **:** having only one combining group

²univalent \\"\\ *n* **:** a univalent chromosome

¹uni·valve \\ˌyünə+\\ *also* **uni·valved** \\"+\\ *adj* [*uni-* + *valve* or *valved*] **:** having or consisting of one valve only ⟨a ~ shell⟩ ⟨a ~ diatom⟩

²univalve \\"+\\ *n* **1 :** a mollusk with a univalve shell; *esp* **:** GASTROPOD — compare BIVALVE **2 :** a mollusk shell consisting of one piece

uni·variant \\ˌyünə+\\ *adj* [ISV *uni-* + *variant*] **:** having one degree of freedom — used of a physical-chemical system; compare BIVARIANT, PHASE RULE

uni·variate \\"+\\ *adj* [*uni-* + *variate*] **:** having or involving one variate only

¹uni·ver·sal \\ˌyünəˈvərsəl, -vōs-, -vəis-\\ *adj* [ME *universel, universal,* fr. MF, fr. L *universalis,* fr. *universus* entire, whole + *-alis* -al — more at UNIVERSE] **1 :** including or covering all or a whole collectively or distributively without limit or notable exception or variation ⟨~ human weakness —T.S.Eliot⟩ ⟨most of the twigs, pearled with water, were patterned very naked against ~ gray —John Galsworthy⟩ **2 a :** present or occurring as indicated throughout the whole world **:** encountered everywhere ⟨~ as the air —Samuel Rogers⟩ **b :** existent or operative as indicated everywhere or under all conditions ⟨far from being infrequent, the crystalline state is almost ~ among solids —K.K.Darrow⟩ **c :** having effectiveness, power, or action through a salient part of the world ⟨a ~ state, in the shape of the Roman Empire —A.J.Toynbee⟩ **3 :** pertinent to or inclusive of all or much of mankind: **a :** practiced, observed, or occurring throughout all peoples or groups or a great many of them **:** commonly or unanimously followed, approved, or subscribed to by a people or group ⟨petty gambling is nearly ~ —W.C.Brownell⟩ ⟨feudalism was not so ~ there . . . as in the north —H.O.Taylor⟩ ⟨~ cultural patterns⟩ **b :** marked by width and inclusiveness **:** embracing a very wide range of interests or pursuits **:** comprehensively broad and versatile ⟨a ~ genius. He wrote . . . logic, rhetoric, poetics, physics, botany, zoology . . . —Frank Thilly⟩ **c :** designed for general or worldwide use or applicability ⟨interested in ideas of ~ citizenship, in Esperanto and Ido and ~ languages —H.G. Wells⟩ **4 :** relatively unrestricted in application **:** of general relevance: as **a** *of a logical proposition* **:** affirming or denying something of all members of a class **b :** constituting a general term capable of denoting every member of a class **c :** common to all members of a class ⟨food is a ~ need of living beings⟩ ⟨color is a ~ attribute of visible objects⟩ **5 :** of, relating to, or involving the totality of a person's legal rights and liabilities ⟨a ~ partnership⟩ — compare UNIVERSAL SUCCESSION **6 :** adapted or adjustable to meet varied requirements (as of use, shape, or size) ⟨a ~ gear cutter⟩ — compare UNIVERSAL JOINT, UNIVERSAL MOTOR, UNIVERSAL VISE **7 :** of, relating to, or constituting a universal

syn COSMIC, ECUMENICAL, CATHOLIC, COSMOPOLITAN: UNIVERSAL is likely to suggest that which is worldwide rather than pertinent to or characteristic of the whole universe; it is often further narrowed to refer to the world of men and human affairs or to important or significant parts of this world. It is likely to indicate a unanimity or conformity of practice or belief or a broad comprehensiveness ⟨no other theory which has won *universal* acceptance —Laurence Binyon⟩ ⟨the *universal* favor with which the New Testament is outwardly received —H.D.Thoreau⟩ ⟨replaced a philosophy which was crude and raw and provincial by one which was, in comparison, catholic, civilized and *universal* —T.S.Eliot⟩ COSMIC is used to suggest matters pertinent to the whole universe as opposed to the earth, esp. in suggestions of infinite vastness, distance, or force ⟨sardonic phantoms, whose vision is *cosmic,* not terrestrial —J.L.Lowes⟩ ⟨the great *cosmic* rhythm of the spirit which sets the currents of life in motion —Laurence Binyon⟩ ECUMENICAL applies to situations involving people throughout the whole world or all people in groups or divisions as indicated, often in religious contexts ⟨the incorporation of all the broken fragments of the former Iranic and Arabic societies into the wholly different structure of a Western World which has grown into an *ecumenical* "Great Society" —A.J.Toynbee⟩ CATHOLIC may stress an attitude involved, as well as a fact, in including, comprehending, or appreciating of all or many peoples, places, or periods ⟨he was a *catholic* nature lover. The tropics, the desert, the tundra, the glaciers and the prairies all found a place in his heart —D.C.Peattie⟩ COSMOPOLITAN may imply an understanding and appreciation of other lands, sections, nations, or cities coming about through personal experience in traveling or living elsewhere; it often contrasts with *provincial* ⟨one of the most entertaining and most *cosmopolitan* of novelists. Born in Tuscany, he was educated in New England, England, Germany, and Italy, became interested in Sanskrit, edited a newspaper in India —Carl Van Doren⟩

syn GENERIC, GENERAL, COMMON: UNIVERSAL implies applicability to each one of a whole and usu. precludes significant exception ⟨a prehistoric and *universal* principle that the burden of defense should rest upon all able-bodied males — G.G.Coulton⟩ ⟨habits both *universal* among mankind and peculiar to individuals —F.H.Allport⟩ GENERIC applies to that which characterizes every individual in a category or group and may suggest further that what is designated may be thought of as a clear and certain classificatory criterion ⟨erect pointed ears are *generic* among foxes⟩ ⟨natural that the preaching of men of all religious categories — except ranters — should have a *generic* likeness —Douglas Bush⟩ GENERAL is used to refer to all, nearly all, or the great majority of a class, type, group, or number; it is less inclusive than *universal* and less precise in suggestion than *generic* ⟨ethylene has come into *general* but not yet universal favor with surgeons —A.C. Morrison⟩ ⟨nightfall brings about a *general* upward movement of the animal species, each striving to attain its optimum illumination —W.H.Dowdeswell⟩ COMMON indicates frequency, applicability to a majority, usu. without being an identifying or classifying attribute; it may suggest a certain participation, sharing, mutual relationship, tendency to group together ⟨the *common,* the perpetually repeated mistake of judging the savage by the standard of European civilization — J.G.Frazer⟩ ⟨crowds . . . swept along by a *common* animating impulse —Laurence Binyon⟩

²universal \\"\\ *n* -S **1 :** the whole of something specified **:** a thing in its entirety — used with *the* **2 :** one that is universal (as in power, currency, interest, scope, or applicability): as **a** (1) **:** a universal proposition in logic — called also *abstract universal;* compare CONCRETE UNIVERSAL (2) **:** a predicable of traditional logic (3) **:** a general concept or something in reality to which it corresponds **:** an abstract and general term or something denoted by such a term **:** the essence of a particular logical genus **:** ABSTRACTION **b** *obs* **:** a remedy affecting or altering the entire bodily mechanism **c** *obs* **:** UNIVERSE **d** (1) **:** a pattern or mode of behavior existing in all cultures ⟨the institution of the family is a ~ in human culture⟩ (2) **:** a culture trait characteristic of all normal adult members of a particular society **3 :** a metaphysical being (as the ego or self) that preserves or evinces an identity of nature through a series of changes or as embodying different relations ⟨self-consciousness, wherein the ~, or self, is the organic total of the facts of consciousness —Josiah Royce⟩ — compare CONCRETE UNIVERSAL

³universal \\"\\ *adv* **:** UNIVERSALLY

universal affirmation *n* **:** a universal proposition that affirms something of all members of a class

universal agent *n* **:** one to whom has been delegated powers to act for the principal in all business and in all matters rather than in a particular business **:** GENERAL AGENT

universal calling *n* **:** the divine summons to all men to repent and accept the gospel

universal cause *n* **:** the ultimate or all-comprehensive cause **:** FIRST CAUSE; *often* **:** GOD

universal chuck *n* **:** a chuck in which the jaws are moved simultaneously to center the workpiece

universal chuck

universal class *n* **:** a class comprising all members of a universe of discourse

universal compass *n* **:** a large compass with hollow adjustable legs each containing a complete bow compass that may be used as a part of the large compass or independently

universal constant *n* **:** a physical constant of wide application and frequent occurrence in physical formulas ⟨the speed of light, *c,* the electronic charge, *e,* and the Planck constant, *h,* are *universal constants*⟩

universal conversion *n* **:** conversion of a proposition in logic into a universal proposition

universal decimal classification *n* **:** an expanded decimal classification widely used in Europe — called also *Brussels classification*

universal dial *n* **:** a sundial with an adjustable gnomon by which the hour may be found in any part of the world or under any elevation of the pole

universal donor *n* **1 :** TYPE O **2 a :** a person with type O blood **b :** the blood of such a person

universal grammar *n* **:** GENERAL GRAMMAR

uni·ver·sa·lian \\ˌyünə(ˌ)vərˈsālyən, -lēən\\ *adj, usu cap* [*¹universal* + *-ian*] **:** UNIVERSALIST

uni·ver·sal·ism \\ˌ⁼ˌ⁼'vərsə,lizəm, -vōs-, -vəis-\\ *n* -S **1** *often cap* **a :** a theological doctrine that all men will eventually be saved or restored to holiness and happiness **b :** the principles and practices of Universalists including centrally the belief that all men will ultimately be saved **2 :** a thing universal in scope; *also* **:** addiction to universal knowledge or pursuits **3 :** the state of being universal **:** UNIVERSALITY **4 a :** a theory according to which the whole is logically or valuationally prior to its parts **b :** an ethical theory that the good of all men should take precedence over that of an individual — contrasted with *individualism* **c :** a social relationship in which behavior is determined by an impersonal code or standard — contrasted with *particularism*

¹uni·ver·sal·ist \\-ləst\\ *n* -S [*¹universal* + *-ist*] **1 a :** one who believes in universalism **b** *usu cap* **:** a member of a Christian denomination founded in America in the 18th century and holding the view that all men will be ultimately saved, employing a modified congregational polity, having at its head a general convention, and using no strictly creedal basis but having members who for the most part acknowledge their common purpose to be the performance of the will of God as revealed by Jesus Christ and the establishment of the kingdom for which he lived and died and who acknowledge belief in God, in the leadership of Jesus Christ, in the supreme worth of every human personality, in the authority of truth now known or to be known, in the power of men of goodwill to overcome evil, and in their power to establish progressively God's kingdom on earth **2 a :** one who affects or is credited with universal knowledge, interests, or aptitudes **b :** one who regards or acts with regard to the whole

²universalist \\"\\ *adj* **1** *usu cap* **:** of or relating to Universalists or their principles and practices **2 :** UNIVERSALISTIC

uni·ver·sal·is·tic \\ˌ⁼ˌ⁼ˌ⁼ˈlistik, -tēk\\ *adj* **1 :** of or relating to the whole **:** universal in scope or nature **2 :** of or relating to universalism or the universal **:** resembling or tending toward universalism **3** *usu cap* **:** UNIVERSALIST 1

universalistic hedonism *n* **:** an ethical theory that the supreme good and the determining consideration of moral conduct is the greatest happiness of the greatest number **:** UTILITARIANISM 1 — contrasted with *egoistic hedonism;* compare PSYCHOLOGICAL HEDONISM

uni·ver·sal·i·ty \\ˌ⁼⁼(ˌ)vərˈsaləd·ē, -lətē, -i\\ *n* -ES [ME *universalite,* fr. LL *universalitas,* fr. L *universalis* universal + *-itas* -ity — more at UNIVERSAL] **1 :** the quality or state of being universal (as in extent, occurrence, or application) **2 :** universal comprehensiveness in range (as of subjects, pursuits, or acquaintances) **:** unrestricted versatility or power of adaptation or comprehension ⟨the ~ of Shakespeare's insight⟩ **3 :** the entire body of a specified group; *sometimes* **:** the mass of the people as distinguished from those deserving (as by reason of class or special notability) to be particularized **4** *obs* **:** GENERALITY

uni·ver·sal·ization \\ˌ⁼⁼ˌ⁼sələ'zāshən, -ə,lī'z-\\ *n* -S **:** the quality or state of being universalized

uni·ver·sal·ize \\ˌ⁼⁼'vərsə,līz\\ *vt* -ED/-ING/-S *see -ize in Explan Notes* [*¹universal* + *-ize*] **:** to make universal (as in character, application, or distribution) **:** GENERALIZE ⟨to observe what is best in the schools and to strive to ~ these qualities —*Amer. Child*⟩ — **uni·ver·sal·iz·er** \\-zə(r)\\ *n* -S

universal joint *or* **universal coupling** *n* **:** a shaft coupling capable of transmitting rotation from one shaft to another not collinear with it and typically consisting of a cross-shaped piece having pivots on its arms so arranged that each pair of pivots engage with the eyes of a yoke on the end of one shaft

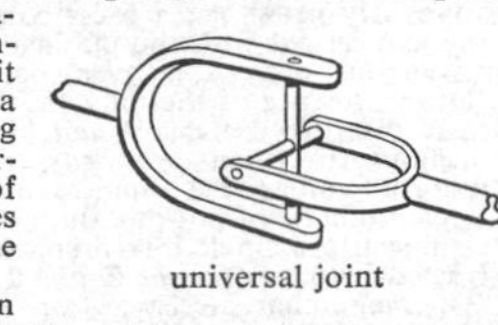

universal joint

universal language *n* **:** an international auxiliary language

universal legacy *n* **:** a legacy under Roman or civil law resembling the residuary legacy of Anglo-American law by which a testator gives to one or more persons all his estate subject to the duty of paying particular legacies and debts and carrying out fideicommissary bequests

uni·ver·sal·ly \\-s(ə)lē, -li\\ *adv* [ME, fr. *universal* + *-ly*] **:** in a universal manner **:** so as to be universal (as in influence or effect) ⟨a ~ applicable rule⟩

universal military service *n* **:** a system under which all male citizens with some specified exceptions are required to serve a prescribed length of time in an active unit of the armed forces

universal military training *n* **:** a system under which all male citizens with some specified exceptions are required to train for a short period in a special organization and a longer period in a reserve unit

universal mill *n* **:** a rolling mill in which metal is acted upon by two sets of rollers commonly horizontal and vertical at each pass and which is used esp. in rolling girder and channel-bar sections

universal milling machine *n* **:** a milling machine having a table fitted with all motions and a dividing head with change gears so that it can perform any type of milling operation

universal motor *n* **:** an electric motor (as for small household and workshop appliances) that can be used on either an alternating or a direct current supply

universal negative *n* **:** a universal proposition that denies something of all members of a class

uni·ver·sal·ness *n* -ES **:** the quality or state of being universal

universal partnership *n* **:** a partnership that includes all the present and future property of the partners and all burdens or losses which without fraud are incurred by either partner and that is exemplified by the community of property between husband and wife under Roman Dutch law or the civil law

universal postulate *n* **:** a criterion of truth: something whose negative is inconceivable must be true

universal quantifier *n* **:** a logical quantifier that asserts all values of a given variable in a formula

universal rule *n* **:** a rule of measurement for the racing of yachts including as factors the waterline length, sail area, and displacement with modifying limitations

universals *pl of* UNIVERSAL

universal scale *n* **:** an architect's or engineer's scale

universal shunt *n* **:** AYRTON SHUNT

universal solvent *n* **:** ALKAHEST

universal stage *n* **:** a small theodolite made in dimensions suitable for a petrographic microscope and used to obtain detailed optical and petrofabric data

universal succession *n* **:** succession under Roman or civil law to the totality of a man's estate including both his rights and liabilities according to the principle that the heir is the same person as the deceased

universal suffrage *n* **:** suffrage of all adults not legally disqualified by the laws of a country: **a :** MANHOOD SUFFRAGE **b :** manhood suffrage together with woman suffrage

universal syllogism *n* **:** a syllogism the conclusion of which is a universal proposition

universal time *n* **:** GREENWICH TIME

universal veil *n* **:** a membrane that initially completely invests the young sporophore of various mushrooms, is ruptured by growth, and is represented in the mature sporophore by a volva about the lower part of the stem and sometimes by scales on the upper surface of the cap — compare PARTIAL VEIL

universal vise *n* **:** a vise (as on some milling machines) that can be swung either horizontally or vertically — compare SWIVEL VISE

uni·verse \ˈyünə͵vərs, -vȳs, -vəis *sometimes* ˈyünē͵-\ *n* -s [L *universum* (trans. of Gk *to holon*), fr. neut. of *universus* entire, whole, fr. *uni-* + *versus*, past part. of *vertere* to turn — more at WORTH] **1 :** the whole body of things and phenomena **:** the totality of material entities **:** COSMOS: as **a :** a systematic whole held to arise by and persist through the direct intervention of divine power **b :** the world of human experience **:** this earth that is the seat of mankind; *also* **:** the inhabitants of earth **:** human beings **c** (1) **:** the entire celestial cosmos **:** the totality of the observed or postulated physical whole — compare EXPANDING UNIVERSE (2) **:** MILKY WAY GALAXY (3) **:** an aggregate of stars comparable to the Milky Way galaxy — see ISLAND UNIVERSE **2 :** a distinct field or province of thought or reality that forms a closed system or self-inclusive and independent organization; *often* **:** UNIVERSE OF DISCOURSE **3 :** POPULATION 4

universe of discourse **1 :** a collection of facts, ideas or entities that is tacitly implied or understood in a given statement, context, or discussion ⟨a proposition concerning "Americans" may be intended to apply only to American aborigines, or to citizens of the U. S., it may include all No. Americans, or be extended to So. Americans as well, the *universe of discourse* in each case being determined by the sense in which the word is taken⟩ **2 :** an inclusive class explicitly containing all the entities to be discussed in a given discourse or investigation or theory ⟨the individual variables of an axiom system may be required to range over members of the class of positive integers, which class is the *universe of discourse* for that system⟩

universe vine *n* **:** BEARBERRY 1

[1]**uni·ver·si·tar·i·an** \¦==͵=səˈterēən, -ta(a)r-, -tār-\ *adj* [*university* + *-arian*] **:** of, relating to, or characteristic of a university

[2]**universitarian** \"\ *n* -s **:** a member of a university

uni·ver·si·tas \͵==ˈ=sə͵tas\ *n, pl* **universita·tes** \͵==͵==ˈtā͵tēz\ [L, lit., totality] **:** something whether in fact composed of one or more than one unit that is treated as an indivisible whole by the law

universitas ju·ris \-ˈju̇rəs\ *n* [L, totality of right] **:** the totality of the rights and liabilities of a person

universitas per·so·na·rum \-͵pərsᵊnˈa(a)rəm, -ˈer-, -ˈār-\ *n* [L, totality of persons] **:** a number of persons (as a college, corporation, or state) functioning together as an independent entity

universitas re·rum \-ˈrērəm, -rār-\ *n* [L, totality of things] **:** a totality of objects treated in one or more respects as a whole in law

uni·ver·si·ty \͵yünəˈvərsəd·ē, -vȳs-,-vəis-, -s(ə)tē, -i\ *n* -ES *often attrib* [ME *universite*, fr. OF *université*, fr. ML, LL, & L; ML *universitat-*, *universitas* university (sense 1), fr. LL, company, corporation, guild, fr. L, totality, universe, fr. *universus* entire, whole + *-itat-*, *-itas* -ity — more at UNIVERSE] **1 a** *archaic* **:** a body of persons gathered at a particular place for the disseminating and assimilating of knowledge in advanced fields of study **b :** an institution of higher learning providing facilities for teaching and research and authorized to grant academic degrees: as (1) **:** an institution in the British Commonwealth authorized to hold examinations and confer degrees and usu. consisting of several affiliated or associated colleges (2) **:** a continental European institution concentrating on or exclusively concerned with advanced or professional study (3) **:** an institution made up of an undergraduate division which confers bachelor's degrees and a graduate division which comprises a graduate school and professional schools each of which may confer master's degrees and doctorates **c :** the physical plant of a university **2** *obs* **a :** UNIVERSE **b :** a body of persons **c :** the mass of the people **3 :** a corporation, guild, association, or other body (as of persons) that is treated as a unit at law **:** UNIVERSITAS

university college *n* **1 :** a college attached to or affiliated with a university **2** *Brit* **:** a college lacking the right to confer its own degrees and for this purpose attached to but physically separate from a university

university extension *n* **:** EXTENSION 6

university press *n* **:** a press connected with a university and esp. concerned with the publication of scholarly works

uni·ver·sol·o·gy \͵==(͵)vərˈsäləjē\ *n* -ES [*universe* + *-o-* + *-logy*] **:** science of the universe

[1]**univ·o·cal** \yüˈnivəkəl\ *adj* [LL *univocus* having only one meaning (fr. L *uni-* + *-vocus*, fr. *voc-*, *vox* voice) + E *-al* — more at VOICE] **1 :** unmistakable in meaning: as **a** *archaic* **:** symptomatic of but one thing **b :** having one meaning only **:** subject to a single interpretation **c :** UNAMBIGUOUS — contrasted with *equivocal* **2** *obs* **a :** UNANIMOUS **b :** UNIFORM **3** *archaic* **:** characteristic of or restricted to things of the same nature — **univ·o·cal·ly** \-vək(ə)lē, -li\ *adv*

[2]**univocal** \"\ *n* **:** a word or term having but one meaning

uni·vocalic \¦yünə+\ *adj* [*uni-* + *vocalic*] **:** having one vowel — compare PLURIVOCALIC

uni·vocality \"+\ *n* **:** the quality or state of being univocal

uni·voc·i·ty \͵yünəˈväsəd·ē\ *n* -ES [*univocal* + *-ity*] **:** the character of being univocal

uni·vol·tine \¦yünə¦vōl͵tēn, -ltᵊn\ *adj* [F *univoltin*, fr. *uni-* + It *volta* time, instance + F *-in* -ine — more at BIVOLTINE] **:** producing one brood in a season and esp. a single brood of eggs capable of hibernating — used of insects; compare BIVOLTINE

un·jaded \¦ən+\ *adj* **:** not jaded **:** FRESH, KEEN ⟨the most lively and ~ fancy may . . . need direction —*Atlantic*⟩

un·jaundiced \"+\ *adj* **:** free from jaundice; *esp* **:** free from hurtful prejudice ⟨good citizens, with well-balanced, ~ minds —Louis Bromfield⟩

un·jelled \"+\ *adj* [[1]*un-* + *jelled*, past part. of *jell*] **:** not stabilized in final or definitive form ⟨an ~ agreement⟩

un·join \"+\ *vt* [ME *unjoinen*, fr. [2]*un-* + *joinen* to join — more at JOIN] **:** to separate from a state of union **:** DIVORCE

un·joined \"+\ *adj* **:** not joined

un·joint \"+\ *vt* [[2]*un-* + *joint*, n.] **:** to sever or dislocate at a joint (as in carving) **:** DISJOINT

un·jointed \"+\ *adj* **:** not jointed

un·joyous \"+\ *adj* **:** deficient in joy **:** lacking the capacity to convey joyous emotion

un·judicial \"+\ *adj* **:** unbecoming or unsuitable to a judge — **un·judicially** \"+\ *adv*

un·judicious \"+\ *adj* **:** INJUDICIOUS

un·just \"+\ *adj* [ME, fr. [1]*un-* + *just*] **1 :** characterized by injustice **:** deficient in justice and fairness **:** WRONGFUL ⟨an ~ judge⟩ ⟨an ~ sentence⟩ ⟨such a proposal was ~ to the consumers⟩ **2** *archaic* **:** DISHONEST, FAITHLESS — **un·justly** \"+\ *adv* — **un·justness** \"+\ *n*

unjust enrichment *n* **:** acquisition of property under such circumstances that one is legally or equitably bound to make restitution of it

un·justice \¦ən+\ *n, chiefly Scot* **:** INJUSTICE

un·justifiable \"+\ *adj* **:** not justifiable **:** lacking in propriety or justice ⟨~ noise⟩ ⟨an ~ decision⟩ — **un·justifiableness** \"+\ *n* — **un·justifiably** \"+\ *adv*

un·justification \"+\ *n* **:** the quality or state of being unjustified

un·justified \"+\ *adj* [[1]*un-* + *justified*, past part. of *justify*] **:** not justified: as **a :** not demonstrably correct or judicious **:** unwarranted in the light of surrounding circumstances ⟨~ abuse⟩ **b** *of a line of type* **:** not adjusted to properly fill the measure

unk *abbr* unknown

un·kar \ˈəŋ͵kär\ *adj, usu cap* [fr. the *Unkar* valley, Arizona] **:** of, relating to, or constituting the lower division of the Algonkian rocks in the Grand Canyon region, Arizona, consisting mainly of sandstone with some limestone and conglomerate and forming a layer nearly 7000 feet in thickness

un·ked *also* **un·kid** \ˈəŋkəd, ˈu̇ŋ-\ *or* **un·ket** \-kət\ *adj* [ME *unkid*, fr. [1]*un-* + *kid*, past part. of *kithen* to make known — more at KITHE] **1** *dial Brit* **:** UNKNOWN, STRANGE, ODD **2** *archaic* **:** UNCOUTH, AWKWARD **3** *dial Brit* **:** DESOLATE, LONELY **4** *dial Brit* **:** UNCANNY, WEIRD, GHASTLY

un·keeled \¦ən+\ *adj* [[1]*un-* + *keel*, n. + *-ed*] **:** having no keel — opposed to *carinate*

un·kempt \"+\ *adj* [[1]*un-* + *kempt*, past part. of *kemb*] **1 a** *of hair* **:** not combed **b :** deficient in order or neatness of person **:** DISHEVELED **2 :** not trimly finished or ordered **:** lacking in formal neatness and order **:** ROUGH ⟨native vistas and ~ rambling paths⟩ **syn** see SLIPSHOD

un·kempt·ly *adv* **:** in an unkempt manner **:** so as to be unkempt

un·kempt·ness *n* -ES **:** the quality or state of being unkempt

un·kenned \¦ən+\ *adj* [ME, fr. [1]*un-* + *kenned*, past part. of *kennen* to ken — more at KEN] *chiefly dial* **:** UNKNOWN, STRANGE

un·kennel \"+\ *vt* **1 a :** to drive (as a fox) from a hiding place or den **b :** to free (dogs) from a kennel **2 :** to cause to come to light **:** bring out into the open **:** DISCOVER, DISCLOSE ⟨seeking to ~ traitors⟩

un·kenning \"+\ *adj* [[1]*un-* + *kenning*, pres. part. of *ken*] *Scot* **:** not knowing **:** IGNORANT

un·kent \"+\ *adj* [[1]*un-* + *kent*, past part. of *ken*] *chiefly Scot* **:** not known or recognized

un·kept \"+\ *adj* [ME, fr. [1]*un-* + *kept*, past part. of *kepen* to keep — more at KEEP] **:** not kept: as **a :** NEGLECTED **b :** DISREGARDED **c :** UNDEFENDED

un·key \"+\ *vt* [[2]*un-* + *key* (insert a keystone)] **:** to remove the key from (as an arch)

un·kind \"+\ *adj* [ME, fr. [1]*un-* + *kind*] **1 a** *of weather or climate* **:** marked by harshness and rigor **:** deficient in pleasant mildness **b** *chiefly dial* **:** exhibiting unfavorable or undesirable qualities **:** inherently bad or unsuitable — used esp. of soil **c** *chiefly dial* **:** not thriving **2** *obs* **a :** deficient in appreciation of or gratitude for benefits **:** UNGRATEFUL **b :** unduly or unnaturally ungenerous or severe **3 :** deficient in humane and kindly feeling, expression, or outlook **:** lacking in sympathy and kindness **:** HARSH, RIGOROUS, CRUEL — **un·kindness** \"+\ *n*

un·kindliness \"+\ *n* [ME *unkindlinesse*, fr. *unkindly* + *-nesse* -ness] **:** the quality or state of being unkindly

[1]**un·kindly** \"+\ *adj* [ME, fr. [1]*un-* + *kindly*] **:** UNKIND

[2]**unkindly** \"\ *also* **un·kind·li·ly** \-lәlē\ *adv* [*unkindly* fr. ME, fr. *unkindly*, adj.; *unkindlily* fr. [1]*unkindly* + *-ly*] **:** in an unkind manner **:** so as to be unkind

un·king \¦ən+\ *vt* [[2]*un-* + *king*, n.] **1 :** to cause to cease to be a king **2 :** to deprive (a monarchy) of having a king

un·kink \¦ən+\ *vt* [[2]*un-* + *kink*] **:** to free from kinks **:** STRAIGHTEN, UNTWIST

unkn *abbr* unknown

un·knit \¦ən+\ *vb* [ME *unknitten*, fr. OE *uncnyttan*, fr. [2]*un-* + *cnyttan* to tie, bind, fasten — more at KNIT] *vt* **1 :** to cause to become undone or unraveled ⟨~ that threatening unkind brow —Shak.⟩ **2 :** to cause to become disunited **:** DISPERSE, DISSOLVE, RELAX ~ *vi* **:** to become unknitted

un·knot \"+\ *vt* [[2]*un-* + *knot*] **:** to undo a knot in; *also* **:** UNTIE, LOOSE

[1]**un·know** \"+\ *vt* [ME *unknowen*, fr. [1]*un-* + *knowen* to know — more at KNOW] **:** to be ignorant of

[2]**unknow** \"\ *vt* [[2]*un-* + *know*] **:** to cease to know **:** FORGET

un·knowability \¦ən+\ *n* **:** the quality or state of being unknowable

[1]**un·knowable** \"+\ *adj* [ME, fr. [1]*un-* + *knowen* to know + *-able*] **:** not knowable **:** of a kind that cannot be comprehended; *esp* **:** lying beyond the limits of human experience or of human powers of apprehension or understanding — **un·knowableness** \"+\ *n* — **un·know·ably** \-əblē, -li\ *adv*

[2]**unknowable** \"\ *n* **:** something that is unknowable: as **a :** absolute reality lying beyond human experience or human understanding **b :** the reality of things as they are in themselves which is outside space and time and underlies phenomena as they appear to human minds **c :** the ultimate reality that we experience but that we can understand only in terms of images and symbols inadequate to its true nature — usu. used with *the*

un·know·en \¦ə(n)¦nōən\ *chiefly dial var of* UNKNOWN

[1]**un·knowing** \¦ən+\ *adj* [ME, fr. [1]*un-* + *knowing*, pres. part. of *knowen* to know — more at KNOW] **1 :** not knowing; *esp* **:** IGNORANT **2 :** UNKNOWN — usu. used with *to* ⟨people who ~ to him had come —James Lerner⟩ — **un·knowingly** \"+\ *adv* — **un·know·ing·ness** \"+\ *n*

[2]**unknowing** \"\ *n* [ME, fr. [1]*un-* + *knowing*, n.] **:** IGNORANCE

[3]**unknowing** \"\ *adv* [ME, fr. *unknowing*, adj.] **:** without knowing

un·knowledgeable \¦ən+\ *adj* **1 :** deficient in or not based on knowledge ⟨an ~ assistant⟩ ⟨such ~ comments⟩ **2 :** UNKNOWABLE ⟨~ splendours —Mary Austin⟩

[1]**un·known** \"+\ *adj* [ME *unknowen*, *unknawen*, fr. [1]*un-* + *knowen*, *knawen* known — more at KNOWN] **1 :** not known: as **a :** STRANGE, UNFAMILIAR **b :** not apprehended **:** not ascertained **c :** INCALCULABLE, INEXPRESSIBLE **d :** lacking an established or normal status **:** having no formal recognition ⟨~ to the court⟩ **2** *obs* **:** not knowing **:** IGNORANT — **un·known·ness** *n* -ES

[2]**unknown** \"\ *n* **1 :** one that is unknown: as **a :** an unknown or unidentified person — usu. used with *the* ⟨the fair ~⟩ **b :** a thing, state, or region that is unknown or imperfectly known or defined ⟨left to seek his fortune in the western ~⟩ ⟨this ~ may alter our plans⟩ **2 :** something requiring to be discovered, identified, or made clear; *esp* **:** a letter or other symbol in a mathematical equation representing a number that is to be found and often consisting of one of the last letters of the alphabet — see UNKNOWN QUANTITY

unknown quantity *n* **1 :** a quantity for which a mathematical value is sought and which is usu. denoted symbolically by a mathematical unknown **2 :** something that constitutes a factor (as in a particular situation) of which the bearing and importance is not apparent

unknown soldier *n, usu cap U&S* **:** an unidentified soldier whose body is selected as a representative of all of the same nation who died in a war and esp. in one of the world wars to receive national honors

un·knownst \¦ə(n)¦nōn(t)st\ *adj* [by alter.] *chiefly dial* **:** UNKNOWN

unl *abbr* unlimited

un·labeled \¦ən+\ *adj* [[1]*un-* + *labeled*, past part. of *label*] **:** not labeled

un·labored \¦ən+\ *adj* [ME *unlaboured*, fr. [1]*un-* + *laboured*, past part. of *labouren* to labor — more at LABOR] **1 :** not cultivated **:** UNTILLED **2 :** produced without labor or toil **3 :** accomplished or attained seemingly without effort **:** NATURAL, SPONTANEOUS ⟨a cheerful, friendly, and ~ book —Harrison Smith⟩

un·laboring \"+\ *adj* [[1]*un-* + *laboring*, pres. part. of *labor*] **:** having no necessity to labor or make an effort

un·laborious \"+\ *adj* **:** not requiring work or striving **:** EFFORTLESS

un·lace \"+\ *vt* [ME *unlacen*, fr. [2]*un-* + *lacen* to lace — more at LACE] **1 a :** to loose by undoing a lacing **:** untie the laces of ⟨*unlaced* her skates⟩ **b** (1) **:** to free by or as if by undoing the laces **:** unloose the dress of (2) *obs* **:** to expose to disgrace ⟨what's the matter that you ~ your reputation thus —Shak.⟩ **2 :** to loose and take off (a bonnet from a sail) **:** cast off (lacing in the rigging) **:** UNTIE

un·laced \"+\ *adj* [ME, fr. past part. of *unlacen*] **:** loosed from laces **:** UNRESTRAINED ⟨~ behavior in a neighborhood pub —Robert Hatch⟩

un·lade \"+\ *vb* [ME *unladen*, fr. [2]*un-* + *laden* to load — more at LADE] *vt* **1 :** to take the load from **:** take out the cargo of ⟨didn't ~ the ponies —C.A.Spring-Rice⟩ **2 :** to have removed (as a load or burden) **:** DISCHARGE, UNLOAD ⟨here freighters . . . lade and ~ cargo with cranes —*Amer. Guide Series: Fla.*⟩ ~ *vi* **:** to discharge cargo ⟨the wharf where the fishing boats ~⟩

un·laden \"+\ *adj* [fr. past part. of *unlade*] **:** UNLOADED

un·ladylike \"+\ *adj* **:** lacking the behavior, manner, or style considered proper for a lady

un·laid \"+\ *adj* [ME *unleyd*, fr. [1]*un-* + *leyd*, *leyed*, past part. of *leyen* to lay — more at LAY] **1 :** not laid or placed **:** not fixed ⟨his supper still ~ —Israel Zangwill⟩ **2 :** not allayed **:** not pacified **:** not laid finally to rest ⟨stubborn, ~ ghost —John Milton⟩ **3 :** not laid out — used esp. of a corpse **4** *of a rope* **:** not twisted

un·lamented \"+\ *adj* [[1]*un-* + *lamented*, past part. of *lament*] **:** not grieved for **:** causing no mourning ⟨interred in an ~ grave —E.J.Mann⟩

un·landed \"+\ *adj* [ME, fr. [1]*un-* + *landed*] **:** possessing no land ⟨uphold the rights of ~ tenants⟩

un·lan·guaged \¦ən¦laŋgwijd\ *adj* [[1]*un-* + *language* + *-ed*] **:** lacking articulateness **:** not expressed in clear articulate speech ⟨the ~ prattling of infants —J.R.Lowell⟩

un·lap \¦ən+\ *vt* [ME *unlappen*, fr. [2]*un-* + *lappen* to lap — more at LAP (to fold over)] **:** to uncover by or as if by the removal of an outer wrapper

un·lash \"+\ *vt* [[2]*un-* + *lash*] **1 :** to detach in order to make use of (something lashed or tied down) **:** untie the lashing of ⟨quickly ~*ed* a sledge he was carrying on the pontoon of his helicopter —Glen Jacobsen⟩ **2 :** LOOSE, UNDO

un·latch \"+\ *vb* [[2]*un-* + *latch*] *vt* **:** to open or loose by lifting the latch ~ *vi* **:** to become loosed or opened

un·latched \"+\ *adj* [[1]*un-* + *latched*] **:** not fastened with a latch or a similar device ⟨went through the ~ gate into the street⟩

un·lat·ined \¦ən¦latᵊnd\ *adj* [[1]*un-* + *Latin* + *-ed*] **:** uninstructed in Latin ⟨the ~ English reader —M.H.Fisch⟩

un·launched \¦ən+\ *adj* [[1]*un-* + *launched*, past part. of *launch*] **:** not launched; *esp* **:** not set afloat ⟨left ~ and dry —John Keats⟩

un·laureled \"+\ *adj* [[1]*un-* + *laureled*, past part. of *laurel*] **:** not crowned with laurel **:** having no acclaim or reward ⟨the ~ heroism of endurance —Francis Parkman⟩

[1]**un·law** \"+\ *n* [ME *unlawe*, fr. OE *unlagu*, of Scand origin; akin to ON *ōlög*, *ūlög* illegality, lawlessness, fr. *ō-*, *ū-* un- + *lög* law — more at LAW] **1 :** a violation of law **:** disregard of the restraints of law **:** ILLEGALITY, LAWLESSNESS ⟨times of ~ alternate with times of law —Frederick Pollock & F.W.Maitland⟩ **2** *Scots law* **:** a fine or amercement for a violation of law

[2]**unlaw** \"\ *vt* [ME (Sc) *unlawen*, fr. *unlawe*, n.] **1** *Scots law* **:** to impose a fine upon **2** [[2]*un-* + *law*, n.] *obs* **:** to deprive of the character of a law **:** ANNUL

un·lawed \"+\ *adj* [[1]*un-* + *lawed*, past part. of *law* (to expeditate)] **:** not expeditated — used esp. of a dog

un·lawful \"+\ *adj* [ME *unlaweful*, fr. [1]*un-* + *laweful* lawful — more at LAWFUL] **1 :** not lawful **:** contrary to or prohibited by law **:** not authorized or justified by law **:** not permitted or warranted by law ⟨~ measures⟩ ⟨~ money⟩ **2 :** acting contrary to or in defiance of the law **:** disobeying or disregarding the law ⟨~ buyer⟩ ⟨~ hunter⟩ **3 :** contrary to normal or acceptable procedure **:** IRREGULAR; *esp* **:** not morally right or conventional ⟨~ love⟩ ⟨~ pleasures⟩ **4 :** born out of wedlock **:** ILLEGITIMATE

unlawful assembly *n* **:** a meeting of three or more persons in pursuance of a common plan and in such a way as to cause a reasonable apprehension that they will disturb the peace tumultuously

un·lawfully \"+\ *adv* [ME *unlawefully*, fr. *unlaweful* + *-ly*] **:** in an unlawful manner ⟨accused of having ~ and willfully entered the waters . . . in search of loot —Frank Yerby⟩

un·law·ful·ness *n* **:** the quality or state of being unlawful

un·lax \¦ən¦laks\ *vb* -ED/-ING/-ES [[2]*un-* + *-lax* (as in *relax*)] *vi* **:** RELAX ⟨lie in the hot sun, feeling yourself gradually ~ —Bennett Cerf⟩ ~ *vt* **:** to gradually relieve the tension in ⟨took only a few minutes of the caressing air of Rome . . . to ~ cramped muscles —Kay Halle⟩

un·lay \¦ən+\ *vb* [[2]*un-* + *lay*] *vt* **:** to untwist the strands of (as a rope) ~ *vi* **:** UNTWIST

un·leached \"+\ *adj* [[1]*un-* + *leached*, past part. of *leach*] **:** not leached — used esp. of wood ashes

un·lead \"+\ *vt* [[2]*un-* + *lead* (to place leads)] **:** to remove lead from (as between lines of type)

un·leaded \"+\ *adj* [in sense 1, fr. past part. of *unlead*; in sense 2, fr. [1]*un-* + *leaded*, past part. of *lead*] **1 :** stripped of lead **2 :** not having leads between the lines in printing

un·leaf \"+\ *vt* [[2]*un-* + *leaf*, n.] **:** to strip of leaves

un·learn \"+\ *vb* [ME *unlernen*, fr. [2]*un-* + *lernen* to learn — more at LEARN] *vt* **1 :** to put out of one's knowledge or memory **:** discard the habit of **:** discover the falsity of ⟨it took him a long time to ~ the puritanism of his childhood —Aldous Huxley⟩ **2 :** UNTEACH ~ *vi* **:** to discard previously acquired habits or knowledge ⟨they do not learn because they cannot or will not ~ —R.G.Vansittart⟩

un·learned *in senses 1, 2 & 4* ¦ən¦lərnəd, -¦lȳn-, -¦ləin- *sometimes* -nd, *in senses 3 & 5* -nd *or* -nt, *dial* ˈlärn- *or* ˈlȧn-\ *adj* [ME *unlerned*, fr. [1]*un-* + *lerned* learned — more at LEARNED] **1 :** possessing little or no learning or education **:** UNSCHOOLED, UNTAUGHT ⟨recounts the experiences of an ~ man in the search for truth and understanding —*Brit. Bk. News*⟩ **2 :** characterized by or revealing ignorance **:** not exhibiting learning ⟨~ speech⟩ **3 :** not gained by study ⟨things better ~⟩ **4 :** lacking in skill or knowledge **:** UNVERSED — usu. used with *in* ⟨~ in the arts of war⟩ ⟨he was not ~ in philosophy⟩ **5 :** independent of experience, training, or the process of learning **:** NATURAL ⟨breathing is an example of man's ~ behavior⟩ **syn** see IGNORANT

un·learned·ly *adv* **:** in an unlearned manner

un·leased \¦ən+\ *adj* [[1]*un-* + *leased*, past part. of *lease*] **:** not leased **:** being without a lease ⟨the house had been ~ for a year⟩

un·leash \"+\ *vt* [[2]*un-* + *leash*] **:** to free from a leash or as if from a leash **:** let loose from control or restraint ⟨a bold and imaginative approach that will ~ the energies of free men —*Nation's Business*⟩ ⟨corruptions of power could ~ great evil in the world —A.M.Schlesinger b. 1917⟩

un·leavened \"+\ *adj* [[1]*un-* + *leavened*, past part. of *leaven*] **:** not leavened **:** containing no leaven ⟨~ bread is usu. flour mixed with water⟩ ⟨these works are tedious, ~ by imaginative power, and cramped in diction —L.N.Richardson⟩

un·led \"+\ *adj* [¹*un-* + *led,* past part. of *lead*] **:** not led **:** lacking leadership or guidance ⟨the ~ or misled welter of a commercial century —John Masefield⟩
un·legal \"+\ *adj* **:** NONLEGAL
un·leisured \"+\ *adj* [¹*un-* + *leisure* + *-ed*] **:** having no leisure ⟨the feverish ~ scrambling lives we live in the big cities —J.C. Powys⟩
¹un·less \(,)ən'les *sometimes* ²n-\ *conj* [ME *unlesse* (*than*), *unless* (*that*), alter. (influenced by ¹*un-*) of *onlesse* (*than*), *onlesse* (*that*), fr. *on* + *lesse* less — more at ON, LESS] **1 :** under any other circumstance than that **:** except on the condition that **:** if . . . not ⟨would have been destroyed ~ a regiment . . . had been sent —J.J.Chapman⟩ ⟨modern man is obsolete . . . ~ he can stop world wars —Stuart Chase⟩ ⟨no person shall be convicted of treason ~ on the testimony of two witnesses —*U. S. Constitution*⟩ **2 :** without the accompanying circumstance or condition that **:** but that **:** BUT ⟨never a day goes by ~ at least one collision occurs —Priscilla Hughes⟩
²unless \"\ *prep* [ME *unlesse* (*than*), alter. of *onlesse* (*than*), fr. *on* + *lesse*] **:** except possibly **:** EXCEPT ⟨no one (~ the psychotherapists who have to deal with the casualties) seems seriously to have considered the dangers —*New Republic*⟩
un·lessened \¦ən+\ *adj* [¹*un-* + *lessened,* past part. of *lessen*] **:** marked by constancy **:** not diminished ⟨in spite of the treatment he received his loyalty was ~⟩
un·lessoned \"+\ *adj* [¹*un-* + *lesson,* n. + *-ed*] **:** lacking lessons or instruction ⟨an ~ girl . . . happy in this, she is not so old but she may learn —Shak.⟩
un·let \"+\ *adj* [¹*un-* + *let,* past part. of *let*] **:** not rented ⟨examined the room . . . which was still ~ —F.W.Crofts⟩
un·lettable \"+\ *adj* **:** not able to be rented
un·lettered \"+\ *adj* [ME, fr. ¹*un-* + *lettered*] **1 a :** not lettered **:** lacking scholarship ⟨regarded as an ~ rhymester —Van Wyck Brooks⟩ **b :** ILLITERATE ⟨many country priests were stupid and ~ —G.B.Sansom⟩ **2 :** not marked with letters ⟨an ~ tombstone⟩ ⟨an ~ police car —*Springfield (Mass.) Daily News*⟩ **syn** see IGNORANT
¹un·level \"+\ *adj* [¹*un-* + *level,* adj.] **:** not level **:** UNEVEN ⟨tennis lawns grown lank and ~ —Adrian Bell⟩
²unlevel \"\ *vt* [²*un-* + *level,* v.] **:** to destroy the level character of **:** make uneven ⟨moles ~*ed* the lawn⟩
un·lev·el·ness *n* **:** the quality or state of being unlevel
un·liable \¦ən+\ *adj* **:** not liable ⟨pictured . . . as being somehow ~ to human frailties —Arnold Bennett⟩
un·licensed \¦ən+\ *adj* **1 a :** unauthorized by license to engage in a specified activity ⟨an ~ airplane pilot⟩ ⟨~ moneylender⟩ **b** *archaic* **:** not granted permission or authority **2 a :** printed without a license — used of a publication **b :** lacking sanction or authorization ⟨imprisoned for ~ preaching —*Dial*⟩ **3 :** lacking restraint **:** LAWLESS ⟨the ~ passions of a guilty people —W.E.Channing⟩
un·licked \"+\ *adj* [¹*un-* + *licked,* past part. of *lick*] **1 :** not licked dry **:** lacking proper form or shape ⟨an ~ bear whelp —Shak.⟩ **2 :** revealing youthful naïveté or crudeness of manner **:** lacking finish or polish ⟨was just an ~ kid when I knew him⟩ ⟨a kind of ~ attempt at civility —Mary Deasy⟩
un·lid \"+\ *vt* [²*un-* + *lid,* n.] **:** to take the lid off **:** UNCOVER ⟨she *unlidded* the second box —T.W.Duncan⟩
un·lidded \"+\ *adj* [¹*un-* + *lid,* n. + *-ed*] **:** not having or equipped with a lid
un·lifelike \"+\ *adj* **:** not lifelike **:** lacking realism
un·light \,ən'līt\ *vi* [²*un-* + *light*] *dial Eng* **:** to get down (as from a vehicle or horse) **:** ALIGHT
un·lighted \¦ən+\ *adj* [¹*un-* + *lighted,* past part. of *light*] **:** not lighted **:** UNLIT
un·lightened \"+\ *adj* [¹*un-* + *lightened,* past part. of *lighten*] **:** not lighted up **:** lacking brightness
un·likable *also* **un·likeable** \¦ən+\ *adj* **:** not likable
¹un·like \"+\ *prep* [ME *unlik,* fr. ¹*un-* + *lik,* prep., like — more at LIKE] **:** not like: as **a** (1) **:** different from **:** dissimilar to ⟨felt strangely ~ a successful lover —Floyd Dell⟩ (2) **:** not characteristic of ⟨it was ~ him to be late⟩ **b** (1) **:** in a different manner from **:** differently from ⟨become, ~ all other human beings, altogether free from personal or class bias —M.R. Cohen⟩ (2) **:** in a manner that is not characteristic of ⟨so many fine men were outside the charmed circle that, ~ most colleges, there was no disgrace in not being a club man —John Reed⟩
²unlike \"\ *adj* [ME *unlik,* fr. *un-* + *lik,* adj., like — more at LIKE] **1 :** not like: as **a :** marked by dissimilarity **:** DISSIMILAR, DIFFERENT ⟨men are profoundly ~ —E.W.Sinnott⟩ **b :** marked by inequality **:** UNEQUAL ⟨contributed ~ amounts⟩ **2** *archaic* **:** UNLIKELY ⟨it's ~ to dry off the grass before midnight —MacKinlay Kantor⟩
³unlike \"\ *n* **:** a person or thing marked by difference
⁴unlike \"\ *conj* **:** in a manner that is different than **:** not as ⟨~ in the gasoline engine, fuel does not enter the cylinder with air on the intake stroke —Irving Frazee⟩
un·likelihood \¦ən+\ *n* **1 :** IMPROBABILITY ⟨his present financial status adds to the ~ of his attending college⟩ **2 :** something improbable
un·likeliness \"+\ *n* **1** *obs* **:** a rank discrepancy **2 :** UNLIKELIHOOD
¹un·likely \"+\ *adj, sometimes* -ER/-EST [ME *unlikli,* fr. ¹*un-* + *likli,* adj., likely — more at LIKELY] **1 :** not likely **:** IMPROBABLE, UNBELIEVABLE ⟨laughed at the . . . description of the ~ animal —C.A.Nicholson⟩ ⟨his nomination seemed an ~ event⟩ **2 :** not such as to inspire liking **:** DISAGREEABLE, OBJECTIONABLE, UNATTRACTIVE ⟨fractured himself with . . . too little work and too many ~ companions —*Time*⟩ **3 :** seemingly lacking in any prospect of success **:** likely to fail **:** UNPROMISING ⟨a place full of good things, but it looked so ~ at first glance —Maristan Chapman⟩ ⟨discovers poetry in the most ~ places —C.D.Lewis⟩
²unlikely \"\ *adv* [ME *unlikli,* fr. ¹*un-* + *likli,* adv., likely — more at LIKELY] **:** in an unlikely manner
un·like·ness *n* [ME *unliknesse,* fr. *unlik,* adj., unlike + *-nesse* -ness] **:** the quality or state of being unlike **:** an instance of dissimilarity **syn** see DISSIMILARITY
un·limber \¦ən+\ *vb* [²*un-* + *limber,* n.] *vt* **1 :** to detach the limber from and so make ready ⟨~ a gun for action⟩ **2 :** to prepare for action **:** arrange for use ⟨~*ed* his cameras . . . and began to work —R.L.Taylor⟩ **~** *vi* **:** to perform the task of preparing something for action
un·lime \"+\ *vt* [²*un-* + *lime,* n.] **:** DELIME
un·limited \¦ən+\ *adj* [ME, fr. ¹*un-* + *limited,* past part. of *limiten* to limit — more at LIMIT] **1 :** lacking any controls **:** UNRESTRICTED, UNCONFINED ⟨to start with a theory of ~ freedom is to end up with ~ despotism —Philip Rahv⟩ ⟨not in favor of ~ experiment; he was in favor of rigid control from above —H.L.Mencken⟩ **2 :** having no bounds **:** wanting limits **:** BOUNDLESS, INFINITE ⟨ceiling ~⟩ ⟨an ~ expanse of ocean⟩ **3 :** not bounded by exceptions **:** UNDEFINED ⟨the ~ and unconditional surrender of the enemy —Sir Winston Churchill⟩
unlimited company *n* **:** a company in which liability of members is not limited
un·lim·it·ed·ly *adv* **:** in an unlimited manner **:** without limitations
un·lim·it·ed·ness *n* **:** the quality or state of being unlimited
unlimited policy *n* **:** an insurance policy covering substantially all hazards or types of loss contemplated under the particular kind of insurance or setting no maximum limitation on the company's liability
¹un·lined \¦ən+\ *adj* [¹*un-* + *lined* (having a lining)] **:** made or constructed without a lining ⟨his jacket was ~⟩
²unlined \"+\ *adj* [¹*un-* + *lined* (marked with lines)] **:** not traced with lines ⟨his cheeks were ~, his speech was soft —J.S. Reeves⟩
un·link \"+\ *vb* [²*un-* + *link*] *vt* **1 :** to unfasten the links of **2 :** to separate by or as if by undoing the links of a chain **~** *vi* **:** to become detached
un·liquid \"+\ *adj* **:** not readily converted into cash
un·liquidated \"+\ *adj* [¹*un-* + *liquidated,* past part. of *liquidate*] **:** not liquidated
un·listed \"+\ *adj* **1 :** not appearing upon a list ⟨telephone number was ~⟩ **2 :** of or relating to a stock or bond not listed on an organized securities exchange
un·listened \"+\ *adj* [¹*un-* + *listened,* past part. of *listen*] not listened to **:** not heard
un·listening \"+\ *adj* **:** not listening **:** lacking sensitivity ⟨his speech fell upon ~ ears⟩
un·lit \"+\ *adj* **:** not lighted: as **a :** not kindled ⟨the table was bare, the fire ~⟩ **b :** not illuminated with or as if with light ⟨through the dark ~ streets —Erskine Caldwell⟩
un·literal \"+\ *adj* **:** not literal **:** lacking complete accuracy
un·literary \¦ən+\ *adj* **:** not literary **:** marked by lack of affectation or pedantry ⟨her talk was very ~ —W.D.Howells⟩
un·literate \"+\ *adj* **:** not literate
un·livable \"+\ *adj* **1 :** unfit to live in or with ⟨~ substandard housing⟩ ⟨~ conditions⟩ **2 :** not conducive to comfortable or easy living ⟨the room was very beautiful, but . . . ~ because there was no place in it where you could settle down —Frances Crane⟩
un·live \"+\ *vt* [²*un-* + *live*] **:** to live down **:** ANNUL, REVERSE ⟨history cannot be *unlived* —*New Republic*⟩
un·lively \"+\ *adj* **:** not lively **:** lacking animation **:** DULL ⟨a particularly ~ session of the Senate⟩
un·livery \"+\ *n* [¹*un-* + *livery*] **:** the unloading or discharge of cargo
un·living \"+\ *adj* **:** LIFELESS ⟨entreat all living and ~ things to weep —Matthew Arnold⟩
¹un·load \"+\ *vb* [²*un-* + *load*] *vt* **1 a** (1) **:** to take off **:** DELIVER, DISCHARGE, REMOVE ⟨call for your car at the port where it is to be ~*ed* —Richard Joseph⟩ (2) **:** to take the cargo from ⟨the whole crew may drop their tools to help ~ an arriving . . . sloop —Stuart Chase⟩ **b :** to give outlet to **:** pour forth ⟨head buried in his mother's lap, he ~*ed* his small problems⟩ **2 a :** to relieve of something burdensome **:** take a load from ⟨~*ed* the pack animals and began making camp⟩ **b :** to relieve from something oppressive or difficult ⟨~*ed* his heart in passionate utterance⟩ **3 :** to draw the charge from ⟨~*ed* the gun⟩ **4 :** to sell esp. in large quantities **:** get rid of **:** DUMP ⟨investors who keep their eyes on fundamental business trends made no move to ~ their holdings —*Newsweek*⟩ ⟨might be able to ~ more of its grain . . . abroad —*Wall Street Jour.*⟩ **5 a :** to discard (worthless or dangerous cards) from one's hand **b :** to meld or discard (high cards) in playing rummy to reduce the count of one's hand **~** *vi* **1 :** to perform the act of unloading ⟨there were certain types of shipping which could ~ in a matter of hours —E.C.R.Lasher⟩ **2 :** to sell large quantities of stock esp. in expectation of a market decline or for an inordinate price **3 :** to meld or discard cards that would be costly if they remained in one's hand at the end of play
²unload \"\ *n* **:** a commodity, consignment, or cargo after it has been unloaded — compare SHIPMENT
un·loader \"+\ *n* **1 a :** one that unloads by hand or by machine **b :** a machine used for unloading **2 :** a valve in an ammonia compressor system that shunts the head pressure so the compressor has less to work against
un·lobed \¦ən+\ *adj* **:** having no lobes
un·localized \"+\ *adj* [¹*un-* + *localized,* past part. of *localize*] **:** lacking a specific location
un·located \"+\ *adj* [¹*un-* + *located,* past part. of *locate*] **1 :** not located or placed **2 :** not surveyed or designated by marks, limits, or boundaries as appropriated ⟨~ lands⟩
un·lock \"+\ *vb* [ME *unlokken,* fr. ²*un-* + *lokken* to lock — more at LOCK] *vt* **1 :** to unfasten the lock of ⟨~*ed* the trunk of his car⟩ **2 a :** to lay open by or as if by undoing a lock ⟨struggle to ~ the lands held by a handful of squatters —*Times Lit. Supp.*⟩ **b :** to gain or grant admission to ⟨how to ~ one of the greatest of all mysteries — photosynthesis —Bruce Bliven b. 1889⟩ ⟨reference books are the keys that quickly ~ the doors to . . . stored knowledge and golden wisdom —G.B. Shaw⟩ **3 :** to cause to open **:** free from restraints or restrictions ⟨the reaction to the shock ~*ed* a flood of emotions⟩ **4 a :** to open by a physical action **:** spread apart ⟨they ~*ed* their cramped fingers from the paddles —Bill Wolf⟩ **b :** to release from immovability ⟨sheer anger finally ~*ed* his tongue and he shouted at the mob⟩ **5 :** to furnish a key to ⟨the three cipher men ~*ed* the whole letter —Fletcher Pratt⟩ **~** *vi* **:** to become unfastened or freed from restraints
un·locked \"+\ *adj* [fr. past part. of *unlock*] **:** not locked ⟨the ~ door⟩
un·lodge \"+\ *vt* [²*un-* + *lodge*] **:** to deprive of lodgment **:** DISLODGE
un·logical \"+\ *adj* **:** ILLOGICAL
un·looked at \¦ən¦lu̇k,tat\ *adj* [¹*un-* + *looked at,* past part. form of the phrase *look at*] **:** lacking attention **:** UNHEEDED ⟨the magazines lay *unlooked at*⟩
un·looked-for \¦ən¦lu̇kt,fȯ(ə)r, -ō(ə)\ *adj* [¹*un-* + *looked for,* past part. form of the phrase *look for*] **:** not observed or foreseen **:** UNEXPECTED ⟨a virtue perhaps *unlooked-for* in a people so full of energy —E.A.Peers⟩
un·looped \¦ən+\ *adj* **:** not looped
un·loose \"+\ *vb* [ME *unloosen, unlosen,* fr. ²*un-* + *loosen, losen* to loose — more at LOOSE] *vt* **1 :** to moderate or relax the strain of ⟨he *unloosed* his grip —I.L.Idriess⟩ **2 :** to release from or as if from restraints **:** set free ⟨a flood of dark memories and fears had been *unloosed* —John Buchan⟩ **3 :** to loosen the ties of ⟨in *unloosing* the traditional social bonds Puritanism awakened aspirations —V.L.Parrington⟩ **~** *vi, obs* **:** to become loose
un·loosen \"+\ *vt* [ME *unlosnen,* fr. ²*un-* + *losnen, loosnen* to loosen — more at LOOSEN] **:** UNLOOSE
un·lopped \"+\ *adj* [¹*un-* + *lopped,* past part. of *lop*] **:** not lopped **:** UNCUT
un·lord \"+\ *vt* [²*un-* + *lord*] **:** to deprive of the rank or position of a lord
un·lordly \"+\ *adj* [¹*un-* + *lordly*] **:** not lordly **:** not arbitrary
un·lost \"+\ *adj* **:** not lost **:** SECURE
un·lovable \"+\ *adj* **:** incapable of inspiring love or admiration ⟨she was in some mysterious way . . . ~ —Joseph Conrad⟩
¹un·love \"+\ *vb* [ME *unloven,* fr. ²*un-* + *loven* to love — more at LOVE] *vt* **:** to cease to love ⟨he must not ~ her but he must certainly leave her —*Delineator*⟩ **~** *vi* **:** to stop loving something ⟨he can . . . ~ so easily —Robert Hichens⟩
²un·love \'ən,ləv\ *n* [¹*un-* + *love,* n.] **:** absence of love **:** HATE ⟨after months of gnawing ~ —Martha Gellhorn⟩
un·loved \¦ən+\ *adj* [ME, fr. ¹*un-* + *loved,* past part. of *loven* to love] **:** not loved ⟨a poet ~ by most critics —C.R.Woodring⟩
un·loveliness \"+\ *n* **:** the quality or state of being unlovely
un·lovely \"+\ *adj, sometimes* -ER/-EST [ME, fr. ¹*un-* + *lovely*] **1 :** lacking the ability to evoke affection **:** possessing qualities that inspire dislike **:** DISAGREEABLE, UNPLEASANT **2 :** not attractive to the senses **:** displeasing in appearance **:** UNSIGHTLY ⟨planked a most ~ boot firmly —Ngaio Marsh⟩
un·loving \"+\ *adj* **:** not loving **:** not giving or reciprocating affection — **un·lov·ing·ly** *adv* — **un·lov·ing·ness** *n*
un·luck \"+\ *n* [¹*un-* + *luck*] *chiefly South* **:** bad luck **:** MISFORTUNE
un·luckily \"+\ *adv* **:** in an unlucky manner **:** UNFORTUNATELY ⟨~ I have lost my memorandum —B.N.Cardozo⟩
un·luckiness \"+\ *n* **:** the quality or state of being unlucky
un·lucky \"+\ *adj* [¹*un-* + *lucky*] **1 :** characterized by adversity or failure ⟨this has been an ~ year for us⟩ **2 :** seemingly presaging misfortune **:** ILL-OMENED ⟨born under an ~ star⟩ **3 :** having or meeting with bad luck ⟨the ~ prisoner was again put in irons —W.H.Prescott⟩ **4** *dial chiefly Eng* **:** causing trouble or mischief **5 :** producing dissatisfaction **:** REGRETTABLE ⟨the ~ fact is that . . . it is not a formal biography —*Times Lit. Supp.*⟩
syn DISASTROUS, ILL-STARRED, ILL-FATED, UNFORTUNATE, LUCKLESS, HAPLESS: UNLUCKY implies that in spite of effort or merit one has bad luck, often chronically, or, as applied to an occasion or action, that it proves to be unfavorable, esp. in outcome or consequences ⟨if you're *unlucky* enough to lose or break your glasses —Richard Joseph⟩ ⟨the loss of over $200,000 in an *unlucky* coffee speculation —H.G.Pearson⟩ ⟨the child who is born on an *unlucky* day —Abram Kardiner⟩ ⟨an *unlucky* throw of the dice⟩ DISASTROUS, applying to anything that is or brings calamity, applies often to anything that has a calamitous fate ⟨a *disastrous* flood⟩ ⟨in so *disastrous* a plight that he died on the following day —W.H.Prescott⟩ ⟨a *disastrous* armaments race —*Current Biog.*⟩ ⟨a *disastrous* expedition against a superior force⟩ ILL-STARRED is interchangeable with DISASTROUS both in the sense of bringing calamity ⟨the *ill-starred* depression year of 1929 —*Springfield (Mass.) Union*⟩ and in the sense of having or doomed to have a calamitous fate ⟨the return trip was *ill-starred:* they narrowly escaped a serious accident —Willa Cather⟩ ⟨the *ill-starred* fellow is pummeled on deck —Herman Melville⟩ ⟨the *ill-starred* lady who perished —Allen Upward⟩ ILL-FATED is ILL-STARRED in the second of the two senses suggested immediately above ⟨an *ill-fated* expedition that perished at sea⟩ UNFORTUNATE, though often interchangeable with UNLUCKY, is weaker in implying mere bad luck ⟨an *unfortunate* day at the races⟩ and stronger in suggesting misfortune, misery, or desolation ⟨expecting some *unfortunate* woman to instruct simultaneously a crowd of fifty urchins of all degrees of ignorance and stupidity —C.H.Grandgent⟩ ⟨assist an *unfortunate* people suffering the calamities of war⟩ though it can often mean only regrettable ⟨the building was completed with *unfortunate* stylistic admixtures —*Amer. Guide Series: N.Y.*⟩ LUCKLESS and HAPLESS usu. apply to a person or thing notably or chronically unfortunate ⟨the *luckless* small investors were ruined —O.S.Nock⟩ ⟨all his speculations had of late gone wrong with the *luckless* old gentleman —W.M.Thackeray⟩ ⟨as the sea dried up, the *hapless* ship sank beneath shifting dunes —*Amer. Guide Series: Calif.*⟩ ⟨these *hapless* creatures now wander as displaced persons —R.H.Jackson⟩
un·lucrative \"+\ *adj* **:** not gainful **:** lacking in profit ⟨made life exciting, but altogether ~ —*Time*⟩
un·luminous \"+\ *adj* **:** lacking illumination **:** not luminous
un·lustrous \"+\ *adj* **:** lacking luster **:** having no brilliance or shine
un·lute \"+\ *vt* [²*un-* + *lute* (to seal)] **:** to take apart (as things cemented) **:** take the clay from
un·luxurious \"+\ *adj* **:** lacking luxury **:** PLAIN, SPARTAN
unm *abbr* unmarried
un·made \¦ən+\ *adj* [ME *unmad,* fr. ¹*un-* + *mad,* past part. of *maken* to make — more at MAKE] **:** not made
unmade-up *adj* [¹*un-* + *made up,* past part. of *make up*] **:** not made or worked up into final form **:** not ready **:** not manufactured
un·magical \¦ən+\ *adj* **:** not magical ⟨life that can be comprehended in ~ terms —*Dial*⟩
un·magnetic \"+\ *adj* **:** not magnetic
un·magnetized \"+\ *adj* [¹*un-* + *magnetized,* past part. of *magnetize*] **:** not magnetized
un·magnified \"+\ *adj* [¹*un-* + *magnified,* past part. of *magnify*] **:** not magnified
un·maidenly \¦ən+\ *adj* [¹*un-* + *maidenly*] **:** not maidenly ⟨high-minded, flat-bosomed young women who embrace world problems with ~ ardor —M.G.Bishop⟩
un·mailable \"+\ *adj* **:** not mailable ⟨found the novel ~ under post office decency clauses —*Newsweek*⟩ — **un·mail·able·ness** *n* -ES
un·maimed \"+\ *adj, archaic* **:** not maimed
un·maintainable \"+\ *adj* **:** not maintainable
un·maintained \"+\ *adj* [¹*un-* + *maintained,* past part. of *maintain*] **:** not maintained
un·make \"+\ *vt* [ME *unmaken,* fr. ²*un-* + *maken* to make — more at MAKE] **1 :** to undo the creation of **:** cause to disappear **:** DESTROY ⟨couldn't ~ the public image his press agents had so carefully built⟩ **2 :** to deprive of rank or office **:** DEPOSE ⟨people have elected me . . . and they can ~ me —John Steinbeck⟩ **3 :** to deprive of essential characteristics **:** change the nature of ⟨enough to ~ any man —Katherine Mansfield⟩ **4 :** to change an attitude of (one's mind) ⟨ladies are allowed to ~ their minds —R.D.Blackmore⟩
un·maker \"+\ *n* [ME *unmakere,* fr. *unmaken* + *-ere* -er] **:** one that unmakes
un·malicious \"+\ *adj* **:** not malicious
un·malleable \"+\ *adj* **:** not malleable
un·malted \"+\ *adj* [¹*un-* + *malted,* past part. of *malt*] **:** not malted ⟨~ barley⟩
un·man \¦ən+\ *vt* [²*un-* + *man,* n.] **1 a** *archaic* **:** to deprive of the characteristics of man ⟨I may put forth angel's plumage, once *unmanned,* but not before —Robert Browning⟩ **b :** to deprive of courage, strength, or vigor **:** cause to become weak or unmanly ⟨the tenderness that threatened to ~ him —Frances G. Patton⟩ ⟨fell prostrate . . . exhausted and *unmanned* —W.H. Hudson †1922⟩ **c** *obs* **:** to place below the level of man **:** DEGRADE ⟨habits of vice ~ men's minds —William Wotton⟩ **2 :** to deprive of sexual or procreative potency **:** CASTRATE, EMASCULATE ⟨*unmanned* themselves during . . . wild transports, which resemble those of dancing dervishes —R.H.Pfeiffer⟩ **syn** see UNNERVE
un·manacle \"+\ *vt* [²*un-* + *manacle*] **:** to free from manacles
un·manageable \"+\ *adj* **:** not manageable **:** UNCONTROLLABLE, INTRACTABLE ⟨became so ~ . . . she was committed to an asylum —H.A.Overstreet⟩ — **un·man·age·able·ness** *n* — **un·manageably** \"+\ *adv*
un·managed \"+\ *adj* [¹*un-* + *managed,* past part. of *manage*] **:** not controlled **:** UNREGULATED ⟨natural ~ populations in excess of a bird per acre —A.S.Leopold⟩
un·manful \"+\ *adj* **:** not manful — **un·manfully** \"+\ *adv*
un·manifest \"+\ *adj* **:** not manifest
un·manifested \"+\ *adj* [¹*un-* + *manifested,* past part. of *manifest*] **:** not manifested
un·manlike \"+\ *adj* **:** not manlike
un·manliness \"+\ *n* **:** the quality or state of being unmanly
¹un·manly \"+\ *adv* [ME, fr. ¹*un-* + *manly,* adv.] *archaic* **:** in an unmanly manner ⟨a dominion so ~ cruel —John Cleveland⟩
²unmanly \"\ *adj* [ME, fr. ¹*un-* + *manly,* adj.] **:** not manly: as **a :** of weak character **:** PUSILLANIMOUS, COWARDLY ⟨~ despair which bids men eat and drink for tomorrow they die —J.R.Green⟩ **b :** EFFEMINATE, SISSY ⟨looked upon the arts as ~ forms of escape —Lewis Mumford⟩
un·manned \¦ən+\ *adj* [¹*un-* + *manned,* past part. of *man*] **1 :** having no men aboard **:** not guided by men on board ⟨an ~, globe-girdling artificial satellite —J.K.Hutchens⟩ ⟨forbade the operation of remotely controlled ~ airplanes —A.R.Weyl⟩ **2** *obs, of a hawk* **:** not trained
un·mannered \"+\ *adj* **1 :** marked by a lack of good manners **:** RUDE, COARSE ⟨a beautiful but ~ people, primitively callous —Rose Macaulay⟩ ⟨resentment flared at such an ~ intrusion —Joseph Hergesheimer⟩ **2 :** characterized by an absence of artificiality or insincerity **:** UNAFFECTED, STRAIGHTFORWARD ⟨the doctor's quiet, ~ entry —Viola Meynell⟩ — **un·man·nered·ly** *adv*
un·mannerliness \"+\ *n* **:** the quality or state of being unmannerly
¹un·mannerly \"+\ *adv* [ME *unmanerly,* fr. ¹*un-* + *manerly,* adv., mannerly] **:** in an unmannerly fashion **:** RUDELY ⟨reformers . . . did not ~ reject those offices of the church —J.J. Blunt⟩
²unmannerly \"\ *adj* [ME *unmanerly,* fr. ¹*un-* + *manerly,* adj., mannerly] **:** not mannerly **:** IMPOLITE, DISCOURTEOUS ⟨disliked for his ~ behavior⟩
un·mantle \"+\ *vt* [²*un-* + *mantle*] **:** to remove a mantle or cover from **:** UNCOVER
un·manufactured \"+\ *adj* [¹*un-* + *manufactured,* past part. of *manufacture*] **:** not manufactured
un·manumitted \"+\ *adj* [¹*un-* + *manumitted,* past part. of *manumit*] **:** not manumitted ⟨we strive with proud, ~ soul —J.W.Watson⟩
un·manured \"+\ *adj* [¹*un-* + *manured,* past part. of *manure*] **1** *obs* **:** UNCULTIVATED, UNTILLED ⟨the soil is wonderfully fruitful, but ~ —John Dryden⟩ **2 :** not fertilized with manure ⟨~ lawns⟩
un·mapped \"+\ *adj* [¹*un-* + *mapped,* past part. of *map*] **:** not mapped **:** UNCHARTED ⟨wild and ~ areas of the physical world —H.G.Rickover⟩
un·marked \¦ən+\ *adj* [ME *unmarked,* fr. ¹*un-* + *marked,* past part. of *merken, marken* to mark — more at MARK] **1 a :** lacking a mark ⟨handed him an ~ card⟩ **b** *of a road* **:** not having a marker giving a street name or route number ⟨an ~, graveled road running parallel with the levee —*Amer. Guide Series: La.*⟩ **2 :** not noticed **:** UNOBSERVED ⟨his retirement . . . was not allowed to go ~ —*Wesfarmers News*⟩ **3 :** not characterized ⟨wrote political articles ~ by a regard for truth⟩
un·marketable \"+\ *adj* **:** not marketable
un·marred \"+\ *adj* [ME *unmerred, unmarred,* fr. ¹*un-* + *merred, marred,* past part. of *merren, marren* to mar — more at MAR] **:** not marred

un·married \"+\ *adj* [ME *unmaried,* fr. ¹*un-* + *maried* married — more at MARRIED] **:** not married **:** **a :** not now or previously married **b :** DIVORCED **c :** WIDOWED

un·marry \"+\ *vb* [²*un-* + *marry*] *vt* **:** to release from marriage **:** cancel the marriage of **:** DIVORCE ~ *vi* **:** to release oneself from marriage

un·martial \"+\ *adj* **:** not martial

un·martyr \"+\ *vt* [²*un-* + *martyr*] **:** to deprive of martyrdom

un·masculine \"+\ *adj* **:** not masculine

un·mask \"+\ *vb* [²*un-* + *mask*] *vt* **1 :** to remove a mask from ⟨a law to ~ the Ku Klux Klan —*Time*⟩ **2 :** to reveal the true nature of **:** remove a false or misleading appearance from **:** EXPOSE ⟨dramatically ~*s* herself on her deathbed when she confesses all —*Irish Digest*⟩ ⟨~ the process of deception —R.W.Southern⟩ ~ *vi* **:** to remove one's mask ⟨at midnight the dancers ~*ed*⟩

un·masker \"+\ *n* **:** one that unmasks

un·mastered \ˌən+\ *adj* [¹*un-* + *mastered,* past part. of *master*] **:** not mastered

un·matchable \"+\ *adj* [¹*un-* + *match,* v. + *-able*] **:** not matchable **:** **a :** INCOMPARABLE, UNEQUALED ⟨state the issue with ~ clarity —R.M.Goldman⟩ **b :** not capable of being paired or duplicated ⟨furniture . . . interspersed with modern and ~ makeshifts —Bret Harte⟩ — **un·match·ably** \-blē\ *adv*

un·matched \"+\ *adj* [¹*un-* + *matched,* past part. of *match*] **1 :** UNMATCHABLE a ⟨infamy . . . ~ in the Western world —H.E.Rieseberg⟩ **2 :** not matching ⟨~ pieces of dinnerware⟩

un·mated \"+\ *adj* [¹*un-* + *mated,* past part. of *mate* (to join)] **:** not mated

un·material \"+\ *adj* [ME *unmateriall,* fr. ¹*un-* + *materiel, material, materiall* material] **:** IMMATERIAL, INSUBSTANTIAL ⟨their . . . almost ~ structure —Simon Newcomb⟩

un·maternal \"+\ *adj* **:** not maternal

un·mathematical \"+\ *adj* **:** not mathematical

un·matted \"+\ *adj* **:** not matted ⟨an ~ watercolor⟩

un·meaning \"+\ *adj* **1 :** lacking intelligence **:** VAPID ⟨an ~ facial expression⟩ **2 :** having no meaning **:** SENSELESS ⟨his response . . . is picayune and ~ —R.B.Pearsall⟩ — **un·mean·ing·ly** *adv* — **un·mean·ing·ness** *n*

un·meant \"+\ *adj* [¹*un-* + *meant,* past part. of *mean*] **:** not meant **:** UNINTENTIONAL ⟨an ~ harshness in her reply⟩

un·measurable \"+\ *adj* [ME *unmesurable,* fr. ¹*un-* + *mesurable* measurable — more at MEASURABLE] **1 :** not measurable **:** of a degree, extent, or amount incapable of being measured **:** INDETERMINABLE ⟨~ reaches of outer space⟩ ⟨satellite is slowing down at an almost ~ rate —J.P.Hagen⟩ **2 :** of an excessive degree or amount **:** IMMODERATE, BOUNDLESS ⟨an ~ desire for fame⟩ ⟨~ enthusiasm⟩ — **un·mea·sur·able·ness** *n* — **un·measurably** \"+\ *adv*

un·measured \ˌən+\ *adj* [ME *unmesured,* fr. ¹*un-* + *mesured,* past part. of *mesuren* to measure — more at MEASURE] **:** not measured **:** LIMITLESS, UNRESTRAINED ⟨~ vastness of our . . . solar system —L.P.Smith⟩ ⟨his hypocrisy and duplicity were ~, almost magnificent —Francis Hackett⟩ ⟨~ scorn⟩; *specif* **:** not metrical ⟨~ verse⟩ — **un·mea·sured·ly** *adv* — **un·mea·sured·ness** *n*

un·mechanical \"+\ *adj* **:** not mechanical; *esp* **:** ignorant of or not interested in mechanics ⟨the difficulty of talking mechanics with an ~ person —C.S.Forester⟩ — **un·mechan·ically** \"+\ *adv*

un·mechanized \"+\ *adj, see -ize in Explan Notes* [¹*un-* + *mechanized,* past part. of *mechanize*] **:** not mechanized ⟨production of furniture remained largely ~ —Gordon Russell⟩

un·meddled \"+\ *adj* [¹*un-* + *meddled,* past part. of *meddle*] **:** not meddled — usu. used with *with* ⟨have the enjoyment of his goods . . . ~ with by others —C.S.C.Bowen⟩

un·meddling \"+\ *adj* [¹*un-* + *meddling,* pres. part. of *meddle*] **:** not meddling

un·mediated \"+\ *adj* [¹*un-* + *mediated,* past part. of *mediate*] **:** not mediated ⟨~ relation between God and the soul of man —*Contemporary Rev.*⟩

un·medical \"+\ *adj* **:** not medical

un·meditated \"+\ *adj* [¹*un-* + *meditated,* past part. of *meditate*] **:** not meditated **:** SPONTANEOUS, UNPREMEDITATED

un·medullated \"+\ *adj* **:** having no medullary sheath ⟨~ nerve fiber⟩

un·meek \"+\ *adj* [ME *unmeoc, unmek, unmeek,* fr. ¹*un-* + *meoc, mek, meek* meek — more at MEEK] **:** not meek

un·meet \ˌən+\ *adj* **:** not meet **:** UNSUITABLE, IMPROPER ⟨would be ~ . . . to pursue that story to its close —A.E. Coppard⟩ — **un·meet·ly** *adv* — **un·meet·ness** *n*

un·mellowed \"+\ *adj* [¹*un-* + *mellowed,* past part. of *mellow*] **:** not mellowed

un·melodious \"+\ *adj* **:** not melodious — **un·me·lo·di·ous·ly** *adv*

un·melted \"+\ *adj* [¹*un-* + *melted,* past part. of *melt*] **:** not melted

un·melting \"+\ *adj* [¹*un-* + *melting,* pres. part. of *melt*] **:** not melting

un·memorable \"+\ *adj* **:** not memorable **:** not worth remembering ⟨an ~ dramatic production⟩

un·mend·able \ˌən¦mendəbəl\ *adj* [¹*un-* + *mendable* capable of being mended, fr. *mend* + *-able*] **:** not capable of being mended

¹**un·mentionable** \ˌən+\ *adj* [¹*un-* + *mentionable*] **:** not mentionable **:** UNSPEAKABLE, HUSH-HUSH ⟨suffered ~ cruelties —M.R.Cohen⟩ ⟨open discussion of formerly ~ topics⟩

²**unmentionable** \"\ *n* -s **:** one that is not to be mentioned or discussed ⟨a long list of advertising ~*s* —*Time*⟩: as **a unmentionables** *pl* **:** TROUSERS ⟨chaste young men in checked ~*s* —Cyril Pearl⟩ **b unmentionables** *pl* **:** UNDERWEAR ⟨having trouble with public laundries shrinking my ~*s* —*Reader's Digest*⟩

un·mentioned \"+\ *adj* [¹*un-* + *mentioned,* past part. of *mention*] **:** not mentioned **:** left out **:** OMITTED ⟨the director was ~ in the program credits⟩

un·mercantile \"+\ *adj* **:** not mercantile

un·mercenary \"+\ *adj* **:** not mercenary

un·merchantable \"+\ *adj* **:** not merchantable **:** not fit for market **:** UNSALABLE

un·merciful \"+\ *adj* **1 :** not merciful **:** MERCILESS ⟨an ~ tyrant⟩ **2 :** EXCESSIVE, EXTREME ⟨sat beside a bore who talked for an ~ period⟩ — **un·mercifully** \"+\ *adv* — **un·mer·ci·ful·ness** *n*

un·merge \"+\ *vt* [²*un-* + *merge*] **:** to dissolve a merger ⟨should be brought under the antitrust laws and *unmerged* —Edward Wimmer⟩

un·meritable \"+\ *adj* **:** not worthy of merit

un·merited \"+\ *adj* **:** not merited **:** UNDESERVED ⟨these defeats, which he believed wholly ~ —J.D.Hicks⟩ ⟨received an ~ honorary degree⟩ — **un·mer·it·ed·ly** *adv*

un·meriting \"+\ *adj* [¹*un-* + *meriting,* pres. part. of *merit*] **:** UNDESERVING

un·mesh \ˌən+\ *vt* [²*un-* + *mesh*] **1 :** to free from a mesh **:** DISENTANGLE **2 :** to release (as gear teeth) from meshing

un·met \"+\ *adj* [¹*un-* + *met,* past part. of *meet*] **1 :** not met **2 :** not yet considered or solved **:** UNANSWERED ⟨find out . . . where ~ needs exist —*New South*⟩

un·metalled \"+\ *adj* [¹*un-* + *metalled,* past part. of *metal*] *chiefly Brit* **:** not provided with road metal ⟨saw an ~, sandy track leading toward some beech woods —M.C.A.Henniker⟩

un·metallic \"+\ *adj* **:** NONMETALLIC

un·metamorphosed \"+\ *adj* [¹*un-* + *metamorphosed,* past part. of *metamorphose*] **:** not metamorphosed ⟨the arrangement of mineral grains in ~ sediments —*Jour. of Geol.*⟩

un·metaphysical \"+\ *adj* **:** not metaphysical

un·methodical \"+\ *adj* **:** not methodical **:** DESULTORY ⟨the project failed through ~ planning⟩ — **un·methodically** \"+\ *adv*

un·methodized \"+\ *adj* [¹*un-* + *methodized,* past part. of *methodize*] **:** not handled methodically

un·metrical \"+\ *adj* **:** not metrical ⟨~ lines of poetry⟩

un·military \"+\ *adj* **:** not military: as **a :** not conforming to military standards or practice ⟨~ posture⟩ ⟨an ~ approach to handling people⟩ **b :** not belonging to or associated with the military ⟨~ circles of government⟩

un·milked \ˌən+\ *adj* [¹*un-* + *milked,* past part. of *milk*] **:** not milked ⟨~ cows⟩

un·milled \"+\ *adj* [¹*un-* + *milled,* past part. of *mill*] **:** not milled

un·minded \"+\ *adj* [¹*un-* + *minded,* past part. of *mind*] *archaic* **:** not attended to **:** UNHEEDED, IGNORED

un·mindful \"+\ *adj* [ME *unmyndeful,* fr. ¹*un-* + *myndeful* mindful — more at MINDFUL] **:** not mindful **:** CARELESS, UNAWARE ⟨while thus ~ of his steps, he stumbled —G.B.Shaw⟩ ⟨not ~ of the heavy responsibility —Ernest Bevin⟩ **syn** see FORGETFUL

un·mined \"+\ *adj* [¹*un-* + *mined,* past part. of *mine*] **:** not mined ⟨deposits of ~ uranium⟩

un·mingled \"+\ *adj* [¹*un-* + *mingled,* past part. of *mingle*] **:** not mingled **:** UNADULTERATED

un·minished \"+\ *adj* [¹*un-* + *minished,* past part. of *minish*] **:** UNDIMINISHED ⟨one everlasting, ~, unchanging joy —E.B. Pusey⟩

un·ministerial \"+\ *adj* **:** not ministerial

un·minted \"+\ *adj* [¹*un-* + *minted,* past part. of *mint*] **:** not minted

un·miraculous \"+\ *adj* **:** not miraculous

un·mirthful \ˌən+\ *adj* **:** not mirthful **:** SERIOUS, HUMORLESS ⟨glanced around a tableful of sober, ~ faces —Caroline Ticknor⟩

un·misgiving \"+\ *adj* [¹*un-* + *misgiving,* pres. part. of *misgive*] **:** not having misgivings **:** CERTAIN, CONFIDENT ⟨a small and unambitious, yet ~ and happy production —Leigh Hunt⟩ — **un·mis·giv·ing·ly** *adv*

un·miss·able \ˌən¦misəbəl\ *adj* [¹*un-* + *miss,* v. + *-able*] **:** that cannot or should not be missed ⟨a large ~ target⟩ ⟨~ tourist attractions⟩

un·missed \ˌən+\ *adj* [ME *unmist,* fr. ¹*un-* + *mist,* past part. of *missen* to miss — more at MISS] **:** not missed ⟨could sneak out and be ~ all night⟩

un·mistakable \"+\ *adj* **:** not capable of being mistaken or misunderstood **:** CLEAR, PLAIN, OBVIOUS, MANIFEST ⟨the ~ odor of alcohol is on his breath —Wayne Hughes⟩ ⟨his opposition to slavery was ~ —Broadus Mitchell⟩ — **un·mis·tak·able·ness** *n* -ES — **un·mistakably** \"+\ *adv*

un·mistrusting \"+\ *adj* [¹*un-* + *mistrusting,* pres. part. of *mistrust*] **:** not mistrusting **:** INGENUOUS

un·miter \"+\ *vt* [²*un-* + *miter*] **:** to deprive of a miter

un·mitigable \"+\ *adj* [¹*un-* + *mitigate* + *-able*] **:** not mitigable ⟨stern and ~ accusations —Sir Walter Scott⟩

un·mitigated \"+\ *adj* [¹*un-* + *mitigated,* past part. of *mitigate*] **1 :** not made less severe or intense **:** UNRELIEVED ⟨the heat is ~ —D.M.Poole⟩ ⟨sounds . . . like an ~ horror of profanity —Agnes Repplier⟩ ⟨had the most ~ contempt —Gertrude Atherton⟩ **2 :** not qualified **:** ARRANT, DOWNRIGHT, OUT-AND-OUT ⟨must think that the . . . public is just a bunch of ~ suckers —R.W.Robey⟩ ⟨an absolutely ~ triumph of wit and writing skill —Brendan Gill⟩ — **un·mit·i·gat·ed·ly** *adv*

un·mix \"+\ *vi* [²*un-* + *mix*] **:** to undergo the separation of a second solid phase from a homogeneous phase ⟨homogeneous synthetic feldspars . . . ~ when held at lower temperatures —*Jour. of Geol.*⟩

un·mixable \"+\ *adj* [¹*un-* + *mix,* v. + *-able*] **:** not mixable **:** INCOMPATIBLE ⟨has brought together in conference . . . apparently ~ groups —Walter Moberly⟩

un·mixed \"+\ *adj* [¹*un-* + *mixed,* past part. of *mix*] **:** not mixed **:** UNADULTERATED, PURE ⟨the course of action . . . is direct and ~ with dissenting viewpoints —F.L.Ryan⟩ ⟨none of them is an ~ blessing —*Modern Industry*⟩ — **un·mixedly** \"+\ *adv*

un·modern \"+\ *adj* **:** not modern **:** OLD-FASHIONED ⟨come from a family too ~ —R.M.Nixon⟩

un·modest \ˌən+\ *adj* **:** IMMODEST

un·modifiable \"+\ *adj* **:** not modifiable **:** UNALTERABLE, INFLEXIBLE ⟨these variations from custom are illogical, incomprehensible, and ~ —*Science News Letter*⟩

un·modified \"+\ *adj* [¹*un-* + *modified,* past part. of *modify*] **:** not modified ⟨the germ cells . . . are ~ by these activities —W.E.Castle⟩ ⟨~ verbs⟩

un·modish \"+\ *adj* **:** UNFASHIONABLE ⟨~ hats⟩ — **un·mo·dish·ly** *adv*

un·modulated \"+\ *adj* [¹*un-* + *modulated,* past part. of *modulate*] **:** not modulated ⟨lectured in an ~ voice edged with hysteria⟩

un·moist \"+\ *adj* **:** not moist

un·moistened \"+\ *adj* [¹*un-* + *moistened,* past part. of *moisten*] **:** not moistened

un·mold \"+\ *vt* [in sense 1, fr. ²*un-* + *mold,* v. (to form); in sense 2, fr. ²*un-* + *mold,* n. (form)] **1 :** to destroy the mold of ⟨'til his very soul ~*s* its essence —S.T.Coleridge⟩ **2 :** to remove from a mold ⟨~ the gelatin on a plate of lettuce or endive⟩

un·molded \"+\ *adj* [¹*un-* + *molded,* past part. of *mold,* (to form)] **:** not molded ⟨envisioned the sculpture latent in the ~ marble⟩

un·molested \"+\ *adj* [¹*un-* + *molested,* past part. of *molest*] **:** not molested **:** not interfered with **:** UNTOUCHED ⟨communities in the Latin-American countries were ~ —Shlomo Katz⟩ ⟨small game . . . roam ~ —*Amer. Guide Series: Maine*⟩ — **un·mo·lest·ed·ly** *adv*

un·monarch \ˌən+\ *vt* [²*un-* + *monarch,* n.] **:** to depose from the position of monarch

un·moneyed \"+\ *adj* **:** not having money **:** PENNILESS ⟨the ~ young man who has married the heiress —Henry James †1916⟩

un·moor \"+\ *vb* [ME *unmooren,* fr. ²*un-* + *mooren, moren* to moor — more at MOOR] *vt* **1 :** to loose from or as if from moorings ⟨~*ed* the punt, leaving the moorings marked with an old tin can —G.G.Carter⟩ ⟨expected to . . . turn the pillows or to ~ the counterpane —Jean Stafford⟩ **2 :** to heave up (an anchor) leaving a second anchor down ~ *vi* **:** to cast off moorings ⟨the ship ~*ed* and swung slowly about⟩

un·moral \"+\ *adj* **1 :** having no moral perception or quality **:** lacking a sense of morality **:** AMORAL ⟨the characters are depicted as being like savages, innocently ~ —Haldeen Braddy⟩ ⟨a triumphant glorification of rascality, the most ~ narrative ever told —Agnes Repplier⟩ **2 :** not influenced or guided by moral considerations or ethical customs ⟨the great ~ power of the modern industrial revolution —F.L.Wright⟩ **3 :** lying outside the bounds of morals or ethics **:** NONMORAL ⟨imagination is, of its very nature, ~ —*Times Lit. Supp.*⟩ — compare IMMORAL

un·morality \"+\ *n* -ES **:** the quality or state of being unmoral ⟨there was something about him, a recklessness, an ~ —Louis Bromfield⟩

un·moralized \"+\ *adj* [¹*un-* + *moralized,* past part. of *moralize*] **:** not influenced or guided by a moral sense ⟨even in his ~ condition he is a social being —James Ford⟩

un·mordanted \"+\ *adj* [¹*un-* + *mordanted,* past part. of *mordant*] **:** not mordanted ⟨~ wool⟩

un·mortared \"+\ *adj* [¹*un-* + *mortared,* past part. of *mortar*] **:** not mortared ⟨roofed with turf and built of ~ stones —R.L. Stevenson⟩

un·mortgaged \"+\ *adj* [¹*un-* + *mortgaged,* past part. of *mortgage*] **:** not mortgaged ⟨an ~ estate⟩

un·mortified \"+\ *adj* [ME, fr. ¹*un-* + *mortified,* past part. of *mortifien* to mortify — more at MORTIFY] **:** not spiritually mortified ⟨an undisciplined and ~ spirit —Jeremy Taylor⟩

un·mothered \ˌən+\ *adj* [¹*un-* + *mother,* n. + *-ed*] **:** deprived of a mother **:** MOTHERLESS ⟨adolescent gosling that, ~, attached itself to him —Della Lutes⟩

un·motherly \"+\ *adj* **:** not motherly

un·motivated \"+\ *adj* [¹*un-* + *motivated,* past part. of *motivate*] **:** lacking an appropriate or understandable motive ⟨began to indulge in odd, ~ behavior⟩

un·motived \"+\ *adj* [¹*un-* + *motive,* n. + *-ed*] **:** UNMOTIVATED

un·mounted \ˌən+\ *adj* **:** not mounted ⟨~ . . . fifteen-inch speakers with integral tweeters —R.S.Lanier⟩ ⟨~ photographs⟩ ⟨~ artillery⟩; *esp* **:** not mounted on or provided with a horse ⟨~ troops⟩

un·mourned \"+\ *adj* [¹*un-* + *mourned,* past part. of *mourn*] **:** not mourned

un·movable \"+\ *adj* [ME *unmevable, unmovable,* fr. ¹*un-* + *mevable, movable* movable — more at MOVABLE] **:** IMMOVABLE — **un·mov·able·ness** \"+\ *n* — **un·movably** \"+\ *adv*

un·moved \ˌən¦müvd\ *adj* [ME *unmeved, unmoved,* fr. ¹*un-* + *meved, moved,* past part. of *meven, moven* to move — more at MOVE] **1 :** not emotionally affected **:** CALM, INDIFFERENT, UNDISTURBED ⟨had always appeared completely ~ and imperturbable —Elinor Wylie⟩ **2 :** remaining in the same place or position **:** FIRM ⟨after 10 years of redevelopment, some houses were still ~⟩ ⟨could be endured . . . with an ~ countenance —W.H. Hudson †1922⟩ — **un·moved·ly** \-vədlē, -vd-\ *adv*

unmoved mover *n* **:** PRIME MOVER 1

un·moving \ˌən+\ *adj* **:** not moving ⟨bade the sun to stay a while ~ —Frederick O'Brien⟩; *esp* **:** not emotionally stirring ⟨only those with an adamant prejudice . . . can find it meaningless or ~ —W.P.Clancy⟩

un·mown \"+\ *adj* [¹*un-* + *mown,* past part. of *mow*] **:** not mown ⟨~ hay⟩

un·muffle \"+\ *vt* [²*un-* + *muffle*] **:** to free from something that muffles ⟨~ a face⟩ ⟨the sunlight seemed . . . to ~ the incessant noise —Osbert Sitwell⟩

un·murmuring \"+\ *adj* [¹*un-* + *murmuring,* pres. part. of *murmur*] **:** not murmuring discontentedly **:** UNCOMPLAINING — **un·mur·mur·ing·ly** *adv*

un·musical \"+\ *adj* **:** not musical: as **a :** not musical in nature **:** HARSH, DISCORDANT ⟨~ call of the bluejay⟩ **b :** not gifted in or appreciative of music ⟨an entirely ~ crooner —Douglas Watt⟩ ⟨too ~ to care for concerts⟩ — **un·musi·cally** \"+\ *adv*

un·mutation \"+\ *n* [trans. of G *rückumlaut*] **:** RÜCKUMLAUT

un·muted \"+\ *adj* **:** not muted ⟨~ trumpets⟩

un·mutilated \"+\ *adj* [¹*un-* + *mutilated,* past part. of *mutilate*] **:** not mutilated ⟨fragile tracery that must be preserved ~ and distinct —B.N.Cardozo⟩

un·muzzle \"+\ *vt* [²*un-* + *muzzle*] **:** to remove a muzzle from ⟨~ the dog after the mailman has left⟩

un·myelinated \"+\ *adj* **:** lacking a myelin sheath ⟨the ~ fiber found in the mammalian central nervous system —H.J.Curtis & K.S.Cole⟩

un·mysterious \"+\ *adj* **:** not mysterious

un·nail \ˌən+\ *vt* [²*un-* + *nail*] **:** to unfasten by removing nails

un·nailed \"+\ *adj* [¹*un-* + *nailed,* past part. of *nail*] **:** not nailed

un·nameable \"+\ *adj* [¹*un-* + *name,* v. + *-able*] **:** not capable of being named or described **:** NAMELESS, UNSPEAKABLE, INEFFABLE ⟨a mongrel, ~ as to breed —*Harper's*⟩ ⟨experienced ~ horrors⟩ ⟨contemplation of ~ transcendence —Evelyn Underhill⟩

un·named \"+\ *adj* **:** not named **:** UNIDENTIFIED, UNSPECIFIED ⟨a gray slate stone marks the grave of two ~ British soldiers —Phyllis Duganne⟩ ⟨domestic gas converted by an ~ process —J.H.Kuney⟩

un·na's boot \ˈünəz-\ *n, usu cap U* [after Paul G. *Unna* †1929 Ger. dermatologist] **:** GELATIN BOOT

un·national \ˌən+\ *adj* **:** not belonging to or characteristic of an individual nation ⟨~, as well as deliberately un-English in style —Osbert Sitwell⟩ — compare SUPRANATIONAL

un·natural \"+\ *adj* [ME, fr. ¹*un-* + *natural*] **1 a :** not innately characteristic of the nature of man ⟨scientific inventions . . . to stimulate depraved appetites, to invent ~ wants —T.L. Peacock⟩ ⟨this secrecy . . . is against my disposition, ~ —Joseph Hergesheimer⟩ **b :** not being in accordance with nature **:** not determined by or consistent with a normal course of events ⟨if idleness is ~ a five-hour work week would be disastrous —Stuart Chase⟩ ⟨nothing impossible or ~ in being in love with two women at the same time —Aldous Huxley⟩ ⟨his abhorrence of men who advocated ~ change —A.S.Link⟩ ⟨shaping her economy along grotesquely ~ lines —O.P. Echols⟩ **2 a :** not being in accordance with normal feelings or behavior **:** PERVERSE, ABNORMAL ⟨she had been vicious and ~ . . . had thrived on hatred —W.H.Wright⟩ ⟨something ~ between him and his now-dead closest friend —*Time*⟩ **b :** not marked by naturalness or genuineness **:** ARTIFICIAL, CONTRIVED ⟨when one . . . is ~ with all who are not intimate friends —W.B. Yeats⟩ ⟨an ~ and not very intelligent simplification of a very complex issue —H.J.Laski⟩ **c :** inconsistent with what is natural or expected **:** STRANGE, IRREGULAR ⟨exaltations in which piety and sensuality kept ~ company —F.J.Mather⟩ ⟨his ~ alliance with the nationalists —Michael Clark⟩ **d :** going beyond what is normal **:** SUPERNATURAL, UNCANNY ⟨an almost ~ gift for winning musical prizes —*Amer. Guide Series: N.J.*⟩ **3 :** not having a natural claim **:** ILLEGITIMATE ⟨the ~ children of my brain that I should wish . . . to disinherit —Ellen Glasgow⟩ — **un·naturally** \"+\ *adv* — **un·nat·u·ral·ness** *n*

unnatural act *n* **:** CRIME AGAINST NATURE

un·naturalize \"+\ *vt* [²*un-* + *naturalize*] **1** *archaic* **:** to deprive of natural characteristics **:** make unnatural **2 :** to deprive of the rights of citizenship

un·naturalized \"+\ *adj* [¹*un-* + *naturalized,* past part. of *naturalize*] **:** not having citizenship

un·navigable \"+\ *adj* **:** not navigable ⟨up rapid-broken, ~ streams —*World's Work*⟩

un·neat \"+\ *adj* **:** not neat ⟨all the edges are ~ —*Nation*⟩

un·necessaries \ˌən+\ *n pl* **:** expendable material **:** needless or unimportant things ⟨nowhere are the ~ of life . . . sold at such extravagant prices —*Quarterly Rev.*⟩

un·necessarily \"+\ *adv* **:** not by necessity **:** to an unnecessary degree ⟨gave an ~ detailed description⟩ ⟨prolonging his journey ~ —Sir Walter Scott⟩

un·necessariness \"+\ *n* **:** the quality or state of being unnecessary

un·necessary \"+\ *adj* [¹*un-* + *necessary*] **:** not necessary **:** USELESS, NEEDLESS ⟨a striker's tent camp . . . was burned with ~ loss of life —F.L.Paxson⟩ ⟨ordered to cut out ~ words —F.P.Donovan⟩

un·necessitated \"+\ *adj* [¹*un-* + *necessitated,* past part. of *necessitate*] **:** not necessitated

un·needed \"+\ *adj* [¹*un-* + *needed,* past part. of *need*] **:** not needed **:** UNNECESSARY ⟨~ public works —*N. Y. Herald Tribune*⟩

un·needful \"+\ *adj* [ME *unnedefull,* fr. ¹*un-* + *nedefull* needful — more at NEEDFUL] **:** not needful **:** UNNECESSARY, NEEDLESS

un·neighbored \"+\ *adj* [¹*un-* + *neighbored,* past part. of *neighbor*] **:** having no neighbors ⟨an ~ isle, and far from all resort of busy man —William Cowper⟩

un·neighborly \"+\ *adj* **:** not neighborly ⟨found the new people on the street an ~ bunch who kept to themselves⟩

un·nerve \"+\ *vt* [²*un-* + *nerve,* n.] **1 :** to deprive of courage and physical strength **:** cause to become weak and ineffective esp. from fear ⟨a steeplejack . . . was exhausted and *unnerved* and could not hold on to his dangerous perch much longer —*Boy Scout Handbk.*⟩ ⟨the sudden revulsion of feeling *unnerved* him —F.W.Crofts⟩ **2 :** to cause to become nervous or discomposed **:** UPSET ⟨a lady . . . so emotional in her acting that she ~*s* me —John McCarten⟩ ⟨waiting for something to happen was starting to ~ everybody⟩ **3 :** DENERVATE ⟨~ a chronically lame leg of a horse⟩

syn UNNERVE, ENERVATE, UNMAN, and EMASCULATE can mean in common to deprive of strength, vigor, or the capacity to advance, to overcome difficulties, or often to stand up under even the normal physical or moral strains of existence. UNNERVE implies marked loss of courage, self-control, or power to act ⟨utterly *unnerved* by her surprise, Fara leaned limply against him —L.C.Douglas⟩ ⟨the magnitude of problems in other fields (education, health, housing, social welfare) is equally *unnerving* —Hal Lehrman⟩ ⟨so *unnerved* . . . that he threw away his pistol —Peter Forster⟩ ENERVATE implies a gradual physical or moral weakening, often as a result of luxury or indolence, until one is too feeble to exert effort ⟨work had not made him strong, but *enervated* him. He was pale and thin, with no chest, no buttocks, not even a stomach —Donald Windham⟩ ⟨such a power does not destroy, but . . . *enervates,* extinguishes, and stupefies a people, till each nation is reduced to nothing better than a flock of timid and industrious animals —Alexis de Tocqueville⟩ ⟨a love of luxury has *enervated* the virile race that swarmed in cabins —Russell Lord⟩ UNMAN implies loss of manly vigor, control, or spirit ⟨debilitated and *unmanned* by factory-produced comforts —*Time*⟩ ⟨every tiny animal he roused in its burrow startled him, *unmanned* him with the noise of its movement —Norman Mailer⟩ ⟨*unmanned* by a woman's tears⟩ EMASCULATE implies a loss of force, esp. by the removal of something essential ⟨a plan *emasculated* by lack of funds⟩ ⟨supporters voted against the treaty . . . rather than have it passed in *emasculated* form —H.S.Quigley⟩ ⟨how to . . . *emasculate* homemade bombs —J.A.Maxwell⟩

un·nest \ˌən+\ *vt* [²*un-* + *nest,* n.] **:** to put out of or as if out of a nest

un·neurotic \"+\ *adj* : not neurotic : well-adjusted ⟨successful mothers — mothers with many ~ children —E.G.Boring⟩
un·neutral \"+\ *adj* [¹*un-* + *neutral*] : not neutral : PARTISAN ⟨regarded the . . . policy as ~ and likely to lead . . . into war —F.M.Russell⟩
un·neutrality \"+\ *n* : the quality or state of being unneutral ⟨his policy of ~ and of assistance to the allies —Dexter Perkins⟩
un·noble \"+\ *adj* [ME, fr. ¹*un-* + *noble*] : not noble : COMMON
un·notched \"+\ *adj* : not notched ⟨~ surface⟩
un·noted \"+\ *adj* [¹*un-* + *noted*, past part. of *note*] : not noted : UNOBSERVED, DISREGARDED ⟨would have lived and died, ~ —S.H.Adams⟩
un·noteworthy \"+\ *adj* : not noteworthy : UNREMARKABLE, COMMONPLACE ⟨the theater season opened with an ~ comedy⟩
un·noticeable \"+\ *adj* [¹*un-* + *notice*, v. + *-able*] : not noticeable : not drawing attention : UNDISTINGUISHED, INSIGNIFICANT ⟨her clothes were simple and ~ —J.G.Cozzens⟩ ⟨an ~ cigarette burn on the rug⟩ — **un·noticeably** \"+\ *adv*
un·noticed \"+\ *adj* [¹*un-* + *noticed*, past part. of *notice*] : not noticed : UNOBSERVED, UNRECOGNIZED ⟨the guests begin to slip away, one by one, ~ —Lafcadio Hearn⟩ ⟨managed to get through the reception line ~⟩
un·noticing \ˌən+\ *adj* [¹*un-* + *noticing*, pres. part. of *notice*] : not noticing
un·nourishing \"+\ *adj* : not nourishing or beneficial ⟨an ~ diet⟩ ⟨the irreligion and the cult of success that were so fatally ~ to . . . the Edwardians —V.S.Pritchett⟩
un·numberable \"+\ *adj* [ME, alter. (influenced by ¹*un-*) of *innumerable*] : INNUMERABLE ⟨with starry globes ~ —P.J. Bailey⟩
un·numbered \"+\ *adj* [ME *unnoumbred*, *unnombred*, fr. ¹*un-* + *noumbred*, *nombred*, past part. of *noumbren*, *nombren* to number — more at NUMBER] : not numbered: as **a** : more than are countable : INNUMERABLE ⟨through my heart's palace thoughts ~ throng —Rupert Brooke⟩ **b** : not having an identifying number ⟨~ page⟩ ⟨you turn west up an ~ dirt road —Bernard DeVoto⟩
un·nurtured \"+\ *adj* [¹*un-* + *nurtured*, past part. of *nurture*] : not nurtured
un·obedient \ˌən+\ *adj* [ME, fr. ¹*un-* + *obedient*] : DISOBEDIENT
un·obeyed \"+\ *adj* [¹*un-* + *obeyed*, past part. of *obey*] : not obeyed : DISOBEYED
un·objected \"+\ *adj* [¹*un-* + *objected*, past part. of *object*] : not objected to
un·objectionable \"+\ *adj* : not objectionable : ACCEPTABLE — **un·objectionableness** \"+\ *n* — **un·objectionably** \"+\ *adv*
un·objective \"+\ *adj* : not possessing or representing objective reality : SUBJECTIVE
un·obligated \"+\ *adj* [¹*un-* + *obligated*, past part. of *obligate*] *of funds* : appropriated but remaining uncommitted by contract at the end of a fiscal period
un·obliging \"+\ *adj* : not obliging : DISOBLIGING
un·obliterated \"+\ *adj* [¹*un-* + *obliterated*, past part. of *obliterate*] : not obliterated ⟨an ~ stain⟩
un·obnoxious \"+\ *adj* [¹*un-* + *obnoxious*] **1** : UNLIABLE **2** : not obnoxious : INOFFENSIVE
un·obscured \"+\ *adj* [¹*un-* + *obscured*, past part. of *obscure*] : not obscured : UNHIDDEN, CLEAR
¹**un·observable** \"+\ *adj* : not observable : INDISCERNIBLE, IMPERCEPTIBLE
²**unobservable** \"\ *n* : something unobservable esp. even in principle ⟨multiply ~*s* and subsistent entities at pleasure —A. E.Duncan-Jones⟩
un·observance \ˌən+\ *n* : want or neglect of observance : NONOBSERVANCE
un·observant \"+\ *adj* : not observant : not noticing — **un·observantly** \"+\ *adv*
un·observed \"+\ *adj* [¹*un-* + *observed*, past part. of *observe*] : not observed : UNPERCEIVED ⟨looking quickly around to be sure she was ~ —Sherwood Anderson⟩ — **un·observedly** \"+\ *adv*
un·observing \"+\ *adj* : not observing : UNNOTICING, INCURIOUS, INATTENTIVE
un·obstinate \"+\ *adj* : not obstinate : ACCOMMODATING, AGREEABLE
un·obstructed \"+\ *adj* [¹*un-* + *obstructed*, past part. of *obstruct*] : not obstructed : CLEAR, UNHINDERED ⟨an ~ view⟩ ⟨~ progress⟩ — **un·ob·struct·ed·ly** *adv* — **un·ob·struct·ed·ness** *n* -ES
un·obtainable \ˌən+\ *adj* : not obtainable
un·obtrusive \"+\ *adj* : not obtrusive : not blatant, immodest, or overly aggressive in manner, action, or appearance ⟨a quiet, ~ life of self-denial —Samuel Butler †1902⟩ — **un·obtrusively** \"+\ *adv* — **un·obtrusiveness** \"+\ *n*
un·obvious \"+\ *adj* : not obvious : not immediately apparent ⟨in mathematical science connections are exhibited which . . . are extremely ~ —A.N.Whitehead⟩
un·occupancy \"+\ *n* : the state of being unoccupied
un·occupied \"+\ *adj* [ME *unoccupyed*, fr. ¹*un-* + *occupyed* occupied] **1** : not busy : UNEMPLOYED **2 a** : not occupied by inhabitants ⟨~ ground⟩ **b** : of, relating to, or being premises on which no one is living although the furniture and fixtures have not been removed — compare VACANT 6 **c** : not occupied by enemy or conquering troops
un·offended \"+\ *adj* [ME, fr. ¹*un-* + *offended*, past part. of *offenden* to offend] : not offended : not given offense — **un·of·fend·ed·ly** *adv*
un·offending \"+\ *adj* [¹*un-* + *offending*, pres. part. of *offend*] : not offending or offensive; *esp* : not harming : HARMLESS, INNOCUOUS
un·offensive \"+\ *adj* : INOFFENSIVE
un·offered \"+\ *adj* [¹*un-* + *offered*, past part. of *offer*] : not offered
un·officered \ˌən+\ *adj* [¹*un-* + *officer* + *-ed*] : not provided with or led by officers
¹**un·official** \"+\ *adj* **1 a** : not belonging to, emanating from, or sanctioned or acknowledged by a government or governing body ⟨a sort of ~ mayor of the village —Siegfried Sassoon⟩ ⟨the ~ capital⟩ ⟨an ~ estimate⟩ **b** *of a drug* : not recognized by the legal standards or government of a country **c** : nominated or elected from among the native inhabitants of a British dependency and holding no appointment from the Colonial Office in the public service ⟨a governor's council with an ~ minority⟩ ⟨there is no legislative council in the Dependent Empire without ~ members —Martin Wight⟩ — compare OFFICIAL **2** : not sanctioned, authorized, or acknowledged by a group, class, or society ⟨proud of their ~ power as mothers —E.H.Erikson⟩ ⟨the custom of awarding prizes . . . substitutes one certified good play for half a dozen ~ good plays —Russell Maloney⟩ — **un·officially** \"+\ *adv*
²**unofficial** \"\ *n* : an unofficial member of a legislature in a British dependency
un·officinal \ˌən+\ *adj* : not commonly kept in stock by pharmacists ⟨~ drugs⟩
un·often \"+\ *adv* : not often : SELDOM
un·oiled \"+\ *adj* : not oiled
uno·na \yəˈnōnə\ *n*, *cap* [NL, alter. of *Anona*] : a genus of tropical Asiatic and African trees, shrubs, or woody vines (family Annonaceae) having flowers with flat spreading petals succeeded by an aggregate of stalked berries
unop *abbr* **1** unopened **2** unopposed
un·open \ˌən+\ *adj* : not open : CLOSED, SHUT, SEALED
un·opened \"+\ *adj* [¹*un-* + *opened*, past part. of *open*] : not opened; *specif* : having adjacent leaves still joined together at the fore edge — used of a book or periodical
un·operated \"+\ *adj* [¹*un-* + *operated*, past part. of *operate*] : not operated upon
un·operative \"+\ *adj* : INOPERATIVE
un·opposable \"+\ *adj* : not opposable
un·opposed \"+\ *adj* : not opposed ⟨~ to earning an honest dollar —R.L.Taylor⟩; *esp* : having no opponent ⟨the incumbent was ~ for the nomination⟩
un·oppressed \"+\ *adj* [¹*un-* + *oppressed*, past part. of *oppress*] : not oppressed esp. emotionally
un·oppressive \"+\ *adj* : not oppressive : MILD, BENEFICENT
un·ordained \"+\ *adj* [¹*un-* + *ordained*, past part. of *ordain*] : not ordained in the ministry or priesthood ⟨an ~ preacher⟩
un·ordered \"+\ *adj* [ME *unordred*, fr. ¹*un-* + *ordred*, past part. of *ordren* to order] **1** : not arranged in order : DISORDERED **2** : not decreed or commanded
un·orderly \"+\ *adj* [ME, fr. ¹*un-* + *order* + *-ly*] : DISORDERLY, DISORDERED
un·ordinary \"+\ *adj* : not ordinary; *esp* : being out of the ordinary : UNUSUAL, EXTRAORDINARY
un·organizable \"+\ *adj* : not organizable
un·organized \"+\ *adj* **1 a** : not brought into a coherent or well-ordered whole **b** : not having a formally organized government ⟨~ territories⟩ **c** : not belonging to a labor union **2** : not having the characteristics of a living organism
un·oriented \"+\ *adj* : not oriented: as **a** : not having a position, direction, and bearing definitely ascertained **b** : of, relating to, or being a texture in igneous rock in which the individual crystals lie crisscross in orientation **c** : lacking a set goal, purpose, or direction ⟨engaged in ~ study⟩
un·original \"+\ *adj* : not original: as **a** : not exerting, capable of exerting, or arising from the use of originality ⟨his life had been ~, conforming completely to the given pattern —Gwethalyn Graham⟩ **b** : not present at the origin ⟨containing ~ emendations⟩ — **un·originality** \"+\ *n*
un·orig·i·nate \ˌənəˈrijənət, -əˌnāt\ *adj* [back-formation fr. *unoriginated*] : UNORIGINATED
un·originated \ˌən+\ *adj* [¹*un-* + *originated*, past part. of *originate*] **1** : not originated : existing from all eternity : UNCREATED **2** : not yet caused to be or to be made
un·originative \ˌən+\ *adj* : having no talent for originating : UNORIGINAL
un·ornamental \"+\ *adj* : not used as or decorated by ornament — **un·ornamentally** \"+\ *adv*
un·ornamented \"+\ *adj* [¹*un-* + *ornamented*, past part. of *ornament*] : not ornamented : UNADORNED, BARE ⟨stark, ~ functional clusters of concrete —*Amer. Guide Series: Minn.*⟩
un·orthodox \"+\ *adj* : not orthodox : not in accord with approved, standardized, or conventional doctrine, method thought, custom, or opinion ⟨~ religious views⟩ ⟨the ~ field of parapsychology —A.G.N.Flew⟩ ⟨an ~ news-gathering tactic —*Newsweek*⟩ — **un·orthodoxly** \"+\ *adv*
un·orthodoxy \"+\ *n* **1** : an unorthodox opinion, doctrine, or method **2** : a group or the body of people holding unorthodox doctrines
un·ossified \"+\ *adj* : not ossified
un·ostentatious \"+\ *adj* : not ostentatious : not showy, forward, flamboyant : quiet and restrained esp. in taste ⟨~ elegance⟩ — **un·ostentatiously** \"+\ *adv* — **un·ostentatiousness** \"+\ *n*
un·owned \ˌən+\ *adj* [¹*un-* + *owned*, past part. of *own*] **1** : having no owner : OWNERLESS **2** : UNACKNOWLEDGED
un·oxygenated \"+\ *adj* [¹*un-* + *oxygenated*, past part. of *oxygenate*] : not oxygenated
unp *abbr* unpaged
un·pacific \ˌən+\ *adj* : not pacific : VIOLENT, WARLIKE
un·pack \"+\ *vb* [ME *unpakken*, fr. ²*un-* + *pakken* to pack] *vt* **1 a** : to remove the contents of ⟨~ a trunk⟩ **b** : to reveal the feelings of : UNBURDEN ⟨must . . . ~ my heart with words —Shak.⟩ **2 a** : to remove or undo from packing or a container ⟨packed and ~*ed* all the gear in traveling —Weston La Barre⟩ **b** : to reveal or decipher (as thought or meaning) by interpretation ⟨the meaning of such statements can be ~*ed* in a series of hypothetical propositions —R.J.Spilsbury⟩ ~ *vi* : to engage in unpacking a container
un·packed \"+\ *adj* [ME *unpakked*, fr. ¹*un-* + *pakked*, past part. of *pakken* to pack] : not packed
un·padded \"+\ *adj* : not padded
un·paged \"+\ *adj* [¹*un-* + *paged*, past part. of *page*] : having no page numbers ⟨an ~ pamphlet⟩ ⟨~ inserts⟩
un·paid \"+\ *adj* [ME *unpayd*, fr. ¹*un-* + *payd*, past part. of *payen* to pay] **1** : not paid : serving without pay ⟨~ officials⟩ **2 a** : not presented as payment ⟨~ wages⟩ **b** : not cleared by payment ⟨an ~ bill⟩ **c** : not purchased or as yet unpurchased by payment — usu. used with *for* ⟨a car partially ~ for⟩ **3** : not paying a salary ⟨an ~ position⟩
unpaid–letter stamp *n* : POSTAGE-DUE STAMP
un·pained \ˌən+\ *adj* [ME *unpeyned*, fr. ¹*un-* + *peyned*, past part. of *peynen* to pain] : having no pain : feeling no pain
un·painful \"+\ *adj* : not painful
un·paintable \"+\ *adj* : not paintable; *esp* : not suitable for artistic representation on canvas — **un·paintableness** \"+\ *n*
un·painted \"+\ *adj* : not painted : not having a coat of paint; *also* : badly in need of a fresh coat of paint
un·paired \"+\ *adj* [¹*un-* + *paired*, past part. of *pair*] **1** : not paired; *esp* : not matched or mated ⟨an ~ shoe⟩ ⟨an ~ electron⟩ **2 a** : situated in the median plane of the body ⟨an ~ fin⟩ **b** : having no mate on the opposite side
un·palatability \"+\ *n* : the quality or state of being unpalatable
un·palatable \"+\ *adj* **1** : not palatable : DISTASTEFUL **2** : UNPLEASANT, DISAGREEABLE ⟨harshly ~ but honest statements —Linton Wells⟩ — **un·palatableness** \"+\ *n* — **un·palatably** \"+\ *adv*
un·palliated \"+\ *adj* [¹*un-* + *palliated*, past part. of *palliate*] : not palliated : SEVERE
un·palpable \"+\ *adj* : IMPALPABLE
un·palped \"+\ *adj* : having no palp
un·paper \"+\ *vt* [²*un-* + *paper*] : to strip paper from
un·papered \"+\ *adj* [¹*un-* + *papered*, past part. of *paper*] : having no paper; *esp* : not covered with wallpaper
un·paradise \"+\ *vt* -ED/-ING/-S [²*un-* + *paradise*, n.] **1 a** : to expel from paradise **b** : to make unhappy **2** : to remove the character of paradise from
un·paragoned \"+\ *adj* [¹*un-* + *paragoned*, past part. of *paragon*] : having no paragon : UNEQUALED, MATCHLESS, PEERLESS
un·parallel \"+\ *adj* : not parallel ⟨~ lines intersect⟩
un·par·al·lel·able \-ləbəl\ *adj* [¹*un-* + *parallel* + *-able*] : not capable of being paralleled; *esp* : that cannot be equalled or matched : INCOMPARABLE
un·paralleled \ˌən+\ *adj* [¹*un-* + *paralleled*, past part. of *parallel*] : having no parallel; *esp* : having no equal or match : UNSURPASSED, UNEQUALED ⟨rains of ~ intensity —W.E. Swinton⟩ ⟨an ~ gift for invective —C.I.Glicksberg⟩
un·paralyzed \"+\ *adj* [¹*un-* + *paralyzed*, past part. of *paralyze*] : not paralyzed
un·pardonable \"+\ *adj* : not admitting of pardon : UNFORGIVABLE, INEXCUSABLE ⟨falsification of results in any way, even by implication is the ~ sin —Jessie Bernard⟩ — **un·pardonableness** \"+\ *n* — **un·pardonably** \"+\ *adv*
un·pardoned \"+\ *adj* [¹*un-* + *pardoned*, past part. of *pardon*] : not pardoned : UNFORGIVEN
un·pardoning \"+\ *adj* [¹*un-* + *pardoning*, pres. part. of *pardon*] : not pardoning : withholding forgiveness
un·par·ent·ed \ˌənˈpa(a)rəntəd, -per-\ *adj* [¹*un-* + *parent* + *-ed*] : having no parent or acknowledged parent : ORPHAN
un·park \ˌən+\ *vt* [²*un-* + *park*] : to remove from a parking place ⟨could ~ the trucks and cars and wagons and mules —William Faulkner⟩
un·parliamentary \"+\ *adj* : not parliamentary : contrary to the practice of parliamentary bodies
un·parted \"+\ *adj* : not parted : UNSEPARATED; *specif* : not subjected to the operation of separating gold from silver — used of gold bullion containing silver or silver bullion containing gold
un·participated \"+\ *adj* [¹*un-* + *participated*, past part. of *participate*] : not participated in : UNEQUALED, UNIQUE
un·partisan \"+\ *adj* : NONPARTISAN — **un·partisanship** \"+\ *n*
un·partitioned \"+\ *adj* [¹*un-* + *partitioned*, past part. of *partition*] : not partitioned : having no partitions
un·passable \"+\ *adj* **1** : IMPASSABLE **2** *obs* : not usable as currency
un·passed \"+\ *adj* [¹*un-* + *passed*, past part. of *pass*] : not passed : still to be crossed
un·passioned \ˌən+\ *adj* : DISPASSIONATE
un·pastoral \"+\ *adj* : not pastoral; *also* : not characteristic of or consonant with the tradition of pastoral verse
un·patentable \"+\ *adj* : not patentable
un·patented \"+\ *adj* [¹*un-* + *patented*, past part. of *patent*] : not patented ⟨~ inventions⟩
un·pathed \ˌənˈpa|tht, -ˈpaa(ə)|, -ˈpai|, -ˈpä|, |t͟hd\ *adj* [¹*un-* + *path* + *-ed*] : not having a path : PATHLESS
un·patient \ˌən+\ *adj* [ME *unpacient*, fr. ¹*un-* + *pacient* patient] : IMPATIENT
un·patriotic \"+\ *adj* : not patriotic : not giving or expressing due regard to one's country or its interests; *esp* : SUBVERSIVE ⟨~ obstruction by any corporation in defense work —F.D. Roosevelt⟩ — **un·patriotically** \"+\ *adv*
un·patrolled \"+\ *adj* [¹*un-* + *patrolled*, past part. of *patrol*] : not patrolled esp. by sentinels or police ⟨an ~ section of the highway⟩
un·patronized \"+\ *adj* [¹*un-* + *patronized*, past part. of *patronize*] : not patronized : having little or no patronage ⟨a restaurant ~ by the elite⟩
un·pausing \"+\ *adj* [¹*un-* + *pausing*, pres. part. of *pause*] : continuing without cease — **un·pausingly** \"+\ *adv*
un·pave \"+\ *vt* [²*un-* + *pave*] : to remove the paving from
un·paved \"+\ *adj* : not paved : not furnished with a pavement
un·pawned \"+\ *adj* [¹*un-* + *pawned*, past part. of *pawn*] : not pawned
un·payable \"+\ *adj* **1** : not capable of being paid **2** : not capable of being profitably worked ⟨~ ore deposits⟩
un·paying \"+\ *adj* [¹*un-* + *paying*, pres. part. of *pay*] : not paying ⟨~ customers⟩
un·peace \"+\ *n* : lack of peace : STRIFE, DISUNITY, DISSENSION
un·peaceable \"+\ *adj* [¹*un-* + *peaceable*] **1** : given to disturbing the peace : DISSENTIENT **2** : lacking peace : DISTURBED, UNPEACEFUL
un·peaceful \"+\ *adj* : not peaceful : INHARMONIOUS, AGITATED, TURBULENT — **un·peacefully** \"+\ *adv*
un·pedantic \"+\ *adj* : not pedantic : not characterized by the dryness and dead mechanical manner of a pedant : LIVELY — **un·pedantically** \"+\ *adv*
un·pedestal \ˌən+\ *vt* [²*un-* + *pedestal*, n.] : to oust from a position of superiority
un·pedigreed \"+\ *adj* [¹*un-* + *pedigreed*, past part. of *pedigree*] **1** : not distinguished by a pedigree **2** *of a domestic animal* : lacking a recorded pedigree : not of the pure blood of a recognized breed — used esp. of a high grade
un·peel \"+\ *vt* [²*un-* + *peel*] : to remove an outer covering (as bark, a rind, or a peel) from ⟨~ a banana⟩
un·peeled ginger \"+-\ *n* : BLACK GINGER
un·peg \"+\ *vt* [²*un-* + *peg*] **1 a** : to remove a peg from **b** : to unfasten by or as if by removing a peg **2** : to cease pegging transactions in (a security or a currency)
un·pen \"+\ *vt* [²*un-* + *pen*] : to release from a pen or from confinement
un·penetrable \"+\ *adj* : IMPENETRABLE
un·penetrated \"+\ *adj* [¹*un-* + *penetrated*, past part. of *penetrate*] : not penetrated
un·penned \"+\ *adj* [¹*un-* + *penned*, past part. of *pen* to enclose & *pen* to write] **1** : not confined by a pen **2** : UNWRITTEN
un·pensioned \"+\ *adj* [¹*un-* + *pensioned*, past part. of *pension*] : not pensioned : having no pension
un·pent \"+\ *adj* : not pent : UNCONFINED, RELEASED
un·people \"+\ *vt* [²*un-* + *people*] : to deprive of inhabitants : DEPOPULATE ⟨the failure of the harvest again produced famine — *unpeopling* farms and hamlets —G.M.Trevelyan⟩
un·peopled \"+\ *adj* [¹*un-* + *peopled*, adj.] : UNPOPULATED, UNINHABITED
un·perceivable \"+\ *adj* [ME, fr. ¹*un-* + *perceivable*] : IMPERCEPTIBLE; *esp* : logically or by nature imperceptible
un·perceived \"+\ *adj* [ME, fr. ¹*un-* + *perceived*, past part. of *perceiven* to perceive] : not perceived, noticed, or remarked
un·perceiving \"+\ *adj* : not perceiving or prone to perceive : UNOBSERVANT
un·perceptive \"+\ *adj* : lacking perception : UNPERCEIVING ⟨as ~ as a boulder —Edmund Wilson⟩
un·perch \ˌən+\ *vt* [²*un-* + *perch*] : to remove from a perch
un·percipient \"+\ *adj* : UNPERCEIVING
un·perfect \"+\ *adj* [alter. (influenced by L *perfectus* perfect) of ME *unperfit*, fr. ¹*un-* + *perfit* perfect] **1** : IMPERFECT **2** *obs* : poorly trained : UNSKILLED — **un·perfectness** \"+\ *n*
un·perfected \"+\ *adj* **1** : not brought to completion : UNFINISHED **2** : poorly trained : INEXPERT
un·perforate \"+\ *adj* : IMPERFORATE
un·perforated \"+\ *adj* : having no perforations : IMPERFORATE
un·performable \"+\ *adj* : not performable; *also* : difficult to perform
un·performed \"+\ *adj* [ME, fr. ¹*un-* + *performed*, past part. of *performen* to perform] : not performed ⟨the author of an ~ play⟩
un·performing \"+\ *adj* : not performing
un·perilous \ˌən+\ *adj* : not perilous : free from danger
un·perishable \"+\ *adj* : IMPERISHABLE
un·perished \"+\ *adj* [ME *unperist*, fr. ¹*un-* + *perist*, *perisshed*, past part. of *perissen*, *perisshen* to perish] : not dead : ALIVE
un·perishing \"+\ *adj* : IMMORTAL
un·perjured \"+\ *adj* : not perjured
un·permanent \"+\ *adj* : IMPERMANENT
un·permissive \"+\ *adj* : not permissive : STRICT
un·permitted \"+\ *adj* : not permitted : DISALLOWED, BANNED
un·perplex \ˌən+\ *vt* [²*un-* + *perplex*] : to free from perplexity
un·perplexed \"+\ *adj* [¹*un-* + *perplexed*, adj.] **1** : not perplexed : UNBAFFLED **2** : SIMPLE, STRAIGHTFORWARD, CLEAR
un·persuadable \"+\ *adj* : not persuadable : ADAMANT — **un·persuadableness** \"+\ *n*
un·persuaded \"+\ *adj* [¹*un-* + *persuaded*, past part. of *persuade*] : not persuaded
un·persuasive \"+\ *adj* : not persuasive — **un·persuasively** \"+\ *adv* — **un·persuasiveness** \"+\ *n*
un·perturbed \"+\ *adj* [ME, fr. ¹*un-* + *perturbed*, past part. of *perturben* to perturb] : not perturbed : unaffected by worry, interruption, disturbance, or disarrangement ⟨a fox who was completely ~ by my appearance —S.P.B.Mais⟩ — **un·perturbedly** \"+\ *adv* — **un·per·turbed·ness** \-b(ə)dnə̇s\ *n* -ES
un·perverted \ˌən+\ *adj* : not perverted
un·petticoated \"+\ *adj* : not wearing a petticoat
un·philosophic \"+\ *or* **un·philosophical** \"+\ *adj* **1** : not in accordance with philosophic knowledge or methods ⟨an ~ judgment⟩ **2** : lacking philosophic breadth, insight, or temperament ⟨the ~ specialist may be a fool in every field not his own —A.L.Guérard⟩ — **un·philosophically** \"+\ *adv*
un·phonetic \"+\ *adj* : characterized by or showing lack of regular correspondence of spelling to sound — **un·pho·net·ic·ness** \-knə̇s\ *n* -ES
un·physical \ˌən+\ *adj* **1** : not physical : MENTAL, SPIRITUAL **2** : not according with the doctrines or methods of physics
un·physiologic \"+\ *also* **un·physiological** \"+\ *adj* : not such as would ordinarily conduce to an organism's normal healthy functioning ⟨an ~ regime⟩ ⟨~ dosage of vitamin D⟩
un·pick \"+\ *vt* [²*un-* + *pick*] : to undo (as sewing, embroidery, or knitting) by taking out stitches
un·pickable \"+\ *adj* : not pickable or easily pickable ⟨an ~ lock⟩
unpicked \"+\ *adj* **1** : UNSORTED **2** : not picked
un·pictorial \"+\ *adj* : not susceptible to pictorial representation — **un·pictorially** \"+\ *adv* — **un·pictorialness** \"+\ *n*
un·picturesque \"+\ *adj* : not picturesque — **un·picturesquely** \"+\ *adv* — **un·picturesqueness** \"+\ *n*
un·pierceable \"+\ *adj* : not pierceable
un·pierced \"+\ *adj* : not pierced
un·pigmented \"+\ *adj* [¹*un-* + *pigmented*, past part. of *pigment*] : not pigmented : having no pigment
un·pile \"+\ *vb* [²*un-* + *pile*] *vt* : to take or disentangle from a pile ⟨waiters *unpiling* the wicker chairs —Cyril Connolly⟩ ~ *vi* : to become separated or disentangled from a pile ⟨at the referee's whistle the players *unpiled*⟩
un·pillared \"+\ *adj* : having no pillar
un·pillowed \"+\ *adj* [¹*un-* + *pillowed*, past part. of *pillow*] : not resting on a pillow
un·piloted \"+\ *adj* [¹*un-* + *piloted*, past part. of *pilot*] : not piloted : being without a pilot ⟨~ missiles⟩

un·pin \"+\ *vt* [ME *unpinnen,* fr. [2]*un-* + *pinnen* to pin] **1 :** to remove a pin from **2 :** to loosen, free, or unfasten by or as if by removing a pin ⟨~ a dress⟩ ⟨~ a frame⟩

unpinion *vt* [[2]*un-* + *pinion*] *obs* **:** to loose from or as if from pinions **:** free from restraint

un·pinioned \¦ən+\ *adj* [[1]*un-* + *pinioned*] **1 :** having no pinions **2 :** not bound by or as if by pinions ⟨perfectly free and ~ —Edward Grey⟩

un·pitiable \¦ən+\ *adj* **:** not pitiable — **un·pitiably** \"+\ *adv*

un·pitied \"+\ *adj* [[1]*un-* + *pitied,* past part. of *pity*] **1 :** not pitied **2** [[1]*un-* + *pity, n.* + *-ed*] *obs* **:** PITILESS, MERCILESS

un·pitiful \"+\ *adj* [ME *unpiteful,* fr. [1]*un-* + *piteful, petefull* pitiful] **:** PITILESS — **un·pitifully** \"+\ *adv*

un·pitying \"+\ *adj* **:** not pitying **:** UNMERCIFUL — **un·pityingly** \"+\ *adv*

un·placed \"+\ *adj* [[1]*un-* + *placed,* past part. of *place*] **1 :** not placed **:** not having a definite or assigned place, position, station, or office **2 :** not winning one of the first three places in a horse race

un·plagued \"+\ *adj* **:** not plagued ⟨a town rich in traditions . . . and ~ by ambition —*Amer. Guide Series: Md.*⟩

un·plait \"+\ *vt* [[2]*un-* + *plait*] **:** to undo the plaits of

un·plaited \"+\ *adj* [[1]*un-* + *plaited*] **:** not plaited

un·planed \"+\ *adj* [[1]*un-* + *planed,* past part. of *plane* to level] **:** not planed ⟨~ planks⟩

un·plank \"+\ *vt* [[2]*un-* + *plank*] **:** to remove the planks from

un·planked \¦ən+\ *adj* [[1]*un-* + *planked,* past part. of *plank*] **:** not planked; *specif* **:** not covered with planks

un·planned \"+\ *adj* **1 :** not planned ⟨an ~ economy⟩ **2 :** UNEXPECTED ⟨accepts an ~ order —J.S.Berliner⟩

un·plant \"+\ *vt* [[2]*un-* + *plant*] **:** to remove from the soil **:** UPROOT

un·plantable \"+\ *adj* **:** not plantable **:** INFERTILE ⟨land hitherto regarded as ~ —*Ulster Yr. Bk.*⟩

un·planted \"+\ *adj* [[1]*un-* + *planted,* past part. of *plant*] **1** *of a plant* **:** growing spontaneously and freely in nature without human intervention **:** UNCULTIVATED **2 :** not colonized **:** UNSETTLED **3 :** not placed in position **:** not set out

un·plastered \"+\ *adj* [[1]*un-* + *plastered,* past part. of *plaster*] **:** not plastered **:** having no plaster ⟨~ walls⟩

un·plastic \"+\ *adj* **:** not plastic; *specif* **:** not amenable to plastic representation

un·plausible \"+\ *adj* **:** IMPLAUSIBLE — **un·plausibly** \"+\ *adv*

un·playable \¦ən+\ *adj* **:** not playable: as **a :** not capable of being played on a musical instrument **b :** being in a position where a stroke or shot is impossible ⟨an ~ lie in golf⟩

un·pleasant \"+\ *adj* **:** not pleasant **:** not amiable or agreeable **:** DISPLEASING, OFFENSIVE ⟨~ odors⟩ ⟨~ repercussions⟩ ⟨an ~ personality⟩ — **un·pleasantly** \"+\ *adv*

un·pleasantness \"+\ *n* **1 a :** the quality or state of being unpleasant **:** DISAGREEABLENESS **b :** an unpleasant situation, experience, or event ⟨murders, bankruptcies, and other *~es* —Charles Spielberger⟩ **2 :** the elementary feeling ordinarily awakened by painful or disagreeable stimuli

un·pleasantry \"+\ *n* **1 :** an unpleasant incident **2 :** an unpleasant remark or speech **:** INSULT ⟨the candidates exchanged *unpleasantries*⟩

un·pleased \"+\ *adj* [ME *unplesed,* fr. [1]*un-* + *plesed* pleased] **:** not pleased **:** DISPLEASED, UNSATISFIED

un·pleasing \"+\ *adj* **:** not pleasing **:** DISAGREEABLE ⟨full of ~ blots and sightless stains —Shak.⟩ — **un·pleasingly** \"+\ *adv*

un·pleasurable \"+\ *adj* **:** not pleasurable **:** not giving pleasure or satisfaction — **un·pleasurably** \"+\ *adv*

un·pleasure \"+\ *n* **1 :** lack of pleasure **2 :** UNPLEASANTNESS 2

un·pleated \"+\ *adj* **:** not pleated **:** having no pleats ⟨an ~ skirt⟩

un·pledged \"+\ *adj* [[1]*un-* + *pledged,* past part. of *pledge*] **:** not bound by a pledge or vow; *specif* **:** not pledged to vote for a specified candidate ⟨the state sent an ~ delegation to the convention⟩

un·pliable \"+\ *adj* **1 :** not liable to persuasion **:** OBSTINATE ⟨the most ~ mind I ever met —H.J.Laski⟩ **2 :** not pliable ⟨~ substances⟩ — **un·pliableness** \"+\ *n*

un·pliancy \"+\ *n* **:** lack of pliancy

un·pliant \"+\ *adj* **1 :** not pliant **2 :** UNPLIABLE, OBSTINATE **3 :** resistant to use **:** not easily managed

un·plowed \"+\ *adj* [[1]*un-* + *plowed,* past part. of *plow*] **:** not plowed

un·plucked \"+\ *adj* [[1]*un-* + *plucked,* past part. of *pluck*] **:** not plucked

un·plug \"+\ *vt* [[2]*un-* + *plug*] **1 a :** to take a plug out of ⟨~ a sink⟩ **b :** to remove an obstruction from ⟨~ the channel⟩ **2 a :** to remove (as an electric plug) from a socket or receptacle **b :** to disconnect from an electric circuit by removing a plug ⟨~ a refrigerator⟩

un·plumbed \"+\ *adj* [[1]*un-* + *plumbed,* past part. of *plumb*] **1 :** not tested with a plumb line **2 a :** not measured with a plumb **b :** not explored in depth, intensity, meaning, or significance ⟨a fascinating variety of ~ possibilities —I.I. Rabi⟩

un·plume \"+\ *vt* [[2]*un-* + *plume*] **1 :** to strip of plumes or feathers **2** *obs* **:** HUMILIATE

un·plumed \"+\ *adj* [[1]*un-* + *plumed,* adj.] **:** not furnished or decorated with plumes

un·plundered \"+\ *adj* [[1]*un-* + *plundered,* past part. of *plunder*] **:** not plundered

un·pocket \"+\ *vt* [[2]*un-* + *pocket*] **:** to remove from a pocket

un·poetic \"+\ *or* **un·poetical** \"+\ *adj* **:** not poetic **:** not having the characteristics of poetry — **un·poetically** \"+\ *adv*

un·pointed \¦ən+\ *adj* **1 :** not pointed **:** having no point **2 :** unprovided with vowel points ⟨an ~ Hebrew text⟩

un·poise \"+\ *vt* [[2]*un-* + *poise*] **:** to upset the equilibrium of

un·poised \"+\ *adj* [[1]*un-* + *poised,* adj.] **:** not poised **:** UNBALANCED

un·poisoned \"+\ *adj* [[1]*un-* + *poisoned,* past part. of *poison*] **:** not poisoned

un·polarized \"+\ *adj* [[1]*un-* + *polarized,* past part. of *polarize*] **:** not polarized ⟨~ light⟩

unpolicied *adj* [[1]*un-* + *policy* + *-ed*] *obs* **:** IMPOLITIC, IMPRUDENT

un·polish \¦ən+\ *vt* [[2]*un-* + *polish*] **:** to deprive of polish

un·polishable \"+\ *adj* **:** not polishable

un·polished \"+\ *adj* [ME *unpolisshed,* fr. [1]*un-* + *polisshed* polished] **1 a :** not smoothed by polishing ⟨an ~ gem⟩ **b :** not coated with polish ⟨~ shoes⟩ **2 a :** not marked by careful reworking and finishing **:** CRUDE ⟨an ~ literary style⟩ **b :** not marked by refinement **:** relatively untouched by urbane or civilizing influences **:** BOORISH, UNCULTURED

unpolished rice *n* **:** rice from which the hulls, germs, and outer bran layers but not the inner bran layers have been removed

un·polite \¦ən+\ *adj* **:** IMPOLITE — **unpolitely** *adv* — **un·politeness** \"+\ *n*

un·politic \"+\ *adj* **:** IMPOLITIC

un·political \"+\ *adj* **1 :** not according with sound political doctrine **2 :** APOLITICAL **3 :** NONPOLITICAL

un·polled \"+\ *adj* [[1]*un-* + *polled,* past part. of *poll*] **1 :** not registered as a voter **2 :** not included or interviewed in a poll

un·polluted \"+\ *adj* **:** not polluted **:** CLEAN, PURE ⟨an ~ water supply⟩

un·polymerized \"+\ *adj* [[1]*un-* + *polymerized,* past part. of *polymerize*] **:** not polymerized

un·pope \"+\ *vt* [[2]*un-* + *pope, n.*] *archaic* **:** to divest of the character, office, or authority of a pope

un·popular \"+\ *adj* **:** not popular **:** viewed or received unfavorably by the public ⟨suspected of ~ ideas —Herbert Agar⟩ — **un·popularity** \"+\ *n*

un·populated \"+\ *adj* [[1]*un-* + *populated,* past part. of *populate*] **:** not populated **:** not occupied or settled **:** not inhabited

un·portable \"+\ *adj* [ME, unbearable, fr. [1]*un-* + *portable*] **:** not portable **:** too bulky or heavy or too complexly or firmly fixed to be easily moved

un·posed \"+\ *adj* [[1]*un-* + *posed,* past part. of *pose*] **:** not posed **:** CANDID ⟨impromptu, ~ portraits —H.L.Mencken⟩

un·possessed \"+\ *adj* **1 :** having no possessor **:** UNOWNED, UNOCCUPIED **2 :** not having a possession — **un·possessedness** \"+\ *n*

unpossessing *adj* [[1]*un-* + *possessing,* pres. part. of *possess*] *obs* **:** not possessing **:** lacking a possession

un·possibility \¦ən+\ *n* **:** IMPOSSIBILITY

un·possible \"+\ *adj* [ME, fr. [1]*un-* + *possible*] **:** IMPOSSIBLE

un·powdered \"+\ *adj* **:** not powdered

un·powered \"+\ *adj* **:** not powered; *specif* **:** not self-powered ⟨an ~ glider⟩ ⟨~ artificial satellites⟩

un·practicable \"+\ *adj* **:** IMPRACTICABLE — **un·practicableness** \"+\ *n*

un·practical \"+\ *adj* **:** IMPRACTICAL — **un·practically** \"+\ *adv* — **un·practicalness** \"+\ *n*

un·practicality \"+\ *n* **:** IMPRACTICALITY

un·practiced \"+\ *adj* **1 :** not put to use or test **:** UNTRIED **2 :** not practiced **:** UNSKILLED, INEXPERT

un·praised \"+\ *adj* [[1]*un-* + *praised,* past part. of *praise*] **:** not praised **:** not extolled in praise

un·prayed \"+\ *adj* [ME *unpreyed,* fr. [1]*un-* + *preyed,* past part. of *preyen* to pray] **1 :** not addressed in prayer **2 :** not sought **:** UNSOLICITED, UNINVITED — often used with *for*

un·preach \"+\ *vt* [[2]*un-* + *preach*] *archaic* **:** to undo or retract by preaching

un·preaching \"+\ *adj* [[1]*un-* + *preaching,* pres. part. of *preach*] **:** not preaching **:** failing to preach

un·precarious \"+\ *adj* **:** not precarious **:** SAFE

un·precedented \"+\ *adj* [[1]*un-* + *precedent* + *-ed*] **:** having no precedent **:** NOVEL, NEW, UNEXAMPLED ⟨inaugurated an ~ expansion in population and industry —*Amer. Guide Series: N.Y.*⟩ — **un·prec·e·dent·ed·ly** *adv* — **un·prec·e·dent·ed·ness** *n* -ES

un·precipitated \¦ən+\ *adj* [[1]*un-* + *precipitated,* past part. of *precipitate*] **:** not precipitated

un·precise \"+\ *adj* **:** IMPRECISE — **un·precisely** \"+\ *adv*

un·predictability \"+\ *n* **:** the quality or state of being unpredictable ⟨the characteristic of the kaleidoscope is ~ —Margery Sharp⟩

[1]un·predictable \"+\ *adj* **:** not predictable **:** not to be foretold ⟨the uncertainty and hazards of bad weather and other ~ factors —H.G.Armstrong⟩ ⟨the very essence of harlequinade to be spontaneous, ~ —*Amer. Guide Series: Calif.*⟩ — **un·pre·dict·able·ness** \-bəlnəs\ *n* -ES — **un·predictably** \¦ən+\ *adv*

[2]unpredictable \"\ *n* -S **:** an unpredictable person, thing, or event ⟨the vocation of her husband, his success, and location are *~s* —L.W.Norris⟩

un·predicted \¦ən+\ *adj* [[1]*un-* + *predicted,* past part. of *predict*] **:** not predicted **:** UNFORESEEN

unpreferred *adj* [ME, fr. [1]*un-* + *preferred,* past part. of *prefer*] *obs* **:** not advanced or promoted

unpregnant *adj, obs* **:** INAPT

un·prejudiced \¦ən+\ *adj* **:** not prejudiced **:** free from undue bias, warp, or prepossession **:** IMPARTIAL ⟨an ~ judge⟩ ⟨an ~ appraisal of the pros and cons —J.L.Lowes⟩ — **un·prej·u·dicedly** \"+\ *adv* — **un·prej·u·diced·ness** *n* -ES

un·prelatical \¦ən+\ *adj* **:** not prelatic

un·premeditated \¦ən+\ *adj* **:** not premeditated — **un·premeditatedly** \"+\ *adv* — **un·premeditatedness** \"+\ *n*

un·premeditation \"+\ *n* **:** lack of premeditation

un·preoccupied \"+\ *adj* **:** not preoccupied

un·prepare \"+\ *vt* [[1]*un-* + *prepare*] **:** to cause to be unprepared **:** make unfit or unready ⟨the purpose . . . is precisely to ~ the reader —W.M.Frohock⟩

un·prepared \"+\ *adj* [[1]*un-* + *prepared,* adj.] **1 a :** not prepared **:** not on the alert or in a state of readiness **:** having made no preparation ⟨our treaty makers approached their immensely difficult problems ~, unsure, inexperienced —R.E.Danielson⟩ **b :** not put into a state of preparedness **:** UNREADY ⟨the machinery was ~ for the extra load⟩ **2 :** happening without preparation **:** arriving or taking place unexpectedly or without warning ⟨the shock was ~⟩ — **un·preparedly** \"+\ *adv* — **un·preparedness** \"+\ *n*

un·prepossessed \"+\ *adj* [[1]*un-* + *prepossessed,* past part. of *prepossess*] **:** having no prior bias or opinion **:** UNPREJUDICED ⟨a mind . . . entirely ~ with any theory or system —John Foster⟩

un·prepossessing \"+\ *adj* **:** not prepossessing **:** creating an unfavorable or neutral first impression ⟨a very ~ lot . . . being fat, skinny, old, young, gawky, commonplace —Rex Ingamells⟩

un·prescient \"+\ *adj* **:** not prescient **:** lacking foresight

un·prescribed \"+\ *adj* [[1]*un-* + *prescribed,* past part. of *prescribe*] **:** not prescribed **:** FREE, VOLUNTARY

un·presentable \"+\ *adj* **:** not presentable; *esp* **:** having a disreputable or unprepossessing character, background, or appearance ⟨~ friends . . . sometimes fleeing from the police —Upton Sinclair⟩ — **un·pre·sent·able·ness** *n* -ES

un·presented \¦ən+\ *adj* [[1]*un-* + *presented,* past part. of *present*] **:** not presented ⟨the meeting adjourned with several proposals ~⟩

un·pressed \"+\ *adj* **:** not pressed

un·presuming \"+\ *adj* **:** not presumptuous **:** keeping to an inherited or appropriate social status **:** MODEST — **un·pre·sum·ing·ness** *n* -ES

un·presumptuous \¦ən+\ *adj* **:** UNPRESUMING — **un·presumptuously** \"+\ *adv*

un·pretended \"+\ *adj* **:** not pretended **:** REAL, GENUINE

un·pretending \"+\ *adj* [[1]*un-* + *pretending,* pres. part. of *pretend*] **:** not pretending; *esp* **:** UNPRETENTIOUS, UNPRESUMING ⟨our mode of living . . . is plain and ~ —Jane Austen⟩ — **un·pre·tend·ing·ly** *adv* — **un·pre·tend·ing·ness** *n*

un·pretentious \¦ən+\ *adj* **:** not pretentious **:** free from ostentation, pomp, elegance, or affectation **:** MODEST ⟨comfortable but ~ homes —*Amer. Guide Series: La.*⟩ ⟨a quiet, frank, and ~ disposition —F.C.Baker⟩ **syn** see PLAIN

un·pretentiously \"+\ *adv* **:** in an unpretentious manner

un·pretentiousness \"+\ *n* **:** the quality or state of being unpretentious

un·prettiness \"+\ *n* **:** lack of prettiness **:** PLAINNESS, UGLINESS

un·pretty \"+\ *adj* **1 :** not pretty **:** lacking in beauty ⟨so ~ she ought to be funny —Eudora Welty⟩ **2 :** not deserving moral approval; *esp* **:** REPREHENSIBLE ⟨as conquerors they make an ~ lot —*Time*⟩

un·prevailing \"+\ *adj* **:** not culminating or not capable of culminating in success **:** INEFFECTIVE

un·preventable \"+\ *adj* **:** not preventable **:** UNAVOIDABLE ⟨~ hysteria⟩ — **un·pre·vent·able·ness** \-bəlnəs\ *n* — **un·pre·vent·ably** \-blē, -li\ *adv*

un·prevented \¦ən+\ *adj* [[1]*un-* + *prevented,* past part. of *prevent*] **:** not prevented

un·pricked \"+\ *adj* **:** not pricked **:** not punctured or wounded by a prick

un·priest \"+\ *vt* [[2]*un-* + *priest*] **:** to deprive of priesthood **:** UNFROCK

un·priestly \"+\ *adj* [[1]*un-* + *priestly,* adj.] **:** not priestly **:** unbefitting a priest

un·prime \"+\ *adj, of a fur* **:** not prime ⟨an ~ fur taken when the animal was molting and growing a new coat⟩

un·primed \"+\ *adj* [[1]*un-* + *primed,* past part. of *prime*] **:** not primed

un·primitive \"+\ *adj* **:** not primitive **:** DEVELOPED ⟨a highly advanced ~ state —*Times Lit. Supp.*⟩

un·princely \"+\ *adj* **:** not princely **:** exhibiting or being characteristics unbefitting a prince

un·principled \"+\ *adj* **:** lacking or exhibiting a lack of moral principles ⟨brash, ~, and conscienceless —J.R.Cominsky⟩ ⟨freedom from coarse, ~ calumny —A.E.Stevenson b. 1900⟩ — **un·prin·ci·pled·ness** *n* -ES

un·printable \¦ən+\ *adj* **:** that cannot be printed specif. because considered offensive to morals or good taste ⟨an ~ epithet⟩ ⟨an ~ picture⟩ — **un·print·able·ness** \-bəlnəs\ *n* — **un·print·ably** \-blē, -li\ *adv*

un·printed \¦ən+\ *adj* [[1]*un-* + *printed,* past part. of *print*] **1 :** not printed upon ⟨would cover . . . the ~ newspaper with charcoal sketches —H.A.Overstreet⟩ **2 :** not transferred to or expressed in print ⟨an ~ manuscript⟩

un·prison \"+\ *vt* [ME, fr. [2]*un-* + *prison*] **:** to free from prison

un·privileged \"+\ *adj* **:** not privileged; not enjoying special rights or benefits ⟨the ~, the disaffected are probably the most amenable recruits —W.E.Moore⟩

un·prized \¦ən+\ *adj* [[1]*un-* + *prized,* past part. of *prize*] *archaic* **:** not valued or properly valued

un·probable \"+\ *adj* **:** IMPROBABLE

un·probed \"+\ *adj* [[1]*un-* + *probed,* past part. of *probe*] **:** not probed **:** not thoroughly investigated or explored

un·problematic \"+\ *adj* **:** not problematic **:** not presenting puzzles or raising questions or doubts

un·processed \"+\ *adj* [[1]*un-* + *processed,* past part. of *process*] **:** not processed; *esp* **:** not altered from an original or natural state

un·proclaimed \"+\ *adj* [[1]*un-* + *proclaimed,* past part. of *proclaim*] **:** not proclaimed **:** UNANNOUNCED

un·produced \"+\ *adj* [[1]*un-* + *produced,* past part. of *produce*] **1 :** not formed, made, or created **2 :** not extended or abnormally extended — **un·pro·duc·ed·ness** \-sədnəs, -stnəs\ *n* -ES

[1]un·productive \¦ən+\ *adj* **:** not productive ⟨elimination of ~ or high-cost industries —Harold Callender⟩ ⟨efforts of early missionaries to proselyte Minnesota Indians were largely ~ —*Amer. Guide Series: Minn.*⟩ — **un·productively** \"+\ *adv* — **un·productiveness** \"+\ *n*

[2]unproductive \"\ *n* -S **:** an unproductive point in a field trial

unproductive consumption *n* **:** consumption of food, fuel, or materials without creation of corresponding values in some other form

un·profane \¦ən+\ *adj* **:** not profane **:** HOLY, SAINTLY

un·profaned \"+\ *adj* [[1]*un-* + *profaned,* past part. of *profane*] **:** not profaned **:** PURE, INVIOLATE

un·professed \"+\ *adj* **:** not professed ⟨an ~ sister⟩

un·professional \"+\ *adj* **1 :** not belonging to or gainfully employed at a particular profession ⟨drawings of the ~ architect, which have commanded the admiration of the critics —C.G.Bowers⟩ **2 :** not characteristic of or befitting a member of a profession ⟨in such ~ language that the high school student could understand it as easily as the lawyer —M.L. Ernst⟩ — **un·professionally** \"+\ *adv*

un·profitability \"+\ *n* **:** the quality or state of being unprofitable ⟨the chaos and ~ of cutthroat price competition —*Economist*⟩

un·profitable \"+\ *adj* [ME, fr. [1]*un-* + *profitable*] **:** not profitable **:** producing no profit, gain, good, or result **:** PROFITLESS, USELESS, VAIN, IDLE ⟨in all this straining after symmetry there is an ~ overcomplication —Robert Humphrey⟩ ⟨miners . . . turned to the deposits that the companies had abandoned as ~ —*Amer. Guide Series: Pa.*⟩ — **un·profitableness** \"+\ *n* — **un·profitably** \"+\ *adv*

un·profited \"+\ *adj* [[1]*un-* + *profited,* past part. of *profit*] **:** PROFITLESS

un·progressive \"+\ *adj* **:** not progressive; *esp* **:** not devoted to or showing economic, social, or political progress **:** BACKWARD ⟨the supposedly volatile but really conservative and, on the whole, industrious but ~ character of the main mass —Samuel Van Valkenburg & Ellsworth Huntington⟩ — **un·progressively** \"+\ *adv* — **un·progressiveness** \"+\ *n*

un·prohibited \"+\ *adj* [[1]*un-* + *prohibited,* past part. of *prohibit*] **:** not prohibited **:** PERMITTED, ALLOWED

un·projected \"+\ *adj* **:** UNPLANNED, UNEXPECTED

un·prolific \"+\ *adj* **:** not prolific **:** INFERTILE

un·promising \"+\ *adj* **:** appearing unlikely to be enjoyable or result favorably ⟨hesitation before an ~ task —M.R. Cohen⟩ ⟨devising beautiful and interesting music for ~ combinations of instruments —Edward Sackville-West & Desmond Shawe-Taylor⟩ — **un·promisingly** \"+\ *adv*

un·prompted \"+\ *adj* [[1]*un-* + *prompted,* past part. of *prompt*] **:** not prompted **:** SPONTANEOUS

un·promulgated \"+\ *adj* [[1]*un-* + *promulgated,* past part. of *promulgate*] **:** not promulgated

un·pronounceable \"+\ *adj* **1 :** not pronounceable **2 :** presenting difficulty in correct pronunciation

un·pronounced \"+\ *adj* [[1]*un-* + *pronounced,* past part. of *pronounce*] **:** not pronounced **:** MUTE

un·prop \"+\ *vt* [[2]*un-* + *prop*] **:** to remove a prop from **:** deprive of support

unproper *adj* [ME *unpropre,* fr. [1]*un-* + *propre* proper] *obs* **:** IMPROPER

un·propertied \¦ən+\ *adj* **:** PROPERTYLESS

un·prophetic \"+\ *adj* **:** not prophetic **:** not foreseeing correctly — **un·prophetically** \"+\ *adv*

un·propitious \"+\ *adj* **:** not propitious ⟨made a by-election necessary at a time highly ~ for the Government —Stewart Cockburn⟩ **syn** see OMINOUS

un·propitiously \"+\ *adv* **:** in an unpropitious manner

un·propitiousness \"+\ *n* **:** the quality or state of being unpropitious

un·proportionable \"+\ *adj* **:** DISPROPORTIONATE — **un·proportionably** \"+\ *adv*

un·proportionate \"+\ *adj* **:** DISPROPORTIONATE — **un·proportionately** \"+\ *adv*

un·proportioned \"+\ *adj* **:** DISPROPORTIONATE

un·propped \"+\ *adj* [[1]*un-* + *propped,* past part. of *prop*] **:** having no prop **:** UNSUPPORTED

un·prosecuted \"+\ *adj* [[1]*un-* + *prosecuted,* past part. of *prosecute*] **:** not prosecuted

un·prospected \"+\ *adj* [[1]*un-* + *prospected,* past part. of *prospect*] **:** not prospected **:** not investigated esp. for minerals

un·prosperous \¦ən+\ *adj* **1 :** not indicative of or resulting in a favorable issue ⟨suggested that some irregular love affair was ~ —Walter Bagehot⟩ **2 :** not prospering with respect to money, health, or general welfare — **un·prosperously** \"+\ *adv* — **un·prosperousness** \"+\ *n*

un·prostituted \"+\ *adj* [[1]*un-* + *prostituted,* past part. of *prostitute*] **:** not prostituted

un·protected \"+\ *adj* **:** lacking protection or defense — **un·pro·tect·ed·ly** *adv* — **un·pro·tect·ed·ness** *n* -ES

un·protestantize \¦ən+\ *vt* [[2]*un-* + *protestantize*] **:** to make other than Protestant **:** cause to change from Protestantism to another form of religion; *also* **:** to deprive of a Protestant characteristic ⟨the attempt to ~ the Church of England —J.A.Froude⟩

un·protested \"+\ *adj* **:** not protested **:** accepted without challenge

un·proud \"+\ *adj* **:** not proud **:** MODEST, MEEK

un·provable \"+\ *adj* [ME, fr. [1]*un-* + *provable*] **:** not provable — **un·provableness** \"+\ *n*

un·proved \"+\ *or* **un·proven** \"+\ *adj* [[1]*un-* + *proved* or *proven,* past part. of *prove*] **:** not proved ⟨~ allegations⟩ ⟨~ assumptions⟩

un·provide \"+\ *vt* [[2]*un-* + *provide*] **:** to deprive of necessary provision

un·provided \"+\ *adj* [[1]*un-* + *provided,* adj.] **1 :** not provided **:** lacking supplies, equipment, or funds ⟨left his family ~ for⟩ **2 :** not warned or made ready **:** UNPREPARED **3 :** not provided for **:** UNEXPECTED — **un·pro·vid·ed·ness** *n* -ES

un·provocative \"+\ *adj* **:** not provocative

unprovoke *vt* [[2]*un-* + *provoke*] *obs* **:** to rid of a motive, desire, or capability

un·provoked \¦ən+\ *adj* [[1]*un-* + *provoked,* past part. of *provoke*] **:** lacking provocation ⟨~ and dastardly attack —F.D.Roosevelt⟩ — **un·pro·vok·ed·ly** \-kədlē, -ktlē, -i\ *adv* — **un·pro·vok·ed·ness** \-nəs\ *n* -ES

un·provoking \¦ən+\ *adj* **:** not provoking **:** not given to provocation

un·pruned \"+\ *adj* [[1]*un-* + *pruned,* past part. of *prune*] **:** not pruned **:** allowed to grow naturally ⟨~ trees⟩ ⟨an ~ vine⟩

un·publicized \"+\ *adj* [[1]*un-* + *publicized,* past part. of *publicize*] **:** not publicized

un·publishable \"+\ *adj* **:** not publishable

un·published \¦ən+\ *adj* [[1]*un-* + *published,* past part. of *publish*] **:** not published ⟨~ memoirs⟩

un·pulled \"+\ *adj* [ME, fr. [1]*un-* + *pulled,* past part. of *pullen* to pull] **:** not pulled

un·pulverized \"+\ *adj* [[1]*un-* + *pulverized,* past part. of *pulverize*] **:** not pulverized

un·pumpable \"+\ *adj* **:** not capable of being pumped esp. for information

un·pumped \"+\ *adj* [[1]*un-* + *pumped,* past part. of *pump*] **:** not pumped

un·punctual \"+\ *adj* **:** not punctual **:** late or habitually late — **un·punctuality** \"+\ *n*

un·punctuated \"+\ *adj* [¹*un-* + *punctuated,* past part. of *punctuate*] : not punctuated : lacking punctuation

un·punishable \"+\ *adj* : not punishable ⟨a sin ~ by law⟩ — **un·punishably** \"+\ *adv*

un·punished \"+\ *adj* [ME *unpunissed,* fr. ¹*un-* + *punissed,* past part. of *punissen* to punish] : not punished ⟨the impious . . . ought not to go ~ —Benjamin Jowett⟩

un·purchasable \"+\ *adj* **1** : not purchasable : too rare or expensive to be or not of a type that can be bought ⟨the ~ beauties of the countryside⟩ **2** : not bribable ⟨it is only the man ~ by society that can create the sound society —O.L. Reiser & Blodwen Davies⟩

un·purchased \"+\ *adj* [¹*un-* + *purchased,* past part. of *purchase*] : not purchased

un·pure \"+\ *adj* [ME, fr. ¹*un-* + *pure*] : IMPURE

un·purged \"+\ *adj* [¹*un-* + *purged,* past part. of *purge*] : not purged

un·purified \"+\ *adj* [¹*un-* + *purified,* past part. of *purify*] : not purified

un·purposed \"+\ *adj* [¹*un-* + *purposed,* past part. of *purpose*] **1** : not done from purpose : UNINTENDED **2** : having no purpose : PURPOSELESS

un·pursued \"+\ *adj* [¹*un-* + *pursued,* past part. of *pursue*] : not pursued

un·put \"+\ *adj* [ME, fr. ¹*un-* + *put,* past part. of *putten* to put] : not put ⟨~ questions⟩ ⟨as yet ~ on the shelf⟩

un·putrefied \"+\ *adj* [¹*un-* + *putrefied,* past part. of *putrefy*] : not putrefied

un·quailing \¦ən+\ *adj* [¹*un-* + *quailing,* pres. part. of *quail*] : not quailing : DAUNTLESS, FEARLESS — **un·quail·ing·ly** *adv*

un·qualifiable \¦ən+\ *adj* [¹*un-* + *qualify* + *-able*] : not capable of qualifying

un·qualified \"+\ *adj* [¹*un-* + *qualified,* adj.] **1** : not fit : not having requisite qualifications **2 a** : not limited by sensible or other qualities or by sensible experience **b** : not modified or restricted by reservations ⟨an ~ denial⟩ — **un·qualifiedly** \"+\ *adv*

un·qualify \"+\ *vt* [²*un-* + *qualify*] : DISQUALIFY

unqualitied *adj, obs* : deprived of the usual faculties

un·quantified \¦ən+\ *adj* [¹*un-* + *quantified,* past part. of *quantify*] : not quantified: **a** : not qualified by a quantifier ⟨an ~ term⟩ **b** : containing no quantifier ⟨an ~ expression⟩

un·quarried \"+\ *adj* : not quarried ⟨~ rock⟩ ⟨~ from the hidden depths of the human mind —*Times Lit. Supp.*⟩

un·queen \"+\ *vt* [²*un-* + *queen*] : to divest of the rank or authority of queen

un·quelled \"+\ *adj* [¹*un-* + *quelled,* past part. of *quell*] : not quelled ⟨~ pockets of resistance left behind the advance⟩

un·quenchable \"+\ *adj* [ME, fr. ¹*un-* + *quenchen* to quench + *-able*] **1** : not quenchable : INEXTINGUISHABLE ⟨an ~ underground fire⟩ **2** : not capable of being satisfied, quelled, or discouraged : INSATIABLE ⟨the author's ~ enthusiasm for his theories —Ralph Linton⟩ — **un·quench·ably** \-əblē, -li\ *adv*

un·quenched \¦ən+\ *adj* [ME *uncwenched,* fr. ¹*un-* + *cwenced,* past part. of *cwencen* to quench, fr. (assumed) OE *cwencan* — more at QUENCH] : not quenched : UNEXTINGUISHED, UNQUELLED, UNSATIATED ⟨~ appetites⟩ ⟨~ curiosity⟩

un·questionable \"+\ *adj* **1** *obs* : averse to questions or conversation **2** : acknowledged as beyond question or doubt ⟨regarded as an ~ legal authority —M.R.Cohen⟩ ⟨~ status as a statesman⟩ **3** : not questionable : INDISPUTABLE, INDUBITABLE ⟨~ evidence⟩ — **un·questionableness** \"+\ *n* — **un·questionably** \"+\ *adv*

un·questioned \"+\ *adj* [¹*un-* + *questioned,* past part. of *question*] **1** : not interrogated : not examined or examined into **2** : not called in question : UNDOUBTED ⟨the claims of literature are no longer supported by an ~ tradition —R.K. Welsh⟩ **3** : not open to question : UNQUESTIONABLE ⟨holds an ~ control over individual members —N.D.Palmer & S.C. Leng⟩ ⟨the ~ masterpieces of our epoch —Herbert Read⟩

un·questioning \"+\ *adj* : not questioning : accepting without examination or hesitation ⟨simple ~ trust in God's loving-kindness toward his children —C.B.Nordhoff & J.N.Hall⟩ ⟨~ obedience to authority⟩ — **un·questioningly** \"+\ *adv* — **un·ques·tion·ing·ness** *n* -ES

un·quickened \¦ən+\ *adj* [¹*un-* + *quickened,* past part. of *quicken*] : not quickened : not infused with life, energy, or spirit

¹**un·quiet** \"+\ *vt* [ME, fr. ²*un-* + *quiet,* n.] : DISQUIET

²**unquiet** \"\ *adj* [¹*un-* + *quiet,* adj.] **1** : not quiet : AGITATED, DISTURBED, TURBULENT ⟨the ~ days of the riots⟩ ⟨was windy and spitting rain and ~ —G.B.Shaw⟩ **2** : physically, emotionally, or mentally restless or perturbed : UNEASY ⟨the human understanding is ~; it cannot stop or rest —Francis Bacon⟩ — **un·quietly** \"+\ *adv* — **un·quietness** \"+\ *n*

³**unquiet** \"\ *n* [¹*un-* + *quiet,* n.] : a state of uneasiness or disturbance : DISQUIET

un·quivering \¦ən+\ *adj* [¹*un-* + *quivering,* pres. part. of *quiver*] : not quivering

un·quote \"+\ *vi* [²*un-* + *quote*] : to end a quotation by or as if by the insertion of closing quotes ⟨the candidate said quote I will not run for office ~⟩

un·quoted \"+\ *adj* [¹*un-* + *quoted,* past part. of *quote*] : not quoted

un·railed \"+\ *adj* [¹*un-* + *railed,* past part. of *rail*] : not equipped with a railing

un·raised \"+\ *adj* : not raised

un·rake \"+\ *vt* [ME *unraken,* fr. ²*un-* + *raken* to rake] : to rake off the top or cover of : expose with raking

un·raked \"+\ *adj* [¹*un-* + *raked,* past part. of *rake*] : not raked

un·rallied \"+\ *adj* [¹*un-* + *rallied,* past part. of *rally*] : not rallied : UNCOLLECTED

un·ransacked \"+\ *adj* [¹*un-* + *ransacked,* past part. of *ransack*] : not ransacked

un·ransomed \"+\ *adj* [¹*un-* + *ransomed,* past part. of *ransom*] : not ransomed

un·raptured \"+\ *adj* [¹*un-* + *raptured,* past part. of *rapture*] : untouched by ecstasy, passion, or transport

un·ratable \"+\ *adj* : not ratable

un·rated \"+\ *adj* [¹*un-* + *rated,* past part. of *rate*] : not rated

un·ratified \"+\ *adj* [¹*un-* + *ratified,* past part. of *ratify*] : not ratified

un·ravaged \"+\ *adj* [¹*un-* + *ravaged,* past part. of *ravage*] : not ravaged or pillaged

un·ravel \"+\ *vb* [²*un-* + *ravel*] *vt* **1** : to disengage or separate the threads of : DISENTANGLE ⟨~*ed* the cord into its separate strands⟩ ⟨~*ed* the woven fabric⟩ **2** : REVERSE, UNDO ⟨many of them have had to ~ their training in this direction —John McDonald⟩ **3** : to resolve the intricacy, complexity, or obscurity of : trace the origin or the elements of : clear up ⟨many attempts have been made to ~ the origin of language —Edward Sapir⟩ ⟨there is always the pleasure of ~*ing* a difficulty —O.W.Holmes †1935⟩ ⟨poking far into the atom to ~ the heart of matter —Norman Cousins⟩ ~ *vi* : to become unraveled : RAVEL ⟨an old rope had frayed and ~*ed*⟩ ⟨a tangled skein of hardly won evidence which gradually ~*s* into strands of horse-doping, blackmail, and fear —Vernon Knowles⟩ **syn** see SOLVE

un·raveler \"+\ *n* : one that unravels

un·ravelment \"+\ *n* : the act of unraveling or the state of being unraveled : DENOUEMENT, DISENTANGLEMENT ⟨he is a shrewd critic of historical ideas and an apt dialectician in the ~ of their intention —Irwin Edman⟩

un·ravished \¦ən+\ *adj* [¹*un-* + *ravished,* past part. of *ravish*] : not ravished

un·razed \"+\ *adj* [¹*un-* + *razed,* past part. of *raze*] : not razed

un·ra·zored \¦ən¦rāzə(r)d\ *adj* [¹*un-* + *razor* + *-ed*] : untouched by a razor : UNSHAVEN

un·reachable \¦ən+\ *adj* : incapable of being reached

un·reached \"+\ *adj* [¹*un-* + *reached,* past part. of *reach*] : not reached

un·reacted \"+\ *adj* [¹*un-* + *reacted,* past part. of *react*] : not having reacted

un·reactive \"+\ *adj* : not reactive; *specif* : INERT 2

un·read \"+\ *adj* [ME *unred,* fr. ¹*un-* + *red,* past part. of *reden* to read] **1** : not read : left unexamined ⟨through sheer mischance the letter remained ~⟩ **2** [¹*un-* + *read*] : lacking the experience or the benefits of reading : having no familiarity with a (specified) field ⟨he seems to have been wholly ~ in political theory —V.L.Parrington⟩

un·readability \"+\ *n* : UNREADABLENESS

un·readable \"+\ *adj* **1** : lacking interest or attraction as reading : alien or dull in vein or spirit ⟨to us, the writings of most of the original 14th and 15th century humanists seem wholly ~ —Aldous Huxley⟩ **2 a** : not clear or plain enough to be read or understood : ILLEGIBLE, UNDECIPHERABLE ⟨penned a page of ~ scribbles⟩ **b** : not open to confident interpretation : INCOMPREHENSIBLE, INDISTINCT, UNINTELLIGIBLE, CONFUSED, OPAQUE ⟨tire tracks in the roadside sand were confused and ~ —E.S.Sullivan⟩ ⟨she raised her eyes, glistening softly in the light with a sort of ~ appeal —Joseph Conrad⟩

un·readableness \"+\ *n* : the quality or state of being unreadable

un·readably \"+\ *adv* : in an unreadable manner

un·readily \"+\ *adv* : not readily or easily : HARDLY

un·readiness \"+\ *n* : the quality or state of being unready

un·reading \"+\ *adj* : little given to reading ⟨the idle and ~ world —Frederic Harrison⟩

un·ready \"+\ *adj* [ME *unredy,* fr. ¹*un-* + *redy* ready] **1** : not ready : UNPREPARED **2** *dial* : being in a state of undress or deshabille **3** : lacking in ready wit, presence, or prompt address ⟨thrice over she cursed her ~ tongue —Josephine Pinckney⟩

un·real \"+\ *adj* **1** : lacking in reality, substance, or genuineness : ARTIFICIAL ⟨considering it in ~ separation from all the other elements with which it actually fuses —E.K.Brown⟩ **2** : lacking in truth : failing to correspond to acknowledged facts, standards, or criteria : FALSE ⟨seems fantastically ~ and utterly remote from the slightest vestige of truth —John Russell b. 1872⟩ **3** : related only to fantasy or fiction : ILLUSORY, IMAGINARY ⟨the idealistic, ~ world of advertising art —Coulton Waugh⟩ ⟨~ as a cinemascope slightly out of focus —E.B.Garside⟩

un·realism \"+\ *n* : lack of realism : failure of verisimilitude : ineptitude in dealing with reality

un·realist \"+\ *n* : one who exhibits unrealism in words or action ⟨neither of them believes anything which has the slightest actual bearing on the course of economic events. They are ~*s,* illusionists, players with ideas —*Nation*⟩

un·realistic \"+\ *adj* : not realistic : inappropriate to reality or fact : DELUSIVE ⟨the school's ~ program —M.H.Fouracre⟩ ⟨prices for both commodities have reached ~ high levels —*Wall Street Jour.*⟩ — **un·realistically** \"+\ *adv*

un·reality \"+\ *n* **1 a** : the quality or state of being unreal : lack of substance or validity : NONEXISTENCE ⟨there is an air of ~ about life among diplomats anywhere —G.S.Gale⟩ **b** : something unreal, insubstantial, or visionary : a figment of imagination ⟨born of silly parents, and trained to *unrealities* —Samuel Butler †1902⟩ **2** : ineptitude or incapacity in recognizing or dealing with reality ⟨the ~ of the ivory-tower attitude of mind —Leslie Rees⟩

un·realizable \"+\ *adj* **1** : incapable of being understood or sensed : INCOMPREHENSIBLE, UNINTELLIGIBLE, UNTHINKABLE **2** : incapable of being brought to reality or given substance or tangible accomplishment ⟨an immense and ~ series of electoral pledges —John Gunther⟩

un·realize \"+\ *vt* : to make unreal : deprive of substance or validity : make fanciful ⟨his fancy . . . ~*s* everything at a touch —J.R.Lowell⟩

un·realized \"+\ *adj* [¹*un-* + *realized,* past part. of *realize*] **1 a** : not reduced to real or actual form : not brought to fruition or accomplishment ⟨an ~ ambition⟩ **b** : not turned into cash by sale : PAPER ⟨an ~ profit⟩ ⟨~ appreciation in the value of property —*U. S. Code*⟩ **2** : not recognized or known : not understood : not brought to conscious awareness ⟨found he had ~ strength and endurance⟩

un·really \"+\ *adv* : in an unreal manner : not genuinely : IMPROBABLY ⟨~ dark shadows —Gilbert Highet⟩

un·reaped \"+\ *adj* [¹*un-* + *reaped,* past part. of *reap*] : not reaped

¹**un·reason** \"+\ *n* [ME *unresoun,* fr. ¹*un-* + *resoun* reason] **1** : an act devoid of rational excuse or justification : conduct based on unconsidered impulse rather than on prudence, calculation, or morality ⟨sought to moderate the new church; to prevent the monstrous riot and ~ which followed —A.D. White⟩ **2 a** : the absence of reason or sanity : disorder of mind : want of rational faculty or competence : IRRATIONALITY, MADNESS ⟨her thoughts went quickly down this ladder of ~ —Jean Stafford⟩ ⟨this hysterical state of ~ —Dorothy C. Fisher⟩ **b** : lack of systematic or intelligible order : absence of arrangement, control, or guidance according to reasoned plan : CHAOS, CONFUSION ⟨waste, ~, moral conflict everywhere abound —J.A.Hobson⟩

²**unreason** \"\ *vt* [²*un-* + *reason,* n.] **1** : to unhinge the reason or sanity of **2** *obs* : DISPROVE

un·reasonable \¦ən+\ *adj* [ME *unresonable,* fr. ¹*un-* + *resonable* reasonable] **1** : lacking equipment of mind on the full human scale : not endowed with reason ⟨the ~ beasts⟩ **2 a** : not governed by or acting according to reason : evincing indifference to reality or appropriate context : ill regulated in behavior **b** : not conformable to reason : ABSURD, INAPPROPRIATE, INCONGRUOUS ⟨the ~ nimbus of romance with which she had encircled that man —Thomas Hardy⟩ **3** : exceeding the bounds of reason or moderation : INORDINATE, UNCONSCIONABLE ⟨the right of the people to be secure in their persons, houses, papers, and effects, against ~ searches and seizures —*U. S. Constitution*⟩ ⟨the general level of their rates was found unjust and ~ —J.C.Nelson⟩ — **un·reasonableness** \"+\ *n* — **un·reasonably** \"+\ *adv*

un·reasoned \"+\ *adj* : not founded on reason or reasoning : UNREASONABLE ⟨~ pity is a passion of weakness —M.R. Cohen⟩

un·reasoning \"+\ *adj* [¹*un-* + *reasoning,* pres. part. of *reason*] **1** : not reasoning; *esp* : swayed by emotion that is uncontrolled by prudence or intelligence ⟨instinctive, ~ as he was, entirely at the mercy of the emotion or impression which, for the moment, had seized upon him —Arthur Symons⟩ **2** : not moderated by reason : not controlled or kept in proportion by intelligence : EXTRAVAGANT ⟨~ terror⟩ ⟨~ prejudice⟩ — **un·rea·son·ing·ly** *adv*

un·reave \¦ən+\ *vt* [²*un-* + *reave*] : UNRAVEL ⟨the web is plaiting which nothing ~*s* —Amy Lowell⟩

un·rebated \"+\ *adj* [¹*un-* + *rebated,* past part. of *rebate*] **1** *obs* : UNDIMINISHED, UNREDUCED **2** : not subject to rebate

un·rebukable \"+\ *adj* : not deserving rebuke or censure : BLAMELESS

un·rebuked \"+\ *adj* [ME, fr. ¹*un-* + *rebuked,* past part. of *rebuken* to rebuke] : not rebuked : UNREPROVED

un·recalled \"+\ *adj* [¹*un-* + *recalled,* past part. of *recall*] : not recalled

un·receivable \"+\ *adj* : not receivable : UNACCEPTABLE

un·received \"+\ *adj* [¹*un-* + *received,* past part. of *receive*] : not received : not acknowledged or accepted

un·receptive \"+\ *adj* : not receptive or responsive : not open : UNSYMPATHETIC

un·recited \"+\ *adj* [¹*un-* + *recited,* past part. of *recite*] : not recited

un·recking \"+\ *adj* [¹*un-* + *recking,* pres. part. of *reck*] : not recking : HEEDLESS

un·reckonable \"+\ *adj* : not reckonable : INCALCULABLE ⟨the prospective candidate himself was the ~ factor —S.H. Adams⟩

un·reckoned \"+\ *adj* [ME *unrekened,* fr. ¹*un-* + *rekened,* past part. of *rekenen* to reckon] : not reckoned, counted, or calculated ⟨whilst time was yet ~, the koala flourished —Bill Beatty⟩

un·reclaimable \"+\ *adj, archaic* : IRRECLAIMABLE

un·reclaimed \"+\ *adj* [¹*un-* + *reclaimed,* past part. of *reclaim*] **1** : UNREFORMED, UNREGENERATE **2** *obs* : UNTAMED **3** : not brought from wildness or desolation into fitness for cultivation or use ⟨water-splotched pastures and ~ prairie lands —*Amer. Guide Series: La.*⟩

un·recognition \"+\ *n* : want of recognition

un·recognizable \"+\ *adj* : not recognizable — **un·rec·og·niz·able·ness** \-nəs\ *n* — **un·recognizably** \¦ən+\ *adv*

un·recognized \¦ən+\ *adj* [¹*un-* + *recognized,* past part. of *recognize*] : not recognized

un·recognizing \"+\ *adj* [¹*un-* + *recognizing,* pres. part. of *recognize*] : not recognizing

un·recognizingly \"+\ *adv* : in an unrecognizing manner

un·recollected \"+\ *adj* : not recollected

un·recompensed \"+\ *adj* [ME, fr. ¹*un-* + *recompensed,* past part. of *recompensen* to recompense] : not recompensed

un·reconcilable \"+\ *adj* : IRRECONCILABLE — **un·reconcilableness** \"+\ *n* — **un·reconcilably** \"+\ *adv*

un·reconciled \"+\ *adj* [ME, fr. ¹*un-* + *reconciled,* past part. of *reconcilen* to reconcile] : not reconciled

un·reconciliable \"+\ *adj* [¹*un-* + L *reconciliare* to reconcile + E *-able* — more at RECONCILE] *obs* : IRRECONCILABLE

un·reconstructed \¦ən+\ *adj* [¹*un-* + *reconstructed,* past part. of *reconstruct*] : not reconstructed; *esp* : adhering to an attitude, position, or standard widely held to be outmoded ⟨the peasants are still ~ small capitalists at heart —W.C.Huntington⟩

un·recorded \"+\ *adj* [¹*un-* + *recorded,* past part. of *record*] **1** : not recorded **2** : not made a matter of official record : UNREGISTERED ⟨an ~ deed to property⟩

un·recoverable \"+\ *adj* [ME, fr. ¹*un-* + *recoverable*] **1** : incapable of being recovered, recaptured, or regained : hopelessly lost : IRRECOVERABLE **2** : INCURABLE, IRREMEDIABLE

un·recovered \¦ən+\ *adj* : not recovered

un·recruited \"+\ *adj* [¹*un-* + *recruited,* past part. of *recruit*] : not recruited

un·rectified \"+\ *adj* [¹*un-* + *rectified,* past part. of *rectify*] : not rectified

un·redeemable \"+\ *adj* : IRREDEEMABLE

un·redeemed \"+\ *adj* [¹*un-* + *redeemed,* past part. of *redeem*] : not redeemed — **un·re·deem·ed·ly** \-mədlē, -li\ *adv*

un·redressed \¦ən+\ *adj* [¹*un-* + *redressed,* past part. of *redress*] : not redressed

un·reduced \"+\ *adj* : not reduced

un·reducible \"+\ *adj* : IRREDUCIBLE

un·reel \"+\ *vb* [²*un-* + *reel*] *vt* : to unwind from or as if from a reel ⟨~*ed* a spectacular 66-yard pass play —*N.Y.Times*⟩ ~ *vi* : to become unwound ⟨one more postwar colonial tragedy has begun to ~ —Denis Healey⟩

un·reelable \"+\ *adj* [¹*un-* + *reel* + *-able*] : incapable of being wound on a reel

un·reeler \"+\ *n* : a textile worker who reels cloth during processing

un·reeve \"+\ *vt* [²*un-* + *reeve*] : to withdraw (a rope) from a ship's block, thimble, or other opening

un·refined \"+\ *adj* : not refined: as **a** : lacking moral or social cultivation or the graces of manners or speech : COARSE, UNCOUTH **b** : not separated from dross, impurity, or unwanted matter ⟨~ ore⟩

un·reflected \"+\ *adj* **1** : not reflected on : UNCONSIDERED **2** : not turned back by physical reflection

un·reflecting \"+\ *adj* : not reflecting : UNTHINKING ⟨the ~ mirth of a sailor when on shore —Sir Walter Scott⟩

un·reflectingly \"+\ *adv* : in an unreflecting manner : THOUGHTLESSLY

un·reflective \"+\ *adj* : not reflective : UNTHINKING, HEEDLESS ⟨the most ~ forms of historical optimism —Reinhold Niebuhr⟩

un·reflectively \"+\ *adv* : in an unreflective manner : THOUGHTLESSLY

un·reformable \"+\ *adj* **1** : INCORRIGIBLE **2** : UNCHANGEABLE

un·reformed \"+\ *adj* **1** : not reformed : UNCORRECTED **2** : not originating with or shaped by the Protestant Reformation ⟨~ churches⟩

un·re·form·ed·ness \-m(ə)dnəs\ *n* : the quality or state of being unreformed

un·refracted \¦ən+\ *adj* [¹*un-* + *refracted,* past part. of *refract*] : not refracted

un·refreshed \"+\ *adj* [¹*un-* + *refreshed,* past part. of *refresh*] : not refreshed

un·refreshing \"+\ *adj* : not refreshing — **un·refreshingly** \"+\ *adv*

un·refusable \"+\ *adj* : not refusable

un·refutable \"+\ *adj* : IRREFUTABLE

un·refuted \"+\ *adj* [¹*un-* + *refuted,* past part. of *refute*] : not refuted

un·regal \"+\ *adj* : not regal

un·regarded \"+\ *adj* [¹*un-* + *regarded,* past. part. of *regard*] : not regarded : IGNORED

un·regardful \"+\ *adj* : not regardful

un·regeneracy \"+\ *n* : the quality or state of being unregenerate

¹**un·regenerate** \"+\ *also* **un·regenerated** \"+\ *adj* [*unregenerate* fr. ¹*un-* + *regenerate,* adj.; *unregenerated* fr. ¹*un-* + L *regeneratus* (past part. of *regenerare* to regenerate) + E *-ed* — more at REGENERATE] **1** : not regenerated : not renewed in heart : remaining or being at enmity with God : UNREPENTANT ⟨sounded a warning of what science could do if it became the mere servant of ~ human nature —Roy Lewis & Angus Maude⟩ **2 a** : unpersuaded by or unconverted to a particular doctrinaire viewpoint, cult, or cause : UNRECONSTRUCTED **b** : persisting in a reactionary stand : OBSTINATE, STUBBORN ⟨in ~ conservatism and unreasoning fear, we supported a regime that had no support among its own people —*New Republic*⟩ — **un·regenerately** \"+\ *adv*

²**unregenerate** \"\ *n* [¹*un-* + *regenerate,* n.] : an unregenerate person

un·regimented \"+\ *adj* [¹*un-* + *regimented,* past part. of *regiment*] **1** : not organized or disciplined in military regiments ⟨~ soldiers roved the countryside⟩ **2** : not dominated by a tightly organized social or economic system : INDEPENDENT, INDIVIDUALISTIC

un·registered \"+\ *adj* [¹*un-* + *registered,* past part. of *register*] : not registered: as **a** : not having entered one's name on a voting list ⟨an ~ citizen⟩ **b** : unrecorded or not filed in the place provided by law ⟨an ~ mortgage⟩ ⟨an ~ trademark⟩ **c** : not recorded with or certified by an appropriate breeders' association ⟨~ dairy cattle⟩

un·regretful \"+\ *adj* : not regretful

un·regretfully \"+\ *adv* : not regretfully

un·regretted \"+\ *adj* [¹*un-* + *regretted,* past part. of *regret*] : not regretted : UNLAMENTED

un·regular \"+\ *adj* : IRREGULAR

un·regulated \"+\ *adj* [¹*un-* + *regulated,* past part. of *regulate*] : not regulated: as **a** : DISORDERLY, CHAOTIC ⟨an ~ mind⟩ **b** : UNCONTROLLED, UNDISCIPLINED, UNGOVERNED ⟨~ traffic⟩

un·rehearsed \"+\ *adj* [ME *unrehersed,* fr. ¹*un-* + *rehersed,* past part. of *rehersen* to rehearse] **1** : not narrated : UNTOLD **2** : not practiced or prepared : SPONTANEOUS ⟨an ~ speech⟩

un·rein \"+\ *vt* [²*un-* + *rein*] : to loosen the reins of : remove restraint from

un·rejoicing \¦ən+\ *adj* [¹*un-* + *rejoicing,* pres. part. of *rejoice*] : not rejoicing

un·related \"+\ *adj* **1** : not connected by birth or family **2** : DISCRETE, DISJOINED, SEPARATE ⟨hard to imagine a rule more completely ~ to the realities of life —B.N.Cardozo⟩ **3** : not told ⟨an ~ tale⟩

un·relatedness \"+\ *n* : the quality or state of being unrelated

un·relative \"+\ *adj* : UNRELATED, DISPROPORTIONATE

un·relaxed \"+\ *adj* [¹*un-* + *relaxed,* past part. of *relax*] : not relaxed ⟨his life was drawing to a close in baffled zeal and ~ strain —U.B.Phillips⟩

un·relaxing \"+\ *adj* [¹*un-* + *relaxing,* pres. part. of *relax*] : not relaxing

un·released \"+\ *adj* [ME *unrelesed,* fr. ¹*un-* + *relesed,* past part. of *relesen* to release] : not released

un·relenting \"+\ *adj* [¹*un-* + *relenting,* pres. part. of *relent*] **1** : not softening, yielding, or swerving in resolution or determination : HARD, STERN ⟨a fierce and ~ partisan leader —*Amer. Guide Series: Tenn.*⟩ **2** : maintaining undiminished speed, vigor, or pace : not letting up or weakening ⟨an intense and ~ struggle is being waged —Sir Winston Churchill⟩

un·relentingly \"+\ *adv* : in an unrelenting manner

un·re·lent·ing·ness *n* -ES : the quality or state of being unrelenting

un·reliability \ˌən+\ *n* : the quality or state of being unreliable

un·reliable \"+\ *adj* : not reliable : UNDEPENDABLE, UNTRUSTWORTHY — **un·reliableness** \"+\ *n* — **un·reliably** \"+\ *adv*

un·relievable \"+\ *adj* [¹*un-* + *relieve* + *-able*] : not relievable

un·relieved \"+\ *adj* [¹*un-* + *relieved*, past part. of *relieve*] **1** : not given relief : furnished no assistance, remedy, or mitigation ⟨drudgery was ~ by labor-saving devices —*Amer. Guide Series: Ind.*⟩ **2** : having or likened to a flat unbroken surface without heights or depths or without lights or shadows : lacking diversity, alternation, or chiaroscuro : MONOTONOUS, UNVARYING ⟨gowns . . . of ~ black —Victoria Sackville-West⟩ ⟨an ~ slum —Gus Tyler⟩ ⟨simple pity that such a career should end in ~ banality —L.B.Gowing⟩ — **un·relievedly** \"+\ *adv*

un·religious \"+\ *adj* [ME, fr. ¹*un-* + *religious*] **1** : IRRELIGIOUS **2** : having no connection with or relation to religion : involving no religious import or idea : NONRELIGIOUS ⟨~ education⟩ — **un·religiously** \"+\ *adv*

un·relinquished \"+\ *adj* [¹*un-* + *relinquished*, past part. of *relinquish*] : not relinquished

un·reluctant \"+\ *adj* : not reluctant

un·reluctantly \"+\ *adv* : not reluctantly

un·remarkable \"+\ *adj* : calling for no notice : lacking interest or distinction : JEJUNE, ORDINARY

un·remarked \"+\ *adj* [¹*un-* + *remarked*, past part. of *remark*] : not remarked : UNNOTICED ⟨the streets were crowded, and we found ourselves wholly ~ —Kenneth Roberts⟩

un·remedied \"+\ *adj* [¹*un-* + *remedied*, past part. of *remedy*] : not remedied

un·rememberable \"+\ *adj* : not worth remembering or likely to be remembered

un·remembered \"+\ *adj* [ME *unremembred*, fr. ¹*un-* + *remembred*, past part. of *remembren* to remember] : not remembered : FORGOTTEN

un·remembering \"+\ *adj* [¹*un-* + *remembering*, pres. part. of *remember*] : not remembering : FORGETFUL, OBLIVIOUS

un·remitted \"+\ *adj* [¹*un-* + *remitted*, past part. of *remit*] **1** : not remitted : UNPARDONED ⟨~ sin⟩ ⟨an ~ debt⟩ **2** : continuously or assiduously maintained : UNBROKEN, UNINTERRUPTED ⟨~ attention⟩

un·re·mit·ted·ly *adv* : in an unremitted manner : without interruption : STEADILY

un·remittent \ˌən+\ *adj* [¹*un-* + L *remittent-*, *remittens*, pres. part. of *remittere* to remit — more at REMIT] : UNREMITTING

un·remitting \"+\ *adj* [¹*un-* + *remitting*, pres. part. of *remit*] : not remitting : CONSTANT, INCESSANT, STEADY, UNINTERRUPTED ⟨exhausted her strength with ~ work —Harrison Smith⟩ ⟨the blatting of automobile horns off yonder, not too loud but variegated and ~ —R.P.Warren⟩ ⟨few other American statesmen have been such careful and ~ students of political thought —Dumas Malone⟩ **syn** see CONTINUAL

un·re·mit·ting·ly *adv* : in an unremitting manner : STEADILY, UNINTERRUPTEDLY

un·remorseful \ˌən+\ *adj* : not remorseful: **a** : REMORSELESS **b** : bringing no remorse : INNOCENT

un·removable \"+\ *adj* **1** *obs* : IMMOVABLE **2** *archaic* : IRREMOVABLE

un·removed \ˌən+\ *adj* [ME, fr. ¹*un-* + *removed*, past part. of *removen* to remove] : not removed: **a** : not eliminated **b** : not moved from one place to another **c** : firmly placed or grounded : IRREMOVABLE, FIXED, STEADFAST

un·remunerated \"+\ *adj* [¹*un-* + *remunerated*, past part. of *remunerate*] : not remunerated : UNPAID

un·remunerative \"+\ *adj* : not remunerative : returning no gain or profit or an inadequate one : UNREWARDING ⟨an ~ occupation⟩ ⟨its first reading is arduous and apparently ~ —T.S.Eliot⟩

un·renderable \"+\ *adj* : not renderable : UNTRANSLATABLE

un·renewed \"+\ *adj* [¹*un-* + *renewed*, past part. of *renew*] : not renewed; *esp* : UNREGENERATE

un·renowned \"+\ *adj* : not renowned : little known : OBSCURE

un·rent \"+\ *adj* [¹*un-* + *rent*, past part. of *rend*] : not rent : UNTORN

un·rentable \"+\ *adj* : incapable of being rented

un·repaid \"+\ *adj* [¹*un-* + *repaid*, past part. of *repay*] : not repaid

un·repair \"+\ *n* : want of repair : DISREPAIR

un·repaired \"+\ *adj* [¹*un-* + *repaired*, past part. of *repair*] : not repaired

un·re·pass·able \ˌən(ˌ)rē¦pasəbəl, -paas-, -pais-, -pås-\ *adj* [¹*un-* + *repass* + *-able*] *archaic* : incapable of being passed again : not to be traversed in returning

unrepealable *adj* : not repealable : IRREVOCABLE

un·repealed \ˌən+\ *adj* [ME *unrepeled*, fr. ¹*un-* + *repeled*, past part. of *repelen* to repeal] : not repealed : remaining in force or effect : UNREVOKED

un·repeatable \"+\ *adj* **1** : not fit to be repeated : offensively coarse : INDECENT **2** : not repeatable : incapable of being duplicated : UNIQUE ⟨dogs, mice, and flies are as individual and ~ as men are —Theodosius Dobzhansky⟩

un·repeated \"+\ *adj* : not repeated

un·repelled \"+\ *adj* [¹*un-* + *repelled*, past part. of *repel*] : not repelled

un·repentance \"+\ *n* [ME *unrepentaunce*, fr. ¹*un-* + *repentaunce* repentance] : IMPENITENCE

un·repentant \"+\ *adj* [ME *unrepentaunt*, fr. ¹*un-* + *repentaunt* repentant] **1** : not repentant : IMPENITENT ⟨~ sinners⟩ **2** : holding to a prior conviction or attitude : OBSTINATE, STUBBORN ⟨an avowed and ~ protectionist —David Thomson⟩

un·repented \"+\ *adj* [¹*un-* + *repented*, past part. of *repent*] : not repented : not regretted and renounced ⟨~ sin⟩

un·repenting \"+\ *adj* [¹*un-* + *repenting*, pres. part. of *repent*] : not repenting

un·repining \"+\ *adj* [¹*un-* + *repining*, pres. part. of *repine*] : not repining : UNCOMPLAINING

un·repiningly \"+\ *adv* : in an unrepining manner : UNCOMPLAININGLY

un·replaceable \"+\ *adj* : IRREPLACEABLE

un·replenished \"+\ *adj* [¹*un-* + *replenished*, past part. of *replenish*] : not replenished

un·replying \ˌən+\ *adj* [¹*un-* + *replying*, pres. part. of *reply*] : not replying

un·reportable \"+\ *adj* **1** *obs* : too extreme or monstrous to report : UNSPEAKABLE **2** : too coarse or indecent to report : UNREPEATABLE

un·reported \"+\ *adj* [¹*un-* + *reported*, past part. of *report*] : not reported

un·representative \"+\ *adj* **1** : not representing an electorate ⟨a parliament which was ~ and corrupt —J.H.Plumb⟩ **2** : not exemplifying a class : ATYPICAL ⟨behavior quite ~ of the profession⟩

un·represented \"+\ *adj* **1** : not represented : having no member or advocate in a legislature ⟨an ~ minority⟩ ⟨an ~ viewpoint⟩ **2** : not exemplified : shown by no instance

un·repressed \"+\ *adj* : not repressed

un·reprieved \ˌən+\ *adj* [¹*un-* + *reprieved*, past part. of *reprieve*] : not reprieved

un·reproachable \"+\ *adj*, *archaic* : IRREPROACHABLE

un·reproached \"+\ *adj* [¹*un-* + *reproached*, past part. of *reproach*] : not reproached

un·reproachful \"+\ *adj* : not reproachful

un·reproaching \"+\ *adj* [¹*un-* + *reproaching*, pres. part. of *reproach*] : not reproaching

un·reproducible \"+\ *adj* : not reproducible

un·re·prov·able \ˌənrə¦prüvəbəl, -rē¦-\ *adj* [*unreprovable* fr. ME, fr. ¹*un-* + *reprovable* open to reproof, fr. *reproven* to reprove + *-able*] : not open to reproof : not meriting censure : BLAMELESS

un·reproved \ˌən+\ *adj* [ME, fr. ¹*un-* + *reproved*, past part. of *reproven* to reprove] : not reproved

un·repugnant \"+\ *adj* : not repugnant : causing or offering no opposition

un·requested \ˌən+\ *adj* [¹*un-* + *requested*, past part. of *request*] : not requested : UNASKED

un·required \"+\ *adj* [ME *unrequered*, fr. ¹*un-* + *requered*, past part. of *requeren* to require] : not required

un·requisite \"+\ *adj* : not requisite

un·re·quit·able \ˌənrə¦kwīd·əbəl, -rē¦-\ *adj* [¹*un-* + *requite* + *-able*] : incapable of being requited : not returnable in kind

un·requited \ˌən+\ *adj* [¹*un-* + *requited*, past part. of *requite*] : not requited : not reciprocated : not returned in kind ⟨~ love⟩

un·resembling \"+\ *adj* [¹*un-* + *resembling*, pres. part. of *resemble*] *archaic* : not resembling : DISSIMILAR

un·resented \"+\ *adj* [¹*un-* + *resented*, past part. of *resent*] : not resented

un·resentful \"+\ *adj* : not resentful

un·resenting \"+\ *adj* [¹*un-* + *resenting*, pres. part. of *resent*] : not resenting

un·reserve \"+\ *n* : absence of reserve : FRANKNESS, OPENNESS

un·reserved \"+\ *adj* **1** : not limited or partial : ENTIRE, FULL, UNQUALIFIED ⟨a book to which one awards an ~ enthusiasm —Carl Van Vechten⟩ **2** : not cautious or reticent : FRANK, OPEN

un·reservedly \"+\ *adv* : in an unreserved manner

un·reservedness \"+\ *n* : the quality or state of being unreserved

un·resistant \"+\ *adj* : not resistant

un·resisted \ˌən+\ *adj* [¹*un-* + *resisted*, past part. of *resist*] : not resisted : not withstood : UNOPPOSED — **un·re·sist·ed·ly** *adv*

un·resistible \"+\ *adj* : IRRESISTIBLE

un·resisting \ˌən+\ *adj* : not resisting : YIELDING — **un·resistingly** \"+\ *adv*

un·resolvable \"+\ *adj* : not resolvable

un·resolve \"+\ *vb* [²*un-* + *resolve*] : to revoke a resolution

un·resolved \"+\ *adj* [¹*un-* + *resolved*, past part. of *resolve*] **1** : UNDECIDED, UNSOLVED ⟨depends upon answers to the many ~ questions —J.A.R.Pimlott⟩ ⟨an ~ conflict⟩ **2 a** : IRRESOLUTE, WAVERING ⟨restless and ~, seeking purpose of some sort from his love —*Times Lit. Supp.*⟩ **b** : unsettled or uncertain in opinion **3** : remaining discordant or dissonant : not modulated to a consonance ⟨~ discords⟩

un·resolvedness \"+\ *n* : IRRESOLUTION

un·resolving \"+\ *adj* [¹*un-* + *resolving*, pres. part. of *resolve*] : not resolving

un·resounding \"+\ *adj* : not resounding

un·respectable \"+\ *adj* : not respectable : unworthy of respect : DISREPUTABLE ⟨says nothing so ~ has happened in years —Louis Bromfield⟩

un·respected \"+\ *adj* [¹*un-* + *respected*, past part. of *respect*] : accorded no respect

un·respectful \"+\ *adj* : not respectful : DISRESPECTFUL

un·respective \"+\ *adj* **1** *archaic* : NEGLIGENT, INATTENTIVE **2** : UNDISCRIMINATING

un·respirable \ˌən+\ *adj* : unfit to breathe ⟨~ air⟩

un·responsible \ˌən+\ *adj* : IRRESPONSIBLE

un·responsive \"+\ *adj* : not responsive — **un·responsively** \"+\ *adv* — **un·responsiveness** \"+\ *n*

un·rest \"+\ *n* [ME, fr. ¹*un-* + *rest*] : want of rest : a disturbed or uneasy state : DISQUIET, TURMOIL ⟨revolt is brewing, there is hatred and ~, and explosion in the atmosphere —Stanley Ross⟩ ⟨social ~⟩ ⟨labor ~⟩

un·rested \"+\ *adj* [¹*un-* + *rested*, past part. of *rest*] : not rested

un·restful \"+\ *adj* [ME, fr. ¹*un-* + *restful*] : not restful: as **a** : not feeling or not conducing to repose **b** : lacking calmness or confidence : DISTURBED, FIDGETY, NERVOUS ⟨one's conducting is apt to become angular and ~ —Warwick Braithwaite⟩

un·resting \"+\ *adj* : not resting : taking no repose : continuing without pause or interruption

un·restored \"+\ *adj* [ME, fr. ¹*un-* + *restored*, past part. of *restoren* to restore] : not restored

un·restrainable \"+\ *adj* [ME *unrestraynable*, fr. ¹*un-* + *restraynen* to restrain + *-able*] : not restrainable : UNCONTROLLABLE — **un·restrainably** \"+\ *adv*

un·restrained \"+\ *adj* **1** : not restrained : IMMODERATE, INTEMPERATE, UNCONTROLLED ⟨~ praise⟩ ⟨~ development resulted in more than 30 subdivisions within the limits of the city —*Amer. Guide Series: Mich.*⟩ **2** : free of constraint, inhibition, or timidity : SPONTANEOUS, UNEMBARRASSED ⟨never before in all her life had she so desired to be spontaneous and ~ —H.G.Wells⟩

un·restrainedly \"+\ *adv* : in an unrestrained manner

un·restrainedness \"+\ *n* : the quality or state of being unrestrained

un·restraint \"+\ *n* : freedom from restraint

un·restricted \ˌən+\ *adj* : not restricted

un·restrictedly \"+\ *adv* : in an unrestricted manner

un·restrictive \"+\ *adj* : not restrictive

un·retaliated \"+\ *adj* [¹*un-* + *retaliated*, past part. of *retaliate*] : not retaliated

un·retarded \"+\ *adj* : not retarded : UNDELAYED

un·retentive \"+\ *adj* : not retentive

un·reticent \"+\ *adj* : not reticent

un·retouched \"+\ *adj* [¹*un-* + *retouched*, past part. of *retouch*] : not retouched

un·retracted \"+\ *adj* : not retracted

un·returnable \"+\ *adj* : not returnable

un·returned \"+\ *adj* [¹*un-* + *returned*, past part. of *return*] : not returned

un·returning \"+\ *adj* : not returning

un·revealed \"+\ *adj* [¹*un-* + *revealed*, past part. of *reveal*] : not revealed

un·revealing \"+\ *adj* : not revealing

un·revenged \"+\ *adj* [¹*un-* + *revenged*, past part. of *revenge*] : not revenged

un·revengeful \"+\ *adj* : not revengeful

un·reverenced \ˌən+\ *adj* [ME, fr. ¹*un-* + *reverenced*, past part. of *reverencen* to reverence] : not reverenced

un·reverend \"+\ *adj* **1** : IRREVERENT **2** : not reverend : not meriting reverence

un·reverent \"+\ *adj* [ME, fr. ¹*un-* + *reverent*] : IRREVERENT

un·reversed \"+\ *adj* : not reversed

un·reviewable \"+\ *adj* : not subject to review (as by superior authority) ⟨discretion may, as a rule, be ~ —*Yale Law Jour.*⟩

un·revised \"+\ *adj* [¹*un-* + *revised*, past part. of *revise*] : not revised

un·revived \"+\ *adj* [¹*un-* + *revived*, past part. of *revive*] : not revived

un·revoked \"+\ *adj* [ME, fr. ¹*un-* + *revoked*, past part. of *revoken* to revoke] : not revoked

un·rewarded \"+\ *adj* [ME, fr. ¹*un-* + *rewarded*, past part. of *rewarden* to reward] : not rewarded

un·rewarding \"+\ *adj* : not rewarding : not repaying effort or attention : UNPROFITABLE ⟨reading him proved to be an ~ labor⟩

un·rhetorical \ˌən+\ *adj* : not rhetorical : LITERAL, PLAIN

un·rhymed \"+\ *adj* [¹*un-* + *rhymed*, past part. of *rhyme*] : not rhymed

un·rhythmic \"+\ *or* **un·rhythmical** \"+\ *adj* : not rhythmic : lacking rhythm : irregular in beat, pulse, or accent

un·ribbed \"+\ *adj* : having no ribs

un·rid \"+\ *adj* [¹*un-* + *rid*, past part. of *rid* (to clear)] *dial Brit* : DISORDERED

un·ridden \"+\ *adj* : not ridden

un·riddle \"+\ *vt* [²*un-* + *riddle*, n.] : to read the riddle of : find the explanation of : SOLVE ⟨patiently *unriddled* a situation of extreme complexity —John Buchan⟩

un·riddler \"+\ *n* : one that unriddles ⟨the poet can no longer be the seer, the ~ of the universe —Peter Viereck⟩

¹un·rifled \"+\ *adj* [¹*un-* + *rifled*, past part. of *rifle* (to rob)] : not rifled : UNDESPOILED, UNROBBED

²unrifled \"\ *adj* [¹*un-* + *rifled*, past part. of *rifle* (to cut grooves)] *of a gun barrel* : not having internal spiral grooves

un·rig \ˌən+\ *vt* [²*un-* + *rig*] **1** : to strip of rigging ⟨~ a ship⟩ **2** : UNCLOTHE, UNDRESS

¹un·right \"+\ *adj* [ME *unriht*, *unright*, fr. OE *unriht*, fr. ¹*un-* + *riht*, adj., right] : WRONG, UNJUST

²unright \"\ *n* [ME *unriht*, *unright*, fr. OE *unriht*, fr. ¹*un-* + *riht*, n., right] : WRONG, INJUSTICE

un·righteous \ˌən+\ *adj* [alter. (influenced by *-eous*) of earlier *unrightwise*, *unrightuous*, fr. ME *unrightwise*, *unrihtwise*, fr. OE *unrihtwīs*, fr. ¹*un-* + *rihtwīs* righteous] **1** : not righteous : EVIL, SINFUL, WICKED ⟨an ~ man⟩ ⟨an ~ act⟩ **2** : UNJUST, INEQUITABLE, UNMERITED ⟨an ~ sentence⟩ — **un·righteously** \"+\ *adv* — **un·righteousness** \"+\ *n*

un·rightful \"+\ *adj* [ME, fr. ¹*un-* + *rightful*] : not rightful : WRONG, UNJUST

un·ringed \"+\ *adj* : not having or wearing a ring

un·rinsed \"+\ *adj* [¹*un-* + *rinsed*, past part. of *rinse*] : not rinsed

un·rip \"+\ *vt* [²*un-* + *rip*] **1** : to rip or slit up : cut or tear open ⟨*unripped* a seam⟩ **2** : DISCLOSE, REVEAL ⟨~ your plan, captain —J.M.Barrie⟩

un·ripe \"+\ *adj* [ME, fr. OE *unrīpe*, fr. ¹*un-* + *rīpe* ripe] **1** : not ripe : less than fully developed : IMMATURE ⟨~ fruit⟩ ⟨an ~ lover⟩ ⟨lived to the not ~ age of 77 —Harvey Graham⟩ **2** : UNREADY, UNPREPARED, UNSEASONABLE ⟨~ for any call to national self-extinction —*Current History*⟩ ⟨the time is ~⟩

un·ripely \"+\ *adv* : in an unripe manner

un·ripened \"+\ *adj* [¹*un-* + *ripened*, past part. of *ripen*] **1** : not ripened : not having attained maturity : UNDEVELOPED **2** *of cheese* : ready for use without curing

un·ripeness \"+\ *n* [ME *unripnes*, fr. *unripe* + *-nes* -ness] : the quality or state of being unripe

un·rippled \"+\ *adj* [¹*un-* + *rippled*, past part. of *ripple*] : not rippled : glassy smooth ⟨~ water⟩

un·risen \"+\ *adj* : not risen

un·rivaled *or* **un·rivalled** \"+\ *adj* [¹*un-* + *rivaled*, *rivalled*, past part. of *rival*] : having no rival : INCOMPARABLE, SUPREME, UNEQUALED, UNPARALLELED ⟨the island offered ~ opportunities for spying —C.S.Forester⟩ ⟨the ~ literary colossus of the age —W.R.Thayer⟩

un·riven \"+\ *adj* [¹*un-* + *riven*, past part. of *rive*] : not riven : UNTORN, UNBROKEN

un·rivet \"+\ *vt* [²*un-* + *rivet*] **1** : to unfasten or separate by removing the rivets of **2** : DETACH, UNDO, UNLOOSE ⟨the diversion ~*ed* his gaze⟩

un·roasted \"+\ *adj* [¹*un-* + *roasted*, past part. of *roast*] : not roasted

un·robbed \"+\ *adj* [ME, fr. ¹*un-* + *robbed*, past part. of *robben* to rob] : not robbed

un·robe \"+\ *vb* [²*un-* + *robe*] : DISROBE, UNDRESS

un·roll \"+\ *vb* [ME *unrollen*, fr. ²*un-* + *rollen* to roll] *vt* **1** : to unwind a roll of : open out : UNCOIL, EXTEND ⟨the limitless exuberance with which America ~*s* the carpet for the imported prodigy —E.O.Hauser⟩ **2** : to spread out like a scroll for reading or inspection ⟨the novel itself ~*s* their previous histories to the reader —Frederic Morton⟩ ~ *vi* : to be unrolled : UNWIND ⟨the landscape ~*s* under the speeding plane⟩

un·rolled \"+\ *adj* : not rolled

un·romantic \"+\ *also* **un·romantical** \"+\ *adj* : not romantic — **un·romantically** \"+\ *adv*

un·roof \"+\ *vt* [²*un-* + *roof*] : to strip off the roof or covering of ⟨would wreck the castle and ~ every house —C.S. Forester⟩

un·roost \"+\ *vb* [²*un-* + *roost*, n.] *vt* : to drive from the roost : DISLODGE ~ *vi* : to leave a roost

un·root \ˌən+\ *vb* [ME *unrooten*, fr. ²*un-* + *rooten* to root] *vt* : to tear up by the roots : ERADICATE, UPROOT ~ *vi* : to become uprooted

un·rooted \"+\ *adj* [¹*un-* + *rooted*, past part. of *root*] **1** : not torn up by the roots — used with *out* **2** : having no roots : ROOTLESS ⟨an ~ and vagrant life —A.L.Kroeber⟩

un·rope \"+\ *vb* [²*un-* + *rope*] *vt* : to remove a rope from : free from a rope ~ *vi* : to detach a rope : loose oneself from a rope ⟨once on gentler slopes we *unroped* and swiftly descended —*Appalachia*⟩

un·rotten \"+\ *adj* : not rotten

un·rouged \"+\ *adj* [¹*un-* + *rouged*, past part. of *rouge*] : not rouged

un·rough \"+\ *adj* : not rough; *esp* : BEARDLESS

un·round \"+\ *vt* [²*un-* + *round*] **1** : to spread (the lips) laterally ⟨necessary to ~ the lips in pronouncing \ē\⟩ **2** : to pronounce (a sound) without lip rounding or with decreased lip rounding

un·rounded \"+\ *adj*, *of a sound* : produced with lips spread laterally

un·roused \"+\ *adj* [¹*un-* + *roused*, past part. of *rouse*] : not roused : UNAWAKENED, DORMANT

un·routed \"+\ *adj* [¹*un-* + *routed*, past part. of *rout*] : not routed

un·royal \ˌən+\ *adj* : not royal

un·rude \"+\ *adj* [ME, alter. (prob. influenced by *rude*) of *unride* rough, violent, fr. OE *ungerȳde*, fr. ¹*un-* + *gerȳde* prepared, easy, fr. *ge-* (perfective prefix) + *-rȳde*, of unknown origin] *dial* : ROUGH, RUDE

un·ruffle \"+\ *vb* [²*un-* + *ruffle*] *vi* : to become calm : quiet down ~ *vt* : CALM, QUIET

un·ruffled \"+\ *adj* [¹*un-* + *ruffled*, past part. of *ruffle*] **1** : emotionally undisturbed : CALM, STEADY, UNFLUSTERED ⟨an efficient organizer, smooth and ~ —Flora Lewis⟩ **2** : not ruffled : SMOOTH ⟨~ water⟩ **syn** see COOL

un·ruffledness \"+\ *n* -ES : the quality or state of being unruffled

un·ruinable \"+\ *adj* [¹*un-* + *ruin* + *-able*] : IMPERISHABLE

un·ruined \"+\ *adj* [¹*un-* + *ruined*, past part. of *ruin*] : not ruined

un·rulable \"+\ *adj* : not rulable : UNGOVERNABLE

un·ruled \"+\ *adj* [ME, fr. ¹*un-* + *ruled*, past part. of *rulen* to rule] **1** : not ruled : UNGOVERNED **2** : lacking ruled lines ⟨~ writing paper⟩

un·rul·i·ness \ˌən¦rülēnəs, -lin-\ *n* -ES : the quality or state of being unruly

un·ruly \-lē, -li\ *adj*, *often* -ER/-EST [ME *unreuly*, fr. ¹*un-* + *reuly*, *ruly* amenable to rule, disciplined, fr. *reule* rule + *-y* (adj. suffix) — more at RULE] **1** : not readily ruled, disciplined, or managed : TURBULENT, UNCONTROLLABLE ⟨began his greatest editorial effort, his battle royal with that stubborn and ~ writer —Harrison Smith⟩ ⟨could imagine no such ~ urgence in man's perfect estate —J.H.Robinson †1936⟩ **2** : STORMY, TEMPESTUOUS, WILD ⟨cleared the land, dug ditches and dammed ~ streams —*Amer. Guide Series: Ariz.*⟩

syn UNGOVERNABLE, INTRACTABLE, REFRACTORY, RECALCITRANT, WILLFUL, HEADSTRONG: UNRULY calls attention to lack of being disciplined; it may suggest incapacity for discipline, turbulence, disorder, or waywardness ⟨*unruly* children⟩ ⟨a wrought-iron collar with three bells attached, used to subdue an *unruly* or runaway slave —*Amer. Guide Series: La.*⟩ ⟨with judicious officers the most *unruly* seamen can at sea be kept in some sort of subjection —Herman Melville⟩ UNGOVERNABLE centers attention on the fact of not being governed, subdued, restrained, or checked; it may apply to whatever has never been subdued or to whatever has thrown off control ⟨in the case of a consistently obstreperous and *ungovernable* slave, he should be sold rather than lashed —C.G.Bowers⟩ INTRACTABLE may suggest a stubborn disposition to resist guidance or restraint ⟨inclined to display a savage, domineering and *intractable* temper —Robert Graves⟩ ⟨to submit to authority — human nature even then remaining so *intractable* that the only assurance of safety against its marauding instincts is subjection to sovereignty —John Dewey⟩ REFRACTORY may connote manifest resistance and rebelliousness, disobedience, and protest ⟨lawlessness is a term applied to the behavior of a social group which is considered to be consistently *refractory* and to be habitually breaking important legal rules —Jerome Frank⟩ ⟨some of them again became most *refractory*, breathing nothing but downright mutiny —Herman Melville⟩ RECALCITRANT may suggest determined resistance, temperamental defiance to authority, or obstinate rebellion ⟨some trouble about a *recalcitrant* miner who wanted to quit work. He shouted something about being a free man. When I ordered him to work, he rushed at me with his pick —John Steinbeck⟩ ⟨the establishment and maintenance of any orderly state generally involves the extermination of some of the *recalcitrant* opposition —M.R.Cohen⟩ WILLFUL implies determination to have one's own will, sometimes capricious, and to flout authority or wise guidance in achieving it ⟨*willful* men whom even the common frontier perils cannot reconcile or make tolerant —V.L.Parrington⟩ ⟨peevish because he called her and she did not come, and he threw his bowl of tea on the ground like a *willful* child —Pearl Buck⟩ HEADSTRONG may suggest obdurate and mulish self-will impatient of restraint, advice, or suggestion ⟨testy and *headstrong* through an excess of will and bias —R.W.Emerson⟩ ⟨*headstrong* enough to make it a very difficult task for him to manage her —Anthony Trollope⟩

un·rumpled \ˌən+\ *adj* [¹*un-* + *rumpled,* past part. of *rumple*] **:** not rumpled **:** SMOOTH

un·rung \"+\ *adj* **:** UNRINGED

un·rusted \"+\ *adj* [¹*un-* + *rusted,* past part. of *rust*] **:** not rusted

un·ruth \"+\ *n* **:** lack of mercy or compassion **:** PITILESSNESS

uns *abbr* unsymmetrical

uns- *or* **unsym-** *comb form, usu ital* [fr. *unsymmetrical*] **:** unsymmetrical — in names of organic compounds ⟨*uns*-dichloro-ethane⟩

un·sabbatical \ˌən+\ *adj* [¹*un-* + *sabbatical*] **:** not suited to the sabbath

un·sack \ˌən+\ *vt* [²*un-* + *sack,* n.] **1 :** to remove the sack from **2 :** to remove from a sack

un·sacred \"+\ *adj* **:** not sacred **:** PROFANE

un·sadden \"\ *vt* [²*un-* + *sadden*] **:** to free from sadness

un·saddle \"+\ *vb* [ME *unsadlen,* fr. ²*un-* + *sadlen* to saddle] *vt* **1 :** to strip of a saddle **:** take the saddle from (as a horse) **2 :** to throw from the saddle **:** UNHORSE ~ *vi* **:** to remove the saddle from a horse

un·saddled \"+\ *adj* [¹*un-* + *saddled,* past part. of *saddle*] **:** not saddled

un·safe \"+\ *adj* **:** not safe **:** exposed or exposing to danger **:** UNRELIABLE ⟨an ~ bridge⟩ ⟨an ~ method⟩ — **un·safely** \"+\ *adv* — **un·safeness** \"+\ *n*

un·safetied \"+\ *adj* [¹*un-* + *safetied,* past part. of *safety*] **:** not made safe

un·safety \"+\ *n* **:** want of safety **:** INSECURITY

un·said \"+\ *adj* [ME, fr. OE *unsægd,* fr. ¹*un-* + *sægd,* past part. of *secgan* to say — more at SAY] **:** not said; *esp* **:** thought but not spoken or expressed in words

un·sailed \"+\ *adj* [¹*un-* + *sailed,* past part. of *sail*] **:** not sailed

un·saint \ˌən+\ *vt* [²*un-* + *saint*] **:** to deprive of status as a saint

un·sainted \"+\ *adj* [¹*un-* + *sainted,* adj.] **:** not sanctified **:** not canonized

un·saintly \"+\ *adj* **:** unbecoming to a saint

un·salability \"+\ *n* **:** the quality or state of being unsalable

un·salable \"+\ *adj* **:** not salable **:** UNMERCHANTABLE ⟨goods which are ~ lose their dollar value —T.W.Arnold⟩ ⟨drama, economics and philosophy were ~ —G.B.Shaw⟩ — **un·sal·ableness** \"+\ *n*

un·salaried \"+\ *adj* **:** not paid a salary ⟨an ~ officer⟩

un·salted \"+\ *adj* [ME, fr. ¹*un-* + *salted,* past part. of *salten* to salt] **:** not salted

un·salutary \"+\ *adj* **:** not salutary **:** HARMFUL, UNHEALTHY

un·saluted \"+\ *adj* [¹*un-* + *saluted,* past part. of *salute*] **:** not saluted

un·salvable \"+\ *adj* **:** not salvable

un·sanctification \"+\ *n* **:** absence or lack of sanctification

un·sanctified \"+\ *adj* [¹*un-* + *sanctified,* adj.] **:** not holy or sanctified **:** not made sacred or holy **:** not reserved for religious use ⟨the daring half-hope is expressed that the lovers' ~ union may be blessed with issue —*New Republic*⟩ — **un·sanc·ti·fi·ed·ly** \-ˌfī(ə)dlē, -li\ *adv*

un·sanctify \ˌən+\ *vt* [²*un-* + *sanctify*] **:** to remove the sanctification from **:** make unsanctified

un·sanctimonious \"+\ *adj* **1 :** not making a show of or giving the appearance of sanctity **2 :** IRRELIGIOUS, UNHOLY — **un·sanctimoniously** \"+\ *adv* — **un·sanctimoniousness** \"+\ *n*

un·sanctioned \"+\ *adj* [¹*un-* + *sanctioned,* past part. of *sanction*] **:** not sanctioned **:** not morally acceptable

un·sandaled \"+\ *adj* **:** not sandaled

un·sane \"+\ *adj* **:** lacking in sanity ⟨people are ~ when their mental maps of reality are slightly out of correspondence with the real world —Martin Gardner⟩ ⟨the noble but somewhat ~ faith that by some principle of truth men can be conditioned to perfectly rational behavior —H.J.Muller⟩

un·sanguinary \"+\ *adj* **:** not sanguinary **:** UNBLOODY ⟨sports-car . . . meet has had a relatively ~ history —J.M. Flagler⟩

un·sanguine \"+\ *adj* **:** not sanguine **:** not optimistic ⟨this ~ appraisal⟩ — **un·sanguineness** \"+\ *n*

un·sanitary \"+\ *adj* **:** not sanitary **:** INSANITARY ⟨~ methods of disposing of sewage —Ellsworth Huntington⟩ ⟨frequently ~ and generally grim conditions —E.G.Harrison⟩ ⟨~ places are placed off limits —*Science News Letter*⟩

un·saponifiable \"+\ *adj* **:** incapable of being saponified — used esp. of the portion of oils and fats other than the glycerides ⟨~ fractions such as steroids or vitamin A⟩

un·saponified \"+\ *adj* [¹*un-* + *saponified,* past part. of *saponify*] **:** not saponified

un·sated \ˌən+\ *adj* **:** not satiated **:** not satisfied **:** INSATIABLE ⟨youth, with its ~ and unbounded desires —Laurence Binyon⟩ ⟨curiosity was still ~ —R.A.Billington⟩

un·satiable \"+\ *adj* [ME *unsaciable,* fr. ¹*un-* + L *satiare* to satiate + E *-able* — more at SATIATE] **:** INSATIABLE — **un·sa·tia·ble·ness** \-bəlnəs\ *n* -ES — **un·sa·tia·bly** \-blē, -li\ *adv*

un·satiate \ˌən+\ *adj* **:** INSATIATE

un·satiated \"+\ *adj* **:** not satiated

un·satisfaction \"+\ *n* **:** absence of satisfaction

un·satisfactorily \"+\ *adv* **:** in an unsatisfactory manner

un·satisfactoriness \"+\ *n* **:** the quality or state of being unsatisfactory

un·satisfactory \"+\ *adj* **:** not satisfactory: as **a :** not yielding content **b :** not meeting the issue or problem **:** not answering the question **c :** failing to make amends or to give satisfaction

un·satisfiable \"+\ *adj* **:** not capable of being satisfied

un·satisfied \"+\ *adj* [ME, fr. ¹*un-* + *satisfied,* past part. of *satisfien* to satisfy] **:** not satisfied ⟨the curiosity was ~ —Sherwood Anderson⟩ ⟨has any claim been left ~ —B.H. Hibbard⟩ ⟨unfilled orders and ~ demand for passenger cars —*Report: General Motors Corp.*⟩ — **un·sat·is·fied·ly** *adv* — **un·sat·is·fied·ness** *n* -ES

unsatisfied judgment fund *n* **:** a state-administered fund for the payment of damages incurred in automobile accidents provided the parties responsible are unable to pay

un·satisfying \ˌən+\ *adj* **:** failing to satisfy ⟨an ~ meal⟩

un·saturate \"+\ *n* -S **:** an unsaturated chemical compound (as an olefinic or acetylenic hydrocarbon)

un·saturated \"+\ *adj* **:** not saturated: as **a :** capable of absorbing or dissolving to a greater degree ⟨an ~ salt solution⟩ **b** *of a chemical compound or mixture* **:** able to form addition products — used esp. of organic compounds containing double or triple bonds between carbon atoms ⟨ethylene, acetylene, and oleic acid are ~ compounds⟩ ⟨hydrogenation of ~ vegetable and marine oils —O.B.J.Fraser⟩ **c :** relating to minerals (as nepheline and leucite) that generally do not form in the same rock with quartz

un·saturation \"+\ *n* **:** the quality or state of being unsaturated

un·savable \"+\ *adj* **:** not savable

un·saved \"+\ *adj* **:** not saved; *esp* **:** not rescued from eternal punishment

un·savorily \"+\ *adv* **:** in an unsavory manner

un·savoriness \"+\ *n* **:** the quality of being unsavory

un·savory \"+\ *adj* [ME, fr. ¹*un-* + *savory*] **1 :** not savory **:** INSIPID, TASTELESS **2 :** unpleasant to taste or smell **:** DISAGREEABLE, DISTASTEFUL ⟨dropped the ~ morsel —John Burroughs⟩ ⟨punishing students . . . by assigning them more work, has made education ~ and unappealing to the average student —H.C.McKown⟩ **3 :** morally offensive ⟨an ~ character . . . could be as harmful to youngsters as a man who beat them or starved them —Ross Annett⟩ ⟨an ~ reputation for providing a friendly haven for pirates —*Amer. Guide Series: R.I.*⟩ ⟨make an example of men around him caught in ~ acts —*New Republic*⟩

un·say \"+\ *vt* [ME *unsayen,* fr. ²*un-* + *sayen* to say] **:** to make as if not said **:** RECANT, RECALL, RETRACT ⟨he would not deny it; he would just ~ it —Nathaniel Peffer⟩ ⟨ten million graves record what youth has said, and cannot now ~ —Alfred Noyes⟩

un·sayable \"+\ *adj* **:** incapable of being said

un·scabbard \ˌən+\ *vt* [²*un-* + *scabbard*] **:** to remove from a scabbard ⟨~ a sword⟩

un·scalable \"+\ *adj* **:** not scalable ⟨an ~ fence⟩ ⟨an ~ barrier⟩

un·scale \"+\ *vt* [²*un-* + *scale,* n.] **:** to divest of scales **:** remove scales from

un·scaled \"+\ *adj* [¹*un-* + *scaled,* past part. of *scale*] **:** not scaled ⟨an ~ mountain⟩

un·scannable \"+\ *adj* **:** not scannable ⟨denouncing his verse as ~ —F.R.Leavis⟩

un·scanned \"+\ *adj* [¹*un-* + *scanned,* past part. of *scan*] **:** not scanned

un·scared \"+\ *adj* **:** not scared

un·scarred \"+\ *adj* [¹*un-* + *scarred,* past part. of *scar*] **:** not scarred ⟨a foot trail leads through heavy, ~ woods —*Amer. Guide Series: Mich.*⟩ ⟨~ by his thirty years as a teacher —H.F. & Katharine Pringle⟩

un·scathed \"+\ *adj* [ME, fr. ¹*un-* + *scathed,* past part. of *scathen* to scathe] **:** wholly unharmed **:** not injured ⟨believed that . . . his devotees pass ~ over this burning charcoal although they actually stamp their feet on it —J.G.Frazer⟩ ⟨emergence from the war physically ~ —A.E.Stevenson †1965⟩

un·scented \"+\ *adj* **:** deprived of scent **:** having no scent ⟨an ~ soap⟩

un·sceptered \ˌən+\ *adj* **:** deprived of a scepter **:** having no scepter

un·scheduled \"+\ *adj* [¹*un-* + *scheduled,* past part. of *schedule*] **:** not scheduled ⟨an ~ airplane flight⟩

un·scholarly \"+\ *adj* **:** not scholarly

un·school \"+\ *vt* [²*un-* + *school*] **:** to make (one) disregard schooling or training

un·schooled \"+\ *adj* [¹*un-* + *schooled,* past part. of *school*] **1 :** not schooled **:** UNTAUGHT, UNTRAINED ⟨comfort and leisure came to people ~ to use them —A.N.Whitehead⟩ **2 :** not artificial **:** NATURAL ⟨employed his ~ talents on vigorous . . . paintings of colonial families —*Amer. Guide Series: N.Y.*⟩

un·scientific \"+\ *adj* **:** not scientific: as **a :** not used in scientific work **b :** not according with the principles and methods of science ⟨essential national resource . . . dwindling from day to day because of ~ management —F.D.Roosevelt⟩ **c :** not showing scientific knowledge or familiarity with scientific methods — **un·scientifically** \"+\ *adv*

un·scorched \"+\ *adj* [¹*un-* + *scorched,* past part. of *scorch*] **:** not scorched

un·scored \"+\ *adj* [¹*un-* + *scored,* past part. of *score*] **:** not scored

un·scorned \"+\ *adj* [¹*un-* + *scorned,* past part. of *scorn*] **:** not scorned

un–scottish \"+\ *adj, usu cap S* **:** not Scottish **:** not characteristic of or consistent with Scottish customs or principles

un·scoured \"+\ *adj* [ME, fr. ¹*un-* + *scoured,* past part. of *scouren* to scour] **:** not scoured

un·scramble \"+\ *vt* [²*un-* + *scramble*] **1 :** to separate (as a conglomeration, mass, or tangle) into original components **:** RESOLVE, CLARIFY ⟨airfreight carriers, are trying to ~ a merger omelet —*Wall Street Jour.*⟩ ⟨the various possible meanings of *di-* and *de-* are so confused that only an expert can ~ them —Charlton Laird⟩ ⟨the *unscrambling* of a composite race into its original pure-race constituents —A.L.Kroeber⟩ ⟨had to ~ the financial operations which had taken place—*Brit. Bk. News*⟩ ⟨no adult can ever successfully ~ his complex mental life —Kathryn Maxwell⟩ ⟨jars or cans dumped on table are instantly *unscrambled* and regimented into a single file —*advt*⟩ **2 :** to restore (a scrambled telephonic, radio, or television transmission) to intelligible form ⟨each process by different methods would enable the home television viewer to ~ special telecast programs —Alvin Shuster⟩

un·scraped \"+\ *adj* [¹*un-* + *scraped,* past part. of *scrape*] **:** not scraped

unscraped ginger *n* **:** BLACK GINGER

un·screen \ˌən+\ *vt* [²*un-* + *screen*] **:** to remove the screen from **:** UNVEIL, REVEAL

un·screened \"+\ *adj* [¹*un-* + *screened,* past part. of *screen*] **1 :** not shut off or protected by a screen ⟨his eyes ~ from the glare⟩ ⟨he now met the college world, ~ —Edmund Wilson⟩ **2 :** not passed through a screening device or procedure ⟨~ sand⟩ ⟨this material was . . . wholly ~ —*Newsweek*⟩

un·screw \"+\ *vb* [²*un-* + *screw*] *vt* **1 :** to draw the screws from **:** loose from screws ⟨~*s* the metal plate⟩ **2 a :** to loosen or withdraw (as a screw or a cover) by turning **b :** to loosen or remove the cover of (as a jar) by turning ~ *vi* **:** to become unscrewed **:** to admit of being unscrewed ⟨vibration often causes the bolts to ~⟩ ⟨the attachment ~*s* easily for removal⟩

un·scripted \"+\ *adj* [¹*un-* + *scripted,* past part. of *script*] **:** not furnished with or using a script ⟨spot interviews, unrehearsed and ~, are the feature of the first part —Roger Manvell⟩ ⟨brought to the microphone . . . for ~ discussion on topics of the moment —Angus Mackay⟩

un·scriptural \"+\ *adj* **:** not in accordance with or in contradiction to the Scriptures ⟨the conservative members were opposed to missionary societies and instrumental music . . . as ~ —Brooke P. Church⟩ ⟨rejected infant baptism as ~ —F.S. Mead⟩ — **un·scripturally** \"+\ *adv* — **un·scripturalness** \"+\ *n*

un·scrupulosity \"+\ *n* **:** UNSCRUPULOUSNESS ⟨at times had a look of cynical ~ —O.W.Holmes †1935⟩

un·scrupulous \"+\ *adj* **1 :** not scrupulous **:** UNPRINCIPLED ⟨~ enough to betray his comrades . . . again and again —Desmond Ryan⟩ ⟨ambitious, ~, and cruel, a master of intrigue —Victor Seroff⟩ ⟨~ politicos who would be happy to sell . . . their country in order to gain power —Green Peyton⟩ **2 :** marked or characterized by unscrupulousness ⟨a witty woman of ~ tongue —Walter Bagehot⟩ ⟨the ~ procession of thieves is led by proud states and lofty statesmen —W.L. Sullivan⟩

un·scrupulously \"+\ *adv* **:** in an unscrupulous manner **:** without scruple ⟨~ uses her personal fascination to make men give her whatever she wants —G.B.Shaw⟩

un·scrupulousness \"+\ *n* **:** the quality or state of being unscrupulous

un·seal \"+\ *vt* [ME *unselen,* fr. ²*un-* + *selen* to seal] **1 :** to break or remove the seal of **:** OPEN ⟨~ the tomb⟩ ⟨~ the letter⟩ **2 a :** to free from constraint or restriction ⟨drink can ~ the shiest tongue⟩ **b :** to release from the necessity of being closed ⟨this event did not ~ her lips —Francis Hackett⟩

un·sealed \"+\ *adj* [ME *unseled,* fr. ¹*un-* + *seled,* past part. of *selen* to seal] **:** not sealed: as **a :** not marked or stamped with a seal ⟨~ goods⟩ **b :** not closed or fastened shut with or as if with a seal ⟨the letter came ~⟩ ⟨passengers should not be flown . . . above 18,000 feet in ~ cabins —H.G.Armstrong⟩ ⟨his lips remain ~⟩ **c :** not verified or confirmed ⟨his doom is as yet ~⟩

un·seam \"+\ *vt* [²*un-* + *seam*] **:** to open the seam of **:** rip open ⟨~ the garment⟩

un·seamanlike \"+\ *adj* **:** not seamanlike ⟨the boats appeared unseaworthy and the men ~ —J.H. & Edward Quick⟩

un·seamed \"+\ *adj* **:** not having any seams **:** SEAMLESS ⟨the dominant expression of his ~ face —B.F.Shambaugh⟩ ⟨an ~ garment made of a plastic⟩

un·searchable \"+\ *adj* [ME *unserchable,* fr. ¹*un-* + *serchen* to search + *-able*] **:** not capable of being explored **:** INSCRUTABLE, HIDDEN, MYSTERIOUS ⟨the ~ ways of Providence⟩ — **un·search·able·ness** \-bəlnəs\ *n* -ES — **un·search·ably** \-blē, -li\ *adv*

un·searched \ˌən+\ *adj* [¹*un-* + *searched,* past part. of *search*] **:** not searched, examined, or investigated ⟨leaving no piece of baggage ~⟩

un·seasonable \"+\ *adj* [ME *unsesounable,* fr. ¹*un-* + *sesounable* seasonable] **1 :** not seasonable **:** being, done, or occurring out of the proper season **:** UNTIMELY, INAPPROPRIATE ⟨you think my intrusion ~ —T.L.Peacock⟩ ⟨their aim . . . to guard the free income of the lesser vested interests against the ~ rapacity of the greater ones —Thorstein Veblen⟩ ⟨lovers will drop in at most ~ hours —Anthony Trollope⟩ **2 :** not being in season ⟨after spawning when the fish . . . are thin, weak, and ~ —C.R.A.Martin⟩ ⟨this partridge was evidently a diseased bird, and the ~ egg was probably due to some abnormal condition —*Country Life*⟩ **3 a :** not usual or normal and usu. undesirable for the season of the year ⟨to forestall losses from sudden ~ northers —*Amer. Guide Series: Texas*⟩ ⟨an ~ April blizzard⟩ **b :** characterized by unseasonable weather ⟨boarding houses . . . had suffered from the ~ summer —Mollie Panter-Downes⟩

un·seasonableness \"+\ *n* **:** the quality or state of being unseasonable

un·seasonably \"+\ *adv* **:** in an unseasonable manner **:** at an unseasonable time **:** not in season ⟨he ~ and precipitously made his decision⟩ ⟨tributes to German generosity fall ~ at this moment on French ears —Sir Winston Churchill⟩ ⟨the night had been ~ hot —Elinor Wylie⟩

un·seasonal \"+\ *adj* **:** not suitable or appropriate for the season **:** UNSEASONABLE ⟨to store . . . the few ~ clothes —Max Steele⟩ ⟨if rains are ~ they may scarcely bloom —*Amer. Guide Series: Texas*⟩ — **un·seasonally** \"+\ *adv*

un·seasoned \"+\ *adj* **:** not seasoned: as **a** *obs* **:** UNSEASONABLE 1 **b :** not matured or developed by growth or passage of time **:** IMMATURE ⟨~ timber⟩ ⟨the stone was often used ~ and without regard for the lie of the strata in the quarry —*Time*⟩ **c :** lacking age or seasoning **:** INEXPERIENCED ⟨~ men who are not used to responsibility because they have never exercised it —Walter Lippmann⟩ ⟨~ artillery volunteers who ought never to have been placed in such a position —H.G.Wells⟩ ⟨~ by any saving knowledge of human nature —V.L.Parrington⟩

un·seat \"+\ *vt* [²*un-* + *seat*] **1 :** to dislodge from one's seat esp. on horseback ⟨gave up horseback riding when a low-hanging limb ~*ed* him⟩ **2 a :** to displace in a political rank or office usu. by an elective process ⟨defeated an attempt . . . to ~ him in the primary —*Current Biog.*⟩ ⟨party caucus that ~*ed* the Old Guard regime —*N. Y. Times*⟩ **b :** to remove or depose from rank or office by legal action or force ⟨by a close vote . . . declined to ~ him —C.A.Berdahl⟩ ⟨had been ~*ed* for bribery —J.A.Froude⟩ ⟨in his second army coup . . . ~*ed* the president of the island republic —*Current Biog.*⟩

un·seated \"+\ *adj* [¹*un-* + *seated,* adj.] **:** not seated: **a :** having been dislodged from one's seat esp. as a rider **:** UNHORSED **b :** having been removed or deposed from political rank or position **c** *of land or territory* **:** not settled or occupied ⟨if all the states rush to claim the ~ lands within the limits of their overlapping —H.R.Warfel⟩

un·seaworthiness \"+\ *n* **:** the quality or state of being unseaworthy

un·seaworthy \"+\ *adj* **:** not seaworthy

un·seconded \"+\ *adj* [¹*un-* + *seconded,* past part. of *second*] **:** not seconded; *esp* **:** not supported or assisted ⟨the motion is ~⟩ ⟨the attempt was ~⟩

¹un·secret \"+\ *adj* [¹*un-* + *secret,* adj.] **:** not secret ⟨ringing his footfalls deliberate and ~ in the hollow silence —William Faulkner⟩

²unsecret *vt* [²*un-* + *secret*] *obs* **:** DISCLOSE, REVEAL

un·sectarian \ˌən+\ *adj* **:** not sectarian **:** not bound to or devoted to the promotion of the interests of a sect ⟨had a wide and ~ interest in religion —Bertrand Russell⟩ — **un·sectarianism** \"+\ *n*

un·secular \"+\ *adj* **:** not secular; *esp* **:** of or relating to religion or the church

un·secularize \"+\ *vt* [²*un-* + *secularize*] **:** to cause to become unsecular ⟨a movement to ~ public education⟩

un·secured \ˌən+\ *adj* [¹*un-* + *secured,* past part. of *secure*] **:** not secured; *esp* **:** not having specific security pledged ⟨~ bond⟩ ⟨~ note⟩

un·seduced \"+\ *adj* [¹*un-* + *seduced,* past part. of *seduce*] **:** not seduced ⟨remains ~ by temptations of personal gain⟩

un·see \"+\ *vt* [¹*un-* + *see*] **:** to fail to see **:** avoid seeing ⟨to prove scientifically the error or unreality of disease, you must mentally ~ the disease —Mary B. Eddy⟩

un·seeable \"+\ *adj* [ME *unseable,* fr. ¹*un-* + *seable* seeable] **:** not seeable **:** INVISIBLE

un·seeded \"+\ *adj* **:** not seeded; *esp* **:** not selectively placed in the draw for a tournament

un·seeing \"+\ *adj* **:** not seeing; *esp* **:** not consciously observing ⟨looking through him with blank ~ eyes⟩ — **un·seeingly** \"+\ *adv* — **un·see·ing·ness** *n* -ES

unseel *vt* [²*un-* + *seel*] *obs* **:** to cause (as the eyes of a hawk) to become uncovered

un·seemliness \ˌən+\ *n* [ME *unsemelines,* fr. *unsemely* unseemly + *-nes* -ness] **:** the quality or state of being unseemly

¹un·seemly \"+\ *adj* [ME *unsemely,* fr. ¹*un-* + *semely* seemly] **:** not seemly: as **a :** not according with established standards of good form or taste **:** UNBECOMING, INDECENT ⟨very ~ to talk in this loose fashion before young men —Willa Cather⟩ ⟨an ~ outbreak of temper —Nathaniel Hawthorne⟩ ⟨one of the *unseemliest* squabbles . . . grew out of the bitterness sowed between a strong administrator and his teaching staff —V.L. Parrington⟩ ⟨rescuing its historic monuments from a century and a half of ~ neglect —Lewis Mumford⟩ **b :** not comely, handsome, or attractive in appearance ⟨a man of ~ aspect⟩ ⟨country farmhouses . . . resembling dingy boxes surrounded by ~ household litter —S.E.Morison & H.S.Commager⟩ **c :** not suitable for time or place **:** INAPPROPRIATE, UNSEASONABLE ⟨at the most ~ hours — eleven at night, four in the morning — alarm clocks shrieked, taps gushed —Jean Stafford⟩ ⟨we demand to know the reason for this ~ intrusion —T.B. Costain⟩ ⟨useless and ~ sorrow for the irrevocable past —W.M.Thackeray⟩

²unseemly \"\ *adv* [ME *unsemely,* fr. ¹*un-* + *semely,* adv., seemly] **:** in unseemly fashion or manner

¹un·seen \ˌən+\ *adj* [ME *unseyn, unsene,* fr. ¹*un-* + *seyn, sene,* past part. of *seen, sen* to see] **1 a** *obs* **:** not hitherto seen or known **:** UNFAMILIAR **b :** SIGHT 1 ⟨an ~ translation⟩ **2 :** not seen or perceived **:** INVISIBLE ⟨~ natural resources⟩ ⟨the visible incarnation of that ~ ideal —Oscar Wilde⟩

²unseen \"\ *n* -S **1 :** something not seen **2** *Brit* **:** a sight translation ⟨was doing an ~ —*Oxford Mag.*⟩

unseen companion star *n* **:** a member of a binary or multiple star system that is known to exist only by its gravitational effect on the visible components whose apparent motions it usu. alters in a cyclic manner

un·segmented \ˌən+\ *adj* [¹*un-* + *segmented,* past part. of *segment*] **:** not divided into or made up of segments

un·segregated \"+\ *adj* **:** free from segregation ⟨Negro students would be admitted . . . on an ~ basis —*New Republic*⟩ ⟨an ~ audience⟩

un·seiz·able \ˌənˈsēzəbəl\ *adj* [¹*un-* + *seize* + *-able*] **:** incapable of being seized ⟨an unshorn lamb . . . now ran round, bleating, terror-stricken, and ~ —Israel Zangwill⟩ ⟨noticed an ~ resemblance between these second cousins —John Galsworthy⟩ ⟨remains as ~ to their wits as a high flight of metaphysics —R.L.Stevenson⟩ — **un·seiz·able·ness** *n* -ES

un·seized \ˌən+\ *adj* [¹*un-* + *seized,* past part. of *seize*] **:** not seized ⟨the ~ opportunity may not return⟩

un·seldom \"+\ *adv* **:** FREQUENTLY — often used with *not* ⟨often becomes tired and not ~ exhausted⟩

un·selected \"+\ *adj* **:** not selected **:** chosen at random

un·selective \"+\ *adj* **:** not selective

un·self \"+\ *vt* [²*un-* + *self,* n.] **:** to do away with selfhood or selfishness in (oneself) ⟨man has the idealism to ~ himself⟩

un·selfconscious \"+\ *adj* **1 :** not self-conscious ⟨the beautifully ~ straight-faced way he plays the scene —Manny Farber⟩ ⟨grew up with him in ~ friendship —G.L.Keynes⟩ **2 :** marked or characterized by unselfconsciousness ⟨the experience of unadorned, ~ goodness —*Times Lit. Supp.*⟩ ⟨she laughed . . . the gayest, most ~ sound in the world —Vincent Sheean⟩

un·selfconsciously \"+\ *adv* **:** in an unselfconscious manner ⟨no choice but ~ to play his role —*School & Society*⟩

un·selfconsciousness \"+\ *n* **:** the quality or state of being unselfconscious ⟨he has the ~ of a child⟩

un·selfish \"+\ *adj* **:** not selfish **:** GENEROUS ⟨his deep devotion and ~ service —W.C.Ford⟩

un·selfishly \"+\ *adv* **:** in an unselfish manner **:** with unselfishness ⟨~ give of their time . . . and money to improve the lot of all farmers —*Farmer's Weekly (So. Africa)*⟩

un·selfishness \"+\ *n* **:** the quality or state of being unselfish

un·sell \"+\ *vt* [²*un-* + *sell*] **1 :** to dissuade from a belief in the truth, value, or desirability of something ⟨has undertaken to ~ the American people on several debatable ideas . . . foisted on them —R.E.Lauterbach⟩ ⟨others won't be able to ~ him on the things he's sold on —*Time*⟩ **2 :** to dissuade one from a belief in the truth, value, or desirability of ⟨comes to

~ the idea that his country wants war⟩ ⟨rushed back before the press release to try to ~ the proposal⟩

unseminared *adj* [¹*un-* + *seminary* + *-ed*] *obs* : deprived of seminal energy

un·sensational \ˌən+\ *adj* : not sensational; *esp* : not of such character as to arouse intense interest, curiosity, or emotional reaction ⟨in a detached ~ fashion he describes the hell of the camps —W.H.Auden⟩ ⟨the text of these two ~ documents discloses no reason why the negotiations should have attracted the world's attention —*Living Age*⟩ — **un·sensationally** \"+\ *adv*

un·sense \"+\ *vt* [²*un-* + *sense*, n.] : to make insensible

un·sensed \"+\ *adj* [¹*un-* + *sensed*, past part. of *sense*] : lacking a distinct meaning : having no certain sense

un·sensible \"+\ *adj* [ME, fr. ¹*un-* + *sensible*] *dial chiefly Brit* : INSENSIBLE

un·sensitive \"+\ *adj* : INSENSITIVE

un·sensualize \"+\ *vt* [²*un-* + *sensualize*] : to elevate from the domain of the senses : PURIFY, SUBLIMATE ⟨~ love and raise it above passion⟩

un·sent \"+\ *adj* [¹*un-* + *sent*, past part. of *send*] : not sent or dispatched ⟨the missive remains unwritten and ~⟩

un·sentenced \"+\ *adj* [¹*un-* + *sentenced*, past part. of *sentence*] : not sentenced; *esp* : not condemned to penalty or punishment

un·sentimental \"+\ *adj* : not sentimental; *esp* : not characterized or dominated by excessive or unwarranted sentiment ⟨a fine, original novel, written with affectionate but ~ understanding of the Norwegians —R.A.Cordell⟩ ⟨much quite ~ appeal to the emotions —M.R.Ridley⟩ ⟨a hard core of ~ intelligence beneath their romantic paganism —Richard Watts⟩ — **un·sentimentality** \"+\ *n* — **un·sentimentally** \"+\ *adv*

un·separable \"+\ *adj* [ME *unseperable*, fr. ¹*un-* + *seperable* separable] : INSEPARABLE

un·separated \ˌən+\ *adj* [¹*un-* + *separated*, past part. of *separate*] : not separated ⟨inevitable that a great deal of bad painting should remain ~ from the good —Walter Pach⟩

un·septate \"+\ *adj* : not septate or partitioned

un·sepulchered \"+\ *adj* [¹*un-* + *sepulchered*, past part. of *sepulcher*] : not buried or entombed

un·serious \"+\ *adj* : not serious ⟨the ~ intermezzi, originally presented between the acts of serious pieces, were . . . put together to form the first light or comic operas —Sheldon Cheney⟩ ⟨flight into an ~ career as an actress —*New Republic*⟩

un·serried \"+\ *adj* : not in close order or array

un·served \"+\ *adj* [ME, fr. ¹*un-* + *served*, past part. of *serven* to serve] : not served: as **a** : not attended to : not furnished with something ⟨many customers waiting ~⟩ ⟨concentrated in the cities, the broadcasting stations leave large rural areas ~⟩ **b** *of a church or parish* : not having a clergyman in attendance **c** *of a legal writ or summons* : not served on a person

un·serviceable \"+\ *adj* **1** : not capable of being used usu. by reason of wear, impairment, or obsolescence ⟨an ~ car was defined as one which had been driven 40,000 miles —*Newsweek*⟩ ⟨~ equipment may be discarded and replaced⟩ **2** : not able to give service or aid : USELESS, INEPT ⟨~ and grossly insolent civil servants —G.B.Shaw⟩ ⟨despite our best efforts, we proved to be quite ~ for his purposes⟩ **3** *chiefly Brit* : incapable of doing military service ⟨ragged, ill-fed, and ~ troops⟩ — **un·serviceableness** \"+\ *n* — **un·serviceably** \"+\ *adv*

¹un·set \"+\ *adj* [ME *unsett*, fr. ¹*un-* + *sett* set] : not set: as **a** *archaic* : not allotted or assigned **b** : not fixed in a setting : UNMOUNTED ⟨auctioning off a collection of ~ stones⟩ ⟨an ~ sawtooth⟩ **c** : not firmed or solidified ⟨~ concrete⟩

²unset \"\ *vt* [²*un-* + *set*] : DISPLACE, UNSETTLE

¹un·setting \ˌən+\ *adj* [¹*un-* + *setting*, pres. part. of *set*] : not setting ⟨where suns ~ light the sky and flowers and fruit abound —J.H.Newman⟩

²unsetting \"\ *n* [¹*un-* + *setting*, n.] : a supporting of the opposite masonry walls of a cut through loose strata by means of buttresses resting on inverted arches

un·settle \ˌən+\ *vb* [²*un-* + *settle*] *vt* **1** : to unfix or loosen from a settled state : DISPLACE ⟨a lusty shock . . . *unsettled* another rock up the mountain —Burtt Evans⟩ **2** : to force or move from a quiet or settled condition : DISTURB ⟨the heavy diet ~*s* his stomach⟩ ⟨this theory, though intended to strengthen the foundations of government, altogether ~*s* them —T.B. Macaulay⟩ ⟨major strikes could ~ 1959 economy —*News Front*⟩ **3 a** : to cause to be doubtful or uncertain : UPSET ⟨new trends ~ old beliefs and opinions⟩ ⟨to ~ the traditional notion —F.R.Leavis⟩ ⟨the cold war has *unsettled* the minds of men —M.B.Travis⟩ **b** : to perturb or agitate mentally or emotionally : DISCOMPOSE ⟨a clumsy driver had *unsettled* the horses —C.S.Forester⟩ ⟨his narratives ~ us, force us to make comparisons in our own terms —E.R.May⟩ ⟨the impact of the momentary glamorous life could ~ a woman —Herbert Mitgary⟩ ~ *vi* : to become unsettled or unfixed ⟨the congregation *unsettled*, produced handkerchiefs, and knelt upon them — James Joyce⟩ **syn** see DISORDER

un·settled \"+\ *adj* [partly fr. ¹*un-* + *settled*; partly fr. past part. of *unsettle*] : not settled: as **a** (1) : not calm or tranquil : DISTURBED, UNQUIET ⟨an ~ air — an echo of turbulence and war — now hangs over every campus —F.E.Robin⟩ ⟨this utterly ~ and uncertain condition —C.S.Peirce⟩ (2) : INCONSTANT, VARIABLE ⟨homebound . . . meeting ~ weather all the way, rain, snow, hail, and sunshine —*Crowsnest*⟩ (3) : remaining in a state of motion or change : not settled down ⟨clouds of ~ dust⟩ ⟨the murky ~ water⟩ **b** (1) : not decided or determined : DOUBTFUL ⟨in an ~ state of mind⟩ (2) : not resolved or worked out : UNDECIDED ⟨~ constitutional questions . . . came up for solution —H.W.H.Knott⟩ ⟨specifications were still ~ —*Fortune*⟩ **c** (1) : not firm or steadfast in disposition or outlook : ERRATIC, UNSTABLE ⟨~ young people without any roots in the past⟩ (2) : characterized by uncertainty, irregularity, or instability ⟨living an ~ life after leaving his family⟩ ⟨the old tribal customs now ~ by modern civilization⟩ **d** (1) : not living or staying in one place ⟨the ~ nomads of the desert⟩ (2) : not inhabited or populated ⟨land within the territory . . . that was then ~ or uncultivated has been peopled or reclaimed —B.N.Cardozo⟩ **e** : mentally unbalanced ⟨minds ~ by excessive ascetic observances —W.G. Sumner⟩ ⟨at one time he was insane or at least ~ —A.B. Guthrie⟩ **f** (1) : not disposed of according to law ⟨the estate remains ~⟩ (2) : not paid or discharged ⟨borrowing money to pay off all ~ debts⟩ — **un·settledness** \"+\ *n*

un·settlement \"+\ *n* **1** : an act, process, or instance of unsettling ⟨in the teaching of foreign languages there has been at least some ~ in consequence of army courses —*Language*⟩ ⟨did not relish the theological ~ that came with the advance of scientific inquiry —V.L.Parrington⟩ **2** : the quality or state of being unsettled ⟨the disturbance and ~ that now marks . . . man's life —John Dewey⟩

un·settling \"+\ *adj* [fr. pres. part. of *unsettle*] : having the effect of upsetting, disturbing, or discomposing ⟨his ornate and exuberant grandiosity that is a bit ~ —R.M.Coates⟩ ⟨the swift pace of scientific discovery . . . has had a profoundly ~ effect upon our modern world view —Melvin Rader⟩ ⟨found even the simplest political questions ~ —R.H.Rovere⟩

un·severed \"+\ *adj* [ME, fr. ¹*un-* + *severed*, past part. of *severen* to sever] : not severed ⟨our ties remain ~⟩

un·sew \"+\ *vt* [ME *unsewen*, fr. ²*un-* + *sewen* to sew] : to take the stitches out of; *also* : to rip apart or separate by removing the sewing

un·sewered \"+\ *adj* [¹*un-* + *sewer* + *-ed*] : not provided with a sewer or drain ⟨~ slums⟩

un·sex \"+\ *vt* [²*un-* + *sex*, n.] **1** : to deprive of sex or sexual power **2** : to remove the qualities typical of one's sex ⟨come you spirits, that tend on mortal thoughts, ~ me here —Shak.⟩ ⟨if she earned money in the one profession that was open to her, the oldest profession of all, she ~*ed* herself —Virginia Woolf⟩

un·sexual \"+\ *adj* : not sexual : lacking sex

unsgd *abbr* unsigned

un·shackle \ˌən+\ *vt* [²*un-* + *shackle*] **1 a** : to loose from a shackle or bond ⟨giving orders to ~ the prisoner and bring him on deck⟩ **b** : to set free from restraint ⟨conversation was *unshackled* —B.M.Bowie⟩ ⟨when the mind has been *unshackled* from ignorance —H.G.Rickover⟩ **2** : to remove a shackle from (as an anchor) ⟨*unshackled* the port anchor and lowered it —H.A.Chippendale⟩

un·shaded \"+\ *adj* : not shaded: as **a** : not darkened or bedimmed by shade : EXPOSED ⟨an ~ meadow⟩ ⟨a bright and ~ lane through the trees⟩ **b** : not having shades in coloring or tone ⟨sharp ~ colors⟩ ⟨a clear ~ voice⟩ **c** : not provided with a shade ⟨an ~ lamp⟩ ⟨~ windows⟩

un·shadow \"+\ *vt* [²*un-* + *shadow*] *archaic* : to rid of shadow

un·shadowed \"+\ *adj* [¹*un-* + *shadowed*, past part. of *shadow*] : not darkened or obscured by shadow ⟨on the rough sea ice you may on an ~ day . . . fall over a chunk of ice that is knee-high —Vilhjalmur Stefansson⟩ ⟨in times of ~ prosperity —Claire Sterling⟩

un·shakable \"+\ *adj* : not shakable : firmly grounded ⟨a sense of deep conviction and ~ faith —*Manchester Guardian Weekly*⟩

un·shak·able·ness *or* **un·shake·able·ness** \-bəlnə̇s\ *n* -ES : the quality or state of being unshakable : FIRMNESS, SOLIDITY

un·shak·ably *or* **un·shake·ably** \-blē, -li\ *adv* : in an unshakable manner : FIRMLY

un·shaked \"+\ *adj* [¹*un-* + *shaked*, dial. past part. of *shake*] *obs* : UNSHAKEN

un·shaken \"+\ *adj* [ME, fr. ¹*un-* + *shaken*, past part. of *shaken* to shake] : not shaken : FIRM, STEADY ⟨although physically only the wreck of a man, his nerve was ~ and his remarkable mental faculties unimpaired —Sir Winston Churchill⟩ — **un·shak·en·ly** *adv* — **un·shak·en·ness** *n* -ES

un·shamed \ˌən+\ *adj* [ME, fr. ¹*un-* + *shamed*, past part. of *shamen* to shame] **1** : not shamed **2** : UNASHAMED

un·shaped \"+\ *adj* : not shaped: as **a** : not dressed or finished to final form ⟨an ~ timber⟩ **b** : imperfect in form or formulation ⟨~ ideas⟩

un·shapeliness \"+\ *n* : the quality or state of being unshapely

un·shapely \"+\ *adj* [ME *unshaply*, *unshaplich*, fr. ¹*un-* + *shap* shape + *-ly*, *-lich* -ly] : not shapely : wanting the beauty of fully realized or developed form ⟨she was a stout, ~ woman —Ellen Glasgow⟩

un·shapen \"+\ *adj* [ME, fr. ¹*un-* + *shapen*] : UNSHAPED

un·shared \"+\ *adj* [¹*un-* + *shared*, past part. of *share*] : not shared

un·sharp \"+\ *adj* : not sharp

unsharp mask *n* : a copy of a photographic image that is intentionally blurred for use over the original image in making final copies which are thereby modified in contrast and edge sharpness

un·sharpness \ˌən+\ *n* : the quality or state of being unsharp; *esp* : a low degree of photographic sharpness

un·shattered \"+\ *adj* [¹*un-* + *shattered*, past part. of *shatter*] : not shattered

un·shaved \"+\ *adj* : not shaved

un·shaven \"+\ *adj* [ME, fr. ¹*un-* + *shaven*] : not shaved : having a beard or the stubble of a beard

un·shawl \"+\ *vi* [²*un-* + *shawl*] : to remove one's shawl

un·sheared \"+\ *adj* : not sheared

un·sheathe \"+\ *vt* [²*un-* + *sheathe*] : to draw from or as if from a sheath or scabbard ⟨*unsheathed* his sword⟩ : BARE, UNCOVER

un·shed \"+\ *adj* : not shed

un·shell \"+\ *vt* [²*un-* + *shell*, n.] : to remove from the shell

un·sheltered \"+\ *adj* [¹*un-* + *sheltered*, past part. of *shelter*] : not sheltered : having or offering no shelter

un·sheltering \"+\ *adj* [¹*un-* + *sheltering*, pres. part. of *shelter*] : not sheltering

un·shent \ˌən+\ *adj* [ME, fr. ¹*un-* + *shent*, past part. of *shenden* to shend] : UNHARMED, UNSPOILED

un·shepherded \"+\ *adj* [¹*un-* + *shepherded*, past part. of *shepherd*] : not shepherded

un·shielded \"+\ *adj* [¹*un-* + *shielded*, past part. of *shield*] : not shielded : UNPROTECTED

un·shiftable \"+\ *adj* [¹*un-* + *shift* + *-able*] : IMMOVABLE

un·shifted \"+\ *adj* [¹*un-* + *shifted*, past part. of *shift*] : unchanged for a fresh article of clothing ⟨a shirt ~⟩

un·ship \"+\ *vb* [ME *unschippen*, fr. ²*un-* + *schippen* to ship] *vt* **1** : to take out of a ship : DISCHARGE, UNLOAD ⟨*unshipped* a cargo⟩ **2** : to remove (as an oar) from position ~ *vi* **1** : to become detached or removed **2** : to become unloaded

un·shipped \"+\ *adj* [¹*un-* + *shipped*, past part. of *ship*] **1** : not shipped ⟨the ~ goods⟩ **2** : having no ship **3** : detached from position in a ship or boat

un·shirted \"+\ *adj* [¹*un-* + *shirted*, past part. of *shirt*] : NAKED, UNDISGUISED, PLAIN — usu. used in the phrase *unshirted hell* ⟨given . . . ~ hell for a speech —Sherman Adams⟩ ⟨old guerrillas were raising ~ hell —*N. Y. Herald Tribune Bk. Rev.*⟩

un·shocked \"+\ *adj* [¹*un-* + *shocked*, past part. of *shock*] : not shocked : not subjected to shocks

un·shod \"+\ *adj* [ME, fr. OE *unscōd*, past part. of *unscōgan* to unshoe, fr. ²*un-* + *scōgan* to shoe — more at SHOE] **1** : wearing no shoes : BAREFOOT **2** *of a horse* : not shod : having cast a shoe **3** : having no tire or rim ⟨an ~ wagon wheel⟩ : lacking a sharp iron point ⟨an ~ pole⟩

un·shoe \"+\ *vt* [²*un-* + *shoe*] : to remove a shoe from

un·shorn \ˌən+\ *adj* [ME, fr. ¹*un-* + *shorn*, past part. of *sheren* to shear] **1** : not cut ⟨his grizzly ~ beard —Anthony Trollope⟩ **2** : not harvested ⟨the ~ fields, boundless and beautiful —W.C.Bryant⟩ **3** : not diminished ⟨hues with all their beams ~ —Lord Byron⟩

un·shortened \"+\ *adj* [¹*un-* + *shortened*, past part. of *shorten*] : not shortened : UNDIMINISHED

un·shot \"+\ *adj* **1** : not shot ⟨an ~ gun⟩ ⟨an ~ arrow⟩ **2** : not hit by a shot **3** : not mingled or variegated : not interwoven ⟨methods of beef preparation . . . not ~ with cunning and imagination —C.H.Baker⟩

un·shoulder \"+\ *vt* [²*un-* + *shoulder*] : to remove from the shoulder ⟨~*ed* their knapsacks⟩

un·shown \"+\ *adj* [¹*un-* + *shown*, past part. of *show*] : not shown

un·showy \"+\ *adj* : not showy

un·shrine \"+\ *vt* [²*un-* + *shrine*] : to remove from a shrine

un·shrinkable \"+\ *adj* [¹*un-* + *shrink* + *-able*] : incapable of being shrunken, diminished, or reduced

un·shrinking \"+\ *adj* [¹*un-* + *shrinking*, pres. part. of *shrink*] : not shrinking

un·shrinkingly \"+\ *adv* : without shrinking

un·shrived \"+\ *adj* [¹*un-* + *shrived*, past part. of *shrive*] : UNSHRIVEN

un·shriven \"+\ *adj* [¹*un-* + *shriven*, past part. of *shrive*] : not shriven

un·shroud \"+\ *vt* [²*un-* + *shroud*] : to remove a shroud from : EXPOSE, UNCOVER

un·shun·na·ble \ˌən¦shənəbəl\ *adj* [¹*un-* + *shun* + *-able*] : not to be shunned or evaded : INESCAPABLE

¹un·shut \ˌən+\ *vb* [ME *unshutten*, fr. ²*un-* + *shutten* to shut] : OPEN

²unshut \"\ *adj* [ME, fr. past part. of *unshutten* to unshut] : not shut : OPEN

un·shutter \ˌən+\ *vt* [²*un-* + *shutter*] : to open or remove the shutters of

un·shy \"+\ *adj* : not shy ⟨they were naked, ~, beautiful, and full of grace —John Cheever⟩

un·shyly \"+\ *adv* : not shyly

un·shyness \"+\ *n* : absence of shyness or timidity

un·sicker \"+\ *adj* [ME *unsiker*, fr. ¹*un-* + *siker* safe, sicker] *Scot* : UNSURE, UNSAFE

un·sifted \"+\ *adj* [¹*un-* + *sifted*, past part. of *sift*] **1** : not passed through a sieve or strainer **2** : not inspected or scrutinized

¹un·sight \"+\ *vt* [²*un-* + *sight*] : to prevent from seeing ⟨a gust of wind blew his . . . hat over his face and ~*ed* him so that he dropped the catch —*N.Y. Times*⟩

²unsight \"\ *adj* [¹*un-* + *sight*, n.] : not sighted or examined ⟨buying the horse ~, unseen⟩

un·sightliness \ˌən+\ *n* : the quality or state of being unsightly

un·sightly \"+\ *adj* : not sightly : not comely ⟨an ~ swamp and dump grounds —*Amer. Guide Series: Minn.*⟩ ⟨a distortion of the back . . . ~ to behold —Herman Melville⟩ **syn** see UGLY

un·signed \"+\ *adj* [¹*un-* + *signed*, past part. of *sign*] : not signed : lacking a signature

un·significant \"+\ *adj* : lacking meaning or significance : INSIGNIFICANT

un·similar \"+\ *adj* : DISSIMILAR — usu. used with *not* ⟨implements . . . not ~ to those still in occasional use —*Economic Geology*⟩ ⟨for reasons not ~ to those cherished —*Current History*⟩

un·sin \"+\ *vt* [²*un-* + *sin*] : to annul (a sin) by subsequent action

un·sinew \"+\ *vt* [²*un-* + *sinew*, n.] : to deprive of sinews or of strength : ENERVATE, ENFEEBLE ⟨seeking every way to ~ the enemy⟩

un·singable \"+\ *adj* : not fitted for singing

un·sinkable \"+\ *adj* : incapable of being sunk ⟨~ ships⟩

un·sizable \"+\ *adj* : of insufficient size or maturity ⟨throwing back all ~ fish he finds in the net⟩

¹un·sized \"+\ *adj* : not fashioned to a size or to regular sizes ⟨~ pieces of slate⟩

²unsized \"\ *adj* [¹*un-* + *sized*, past part. of *size* to treat with size] : not treated with size ⟨~ paper⟩

un·skill \ˌən+\ *n* : lack of skill or proficiency ⟨his failure could only be a matter of technical ~ —Samuel Alexander⟩

un·skilled \"+\ *adj* **1** : not skilled or proficient ⟨~ copyists cannot be relied on in matters of punctuation —R.P.Blackmur⟩ ⟨is ~ in parliamentary debate⟩; *specif* : not skilled in a specified branch of work : lacking technical training ⟨all workers — skilled, semiskilled, and ~ —G.S.Watkins⟩ **2** : not requiring or involving skill ⟨the book lists all skilled and ~ occupations⟩ **3** : displaying lack of skill or proficiency ⟨a rude and comparatively ~ poem —Gilbert Highet⟩

unskilled labor *n* : labor that requires relatively little or no training or experience for its satisfactory performance; *also* : workers or personnel engaged in such labor ⟨an accident attributed to the use of *unskilled labor* —*Current Biog.*⟩

un·skillful \ˌən+\ *adj* [ME *unskilful*, fr. ¹*un-* + *skilful*] **1** : not skillful : lacking in skill or proficiency ⟨although a keen mountaineer, I am a pretty ~ one —Wynford Vaughan-Thomas⟩ **2** : displaying lack of skill or proficiency ⟨an ~ attempt⟩ ⟨~ manner⟩ — **un·skillfully** \"+\ *adv* — **un·skillfulness** \"+\ *n*

un·skimmed \"+\ *adj* [¹*un-* + *skimmed*, past part. of *skim*] **1** : not skimmed ⟨~ milk⟩ **2** : not covered with a skim coat ⟨~ plaster⟩

un·slacked \"+\ *adj* [¹*un-* + *slacked*, past part. of *slack*] **1** : not slackened or relaxed **2** : UNSLAKED 1

un·slaked \"+\ *adj* [¹*un-* + *slaked*, past part. of *slake*] **1** *of lime* : not slaked **2** : not lessened or brought to an end ⟨~ thirst⟩ ⟨demonstrators went home with their wrath ~ —*Newsweek*⟩ ⟨would leave human longing ~ —F.R.Leavis⟩

un·slate \"+\ *vt* [²*un-* + *slate*] : to remove the slate from ⟨the wind can ~ the roof⟩

un·sleeping \"+\ *adj* [¹*un-* + *sleeping*, pres. part. of *sleep*] : not sleeping or resting : WAKEFUL, WATCHFUL, ACTIVE ⟨~ waters of the ocean⟩ ⟨face and eyes of ~ passion —S.H. Adams⟩ ⟨that ~ interest in everything about him —B.J. Hendrick⟩

un·slept \"+\ *adj* [¹*un-* + *slept*, past part. of *sleep*] **1** : not having slept ⟨arose early ~⟩ **2** : not used for sleeping — usu. used with *in* ⟨his bed is ~ in⟩

un·sling \"+\ *vt* [²*un-* + *sling*] : to remove from being slung : DETACH, UNHITCH ⟨would ~ the yellow tape from his shoulders and measure . . . the man's waist —Michael McLaverty⟩ ⟨having dismounted he *unslung* his binoculars —J.T. McNish⟩; *specif* : to take off the slings of or remove from a sling esp. aboard ship ⟨climbing the rigging to ~ the sail⟩ ⟨lowered the cask into the hold and *unslung* it⟩ ⟨was ordered to ~ his hammock⟩

un·slip \"+\ *vt* [²*un-* + *slip*] : to set loose : FREE ⟨~*s* the yelping pack of hounds⟩

un·slotted \ˌən+\ *adj* : not slotted

un·sluice \"+\ *vt* [²*un-* + *sluice*] *archaic* : to open the sluice of : let flow : SLUICE

un·smart \"+\ *adj* : not smart ⟨is a young accountant — hard up, shy, ~ —R.P.Fleming⟩

un·smeared \"+\ *adj* [¹*un-* + *smeared*, past part. of *smear*] : not smeared

un·smiling \"+\ *adj* [¹*un-* + *smiling*, pres. part. of *smile*] : not smiling — **un·smilingly** \"+\ *adv*

un·smirched \"+\ *adj* [¹*un-* + *smirched*, past part. of *smirch*] : not smirched

un·smoked \"+\ *adj* [¹*un-* + *smoked*, past part. of *smoke*] **1** : not smoked or exposed to smoke ⟨there is no industry here and that's . . . why it's so calm, so ~ and unsoiled —Richard Joseph⟩ **2** : not used up by smoking ⟨leaving his cigar ~ in the ashtray⟩

¹un·smooth \"+\ *adj* [¹*un-* + *smooth*, adj.] : not smooth : ROUGH, HARSH ⟨strokes his ~ face⟩ ⟨awkward and ~ writing⟩ — **un·smoothly** \"+\ *adv*

²unsmooth \"\ *vt* [²*un-* + *smooth*] : to make unsmooth or uneven : ROUGHEN ⟨the passing ship ~*s* the water⟩

un·smoothed \ˌən+\ *adj* [¹*un-* + *smoothed*, past part. of *smooth*] : not smoothed

un·snap \"+\ *vt* [²*un-* + *snap*] : to loosen or free by or as if by undoing a snap : UNDO, RELEASE ⟨the groom ~*s* the halter⟩ ⟨the great beast ~*s* its jaws⟩

un·snarl \"+\ *vt* [²*un-* + *snarl*] : to disentangle a snarl in ⟨helping ~ the yarn⟩ ⟨worked hard to ~ the company's affairs⟩

un·snuffed \"+\ *adj* [¹*un-* + *snuffed*, past part. of *snuff*] : not snuffed

un·sober \"+\ *adj* [ME *unsober*, *unsobre*, fr. ¹*un-* + *sober*, *sobre* sober] : not sober: as **a** *obs* : marked by extremes : IMMODERATE, EXCESSIVE **b** : not serious or sober-minded : undisciplined in conduct or thought ⟨an ~, temperamental person⟩ **c** : given to drinking : INTOXICATED ⟨comes often ~ from the taproom⟩ — **un·soberly** \"+\ *adv*

un·sociability \"+\ *n* : the quality or state of being unsociable

un·sociable \"+\ *adj* **1 a** : not inclined to society or conversation : SOLITARY, RESERVED, WITHDRAWN ⟨is generally ~ except with intimate friends⟩ ⟨my ~ nature . . . shy, awkward, reserved —Havelock Ellis⟩ **b** : marked by or resulting from unsociability ⟨~ behavior⟩ ⟨~ demeanor⟩ **2** *archaic* : not mutually accordant : INCOMPATIBLE, DISCORDANT **3** : lacking or preventing social intercourse ⟨living an ~ distance apart⟩ — **un·sociableness** \"+\ *n* — **un·sociably** \"+\ *adv*

un·social \"+\ *adj* **1 a** : not social : not seeking or given to association ⟨as Christians, they are ~, since they find themselves unable to go along with any . . . organized groups —Katharine F. Gerould⟩ **b** : marked by or resulting from an unsocial quality or state ⟨the ~ disposition to neglect one's neighbor's appreciations —W.C.Brownell⟩ ⟨his desire to escape notoriety . . . did not denote an ~ nature —Caroline Ticknor⟩ **2** : ANTISOCIAL 1b ⟨hoarding of money, lending it on interest, cornering of foodstuffs — all these ~ tendencies are sternly prohibited —P.G.Waris⟩ ⟨a margin . . . such as would make for ~ profits and induce to a larger capital formation than might be proper —S.E.Harris⟩ — **un·socially** \"+\ *adv*

un·socialized \"+\ *adj* [¹*un-* + *socialized*, past part. of *socialize*] : not socialized; *specif* : not sufficiently socialized to adjust to societal norms ⟨~ and aggressive delinquents⟩

un·socket \"+\ *vt* [²*un-* + *socket*] : to loose or take from a socket ⟨a severe twist can ~ the bone⟩

un·sodden \ˌən+\ *adj* : not sodden; *esp* : not wet or soaked : not weighed down by moisture ⟨the wet leaves are rendered ~ by the drying wind⟩

un·soil \"+\ *vb* [²*un-* + *soil*, n.] *vt* : to strip the top layer of soil or mold from ~ *vi* : to remove the soil (as in opening a deposit of clay for brickmaking)

un·soiled \"+\ *adj* [¹*un-* + *soiled*, past part. of *soil*] : not soiled or dirtied ⟨an ~ towel⟩ : not sullied ⟨his ~ name⟩

un·sold \"+\ *adj* [ME, fr. ¹*un-* + *sold*, past part. of *sellen* to sell] : not sold; *esp* : not disposed of by purchase

un·solder \"+\ *vt* [²*un-* + *solder*] : to separate or disunite (something that has been soldered) : DIVIDE, SUNDER ⟨~ all electrical connections⟩ ⟨nothing would ~ fraternal bonds⟩

un·soldierly \"+\ *adj* : not characteristic of or befitting a soldier ⟨~ maneuver⟩ ⟨~ appearance and conduct⟩

un·solemn \"+\ *adj* **1 :** not solemn **:** not solemnized by formalities **2** *of a will* **:** lacking the name of an executor
un·solicited \"+\ *adj* [1*un-* + *solicited*, past part. of *solicit*] **:** not solicited: as **a :** not subjected to solicitation ⟨the old pastor sent for him and ~ granted him the request —Willa Cather⟩ ⟨half the block is as yet ~ for contributions⟩ **b :** not asked for **:** granted or given without request ⟨his early adherence to the principles . . . brought him an ~ nomination and election to Congress —J.D.Hicks⟩ ⟨some information . . . was obtained ~ from anonymous sources —W.E.Welmers⟩
un·solicitous \"+\ *adj* **:** not solicitous; *esp* **:** not manifesting anxiety or concern ⟨is ~ about the welfare of others⟩
un·solid \"+\ *adj* **1 :** not solid ⟨~ materials crumble⟩ **2 :** lacking a sound or substantial basis ⟨an ~ argument⟩ ⟨~ thinking⟩
un·solidified \ˌən+\ *adj* [1*un-* + *solidified*, past part. of *solidify*] **:** not solidified
un·soluble \"+\ *adj* **:** INSOLUBLE
un·solvable \"+\ *adj* **:** not solvable **:** INSOLUBLE ⟨public finance . . . had long presented problems ~ or at least unsolved —C.L.Jones⟩
un·solved \"+\ *adj* [1*un-* + *solved*, past part. of *solve*] **:** not solved ⟨many crimes remain ~⟩ ⟨an ~ *x* in all equations —Ralph Linton⟩ ⟨~ problems⟩
un·son \"+\ *vt* **unsonned; unsonned; unsonning; unsons** [2*un-* + *son*] **:** to dispossess of the station or character of a son ⟨denied his heritage and took steps to ~ himself⟩
un·sonsy \"+\ *adj* **1** *dial Brit* **:** boding or causing misfortune **:** UNLUCKY, FATAL **2** *dial Brit* **:** UNPLEASANT, DISAGREEABLE
un·sophisticate \"+\ *adj* **:** UNSOPHISTICATED ⟨a simple, genuine ~ nature⟩
un·sophisticated \"+\ *adj* **:** not sophisticated: as **a** (1) **:** not altered in substance **:** UNADULTERATED (2) **:** not changed or corrupted **:** GENUINE ⟨pure loyalty ~ by hypocrisy⟩ **b** (1) **:** not worldly-wise **:** lacking sophistication **:** NAIVE, ARTLESS, INGENUOUS ⟨~ Indians who would barter bales of furs for a handful of trinkets —R.A.Billington⟩ ⟨has scaled the Hollywood heights but remains essentially ~, untouched by it all —Donald Foley⟩ ⟨were either too ~ or too honest to promise . . . more than they thought they could reasonably deliver —*Newsweek*⟩ (2) **:** lacking adornment or complexity of structure **:** PLAIN, SIMPLE ⟨the earliest buildings in Philadelphia and its vicinity were . . . ~ with gable or sometimes gambrel roofs —*Amer. Guide Series: Pa.*⟩ ⟨his rhythms are basic, regular, and generally ~ —Harold Rogers⟩ ⟨is dealing with a relatively ~ problem⟩ **syn** see NATURAL
un·sophistication \"+\ *n* **:** a lack of or freedom from sophistication
un·sordid \"+\ *adj* **:** not sordid
un·sorted \"+\ *adj* [1*un-* + *sorted*, past part. of *sort*] **1 :** not sorted or classified ⟨a lot of ~ goods⟩ **2** *obs* **:** not well selected or chosen
un·sought \ˌən+\ *adj* [ME *unsouht, unsought*, fr. 1*un-* + *souht, sought*, past part. of *seken* to seek] **:** not sought: as **a :** not searched for or sought out ⟨kindness receives ~ compliments⟩ **b :** not acquired by effort or search ⟨help ~ may sometimes come when all seeking has failed⟩ **c :** not requested **:** UNSOLICITED ⟨reads the mind's desires and grants favors ~⟩ **d** *obs* **:** not explored or examined
un·soul \"+\ *vt* [2*un-* + *soul*] **:** to deprive of soul or spirit
un·sound \"+\ *adj* [ME, fr. 1*un-* + *sound*] **:** not sound: as **a** (1) **:** not physically healthy or whole **:** UNHEALTHY, DISEASED ⟨an ~ limb⟩ ⟨the teeth were ~⟩; *esp* **:** having a disease, abnormality, or defect of such a nature or to such a degree as to impair usefulness — used esp. of a horse (2) **:** not in good or edible condition **:** STALE, ROTTEN ⟨poultry in a state of decomposition must be regarded as ~ —C.R.A.Martin⟩ ⟨all ~ produce is refused at the market⟩ (3) **:** not mentally sound or normal **:** not wholly or consistently sane ⟨is said to be of ~ mind⟩ **b :** not morally sound **:** CORRUPT, EVIL ⟨a strong nation cannot be built of an ~ people⟩ **c :** not firmly made, placed, or fixed ⟨if pure copper . . . was cast thinly, the ingots proved ~ —John Craig⟩ ⟨in detail design it was fundamentally ~ —O.S.Nock⟩ **d** (1) **:** not based on logical reasoning or established fact **:** FALSE, INVALID, SPECIOUS ⟨it is doubtless ~ to argue that what can be done by the government in time of war can also be effected in time of peace —M.R.Cohen⟩ ⟨contained exaggerated statements and ~ prophecies —W.O.Lynch⟩ (2) **:** not based on proven practice, established procedure, or practical knowledge ⟨the economic collapse . . . brought on by ~ banking and wild speculation in public utilities —*Amer. Guide Series: Nev.*⟩ ⟨the present arrangement is obviously a precarious and ~ one, dangerous to the long-term stability of the . . . area —G.F.Kennan⟩ — **un·soundly** \"+\ *adv*
unsoundable \"+\ *adj* [1*un-* + *sound* + *-able*] **:** not capable of being sounded or fathomed ⟨a silence ~ —Thomas Carlyle⟩ ⟨~ depths⟩
1**un·sounded** \"+\ *adj* [1*un-* + *sounded*, past part. of *sound*] **:** not pronounced or spoken **:** not made to sound ⟨the words stopped at her lips ~⟩ ⟨in French certain letters are often ~⟩
2**unsounded** \"\ *adj* [1*un-* + *sounded*, past part. of *sound* to fathom] **:** not fathomed or probed ⟨remote and ~ caverns —S.A.Coblentz⟩ ⟨the ~ depths of human misery⟩
un·soundness \ˌən+\ *n* **1 :** the quality or state of being unsound ⟨recognize the substantial ~ of certain conclusions —M.R.Cohen⟩ ⟨the ~ of the island's economy⟩ **2 :** something (as a disease) that causes one to be unsound ⟨heaves is an ~ in the horse⟩
un·soured \"+\ *adj* [1*un-* + *soured*, past part. of *sour*] **:** not soured ⟨giving him the taste of opulence ~ by satiety —Norman Lewis⟩
un·sown \"+\ *adj* [1*un-* + *sown*, past part. of *sow*] **1 :** not sown in the ground ⟨it is so cold this year that the seed is still ~⟩ **2 :** not planted with seed ⟨farmland . . . still ~ —Benjamin Waife⟩
un·spaced \"+\ *adj* **:** not spaced
un·spar \"+\ *vt* [ME *unsperren*, fr. 2*un-* + *sperren* to bolt, spar] *archaic* **:** to take the spars, stakes, or bars from **:** OPEN
un·sparing \"+\ *adj* [1*un-* + *sparing*, pres. part. of *spare*] **1 :** not merciful or forbearing **:** HARD, RUTHLESS ⟨portrait, at once ~ and compassionate —Coleman Rosenberger⟩ ⟨both artists have been ~ with their social comments —*Amer. Guide Series: Minn.*⟩ ⟨become an ~ critic of himself and of others —Walter Silz⟩ **2 :** not frugal **:** LIBERAL, PROFUSE ⟨worked and expected others to work with the same ~ energy —Roger Cary⟩ ⟨has periods of niggardliness followed by impulses of ~ generosity⟩
un·sparingly \"+\ *adv* **:** in an unsparing manner ⟨drove himself ~ and often beyond his strength —J.C.Fitzpatrick⟩ ⟨~ portrayed the money-grabbing society of the Gilded Age —*Amer. Guide Series: N.Y.*⟩ ⟨his book . . . is ~ comprehensive —F.P.Rous⟩
unspeak *vt* [2*un-* + *speak*] *obs* **:** UNSAY
un·speakable \ˌən+\ *adj* [ME *unspekeable*, fr. 1*un-* + *speken* to speak + *-able*] **1 a :** not capable of being verbally expressed **:** UNUTTERABLE, INDESCRIBABLE ⟨watching the ~ beauties of that wondrous bay —Martha Kean⟩ ⟨with ~ delight . . . took and divided the gifts —Francis Parkman⟩ ⟨all creative work starts as a feeling . . . or some other ~ affective state —A.H.S.Korzybski⟩ **b :** indescribably objectionable or hateful ⟨that ~ odor came sweeping into the room, wave upon wave of the breath of all corruption —Arthur Grimble⟩ ⟨so likable as a man, so ~ as a politician —Francis Biddle⟩ ⟨those poor painted females . . . plied their ~ trade —D.B.Chidsey⟩ **2 :** that may not or cannot be uttered or spoken ⟨oddest of all are the bawdy thoughts that come into one's head — the ~ words —L.P.Smith⟩ ⟨our job to see that a speaker does not have to contend with ~ collections of consonants —Rosemary Jellis⟩
un·speakableness \"+\ *n* **:** the quality or state of being unspeakable
un·speakably \"+\ *adv* **:** UNUTTERABLY, INEXPRESSIBLY ⟨~ glad⟩ ⟨~ obnoxious⟩
un·specialized \"+\ *adj* **:** not specialized; *esp* **:** not adapted or modified in form or structure for a particular purpose or function **:** GENERALIZED
un·specific \"+\ *adj* **:** not specific ⟨the statement of his hero's disillusionment is ~ —H.E.Clurman⟩ ⟨is deterred . . . by an ~ dread which is not placed in any time sequence of rewards and punishments —Margaret Mead⟩
un·specificness \"+\ *n* **:** the quality or state of being unspecific
un·specified \"+\ *adj* [1*un-* + *specified*, past part. of *specify*] **:** not specified
un·spectacular \"+\ *adj* **:** not spectacular ⟨studious and ~ . . . one of labor's ablest parliamentarians —*Current Biog.*⟩ ⟨does well an ~ but necessary task⟩ — **un·spectacularly** \"+\ *adv*
un·speculative \"+\ *adj* **:** not speculative: as **a :** not pondering or given to thought ⟨exhibits a facile and ~ mind⟩ **b :** not risky **:** of a conservative nature **:** SOUND ⟨containing a large number of bonds and blue-chip stocks, his investment portfolio is clearly ~⟩
un·sped \"+\ *adj* [ME, fr. 1*un-* + *sped*, past part. of *speden* to succeed — more at SPEED] **:** not performed or accomplished ⟨returns with his mission ~⟩
un·spell \ˌən+\ *vt* [2*un-* + *spell*, n.] **:** to break the power of or release from a spell
un·spent \"+\ *adj* [ME, fr. 1*un-* + *spent*] **1 :** not spent or used **:** UNEXPENDED ⟨a corresponding amount of income will be left ~ —W.M.Dacey⟩ **2 :** not consumed or used up ⟨continuing on with ~ momentum⟩
un·sphere \"+\ *vt* [2*un-* + *sphere*] **:** to remove (as a planet) from its sphere **:** DISPLACE
un·spike \"+\ *vt* [2*un-* + *spike*, n.] **:** to remove a spike from (as the vent of a cannon)
un·spin \"+\ *vt* [2*un-* + *spin*] **:** UNTWIST
unspirited *adj* [1*un-* + *spirited*, adj.] *obs* **:** lacking in spirit **:** SPIRITLESS
un·spiritual \ˌən+\ *adj* **:** not spiritual ⟨the ~ man does not welcome the teachings of the Spirit of God —W.F.Howard⟩ — **un·spiritually** \"+\ *adv* — **un·spiritualness** \"+\ *n*
un·spiritualize \"+\ *vt* [2*un-* + *spiritualize*] **:** to remove spiritual qualities from ⟨materialism can ~ man⟩
un·spit \"+\ *vt* [2*un-* + *spit*] *archaic* **:** to take or release from a spit
un·split \"+\ *adj* **:** not split or divided
un·spoiled \"+\ *adj* [1*un-* + *spoiled*, past part. of *spoil*] **1 a :** not pillaged or plundered ⟨the land is ~ by war⟩ **b :** not spoiled or decayed **2 a :** not worn or damaged ⟨stamps . . . in perfect condition with the gum ~ —Barbara Hooper⟩ **b :** not marred or altered from a natural or original state esp. by industry, commerce, or tourism ⟨a paradise of color and silence which has somehow remained ~ and uncommercialized —Guy Priest⟩ ⟨primitive, ~, breathtaking in the ruggedness of its mountains and the simplicity of its people —T.H.Fielding⟩ ⟨magnificent coast . . . is ~ by industry —L.D.Stamp⟩ **c :** not deteriorated or impaired in character or disposition by excessive pampering or indulgence or contaminating influences ⟨thanks to the sturdy simplicity of their parents, quite ~ —Nevil Shute⟩ ⟨liked each other at once, both being good-humored . . . and ~ by fame —*Irish Digest*⟩
un·spoken \"+\ *adj* [ME, fr. 1*un-* + *spoken*, past part. of *speken* to speak] **1 :** not spoken or uttered **:** TACIT, UNEXPRESSED ⟨the ~ conclusion is obvious —M.W.Straight⟩ ⟨by some sort of ~ agreement, they patronize a less pretentious shop in the opposite direction —Cabell Phillips⟩ **2 :** not spoken to or addressed — often used with *to* ⟨sitting for hours ~ to⟩ **3 :** not speaking **:** SILENT
un·sporting \"+\ *adj* **:** not sportsmanlike ⟨had beaten . . . at tennis with a nasty, ~ serve —Sinclair Lewis⟩
un·sportsmanlike \"+\ *adj* [1*un-* + *sportsman* + *like*] **:** not sportsmanlike **:** not characteristic of or exhibiting good sportsmanship ⟨to shoot down a bear . . . when he is off his guard is too ~ —A.W.Long⟩
un·spotted \"+\ *adj* [ME, fr. 1*un-* + *spotted*] **:** not spotted **:** free from spot or stain; *esp* **:** free from moral stain ⟨~ by such alleged vices as drinking, smoking, card playing —F.L. Allen⟩ — **un·spottedness** \"+\ *n*
un·spring \"+\ *vt* [2*un-* + *spring*, n.] **:** to loosen or release by or as if by pressing a spring
un·sprung \"+\ *adj* [1*un-* + *sprung*, past part. of *spring*] **:** not sprung; *esp* **:** not equipped with springs ⟨~ parts and units . . . depend entirely upon the resiliency of the tires for protection from road shock —Joseph Heitner⟩
unsprung weight *n* **:** weight (as of a vehicle) not supported by springs
un·spun \ˌən+\ *adj* [1*un-* + *spun*, past part. of *spin*] **:** not spun
un·stability \"+\ *n* [ME *unstabilite*, fr. 1*un-* + *stabilite* stability] **:** INSTABILITY
un·stable \"+\ *adj* [ME, fr. 1*un-* + *stable*] **:** not stable: as **a** (1) **:** not firm or fixed in one place **:** apt to move **:** MOVABLE ⟨snow as ~ as aspic trembled on the steep slope —R.L.Neuberger⟩ ⟨the ~ shifting sands of the desert⟩ (2) **:** lacking steadiness **:** apt to sway or fall ⟨the tower proved to be ~ in a high wind⟩ ⟨the bird flutters on its ~ perch⟩ (3) **:** not steady in movement **:** IRREGULAR ⟨felt the ~ tripping beat of his heart⟩ (4) **:** not firm or substantial **:** WEAK, INSECURE ⟨the young earth was yet ~, the molten forces within were constantly looking for escape —W.E.Swinton⟩ ⟨the road may become so ~ as to compel the imposition of a speed limit —O.S.Nock⟩ ⟨built on an ~ foundation⟩ **b** (1) **:** wavering in purpose or intent **:** VACILLATING ⟨an ~ and uneasy class of yeomen —S.E.Morison & H.S.Commager⟩ ⟨his rather ~ religious convictions —H.E.Starr⟩ ⟨woman's love . . . is volatile, insoluble, ~ —Marcia Anderson⟩ (2) **:** exhibiting or characterized by emotional instability ⟨an ~ temperament —Rex Ingamells⟩ ⟨the ~ prisoners . . . placed in the vague but convenient category of psychopaths —A.H.MacCormick⟩ ⟨had brought an inherently ~ nature to the point of mental and emotional collapse —E.J.Simmons⟩ **c** (1) **:** variable in character or condition **:** liable to change or alteration **:** CHANGEABLE ⟨an ~ world economy . . . subjected to periods of wars, inflation, and depression —*Farmer's Weekly (So. Africa)*⟩ ⟨the wind might change; for it is an ~ world —Charles Kingsley⟩ ⟨~ climate⟩ ⟨~ relationship⟩ (2) **:** readily decomposing or changing otherwise in chemical composition or biological activity — compare LABILE 3, SENSITIVE 4e (3) **:** readily changing in physical state or properties ⟨~ emulsions tend to separate into layers⟩ (4) **:** spontaneously radioactive **syn** see INCONSTANT
unstable equilibrium *n* **:** a state of equilibrium of a body (as a pendulum standing directly upward from its point of support) such that when the body is slightly displaced it departs further from the original position — compare STABLE EQUILIBRIUM
un·stableness \ˌən+\ *n* [ME *unstablenesse*, fr. *unstable* + *-nesse* -ness] **:** the quality or state of being unstable
unstable oscillation *n* **:** an oscillation (as of an airplane) whose amplitude increases continuously until an altitude is reached from which there is no tendency to return toward the original altitude, the motion becoming a steady divergence — compare STABLE OSCILLATION
un·stably \ˌən+\ *adv* [ME, partly fr. 1*un-* + *stably* & partly fr. *unstable* + *-ly*] **:** in an unstable manner **:** without steadiness
un·stack \"+\ *vt* [2*un-* + *stack*] **:** to remove from a stack or pile
un·staid \"+\ *adj* **1** *obs* **:** not demure, reserved, or well ordered in behavior **2 :** UNCONTROLLED, UNRESTRAINED ⟨~ thoughts⟩ ⟨~ delights⟩ **3** *obs* **:** CHANGEABLE, VACILLATING, UNSTABLE
un·stained \"+\ *adj* **1 :** not stained or discolored **:** not spotted ⟨keeps his clothing ~⟩ **2 :** not morally blemished or stained **:** UNSULLIED ⟨his thoughts were ~ with selfishness and lust —John Steinbeck⟩ ⟨felt a wild longing for the ~ purity of his boyhood —Oscar Wilde⟩
un·stalked \"+\ *adj* **:** lacking a stalk or stem
un·stamped \"+\ *adj* [1*un-* + *stamped*, past part. of *stamp*] **:** not stamped with an official device or impression; *also* **:** not affixed with an official stamp or adhesive label to certify payment of a tax or duty
un·starred \"+\ *adj* **:** not starred; *esp* **:** not marked or decorated with a star or asterisk
un·state \"+\ *vt* [2*un-* + *state*] **:** to deprive of state dignity or rank ⟨Caesar will ~ his happiness —Shak.⟩
un·stated \"+\ *adj* [1*un-* + *stated*, adj.] **:** not stated or set forth ⟨his action is clear but his reason remains ~⟩
un·statesmanlike \"+\ *adj* [1*un-* + *statesman* + *like*] **:** not statesmanlike ⟨~ procedure⟩
un·statutable \"+\ *adj* [1*un-* + *statute* + *-able*] **:** contrary to or not according with a statute ⟨an ~ procedure⟩
1**un·stayed** \"+\ *adj* [1*un-* + *stayed*, past part. of *stay* to hinder] **:** not hindered or checked **:** UNIMPEDED ⟨goes his way ~ by any minor obstacles⟩
2**unstayed** \"\ *adj* [1*un-* + *stayed*, past part. of *stay* to support] **:** not steadfast **:** not firmly supported ⟨~ in his weakness except by faith⟩
3**unstayed** \"\ *adj* [1*un-* + *stay*, n. + *-ed*] **:** not fastened or secured with stays ⟨the bowsprit was a makeshift sort of spar, crooked and ~ —Alan Moore⟩
unstdy *abbr* unsteady
un·steadfast \ˌən+\ *adj* [ME *unstedefast*, fr. 1*un-* + *stedefast* steadfast] **1 :** not steadfast in thought or action **:** VACILLATING ⟨an ~ backslider⟩ ⟨a man of ~ heart⟩ **2 :** UNSTABLE a(1) ⟨the ~ waters of the ocean⟩ — **un·steadfastness** \"+\ *n*
un·steadily \"+\ *adv* [1*un-* + *steadily*] **:** in an unsteady or unstable manner
un·steadiness \"+\ *n* **:** the quality or state of being unsteady
1**un·steady** \"+\ *vt* [2*un-* + *steady*] **:** to make unsteady ⟨joy *unsteadies* his voice⟩ ⟨the drop in ammunition *unsteadied* the artillery action⟩ ⟨he was *unsteadied* by the sudden turn of events⟩
2**unsteady** \"\ *adj* [1*un-* + *steady*, adj.] **:** not steady: as **a :** not firm or solid **:** not fixed in position ⟨the man's hand was ~ as he poured the wine —George Meredith⟩ ⟨climbing carefully up the ~ ladder⟩ **b :** UNSTABLE b(1) ⟨were excited and ~ and . . . required time to collect themselves —J.A. Froude⟩ ⟨his mind becomes ~ in a crisis⟩ **c :** marked by change or fluctuation **:** CHANGEABLE ⟨a new and yet ~ world of discovery, hope, failure, glory —H.A.L.Craig⟩ ⟨~ business conditions⟩ ⟨this ~ time⟩ **d :** not uniform or even **:** IRREGULAR ⟨the gas jet . . . threw an ~ light on her features —Ellen Glasgow⟩ ⟨the lady feels her pulse's beat ~ —Elinor Wylie⟩ ⟨a decade . . . of somewhat ~ growth —F.A.Ogg & Harold Zink⟩
un·steel \ˌən+\ *vt* [2*un-* + *steel*] **:** to make soft or penetrable **:** DISARM ⟨the gentle appeal ~*ed* his heart⟩
un·stemmed \"+\ *adj* **:** not having the stem removed
un·step \"+\ *vt* [2*un-* + *step*] **:** to remove (a mast) from its step ⟨the canvas came down with a rush, and the mast was *unstepped* —Luis Marden⟩
un·sterilized \"+\ *adj* [1*un-* + *sterilized*, past part. of *sterilize*] **:** not sterilized ⟨~ milk⟩
un·stick \"+\ *vt* [2*un-* + *stick*] **:** to cause to draw apart **:** RELEASE, UNFASTEN
un·stiffen \"+\ *vt* [2*un-* + *stiffen*] **:** to remove the stiffness from **:** make limp or flexible ⟨the penetrating heat ~*s* his joints⟩ ⟨pragmatism ~*s* all our theories, limbers them up and sets each one at work —William James⟩
un·stimulating \"+\ *adj* [1*un-* + *stimulating*, pres. part. of *stimulate*] **:** not stimulating
un·sting \"+\ *vt* [2*un-* + *sting*] **:** to remove the sting of
un·stinted \"+\ *adj* [ME, fr. 1*un-* + *stinted*, past part. of *stinten* to stint] **:** not restrained or restricted **:** generously or freely given ⟨his bravery and resourcefulness won him . . . ~ praise —E.M.Coulter⟩ ⟨the deep civic convictions, the integrity, and the ~ devotion —C.T.Lanham⟩ — **un·stintedly** \"+\ *adv*
un·stinting \"+\ *adj* [1*un-* + *stinting*, pres. part. of *stint*] **:** not restricting or holding back **:** giving or contributing freely or generously ⟨teachers who sent in reports on his model lessons were ~ in their praise —Robertson Davies⟩ ⟨called for ~ support of the United Nations —I.G.Blake⟩ ⟨gave his unqualified backing to . . . ~ aid to Britain —Roscoe Drummond⟩ — **un·stintingly** \"+\ *adv*
un·stirred \ˌən+\ *adj* [ME *unstired*, fr. 1*un-* + *stired*, past part. of *stiren* to stir] **:** not stirred
un·stitch \"+\ *vt* [2*un-* + *stitch*] **:** to take out the stitches of; *also* **:** to undo or separate by removing the stitches
un·stock \"+\ *vt* [2*un-* + *stock*] **:** to remove the stock from (as a gun)
un·stocked \"+\ *adj* [ME *unstokked*, fr. 1*un-* + *stokked*, past part. of *stokken* to stock] **:** not stocked: as **a :** not equipped or provided with a stock ⟨~ rifle⟩ **b :** not furnished with animals, fish, or livestock ⟨~ woods⟩ ⟨~ pond⟩
un·stop \"+\ *vt* [ME *unstoppen*, fr. 2*un-* + *stoppen* to stop] **1 :** to free from any obstruction **:** OPEN **2 :** to remove the stopper or plug from (as a bottle, cask, or vent) ⟨~ this flask —William Alfred⟩
un·stoppable \"+\ *adj* [1*un-* + *stop* + *-able*] **:** not stoppable ⟨as ~ as the wind —Han Suyin⟩ ⟨at his present pace, he may just be ~ —*Newsweek*⟩ — **un·stop·pa·bly** \-blē, -li\ *adv*
un·stopped \ˌən+\ *adj* [ME, fr. 1*un-* + *stopped*] **:** not stopped: as **a :** not stoppered or plugged **:** not closed ⟨an ~ rabbit hole⟩ **b :** not prevented or hindered ⟨is coming on ~⟩ **c** *of a consonant* **:** OPEN, CONTINUANT **d :** RUN-ON ⟨~ lines often occur in his verse⟩
un·stopper \"+\ *vt* [2*un-* + *stopper*] **:** to remove the stopper from **:** UNSTOP ⟨~*ed* the decanter —William Faulkner⟩ ⟨will ~ the economy so that the forces for full employment . . . are freed —*Time*⟩
un·storied \"+\ *adj* **:** not having a history **:** not told or celebrated in story ⟨the land . . . still ~ —Robert Frost⟩
un·stow \"+\ *vt* [2*un-* + *stow*] **:** to empty of cargo or contents **:** UNLOAD ⟨~ the ship⟩ ⟨~ the goods in the hold⟩ ⟨began to ~ the panniers —Henry Green⟩
un·strain \"+\ *vt* [2*un-* + *strain*] **:** to relieve from strain
un·strained \"+\ *adj* [ME *unstreined*, fr. 1*un-* + *streined*, past part. of *streinen* to strain] **:** not strained: as **a :** not placed under a strain **:** not stretched ⟨the campaign would not leave party loyalties ~⟩ ⟨~ iron⟩ **b :** not forced or resulting from undue effort ⟨his playing is facile and ~⟩ **c :** not put through a strainer ⟨~ juice⟩ **:** not cleared or purified by straining ⟨~ oil⟩
un·strap \"+\ *vt* [2*un-* + *strap*] **:** to unfasten, remove, or loose a strap from ⟨~*s* the trunk⟩ ⟨the hikers ~ their packs⟩ ⟨the cowboy ~*s* his gun belt⟩
un·stratified \"+\ *adj* [1*un-* + *stratified*, past part. of *stratify*] **:** not stratified; *specif* **:** not deposited in layers ⟨glacial till is ~⟩
un·strengthen \"+\ *vt* [2*un-* + *strengthen*] **:** to make weak **:** WEAKEN
un·stress \"+\ *n* **:** a syllable having relatively weak stress or lacking in phonetic prominence
un·stressed \"+\ *adj* [1*un-* + *stressed*, past part. of *stress*] **:** not stressed or emphasized; *specif* **:** not bearing a stress or accent
un·stretch \ˌən+\ *vb* [2*un-* + *stretch*] *vt* **:** to release the tension of **:** RELAX ~ *vi* **:** SLACKEN
un·string \"+\ *vt* [2*un-* + *string*] **1 a :** to loosen or remove the string from (a bow or musical instrument) **b :** to untie the strings of (a purse) **2 :** to remove from a string ⟨~*s* the beads⟩ **3 :** to make weak, disordered, or unstable ⟨the news *unstrung* his nerves⟩ ⟨getting married ~*s* some men —Owen Wister⟩
un·striped \"+\ *adj* **:** not striped or striated ⟨~ muscle⟩
un·stripped \"+\ *adj* [1*un-* + *stripped*, past part. of *strip*] **:** not stripped **:** not detached by stripping
un·structured \"+\ *adj* **:** lacking structure or organization: as **a** (1) **:** not having an integrated system or hierarchy of the roles, functions, or statuses of an organized society ⟨the situation was ~, for there were no persons vested with authority by virtue of station or public office —*Amer. Anthropologist*⟩ ⟨were experiencing a permissive and relatively ~ situation that included strong demands for individual participation —G.E. Swanson⟩ ⟨in a neighborhood gang . . . with a relatively ~ system —*Jour. of Social Issues*⟩ (2) **:** not forming a part of such an integrated system or hierarchy ⟨the position of the poet is ~ . . . in our society —*Report: Harvard Laboratory of Social Relations*⟩ ⟨the defeated candidate has an extremely ~ status —R.M.Goldman⟩ **b :** not formally organized into a set or conventional pattern **:** AMBIGUOUS ⟨questions on the effect of price and flavor were ~ . . . purposely vague to encourage respondents to give an answer —*Australian Jour. of Dairy Tech.*⟩ ⟨in an ~ or new situation the person feels insecure because the psychological directions are not defined —Kurt Lewin⟩ ⟨an ~ situation . . . with no frame of reference except such as may be created by the subject himself —W.S.Ray⟩
un·strung \"+\ *adj* [1*un-* + *strung*, past part. of *string*] **1 :** having the strings loosened or detached **2 :** nervously relaxed or weakened **:** UNNERVED, DISCOMPOSED ⟨the nerves of the men were much ~ —H.A.Chippendale⟩ ⟨felt weak, ~, incapable of rational effort —Ellen Glasgow⟩

un·stuck \"+\ *adj* [¹*un-* + *stuck*, past part. of *stick*] **1 :** released from being glued, fastened, or bound ⟨glancing through the photographs one day . . . she had found that one beginning to come ~ —Elizabeth Taylor⟩ ⟨the gears locked in second and would not come ~ —Herbert Passin⟩ **2 :** brought to a state of disorder, disorganization, or incoherence ⟨the government's stabilization program . . . has recently shown signs of coming ~ —*N.Y.Times*⟩ ⟨price programs became ~ because little grain was available —*Newsweek*⟩ ⟨projects were always coming ~ at the last minute —Bruce Catton⟩

un·studied \"+\ *adj* [ME, fr. ¹*un-* + *studied*, past part. of *studien* to study] **1** *obs* **:** not studied or contemplated **:** NEGLECTED **2 :** lacking knowledge gained by study often in a specified field **:** UNLEARNED ⟨is ~ in Latin as he is in many other matters⟩ **3 :** not forced or unnecessarily elaborated by study or artifice: as **a :** UNAFFECTED, NATURAL ⟨the clusters of houses set beside these winding lanes have a simple ~ charm —*Amer. Guide Series: Mich.*⟩ ⟨was possessed of a nervous temperament and his gestures were rapid and ~ —Marie B. Owen⟩ **b :** CASUAL, OFFHAND, IMPROMPTU ⟨an air of ~ spontaneous utterance is apt to be as painstakingly achieved as any other quality in the poetic fiction —Susanne K. Langer⟩

un·studious \"+\ *adj* **:** not studious

un·stuff \"+\ *vt* [²*un-* + *stuff*] **:** to take the stuffing from or out of

un·stylish \"+\ *adj* **:** not stylish ⟨wearing ~ clothes⟩ — **un·stylishly** \"+\ *adv* — **un·stylishness** \"+\ *n*

un·subdued \ˌən+\ *adj* **:** not subdued — **un·subduedness** \"+\ *n*

un·suberized \"+\ *adj* [¹*un-* + *suberized*, past part. of *suberize*] **:** not corky **:** not converted into phellem

un·subsidized \"+\ *adj* [¹*un-* + *subsidized*, past part. of *subsidize*] **:** not subsidized ⟨the shipping industry . . . is not only privately owned and managed but ~ —E.K.Lindley⟩

un·substantial \"+\ *adj* [ME, fr. ¹*un-* + *substantial*] **:** not substantial: as **a :** lacking a basis in fact ⟨an ~ argument⟩ ⟨an ~ hope⟩ ⟨~ speculation⟩ **b :** not having matter or substance **:** VISIONARY, UNREAL ⟨an ~ phantom . . . luring men away from safety and ease —Bertrand Russell⟩ ⟨remote and ~ as the most distant nebulae —G.W.Russell⟩ ⟨pale and ~ in the moonlight, the shadowy figure of a man was moving —C.B.Nordhoff & J.N.Hall⟩ **c :** lacking firmness or strength in construction **:** WEAK, UNSTABLE ⟨a chipping sparrow . . . collecting stray hairs from the farm horses' tails for lining her very ~ nest —W.P.Smith⟩ ⟨a child of wax, delicate and charming and ~ —H.G.Wells⟩ ⟨birds and butterflies and such ~ things —W.H. Hudson †1922⟩ — **un·substantially** \"+\ *adv*

un·substantiality \"+\ *n* **:** the quality or state of being unsubstantial **:** INSUBSTANTIALITY

un·substantiate \"+\ *vt* [²*un-* + *substantiate*] **:** to divest of substantiality **:** make unsubstantial

un·substantiated \"+\ *adj* [¹*un-* + *substantiated*, past part. of *substantiate*] **:** not substantiated; *esp* **:** not supported or borne out by fact ⟨another example of making an ~ assertion and then treating it as an established fact —Ruth P. Randall⟩

un·substituted \ˌən+\ *adj* [¹*un-* + *substituted*, past part. of *substitute*] **:** not substituted

un·subtle \"+\ *adj* **:** not subtle ⟨thinks these characteristics are rather barbarian and ~ —Owen & Eleanor Lattimore⟩ ⟨the ~ statement that love and years are the only tragedy —Malcolm Cowley⟩ ⟨weaves a light romance with all the direct charm of a strong and ~ plot —*Times Lit. Supp.*⟩

un·subtly \"+\ *adv* **:** in an unsubtle manner

un·success \"+\ *n* **:** lack of success **:** FAILURE ⟨effort which has been waged . . . for over 15 years usually with disheartening ~ —H.L.Varney⟩ ⟨~*es* and futilities —D.C.Peattie⟩

un·successful \"+\ *adj* **:** not successful **:** not meeting with or producing success ⟨his early efforts to raise capital were ~ —Frank Monaghan⟩ ⟨attempted some short stories and novels which were ~ —Witmer Stone⟩ ⟨was the son of an illiterate and ~ . . . immigrant —F.L.Paxson⟩ ⟨was an ~ . . . candidate for congress —H.K.Beale⟩

un·successfully \"+\ *adv* **:** in an unsuccessful manner **:** without success

un·successfulness \"+\ *n* **:** the quality or state of being unsuccessful

un·successive \"+\ *adj* **:** not successive **:** not following in order or in series

un·sufferable \"+\ *adj* [ME, fr. ¹*un-* + *sufferable*] **1 :** not to be suffered or borne with patience or composure **:** INTOLERABLE, INSUFFERABLE ⟨an ~ wrong⟩ ⟨~ pride⟩ ⟨an ~ snob⟩ **2 :** so painful or severe as to be physically unbearable ⟨~ cold⟩ ⟨~ torment⟩ ⟨~ pain⟩ — **un·sufferably** \"+\ *adv*

un·sufficient \"+\ *adj* [ME, fr. ¹*un-* + *sufficient*] **1** *obs* **:** INSUFFICIENT **a 2 :** lacking in the required strength, quality, or amount **:** INADEQUATE ⟨the present aid is quite ~ to meet the requirements —*Dawn*⟩ — **un·sufficiently** \"+\ *adv*

un·suggestive \"+\ *adj* **:** not suggestive **:** UNSTIMULATING ⟨his walk was curiously uninspiring and ~ —Willa Cather⟩

un·suit \ˌən+\ *vt* [²*un-* + *suit*] **:** to make unfit ⟨long periods of staff duty tend to disqualify and ~ the once promising commander —H.H.Arnold & I.C.Eaker⟩

un·suitability \"+\ *n* **:** UNSUITABLENESS

un·suitable \"+\ *adj* **:** not suitable or fitting **:** UNBECOMING, INAPPROPRIATE ⟨a new element in life renders . . . the operation of the old instincts ~ —A.N.Whitehead⟩ ⟨in certain conditions alcohol is ~ as an antifreeze⟩ — often used with *to* or *for* ⟨compositions most ~ to this medium —Osbert Sitwell⟩ ⟨an ~ article for export —Vernon Bartlett⟩

un·suitableness \"+\ *n* **:** the quality or state of being unsuitable

un·suitably \"+\ *adv* **:** in an unsuitable manner **:** without suitability

un·suited \"+\ *adj* [¹*un-* + *suited*, past part. of *suit*] **:** not suited or fit **:** not adapted **:** UNFIT ⟨a mental and physical fatigue . . . will break down the less rugged and the temperamentally ~ —H.H.Arnold & I.C.Eaker⟩ ⟨a material utterly ~ for such use —Lafcadio Hearn⟩ ⟨thinks your hobby ~ to your position in life —Dorothy Sayers⟩

un·sullied \"+\ *adj* [¹*un-* + *sullied*, past part. of *sully*] **:** not sullied or stained **:** spotlessly clean **:** IMMACULATE ⟨the ~ snow of mountains —L.P.Smith⟩ ⟨the ~ splendor of eternal youth —Oscar Wilde⟩ ⟨~ name⟩ ⟨~ reputation⟩

un·sulliedness \"+\ *n* -ES **:** the quality or state of being unsullied

un·summed \"+\ *adj* [ME *unsumed*, fr. ¹*un-* + *sumed*, past part. of *sumen* to sum] **:** UNCOUNTED

un·sung \"+\ *adj* [¹*un-* + *sung*, past part. of *sing*] **1 :** not sung **:** not rendered in song **2 :** not celebrated in song or verse or otherwise praised ⟨our writers, artists, and musicians . . . go ~ —Cornelia O. Skinner⟩ ⟨the creator of infiltration is the ~ prophet of the new age in warfare —S.L.A.Marshall⟩ ⟨massed infantry to do the bloody ~ job of mopping up the enemy —*Time*⟩

un·sunned \"+\ *adj* [¹*un-* + *sunned*, past part. of *sun*] **1 a :** not exposed to sunlight ⟨the ~ northerly face of the cliff⟩ **b :** not affected or changed by the sun's light or heat ⟨a creeping chilliness . . . probably caused by the ~ morning air —Thomas Hardy⟩ **c :** not burned or tanned by the sun ⟨the pale ~ features of the city dweller⟩ **d :** unlighted by the sun ⟨the ~ landscape⟩ **2 :** not conveyed or open to the public ⟨the ~ art treasures kept locked up in a private gallery⟩

un·supervised \"+\ *adj* [¹*un-* + *supervised*, past part. of *supervise*] **:** not supervised **:** not under constant observation ⟨the school maintains ~ study halls during free periods⟩ ⟨reliable workers are generally ~⟩

un·supplied \"+\ *adj* [¹*un-* + *supplied*, past part. of *supply*] **:** not supplied: as **a** *archaic* **:** not furnished or provided with **b :** not satisfied **:** UNFILLED ⟨a tremendous ~ book demand —Edward Bok⟩ ⟨the ~ needs of the poor⟩

un·supportable \"+\ *adj* **:** not supportable: as **a** *archaic* **:** OFFENSIVE, VEXATIOUS **b :** hardly to be suffered or borne **:** INTOLERABLE, INSUPPORTABLE ⟨war would be ~ to the human conscience —H.C.Dillard⟩

un·supported \"+\ *adj* [¹*un-* + *supported*, past part. of *support*] **1 a :** not supported or verified **:** UNSUBSTANTIATED ⟨his assumption . . . is an ~ hypothesis —W.G.Byron⟩ **b :** not backed up or assisted ⟨the artillery rolled off leaving the infantry ~⟩ **2 :** not held up or sustained ⟨removal of the center post will leave the roof ~⟩ ⟨~ portions of the body, due to their inertia, may tend to lag behind —H.G.Armstrong⟩ — **un·sup·port·ed·ly** *adv* — **un·sup·port·ed·ness** *n* -ES

un·suppressed \"+\ *adj* [¹*un-* + *suppressed*, past part. of *suppress*] **:** not suppressed ⟨~ feelings⟩ ⟨~ rage⟩

un·sure \"+\ *adj* [ME, fr. ¹*un-* + *sure*] **1** *obs* **:** not safe from danger or mishap **:** INSECURE **b :** lacking in security or safety **:** DANGEROUS, UNSAFE **2 a :** lacking confidence or assurance **:** UNCERTAIN ⟨approached their . . . problems unprepared, ~, inexperienced —R.E.Danielson⟩ ⟨a young man . . . ~ of himself and of his future —L.A.G.Strong⟩ **b :** not having certain knowledge ⟨was still ~ whether they were human or not —J.D. Beresford⟩ — often used with *of* ⟨~ of public support —Paul Rosenfeld⟩ ⟨is ~ of the results of his calculations⟩ **c :** marked by lack of confidence, assurance, or certainty ⟨his memory was curiously ~ —H.G.Wells⟩ ⟨moving with ~ steps⟩ ⟨the place of either manifestation in a cultural sequence remains ~ —A.L. Kroeber⟩ **3 a :** not steadfast or stable **:** CONTINGENT, PRECARIOUS ⟨the ~ state of our existence⟩ **b** *archaic* **:** of doubtful or uncertain prospect **4 :** not reliable **:** UNTRUSTWORTHY ⟨an ~ deceitful man⟩

un·sureness \"+\ *n* [ME *unsurenesse*, fr. *unsure* + *-nesse* -ness] **:** the quality or state of being unsure ⟨his ~ of himself —Osbert Sitwell⟩

un·surety \"+\ *n* [ME *unsuirte*, fr. ¹*un-* + *suirte*, *surete* surety] **:** lack of surety **:** UNCERTAINTY, INSECURITY ⟨the forced jocularity which is really ~ masquerading —H.M.Reynolds⟩

un·surmountable \"+\ *adj* **:** INSURMOUNTABLE ⟨an ~ barrier⟩ ⟨an ~ obstacle⟩ — **un·sur·mount·able·ness** *n* -ES

un·sur·pass·able \ˌənsərˈpasəbəl, -paas-, -pais-, -pȧs-\ *adj* [¹*un-* + *surpass* + *-able*] **:** incapable of being surpassed **:** not to be exceeded ⟨was hailed with ~ enthusiasm —Fred Whishaw⟩ ⟨~ standards of workmanship⟩ ⟨~ skill⟩ — **un·sur·pass·ably** \-blē, -li\ *adv*

un·surpassed \ˌən+\ *adj* [¹*un-* + *surpassed*, past part. of *surpass*] **:** not surpassed or exceeded usu. in excellence ⟨as a teacher of practical chemistry he was ~ by his contemporaries —L.C.Newell⟩ ⟨the swamp is an ~ laboratory for biologists —*Amer. Guide Series: La.*⟩ ⟨the ~ beauty of the scenes —Matthew Arnold⟩

un·surprised \"+\ *adj* [¹*un-* + *surprised*, past part. of *surprise*] **:** not surprised **:** not expressing surprise ⟨~ . . . at such gaps in his vocabulary —Jack London⟩ ⟨that ~ obstinate look of his —Edith Sitwell⟩

un·surprising \"+\ *adj* [¹*un-* + *surprising*, pres. part. of *surprise*] **:** not surprising or unexpected ⟨the ~ findings of the report⟩ ⟨his violent reaction was ~⟩ — **un·surprisingly** \"+\ *adv*

un·susceptibility \"+\ *n* **:** the quality or state of being unsusceptible

un·susceptible \"+\ *adj* **:** not susceptible **:** not able to be moved, affected, or impressed ⟨is generally ~ to disease⟩ ⟨such a missile . . . must also be ~ to electronic countermeasures —*Scientific Monthly*⟩

un·suspected \ˌən+\ *adj* [¹*un-* + *suspected*, past part. of *suspect*] **1 :** not being suspected ⟨observing ~ all their secret plottings⟩ **2 :** not regarded or considered suspiciously ⟨remaining ~ as the head of the spy ring⟩ **3 :** not known to exist **:** UNEXPECTED, UNKNOWN ⟨saw myriads of minute living creatures, the existence of which had hitherto been ~ —R.W. Miner⟩ ⟨things obscurely felt surged up from ~ depths in her —Edith Wharton⟩ ⟨~ turnings in roadways —Ludwig Lewisohn⟩

un·suspectedly \"+\ *adv* **:** in an unsuspected manner **:** without being suspected

un·suspectedness \"+\ *n* **:** the quality or state of being unsuspected ⟨the ~ of the evidence is as bad a shock as the immediate effects⟩

un·suspecting \"+\ *adj* [¹*un-* + *suspecting*, pres. part. of *suspect*] **:** not suspecting **:** not being suspicious ⟨took refuge . . . in the doorway of Mount Vernon church, all ~ of the fact that I would one day be its minister —Sidney Lovett⟩ ⟨deceiving the ~ public —A.E.Wiggam⟩

un·sus·pect·ing·ly *adv* **:** without suspicion ⟨you couldn't all at once ~ have been caught —Mary Austin⟩

un·suspicion \ˌən+\ *n* **:** lack of suspicion ⟨sometimes a man's ~ is wiser —Booth Tarkington⟩

un·suspicious \"+\ *adj* **:** not suspicious **:** UNSUSPECTING ⟨as long as one remains inside the car, the animals are ~ —Jan Juta⟩ ⟨a carefree ~ fellow —C.B.Nordhoff & J.N.Hall⟩ — **un·suspiciously** \"+\ *adv* — **un·suspiciousness** \"+\ *n*

un·sustainable \"+\ *adj* [¹*un-* + *sustain* + *-able*] **:** not capable of being sustained

un·sustained \"+\ *adj* [¹*un-* + *sustained*, past part. of *sustain*] **:** not sustained: as **a** *obs* **:** not physically sustained or supported **b :** not kept up or supported by some aid ⟨leaving the station feeling empty and ~ —S.H.Adams⟩ ⟨~ any longer by loans, the business failed⟩ **c :** not kept or continued at a consistently high level ⟨a convolution of plots makes for ~ interest —*Current Biog.*⟩

un·swaddle \"+\ *vt* [²*un-* + *swaddle*] **:** to free or take from a swaddle **:** UNSWATHE

un·swallowable \"+\ *adj* [¹*un-* + *swallow* + *-able*] **:** not able to be swallowed

un·swallowed \"+\ *adj* [¹*un-* + *swallowed*, past part. of *swallow*] **:** not swallowed

un·swathe \"+\ *vt* [ME *unswathen*, fr. ²*un-* + *swathen* to swathe] **:** to take a swathe from **:** relieve from a bandage ⟨~ the child⟩

un·swayed \"+\ *adj* [¹*un-* + *swayed*, past part. of *sway*] **:** not moved or affected **:** not influenced ⟨~ by personal considerations⟩

un·swear \"+\ *vb* [²*un-* + *swear*] *vi* **:** to unsay or retract something sworn or firmly stated ⟨the false swear and ~ easily⟩ ~ *vt* **:** to recant or recall (as an oath) esp. by a second oath ⟨he swore his oath only to ~ it next day⟩

un·sweet \"+\ *adj* [ME *unswete*, fr. OE *unswēte*, fr. ¹*un-* + *swēte* sweet] **:** not sweet: as **a :** not pleasant or agreeable **:** DISTASTEFUL ⟨he sometimes finds life ~⟩ **b** (1) **:** not sweet or pleasing to the taste ⟨~ fruit⟩ (2) **:** DRY 16a, 16b **c :** not pleasant to hear ⟨has a fine voice . . . not ~ in its lower ranges —*Theatre Arts*⟩ **d :** having an unpleasant smell **:** FOUL ⟨the ~ sewers of the city⟩

un·sweetened \"+\ *adj* [¹*un-* + *sweetened*, past part. of *sweeten*] **:** not sweet **:** not made sweet

un·swell \"+\ *vb* [ME *unswellen*, fr. ²*un-* + *swellen* to swell] *vi, archaic* **:** to reduce from swelling **:** SUBSIDE ~ *vt, archaic* **:** to reduce the swelling of

un·swelled \"+\ *adj* [¹*un-* + *swelled*, past part. of *swell*] **:** not swelled or swollen

un·swept \"+\ *adj* [¹*un-* + *swept*, past part. of *sweep*] **:** not swept

un·swerving \"+\ *adj* [¹*un-* + *swerving*, pres. part. of *swerve*] **1 :** not swerving or turning aside ⟨a straight narrow clay road . . . tree-lined and ~ across the far-reaching lowlands —*Amer. Guide Series: Vt.*⟩ **2 :** STEADY, UNREMITTING ⟨~ loyalty⟩ ⟨~ integrity⟩ ⟨holds an ~ belief in the democratic form of government —Victor Lewis⟩

un·swerv·ing·ly *adv* **1 :** without swerving or turning aside ⟨the ship drives ~ through the night⟩ ⟨the businessman who goes ~ to business —J.W.Aldridge⟩ **2 :** STEADILY, UNREMITTINGLY ⟨an ~ loyal man —*Current Biog.*⟩ ⟨~ supported . . . foreign policy —R.J.Kerner⟩ ⟨these compulsions do not operate ~ —Max Lerner & Edwin Mims⟩

un·swerv·ing·ness *n* -ES **:** the quality or state of being unswerving

un·swoll·en \ˌən+\ *adj* **:** not swollen

un·sworn \"+\ *adj* **1 :** not sworn in or bound by oath ⟨the witness stands ~⟩ **2 :** not verified or stated on oath ⟨~ testimony⟩

un·syllabic \"+\ *adj* **:** NONSYLLABIC

un·syllabled \"+\ *adj* [¹*un-* + *syllabled*, past part. of *syllable*] **:** not articulated in syllables

unsym- — see UNS-

un·symbolic \"+\ *adj* **:** not symbolic — **un·symbolically** \"+\ *adv*

un·symmetrical \"+\ *also* **un·symmetric** \"+\ *adj* **1 :** not symmetrical **:** lacking symmetry **:** ASYMMETRIC **2** *of an equation or logical proposition* **:** of such a structure that its terms may not be interchanged without altering its value, character, or truth — **un·symmetrically** \"+\ *adv*

un·sympathetic \ˌən+\ *adj* **:** not sympathetic **:** UNRESPONSIVE ⟨his dignity made of him an aloof and ~ figure —Stringfellow Barr⟩ ⟨could tackle a theme that was temperamentally ~ to him —Eric Newton⟩ ⟨the revolt was directed against an unrepresentative and ~ officialdom —G.M.Trevelyan⟩ — **unsympathetically** \"+\ *adv*

un·sympathizing \"+\ *adj* [¹*un-* + *sympathizing*, pres. part. of *sympathize*] **:** not sympathizing ⟨an uncharitable and ~ attitude⟩ — **un·sympathizingly** \"+\ *adv*

un·systematic \"+\ *also* **un·systematical** \"+\ *adj* **:** not systematic **:** lacking systematic arrangement, method, or organization ⟨the ~ and fragmentary records that have come down to us —J.G.Edwards⟩ ⟨does his work in an ~ manner⟩ — **un·systematically** \"+\ *adv*

un·systematized \"+\ *adj* [¹*un-* + *systematized*, past part. of *systematize*] **:** not systematized **:** not planned, ordered, or done according to a system ⟨an ~ procedure⟩ ⟨in an ~ fashion⟩

unt \ˈənt\ *n* -S [origin unknown] *dial Eng* **:** a European mole (*Talpa europaeus*)

un·tackle \ˌən·+\ *vt* [²*un-* + *tackle*] **:** to take the tackle from **:** rid of tackling or harness

un·tactful \"+\ *adj* **:** lacking in tact ⟨an intelligent but overzealous and ~ officer —*Nation*⟩ — **un·taotfully** \"+\ *adv* — **un·tact·ful·ness** *n*

un·tainted \"+\ *adj* [¹*un-* + *tainted*, past part. of *taint*] **1 :** not corrupted or infected **:** not spoiled **:** free from taint **:** UNBLEMISHED ⟨a young dreamer with ~ senses —W.J.Fisher⟩ ⟨is gratifyingly ~ by . . . stuffy critical phraseology —Henri Peyse⟩ **2** *obs* **:** not attainted ⟨~, unexamined, free, at liberty —Shak.⟩ — **un·taint·ed·ly** *adv* — **un·taint·ed·ness** *n* -ES

un·takable \"+\ *adj* **:** not capable of being taken ⟨an ~ fortress⟩

un·taken \"+\ *adj* [ME, fr. ¹*un-* + *taken*, past part. of *taken* to take] **:** not taken ⟨an ~ city⟩ ⟨left no opportunity ~⟩

un·talented \"+\ *adj* **:** not talented **:** not endowed with superior talent ⟨the talented child of ~ parents⟩

un·talked-of \ˌən·ˈtȯk,təv, -ˌtäv\ *adj* [¹*un-* + *talked of*, past part. form of the phrase *talk of*] **:** not talked about **:** not mentioned

un·tamable \ˌən·+\ *adj* **:** not capable of being tamed ⟨an ~ animal⟩ ⟨sweeps along the ~ flood —J.C.Mangan⟩ — **un·tam·able·ness** *n* — **un·tam·ably** \-blē\ *adv*

un·tamed \"+\ *adj* [¹*un-* + *tamed*, past part. of *tame*] **:** not tamed **:** UNSUBDUED, WILD ⟨the ~ background of forest and prairie —Dorothy Dondore⟩ ⟨a haughty, almost fierce, uneasy look — an ~ look —John Galsworthy⟩ — **un·tamed·ly** *adv* — **un·tamed·ness** *n* -ES

un·tangible \"+\ *adj* **:** INTANGIBLE

un·tangle \"+\ *vt* [²*un-* + *tangle*] **:** to loose from tangles **:** straighten out **:** DISENTANGLE ⟨drank, set down his glass, and *untangled* his legs —Hamilton Basso⟩ ⟨aided in the reorganization of municipal administration, *untangled* financial difficulties —T.H.Jack⟩ **syn** see EXTRICATE

un·tanned \"+\ *adj* **:** not put through a tanning process ⟨~ leather⟩

un·tapped \"+\ *adj* [¹*un-* + *tapped*, past part. of *tap*] **1 :** not subjected to tapping ⟨an ~ sugar maple⟩ ⟨an ~ keg⟩ **2 :** not drawn upon or utilized ⟨the ~ stockrooms of our minds —G.R.Harrison⟩ ⟨~ natural resources⟩

un·tarnished \"+\ *adj* [¹*un-* + *tarnished*, past part. of *tarnish*] **:** not tarnished **:** free from stain or blemish ⟨an ~ reputation⟩

un·tarred \"+\ *adj* [¹*un-* + *tarred*, past part. of *tar*] **:** not tarred

un·tasted \"+\ *adj* [¹*un-* + *tasted*, past part. of *taste*] **:** not tasted ⟨~ food⟩ **:** not sampled or tried out ⟨all his virtues . . . are like to rot ~ —Shak.⟩

un·taught \"+\ *adj* [ME *untaght*, fr. ¹*un-* + *taght*, past part. of *techen* to teach] **1 :** not instructed or trained **:** IGNORANT, UNTUTORED ⟨unusually interesting . . . not only for the music lover, but also for many who think they know a thing or two —Richard Aldrich⟩ **2 :** NAÏVE, NATURAL, SPONTANEOUS ⟨~ kindness⟩ **syn** see IGNORANT

un·taught·ness *n* **:** the quality or state of being untaught

un·tax \ˌən·+\ *vt* [²*un-* + *tax*] **:** to take a tax from **:** remove from taxation

un·taxed \"+\ *adj* [¹*un-* + *taxed*, past part. of *tax*] **:** not subjected to taxation ⟨an ~ expense account⟩

un·teach \"+\ *vt* [²*un-* + *teach*] **1 :** to cause to unlearn something ⟨an employee who has learned outmoded procedures on previous jobs must first be *untaught*⟩ **2 :** to demonstrate the falsity of **:** teach the contrary of something previously believed or accepted ⟨will take a generation to ~ this monstrous lie —Upton Sinclair⟩

un·teachable \"+\ *adj* [ME, fr. ¹*un-* + *techen* to teach + *-able*] **1 :** not teachable **:** resisting guidance or instruction **:** STUBBORN ⟨is opinionated and rather ~ —Stephen Haggard⟩ **2 :** not capable of being conveyed or developed by teaching ⟨an ~ skill⟩ — **un·teach·able·ness** *n*

un·team \"+\ *vt* [²*un-* + *team*] *archaic* **:** to unyoke a team from

un·technical \"+\ *adj* **1 :** lacking technical training or skill ⟨may seem wearisome to an ~ reader —*Amer. Mercury*⟩ **2 :** not technical in meaning or style ⟨in clear, ~, effective style —*School & Society*⟩ — **un·technically** \"+\ *adv*

untell *vt* [²*un-* + *tell*] *obs* **:** to make as if not counted **:** nullify the passage of ⟨that time could turn up his swift sandy glass, to untell the days —Thomas Heywood⟩

un·tell·able \ˌən·ˈteləbəl\ *adj* [ME, fr. ¹*un-* + *tellen* to tell + *-able*] **:** INEXPRESSIBLE ⟨a thing of ~ splendor —Lucius Beebe⟩ ⟨the ecstasy of this experience is ~ —A.J.Russell⟩ — **un·tell·ably** \-blē\ *adv*

un·tempered \ˌən·+\ *adj* [ME, fr. ¹*un-* + *tempered*] **1 a :** lacking in moderation **:** INTEMPERATE, UNCONTROLLED ⟨the inhumanity of his ~ principles —M.S.Dworkin⟩ **b :** not made less extreme **:** UNMODIFIED ⟨individualism ~ by social responsibilities and loyalties —F.M. & Marie Keesing⟩ **2 :** not brought to a proper consistency ⟨~ mortar⟩ **:** not hardened ⟨~ steel⟩ **3** *of a musical scale* **:** PURE 1b(2)

un·tempting \"+\ *adj* **:** UNATTRACTIVE, UNINVITING ⟨~ food⟩ ⟨find the night dark and windy and ~ —F.A.Swinnerton⟩ — **un·tempt·ing·ly** *adv*

un·tenability \"+\ *n* **:** the quality or state of being untenable

un·tenable \"+\ *adj* **1 :** not able to be defended or maintained **:** INDEFENSIBLE ⟨an ~ position⟩ ⟨their arguments were found so ~ that they themselves renounced them —Samuel Butler †1902⟩ **2 :** not able to be occupied ⟨found the place ~ —Edith Wharton⟩ — **un·ten·able·ness** *n*

un·tenant \"+\ *vt* [²*un-* + *tenant*] **1 :** to remove a tenant from **2 :** LEAVE, QUIT

un·ten·ant·able \"+əbəl\ *adj* **:** incapable of being occupied or lived in ⟨an ~ house⟩ ⟨an ~ island⟩

un·tenanted \ˌən·+\ *adj* [¹*un-* + *tenanted*, past part. of *tenant*] **:** not tenanted **:** not leased to or occupied by a tenant ⟨very little unclaimed and ~ land —*Amer. Guide Series: Mich.*⟩ ⟨look up at the ~ air —Sidney Alexander⟩

un·tended \"+\ *adj* [¹*un-* + *tended*, past part. of *tend*] **:** not tended or cared for **:** NEGLECTED ⟨the candles may gutter out at their own greasy will — unsnuffed, ~ —Israel Zangwill⟩

un·tender \"+\ *adj* **1 :** not tender in manner or approach **:** not gentle or sympathetic ⟨an amusing companion . . . but fundamentally an unloving, ~ woman —C.D.Lewis⟩ ⟨so young and so ~ —Shak.⟩ **2** *archaic* **:** not guided or influenced by religious feelings **3 :** not soft or fragile **:** not easily hurt **:** TOUGH ⟨my throat was stiff and my jaw was not ~ —Raymond Chandler⟩ — **un·ten·der·ly** *adv* — **un·ten·der·ness** *n*

un·tent \"+\ *vt* [²*un-* + *tent*, n.] **:** to bring out of a tent

¹un·tented \"+\ *adj* [¹*un-* + *tented*, past part. of *tent* to probe] **:** not probed or attended to ⟨the ~ woundings of a father's curse —Shak.⟩

²untented \"+\ *adj* [¹*un-* + *tented*, past part. of *tent* to attend to] *archaic* **:** UNHEEDED

un·tenty \"+\ *adj, Scot* **:** INATTENTIVE, INCAUTIOUS

un·terrified \"+\ *adj* **:** UNDAUNTED ⟨the committee's most ~ man on any political question —W.S.White⟩

un·terrifying \"+\ *adj* **:** not arousing terror

un·tested \"+\ *adj* **:** not put to a test **:** not proved by trial or experience ⟨an ~ theory⟩

un·thanked \ˌən+\ *adj* [¹*un-* + *thanked*, past part. of *thank*] **:** not thanked **:** UNAPPRECIATED ⟨performs its dreary and ~ job —T.O.Heggen⟩

un·thankful \"+\ *adj* [ME, fr. ¹*un-* + *thankful*] **1 :** not such as to call for thanks **:** DISAGREEABLE, THANKLESS, UNPLEASANT ⟨an ~ assignment⟩ **2 :** not giving thanks **:** UNAPPRECIATIVE ⟨an ~ child⟩ — **un·thankfully** \"+\ *adv* — **un·thank·ful·ness** *n*

un·thatch \"+\ *vt* [²*un-* + *thatch*] **:** to remove the thatch of ⟨a haystack which had been ~*ed*, ready for removal —Flora Thompson⟩

un·thatched \"+\ *adj* [¹*un-* + *thatched*, past part. of *thatch*] **:** not thatched ⟨an ~ cottage⟩

un·thaw \"+\ *vb* [²*un-* + *thaw*] **:** THAW

un·thawed \"+\ *adj* [¹*un-* + *thawed*, past part. of *thaw*] **:** not thawed **:** FROZEN

un·theatrical \"+\ *adj* **1 :** not suited to the stage ⟨a beautifully written but ~ play⟩ **2 :** not of a nature or quality characteristic of the stage ⟨an ~ personality⟩

un·think \"+\ *vb* [²*un-* + *think*] *vi* **:** to terminate or reverse a thought process ⟨learned how to think and how to ~ —Peggy Bennett⟩ ~ *vt* **:** to put out of mind ⟨~ your speaking and . . . say so no more —Shak.⟩

un·think·abil·i·ty \ˌən,thiŋkə¦bilәd·ē\ *n* **:** the quality or state of being unthinkable

¹**un·thinkable** \ˌən+\ *adj* [ME, fr. ¹*un-* + *thinken* to think + *-able*] **1 :** EXTRAORDINARY, UNIMAGINABLE ⟨~ joy⟩ **2 a :** incapable of being thought **:** not conceivable by the mind ⟨either alternative is ~⟩ **b :** contrary to what is reasonable or probable **:** INCREDIBLE ⟨it seemed ~ that this quiet and apparently worthy citizen should be connected with crimes —F.W.Crofts⟩ **3 :** not to be considered **:** being out of the question ⟨the average tenor was ~ in these youthful parts —James Joll⟩ — **un·think·able·ness** *n* — **un·thinkably** \"+\ *adv*

²**unthinkable** \"\ *n* **:** something unthinkable ⟨the realm of the disharmonic ~*s* —A.E.Wiggam⟩

un·thinking \"+\ *adj* **1 :** not taking thought **:** HEEDLESS, INATTENTIVE, UNMINDFUL ⟨an exploit performed thousands of times a day by ~ New Yorkers —Bennett Cerf⟩ **2 :** not indicating thought or reflection **:** VACANT ⟨with earnest eyes, and round ~ face —Alexander Pope⟩ **3 :** not having the power of thought ⟨vicious ~ animal —Richard Sale⟩ — **un·think·ing·ly** *adv* — **un·think·ing·ness** *n*

un·thorough \"+\ *adj* **:** not thorough **:** SLIPSHOD ⟨incapable of an ~ or conscienceless job —Olin Downes⟩

¹**un·thought** \"+\ *adj* [¹*un-* + *thought*, past part. of *think*] **1 :** not anticipated **:** UNEXPECTED ⟨shooting off at ~ angles —William Sansom⟩ — often used with *of* or *on* **2 :** not thought **:** UNPREMEDITATED

²**unthought** \"\ *n* [¹*un-* + *thought*, n.] **:** lack of thought

un·thoughted \"+\ *adj* **1 :** not thought of **2** *dial* **:** ill-considered **:** THOUGHTLESS

un·thoughtful \"+\ *adj* **1 :** not thoughtful **:** lacking in thought ⟨a mechanical, ~ process —W.H.Hale⟩ **2 :** THOUGHTLESS ⟨careless, ~ behavior⟩ — **un·thoughtfully** \"+\ *adv* — **un·thought·ful·ness** *n*

un·thread \ˌən+\ *vt* [²*un-* + *thread*] **1 :** to draw or take out a thread from ⟨~ a needle⟩ **2 :** to loosen the threads or connections of ⟨he with his bare wand can ~ thy joints —John Milton⟩ **3 :** to make one's way through ⟨~*ed* the maze⟩

un·threaded \"+\ *adj* [¹*un-* + *threaded*, adj.] **:** lacking a thread ⟨~ pipe⟩

un·threshed \"+\ *adj* [¹*un-* + *threshed*, past part. of *thresh*] **:** not threshed

¹**un·thrift** \"+\ *n* [ME, fr. ¹*un-* + *thrift*] **1 :** lack of thrift **:** EXTRAVAGANCE, WASTEFULNESS ⟨the repression of ~ and dissipation —James Ford⟩ **2 :** an extravagant person **:** SPENDTHRIFT, WASTREL ⟨like ~*s*, having spent your stock, and needy grown —John Drinkwater⟩

²**unthrift** \"\ *adj* **:** EXTRAVAGANT, LAVISH, UNTHRIFTY ⟨in an ~ generosity, has given it with a much more valuable present —J.G.Lockhart⟩

un·thriftily \"+\ *adv* [ME, fr. *unthrifty* + *-ly*] **:** in an unthrifty manner

un·thriftiness \"+\ *n* [ME *unthriftinesse*, fr. *unthrifty* + *-nesse* -ness] **:** the quality or state of being unthrifty

un·thrifty \"+\ *adj* [ME, fr. ¹*un-* + *thrifty*] **1 :** marked by lack of thrift **:** of little value or effect in proportion to the effort or expenditure involved **:** UNPROFITABLE, WASTEFUL ⟨nothing is cooked, and nobody is warmed — a most ~ fire —Edna S. V. Millay⟩ **2** *obs* **:** DISSOLUTE, PROFLIGATE ⟨can no man tell me of my ~ son —Shak.⟩ **3 a :** not thriving or prospering ⟨an ~ tree⟩ **b** *of livestock* **:** lacking in vigor or bloom **:** constitutionally unsound ⟨the intelligent buyer of choice feeders rejects all lambs that appear in the least ~ —W.C.Coffey⟩ **4 :** not given to thrift or saving **:** EXTRAVAGANT, IMPROVIDENT, PRODIGAL

un·thriven \"+\ *adj* [¹*un-* + *thriven*, past part. of *thrive*] *Scot* **:** UNTHRIVING

un·thriving \"+\ *adj* **:** not thriving

un·throne \"+\ *vt* [²*un-* + *throne*] **:** to remove from or as if from a throne **:** DETHRONE ⟨the dahlias that flaunted for so many royal weeks to be *unthroned* in a single night —C.G. Glover⟩

un·tidily \ˌən+\ *adv* **:** in an untidy manner

un·tidiness \"+\ *n* **:** the quality or state of being untidy

¹**un·tidy** \"+\ *adj* [ME, fr. ¹*un-* + *tidy*, adj.] **1 :** UNFIT, UNSUITABLE ⟨is an ~ walk on a glaring afternoon in July —Michael Arlen⟩ **2 a :** not neat in appearance **:** CARELESS, SLOVENLY ⟨~ tufts of grizzled hair —Walter de la Mare⟩ **b :** not neat in habits or procedure **:** not orderly ⟨was ~ and casual about money —Frank O'Connor⟩ **3 a :** not neatly organized or carried out **:** having loose ends ⟨convert an ~ manuscript into a great book —S.E.Harris⟩ ⟨instinct for illogical and ~ but highly effective compromise —G.B. Baldwin⟩ **b :** marked by or conducive to a lack of neatness ⟨~ tasks like bathing the baby —*New Yorker*⟩

²**untidy** \"\ *vt* [²*un-* + *tidy*] **:** DISARRANGE, DISORDER

un·tie \"+\ *vb* [ME *untyen*, fr. OE *untīegan*, fr. ²*un-* + *tīegan* to tie — more at TIE] *vt* **1 :** to detach from something by loosing a connecting rope or other tie ⟨*untied* the horse from the fence⟩ **2 :** to free from something that fastens or restrains **:** let loose **:** UNBIND ⟨*untied* him from his promise⟩; *specif* **:** to set free from a rope or other confining bond ⟨*untied* his hands⟩ ⟨*untied* the package⟩ **3 a :** to disengage the knotted parts of ⟨*untied* his tie, took it off, and opened his collar⟩ ⟨found it hard to ~ the knot⟩ **b :** DISENTANGLE, RESOLVE ⟨the worst traffic tangle . . . when 75,000 cars choked all roads leading out of the city, was *untied* —*Sydney (Australia) Bull.*⟩ **c :** DISSOLVE, UNDO ⟨~ the spell —Shak.⟩ ~ *vi* **1 :** to become loosened or unbound ⟨all cords easily *untied* but the one binding me to what I loved —Anaïs Nin⟩ **2 :** to unfasten a knot or loosen a bond ⟨those who tangled must ~ —Robert Browning⟩

un·tied \"+\ *adj* [ME *untyed*, fr. ¹*un-* + *tyed*, past part. of *tyen* to tie] **:** not tied; *specif* **:** not limited or restricted ⟨an ~ loan⟩

un·tight \"+\ *adj* [¹*un-* + *tight*, adj.] **:** not tight **:** LOOSE, LEAKY

un·tighten \"+\ *vt* [²*un-* + *tighten*] **:** to make less tight **:** LOOSEN ⟨an expulsion of breath ~*s* the chest —William Faulkner⟩

¹**un·til** \(ˌ)әn·¦til, әn¦tᵊl, *often* ᵊn| *after* t, d, s, z, *often* ᵊm *after* p, b, *often* ᵊŋ *after* k, g; *sometimes* ˈәn·tᵊl *or* ˈәn·ˌtil *or* |ˌtel\ *prep* [ME, fr. *un-* unto, until (akin to OE *ōth*, prep. & conj., to, up to, until, OHG *unt*, prep., unto, until, ON & Goth *und*, prep., unto, until, OE *end* end) + *til* till — more at END, TILL] **1** *chiefly Scot* **a** — used as a function word to indicate movement to and arrival at a destination **b** — used as a function word to indicate movement reaching as far as a limit or stopping point **c :** AGAINST **2** *chiefly Scot* **:** TO, TOWARD **3** — used as a function word to indicate continuance (as of an action, condition, or state) up to a particular time ⟨a tedious task which took ~ almost ten o'clock that night —M.M.Musselman⟩ ⟨the accident remained undiscovered ~ morning⟩ **4 a** — used as a function word after a negative expression to indicate performance or occurrence at a specified time ⟨the final ordering cannot be achieved ~ page proof —*Amer. Institute of Physics*⟩ **b :** BEFORE ⟨had barely heard of the mayor ~ this evening —Nigel Dennis⟩

²**until** \"\ *conj* [ME, fr. *until*, prep.] **1 :** up to the time that **:** till such time as ⟨the game continued ~ it got dark⟩ **2 :** before the time that ⟨often years pass by ~ the new ruler is found —Heinrich Harrer⟩ — often used after a negative or qualified statement ⟨had never been able to relax ~ he took up fishing⟩ **3 :** to the point or degree that **:** so long or so far that ⟨would clamber up the stairs ~ he was breathless —Martha Gellhorn⟩

un·tile \ˌən·+\ *vt* [ME *untilen*, fr. ²*un-* + *tilen* to tile] **:** to take the tiles from ⟨the storm *untiled* part of the roof⟩

un·tiled \"+\ *adj* [¹*un-* + *tiled*, adj.] **:** not supplied with tiles

un·tillable \"+\ *adj* **:** not tillable **:** BARREN, UNPRODUCTIVE

un·tilled \"+\ *adj* [ME *untiled*, fr. ¹*un-* + *tiled*, past part. of *tilen* to till] **:** not tilled **:** not cultivated ⟨~ land⟩

until that *conj* [ME] *archaic* **:** UNTIL

un·timbered \ˌən+\ *adj* **1 :** lacking timbers ⟨an ~ boat⟩ **2 :** TREELESS, UNWOODED ⟨an ~ area⟩

un·timeliness \"+\ *n* **:** the quality or state of being untimely

¹**un·timely** \"+\ *adv* [ME *untimliche*, *untimely*, fr. ¹*un-* + *timliche*, *timely*, adv., timely] **1 :** at an inopportune time **:** UNSEASONABLY ⟨thought I was mad, or most ~ merry —T.E. Lawrence⟩ **2 :** PREMATURELY ⟨died ~ a few months ago at the age of thirty-nine —Gerald Bullett⟩

²**untimely** \"\ *adj* [¹*un-* + *timely*, adj.] **1 :** occurring or done before the due, natural, or proper time **:** too early **:** PREMATURE ⟨come to an ~ end through passion —Cyril Connolly⟩ **2 :** INOPPORTUNE, UNSEASONABLE ⟨an ~ joke⟩ ⟨the only passenger who came on board at that ~ hour —Charles Dickens⟩ ⟨an ~ frost⟩ **3 :** not observing fitness of time or occasion ⟨during the performance of music when ~ people come in or go out —Owen Wister⟩

un·timeous \"+\ *adj*, *chiefly Scot* **:** UNTIMELY — **un·time·ous·ly** *adv*, *chiefly Scot*

un·tinged \"+\ *adj* [¹*un-* + *tinged*, past part. of *tinge*] **:** not tinged **:** not colored or affected ⟨based on a two-year study, ~ by politics —*N.Y. Times*⟩ ⟨their cheeks ~ by shame —William Blacker⟩

un·tir·abil·i·ty \ˌən·ˌtīrә¦bilәd·ē\ *n* **:** the quality or state of being untirable

un·tir·able \ˌən·¦tīrәbәl\ *adj* [¹*un-* + *tire* + *-able*] **:** incapable of being tired ⟨seemed invigorated and ~ —H.H.Johnston⟩

un·tire \ˌən·+\ *vt* [²*un-* + *tire*] **:** to give rest to **:** REFRESH ⟨a bench or two on which the drinkers ~ themselves —Richard Ford⟩

un·tired \"+\ *adj* [¹*un-* + *tired*, adj.] **:** not tired or worn out ⟨his head was hot, but he was singularly ~ —Stephen McKenna⟩ — **un·tired·ly** *adv*

un·tiring \"+\ *adj* [¹*un-* + *tiring*, pres. part. of *tire*] **:** incapable of tiring **:** INDEFATIGABLE, UNWEARYING ⟨to the end of his life he was an ~ worker —A.C.McGiffert⟩ — **un·tir·ing·ly** *adv*

un·titled \"+\ *adj* **1 :** having no title or right ⟨O nation miserable, with an ~ tyrant —Shak.⟩ **2 :** not named ⟨still ~ autobiography —*Publishers' Weekly*⟩ **3 :** not called by a title ⟨a dignity and prestige which can never be maintained among ~ civilians —Eugene Field⟩

un·to \ˌәntә, -n·tů, -n·(ˌ)tü, +V *often* -ntәw\ *prep* [ME, fr. *un-* unto, until + *to* — more at UNTIL, TO] **1 a** — used as a function word to indicate direction and completion of movement toward a place, destination, or object ⟨come ~ these yellow sands —Shak.⟩ ⟨they had gone ~ the wars —E.A.Poe⟩ **b** — used as a function word to indicate movement, inclination, or tendency toward an unreached object ⟨we stretch our hands ~ the Egyptians —John Donne⟩ ⟨my inwardness and love is very much ~ the prince —Shak.⟩ **c** *archaic* **:** AT **2 a** — used as a function word to indicate a limit of reach or extension ⟨my nails can reach ~ thine eyes —Shak.⟩ **b** — used as a function word to indicate a limit of contact, juxtaposition, or union ⟨pressed his dead child ~ his heart —Robert Browning⟩ **c** — used as a function word to indicate a limit in amount, extent, or degree ⟨lay sick almost ~ death —H.J.Johnson⟩ ⟨assume the configuration of a balancer, even ~ the finer details —V.C.Twitty⟩ **d** *obs* **:** next to **:** in front of ⟨flout me thus ~ my face —Shak.⟩ **3** — used as a function word to indicate the end of an interval of time or continuance ⟨her sentence that subsists ~ this day —Robert Browning⟩ **4 a** — used as a function word to indicate aim, purpose, or destiny ⟨went ~ his doom⟩ **b** — used as a function word to indicate a result, condition, or situation achieved or imposed ⟨our wars will turn ~ a peaceful comic sport —Shak.⟩ ⟨dust thou art, and ~ dust shalt thou return —Gen 3:19 (AV)⟩ **5 a** — used as a function word to indicate a person spoken to ⟨the serpent said ~ the woman, ye shall not surely die —Gen 3:4 (AV)⟩ **b** (1) — used as a function word to indicate the recipient of an action, benefit, or feeling or the person affected by an event ⟨and ~ thy seed, I will give all these countries —Gen 26:3 (AV)⟩ ⟨~ you is born this day . . . a Savior —Lk 2:11 (AV)⟩ (2) — used as a function word to indicate reference, concern, or interest ⟨is a law ~ himself —Raymond Daniell⟩ ⟨each town lived ~ itself —*Amer. Guide Series: Conn.*⟩ **c** — used as a function word to indicate the recipient of care, regard, faith, or reverence ⟨attended ~ his friend⟩ ⟨hearkened ~ his words⟩ ⟨trusted ~ his good fortune⟩ **6** — used as a function word to indicate comparison, agreement, or relationship ⟨are dangerously like ~ cancerous cells in the social organism —B.M.Beck⟩: as **a :** with respect to ⟨as strange ~ your town as to your talk —Shak.⟩ ⟨the effort of the individual reader to live ~ God —L.A.Weigle⟩ **b :** in agreement with ⟨and ~ this he frames his song —William Wordsworth⟩ **c :** in comparison with ⟨as water ~ wine —Alfred Tennyson⟩ **7** — used as a function word to indicate possession, belonging, or relationship ⟨documents pertaining ~ the case⟩ ⟨servant ~ the king⟩ ⟨cousin ~ his wife⟩ **8 a** — used as a function word to limit or direct the application of a quality or attribute to a specific individual or group ⟨forgiving ~ his enemies⟩ ⟨liberties which are designed to be available even ~ the most iconoclastic —*New Republic*⟩ **b** — used as a function word to indicate range of perception or knowledge ⟨a secret known ~ few⟩ ⟨a name known ~ many⟩ **9** — used as a function word to indicate something arousing a response or responsive action ⟨yielded ~ their prayers⟩ ⟨bowed ~ their demands⟩ **10 :** BESIDES ⟨should have given him tears ~ entreaties —Shak.⟩

un·toggle \ˌən·+\ *vt* [²*un-* + *toggle*] **:** to unfasten by removing a toggle from its loop

un·told \"+\ *adj* [ME, fr. OE *unteald*, fr. ¹*un-* + *teald*, past part. of *tellan* to tell] **1 a** *obs* **:** not numbered or counted ⟨in the number let me pass ~ —Shak.⟩ **b :** too great or numerous to count **:** VAST ⟨~ wealth⟩ ⟨destroy ~ quantities of fish —Tom Marvel⟩ ⟨the boulder, product of ~ ages —*Amer. Guide Series: Mich.*⟩ **c :** being without limit **:** IMMEASURABLE ⟨~ happiness⟩ ⟨~ suffering⟩ ⟨~ damage⟩ **2 a :** not related **b :** kept secret **:** UNREVEALED ⟨the effect of mystery, of ~ implications —C.D.Lewis⟩

un·tomb \"+\ *vt* [²*un-* + *tomb*] **:** to take from a tomb **:** DISENTOMB, DISINTER

un·tombed \"+\ *adj* [¹*un-* + *tombed*, past part. of *tomb*] **:** not supplied with a tomb **:** UNBURIED

un·tone \"+\ *vt* [²*un-* + *tone*] **:** to put out of tone

un·tooth \"+\ *vt* [²*un-* + *tooth*] **:** to take out the teeth of

un·torn \"+\ *adj* [¹*un-* + *torn*, past part. of *tear*] **:** not torn **:** unmarred by tears **:** WHOLE

un·touch·abil·i·ty \ˌən·ˌtәchә¦bilәd·ē\ *n* **:** the quality or state of being untouchable; *specif* **:** the state of being an untouchable

¹**un·touchable** \ˌən·+\ *adj* [¹*un-* + *touch* + *-able*] **1 a :** forbidden to the touch **:** not to be handled ⟨in most museums such articles are ~⟩ **b :** exempt from criticism or control ⟨for the first time criticism was directed at a hitherto ~ target —*Newsweek*⟩ **2 :** lying beyond the reach **:** being out of reach ⟨~ resources buried deep within the earth⟩ **3 :** disagreeable or defiling to the touch — **un·touch·ably** \-blē\ *adv*

²**untouchable** \"\ *n* -s **:** one that is untouchable; *specif* **:** a member of a large hereditary group in India having in traditional Hindu belief and practice the quality of defiling by contact the person, food, or drink of a member of a higher caste and formerly being strictly segregated and restricted to menial work

un·touched \"+\ *adj* [ME, fr. ¹*un-* + *touched*, past part. of *touchen* to touch] **1 a :** not subjected to touching **:** not handled ⟨the new piano stood ~ for weeks⟩ **b :** not traveled or explored ⟨free to pursue their explorations in almost ~ territory —*Times Lit. Supp.*⟩ **c :** not reached ⟨an enormous and hitherto ~ audience —Harrison Smith⟩ **2 :** not described or dealt with ⟨in the second volume he left few areas of our life ~ —J.D.Adams⟩ **3 a :** left in an intact state or condition **:** not damaged or injured ⟨it refreshed him to see something ~, unscarred, unhardened by suffering —Joseph Conrad⟩ **b :** UNTASTED ⟨stood at the edge of the group with an ~ cocktail in her hand —Louis Auchincloss⟩ **c** (1) **:** being in the first state or condition **:** not altered, treated, or worked on ⟨this small cherrywood chest-on-chest . . . is in its original ~ condition —*Antiques*⟩ ⟨published the full and ~ text of his father's diary —W.C.Ford⟩ (2) **:** ABORIGINAL, PRIMEVAL ⟨its brooding magic of an ~ world —Anita Leslie⟩ ⟨a very early human being, standing upon an ~ earth —Emma Hawkridge⟩ **4 a :** not influenced **:** UNAFFECTED ⟨stewed in its petty provincialism ~ by the brisk debates that stirred the old world —V.L.Parrington⟩ **b :** not disturbed or swayed by emotion **:** CALM, UNMOVED ⟨the difficulty is to keep oneself ~ in a crowd —Lewis Vogler⟩ **5 :** UNEQUALED ⟨a perfection of form . . . ~ in English letters —H.J.Laski⟩ — **un·touched·ness** *n* -ES

un·toward \ˌәn·¦tō(ә)rd, |ō(ә)rd, |ōd, |ō(ә)d *also* -tw| *or* -ntә¦wō(ә)rd *or* -ntә¦wō(ә)d\ *adj* [¹*un-* + *toward*, adj.] **1 a :** difficult to guide, manage, or influence **:** UNRULY ⟨an ~ wife⟩ **b :** resistant to manipulation, treatment, or use ⟨~ land⟩ ⟨~ material⟩ **c** *archaic* **:** AWKWARD, UNGRACEFUL **2 a :** marked by or causing trouble or unhappiness **:** UNFORTUNATE, UNLUCKY ⟨the oppressive realities of an ~ life —*Times Lit. Supp.*⟩ ⟨an ~ accident⟩ ⟨~ circumstances plunged it into bankruptcy —*Amer. Guide Series: Oregon*⟩ **b :** not favoring or assisting **:** ADVERSE, UNPROPITIOUS ⟨have managed to make a place for themselves under the most ~ conditions —M.F.A.Montagu⟩ **c :** not usual or expected **:** OUT-OF-THE-WAY ⟨~ scrap losses —Harold Koontz & Cyril O'Donnell⟩ ⟨some ~ and amusing incident —*Spectator*⟩ **3 :** not in accordance with propriety **:** IMPROPER, INDECOROUS ⟨moving to curb the ~ enthusiasm of the standees —Irving Kolodin⟩ — **un·toward·ness** *n*

¹**un·toward·ly** *adj* [¹*un-* + *towardly*, adj.] **1** *archaic* **:** OBSTINATE, PERVERSE **2** *archaic* **:** UNFAVORABLE

²**un·toward·ly** *adv* [*untoward* + *-ly*] **:** in an untoward manner

un·trace \ˌən·+\ *vt* [²*un-* + *trace*, n.] **:** to loose from a trace

un·traceable \"+\ *adj* [¹*un-* + *trace* + *-able*] **:** not traceable — **un·trace·able·ness** *n* — **un·traceably** \"+\ *adv*

un·track \"+\ *vt* [²*un-* + *track*] **:** to cause to move out of one's tracks **:** cause to get going ⟨the eventual victors were unable to ~ themselves right away —*N.Y.Times*⟩

un·tracked \"+\ *adj* [¹*un-* + *tracked*, past part. of *track*] **1 :** not provided with a track **:** TRACKLESS ⟨the ~ wilderness⟩ **2 :** not traced ⟨the getaway car is still ~⟩

untraded *adj* [¹*un-* + *traded*, past part. of *trade*] *obs* **:** not common or hackneyed **:** UNUSUAL ⟨mock not that I affect the ~ oath —Shak.⟩

un·train \ˌən+\ *vt* [²*un-* + *train*] **:** to undo the training of ⟨~ a badly trained painter⟩

un·trained \ˌən·¦trānd\ *adj* [¹*un-* + *trained*, adj.] **1 :** not trained **:** not made adept or expert by instruction or experience ⟨the afflicted person is ~ in the habit of concentration —H.A. Overstreet⟩ ⟨an ~ listener⟩ ⟨~ troops⟩ ⟨an ~ voice⟩ **2 :** not based on training or knowledge **:** INEXPERT ⟨an ~ diagnosis —Leon Gellert⟩ — **un·trained·ly** \-nәdlē, -nd-\ *adv* — **un·trained·ness** \-nәdnәs, -n(d)n-\ *n* -ES

un·trammeled \ˌən·+\ *adj* [¹*un-* + *trammeled*, past part. of *trammel*] **1 :** not confined or limited **:** not hindered ⟨melted with the same ~ rush that the snows had shown in the first spring sun —Farley Mowat⟩ ⟨the gift of a fresh eye and an ~ curiosity —Russell Lord⟩ ⟨command ~ by orders from committees of weak and treacherous noblemen —J.A.Froude⟩ **2 :** being free and easy ⟨the old ~ days —D.W.Brogan⟩ — **un·tram·meled·ness** *n* -ES

un·tranquil \"+\ *adj* **:** DISTURBED, RESTLESS ⟨despite my ~ night —A.J.Liebling⟩

un·tranquilize \"+\ *vt* [²*un-* + *tranquilize*] **:** to make untranquil **:** disturb the quiet of

un·transcended \"+\ *adj* [¹*un-* + *transcended*, past part. of *transcend*] **:** not transcended **:** not surpassed **:** not risen above or gone beyond

un·transferable \"+\ *adj* **:** not subject to transfer **:** incapable of being transferred

un·transformed \"+\ *adj* [¹*un-* + *transformed*, past part. of *transform*] **:** not transformed **:** not changed in form

un·translatability \"+\ *n* **:** the quality or state of being untranslatable

un·translatable \"+\ *adj* [¹*un-* + *translate* + *-able*] **:** not translatable **:** not capable of being put into another form, style, or language ⟨an ~ idiom⟩ ⟨an ~ art⟩ — **un·trans·lat·able·ness** *n* -ES — **un·trans·lat·ably** \-blē\ *adv*

un·translated \"+\ *adj* [¹*un-* + *translated*, past part. of *translate*] **1 :** not put into another language **2 :** not removed to another place or condition

un·transparent \"+\ *adj* **:** OPAQUE

un·traveled \ˌən·+\ *adj* **1 :** not having traveled **:** lacking direct knowledge of other countries or regions ⟨an intelligent but ~ inland girl —Carl Van Doren⟩ **2 :** not passed over or through by travelers **:** UNTRAVERSED ⟨an ~ desert⟩

un·traversed \"+\ *adj* [¹*un-* + *traversed*, past part. of *traverse*] **:** not traversed; *esp* **:** not journeyed **:** not traveled over or through ⟨an ~ region⟩

un·tread \"+\ *vt* [²*un-* + *tread*] **:** to tread back **:** RETRACE ⟨treads the path that she ~*s* again —Shak.⟩

un·treasure \"+\ *vt* [²*un-* + *treasure*] **1 :** to rob or deprive of a treasure ⟨found the bed *untreasured* of their mistress —Shak.⟩ **2 :** to bring forth (something precious) **:** EXHIBIT ⟨*untreasured* . . . the stores of his memory —John Mitford⟩

un·treatable \"+\ *adj* [ME *untretable*, fr. ¹*un-* + *tretable*] **:** incapable of being treated; *specif* **:** not susceptible of medical treatment ⟨its striking effectiveness against types of the disease previously ~ —*Newsweek*⟩

un·treated \"+\ *adj* [¹*un-* + *treated*, past part. of *treat*] **:** not subjected to treatment ⟨an ~ disease⟩ ⟨an ~ fabric⟩

un·tremulous \"+\ *adj* **:** not tremulous **:** STEADY

un·trenched \"+\ *adj* **:** not trenched

un·tressed \"+\ *adj* [ME, fr. ¹*un-* + *tressed*] **:** not tied up in tresses ⟨~ hair⟩

un·tried \"+\ *adj* [¹*un-* + *tried*, past part. of *try*] **1 :** not tested or proved by experience or trial ⟨an illustrator ~ in monumental painting —F.J.Mather⟩ **2** *obs* **:** not noted or examined **:** not commented on ⟨slide o'er sixteen years and leave the growth ~ —Shak.⟩ **3 :** not tried in court ⟨had accompanied us as an ~ prisoner —R.H.Davis⟩

untried horse *n* **:** a horse whose get are maidens in racing

un·trim \ˌən·+\ *vt* [²*un-* + *trim*] **:** to strip of trimming **:** put in disorder

un·trimmed \"+\ *adj* [¹*un-* + *trimmed*, past part. of *trim*] **:** not made or kept neat **:** DISORDERED ⟨by chance, or nature's changing course, ~ —Shak.⟩; *specif* **:** not cut for trimness ⟨style is often ~ to the point of tediousness —Duncan Aikman⟩ ⟨the black hair was tangled and unkempt and the beard ~ —Israel Zangwill⟩ — **un·trimmed·ness** *n* -ES

un·tripe \"+\ *vt* -ED/-ING/-S [²*un-* + *tripe*] **:** DISEMBOWEL

un·trod *or* **un·trodden** \"+\ *adj* [¹*un-* + *trod* or *trodden*, past part. of *tread*] **:** not trod **:** UNTRAVERSED ⟨~ snow⟩ ⟨~ wilderness⟩

un·troubled \"+\ *adj* [ME, fr. ¹*un-* + *troubled*] **1 :** not given trouble **:** not made uneasy ⟨could pursue my hobby ~ by the dislike of needless waste —Francis Birtles⟩ **2 :** CALM, TRANQUIL ⟨the pictorial value of the large ~ rectangular spaces —Roger Fry⟩ ⟨a huge stretch of ~ harbor, sheltered from the winds —Julian Dana⟩ — **un·trou·bled·ness** *n*

un·troublesome \"+\ *adj* **:** not troublesome **:** EASY ⟨an ~ guest⟩ ⟨an ~ procedure⟩ — **un·trou·ble·some·ness** *n*

¹**un·true** \"+\ *adj* [ME *untrewe*, fr. OE *untrēowe*, fr. ¹*un-* + *trēowe* true] **1 :** not true to an obligation, love, or trust **:** DISLOYAL, UNFAITHFUL ⟨is ~ to his highest opportunity and duty —Bruno Lasker⟩ ⟨finally locates her lover, finds that he has been ~ and shoots him —W.E.Roberts⟩ **2 :** not according with a standard of correctness **:** not level or exact ⟨unsightly cracks, off-level floors, and ~ doors and windows —*Building, Estimating & Contracting*⟩ **3 :** not according with the facts **:** FALSE ⟨the claim presented to the government contained an ~ statement —R.L.Taylor b. 1889⟩ **4 :** not honest or fair **:** WRONG ⟨~ methods⟩ — **un·true·ness** *n*

²untrue *adv* [ME *untrewe*, fr. *untrewe*, adj.] *obs* : UNTRULY
un·truism \ˌən+\ *n* : something obviously not true ⟨revel in platitudes, truisms, and ~ —Anthony Trollope⟩
un·truly \"+\ *adv* [ME *untrewely*, fr. OE *untrēowlīce*, fr. ¹*un-* + *trēowlīce* truly] : in an untrue manner
un·truss \"+\ *vb* [ME *untrussen*, fr. ²*un-* + *trussen* to truss] *vt* **1** *archaic* : to loose from a fastening : set free **2** *archaic* **a** : UNTIE, UNFASTEN, UNDO — used in the phrase *untruss one's points*, compare ¹POINT 10a **b** : UNDRESS ~ *vi*, *archaic* : to unfasten or take off one's clothes and esp. one's breeches ⟨is condemned for ~*ing* —Shak.⟩
un·trust \"+\ *n* [ME, fr. ¹*un-* + *trust*] *archaic* : DISTRUST
un·trustworthiness \"+\ *n* : the quality or state of being untrustworthy
un·trustworthy \"+\ *adj* : not trustworthy : UNRELIABLE ⟨an ~ person with whom, when I discovered his true character, I had no wish to associate —Eric Linklater⟩
un·trusty \"+\ *adj* [ME, fr. ¹*un-* + *trusty*] : UNTRUSTWORTHY
un·truth \"+\ *n* [ME *untreuth*, fr. OE *untrēowth*, fr. ¹*un-* + *trēowth* truth] **1** *archaic* : DISLOYALTY, UNFAITHFULNESS **2** : lack of truthfulness : FALSITY ⟨literary art may be associated with ~ —Aldous Huxley⟩ **3** : something that is untrue : FALSEHOOD, MISSTATEMENT ⟨motivated to cling to these childish ~*s* —Weston La Barre⟩ ⟨told you ~*s* yesterday morning merely to cheer you up —Arnold Bennett⟩
un·truth·ful \"+\ *adj* : not truthful : FALSE, INACCURATE ⟨an ~ report⟩ **syn** see DISHONEST
un·truthfully \"+\ *adv* : in an untruthful manner
un·truth·ful·ness *n* : the quality or state of being untruthful
unts *pl of* UNT
un·tuck \ˌən+\ *vt* [²*un-* + *tuck*] : to release from a tuck or from being tucked up ⟨stooping to ~ the rug —Clive Arden⟩ ⟨~*ed* her legs, and stuck her feet into her shoes —Frances G. Patton⟩
un·tufted \"+\ *adj* [¹*un-* + *tufted*, past part. of *tuft*] : not tufted : not having tufts ⟨~ ears⟩
un·tunable \"+\ *adj* : not melodious : DISCORDANT, HARSH — **un·tun·able·ness** *n* — **un·tun·ably** \-blē\ *adv*
un·tune \"+\ *vt* [²*un-* + *tune*] **1** : to put out of tune : make incapable of harmony or harmonious action ⟨~ that string, and hark, what discord follows —Shak.⟩ **2** : DISARRANGE, DISCOMPOSE ⟨his troubles had *untuned* his mind⟩
un·tuned \"+\ *adj* [¹*un-* + *tuned*, adj.] **1** : made untuneful or discordant ⟨with ~ tongue she hoarsely calls her maid —Shak.⟩ **2** : not tuned : being out of tune ⟨an ~ violin⟩
un·tuneful \"+\ *adj* : not pleasing in sound : HARSH — **un·tunefully** \"+\ *adv* — **un·tune·ful·ness** *n*
un·turn \"+\ *vt* [²*un-* + *turn*] : to turn in a reverse way
un·turned \"+\ *adj* [¹*un-* + *turned*, past part. of *turn*] : not turned ⟨would leave no stone ~ to secure its success —W.B. Shaw⟩
un·tutored \"+\ *adj* [¹*un-* + *tutored*, past part. of *tutor*] **1 a** : having no formal learning or training : UNEDUCATED ⟨~ in local history and Moslem architecture —Douglas Carruthers⟩ ⟨to the ~ ear they are meaningless — these queer noises —Waldemar Kaempffert⟩ **b** : NAÏVE, SIMPLE, UNSOPHISTICATED ⟨a growing and powerful, if politically ~, body of industrial workers —T.H.White b.1915⟩ **2** : owing nothing to education : not produced or developed by instruction ⟨the ~ ethical judgment of the individual —Alfred Cobban⟩ **syn** see IGNORANT
un·twine \"+\ *vb* [ME *untwinen*, fr. ²*un-* + *twinen* to twine] *vt* **1 a** : to break up : DISSOLVE ⟨~ the ties of custom which bind a people to the established and the old —William Hamilton †1856⟩ **b** : to unwind the twisted or tangled parts of ⟨~*s* the ball of thread⟩ **c** : DISENTANGLE, UNCLASP **2** : to remove by unwinding ~ *vi* : to become disentangled or unwound
un·twist \"+\ *vb* [²*un-* + *twist*] *vt* **1 a** : to separate the twisted parts of : UNTWINE ⟨~ a knot⟩ **b** *archaic* : DISENTANGLE **2** : to bring to nothing : FRUSTRATE ⟨able to overcome prejudices and vested interests, to ~ wrong purposes and unmask false ideals —G.A.L.Sarton⟩ **3** *archaic* : to let loose : FREE ~ *vi* : to become separated : become untwined
un·twisted \"+\ *adj* [¹*un-* + *twisted*, past part. of *twist*] : not twisted
untwisting *n* [fr. gerund of *untwist*] : the act or action of untwisting
un·typical \ˌən+\ *adj* : not typical : not representative ⟨too small and ~ to serve as a cross section of national opinion —E.K.Lindley⟩ — **un·typically** \"+\ *adv*
un·understandable \ˌən+\ *adj* : not understandable : PUZZLING, UNINTELLIGIBLE
un·understanding \"+\ *adj* : lacking in understanding : UNCOMPREHENDING
un·understood \"+\ *adj* : not understood ⟨should not tamely submit to the unpredictable and ~ cycles of wars —*Psychiatry*⟩
un·uniform \"+\ *adj* : not uniform — **un·uni·form·ly** *adv*
un·uniformed \"+\ *adj* : not dressed in uniform
un·united \"+\ *adj* : DISUNITED
un·upbraided \"+\ *adj* [¹*un-* + *upbraided*, past part. of *upbraid*] *archaic* : not accused : UNREPROACHED
un·upbraiding \"+\ *adj* [¹*un-* + *upbraiding*, pres. part. of *upbraid*] *archaic* : not reproachful
un·upholstered \"+\ *adj* : not upholstered
un·urbane \"+\ *adj* : not urbane : CHURLISH, VULGAR
un·urged \ˌən+\ *adv* [¹*un-* + *urged*, past part. of *urge*] : without being urged : VOLUNTARILY ⟨goes ~ for the mail because it's his birthday⟩
un·usable \"+\ *adj* : not serviceable : USELESS — **un·usably** \"+\ *adv*
un·use \"+\ *n* [¹*un-* + *use*] : lack of usage
un·used \"+\ *adj* [ME, fr. ¹*un-* + *used*, past part. of *usen* to use] **1** : not habituated : UNACCUSTOMED ⟨a country boy ~ to city ways⟩ **2** : not used: as **a** : recently made or acquired : FRESH, NEW ⟨set an ~ canvas on the easel and got out a fresh brush⟩ **b** : not being in use : IDLE, VACANT ⟨stay in a friend's ~ apartment⟩ **c** : waiting to be used : ACCRUED, ACCUMULATED ⟨~ annual leave⟩ **d** *of a postage stamp* : not canceled **3** *archaic* : not familiar : STRANGE ⟨strange dainty things they ate, of ~ savor —William Morris⟩
un·useful \"+\ *adj* : of no practical value : UNHELPFUL, USELESS ⟨nameless and ~ plants such as flourish under barrels —Thomas Wolfe⟩ — **un·usefully** \"+\ *adv*
un·use·ful·ness *n* : the quality or state of being impractical or worthless
un·usual \ˌən+\ *adj* **1 a** : being out of the ordinary : EXCEPTIONAL, REMARKABLE ⟨a scholar of ~ ability⟩ ⟨a scene of ~ beauty⟩ **b** : deviating from the normal : PECULIAR, STRANGE ⟨devoted to all that was strange, ~ and exotic in humanity —B.K.Malinowski⟩ ⟨excessive bail shall not be required . . . nor cruel and ~ punishments inflicted —*U.S.Constitution*⟩ **2** : being unlike others : DIFFERENT, UNIQUE ⟨~ and highly entertaining variations of the . . . trick-ending story —William Peden⟩ ⟨discovered an ~ meteorite —Walter Granger⟩ — **un·usually** \"+\ *adv*
un·u·su·ali·ty \ˌən,yüzhəˈwalәd·ē\ *n* -ES **1** : UNUSUALNESS **2** : something unusual
unu·su·al·ness *n* : the quality or state of being unusual
un·utilized \ˌən+\ *adj* [¹*un-* + *utilized*, past part. of *utilize*] : not utilized
un·utterable \"+\ *adj* : being beyond the powers of description : INEXPRESSIBLE, UNSPEAKABLE ⟨longed with ~ longing . . . for those nights in the wagon on the prairie —Edna Ferber⟩ ⟨the ~ miseries and wretchedness of mankind —M.R.Cohen⟩ — **un·ut·ter·ably** \-blē, -li\ *adv*
un·utterables \"+\ *n pl*, *archaic* : UNMENTIONABLES
un·uttered \"+\ *adj* [¹*un-* + *uttered*, past part. of *utter*] : not expressed in words : UNSPOKEN ⟨meeting glances tell the ~ tale of love —Amelia Welby⟩
un·vaccinated \"+\ *adj* [¹*un-* + *vaccinated*, past part. of *vaccinate*] : not vaccinated
un·valuable \"+\ *adj* **1** *obs* : INVALUABLE **2 a** : not valuable **b** : having negative value
un·value \"+\ *n* : a negative value; *esp* : ethical or aesthetic badness ⟨truth, goodness, and beauty . . . contrast with their ~*s* of error, evil, and ugliness —Samuel Alexander⟩
un·valued \"+\ *adj* [¹*un-* + *valued*, past part. of *value*] **1** *obs* : of inestimable worth : INVALUABLE **2 a** : not important or prized : DISREGARDED, INSIGNIFICANT ⟨the inestimable, tho' ~ benefit of health —Edward Hyde⟩ ⟨he may not, as ~ persons do, carve for himself —Shak.⟩ **b** : not appraised ⟨an ~ estate⟩
unvalued policy *n* : an insurance policy in which absence of prior agreement leaves losses to be settled on the basis of indemnity
un·van·quish·able \ˌən¦vaŋkwishəbəl, -ank-\ *adj* [ME *unvenkusable*, fr. ¹*un-* + *venkussen*, *venquissen* to vanquish + *-able*] : incapable of being subdued : UNCONQUERABLE
un·vanquished \ˌən+\ *adj* [ME *unvenquissed*, fr. ¹*un-* + *venquissed*, past part. of *venquissen* to vanquish] : not vanquished : UNDEFEATED
un·vaporized \"+\ *adj* [¹*un-* + *vaporized*, past part. of *vaporize*] : not vaporized
un·variable \"+\ *adj* [ME, fr. ¹*un-* + *variable*] : INVARIABLE
un·varied \"+\ *adj* : not varied : MONOTONOUS, UNDIVERSIFIED
un·variegated \"+\ *adj* : not variegated : PLAIN, UNIFORM
un·varnished \"+\ *adj* [¹*un-* + *varnished*, past part. of *varnish*] **1 a** : free from ambiguity or subterfuge : PLAIN, STRAIGHTFORWARD ⟨straight talk to the Turks, who appreciate ~ discourse —Welles Hangen⟩ ⟨more concerned with making himself look good . . . than he was with telling the ~ truth —K.S.Davis⟩ **b** : free from affectation : ARTLESS, FRANK ⟨the thought of that other woman, so ~, so undefended —Ida A. R. Wylie⟩ ⟨the ~ candor of old people and children —Janet Flanner⟩ **2** : not coated with or as if with varnish : CRUDE, UNFINISHED ⟨an ~ floor⟩ ⟨legal methods shall be substituted for ~ use of force —P.C.Nash⟩
un·varying \"+\ *adj* [¹*un-* + *varying*, pres. part. of *vary*] : not varying : CONSTANT, UNCHANGING ⟨principles of ~ validity —B.N.Cardozo⟩ ⟨Latin as an artificial, ~ language —R.A.Hall b. 1911⟩ — **un·vary·ing·ly** *adv*
un·vaulted \"+\ *adj* [¹*un-* + *vaulted*, past part. of *vault*] : not vaulted
un·veil \"+\ *vb* [²*un-* + *veil*] *vt* **1 a** : to divest of or as if of a veil ⟨ended child marriage, ~*ed* the women —*Time*⟩ ⟨~*ed* Olympus before my enraptured vision —W.J.Locke⟩ **b** : to expose by or as if by removing a veil : UNMASK ⟨~*s* a hidden alter ego by playing the piccolo for his astonished guests⟩ ⟨the physicist, wishing to ~ the . . . architecture of the atom —G.W. Gray b. 1886⟩ **c** (1) : to display publicly for the first time by drawing aside a curtain or covering ⟨~ a statue⟩ (2) : to make public for the first time : INTRODUCE ⟨brought from London by the Theater Guild and ~*ed* here last Thursday —John Lardner⟩ **2 a** : to disclose to the public : DIVULGE, REVEAL ⟨these addresses ~ as do no other writings of the great preacher his own personal experiences —C.A.Dinsmore⟩ ⟨~*ed* a vision of society in the twentieth century —R.M.Lovett⟩ **b** : to present to the eye : EXHIBIT, SHOW ⟨in its wide windows and slender piers . . . unconventional verticality is frankly ~*ed* —*Amer. Guide Series: N.Y.*⟩ ~ *vi* : to remove a veil : discard a protective cloak ⟨~*ed* before each other concerning it —Richard Blaker⟩
un·veiled \"+\ *adj* [¹*un-* + *veiled*, past part. of *veil*] : not veiled : OPEN, REVEALED
unveiling *n* [fr. gerund of *unveil*] : an act or instance of revealing or putting on display esp. for the first time : EXPOSURE, PRESENTATION ⟨the ~ of some of nature's most precious secrets —Johnny Antillon⟩ ⟨~ of his latest film —A.H.Weiler⟩ ⟨~*s* of the new models⟩
un·vendible \"+\ *adj* : not salable
un·venerable \"+\ *adj* : unworthy of veneration ⟨forever ~ be thy hands, if thou tak'st up the princess —Shak.⟩
un·vented \"+\ *adj* [¹*un-* + *vented*, past part. of *vent*] : not vented
un·ventilated \"+\ *adj* [¹*un-* + *ventilated*, past part. of *ventilate*] : not ventilated
un·ventured \"+\ *adj* [¹*un-* + *ventured*, past part. of *venture*] : not ventured
un·veracious \"+\ *adj* : not veracious : FALSE
un·veracity \"+\ *n* : lack of truthfulness : FALSEHOOD, MENDACITY
un·verbalized \"+\ *adj* [¹*un-* + *verbalized*, past part. of *verbalize*] : not put into words or given conscious expression ⟨the ~ resentment the patient might have —M.M.Gill & Margaret Brenman⟩ ⟨deep ~ levels of the mind —Lilian Smith⟩
un·verifiability \ˌən+\ *n* : the quality or state of being unverifiable
un·verifiable \"+\ *adj* : incapable of being verified ⟨~ reports of flying saucers⟩ — **un·ver·i·fi·a·bly** \-blē\ *adv*
un·verified \"+\ *adj* [¹*un-* + *verified*, past part. of *verify*] : not verified : lacking substantiation
un·vernalized \"+\ *adj* [¹*un-* + *vernalized*, past part. of *vernalize*] : not subjected to vernalization
un·versed \"+\ *adj* : displaying lack of knowledge or proficiency : IGNORANT, INEXPERIENCED ⟨~ in the jargon of the social scientist —*Dun's Rev.*⟩
un·vest \"+\ *vi* [²*un-* + *vest*] : to take off ecclesiastical vestments
un·vexed \"+\ *adj* [ME *unvext*, fr. ¹*un-* + *vext*, past part. of *vex*] : free from disturbance : CALM, SERENE
un·viable \"+\ *adj* : incapable of growth or development
un·vicious \"+\ *adj* : not vicious : GENTLE, TRACTABLE
un·victorious \"+\ *adj* : not victorious : DEFEATED
un·viewed \ˌən+\ *adj* [¹*un-* + *viewed*, past part. of *view*] : not viewed : UNSEEN
un·vigilant \"+\ *adj* : not vigilant : INATTENTIVE, UNWARY
un·vindicated \"+\ *adj* [¹*un-* + *vindicated*, past part. of *vindicate*] : not vindicated
un·vindictive \"+\ *adj* : not vindictive : FORGIVING, MERCIFUL
un·violated \ˌən+\ *adj* [¹*un-* + *violated*, past part. of *violate*] : not violated : INTACT, UNBROKEN
un·violent \"+\ *adj* : not violent : MILD, SUBDUED
un·virtuous \"+\ *adj* [ME *unvertuous*, fr. ¹*un-* + *vertuous* virtuous] : lacking in honor or integrity : IMMORAL, WICKED — **un·vir·tu·ous·ly** *adv*
un·visited \"+\ *adj* [¹*un-* + *visited*, past part. of *visit*] **1** : not attracting visitors : BYPASSED, NEGLECTED ⟨remains astonishingly ~ by Americans —S.P.B.Mais⟩ **2** : not attended : UNACCOMPANIED — usu. used with *by* ⟨many a night ~ by sleep —W.C.Bryant⟩
un·visored \"+\ *adj* : not having or wearing a visor ⟨an ~ helm⟩ ⟨see the face of an ~ foe⟩
un·vital \"+\ *adj* **1** : not vital : INANIMATE **2** : INCONSEQUENTIAL
un·vitiated \"+\ *adj* [¹*un-* + *vitiated*, past part. of *vitiate*] *archaic* : not vitiated : UNCONTAMINATED
un·vit·ri·fi·a·ble \ˌən¦vi·trə¦fīəbəl\ *adj* [¹*un-* + *vitrify* + *-able*] : incapable of being vitrified
un·vitrified \ˌən+\ *adj* [¹*un-* + *vitrified*, past part. of *vitrify*] : not vitrified
un·vocal \"+\ *adj* : not eloquent or outspoken : INARTICULATE ⟨plight of the ~ agricultural worker —H.L.Hoskins⟩; *esp* : UNMUSICAL ⟨~ progressions —M.F.Bukofzer⟩
un·vocalized \"+\ *adj* [¹*un-* + *vocalized*, past part. of *vocalize*] : not vocalized
un·voice \"+\ *vt* [²*un-* + *voice*] : DEVOICE
un·voiced \"+\ *adj* [¹*un-* + *voiced*, past part. of *voice*] **1** : not verbally expressed : SILENT, STIFLED ⟨an ~ pact between us —H.V.Gregory⟩ ⟨this ~ aspect of Italy has made itself heard in our days through . . . poetry —Serge Hughes⟩ **2** : VOICELESS 2
un·vouched \"+\ *adj* [¹*un-* + *vouched*, past part. of *vouch*] : not attested : UNVERIFIED
un·vowed \"+\ *adj* [¹*un-* + *vowed*, past part. of *vow*] : not bound by an oath : UNSWORN
un·vowelled \"+\ *adj* : having no vowel sounds or signs
un·voy·age·able \ˌən¦vȯi·ijəbəl\ *adj* [¹*un-* + *voyage* + *-able*] : incapable of being traversed : IMPASSABLE, UNNAVIGABLE
un·vulcanized \ˌən+\ *adj* [¹*un-* + *vulcanized*, past part. of *vulcanize*] : not vulcanized
un·vulgar \"+\ *adj* : free from crudity : REFINED
un·waked *or* **un·wakened** \ˌən+\ *adj* [¹*un-* + *waked* (past part. of *wake*) or *wakened* (past part. of *waken*)] : not awakened
un·walked \"+\ *adj* [¹*un-* + *walked*, past part. of *walk*] **1** : not walked **2** *of a gamecock* : not having the leg muscles hardened by roadwork
un·wall \"+\ *vt* [²*un-* + *wall*] : to expose by demolishing a wall ⟨~ a bricked-up fireplace⟩
un·walled \"+\ *adj* [ME, fr. ¹*un-* + *walled*, past part. of *wallen* to wall] : not enclosed by or as if by a wall : OPEN, EXPOSED ⟨an ~ garden⟩ ⟨the round ~ horizon of the open sea —O.W.Holmes †1894⟩
un·wandered \"+\ *adj* [¹*un-* + *wandered*, past part. of *wander*] : UNTRAVELED
un·wandering \"+\ *adj* [¹*un-* + *wandering*, pres. part. of *wander*] : not devious or vagrant : FIXED, UNSWERVING
un·waning \"+\ *adj* [¹*un-* + *waning*, pres. part. of *wane*] : not diminishing : CONSTANT, PERPETUAL ⟨the miracle of the ~ oil in the temple —Israel Zangwill⟩
un·wanted \"+\ *adj* [¹*un-* + *wanted*, past part. of *want*] **1** : not wanted ⟨sits at home ~⟩ **2** : not needed or useful : SUPERFLUOUS, UNNECESSARY ⟨give away ~ kittens⟩ ⟨ignore ~ advice⟩ **3** : detrimental in character : FAULTY, UNDESIRABLE ⟨not likely to leave descendants to preserve his . . . ~ qualities —S.A.Coblentz⟩ ⟨~ shadows distort the picture⟩
un·ware \ˌən¦wa(a)(ə)r, -we(ə)r\ *adv* [ME *unwar*, fr. OE *unwær*, fr. *unwær*, adj., unaware, fr. ¹*un-* + *wær* wary — more at WARY] *obs* : UNAWARES
un·wares \-rz\ *adv* [ME, fr. *unwar*, adj., unaware (fr. OE *unwær*) + *-es*, adv. suffix (fr. *-es*, gen. sing. ending of nouns) — more at ¹*s*] *archaic* : UNAWARES
un·warily \ˌən+\ *adv* : in an unwary manner : CARELESSLY, INCAUTIOUSLY
un·wariness \"+\ *n* : the quality or state of being unwary : HEEDLESSNESS, INDISCRETION
un·warlike \"+\ *adj* : disinclined to wage war : NONBELLIGERENT, PACIFIC
un·warmed \"+\ *adj* [¹*un-* + *warmed*, past part. of *warm*] : not subjected to heat or stimulation ⟨~ rolls⟩ ⟨a heart ~ by affection⟩
un·warming \"+\ *adj* [¹*un-* + *warming*, pres. part. of *warm*] : not exuding warmth : COLD ⟨the moon's ~ light⟩
un·warned \"+\ *adj* [ME, fr. OE *unwarnod*, fr. ¹*un-* + *warnod*, past part. of *warnian* to warn] : receiving no warning : not cautioned or rebuked ⟨stepped ~ into the path of an oncoming car⟩ ⟨wickedness ~ and wrong unredressed —Margaret Oliphant⟩
un·warp \"+\ *vt* [²*un-* + *warp*] : to straighten out : UNTWIST
un·warped \"+\ *adj* [¹*un-* + *warped*, past part. of *warp*] : not warped : UNDISTORTED
un·warrantable \"+\ *adj* [¹*un-* + *warrant* + *-able*] : not justifiable : INEXCUSABLE ⟨~ liberties . . . taken with ancient works of art —Norman Douglas⟩ — **un·war·rant·ably** \-blē\ *adv*
un·war·rant·able·ness *n* : the quality or state of being unwarrantable
un·warranted \ˌən+\ *adj* [¹*un-* + *warranted*, past part. of *warrant*] : lacking adequate or official support : UNJUSTIFIED, UNAUTHORIZED ⟨an ~ restriction of personal freedom —J.V.L. Casserley⟩ ⟨leap to sensational and ~ conclusions —R.W. Murray⟩ ⟨~ search and seizure⟩ — **un·war·rant·ed·ly** *adv*
un·wary \"+\ *adj* **1** *obs* : UNEXPECTED **2 a** : not alert : easily fooled or surprised : HEEDLESS, GULLIBLE ⟨seduce the ~ reader into easy acquiescence —O.J.Campbell⟩ **b** : careless of consequences : IMPRUDENT, RASH ⟨an ~ step may plunge them waist deep into a hidden hole —Hugh Cave⟩
¹un·washed \"+\ *adj* [ME *unwasched*, fr. ¹*un-* + *wasched*, past part. of *waschen* to wash] **1** : not cleaned with or as if with soap and water ⟨a sink full of ~ dishes⟩ **2** : belonging to or characteristic of the common herd : IGNORANT, PLEBEIAN ⟨the country is intellectually ~ —George Moore⟩ ⟨popular support . . . lay in the ~ social stratum —*Time*⟩
²unwashed \"\ *n* -s : an ignorant or underprivileged group : RABBLE ⟨spreading . . . sunshine among the ~ as well as the nobility —C.W.Ferguson⟩ — often used in the phrase *the great unwashed* ⟨from the society woman down to numbers of the great ~ —*Sydney (Australia) Mail*⟩
un·washen \"+\ *adj* [ME *unwaschen*, fr. OE *unwæscen*, fr. ¹*un-* + *wæscen*, past part. of *wascan* to wash] *archaic* : UNWASHED
un·wasted \"+\ *adj* [ME, fr. ¹*un-* + *wasted*, past part. of *wasten* to waste] **1** *archaic* : not decreased by consumption or erosion : UNDIMINISHED **2** *archaic* : not sacked : UNRAVAGED
un·wasteful \"+\ *adj* : not wasteful : FRUGAL — **un·waste·fully** \"+\ *adv*
un·wasting \"+\ *adj* [ME, fr. ¹*un-* + *wasting*, pres. part. of *wasten* to waste] *archaic* : not diminishing : remaining constant
un·watched \"+\ *adj* [ME *unwached*, fr. ¹*un-* + *wached*, past part. of *wachen*, *wacchen* to watch] : not watched : NEGLECTED, UNATTENDED ⟨that applied science, ~, improperly handled, and not understood by men —Harrison Brown⟩
un·watchful \"+\ *adj* : not watchful : INATTENTIVE, UNOBSERVANT — **un·watchfully** \"+\ *adv*
un·watch·ful·ness *n* : the quality or state of being unwatchful
un·water \ˌən+\ *vt* [²*un-* + *water*] : to draw off water from : empty of moisture : DRAIN ⟨~ a mine shaft by bucket or pump⟩ ⟨~ a rice field for harvesting⟩
un·watered \"+\ *adj* [ME *unwattred*, fr. ¹*un-* + *wattred*, past part. of *wattren*, *wateren* to water] **1 a** : not supplied with water either naturally or artificially : ARID, DRY ⟨~ desert⟩ ⟨an ~ lawn⟩ **b** : emptied of moisture ⟨an ~ mine⟩ **2** : not diluted with water ⟨~ alcohol⟩
un·watermarked \"+\ *adj* [¹*un-* + *watermarked*, past part. of *watermark*] : not watermarked
un·waved \"+\ *adj* [¹*un-* + *waved*, past part. of *wave*] : not waved : STRAIGHT ⟨~ hair⟩
un·wavering \"+\ *adj* [¹*un-* + *wavering*, pres. part. of *waver*] : characterized by absence of fluctuation : FIXED, STEADFAST ⟨an ~ gaze⟩ ⟨~ concentration⟩ ⟨~ faith in God⟩ ⟨complexity of form is handled with ~ conviction and taste —J.T.Soby⟩ — **un·wa·ver·ing·ly** *adv*
un·waving \"+\ *adj* [¹*un-* + *waving*, pres. part. of *wave*] : not waving
un·waxed \"+\ *adj* [¹*un-* + *waxed*, past part. of *wax*] : not waxed ⟨an ~ floor⟩
un·weakened \"+\ *adj* [¹*un-* + *weakened*, past part. of *weaken*] : not weakened
un·wealthy \"+\ *adj* [ME *unwelthy*, fr. ¹*un-* + *welthy* wealthy] : not wealthy : POOR
un·weaned \"+\ *adj* [¹*un-* + *weaned*, past part. of *wean*] : not weaned
unweapon *vt* [²*un-* + *weapon*] *obs* : DISARM
un·weaponed \ˌən+\ *adj* [ME *unwepned*, fr. ¹*un-* + *wepned*, past part. of *wepnen* to arm — more at WEAPON] *archaic* : not armed with or as if with a weapon
un·wearable \"+\ *adj* [¹*un-* + *wear* + *-able*] : not wearable : UNBECOMING, WORN-OUT ⟨an ~ style⟩ ⟨shoes so dilapidated as to be ~⟩
un·wea·ri·a·ble \ˌən¦wirēəbəl\ *adj* [¹*un-* + *weary* + *-able*] : incapable of being wearied : persevering despite fatigue : INDEFATIGABLE, TIRELESS — **un·wea·ri·a·bly** \-blē\ *adv*
un·wearied \ˌən+\ *adj* [¹*un-* + *wearied*, past part. of *weary*] : not tired or jaded : FRESH, DILIGENT ⟨must be skilled, persistent, and ~ —J.B.Gallagher⟩ — **un·wea·ried·ly** *adv*
un·wea·ried·ness *n* : the quality or state of being unwearied : DILIGENCE, ENDURANCE
un·weary \"+\ *adj* [ME *unwery*, fr. OE *unwērig*, fr. ¹*un-* + *wērig* weary] : UNWEARIED
un·wearying \"+\ *adj* [¹*un-* + *wearying*, pres. part. of *weary*] **1** : UNWEARIABLE **2** : not causing fatigue or boredom — **un·wea·ry·ing·ly** *adv*
un·weathered \"+\ *adj* : not showing the effects of exposure to the weather ⟨~ stone⟩ ⟨~ shingles⟩
un·weave \"+\ *vt* [²*un-* + *weave*] : to dismantle or extract from or as if from a mesh : DISENTANGLE, RAVEL ⟨~ a knot⟩ ⟨cannot be *unwoven* and analyzed independently —S.L.Payne⟩
un·webbed \"+\ *adj* [¹*un-* + *webbed*, past part. of *web*] : not webbed
un·wed *or* **un·wedded** \"+\ *adj* [*unwed* fr. ¹*un-* + *wed*, past part. of *wed*; *unwedded* fr. ME, fr. ¹*un-* + *wedded*, past part. of *wedden* to wed] : not married
un·wedge \"+\ *vt* [²*un-* + *wedge*] **1** : to remove a wedge from ⟨~ a door and let it swing shut⟩ **2** : to release from a tight position ⟨*unwedged* his bulk from the telephone booth⟩

un·wedge·able \"+əbəl\ *adj* [1*un-* + *wedge* + *-able*] **:** impervious to wedges **:** HARD, IMPENETRABLE ⟨the ~ and gnarled oak —Shak.⟩
un·weeded \ˌən+\ *adj* [1*un-* + *weeded*, past part. of *weed*] **:** not weeded or culled
un·weeting \"+\ *adj* [ME *unweting*, fr. 1*un-* + *weting*, pres. part. of *weten* to know — more at WEET] *archaic* **:** UNWITTING — **un·weet·ing·ly** *adv, archaic*
un·weighed \"+\ *adj* [ME *unweyed*, fr. 1*un-* + *weyed*, past part. of *weyen* to weigh] **:** not weighed on or as if on a scale **:** INJUDICIOUS ⟨what an ~ behavior hath this . . . drunkard —Shak.⟩
un·weighted \"+\ *adj* [1*un-* + *weighted*, past part. of *weight*] **1 :** not encumbered **:** UNBURDENED ⟨to change . . . direction the ~ ski is turned —George Gallowhur⟩ ⟨plots . . . ~ by great profundity of thought —*Americana Annual*⟩ **2 :** obtained from statistical data not distinguished as to relative importance ⟨~ mean⟩
1un·welcome \"+\ *adj* [ME, fr. 1*un-* + *welcome*, adj.] **:** not welcome **:** DISTASTEFUL, UNWANTED ⟨~ disturbance of routine —J.H.Robinson †1936⟩ ⟨in the city you are more free from ~ intimacy —M.R.Cohen⟩ ⟨forced the ~ truth out of his mind —Gordon Merrick⟩ — **un·wel·come·ly** *adv*
2unwelcome \"\ *n* [1*un-* + *welcome*, n.] **:** lack of cordiality ⟨unmeant smiles . . . strengthened the irritant feeling of ~ —Richard Llewellyn⟩
3unwelcome \"\ *vt* [2*un-* + *welcome*] **:** to receive without enthusiasm ⟨plowing through his manuscripts *unwelcomed* —H.J.Laski⟩
un·wel·come·ness *n* **:** the quality or state of being unwelcome
un·welded \ˌən+\ *adj* [1*un-* + *welded*, past part. of *weld*] **:** not welded
un·well \"+\ *adj* [ME *unwel*, fr. 1*un-* + *wel* well] **1 :** being in poor health **:** AILING, SICK ⟨felt ~ . . . and went to bed —*N. Y. Times*⟩ **2 :** undergoing menstruation
un·well·ness *n* **:** the quality or state of being unwell
unwemmed *adj* [ME, fr. OE, fr. 1*un-* + *wemman* to stain — more at WEM] *obs* **:** having no stain or blemish **:** FLAWLESS, PURE
un·wept \ˌən+\ *adj* [1*un-* + *wept*, past part. of *weep*] **:** not mourned **:** UNLAMENTED ⟨go down to the vile dust . . . ~, unhonored, and unsung —Sir Walter Scott⟩
un·wet \"+\ *adj* [ME, fr. 1*un-* + *wet*, adj.] **:** not wet; *esp* **:** not suffused with tears ⟨with eyes ~ —John Dryden⟩
un·wetted \"+\ *adj* [1*un-* + *wetted*, past part. of *wet*] **:** UNWET
un·wheel \"+\ *vt* [2*un-* + *wheel*] **:** to deprive of wheels
un·whetted \"+\ *adj* [1*un-* + *whetted*, past part. of *whet*] **:** not whetted
un·whipped \"+\ *adj* [1*un-* + *whipped*, past part. of *whip*] **:** not whipped **:** UNPUNISHED ⟨crimes ~ of justice —Shak.⟩
un·whiskered \"+\ *adj* **:** not having whiskers
un·whispered \"+\ *adj* [1*un-* + *whispered*, past part. of *whisper*] **:** not whispered ⟨something that passed ~ with his breath —E.A.Robinson⟩
un·whitewashed \"+\ *adj* [1*un-* + *whitewashed*, past part. of *whitewash*] **:** not whitewashed
un·wholesome \"+\ *adj* [ME *unholsum*, fr. 1*un-* + *holsum* wholesome] **1 :** detrimental to physical, mental, or moral well-being **:** UNHEALTHY ⟨~ food⟩ ⟨~ pastimes⟩ ⟨keep your soul perpetually in the ~ region of remorse —Nathaniel Hawthorne⟩ **2 a :** marked by lack of integrity or dependability **:** CORRUPT, UNSOUND ⟨the people muddied . . . ~ in their thoughts and whispers —Shak.⟩ ⟨wild speculation and ~ overexpansion —*Amer. Guide Series: N. C.*⟩ **b :** offensive to the senses **:** LOATHSOME, REPULSIVE ⟨bluebottles, swollen and ~, crawled and buzzed —Mary Webb⟩
syn UNWHOLESOME, MORBID, SICKLY, DISEASED, and PATHOLOGICAL apply to what is unhealthy in various ways; UNWHOLESOME applies not only to what is physically and mentally unhealthy but also to what is morally corruptive ⟨an *unwholesome* diet⟩ ⟨an *unwholesome* environment for children⟩ ⟨an aura about him of *unwholesome* cleverness —J.V.Baker⟩ ⟨*unwholesome* thoughts⟩ ⟨an *unwholesome* exaltation and relaxing revery —P.E.More⟩ MORBID applies not only to what is diseased, markedly unwholesome, deranged or similarly abnormal, or notably decadent but also to the fancies, feelings, or behavior resulting from or suggesting such conditions ⟨a *morbid* condition of the liver⟩ ⟨the *morbid* mental habit of dwelling on death and physical decay⟩ ⟨a *morbid* fascination for crime and violence⟩ SICKLY applies to what is a sign of or shows signs of marked lack of health, typically wanness, weakness, and marked general and often chronic absence of vigor, robustness, virility; it applies widely, for example to persons, animals, plants, feelings, behavior, and colors ⟨the child was puny, white and *sickly*, so they sent continually for the doctor —Samuel Butler †1902⟩ ⟨movie attendance is at the *sickliest* level in four years —*Wall Street Jour.*⟩ ⟨a dark, tunnellike passage, through which came a deathly, *sickly* odor —Bram Stoker⟩ ⟨the *sickly* yellow of the sea lamps —Jack London⟩ ⟨a *sickly* smile⟩ ⟨*sickly* vines withering on the trellis⟩ DISEASED applies not only to what has been attacked by disease but, like MORBID, also to what is deranged or similarly abnormal, or markedly unwholesome ⟨a *diseased* liver⟩ ⟨a *diseased* mind subject to self-deception⟩ ⟨the paralysis of a *diseased* will⟩ PATHOLOGICAL applies to physical, mental, or moral conditions which have their origin in disease or marked abnormality ⟨a *pathological* wasting away⟩ ⟨*pathological* moods of depression⟩ ⟨a *pathological* fear of crowds⟩ ⟨almost *pathological* desire to cling to the ideal of unstained innocence —Charles Weir⟩
un·whole·some·ly *adv* [ME *unholsumly*, fr. *unholsum* + *-ly*] **:** in an unwholesome manner **:** INJURIOUSLY, NOXIOUSLY ⟨air . . . ~ close and foul —Florence Nightingale⟩ ⟨the vegetation was . . . ~ green —Mary S. Watts⟩
un·whole·some·ness *n* **:** the quality or state of being unwholesome
un·wield·i·ly \ˌən¦wēldəlē, -li\ *adv* **:** in an unwieldy manner
un·wield·i·ness \-dēnəs, -din-\ *n* -ES **:** the quality or state of being unwieldy **:** AWKWARDNESS
un·wieldy \-dē, -di\ *also* **un·wield·ly** \-dlē, -li\ *adj* [*unwieldy* fr. ME *unweldy*, fr. 1*un-* + *weldy* wieldy; *unwieldly* alter. (influenced by *-ly*) of *unwieldy*] **1** *obs* **:** characterized by debility **:** FEEBLE, INFIRM ⟨time the taste destroys, with sickness and ~ years —John Dryden⟩ **2 a :** hard to handle or control **:** AWKWARD, CUMBERSOME ⟨the increasingly ~ colonial organization —Marjory S. Douglas⟩ ⟨on the ~ circus train the going is tedious and filled with fits and starts —R.L. Taylor⟩ **b :** not useful or workable **:** INVOLVED, IMPRACTICAL ⟨some of its rules are so ~ that many of the simplest things . . . are often the most difficult to prove —B.N.Cardozo⟩ ⟨brilliant hypotheses and all too often ~ ideas —D.M.Schneider⟩ **3 a :** disproportionately large or clumsy **:** UNGAINLY ⟨his ~ mouth wearing the jealous leer proper to his profession —Herbert Gold⟩ ⟨any word becomes ~ . . . when its spread of emotional sail overbalances the lead and oak that ought to carry cargo —Archibald MacLeish⟩ **b :** massive in size **:** HUGE, HULKING ⟨heaved his ~ figure out of his chair —Moray Firth⟩ ⟨discourage ~ . . . corporate surpluses —F.D.Roosevelt⟩
un·wifely \ˌən+\ *adj* **:** not wifely
un·wig \"+\ *vt* [2*un-* + *wig*] **:** to divest of a wig
un·wigged \"+\ *adj* [1*un-* + *wigged*, adj.] **:** not wearing a wig
un·will \"+\ *vt* -ED/-ING/-S [2*un-* + *will*] **:** to change the mind with regard to **:** CONTRADICT ⟨~*s* what he willed —J.A. Carlyle⟩
un·willed \"+\ *adj* [1*un-* + *willed*, past part. of *will*] **:** not willed **:** INVOLUNTARY, UNINTENTIONAL ⟨my heart with ~ love grew warm —George Macdonald †1905⟩
un·willing \"+\ *adj* **1 a :** withholding consent **:** AVERSE, OPPOSED ⟨the radicals were ~ to this —R.W.Winston⟩ ⟨the judge was ~ that the witness be recalled⟩ **b :** UNWILLED ⟨'twas a fault ~ —Shak.⟩ ⟨the ~ honor of being the most talked-of man in the musical world —George Copeland⟩ **c :** not favorably inclined **:** LOATH, RELUCTANT ⟨pride makes them ~ to appear to be in any way subordinate —James Bryce⟩ ⟨could not dance and was ~ to learn⟩ ⟨his ~ accomplice from beginning to end —G.G.Coulton⟩ **2 :** offering opposition **:** OBSTINATE, REFRACTORY ⟨two horses, one of which is . . . sluggish, lazy and ~ —Rex Warner⟩ ⟨fought against nature and an ~ soil —W.C.Dickinson⟩ — **un·will·ing·ly** *adv*
un·will·ing·ness *n* **:** the quality or state of being unwilling **:** DISINCLINATION, REFUSAL
un·wilted \ˌən+\ *adj* [1*un-* + *wilted*, past part. of *wilt*] **:** not wilted
un·wily \"+\ *adj* [ME, fr. 1*un-* + *wily*] **:** not wily **:** GUILELESS, SIMPLE
un·wincing \"+\ *adj* [1*un-* + *wincing*, pres. part. of *wince*] **:** not marked by hypersensitivity **:** FEARLESS, UNFLINCHING ⟨a veteran without hands . . . and his story is told with ~ documentary touches —Parker Tyler⟩
un·wind \"+\ *vb* [ME *unwinden*, fr. 2*un-* + *winden* to wind] *vt* **1 a :** to free from convolution or cause to uncoil **:** wind off **:** UNROLL ⟨~ a bedroll⟩ ⟨*unwound* her arms from his neck⟩ ⟨~ thread from a spool⟩ **b :** to free from or as if from a binding or knot **:** DISENGAGE, UNDO ⟨~ a bandaged arm⟩ ⟨*unwound* himself from his machine only to fall . . . into an exhausted sleep —W.B.Ready⟩ ⟨an awful lot of red tape to ~ —S.E. White⟩ **c :** to release from tension **:** RELAX ⟨try to let yourself go . . . ~ yourself —Claud Cockburn⟩ **2** *archaic* **:** to traverse in the opposite direction **:** RETRACE ⟨~*ing* the labyrinth and bringing the hero . . . to a state of rest —Laurence Sterne⟩ ~ *vi* **1 a :** to become uncoiled or disentangled **:** UNFOLD, UNREEL ⟨the dance record went on and on . . . as the machine *unwound* —Millen Brand⟩ ⟨the narrative ~*s* slowly⟩ ⟨a vague, unraveling, final tune like a long ~*ing* silk cocoon —Vachel Lindsay⟩ **b :** to throw off restraint **:** cut loose ⟨wanted to be ready to ~ with the race of his life —*Time*⟩ **2 :** to become released from tension **:** RELAX ⟨this ability to block official worries out of his range of thought . . . enables him to ~ —Russell Baker⟩
un·winder \"+\ *n* **:** UNREELER
un·windy \"+\ *adj* **:** not windy **:** CALM, STILL
un·winged \"+\ *adj* [1*un-* + *winged*, past part. of *wing*] **:** not having wings **:** WINGLESS
un·winking \"+\ *adj* [1*un-* + *winking*, pres. part. of *wink*] **:** not winking **:** UNWAVERING ⟨an ~ stare⟩ — **un·wink·ing·ly** *adv*
un·winnable \ˌən+\ *adj* [1*un-* + *win* + *-able*] **:** incapable of being won ⟨an ~ contest⟩; *esp* **:** IMPREGNABLE ⟨an ~ fortress⟩
un·winnowed \"+\ *adj* [1*un-* + *winnowed*, past part. of *winnow*] **:** not winnowed
un·wiped \ˌən+\ *adj* [1*un-* + *wiped*, past part. of *wipe*] **:** not wiped **:** SMEARY
un·wired \"+\ *adj* [1*un-* + *wired*, past part. of *wire*] **:** not wired; *esp* **:** not equipped with electric circuits ⟨a totally unheated, ~ and bathroomless house —Joanna Spencer⟩
un·wisdom \"+\ *n* [ME, fr. OE *unwīsdōm*, fr. 1*un-* + *wīsdōm* wisdom] **:** lack of wisdom **:** FOOLISHNESS, RECKLESSNESS ⟨aesthetically vital but unsound . . . a superb expression of ~ —Norman Foerster⟩ ⟨regarded the attack . . . as almost inept in its ~ —*Country Life*⟩
un·wise \"+\ *adj* [ME, fr. OE *unwīs*, fr. 1*un-* + *wīs* wise] **1 :** lacking in wisdom or good sense **:** FOOLISH, IMPRUDENT ⟨~ to pass another car on a curve⟩ ⟨an ~ investor is soon impoverished⟩ **2 :** characterized by lack of wisdom **:** ILL-ADVISED, SENSELESS ⟨held that the action was "hasty" and "~" at a time of great tension —George Dugan⟩ ⟨these revolting and most ~ persecutions —Anne Marsh⟩ — **un·wise·ly** *adv*
un·wise·ness *n* **:** UNWISDOM
un·wish \ˌən+\ *vt* [2*un-* + *wish*] **1 :** to revoke as a wish **:** CANCEL, WITHDRAW ⟨~ a wish⟩ **2** *obs* **:** to wish away **:** obliterate by wishing ⟨now thou hast ~*ed* five thousand men —Shak.⟩
un·wished \"+\ *adj* [1*un-* + *wished*, past part. of *wish*] **:** UNWANTED, UNWELCOME
un·wished-for \ˌən¦wisht,fȯ(ə)r, -ō(ə)\ *adj* [1*un-* + *wished for*, past part. form of the phrase *wish for*] **:** UNWISHED
un·wishful \ˌən+\ *adj* **:** not wishful **:** RELUCTANT
un·wist \ˌən¦wist\ *adj* [ME, fr. 1*un-* + *wist*, past part. of *witten* to know] *archaic* **:** not known **:** UNDETECTED, UNRECOGNIZED
un·wit \ˌən+\ *vt* [2*un-* + *wit*, n.] *obs* **:** to deprive of wit **:** DERANGE ⟨as if some planet had *unwitted* men —Shak.⟩
un·witch \"+\ *vt* [2*un-* + *witch*] **:** to free from or as if from a magic spell **:** UNBEWITCH
un·withdrawn \"+\ *adj* **:** not withdrawn
un·withered \"+\ *adj* [1*un-* + *withered*, past part. of *wither*] **:** not withered **:** FRESH, VIGOROUS
un·withering \"+\ *adj* [1*un-* + *withering*, pres. part. of *wither*] **:** remaining fresh and unfaded
un·withstood \"+\ *adj* [1*un-* + *withstood*, past part. of *withstand*] **:** not withstood **:** VICTORIOUS
un·witnessed \"+\ *adj* [ME, fr. 1*un-* + *witnessed*, past part. of *witnessen* to witness] **1 :** not discerned by the senses **:** UNPERCEIVED ⟨trifles, ~ with eye or ear —Shak.⟩ **2 :** not bearing the signature of a witness ⟨an ~ legal document⟩
un·witting \"+\ *adj* [ME, fr. 1*un-* + *witting*, pres. part. of *witten*, *witen* to know — more at WIT] **1 :** not intended **:** ACCIDENTAL, INADVERTENT ⟨probable that any ~ mistake may be overlooked or regarded as ignorance on the part of a stranger —*Notes & Queries on Anthropology*⟩ **2 a :** being unaware **:** OBLIVIOUS ⟨carried home washings to the best families and also, her father ~, to . . . the parlor houses on alleys —Mary Ross⟩ **b :** exhibiting lack of knowledge or awareness **:** IGNORANT, UNCONSCIOUS ⟨man is born the most helpless and ~ of animals —R.M.MacIver⟩ ⟨the lyrical impulse swollen to epical proportions produces either conscious irony or ~ absurdity —L.A.Fiedler⟩ — **un·wit·ting·ly** *adv*
un·wit·ting·ness *n* -ES **:** the quality or state of being unwitting
un·witty \ˌən+\ *adj* [ME, fr. OE *unwittig*, fr. 1*un-* + *wittig* witty] **:** not wise or clever **:** SENSELESS, SILLY
un·wive \"+\ *vt* [2*un-* + *wive*] **:** to deprive of a wife
un·wived \"+\ *adj* [1*un-* + *wived*, past part. of *wive*] **:** being without a wife **:** WIFELESS
unwmkd *abbr* unwatermarked
un·woman \ˌən+\ *vt* [2*un-* + *woman*] **:** to deprive of womanly qualities
1un·womanly \"+\ *adv* [ME, fr. 1*un-* + *womanly*, adv.] **:** in an unwomanly manner
2unwomanly \"\ *adj* [1*un-* + *womanly*, adj.] **:** not womanly **:** MANNISH, UNGENTLE
un·won \"+\ *adj* [1*un-* + *won*, past part. of *win*] **:** not won; *esp* **:** courted unsuccessfully ⟨the lost dinner and ~ lady —William Maginn⟩
un·wont \"+\ *adj* [ME *unwount*, fr. 1*un-* + *wount*, *wunt* wont] *archaic* **:** UNWONTED, UNACCUSTOMED
un·wonted \"+\ *adj* **1 :** being out of the ordinary **:** RARE, UNUSUAL ⟨an ~ softness had invaded her face —William McFee⟩ ⟨this ~ substitution of warm for cool waters had disastrous effects upon the fish —R.E.Coker⟩ **2** *archaic* **:** not accustomed by experience **:** UNUSED ⟨boys ~ to the tasks of war —W.C.Bryant⟩ — **un·wont·ed·ly** *adv*
un·wont·ed·ness *n* **:** the quality or state of being unwonted **:** SINGULARITY, STRANGENESS
un·wooded \ˌən+\ *adj* [1*un-* + *wooded*, past part. of *wood*] **:** not wooded **:** TREELESS
un·wooed \"+\ *adj* [1*un-* + *wooed*, past part. of *woo*] **:** not wooed
un·wordable \"+\ *adj* [1*un-* + *word* + *-able*] **:** inexpressible in words
un·wordy \ˌən¦wərdi\ *adj* [by alter.] *Scot* **:** UNWORTHY
un·workability \"+\ *n* **:** the quality or state of being unworkable **:** IMPRACTICALITY
un·workable \"+\ *adj* **:** not workable **:** IMPRACTICAL
un·work·able·ness *n* **:** UNWORKABILITY
un·worked \ˌən+\ *adj* [1*un-* + *worked*, past part. of *work*] **1 :** not shaped by working **:** CRUDE, RAW ⟨one single ~ flint —John Lubbock⟩ **2 :** not put to use **:** UNEXPLORED, UNTAPPED ⟨allowing so important a clue to remain ~ —F.W.Crofts⟩ ⟨an ~ inventory⟩ ⟨an ~ mine⟩
un·working \"+\ *adj* [1*un-* + *working*, pres. part. of *work*] **:** not working **:** IDLE
un·workmanlike \"+\ *adj* [1*un-* + *workman* + *like*] **:** not characteristic of or suited to a good workman **:** INCOMPETENT, INEFFICIENT ⟨an ~ result⟩ ⟨an ~ tool⟩
un·worldliness \"+\ *n* **:** the quality or state of being unworldly
un·worldly \"+\ *adj* **1 :** not of this world **:** UNEARTHLY ⟨an ~ stillness in the cloud —Ira Wolfert⟩; *specif* **:** SPIRITUAL **2 a :** not wise in the ways of the world **:** NAÏVE, UNSOPHISTICATED ⟨this helplessly ~ woman —Kate O'Brien⟩ **b :** not swayed by mundane considerations (as of wealth) ⟨was ~, and did not greatly miss worldly rewards —Sheldon Cheney⟩
un·worn \"+\ *adj* **1 :** unimpaired by use **:** not eroded or worn away **2 a :** not jaded **:** FRESH, ORIGINAL **b :** not worn **:** NEW, PRISTINE
un·worried \"+\ *adj* [1*un-* + *worried*, past part. of *worry*] **:** not worried
un·worshiped \"+\ *adj* [ME *unworschiped*, fr. 1*un-* + *worschiped*, past part. of *worschipen* to worship] **:** not worshiped
1un·worth \"+\ *adj* \1*un-* + *worth*, adj.] **:** UNWORTHY
2unworth \"\ *n* [1*un-* + *worth*, n.] **:** lack of value or merit **:** POVERTY, UNWORTHINESS
un·wor·thi·ly \ˌən¦wərthəlē, -li\ *adv* [ME, fr. *unworthy* + *-ly*] **:** in an unworthy manner
un·wor·thi·ness \-thēnəs, -thin-\ *n* [ME *unworthines*, fr. *unworthy* + *-nes* -ness] **:** the quality or state of being unworthy
1un·worthy \ˌən+\ *adj* [ME, fr. 1*un-* + *worthy*] **1 a :** lacking in excellence or value **:** POOR, WORTHLESS ⟨the precincts of the Minister are quite clear of any ~ building —S.P.B.Mais⟩ ⟨the tremendous advances of science and technology have somehow led us to believe that other kinds of knowledge are ~ —C.S.Kilby⟩ **b :** of a contemptible nature **:** BASE, DISHONORABLE ⟨no right to employ other men on ~ tasks, whether we pay them well or not —W.R.Inge⟩ ⟨the right to dismiss or expel . . . a student whose conduct is deemed ~ —*Villanova College Cat.*⟩ **2 :** not meritorious **:** UNDESERVING ⟨ration cards to citizens previously held politically ~ —Frank Gorrell⟩ — often used with *of* or *to* ⟨~ of continued confidence —H.S.Drinker⟩ ⟨a vile man . . . deemed ~ to discharge the duty —J.G. Frazer⟩ **3 :** not corresponding to desert **:** UNMERITED, UNJUSTIFIED ⟨an ~ treatment of a potentially fine subject —Anthony Boucher⟩ **4 :** UNBECOMING — usu. used with *of* ⟨such bargaining seemed ~ of a self-respecting nation —S.E.Morison & H.S.Commager⟩
2unworthy \"\ *n* **:** an unworthy person ⟨a whole gallery of . . . worthies and *unworthies* come to life —*Times Lit. Supp.*⟩
3unworthy \"\ *adv, archaic* **:** UNWORTHILY
un·wound \"+\ *adj* [1*un-* + *wound*, past part. of *wind*] **1 :** not wound ⟨an ~ clock⟩ **2 :** released from a coiled state ⟨the bobbin has come ~⟩
un·wound·able \"+əbəl\ *adj* [1*un-* + *wound* + *-able*] **:** incapable of being wounded **:** INVULNERABLE
un·wounded \ˌən+\ *adj* [ME *unwunded*, fr. OE *unwundod*, fr. 1*un-* + *wundod*, past part. of *wundian* to wound] **:** not wounded **:** INTACT, WHOLE
un·woven \"+\ *adj* [ME, fr. 1*un-* + *woven*, past part. of *weven* to weave] **:** not woven ⟨~ fabrics are made by combining textile fibers . . . with a binder by means of heat and pressure —*Amer. Fabrics*⟩
un·wrap \"+\ *vt* [ME *unwrappen*, fr. 2*un-* + *wrappen* to wrap] **1 :** to open to view by or as if by removing a wrapping **:** DISCLOSE, REVEAL ⟨~ a package⟩ ⟨~ . . . the evidence in a criminal case —*Newsweek*⟩ **2 :** UNFOLD, UNROLL ⟨*unwrapped* his blankets, spread them on the bed —Andrew Robertson⟩
un·wreaked \"+\ *adj* [1*un-* + *wreaked*, past part. of *wreak*] **:** not wreaked **:** UNAVENGED
un·wreathe \"+\ *vt* [2*un-* + *wreathe*] **:** UNCOIL, UNTWIST
un·wreathed \"+\ *adj* [1*un-* + *wreathed*, past part. of *wreathe*] **:** lacking or divested of a wreath ⟨the Empire's ~ laureate —*Time*⟩
un·wrench \"+\ *vt* [2*un-* + *wrench*] *archaic* **:** to yank off or open
un·wrinkle \"+\ *vt* [2*un-* + *wrinkle*] **:** to free from wrinkles **:** smooth out
un·wrinkled \"+\ *adj* [1*un-* + *wrinkled*, past part. of *wrinkle*] **:** not wrinkled **:** SMOOTH
un·writable \"+\ *adj* **:** incapable of being put into writing ⟨an ~ sound⟩
un·write \"+\ *vt* [2*un-* + *write*] **:** to obliterate from writing **:** EXPUNGE, RESCIND ⟨it is easier to unsay than to ~ cross words —*Court Life at Naples*⟩
un·written \"+\ *adj* [ME *unwriten*, fr. 1*un-* + *writen*, past part. of *writen* to write] **1 :** not reduced to writing **:** ORAL, TRADITIONAL ⟨an ~ code⟩ ⟨rites . . . so ancient that they well might have had their ~ origins in Aurignacian times —J.L.T.C. Spence⟩ **2 :** containing no writing **:** BLANK ⟨an ~ page⟩
unwritten constitution *n* **:** a constitution not embodied in a single document but implied in the institutions and customs of the country as expressed in long-accepted statutes and the body of the common law — called also *customary constitution*
unwritten law *n* **1 :** law (as the common law of England or the U.S.) originating in custom or otherwise than as formally made and declared by the sovereign legislative power and not committed to writing at its origin **2 :** the custom of granting a measure of immunity to persons guilty of certain criminal acts justified in the eyes of the public esp. in avenging injury to family honor arising from seduction or adultery — usu. used with *the*
un·wronged \ˌən+\ *adj* [1*un-* + *wronged*, past part. of *wrong*] **:** not wronged
un·wrought \"+\ *adj* [ME, fr. 1*un-* + *wrought*] **1 :** not shaped into finished form **:** ROUGH ⟨~ steel⟩ ⟨the mass of notes he had made remained ~ —Isabel Paterson⟩ **2 a :** not processed for use **:** still in a natural state **:** RAW, VIRGIN ⟨~ rock⟩ ⟨~ land⟩ **b :** not worked **:** UNDEVELOPED ⟨an ~ mine⟩
un·wrung \"+\ *adj* [1*un-* + *wrung*, past part. of *wring*] **:** not painfully affected **:** UNMOVED ⟨let the gall'd jade winch; our withers are ~ —Shak.⟩
un·yeaned \"+\ *adj* [1*un-* + *yeaned*, past part. of *yean*] **:** UNBORN — used esp. of a lamb
un·yielded \"+\ *adj* [1*un-* + *yielded*, past part. of *yield*] **:** not yielded **:** not surrendered
un·yielding \"+\ *adj* [1*un-* + *yielding*, pres. part. of *yield*] **1 a :** characterized by lack of softness or flexibility **:** HARD, STIFF ⟨an ~ horsehair sofa⟩ **b :** refusing to give way **:** RESOLUTE, OBSTINATE ⟨remove your siege from my ~ heart —Shak.⟩ ⟨the steady, swift, ~ stream of parkway traffic —E.J.Kahn⟩ **c :** not subject to amelioration or development **:** FIXED, RIGID ⟨the music was . . . acrobatic, ~ and overdissonant —*Time*⟩ ⟨the farms look ~, the buildings drab —*Amer. Guide Series: Vt.*⟩ **2 :** characterized by firmness or obduracy **:** ADAMANT, FLINTY ⟨~ determination⟩ ⟨looks strong-minded and dignified . . . with his ~ mouth and glassy eyes —Marchette Chute⟩ — **un·yield·ing·ly** *adv*
un·yield·ing·ness *n* **:** the quality or state of being inflexible **:** PERTINACITY, RIGIDITY
un·yoke \ˌən+\ *vb* [ME *unyoken*, fr. OE *ungeocian*, fr. 2*un-* + *geocian* to yoke] *vt* **1 a :** to free (a draft animal) from a yoke or harness **:** OUTSPAN, UNHITCH **b** *obs* **:** to liberate as if from a yoke **:** RELEASE ⟨the property of truth is . . . to ~ and set free the minds and spirits of a nation —John Milton⟩ **2 :** to take apart **:** DISJOIN, UNLINK ⟨at the rapids the large rafts are . . . *unyoked*, and divided into small portions —Anthony Trollope⟩ ~ *vi* **1** *archaic* **:** to unharness a draft animal **2** *archaic* **:** to stop work **:** slack off
un·yoked \"+\ *adj* [in sense 1, fr. 1*un-* + *yoked*, past part. of *yoke*; in sense 2, fr. past part. of *unyoke*] **1 :** not yoked **:** UNRESTRAINED **2 :** freed from or as if from a yoke
un·zealous \"+\ *adj* **:** not zealous — **un·zeal·ous·ly** *adv*
un·zip \"+\ *vb* [2*un-* + *zip*] *vt* **:** to zip open ⟨~ a zipper⟩ ⟨*unzipped* a pocket in his black nylon parka —E.S.Hatch⟩ ~ *vi* **:** to open by means of a zipper ⟨~*s* to hold full pack —*Mademoiselle*⟩
un·zipper \"+\ *vb* **:** UNZIP
un·zoned \"+\ *adj* [1*un-* + *zoned*, past part. of *zone*] **1 :** not zoned **:** UNRESTRICTED **2** *archaic* **:** not cinctured
1up \(ˈ)əp\ *adv* [partly fr. ME *up* upward, fr. OE *ūp*; partly fr. ME *uppe* on high, fr. OE; both akin to OHG *ūf* up, ON *upp* up, upward, *uppi* on high, Goth *iup* upward, *uf* under, L *sub* under, below, Gk *hypo* under, Skt *upa* towards, near to, at, under, *upari* over — more at OVER] **1 a (1) :** toward the sky **:** toward a higher position **:** away from the center of the earth ⟨pushes the boy ~ to the top of the fence so he can see⟩ ⟨the oil shoots ~ 200 feet⟩ ⟨has breakfast brought ~ to her bedroom⟩ ⟨ordered ~ searchlights to stab the sky —Noel Houston⟩ — often used as an intensive ⟨lift ~ your eyes⟩ ⟨raised ~ the ceiling a few feet⟩; often used in commands or exclamations calling for upward motion ⟨hands ~⟩ ⟨~ periscope —E.L.Beach⟩; formerly used in combination with a verb, esp. an

auxiliary ⟨we will, fair Queen, ~ to the mountain's top —Shak.⟩ (2) **:** from beneath the ground or water to the surface ⟨digs ~ arrowheads in his backyard⟩ ⟨the fish swim ~ for crumbs⟩ (3) **:** from below the horizon ⟨sees the moon come ~⟩ (4) **:** toward a slightly higher level ⟨fishermen pulling boats ~ onto a beach⟩; *specif* **:** to or near the putting green of a golf course ⟨hits the ball well ~⟩ (5) **:** toward a point (as on a river) that is farther away from the ocean ⟨must time everything exactly — ~ with the flood tide, arriving . . . precisely at slack water —C.S.Forester⟩ (6) **:** from a prone, sitting, slanting, or stooped position to an upright position ⟨helps ~ a man who has fallen⟩ ⟨draws himself ~ to his full height⟩; *specif* **:** out of bed ⟨stayed ~ all night long⟩ — sometimes used in commands or exclamations ⟨~, ~, my friend, and quit your books —William Wordsworth⟩ **b :** upward from the ground or other surface so as to be detached ⟨pulls ~ all the tulips⟩ **c** *archaic* **:** to a condition of being open ⟨have broken ~ my packet again to insert this letter —Edmund Verney⟩ **d :** so as to expose fully a particular side or surface ⟨turns the ace of spades ~⟩ **2 a :** in a relatively high position ⟨~ in the mountains⟩ ⟨brings in a mirror-sharp picture 35,000 feet ~ —*advt*⟩ ⟨wants to see her name ~ in lights⟩ ⟨only a kid . . . with that flaming hair of hers just ~ —Mary Deasy⟩ ⟨the ball is ~ on the green⟩ **b :** at a point (as on a river) that is farther away from the ocean ⟨camps ~ above the rapids⟩ **c :** in an upright position; *specif* **:** on one's feet ⟨standing ~ in front of a judge —Kay Boyle⟩ **3 a :** so as to cause sound to rise in volume or to be heard ⟨speak ~ so that she can hear⟩ ⟨turns ~ the radio too loud⟩ **b :** so as to cause light to become brighter ⟨turns ~ the lamp on the desk⟩ **4 a :** to or in a higher or better condition or status ⟨on his way ~ as a junior member of a law firm —Sara H. Hay⟩ ⟨pressure on manufacturers to keep quality ~ —*Current Biog.*⟩ ⟨keeps him ~ out of sentimental estheticism —Clive Bell⟩ — sometimes used in exclamations ⟨~ the workers —Liam O'Flaherty⟩ **b :** to or toward an advanced state (as of maturity or skill) ⟨grew ~ in the city⟩ **c :** to or in a state of greater resolution or cheerfulness ⟨brace ~ and keep going⟩ ⟨only buoyed ~ by the hope . . . of seeing a junk —Osbert Lancaster⟩ — sometimes used in commands or exclamations **d** (1) **:** to or in a state of greater activity or excitement ⟨stirs ~ crowds⟩ ⟨the type that boiled ~ inside sometimes —E.V.Roberts⟩ (2) — used as a function word usu. in combination with *it* to indicate marked or intense activity ⟨singing and laughing it ~ with the boys —Arthur Godfrey⟩ **e :** to or at a greater speed, rate, or amount ⟨an effort to bring military plane production ~ —*Current Biog.*⟩ ⟨rents would move ~ or down —S.L.Payne⟩ **f :** to or at a higher musical pitch ⟨transposes the melody ~ a fifth⟩ ⟨singing easily ~ above high C⟩ **g :** in continuance (as in time or a series) ⟨indefatigable labors from youth ~ —D.S. & Jessie K. Jordan⟩ ⟨boys from fourth grade ~ —Gladys Skelley⟩ ⟨rent from $50 ~ —Warner Olivier⟩ ⟨highly alert during the night and ~ through dawn —P.W.Thompson⟩ ⟨from early childhood ~ until the age of 20⟩ **h :** into greater prominence or a higher status or estimation (as by means of a specific action) ⟨talks ~ all the new styles⟩ ⟨the quality of the beef is what counts, and the brown sugar is the touch to point it ~ —C.H.Baker⟩ **i :** to or in a state of expansion ⟨a fish that puffs itself ~⟩ ⟨the ingenious folly of pumping ~ a poem till it means everything —N.E. Nelson⟩ **5 a :** into existence, evidence, prominence, or prevalence **:** into operation or practical form ⟨drawings . . . worked ~ in the office by several draftsmen —F.J.Mather⟩ ⟨saloons went ~ rapidly —D.D.Martin⟩ ⟨a skillful building ~ of suspense —C.W. Shumaker⟩ ⟨the money will turn ~ somewhere⟩ ⟨stokes the fire to get steam ~⟩ **b :** to the consideration or attention of a person so that a decision or disposition can be made ⟨put the problem squarely and finally ~ to the states and cities whose immediate concern it is —F.E. Johnson⟩ ⟨senators come ~ for reelection —T.R.Ybarra⟩ ⟨the unmanageable gelding went ~ for raffle —*Time*⟩ **c :** to or at bat ⟨comes ~ twice in the same inning⟩ **6 a :** into the hands of another ⟨yielded himself ~ a prisoner —Maria Edgeworth⟩ **b :** into one's possession ⟨their licenses can be taken ~ and returned to authorities in their own state —*Birmingham (Ala.) News*⟩ **c :** in disclosure or confession — used with *own*, *show*, or *give* **7 a :** to or toward a total number or quantity ⟨counts ~ all the factors⟩ ⟨ran ~ a big bill⟩ ⟨sums ~ the whole situation⟩ **b** (1) **:** to a state of completeness or finality ⟨eats ~ the cake⟩ ⟨finds that the land he is interested in is leased ~ —J.L.Harnon⟩ ⟨charge it ~ to experience⟩ — often used as a function word for emphasis with little addition of meaning ⟨might wake even the bomber boys ~ —J.G.Cozzens⟩ ⟨the pipe is stopped ~ with dirt⟩ ⟨the black water had swallowed me ~ —O.S.J.Gogarty⟩ ⟨to fright the animals and to kill them ~ —Shak.⟩ (2) **:** to a degree approaching completeness **:** to a marked degree ⟨show houses were being bought ~ by the moving picture interests —C.F.Wittke⟩ ⟨clean ~ the house⟩ ⟨softening ~ the enemy with artillery before making the final attack⟩ — often used as a function word for emphasis ⟨the plane's fueling ~ —Kay Boyle⟩ ⟨the roads empty magically while the drivers chow ~ —Barrett McGurn⟩ **8 a :** in or into a storage place ⟨lays ~ supplies for the winter⟩ ⟨putting ~ preserves⟩ **b :** in or into a condition of closure or confinement ⟨buttoned himself ~ —John Buchan⟩ ⟨wrapped ~ in a dressing gown —H.A.L.Craig⟩ ⟨a fine time to pot ~ bulbs for forcing —*Catalog: Holland Bulb Gardens*⟩ ⟨cork the bottle ~⟩ ⟨have locked ~ and gone home —Brooks Atkinson⟩ **c :** in or into a condition of union or combination ⟨sews ~ the rip⟩ ⟨joins ~ with his friends⟩ **d :** by way of remedying or eliminating a defect (as a break) ⟨patched ~ his old pants⟩ ⟨a rather battered sign . . . we ought to paint it ~ —*Holiday*⟩ **9 a :** so as to arrive or approach ⟨comes driving ~ in a new car⟩ ⟨an avenue of trees leads ~ to the house⟩ **b :** in a direction that is conventionally the opposite of *down* regardless of difference in elevation **:** toward, to, or at a place that is regarded as higher: as (1) *chiefly Brit* **:** toward or in a more important place (as a large city, university, or headquarters) ⟨went ~ to London as professor of surgery —Harvey Graham⟩ (2) **:** toward the direction from which the wind is blowing **:** to windward (3) **:** toward or in the north ⟨peach cultivation is slowly extending ~ from the south —*Amer. Guide Series: Ark.*⟩ (4) **:** toward or near the top (as of a sheet of paper) ⟨your rapid pen moved ~ and down —Edna S.V. Millay⟩ (5) **:** toward or in an outlying district ⟨went ~ to the farm for a rest⟩ (6) **:** toward or at the rear of a theatrical stage — used chiefly in stage directions ⟨offended, walks ~ —W.S.Gilbert⟩ (7) **:** to prison ⟨went ~ in the 1920's . . . for 20 years —D.W.Maurer⟩ **c :** toward or at a forward position ⟨hold their positions ~ in the trenches⟩ **d :** so as to be even with, overtake, find, or arrive at ⟨his horse was fourth but then came ~ and won⟩ ⟨may be traced ~ to the first beginnings of Greek speculation —Walter Pater⟩ **10 :** in or into separated parts ⟨break ~ the road before widening it⟩ ⟨tears ~ newspapers⟩ — often used as a function word for emphasis ⟨the country was divided ~ into two spheres of interest —A.T. Bouscaren⟩ **11 a :** to a stop — usu. used with *draw*, *bring*, *fetch*, or *pull* **b :** without delay **:** PROMPTLY ⟨didn't wait for recognition but spoke right ~⟩ ⟨answers ~ to every question⟩ **12 a :** in advance (as of one's opponent) **:** AHEAD ⟨on the next hole he shot a birdie three to go two ~ —*Time*⟩ ⟨the intellectual's game of being one ~ on the prevailing interpretation —W.L.Miller⟩ **b :** for each side **:** EACH ⟨the score is 15 ~⟩ **13 a :** in multiples (as copies printed on a single sheet from identical plates at a single impression) ⟨when circulars are ordered in large quantities, it is common to print them two ~ or four ~ —Daniel Melcher & Nancy Larrick⟩ — compare [1]GANG 3a(2) **b :** in capital letters **:** with a capital initial letter ⟨put all of these words ~⟩ **c :** on a recto page and with the head next to the binding edge — used of the facing of an illustration; compare [2]FACE 9

[2]up \'əp\ *adj* [ME *uppe*, fr. OE, fr. *uppe*, adv.] **1 a :** risen above the horizon esp. so as to be visible **:** present in the sky ⟨the sun is still ~⟩ **b** (1) **:** standing on one's feet (2) *chiefly Brit* **:** standing and delivering a speech ⟨the chancellor of the exchequer's ~ —Charles Dickens⟩ **c :** risen from bed **:** being out of bed ⟨is ~ every morning at six⟩ ⟨a man who was just ~ from an attack of the measles —A.W.Long⟩ ⟨was ~ all last night —Kay Boyle⟩ **d :** high with respect to the bank of a stream or a shore ⟨the river is dangerously ~⟩ **e :** being in a raised position **:** RAISED, LIFTED ⟨all the windows are ~⟩ ⟨with the thumbscrew in the ~ position —H.G.Armstrong⟩ ⟨her defenses were ~ —Ethel Wilson⟩ **f :** standing above the ground **:** CONSTRUCTED, BUILT ⟨the two temporary bridges are ~ —Kay Boyle⟩ **g** (1) **:** having the face uppermost and exposed **:** facing upward (2) **:** fried on one side ⟨ordered two eggs ~⟩ **h :** mounted on the back of a horse ⟨with a new jockey ~⟩ ⟨is ~ on a long shot —Walter Bernstein⟩ **i :** grown or moved above a surface (as of the ground) so as to be visible ⟨the corn is ~ now⟩ **j :** cut and placed suitably (as in storage) ⟨the hay is ~, and the turnips thinned —Padraic Fallon⟩ **k** (1) **:** having the surface broken (as for repairs) ⟨began to unload poles and warning notices of "Road *Up*" —Adrian Bell⟩ (2) **:** REMOVED ⟨finds the track ~ for several hundred feet⟩ **l :** moving, inclining, or directed upward ⟨the ~ escalator⟩ ⟨looked at him with an ~ glance⟩ **m** (1) **:** set with a capital initial letter or all in capitals ⟨all genus names are ~⟩ (2) **:** marked by the use of more capital letters than is usual ⟨the style of this magazine is ~⟩ **n :** held or brushed up toward the top of the head ⟨a new ~ hairdo, a little fancy for daytime —Budd Schulberg⟩ **2 a** (1) **:** marked by a state of revolt, agitation, or excitement ⟨they say the tribes are ~ —John Masefield⟩ ⟨their fighting blood was ~ —S.H.Adams⟩ (2) **:** marked by activity **:** ACTIVE ⟨let's be ~ and doing⟩ **b :** marked by confidence and good spirits ⟨in his ~ periods he joked and talked —Cyril Connolly⟩ **c :** increased above a former level (as of quantity or price) ⟨bank loans were ~ six percent —Harvey Walker⟩ ⟨Sunday school enrollment is ~ —Ben Bradford⟩ ⟨fever was down, appetite was ~ —G.W.Gray b. 1886⟩ **d** (1) **:** marked by greater than usual power or strength ⟨haunts the sandbar now and growls when the wind is ~ —Laurence Critchell⟩ ⟨the lights in the drawing room on the first floor . . . were ~ —Margery Allingham⟩ (2) **:** exerting enough force or power (as for operation) ⟨the ship will sail as soon as steam is ~⟩ ⟨I'll make a pot of tea. The fire is just ~ —Katharine Shattuck⟩ **e :** sailing on the way **:** BOUND ⟨a ship now ~ for the tropics⟩ **f :** EFFERVESCENT ⟨took a sip to see if the champagne was still ~⟩ **g :** READY ⟨was ~ to any party of pleasure —W.M.Thackeray⟩; *specif* **:** marked by a high degree of physical and psychological preparedness ⟨players will be ~ for the conference opponents and traditional rivals —H.O. Crisler⟩ **h** (1) **:** going on **:** taking place ⟨went out to see what was ~ —Francis Shean⟩ ⟨begins to realize something is ~ —Anne Brooks⟩ (2) **:** WRONG, AMISS ⟨there was something ~ with her voice —Richard Llewellyn⟩ **3 a :** come to an end **:** COMPLETED, ENDED, TERMINATED ⟨the ringing of a bell in the classroom means that the hour is ~ —Ralph Linton⟩ ⟨his term of duty is nearly ~ —A.H.Townsend⟩ ⟨the game is ~ at 15 points⟩ **b** *Brit* **:** ADJOURNED ⟨Parliament was ~ —C.E. Robinson⟩ **c :** come to an undesired end ⟨the game's all ~ with him⟩ ⟨the hunt was now fairly ~ and a crowd nearly 50 strong was racing down the wharf after them —Max Peacock⟩ **d :** set in type ⟨the editorial is all ~⟩ **4 a :** standing high (as in status or fortune) **:** having risen from a lower position ⟨at graduation he was well ~ in his class⟩ ⟨can almost tell which industries are down and which are ~, from the gifts —Sanford Brown⟩ ⟨choose management material not from men ~ from the bench but from young college-trained technicians —*Time*⟩ **b :** situated forward with respect to others ⟨his horse is well ~⟩ **c** *archaic* **:** much spoken about **d :** being or having arrived on the same level or at the same point **:** EQUAL, EVEN ⟨there were no dragging ends in the rear . . . nobody complaining that food or ammunition was not ~ —*Everybody's Mag.*⟩ — often used with *to* or *with* ⟨was well ~ to the average of her class —F.W. Crofts⟩ ⟨did not feel quite ~ to par and proposed to rest —Alexander MacDonald⟩ ⟨discovers he is ~ with the best of them⟩ **e :** advanced in age ⟨lived until she was ~ in the eighties⟩ **f** (1) **:** well informed through study or experience **:** quite familiar **:** ABREAST — usu. used with *on* ⟨his friends are ~ on the very latest things in the arts —Geoffrey Gorer⟩; also used with *in* or *to* ⟨well ~ in these things —J.B.Smyth⟩ (2) **:** being on schedule **:** not fallen behind — usu. used with *on* or *in* ⟨said he was ~ on his homework⟩ **g :** ahead of one's opponent (as in a game) ⟨in spite of being set four tricks they were still ~⟩ ⟨was three ~ on the second hole⟩ ⟨black is a pawn ~⟩ **h :** being at or near the top (as of a list) ⟨rehashing . . . the rumors of names ~ for rotation —T.H.Phillips⟩ **i :** being the higher pair in a poker hand consisting of two pairs ⟨queens ~⟩ **5 a** (1) **:** bound in a direction regarded as up (as toward the north, an important city, or the source of a river) ⟨caught the ~ train to town⟩ ⟨a very small fraction of the ~ traffic —Werner Mangold⟩ (2) **:** of or relating to traffic bound in a direction regarded as up ⟨checked his suitcase on the ~ side of the station⟩ **b** *chiefly Brit* (1) **:** staying temporarily in a more important place (as London) (2) **:** resident at a university or a school ⟨was ~ . . . with my wife as an undergraduate —W.B.Millen⟩ ⟨was still the depth of the vacation, and there were only a few scholars ~ —C.P.Snow⟩ **c :** placed so as to hold the rudder far to leeward ⟨the tiller is ~⟩ **d :** blowing from a mark used in archery toward the shooter ⟨a strong ~ wind⟩ **e :** confined to prison **6 a** (1) **:** being under consideration (as for the making of a decision) ⟨the bill is now ~ before Congress⟩ ⟨the question is now ~ to the full cabinet and a decision is expected —H.T.Simmons⟩ (2) **:** presented for consideration (as for the making of a decision) **:** due to be considered ⟨is ~ for reelection —Elmer Davis⟩ ⟨is now ~ for sale —S.P.B.Mais⟩ ⟨a labor contract is ~ for negotiation —*Securities Outlook*⟩; *specif* **:** present (as in a court) and charged with an offense ⟨is ~ for rape —Charles Oldfather⟩ **b :** placed at stake **:** BET, WAGERED ⟨many thousands of dollars were ~ on the match⟩ — **up against :** confronted with **:** face-to-face with ⟨realized that they were *up against* a major difficulty —Nevil Shute⟩ ⟨really took a professional to understand what he was *up against* —Robertson Davies⟩ — **up against it :** face-to-face with a seemingly insuperable obstacle **:** in desperate straits ⟨a first-rate story of people who happen to be *up against it* —J.R.Chamberlain⟩ — **up to 1 a :** capable of performing or dealing with **:** competent or able to cope with **:** capable of ⟨feels she is *up to* her role in the play⟩ ⟨is now *up to* seeing visitors⟩ ⟨was *up to* doing the job in a little over six days —Robert Bendiner⟩; *specif* **:** capable of carrying without strain ⟨require a horse *up to* 13 stone —F.C.Hitchcock⟩ **b :** aware of and prepared for ⟨should certainly be *up to* his tricks by this time⟩ **2 :** engaged in esp. secretly and with intentions that are bad or not altogether good ⟨ferreting out clues as to what he was *up to* —R.H.Popkin⟩ ⟨was always *up to* something —H.G.Wells⟩ **3 :** incumbent on **:** devolving on **:** being the responsibility of ⟨it was *up to* the parent to educate his child —Benjamin Fine⟩ ⟨left the next move *up to* the Russians —*Current History*⟩ ⟨the amount you give is entirely *up to* you —Agnes M. Miall⟩

[3]up \"\ *vb* **upped** *or in vi 1* **up; upped; upping; ups** *or in vi 1* **up** [[1]*up*] *vi* **1 :** to act abruptly or surprisingly — usu. followed by *and* and another verb ⟨he ~ and married a show girl —Michael Mackay⟩ ⟨the jackass *upped* and died —*Springfield (Mass.) Union*⟩ ⟨no sooner is a girl qualified to be a doctor than she ~*s* with some white-jacketed junior bandage wrapper and is off with him to a suburban villa —R.P.Lister⟩ **2 :** to rise from a lying or sitting position **:** get up **3 :** to move upward **:** RISE, ASCEND **4 :** to raise one's hand or arm esp. quickly and aggressively — followed by *with* ⟨*upped* with a shotgun and opened some rain holes in the cloth top —F.B. Gipson⟩ ~ *vt* **1 :** to catch a swan in order to put the owner's mark on the beak **2 a :** to move to a physically higher position **:** RAISE, LIFT ⟨~*s* flukes and goes down again —W.J.Hopkins⟩ ⟨*upped* sail —John Buchan⟩ **b** (1) **:** to raise to a higher level **:** INCREASE, ADVANCE ⟨*upped* the fare from 10 cents to 15 cents a ride —Gus Tyler⟩ ⟨cattle growers *upped* meat production —*N.Y. Times*⟩ (2) **:** to put into a higher occupational position **:** PROMOTE ⟨has been *upped* to general merchandising director —Bennett Cerf⟩ (3) **:** RAISE 17 **3 :** to put (the helm) up

[4]up \(¦)əp\ *prep* [[1]*up*] **1 a :** from a lower to a higher place on or along **:** to, toward, or at a higher point of ⟨climbing ~ a tree⟩ ⟨building a cogwheel railway ~ the mountain —*Amer. Guide Series: N.H.*⟩ ⟨the heat which is normally wasted ~ the chimney —Ronald Robson⟩ ⟨a child can be shifted horizontally as he progresses ~ the school —G.B.Jeffery⟩ ⟨it might be snowing ~ the mountain —J.M.Brinnin⟩ **b :** up into or in the ⟨go ~ garret and play —B.F.Taylor⟩ ⟨asked was there anything ~ attic —Robert Frost⟩ **2 :** in a direction regarded as being toward or near the upper end or part of ⟨a journey ~ one of the valleys —L.D.Stamp⟩: as **a :** toward or at a point that is closer to the source or beginning of ⟨a steamer groping her way ~ river —Cicely F. Smith⟩ ⟨these fish winter ~ the river —*Biol. Abstracts*⟩ **b :** toward or near the inner part of ⟨walks ~ the walk —Edna S.V.Millay⟩ ⟨advanced ~ the room —J.G.Cozzens⟩ ⟨will find himself trapped ~ a dead end —H.A.Burr⟩ **c :** to, toward, or in the interior of (as a region) ⟨traveling ~ the country⟩ ⟨~ country in the coffee and cotton plantations . . . life is rougher — William Tate⟩ **d :** toward the north along or through ⟨lives a few miles ~ the coast⟩ ⟨withdrew his army ~ the island — H.E.Scudder⟩ — often used in combination with a following noun to form adjectives and adverbs ⟨an auction of *up*county farm land — Lonnie Coleman⟩ ⟨the water would then flow *up*dip through the more porous strata —C.G.Lalicker⟩ **3 :** in the direction opposite to **:** AGAINST ⟨~ the wind⟩ **4 a :** in a direction parallel to the length of **:** ALONG ⟨took his arm and they began to walk together ~ the street —William Fay⟩ **b :** nearby on ⟨as familiar as the man who lives ~ the street⟩

[5]up \'əp\ *n* -s [[1]*up* & [2]*up*] **1 :** one that is in a high or advantageous position ⟨the savor of the book lies in . . . figures in the crowd, in the downs as well as the ~*s* —Ernestine Evans⟩ **2 :** an upward slope **3 :** a period or state of prosperity or success ⟨unions always thrive most in times of business ~*s* or business downs —*Kiplinger Washington Letter*⟩ ⟨has had downs as well as ~*s* since he became . . . commander of the northern expeditionary forces —*New Republic*⟩ **4 :** a rise in value or price — **in two ups** *Austral* **:** in a jiffy — **on the up :** moving upward ⟨is *on the up* in any case. Thirteen miles away . . . the world's largest molybdenum mine is booming —*Time*⟩ ⟨the curve is steadily *on the up* —B.M.Beck⟩

up *abbr* upper

UP *abbr* underproof

up-a-daisy *var of* UPSY-DAISY

upaith·ric \(')yü¦pīthrik\ *adj* [irreg. fr. Gk *hypaithros* in the open air, uncovered + E *-ic* — more at HYPAETHRAL] **:** HYPAETHRAL

up-anchor \¦=¦==\ *vi* [[3]*up* + *anchor*, n.] **:** to pull up the anchor esp. before getting under way ⟨we *up-anchored*, southbound for the canal —*Blue Bk.*⟩

up-and-comer \'=='==\ *n* [*up-and-coming* + *-er*] **:** COMER 2

up-and-coming \¦==¦==\ *adj* [[2]*up*] **:** alertly active and likely to advance or succeed **:** ENTERPRISING, PROMISING ⟨gave encouragement, contracts, and advances to *up-and-coming* young songwriters —Hal Levy⟩ ⟨an *up-and-coming* new town⟩

[1]up and down *adv* [ME *up and down*] **1 :** to and fro **:** backward and forward ⟨spent the night pacing *up and down*⟩ **2 :** here and there esp. throughout an area ⟨looking for him *up and down*⟩ **3 a :** with regard to every particular **:** THOROUGHLY, COMPLETELY ⟨his home state which he knows *up and down*⟩ ⟨looked her *up and down* before speaking⟩ **b :** without holding back **:** BLUNTLY, DIRECTLY ⟨told him *up and down* he was a fool⟩ **4 :** into or in a vertical position — used of a cable when the anchor is under or nearly under the bow

[2]up and down *n, pl* **ups and downs 1** *ups and downs pl* **a :** alternating rise and fall esp. in fortune or degree of success **:** ALTERNATION, FLUCTUATION, VICISSITUDE ⟨jogging along with *ups and downs* and plenty of worries and some satisfactions —F.M.Ford⟩ ⟨a little weary of the perpetual *ups and downs* of her mood —J.W.Krutch⟩ **b :** an undulation or irregularity (as on the surface of the ground) ⟨a difficult route with many *ups and downs*⟩ **2 :** a quick examining look ⟨gave me the *up and down*, and I saw that he remembered me —*Popular Mag.*⟩ **3 :** a design or texture that changes in appearance when the material is viewed from a different angle and that must be placed upright in order to obtain the desired effect ⟨the pieces of a pattern can be placed closely on this solid-color fabric because it has no *up and down*⟩

up-and-down \¦==¦=\ *adj* [[1]*up and down*] **1 :** marked by alternate upward and downward movement or action ⟨an odd *up-and-down* gait⟩ ⟨in his natural *up-and-down* voice —I.S. Cobb⟩ ⟨many such *up-and-down* years —Thomas Hughes⟩ **2 a :** very steep **:** PERPENDICULAR ⟨in the deep sand about a foot from a straight *up-and-down* bank —Ring Lardner⟩ **b :** DIRECT, DOWNRIGHT ⟨an *up-and-down* quarrel⟩ **3 :** marked by irregularity of surface; *esp* **:** having an irregular terrain **:** HILLY, MOUNTAINOUS ⟨an *up-and-down* place where the hotel has seven main entrances, each on a different floor —*Geog. School Bull.*⟩ **4** *Brit* **:** ROUGH-AND-TUMBLE ⟨savage, desperate, *up-and-down* fighting —Charles Kingsley⟩ — **up-and-downness** *n* -ES

up-and-down indicator *n* **:** a device for showing to what extent a timepiece has run down

up-and-up \'=='=\ *n* [[1]*up*] **1 :** an honest or respectable course — used chiefly in the phrase *on the up-and-up* ⟨it's on the *up-and-up*. Go ahead and start your investigation —Erle Stanley Gardner⟩ ⟨an occupation of free love considered strictly on the *up-and-up* —Hendrik de Leeuw⟩ **2 :** an upward course esp. toward an improved state — used chiefly in the phrase *on the up-and-up* ⟨business was on the *up-and-up* all through 1936 —Benjamin Stolberg⟩

upan·i·shad *also* **upan·i·sad** \ü'pänē,shäd, ü'panē,shad\ *n* -s *usu cap* [Skt *upaniṣad* act of sitting down near something, secret session, secret doctrine, fr. *upa* toward, near to, under + *ni* down + *sīdati* he sits — more at UP, NETHER, SIT] **:** one of a late class of Vedic treatises dealing with broad philosophic problems (as the nature of ultimate reality, man, and the universe) — **upan·i·shad·ic** *also* **upan·i·sad·ic** \=¦==¦shädik, -shad-\ *adj, usu cap*

upa·pu·ra·na \¦üpəpü¦ränə\ *n* -s *often cap* [Skt *upapurāṇa* secondary purana, fr. *upa* toward, near to, under, secondary + *purāṇa* — more at PURANA] **:** a minor purana

uparching \¦=¦==\ *n* [[1]*up* + *arching*, pres. part. of *arch*] **:** the bending of rocks into an anticline or a dome

upas \'yüpəs\ *n* -ES [Malay *(pohon) upas*, fr. *pohon* tree + *upas* poison, fr. Jav] **1 a** *or* **upas tree :** a very large evergreen tree (*Antiaris toxicaria*) formerly believed to be so poisonous as to destroy any living thing in its vicinity that grows in lowland areas of southeastern Asia and eastward to the Philippines, that is closely related to the breadfruits, that yields a latex containing poisonous glucosides which act on the heart and are used in arrow and dart poisons, and that has an inner bark which is a locally important source of bark cloth **b :** any of various poisonous plants of the genus *Strychnos* that are used with or similarly to the upas in arrow poisons; *esp* **:** a Javanese vine (*S. tieute*) **2 :** a poisonous mixture that usu. contains the juice or latex of a upas, is commonly boiled down to a thick tarry consistency, and is used esp. on arrows or darts **3 :** a poisonous or harmful influence or institution ⟨the ~ of contemporary public life —W.R.Thayer⟩

upbank thaw \'=,=-\ *n* [[4]*up* + *bank*] **:** a thaw on hills while the frost is unbroken in the valley below

upbear \¦=¦=\ *vt* [ME *upberen*, fr. *up* + *beren* to bear — more at BEAR] **:** to bear up **:** SUPPORT, RAISE

[1]upbeat \'=,=\ *n* [[2]*up* + *beat*] **1 a :** an unaccented beat in a musical measure; *specif* **:** the last beat of the measure **b :** PICKUP 4g **2 a :** ANACRUSIS 1 **b :** a weak or slack element or syllable in a metrical foot **:** THESIS **3 :** an increase in activity or prosperity ⟨find the town on the ~ after a local recession —S.W.Taylor⟩

[2]upbeat \"\ *adj* **:** marked by optimism **:** OPTIMISTIC, CHEERFUL, HAPPY ⟨there is no reason why realistic drama must invariably have a downbeat ending — especially in so ~ an era —Walter Goodman⟩

upbend \'=,=\ *n* [[2]*up* + *bend*] **:** the fore part of a ski that curves upward and terminates at the point

upblast \'=,=\ *n* [[2]*up* + *blast*] **:** a blast that exerts force upward

upblown \¦=¦=\ *adj* [[1]*up* + *blown*, past part. of *blow* (after *blow up*)] **:** blown up; *esp* **:** INFLATED

upboil \¦=¦=\ *vi* [ME *upboilen*, fr. [1]*up* + *boilen* to boil — more at BOIL] **:** to boil up

upbound \'=¦=\ *adj* [[1]*up* + *bound*] **:** traveling or leading in a direction that is regarded as up ⟨~ freighters⟩ ⟨~ shipping lanes⟩

up-bow \'=,bō\ *n* [[1]*up* + *bow*] **:** a stroke in playing a bowed instrument (as a violin) made toward the heel of the bow — contrasted with *down-bow;* symbol V

up·braid \¦əp¦brād *sometimes* ,əp'b-\ *vt* -ED/-ING/-S [ME *upbreyden*, fr. OE *ūpbregdan*, prob. fr. *ūp* up + *bregdan* to move suddenly, snatch, weave together — more at UP, BRAID] **1** *obs* **:** to bring forth as a cause for censure ⟨there will come a time when this shall be ~*ed* to us —Jeremy Taylor⟩ **2 a :** to criticize severely **:** find fault with ⟨~*s* all forms of ceremony —W.B.Yeats⟩ **b :** to reproach severely **:** scold vehemently ⟨saw the priest go over to the parents and ~ them for bringing their children to such a place —Francis Stuart⟩ **3** *archaic* **:** to make queasy **:** NAUSEATE **syn** see SCOLD

up·braid·er \-də(r)\ *n* -s **:** one that upbraids

up·braid·ing·ly *adv* **:** in an upbraiding manner

1upbreak \¦=¦=\ *vb* [ME *upbreken*, fr. *up* + *breken* to break — more at BREAK] *vt* **:** to break up or open ~ *vi* **:** to force a way up (as through the surface)

2upbreak \ˈ=,=\ *n* **:** an act or instance of breaking up; *esp* **:** ERUPTION, OUTBURST

upbreathe \¦=¦=\ *vt* [1*up* + *breathe*] *archaic* **:** to breathe up or out **:** EXHALE

upbringing \ˈ=,==\ *n* -s [fr. gerund of obs. *upbring* to bring up fr. ME *upbringen*, fr. *up* + *bringen* to bring] **:** the process of bringing up **:** early training ⟨by ~ and temperament he is at home in high politics —Alan Campbell-Johnson⟩; *esp* **:** a particular way of bringing up a child ⟨had a strict old-fashioned ~ —A.W.Barkley⟩

upbuild \¦=¦=\ *vt* [1*up* + *build*] **:** to build up ⟨man . . . who can ~ or destroy his home, the earth —Van Wyck Brooks⟩ ⟨an atmosphere favorable to the development of a sense of responsibility and the ~*ing* of character —*Villanova College Cat.*⟩ — **up·build·er** \"+ə(r)\ *n*

up·by *also* **up·bye** \¦əp¦bī\ *adv* [1*up* + *by*] *chiefly Scot* **:** up there

upcard \ˈ=,=\ *n* [2*up* + *card*] **1 a :** the card turned up to start the play (as in rummy and stops games) — called also *starter*, *turnup* **b :** the card at the top of a discard pile or talon **2 :** any card properly dealt faceup; *specif* **:** the first card dealt faceup to a player in stud poker

1upcast \¦=¦=\ *vt* [ME *upcasten*, fr. *up* + *casten* to cast — more at CAST] **:** to cast up

2upcast \ˈ=,=\ *adj* [ME, fr. past part. of *upcasten*] **1 :** turned or directed upward ⟨saw that she was blind, her face slightly ~ to her companion's —Lawrence Durrell⟩ **2 :** having an upward draft (as in a mine) ⟨the proposed ~ airway —*Economist*⟩

3upcast \"\ *n* [1*upcast*] **1 :** ACCIDENT, CHANCE ⟨kissed the jack upon an ~ —Shak.⟩ **2** *chiefly Scot* **:** REPROACH, TAUNT **3 :** an upward dislocation of a stratum **4 :** the ventilating shaft (as in a mine) up which the air passes after circulation **5 :** material that has been thrown up (as by digging)

upcheck \ˈ=,=\ *n* [2*up* + *check*] **:** a satisfactory mark in a test and esp. in a check flight

upchuck \ˈ=,=\ *vb* [1*up* + *chuck*] **:** VOMIT

upclimb \¦=¦=\ *vb* [1*up* + *climb*] **:** to climb up **:** ASCEND — **up·climb·er** \"+ə(r)\ *n*

upclose \¦=¦=\ *vb* [ME *upclosen*, fr. *up* + *closen* to close — more at CLOSE] **:** to close up **:** SHUT

upcoast \ˈ=¦=\ *adj* [4*up* + *coast*] **:** situated or going up the coast ⟨the isolated ~ cannery will soon be a thing of the past —*Canadian Geog. Jour.*⟩

upcome \ˈ=,=\ *n* [2*up* + *come*] **1** *Scot* **:** the outward appearance of a person **2** *Brit* **:** RESULT, PRODUCT

1upcoming \ˈ=,==\ *n* -s [ME, fr. *up* + *coming*, gerund of *comen* to come (after *comen up* to come up)] **:** the action or process of coming up

2upcoming \ˈ=¦==\ *adj* [1*up* + *coming*, pres. part. of *come* (after *come up*, v.)] **:** coming up; *esp* **:** being in the near future **:** FORTHCOMING, APPROACHING ⟨the ~ musicals and plays —J.E.Booth⟩

1up-country \ˈ=¦==\ *adj* [4*up* + *country*, n.] **:** of, relating to, or characteristic of the interior of a country or a region ⟨lying out there in that *up-country* hospital —John Galsworthy⟩ ⟨the representatives of the *up-country* interests —C.H.Wesley⟩ ⟨the great *up-country* fireplace —Miles Franklin⟩

2up-country \"\ *adv* [4*up* + *country*, n.] **:** to or in the interior of a country or a region ⟨marched *up-country* with Indian guides —S.E.Morison⟩ ⟨live *up-country* in comparative isolation —R.J.G.Boothby⟩

3up-country \"\ *n* [2*up* + *country*] **:** the interior of a country or a region

upcropping \ˈ=,==\ *n* [2*up* + *cropping*, gerund of *crop* (after *crop up*, v.)] **:** an act or instance of cropping up **:** APPEARANCE, OUTCROP ⟨the healthy ~ of sizable plants in modest towns —B.M.Bowie⟩

upcurl \¦=¦=\ *vb* [1*up* + *curl*] **:** to curl up ⟨his boots . . . had ~*ing* toes —T.B.Costain⟩

upcurve \ˈ=,=\ *n* [2*up* + *curve*] **:** an upward curve

upcurved \ˈ=¦=\ *adj* [1*up* + *curved*, past part. of *curve*] **:** curving upward ⟨has an ~ bill, which he sweeps back and forth through the shallows —*Amer. Guide Series: Wash.*⟩

1upcut \¦=¦=\ *vt* [1*up* + *cut*, v.] **:** to cut (machine work) while the tool is moving upward

2upcut \ˈ=,=\ *n* [2*up* + *cut*, n.] **:** an upward cut

update \¦=¦=\ *vt* [1*up* + *date*] **:** to bring up to date ⟨the last four chapters read like filler designed to round out, ~, and lengthen a longish article —Carlos Baker⟩ ⟨the motel is like the roadside inn of old, *updated* and lavished with glamour —C.L.Biemiller⟩ — **up·dat·er** \"+ə(r)\ *n*

up·do \ˈəp,dü\ *n* -s [*up*swept hair*do*] **:** an upswept hairdo

updraft \ˈ=,=\ *n* [2*up* + *draft*] **:** an upward movement of air or other gas

updraft kiln *n* **:** a vertical kiln in which the heat is blown or directed upward through the kiln

1updraw \¦=¦=\ *vb* [ME *updrawen*, fr. *up* + *drawen* to draw] **:** to draw up **:** pull up

2updraw \ˈ=,=\ *n* **:** an act or process of drawing up ⟨with a quick ~ of his knees to the other's chest, broke the grip —Jack London⟩

upend \,=ˈ=\ *vb* -ED/-ING/-S [1*up* + *end*, n.] *vt* **1 :** to set on end **:** turn up an end of ⟨~*ed* a reed basket and sat down —L.C. Douglas⟩ ⟨was caught by a giant wave which ~*ed* him —Leonard Lyons⟩ **2 a :** to affect radically **:** turn upside down ⟨a painstakingly executed literary shocker, designed to ~ the credulous matrons —Wolcott Gibbs⟩ **b :** BEAT 4a, 4b ⟨one world record and one world champion were ~*ed* during the . . . championships —*Newsweek*⟩ ~ *vi* **:** to rise on an end **:** move so as to expose an end ⟨the great fish would then ~ — head up, tail straight down in mid-water —William Beebe⟩ ⟨would ~ like ducks and begin to graze —William Beebe⟩

upey·gan \üˈpāgən\ *n* -s [Shona] **:** BLACK RHINOCEROS

upfeed \ˈ=,=\ *adj* [1*up* + *feed*, v.] **:** supplied with a material (as hot water) that is forced upward ⟨an ~ heating system⟩

upfill \¦=¦=\ *vt* [ME *upfillen*, fr. *up* + *fillen* to fill] *archaic* **:** to fill up

upfitter \ˈ=,==\ *n* [2*up* + *fitter* (after *fit up*, v.)] **1 :** one that attaches hardware and trim to wooden furniture — called also *fitter* **2 :** one that fits and assembles tops to casket bodies and puts in the hinges and other hardware — called also *fitter* **3 :** an assembly line worker who installs door handles and other hardware in automobile bodies

upflare \ˈ=,=\ *n* [2*up* + *flare* (after *flare up*, v.)] **:** FLARE-UP

upfling \¦=¦=\ *vt* [1*up* + *fling*] **:** to fling up

upflow \ˈ=,=\ *n* [2*up* + *flow* (after *flow up*, v.)] **:** an upward flow

upfly \¦=¦=\ *vi* [1*up* + *fly*] **:** to fly up

1upfold \¦=¦=\ *vt* [ME *upfolden*, fr. *up* + *folden* to fold] **:** to fold up

2upfold \ˈ=,=\ *n* [2*up* + *fold*, n.] **:** stratified rocks that are folded upward to a crest **:** ANTICLINE

upfurled \¦=¦=\ *adj* [1*up* + *furled*, past part. of *furl* (after *furl up*, v.)] **:** furled upward

up·gang \ˈəp,gaŋ\ *n* [ME (Sc), fr. *up* + *gang* (going)] *chiefly Scot* **:** ASCENT

upgather \¦=¦==\ *vb* [1*up* + *gather*] **:** to gather up

upglide \ˈ=,=\ *n* [2*up* + *glide*] **:** an upward glide

upgliding \ˈ=¦==\ *adj* [1*up* + *gliding*, pres. part. of *glide* (after *glide up*, v.)] **:** outgliding with an upward glide (as the vocalic parts of *day* and *dough* when these parts are diphthongal)

1upgo \¦=¦=\ *vi* [ME *upgon*, *upgan*, fr. *up* + *gon*, *gan* to go — more at GO] **:** to go up **:** ASCEND

2upgo \ˈ=,=\ *n* **:** ASCENT

1upgrade \ˈ=,=\ *n* [2*up* + *grade*, n.] **1 :** an upward grade (as of a road) ⟨ran beside his dogs on the ~*s* —Farley Mowat⟩ **2 a :** INCREASE ⟨thefts and forgeries have been on the ~ —*New Orleans (La.) Times-Picayune*⟩ **b :** a rise toward a better state ⟨on the ~ with nothing more than the occasional discomfort —O.W.Holmes †1935⟩

2upgrade \ˈ=¦=\ *adv* [4*up* + *grade*, n.] **:** toward a higher level on an incline ⟨a locomotive going ~ —Danforth Ross⟩

3upgrade \¦=¦=\ *vt* [1*up* + *grade*, v.] **:** to raise the grade of: as **a :** to improve (as livestock) by the use of purebred sires **b :** to advance to a job requiring a higher level of skill esp. as part of a training program **:** advance in professional rank **c :** to raise the quality of (as a manufactured product) **d :** to raise the classification and usu. the price of (a product) without improving the quality — **up·grad·er** \"+ə(r)\ *n*

upgrow \¦=¦=\ *vi* [ME *upgrowen*, fr. *up* + *growen* to grow] **:** to grow up

upgrowth \ˈ=,=\ *n* **1 :** the process of growing up **:** upward growth **:** DEVELOPMENT ⟨the ~ of the atolls during a rising sea level —F.P.Shepard⟩ ⟨a tremendous ~ of science and practical arts —I.J.Fellner⟩ **2 :** a result of upward growth or development; *specif* **:** PROCESS 4

1upgushing \ˈ=¦==\ *adj* [1*up* + *gushing*, pres. part. of *gush*] **:** gushing upward

2upgushing \ˈ=,==\ *n* -s [2*up* + *gushing*, gerund of *gush*] **:** an act or instance of gushing upward

uphang \¦=¦=\ *vt* [ME *uphongen*, fr. *up* + *hangen*, *hongen* to hang — more at HANG] **:** to hang up

up·haud \,əˈpȯd\ *chiefly Scot var of* UPHOLD

up-headed \ˈ=¦==\ *adj* [1*up* + *headed*] **:** holding the head upright

upheaped \ˈ=¦=\ *adj* [ME *upheped*, fr. *up* + *heped*, past part. of *hepen* to heap — more at HEAP] **:** heaped up **:** ACCUMULATED

up·heav·al \¦əp¦hēvəl, (,)əˈpē- *sometimes* ˌəpˈhē-\ *n* -s **1 a :** the action of upheaving esp. of part of the earth's crust (as by volcanic action) **b :** an instance of upheaving esp. of the earth's crust **2 a :** extreme agitation and disorder (as of society) **:** radical change **:** CONVULSION ⟨unless immediate steps are taken . . . the seven-year-old federation will succumb to violent ~ —Leonard Ingalls⟩ **b :** an instance of extreme disorderly agitation or radical change ⟨the world's peoples are churning in one of history's greatest ~*s* —A.E.Stevenson †1965⟩ ⟨lived through an emotional ~ as shattering as an earthquake —Elizabeth Goudge⟩ **syn** see COMMOTION

up·heav·al·ist \-ləst\ *n* -s **:** an advocate of the theory that upheaval explains geological changes

up·heave \-ēv\ *vb* [ME *upheven*, fr. *up* + *heven* to heave — more at HEAVE] *vt* **1 a :** to heave up **:** LIFT, RAISE ⟨great boulders were *upheaved* by the gold-seekers in their first eager rush —Mary S. Broome⟩ **b :** to force or throw upward with great power or violence ⟨other parts of the coast . . . may be *upheaved* by deep-seated geologic forces —R.W.Miner⟩ **2 :** to disturb extremely **:** throw into disorder ⟨the coming of the troops *upheaved* the whole province⟩ ~ *vi* **:** to move upward esp. with power ⟨the surface of the bay . . . *upheaved* with a slow majestic movement —Bayard Taylor⟩ — **up·heav·er** \-və(r)\ *n*

up·heave·ment \-vmənt\ *n* -s **:** UPHEAVAL

up-hel·ly-aa \ˈəp,helē,ä\ *n* -s *usu cap U & H & A* [ME *uphaliday*, fr. *up* + *haliday*, *holiday* holiday] **:** a festival held in Shetland usu. on the last Tuesday night of January to mark the end of the yule season

1uphill \ˈ=,=\ *n* [4*up* + *hill*, n.] **:** rising ground **:** ASCENT ⟨on the ~ our pace was dragging and stiff —Eve Langley⟩

2uphill \ˈ=¦=\ *adv* [4*up* + *hill*, n.] **1 :** upward on a hill or incline ⟨the heavy material . . . is guided ~ —A.M.Gaudin⟩ ⟨these side streets lay ~ —Sacheverell Sitwell⟩ **2 :** against difficulties ⟨seemed to be talking ~ —Willa Cather⟩

3uphill \"\ *adj* **1 :** situated on elevated ground ⟨an ~ city⟩ **2 :** ascending or directed toward higher ground **:** going up ⟨the trail was ~ and steep —Zane Grey⟩ **3 a :** presenting difficulties **:** requiring much effort **:** DIFFICULT, LABORIOUS ⟨the ~ fight for the abolition of slavery —*London Calling*⟩ ⟨the conversation was all ~ —Irwin Shaw⟩ **b :** struggling against difficulties

uphlstg *abbr* upholstering

uphoard *vt* [1*up* + *hoard*] *obs* **:** to hoard up

uphol *abbr* upholsterer; upholstering; upholstery

1up·hold \ˈə,pōd\ *n* [ME (Sc) *uphald*, fr. OE *ūpheald*, fr. *ūp* up + *heald* hold — more at UP, HOLD] *chiefly Scot* **:** SUPPORT, STAY

2up·hold \¦əp¦hōld, (,)əˈpō- *sometimes* ˌəpˈhō-\ *vt* **up·held** \¦əp¦held, (,)əˈpe- *sometimes* ˌəpˈhe-\ **upheld; upholding; upholds** [ME *uphalden*, *upholden*, fr. *up* + *halden*, *holden* to hold — more at HOLD] **1 a :** to give support to (as by help or action) **:** SUSTAIN, MAINTAIN ⟨tried to ~ the morale of the occupied capital —F.L.Paxson⟩ ⟨the patrol went on . . . after the earthquake, thus ~*ing* the finest traditions of this force —Francis Kingdon-Ward⟩ **b** (1) **:** to support against an opponent **:** DEFEND ⟨enough to ~ . . . the air generals against a strong and well-seated opposition —J.G.Cozzens⟩ (2) *dial Brit* **:** AFFIRM, WARRANT, GUARANTEE ⟨will ~ that you are the coolest hand that I ever came nigh —George Borrow⟩ (3) **:** to adjudge constitutional or legally valid ⟨his language toward a witness was censured by the court of appeals but his decision *upheld* —*Current Biog.*⟩ **c** *chiefly Brit* **:** to keep in good repair **:** keep on the same level **2 a :** to give physical support to **:** keep elevated ⟨slender Corinthian columns ~ the hipped roof —*Amer. Guide Series: La.*⟩ **b :** to lift up **:** RAISE ⟨*upheld* their clenched hands —F.W.Farrar⟩

up·hold·er \-də(r)\ *n* [ME *upholdere*, fr. *upholden* (to repair) + *-ere* -er] **1** *archaic* **a** (1) **:** a dealer in small goods (2) **:** a repairer or maker of small goods **b :** UPHOLSTERER **c :** UNDERTAKER 4 **2 :** one that upholds: as **a :** a physical support **b :** SUPPORTER, MAINTAINER, DEFENDER ⟨a stout ~ of authority —V.L.Parrington⟩

1up·hol·ster \(,)əpˈhōlztə(r), (,)əˈpō-, -l(t)st-\ *n* -s [ME *upholdester*, fr. *upholden* to uphold (repair) + *-estere*, *-ester* -ster] **1** *archaic* **a :** one who deals in small goods **b :** one who repairs or makes small goods **2** *obs* **:** UPHOLSTERER

2upholster \"\ *vt* **upholstered; upholstered; upholstering** \-t(ə)riŋ\ **upholsters** [back-formation fr. *upholsterer* & *upholstery*] **:** to furnish with or as if with upholstery ⟨the classic broadcloths . . . that were used to ~ carriages —*Amer. Fabrics*⟩ ⟨a very fat woman ~*ed* in pink satin —S.E.White⟩; *esp* **:** to cover (a seat) with padding and fabric that is fastened over the padding

up·hol·stered \-(r)d\ *adj* **:** furnished with or as if with upholstery: as **a** (1) **:** containing furniture or fittings that are padded and covered with fabric (2) **:** marked by a high degree of comfort **:** providing luxury **:** LUXURIOUS ⟨crossed on the ~ route —Horace Sutton⟩ **b :** marked by fullness of style ⟨the more lightly and swiftly moving writers of the 17th century rather than the more heavily ~ ones of the earlier Renaissance —Edmund Wilson⟩ **c :** FAT, FLESHY ⟨~ old dowagers —*Harper's*⟩

up·hol·ster·er \-t(ə)rə(r)\ *n* -s [1*upholster* + *-er*] **:** one that upholsters; *specif* **:** one whose occupation is the making or supplying of upholstery

upholsterer bee *n* **:** LEAF-CUTTING BEE

up·hol·ster·ess *also* **up·hol·stress** \-t(ə)rəs\ *n* -ES **:** a female upholsterer

upholstering *n* -s **:** UPHOLSTERY

up·hol·stery \-t(ə)rē, -ri\ *n* -ES [1*upholster* + *-y*] **:** the materials (as fabric, padding, and springs) used to make a soft covering esp. for a seat; *specif* **:** the fabric used to cover a seat

upholstery leather *n* **:** leather made from cattlehides tanned in the whole hide and used esp. for upholstering furniture, automobiles, or airplanes

uphung \¦=¦=\ *adj* [1*up* + *hung*, past part. of *hang*] **:** hung up **:** SUSPENDED

up jen·kins \-ˈjeŋkənz\ *n*, *usu cap J* [*jenkins* fr. the name *Jenkins*] **:** a game in which the players seated on one side of a table pass a coin along under the table and the captain of the opposing team seated on the other side of the table commands them with the words *up Jenkins* and *down Jenkins* to show their hands and tries to guess which hand holds the coin

1upkeep \ˈ=,=\ *n* [2*up* + *keep* (after *keep up*, v.)] **1 a :** the act of maintaining in good condition **:** MAINTENANCE ⟨the building and ~ of roads⟩ **b :** the state of being maintained in good condition **2 :** the cost of maintaining in good condition or supporting ⟨his parents had no feeling that he ought to contribute to their ~ —Rebecca West⟩

2upkeep \¦=¦=\ *vt*, *chiefly Brit* **:** to maintain in good condition **:** keep up ⟨found it hard to ~ his family seat — a 45-room twin-turreted castle —*Irish Digest*⟩

1up·land \ˈəplənd, -,land, -,laa(ə)nd\ *n* [ME *uppeland*, *upland*, fr. *uppe land* in the country, fr. *uppe* on (fr. OE, fr. *uppe*, adv., on high) + *land* — more at UP, LAND] **:** the rural parts of a country **:** COUNTRY

2upland \"\ *adj* [ME *upland*, fr. *uppeland*, *upland*, n.] *archaic* **:** of or relating to the country **:** RUSTIC, PROVINCIAL ⟨Christianity was still an exotic religion, professed by the court, but resisted by a stubborn ~ heathenism —F.M.Stenton⟩

3upland \"\ *n* [2*up* + *land*] **1 a :** high land esp. far from the sea **:** PLATEAU **b :** a region of high land **2 a :** ground elevated above the lowlands along rivers or between hills **:** land above flood level **b :** an area of land above flood level **3 :** UPLAND COTTON — usu. used in pl. but sing. or pl. in constr.

4upland \"\ *adj* **:** of or relating to high land: as **a :** situated on high land esp. away from the sea ⟨an ~ village⟩ ⟨~ provinces⟩ **b** (1) **:** living in a relatively high region esp. away from water **:** frequenting high ground ⟨the woodcock is considered an ~ bird though in reality he belongs to the shore bird family —*Handbk. on Shotgun Shooting*⟩ (2) **:** of or relating to upland game ⟨~ hunting⟩ ⟨used their favorite ~ guns —*Catalog: Remington Trap & Skeet Equipment*⟩ **c :** growing, occurring, or developed on high land ⟨~ floras —*Jour. of Geol.*⟩ ⟨pollens seem likely to bring into a deposit a representation of forms farther from the sedimentary basin and more ~ to it —S.A. Cain⟩

5upland \"\ *adv* [4*up* + *land*] **:** in the interior or higher regions

upland boneset *n* **:** a boneset (*Eupatorium sessilifolium*) of eastern No. America with slender stems and nearly sessile and usu. opposite leaves

upland cotton *n*, *often cap U* **:** any of various usu. short-staple cottons that are cultivated esp. in the U.S. and derived chiefly from a prob. tropical American wild cotton (*Gossypium hirsutum*) — called also *American upland cotton*

upland cranberry *n* **:** BEARBERRY 1

upland cress *n* **:** WINTER CRESS

up·land·er \-də(r)\ *n* -s [3*upland* + *-er*] **:** a native or an inhabitant of an upland

upland goose *n* **:** a wild goose (*Chloëphaga leucoptera*) of Patagonia and the Falkland islands

upland hickory *n* **:** SHAGBARK HICKORY 1

1up·land·ish \¦əp¦landish, -aan-, -dēsh\ *adj* [ME *uplondish*, fr. *up* + *land*, *lond* land, country + *-ish*] *archaic* **:** 4UPLAND a

2uplandish \"\ *adj* [ME, fr. *uppeland*, *upland* + *-ish*] **1** *obs* **:** PROVINCIAL, RUSTIC, CRUDE ⟨the rude and ~ plowmen —Thomas More⟩ **2** *obs* **:** OUTLANDISH

upland moccasin *n* **:** a snake of the southern U. S. that is prob. a dark variety of the copperhead

upland plover *also* **upland sandpiper** *n* **:** a large sandpiper (*Bartramia longicauda*) of eastern No. America that frequents fields and uplands, resembles a plover in habits and in appearance esp. in its short bill, is a fine game bird, and has been nearly exterminated in some states

upland rice *n* **:** any of several rices that can be grown (as in high-rainfall areas) without irrigation — called also *dry rice;* compare LOWLAND RICE

upland speedwell *n* **:** a speedwell (*Veronica officinalis*)

upland white aster *n* **:** a tufted rigid No. American perennial herb (*Aster ptarmicoides*) with rather open loose clusters of white-rayed heads

upland willow oak *n* **:** BLUEJACK

uplay \¦=¦=\ *vt* [1*up* + *lay*] **:** to lay up **:** STORE

1upleap \¦=¦=\ *vi* [ME *uplepen*, fr. *up* + *lepen* to leap — more at LEAP] **:** to leap up

2upleap \ˈ=,=\ *n* **:** an upward leap

1uplift \¦=¦=\ *adj* [ME, fr. *up* + *lift*, past part. of *liften* to lift] *archaic* **:** UPLIFTED

2up·lift \¦əp¦lift *sometimes* ˌəpˈl-\ *vb* [ME *upliften*, fr. *up* + *liften* to lift] *vt* **1 :** to raise to a higher physical position **:** lift up; *specif* **:** to push up (a part of the earth's surface) above the surrounding area **2 :** to improve or attempt to improve the condition of esp. spiritually, socially, culturally, or intellectually ⟨love ~*s* the lover's being —H.O.Taylor⟩ ⟨stirring to ~ their masses from age-old conditions of squalor and ignorance —Howard M. Jones⟩ **3** *Scot* **:** to take (as money that is owed) into one's possession **:** COLLECT **4 :** RAISE 5 ⟨~*ed* their voices in song⟩ ~ *vi* **:** to rise esp. because of geologic forces

3uplift \ˈ=,=\ *n*, *often attrib* **:** an act, process, result, or cause of uplifting: as **a** (1) **:** the uplifting of a part of the earth's surface either uniform throughout a region or differential (as in tilting) ⟨the ~ of continents drained vast areas of land —W.E.Swinton⟩ (2) **:** an uplifted mass of land ⟨beyond the desert rise the mountains, the first outlying ranges of that vast ~ —Douglas Carruthers⟩ **b :** the upward pressure of water (as on the base of a structure) **c :** an elevation of spirit or emotion ⟨should have brought a larger mentality, a more vital ~ —*Cosmopolitan*⟩ **d :** a bettering of condition **:** IMPROVEMENT ⟨did for their ~ all that the custom of the times permitted —C.G. Woodson⟩ **e** (1) **:** influences that are intended to improve esp. morally or culturally **:** the ideas of active participants in programs for improvement esp. of moral and cultural standards ⟨night life . . . is conducted in an atmosphere of furious rectitude, fashionable economy, and intellectual ~ —Gilbert Millstein⟩ ⟨all this bosh sounds like ~; I teach my students English —W.G.Perry⟩ ⟨had been delighted when his daily poem and his ~ editorials first proved successful —Willa Cather⟩ (2) **:** a social movement to improve esp. morally or culturally **:** the work or cause of uplifting ⟨goes in for public things — very strong on woman suffrage, charities, ~, and pacifism —O.M.Johnson⟩ ⟨owns all the ~ papers —John Buchan⟩ **f :** a brassiere designed to hold the breasts up

uplifted \¦=¦==\ *adj* [ME, fr. *up* + *lifted*, past part. of *liften* to lift] **1 :** RAISED, ELEVATED, IMPROVED **2** *archaic* **:** ELATED, PROUD — **up·lift·ed·ness** *n* -ES

up·lift·er \,əpˈliftə(r)\ *n* **:** one that uplifts; *esp* **:** a person engaged in or devoted to the improvement of society

up·lift·ment \-tmənt\ *n* -s **:** UPLIFT c, d

uplock *vt* [1*up* + *lock*] **:** to lock up

up lock *n* [1*up*] **:** a locking device in airplanes that keeps the landing gear up in the retracted position

1uplook \¦=¦=\ *vi* [ME *uploken*, fr. *up* + *loken*, *looken* to look — more at LOOK] **:** to look upward — **up·look·er** \"+ə(r)\ *n*

2uplook \ˈ=,=\ *n* [2*up* + *look*, n.] **:** an upward look

uplying \¦=¦==\ *adj* [1*up* + *lying*, pres. part. of *lie*] **:** situated or growing on high land

1upmaking \ˈ=,==\ *n* [fr. gerund of obs. Sc *upmake* to make up, fr. ME (Sc) *upmaken*, fr. *up* + *maken* to make — more at MAKE] **:** an act or action of making up

2upmaking \"\ *adj* [fr. pres. part. of obs. Sc *upmake* to make up] *Scot* **:** making up for a shortcoming **:** COMPENSATING

up·most \ˈəp,mōst *also chiefly Brit* -ˌməst\ *adj* **:** UPPERMOST

up·ness \ˈəpnəs\ *n* -ES **:** the state or quality of being up

up north *adv*, *often cap N* [4*up*] **:** in or into a more northerly location; *esp* **:** in or into the part of the U.S. that lies north of Mason and Dixon's Line and the Ohio river

upo \əˈpō\ *prep* [ME *uppo*, *upo*, fr., *uppe* & *up* up + *o* on — more at O'] *archaic* **:** UPON

1upon \ə¦pȯn, ə¦pän, ə(¦)pən *sometimes* ,ə¦p-\ *prep* [ME *uppon*, *upon*, fr. *uppe* & *up* up + *on*, prep. — more at UP, ON] **1 :** ON **2 a :** upward so as to be on ⟨jumped ~ the horse⟩ **b :** in a high position on ⟨built a house ~ the hill⟩ **3 :** having a powerful influence on **:** lying heavily on ⟨the enchantment of the beautiful scenery was still ~ me —Scott Fitzgerald⟩ ⟨the hush ~ the dinner table —Maurice Hewlett⟩ **4** — used as a function word to indicate the one by which an oath is taken or by which one swears ⟨~ my word⟩ **5** *obs* **:** IN 3b ⟨was ~ this fashion bequeathed me by will —Shak.⟩ **6 a** (1) **:** in or into close proximity or contact with by way of or as if by way of attack ⟨the enemy is ~ us⟩ ⟨despondency fell ~ me —O.S.J. Gogarty⟩ ⟨summer holidays are ~ us —Alex Atkinson⟩ (2) **:** into sudden esp. unexpected contact with ⟨came ~ the letter in an old desk⟩ ⟨hits ~ a solution⟩ **b** *archaic* (1) **:** on the point of ⟨talk with him on this subject, for I see he is ~ settling one —Thomas Gray⟩ (2) **:** coming close to a specified number ⟨has the largest single group . . . in the world (just ~

70 millions) —*Spectator*⟩ **7 :** against in vengeance or punishment ⟨perform ~ the unguarded —Shak.⟩ **8** — used as a function word to indicate (1) a beginning course of action or an action or condition that is beginning ⟨students desiring to enter ~ graduate training —*College of William & Mary Cat.*⟩ or (2) an area of activity or being ⟨a dashing young ensign just come ~ the town —Washington Irving⟩ **9 a :** at the risk of ⟨are hereby charged, ~ your peril, to pay strict attention —C.S.Forester⟩ **b** *obs* **:** on the condition of ⟨~ my blessing I command thee go —Shak.⟩ **10 a** (1) **:** immediately following on **:** very soon after ⟨~ his death, she went on the . . . stage —Marie A. Kasten⟩ (2) **:** in answer to **:** in satisfaction of ⟨~ the demand of government leaders . . . arrangements were made this year —Wheeler McMillen⟩ ⟨transcripts are sent ~ the request of the particular student —*Bull. of Meharry Med. Coll.*⟩ **b :** on the occasion of **:** at the time of ⟨tells us what combinations of traits occur ~ the mixture of two racial types —Ruth Benedict⟩ ⟨a yoke which men of spirit will throw off ~ the first favorable opportunity —*Harper's*⟩ **11** *archaic* **:** by means of ⟨to die ~ the hand I love so well —Shak.⟩ **12** *chiefly Scot* **:** TO ⟨was married . . . ~ my Uncle Robin —R.L.Stevenson⟩

²upon \"\ *adv* [ME *uppon, upon,* fr. *uppon, upon,* prep.] **1 a** *obs* **:** on the surface **:** on it ⟨a coin that bears the figure of an angel stamped in gold, but that's insculped ~ —Shak.⟩ **b** *archaic* **:** on the body or something that resembles a body **2** *obs* **:** THEREAFTER, THEREON ⟨followed hard ~ —Shak.⟩

upped *past of* UP

¹up·per \ˈəpə(r)\ *adj* [ME, fr. *uppe* up + *-er* — more at UP] **1 :** relatively high in physical position: as **a** (1) **:** occupying high ground ⟨keep the hills and ~ regions —Shak.⟩ (2) **:** farther inland ⟨the ~ Mississippi⟩ ⟨carried squared timbers from the ~ lakes lumber ports to the St. Lawrence —*Amer. Guide Series: Mich.*⟩ (3) *usu cap* **:** living on higher ground, farther inland, farther upstream, or farther north than others of the same group ⟨the *Upper* Creek⟩ **b** (1) **:** being a higher part esp. of a pair or a set ⟨~ lip⟩ ⟨the ~ stories of the building⟩ (2) **:** worn over a part of the body above the waist ⟨his ~ clothes were black and his lower clothes red —J.G.Frazer⟩ **c :** directed upward **d :** being above or on the earth's surface rather than below it or in nether regions ⟨those appointed to sit there had . . . flown to the ~ world —John Milton⟩ **e** (1) **:** being or occurring on a higher level with respect to the earth's surface ⟨the ~ atmosphere⟩ ⟨~ plankton —R.E.Coker⟩ (2) **:** constituting a stratum relatively near the earth's surface (3) *usu cap* **:** being a later epoch or series of the period or series named ⟨*Upper* Carboniferous⟩ ⟨*Upper* Cretaceous⟩ ⟨*Upper* Permian⟩ ⟨*Upper* Silurian⟩ — contrasted with *Lower* **2 a :** higher in rank or order **:** superior in position ⟨senates were substituted for councils as the ~ house —Harvey Walker⟩ ⟨the . . . club was generally restricted to the ~ social brackets —*Current Biog.*⟩; *specif* **:** being on a more advanced level in an educational system ⟨the ~ school⟩ ⟨~ freshmen⟩ **b :** being of superior quality ⟨the ~ grades of lumber⟩ **3** *archaic* **:** worn on top of another garment **:** OUTER **4 :** situated farther from the door **:** INNERMOST ⟨the ~ end of the hall⟩ **5 :** of or relating to higher musical pitch ⟨although entirely different in their ~ parts, they share the same bass —P.H. Lang⟩ ⟨the most securely brilliant ~ registers heard in the vast house in many years —*Newsweek*⟩ **6 :** EARLIER ⟨determines the ~ limit of date⟩ **7 :** being the northern part of an area ⟨cut across ~ New York to the Vermont state line —Budd Schulberg⟩ ⟨~ Manhattan⟩

²upper \"\ *n* -s **:** one that is upper: as **a :** the parts of a shoe or boot that are above the sole **b uppers** *pl but sometimes sing in constr* **:** the best grade of lumber **:** FINISH **c** (1) **:** an upper tooth ⟨has two ~s missing⟩ (2) **:** an upper denture **d :** an upper berth **e :** a drill hole driven upward in a mine **f :** a piece of clothing worn above the waist **:** TOP ⟨were allowed to remove their pink pajama ~s —Earle Birney⟩ — **on one's uppers :** in straitened circumstances **:** at the end of one's means ⟨doing his own laundry, and that . . . indicates he was *on his uppers* —Hal White⟩

³upper \"\ *n* -s [¹*up* & ³*up* + *-er*] **:** one that ups — sometimes used in combination ⟨builder-*upper*⟩ ⟨coffee, which he finds the best of all toner-*uppers* —H.W.Wind⟩

upper alveolar index *n* **:** the ratio of the maximum external breadth to the external length of the upper jaw multiplied by 100

upper angle *n* **:** FIRST ANGLE

upper austral *adj, usu cap U&A* **:** of, relating to, or being a division of the Austral zone comprising the Carolinian and Upper Sonoran areas

upper bench *n, usu cap U&B* **:** COURT OF KING'S BENCH — used during the Cromwellian period

upper bridge *n* **:** the higher platform of a ship's bridge having two levels

upper case *n* **:** the upper one of a pair of type cases that contains capitals and usu. also small capitals, fractions, symbols, accents — compare LOWER CASE

¹uppercase \ˌ=ˈ=\ *adj* [*upper case*] **1** *of a letter* **:** having as its typical form AFG or *BNI* or **QZR** rather than afg or *bni* or **qzr** — abbr. *uc*; compare CAPITAL **2 :** set, printed, written, or otherwise rendered in uppercase letters — abbr. *uc*

²uppercase \"\ *n* **:** uppercase letters — abbr. *uc*; compare LOWERCASE

³uppercase \"\ *vt* **:** to print or set in uppercase; *also* **:** to change (as a lowercase letter) to an uppercase letter — abbr. *uc*

upper chinook *n, usu cap U&C* **:** a Chinookan language of the Clackamas, Wasco, Wishram, and neighboring peoples

upper class *n* **1 :** the highest stratum of society usu. composed of people with the greatest wealth, education, and prestige **2 upper classes** *pl* **:** an aggregate of social groupings comprising subdivisions of the upper class

upper-class \ˌ=ˈ=\ *adj* [*upper class*] **1 a :** of or relating to the upper class **b :** belonging to or having the characteristics of the upper class ⟨frightfully *upper-class* and having all the glorious self-confidence that comes of having been born rich —Aldous Huxley⟩ — compare LOWER-CLASS, MIDDLE-CLASS **2 :** of or relating to the junior or senior class in a college or a high school

up·per·class·man \ˌ=ˈ==mən\ *n, pl* **upperclassmen** [fr. the phrase *upper class* "junior or senior class" + *man*] **:** a member of the junior or senior class in a college or a high school

upper crust *n* [ME] **1 :** the top crust (as of a loaf of bread or a pie) **2 :** the highest segment of a social class or group ⟨the *upper crust* of the underworld —D.W.Maurer & V.H.Vogel⟩; *esp* **:** the highest circle of the upper classes ⟨a smart specialty shop for the *upper crust* —McKenzie Porter⟩

upper-crust \ˌ=ˈ=\ *adj* [*upper crust*] **:** of, relating to, or having the characteristics of the highest class of society ⟨one was of low condition, the other, *upper-crust* —W.S.Gilbert⟩ ⟨her best *upper-crust* voice —Marian Castle⟩

upper-crust·er \"+ə(r)\ *n, pl* **upper-crusters** [*upper crust* + *-er*] **:** a member of the upper crust

¹uppercut \ˈ==ˌ=\ *n* [¹*upper* + *cut*] **:** a swinging blow (as in boxing) directed upward with a bent arm

²uppercut \"\ *vt* **:** to hit with an uppercut **~** *vi* **:** to deliver or attempt to deliver an uppercut

upper deck *n* **1 :** the topmost full-length deck of a ship **:** a full-length deck above the main deck — see DECK illustration **2 :** a partial deck above the main deck in a naval vessel

upperdog \ˈ==ˌ=\ *n* **:** TOP DOG

upper facial index *n* **:** the ratio of the distance between nasion and prosthion to the bizygomatic breadth multiplied by 100

upper german *n, usu cap U&G* **:** the southern dialects of High German including Alemannic and Bavarian

upper hand *n* **1 :** CONTROL, MASTERY, ADVANTAGE ⟨finally got the *upper hand* of the situation⟩ ⟨at first the Liberals held the *upper hand* —C.L.Jones⟩ **2** *archaic* **:** the position of honor or authority

upper house *or* **upper chamber** *n* **:** the house of more restricted membership in a legislative body having two chambers

upper jewel *n* **:** a jewel bearing set into the bridge, cock, or upper plate of a watch

upper leather *n* **1 a :** the leather that forms the upper of a shoe or boot **b :** ²UPPER a **2 :** leather suitable for making uppers

upper limb *n* **:** the edge of a celestial body that is nearest the zenith ⟨the *upper limb* of the rising sun⟩

upper mars *n, usu cap U&M* **:** a Mount located on the percussion below the Mount of Mercury and above the Mount of Luna that when well developed is usu. held by palmists to indicate passive courage, strength of resistance, and self-control — compare LOWER MARS

upper mordent *n* **:** PRALLTRILLER

¹up·per·most \ˈəpə(r),mōst *also chiefly Brit* -ˌməst\ *adv* [ME, fr. *upper* + *most*] **1 :** in or into the highest physical position ⟨the blade turned ~⟩ **2 :** in or into the most prominent position (as in the mind) ⟨says whatever comes ~⟩

²uppermost \"\ *adj* **1 a :** situated in the highest physical position **:** farthest up ⟨the ~ falls of the river⟩ **b :** OUTERMOST ⟨the ~ skin⟩ **2 a :** highest in rank or power ⟨prominent in its ~ councils —*Current Biog.*⟩ ⟨whatever faction happens to be ~ —Jonathan Swift⟩ **b :** occupying the most prominent or most important position ⟨the thoughts that were ~ in my mind —R.B.Merriman⟩ ⟨essays in which philosophical considerations are ~ —J.E.Smith⟩

upperpart \ˈ==ˌ=\ *n* **:** a part lying on the upper side esp. of an animal

upper partial *n* **:** OVERTONE 1

upper pharyngeal *n* **:** PHARYNGOBRANCHIAL

upper republican *adj, usu cap U&R* [*Upper Republican,* river in Kansas and Nebraska] **:** of or relating to a culture of the plains and esp. of Kansas and Nebraska about 1300–1600 characterized by earth-covered pit houses, cultivation of gardens in creek bottoms, and hard gray pottery decorated externally by the application of a cord-wrapped paddle and on the rims with incised geometric designs

uppers *pl of* UPPER

upper sonoran *adj, usu cap U&S* **:** of, relating to, being, or native to the cooler part of the Sonoran life zone that adjoins the Transition zone — compare LOWER SONORAN

upperstock \ˈ==ˌ=\ *n* **:** STOCKING; *specif* **:** a 16th century stocking reaching below the knee and worn with netherstocks and trunk hose

upper story *n* **1 :** a story (as of a house) that is above the ground floor **2** *slang* **:** BRAIN ⟨a little off in the *upper story* —Erle Stanley Gardner⟩

upper ten *or* **upper ten thousand** *n* **:** the members of the highest social class **:** UPPER CLASS

up·per·ten·dom \ˌəpə(r)ˈtendəm\ *n* -s **:** the highest social class

upper transit *also* **upper culmination** *n* **:** the passage of a celestial body over the celestial meridian at the higher of its two crossings; *also* **:** the point at which such a crossing takes place

upper vol·ta \ˌ==ˈvōltə, -ˈväl-\ *adj, usu cap U&V* [*Upper Volta,* republic in western Africa] **:** of or relating to the Republic of Upper Volta **:** of the kind or style prevalent in Upper Volta

upperworks \ˈ==ˌ=\ *n pl* **1 a :** all the parts of the hull of a ship that are above the load waterline **b** (1) **:** the sides of a ship from the waterline to the plank-sheer of the upper deck (2) **:** SUPERSTRUCTURE 1b **2** *slang* **:** BRAINS

upperworld \ˈ==ˌ=\ *n* **:** the respectable law-abiding part of society — contrasted with *underworld*

upping *pres part of* UP

up·pish \ˈəpish, -pēsh\ *adj* [¹*up* + *-ish*] **1** *archaic* **:** being in high spirits **:** ELATED **2 :** UPPITY ⟨very full of himself, ~ —A. J.Cronin⟩ **3** *archaic* **:** taking offense easily **4 :** somewhat up in position or direction — **up·pish·ly** *adv* — **up·pish·ness** *n* -ES

up·pi·ty \ˈəpəd·ē, -ətē, -i\ *adj* [prob. fr. ¹*up* + *-ity* (as in *biggity,* var. of *biggety*)] **:** marked by airs of superiority **:** ARROGANT, PRESUMPTUOUS, PUSHING ⟨were so rich and ~ because the government was trying to make everybody equal —Marya Mannes⟩ ⟨her family laughed at her ~ notions —Peter Cansdale⟩ — **up·pi·ty·ness** *n* -ES

up·po·woc \ˌəˈpōˌwäk\ *n* [fr. *uppówoc, uhpooc* (in some Algonquian language of Virginia)] *archaic* **:** TOBACCO

upputting \ˈ=ˌ==\ *also* **upput** \ˈ=ˌ=\ *n* [²*up* + *putting* (gerund of *put*) or *put* (after *put up,* v.)] *Scot* **:** LODGING

¹upraise \ˌ=ˈ=\ *vt* [ME *upreisen, upraisen,* fr. *up* + *reisen, raisen* to raise — more at RAISE] **1 :** to raise up **:** LIFT, ELEVATE; *specif* **:** to raise by geologic upheaval **2 :** to raise from a depressed state **:** CHEER — **up·rais·er** \"+ə(r)\ *n*

²upraise \ˈ=ˌ=\ *n* **:** RAISE 4

uprear \ˌ=ˈ=\ *vb* [ME *upreren,* fr. *up* + *reren* to raise — more at REAR] *vt* **1 a :** to lift up **:** RAISE ⟨commands that . . . be ~*ed* his mighty standard —John Milton⟩ **b :** ERECT ⟨by adding stone to stone had ~*ed* this monument —Arnold Bennett⟩ **2 :** to raise the dignity of **:** EXALT **~** *vi* **:** RISE

¹upright \ˈ=ˌ=\ *adj* [ME, fr. OE *ūpriht,* fr. *ūp* up + *riht* right — more at UP, RIGHT] **1 a :** standing up straight on the feet or on one end **:** being in a vertical position **:** PERPENDICULAR, ERECT ⟨Sinanthropus was of medium stature and certainly ~ —R.W. Murray⟩ **b :** marked by erectness of carriage **:** having good posture ⟨a tall dark girl with that bold ~ well-poised figure —Anthony Trollope⟩ **c** (1) **:** having the main axis or a main part perpendicular ⟨designs of freezers . . . center around the alternatives of chest and ~ freezers —J.A.Mixon & H.D. Johnson⟩ ⟨the scribe wrote a large flowing hand . . . with the individual letters ~ and square in formation —Jack Finegan⟩ (2) **:** not slanting or upside-down **:** having the right side up ⟨had to have a gyroscope . . . inside it in order to keep it ~ —Edward Sackville-West & Desmond Shawe-Taylor⟩ **2** *obs* **:** SUPINE 1 **3 :** marked by strong moral rectitude **:** morally correct ⟨~ women shall associate with no men who drink alcohol —Waldo Frank⟩ ⟨his unquestioned integrity and ~ innocence —J.G.Cozzens⟩ **4** *archaic* **:** BIG, STRONG — used chiefly of a vagrant **5** *obs* **:** straight so as to fit either foot ⟨an ~ shoe —Robert Burton⟩ **6 :** having a vertical or upward course **7 :** having greater height than width ⟨a very decorative antique Sheraton ~ wall mirror —*Antiques*⟩ ⟨~ books⟩

syn HONEST, JUST, CONSCIENTIOUS, SCRUPULOUS, HONORABLE: UPRIGHT may imply strict regard for the right and resolute, thoughtful adherence to high moral principles ⟨they hate all chicanery, all evasiveness and slipperiness. They are *upright* and downright —H.S.Commager⟩ ⟨best described by the old-fashioned word *upright.* It's a good word, comprises a good many things—all the straight qualities, like loyalty, truthfulness, the right sort of pride —Elizabeth Goudge⟩ HONEST may describe adherence to truth, candor, straightforwardness, sincerity, fairness, and freedom from fraud and duplicity ⟨the idealism that would build peace and content on *honest* foundations, and would deny them to none —V.L.Parrington⟩ ⟨only a careful study of the evidence will enable us to give an *honest* answer —M.R.Cohen⟩ ⟨the *honest* heart that's free frae a' intended fraud or guile —Robert Burns⟩ JUST may stress choice of the righteous and equitable ⟨a life unblamable and *just* —William Cowper⟩ ⟨nor shall private property be taken for public use without *just* compensation —*U.S.Constitution*⟩ ⟨crime sometimes pays. The *just* man . . . continues unaccountably to suffer, and the wicked to flourish like the green bay tree —Weston La Barre⟩ CONSCIENTIOUS may indicate habitual painstaking dutiful effort to accord with moral law ⟨the skillful, *conscientious* schoolmistresses whose lives were spent in trying to inculcate real knowledge —C.H.Grandgent⟩ ⟨she took to religion, and her *conscientious* Christian virtues, practiced with stern inclemency, were the canker of the family —Arnold Bennett⟩ SCRUPULOUS describes a very careful, meticulous, and sometimes even anxious adherence to dictates of morality and conscience ⟨not one word that I have said runs counter to the demands of delicate and penetrating accuracy of observation, or of *scrupulous* fidelity to fact as it appears —J.L.Lowes⟩ ⟨the delicate equipoise and *scrupulous* objectivity which the judge must try to preserve at all times —R.M.Dawson⟩ HONORABLE indicates a holding to codes of honor and sanctioned proprieties ⟨too *honorable* to lend himself to an accusation which he knew to be false —J.A.Froude⟩ ⟨he avoided the mean and tricky: he was always an *honorable* foe —W.C.Ford⟩

²upright \ˈ=ˌ=\ *vt* [ME *uprighten,* fr. *upright,* adj.] **:** to make upright

³upright \ˌ=ˈ=\ *adv* [¹*upright*] *archaic* **:** vertically upward ⟨for all beneath the moon would I not leap ~ —Shak.⟩

⁴upright \ˈ=ˌ=\ *n* [¹*upright*] **1 a** *obs* **:** a vertical face (as of a building) **b** *archaic* **:** ELEVATION 5 **2 :** the state of being upright **:** PERPENDICULAR ⟨a pillar out of ~⟩ **3 :** something that stands upright: as **a :** a vertical piece of timber in a building **b :** a perpendicular stone, post, or stake **c :** a vertical structural member of a piece of furniture (as a chair) — usu. used in pl. **d :** the wall down the middle of a brick clamp **e :** a goal-post esp. on a football field — usu. used in pl. **4 :** an upright geologic stratum **5 :** UPRIGHT PIANO

upright drill *n* **:** a drilling machine with a vertical spindle

uprighteously *adv* [blend of ¹*upright* and *righteously*] **:** in a morally correct manner **:** UPRIGHTLY

up·righ·teous·ness \ˌəpˈrīchəsnəs\ *n* [blend of ¹*upright* and *righteousness*] **:** the state or quality of being morally correct **:** UPRIGHTNESS

uprighting *n* -s **:** the process of placing the pivot holes in the plates of a timepiece so that the arbors will be perpendicular to the plates

up·right·ly *adv* **:** in an upright manner or position

up·right·ness *n* **:** the state or quality of being upright

upright piano *n* **:** a piano whose strings run vertically — contrasted with *grand piano*

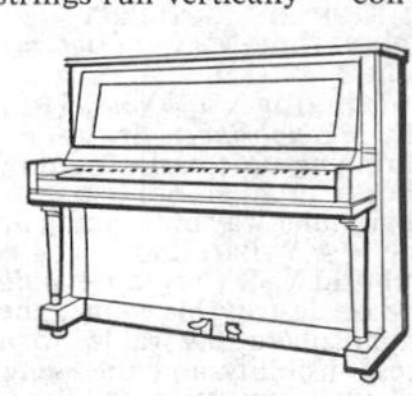

upright piano

upright tomato *n* **:** any of various stout erect compact tomatoes with the leaves crowded and curled that prob. have developed in cultivation and are usu. considered a distinct variety (*Lycopersicon esculentum validum*)

upright yellowwood *n* **:** a tall tree (*Podocarpus latifolius* syn. *P. thunkergii*) widely distributed in southern Africa where it is an important timber tree

up·ris·al \ˌəpˈrīzəl\ *n* **:** an act or instance of rising up **:** UPRISING

¹up·rise \ˌəpˈrīz\ *vi* **up·rose** \-rōz\ *also archaic* **up·rist** \-rist\ **up·ris·en** \-ˈrizᵊn\ *also archaic* **uprist; uprising; uprises** [ME *uprisen,* fr. *up* + *risen* to rise — more at RISE] **1 a :** to rise to a higher position ⟨the lands were *uprising* and new mountains were rearing their heads —W.E.Swinton⟩ **b** (1) **:** to get up on one's feet **:** stand up (2) **:** to get out of bed **c :** to come into view from below; *esp* **:** to come into view from below the horizon ⟨the glorious sun *uprist* —S.T.Coleridge⟩ **2 :** to rise from the dead or the underworld **3 :** to rise up in or as if in rebellion **4 :** to become existent ⟨since earth *uprose* —P.B.Shelley⟩ **5 :** to rise up in sound ⟨the whisper of gongs and trumpets *uprose* again —James Hilton⟩ — **up·ris·er** \-zə(r)\ *n*

²uprise \ˈ=ˌ=\ *n* **1 :** an act or instance of uprising: as **a :** the rising of a celestial body (as the sun) **:** DAWN **b :** an act or instance of rising to a higher position ⟨the ~ of the flood waters⟩ **c :** an act or instance of becoming existent or prominent **:** RISE ⟨the ~ of a new school of painters⟩ **d :** a direct rise from the end of a backward swing to a position of rest on a gymnastic apparatus (as the horizontal bar or flying rings) **2 :** the beginning of a rise in the land **:** an increase in elevation ⟨the horizon at which the plains end and, with a swift dramatic ~, the world of the mountains begins —Wynford Vaughan-Thomas⟩

uprising \ˈ=ˌ==\ *n* [ME, fr. *up* + *rising,* gerund of *risen* to rise (after *risen up* to rise up)] **:** an act or instance of rising up; *esp* **:** INSURRECTION, REVOLT **syn** see REBELLION

upriver \ˈ=ˈ==\ *adv (or adj)* [⁴*up* + *river*] **:** toward, at, or from a point nearer the source of a river ⟨proceeded ~ —R.P.Warren⟩ ⟨an ~ voyage —John Hersey⟩

¹up·roar \ˈəp,rō(ə)r, -,rȯ(ə)r, -ōə, -ȯ(ə)\ *n* -s [by folk etymology fr. D *oproer,* fr. MD, fr. *op* up + *roere, roer* motion; akin to OE *ūp* up and to OE *hrēran* to stir — more at UP, CRATER] **1** *archaic* **:** INSURRECTION, REVOLT **2 a :** a loud roaring usu. disorderly noise of some duration ⟨the students were making a terrific ~ in the hall⟩ ⟨storms and ~s and all such movie wonderments —John McCarten⟩ **b :** a state of commotion or excitement **:** violent disturbance **:** TUMULT, TURMOIL ⟨the recent ~ created by war-scare statements —*Newsweek*⟩ **syn** see DIN

²uproar \ˌ=ˈ=\ *vt* -ED/-ING/-S **:** to throw into an uproar

up·roar·i·ous \ˌəpˈrōrēəs, -ˈrȯr- *sometimes* ˌəpˈr-\ *adj* [¹*uproar* + *-ious*] **1 :** marked by a great deal of noise and disorder ⟨fights between heavyweight personalities fought to a finish ~ with the shouts of attendant partisans —*Times Lit. Supp.*⟩ **2 :** very noisy and full ⟨burst into the most ~ laughter —R.H. Davis⟩ ⟨an ~ cough —Frank O'Connor⟩ **3 :** productive of loud laughter **:** extremely funny ⟨an ~ comedy⟩ — **up·roar·i·ous·ly** *adv* — **up·roar·i·ous·ness** *n* -ES

uproll \ˌ=ˈ=\ *vb* [¹*up* + *roll*] *vt* **1 :** to move upward by rolling **2 :** to form into a roll **:** wind up **~** *vi* **:** to roll up

¹uproot \ˌ=ˈ=\ *vb* [¹*up* + *root,* n.] *vt* **1 :** to pull up by or as if by the roots ⟨~*ed* the vine —V.L.Parrington⟩ ⟨one signal light tower was ~*ed* when struck by the flying truck —*Springfield (Mass.) Daily News*⟩ **2 :** to remove as if by pulling up the roots **:** ERADICATE, DESTROY ⟨all vestiges of political democracy were soon ~*ed* —C.E.Black & E.C.Helmreich⟩ ⟨the vulgarity of his age . . . is what he has violently ~*ed* from his own being —Albert Dasnoy⟩ **3 :** to displace from a country or traditional habitat **:** tear away from established cultural patterns and values ⟨millions of people were ~*ed* by the war⟩ ⟨automation would ~ millions of laborers —John Lear⟩ **~** *vi* **:** to change one's place of residence and way of life ⟨he's nearly 60, and that's awfully old to ~ and leave everything and everyone you know —Nevil Shute⟩ **syn** see EXTERMINATE

²uproot \"\ *vt* [¹*up* + *root* (to dig up)] **:** to dig up with the snout

up·root·ed·ness *n* **:** the state or quality of being uprooted ⟨a sense of insecurity and ~ —Dixon Wecter⟩

up·root·er \"+ə(r)\ *n* **:** one that uproots

uprouse \ˌ=ˈ=\ *vt* [¹*up* + *rouse*] **:** to rouse up

¹uprush \ˌ=ˈ=\ *vi* [¹*up* + *rush*] **:** to rush upward

²uprush \ˈ=ˌ=\ *n* **1 :** an upward rush of gas or liquid ⟨that vigorous ~ of the atmosphere essential to the thunderstorm —W.J.Humphreys⟩ **2 a :** a sudden rising esp. from the subconscious ⟨an ~ of fear —J.M.Cohen⟩ ⟨was the triumph of irrationalism and betokened an ~ of forces from the psychic underworld —Walter Moberly⟩ **b :** a sudden increase ⟨an ~ in government debt —Stuart Chase⟩

ups *pres 3d sing of* UP, *pl of* UP

ups–a–daisy *var of* UPSY-DAISY

up–saddle \ˌ=ˈ==\ *vi* [¹*up* + *saddle*] **:** to saddle a horse or a mule ⟨sleepy muleteers . . . *up-saddled,* thinking dawn had come —*Spectator*⟩

ups and downs *pl of* UP AND DOWN

upscuddle \ˌ=ˈ==\ *n* -s [²*up* + *scuddle* (origin unknown)] *South* **:** QUARREL

upsee–daisy *var of* UPSY-DAISY

upseeking \ˌ=ˈ==\ *adj* [¹*up* + *seeking,* pres. part. of *seek*] **:** seeking by looking upward

upsend \ˌ=ˈ=\ *vt* [¹*up* + *send*] **:** to send upward

¹up·set \ˌəpˈset *sometimes* ˌəpˈs-; *usu* -ed·+V\ *adj* [ME, fr. *up* + *set,* past part. of *setten* to set — more at SET] **1** *archaic* **:** set up **:** RAISED, ERECTED **2** [fr. past part. of ²*upset*] **:** emotionally disturbed **:** affected by an emotional disturbance ⟨was too ~ to say anything —Frank Sargeson⟩ ⟨her nerves were more ~ than usual —Arnold Bennett⟩

²upset \ˌəpˈset *sometimes* ˌəpˈs-; *usu* -ed·+V\ *vb* **upset; upset; upsetting; upsets** *see vt 1b* [ME *upsetten,* fr. *up* + *setten* to set] *vt* **1 a** *obs* **:** to set up **:** put upright **:** RAISE **b** *also past & past part* **upsetted** (1) **:** to turn the outer ends of (stakes) upward so as to make a foundation (as for the side of a basket) (2) **:** to form (the side of a basket) by upsetting the stakes **2 a :** to thicken and shorten (as a heated bar of iron) by the application of pressure on an end (as by hammering) **:** SWAGE **b :** to shorten (a metal tire on a wooden wheel) by cutting and hammering on the ends or by treating in a special machine without cutting **3 :** to force out of the usual upright, level, or proper position **:** CAPSIZE ⟨~ his chair —John Buchan⟩ ⟨the winds have torn and ~ the mossy structures in the bushes —Richard Jefferies⟩ **4 a :** to disturb the equilibrium of **:** cause an emotional disturbance in **:** DISCOMPOSE ⟨the least little thing ~ her —Elizabeth Schutt⟩ **b :** to throw into disorder **:** put out of kilter **:** DISARRANGE ⟨any effort that ~s the routine of daily life may bring about a restless night —Morris Fishbein⟩ ⟨the financial stability of the country was ~ —P.E.James⟩ **c** (1) **:** to make invalid by or as if by intervention ⟨have enough pigheaded individual ways of their own to ~ any calculation that they will give a certain exact response —C.E.Montague⟩ ⟨induced the jury to ~ a will under unusual circumstances —H.W.H.Knott⟩ (2) **:** to defeat unexpectedly (as in an athletic or political contest) ⟨strong enough to ~ the candidates of the major parties —I.G.Blake⟩ **5 :** to cause a physical disorder in **:** make somewhat ill esp. in the digestive tract ⟨some children are unable to eat certain foods without being ~ by them —H.R.Litchfield & L.H.Dembo⟩ **~** *vi* **1 :** to turn over **:** CAPSIZE ⟨a chafing dish . . . which may be held in the hands yet cannot possibly ~ —G.G.Coulton⟩ **2** *of a bullet* **:** to expand laterally while moving through a rifled bore and upon striking an object **3 :** to upset the stakes in making a basket **syn** see DISCOMPOSE, OVERTURN

³upset \'ₛ,ₛ\ *n* -s **1 :** a physical overturning **:** OVERTURN ⟨bruised by the ~ of his gig while viewing lands —W.L.Whittlesey⟩ **2 a** (1) **:** an act of throwing into disorder **:** DERANGEMENT, OVERTHROW ⟨the ~ of price levels in the inflation period —C.L.Jones⟩ ⟨a radical innovation, an ~, a reversal of patterns in American domestic life —*Harper's*⟩ (2) **:** a state of disorder **:** CONFUSION ⟨produced less profound changes . . . but also much less ~ and clash —A.L.Kroeber⟩ **b :** QUARREL **c :** an unexpected defeat (as in an athletic or political contest) ⟨cut loose with a dazzling passing attack today to effect one of the most startling ~*s* of the college football season —*N.Y. Times*⟩ ⟨ran for mayor a second time . . . and scored an ~ victory —*Current Biog.*⟩ **3 a :** a physical disorder **:** a slight illness ⟨a stomach ~⟩ ⟨would become disturbed about every single ~ as if it were a major illness —Evelyn Barkins⟩ **b :** an emotional disturbance ⟨went through a big ~ after her father's death⟩ **4 a :** a part of a rod or similar object (as the head on a bolt) that is upset **b :** the buckling of wood fibers due to crushing **c :** the expansion of a bullet that is the result of upsetting **5 :** the rods plaited or woven around the bottoms of the stakes of a basket immediately after upsetting so that they will stay in position — see BASKET illustration **6 :** a swage used in upsetting

upset butt welding *n* **:** butt welding in which a continuous pressure is applied until the work is plastic and is then followed by a pressure high enough to produce an upset joint

upset price *n* **:** the minimum price set by a seller or auctioneer at which property will be offered or sold at auction or public sale

up·set·ter \,əp'sed·ə(r)\ *n* -s **:** one that upsets: as **a :** a person who causes upsets ⟨the businessman . . . is the great ~ on the contemporary scene —M.S.Rukeyser⟩ **b :** an upsetting machine **c :** a forging press operator who increases the breadth of a piece of metal by heating and pressing it so that it spreads

up·set·ter·man \-(r)mən\ *n, pl* **upsettermen :** UPSETTER c

upsetting *adj* **1** *Scot* **:** PRESUMPTUOUS, CONCEITED, ASSUMING **2 :** producing an upset; *esp* **:** causing an emotional disturbance **:** DISTURBING ⟨the hurly-burly of politics is ~ to a sensitive mind and nature —John Lodge⟩ — **up·set·ting·ly** *adv*

¹upshift \'ₛ,ₛ\ *vi* [¹*up* + *shift*] **:** to shift into a higher automotive gear ⟨the car . . . automatically ~*s* to the cruising range as speed increases —*Report: General Motors Corp.*⟩ ⟨the driver ~*ed* into second⟩

²upshift \"\ *n* **:** a shift into a higher automotive gear ⟨the ~ to second speed in the low range is produced by the automatic controls —Joseph Heitner⟩

¹upshoot \'ₛ,ₛ\ *n* [²*up* + *shoot*, n.] **1** *archaic* **:** OUTCOME, UPSHOT **2 :** an act or result of shooting up ⟨the volcanic ~ of fire lasted but a second or two —Russell Grenfell⟩

²upshoot \ₛ'ₛ\ *vb* [¹*up* + *shoot*, v.] *vi* **:** to shoot upward **:** grow upward **~** *vt* **:** to send up **:** RAISE

upshot \'ₛ,ₛ\ *n* [²*up* + *shot*] **1 a :** a final shot in an archery match **b :** the best shot up to the moment in an archery match **2 a :** the final result (as of a series or group of actions or events) **:** OUTCOME ⟨the ~ of all this has been a growth of hostility —Sidney Hook⟩ ⟨in the ~ his ideal white man's country . . . has been overtaken by the march of world events —W.M.Macmillan⟩ **b :** the conclusion reached in a reasoning process (as a discussion or an analysis) **:** GIST, ESSENCE ⟨the ~ of the argument⟩ ⟨the ~ of these paragraphs —A.L.Kroeber⟩ **c** *archaic* **:** LIMIT **syn** see EFFECT

upsidaisy *var of* UPSY-DAISY

upside \'ₛ,ₛ\ *n* [²*up* + *side*] **1 :** the upper side or part **2 :** an upward trend (as of prices) ⟨this issue has emerged on the ~ —*Stock Trend Service*⟩ ⟨appreciable ~ progress —*Wall Street Jour.*⟩

upside down *adv* [by folk etymology fr. earlier *up so down, upsedown*, fr. ME *up so doun, upsedoun*, fr. *up* + *so* + *doun* down] **1 :** in such a way that the upper and the lower parts are reversed in position ⟨turned the table *upside down*⟩ **2 :** in or into a state of great disorder ⟨turned the world *upside down* —Dorothy Witton⟩

upside-down \'ₛₛ'ₛ\ *adj* [*upside down*] **1 :** having the upper and the lower parts reversed in positon **:** INVERTED ⟨*upside-down* letters⟩ **2 :** marked by confusion; *esp* **:** marked by an inversion of the usual or the reasonable ⟨that *upside-down* snobbery of the café chantant —Edmund Wilson⟩ ⟨a fine case of *upside-down* logic —Janet Flanner⟩ — **upside-down·ness** *n*

upside-down cake *n* **:** a cake baked with its batter covering a close arrangement of pieces of fruit in a syrup in the bottom of the pan and served fruit side up

up·sides \,əp'sīdz\ *adv (or adj)* [*upside* + -*s*] **1** *dial Brit* **:** on the same level (as in retaliation) **:** EVEN, SQUARE — usu. used with *with* **2** *Brit* **:** in an equally advanced position (as in a horse race)

up·si·lon \'yüpsə,län, 'əp-, -,lən, *Brit* yüp'sīlən\ *n* -s [MGk *y psilon, ypsilon*, lit., simple upsilon, fr. Gk *y* upsilon + *psilon*, neut. of *psilos* simple, mere, bare; fr. the desire to distinguish between graphic *y* and graphic *oi*, pronounced the same in later Greek — more at PSIL-] **:** the 20th letter of the Greek alphabet — symbol Υ or υ; see ALPHABET table

upsitten \ₛ'ₛₛ\ *adj* [¹*up* + *sitten*, archaic past part. of *sit*] *Scot* **:** INDIFFERENT

upsitting \'ₛ,ₛₛ\ *n* [²*up* + *sitting*, gerund of sit (after *sit up*, v.)] **1 a** *archaic* **:** the first time a woman sits up to receive company after having a baby **b** *obs* **:** the first time one sits up after an illness **2** *chiefly Africa* **:** the act of sitting up at night in courtship

upski \'ₛ,ₛ\ *n* [¹*up* + *ski*] **:** a ski lift that is pulled uphill like a sled by a cable

upslip \'ₛ,ₛ\ *n* [²*up* + *slip*] **:** an upward displacement on one side of a fault without there being a downward slip on the other side to the full extent of the total displacement

¹upslope \'ₛ,ₛ\ *n* [²*up* + *slope*] **:** a slope that lies upward **:** UPHILL

²upslope \ₛ'ₛ\ *adv* [⁴*up* + *slope*, n.] **:** in an upward direction **:** UPHILL ⟨the fire . . . was working ~ toward us —G.R.Stewart⟩

upslope fog *n* **:** fog produced by the flow of moist air along upward sloping terrain

upsoar \ₛ'ₛ\ *vi* [¹*up* + *soar*] **:** to soar upward

¹upspring \'ₛ,ₛ\ *n* [ME, fr. OE *ūpspring*, fr. *ūp* up + *spring*] **1** *archaic* **:** an act or instance of springing up; *esp* **:** ORIGIN, DEVELOPMENT, GROWTH **2** *obs* **:** a wild dance

²upspring \ₛ'ₛ\ *vi* [ME *upspringen*, fr. *up* + *springen* to spring — more at SPRING] **1 a :** to spring up (as of a plant) **:** GROW **b :** to come into existence **:** ARISE ⟨a little corps of heroes has *upsprung* among us —*Lippincott's Mag.*⟩ **2 :** to spring upward **:** RISE; *specif* **:** to jump to one's feet

¹upstage \ₛ'ₛ\ *adv* [⁴*up* + *stage*] **:** toward or at the rear of a theatrical stage or the part away from the footlights — compare DOWNSTAGE, LEFT STAGE, RIGHT STAGE

²upstage \"\ *adj* **1 :** of or relating to the rear of a theatrical stage **2 a :** occupying the rear of a theatrical stage esp. in such a way as to cause other actors to turn their backs to the audience **b :** marked by superiority of manner **:** HAUGHTY, SNOBBISH, HIGH-CLASS ⟨still thinks he's someone and is very ~ if you start to kid him —H.L.Wilson⟩

³upstage \'ₛ,ₛ\ *n* **:** the part of a theatrical stage away from the footlights

⁴upstage \ₛ'ₛ\ *vt* **1 :** to put (an actor) at the disadvantage of having to face away from the audience by staying upstage ⟨two men and a ballerina maneuver to ~ each other —*Time*⟩ **2 :** to steal the show from ⟨the . . . chimpanzee who has been *upstaging* human actors —*Newsweek*⟩ **3 :** to treat snobbishly **:** put in one's place ⟨properly *upstaged* me by showing me how to shut the door —John Logan⟩

¹upstairs \ₛ'ₛ\ *adv* [⁴*up* + *stairs*, pl. of *stair*] **1 a :** up the stairs **:** to or on a higher floor or level **b :** up into or up in the air; *esp* **:** to or at a high altitude ⟨take a new fighter plane ~ —*Business Week*⟩ **2 :** to or in a higher position; *esp* **:** to or in a technically or ostensibly higher position that is less desirable esp. because of diminished authority ⟨began organizing for victory by kicking the commander . . . ~ to the viceroyalty —O.S.J.Gogarty⟩ ⟨quietly moved him ~ to board chairman —*Newsweek*⟩ **3** *slang* **:** in the head ⟨she's all vacant ~ —J.T. Farrell⟩

²upstairs \"\ *adj* **1** *also* **upstair** \"\ **a :** situated above the stairs esp. on an upper floor ⟨an ~ room⟩ **b :** of or relating to the upper floors ⟨an ~ maid⟩ **2 :** placed at or occupying a higher level ⟨skilled in ~ politics —C.S.Bluemel⟩ ⟨the ~ ultra-high-frequency area allocated to television —*Telephone Engineer & Management*⟩

³upstairs \ₛ'ₛ\ *n pl but sing or pl in constr* **:** the part of a building that is above the ground floor

upstairs man *n* **:** a dining-car waiter who serves meals outside the diner

¹upstand \ₛ'ₛ\ *vi* [ME *upstanden*, fr. *up-* + *standen* to stand — more at STAND] **:** to stand up on one's feet **:** rise to a standing position

²upstand \"\ *n, Brit* **:** one that stands up; *esp* **:** an upright structural part

up·stand·er \"+ə(r)\ *n* **:** one of the handlebars of an Eskimo sledge

up·stand·ing \,əp'standiŋ, -aan-, -dēŋ\ *adj* [ME, fr. pres. part. of *upstanden*] **1 :** standing up esp. so as to project **:** ERECT ⟨kept his ~ hair and the grin —Edmund Wilson⟩ ⟨one of the most ~ collars in town surmounts a straight coat —Lois Long⟩ **2 :** marked by erect carriage **:** UPRIGHT ⟨a rather ~ horse with strong closely coupled body —G.M.Rommel⟩ ⟨an ~ stalwart figure of a man —*Boston Sunday Herald*⟩ **3 :** marked by integrity and independence **:** STRAIGHTFORWARD ⟨a fine ~ gentleman of the old school —Sinclair Lewis⟩ — **up·stand·ing·ness** *n* -ES

upstaring \ₛ'ₛₛ\ *adj* [¹*up* + *staring*, pres. part. of *stare*] *obs* **:** standing up on end ⟨the king's son . . . with hair ~ —Shak.⟩

¹upstart \ₛ'ₛ\ *vi* [ME *upsterten*, fr. *up* + *sterten* to start — more at START] **1 :** to start up **:** jump up (as to one's feet) **2** *obs* **:** to rise up on end **3 :** to come into being or notice

²upstart \'ₛ,ₛ\ *n* **1 :** one that has risen suddenly (as from a low position to wealth or power); *esp* **:** one that has risen from a lower position and presumes on his success **:** PARVENU **2 :** ⁵KIP 1a

³upstart \"\ *adj* [²*upstart*] **1 :** recently come into existence **:** NEW ⟨all this material was of neolithic antiquity. . . . By comparison the taking of peyote was an ~ ceremony —Alice Marriott⟩ **2 a :** recently or suddenly risen to a higher position or greater prominence ⟨a mésalliance with a little nobody — a little ~ governess —W.M.Thackeray⟩ **b :** characteristic of an upstart **:** FORWARD, PRESUMPTUOUS ⟨the ~ pretensions of a young woman without family, connections, or fortune —Jane Austen⟩ — **up·start·ness** *n* -ES

¹upstate \ₛ'ₛ\ *adv* [⁴*up* + *state*, n.] **:** to or in a part of a state designated as upstate ⟨must run ~ and see her —Zona Gale⟩

²upstate \"\ *adj* **:** of, relating to, originating or being in, or characteristic of a part of a state designated as upstate ⟨~ New York⟩ ⟨an ~ resort —William Peden⟩ ⟨his ~ political organization —Hastings Lyon⟩ ⟨~ pronunciation —H.L. Mencken⟩

³upstate \"\ *n* **:** the more northerly part of a state of the U.S. as distinguished from a southerly part conventionally designated as *downstate* ⟨the state was again divided: . . . downstate versus ~ —*Our State & Local Gov't of N.Y.*⟩

up·stat·er \ₛ'stād·ə(r)\ *n* -S [*upstate* + -*er*] **:** an inhabitant or a native of an upstate region

upstay \ₛ'ₛ\ *vt* [¹*up* + *stay*] **:** SUSTAIN, SUPPORT

upstir \ₛ'ₛ\ *vt* [¹*up* + *stir*] **:** to stir up **:** INCITE, STIMULATE

upstraight \ₛ'ₛ\ *adj* [¹*up* + *straight*] **:** ERECT

¹upstream \ₛ'ₛ\ *adv* [⁴*up* + *stream*, n.] **:** in a direction nearer the source of a stream ⟨traveled ~⟩ ⟨an extensive tract a few miles ~ —*Amer. Guide Series: La.*⟩

²upstream \"\ *adj* **1 :** directed upstream ⟨an ~ course⟩ **2 :** situated or occurring upstream ⟨the ~ countries —F.W. Morgan⟩

upstreet \'ₛ,ₛ\ *adv* [⁴*up* + *street*] **:** up the street

upstretched \ₛ'ₛ\ *adj* [¹*up* + *stretched*, past part. of *stretch*] **:** stretched upward

upstroke \'ₛ,ₛ\ *n* [²*up* + *stroke*] **:** an upward stroke esp. of a pen

¹upsun \'ₛ,ₛ\ *n* [ME (Sc) *upson*, fr. *up* + *sunne, sonne, son* sun — more at SUN] *Scot* **:** the time between sunrise and sunset — **with upsun** *adv, Scot* **:** while the sun is up

²upsun \ₛ'ₛ\ *adv* [⁴*up* + *sun*, n.] **:** in a direction toward the sun **:** with the sun in one's eyes

¹upsurge \ₛ'ₛ\ *vi* [¹*up* + *surge*] **:** to surge up **:** RISE, INCREASE

²upsurge \'ₛ,ₛ\ *n* **:** an act or instance of surging up; *esp* **:** a rapid increase **:** a sudden rise ⟨a big ~ of wage claims —Margaret Stewart⟩ ⟨the present ~ of concern for the quality of . . . teaching —Ellsworth Barnard⟩

up·sur·gence \,əp'sərjən(t)s\ *n* -S **:** UPSURGE

¹upsweep \ₛ'ₛ\ *vi* [¹*up* + *sweep*] **:** to sweep upward

²upsweep \'ₛ,ₛ\ *n* **:** an upward sweep: as **a :** the upward curving of the underjaw of an animal (as the bulldog) **b :** an increase in elevation; *esp* **:** a steep slope ⟨the thousand-foot ~ of usually frowning scree and cliff on the other side of the water —F.W.Rothwell⟩ **c :** a hairdo in which the hair is brushed up to the top of the head and held in position by pins or combs **d :** a marked increase of activity ⟨this ~ continues to the end of the base period —*Jour. of Accountancy*⟩

upsweep c

upswell \ₛ'ₛ\ *vb* [ME *upswellen*, fr. *up* + *swellen* to swell — more at SWELL] **:** to swell up

upswelling \ₛ'ₛₛ\ *n* **:** an act or instance of swelling upward ⟨the ~ of the seed in the earth —Walter Pater⟩

upswept \ₛ'ₛ\ *adj* [fr. past part. of *upsweep*] **:** swept upward: as **a :** brushed up to the top of the head and held in position by pins or combs ⟨a statuesque young lady with ~ platinum hair —Douglas Watt⟩ **b :** curved upward **:** sloped upward ⟨an ~ flourish of mustachios —Frank Yerby⟩ ⟨~ rear fenders⟩

upswing \'ₛ,ₛ\ *n* [²*up* + *swing*] **:** an upward swing; *esp* **:** an upward movement of considerable strength (as in activity or prices) **:** a marked increase ⟨business activity is still on the ~ —*Amer. Guide Series: Maine*⟩ ⟨a tremendous ~ in technological progress —H.H.Curtice⟩

up·sy-dai·sy \'əpsē,dāzē\ *also* **up-a-dai·sy** \-pə,-\ *or* **ups-a-dai·sy** \-psə,-\ *or* **up·see-dai·sy** *or* **up·si·dai·sy** \-sē,-\ *interj* [irreg. fr. ¹*up*] — used to express reassurance typically to a small child when it is being lifted

up·sy-down \'əpsē'daùn\ *archaic var of* UPSIDE DOWN

upsy dutch *adv, usu cap D, obs* **:** UPSY FREEZE

upsy freeze *adv* [D *op zijn Fries*, lit., in the Frisian manner] *obs* **:** to an excessive degree (as in drinking) **:** HEAVILY

¹uptake \ₛ'ₛ\ *vt* [ME *uptaken*, fr. *up* + *taken* to take — more at TAKE] **1** *obs* **:** to take up **:** LIFT, RAISE **2** *chiefly Scot* **:** UNDERSTAND, COMPREHEND

²uptake \'ₛ,ₛ\ *n* **1 :** UNDERSTANDING, COMPREHENSION ⟨quick on the ~⟩ ⟨slow in the ~ —Arnold Bennett⟩ ⟨prided herself upon being sharp at the ~ —Victoria Sackville-West⟩ **2 a :** the pipe leading upward from the smokebox of a steam boiler to the chimney or smokestack **:** a flue leading upward **b :** a shaft or tube up which a current of air passes esp. for ventilation **:** UPCAST **3 :** TAKE-UP ⟨the loom's ~⟩ **4 :** an act or instance of absorbing and incorporating esp. into a living organism ⟨the ~ of inorganic phosphate normally associated with respiration —P.A.Harvey & Wei Yang⟩ ⟨thyroid function should be determined by radioiodine ~ studies —*Jour. Amer. Med. Assoc.*⟩

uptear \ₛ'ₛ\ *vt* [¹*up* + *tear*] **:** to tear up by or as if by the roots **:** DESTROY

up-tempo \'ₛ'(,)ₛ\ *n* [²*up* + *tempo*] **:** a fast-moving tempo (as in jazz or popular music)

¹upthrow \ₛ'ₛ\ *vt* [¹*up* + *throw*] **:** to throw upward **:** cast up

²upthrow \'ₛ,ₛ\ *n* **1 a :** an upward displacement (as of a stratum or a seam in a mine) **b :** the body of rock on the side of a fault that has moved or appears to have moved upward during the faulting in relation to that on the other side of the fault **c :** an upheaval of the earth's crust **2 :** the amount of upward displacement in a fault — compare THROW

upthrown \ₛ'ₛ\ *adj* [fr. past part. of ¹*upthrow*] **:** thrown upward; *specif* **:** displaced upward in a geologic fault

¹upthrust \ₛ'ₛ\ *vb* [¹*up* + *thrust*] *vt* **:** to thrust up; *specif* **:** to push up in an upthrust ⟨before the mountains were ~ —E.E. Slosson⟩ **~** *vi* **:** to rise with an upward thrust

²upthrust \'ₛ,ₛ\ *n* **:** an upward thrust; *specif* **:** an uplift of part of the earth's crust commonly with faulting

uptie \ₛ'ₛ\ *vt* [ME *uptien*, fr. *up* + *tien* to tie — more at TIE] **:** to tie up

up till *prep* [ME] **1** *obs* **:** up to **:** AGAINST **2 :** TILL, UNTIL ⟨*up till* the moment when bullets and stones began to fly —*Contemporary Rev.*⟩

uptilt \ₛ'ₛ\ *vt* [¹*up* + *tilt*] **:** to tilt upward

up to *prep* [ME] **1 :** as far as a designated part (as of the body or a weapon that penetrates) ⟨sank in quicksand *up to* his armpits⟩ ⟨pushed the knife in *up to* the hilt⟩ ⟨was walking right into hot water . . . *up to* her neck —Elizabeth Headley⟩ **2 :** to or in fulfillment of **:** in complete accordance with **:** so as to make full use of ⟨unable to write *up to* their high standards⟩ ⟨practices *up to* his knowledge⟩ **3 a :** to the limit of ⟨guesses on the size of his wealth ran *up to* $2 billion —Joseph Nolan⟩ ⟨sick leave may be accumulated *up to* 150 days —*Careers for College Graduates*⟩ ⟨golden perch, *up to* a few pounds in weight, bit readily —Francis Birtles⟩ ⟨come in sizes *up to* 10 cups —Jane Nickerson⟩ **b :** as many as **:** as much as ⟨freighters carry *up to* 12 passengers —Richard Joseph⟩ ⟨would exempt tickets costing *up to* 60 cents —*Wall Street Jour.*⟩ ⟨carelessness may mean great agony and *up to* weeks in bed —J.L.B.Smith⟩ **4 :** TILL, UNTIL ⟨*up to* that date they had been generally successful —*Amer. Guide Series: Mich.*⟩ ⟨*up to* the war rural areas were always the dwelling place of the surplus population —S. E.Harris⟩ **5 :** as far as a designated point ⟨painted the wall green *up to* the side door⟩ ⟨*up to* this point we have discussed chiefly the material factors —W.C.Huntington⟩

up-to-date \ₛₛ'ₛ\ *adj* **1 :** extending up to the present time **:** including the latest facts ⟨the new 10th edition is *up-to-date* —*Infantry Jour.*⟩ ⟨*up-to-date* maps —George Milburn⟩ **2 :** abreast of the times (as in style or technique) **:** MODERN ⟨the stores . . . are as *up-to-date* as those of any big city —Corey Ford⟩ ⟨the most *up-to-date* methods of cultivation —J.H.Plumb⟩ ⟨a curiously *up-to-date* malaise —Frederic Morton⟩ — **up-to-date·ly** *adv* — **up-to-date·ness** *n* -ES

up-to-the-minute \ₛₛₛ'ₛₛ\ *adj* **1 :** extending up to the immediate present **:** including the very latest information ⟨the facts are *up-to-the-minute* —*New Republic*⟩ **2 :** marked by complete up-to-dateness **:** entirely modern ⟨will be remodeled into an *up-to-the-minute* flour mill —*Nat'l Miller*⟩

¹uptown \'ₛ'ₛ\ *adv* [⁴*up* + *town*, n.] **1 :** toward, to, or in the upper part of a town or city ⟨walked ~ behind two strangers —Sinclair Lewis⟩ **2 :** toward, to, or in the residential section of a city

²uptown \"\ *adj* **1 :** situated in or belonging to the upper part of a town or city ⟨~ streets⟩ ⟨~ theaters⟩ ⟨~ society⟩ **2 :** situated in or belonging to the residential section of a city

³uptown \"\ *n* **1 :** the upper part of a town or city **2 :** the residential section of a city

up·town·er \ₛ'taùnə(r)\ *n* [¹*uptown* + -*er*] **:** one who lives uptown

uptrain *vt* [¹*up* + *train*] *obs* **:** to train up **:** bring up **:** REAR

uptrend \'ₛ,ₛ\ *n* [²*up* + *trend*] **:** a tendency upward esp. in the development of economic factors

¹upturn \ₛ'ₛ\ *vb* [¹*up* + *turn*] *vt* **1 a :** to turn up **:** turn upside down **:** OVERTURN ⟨his plate had been ~*ed* —Marguerite Young⟩ **b :** to throw into great disorder **:** UPHEAVE ⟨a treeless volcanic ~*ed* region —A.W.Greely⟩ **2 :** to direct upward ⟨~*ed* his nostril —John Milton⟩ **~** *vi* **:** to turn upward

²upturn \'ₛ,ₛ\ *n* **1 :** extreme disorder (as of society) **:** CONVULSION, UPHEAVAL ⟨a truth about violent social ~ —Richard Watts⟩ **2 :** an upturned part **3 :** an upward turn esp. toward better conditions or higher prices ⟨an ~ in the economy —*Wall Street Jour.*⟩ ⟨a gradual ~ in living standards —B.M.Jones⟩ ⟨the exceptional ~ of strikes —A.E.Rees⟩

up-twister \'ₛ,ₛₛ\ *n* **:** a textile machine with upward feeds that is used to add twist to single yarns without plying them — compare DOWN-TWISTER

upu·pa \'yüpyəpə\ *n, cap* [NL, fr. L, hoopoe, prob. of imit. origin] **:** a small genus (the type of the family Upupidae of the order Coraciiformes) of nonpasserine birds comprising the typical hoopoes

¹up·ward \'əpwə(r)d\ *or* **up·wards** \-dz\ *adv* [*upward* fr. ME, fr. OE *ūpweard*, fr. *ūp* up + *-weard* -ward; *upwards* fr. ME *upwardes*, fr. OE *ūpweardes*, fr. *ūpweard* + *-es* (adverbially functioning gen. sing. ending of nouns) — more at UP, ¹-S] **1 a :** toward a higher position **:** in a direction from a lower to a higher place ⟨the land gradually rose ~ —J.P.Marquand⟩ ⟨his hands were groping ~ —James Hilton⟩ **b :** toward the source of a stream or the interior of a region ⟨an explorer moving ~ from a river mouth finds a place at which the stream divides —A.H.Hill⟩ **c :** in a higher or the highest relative position ⟨holding out her right hand, palm *upwards* —*Tomorrow*⟩ **d :** in the upper parts esp. of the body **:** toward the head **:** ABOVE ⟨from the waist ~⟩ ⟨sea monster, ~ man and downward fish —John Milton⟩ **2** *archaic* **:** toward the past **3 :** toward a higher or better condition, status, or level ⟨forced his way steadily *upwards* by his mere soldierlike qualities —J.A.Froude⟩ ⟨both man and the manlike apes have developed *upwards* from a common prehistoric ancestral stock —R.W.Murray⟩ ⟨the Senate has amended its opinion of him ~ —*Time*⟩ **4 a :** to an indefinitely greater amount, figure, or rank ⟨from $5 ~⟩ ⟨each claiming as his own anywhere from 100 head ~ —Agnes M. Cleaveland⟩ **b :** toward a greater amount or higher number, degree, or rate ⟨family incomes shot swiftly ~ —Oscar Handlin⟩ ⟨building costs have proved flexible ~ but not downward —T.W.Arnold⟩ **5 :** toward or into later years ⟨from his youth ~⟩ **6 :** toward a large city **7 :** toward the top (as of a sheet of paper) ⟨this stroke . . . is written ~ —Dwight McEwen⟩

²upward \"\ *prep* [ME, fr. *upward*, adv.] *archaic* **:** up along ⟨~ ragged precipices flit to save poor lambkins —John Keats⟩

³upward \"\ *adj* [¹*upward*] **1 a :** directed toward a higher place **:** ASCENDING ⟨the drive along that winding ~ track —Norman Douglas⟩ ⟨a general ~ movement of fish⟩ **b :** situated in a higher place or position ⟨scaling the ~ sky —P.B. Shelley⟩ **2 :** marked by improvement or progress ⟨the line of ~ development which led to the anthropoid —R.W.Murray⟩ **3 :** UPSTREAM ⟨discovered and named the falls . . . which they had barely missed on the ~ journey —*Amer. Guide Series: Minn.*⟩ **4 :** rising to a higher pitch ⟨her words had an ~ inflection —Ethel Wilson⟩ **5 :** marked by an increase **:** RISING ⟨prices . . . continued their ~ movement —N.H.Brown⟩ ⟨struggling . . . against the ~ trend of wages —Alzada Comstock⟩ ⟨look forward to an unending ~ market —K.D. Burke⟩ **6 :** directed toward the top (as toward the top of a sheet of paper) ⟨an ~ stroke —J.R.Gregg⟩ — **up·ward·ly** *adv* — **up·ward·ness** *n* -ES

⁴upward \"\ *n, obs* **:** TOP, CROWN ⟨extremest ~ of thy head —Shak.⟩

upwards of *also* **upward of** *adv* **1 :** more than **:** in excess of ⟨signed *upwards of* 10,000 bills into law and vetoed more than 1500 —Beverly Smith⟩ **2 :** a little less than **:** not quite **:** ALMOST, APPROXIMATELY, ABOUT ⟨outlined *upwards of* a thousand words by means of which he maintained almost anything could be expressed —Louise Pound⟩

¹upwarp \'ₛ,ₛ\ *n* [²*up* + *warp*, n.] **:** a very broad anticline with gently dipping limbs that is due to differential uplift

²upwarp \ₛ'ₛ\ *vt* [¹*up* + *warp*, v.] **:** to uplift differentially so as to produce an upwarp or a broad low arching of the surface ⟨the land to the northward had been ~*ed* —*Jour. of Geol.*⟩

upwash \'ₛ,ₛ\ *n* [²*up* + *wash*] **:** the upward flow of air directly ahead of the leading edge of a moving airfoil

upwell \ₛ'ₛ\ *vi* [¹*up* + *well*] **:** to well up; *specif* **:** to move or flow upward

upwent *past of* UPGO

upwhirl \ₛ'ₛ\ *vb* [¹*up* + *whirl*] *vt* **:** to cause to whirl upward **~** *vi* **:** to whirl upward

¹upwind \ₛ'ₛ\ *vb* [¹*up* + *wind*] *vt, obs* **:** to wind up **:** ROLL, COIL **~** *vi* **:** to wind upward

²**upwind** \ˈ=ˌ=\ *adv* [⁴*up* + *wind*, n.] **1 :** with face or course against the wind ⟨stalked cautiously ~⟩ ⟨the slim and beautiful jets . . . roared ~ —J.A.Michener⟩ **2 :** in a position toward the direction from which the wind is blowing ⟨are dropped ~ and will drift down upon the survivors —*Nat'l Geographic Mag.*⟩

³**upwind** \ˈ=ˌ=\ *n* [²*up* + *wind*, n.] **1 :** a wind blowing against one's course **2 :** a wind blowing up a slope

⁴**upwind** \ˈ=ˌ=\ *adj* [²*upwind*] **:** being toward or in the direction from which the wind is blowing ⟨the infamous ~ turn which calls for the most precise piece of instrument flying —G.G. O'Rourke⟩ ⟨sent to the ~ side —James Stevenson-Hamilton⟩

¹**up·with** \ˈəpˌwith\ *adv* [¹*up* + obs. *with*, adv., together, fr. ME — more at DOWNWITH] *chiefly Scot* **:** UPWARD

²**upwith** \"\ *adj, chiefly Scot* **:** sloping upward **:** RISING

¹**ur** \(ˌ)ü(ə)r, (ˌ)ür\ *dial var of* OUR

²**ur** *like* ER\ *interj* **:** ER

¹**ur-** *or* **uro-** *comb form* [NL, fr. Gk *our-, ouro-*, fr. *ouron* urine — more at URINE] **1 :** urine ⟨*ur*analysis⟩ ⟨*uro*bilin⟩ **2 :** urinary tract ⟨*uro*gram⟩ **3 :** urination ⟨*uro*lagnia⟩ **4 :** urinal and ⟨*uro*genital⟩ **5 :** urea ⟨*ur*ethane⟩ ⟨*ur*acil⟩ **6 :** uric acid ⟨*ur*oxanic⟩

²**ur-** *or* **uro-** *comb form* [NL, fr. Gk *our-, ouro-*, fr. *oura*, akin to Gk *orrhos* buttocks — more at ASS] **1 :** tail **:** taillike ⟨*uro*steon⟩ ⟨*Uro*glena⟩ ⟨*uro*pod⟩ **2 :** posterior segment, region, or process **:** caudal ⟨*ur*ite⟩ ⟨*uro*hyal⟩ ⟨*uro*some⟩

ur *abbr* urinal; urine

UR *abbr* **1** uniform regulations **2** unsatisfactory report **3** upper right

-u·ra \(y)ürə, (y)ürə\ *n comb form, pl* **-ura** [NL, fr. fem. sing. and neut. pl. of *-urus* -urous] **:** one having (such) a tail ⟨*Chel*ura⟩ **:** ones having (such) a tail ⟨*Brachy*ura⟩ — in taxonomic names in zoology

ura·chal \ˈyůrəkəl\ *adj* [NL *urachus* + E *-al*] **:** of, relating to, or being a urachus

ura·chus \-kəs\ *n* -ES [NL, fr. Gk *ourachos*, fr. *our-* ¹ur- + *-achos* (fr. *echein* to hold) — more at SCHEME] **:** a cord of fibrous tissue extending from the bladder to the umbilicus and constituting the functionless remnant of a part of the duct of the allantois of the embryo

ura·cil \ˈyůrəˌsil\ *n* -S [ISV ¹*ur-* + *acetic* + *-il*] **:** a crystalline heterocyclic compound $C_4H_4N_2O_2$ that is capable of salt formation with sodium hydroxide and is obtained by hydrolysis of ribonucleic acid or by reaction of urea with ethyl formyl-acetate; 2,4-dihydroxy-pyrimidine; *also* **:** any of various derivatives of this compound — compare THYMINE

urad \ˈürəd\ *n* -S [Hindi *urd, urad*] **:** a small-seeded Indian pulse (*Phaseolus radiatus*) resembling the related mung bean and often cultivated as a small grain crop

uraemia *var of* UREMIA

urae·us \yəˈrēəs, yüˈr-\ *n, pl* **uraei** \-ēˌī\ [NL, fr. LGk *ouraios*, a snake, perh. asp] **:** a stylized representation of the sacred asp (*Naja haje*) appearing on the headdress of ancient rulers esp. just over the forehead and serving as a symbol of sovereignty

uraeus

u rail *n, cap U* **:** a U-shaped rail

ural \ˈyůrəl, ˈyürəl, *Russian* ůˈrälʹ\ *adj, usu cap* [fr. *Ural* mountains & *Ural* river, western Asia] **:** of, relating to, or constituting the Ural mountain range running north and south and forming for the most part the eastern boundary of the U.S.S.R. in Europe or the Ural river of southern Russia and Asia

¹**ural-altaic** \ˈ=|=ˌ=|=\ *adj, usu cap U&A* **:** of, relating to, or constituting Uralic, Altaic, or other agglutinating languages

²**ural-altaic** \"\ *n* -S *cap U&A* **1 :** a postulated language group comprising the Uralic and Altaic languages **2 :** a language type showing agglutination and vowel harmony and occurring esp. in languages of Eurasia

urali *var of* OORALI

urali·an \yəˈrālēən, yüˈr-, -ral-\ *adj, usu cap* [*Ural* mountains, northwestern Asia + E *-an*] **1 :** of or relating to the Ural mountains or to the people dwelling in or near them **2 :** constituting or relating to the Finno-Ugric or the Finno-Ugric and Samoyed languages

uralian emerald *n, usu cap U* **:** DEMANTOID

¹**ural·ic** \-ralik\ *adj, usu cap* [*Ural* mountains + E *-ic*] **:** URALIAN

²**uralic** \"\ *n, cap* **:** a language family comprising the Finno-Ugric and Samoyed languages

URALIC LANGUAGES

SUBFAMILY	BRANCH	LANGUAGES	CHIEF LOCALITIES
FINNO-UGRIC		Lapp	northern Scandinavia, Finland, the Kola peninsula of Russia
	Finnic	Finnish, Karelian, Estonian, Livonian, Veps	Finland, Estonia, Latvia, adjacent parts of Russia
		Mordvin	middle Volga region
		Cheremis	middle Volga region
		Votyak, Zyrian	northeastern European Russia
	Ugric	Ostyak, Vogul	Ob valley of northwestern Siberia
		Magyar	Hungary, Romania
SAMOYED		Kamasin, Tavgi, Yenisei, Yurak, Ostyak Samoyed	northwestern Siberia

ural·ite \ˈyůrəˌlīt\ *n* -S [G *uralit*, fr. *Ural* mountains, its locality + G *-it* -ite] **:** a usu. fibrous and dark-green amphibole resulting from alteration of pyroxene — **ural·it·ic** \ˌ==ˈlid·ik\ *adj*

urali·ti·za·tion \yəˌraləd·əˈzāshən, yüˌr-, -ləˌtīˈz-\ *n* -S [ISV *uralitize* + *-ation*] **:** the development of amphibole from pyroxene

ural·i·tize \ˈ=ləˌtīz\ *vt* -ED/-ING/-S [*uralite* + *-ize*] **:** to alter (pyroxene) so as to form uralite

ura·mil \ˈyůrəˌmil, yəˈraməl\ *n* -S [ISV ¹*ur-* + *-am* + *-il*; prob. orig. formed in G] **:** a nitrogenous cyclic compound CO-$(NHCO)_2CHNH_2$ obtained from alloxantin and other derivatives of uric acid or urea in colorless crystals that redden on exposure; 5-amino-barbituric acid — called also *murexan*

uran \(y)əˈran\ *n* -S [F *ouran, varan*, fr. Ar *waran*] **:** a monitor lizard

¹**uran-** *or* **urano-** *comb form* [NL, fr. L, fr. Gk *ouran-, ourano-*, fr. *ouranos* sky, heaven, roof of the mouth] **1 :** sky **:** heaven ⟨*urano*graphy⟩ **2 :** palate ⟨*urano*plasty⟩ ⟨brachy*uranic*⟩

²**uran-** *or* **urano-** *comb form* [F, fr. NL *uranium*] **:** uranium ⟨*urano*thorite⟩ ⟨*uran*yl⟩

uranalysis *var of* URINALYSIS

ura·nate \ˈyůrəˌnāt\ *n* -S [ISV ²*uran-* + *-ate*] **:** a compound [as calcium uranate $CaUO_4$ or ammonium di-uranate $(NH_4)_2$-U_2O_7] formed by reaction of a uranyl salt with a base or by fusion of uranium trioxide or tri-uranium oct-oxide with a metal chloride

ura·nia \yəˈrānēə, yüˈr-, -nyə\ *n, cap* [NL, fr. Gk *ourania*, fem. of *ouranios* heavenly, fr. *ouranos* heaven] **:** a genus (the type of the family Uraniidae) of large brilliantly colored moths that are native to the West Indies and So. America and have tailed hind wings and diurnal flight which cause them to resemble butterflies — **ura·ni·id** \-ēəd\ *n or adj*

¹**ura·nian** \-nēən, -nyən\ *adj, usu cap* [n sense 1, fr. ML *uranius* heavenly, celestial (fr. Gk *ouranios*) + E *-an*; in sense 2, fr. L *Urania* (fr. Gk *Ourania*, one of the muses, fr. fem. of *ouranios*) + E *-an*] **1 :** of, relating to, or concerned with the heavens **:** HEAVENLY, CELESTIAL **2 a :** of or relating or dedicated to Urania, the muse of astronomy **b :** of or relating to the science of astronomy **:** ASTRONOMICAL

²**uranian** \"\ *adj, usu cap* [*Uranus*, seventh planet from the sun + E *-an* — more at URANIUM] **:** of or relating to the planet Uranus

³**uranian** \"\ *n* -S *usu cap* **:** a hypothetical inhabitant or native of the planet Uranus

⁴**uranian** \"\ *adj or n* [*Urania*, the Greek goddess of love Aphrodite + E *-an*] **:** HOMOSEXUAL

¹**uran·ic** \yəˈranik, yüˈr-\ *adj* [ISV ²*uran-* + *-ic*] **:** of, relating to, or containing uranium — used esp. of compounds in which this element has a valence higher than in uranous compounds

²**uranic** \"\ *adj* [¹*uran-* + *-ic*] **:** URANIAN 2b

urani·cen·tric \ˌyůrənəˈsen·trik, yəˌrān-, yüˌr-, -ˌran-\ *adj, often cap* [*Uranus* + *-i-* + *-centric*] **:** referred to the planet Uranus as a center

ura·nide \ˈyůrəˌnīd\ *n* -S [²*uran-* + *-ide*] **1 :** URANIUM **2 :** a transuranium element — compare ACTINIDE

ura·nif·er·ous \ˌyůrəˈnif(ə)rəs\ *adj* [ISV ²*uran-* + *-iferous*] **:** containing uranium

ura·nin \ˈyůrənən, yəˈrān-, yüˈrān-\ *n* -S [²*uran-* + *-in*, *-ine*; fr. its fluorescence resembling that of uranium glass] **:** the sodium salt of fluorescein — see DYE table I (under *Acid Yellow 73*)

ura·nin·ite \-əˌnīt, yəˈranə-, yüˈr-\ *n* -S [G *uranin* uraninite (fr. ²*uran-* + *-in*) + E *-ite*] **:** a mineral UO_2 that is a black octahedral or cubic oxide of uranium, that contains also thorium, the cerium and yttrium metals, and lead, that often yields when heated a gas consisting chiefly of helium, and that is the chief ore of uranium (hardness 6.6, sp. gr. 9.7 when unaltered) — called also CLEVEITE; see BRÖGGERITE, NIVENITE, PITCHBLENDE

ura·nism \ˈyůrəˌnizəm\ *n* -S [G *uranismus*, fr. *Urania*, the Greek goddess of love Aphrodite (fr. Gk *Ourania*, fr. fem. of *ouranios* heavenly) + G *-ismus* -ism] **:** a homosexual condition esp. when involving physically normal males

ura·nist \-ˌnəst\ *n* -S [ISV *uran-* (in *uranism*) + *-ist*] **:** HOMOSEXUAL

ura·nium \yəˈrānēəm, yüˈr- *also* -nyəm\ *n* -S [NL, fr. *Uranus*, seventh planet from the sun discovered in the same decade as uranium (after *Uranus*, in Greco-Roman mythology the personification of heaven and husband of Earth, fr. L, fr. Gk *Ouranos*, fr. *ouranos* sky, heaven) + NL *-ium*] **:** a lustrous silvery heavy radioactive polyvalent metallic element of the actinide series that occurs in concentrated form in pitchblende, carnotite, and autunite and in traces of 0.2 to 200 parts per million in most igneous rocks, phosphate rocks, lignites, and oil shales, that is prepared from its halides by reduction with alkali or alkaline earth metals or from its oxides by reduction with hot carbon, aluminum, or calcium, that exists naturally as a mixture of three isotopes of mass numbers 238, 235, and 234 in the proportions 99.28 percent, 0.71 percent, and 0.006 percent respectively, that undergoes very slow radioactive decay and captures neutrons in a nuclear reactor to produce a heavier isotope of mass number 239 which decomposes by beta emissions into neptunium and then plutonium, and that is used primarily in atomic energy programs to sustain chain-reaction piles, to provide a source of the light isotope uranium 235, and to make plutonium — symbol *U*; see THORIUM, URANIUM SERIES; ELEMENT table

ura·nium·aire \=ˌrānēəˈma(a)(ə)r, -nyəˈm-, =ˈ=(=)=ˌ=\ *n* -S [*uranium* + *-aire* (as in *millionaire*)] **:** a person making a fortune from uranium and esp. from the discovery of new deposits

uranium fluoride *n* **:** a fluoride of uranium: as **a :** URANIUM TETRAFLUORIDE **b :** URANIUM HEXAFLUORIDE

uranium glass *n* **:** a fluorescent yellow glass colored by adding uranium compounds

uranium hexafluoride *n* **:** a pale yellow deliquescent crystalline compound UF_6 that sublimes at 56.5°C, that is made usu. from uranium tetrafluoride or uranium by direct action of fluorine, and that is used in the gaseous diffusion process for separation of uranium 235 from ordinary uranium

uranium lead *n* **:** lead consisting essentially of the isotope of mass number 206 formed as the final product of the uranium series

uranium nitrate *n* **:** URANYL NITRATE

uranium-ocher \=ˈ=(ə)=ˈ=\ *n* **:** GUMMITE

uranium oxide *n* **:** any of a series of oxides of uranium that are usu. regarded as definite compounds but are better considered phases with a range of compositions: as **a :** the dioxide UO_2 or approximately $UO_{2.0\text{-}2.6(?)}$ obtained as a brown to black crystalline powder by heating uranium trioxide or tri-uranium oct-oxide in hydrogen or carbon monoxide and formerly used in gas mantles and in ceramic glazes — compare URANINITE **b :** the most stable of the oxides U_3O_8 that occurs in pitchblende, that is obtained as a green to black crystalline compound by treating pitchblende successively with acids, bases, and dilute acids or by igniting other uranium oxides or most other uranium compounds in air, that is reduced to metallic uranium by heating with carbon or aluminum, and that is a primary source of uranium for atomic energy work **:** tri-uranium oct-oxide **c :** the trioxide UO_3 that is obtained as a light yellow to orange to brick-red amorphous or crystalline substance usu. by heating uranyl nitrate or ammonium di-uranate, that loses oxygen on heating to form tri-uranium oct-oxide, and that is sometimes used as a pigment for green-yellow colors in glass

uranium ray *n* **:** BECQUEREL RAY

uranium series *or* **uranium-radium series** *n* **:** a radioactive series beginning with uranium I of mass number 238 and ending with radium G constituting the nonradioactive isotope of lead of mass number 206: uranium I, at. no. 92 → uranium X_1 at. no. 90 (syn. thorium 234) → uranium X_2, at. no. 91 (syn. protactinium 234) → uranium II, at. no. 92 (syn. uranium 234) → ionium, at. no. 90 (syn. thorium 230) → radium 226, at. no. 88 → radon 222, at. no. 86 → radium A, at. no. 84 (syn. polonium 218) → radium B, at. no. 82 (syn. lead 214) [or astatine 218] → radium C, at. no. 83 (syn. bismuth 214) → radium C′, at. no. 84 (syn. polonium 214) [or radium C″, at. no. 81 (syn. thallium 210)] → radium D, at. no. 82 (syn. lead 210) → radium E, at. no. 83 (syn. bismuth 210) → radium F, at. no. 84 (syn. polonium 210) → radium G, at. no. 82 (syn. lead 206) — called also *radium series*

uranium tetrafluoride *n* **:** a green crystalline nonvolatile compound UF_4 that is usu. made from uranium dioxide and hydrogen fluoride above 500°C or from uranium metal and fluorine and that is used in making uranium hexafluoride

uranium 235 *n* **:** a light isotope of uranium of mass number 235 that is physically separable from natural uranium or is formed from plutonium by emission of a helium nucleus, that as the parent of the actinium series undergoes very slow radioactive disintegration, and that when bombarded with slow neutrons undergoes rapid fission into smaller atoms (as strontium and xenon or barium and krypton) together with much radiation and atomic energy, and that is used in power plants and atom bombs — symbol U^{235} or ^{235}U; called also ACTINOURANIUM

uranium yellow *n* **:** a yellow salt $Na_2U_2O_7.6H_2O$ used esp. formerly in ceramic glazes and fluorescent glass **:** sodium di-uranate

urano- — see URAN-

ura·no·cir·cite \ˌyůrənōˈsərˌsīt, yəˌran-\ *n* -S [G *uranocircit*, fr. ²*uran-* + Gk *kirkos* hawk (trans. of G *falken* in *Falkenstein*, city in central Germany, its locality) + G *-it* -ite — more at CIRCAETUS] **:** a mineral $Ba(UO_2)_2(PO_4)_2.8H_2O$ that is a hydrous barium uranium phosphate in yellow-green crystals and is isomorphous with torbernite, autunite, saléeite, zeunerite, and uranospinite

ura·nog·ra·pher \ˌyůrəˈnägrəfə(r)\ *also* **ura·nog·ra·phist** \-fəst\ *n* -S **:** an expert in or student of uranography

ura·no·graph·ic \ˌyůrənōˈgrafik\ *or* **ura·no·graph·i·cal** \-fəkəl\ *adj* **:** of or relating to uranography

ura·nog·ra·phy \ˌyůrəˈnägrəfē\ *n* -ES [Gk *ouranographia*, fr. *ouran-* ¹uran- + *-graphia* -graphy] **1 :** description of the celestial regions and the divine abode **2 a :** a branch of science dealing with the description of the heavens and the celestial bodies **:** URANOLOGY **b :** the construction of celestial representations (as maps or globes)

ura·no·log·i·cal \ˌyůrənəˈläjəkəl\ *adj* **:** of or relating to uranology

ura·nol·o·gy \ˌyůrəˈnäləjē\ *n* -ES [prob. fr. (assumed) NL *uranologia*, fr. NL ¹*uran-* + *-logia* -logy] **1 :** the study of the heavens **:** ASTRONOMY **2 :** a discourse or treatise on the heavens and the celestial bodies

ura·no·met·ri·cal \ˌyůrənōˈme·trəkəl\ *adj* [NL *uranometria* uranometry + E *-ical*] **:** of or relating to uranometry

ura·nom·e·try \ˌyůrəˈnäm·ə·trē\ *n* -ES [NL *uranometria*, fr. ¹*uran-* + *-metria* -metry] **1 :** a chart or catalog of celestial bodies and esp. of visible fixed stars **2 :** the measurement of the heavens

uran·o·phane \yəˈranəˌfān\ *n* -S [G *uranophan*, fr. ²*uran-* + *-phan* -phane] **:** a mineral $Ca(UO_2)_2Si_2O_7.6H_2O$ that is a hydrous uranium calcium silicate, occurs in yellow fibrous masses, and is possibly identical with uranotil (sp. gr. 3.81–3.90)

ura·nopi·lite \ˌyůrəˈnōpəˌlīt, -ˈnäpəˌlīt\ *n* -S [G *uranopilit*, fr. ²*uran-* + Gk *pilos* felt + G *-it* -ite — more at PILE (hair)] **:** a mineral $(UO_2)_6(SO_4)(OH)_{10}.12H_2O$ that is a hydrous basic sulfate of uranium and occurs in yellow velvety incrustations composed of microscopic needlelike crystals

ura·nos·co·pid \ˌyůrəˈnäskəpəd\ *adj* [NL *Uranoscopidae*] **:** of or relating to the Uranoscopidae

ura·no·scop·i·dae \ˌyůrənōˈskäpəˌdē\ *n pl, cap* [NL, fr. *Uranoscopus*, type genus (fr. L *uranoscopus*, a fish, fr. Gk *ouranoskopos*, fr. *ouranoskopos*, adj., observing the heavens, fr. *ouranos* sky, heaven + *-skopos* observing, fr. *skopein* to observe, look at) + *-idae* — more at SPY] **:** a family of percoid fishes comprising the stargazers

uranoso- *comb form* [ISV, fr. NL *uranosus* uranous] **:** uranous ⟨*uranoso*potassic⟩

ura·no·so·uranic oxide \ˌyůrəˌnōˌsō + . . .-\ *n* [*uranoso-* + ¹*uranic*] **:** URANIUM OXIDE b

ura·no·sphae·rite *also* **ura·no·sphe·rite** \ˌyůrənōˈsfiˌrīt\ *n* -S [G *uranosphaerit*, fr. ²*uran-* + *sphaer-* + *-it* -ite] **:** a mineral $(BiO)_2U_2O_7.3H_2O$ that is a hydrous bismuth uranate and occurs in orange-yellow to brick-red half-globular aggregates

ura·nos·pi·nite \ˌyůrəˈnäspəˌnīt\ *n* -S [G *uranospinit*, fr. ²*uran-* + Gk *spinos* chaffinch (taken to mean siskin) + G *-it* -ite; fr. its color resembling that of the siskin — more at FINCH] **:** a mineral $Ca(UO_2)_2(AsO_4)_2.8H_2O$ that is a hydrous calcium uranium arsenate, occurs in green tabular crystals, and is isomorphous with zeunerite, torbernite, autunite, saléeite, and uranocircite

ura·no·tan·ta·lite \ˌyůrənōˈtantᵊlˌīt\ *n* [G *uranotantal* uranotantalite (fr. ²*uran-* + *tantal* tantalite) + E *-ite*] **:** SAMARSKITE

ura·no·thal·lite \-ˈthaˌlīt\ *n* -S [G *uranothallit*, fr. ²*uran-* + *thall-* + *-it* -ite; fr. its color] **:** LIEBIGITE

ura·no·thorianite \ˌyůrənō+\ *n* [²*uran-* + *thorianite*] **:** a mineral that is an intermediate member in the isomorphous series from uraninite to thorianite

ura·no·thorite \"+\ *n* [²*uran-* + *thorite*] **:** a uraniferous variety of thorite

uran·o·til \yəˈranəˌtil\ *or* **uran·o·tile** \-ˌtīl\ *n* -S [G *uranotil*, fr. ²*uran-* + Gk *tilos* fiber] **:** URANOPHANE

ura·nous \ˈyůrənəs, yəˈrān-, yüˈrān-\ *adj* [NL *uranosus*, fr. ²*uran-* + L *-osus* -ose] **:** of, relating to, or containing uranium — used esp. of compounds in which this element has a lower valence than in uranic compounds

ura·nyl \ˈyůrəˌnil\ *n* -S [ISV ²*uran-* + *-yl*] **:** the bivalent radical UO_2 or ion UO_2^{++} formed by uranium trioxide in acid solution; di-oxo-uranium(VI)

uranyl nitrate *n* **:** a yellow salt $UO_2(NO_3)_2$ that is soluble in many organic solvents as well as in water, that is obtained by reaction of uranium oxides with nitric acid, and that is now used chiefly in the purification of uranium and in nuclear reactions

¹**ura·re** *or* **ura·ri** \(y)üˈrärē\ *n* -S [Carib *urari*] **:** CURARE

²**urare** \"\ *n* -S [AmerSp] **:** SPINY RAT 1

urate \ˈyůˌrāt\ *n* -S [F, fr. *ur-* (in *urique* uric, fr. E *uric*) + *-ate*] **:** a salt of uric acid

urate cell *n* **:** a specialized cell in an insect fat body containing uric acid salts

urat·ic \yəˈrad·ik\ *adj* [ISV *urate* + *-ic*] **:** of, relating to, or containing urates

ura·wa \üˈräwə, -ˌwä\ *adj, usu cap* [fr. *Urawa*, Japan] **:** of or from the city of Urawa, Japan **:** of the kind or style prevalent in Urawa

ura·zine \ˈyůrəˌzēn, -ˌzən\ *n* -S [ISV ¹*ur-* + *az-* + *-ine*; orig. formed as G *urazin*] **1 :** a crystalline compound $C_2H_4N_4O_2$ that is an amino derivative of urazole **2 :** an isomeric crystalline compound $C_2H_4N_4O_2$ derived from tetrazine or theoretically as a condensation product of two molecules of urea — called also *para-urazine*

ura·zole \ˈyůrəˌzōl\ *n* -S [ISV ¹*ur-* + *az-* + *-ole*, orig. formed as G *urazol*] **:** a crystalline acidic compound $C_2H_3N_3O_2$ derived from triazole and made esp. by heating urea with hydrazine sulfate; *also* **:** a derivative of it

ur·ban \ˈərbən, ˈəb-, ˈəib-\ *adj* [L *urbanus*, fr. *urb-, urbs* city + *-anus* -an] **1 a :** of, relating to, characteristic of, or taking place in a city ⟨~ affairs⟩ ⟨~ manners⟩ ⟨~ life⟩ **b :** constituting or including and centered on a city ⟨an ~ area⟩ **c :** of, relating to, or concerned with an urban and specif. a densely populated area ⟨~ sociology⟩ ⟨~ biology⟩ **2 :** having authority, property, or residence in a city or urban area ⟨an ~ magistrate⟩ ⟨~ property owners⟩ **3 :** belonging or having relation to buildings that are characteristic of cities ⟨an ~ lease⟩

urban district *n* **:** a subdivision of an administrative county esp. in England, Wales, and Northern Ireland comprising thickly populated communities, distinguished from a borough in not possessing a borough charter, and governed by an urban district council with local jurisdiction in matters of roads, housing, and policing and to some extent sanitation and education — compare RURAL DISTRICT

ur·bane \ˌərˈbān, (ˈ)əˈb-, (ˈ)əiˈb-\ *adj, sometimes* -ER/-EST [L *urbanus*] **1** *archaic* **:** URBAN 1, 2 **2 :** evincing the polish and suavity characteristic of social life in large cities **:** smoothly courteous **:** notably polite or finished in manner **syn** see SUAVE

ur·bane·ly *adv* **:** in an urbane manner **:** with urbanity

ur·ban·ism \ˈərbəˌnizəm, ˈəb-, ˈəib-\ *n* -S [F *urbanisme*, fr. L *urbanus* urban + F *-isme* -ism] **1 :** the condition or characteristic way of life of those who live in an urban area **2 :** the study and theory of building and other physical needs in cities or predominantly urban cultures **:** city planning **3 :** URBANIZATION

ur·ban·ist \-ˌnəst\ *n* -S [ISV *urban* + *-ist*] **:** a specialist in city planning — compare URBANISM 2

ur·ban·is·tic \ˌ=bəˈnistik\ *adj* [fr. *urbanism*, after such pairs as E *optimism*: *optimistic*] **:** of or relating to urbanism — **ur·ban·is·ti·cal·ly** \-tək(ə)lē\ *adv*

ur·ban·ite \ˈ=bəˌnīt\ *n* -S **:** one who lives in a city

ur·ban·i·ty \ˌərˈbanəd·ē, ˌəˈb-, ˌəiˈb-, -nətē, -i\ *n* -ES [MF & L; MF *urbanité* quality of being urbane, fr. L *urbanitat-, urbanitas* urban life, fr. *urbanus* urban + *-itat-, -itas* -ity] **1 a :** the quality or state of being urbane **b urbanities** *pl* **:** suavely gracious acts or conduct **2 :** the condition of being urban; *also* **:** urban life **3 :** well-bred and polished conversation esp. when light and witty

ur·ban·iza·tion \ˌərbənəˈzāshən, ˌəb-, ˌəib-, -ˌnīˈz-\ *n* -S **:** the quality or state of being or becoming urbanized

ur·ban·ize \ˈ=bəˌnīz\ *vt* -ED/-ING/-S *see -ize in Explan Notes* [ISV *urban* + *-ize*] **1 :** to cause (as a rural area) to take on urban characteristics **:** convert to or incorporate into an urban area ⟨the eastern states were gradually *urbanized*⟩ **2 :** to impart to or force upon (as persons) urban habits, ways of life, or responsibilities ⟨the need to ~ a peasant population is a factor in delaying industrialization⟩

urban quaestor *n* **:** an ancient Roman quaestor in charge of the public treasure

urban revolution *n* **:** a period in the growth of a culture characterized by the development of cities **:** an initial period of urbanization

urban servitude *n* **:** a servitude under Roman, civil, and Scots law affecting a building wherever located with respect to various rights (as of inserting a beam in another's wall, of support by another's wall, of eavesdrip, of drainage of rainwater collected and drained onto another's land, and of light and prospect)

urban society *or* **urban culture** *n* **:** a society that is typical of modern industrial civilization and heterogeneous in cultural tradition, that emphasizes secular values, and that is individualized rather than integrated — contrasted with *folk society*

urban sociology *n* **:** a branch of sociology dealing with the development of urban communities and their effect upon society — compare RURAL SOCIOLOGY

ur·bi·car·i·an \ˌərbəˈka(a)rēən\ *adj* [LL *urbicarius* of the city + E *-an* — more at SUBURBICARIAN] : SUBURBICARIAN

ur·bic·o·lae \ˌərˈbikəˌlē, -ˌlī\ [NL, fr. pl. of *urbicola* city dweller, fr. L *urb-*, *urbs* city + NL *-i-* + *-cola*] *syn of* HESPERIDAE

ur·bi·cul·ture \ˈərbəˌkəlchər\ *n* [L *urb-*, *urbs* city + E *-i-* + *culture*] : the practices and problems peculiar to cities or to urban life

URC *abbr* upper right center

ur·cei·form \ˈərsēəˌfȯrm\ *adj* [F *urcéiforme*, fr. L *urceus* + F *-iforme* -iform] : shaped like an urceus

ur·ce·o·lar \ˌərˈsēələr\ *adj* [ISV *urceol-* (fr. NL *urceolus*) + *-ar*] : URCEOLATE

ur·ce·o·late \-lət\ *adj* [NL *urceolatus*, fr. L *urceolus* little pitcher + *-atus* -ate] : swollen below and contracted toward the orifice : shaped like an urn

ur·ce·ole \ˈərsēˌōl\ *n* -s [L *urceolus* little pitcher, dim. of *urceus* jar, pitcher] : a vessel for water for washing the hands (as after consecration of the Host in Roman Catholic mass); *also* : one to hold wine or water : CRUET

ur·ce·o·li·na \ˌər(ˌ)sēəˈlīnə, -lēnə\ *n, cap* [NL, fr. L *urceolus* little pitcher + NL *-ina*; fr. the shape of the flowers] : a small genus of So. American herbs (family Amaryllidaceae) that are often cultivated as ornamentals and that have usu. yellow and green urceolate flowers and broad leaves produced from a bulb

ur·ce·o·lus \ˌərˈsēələs\ *n, pl* **urceo·li** \-ˌlī\ [NL, fr. L, little pitcher] **1** : an urn-shaped organ or part of a plant **2** : the external tube of some rotifers

ur·ce·us \ˈərsēəs\ *n, pl* **ur·cei** \-ēˌī\ [L — more at URN] : an ancient Roman jug or pitcher with one handle

[1]**ur·chin** \ˈərchən, ˈəch-, ˈəich-\ *n* -s [ME *urchin*, *urchon*, *hurcheoun*, *hirchoun* hedgehog, fr. MF *herichon*, *heriçon*, fr. L *ericius*, fr. *er*, *eris*; akin to Gk *chēr* hedgehog — more at HORROR] **1** : HEDGEHOG **2** *dial* : HUNCHBACK **3** : a pert or roguish youngster; *esp* : a mischievous boy **4** *obs* : a mischievous elf that sometimes takes the form of a hedgehog **5** : SEA URCHIN **6** : either of two small card cylinders around the large drum of a carding machine

[2]**urchin** \"\ *adj* **1** *obs* : inclined to make mischief : ELFISH **2** : of, relating to, or like an urchin; *esp* : PRICKLY

ur·chin·ess \-ənəs\ *n* -ES : a female urchin (sense 3)

urchin fish *n* : PORCUPINE FISH

ur·chin·ly \-ənlē\ *adj* : of, relating to, having the character of, or being an urchin

urd \ˈu̇(ə)rd, ˈərd\ *or* **urd bean** *n* -s [Hindi *urd*, *urad*] : a spreading hairy annual bean (*Phaseolus mungo*) that is native to India, is widely cultivated in warm regions for its edible blackish seed, for green manure, or for forage, and is closely related to but less erect in growth than the mung bean — called also *black gram*, *woolly pyrol*

ur·dée *also* **ur·dé** \ˈərdē, ˌərˈdā\ *or* **ur·dy** \ˈərdē\ *adj* [origin unknown] *of a cross* : having each arm expanding at the end into a form like a lozenge with slightly concave edges

ur·du \ˈu̇r(ˌ)dü, ˈər- *sometimes* (ˌ)=ˈ=\ *n* -s *cap* [Hindi *-urdū*, *urdū-* (in *zabān-i-urdū*, *urdū-zabān* language of the camp, fr. Per *zabān* language + *urdū* camp, army, fr. Turk *ordu*); akin to Mongolian *ordu*, *orda* court, camp, horde — more at HORDE] : an Indic language that is an official literary language of Pakistan and widely used particularly by Indians in India, has a colloquial basis very similar to that of Hindi but has developed under strong Persian rather than Sanskrit influence, and is generally written in Persian script

[1]**ure** *n* -s [ME, fr. MF *uevre*, *oeuvre* work, practice, fr. L *opera* — more at OPERA] *obs* : USE, CUSTOM, PRACTICE, EXERCISE

[2]**ure** \ˈe̅r\ *n* -s [of Scand origin; akin to Dan & Norw *øre* öre, ON *aur-*, *eyrir* ounce — more at ÖRE, ORA] : an old unit of land area used in the Shetland and Orkney islands equal to the area rentable for ⅛ mark : ⅛ markland

[3]**ure** \"\ *n* [of Scand origin; akin to Norw dial. *ur* rain cloud, ON *ūr* drizzle — more at URINE] *chiefly Scot* : MIST, HAZE

ure- *or* **ureo-** *comb form* [ISV, fr. NL *urea*] : urea ⟨*ureide*⟩

-ure \ə(r), ˌ(y)u̇(ə)r, -üə\ *n suffix* -s [ME, fr. OF, fr. L *-ura*] **1** : act : process : being ⟨*tubulature*⟩ ⟨*exposure*⟩ ⟨*composure*⟩ **2 a** : office : function ⟨*judicature*⟩ **b** : body for (such) an activity ⟨*legislature*⟩

urea \yəˈrēə, yüˈr- *sometimes* ˈyu̇rēə *or* ˈyür-\ *n* -s [NL, fr. F *urée*, fr. *urine*, fr. MF — more at URINE] **1** : a highly soluble crystalline nitrogenous compound $CO(NH_2)_2$ that is formed in nature by the decomposition of protein and synthesized commercially usu. by heating ammonia and carbon dioxide under pressure, constitutes the chief solid component of the urine of man and other mammals and is also present in the urine of various lower animals and in small quantities in the blood and other body fluids and in the liver, is a very weak base and forms salts only with strong acids, and is used esp. in various chemical syntheses and in fertilizers and animal rations — called also *carbamide*; compare BIURET, ORNITHINE, PSEUDOUREA **2** : any of various derivatives of urea — usu. used in combination ⟨alkylated *~s*⟩

urea·form \-ˌfȯrm\ *n* -s [*urea* + *form*aldehyde] : a synthetic fertilizer compounded of urea and formaldehyde and designed to release nitrogen slowly in usable form through the action of soil bacteria

urea-formaldehyde resin *n* : a thermosetting synthetic resin made by condensing urea with formaldehyde and used esp. in wood-bonding adhesives, colored molded articles, and for finishes (as of textiles, paper, and metals)

ure·al \yəˈrēəl *sometimes* ˈyu̇rē-\ *adj* [*ure-* + *-al*] : of or relating to urea : containing or consisting of urea

ure·am·e·ter \ˌyu̇rēˈaməd·ə(r)\ *n* [by alter.] : UREOMETER

urea peroxide *n* : a crystalline addition compound $CO(NH_2)_2 \cdot H_2O_2$ of urea and hydrogen peroxide used chiefly as a solid source of hydrogen peroxide

urea resin *n* : a resin made from urea and an aldehyde; *esp* : UREA-FORMALDEHYDE RESIN

ure·ase \ˈyu̇rēˌās, -āz\ *n* -s [ISV *ure-* + *-ase*] : a crystallizable enzyme that promotes the hydrolysis of urea into ammonia and carbon dioxide, is present in the alkaline fermentation of urine, and is produced by many bacteria and found in various seeds (as the jack bean and soybean)

ure·chis \ˈyu̇rəkəs, yəˈrek-\ *n, cap* [NL, fr. [2]*ur-* + Gk *echis* viper — more at ECHIS] : a genus (the type of the family Urechidae) of large echiuroid worms which are common in mud along the California seacoast and in which a circulatory system is completely lacking so that the blood corpuscles float free in the coelomic fluid

uredia *pl of* UREDIUM

ure·di·al \yəˈrēdēəl\ *adj* [NL *uredium* + E *-al*] : of, relating to, or constituting a uredium ⟨~ stages⟩

uredi·na·les \yəˌredᵊnˈā(ˌ)lēz, -rēd-\ *n pl, cap* [NL, fr. *Uredin-*, *Uredo* + *-ales*] : an order of parasitic fungi (class Basidiomycetes) that cause rusts in plants, have complex life cycles involving usu. pycnial, aecial, uredinial, and telial stages often on different hosts, and are distinguished from the smuts by producing on a sterigma basidiospores which germinate not by budding but by growing out into an infective hypha

uredinales im·per·fec·ti \-ˌimpə(r)ˈfekˌtī\ *n pl, cap U & sometimes cap I* [NL, lit., imperfect Uredinales] *in some classifications* : a group of form genera of rust fungi including those in which the telial stage is either unknown or cannot be definitely predicted

ure·din·e·ae \ˌyu̇rəˈdinēˌē\ [NL, fr. *Uredin-*, *Uredo* + *-eae*] *syn of* UREDINALES

ure·din·i·al \ˌyu̇rəˈdinēəl\ *adj* [NL *uredinium* + E *-al*] : of, relating to, or being a uredinium

ure·din·i·op·sis \ˌyu̇rəˌdinēˈäpsəs\ [NL, fr. *uredinium* + *-opsis*] *syn of* UREDINOPSIS

ure·din·i·um \ˌyu̇rəˈdinēəm\ *n, pl* **uredin·ia** \-ēə\ [NL, fr. L *uredin-*, *uredo* blast, blight + NL *-ium*] : the crowded usu. yellow or brownish aggregation of spore-bearing hyphae and urediospores of a rust forming pustules or sori that become exposed by rupture of the host's cuticle or epidermis beneath which they develop

uredi·noid \yəˈredᵊnˌȯid, -rēd-\ *adj* [NL *Uredin-*, *Uredo* + E *-oid*] **1** : resembling or related to the Uredinales **2** [NL *uredinium* + E *-oid*] : similar to or having the form or function of a uredinium

uredi·nol·o·gy \=ˌ==ˈäləjē\ *n* -ES [NL *Uredin-*, *Uredo* + E *-o-* + *-logy*] : a branch of mycology dealing with the rusts

uredi·nop·sis \-ˈäpsəs\ *n, cap* [NL, fr. *uredinium* + *-opsis*] : a genus of rusts that is related to *Melampsora* and has solitary sessile teliospores formed within the mesophyll of the leaves of the host

uredi·nous \yəˈredᵊnəs, -rēd-\ *adj* [NL *Uredin-*, *Uredo* + E *-ous*] : of, relating to, or being fungi of the order Uredinales

ure·dio·spore \yəˈrēdəˌspō(ə)r\ *or* **ure·do·spore** \-dəˌs-\ *or* **ure·din·io·spore** \ˌyu̇rəˈdinēəˌs-\ *n* [*urediospore* alter. (influenced by NL *uredium*) of *uredospore*; *uredospore* fr. NL *Uredin-*, *Uredo* + E *-spore*; *urediniospore* alter. (influenced by NL *uredinium*) of *uredospore*] : one of the thin-walled yellow, orange, or reddish spores that are usu. produced by the uredinia of rust fungi in repeated crops, are readily disseminated and quickly germinate to produce a vegetative mycelium which may give rise to other urediospores and thus further rapid spread of the fungus or esp. later in the growing season may produce telia

ure·di·um \yəˈrēdēəm\ *n, pl* **ure·dia** \-ēə\ [NL, fr. *Uredo* + *-ium*] : UREDINIUM

ure·do \yəˈrē(ˌ)dō\ *n* [NL, fr. L, blast, blight, burning itch, fr. *urere* to burn — more at EMBER] **1** -s : the uredostage of a rust formerly regarded as a distinct genus **2** *cap* : a form genus of rusts including forms having either a uredostage only or having a uredostage together with pycnial and aecial stages

ure·do·sorus \yəˈrēdō+ˌ-\ *n, pl* **uredosori** [NL, fr. *Uredin-*, *Uredo* + *sorus*] : UREDINIUM

ure·do·stage \yəˈrēdō+\ *n* [NL *uredo* + E *stage*] : the uredinial stage of a rust

ure·ic \yəˈrēik\ *adj* [ISV *ure-* + *-ic*] : of, relating to, or containing urea

ure·ide \ˈyu̇rēˌīd, -ēəd\ *n* -s [ISV *ure-* + *-ide*] : an acyl derivative of urea whether acyclic (as acetyl-urea) or cyclic (as parabanic acid, alloxan, or barbituric acid)

ure·ido \yəˈrēəˌdō\ *adj* [*ureido-*] : containing the radical NH_2CONH-

ureido- *comb form* [*ureide* + *-o-*] **1** : UREYLENE **2** : containing the univalent radical NH_2CONH- ⟨*ureido*-benzene-arsonic acid⟩

ure·mia *or* **urae·mia** \yəˈrēmēə, yüˈr-, -myə\ *n* -s [NL, fr. [1]*ur-* + *-emia*] : accumulation in the blood of constituents normally eliminated in the urine producing a toxic condition marked by headache, gastrointestinal disorders and esp. vomiting, coma, and convulsions and commonly associated with severe kidney disorder — **ure·mic** *or* **urae·mic** \-mik, -mēk\ *adj*

ure·na \yəˈrēnə\ *n* [NL, fr. Malayalam *uren* urena] **1** *cap* : a small genus of tropical herbs or shrubs (family Malvaceae) having small yellow flowers with five connate bracts, bearing fruit with hooked bristles, yielding a medicinal mucilaginous juice, and including a coarse weedy herb (*U. lobata*) sometimes cultivated for its fiber which is comparable to jute **2** -s **a** : any plant of the genus *Urena* (esp. *U. lobata*) **b** *or* **urena lo·ba·ta** \-lōˈbād·ə, -bäd·ə\ : the cordage fiber derived from the urena (*U. lobata*)

ureo- — see URE-

ure·om·e·ter \ˌyu̇rēˈäməd·ə(r)\ *n* [ISV *ure-* + *-meter*] : an apparatus for the detection and measurement of urea (as in blood or urine)

ureo·secretory \yəˌrēō, ˌyu̇rē(ˌ)ō+\ *adj* [ISV *ure-* + *secretory*] : of or relating to the secretion of urea

ure·ox \ˈyü(ə)ˌräks\ *n, pl* **ure·oxen** [part trans. of obs. G *urochs* (now *auerochs*) — more at AUROCHS] : URUS

ures *pl of* URE

-ures *pl of* -URE

ure·sis \yəˈrēsəs\ *n* -ES [NL, fr. Gk *ourēsis*, fr. *ourein* to urinate] : excretion of urine : URINATION

-u·ret \(y)əˌrelt, *usu* |d·+V; *in "carburet" often* -rā|\ *n comb form* -s [NL *-uretum*, fr. F *-ure*, fr. L *-ur* (in *sulfur*)] : -IDE 1 ⟨carb*uret*⟩ ⟨bi*uret*⟩

ure·ter \yəˈrē|d·ə(r), yüˈrē|, |tə- *also* ˈyu̇rə| *or* ˈyürə|\ *n* -s [NL, fr. Gk *ourētēr*, fr. *ourein* to urinate — more at URINE] : either of the paired ducts that carry away urine from a kidney to the bladder or cloaca, that in man are slender membranous epithelium-lined flat tubes about sixteen inches long which open above into the pelvis of a kidney and below into the back part of the same side of the bladder at a very oblique angle and in other mammals except monotremes open into the bladder and in lower vertebrates into the cloaca, and that in the lower vertebrates are mesonephric ducts and often serve also as sperm ducts in the male — **ure·ter·al** \yəˈrēd·ərəl, yüˈr-, -ētə-\ *or* **ure·ter·ic** \ˌyu̇rəˈterik, ˌyür-, -erēk; yəˈrēd·ərik, yüˈr-, -ētə-\ *adj*

ure·ter·itis \yəˌrēd·əˈrīd·əs *also* ˌyu̇rəd·-\ *n* -ES [NL, fr. *ureter* + *-itis*] : inflammation of the ureter usu. secondary to pyelonephritis

uretero- *comb form* [ISV *ureter* + *-o-*] **1** : ureter ⟨*ureterography*⟩ **2** : ureteral and ⟨*uretero*cervical⟩

ure·ter·o·gram \yəˈrēd·ərəˌgram\ *n* [ISV *uretero-* + *-gram*] : an X-ray photograph of the ureters after injection of a radiopaque substance

ure·ter·o·graph \-ˌgraf, -ˌgráf\ *n* [*uretero-* + *-graph*] : URETEROGRAM

ure·ter·og·ra·phy \yəˌrēd·əˈrägrəfē *also* ˌyu̇rəd·-\ *n* [ISV *uretero-* + *-graphy*] : the art, practice, or act of making ureterograms

ure·tero·intestinal \yəˌrēd·ə(ˌ)rō+\ *adj* [*uretero-* + *intestinal*] : of, relating to, or involving both the intestine and a ureter

ure·tero·lithotomy \"+\ *n* [ISV *uretero-* + *lithotomy*] : removal of a calculus by incision of a ureter

ure·tero·pelvic \"+\ *adj* [*uretero-* + *pelvic*] : of, relating to, or involving a ureter and the adjoining renal pelvis ⟨~ obstruction⟩

ure·tero·pyelogram \"+\ *n* [*uretero-* + *pyelogram*] : an X-ray photograph of the pelves of the kidneys and the ureters made after filling them by injection with a radiopaque substance

ure·tero·pyelography \"+\ *n* [ISV *uretero-* + *pyelography*] : the making of pyelograms

ure·tero·stenosis \"+\ *n* [NL, fr. *uretero-* + *stenosis*] : stricture of a ureter

ure·thane \ˈyu̇rəˌthān, yəˈreˌth-\ *or* **ure·than** \-an\ *n* -s [F *uréthane*, fr. [1]*ur-* + *éth-* eth- + *-ane* -ane, -an] **1 a** : a crystalline ester-amide $NH_2COOC_2H_5$ made usu. by the action of ammonia on ethyl carbonate or ethyl chloroformate or by heating urea nitrate and ethyl alcohol and used chiefly in medicine, for anesthetizing laboratory animals, and as a gelatinizing agent for cellulose acetate or cellulose nitrate — called also *ethyl carbamate* **b** : an ester of carbamic acid other than the ethyl ester **2 a** : an ester (as phenylurethane or other ethyl esters) of a substituted carbamic acid — compare PHENYLURETHANE **b** : POLYURETHANE ⟨~ foams⟩

ure·than·ize \-āˌnīz, -aˌn-\ *vt* -ED/-ING/-S : to treat and esp. to anesthetize with urethane

urethr- *or* **urethro-** *comb form* [NL, fr. LL *urethra*] : urethra ⟨*urethr*ectomy⟩

ure·thra \yəˈrēthrə, yüˈr-\ *n, pl* **urethras** \-thrəz\ *or* **ure·thrae** \-(ˌ)thrē\ [LL, fr. Gk *ourēthra*, fr. *ourein* to urinate — more at URINE] : the canal that in most mammals carries off the urine from the bladder and in the male serves also as a genital duct — **ure·thral** \-thrəl\ *adj*

ure·thri·tis \ˌyu̇rəˈthrīd·əs\ *n, pl* **ure·thrit·i·des** \-thridəˌdēz\ [NL, fr. *urethr-* + *-itis*] : inflammation of the urethra

ure·thro·cele \yəˈrēthrəˌsēl\ *n* -s [ISV *urethr-* + *-cele*] : a pouched protrusion of urethral mucous membrane in the female

ure·thro·gram \-thrəˌgram\ *n* [ISV *urethr-* + *-gram*] : a roentgenogram of the urethra made after injection of a radiopaque substance

ure·thro·graph \-raf, -ráf\ *n* [*urethr-* + *-graph*] : URETHROGRAM

ure·thro·scope \-thrəˌskōp\ *n* [ISV *urethr-* + *scope*] : an instrument designed to permit visual inspection of the urethra by means of lighting and optical attachments — **ure·thro·scop·ic** \=ˌ=ˈskäpik\ *adj*

ure·throt·o·my \ˌyu̇rəˈthräd·əmē, ˌyu̇ˌrēˈth-, yəˌrēˈth-\ *n* -ES [ISV *urethr-* + *-tomy*] : surgical incision into the urethra esp. for the relief of stricture

uret·ic \yəˈred·ik\ *adj* [LL *ureticus*, fr. Gk *ourētikos*, fr. (assumed) *ourētos* (verbal of *ourein* to urinate) + *-ikos* -ic — more at URINE] : of, relating to, or occurring in the urine : URINARY ⟨~ solids⟩; *esp* : DIURETIC ⟨~ medicine⟩

ure·yl·ene \yəˈrēəˌlēn\ *n* -s [*ure-* + *-ylene*] : a bivalent radical $-NHCONH-$ derived from urea

'urf \ˈu̇(ə)rf\ *n* -s [Ar, custom] : Persian customary law — compare ADAT

ur·fir·nis \ˈu̇(ə)rˌfirnəs\ *n* -ES [G, fr. *ur-* primitive, original (fr. OHG *ur-*, *ur* out of) + *firnis* varnish, fr. MHG *vernis*, fr. MF *vernis* — more at ABEAR, VARNISH] : a lustrous paint varying from black to red and found on some prehistoric Greek pottery

ur·ga \ˈu̇rgə, -ˌgä\ *adj, usu cap* [fr. *Urga*, Outer Mongolia] : of or from Urga, the capital of Outer Mongolia : of the kind or style prevalent in Urga

[1]**urge** \ˈərj, ˈə̄j, ˈəij\ *vb* -ED/-ING/-S [L *urgēre* to press, drive, urge — more at WREAK] *vt* **1** : to present in an earnest or pressing manner : press upon attention : insist upon : plead or allege in or as if in argument or justification : advocate or demand with importunity ⟨the psychiatrist *urged* greater cooperation between the psychiatrist and the general practitioner —*Current Biog.*⟩ ⟨opportunity to ~ her point of view —Samuel Van Valkenburg & Ellsworth Huntington⟩ ⟨alert observers *urged* more forcefully that our country must hurry to develop its military power —Herbert Feis⟩ ⟨let me ~ this thought upon you —Dean Acheson⟩ **2** : to undertake the accomplishment of with energy, swiftness, or enthusiasm : prosecute vigorously ⟨the attack . . . is being violently *urged* wherever the winter conditions permit —*Manchester Guardian Weekly*⟩ **3 a** : to press the mind or will of : ply with motives, arguments, persuasions, or importunity : solicit or entreat earnestly ⟨they ~ us to stop thinking and do something —M.R.Cohen⟩ **b** : to be a compelling, impelling, or constraining influence upon : serve as a motivating impulse or reason for ⟨men . . . living in much the same way, *urged* by the same hungers —Marjory S. Douglas⟩ ⟨three general purposes have *urged* me to the task —R.E.Coker⟩ **4 a** : to force or impel in an indicated direction or to an indicated place ⟨*urged* on by a pair of automatic pistols —Eric Linklater⟩ ⟨mustered the ladies together and *urged* them into another room —Maurice Cranston⟩ ⟨wedges are driven in to ~ the trunk in the required direction —F.D.Smith & Barbara Wilcox⟩ **b** (1) : to accelerate or urgently maintain the speed of : HASTEN ⟨through the thick deserts headlong *urged* his flight —Alexander Pope⟩ (2) *archaic* : to travel rapidly or diligently upon or over **c** : to force or impel to motion or to greater speed ⟨red-jacketed dragoons *urged* their horses in furious pursuit —F.V.W.Mason⟩ **5** : to rouse from a dormant state or into life, expression, or action : STIMULATE, PROVOKE ⟨~ not my father's anger —Shak.⟩ ⟨men *urged* their land with perpetual stinking fertilizing —Pearl Buck⟩ ~ *vi* **1** : to declare, advance, or press earnestly a statement, argument, charge, or claim ⟨appeared before the House Banking Committee to ~ against the adoption of an amendment —*Current Biog.*⟩ **2** : to advance with speed or force : HASTEN ⟨she *urged* toward him —Maurice Hewlett⟩ **3** : to exercise an inciting, constraining, or stimulating influence

syn EGG, EXHORT, GOAD, PROD, SPUR, PRICK, SIC: URGE indicates a pressing, impelling, seeking to influence, or overcoming some obstacle, check, or drawback to a certain course ⟨the American tendency to *urge* youngsters to early independence was contrasted with the French practice of encouraging the young to remain dependent for a longer time upon parental guidance —Dorothy Barclay⟩ ⟨the old president *urged* the new president to take it easy, not to destroy himself with zeal —H.F.Wilkins⟩ EGG suggests encouraging, stimulating, or whetting a will or inclination that is hesitant, laggard, or dull ⟨*egged* me to borrow the money —Rudyard Kipling⟩ ⟨*egg* on one of their number to sing —Edmund Wilson⟩ EXHORT may suggest the ardent urging or admonishing of an orator or preacher ⟨*exhorted* his friend to confess, and not to hide his sin any longer —George Eliot⟩ ⟨the situation was of the strangest and gravest description, but the public was *exhorted* to avoid and discourage panic —H.G.Wells⟩ GOAD may suggest an exciting, driving, or irritating to action suggestive of driving animals with pointed sticks ⟨the harsh ruling only *goaded* the Indians into fiercer resistance —R.A.Billington⟩ ⟨must *goad* the slack part of his orchestra by the constant implied threat of dismissal —J.N.Burk⟩ PROD may suggest a driving to action as if with a stick or rod but is gentler in suggestion than GOAD ⟨Indians grew hungry and hatred of the white man *prodded* them into open hostilities —Julian Dana⟩ ⟨enough public support to *prod* congressmen on both sides to furnish the necessary votes —*Newsweek*⟩ SPUR often suggests the use of a spur or sharp spike on the flanks of a lagging horse ⟨*spurred* to earnest effort —M.L.Bonham⟩ ⟨an aching conscience was the chief thing that *spurred* me on —John McNulty⟩ PRICK, similar to SPUR, may refer to inciting or impelling as if by something with a sharp point ⟨tries only to *prick* the student into a desire for the truth —Barbara Buckley⟩ ⟨rely on their animal instinct and developed reflexes to *prick* them into awareness when danger threatened —Fred Majdalany⟩ SIC, orig. used as a command to a dog, may indicate an inciting to attack or worry ⟨a civilized nation *sicced* on the Barbary whelps to tear the peaceful passerby —J.R.Spears⟩

[2]**urge** \"\ *n* -s **1** : the act or process of urging **2** : a force or impulse that urges ⟨many young men had the ~ to participate in the new venture —R.J.Dubos⟩; *esp* : a continuing impulse or tendency toward some activity or goal ⟨that almost mystic ~ to climb can dominate your whole life —Wynford Vaughan-Thomas⟩ **syn** see DESIRE

urged *past of* URGE

ur·gence \-jən(t)s\ *n* -s [MF, fr. LL *urgentia* pressure] : URGENCY

ur·gen·cy \ˈərjənsē, ˈə̄j-, ˈəij-, -si\ *n* -ES [LL *urgentia* pressure, urgency, fr. L *urgent-*, *urgens*, pres. part. + *-ia* -y] **1** : the quality or state of being urgent : INSISTENCE, PRESSURE ⟨the ~ of a petitioner⟩ ⟨the ~ of his need⟩ **2** : an urgent stress (as of wind or need) **3** : a force or impulse that impels or constrains : URGE; *esp* : a compelling desire to urinate or defecate due to some abnormal stress (as inflammation or infection) **4** : IMPORTUNITY, ENTREATY

ur·gent \-nt\ *adj* [ME, fr. MF, fr. L *urgent-*, *urgens*, pres. part. of *urgēre* to press, urge — more at WREAK] **1 a** : calling for or demanding immediate attention : of a kind to urge to action ⟨~ appeals for help⟩ ⟨problems of an ~ nature⟩ **b** : conveying a sense of urgency ⟨an ~ and determined manner⟩ **2** : impelling onward ⟨borne by the mastery of its ~ wings —Robert Bridges †1930⟩ **3** *obs* : passing quickly **4** : SOLICITOUS, IMPORTUNATE ⟨an ~ lover⟩ **5** : serving to impel or constrain ⟨~ affections⟩ **6** *obs* : OPPRESSIVE **syn** see PRESSING

ur·gent·ly *adv* : in an urgent manner : with urgency

urg·er \ˈərjər, ˈə̄jə(r, ˈəijə(r\ *n* -s : one that urges

urges *pres 3d sing of* URGE, *pl of* URGE

ur·gin·ea \ˌərˈjinēə\ *n* [NL, fr. Ben *Urgin*, Arab tribe near Bône, northeastern Algeria, where plants of the genus were orig. found] **1** *cap* : a genus of bulbous herbs (family Liliaceae) native to the Old World and esp. to the Mediterranean region with a deciduous perianth and 3-angled capsule — see SQUILL **2** -s **a** *often cap* : the younger bulbs of a plant (*Urginea indica*) that have action and uses which are the same as those of squill — used in the British Pharmacopoeia **b** : any plant of the genus *Urginea*

urging *pres part of* URGE

urg·ing·ly *adv* : so as to urge : in an urging manner

ur·grund \ˈu̇(ə)rˌgrünt\ *n* -s [G, fr. *ur-* primal, original (fr. OHG *ur-*, *ur* out of) + *grund* ground, bottom, foundation, cause, fr. OHG *grunt* ground, bottom — more at ABEAR, GROUND] : a primal cause or ultimate cosmic principle

-ur·gy \ˌə(r)jē, ˌərj-, ˌə̄j-, ˌəij-, -ji *sometimes* ˈ=ə=\ *n comb form* -ES [NL *-urgia*, fr. Gk *-ourgein* to work (fr. *ergon* work) + L *-ia* -y — more at WORK] : technique or art of dealing or working with (such) a product, matter, or tool ⟨chem*urgy*⟩ ⟨micr*urgy*⟩

ur·heen *or* **ur·hien** *or* **urh·heen** \ˈərˈhē(ə)n\ *n* -s [modif. of Chin (Pek) *êr*[4]*-hsien*[2], lit., two strings] : a Chinese fiddle consisting of two strings usu. of silk tuned a fifth apart, stretched across a small mallet-shaped hollow block, and fastened at the other end to tuning pegs set in a long stick

uria \ˈyu̇rēə\ *n, cap* [NL, fr. Gk *ouria*, a water bird; akin to Gk *ouron* urine] : a genus of guillemots comprising the murres

-uria \ˈ(y)u̇rēə, ˈ(y)ür-\ *n comb form* -s [NL, fr. Gk *-ouria*, fr.

ouron urine + *-ia* -y — more at URINE] **1 :** presence of (a specified substance) in urine ⟨aceton*uria*⟩ ⟨albumin*uria*⟩ **2 :** condition of having (such) urine ⟨poly*uria*⟩; *esp* **:** abnormal or diseased condition that is marked by the presence of (a specified substance) ⟨py*uria*⟩

uri·al *or* **oo·ri·al** \ˈu̇rēəl, -ēˌäl\ *n* -S [Panjabi *hureāl*] **:** a wild sheep (*Ovis vignei*) of the uplands of southern and central Asia that is possibly one of the ancestors of domesticated breeds of sheep and is reddish brown with a white neck and a dark beard from the chin to the chest

uric \ˈyu̇rik, -rēk\ *adj* [¹*ur-* + *-ic*] **1 :** of or relating to urine **2 :** obtained from or occurring in urine

uric- *or* **urico-** *comb form* [*uric* (in *uric acid*)] **:** uric acid ⟨*uricolytic*⟩

-u·ric \ˌ(y)u̇rik, ˈ(y)u̇r-, -rēk\ *adj suffix* [*uric*] **1 :** related to uric acid, urea, or both uric acid and urea ⟨allanto*uric*⟩ **2 :** occurring in urine ⟨hipp*uric*⟩

uric acid *n* **:** a white odorless tasteless nearly insoluble dibasic acid $C_5H_4N_4O_3$ that is present in small quantity in the urine of man and most mammals and abundantly in the form of urates in the excrement of birds, reptiles, and invertebrates in whom it constitutes the chief nitrogenous excretion product, that is a common component either as the free acid or as a urate of urinary or renal calculi and of the so-called gouty concretions, and that is capable of being made synthetically; 2,6,8-trihydroxy-purine

uri·case \ˈyu̇rəˌkās, -āz\ *n* -S [ISV *uric-* + *-ase*] **:** an enzyme that promotes oxidation of uric acid to allantoin, carbon dioxide, and other products and that is found esp. in the liver, kidney, and brains of most animals other than primates

uri·col·y·sis \ˌyu̇rəˈkäləsəs\ *n* [NL, fr. *uric-* + *-lysis*] **:** breakdown of uric acid esp. in the animal body

uri·co·lyt·ic \ˌyu̇rəkōˈlid·ik\ *adj* [*uric-* + *-lytic*] **:** of, relating to, or functioning in uricolysis ⟨a ~ enzyme⟩

uri·co·su·ric \ˌyu̇rəkōˈsu̇rik\ *adj* [*uric-* + connective *-s-* + *-uric*] **:** relating to or promoting the excretion of uric acid in the urine

uri·dine \ˈyu̇rəˌdēn, -ˌdən\ *n* -S [ISV ¹*ur-* + *-idine*] **:** a crystalline nucleoside $C_9H_{12}N_2O_6$ that is obtained by hydrolysis of ribonucleic acid and uridylic acid and that in the form of phosphate derivatives (as the coenzyme uridine diphosphate glucose) plays an important role in carbohydrate metabolism; 1-D-ribosyl-uracil

uri·dyl·ic acid \ˌyu̇rəˈdilik-\ *n* [ISV *uridine* + *-yl* + *-ic*] **:** a crystalline nucleotide $C_9H_{13}N_2O_9P$ known in three isomeric forms obtained by hydrolysis of ribonucleic acid **:** uridine mono-phosphate

urim and thum·mim \ˈ(y)u̇rəmənˈthəməm, ˈu̇ˌrēmənˈtu̇ˌmēm\ *n pl, usu cap U&T* [part trans. of Heb *ūrīm wĕthummīm*] **:** sacred lots possibly in the form of precious stones mentioned in the Old Testament as objects cast by a priest for the purpose of obtaining an oracle interpreted as the will of God

urin \ˈu̇rən\ *n* -S [Panjabi *huren*] **:** URIAL

urin- *or* **urino-** *comb form* [ME, fr. OF, fr. L, fr. *urina* urine — more at URINE] **:** urine **:** ¹UR- ⟨*urinogenital*⟩ ⟨*urinology*⟩

uri·nal \ˈyu̇rənᵊl, ˈyür-. *Brit also* yu̇ˈrīnᵊl\ *n* -S [ME, fr. OF, fr. LL, fr. L *urinalis* of urine, fr. *urina* urine + *-alis* -al] **1 a :** a vessel so constructed that it can be used for urination by a bedfast patient **b :** a container worn by one with urinary incontinence **2 :** a building, enclosure, or fixture for urinating purposes

uri·nal·y·sis *also* **uranalysis** \ˌyu̇rəˈnaləsəs, ˌyür-\ *n* [*urinalysis* fr. NL, irreg. fr. *urin-* + *analysis*; *uranalysis* fr. NL, fr. ¹*ur-* + *analysis*] **:** chemical analysis of urine

uri·nant \ˈyu̇rənənt\ *adj* [L *urinant-, urinans*, pres. part. of *urinari* to plunge under water, dive — more at URINE] *heraldry, of a fish or water animal* **:** being in pale with the head down — compare HAURIANT

uri·nar·i·um \ˌyu̇rəˈnerēəm\ *n* -S [ML, fr. L *urin-* + *-arium* -ary] **:** a reservoir into which urine drains from a stable and from which it is drawn to fertilize a field

¹**uri·nary** \ˈyu̇rəˌnerē, ˈyür-, -eri\ *adj* [NL *urinarius*, fr. *urin-* + *-arius* -ary] **1 :** relating to, occurring in, or constituting the organs concerned with the formation and discharge of urine **2 :** of, relating to, or for urine **3 :** excreted as or in urine ⟨~ nitrogen⟩

²**urinary** \"\ *n* -ES [*urin-* + *-ary*, n. suffix] **:** URINAL 2

urinary bladder *n* **:** a distensible membranous sac in many vertebrates that serves for the temporary retention of the urine, that in man is situated in the pelvis in front of the rectum, receives the urine from the two ureters and discharges it at intervals into the urethra through an orifice closed by a sphincter, is lined with transitional hypoblastic epithelium, and develops from the proximal part of the allantois of the embryo, that in the lowest mammals and in birds, reptiles, and amphibians opens separately into the cloaca, and that in fishes if present is not homologous with that of the higher vertebrates but is a dilatation of a ureter or of the united ureters

urinary calculus *n* **:** a calculus occurring in any portion of the urinary tract and esp. in the pelvis of the kidney

urinary pigment *n* **:** any of several coloring materials (as urobilin) present in the urine together with indican

urinary tract *n* **:** the tract conducting urine **:** the renal tubules and pelvis of the kidney, the ureters, the bladder, and the urethra

uri·nate \ˈyu̇rəˌnāt, ˈyür-, *usu* -ād.+V\ *vb* -ED/-ING/-S [ML *urinatus*, past part. of *urinare* to urinate, fr. L *urina* urine] *vi* **:** to discharge urine **:** make water **:** MICTURATE ~ *vt* **1 :** to wet with urine **2 :** to pass as or in the urine ⟨*urinated* a bloody fluid⟩ — **uri·na·tion** \ˌ==ˈnāshən\ *n* -S

urinator *n* -S [L, fr. *urinari* to plunge under water + *-ator*] *obs* **:** one who dives under water for something **:** DIVER

urine \ˈyu̇rən, ˈyür-\ *n* -S [ME, fr. MF, fr. L *urina*; akin to Gk *ouron* urine, *ourein* to urinate, L *urinari* to plunge under water, dive, Skt *vār* water, ON *ūr* drizzle, *ver* sea, OE *wær* sea, *wæter* water — more at WATER] **:** liquid to semisolid matter that is produced in the kidney and discharged through the urinary organs, that is typically (as in normal man) a clear transparent amber-colored slightly acid fluid which is essentially a watery solution of end products (as urea, uric acid, and creatinine) of protein metabolism, inorganic salts, and complex pigments, and that constitutes the major true excretion of the vertebrate body

uri·nif·er·ous tubule \ˌyu̇rəˈnif(ə)rəs-\ *n* [*uriniferous* fr. *urin-* + *-iferous*] **:** a vertebrate nephron

urino- — see URIN-

uri·no·genital ridge \ˈyu̇rənō+ . . . -\ *n* [*urinogenital* fr. *urin-* + *genital*] **:** a pair of dorsolateral mesodermal ridges in the vertebrate embryo out of which the urogenital organs are developed

urinogenital sinus *n* **:** a pouch or cavity communicating with the exterior or with the cloaca of which it may be a part and receiving the urinary and genital canals

uri·nom·e·ter \ˌyu̇rəˈnäməd·ə(r)\ *n* [ISV *urin-* + *-meter*] **:** a small hydrometer for determining the specific gravity of urine — **uri·no·met·ric** \ˌyu̇rənōˈme·trik\ *adj* — **uri·nom·e·try** \ˌyu̇rəˈnäməˌtrē\ *n* -ES

uri·nous \ˈyu̇rənəs, ˈyür-\ *adj* [NL *urinosus*, fr. L *urin-* + *-osus* -ous] **:** of, relating to, like, or having the qualities or odor of urine

urins *pl of* URIN

urisk \ˈu̇risk\ *n* -S [ScGael *ūruisg*, fr. *uisge* water; akin to OIr *uisce* water — more at WHISKEY] **:** a brownie held in Scottish folklore to frequent sequestered places and waterfalls

urite \ˈyu̇ˌrīt\ *n* -S [ISV ²*ur-* + *-ite*] **:** one of the segments of the abdomen or postabdomen of an arthropod

ur·man \(ˈ)u̇rˈmän, -man\ *n* -S [Russ, fr. Kazan Tatar, forest] **:** TAIGA 1

¹**urn** \ˈərn, ˈən, ˈəin\ *n* -S [ME *urne*, fr. L *urna*, prob. of non-IE origin; akin to the source of L *urceus* pitcher, ewer, Gk *hyrchē* jar] **1 a :** a vessel (as a vase) of various forms usu. furnished with a foot or pedestal and employed for holding liquids, for ornamental uses, for preserving the ashes of the dead after cremation, for holding lots to be drawn, for receiving ballots, or for other purposes **b :** a closed vessel usu. with a heating device and a spigot used in making and serving a hot beverage ⟨coffee ~⟩ ⟨tea ~⟩ **2 :** a sculptured ornament or decoration in the shape of a footed and usu. covered urn **3** *archaic* **:** a spring, fountain, or watercourse that is the source of a flow of liquid **4 :** the theca of a moss

urn 1a

²**urn** \"\ *vt, archaic* **:** INURN

ur·na·tel·la \ˌərnəˈtelə\ *n, cap* [NL, irreg. fr. L *urna* urn + *-ella*] **:** a genus (the type of a family Urnatellidae) of eastern No. American colonial freshwater entoproctans that form small colonies of bell-shaped zooids on the underside of stones in running water

urn burial *n* **:** burial in which a pottery vessel is used as a grave repository for the ashes and bones of the corpse

urnfield \ˈ=ˌ=\ *n* **:** a Bronze Age cemetery of urn burials

urnflower \ˈ=ˌ=\ *n* **:** a plant of the genus *Urceolina*

ur·ning \ˈu̇rniŋ\ *n* -S [G, irreg. fr. *Urania*, the love goddess Aphrodite (fr. Gk *Ourania*) + G *-ing* ²-ing — more at URANISM] **:** a male or female homosexual

ur·ning·ism \-ŋˌizəm\ *n* -S **:** HOMOSEXUALITY

urn moss *n* **:** any of several mosses (as members of the genus *Physcomitrium* and esp. *P. turbinatum*) having an urn-shaped theca

urn schemata *n pl* **:** the representation of frequency distributions by means of withdrawals of different-colored balls from one or more vessels or urns containing the balls in various numbers and proportions

uro- — see UR-

uro·bi·lin \ˌyu̇rəˈbīlən\ *n* -S [ISV ¹*ur-* + *-bilin* (as in *stercobilin*)] **:** any of several brown bile pigments formed from urobilinogens and found in normal feces, in normal urine in small amounts, and in pathological urines in larger amounts — compare STERCOBILIN

uro·bi·lin·o·gen \-ˌbīˈlinəjən, -ˌjen\ *n* -S [ISV *urobilin* + *-ogen* (as in *stercobilinogen*)] **:** any of several chromogens that are reduction products of bilirubin and yield urobilins on oxidation — called also *stercobilinogen*

uro·bi·lin·o·gen·uria \-ˌlinəjəˈn(y)u̇rēə\ *n* -S [NL, fr. ISV *urobilinogen* + NL *-uria*] **:** the presence of urobilinogen in the urine esp. in excess

uro·bi·lin·uria \-ˌbīləˈn(y)u̇rēə\ *n* -S [NL, fr. ISV *urobilin* + NL *-uria*] **:** the presence of urobilin in the urine esp. to an excessive degree

uro·canic acid \ˌyu̇rəˌkanik-, -kānik-\ *n* [¹*ur-* + *canine* + *-ic*] **:** a crystalline acid $C_3H_3N_2CH{=}CHCOOH$ obtained first from the urine of a dog and formed by the enzymic deamination of histidine; 4(or 5)-imidazole-acrylic acid

¹**uroc·er·id** \yəˈräsərəd\ *adj* [NL *Uroceridae*] **:** SIRICID

²**urocerid** \"\ *n* -S **:** SIRICID

uro·cer·i·dae \ˌyu̇rəˈserəˌdē\ [NL, fr. *Urocerus*, genus of siricids (fr. ²*ur-* + *-cerus*) + *-idae*] *syn of* SIRICIDAE

uro·chlo·ral·ic acid \ˌyu̇rə(ˌ)klōˈralik-\ *n* [ISV ¹*ur-* + *chloral* + *-ic*] **:** a crystalline glycoside $C_8H_{11}Cl_3O_7$ of trichloro-ethyl alcohol and glucuronic acid found in the urine after administering chloral hydrate

uro·chord \ˈyu̇rəˌkȯrd\ *n* [²*ur-* + *chord*; fr. its being chiefly confined to the tail region] **1 :** the notochord of larval ascidians and of various adult tunicates **2** [NL *Urochorda*] **:** an animal of the group Urochorda **:** TUNICATE

uro·chor·da \ˌ==ˈkȯrdə\ *n pl, cap* [NL, fr. ²*ur-* + *chorda*] **:** a subphylum or sometimes a class of marine animals (phylum Chordata) comprising the tunicates, including the orders Ascidiacea, Thaliacea, and Larvacea, and being distinguished by clefts in the vascular walls of the pharyngeal gills, by the secretion of a thick outer covering of tunicin for the body, by the reduction of the nervous system to little more than a single dorsally placed ganglion, and by a heart that so changes its contractions as to reverse the direction of the blood flow at intervals

uro·chor·dal \ˌ==ˈkȯrdᵊl\ *adj* [NL *Urochorda* + E *-al*] **1 :** of or relating to the Urochorda **2** [*urochord* + *-al*] **:** having a notochord in the tail region only

uro·chordata \ˌyu̇rə+\ [NL, fr. ²*ur-* + *Chordata*] *syn of* UROCHORDA

¹**uro·chor·date** \ˌyu̇rəˈkȯrdət, -ˌdāt\ *adj* [*urochord* + *-ate*] **:** having a urochord

²**urochordate** \"\ *n* -S [NL *Urochordata*] **:** UROCHORD 2

uro·chrome \ˈyu̇rəˌkrōm\ *n* -S [¹*ur-* + *-chrome*] **:** a yellow pigment to which the yellow color of normal urine is principally due

urochs \ˈ(y)u̇ˌräks\ *n* [obs. G *urochs* (now *auerochs*), fr. MHG *ūrochse*, fr. OHG *ūrohso* — more at AUROCHS] **1** *archaic* **:** URUS **2** *archaic* **:** WISENT

¹**uro·cop·tid** \ˌyu̇rəˈkäptəd\ *adj* [NL *Urocoptid-, Urocoptis*] **:** of or relating to the genus *Urocoptis* or the family Urocoptidae

²**urocoptid** \"\ *n* -S **:** a land snail of the genus *Urocoptis* or the family Urocoptidae

uro·cop·tis \ˌ==ˈtəs\ *n, cap* [NL, fr. ²*ur-* + *-coptis* (fr. Gk *koptein* to cut off) — more at CAPON] **:** a large genus (the type of the family Urocoptidae of the order Pulmona) of land snails of southern Florida, the West Indies, and Mexico found only on limestone cliffs and outcrops

uroc·y·on \yəˈräsēən, -ēˌän\ *n, cap* [NL, fr. ²*ur-* + Gk *kyōn* dog — more at HOUND] **:** a genus of mammals (family Canidae) comprising the American gray foxes

uro·cyst \ˈyu̇rəˌsist\ *n* [¹*ur-* + *-cyst*] **:** the urinary bladder — **uro·cys·tic** \ˌ==ˈsistik\ *adj*

uro·cys·tis \ˌ==ˈsistəs\ *n, cap* [NL, fr. ²*ur-* + *-cystis*] **:** a genus of smuts (family Tilletiaceae) having compound chlamydospores with the dark central cells fertile and the outer sterile — see FLAG SMUT, ONION SMUT

uro·dae·al *or* **uro·de·al** \ˌyu̇rəˈdēəl\ *adj* [NL *urodaeum* + E *-al*] **:** of or relating to the urodaeum

uro·dae·um \ˌ==ˈdēəm\ *n* -S [NL, fr. ¹*ur-* + *-odaeum* (fr. Gk *hodaion*, neut. of *hodaios* on the way, fr. *hodos* way) — more at CEDE] **:** the part of the cloaca (as of a bird) into which the ureters and genital ducts empty

uro·de·la \ˌyu̇rəˈdēlə\ [NL, fr. ²*ur-* + Gk *dēlos* visible — more at ADEL-] *syn of* CAUDATA

¹**uro·dele** \ˈ==ˌdēl\ *also* **uro·de·lan** \ˌ==ˈdēlən\ *n* -S [*urodele* fr. F *urodèle*, fr. NL *Urodela*; *urodelan* fr. NL *Urodela* + E *-an*] **:** CAUDATE

²**urodele** *also* **uro·de·lous** \ˌ==ˈdēləs\ *adj* [*urodele* fr. ¹*urodele*; *urodelous* fr. ¹*urodele* + *-ous*] **:** of or relating to the Caudata

uro·erythrin \ˌyu̇rō+\ *n* [¹*ur-* + *erythrin*] **:** a pink or reddish pigment found in many pathological urines and also frequently in normal urine in very small quantity

uro·gas·ter \ˌyu̇rəˈgastə(r)\ *n* -S [NL, fr. ¹*ur-* + *-gaster*] **1 :** the urinary tract (as of the embryo) including the allantoic cavity **2** [NL, fr. ²*ur-* + *-gaster*] **:** the posterior division of the gastric region of a crustacean (as a crab) — **uro·gas·tric** \-strik\ *adj*

uro·gas·trone \ˌyu̇rəˈgaˌstrōn\ *n* -S [¹*ur-* + *-gastrone* (as in *enterogastrone*)] **:** a substance obtained from the urine of man and other mammals as an amorphous buff-colored powder resembling enterogastrone in physiological activity

uro·gen·i·tal \ˌyu̇rōˈjenəd·ᵊl, ˌyür-, -rō¦j-, -nətᵊl\ *also* **uro·gen·i·tary** \-nəˌterē, -ri\ *adj* [*urogenital* ISV ¹*ur-* + *genital*; *urogenitary* fr. ¹*ur-* + L *genitalis* genital + E *-ary*] **:** of, relating to, or being the organs or functions of excretion and reproduction

urogenital diaphragm *n* **:** a double layer of pelvic fascia with its included muscle that is situated between the ischial and pubic rami, supports the prostate in the male, is traversed by the vagina in the female, gives passage to the membranous part of the urethra, and encloses the sphincter of the urethra

urog·e·nous \yəˈräjənəs\ *adj* [ISV ¹*ur-* + *-genous*] **:** derived from or occurring in urine ⟨~ salts⟩

uro·gle·na \ˌyu̇rəˈglēnə\ *n, cap* [NL, fr. ²*ur-* + Gk *glēnē* socket of a joint — more at GLENOID] **:** a genus of colonial plantlike flagellates (order Chrysomonadina) with numerous biflagellate individuals united in a spherical colony by gelatinous strands

uro·gom·phus \ˌyu̇rəˈgäm(p)fəs\ *n, pl* **urogom·phi** \-mˌfī, -mˌfē\ [NL, fr. ²*ur-* + L *gomphus* nail, peg, fr. Gk *gomphos* tooth, bolt, peg — more at COMB] **:** PSEUDOCERCUS

uro·gram \ˈyu̇rəˌgram\ *n* [¹*ur-* + *-gram*] **:** a roentgenogram made by urography

uro·graph·ic \ˌ==ˈgrafik\ *adj* [*urography* + *-ic*] **:** of or relating to urography

urog·ra·phy \yəˈrägrəfē\ *n* -ES [ISV ¹*ur-* + *-graphy*] **:** roentgenography of a part of the urinary tract (as a kidney or ureter) after injection of an opaque medium — compare CYSTOGRAPHY, PYELOGRAPHY, RETROGRADE PYELOGRAM

¹**uro·hy·al** \ˌyu̇rōˈhīəl\ *adj* [ISV ²*ur-* + *hy-* + *-al*] **1 :** of, relating to, or being a median posterior bony element of the hyoid arch attached between the hypohyals of a fish **2 :** of, relating to, or being a median posterior process or a separate piece extending backward from the basihyal and forming a basibranchial element of a bird

²**urohyal** \"\ *n* -S **:** a urohyal element

urol *abbr* urological; urology

uro·lag·nia \ˌyu̇rōˈlagnēə\ *n* -S [NL, fr. ¹*ur-* + *-lagnia*] **:** sexual excitement associated with urine or with urination

uro·leu·cic acid \ˌyu̇rōˈlüsik-\ *or* **uro·leu·cin·ic acid** \ˌyu̇rōˌlü¦sinik-\ *n* [*uroleucic* fr. ¹*ur-* + *leuc-* + *-ic*; *uroleucinic* fr. G *uroleucin* (fr. ¹*ur-* + *leuc-* + *-in*) + E *-ic*; fr. its color] **:** a crystalline acid $C_9H_{10}O_5$ that is found in abnormal urine and is similar to homogentisic acid

uro·lith \ˈyu̇rəˌlith\ *n* -S [ISV ¹*ur-* + *-lith*] **:** URINARY CALCULUS — **uro·lith·ic** \ˌ==ˈlithik\ *adj*

uro·li·thi·a·sis \ˌyu̇rələˈthīəsəs\ *n* [NL, fr. ¹*ur-* + *lithiasis*] **:** the condition characterized by the formation or presence of calculi in any part of the urinary tract

uro·log·ic \ˌyu̇rəˈläjik, ˌyür-, -jēk\ *also* **uro·log·i·cal** \-jəkəl, -jēk-\ *adj* [*urologic* ISV ¹*urology* + *-ic*; *urological* fr. *urology* + *-ical*] **:** of or relating to the urinary tract or to urology

urol·o·gist \yəˈräləjəst, yu̇ˈr-\ *n* -S [ISV *urology* + *-ist*] **:** a physician who specializes in urology

urol·o·gy \-jē, -ji\ *n* -ES [¹*ur-* + *-logy*] **:** a branch of medicine that concerns itself with the urogenital tract in the male and the urinary tract in the female

uro·mere \ˈyu̇rəˌmi(ə)r\ *n* -S [²*ur-* + *-mere*] **:** an abdominal segment of an arthropod — **uro·mer·ic** \ˌ==ˈmerik, -ˈmir-\ *adj*

uro·my·ces \ˌyu̇rəˈmī(ˌ)sēz\ *n, cap* [NL, fr. ²*ur-* + *-myces*] **:** a genus of rusts (family Pucciniaceae) having one-celled teliospores — see CARNATION RUST

uro·my·cla·di·um \-ˌmīˈklādēəm\ *n, cap* [NL, fr. *Uromyces* + *clad-* + *-ium*] **:** a genus of chiefly Australian rusts (family Pucciniaceae) distinguished by teliospores clustered at the top of a stalk with usu. a colorless cyst just below and including several forms (as *U. tepperianum*) that disfigure and destroy wattles in Australia

uro·mys \ˈyu̇rəˌmis\ *n, cap* [NL, fr. ²*ur-* + *-mys*] **:** a genus of murid rodents of southeastern Asia and Australia — see MOSAIC-TAILED RAT

-u·ron·ic \(y)ə¦ränik, (y)u̇¦r-, -nēk\ *adj suffix* [Gk *ouron* urine + ISV *-ic* — more at URINE] **:** urine — in names of certain aldehyde-acids derived from sugars or compounds of such acids ⟨ald*uronic*⟩ ⟨hyal*uronic*⟩

uron·ic acid \yə¦ränik-, yü¦, -nēk\ *n* [*uronic* ISV, fr. *-uronic*] **:** any of a class of aldehyde-acids HOOC(CHOH)ₙCHO that are oxidation products of sugars and that occur combined in many polysaccharides and in urine — see HEXURONIC ACID, POLYURONIC ACID, POLYURONIDE

uro·nide \ˈyu̇rəˌnīd, -ˌnəd\ *n* -S [*uronic* (in *uronic acid*) + *-ide*] **:** a glycosidic compound that yields a uronic acid on hydrolysis; *esp* **:** POLYURONIDE

uro·patagium \ˌyu̇(ˌ)rō+\ *n* [NL, fr. ²*ur-* + *patagium*] **1 :** the membrane that extends between the thighs of a bat and commonly includes the tail **2 :** one of two plates bounding the sides of the anus in insects

uro·path·ic \ˌyu̇rəˈpathik\ *adj* **:** of or relating to uropathy

urop·a·thy \yəˈräpəthē\ *n* -ES [¹*ur-* + *-pathy*] **:** a disease of the urinary or urogenital organs

¹**uro·pel·tid** \ˌyu̇rəˈpeltəd\ *adj* [NL *Uropeltidae*] **:** of or relating to the Uropeltidae

²**uropeltid** \"\ *or* **uro·pelt** \ˈyu̇rəˌpelt\ *n* -S [*uropeltid* fr. NL *Uropeltidae*; *uropelt* fr. NL *Uropeltis*] **:** a snake of the family Uropeltidae

uro·pel·ti·dae \ˌyu̇rəˈpeltəˌdē\ *n pl, cap* [NL, fr. *Uropeltis*, type genus (fr. ²*ur-* + Gk *peltē* shield) + *-idae* — more at PELTA] **:** a family of small harmless Oriental burrowing snakes having an enlarged scale or shield at the end of the tail

uro·pepsin \ˌyu̇rə+\ *n* [¹*ur-* + *pepsin*] **:** a proteolytic hormone found in urine esp. in cases of peptic ulcers and other disorders of the digestive tract

uro·phlyc·tis \ˌyu̇rəˈfliktəs\ *n, cap* [NL, fr. ²*ur-* + Gk *phlyktis* blister, boil, fr. *phlyein, phlyzein* to boil over — more at FLUID] **:** a genus of lower fungi (order Chytridiales) having a thallus made up of a series of top-shaped cells each with a crown of fingerlike haustoria and connected by slender hyphae — see CROWN WART

uro·pod \ˈyu̇rəˌpäd\ *n* -S [ISV ²*ur-* + *-pod*] **:** either of the flattened leaflike appendages of the last abdominal segment of various crustaceans (as the lobster) that with the telson forms the tail fan; *sometimes* **:** any abdominal appendage of a crustacean — **urop·o·dal** \yəˈräpədᵊl\ *or* **urop·o·dous** \-dəs\ *adj*

uro·poi·e·sis \ˌyu̇rəˌpȯiˈēsəs\ *n* [NL, fr. ¹*ur-* + *-poiesis*] **:** production of urine

uro·poi·et·ic \ˌ==pȯiˈed·ik\ *adj* [ISV ¹*ur-* + *-poietic*] **:** of or relating to uropoiesis

uro·por·phy·rin \ˌyu̇rō+\ *n* [ISV ¹*ur-* + *porphyrin*] **:** any of four isomeric porphyrins $C_{20}H_6N_4(CH_2COOH)_4(CH_2CH_2COOH)_4$ which contain acetic acid and propionic acid groups on the porphin nucleus and are closely related to the coproporphyrins and of which types I and III are found in urine esp. in porphyria and type III is found also as the copper complex turacin

uro·py·gi \ˌyu̇rəˈpīˌjī\ *n pl, cap* [NL, fr. ²*ur-* + Gk *pygē* rump, buttocks] **:** a division of Pedipalpida including those (as the whip scorpions) with a tail

¹**uro·pyg·i·al** *also* **uro·pyg·e·al** \ˌyu̇rəˈpijēəl\ *adj* [*uropygial* ISV *uropyg-* (fr. NL *uropygium*) + *-ial*; *uropygeal* irreg. fr. NL *uropygium* + E *-al*] **:** of or relating to the uropygium ⟨~ fat⟩

²**uropygial** \"\ *n* -S **:** a uropygial feather **:** a tail feather

uropygial gland *n* **:** a large gland that opens on the back at the base of the tail feathers in most birds, secretes an oily fluid which the bird uses in preening its feathers, and is esp. developed in waterfowl and helps to make the plumage shed water — called also *preen gland*

uro·pyg·i·um \ˌyu̇rəˈpijēəm\ *n* -S [NL, fr. Gk *ouropygion*, fr. *ouro-* ²ur- + *pygē* rump, buttocks — more at FOG] **:** the fleshy and bony prominence at the posterior extremity of a bird's body that supports the tail feathers and contains the free caudal vertebrae and the pygostyle

uro·pyloric \ˌyu̇rō+\ *adj* [²*ur-* + *pyloric*] **:** of, relating to, or being a posterior division of the stomach in various crustaceans

uro·sacral \"+\ *adj* [²*ur-* + *sacral*] **:** of or being the caudal and sacral parts of the vertebral column; *specif* **:** of, relating to, or being the anterior caudal vertebrae of a bird that is consolidated with the true sacral vertebrae and pelvic bones

uro·sal·pinx \ˌyu̇rōˈsal()piŋ(k)s\ *n, cap* [NL, fr. ²*ur-* + Gk *salpinx* trumpet] **:** a genus of small carnivorous gastropod mollusks (family Muricidae) comprising the oyster drill (*U. cinerea*) and related forms

uros·co·py \yəˈräskəpē\ *n* -ES [NL *uroscopia*, fr. ¹*ur-* + *-scopia* -scopy] **:** examination or analysis of the urine (as for the purpose of medical diagnosis)

uro·somite \ˌyu̇rə+\ *n* -S [²*ur-* + *somite*] **:** UROMERE

uroste·gal \yəˈrästigəl, ˌyu̇rəˈstēg-\ *adj* [*urostege* + *-al*] **:** of or relating to a urostege

uro·stege \ˈyu̇rəˌstēj\ *also* **uros·te·gite** \yəˈrästəˌjīt\ *n* -S [*urostege* fr. ²*ur-* + *-stege*; *urostegite* fr. ²*ur-* + *-stege* + *-ite*] **:** a scale on the underside of the tail of a snake

uros·te·on \yəˈrästēˌän\ *n, pl* **uros·tea** \-ēə\ [NL, fr. ²*ur-* + *-osteon*] **:** a median ossification at the back of the lophosteon in the sternum of some birds

uro·sternite \ˌyu̇rō+\ *n* [²*ur-* + *sternite*] **:** the sternite of a uromere

uro·sty·lar \ˌyu̇rəˈstīlə(r)\ *adj* **:** of or relating to a urostyle

uro·style \ˈ==ˌstīl\ *n* -S [ISV ²*ur-* + *-style*] **1 :** a long rodlike unsegmented bone representing a number of fused vertebrae that forms the posterior part of the vertebral column of frogs and toads **2 a :** the hypural bone of a fish **b :** a similar bone formed by the fusion of two or more caudal vertebrae at the end of the tail in various extinct turtles

uro·toxic \ˌyu̇rə+\ *adj* [ISV ¹*ur-* + *toxic*, orig. formed as F *urotoxique*] **:** of or relating to the toxicity or the toxic constituents of urine

Urot·ro·pine \yəˈrä·trəˌpēn, -ˌpən\ *trademark* — used for a preparation of hexamethylenetetramine

-u·rous *or* **-ou·rous** \ˈ(y)u̇rəs, ˈ(y)ür-\ *adj comb form* [NL *-urus, -ourus*, fr. Gk *-ouros*, fr. *oura* tail; akin to Gk *orrhos* buttocks — more at ASS] **:** tailed ⟨xiphurous⟩ ⟨anourous⟩

urox·an·ic acid \ˌyu̇ˌräkˈsanik\ *n* [ISV ¹*ur-* + alloxan + *-ic*] **:** a crystalline acid $C_5H_8N_4O_6$ derived from imidizole and obtained by the slow oxidation of uric acid in alkaline solution

¹**ursid** \ˈərsəd\ *adj* [NL *Ursidae*] **:** of or relating to the Ursidae

²**ursid** \"\ *n* -s **:** a mammal of the family Ursidae

ur·si·dae \-səˌdē\ *n pl, cap* [NL, fr. *Ursus*, type genus + *-idae*] **:** a family of large powerful plantigrade carnivores including the bears and extinct related forms

ur·si·form \-səˌfȯrm\ *adj* [L *ursus* bear + E *-iform*] **:** having the shape of a bear

ur·si·gram \-səˌgram\ *n* [ISV *ursi-* (fr. F *Union Radiophonique Scientifique Internationale*, organization which inaugurated the broadcast in 1930) + *-gram*] **:** a message broadcast by radio or otherwise giving scientific data (as on terrestrial magnetism, radio transmission, or sunspots)

ur·sine \ˈərˌsīn, -ˌsēn, -sᵊn, -ˌsin\ *adj* [L *ursinus*, fr. *ursus* bear + *-inus* -ine — more at ARCTIC] **1 :** of, relating to, or characteristic of a bear or the Ursidae **2 :** resembling a bear or that of a bear ⟨the ~ indignation that set him on the path toward his final intellectual disaster —*Time*⟩

ursine baboon *n* **:** CHACMA

ursine dasyure *n* **:** TASMANIAN DEVIL

ursine howler *n* **:** HOWLER MONKEY

ursine seal *n* **:** FUR SEAL b

ur·sin·ia \ˌəˈrsinēə\ *n* [NL, fr. Johann Heinrich *Ursinus* (Latinization of G *Bär*) †1667 Ger. theologian + NL *-ia*] **1** *cap* **:** a genus of annual or perennial southern African herbs or subshrubs (family Compositae) used as ornamentals with usu. yellow flowers and fruit with a white enlarged pappus **2** -s **:** any plant of the genus *Ursinia*

ur·soid \ˈərˌsȯid\ *adj* [L *ursus* bear + E *-oid*] **:** resembling a bear or that of a bear

ur·solic acid \ˌərˈsäl|ik-, -sō|\ *n* [¹uva-*ursi* + *-ol* + *-ic*] **:** a crystalline triterpenoid acid $C_{30}H_{48}O_3$ found in various esp. ericaceous plants (as the bearberry)

ur·spra·che \ˈu̇(ə)rˌshpräkə\ *n* -s *usu cap* [G, fr. *ur-* primitive, original (fr. OHG *ur-*, *ur* out of) + *sprache* language, fr. OHG *sprāhha* speech — more at ABEAR, SPEECH] **:** a parent language; *esp* **:** one reconstructed from the evidence of later languages

ur·su·la butterfly \ˈərsələ-\ *n, usu cap U* [fr. *Ursula*, feminine name] **:** RED-SPOTTED PURPLE

¹**ur·su·line** \-lən, -ˌlīn, -ˌlēn\ *n* -s *usu cap* [NL *Ursulina*, fr. *Ursula* St. Ursula 3d or 5th cent. A.D. legendary Christian martyr + L *-inus* -ine] **:** a member of a teaching order of nuns founded by St. Angela Merici at Brescia, Italy, about 1537

²**ursuline** *adj, usu cap* **:** of, relating to, or being a member of the Ursulines ⟨~ nuns⟩ ⟨an ~ convent⟩

ur·sus \ˈərsəs\ *n, cap* [NL, fr. L, bear — more at ARCTIC] **:** a genus (the type of the family Ursidae) of bears held by some authorities to include all recent bears except the sloth bear and restricted by others to the European brown bear and immediately related forms or subdivided in various ways — compare SELENARCTOS, THALARCTOS

urta-juz \ˌu̇rdəˈjüz\ *n pl, usu cap U&J* [Kirghiz] **:** MIDDLE HORDE

ur·ti·ca \ˈərd·əkə\ *n* [NL, fr. L, nettle; prob. akin to L *urere* to burn; fr. its sting — more at EMBER] **1** *cap* **:** a genus (the type of the family Urticaceae) of widely distributed plants having opposite stipulate leaves with stinging hairs and small greenish tetramerous flowers **2** -s **:** any plant of the genus *Urtica*

ur·ti·ca·ce·ae \ˌərd·əˈkāsēˌē\ *n pl, cap* [NL, fr. *Urtica*, type genus + *-aceae*] **:** a family of herbs, shrubs, and trees (order Urticales) including many with stinging hairs and having small monoecious, dioecious, or polygamous apetalous flowers followed by fruits that are usu. achenes — see STRAWBERRY NETTLE — **ur·ti·ca·ceous** \ˌ==ˈkāshəs\ *adj*

ur·ti·ca·les \ˌ==ˈkā(ˌ)lēz\ *n pl, cap* [NL, fr. *Urtica* + *-ales*] **:** an order of dicotyledonous plants usu. including the Urticaceae, Ulmaceae, and Moraceae and being characterized mainly by the free apetalous perianth and one-celled superior ovary

ur·ti·cant \ˈərd·əkənt\ *adj* [F, fr. ML *urticant-, urticans*, pres. part. of *urticare* to sting] **:** producing itching or stinging **:** URTICATING, STINGING; *esp* **:** producing an itching swelling ⟨a caterpillar with ~ hairs⟩

ur·ti·car·ia \ˌərd·əˈka(a)rēə\ *n* -s [NL, fr. L *urtica* nettle] **:** a transient skin eruption characterized by itching red or pale smooth slightly raised patches and caused by irritation (as by food or an inhalant) of the gastrointestinal, pulmonary, or urinary mucous membranes or from contact with an external agent (as a plant, sun, or cold) and found in individuals with a peculiar sensitivity — called also *hives;* compare DERMOGRAPHIA — **ur·ti·car·i·al** \ˌ==ˈ==ēəl\ *adj*

ur·ti·cate \ˈərd·əˌkāt\ *vb* -ED/-ING/-S [ML *urticatus*, past part. of *urticare* to sting, fr. L *urtica* nettle] *vi* **:** to sting in the manner of a nettle; *specif* **:** to produce urticaria ⟨an *urticating* caterpillar⟩ ~ *vt* **:** to afflict with urtication or urticaria **:** cause nettle rash

ur·ti·ca·tion \ˌ==ˈkāshən\ *n* -s [ML *urtication-, urticatio*, fr. *urticatus* (past part.) + L *-ion-, -io* -ion] **1 :** an itching and stinging sensation (as from contact with nettles) **2** [*urtic-* (in NL *urticaria*) + *-ation*] **:** wheal formation in urticaria

ur·ti·cose \ˈərd·əˌkōs\ *adj* [NL *urticosus*, fr. L *urtica* nettle + *-osus* -ose] **:** abounding with nettles

uru·bu \ˌu̇rəˈbü\ *n* -s [Sp & Pg *urubu, urubú*, fr. Tupi *urubú*] **:** BLACK VULTURE

uru·cú \ˌu̇rəˈkü\ *n* -s [Pg, fr. Tupi] **:** ANNATTO 1

urucu-rana \ˌu̇rəkəˈranə\ *n* -s [Pg *urucurana*, fr. Tupi, fr. *urucú* annatto + *rana* false] **1 :** a tropical So. American timber tree (*Hieronyma alchorneoides*) of the family Euphorbiaceae **2 :** the deep reddish brown hard wood of the urucu-rana used for construction and cabinet work

uru·cu·ri iba \ˌu̇rəkəˌrēˈēbə\ *n* -s [Tupi, lit., ouricury tree] **:** OURICURY 1

uru·guay \ˈu̇rəˌgwī, ˈyu̇rəˌgwā *also* ˈyu̇rəˌgwī *sometimes* ˈu̇rəˌgwā\ *adj, usu cap* [fr. *Uruguay*, country in So. America] **:** of or from Uruguay **:** of the kind or style prevalent in Uruguay **:** URUGUAYAN

¹**uru·guay·an** \ˌ==ˈgwīən, -ˈgwāən\ *adj, usu cap* [Sp *uruguayano*, adj. & n., fr. *Uruguay*, country in So. America + Sp *-ano* -an] **:** of or relating to Uruguay or its inhabitants

²**uruguayan** \"\ *n* -s *cap* [Sp *uruguayano*] **:** a native or inhabitant of Uruguay

uruguay potato *n, usu cap U* **1 :** a So. American plant (*Solanum commersonii*) **2 :** the tuber of the Uruguay potato resembling the common potato

uruk \ˈu̇rək\ *adj, usu cap* [fr. *Uruk* (Erech), ancient Sumerian city on the Euphrates in Babylonia (now *Warka*, locality in southeastern Iraq), site of the culture's remains] **:** of or relating to a Sumerian early Bronze Age culture characterized by temples of stone, sculpture in the round, writing on clay, engraved cylinder seals, and plain red or gray pottery often having a polished surface

urun·day \ˌu̇rənˈdī\ *n* -s [Sp, fr. Guarani *urundai*] **:** any of several timber trees (as *A. urundeuva*) of the genus *Astronium* (family Anacardiaceae) of southern So. America that have hard fine wood used for a variety of purposes

urus \ˈyu̇rəs\ *n* -ES [L, of Gmc origin; akin to OHG *ūrohso* urus — more at AUROCHS] **:** an extinct large long-horned wild ox (*Bos primigenius*) of the German forests believed to be a wild ancestor of domestic cattle

-u·rus \ˈ(y)u̇rəs, ˈ(y)ür-\ *n comb form* [NL, fr. Gk *oura* — more at -UROUS] **:** one having (such) a tail — esp. in generic names ⟨*Brachyurus*⟩ ⟨*Dasyurus*⟩ ⟨*Saururus*⟩

uru·shi \ˈrüshē\ *n* -s [Jap] **:** LACQUER

uru·shic acid \(y)u̇ˈrüshik-\ *or* **uru·shin·ic acid** \ˌ(y)u̇rəˌshinik-\ *n* [*urushic* ISV *urushi* (fr. Jap) + *-ic*; *urushinic* fr. *urushi* + *-in* + *-ic*] **:** URUSHIOL

uru·shi·ol \(y)u̇ˈrüshēˌȯl, -ēˌōl\ *n* -s [ISV *urushi* + *-ol*] **:** a poisonous oily liquid phenolic compound $C_{15}H_{27}C_6H_3(OH)_2$ in the sap of Oriental lacquer trees (*Rhus verniciferi* and *R. succedanea*) and present also as one of the principal blistering substances in poison ivy, poison oak, and poison sumac that hardens and becomes colored by atmospheric oxidation and serves as the chief component of Japanese and Chinese lacquers; 3-pentadeca-trien-yl-pyrocatechol

uru·shi·ye \əˈrüshē(ˌ)yā\ *n* -s [Jap] **:** a Japanese color print in which the dark colors are printed with a lustrous medium commonly considered to be lacquer

uru·tu \ˌu̇rəˈtü\ *n* -s [Pg, fr. Tupi] **:** any of several So. American pit vipers; *esp* **:** a showy viper (*Bothrops alternatus*) with a series of dark brown lateral crescents on a cream ground

ur·va \ˈu̇rˈvä, ər-\ *n* -s [Nepali *urvā, arvā*] **:** a common mongoose (*Herpestes urva*) of southeastern Asia having fur like that of the badger in appearance with a white stripe extending from throat to shoulder, the back grizzled black and white, and the feet and chest black

us \(ˈ)əs\ *pron, objective case of* WE [ME, fr. OE *ūs;* akin to OHG & Goth *uns* us, ON *oss*, L *nos*, Gk *hēmas* (Aeolic *amme*), Skt *nas, asmān*] **1 :** ¹WE 1: **a** (1) — used as indirect object of a verb ⟨give ~ this day our daily bread —Mt 6:11 (AV)⟩ (2) *obs* — used as a vague indirect object simply to suggest the concern or involvement of a group including the one speaking or writing ⟨they wounded ~ only one man —*London Gazette*⟩ **b** — used as object of a preposition ⟨walking away from ~⟩ ⟨men, women, all of ~, just because we are human —Walter de la Mare⟩ **c** — used as direct object of a verb ⟨they were visiting ~⟩ **d** — used in comparisons after *than* and *as* when the first term in the comparison is the direct or indirect object of a verb or the object of a preposition ⟨the march tired the other platoon more than ~⟩ ⟨the bank would rather give you a loan than ~⟩ ⟨time has dealt as harshly with them as ~⟩ **e** — used in absolute or elliptical constructions ⟨who, ~⟩, esp. together with a prepositional phrase, adjective, or participle ⟨it is best not to speak to him, ~ not knowing to what ideology his loyalty might or might not belong —Peggy Bennett⟩ **f** — used by speakers on all educational levels and by many reputable writers though disapproved by some grammarians in the predicate after forms of *be*, in comparisons after *than* and *as* when the first term in the comparison is the subject of a verb, and in other positions where it is itself neither the subject of a verb nor the object of a verb or preposition ⟨the miraculous generation which is ~ —Arnold Bennett⟩ ⟨you are bigger and stronger than ~ women —K.A.Menninger⟩ ⟨~ and our little problems⟩ **g** (1) — used chiefly in substandard speech and formerly also by reputable writers as part of the compound subject of a verb or esp. with an immediately following appositive noun as the subject of a verb which it does not immediately precede ⟨our neighbors and ~ don't like that⟩ ⟨~ kids were always given a swallow —Walter Karig⟩ (2) *chiefly dial* — used as the subject of a verb from which it is not separated by other words ⟨~ lived in a two-story house —Ralph Ellison⟩ **h** — used like the adjective *our* with a gerund by speakers and writers on all educational levels though disapproved by some grammarians ⟨she approved of ~ getting summer jobs⟩ **2 :** OURSELVES, OURSELF — used reflexively as indirect object of a verb ⟨we built ~ a shack by the lake⟩, object of a preposition ⟨we'll take you with ~⟩, or direct object of a verb ⟨now we will divest ~ . . . of rule, interest of territory, cares of state —Shak.⟩ **3 a :** ¹ME 1 — used by kings and other sovereigns and by editors and other writers when *we* is used instead of *I* ⟨what touches ~ ourself shall be last served —Shak.⟩; compare ¹WE 2 **b :** ¹ME 1 — used in ordinary situations by a speaker of any kind in reference to himself ⟨give ~ a goodnight kiss —Richard Llewellyn⟩ **4 :** our ship ⟨about to board ~⟩

US *abbr* **1** *often not cap* [L *ubi supra*] where above mentioned **2** undersecretary **3** united service **4** unserviceable **5** *often not cap* [L *ut supra*] as above

u's *or* **us** *pl of* U

us·abil·i·ty \ˌyüzəˈbiləd·ē, -lətē, -i\ *n* **:** the quality or state of being usable

us·able *also* **use·able** \ˈyüzəbəl\ *adj* [ME, fr. MF *usable*, fr. *user* to use + *-able*] **1 :** that can be used ⟨a small lake comprises approximately 20 acres, leaving 140 acres ~ for burial purposes —*U.S.Code*⟩ **2 :** that is convenient and practicable for use ⟨the short story, as a ~ form of art, will nevertheless survive —G.H.Genzmer⟩ — **us·able·ness** *n* -ES — **us·ably** \-blē, -li\ *adv*

us·age \ˈyüs|ij, |ēj *also* -üz|\ *n* -s [ME, fr. OF, fr. *user* to use + *-age*] **1 :** habitual or customary practice or use: **a** (1) **:** the prevailing mode of procedure (as of a craft, business, liturgical tradition) **:** a principle or method of action or body of these commonly followed within a group ⟨these principles and rules grew up entirely on the basis of ~ (sometimes reenforced by judicial decision), and were never enacted by Parliament —F.A.Ogg & Harold Zink⟩ ⟨the chapel services follow the ~ of the Episcopal church —*Bard College Bull.*⟩ (2) **:** a uniform certain reasonable practice not contrary to law which exists in a particular locality or among those engaged in a particular occupation or business and by which those entering into consensual transactions are bound either by express assent or by implied acquiescence on the basis of presumed familiarity — compare CUSTOM, PRESCRIPTION **b :** the habitual practice of a person **:** usual behavior **:** HABIT ⟨propping oneself on one's elbows to drink a cup of tea . . . is still an ill-bred ~ —Agnes M. Miall⟩ **c :** the way in which words and phrases are actually used (as in a particular form or sense) generally or among a community or group of persons **:** customary use of language ⟨like all grammarians, he professed to base his work on actual ~; in fact, however, he . . . gave his approval only to such constructions as met his rigid notions of logic and propriety —G.H.Genzmer⟩ ⟨instruct pupils in the rules of good ~⟩ **2 a :** the action, amount, or mode of using **:** USE ⟨the corners somewhat smashed and broken as by long, rough ~ —R.L.Stevenson⟩ ⟨steadily increasing ~ of the nation's highways —J.C.Nelson⟩ ⟨freshmen students are given a brief period of instruction in library ~ —*Bull. of Meharry Med. Coll.*⟩ **b :** manner of conduct toward a person **:** TREATMENT ⟨complained of ill ~ at the hands of his jailors — threats, scanty food, beatings⟩ **3 :** UTILITY, ADVANTAGE ⟨we can fell trees and put them to our ~ —George Moore⟩ **syn** see FORM, HABIT

us·ag·er \ˈyüzijə(r)\ *n* -s *usu cap* [*usage* + *-er*] **:** a member of a party of nonjurors in the Church of England and Scottish Episcopal Church accepting the ritual usages of a Communion service published in 1718 including dilution of the Eucharistic wine, a prayer for the descent of the Holy Spirit on the consecrated elements, an oblatory prayer, and prayers for the dead

usam·ba·ra violet \ˌüsəmˈbärə-\ *n, usu cap U* [fr. *Usambara*, district of northeast Tanganyika, Africa] **:** AFRICAN VIOLET

us·ance \ˈyüzᵊn(t)s\ *n* -s [ME *usaunce*, fr. ML *usantia*, fr. *usant-, usans* (pres. part. of *usare* to use) + L *-ia* -y] **1 :** USAGE 1a,1b **2 :** the action of using or fact of being used **:** USE **3 a** *obs* **:** USURY ⟨many a time . . . you have rated me about my monies and my ~s —Shak.⟩ **b :** INTEREST ⟨make an investment of any spare monies as may render some ~ —Lord Byron⟩ **4 :** the time allowed exclusive of grace for the payment of a bill of exchange or note as fixed by custom or by law

usar \ˈüˌsär\ *n* -s [Hindi *ūsar*, fr. Skt *ūṣara*, fr. *ūṣara* containing salt] **:** REH

usara root *var of* UZARA ROOT

usar grass *n* **:** an East Indian perennial grass of the genus *Sporobolus* (*S. orientalis*) that is useful for forage in alkali or saline situations

u. s. army black \ˈyüˈes-\ *n, usu cap U&S&A* **:** a nearly neutral very slightly bluish black

u. s. army brick red *n, usu cap U&S&A* **:** a dark red

u. s. army brown *n, usu cap U&S&A* **:** a moderate brown

u. s. army buff *n, usu cap U&S&A* **:** a light yellowish brown

u. s. army cobalt blue *n, usu cap U&S&A* **:** a dark blue that is redder and stronger than U.S. Army sky blue

u. s. army color *n, usu cap U&S&A* **:** a color standardized for the United States Army by the Textile Color Card Association of the U.S. and calibrated by measurements in the National Bureau of Standards

u. s. army crimson *n, usu cap U&S&A* **:** a deep purplish red

u. s. army dark blue *n, usu cap U&S&A* **:** a slightly bluish black

u. s. army golden orange *n, usu cap U&S&A* **:** a strong orange

u. s. army golden yellow *n, usu cap U&S&A* **:** a vivid yellow

u. s. army green *n, usu cap U&S&A* **:** a dark yellowish green

u. s. army light blue *n, usu cap U&S&A* **:** a moderate greenish blue to grayish blue

u. s. army maroon *n, usu cap U&S&A* **:** a dark grayish red

u. s. army mosstone *n, usu cap U&S&A* **:** a moderate yellow green

u. s. army old gold *n, usu cap U&S&A* **:** a moderate yellow

u. s. army orange *n, usu cap U&S&A* **:** a vivid reddish orange that is redder and paler than international orange, redder and darker than chrome orange, and redder and duller than golden poppy

u. s. army pansy *n, usu cap U&S&A* **:** a strong violet

u. s. army scarlet *n, usu cap U&S&A* **:** a strong red

u. s. army silver gray *n, usu cap U&S&A* **:** a medium slightly yellowish gray

u. s. army sky blue *n, usu cap U&S&A* **:** a dark blue

u. s. army ultramarine blue *n, usu cap U&S&A* **:** a vivid blue to purplish blue

u. s. army white *n, usu cap U&S&A* **:** a yellowish gray to yellowish white

u. s. army yellow *n, usu cap U&S&A* **:** a strong orange yellow that is redder and deeper than Spanish yellow, bright maize, or nasturtium yellow (sense 2)

usbek *or* **usbeg** *cap, var of* UZBEK

USC *abbr* under separate cover

¹**use** \ˈyüs\ *n* -s [ME *us, use*, fr. OF *us*, fr. L *usus* use, employment, custom, fr. *usus*, past part. of *uti* to use, employ] **1 a :** the act or practice of using something **:** EMPLOYMENT ⟨a ~ of his public post to secure a favor for a friend⟩ ⟨become familiar with algebra through the ~ of a good text⟩ ⟨an increase in the ~ of intoxicating liquors⟩ ⟨the ~ of subsidies to hold food prices down —*Current Biog.*⟩ **:** APPLICATION ⟨knowledge . . . to be valuable must be ready for ~ —C.H.Grandgent⟩ **b :** the fact or state of being used ⟨a lamp in daily ~ for over 50 years⟩ ⟨put the new broom to ~⟩ ⟨expressions out of ~ except in dialect⟩ ⟨when fountain pens first came into ~⟩ **c :** continued or repeated exercise or employment ⟨worn out through long ~⟩ **d :** a method or manner of using something ⟨the water in the font, having once been consecrated, tempted folk to superstitious ~s —G.G.Coulton⟩ ⟨gain proficiency in the ~ of the typewriter⟩ **2 a** (1) **:** habitual or customary practice **:** accustomed or usual procedure (2) **:** an individual habit or group custom ⟨it had been a family ~ . . . to make a point of saving for him anything which he might possibly eat —Mary Austin⟩ **b :** a liturgical form or observance ⟨ferial ~⟩ ⟨festal ~⟩; *esp* **:** a liturgy having modifications peculiar to a local church or diocese (as in England before the Reformation) or a religious order ⟨the celebration of Mass in those religious orders . . . whose ~ differs from the standard Roman rite —*advt*⟩ ⟨from henceforth all the whole realm shall have but one ~ —*Bk. of Com. Prayer*⟩ **c** *obs* **:** common occurrence **:** ordinary experience ⟨these things are beyond all ~ —Shak.⟩ **3 a :** the privilege or benefit of using something ⟨offered him the ~ of his pen for signing⟩ ⟨had the ~ of the usual class time for study⟩ ⟨nor shall private property be taken for public ~ without just compensation —*U.S.Constitution*⟩ ⟨the Lord bless this food to our ~, and us to His service —*Bk. of Com. Worship*⟩ **b :** the ability or power to use something (as a limb or faculty) ⟨regained the ~ of his arm⟩ ⟨still has the ~ of his speech⟩ **c :** the legal enjoyment of property that consists in its employment, occupation, exercise, or practice ⟨~ of the automobile is covered by insurance⟩ **d :** a personal servitude under Roman and civil law consisting in a jus utendi as distinguished from the usufruct **4 a :** a particular service or end **:** PURPOSE, OBJECT, FUNCTION ⟨put his learning to a good ~⟩ ⟨the river waters were dammed for power ~ —*Amer. Guide Series: Mich.*⟩ ⟨develop the industrial ~s of atomic energy⟩ **b** (1) **:** the quality of being suitable for employment **:** capability of filling a need or promoting an advantage **:** USEFULNESS, UTILITY ⟨being ready first was of little ~, since you were then called on to button the others —Natacha Stewart⟩ ⟨old clothes that might be of some ~ to refugees⟩ (2) **:** something that fills a need or gives a benefit or advantage — used predicatively ⟨the thing that any artist must have to go on: the feeling . . . that he's some ~ in the world —Deems Taylor⟩ ⟨small ~ to argue if he's already made up his mind⟩ esp. in negative constructions ⟨it is no ~ reading this article any further until you have settled this first point for yourself —J.B.Nettleship⟩ **c :** the occasion or need to employ **:** NECESSITY, DEMAND ⟨took only what he had ~ for⟩ ⟨found little ~ for his rifle⟩ **5 a :** the benefit in law of one or more persons; *specif* **:** the benefit of or the profit arising from lands and tenements to which legal title is held by a person in whom a trust or confidence is reposed that another person should take and enjoy — compare CESTUI QUE USE **b :** a legal arrangement that is a right in equity by which such benefits and profits are established in one other than the legal possessor of the property — compare TRUST **6** *chiefly dial* **:** money paid for the use of a loan **:** INTEREST **7 :** a part of a sermon in which a doctrine is applied to life **:** practical application ⟨the discourse . . . was divided into fifteen heads, each of which was garnished with seven ~s of application —Sir Walter Scott⟩ **8 :** a rough block of iron or steel suitable for working up into small forgings or for welding in making large ones **9 :** a favorable attitude toward a person or thing as having worth or use **:** ESTEEM, LIKING — used with *for* in negative constructions ⟨had no ~ for most sales managers —*Time*⟩ ⟨had very little ~ for the music of most of his contemporaries —Deems Taylor⟩

syn SERVICE, ADVANTAGE, PROFIT, ACCOUNT, AVAIL, and USE have in common a sense of a useful or valuable end, result, or purpose. USE stresses the practicality of the end, result, or purpose for which something is employed ⟨a tool with many *uses*⟩ ⟨put a gift of money to good *use* in paying off debts⟩ SERVICE is used more frequently of persons or animals or their work or activities than of inanimate things; in relation to persons it usu. suggests self-abnegation ⟨a man of great *service* to the community⟩ ⟨put a horse to good *service* in hauling logs⟩ ADVANTAGE puts stress upon improvement of one's position or enhancement of something one considers of value, esp. personal value ⟨gain the *advantage* of a steady income⟩ ⟨offer valuable educational *advantages* —*Amer. Guide Series: Minn.*⟩ ⟨find some *advantage* in even the worst circumstances⟩ PROFIT is more particular in usu. implying reward, often the rewarding character of what is attained but commonly pecuniary gain ⟨whether or not they found the sources of the gold they were seeking, they certainly drew other *profits* from their venture —*Brit. Bk. News*⟩ ⟨pursue graduate studies with *profit* —*Official Register of Harvard Univ.*⟩ ⟨coal and steel interests were merging with mutual *profit* —*Amer. Guide Series: Pa.*⟩ ACCOUNT usu. suggests a calculated value; it occurs commonly in fixed phrases ⟨turn every talent to good *account*⟩ ⟨consider a small loss of no *account* in the long run⟩ AVAIL strongly suggests effectualness or effectiveness, occurring usu. in idiomatic phrases mostly in the negative ⟨medicine that is of no *avail* in curing a given disease⟩ ⟨of what *avail* is it to spend time dreaming⟩ **syn** see in addition HABIT

— **in use** *or* **into use :** in heat ⟨conception can only occur at the precise time when the mare is fully *in use* —Henry Wynmalen⟩

²**use** \ˈyüz, *in vi sense 1* ˈyüs *sometimes* ˈyüz\ *vb* **used** \ˈyüzd, *in vi sense 1* ˈyüst (ˈyüs *when "to" follows immediately*) *sometimes* ˈyüz(d)\ **used; using; uses** [ME *usen*, fr. OF *user*, fr. ML *usare*, fr. L *usus*, past part. of *uti* to use, employ, enjoy; akin to Oscan *úittiuf* uses (acc. pl.)] *vt* **1 a** *archaic* **:** to observe or follow as a custom ⟨the like custom is *used* throughout the dominions —Samuel Purchas⟩ ⟨it was in old times *used* . . . for men to shave themselves —Richard Montagu⟩ **b** *archaic* **:** to follow or practice regularly as a mode of life or action ⟨then let them ~ the office of a deacon —1 Tim. 3:10 (AV)⟩ **c** *archaic* **:** to make familiar by repeated or continued practice or experience **:** ACCUSTOM, HABITUATE, INURE ⟨spoke near the sea in storms . . . to ~ himself to speak aloud —Earl of Chesterfield⟩ **d** *chiefly dial* **:** to resort to regularly **:** FREQUENT ⟨it ~s more the low sandy inland parts than the plovers —Hans Sloane⟩ **2 :** to put into action or service **:** have recourse to or enjoyment of **:** EMPLOY ⟨the pronunciations that people from different parts of the country ~⟩ ⟨wondered whether he would ever ~ the tie she had given him⟩ **:** EXERCISE ⟨examiners will ~ judgment and discretion in applying the exercise test —H.G.

Armstrong⟩ ⟨~ his political influence to get the job⟩: as **a** : to speak or write in (a language) ⟨they speak little Welsh — only forty or so in a thousand ~ the tongue —Wilfrid Goatman⟩ **b** : to consume or take (as liquor or drugs) regularly ⟨does not give scholarships to students who ~ tobacco⟩ ⟨do you ~ sugar in your coffee⟩ **c** *archaic* : to have sexual relations with ⟨. . . did carnally know and ~ his wife —Francis Hackett⟩ **d** *archaic* : to practice or exercise upon or toward others ⟨I guess by the . . . waspish action which she did ~ —Shak.⟩ ⟨with their tongues they have *used* deceit —Rom 3:13 (AV)⟩ **3** : to carry out a purpose or action by means of : make instrumental to an end or process : apply to advantage : turn to account : UTILIZE ⟨carried air mail *using* two small single-engined planes and five employees —*Current Biog.*⟩ ⟨some of the best tests . . . can be *used* only by professional psychologists —Bruce Payne⟩: as **a** : to spend (time) in some occupation, interest, or activity : PASS ⟨they ~ 30 days in traveling . . . about 1,000 miles —F.C.Lincoln⟩ ⟨stop by the way . . . to chase a rabbit, or merely to ~ time —Joyce Cary⟩ **b** : to make an involuntary or concealed means to one's own ends ⟨he is being *used* and manipulated by the knowing men around him —T.R.Ybarra⟩ ⟨juries . . . may be *used* to suppress writings in opposition to the government —Zechariah Chafee⟩ **c** : to employ a word, phrase, or sentence to refer ⟨to say "*life* is a short word" is to mention the word *life* . . . but to say "Life is short" is to ~ it —R.G.F.Robinson⟩ **4** : to expend or consume by putting to use ⟨percent of the world's population . . . produces and ~*s* almost one half of the industrial goods and services —C.C.Furnas⟩ **5 a** *archaic* : to bear (oneself) in relations with others : BEHAVE, CONDUCT ⟨he *used* himself more like a fellow to your Highness than like a subject —Edward Herbert⟩ **b** : to behave toward : act with regard to : TREAT ⟨had been taken prisoner by . . . partisans, who had *used* him with some brutality —Eric Linklater⟩ **6** : to apply or have applied as the usual designation (as a title or surname) of a person ⟨took his friends a while to acquire the habit of *using* the "*doctor*" after he received his Ph.D.⟩ ⟨a woman who ~*s* her maiden name professionally⟩ **7** : to benefit from the use of ⟨houses that could ~ a paint job —J.W.Ellison b.1929⟩ ⟨I can ~ some of that gold —E.B.Lung⟩ **~** *vi* **1 a** : to be in the habit or custom : make a practice of doing something : be wont ⟨sit here by the window with your hand in mine . . . both of one mind, as married people ~ —Robert Browning⟩ ⟨he does not ~ to be last on these occasions —George Lillo⟩ ⟨the black coachman, who had *used* to drive . . . the carriage —Marguerite Young⟩ ⟨patrons who *used* to do their banking on Friday⟩ ⟨~ to have tallyho parties out on the . . . pike when we were young —Anne G. Winslow⟩ ⟨*used* you to beat your mother —G.B.Shaw⟩ **b** — used in the past with *to* to indicate a former fact or state ⟨claims the winters *used* to be harder⟩ ⟨isn't going to take as long as it *used* to⟩ ⟨didn't ~ to have a car⟩ **2** *chiefly dial* **a** : to make a practice of going to a place : resort to customarily : go regularly ⟨if he didn't quit *using* around there she would make trouble for him —Mark Twain⟩ **b** : to occupy a place as a settled residence or habitat : DWELL, LIVE — usu. used of an animal ⟨I know where the gray fox ~*s* up yonder —R.A.Helton⟩

syn EMPLOY, UTILIZE, APPLY, AVAIL: USE is general and indicates any putting to service of a thing, usu. for an intended or fit purpose or person, in this latter reference with implications of inconsiderate or high-handed treatment ⟨*use* a jack to raise a car⟩ ⟨*use* a knife blade to pry up a lid⟩ ⟨*use* money wisely⟩ ⟨*used* his business experience to place the country in a better financial position —S.G.Inman⟩ ⟨his sense of being *used* rose suddenly above the treacherous sympathy he had begun to feel for her —Booth Tarkington⟩ EMPLOY may imply purposive selection, continued use or utilization, or smart turning to account ⟨by the dialect which he *employs* the author betrays that he was an Ionian Greek —Benjamin Farrington⟩ ⟨frequently lotteries were *employed* to raise funds for channel clearing —*Amer. Guide Series: Tenn.*⟩ UTILIZE may indicate finding a new, profitable, or practical use for something ⟨it was now charged against him that he *utilized* his military office for private gain —R.G.Adams⟩ ⟨all civilized governments have *utilized* the Indians as military allies —M.M.Quaife⟩ ⟨a huge wine bottle, *utilized* as a pivot for the rooster weather vane when no other instrument would hold —*Amer. Guide Series: Mich.*⟩ APPLY may imply a using or employing especially for a particular purpose or in a particular situation, sometimes with the suggestion of bringing into contact or relationship ⟨*apply* salve to a burn⟩ ⟨*apply* pressure at a crucial point⟩ ⟨the value of *applying* statistical methods to the data⟩ ⟨undertakes to *apply* the findings of science to personal problems —*Amer. Guide Series: Mich.*⟩ AVAIL in reflexive uses applies to a using or taking advantage of something one might waive or leave untouched ⟨I doubt if I should abuse the permission. It is a hundred to one if I should *avail* myself of it four times a year —Charles Dickens⟩ ⟨takes us thus directly into the consciousness of his characters, and in order to do so, he has *availed* himself of methods of which Flaubert never dreamed —Edmund Wilson⟩

— **use language** : to use profanity : SWEAR ⟨her husband's *using language* before ladies showed him to be in high good humor —Edith Wharton⟩

useable *var of* USABLE

use and occupancy insurance *n* [¹*use*] : BUSINESS INTERRUPTION INSURANCE

use and occupation *n* : a legal action of the character of an assumpsit that may be maintained by the owner of real property against a person who has had the use and occupation of it under express or implied contract to pay therefor but without a written lease or beyond the term of the written lease

use and wont *n* : USE 2a(1) ⟨life is an affair of *use and wont* and persists substantially unchanged —Walter Moberly⟩

used \ˈyüzd, *in sense 3* ¦yüst (¦yüs *when "to" follows immediately*) *sometimes* ¦yüz(d)\ *adj* [ME, fr. past part. of *usen* to use] **1** : employed in accomplishing something ⟨his most ~ name⟩ ⟨the principle of surprise is the most ~ and misused of all the principles of war —H.H.Arnold & I.C.Eaker⟩ **2** : that has endured considerable use : that has been utilized according to its nature or purpose: as **a** : partly worn-out : SECONDHAND ⟨bought a ~ car because he couldn't afford a new one⟩ ⟨collect ~ clothing for overseas relief⟩ **b** *of a stamp* : that has served as postage on a piece of mail **3** : ACCUSTOMED, HABITUATED, EXPERIENCED ⟨showing how ~ he was to papers with lies on them —Gilbert Millstein⟩

use district *n* [¹*use*] : a zone or area in a city or town within which the types of usage to which buildings are put are regulated by law

used·n't *or* **use·n't** \ˈyüsᵊn(t)\ [by contr.] *chiefly Brit* : used not

used to \¦yüs *sometimes* ¦yüz + *pronunc at* TO\ *adv* [fr. the verb phrase *used to*, fr. *used*, past of ²*use* + *to*, function word normally indicating that the following verb is an infinitive] *dial* : FORMERLY, ONCE ⟨he ain't as popular now as he *used to* was —Mark Twain⟩ ⟨I can't do the hard day's work I *used to* could —Erskine Caldwell⟩ ⟨*used to* Pa wouldn't a done a thing like this —J.H.Stuart⟩

us·ee \¦yü¦zē\ *n* -s [²*use* + -*ee*] : one to or for whose use a thing is done or given; *esp* : one for whose benefit a suit is brought : use plaintiff

use·ful \ˈyüsfəl\ *adj* [¹*use* + -*ful*] : capable of being put to use : having utility : ADVANTAGEOUS ⟨the Communists find him just as ~ as an opponent —*Time*⟩; *esp* : producing or having the power to produce good : serviceable for a beneficial end or object ⟨all sorts of ~ implements such as axes, chisels, gouges, arrowheads —*Amer. Guide Series: R.I.*⟩ ⟨~ to remind ourselves occasionally of our limitations⟩ ⟨no ~ rain had fallen for five or six months —*Sydney (Australia) Bull.*⟩

useful load *n* : the excess of the full load including the crew and passengers, oil and fuel, auxiliary power system, and communication, navigation, and other equipment over the dead weight of an aircraft itself — compare DEAD LOAD

use·ful·ly \-fəlē, -li\ *adv* : in a useful manner

use·ful·ness *n* -ES : the quality or state of being useful : conduciveness to an end : UTILITY

use inheritance *n* [¹*use*] : supposed inheritance by offspring of characters acquired by the parent through use or disuse of structures — compare LAMARCKISM

use·less \ˈyüsləs\ *adj* [¹*use* + -*less*] : having or being of no use : producing no good end : answering no desired purpose : INEFFECTUAL, INEFFICIENT, UNSERVICEABLE ⟨attempts . . . to sterilize the seawater at swimming beaches are ~ because the seawater itself is a sterilizing agent —G.E. & Nettie MacGinitie⟩ — **use·less·ly** *adv* — **use·less·ness** *n* -ES

us·en \ˈyüsᵊn\ *dial var of* USED

¹**us·er** \ˈyüzə(r)\ *n* -s [ME, fr. *usen* to use + -*er*] : one that uses; *specif* : a person who uses alcoholic beverages or narcotics

²**user** \"\ *n* -s [back-formation fr. ¹*non-user*] : enjoyment of a right of use : a right to use resulting from long-continued use ⟨claims to arms by ~ could be allowed only if they went back before 1530 —L.G.Pine⟩

uses *pl of* USE, *pres 3d sing of* USE

use tax *n* [¹*use*] : a supplement to a retail sales tax designed to reach goods purchased in a state that does not tax them and brought or shipped in to the taxing jurisdiction for use, storage, or consumption

use up *vt* [²*use*] **1** : to leave nothing of as a result of continued expenditure : consume completely ⟨soon *used up* his supplies and had nothing to eat⟩ **2** : to leave no capacity of force or use in : exhaust of strength or useful properties ⟨who at the age of 53 was pretty well *used up* by fighting —S.E.Morison & H.S.Commager⟩ **3** : to subject to thorough and abusive treatment : attack physically or verbally : work over ⟨the summary and effectual manner in which the argument is put and his opponent *used up* —P.T.Barnum⟩

ush \ˈəsh\ *vi* -ED/-ING/-ES [back-formation fr. ¹*usher*] *slang* : USHER

ushab·ti \(y)üˈshabtē\ *also* **sha·wab·ti** \shəˈwa-\ *n, pl* **ushabti** \-tē\ *or* **ushabtis** \-tēz\ *or* **ushabtiu** \-tē,ü\ [Egypt *wšbty*, lit., answerer] : a small figure deposited in an ancient Egyptian tomb with the mummy generally bearing inscriptions from the Book of the Dead and representing servants expected to do certain agricultural labors required of the deceased in the land of the dead

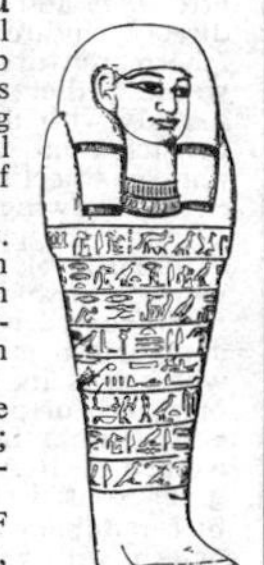

ushabti

ushak *or* **ou·shak** \üˈshäk\ *n* -s *usu cap* [fr. *Ushak, Oushak* (Usak), manufacturing town of western Turkey in Asia] : a heavy woolen oriental rug tied in Ghiordes knots and characterized by bright primary colors and an elaborate medallion pattern

u-shaped \ˈ=,=\ *adj, cap U* : having the shape of a capital U ⟨a *U-shaped* statistical curve⟩; *specif* : resembling a broad U in cross profile ⟨a *U-shaped* valley⟩

¹**ush·er** \ˈəshə(r)\ *n* -s [ME *ussher*, fr. MF *ussier*, fr. (assumed) VL *ustiarius* doorkeeper, fr. L *ostium, ustium* door, mouth of a river + -*arius* -ary; akin to Skt *oṣṭha* lip, Lith *uostas* mouth of a river, L *or-, os* mouth — more at ORAL] **1 a** : an officer or servant who has the care of the door of a court, hall, or chamber **b** (1) : an officer whose business it is to introduce strangers or to walk before a person of rank ⟨various ~*s* attached to the royal household in England including the Gentleman-Usher of the Black Rod⟩ (2) *obs* : something that precedes or gives indication of the approach of a person or thing : HARBINGER **c** : a minor official of an English court of law (as formerly the Court of Chancery) charged with maintaining silence and order **d** : one who escorts persons to seats at an assemblage (as in a theater, church, or hall) **e** : one employed to direct or assist patrons (as of a store) or visitors (as to a public building) **2** *archaic* : an assistant teacher in a private school **3** *obs* : a male attendant accompanying a lady

²**usher** \"\ *vb* **ushered**; **ushered**; **ushering** \-sh(ə)riŋ\ **ushers** *vt* **1** : to conduct to a place ⟨~ the bride's mother to her seat⟩ **2** : to precede as a herald or harbinger **3** : to serve as introduction for (as a discourse, essay, book) : PREFACE **4** : to cause to enter : INTRODUCE ⟨even before the child was ~*ed* into the world —J.H.Cornyn⟩ **~** *vi* : to serve as an usher ⟨asked him to ~ at his wedding⟩

ush·er·er \-shərə(r)\ *n* -s [²*usher* + -*er*] : one that ushers : USHER

ush·er·ette \¦əshə¦ret, *usu* -ed+V\ *n* -s [¹*usher* + -*ette*] : a woman employed to show patrons to seats (as in a theater) : female usher

usher in *vt* [²*usher*] **1** : to serve to bring into being : INAUGURATE ⟨a truce would *usher in* a period of great uncertainty —*N.Y.Times*⟩ **2** : to bring in or observe the entry of with ceremony ⟨already the town boys were *ushering in* the month of May —A.T.Quiller-Couch⟩ **3** : to mark the beginning or occurrence of ⟨1879 did indeed *usher in* a renaissance —W.V. Quine⟩

ush·er·less \ˈəshə(r)ləs\ *adj* : having no usher

usher of the black rod : BLACK ROD

ush·er·ship \-(r),ship\ *n* **1** : the office of an usher **2** : a position as an usher

using *adj* [fr. gerund of ²*use*] *of a saddle horse* : trained for utility service (as herding or roping) rather than as a pleasure mount

using-ground \ˈ==,=\ *n* : a place frequented by game (as wild fowl)

us·kok \ˈü,skäk\ *n* -s *cap* : a Slav of Dalmatian origin orig. fugitive from Turkish rule

us·nea \ˈəsnēə\ *n* [NL, fr. Ar *ushnah* moss] **1** *cap* : a genus of widely distributed lichens of the family Usneaceae usu. having a grayish or yellow pendulous freely branched thallus — see BEARD LICHEN **2** -s : any lichen of the genus *Usnea*

us·ne·a·ceae \,əsnēˈāsē,ē\ *n pl, cap* [NL, fr. *Usnea*, type genus + -*aceae*] : a family of fruticose lichens characterized by prostrate, erect, or pendulous thalli that are generally radially symmetrical and including the genera *Usnea, Evernia, Ramalina*, and *Alectoria* — **us·ne·a·ceous** \¦==¦āshəs\ *adj*

us·ne·oid \ˈəsnē,ȯid\ *adj* [NL *Usnea* + E -*oid*] : resembling or related to the genus *Usnea*

us·nic acid \ˈəsnik-\ *n* [NL *Usnea* + E -*ic*] : a yellow crystalline antibiotic $C_{18}H_{16}O_7$ that is a heterocyclic keto phenol related to dibenzo-furan and is obtained from various lichens (as of the genera *Usnea* and *Parmelia*)

us·pan·tec \üˈspan,tek\ *n, pl* **uspantec** *or* **uspantecs** *usu cap* **1 a** : an Indian people of Uspantan in central Guatemala **b** : a member of such people **2** : a Mayan language of the Uspantec people

us·que ad coe·lum \ˈüskwäädˈkȯiləm, ˈəskwēadˈsēləm\ [NL] : up to the heavens : as far as heaven — referring to a rule in law that the owner of land owns the air space above it indefinitely upward ⟨the Swiss Government announced that it adopted the principle of territoriality *usque ad coelum* —*Times Hist. of the War*⟩

usque ad fi·lum aquae \-ˈfēləˈmä,kwī, ˈfīləˈmā,kwē\ [ML, lit., as far as the thread of water] : as far as the middle of the stream — referring to a rule in law that when a boundary of a real property is formed by a nontidal stream, unless otherwise evident, the title extends to an imaginary line along the middle of the stream subject to the rights of the public

us·que·baugh *also* **us·que·bagh** \ˈəskwə,bä, -bȯ\ *or* **us·qua·bae** *or* **us·que·bae** \-bā\ *n* -s [*usquebaugh, usquebagh* fr. IrGael *uisce beathadh; usquabae, usquebae* fr. ScGael *uisge beatha* — more at WHISKEY] **1** *Irish & Scot* : WHISKEY **2** : a strong Irish cordial flavored with spice (as cinnamon or clove)

USS *abbr* **1** United States ship **2** United States standard

ussh·er·i·an \¦ə¦shirēən\ *adj, usu cap* [James *Ussher* †1656 Irish Archbishop + E -*ian*] : of or relating to Archbishop Ussher or to his biblical chronology in which 4004 B.C. is taken as the date of the world's creation

us·sing·ite \ˈəsiŋ,īt\ *n* -s [Dan *ussingit*, fr. Niels V. *Ussing* †1911 Dan. mineralogist + Dan -*it* -ite] : a mineral $Na_2AlSi_3O_8(OH)$ consisting of a basic sodium aluminum silicate related to the zeolites and occurring in reddish violet masses (hardness 6–7, sp. gr. 2.5)

us·ta·ra·na *also* **ush·ta·ra·na** \ˈüshtərənə\ *n, pl* **ustarana** *or* **ustaranas** *usu cap* **1** : a Pathan people on the west side of the middle Indus in Pakistan **2** : a member of the Ustarana people

us·ti·lag·i·na·ce·ae \,əstə,lajəˈnāsē,ē\ *n pl, cap* [NL, fr. *Ustilagin-, Ustilago*, type genus + -*aceae*] : a large and economically important family of smut fungi (order Ustilaginales) that produce chlamydospores which germinate to form a several-celled promycelium either bearing terminal and lateral sporidia or forming an infection hypha — **us·ti·lag·i·na·ceous** \¦==¦==¦nāshəs\ *adj*

us·ti·lag·i·na·les \,==,==ˈnā(,)lēz\ *n pl, cap* [NL, fr. *Ustilagin-, Ustilago* + -*ales*] : an order of parasitic basidiomycetous fungi that cause smuts of various plants and esp. of cereal grasses and have a complex life cycle which may include conidia production and in which sessile haploid basidiospores ultimately yield thick-walled dark-colored chlamydospores which typically replace the ovaries of an infected plant in a smutty mass and germinate with a meiosis to form a promycelium and begin a new basidial generation — compare UREDINALES, USTILAGO; see TILLETIACEAE

us·ti·lag·i·noi·dea \-ˈnȯidēə\ *n, cap* [NL, fr. *Ustilagin-, Ustilago* + -*oidea*] : a genus of imperfect fungi (family Dematiaceae) forming conidia-bearing sclerotia which replace the grain in grasses and later produce ascigerous heads similar to those in *Claviceps* — see GREEN SMUT

us·ti·la·go \,əstəˈlā(,)gō\ *n, cap* [NL *Ustilagin-, Ustilago*, fr. LL, a thistle, fr. L *ustus*, past part. of *urere* to burn; so called from its scorched appearance — more at EMBER] : a genus (the type of the family Ustilaginaceae) of smut fungi comprising the loose smuts — compare TILLETIA

us·tion \ˈəs(h)chən\ *n* -s [MF, fr. L *ustion-, ustio*, fr. *ustus* (past part. of *urere* to burn) + -*ion-, -io* -ion] **1** : the action of burning **2** *obs* : CAUTERIZATION

u-stirrup \ˈ=,==\ *n, cap U* : a stirrup for reinforced concrete bent in the form of a U

us·tu·la·tion \,əs(h)chəˈlāshən\ *n* -s [ML *ustulation-, ustulatio*, fr. L *ustulatus* (past part. of *ustulare* to burn slightly, scorch, fr. assumed L *ustulus* slightly burned, fr. L *ustus*, past part. of *urere* to burn) + -*ion-, -io* -ion] **1** : the action of burning or searing **2** : an operation formerly used in chemistry of expelling one substance from another (as sulfur from an ore) by heat in a muffle

us·tu·li·na \,əs(h)chəˈlīnə\ *n, cap* [NL, fr. L *ustulare* to scorch + NL -*ina*] : a genus of fungi (family Xylariaceae) distinguished by stromata indefinite in form and often spreading and undulate and including a fungus (*U. zonata*) that causes a common root disease of tea

usu *abbr* usual; usually

¹**usu·al** \ˈyüzh(ə)wəl, -zhəl\ *adj* [ME, fr. MF or L; MF *usuel*, fr. LL *usualis* that is for use, usual, fr. L *usus* use, custom + -*alis* -al] **1** : such as accords with usage, custom, or habit : of the character or amount in common use : PREVALENT, ACCUSTOMED ⟨it is ~ to give way to the vehicle on one's right —Richard Joseph⟩ ⟨charged only half his ~ fee in view of their poverty⟩ **2** : commonly or ordinarily employed ⟨tried a short cut instead of following the ~ route⟩ ⟨sent someone strange instead of the ~ substitute⟩ **3** : such as occurs in ordinary practice or in the ordinary course of events : ORDINARY, COMMON ⟨the characters were better drawn than is ~ in romantic drama —A.H.Quinn⟩ ⟨all the facilities ~ to a military base —*Amer. Guide Series: Nev.*⟩

syn CUSTOMARY, HABITUAL, WONTED, ACCUSTOMED: USUAL describes that which happens frequently in the normal course of events and lacks any element of strangeness ⟨it is with the domestic artist as with artists at large — painters, architects, and others — the *usual* error lies in excess prompted by undue desire for admiration —Herbert Spencer⟩ ⟨it is *usual*, when visiting a new mother for the first time, to take a little present for the baby —Agnes M. Miall⟩ CUSTOMARY describes what characteristically accords with the practices or usages of a particular individual or community ⟨no idea how men behave when their *customary* way of life is disrupted and their familiar habits are disordered —Walter Lippmann⟩ ⟨settle down to his *customary* occupations or amusements —W.M.Thackeray⟩ ⟨the *customary* arts of the pleader, the appeal to the sympathies of the public, the introduction into court of weeping wife and children —G.L.Dickinson⟩ HABITUAL applies to what is settled by long repetition into a habit, followed or conformed to without thoughtful intent ⟨the appearance of self-possession or poise that comes from an *habitual* attention to what is graceful and becoming —D.C.Hodges⟩ ⟨then I stop ashamed, for I am talking *habitual* thoughts, and not adapting them to her ear, forgetting beauty in the pursuit of truth —W.B.Yeats⟩ WONTED may apply to that favored, sought, or purposefully cultivated ⟨his nerve steadied itself back into its *wonted* control —C.G.D.Roberts⟩ ⟨threw himself with his *wonted* zest into appreciating the thoughts and feelings of his artistic friends —R.F.Harrod⟩ ACCUSTOMED may refer to that long practiced, now habitual or customary, and noticed, looked for, or expected by others ⟨will be long before I recover my *accustomed* cheerfulness —W.S.Gilbert⟩ ⟨pausing to fling out an arm with some familiar *accustomed* gesture in a House of Commons —A.T.Quiller-Couch⟩

— **as usual** *adv* : in the accustomed or habitual way ⟨*as usual* he was late⟩

²**usual** \"\ *n* -s : something usual ⟨old tabbies would begin asking questions of me, like what my name was, where was my folks, and the ~ —Helen Eustis⟩ ⟨a reserve of available funds in case their customers should happen to require more than their ~ —J.A.Todd⟩

usual covenant *n* **1** : one of the covenants for title usu. inserted in a deed conveying land to secure to the grantee the benefit of the title purported to be conveyed **2** : a covenant by the lessor for quiet enjoyment so far as concerns his own acts and those of persons claiming under or through him, or one of the covenants by the lessee to pay rent, to pay taxes except those expressly payable by the lessor, to keep and deliver up the premises in repair, and to allow the lessor to enter and view the state of repair

usu·al·ly \ˈyüzh(ə)wəlē, -zh(ə)wəlē, -li *sometimes* -üz(ə)l-\ *adv* [ME, fr. *usual* + -*ly*] **1** : by or according to habit or custom : HABITUALLY, CUSTOMARILY ⟨a banqueting house is ~ secluded from the street —Lafcadio Hearn⟩ **2** : more often than not : most often : as a rule : ORDINARILY ⟨the dragonfly is ~ seen near small streams —*Word-List From South Carolina*⟩ ⟨delivered from more than ~ black thoughts —R.L.Stevenson⟩

us·u·al·ness *n* -ES : the quality or state of being usual

us·u·ary \ˈyüzhə,werē\ *n* -ES [LL *usuarius*, fr. L *usus* use + -*arius* -ary] *Roman & civil law* : the beneficiary of a use

usu·ca·pi·ent \,yüzəˈkāpēənt, ,yüsə-\ *n* -s [L *usucapient-, usucapiens*, pres. part. of *usucapere* to usucapt] *Roman law* : one who claims title by usucapion — called also *usucaptor*

usu·ca·pio \-ē,ō\ *n* -s [L *usucapion-, usucapio*] : USUCAPION

usu·ca·pi·on \-ē,än\ *also* **usu·cap·tion** \-ˈkapshən\ *n* -s [*usucapion* fr. L *usucapion-, usucapio*, fr. *usucapere* to usucapt + -*ion-, -io* -ion; *usucaption*, alter. (influenced by *caption*) of *usucapion*] *Roman law* : a mode of acquiring title to property by uninterrupted possession of it for a definite period (as one year for movables or two for immovables) under a title acquired in good faith — **usu·ca·pi·on·ary** \¦==¦kāpēə,nerē\ *adj*

usu·capt \ˈ==,kapt\ *vt* -ED/-ING/-S [L *usucaptus*, past part. of *usucapere* to usucapt, fr. *usu capere*, lit., to take by use, fr. *usu* (abl. sing. of *usus* use) + *capere* to take — more at HEAVE] : to claim or acquire the title to by usucapion

usu·capt·able *or* **usu·capt·ible** \¦==¦kaptəbəl\ *adj* [*usucapt* + -*able* or -*ible*] : capable of being acquired by usucapion

usu·cap·tor \,==ˈkaptə(r)\ *n* -s [*usucapt* + -*or*] : USUCAPIENT

¹**usu·fruct** \ˈyüzə,frəkt, ˈyüsə,-\ *n* -s [L *ususfructus*, fr. *usus (et) fructus* use and enjoyment, fr. *usus* use + *et* and + *fructus* enjoyment — more at USE, FRUIT] **1** : the right of using and enjoying the fruits or profits of an estate or other thing belonging to another generally treated as a personal servitude ⟨the land is held to be the property of the tribe . . . and the individual only enjoys the ~ of a certain piece as long as he continues to cultivate it —G.B.Masefield⟩ ⟨an estate given in ~⟩ — see IMPERFECT USUFRUCT, PERFECT USUFRUCT **2** : the right to use or enjoy something ⟨like the skeptical miser you lost the ~ of heaven —Denis Devlin⟩

²**usufruct** \"\ *vt* -ED/-ING/-S : to hold (property) in usufruct

¹**usu·fruc·tu·ary** \,==ˈfrəkchə,werē, -ksh-\ *n* -ES [L *usufructuarius*, fr. *ususfructus* usufruct + -*arius* -ary] **1** : one having the usufruct of property **2** : one having the use or enjoyment of something

²**usufructuary** \¦==¦==¦==\ *adj* : of or relating to a usufruct : having the character of or possessing in the character of a usufruct

usun \ˈüˈsün\ *n, pl* **usun** *or* **usuns** *usu cap* **:** a member of an ancient people of central Asia said to have been blond and blue-eyed

usu·ra \yüˈsürə\ *n, pl* **usurae** [L] **:** interest paid on borrowed money

usu·rae usu·ra·rum \yüˈsü,rī,yüsəˈrärəm, -rē...ˈrärəm\ *n pl* [NL, lit., interests on interests] *Roman law* **:** COMPOUND INTEREST

usure *n* -s [ME, fr. MF, fr. L *usura* use, interest, usury — more at USURY] *obs* **:** USURY

usu·rer \ˈyüzhərə(r)\ *n* -s [ME, fr. AF, fr. ML *usurarius*, fr. L *usura* interest, usury + *-arius* -ary] **:** one that lends money and takes interest for it **:** MONEYLENDER; *specif* **:** one that lends money at a rate of interest beyond that established by law or at an exorbitant rate

usu·ri·ous \yüˈzhürēəs\ *adj* [*usury* + *-ous*] **1 :** practicing usury **:** taking illegal or exorbitant interest for the use of money ⟨a ~ old pawnbroker⟩ **2 :** involving usury **:** of the character of usury ⟨a ~ rate of interest⟩ — **usu·ri·ous·ly** *adv* — **usu·ri·ous·ness** *n* -ES

usu·rous \ˈyüzhərəs\ *adj* [*usure* + *-ous*] *obs* **:** USURIOUS

usurp \yüˈsərp, -ˈzəp, -ˈzəip *sometimes* -ˈz\ *vb* -ED/-ING/-S [ME *usurpen*, fr. MF *usurper*, fr. L *usurpare* to take possession of by use, employ, usurp, fr. *usu* (abl. of *usus* use) + *rapere* to seize — more at USE, RAPID] *vt* **1 :** to seize and hold (as office, place, functions, powers, or rights) in possession by force or without right ⟨~ a throne⟩ ⟨by use of the treaty-making power, the president can ~ legislative powers that do not belong to him —J.J.Del Castillo⟩ **2 :** to occupy (as land or a city) by or as if by force **:** take possession of ⟨the bogs, like inland seas, ~ the earth —Sacheverell Sitwell⟩ **3 :** to employ wrongfully **:** use without authority **4 :** to take the place of by or as if by force **:** SUPPLANT ⟨gloom was beginning to ~ mirth —O.S.J. Gogarty⟩ **5** *archaic* **:** to appropriate (a word or expression) for use ~ *vi* **:** to act as a usurper: **a :** to seize or exercise authority or possession wrongfully **b :** to practice usurpation upon a person — used with *on* or *upon* **c :** to encroach or infringe upon a right or privilege — used with *on* or *upon* **syn** see APPROPRIATE

usur·pa·tion \,yüsə(r)ˈpāshən *sometimes* ,yüzə(-\ *n* -s [ME, fr. MF, fr. L *usurpation-, usurpatio* act of using, fr. *usurpatus* (past part. of *usurpare* to use) + *-ion-, -io* -ion] **1 :** the act of usurping **:** unauthorized arbitrary assumption and exercise of power esp. as infringing on others' rights ⟨dictatorial ~ of Congressional power —*Current History*⟩; *specif* **:** the illegal seizure of sovereign power — usu. used with *of* or sometimes with *on* or *upon* **2 :** an act or an instance of encroachment ⟨protect the executive branch from any legislative ~*s* —Sidney Hyman⟩ **3 :** the dispossession of the patron of a church by a stranger presenting to a vacant benefice a clerk who is thereupon admitted and instituted **4** *Roman law* **:** an interruption of use or possession (as in usucapion or in cohabitation)

usur·pa·tive \yüˈsərpəd·iv *sometimes* -ˈzər-\ *adj* [LL *usurpativus* wrongly used, fr. L *usurpatus* (past part. of *usurpare* to usurp) + *-ivus* -ive] **:** of or constituting usurpation **:** USURPING ⟨the tyranny of some ~ minority —*Nineteenth Century & After*⟩

usur·pa·to·ry \-pə,tōrē\ *adj* [LL *usurpatorius*, fr. L *usurpatus* + *-orius* -ory] **:** USURPATIVE

usurp·a·ture \-pə,chü(ə)r, ,yüzərˈpā,-\ *n* -s [L *usurpatus* + E *-ure*] **:** USURPATION

usurp·er \yüˈsərpər, -ˈzəpə(r, -ˈzəipə(r *sometimes* -ˈz\ *n* -s [ME, fr. *usurpen* to usurp + *-er*] **:** one that usurps: as **a :** one that seizes illegally on sovereign power ⟨a ~ who should make himself master of the relics would be acknowledged king without dispute —J.G.Frazer⟩ **b :** one that infringes or encroaches upon the rights or property of another **c :** one that without proper authority assumes public office and performs official acts

usurp·ing·ly *adv* [*usurping* (pres. part. of *usurp*) + *-ly*] **:** by usurpation

usur·press \-prəs\ *n* -ES [*usurper* + *-ess*] *archaic* **:** a woman usurper

usu·ry \ˈyüzh(ə)rē, -ri\ *n* -ES [ME, fr. ML *usuria*, fr. L *usura* use, interest, usury (fr. *usus* — past part. of *uti* to use — + *-ura* -ure) + *-ia* -y — more at USE] **1** *archaic* **:** a premium or increase paid or stipulated for a loan of money or goods **:** INTEREST ⟨thou shalt not lend upon ~ to thy brother —Deut. 23:19 (AV)⟩ **2 :** the lending out of money with an interest charge for its use **:** the taking or practice of taking interest **3 :** an unconscionable or exorbitant rate or amount of interest; *specif* **:** interest in excess of a legal rate charged to a borrower for the use of money

usus \ˈyüsəs\ *n* -ES [L — more at USE] **1** *Roman law* **:** the act of making use of something **:** USE **2** *Roman law* **:** the personal and inalienable servitude of the usuary of making the bare use of real or personal property without enjoying its income, profit, or produce

USW *abbr* **1** ultrashort wave **2** *often not cap* [G *und so weiter*] and so forth

us·ward \ˈəswə(r)d\ *adv* [ME (*to*) *usward*, fr. *to* + *us* + *-ward*] **:** toward us ⟨bending ~ with memorial urns the most high Muses . . . weep —A.C.Swinburne⟩ ⟨the Lord . . . is longsuffering to ~ —2 Pet 3:9 (AV)⟩

ut \ˈət, ˈüt\ *n* -s [ME, lowest note of Guido's scale, fr. ML, fr. L, that, in order that, a word sung to this note in a medieval hymn to St. John the Baptist] **:** the musical tone *C* in the French fixed-do system replaced in solmization by *do*

ut *abbr* utility

UT *abbr* universal time

¹uta \ˈyüd·ə\ *n* [NL, fr. E ¹*ute*] **1** *cap* **:** a large genus of iguanid lizards found from New Mexico to Lower California — compare SWIFT 1a **2** -s **:** any lizard of *Uta* or a related genus

²uta \ˈüd·ə\ *n* -s [fr. native name in Peru] **:** a leishmaniasis of the skin occurring in Peru **:** ESPUNDIA

¹utah \ˈyü,tȯ, -tä\ *n, pl* **utah** *or* **utahs** *usu cap* **:** ¹UTE

²utah \ˈ"\ *adj, usu cap* [fr. *Utah*, state in the western U.S. fr. Ute *Yuta* Ute] **:** of or from the state of Utah ⟨*Utah* mines⟩ **:** of the kind or style prevalent in Utah **:** UTAHAN

¹utah·an \-ōən, -äən\ *adj, usu cap* [*Utah*, state in the western U.S. + E *-an*] **1 :** of, relating to, or characteristic of the state of Utah **2 :** of, relating to, or characteristic of the people of Utah

²utahan \ˈ"\ *also* **utahn** \-ōn, -än\ *n* -s *cap* **:** a native or resident of the state of Utah

utah juniper *n, usu cap U* **:** a small tree (*Juniperus osteosperma*) of the midwestern and Rocky Mountain regions of No. America with gray fibrous shreddy bark and yellow-green leaves

utah·lite \-ō,līt, -ä,-\ *n* -s [fr. *Utah*, state + *-lite*] **:** VARISCITE

utas \ˈyü,tas\ *n* -ES [ME, contr. of *utaves*, fr. MF *huitaves*, pl. of *huitave* octave, fr. ML *octava* — more at OCTAVE] *archaic* **:** the octave of a church feast

ut dict \ˈətˈdikt\ *abbr* [L *ut dictum*] as directed

¹ute \ˈyüt, *usu* -üd·+V; ˈyüd·|ē, -üt|, |i\ *n, pl* **ute** *or* **utes** *usu cap* [Ute *Yuta*] **1 a :** a group of Shoshonean peoples of Colorado, Utah, and New Mexico **b :** a member of any of such peoples **2 :** the language of the Ute people

²ute \ˈyüt\ *n* -s [by shortening & alter.] **:** a truck adaptable to numerous uses **:** a utility truck ⟨while I'm loading the ~ —R.M.Daw⟩

uten·sil \yüˈten(t)səl\ *n* -s [ME *utensele, utensil* collection of domestic articles, fr. MF *utensile*, fr. L *utensilia* utensils, fr. neut. pl. of *utensilis* useful, fr. *uti* to use — more at USE] **1 a :** an article useful or necessary in a household; *esp* **:** an implement, instrument, or vessel used in a kitchen ⟨household ~*s*⟩ **b :** an article (as a tool, implement, or vessel) serving a useful purpose ⟨providing his chums with the ~*s* of smoking —Arnold Bennett⟩ ⟨writing ~*s*⟩ ⟨farming ~*s*⟩ **2 :** a vessel, ornament, or furnishing belonging to a church; *esp* **:** one used in religious service ⟨consecration of the altar and its ~*s*⟩ **3 :** a person that is useful or is made use of ⟨a lackey and serf, the merest ~ of his master's will —Sir Winston Churchill⟩ **4** *archaic* **:** CHAMBER POT **syn** see IMPLEMENT

uter- *or* **utero-** *comb form* [L *uterus*] **1 :** uterus ⟨*uter*algia⟩ ⟨*uter*ectomy⟩ ⟨*utero*cele⟩ ⟨*utero*logy⟩ **2 :** uterine and ⟨*utero*abdominal⟩ ⟨*utero*ovarian⟩ ⟨*utero*vaginal⟩

uteri *pl of* UTERUS

uter·ine \ˈyüd·ərən, -ütə-, -ə,rīn\ *adj* [ME, fr. LL *uterinus*, fr. L *uterus* + *-inus* -ine] **1 a :** born of the same mother but by a different father ⟨~ brothers⟩ **b** (1) **:** related by blood through the mother **:** having relationship traced entirely through females ⟨~ uncle⟩ ⟨~ kin⟩ (2) **:** based upon such relationship ⟨a ~ system of descent⟩ **2 :** suited for use in or on the uterus ⟨~ probe⟩ ⟨~ speculum⟩ **3 :** of, relating to, or situated in the uterus **:** affecting or taking place in the uterus ⟨~ diseases⟩

uterine artery *n* **:** an artery that is derived from the hypogastric artery and that following a course between the layers of the broad ligament reaches the uterus at the cervix and supplies the uterus and adjacent parts and during pregnancy the placenta — see UTERINE PLEXUS

uterine gland *n* **:** any of the branched tubular glands in the mucous membrane of the uterus

uterine milk *n* **:** a nutritive secretion that is produced by uterine glands esp. during early phases of mammalian gestation and that nourishes the young mammalian embryo prior to implantation

uterine plexus *n* **:** a plexus of veins tributary to the hypogastric vein by which blood is returned from the uterus — compare UTERINE ARTERY

uterine tube *n* **:** FALLOPIAN TUBE

utero·gestation \ˌyüd·ə(ˌ)rō+\ *n* [*uter-* + *gestation*] **1 :** the part of the gestation period that is passed within the uterus **2 :** the entire normal mammalian gestation period

uter·o·gram \ˈyüd·ərə,gram\ *n* [*uter-* + *-gram*] **:** an X-ray photograph of the uterine cavity made after the injection of a radiopaque substance

uter·og·ra·phy \,yüd·əˈrägrəfē\ *n* -ES [ISV *uter-* + *-graphy*] **:** the art, practice, or action of making uterograms

utero·ma·nia \,yüd·ərōˈmānēə\ *n* [NL, fr. *uter-* + *mania*] **:** NYMPHOMANIA

utero·sal·pin·gog·ra·phy \,≈≈≈,sal,piŋˈgägrəfē\ *n* [ISV *uter-* + *salpingo-* + *-graphy*] **:** HYSTEROSALPINGOGRAPHY

uter·o·tub·al \ˌ≈≈≈ˈtübəl, -ˌtyü-\ *adj* [*uter-* + *tube* + *-al*] **:** of or relating to the uterus and Fallopian tubes ⟨a ~ insufflation of air in which air injected into the uterus is forced through the tubes⟩

uter·us \ˈyüd·ərəs, -ütər-\ *n, pl* **uteri** \-ə,rī\ [L, womb, belly; perh. akin to Gk *hoderos* belly, Skt *udara*] **1 :** an organ in female mammals for containing and usu. for nourishing the young during development previous to birth that consists of a greatly modified and enlarged section of an oviduct or of the two oviducts united, that has thick walls consisting of an external serous coat, a very thick muscular coat of nonstriated muscle, and a mucous coat containing numerous glands, and that during pregnancy undergoes remarkable increase in size and change in the condition of its walls **:** WOMB — compare CERVIX, FALLOPIAN TUBE, PLACENTA **2 a :** a section or diverticulum of an oviduct of any of various vertebrate or invertebrate animals other than the mammals that is enlarged or modified to serve as a place of development of the eggs or of the young **b :** the glandular part of the oviduct that secretes the eggshell

utes *pl of* UTE

ut·fang·thief *or* **ut·fang·thef** \ˈətfaŋ,thēf\ *n* [OE *ūtfangenethēof* — more at OUTFANGTHIEF] **:** OUTFANGTHIEF

utia \üˈtēə\ *n* -s [Sp *hutia* — more at HUTIA] **:** HUTIA

uti·ca \ˈyüd·|əkə, -üt|, |ēkə\ *adj, usu cap* [fr. *Utica*, manufacturing city of central New York] **:** of or from the city of Utica, N.Y. ⟨*Utica* knitting mills⟩ **:** of the kind or style prevalent in Utica

utick \ˈyütik\ *n* -s [prob. of imit. origin] *dial Eng* **:** WHINCHAT

util *or* **utile** \ˈyüd·ᵊl, -ütᵊl, -ü(,)til\ *n* -s [back-formation fr. ¹*utility*] **:** a hypothetical unit of utility

utile \ˈ"\ *adj* [MF, fr. L *utilis* — more at UTILITY] **:** having utility **:** productive of profit or advantage **:** PRACTICAL, USEFUL ⟨~ metals such as copper and tin —R.E.M.Wheeler⟩ ⟨ready-made and ~ substitutes —Parker Tyler⟩ ⟨a ~ agent⟩

¹util·i·tar·i·an \(ˌ)yü,tiləˈterēən, -ˈta(a)r-, -ˈtär-\ *n* -s [*utility* + *-arian*] **1 :** one that believes in, advocates, or follows the doctrine of utilitarianism ⟨the original ~*s* . . . believed that each individual was the best judge of his own welfare —E.S. Griffith⟩ **2 :** a person who has a utilitarian outlook

²utilitarian \(ˈ)≈¦≈¦≈≈≈\ *adj* **1 a :** of, relating to, or based upon the doctrine of utilitarianism ⟨on the ~ theory of obligation all duties are subordinate to one: maximize good consequences —O.A.Johnson⟩ ⟨first exponent of ~ political theory —*Times Lit. Supp.*⟩ **b :** believing in, advocating, or supporting the doctrine of utilitarianism ⟨~ philosophers⟩ **2 :** marked by a prevalence of the doctrines, principles, or views of utilitarianism ⟨love of truth for its own sake is . . . becoming rarer in this hasty ~ age —M.R.Cohen⟩ ⟨a ~ culture⟩ **3 a :** of or relating to utility **:** concerned with practical things or material interests ⟨humanistic vs. ~ education —J.E.Tobin⟩ ⟨a ~ point of view⟩ **b** (1) **:** characterized by or aiming at utility as distinguished from beauty or ornament ⟨her dark abundant hair was skewered into a ~ knob —Edna Ferber⟩ ⟨an essentially ~ and only accidentally aesthetic end —Stanley Morison⟩ ⟨~ steel tables⟩ (2) **:** evincing or characterized by a regard for utility of a lower kind **:** marked by a sordid spirit ⟨~ narrowness⟩ ⟨a ~ indifference to art⟩ **c :** preferring such utility ⟨a ~ people who are concerned more with getting on in the world and seducing women than with theology and a decent meal —Thomas Sugrue⟩

util·i·tar·i·an·ism \(ˌ)≈¦≈¦≈ˈterēə,nizəm, -ta(a)r-, -tär-\ *n* -s [¹*utilitarian* + *-ism*] **1 a :** a doctrine that the useful is the good and that the determining consideration of right conduct should be the usefulness of its consequences; *specif* **:** a theory elaborated by Jeremy Bentham and James and John Stuart Mill that the aim of moral, social, and political action should be the largest possible balance of pleasure over pain or the greatest happiness of the greatest number — compare BENTHAMISM, HEDONISM 1 **b :** one of a group of primarily 20th century ethical theories based not or not only on a conception of pleasure as an intrinsic good but on other intrinsic goods (as beauty, harmony, or affection) ⟨enunciates the general principle of ~ in the formula that it is right to aim at whatever will promote the increasingly full realization of increasingly high values —C.D.Broad⟩ — called also *ideal utilitarianism* **2 :** utilitarian character, spirit, or quality ⟨the ~ of commercial industry —Bertrand Russell⟩ ⟨the forthright ~ of the superb . . . aqueduct —*Amer. Guide Series: N.Y.*⟩

¹util·i·ty \yüˈtiləd·ē, -ətē, -i\ *n* -ES [ME *utilite*, fr. MF *utilité*, fr. L *utilitat-, utilitas*, fr. *utilis* useful (fr. *uti* to use + *-ilis* -ile) + *-itat-, -itas* -ity — more at USE] **1 :** the quality or state of being useful **:** fitness for some purpose **:** profitability to some desired end **:** SERVICEABLENESS, USEFULNESS ⟨demonstrated the ~ of hard coal as a domestic fuel —*Amer. Guide Series: Pa.*⟩ ⟨the design . . . is based on ~ rather than artistic embellishment —*Amer. Guide Series: Minn.*⟩ ⟨a road whose ~ was proved —*Amer. Guide Series: Ark.*⟩ — sometimes used with *of* ⟨more of ostentation than of real ~ in ships of this . . . burthen —Henry Fielding⟩ **2 :** something useful or designed primarily for use: as **a :** a useful factor or feature ⟨their views of the relative *utilities* of . . . democracy and communism —H.A.Steiner⟩ ⟨many of the admitted *utilities* and amenities from social services —J.A.Hobson⟩ **b :** a tool, device, or other implement; *esp* **:** one used as an adjunct to a more important machine **c :** a service provided by a public utility **d** *chiefly Austral* **:** a versatile motor vehicle **:** one having or adaptable to a number of uses (as both a truck and a car) **e :** a unit composed of one or more pieces of equipment usu. connected to or part of a structure and designed to provide a service (as heat, light, power, water, or sewage disposal) ⟨the price of the house included all *utilities*⟩ **3 :** the capacity to satisfy human wants or desires — see MARGINAL UTILITY, SUBJECTIVE UTILITY **4 a :** PUBLIC UTILITY 1 ⟨the *utility's* regular residential . . . customers —*N.Y. Times*⟩ ⟨effective public regulation of *utilities* —*Amer. Polit. Sci. Rev.*⟩ **b utilities** *pl* **:** stocks or bonds of utility companies ⟨*utilities* . . . displayed an easier tone —*Brookmire Investment Reports*⟩

²utility \ˈ"\ *adj* **1 :** capable of serving as a substitute in any of various roles or positions ⟨a ~ actor⟩ ⟨~ workers⟩ — compare UTILITY MAN **2 a :** kept for the production of an economically valued product (as meat, eggs, or milk) rather than for show or as pets ⟨~ livestock⟩ ⟨~ poultry⟩ ⟨~ sheep⟩ **b :** of, belonging to, or constituting an inferior grade of market cattle ⟨~ cows⟩ **c :** of, belonging to, or constituting a low grade of meat or other food products ⟨~ beef⟩ ⟨~ grades of lamb⟩ **3 :** serving primarily for utility rather than beauty **:** designed primarily for usefulness often at the expense of beauty, taste, or good quality **:** FUNCTIONAL, UTILITARIAN ⟨~ furniture⟩ ⟨~ clothes⟩ ⟨~ art⟩ ⟨~ goods⟩ **4 :** having or designed for a number of useful and practical purposes **:** adapted or adaptable for general use esp. in place of something specialized ⟨~ bag⟩ ⟨~ knife⟩ ⟨~ chair⟩ ⟨~ boat⟩ **5 :** of, relating to, or based upon philosophical utility ⟨~ calculus⟩ ⟨~ concepts⟩ **6 :** playing a usu. minor part incidental to the plot but often of considerable technical or expository usefulness ⟨a ~ character in a story or play⟩ **7 a :** of, relating to, or constituting a public utility ⟨~ companies⟩ ⟨~ regulation⟩ ⟨~ mergers⟩ ⟨a ~ meter⟩ **b :** of, relating to, or based on the prices of shares of public utility stocks ⟨the ~ average climbed 1.2 points in heavy trading⟩

utility man *n* **:** a man available for service in various positions: as **a :** an actor who performs minor parts and does odd jobs in a theater **b :** a member of a baseball team who plays various positions in the absence of regular players **c :** a kitchen helper or busboy on a ship — called also *galley man* **d :** JUMPER 1f **e :** one (as a handyman, houseman, or man-of-all-work) who is available for a variety of jobs

utility pole *n* **:** one of a series of poles usu. located at the side of a street or road and used to support wires and other equipment used by utilities (as telephone and electric companies) ⟨his car sideswiped a *utility pole* —*Springfield (Mass.) Union*⟩

utility principle *n* **:** GREATEST HAPPINESS PRINCIPLE

utility room *n* **:** a room (as in a dwelling) designed or used to house heating, laundry, or general maintenance equipment

uti·liz·able \ˈyüd·ᵊl,īzəbəl, -ütᵊl-, ,≈≈ˈ≈≈≈\ *adj* **:** capable of being utilized ⟨a two-seated bomber . . . ~ for the launching of torpedoes —*New Republic*⟩

uti·li·za·tion \,yüd·ᵊləˈzāshən, -ütᵊl-, -ᵊl,īˈ-\ *n* -s [F *utilisation*, fr. *utiliser* to utilize + *-ation*] **:** the action of utilizing or the state of being utilized ⟨the ~ of quotations from archives —C.H.Driver⟩ ⟨~ of glucose in the liver⟩ ⟨the disparity between the established drawing rights and their rate of ~ —R.F.Mikesell⟩

utilization coefficient *n* **:** the fraction of the total luminous flux from the lighting equipment of a room or office that falls upon areas (as desks or tables) where it is actually utilized

utilization factor *n* **:** the ratio of the maximum demand on a generator or generating station to the capacity of the generators

uti·lize \ˈyüd·ᵊl,īz, -ütᵊl-\ *vt* -ED/-ING/-S *see -ize in Explan Notes* [F *utiliser*, fr. *utile* useful (fr. L *utilis*) + *-iser* -ize — more at UTILITY] **:** to make useful **:** turn to profitable account or use **:** make use of **:** convert to use ⟨a cheese factory ~*s* milk from scores of farms —*Amer. Guide Series: Ark.*⟩ ⟨the ability of an organism to ~ oxygen —H.G.Armstrong⟩ ⟨~ the services of existing agencies —Frederick Graham⟩ **syn** see USE

uti·liz·er \-zə(r)\ *n* -s **:** one that utilizes

uti pos·si·de·tis \ˈü,tē,päsəˈdād·əs, ˈyü,tī,päsəˈdēd·əs\ *n* [L, as you (now) possess (fr. the wording of the formula of interdiction)] **1 :** an interdict in Roman and civil law for deciding the right to the possession of immovables and preserving things in statu quo pending the decision — compare UTRUBI **2 :** a principle in international law that a conclusion or treaty of peace between belligerents vests in them respectively as absolute property the territory under their actual control and the things attached to it and the movables then in their possession except as otherwise stipulated (as by treaty)

ut·man khel \ˈütmənˈkā(ə)l\ *n, pl* **utman khel** *or* **utman khels** *usu cap U&K* **1 :** an independent Pathan people in the country southwest of the junction of the Swat and the Panjkora **2 :** a member of the Utman Khel

¹ut·most \ˈət,mōst *also chiefly Brit* -,məst\ *adj* [ME, alter. (influenced by *most*) of *utmest*, fr. OE *ūtmest*, superl. adj. fr. *ūt* out (adv.) — more at OUT] **1 :** situated at the farthest point or extremity **:** most distant or remote in location **:** EXTREME ⟨the ~ point of the earth —John Hunt⟩ ⟨the ~ island⟩ **2 :** of the greatest or highest degree **:** of the largest quantity, number, or amount ⟨a matter calling for the ~ secrecy —E.S. McCartney⟩ ⟨living in the ~ misery —Angélica Mendoza⟩ ⟨separated with the ~ clearness of distinction —R.M.Weaver⟩ **3 :** final in order or time **:** LAST ⟨obtain the ~ penny of his debt —Maria Edgeworth⟩ **4** *archaic* **:** furthest extended **:** greatest in length, measure, or extent ⟨put forth your hand to the ~ stretch —Henry Felton⟩

²utmost \ˈ"\ *n* [ME, fr. OE *ūtmest*, fr. *ūtmest*, adj.] **1** *archaic* **:** something that is most outward, distant, or remote **:** the farthest limit, part, or district (as of an extent or area) ⟨a city . . . on the ~ of the ridge of a hill —George Sandys⟩ **2 a :** the most possible **:** the extreme limit **:** the highest attainable point or degree ⟨designed to provide the ~ in comfort —*advt*⟩ ⟨the modeling of individual figures was . . . the ~ they attempted —O. Elfrida Saunders⟩ — used esp. in the phrase *to the utmost* ⟨decentralizing authority . . . to the ~ —A.L. Nickerson⟩ ⟨taxing my resources to the ~ —E.S.McCartney⟩ **b :** the highest, greatest, or best of one's abilities, powers, and resources ⟨doing his ~ for a woman confided to his protection —Thomas De Quincey⟩ ⟨after society and culture have done their ~ —Ralph Linton⟩

uto-aztecan \ˈyü(ˌ)tō+\ *n, usu cap U&A* [*Ute* + *-o* + *Aztec* + *-an*] **1 :** a language phylum comprising the Nahuatlan, Taracahitian, Piman, and Shoshonean families **2 a :** a people speaking a Uto-Aztecan language **b :** a member of such people

uto·pia \yüˈtōpēə\ *n* -s [fr. *Utopia* an imaginary country with ideal laws and social conditions (fr. Gk *ou* not, no + *topos* place) described in the book *Utopia* (1516) by Sir Thomas More †1535 English statesman and author — more at TOPIC] **1 :** a place (as a region, island, country, or locality) that is imaginary and indefinitely remote **2** *often cap* **:** a place, state, or condition of ideal perfection esp. in laws, government, and social conditions ⟨that workers' ~ . . . in which there are more jobs than men seeking them —S.E.Harris⟩ — often used without article ⟨many were persuaded that independence would usher in ~ —A.E.Stevenson b. 1900⟩ **3 :** an impractical and usu. impossibly ideal scheme esp. for social improvement **4 :** a romance or other work describing a utopia ⟨a ~ written for girls —Emory Holloway⟩

¹uto·pi·an \(ˈ)yüˈtōpēən\ *adj, often cap* [NL *utopianus*, fr. *Utopia*, Sir Thomas More's imaginary country + L *-anus* -an] **1 :** of, relating to, or having the characteristics of a utopia; *specif* **:** having impossibly ideal conditions (as in politics, economics, and social customs and organization) ⟨the dim ~ future —J.G.Colton⟩ ⟨a ~ commonwealth⟩ **2 :** proposing or advocating visionary and usu. impractically ideal schemes esp. for the perfection of social and political conditions ⟨~ idealists⟩ **3 :** involving or founded upon imaginary perfection **:** impossibly ideal **:** CHIMERICAL, VISIONARY ⟨those who react adversely to secrecy often propose ~ alternatives —R.A. Dahl⟩ ⟨branded as a ~ objective —M.K.Dziewanowski⟩ ⟨recognized the ~ nature of his hopes —C.S.Kilby⟩ **4 :** believing in, advocating, or having the characteristics of utopian socialism ⟨~ socialists⟩ ⟨~ doctrines⟩

²utopian \≈ˈ≈≈≈\ *n* -s *sometimes cap* **1 :** a native or inhabitant of a utopia **2 a :** one that believes in the perfectibility of human society **:** IDEALIST, VISIONARY ⟨a consistent ~, expecting the future to realize her hopes —Van Wyck Brooks⟩ **b :** one that proposes or advocates plans usu. of an impractical kind for social improvement and esp. toward ideal social and political conditions ⟨the attempts of ~*s* to impose an impossible social order —N.S.Timasheff⟩ **c :** one that believes in or advocates utopian socialism

uto·pi·an·ism \-ēə,nizəm\ *n* -s **1 :** a utopian idea or theory ⟨mixes a good deal of hard sense with some curious ~*s* —*New Republic*⟩ **2** *often cap* **:** the body of ideas, views, or aims of a utopian **:** impracticable and usu. impossibly ideal schemes of human perfection or social improvement ⟨the somewhat impractical ~ . . . naturally found among socialists —Woodrow Wyatt⟩

uto·pi·an·ist \-,nəst\ *n* -s *often cap* [¹*utopian* + *-ist*] **:** UTOPIAN 2

uto·pi·an·ize \-ēə,nīz\ *vt* -ED/-ING/-S *sometimes cap* **:** to render utopian **:** make a utopia of ⟨~ society⟩

utopian socialism *n, sometimes cap U&S* **:** socialism based on a belief that elimination of unemployment and the attainment of economic security by means of social ownership of the means of production could be achieved by a voluntary and peaceful surrender of their holdings by propertied groups — compare MARXIAN SOCIALISM

uto·pism \'yüd·ə,pizəm\ *n* -s [*utopia* + *-ism*] : UTOPIANISM 2 ⟨unrealistic ~ . . . dominated Italian ideals in the nineteenth and twentieth centuries —R.A.Hall b. 1911⟩

uto·pist \-,pəst\ *n* -s [*utopia* + *-ist*] : UTOPIAN ⟨that world directorate of which ~s dream —Elmer Davis⟩

uto·pis·tic \¦==¦pistik\ *adj* : having a utopian quality or character ⟨a ~ dream of a federated Italy —R.A.Hall b. 1911⟩ ⟨such idealistic ~ . . . self-righteousness —Violet Paget⟩

u trap *n, cap U* : a U-shaped running trap

utra·quism \'yü·trə,kwizəm\ *n* -s *usu cap* [*utraquist* + *-ism*] : the doctrines or practices of the Calixtins

utra·quist \-,kwəst\ *n* -s *usu cap* [NL *utraquista*, fr. L *utraque* (abl. sing. fem. of *uterque* each of two, both, fr. *uter* which of two + *-que* generalizing particle akin to L *-que* and) (in the ML phrase *sub utraque specie* under each kind) + *-ista* -ist — more at WHETHER, SESQUI-] : CALIXTIN

utrecht \'yü·,trekt\ *adj, usu cap* [fr. *Utrecht*, city of western Netherlands] : of or from the city of Utrecht, Netherlands : of the kind or style prevalent in Utrecht

utrecht velvet *n, usu cap U* : a velvet consisting primarily of cotton and mohair and used for upholstery ⟨two large armchairs upholstered in shabby *Utrecht velvet* —Dorothy M. Richardson⟩

utri·cle \'yü·trəkəl, -rēk-\ *n* -s [L *utriculus* small bag, dim. of *uter* leather bag] : any of various small pouches or saccate parts of an animal or plant body: as **a** (1) : an air cell of a fucoid seaweed (2) : one of the bladders of a bladderwort (3) : a saclike terminal branch of an alga of the genus *Codium* **b** (1) : the part of the membranous labyrinth of the ear into which the semicircular canals open — compare SACCULE (2) : UTRICULUS b **c** : a small one-celled usu. indehiscent one-seeded or few-seeded achene (as that of a goosefoot or amaranth) with thin membranous pericarp — see FRUIT illustration

utricul- *or* **utriculo-** *comb form* [L *utriculus* small bag] : utricle ⟨*utriculo*plastic⟩ ⟨*utriculo*plasty⟩ ⟨*utriculi*ferous⟩ : utricular and ⟨*utriculo*saccular⟩

[1]**utric·u·lar** \(')yü·¦trikyələ(r)\ *adj* [L *utriculus* small bag + E *-ar*] **1 a** : of or relating to a utricle **b** : containing one or more utricles **2** : resembling a utricle — used esp. of such substances as sulfur and selenium when condensed from vapor and deposited on cold bodies in small globules filled with liquid

[2]**utricular** \"\ *adj* [L *utriculus* (dim. of *uterus* womb) + E *-ar*] : UTERINE 3 ⟨~ glands⟩

utric·u·lar·ia \yü,trikyə'la(a)rēə\ *n* [NL, fr. L *utriculus* small bag + NL *-aria*] **1** *cap* : a large widely distributed genus of aquatic plants (family Lentibulariaceae) having saclike ascidia that serve as animal traps, floating stems with finely dissected leaves, and scapose often showy flowers with a very irregular spurred bilabiate corolla **2** -s : any plant of the genus *Utricularia*

utric·u·lar·i·a·ce·ae \=,==,la(a)rē'āsē,ē\ [NL, fr. *Utricularia* + *-aceae*] *syn of* LENTIBULARIACEAE

utric·u·lif·er·ous \(¦)yü·¦trikyə¦lif(ə)rəs\ *adj* [*utricul-* + *-iferous*] : bearing or producing utricles

utric·u·li·form \(')yü·¦trikyələ,fȯrm\ *adj* [ISV *utricul-* + *-iform*] **1** : resembling a utricle **2** : UTRICULOID

utric·u·loid \-yə,lȯid\ *adj* [*utricul-* + *-oid*] : resembling a bladder

utric·u·lo·saccular \yü·¦trikyə(,)lō+\ *adj* [*utricul-* + NL *sacculus* + E *-ar*] : of or relating to the utriculus and sacculus of the inner ear; *specif* : constituting a duct connecting the two

utric·u·lose \(')yü·¦trikyə,lōs\ *adj* [*utricul-* + *-ose*] : UTRICULOID

utric·u·lus \yü·'trikyələs\ *n, pl* **utricu·li** \-yə,lī\ [L, small bag; in sense b, partly fr. L *utriculus* small uterus — more at UTRICULAR] : UTRICLE: as **a** : the utricle of the ear **b** : a small blind pouch directed dorsally from the urethra into the prostate and regarded as a vestige of the fused lower ends of the Müllerian ducts and therefore the homologue in the male of the uterus and vagina in the female

ut·ru·bi \'ə·trə,bī\ *n* -s [L, in which of two places, fr. *uter* which of two + *ubi* where, in what place; fr. the wording of the interdict — more at WHETHER, UBIQUITY] : an interdict in Roman and civil law for deciding the right of possession of movables and preserving things in statu quo pending the decision — compare UTI POSSIDETIS

uts *pl of* UT

UTS *abbr* ultimate tensile strength

[1]**ut·ter** \'əd·ə(r), 'ətə-\ *adj* [ME, fr. OE *ūtera ūterra* outer, compar. adj. fr. *ūt* out, adv. — more at OUT] **1** : situated on the outside or extreme limit : remote and often most remote from the center ⟨through ~ and through middle darkness borne —John Milton⟩ **2** : carried to the utmost point or highest degree : ABSOLUTE, COMPLETE, ENTIRE, TOTAL ⟨a scene of ~ destruction —F.D.Roosevelt⟩ ⟨the ~ clarity of these winter dawns —Florence Jaques⟩ ⟨an ~ impossibility⟩ ⟨~ strangers⟩ **3** : extreme to the point of strangeness or abnormality : UNUSUAL

[2]**utter** \"\ *vb* -ED/-ING/-S [ME *uttren*, fr. *utter* outside, adv., fr. OE *ūtor*, compar. of *ūt* out] *vt* **1** : to place on the market : offer for sale or barter : dispose of in trade : SELL, VEND **2 a** : to send forth as a sound : give out in an audible voice : give vent or expression to : burst out with ⟨the meadowlark ~*ed* her strong but tender note —John Burroughs⟩ ⟨~*ed* a contemptuous laugh —Zane Grey⟩ ⟨~*ed* a wolf whistle —F.V.W.Mason⟩ **b** : to give utterance to : PRONOUNCE, SAY, SPEAK ⟨beyond all the words she could ~ —William Black⟩ ⟨if I could ~ his name on this occasion —Edmund Burke⟩ **c** : to give public expression to : express, describe, or report in words : speak of or about ⟨would ~ opinions on all passing affairs —R.W.Emerson⟩ ⟨visions of splendor which it is not lawful to ~ —W.L.Sullivan⟩ ⟨if one had to ~ any criticism of her book —Sean O'Faolain⟩ **3** *obs* : to make known or manifest (something unknown, secret, or hidden) : DISCLOSE, DIVULGE, REVEAL ⟨his tongue and pen ~*ed* heavenly mysteries —Izaak Walton⟩ **4** : to put (as notes or currency) into circulation; *specif* : to circulate (as a forged or counterfeit note) as if legal or genuine ⟨having possession of 745 counterfeit sovereigns, with intent to ~ them —*Numismatist*⟩ **5** : to put forth or out : pour, thrust, or shoot out : DISCHARGE, EJECT, EMIT, EXHALE ⟨fountains that ~*ed glittering* streams of water⟩ **6** : to express (oneself) in words ⟨meant . . . to ~ himself upon that theme —Nathaniel Hawthorne⟩ ~ *vi* **1** : to exercise the faculty of speech : make a statement or sound : SPEAK, TALK ⟨give me the liberty to know, to ~, and to argue freely —John Milton⟩ ⟨the parrot would never ~ —Osbert Sitwell⟩ **2** : to undergo utterance : become spoken ⟨words that will not ~ —James Hamilton⟩ **syn** see EXPRESS

ut·ter·able \-ərəbəl-\ *adj* : capable of being uttered (as in words or statements)

[1]**ut·ter·ance** \'əd·ərən(t)s, 'ətər- *sometimes* 'ə·trən-\ *n* -s [ME *utteraunce, uttraunce*, modif. (influenced by [1]*utter*) of MF *outrance* — more at OUTRANCE] : an extreme degree : the last extremity : BITTER END ⟨come, Fate, . . . champion me to th' ~ —Shak.⟩

[2]**utterance** \"\ *n* -s [ME, fr. *utteren* to utter + *-ance*] **1** *obs* : the sale or disposal (as of goods or commodities) to the public **2** : something that is uttered: **a** : an oral or written statement : a stated or published expression : an articulated sound ⟨seditious oral ~*s* —J.L.O'Brian⟩ ⟨delivers some gemlike ~*s* —Anthony Quinton⟩ ⟨the speech will rank as one of his greater ~*s* —*Manchester Guardian Weekly*⟩ **b** : a continuous stretch of speech activity esp. when regarded as grammatically independent of preceding and following stretches whether by the same or another speaker ⟨a sequence of ~*s* by the same speaker is often called a discourse⟩ **3** : the action of uttering with the voice : vocal expression : ARTICULATION, SPEECH ⟨at length gave ~ to these words —John Milton⟩ ⟨gave ~ to a yell —Rachel Henning⟩ **4 a** : the faculty or power of speech ⟨one who had no gift of ~ —John Buchan⟩ **b** : the style or manner of speaking ⟨a model . . . of beautiful English ~ —George Sampson⟩ ⟨a tall thin man with . . . a sententious ~ —Donn Byrne⟩

utter barrister *n* : a barrister of the outer bar — compare BENCHER b

ut·ter·er \'əd·ərə(r), 'ətər-\ *n* -s : one that utters ⟨~*s* of unknown tongues —H.H.Johnston⟩ ⟨the ~ of a bad note was put to death —Charles Dickens⟩

ut·ter·less \'==ləs\ *adj* [[2]*utter* + *-less*] : incapable of being uttered ⟨pangs of ~ desire —Christina Rossetti⟩ ⟨~ dishonor⟩

ut·ter·ly *adv* [ME, fr. [1]*utter* + *-ly*] : in an utter manner : to an absolute or extreme degree : to the full extent : ABSOLUTELY, ALTOGETHER, ENTIRELY, FULLY, THOROUGHLY, TOTALLY ⟨Congress defeated ~ the administration civil rights program —T.K.Finletter⟩ ⟨this whole harmony . . . is ~ destroyed —P.E.James⟩ ⟨an ~ fantastic notion⟩

[1]**ut·ter·most** \'əd·ə(r),mōst, 'ətə- *also chiefly Brit* -,məst\ *adj* [ME, alter. (influenced by *most*) of *uttermest*, fr. [1]*utter* + *-mest* (as in *utmest* utmost)] **1** : farthest out : most remote : OUTERMOST ⟨to the ~ parts of the earth —Kemp Malone⟩ ⟨from the extreme west to the ~ east —Douglas Carruthers⟩ **2** : being in the farthest, greatest, or highest degree : EXTREME, UTMOST 2 ⟨she had the ~ confidence in the rogue —O.S.J.Gogarty⟩ ⟨reach the ~ peak of position —Irving Stone⟩ ⟨in the ~ distress⟩ **3** *archaic* : LAST — used chiefly in the phrase *the uttermost farthing*

[2]**uttermost** \"\ *n* [ME, fr. [1]*uttermost*] : UTMOST ⟨done her ~ to encourage him —Edith Sitwell⟩ ⟨to the ~ of our capacity —H.S.Truman⟩

ut·ter·ness *n* -ES : the quality or state of being utter : ABSOLUTENESS, COMPLETENESS

utu \'ü,tü\ *n* -s [Maori] : satisfaction for injuries received (as by retaliation in kind or by payment) in Maori law and custom

u-tube \'=,=\ *n, cap U* : a U-shaped tube

u-turn \'=,=\ *n, cap U* **1** : a turn resembling the letter U; *specif* : one made by a vehicle traveling along one side of a way by crossing the lane of oncoming traffic and turning into and proceeding along a lane on the other side of the way in a direction exactly opposite to the direction of movement at the start of the turn **2** : something held to resemble a U-turn (as a reversal of policy) ⟨stated that the Administration is making an economic *U-turn* —T.R. Ybarra⟩

U-tube

UV *abbr* **1** ultraviolet **2** under voltage

uva \'yüvə\ *n, pl* **uvas** \-əz\ *or* **uvae** \-,vē\ [NL, fr. L, grape, bunch of grapes — more at UVULA] : a pulpy indehiscent fruit (as a grape) with a central placenta

uva grass \'üvə-\ *n* [AmerSp, fr. Tupi *ubá, ubiá*] : an ornamental tropical American grass (*Gynerium sagittatum*) reaching a height of 30 feet or more and having huge pale tan or cream-colored panicles resembling plumes — called also *cana brava*

uva·la \'üvələ\ *n* -s [Serbo-Croatian] : a large elongate sinkhole resulting from enlargement and coalescence of a linear group of small sinkholes

u-valley \'=,==\ *n, cap U* : a valley of U-shaped cross section such as results from erosion by a valley glacier

uvan·ite \'yüvə,nīt\ *n* -s [*u*ranium + *van*adium + *-ite*] : a hydrous uranium vanadate $U_2V_6O_{21}.15H_2O$ occurring as a brownish yellow powder

uva·rov·ite *also* **uwa·rowite** *or* **ouva·rovite** \ü'vārə,vīt, yü-\ *n* -s [G *uwarowit*, fr. Count Sergei S. *Uvarov* †1855 Russ. statesman + G *-it* -ite] : an emerald green calcium-chromium garnet $Ca_3Cr_2(SiO_4)_3$

[1]**uva-ur·si** \¦yüvə'ərsē\ [NL, fr. *uva ursi* bearberry] *syn of* ARCTOSTAPHYLOS

[2]**uva-ursi** \"\ *n* -s [NL *uva ursi*, lit. bear's grape] : BEARBERRY

[1]**uvea** \'yüvēə\ *n* -s [ML, fr. L *uva* grape, bunch of grapes — more at UVULA] **1** : the posterior pigmented layer of the iris of the eye **2** : the portion of the eye composed of the iris and ciliary body together with the choroid coat

[2]**uvea** \ü'vāə\ *n* -s *usu cap* [fr. *Uvea*, main island of Wallis islands] : the Polynesian language of the Wallis islands

uve·al \'yüvēəl\ *adj* [[1]*uvea* + *-al*] : of, relating to, or affecting the uvea : constituting or consisting of the uvea ⟨~ layer⟩ ⟨~ tract⟩

[1]**uve·an** \ü'vāən\ *adj, usu cap* [*Uvea*, main island of the Wallis islands + E *-an*] **1** : of or relating to Uvea Island **2** : of or relating to the people of Uvea Island **3** : of or relating to Uvea

[2]**uvean** \"\ *n* -s *usu cap* **1** : a Polynesian of Uvea Island **2** : [2]UVEA

uve·i·tis \,yüvē'īd·əs\ *n* -ES [NL, fr. [1]*uvea* + *-itis*] : inflammation of the uvea of the eye

uveo·parotid fever \'yüvē(,)ō+. . .-\ *n* [[1]*uvea* + *-o-* + *parotid*] : chronic inflammation of the parotid gland and uvea marked by low-grade fever, lassitude, and bilateral iridocyclitis and often associated with sarcoidosis or other conditions

uveo·parotitis \"+\ *n* -ES [NL, fr. [1]*uvea* + *parotis* + *-itis*] : UVEOPAROTID FEVER

uveous *adj* [[1]*uvea* + *-ous*] *obs* : UVEAL

uvi·ol glass \'yüvē,ōl-, -,ȯl-\ *n* [fr. *Uviol*, a trademark] : a glass particularly transparent to ultraviolet rays

uvit·ic acid \(')yü¦vid·ik-\ *n* [L *uva* grape + ISV *-itic*: fr. its being producible from tartaric acid] : a crystalline acid $CH_3C_6H_3(COOH)_2$ obtained esp. by partial oxidation of mesitylene; 5-methyl-isophthalic acid

uvi·ton·ic acid \¦yüvə¦tänik-\ *n* [*uvit-* (as in *uvitic*) + *-onic*] : a crystalline acid $CH_3C_5H_2N(COOH)_2$ obtained by the action of ammonia on pyruvic acid; 6-methyl-2, 4-pyridine-dicarboxylic acid

uvu·la \'yüvyələ\ *n, pl* **uvulas** \-ləz\ *or* **uvu·lae** \-yə,lē\ [ML, dim. of L *uva* grape, bunch of grapes, uvula; akin to Gk *oa* (Ionic *oiē*) service tree, OE *īw* yew — more at YEW] **1** : the pendent fleshy lobe in the middle of the posterior border of the soft palate **2** : an elevation of the mucous membrane lining the lower anterior part of the bladder **3** : a lobe of the vermiform process of the lower surface of the cerebellum located in front of the pyramid

[1]**uvu·lar** \-lə(r)\ *adj* [NL *uvularis*, fr. ML *uvula* + L *-aris* -ar] : of or relating to the uvula ⟨~ glands⟩; *specif* : produced with the aid of the uvula — **uvu·lar·ly** *adv*

[2]**uvular** \"\ *n* -s : a uvular sound

uvu·lar·ia \,yüvyə'la(a)rēə\ *n* [NL, fr. *uvula* + *-aria*] **1** *cap* : a genus of No. American herbs (family Liliaceae) having erect stems, sessile or perfoliate leaves, and yellowish drooping bell-shaped flowers **2** -s : any plant of the genus *Uvularia*

uvular r *n* : a sound formed by trilling the uvula against the back of the tongue or by friction of the breath between the back of the tongue and the uvula or the velum

UW *abbr* underwriter

uwarowite *var of* UVAROVITE

ux *abbr* [L *uxor*] wife

UXB *abbr* unexploded bomb

ux·o·ri·al \,ək¦s¦ōrēəl, ¦əg¦z¦, ¦ȯr-\ *adj* [L *uxorius* uxorial + E *-al* — more at UXORIOUS] : of, relating to, or having the characteristics of a wife

[1]**ux·or·i·cide** \,ək'sōrə,sīd, ,əg'z¦, ¦ȯr-\ *n* -s [ML *uxoricidium*, fr. L *uxor* wife + *-i-* + *-cidium* -cide (killing) — more at UXORIOUS] : the murder of a wife by her husband

[2]**uxoricide** \"\ *n* -s [L *uxor* + *-i-* + E *-cide* (killer)] : one that murders his wife

ux·ori·local \,ək¦sōrə+\ *adj* [L *uxor* + *-i-* + E *local*] : MATRILOCAL ⟨the Yao are matrilineal and predominantly ~ —*African Abstracts*⟩ — contrasted with *virilocal*

ux·o·ri·ous \,ək¦sōrēəs, ¦əg¦z¦, ¦ȯr-\ *adj* [L *uxorius* uxorial, uxorious, fr. *uxor* wife; prob. akin to Skt *ukṣati* he sprinkles — more at HUMOR] : characterized by doting and usu. excessive fondness for and often submission to a wife ⟨an ~ husband⟩

ux·o·ri·ous·ly *adv* : in an uxorious manner : to an uxorious degree

ux·o·ri·ous·ness *n* -ES : the quality or state of being uxorious ⟨a prince whose manhood was . . . molten down in mere ~ —Alfred Tennyson⟩

uza·ra root \ü'zärə-\ *or* **u·sa·ra root** \ü'särə-\ *n* [origin unknown] : the root of a So. African woody herb (*Dicoma anomala*) of the family Compositae that yields uzarin and that is dried and used by the natives as a masticatory for dysentery

uzar·i·gen·in \ü,zärə'jenən\ *n* -s [*uzarin* + *-genin*] : a crystalline steroid lactone $C_{23}H_{34}O_4$ that is the aglucon of uzarin and is structurally similar to digitoxigenin

uza·rin \ü'zärən\ *n* -s [ISV *uzara* + *-in*] : a crystalline glucoside $C_{35}H_{54}O_{14}$ that constitutes the active principle of uzara root and is used as an arrow poison by some southeast African peoples

uz·bek \'üz,bek, 'əz-\ *or* **uz·beg** \-eg\ *also* **uz·bak** \-bak\ *or* **us·bek** \'üs,bek, 'əs-\ *or* **us·beg** \-eg\ *n, pl* **uzbek** *or* **uzbeks** *or* **uzbeg** *or* **uzbegs** *usu cap* **1 a** : a Turkic people of Turkistan and esp. of the Uzbek Republic of the U.S.S.R. that are Sunnite Muslims and are characterized chiefly by agricultural pursuits and life in towns rather than being nomads **b** : a member of such people **2** : the Turkic language of the Uzbek people

¹v \'vē\ *n, pl* **v's** *or* **vs** \'vēz\ *often cap, often attrib* **1 a :** the 22d letter of the English alphabet **b :** an instance of this letter printed, written, or otherwise represented **c :** a speech counterpart of orthographic *v* (as *v* in *vivid, hive,* or Spanish *vivo*) **2 :** FIVE — see NUMBER table **3 :** a printer's type, a stamp, or some other instrument for reproducing the letter *v* **4 :** someone or something arbitrarily or conveniently designated *v* esp. as the 21st or when j is used for the 10th the 22d in order or class **5 :** something having the shape of the letter V: as **a :** a V-shaped neck of a dress, sweater, or blouse **b :** a rib, guiding strip, or groove having sloping sides like a V ⟨the *V's* on the bed of a turning lathe on which the carriage slides⟩

²v *abbr, often cap* **1** vacuum tube **2** vagabond **3** value **4** valve **5** van **6** vapor **7** variable; variation **8** vector **9** vein **10** velocity **11** venerable **12** vent **13** ventilator **14** ventral **15** Ventzke **16** verb **17** verse **18** versicle **19** version **20** verso **21** versus **22** [L *verte*] turn over **23** vertex **24** vertical **25** very **26** vicar **27** vice **28** vicinal **29** victory **30** [L] vide **31** village **32** violin **33** virgin **34** viscosity **35** viscount **36** visibility **37** vision **38** visual acuity **39** vocative **40** voice **41** volt; voltage **42** [It *volti*] turn **43** voltmeter **44** volume **45** volunteer **46** von **47** vowel

³v *symbol, cap* **1** vanadium **2** potential difference

va *abbr* **1** variance **2** viola

VA *abbr* **1** *often not cap* verb active **2** *often not cap* verbal adjective **3** vicar apostolic **4** vice admiral **5** visual aid **6** [L *vixit annas*] he (she) lived . . . years. **7** *often not cap* volt-ampere

va·ad \'vä,äd, ˌ=ˈ=\ *n, pl* **vaa·dim** \ˌvä,äˈdēm, ˈ=,=,=\ [LHeb *waʿad*] **:** an authorized Jewish representative body that serves in an advisory or supervisory capacity for activities (as the production and sale of kosher food products) of the Jewish community

vaal \'väl\ *n* -s [Afrik, lit., fallow, fr. MD *vale*; akin to OHG *falo* pale, fallow — more at FALLOW] **:** RHEBOK

vaal·haai \'väl,hī\ *n* -s [Afrik, fr. *Vaal*, river in So. Africa + Afrik *haai* shark, fr. D] *southern Africa* **:** TOPE

vac \'vak\ *n* -s [by shortening] *Brit* **:** VACATION 3c

vac *abbr* **1** vacant **2** vacation **3** vacuum

va·cance \'vākən(t)s\ *n* -s [MF, fr. ML *vacantia*] *Scot* **:** VACATION

va·can·cy \'vākənsē, -si\ *n* -ES [ML *vacantia*, fr. L *vacant-, vacans* (pres. part. of *vacare* to be empty, be free) + *-ia* -y] **1** *archaic* **:** time of freedom from occupation **:** an interval of leisure **:** LEISURE, VACATION ⟨those little *vacancies* from toil are sweet —John Dryden⟩ **2 :** the state or fact of being free from occupation or from mental preoccupation **:** physical or mental inactivity or relaxation **:** IDLENESS **3 a :** a vacating of an office, post, or piece of property **b :** the state of such when vacated or vacant **c :** the time such office or property is vacant ⟨the death of the incumbent has caused a ~⟩ ⟨in case of ~ of the property⟩ **4 :** a vacant office, post, or tenancy ⟨three *vacancies* in this apartment house⟩ ⟨the president shall have power to fill up all *vacancies* that may happen during the recess of the senate —*U. S. Constitution*⟩ **5 :** empty space **:** VOID, VACUUM, BLANK **6 :** the state of being vacant **:** BARRENNESS, LONELINESS, VACUITY ⟨a ~ of sound after the train had left —J.P.Marquand⟩ **7 :** a defect existing in a crystal due to the absence of an atom or ion from a normal lattice position — called also *hole*

vacancy clause *or* **vacancy permit** *n* **:** a special endorsement in property insurance permitting premises to be vacant or unoccupied beyond the period stipulated in the original contract and insured during the extension period either for the full or a reduced amount

va·cant \'vākənt\ *adj* [ME, fr. OF, fr. L *vacant-, vacans*, pres. part. of *vacare* to be empty, be free; perh. akin to L *vanus* empty, vain — more at WANE] **1 :** not filled or occupied by an incumbent, possessor, or officer ⟨appointed to the ~ office⟩ **2 :** being without content or occupant ⟨a ~ seat in a bus⟩ ⟨a ~ room⟩ **3 :** DEVOID, DESTITUTE — usu. used with *of* ⟨the past, the future, majesty, love . . . you are ~ of them —Walt Whitman⟩ **4 :** free from activity ⟨amid the stillness of the ~ night —William Cowper⟩ **:** free from work or occupation **:** UNOCCUPIED ⟨obliged to spend his ~ hours in a comfortless hotel —Jane Austen⟩ **5 :** characterized by absence of thought and reflection: as **a :** STUPID, FOOLISH, SILLY, DULL **b :** EXPRESSIONLESS ⟨she would forget altogether what she was about, and would sit down with a peculiarly ~ look on her face —O. E.Rölvaag⟩ ⟨~ serenity of a . . . marble athlete —Edith Wharton⟩ **c :** marked by a respite from coherent purposive thought and reflection or by freedom from care ⟨when on my couch I lie in ~ or in pensive mood —William Wordsworth⟩ **6 :** of, relating to, or being premises which are not lived in and from which the furniture and fixtures have been removed — compare UNOCCUPIED b **7 a :** not occupied or put to use ⟨~ land⟩ **b :** having no heir or claimant **:** ABANDONED ⟨a ~ estate⟩ **c :** not granted away — used esp. of state lands **syn** see EMPTY

va·can·tia \vāˈkanshēə\ *or* **vacantia bo·na** \-ˈbōnə\ *n pl but sing or pl in constr* [*vacantia* short for *vacantia bona*; *vacantia bona* fr. NL, lit., vacant goods] **:** goods without an owner or claimant; *specif* **:** the inheritance of a deceased person when there is no one able and willing to enter

va·cant·ly *adv* **:** in a vacant manner **:** IDLY, INANELY

va·cant·ness *n* -ES **:** the quality or state of being vacant

va·cat·able *pronunc at* VACATE + əbəl\ *adj* **:** that can be vacated

va·cate \'vā,kāt, =ˈ=, *usu* -kād.+V; *chiefly Brit* vəˈk-\ *vb* -ED/-ING/-S [L *vacatus*, past part. of *vacare* to be empty, be free] *vt* **1 :** to make of no authority or validity **:** make void **:** ANNUL ⟨~ a charter⟩ **2 :** to make useless, ineffectual, or without force or significance ⟨he ~*s* my revenge —John Dryden⟩ **3 :** to make vacant (as an office, post, or house) **:** deprive of an incumbent or occupant; *also* **:** to give up the incumbency or occupancy of ⟨the throne was *vacated* by the exile of the royal family⟩ ⟨*vacated* his seat in Congress by resignation⟩ **4 :** to make free (as from care) ⟨its problems, indeed, *vacated* my mind of her —Edgar Saltus⟩ ~ *vi* **1 :** to vacate an office, post, or tenancy **2 :** to give one's time **:** devote oneself **3** *slang* **a :** to go away **:** LEAVE **b :** to take a vacation

¹va·ca·tion \vāˈkāshən, vəˈk-\ *n* -S *often attrib* [ME *vacacioun*, fr. MF *vacation*, fr. L *vacation-, vacatio* freedom, exemption, immunity, fr. *vacatus* (past part. of *vacare*) + *-ion-, -io* -ion — more at VACANT] **1 :** a respite or a time of respite from something **:** INTERMISSION, REST ⟨on a ~ from acting on the screen, she appeared as a singing and dancing star in . . . vaudeville —*Current Biog.*⟩ **2** *obs* **a :** freedom from work or cares **:** LEISURE **b :** time free for something else; *specif* **:** time for contemplation **3 a :** a scheduled period during which activity or work is suspended **:** RECESS **b :** a period of exemption from work granted to each employee of an industry or business **:** a leave of absence for rest and relaxation ⟨students hired to fill in for workers on ~⟩ ⟨allowed to take two weeks of ~ with pay annually⟩ **c :** an intermission in the regular teaching and studying at an educational institution (as between terms) **d :** intermission of judicial proceedings **:** the interval between the end of one term and the beginning of the next **:** NONTERM, RECESS **4 :** a period spent away from home or business in travel or recreation **:** HOLIDAYS ⟨had a restful ~ at the beach⟩ **5 :** an act or an instance of vacating (as an office, post, or house) ⟨the chief of staff, while holding office as such, shall have the grade of general, without ~ of his permanent grade in the Air Force —*U.S. Code*⟩ **6 :** the act of vacating an order or legal proceeding **:** ANNULMENT

²vacation \"\ *vi* **vacationed; vacationed; vacationing** \-sh(ə)niŋ\ **vacations :** to take a vacation **:** pass one's vacation ⟨~*ed* in Europe last summer⟩

vacation church school *or* **vacation bible school** *n, usu cap V&C&B&S* **:** a weekday program of Christian education for children featuring religious study courses, arts and crafts, and recreation conducted by local Protestant Christian churches for one or more weeks during the summer vacation — called also *Daily Vacation Bible School*

va·ca·tion·er \-sh(ə)nə(r)\ *n* -S **:** VACATIONIST

va·ca·tion·ist \-nəst\ *n* -S **:** a person taking a vacation; *esp* **:** one traveling for pleasure or passing a vacation at a summer resort

vacationland \=ˈ==,=\ *n* **:** an area with recreational attractions and facilities for vacationists

va·ca·tion·less \-.ləs\ *adj* **:** having no vacation

va·ca·tur \vāˈkād.ə(r\ *n* -S [NL, it is vacated, 3d pers. pres. indic. pass. of *vacare* to be empty] **:** an order of court vacating a legal proceeding

vac·car·ia \vaˈka(a)rēə\ *n, cap* [NL, fr. ML, cow pasture; fr. its value as fodder] *in some classifications* **:** a small genus of Eurasian annual herbs (family Caryophyllaceae) having opposite acute leaves and rather small red or pink flowers in terminal cymes followed by 5-angled much inflated capsules and being usu. included in the genus *Saponaria*

vac·ca·ry \'vakərē\ *n* -ES [ME *vaccarie*, fr. ML *vaccaria*, fr. L *vacca* cow + *-aria* -ary — more at VACCINE] **:** a place where cows or cattle are kept **:** cow pasture **:** dairy farm

vac·cen·ic acid \(ˈ)vakˈsenik-\ *n* [L *vacca* cow + E *-en* (in *octadecenoic*) + *-ic*] **:** a crystalline unsaturated acid C_6H_{13}-$CH{=}CH(CH_2)_9COOH$ that is isomeric with elaidic acid and oleic acid and that is obtained esp. in the trans form from beef fat and other animal fats and in the cis form from bacterial fats; 11-octadecenoic acid

vac·ci·nal \'vaksənəl\ *adj* [ISV ²*vaccine* + *-al*; orig. formed in F] **:** of or relating to vaccine or vaccination ⟨~ control of a disease⟩

¹vac·ci·nate \'vaksə,nā|t, *usu* |d.+V\ *vb* -ED/-ING/-S [back-formation fr. *vaccination*] *vt* **1 :** to inoculate (a person) with cowpox virus in order to produce immunity to smallpox **2 :** to administer a vaccine to (a person or animal) usu. by injection ~ *vi* **:** to perform or practice vaccination

²vac·ci·nate \", -nə̇t\ *n* -S [²*vaccine* + *-ate*] **:** a vaccinated individual

vac·ci·na·tion \ˌ==ˈnāshən\ *n* -S [F, fr. *vaccine*, adj. (fr. NL *vaccinus*) + *-ation*] **:** the introduction into man or domestic animals of microorganisms that have previously been treated to make them harmless for the purpose of inducing the development of immunity ⟨oral ~⟩ ⟨~ against smallpox⟩ ⟨~ for whooping cough⟩

vac·ci·na·tor \'==,nād.ə(r), -ātə-\ *n* -S [ISV *vaccine* + *-ator*] **:** one that vaccinates

¹vac·cine \(ˈ)vakˈsēn *sometimes* ˈvaksən\ *adj* [L *vaccinus* of or from cows, fr. *vacca* cow + *-inus* -ine; akin to Skt *vaśa* cow] **1 :** of, relating to, or derived from cows; *esp* **:** derived from cows infected with cowpox or inoculated with its virus ⟨~ lymph⟩ **2** [NL *vaccinus*, fr. L] **:** of or relating to vaccinia or vaccination ⟨a ~ pustule⟩

²vaccine \"\ *n* -S **1 :** matter or a preparation containing the virus of cowpox or vaccinia in a form used for vaccination **2 :** a preparation of killed microorganisms, living attenuated organisms, or living fully virulent organisms that is administered to produce or artificially increase immunity to a particular disease — compare ANTIGEN, SERUM

vac·cin·ia \vakˈsinēə\ *n* -S *often attrib* [NL, fr. *vaccinus* + *-ia*] **:** COWPOX; *esp* **:** the mild systemic reaction of a human being to cowpox virus constituting the take that signals immunization following vaccination against smallpox

vac·cin·i·a·ce·ae \(ˌ)vak,sinēˈāsē,ē\ *n pl, cap* [NL, fr. *Vaccinium* + *-aceae*] *in some classifications* **:** a family of widely distributed shrubs and trees (order Ericales) including among its genera *Vaccinium, Gaylussacia,* and *Oxycoccus*, comprising the huckleberries, blueberries, and cranberries, and set off from the Ericaceae chiefly on the basis of the inferior ovary which forms in fruit a many-seeded berry or drupe — **vac·cin·i·a·ceous** \(ˌ)ˌ==ˈāshəs\ *adj*

vac·cin·i·al \(ˈ)vakˈsinēəl\ *adj* **:** of, relating to, or characteristic of vaccinia

vac·cin·iform \(ˈ)vakˈsinə,fȯrm\ *adj* **:** resembling vaccinia

vac·cin·i·um \vakˈsinēəm\ *n* [NL, fr. L, blueberry, whortleberry, prob. of non-IE origin; akin to the source of Gk *hyakinthos* hyacinth] **1** *cap* **:** a large widely distributed genus of shrubs (family Ericaceae) including the blueberries and cranberries and distinguished by the 4- to 5-celled ovary and the usu. many-seeded baccate fruit — compare OXYCOCCUS **2** -S **:** any plant of the genus *Vaccinium*

vac·ci·noid \'vaksə,nȯid\ *adj* [ISV *vaccin-* (fr. NL *vaccinia*) + *-oid*] **:** VACCINIFORM

va·chette clasp \(ˈ)vaˈshet-\ *n* [*vachette* prob. fr. F, cowhide leather (used for ligatures), lit., small cow, fr. *vache* cow + *-ette*] **:** a piece of strong steel wire with the ends curved and pointed used on toe or quarter cracks of a horse's hoof to bind the edges together and facilitate healing

vac·il·lan·cy \'vasələnsē\ *n* -ES [L *vacillare* to sway, waver + E *-ancy*] **:** VACILLATION

vac·il·lant \-nt\ *adj* [L *vacillant-, vacillans*, pres. part. of *vacillare*] **:** VACILLATING

vac·il·late \'vasə,lāt, *usu* -ād.+V\ *vi* -ED/-ING/-S [L *vacillatus*, past part. of *vacillare* to sway, waver; akin to MIr *feccaid* he kneels, Skt *vañcati* he goes crooked — more at PREVARICATE] **1 a :** to sway through lack of equilibrium **:** WAVER, TOTTER **b** FLUCTUATE, OSCILLATE **2 :** to waver in mind, will, or feeling **:** hesitate in choice of opinions or courses **:** be variable in one's emotions or judgments ⟨faced this choice, *vacillated*, and plunged for one or other disagreeable alternative —Peter Wiles⟩ ⟨throughout the book the professor ~*s* between humility and arrogance —Therese Pol⟩ **syn** see HESITATE

vac·il·lat·ing·ly *adv* **:** in a vacillating manner

vac·il·la·tion \ˌ==ˈlāshən\ *n* -S [F, fr. L *vacillation-, vacillatio* action of swaying, fr. *vacillatus* (past part.) + *-ion-, -io* -ion] **1 :** an act or instance of vacillating (as in conduct, purpose, policy) **:** WAVERING **2 :** the quality or state of one that vacillates **:** inability to take a stand **:** IRRESOLUTION, CHANGEABLENESS, INDECISION

vac·il·la·tor \'==,lād.ə(r)\ *n* -S **:** one that vacillates

vac·il·la·to·ry \'==.lə,tōrē, -tȯrē, -ri\ *adj* **:** manifesting vacillation

va·coa \vəˈkōə\ *n* -S [native name in Mauritius] **:** a screw pine (*Pandanus utilis*)

vac·re·a·tion \ˌvakrēˈāshən\ *n* -S **:** the act or process of using a Vacreator machine

Vac·re·a·tor \'==,ād.ə(r)\ *trademark* — used for a machine by means of which dairy fats are pasteurized by a vacuum process

vacua *pl of* VACUUM

vac·u·ate \'vakyə,wāt\ *vt* -ED/-ING/-S [L *vacuatus*, past part. of *vacuare* to empty, fr. *vacuus* empty] *archaic* **:** EVACUATE

vac·u·ist \-yəwəst\ *n* -S [NL *vacuista*, fr. L *vacuum* + *-ista* -ist] **:** one who maintains that there are vacuums in nature ⟨by 1660 learned men were lining up on two opposing sides, the ~*s* and the plenists —*Amer. Scientist*⟩ — compare PLENIST

va·cu·i·ty \vaˈkyüəd.ē, vəˈ-, -ətē, -i\ *n* -ES [L *vacuitas*, fr. *vacuus* empty + *-itas* -ity — more at VACUUM] **1 :** an empty space: as **a :** an unfilled cavity, interstice, or hollow within a body or substance **b :** an empty open space **:** VOID, GAP **c :** an extent devoid throughout of content, substance, or activity **:** a dull or monotonous stretch ⟨the long ~ of an arctic night⟩ ⟨smoking fills the *vacuities* of life —Bergen Evans⟩ **2 :** space wholly or approximately devoid of matter **:** VACUUM **3 :** the condition, fact, or quality of being empty or unfilled either physically or spiritually **:** VACANCY, EMPTINESS, HOLLOWNESS ⟨the ~ of the arteries after death⟩ ⟨the ~ of a desert⟩ **4 :** vacancy of mind **:** the state or fact of being temporarily or characteristically free of ideas, reflections, cares **:** mental emptiness or inactivity ⟨fatigued his mind into an agreeably grave ~ —Arnold Bennett⟩ ⟨a cunning gravity of manner concealing mere ~ —J.A.Froude⟩ **5 :** INANITY, BLANKNESS, VACUOUSNESS ⟨the ~ of his face⟩ **6 :** a vacuous or inane thing ⟨fill up a speech with *vacuities*⟩ **7 :** the quality or state of being completely free or devoid of something ⟨his lesser verse seems . . . full of empty conceits whose virtuosity and lavish display only emphasize their intellectual and emotional ~ —R.A.Hall b. 1911⟩ **8 :** NIHILITY, NOTHINGNESS

vac·u·o·lar \ˌvakyəˈwōlə(r), ˈvakyə(wə)l-\ *adj* [ISV *vacuole* + *-ar*] **:** of, relating to, or of the character of a vacuole

vacuolar membrane *n* **1 :** TONOPLAST **2 :** any differentiated layer surrounding a vacuole (as the osmophilic surface of a protozoan contractile vacuole)

vacuolar system *n* **:** the vacuole of the plant cell with all identifiable precursors and derivatives that constitute a fundamental system of organelles comparable to the plastids — compare VACUOME

¹vac·u·o·late \'vakyə(wə),lāt, ¦vakyəˈwōlət\ *or* **vac·u·o·lat·ed** \'vakyə(wə),lād.əd, -yə,wō,l-\ *adj* [*vacuole* + *-ate* or *-ate* + *-ed*] **:** containing one or more vacuoles

²vac·u·o·late \'vakyə(wə),lāt\ *vi* -ED/-ING/-S [*vacuole* + *-ate*, vb. suffix] **:** to form vacuoles

vac·u·o·la·tion \ˌ==(=)ˈlāshən\ *n* -S [*vacuole* + *-ation*] **:** the development or formation of vacuoles

vac·u·ole \'vakyə,wōl\ *n* -S [F, fr. lit., small vacuum, fr. L *vacuum* + F *-ole*] **1 :** a small space in the tissues of an organism containing air or fluid **2 :** a cavity in the cytoplasm of a cell that is bounded by a distinct membrane, that is characteristic of plant cells and protozoans but may occur in higher animals, that in higher plant cells occupies most of the space of the cell, contains cell sap, and is often interpreted as a droplet of fluid enclosed by a membrane rather than as a vacuity, and that in protozoans is one of the most prominent organelles, performs various digestive, excretory, hydrostatic, and secretory functions, and may be either a transitory or an essentially permanent part of the protoplast — see CONTRACTILE VACUOLE, FOOD VACUOLE, TONOPLAST; AMOEBA illustration, CELL illustration

vac·u·ol·iza·tion \ˌ=,=wōlәˈzāshən, -ˌlīˈz-\ *n* -S [*vacuole* + *-ization*] **:** VACUOLATION

vac·u·ome \'vakyə,wōm\ *n* -S [F, fr. *vacu-* (in *vacuole*) + *-ome*] **1 :** VACUOLAR SYSTEM **2 :** any of various substances or structures in plant or animal cells that resemble the vacuolar system in their staining with vital dyes (as neutral red): as **a :** GOLGI APPARATUS **b :** CHONDRIOME

vac·u·om·e·ter \ˌvakyəˈwämәd.ə(r)\ *n* [ISV *vacuum* + *-o-* + *-meter*] **:** an apparatus for measuring low pressures

vac·u·ous \'vakyəwəs\ *adj* [L *vacuus*] **1 :** emptied of or lacking content (as of air or gas) ⟨~ spaces⟩ **2 :** marked by or indicative of mental vacuity or lack of ideas or intelligence **:** lacking substance **:** thin in intellectual content **:** DULL, STUPID, INANE ⟨a ~ mind⟩ ⟨a ~ expression⟩ ⟨a ~ play⟩ **3 :** devoid of serious occupation **:** spent in inanities or frivolity **:** IDLE **4 :** containing no element, point, or member **:** NULL — used of a class in mathematics or logic **syn** see EMPTY

vac·u·ous·ly *adv* **:** in a vacuous manner

vac·u·ous·ness *n* -ES **:** the quality or state of being vacuous

¹vac·u·um \'vaky(əw)əm, -(ˌ)yüm\ *n, pl* **vacuums** \-mz\ *or* **vac·ua** \-yəwə\ [L, fr. neut. of *vacuus* empty; akin to L *vacare* to be empty — more at VACANT] **1 :** emptiness of space ⟨flames . . . mounting on high into ~, into nonentity —William Blake⟩ **2 a :** a space absolutely devoid of matter — opposed to *plenum* **b :** a space (as the interior of a closed vessel) partially exhausted (as to the highest degree possible) by an air pump or by any of various other artificial means ⟨a reaction carried out in ~⟩ **c :** a degree of rarefaction below atmospheric pressure **:** NEGATIVE PRESSURE ⟨a ~ of two millimeters of mercury⟩ ⟨pumps that pull too high a ~ for gages to measure⟩ ⟨spray milk under ~ into a pan⟩ **3 a :** an unfilled or empty space or extent **:** something devoid of content **:** VOID, GAP ⟨his death has left a ~ in their lives⟩ ⟨the music stopped and the voices rose into the ~ it left —Hamilton Basso⟩ **b :** a state of isolation from outside influences or factors ⟨people who live in a ~ . . . so that the world outside them is of no moment —W.S. Maugham⟩ **4 :** a device creating or utilizing a partial vacuum; *specif* **:** VACUUM CLEANER

²vacuum \"\ *adj* **1 :** of, relating to, or associated with a vacuum or vacuum system ⟨~ pressure⟩ ⟨~ controls⟩ ⟨~ hose⟩ **2 :** used in producing a vacuum ⟨~ equipment⟩ ⟨~ sealing grease⟩ **3 a** (1) **:** partly exhausted of air or gas **:** containing a vacuum ⟨a ~ cylinder⟩ ⟨a ~ oven⟩ (2) **:** made nonconducting by means of a vacuum; *esp* **:** being or containing a usu. glass vessel or casing with double walls enclosing a vacuum for temperature insulation (as of liquids) ⟨a ~ flask⟩ ⟨a ~ jug⟩ ⟨*vacuum*-jacketed apparatus⟩ ⟨a ~ pitcher⟩ **b :** carried on under partial vacuum or by means of suction ⟨~ distillation⟩ ⟨~ metallurgy⟩ ⟨~ spectroscopy⟩ ⟨~ filling of milk bottles⟩ **c :** being or used in a canning, bottling, or packaging process in which much of the air in the container is extracted before sealing for better preservation of contents ⟨~ canning⟩ ⟨a ~ jar⟩ **d :** mounted in a vacuum ⟨a ~ filament lamp⟩ ⟨~ contacts⟩ **4 :** being or incorporating a device producing a partial vacuum (as for drawing off or holding fast) ⟨a ~ dryer⟩ ⟨a ~ filter⟩ ⟨a ~ ash conveyer⟩ ⟨a ~ chuck for holding delicate materials on a lathe⟩ ⟨a ~ pad for hoisting concrete slabs⟩ ⟨~ impregnating apparatus⟩ **5 :** produced by a process utilizing a vacuum (as for evaporation) ⟨~ salt⟩

³vacuum \"\ *vb* -ED/-ING/-S *vt* **1 :** to use a vacuum device upon **2** *or* **vacuum-clean :** to clean or remove by means of a vacuum cleaner ⟨~ the rug⟩ ⟨~ the crumbs⟩ ~ *vi* **1 :** to operate a vacuum device (as a vacuum drier) **2** *or* **vacuum-clean** \'=(=)=ˌ=, '=(ˌ)=ˈ=\ **:** to clean a surface with a vacuum cleaner ⟨hired a woman to scrub, dust, and ~⟩

vacuum back *n* **:** a vacuum platen used in the focal plane of a camera to hold the film during exposure

vacuum booster *n* **:** a piston actuated by the vacuum of the intake manifold and attached to the brake pedal of an automotive vehicle to apply added pressure on the brake cylinder

vacuum bottle *n* **:** a cylindrical container having a usu. glass liner made on the principle of the Dewar vessel for keeping liquids either hot or cold for several hours

vacuum brake *n* **:** a brake using a partial vacuum in its operation; *specif* **:** an automobile brake in which the braking pressure applied by the operator is augmented by the negative pressure of the suction on the intake manifold

vacuum breaker *n* **:** a device admitting (as into a water supply line) air or other gas to vitiate a vacuum (as for preventing back siphonage)

vacuum cleaner *also* **vacuum sweeper** *n* **:** an electrical appliance for cleaning (as floors, carpets, tapestry, or upholstered work) by suction

vacuum coffee maker *n* **:** a coffee maker consisting of an upper bowl that holds ground coffee and a filtering device and is fitted by a tight seal into a lower bowl that holds water which on boiling rises into the upper bowl from which it is drawn through the coffee back into the lower bowl by the suction caused by the reduced pressure upon removal of the heat

vacuum coffee maker

vacuum concrete *n* **:** concrete that has had a vacuum applied through special mats, pads, or forms shortly after placement for the purpose of removing a portion of the mixing water not needed for the hydration of the cement

vacuum cup *n* **:** a hollow hemisphere (as of rubber) that can adhere to a smooth surface or agitate a fluid by suction **:** SUCTION CUP ⟨*vacuum cups* for hanging suits on car windows⟩

vacuum distillation *n* **:** distillation carried on under reduced pressure so that the liquid being distilled boils at a lower temperature than under atmospheric pressure and consequently with less chance of decomposition — compare MOLECULAR DISTILLATION

vacuum filter *n* **:** a filter in which the pressure on the outlet side of the filter medium is less than that of the atmosphere

vacuum frame *n* **:** a contact printing device using a vacuum to create a uniform pressure during exposure of a photographic film or paper

vacuum gauge *n* **:** a gauge indicating degree of negative pressure

vac·u·um·ize *pronunc at* VACUUM + ˌīz\ *vt* -ED/-ING/-S **1 :** to produce a vacuum in **2 :** to clean, dry, or pack by a vacuum mechanism or in a vacuum container

vacuum-packed *adj* **:** packed in a container that has much of the air removed before being hermetically sealed ⟨*vacuum-packed* coffee⟩

vacuum pan *n* **:** a tank with a vacuum pump and condenser for rapid evaporation and condensation (as of salt brine, sugar syrup, milk) by boiling at a low temperature ⟨vacuum pans . . . enable the sugar solution to boil at a low temperature, without burning —*Story of Cane Sugar*⟩

vacuum pump *n* **1 :** PULSOMETER **2 :** a pump for exhausting air or other gas from an enclosed space to a desired degree of vacuum

vacuum tank *n* **:** a tank which is used with some internal-combustion engines, into which the fuel (as gasoline) is sucked from the main tank, and from which it flows by gravity to the carburetor usu. directly below

vacuum tube *n* **:** an electron tube evacuated to a high degree of vacuum

vacuum–tube voltmeter *n* **:** a voltmeter employing vacuum tubes and useful because of its very high input impedence for measurements in circuits (as vacuum-tube circuits) from which only very small currents can be drawn without altering the voltages being measured

vacuum valve *n* **1 :** SAFETY VALVE 1b **2** *chiefly Brit* **:** VACUUM TUBE **3 :** a vacuum-tube rectifier

vacuum ventilation *n* **:** ventilation using an exhaust fan so that air is drawn in from outside

vacuum weight *n* **:** a weight equivalent to the one obtained by weighing a body in a vacuum but actually computed from ordinary weighing by vacuum correction using the known volume of body and weights and the known density of the air

VAD *abbr* voluntary aid detachment

vade *vi* -ED/-ING/-S [ME *vaden*, alter. (prob. influenced by L *vadere* to go) of *faden* to fade — more at WADE, FADE] *obs* **:** FADE

va·de me·cum \ˌvādēˈmēkəm, ˌväd-\ *n, pl* **vade mecums** [L, go with me] **1 :** a book for ready reference **:** HANDBOOK, MANUAL ⟨his first treatise . . . became a *vade mecum* for the local magistrates —V.L.Wilkinson⟩ **2 :** something regularly carried about by a person ⟨the small wooden bowl, the indispensable *vade mecum* of all Tartars —William Hazlitt †1893⟩

vades *pl of* VAS

vad·i·mo·ni·um \ˌvadəˈmōnēəm\ *n, pl* **vadimo·nia** \-ēə\ [L, fr. *vad-, vas* bail, pledge, security — more at WED] **:** any of several legal pledges or securities: as **a :** a contract of suretyship in Roman and civil law used in sales to secure the payment of the purchase price **b :** a bond or pledge in early English law for appearance before a judge on a certain day

vad·i·mo·ny \ˈ==ˌmōnē\ *n* -ES [L *vadimonium*] **:** VADIMONIUM b

vadium mortuum *n* [ML, lit., dead pledge] **:** MORTUUM VADIUM

va·di·um vi·vum \ˈwädēˌüm ˈwīˌwüm\ *n* [ML] **:** LIVING PLEDGE

va·dose \ˈvāˌdōs\ *adj* [L *vadosus* shallow, fr. *vadum*, n., shallow, ford + *-osus* -ose; akin to L *vadere* to go, walk — more at WADE] **:** of, relating to, or resulting from water or solutions in the part of the earth's crust that is above the permanent groundwater level ⟨~ circulation⟩ ⟨~ deposits⟩

vadose water *n* **:** groundwater suspended or in circulation above the water table

vaes·ite \ˈväˌsīt\ *n* -S [Johannes *Vaes*, 20th cent. Belgian mineralogist + E *-ite*] **:** a mineral NiS_2 consisting of sulfide of nickel and belonging to the pyrite group

¹vag \ˈvag, -aa(ə)g, -aig\ *n* -S [by shortening] **:** VAGRANT ⟨a society of homeless men . . . the *~s* and strays —J.J.Maloney⟩

²vag \"\ *vt* **vagged; vagged; vagging; vags :** to arrest as a vagrant ⟨have them all *vagged* . . . in a week —John Lardner⟩

vag- *or* **vago-** *comb form* [ISV, fr. NL *vagus*] **1 :** vagus nerve ⟨*vago*gram⟩ ⟨*vag*al⟩ ⟨*vago*lysis⟩ **2 :** vagal and ⟨*vago*accessorius⟩ ⟨*vago*glossopharyngeal⟩

¹vag·a·bond \ˈvagəˌbänd, ˈvaig-, *chiefly Brit* -ˌbənd\ *adj* [ME *vagabound*, fr. MF *vagabond*, fr. L *vagabundus*, fr. *vagari* to move about, wander — more at VAGARY] **1 :** moving from place to place without a fixed home **:** WANDERING, NOMADIC ⟨~ minstrels⟩ ⟨a ~ people⟩ **2 a :** of, relating to, or characteristic of a wanderer ⟨those ~ moods that visit husbands in April and November —Ellen Glasgow⟩ **b :** leading an unsettled, irresponsible, or disreputable life **:** WORTHLESS ⟨a thoroughly ~ outcast —Bret Harte⟩ **3 :** not having a fixed course **:** following an irregular or vagrant course ⟨runs ~ sailings out of Montreal —*N.Y.Times*⟩

²vagabond \"\ *n* -S [ME *vagabound*, fr. *vagabound*, adj., vagabond] **1 a :** one who wanders about from place to place ⟨a fugitive and a ~ shalt thou be in the earth —Gen 4:12 (AV)⟩ **b** (1) **:** one who wanders from place to place with no fixed dwelling or if he has one not abiding in it and who is without visible means of support (2) **:** one who is by statute declared a vagabond; *esp* **:** one other than a rogue accountable under British vagrancy statutes for specific offenses **c** (1) **:** an idle beggar **:** TRAMP (2) **:** an idle carefree roamer **2 :** an irresponsible, worthless, or disreputable person ⟨such a ~ of a husband —Hall Caine⟩ **3** *or* **vagabond green :** DUCK GREEN

syn VAGABOND, VAGRANT, TRUANT, TRAMP, HOBO, BUM, STIFF, SWAGMAN, and SUNDOWNER designate a person who wanders at will or habitually. VAGABOND usu. implies only a carefree fondness for a roaming life ⟨militiamen fleeing from Washington's army wandered like homeless *vagabonds* on all the roads —Kenneth Roberts⟩ VAGRANT implies disreputableness and in its common legal use applies to a person with no fixed or known residence who is likely to become a public menace or public charge ⟨by no means a *vagrant* but he was an itinerant: at the time of his arrest he peddled fish from a pushcart in the poorer sections of Boston —Phil Stong⟩ ⟨the depression had left a number of them indigent, without state or federal relief. Some had become *vagrants*, tramping the highways of South Texas, living in hobo jungles —Green Peyton⟩ TRUANT applies chiefly to pupils absent from school without permission or authorization ⟨played *truant* from their Dublin school —*London Calling*⟩ ⟨employers were now obliged . . . to discharge *truants* without notice; and one day of unjustified absence sufficed —S.M.Schwarz⟩ TRAMP is the ordinary, generally derogatory term for one who lives by wandering whether in search of transient work or engaged in beggary or petty thievery, and is also often applied to a morally disreputable woman ⟨wandering fruit *tramps* who drift through California's central valley, following the crop seasons —*Time*⟩ ⟨a distinct class of these gentlemen *tramps*, young men no longer young, who wouldn't settle down, who disliked polite society and the genteel conventions —George Santayana⟩ ⟨*tramps* who had been fed at the kitchen door —Sherwood Anderson⟩ ⟨don't take it so hard . . . she's just a *tramp* —Chandler Brossard⟩ BUM stresses worthlessness with implications of laziness and often drunkenness or general moral disreputableness and applies chiefly to one who would rather sponge on others than work ⟨paging the town *bum*, and soon he appeared, barefooted, his pants falling away from his hips, his face a thicket of whiskers —J.A.Michener⟩ ⟨a young reporter working on a story about down-and-out *bums* —J.A.Morris b.1904⟩ HOBO sometimes implies a willingness to work, sometimes suggests travel by freight trains, and is often applied to a migratory worker who follows seasonal occupations ⟨a *hobo* works and wanders, a tramp dreams and wanders, and a bum drinks and wanders —S.H.Holbrook⟩ ⟨a swarm of crop *hoboes* had come in on it to work in the back-country lambing camps —H.L. Davis⟩ ⟨a piano *hobo*, knocking around the Mexican border with a four-piece band —*Lamp*⟩ ⟨most distressing of all was the large number of young people who had virtually become *hoboes* —F.D.Roosevelt⟩ STIFF applies chiefly to workers, esp. migratory workers or roustabouts; the term is usu. limited by a modifier ⟨the pay envelopes of the working *stiffs* of the smoky little towns of western Pennsylvania, Ohio and Indiana —E.A. Lahey⟩ ⟨after sixteen years of being homeless, of working with harvest *stiffs*, hockey players and sailors —Hugh MacLennan⟩ ⟨a cattle *stiff*⟩ ⟨a bindle *stiff*⟩ SWAGMAN is Australian for a hobo or migratory worker in the bush who carries his clothing and bedding with him in a roll and SUNDOWNER is Australian and South African for a bum or swagman who makes a practice of arriving at a bush station at sundown to ask for free food and shelter, traditionally unrefusable ⟨bundle of belongings *swagmen* carry as they tramp about the land —*Time*⟩ ⟨the *swagman*, a born wanderer who moves steadily on and occasionally takes a casual job —*Times Lit. Supp.*⟩ ⟨some swagmen were known as *sundowners*, because they arrived in time to eat the evening meal but not to earn it —William Power⟩

³vagabond \"\ *vi* -ED/-ING/-S **:** to wander in the manner of a vagabond **:** roam about ⟨a young ex-typist *~ing* in the Far East —Ida Hurst⟩

vag·a·bond·age \-ˌbändij, -dēj\ *n* -S [F, fr. *vagabond* + *-age*] **1 :** the act, condition, or practice of a vagabond **:** the state or habit of wandering about ⟨winter cruising . . . was the nature of our ~ —*Everybody's Mag.*⟩ **2 :** VAGABONDS ⟨roads were thronged with ~ —John Buchan⟩

vag·a·bon·dia \ˌ==ˈbändēə\ *n* -S [*vagabond* + *-ia* (as in *bohemia*)] **:** the life of a vagabond **:** VAGABONDAGE ⟨his departure from Leyden on the road to ~ —*No. Amer. Rev.*⟩

vag·a·bond·ish \-ˌbändish, -dēsh\ *adj* **:** of, resembling, or characteristic of a vagabond ⟨a lazy ~ itinerant farmer moving from one failure to another —B.J.Hendrick⟩

vag·a·bond·ism \-ˌbänˌdizəm, *chiefly Brit* -ˌbən-\ *n* -S **:** VAGABONDAGE

vag·a·bond·ize \-ˌdīz\ *vi* -ED/-ING/-S **:** VAGABOND

vagabonds *pl of* VAGABOND, *pres 3d sing of* VAGABOND

vagabond's disease *n* **:** a condition of pigmentation of the skin caused by long continued exposure, uncleanliness, and esp. by scratch marks and other lesions due to the presence of body lice

va·gal \ˈvāgəl\ *adj* [ISV *vag-* + *-al*] **:** of, relating to, involving the action of, or being the vagus nerve ⟨~ inhibition⟩ ⟨~ impulses⟩

va·gar·i·ous \vāˈgerēəs, vəˈg-, -ga(a)r-, -gär-\ *adj* **:** marked by vagaries **:** CAPRICIOUS, WHIMSICAL ⟨a ~ American leadership dependent upon the clash of domestic interests —Herbert Elliston⟩ — **va·gar·i·ous·ly** *adv*

va·gary \ˈvāgərē, -ri; vəˈger-, vāˈg-, -ˈga(a)r-, -ˈgär- *sometimes* ˈvāˌg-; *sometimes* ˈvagər- *or* ˈvaigər-\ *n* -ES [prob. fr. L *vagari* to move about, wander; akin to L *vagus* wandering, OIr *fān* slope, bend, Skt *vañcati* he goes crooked — more at PREVARICATE] **1** *archaic* **:** JOURNEY, EXCURSION, TOUR ⟨permitted to make a walking ~ throughout all London —W.E.Andrews⟩ **2** *archaic* **:** an aimless digression ⟨presently would fall into a wordy ~ —Richard Baxter⟩ **3 a** *obs* **:** a departure from the regular, lawful, or proper course of conduct **b :** CAPER, FROLIC ⟨into strange *vagaries* fell, as they would dance —John Milton⟩ **4 :** a departure from an expected, normal, or logical order or course: **a :** a capricious, eccentric, or unpredictable action ⟨fearing to entrust his person to the *vagaries* of some erratic cabdriver —David Walden⟩ **b :** a change that is hard to predict or explain ⟨dependence of the schooner men upon the *vagaries* of weather —*Amer. Guide Series: Mich.*⟩ ⟨made the best of the *vagaries* of circumstance —Rose Macaulay⟩ ⟨these prospects . . . hinge on the *vagaries* of politics —*Fortune*⟩ ⟨independent of the *vagaries* of the international market —Vicki Baum⟩ ⟨passes through a series of *vagaries* and vicissitudes —John Barkham⟩ **c :** a whimsical, fanciful, or extravagant idea or notion ⟨his mind seemed . . . to be abandoned to *vagaries* —S.H.Adams⟩

vagation *n* -S [ME *vagacion*, fr. MF *vagation*, fr. L *vagation-*, *vagatio* action of wandering, fr. *vagatus* (past part. of *vagari*) + *-ion-*, *-io* -ion] *obs* **:** an act or instance of departing from an expected or regular course

vagged *past of* VAG

vagging *pres part of* VAG

vagi *pl of* VAGUS

vag·ile \ˈvajəl, -aˌjīl, -a(ˌ)jil\ *adj* [ISV *vag-* (fr. L *vagus* wandering) + *-ile*; prob. orig. formed as G *vagil*] **:** free to move about ⟨~ aquatic animals⟩ — compare SESSILE

va·gil·i·ty \vəˈjiləd-ē, -ətē, -i\ *n* -ES **:** the quality or state of being vagile; *broadly* **:** the capacity of an organism to compete successfully in the struggle for existence

vagin- *also* **vagini-** *comb form* [NL, fr. L *vagina*] **:** vagina ⟨*vagin*ectomy⟩ ⟨*vagini*coline⟩

va·gi·na \vəˈjīnə\ *n, pl* **vagi·nae** \-ī(ˌ)nē\ *or* **vaginas** [L, scabbard, sheath, vagina; prob. akin to Lith *vožti* to cover over with something hollow] **1 a :** a canal that leads from the uterus of a female mammal to the external orifice of the genital canal **b :** a canal of similar function or location in any of various other animals **2 :** a sheathlike part **:** SHEATH; *specif* **:** the expanded or ensheathing part of the base of a leaf **3 :** the upper part of the shaft of a terminus from which the bust or figure seems to rise

¹vagi·nal \ˈvajənᵊl, vəˈjīnᵊl\ *adj* [NL *vaginalis*, fr. L *vagina* + *-alis* -al] **1 :** of, relating to, or resembling a vagina **:** THECAL ⟨a ~ synovial membrane surrounding a tendon⟩ ⟨the ~ branches of the hepatic artery⟩ **2 :** of, relating to, or affecting the vagina of the genital canal ⟨the ~ plexus of nerves or veins⟩

²vaginal \"\ *n* -S **:** a vaginal artery or muscle

vaginal artery *n* **:** any of the several branches of the iliac artery supplying the vagina

vaginal process *n* **1 :** a projecting lamina of bone on the inferior surface of the petrous portion of the temporal bone that is continuous with the tympanic plate and surrounds the root of the styloid process **2 :** either of a pair of projecting laminae on the inferior surface of the sphenoid that articulate with the alae of the vomer

vaginal smear *n* **:** a smear taken from the vaginal mucosa for cytologic diagnosis

vag·i·nant \ˈvajənənt\ *adj* [NL *vaginant-*, *vaginans*, fr. *vagin-* + L *-ant-*, *-ans* -ant] **:** SHEATHING ⟨~ culm of grass⟩

vagina syn·o·vi·a·lis \-səˌnōvēˈāləs, -ˈāl-, -ˈäl-\ *n* [NL, synovial sheath] **:** VAGINA TENDINIS

vag·i·nate \ˈvajəˌnāt, -ˌnət\ *or* **vag·i·nat·ed** \-ˌnād-əd\ *adj* [*vaginate* prob. fr. (assumed) NL *vaginatus*, fr. NL *vagin-* + L *-atus* -ate; *vaginated* prob. fr. (assumed) NL *vaginatus* + E *-ed*] **:** invested with or as if with a sheath

vagina ten·di·nis \-ˈtendənəs\ *n* [NL, tendinous sheath] **:** the synovial sheath of a tendon esp. of the hand or foot

vag·i·nic·o·la \ˌvajəˈnikələ\ *n, cap* [NL, fr. *vagin-* + *-cola*] **:** a genus of ciliate protozoans that form minute vaselike or tubular cases in which they dwell

vag·i·nic·o·lous \ˌ==ˈnikələs\ *adj* [*vagin-* + *-colous*] **:** secreting and inhabiting a theca

vag·i·nif·er·ous \-if(ə)rəs\ *adj* [ISV *vagin-* + *-ferous*] **:** THECATE

vag·i·nis·mus \ˌvajəˈnizməs\ *n* -ES [NL, fr. *vagin-* + L *-ismus* -ism] **:** a painful spasmodic contraction of the vagina

vag·i·ni·tis \-ˈnīd-əs\ *n* -ES [NL, fr. *vagin-* + *-itis*] **1 :** inflammation of the vagina **2 :** inflammation of a sheath (as a tendon sheath)

va·ginu·la \vəˈjinyələ, -jīn-\ *n, pl* **vaginu·lae** \-əˌlē\ [NL, fr. L, dim. of *vagina* sheath, vagina] **1 :** the part of the archegonium of a moss enveloping the base of the embryo or seta after the upper part has been torn away **2 :** a small theca — **va·ginu·late** \-ˌlāt, -ˌlət\ *adj*

vag·i·nule \ˈvajəˌn(y)ül\ *n* -S [NL *vaginula*] **:** VAGINULA

Vag·nera \ˈvagnərə\ [NL, prob. modif. of the name *Wagner*] *syn of* SMILACINA

vago- — see VAG-

va·go·depressor \ˌvāgō+\ *adj* [*vag-* + *depressor*] **:** depressing to the vagus nerve — used chiefly of drugs or their action

va·go·sympathetic \"+\ *n* [*vag-* + *sympathetic*] **:** the vagus and a cervical sympathetic nerve when enclosed in the same sheath (as in a dog)

va·got·o·mize \vāˈgäd-əˌmīz\ *vt* -ED/-ING/-S **:** to perform a vagotomy on

va·got·o·my \-ˌmē, -mi\ *n* -ES [ISV *vag-* + *-tomy*] **:** surgical division of the vagus nerve

va·go·to·nia \ˌvāgəˈtōnēə\ *also* **va·goto·ny** \ˈvāgəˌtōnē, vāˈgätᵊnē\ *n, pl* **vagotonias** *also* **vagotonies** [*vagotonia* fr. NL, fr. *vag-* + *-tonia*; *vagotony* ISV *vag-* + *-tony*] **:** excessive excitability of the vagus nerve resulting typically in vasomotor instability, constipation, and sweating — **va·go·ton·ic** \ˌvāgəˈtänik\ *adj*

va·go·trop·ic \ˌvāgəˈträpik\ *adj* [*vag-* + *tropic*] **:** acting selectively upon the vagus nerve ⟨~ drugs⟩

vagous *adj* [L *vagus* — more at VAGARY] *obs* **:** WANDERING, UNSETTLED

va·grance \ˈvāgrən(t)s\ *n* -S **:** VAGRANCY

va·gran·cy \-nsē, -si\ *n* -ES **1 :** VAGARY 4 ⟨the *vagrancies* of the heart —John Tulloch⟩ **2 :** the state or action of wandering about from place to place ⟨happier life I cannot imagine than this ~ if the weather were but tolerable —Thomas De Quincey⟩ **3 :** the state or offense of being a vagrant

va·grant \-nt\ *n* -S [ME *vagraunt*, prob. modif. (influenced by MF *vagant* vagrant, fr. pres. part. of *vaguer* to wander) of MF *waucrant*, *wacrant* wandering, fr. OF, fr. pres. part. of *waucrer*, *wacrer*, *walcrer* to roll, roam, wander, of Gmc origin; akin to OE *wealcan* to roll, turn, revolve — more at VAGUE, WALK] **1 a** (1) **:** a person who has no established residence and wanders idly from place to place without lawful or visible means of support (2) **:** one whose conduct constitutes statutory vagrancy; *esp* **:** one (as an itinerant peddler trading without a license, a common prostitute wandering in the public streets, one begging in a public place, a fortune teller, one exhibiting an obscene picture in a public place, one guilty of indecent exposure, one playing or betting in a public place at or with a gambling table or instrument, and formerly a pimp) whose conduct constitutes vagrancy under British law **b :** one who leads a wandering life **:** WANDERER ⟨a chronic ~ from the spirit's home —Edward Sapir⟩ **2 :** an insect or other small arthropod that produces no web, nest, gall, or other protective structure but wanders at large where suitable food is to be found **syn** see VAGABOND

²vagrant \"\ *adj* [ME *vagraunt*, prob. modif. of MF *waucrant*, *wacrant*] **1 a :** wandering about from place to place usu. with no means of support ⟨his house was known to all the ~ train —Oliver Goldsmith⟩ **b :** tied to or as if to no home or country **:** ROVING ⟨administer the government in the name of ~ and mendicant Kings —T.B.Macaulay⟩ **2 a :** having a fleeting, wayward, or inconstant quality ⟨had cleared my soul of sundry ~ impulses —Mary Austin⟩ ⟨his ~ attention was caught —Dorothy Sayers⟩ ⟨hummed snatches of some ~ melody —H.A.Sinclair⟩ **b :** having no fixed course, direction, or aim **:** RANDOM ⟨the ~ breeze . . . died down again —Ellen Glasgow⟩ ⟨a ~ shaft of sunlight struck the ocean —Jack London⟩ **3 :** of, relating to, or characteristic of a wanderer ⟨go down to the seas again to the ~ gypsy life —John Masefield⟩

va·grant·ly *adv* **:** in the manner of a vagrant

va·grom \ˈvāgrəm\ *adj* [by alter.] **:** VAGRANT ⟨a ~ . . . thought ran through my head —H.L.Mencken⟩

vags *pl of* VAG, *pres 3d sing of* VAG

¹vague \ˈvāg\ *vi* -ED/-ING/-S [ME (Sc) *vagen*, fr. MF *vaguer*, fr. L *vagari* — more at VAGARY] *archaic* **:** WANDER, ROAM

²vague \"\ *adj* -ER/-EST [MF, fr. L *vagus* wandering, unsettled, uncertain, vague — more at VAGARY] **1 a :** not clearly expressed **:** stated in general or indefinite terms ⟨sign a very ~ treaty of friendship —William Clark⟩ ⟨~ chatter about the higher things —D.W.Brogan⟩ ⟨distrust of ~ beliefs in social service —M.R.Cohen⟩ **b :** not having an exact or precise meaning ⟨a ~ term of abuse for any style that is bad —T.S. Eliot⟩ ⟨statement . . . is so ~ as to be really meaningless —Havelock Ellis⟩ **2 a :** not clearly defined, grasped, or understood **:** INDISTINCT ⟨owed only ~ allegiance to some overlord —Roger Burlingame⟩ ⟨knows . . . in a ~ way what he wants from a book —Bliss Perry⟩ ⟨a ~ idea of the existence of an all=powerful spirit —P.T.Etherton⟩ **b :** not clearly or sharply felt or sensed **:** somewhat subconscious ⟨a ~ longing for common deliverance —J.R.Green⟩ ⟨the ~ unrest of a husband whose infidelities are imaginary —Ellen Glasgow⟩ ⟨a ~ desire for change —Will Irwin⟩ **3 :** not thinking or expressing one's thoughts clearly or precisely **:** characterized by looseness or haziness of thought or expression ⟨was very ~ about when he could see her again —Irwin Shaw⟩ ⟨somewhat ~ but possessing her own peculiarly feminine brand of common sense —C.V.Woodward⟩ ⟨kept no diary . . . was ~ about dates —Valentine Williams⟩ **4 :** lacking expression **:** VACANT ⟨danced along with ~ regardless eyes —John Keats⟩ **5 :** not sharply outlined **:** dim or indistinct in form or character **:** SHADOWY, HAZY ⟨met by ~ figures with shaded torchlights —Earle Birney⟩ ⟨the pattern is ~ and indecisive —A.N.Whitehead⟩ ⟨the ~ world of sleep —Edmund Wilson⟩ **syn** see OBSCURE

³vague \"\ *n* -S **1 a :** an indefinite or unsettled state — often used in the phrase *in the vague* ⟨plans are still in the ~ —Jane W. Carlyle⟩ **b :** a haze of thoughts or sensations ⟨am wondering in a vast ~ about her —Thomas Wolfe⟩ **2 :** an indefinite expanse ⟨the gray ~ of unsympathizing sea —J.R.Lowell⟩

⁴vague \"\ *adv* **:** VAGUELY — usu. used in combination ⟨*vague*=shining⟩

vague·ly *adv* **:** in a vague manner or form

vague·ness *n* -ES **1 :** the quality or state of being vague ⟨the ~ of a dream that is half forgotten —Elizabeth Goudge⟩ **2 :** something that is vague ⟨paintings . . . grew touch by touch into *~es* at which I shuddered —E.A.Poe⟩

vague year *n* [prob. so called fr. the fact that in a cycle of 1507 vague years any date in it passed through all the seasons] **:** a year of 365 days used by the ancient Egyptians before the Roman conquest

va·guish \ˈvāgish, -gēsh\ *adj* **:** somewhat vague

va·gus nerve \ˈvāgəs-\ *also* **va·gus** *n, pl* **vagus nerves** *also* **vagi** [*vagus nerve* part trans. of NL *vagus nervus*, lit., wandering nerve; *vagus* fr. NL, fr. L, wandering; fr. its length and wide distribution in the brain — more at VAGARY] **:** either of the 10th pair of cranial nerves being a mixed nerve with sensory fibers that have cell bodies in the ganglion nodosum and jugular ganglion and central connections through the lateral wall of the medulla and with motor fibers that pass from the medulla in company with those of the 9th nerve and supplying chiefly the viscera esp. with autonomic fibers

va·hi·ne \väˈhē(ˌ)nā\ *n* -S [Tahitian] **:** a woman of Central Polynesia

vai *also* **vei** \ˈvī\ *n, pl* **vai** *or* **vais** *usu cap* **1 a :** a Negro people of Liberia **b :** a member of such people **2 :** a Mande language of the Vai people **3 :** a syllabic script invented about 1834 for use with the Vai language

vai·bha·si·ka \vīˈbäs(h)əkə\ *n* -S *usu cap* [Skt *vaibhāṣika*, fr. *Vibhāṣā*, a commentary on the Buddhist scriptures, fr. *vibhāṣate* it shines brightly, fr. *vi* apart, asunder + *bhāṣate* it shines; akin to Skt *bhāti* it shines — more at WITH, FANCY] **:** a Hinayana Buddhist philosophical school of realism derived from the Sarvastivadin and found chiefly in Gandhara and Kashmir

¹vail \ˈvāl, *esp before pause or consonant* -āəl\ *vb* -ED/-ING/-S [ME *vailen*, fr. OF *vail-*, *vaill-*, stem of *valoir* to be of worth, fr. L *valēre* to be strong, be of worth — more at WIELD] *archaic* **:** AVAIL

²vail \"\ *vb* -ED/-ING/-S [ME *valen*, partly fr. MF *valer* (short for *avaler* to fall, let fall) & partly short for ME *avalen* to fall, let fall — more at AVALE] *vt* **1 a :** to let fall **:** cause to descend or sink ⟨*~ed* her handkerchief and drew a breath of air —Aldous Huxley⟩ **b :** to lower as a sign of respect or submission ⟨had no intention of *~ing* their crest —Louis Golding⟩ **2** *archaic* **:** to take off esp. as a sign of respect or submission **:** DOFF ⟨acknowledged their greeting by *~ing* his plumed cap —E.G.Bulwer-Lytton⟩ **3** *obs* **a :** HUMBLE, ABASE ⟨now ~ your pride . . . and kneel for mercy —Christopher Marlowe⟩ **b :** YIELD, SUBMIT ⟨~ their faith and understanding to his dictates —John Owen⟩ **~** *vi* **1 a** *archaic* **:** to become lowered esp. as a sign of respect or submission **b** *obs* **:** to lower a sail as a sign of respect or submission **2** *archaic* **:** to take off one's hat esp. as a sign of respect or submission **3** *archaic* **:** YIELD

³vail \"\ *n* -S [ME, fr. *vailen* to avail — more at ¹VAIL] **1 a** *archaic* **:** an occasional fee or offering usu. attached to an office ⟨his revenue besides *~s* amounted to about thirty pounds —Jonathan Swift⟩ **b vails** *pl* **:** a perquisite held or claimed as a customary right or possession ⟨the upper garment is the *~s* of the executioner —John Cleveland⟩ **2** *also* **vale :** a gratuity given esp. to a servant **:** TIP

¹vain \ˈvān\ *adj* -ER/-EST [ME *vain*, *vein*, fr. OF, fr. L *vanus* empty, vain — more at WANE] **1 :** having no real value, meaning, or foundation **:** EMPTY, IDLE, WORTHLESS ⟨~ pomp and glory of this world —Shak.⟩ ⟨~ pretensions⟩ ⟨~ promises⟩ **2 :** marked by futility or ineffectualness **:** FRUITLESS, UNSUCCESSFUL ⟨our ~ quest for a utopian equilibrium —W.H.Whyte⟩ ⟨a ~ effort to stop the decay —H.I.Priestley⟩ **3** *archaic* **:** having or showing little sense or wisdom **:** FOOLISH, SILLY ⟨all that ~ men imagine or believe —P.B.Shelley⟩ **4 :** having or showing undue or excessive pride esp. in one's appearance or achievements **:** CONCEITED ⟨was ~ about his clothes —Hugh Walpole⟩ ⟨was ~ of the honor which he had won —J.A. Froude⟩ ⟨~ of his family's long history —P.L.Fermor⟩

syn NUGATORY, OTIOSE, IDLE, EMPTY, HOLLOW: VAIN describes that which is either absolutely lacking in value and worth or relatively insignificant and unavailing in comparison or contrast to other things vastly more significant, valuable, or powerful ⟨a good deal of the older speculation on life and destiny was *vain* and insipid because of the theologic bias —M.R.Cohen⟩ ⟨unless the forces of destruction now set loose in the world are brought under control, it is *vain* to plan for the future —Clement Attlee⟩ NUGATORY may apply to the completely insignificant or to the inoperative, ineffective, void, or null ⟨this book is so one-sided that as a constructive contribution it is *nugatory* —*Times Lit. Supp.*⟩ ⟨make the indictment void and *nugatory*⟩ OTIOSE describes that which is purposeless, profitless, or useless and is therefore at best superfluous and at worst encumbering and productive of unnecessary expense or difficulty ⟨what kinds of criticism are useful and what are *otiose* —T.S.Eliot⟩ ⟨mummified customs that have long outlasted their usefulness, and *otiose* dogmas that have long lost their vitality —W.R.Inge⟩ IDLE may suggest lack of basis or solid foundation and hence may describe that which is incapable of use or effect ⟨in the light of our present very limited knowledge of psychological processes it seems *idle* to speculate as to the origins of this need —Ralph Linton⟩ ⟨living in an age of transition in everything and it is *idle* to deny that it is uncomfortable —S.P.B.Mais⟩ EMPTY applies to what lacks content or substance and hence significance although perhaps apparently consequential ⟨if the right of the states to tax the means employed by the general government be conceded, the declaration that the constitution, and the laws made in pursuance thereof, shall be the supreme law of the land, is *empty* and unmeaning declamation —John Marshall⟩ ⟨they have offered not a shred of evidence — nothing but bald assertion. And on the basis of this *empty* vociferation school programs and college admission requirements are overturned —C.H.Grandgent⟩ HOLLOW may suggest a deceiving lack of substance perceptible after examination or trial ⟨the fight for the extension of the franchise is one of the most thrilling chapters in the history of political liberties, but its final triumph in the extension of the franchise to women came too late to conceal the fact that the victory was a *hollow* one, since political reforms could have little or no efficacy without corresponding economic reforms —F.B.Millett⟩ ⟨the old Georgian mansions were converted into rooming houses. Trees were chopped down, so that the streets could be widened. The title of "most beautiful city" became *hollow* —*Amer. Guide Series: Mich.*⟩

—in vain *adv* [ME; trans. of OF *en vein* & ML *in vanum*] **1 :** to no end : without success or result ⟨protests made *in vain* by county councils —S.P.B.Mais⟩ **2 :** in an irreverent, disrespectful, or blasphemous manner ⟨the Lord will not hold him guiltless who takes his name *in vain* —Deut 5:11 (RSV)⟩

²vain *n* -s [ME *vein*, fr. OF, fr. *vein*, adj., vain] *obs* : VANITY

vainglorious \(ˈ)═¦═══\ *adj* [ME *vanegloreous*, fr. MF, fr. ML *vaniglorius*, fr. L *vanus* vain + *gloria* glory, vainglory] **:** marked by vainglory : BOASTFUL, VAIN ⟨was rather ~ about his own war record —Gideon Tode⟩ ⟨had a bombastic almost ~ air —*New Yorker*⟩ — **vaingloriously** *adv* — **vaingloriousness** *n*

¹vainglory \ˈ═¦══ *also* ═ˈ═══\ *n* [ME *vain glory, vein glory*, fr. OF *vaine gloire, veine gloire*, fr. *vaine, veine* (fem. of *vain, vein* vain) + *gloire* glory, vainglory, fr. L *gloria*] **1 :** excessive or ostentatious pride esp. in one's achievements ⟨is neither ~ nor vaunting in this little chronicle —J.T.Winterich⟩ **2 :** vain display or show : VANITY ⟨these feasts, pomps, and *vainglories* —Shak.⟩ **syn** see PRIDE

²vainglory \"\ *vi* **:** to indulge in or show vainglory

vain·ly *adv* [ME *vainly, veinly*, fr. *vain, vein* vain + *-ly* — more at VAIN] **:** in a vain manner : in vain

vain·ness *n* -ES **:** the quality or state of being vain

¹vair \ˈva(a)(ə)r, ˈve(, |ə\ *n* -s [ME *veir*, fr. OF *vair*, fr. *vair*, adj., variegated, fr. L *varius* variegated, various — more at VARIOUS] **1 :** a squirrel skin widely used in medieval times as fur trimming or lining for the garments of kings, nobles, and prelates — see MINIVER **2 a** *obs* : VAIR ANCIENT **b :** a heraldic fur consisting of rows of interlocking upright and inverted shield-shaped or bell-shaped panes alternately argent and azure unless other tinctures are specified with the rows being so placed one beneath another that each pane stands broad edge to broad edge or point to point with one of the opposite tincture **c** (1) **:** a fur made up of panes typically found in vair — see COUNTERVAIR, VAIR IN PALE, VAIR UNDY (2) **:** a fur or other repeat pattern known or believed to be historically a variety, variant, or modification of vair in its original medieval form

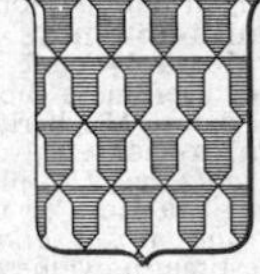
vair 2b

²vair \"\ *adj* **1 :** of the heraldic vair **2 :** VAIRÉ

¹vair ancient *n* [part trans. of F *vair ancien*] **:** a heraldic vair consisting of horizontal bands each of which is divided per fess wavy argent and azure unless other tinctures are specified

²vair ancient *adj* **:** of the heraldic vair ancient

¹vairé *or* **vairy** \ˈva(a)rē,-erē\ *adj* [*vairé* fr. F, fr. OF *vair*; *vairy* fr. ME *varri*, fr. MF *vairy*, fr. OF *vair*] **1 :** having the pattern of a heraldic vair — used when the tinctures are other then argent and azure ⟨a fess ~ or and gules⟩ **2 :** VAIR 1

²vairé *or* **vairy** \"\ *n* -s **:** a heraldic vair consisting of tinctures other than argent and azure

vair-en-point \¦═ə̇n¦═\ *n* [F, lit., vair in point] : VAIR IN PALE

vair in pale *n* **:** a heraldic vair in which each pane stands broad edge to point or point to broad edge with one of the same tincture above or below it

vair undy *n* **:** a heraldic vair in pale in which each pane stands broad edge to point or point to broad edge with one of the other tincture above or below it

vais *usu cap, pl of* VAI

vai·she·shi·ka *also* **vai·se·si·ka** \vīˈshāshə̇kə, -ˈsāsə̇-\ *n* -s *usu cap* [Skt *vaiśeṣika* distinction, distinct nature of the eternal substances, fr. *viśeṣa* distinction, fr. *viśiṣyate* it is distinguished, fr. *vi* apart, asunder + *śiṣyate* it is left — more at WITH] **:** an orthodox philosophical system in Hinduism distinguished by its atomic theory of cosmology

vaish·na·va *also* **vais·na·va** \ˈvīs(h)nəvə\ *n* -s *usu cap* [Skt *vaiṣṇava* of Vishnu, fr. *Viṣṇu*, second god of the supreme triad of Hindu gods consisting of Brahma, Vishnu and Siva] **:** a worshiper of Vishnu in any of his forms or incarnations

vaish·na·vism *also* **vais·na·vism** \-ə,vizəm\ *n* -s *usu cap* **:** the worship of Vishnu

vaish·na·vite \-,vīt\ *n* -s *usu cap* [Skt *vaiṣṇava* + E *-ite*] : VAISHNAVA

vais·ya *also* **vaish·ya** \ˈvīs(h)yə\ *n* -s *usu cap* [Skt *vaiśya*, fr. *viś* settlement — more at VICINITY] **1 :** a twice-born Hindu of the third ancient varna assigned by classical law to an agricultural or commercial occupation **2 :** a twice-born Hindu belonging to one of a large group of modern upper castes traditionally derived from the ancient Vaisya varna — compare BRAHMAN, KSHATRIYA, SUDRA

vai·vode \ˈvī,vōd\ *or* **voi·vode** *also* **voi·vod** \ˈvȯi,-\ *n* -s [*vaivode* fr. NL & It *vaivoda*, fr. obs. Hung *vajvoda*, fr. Serb & Slovene *vojvoda*, fr. OBulg *vojevoda*, lit., chieftain, fr. *voinŭ* warrior, soldier (akin to Lith *vyti* to pursue, hunt) + *voditi* to lead; *voivode* fr. Russ *voevoda*, fr. OBulg — more at VIM] **:** a military commander or governor of a town or province in various Slavic countries

vaj·ra·ya·na \,vəjrəˈyänə, -rēˈä-\ *n* -s *usu cap* [Skt *vajrayāna*, lit., vehicle of thunderbolt, fr. *vajra* thunderbolt + *yāna* vehicle] **:** tantric Buddhism : TANTRISM 2

va·kass \ˈvä,käs\ *n* -ES [Arm *vagas*] **:** an amice worn by priests of the Armenian Church

va·keel *or* **va·kil** \vəˈkē(ə)l\ *n* -s [Hindi *vakel*, fr. Ar *wakīl*] **1 :** an agent or representative esp. of a person of political importance in India **2 :** an authorized public pleader in a court of justice in India

val \ˈval\ *or* **val lace** *n* -s *often cap V* [by shortening] : VALENCIENNES

val *abbr* **1** valentine **2** valuation **3** value; valued

val·ance *also* **val·lance** \ˈvalən(t)s, ˈvāl-\ *n* -s [ME *valaunce, vallance*, perh. fr. *Valence*, textile manufacturing commune of southeast France] **1 a :** a usu. gathered or pleated drapery attached along the edge of a bed, table, altar, canopy, or shelf and hanging straight and loosely often to the floor for concealment and decoration **b :** a similar decoration of leather, metal, wood esp. on furniture **c :** a short usu. shaped or pleated drapery or a short wood or metal frame used as a decorative heading to conceal the top of curtains and fixtures **2 :** something resembling a valance: as **a :** a flap on the back of a cap **b :** a fringe of hair (as a mustache) **c :** a decorative treatment in the form of balancing scrolls that resemble a drapery valance

val·anced \-st\ *adj* [*valance* + *-ed*] **:** provided or decorated with a valance ⟨an old set-stitched chair, ~ and fringed around —Laurence Sterne⟩

valdenses *usu cap, var of* WALDENSES

val·de·pe·nas \,väldəˈpānyəs\ *n, usu cap* [fr. *Valdepeñas*, commune of south central Spain] **:** a table wine usu. red but occas. white from the village of Valdepeñas south of Madrid, Spain

¹vale \ˈvāl, *esp before pause or consonant* -āəl\ *n* -s [ME, fr. OF *val*, fr. L *valles, vallis* valley; akin to L *volvere* to roll — more at VOLUBLE] **1 :** a low-lying country or tract usu. containing a brook or a stream ⟨a prospect of the city in the ~ below —Thomas Gray⟩ ⟨the pattern of parallel strips made by the alternation of ~*s* and cuesta ridges —O.D.Von Engeln⟩ **2 a :** the earth, world, or earthly life in contrast to heaven or eternity ⟨this ~ of tears⟩ ⟨this mortal ~⟩ ⟨the tortured route through the ~ of foreign policy —E.E.Morison⟩ **b :** the scene or place of life ⟨the ~ of time⟩ ⟨the cool sequestered ~ of life —Thomas Gray⟩

²vale *var of* VAIL

³va·le \ˈv|ä(,)lā, ˈw|, |ä(-\ *n* -s [L, farewell, interj., fr. 2d sing. imper. of *valēre* to be strong, be well — more at WIELD] **:** a salutation of leave-taking — often used interjectionally

val·e·dic·tion \,valəˈdikshən\ *n* -s [L *valedictus* (past part. of *valedicere* to say farewell, fr. *vale* farewell + *dicere* to say) + E *-ion* — more at DICTION] **1 :** an act or instance of bidding farewell ⟨each departing with a brief ~⟩ **2 :** VALEDICTORY

¹val·e·dic·to·ri·an \,valə,dikˈtōrēən, -tȯr-\ *n* -s [²*valedictory* + *-an*] **:** the student usu. of the highest rank in a graduating class who delivers the valedictory oration at the commencement exercises

²valedictorian \¦══¦═══\ *adj* **:** of, relating to, or having the characteristics of a valedictory or valedictorian ⟨the ~ speech⟩ ⟨~ gush about gleams, goals, ideals —H.N.Fairchild⟩

¹val·e·dic·to·ry \¦valə¦dikt(ə)rē, -ri\ *adj* [L *valedictus* (past part. of *valedicere*) + E *-ory*] **1 :** spoken or given at a time or ceremony of farewell or leave-taking esp. from an office or an educational institution ⟨a ~ address⟩ ⟨~ praise for his courtesy and uniformly manly course —Dixon Wecter⟩ **2 :** performed or carried out by way of valediction ⟨has settled his hopes on a spectacular Asian compromise as a suitable ~ gesture —*Time*⟩

²valedictory \"\ *n* -ES **:** a valedictory oration or statement; *specif* **:** the speech of farewell usu. given at the commencement exercises of a school or college

va·lence \ˈvālən(t)s\ *n* -s [LL *valentia* power, capacity, fr. L *valent-, valens* (pres. part. of *valēre* to be strong) + *-ia* -y — more at WIELD] **1 a :** the degree of combining power of an element or radical **:** the number of atoms of hydrogen, sodium, fluorine, or other univalent element with which an atom of the element or a molecule of the radical will combine by means of bonds or for which it can be substituted or with which it can be compared **:** the oxidation state of an element in a compound ⟨potassium has a ~ of one because a gram atom combines with a gram atom of hydrogen to form potassium hydride KH or with a gram atom of fluorine to form potassium fluoride KF⟩ ⟨iron has a variable ~: two in ferrous chloride $FeCl_2$ and three in ferric chloride $FeCl_3$⟩ — see COVALENCE, ELECTROVALENCE; compare COORDINATE BOND, POLAR VALENCE 2 **b :** a unit of valence ⟨the four ~*s* of carbon⟩ **2 a :** relative capacity to unite, react, or interact (as with antigens or a biological substrate) **b :** the degree of attractiveness an individual, activity, or object possesses as a behavioral goal ⟨the group may have a positive ~ for member A because he has friends in it —Neal Gross & W.E.Martin⟩

valence electron *n* **:** a single electron or one of two or more electrons contained in the outer incomplete shell of an atom and responsible for the chemical properties of the atom ⟨sodium and other alkali metals have only one *valence electron*⟩

valence number *n* : OXIDATION STATE

valence shell *n* **:** the outermost shell of an atom containing the valence electrons

va·len·cia \vəˈlench(ē)ə, -n(t)sēə\ *adj, usu cap* **1** [fr. *Valencia*, commune of eastern Spain] **:** of or from the city of Valencia, Spain **:** of the kind or style prevalent in Valencia **2** [fr. *Valencia*, commercial city of northern Venezuela] **:** of or from the city of Valencia, Venezuela **:** of the kind or style prevalent in Valencia

valencia cocktail *n, usu cap V* **:** a cocktail made from apricot brandy and orange juice and flavored with several dashes of orange bitters

¹va·len·cian \-nch(ē)ən, -n(t)sēən\ *adj, usu cap* [*Valencia*, province & commune of eastern Spain + E *-an*] **1 :** of, relating to, or characteristic of Valencia province or city **2 :** of, relating to, or characteristic of the Valencians

²valencian \"\ *n* -s *cap* **:** a native or resident of Valencia province or city in Spain

va·len·ci·ennes \və;len(t)sēˈen(z) *sometimes* ¦valənsēˈen(z) *or* ¦valən¦sēnz\ *also* **valenciennes lace** *n, usu cap V* [fr. *Valenciennes*, industrial city of northern France] **:** a fine bobbin lace having a ground with a square or diamond-shaped mesh which is plaited rather than twisted and a pattern made together with the ground and of the same kind of thread

va·len·cy \ˈvālənsē, -si\ *n* -ES [LL *valentia* power, capacity — more at VALENCE] : VALENCE

va·lent \ˈvālənt *sometimes* ,vələnt; *the second pronunc is not shown at the entries of compounds*\ *adj* [back-formation fr. *valence* or *valency*] **:** having valence — usu. used in combination ⟨*bivalent*⟩ ⟨*multivalent*⟩

val·en·tine \ˈvalən,tīn, *dial* ˈväl- *or* ˈvȯl-\ *n* -s [ME, after Saint Valentine's Day] **1 :** a sweetheart chosen or complimented on St. Valentine's Day **:** one's beloved **2** *dial Brit* **:** one of a number of folded papers containing a name to be drawn as a valentine **3 a :** something sent or given esp. to a sweetheart on St. Valentine's Day; *specif* **:** an ornamental engraved or printed greeting of a mock sentimental or comic character sent often anonymously on this day **b :** a piece of writing or a literary work expressing praise or affection for something ⟨toss a nostalgic ~ to his Bronx boyhood in his novel —*Time*⟩ — usu. used with *to* ⟨one of the finest American plays . . . is a radiant personal mirror of life and a ~ to humanity —T.J.Panter⟩ ⟨this ~ to the pioneer jazz-makers of the Twenties —Lee Rogow⟩ **4** *usu cap* : LOVE SONG

valentine day *or* **valentine's day** *n, usu cap V&D* : SAINT VALENTINE'S DAY

¹val·en·tin·i·an \,valən·ˈtinēən\ *n* -s *usu cap* [ME, fr. *Valentinus*, 2d cent. A.D. Roman Gnostic philosopher and teacher + ME *-an*] **:** an adherent of Valentinianism

²valentinian \¦══¦═══\ *adj* **:** of or relating to Valentinus or his system of gnosticism

val·en·tin·i·an·ism \,══ˈ══ə,nizəm\ *n* -s *usu cap* [*valentinian* + *-ism*] **:** gnosticism in which the divine pleroma is conceived as being made up of aeons that are held to be aspects of the nature and activity of God

val·en·ti·nite \ˈvalən·,tē,nīt\ *n* -s [G *valentinit*, fr. Basil *Valentine*, 15th cent. Ger. alchemist + G *-it* -ite] **:** a mineral Sb_2O_3 consisting of antimony oxide in orthorhombic crystals polymorphous with senarmontite

val·en·tin's knife \ˈvalən·,tēnz-\ *n, usu cap V* [prob. after Gabriel G. *Valentin* †1883 Ger. physiologist] **:** a knife made with two parallel adjustable blades and used to cut thin slices of fresh tissues

vale of years [¹*vale*] **:** the declining years of life

valer- *or* **valero-** *comb form* [*valeric* (*acid*)] **:** valeric acid ⟨*valeraldehyde*⟩ ⟨*valerolactone*⟩

val·er·aldehyde \¦valər+\ *n* [ISV *valer-* + *aldehyde*] **:** any of four liquid aldehydes C_4H_9CHO corresponding to the valeric acids; *esp* **:** the normal aldehyde $CH_3(CH_2)_3CHO$

val·er·amide \"+\ *n* [ISV *valer-* + *-amide*] **:** any of four crystalline amides $C_4H_9CONH_2$ derived from the valeric acids; *esp* **:** the normal amide $CH_3(CH_2)_3CONH_2$

val·er·ate \ˈvalə,rāt\ *n* -s [ISV *valer-* + *-ate*] **:** a salt or ester of valeric acid

va·le·ri·an \vəˈlirēən\ *n* -s [ME, fr. MF or ML; MF *valeriane*, fr. ML *valeriana*, prob. fr. fem. of *valerianus* of Valeria, fr. *Valeria*, Roman province formerly part of Pannonia + L *-anus* -an] **1 :** a plant of the genus *Valeriana* (esp. *V. officinalis*) — compare GREEK VALERIAN **2 a :** a drug consisting of the dried rhizome and roots of the garden heliotrope (*Valeriana officinalis*) formerly used as a carminative and sedative esp. in nervous conditions **b :** the dried rhizome and roots of an East Indian valerian (*V. wallichii*) used in incense and perfumes

va·le·ri·ana \və,lirēˈanə, -ˈä-,-ˈā-\ *n* [NL, fr. ML, valerian] **1** *cap* **:** a large genus of widely distributed perennial herbs (family Valerianaceae) having lobed or dissected leaves and cymose white or pink flowers with spurless corollas **2** -s **:** any plant of the genus *Valeriana*

va·le·ri·a·na·ce·ae \və,lirēəˈnāsē,ē\ *n pl, cap* [NL, fr. *Valeriana*, type genus + *-aceae*] **:** a family of herbs (order Rubiales) chiefly of temperate regions having opposite leaves and mostly cymose flowers, a regular or irregular corolla and free anthers, and an achene fruit crowned with a persistent calyx border — **va·le·ri·a·na·ceous** \═¦═══ˈnāshəs\ *adj*

va·le·ri·a·na·les \-ā(,)lēz\ *n pl, cap* [NL, fr. *Valeriana* + *-ales*] *in some classifications* **:** an order of dicotyledonous plants consisting of the two families Valerianaceae and Dipsacaceae characterized by a gamopetalous corolla and an inferior ovary

va·le·ri·a·nel·la \-ˈnelə\ *n, cap* [NL, fr. *Valeriana* + *-ella*] **:** a genus of annual herbs (family Valerianaceae) that are natives of the Old World but naturalized widely (as in the U. S.) and are distinguished by the variously appendaged but not pappose calyx — compare CORN SALAD

valerian family *n* : VALERIANACEAE

valerian oil *n* **:** a yellowish green to brownish essential oil that has an unpleasant odor and is obtained from the roots and rhizomes of the garden heliotrope

va·ler·ic acid \vəˈlirik-, -lerik-\ *also* **va·le·ri·an·ic acid** \-¦lirē¦anik-\ *n* [*valerian* + *-ic*; fr. its occurrence in the root of valerian] **:** any of four isomeric fatty acids C_4H_9COOH or a mixture of two or more of them: **a :** a liquid normal acid $CH_3(CH_2)_3COOH$ that has a disagreeable odor, that is found in pyroligneous acid and petroleum distillates, that is made synthetically (as by oxidation of normal pentyl alcohol or by fermentation), and that is used in organic synthesis — called also *pentanoic acid* **b :** ISOVALERIC ACID **c :** a liquid acid $CH_3CH_2CH(CH_3)COOH$ existing in three optically isomeric forms and occurring usu. in the dextrorotatory form in a few essential oils; α-methyl-butyric acid **d :** PIVALIC ACID

va·le·ro·lactone \vəˈli(,)rō, ¦valərō+\ *n* [ISV *valer-* + *lactone*] **:** the lactone $C_5H_8O_2$ of any hydroxy derivative of valeric acid; *esp* **:** the γ-lactone found in pyroligneous acid, made synthetically, and used chiefly as a solvent

va·le·ryl \vəˈlirəl, ˈvalə,ril\ *n* -s [ISV *valer-* + *-yl*] **:** the univalent radical C_4H_9CO of a valeric acid; *esp* **:** the normal radical $CH_3(CH_2)_3CO$–

vales *pl of* VALE

¹valet \ˈvalə̇t (*usu* -ə̇d-+V) *also* ˈva,lā *or* vaˈlā *sometimes* vəˈlā *or* ˈvalē *or* ˈvalə̇\ *n* -s [MF *vaslet, vallet, valet, varlet* young nobleman, page, squire, domestic servant, fr. (assumed) ML *vassellittus*, dim. of *vassus* servant, vassal — more at VASSAL] **1 a :** a man's male servant who performs personal services (as taking care of clothing and doing errands) for his employer — called also *manservant* **b :** an employee of a hotel, ship, or other public facility who performs personal services (as the cleaning and repair of clothing) for guests **2 :** a goad or stick with a point of iron **3 :** any of various contrivances usu. of a metal framework designed for holding clothing or personal effects

valet 3

²valet \"\ *vt* -ED/-ING/-S **:** to serve as a valet ⟨he . . . was waited upon and ~*ed* by the staff —Dorothy Sayers⟩

va·let de cham·bre \,va,lādəˈshäⁿbr(ᵊ), -b(rə)\ *n, pl* **valets de chambre** \-ā(z)d-\ [F, lit., chamber valet] : VALET 1a

valet de place \-dəˈpläs, -las\ *n, pl* **valets de place** \-ā(z)d-\ [F, lit., valet of the locality] **:** a valet who serves transient travelers or strangers by acting as guide ⟨the people the traveler naturally sees most — the tavern keepers, *valets de place*, and postilions —C.G.Bowers⟩

val·et·ry \ˈvalə̇trē\ *n* -ES [*valet* + *-ry*] **:** the occupation or service of a valet; *also* : VALETS

¹val·e·tu·di·nar·i·an \,valə,tüdᵊnˈerēən, -lə·,tyü-, -ˈa(a)r-, -ˈär-\ *n* -s [¹*valetudinary* + *-an*] **:** a person of a weak or sickly constitution; *esp* **:** one whose chief concern is his invalidism ⟨was a ~ and believed that no other physician could keep him in health —Bertrand Russell⟩

²valetudinarian \¦══,══¦═══\ *adj* **:** of, relating to, or characteristic of a valetudinarian : SICKLY, WEAK, INFIRM ⟨become slight-limbed, puny, and ~ —William Cowper⟩ ⟨the virtue which the world wants is a healthful virtue, not a ~ virtue —T.B.Macaulay⟩

val·e·tu·di·nar·i·an·ism \,══,══ˈ══ə,nizəm\ *n* -s [¹*valetudinarian* + *-ism*] **:** the condition or state of mind of a valetudinarian

¹val·e·tu·di·nary \,valə¦tüdᵊn,erē, -lə·¦tyü-, -ri\ *adj* [L *valetudinarius*, fr. *valetudin-, valetudo* health, state of health, sickness (fr. *valēre* to be well + *-tudin-, -tudo* -tude) + *-arius* -ary — more at WIELD] : VALETUDINARIAN

²valetudinary \"\ *n* -ES : VALETUDINARIAN

val·gus \ˈvalgəs\ *n* -ES [NL, adj., turned outward to an abnormal degree, fr. L, bowlegged — more at WALK] **:** a position of a joint's being turned outward to an abnormal degree ⟨the heel is in ~ —*Yr. Bk. of Orthopedics & Traumatic Surgery*⟩

val·hal·la \valˈhalə, välˈhälə, vălˈhälə\ *also* **wal·hal·la** \wȯl-, wäl-\ *n* -s *usu cap* [fr. *Valhalla, Walhalla*, in Norse mythology the hall of Odin into which he receives the souls of heroes slain in battle, fr. G & ON; G *Walhalla*, fr. ON *Valhöll*, lit., hall of the slain, fr. *valr* the slain + *höll* hall; akin to OE *wæl* slaughter, the slain, OHG *wal*, OIr *fuil* blood — more at HALL] **:** a place of honor or glorification : SHRINE ⟨announced that later a pantheon will replace the present tomb . . . as a *Valhalla* for all the fallen heroes —*Newsweek*⟩ ⟨has made the . . . city a gourmet's *Valhalla* and lures lovers of fine food from all over the world —J.A.Maxwell⟩

va·li \ˈvälē\ *n* -s [Turk *vāli*, fr. Ar *wālīy* wali] **1 :** a governor-general of a vilayet **2 :** WALI 1

val·iance \ˈvalyən(t)s\ *n* -s [ME *valiaunce*, fr. MF *vaillance*, fr. OF, fr. *vaillant* valiant] : VALIANCY ⟨on that . . . day there were terror and ~ and devotion —Adria Langley⟩

val·ian·cy \-nsē,-nsi\ *n* -ES [*valiant* + *-cy*] **:** the quality or state of being valiant : BRAVERY, VALOR

¹val·iant \ˈvalyənt\ *adj* [ME *valiaunt*, fr. MF *vaillant*, fr. OF, fr. pres. part. of *valoir* to be strong, be worth, fr. L *valēre* — more at WIELD] **1** *obs* : FIRM, STRONG, ROBUST **2 :** possessing or acting with bravery or boldness : COURAGEOUS, INTREPID, STOUTHEARTED ⟨~ he was, cunning and skilled in war —Charles Kingsley⟩ ⟨a ~ and energetic lot whose legends described their long migration —Marjory S. Douglas⟩ ⟨was . . . an ardent lover of mankind and a passionate and ~ idealist —J.H. Holmes⟩ — sometimes used ironically ⟨became this chieftain's guest, crony, and ~ drinking companion —Alan Devoe⟩ ⟨was as ~ a trencherman —B.A.Williams⟩ **3 :** marked by, exhibiting, or carried out with courage, persistence, or determination : HEROIC ⟨had a ~ war record —F.C.Brady⟩ ⟨is prepared to make a ~ fight —Douglass Cater⟩ ⟨made a ~ effort to relieve the distress of the people —Hallie Farmer⟩ ⟨against all these . . . forces the critic and the historian must make a ~ struggle —L.P.Smith⟩ — sometimes used ironically ⟨his contribution had been a ~ plan to send a thousand men to die gloriously in a futile attack —Leslie Rees⟩ **4 :** possessing merit or worth : EXCELLENT, NOTEWORTHY ⟨wrote two most ~ and revelatory works of realism —Sinclair Lewis⟩ ⟨the six-volume series began . . . with his ~ and lovely impressions of childhood —Brooks Atkinson⟩ **syn** see BRAVE

²valiant \"\ *n* -s **:** a valiant person ⟨the first white comers . . . were two ~*s* of Cortez's band —Julian Dana⟩

val·iant·ly *adv* **:** in a valiant manner : BRAVELY, COURAGEOUSLY, DETERMINEDLY

val·iant·ness *n* -ES [ME *valiauntnesse*, fr. *valiaunt* valiant + *-nesse* -ness] *obs* **:** the quality or state of being valiant

val·id \ˈvalə̇d\ *adj* [MF or ML; MF *valide*, fr. ML *validus*, fr. L, strong, fr. *valēre* to be strong — more at WIELD] **1 a :** having legal strength or force : incapable of being rightfully overthrown or set aside : sanctioned or authorized by sovereign temporal or spiritual power ⟨a ~ deed⟩ ⟨a ~ covenant⟩ ⟨a ~ title⟩ ⟨where a client has no ~ ground for divorce —H.S. Drinker⟩ ⟨exempt from the natural laws which may be ~ for lesser creatures —Ritchie Calder⟩ **b :** conforming to conditions essential to sacramental efficacy ⟨the synod also declared that the only ~ baptism was by immersion —K.S.Latourette⟩ **2 a :** well grounded or justifiable : applicable to the matter at hand : PERTINENT, SOUND ⟨the above theory was tested experimentally . . . and was proved to be ~ —H.G.Armstrong⟩ ⟨particular grievances call . . . for the formulation of universally ~ reasons why they should be redressed —Aldous Huxley⟩ ⟨find no ~ evidence for such suspensions —W.R.Inge⟩ ⟨a ~ argument⟩ ⟨a ~ purpose⟩ **b** *of an inference* : correctly derived from its premises; *specif* : true in terms of the logical principles of the logistic system to which the inference belongs **3 a** : able to effect or accomplish what is designed or intended : EFFECTIVE, EFFICACIOUS ⟨literary scholarship has its own ~ methods —René Wellek & Austin Warren⟩ ⟨the written word was no longer a ~ medium, the motion picture having supplanted it —Alexander Klein⟩ ⟨in finally finding her courage ~ it had in the same moment vanished —Janet Terrace⟩ **b** : capable of measuring, predicting, or representing according to intention or design ⟨if the results of university matriculation examinations are a ~ test —B.K.Sandwell⟩ — compare RELIABLE **4 a** : STRONG, POWERFUL **b** : HEALTHY, ROBUST **5 a** *of a taxon* : based on distinctive characters of recognized importance : founded on an adequate basis of classification; *also* : validly published **b** *of the publication of a taxon* : effective and accompanied by a description of the taxon or a reference to a previous description

syn SOUND, COGENT, CONVINCING, TELLING may be compared with VALID in being applied to arguments, reasonings, principles, ideas which have such force that they compel acceptance. Both VALID and SOUND imply that the force is inherent in the rationality of the thought apart from its presentation. A VALID argument or principle is supported either by objective truth or a generally accepted standard or authority ⟨mathematical symbols, which are *valid* whether there is anything corresponding to them in nature or not —W.R.Inge⟩ ⟨charges always *valid* in every age and country —J.A.Hobson⟩ although a VALID concept may have certain especially psychological limits ⟨a "psychological fact" is *valid* for the person who holds it if for no other —F.J.Hoffman⟩ SOUND, which may be applied to both persons and concepts, implies avoidance of fallacies, insufficient evidence, and hasty conclusions, and stresses solid foundation in fact or in reason or both, as well as the habit of clear and deliberate thought, often with an admixture of shrewd practical sense ⟨much too *sound* a political thinker and too sagacious a party leader to rest his case upon abstract theory —V.L.Parrington⟩ ⟨good, *sound* reasons against the passionate conclusions of love —Joseph Conrad⟩ COGENT and CONVINCING apply to ideas (less frequently, to persons) compelling mental assent, but COGENT stresses a force resident in the argument or reasoning, as inevitability or conclusiveness, as well as succinct and lucid presentation ⟨the most *cogent* argument for freedom — man's tremendous innate variability —E.W.Sinnott⟩ ⟨the most *cogent* political comment of the year —G.W.Johnson⟩ whereas a convincing argument, speaker, or book may convince by either sound reasoning or by skillful selection and presentation ⟨there are other ways of making a thing . . . *convincing* . . . besides merely appealing to one's logic and sense of fact —Irving Babbitt⟩ CONVINCING is often applied to fictional creations having the flavor of reality ⟨in Aristophanes you have the *convincing* hurly-burly, the sweating, mean, talented, scrambling, laughing life of the Mediterranean —J.J.Chapman⟩ TELLING suggests an immediate and crucial effect striking at the essence of the point, idea, or sentiment to be conveyed regardless of the validity of the cause ⟨certainly makes some *telling* points . . . with a deftness that will disarm orthodox heresy-hunters —M.R.Cohen⟩ ⟨paused as if to edit his woes and select the most *telling* ones —Norman Mailer⟩

val·i·date \ˈvaləˌdāt, *usu* -ād.+V\ *vt* -ED/-ING/-S [ML *validatus*, past part. of *validare* to validate, fr. *validus* valid] **1 a** : to make legally valid : confirm or declare formally or officially : RATIFY ⟨requires legislation by the whole Congress to ~ every treaty —*Civil Liberties*⟩ ⟨*validated* the marriages of former slaves —*Amer. Guide Series: N. C.*⟩ **b** : to grant official sanction to by or as if by stamping or marking ⟨the Coast Guard would ~ seamen's papers —Frank O'Leary⟩ **c** : to confirm the validity of (an election); *also* : to declare (a person) elected **2** : to corroborate or support on a sound basis or authority : VERIFY, SUBSTANTIATE ⟨true ideas are those that we can assimilate, ~, corroborate —William James⟩ ⟨the freedom . . . to worry through with a theory until it is *validated* or disproved —*Science*⟩ ⟨describe, define, and ~ the doctrinal distinctions between church and chapel —W.L.Sperry⟩ **syn** see CONFIRM

val·i·da·tion \ˌvaləˈdāshən\ *n* -S [*validate* + *-ion*] : an act, process, or instance of validating ⟨meeting to discuss ~ of the contract⟩ ⟨stamping the ~ on the passport⟩; *specif* : the process of determining the degree of validity of a measuring device ⟨many . . . criteria require almost as much ~ as the tests they are supposed to validate —Herbert Goldhamer⟩

val·i·da·to·ry \ˈvalədəˌtōrē\ *adj* [*validate* + *-ory*] : of or relating to validation

va·lid·i·ty \vəˈlidəd·ē, -idətē, -i *sometimes* vaˈl-\ *n* -ES [MF or ML; MF *validité*, fr. ML *validitat-, validitas*, fr. L, strength, fr. *validus* strong + *-itat-, -itas* -ity — more at VALID] : the quality or state of being valid ⟨the ~ of marriages celebrated in accordance with polygamous forms . . . is a question of considerable difficulty —J.H.C.Morris⟩ ⟨you can travel any time . . . during the nine-day ~ of the ticket —Richard Joseph⟩ ⟨a defender of the ~ of Presbyterian ordination —H.E.Starr⟩ ⟨dared question the ~ of the esthetic or moral principles —Manès Sperber⟩ ⟨the ~ of a test is a relative matter, depending upon the criterion used —J.B.Carroll⟩

val·id·ly *adv* : in a valid manner : with validity ⟨to do by exposure and publicity what . . . may not ~ be done by legislation —*New Republic*⟩ ⟨could not ~ oppose the journey —Arnold Bennett⟩ ⟨a name that has not been ~ published has no standing in nomenclature —*Internat'l Bull. of Bacteriological Nomenclature & Taxonomy*⟩

val·id·ness *n* -ES : VALIDITY

val·i·en·te \ˌvalēˈentē\ *n, pl* **valiente** *or* **valientes** *usu cap* **1 a** : a Chibchan people of western Panama **b** : a member of such people **2** : a language of the Valiente people

valine \ˈvaˌlēn, ˈvā-, -ˌlən\ *n* -S [ISV *val-* (fr. *isovaleric acid*) + *-ine*] : a crystalline amino acid $(CH_3)_2CHCH(NH_2)COOH$ that in the dextrorotatory L form is essential in the nutrition of lower animals and man and that is obtained in this form by the hydrolysis of proteins (as casein or zein) and in the racemic form by synthesis; α-amino-isovaleric acid

valis *pl of* VALI

va·lise \vəˈlēs, *chiefly Brit* -ēz\ *n* -S [F, fr. It *valigia*] : TRAVELING BAG

val·kyr \ˈvalkə(r)\ *n* -S *usu cap* [by shortening] : VALKYRIE

val·kyr·i·an \(ˈ)valˈkirēən, -kīr-\ *adj, usu cap* [*valkyrie* + *-an*] : of or relating to the Valkyries or to battle ⟨like some *Valkyrian* hero lighting a fire in a black forest —Anais Nin⟩

val·kyr·ie \valˈkirē, -ˈkīr, -ri, ˈ=ˌ==; ˈvalkər-\ *also* **wal·kyr·ie** \wȯl-, wäl-\ *n* -S *usu cap* [G & ON; G *walküre*, fr. ON *valkyrja*, lit., chooser of the slain; akin to OE *wælcyrige* witch, sorceress; both fr. a prehistoric WGmc-NGmc compound whose first constituent is represented by ON *valr* the slain and whose second constituent is akin to ON *kjōsa* to choose — more at VALHALLA, CHOOSE] : one of the maidens of the mythological Norse god Odin who hover over the field of battle choosing those to be slain and conducting the worthy heroes to Valhalla

valla *pl of* VALLUM

val·la·bha·char·ya \ˌvələˌbäˈchäryə\ *n* -S *usu cap* [Skt *vallabhācārya*, fr. *Vallabha* fl1520 Hindu religious leader + *ācārya* teacher — more at ACHARYA] : one of a Hindu Vaishnava sect founded by the Brahmin Vallabha

val lace *often cap V, var of* VAL

val·la·do·lid \ˌvalədəˈlid -ˈlē; ˌvä(l)yədəˈlē, -yəthə-\ *adj, usu cap* [fr. *Valladolid*, commune of northwest central Spain] : of or from the city of Valladolid, Spain : of the kind or style prevalent in Valladolid

vallance *var of* VALANCE

val·la·ry *also* **val·lery** \ˈvalərē\ *adj* [L (*corona*) *vallaris* mural crown, fr. *vallum* wall, rampart + *-aris* -ar] *heraldry* : formed of a gold circlet surmounted by flat pointed or curved strips

val·late \ˈvaˌlāt\ *adj* [L *vallatus*, past part. of *vallare* to surround with a wall, fr. *vallum* wall, rampart — more at WALL] : having a raised edge surrounding a depression

vallate papilla *n* : CIRCUMVALLATE PAPILLA

val·la·tion \vaˈlāshən\ *n* -S [LL *vallation-, vallatio*, fr. L *vallatus* + *-ion-, -io* -ion] *archaic* : an earthwork wall : RAMPART, ENTRENCHMENT

val·lec·u·la \vəˈlekyələ, vaˈl-\ *n, pl* **vallecu·lae** \-yəˌlē, -lī\ [NL, fr. LL, little valley, depression, dim. of *valles* valley — more at VALE] : an anatomical groove, channel, or depression: as **a** (1) : a groove on the stem of a plant of the genus *Equisetum* (2) : a groove on the fruit of a various plant of the family Ammiaceae **b** : a groove between the base of the tongue and the epiglottis **c** : a fossa on the underside of the cerebellum separating the hemispheres and including the inferior vermis

val·lec·u·lar \-yələ(r)\ *adj* [NL *vallecula* + E *-ar*] : of or relating to a vallecula

vallecular canal *n* : one of the large intercellular passages of the cortical parenchyma alternating with the vascular bundles in the stems of plants of the genus *Equisetum*

vallecula syl·vii \-ˈsilvēˌī, -vēˌē\ *n, usu cap S* [NL, lit., vallecula of Sylvius, after Franciscus *Sylvius* (Franz de la Boë) †1672 Ger. anatomist] : the depression in the brain in which the lateral fissure begins

val·lec·u·late \-lət, -ˌlāt\ *adj* [NL *vallecula* + E *-ate*] : having valleculae

val·le·ri·ite \vəˈlirēˌīt\ *n* -S *usu cap* [Sw, *valleriit*, fr. G. *Wallerius* (*Vallerius*) †1742 Swed. mineralogist + Sw *-it* -ite] : a mineral $Cu_2Fe_4S_7$ consisting of sulfide of copper and iron perhaps identical with the artificial compound $Cu_3Fe_4S_6$

val·ley \ˈvalē, -li\ *n, pl* **valleys** *often attrib* [ME *valeie, valey*, fr. OF *valee*, fr. *val* valley, vale — more at VALE] **1 a** : an elongate depression of the earth's surface commonly situated between ranges of hills or mountains and often comprising a drainage area — compare CANYON, GULLY, RAVINE; see RIFT VALLEY, SYNCLINAL VALLEY **b** : an area of generally flat land extending many miles inland and drained or watered by a large river and its tributary streams **2 a** : a low, gloomy, or fearsome place or situation ⟨the ~ of the shadow of death⟩ ⟨a ~ of misery without parallel in industrial history —Roger Burlingame⟩ **b** : a low point in a course of development esp. as represented or capable of being represented on a graph ⟨peaks of inflation and . . . ~*s* of extreme depression —F.D.Roosevelt⟩ ⟨a sequence of sounds . . . is therefore characterized by successive peaks and ~*s* of sonority —Bernard Bloch & G.L.Trager⟩ **3** : a hollow or depression resembling or suggestive of a valley: as **a** : a trough between waves **b** : the place of meeting of two slopes of a roof that form on the plan a reentrant angle; *also* : the material (as sheet metal or tile) placed in a roof valley to shed water **c** : VALLECULA **4** : LILY OF THE VALLEY

valley 3b

valley board *n* : a board placed for the reception of the lead gutter in the valley of a roof

valley breeze *n* : a breeze that blows up valleys or mountain slopes on clear days

valley fever *n* [so called fr. its prevalence in the San Joaquin valley of central California] : COCCIDIOIDOMYCOSIS

valley flat *n* : the low flat land bordering the channel of a stream

valley glacier *n* : a glacier usu. originating in a cirque at a valley head or in a plateau ice cap and flowing downward between the walls of a valley

valley lily *n* : LILY OF THE VALLEY

valley oak *n* : CALIFORNIA WHITE OAK

valley quail *also* **valley partridge** *n* : CALIFORNIA QUAIL; *esp* : a bird of a distinct variety (*Lophortyx californica californica*) that is distinguished by pale plumage and is found chiefly in dry interior valleys below 5000 feet

valley rafter *n* : the rafter running from the wall plate to the ridge and along the valley of a valley roof

valley tile *n* : roofing tile shaped to fit in the valley of a roof

valley train *n* : a deposit of glaciofluvial sand and gravel extending along the floor of a valley : TRAIN

valley white oak *n* : CALIFORNIA WHITE OAK

valley wind *n* : a breeze of diurnal period depending on the unevenness of land surfaces that blows up the slope by day — compare MOUNTAIN WIND

val·lis \ˈvaləs\ *n* -ES [NL, fr. L, valley — more at VALE] : VALLECULA C

val·lis·ne·ria \ˌvaləˈsnirēə, -ləzˈn-\ *n, cap* [NL, fr. Antonio *Vallisnieri* †1730 Ital. naturalist + NL *-ia*] : a genus of submerged aquatic plants (family Hydrocharitaceae) with ribbonlike leaves and pistillate spathes on long finally spiral scapes

val·lis·ne·ri·a·ce·ae \ˌ==ˌ==ˈāsēˌē\ *n pl, cap* [NL *Vallisneria*, type genus + *-aceae*] *in some classifications* : a family comprising monocotyledonous aquatic herbs (order Naiadales) that are distinguished by having flowers with the tube of the perianth more or less adnate to the ovary and the carpels united in fruit and that are now usu. included in Hydrocharitaceae — **val·lis·ne·ri·a·ceous** \ˌ==ˌ==ˈāshəs\ *adj*

val·lo·ta \vəˈlōd·ə, va-\ *n, cap* [NL, after Antoine *Vallot* †1671 Fr. physician and botanist] : a genus of southern African bulbous herbs (family Amaryllidaceae) with a long funnel-shaped perianth tube and winged seeds — see SCARBOROUGH LILY

val·lum \ˈvaləm, ˈwäˌlu̇m\ *n, pl* **val·la** \-lə, -(ˌ)lä\ *or* **vallums** [L — more at WALL] : a defensive wall of earth, sod, or stone : RAMPART; *specif* : an earthwork surmounted by a palisade esp. as constructed by the ancient Romans from dirt thrown up from a surrounding fosse

valn *abbr* valuation

va·lois \ˈvalˌwä, ˈ=ˈ=\ *adj, usu cap* [*Valois*, French royal house] : of or relating to a French royal family furnishing the rulers of France from 1328 to 1589

¹va·lo·nia *also* **va·lo·nea** *or* **val·lo·nia** \vəˈlōnēə\ *n* -S [It *vallonia, vallonea*, fr. MGk *balanidia*, pl. of *balanidion*, dim. of Gk *balanos* acorn — more at GLAND] : dried acorn cups that are obtained from the valonia oak or sometimes various other oaks, contain from 20 to 40 percent of tannin, and are used esp. in tanning or dressing leather — compare CAMATA

²valonia \"\ *n, cap* [NL] : a genus (coextensive with the family Valoniaceae) of marine green algae having a thallus that is a single oval or cylindrical multinucleate cell often an inch long — compare SEA BOTTLE

va·lo·ni·a·ce·ae \vəˌlōnēˈāsēˌē\ *n pl, cap* [NL *Valonia*, type genus + *-aceae*] : a family of coenocytic green algae usu. classed among the Siphonocladales but sometimes esp. formerly among the Siphonales — see ²VALONIA — **va·lo·ni·a·ceous** \vəˌlōnēˈāshəs\ *adj*

valonia oak *n* [¹*valonia*] : a tall evergreen oak (*Quercus aegilops*) of southwestern Europe and Asia Minor whose immature fruit yields valonia and camata and whose wood is used for furniture

val·or \ˈvalə(r)\ *n* -S *see -or in Explan Notes* [ME *valour, valor*, fr. MF *valor, valour, valeur*, fr. ML *valor*, fr. L *valēre* to be strong, be worth — more at WIELD] **1** *obs* : VALUE, WORTH **2** : the quality or state of mind with which a person faces danger or hardship boldly or firmly : BRAVERY, COURAGE ⟨the fortitude and ~ of her sons —William Laurence⟩ ⟨to stay there . . . required a ~ which is an essential part of sheer nobility and integrity —*advt*⟩ ⟨perhaps it would have been the better part of ~ to have come back later —John Cogley⟩

val·o·ri·za·tion \ˌvalərəˈzāshən, -ˌrīˈz-\ *n* -S [Pg *valorização*, fr. *valorizare* to valorize, boost prices (fr. *valor* value, price — fr. ML — + *-izare* -ize, fr. LL) + *-ação* -ation, fr. L *-ation-, -atio*] : the act or process of attempting to give an arbitrary market value or price to a commodity usu. by governmental intervention (as by maintaining a purchasing fund to buy up surpluses or making loans to producers to enable them to store their products); *specif* : price fixing by cartels or agreements — compare TRUST

val·o·rize \ˈvaləˌrīz\ *vt* -ED/-ING/-S [back-formation fr. *valorization*] : to determine or set the price of by valorization ⟨the coffee crisis came, and our main product was *valorized*; we tried to protect its price —G.D.Vargas⟩

val·or·ous \ˈvalərəs\ *adj* [ML *valorosus*, fr. *valor* + L *-osus* -ous] **1** : possessing or exhibiting valor : BRAVE, COURAGEOUS ⟨~ men continued the struggle against overwhelming odds⟩ **2** : characterized by or performed with valor ⟨his thoughts would be full of ~ deeds —Joseph Conrad⟩ ⟨the ~ days of 1945 —Byron Price⟩ **syn** see BRAVE

val·or·ous·ly *adv* : in a valorous manner : with valor

val·or·ous·ness *n* -ES : the quality or state of being valorous

val·pa·rai·so *or* **val·pa·ra·íso** \ˌvalpəˈrī(ˌ)zō, -pəˈrā(-, ˌvalˌpärəˈē(ˌ)sō\ *adj, usu cap* [fr. *Valparaiso*, seaport of central Chile] : of or from the city of Valparaiso, Chile : of the kind or style prevalent in Valparaiso

valparaiso oak *n, usu cap V* : CANYON LIVE OAK

val·po·li·cel·la \ˌvälˌpōləˈchelə\ *n, usu cap* [fr. *Valpolicella*, valley of northern Italy] : a dry red table wine from vineyards near Lake Garda in Venetia in Italy

vals *pl of* VAL

val·sa \ˈvalsə\ *n, cap* [NL] : a genus (the type of the family Valsaceae) of fungi having perithecia immersed in a stroma and usu. with elongated necks converging toward the center — compare DIAPORTHE

val·sa·ce·ae \valˈsāsēˌē\ *n pl, cap* [NL, fr. *Valsa*, type genus + *-aceae*] : a family of ascomycetous fungi (order Sphaeriales) sharing the characters of the genus *Valsa*

val·sal·va maneuver \(ˌ)valˌsalvə-\ *n, usu cap V* [after Antonio *Valsalva* †1723 Ital. anatomist] : the inflation of the middle ear by closing the mouth and nostrils and blowing so as to puff out the cheeks

valse \väls\ *n* -S [F, fr. G *walzer* — more at WALTZ] : WALTZ; *specif* : a concert waltz

val·soid \ˈvalˌsȯid\ *adj* [NL *Valsa* + E *-oid*] : of, resembling, or having perithecia like fungi of the genus *Valsa*

¹val·u·able \ˈvalyəbəl *also* -yəwəbəl\ *adj* [²*value* + *-able*] **1** : possessing monetary value in use or exchange ⟨disposing of a ~ store of furs —I.B.Richman⟩ ⟨contains the most ~ minerals in a profuse variety —H.T.Buckle⟩ ⟨started the very ~ ostrich feather industry —Carveth Wells⟩ **2 a** : having or exhibiting desirable or esteemed characteristics or qualities esp. of an intrinsic nature : VALUED ⟨another human being equally ~ in the sight of . . . God —W.R.Harris⟩ ⟨both are unquestionably ~ as literature —*Americas*⟩ ⟨a continual surrender of himself . . . to something which is more ~ —T.S. Eliot⟩ **b** : characterized by usefulness, worth, or serviceableness usu. for a specific purpose ⟨experience . . . made him a ~ member of committees —*Current Biog.*⟩ ⟨food is ~ to the animal and moisture to the plant —Samuel Alexander⟩ ⟨the author's illustrations are highly ~ to the text —Irene Smith⟩ ⟨~ information⟩ ⟨~ advice⟩ ⟨~ contributions⟩ **3** *obs, of a person* : ESTIMABLE, WORTHY **syn** see COSTLY 2

²valuable *n* -S : something of worth or value usu. of the nature of personal effects — usu. used in pl. ⟨the man . . . told me to check my ~*s* —Andy Logan⟩ ⟨they contracted to carry ~*s*, securities, and bundles —R.J.Purcell⟩

valuable consideration *n* : an equivalent or compensation having value that is given for something (as money, marriage, services) acquired or promised and that may consist either in some right, interest, profit, or benefit accruing to one party or some responsibility, forbearance, detriment, or loss exercised by or falling upon the other party — compare CONSIDERATION 8

val·u·able·ness *n* -ES : the quality or state of being valuable

val·u·ably \-blē, -bli\ *adv* : in a valuable manner : with value or usefulness ⟨he adds ~ to the record of our national life —George Mayberry⟩

val·u·ate \ˈvalyəˌwāt\ *vt* -ED/-ING/-S [back-formation fr. *valuation*] : to place a value on : VALUE, APPRAISE

val·u·a·tion \ˌvalyəˈwāshən\ *n* -S [MF, fr. *valuer* to value (fr. *value*, n.) + *-ation*] **1** : the act or process of valuing or of estimating value or worth: as **a** : the act or process of setting or determining the price of something : APPRAISAL **b** : the determination of the present value of a life insurance policy as measured by the difference between the present value of the benefits promised and the present value of all the premiums expected to be received on the policy **2** : the value or price set upon something as its estimated or determined market value ⟨if the final bid is below the reserve ~ of the wool, the sale may be closed⟩ ⟨the property is valued by local assessors . . . to determine the ~ on which the owners' tax obligations shall be computed —F.A.Ogg & P.O.Ray⟩ **3** : the appreciation or usu. personal estimation of the merit, excellence, or character of something ⟨the private ~ of a person's worth —M.O.Purcell⟩ ⟨children whose ~ of fighting is simple and absolute —Margaret Mead⟩ ⟨the traditional British ~ of high scholastic attainment —A.T.M.Wilson⟩

valuation account *n* : RESERVE ACCOUNT 1

val·u·a·tion·al \ˌvalyəˈwāshənᵊl, -shnəl\ *adj* : of, relating to, or concerned with valuation ⟨all judgments are ~ —Herbert Fingarette⟩ ⟨advances a number of ~ and moral arguments —Frank Thilly⟩ ⟨aspects which determine . . . our ~ attitudes —Eliseo Vivas⟩ — **val·u·a·tion·al·ly** \-ᵊlē, -əlē\ *adv*

valuation survey *n* : the survey of the stand of trees upon an average area of forest selected for detailed measurement and valuation

val·u·a·tive \ˈvalyəˌwād·iv, -ˌwəd· -\ *adj* [²*value* + *-ative*] : VALUATIONAL, EVALUATIVE — **val·u·a·tive·ly** \-d·əvlē\ *adv*

val·u·a·tor \-ˌwād·ə(r)\ *n* -S [²*value* + *-ator*] : one that valuates; *specif* : APPRAISER

¹val·ue \ˈval(ˌ)yü, -yə (*this pronunc before a vowel or pause is esp South*); *often* -yəw+V; *dial* -lē *or* -li\ *n* -S *often attrib* [ME, fr. MF, fr. (assumed) VL *valuta*, fr. fem. of (assumed) VL *valutus*, past part. of L *valēre* to be worth — more at WIELD] **1 a** : the amount of a commodity, service, or medium of exchange that is the equivalent of something else : a fair return in goods, services, or money ⟨the method of merchandising is to give the buyer good ~ at the right price —*Wall Street Jour.*⟩ ⟨I take his wages because I give good ~ for them —John Buchan⟩ — often used in pl. ⟨priced at levels that reflect . . . policy of passing on to the customer the ever greater ~*s* resulting from technological progress —A.P.Sloan & H.H. Curtice⟩ ⟨the store advertises great ~*s* at large savings⟩ **b** : VALUABLE CONSIDERATION ⟨for ~ received⟩ ⟨a holder or purchaser for ~⟩ **2** : the monetary worth of something : marketable price usu. in terms of a medium of exchange ⟨his holdings increase in ~⟩ ⟨has the same ~ as the U.S. dollar —S.G.Inman⟩ ⟨fool's gold is of practically no ~⟩ ⟨having a ~ of $5⟩ **3 a** : relative worth, utility, or importance : degree of excellence : status in a scale of preferences ⟨we know the ~ of a thing by the way it is sought, shunned, protected —H.N. Wieman⟩ ⟨he knew the precise ~ of men and could marshal them —A.H.Meneely⟩ ⟨learned the ~ of rest in the treatment of . . . tuberculosis —J.F.Fulton⟩ ⟨the physicist has become a military asset of such ~ —I.I.Rabi⟩ ⟨only a few . . . have anything of ~ to say —Edward Clodd⟩ **b** : a liking or regard for a person or thing ⟨she had a ~ for rank and consequence —Jane Austen⟩ ⟨a sad man who, for all his gaiety . . . had little ~ for life —Joyce Cary⟩ **4 a** : a particular quantitative determination in mathematics ⟨as the ~ of *a* increases, *b* decreases⟩ ⟨the ~*s* of the angles vary proportionately⟩ **b** : the amount or extent of a specified measurement of time, space, or quantity ⟨~*s* of the age of the earth determined by the geologists —S.F.Mason⟩ ⟨gives a fairly exact ~ of the constant temperature deeper down —Valter Schytt⟩ ⟨pressure maintained at sea level ~*s* —H.G.Armstrong⟩ **5** : the relative length or duration of a musical tone or note ⟨a quarter note has the ~ of two eighth notes⟩ **6** : the relative rank, importance, or numerical worth of a playing card, chessman, or other game component ⟨the ace is often given a different ~ in different forms of rummy⟩ **7 a** : ¹LIGHTNESS 2 **b** : value in the Munsell system — used in psychophysics; see the Color Charts explanation at COLOR **c** : the relation of one part or detail in a picture to another with respect to lightness and darkness **8** : something (as a principle, quality, or entity) intrinsically valuable or desirable ⟨may call food a ~ for the animal —Samuel Alexander⟩ ⟨the devotee of . . . education and religion was keenly aware of ~ —A.H.Johnson⟩ — often used in pl. ⟨defending the ~*s* of the classical . . . tradition —*Current Biog.*⟩ ⟨all ~*s* are only relative to a given culture —Erich Fromm⟩ ⟨the business world with its regulated system of ~*s* —D.H.Lawrence⟩ ⟨for the sensate mentality . . . human ~*s* are hedonistic and utilitarian —David Bidney⟩ **9** : the precious metals contained in rock, gravel, or earth — usu. used in pl. ⟨the vein carries good ~*s*⟩ ⟨~*s* were discovered here in 1864 and a 10-stamp mill was soon at work —*Amer. Guide*

Series: Nev.⟩ **10** : DENOMINATION 4 ⟨a new airmail ~ is to be issued here soon —*Nat'l Stamp News*⟩ **11** : the distinctive character or quality of a speech sound ⟨an alphabet made up of letters with phonetic ~*s* —Charlton Laird⟩ ⟨in . . . *Elhua* the *h* really has the ~ of *ch* in the Scottish word *loch* —T.H. Gaster⟩ **12** : a term or an expression in logic that may replace a variable in a propositional function so that the resultant is a true or false statement ⟨*man* is a ~ for *x* in the function *x is rational*⟩

syn WORTH: VALUE and WORTH are frequently differentiated more often by the demands of idiom than by differences in meaning or connotation. VALUE may sometimes suggest an evaluation made from an individual or specific point of view or in an individual or special situation ⟨have to comprehend the artist's own *values* —Havelock Ellis⟩ ⟨the ability of an ordinary Englishman to measure up to the times even though he must change his *values* —J.D.Hart⟩ WORTH may suggest more lasting genuine merit resting on deeper, intrinsic, and enduring qualities ⟨those qualities of the human personality which have an abiding *worth* under the tests of our civilization —Henry Suzzallo⟩ ⟨having gained a more judicious knowledge of the *worth* and dignity of individual man —William Wordsworth⟩ ⟨this book on navigation has chapters of varying *worth*⟩

— **at value** *adv* : at the value fixed by the ruling or current market price — used where goods are sold subject to the price being fixed at some time later than the sale or when shipment is made

²**value** \"\ *vt* -ED/-ING/-S **1 a** : to estimate or assign the monetary worth of : APPRAISE ⟨gave me a piece of his amethyst and I planned to have it properly *valued* —Edwin Corle⟩ ⟨merchandise inventories will be *valued* at the end of the year⟩ — often used with *at* ⟨~*s* his holdings at $3,000,000⟩ ⟨the institution ~*s* its plant and endowment at several million⟩ **b** : to rate or scale in usefulness, importance, or general worth : EVALUATE ⟨impresssions which she had long since arranged and *valued* in her mind —Mary Deasy⟩ ⟨search and ~ every element in the conflict before him —Thomas De Quincey⟩ **2** : to consider or rate highly : PRIZE, ESTEEM ⟨from his parents . . . he learned to ~ education —*Current Biog.*⟩ ⟨responded to and *valued* pleasant friendships —Ruth P. Randall⟩ ⟨*valued* himself on his tolerance of heresy in great thinkers —Robert Frost⟩ **3** *archaic* : to show concern for : HEED **syn** see APPRECIATE, ESTIMATE

value added *n* : the value added to or created in a product or commodity by the manufacturing or marketing process exclusive of the cost of materials, supplies, packaging, or overhead

val·ued \ˈval(ˌ)yüd, -yəd\ *adj* [¹*value* + *-ed*] : having such or so many values — usu. used in combination ⟨multi*valued*⟩ ⟨two-*valued*⟩

value date *n, chiefly Brit* : the date when the proceeds of a credit instrument (as a check) or of a foreign exchange transaction (as the sale of dollars for sterling) become available for use

valued policy *n* [fr. past part. of ²*value*] : an insurance policy in which the insurer and insured agree upon a stated value in advance of a loss to be accepted as the measure of liability in case of a total loss

valued policy law *n* : a law requiring insurance companies to pay to the insured in case of total loss the full amount of the insurance regardless of the actual value of the property at the time of the loss

value judgment *n* : a judgment attributing a value (as good, evil, beautiful, desirable) to a thing, action, or entity ⟨even where there are protestations of tolerance and avowed lack of prejudice, *value judgments* creep in —F.J.Brown & J.S.Roucek⟩

val·ue·less \ˈvalyüləs, -yəl-\ *adj* **1** : having no value : WORTHLESS ⟨hemlock, at first considered ~, was ruthlessly destroyed —*Amer. Guide Series: Pa.*⟩ **2** : lacking in values — **val·ue·less·ness** *n* -ES

value of service : the highest sum in transportation charges that any particular class of shippers can afford or will consent to pay

val·u·er \ˈvalyəwə(r)\ *n* -S : one that values: as **a** *Brit* : APPRAISER **b** : CRUISER 4a

values *pl of* VALUE, *pres 3d sing of* VALUE

value system *n* : the system of established values, norms, or goals existing in a society

va·lu·ta \vəˈlüd·ə\ *n* -S [It, value, coin, commercial paper, fr. (assumed) VL *valuta* value — more at VALUE] **1** : the value of a currency (as of a European country) as agreed upon or its exchange value with reference to the currency of another country **2** : foreign exchange in available or usable form

val·va \ˈvalvə\ *n, pl* **val·vae** \-ˌlˌvē, -lˌvī\ [NL, fr. L, leaf of a double door — more at VALVE] : VALVE 2a,3,4

val·val \ˈvalvəl\ *or* **val·var** \-alvə(r)\ *adj* [*valve* + *-al* or *-ar*] : VALVULAR

valvasor *or* **valvassor** *var of* VAVASOR

val·va·ta \valˈväd·ə, -ˈvād·ə\ *n* [NL, fr. fem. of *valvatus* valvate] **1** *cap* : a genus of freshwater operculate snails (suborder Taenioglossa) having the gill attached only by the base so that it forms a process like a feather outside the shell when extended **2** -S : any snail of the genus *Valvata*

val·vate \ˈvalˌvāt\ *adj* [NL *valvatus*, fr. L, having folding doors, fr. *valva* leaf of a folding door + *-atus* -ate — more at VALVE] : having valves or parts resembling a valve: **a** : meeting at the edges without overlapping ⟨~ sepals⟩ ⟨~ leaves⟩ **b** : opening as if by doors or valves ⟨~ capsules⟩ ⟨~ anthers⟩

valve \ˈvalv, ˈvau̇v\ *n* -S *often attrib* [L *valva* leaf of a folding or double door; akin to L *volvere* to roll, turn around — more at VOLUBLE] **1 a** *archaic* : a leaf or a half of a folding or double door **b** : the door or gate used for regulating the flow of water in a sluice **2** : something resembling or suggestive of a valve or stop esp. in regulating, checking, or permitting flow or movement through a passage: as **a** [NL *valva*] : any of various bodily structures esp. in the veins and lymphatics whose function is to close temporarily a passage or orifice or permit a movement of fluid in one direction only and that may consist of a sphincter muscle or of two or sometimes three membranous folds inclined in the normal direction of flow — see MITRAL VALVE, SEMILUNAR VALVE, TRICUSPID VALVE **b** (1) : any of numerous mechanical devices by which the flow of liquid, air or other gas, or loose material in bulk may be started, stopped, or regulated by a movable part that opens, shuts, or partially obstructs one or more ports or passageways; *also* : the movable part of such a device — compare COCK 2; see CHECK VALVE, GATE VALVE, PISTON VALVE, SAFETY VALVE (2) : such a device in a brass wind instrument that is designed for quickly varying the tube length in order to change the fundamental tone by some definite interval and usu. consists of a piston or rotary valve **c** *chiefly Brit* : ELECTRON TUBE, VACUUM TUBE **3** [NL *valva*] **a** : one of the distinct and usu. movably articulated pieces of which the shell of lamellibranch mollusks, brachiopods, barnacles, and some other shell-bearing animals consists **b** : one of the pieces forming the sheath of the ovipositor or external genital organs of many insects **4** [NL *valva*] **a** : one of the segments or pieces into which a dehiscing capsule or legume separates **b** : the portion of various anthers (as of the barberry) resembling a lid **c** : one of the two silicified shells or encasing membranes of a diatom **5** : one of the two halves of a stone or clay mold used by primitive or ancient peoples for casting bronze objects

valve chest *also* **valve box** *n* : a chamber in which a valve works; *specif* : STEAM CHEST

valved \-vd\ *adj* [*valve* + *-ed*] **1** : VALVATE **2** : provided or equipped with valves ⟨~ outlets⟩ ⟨~ musical instruments⟩

valve gear *n* : any of numerous gears by which motion is given to the valves of an engine and esp. a steam engine; *specif* : such a gear for a steam engine by which the cutoff may be varied while the engine is running and the engine started, stopped, or reversed

valve-in-head engine \ˈ=-=,=-\ *n* : an internal-combustion engine in which both inlet and exhaust valves are located in the cylinder head

valve·less \ˈ=ləs\ *adj* : having no valves; *specif* : having no separate valve ⟨a ~ engine⟩

valve lifter *n* : a device used esp. in the internal-combustion engine for opening the valve of a cylinder

valve·man \ˈ=mən, -ˌman\ *n, pl* **valvemen** : a valve operator

valve motion *n* : VALVE GEAR

valve of bau·hin \-bōˈaⁿ\ *usu cap B* [after Gaspard *Bauhin* †1624 Swiss botanist and anatomist] : ILEOCECAL VALVE

valve of ger·lach \-ˈgerˌläk\ *usu cap G* [after Joseph *Gerlach* †1896 Ger. anatomist] : an inconstant fold of mucous membrane resembling a valve at the cecal end of the vermiform appendix

valve of has·ner \-ˈhäsnə(r), -äz-\ *usu cap H* [after Joseph Ritter von Artha *Hasner* †1892 Austrian oculist] : an imperfect valve at the opening of the nasolacrimal duct into the inferior meatus of the nose

valve of hei·ster \-ˈhīstə(r)\ *usu cap H* [after Lorenz *Heister* †1758 Ger. surgeon] : VALVULA SPIRALIS

valve of hous·ton \-ˈ(h)yüstən, -ˈhüs-,-ˈhau̇s-\ *usu cap H* [after John *Houston* †1845 Irish physician] : RECTAL VALVE

valve of kerck·ring \-ˈkerkriŋ\ *usu cap K* [after Theodor *Kerckring* †1693 Du. anatomist] : PLICA CIRCULARIS

valve of the·be·si·us \-tāˈbāzēəs\ *usu cap T* [after Adam C. *Thebesius* †1732 Ger. physician] : CORONARY VALVE

valve of vieus·sens \-ˌvyə(r)ˈsäⁿs, -vyə̄ˈs-\ *usu cap 2d V* [after Raymond *Vieussens* †1716 Fr. anatomist] : the anterior medullary velum

valve pilot *n* : a device used on a steam locomotive to inform the engineman by visual indication on a dial the proper percentage of cutoff to use in admitting steam to the cylinders

valve ring *n* : RELIEF FRAME

valve seat *n* : a circular ring of heat-resistant bronze or steel on which a valve of an internal-combustion engine rests when closed

valve snail *n* : a snail of the genus *Valvata*

valve trombone *n* : a trombone having three piston valves

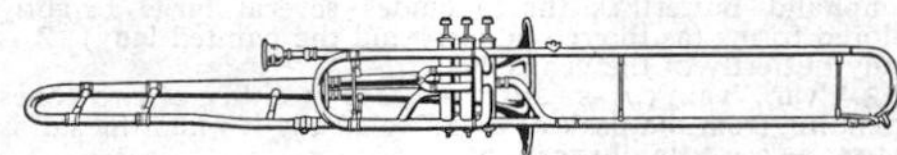

valve trombone

instead of a slide to alter the tone or pitch

val·vi·fer \ˈvalvəfə(r)\ *n* -S [NL, fr. *valva* + *-i-* + *-fer*] : any of the basal plates of an insect's ovipositor arising from the eighth and ninth abdominal segments — compare VALVULA 2

val·vif·er·ous \(ˈ)valˈvif(ə)rəs\ *adj* [*valve* + *-iferous*] : having valves

val·vi·form \ˈvalvəˌfȯrm\ *adj* [*valve* + *-iform*] : shaped or formed like a valve

valv·ing \ˈvalviŋ\ *n* -S [*valve* + *-ing*] : a system or arrangement of valves ⟨changed the angle and the ~ on the rear shocks —Walt Woron⟩ ⟨the ~ can be opened to the pump line —George Hofferkamp & John Zich⟩

val·vot·o·my \valˈväd·əmē\ *n* -ES [*valve* + *-o-* + *-tomy*] : VALVULOTOMY

valvul- *or* **valvulo-** *comb form* [NL *valvula*] : small valve : valvule : fold ⟨*valvul*itis⟩ ⟨*valvulo*tome⟩

val·vu·la \ˈvalvyələ\ *n, pl* **valvu·lae** \-ˌlē, -ˌlī\ [NL, dim. of *valva*] **1** : a small valve or fold **2** : any of the six processes forming the blades and enclosing the lobes of an insect's ovipositor

valvula co·li \-ˈkōˌlī, -ˈkōˌlē\ *n* [NL, lit., valvula of the colon] : ILEOCECAL VALVE

valvula con·ni·vens \-kəˈnīˌvenz, -nēˌven(t)s\ *n, pl* **valvulae conniven·tes** \-ˌkänəˈvenˌtēz, -enˌtās\ [NL, lit., closing valvula] : PLICA CIRCULARIS

val·vu·lar \ˈvalvyələ(r)\ *adj* [*valvule* + *-ular*] **1** : resembling or having the function of a valve esp. of a plant or animal body ⟨a ~ opening⟩ ⟨~ divisions of the heart⟩ **2** : of or relating to a valve esp. of the heart ⟨~ defect⟩ ⟨~ disease⟩ ⟨~ stenosis⟩

valvula spi·ra·lis \-ˌspīˈraləs, -rāl-; spəˈräl-\ *n, pl* **valvulae spira·les** \-a(ˌ)lēz, -ā(ˌ)lēz, -ä(ˌ)lās\ [NL, lit., spiral valvula] : a series of crescentic folds of mucous membrane somewhat spirally arranged on the interior of the gallbladder and continuing into the cystic duct — called also *valve of Heister*

val·vu·late \ˈvalvyəˌlāt, -ˌlət\ *adj* [*valvul-* + *-ate*] : having valvules

val·vule \ˈval(ˌ)vyül\ *n* -S [NL *valvula*] : a small valve or structure resembling a valve

val·vu·li·tis \ˌvalvyəˈlīd·əs\ *n* -ES [NL, fr. *valvul-* + *-itis*] : inflammation of a valve esp. of the heart ⟨mitral ~⟩

val·vu·lo·plas·ty \ˈvalvyəlōˌplastē\ *n* -ES [*valvul-* + *-plasty*] : VALVULOTOMY

val·vu·lo·tome \ˈvalvyəlōˌtōm\ *n* -S [*valvul-* + *-tome*] : a surgical blade designed for valvulotomy or commissurotomy

val·vu·lot·o·my \ˌvalvyəˈläd·əmē\ *n* -ES [*valvul-* + *-tomy*] : the operation of enlarging a narrowed heart valve by cutting through the mitral commissures to relieve the symptoms of mitral stenosis — compare COMMISSUROTOMY

valyl \ˈvalə̇l, ˈvālə̇l\ *n* -S [ISV *valine* + *-yl*] : the univalent acyl radical $(CH_3)_2CHCH(CH_2)CO$— of valine

vam·brace \ˈvamˌbrās\ *n* [ME *vambras, vambrace*, fr. AF *vauntbras*, fr. *vaunt-* fore- (fr. OF *avant-*) + *bras* arm (fr. OF) — more at VANGUARD, BRACELET] : a piece of medieval armor designed to protect the forearm

vam·braced \-st\ *adj* [*vambrace* + *-ed*] : wearing a vambrace — used chiefly in heraldic description

va·moose \vaˈmüs, vəˈm- *sometimes* -mōs\ *vb* -ED/-ING/-S [Sp *vamos* let us go, suppletive 1st pl. imper. (fr. L *vadere* to go) of *ir* to go — more at WADE] *vi, slang* : to depart quickly : DECAMP ~ *vt, slang* : to depart from ⟨~ the ranch⟩

¹**vamp** \ˈvamp, -aa(ə)-, -ai-\ *n* -S [ME *vaumpe, vampe*, fr. OF *avantpié*, fr. *avant-* fore- + *pié* foot, fr. L *ped-, pes* — more at VANGUARD, FOOT] **1** *dial* : a short hose coming to the calf formerly sometimes worn over a stocking : SOCK **2** : the part of a shoe upper or boot upper covering esp. the forepart of the foot and sometimes also extending forward over the toe or backward to the back seam of the upper — see BROGUED VAMP, CIRCULAR VAMP, THREE-QUARTER VAMP, WHOLE VAMP; SHOE illustration **3** [²*vamp*] **a** : a simple musical accompaniment improvised for the occasion **b** : an introductory section of two or four measures often played several times (as in vaudeville) before a solo or between verses while the soloist is preparing to sing or is indulging in byplay **4** [²*vamp*] : something vamped or patched up; *esp* : a literary composition based on old material

²**vamp** \"\ *vb* -ED/-ING/-S *vt* **1 a** : to provide (a shoe) with a new vamp : REVAMP **b** : to piece (something old) with a new part : PATCH — used often with *together* or *up* ⟨~ up old sermons⟩ ⟨a ~*ed* play⟩ **2** : INVENT, CONCOCT, FABRICATE — usu. used with *up* ⟨~ up an excuse⟩ ⟨hastily *vamped*-up pretext⟩ **3** *obs* : to make or present (one) as something else **4** *dial* : to walk or tramp over or along **5** : to make a vamp to : improvise (an accompaniment) for a solo ~ *vi* **1** *dial* : to go on foot : TRAMP, PLOD **2** : to play a vamp or a vamped accompaniment

³**vamp** \"\ *n* -S [origin unknown] : a volunteer fireman

⁴**vamp** \"\ *n* -S [short for *vampire*] : a woman who uses her charm or wiles to seduce and exploit men : FLIRT, ADVENTURESS ⟨uncle who confronts a ~ to rescue a foolish nephew from her clutches —*Theatre Arts*⟩

⁵**vamp** \"\ *vt* -ED/-ING/-S : to practice seductive wiles on : capture or seduce by coquetry

vamped \-m(p)t\ *or* **vamped-up** \ˈ=ˌ=\ *adj* [fr. past part. of ²*vamp*] **1** : patched up : REPAIRED **2** : made up of old materials : not fresh or original ⟨~ adventure story⟩ **3** : trumped-up : FABRICATED

vamp·er \-mpə(r)\ *n* -S **1** [²*vamp* + *-er*] : one that vamps **2** [¹*vamp* + *-er*] : a shoe worker who stitches vamps to quarters

vamphorn \ˈ=ˌ=\ *n* [²*vamp* + *horn*; fr. its use by the choir leader to amplify his voice as an accompaniment to the rest of the choir] : a megaphone used in churches during the 18th and early 19th centuries

vamphorn

vam·pire \ˈvamˌpī(ə)r, ˈvaam-, -īə\ *n* -S [F, fr. G *vampir*, of Slav origin; akin to Serb *vampir* vampire, Russ *upyr'*] **1** : a bloodsucking ghost or reanimated body of a dead person believed to come from the grave and wander about by night sucking the blood of persons asleep and causing their death **2 a** : one who lives by preying mercilessly on others : EXTORTIONER, BLOODSUCKER **b** : a mercenary unscrupulous woman who seduces, exploits, and ruins her lover: as (1) : a stage character of this kind (2) : an actress playing such roles **3** *also* **vampire bat** : any of various bats reputed to feed on blood: as **a** : any of several large So. and Central American leaf-nosed bats (as a false vampire or spearnose bat) that in fact feed on insects rather than blood **b** : any of various So. American bats constituting the genera *Desmodus* and *Diphylla* of the family Desmodontidae that are structurally adapted for subsisting on blood with incisor and canine teeth modified for slitting the skin, with the stomach small and tubular, and with the intestine short and are dangerous to man and domestic animals esp. because they are vectors of equine trypanosomiasis and of rabies in some regions **c** : any large bat (as a fruit bat) of the Old World supposed to suck blood but actually either insectivorous or frugivorous **4** : a stage trapdoor for sudden disappearances

vam·pir·ic \(ˈ)=ˈpirik\ *adj* [*vampire* + *-ic*] : BLOODSUCKING, PARASITIC

vam·pir·ish \ˈ=ˌpī(ə)rish, -rēsh\ *adj* : of, relating to, resembling, or characteristic of a vampire ⟨a mischievous flirtatious girl rather than a ~ woman of the world —W.C.Smith⟩

vam·pir·ism \-ˌrizəm\ *n* -S **1** : belief in vampires **2** : the actions of a vampire : the act or practice of bloodsucking : the practice of preying upon another (as a lover)

vam·pir·ize \-ˌrīz\ *vb* -ED/-ING/-S *vi* : to play the vampire ~ *vt* : to exhaust or prey upon in the manner of a vampire ⟨parents who ~ their children⟩

vamp·ish \ˈvampish\ *adj* [⁴*vamp* + *-ish*] : having the characteristics of a vamp ⟨~ actress⟩

vam·plate \ˈvamˌplāt\ *n* [ME, *vaunplate*, fr. AF *vaunt-* fore- (fr. OF *avant-*) + *plate* — more at VANGUARD] : a round plate of iron mounted on the shaft of a lance or tilting spear to protect the hand

vamps *pl of* VAMP, *pres 3d sing of* VAMP

vamp trap *n* [*vamp* (short for *vampire*) + *trap*] : VAMPIRE 4

vam·py·rel·la \ˌvampəˈrelə, -ˌpīˈr-\ *n, cap* [NL, fr. *vampyrus* vampire + *-ella* — more at VAMPYRUM] : a genus of protozoans (order Amoebina) comprising small amoeboid forms that are ectoparasitic on algae

vam·py·rum \(ˈ)vamˈpīrəm\ *n, cap* [NL, fr. *vampyrus* vampire, fr. F *vampire*] : a genus of So. and Central American bats (family Phyllostomatidae) that includes various harmless insectivorous usu. spearnose bats — compare VAMPIRE 3a

¹**van** \ˈvan, ˈvaa(ə)n\ *n* -S [ME, fr. MF, fr. L *vannus* — more at WINNOW] **1** *dial Eng* : a fan or other winnowing device **2 a** : the wing of a bird or insect ⟨the bird . . . leant on the wind and then swung into it on taut ~*s* —Alan Duncan⟩ **b** : a windmill's sail **3 a** : a shovel used in dressing ore **b** *dial Eng* : the process of testing ore on such a shovel

²**van** \"\ *n* -S [short for *vanguard*] **1** : the leading unit or division of an advancing army, fleet, or other group ⟨battling its way . . . through the high steep seas of a levanter with the red-crossed admiral's flag in the ~ —C.S.Forester⟩ **2** : the group taking the lead or occupying the front position in a moving company : the first part of a procession : HEAD ⟨the paper would be in the ~ of progressive thought —John Buchan⟩ ⟨led the ~ in solving problems —G.C.Sellery⟩ ⟨stocks . . . which have been in the ~ of the market —*Wall Street Jour.*⟩

³**van** \"\ *n* -S [short for *caravan*] **1** : a wagon or motortruck usu. enclosed and used for transportation of goods or animals ⟨route ~⟩ ⟨horse ~⟩ ⟨great ~*s* carrying enormous piled-up loads advanced swaying like mountains —Joseph Conrad⟩ **2** *chiefly Brit* : an enclosed railroad freight or baggage car ⟨the train, consisting of three carriages and a ~ —G.B.Shaw⟩ **3** : a small general store in a lumber camp and sometimes on wheels at which clothing, tobacco, and other small articles for the crew are kept for sale

livestock van

⁴**van** \"\ *vt* **vanned; vanned; vanning; vans** : to carry or forward in a van ⟨it would be possible to ~ the horses each day from one track to the other —*Springfield (Mass.) Union*⟩

⁵**van** \"\ *n* -S [by shortening] *Brit* : ADVANTAGE 5

vanad- *or* **vanado-** *comb form* [NL *vanadium*] : vanadium ⟨*vanad*yl⟩ ⟨*vanado*silicate⟩

van·a·date \ˈvanəˌdāt\ *n* -S [ISV *vanad-* + *-ate*] : a salt or ester derived from vanadium pentoxide and containing pentavalent vanadium — compare METAVANADATE

va·nadic \vəˈnādik, -nad-\ *adj* [NL *vanadium* + ISV *-ic*] : of, relating to, or containing vanadium — used esp. of compounds in which this element has a relatively higher valence than in vanadous compounds

vanadic acid *n* **1** : any of various acids that are hydrates of vanadium pentoxide or known esp. in the form of salts and esters — compare METAVANADIC ACID **2** : VANADIUM PENTOXIDE — not used systematically

vanadic oxide *n* : VANADIUM PENTOXIDE

van·a·dif·er·ous \ˌvanəˈdif(ə)rəs\ *adj* [ISV *vanad-* + *-iferous*] : containing or yielding vanadium

va·na·di·nite \vəˈnādᵊnˌīt; ˌvanəˈdēˌnīt, ˈvanədəˌn-\ *n* -S [G *vanadinit*, fr. *vanadin* vanadium (fr. NL *vanadium* + G *-in* -ine) + *-it* -ite] : a mineral consisting of a lead vanadate and chloride of the opatite group and occurring in yellowish, brownish, or ruby-red hexagonal crystals (hardness 2.75–3, sp. gr. 6.66–7.10)

van·a·dite \ˈvanəˌdīt\ *n* -S [G *vanadit*, fr. *vanad-* + *-it* -ite] : HYPOVANADATE

va·na·di·um \vəˈnādēəm\ *n* -S [NL, fr. ON *Vanadīs* (Freya, Scandinavian goddess) + NL *-ium*] : a gray or white malleable ductile polyvalent metallic element that is resistant to air, seawater, alkalies, and reducing acids except hydrofluoric acid, that occurs widely but for the most part in small amounts in combination in minerals (as vanadinite, patronite, carnotite, roscoelite), in the ashes of many plants, in coals, petroleums, and asphalts, and in the blood of tunicates and other marine animals, that is usu. obtained in the form of ferrovanadium or other alloys or in almost pure metallic form containing small amounts of oxygen, carbon, or nitrogen by reduction of ores, slags, or vanadium pentoxide, and that is used chiefly as a constituent of vanadium steel — symbol *V*; see ELEMENT table

vanadium bronze *n* : any of various yellow or orange pigments said to be metavanadic acid or a salt containing vanadium in the anion

vanadium oxide *n* : an oxide of vanadium: as **a** : the sesquioxide V_2O_3 obtained as a black crystalline powder by reducing vanadium pentoxide : di-vanadium trioxide **b** : the dioxide VO_2 or V_2O_4 obtained as blue-black crystals by partially reducing vanadium pentoxide **c** : VANADIUM PENTOXIDE

vanadium pentoxide *n* : a yellowish red crystalline compound V_2O_5 that forms yellow colloidal solutions, that is obtained by roasting ammonium metavanadate in oxygen or as a by-product of smelting operations or from the soot of some petroleum fuel oils, and that is used in glass manufacture and as a catalyst for oxidations and other reactions; di-nitrogen pentoxide

vanadium steel *n* **1** : steel alloyed with vanadium which strengthens the steel and serves to remove oxygen and possibly nitrogen **2** : steel alloyed with vanadium and other elements (as chromium)

va·na·do·an \vəˈnādəwən\ *adj* [obs. E *vanado*-magnetite coulsonite (fr. E *vanad-* + *magnetite*) + E *-an*] : containing vanadous vanadium and esp. bivalent vanadium

vana·dous \vəˈnādəs, ˈvanəd-\ *adj* [*vanad-* + *-ous*] : of, relating to, or containing vanadium — used esp. of compounds in which this element has a lower valence than in vanadic compounds

vana·dyl \vəˈnādᵊl, ˈvanəˌdil\ *n* -S [*vanad-* + *-yl*] : either of two radicals composed of vanadium and oxygen: **a** : the univalent, bivalent, or trivalent radical VO ⟨~ sulfate $VOSO_4$⟩ **b** : the univalent radical VO_2

van al·len radiation belt \vaˈnalən-, vəˈn-\ *n, usu cap V&A* [after James A. *Van Allen* *b*1914 Am. physicist] : a belt of intense ionizing radiation that surrounds the earth in the outer atmosphere, has particles carrying energies of from approximately 20,000 electron volts to several million electron volts or more, and has an outer zone that extends into space to a distance of about 55,000 kilometers

va·na·pras·tha \ˌvänəˈprəstə\ *n* -s [Skt, lit., one who departs to the forest, fr. *vana* forest + *pratiṣṭhati* he sets forth, fr. *pra-* forward, forth + *tiṣṭhati* he stands — more at BANDAR, FOR, STAND] : a forest-dwelling Hindu hermit; *esp* : one in the third stage of the Brahmanic scheme of life

va·nas·pa·ti \vəˈnəspəd·ē\ *n* -s [Skt *vanaspati* forest tree, soma plant, lit., lord of the forest, fr. *vana* forest + *pati* lord, master — more at BANDAR, POTENT] : a hydrogenated vegetable fat used as a butter substitute in India

van·courier \(ˈ)van + *pronunc at* COURIER\ *n* [modif. (influenced by *courier*) of MF *avant-coureur*, fr. *avant-* fore- + *coureur* runner, fr. OF *courre* to run + *-eur* -or — more at VANGUARD, CURRENT] : a scout or herald sent in advance : FORERUNNER, PRECURSOR

van·cou·ver \(ˈ)van¦küvə(r), (ˈ)vaan-\ *adj, usu cap* [fr. *Vancouver*, city of southern British Columbia, Canada] : of or from the city of Vancouver, B.C. : of the kind or style prevalent in Vancouver

van·cou·ve·ria \ˌvankü'virēə\ *n, cap* [NL, prob. fr. George *Vancouver* †1798 Eng. navigator + NL *-ia*] *in some classifications* : a genus of western No. American herbs (family Berberidaceae) that have dissected basal leaves and small panicled white flowers with numerous sepals and six petals and are usu. included in the genus *Epimedium*

van·cou·ver·ite \=ˈküvə,rīt\ *n* -s *cap* [*Vancouver*, British Columbia + E *-ite*] : a native or resident of Vancouver, B.C.

van·da \ˈvandə\ *n* [NL, fr. Hindi *vandā* mistletoe, fr. Skt, a parasitic plant] **1 a** *cap* : a genus of Indo-Malayan epiphytic orchids having loose racemes of large flowers with spreading perianth and a lip saccate at the base **b** -s : any plant of the genus *Vanda* **2** -s : a pale purple to pale reddish purple

¹van·dal \ˈvandᵊl, ˈvaan-\ *n* -s [L *Vandalus* (sing.), *Vandalii* (pl.), of Gmc origin] **1** *usu cap* : one of a Germanic people anciently dwelling south of the Baltic between the Vistula and the Oder, overrunning Gaul, Spain, and northern Africa in the 4th and 5th centuries A.D. and in 455 entering Italy, sacking Rome, and destroying many monuments of art and literature, and being overthrown in their final stronghold in No. Africa by Belisarius in 534 — see HERMINONES **2 a** : one who willfully destroys or mars something beautiful (as a work of art) **b** : a wanton or ignorant destroyer or defacer of a building or monument that should be preserved ⟨although abandoned and exposed to the elements and to ~*s* for centuries, the walls of these buildings stand strong —R.W.Murray⟩

²vandal \"\ *adj* **1** *usu cap* : of, relating to, or characteristic of the Vandals **2** : carelessly or ignorantly destructive : given to vandalism

van·dal·ic \(ˈ)=¦dalik\ *adj* [¹*vandal* + *-ic*] **1** : VANDAL 2 **2** *usu cap* : VANDAL 1

van·dal·ish \ˈ= dəlish\ *adj* [¹*vandal* + *-ish*] : VANDALISTIC

van·dal·ism \-ˌlizəm\ *n* -s [F *vandalisme*, fr. *vandale* vandal, Vandal (fr. L *Vandalus*) + *-isme* -ism] : willful or malicious destruction or defacement of things of beauty or of public or private property

van·dal·is·tic \¦=ˌ=¦listik, -tēk\ *adj* [¹*vandal* + *-istic*] : of, relating to, or perpetrating vandalism

van·dal·iza·tion \ˌ=dələˈzāshən, -ˌlīˈz-\ *n* -s : the act of vandalizing or state of being vandalized

van·dal·ize \ˈ==ˌlīz\ *vt* -ED/-ING/-S [¹*vandal* + *-ize*] : to subject to vandalism ⟨youths *vandalized* the shop —*N.Y.Times*⟩

vandalroot \ˈ==ˌ=\ *n* **1** : GARDEN HELIOTROPE 1 **2** : VALERIAN 2a

van de graaff generator \ˈvandəˌgraf-\ *n, usu cap V & 1st G* [after Robert J. *Van de Graaff* †1967 Am. physicist] : ELECTROSTATIC GENERATOR

¹van·de·mo·ni·an \ˌvandəˈmōnēən, -dēˈm-\ *also* **van·die·me·ni·an** \-ˈmēnē-\ *or* **van·die·mo·ni·an** \-ˈmōnē-\ *n* -s *usu cap* [irreg. (influenced by E ¹*demon*) fr. *Van Diemen's Land* (now Tasmania) (fr. Anton *Van Diemen* †1645 Du. statesman) + E *-an*] : a white inhabitant of Tasmania; *esp* : one penally transported there before 1853

²vandemonian \¦==¦===\ *adj, usu cap* **1** : of or relating to a Vandemonian **2** : RUFFIANLY, VIOLENT

van den bergh test \ˈvandənˌbərg-\ *n, usu cap B* [after A. A. H. *van den Bergh* †1943 Du. physician] : a test indicating presence of bilirubin in the blood when a diazotizing reagent added to blood serum turns it red (as in jaundice and destructive diseases of the liver)

van·den·bran·de·ite \ˌvandənˈbrandēˌīt\ *or* **van·den·bran·dite** \-ˌbranˌdīt\ *n* -s [F *vandenbrandeite*, fr. P. *Van den Brande*, 20th cent. Belg. geologist + F *-ite*] : a mineral $CuUO_4.2H_2O$ consisting of a hydrous uranium and copper oxide in very dark green flattened crystals

van·der·bilt club convention \ˈva|ndə(r)ˌbilt-, ˈvaa|\ *n, usu cap V* [after Harold S. *Vanderbilt* †1970 Am. capitalist, its inventor] : CLUB CONVENTION

van der waals adsorption \ˈvandə(r)ˌwȯlz-\ *n, usu cap W* : adsorption due to van der Waals forces between the adsorbed molecules and the adsorbing material — opposed to *chemisorption*

van der waals equation *n, usu cap W* [after Johannes D. *van der Waals* †1923 Dutch physicist] : an equation that defines the physical state of a homogeneous gas, is a modification of the ideal-gas equation, and more nearly describes the properties of actual gases: $(p+\frac{a}{v^2})(v-b)=RT$ where *p* is the pressure, *v* the specific volume, *R* the gas constant, *T* the absolute temperature, and *a* and *b* are constants depending respectively on the cohesion between the molecules and the volume occupied by the molecules — compare GAS LAW c

van der waals forces *n pl, usu cap W* [after Johannes D. *van der Waals* †1923 Du. physicist] : the relatively weak attractive forces operative between neutral atoms and molecules, arising because of the electric polarization induced in each of the particles by the presence of other particles, and effective at relatively great distances

V and M *abbr* virgin and martyr

V and T *abbr* volume and tension

¹van·dyke *or* **van·dyck** \(ˈ)van¦dīk, (ˈ)vaan- *also* vənˈd-\ *n* -s [after Sir Anthony *Vandyke* or *Van Dyck* †1641 Flem. painter] **1** *usu cap* [so called fr. its frequent appearance in paintings by Vandyke] **a** : a wide collar made to resemble that of a cape with a deeply indented edge and worn by men and women in the 17th century and later by women only **b** : one of several deeply indented, pointed, or scalloped sections of a decorative edging (as on a collar) **c** : a border or edging with such indentations **2** *usu cap* : VANDYKE BEARD

²vandyke \"\ *vb* -ED/-ING/-S *vt* : to finish (an edge) with vandykes : make or shape with deep indentations ⟨a *vandyked* apron⟩ ~ *vi* : to stagger, weave, or wander in the zigzag course of one drunken or irresolute

Van Dyke \"\ *trademark* — used for a photographic print that is similar to a blueprint but has white translucent lines on a brown opaque background and is used as a master print from which blueprints with blue lines on a white background are made

vandyke beard *n, often cap V* [so called from its frequent appearance in paintings by Vandyke] : a trim pointed beard

vandyke brown *n* [so called from its use by Vandyke] **1** *usu cap V* **a** : a deep-brown pigment of uncertain identity **b** : a natural brown-black pigment of poor light fastness obtained from bog earth or peat or lignite deposits, composed chiefly of organic matter with a small amount of ferric oxide, and used chiefly as an artist's color and stain — called also *Cassel brown, Cologne brown* **c** : any of various synthetic brown pigments (as a mixture of a carbon black with an iron-oxide red) **2** *often cap V* : a moderate brown that is redder, lighter, and slightly stronger than coffee, slightly redder, lighter, and stronger than chestnut brown, slightly yellower than auburn, and yellower and paler than bay — called also *Cassel brown, Cologne brown, Cullen earth, Roman sepia, Verona brown*

vandyke beard

vandyke red *n* [after Sir Anthony *Vandyke* †1641 Flem. painter] **1** *often cap V* : a grayish red that is bluer and deeper than Pompeian red, bluer and darker than bois de rose, and yellower and deeper than appleblossom — called also *Florence brown* **2** : a synthetic red to brown pigment consisting of copper ferrocyanide $Cu_2Fe(CN)_6$

vane \ˈvān\ *n* -s [ME (southern dial.), fr. OE *fana* flag, banner; akin to OHG *fano* cloth, gund*fano* war flag, gonfalon, ON gunn*fani*, Goth *fana* piece of cloth, rag, L *pannus*, Gk *pēnē* thread on a bobbin, woof, web] **1 a** : a movable device attached to a spire, mast, or other elevated object for showing the direction of the wind **b** : one that is changeable or inconstant **2** : a flat or curved surface exposed to a flow of air, gas, or liquid so as to be impelled to move or to rotate about an axis, to redirect the flow (as in a turbine), or itself to be the impeller ⟨the ~*s* of a windmill⟩ ⟨the ~*s* of a fan blower⟩ ⟨the ~*s* of a ship's screw⟩ ⟨the ~*s* of a washing machine agitator⟩ ⟨the ~*s* of an aerial bomb⟩ **3** : the web or flat expanded part of a feather formed of the barbs and their appendages **4** : a feather fastened to the shaft near the nock of an arrow **5 a** : the target of a leveling rod **b** : one of the sights of a compass or quadrant

vaned \ˈvānd\ *adj* [*vane* + *-ed*] : having vanes

va·nel·lus \vəˈneləs\ *n, cap* [NL, fr. F *vanneau* lapwing, fr. OF *vaniel*, fr. *van* winnowing fan — more at VAN] : a genus of birds (family Charadriidae) including the Eurasian lapwing

va·nes·sa \vəˈnesə\ *n* [NL] **1** *cap* : a cosmopolitan genus of nymphalid butterflies that includes several large brightly colored forms (as the red admiral and the painted lady) **2** -s : any butterfly of the genus *Vanessa*

vang \ˈvaŋ, ˈvaiŋ\ *n* -s [alter. of ²*fang*] : either of two ropes extending from the peak of a gaff to steady it when the sail is not set — see SHIP illustration

van·guard \ˈvanˌgärd, ˈvaan-, -gȧd\ *n* [ME *avaunt garde*, *vantgard*, fr. MF *avant-garde*, fr. OF, fr. *avant-* fore- (fr. *avant* before, forward, fr. L *abante*) + *garde* guard — more at ADVANCE, GUARD] **1** : the troops who march at the head of an army : VAN **2** : the leaders of thought, taste, or opinion in a field (as art, letters, or politics) : the forefront of a school or movement ⟨the educators may be in the ~, but . . . they are bucking no trends —W.H.Whyte⟩

van guard \"\ *n* [³*van* + *guard*] : a guard for a railway van or a motortruck

van·guard·ism \-ˌdizəm\ *n* -s : the attitudes, ideas, or activities of persons regarding themselves as members of a vanguard

van·guard·ist \-ˌdəst\ *n* -s : a member of a vanguard

van·gue·ria \vanˈg(w)irēə\ *n, cap* [NL, fr. Malagasy *voa*= *vanguer*, a tree of the genus + NL *-ia*] : a genus of tropical African and Asiatic trees or shrubs (family Rubiaceae) having axillary clusters of small whitish flowers with five stamens and a 3- to 5-celled ovary and drupaceous fruit

van hoorne's canal \va|nˈhō(ə)rnz- *also* və|\ *n, usu cap H* [after Jean *van Hoorne* †1670 Du. anatomist] : THORACIC DUCT

va·nil·la \vəˈnilə, -nelə\ *n* -s *often attrib* [in sense 1a, fr. NL, fr. Sp *vainilla* vanilla; in other senses fr. Sp *vainilla* pod, vanilla, dim. of *vaina* sheath, fr. L *vagina* — more at VAGINA] **1 a** *cap* : a genus of tropical American climbing orchids (family Orchidaceae) having fleshy distichous leaves, numerous aerial roots, and flowers in axillary racemes with a spreading perianth and the labellum united to the column **b** -s : any plant of this genus **2** -s **a** : a capsule that is the fruit of a vanilla (*Vanilla planifolia*) widely distributed from Florida southward throughout tropical America, that has the form of an elongated pod, and that is an important article of commerce for the flavoring extract that it yields; *broadly* : any of several capsules that are the fruits of other vanillas — compare VANILLON **b** : a flavoring extract made by soaking comminuted vanilla pods in a mixture of water and grain alcohol

vanilla bean *n* : VANILLA 2a

vanilla grass *n* : SWEET GRASS 1b(1)

vanill·aldehyde \ˌvanᵊl, vəˌnil+\ *n* [*vanilla* + *aldehyde*] : VANILLIN

vanilla leaf *n* **1** : WILD VANILLA **2** : a perennial herb (*Achlys triphylla*) of the barberry family that occurs along coastal northwestern North America and has fan-shaped trifoliolate leaves and spikes of small flowers terminating leafless stems

vanilla plant *n* **1** : a plant (*Vanilla planifolia*) of Florida and tropical America that is widely cultivated **2** : WILD VANILLA

vanil·late \ˈvanᵊlˌāt; vəˈnilət, -ˌlāt\ *n* -s [ISV *vanillic (acid)* + *-ate*] : a salt or ester of vanillic acid

va·nille \vaˈnē, vəˈnē\ *n* -s [F, fr. Sp *vainilla*] **1** : VANILLA 2b **2** *or* **vanille ice** : vanilla ice cream

va·nil·lery \vəˈnilərē\ *n* -ES [F *vanillerie*, fr. *vanille* vanilla + *-erie* -ery] : a plantation of vanilla

va·nil·lic acid \vəˈnilik-\ *n* [*vanillic* ISV *vanilla* + *-ic*] : an odorless crystalline phenolic acid $CH_3O(OH)C_6H_3COOH$ found in some varieties of vanilla, formed by oxidation of vanillin, and used chiefly in the form of esters as food preservatives

va·nil·lin \ˈvanᵊlən, vəˈnilən\ *n* -s [ISV *vanilla* + *-in*] **1** : a crystalline phenolic aldehyde $CH_3O(OH)C_6H_3CHO$ that is the principal fragrant component of vanilla and occurs in many other plants (as the tonka bean), that is usu. made synthetically, and that is used chiefly in flavoring and in perfumery; 4-hydroxy-3-methoxy-benzaldehyde **2** : an aldehyde isomeric with vanillin; *esp* : the ortho isomer; 2-hydroxy-3=methoxy-benzaldehyde

vanil·lism \vəˈniˌlizəm, ˈvanᵊlˌi-\ *n* -s [*vanilla* + *-ism*; fr. its being caused by excessive handling of vanilla] : GROCER'S ITCH

va·nil·lon \ˌva¦nē¦yōⁿ\ *n* -s [F, fr. *vanille* vanilla] : any of various usu. large coarse vanillas of inferior flavor and aroma that are obtained esp. from uncultivated vanilla vines

va·nil·lo·yl \vəˈniləˌwil\ *n* -s [*vanillic (acid)* + *-oyl*] : the univalent radical $CH_3O(OH)C_6H_3CO$— of vanillic acid

vanil·lyl \ˈvanᵊlˌil, vəˈniləl\ *n* -s [*vanillin* + *-yl*] : the univalent radical $CH_3O(OH)C_6H_3CH_2$— derived from vanillyl alcohol

vanillyl alcohol *n* : a crystalline phenolic alcohol $CH_3O(OH)C_6H_3CH_2$— obtained by reducing vanillin

¹van·ish \ˈvanish, -nēsh, *esp in pres part* -nəsh\ *vb* -ED/-ING/-ES [ME *vanisshen*, fr. MF *evaniss-*, stem of *esvanir*, *evanir*, fr. (assumed) VL *exvanire*, alter. of L *evanescere* to evaporate, die away, vanish, fr. *e-* + *vanescere* to vanish, fr. *vanus* empty — more at WANE] *vi* **1 a** : to disappear entirely : pass altogether out of sight : become invisible ⟨straightway ~*ed* beneath his blankets —John Muir †1914⟩ ⟨the last traces of respectability had ~*ed* —Marcia Davenport⟩ **b** : to disappear by departing : go away ⟨he ~*ed* into the bathroom —Scott Fitzgerald⟩ ⟨as each member of our family finished eating dinner he would excuse himself and ~ —*Parents' Mag.*⟩ ⟨takes her to a social and ~*es* with the boys to the bar —Marjorie Proops⟩ **c** : to disappear by passing out of existence : cease to be ⟨two dozen cheeses, as big as cartwheels, ~*ed* into the void every day —Van Wyck Brooks⟩ ⟨her resolution ~*ed* —Ellen Glasgow⟩ ⟨many human ills . . . will run their course and ~ without treatment of any sort —Martin Gardner⟩ **2** : to assume the value zero ⟨by definition a fluid is called ideal if, and only if, the viscosity tensor ~*es* —*Mathematics Mag.*⟩ ~ *vt* : to cause to disappear ⟨you can ~ the coin completely —Jean Hugard⟩ — **van·ish·er** *n* -s

syn VANISH, EVANESCE, EVAPORATE, DISAPPEAR, and FADE agree in meaning to pass from view or out of existence. VANISH usu. suggests a total, often mysterious, sudden passing, commonly leaving no trace ⟨his grandmother's fortune *vanished* in a bank failure —Catharine Brody⟩ ⟨many of the wild creatures of early times have *vanished* or are almost extinct —*Amer. Guide Series: Texas*⟩ ⟨his smile quickly *vanished* —Kenneth Roberts⟩ ⟨the apparition appeared for a moment, then *vanished*⟩ EVANESCE usu. suggests a gradual effacement or dissipation to a final complete dissolution ⟨their hopes *evanesced* as money and food became scarcer⟩ ⟨the beauty of youth *evanesced* before the hardships of existence⟩ EVAPORATE suggests a vanishing as silently and inconspicuously as that of a vapor ⟨nothing can insure the continuance of love. It will *evaporate* like a spirit —Thomas Hardy⟩ ⟨his anger did not *evaporate* in words —George Meredith⟩ ⟨invested capital *evaporates* even with watchful care —W.C.Allee⟩ DISAPPEAR usu. suggests only the passing from sight or thought, other implications depending on context, although it is often interchangeable with VANISH ⟨the man seemed to *disappear* before his eyes⟩ ⟨what caused the Hohokam culture to *disappear* suddenly around 1400 . . . is a mystery —R.W.Murray⟩ ⟨farming is rapidly *disappearing* because of poor marketing conditions —*Amer. Guide Series: N.H.*⟩ ⟨this document has *disappeared* from the files — R.M.Lovett⟩ FADE, often with *out* or *away*, stresses a gradual diminution in clearness or distinctness, usu. to an ultimate disappearance ⟨the old myth . . . had *faded* from the minds of men —Agnes Repplier⟩ ⟨the shouting on shore *faded* to a whispering —Kenneth Roberts⟩ ⟨the trade routes fell into disuse and the towns *faded* out of existence —Anne Dorrance⟩ ⟨the earlier beauty of the piece had *faded* away over the years⟩

²vanish \"\ *n* -ES **1** : a disappearance or an act of causing something to disappear ⟨this ~ . . . has been used by generations of magicians —Jean Hugard⟩ **2** : the relatively faint latter part of a speech sound (as a falling diphthong)

vanished *past of* VANISH

vanishes *pres 3d sing of* VANISH

vanishing *pres part of* VANISH

vanishing cream *n* [*vanishing* (pres. part. of ¹*vanish*) + *cream*] : a cosmetic preparation that is less oily than cold cream, that typically contains an excess of stearic acid emulsified by a stearate soap in a high percentage of water, and that is used chiefly as a foundation for face powder ⟨*vanishing creams* do not actually disappear into the skin, but simply spread a thin smooth film over it —Florence E. Wall⟩ — compare COLD CREAM

vanishing line *n* : one of the lines converging to a vanishing point in a pictorial perspective

van·ish·ing·ly *adv* : in a vanishing manner : so as to disappear or to approach or become zero ⟨their mass is ~ small in proportion to their bulk —Agnes M. Clerke⟩

vanishing point *n* [*vanishing* (gerund of ¹*vanish*) + *point*] **1** : a point at which a group of receding parallel lines seems to meet when represented in linear perspective **2** : a point at which something disappears or ceases to exist ⟨cut down the incidence of tuberculosis in cattle to the *vanishing point* —Morris Fishbein⟩

vanishing trace *n* : a line containing the vanishing points of all systems of parallels in a picture in linear perspective

van·ish·ment \-mənt\ *n* -s [¹*vanish* + *-ment*] : an act of vanishing or state of having vanished

van·ist \ˈvānəst\ *n* -s *usu cap* [Sir Henry *Vane* †1662 governor of Massachusetts (1636–37) + E *-ist*] : a follower of Sir Henry Vane who as governor of Massachusetts colony defended Anne Hutchinson on charges of antinomianism

van·i·to·ry \ˈvanəˌtōrē\ *n* -ES [fr. *Vanitory*, a trademark] : a combined bathroom lavatory basin and dressing table ⟨full room-size master bathroom with ~ —*advt*⟩

van·i·tous \ˈvanəd·əs\ *adj* [*vanity* + *-ous*] : INFLATED, VAIN

van·i·ty \ˈvanəd·ē, -ətē, -i\ *n* -ES [ME *vanite*, fr. OF *vanité*, fr. L *vanitat-*, *vanitas* quality of being empty or vain, fr. *vanus* empty, idle, vain + *-itat-*, *-itas* -ity — more at WANE] **1 a** : something that is empty, vain, or valueless : something idle, objectless, or unprofitable ⟨the powerlessness of man before the blind hurry of the universe from ~ to ~ —Bertrand Russell⟩ ⟨he had ceased then to be an egotism, a ~ —H.G.Wells⟩ ⟨the pomps and *vanities* of the great world —C.E.Montague⟩ **b** *obs* : trivial or unprofitable activity : blind frittering away of time **c** : the quality of being vain or empty : HOLLOWNESS, WORTHLESSNESS ⟨knew the ~ of her own attainments —G.B. Shaw⟩ **2 a** : exaggerated self-love : inflated pride in oneself or in one's appearance, attainments, performance, possessions, or successes : hunger for praise or admiration : CONCEIT, VAINGLORY ⟨love of the good opinion of others (which we may call ~) is a desire which man shares with many animals —Bertrand Russell⟩ ⟨the epitome of maleness with all its ~ and self=importance —Carl Van Vechten⟩ ⟨his wounded ~ turned and turned upon itself —J.C.Powys⟩ **b** : an instance or example of such vanity : something of which one is proud or which exhibits his self-love ⟨one of his hidden *vanities* was to be the first man on the subscription paper with the largest donation —W.A.White⟩ **3** : the ostentation of fashion, wealth, or power regarded as an occasion of empty pride or a vain show ⟨takes for granted . . . all the privileges and appurtenances of wealth, and there emerges the 16-year-old boy caught up in *vanities* —Gene Baro⟩ **4** : a fashionable trifle or knicknack : GAUD ⟨such *vanities* as gloves, a wristwatch, a silver cigarette case —John Morrison⟩ **5 a** : ³COMPACT 2 **b** : a small case or handbag for toilet articles used by women ⟨room beneath your chair for small luggage like a briefcase or ~ —*Welcome Aboard*⟩ **6** : DRESSING TABLE **7** : SANDUST **syn** see PRIDE

vanity bag *or* **vanity case** *n* : VANITY 5b

vanity fair *n, often cap V&F* [fr. *Vanity-Fair*, a fair held in the frivolous town of Vanity in *Pilgrim's Progress* (1678) by John Bunyan †1688 Eng. preacher and writer] : a place of busy pride and empty ostentation ⟨a meretricious *vanity fair* of the gaudy commonplace —Rose Macaulay⟩ ⟨the *Vanity Fair* of Washington society —C.G.Bowers⟩

vanity press *or* **vanity publisher** *n* : a press that publishes books at the author's expense — compare AUTHOR'S EDITION

van·john \(ˈ)van¦jän\ *n* [modif. of F *vingt-et-un*] *Brit* : ³TWENTY-ONE 5

van·man \ˈvanˌman, -ˌmən\ *n, pl* **vanmen** [³*van* + *man*] : a van driver

van·nal \ˈvanᵊl\ *adj* [NL *vannus* + E *-al*] : of, relating to, or constituting a vannus and esp. a fold between the remigium and vannus of the wings of some insects

vanned *past of* VAN

¹van·ner \ˈvanə(r)\ *n* -s [E dial. *van* to separate ore with a van (fr. ¹*van*) + E *-er*] **1** : a miner who separates ore with a shovel or pan **2** : SHAKING TABLE

²vanner \"\ *n* -s [³*van* + *-er*] *chiefly Brit* : a horse used or suitable for use in hauling vans

van·ner·man \-mən\ *n, pl* **vannermen** [¹*vanner* + *man*] : one who operates an ore vanner

vanning *pres part of* VAN

van·nus \ˈvanəs\ *n* -ES [NL, fr. L, winnowing fan — more at WINNOW] : the anal lobe of an insect's wing esp. when large and fanlike

van·ox·ite \(ˈ)va¦näkˌsīt\ *n* -s [*vanadium oxide* + *-ite*] : a mineral $V_6O_{13}.8H_2O$(?) consisting of a hydrous oxide of vanadium

¹van·quish \ˈvaŋkwish, -ank-, -wēsh, *esp in pres part* -wəsh\ *vb* -ED/-ING/-ES [ME *venquissen, vainquisshen; venquissen* fr. MF *venquis*, preterit of *veintre* to conquer, fr. OF, fr. L *vincere*; ME *vainquisshen* fr. MF *vainquiss-*, stem of *vainquir* to conquer, fr. OF *vainkir*, alter. of *veintre* — more at VICTOR] *vt* **1** : to conquer or overcome in battle : win dominion over : SUBJUGATE **2** : to defeat (an antagonist) in a conflict or contest of any kind : emerge as victor over **3** : to gain mastery over (an emotion, passion, or temptation) : CONTROL, SUBDUE ~ *vi* : to be victorious **syn** see CONQUER

²vanquish \"\ *n* -ES *Scot* : ¹PINE 3

van·quish·able \-shəbəl\ *adj* : capable of being vanquished : VINCIBLE

van·quish·er \-shə(r)\ *n* -s [ME *vainquissheur*, fr. *vainquisshen* to vanquish + *-eur* -or] : one that vanquishes : CONQUEROR

van·quish·ment \-shmənt\ *n* -s [¹*vanquish* + *-ment*] **1** : an act of vanquishing : CONQUEST, VICTORY **2** : the state of being vanquished : DEFEAT

vans *pl of* VAN

van·sit·tart·ism \vanˈsid·ə(r)d·ˌizəm *also* vən-\ *n* -s *usu cap* [Sir Robert *Vansittart*, 1st Baron Vansittart of Denham †1957 Brit. diplomat + E *-ism*] : a doctrine holding that the conduct of German war leaders from the Franco-Prussian war on has had the wholehearted support of the majority of Germans and that Germany must be demilitarized during a protracted period of occupation and reeducation to insure against her undertaking further wars of conquest

van slyke method \va|nˈslīk- *also* və|\ *n, usu cap V&S* [after Donald D. *Van Slyke* †1971 Am. biochemist] : any of several analytical methods; *esp* : the determination of free amino groups (as in amino acids, peptides, or proteins) by measuring the volume or pressure of nitrogen gas formed by reaction with nitrous acid

[1]**van·tage** \'vantij, -aan-,-ain-,-ån-, -tēj\ *n* -s [ME, fr. AF, fr. MF *avantage* — more at ADVANTAGE] **1** *archaic* **:** BENEFIT, GAIN **2 a :** an advantage in a contest **:** SUPERIORITY **b :** something (as strategic position or superior force) that gives an advantage to one of two contenders ⟨attempts to secure ~ ground south of the river —*Amer. Guide Series: Va.*⟩ ⟨manipulation of the machinery of the convention from his ~ point as chairman —C.R.Erdman⟩ **c :** a place esp. suited to give a comprehensive view or a commanding perspective **:** COIGN OF VANTAGE ⟨looking back on her life from the ~ of her 80th birthday —*Newsweek*⟩ ⟨from the ~ point of a window seat, one surveys the slums —*Amer. Guide Series: N.Y. City*⟩ **3 :** something thrown in for good measure **:** an additional sum or quantity **:** BOOT **4** [by shortening] *Brit* **:** ADVANTAGE 5 — **to the vantage** *adv*, *obs* **:** in addition **:** to boot

[2]**vantage** \"\ *vt* -ED/-ING/-S [ME *vantagen*, fr. [1]*vantage*] **:** ADVANTAGE, PROFIT

vantguard *n* [ME *avaunt garde, vantgard* — more at VANGUARD] *obs* **:** VANGUARD

vant·hoff·ite \vant'hȯ,fīt, vän-, -hä,f-\ *n* -s [Jacobus H. *van't Hoff* †1911 + E *-ite*] **:** a mineral consisting of a sulfate of sodium and magnesium that occurs in granular or layered aggregates

van't hoff's law \-ȯfs-,-äfs-\ *n, usu cap H* [after Jacobus H. *van't Hoff* †1911 Du. physical chemist] **:** a statement in physical chemistry: for a system in equilibrium an increase in temperature increases the rate of the reaction absorbing heat — compare LE CHATELIER'S LAW

van tie·ghem cell \van·'tēgəm-, ¦van·(,)tyā¦gem-\ *n, usu cap V&T* [after P.E.L. *Van Tieghem* †1914 Fr. botanist] **:** a device used for the microscopic observation of microorganisms usu. in hanging-drop cultures and consisting of a ring or short tube fixed to a glass slide or Petri dish and capped with a cover glass

[1]**van·ward** \'vanwə(r)d, 'vaan-\ *adj* [[2]*van* + *-ward*, adj. suffix] **:** located in the van **:** taking the lead **:** ADVANCED ⟨a ~ woman —George Meredith⟩

[2]**vanward** \"\ *adv* [[2]*van* + *-ward*, adv. suffix] **:** to or toward the van **:** FORWARD

van-winged hawk \'=,=-\ *n* [[1]*van* + *winged*] *dial Eng* **:** [3]HOBBY

vap·id \'vapəd *also* 'vāp-\ *adj* [L *vapidus* flat tasting, spiritless; akin to L *vappa* vapid wine and prob. to L *vapor* steam — more at COVET] **:** lacking flavor, zest, animation, or spirit **:** having lost the appeal of liveliness, tang, briskness, or force **:** FLAT, INSIPID, UNINTERESTING, POINTLESS, TRITE ⟨~ beer⟩ ⟨a fixed, ~ smile —Roger Eddy⟩ ⟨expressed a mild, ~ surprise at things told her —Arnold Bennett⟩ **syn** see INSIPID

va·pid·i·ty \və'pidəd·ē, va'-, -ətē, -i\ *n* -ES [*vapid* + *-ity*] **1 :** VAPIDNESS ⟨unblushing acceptance of a total ~ of soul —Albert Dasnoy⟩ **2 :** something vapid ⟨the *vapidities* of everyday conversation⟩

vap·id·ly *adv* **:** in a vapid manner ⟨~ smiling little man —Richard Blaker⟩

vap·id·ness *n* -ES **:** the quality or state of being vapid

vapo- *comb form* [*vapor*] **:** vapor ⟨*vapo*cauterization⟩ ⟨*vapog*raphy⟩

va·po-dusting \'vāpō+,-\ *n* [*vapo-* + *dusting*, gerund of *dust*] **:** a method of dispersing insecticides in which the insecticide solution is broken up into fine particles and carried to the foliage in an air stream

va·pog·ra·phy \vā'pägrəfē\ *n* -ES [*vapo-* + *-graphy*] **:** the process of obtaining a developable image by permitting a sensitive film or plate to remain in contact with a substance (as zinc or printer's ink) that gives off vapors or emanations affecting it without exposure to light

[1]**va·por** \'vāpə(r)\ *n* -s *see -or in Explan Notes* [ME *vapour*, fr. MF *vapeur*, fr. L *vapor* steam, vapor — more at COVET] **1 :** diffused matter (as smoke, fog, mist, steam, or an exhalation) suspended floating in the air and impairing its transparency ⟨cold motors turning over and the ~ from the exhausts steaming —R.H.Newman⟩ **2 a :** a substance in the gaseous state as distinguished from the liquid or solid state **:** a gasified liquid or solid **:** a gaseous substance that is at a temperature below its critical temperature and therefore liquefiable by pressure alone **b :** a substance (as gasoline, alcohol, mercury, or benzoin) vaporized for industrial, therapeutic, or military uses; *also* **:** a mixture (as in an internal-combustion engine) of such a vapor with air **3 a** *archaic* **:** something unsubstantial or transitory ⟨beyond the ~*s* of her sleep she would hear a night-passer, . . . a car on the road —Elizabeth M. Roberts⟩ **b :** a foolish or fanciful notion **:** a fantastic idea ⟨his realities may seem most impalpable ~*s* —G.W.Brace⟩ ⟨what amazing ~*s* a lonely man may get into his head —H.G.Wells⟩ **4 vapors** *pl* **a** *archaic* **:** exhalations of bodily organs (as the stomach) held to affect the physical or mental condition **b :** a depressed or hysterical nervous condition formerly held to be caused by bodily exhalations ⟨neurotic women subject to the ~*s* —Lois & Don Thorburn⟩ ⟨had a fit of the ~*s* shortly after breakfast —James Reynolds⟩ **5 :** a medicinal agent designed for administration in the form of inhaled vapor

[2]**vapor** \"\ *vb* -ED/-ING/-S [ME *vapouren*, fr. *vapour* vapor] *vt* **1 :** to send in or as if in vapor **:** cause to evaporate **:** reduce to vapor ⟨~ away a heated fluid⟩ **2 a :** to assert or boast loudly or foolishly **:** utter in high-flown language **b** *archaic* **:** to overcome by highflown or bombastic language **:** BULLY **3** *archaic* **:** to affect with the vapors **:** DEPRESS, BORE ~ *vi* **1 a :** to rise in vapor **:** pass off as vapor **:** EVAPORATE ⟨could see his breath and my own ~*ing* . . . in the freezing air —H.E.Bates⟩ **b :** to emit vapor **:** FUME, STEAM ⟨running waters ~ not so much as standing waters —Francis Bacon⟩ **2 :** to indulge in bragging, blustering, or idle talk **:** speak or write in a pompous or inflated style

va·por·abil·i·ty \,vāpərə'biləd·ē\ *n* **:** the quality of being vaporable

va·por·able \'vāpərəbəl\ *adj* [ME, fr. ML *vaporabilis*, fr. L *vaporare* to steam (fr. *vapor* steam, vapor) + *-abilis* -able] **:** that can be vaporized **:** VAPORIZABLE

vapor barrier *n* **:** a layer of material (as of paint, building paper, or felt) used to retard or prevent the absorption of moisture (as into a wall or floor) and its subsequent condensation therein

vapor density *n* **:** the relative density of a gas or vapor as compared with some specific standard (as hydrogen)

vapor engine *n* **:** an engine in which the working fluid is a vapor esp. other than steam

va·por·er \'vāpərə(r)\ *n* -s [[2]*vapor* + *-er*] **:** one that vapors; *esp* **:** BRAGGART

va·po·ret·to \,väpə'red·(,)ō\ *n* -s [It, dim. of *vapore* steamboat, fr. F *vapeur*, fr. *bateau à vapeur* steamboat, fr. *bateau* boat + *à* to (fr. L *ad*) + *vapeur* steam, fr. L *vapor* — more at BATEAU, AT, COVET] **:** a small steamboat used as a canal bus in Venice, Italy

vapor heating *n* **:** steam heating in which the steam has a pressure slightly above that of the atmosphere **:** very low-pressure steam heating

vapori- *comb form* [L *vapor*] **:** vapor ⟨*vapori*form⟩ ⟨*vapor*imeter⟩

va·por·if·ic \¦vāpə¦rifik\ *adj* [*vapori-* + *-fic*] **:** producing vapor **:** tending to pass or to cause to pass into vapor **:** VAPOROUS

va·por·im·e·ter \,vāpə'rimad·ə(r)\ *n* [ISV *vapori-* + *-meter;* orig. formed in G] **:** an instrument for measuring the volume or the pressure of a vapor; *specif* **:** one used in alcoholometry

[1]**vaporing** *n* -s [fr. gerund of [2]*vapor*] **:** the act or speech of one that vapors **:** an idle, extravagant, or high-flown expression or speech **:** a vapid remark or statement ⟨a minimum of nationalistic ~ —*Newsweek*⟩ ⟨not mere academic ~ —Raymond Moley⟩ — usu. used in pl. ⟨like the juvenile ~*s* of an immature mind —Mary R. Rinehart⟩ ⟨unmistakable warnings against grandiose ~*s* —E.H.Eby⟩

[2]**vaporing** *adj* [fr. pres. part. of [2]*vapor*] **:** that vapors **:** spouting forth vapors **:** VAUNTING — **va·por·ing·ly** *adv*

va·por·ish \'vāpərish, -rēsh\ *adj* [[1]*vapor* + *-ish*] **1 :** resembling or suggestive of vapor **:** VAPOROUS, MISTY, THIN ⟨her pure white and ~ hair —Antonio Barolini⟩ ⟨an old man's ideas were apt to be wild and ~ —H.L.Davis⟩ ⟨stories . . . are ~ and sad, without much core —*New Yorker*⟩ **2 :** affected by the vapors **:** given to fits of depression or hysteria — **va·por·ish·ness** *n* -ES

va·por·iz·able \'vāpə,rīzəbəl, ,=='===\ *adj* **:** capable of being vaporized

va·por·iza·tion \,vāpərə'zāshən, -,rī'-\ *n* -s [*vaporize* + *-ation*] **:** the act or process of vaporizing or state of being vaporized **:** artificial formation of vapor; *specif* **:** conversion of water into steam (as in a steam boiler)

va·por·ize \'vāpə,rīz\ *vb* -ED/-ING/-S [[1]*vapor* + *-ize*] *vt* **1 :** to convert into vapor either naturally or artificially (as by the application of heat or by spraying) **2 :** to reduce to a vaporous state or form **:** cause to become ethereal or dissipated ⟨*vaporized* by a nuclear explosion⟩ ~ *vi* **1 :** to become converted into vapor or reduced to a vaporous state **2 :** to indulge in vaporing

va·por·iz·er \-zə(r)\ *n* -s **:** one that vaporizes: as **a :** ATOMIZER **b :** an apparatus for vaporizing a heavy oil (as petroleum) for the explosive charge of an internal-combustion engine; *also* **:** a simple form of carburetor **c :** a device for converting a medicated liquid into a vapor for inhalation **d :** one who prepares plastics material for finishing by treating it with solvent vapors in a vaporizing machine

vaporizing *n* -s [fr. gerund of *vaporize*] **:** VAPORING ⟨the ~*s* of latter-day romancers —*New Yorker*⟩

vapor jacket *n* **:** a closed glass or metal case surrounding a bulb or other apparatus and often containing a vapor at a known temperature

vapor lamp *n* **1 :** a lamp burning a vapor (as of alcohol) **2 :** a lamp in which an electric discharge takes place through a metallic vapor — compare MERCURY-VAPOR LAMP

va·por·less \'vāpə(r)ləs\ *adj* **:** devoid of vapor

vapor lock *n* **:** partial or complete interruption of fuel flow in an internal-combustion engine caused by the formation of bubbles of vapor or gas in the fuel-feeding system

va·por·ous \'vāp(ə)rəs\ *adj* [L *vaporosus* full of steam or vapor, fr. *vapor* + *-osus* -ous] **1 :** consisting or characteristic of vapor **:** having the form or nature of vapor ⟨a ~ substance⟩ ⟨~ consistency⟩ **2 a** *obs* **:** causing flatulence ⟨~ foods⟩ **b :** producing vapors **:** VOLATILE ⟨a ~ paint⟩ **3 :** full of vapor **:** containing or obscured by vapors **:** FOGGY, MISTY ⟨a ~ atmosphere⟩ ⟨shady vales between the ~ mountains —H.D. Thoreau⟩ ⟨faint beacon, ~ in the rainy darkness —A.J.Cronin⟩ **4 a :** ETHEREAL, UNSUBSTANTIAL, VAGUE ⟨a score of ~ twilight landscapes —*Time*⟩ **b :** FILMY ⟨~ silks⟩ **c :** consisting of or indulging in vaporings ⟨such ~ speculations were inevitable —Thomas Carlyle⟩ ⟨~ realms of conjecture and hyperbole —H.E.Clurman⟩ ⟨give himself up to ~ dreams —Sherwood Anderson⟩ — **va·por·ous·ly** *adv* — **va·por·ous·ness** *n* -ES

vapor pressure *or* **vapor tension** *n* **:** the pressure exerted by a vapor that is in equilibrium with a solid or liquid

vapor-pressure thermometer *n* **:** a thermometer in which the variable saturated vapor pressure of a volatile liquid is used as a measure of the temperature and which thus has the advantage over some other types of thermometers of being free from errors due to bulb expansion

vaporproof \¦==¦=\ *adj* **:** impervious to the penetration of vapor

vapors *pl of* VAPOR, *pres 3d sing of* VAPOR

vapor seal *n* **:** VAPOR BARRIER

vapor trail *n* **:** CONTRAIL

va·pory \'vāp(ə)rē, -ri\ *adj* [[1]*vapor* + *-y*] **:** consisting of, full of, characterized by, or resembling vapor **:** VAPOROUS, MISTY

va·pour·er \'vāpərə(r\ *or* **vapourer moth** *n* -s *Brit* **:** a tussock moth (*Orgyia antiqua*) the female of which has vestigial wings; *also* **:** any of several related moths

va·que·ro \vä'ke(,)rō, vȧ'-\ *n* -s *see sense 2* [Sp — more at BUCKAROO] **1 :** HERDSMAN, COWBOY **2** *or pl* **vaquero** *usu cap* **:** APACHE; *esp* **:** QUERECHO

va·quez's disease \vä'kezəz-\ *n, usu cap V* [after Louis Henri *Vaquez* †1936 Fr. physician] **:** POLYCYTHEMIA

va·qui·ta \vä'kēd·ə\ *n* -s [AmerSp, dim. of Sp *vaca* cow, fr. L *vacca* — more at VACCINE] **:** a West Indian weevil (*Diaprepes abbreviatus*) of which the larvae feed on the roots esp. of trees and the adults on the leaves

var \'vär\ *n* -s [*v*olt-*a*mpere *r*eactive] **:** the reactive volt-ampere unit

var *abbr* **1** variable **2** variant **3** variation **4** variegated **5** variety **6** variometer **7** various

VAR *abbr* **1** visual-aural radio range; visual-aural range **2** volt-ampere reactive

va·ra \'värə\ *n* -s [Sp & Pg, rod, pole, a unit of length, fr. L, forked pole, fr. fem. of *varus* bent, crooked — more at PREVARICATE] **1 :** any of various Spanish and Portuguese units of length used in Latin America and southwestern U. S. equal to between 31 and 34 inches; *esp* **:** a Texas unit equal to 33.33 inches **2 :** a staff or cane used in Spanish-American countries as a badge of office **3 :** [5]PIC 1

var·an \'varən\ *n* -s [NL *Varanus*] **:** MONITOR LIZARD

[1]**va·ran·gi·an** \və'ranjēən\ *adj, usu cap* [MGk *Barangoi*, pl. + E *-an*, adj. suffix] **:** of, relating to, or characteristic of the Varangians

[2]**varangian** \"\ *n* -s *cap* [MGk *Barangoi*, pl., Varangians (of Scand origin; akin to ON *Væringjar* Varangians, fr. pl. of *væringi* confederate, fr. *vārar*, pl., pledge) + E *-an*, n. suffix — more at VERY] **1 :** one of the Scandinavians who founded a dynasty in Russia in the 9th century **2 :** a member of the bodyguard of the Byzantine emperors esp. in the 11th and 12th centuries composed chiefly of Russians or later of Scandinavians or other northern Europeans

[1]**var·a·nid** \'varənəd\ *adj* [NL *Varanidae*] **:** of or relating to the Varanidae

[2]**varanid** \"\ *n* -s **:** a lizard of the family Varanidae

va·ran·i·dae \və'ranə,dē\ *n pl, cap* [NL, fr. *Varanus*, type genus + *-idae*] **:** a family of large tropical Old World lizards comprising the monitors, having an elongated neck and tail and well-developed limbs, and being terrestrial or semiaquatic and voraciously carnivorous — compare KOMODO DRAGON

var·a·nus \'varənəs\ *n, cap* [NL, fr. Ar *waran, waral* monitor lizard] **:** a genus (the type and sole recent genus of the family Varanidae) of Old World lizards

vardapet *var of* VARTABED

vare \'va(a)(ə)r\ *n* -s [ME *veir* squirrel fur, weasel — more at VAIR] *dial Eng* **:** WEASEL

var·ec *also* **var·ech** \'va,rek\ *n* -s [F, fr. AF *warec* wreck, seaweed — more at WRECK] **1 :** SEAWEED **2 :** the calcined ashes of coarse seaweeds used for the manufacture of iodine, potash, and formerly soda **:** KELP 2

var·gue·no \vär'gān(,)yō\ *n* -s [Sp *bargueño*, fr. *bargueño* of Bargas, fr. *Bargas*, village near Toledo, Spain] **:** a decorative writing cabinet of a form originating in Spain, composed of a rectangular chest supported on legs or a decorative framework, and having the front opening downward on hinges to serve as a writing desk

vargueno

va·ri \vä'rē\ *n* -s [Malagasy *varika*] **:** RUFFED LEMUR

vari- *or* **vario-** *comb form* [L *varius* — more at VARIOUS] **:** varied **:** diverse ⟨*vari*form⟩ ⟨*vario*coupler⟩

var·ia \'va(a)rēə\ *n pl* [NL, fr. L, neut. pl. of *varius* various] **:** various things **:** MISCELLANY; *esp* **:** a literary miscellany

var·i·a·bil·i·ty \,verēə'biləd·ē, ,va(a)r-, ,vär-, -lətē, -i\ *n* **1 :** the quality or fact of being variable or subject to variation **:** VARIABLENESS ⟨apparently unlimited ~ of individual behavior —Edward Sapir⟩ ⟨free intellectual ~ which is the source of genuine progress in science —M.R.Cohen⟩ **2 :** the quality or attribute of animals and plants that causes them to exhibit variation **:** the ability to vary from whatever cause — compare VARIATION 6a **3 :** DISPERSION 2a

[1]**var·i·a·ble** \'verēəbəl, 'va(a)r-, 'vär-\ *adj* [ME, fr. MF, fr. L *variabilis*, fr. *variare* to vary + *-abilis* -able] **1 a :** able or apt to vary or change **:** susceptible or subject to variation or changes **:** CHANGEABLE, SHIFTING ⟨~ winds⟩ ⟨a ~ climate⟩ ⟨a ~ speech habit —Stanley Newman⟩ ⟨~ manufacturing expenses —*Cost Accounting*⟩ **b :** FICKLE, UNSTEADY, INCONSTANT ⟨lest thy love prove likewise ~ —Shak.⟩ **2 :** characterized by variations or by varying **:** marked by diversity or difference ⟨nature is infinitely ~ —John Burroughs⟩ ⟨the ~ and tuneful warblings of the nonpareil —William Bartram⟩ **3 :** admitting change or variation **:** ALTERABLE ⟨a ~ period of three days to two weeks⟩ ⟨the annual fair begins on a ~ date in October⟩ ⟨a ~ angle⟩ **4 :** being or having the characteristics of a variable ⟨a ~ number⟩ **5 :** not true to type **:** ABERRANT, INCONSTANT — used of a biological group or a biological character

[2]**variable** \"\ *n* -s **1 :** something that is variable **:** something that varies, may vary, or is liable to vary **:** something subject to change **2 a :** a quantity that may assume any one of a specified set of values — see DEPENDENT VARIABLE, INDEPENDENT VARIABLE, STATISTICAL VARIABLE **b** (1) **:** a symbol in a mathematical formula representing a variable **:** PLACEHOLDER ⟨the value of the function $f(x)$ is determined by the value of the ~ x⟩ (2) **:** a symbol in a logistical formula that stands for any one of a class of things; *esp* **:** FREE VARIABLE — see BOUND VARIABLE, INDIVIDUAL VARIABLE, PREDICATE VARIABLE **3 variables** *pl* **:** an area or belt of ocean where the winds do not usu. blow steadily **:** a region of calm; *specif* **:** DOLDRUMS **4 :** VARIABLE STAR **5 :** a course in a school curriculum that may or may not be included in a pupil's program — contrasted with *constant*

variable-area \¦====¦===\ *adj* **:** being or relating to a motion-picture sound track in which the sounds are represented by an opaque line of varying width that runs parallel to the length of the film ⟨*variable-area* track⟩ — compare VARIABLE-DENSITY

variable condenser *or* **variable capacitor** *n* **:** a condenser whose capacitance may be varied for circuit-tuning or other purpose

variable cost *n* **:** cost that fluctuates directly with changes in output — compare FIXED COST

variable-density \¦====¦===\ *adj* **:** being or relating to a motion-picture sound track in which the sounds are represented as parallel lines that are at right angles to the length of the film and that vary in density in accordance with the volume and pitch of the recorded sound ⟨*variable-density* track⟩ — compare VARIABLE-AREA

variable error *n* **:** the variability of a subject's estimates of an objective magnitude measured by their average deviation

variable gear *or* **variable gearing** *n* **:** a gear wheel of irregular outline gearing with a corresponding wheel so that the velocity ratio changes one or more times throughout a single revolution

variable inductor *n* **:** an inductor or reactor whose inductance is continuously adjustable

variable nebula *n* **:** a nebula whose light is subject to fluctuations

var·i·able·ness *n* -ES [ME *variablenesse*, fr. [1]*variable* + *-nesse* -ness] **:** the quality of being variable **:** tendency to vary **:** CHANGEABLENESS

variable oak leaf caterpillar *n* **:** a caterpillar that is the larva of a notodontid moth (*Heterocampa manteo*) and that feeds on many deciduous trees in the eastern U.S.

variable spacer *n* **:** a control on the left-hand platen knob of a typewriter that disengages the line space lever to allow writing at positions other than those normally turned up by the ratchet

variable-speed gear *n* **:** CHANGE GEAR

variable star *n* **:** a star whose brightness changes usu. in more or less regular periods — compare CEPHEID, ECLIPSING VARIABLE, PULSATING STAR

variable time fuze *n* **:** PROXIMITY FUZE

variable toad *n* **:** GREEN TOAD

var·i·a·bly \'verēəblē, 'va(a)r-, 'vär-, -li\ *adv* [[1]*variable* + *-ly*] **:** in a varying manner **:** with frequent variation ⟨~ strong winds⟩ ⟨highway is . . . ~ macadam, concrete, and blacktop —*Amer. Guide Series: Vt.*⟩

Var·i·ac \'verē,ak, 'va(a)r-\ *trademark* — used for an adjustable-ratio transformer for test and calibration work

var·i·ad \-,ad\ *n* -s [*vari-* + *-ad*] **:** one of the slightly differentiated subforms that make up a phylogenetic stock or species

va·ri·ag \'värē,äg\ *n, cap* [Russ *Varyag*, of Scand origin; akin to ON *Væringjar* Varangians — more at VARANGIAN] **:** VARANGIAN

var·i·ance \'verēən(t)s, 'va(a)r-, 'vär-\ *n* -s [ME *variaunce*, fr. MF, fr. L *variantia*, fr. *variant-, varians* (pres. part. of *variare*) + *-ia* -y] **1 a :** the fact, quality, or state of being variable or variant **:** VARIATION, DIFFERENCE, DEVIATION ⟨account for the ~ in crops⟩ ⟨a daily ~ of one degree Fahrenheit⟩ ⟨the ~ between reports⟩ **b :** an instance of variableness **:** a degree of difference **:** DISCREPANCY ⟨a ~ in the testimony⟩ ⟨send the bill to conference to iron out ~*s* in House and Senate bills —*Springfield* (*Mass.*) *Union*⟩ **c :** a difference between what has been expected or predetermined and what actually occurs; *specif* **:** a difference between a standard and an historical cost or between a budgeted and an actual expense **2 a :** the fact or state of being in disagreement **:** a difference of opinion producing dispute or controversy **:** DISSENSION, DISCORD ⟨forestall ~ among the heirs⟩ **b :** an instance of this ⟨friends who have never had a ~⟩ **3 a :** a disagreement or difference between two parts (as the writ and the declaration, or the allegation and the proof) of the same legal proceeding that to be effectual ought to agree **b :** a permission or license to do some act contrary to the usual rule and used esp. of grants of permission or authorizations to build contrary to the provisions of an otherwise applicable zoning ordinance or building code **4 :** the number of degrees of freedom possessed by a physical-chemical system esp. when it is in equilibrium — compare PHASE RULE **5 :** the square of the standard deviation **:** the mean square of the deviations from the arithmetic mean of a frequency distribution — symbol σ^2 **syn** see DISCORD — **at variance 1 :** in a state of difference **:** not in harmony or agreement ⟨may find his pecuniary advantage *at variance* with his professional duty —R.M.MacIver⟩ **2 :** in a state of dissension or controversy ⟨*at variance* with himself —John Milton⟩

[1]**var·i·ant** \-nt\ *adj* [ME, fr. MF, fr. L *variant-, varians*, pres. part. of *variare* to vary] **1** *obs* **:** tending to, undergoing, or exhibiting change **:** not constant, unchanging, or uniform **:** VARIABLE, FICKLE **2 :** manifesting variety **:** marked by diversity **:** VARIEGATED, VARIED ⟨long strip of ~ country —M.H.Ellis⟩ **3 a :** different from others of its kind or class **:** exhibiting slight difference, alteration, or disagreement ⟨the principal ~ points of view —A.T.Weaver⟩ ⟨a phrase . . . subject to ~ interpretation by successive scholars —*Language*⟩ ⟨development of these ~ religious groups —E.T.Thompson⟩ **b :** not definitive, generally accepted, or commonly found **:** MODIFIED ⟨an appendix which contains some ~ readings —B.R.Redman⟩ ⟨rare and elusive ~ editions —L.C.Wroth⟩

[2]**variant** \"\ *n* -s **1 a :** one of two or more persons or things exhibiting usu. slight differences **:** VARIATION ⟨~*s* of a folk song⟩ ⟨that all societies are but ~*s* of one another —Thornton Wilder⟩ **b :** one that varies from the original or archetype ⟨most military campaigns are . . . ~*s* on a historical pattern —*New Republic*⟩ **c :** one that exhibits variation from a type or norm **:** MUTATION; *often* **:** one whose behavior is at variance with societal norms — compare DEVIANT **2 a :** one of two or more different spellings (as *labor* and *labour* or *indexes* and *indices*) or pronunciations (as of *economics* \ek-, ēk-\) of the same word **b :** one of two or more words or word elements (as *biologic* and *biological* or *stomat-* and *stomato-*) of essentially the same meaning differing only in the presence or absence of an affix **3 :** ALLOPHONE **4 :** a cipher element or code group having the same significance as another and used to impede cryptanalysis

[1]**var·i·ate** \-ē,āt\ *vt* -ED/-ING/-S [L *variatus*, past part. of *variare* to vary] **:** to make varied or irregular **:** BREAK ⟨the *variated* melody of the first three measures —*Down Beat*⟩ ⟨a *variated* ceiling⟩

[2]**var·i·ate** \-ēət, -ē,āt\ *n* -s [L *variatus*, past part. of *variare* to vary] **1 :** VARIANT **2 a :** a particular value of a mathematical variable **:** the quantitative measure of a characteristic **b :** VARIABLE **3 :** RANDOM VARIABLE

var·i·a·tion \,verē'āshən, ,va(a)r-, ,vär-\ *n* -s [L *variation-, variatio*, fr. *variatus* (past part. of *variare* to vary) + *-ion-, -io* -ion] **1 a :** the act of varying **:** the process, state, or fact of being varied **:** change in the form, position, state, or quality of something **:** MODIFICATION, ALTERATION, MUTATION, DIVERSIFICATION ⟨things incapable of ~⟩ **b :** an instance of varying ⟨long for a ~ in our routine⟩ ⟨an agreeable ~ in weather⟩

c : an embellishing change ⟨telling his story again with ~*s*⟩ d : extent to which or range in which a thing varies : degree of departure from norm or type : amount or rate of change ⟨great ~*s* in speed⟩ ⟨within the limits of barometric ~⟩ 2 a : the compass error caused by the earth's magnetic field and measured as the angle between true north and north as indicated by a compass needle unaffected by any other influence b : DECLINATION 6 3 : a change in the mean motion or mean orbit of a planet or other celestial body ⟨the ~ of the moon depending on its angular distance from the sun⟩ 4 a : PERMUTATION 3b b : the sequence +− or −+ in a row of such signs or of terms affected by them — opposed to *permanence* c : lack of uniformity in statistical observations or measures 5 a : the repetition of a theme or melody with embellishments or modifications in rhythm, tune, harmony, or key b **variations** *pl* : the varied repetitions of a theme in a theme and variations 6 a : divergence in structural or functional qualities of an organism or biotype from those typical or usual to the group of which it is a part (as divergence of offspring from parent) usu. including fundamental hereditary changes through which natural selection works to induce evolutionary development as well as purely individual fluctuations that lack evolutionary significance — compare ADAPTATION, MUTATION b : an individual or group exhibiting variation : VARIANT 7 a : a continuation (as in notes to a tournament game) from a given position different from that actually played in a chess game b : one of a family of opening continuations branching off from an initial common sequence 8 : the maximum angular displacement in electrical degrees between the voltage wave of an alternating-current circuit or machine and a wave whose constant frequency is the average frequency of the circuit or machine 9 : the maximum angular or phase displacement of the revolving member or armature of a machine from the position of uniform rotation — compare PULSATION 3 10 a : a solo dance in ballet b : a repetition in modern dance composition of a movement sequence with changes

var·i·a·tion·al \ˌ==ˈāshənᵊl, -shnəl\ *adj* : of or relating to variation : characterized by variation — **var·i·a·tion·al·ly** \-shənᵊlē, -shnəlē, -i\ *adv*

var·i·a·tion·ist \ˌ==ˈāshənəst\ *n* -s : a composer of musical variations

variation of latitude : a small periodic change in the observed latitude of any place resulting from wandering of the poles

variation of parameters : a method for solving a differential equation by first solving a simpler equation and then generalizing this solution properly so as to satisfy the original equation by treating the arbitrary constants not as constants but as variables

var·i·a·tive \ˈverēˌād·iv, ˈva(a)r-, -ēəd·iv\ *adj* [L *variatus* (past part. of *variare* to vary) + E *-ive*] : of, relating to, or showing variation — **var·i·a·tive·ly** \-d·əvlē\ *adv*

var·i·a·tor \-ēˌād·ə(r)\ *n* -s [L *variatus* + E *-or*] : one that variates ⟨a speed ~⟩; *specif* : a joint that compensates for variations in length due to temperature changes : EXPANSION JOINT

var·i·a·tus \ˌverēˈād·əs, ˌva(a)r-\ *n* -ES [NL *variatus* (specific epithet of *Platypoecilus variatus*), fr. L, past part. of *variare* to vary] : a fish (*Platypoecilus variatus*) related to the common platy and often kept in the tropical aquarium

varic- *or* **varico-** *comb form* [NL, fr. *varic-, varix* — more at VARICOSE] : varix ⟨*varicosis*⟩ ⟨*varicocele*⟩

var·i·cel·la \ˌvarəˈselə\ *n* -s [NL, irreg. dim. of *variola*] : CHICKEN POX — **var·i·cel·lar** \ˌ==ˈselə(r)\ *adj*

var·i·cel·late \ˌ==ˈselət, -eˌlāt\ *adj* [NL *varicella* (dim. of *varic-, varix*) + E *-ate*] *of a shell* : having small or indistinct varices

var·i·cel·li·form \ˌ==ˈseləˌfȯrm\ *adj* [NL *varicella* chicken pox + ISV *-iform*] : resembling chicken pox

varices *pl of* VARIX

var·i·co·cele \ˈvarəkōˌsēl\ *n* -s [NL, fr. *varic-* + *-cele*] : a varicose enlargement of the veins of the spermatic cord producing a soft compressible tumor mass in the scrotum

var·i·coid \ˈvarəˌkȯid\ *adj* [*varic-* + *-oid*] : resembling a varix

vari·colored \ˈverēˌkələ(r)d, ˈva(a)r-, ˈvār-, -riˌ-\ *adj* [*vari-* + *colored*] : having various colors : VARIEGATED ⟨~ marble⟩

var·i·cose \ˈvarəˌkōs, ˈver-\ *adj* [L *varicosus* full of dilated veins, fr. *varic-, varix* dilated vein + *-osus* -ose; prob. akin to L *varus* pimple, *verruca* wart — more at WART] 1 a *also* **var·i·cosed** \-st\ : abnormally swollen or dilated ⟨~ veins⟩ ⟨~ lymph vessels⟩ b : causing abnormal swelling ⟨~ stasis⟩ 2 : of, relating to, or exhibiting varices ⟨~ mollusks⟩ ⟨puffy and ~ men —C.W.Ferguson⟩

var·i·cose·ness *n* -ES : the condition of being varicose

varicose vein *n* : VARIX 1b

var·i·co·sis \ˌ==ˈkōsəs\ *n, pl* **varico·ses** \-ōˌsēz\ [NL, fr. *varic-* + *-osis*] 1 : the condition of being varicose 2 : VARIX

var·i·cos·i·ty \ˌ==ˈkäsəd·ē, -ətē, -i\ *n* -ES [*varicose* + *-ity*] 1 : the quality, state, or condition of being varicose 2 : VARIX ⟨a hemorrhoid is a ~ within the anal canal⟩

var·ied \ˈverēd, ˈva(a)r-, ˈvār-, -rid\ *adj* [fr. past part. of *vary*] 1 : CHANGED, ALTERED 2 : having numerous forms or types : VARIOUS, DIVERSIFIED, DIVERSE ⟨a ~ experience⟩ ⟨~ interests⟩ ⟨~ scenery⟩ 3 : marked conspicuously or contrastingly with several colors : VARIEGATED

varied bunting *n* : a bunting (*Passerina versicolor*) of eastern Mexico and southern Texas the male of which is handsomely colored with the plumage largely of shades of purple and red

varied carpet beetle *n* : a mottled brown and white dermestid beetle (*Anthrenus verbasci*) that feeds as both larva and adult on dry organic matter (as wool, skin, or hair) and is often a household pest

var·ied·ly *adv* : in a varied manner

varied thrush *n* : a thrush (*Ixoreus naevius*) of western No. America similar in form and size to the robin but reddish or orange brown underneath and with a black mark on the breast

var·ie·gate \ˈver(ē)əˌgāt, ˈva(a)r-, ˈvār-, -rēˌ-, -riˌ-, *usu* -gād·+V\ *vt* -ED/-ING/-S [L *variegatus*, past part. of *variegare* to variegate, fr. *varius* varied, various + *-egare* (akin to L *agere* to drive) — more at VARIOUS, AGENT] : to diversify esp. in external appearance (as with different colors) : enliven or impart interest to by means of variety ⟨as a woman saves odd moneys to ~ her wardrobe with a gown —Freya Stark⟩ ⟨the irresolution, precipitation, regret and so on that ~ a character through its forties and fifties —Donald Sutherland⟩

var·ie·gat·ed \-gād·əd, -gātəd\ *adj* [fr. past part. of *variegate*] : VARIED ⟨a ~ throng —Adrian Bell⟩; *esp* : marked with different colors or tints in spots, streaks, or stripes ⟨a ~ tulip⟩

syn PARTI-COLORED, MOTLEY, CHECKERED, CHECKED, PIED, PIEBALD, SKEWBALD, DAPPLED, FREAKED: VARIEGATED indicates only variation in the color of a single piece, object, or specimen without indication of what colors or what forms — spots, streaks, blotches — are involved ⟨disliked the *variegated* hues of the buildings — they reminded him of the garish brilliance in the lower town —Norman Douglas⟩ PARTI-COLORED may stress not so much the presence of different colors as their clear and distinct presentation. MOTLEY in most uses is likely to suggest presence of three or more colors in very noticeable diversity in a chance or very capricious arrangement ⟨birds of *motley* colors and varied cries —G.K.Chesterton⟩ ⟨the *motley* dress of a court jester⟩ CHECKERED indicates a regular alternation of rectangular shapes different in color or shade like a checkerboard, esp. an alternation between black and white or dark and light ⟨the *chequered* fabric of Constable's pictures, their deep undertones overlaid with variegated passages of crumbling impasto and strewn with particles of white light —Robin Ironside⟩ CHECKED indicates much the same thing but is admissible in situations where figures are less certainly rectangular; it is common in reference to fabrics ⟨a gambler's *checked* vest⟩ PIED suggests patches, blotches, or spots of colors on a contrasting background, esp. the white on black of a magpie's plumage. PIEBALD suggests the same coloration, esp. in reference to the markings of a horse or dog, and SKEWBALD indicates an arrangement of spots and background involving white and some color other than black ⟨*piebald* strictly means spotted white and black and *skewbald* white and any color but black —G.G.Simpson⟩ DAPPLED describes a marking with small spots, patches, or specks of color or shade differing from that of the background ⟨it lay *dappled* with sun and shade, still, clear, and irresistible —Susan Ertz⟩ FREAKED may suggest bold streaks of contrasting color ⟨tall bare fells, capped and *freaked* with snow —John Brophy⟩ ⟨the woods were *freaked* and pied with fresh transparent leaves and flowers —Elinor Wylie⟩

variegated copper ore *n* : BORNITE

variegated cutworm *n* : a widespread and destructive cutworm (*Peridroma saucia*)

variegated grass *n* : RIBBON GRASS

variegated sheldrake *n* : PARADISE DUCK

variegated spider monkey *n* : a black, white, and yellow So. American spider monkey (*Ateles variegatus*)

variegated spurge *n* : SNOW-ON-THE-MOUNTAIN 2

variegated thistle *n, NewZeal* : MILK THISTLE 1

var·ie·ga·tion \ˌ==(=)ˈgāshən\ *n* -s [*variegate* + *-ion*] 1 : the act of variegating or state of being variegated; *esp* : diversity of colors or tints 2 : the presence of two or more colors in leaves, flowers, or stems due to localized distribution of pigments or to absence of pigments in some areas

var·ie·ga·tor \ˈ==(=)ˌgād·ə(r)\ *n* -s [*variegate* + *-or*] : one that variegates

var·i·er \ˈverēə(r), ˈva(a)r-\ *n* -s : one that varies

varies *pres 3d sing of* VARY

va·ri·e·tal \vəˈrīəd·ᵊl, -ətᵊl\ *adj* [*variety* + *-al*] : of, relating to, or characterizing a variety ⟨~ name⟩ : being a variety in distinction from an individual or species : SUBSPECIFIC — **va·ri·e·tal·ly** \-ᵊlē, -ᵊli\ *adv*

varietal wine *also* **varietal** *n* -s : a wine bearing the name of the principal grape from which it is produced ⟨Cabernet is a California *varietal wine*⟩ — compare GENERIC WINE

va·ri·e·tas \vəˈrīəˌtas\ *n, pl* **varieta·tes** \ˌ=ˌ==ˈtād·ˌēz\ [L *varietat-, varietas*] : VARIETY

va·ri·e·tist \vəˈrīəd·əst\ *n* -s [*variety* + *-ist*] : one who varies from the norm (as in aptitudes, desires, or appetites)

va·ri·e·ty \vəˈrīəd·ē, -ətē, -i\ *n* -ES [MF or L; MF *varieté*, fr. L *varietat-, varietas*, fr. *varie-* (fr. *varius* various) + *-tat-, -tas* -ty] 1 : the quality or state of having numerous forms or types : the quality or state of being various or varied : MULTIFARIOUSNESS ⟨astonishing grasp of the multiplicity and ~ of life —René Wellek⟩ ⟨his imagination is ensnared by her endless ~ —Edwin Mims⟩ ⟨the ~ of the city's musical life⟩ 2 : an intermixture or succession of different things, forms, or qualities : a number or collection of different things esp. of a particular class : ASSORTMENT ⟨worked at a ~ of occupations —*Current Biog.*⟩ ⟨fought for a ~ of local improvements —Frank Monaghan⟩ ⟨region has a wide ~ of plant life —*Amer. Guide Series: Ark.*⟩ 3 : something differing from others of the same general kind : one of a number of things that are related : SORT ⟨army of foremen, clerks, shopkeepers and middlemen of every ~ —G.M.Trevelyan⟩: as a : any of various infraspecific groups of plants or animals: as (1) *archaic* : a group or kind of individual distinguished by characters too inconstant or too trivial to justify specific rank (2) : SUBSPECIES a (3) : a category immediately inferior to a subspecies and not resulting from geographic isolation (4) : a specified biotype (as a color phase) (5) : HORTICULTURAL VARIETY b : one of the forms in which a species of mineral may occur differing in minor characteristics esp. of structure, color, or purity of composition ⟨sapphire is a blue ~ of corundum⟩ 4 : VARIETY STORE ⟨operates a ~ and luncheonette —*Springfield (Mass.) Daily News*⟩ ⟨a ~ chain⟩ 5 a : entertainment consisting of successive unrelated performances (as songs, dances, skits, acrobatic feats, and trained animal acts) ⟨~ program⟩ ⟨~ turn⟩ ⟨~ house⟩ ⟨the wireless blares out ~ and swing music —Flora Thompson⟩ — see VARIETY SHOW; compare VAUDEVILLE b : the production of or performance in variety shows : variety performances 6 : the effect of multiplicity and continuous discovery in form as opposed to aesthetic monotony

syn SUBSPECIES, RACE, BREED, STRAIN, STOCK: these words show variable uses according to the period of scientific writing in which they appear and have been used to designate closely related groups of plants or animals narrower in scope than a species. VARIETY and SUBSPECIES often apply to a group distinguished from others in a general class by characteristics too minor to constitute criteria of a species. Sometimes VARIETY designates a group produced by human research and control ⟨a new *variety* of apples⟩ SUBSPECIES indicates a subdivision of a species set off from the rest by minor or unstable differences. RACE, often a bitterly controversial word in both scientific and lay discussions, may designate a group whose distinctive characteristics set it off from other groups of the same ancestry and are likely to be inherited from generation to generation with a degree of stability ⟨the darker *races* of mankind are made up of those having skins rich in melanin⟩ BREED may refer to an established group within a species sharing inheritable characteristics and usu. developed or maintained through human control (as Jersey cows or beagle dogs). STRAIN may refer to a group smaller than a breed and linked by common quite specific ancestry or identifying characteristic ⟨a *strain* of Shorthorn cattle known as the Milking Shorthorn⟩ ⟨a resistant *strain* of bacteria⟩ STOCK may suggest a genetically close relationship and a general similarity of origin, environment, and development, but its range of reference is not clearly defined ⟨coming from a healthy *stock*⟩

syn VARIETY, DIVERSITY: VARIETY usu. applies to a multiplicity of things within the same class or category that can be distinguished, often by marked differences ⟨the *variety* of feelings which bore me onward —Mary W. Shelley⟩ ⟨a *variety* of competing sects —Stringfellow Barr⟩ ⟨a *variety* of styles⟩ ⟨a *variety* of pleasures⟩ DIVERSITY, though often interchangeable with VARIETY, more usu. stresses a marked difference or divergence among individuals, parts, or elements, seldom implying also or putting much stress on a class likeness ⟨the range and *diversity* of their interests and activities —Dumas Malone⟩ ⟨man's genetic *diversity* —Curt Stern⟩ ⟨has a better eye for similarities among cultures than for *diversities* —Raphael Demos⟩ ⟨absorbed in the *diversity* resulting where immigration plays an important role, as in religion and personal names —B.A.Botkin⟩

variety meat *n* : an edible part of a slaughter animal other than skeletal muscle usu. including organ meats (as liver, heart, tripes, or kidneys) and various other structures (as tongues, ears, or skin); *broadly* : any of various edible meat products or meat by-products that do not consist predominantly of skeletal muscle (as feet) and that are often sold partially processed (as in sausage)

variety show *n* : a theatrical entertainment of successive separate performances (as of songs, dances, comic routines, and acrobatic feats, short dramatic sketches) ⟨*variety shows* on television⟩

variety store *also* **variety shop** *n* : a retail establishment dealing in a large variety of merchandise esp. of low unit value — compare FIVE-AND-TEN, GENERAL STORE

vari·focal lens \ˌverē, ˌva(a)rē+. . . -\ *n* [*vari-* + *-focal*] : ZOOM LENS

var·i·form \ˈva(a)rəˌfȯrm, ˈver-, -fȯ(ə)m\ *adj* [*vari-* + *-form*] : having various forms : varied or different in form : DIVERSIFORM — **var·i·form·ly** *adv*

vario- — see VARI-

var·io·coupler \ˌverē(ˌ)ō, ˌva(a)rē(ˌ)ō+\ *n* [*vari-* + *coupler*] : an inductive coupler the mutual inductance of which is adjustable by moving one coil with respect to the other

va·ri·o·la \vəˈrīələ\ *n* -s [NL, fr. ML, pustule, pox, fr. LL, pustule; prob. akin to L *varus* pimple — more at VARICOSE] : any of several virus diseases marked by a pustular eruption: as a : SMALLPOX 1 b : COWPOX 1 c : HORSEPOX d : FOWL POX a

variola equi·na \-ēˈkwīnə\ *n* [NL] : HORSEPOX

va·ri·o·lar \vəˈrīələ(r)\ *adj* [NL *variola* + E *-ar*] : VARIOLOUS

var·i·o·late \ˈverēələt, ˈva(a)r-, -əˌlāt\ *adj* [NL *variola* + E *-ate*] : having lesions or marks resembling those of smallpox

variola vac·cin·ia \-vakˈsinēə\ *n* [NL] : COWPOX

var·i·ole \ˈverēˌōl, ˈva(a)r-\ *n* -s [ML *variola* pustule, pox] 1 : FOVEOLA 2 : a spherule of a variolite

var·i·ol·ic \ˌ==ˈälik\ *adj* [NL *variola* + E *-ic*] : VARIOLOUS

var·i·ol·i·form \ˌ==ˈäləˌfȯrm\ *adj* [NL *variola* + ISV *-iform*] : resembling smallpox

var·i·o·lite \ˈverēəˌlīt, ˈva(a)r-\ *n* -s [prob. fr. NL *variolites*, fr. ML *variola* pustule, pox + L *-ites* -ite] : a basic rock embedded with whitish spherules

var·i·o·lit·ic \ˌ===ˈlid·ik\ *adj* [ISV *variolite* + *-ic*] : of, relating to, or resembling variolite

var·i·o·lit·iza·tion \ˌ===ˌlid·əˈzāshən\ *n* -s [*variolite* + *-ization*] : conversion into variolite : production of variolitic structure

var·i·o·loid \ˈverēəˌlȯid, ˈva(a)r-\ *n* -s [NL *variola* + E *-oid*] : a modified mild form of smallpox occurring in persons who have been vaccinated or who have had smallpox

va·ri·o·lous \vəˈrīələs\ *adj* [in sense 1, fr. NL *variola* smallpox + L *-osus* -ous; in sense 2, fr. ML *variolosus* pockmarked, fr. *variola* pustule, pox + L *-osus* -ous] 1 : of or relating to smallpox 2 : FOVEATE

var·i·om·e·ter \ˌverēˈäməd·ə(r), ˌva(a)r-\ *n* [*vari-* + *-meter*] 1 : VARIOCOUPLER; *esp* : one provided with an arbitrary scale 2 : DECLINOMETER 3 : an aeronautical instrument for indicating rate of climb

¹**var·i·o·rum** \ˌverēˈōrəm, ˌva(a)rē-, ˌvārē-, -ˈȯr-\ *or* **variorum edition** *n* -s [L *variorum* of various persons (gen. pl. masc. of *varius* various), in the phrase *cum notis variorum* with the notes of various persons] 1 : an edition or text esp. of a classical author with notes by different persons 2 : an edition of a publication containing variant readings of the text ⟨a *variorum edition* is indicated whenever a great literary work has had a long and complex editorial history —L.P.G.Peckham⟩

²**variorum** \ˌ==ˈ==\ *adj* 1 : relating to or being an edition or text containing notes of various commentators and editors ⟨The Dunciad *Variorum*⟩ 2 : drawn or derived from various sources ⟨~ illustrations⟩ ⟨this last charge, as it flew from tongue to tongue, acquired ~ readings —H.L.Mencken⟩

¹**var·i·ous** \ˈverēəs, ˈva(a)r-, ˈvār-\ *adj* [L *varius*; prob. akin to L *varus* bent, crooked — more at PREVARICATE] 1 *archaic* : subject to change or undergoing changes : VARIABLE, CHANGEABLE, INCONSTANT 2 : of varied color : VARICOLORED ⟨birds of ~ plumage —H.W.Longfellow⟩ 3 a : of differing kinds : being a varied assortment : MULTIFARIOUS ⟨doors had been blocked open with ~ mine equipment —J.E.Summers⟩ ⟨engaging at times in ~ business enterprises —E.E.Dale⟩ b : UNLIKE ⟨animals as ~ as the jaguar, the cavy, and the sloth⟩ 4 : having or manifesting a number of different aspects or characteristics ⟨a most ~ genius —F.J.Mather⟩ ⟨the story is lively and ~ —James Gray⟩ ⟨ready, cheerful, ~, and illuminating conversation —J.B.Holroyd⟩ 5 : VARIANT ⟨~ readings of the Bible⟩ 6 : consisting of an indefinite number greater than one : SUNDRY, DIVERS ⟨inspection trips to ~ manufacturing plants —*Current Biog.*⟩ 7 : being one of a group : INDIVIDUAL, SEPARATE ⟨refunds to the ~ club members⟩ ⟨distribute taxes equitably among the ~ economic groups —R.G.Woolbert⟩ ⟨the twelve ~ departments of the Clinic —Terry Southern⟩ **syn** see DIFFERENT

²**various** \"\ *pron, pl in constr* : several different ones ⟨I questioned ~ of them⟩

var·i·ous·ly *adv* 1 : in various ways : at various times : DIVERSELY ⟨was ~ occupied teaching school, farming, clerking in a store⟩ ⟨the family name is ~ spelled —*Current Biog.*⟩ ⟨artists speaking languages ~ alien to our own —Irwin Edman⟩ ⟨the most ~ stored mind of his age —Robert Lynd⟩ 2 : by various designations ⟨insects ~ known as sandflies, biting midges, punkies —*Jour. of Economic Entomology*⟩ 3 : in a varied selection or arrangement ⟨scattered on top of the outmoded square piano, I could see ~: a large family album, several daguerreotypes, an assortment of seashells —Ruby Tartt⟩

var·i·ous·ness *n* -ES : the quality or state of being various ⟨the infinite ~ of the world —John Buchan⟩

var·is·cite \ˈvarəˌsīt\ *n* -s [G *variscit*, fr. ML *Variscia*, ancient name of the Vogtland district, Saxony, Germany + G *-it* -ite] : a bluish to greenish gem mineral sometimes confused with or substituted for turquoise — called also *utahlite;* see AMATRICE

variscite green *n* : a light green that is yellower and less strong than average mint green and yellower and paler than serpentine

vari·sized \ˈverēˌsīzd, ˈva(a)r-, ˈvār-, -ri\ *adj* [*vari-* + *sized*] : of various sizes ⟨swirls of ~ navy polka dots —*New Yorker*⟩

var·is·tor \vaˈristə(r), veˈ-\ *n* -s [*vari-* + *resistor*] : an electrical resistor whose resistance depends on the applied voltage

¹**var·i·type** \ˈverēˌtīp, ˈva(a)r-, ˈvār-, -rəˌ-\ *n* [back-formation fr. *VariTyper*] 1 : a VariTyper machine 2 : the process of composing text matter by means of a VariTyper machine

²**varitype** \"\ *vt* : to set by varitype ~ *vi* : to operate a VariTyper machine

Var·i·Typ·er \-pə(r)\ *trademark* — used for a machine for composing text matter often in justified lines that is similar in operation to a typewriter but has changeable type

var·i·typ·ist \-pəst\ *n* [¹*varitype* + *-ist*] : an operator of a VariTyper machine

var·ix \ˈva(a)riks, ˈver-, -rēks\ *n, pl* **vari·ces** \-rəˌsēz\ [L *varic-, varix* — more at VARICOSE] 1 a : an abnormally dilated and lengthened vein, artery, or lymph vessel ⟨esophageal ~⟩ b : an abnormal swelling and tortuosity esp. of the superficial veins of the legs 2 : one of the prominent ridges across each whorl of various univalves showing a former position of the outer lip of the aperture

var lect *abbr* [L *varia lectio*] variant reading

var·let \ˈvärlət, ˈväl-, *usu* -əd·+V\ *n* -s [ME, fr. MF *vallet, varlet, vaslet* young nobleman, page, squire — more at VALET] 1 *archaic* a : ATTENDANT, MENIAL, SERVANT b : a knight's page 2 : a low fellow : a base unprincipled person ⟨some ~ put a parking ticket on the . . . car —Claudia Cassidy⟩

var·let·ry \-trē\ *n* -ES [*varlet* + *-ry*] *archaic* : a group of menials : RABBLE, CROWD, MOB

var·ley loop \ˈvärlē-\ *n, usu cap V* [after C. F. *Varley* †1883 Eng. electrical engineer] : a bridge circuit in wire line work to determine the distance to a fault on the line

var·ley's gray \ˈvärlēz-\ *n, usu cap V* [after John *Varley* †1842 Eng. landscape painter] : a purplish gray to grayish purple

var·meter \ˈvärˌmēd·ə(r)\ *n* [²*var* + *-meter*] : an instrument for indicating volt-amperes reactive

¹**var·mint** *also* **var·ment** \ˈvärmənt, ˈvȧm-\ *n* [alter. of *vermin*] 1 *pl* **varmints** *also* **varmint** a *dial* : VERMIN b : an animal classed as vermin and unprotected by game laws ⟨coyotes, prairie dogs, or other hard-to-stalk ~*s* —*Amer. Rifleman*⟩ c *dial* : an esp. wild animal or bird considered as a pest or nuisance ⟨old dog running out to bark at some ~ above in the brush —*Amer. Mercury*⟩ 2 -s : an obnoxious, vexing, or contemptible person : RASCAL, ROGUE; *broadly* : PERSON, FELLOW, CHAP

²**varmint** *or* **varment** \"\ *adj* [fr. obs. *varmint, varment* an amateur in sports with professional skill, of unknown origin] 1 *archaic* : SPORTING, DASHING 2 *dial* : CLEVER, SHARP, CUNNING

var·mint·er \-tə(r)\ *n* -s [¹*varmint* + *-er*] : a rifle designed esp. for hunting varmints

varmint gun *or* **varmint rifle** *n* : VARMINTER

var·na \ˈvərnə\ *n* -s [Skt *varṇa*, lit., color, sort, class, fr. *vṛṇoti* he covers, envelops — more at WEIR] 1 : one of the four ancient Hindu social groups assigned by classical law to specific occupational duties and including the twice-born Brahmans, Kshatriyas, and Vaisyas and the chiefly aboriginal Sudras 2 : one of four groupings of modern Hindu castes traditionally derived from the ancient varnas : CLASS

var·nash·ra·ma \ˌvərˈnäshrəmə\ *n* -s [Skt *varṇāśrama*, lit., caste and stage of life, fr. *varṇa* varna + *āśrama* ashrama] : the institution of caste

¹**var·nish** \ˈvärnish, ˈvȧn-, -nēsh\ *n* -ES *see sense 4* [ME *vernisch*, fr. MF *vernis*, fr. OIt or ML; OIt *vernice*, fr. ML *veronice, veronic-, veronix* sandarac (resin), fr. Gk *berenikē*, prob. fr. *Berenikē* Berenice (now Benghazi), city in Cyrenaica] 1 a : a liquid preparation that when spread upon a surface dries by evaporation or oxidation forming a hard lustrous coating that is more or less transparent unless pigments have been added and serves for decoration and protection — see OIL VARNISH, SPIRIT VARNISH; JAPAN, LACQUER, SHELLAC; compare ENAMEL 3 b : the covering, coating, or glaze given by the application of varnish ⟨seemed to be like a painting cleaned of later restorations and ~*es*—Erwin Rosenthal⟩ c : the act of applying this substance to a surface d : something that resembles or suggests varnish by its gloss ⟨the ~ of the holly and ivy —T.B.Macaulay⟩ 2 : an artificial covering to

give a pleasing or conventional appearance to action or conduct : an embellishing feature : outside show : GLOSS ⟨absence of literary ~ —Frederic Morton⟩ ⟨concealed, under a ~ of conventionality . . . a nature throbbing with passion —Norman Douglas⟩ **3 a :** thickened linseed oil with which pigments are ground to form the ink used in lithography **b :** GROUND 3g **4** *pl* **varnish** *slang* **a :** a through passenger train or car ⟨ride the ~⟩ ⟨a ~ conductor⟩ **b :** a highly varnished wooden passenger car ⟨the last such ~ ever to roll over the Carson meadows —Lucius Beebe & C.M.Clegg⟩ **5** *chiefly Brit* **:** NAIL POLISH **6 :** a deposit formed in engines by oxidation and polymerization of fuels and lubricants

²**varnish** \ˈ", *esp in pres part* -nəsh\ *vb* -ED/-ING/-ES [ME *vernischen*, fr. MF *vernisser*, fr. *vernis* varnish] *vt* **1 :** to apply varnish to : cover with a thin coating of a liquid that when dry produces a hard glossy surface ⟨~ a table⟩ ⟨~ a painting⟩ — often used with *over* ⟨~ over a surface⟩ **2 :** to coat over with something resembling or likened to varnish : cover or conceal with something that gives a fair appearance : gloss over ⟨a manner highly ~*ed*, a blend of cool bluff and right thinking —Francis Hackett⟩ ⟨never imagine that anything you can say yourself will ~ your defects —Earl of Chesterfield⟩ ⟨one that degraded art, and ~*ed* vice —Robert Bridges †1930⟩ **3 :** ADORN, EMBELLISH ⟨beauty doth ~ age —Shak.⟩ ~ *vi* **:** to apply varnish

varnished *adj* [fr. past part. of ²*varnish*] **1 :** covered with or as if with varnish ⟨a ~ table⟩ ⟨a ~ reputation⟩ **2 :** VERNICOSE

varnished willow *n* **:** CRACK WILLOW 1

var·nish·er \-shə(r)\ *n* -s **:** one that varnishes

varnish gum *n* **:** a natural or synthetic resin used in making varnish

varnishing day *n* [*varnishing* (gerund of ²*varnish*) + *day*] **1 :** a day before the opening of an exhibition of paintings reserved for the painters to varnish or put on finishing touches **2 :** the opening day of an art exhibition

varnish tree *n* **:** any of various trees yielding a milky juice from which in some cases varnish or lacquer is prepared: as **a :** JAPANESE VARNISH TREE 1 **b :** LACQUER TREE **c :** BLACK-VARNISH TREE **d :** MARKING NUT **e :** AILANTHUS 2 **f :** GOLDENRAIN TREE **g :** CANDLENUT 2

var·nishy \-shē\ *adj* [¹*varnish* + *-y*] **:** of, relating to, or resembling varnish : having a varnished surface ⟨a ~ smell⟩ ⟨a ~ appearance⟩

va·ro·hío \ˌvärəˈhē(ˌ)ō\ *n, pl* **varohío** *or* **varohíos** *usu cap* **1 :** a Taracahitian people of the Río Mayo valley between the states of Chihuahua and Sonora, Mexico **2 :** a member of the Varohío people

va·ro·li·an \vəˈrōlēən\ *adj, usu cap* [NL (*pons*) *varolii* + E *-an*] **:** of or relating to the pons Varolii

var·ro·nia \vəˈrōnēə\ *n, cap* [NL, fr. *Varron-, Varro* (Marcus Terentius *Varro* †27 B.C. Roman scholar) + NL *-ia*] **:** a large genus of tropical American shrubs and trees (family Boraginaceae) having pubescent or scabrous foliage and small usu. white flowers with a 4-lobed or 5-lobed limb followed by fruit that is a small slightly fleshy drupe

var·ro·ni·an \-ēən\ *adj, usu cap* [L *varronianus*, fr. the Roman surname *Varron-, Varro*] **:** of or relating to a person having the surname Varro (as Marcus Terentius Varro)

varronian satire *n, usu cap V* **:** a form of dramatic satire practiced by Marcus Terentius Varro

vars *pl of* VAR

var·sha \ˈvərshə\ *n* -s [Skt *varṣa* rain, rainy season; akin to Skt *varṣati* it rains, *vār* water — more at URINE] *India* **:** the rainy season : MONSOON

var·si·ty \ˈvärsəd-ē, ˈväs-, -ətē, -i\ *n* -ES *often attrib* [by shortening & alter. fr. *university*] **1** *chiefly Brit* **:** UNIVERSITY **2 :** a first team or group of players capable of playing on the first team representing a university, college, school, or club in a sport or other form of competition in contests with teams of equal standing from other universities, colleges, schools, or clubs

¹**var·so·vi·an** \(ˈ)värˈsōvēən\ *adj, usu cap* [fr. (assumed) ML *varsovianus*, fr. *Varsovia* Warsaw, capital of Poland + L *-anus* -an] **:** of, relating to, or characteristic of Warsaw, Poland

²**varsovian** \"\ *n* -s *cap* **:** a native or resident of Warsaw, Poland

var·so·via·na *also* **var·sou·via·na** \ˌvärsōˈvyänə\ *n* -s [prob. fr. Sp *varsoviana*, fr. fem. of *varsoviano* Varsovian, fr. (assumed) ML *varsovianus*] **1 :** a graceful dance similar to a mazurka and popular in many European countries, Mexico, and the U. S. **2 :** music for the varsoviana characterized by a slow triple meter and a strong initial accent in every second measure

var·so·vienne \-ˈvyen\ *n* -s [F, fr. fem. of *varsovien* Varsovian, fr. (assumed) ML *varsovianus*] **:** VARSOVIANA

var·ta·bed \ˌvärtäˈbed\ *or* **var·da·pet** \-däˈpet\ *or* **var·ta·bet** \-täˈbet\ *n* -s [Arm *vartabed*, lit., teacher] **:** a member of an order of celibate preachers in the Armenian clergy corresponding to the archimandrite in the Greek church

va·ru·lite \ˈvärəˌlīt\ *n* -s [Sw *varulit*, fr. *Varuträsk*, locality in northern Sweden + Sw *-lit* -lite] **:** a mineral $(Na,Ca)(Mn,Fe)_2(PO_4)_2$ consisting of manganese, sodium, and calcium with minor amounts of iron, isomorphous with hühnerkobelite, and isostructural with triphylite and lithiophilite

var·us \ˈva(a)rəs, ˈver-\ *n* -ES [NL, adj., turned inward to an abnormal degree, fr. L, knock-kneed — more at PREVARICATE] **:** the position of a joint's being turned inward to an abnormal degree ⟨the foot must turn into ~ to keep in line with the knee joint —*Yr. Bk. of Orthopedics & Traumatic Surgery*⟩

varve \ˈvärv, ˈväv\ *n* -s [Sw *varv* turn, revolution, layer; akin to OE *hweorfan* to turn — more at WHARF] **:** a pair of layers of alternately finer and coarser silt or clay believed to comprise an annual cycle of deposition in a body of still water (as a glacial lake) and used to measure the time involved in the deposition of the entire group of sediments and to construct a time scale in a manner similar to that employed in the study of annual rings in trees ⟨~ chronology⟩

varved \-vd\ *adj* [*varve* + *-ed*] **:** stratified in paired layers of annual deposition ⟨~ clays⟩

varvel *var of* VERVEL

var·vi·ty \ˈvärvəd-ē\ *n* -ES [*varve* + *-ity*] **:** stratification in varves

vary \ˈverē, ˈva(a)r-, ˈvär-, -ri\ *vb* -ED/-ING/-ES [ME *varien*, fr. MF or L; MF *varier*, fr. L *variare*, fr. *varius* diverse, various — more at VARIOUS] *vt* **1 :** to bring about differences in: **a :** to make an esp. minor or partial change in : make different in some attribute or characteristic ⟨this is not a proceeding which may be *varied* —John Marshall⟩ **b :** to make differences between items in : insure variety in : make unlike in some particular : VARIEGATE, DIVERSIFY ⟨a program that was *varied* enough to avoid monotony —Katharine Amend⟩ ⟨the days were not crowded, but they were enviably *varied* —Virginia Woolf⟩ **2 :** to present under new aspects ⟨~ the rhythm and harmonic treatment⟩ ~ *vi* **1 :** to exhibit or undergo change : break from sameness or uniformity : DIFFER ⟨a constantly ~*ing* terrain —Shipley Thomas⟩ ⟨chapters of ~*ing* worth —F.N.Robinson⟩ ⟨historical allusions of ~*ing* degrees of accuracy —T.D.McCormick⟩ **2 :** DEVIATE, DEPART, SWERVE ⟨~ from the law⟩ ⟨~ from the mean⟩ **3 :** to exhibit differing qualities or attributes in alternation or succession with something else ⟨one mathematical quantity may ~ inversely with another⟩ **4 :** to exhibit divergence in structural or physiological characters from those typical or usual in the group **syn** see CHANGE, DIFFER

varying hare *n* [*varying* (pres. part. of *vary*) + *hare*] **:** any of several hares having white fur in winter; *esp* **:** SNOWSHOE RABBIT

varying lemming *n* **:** an arctic lemming esp. of the genus *Dicrostonyx* in which the pelage is more or less completely white in winter

vary·ing·ly *adv* **:** in a varying manner

¹**vas** \ˈvas\ *n, pl* **vasa** \ˈvasə, ˈväsə, ˈväzə, ˈväsə, ˈväzə\ [NL, fr. L, vessel — more at VASE] **:** an anatomical vessel : DUCT

²**vas** \ˈwäs, ˈvas\ *n, pl* **va·des** \ˈwä(ˌ)dās, ˈvä(ˌ)dēz\ [L — more at WED] *Roman & civil law* **:** a pledge or surety for another's appearance in court

vas- *or* **vasi-** *or* **vaso-** *comb form* [NL, fr. L *vas*] **1 :** duct : channel : vessel (*vasi*centric): as **a :** blood vessel ⟨*vaso*formative⟩ ⟨*vaso*constriction⟩ **b :** vas deferens ⟨*vas*ectomy⟩ **2 :** vascular and ⟨*vaso*vagal⟩ **3 :** vasomotor ⟨*vaso*inhibitor⟩

vasa *n* -s [L, pl., vessels] *obs* **:** VASE

vas ab·er·rans \ˈvaˈsabəˌranz\ *n, pl* **vasa aberran·tia** \ˈ⸗⸗-ˌabəˈranch(ē)ə\ [NL, lit., deviating vessel] **1 :** a blind tube that is occas. present parallel to the first part of the vas deferens with which or with the epididymis it may communicate **2** *vasa aberrantia pl* **:** slender arteries that are only occas. present and that connect the axillary or brachial artery and the radial or other artery of the forearm or the subclavian artery and the thoracic aorta

vasa bre·via \ˌ⸗⸗ˈbrēvēə\ *n pl* [NL, lit., short vessels] **:** short branches of the splenic artery and vein that run to the greater curvature of the stomach

vasa deferentia *pl of* VAS DEFERENS

vasa ef·fer·en·tia \-ˌefəˈrench(ē)ə\ *n pl* [NL, lit., efferent vessels] **:** the 12 to 20 tubes that lead from the rete of the testis to the vas deferens and except near their commencement are greatly convoluted and form the compact head of the epididymis

vasal \ˈvāsəl, ˈvāzəl, ˈvasəl\ *adj* [*vas-* + *-al*] **:** of, relating to, or constituting an anatomical vessel

vasa mur·rhi·na \-məˈrīnə, -rēnə\ *n, usu cap V&M* [NL, lit., murrhine dish] **:** a late 19th century American glassware of variegated color and often with metallic flecking

va·sa parrot \ˈväsə-, ˈäzə-\ *n* [Malagasy *vàza* vasa parrot, lit., loud-voiced] **:** any of several blackish brown Madagascan parrots of the genus *Coracopsis* (esp. *C. vasa*)

va·sa·tes \vəˈsād·(ˌ)ēz\ *n, cap* [NL] **:** a genus of plant-feeding mites containing some that are destructive to many crop plants — see TOMATO RUSSET MITE

vasa va·so·rum \-ˌvaˈsōrəm, -ˌväl, -ˌväl, ˈzō-\ *n pl* [NL, lit., vessels of vessels] **:** small blood vessels that are distributed to the walls of the larger arteries and veins and arise from a branch of the same vessel or from a neighboring vessel

vas·con \ˈvaskən, -skän\ *n, pl* **vascons** \-nz\ *or* **vasco·nes** \-skəˌnēz\ *cap* [L *Vascon-, Vasco*] **:** BASQUE 1

vascul- *or* **vasculo-** *comb form* [NL, fr. L *vasculum* small vessel] **:** vessel; *esp* **:** blood vessel ⟨*vasculo*motor⟩

vas·cu·lar \ˈvaskyələ(r), ˈvaas-\ *adj* [NL *vascularis*, fr. L *vasculum* small vessel (dim. of *vas* vessel) + *-aris* -ar — more at VASE] **1 a :** of, relating to, or affecting a tube for the conveyance of a body fluid (as the blood of an animal or the sap of a plant); *often* **:** of, relating to, or constituting a system of such tubes ⟨lymph ~ degeneration⟩ — compare WATER-VASCULAR SYSTEM **b :** supplied with or containing ducts and esp. blood vessels ⟨a ~ tumor⟩ ⟨the ~ layer of the skin⟩ **2 :** marked by vigor and ardor : SPIRITED, PASSIONATE ⟨writing must be done with gusto, must be ~ —S.E.Hyman⟩ ⟨the most ~ and virile thus far printed —Mark Sullivan⟩

vascular bed *n* **:** the intricate meshwork of minute blood vessels that ramifies through the tissues of the body or of one of its parts

vascular bundle *also* **vascular strand** *n* **:** a unit strand of the vascular system of a higher plant consisting usu. of vessels and sieve tubes commonly in association with elongated parenchyma cells and fibers that may surround the strand as a sheath — called also *fibrovascular bundle;* see AMPHICRIBRAL, AMPHIVASAL; compare STELE

vascular cambium *n* **:** the lateral meristem from which vascular tissue is differentiated and which is distinguished from phellogen

vascular cryptogam *n* **:** a cryptogamic plant (as a fern or moss) that has a vascular system — compare CELLULAR CRYPTOGAM

vascular cylinder *n* **:** the cylinder of vascular tissue between cortex and pith of a vascular plant : STELE

vas·cu·lar·i·ty \ˌ⸗⸗ˈlarəd-ē\ *n* -ES [ISV *vascular* + *-ity*] **:** the quality or state of being vascular

vas·cu·lar·iza·tion \ˌ⸗⸗ˌlərəˈzāshən, -ˌrīˈz-\ *n* -s [ISV *vascular* + *-ization*] **:** the process of becoming vascular; *often* **:** abnormal or excessive formation of blood vessels (as in the retina or on the cornea)

vas·cu·lar·ize \ˈ⸗⸗⸗ˌrīz\ *vt* -ED/-ING/-S [*vascular* + *-ize*] **:** to make vascular ⟨gradually *vascularizing* the yolk sac⟩

vas·cu·lar·ly *adv* **:** in a vascular manner : by vessels

vascular plant *n* **:** a plant having a specialized conducting system that includes xylem and phloem : TRACHEOPHYTE

vascular ray *n* **:** a ray of cambial origin that occurs in the stele of many vascular plants and often separates the vascular bundles — see PHLOEM RAY, XYLEM RAY; compare MEDULLARY RAY

vascular system *n* **:** the part of the body of a vascular plant that is made up of vascular tissue

vascular tissue *n* **:** tissue concerned mainly with conduction in plants; *esp* **:** the highly specialized tissue found in the higher plants consisting essentially of phloem and xylem and forming a continuous system throughout the plant body — compare VASCULAR BUNDLE

vas·cu·la·tion \ˌvaskyəˈlāshən\ *n* -s [*vascul-* + *-ation*] **:** formation or arrangement of vessels in a plant

vas·cu·la·ture \ˈvaskyələˌchů(ə)r, -ˌchər\ *n* -s [*vascul-* + *-ature* (as in *musculature*)] **:** the disposition or arrangement of blood vessels in an organ or part

vas·cu·lo·genesis \ˌvaskyəlō+\ *n* [NL, fr. *vascul-* + *genesis*] **:** embryonic formation and differentiation of the blood-vascular system

vas·cu·lum \ˈvaskyələm\ *n, pl* **vascu·la** \-lə\ [NL, fr. L, small vessel — more at VASCULAR] **1 :** ASCIDIUM **2 :** a usu. metal and commonly cylindrical or flattened box with a cover opening lengthwise that is used in collecting plants

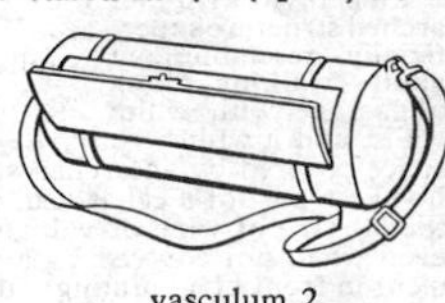
vasculum 2

vas def·er·ens \-ˈdefərənz, -ˌrenz\ *n, pl* **vasa deferen·tia** \-ˌdefəˈrench(ē)ə\ [NL, lit., deferent vessel] **:** a spermatic duct esp. of a higher vertebrate that in man is a small but thick-walled tube about two feet long formed by the union of the vasa efferentia, is greatly convoluted in its proximal portion where it forms the body and tail of the epididymis, runs in the spermatic cord through the inguinal canal, and descends into the pelvis where it joins the duct of the seminal vesicle to form the ejaculatory duct

vase \ˈvās *also* ˈvāz *sometimes* ˈvä|z *or* ˈvä| *or* |s, *archaic Brit* ˈvōz\ *n* -s [F, fr. L *vas;* akin to Umbrian *vasor* vessels] **1 :** a vessel that is usu. rounded and of greater depth than width, is commonly decorative, and is used chiefly for ornament or for flowers though also adapted for various domestic purposes and used anciently in religious rites ⟨a porcelain ~⟩ ⟨a Grecian ~⟩ **2 :** an ornament (as on furniture) having the form of a vase

vase clock *n* **:** a clock whose decorative case has the general form of a vase; *esp* **:** one in which there is no dial of the usual form but in which a part of a vase revolves while a single stationary indicator serves as a hand

vas·ec·to·mize \vaˈsektəˌmīz, vaˈze-, väˈze-, väˈse-\ *vt* -ED/-ING/-S **:** to perform a vasectomy on

vas·ec·to·my \-mē\ *n* -ES [ISV *vas-* + *-ectomy*] **:** surgical excision of the vas deferens usu. to induce permanent sterility

vase·ful *pronunc at* VASE + ˌfu̇l\ *n* -s **:** as much as a vase will hold

vaselike \ˈ⸗ˌ⸗\ *adj* **:** resembling or suggesting a vase esp. in outline

vas·e·line \ˈvasəˌlēn, ˌ⸗⸗ˈ, *sometimes* -azə-\ *vt* -ED/-ING/-S [*Vaseline*] **:** to apply petrolatum to

Vas·e·line \"\ *trademark* — used for petrolatum

vase rug *n* **:** an uncommon 16th century Persian rug woven over a double warp in striking and severe floral designs with which a vase motive is often combined

vase splat *n* **:** a splat of a chair back having the outline of a vase and being common in the Queen Anne period

vase splat

vase-vine \ˈ⸗ˌ⸗\ *n* **:** LEATHERFLOWER

va·sey grass \ˈvāzē, -āsē-\ *n, usu cap V* [after George *Vasey* †1893 Am. physician and botanist] **:** an erect perennial grass (*Paspalum urvillei*) native to Argentina and grown for pasture from No. Carolina to Texas

vas·hegy·ite \ˈväsh.heˌjīt, ˈvōsh-\ *n* -s [G *vashegyit*, fr. *Vashegy*, village formerly in Hungary, now in southern Czechoslovakia, its locality + G *-it* -ite] **:** a mineral $2Al_4(PO_4)_3(OH)_3.27H_2O$ (?) that is hydrated basic aluminum phosphate and occurs in white to yellow masses (hardness 2–3, sp. gr. 1.96)

vasi- — see VAS-

vasi·cen·tric \ˌvāzəˈsen·trik, ˌväsə-, ˌvasə-, ˌvazə-\ *adj* [*vas-* + *-centric*] **:** forming a distinct round to oval sheath about a vessel in wood ⟨~ parenchyma⟩ — see VASICENTRIC TRACHEID; compare APOTRACHEAL, METATRACHEAL, PARATRACHEAL

vasicentric tracheid *n* **:** any of the short tracheids found in the vicinity of wood vessels and not arranged in definite longitudinal rows

vas·i·cine \ˈvasəˌsēn, -azə-\ *n* -s [ISV *vasic-* (fr. NL *vasica* — specific epithet of the Malabar nut *Adhatoda vasica* — , fr. Skt *vāsikā, vāsaka* Malabar nut, fr. *vāsayati* it perfumes, makes fragrant) + *-ine*] **:** a crystalline alkaloid $C_{11}H_{12}N_2O$ that is found in the leaves of the Malabar nut and seeds of the harmal and is thought to poison lower plants and animals but not higher animals

vasi·fac·tive \ˌvāz|əˈfaktiv, ˌväs|, ˌvas|, ˌvaz|\ *or* **vaso·fac·tive** \|ō|-\ *adj* [*vas-* + *-factive*] **:** VASOFORMATIVE

vasi·form \ˈvāzəˌfȯrm, ˈväsə-,ˈvasə-,ˈvazə-\ *adj* [NL *vasiformis*, fr. L *vas* + *-iformis* -iform — more at VASE] **1 :** having the form of a hollow tube : resembling or consisting of a duct **2 :** having the form of a vase ⟨porcelain ~ lamp, with shade —*Parke-Bernet Galleries Cat.*⟩

vaso- — see VAS-

vaso·constricting \ˌvā(ˌ)zō, ˌvā(ˌ)sō, ˌva(ˌ)sō, ˌva(ˌ)zō+\ *adj* [*vasoconstriction* + *-ing*] **:** VASOCONSTRICTIVE

vaso·constriction \"+\ *n* [ISV *vas-* + *constriction*] **:** narrowing of the lumen of blood vessels esp. as a result of vasomotor nervous action

vaso·constrictive \"+\ *adj* [*vas-* + *constrictive*] **:** inducing vasoconstriction

vaso·constrictor \"+\ *n* [ISV *vas-* + *constrictor*] **:** an agent (as a sympathetic nerve fiber or a drug) that induces or initiates vasoconstriction

vaso·corona \"+\ *n* [NL, fr. *vas-* + *corona*] **:** the system of peripheral blood vessels of the spinal cord sending branches toward the central canal

vaso·dentin \"+\ *n* [*vas-* + *dentin*] **:** a modified dentin permeated by blood capillaries and common in the teeth of the lower vertebrates

vaso·depressor \"+\ *n, often attrib* [*vas-* + *depressor*] **:** VASODILATOR

vaso·dilatation \"+\ *n* [ISV *vas-* + *dilatation*] **:** widening of the lumen of blood vessels whether due to vasodilator action or to the failure of vasoconstrictor activity

vaso·dil·a·tin \"+ˌdīlətən\ *n* -s [ISV *vasodilat*ation + *-in*] **:** a substance (as acetylcholine) that induces vasodilatation

vaso·dilating \"+\ *adj* [*vasodilation* + *-ing*] **:** inducing or initiating vasodilatation

vaso·dilation \"+\ *n* [*vas-* + *dilation*] **:** VASODILATATION

vaso·dilator \"+\ *n* [*vas-* + *dilator*] **:** an agent (as a parasympathetic nerve fiber or a drug) that induces or initiates vasodilatation

vaso·excitor \"+\ *n* **:** VASOCONSTRICTOR

vaso·formative \"+\ *adj* [ISV *vas-* + *formative*] **:** functioning in the development and formation of vessels and esp. blood vessels ⟨~ cells⟩

vaso·ganglion \"+\ *n* [NL, fr. *vas-* + *ganglion*] **:** a dense knot of blood vessels

vaso·inhibitor \"\ *n* [*vas-* + *inhibitor*] **:** an agent (as a drug) that depresses or inhibits the vasomotor and esp. the vasoconstrictor nerves — **vaso·inhibitory** \"+\ *adj*

vaso·ligation \"+\ *n* [*vas-* + *ligation*] **:** surgical ligation of a vessel and esp. of the vas deferens

vaso·motion \"+\ *n* [*vas-* + *motion*] **:** alteration in the caliber of blood vessels

vaso·motor \"+\ *adj* [ISV *vas-* + *motor*] **1 :** controlling the size of blood vessels **2 :** of, relating to, affecting, or being those nerves or the centers (as in the medulla and spinal cord) from which they arise that supply the muscle fibers of the walls of blood vessels, include sympathetic vasoconstrictors and parasympathetic vasodilators, and by their effect on vascular diameter regulate the amount of blood passing to a particular body part or organ

vasomotor rhinitis *n* **:** allergic rhinitis

vaso·neurosis \ˌvā(ˌ)zō, ˌvā(ˌ)sō, ˌva(ˌ)sō, ˌva(ˌ)zō+\ *n* [NL, fr. *vas-* + *neurosis*] **:** a disorder of blood vessels (as a vascular spasm) that is of basically neural origin : pathology arising in the vasomotor structures

vaso·neurotic \"+\ *adj* [fr. NL *vasoneurosis*, after NL *neurosis:* E *neurotic*] **:** of, relating to, or constituting a vasoneurosis

vaso·pres·sin \ˌvāzōˈpresᵊn, -āsō-, ˌvazo-, ˌvasō-\ *n* -s [fr. *Vasopressin*, a trademark] **:** a polypeptide hormone that is secreted together with oxytocin by the posterior lobe of the pituitary, that is also obtained synthetically, that increases blood pressure in mammals and exerts an antidiuretic effect, and that is used esp. in treating diabetes insipidus

¹**vaso·pressor** \ˌvā(ˌ)zō, ˌvā(ˌ)sō, ˌva(ˌ)zō, ˌva(ˌ)sō+\ *adj* [*vas-* + *pressor*] **:** causing a rise in blood pressure : exerting a vasoconstrictor effect

²**vasopressor** \"\ *n* -s **:** a vasopressor agent : VASOCONSTRICTOR

vaso·reflex \ˌvā(ˌ)zō, ˌvā(ˌ)sō, ˌva(ˌ)sō, ˌva(ˌ)zō+\ *n* [*vas-* + *reflex*] **:** a reflex reaction of a blood vessel

vaso·spasm \ˈ⸗⸗+ˌ-\ *n* [ISV *vas-* + *spasm*] **:** sharp and often persistent contraction of a blood vessel resulting in a reduction of its caliber and blood flow : ANGIOSPASM

vaso·spastic \ˌ⸗(ˌ)⸗+\ *adj* [fr. *vasospasm*, after E *spasm: spastic*] **:** of, relating to, or tending to induce vasospasm

vaso·tonic \"+\ *adj* [*vas-* + *tonic*] **:** of, relating to, or promoting tone of blood vessel walls

vaso·vagal \"+\ *adj* [*vas-* + *vagal*] **:** of, relating to, or involving both vascular and vagal factors

vasovagal syncope *n* **:** a usu. transitory condition marked by anxiety, nausea, and respiratory distress and believed due to joint vasomotor and vagal disturbances

¹**vas·sal** \ˈvasəl, ˈvaas-\ *n* -s [ME, fr. MF, fr. ML *vassallus*, fr. *vassus* servant, vassal, of Celt origin; akin to W *gwas* boy, servant, Bret *gwaz* man, OIr *foss* servant] **1 a :** a person who is under the protection of another as his feudal lord and is vowed to homage and fealty to that other : a feudal tenant : FEUDATORY **b** *Scots law* **:** a tenant entitled to the beneficial enjoyment of land and holding of a lord or other superior owning the legal title thereto conditionally upon the rendering of an annual service or payment — compare FEU-DUTY **2 :** one in a position or status felt to resemble that of a feudal vassal to his lord : one who owes or is forced to give allegiance and service to another as a superior ⟨the Baltic states that became ~*s* of Russia⟩ **3 a :** a person in a humble and subordinate or suppliant position : DEPENDENT, SERVANT, SLAVE **b :** one wholly subordinated to some controlling influence ⟨a ~ to his fears⟩ ⟨interest rates became the ~ of central banking and treasury policy —R.I.Robinson⟩

²**vassal** \"+\ *adj* **1 :** of, relating to, or typical of a vassal **2 :** occupying the position or relation of a vassal; *broadly* **:** SERVILE SUBSERVIENT ⟨a tenuous ~ relationship to the Chinese court —J.F.Cady⟩

³**vassal** \"\ *vt* **vassaled** *or* **vassalled; vassaled** *or* **vassalled; vassaling** *or* **vassalling; vassals** *archaic* **:** VASSALIZE ⟨~*ed* themselves to the great Mongol —Peter Heylin⟩

vas·sal·age \-ij\ *n* -s [ME, fr. MF, fr. *vassal* + *-age*] **1 a** *archaic* **:** conduct becoming to a vassal; *esp* **:** courage and prowess under difficulties (as on the field of battle) **b** *obs* **:** a valiant or chivalrous act **2 :** the condition or status of a vassal : the relation of a vassal to his lord; *also* **:** the specific homage, fealty, or services due from vassal to lord **3 :** a position of subordination or submission (as to a political power or a detrimental influence) : SERVITUDE, SUBJECTION ⟨~ of the states through increasing centralization of power in the federal government⟩ ⟨a mind in ~ to passion⟩ **4 :** vassals as a group or of a particular lord : VASSALRY

vas·sal·ic \(ˈ)vaˈsalik\ *adj* **:** of or relating to or having the nature of a vassal or the vassal system

vas·sal·ize \ˈvasəˌlīz, ˈvaas-\ *vt* -ED/-ING/-S **:** to make a vassal of **:** bring into a condition of subordination to someone or something ⟨~ a people⟩

vas·sal·ry \-səlrē, -ri\ *n* -ES **:** the whole body or estate of vassals

vassal state *n* **:** a state with varying degrees of independence in its internal affairs but dominated by another state in its foreign affairs and potentially wholly subject to the dominating state

vas·sar rose \ˌvasəˌrōz, ˈvaas-\ *n, often cap V* [fr. *Vassar* College, Poughkeepsie, N.Y.] **1 :** a dark pink to grayish red **2** *of textiles* **:** a moderate purplish pink that is redder and paler than fuchsia pink

vassar tan *n, often cap V* [fr. *Vassar* College] **:** a moderate to strong brown that is redder and slightly lighter than oak, lighter than Arabian brown, and redder and slightly lighter than Sudan brown

¹vast \ˈvast, -aa(ə)-, -ai-, -ȧ-\ *adj* -ER/-EST [L *vastus;* akin to OIr *fot, fut* length] **:** characterized by greatness in size, bulk, amount, numbers, degree, intensity, or esp. in extent, range, and comprehensiveness ⟨stimulate consumption in these ~ areas of low-paid labor, China, India, Russia, Africa —J.A. Hobson⟩ ⟨the ~ accumulation of knowledge, and of mechanical appliances, which we call civilization —W.R.Inge⟩ ⟨the dog with ~ unconcern, curled up on the floor and went to sleep —Jan Struther⟩ **syn** see HUGE

²vast \"\ *n* -S **1 :** a boundless compass or space **:** IMMENSITY ⟨the ~ of heaven —John Milton⟩ ⟨the dead ~ and middle of the night —Shak.⟩ **2** *chiefly dial* **:** a great quantity, amount, or number ⟨took a ~ of pains to have everything ready for the fair⟩

³vast \"\ *adv, chiefly dial* **:** VASTLY

vas·ta·tion \vaˈstāshən\ *n* -S [L *vastation-, vastatio,* fr. *vastatus* (past part. of *vastare* to lay waste, fr. *vastus* empty, waste) + *-ion-, -io* -ion — more at WASTE] **1** *obs* **:** DEVASTATION **2 :** a renewal or purification through the burning away or destruction of evil attributes

vas·tid·i·ty \vaˈstidəd·ē\ *n* -ES [alter. of *vastity*] *archaic* **:** VASTNESS ⟨through all the world's ~ —Shak.⟩

vas·ti·tude \ˈvastəˌtüd, ˈvaas-,ˈvais-,ˈvȧs-, -stə-,tyüd\ *n* -S [L *vastitudo,* fr. *vastus* vast + *-tudo* -tude] **1 :** the quality or state of being vast **:** IMMENSITY ⟨the ~ of the concept held him spellbound⟩ **2 :** a vast extent or space ⟨all that ~ of wilderness —Walter O'Meara⟩

¹vas·ti·ty \-stəd·ē, -ətē, -i\ *n* -ES [MF *vastité,* fr. L *vastitat-, vastitas,* fr. *vastus* empty, waste + *-itat-, -itas* -ity] *archaic* **:** a waste or desolate condition ⟨all the ~ of the Arabian peninsula —C.M.Doughty⟩

²vastity \"\ *n* -ES [L *vastitas,* fr. *vastus* vast + *-itas* -ity] **:** VASTITUDE ⟨the dreadful ~ of the stars —Rose Macaulay⟩

vast·ly *adv* **:** to a vast extent or degree **:** IMMENSELY; *often* **:** very greatly ⟨I shall be ~ obliged⟩

vast·ness \-s(t)nəs\ *n* -ES **1 :** the quality or state of being vast **2 :** a vast expanse or region ⟨watching the ~*es* of the mountains unfold⟩

vas·tus ex·ter·nus \ˌvastəˌsekˈstərnəs\ *n* [NL, lit., great external (muscle)] **:** VASTUS LATERALIS

vastus in·ter·me·di·us \-ˌsintərˈmēdēəs\ *n* [NL, lit., great intermediate (muscle)] **:** the division of the quadriceps muscle that arises from and covers the front of the shaft of the femur

vastus in·ter·nus \-ˌsinˈtərnəs\ *n* [NL, lit., great internal (muscle)] **:** VASTUS MEDIALIS

vastus lat·er·alis \-ˌslad·əˈraləs, -rāl-,-räl-\ *n* [NL, lit., great lateral (muscle)] **:** a division of the quadriceps muscle covering the outer anterior aspect of the femur, arising chiefly from that bone and inserted into the outer border of the patella by a flat tendon which blends with that of the other divisions of the muscle and sends an expansion to the knee capsule

vastus me·di·alis \-ˌsmēdēˈaləs, -ˈāl-,-ˈäl-\ *n* [NL, lit., great medial (muscle)] **:** a division of the quadriceps muscle covering the inner anterior aspect of the femur, arising chiefly from that bone and the adjacent intermuscular septum, inserted into the inner border of the patella and into the tendon of the other divisions of the muscle, sending also a tendinous expansion to the capsule of the knee joint and being closely united and in the upper part often inseparably with the vastus intermedius

vasty *pronunc at* ¹VAST + ē *or* i\ *adj* -ER/-EST [¹*vast* + *y*] **:** VAST, IMMENSE ⟨call spirits from the ~ deep —Shak.⟩

va·su \ˈvä(ˌ)sü, -)zü\ *n* -S [Fijian] **:** a child of a sister of a Fijian male upon whom the child has particular claims (as for food, portable property, or land); *also* **:** the peculiar right or claim of a vasu

¹vat \ˈvat, *usu* -ad·+V\ *n* -S [ME *vat, fat,* fr. OE *fæt;* akin to OHG *vaz* vessel, cask, vat, ON *fat* vessel, Lith *puodas* pot and perh. to Skt *palla* granary, barn] **1 :** a large cistern, tub, barrel, or other vessel; *esp* **:** one used to hold or store liquids ⟨soups fresh from the big fifty-gallon soup ~*s* —Jack Alexander⟩ **2 a :** a large vessel for holding preparations for dyeing **b :** a liquor or bath containing a dye that has been converted by reduction usu. with sodium hydrosulfite and alkali into a soluble leuco form that does not dye **3 :** TAN VAT **4 a :** a tank used in papermaking that contains the stock from which handmade papers are dipped by a mold **b :** one of the tanks in which the cylinders of a cylinder machine rotate **c :** a tank used to hold tub sizing **d :** a tank in which paper stock is bleached **5 :** a wooden tub in which to wash ores and minerals **6 a :** SALT PIT **b** *Southwest* **:** an incrusted dried margin around a water hole

²vat \"\ *vt* **vatted; vatted; vatting; vats 1 :** to put into or treat in a vat **2 :** to prepare a vat (sense 2b) **:** reduce (a vat dye) to form a solution of a leuco compound

va·tair·eop·sis \vəˌta(a)rēˈäpsəs\ *n, cap* [NL, fr. *Vatairea,* genus of unarmed trees (perh. alter. of *Vateria*) + *-opsis*] **:** a small genus of unarmed Brazilian trees (family Leguminosae) with large panicles of violet flowers — see GOA POWDER

vat dye *or* **vat color** *n* **:** any of a large and widely used class of water-insoluble generally fast dyes (as indigoid dyes and many anthraquinone dyes) that are formed on and in textile fibers by oxidation of a soluble reduced leuco form either prepared previously in a vat (sense 2b) or produced on the fibers by treating with a suspension or paste containing the unreduced dye and then reducing — see DYE table I, SOLUBILIZED VAT DYE

vat-dyed \ˈ=ˌ=\ *adj* **:** dyed with one or more vat dyes

va·te·ria \vəˈtirēə\ *n, cap* [NL, fr. Abraham *Vater* †1751 Ger. anatomist and botanist + NL *-ia*] **:** a genus of Asiatic trees (family Dipterocarpaceae) having entire small coriaceous leaves and white or yellow flowers with about 15 stamens — see PINEY TREE

va·ter·ite \ˈväd·əˌrīt, ˈfä-\ *n* -S [Heinrich *Vater,* 20th cent. Ger. mineralogist + E *-ite*] **:** a mineral $CaCO_3$ that consists of a relatively unstable form of calcium carbonate and is polymorphous with calcite and aragonite

vater's ampulla *n, usu cap V* **:** AMPULLA OF VATER

va·ter's corpuscle \ˈfä|tə(r)z-, -ä|\ *n, usu cap V* [after Abraham *Vater* †1751] **:** PACINIAN CORPUSCLE

vat·ic \ˈvad·ik\ *adj* [L *vates* seer, prophet + E *-ic;* akin to OIr *fáith* seer, poet, OE *wōth* voice, song, poetry, *wōd* mad, raging, OHG *wuot* frenzy, madness, ON *ōthr,* n., song, poetry, *ōthr,* adj., frantic, mad, Goth *woths* possessed] **:** of, relating to, or characteristic of a prophet **:** PROPHETICAL, ORACULAR ⟨any poet . . . has his stuffy moments, especially when he is being consciously ~ —Dudley Fitts⟩

vat·i·can \ˈvad·ə̇kən, -at|, |ēk-\ *adj, usu cap* [fr. The *Vatican,* official residence of the pope situated upon Vatican Hill in Vatican City, Rome, fr. ML *Vaticanus,* fr. L, Vatican Hill] **:** of or relating to the Vatican esp. as symbolizing the Papacy or its policies ⟨a *Vatican* announcement⟩

vatican city *adj, usu cap V&C* [fr. *Vatican City,* independent papal state within Rome, Italy] **:** of or relating to Vatican City

vat·i·can·ism \-kəˌnizəm\ *n* -S *usu cap* **:** the doctrine of absolute papal supremacy

vat·i·can·ist \-ˌnəst\ *n* -S *usu cap* **:** a supporter of Vaticanism

vat·i·cide \ˈvad·əˌsīd\ *n* -S [L *vates* prophet + E *-cide*] **:** the murderer of a prophet

va·tic·i·nal \vəˈtisᵊnᵊl, vaˈt-\ *adj* [L *vaticinus* prophetic (fr. *vaticinari* to prophesy) + E *-al*] **:** of, relating to, or containing prophecy **:** PROPHETIC ⟨credited with very solid ~ powers —Wilder Hobson⟩

va·tic·i·nate \-ˌnāt\ *vb* -ED/-ING/-S [L *vaticinatus,* past part. of *vaticinari* to prophesy, fr. *vates* prophet + *-cinari* (akin to L *canere* to sing, prophesy) — more at CHANT] *vi* **:** to prophesy things to come **:** behave like a seer and a prophet ⟨it is very seldom that we can . . . ~ on such subjects —George Saintsbury⟩ ~ *vt* **:** to predict about **:** FORETELL ⟨the revolution *vaticinated* by Marx —R.M.MacIver⟩

va·tic·i·na·tion \vəˌtisᵊnˈāshən, (ˌ)vaˌt-\ *n* -S [L *vaticination-, vaticinatio,* fr. *vaticinatus* (past part.) + *-ion-, -io* -ion] **1 :** something foretold **:** PREDICTION, PROPHECY ⟨had been wont to smile at these annual ~*s* of his mother's —Edith Wharton⟩ **2 :** the act of prophesying ⟨rejected ~ along with the Victorian tendency to preach —Van Wyck Brooks⟩

va·tic·i·na·tor \ˈ=ˈ==ˌād·ə(r)\ *n* -S [L, fr. *vaticinatus* (past part. of *vaticinari* to prophesy) + *-or*] **:** one that vaticinates **:** PROPHET

vat jade green *n, usu cap V&J&G* **:** an anthraquinone vat dye — see DYE table I

vat-lined \ˈ=ˌ=\ *adj* **:** having liners affixed by a cylinder machine

vat machine *n, Brit* **:** CYLINDER MACHINE

vat·man \ˈvatmən\ *n, pl* **vatmen :** a worker who washes, dyes, cooks, or chemically treats products in a vat: as **a :** a workman who forms sheets of handmade paper by dipping a mold into a vat of stock **b :** one who saturates logs and flitches with hot water or steam to soften the fibers prior to veneer cutting — called also *wood cooker* **c :** an operator of a dye reel or jig **:** JIGGER **d :** PLATER 1a(2) **e :** one who pasteurizes and ripens cream for use in making butter

vat paper *n* **:** handmade paper

vats *pl of* VAT, *pres 3d sing of* VAT

vatted *past of* VAT

vatting *pres part of* VAT

vau \ˈvau̇, ˈvō\ *n* -S [L, fr. Gk *wau,* of Sem origin; akin to Heb *wāw* waw] **:** DIGAMMA

vau·che·ria \vōˈshirēə, vōˈsh-\ *n* [NL, fr. Jean Pierre Étienne *Vaucher* †1841 Swiss botanist + NL *-ia*] **1** *cap* **:** a genus of green algae (family Vaucheriaceae) that have a thallus consisting of a single elongated irregularly branched multinucleate cell attached to the substratum by rhizoids, reproduce both sexually and asexually, and live in fresh or brackish water or on damp ground where they often form a green tangled mat **2** -S **:** any green alga of the genus *Vaucheria*

vau·che·ri·a·ce·ae \(ˌ)=ˌ==ˈāsēˌē\ *n pl, cap* [NL, fr. *Vaucheria,* type genus + *-aceae*] **:** a family of oogamous green algae (order Siphonales) of which *Vaucheria* is the chief and type genus — **vau·che·ri·a·ceous** \(ˌ)=ˈ==ˈāshəs\ *adj*

vaude \ˈvōd *also* ˈvȯd *or* ˈväd\ *n* -S [by shortening] **:** VAUDEVILLE

vaude·ville \ˈvōd(ə)vəl, -)vil *also* ˈvȯd- *or* ˈväd-\ *n* -S [F, fr. MF, alter. (influenced by *ville* town, city, fr. L *villa* village) of *vaudevire* popular satirical song, fr. *vau-de-Vire* valley of Vire, locality near Vire, town in northwestern France where such songs were first composed in the 15th century, fr. *vau, val* valley + *de* from, of (fr. L) + *Vire* — more at VILLAGE, DE-, VALE] **1 :** a popular song often satirical in character **2 :** a light often comic theatrical piece frequently combining pantomime, dialogue, dancing, and song ⟨an aria apiece for the rival ladies . . . and a concluding ~ in which all express their desire to cooperate for the greater glory of art —Edward Sackville-West & Desmond Shawe-Taylor⟩ **3 a :** a stage entertainment esp. popular in theaters in the early decades of the 20th century that consisted of various unrelated acts following one another in succession and that might include performing animals, acrobats, comedians, dancers, singers, or magicians **b :** something resembling the lightness and frivolity of vaudeville ⟨I have also written three novels . . . but they are none of them ~ —Sinclair Lewis⟩

¹vaude·vil·lian \(ˈ)vōdˈvilyən, ˌvōdəˈv- *also* -vȯd- *or* -väd-\ *also* **vaude·vill·ist** *pronunc at* VAUDEVILLE +əst\ *n* -S [*vaudevillian* fr. *vaudeville* + *-an,* n. suffix; *vaudevillist* fr. F *vaudevilliste* vaudeville writer, fr. *vaudeville* + *-iste* -ist] **:** a vaudeville writer, actor, singer, or performer ⟨never ceased to wonder at the showmanship of the old-time ~*s* —Philip Hamburger⟩

²vaudevillian \"\ *adj* [*vaudeville* + *-an* (adj. suffix)] **:** of, relating to, or characteristic of vaudeville ⟨a certain ~ flavor has crept in —Amy Lowell⟩

¹vau·dois \(ˈ)vōˈdwä\ *n pl, usu cap* [MF *Vaudois, Valdois,* fr. ML *Valdenses* — more at WALDENSES] **:** WALDENSES

²vaudois \"\ *n, pl* **vaudois** *cap* [F, fr. *Vaud,* Switzerland + F *-ois* -ese (fr. L *-ensis*)] **1 :** a native or inhabitant of the Swiss canton of Vaud **2 :** the French dialect of Vaud

vau·dy \ˈvȯdi\ *adj* [origin unknown] **1** *Scot* **:** CHEERFUL, ELATED **2** *Scot* **:** gaudy in appearance

¹vault \ˈvȯlt, *chiefly Brit* ˈvält\ *n* -S [ME *vout, voute,* fr. MF *voute, volte,* fr. (assumed) VL *volvita* turn, vault, prob. fr. *volvitare* to turn, leap, vault — more at ³VAULT] **1 a :** an arched structure of masonry usu. forming a ceiling or roof but sometimes carrying a separate roof, a floor, or a staircase — see BARREL VAULT, GROIN 2, RIBBED VAULT **b :** an arched structure superficially resembling a vault ⟨walking along a passage with white walls, and a white ~ above —W.C.Bryant⟩ **2 a :** a room or space covered by an arched structure esp. when underground **b** (1) **:** a part of a cellar usu. devoted to a special purpose (as the storage of wine or valuables) (2) **:** such a compartment even when not covered by a vault (as below the street pavement in front of a building) **c** (1) **:** a room for the safekeeping of valuables and commonly built of steel (2) **:** a special compartment usu. in a piece of office equipment for the safekeeping of money **3 :** a place (as a cavern, the crater of a volcano, a great pit) resembling or suggesting a vault ⟨the ~*s* of Mt. Vesuvius⟩ **4 a :** a burial chamber with or without an arched roof esp. when partially or entirely underground **b :** a prefabricated container typically of metal or concrete into which a casket is placed at burial **5 :** the canopy of heaven **:** SKY ⟨a falling star streamed down the blue ~ —O.S.J.Gogarty⟩ **6 :** an arched or dome-shaped anatomical structure: as **a :** SKULLCAP, CALVARIUM **b :** the arched roof of the nasopharynx **c :** the combined hard and soft palate forming the roof of the mouth **d :** FORNIX 1d **7 :** the pit of a privy **8 :** an arched covering of calcareous plates between the arms of Paleozoic crinoids

vaults 1a: *1* barrel, *2* cross, *3* Welsh, *4* cloister

²vault \"\ *vb* -ED/-ING/-S [ME *vouten,* fr. MF *vouter, volter,* fr. *voute, volte* vault] *vt* **1 a :** to form with or to cover with a vault **:** give the shape or the character of a vault to **:** ARCH ⟨~ a roof or ceiling⟩ **b :** to overarch or extend over in the fashion of a vault ⟨tall elms ~*ed* the quiet street⟩ **2** *chiefly dial* **:** to place in or as if in a vault **:** BURY ~ *vi* **:** to arch, bend, or curve in the shape of a vault

³vault \"\ *vb* -ED/-ING/-S [MF *volter,* fr. OIt *voltare,* fr. (assumed) VL *volvitare* to turn, leap, vault, freq. of L *volvere* to roll, turn, revolve — more at VOLUBLE] *vi* **1 :** to bound vigorously; *esp* **:** to execute a leap using the hands or a pole — see POLE-VAULT ⟨put his hand on the counter and ~*ed* over, landing heavily on the other side —Josephine Johnson⟩ ⟨~*ed* out of the hole and moved across the clearing —W.F.Davis⟩ ⟨~*ed* into the saddle —L.C.Douglas⟩ **2 :** to do or achieve something that resembles a leap ⟨the rapidity with which we ~*ed* to the position of world leadership —Reinhold Niebuhr⟩ ~ *vt* **:** to leap over; *esp* **:** to leap over by or as if by aid of the hands or a pole ⟨~ a fence⟩ ⟨have ~*ed* price levels beneath which they hovered for . . . years —J.T.Soby⟩ **syn** see JUMP

⁴vault \"\ *n* -S [MF *volte* turn, vault, fr. OIt *volta,* fr. *voltare* to turn, vault] **1 :** an unusually vigorous leap **:** BOUND; *esp* **:** a leap over or upon something made by aid of the hands or of a pole **2 :** the leap of a horse **:** CURVET **syn** see JUMP

vault·age \-ij\ *n* -S **:** a vaulted place **:** an arched cellar

vaulted *adj* [fr. past part. of ²*vault*] **1 a :** built in the form of a vault **:** ARCHED ⟨a ~ roof⟩ ⟨on its ~ blue dome are gold stars —*Amer. Guide Series: La.*⟩ **b :** having a form resembling a vault ⟨the spacious ~ reaches of the sky⟩ **2 :** covered with a vault ⟨~ centrally planned buildings of Christian practice —J.B.Ward-Perkins⟩

vault·er \ˈvȯltə(r)\ *n* -S [³*vault* + *-er*] **:** one that vaults; *esp* **:** POLE-VAULTER

¹vaulting *n* -S [fr. gerund of ²*vault*] **1 :** the act, practice, or art of building vaults ⟨method of ~⟩ **2 :** vaulted construction ⟨arches and ~⟩

²vaulting *adj* [fr. pres. part. of ³*vault*] **1 :** leaping upwards **:** reaching or stretching for the heights ⟨achieve a quiet serenity if not a ~ happiness —D.L.Cohn⟩ ⟨the calm aggressive flash . . . of ~ ambition —Liam O'Flaherty⟩ **2** [fr. gerund of ³*vault*] **:** designed for use in vaulting or in gymnastic exercises ⟨a ~ block⟩ ⟨a ~ bar⟩

vaulting capital *n* **:** the capital of a vaulting shaft

vaulting cell *n* **:** a compartment of a vault contrived (as in ribbed structure) to permit the building of an entire part at a time

vaulting course *n* **:** a course consisting of the springers of a vault usu. set with horizontal beds and in projection or corbeled out

vaulting horse *n* **1 :** LONG HORSE 1 **2 :** SIDE HORSE

vaulting shaft *or* **vaulting pillar** *n* **:** an upright member (as a pilaster or column) from which springs a rib of a vault and that is commonly one of a cluster or forms part of a larger pier

vault·man \ˈ=mən, -ˌman\ *n, pl* **vaultmen** [¹*vault* + *man*] **1 :** a boxman in an ice or dairy products plant who removes goods as needed for delivery **2 :** a custodian of the vault in which motion-picture negatives are kept

vault mount *n* **:** a leap in gymnastics onto a piece of apparatus made by aid of the hands

vault rib *n* **:** one of the arches carrying a vault

vaults *pl of* VAULT, *pres 3d sing of* VAULT

vaulty \ˈvȯltē\ *adj, sometimes* -ER/-EST **:** resembling a vault **:** ARCHED, CONCAVE ⟨the ~ heaven so high above our heads —Shak.⟩

¹vaunt \ˈvȯnt, -ä-,-ȧ-\ *vb* -ED/-ING/-S [ME *vaunten,* fr. MF *vanter,* fr. LL *vanitare,* fr. L *vanitas* vanity — more at VANITY] *vi* **:** to make a vain display esp. of one's own worth or attainments **:** talk vaingloriously **:** BRAG ⟨strutted and ~*ed* before the girls⟩ ~ *vt* **:** to boast of **:** make a vainglorious display of **:** put forward boastfully ⟨propaganda literature ~*ed* the successes of . . . scientists —F.L.O'Dea⟩ ⟨ye ~*ed* your fathomless power, and ye flaunted your iron pride —Rudyard Kipling⟩ **syn** see BOAST

²vaunt \"\ *n* -S **1 :** a vainglorious display of what one is or has or has done **:** OSTENTATION **2 :** a bragging assertive speech **:** loud boast ⟨may the ~*s* and menace of the vengeful enemy pass like the gust —S.T.Coleridge⟩

³vaunt \"\ *n* -S [MF *avant* before, forward — more at AVAUNT (hence)] **1** *obs* **:** the front part **2** *obs* **:** the foremost ranks of an army **:** VAN

vaunt-courier \(ˈ)=+\ *n* [MF *avant-courrier,* lit., advance courier] **1** *obs* **:** AVANT COURIER 1 **2 :** one sent in advance **:** FORERUNNER

vaunted *adj* [fr. past part. of ¹*vaunt*] **:** boasted about **:** praised to the skies ⟨the ~ Southern hospitality —Marjorie K. Rawlings⟩ ⟨our ~ industrial economy which makes this population possible —Marston Bates⟩

vaunt·er \ˈvȯntə(r), ˈvän-,ˈvȧn-\ *n* -S [ME *vauntour,* fr. MF *vanteur,* fr. *vanter* to boast + *-eur* -or] **:** one that boasts ⟨men are . . . ~*s* about what they can't do —Bruce Marshall⟩

vaunt·ery \-tərē\ *n* -ES [¹*vaunt* + *-ery*] **1 :** an overweening vaunting **:** BRAVADO **2** *obs* **:** BOAST

vaunt·ful \ˈvȯntfəl, ˈvän-,ˈvȧn-\ *adj* **:** BOASTFUL, VAINGLORIOUS

¹vaunting *n* -S [ME, fr. gerund of *vaunten* to vaunt] **:** the act of boasting **:** BRAGGING ⟨make your ~ true —Shak.⟩

²vaunting *adj* [fr. pres. part. of ¹*vaunt*] **1 :** inclined or given to vainglorious boasting ⟨a ~ Spaniard —Francis Hackett⟩ **2 :** of or characterized by boastfulness ⟨~ smile appeared on his lips —Mary McCarthy⟩

vaunt·ing·ly *adv* **:** in a vaunting manner

vaunt·lay \ˈvȯntˌlā, ˈvän-,ˈvȧn-\ *n* -S [³*vaunt* + *-lay* (as in *relay*)] **:** the releasing of a relay of hunting dogs after the quarry has passed and before the rest of the pack has come up; *also* **:** the relay of dogs released in this manner

vaunty *also* **vaunt·ie** \-ti\ *adj, Scot* **:** BOASTFUL, PROUD, VAIN ⟨your letter made me ~ —Robert Burns⟩

vau·que·lin·ite \ˈvōk(ə)ləˌnīt\ *n* -S [Sw *vauquelinit,* fr. Louis N. *Vauquelin* †1829 Fr. chemist + Sw *-it* -ite] **:** a mineral $(Pb,Cu)_3(CrO_4,PO_4)_2$(?) consisting of a green to brown lead copper phosphate and chromate

vaux·ite \ˈvȯkˌsīt, ˈväk-\ *n* -S [George *Vaux* †1927 Am. lawyer and naturalist + E *-ite*] **:** a mineral $FeAl_2(PO_4)_2(OH)_2.7H_2O$ consisting of a hydrous basic phosphate of iron and aluminum in triclinic crystals

vav *var of* WAW

vav·a·sor *or* **vav·a·sour** *also* **vav·as·sor** \ˈvavəˌsō(ə)r, -sü(-, -sō(-\ *or* **val·va·sor** *or* **val·vas·sor** \ˈvalv-\ *n* -S [ME *vavasour,* fr. OF *vavassor, vavassour,* prob. fr. ML *vassus vassorum* vassal of vassals, fr. *vassus* vassal + *vassorum* of vassals, gen. pl. of *vassus* — more at VASSAL] **:** a feudal tenant ranking directly below a peer or baron

vav·a·so·ry \-sōrē\ *n* -ES [OF *vavassourie,* fr. *vavassour* + *-ie* -y] **:** the tenure of a fee or the lands held by a vavasor

va·ward \ˈvau̇ˌ(w)ȯrd\ *n* -S [ME *vauntwarde, vaward,* fr. ONF *avantwarde,* fr. *avant* forward, before (fr. L *abante*) + *warde* guard, guardian, fr. *warder* to guard — more at AVAUNT, REWARD] **:** the foremost part **:** FOREFRONT ⟨the ~ of our youth —Shak.⟩

vb *abbr* verb; verbal

VB *abbr* **1** valve box **2** vertical beam **3** volunteer battalion

v-beam radar \ˈ=ˌ=-\ *n, cap V* **:** a height-finding radar emitting a vertical beam and another beam at a 45-degree angle each of which receives separate signals that can be measured against the range of target to obtain an accurate measurement of its height

v-belt \ˈ=ˌ=\ *cap V, also* **vee belt** \"\ *n* **:** a belt of V-shaped cross section engaging a V-shaped groove in a pulley for wedging and better traction

vbl *abbr* verbal

v-block \ˈ=ˌ=\ *n, cap V* **:** a steel block having a V-shaped groove in one side and used in machine tooling esp. as a support for round work

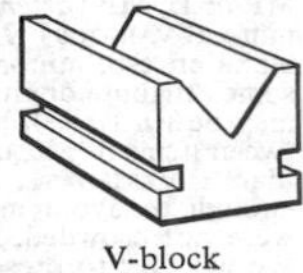
V-block

v-bob \ˈ=ˌ=\ *n, cap V* **:** a strong frame shaped like an isosceles triangle, turning on a pivot at its apex, and used as a bell crank to change the direction of a main pump rod

v-bomb \ˈ=ˌ=\ *n, usu cap V* [*v* (as in *V-1, V-2*) + *bomb*] **:** a V-1, V-2, or similar weapon used esp. by the Germans in World War II

v-bottom \ˈ=ˌ==\ *cap V, also* **vee bottom** \"\ *n* **1 :** a sailboat that is usu. broad and shoal and has the bottom in the form of a flat V joined by a chine to vertical or flaring sides **2 :** a usu. high-speed powerboat developed from the sailing type of V-bottom

vc *abbr* violoncello

VC *abbr* **1** valuable cargo **2** valuation clause **3** veterinary corps **4** vice-chairman **5** vice-chancellor **6** vice-consul **7** vigilance committee **8** visible capacity **9** [vision color] color vision **10** volunteer corps

v-connection \ˈ=ˌ==\ *n, cap V* **:** OPEN-DELTA CONNECTION

vct *abbr* victor

VD \ˈ=ˈ=\ *abbr or n* -S *sometimes not cap* venereal disease

VD *abbr* **1** vapor density **2** various dates

v-day \ˈ=ˌ=\ *n, cap V* [²*v* (abbr. for *victory*)] **:** a day of victory — compare D DAY, M-DAY

VDH *abbr* valvular disease of the heart

VDM *abbr* vasodepressor material

ve *var of* VEE

VE *abbr* vesicular exanthema

've \(ə)v\ *vb* [by contr.] **:** HAVE ⟨we've been there⟩ ⟨I've the book⟩

ve·adar *or* **we·adar** \ˌvā(ˌ)äˈdär\ *n* -S *usu cap V&W&A* [Heb *wĕ-ădhār,* lit., and Adar (i.e., the second Adar)] **:** the intercalary month of the Jewish year having 29 days and in leap years following Adar — called also *Adar Sheni;* see MONTH table

[1]**veal** \ˈvēl, *esp before pause or consonant* -ēəl\ *n* -S *often attrib* [ME *vel, veel,* fr. MF *veel,* fr. L *vitellus* small calf, dim. of *vitulus* calf — more at WETHER] **1 :** CALF; *esp* **:** one suitable for or used for food **2 :** the flesh of a calf a few days to 12 or 14 weeks of age — see BOB VEAL, VEALER

[2]**veal** \ˈ"\ *vt* -ED/-ING/-S **:** to kill and dress (a calf) for veal

veal bird *n* **:** a small thin slice of veal rolled around stuffing, seared, and stewed

veal cutlet *n* **:** a slice from a leg of veal cut into small portions and fried plain or breaded

veal·er \ˈvēlə(r)\ *n* -S **:** a calf suitable for veal; *esp* **:** one less than three months old and largely or wholly milk-fed

veal·i·ness \-lēnə̇s\ *n* -ES **:** the quality or state of being vealy **:** IMMATURITY

vealskin \ˈ≈,≈\ *n* **:** a large calfskin — compare KIP 2

vealy \ˈvēlē\ *adj* -ER/-EST **:** resembling or suggesting veal or a calf ⟨white ~ face —John Dos Passos⟩; *esp* **:** IMMATURE ⟨a ~ graduate⟩

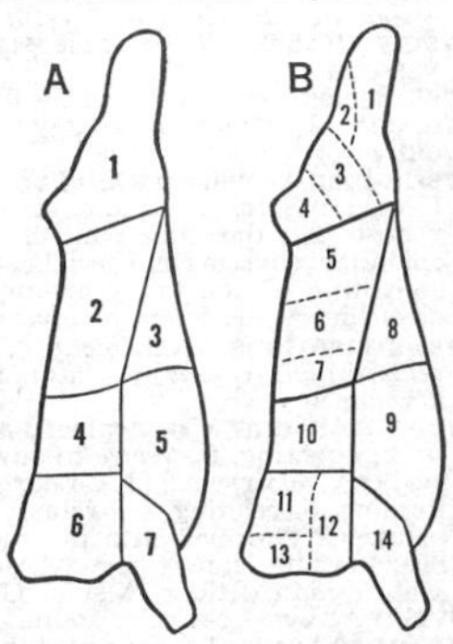

A B 1 2 3 4 5 6 7 1 2 3 4 5 6 7 8 9 10 11 12 13 14

veal 2: *A*, wholesale cuts: *1* leg, *2* loin, *3* flank, *4* rib, *5* breast, *6* shoulder, *7* shank; *B* retail cuts: *1* hind shank, *2* heel of round, *3* round, *4* rump roast, *5* sirloin steak, *6* loin chops, *7* kidney chops, *8* flank, *9* breast, *10* rib roast, *11* blade steak, *12* arm steak, *13* shoulder roast, *14* fore shank

veatch·ite \ˈvē,chīt\ *n* -S [John A. *Veatch,* 19th cent. Am. mineralogist + E *-ite*] **:** a mineral $Sr_3B_{16}O_{27}.5H_2O$(?) consisting of a hydrous strontium borate but orig. thought to be a calcium borate

veb·le·ni·an \(ˈ)veˈblēnēən\ *adj, usu cap* [Thorstein B. *Veblen* †1929 Am. social scientist + E *-an*] **:** of or relating to the social scientist Veblen or his theories

veb·len·ism \ˈveblə,nizəm\ *n* -S *usu cap* [Thorstein *Veblen* + E *-ism*] **:** the theories of Veblen

veb·len·ite \-nīt\ *n* -S *usu cap* [Thorstein *Veblen* + E *-ite*] **:** a supporter of Veblen

vec·to·graph \ˈvektə,graf, -rȧf\ *n* [*vector* + *-graph*] **:** a picture composed of two superposed stereoscopic images polarized at right angles to each other and giving a three-dimensional effect when viewed through appropriate polarizing spectacles — compare STEREOGRAPH — **vec·to·graph·ic** \ˌ≈≈ˈgrafik\ *adj*

[1]**vec·tor** \ˈvektə(r) *sometimes* -,tȯ(ə)r *or* -ȯ(ə)\ *n* -S [NL, fr. L, carrier, fr. *vectus* (past part. of *vehere* to carry) + *-or* — more at WAY] **1 a :** RADIUS VECTOR 2 **b** *or* **vector quantity :** a quantity that requires for its complete specification a magnitude, direction, and sense and that is commonly represented by a line segment the length of which designates the magnitude of the vector, the orientation of which designates the direction of the vector, and the sense of which is designated by an arrowhead at one end of the segment **:** a quantity having both magnitude and direction **c :** a course or compass direction esp. of an airplane **2 :** an agent capable of transmitting a pathogen from one organism to another either mechanically as carrier (as houseflies that transport typhoid bacteria) or biologically by playing a specific role in the life cycle of the pathogen (as mosquitoes in relation to the malaria parasite) ⟨fleas are ~*s* of plague⟩ ⟨aphids are ~*s* of plant viruses⟩ **3 :** a behavioral field of force toward or away from the performance of various acts; *broadly* **:** DRIVE

[2]**vector** \ˈ"\ *vt* -ED/-ING/-S **:** to guide (as an airplane or a missile) in flight by means of a radioed vector ⟨system to ~ night fighters to attack approaching airplanes —*Flying*⟩ ⟨was ~*ed* into radar contact with these aircraft —Guy Bordelon⟩ ⟨the pilots were ~*ed* through the storm by the flight controller —*Science*⟩

vector addition *n* **:** the process of finding the geometric sum of a number of vectors by repeated application of the parallelogram law

vector algebra *n* **:** an algebra for which the elements involved may represent vectors and the assumptions and rules are based on the behavior of vectors

vector analysis *n* **:** a branch of mathematics that treats of vectors

vector calculus *n* **:** the application of the calculus to vectors

vec·tor·cardiogram \ˌ≈(,)≈+\ *n* [*vector* + *cardiogram*] **:** the graphic record made by vectorcardiography

vec·tor·cardiographic \"+\ *adj* [*vectorcardiography* + *-ic*] **:** relating to, employing, or obtained by means of vectorcardiography ⟨~ systems that employ a limited number of body surface electrodes —D.A.Brody⟩

vec·tor·cardiography \"+\ *n* [*vector* + *cardiography*] **:** a method of recording the direction and magnitude of the electrical forces of the heart by means of a continuous series of vectors that form a curving line around a center

vector diagram *n* **:** a diagram involving vectors

vector field *or* **vector point** *n* **:** an aggregate of vectors which is defined at the various points of a curve or surface or region of space and in which one of the aggregate is associated with each point of the curve, surface, or region

vec·to·ri·al \(ˈ)vekˈtōrēəl\ *adj* [ISV *vector* + *-ial*] **:** of or relating to a vector or vector quantity

vectorial angle *n* **:** the angle from the polar axis to the radius vector

vec·to·ri·al·ly \-ēəlē\ *adv* **:** in a vectorial way

vector multiplication *n* **:** the product of vectors

vector potential *n* **:** a vector field so distributed in space as to represent by means of its curl some physically important vector

vector product *also* **vector cross product** *n* **:** a vector that is the product of the magnitude of two vectors A and B and the sine of the included angle and that has a direction perpendicular to the plane of the two vectors A and B and a sense that is determined by the right-handed screw convention

vector psychology *n* **:** TOPOLOGICAL PSYCHOLOGY

vector sum *n* **:** the sum obtained in vector addition

vec·tu·rist \ˈvekchərə̇st\ *n* -S [L *vectura* vehicle (fr. *vectus* + *-ura* -ure) + E *-ist* — more at VECTOR] **:** a collector of transportation tokens

ve·da \ˈvādə *sometimes* ˈvēdə\ *n* -S *usu cap* [Skt, knowledge, sacred lore, Veda; akin to Skt *veda* I know — more at WIT] **:** any of a class of the most ancient sacred writings of the Hindus; *specif* **:** any of the four Samhitas — compare ARANYAKA, BRAHMANA, SUTRA, UPANISHAD

ve·da·ic \vəˈdāik, vāˈd-\ *adj, usu cap* **:** of or relating to the Vedas **:** VEDIC

[1]**ve·da·lia** \vəˈdālyə, -lēə\ [NL] *syn of* RODOLIA

[2]**vedalia** \"\ *n* -S [NL] **:** an Australian ladybug (*Rodolia cardinalis*) that has been introduced to many countries to control scale (as the cottony-cushion scale)

ve·dan·ga \vāˈdäŋgə\ *n* -S *usu cap* [Skt *vedāṅga,* lit., limb of the Veda, fr. *veda* + *aṅga* limb — more at ANGLE] **:** any one of six classes of Sanskrit works written in the sutra style including phonetics, meter, grammar, etymology, religious ceremony, and the ritualistic calendar and designed to teach how to recite, understand, and apply Vedic texts

ve·dan·ta \vāˈdäntə, vəˈdan-\ *n* -S *usu cap* [Skt *vedānta,* lit., end of the Veda, fr. *veda* + *anta* end — more at END] **:** an orthodox Hindu philosophy based on the latter part of the Vedas as concerned with the ultimate goal of contemplation — compare BRAHMAN, MIMAMSA

ve·dan·tic \-tik\ *adj, usu cap* **1 :** of or relating to the Vedanta philosophy **2 :** VEDIC

ve·dan·tism \-n-,tizəm\ *n* -S *usu cap* **:** Vedantic philosophy

[1]**ve·dan·tist** \-ntə̇st\ *adj, usu cap* **:** VEDANTIC

[2]**vedantist** \"\ *n* -S **:** an adherent of Vedantism

ved·da *also* **ved·dah** \ˈvedə\ *n, pl* **vedda** *or* **veddas** *usu cap* [Sinhalese *vedda* hunter] **1 :** an aboriginal people of Ceylon characterized by slender build, small stature, dark complexion, and profuse wavy hair and often held to be intermediate between the Australian blacks and the Dravidians of Hindustan **2 :** a member of the Vedda people

[1]**ved·doid** \ˈveˌdȯid\ *adj, usu cap* [*Vedda* + E *-oid*] **1 :** resembling or related to the Veddas **2 :** of or relating to the Veddoids

[2]**veddoid** \"\ *n* -S *usu cap* **:** a member of an ancient race of southern Asia characterized by wavy to curly hair, chocolate-brown skin color, linear build, and fine features and represented by the Vedda of Ceylon, the Shom Pen of the Nicobars, the Toala of Celebes, and aborigines of northern Australia

veddoid–australoid \ˌ≈≈ˈ≈≈,≈\ *n* -S *usu cap V&A* **:** VEDDOID

ve·dette *or* **vi·dette** \vəˈdet\ *n* -S [F, fr. It *vedetta,* alter. (influenced by *vedere* to see, fr. L *vidēre*) of *veletta,* prob. fr. Sp *vela* watch (fr. *velar* to keep watch, fr. L *vigilare* to wake, watch, fr. *vigil* awake, watchful) + It *-etta* -ette (fr. LL *-ita*) — more at WIT, VIGIL] **:** a mounted sentinel stationed in advance of pickets to watch an enemy and give notice of danger

vedette post *n* **:** an outpost of two or more vedettes one of whom is constantly on the alert

[1]**ve·dic** \ˈvādik *sometimes* ˈvēd-\ *adj, usu cap* [*Veda* + *-ic*] **:** of or relating to the Vedas, the language in which they are written, or the period and culture that they represent

[2]**vedic** \"\ *or* **vedic sanskrit** *n, cap V&S* **:** the Indic language of the Vedas

ve·dro \vəˈdrō, -rȯ\ *n* -S [Russ, lit., bucket] **:** a Russian unit of liquid capacity equal to 3.25 U.S. gallons or 2.71 imperial gallons

[1]**vee** *also* **ve** \ˈvē\ *n* -S *often attrib* **1 :** the letter *v* **2 a :** something having the shape of the letter V ⟨~ formation of flying geese⟩ ⟨make the sign ~ for victory⟩ ⟨dropped it inside the ~ of his shirt —Howard Hunt⟩ ⟨~ neck of a sweater⟩ ⟨the vast, gloomy ~ of the gorge —John Hersey⟩ **b :** a groove with a V-shaped section

[2]**vee** \"\ *vt* -ED/-ING/-S **:** to form into a vee ⟨~ boards to make a trough⟩

vee belt *var of* V-BELT

vee bottom *var of* V-BOTTOM

vee engine *var of* V-ENGINE

veep \ˈvēp\ *n* -S [fr. *v.p.* (abbr. for *vice-president*)] **:** VICE-PRESIDENT

[1]**veer** \ˈvi(ə)r, -iə\ *vt* -ED/-ING/-S [ME *veren,* of LG or D origin; akin to MD *vieren* to let out, slacken, MLG *vīren* to slacken; prob. akin to OHG *fiaren* to give direction to, OFris *firia* to be far and prob. to OE *feorr* far — more at FAR] **:** to let or pay out (as a rope or anchor chain) ⟨~ the mainsheet⟩ — **veer and haul :** to pay out and haul in alternately or to pay out and haul in simultaneously on various parts

[2]**veer** \"\ *vb* -ED/-ING/-S [MF *virer,* prob. of Celt origin; akin to W *gwyro* to shift, deviate, Bret *goara* to curve, OIr *fiar* slanting, oblique; akin to OE *wīr* wire — more at WIRE] *vi* **1 :** to change direction **:** shift from one direction, position, condition, or inclination to another **:** be variable **:** TURN ⟨the highway ~*s* inland at this point⟩ ⟨his ~*ing* gait —William Wordsworth⟩ ⟨he ~*ed* aside when he heard the train moving —J.C.Powys⟩ ⟨my attention ~*ed* aimlessly around —Anne S. Mehdevi⟩ ⟨his mind ~*ed* away from the memory —Marcia Davenport⟩ **2** *of the wind* **:** to shift in a clockwise direction — opposed to *back* **3 :** to wear ship **:** alter course by turning away from the direction of the wind **~** *vt* **:** to direct to a different course ⟨pressures ~*ing* him from his purpose⟩ **:** TURN, SHIFT; *specif* **:** WEAR 8 ⟨~ a ship⟩ **syn** see SWERVE — **veer and haul :** to vary the course or direction ⟨a wind that *veers* aft *and hauls* forward⟩

[3]**veer** \"\ *n* -S **:** an act of veering **:** a change in course, direction, or inclination ⟨took a sharp ~ to the left⟩ ⟨a ~ toward ultraconservatism⟩ ⟨a ~ in our policy —*Kiplinger Washington Letter*⟩

veer away *or* **veer out** *vt* **1 :** to let out **:** slacken and let run **:** pay out ⟨*veer away* the cable⟩ ⟨*veer out* a rope⟩ **2 :** to permit to drift off by letting out a line ⟨*veer* the ship *away*⟩

[1]**veering** *adj* [fr. pres. part. of [2]*veer*] **:** TURNING, SHIFTING, VARIABLE ⟨snakelike, ~ dances —Richard Wright⟩ ⟨such a ~ record . . . would seem to support the charges of inconsistency often brought against him —John Mason Brown⟩; *esp* **:** shifting in a clockwise direction ⟨a ~ wind⟩

[2]**veering** *n* -S [fr. gerund of [2]*veer*] **:** a shifting esp. in a clockwise direction; *specif* **:** an altering of a ship's course by turning away from the direction of the wind

veer·ing·ly *adv* **:** in a veering manner

vee·ry \ˈvirē, -ri\ *n* -ES [perh. imit. of one of its notes] **:** a thrush (*Hylocichla fuscescens*) common in the eastern U.S. that is light tawny brown above, pale buff below, rather indistinctly spotted with brown, and grayish white on the sides — called also *tawny thrush, Wilson's thrush*

vee tail *also* **v tail** *n, cap 2d V* **:** an airplane tail in which longitudinal and directional stability and control are provided by two surfaces inclined to each other and to the plane of symmetry so that in section they form a V — see RUDDERVATOR

vee thread *var of* V THREAD

ve·ga \ˈvāgə\ *n* -S [Sp, prob. of Basque origin; akin to Basque *ibaiko* of the river, *ibai* river] **:** an open tract of ground **:** PLAIN; *esp* **:** a moist or boggy meadow

[1]**veg·e·ta·ble** \ˈvejtəbəl *also* -jəd·əb- *or* -jətəb-\ *adj* [ME, fr. ML *vegetabilis* capable of growth, vegetative, fr. *vegetare* to grow, flourish (fr. L, to enliven, animate, fr. *vegetus* lively, animated, fr. *vegēre* to rouse, excite, be active) + L *-abilis* -able — more at WAKE] **1** *obs* **:** living or growing in the manner of simple living things (as plants) **:** VEGETATIVE **2 a :** of or relating to plants **:** having the nature of or produced by plants **:** growing in the manner of a plant ⟨~ growths⟩ ⟨~ matter⟩ ⟨high pointed tower . . . seems . . . to have grown up in an inevitable, ~ way from the three tall arches —Eleanor Clark⟩ **b :** consisting of plants **:** VEGETATIONAL ⟨~ cover⟩ **3 :** made from plant matter ⟨~ color⟩ ⟨insulation used in houses can be grouped into three general classes, ~, mineral, and metallic —*Building, Estimating & Contracting*⟩; *often* **:** made chemically from plant tissue or substance to resemble an animal product ⟨~ wool⟩ ⟨~ fat⟩ **4 :** resembling or suggesting a plant (as in lowliness, monotony of existence attached to one place, or inexpressiveness) **:** MONOTONOUS, DULL, STUPID ⟨great stretch of empty time . . . in which I lived an essentially ~ existence —J.P.Roche⟩ ⟨gossip, the necessary continuum of corruption and violence in otherwise ~ lives —Harvey Manning⟩

[2]**vegetable** \"\ *n* -S **1 a :** PLANT 1c — not used technically **b :** a usu. herbaceous plant (as the cabbage, potato, bean, or turnip) that is cultivated for an edible part which is used as a table vegetable **2 :** an edible part of a plant (as seeds, leaves, or roots) that is used for human food and usu. eaten cooked or raw during the principal part of a meal rather than as a dessert — contrasted with *fruit* ⟨the tomato though botanically a fruit is usu. eaten as a ~⟩

vegetable bezoar *n* **:** a concretion formed of the hairs of crimson clover, the awns of oats, or similar vegetable matter in the stomach of a ruminating animal to which it is sometimes fatal

vegetable black *n* **1 :** a fine lampblack made by the combustion of vegetable oils **2 :** any of various black pigments resembling lampblacks but made by charring vegetable matter (as vine twigs, willow wood, or wood-pulp waste) and used chiefly in printing inks, cements, and mortars — compare CARBON BLACK, VINE BLACK

vegetable brain *n* **:** the aril of the akee

vegetable butter *n* **1 :** a vegetable fat (as cocoa butter or shea butter) that resembles butter or lard esp. in consistency — compare VEGETABLE TALLOW **2 :** AVOCADO

vegetable caterpillar *n* **:** AWETO

vegetable color *n* **:** a coloring matter of plant origin

vegetable dye *n* **:** a natural dye (as logwood) obtained from a plant

vegetable egg *n* **1 :** EGGPLANT **2 :** the fruit of the marmalade tree

vegetable fat *n* **:** a fat of vegetable origin that is obtained naturally from plants or by hydrogenation of a vegetable oil

vegetable glue *n* **:** an adhesive made from vegetable material; *esp* **:** one made by treating starch (as from cassava root) with alkali and used in plywood and veneered products

vegetable hair *or* **vegetable horsehair** *n* **:** a fiber from a European dwarf fan palm (*Chamaerops humilis*) used for furniture stuffing

vegetable ivory *n* **1 :** the hard white opaque endosperm of the ivory nut that takes a high polish and is used as a substitute for ivory esp. in the manufacture of buttons **2 :** IVORY NUT

vegetable kingdom *n* **:** PLANT KINGDOM

vegetable lamb *n* **1 :** SCYTHIAN LAMB 1 **2 :** the cotton plant

vegetable leather *n* **:** a shrubby West Indian spurge (*Euphorbia punicea*) having leathery foliage and crimson bracts

vegetable marrow *n* **:** any of various smooth-skinned cylindrical to oval summer squashes (as a cocozelle or zucchini) that usu. have creamy white to deep green skins often mottled or streaked with darker color

vegetable mold *n* **:** HUMUS

vegetable oil *n* **:** an oil obtained from a plant; *esp* **:** a fatty oil obtained usu. from seeds or nuts — compare DRYING OIL, ESSENTIAL OIL

vegetable orange *n* **:** MANGO MELON

vegetable oyster *n* **1 :** SALSIFY **2 :** BLACK SALSIFY

vegetable parchment *n* **:** a highly grease-resistant and water-resistant paper resembling parchment, often used as a food wrapper, and made by passing unsized paper through sulfuric acid to gelatinize its surface and then washing and drying it — called also *parchment paper*

vegetable pathology *n* **:** PLANT PATHOLOGY

vegetable pear *n* **:** CHAYOTE

vegetable plate *n* **:** a main course without meat consisting of several vegetables cooked separately and served on one plate

vegetable rennet *n* **:** a plant that has the power of coagulating milk: as **a :** BUTTERWORT **b :** a shrub (*Withania coagulans*) of Afghanistan whose seeds are used in place of rennet

vegetable rouge *or* **vegetable red** *n* **:** CARTHAMUS RED

vegetable satyr *n* **:** SATYR ORCHID

vegetable sheep *n* **:** SHEEP PLANT

vegetable silk *n* **:** a cottony fibrous material obtained from the coating of the seeds of any of various trees (as the floss-silk) and used esp. for stuffing cushions — compare SILK COTTON

vegetable soul *n* **:** the soul that in the scholastic tradition controls the nutritive and reproductive functions of human life and is held to be lower or less complete than the animal soul and rational soul

vegetable sponge *n* **:** LUFFA 3

vegetable stock *n* **:** vegetable pot liquor

vegetable sulfur *n* **:** LYCOPODIUM POWDER 2

vegetable tallow *n* **:** a fatty substance (as Chinese tallow) that is obtained from plants and resembles tallow in consistency

vegetable–tallow tree *or* **vegetable tallow** *n* **:** WAX MYRTLE

vegetable tanning *n* **:** the process of tanning by impregnating (an animal skin) with plant infusions

vegetable wax *n* **:** a waxy product (as Japan wax) that is secreted by various plants commonly in thin flakes by the walls of the epidermal cells and that sometimes forms a bloom

vegetable weevil *n* **:** a So. American weevil (*Listroderes obliquus*) that has been introduced into No. America, Australia, Africa, and Hawaii and is very destructive to many vegetable and other crop plants

veg·e·ta·blize \ˈvejtəbə,līz *also* -jəd·əb- *or* -jətəb-\ *vt* -ED/-ING/-S **:** to transform into or cause to take the properties of a vegetable

veg·e·ta·bly \ˈvejtəblē, -bli *also* -jəd·əb- *or* -jətəb-\ *adv* **:** in the manner of or like a vegetable **:** with the characteristics of a vegetable ⟨living ~ and intuitively —Aldous Huxley⟩

[1]**vegetal** *n* -S [MF, fr. *vegeter* to grow as a plant, fr. ML *vegetare* to grow, flourish] *obs* **:** VEGETABLE

[2]**veg·e·tal** \ˈvejəd·ᵊl, -jətᵊl\ *adj* [ML *vegetare* to grow, flourish + E *-al*] **1** *obs* **:** having or showing plantlike life and growth **2 :** relating to vegetables or to vegetation **:** of the nature of a vegetable (as in growth and development) as contrasted with that of an animal **:** VEGETABLE **3 :** composed of or derived from vegetables ⟨a ~ diet⟩ ⟨a ~ remedy⟩ ⟨regions rich in ~ and mineral products —*Canadian Mining Jour.*⟩ **4 :** VEGETATIVE 1 **5 :** of or relating to the vegetal pole of an egg or to that part of an egg from which the endoderm normally develops — compare ANIMAL 5

veg·e·tal·ize \-,īz\ *vb* -ED/-ING/-S *vt* **:** to cause (embryonic cells) to exhibit vegetal characters **~** *vi, of embryonic cells* **:** to exhibit vegetal characters

vegetal pole *n* **:** the point on the surface of an egg that is diametrically opposite to the animal pole and usu. marks the center of the protoplasm containing more yolk, dividing more slowly and forming larger blastomeres than that about the animal pole, and giving rise to the hypoblast of the embryo — see BLASTULA illustration

[1]**veg·e·tar·i·an** \ˌvejəˈterēən, -ta(a)r-, -tär-\ *n* -S [[2]*vegetable* + *-arian*] **1 :** one who believes in or practices vegetarianism **2 :** a phytophagous animal **:** HERBIVORE

[2]**vegetarian** \ˌ≈≈ˈ≈≈≈\ *adj* **1 :** of or relating to vegetarianism **2 :** consisting wholly of vegetables ⟨a ~ diet⟩

veg·e·tar·i·an·ism \ˌ≈≈ˈ≈≈ə,nizəm\ *n* -S **:** the theory or practice of living solely upon vegetables, fruits, grains, and nuts

veg·e·tate \ˈvejə,tāt, *usu* -ād·+V\ *vb* -ED/-ING/-S [ML *vegetatus,* past part. of *vegetare* to grow, flourish — more at VEGETABLE] *vi* **1 a :** to grow as a plant or after the fashion of plants ⟨the algae usually ~ vigorously —Florence Chase⟩ **b :** to produce vegetation ⟨fields permitted to ~ for a given time⟩ **c :** to propagate vegetatively as distinguished from sexually ⟨a bacterial growth . . . was *vegetating* along with the fungus —*Chronica Botanica*⟩ **2 :** to lead a passive existence without initiative or exertion of body or mind **:** do little but eat and grow ⟨a dull, ambitionless, *vegetating* individual —J.A.Brussel⟩ ⟨left to ~ back to a robust physical health —William Manchester⟩ ⟨~ in luxurious subtropical surroundings —Jack Westeyn⟩ ⟨perfectly content to ~, to continue leading a humdrum, uneventful life —A.H. & Ruth Verrill⟩ **3 :** to grow exuberantly **:** produce fleshy or warty outgrowths ⟨a *vegetating* tumor⟩ **~** *vt* **1** *obs* **:** to cause to grow **2 :** to establish vegetation in or on **:** provide the vegetation of ⟨~ a hillside or ravine⟩ ⟨~ a meadow with native grasses⟩ ⟨dominant types of trees that ~ a coral island —T.C.Roughley⟩

veg·e·ta·tion \ˌvejəˈtāshən\ *n* -S [ML *vegetation-, vegetatio,* fr. *vegetatus* (past part. of *vegetare* to grow, flourish) + L *-ion-, -io* -ion] **1 :** the act or process of growing as a plant does **:** vegetable growth, development, or activity **2 :** inert existence **:** life removed from the stimulation of social and intellectual activity **:** dull and stagnant living ⟨lived a life of serene ~ —William Faulkner⟩ **3 :** plant life or total plant cover (as of an area, forest, or prairie) ⟨all life depends on the photosynthetic action of ~⟩ — sometimes distinguished from *flora* as concerned with mass effects or individuals rather than kinds of plants ⟨though the flora was small at this time it formed a heavy ~ chiefly of tree ferns and primitive gymnosperms⟩ **4 :** an abnormal outgrowth upon a part resembling in form a plant or sponge; *specif* **:** one of the warty excrescences on the valves of the heart that are composed of fibrin, collagen, and other tissue elements and are typical of endocarditis

veg·e·ta·tion·al \ˌ≈≈ˈtāshənᵊl, -shnəl\ *adj* **:** relating to, composed of, or suggesting vegetation ⟨~ cover⟩

veg·e·ta·tion·less \ˌ≈≈ˈtāshənlə̇s\ *adj* **:** destitute of or free from vegetation

vegetation type *also* **vegetational type** *n* **:** the life form (as grass, shrub, submerged aquatic) that gives its character to a plant community

veg·e·ta·tive \ˈvejə,tād·|iv, -āt|, |ēv *also* |əv, *chiefly Brit* -jətətiv\ *adj* [ME *vegetatif,* fr. ML *vegetativus,* fr. *vegetatus* (past part. of *vegetare*) + L *-ivus* -ive] **1 a :** growing or having the power of growing **:** of, relating to, or engaged in nutritive and growth functions (as of a plant) as contrasted with reproductive functions ⟨a ~ stage in the life history of a plant⟩ ⟨a ~ nucleus⟩ ⟨roots, stems, and leaves are termed the ~ organs of a seed plant's body —H.J.Fuller & Oswald Tippo⟩ ⟨concerned with the ~ activities of the plant —E.W. Sinnott⟩ **b :** having the power to induce growth in plants **:** PRODUCTIVE ⟨the ~ properties of soil⟩ **c :** of or relating to the propagation esp. of plants by nonsexual processes (as gemmation or the formation of runners or tubers) or methods (as division, cuttings, or grafting) **2 :** VEGETATIONAL ⟨~ cover⟩ ⟨the ~ layer of forest duff —Russell Lord⟩ **3 :** of or relating to the division of nature comprising the vegetable kingdom ⟨the ~ as contrasted with the animal world⟩ **4 :** affecting, arising from, or relating to involuntary bodily functions or esp. the parasympathetic nervous system **:** AUTONOMIC ⟨a ~ neurosis⟩ ⟨~ symptoms⟩ ⟨circulation, respiration, digestion, excretion, and related ~ functions —F.A.Geldard⟩ **5 :** leading a secluded or passive existence without social or intellectual

activity : VEGETABLE 4 — **veg·e·ta·tive·ly** *adv* — **veg·e·ta·tive·ness** *n* -ES
vegetative cell *n* : SOMATIC CELL; *specif* : TUBE CELL
vegetative cone *n* : the conical protuberance that commonly forms the apex of a growing shoot : the apical point of a shoot
vegetative mutation *n* : SOMATIC MUTATION
vegetative nervous system *n* : SYMPATHETIC NERVOUS SYSTEM
vegetative pole *n* : VEGETAL POLE
ve·gete \vəˈjēt\ *adj* [L *vegetus* — more at VEGETABLE] *archaic* : LIVELY, HEALTHY, FLOURISHING ⟨when my brain is ~ and apt for thought —R.W.Emerson⟩
veg·e·tive \ˈvejəd·iv\ *adj* [ML *vegetare* to grow + E *-ive* — more at VEGETABLE] : VEGETABLE, VEGETATIVE
ve·he·mence \ˈvēəmən(t)s *sometimes* ˈvēhəm- *or* ˈvāəm-, *chiefly in substand speech* vəˈhēm- *or* vēˈh-, *in substand speech* -ˈhēəm-\ *n* -S [MF, fr. L *vehementia*, fr. *vehement-, vehemens* impetuous, vehement + *-ia -y*] : the quality or state of being vehement : INTENSITY, VIOLENCE
ve·he·men·cy \-nsē, -nsi\ *n* -ES [L *vehementia*] *archaic* : VEHEMENCE
ve·he·ment \-nt\ *adj* [MF, fr. L *vehement-, vehemens*; akin to L *vehere* to carry — more at WAY] **1 a** *archaic* : immoderate in strength or degree : INTENSE, SEVERE ⟨his pain was very ~ —Nicholas Robinson⟩ ⟨requires a ~ fire to flux it —Robert Boyle⟩ **b** *archaic* : marked by excessive vigor or turbulence : FURIOUS, VIOLENT ⟨~ deluges of rain —John Morgan⟩ **c** : having a strong physical effect : POTENT ⟨produces a ~ kind of whiskey known as tanglefoot —Joseph Mitchell⟩ **2** : strongly entertained : EMPHATIC, PRONOUNCED ⟨any denial . . . was thenceforward sufficient to justify ~ suspicion of heresy —G.G.Coulton⟩ **3 a** : warmly emotional : ARDENT, PASSIONATE ⟨the affections of an only child of fourteen are as concentrated as they are ~ —Ngaio Marsh⟩ ⟨~ patriotism and poetic style —E.E.Allen⟩ **b** : scathingly hostile : RANCOROUS, TRUCULENT ⟨that ~, that furious obsession of animosity —Van Wyck Brooks⟩ **4 a** : full of energy : LIVELY, STRENUOUS ⟨~ applause⟩ ⟨against his ~ opposition, the war . . . was precipitated —U.B.Phillips⟩ **b** : strikingly colorful : SHOWY, VIVID ⟨a tall, pale apparition, equipped with a ~ red wig and a police whistle —Wolcott Gibbs⟩ **5 a** : expressive of strong emotion or conviction : IMPASSIONED ⟨~ utterances in opposition to slavery —H.A.Bridgman⟩ **b** : characterized by active conviction or enthusiasm : FERVENT, ZEALOUS ⟨a ~ extremist⟩ ⟨a fine . . . scholar and ~ teacher —W.B.Yeats⟩ **c** : characterized by bitter antagonism : HEATED ⟨a ~ debate⟩ — **ve·he·ment·ly** *adv*
ve·hi·cle \ˈvē,ikəl *also* ˈvē,hik- *or* ˈvēək- *sometimes* vēˈhik- *or* viˈh-\ *n* -S *often attrib* [F *véhicule* transmitting agent, vehicle, fr. L *vehiculum* carriage, conveyance, fr. *vehere* to carry — more at WAY] **1 a** : an inert substance (as syrup, lard, or liquid petrolatum) in a medicinal compound through which an active agent is administered or by which other ingredients are held together : DILUENT, EXCIPIENT **b** : a liquid ingredient of other mixtures: as (1) : a fluid in which something is dissolved or held in suspension ⟨filled his glass of tomato juice half full of salt so that . . . the juice became scarcely more than a ~ for the salt —C.P.Richter⟩ ⟨lapping abrasive has been used successfully with ~s of all kinds: water, soluble oils, cottonseed oil —E. Leslie Anderson⟩ (2) : the binder and volatile thinners of a finishing material (as paint or lacquer) (3) : the varnish in printing ink (4) : a fluid or other substance in which light-sensitive salts for coating photographic plates are contained **c** : MEDIUM 9b **2 a** : an agent of transmission : CARRIER ⟨water, food, insects, and inanimate objects may be ~s of infection —V.M.Ehlers & E.W.Steel⟩ ⟨the conception of blood as the ~ of life —J.G.Frazer⟩ ⟨man . . . as a ~ of culture —A.L. Kroeber⟩ **b** : the literal content of a metaphorical statement — compare TENOR 1c **3 a** : a mode of expression : FORM, STYLE ⟨words, pictures, and other ~s of expression —H.O.Taylor⟩ ⟨find a new form of verse which shall be as satisfactory a ~ for us as blank verse was for the Elizabethans —T.S.Eliot⟩ **b** : MEDIUM 3c ⟨the organ had been for centuries the ~ of sacred music —A.E.Wier⟩ ⟨public schools remain the primary ~ for the education of our youth —J.B.Conant⟩ ⟨using a program of slum clearance as a ~ . . . to secure the adoption of other and extraneous legislation —*New Republic*⟩ ⟨the United Nations as the principal ~ by which world peace may . . . be reached —Patrick McMahon⟩; *specif* : an artistic composition serving to convey a particular conception ⟨these pictures are the ~s of this spirit —Herbert Read⟩ **c** : a Buddhist path to salvation — compare HINAYANA, MAHAYANA **d** : an outlet for artistic talent ⟨the American minstrel show . . . as a ~ for amateurs —C.F.Wittke⟩; *specif* : a work created esp. to display the powers of a particular performer ⟨a play intended as a starring ~ for an actress⟩ ⟨a piano concerto composed as a ~ for a famous virtuoso⟩ **4** : a material embodiment or repository ⟨capable of exercising choice in the matter of reincarnation ~s —H.B.Piper⟩ **5** : a means of carrying or transporting something : CONVEYANCE: as **a** : a carrier of goods or passengers ⟨the most used ~ was the mule —James Bird⟩ ⟨the locomotive is well under way by the time the last ~s are started from rest —O.S.Nock⟩ ⟨aerial ~s such as airplanes, and submerged ~s such as . . . submarines —Fritz Zwicky⟩ ⟨for summer hunting . . . the kayak is their indispensable ~ —C.D.Forde⟩; *specif* : MOTOR VEHICLE ⟨exhaust from road ~s⟩ ⟨the turning radii of the transit ~ determines the length of the bus stop —B.H. Sexton⟩ **b** : a container in which something is conveyed ⟨the research ~s — the satellites and the lunar probes —H.H.Martin⟩ ⟨have the space ~ tracked from the earth —L.S.Brown⟩ **c** : a piece of mechanized equipment ⟨tractors and farm ~s —*Statesman's Yr. Bk.*⟩ ⟨tanks, half-tracks and other combat ~s —*Time*⟩ **d** : a propulsive device ⟨launching ~ lifts the satellite into orbit —*Space Talk*⟩ **syn** see MEAN
ve·hic·u·lar \(ˈ)vēˈhikyələ(r) *sometimes* -ēˈi-\ *adj* [LL *vehicularis*, fr. L *vehiculum* vehicle + *-aris* -ar] **1 a** : of, relating to, or designed for vehicles and esp. for motor vehicles ⟨~ traffic volume⟩ ⟨a ~ tunnel⟩ **b** : transported by vehicle ⟨~ . . . public address systems —*Armed Forces Talk*⟩ **2** : serving as a vehicle ⟨speak . . . at least one of the three ~ languages —*N. Y. Herald Tribune*⟩
vei *usu cap, var of* VAI
v-eight \ˈ=ˈ=\ *n, cap V* : an internal-combustion engine (as in an automobile) having two banks of four cylinders each with the banks at an angle to each other; *also* : an automobile having such an engine
¹veil \ˈvāl, *chiefly before pause or consonant* -āəl\ *n* -S [ME *veile*, fr. ONF, fr. L *vela*, pl. of *velum* cloth, covering, curtain, veil] **1 a** (1) : a length of cloth worn by women from ancient times as a covering for the head and shoulders and often used also in eastern countries to conceal the face esp. of a married woman ⟨Jewish women wore ~s . . . in token of reverence and submission —Mary B. Eddy⟩; *specif* : the outer covering of a nun's headdress (2) : the cloistered life of a nun ⟨make a choice between the world and the ~ —Sir Walter Scott⟩ **b** : a length of veiling or netting worn over the head or face or attached for protection or ornament to a hat or headdress ⟨bridal ~⟩ ⟨tiny black velvet hat has a visor ~ ending at the temples —*Women's Wear Daily*⟩ **2 a** (1) : a hanging used to curtain off a sacred enclosure ⟨~ of the sanctuary⟩ (2) : the limit of sense perception dividing the living from the dead ⟨when you and I behind the ~ are past —Edward FitzGerald⟩ (3) : a hidden sanctuary; *esp* : the mysterious realm of the dead ⟨passed on within the ~ —A.J.Ross⟩ **b** : a liturgical cloth used to cover or shroud a religious object (as a crucifix or chalice) esp. during Lent : PALL **c** : HUMERAL VEIL **3 a** : a deceptive appearance or masking layer : CLOAK, COVER ⟨expressing daring criticism under the ~ of . . . buffoonery —R.A.Hall b. 1911⟩ ⟨against the first ~s of twilight the flashing of the guns was faintly . . . orange —Eric Linklater⟩ ⟨tear away the ~ of mystery that shrouds human sleep —Webb Garrison⟩ **b** : a curtain of silence or reticence ⟨the few sketches of his career draw a ~ over the nature of his pranks —Lindsay Rogers⟩ ⟨the first lifting of the ~ on the privacy of . . . royalty —Sheila O'Callaghan⟩ **c** : a slight obscuration of the voice in singing (as from a peculiarity of the larynx or a natural huskiness) ⟨sang . . . handsomely, though her voice has a ~ on it —Virgil Thomson⟩ **d** : a slight darkening of the lighter portions of a photographic image and the unexposed areas usu. due to chemical fog and resulting in loss of contrast **4 a** (1) : PARTIAL VEIL (2) : UNIVERSAL VEIL **b** : CALYPTRA 1 **c** : VELUM **d** : a part of the amnion sometimes covering the face of a newborn child : CAUL
²veil \"\ *vb* -ED/-ING/-S [ME *veilen*, fr. *veile* veil] *vt* **1 a** : to conceal or curtain off with or as if with a veil : HIDE, OBSCURE ⟨lace appliqués . . . ~*ed* by nylon tulle —*Women's Wear Daily*⟩ ⟨evasiveness . . . ~*ed* her face —Marcia Davenport⟩ ⟨rain and mist often ~*ed* the passage —Elsie M. B. Grosvenor⟩ ⟨~*s* his toughness with soft speech —*Newsweek*⟩ **b** : to withhold from public knowledge ⟨profound secrecy ~*ed* this undertaking —C.F.Cochran⟩ **2** *archaic* : to admit into membership in a convent ⟨she had surely been sainted if ~*ed* —Thomas Fuller⟩ ~ *vi* : to put on or wear a veil : become veiled ⟨many eastern women ~ in the presence of men⟩ ⟨his ice-clear eye gradually ~*ed* . . . his powers slipped —*Time*⟩
veiled \ˈvā(ə)ld\ *adj* [fr. past part. of ²*veil*] **1 a** : having or wearing a veil or concealing cover ⟨a ~ hat⟩ ⟨a ~ dancer⟩ ⟨a rose-*veiled* five-room cottage —Sinclair Lewis⟩ ⟨snowflakes from the ~ immensity of the sky —Ellen Glasgow⟩ **b** : characterized by a softening tonal distortion : BLURRED, MUFFLED ⟨strive for a little more sharpness of detail; the sound here is sometimes a bit ~ —Irving Kolodin⟩ **c** : lacking in contrast : CLOUDY ⟨if negative appears ~ or fogged —*Map Reproduction in the Field*⟩ **2** : obscured as if by a veil : DISGUISED, HIDDEN ⟨announcement of the capabilities of the new missile constitutes a ~ threat⟩ ⟨penned a ~ letter . . . hinting that French traders would be kindly received —R.A.Billington⟩ ⟨~ by this genial brogue . . . was a cold and analytical mind —*Irish Digest*⟩ — **veil·ed·ly** \ˈvālədlē\ *adv*
veiled medusa *n* : a velate typically Hydrozoan jellyfish having a diaphragm that partially closes the subumbrellar cavity
veiling *n* -S [fr. gerund of ²*veil*] **1 a** : VEIL ⟨no jungle tree . . . can withstand the blasting of violent sun after the ~ of emerald foliage is torn away —William Beebe⟩ **b** : an act or instance of covering with or as if with a veil ⟨the ~ of the cross on Good Friday⟩ ⟨color can be applied by . . . spray ~ —S.W.Menefee⟩ **2** : any of various light sheer fabrics (as net, lace, or chiffon) suitable for veils and used also for making dresses, hats, and scarves
veil·less \ˈvā(ə)lləs\ *adj* : not veiled : EXPOSED, UNSCREENED ⟨drove the dust against her ~ eyes —Alfred Tennyson⟩ ⟨the sun's hard ~ stare —Rhoda Broughton⟩
veillike \ˈ=,=\ *adj* : resembling a veil
veiltail \ˈ=,=\ *n* : a variety of domesticated goldfish with a very long, nearly transparent, veillike tail
¹vein \ˈvān\ *n* -S [ME *veine*, fr. OF, fr. L *vena* blood vessel, watercourse, natural bent, trait, vein] **1 a** (1) : a narrow water channel in rock, earth, or ice ⟨shooting, more often than not, collapses the ceiling and sides of the water ~ —Gaston Burridge⟩ (2) : a stream of water flowing through such a channel ⟨learned that several ~s of water . . . originated from one central dome and spread out in all directions —Kenneth Roberts⟩ **b** : a venous sinus of an invertebrate animal **c** : BLOOD VESSEL — not used technically ⟨had ice water in his ~s⟩ **d** : something likened to a vein or system of veins ⟨across the face of the . . . new map of the United States runs a significant network of fine scarlet ~s —*Nat'l Geographic*⟩ **2 a** : one of the tubular branching vessels that carry blood from the capillaries toward the heart in man and other vertebrates and have thinner walls than the arteries and often valves at intervals to prevent reflux of the blood which flows in a steady stream and is in most cases dark-colored due to the presence of reduced hemoglobin — compare CIRCULATION, PORTAL VEIN, VENAE COMITES **b** (1) : a body of ore filling a rock fissure and usu. deposited there from solution by underground water : LODE — compare DIKE (2) : a mineral bed or deposit ⟨a ~ of coal⟩ **c** : something that resembles a lode ⟨this . . . novel is by no means a pursuit of a worn-out ~; the author has discovered a new gold mine —Harrison Smith⟩ **d** : a strip of land differentiated by quality (as by special fertility) from its surroundings **e** *archaic* : the channel or flow of a stream : CURRENT, LANE ⟨whales . . . mostly swim in ~s —Herman Melville⟩ ⟨a whirlwind . . . directed its course toward the east, in a ~ of near half a mile wide —Jeremy Belknap⟩ **3 a** : one of the vascular bundles forming the framework of fibrous tissue of a leaf — called also *nerve, rib* **b** : a line of a different color or texture from the main body : STREAK, STRIPE; *esp* : a wavy variegation in marble and other stones **c** : one of the thickened cuticular ribs that serve to stiffen the wings of an insect **d** : the intestine and associated structures of a shrimp or prawn that appear as a dark line on the convex surface of the shellfish after it has been cooked and shelled **4 a** : a distinctive mode of expression : MANNER, STYLE ⟨produced some fifty ballets . . . in the romantic ~ characteristic of his generation —Anatole Chujoy⟩ ⟨a small masterpiece . . . in his best ~ —Mary A. Hamilton⟩ ⟨written . . . in the appropriate ~ for commercial correspondence —G.B.Shaw⟩ **b** : a distinctive thread : STRAIN ⟨a ~ of comedy weaves in and out of a great tragedy —R.M.Weaver⟩ **c** : a predominant line : general direction : TENOR ⟨statesmen whose hopes ran in this ~ —Oscar Handlin⟩ ⟨have no intention of continuing my comment . . . in this ~ —A.P.d'Entrèves⟩ **5 a** : a quality of character : TRAIT ⟨in the mother there was a deep ~ of mystical piety —Stewart Means⟩ **b** : a special aptitude : TALENT ⟨in her youth had no comedy ~ —Athene Seyler & Stephen Haggard⟩ **c** (1) : a frame of mind : HUMOR ⟨in your happiest ~ —H.J.Laski⟩ ⟨seemed to feel in the ~ to justify himself —Maurice Hewlett⟩ (2) : top form : FETTLE ⟨I am in ~ tonight . . . I have just got a third good idea —Angela Thirkell⟩ ⟨in the ~, there is probably no one . . . who can match the power and splendor of her singing —*N.Y. Post*⟩ **syn** see MOOD
²vein \"\ *vt* -ED/-ING/-S **1** : to pattern with or as if with veins : STRIATE ⟨the backs of her hands . . . were ~*ed* and worn —Kay Boyle⟩ ⟨goat paths ~*ing* its slopes —Josephine Pinckney⟩ ⟨was ~*ed* by railroads —W.A.White⟩ ⟨their works are ~*ed* with insinuations —Laurent Le Sage⟩ **2** : to diffuse in ramified form : SPREAD ⟨quartz crystals ~*ed* abundantly through its sandstone —*Amer. Guide Series: Ark.*⟩
vein·al \ˈvānᵊl\ *adj* : of or relating to the veins ⟨leaves affected with ~ mosaic⟩
veinbanding \ˈ=,==\ *n* [¹*vein* + *banding*] **1** : an evanescent abnormality of leaves commonly associated with virus diseases and characterized by veins standing out clearly because of either a chlorotic or a dark green bounding band that often sets off more clearly the adjacent interveinal tissue **2** : a plant disease of which veinbanding is a symptom — compare RUGOSE MOSAIC, VEINCLEARING
veinclearing \ˈ=,==\ *n* [¹*vein* + *clearing*] : an early and usu. evanescent symptom of plant diseases esp. of virus origin in which the veins stand out clearly because the tissue close to them is more or less translucent — compare VEINBANDING
veined \ˈvānd\ *adj* [¹*vein* + *-ed*] : marked or shot through with or as if with veins ⟨black hair, ~ with silver —Gordon Bottomley⟩ ⟨the terrain is finely ~ with roads —A.J.Liebling⟩ ⟨a beautiful book; heartbreaking, and at the same time ~ with humor —C.J.Rolo⟩; *specif* : showing venation ⟨a ~ leaf⟩
vein ending *n* : VEINLET
vein·er \ˈvānə(r)\ *n* -S : one that veins; *specif* : a small V gouge used in wood carving
veining *n* -S [fr. gerund of ²*vein*] **1** : the act or process of marking with or as if with veins ⟨use it for . . . mortising, ~, beading and for hundreds of other different cuts —*advt*⟩ **2 a** : a vein or pattern of veins ⟨an enchanting . . . watercolor, all delicate ~ and spongy texture —Carlyle Burrows⟩; *specif* : VENATION **b** : BEADING c
vein islet *n* : AREOLA a
vein·less \ˈvānləs\ *adj* : having no veins
vein·let \ˈvānlət\ *n* -S : a small vein; *specif* : the smallest or terminal branch of a vein (as of a leaf) — compare VENULE
veinlike \ˈ=,=\ *adj* : resembling a vein
vein of galen *usu cap G* : GALEN'S VEIN 1
vein·ous \ˈvānəs\ *adj* **1** : having veins that are esp. prominent : VEINED ⟨clasped her ~ and knotted hands —Charles Dickens⟩ **2** : VENOUS ⟨less evidence of a ~ stasis —*Diseases of the Nervous System*⟩
vein quartz *n* : quartz occurring as gangue in a vein
vein rot *n* : a pole rot of tobacco involving principally the main veins and larger lateral veins
veins *pl of* VEIN, *pres 3d sing of* VEIN
veinstone \ˈ=,=\ *n* [¹*vein* + *stone*] : GANGUE
veinstuff \ˈ=,=\ *n* [¹*vein* + *stuff*] : GANGUE
vein·ule \ˈvā(,)nyül\ *also* **vein·u·let** \ˈvānyələt\ *n* -S [¹*vein* + *-ule* or *-ulet* (fr. *-ule* + *-et*)] : VEINLET
veiny \ˈvānē\ *adj, sometimes* -ER/-EST : full of veins : VEINED, VEINOUS
vel- *comb form* [NL, fr. *velum*] : velum ⟨*veliform*⟩
vel *abbr* **1** vellum **2** velocity
vela *pl of* VELUM
ve·la·men \vəˈlāmən\ *n, pl* **ve·lam·i·na** \-lamənə\ [NL, fr. L, covering, fr. *velare* to cover, fr. *velum* veil] **1** : MEMBRANE, VELUM **2** : the thick whitish or greenish multiseriate corky epidermis covering the aerial roots of an epiphytic orchid and consisting of compactly arranged nonliving cells capable of absorbing water from the atmosphere
vel·a·men·tous \ˌveləˈmentəs\ *adj* [ISV *velament-* (fr. NL *velamentum*) + *-ous*] : relating to, resembling, or constituting a velamen
vel·a·men·tum \ˌ==ˈmentəm\ *n, pl* **velamen·ta** \-tə\ [NL, fr. L, covering, fr. *velare* to cover] : MEMBRANE
¹ve·lar \ˈvēlə(r)\ *adj* [NL *velaris*, fr. *velum* + *-aris* -ar] **1** : of, forming, or relating to a velum; *esp* : of or relating to the soft palate **2** : formed with the back of the tongue touching or near the soft palate ⟨the ~ \k\ of \ˈkül\ *cool*⟩ ⟨the ~ \g\ of \ˈgüs\ *goose*⟩ ⟨the ~ \k̟\ of German \ˈbük̟\ *Buch*⟩
²velar \"\ *n* -S : a velar sound
ve·lar·ic \vəˈlarik\ *adj* : having velar inner closure — used of a stop or stop articulation; compare GLOTTALIC, PULMONIC
ve·lar·i·um \vəˈla(a)rēəm\ *n, pl* **velar·ia** \-ēə\ [L, fr. *velum* veil] **1** : an awning over an ancient Roman theater or amphitheater **2** [NL, fr. L] : the velum that occurs in various scyphozoans and cubomedusans and that differs from that of hydrozoa in containing endoderm-lined canals
ve·lar·iza·tion \ˌvēlərəˈzāshən, -ˌrīˈ-\ *n* -S : the act of velarizing
ve·lar·ize \ˈvēlə,rīz\ *vt* -ED/-ING/-S [¹*velar* + *-ize*] : to modify (as the \l\ of \ˈpül\ *pool*) by a simultaneous velar articulation as a result of the assimilative influence of the vowel
velar r *n* : UVULAR R; *specif* : uvular r formed by friction
ve·late \ˈvēlət, -ē,lāt, *usu* -d.+V\ *adj* [partly fr. L *velatus*, past part. of *velare* to veil & partly fr. NL *velatus*, fr. *vel-* + L *-atus* -ate] : having a veil or velum
ve·lat·ed \-ē,lād·əd\ *adj* [L *velatus* & NL *velatus* + E *-ed*] : VEILED, VELATE
ve·la·tion \vəˈlāshən\ *n* -S [L *velation-, velatio* action of veiling, fr. *velatus* (past part. of *velare* to veil) + *-ion-, -io* -ion] **1** : the act or process of veiling or the state of being veiled **2** : the formation of a velum
veld *or* **veldt** \ˈvelt, *in S. Africa* ˈfe-\ *n* -S [Afrik *veld*, fr. MD *velt, veld* field; akin to OE & OHG *feld* field — more at FIELD] **1** : African grassland that is usu. nearly level, is often intermixed with scattered shrubs or trees, and is chiefly located in eastern and southern Africa — see SOURVELD, SWEETVELD; compare TREE STEPPE **2** : grassland similar to African veld (as in parts of California or elevated plains of the Russian steppes)
veld·schoen \ˈvelt,skün, ˈfe-\ *n, pl* **veldschoens** \-nz\ *or* **veldschoen** \-n\ [modif. of Afrik *velskoen*, fr. *vel* skin (fr. MD) + *skoen* shoe, fr. MD *schoe, schoen*; akin to OHG *fel* skin and to OE *scōh* shoe — more at FELL (skin), SHOE] : a heavy rawhide shoe made without nails and usu. without insole
veld sore *n* : DESERT SORE
veldtgrass *or* **veldgrass** \ˈ=,=\ *n* : a southern African grass (*Leersia calycina*) that is naturalized in western Australia and is used in the southwestern U.S. esp. to anchor light soils
veldt·schoen *Brit var of* VELDSCHOEN
ve·lel·la \vəˈlelə\ *n* [NL, fr. L *velum* sail + *-ella*] **1** *cap* : a genus of floating oceanic siphonophores widely distributed in warm seas and closely related to those of the genus *Porpita* but having an oblique crest which acts as a sail and often causes the animal to be drifted to coasts remote from its native habitat **2** -S : any animal of the genus *Velella* — **ve·lel·li·dous** \-elədəs\ *adj*
ve·le·ta \vəˈlād·ə\ *n* -S [Sp, weathervane, fr. *vela* cloth, veil, fr. L *vela*, pl. of *velum* veil] : a ballroom round dance of English origin in waltz time
ve·lic \ˈvēlik\ *adj* [*vel-* + *-ic*] : being or relating to the narrow passage located between the pharynx and the nasal passages and closable by raising the velum
ve·li·form \ˈvēlə,fȯrm, ˈvel-\ *adj* [ISV *vel-* + *-iform*] : resembling a velum in form
ve·li·ger \ˈvēləjə(r), ˈvel-\ *n* -S [NL, fr. *vel-* + L *-iger* -igerous] : a larval mollusk in the stage when it has developed the velum
ve·li·idae \vəˈlīə,dē\ *n pl, cap* [NL, fr. *Velia*, type genus + *-idae*] : a family of aquatic bugs that is closely related to Gerridae and is distinguished chiefly by details of the form and placement of the legs and by a 3-jointed proboscis — see WATER STRIDER
vel·i·ta·tion \ˌveləˈtāshən\ *n* -S [L *velitation-, velitatio*, fr. *velitatus* (past part. of *velitari* to skirmish, fr. *velit-, veles* light-armed foot soldier) + *-ion-, -io* -ion — more at VELOCITY] : a dispute or slight contest : SKIRMISH
¹vell \ˈvel\ *vt* -ED/-ING/-S [E dial. *vell*, n. fleece, skin, var. of ¹*fell*] *dial Eng* : to cut the turf from (as for burning)
²vell \"\ *n* -S [origin unknown] *Brit* : the stomach of a calf used in making rennet
vel·la·la *or* **vel·lal·la** \vəˈlälə\ *n, pl* **vellala** *or* **vellalas** *or* **vellalla** *or* **vellallas** *usu cap* [Tamil *veḷḷāḷaṉ*] : a member of a Tamil caste of the highest Sudra rank whose members are numerous in Madras and consist chiefly of landowners and cultivators
vel·le·da moth \ˈveləda-\ *n* [NL *velleda*, fr. *Veleda, Velleda*, legendary German prophetess of the 1st cent. A.D. fr. L] : a lappet moth (*Tolype velleda*) having the body chiefly white and wings dusky gray with white markings and having a larva that feeds on the apple, poplar, and other trees
vel·le·i·ty \vəˈlēəd·ē, veˈ-, -lēətē, -i\ *n* -ES [NL *velleitas*, fr. L *velle* to wish, will + *-itas* -ity — more at WILL] **1** : the lowest degree of desire : imperfect or incomplete volition ⟨~, which is only a . . . faint, imperfect volition of an end, without regard to the means —Theophilus Gale⟩ **2** : a slight wish : a faint hope : DESIRE, INCLINATION ⟨every wish, every ~ of his had only to be expressed to be at once Victoria's —Lytton Strachey⟩ ⟨I have a secretary who has socialistic *velleities* —O.W. Holmes †1935⟩ ⟨his *velleities* toward the good life, true taste, beautiful women . . . weakened as he drew on toward middle age —*Time*⟩
vel·li·cate \ˈvelə,kāt, *usu* -ād·+V\ *vb* -ED/-ING/-S [L *vellicatus*, past part. of *vellicare* to twitch, fr. *vellere* to pluck, pull — more at VULNERABLE] *vt* **1** : TWITCH, NIP, PINCH; *also* : to cause to twitch **2** : TICKLE, TITILLATE ~ *vi* : to move spasmodically : TWITCH
vel·li·ca·tion \ˌ==ˈkāshən\ *n* -S [L *vellication-, vellicatio*, fr. *vellicatus* (past part.) + *-ion-, -io* -ion] : the act of twitching or of causing to twitch; *also* : a local twitching of a group of muscle fibers
vel·linch \ˈvelinch\ *n* -ES [alter. of earlier *valinch*, alter. of *valentia*, modif. of Sp *venencia* fr. *avenencia* agreement, transaction, fr. *avenir* to come to (fr. L *advenire*) + *-encia* -ency (fr. L *-entia*) — more at ADVENE] : an instrument for drawing a sample from a cask through the shive hole — called also *flincher*
ve·llon \ve(l)ˈyōn\ *n* -S [Sp *vellón*, modif. (influenced by *vellón* fleece) of F *billon* — more at BILLON] : debased silver esp. when alloyed with considerable copper : BILLON
ve·llo process \ˈvel(,)yō-\ *n, usu cap V* [after Leopoldo Sanchez-*Vello*, 20th cent. Span. inventor] : a process for producing glass tubing by dropping molten glass through an annular space surrounding a rotating hollow pipe, the diameter of the tubing being determined by pressure of the air passed through the pipe, drawing speed, and temperature of the glass
vel·lo·zia \vəˈlōzēə\ *n, cap* [NL, fr. José *Velloso* Xavier †1811 Brazilian botanist + NL *-ia*] : a genus (the type of the family Velloziaceae) of Brazilian plants having branching stems clothed with the bases of the stiff linear pointed leaves and including some that are cultivated for their bell-shaped flowers
vel·lo·zi·a·ce·ae \və,lōzēˈāsē,ē\ *n pl, cap* [NL, fr. *Vellozia*, type genus + *-aceae*] : a family of African and Brazilian plants (order Liliales) distinguished from Amaryllidaceae

by woody stems, one-flowered peduncles, commonly persistent perianth, and more numerous stamens — **vel·lo·zi·a·ceous** \ˌ≈ˌ≈ˈāshəs\ *adj*

[1]**vel·lum** \ˈveləm\ *n* -s [ME *velim*, fr. MF *velin, veelin*, fr. *velin, veelin*, adj., of a calf, fr. *veel* calf — more at VEAL] **1 a :** a thin calfskin specially prepared for uses similar to those of parchment (as for writing upon and binding books) **b :** a fine-grained unsplit lambskin, kidskin, or calfskin prepared for these uses **2 :** a manuscript written or printed on vellum **3 a :** VELLUM PAPER **b :** VEGETABLE PARCHMENT **c :** paper that has been made sufficiently translucent for tracing purposes ⟨a blueprint made from a drawing on ∼⟩ **d :** a usu. glazed and embossed cotton book cloth made to imitate calfskin parchment **4 :** MEMBRANE

[2]**vellum** \"\ *adj* **1 :** of, resembling, or bound in vellum **2 :** resembling the finish of eggshell paper but having a finer grain ⟨paper having a ∼ finish⟩

vellum paper *n* **:** a strong cream-colored paper resembling parchment from calfskin in appearance but not parchmentized

vel non \ˈvelˈnän\ *adv* [L, or not] **:** whether or not — used to express a legal situation where something must be done or a given determination must be made or not with no third alternative; see DEVISAT VEL NON

ve·lo \ˈvē(ˌ)lō\ *n* -s [F *vélo*, short for *vélocipède* velocipede] **:** VELOCIPEDE; *specif* **:** TRICYCLE ⟨bikes and ∼*s*⟩

ve·lo·ce \vəˈlōchē\ *adj* [It, fr. L *veloc-, velox* quick — more at VELOCITY] **:** rapid in tempo — used as a direction in music

ve·lo·ci·man \vəˈläsəmən\ *n* -s [F *vélocimane*, fr. *véloci-* (as in *vélocipède*) + L *manus* hand — more at MANUAL] **:** an obsolete hand-driven vehicle like a velocipede

vel·o·cim·e·ter \ˌveləˈsimədə(r)\ *n* [*velocity* + *-meter*] **:** an apparatus for measuring speed (as of machinery, vessels, projectiles, or sound)

ve·lo·cious \vəˈlōshəs\ *adj* [L *veloc-, velox* quick + E *-ious*] **:** SPEEDY, FAST

[1]**ve·loc·i·pede** \vəˈläsəˌpēd\ *n* -s [F *vélocipède*, fr. *véloci-* (as in *vélocité* velocity) + L *ped-, pes* foot — more at FOOT] **:** a lightweight wheeled vehicle propelled by the rider: as **a :** DANDY HORSE **b :** BICYCLE — used of early forms **c :** TRICYCLE a(2)

[2]**velocipede** \"\ *vi* -ED/-ING/-S **:** to ride on a velocipede

velocipede car *n* **:** a lightweight hand-propelled 3-wheeled railway inspection car used mainly by telegraph linemen and maintenance personnel

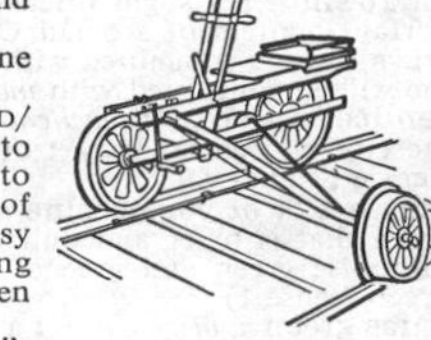
velocipede car

ve·loc·i·ped·ist \-dəst\ *n* -s **:** one who rides a velocipede

ve·loc·i·tize \vəˈläsəˌtīz\ *vt* -ED/-ING/-S [*velocity* + *-ize*] **:** to cause (an automobile driver) to misjudge or become unaware of true speed or to become drowsy as a result of prolonged traveling at a high speed (as on an open highway)

ve·loc·i·ty \vəˈläsəd·ē, -ətē, -i\ *n* -ES [MF *velocité*, fr. L *velocitat-, velocitas*, fr. *veloc-, velox* quick + *-itat-, -itas* -ity; akin to L *veles* light-armed foot soldier, *vehere* to carry, convey — more at WAY] **1 :** quickness of motion **:** SWIFTNESS, SPEED, CELERITY, RAPIDITY — used chiefly of inanimate things ⟨the ∼ of a bullet⟩ ⟨the ∼ of flow of water⟩ ⟨∼ of a train⟩ ⟨the ∼ of sound⟩ **2 a** (1) **:** time rate of linear motion in a given direction **:** a vector quantity equal to speed in a particular direction and relative to a stated frame of reference — compare SPEED 2b (2) **:** ANGULAR VELOCITY **b :** the rate at which a chemical reaction progresses **3 :** rate of occurrence or action **:** RAPIDITY ⟨*velocities* of inhibition of bacterial growth by sulfonamide —*Jour. Amer. Med. Assoc.*⟩ ⟨if the blood vessels were in a dilated condition the ∼ of heat transfer was reduced —F.A.Geldard⟩ ⟨a book having a high sales ∼⟩ **:** rate of turnover ⟨∼ of money⟩

velocity function *n* **:** the distribution of the velocities of the stars in a given region of space

velocity head *n* **:** the vertical distance through which a liquid would have to fall to attain a given velocity

velocity microphone *n* **:** a microphone (as the ribbon microphone) whose very light and flexible diaphragm follows almost without phase lag the air movements in the sound waves that actuate it

velocity modulation *n* **:** modification of the velocity of a stream of electrons by imparting alternate accelerations and decelerations to the electrons in such a way that they are caused to bunch together with the result that each bunch causes a cycle of current as it passes an output electrode

velocity of circulation : the average number of times that a unit of currency circulates during a given period of time **:** the rate of turnover of money

velocity of escape : a velocity that if attained by a moving body (as a rocket) would enable it to escape from the gravitational field of the earth or a celestial body and move outward in space ⟨the ability of a celestial body to retain an atmosphere around it depends on the *velocity of escape* at its surface —R. H.Baker⟩ ⟨this critical speed of seven miles a second is known as the earth's *velocity of escape* —P.A.Moore⟩

velocity of light : a fundamental constant that represents the speed of electromagnetic radiation in a vacuum and equals approximately 2.9979×10^{10} centimeters per second

velocity potential *n* **:** the scalar quantity whose negative gradient equals the velocity in the case of irrotational flow of a fluid

velocity ratio *n* **:** the ratio of the distance through which any part of a machine moves to that through which the driving part moves during the same time

velocity stage *n* **:** the stage in the process of expansion and of energy transformation in which there is no pressure drop and in which the velocity of steam flow in a steam turbine decreases the kinetic energy of the steam being imparted to the moving blades — compare PRESSURE STAGE

ve·lo·drome \ˈvēləˌdrōm, ˈvel-\ *n* -s [F *vélodrome*, fr. *vélo* velo + *-drome*] **:** a building containing a track designed for cycling

Ve·lom·e·ter \vēˈläməd·ə(r)\ *trademark* — used for a meter for measuring the velocity of air

velos *pl of* VELO

ve·lour *or* **ve·lours** \vəˈlu̇(ə)r, -ú(ə)\ *n, pl* **velours** \-ú(ə)r(z), -ú(ə)(z)\ *often attrib* [F *velours* velvet, velour, fr. MF *velours*, *velour* — more at VELURE] **1 :** any of various fabrics with a pile or napped surface resembling velvet made usu. of cotton, rayon, silk, or wool and used in heavy weights for upholstery and curtains and in light weights for coats and jackets **2 :** a fur felt usu. of rabbit, hare, beaver, or nutria finished with a long velvety nap and used esp. for hats

ve·lou·té \vəˌlüˈtā\ *also* **velouté sauce** *n* -s [F *velouté*, lit., velvety, fr. MF, fr. *velours* velvet] **:** a white sauce made of chicken or veal stock and cream and thickened with butter and flour — compare BÉCHAMEL, POULETTE

velt-marshal \ˈfelt+ˌ-\ *n* [part trans., part modif. (influenced by obs. D *velt* field, fr. MD) of G *feldmarschall* (trans. of F *maréchal de camp*), fr. *feld* field (fr. OHG) + *marschall* marshal, fr. OHG *marahscalc* — more at VELD, MARSHAL] **:** FIELD MARSHAL

ve·lum \ˈvēləm\ *n, pl* **ve·la** \-lə\ [NL, fr. L, covering, curtain, veil] **:** a membrane or membranous part likened to a veil or curtain: as **a :** SOFT PALATE **b :** an annular membrane projecting inward from the margin of the umbrella in hydromedusans and a few other jellyfishes **c :** a delicate membranelle bordering the mouth of various infusorians **d** (1) **:** PARTIAL VEIL (2) **:** UNIVERSAL VEIL **e :** the thin membrane that envelops a sporocarp in plants of the genus *Isoetes* **f :** a larval swimming organ that is esp. well developed in the later larval stages of many marine gastropods but occurs also in those of many lamellibranchs, that is developed from the preoral ciliate ring of the trochophore with the ring of cilia becoming raised on a more or less prominent and contractile collar-shaped ridge which in typical cases is produced into large lateral lobes bordered with long cilia, and that prob. serves also for respiration

ve·lu·men \vəˈlümən\ *n, pl* **velumi·na** \-mənə\ [L, fleece; prob. akin to L *vellere* to pluck, pull — more at VULNERABLE] **:** the velvety covering of various parts of plants or animals

velure *n* -s [modif. (influenced by *-ure*) of MF *velours, velour*, fr. OF *velous, velos*, fr. L *villosus* hairy, shaggy, fr. *villus* hair + *-osus* -ose — more at VELVET] *obs* **:** velvet or a fabric resembling it

vel·u·ti·na \ˌveləˈtīnə\ *n* [NL, fr. fem. of *velutinus* velutinous] **1** *cap* **:** a genus of marine gastropods related to the moon shells but having a shell with few whorls and a thick periostracum **2** -s **:** any member of the genus *Velutina*

ve·lu·ti·nous \vəˈlütᵊnəs\ *adj* [NL *velutinus*, fr. ML *velutum* velvet (prob. fr. OIt *velluto* shaggy, fr. — assumed — VL *villutus*) + L *-inus* -ine] **:** covered with a fine and dense silky pubescence **:** VELVETY

vel·ver·et \ˌvelvəˈret\ *n* -s [alter. of [1]*velvet*] **:** a velveteen often having printed designs

[1]**vel·vet** \ˈvelvət, *usu* -əd·+V\ *n* -s [ME *veluet, velvet*, fr. MF *velu* shaggy (fr. — assumed —VL *villutus*, fr. L *villus* shaggy hair) + ME *-et*; akin to L *vellus* fleece — more at WOOL] **1 :** a clothing and upholstery fabric in a wide range of constructions and weights made of silk, rayon, cotton, nylon, or wool and characterized by a short soft dense pile produced by weaving into a single cloth an extra warp which is looped over wires and later cut or by weaving a double cloth with an extra warp connecting the two fabrics which are later cut apart — see UNCUT VELVET **2 a :** something like or suggesting velvet (as in softness or luster) **b :** a characteristic of velvet: as (1) **:** SOFTNESS ⟨the stars are studded in the warm intimate ∼ of the night —Norman Mailer⟩ (2) **:** SMOOTHNESS ⟨fine old cognac loses its ∼ when chilled —Jerry Thomas⟩ **3 :** the soft and highly vascular hairy skin that envelops and nourishes the antlers of deer during their rapid growth but later peels off or is rubbed off by the animal **4 a :** the cash or chips a player is ahead in a gambling game **:** WINNINGS **b :** a profit or gain esp. when beyond ordinary expectation ⟨the rest of the collection . . . would cost him nothing; whatever he could sell it for would be ∼ —S.N.Behrman⟩ ⟨if one of them is real lucky and has the breaks and finally gets to be well known and makes some money, well, it's so much ∼ then —Louis Armstrong⟩ **5 :** a drink that is half champagne and half porter — compare BLACK VELVET 2 **6 :** VELVET SPONGE — **on velvet 1 :** in the position of having or operating with money previously won (as in gambling or speculating) **2 :** in an easy, safe, prosperous, or otherwise desirable position ⟨we were *on velvet* financially —J.C.Snaith⟩

[2]**velvet** \"\ *adj* **1 :** made of or covered with velvet; *sometimes* **:** clad in velvet **2 :** resembling or suggesting velvet **:** VELVETY ⟨the callous soles of the passersby made the merest ∼ shuffling —William Beebe⟩ ⟨the horse had a ∼ gait —Edna Ferber⟩ ⟨the apple-green twilight deepened into emerald and then into a ∼ darkness —John Buchan⟩ ⟨∼ lawns⟩

[3]**velvet** \"\ *vt* -ED/-ING/-S [ME, fr. *velvet*, n.] **:** to make like or cover with velvet ⟨bald mountains that ∼ their own sides with shadows —*New Republic*⟩

velvet ant *n* **:** any of various solitary fossorial wasps that constitute the family Mutillidae, have a wingless female and a body usu. covered with fine soft hair often of bright red or some other conspicuous color, are able to sting, in many cases are parasitic in the nests of bees or other hymenopterous insects and in such cases feed while young on the larvae of the host

velvet ash *n* **:** a forest tree (*Fraxinus velutina*) of New Mexico and Arizona

velvet bean *n* **1 :** an annual legume (*Stizolobium deeringianum* syn. *Mucuna deeringiana*) that is related to the cowage and cultivated esp. in the southern U. S. for green manure and grazing **2 :** the seed of the velvet bean which is often used as cattle and hog feed — called also *Florida velvet bean*

velvet bean caterpillar *n* **:** a caterpillar that is the larva of a noctuid moth (*Anticarsia gemmatilis*) and feeds on velvet beans, soybeans, and other leguminous crops in southern U. S.

velvet bent *n* **:** DOG BENT

velvetbreast \ˈ≈≈ˌ≈\ *n* -s **:** AMERICAN MERGANSER

velvet brown *n* **:** BURNT UMBER 2

velvet bur *n* **:** a tropical American perennial herb (*Priva lappulacea*) of the family Verbenaceae whose fruiting calyx is beset with small hooked bristles

velvet carpet *or* **velvet rug** *n* **:** a carpet or rug having a cut pile; *esp* **:** TAPESTRY VELVET CARPET

velvet crab *n* **:** a small stoutly built Australian spider crab (*Paratymolus latipes quadridentata*) that is densely covered with short velvety hairs

velvet dock *n* **1 :** a common mullein (*Verbascum thapsus*) **2 :** ELECAMPANE

velveted *adj* **:** covered with velvet **:** having the texture of velvet **:** made to resemble velvet (as in softness or smoothness)

vel·vet·een \ˌvelvəˈtēn\ *n* -s *often attrib* [[1]*velvet* + *-een*] **1 :** a clothing fabric usu. of cotton in twill or plain weaves made with a short close weft pile in imitation of velvet **2 velveteens** *pl* **:** clothes made of velveteen; *esp* **:** trousers made of it

velvet fish *n* **:** any of various Australian fishes having a velvety skin; *esp* **:** a fish (*Aploactis milesii*) related to the scorpion fishes

velvet flower *n* **:** SALPIGLOSSIS 2

velvet glove *n* **:** superficial gentleness and courtesy masking a strong and unyielding will or determination ⟨the communists were on the . . . Peninsula only six months in any force, so the people did not have a chance to feel the iron beneath their *velvet glove* —Darrell Berrigan⟩

velvet grass *n* **:** a tall European grass (*Holcus lanatus*) having a velvety stem, naturalized in the U. S., and used for forage

velvet green *n* **:** a moderate olive green that is yellower, lighter, and stronger than cypress green, greener and stronger than holly green (sense 2), and greener, lighter, and stronger than Lincoln green

velvet groundsel *n* **:** CALIFORNIA GERANIUM

velvet guard *n, obs* **:** velvet trimming or one wearing it

vel·vet·i·ness \ˈvelvəd·ēnəs\ *n* -ES **:** quality of velvet **:** velvety appearance, feeling, or taste

velveting *pres part of* VELVET

velvetleaf \ˈ≈≈ˌ≈\ *n* **:** any of various plants that have soft velvety leaves: as **a :** a tropical vine (*Cissampelos pareira*) with roots that constitute the false pareira of commerce **b :** INDIAN MALLOW 1 **c :** TREE MALLOW **d :** MULLEIN

velvet loom *n* **1 :** a loom for weaving velvet fabric **2 :** a loom for weaving velvet carpet

velvet moss *n* **:** a northern European lichen (*Gyrophora murina*) used in dyeing

velvet osier *n* **:** OSIER 1a

velvet plant *n* **1 :** GREAT MULLEIN **2** *also* **velvet tree :** a Javanese foliage plant (*Gynura aurantiaca*) with handsome velvety leaves with violet-purple hairs

velvets *pl of* VELVET, *pres 3d sing of* VELVET

velvet scoter *or* **velvet duck** *n* **1 :** a large scoter (*Melanitta fusca*) of northern Europe and Asia closely resembling the white-winged scoter of America **2 :** WHITE-WINGED SCOTER

velvetseed \ˈ≈≈ˌ≈\ *n* **1 :** a shrub or small tree (*Guettarda elliptica*) of the family Rubiaceae of the West Indies and Florida with yellowish white flowers and black fruit **2 :** SEVEN-YEAR APPLE 1

velvet shell *n* **:** a marine gastropod of *Velutina* or a related genus

velvet sponge *n* **:** a fine soft commercial sponge (*Hippiospongia equina meandriformis*) typically of flat rounded form occurring in the Gulf of Mexico and off the West Indies

velvet sumac *n* **:** STAGHORN SUMAC

velvet tamarind *n* **:** a western African tree (*Dialium guineënse*) of the family Leguminosae with velvety black pods containing an acid pulp that is chewed to relieve thirst or macerated in water to form a beverage — called also *black tamarind*

velvet violet *n* **:** PANSY VIOLET 1

velvetweed \ˈ≈≈ˌ≈\ *n* **:** INDIAN MALLOW

velvet willow *n* **:** SITKA WILLOW

vel·vety \ˈvelvəd·ē, -ətē, -i\ *adj* **1 :** having the character of velvet **:** soft and smooth (as in appearance or to the sight, hearing, touch) ⟨the shadows in the valleys and gorges of ∼ blackness —Bram Stoker⟩ ⟨his tone is not as ∼ as that of some other cellists —*N.Y. Times*⟩ ⟨how I loved the ∼ highway dust —W.A.White⟩ **2 a :** smooth to the taste **:** MILD ⟨∼ rum⟩ **b :** giving a contact like that of velvet ⟨the ∼ touch of a piano player⟩

VEM *abbr* vasoexciter material

ven \ˈven\ *chiefly dial var of* FEN

ven- *or* **veni-** *or* **veno-** *comb form* [L *vena*] **1 :** vein ⟨*veni*puncture⟩ ⟨*veno*clysis⟩ ⟨*veni*section⟩ **2 :** of or relating to the vena cava **:** caval and ⟨*veno*atrial⟩

ven *abbr, often cap* venerable

ve·na \ˈvēnə\ *n, pl* **ve·nae** \-ˌnē, -ˌnī\ [ME, fr. L] **:** VEIN

ve·na ca·va \ˌvēnəˈkāvə\ *n, pl* **ve·nae ca·vae** \ˌvēnēˈkā(ˌ)vē\ [NL, fr. L, hollow vein] **:** one of the large veins by which in air-breathing vertebrates the blood is returned to the right atrium of the heart, which develop in part from and replace in function the cardinal veins and ducts of Cuvier of the embryo, and which commonly occur as two anterior venae cavae returning blood from the head and forelimbs and one posterior vena cava returning blood from the posterior parts of the body and the viscera

vena co·mes \-ˈkōˌmēz, -mes\ *n, pl* **venae com·i·tes** \-ˈkäməˌtēz, -tās\ [NL, companion vein] **:** a vein accompanying an artery

vena con·trac·ta \-kənˈtraktə\ *n, pl* **venae contrac·tae** \-kˌtē, -ˌtī\ [NL, contracted vein] **:** any of the contracted parts of minimum cross section of a jet of fluid discharging from an orifice; *esp* **:** the one nearest the orifice

venae vor·ti·co·sae \-ˌvȯ(r)d·əˈkōˌsē, -ˌsī\ *n pl* [NL, lit., eddying veins] **:** the veins of the outer layer of the choroid coat of the eye

[1]**ve·nal** \ˈvēnᵊl\ *adj* [L *vena* + E *-al*] *archaic* **:** VENOUS

[2]**venal** \"\ *adj* [L *venalis*, fr. *venus, venum* sale + *-alis* -al; akin to Gk *ōnos* price, Skt *vasna*] **1 :** capable of being bought or obtained for money or other valuable consideration **:** made matter of trade or barter **:** PURCHASABLE; *esp* **:** open to corrupt influence and esp. bribery ⟨a ∼ legislator⟩ ⟨∼ services⟩ ⟨∼ votes⟩ **2 :** originating in, characterized by, or associated with corrupt bargaining ⟨a ∼ throne⟩ ⟨a ∼ arrangement with the police⟩

ve·nal·i·ty \vēˈnaləd·ē, vəˈ-, -lətē, -i\ *n* -ES [F or LL; F *venalité*, fr. LL *venalitat-, venalitas*, fr. L *venalis* venal + *-itat-, -itas* -ity] **:** the quality or state of being venal esp. in the prostitution of talents, offices, or services for reward **:** willingness to be influenced improperly (as by bribery or corrupt measures) ⟨the ∼ of a judge⟩

ve·nal·ly \ˈvēnᵊlē, -li\ *adv* [[2]*venal* + *-ly*] **:** in a venal manner **:** so as to be venal

ve·nal·ness *n* -ES **:** VENALITY

ve·nan·tes \vəˈnan·(ˌ)tēz\ *n pl, cap* [NL, fr. L *venant-, venans*, pres. part. of *venari* to hunt] *in some classifications* **:** a group comprising the hunting spiders

vena sal·va·tel·la \-ˌsalvəˈtelə\ *n, pl* **venae salvatel·lae** \-e(ˌ)lē, -ˌlī\ [NL, lit., little saver vein; fr. the former belief that bleeding from it saved one from disease] **:** a superficial vein on the back of the hand coming from the little finger

ve·nat·ic \vəˈnad·ik, vēˈ-\ *also* **ve·nat·i·cal** \-d·əkəl\ *adj* [*venatic* fr. L *venaticus*, fr. *venatus* (past part. of *venari* to hunt) + *-icus* -ic; *venatical* fr. L *venaticus* + E *-al* — more at VENISON] **1 :** of, relating to, or used in hunting ⟨∼ sport⟩ ⟨∼ equipment⟩ **2 :** fond of or living by hunting ⟨the ∼ tribes of ancient Europe⟩ — **ve·nat·i·cal·ly** \-k(ə)lē\ *adv*

[1]**ve·na·tion** \vēˈnāshən, vəˈ-\ *n* -s [L *venation-, venatio*, fr. *venatus* (past part.) + *-ion-, -io* -ion] *archaic* **:** HUNTING

[2]**venation** \"\ *n* -s [*ven-* + *-ation*] **:** an arrangement or system of veins ⟨the ∼ of the hand⟩: as **a :** the arrangement of veins in the tissue of a leaf blade **b :** the arrangement of veins in the wing of an insect

venation: *1* pinnate, *2* palmate, *3* base to tip, *4* base to midrib, *5* midrib to margin

ve·na·tion·al \-shənᵊl, -shnəl\ *adj* [[2]*venation* + *-al*] **:** of or relating to venation

ven·a·to·ri·al \ˌvenəˈtōrēəl, -tȯr-\ *or* **ven·a·to·ry** \ˈ≈≈ˌtōrē, -tȯrē, -ri\ *adj* [*venatorial* fr. L *venatorius* venatic (fr. *venatus*, past part. + *-orius* -ory) + E *-al*; *venatory* fr. L *venatorius*] **:** VENATIC

ven·co·la \ˈveŋkələ\ *n* -s [AmerSp] **:** QUIRA

[1]**vend** \ˈvend\ *vb* -ED/-ING/-S [L *vendere*, contr. of *venumdere*, fr. *venum* sale + *-dere* (fr. *dare* to give) — more at VENAL, DATE] *vi* **:** to become an object of commerce **:** change hands through sale ⟨a product that should ∼ well⟩; *also* **:** to engage in selling ⟨merchants planning to ∼ abroad⟩ ∼ *vt* **1 a :** to transfer to another for a pecuniary equivalent ⟨planned to ∼ his household goods **b :** to engage in the sale of often by hawking or peddling ⟨∼*ed* fruit on that corner for many years⟩ ⟨developed a machine for ∼*ing* hot coffee⟩ **2 :** to put forth in or as a statement **:** utter publicly **:** publish abroad ⟨uttering such comments as ought not to have been ∼*ed* from a pulpit⟩

[2]**vend** \"\ *n* -s *Brit* **:** an occasion or act of vending **:** SALE; *esp* **:** the total sales of a colliery esp. as restricted by annual agreement

[3]**vend** \"\ *or* **ve·ned** \vəˈned\ *n, pl* **vends** \-n(d)z\ *or* **ve·ne·di** \vəˈnedē\ *cap* [*vend* alter. (influenced by L *Venedi* Vends) of [2]*wend*; *vened* fr. L *Venedi, Veneti*, pl., Vends] **:** WEND

ven·da \ˈvendə\ *n, pl* **venda** *or* **vendas** *usu cap* **1 a :** a people of the northern Transvaal, Africa **b :** a member of such people **2 :** a Bantu language of the Venda people

ven·dace \ˈvendəs *also* -ˌdās\ *n, pl* **vendace** *also* **vendaces** [NL *vandesius*, fr. MF *vandoise*, prob. of Celt origin; akin to OIr *find* white — more at FINNOCK] **:** a whitefish (*Coregonus vandesius*) native to various lakes of Scotland and England

ven·dage \ˈvendij\ *n* -s [ME — more at VINTAGE] **:** the harvesting or harvest time of grapes **:** VINTAGE

ven·da·val \ˌvendəˈval, -ˈväl\ *n* -s [Sp, fr. F *vent d'aval* westerly wind, lit., downstream wind, fr. *vent* wind (fr. L *ventus*) + *d'* of (contr. of *de*, fr. L) + *aval* downstream, downward — more at WIND, DE-, AVALE] **1 :** a gusty southwest wind occurring chiefly in winter about the strait of Gibraltar **2 :** an autumnal thundersquall on the coast of Mexico

[1]**ven·de·an** \(ˈ)venˈdēən\ *adj, usu cap* [La *Vendée*, region in western France + E *-an*] **:** of or relating to La Vendée, France

[2]**vendean** \"\ *n* -s *usu cap* **:** one of the people of La Vendée; *esp* **:** one of those taking part in the Wars of the Vendée during the French Revolution

vend·ee \(ˈ)venˈdē\ *n* -s [[1]*vend* + *-ee*] **:** one to whom a thing is sold **:** BUYER, PURCHASER

vend·er \ˈvendə(r)\ *n* -s [by alter.] **:** VENDOR

ven·det·ta \venˈded·ə, -etə\ *n* -s [It, lit., revenge, fr. L *vindicta*, fr. *vindicare* to avenge — more at VINDICATE] **1 :** BLOOD FEUD ⟨should have disappeared from civilized society along with ∼*s* and black magic —Lucius Garvin⟩ **2 :** a prolonged feud marked by bitter hostility ⟨waging a literary ∼ of his own —C. I.Glicksberg⟩ ⟨would neither conduct partisan ∼*s* nor indulge in political patronage —*Newsweek*⟩

ven·deuse \(ˈ)väⁿˈdə(r)z, -dəz, ˈvänˌdüz, *F* väⁿdœzˈ\ *n* -s [F, fem. of *vendeur* salesman — more at VENDOR] **:** SALESWOMAN

vend·ibil·i·ty \ˌvendəˈbiləd·ē\ *n* -ES **:** the quality or state of being vendible

[1]**vend·ible** *or* **vend·able** \ˈ≈dəbəl\ *adj* [*vendible* fr. ME, fr. L *vendibilis*, fr. *vendere* to sell + *-ibilis* -ible; *vendable* fr. ME, fr. MF, fr. *vendre* to sell (fr. L *vendere*) + *-able* — more at VEND] **1 :** available or suitable for sale ⟨∼ produce⟩ **:** of a kind to command a cash return ⟨∼ beauty⟩ **2** *obs* **:** open to corrupt bargaining **:** VENAL **3 :** generally acceptable **:** passing as current

[2]**vendible** \"\ *n* -s **:** a vendible article — usu. used in pl.

vending *pres part of* VEND

vending machine *n* **:** a slot machine for vending merchandise mechanically

ven·di·tion \venˈdishən\ *n* -s [L *vendition-, venditio*, fr. *venditus* (past part. of *vendere* to sell) + *-ion-, -io* -ion] **:** the act of selling **:** SALE

ven·dor \ˈvendə(r); (ˈ)venˈdȯ(ə)r, -ȯ(ə)\ *n* -s [MF *vendeor*, *vendeur*, fr. *vendre* to sell (fr. L *vendere*) + *-eor, -eur* -or] **:** one that offers goods for sale esp. habitually or as a means of livelihood : SELLER: **a** (1) : an independent seller in a small way of business; *esp* : PEDDLER (2) : a person that hawks and sells merchandise (as refreshments, programs, or souvenirs) to patrons of a public gathering **b** : VENDING MACHINE

vendor's lien *n* : an implied lien given in equity to a vendor of lands for unpaid purchase money as against the vendee and volunteers under him

vendor's share *n* : a security taken instead of cash payment by one transferring property to a corporation

vends *pres 3d sing of* VEND, *pl of* VEND

ven·due \(ˈ)venˌd(y)ü, (ˈ)van-, (ˈ)vän-\ *n* -s [obs. F, fr. MF, fr. *vendu*, past part. of *vendre* to sell] : a public sale at which goods are sold to the highest bidder : AUCTION

vendue crier *or* **vendue master** *n* : AUCTIONEER

vened *usu cap, var of* VEND

¹ve·neer \vəˈni(ə)r, -iə\ *n* -s [G *furnier*, fr. *furnieren* to veneer] **1 a** : a thin sheet of wood cut or sawed from a log and adapted for adherence to a smooth surface (as of wood) ⟨cut the log into ~s⟩: as (1) : a layer of wood of superior value or excellent grain for overlaying an inferior wood (as in cabinetmaking) usu. by gluing (2) : any one of the thin layers that are glued or otherwise bonded together to form plywood **b** : material (as sheets of wood) for veneering; *sometimes* : thin highly glazed colored paperboard for such use **2** : something felt to resemble or functioning in the manner of a veneer of wood esp. in forming a superficial layer: as **a** : a superficial or meretricious show : GLOSS **b** : a protective or ornamental facing (as of brick or stone) for a wall **c** (1) : a thin but extensive covering of an older geologic formation or surface ⟨a ~ of till⟩ (2) : a weathered or otherwise altered surficial part of a rock

²veneer \"\ *vt* -ED/-ING/-S [earlier *fineer*, fr. G *furnieren*, fr. F *fournir* to furnish, fr. MF *furnir, fournir* to complete, equip — more at FURNISH] **1 a** : to overlay or plate (as a common sort of wood) with a thin layer of finer wood for outer finish or decoration ⟨~ gumwood furniture with mahogany⟩; *broadly* : to face with a material giving a superior surface ⟨a wall ~*ed* with brick⟩ **b** : to glue together (thin pieces of wood) into plywood **2** : to cover like a veneer of wood : give an attractive surface appearance to; *esp* : to conceal (as a defect of character) under a superficial and specious attractiveness

ve·neer·er \vəˈnirə(r)\ *n* -s : one that veneers

veneer graft *n* : a plant graft made by chamfering the surfaces of scion and stock and applying the one to the other

ve·neer·ing \-riŋ, -rēŋ\ *n* -s [¹*veneer* + *-ing*] **1** : VENEER 1b **2** : a surface covered by veneer : a veneered surface

veneer moth *n* : any of various small moths of the family Pyralididae with mottled colors that suggest those of some veneering

¹ven·e·nate \ˈvenəˌnāt\ *vb* -ED/-ING/-S [L *venenatus*, past part of *venenare* to poison, fr. *venenum* poison — more at VENOM] *vt* : POISON; *specif* : to inject a toxic substance into ⟨blood-sucking insects that ~ the wounds they form⟩ ~ *vi* : to use a toxic substance in preying or feeding ⟨*venenating* arthropods⟩

²ven·e·nate \-nət, -ˌnāt\ *adj* [L *venenatus*, past part. of *venenare*] : POISONED, POISONOUS ⟨a ~ zone surrounding the primary lesion in the leaf⟩

ven·e·na·tion \ˌ==ˈnāshən\ *n* -s [L *venenatus* + E *-ion*] : the course or process of being poisoned esp. by a venom of animal origin

¹ve·nene \vəˈnēn, veˈn-\ *adj* [irreg. fr. L *venenum* poison] *archaic* : POISONOUS

²venene *var of* VENIN

ven·e·nif·er·ous \ˌvenəˈnif(ə)rəs\ *adj* [L *venenifer* veneniferous (fr. *venenum* + *-fer* -ferous) + E *-ous*] : bearing or transmitting poison and esp. a natural venom

ven·e·nous \ˈvenənəs\ *adj* [LL *venenosus*, fr. L *venenum* poison + *-osus* -ose] : POISONOUS, VENOMOUS

venepuncture *var of* VENIPUNCTURE

ven·er·abil·i·ty \ˌvən(ə)rəˈbiləd·ē, -lətē, -i\ *n* [ML *venerabilitas*, fr. L *venerabilis* venerable + *-itas* -ity] : the quality or state of being venerable

¹ven·er·able \ˈvenər(ə)bəl, -nrəb-\ *adj* [ME, fr. L *venerabilis*, fr. *venerari* to venerate + *-abilis* -able] **1** : deserving to be venerated : worthy of honor and respect usu. by reason of prolonged testing (as of character or in office) ⟨a ~ judge⟩ — used as a title or in a respectful form of address to an archdeacon of a church of the Anglican Communion or a person recognized by Roman Catholics as having attained the lowest of three degrees of sanctity **2** : made sacred by religious, historic, or other associations : meriting to be regarded with awe and treated with reverence ⟨the ~ walls of a church⟩ ⟨~ relics of our forefathers⟩ ⟨the ~ silence of the library —Ernst Krenek⟩ **3 a** : calling forth respect through age, character, and attainments ⟨~ sages⟩ ⟨a ~ leader⟩; *broadly* : conveying an impression of aged goodness and benevolence ⟨his ruddy features and snow-white hair gave him a ~ appearance⟩ **b** : impressive by reason of age ⟨under ~ pines⟩ ⟨that ~ coat had sheltered three generations⟩ **4** *obs* : showing or giving deep respect : REVERENTIAL **syn** see OLD

²venerable \"\ *n* -s : a venerable individual; *esp* : one entitled (as by position) to the title of venerable

ven·er·able·ness *n* -ES : VENERABILITY

ven·er·ably \-blē, -li\ *adv* : in a venerable manner : so as to be venerable

ven·er·a·cea \ˌvenəˈrāshēə\ *n pl, cap* [NL, fr. *Vener-*, *Venus*, included genus + *-acea*] : a suborder of Eulamellibranchia comprising bivalve mollusks with the foot compressed, the siphons generally short, and both adductor muscles present and including the families Veneridae and Petricolidae — **ven·er·a·cean** \ˌ==ˈrāshən\ *adj or n* — **ven·er·a·ceous** \-shəs\ *adj*

ven·er·ate \ˈvenəˌrāt, *usu* -ād·+V\ *vt* -ED/-ING/-S [L *veneratus*, past part. of *venerari* to venerate — more at WIN] : to regard with reverential respect or with admiration and deference as being hallowed or as having nobility esp. if accompanied with age : REVERE ⟨we ~ noble parents⟩ ⟨do not know a man more to be *venerated* for uprightness of heart and loftiness of genius —Sir Walter Scott⟩ **syn** see REVERE

ven·er·a·tion \ˌ==ˈrāshən\ *n* -s [ME *veneracion*, fr. L *veneration-*, *veneratio*, fr. *veneratus* (past part. of *venerari*) + *-ion-*, *-io* -ion] **1** : a feeling of respect mingled with awe excited by the dignity, wisdom, or superiority of a person, by sacredness of character, by consecrated state, or by hallowed association ⟨the tremendous ~ in which art and artists have been held —Huntington Hartford⟩ ⟨regarded their teachers and institutions with the deepest ~⟩ **2 a** : the act of venerating esp. by the expressing of deeply reverent feeling — compare ADORATION **b** : the face of admiring humbly and respectfully **3** : the condition of one that is venerated ⟨hoping to attain ~ from his subjects⟩ **4** : the phrenologic faculty of reverence — **ven·er·a·tion·al** \ˌ==ˈrāshənᵊl, -shnəl\ *adj*

ven·er·a·tor \ˈ==ˌrād·ə(r), -ātə-\ *n* -s [L, fr. *veneratus* (past part.) + *-or*] : one that venerates ⟨a ~ of tradition⟩

ve·ne·re·al \vəˈnirēəl\ *adj* [ME *venereall*e, fr. L *venereus* venereal (fr. *vener-*, *venus* love, sexual desire) + ME *-alle*, *-al* -al — more at WIN] **1 a** : of or relating to sexual pleasure or indulgence : of, relating to, or preoccupied with sexual intercourse **b** *obs, of persons* : inclined to be lascivious **2** : adapted or likely to excite sexual desire : APHRODISIAC **3 a** : resulting from or contracted during sexual intercourse ⟨a ~ inflammation⟩ ⟨~ transmission of disease⟩ ⟨~ infections⟩ **b** (1) : of or relating to venereal disease ⟨a ~ clinic⟩ ⟨a high ~ rate⟩ ⟨newer ~ treatments⟩ (2) : affected with venereal disease ⟨the ~ patient⟩ **c** : occurring on or affecting the genital organs ⟨a ~ sarcoma⟩

venereal disease *n* : a contagious disease that is typically acquired in sexual intercourse ⟨cloacitis of fowls is a *venereal disease*⟩ — compare CHANCROID, GONORRHEA, GRANULOMA INGUINALE, LYMPHOGRANULOMA, SYPHILIS

venereal wart *n* : CONDYLOMA

ve·ne·re·an \-rēən\ *adj* [L *venereus* venerean (fr. *Vener-*, *Venus*, Roman goddess of love, 2d planet from the sun — fr. *vener-*, *venus* love, sexual desire — + *-eus* -eous) + E *-an*] **1** : of or relating to the ancient goddess Venus or to the planet Venus : VENUSIAN ⟨the strange ~ landscape⟩ **2** *obs* : VENEREAL

ve·ne·re·ol·o·gist \vəˌnirēˈäləjəst\ *n* -s [*venereology* + *-ist*] : a physician specializing in venereal diseases

ve·ne·re·ol·o·gy \-jē\ *or* **ven·er·ol·o·gy** \ˌvenəˈräləjē\ *n* -ES [*venereology* ISV *venereal* + *-o-* + *-logy*; *venerology* ISV *venereal* (fr. ML *veneralis*, fr. L *vener-*, *venus* love, sexual desire + *-alis* -al) + *-o-* + *-logy*] : a branch of medical science concerned with venereal diseases

ve·ne·re·ous \vəˈnirēəs\ *adj* [L *venereus*] : VENEREAL; *esp* : LASCIVIOUS

ven·er·er \ˈvenərə(r)\ *n* -s [¹*venery* + *-er*] : HUNTER 1

veneres *pl of* VENUS

¹venerian *adj* [ME *venerien*, fr. MF, fr. L *venerius*, *venereus* venerean + MF *-en* -an] *obs* : VENEREAN

²ve·ne·ri·an \vəˈnirēən\ *n* -s *usu cap* [L *Vener-*, *Venus*, 2d planet from the sun + E *-an*] : VENUSIAN 2

ve·ner·i·dae \vəˈnerəˌdē\ *n pl, cap* [NL, fr. *Vener-*, *Venus*, type genus + *-idae*] : a family of bivalve mollusks (order Eulamellibranchia) mostly having a solid equivalve shell, short siphons, and a narrow foot and sometimes a strikingly sculptured shell

ve·ner·i·form \-rəˌfȯrm\ *adj* [NL *Vener-*, *Venus* + E *-iform*] : resembling a mollusk of the family Veneridae

¹ven·ery \ˈvenərē, -ri\ *n* -ES [ME *venerie*, fr. MF, fr. *vener* to hunt (fr. L *venari*) + *-ie* -y — more at VENISON] **1** : the activity or practice of hunting esp. when developed into or carried out as a highly stylized art (as during the middle ages in Europe) or when forming a professional craft **2** : animals that are hunted : GAME; *specif* : BEASTS OF VENERY

²ven·ery \" *sometimes* ˈvēn-\ *n* -ES [ME *venerie*, fr. ML *veneria*, fr. L *vener-*, *venus* love, sexual desire, venery + *-ia* -y — more at WIN] : SEXUAL INTERCOURSE, COITUS; *often* : pursuit of or indulgence in sexual pleasures

ven·e·sect \ˈvenəˌsekt, ˌ==ˈ=\ *vt* -ED/-ING/-S [back-formation fr. *venesection*] : to perform venesection on

ven·e·sec·tion *or* **ven·i·sec·tion** \ˌ==ˈsekshən\ *n* [*venesection* fr. L *venae* (gen. of *vena* vein) + E *section*; *venisection* fr. *ven-* + *section*] : the operation of opening a vein for letting blood : PHLEBOTOMY

ven·e·ti \ˈvenəˌtī\ *also* **ven·e·tes** \-əˌtēz\ *n pl, usu cap* [L *Veneti*] **1** : an ancient people in Gaul conquered by Caesar 56 B.C. **2** : an ancient people in northeastern Italy allied politically to the Romans

¹ve·ne·tian \vəˈnēshən *sometimes* -nish-\ *n* -s [alter. (influenced by L *Venetia*) of ME *venicien*, fr. MF, fr. ML *venetianus*, fr. *Venetia* Venice, city in northeastern Italy (fr. L, land of the Veneti in northern Italy) + L *-anus* -an] **1** *cap* **a** : a native or resident of Venice **b** : the Italian dialect of Venice **2** *or* **venetian cloth** [F *vénitienne*, fr. fem. of *vénitien* native of Venice, fr. MF *venicien*] **a** : a fine worsted fabric used esp. for suits, coats, or dresses and made in twill or satin weave with a napped or clear surface and a lustrous finish **b** : a lustrous sateen used esp. for linings **3** : VENETIAN BLIND

²venetian \"\ *adj, usu cap* [ML *venetianus*, fr. *Venetia* Venice + L *-anus* -an] : of or relating to Venice in Italy : of the kind or style typical of Venice

venetian arch *n, usu cap V* : a usu. pointed arch with a band wider at the peak than at the spring

venetian ball *n, usu cap V* : a ball of glass made decorative by colored patterns or by objects enclosed within its mass and used esp. as a toy or paperweight

venetian blind *n, sometimes cap V* : a blind (as for a window) made of numerous horizontal slats suspended one above another so that they may be set simultaneously at one of several angles permitting various degrees of overlapping or may be drawn together and raised

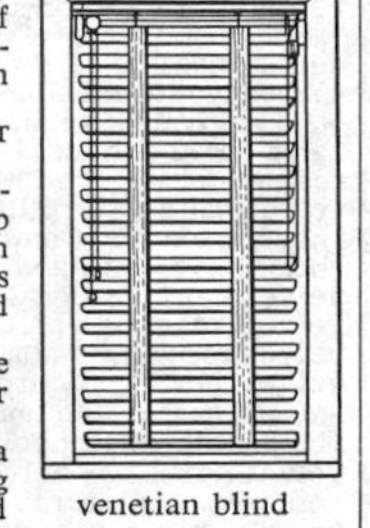

venetian blind

venetian blue *n, often cap V* : COBALT BLUE 2

venetian carpet *n, usu cap V* : an inexpensive carpet having a worsted warp which conceals the weft and a pattern commonly made up of simple stripes and used esp. formerly for passages and stairs

venetian chalk *n, usu cap V* : a white compact talc or steatite used esp. for marking on cloth

venetian dentil *n, usu cap V* : one of a series of cubical projections alternating with splayed surfaces that may be formed along the edge of a projecting band by cutting bevels at intervals to produce notches with the dentils between; *also* : the ornament or ornamentation so produced

venetian door *n, sometimes cap V* : a door with sidelights like those of a Palladian window

ve·ne·tianed \-nd\ *adj, sometimes cap* : having or furnished with venetian blinds

venetian glass *n, often cap V* **1** : a dainty delicate and artistic glassware made at Murano near Venice **2** : a decorative glass made by the combination of pieces of glass of different colors fused together and wrought into various ornamental patterns

venetian green *n, often cap V* : a moderate bluish green that is greener and darker than porcelain green and greener and duller than sea blue

venetian lake *n, often cap V* : CARMINE 2

venetian pearl *n, often cap V* : an imitation pearl made of solid glass

venetian pink *n, often cap V* : BLOSSOM 5

venetian point *n, often cap V* : needlepoint lace (as raised point or rose point) of Venetian origin

venetian red *n* **1** *usu cap V* **a** : an earthy hematite used as a pigment **b** : a synthetic iron oxide pigment that is made usu. by calcining copperas with lime and consists essentially of ferric oxide and calcium sulfate — compare INDIAN RED 1 **2** *often cap V* **a** : a strong reddish brown that is yellower and slightly lighter than Indian red and yellower, stronger, and very slightly darker than Morocco red — called also *Siena*, *Sierra* **b** : a moderate reddish brown that is yellower and deeper than mahogany (sense 5)

venetian rose *n, often cap V* : a moderate to deep red that is bluer than cadmium purple or burnt carmine

venetian scarlet *n, often cap V* : SCARLET 2b

venetian soap *n, usu cap V* : a soap made from olive oil — compare CASTILE

venetian sumac *n, usu cap V* : SMOKE TREE 1a

venetian swell *n, often cap V* : a swell organ with blinds patterned on venetian blinds closing the swell box

venetian turpentine *n, usu cap V* : VENICE TURPENTINE

venetian white *n, usu cap V* : a pigment consisting of a mixture of white lead and barium sulfate usu. in equal parts

venetian window *n, sometimes cap V* : PALLADIAN WINDOW

venetian yellow *n, often cap V* : AMBER YELLOW

¹ve·net·ic \vəˈned·|ik, -et|, |ēk\ *adj, often cap* [L *veneticus*, fr. *Veneti* + L *-icus* -ic] : of or relating to the ancient Veneti of Italy or their language

²venetic \"\ *n* -s *usu cap* : the Italic language of the Venetic people known from a small body of inscriptions and formerly classified as Illyrian

ve·neur *R* vəˈnər, + *vowel* -ˈnər·; *–R* -ˈnə̄, + *vowel in a word following without pause* -ˈnər· *or* -ˈnə̄ *also* -ˈnər\ *n* -s [MF, fr. OF, hunter, fr. L *venator*, fr. *venatus* (past part. of *venari* to hunt) + *-or* — more at VENISON] : a person acting as superintendent of the chase and esp. of hounds in French medieval venery and being an important officer of the royal household

ven·e·zu·e·la \ˌvenəz(ə)ˈwālə, -wēlə\ *adj, usu cap* [fr. *Venezuela*, republic of So. America] : of or from Venezuela : of the kind or style prevalent in Venezuela : VENEZUELAN

venezuela grass *n, usu cap V* : MOLASSES GRASS

¹ven·e·zu·e·lan \ˌvenəz(ə)ˈwālən, -wēl-\ *adj, usu cap* [*Venezuela* + E *-an*] : of or relating to Venezuela or its people : VENEZUELA

²venezuelan \"\ *n* -s *cap* : a native or inhabitant of Venezuela

venge \ˈvenj\ *vb* -ED/-ING/-S [ME *vengen*, fr. OF *venger*, *vengier*] : AVENGE

venge·able *or* **veng·ible** \ˈvenjəbəl\ *adj* [*vengeable* fr. ME, fr. *vengen* to avenge + *-able*; *vengible* fr. *venge* + *-ible*] **1** *chiefly dial* **a** : able. apt, or of a kind to take vengeance **b** : MISCHIEVOUS, DESTRUCTIVE **2** *obs* : very great : TREMENDOUS, EXTRAORDINARY

ven·geance \ˈvenjən(t)s\ *n* -s [ME, fr. OF, fr. *venger*, *vengier* to avenge (fr. L *vindicare* to lay claim to, avenge) + *-ance* — more at VINDICATE] **1 a** : the taking of revenge : infliction of punishment in return for an injury or offense : retributive action ⟨to me belongeth ~ and recompense —Deut 32:35 (AV)⟩ **b** : a particular act or instance of such vengeance ⟨plagued with petty spites and ~s⟩ **2** *obs* : HARM, MISCHIEF, EVIL ⟨do no ~ to me —Shak.⟩ **3** *archaic* : a harsh or blasphemous utterance : CURSE, OATH, IMPRECATION ⟨a ~ on't —Shak.⟩ — usu. used with *with* — **with a vengeance** *adv* (*or adj*) **1** : in a markedly violent, forceful, or urgent manner ⟨the wind blew *with a vengeance*⟩ ⟨finally beat him *with a vengeance*⟩ **2** : in an abundant or excessive amount or to such a degree ⟨leading a double life *with a vengeance* —John McCarten⟩ ⟨this was understatement *with a vengeance*⟩

ven·geant \ˈvenjənt\ *adj* [ME *vengaunt*, fr. MF *vengant*, pres. part. of *venger* to avenge] : AVENGING

venge·ful \ˈvenjfəl\ *adj* [obs. E *venge* revenge (fr. E *venge*, v.) + E *-ful*] : REVENGEFUL: as **a** : seeking to avenge **b** : serving to gain vengeance **c** : caused by the desire to gain vengeance : inspired by desire to avenge **syn** see VINDICTIVE

venge·ful·ly \-fəlē\ *adv* : in a vengeful manner : so as to be vengeful : REVENGEFULLY

venge·ful·ness *n* -ES : the quality or state of being vengeful

veng·er \ˈvenjə(r)\ *n* -s [ME, modif. (influenced by *-er*) of MF *vengeor*, *vengeur*, fr. *venger* to avenge + *-eor*, *-eur* -or] : AVENGER

v–engine *cap V, also* **vee engine** \ˈvē-\ *n* : an internal-combustion engine the cylinders of which are arranged in two banks forming an acute angle or a 90-degree angle

veni- — see VEN-

ve·nia ae·ta·tis \ˈvēnēəēˈtād·əs\ *n* [L, lit., privilege of age] : the privilege of age sometimes granted a minor under Roman or civil law, entitling him to the rights and liabilities of a person of full age, and resembling emancipation in modern law

ve·nial \ˈvēnēəl, -nyəl\ *adj* [ME, fr. OF, fr. LL *venialis*, fr. L *venia* indulgence, grace, privilege, pardon + *-alis* -al; akin to L *venus* love — more at WIN] **1 a** : of a kind that can be forgiven or remitted : not heinous nor damning — see VENIAL SIN **b** : meriting no particular censure or notice : minor or trivial in comparison with the whole in question : EXCUSABLE, INSIGNIFICANT ⟨the faults of this book . . . are few and ~ —Dudley Fitts⟩ ⟨the fastidious could carp at many minor slips . . . but they seem fairly ~ —R.H.Bowers⟩ **2** *obs* : of a kind to be permitted : ALLOWABLE, UNOBJECTIONABLE — **ve·nial·ly** \-əlē, -li\ *adv* — **ve·nial·ness** *n* -ES

venial sin *n* : a slight offense against divine law in less important matters of Roman Catholic belief or an offense in grave matters committed without reflection or full consent of the will — contrasted with *mortal sin*

¹ven·ice \ˈvenəs\ *adj, usu cap* [fr. *Venice*, Italy] : of or from the city of Venice, Italy : of the kind or style prevalent in Venice : VENETIAN

²venice \"\ *or* **venice blue** *n* -s *often cap V* : a light bluish green that is bluer and duller than Venice green or average turquoise green and greener and deeper than average aqua green (sense 1)

venice green *n, often cap V* : a light bluish green that is greener and deeper than average aqua green (sense 1), deeper and slightly bluer than robin's-egg blue (sense 2), and greener, stronger, and slightly darker than average turquoise green

venice red *n, often cap V* : BOLE 3

venice treacle *n, usu cap V* : a long-disused universal antidote or cure-all : THERIACA 1

venice turpentine *n, usu cap V* **1** : a yellowish or yellowish green viscous oleoresin from the European larch (*Larix decidua*) used chiefly for lithographic work, in sealing wax, and in varnishes — called also *larch turpentine*, *Venetian turpentine* **2** : a mixture of rosin and turpentine oil — called also *artificial Venice turpentine*

ve·nid·i·um \vəˈnidēəm\ *n* [NL, fr. *ven-* + *-idium*; prob. fr. the veined achenes] **1** *cap* : a genus of southern African annual or perennial tomentose herbs (family Compositae) that are used as ornamentals and have solitary chiefly yellow or creamy flower heads with involucral bracts in several rows **2** -s : any plant of the genus *Venidium*

ven·in \ˈvenən\ *also* **ven·ene** \ˈveˌnēn\ *n* -s [*venin* fr. ¹*venom* + *-in*; *venene* fr. L *venenum* poison] : any of various toxic substances in snake venom

veni·puncture *also* **vene·puncture** \ˈvenə, ˈvēnə, ˈvānə+ˌ-\ *n* [*venipuncture* fr. *ven-* + *puncture*; *venepuncture* fr. *vene-* (as in *venesection*) + *puncture*] : surgical puncture of a vein usu. with a hypodermic needle for the purpose of withdrawing blood or for intravenous injection of medication

ve·nire \vəˈnīrē, -nirē\ *n* -s [short for *venire facias*, fr. ME, fr. ML, you should cause to come, fr. L *venire* to come + *facias* you should cause, should make, 2nd pers. sing. pres. subj. of *facere* to make, do, cause; fr. the words in the writ — more at COME, DO] **1** *or* **venire fa·ci·as** \-ˈfāshēˌas\ **a** : a judicial writ directed to a sheriff and requiring him to cause an indicated number of qualified persons to appear in court at a specified time for service as jurors **b** : a writ under English law that is a summons to a person indicted on a penal statute to appear in court **2** : an entire panel which is drawn for jury duty and from which a jury is to be selected

venire facias de novo *also* **venire de novo** *n* [*venire facias de novo* fr. NL, lit., you cause to come anew; *venire de novo* fr. NL, lit., to come anew] : a new writ of venire issued to summon a jury anew on some irregularity or defect in the proceeding under the first venire; *also* : an order granting a new trial for any reason

venire·man \-ˈ==mən\ *n, pl* **veniremen** [*venire* + *man*] : a member of a venire : JUROR

venisection *var of* VENESECTION

ve·nise lace \vəˈnēs, ˈvenəs-\ *also* **venise** *n* -s *usu cap V* [*venise* fr. F, fr. *Venise* Venice, fr. It *Venezia*, fr. L *Venetia*] **1** : VENETIAN POINT **2** : a machine-made imitation of Venetian point made by the burnt-out process

ven·i·son \ˈvenəsən, -əzən *chiefly Brit* -nzən\ *n, pl* **venisons** *also* **venison** *often attrib* [ME *venison*, *veneison*, fr. OF *veneison*, fr. L *venation-*, *venatio* hunt, chase, quarry, prey, fr. *venatus* (past part. of *venari* to hunt, pursue) + *-ion-*, *-io* -ion; akin to Skt *vanati* he loves, desires — more at WIN] **1 a** : the edible flesh of a wild mammal or sometimes bird or one taken by hunting (as in the chase); *esp* : the edible flesh of a beast of venery **b** : the flesh of a deer ⟨elk ~⟩ **2 a** *archaic* : a game animal (as a beast of chase or beast of venery) **b** : a mammal of the family Cervidae : DEER ⟨bought ~ skins to make gloves of⟩

venison bird *or* **venison hawk** *n* : CANADA JAY

venn \ˈven\ *dial var of* FEN

venn diagram \ˈven-\ *or* **venn's diagram** *n, usu cap V* [after John *Venn* †1923 Eng. logician] : a graphic method employing circles or ellipses to represent relations in logic between and operations on classes and the terms of propositions by the inclusion, exclusion, or intersection of these figures and by the use of shading to indicate empty areas, crosses for those that are not empty, and blank spaces for those that may be either

ven·nel \ˈvenᵊl\ *n* -s [ME, fr. MF *vanelle*, *venelle*, fr. ML *venella*, fr. L *vena* vein, duct + *-ella*] **1** *chiefly Scot* : a narrow urban passage (as a lane or alley) **2** *dial Brit* : GUTTER, SEWER

veno- —see VEN-

veno·clysis \ˈvēnə, ˌvenə+\ *n* [NL, fr. *ven-* + *clysis*] : clysis into a vein

veno·gram \ˈ==ˌgram\ *n* [ISV *ven-* + *-gram*] : a roentgenogram that is made after the injection of an opaque substance into a vein

veno·graph·ic \ˌ==ˈgrafik\ *adj* : of or relating to venography or a venogram

ve·nog·ra·phy \vēˈnägrəfē, vəˈ-\ *n* -ES [ISV *ven-* + *-graphy*] : roentgenography of a vein after the injection of an opaque substance

¹ven·om \ˈvenəm\ *n* -s [ME *venom*, *venum*, *venim*, fr. OF *venim*, fr. (assumed) VL *venimen*, alter. of L *venenum* drug, poison, magic potion, charm; akin to L *venus* love, sexual desire — more at WIN] **1** : poisonous matter normally secreted by some animals (as snakes, scorpions, or bees) used chiefly in the taking of prey and in defense and communicated chiefly by biting or stinging; *broadly* : material that is poisonous : matter fatal or injurious to life **2** : something that embitters or blights the mind or spirit as a poison blights the body: as **a** : a spiteful malicious feeling or state of mind : MALIGNITY ⟨their belief in ~ and jealousy behind the war

—F.L.Paxson⟩ **b** : a venomous utterance ⟨spouting ~ —Kenneth Roberts⟩ **syn** see POISON

²**venom** \"\ *vb* -ED/-ING/-S [ME *venomen, venimen,* fr. MF *venimer,* fr. OF, fr. *venim* venom] *vt* **1** : to inject or injure with venom : CORRUPT, POISON **2** *archaic* : to make venomous by or as if by application of a venom ~ *vi, obs* : to become envenomed

ven·om·ness *n* -ES : the quality or state of being venomous

ven·o·mo·salivary \ˌvenəmō+\ *adj* [¹*venom* + *-o-* + *salivary*] **1** : of or relating to venom and saliva **2** *of a salivary gland* : modified to secrete venom instead of saliva

ven·om·ous \ˈvenəməs\ *adj* [ME *venimous,* fr. OF *venimos, venimeux,* fr. *venim* venom + *-os, -eux* -ous] **1 a** : full of venom : noxious to animal life by means of venom ⟨a ~ sting⟩; *broadly* : POISONOUS **b** : VIRULENT, BANEFUL ⟨a ~ doctrine⟩ **2** : characterized by or having the nature of venom; *often* : MISCHIEVOUS, MALIGNANT, SPITEFUL ⟨a ~ writer⟩ ⟨~ criticism⟩ **3** : having a gland for the secretion of venom : able to inflict a poisoned bite, sting, or wound **4** : tipped with or dipped in poison : POISONED, ENVENOMED ⟨~ darts⟩ — **ven·om·ous·ly** *adv* — **ven·om·ous·ness** *n* -ES

ven·om·some \ˈ==səm\ *adj* [¹*venom* + *-some*] *dial Eng* : VENOMOUS

ve·no·pressor \ˌvēnə, ˌvenə+\ *adj* [*ven-* + *pressor*] : of, relating to, or controlling venous blood pressure

ve·nose \ˈvēˌnōs\ *adj* [L *venosus*] : VENOUS; *esp* : having numerous or conspicuous veins ⟨insects with ~ wings⟩

ve·nos·i·ty \vəˈnäsəd·ē, vē-\ *n* -ES : the quality or state of being venous

ve·nos·ta·sis \vēˈnästəsəs, vəˈ-\ *n* [NL, fr. *ven-* + *-stasis*] : an abnormal slowing or stoppage of the flow of blood in a vein

ve·nous \ˈvēnəs\ *adj* [L *venosus,* fr. *vena* vein + *-osus* -ose] **1 a** : full of or characterized by veins : VEINY, VEINED ⟨a ~ rock⟩ **b** : made up of or carried on by veins ⟨the ~ circulation⟩ ⟨an open ~ system⟩ **2** : of, relating to, or performing the functions of a vein ⟨a ~ inflammation⟩ ⟨~ arteries⟩ **3** *of blood* : having passed through the capillaries and given up oxygen for the tissues and become charged with carbon dioxide and ready to pass through the respiratory organs to release its carbon dioxide and renew its oxygen supply : dark red from reduced hemoglobin : UNOXYGENATED — compare ARTERIAL — **ve·nous·ly** *adv*

venous sinus *n* **1 a** : a large vein or passage (as in the dura mater) for venous blood **b** : SINUS VENOSUS **2** : one of the ill-defined spaces among the tissues of many invertebrates that is functionally equivalent to a vertebrate vein

¹**vent** \ˈvent\ *vb* -ED/-ING/-S [ME *venten,* prob. fr. MF *eventer, esventer,* to blow out, fr. *e-, es-* out, forth (fr. L *ex-* ¹ex-) + *venter* to blow, fr. (assumed) VL *ventare* to blow, be windy, fr. L *ventus* wind — more at WIND] *vt* **1** : to provide with an opening for the discharge of gases or the relief of pressure ⟨~ a plumbing system⟩ : equip with a vent or venting **2 a** : to serve as a vent for ⟨tall chimneys ~*ed* the smoke⟩ **b** (1) : to cause to flow or drain away : cast out : EXPEL ⟨~*ing* off the excess fluid through a series of conduits⟩ (2) *archaic* : to eject from the body : EVACUATE **c** (1) : to give expression to : release by expressing : LOOSE ⟨~*ed* his fury on the hapless dog⟩ (2) : to give utterance to : make public ⟨~*ing* his grievance before them all⟩ **3** : to relieve by venting ⟨some could ~ themselves in grief⟩ ⟨a valve to ~ the pressure in the boiler⟩ ~ *vi* **1** : to issue forth by or as if by a vent : go away or out through a vent **2** : to come to the surface to breathe — used esp. of an otter **3 a** : to have a vent (as for the escape of gases) ⟨an old-fashioned toilet ~*ing* through the chimney⟩ **b** *chiefly Scot* : to have draft : DRAW ⟨the chimney ~*s* well⟩ **syn** see EMIT, EXPRESS

²**vent** \"\ *n* -S [ME *vente,* alter. (prob. influenced by MF *vent* wind, fr. L *ventus*) of *fente, fent,* fr. MF *fente* slit, fissure, fr. *fendre* to split, fr. L *findere* — more at BITE] : a slit in a garment; *specif* : an opening in the lower part of a seam (as of a jacket, coat, skirt, or sleeve)

³**vent** \"\ *vb* [ME *venten,* fr. MF *vente* sale — more at ⁵VENT] *archaic* : VEND, SELL

⁴**vent** \"\ *n* -S *often attrib* [partly fr. ¹*vent* & partly fr. MF *event, esvent* opening, vent, fr. *eventer, esventer* to blow out, vent — more at ¹VENT] **1** *obs* : the act or fact of emitting something (as words) **2 a** : an opportunity or way of escape or passage : OUTLET ⟨the gases found ~ through fissures in the rock⟩ ⟨his writing gives ~ to his unused talents⟩ **b** : an opening or hole for the escape or passage of something (as of a gas or liquid) or for the relief of pressure within something (as a boiler) ⟨the ~ of a cask⟩ ⟨a hot-water system with a relief tank as ~⟩: as (1) : the external opening of the rectum or cloaca : ANUS — used esp. of a nonmammalian vertebrate (as a fish or bird) (2) : PIPE 3b(3), FUMAROLE (3) : an opening at the breech of a gun through which fire is communicated to the powder (as a hole from the top of the breech to the chamber of a muzzle-loading gun or a hole in the axis of the breechblock of a breech-loading gun) (4) *chiefly Scot* : CHIMNEY, FLUE (5) : an opening (as in a room or building) for ventilation esp. when not such as would ordinarily be classed as a window or door ⟨a poultry house with adjustable ~*s* under the eaves⟩ **3** : the coming of an otter to the surface of the water in order to breathe

⁵**vent** \ˈvent\ *n* -S [MF *vente,* fr. (assumed) VL *vendita,* fr. fem. of L *venditus,* past part. of *vendere* to sell — more at VEND] *archaic* : SALE: as **a** : the act of selling **b** : opportunity to sell : MARKET

⁶**vent** *or* **vent brand** \"\ *n* -S [Sp *venta* sale, inn, fr. (assumed) VL *vendita* sale] *West* : a brand indicating the sale of the animal branded that sometimes takes the form of a special mark but is commonly a bar across the seller's brand

⁷**vent** \"\ *vt* -ED/-ING/-S *West* : to cancel (a brand) by a vent mark

vent *abbr* ventilate; ventilating; ventilation; ventilator

ven·ta \ˈventə\ *n* -S [Sp] : a rural inn esp. in a Spanish-speaking area

vent·age \ˈventij\ *n* -S [⁴*vent* + *-age*] **1** : a small hole (as a flute stop) : VENT **2** : arrangement for or means of venting something

ven·tail \ˈvenˌtāl\ *n* -S [ME, fr. MF *ventaille* sluice, ventail, fr. *vent* wind, air] : the lower movable front of a medieval helmet designed for the admission of air and usu. restricted to the part below the visor but sometimes including the visor

vent disease *n* : RABBIT SYPHILIS

vent drill *or* **vent gimlet** *n* : an instrument for freeing the vent of a cannon from obstructions — called also *vent punch*

vented *past of* VENT

¹**ven·ter** \ˈventə(r)\ *n* -S [AF, fr. L, abdomen, womb; akin to L *vensica, vesica* bladder, OHG *wanast, wenist* paunch, Icel *vinstr* omasum, Skt *vasti* bladder] **1** : a wife or mother that is a source of offspring ⟨had a son by one ~ and two daughters by another⟩ ⟨children of the same ~⟩ **2** : an anatomical structure that is protuberant and often hollow: as **a** : ABDOMEN; *also* : a large bodily cavity (as in the head, thorax, or abdomen) containing organs **b** : BELLY 5c ⟨a muscle with a double ~⟩ **c** : the undersurface of the abdomen of an arthropod **d** : a broad shallow concavity of a bone ⟨the ~ of the scapula⟩ **e** : the outer and convex part of the shell of a curved or coiled cephalopod or gastropod **f** : the swollen basal portion of an archegonium in which the egg of a vascular cryptogam is developed

²**vent·er** \ˈventə(r)\ *n* -S [¹*vent* + *-er*] : one that vents; *esp* : one that gives utterance or publicity to personal ideas, doctrines, or grievances

vent feather *n* : a crissal feather

vent gleet *n* : CLOACITIS

venthole \ˈ=ˌ=\ *n* [⁴*vent* + *hole*] : an opening that is a vent or is used for venting ⟨an otter's ~ in the ice⟩

venti- *or* **vento-** *comb form* [L *ventus* wind + E *-i-* or *-o-*] : wind ⟨*venti*fact⟩

ven·ti·duct \ˈventəˌdəkt\ *n* [*venti-* + *-duct* (as in *aqueduct*)] : a passage for wind or air (as for ventilating an apartment)

ven·ti·fact \ˈ=əˌfakt\ *n* [*venti-* + *-fact* (as in *artifact*)] : a stone worn, polished, or faceted by windblown sand — called also *glyptolith, rillstone*

ven·til \ˈventᵊl\ *n* -S [G, prob. fr. F *ventelle* small valve, sluice, fr. MF *ventaille* sluice — more at VENTAIL] : a valve in various wind musical instruments

ven·tila·gin \venˈtiləjən; ˌventᵊlˈāj-, -ᵊlˈaj-\ *n* -S [ISV *ventilag-* (fr. NL *Ventilago* — genus name of *Ventilago maderaspatana* —, irreg. fr. L *ventulus* + *agere* to drive) + *-in* — more at AGENT] : a reddish brown resinous coloring matter $C_{15}H_{14}O_6$ derived from anthraquinone and obtained from the root bark of an East Indian woody vine (*Ventilago maderaspatana*) of the family Rhamnaceae

ven·ti·late \ˈventᵊlˌāt, *usu* -ād·+V\ *vb* -ED/-ING/-S [LL *ventilatus,* past part. of *ventilare* to ventilate, fr. L, to toss, brandish in the air, winnow, fan, fr. *ventulus* slight wind, breeze, fr. *ventus* wind + *-ulus* — more at WIND] *vt* **1 a** : to open for consideration and discussion : examine, discuss, or investigate freely, fully, and usu. publicly ⟨*ventilating* family quarrels before strangers⟩ **b** : to make public or known to others : give expression to : UTTER ⟨continued to ~ his complaints⟩ **2 a** *archaic* : to free (as grain) from chaff by fanning or winnowing **b** *obs* : to enliven (as a fire) by or as if by blowing or fanning **c** *archaic* : to cause (air) to move as by fanning or blowing **3** : to expose to air and esp. to a current of fresh air (as for cooling, purifying, or refreshing): as **a** : to expose (blood) to air (as in a lung or gill) to permit uptake of oxygen and release of carbon dioxide : OXYGENATE, AERATE **b** : to expose (as grain or hay) to a current of air usu. to dry or cure **4 a** *of a current of air* : to pass or circulate through so as to freshen and to dissipate vitiated or contaminated air **b** : to cause fresh air to circulate through and vitiated or contaminated air to be simultaneously withdrawn from (as a room or mine) ⟨powerful blowers ~ the long passages⟩ **5 a** : to plan the ventilation of or provide with vents or other openings through which air or other gas may pass or circulate ⟨an attic *ventilated* with louvers under the eaves⟩ ⟨diagrams showing how to ~ a founder's mold⟩ **b** : to induce ventilation of by manipulation of facilities provided ⟨threw open the windows and *ventilated* the long-closed house⟩ **c** : to make (as a wig) by knotting individual hairs to a lace net foundation **d** : to provide an opening in (a burning structure) to permit escape of smoke and heat ~ *vi* : to undergo ventilation : become ventilated ⟨surfacing at night to recharge her batteries and ~ —J.P.Baxter b.1893⟩ **syn** see EXPRESS

ventilated car *n* : a boxcar having openings at the top, sides, and often ends for ventilation

ventilated rib *n* : a shotgun rib that is supported over the barrel by a series of fastenings to provide better cooling as well as a straight sighting plane

ventilating *adj* : serving to ventilate : used in the provision or production of ventilation ⟨~ skylights⟩ ⟨~ devices⟩

ventilating brick *n* : a cored-out brick providing an air passage (as for ventilation)

ventilating jack *n* : a sheet-metal hood placed over the inlet of a ventilating pipe to cause the induction of an increased air volume into the pipe

ventilating millstone *n* : a millstone having a device for inducing a strong current of air through its grooves

ven·ti·la·tion \ˌventᵊlˈāshən\ *n* -S [ME *ventulacioun,* modif. (influenced by L *ventulus* breeze) of L *ventilation-, ventilatio,* fr. *ventilatus* (past part. of *ventilare* to brandish in the air) + *-ion-, -io* -ion] **1** *obs* : a current of air (as a breeze) **2** : an act or instance of ventilating: as **a** *archaic* : an act or action of fanning or blowing; *esp* : the winnowing of grain **b** : a movement and esp. circulation of air (as in an enclosed space) ⟨a mine with poor ~⟩; *often* : the circulation and exchange of gases in the lungs that is basic to respiration **c** (1) : a making public or openly uttering : VENT ⟨his ~ of these views alienated popular sympathy⟩ (2) : free and open discussion (as of a matter of public interest) ⟨such a proposal deserves thorough ~⟩ (3) : verbal expression of mental or emotional conflicts leading to reduction of inner tensions — compare CATHARSIS 3a **3** : provision of facilities or the facilities available to ensure an adequate or a particular sort of circulation (as of air) ⟨a cave with good natural ~⟩ ⟨planned a complex ~ system of blowers and ducts⟩ ⟨the ~ broke down⟩

ven·ti·la·tive \ˈ==ˌād·iv\ *adj* : of or relating to ventilation : adapted to secure ventilation

ven·ti·la·tor \-ˌād·ə(r)\ *n* -S : one that ventilates: as **a** : a contrivance (as a shutter device forming an adjustable aperture or a machine causing movement of air) used for introducing fresh air or expelling foul or stagnant air to or from an enclosed space (as a building) **b** : one responsible for ventilating some place

ven·ti·la·to·ry \-əˌtōrē, -tȯrē, -ri\ *adj* **1** : provided with ventilation **2** : of, relating to, or involved in pulmonary ventilation ⟨the ~ response to carbon dioxide⟩ ⟨~ efficiency⟩ ⟨~ thoracic pressure changes⟩

Ven·tile \ˈventᵊl, -nˌtīl\ *trademark* — used for woven textile piece goods made of cotton

venting *pres part of* VENT

vent·less \ˈventləs\ *adj* [⁴*vent* + *-less*] : having no vent

vento- — see VENTI-

ven·tom·e·ter \venˈtämәd·ə(r)\ *n* [*venti-* + *-meter*] : an instrument for indicating the velocity of the wind esp. as designed for use on target ranges — compare ANEMOMETER

ven·tose \ˈvenˌtōs, =ˈ=\ *adj* [L *ventosus,* fr. *ventus* wind + *-osus* -ose — more at WIND] *archaic* : FLATULENT, WINDY

ven·tos·i·ty \venˈtäsəd·ē\ *n* -ES [ME *ventosite,* fr. MF *ventosité,* fr. LL *ventositat-, ventositas,* fr. L *ventosus* windy, flatulent + *-itat-, -itas* -ity] **1** *obs* : flatulence or its cause **2** : pompous inflated conceit or boasting

vent punch *n* : VENT DRILL

ventr- *or* **ventri-** *or* **ventro-** *comb form* [F, fr. L *ventr-, venter* — more at VENTER] **1** : abdomen : ventral ⟨*ventr*ic⟩ ⟨*ventro*tomy⟩ ⟨*ventri*columna⟩ **2** : ventral and ⟨*ventro*dorsal⟩ **3** : ventricose : round ⟨*ventri*pyramid⟩

ven·trad \ˈvenˌtrad\ *adv* [*ventr-* + *-ad*] : toward the ventral side : VENTRALLY ⟨tracing the nerve ~⟩

¹**ven·tral** \ˈventrəl\ *adj* [F, fr. L *ventralis,* fr. *ventr-, venter* + *-alis* -al] **1** : of or relating to the belly : ABDOMINAL; *usu* : belonging to or situated near or on the anterior or lower surface of an animal or one of its parts that is opposite the back — opposed to DORSAL ⟨a ~ scale of a snake⟩ ⟨the liver is somewhat ~ in position⟩ ⟨the ~ aspect of the body⟩ **2 a** : AXIAL **b** : belonging to or located on the lower surface usu. of a creeping dorsiventral structure (as a thallus)

²**ventral** \"\ *n* -S : a ventral part (as a scale or plate); *esp* : VENTRAL FIN

ventral canal cell *n* [trans. of G *bauchkanalzelle*] : a small cell that is cut off from the central cell of an archegonium just below the neck and above the oosphere

ventral column *n* : either of a pair of gray columns situated one on each side in the ventral aspect of the spinal column and containing neurons that give rise to motor fibers of the ventral roots of spinal nerves

ventral diaphragm *n* : a muscular membrane present in the ventral part of the abdomen of some insects

ventral fin *n* **1 a** : either of the pair of fins of a fish that correspond to the hind limbs of quadrupeds : PELVIC FIN **b** : ANAL FIN **2** : a fixed stabilizing surface attached to the rear undersurface of an airplane

ven·tral·ly \ˈven·trəlē, -li\ *adv* : in a ventral direction or position ⟨attached ~ to the mesentery⟩ — see VENTRAD

ventral nerve cord *n* : a chain of connected segmental ganglia lying against the body wall in an arthropod or annelid

ventral plate *n* : a thickening of the blastoderm in an early embryo of an insect or other arthropod on the underside of the egg that is destined to develop into the body of the embryo proper

ventral root *n* : the one of the two roots of a spinal nerve that passes ventrally from the spinal cord and consists of motor fibers — compare DORSAL ROOT

ventral segment *n* : the portion of a vibrating medium between two successive nodes

ventral sinus *n* : a cavity of the abdomen of an insect between the ventral diaphragm and the ventral body wall

ventral tube *n* : COLLOPHORE

ventral·ward \ˈ==wə(r)d\ *also* **ventral·wards** \-dz\ *adv* [¹*ventral* + *-ward, -wards*] : toward the ventral aspect or surface

ven·tri·cle \ˈven·trəkəl, -rēk-\ *n* -S [ME, fr. L *ventriculus* stomach, ventricle of the heart, dim. of *venter* abdomen — more at VENTER] : a cavity of a bodily part or organ: as **a** : a chamber or one of the chambers of the heart which receives blood from a corresponding atrium and from which blood is forced into the arteries **b** : one of the system of communicating cavities in the brain that are continuous with the central canal of the spinal cord, that like it are derived from the medullary canal of the embryo, that are lined with an epithelial ependyma, and that contain a serous fluid **c** : a fossa or pouch on each side of the larynx between the false vocal cords above and the true vocal cords below — called also *ventricle of Morgagni* **d** : STOMACH, VENTRICULUS **e** *obs* : BELLY, WOMB

ven·tri·columna \ˌven·trə+\ *n* [NL, fr. *ventr-* + *columna*] : VENTRAL COLUMN — **ven·tri·columnar** \"+\ *adj*

ven·tri·cornu \"+\ *n* [NL, fr. *ventr-* + *cornu*] : VENTRAL COLUMN

ven·tri·cose \ˈven·trəˌkōs\ *adj* [NL *ventricosus,* fr. (assumed) NL *ventricus* of the abdomen (fr. L *ventr-, venter* + *-icus* -ic) + L *-osus* -ose] : DISTENDED, INFLATED; *esp* : markedly swollen on one side

ventricose shell *n* **1** : a spiral shell having the body whorls rounded or swollen in the middle **2** : a bivalve shell in which the valves are strongly convex

ven·tri·cos·i·ty \ˌ==ˈkäsəd·ē\ *n* -ES : the quality or state of being ventricose : CONVEXITY

ven·tric·u·lar \(ˈ)venˌtrikyələ(r)\ *adj* [NL *ventricularis,* fr. L *ventriculus* stomach, ventricle + *-aris* -ar] **1 a** : of or relating to the stomach or belly : ABDOMINAL **b** : of, relating to, or constituting a ventriculus **2** : of or relating to a ventricle (as of the heart or brain)

ventricular fibrillation *n* : very rapid uncoordinated contractions of the ventricles of the heart resulting in loss of synchronization between heartbeat and pulse beat

ventricular fold *n* : FALSE VOCAL CORD

ven·tric·u·lar·is \(ˌ)venˌtrikyəˈla(a)rəs\ *n* -ES [NL, fr. *ventricularis* ventricular] : a part of the thyroarytenoideus that enters the false vocal cord on either side

ven·tric·u·lite \venˈtrikyəˌlīt\ *n* -S [NL *Ventriculites*] : a fossil sponge of *Ventriculites* or related genus — **ven·tric·u·lit·ic** \(ˈ)=ˌ==ˈlid·ik\ *adj*

ven·tric·u·li·tes \=ˌ==ˈlīd·ˌēz\ *n, cap* [NL, fr. L *ventriculus* ventricle + NL *-ites*] : a genus (the type of the family Ventriculitidae of the class Hyalospongiae) of fossil often vase-shaped or mushroom-shaped chiefly Cretaceous sponges having a latticed skeleton in which the nodes formed by the crossing of the spicular threads are perforated

ven·tric·u·lo·gram \=ˈ==ləˌgram\ *n* [ISV *ventriculo-* (fr. L *ventriculus* ventricle) + *-gram*] : an X-ray photograph of the ventricles of the brain made after withdrawing fluid from the ventricles and replacing it with air or a radiopaque substance

ven·tric·u·log·ra·phy \=ˌ==ˈlägrəfē\ *n* -ES [ISV *ventriculo-* + *-graphy*] : the act or process of making ventriculograms

ven·tric·u·lus \=ˈ==ləs\ *n, pl* **ventricu·li** \-ˌlī\ [NL, fr. L, stomach, ventricle of the heart — more at VENTRICLE] : a ventricle that functions or is viewed as functioning in digestion: as **a** : STOMACH **b** : GIZZARD 1a **c** : the digestive part of an insect's stomach usu. immediately behind the proventriculus

ven·tri·lo·qui·al \ˌven·trəˈlōkwēəl\ *adj* : of, relating to, resembling, or using ventriloquism ⟨in his place, a disembodied, ~ voice spoke for the Soviet leadership in carefully drafted ... statements —Strobe Talbott⟩ — **ven·tri·lo·qui·al·ly** \-əlē, -li\ *adv*

ven·tril·o·quism \venˈtriləˌkwizəm\ *n* -S [LL *ventriloquus* ventriloquist (fr. L *ventr-, venter* abdomen + *loqui* to speak) + E *-ism;* fr. the belief that the voice is produced in the ventriloquist's stomach — more at VENTER] : the act, art, or practice of speaking in such a manner that the voice appears to come from some source other than the vocal organs of the speaker and esp. with little or no movement of the lips so as to create the illusion that the voice may be coming from a source other than the speaker (as from a dummy whose lip movements are produced mechanically by the speaker)

ven·tril·o·quist \-ˌkwəst\ *n* -S [*ventriloquy* + *-ist*] : one who uses or is skilled in ventriloquism; *esp* : one who entertains by ventriloquism usu. through holding a wooden dummy and apparently carrying on a conversation with it

ven·tril·o·quis·tic \(ˌ)=ˌ==ˈkwistik\ *adj* **1** : of or relating to ventriloquism or ventriloquists : practicing ventriloquism **2** *of a sound* : seeming to originate at other than the actual point of origin

ven·tril·o·quize \=ˈ==ˌkwīz\ *vb* -ED/-ING/-S [*ventriloquy* + *-ize*] *vi* : to use ventriloquism ~ *vt* : to utter (as a speech or opinion) in the manner of a ventriloquist

ven·tril·o·quous \=ˈ==kwəs\ *adj* [LL *ventriloquus* + E *-ous*] : VENTRILOQUISTIC

ven·tril·o·quy \venˈtriləkwē\ *n* -ES [LL *ventriloquus* + E *-y*] : VENTRILOQUISM

ven·trip·o·tent \venˈtripəd·ənt *also* -əˈtᵊnt\ *adj* [F, fr. *ventri-* (fr. L, fr. *ventr-, venter* abdomen) + L *potent-, potens,* pres. part. of (assumed) OL *potēre* to be powerful — more at POTENT] : having a large belly; *also* : GLUTTONOUS

ven·tri·pyramid \ˌven·trə+\ *n* [*ventr-* + *pyramid*] : the pyramid of the medulla oblongata

ventro- — see VENTR-

ven·tro·lateral \ˌven·(ˌ)trō+\ *adj* [*ventr-* + *lateral*] : ventral and lateral; *usu* : situated or occurring ventrally and somewhat laterally — **ven·tro·laterally** \"+\ *adv*

ven·tro·medial \"+\ *also* **ven·tro·median** \"+\ *adj* [*ventr-* + *medial* or *median*] : ventral and medial : situated or occurring in the median ventral line — **ven·tro·medially** \"+\ *adv*

ven·tro·mesial \"+\ *adj* [*ventr-* + *mesial*] : ventral and mesial

¹**vents** *pres 3d sing of* VENT, *pl of* VENT

²**vents** \ˈvents\ *var of* FEN

vent stack *n* : a pipe placed vertically or nearly so and connected to the traps of plumbing fixtures in such a manner as to ventilate them and prevent the water seal from being siphoned out of them

vent tank *n* : a primary still used in the manufacture of natural gasoline to remove absorbed gases that are too volatile for gasoline

¹**ven·ture** \ˈvenchə(r)\ *vb* -ED/-ING/-S [ME *venteren,* by shortening & alter. fr. *aventuren* to venture — more at ADVENTURE] *vt* **1** : to expose to risk or hazard: as **a** : to lay (as oneself) open to danger **b** : to put or send on a venture esp. when involving unusual risks : gamble or speculate with : HAZARD ⟨~ a ship in the coastal trade⟩ ⟨*ventured* more than he could afford on speculative stocks⟩ **2 a** : to face or undertake the risks and dangers of : dare to encounter, undertake, or embark on : BRAVE ⟨a band of Puritans ... *ventured* in 1620 a settlement at Plymouth —Stringfellow Barr⟩ ⟨unwilling to ~ the elements in such a storm⟩ **b** *archaic* : to risk giving one's confidence to : rely on : TRUST **3** : to dare or have the courage or boldness to advance, offer, or put forward esp. when rebuff, rejection, or censure seems likely to ensue ⟨*ventured* a hint of doubt —H.J.Laski⟩ ⟨upon the irresponsible taxation he does ~ to speak plainly —G.G.Coulton⟩ ⟨I ~ to say that 5000 people were present⟩ ~ *vi* : to proceed accepting risks : go ahead with something uncertain or risky despite danger and trepidation : dare or show the courage to go ⟨explorers by sea, *venturing* uneasily northward along the shores in pygmy galleons —*Amer. Guide Series: Calif.*⟩ ⟨strikebreakers were compelled to remain in the shops for weeks before *venturing* to their homes —*Amer. Guide Series: Del.*⟩ ⟨too old to ~ on a new way of life⟩

syn HAZARD, RISK, CHANCE, ENDANGER, IMPERIL, JEOPARDIZE: VENTURE indicates an exposing to risk of losing in speculation, gambling, or other matters of chance either boldly or timorously ⟨*venture* one's capital⟩ and it may suggest a proceeding that calls for caution or an offering liable to rejection or contradiction ⟨hazardous to approach too near to the snow or *venture* beneath it —*Amer. Guide Series: N.H.*⟩ ⟨I *venture* to predict —F.D.Roosevelt⟩ HAZARD may occas. more strongly suggest utter chance, as of the turn of a card or spin of a wheel, as a determining factor, and consequently suggest more uncertainty and less calculation than VENTURE ⟨able young men have been willing to *hazard* their chances of professional advancement in order to engage in academic experiments —G.F. Whicher⟩ RISK may stress the fact of danger of loss, damage, or defeat without undue implication of reasons, motives, degrees of danger ⟨Poland did not hesitate ... to *risk* all the progress she had made —Sir Winston Churchill⟩ ⟨not *risking* a landing because of the fierce aspect of the natives —V.G.Heiser⟩ CHANCE may suggest more inclination to trust to luck and less considering or reckoning. ENDANGER, IMPERIL, and JEOPARDIZE heighten notions of exposure to danger. IMPERIL may occas. suggest exposure to greater or inseparable danger and may be preferred in figurative uses ⟨floods *endangering* the building in 1866, Fort Lyon was moved up the river —L.R.Hafen⟩ ⟨kings in Europe were sometimes shot at by passersby, there being hardly a monarch who had not been so *imperiled* —G.B. Shaw⟩ JEOPARDIZE may be somewhat stronger and imply even chances of success or failure, preservation or loss, or suggest greater imminence of danger or inexorability of decision ⟨to settle for merely another temporary respite would surely *jeopardize* the future security of all the world —H.S.Truman⟩

²**venture** \"\ *n* -s [ME, short for *aventure* adventure — more at ADVENTURE] **1** *obs* **:** FORTUNE, HAP, CONTINGENCY; *also* **:** PERIL, JEOPARDY **2 a :** an undertaking involving chance, risk, or danger **:** an undertaking of uncertain outcome or unforeseen conditions; *esp* **:** a business enterprise of speculative nature **:** SPECULATION ⟨a trading ~⟩ ⟨took a ~ in oil⟩ **b :** an act of venturing (as in speech or action) **:** venturesome conduct ⟨his ~ into honest living⟩ ⟨this ~ in plain speaking cost us dear⟩ **c :** an entire voyage (as of a trading ship) from home port to home port **3 :** something at hazard in a speculative venture (as of trade by sea) ⟨lost his first ~ in the China trade⟩; *usu* **:** the property, money, or other thing of value that is risked in a business enterprise or speculation ⟨my ~*s* are not in one bottom trusted —Shak.⟩ **4** *dial Brit* **:** an adventurous spirit **:** a willingness to take risks or run dangers **:** COURAGE ⟨what in the world wide put ~ into you that made you go face the dog —Augusta Gregory⟩ — **at a venture** *adv* **:** at hazard or random **:** without seeing the mark or foreseeing the issue

venture capital *n* **:** money invested or available for investment in stocks; *esp* **:** funds invested in stock of newer unseasoned enterprises — called also *equity capital, risk capital*

ven·tur·er \'venchərər, -ch(ə)rə\ *n* -s **:** one that ventures or puts to hazard **:** ADVENTURER; *specif* **:** a person (as a merchant) who engages in business ventures

ven·ture·some \-chə(r)səm\ *adj* **1 :** disposed to court or incur risk or danger **:** inclined to undertake hazardous ventures **:** bold or daring in new enterprises ⟨a ~ hunter⟩ ⟨a chance for ~ investors⟩ ⟨a ~ outlook on life⟩ **2 :** resembling or characteristic of a venture involving risk **:** HAZARDOUS ⟨a ~ journey in wintertime⟩ ⟨planned to do something ~⟩ **syn** see ADVENTUROUS

ven·ture·some·ly *adv* **:** in a venturesome manner **:** so as to be venturesome

ven·ture·some·ness *n* -ES **:** the quality or state of being venturesome

ven·tu·ri \ven·'tu̇rē\ *or* **venturi tube** *n* -s *sometimes cap V* [after G. B. *Venturi* †1822 Ital. physicist] **:** a short tube that is inserted in a pipeline, that has flaring ends connected by a constricted middle section forming a throat, that depends for operation upon the fact that as the velocity of flow of a fluid increases in the throat the pressure decreases, that is used for measuring the quantity of a fluid flowing, in connection with other devices for measuring airspeed, and for producing suction esp. for driving aircraft instruments by means of a branch tube joined at the throat

ven·tu·ria \ven·'t(y)u̇rēə\ *n, cap* [NL, fr. A. *Venturi*, 19th cent. Ital. botanist + NL *-ia*] **:** a genus of fungi (family Mycosphaerellaceae) having generally sunken dark-colored perithecia with a bristly apex and olive green unequally 2-celled ascospores — see APPLE SCAB, PEAR SCAB

ven·tu·rine \'venchə,rēn, -,rən\ *n* -s [F *aventurine* — more at AVENTURINE] **:** a gold powder for varnished surfaces

venturing *pres part of* VENTURE

ven·tur·ous \'vench(ə)rəs\ *adj* [short for *adventurous*] **1 :** courting or oblivious of danger **:** ready to meet risks **:** DARING, BOLD, VENTURESOME, ADVENTUROUS ⟨a ~ spirit⟩ **2 :** involving danger or risk **:** HAZARDOUS, DANGEROUS, RISKY ⟨a ~ enterprise⟩ **syn** see ADVENTUROUS

ven·tur·ous·ly *adv* **:** in a venturous manner

ven·tur·ous·ness *n* -ES **:** the quality or state of being venturous

vent wire *n* **:** a pointed wire for making vents in foundry molds

ven·ue \'ven(,)yü *also* 've(,)nü *sometimes* 'vā(-\ *n* -s [MF, fr. fem. of *venu*, past part. of *venir* to come, fr. L *venire* — more at COME] **1** *obs* **a :** a thrust, hit, or lunge in or as if in fencing **b :** an encounter, bout, or match in or as if in fencing or cudgel play **2 a** (1) **:** a place (as a county) in which alleged events from which a legal action arises take place (2) **:** the place from which the jury is drawn and in which trial is held in such an action **b :** the locale of a past or projected real or imaginary event; *esp* **:** a place designated to be the scene of a proposed gathering (as for a sports event or a political conference) **c :** the position, side, or line of argument assumed by an individual in debate or discussion **:** GROUND **3 a :** a statement forming part of a declaration at law and alleging the residence of the parties, where the injury occurred, or other information that shows the case to be brought to the proper court or authority **b :** a clause or acknowledgment in an affidavit indicating the locality of execution

ven·u·la \'venyələ\ *n* -s [L] **:** a small vein **:** VENULE

ven·u·lar \-lə(r)\ *adj* **:** of, relating to, or involving venules ⟨~ disorders⟩

ven·ule \'ven(,)yül\ *n* -s [L *venula*, dim. of *vena* vein] **:** a small vein: as **a :** one of the small branches of a vein of an insect's wing **b :** a minute vein connecting the capillary bed with the larger systemic veins

ven·u·lose \'venyə,lōs\ *or* **ven·u·lous** \-ləs\ *adj* [*venule* + *-ose* or *-ous*] **:** full of venules

ve·nus \'vēnəs\ *n* [after *Venus*, Roman goddess of love, 2d planet from the sun, fr. L *Vener-, Venus*, fr. *vener-, venus* love — more at WIN] **1** -ES *usu cap* **:** a woman felt to resemble the Roman goddess of love and beauty; *broadly* **:** a beautiful and charming woman or one who exemplifies feminine grace and charm **2** -ES *usu cap* [ME *Venus*, 2d planet from the sun, fr. L *Vener-, Venus*] **:** the lesser astrological fortune **:** a feminine temperately cold and moist nocturnal planet the mansions of which are Taurus and Libra, the exaltation 27 degrees Pisces, the depression 27 degrees Virgo, and the orb 7 degrees **3** -ES [ME *Venus*, fr. ML *Vener-, Venus*, fr. L, 2d planet from the sun] **:** COPPER **4** [NL, fr. L] **a** *cap* **:** a large genus of marine bivalve mollusks (family Veneridae) having a thick oval usu. inflated shell with often prominent concentric ridges and with the internal margins finely denticulate **b** *pl* **venuses** \-əsəz\ *also* **ven·er·es** \'venə,rēz\ **:** any mollusk of *Venus* or a related genus

venus and adonis stanza *usu cap V & 2d A* [fr. *Venus and Adonis* (1593), poem in this stanza by William Shakespeare †1616 Eng. dramatist and poet] **:** a stanza consisting of an iambic pentameter quatrain and couplet with the rhyme scheme *ababcc*

venus calendar *n, usu cap V* [*Venus*, 2d planet from the sun] **:** a Maya ritualistic calendar based on the lowest common factor of the synodical revolution of the planet Venus reckoned as 584 days and the year of 365 days

venus clam *n, often cap V* [NL *Venus*] **:** a bivalve mollusk of the family Veneridae

venus flytrap *n, sometimes cap V* **:** VENUS'S-FLYTRAP

venushair \'⸗⸗,⸗\ *or* **venus'-hair fern** *n, usu cap V* [*Venus*, Roman goddess of love + *hair*] **:** a delicate maidenhair fern (*Adiantum capillus-veneris*) having a slender black and shining stipe and branches

¹**ve·nu·sian** \və'n(y)üsēən, -sh(ē)ən\ *adj, usu cap* [*Venus*, 2d planet from the sun + E *-an*] **:** relating to the planet Venus **:** of or belonging to the planet Venus

²**venusian** \"\ *n* -s *usu cap* [*Venus*, Roman goddess of love + E *-an*] **1 :** one that has a prominent and well-developed Mount of Venus often marked with many lines and that is usu. held by palmists to be characterized by warmth of personality, strong sexual attraction, and personal attractiveness and beauty **2** [¹*venusian*] **:** a hypothetical native or inhabitant of the planet Venus

venus's-basket \'vēnəs(əz)'⸗⸗\ *n, pl* **venus's-baskets** *usu cap V* **:** VENUS'S-FLOWER-BASKET

venus's-chariot *n, pl* **venus's-chariots** *usu cap V* **:** a monkshood (*Aconitum napellus*)

venus's-comb *also* **venus comb** *n, pl* **venus's-combs** *usu cap V* **1 :** LADY'S-COMB **2 :** a marine snail (*Murex tenuispina*) having a long tubular canal with a row of long slender spines along both of its borders and rows of similar spines on the body of the shell

venus's-cup *n, pl* **venus's-cups** *usu cap V* **1 :** a yellow lady's slipper (*Cypripedium parviflorum*) **2 :** WILD TEASEL

venus's-ear *n, pl* **venus's-ears** *usu cap V* **:** ABALONE

venus's-fan *n, pl* **venus's-fans** *usu cap V* **:** a reticulated fan-shaped gorgonian (*Gorgonia flabellum*) native to Florida and the West Indies commonly purple or yellow or a mixture of the two while living

venus's-flower-basket *n, pl* **venus's-flower-baskets** *usu cap V* **:** a delicate tubular or cornucopia-shaped hexactinellid sponge (genus *Euplectella*) native to the East Indies and the eastern coast of Asia and having a skeleton of glassy transparent siliceous fibers interwoven into a firm network with long slender divergent anchoring fibers at the base by means of which the sponge stands erect in the soft mud at the bottom of the sea

venus's-flytrap *n, pl* **venus's-flytraps** *usu cap V* **:** an insectivorous plant (*Dionaea muscipula*) of the family Droseraceae found on the coast of the Carolinas and having the leaf apex modified into a ciliate margined insect trap of which the inner surface is provided with hairs that are sensitive to contact and cause the halves of the leaf to come together when touched

venus's-girdle *n, pl* **venus's-girdles** *usu cap V* **:** any of various ctenophores constituting the genus *Cestum* and having the body greatly compressed transversely and elongated in a sagittal plane so that it is ribbonlike with the mouth at the middle of one border

venus's-hairstone *or* **venus hairstone** *n, pl* **venus's-hairstones** *usu cap V* **:** quartz penetrated by acicular crystals of rutile

venus's looking-glass *n, usu cap V* **:** a plant of the genus *Specularia* (esp. *S. speculum-veneris*)

venus's-navelwort *n, pl* **venus's-navelworts** *usu cap V* **:** NAVELWORT 1,2

venus's-pride *n, pl* **venus's-prides** *usu cap V* **:** a bluet of the genus *Houstonia*

venus's-shell *n, pl* **venus's-shells** *usu cap V* **1 :** COWRIE **2 :** VENUS'S-COMB 2 **3 :** a mollusk of the family Veneridae; *also* **:** its shell

venus's-shoe *or* **venus's-slipper** *n, pl* **venus's-shoes** *or* **venus's-slippers** *usu cap V* **:** an American orchid of the genus *Cypripedium* — compare LADY'S SLIPPER

ve·nust \və'nəst\ *adj* [L *venustus*; akin to L *vener-, venus* love, charm — more at WIN] *archaic* **:** BEAUTIFUL, COMELY, GRACEFUL, ELEGANT

ve·nu·tian \və'n(y)üshən\ *n* -s *usu cap* [*Venus*, 2d planet from the sun + E *-tian* (as in *Martian*)] **:** VENUSIAN 2

ven·ville \'ven,vil\ *n* -s [alter. (influenced by *-ville*, suffix of place names, fr. OF *ville* town, village) of ME *venneféld, wengefeld*, fr. *venne, wenge* (of unknown origin) + *feld* field — more at VILLAGE, FIELD] **:** a tenure under English law peculiar to the neighborhood of Dartmoor forest by which the tenants have some rights in the forest

veny *obs var of* VENUE

veps \'veps\ *also* **vep·se** \'vepsə\ *n, pl* **veps** *also* **vep·ses** *cap* [Finn *vepsä*] **1 a :** a Finnish people of Russia now merged in the general population of the area between the Dnieper and the Volga **b :** a member of such people **2 :** a Finno-Ugric language of the Veps people — see URALIC LANGUAGES table

vep·si·an \'vepsēən\ *n* -s *usu cap* [*Veps* + *-ian*] **:** VEPS 2

ver *n* -s *usu cap* [ME, fr. L — more at VERNAL] *obs* **:** SPRINGTIME

ver *abbr* **1** verse **2** version **3** vertex

¹**vera** \'verə, 'varə, 'vərə\ *Scot var of* VERY

²**ve·ra** \'vārə\ *n* -s [AmerSp, prob. fr. Sp, edge, border, fr. Pg *beira*] **1 :** a timber tree (*Bulnesia arborea*) of the family Zygophyllaceae of northwestern So. America **2 :** the very hard brownish yellow wood of the vera tree that is used as a substitute for lignum vitae

ve·ra·cious \və'rāshəs\ *adj* [L *verac-, verax* + E *-ious*] **1 :** observant of the truth **:** habitually speaking the truth **:** TRUTHFUL ⟨fish, flesh, and fowl . . . have been picked up by ~ people after a storm —John Burroughs⟩ **2 a :** marked by truth **:** ACCURATE, TRUE ⟨efforts to call up before us ~ images of a bedroom, a bed, pillows, a lighted candle —C.E.Montague⟩ ⟨a striving toward the ~ depiction of reality —*Encyc. Americana*⟩ **b :** not deceitful **:** DIRECT, HONEST, SINCERE ⟨the clear ~ glance of the brown eyes —George Eliot⟩ — **ve·ra·cious·ly** *adv* — **ve·ra·cious·ness** *n* -ES

ve·rac·i·ty \və'rasəd·ē, -raas-, -sətē, -i\ *n* -ES [NL *veracitas*, fr. L *verac-, verax* true, truthful + *-itas* -ity — more at VERY] **1 :** devotion to the truth **:** TRUTHFULNESS ⟨have no confidence in the ~ of this witness⟩ **2 :** power of conveying or perceiving truth **:** CORRECTNESS ⟨the ~ of his vision⟩ **3 :** conformity with truth or fact **:** ACCURACY ⟨any fool may write a most valuable book by chance, if he will only tell us what he heard and saw with ~ —Thomas Gray⟩ **4 :** something that is true ⟨a convincing speaker who can make lies sound like *veracities*⟩ **syn** see TRUTH

ve·ra·cruz \,verə¦krüz\ *adj, usu cap* [fr. *Veracruz*, Mexico] **:** of or from the city of Veracruz, Mexico **:** of the kind or style prevalent in Veracruz

ve·ra·cru·za·no \,⸗⸗,krü'zä(,)nō\ *n* -s *cap* [Sp, fr. *Veracruz*, Mexico + Sp *-ano* -an (fr. L *-anus*)] **:** a native or resident of Veracruz, Mexico

ve·ran·da *or* **ve·ran·dah** \və'randə, -raan-\ *n* -s [partly fr. Hindi *varaṇḍā, baraṇḍā*; akin to Beng *bāraṇḍā* veranda, lexical Skt *varaṇḍa*; partly fr. Pg *varanda*; akin to Sp *baranda* railing, balustrade, Prov *barando*, Catal *barana*] **:** a usu. roofed open gallery or portico attached to the exterior of a building and used for sitting out of doors **:** PIAZZA, PORCH — compare LOGGIA **syn** see BALCONY

ve·ran·daed *also* **ve·ran·dahed** \-dəd\ *adj* **:** having a veranda ⟨an old-fashioned wide ~ house —*Living Church*⟩

ver·a·scope \'verə,skōp\ *n* [ISV *vera* (fem. of L *verus* true) + *-scope* — more at VERY] **:** a small stereoscopic camera made of metal and taking plates 45 to 107 millimeters in size

veratr- *or* **veratro-** *comb form* [NL, fr. *Veratrum*] **:** veratrine **:** veratric acid ⟨*veratrize*⟩ ⟨*veratroyl*⟩

ver·a·tral·de·hyde \,verə'traldə,hīd\ *n* [*veratr-* + *aldehyde*] **1 :** a crystalline compound $(CH_3O)_2C_6H_3CHO$ made usu. by methylating vanillin; 3,4-dimethoxy-benzaldehyde **2 :** a crystalline compound isomeric with veratraldehyde; 2,3-dimethoxy-benzaldehyde — called also *ortho-veratraldehyde*

ver·a·tram·ine \-'tra,mēn, -mən, və'ra·trəmən\ *n* [*veratr-* + *amine*] **:** a crystalline alkaloid $C_{27}H_{39}NO_2$ obtained from hellebore and esp. American hellebore

vera·trate \'verə,trāt\ *n* -s [ISV *veratr-* + *-ate*] **:** a salt or ester of veratric acid

ve·rat·ric acid \və'ra·trik-\ *n* [ISV *veratr-* + *-ic*] **1 :** a crystalline acid $(CH_3O)_2C_6H_3COOH$ occurring in sabadilla seed and also formed by decomposition of veratridine and other alkaloids; 3,4-dimethoxy-benzoic acid **2 :** a crystalline acid isomeric with veratric acid; 2,3-dimethoxy-benzoic acid — called also *ortho-veratric acid*

ve·rat·ri·dine \-rə,dēn, -dən\ *n* -s [*veratr-* + *-idine*] **:** a poisonous amorphous alkaloid $C_{36}H_{51}NO_{11}$ occurring in sabadilla seed and in some hellebores (as American hellebore)

ver·a·trine \'verə,trēn, -trən\ *n* -s [NL *veratrina*, fr. *Veratrum* + *-ina* -ine] **1 :** a mixture of alkaloids including cevadine, veratridine, and cevine that is obtained as a white or grayish powder from sabadilla seeds, that is an intense local irritant and a powerful muscle and nerve poison, and that has been used as a counterirritant in neuralgia and arthritis **2 a :** VERATRIDINE **b :** CEVADINE

ver·a·trole \-,trōl\ *n* -s [ISV *veratr-* + *-ole*] **:** a crystalline or liquid ether $C_6H_4(OCH_3)_2$ made by methylating guaiacol or pyrocatechol; *ortho*-dimethoxy-benzene

ver·a·tro·yl \və'ra·trə,wil\ *n* -s [ISV *veratr-* + *-yl*] **:** the univalent radical $(CH_3O)_2C_6H_3CO—$ of veratric acid

ve·ra·trum \və'rā·trəm\ *n* [NL, fr. L, hellebore] **1 a** *cap* **:** a genus of coarse herbs (family Liliaceae) having short poisonous rootstocks, large plicate clasping leaves in three vertical ranks, and panicled flowers with the perianth segments adnate to the ovary — compare VERATRINE **b** -S **:** any plant of the genus *Veratrum* **2** -S **:** the dried rhizome and roots of the American hellebore (*Veratrum viride*) or the European white hellebore (*V. album*) used in the treatment of hypertension

ver·a·tryl \'verə,tril, -ēl\ *n* -s [*veratr-* + *-yl*] **:** the univalent radical $(CH_3O)_2C_6H_3CH_2—$ of the alcohol corresponding to veratraldehyde and veratric acid; 3,4-dimethoxy-benzyl

ver·a·tryl·i·dene \,⸗⸗'trilə,dēn\ *n* -s [*veratryl* + *-idene*] **:** the bivalent radical $(CH_3O)_2C_6H_3CH=$ derived from veratraldehyde by removal of the aldehydic oxygen

verb \'vərb, 'vəb, 'vəib\ *n* -s *often attrib* [ME *verbe*, fr. MF, fr. L *verbum* word, verb; trans. of Gk *rhēma* — more at WORD] **:** a word belonging to that part of speech that characteristically is the grammatical center of a predicate and expresses an act, occurrence, or mode of being and that in various languages is inflected for agreement with the person and number of the subject, for tense, for voice, for mood, or for aspect and that typically has rather full descriptive meaning and characterizing quality but is in some instances nearly devoid of such meaning and quality esp. in use as an auxiliary or copula

¹**ver·bal** \'vərbəl, 'vəb-, 'vəib-\ *adj* [MF or LL; MF *verbal*, fr. LL *verbalis*, fr. L *verbum* word, verb + *-alis* -al] **1 a :** expert or facile in the use of words ⟨the most painstaking and elaborate ~ artist among the . . . poets of today —H.M.Green⟩ **b :** concerned with or using words for effect rather than meaning ⟨a merely ~ writer who sacrifices content to sound⟩ **c** *obs* **:** VERBOSE, WORDY ⟨you put me to forget a lady's manners by being so ~ —Shak.⟩ **2 a :** of or relating to words **:** consisting in or having to do with words ⟨few poets of the twentieth century have written ~ music with deeper sensibility —H.V. Gregory⟩ ⟨a table of proportional dimensions for various widths is reproduced, and detailed ~ instructions are given —*Experiment Station Record*⟩ **b :** of, relating to, or involving words only **:** having to do with words rather than meaning or substance ⟨a consistency that is merely ~ and scholastic —B.N.Cardozo⟩ ⟨an outward conformity with its precepts and a ~ profession of its tenets —J.G.Frazer⟩ **c :** consisting of or using words only and not effective action ⟨confined himself to a mere ~ protest⟩ **3 :** of, relating to, or formed from a verb ⟨occurs not less than ten times (eight times as a noun and twice in its ~ form) —*Lutheran Quarterly*⟩ ⟨a ~ adjective⟩ **4 :** spoken rather than written **:** ORAL ⟨invitations to them may be ~ or by way of a short, informal note —Noreen Routledge⟩ ⟨the employer's consent, ~ or written —Jacob Loft⟩ **5 :** word for word **:** LITERAL, VERBATIM ⟨a ~ translation⟩ **6 a :** of or relating to facility in the use and comprehension of words ⟨~ aptitude⟩ ⟨the ~ factor of a test⟩ — compare NUMERICAL 1e **b :** depending on the medium of words ⟨~ communication⟩ ⟨~ arts⟩ **7 a :** involving the use of words rather than action or performance ⟨the ~ IQ⟩ **b :** expressed merely through words **:** lacking in conceptual or emotional grasp — **ver·bal·ly** \-bəlē, -li\ *adv*

²**verbal** \"\ *n* -s **:** a word that combines characteristics of a verb with those of a noun or adjective — compare GERUND, INFINITIVE, PARTICIPLE

verbal auxiliary *n* **:** an auxiliary verb

verbal definition *n* **:** NOMINAL DEFINITION

verbal fallacy *n* **:** unsound reasoning that uses words ambiguously or otherwise violates a condition for the proper use of language in argument — compare AMPHIBOLOGY, FALLACY OF COMPOSITION, FALLACY OF DIVISION, FORMAL FALLACY

verbal image *n* **:** a mental image representing a word as heard, as seen, or as felt when pronounced

verbal inspiration *n* **:** the theological doctrine that a divine inspiration extends to every word of a particular text ⟨those who defend the *verbal inspiration* of the Bible⟩

ver·bal·ism *pronunc at* ¹VERBAL + ,izəm\ *n* -s **1 a :** something expressed verbally **:** TERM, WORD ⟨the ~*s* so frequently considered amusing in published lists of pupils' boners —*Textbooks in Education*⟩ **b :** PHRASING, WORDING ⟨himself reasonably discriminating in his ~, he is apt to quote less carefully phrased expressions from the writings of others —*Times Lit. Supp.*⟩ **2 :** words used as or as if a substitute for or more significant than things **:** the equating of verbal quality with reality ⟨the emancipation of science from ~ —G.A.L.Sarton⟩ ⟨for the normal person every experience, real or potential, is saturated with ~ —Edward Sapir⟩ **3 a :** an empty form of words **:** a wordy expression of little meaning ⟨has produced grandiose theories and pretentious ~*s* —Austin Warren & René Wellek⟩ **b :** WORDINESS ⟨no time is wasted with superfluous ~ —M.W.Smith⟩

ver·bal·ist \-ləst\ *n* -s **1 :** one who places a special or undue emphasis on words ⟨we ~*s* and theorists often lack the simple faith of the concretizing mind —R.L.Shayon⟩ **2 :** a person skilled in the use of words ⟨the best ~ in his class⟩ — **ver·bal·is·tic** \,⸗⸗¦listik, -tēk\ *adj*

ver·bal·i·ty \,vər'baləd·ē, -lətē, -i\ *n* -ES **1 :** VERBIAGE ⟨prolix, drawling stuff, full of stale, puling ~ —G.T.Buckley⟩ **2 :** a verbal statement or formulation ⟨if they agree with these *verbalities* and effects, we can know that our ideas of the past are true —William James⟩ **3 :** the quality or nature of a verb

ver·bal·iza·tion \,vərbələ'zāshən, ,vəb-, ,vəib-, -ə,lī'z-\ *n* -s **:** the act or an instance of verbalizing

ver·bal·ize \'⸗⸗,līz\ *vb* -ED/-ING/-S [*verbal* + *-ize*] *vi* **1 :** to speak or write verbosely **2 :** to state something in words **:** make a verbal statement ⟨this wondrous ability of each character to ~, to articulate so clearly and precisely his point of view —Arthur Knight⟩ ~ *vt* **1 :** to convert into a verb **:** VERBIFY ⟨a language in which nouns are freely *verbalized*⟩ **2 :** to express in speech **:** name or describe in words ⟨doesn't ~ his cockiness, but he has a kind of negative confidence —A. J.Liebling⟩ ⟨difficult to ~ these pain experiences —Fredric Wertham⟩

ver·bal·iz·er \-zə(r)\ *n* -s **:** one that verbalizes

verbal note *n* **:** an unsigned diplomatic memorandum serving as an informal reminder of an unanswered question or request

verbal noun *n* **:** a noun derived directly from a verb or verb stem and in certain uses partaking of the sense and constructions of a verb — see GERUND

verbal proposition *n* **:** a proposition in which the subject and predicate are only verbally different and which conveys no real information unless about the meaning of words

ver·bar·i·um \(,)vər'ba(a)rēəm\ *n* -s [NL, fr. L *verbum* + *-arium*] **:** ANAGRAMS

ver·bas·cose \(,)⸗'ba,skōs\ *n* -s [ISV *verbasc-* (fr. NL *Verbascum*) + *-ose*] **:** a crystalline sugar $C_{30}H_{56}O_{26}$ obtained from mullein root

ver·bas·cum \-,skəm\ *n, cap* [NL, fr. L, mullein] **:** a genus of coarse widely distributed herbs (family Scrophulariaceae) having large often woolly leaves and terminal spikes of yellow, white, or purplish flowers with a rotate corolla and five perfect stamens — see MULLEIN

¹**ver·ba·tim** \və(r)'bā¦d·əm, ,vər'b-,və̄'b-,vəi'b-, ¦təm *sometimes* -ba¦\ *adv* [ME, fr. ML, fr. L *verbum* word — more at WORD] **1 :** word for word **:** in the same words ⟨that irritating and unforgivable habit of reporting conversations ~ —*Times Lit. Supp.*⟩ **2 :** note for note ⟨in ragtime are often repeated ~ or else varied by slight changes in figuration —Rudi Blesh⟩

²**verbatim** \"\ *adj* **1 :** reproduced from or repeating an original source word for word **:** following the original exactly ⟨the stenographers who take down the ~ record —J.F.J.Gillen⟩ **2 :** skilled in taking down a speech, report, or proceedings word for word ⟨a ~ reporter⟩

³**verbatim** \"\ *n* -s **:** an account, translation, or report that follows an original word for word

ver·be·na \və(r)'bēnə, ⸗·nyə\ *n* [NL, fr. L, sing. of *verbenae* sacred boughs of laurel or olive or myrtle, class of medicinal plants — more at VERVAIN] **1** *cap* **:** a genus (the type of the family Verbenaceae) of chiefly American herbs or subshrubs having bracted flowers in heads or spikes, a regular corolla with a 5-lobed limb, and four one-seeded nutlets **2** -S **a :** VERVAIN 1; *esp* **:** any of numerous garden plants of hybrid origin but treated as a hybrid species (*Verbena* × *hybrida*) that are widely cultivated usu. as annuals for their showy spikes of white, pink, red, or blue flowers which are borne in profusion over a long season — see BLUE VERVAIN **b :** any of various plants felt to resemble verbenas — usu. used in combination; see LEMON VERBENA, SAND VERBENA **3** *or* **verbena violet** -s **:** a pale violet to pale purple — called also *vervain*

verbena

ver·be·na·ce·ae \,vərbə'nāsē,ē\ *n pl, cap* [NL, fr. *Verbena*, type genus + *-aceae*] : a family of herbs, shrubs, and trees (order Polemoniales) having opposite leaves, chiefly irregular flowers, and entire ovary — **ver·be·na·ceous** \ˌ⸗⸗ˈnāshəs\ *adj*

verbena family *n* : VERBENACEAE

ver·be·na·lin \və(r)ˈbēnᵊlən\ *n* -s [ISV *verben-* (fr. NL *Verbena*) + *-alin* (as in *digitalin*)] : a bitter crystalline glucoside $C_{17}H_{24}O_{10}$ in the flowers of the common vervain (*Verbena officinalis*)

verbena oil *n* **1** : a fragrant essential oil obtained esp. from lemon verbena and used in perfumery **2** : LEMONGRASS OIL

ver·be·none \ˈvərbəˌnōn\ *n* -s [ISV *verben-* (fr. NL *Verbena*) + *-one*] : a liquid ketone $C_{10}H_{14}O$ found in verbena oil from Spain; 2-pinen-4-one

ver·ber·ate \ˈvərbəˌrāt\ *vt* -ED/-ING/-S [L *verberatus*, past part. of *verberare* to lash, whip, beat — more at REVERBERATE] : BEAT, STRIKE

ver·ber·a·tion \ˌ⸗⸗ˈrāshən\ *n* -s [LL *verberation-*, *verberatio*, fr. L *verberatus* (past part.) + *-ion-*, *-io* -ion] : the act or action of beating or striking; *specif* : the impulse or vibration of a body that causes sound

ver·be·si·na \ˌvərbəˈsīnə, -sēnə\ *n* [NL, modif. (influenced by *Verbena*) of It dial. *forbesina* verbesina] **1** *cap* : a small genus of herbs (family Compositae) having yellow or white heads of tubular and radiate flowers — see GRAVELWEED, VIRGINIA CROWNBEARD **2** -s : any plant of the genus *Verbesina* — called also *crownbeard*

ver·bi·age \ˈvərbēij, ˈvəb-, ˈvəib- *sometimes* -bij *or* -bēj\ *n* -s [F, fr. MF *verbier* to chatter (fr. *verbe* word) + *-age* — more at WORD] **1** : excessive use of words : superfluity of language in proportion to sense or content : PROLIXITY, VERBOSITY, WORDINESS ⟨his concise and well-informed speeches were welcomed amid the common ~ of debate —John Buchan⟩ **2** : manner of expressing oneself in words : DICTION, WORDING ⟨messages and orders must use concise military ~ —G.S.Patton⟩

ver·bi·cide \-bəˌsīd\ *n* -s [L *verbi-* (fr. *verbum* word) + E *-cide*] **1** : deliberate distortion or destruction of the sense of a word (as in punning) ⟨raises the humor above the exasperation of sheer ~ —P.E.More⟩ **2** : one who distorts or destroys the sense of a word ⟨is not a true humorist but a dull ~⟩

ver·bid \ˈvərbəd\ *n* -s [*verb* + *-id*] : VERBAL

verb·ifi·ca·tion \ˌvərbəfəˈkāshən\ *n* -s [fr. *verbify*, after such pairs as E *ossify: ossification*] : the act of making into a verb

verb·ify \ˈ⸗⸗ˌfī\ *vb* -ED/-ING/-ES [*verb* + *-ify*] *vt* : to make into a verb : use as a verb ⟨elements used to ~ nouns are suffixed to noun stems —Edward Sapir⟩ ~ *vi* : to create a verb

ver·big·er·ate \(ˌ)vərˈbijəˌrāt\ *vi* -ED/-ING/-S [L *verbigeratus*, past part. of *verbigerare* to talk, fr. *verbum* word + *-gerare* (fr. *gerere* to carry) — more at CAST] : to repeat a word or sentence endlessly and meaninglessly ⟨never varied his ideas, seldom his expressions . . . he went on stubbornly *verbigerating* in the face of history —Vincent Sheean⟩

ver·big·er·a·tion \(ˌ)⸗ˌ⸗⸗ˈrāshən\ *n* -s [ISV *verbigerate* + *-ion*] : continual repetition of stereotyped phrases (as in schizophrenia)

ver·bile \ˈvərˌbīl\ *n* -s [L *verb*um word + E *-ile* (as in *audile*)] : one whose mental imagery consists of words — compare AUDILE

verb·less \ˈ⸗ləs\ *adj* : lacking a verb

ver·bo·mania \ˌvərbə+\ *n* [NL, fr. *verbo-* (fr. L *verbum* word) + *mania*] : a mania for words : excessive use of or obsession with words

ver·bo·maniac \ˈ⸗⸗+\ *n* [ISV, fr. NL *verbomania*, after LL *mania:* ISV *maniac*] : one afflicted with verbomania

ver·bose \və(r)ˈbōs, ˌvərˈb-,vəˈb-,vəiˈb-\ *adj* [L *verbosus*, fr. *verbum* word + *-osus* -ose — more at WORD] **1** : abounding in words : containing more words than necessary : PROLIX, TEDIOUS ⟨his arguments, clear, logical, never ~ —H.W.H. Knott⟩ **2** : given to wordiness : using words excessively : tediously long in speaking or writing ⟨a ~ orator⟩ **syn** see WORDY

ver·bose·ly *adv* : in a verbose manner

ver·bose·ness *n* -ES : VERBOSITY

ver·bos·i·ty \-ˈbäsəd·ē, -ətē, -i\ *n* -ES [MF or LL; MF *verbosité*, fr. LL *verbositat-*, *verbositas*, fr. L *verbosus* verbose + *-itat-*, *-itas* -ity] : the quality or state of being verbose : PROLIXITY, WORDINESS ⟨produced fifty-nine volumes of lachrymose ~ —*Amer. Guide Series: Conn.*⟩

1ver·bo·ten \və(r)ˈbōtᵊn, fə(r)ˈb-, ferˈb-, feəˈb-\ *adj* [G, fr. OHG *farbotan*, past part. of *farbiotan*, *firbiotan* to forbid — more at FORBID] : FORBIDDEN; *esp* : prohibited by dictate ⟨hanging onto the steps is ~ —J.F.Dobie⟩

2verboten \"\ *n* -s : something forbidden by authority ⟨the duties are mostly negative, in the form of standard, well-understood ~*s* —*Commonweal*⟩

verbs *pl of* VERB

verb sap \ˈvərbˈsap\ *or* **ver·bum sap** \ˌvərbəmˈs-\ [short for L *verbum sapienti sat est* a word to the wise is sufficient] : enough said — used terminally and often responsively to indicate that something left unsaid may or should be inferred

verd \ˈvərd\ *n* -s [obs. F *verd* (now *vert*), fr. OF, fr. L *viridis*] *archaic* : GREEN, GREENNESS

verd- *or* **verdo-** *comb form* [MF *verd-*, fr. OF *verd*, *vert* green] : green-colored ⟨*verdo*hemoglobin⟩

ver·dac·cio \verˈdä(ˌ)chō, -ˌchēˌō\ *n* -s [It, fr. *verde* green (fr. L *viridis*) + *-accio* (fr. L *-aceus* -aceous)] : a green color popular in late medieval Italy for fresco painting

ver·dan·cy \ˈvərdᵊnsē, ˈvəd-,ˈvəid-, -si\ *n* -ES : the quality or state of being verdant

ver·dant \-nt\ *adj* [MF *verdoyant*, fr. pres. part. of *verdoyer* to be verdant, to grow green, fr. OF *verdier*, *verdoier*, fr. *verd*, *vert* green, fr. L *viridis*, fr. *virēre* to be green] **1 a** : green in tint or color ⟨~ grass⟩ **b** : green with growing plants : covered with fresh vegetation ⟨~ fields⟩ **2** : unripe in knowledge or judgment : UNSOPHISTICATED, RAW — **ver·dant·ly** *adv*

verdant green *n* : a moderate yellow green that is yellower and less strong than average pea green, yellower and duller than apple green (sense 1), and greener and lighter than average moss green

verd an·tique *or* **verde antique** \ˈvərˌdan·ˈtēk\ *n* [It *verde antico*, lit., ancient green] **1** : a green mottled or veined serpentine marble or calcareous serpentine much used for indoor decoration esp. by the ancient Romans : OPHICALCITE **2** : an andesite porphyry showing crystals of feldspar in a dark green groundmass

verdant zone *n* : THERMAL BELT

ver·der·er *or* **ver·der·or** \ˈvərdərər, ˈvədərə(r, ˈvəidərə(r\ *n* -s [AF *verderer*, fr. OF *verdier* (fr. *verd* green + *-ier* -er) + E *-er*] : an English judicial officer having charge of the king's forest who is sworn to preserve the vert and venison, keep the assizes, and to view, receive, and enroll attachments and presentments of all manner of trespasses

ver·der·er·ship \-ˌship\ *n* : the office or position of a verderer

ver·det \ˌvərˈdā, -det\ *n* -s [MF, fr. *verd* green + *-et*] : VERDIGRIS 4

ver·det constant \ˌvərˈdā-\ *n, usu cap V* [after Marcel Emile *Verdet* †1866 Fr. mathematician] : a constant that expresses the effect of a magnetic field in rotating the plane of polarization of plane polarized light when it traverses a transparent substance placed in the field and that is equal to the rotation produced in one centimeter length of the substance by a magnetic field of one gauss

verd gay \ˈvərdˈgā\ *n* [F *vert gai*] : PARROT GREEN

ver·dict \ˈvər|(ˌ)dikt, ˈvə|, |ˈvəi|, |ˌdēkt\ *n* -s [alter. (influenced by ML *verdictum*, *veredictum* verdict, fr. L *vere dictum* truly said, fr. *vere* truly — fr. *verus* true — + *dictum* something said, saying) of ME *verdit*, fr. AF, fr. OF *ver*, *veir* true (fr. L *verus*) + *dit* saying, fr. past part. of *dire* to say, fr. L *dicere* — more at DICTUM, VERY, DICTION] **1** : the answer of a jury given to a court concerning a matter of fact in a civil or criminal cause committed to their examination and determination : the finding or decision of a jury on the matter legally submitted to them in the course of the trial of a cause that ordinarily in civil actions is for the plaintiff or for the defendant and in criminal actions guilty or not guilty — see DIRECTED VERDICT, SCOTCH VERDICT, SEALED VERDICT, SPECIAL VERDICT **2** : an opinion pronounced or felt : DECISION, JUDGMENT ⟨rejected the general ~ on her looks —Edith Wharton⟩ ⟨that a given novel satisfies the criterion entails a favorable critical ~ —C.W.Shumaker⟩

1ver·di·gris \ˈvərdəˌgrēs, ˈvəd-,ˈvəid-, -ˌgris *sometimes* -ˌgrē\ *n* -ES [alter. (influenced by MF *verdegris*, alter. — influenced by *gris* gray — of OF *verte grez*) of ME *vertegrez*, fr. OF *verte grez*, *vert de Grice*, lit., green of Greece, fr. *vert* green + *de* of, from (fr. L) + *Grice*, *Grece* Greece, fr. L *Graecia* — more at GRIZZLE, VERDANT, DE-, GRECIAN] **1** : a green or greenish blue poisonous pigment obtained by the action of acetic acid on copper and used chiefly in antifouling paints and formerly in medicine: as **a** : a light blue powder or silky blue crystalline product $Cu(C_2H_3O_2)_2.CuO.6H_2O$ — called also *blue verdigris* **b** : a green product $2Cu(C_2H_3O_2)_2.CuO.6H_2O$ — called also *green verdigris* **2** : the poisonous normal copper acetate $Cu(C_2H_3O_2)_2.H_2O$ obtained as a green powder or dark green efflorescent crystals (as by the action of acetic acid on copper oxide [sense b]) and used chiefly in making Paris green — called also *crystallized verdigris*, *neutral verdigris* **3** : a green or bluish deposit esp. of copper carbonates formed on copper, brass, or bronze surfaces — compare PATINA 2 **4** *or* **verdigris green** : a moderate yellowish green that is greener, lighter, and stronger than tarragon or average almond green and paler and slightly greener than malachite green — called also *distilled green*, *Montpellier green*, *Spanish green*, *verdet*

2verdigris \"\ *vb* -ED/-ING/-ES *vt* : to cover or coat with verdigris ⟨a rusty lantern or a ~*ed* cannonball —Nike Anderson⟩ ~ *vi* : to become spotted or stained with verdigris — used of an insect mounted on a pin

ver·di·grisy \-ēsē, -isē, -si\ *adj* : resembling or suggesting verdigris (as in color)

ver·din \ˈvərdᵊn, vərˈdan\ *n* -s [F, yellowhammer] : a very small yellow-headed titmouse (*Auriparus flaviceps*) found from Texas to California and southward that builds a large globular nest

ver·dit \ˈvərdət, ˈvär-\ *dial var of* VERDICT

ver·di·ter \ˈvərdəd·ə(r), ˈvəd-,ˈvəid-, -dətə-\ *n* -s [MF *verd de terre*, lit., green of earth] **1** : BLUE VERDITER **2** : GREEN VERDITER

verditer blue *n* : AZURITE BLUE

verditer green *n* : MALACHITE GREEN 3

verdo- — see VERD-

ver·do·globin \ˈvərdə+\ *n* [*verd-* + *globin*] : any of several green compounds (as choleglobin and sulfhemoglobin) derived from hemoglobin or related compounds by cleavage of the porphyrin ring

ver·do·la·ga \ˌvərdəˈlägə, ˌver-\ *n* -s [Sp, fr. Ar *bardilāga*, fr. L *portulaca* purslane — more at PORTULACA] : a common purslane (*Portulaca oleracea*)

ver·do·peroxidase \ˈvərdə+\ *n* [*verd-* + *peroxidase*] : a green-colored peroxidase obtained from leukocytes

verds *pl of* VERD

ver·dure \ˈvərjər, ˈvəjə(r, ˈvəijə(r\ *n* -s [ME, fr. MF, fr. *verd* green + *-ure* — more at VERDANT] **1** : the greenness and freshness of growing vegetation; *also* : such vegetation itself : a green growth **2** : a tapestry having a design made up of foliage, trees, or flowers often in the form of formal gardens **3** : a dark to deep yellowish green **4** : a vigorous condition suggesting fresh growth of vegetation : good health : freshness and strength

ver·dured \-jə(r)d\ *adj* : covered with verdure

ver·dure·less \ˈ⸗⸗ləs\ *adj* : having no verdure : lacking vegetation

ver·dur·ous \-jərəs\ *adj* : clothed with the fresh green of vegetation : VERDURED, VERDANT

verd ves·sie \-ˈvesē\ *n* [F *vert de vessie*] : SAP GREEN 2b

ver·ein \vəˈrīn, fə-\ *n* -s [G, fr. MHG *vereine* union, association, fr. *vereinen* to unite, fr. *ver-* for- (fr. OHG *far-*) + *einen* to make one, fr. *ein* one, fr. OHG — more at FOR-, ONE] : a usu. social or political organization or association

ver·ek \ˈfeˌrek\ *n* -s [NL (specific epithet of *Acacia verek*, syn. of *Acacia senegal*), fr. Berber *afarak*, fr. Hausa *farak k'aya*, fr. *farar* white + *k'aya* thorn] : an acacia (*Acacia senegal*)

ver·e·til·lum \ˌverəˈtiləm\ *n* [NL, fr. L, dim. of *veretrum* genitals; akin to L *vereri* to fear — more at WARY] **1** *cap* : a genus of club-shaped pennatulaceans with zooids distributed irregularly all round the rachis that occur at moderate depths in the Mediterranean and Atlantic **2** -s : any animal of the genus *Veretillum*

1verge \ˈvərj, ˈvəj, ˈveij\ *n* -s [ME, fr. MF, fr. L *virga* twig, rod, streak, stripe — more at WHISK] **1 a** (1) : a rod or staff carried as an emblem of authority or as a symbol of office (2) *obs* : a stick or wand held by a person being admitted to tenancy while he swears fealty **b** (1) : the spindle of a watch balance; *esp* : a spindle with pallets in an old vertical escapement (2) *or* **verge watch** : a watch with a vertical escapement **c** : the male intromittent organ of any of various invertebrates **d** (1) : a needle guide in a stocking machine (2) : a bobbin guide in a lace machine **2 a** : something that borders, limits, or bounds: as (1) : an outer often decorated or inscribed margin of an object or structural part ⟨electric candles . . . around the ~ between walls and ceiling —Clifton Daniel⟩ (2) *obs* : an enclosing band : CIRCLET, RING ⟨the inclusive ~ of golden metal that must round my brow —Shak.⟩; *also* : RIM, BRIM (3) : the outermost edge or a part of the edge of an extended area ⟨a row of white palings, which marked the ~ of the heath —Thomas Hardy⟩ ⟨the southern ~ of the Lake District —E.B. Ford⟩ ⟨the ~ of the sea⟩ (4) : the bottom or usu. the upper margin of a precipice ⟨the child crept to the edge, and was balanced on the very ~ —Richard Jefferies⟩ (5) : the edge of a bed or border esp. of flowers (6) : a strip of vegetation adjoining a walk, road, or railway line ⟨grass ~*s* also lose their correct level above the path —*Gardeners' Chronicle*⟩ (7) : HORIZON ⟨the sky was clear from ~ to ~ —Thomas Hardy⟩ (8) : the edge of the tiling projecting over the gable of a roof (9) *Brit* : the paved, unpaved, or planted shoulder of a road or walk ⟨the graveled ~*s* of the path —Lionel Shapiro⟩ ⟨the road narrows and . . . the edges of the ~*s* are not surfaced —R.J.P. Mortished⟩ **b** : the point marking the beginning of a new or different state, condition, or action : BRINK, THRESHOLD ⟨the country was on the ~ of bankruptcy —*London Calling*⟩ ⟨on the ~ of asking to be relieved —John Mason Brown⟩ ⟨vocabulary and grammar are both bad to the ~ of illiteracy —M.M. Rossi⟩ **c** : the outermost margin or marginal area of a state, concept, class, or jurisdiction : FRINGE ⟨the mob operates on the ~ of the confidence rackets —D.W.Maurer⟩ ⟨not enough that a statute goes to the ~ of constitutional power —O.W. Holmes †1935⟩ **3 a** (1) : the area or limit within 12 miles of the place of the court of an English sovereign formerly delimited as under the king's peace (2) : either of two former English courts under the special jurisdiction of the lord steward and marshal of the king's household **b** (1) *obs* : the area of application of a category or concept : RANGE, SCOPE (2) *obs* : the entities that fall within the area of a category or concept : CLASS (3) *obs* : CONTROL, JURISDICTION **c** : the actual area covered by or the immediate environs of a place **4** : the scope permitted by a limiting line or condition ⟨anyone who has figured prominently in the social consciousness . . . should be given ~ and room —Allan Nevins⟩ **syn** see BORDER

2verge \"\ *vb* -ED/-ING/-S *vt* **1** : to provide with a verge : BORDER, EDGE, TRIM ⟨shores . . . *verged* with floating lawns of . . . aquatic plants —William Bartram⟩ **2** : to constitute the verge of : act as a border for ⟨a file of trees *verging* the road —Richard Wilbur⟩ ~ *vi* **1** : to be in the next or neighboring place : be contiguous **2** : to be on the verge : be at or approach the border or start of condition, state, or event ⟨a personality who at least *verged* on greatness —George Woodcock⟩ ⟨a courage that *verged* on foolhardiness —Agnes M. Cleaveland⟩ ⟨already *verging* on old age —W.H.Hudson †1922⟩

3verge \"\ *vi* -ED/-ING/-S [L *vergere* to bend, incline — more at WRENCH] **1 a** *of the sun* : to incline toward the horizon : SINK **b** : to move, extend, or incline in a particular direction or toward a point, goal, or condition ⟨the hill ~*s* to the north⟩ ⟨the declining civilization ~*s* to its fall —A.J.Toynbee⟩ **2** : to be in or as if in transition from one state to another : be in the process of changing or merging ⟨gradations from azures to hues *verging* on black —H.E.Riesebery⟩

vergeboard \ˈ⸗ˌ⸗\ *n* [by alter.] : BARGEBOARD

ver·gence \ˈvərjən(t)s\ *n* -s [3*verge* + *-ence*] : a turning movement of the eyeballs

ver·gen·cy \-nsē, -si\ *n* -ES [3*verge* + *-ency*] **1** *obs* : the act or process of verging, approaching, or bordering on something : TENDENCY, INCLINATION **2** : a measure of convergence or divergence of a pencil of rays entering or issuing from a lens or mirror that is expressed as the reciprocal of the distance from lens or mirror to the focus of the rays and for rays through a principal focus is equal to the focal power of the lens or mirror

verg·er \ˈvərjər, ˈvəjə(r, ˈvəijə(r\ *n* -s [ME, fr. MF *verge* + ME *-er* — more at VERGE] **1** *Brit* : an attendant that carries a verge before a bishop, dean, or other official **2** : a church official who serves as a sacristan, as an attendant who keeps order during services, or as an usher

verge rafter *n* [*verge* short for *vergeboard*] : BARGEBOARD

verges *pl of* VERGE, *pres 3d sing of* VERGE

verge watch *n* : VERGE 1b(2)

ver·gi·form \ˈvərjəˌfȯrm\ *adj* [1*verge* + *-iform*] : RODLIKE

ver·gil·ian *or* **vir·gil·ian** \ˌvərˈjilēən, vəˈj-, vəiˈj-, -lyən\ *adj, usu cap* [*vergilian* fr. L *vergilianus*, fr. Publius *Vergilius* Maro †19 B.C. Roman poet + L *-anus* -an; *virgilian* fr. LL *virgilianus*, alter. of L *vergilianus*] : of or relating to Vergil; *esp* : characteristic of the style of Vergil

ver·glas \(ˈ)verˈglä\ *n, pl* **verglases** \-ä(z)\ [F, fr. MF, fr. OF *verre-glaz* lit., glass-ice, fr. *verre* glass (fr. L *vitrum* glass, woad) + *glaz*, *glace* ice, fr. LL *glacia* — more at WOAD, GLACIER] : a thin film of ice on rock

veridian *var of* VIRIDIAN

ve·rid·i·cal \vəˈridəkəl, -dēk-\ *adj* [L *veridic*us veracious (fr. *verus* true + *-dicus*, fr. *dicere* to say) + E *-al* — more at VERY, DICTION] **1** : conforming to the truth : TRUTHFUL, VERACIOUS ⟨tried . . . to supply . . . a ~ background to the events and people portrayed —Laura Krey⟩ **2** : not illusory : GENUINE, REAL, ACTUAL, TRUE ⟨perceptual error . . . has a surprising resemblance to ~ perception —F.A.Olafson⟩ — **ve·rid·i·cal·ly** \-k(ə)lē, -li\ *adv*

veridical hallucination *n* : a hallucination corresponding to a real event (as when the apparition of an image of an absent person is coincident with his death)

ve·rid·i·cal·i·ty \vəˌridəˈkaləd·ē\ *n* -ES : the quality or state of being veridical : TRUTHFULNESS, GENUINENESS

verier *comparative of* VERY

veriest *superlative of* VERY

ver·i·fi·abil·i·ty \ˌverəˌfīəˈbiləd·ē, -lətē, -i\ *n* : the quality or state of being confirmable

verifiability principle *or* **verifiability theory** *n* : a proposal or claim of early logical positivists according to which a requirement or criterion for the meaningfulness of a factual statement is its susceptibility to the possibility of being either theoretically or actually proved true or false by reference to empirical facts — compare CONFIRMABILITY THEORY

ver·i·fi·able \ˈverəˌfīəbəl\ *adj* **1** : capable of being verified **2** : susceptible to the possibility of being either theoretically or actually proved true or false by reference to empirical facts — compare CONFIRMABLE 2 — **ver·i·fi·able·ness** *n* -ES

ver·i·fi·ca·tion \ˌverəfəˈkāshən\ *n* -s [MF, fr. ML *verification-*, *verificatio*, fr. *verificatus* (past part. of *verificare* to verify) + L *-ion-*, *-io* -ion] **1 a** : the act or process of verifying or the state of being verified : the authentication of truth or accuracy by such means as facts, statements, citations, measurements, or attendant circumstances **b** (1) : confirmation by evidence in law (2) : confirmation by oath or affidavit **c** : the procedure required for the establishment of the truth or falsity of a statement **2** : an averment used in concluding a plea that states that the pleader is prepared to prove his allegations **3** : an oath to the truth of a pleading in code pleading **4** : the ceremony of subscribing statements as true under oath and the certification of the ceremony by the notary or other officer administering the oath **5** : RATIFICATION

verification principle *or* **verification theory** *n* : VERIFIABILITY PRINCIPLE

ver·i·fi·ca·to·ry \ˈverəfəˌkād·ərē, -ātərē, -ā·trē, -i\ *adj* [*verification* + *-ory*] : that is capable of verification or serves to verify : VERIFYING, AUTHENTICATING, CONFIRMING

ver·i·fied \ˈverəˌfīd\ *adj* [ME, fr. past part. of *verifien* to verify] **1** : authenticated by affidavit ⟨a ~ motion⟩ **2** : substantiated by competent proof ⟨a ~ case⟩ ⟨a ~ claim⟩

ver·i·fi·er \-ˌfī(ə)r, -īə\ *n* -s **1** : one that searches for or discovers verification **2** : one that serves as verification ⟨the problem of verifying beliefs . . . where the ~ lies beyond experience —J.W.Yolton⟩ **3** : a machine used to check the correctness of the previous recording of data (as by punching cards or magnetizing tape)

ver·i·fy \-ˌfī\ *vt* -ED/-ING/-ES [ME *verifien*, fr. MF *verifier*, fr. ML *verificare*, fr. L *verus* true + *-ficare* -fy — more at VERY] **1 a** : to confirm or substantiate in law by oath or proof : add the legal verification to (a pleading or petition) **b** (1) : to swear to or affirm the truth of (2) *obs* : to second the testimony of : affirm the truthfulness of **2** : to prove to be true : establish the truth of : conclusively demonstrate by presentation of facts or by sound reasoning or argument ⟨have continually *verified* their own position by an appeal to the arts of the past —Bernard Smith⟩ **3** : to serve as conclusive evidence, argument, proof, or demonstration of ⟨observations of the research team *verified* the foreman's statement —*Management Behavior & Foreman Attitude*⟩ ⟨admirably adapted to an aquarium life, as the following account will ~ —G.E. & Nettie MacGinitie⟩ **4** : to check or test the accuracy or exactness of : confirm the truth or truthfulness of by or as if by comparison with known data or a recognized standard or authority ⟨sought out and *verified* the scientific names of birds mentioned in the text —E.A.Armstrong⟩ ⟨a government survey party was ~*ing* the neighboring landmarks —Joseph Furphy⟩ **5** : to confirm or establish the authenticity or existence of by examination, investigation, or competent evidence **syn** see CONFIRM

ver·i·ly \ˈverəlē, -li\ *adv* [ME *verraily*, fr. *verray* very + *-ly* — more at VERY] **1** : in very truth : beyond doubt or question : in fact : CERTAINLY ⟨trust in the Lord and do good . . . and ~ thou shalt be fed —Ps 37:3 (AV)⟩ **2** : TRULY, CONFIDENTLY, REALLY ⟨I ~ think so⟩

veri·sim·i·lar \ˈverəˈsimələ(r)\ *adj* [L *verisimil*is verisimilar + E *-ar*] : having the appearance of truth : PROBABLE, LIKELY — **veri·sim·i·lar·ly** *adv*

veri·si·mil·i·tude \ˌ⸗⸗səˈmiləˌtüd, -ə·ˌtyüd\ *n* [L *verisimilitudo*, fr. *verisimilis*, *veri similis* having the appearance of truth (fr. *veri* — gen. of *verum*, neut. of *verus* true — + *similis* like, similar) + *-tudo* -tude — more at VERY, SAME] **1** : the quality or state of being verisimilar : the appearance of truth : PROBABILITY, LIKELIHOOD ⟨the dialogue is too abstract and self-conscious for ~ —Paul Pickrel⟩ **2** : that which is verisimilar : a statement apparently true **syn** see TRUTH

veri·si·mil·i·ty \-əd·ē\ *n* -ES [L *verisimil*is + E *-ity*] : VERISIMILITUDE

veri·sim·i·lous \ˈ⸗⸗ˈsiməlәs\ *adj* [L *verisimil*is + E *-ous*] : VERISIMILAR

ve·rism \ˈviˌrizəm, ˈveˌr-\ *n* -s [It *verismo*, fr. *vero* true (fr. L *verus*) + *-ismo* -ism] **1** : artistic use of contemporary everyday material esp. in opera in preference to the heroic, the mythical and legendary, or the historical **2** : a realistic or objective style of musical composition or of painting appropriate to the treatment of everyday material

1ve·rist \-ˌrəst\ *n* -s [It *verista*, fr. *vero* true + *-ista* -ist] : one who practices or advocates verism

2verist \"\ *or* **ve·ris·tic** \vəˈristik\ *adj* [*verist* fr. F *vériste*, fr. It *verista* verist, n.; *veristic* fr. 1*verist* + *-ic*] : having the qualities or character of verism

ver·i·ta·ble \ˈverəd·əbəl, -rətə-\ *adj* [MF *veritable*, fr. *verité* verity + *-able*] : being actually that which is named : possessing the characteristics applied : not false, unreal, imaginary, or metaphorical ⟨shots taken in a ~ bull ring —John McCarten⟩ ⟨the only guts that are mentioned . . . are the ~ entrails of a fish —Mark Schorer⟩ ⟨spiritual heights which may be just as ~ as the streets and gutters —H.O.Taylor⟩ — often used to stress the aptness of a metaphor ⟨whose conversation was a ~ memo pad of given names, connections, ties, appointments —Mary McCarthy⟩ ⟨a ~ mountain of newspaper material —T.D.Clark⟩ **syn** see AUTHENTIC

ver·i·ta·ble·ness *n* -ES : the quality or state of being veritable

ver·i·ta·bly \-blē, -li\ *adv* : in a veritable manner : TRULY

ver·i·tism \ˈverəˌtizəm\ *n* -s [*verity* + *-ism*] : VERISM

ver·i·tist \-rəd·əst\ *n* -s [*verity* + *-ist*] : VERIST

ver·i·ty \ˈverəd·ē, -rətē, -i\ *n* -ES [ME *verite*, fr. MF *verité*, fr. L *veritat-*, *veritas*, fr. *verus* true + *-itat-* *-itas* -ity — more at VERY] **1 a** : the quality or state of being true or real: (1) : the consonance of a statement, proposition, or representation with fact ⟨the ~ of his recollection of the castle⟩ (2) : faithfulness or correspondence to aesthetic truth ⟨the ~ of a symphony to the composer's conception⟩ **b :** the quality or state of being eternally or necessarily true and not merely true as a matter of fact **2 :** something that is true **:** a true fact or statement; *esp* **:** a statement true in all circumstances **:** a necessary esp. ethical, religious, or aesthetic truth **3 :** HONESTY, VERACITY **syn** see TRUTH

¹ver·juice \ˈvər,jüs\ *n* [ME *verjuis, verjus*, fr. MF *verjus, vert jus*, lit., green juice, fr. OF, fr. *vert* green + *jus* juice — more at VERDANT, JUICE] **1 :** the sour juice of crab apples or of green or unripe grapes, apples, or other fruit; *also* **:** an acid liquor made from verjuice **2** *archaic* **:** acidity of disposition, manner, or temperament

²verjuice \"\ *vt, archaic* **:** to acidify as if with verjuice **:** EMBITTER

ver macaque \ˈver-\ *n* [F, lit., macaque worm] **:** TORSALO

¹ver·meil \ˈvərməl, -,māl, ,vərˈmā(ə)l\ *adj* [ME *vermail*, fr. MF *vermeil, vermail*, fr. OF — more at VERMILION] **:** bright red

²vermeil \"\ *n* -s [MF, fr. *vermeil*, adj.] **1 :** VERMILION **2 a :** an orange-red garnet **b :** SPINEL **c :** RUBY **3 :** a red varnish applied to a gilded surface to give luster **4 :** gilded silver, bronze, or copper

³vermeil \"\ *vt* -ED/-ING/-s **:** to color or stain with or as if with vermilion

¹ver·mes \ˈvər(,)mēz\ *n pl, cap* [NL, fr. pl. of L *vermis* worm] **:** any of several major divisions of the animal kingdom: as **a** *in former classifications* **:** a group containing all invertebrates with the exception of the arthropods **b** *in some esp former classifications* **:** a group comprising the typically soft-bodied and more or less vermiform invertebrates, including the flatworms, roundworms, annelid worms, and minor forms, and usu. held to be a purely artificial assemblage

²vermes *pl of* VERMIS

¹ver·me·tid \ˈvərmədəd\ *adj* [NL *Vermetidae*, family of mollusks, fr. *Vermetus*, type genus + *-idae*] **:** of or relating to the Vermetidae

²vermetid \"\ *n* -s [NL *Vermetidae*] **:** a mollusk of the family Vermetidae **:** WORM SHELL

ver·met·i·dae \,vərˈmed·ə,dē\ *n pl, cap* [NL, fr. *Vermetus*, type genus + *-idae*] **:** a small family of marine mollusks (suborder Taenioglossa) comprising *Vermetus* and closely related genera — see SILIQUARIA

ver·me·tus \,=ˈmēd·əs\ *n* [NL, fr. L *vermis* worm] **1** *cap* **:** a genus (the type of the family Vermetidae) of marine gastropod mollusks having when young regularly spiral shells and being free to creep about and later becoming permanently attached to an object and developing separate whorls often irregularly bent and contorted like a worm tube **2** -ES **:** VERMETID

vermi- *comb form* [NL, fr. LL, fr. L *vermis* — more at WORM] **:** worm ⟨*vermi*form⟩ ⟨*vermi*parous⟩

ver·mi·an \ˈvərmēən\ *adj* [ISV *vermi-* + *-an*] **1 :** of, relating to, or resembling the worms **2 :** of or relating to the vermis of the cerebellum

¹ver·mi·cel·li \,vərməˈselē, ,vəm-, ,vəim-, -məˈche-\ *n* -s [It, fr. pl. of *vermicello*, dim. of *verme* worm, fr. L *vermis*] **:** alimentary paste made in long thin solid strings smaller in diameter than spaghetti — compare MACARONI

²vermicelli \"\ *adj* **1 :** composed of or containing vermicelli ⟨~ soup⟩ **2 :** resembling vermicelli ⟨~ designs⟩

ver·mi·ci·dal \;==ˈsīdᵊl\ *adj* **1 :** destroying worms **2 :** of or relating to a vermicide

ver·mi·cide \ˈ==,sīd\ *n* -s [*vermi-* + *-cide*] **:** an agent that destroys worms, esp. those that are intestinally parasitic — compare ANTHELMINTIC

ver·mi·cle \ˈvərməkəl\ *n* -s [L *vermiculus*] **:** a small worm or wormlike larva

ver·mic·u·lar \(,)vərˈmikyələr\ *adj* [NL *vermicularis*, fr. L *vermiculus* little worm + *-aris* -ar] **1 a :** resembling a worm in form or motion **:** VERMIFORM **b :** VERMICULATE **2 :** of, relating to, or caused by worms

ver·mic·u·lar·ia \(,)vər,mikyəˈla(a)rēə\ *n, cap* [NL, fr. L *vermiculus* + NL *-aria*] **:** a genus of imperfect fungi (family Melanconiaceae) characterized by setose pycnidia and unicellular vermiform pycnospores

ver·mic·u·late \və(r)ˈmikyələ̇t, -,lāt, *usu* |d+V\ *adj* [L *vermiculatus*, past part. of *vermiculari* to be wormy, fr. *vermiculus* little worm — more at VERMILION] **1 a :** wormlike in shape **b :** covered with wormlike elevations **:** marked with irregular fine lines of color or with irregular wavy impressed lines like worm tracks ⟨a ~ nut⟩ **2 :** TORTUOUS, INVOLUTE **3 :** full of worms **:** WORM-EATEN

ver·mic·u·lat·ed \-,lād·əd, -ātəd\ *adj* [L *vermiculatus* + E *-ed*] **:** VERMICULATE

vermiculated work *or* **vermicular work** *n* **:** stonework wrought to have the appearance of convoluted worms or of having been eaten into by or covered with tracks of worms

vermiculated work

ver·mic·u·la·tion \=,==ˈlāshən\ *n* -s [L *vermiculation-, vermiculatio*, fr. *vermiculatus* (past part. of *vermiculari*) + *-ion-, -io* -ion] **1 :** penetration by worms **:** the state of being worm-eaten **2 :** the act or process of moving like a worm **:** WRITHING, TWISTING ⟨the ~ of the intestines⟩ **3 :** an esp. ornamental narrow and wavy or tortuous marking or system of markings

ver·mi·cule \ˈvərmə,kyül\ *n* -s [L *vermiculus* little worm] **:** a wormlike body; *specif* **:** OOKINETE

ver·mic·u·lite \və(r)ˈmikyə,līt, *usu* -īd+V\ *n* -s [L *vermiculus* + E *-ite*] **:** any of a number of micaceous minerals (as maconite) that are hydrous silicates derived generally from the alteration of mica which do not burn, are not harmed by water, and whose granules expand greatly at high temperatures to give a lightweight highly water-absorbent material that is used in seedbeds as a mulch, in plaster, mortar, and concrete as a substitute for sand, and as an insulating material in walls, floors, and ceilings

ver·mi·form \ˈvərmə,fȯrm\ *adj* [NL *vermiformis*, fr. *vermi-* + *-formis* -form] **:** WORMLIKE, VERMICULAR

vermiform appendix *n* [trans. of NL *appendix vermiformis*] **:** a narrow blindly ending tube usu. about three or four inches long that extends from the cecum in the lower right-hand part of the abdomen in a direction which varies in different individuals, that has much lymphoid wall tissue, that normally communicates with the cavity of the cecum, and that represents an atrophied terminal part of the cecum — called also *vermiform process;* compare APPENDICITIS; see DIGESTION illustration

ver·mi·for·mis \,vərməˈfȯrmə̇s\ *n* -ES [NL, short for *appendix vermiformis*] **:** VERMIFORM APPENDIX

vermiform process *n* **1 :** the vermis of the cerebellum **2 :** VERMIFORM APPENDIX

ver·mif·u·gal \;vərˈmifyəgəl, ;vərməˈfyüg-\ *adj* [²*vermifuge* + *-al*] **:** VERMIFUGE

¹ver·mi·fuge \ˈvərmə,fyüj\ *adj* [prob. fr. (assumed) NL *vermifugus*, fr. NL *vermi-* + (assumed) NL *-fugus* expelling (fr. L *fugare* to put to flight) — more at -FUGE] **:** serving to destroy or expel parasitic worms esp. of the intestine **:** ANTHELMINTIC

²vermifuge \"\ *n* -s [*vermi-* + *-fuge*] **:** a vermifuge agent

ver·mi·lin·gua \,vərməˈliŋgwə\ *n pl, cap* [NL, fr. *vermi-* + L *lingua* tongue — more at TONGUE] *in some esp former classifications* **:** a superfamily comprising the American anteaters or sometimes these together with the pangolins and aardvark

¹ver·mi·lin·guia \-gwēə\ *also* **vermilin·gues** \-(,)gwēz\ [NL, fr. *vermi-* + *-linguia* or *-lingues* (fr. L *lingua* tongue)] *syn of* VERMILINGUA

²vermilinguia \"\ *n pl, cap* [NL, fr. *vermi-* + *-linguia* (fr. L *lingua* tongue)] **:** a division of lizards consisting of the chameleons — **ver·mi·lin·gui·al** \;=;=ˈgwēəl\ *adj*

¹ver·mil·ion *or* **ver·mil·lion** \və(r)ˈmilyən\ *n* -s [ME *vermilioun*, fr. OF *vermeillon*, fr. *vermeil*, adj., bright red, fr. LL *vermiculus* kermes (scale from which red dyestuff is derived), fr. L, little worm, dim. of *vermis* worm — more at WORM] **1 a :** a bright red pigment consisting of mercuric sulfide formerly obtained from the mineral cinnabar but now always prepared synthetically (as by reaction of mercury, sulfur, and sodium hydroxide), that varies from crimson when coarse-grained to nearly orange when finely divided, and that is used chiefly as an artist's color and in rubber — called also *Chinese vermilion;* see ENGLISH VERMILION **b :** any of various other red pigments: as (1) **:** AMERICAN VERMILION (2) **:** ANTIMONY VERMILION **2 a :** GOYA **b :** a variable color averaging a vivid reddish orange that is redder, darker, and slightly stronger than chrome orange, redder and darker than golden poppy, and redder and lighter than international orange **3 :** VERMEIL 2a **4 :** AMBOYNA 1

²vermilion *or* **vermillion** \"\ *vt* -ED/-ING/-s **:** to color or tint with or as if with vermilion

ver·mil·ion·ette \=,==ˈnet\ *n* -s [ISV *vermilion* + *-ette*] **:** any of various brilliant red organic pigments made by precipitating eosin or a similar dye upon a base (as barium sulfate or white lead)

vermilion flycatcher *n* **:** any of several American flycatchers of the genus *Pyrocephalus* which have in the adult male bright scarlet and brownish gray or black plumage and one (*P. rubinus mexicanus*) of which is found as far north as southern Texas and Arizona

ver·mil·ion·ize \və(r)ˈmilyə,nīz\ *vt* -ED/-ING/-s **:** to make vermilion in color

vermilion rockfish *n* **:** a common commercially important red rock cod (*Sebastodes miniatus*) of the Pacific coast of No. America that is vermilion to brick red above shading to pink and light red on the sides and belly and liberally speckled with black on the back and sides

ver·min \ˈvərmə̇n, ˈvəm-, ˈvəim-\ *n, pl* **vermin** *usu pl in constr* [ME, fr. MF *vermin, vermine*, fr. L *vermis* worm] **1 :** animals obnoxious to man: as **a :** small animals (as lice, bedbugs, mice) that tend to occur in great numbers, are difficult to control, and are offensive as well as injurious **b :** birds and mammals (as owls and weasels) that prey upon game **c :** animals that at a particular time and place compete with man or his domestic animals (as for food) ⟨deer are considered ~ in New Zealand⟩ **2 :** a noxious or offensive person or persons

ver·mi·nate \-mə,nāt, *usu* -ād·+V\ *vi* -ED/-ING/-s [L *verminatus*, past part. of *verminare* to have worms, fr. *vermis* worm] **1** *archaic* **:** to breed vermin **2 :** to become infested with vermin

ver·mi·na·tion \,==ˈnāshən\ *n* -s [L *vermination-, verminatio* disease caused by botflies or worms, fr. *verminatus* (past part.) + *-ion-, -io* -ion] *obs* **:** the growth of vermin **:** the multiplication of vermin by breeding

ver·mi·no·sis \,vərməˈnōsə̇s\ *n, pl* **vermino·ses** \-ō,sēz\ [NL, fr. L *vermin-* (as in *verminare*) + *-osis*] **:** infestation with or disease caused by parasitic worms

ver·min·ous \ˈvərmənəs, ˈvəm-, ˈvəim-\ *adj* [L *verminosus*, fr. *vermin-* (as in *verminare*) + *-osus* -ous] **1 :** consisting of vermin **:** being vermin **:** NOXIOUS ⟨a ~ brood⟩ **2 :** tending to be a breeding place of vermin; *also* **:** infested by vermin **:** FILTHY, OFFENSIVE ⟨~ garbage⟩ ⟨a dirty ~ cellar⟩ **3 :** caused by or characterized by the presence of vermin ⟨~ disease⟩ — **ver·min·ous·ly** *adv*

ver·mip·a·rous \(ˌ)vərˈmipərəs\ *adj* [prob. fr. (assumed) NL *vermiparus*, fr. LL *vermi-* (fr. L *vermis*) + L *-parus* -parous] **:** producing wormlike young ⟨blowflies are ~⟩

ver·mis \ˈvərmə̇s\ *n, pl* **ver·mes** \-r,mēz\ [NL, fr. L, worm] **1 :** either of two parts of the median lobe of the cerebellum: **a :** one slightly prominent on the upper surface — called also *superior vermis* **b :** one on the lower surface sunk in the vallecula — called also *inferior vermis* **2 :** the median lobe or part of the cerebellum

ver·miv·o·rous \(ˌ)vərˈmivərəs\ *adj* [ISV *vermi-* + *-vorous*] **:** feeding on worms

ver·mix \ˈvərmiks\ *n* -ES [*vermi*form append*ix*] **:** VERMIFORM APPENDIX

¹ver·mont \və(r)ˈmänt *also* ,vərˈm- *or* vəˈm- *or* vəiˈm- *sometimes* -mȯnt *in NE*\ *adj, usu cap* [fr. *Vermont*, state in the northeastern U.S., irreg. fr. F *vert* green + *mont* mountain; intended as trans. of E *Green Mountains* — more at VERDANT, MOUNT] **:** of or from the state of Vermont ⟨*Vermont* marble⟩ **:** of the kind or style prevalent in Vermont **:** VERMONTESE

²vermont \"\ *n* -s *usu cap* [so called fr. its having been orig. imported into Vermont and bred there] **:** a Merino sheep having the skin folds greatly exaggerated

ver·mont·er \-ntə(r)\ *n* -s *cap* [*Vermont*, state in the northeastern U.S. + E *-er*] **:** a native or resident of the state of Vermont

¹ver·mont·ese \(,)=ˌmänt-ˈēz, -mȯn-, -ēs\ *adj, usu cap* [*Vermont* state + E *-ese*] **1 :** of, relating to, or characteristic of the state of Vermont **2 :** of, relating to, or characteristic of the people of Vermont

²vermontese \"\ *n, pl* **vermontese** *cap* **:** VERMONTER

vermont snakeroot *n, usu cap V* **:** WILD GINGER 2a

ver·mo·rel \;vərməˈrel, ;verm-\ *adj* [after Victor B. *Vermorel* †1927 Fr. industrialist and author] **:** of, relating to, or being a spray nozzle for projecting liquid insecticides in a fine spray with considerable force

ver·mouth *also* **ver·muth** \və(r)ˈmüth\ *n* -s [modif. of F *vermout*, fr. G *wermut* wormwood, absinthium, fr. MHG *wermuot, wermuote* wormwood, fr. OHG *wermuota* — more at WORMWOOD] **:** a white wine flavored esp. with herbs (as coriander, orris root, cinchona, calamus, elder flowers, angelica, cloves, nutmeg, or sage) that is used principally as an aperitif or in mixed drinks and that is produced chiefly in (1) a pale amber and dry variety and in (2) a dark amber and sweet variety — called also respectively (1) *French vermouth*, (2) *Italian vermouth*

vermouth cassis *n* **:** a mixed drink consisting of French vermouth, crème de cassis, and carbonated water

vernacle *var of* VERNICLE

¹ver·nac·u·lar *R* və(r)ˈnakyələr, *-R* vəˈnakyələ(r\ *adj* [L *vernaculus* homeborn, native (fr. *verna* homeborn slave, native) + E *-ar*] **1 a :** using a language or dialect native to a region or country rather than a literary, cultured, or foreign language ⟨~ speakers⟩ ⟨Ceylon had 336 English and 4701 ~ schools — *Origins & Purpose*⟩ ⟨in . . . this ~ poetry, the effect of Latin verse forms appears —H.O.Taylor⟩ **b :** belonging to or being a language or dialect developed in and spoken and used by the people of a particular place, region, or country in a form (as a dialect or a variety of cant, slang, jargon, or argot) considered nonstandard or substandard usu. as contrasted with a literary or cultured form ⟨his freedom from eccentricity, his gumption, to use the ~ word —William James⟩ ⟨only when a language . . . has ceased to be ~, does its form become unchanging —L.H.Gray⟩ ⟨slang widely used by . . . adults in the ~ speech of the street and country —H.D.Rinsland⟩ ⟨Hebrew . . . translated into the ~ Aramaic —J.R.Dummelow⟩ ⟨the various ~ languages of the region —Cecil Hobbs⟩ **c :** of, relating to, expressed in, or being a dialect or variety of a language normally or naturally spoken by all the speakers of a language ⟨crudely written, in a ~ style that is often tiring —Granville Hicks⟩ **d :** being the name of a plant or an animal in the vernacular language or common native speech as distinguished from the Latin nomenclature of scientific classification ⟨black alder and winterberry are ~ names of *Ilex verticillata*⟩ **2 :** of, relating to, characteristic of, or expressed in the style of a place, period, or group ⟨the ~ culture of our people —L.R. Beltran⟩; *esp* **:** of, relating to, or being the common building style of a period or place **:** employing the commonest or most typical architectural forms and decorations ⟨thatch and half=timber construction . . . of English ~ building —Harry Batsford & Charles Fry⟩ — **ver·nac·u·lar·ly** *adv*

²vernacular \"\ *n* -s **1 :** a vernacular language, expression, or mode of expression: as **a :** the native language or dialect of a country, region, or person ⟨autobiography of a Nigerian woman was dictated in the ~ —*Brit. Bk. News*⟩ ⟨the English ~ of Ireland⟩ **b :** a language that is spoken or written naturally at a particular period **:** LIVING LANGUAGE ⟨read Greek and Latin as energetically as he read Italian and French and other ~s —Gilbert Highet⟩ ⟨an imported ~ was widely current —Ruth Dean⟩ **c :** an expression or mode of expression natural to or used by a group or class ⟨has become a part of ethnological, even . . . of literary ~ —Gladys A. Reichard⟩ ⟨the findings of accredited biblical scholarship are translated into the ~s of childhood and youth —W.L.Sperry⟩ ⟨believed signs were the ~ of the deaf —J.S.Long⟩ **d :** the variety of a language or an expression in this variety commonly spoken by all or a part of the users of the language as distinguished from a written, literary, or cultured variety ⟨state the problem in simple ~ —Anthony Leviero⟩ ⟨in the inelegant ~, "So what?" —C.R.Rogers⟩ **e :** a vernacular name of a plant or animal **2 :** a style of artistic or technical and esp. architectural expression employing the commonest forms, materials, and decorations of a place, period, or group ⟨an impressive structure of white marble, expressed in a Renaissance ~ —*Amer. Guide Series: Minn.*⟩ ⟨builders, masons, and thatchers developed their forms of ~ in response to climatic conditions —Norman Wymer⟩ **syn** see DIALECT

ver·nac·u·lar·ism \-lə,rizəm\ *n* -s **:** a vernacular word or idiom

ver·nac·u·lar·i·ty \=,==ˈlarəd·ē\ *n* -ES **1 :** the use of or adherence to the vernacular in literary composition **2 :** VERNACULARISM

ver·nac·u·lar·ize \=ˈ=yələ,rīz\ *vt* -ED/-ING/-s **:** to render into or express in a vernacular

ver·nad·skite \və(r)ˈnadz,kīt, -d,sk-\ *n* -s [Vladimir I. *Vernadsky* †1945 Russ. geologist + E *-ite*] **:** a mineral $Cu_4(SO_4)_3(OH)_2.4H_2O$ consisting of a hydrous basic sulfate of copper

ver·nal \ˈvərnᵊl, ˈvən-, ˈvəin-\ *adj* [L *vernalis*, fr. *vernus* vernal (fr. *ver* spring) + *-alis* -al; akin to Gk *ear* spring, OIr *errach*, OSlav *vesna*, Skt *vasanta* and prob. to ON *vār* spring and perh. to L *aurora* dawn — more at EAST] **1 a :** appearing or occurring in the spring ⟨~ flora⟩ ⟨~ catarrh⟩ **b** *of migratory birds* **:** arriving at the breeding range in spring **2 :** of, relating to, or characteristic of the spring ⟨~ sunshine⟩ ⟨the ~ softness of first bloom —Claudia Cassidy⟩ **3 :** resembling or suggesting the spring of the year esp. in freshness, gentleness, or newness **:** SPRINGLIKE ⟨~ freshness of a child —Coulton Waugh⟩ — **ver·nal·ly** \-nᵊlē, -li\ *adv*

vernal grass *n* **:** SWEET VERNAL GRASS

ver·nal·i·za·tion \,=nᵊləˈzāshən, -nᵊl,īˈz-\ *n* -s [ISV ²*vernalize* + *-ation*] **:** the act or process of vernalizing

¹ver·nal·ize \ˈ=nᵊl,īz\ *vt* -ED/-ING/-s **:** to make vernal **:** give freshness to

²vernalize \"\ *vt* -ED/-ING/-s [ISV *vernal* + *-ize*] **:** to hasten the flowering and fruiting of (plants) by treating seeds, bulbs, or seedlings by a method (as exposing sometimes partially sprouted seed to low or high temperatures for a period) that induces a shortening of the vegetative period **:** JAROVIZE

vernal sedge *n* **:** a Eurasian sedge (*Carex caryophyllea*) with stoloniferous habit and early-blooming spikes that is naturalized in the eastern U.S. — called also *iron grass*

vernal witch hazel *n* **:** a fragrant witch hazel (*Hamamelis vernalis*) native to the lower Mississippi valley with very small flowers that appear from midwinter to spring

ver·nant \ˈvərnənt\ *adj* [ME *vernand*, fr. L *vernant-, vernans*, pres. part. of *vernare* to flourish, be verdant, fr. *ver* spring] *archaic* **:** VERNAL

ver·na·tion \,vərˈnāshən\ *n* -s [NL *vernation-, vernatio*, fr. L *vernatus* (past part. of *vernare* to flourish, be verdant) + *-ion-, -io* -ion] **:** the arrangement of foliage leaves within the bud — compare AESTIVATION

ver·ner's law \ˈver|nərz-, ˈvər|\ *n, usu cap V* [after Karl A. *Verner* †1896 Dan. philologist, its formulator] **:** a statement in historical linguistics: in medial or final position in voiced environments and when the immediately preceding vowel did not bear the principal accent in Proto-Indo-European, the Proto=Germanic voiceless fricatives *f*, *þ*, and *χ* which came from the Proto-Indo-European voiceless stops *p*, *t*, and *k* respectively, and the Proto-Germanic voiceless fricative *s* which came from Proto-Indo-European *s*, became the voiced fricatives *b*, *ð*, *g*, and *z* respectively, represented in many of the recorded Germanic languages by *b*, *d*, *g*, and *r* respectively ⟨the *b* of Gothic *þaurbum* "we need" as contrasted with the *f* of Gothic *þarf* "I need," the final *d* of English *dead* as contrasted with the final *th* of English *death*, the *g* of Old High German *zugum* "we pulled" as contrasted with the *h* of Old High German *ziohan* "to pull," and the *r* of English *were* as contrasted with the *s* of English *was*, are examples of *Verner's law*⟩ see GRAMMATICAL CHANGE; compare GRIMM'S LAW

ver·neuil process *or* **verneuil method** \(ˈ)verˈnər-, -nœ̄, *F* vernœy\ *n* [after A. V. L. *Verneuil*, 19th cent. Fr. mineralogist] **:** a procedure for growing large crystals (as of sapphire, ruby, spinel, or rutile) by adding the powdered material to the top of a rod the end of which is maintained at or close to the melting point by a flame directed vertically downward upon it

ver·neuk \və(r)ˈnük\ *vt* [Afrik, fr. D dial. *verneuken* to hinder, cheat, fr. D *ver-* for- (akin to OHG *far-, fir-*) + D dial. *neuken* to nag — more at FOR-] *southern Africa* **:** HUMBUG, CHEAT, SWINDLE

ver·ni·cle *or* **ver·na·cle** *n* -s \ˈvərnəkəl\ [ME *vernicle*, fr. MF *vernicle, veronique*, fr. ML *veronica* — more at VERONICA] **:** ²VERONICA

ver·ni·cose \ˈvərnə,kōs\ *adj* [ML *vernic-, vernix, veronic-, veronix* varnish + E *-ose* — more at VARNISH] **:** brilliantly polished ⟨~ leaves⟩

¹ver·ni·er \ˈvərnēər, ˈvənēə, ˈvəinēə(r\ *also* **vernier scale** *n* -s [after Pierre *Vernier* †1637 Fr. mathematician] **1 :** a short scale made to slide along the divisions of a graduated instrument (as the limb of a sextant or the scale of a barometer) for indicating parts of divisions and so graduated that a convenient number of its divisions are just equal in length to a number (either one less or one more) of the divisions of the instrument and so that parts of a division are determined by observing what line on the vernier coincides with a line on the instrument **2 :** a small auxiliary device (as a variable condenser of very small capacity in parallel with another condenser) used with a main device to obtain fine adjustment

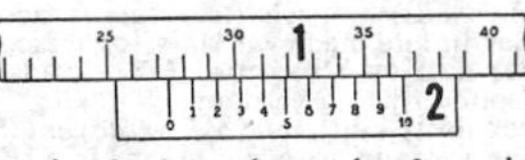

vernier 1: *1* regular scale, *2* vernier scale indicating measurement of 27.4

²vernier \"\ *adj* **:** having or comprising a vernier ⟨~ comparator⟩

vernier caliper *or* **vernier micrometer** *n* **:** a caliper rule with vernier attachment and adjusting screw for very fine measurement

vernier compass *n* **:** a surveyor's compass with a vernier by means of which a compensating adjustment may be made for magnetic variation to enable the reading of the correct bearings directly from the compass

vernier gage *n* **:** an adjustable gage (as a height or depth gage) having a vernier scale on it

ver·nis mar·tin \,verˈnē,märˈtan\ *n, usu cap M* [F, lit., Martin varnish, after Robert *Martin* †1765 and his brothers Guillaume, Simon-Étienne, & Julien *Martin*, 18th cent. Fr. furniture makers and decorators] **:** a preparation of green varnish with gold powder used to finish furniture; *also* **:** furniture finished with vernis Martin

ver·nis·sage \;ver(,)nēˈsäzh\ *n* -s [F, fr. *vernis* varnish + *-age* — more at VARNISH] **:** VARNISHING DAY

ver·nix \ˈvərniks\ *or* **vernix ca·se·o·sa** \-,kāsēˈōsə, -zēˈōzə\ *n* -ES [NL *vernix*, short for *vernix caseosa*, lit., cheesy varnish] **:** a pasty covering chiefly of dead cells and sebaceous secretions that protects the skin of the fetus

ver·no·nia \,vərˈnōnēə\ *n* [NL, fr. William *Vernon* †1711 Eng. botanist + NL *-ia*] **1** *cap* **:** a genus of chiefly tropical herbs or shrubs (family Compositae) occurring chiefly in So. America but including some that are native to No. America and having alternate leaves mostly red or purple and terminal cymose heads of perfect tubular flowers — see IRONWEED **2** -s **:** any plant of the genus *Vernonia*

vernonia purple *n* [NL *Vernonia*] **:** a grayish purplish red that is redder and deeper than average rose plum, bluer, stronger, and slightly lighter than Aztec maroon, and redder and darker than tourmaline pink

ver·no·nin \ˈvərnənə̇n, -ə,nin, vərˈnōnə̇n\ *n* -s [*vernon-* (fr. NL *Vernonia*) + *-in*] **:** a poisonous glucoside $C_{10}H_{24}O_7$ extracted from batiator root (*Vernonia nigritiana*) as a deliquescent powder

ver·nunft \ferˈnu̇nft, fər-, -ùm(p)ft\ *n* -s *usu cap* [G, fr. OHG *firnunft* perception, understanding, fr. *firneman* to perceive, understand, fr. *fir-* for- + *neman* to take — more at NIMBLE] : REASON 2f — distinguished from *verstand*

ve·ro·na \və'rōnə\ *adj, usu cap* [fr. *Verona*, Italy] : of or from the city of Verona, Italy : of the kind or style prevalent in Verona

verona brown *n, often cap V* : VANDYKE BROWN 2

verona earth *n, often cap V* : GREEN EARTH 2

verona green *n, often cap V* : TERRE VERTE

Ver·o·nal \'verə,nȯl, -,nᵊl, -,nal\ *trademark* — used for barbital

verona orris *n, usu cap V* : orrisroot from a German iris (*Iris germanica*) grown in central and southern Europe or from an iris (*Iris pallida*) indigenous to the eastern Mediterranean countries

verona yellow *n* **1** *usu cap V* : CASSEL YELLOW 1 **2** *often cap V* : ORPIMENT 2

¹ver·o·nese \¦verə¦nēz, -nēs\ *adj, usu cap* [It, fr. (assumed) VL *veronesis*, fr. L *veronensis*, fr. *Verona*, city in northeastern Italy + L *-ensis* -ese] : of or relating to Verona, Italy

²veronese \"\ *n, pl* **veronese** *cap* [It, fr. *veronese*, adj.] : a native or resident of Verona

veronese green *n, often cap V* [*veronese* in sense 1, fr. ¹*veronese*; in sense 2, after Paolo *Veronese* †1588 Ital. painter born in Verona; trans. of F *vert véronèse*] **1** : VIRIDIAN 2 **2** : EMERALD 2a

veronese yellow *n, often cap V* : ORPIMENT 2

¹ve·ron·i·ca \və'ränəkə\ *n* [NL, prob. modif. (influenced by the feminine name *Veronica*) of LGk *berenikion*, a plant, fr. Gk *Berenikē, Pherenikē* Berenice, feminine name] **1** *cap* : a genus of herbs and sometimes shrubs or trees (family Scrophulariaceae) of wide distribution, with small pink, white, blue, or purple flowers with a 4-lobed rotate corolla, two stamens, and a compressed capsule — see HEBE, SPEEDWELL **2** -s : any plant of the genus *Veronica*

²veronica \"\ *n* -s *sometimes cap* [ML, fr. *Veronica* St. Veronica, legendary saint of the 1st cent. A.D.] : a portrait or representation of the image of Christ's face said to have been impressed on the handkerchief that St. Veronica gave him to wipe his face as he passed on the way to his crucifixion; *also* : a handkerchief or cloth resembling the legendary one of St. Veronica — called also *vernicle*

³veronica \"\ *n* -s [Sp, fr. *Veronica*, feminine name] : a pase in bullfighting in which the cape is swung slowly away from the charging bull while the matador keeps his feet in the same position

ve·ron·i·cas·trum \=,=nə'kastrəm\ *n, cap* [NL, fr. *Veronica* + L *astrum* star, fr. Gk *astron* — more at STAR] : a small genus of tall herbs (family Scrophulariaceae) that resemble speedwells — see CULVER'S ROOT

ve·ron·i·cel·la \və,ränə'selə\ *n, cap* [NL, prob. fr. the name *Veronica* + NL *-ella*] : a genus (the type of the family Veronicellidae) of sluglike pulmonate gastropods having the body covered by a thick coriaceous mantle beneath which the head may be retracted

ver·pa \'vərpə\ *n, cap* [NL, fr. L, penis] : a genus of fungi (family Helvellaceae) with a bell-shaped cap attached only at the top of the stipe

ver·ra \'verə\ *Scot var of* VERY

ver·rel \'verəl\ *archaic var of* FERRULE

ver·ric·u·late \və'rikyələt, ve'-, -ə,lāt\ *or* **ver·ric·u·lat·ed** \-,lād·əd\ *adj* [L *verriculum* dragnet, seine + E *-ate* or *-ated* (fr. *-ate* + *-ed*)] : having verricules

ver·ri·cule \'verə,kyül\ *n* -s [L *verriculum* dragnet, fr. *verrere* to sweep — more at WAR] : a close tuft of nearly parallel upright hairs, bristles, or other slender filaments

¹ver·ru·ca \və'rükə, ve'r-\ *n, pl* **ver·ru·cae** \-ü(,)kē, -ü,kī, -ü(,)sē\ [L — more at WART] **1 a** : WART **b** : any of numerous warty skin lesions — usu. used in combination **2** : a warty elevation on a plant or animal surface; *specif* : a large tubercle bearing a tuft of bristles or spines in some caterpillars

²verruca \"\ *n, cap* [NL, fr. L, wart] : a nearly cosmopolitan genus (the type of the family Verrucidae) of sessile barnacles

verruca acu·mi·na·ta \-ə,kyümə'nād·ə, -nād·ə\ *n* [NL, acuminate wart] : a venereal wart

ver·ru·car·ia \,ver(y)ə'ka(a)rēə\ *n, cap* [NL, fr. L *verruca* wart + NL *-aria*] : a genus (the type of the family Verrucariaceae) of chiefly rock-inhabiting crustose lichens having small immersed globular apothecia

ver·ru·cat·ed \'ver(y)ə,kād·əd\ *adj* [NL *verrucatus* (fr. L *verruca* + *-atus* -ate) + E *-ed*] : VERRUCOSE

verruca vul·ga·ris \-,vəl'ga(a)rəs\ *n* [NL] : WART 1a

ver·ru·cose \'ver(y)ə,kōs\ *adj* [L *verrucosus*, fr. *verruca* wart + *-osus* -ose] : covered with wartlike elevations : WARTY ⟨a ~ capsule⟩ — **ver·ru·cose·ness** *n* -es

ver·ru·co·sis \,=='kōsəs\ *n, pl* **verruco·ses** \-ō,sēz\ [NL, fr. L *verruca* + *-osis*] : CITRUS SCAB

ver·ru·cous \və'rükəs, ve'r-\ *adj* [L *verruca* + E *-ous*] : of, relating to, or resembling a wart : characterized by warts

verrucous endocarditis *n* : endocarditis marked by the formation or presence of warty nodules of fibrin on the lips of the heart valves

ver·ru·cu·lose \və'rükyə,lōs, ve'r-\ *adj* [NL *verruculosus*, fr. L *verrucula* (dim. of *verruca* wart) + *-osus* -ose] : minutely verrucose

ver·ru·ga \və'rügə, ve'r-\ *n* -s [Sp, fr. L *verruca* — more at WART] **1** : VERRUCA **2** : VERRUGA PERUANA

verruga per·u·a·na \-,perə'wänə\ *also* **verruga pe·ru·vi·ana** \-pə,rüvē'anə, -'änə, -'änə\ *n* [*verruga peruana* fr. Sp, lit., Peruvian wart; *verruga peruviana* fr. NL, part trans. of Sp *verruga peruana*] : the second stage of bartonellosis characterized by warty nodules tending to ulcerate and bleed

ver·ry \'verē\ *archaic var of* VAIRÉ

vers *abbr* versed sine

ver·sa·bil·i·ty \,vərsə'biləd·ē\ *n* [LL *versabilitat-, versabilitas*, fr. L *versabilis* capable of being turned, changeable (fr. *versare, versari* to turn + *-bilis* capable of being acted upon) + *-tat-, -tas* -ty — more at -ABLE] *archaic* : capability of being turned

¹ver·sal \'vərsəl\ *adj* [short for *universal*] *archaic* : ENTIRE, UNIVERSAL ⟨looks as pale as any clout in the ~ world —*Shak.*⟩

²vers·al \"\ *n* -s [¹*verse* + *-al*] : an often elaborate and ornate capital letter used (as in illuminated manuscripts) at the beginning of a verse, paragraph, section, or chapter

¹ver·sant \'vərsᵊnt, 'vəs-, 'vəis-\ *adj* [L *versant-, versans*, pres. part. of *versare, versari* to turn, occupy oneself, meditate, be busy with] **1** : mentally engaged or occupied : CONCERNED, INTERESTED **2** : EXPERIENCED, PRACTICED **3** : closely acquainted : CONVERSANT ⟨men not ~ with courts of justice will not believe it —Sydney Smith⟩

²versant \"\ *n* -s [F, fr. pres. part. of *verser* to turn, incline, fr. L *versare* to turn] **1** : the slope of a side of a mountain chain **2** : the general slope of a country : INCLINATION

ver·sa·tile \'vərsəd·ᵊl, 'vəs-, 'vəis-, -sətᵊl, -sə(,)til *sometimes* -stᵊl *or* -(,)stil, *chiefly Brit* -sə,tīl\ *adj* [F or L; F *versatile*, fr. L *versatilis*, fr. *versatus* (past part. of *versare, versari* to turn, change, overturn, occupy oneself, be busy with, freq. of *vertere* to turn) + *-ilis* -ile — more at WORTH] **1 a** : marked by a tendency to change : fluctuating readily : CHANGEABLE, VARIABLE ⟨a ~ disposition⟩ **b** : easily swayed : FICKLE ⟨a ~ faction⟩ **2 a** : adapted to or embracing a variety of subjects, fields, or skills ⟨his steady political wisdom and his vast and ~ erudition —*Amer. Guide Series: Ind.*⟩ **b** : having a capacity for turning with ease from one thing to another : having a wide range of skills, aptitudes, or interests : MANY-SIDED ⟨extremely ~ in the sense that he was a painter of portraits, of genre, of still life, and of landscape —Eliot Clark⟩ ⟨the most ~ soprano now active —Irving Kolodin⟩ **3 a** (1) : capable of turning forward or backward : REVERSIBLE ⟨a ~ toe of a bird⟩ (2) : capable of moving laterally and up and down ⟨~ antennae⟩ **b** *of an anther* : having the filaments attached at or near the middle so as to swing freely — compare BASIFIXED **4 a** : having many uses or applications ⟨a handy, ~ material which you will find as veneer base and drawers in furniture, as cabinets and shelving —*Monsanto Mag.*⟩ **b** : capable of being worn in varied combinations or ways ⟨~, packable separates —*Woman's Home Companion*⟩ ⟨has evolved a ~ topcoat for a man who does a lot of traveling —*New Yorker*⟩ **5** : DIVERSIFIED ⟨a ~ line of over 100 different papers —*advt*⟩

syn VERSATILE, MANY-SIDED, and ALL-AROUND can all suggest being marked by or showing skill or ability or capacity or usefulness of many different kinds. When applied to persons, VERSATILE stresses aptitude and facility in many different activities requiring skill or ability, esp. the ability to turn with no diminution in skill from one activity to another without a hitch; applied to things, it stresses their multiple and diverse qualities, uses, or possibilities ⟨a *versatile* student⟩ ⟨a *versatile* athlete⟩ ⟨*versatile* interests⟩ ⟨a *versatile* combat weapon⟩ ⟨a *versatile* building material⟩ MANY-SIDED applied to persons stresses breadth or diversity of interests or accomplishments; applied to things, their diversity of aspects, attributes, or uses ⟨a *many-sided* scholar and citizen⟩ ⟨a *many-sided* and truly civilized life —G.M.Trevelyan⟩ ⟨a *many-sided* personality⟩ ⟨a *many-sided* agreement —*Manchester Guardian Weekly*⟩ ALL-AROUND implies completeness or symmetry in development, generally or within a single activity with many phases, not necessarily implying any special or great attainments but rather a general ability to do oneself credit; when applied to things, it implies an analogous general usefulness ⟨many observers have called him the best *all-around* reporter in the country —Stanley Walker⟩ ⟨the *all-around* adaptability and quality of our men —A.B.Vosseller⟩

ver·sa·tile·ly \-l(l)ē, -i\ *adv* : in a versatile manner

ver·sa·tile·ness *n* -es : VERSATILITY

ver·sa·til·i·ty \,==='tiləd·ē, -lətē, -i\ *n* -es [F *versatilité*, fr. *versatile* + *-ité* -ity] : the quality or state of being versatile ⟨a man of great ~, an explorer in all the sciences underlying agriculture —R.H.Chittenden⟩ ⟨a metal valued for its ~⟩

ver·sa·tion \,vər'sāshən\ *n* -s [L *versation-, versatio*, fr. *versatus* (past part. of *versare* to turn) + *-ion-, -io* -ion] *archaic* : the act or action of turning something over

vers de so·cié·té \,verdə,sōs,yā'tā, -ōsēə'tā\ *n* [F, society verse] : witty and typically ironic light verse written to amuse a sophisticated circle of readers

¹verse \'vərs, 'vōs, 'vəis\ *n* -s [ME *vers, fers*, fr. OF *vers* & OE *fers*, both fr. L *versus* row, line, verse; akin to L *vertere* to turn — more at WORTH] **1** : a line of metrical writing ⟨in English the caesura . . . can occur after any syllable, even the first or the ninth of a ten-syllable ~ —Malcolm Cowley⟩ **2** : VERSICLE 1 **3 a** (1) : metrical language : speech or writing distinguished from ordinary language by its distinctive patterning of sounds and esp. by its more pronounced or elaborate rhythm (2) : metrical writing that is distinguished from poetry esp. by its lower level of intensity and its lack of essential conviction and commitment ⟨many writers of ~ who have not aimed at writing poetry —T.S.Eliot⟩ (3) : POETRY 2 ⟨~ that gives immortal youth to mortal maids —W.S.Landor⟩ **b** : a particular example of metrical writing : POEM ⟨using some of her ~s as exercises in one of his textbooks —Antony Alpers⟩ **c** : a body of metrical writing (as of a single author, a period, or a country) ⟨Shakespearean ~⟩ ⟨Renaissance ~⟩ ⟨English ~⟩ **4 a** (1) : a unit of metrical writing larger than a single line : STANZA (2) : the portion of a song preceding the refrain or chorus and excluding any introduction ⟨sing the first and last ~s only⟩ **b** : a portion of an anthem or musical service to be performed by a single voice to each part **5** : one of the short divisions into which a chapter of the Bible is traditionally divided ⟨the first ~ of the first chapter of Genesis⟩

²verse \"\ *adj* : of, relating to, or written in verse ⟨~ technique⟩ ⟨a ~ drama⟩

³verse \"\ *vb* -ED/-ING/-s [ME *versen*, partly fr. *vers, fers* verse & partly fr. OE *fersian* to versify, fr. *fers* verse] *vi* : to make verse : write poetry : VERSIFY ~ *vt* **1** : to tell or celebrate in verse **2** : to turn into verse

⁴verse \"\ *vt* -ED/-ING/-s [back-formation fr. *versed*] : to familiarize by close association, study, or experience ⟨*versed* himself in the theater⟩

verse anthem *n* [¹*verse*] : an anthem in use in the English Church for solo voices or having a passage for solo voices — compare FULL ANTHEM

versecraft \'=,=\ *n* : the art or practice of writing verse

versed \'vərst, 'vōst, 'vəist\ *adj* [L *versatus* (past part. of *versare, versari* to turn, overturn, occupy oneself, be busy with) + E *-ed* — more at VERSATILE] : acquainted or familiar from experience, study, or practice : PRACTICED, SKILLED — usu. used with *in* ⟨~ in magnetism and familiar with compasses —K.K.Darrow⟩ ⟨was better ~ in diplomatic usage than any of his colleagues —F.A.Ogg & Harold Zink⟩

versed sine *n* [*versed* fr. NL *versus* turned (fr. past part. of L *vertere* to turn) + E *-ed*] : 1 minus the cosine of an angle

verse·let \'=lət\ *n* -s : a little verse

verse·man \'=mən\ *n, pl* **versemen** : a maker of verses : VERSIFIER

versemonger \'=,==\ *n* [¹*verse* + *monger*] : POETASTER

vers·er \'vərsər, 'vōsə(r, 'vəisə(r\ *n* -s : VERSIFIER

verse service *n* : a service in the English Church sung by solo voices

versesmith \'=,=\ *n* [¹*verse* + *smith*] : VERSIFIER

verse-speaking choir \'=¦==-\ *n* : a group organized for the choral speaking of poetry

vers·et \'vərsət, ¦vər¦set\ *n* -s [ME, fr. OF, fr. *vers* verse + *-et* — more at VERSE] **1 a** *archaic* : VERSICLE **b** : a short verse esp. from a sacred book ⟨sat . . . with an open Koran on his knees and chanted the ~s —Joseph Conrad⟩ **2** : a short interlude or prelude for the pipe organ

ver·si·cle \'vərsəkəl\ *n* -s [ME, fr. L *versiculus* short line, dim. of *versus* line, verse — more at VERSE] **1 a** : a short verse or sentence said or sung in public worship by a priest or minister and followed by a response from the people — symbol ℣ **b** : a suffrage taken from the Psalms in the Anglican Communion **2** : a little verse: as **a** : a line of verse ⟨here are some ~s, which I made one sleepless night —Lord Byron⟩ **b** : a brief poem or set of verses ⟨a little ~ that most of us learned when we were very young —Kenneth MacKenzie⟩

ver·si·col·or *or* **ver·si·colored** \¦vərsə+\ *adj* [*versicolor* fr. L, fr. *versus* (past part. of *vertere* to turn, change) + *color*; *versicolored* fr. L *versicolor* + E *-ed* — more at WORTH] **1** : having various colors : PARTI-COLORED, VARIEGATED ⟨~ flowers⟩ **2** : changeable in color : IRIDESCENT ⟨~ silk⟩

ver·sic·u·lar \(¦)vər¦sikyələr\ *adj* [L *versiculus* + E *-ar*] : of or relating to verses or versicles; *esp* : of or relating to biblical verses

ver·si·cule \'vərsə,kyül\ *n* -s [F, fr. L *versiculus*, dim. of *versus* line, verse] : a short poem : VERSICLE

ver·sic·u·lus \,vər'sikyələs\ *n, pl* **versicu·li** \-ə,lī\ [L] : VERSICLE

ver·si·fi·ca·tion \,vərsəfə'kāshən, ,vəs-, ,vəis-\ *n* -s [L *versification-, versificatio*, fr. *versificatus* (past part. of *versificare* to versify) + *-ion-, -io* -ion] **1** : the making of verses : the act, art, or practice of metrical composition ⟨~ based on . . . strict rules —H.A.Grubbs⟩ **2 a** : metrical structure **b** : a particular metrical structure or style ⟨commending her poem . . . for its ~ —Bertha Stearns⟩ **3** : a version in verse of something orig. in prose

ver·si·fi·ca·tor \'==fə,kād·ə(r)\ *n* -s [L, fr. *versificatus* (past part.) + *-or*] : VERSIFIER

ver·si·fi·er \'==,fī(ə)r, -īə\ *n* -s [ME, fr. *versifien* to versify + *-er*] **1** : one that makes verses; *esp* : a writer of light or poor verse ⟨the art of putting words on the line so that they create rhythms independent of the steady beat . . . distinguishes the poet from the ~ —Ronald McCraig⟩ **2** : one that converts into verse; *esp* : one that versifies prose

ver·si·fy \'==,fī\ *vb* -ED/-ING/-s [ME *versifien*, fr. MF *versifier*, fr. L *versificare*, fr. *versus* line, verse + *-ficare* -fy — more at VERSE] *vi* : to make verses : write poetry ~ *vt* **1** : to relate or describe in verse : compose in verse **2** : to turn into verse : render into metrical form

ver·sine *or* **ver·sin** \'vər,sīn\ *n* -s [by contr.] : VERSED SINE

versing *pres part of* VERSE

¹ver·sion \'vər\|zhən, 'vō\|, 'vəi\| *also* \|shən\ *n* -s [MF, fr. ML *version-, versio* action of turning, fr. L *versus* (past part. of *vertere* to turn) + *-ion-, -io* -ion — more at WORTH] **1 a** : something rendered from another language : TRANSLATION ⟨comparison of the original text with the English ~ —Milton Hindus⟩; *esp* : a free rendering of a literary work and esp. a poem into another language that endeavors to express the spirit rather than the literal sense of the original **b** : a translation or rendering of the Bible or a part of it **2 a** : an account or description from a particular point of view esp. as contrasted with another account ⟨each came . . . to give his separate ~ of the event —H.J.Laski⟩ ⟨their ~ of economic history —W.H.Whyte⟩; *broadly* : one of a set of related intellectual constructions ⟨the senate . . . passed its ~ of the excise tax bill —*Wall Street Jour.*⟩ ⟨his fictional ~ of what he saw —*Yankee*⟩ ⟨the printed problem or the teacher's blackboard ~ —I.G.Ellson⟩ ⟨the full ~ of the journals —Bernard De Voto⟩ **b** : one from a set of related artistic productions without one among them having a special status or with an original excluded from the set or with an original included among the set: as (1) : an adaptation of a literary work ⟨a stage ~ of the novel⟩ (2) : a distinct form of something regarded by its creator or others as one work ⟨published a shortened ~ myself —G.W.Knight⟩ ⟨the original ~s written piecemeal for a monthly publication —Peter Blake⟩ (3) : a musical composition adapted or arranged for a new purpose ⟨a ~ of a symphony arranged as a ballet suite⟩ ⟨a concert ~ of an opera⟩ (4) : a performance or interpretation of a work of art esp. when thought to have a marked character or excellence ⟨several recorded ~s of the opera⟩ ⟨his ~ of the role has matured⟩ (5) : an artistic production expressing an artist's or period's interpretation of a theme or style ⟨a modern ~ of Italian Renaissance architecture —*Amer. Guide Series: N. Y.*⟩ ⟨a swing ~ of a blues tune⟩ (6) : EDITION 2 **3** : a form, variant, species, or copy of a type or original ⟨an experimental night-fighter ~ of the plane⟩ ⟨the emery wheel — an improved ~ of the age-old grindstone —Howell Walker⟩ ⟨modern ~s of old-time medicine shows —*Amer. Guide Series: Texas*⟩ ⟨radioactive ~s of the ordinary elements —S.F.Mason⟩ ⟨in front of the three-folded mirror so that she could see three separate ~s of her . . . face—Virginia Woolf⟩ **4 a** : a condition of an organ or part (as the uterus) of being turned from its normal position **b** : the manual operation of turning a fetus in the uterus to aid delivery

²version \"\ *vt* -ED/-ING/-s : to make a translation of

ver·sion·al \¦zhənᵊl, ¦zhnəl, ¦sh-\ *adj* : of or relating to a version of the Bible

vers li·bre \ver'lēbr(ᵊ), -b(rə)\ *n, pl* **vers libres** \", -b(rə)z\ [F] : FREE VERSE

vers-librist \-brəst\ *also* **vers-libriste** \", ¦verlē¦brēst\ *n* -s [F *vers-libriste*] : a writer of free verse

ver·so \'vər(,)sō, 'vō(-, 'vəi(-\ *n* -s [NL *verso (folio)* the page being turned] **1** : the side of a leaf (as of manuscript) that is to be read second — contrasted with *recto* **2** : a left-hand page (as of a book) usu. carrying an even page number **3** : the back cover of a book and esp. the outside back cover; *also* : the corresponding part of a book jacket

verst *also* **verste** *or* **werst** \'vərst\ *n* -s [F *verste* & G *werst*, fr. Russ *versta* row, line, verst; akin to Lith *versti* to turn — more at WORTH] : a Russian unit of distance equal to 500 sagenes or 0.6629 miles

ver·stand \fer'shtänt, fər-\ *n* -s [G, fr. MHG *verstant*, fr. *verstan* to understand, fr. OHG *farstān*, fr. *far-* for- + *stān* to stand — more at FOR-, STAND] : UNDERSTANDING 3c — distinguished from *vernunft*

ver·ste·hen \fer'shtāən, fər-\ *n* -s *usu cap* [G, fr. *verstehen* to understand, fr. MHG *versten, verstan*] : an intuitive doctrine or method of interpreting human culture esp. in its subjective motivational and valuational aspects through the understanding of symbolic relationships

ver·sus \'vərsəs, 'vōs-, 'vəis-, -səz\ *prep* [L, towards, fr. *versus*, past part. of *vertere* to turn] **1** : AGAINST ⟨John Doe ~ Richard Roe⟩ ⟨the varsity ~ the scrubs⟩ ⟨the champion ~ the challenger⟩ **2** : in contrast to or as the alternative of ⟨free trade ~ protection⟩ — abbr. *v, vs*

versus cau·da·ti \'versə,skau'däd·(,)ē\ *n* [NL] : TAIL RHYME

¹vert \'vərt, 'vōt, 'vəit, *usu* -d·+V\ *n* -s [ME *veert, verte*, fr. MF *vert* green, fr. L *viridis* — more at VERDANT] **1 a** : the green and growing things of a forest esp. when forming cover or providing food for deer **b** : the right or privilege (as in England) of cutting living wood or sometimes of pasturing animals in a forest **2** : the color green esp. as an heraldic tincture

²vert \"\ *vt* -ED/-ING/-s [L *vertere*] : to cause to turn or bend from one direction to another

³vert \"\ *n* -s [short for *convert*] : one who changes his affiliation or orientation esp. in religion

⁴vert \"\ *vi* -ED/-ING/-s : to become a convert

vert *abbr* **1** vertebra; vertebrate **2** vertical

vertebr- *or* **vertebro-** *comb form* [NL, fr. L *vertebra*] **1** : vertebra : vertebrae ⟨*vertebri*form⟩ ⟨*vertebr*ectomy⟩ **2** : vertebral and ⟨*vertebro*femoral⟩

ver·te·bra \'vər\|d·əbrə, 'vō\|, 'vəi\|, \|təb-, ÷ -,brā\ *n, pl* **vertebrae** \-(,)brē, ÷ -,brā\ *also* **vertebras** [L, joint, vertebra; akin to L *vertere* to turn — more at WORTH] **1** : one of the bony or in young or primitive individuals more or less cartilaginous elements that together make up the spinal column of a vertebrate, that in lower forms consists of several imperfectly fused elements, and that in higher vertebrates is a solidly fused structure consisting of a cylindrical centrum articulated with adjacent centra by cartilaginous or elastic pads, a dorsal arch arising from the centrum and providing a protected passage for the spinal cord, and various spinous and articular processes by which the spinal column is stiffened and attached to muscles and other bones (as the ribs) **2** *vertebrae pl* : SPINAL COLUMN, BACKBONE **3** : any of a series of ossicles that resemble the centrum of a vertebra and form the axis of the arm in most ophiurans

¹ver·te·bral \-,brəl, (,)vər'tēb-, vē-, vei-\ *adj* [NL *vertebralis*, fr. L *vertebra* + *-alis* -al] **1** : of, relating to, or constituting vertebrae or the vertebral column : SPINAL **2** : composed of or having vertebrae **3** : situated near or in the median dorsal plane of a vertebrate animal

²vertebral \"\ *n* -s : a vertebral part or element (as an artery or a vein or plate); *esp* : a median dorsal plate in the carapace of a turtle

vertebral aponeurosis *n* : a fascia of the back separating the muscles that hold erect the spinal column and head from those that move the arm and shoulders and extending from the spinous processes to the angles of the ribs

vertebral artery *n* : a large branch of the subclavian artery that ascends through the foramina in the transverse processes of each of the cervical vertebrae except the last one or two, enters the cranium through the foramen magnum, and unites with the corresponding artery of the opposite side to form the basilar artery

vertebral canal *n* : SPINAL CANAL

vertebral column *n* : SPINAL COLUMN

ver·te·bral·ly \-brəlē\ *adv* : toward, upon, or with the vertebrae

vertebral plate *n* **1** : the part of the mesoblast that in most craniate vertebrate embryos lies near the notochord and forms somites **2** : a vertebral plate of a turtle

vertebral rib *n* : FLOATING RIB

vertebral vein *n* : a tributary of the innominate vein formed by the union of branches which originate in the occipital region and form a plexus about the vertebral artery in its passage through the foramina of the cervical vertebrae and receiving various branches which join it near its termination

ver·te·brar·ia \,vərd·ə'bra(a)rēə\ *n, cap* [NL, fr. *vertebr-* + *-aria*] : a genus of fossil plants based upon rootlike remains of Triassic age that resemble a vertebral column

ver·te·bra·ta \,=='bräd·ə, -rād·ə\ *n pl, cap* [NL, fr. neut. pl. of *vertebratus* vertebrate] **1** : a major division of animals that is usu. a subphylum of Chordata, that comprises bilaterally symmetrical animals with a segmented spinal column or in primitive forms with a persistent notochord, a tubular dorsal nervous system divisible into brain and spinal cord, an anterior head bearing a mouth and the major sense organs, an internal articulated skeleton of bone or cartilage, respiration by gills or lungs, and not more than two pairs of limbs which may be modified as grasping, walking, swimming, or flying organs in different members of the division, and that includes the mammals, birds, reptiles, amphibians, fishes, elasmobranchs, and cyclostomes and sometimes the lancelets — compare ACRANIA **2** *in some classifications* : CHORDATA

¹ver·te·brate \'== brə\|t, -,brā\|, *usu* \|d·+V\ *adj* [NL *vertebratus*, fr. L, jointed, fr. *vertebra* joint, vertebra + *-atus* -ate] **1 a** : having a spinal column **b** (1) : of or relating to the Vertebrata (2) : characteristic of or found in an animal belonging to the Vertebrata **2** : having a strong framework suggesting vertebrae **3** : organized or constructed in orderly or developed form ⟨a ~ piece of composition⟩

²**ver·te·brate** \-,brāt, *usu* -ād·+V\ *vt* -ED/-ING/-S : to link together in a manner suggesting vertebrae
³**vertebrate** *same as* ¹VERTEBRATE\ *n* -S [NL *Vertebrata*] : a vertebrate animal
ver·te·brat·ed \'≈≈,brād·əd\ *adj* [NL *vertebratus* + E *-ed*] **1** : VERTEBRATE **2** : composed of or having vertebrae or segments resembling vertebrae ⟨a fish with a ~ tail⟩
ver·te·bra·tion \,≈≈'brāshən\ *n* -S [¹*vertebrate* + *-ion*] : strength as if from a firm spinal column : FIRMNESS ⟨the solid ~ of his logic⟩
ver·te·bre \'vərd·əbə(r)\ *n* -S [MF, fr. L *vertebra*] *archaic* : VERTEBRA
vertebro- — see VERTEBR-
ver·te·bro·chondral \¦vərd·əbrō+\ *adj* [*vertebr-* + *chondral*] : of, relating to, or involving a vertebra and a costal cartilage
ver·te·bro·sternal \"+\ *adj* [*vertebro-* + *sternal*] : of, relating to, or extending between the vertebrae and the sternum
verted *past of* VERT
ver·tep \vər'tep\ *n* -S [Russ, lit., cavern, den] : an early Russian puppet show
ver·tex \'vər,teks, 'vəl, 'vəil\ *n, pl* **verti·ces** \ld·ə,sēz, ¦tə-\ *also* **vertexes** \¦,teksəz\ [L *vertex, vortex* whirl, whirlpool, highest point, peak, fr. L *vertere* to turn — more at WORTH] **1 a** (1) : the point opposite to and farthest from the base in a figure (2) : the termination or intersection of lines or curves ⟨the ~ of an angle⟩ (3) : a point where an axis of an ellipse, parabola, or hyperbola intersects the curve itself **b** : the point of intersection of an axially symmetrical optical surface with its axis of symmetry **c** (1) : ZENITH 1; *also* : the point on the limb of a celestial body nearest the zenith (2) : a point on the celestial sphere toward which star streaming is directed **2** : the top of the head: as **a** : the upper part of the head of an insect in front above the antennae and between the compound eyes **b** (1) : the highest point of the human skull when held in the eye-ear plane (2) : the highest median point of the head of the living human when in a natural position **3** : a principal or highest point : SUMMIT, APEX ⟨a monument on the ~ of the hill commands a breathtaking view⟩; *often* : the high point of an arch : CROWN, KEYSTONE
¹**ver·ti·cal** \'vər¦d·ə̇kəl, 'vəl, 'vəil, ¦t¦, ¦ēk-\ *adj* [MF or LL; MF *vertical*, fr. LL *verticalis*, fr. L *vertic-, vertex* peak + *-alis* -al] **1 a** : of or relating to the vertex : situated at the highest point : directly overhead or in the zenith **b** *obs* : being or relating to a high point (as of a life, of eminence, or of excellence) **c** : of or relating to the vertex of the head **d** : of, relating to, or being an aerial photograph taken with the camera pointing straight down or nearly so **2 a** : perpendicular to the plane of the horizon or to a primary axis : UPRIGHT, PLUMB ⟨a ~ line⟩ **b** (1) : located at right angles to the plane of a supporting surface (2) : lying in the direction of an axis : LENGTHWISE **c** : directed upward or downward at a right angle to the plane of the body or part of the surface of the earth ⟨~ fins of a fish⟩ **3** : relating to, involving, or integrating discrete elements (as from lowest to highest or from first to last): as **a** : consisting of two or more economic units on different levels of production or distribution ⟨a ~ business organization⟩ ⟨a completely ~ manufacturing operation —*N.Y. Times*⟩ **b** : of, relating to, or comprising persons of different status ⟨the ~ arrangement of society⟩ ⟨race, religion, and nation are examples of ~ groups —C.M.Panunzio⟩ — compare INDUSTRIAL UNION **4** : relating to harmony esp. in a homophonic composition as contrasted with a contrapuntal one — compare HORIZONTAL 2b(3) **5** *of a stamp* : having a rectangular shape with the shorter sides forming the top and bottom **6** : coming from or involving action from above and specif. from the air ⟨~ warfare⟩; *esp* : constituting aerial bombing from a craft flying parallel with the earth
syn PERPENDICULAR, PLUMB: VERTICAL in general nontechnical use may suggest a line or direction rising upward toward a zenith ⟨the design is the characteristic American perpendicular skyscraper style, with horizontal lines subdued and the *vertical* lines emphasized —*Amer. Guide Series: Minn.*⟩ ⟨the *vertical*, or conventional, approach, was to begin at a designated place and time in history, and then climb the chronological ladder until you reached the present —Norman Cousins⟩ and it may also be applied to a straight downward direction but is so used less frequently ⟨face, as many have done and are doing, the level as opposed to the *vertical* fire of the enemy —Sir Winston Churchill⟩ PERPENDICULAR may suggest a stiff straightness; it is somewhat more likely than VERTICAL to suggest a downward line or straight drop or descent ⟨it appears that the water is broken nowhere by striking against the rocks, and that therefore the descent is *perpendicular* —Anthony Trollope⟩ ⟨the trail led under the foot of a high, almost *perpendicular* rock —C.G.D.Roberts⟩ PLUMB in this sense is mainly an artisan's or builder's term indicating exact verticality capable of being ascertained by plumb line ⟨the wall was not *plumb*⟩
²**vertical** \"\ *n* -S : something that is vertical: as **a** *obs* : VERTEX, HEIGHT, SUMMIT **b** : a vertical line, plane, or circle; *esp* : PERPENDICULAR **c** : a vertical member in a truss **d** : a vertical photograph : an aerial photograph taken with the camera pointed straight downward **e** : UPRIGHT PIANO
vertical angle *n* **1** : an angle measured on a vertical circle either upward or downward from the horizon **2** : either of two angles lying on the opposite sides of two intersecting lines or planes
vertical bank *n* : a flight maneuver in which an airplane is so steeply banked that its lateral axis approaches the vertical
vertical circle *n* **1 a** : a great circle of the celestial sphere whose plane is perpendicular to that of the horizon : AZIMUTH CIRCLE **b** : an astronomical observational circle so mounted as to turn to any azimuth **2** : a theodolite having a finely divided circle on its horizontal axis and used for measuring altitudes
vertical combination *or* **vertical integration** *n* : a combining of business firms engaged in different phases of the manufacture and distribution of a product into an interacting whole
vertical curve *n* : an easement curve in railroad track to connect intersecting grade lines
vertical engine *n* : an engine in which the piston moves vertically up and down and the crankshaft is usu. below the cylinder
vertical envelopment *n* : envelopment of a military enemy from the air (as with troops dropped by parachute or landed by gliders, helicopters, or airplanes) usu. to seize key objectives in the enemy's rear
vertical-fiber brick *n* : a wire-cut vitrified paving brick laid in a pavement with a wire-cut face up
vertical file *n* **1** : a file the records of which are placed upright or on edge **2** : a collection of pamphlets, clippings, and ephemera (as in a library) that is maintained to answer brief questions quickly or to provide points of information not easy to locate elsewhere

vertical file 1

vertical fin *n* : any of the median fins of a fish : a dorsal, anal, or caudal fin
vertical flute *n* : RECORDER
vertical gradient *n* : LAPSE RATE
vertical grain *n* : quarter-sawed lumber
vertical-grained \¦≈≈≈¦≈\ *adj* : QUARTER-SAWED
vertical index *n* : the ratio of the height of the cranium to its length multiplied by 100
vertical interval *or* **vertical distance** *n* : CONTOUR INTERVAL
ver·ti·cal·ism \'≈≈kə,lizəm\ *n* -S [ISV *vertical* + *-ism*] : VERTICALITY
ver·ti·cal·i·ty \,≈≈'kaləd·ē\ *n* -ES : the quality or state of being vertical : PERPENDICULARITY ⟨the principle of ~ which makes tall towers seem to soar — Sheldon & Martha C. Cheney⟩
vertical keel *n* **1** : KEELSON b **2** : ³KEEL 1a(2)
vertical lift bridge *n* : a drawbridge of which the moving parts rise vertically
vertical-lift mower *n* : a mowing machine so designed that the cutter bar can be lifted to nearly a vertical position permitting the machine to pass close to an obstacle
vertical limb *n* : a graduated arc attached to an instrument (as a theodolite), for measuring vertical angles
vertical line *n* : a line perpendicular to a surface or to another line considered as a base: as **a** : a line perpendicular to the horizon **b** : a line parallel to the sides of a page or sheet as distinguished from a horizontal line **c** : the direction of a plumb line **2** : a line normal to the surface of still water
ver·ti·cal·ly \'≈≈k(ə)lē, -li\ *adv* : so as to be vertical : in respect to the vertical
ver·ti·cal·ness *n* -ES : VERTICALITY
vertical plane *n* **1** : a plane that passes through a vertical line **2** : a plane of perspective passing through the point of sight and perpendicular to the ground plane and to the picture
vertical renversement *n* : an air maneuver in which an airplane reverses its direction of flight by pulling up in a vertical climb until stall, dropping the nose in a wingover, and doing a half-roll
vertical sash *n* : a sash sliding up and down — compare FRENCH SASH
vertical saw *n* **1** : a saw (as a muley saw) whose supporting frame moves in vertical guides **2** : a circular saw operating in a vertical plane
vertical section *n* : a mechanical drawing showing an interior, wall thicknesses, and similar relations as if made on a vertical plane passing through the object (as a building) depicted
vertical south dial *n* : a sundial (as on the south wall of a building) in the vertical plane facing south
vertical structure *n* : music composed or viewed as a succession of harmonies or chordal units in contrast to simultaneous independent melodies — compare HORIZONTAL STRUCTURE
vertical trust *n* : a trust formed by vertical combination
vertical union *n* : INDUSTRIAL UNION
vertices *pl of* VERTEX
ver·ti·cil \'vərd·ə,sil\ *n* -S [NL *verticillus*, fr. L, whorl of a spindle] : a circle or whorl of similar body parts (as flowers about a point on an axis or sensory hairs about an antennal joint)
verticil- *comb form* [NL, fr. *verticillus*, fr. L, whorl of a spindle, dim. of *vertic-, vertex* whirl — more at VERTEX] : whorl : verticil ⟨*verticill*ary⟩
ver·ti·cil·las·ter \,vərd·əsə'lastə(r)\ *n* -S [NL, fr. *verticill-* + *-aster*] : a mixed inflorescence (as in many labiates) consisting of a pair of much-condensed nearly sessile cymes arranged around an axis like a true verticil — see INFLORESCENCE illustration
ver·ti·cil·las·trate \¦≈≈≈¦la,strāt, -astrət\ *adj* [NL *verticillaster* + E *-ate*] : bearing or arranged in verticillasters
ver·ticil·la·tae \,vərd·əsə'lād·(,)ē, (,)vər,tis-\ [NL, fr. fem. pl. of *verticillatus* verticillate] *syn of* CASUARINALES
ver·ticil·late \¦vərd·ə¦silət, (,)vər'tisə,lāt\ *adj* [NL *verticillatus*, fr. *verticillus* + L *-atus* -ate] : arranged in verticils : WHORLED; *esp* : arranged in a transverse whorl like the spokes of a wheel ⟨~ leaves⟩ ⟨a ~ shell⟩ — **ver·ticil·late·ly** \-lē\ *adv* — **ver·ticil·la·tion** \,vərd·əsə'lāshən, (,)vər,tisə'l-\ *n* -S
ver·tic·il·lat·ed \-,lād·əd\ *adj* [NL *verticillatus* + E *-ed*] : VERTICILLATE
verticilli- *comb form* [NL *Verticillium*] : *Verticillium* ⟨*verticilli*osis⟩
ver·ti·cil·li·ose \,vərd·ə'silē,ōs\ *n* -S [ISV *verticilli-* + *-ose*] : VERTICILLIOSIS
ver·ti·cil·li·o·sis \,≈≈,silē'ōsə̇s\ *n, pl* **verticillio·ses** \-ō,sēz\ [NL, fr. *verticilli-* + *osis*] : a wilt disease of various plants caused by soil-borne fungi of the genus *Verticillium*
ver·ti·cil·li·um \,≈≈'silēəm\ *n* [NL, fr. *verticill-*] **1** *cap* : a genus of imperfect fungi (order Moniliales) having conidia borne singly at the apex of whorled branchlets and including several that cause destructive wilts in plants — see VERTICILLIOSIS **2** -S : a fungus of the genus *Verticillium*
verticillium wilt *n* : VERTICILLIOSIS
ver·tic·i·ty \,vər'tisəd·ē\ *n* -ES [NL *verticitat-, verticitas*, fr. L *vertic-, vertex* highest point, peak + *-itat-, -itas* -ity — more at VERTEX] : a tendency (as shown by a magnetized needle) to turn toward a magnetic pole ⟨the old window stanchions had become magnetic, proving, as he thinks, that iron acquires ~ —Walter Pater⟩
ver·tig·i·nate \,vər'tijə,nāt\ *vi* -ED/-ING/-S [LL *vertiginatus*, past part. of *vertiginare* to whirl around, fr. L *vertigin-, vertigo* action of whirling] : to whirl dizzily around : TWIRL
ver·tig·i·nous \-nəs\ *adj* [L *vertiginosus* one suffering from dizziness, vertiginous, fr. *vertigin-, vertigo* + *-osus* -ose] **1** : characterized or accompanied by vertigo ⟨a ~ dream⟩ ⟨~ disorders⟩ **2 a** : suffering from vertigo : afflicted with dizziness : GIDDY **b** : having a light or silly mind : deficient in steadfastness or constancy : inclined to frequent and often pointless or foolish change **3** : causing or tending to cause dizziness : of a kind likely to cause vertigo ⟨~ heights⟩ ⟨a ~ speed⟩ **4** : involving or marked by turning : ROTARY ⟨the ~ motion of the earth⟩ — **ver·tig·i·nous·ly** *adv*
ver·ti·go \'vər¦d·ə̇,gō, 'vəl, 'vəil, ¦t¦, ¦ē,gō *sometimes* (,)vər'tē(,)gō *or* (,)vər'tī(,)gō\ *n* [L, action of whirling, fr. *vertere* to turn — more at WORTH] **1** *pl* **vertigoes** \-ōz\ *or* **vertig·i·nes** \,vər'tijə,nēz\ **a** (1) : a disturbance which is associated with various known diseases or due to unknown causes and in which the external world seems to revolve around the individual or in which the individual seems to revolve in space — called also respectively *objective vertigo, subjective vertigo* (2) : DIZZINESS **b** : a dizzy confused condition of mind : a state in which all things seem to be whirling around : mental bewilderment or confusion **c** : disordered equilibration or vertiginous movements in a lower animal often forming a symptom of a specific disease; *also* : a disease (as gid or staggers) marked by such vertigo **2** *cap* [NL, fr. L] : a genus that comprises very small cylindrical land snails usu. found under stones and dead wood and is included in the family Pupillidae or made the type of a separate family
verting *pres part of* VERT
vert russe \¦ver¦rüs\ *n* [F] : RUSSIAN GREEN
verts *pl of* VERT, *pres 3d sing of* VERT
vertu *var of* VIRTU
ver·u·la·mi·an \,verə'lāmēən\ *adj, usu cap* [Baron *Verulam* (title of Francis Bacon †1626 Eng. philosopher and author) + E *-an*] : of, relating to, or like that of Francis Bacon
ver·u·mon·ta·num \,≈≈,män·'tānəm\ *n* -S [NL, fr. L *veru* spit, dart + *montanum*, neut. of *montanus* mountainous — more at SAUERKRAUT, MOUNTAIN] : an elevation in the floor of the prostatic portion of the urethra where the seminal ducts enter
ver·vain \'vər,vān\ *n* -S [ME *verveine*, fr. MF, fr. L *verbena*, sing. of *verbenae* sacred boughs of laurel, olive, or myrtle, class of medicinal plants; akin to L *verber* rod, Gk *rhabdos* rod, *rhamnos* buckthorn and prob. to Gk *rhembein* to whirl, OHG *werfan* to throw — more at WARP] **1** : a plant of the genus *Verbena; esp* : one having small spicate flowers — see BLUE VERVAIN **2** : VERBENA 3
vervain family *n* : VERBENACEAE
vervain hummingbird *n* : a very small hummingbird (*Mellisuga minima*) of Hispaniola and Jamaica
vervain mallow *n* : a European mallow (*Malva alcea*) often cultivated for its rose-colored flowers
vervain sage *n* : WILD SAGE 1
vervain thoroughwort *n* : a rough-foliaged perennial herb (*Eupatorium pilosum*) of the eastern U.S. having opposite mostly oblong leaves and an open cymose cluster of white flower heads
verve \'vərv, 'vav,'vaiv, 've(ə)rv, 'veav\ *n* -S [F, fr. MF, caprice, fantasy, fr. OF, proverb, delivery, verbosity, fr. L *verba*, pl. of *verbum* word — more at WORD] **1** *archaic* : special ability or talent **2 a** : a forceful and lively quality or manner of composition or performance (as of a poem, painting, musical work) : DASH, VIVACITY ⟨the animals were drawn with such ~ that they seemed ready to leap straight out of the scroll —*New Yorker*⟩ ⟨performing with matchless ~ and gusto —Barry Carman⟩ **b** : ENERGY, VITALITY ⟨with the ~ of a girl under twenty, she recovered her spirits —Francis Hackett⟩ **syn** see VIGOR
ver·veine \'vər,vān\ *n* -S [F, fr. MF] : VERVAIN
ver·vel \'vərvəl\ *also* **var·vel** \'vär-\ *n* -S [MF *vervelle*, fr. LL *vertibulum* joint of the spine; akin to L *vertebra* — more at VERTEBRA] : a ring or one of several rings attached to a bird's leg for securing the bird to its perch
ver·velle \,vər'vel\ *n* -S [obs. F, fr. MF, vervelle, vervel] : a staple or small loop used in medieval armor esp. for lacing a camail to the headpiece
ver·ver \(')vā¦vā, (')ve¦ve\ *n* -S [Haitian Creole] : a voodooistic ritual design commonly traced on the ground
ver·vet \'vərvə̇t\ *n* -S [F, fr. MF, fr. *vert* green + *-vet* (as in *grivet*); fr. its color — more at VERT] : a southern and eastern African guenon monkey (*Cercopithecus pygerythrus*) related to the grivet but having the face, chin, hands, and feet black
¹**very** \'verē, -ri\ *adj* -ER/-EST [ME *verray, verry*, fr. OF *verai*, fr. (assumed) VL *veracus*, fr. L *verac-, verax* true, truthful, fr. *verus* true; akin to OE *wǣr* true, correct, *wǣr* faith, care, bond of friendship, OHG *wāra* bond, trust, care, ON *vārar* pledge, OIr *fír* true, Gk *ēra* (acc.) favor, OSlav *vēra* faith; basic meaning: care, loyalty] **1 a** : properly entitled to the name or designation : TRUE ⟨~ God of ~ God, begotten not made —*Nicene Creed*⟩ ⟨the fierce hatred of a ~ woman —J.M. Barrie⟩ **b** : ACTUAL, REAL, VERITABLE ⟨whether thou be my ~ son . . . or not —Gen 27:21 (AV)⟩ ⟨the ~ blood and bone of our grammar —H.L.Smith b. 1913⟩ **c** : SIMPLE, PLAIN ⟨in ~ truth, life is short —Benjamin Farrington⟩ **2 a** : EXACT, PRECISE ⟨might be the ~ condition we seek —H.H.Curtice⟩ ⟨is in the ~ heart of the Irish capital —Gerard MacGowan⟩ **b** : exactly suitable or necessary ⟨may be the ~ thing for the purpose —C.K.Ogden⟩ **3 a** : ABSOLUTE, UTTER ⟨the *veriest* idiot that ever lived —Joseph Conrad⟩ **b** : SHEER, UNQUALIFIED ⟨the sailors mutinied from ~ hunger —T.B.Macaulay⟩ **4** — used as an intensive esp. to emphasize identity ⟨my ~ chains and I grew friends —Lord Byron⟩ ⟨cause the ~ rocks to tremble —*Amer. Guide Series: Maine*⟩ ⟨the ~ language of the churches is becoming unintelligible to them —W.R.Inge⟩ **5** : MERE, BARE ⟨the *veriest* shadow of a mighty dynasty —W.E. Swinton⟩ ⟨the ~ thought of thee with sweetness fills the breast —Edward Caswall⟩ **6** : SELFSAME, IDENTICAL ⟨her own mother had once used that ~ word —Helen Howe⟩ **7** : SPECIAL, PARTICULAR ⟨the path that led across the roots of his ~ tree —Nathaniel Hawthorne⟩ **syn** see SAME
²**very** \"\ *adv* [ME *verray*, fr. *verray*, adj.] **1** : to a high degree : EXTREMELY, EXCEEDINGLY ⟨a ~ hot day⟩ ⟨sun is ~ bright⟩ ⟨is ~ much a believer in reason —F.A.Pottle⟩ ⟨saw the four of them ~ plainly —Carson McCullers⟩ ⟨is ~ pleased to edit the . . . magazine —H.M.McLuhan⟩ ⟨towns were ~ separated from one another —L.D.Stamp⟩ ⟨round the corner came a ~ ~ nice old lady —Lilian Balch⟩ **2** : in actual fact : REALLY, TRULY ⟨the ~ best store in town⟩ ⟨on the ~ next page⟩ ⟨the ~ same statement made in different ways —*Times Lit. Supp.*⟩ ⟨expected the ~ opposite result⟩ **3** *archaic* : EXACTLY, PRECISELY ⟨looked as though in her heart she was now, ~ now, singing the old lines —Llewelyn Powys⟩
very high frequency *n* **1** : a radio frequency in the range of the radio spectrum above high frequency — see RADIO FREQUENCY table **2** : a radio frequency in the part of the very high frequency band between 100 and 156 megacycles used for radio aids to airplane navigation and communication
very-high-frequency *adj* : of or relating to very high frequency or to a radio wave having such a frequency
very light \'verē, -ri-\ *n, usu cap V* [after Edward W. *Very* †1910 Am. naval officer] : one of the flares used in the Very system of signaling — compare STAR SHELL, VERY'S NIGHT SIGNALS
very low frequency *n* : a radio frequency in the lowest range of the radio spectrum — see RADIO FREQUENCY table
very-low-frequency *adj* : of or relating to very low frequency or to a radio wave having such a frequency
very pistol *n, usu cap V* [after Edward W. *Very* †1910] : a pistol designed to fire Very lights
very reverend — used as a courtesy title for various ecclesiastical officials (as Roman Catholic and Anglican deans, rectors of Roman Catholic colleges and seminaries, superiors of religious houses, monsignor with the rank of papal chamberlain)
very's night signals *also* **very night signals** *n pl, usu cap V* [after Edward W. *Very* †1910 Am. naval officer] : a system of signaling in which balls of red and green fire are fired from a pistol and their arrangement in groups denotes numbers having a code significance
ves *pl of* VE
ves *abbr* **1** [L *vesica*] bladder **2** vesicular **3** vessel **4** vestry
ve·si \'vāsē, -āzē\ *n* -S [Fiji] : IPIL
vesic *abbr* [L *vesicula*] blister
vesi·ca \və'sēkə, və'sīkə, 'vesə̇kə\ *n, pl* **vesi·cae** \-ē,kī, -ī(,)kē, -ī(,)sē, -ə,kē, -ə,kī, -ə,sē\ [L *vesica, vensica*; akin to L *venter* belly — more at VENTER] **1** : BLADDER **2** *obs* : a large vessel for distilling liquor **3** : VESICA PISCIS ⟨the ~ and festoons common in Irish cut glass⟩
ves·i·cal \'vesə̇kəl, -sēk-\ *adj* [F *vésical*, fr. MF *vesical*, fr. L *vesica* + MF *-al*] **1** : of or relating to a bladder; *esp* : of or relating to the urinary bladder **2** : of the shape of a bladder : having the form of a pointed oval
vesical artery *n* : any of several arteries derived from the anterior trunk of the hypogastric artery and distributed to the urinary bladder and adjacent parts
vesical neck *n* : the part of the urinary bladder immediately surrounding the internal orifice of the urethra
vesical plexus *n* **1** : a plexus of nerves at the base of the bladder comprising preganglionic fibers chiefly from the hypogastric plexus and lodging postganglionic neurons whose fibers are distributed to the bladder **2** : a venous plexus between the muscular wall of the bladder and the overlying peritoneum draining into the pudendal plexus
¹**ves·i·cant** \'vesə̇kənt\ *n* -S [NL *vesica* bladder, blister + E *-ant*, n. suffix] **1** : an agent (as a drug or a plant substance) that induces blistering **2** : a vesicant war gas (as mustard gas or lewisite) — called also *blister gas*
²**vesicant** \"\ *adj* [L *vesica* + E *-ant*, adj. suffix] : producing or tending to produce blisters
vesica pis·cis \-'piskə̇s, 'pisə̇s, 'pīsə̇s, 'pēsə̇s\ *n* [NL, lit., fish bladder] : a pointed oval figure typically composed of two intersecting arcs; *specif* : an aureole of this shape surrounding a representation of a sacred personage
ves·i·car·ia \,vesə'ka(a)rēə\ *n, cap* [NL, fr. L *vesica* + NL *-aria*] : a small genus of chiefly Mediterranean annual or perennial herbs (family Cruciferae) with inflated seed pods
ves·i·cate \'vesə,kāt\ *vb* -ED/-ING/-S [back-formation fr. *vesication*] : BLISTER
ves·i·ca·tion \,≈≈'kāshən\ *n* -S [MF, fr. L *vesica* bladder, blister + MF *-ation*] **1** : an instance or the process of blistering **2** : BLISTER
ves·i·ca·to·ry \'vesə̇kə,tōrē, və'sik-\ *adj or n* [MF *vesicatoire*, fr. *vesication* + *-oire* -ory] : VESICANT

vesica piscis

vesicatory gas *n* : a war gas that causes blistering
ves·i·cle \'vesə̇kəl, -sēk-\ *n* -S [MF *vesicule*, fr. L *vesicula* small bladder, small blister, dim. of *vesica* bladder, blister — more at VESICA] : a body felt to resemble a bladder esp. in constituting a small thin-walled cavity: as **a** : a plant or animal structure (as a cyst, vacuole, or cell) having the general form of a membranous cavity : a thin sac esp. when filled with fluid **b** : minute bubbles formerly held to make up the substance of a cloud or fog **c** : a small and more or less circular elevation of the cuticle of the skin containing a clear watery fluid : BLISTER **d** : a small cavity in a mineral or rock and esp. in a basaltic lava produced originally by the expansion of vapor in the molten mass
vesicul- *or* **vesiculo-** *comb form* [NL *vesicula*] : vesicle ⟨*Vesicularia*⟩ : vesicular and ⟨*vesiculo*papular⟩
ve·sic·u·la \və'sikyələ\ *n, pl* **vesicu·lae** \-ə,lē, -lī\ *also* **vesiculas** [NL, fr. L, small bladder, small blister — more at VESICLE] : VESICLE
ve·sic·u·lar \-lə(r)\ *adj* [*vesicul-* + *-ar*] **1 a** : formed or constructed like a vesicle : constituting a vesicle ⟨a ~ cavity⟩ **b** : containing, made up of, or characterized by the presence of vesicles ⟨~ lava⟩ ⟨a ~ texture in rock⟩ **2** : of, relating to, or involving a vesicular structure (as the alveoli of the lungs) or the presence or formation of vesicles ⟨a ~ eczema⟩ ⟨normal ~ breathing in which air has free access to the individual alveoli⟩ **3** *of a cell nucleus* : appearing to have the chromatin in discrete

stainable particles embedded in a clear nuclear sap — **ve·sic·u·lar·ly** *adv*

vesicular exanthema *n* **:** an acute virus disease of swine that closely resembles foot-and-mouth disease but is not transmissible to cattle, sheep, or goats and may occur in epizootic proportions in outbreaks which are usu. traceable to the feeding of contaminated garbage

vesicular gland *n* **:** a subepidermal gland in a plant containing essential oil

ve·sic·u·lar·ia \və̇ˌsikyəˈla(a)rēə\ *n, cap* [NL, fr. *vesicul-* + *-aria*] **:** a genus of marine bryozoans (order Ctenostomata) that have delicate tubular cells clustered on slender flexible stems

vesicular stomatitis *n* **:** an acute virus disease of horses and mules and sometimes also of cattle or rarely of swine much resembling foot-and-mouth disease and marked by erosive blisters in and about the mouth and esp. on the tongue which may prevent eating

¹ve·sic·u·late \və̇ˈsikyə‚lāt, -‚lə̇t, *usu* -d·+V\ *adj* [*vesicul-* + *-ate*, adj. suffix] **1 :** containing or covered with vesicles **2 :** VESICULAR 1a

²ve·sic·u·late \-‚lāt, *usu* -ād·+V\ *vb* -ED/-ING/-S [*vesicul-* + *-ate*, v. suffix] *vt* **:** to cause to become vesicular ∼ *vi* **:** to become vesicular ⟨chromosome fragments ∼ at metaphase —*Amer. Naturalist*⟩

ve·sic·u·la·tion \-‚══ˈlāshən\ *n* -S **1 :** the condition of having or process of forming vesicles **:** the presence or formation of vesicles **2 :** distribution or arrangement of vesicles ⟨a variable ∼ of the affected skin⟩ ⟨∼ of the two types of lava differs considerably —G.W.Tyrrell⟩

ve·sic·u·li·na \-ˈlīnə\ *n, cap* [NL, fr. *vesicul-* + *-ina*] *in some classifications* **:** a genus of American herbs comprising New World forms (as the purple bladderwort) that are usu. assigned to the genus *Utricularia*

ve·sic·u·lo·papular \və̇ˈsikyəlō+\ *adj* **:** of, relating to, or marked by both vesicles and papules ⟨a ∼ inflammation⟩

ve·sic·u·lo·pustular \"+\ *adj* **:** of, relating to, or marked by both vesicles and pustules ⟨a ∼ eruption⟩

ve·sic·u·lose \və̇ˈsikyə‚lōs\ *adj* [*vesicul-* + *-ose*] **:** VESICULATE

ve·sic·u·lus \-ləs\ *n, pl* **vesicu·li** \-‚lī, -‚lē\ [NL, alter. of *vesicula*] **:** VESICLE

ves·kit \ˈveskə̇t, *usu* -ə̇d·+V\ *dial var of* WAISTCOAT

ves·pa \ˈvespə\ *n* [NL, fr. L, wasp — more at WASP] **1** *cap* **:** the type genus of Vespidae including various hornets and yellow jackets **2** -S **:** any insect of the genus *Vespa*

ves·pa·cide \-‚sīd\ *n* -S [L *vespa* wasp + E *-cide*] **:** one that kills wasps

ves·pal \ˈvespəl\ *adj* [L *vespa* wasp + E *-al*] **:** of or relating to wasps

¹ves·per \ˈvespə(r)\ *n* -S [ME, fr. L, evening, evening star — more at WEST] **1** *usu cap* **:** EVENING STAR 1 **2 vespers** *pl* [modif. of ML *vesperia*, fr. L *vesper* + *-ia* -y] **:** public ceremonies or disputations formerly preceding commencement at an English university; *also* **:** the time of such ceremonies **:** the eve of commencement **3 vespers** *pl, often cap* [F *vespres*, fr. ML *vesperae*, fr. pl. of L *vespera* evening — more at WEST] **a :** the sixth and next to the last of the canonical hours **b :** a religious office or service for this time: as (1) **:** an office formerly said or sung before nightfall (2) **:** the evening prayer or evensong of churches of the Anglican communion compiled from the ancient offices of vespers and compline (3) *or* **vesper service :** a late afternoon or evening religious service that is often largely musical **4 :** a vesper bell **5** *archaic* **:** EVENING, EVENTIDE

²vesper \"\ *adj* **1 :** of, relating to, or used in connection with religious vespers ⟨∼ music⟩ **2 :** of or relating to the evening **:** VESPERTINE

¹ves·per·al \-p(ə)rəl\ *adj* [LL *vesperalis*, fr. L *vesper* evening + *-alis* -al] **:** VESPER ⟨a ∼ breeze⟩; *esp* **:** CREPUSCULAR 2 ⟨∼ insects⟩

²vesperal \"\ *also* **ves·per·a·le** \‚vespəˈra(‚)lē, -ˈrāl-, -ˈräl-\ *n* -S [F *vespéral*, fr. LL *vesperalis*, adj.] **1 :** a book containing the office and music for vespers **2 :** a generally colored altar cover that is used to protect the white altar cloths between ceremonies

ves·per·ing \ˈvesp(ə)riŋ, -rēŋ\ *adj* [¹*vesper* + *-ing*] **:** singing vesper songs ⟨a hush of ∼ birds —Thomas Moult⟩

vesper iris *n* **:** a late-flowering and very free-blooming Asian fibrous-rooted iris (*Iris dichotoma*) that is sometimes cultivated for its predominantly lavender and white flowers which open only toward dusk

vesper mouse *n* **:** WHITE-FOOTED MOUSE

vesper sparrow *also* **vesper bird** *n* **:** a common American sparrow (*Pooecetes gramineus*) having the outer tail feathers white and singing esp. in the evening

vespertide \ˈ══‚═\ *n* **:** the time of vespers

ves·per·til·ian \‚vespə(r)ˈtilēən, -lyən\ *adj* [L *vespertilio* bat + E *-an*] **:** of, relating or suitable to, or resembling a bat ⟨∼ habits⟩ ⟨∼ anatomy⟩

ves·per·til·io \‚══ˈtilē(‚)ō\ *n* [NL, fr. L, bat, fr. *vesper* evening — more at WEST] **1** *cap* **:** the type genus of Vespertilionidae formerly comprehensive but now comprising solely the frosted bat (*V. murinus*) or slightly extended to include the serotine and the American brown bats which are more often placed in the genus *Eptesicus* **2** -S **:** any bat of the genus *Vespertilio*; *broadly* **:** BAT

¹ves·per·til·i·o·nid \‚══ˈtilēō‚nid\ *adj* [NL *Vespertilionidae*] **:** of or related to the Vespertilionidae

²vespertilionid \"\ *n* -S **:** a bat of the family Vespertilionidae

ves·per·til·i·on·i·dae \‚══‚tilēˈänə‚dē\ *n pl, cap* [NL, fr. *Vespertilion-, Vespertilio*, type genus + *-idae*] **:** a very large family of bats (suborder Microchiroptera) found in most parts of the world, including the majority of the common bats of temperate regions, and having separate ears with well-developed tragal lobes, a simple nose without appendages, and a tail that extends to the border of the posterior part of the volar membrane which stretches between the thighs — see VESPERTILIO

ves·per·ti·nal \‚══ˈtīnᵊl\ *adj* [LL *vespertinalis*, fr. L *vespertinus* + *-alis* -al] **:** VESPERTINE ⟨became purely ∼, never stirring abroad till after dark —J.R.Lowell⟩

ves·per·tine \ˈ══‚tīn, -‚tin, -‚tēn\ *adj* [L *vespertinus*, fr. *vesper* evening + *-tinus* (as in *matutinus* of the morning) — more at WEST] **1 :** of, relating to, or occurring in the evening **:** resembling that of evening ⟨∼ shadows⟩ **2** *of a planet* **:** setting with or just after the sun **3 :** active or flourishing in the evening **:** CREPUSCULAR: as **a :** feeding or flying in early evening **b :** blossoming in the evening

ves·pe·tro \ˈvespə‚trō\ *n* -S [F *vespétro*, fr. *vesser* to break wind noiselessly + *péter* to break wind + *roter* to belch] **:** a liqueur consisting of brandy flavored with anise, fennel, coriander, and angelica and sweetened with sugar

ves·pi·ary \ˈvespē‚erē\ *n* -ES [L *vespa* wasp + E *-iary* (as in *apiary*) — more at WASP] **:** a nest of social wasps; *also* **:** a colony of wasps inhabiting such a nest

¹ves·pid \ˈvespə̇d\ *adj* [NL *Vespidae*] **:** of or relating to the Vespidae

²vespid \"\ *n* -S **:** a wasp of the family Vespidae

ves·pi·dae \-pə‚dē\ *n pl, cap* [NL, fr. *Vespa*, type genus + *-idae*] **:** a widely distributed family of wasps (superfamily Vespoidea) containing the social wasps that live in colonies like bees, produce workers as well as perfect females and males, feed on various animal or vegetable matter but usu. do not store up supplies since their colonies are destroyed by the cold season, and build nests which generally consist of or contain one or more combs of papery material that is usu. horizontally placed so that the cells are vertical and with the open end down — compare POLISTES, VESPA, VESPULA; HORNET, YELLOW JACKET

ves·pine \ˈve‚spīn, -‚spə̇n\ *adj* [L *vespa* wasp + E *-ine* — more at WASP] **:** of, relating to, characteristic of, or resembling wasps esp. of the family Vespidae

ves·poid \ˈve‚spȯid\ *adj* [L *vespa* wasp + E *-oid*] **1 :** resembling or related to the wasps **2** [NL *Vespoidea*] **:** of or related to the Vespoidea

ves·poi·dea \veˈspȯidēə\ *n pl, cap* [NL, fr. *Vespa* + *-oidea*] **:** a superfamily of Hymenoptera comprising the true wasps, hornets, and related insects and consisting of the family Vespidae often together with other families (as Pompilidae and Mutillidae)

ves·pu·la \ˈvespyələ\ *n, cap* [NL, fr. *Vespa* + *-ula*] **:** a genus of social wasps that includes various hornets and yellow jackets and is sometimes treated as a subgenus of *Vespa*

¹ves·sel \ˈvesəl\ *n* -S [ME *vessel, vesselle*, fr. OF *vessel, vaissel, vessel* receptacle, container (fr. LL *vascellum*, dim. of L *vas* vessel, vase) & *vassele, vaissele, vessele* domestic receptacles collectively, fr. (assumed) VL *vascella*, fr. LL, pl. of *vascellum* — more at VASE] **1 a** *obs* **:** domestic containers or utensils; *specif* **:** PLATE 3a **b** *dial Brit* **:** cutlery, dishes, and other table furnishing ⟨had to wash up the ∼ before she could leave⟩ **2 a :** a hollow and usu. cylindrical or concave utensil (as a hogshead, bottle, kettle, cup, or bowl) for holding something and esp. a liquid **:** a receptacle of tight construction sometimes as distinguished from one (as a basket) of slack or open construction ⟨set a large copper ∼ over the fire⟩ ⟨alchemists' flasks and similar ∼s⟩ **b :** a person that is the receptacle of something; *esp* **:** one in whom a divine action is manifested **c** *dial Eng* **:** the udder of a cow **3 a :** a usu. hollow structure used on or in the water for purposes of navigation **:** a craft for navigation of the water; *esp* **:** a watercraft or structure with its equipment whether self-propelled or not that is used or capable of being used as a means of transportation in navigation or commerce on water and that usu. excludes small rowboats and sailboats **b :** any of various aircraft; *esp* **:** an airplane (as a hydroplane) that is capable of being used on water **4 a :** a tube or canal (as an artery, vein, or lymphatic) in which a body fluid (as blood or lymph) is contained and conveyed or circulated **b :** a conducting tube in a vascular plant formed in the xylem by the fusion and loss of end walls of a series of cells — compare TRACHEID

²ves·sel \ˈvesəl\ *n* -S [origin unknown] **:** a piece of paper ⅛ of a sheet of foolscap (about 7 in. x 4½ in.)

vessel element *or* **vessel member** *n* **:** one of the individual cells making up a vessel of the plant vascular system

vessel ton *n* **:** TON 2a

¹vest \ˈvest\ *vb* -ED/-ING/-S [ME *vesten*, fr. MF *vestir* to clothe, invest with ecclesiastical vestments, fr. L *vestire* to clothe, fr. *vestis* garment, attire — more at WEAR] *vt* **1 a :** to place or give into the possession or discretion of some person or authority ⟨the regulation of the waterways . . . was ∼*ed* in the corporation —Edwin Benson⟩; *esp* **:** to give to a person a legally fixed immediate right of present or future enjoyment of (as an estate) ⟨a deed that ∼*s* a life estate in the grantee and a remainder in his children⟩ **b :** to grant, endow, or clothe with a particular authority, right, or property ⟨∼ a court with the right to try criminal cases⟩ ⟨the retirement plan ∼*ed* the workers absolutely with the company's contribution after 10 years of continuous employment⟩ **c :** to put (a person) in possession of land by the feudal ceremony of investiture **:** ENFEOFF **2 :** to clothe with or as if with a garment; *esp* **:** to garb in ecclesiastical vestments ⟨came ∼*ed* all in white, pure as her mind —John Milton⟩ **3 :** to lay out (money) **:** INVEST ∼ *vi* **1 :** to become legally vested ⟨normally title to real property ∼*s* in the holder of a properly executed deed⟩ **2 :** to put on garments; *esp* **:** to robe formally for or as if for a ceremonial occasion ⟨the little room where the priests ∼*ed* for mass⟩

²vest \"\ *n* -S [F *veste*, fr. It, fr. L *vestis* garment, attire] **1** *archaic* **a** (1) **:** a loose outer garment worn by men (as in ancient times or eastern countries) **:** ROBE, GOWN (2) **:** a similar garment worn by women **b :** VESTURE, CLOTHING, GARB **c :** an ecclesiastical vestment **2 a :** a man's garment for wear under a coat made in varying styles and lengths; *esp* **:** a sleeveless collarless close-fitting coat reaching just below the waist, having four small pockets, and buttoned up to a V neck **b :** a garment of similar design for women **:** WAISTCOAT **c :** a protective or safety garment shaped like a man's vest and worn esp. by military personnel on active duty or people in or on the water **3 a** *chiefly Brit* **:** a man's undershirt **b :** a knitted sleeved or sleeveless undershirt for women or sometimes children **4 :** a plain or decorative piece used to fill in the front neckline of a woman's outer garment (as a waist, coat, or gown) — compare DICKEY

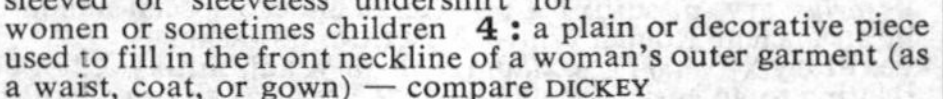

vest 2a

vest *abbr* vestibule

ves·ta \ˈvestə\ *n* -S [after *Vesta*, ancient Roman goddess of the hearth, fr. L] **:** a short match with a shank of wax-coated threads; *also* **:** a short wooden match

¹ves·tal \ˈvestᵊl\ *adj* [ME *vestalle*, fr. L *vestalis*, fr. *Vesta* + *-alis* -al] **1 :** of or relating to the Roman goddess Vesta **2 a :** of or relating to a vestal virgin **b :** CHASTE ⟨who, even in pure and ∼ modesty, still blush —Shak.⟩ — **ves·tal·ly** \-tᵊlē, -li\ *adv*

²vestal \"\ *n* -S [L *vestalis*, fr. *vestalis*, adj.] **1** *also* **vestal virgin** [*vestal virgin* part trans. of L *vestalis virgo*] **a :** a virgin consecrated to the Roman goddess Vesta and to the service of watching the sacred fire perpetually kept burning upon her altar **b :** a pure and chaste woman (as a virgin or nun) **2 a :** grayish purple to grayish reddish purple

vested interest *n* **1 a :** an interest (as a right or title to an estate) carrying a legal right of present or future enjoyment and of present alienation **b :** an interest (as in an existing political, economic, or social arrangement) in which the holder has a strong personal commitment as a result sometimes of long association but more often of present or future benefits ⟨those who have a *vested interest* in the educational status quo —A.E.Bestor⟩ ⟨to continue in existence it must create *vested interests* in its survival —Paul Johnson⟩ **c :** a right vested in an employee under a pension plan **2 :** one having a vested interest in something; *specif* **:** a group closely associated with and enjoying benefits from an existing economic or political privilege ⟨vacant land . . . is bought up by speculators or held by *vested interests* —A.J.Bruwer⟩ ⟨the free press, so integral to the self-maintenance and growth of free society, was brought into subservience to the *vested interests* —H.M.Kallen⟩

vested remainder *n* **:** a remainder granted or devised by the owner of a fee to a then ascertainable existing person who has or whose heirs or devisees have the present legal right to enter into possession and enjoy the estate upon the termination of a preceding freehold estate (as a life estate fee tail)

vested right *n* **:** a right belonging so absolutely, completely, and unconditionally to a person that it cannot be defeated by the act of any private person and that is entitled to governmental protection usu. under a constitutional guarantee ⟨the contract clause remained extremely important for the protection of *vested rights* against state legislation —C.B.Swisher⟩

vest·ee \(ˈ)veˈstē\ *n* -S [²*vest* + *-ee*] **1 :** DICKEY; *esp* **:** one that is made to resemble a vest and is worn under a coat **2 :** VEST 4

ves·ti·ar·i·an \‚vesteˈa(a)rēən\ *adj, often cap* [L *vestiarius* vestiary + E *-an*] **:** of, relating to, or constituting a controversy over ecclesiastical vestments in 16th century England ⟨at present a refugee in consequence of the Vestiarian controversy —J.Y.Evans⟩

¹ves·ti·ary \ˈvestē‚erē, -ri\ *n* -ES [ME *vestiarie*, fr. OF *vestiaire, vestiarie*, fr. ML *vestiarium*, fr. L *vestire* to clothe, put on + *-arium* -ary, n. suffix — more at VEST] **1 a :** a robing room (as of a church) **:** VESTRY **b :** a room (as in a monastery) where clothing is stored and attended; *also* **:** CLOAKROOM **c :** a storage chest (as for clothing) **2 :** CLOTHING, RAIMENT; *esp* **:** a set of clerical vestments **3 :** any of various medieval officials or household officers; *specif* **:** an ecclesiastical dignitary who is charged in some cathedrals with the robing of the canons

²vestiary \"\ *adj* [L *vestiarius*, fr. *vestis* garment, attire + *-arius* -ary, adj. suffix — more at WEAR] **:** of or relating to clothes and esp. vestments

ves·tib·u·lar \(ˈ)veˈstibyələ(r)\ *adj* [*vestibule* + *-ar*] **1 :** of or relating to a vestibule **:** resembling or sharing the nature of a vestibule **2 :** of, relating to, mediating, constituting, or affecting the vestibular sense

vestibular apparatus *n* **:** the vestibule of the inner ear together with the end organs and nerve fibers that mediate the vestibular sense

vestibular nerve *n* **:** a branch of the auditory nerve that supplies the vestibule of the inner ear and the ampullae of the semicircular canals

vestibular nucleus *n* **:** a neural nucleus in which the fibers of the vestibular nerve terminate and of which the upper part is continuous with Deiters' nucleus

vestibular sense *n* **:** a sense mediated by end organs in the vestibule of the internal ear that contain otoliths and are stimulated by the pull of gravity and by the starting and stopping of rectilinear head movements; *broadly* **:** LABYRINTHINE SENSE

ves·tib·u·late \(ˈ)veˈstibyələ̇t, -‚lāt\ *adj* [*vestibule* + *-ate*] **:** having or resembling a vestibule

¹ves·ti·bule \ˈvestə‚byül\ *n* -S [F & L; F *vestible, vestibule*, fr. L *vestibulum*] **1 a :** an entrance court (as of an ancient Roman building) **b :** a passage, hall, or chamber between the outer door and the interior of a building **:** a porch or entrance into a house **:** LOBBY, NARTHEX **c :** an enclosed entrance to a railway passenger car fitted with side doors for ingress to and egress from the train and with a flexible side wall and roof attached to the end of the car **2 :** any of various bodily cavities esp. when serving as or resembling an entrance to some other cavity or space: as **a** (1) **:** the central cavity of the bony labyrinth of the ear (2) **:** the parts of the membranous labyrinth comprising the utricle and the saccule and contained in the cavity of the bony labyrinth — see EAR illustration **b :** the space between the labia minora containing the orifice of the urethra **c :** the part of the left ventricle of the heart immediately below the aortic orifice **d :** the part of the mouth cavity outside the teeth and gums **e :** the part of the larynx above the false vocal cords **f :** a more or less tubular depression leading to the mouth of an infusorian **g :** the space within the circle of tentacles in bryozoans esp. of the group Entoprocta

²vestibule \"\ *vt* -ED/-ING/-S **1 :** to furnish with a vestibule **2 :** to join (railroad cars) by vestibules

vestibule car *n* **:** a railway car with a vestibule at each end

ves·ti·buled \-ld\ *adj* **:** having a vestibule

vestibule latch *n* **:** a lock actuated from outside by a key and from inside by a knob and having no dead bolt

vestibule school *n* **:** a school organized in an industrial plant to train new workers in specific skills before starting them on the actual working routine

vestibule train *n* **:** a railway train that is made up of vestibule cars

vestibule training *n* **:** in-service training in a vestibule school

ves·ti·bu·li·tis \‚vestəbyəˈlīd·ə̇s\ *n* -ES [NL, fr. *vestibulum* + *-itis*] **:** inflammation of a bodily vestibule

ves·tib·u·lo·spinal \veˈstibyəlō+\ *adj* [*vestibule* + *-o-* + *spinal*] **:** of, relating to, or being a nerve tract passing from the nuclei of the vestibular nerve in the medulla down the spinal cord

vestibulo-urethral \"+\ *adj* [*vestibule* + *-o-* + *urethral*] **:** of or relating to the vestibule of the vagina and the urethra

ves·tib·u·lum \veˈstibyələm\ *n, pl* **vestibu·la** \-lə\ [NL & L; NL (in anatomical senses), fr. L (in other senses)] **:** VESTIBULE

ves·tige \ˈvestij, -tēj\ *n* -S [F, fr. L *vestigium*] **1 a :** a trace, mark, or visible sign left by a material thing (as a building) formerly present but now otherwise lost or unknown ⟨digging for the ∼*s* of past civilizations⟩ ⟨fossil bones and other ∼*s*⟩ **b :** the mark of a foot left on the earth **:** FOOTSTEP, TRACK **2 a :** a remaining bit that constitutes a memorial or trace of something formerly present or assumed to be present ⟨a manner showing ∼*s* of past culture⟩ ⟨could detect ∼*s* of beauty in her aging face⟩; *broadly* **:** a minute amount **:** the smallest quantity or trace ⟨lost all remaining ∼*s* of self-control —Evelyn Barkins⟩ ⟨the lack of a ∼ of hair on his pate —Leonard Wibberley⟩ ⟨not a ∼ of sugar in the house⟩ **b :** a small and degenerate or imperfectly developed bodily part or organ that remains from one more fully developed in an earlier stage of the individual, in a past generation, or in closely related forms

ves·tig·ial \(ˈ)veˈstij(ē)əl\ *adj* [L *vestigium* + E *-al*] **:** of, relating to, or being a vestige **:** resembling or having the form of a vestige — **ves·tig·ial·ly** \-əlē, -li\ *adv*

vestigial side band *n* **:** the transmitted portion of a partially suppressed side band utilized with the corresponding unsuppressed side band in signal transmission

ves·tig·i·um \veˈstijēəm\ *n, pl* **vestig·ia** \-jēə\ [L] **:** VESTIGE

ves·ti·ment \ˈvestəmənt\ *archaic var of* VESTMENT

vesting *n* -S [fr. gerund of ¹*vest*] **1 :** the conveying to an employee of inalienable rights to share in a pension fund and esp. to recover his own and his employer's contribution on his behalf in the event of termination of employment prior to the normal retirement age; *also* **:** the right so conveyed **2 :** the taking over of private property by a government usu. in return for compensation ⟨∼ of foreign security holdings in time of war⟩

vesting order *n* **:** an order of a court, an administrative agency, or public officer passing the legal title in lieu of a legal conveyance

ves·ti·ni \veˈstī‚nī, -tē(‚)nē\ *n pl, usu cap* [L] **:** an ancient Sabine people of central Italy allied with the Romans about 300 B.C.

ves·ti·ni·an \veˈstinēən\ *n* -S *usu cap* **:** a Sabellian dialect

ves·ti·ture \ˈvestə‚chù(ə)r, -‚chùə, -‚chə(r), -tə‚tù-, -tə-‚tyù-\ *n* -S [ML *vestitura*, fr. L *vestitus* (past part. of *vestire* to clothe, put on) + *-ura* -ure — more at VEST] **1 :** INVESTITURE ⟨a ∼ of power in the proletariat —Philip Wylie⟩ **2 :** CLOTHING, GARB, DRESS **3 :** something that covers a surface like a garment; *esp* **:** a covering (as of scales, hairs, or spines) on an insect's body or wings

vest·less \ˈ═ləs\ *adj* **:** having no vest

vest·let \-lə̇t\ *n* -S [²*vest* + *-let*] **:** any of various actinians (genus *Cerianthus*) that secrete a tough tube about the body

vestlike \ˈ═‚═\ *adj* **:** resembling a vest

vest·ment \ˈves(t)mənt\ *n* -S [ME *vestement, vestiment*, fr. OF, fr. L *vestimentum*, fr. *vestire* to clothe, put on + *-mentum* -ment — more at VEST] **1 a :** a covering or outer garment; *esp* **:** a garment or robe of ceremony or office **b vestments** *pl* **:** CLOTHING, GARB, DRESS **2 :** a covering felt to resemble a garment ⟨the verdant ∼ which spring spreads over the land⟩ **3 :** a liturgical garment **:** an article of the ceremonial attire and insignia that are worn by ecclesiastical officiants and assistants during divine service as appropriate to the rite and indicative of their hierarchical rank — **vest·men·tal** \(ˈ)═ˈmentᵊl\ *adj*

vest·ment·ed \ˈ═‚mentə̇d\ *adj* **1 :** arrayed in vestments **2** *of a ceremony or service* **:** conducted by clergy in vestments

ves·to·ri·an blue \(ˈ)veˈstōrēən, -tȯr-,-\ *n, usu cap V* [part trans. of L *caeruleum vestorianum*, fr. *caeruleum* blue + *vestorianum*, neut. of *vestorianus* of Vestorius, perh. fr. *Vestorius fl* 44 B.C. Roman banker + L *-anus* -an] **:** EGYPTIAN BLUE

vest-pocket \ˈ═ˈ══\ *adj* **1 :** designed or adapted to fit into the vest pocket ⟨a *vest-pocket* dictionary⟩ **2 :** of very small size or scope ⟨a *vest-pocket* war⟩

vest-pocket camera *n* **:** a camera taking pictures 1⅝ by 2½ inches in size

vest-pocket veto *n* **:** POCKET VETO

ves·tral \ˈvestrəl\ *adj* [*vestry* + *-al*] **:** of or relating to a vestry

ves·try \-trē, -ri\ *n* -ES [ME *vestrie*, prob. modif. of MF *vestiarie, vestiaire* — more at VESTIARY] **1** *or* **vestry room a** (1) **:** a room within or attached to a church building in which the vestments of the clergy, the altar linen and hangings, and the sacred vessels and often church records are kept — called also *sacristy* (2) **:** a room corresponding to a church vestry in a non-Christian temple **b :** a storage place (as a room or closet) for clothing or formerly other valuables **c :** a room within or a building attached to a church building used variously as a chapel, church-school room, or prayer-meeting room **2 :** a body of persons entrusted with the administration of the temporal affairs of a parish in the Church of England or in the Protestant Episcopal Church; *also* **:** a parish meeting or a meeting of a vestry esp. in England

ves·try·man \'‑‑mən\ *n, pl* **vestrymen** : one of a vestry
vests *pres 3d sing of* VEST, *pl of* VEST
ves·tur·al \'veschərəl\ *adj* : of or relating to vesture or clothing
¹ves·ture \'veschə(r)\ *n* -s [ME, fr. MF, fr. *vestir* to clothe + *-ure* — more at VEST] **1** : something that covers the body: **a** : a covering garment (as a robe or vestment) **b** : CLOTHING, APPAREL, COSTUME **2** : something that covers like a garment: as **a** : the covering vegetation (as crops) other than trees on land **b** : a covering (as of data, style, and language) in which a theme or topic is enveloped in being developed or elaborated **3** : INVESTITURE, SEISIN
²vesture \"\ *vt* -ED/-ING/-S : to cover with vesture : CLOTHE, ENVELOP
vestured pit *n* : a bordered pit with minute outgrowths projecting into the pit cavity from the secondary wall around the pit
ves·tur·er \-chərə(r)\ *n* -s : SEXTON; *esp* : one in charge of church vestments and ornaments
¹ve·su·vian \və'süvēən, -vyən\ *adj, usu cap* [*Vesuvius*, volcano near Naples, Italy + E *-an*] **1** : of, relating to, or resembling the volcano Vesuvius **2** : marked by uncertainty or sudden outbursts : FURIOUS ⟨a *Vesuvian* rage⟩ ⟨*Vesuvian* language⟩
²vesuvian \"\ *n* -s [in sense 1, fr. G, fr. *Vesuv* Vesuvius + G *-ian* (fr. L *-ianus* -ian); in sense 2, fr. ¹*vesuvian*] **1** : IDOCRASE **2** : a match or fusee used esp. formerly for lighting cigars
ve·su·vi·an·ite \-ə,nīt\ *n* -s [²*vesuvian* + *-ite*] : IDOCRASE
ve·su·vin \və'süvən\ *n* -s [G, fr. *Vesuv* Vesuvius + G *-in*] : BISMARCK BROWN
ve·szel·yite \'vesəl,yīt, 'vesē,īt; və's|ālē,īt, 'z|, |el-\ *n* -s [G *veszelyit*, fr. A. *Veszely*, 19th cent. Hung. mining engineer + G *-it* -ite] : a mineral $(Cu,Zn)_3PO_4(OH)_3.2H_2O$ that is a hydrous basic copper zinc phosphate occurring mostly in greenish blue incrustations (hardness 3.5–4, sp. gr. 3.5)
¹vet \'vet, *usu* -ed·+V\ *n* -s [by shortening] : VETERINARIAN, VETERINARY
²vet \"\ *vb* **vetted; vetted; vetting; vets** *vt* **1 a** : to provide veterinary care for (an animal) : subject to veterinary examination and care and esp. to a general physical examination **b** : to provide (a person) with medical care; *esp* : to subject to a physical examination or checkup **2** : to inspect or examine with careful thoroughness and esp. in the quality of an expert ⟨spent the evening *vetting* the report⟩ ⟨it is wise to have an experienced person ~ old silver before you buy⟩ ~ *vi* : to practice as a veterinarian ⟨*vetted* for the track since its opening season⟩
³vet \"\ *adj or n* [by shortening] : VETERAN
ve·ta \'vād·ə\ *n* -s [AmerSp] : MOUNTAIN SICKNESS
¹vetch \'vech\ *n* -ES [ME *fecche, vecche*, fr. ONF *veche*, fr. L *vicia*; akin to OE *wicga* insect, MHG *gewige* antlers, Goth *waihsta* corner, L *vincire* to bind, tie, Gk *eikein* to yield, retreat, Skt *vejate, vijate* he flees from, retreats, OE *wīr* wire — more at WIRE] **1** : any of various annual, biennial, or perennial herbaceous twining plants constituting the genus *Vicia* and including valuable fodder and soil-building plants as well as a few that are toxic; *also* : any of several other herbaceous legumes that resemble or are used like vetch — often used with a qualifying term; see BITTER VETCH, HORSESHOE VETCH, KIDNEY VETCH, MILK VETCH **2** : the seed of a vetch; *esp* : the small edible dark brown seed of a Eurasian vetch (*Vicia sativa*)
²vetch \"\ *dial Eng var of* FETCH
vetch bruchid *n* : a widely distributed bruchid weevil (*Bruchus brachialis*) that is destructive to the seeds of various vetches
vetch·ling \'vechliŋ, -lēŋ\ *n* -s [¹*vetch* + *-ling*] : any of various small plants of the genus *Lathyrus* (esp. *L. pratensis*)
vetchworm \'‑,‑\ *n* : CORN EARWORM
¹vet·er·an \'ved·ərən, 've·trən, 'ved·ərn, 'vetərən\ *n* -s [L *veteranus*, fr. *veteranus*, adj.] **1 a** (1) : a person with long experience in military service : an old soldier (2) : a former member of armed forces who by length and type of service, honorable discharge or release, or degree of disablement qualifies under a statute (as of the U. S. or one of its states) for benefits or privileges provided by law for ex-servicemen **b** : one grown old in service (as in politics, a profession, or an industry or art) or experienced through length of service ⟨depended on the ~*s* to help the novices on the assembly line⟩ ⟨a ~ of 20 years' service⟩ **c** : one seasoned by intensity of experience or service however brief either in or out of military life ⟨the ~*s* of a battle⟩ **2** : an old tree (as from a former stand); *specif* : a tree over two feet in diameter breast high
²veteran \"\ *adj* [L *veteranus* old, veteran, fr. *veter-, vetus* old + *-anus* -an — more at WETHER] **1** : grown old and skilled through experience : attained to competence through long practice (as of military life) ⟨a ~ officer⟩ ⟨the team depended on its ~ fielder⟩ **2** : extending over a great period : PROLONGED ⟨~ service to his country⟩ **3** : of, relating to, or characteristic of a veteran : available to veterans : dealing with veterans ⟨~ steadiness⟩ ⟨a ~ administrator⟩ ⟨~ benefits⟩ ⟨a ~ camp⟩
vet·er·an·ize \-ə,nīz\ *vb* -ED/-ING/-S *vi* : to make a veteran of oneself by reenlisting in a military service ~ *vt* : to cause (as soldiers) to become seasoned usu. by exposure to active service
veterans day *n, usu cap V&D* : ARMISTICE DAY
veterans' preference *n* : preferential treatment (as in employment, securing of housing, or credit) given qualified veterans (as of the U. S. armed forces) under a federal or state statute; *specif* : special consideration (as by allowance of points) on a civil service examination
vet·er·i·nar·i·an \,ved·ərə'n|erēən, ,vetərə'n|, ,ve·trə'n|, ÷,ved·ə(r)'n|, ÷,vetə(r)'n|, ÷,vet'n'|, |a(ə)r-, |ār-\ *n* -s [L *veterinarius* veterinarian + E *-an*] : one skilled in or treating diseases and injuries of animals : one qualified and duly authorized to treat diseases of animals : a doctor of veterinary medicine
¹vet·er·i·nary \'ved·ərə,nerē, 'vetərə,ne-, 've·trə,ne-, ÷'ved·ə(r)ne-, ÷'vetə(r)ne-, ÷'vet'n,e-, -eri\ *adj* [L *veterinarius*, fr. *veterinae, veterina* beasts of burden, domestic animals (fr. fem. pl. & neut. pl. respectively of *veterinus* suitable for a beast of burden, of a beast of burden) + *-arius* -ary; akin to L *veter-, vetus* old — more at WETHER] : of, relating to, or constituting a branch of science and art dealing with the prevention, cure, or alleviation of disease and injury in animals and esp. domestic animals and including the normal biology (as anatomy and physiology) as well as the pathology of such animals
²veterinary \"\ *n* -ES [L *veterinarius*, fr. *veterinarius*, adj.] : VETERINARIAN
veterinary surgeon *n, Brit* : VETERINARIAN
vet·i·vene \'ved·ə,vēn\ *n* -s [ISV *vetiver* + *-ene*] : a liquid mixture of sesquiterpenes $C_{15}H_{24}$ obtained from vetiver oil
vet·i·ven·ol \-,nōl, -,nŏl\ *n* -s [ISV *vetivene* + *-ol*] : VETIVEROL
vet·i·ver \'ved·əvə(r)\ *also* **vet·i·vert** \-və(r)t\ *n* -s [F *vétiver, vétyver*, fr. Tamil *veṭṭivēr*, fr. *veṭṭi* khuskhus + *vēr* root] : KHUSKHUS
vetiver green *n* : a light grayish olive color that is deeper than Quaker gray or twine, greener and slightly duller than hemp, and redder and deeper than average citron gray
vet·i·ve·ria \,‑‑'virēə\ *n, cap* [NL, fr. ISV *vetiver* + NL *-ia*] *in some classifications* : a small genus of perennial grasses found in the Old World tropics, having narrow panicles of slender spikelike racemes, including some cultivated for the aromatic roots or oil, and being usu. placed in the genus *Andropogon*
vetiver oil *also* **vetivert oil** *n* : a brown to reddish brown essential oil obtained from the roots of khuskhus and used in perfumes, cosmetics, and soaps
vet·i·ver·ol \,ved·ə'vē,rōl, -,rŏl\ *n* -s [ISV *vetiver* + *-ol*] : a liquid mixture of sesquiterpenoid alcohols $C_{15}H_{23}OH$ obtained from vetiver oil and used often in the form of the acetate in perfumes — called also *vetivenol*
vet·i·vone \'ved·ə,vōn\ *or* **vet·i·ver·one** \,‑‑'ve,rōn\ *n* -s [*vetivone* fr. *vetiver* + *-one*; *vetiverone* ISV *vetiver* + *-one*] : a bicyclic sesquiterpenoid ketone $C_{15}H_{22}O$ that is an odorous component of vetiver oil and is known in two crystalline stereoisomeric forms
vet·kou·sie \'fet,kōsē\ *n* -s [Afrik, lit., fat wick, fr. *vet* fat, grease (fr. MD) + *kousie* wick, fr. D *kousje*, dim. of *kous* stocking, fr. MD *couse* chausses, fr. OF dial. (Picardy) *cauce*, fr. ML *calcea*; akin to OE *fǣtt* fat — more at FAT, CHAUSSES] : a southern African fig marigold (*Mesembryanthemum pomeridianum*) the young foliage of which is used like spinach
¹ve·to \'vē(,)tō, -ēd·(,)ō *sometimes* -ēd·ə *or* (+V) -ēd·əw\ *n* -ES [L, I forbid, 1st pers. sing. pres. indic. of *vetare* to forbid] **1** : an authoritative prohibition or negative : an act or instance of forbidding something proposed ⟨mother's ~ of our plans⟩ **2 a** *or* **veto power** : a right or power possessed by one department or branch of a government to forbid or prohibit finally or provisionally the carrying out of projects attempted by another department; *esp* : a power vested in a chief executive to prevent permanently or temporarily the enactment of measures passed by a legislature — see POCKET VETO, SUSPENSIVE VETO **b** (1) : the exercise of such authority : an act of prohibition or prevention ⟨a ~ is probable if the bill passes⟩ (2) *or* **veto message** : a document or message communicating the reasons of an executive (as the president of the U. S.) for not officially approving a proposed law
²veto \"\ *vt* -ED/-ING/-ES : to refuse to admit or approve : NEGATIVE, PROHIBIT; *also* : to refuse assent to (a legislative bill) so as to prevent enactment or cause reconsideration
ve·to·er \-ōə(r) *sometimes* -əwə-\ *n* -s : one that vetoes
vets *pl of* VET, *pres 3d sing of* VET
vetted *past of* VET
vetting *pres part of* VET
vet·tu·ra \ve'türə\ *n, pl* **vettu·re** \-ü(,)rā\ [It, fr. L *vectura* transportation, conveyance, fr. *vectus* (past part. of *vehere* to carry, convey) + *-ura* -ure — more at WAY] : an Italian four-wheel carriage usu. for hire
vet·tu·ri·no \,ved·ə'rē(,)nō\ *n, pl* **vetturi·ni** \-nē\ [It, dim. of *vettura*] : one who lets or drives a vettura
veuve \vœv\ *n, pl* **veuves** \"\ *n* -s [F, lit., widow, fr. L *vidua*; fr. the somber plumage — more at WIDOW] : WHYDAH
¹vex \'veks\ *vb* **vexed** *also* **vext** \'vekst\; **vexed** *also* **vext; vexing; vexes** [ME *vexen*, fr. MF *vexer*, fr. L *vexare* to shake, injure, annoy, prob. fr. *vehere* to carry, convey — more at WAY] *vt* **1** : to bring trouble or distress to: as **a** : to subject to mental suffering : cause agitation or anxiety to : interfere with the peace and quiet of by or as if by encroachment ⟨~*ing* his mind to recall the address⟩ ⟨~*ed* by a restless desire for change⟩ ⟨tasks that ~ our quiet days⟩ **b** : to bring physical distress to : cause bodily pain or anguish ⟨~*ed* with a rheumatic disorder⟩ ⟨a headache had ~*ed* him all day⟩ **c** : to irritate or annoy by or as if by petty provocations : harass to anger : PLAGUE ⟨a lazy stubborn boy who ~*ed* his father daily⟩ ⟨was ~*ed* with the heedless crowds⟩ **d** : to cause difficulty to in respect to finding a solution or answer ⟨a puzzle to ~ the keenest wit⟩ **e** : TEASE, TORMENT ⟨don't ~ the cat⟩ **2** : to go over in careful and minute detail : debate or discuss at length ⟨many men have ~*ed* this question without reaching a solution⟩ **3** : to perturb by physical agitation : shake or toss about : BATTER, BELABOR ⟨wintry winds ~*ing* the forest giants⟩ ⟨a coast ~*ed* by waves⟩ ~ *vi* : to suffer distress (as of mind) : become irritated : FRET, WORRY ⟨how foolish to ~ over such trivia⟩ **syn** see ANNOY
²vex \"\ *n* -ES *Scot* : VEXATION, ANNOYANCE, DISTURBANCE
vex·a·tion \vek'sāshən\ *n* -s [ME *vexacioun*, fr. MF *vexation*, fr. L *vexation-, vexatio* shaking, agitation, annoyance, fr. *vexatus* (past part. of *vexare*) + *-ion-, -io* -ion] **1** : the quality or state of being vexed : IRRITATION ⟨have found continual ~ in my work⟩ **2** : the act of harassing or vexing : TROUBLING; *esp* : harassment by process of law **3** : a cause of trouble or disquiet : AFFLICTION ⟨your children were ~ to your youth —Shak.⟩
vex·a·tious \(')vek'sāshəs\ *adj* [*vexation* + *-ous*] **1 a** : causing or likely to cause vexation : DISTRESSING, AFFLICTIVE ⟨a ~ child⟩ ⟨nothing is more ~ than to find that one is wrong⟩ **b** : lacking justification and intended to harass ⟨the company's ~ refusal to pay a patently valid claim⟩ ⟨a ~ suit at law⟩ **2** : lacking in peace or calm : full of disorder or stress : UNQUIET, DISORDERED, TROUBLED ⟨a ~ period in his life⟩ ⟨a very ~ interview⟩ — **vex·a·tious·ly** *adv* — **vex·a·tious·ness** *n* -ES
vex·ed·ly \'veksədlē, -li\ *adv* : in a vexed manner : with vexation
vex·ed·ness \-nəs\ *n* -ES : the quality or state of being vexed
vex·er \'veksə(r)\ *n* -s : one that vexes
¹vex·il·lary \'veksə,lerē, -ri\ *n* -ES [L *vexillarius*, fr. *vexillum* + *-arius* -ary, n. suffix] **1** : a veteran under a special standard in an ancient Roman army **2** : STANDARD-BEARER
²vexillary \"\ *adj* [L *vexillum* + E *-ary*, adj. suffix] **1** : of or relating to an ensign or standard **2** : relating to or constituting a vexillum
vexillary aestivation *n* : aestivation (as in most pea flowers) in which one large upper petal folds over and covers the other smaller petals
vex·il·late \'veksə,lāt, vek'silət, 'veksələt\ *adj* [NL *vexillum* + E *-ate*] : having a vexillum
vex·il·la·tion \,veksə'lāshən\ *n* -s [L *vexillation-, vexillatio*, fr. *vexillum* + *-ation-, -atio* -ation] **1** : a company of ancient Roman troops under one vexillum and detached for special service from a main body of soldiers **2** : a regular troop of Roman cavalry; *also* : a company of veterans of a legion
vex·il·lum \vek'siləm\ *n, pl* **vexil·la** \-lə\ [L, prob. fr. *velum* cloth, sail, veil — more at VEIL] **1 a** : a square flag hanging transversely by a wooden crosspiece from a spear and used esp. by ancient Roman cavalry **b** : a processional standard, banner, or cross **2** : STANDARD 16a **3** [NL, fr. L] : the web or vane of a feather **4** : a company of ancient Roman troops and esp. of vexillaries serving under one standard
vex·ing·ly *adv* : so as to vex : in a manner designed or likely to produce vexation
vext *past of* VEX
VF *abbr* **1** vertical file **2** very fair; very fine **3** vicar forane **4** video frequency **5** visual field **6** voice frequency
VFO *abbr* variable frequency oscillator
VFR *abbr* visual flight rules
VG *abbr* **1** *often not cap* [L *verbi gratia*] for example **2** vertical grain **3** very good **4** vicar-general
v-girl *n, usu cap V* [*victory girl*] : VICTORY GIRL
VHC *abbr* very highly commended
VHF *abbr, often not cap* very high frequency
v-hut \'‑,‑\ *n, cap V* : a primitive hut having a cross section like an inverted letter V
vi *var of* VI APPLE
VI *abbr* **1** *often not cap* verb intransitive **2** vertical interval **3** *often not cap* [L *vide infra*] see below **4** viscosity index **5** volume indicator
¹via \'vīə *also* 'vēə\ *prep* [L, abl. of *via* way; akin to Gk *hiesthai* to hurry — more at VIM] **1** : by way of : by a route passing through ⟨shipped to New York ~ the Panama Canal⟩ ⟨arrived ~ the back door of the inn —Adrian Bell⟩ ⟨excretion of absorbed aluminum is ~ liver and kidney —C.H.Thienes⟩ **2** : through the medium of ⟨an increase in number of shareholders ~ lower-priced stock —*Wall Street Jour.*⟩ ⟨the central role which communication, especially ~ the mass media, plays —F.S.Fearing⟩ : by means of ⟨ability to harness . . . neighbor states to its war machine ~ blitz attack —S.L.A. Marshall⟩ ⟨trying to woo his reader, ~ heavy humor —Frances Keene⟩
²via \'vīə; 'vēə\ *n, pl* **vias** \-əz\ *or* **vi·ae** \-ī,ē; -ē,ī\ [L] **1 a** : ROAD, PASSAGE, RIGHT-OF-WAY **b** *pl* **viae** [NL, fr. L] : an anatomical passage (as a blood vessel or lymph channel) **2** : a right under Roman law to pass over the land of another in any manner — compare ACTUS
vi·a·bil·i·ty \,vīə'biləd·ē, -lətē, -i\ *n* [F *viabilité*, fr. *viable* + *-ité* -ity] **1** : the quality or state of being viable : the ability to live, grow, and develop ⟨the ~ of seeds under dry conditions⟩ ⟨~ of a fetus⟩ ⟨the ~ of small, new states is uncertain —R.A. Newhall⟩ ⟨serious questions as to the ~ of the economic plans —Vera M. Dean⟩
vi·a·ble \'vīəbəl\ *adj* [F, fr. MF, fr. *vie* life (fr. L *vita*) + *-able* — more at VITAL] **1 a** : capable of living ⟨the skin graft was ~⟩ ⟨~ cancer cells⟩ ⟨a ~ infant⟩ **b** *of a fetus* : having attained such form and development of organs as to be normally capable of living outside the uterus ⟨a 7-month ~ fetus⟩ **2** : capable of growing or developing ⟨~ seeds⟩ ⟨~ eggs⟩ **3** : affecting the imagination, mind, or senses as real, genuine, artistically whole, or important : LIVING ⟨make the life of industry and the city ~ to the imagination —L.A.Fiedler⟩ ⟨make ~ for their students the great cultural heritage —J.W. Dodds⟩ ⟨the poet . . . is to make philosophic content more ~ by addition of sensuous and emotional qualities —John Dewey⟩ **4 a** : capable of being put into practice : WORKABLE ⟨a ~ middle road . . . between the grim alternatives of appeasement and all-out war —F.W.Riggs⟩ ⟨even brigands can make a ~ agreement provided it embodies a common purpose —*New Republic*⟩ **b** : not self-contradictory : not lacking significance or consequences : capable of conceptual or aesthetic development ⟨offers a ~ alternative to other world views —J.W.Nixon⟩ ⟨anthropology is a ~ science —E.A. Hoebel⟩ ⟨if skepticism is a ~ enterprise —F.A.Olafson⟩ ⟨the novel is the only major art form that has come down to us from the nineteenth century in a ~ condition —Arnold Hauser⟩ **5** : capable of existence and development as a relatively independent social, economic, or political unit ⟨adopted the politically and economically superior culture . . . and set about transforming it into a ~ tropical civilization —Gilberto Freyre⟩ ⟨an artificial and hardly ~ state —E.K. Lindley⟩ ⟨reapportioning the country into 14 large and ~ states —*Time*⟩ — **vi·a·bly** \-blē, -li\ *adv*
via do·lo·ro·sa \-,dälə'rōsə, -,dōl-\ *n* [fr. *Via Dolorosa* (fr. L, lit., sorrowful road), Jesus' route from Pilate's judgment hall to Golgotha to be crucified] : a painfully difficult route, passage, or series of experiences ⟨an epoch which condemns its children to a *via dolorosa* of examinations —Herbert Read⟩
vi·a·duct \'vīə,dəkt *sometimes* 'vēə,\ *n* [L *via* way, road + E *-duct* (as in *aqueduct*)] **1** : a bridge esp. when resting on a series of narrow reinforced concrete or masonry arches, having high supporting towers or piers, and carrying a road or railroad over a valley, river, road, or other low-lying obstruction — compare TRESTLE **2** : a steel bridge made up of short spans carried on high steel towers

viaduct 1

via·ja·ca \vyə'häkə\ *n* -s [AmerSp (Cuba) *viajaca, biajaca*, modif. of Carib *diahaca*] : a small Cuban freshwater food fish (*Parapetenia tetracantha*) of the family Cichlidae
vi·al \'vī(ə)l\ *n* -s [ME *viole, fiole* — more at PHIAL] **1** : a small vessel for liquids: as **a** : a small glass or plastic bottle for a medicine or chemical **b** : the glass tube containing the liquid in a spirit level **2** : something regarded as a container or receptacle esp. of something immaterial ⟨pour out the ~*s* of the wrath of God upon the earth —Rev 16:1 (AV)⟩
via lac·tea \-'laktēə\ *n, usu cap V&L* [L] : MILKY WAY
via la·sci·via \-lə'sivēə\ *n, usu cap V&L* [NL, lit., lascivious path] : a line on the palm that appears as a sister line to the line of Mercury and is usu. held by palmists to indicate intensity of sentiments and sometimes sensuality
via me·dia \-'mēdēə, -'mādēə\ *n* [L] : a middle way or ground : a mediating conception ⟨a *via media* between dogmatism and skepticism —W.T.Jones⟩
vi·and \'vīənd *sometimes* 'vēə-\ *n* -s [ME *viaunde*, fr. MF *viande*, fr. (assumed) VL *vivanda*, alter. of L *vivenda*, neut. pl. of *vivendus*, gerundive of *vivere* to live — more at QUICK] **1** : an article of food **2** : **viands** \-n(d)z\ *pl* : PROVISIONS, FOOD, FARE
vi antigen \'vē,ī-\ *n, usu cap V* [*virulent antigen*] : a heat-labile somatic antigen associated with virulence in some bacteria (as of the genus *Salmonella*) and esp. in the typhoid fever bacterium and used to detect typhoid carriers through the presence in their serum of agglutinins against this antigen
vi apple \'vē-\ *also* **vi** *n* -s [*vi* fr. Tahitian] : OTAHEITE APPLE 1
vias *pl of* VIA
vi·at·i·cum \vī'ad·|ə̇kəm, -at|, |ēk-\ *n, pl* **viaticums** \-mz\ *or* **viati·ca** \-kə\ [L — more at VOYAGE] **1 a** : an allowance (as of transportation or supplies and money) for traveling expenses **b** : provisions for a journey ⟨prepared for me a ~ in the shape of a small loaf —C.B.Fairbanks⟩ **2** [LL, fr. L] : the Christian Eucharist or communion given to a person in danger of dying — compare EXTREME UNCTION
vi·a·tor \vī'ād·ə(r)\ *n* -s [L, fr. *viatus* + *-or*] : TRAVELER, WAYFARER
vib *abbr* vibrate; vibration
vibes \'vībz\ *n pl but usu sing in constr, also* **vibe** \-b\ [by shortening & alter.] : VIBRAPHONE
vi·bex \'vī,beks\ *n, pl* **vib·i·ces** \-ībə,sēz\ [L, mark of a blow, weal; prob. akin to Latvian *wibele* weals, *wile* seam, weal, scar, and perh. to L *vibrare* to shake, vibrate — more at WIPE] : a linear subcutaneous extravasation of blood
vib·ist \'vībəst\ *n* -s [*vibes* + *-ist*] : VIBRAPHONIST
vi·brac·u·lar \vī'brakyələ(r)\ *adj* [NL *vibraculum* + E *-ar*] : of, relating to, or furnished with vibracula
vi·brac·u·lar·i·um \vī,brakyə'la(a)rēəm\ *n* -s [NL, fr. *vibraculum* + *-arium*] **1** : VIBRACULUM **2** : a cell containing the motive cells of a vibracularium
vi·brac·u·loid \‑'‑‑,lȯid\ *adj* [NL *vibraculum* + E *-oid*] : of, relating to, or resembling a vibraculum
vi·brac·u·lum \-yələm\ *n, pl* **vibracula** [NL, fr. L *vibrare* to shake, vibrate + *-culum* -cle] : one of the movable slender spinelike organs or parts with which bryozoans are furnished and which are specially modified zooids of nearly the same nature as avicularia
vi·brance \'vībrən(t)s\ *n* -s : VIBRANCY
vi·bran·cy \-nsē, -si\ *n* -ES : the quality or state of being vibrant : RESONANCE, VIBRATION
vi·brant \-nt\ *adj* [L *vibrant-, vibrans*, pres. part. of *vibrare* to shake, vibrate — more at WIPE] **1 a** (1) : oscillating or pulsating rapidly : VIBRATING, PULSING ⟨~ quivering telegraph wires —J.C.Powys⟩ (2) : pulsating with life, vigor, or activity : ALIVE, VITAL ⟨the ~ atmosphere of a new age and a new world —I.M.Price⟩ ⟨a ~, active force, refusing to cede the dominion he had won —E.M.Lustgarten⟩ ⟨his ~ personality⟩ (3) : actively affected by an influence ⟨enfeebled but still ~ with her memories —*Newsweek*⟩ **b** (1) : readily set in vibration (2) : open and responsive to or easily affected by environment, events, other people, or stimuli : SENSITIVE ⟨hungry for ideas, intellectually and emotionally ~ —V.L.Parrington⟩ ⟨mind was—rather than deeply original—L.H.Butterfield⟩ **2 a** : sounding as a result of vibration **b** : having, exhibiting, or being a vital resonant sound : SONOROUS, RESONANT, RESOUNDING ⟨~ baritone voice —William Fifield⟩ **c** : resonant or echoing with the sounds of life and activity **3** : having the effect of or enlivened by sparkling light, color, or texture ⟨a painting ~ with color and action —F.J.Mather⟩ **syn** see RESONANT
vi·brant·ly *adv* : in a vibrant manner
vi·bra·phone \'vībrə,fōn\ *n* [ISV *vibra-* (fr. L *vibrare* to shake, vibrate) + *-phone*] : a percussion musical instrument resembling the xylophone but having metal bars and motor-driven resonators for sustaining the tone and producing a vibrato effect
vi·bra·phon·ist \-,nəst\ *n* -s : one that plays the vibraphone
vi·brate \'vī,brāt, *usu* -ād·+V\ *vb* -ED/-ING/-S [L *vibratus*, past part. of *vibrare* to shake, vibrate — more at WIPE] *vt* **1** : THROW, CAST, LAUNCH **2** : to emit with or as if with a vibratory motion **3** : to mark or measure by oscillation ⟨a pendulum *vibrating* seconds⟩ **4** : to set in vibration ⟨*vibrated* their open hands in imitation of the quivering sunlight —Philippa Pollenz⟩ **5** : to treat by vibration; *specif* : to compress or compact by vibration ~ *vi* **1 a** : to move to and fro or from side to side : OSCILLATE **b** : ALTERNATE ⟨*vibrated* for some years between art and literature —G.F.Whicher⟩ **2** : to have an effect or move by or as if by vibration **3 a** : to be in a state of vibration : oscillate very rapidly : QUIVER ⟨the eardrum ~*s* and transmits the vibrations —Morris Fishbein⟩ ⟨the lower lip *vibrated* with a delicate flabbiness —R.P. Warren⟩ **b** : to act in or as if in acoustic sympathy ⟨strings . . . which ~ when a chord is struck —R.W.Sockman⟩ ⟨an intellectual who ~*s* intuitively to ideas —William Barrett⟩ ⟨the scrapbook fairly ~*s* with enthusiasm —Virginia D. Dawson & Betty D. Wilson⟩ **syn** see SWING
vibrated concrete *n* : concrete that has been vibrated either

internally or externally after it has been placed in order to produce a denser mass

vi·bra·tile \ˈvībrəd·ᵊl, -ət³l, -əˌtīl, -ə(ˌ)til\ *adj* [F, fr. L *vibratus* + F *-ile*] **1 :** characterized by vibration **:** VIBRATORY, OSCILLATING **2 :** adapted to or used in vibratory motion ⟨the ~ organs of insects⟩ — **vi·bra·til·i·ty** \ˌvībrəˈtiləd-ē, -lətē, -i\ *n* -ES

vi·brat·ing·ly *adv* **:** in a vibrating manner

vibrating screen *n* **:** a device made with a screening surface vibrated mechanically at high speeds and used esp. for screening ore, coal, or other fine dry materials

vi·bra·tion \vīˈbrāshən\ *n* -S [L *vibration-, vibratio,* fr. *vibratus* (past part. of *vibrare* to shake, vibrate) + *-ion-, -io* -ion — more at WIPE] **1 a :** a periodic motion of the particles of an elastic body or medium in alternately opposite directions from the position of equilibrium when that equilibrium has been disturbed (as when a stretched cord or other body produces musical tones or particles of air transmit sounds to the ear) **b :** the action of vibrating or the state of being vibrated or in vibratory motion: as (1) **:** OSCILLATION (2) **:** a quivering or trembling motion **:** QUIVER **2 :** an instance of vibration: as **a :** the complete movement described by a particle of an elastic body or medium until the periodic motion begins to repeat itself **b :** one half of the periodic motion of a particle **c** *obs* **:** a hypothetical motion of the nerves serving as a means of transmission of sensory impressions **d :** an occult or supernatural entity that exerts a harmful or beneficial influence and is sensible to a person psychically attuned to it ⟨the evil act has set millions of ~s going —Margery Allingham⟩ ⟨got ~s that you fellows were close —W.T.Brannon⟩ **3 :** vacillation in opinion, doctrine, or conduct **4 a :** a characteristic emanation, aura, or spirit that infuses or vitalizes and that can be intuitively sensed or experienced ⟨what was most stimulating . . . depended largely on the ~s of his time and country —Sean O'Faolain⟩ ⟨the ~ of human kinship —Jean S. Untermeyer⟩ **b :** a psychological response esp. to aesthetic or emotional stimuli ⟨could . . . the memory of his smile awake the familiar ~s —Ellen Glasgow⟩

vi·bra·tion·al \(ˈ)vīˈbrāshənᵊl, -shnəl\ *adj* **1 :** of or relating to vibration **2 :** having a periodic or harmonic motion

vibrational quantum number *n* **:** a scalar quantum number that defines the energy state of a harmonic or approximately harmonic vibrating atomic system

vibrational specific heat *n* **:** the contribution made by the energy of internal vibration of the molecules of a substance to the total specific heat of the substance — compare ROTATIONAL SPECIFIC HEAT

vibrational spectrum *or* **vibration spectrum** *n* **:** the part of a molecular spectrum in which the bands arise from quantized changes in the energy of mutual atomic vibrations within the molecule — compare ROTATIONAL SPECTRUM

vi·bra·tion·less \-shənləs\ *adj* **:** having no vibration

vibration number *or* **vibrational number** *n* **:** the number of vibrations per second of a musical tone — compare ⁴PITCH 4b(1)

vi·bra·ti·un·cle \vīˈbrāshēˌəŋkəl\ *n* -S [*vibration* + *-uncle* (fr. L *-uncula,* dim. suffix)] **:** a slight vibration

vi·bra·tive \ˈvībrəd·iv\ *adj* [*vibrate* + *-ive*] **:** VIBRATORY

vi·bra·to \vēˈbräd·(ˌ)ō, vī-, -ä(ˌ)tō\ *n* -S [It, past part. of *vibrare* to vibrate, fr. L, to shake, vibrate — more at WIPE] **1 :** a slightly tremulous effect imparted to vocal or instrumental tone for added warmth and expressiveness and consisting of slight and rapid variations in the pitch of the tone being produced **2 :** TREMOLO 1b **3 :** a periodic fluctuation of sustained tones or of tones of steadily changing pitch in speech and esp. in emotional speech

vi·bra·tor \ˈvīˌbrād·ə(r), -ātə-\ *n* -S **1 :** a device, instrument, mechanism, attachment, or organ that vibrates or causes vibration or oscillation: as **a :** a vibrating object (as a violin string or a reed in an organ) that produces a tone **b :** an ink-distributing roller in a printing press that has end-to-end vibratory motion as well as rotary motion **c :** a vibrating electrical apparatus used in massage **d :** a usu. pneumatic attachment in a molding machine to shake the pattern or match plate loose **e :** a vibrating device (as in an electric bell or buzzer) for opening or closing an electric circuit **f :** a device for vibrating concrete **2 :** a device that consists of a standard balance and standard balance spring and is used for determining the strength of balance springs by a comparison of the vibrations **3 :** an electromagnetic device that converts low direct current to pulsating direct current or alternating current

vi·bra·to·ry \ˈvībrəˌtōrē, -tȯr-, -ri\ *adj* [*vibrate* + *-ory*] **1 a :** consisting in, capable of, or causing vibration or oscillation **b :** characterized by vibration **:** VIBRANT, VIBRATING **2 :** of, relating to, affecting, or constituting a sense responsive to vibrations and believed by some to be distinct from the sense of touch

vib·rio \ˈvibrēˌō\ *n* [NL, fr. L *vibrare* to shake, vibrate — more at WIPE] **1** *cap* **:** a genus of short rigid motile bacteria (family Spirillaceae) having a polar flagellum or sometimes two or three, being typically shaped like a comma or an S that occur singly or united into spirals, and including various saprophytes and a few important pathogens (as *V. comma* and *V. fetus* that are the cause of Asiatic cholera and of abortion in cattle and sheep respectively) — compare SPIRILLUM **2** -S **:** any bacterium of the genus *Vibrio; broadly* **:** a curved rod-shaped bacterium — **vib·ri·oid** \-ēˌȯid\ *adj*

vib·ri·on \-ēˌän\ *n* -S [NL *Vibrion-, Vibrio*] **:** VIBRIO; *also* **:** a motile bacterium

vib·ri·on·ic \ˌ==ˈänik\ *adj* [NL *Vibrion-, Vibrio* + E *-ic*] **:** caused by a vibrio ⟨~ dysentery⟩

vibrionic abortion *n* **:** abortion in sheep and cattle caused by a bacterium (*Vibrio fetus*) that invades the uterine and placental capillaries, interferes with fetal nutrition, and causes the death of the developing fetus

vib·ri·o·sis \ˌ==ˈōsəs\ *n, pl* **vibrio·ses** \-ōˌsēz\ [NL, fr. *Vibrio* + *-osis*] **:** infestation with or disease caused by bacteria of the genus *Vibrio; specif* **:** VIBRIONIC ABORTION

vi·bris·sa \vīˈbrisə\ *n, pl* **vibris·sae** \-iˌsē\ [NL, fr. L *vibrissae,* pl., hairs in the nostrils, prob. fr. *vibrare* to shake, vibrate — more at WIPE] **1 :** one of the stiff hairs that grow about the nostrils or on other parts of the face in many mammals (as the whiskers of a cat or the hairs of the nostrils of man) and that are not themselves sensitive but often serve as tactile organs; *also* **:** a similar stiff tactile hair growing elsewhere on some mammals (as in a small tuft at the wrist) **2 :** one of the feathers that resemble bristles near the mouth of many birds and esp. of some insectivorous birds and that may help to prevent the escape of insects **3 :** either of a pair of stout bristles situated on either side of the mouth of some two-winged flies

vi·bris·sal \-səl\ *adj* [NL *vibrissa* + E *-al*] **:** of or relating to a vibrissa

vibro- *comb form* [ISV, fr. L *vibrare* to shake, vibrate] **:** vibration ⟨*vibro*massage⟩

vi·bro·graph \ˈvībrəˌgraf, -ràf\ *n* [ISV *vibro-* + *-graph*] **:** an instrument to observe, measure, and record vibrations

vi·brom·e·ter \vīˈbräməd·ə(r)\ *n* [*vibro-* + *-meter*] **:** VIBROGRAPH

vi·bur·num \vīˈbərnəm, -ˈbən-, -ˈbəin-\ *n* [NL, fr. L, wayfaring tree] **1** *cap* **:** a large genus of widely distributed shrubs or trees (family Caprifoliaceae) having simple leaves and white or rarely pink cymose flowers with a regular 5-lobed corolla, a 3-lobed style, and a 1- to 3-celled ovary that becomes in fruit a one-seeded drupe — see BLACK HAW, CRANBERRY BUSH, DOCKMACKIE, LAURUSTINE, WAYFARING TREE, WITHE ROD **2** -S **:** any plant of the genus *Viburnum*

¹**vic** \ˈvik\ *n* -S [short for *victrola*] **:** PHONOGRAPH

²**vic** \"\ *n* -S [fr. British signalmen's telephone pron. of the letter *V*] *Brit* **:** a V-shaped formation of airplanes

vic- *comb form, usu ital* [*vicinal*] **:** vicinal — in names of organic chemical compounds ⟨*vic*-triazine or 1,2,3-triazine⟩ ⟨*vic-, as-,* or 1,2-dinitro-ethane⟩

vic *abbr* **1** vicar; vicarage **2** vicinity

vic·ar \ˈvikə(r)\ *n* -S [ME *vicare, vicair, viker,* fr. LL *vicarius,* fr. L, substitute, deputy, fr. *vicarius,* adj., substituting, delegated, vicarious — more at VICARIOUS] **1 :** a human representative or agent of God on earth ⟨those who regard the pope as being God's ~⟩ **2 a :** the incumbent of an impropriated or formerly appropriated benefice of the Church of England **:** the priest of a parish of which the tithes are owned by a layman or formerly a spiritual corporation **:** an incumbent of a Church of England parish not a rector **b :** a Protestant Episcopal clergyman in charge of a dependent chapel as the deputy of another clergyman **c :** an ecclesiastic who acts as the substitute or representative of another in the Roman Catholic Church **3 a :** an administrative deputy **:** VICEGERENT **b :** someone or something that serves as a substitute ⟨there is no ~ for poetry on earth —R.P.Blackmur⟩

Vi·cara \vīˈkarə\ *trademark* — used for a woolly protein textile fiber from corn zein used esp. in blends with other fibers

vic·ar·age \ˈvikərij, -rēj\ *n* -S [ME *vicarage, vikerage,* fr. *vicar, vicair, viker* vicar + *-age*] **1 a :** the benefice of a vicar **b** *Scot* **:** tithes or dues paid to a vicar **2 :** the house or household of a vicar **3 :** the office, function, or duty of a vicar **:** VICARSHIP

vicar apostolic *n, pl* **vicars apostolic :** a titular bishop who acts as a delegate of the Roman Catholic pope in administering an ecclesiastical district in a missionary region

vic·ar·ate \-kərət, -kəˌrāt\ *n* -S **:** VICARIATE

vicar capitular *n, pl* **vicars capitular :** an ecclesiastic selected by a Roman Catholic cathedral chapter to administer the affairs of a vacant see until a new bishop is appointed

vicar choral *n, pl* **vicars choral :** one of a number of clergy or laymen in an Anglican cathedral whose duty is to sing a portion of the music of the services

vic·ar·ess \-kərəs\ *n* -ES **1 :** a nun whose official rank is immediately below that of the superior of a convent **2 :** a woman who is the representative or vicegerent of someone else **3 :** a vicar's wife

vicar fo·rane \-fōrˈān\ *n, pl* **vicars forane** [*forane* fr. LL *foranus* situated on the outside — more at FOREIGN] **:** DEAN 2c

vicar–general \ˈ==ˈ=(=)=\ *n, pl* **vicars–general** [ME; trans. of ML *vicarius generalis*] **1 a :** the deputy of a Roman Catholic or Anglican bishop assisting in the jurisdiction of the diocese **b :** an administrative deputy of the head of a religious order **2 :** a lay legal officer who is deputy of a bishop of the Church of England in some matters

vicar–general·ship \"+ˌship\ *n* **:** the office of vicar-general

vi·car·i·al \(ˈ)vīˈka(a)rēəl, vəˈk-, -ker-, -kär-\ *adj* [L *vicarius* + E *-al*] **1 :** DELEGATED, DEPUTED **2 :** of or relating to a vicar ⟨~ duties⟩

¹**vi·car·i·ate** \-ēət, -ēˌāt, *usu* -d.+V\ *n* -S [ML *vicariatus,* fr. LL *vicarius* vicar + L *-atus* -ate, n. suffix — more at VICAR] **1 a :** the office, authority, or jurisdiction of a vicar **:** VICARSHIP **b :** the period of a vicar's incumbency **2 a :** a governmental or administrative office held by a deputy **b :** a district governed or administered by a deputy **3 :** SUBSTITUTION ⟨the ~ seemingly exercised by the sharpened remaining senses of a blind man⟩

²**vicariate** \"\ *adj* [L *vicarius* + E *-ate,* adj. suffix] **:** having delegated power **:** VICARIOUS

vicariate apostolic *n, pl* **vicariates apostolic :** a Roman Catholic missionary district over which a vicar apostolic exercises jurisdiction

vi·cari·ism \vīˈka(a)rēˌizəm\ *n* -S [*vicarious* + *-ism*] **:** the quality or state of being vicarious ⟨the tendency of some genera to exhibit ~⟩

vi·car·i·ous \(ˈ)vīˈka(a)rēəs, -ker-, -kär- *sometimes* vəˈk-\ *adj* [L *vicarius,* fr. *vicis* change, alternation, stead + *-arius* -ary — more at WEEK] **1 :** having the function of a substitute **:** serving instead of someone or something else **:** acting for a principal **:** representing or taking the place of something primary or original **:** DELEGATED ⟨memory is ~ experience in which there is all the emotional value of actual experience —John Dewey⟩ **2 :** performed or suffered by one person as a substitute for another or to the benefit or advantage of another **:** SUBSTITUTIONARY ⟨~ sacrifice⟩ **3 :** experienced or realized through imaginative or sympathetic participation in the experience of another ⟨was getting a ~ kick out of watching a fellow female preening herself over the capitulation of the male —Helen Howe⟩ **4 :** occurring in an unexpected or abnormal part of the body instead of the usual one ⟨bleeding from the gums sometimes replaces the discharge from the uterus in ~ menstruation⟩ **5 a :** of, relating to, or being closely related kinds of organisms that occur in similar environments or as fossils in corresponding strata but in distinct and often widely separated areas **b :** made up of or characterized by the presence of such organisms ⟨~ pairs⟩ ⟨a ~ area⟩

vi·car·i·ous·ly *adv* **:** in a vicarious manner **:** as, by, or through a substitute ⟨we want ~ and temporarily to be other people in other worlds —C.A.Smart⟩

vi·car·i·ous·ness *n* -ES **:** the quality or state of being vicarious

vicar of bray \-ˈbrā\ *usu cap B* [after the *Vicar of Bray,* semilegendary 16th cent. Eng. vicar of the village of Bray, Berkshire county, England, who gave allegiance to Protestantism or Roman Catholicism according to the religion of the reigning monarch, and is said to have been twice a Protestant and twice a Roman Catholic vicar] **:** a man of changeable allegiance **:** OPPORTUNIST, TURNCOAT

vicar of christ *cap C* **:** a Roman Catholic pope

vicars *pl of* VICAR

vic·ar·ship \ˈvikə(r)ˌship\ *n* **:** the office or tenure of a vicar

vi·cat apparatus \(ˈ)vēˈkä-\ *n, usu cap V* [after Louis J. *Vicat* †1861 Fr. engineer] **:** a device for determining the normal consistency and time of setting of portland cements that consists of a rod weighing 300 grams, having a needle in each end, and supported in a frame with a graduated scale to measure the distance to which the needle penetrates the cement

¹**vice** \ˈvīs\ *n* -S [ME, fr. OF, fr. L *vitium* fault, blemish, crime, vice — more at WITH] **1 a :** moral depravity or corruption **:** evil conduct or habits **:** indulgence of degrading appetites **:** WICKEDNESS ⟨the true lover of the human race is surely he who can put up with it in all its forms, in ~ as well as in virtue —John Galsworthy⟩ **b :** a wrong, degrading, or immoral habit or practice **:** evil behavior of a particular or accustomed kind ⟨tainted with the ~ of homosexuality —R.A.Hall b.1911⟩ **c :** a fault or shortcoming that becomes a foible **:** a constitutional failing **:** a moral flaw ⟨the local ~ of overstatement —W.L.Sperry⟩ **2 a :** a blemish or imperfection in something **:** DEFECT ⟨the ~ of his conception is that it overlooks the serious consequences⟩ **b** (1) **:** an imperfection in merchandise or in a contract serious enough to invalidate the contract or a sale of the goods (2) **:** a fault or imperfection which because inherent in the nature of the goods or material often cannot be insured against **3 :** a physical imperfection, deformity, or taint **4 a** *often cap* **:** a character representing one of the vices in an English morality play **b :** BUFFOON, JESTER **5 :** habitual undesirable conduct in a domestic animal; *specif* **:** an abnormal behavior pattern (as in cannibalism of poultry or the sucking vice of calves) detrimental to the health or usefulness of an individual or group and commonly representing perversion or overdevelopment of normal instincts or reflexes — compare CRIB-BITING **6 :** an incapacity **:** HARMFULNESS **7 :** sexual immorality; *esp* **:** PROSTITUTION **syn** see FAULT

²**vice** \"\ *n* -S [ME *vis, vice,* fr. MF *vis, viz* — more at VISE] **1 :** a winding stairway **2** *obs* **a :** a mechanical device working an apparatus **b :** SCREW **c :** a stopper that screws into an opening (as of a cask) **3** *chiefly Brit* **:** VISE **4 :** a device for making the leads for leaded windows

³**vice** \"\ *vt* -ED/-ING/-S *chiefly Brit* **:** VISE

⁴**vice** \"\ *n* -S [*vice-*] **:** PROXY, SUBSTITUTE

⁵**vi·ce** \ˈvīsē, -si\ *n* -S [L, abl. of *vicis* change, alternation, stead — more at WEEK] **1** *chiefly Scot* **:** PLACE, STEAD **2** *chiefly Scot* **:** a turn in sequence

⁶**vice** \"\ *prep* [L, abl. of *vicis*] **:** in the place of **:** in the stead of **:** SUCCEEDING ⟨John Doe was appointed postmaster ~ Richard Roe, resigned⟩

vice- *prefix* [ME *vis-, vice-,* fr. MF, fr. LL *vice-,* fr. L *vice,* abl. of *vicis*] **:** one that takes the place of ⟨*vice*-consul⟩ ⟨*vice*-chairman⟩ ⟨*vice*-principal⟩

vice admiral \ˈvīs+\ *n* [MF *visamiral,* fr. *vis-* vice + *amiral* admiral — more at ADMIRAL] **1 :** a commissioned naval officer ranking just below an admiral and above a rear admiral — abbr. *VA* **2** *obs* **:** a ship of war commanded by a vice admiral

vice admiralty \"+\ *n* **1 :** the office of a vice admiral **2 :** the district under the jurisdiction of a vice admiral

vice–admiralty court *n* **:** a British Admiralty court established in a colony beyond the seas in which the governor of the colony in his capacity as vice admiral exercises his judicial authority for the trial of maritime cases of a civil nature including prize cases

vice–chairman \ˈvīs+\ *n* [*vice-* + *chairman*] **:** one that assists a chairman or acts as his deputy in his absence

vice–chamberlain \"+\ *n* [*vice-* + *chamberlain*] **:** a deputy of a chamberlain

vice–chancellor \"+\ *n* [ME *vichauncellor,* fr. MF *vischancelier,* fr. *vis-* vice- + *chancelier* chancellor — more at CHANCELLOR] **:** an officer ranking next below a chancellor **:** a chancellor's deputy ⟨the *vice-chancellor* of a university⟩; *esp* **:** a judge appointed to act for or to assist a chancellor

vice–chancellorship \"+\ *n* **:** the office or term of a vice-chancellor

vice–consul \"+\ *n* [*vice-* + *consul*] **:** a consular officer subordinate to a consul general or to a consul

vice–count *n* [ME *viscounte, vicecount* — more at VISCOUNT] *obs* **:** VISCOUNT

vice–county \ˈvīs+\ *n* [*vice-* + *county*] *Brit* **:** a subdivision of a county

viced *past of* VICE

vice·ge·ren·cy \vīsˈjirənsē, -si\ *also* **vice·ge·rence** \-n(t)s\ *n, pl* **vicegerencies** *also* **vicegerences :** the office or jurisdiction of a vicegerent

vice·ge·rent \-nt\ *n* [ML *vicegerent-, vicegerens,* fr. L *vice-* + *gerent-, gerens,* pres. part. of *gerere* to bear — more at CAST] **1 :** an administrative deputy **:** a person appointed to perform functions of a king or magistrate **:** DEPUTY, LIEUTENANT **2 :** a person deputed by God to exercise his authority in government or religious matters ⟨kings who considered themselves God's ~s in their dominions⟩ **3 :** someone or something that substitutes for another

vice–god \ˈvīs+\ *n, often cap V&G* [*vice-* + *god*] **:** a deputy of God — usu. used disparagingly

vice–governor \"+\ *n* [*vice-* + *governor*] **:** a governor's assistant or deputy

vice–king \"+\ *n* [*vice-* + *king*] **:** VICEROY

vice–legate \"+\ *n* [*vice-* + *legate*] **:** the deputy of a legate

vice·less \ˈvīsləs\ *adj* [¹*vice* + *-less*] **:** having no vices

vicelike \ˈ=ˌ=\ *adj* [²*vice* + *-like*] **:** VISELIKE

vice–master \ˈvīs+\ *n* [*vice-* + *master*] **:** a master's deputy or assistant

vic·e·nary \ˈvisəˌnerē, -ri\ *adj* [L *vicenarius,* fr. *viceni* twenty each + *-arius* -ary; akin to L *viginti* twenty; akin to OIr *fiche* twenty, Gk *eikosi* (Doric *ϝikati*), Skt *viṁśati*; all fr. an IE compound whose 1st constituent was an IE word meaning "two" (represented by Skt *vi* apart), and whose 2d constituent is represented by L *decem* ten — more at WITH, TEN] **1 :** containing 20 **2 :** based on the number 20 **:** VIGESIMAL

vi·cen·ni·al \(ˈ)vīˈsenēəl\ *adj* [LL *vicennium* period of 20 years (fr. L *vicies* 20 times + *-ennium,* fr. *annus* year) + E *-al;* akin to L *viginti* twenty — more at ANNUAL] **:** occurring once every 20 years

vice–premier \ˈvīs+\ *n* [*vice-* + *premier*] **:** a premier's deputy or assistant

vice–presidency \"+\ *n* **:** the office of vice-president

vice–president \"+\ *n* [*vice-* + *president*] **1 :** an officer next in rank below a president and acting as president in case of that officer's absence or disability **2 :** one of several officers serving as a president's deputies in charge of particular locations or functions ⟨eastern regional *vice-president*⟩ ⟨*vice-president* and plant manager⟩ ⟨*vice-president* in charge of sales⟩ ⟨*vice-president* in charge of engineering⟩ — **vice–presidential** \"+\ *adj*

vice–queen \"+\ *n* [*vice-* + *queen*] **1 :** VICEREINE 2 **2 :** a viceroy's wife

viceregal \"+\ *adj* [*vice-* + *regal*] **:** of or relating to a viceroy

vice–regent \"+\ *n* [*vice-* + *regent*] **:** a regent's deputy or assistant

vice·reine \ˈvīsˌrān\ *n* -S [F, fr. *vice-* + *reine* queen, fr. L *regina* — more at REINA] **1 :** the wife of a viceroy **2 :** a woman viceroy

vice·roy \ˈvīsˌrȯi\ *n* -S [MF *vice-roi,* fr. *vice-* + *roi* king, fr. L *reg-, rex* — more at ROYAL] **1 :** the governor of a country or province who rules as the representative of his king or sovereign and has power to act generally in the name and behalf of his sovereign **2 :** a showy American butterfly (*Limenitis archippus*) closely mimicking the monarch butterfly in coloration but smaller and having larvae that feed on willow, poplar, and apple trees

vice·royalty \ˈvīs+ˌ-\ *n* [*vice-* + *royalty;* trans. of F *vice-royauté*] **:** the office, jurisdiction, or term of service of a viceroy

vice·roy·ship \ˈ==ˌship\ *n* [*viceroy* + *-ship*] **:** VICEROYALTY

vices *pl of* VICE, *pres 3d sing of* VICE

vicesimo–quarto *var of* VIGESIMO-QUARTO

vice–skip \ˈvīs+\ *n* [*vice-* + *skip*] **:** the third man on a curling team

vice squad *n* **:** a police squad charged with enforcement of laws concerning vice

vice–treasurer \ˈvīs+\ *n* [*vice-* + *treasurer*] **:** a treasurer's deputy or assistant

vice–treasurer·ship \"+ˌship\ *n* **:** the office or tenure of a vice-treasurer

vice ver·sa \ˌvīsəˈvərsə, -sē-, -si'-, -ˈvəsə, -ˈvəisə, (ˈ)vīsˈ-\ *adv* [L] **:** with the alternation or order changed **:** with the relations reversed **:** CONVERSELY ⟨it was with vast relief that we came upon a man pretending to be a machine, rather than *vice versa* —*New Yorker*⟩

vice–warden \ˈvīs+\ *n* [*vice-* + *warden*] **:** a warden's deputy or assistant

vich·i·an \ˈvikēən\ *adj, usu cap* [It *vichiano,* fr. G. B. *Vico* + It *-iano* -ian — more at VICONIAN] **:** VICONIAN

vi·chy·ite \ˈvishēˌīt, ˈvēsh-, -shi-, *usu* -īd-+V\ *n* -S *usu cap* [fr. *Vichy,* France, capital of unoccupied France in World War II + E *-ite*] **:** a member or supporter of the authoritarian regime of Marshal Henri Pétain governing unoccupied France during the earlier part of World War II under an agreement calling for economic collaboration with the Nazis

vi·chys·soise \ˌvishēˈswäz, ˌvēsh-, -shi'-\ *n* -S [F (short for *crème vichyssoise glacée,* lit., ice-cold Vichy cream), fr. fem. of *vichyssois* of Vichy, fr. *Vichy,* France] **:** a soup made of pureed leeks or onions and potatoes, cream, chicken stock, and seasoning and usu. served cold

vi·chy water \ˈviˌshē- ˈvē-, -shi-\ *n, often cap V* [fr. *Vichy,* France] **:** SODA WATER 2a

Vi·ci \ˈvīˌsī\ *trademark* — used for leather used esp. for the uppers of shoes

vi·cia \ˈvis(h)ēə\ *n, cap* [NL, fr. L, vetch — more at VETCH] **:** a widely distributed genus of often climbing herbs (family Leguminosae) having pinnate leaves and blue, purple, or yellow flowers either solitary or in axillary racemes, the style usu. beaked or tufted, and the ovary containing numerous ovules — see HAIRY VETCH, VETCH

vi·ci·a·nin \-ənən\ *n* -S [ISV *vician-* (fr. NL *Vicia angustifolia*) + *-in*] **:** a crystalline glycoside $C_{19}H_{25}NO_{10}$ found in the seeds of a vetch (*Vicia angustifolia*) that yields vicianose, benzaldehyde, and hydrogen cyanide on hydrolysis

vi·ci·a·nose \-əˌnōs\ *n* -S [ISV *vicianin* + *-ose*] **:** a crystalline disaccharide sugar $C_{11}H_{20}O_{10}$ that is obtained by hydrolysis of vicianin and that yields L-arabinose and D-glucose on hydrolysis

vic·i·lin \ˈvisələn\ *n* -S [L *vicia* vetch + E *globulin*] **:** a globulin associated with legumin (as in the pea, lentil, or broad bean)

vic·i·nage \ˈvis(ᵊ)nij, -(ᵊ)nēj\ *n* -S [ME *vesinage,* fr. MF *vesinage, vicenage, voisinage,* fr. *vesin, vicin, voisin* neighboring (fr. L *vicinus*) + *-age* — more at VICINITY] **1 a :** an adjacent, neighboring, or surrounding district **:** a limited nearby area **:** NEIGHBORHOOD, VICINITY **b :** the residents of a vicinage **2 :** a right of common arising to neighboring tenants of the same barony and fee

vic·i·nal \-(ᵊ)nəl\ *adj* [L *vicinalis,* fr. *vicinus* neighbor (fr. *vicinus* neighboring) + *-alis* -al] **1 :** of, relating to, or confined to a limited district or neighborhood **:** belonging to or restricted to a vicinity **:** LOCAL ⟨~ roads are distinguished from through highways⟩ **2 :** of, relating to, or being the subordinate forms or faces on a crystal which sometimes take the place of the fundamental ones, approach them very closely in angle, and have in general very complex symbols **3 :** relating to, characterized by, or being adjoining positions in an organic chemical compound ⟨the three ~ 1,2,3-positions in benzene⟩ — abbr. *v;* compare NEIGHBORING 2, ¹ORTHO 2

vic·ine *also* **vic·in** \ˈvīsən\ *n* -s [L *vicia* vetch + ISV *-ine*] **:** a crystalline glucoside $C_{10}H_{16}N_4O_7$ obtained esp. from seeds of vetches (genus *Vicia*) and beets that yields glucose and a pyrimidine on hydrolysis

vicing *pres part of* VICE

vic·i·nism \ˈvisə,nizəm\ *n* -s [ISV *vicin-* (fr. L *vicinus* neighbor) + *-ism*] **:** natural cross-pollination between two species or two varieties of a plant

vi·cin·i·ty \vəˈsinəd·ē, -ətē, -i *sometimes chiefly Brit* vīˈ-\ *n* -ES [MF *vicinité,* fr. L *vicinitat-, vicinitas,* fr. *vicinus* neighboring (fr. *vicus* row of houses, village + *-inus* -ine) + *-itat-, -itas* -ity; akin to Goth *weihs* village, Gk *oikos* house, dwelling, Skt *viś* settlement, dwelling, house] **1 :** the quality or state of being near **:** NEARNESS, PROPINQUITY, PROXIMITY ⟨might well dread the immediate ~ of a monarch so great, so ambitious, and so unscrupulous —T.B.Macaulay⟩ ⟨so near a ~ to her mother . . . was not desirable —Jane Austen⟩ **2** *obs* **:** close relationship or resemblance **3 :** a surrounding area or district **:** LOCALITY, NEIGHBORHOOD ⟨in the ~ of his home⟩ ⟨old residents of the ~ —John DeMeyer⟩ **4 :** NEIGHBORHOOD 3b ⟨invitations which he receives average in the ~ of 300 a month —Philip Hamburger⟩

vi·cious \ˈvishəs\ *adj* [ME, fr. MF *vicieus,* fr. L *vitiosus* full of faults, bad, corrupt, fr. *vitium* blemish, crime, vice + *-osus* -ous — more at WITH] **1 a :** having the nature or quality of vice **:** violative of moral rectitude **:** contrary to accepted standards of right or good **:** DEBASED, DEPRAVED ⟨a great university, in a few months, became a ~ political tool —R.A.Smith⟩ **b :** addicted to vice, immorality, or depravity **:** corrupt or dissolute in conduct **:** EVIL, REPROBATE ⟨a family with a good mother can withstand a feckless or even a ~ father —*Times Lit. Supp.*⟩ **2 a :** missing or incompatible with a norm of excellence **:** failing to meet a test or criterion **:** BAD, FAULTY, POOR, REPREHENSIBLE ⟨discriminate between thoroughly ~ ideas and those which should have a chance to be heard —Zechariah Chafee⟩ ⟨criticism at its most ~ —C.D.Lewis⟩ **b :** marred or nullified by imperfection **:** voided before the law by inherent defect **:** UNLAWFUL ⟨a badly drawn or ~ bill —Allan Nevins⟩ **c :** ruined or invalidated by defect ⟨a ~ argument⟩ **:** inferior in form or taste **:** stunted in development **:** IMPAIRED, TRIVIAL ⟨a ~ line of reasoning⟩ ⟨~ and ephemeral light verse⟩ ⟨~ spelling⟩ **3 a :** FOUL, IMPURE, NOXIOUS **b :** DISEASED, MALIGNANT, MORBID ⟨a gastric carcinoma is a very ~ tumor —W.H.Cole⟩ **4 a :** having dangerous or refractory habits **:** SAVAGE, UNTAMED ⟨a particularly ~ dog which snapped at every passerby —*Amer. Guide Series: R. I.*⟩ **b :** marked by violence or ferocity **:** FIERCE, SHARP, WILD ⟨took a ~ swing at him with the pick —Rex Ingamells⟩ ⟨~ animosity of political opponents —*Amer. Guide Series: Tenn.*⟩ **c :** of or relating to perverse or abnormal behavior of domestic animals ⟨the ~ habit of picking feathers —*Poultry Science*⟩ **5 :** MALICIOUS, SPITEFUL ⟨ugly and ~ stories invented and repeated by respectable lawyers and college professors —A.M. Schlesinger b. 1917⟩ **6 :** INTENSE, SEVERE ⟨there have been unusually ~ windstorms —Janet Flanner⟩ **7 :** painfully strenuous or extreme ⟨the alternative of a ~ tightening of . . . belts later in the year —*Economist*⟩ **8 :** having a sequence or progression analogous to that of a vicious circle **:** intensified, worsened, or accelerated by internal causes that reciprocally aggravate each other's bad effects ⟨you can see in all this wage business the ~ spiral at work. The miners got more pay, so coal prices went up, so the railways raised their freight charges, so coal prices went up again to meet dearer transport, so the miners asked for more pay to meet the higher cost of living —Margaret Stewart⟩ ⟨a ~ cycle⟩

syn VILLAINOUS, INIQUITOUS, NEFARIOUS, FLAGITIOUS, INFAMOUS, CORRUPT, DEGENERATE: VICIOUS may suggest addiction to or exemplification of vice, immorality, or depravity; it may connote violence, deliberate cruelty, or effective malignancy ⟨she had been *vicious* and unnatural; she had thriven on hatred, and had made life a hell for everyone about her —W.H. Wright⟩ ⟨protect the community from even its thoroughly *vicious* young criminals —Bruce Smith⟩ ⟨*vicious* accusations in the press that Jews had poisoned water supplies —Shlomo Katz⟩ VILLAINOUS is a forceful general descriptive term for anything depraved, scoundrelly, evil, or vile ⟨certain *villainous* government officials had plotted to murder the Count —Edmund Wilson⟩ ⟨nor does great creative Nature pause for one minute to discourage such scoundrels in their *villainous* malpractice —J.C.Powys⟩ INIQUITOUS applies to an utter lack of justice or fairness, a callous disregard for decent conduct or procedure ⟨they now appeared to him everything that was *iniquitous* and bad. Secret murder was their object — black, foul, midnight murder —Anthony Trollope⟩ ⟨that quenchless hunger for raw, quick, dirty money in American politics, which hardly sugarcoats its bribes, which glazes over its most *iniquitous* corruption —W.A.White⟩ NEFARIOUS sometimes suggests impiety or flagrantly countering established laws and social principles ⟨he kills devotion with an almost infallible aim. Charity turns into a lump of ice under his *nefarious* gaze —Julien Green⟩ ⟨our politicians would not dare to sacrifice the life and happiness of innumerable children to their *nefarious* schemes of bloodshed and oppression —Bertrand Russell⟩ FLAGITIOUS may describe whatever is disgracefully or scandalously wicked ⟨the most *flagitious* villain upon earth —Henry Fielding⟩ INFAMOUS is a general adjective for anything very bad, abhorrent, base, and deserving of evil fame ⟨this man is of a character so *infamous* that he will stick at no falsehood, or hesitate at no crime —W.M.Thackeray⟩ ⟨the *infamous* Luboff, who, as chief of the secret police at Odessa after the defeat of Denikin's army, put thousands of innocent people to death —Valentine Williams⟩ CORRUPT applies to what has lost integrity, honesty, and virtue and become degraded and depraved ⟨now known to have been a traitor to the United States, a pensioner of Spain, and an accomplice of Aaron Burr: *corrupt,* profligate, and insubordinate —Allan Nevins & H.S.Commager⟩ ⟨a disordered and competitive mob, bent only on turning each to his own personal advantage the now *corrupt* machinery of administration and law —G.L. Dickinson⟩ DEGENERATE may suggest retrogression and corruption into an especially vicious or enervated condition ⟨the *degenerate* practices of the court of the Caesars⟩ ⟨the *degenerate* physique as a whole is often marked by diminished stature and inferior vigor —H.G.Armstrong⟩

vicious circle *n* **1 :** a chain of circumstances constituting a situation in which the process of solving one difficulty creates a new problem involving increased difficulty in the original situation **2 :** an argument or definition that is valueless because it either overtly or covertly assumes as true or as understood something which is to be proved or defined **3 :** a chain of abnormal processes in which a primary disorder leads to a second which in turn aggravates the first one ⟨the *vicious circle* of fatigue-anxiety-fatigue⟩

vicious circle principle *n* **:** a principle in logic: whatever is defined in terms of all of a collection or of a totality cannot be a member thereof — compare RUSSELL'S PARADOX

vicious intromission *n* **:** an intromission made unjustifiably under Scots law by an heir with his ancestor's movable estate — compare EXECUTOR DE SON TORT, LEGAL INTROMISSION

vi·cious·ly *adv* [ME, fr. *vicious* + *-ly*] **:** in a vicious manner

vi·cious·ness *n* -ES [ME *viciousnesse,* fr. *vicious* + *-nesse* -ness] **:** the quality or state of being vicious

vi·cis·si·tude \vəˈsisə,tüd, -ə,tyüd *sometimes chiefly Brit* vīˈ-\ *n* -s [MF, fr. L *vicissitudo,* fr. *vicissim* in turn (fr. *vicis* change, alternation, stead) + *-tudo* -tude — more at WEEK] **1 a :** the quality or state of being changeable or in flux **:** MUTABILITY ⟨the ~ of human condition⟩ **b :** natural change or mutation **:** the rise and decline of phenomena **:** the successive alternations visible in nature or in human affairs ⟨the ~*s* of time and chance have left only 9 of the 30 trees —*Amer. Guide Series: Mich.*⟩ **2 a :** an accident of fortune **:** a shift of luck or vagary of chance **:** a fluctuation in condition (as of wealth, prosperity, or happiness) ⟨lovers not only faithful but patient in the face of remarkable ~*s* —Claudia Cassidy⟩ **b :** alternating change **:** SUCCESSION ⟨such alternations of energy and inertia, such sudden ~*s* of greatness and decay —Irving Babbitt⟩

syn see DIFFICULTY

vi·cis·si·tu·di·nous \=¦==¦tüdᵊnəs, -¦tyü-\ *adj* [L *vicissitudin-, vicissitudo* + E *-ous*] **:** marked by or filled with vicissitudes **:** undergoing alternations of fortune or condition

vick·ers hardness test \ˈvikə(r)z-\ *n, usu cap V* [prob. fr. *Vickers* Armstrong Ltd., Brit. steel-manufacturing concern] **:** an indentation hardness test for metals in which a 136-degree diamond pyramid is pressed into the surface of the metal being tested by a load of 5 to 120 kilograms

vi·co·ni·an \vēˈkōnēən\ *adj, usu cap* [fr. Giovanni *Vico* †1744 Ital. philosopher + connective *-n-* + E *-ian*] **:** of, relating to, or typical of the philosopher Vico or his cyclical theory of history

vi·con·ti·el \(ˈ)vī¦käntēəl\ *adj* [AF *viscontiel, vicontiel,* fr. MF *visconte* viscount + *-iel* -ial — more at VISCOUNT] **:** of or relating to a viscount or sheriff

vicontiel rents *n pl* **:** royal farm rents collected and paid by a viscount or sheriff

vi·con·ti·els \vīˈkäntēəlz\ *n pl* **:** money payable by a viscount or sheriff to the English crown; *esp* **:** VICONTIEL RENTS

vicontiel writs *n pl* **:** writs triable in the old county court before the sheriff

vics *pl of* VIC

vic·tim \ˈviktəm\ *n* -s [L *victima;* akin to OE *wīh, wēoh, wīg* idol, image, OHG *wīh, wihi* holy, ON *vē* temple, Goth *weihs* holy, Skt *vinakti* he separates, sets apart; basic meaning: to set apart, single out] **1 :** a living being sacrificed to some deity or in the performance of a religious rite **2 :** someone put to death, tortured, or mulcted by another **:** a person subjected to oppression, deprivation, or suffering ⟨a ~ of war⟩ ⟨a ~ of intolerance⟩ ⟨fell a ~ to prohibition era gangsters⟩ **3 :** someone who suffers death, loss, or injury in an undertaking of his own ⟨became a ~ of his own ambition⟩ **4 :** someone tricked, duped, or subjected to hardship **:** someone badly used or taken advantage of ⟨felt himself the ~ of his brother's shrewdness —W.F.Davis⟩ ⟨little boys, as well as adolescent girls, became the willing ~*s* of sailors and marines —R.M.Lovett⟩

syn PREY, QUARRY: VICTIM applies to anyone who suffers either as a result of ruthless design or incidentally or accidentally ⟨the *victim* sacrificed on these occasions is a hen, or several hens —J.G.Frazer⟩ ⟨was the girl born to be a *victim;* to be always disliked and crushed as if she were too fine for this world —Joseph Conrad⟩ ⟨lest such a policy precipitate a hot war of which western Europe would be the *victim* —Quincy Wright⟩ PREY may designate a victim clutched, seized, captured by or as if by an enemy, hunter, or wild beast ⟨others hold the battleship to be an obsolete arm, expensive beyond its worth, useful only for fighting other battleships and the easy *prey* of the submarine and the airplane —R.L.Buell⟩ ⟨an old castle from which the robber barons in the old days could see their *prey* coming and rush down upon the caravan to overpower it —W.A.White⟩ ⟨she still went recklessly on, her eyes confused by the rain, her brain a *prey* to wild and despairing thoughts —William Black⟩ QUARRY is applicable to the object of a chase, esp. by hounds, or to a person or thing relentlessly pursued or vigorously quested after ⟨with grain in their storerooms, and mountain sheep and deer for their *quarry,* they rose gradually from the condition of savagery —Willa Cather⟩ ⟨government agents tracking their *quarry* through the underworld of several cities⟩

vic·tim·hood \ˈviktəm,hu̇d\ *n* **:** the state or condition of being a victim

vic·tim·iza·tion \,viktəməˈzāshən, -tə,mīˈ-\ *n* -s **:** the act or process of victimizing or the state of being victimized

vic·tim·ize \ˈviktə,mīz\ *vt* -ED/-ING/-s *see -ize in Explan Notes* [*victim* + *-ize*] **1 a :** to make a victim of **:** SACRIFICE ⟨as a family they were flogged, defrauded, *victimized* —Ann Petry⟩ **b :** to slaughter as a sacrificial victim **2 :** to subject to deception or fraud **:** CHEAT, DUPE, TRICK ⟨fearing to be *victimized* we are inclined not to believe at all —N.M.Pusey⟩ ⟨relentlessly *victimized* by every piece of mischief known to the young —Paul Pickrel⟩ **3 :** to destroy (plants) entirely ⟨the red spores of the parasite . . . ~ winter wheat —*Current Biog.*⟩

vic·tim·iz·er \-zə(r)\ *n* -s **:** one that victimizes

¹**vic·tor** \ˈviktə(r)\ *n* -s [ME, fr. L, fr. *victus* (past part. of *vincere* to conquer) + *-or;* akin to OE & OHG *wīgan* to fight, ON *vīg* fight, Goth *weihan* to fight, OIr *fichid* he fights, OSlav *věků* strength, power; basic meaning: strength, manifestation of strength] **1 :** one that defeats an enemy **:** the winner in a battle, war, or fight **2 :** the winner in a conflict or struggle **:** a successful contender ⟨emerged ~ at the polls⟩ ⟨~ in a series of intramural contests⟩

²**victor** \"\ *adj* **:** VICTORIOUS, TRIUMPHANT

³**victor** \"\ *usu cap* — a communications code word for the letter *v*

victorfish \ˈ==,=\ *n* **:** OCEANIC BONITO

¹**vic·to·ria** \vikˈtōrēə, -tȯr-\ *n* -s [after *Victoria* †1901 queen of England] **1 a :** a low four-wheel pleasure carriage for two with a calash top and a raised seat in front for the driver **b :** an open passenger automobile with a calash top that usu. extends over the rear seat only **2** [NL, after Queen *Victoria*] **a** *cap* **:** a genus of immense So. American aquatic plants (family Nymphaeaceae) with large spreading leaves that are often over 5 feet in diameter and have a rim from 3 to 8 inches high, extremely large rose-white flowers opening for several successive evenings, and edible seeds **b** -s **:** any plant of this genus — see VICTORIA REGIA

victoria 1a

²**victoria** \(ˈ)=¦==\ *adj, usu cap* [fr. *Victoria,* Australia & *Victoria,* British Columbia] **1 :** of or from the state of Victoria, Australia **:** of the kind or style prevalent in the state of Victoria **2 :** of or from Victoria, the capital of British Columbia **:** of the kind or style prevalent in Victoria, B. C.

victoria blight *n, usu cap V* [fr. *Victoria,* a variety of oats, after Queen *Victoria*] **:** a fungous disease that is peculiar to oats which have Victoria variety in their parentage, is caused by a fungus (*Helminthosporium victoriae*), and is characterized by seed and root rot, seedling stunt, and orange or orange-brown streaking esp. of the leaf margins and blackening and breaking at the nodes

victoria blue *n* [after Queen *Victoria*] **1** *usu cap V & often cap B* **:** any of several basic dyes derived from diphenyl-naphthyl-methane that dye wool and silk royal blue and are used also as biological stains and organic pigments: as **a** *or* **victoria blue B :** a dye made from Michler's ketone and *N*-phenyl-alpha-naphthylamine — see DYE table I (under *Basic Blue 26, Pigment Blue 2, Solvent Blue 4*) **b** *or* **victoria blue R :** a dye made from Michler's ketone and *N*-ethyl-alpha-naphthylamine — see DYE table I (under *Basic Blue 11, Solvent Blue 6*) **c :** VICTORIA PURE BLUE B **2** *often cap V* **:** a strong blue that is redder and duller than Sèvres, cerulean blue (sense 1b), or cyanine blue (sense 1a)

victoria day *n, usu cap V&D* [after Queen *Victoria*] **1 :** formerly May 24 and now the Monday preceding May 25 observed in Canada as a legal holiday **2 :** EMPIRE DAY

victoria fast violet RR *n, usu cap both Vs & F* [after Queen *Victoria*] **:** an acid dye — see DYE table I (under *Acid Violet 1*)

victoria green *n, usu cap V & often cap G* [after Queen *Victoria*] **:** MALACHITE GREEN 2

victoria lake *n, often cap V* [fr. *Victoria Lake,* east-central Africa] **:** PUCE

victoria lily *n, usu cap V* [after Queen *Victoria*] **:** VICTORIA 2b

¹**vic·to·ri·an** \(ˈ)vik¦tōrēən, -tȯr-\ *adj, usu cap* [Queen *Victoria* + E *-an*] **1 :** of or relating to the reign of Queen Victoria of England **:** representative of the art, letters, or taste of Victoria's reign ⟨*Victorian* novels⟩ **2 :** typical of the moral standards or conduct of the age of Victoria esp. when stuffy or hypocritical ⟨the bohemian was always at war in him with the *Victorian* gentleman —G.S.Haight⟩

²**victorian** \"\ *n* -s *usu cap* **:** a person living during Queen Victoria's reign; *esp* **:** a representative author of that time

³**victorian** \"\ *adj, usu cap* [fr. *Victoria,* Australia & *Victoria* British Columbia + E *-an*] **1 :** of, relating to, or characteristic of the state of Victoria, Australia, or the city of Victoria, British Columbia **2 :** of, relating to, or characteristic of the people of Victoria, Australia, or Victoria, B. C.

⁴**victorian** \"\ *n* -s *cap* **:** a native or inhabitant of Victoria

victorian box *or* **victorian laurel** *n, usu cap V* [³*Victorian* (of Victoria, Australia)] **:** NATIVE LAUREL 1

victorian gothic *n, usu cap V&G* [¹*Victorian*] **:** an architectural style belonging to the later Gothic Revival of Victoria's reign and combining French, Italian, and English elements with a free use of parti-colored materials

victorian hazel *n, usu cap V* [³*Victorian* (of Victoria, Australia)] **:** a shrub of the genus *Pomaderris*

vic·to·ri·an·ism \vikˈtōrēə,nizəm, -tȯr-\ *n* -s *usu cap* [¹*Victorian* + *-ism*] **1 :** the quality or state of being Victorian esp. in taste, habits of thought, or conduct **2 :** a typical instance or product of Victorian expression, taste, or conduct ⟨a scrolly piece of ~ just big enough to hold his papers and his typewriter —Clemence Dane⟩

vic·to·ri·an·ize \-,nīz\ *vt* -ED/-ING/-s *often cap* [¹*Victorian* + *-ize*] **:** to make Victorian (as in style or taste)

victorian rosemary *n, usu cap V* [³*Victorian* (of Victoria, Australia)] **:** an Australian shrub (*Westringia rosmariniformis*) of the family Labiatae with silvery-white fragrant foliage and small axillary flowers

victoria pigeon *n, usu cap V* [fr. *Victoria,* Australia] **:** a crowned pigeon (*Goura victoria*)

victoria pure blue B *or* **victoria pure blue BO** *n, usu cap V&P&B* [after Queen *Victoria*] **:** a Victoria blue dye made from the ethyl analogue of Michler's ketone and *N*-ethyl-alpha-naphthylamine — see DYE table I (under *Basic Blue 7, Pigment Blue 1, Solvent Blue 5*)

victoria red *n, often cap V* [after Queen *Victoria*] **:** vermilion or a color resembling it

victoria re·gia \-ˈrējēə\ *n* [NL, lit., royal Victoria; after Queen *Victoria*] **:** ROYAL WATER LILY

victorias *pl of* VICTORIA

vic·to·ri·ate \vikˈtōrēət, -ˈtȯr-, -ēāt\ *n* -s [L *victoriatus,* fr. *victoria* victory + *-atus* -ate — more at VICTORY] **:** a silver coin of the ancient Roman republic orig. worth ¾ denarius, having on the reverse a figure of Victory crowning a trophy, and struck for use in foreign trade

victoria violet 4BS *n, usu cap both Vs* [after Queen *Victoria*] **:** an acid dye — see DYE table I (under *Acid Violet 3*)

¹**vic·to·rine** \¦viktə¦rēn\ *n* -s [prob. fr. Queen *Victoria* + E *-ine*] **:** a woman's fur tippet with long ends

²**victorine** \"\ *n, usu cap* [F *victorin,* fr. the Abbey of St. *Victor* near Paris, France + F *-in* -ine] **:** a canon regular of the Order of St. Victor founded in Paris in 1110, widespread during the medieval period, famous for its learning, and extinct since the French Revolution

vic·to·ri·ous \(ˈ)vik¦tōrēəs, -tȯr-\ *adj* [ME, fr. MF *victorieus,* fr. L *victoriosus,* fr. *victoria* victory + *-osus* -ous] **1 a :** having defeated an enemy or antagonist **:** having won a battle or contest **:** CONQUERING, TRIUMPHANT ⟨a ~ army⟩ ⟨a ~ fighter⟩ ⟨a ~ candidate⟩ **b :** of, relating to, or characteristic of victory **:** emblematic or suggestive of a winner or a success ⟨a ~ flag⟩ ⟨a ~ air⟩ **2 :** having displaced a rival **:** having won approval or acceptance instead of another ⟨an urban industrial society was ~ over historic agrarian forms⟩ **3 a :** evincing moral harmony or other attainment **:** consummating an endeavor **:** FULFILLED ⟨a robust, thoroughly healthy, and withal, very prosperous and ~ man —Thomas Carlyle⟩ **b :** achieving a perfection of form, grace, or vision (as in artistic performance)

vic·to·ri·ous·ly *adv* **:** in a victorious manner

vic·to·ri·ous·ness *n* -ES **:** the quality or state of being victorious

victors *pl of* VICTOR

vic·to·ry \ˈvikt(ə)rē, -ri\ *n* -ES [ME, fr. MF *victorie,* fr. L *victoria,* fr. fem. of (assumed) L *victorius* victorious, fr. L *victus* (past part. of *vincere* to conquer) + *-orius* -ory — more at VICTOR] **1 :** the overcoming of an enemy in battle or of an antagonist in a contest ⟨won ~ at last in a protracted war⟩ ⟨scored a knockout ~⟩ ⟨earned a significant political ~⟩ — opposed to *defeat* **2 a :** the gaining of superiority or success in any struggle or endeavor ⟨his new model represented a ~ of constructive imagination⟩ **b :** a moral or spiritual triumph of any kind ⟨yet his mental ~ over this cruel illness is complete as well as inspiring —Ellen Patterson⟩

syn CONQUEST, TRIUMPH: although VICTORY can be used to imply no more than the defeat of an opponent in a contest or struggle, in applying to certain kinds of struggle it often inevitably suggests a certain satisfaction or praise accruing to the victor ⟨a new concept of *victory* in war —R.J.Bunche⟩ ⟨*victory* without peace —Archibald MacLeish⟩ ⟨the *victory* over Everest was a fit coronation present for the Queen —W.O.Douglas⟩ CONQUEST implies a mastery over or subjugation of the opponent, whether a group of human beings or a difficult undertaking ⟨the Roman *conquest* of the Greeks⟩ ⟨the *conquest* of the Atlantic by air —*Irish Digest*⟩ ⟨the education of women was in large part a feminine *conquest* —H.M. Parshley⟩ TRIUMPH suggests great acclaim or personal satisfaction accruing to the victor as from a brilliant or decisive victory or an overwhelming conquest ⟨it is surely questionable whether we as noncombatant individuals should desire their *triumph,* a degree of success that clearly implies the full accomplishment of all their ends, good and bad —*Commonweal*⟩ ⟨the battle . . . marked the beginning of final Union *triumph* in the Chattanooga campaign —A.P.James⟩ ⟨achieved a diplomatic *triumph* in bringing about the adoption of treaties —G.E. Rines⟩ ⟨that she did as well as she did was a *triumph* of experience over inadequate means —Irving Kolodin⟩

victory garden *n, often cap V* **:** a wartime vegetable garden developed to increase food production esp. by home gardeners

victory girl *n, often cap V* **:** a wartime amateur camp follower or pickup girl — called also *V-girl*

vic·tress \ˈviktrəs\ *n* -ES [*victor* + *-ess*] **:** a female victor

vic·trix \-riks\ *n, pl* **victri·ces** \-rə,sēz\ [L, fem. of *victor*] **:** VICTRESS

Vic·tro·la \vikˈtrōlə\ *trademark* — used for a phonograph

¹**vict·ual** \ˈvid·ᵊl, -itᵊl\ *n* -s [alter. (influenced by LL *victualia*) of ME *vitaile, vitaille,* fr. MF, fr. LL *victualia,* pl., provisions, victuals, fr. neut. pl. of *victualis* of nourishment, fr. L *victus* nourishment, sustenance (fr. *victus,* past part. of *vivere* to live) + *-alis* -al — more at QUICK] **1 a :** food usable by man ⟨drinks and cakes and pastry, but . . . no substantial ~ —Nathaniel Hawthorne⟩ **b** *archaic* **:** vegetable produce **c** *Scot* **:** GRAIN **2 victuals** *pl* **:** supplies of food **:** PROVISIONS ⟨the navy's ships provided artillery support 10 miles deep, besides ~*s* and supplies for the advancing army —Walter Karig⟩ ⟨worker's wives switching to the less costly kinds of ~*s* —J.A. Lack⟩ ⟨tempting tales of appetizing ~*s* —Green Peyton⟩

²**victual** \"\ *vb* **victualed** *or* **victualled; victualed** *or* **victualled; victualing** *or* **victualling** \-d·ᵊliŋ, -t(ᵊ)l-\ **victuals** [ME *vitailen, vitaillen,* fr. MF *vitailler, vitailler,* fr. *vitaile, vitaille,* n.] *vt* **:** to supply with food ⟨this population was ~*ed* with goods brought by rail —H.W.H.King⟩ ~ *vi* **1 a :** EAT **b :** FEED, PASTURE — used of domestic animals **2 :** to lay in provisions ⟨the ship was ~*ing*⟩

vict·ual·age \-ᵊlij\ *n* -s **:** VICTUALS

victualing bill *n* **:** a list of bonded or drawback goods taken aboard for use as ship's stores that when signed by a customs officer becomes one of the master's clearance papers

vict·ual·ler *or* **vict·ual·er** \ˈvid·ᵊlə(r), -it(ᵊ)l-\ *n* -s [ME *vitailer, vitailler,* fr. MF *vitaillier, vitaillier,* fr. *vitaile, vitaille* + *-ier*] **1 :** the keeper of a restaurant or tavern **:** one who serves meals or liquors in a public house ⟨held a common ~*'s* license⟩ **2 :** one that provisions an army, a navy, or a ship with supplies of food **:** SUTLER **3 :** an army or navy provision ship

vicuña

vi·cu·ña *or* **vi·cu·na** *also* **vi·cu·gna** \vīˈk(y)ünə, vəˈ-, vəˈkünyə\ *n* -s [Sp *vicuña,* fr. Quechua *wikúña*] **1 :** a wild ruminant (*Lama vicugna*) of the Andes from Ecuador to Bolivia that is related to the domesticated llama and alpaca, is light brown, paler on the underparts and with light markings on legs and head, is smaller than the guanaco but like it lives in herds and is fleet-footed, and has been much hunted for its wool and fur **2 a :** the woollike fiber from the vicuña's fine lustrous undercoat **b** (1) **:** a fabric made of vicuña fiber (2) **:** woolen fabric made to imitate this

vid *abbr* **1** [L *vide*] see **2** video **3** [L *vidua*] widow

vida finch \ˈvīdə-\ *n* [*vida* modif. of NL *Vidua*] **:** WHYDAH

vi·dame \vēˈdam\ *n* -s [MF, fr. ML *vice-dominus*, fr. LL *vice-* + L *dominus* lord, master — more at DAME] **:** one of a class of French feudal temporal officers or advocates who orig. represented the abbeys or bishops but later erected their offices into fiefs — used as an hereditary title of nobility which was recognized to the end of the ancien régime

vid·dhal \vəˈdäl\ *n, pl* **viddhal** *or* **viddhals** *usu cap* **:** a member of a Turkoman people on the east shore of the Caspian sea

vid·dui \vəˈdüē\ *n* [Heb *widdūy*] *Jewish relig* **:** a confession of sin alphabetically arranged and recited as part of the Yom Kippur liturgy in the synagogue; *also* **:** a confession of sin recited privately by a person approaching death

¹vi·de \ˈvīdē, -di, ˈvēdā\ *v imper* [L, 2d pers. sing. imper. of *vidēre* to see] **:** SEE — used to direct a reader to another item

²vide \ˈvēd\ *adj* [F, fr. OF *vuit, voit* — more at VOID] **1 :** OPEN, EMPTY — used of strings on musical instruments **2 :** CUT, OMITTED — used as a direction on musical scores with *vi* indicating the beginning of a passage to be cut and *de* its close

vi·de·li·cet \vəˈdeləˌset, -ˌsət; vəˈdāləˌket, wēˈd-\ *adv* [L, fr. *vidēre* to see + *licet* it is permitted, 3d pers. sing. pres. indic. of *licēre* to be permitted — more at WIT, LICENSE] **:** that is to say **:** NAMELY — abbr. *viz.*

¹vid·eo \ˈvidēˌō\ *adj* **:** relating to or used in the transmission or reception of the television image ⟨~ channel⟩ ⟨~ frequency⟩ — compare AUDIO

²video \"\ *n* -s [L *vidēre* to see + E *-o* (as in *audio*)] **:** TELEVISION

vid·e·o·gen·ic \ˌvidēōˈjenik\ *adj* [*video* + *-genic*] **:** TELEGENIC

video recording *n* **1 :** a motion picture of a television production made by photographing the kinescope tube **2 :** VIDEO TAPE RECORDING

video signal *n* **:** PICTURE SIGNAL

video tape recording *n* **:** a recording of a television production made by recording sound and video signals on magnetic tape

vi·dette \və-\ *var of* VEDETTE

vid·i·an \ˈvidēən\ *adj, usu cap* [Vidus *Vidius* (Guido Guidi) †1569 Ital. anatomist + E *-an*] **:** of or relating to the anatomist Guidi

vidian artery *n, usu cap V* **:** a branch of the internal maxillary artery passing through the pterygoid canal of the sphenoid bone

vidian canal *n, usu cap V* **:** PTERYGOID CANAL

vidian nerve *n, usu cap V* **:** a nerve formed by the union of the greater superficial petrosal and the deep petrosal nerves and passing forward through the pterygoid canal in the sphenoid bone and joining the sphenopalatine ganglion

vid·i·con \ˈvidəˌkän\ *n* -s *often cap* [*video* + *iconoscope*] **:** a small camera tube containing an electron gun and a photoconductor on which an optical image is focused so that a beam of electrons from the gun is collected by the photoconductor and transformed into current whose rapid fluctuations representing the light and shade of the image are subsequently amplified and transmitted as television picture signals

vi·di·mus \ˈvīdəməs, ˈvid-\ *n* -ES [L, we have seen, 1st pers. pl. perf. indic. of *vidēre* to see] **:** an official or legal inspection (as of a document); *also* **:** an attested copy of a document

vid·ua \ˈvijəwə\ *n, cap* [NL, fr. L, widow] **:** a genus of African weaverbirds comprising various typical whydahs

vidual *adj* [LL *vidualis*, fr. L *vidua* widow + *-alis* -al] *obs* **:** of or relating to widowhood or widows

vi·du·i·ty \vəˈd(y)üəd·ē\ *n* -ES [ME (Sc) *viduite*, fr. MF *viduité*, fr. L *viduitat-, viduitas*, fr. *vidua* widow + *-itat-, -itas* -ity] **:** WIDOWHOOD

¹vie *n* -s [modif. of MF *envi*, fr. OF, invitation, challenge, wager, fr. *envier* to invite, challenge, wager a sum at cards] *obs* **:** CHALLENGE, WAGER

²vie \ˈvī\ *vb* **vied; vied; vying; vies** [modif. of MF *envier*, fr. OF, to invite, challenge, wager a sum at cards, fr. L *invitare* to invite, challenge — more at INVITE] *vi* **:** to strive for superiority **:** CONTEND ⟨politicians *vying* with each other⟩ ⟨nations *vying* for international trade⟩ ~ *vt* **:** to hazard, stake, or wager ⟨~ money on the turn of a card⟩; *also* **:** to exchange in rivalry **:** MATCH ⟨~ accusation against accusation⟩

vie·ji·tos \vyāˈhēˌtōs\ *n pl but sing in constr* [MexSp, fr. Sp, little old men, pl. of *viejito* old man, dim. of *viejo* old man, fr. *viejo*, adj., old, fr. L *vetulus*, fr. *vetus* old — more at WETHER] **:** a comic dance of the Tarascan Indians performed by young men dressed and masked as old men

vielle \ˈvyel\ *n* -s [F — more at VIOL] **1 :** a large medieval viol of the 12th and 13th centuries **2 :** HURDY-GURDY 1

vi·en·na \vēˈenə\ *adj, usu cap* [fr. *Vienna*, Austria] **:** of or from Vienna, the capital of Austria **:** of the kind or style prevalent in Vienna

vienna brown *n, often cap V* **:** GOLD BRONZE 2

vienna coup *n, usu cap V* **:** a squeeze in bridge or whist that is introduced by the cashing of a winning card that establishes an opponent's card

vienna green *n, often cap V* **:** EMERALD 2a

vienna lake *n, often cap V* **:** CARMINE 2

vienna lime *n, usu cap V* **:** a high-magnesia lime specially prepared from calcined dolomite for use as a buffing and polishing material esp. for metals, plastics, and glass

vienna red *n, often cap V* **:** vermilion or a color resembling it

vienna sausage *n, usu cap V* **:** a short slender frankfurter in a thin casing usu. having the ends cut off

vienna smoke *n, often cap V* **:** SMOKE BROWN

vienna system *n, usu cap V* **:** a method of bidding in contract bridge that is a modification of the club convention

¹vi·en·nese \ˌvēəˈnēz, -ēs\ *adj, usu cap* [*Vienna*, Austria + E *-ese*] **1 :** of or belonging to Vienna, Austria **2 :** characteristic of Vienna or the Viennese

²viennese \"\ *n, pl* **viennese** *cap* **1 :** a native or resident of Vienna, Austria **2 :** the dialect of German spoken in Vienna

vien·tiane \(ˈ)vyenˈtyän\ *adj, usu cap* [fr. *Vientiane*, Laos] **:** of or from Vientiane, the capital of Laos **:** of the kind or style prevalent in Vientiane

vi·er \ˈvī(ə)r\ *n* -s [²*vie* + *-er*] **:** one that vies (as for supremacy)

vie·ren·deel truss \ˈvirənˌdāl-\ *or* **vierendeel girder** *n, usu cap V* [after M. *Vierendeel*, Belgian engineer who invented it in 1896] **:** an open-web truss with vertical members but without diagonals and with rigid joints

viet \vēˈet, ˈvyet\ *n* -s *usu cap* [short for *Vietminh*] **:** a member of the Vietminh

vi et armis \ˈvīēˈtärməs\ *adv* [L] **:** with force and arms — used of a trespass to person or property which is the immediate cause of damage; compare MANU FORTI

viet·cong \vēˈetˌkäŋ, ˈvyet-, -kȯŋ; *also* \vēət- *or* ˈvēt-\ *n, pl* **vietcong** *usu cap* **:** an adherent of the Vietnamese communist movement supported by North Vietnam and engaged esp. in guerrilla warfare in South Vietnam

viet·minh \vēˈetˌmin, ˈvyet-, *also* \vēət- *or* -mēn *or* ˈvētˌmin\ *n, pl* **vietminh** *or* **vietminhs** *usu cap* **:** an adherent of the Vietnamese communist movement

viet·nam \-ˈnäm, -nam, -nȧm\ *adj, usu cap* [fr. *Vietnam*, country in Indochina] **:** of or from Vietnam **:** of the kind or style prevalent in Vietnam **:** VIETNAMESE

¹viet·nam·ese \vēˌetnəˈmēz, ˌvyet-, -t(ˌ)naˈm-, -t(ˌ)näˈm-, -mēs *also* \vēət- *or* ˈvēt-\ *adj, usu cap* [*Vietnam* + E *-ese*] **1 a :** of, relating to, or characteristic of Vietnam **b :** of, relating to, or characteristic of the people of Vietnam **2 :** of, relating to, or characteristic of the Vietnamese language

²vietnamese \"\ *n, pl* **vietnamese** *cap* **1 :** a native or inhabitant of Vietnam **2 :** the language of the largest group in Vietnam and the official language of the country — compare MUONG

¹view \ˈvyü\ *n* -s [ME *vewe*, fr. MF *veue, vue*, fr. OF, fr. fem. of *veu, vu*, past part. of *veeir, veoir, voir* to see, fr. L *vidēre* — more at WIT] **1 :** the act of seeing or beholding; *specif* **:** an inspection by the jury of a court of law of a place where a litigated transaction (as a crime or tort) occurred or of premises or some other object (as a corpse) involved in a legal proceeding **2 :** a formal examination **:** INSPECTION ⟨a close ~ of all details⟩ **:** SURVEY ⟨a ~ of German literature⟩ **3 :** mode or manner of looking at or regarding something **:** CONCEPTION, GRASP ⟨an imperfect ~ of parliamentary government⟩ **4 :** an overall survey **:** complete summary ⟨a columnist's ~ of the world crisis⟩ **5 :** what is revealed to the vision or can usu. be seen ⟨the ~ from a picture window⟩; *also* **:** an extensive or imposing prospect **:** PANORAMA ⟨Alpine ~s⟩ **6 :** extent or range of vision **:** SIGHT ⟨no ships in ~⟩ **7 a :** something that is looked toward or kept in sight **:** OBJECT, AIM ⟨with no ~ in mind⟩ ⟨diplomatic maneuvers with a ~ to establishing a clear case⟩ **b :** something that is expected **:** PROSPECT ⟨no hope in ~⟩ **8 a :** a pictorial representation **:** SKETCH ⟨a photographic ~⟩ ⟨a ~ of the local town hall⟩; *also* **:** DIAGRAM **b :** the graphic projection of an object upon a plane obtained by finding the intersections with the plane of parallel lines drawn through the points of the object **9** *dial* **:** APPEARANCE, ASPECT ⟨if you're an ugly man to be looking at, I'm thinking your tongue's worse than your ~ —J.M.Synge⟩ **10 :** intellectual makeup **:** spiritual and cultural nature ⟨literary themes which reveal the ~ of their author⟩ **syn** see OPINION — **at the view** *adv* **:** by sight — usu. used in the phrase *hunt at the view* — **in view of** *prep* **:** in regard to **:** in consideration of ⟨a failure *in view of* financial returns⟩ — **on view :** on exhibition **:** open to public inspection ⟨model homes *on view*⟩

²view \"\ *vt* -ED/-ING/-S **1 a :** to examine carefully or officially **:** INSPECT ⟨~ evidence⟩ ⟨~ records⟩ **b** *archaic* **:** EXPLORE **2 :** to look at attentively **:** SCRUTINIZE, OBSERVE ⟨~ a landscape⟩ **3 :** to consider esp. with earnest attention or with an attempt at wide or overall comprehension ⟨~ a problem⟩ **:** take under consideration ⟨~ applications for membership⟩ **syn** see SEE

view·able \-üəbəl\ *adj* **1 :** capable of being seen or inspected ⟨~ evidence⟩ **2 :** likely to be or possessing enough appeal to be viewed ⟨a ~ television show⟩

view angle *n* **:** the angle included by a photographic lens as determined from the ratio of the focal length to the diameter of the field **:** ANGLE OF VIEW

view camera *n* **:** a camera having a rising, tilting, and swinging front, a removable lens board, a long bellows, a focusing cloth, a ground-glass focusing screen, a tilting and swinging back, a plate or film holder, and a rack-and-pinion adjustment

view·er \ˈvyüə(r), -yü(ə)r, -yüə\ *n* -s [ME *vewer*, fr. *vewe* view + *-er* — more at VIEW] **:** one that views: as **a :** a person legally appointed to inspect and report on property (as highways) **b :** an optical device of any of several forms used to assist in viewing (as photographic transparencies) **c :** a person who watches television

viewfinder \ˈ=ˌ==\ *n* **:** FINDER 5

view halloo *also* **view hallo** *or* **view halloa** *n* **:** a shout uttered by a hunter on seeing a fox break cover; *also* **:** a shout indicating or announcing the appearance of something

viewing *n* -s [fr. gerund of ²*view*] **1 :** an act of seeing or taking a look (as at scenery or an exhibition) ⟨the ~ of the new models⟩; *specif* **:** a period when visitors may view a body in a funeral parlor **2 :** the watching of television

viewing glass *n* **:** a colored filter used in viewing the scene to be photographed in order to anticipate how the scene will be reproduced

view·less \ˈvyüləs\ *adj* **1 :** affording no view **2 :** expressing no views or opinions **3 :** not perceivable **:** INVISIBLE

view·less·ly *adv* [*viewless* + *-ly*] **:** INVISIBLY

view of frankpledge [ME, trans. of AF *vewe de fraunq plege*] **:** the gathering and inspection in the court leet at least once a year of all the men who were or ought to be in frankpledge

viewpoint \ˈ=ˌ=\ *n* **1 :** an attitude of mind from which something is considered ⟨incapable of comprehending another person's ~ —Ruth Park⟩ **2 :** a position from which something is observed ⟨describes his own method of photographing motor races, and gives hints on the choice of subjects and ~s —*Eastman Kodak Monthly Abstract Bull.*⟩

views *pl of* VIEW, *pres 3d sing of* VIEW

view window *n* **:** PICTURE WINDOW

viewy \ˈvyüē, -üi\ *adj* -ER/-EST **1 :** possessing visionary, impractical, or fantastic views **2 :** spectacular or arresting in appearance **:** SHOWY ⟨a ~ little socialite⟩

vi·ga \ˈvēgə\ *n* -s [Sp, beam, rafter] **:** one of the heavy rafters that is often a log and that supports the roof in the native Indian and Spanish colonial architecture of the Southwest

vi·ge·nère cipher \ˌvēzhəˈne(ə)r-\ *n, usu cap V* [after Blaise de *Vigenère* †1596 Fr. diplomat and student of cryptography] **:** polyalphabetic substitution with alphabets derived from one pair of primary alphabets by sliding (as in the Vigenère tableau) for which the usual keying formula is P+K=C where P is the position of the plaintext letter in the plain component, C that of the ciphertext letter in the cipher sequence, and K that of the key letter in the normal alphabet and where positions are numbered from 0 to 25 and 26 is subtracted from sums above 25 — compare BEAUFORT CIPHER, PROGRESSIVE-ALPHABET CIPHER

vigenère tableau *also* **vigenère table** *or* **vigenère square** *n, usu cap V* [after B. de *Vigenère*] **:** a square cipher table formed by placing the same normal or mixed primary alphabet one step farther to the left on each successive line and used by reading the ciphertext letter within the table in the row and column defined by key and plaintext letters in alphabets in the left and top margins respectively

¹vi·gen·ten·ni·al \ˌvījenˈtenēəl\ *adj* [L *vigeni, viceni* twenty each + E *-tennial* (as in *centennial*) — more at VICENARY] **:** occurring once every 20 years **:** relating to a 20th anniversary

²vigentennial \"\ *n* -s **:** a 20th anniversary or its celebration

vi·ges·i·mal \(ˈ)vīˈjesəməl\ *adj* [L *vigesimus, vicesimus* twentieth + E *-al*; akin to L *viginti* twenty — more at VICENARY] **:** based on the number 20

vi·ges·i·mo-quarto \(ˈ)vīˈjesə(ˌ)mō+\ *or* **vi·ces·i·mo-quarto** \-ˈīse-+\ *n* [L, abl. of *vigesimus-quartus, vicesimus-quartus* twenty-fourth, fr. *vigesimus, vicesimus* twentieth + *quartus* fourth — more at QUART] **:** TWENTY-FOURMO — see BOOK tables

vi·gia \vəˈjēə, vēˈhēə\ *n* -s [Sp *vigía* watch, vigil, rock, reef, fr. Pg *vigia*, fr. *vigiar* to watch, keep vigil, fr. L *vigilare* — more at VIGILANT] **:** a mark made on a nautical chart indicating a dangerous rock or shoal and used chiefly on Spanish charts

vig·il \ˈvijəl\ *n* -s [ME *vigile*, fr. OF, fr. LL & L; LL *vigilia* watch on the eve of a religious festival, fr. L, wakefulness, watch, fr. *vigil* awake, alert; akin to L *vigēre* to be vigorous, flourish, *vegēre* to rouse, excite, be active — more at WAKE] **1 a :** a watch formerly kept on the night before a religious feast and customarily spent in prayer or other devotions **b :** the day before a religious feast observed as a day of spiritual preparation **c :** a religious service on the morning of the day before a holy day **2 a :** evening or nocturnal devotions or prayers — usu. used in pl. **b :** devotional watching ⟨nobles standing ~ by the coffin of their dead monarch⟩ **3 a :** the act or action of keeping awake esp. at times when sleep is customary; *also* **:** a period of wakefulness ⟨an all-night ~ spent awaiting the arrival of a celebrity⟩ **b :** unrelenting, hostile, or oppressive observation ⟨guards keeping ~ over a noisy mob⟩; *also* **:** a steady gaze or stare **4 a :** an act or action of wakeful watching **:** WATCH ⟨keep ~ all night beside a sickbed⟩; *also* **:** the period spent in wakeful watching **b :** a protracted and usu. lonely stay or sojourn ⟨a five-month ~ near the polar ice pack⟩

vig·i·lance \ˈvijələn(t)s\ *n* -s [MF, fr. L *vigilantia* wakefulness, vigilance, fr. *vigilant-, vigilans* + *-ia* -y] **1 :** the quality or state of being vigilant **:** watchfulness in respect of danger or hazard ⟨constant ~ against the spread of disease⟩ **2 :** readiness or alertness esp. to respond to stimuli ⟨the ~ of a person's nerves⟩

vigilance committee *n* **:** a volunteer committee of citizens for the oversight and protection of an interest; *esp* **:** a committee organized to suppress and punish crime summarily (as when the processes of law appear inadequate) — compare VIGILANTE

vig·i·lant \-nt\ *adj* [ME, fr. MF, fr. L *vigilant-, vigilans*, fr. pres. part. of *vigilare* to be awake, watch, keep vigil, fr. *vigil* awake, alert — more at VIGIL] **:** alertly or watchfully awake; *esp* **:** alert or watchful to discover and avoid danger ⟨a ~ mountain climber⟩ ⟨a ~ treasurer⟩ **syn** see WATCHFUL

vig·i·lan·te \ˌvijəˈlantē, -län-, -tī\ *n* -s *often attrib* [Sp, watchman, guard, fr. *vigilante*, adj., watchful, vigilant, fr. L *vigilant-, vigilans*] **:** a member of a vigilance committee ⟨~ work⟩ ⟨a ~ system⟩

vig·i·lan·tism \-nˌtizəm\ *n* -s [*vigilante* + *-ism*] **:** the policy or practice of vigilantes

vig·i·lant·ly *adv* **:** in a vigilant manner **:** ALERTLY, WATCHFULLY

vig·i·lant·ness *n* -ES **:** the quality or state of being vigilant

vigil light *n* **1 :** a candle lighted by a worshiper in a Roman Catholic church for a specific religious purpose (as the veneration of a saint) **2 :** a candle or small lamp burning before a shrine, memorial, statue, or image

vi·gin·ten·ni·al \ˌvījinˈtenēəl\ *adj or n* [L *viginti* twenty + E *-ennial* (as in *centennial*) — more at VICENARY] **:** VIGENTENNIAL

vi·gin·til·lion \ˌ=ˈtilyən\ *n* -s *often attrib* [L *viginti* twenty + E *-illion* (as in *million*)] — see NUMBER table

vig·na \ˈvignə\ *n, cap* [NL, after Domenico *Vigna* †1647 Ital. botanist] **:** a genus of vines or erect herbs (family Leguminosae) found in warm or tropical regions and having trifoliolate leaves, yellowish or purplish flowers with an eared vexillum, and a linear and 2-valved pod — see COWPEA

vi·gne·ron \ˌvēnyəˈrōn\ *n* -s [ME *vigneroun*, fr. MF *vigneron*, fr. OF *vineron*, fr. *vine, vigne* vine, vineyard — more at VINE] **:** WINEGROWER, VITICULTURIST

¹vi·gnette \(ˈ)vinˈyet, (ˈ)vēn-, *usu* -ed·+V\ *n* -s [F, fr. MF *vignete* young vine, vignette, dim. of *vigne* vine — more at VINE] **1 :** a running ornament (as of vine leaves, tendrils, and grapes) put on or just before the title page or at the beginning or end of a chapter of a manuscript or book; *also* **:** a small decorative design or picture so placed **2 a :** a picture (as an engraving or photograph) that shades off gradually into the surrounding ground or the unprinted paper; *also* **:** the rough or serrated edged mask used to print the picture **b :** a picture on a postage stamp **:** the pictorial part of a stamp design as distinguished from the frame and lettering **3 :** a short literary sketch chiefly descriptive and characterized usu. by delicacy, wit, and subtlety

²vignette \"\ *vt* -ED/-ING/-S **1 :** to apply a vignette to ⟨*vignetted* plates⟩ **2 :** to finish (as a photograph) in the manner of a vignette **3 :** to describe or sketch delicately or subtly

vi·gnet·ter \-ed·ə(r)\ *n* -s **1 :** one who makes vignettes **:** VIGNETTIST **2 :** a photographic device for vignetting (as a screen with an aperture the edges of which insensibly become opaque)

vignetting *n* -s **1 :** a reduction in intensity of illumination at the edges of a field of view of an optical instrument due to the restrictive action of the edge of the aperture for rays that are not axial **2 :** the progressive reduction in the illumination falling on a photographic film towards the corners of the picture due to the obstruction of oblique light beams by the lens mount

vi·gnet·tist \-ed·əst\ *n* -s **:** an artist, designer, or author who produces vignettes

vi·gnoles rail \(ˈ)vinˈyōlz-\ *n, usu cap V* [after Charles B. *Vignoles* †1875 Eng. engineer] **:** T RAIL

vi·gogne yarn \vēˈgōnʸ-, -ōn-\ *n* [*vigogne* fr. F, vicuña, fabric made from vicuña wool, fr. Sp *vicuña* — more at VICUÑA] **:** a yarn spun from a blend of cotton and wool and used chiefly for clothing fabrics

vig·or \ˈvigə(r)\ *n* -s *see -or in Explan Notes* [ME *vigour*, fr. MF *vigeur*, fr. L *vigor*, fr. *vigēre* to be vigorous, flourish + *-or* — more at VIGIL] **1 :** active strength or force of body or mind **:** capacity for physical, intellectual, or moral exertion **:** effective energy or power ⟨the ~ of youth⟩ ⟨the ~ of a storm⟩ **2 :** strength or force in animal or vegetable nature or action ⟨a plant grows with ~⟩ **3 :** intensity of action or effect **:** FORCE, ENERGY ⟨the ~ of an argument⟩ ⟨commanding a troop with ~⟩ ⟨a drug that acts with ~⟩ **4 :** effective legal status **:** VALIDITY ⟨laws that are still in ~⟩

syn VIGOR, VIM, SPIRIT, DASH, ESPRIT, VERVE, PUNCH, ÉLAN, and DRIVE denote, in common, a quality of force, forcefulness, or energy. VIGOR implies active good health and native robustness or a display of energy or forcefulness deriving from it or befitting it ⟨the physical and intellectual *vigor* and toughness which the trial lawyer needs —Robert Hale⟩ ⟨the *vigor* and inventiveness that American business has shown in many other fields —*Defense Against Recession*⟩ ⟨burst into leaf with exceptional *vigor* —*Amer. Guide Series: Md.*⟩ ⟨a wonderfully witty book, with an intellectual *vigor* —Paul Pickrel⟩ VIM stresses the display of usu. enthusiastic energy in doing or making something ⟨enter into an enterprise with a good deal of *vim*⟩ ⟨the *vim* and energy with which he spoke was exhausting to the audience⟩ SPIRIT stresses a driving vivacity, liveliness, or animated interest usu. deriving from disposition or temperament ⟨enter into a campaign with *spirit*⟩ ⟨on the eve of a match the players worked up *spirit* by celebrations —*Amer. Guide Series: Fla.*⟩ DASH implies a bold, devil-may-care force, often tending to stress the impact upon the observer, reader, or listener ⟨the picture really captures the obsessive *dash* of professional airmen —*Time*⟩ ⟨their lineaments and general contours to be drawn with Düreresque vigor and *dash* —Thomas Hardy⟩ ⟨his study . . . aspiring to make up in liveliness, *dash*, and clarity what it is bound to lack in analytical rigor —Clifton Fadiman⟩ ⟨lack of oratorical *dash* —N.F.Busch⟩ ESPRIT is a quality of interest or energy of mind or disposition more subtly manifest than spirit and often strongly implying active cleverness or wit ⟨there are men of *esprit* who are excessively exhausting to some people —O.W.Holmes †1894⟩ ⟨acquire the industrial *esprit* that could spark general economic advance —David Riesman⟩ VERVE suggests strongly a characteristic or peculiar active energy or interest ⟨writing with the *verve* and gusto dear to the mid-nineteenth century —Mary Ross⟩ ⟨both sing with shattering *verve* —Herbert Weinstock⟩ ⟨the dancers performed with *verve* —Douglas Watt⟩ ⟨tells his story . . . with unquenchable *verve* and enthusiasm —*Times Lit. Supp.*⟩ ⟨recited King Henry V's speech before the battle of Agincourt with such *verve* that she brought the house down —Bruce Marshall⟩ PUNCH stresses forcefulness of impact or immediate effectiveness ⟨a speech with very little *punch*⟩ ⟨the poem which I have chosen seems to me . . . to be crisp in its language and also to carry a considerable *punch* —Louis MacNeice⟩ ⟨coconut sap is poured to make toddy — which looks like milk but has a *punch* —*N. Y. Times Mag.*⟩ ÉLAN stresses a spirit or quality marked by ardor or spiritedness in action ⟨marching in perfect formation and with military *élan* —Philip Hamburger⟩ ⟨clears his hurdles with agility and *élan* —*Times Lit. Supp.*⟩ ⟨a real victory would give them a great *élan* for the sterner tests yet to come —D.D.Eisenhower⟩ DRIVE stresses an unremitting purposive action or forcefulness resulting from a large reservoir of energy ⟨lack the *drive*, the initiative, and the sense of aggression necessary to carry out a planned crime of violence —D.W.Maurer & V.H.Vogel⟩ ⟨this titan's spirit which gave such *drive* and strength to the mightiest of his plays —John Mason Brown⟩ ⟨enough *drive* to achieve success in almost any field⟩

vig·or·ish \ˈvigərish\ *n* -ES [prob. fr. Yiddish, fr. Russ *vyigrysh* winnings, profit] **1 :** a charge taken (as by a bookie or gambling house) on bets; *also* **:** the degree of such a charge ⟨a ~ of 5 percent⟩ **2 :** interest paid to a moneylender

vig·or·less \ˈvigə(r)ləs\ *adj* **:** lacking vigor **:** LISTLESS, WEAK

vi·go·ro·so \ˌvēgəˈrō(ˌ)sō\ *adj (or adv)* [It, vigorous, fr. OIt, fr. MF *vigoros*] **:** energetic in style — used as a direction in music

vig·or·ous \ˈvig(ə)rəs\ *adj* [ME, fr. MF, fr. OF, fr. *vigour, vigeur* vigor + *-ous*] **1 :** possessing vigor **:** full of physical or mental strength or active force **:** STRONG ⟨a ~ youth⟩ ⟨a ~ plant⟩ **2 :** exhibiting strength either of body or mind **:** POWERFUL, STRONG ⟨~ exertions⟩ ⟨a ~ prosecution of a war⟩ ⟨a ~ protest⟩ **3 :** done with vigor **:** carried out forcefully and energetically **:** enforced strictly ⟨took ~ measures to stop the practice⟩ ⟨~ enforcement of the country's laws⟩

syn ENERGETIC, STRENUOUS, LUSTY, NERVOUS: VIGOROUS suggests active strength, force, reserve vitality, and undiminished or pulsing robustness of body or freshness and ability of mind ⟨the *vigorous* mother of a large family⟩ ⟨his *vigorous* industry that produced so many full-bodied books before his death at forty-four —H.T.Moore⟩ ⟨a *vigorous* critic of materialism, complacency, and hazy thinking —*Current Biog.*⟩ ENERGETIC may apply to display of or capacity for great activity, sometimes bustling or ambitious ⟨displayed a highly cultivated and *energetic* mind, full of impassioned schemes of liberty, and impatience of masculine usurpation —T.L. Peacock⟩ ⟨restless, *energetic*, impetuous, temperamental, and at times a little irascible —A.W.Long⟩ STRENUOUS suggests the constantly energetic; used of persons and their inclinations, it may indicate a pleasure in or preference for coping with the arduous or vigorous ⟨if you want an incentive to act, if you want to live the *strenuous* life —Alfred Buchanan⟩ ⟨attribute the winning of the West principally to the *strenuous* virtues of Teutonic males —Howard M. Jones⟩ ⟨a *strenuous* and sometimes violently abusive opponent of every political movement that threatens to curtail her leisure —G.B.Shaw⟩ LUSTY suggests a healthy vitality and exuberant energy, with a robust and unrestrained inclination for enjoyment ⟨the native men and half a dozen *lusty* girls shouting and laughing as they put their backs into the work —C.B.Nordhoff & J.N.Hall⟩ ⟨the *lusty* American spirit of active, vigorous living —Bud Wilson⟩ NERVOUS may suggest continuing activity, often forceful, arising from an energetic temperament ⟨his rhythm has a pulsating and *nervous* vitality —Robert Collet⟩ ⟨the suppleness of youthful fingers, the *nervous* alertness of youthful brains, and the stamina of youthful bodies —*Amer. Guide Series: Mich.*⟩ ⟨the *nervous* new civilization of the Texas cities —T.H.White b. 1915⟩

vig·or·ous·ly *adv* [ME, fr. *vigorous* + *-ly*] **:** in a vigorous manner **:** FORCEFULLY

vig·or·ous·ness *n* -ES [ME *vigorousnesse*, fr. *vigorous* + *-nesse* -ness] **:** the quality or state of being vigorous **:** FORCEFULNESS

vigour *chiefly Brit var of* VIGOR

vi·gou·reux \ˌvēgəˈrə̄\ *n, pl* **vigoureux** \"\ *often attrib* [*vigoureux (printing)*] **:** a yarn or fabric colored by vigoureux printing

vigoureux printing *n* [after *Vigoureux*, 19th cent. Fr. textile printer who invented it] **:** a method of printing woolen sliver before spinning to produce a mixed usu. black and white color effect in yarn and fabric

vi·greux column \vēˈgrə̄-\ *n, usu cap V* [prob. after Léon *Vigreux* †1891 Fr. hydraulic engineer] **:** a long unpacked glass tube for use in laboratory fractional distillation that is characterized by many deep pointed indentations in its sidewall and has an opening at the top for a thermometer and a side arm near the top for attachment to a condenser

vi·ha·ra \vəˈhärə\ *n* -S [Skt *vihāra*, lit., place of recreation, fr. *viharati* he spends time, he walks about for pleasure, fr. *vi* apart, asunder + *harati* he takes, carries — more at WITH, YARD] **:** a Buddhist monastery or temple

vi·hue·la \vēˈwālə\ *n* -S [Sp] **1 :** the early Spanish viol **2 :** the Spanish lute

vi·jao \vēˈhä(ˌ)ō\ *n* -S [Sp *vijao, bijao, vihao, bihao*, fr. Taino *bihao*] **:** a tropical herb (*Amomum exaltatum*) whose seeds are used in Puerto Rico as a source of black coloring matter

vij·na·na·va·da \ˌvijˌnänəˈvädə\ *n* -S *usu cap* [Skt *vijñānavāda*, fr. *vijñāna* discrimination, intelligence (fr. *vijānāti* he distinguishes, understands, fr. *vi* apart + *jānāti* he knows) + *vāda* speech, discourse, doctrine, fr. *vadati* he speaks, says — more at WITH, KNOW, ODE] **:** the subjective idealism taught by the Yogacara school of Buddhist philosophy

vi·king \ˈvīkiŋ, -kēŋ\ *n* -S [ON *víkingr*, prob. fr. *vík* small inlet, creek, bay + *-ingr* -ing — more at WICK (creek)] **1 a** *usu cap* **:** one belonging to the pirate crews from among the Northmen plundering the coasts of Europe in the 8th to 10th centuries **b :** SEA ROVER **2** *usu cap* **:** SCANDINAVIAN

vil *abbr* village

vi·la \ˈvēlə\ *n, pl* **vilas** \-əz\ *or* **vi·ly** \-lē\ [Slovenian & Serbo-Croatian; akin to ORuss & Bulg *vila* and perh. to Lith *vyti* to chase, pursue, Skt *veti* he goes, advances — more at VIM] **:** a supernatural being of Slavonic lands sometimes held to inhabit hills and woods and appear in the form of a beautiful young woman **:** FAIRY

vi·la·yet \vēˈläˌyet, ˌvēləˈyet\ *n* -S [Turk *vilâyet*, fr. Ar *wilāyat*, fr. *walīy* governor] **:** one of the chief administrative divisions of Turkey having as head a vali who represents the government and is assisted by an elective council and being subdivided into cazas

vild \ˈvīld\ *adj* [by alter.] *archaic* **:** VILE

¹vile \ˈvīl, *esp before pause or consonant* -īəl\ *adj* -ER/-EST [ME *vil, vile*, fr. OF *vil*, fr. L *vilis* cheap, base, vile; perh. akin to L *venus, venum* sale — more at VENAL] **1 :** of small worth or account ⟨the sea, wherein he counts not one inch of ~ dominion —Robert Browning⟩ **:** of inferior quality or state **:** COMMON ⟨Savior . . . shall change our ~ body, that it may be fashioned like unto his glorious body —Phil 3:21 (AV)⟩ **:** MEAN ⟨wrapped in a ~ disguise —P.B.Shelley⟩ **2 a :** morally despicable or abhorrent ⟨instills ~ suspicions into her confiding soul —Karl Polanyi⟩ ⟨the *vilest* specimens of human nature are to be found among demagogues —T.B.Macaulay⟩ **b :** physically repulsive (as from filth or corruption) **:** FOUL ⟨the plagues that came from the ~ unsanitary quarters of the industrial city —Lewis Mumford⟩ **3 :** tending to degrade a person **:** HUMILIATING, IGNOMINIOUS ⟨a slave, in the *vilest* of all positions —F. W.Farrar⟩ **4 a :** disgustingly bad or inferior **:** highly objectionable ⟨in a ~ temper⟩ **:** CONTEMPTIBLE ⟨the ~ habit of thinking that the latest is always the best —M.R.Cohen⟩ ⟨a ~ climate⟩ ⟨~ handwriting⟩ ⟨writes ~ verse⟩ **b :** GREAT, EXTREME — used intensively with nouns denoting a bad quality or state ⟨protecting her against the *vilest* evil Europe has yet produced —Beverley Nichols⟩ **syn** see BASE

²vile \"\ *adv* [ME *vil, vile*, fr. *vil, vile*, adj.] **:** VILELY — used chiefly in combination ⟨*vile*-born⟩

vi·le·la \vēˈlālə\ *n, pl* **vilela** *or* **vilelas** *usu cap* [Sp, of Amer-Ind origin] **1 :** a group of peoples of northwestern Argentina **2 :** a member of a Vilela people

vile·ly \ˈvī(ə)llē, -il\ *adv* [ME *vily*, fr. *vil, vile* + *-ly*] **:** in a vile manner ⟨the suit was ~ botched and skimped —Thomas Wolfe⟩

vile·ness *n* -ES **1 :** the quality or state of being vile **2 :** an instance of vileness **3 :** something vile ⟨addressed a final ~ at the cabdriver —D.C.Loughlin⟩

vil·i·fi·ca·tion \ˌviləfəˈkāshən\ *n* -S [ML *vilification-, vilificatio*, fr. LL *vilificatus* (past part. of *vilificare*) + L *-ion-, -io* -ion] **1 :** the act of vilifying **:** ABUSE **2 :** an instance of vilifying **:** defamatory utterance

vil·i·fi·er \ˈviləˌfī(ə)r, -īə\ *n* -S **:** one that vilifies

vil·i·fy \-ˌfī\ *vb* -ED/-ING/-S [ME *vilifien*, fr. LL *vilificare*, fr. L *vilis* cheap, base, vile + *-ficare* -fy — more at VILE] *vt* **1 a :** to make less valuable or important **:** lower in estimation ⟨declare that opposition to the established system was an effort to destroy and ~ religion —C.L.Jones⟩ **b** *obs* **:** to make morally despicable or abhorrent **:** DEGRADE ⟨themselves they *vilified* to serve ungoverned appetite —John Milton⟩ **2 a** *obs* **:** to speak slightingly or contemptuously of ⟨the disposition of vulgar minds to ridicule and ~ what they cannot comprehend —Samuel Johnson⟩ **b :** to utter slanderous and abusive statements against **:** denounce unjustly or abuse as hateful or vile **:** DEFAME, TRADUCE ⟨his policies . . . attacked; his personal character *vilified* —William Peden⟩ **~** *vi* **1 :** to cause a person to become vile ⟨nothing *vilifies* and degrades more than pride —Earl of Chesterfield⟩ **2 :** to utter or publish slander **syn** see MALIGN

vil·i·fy·ing·ly *adv* **:** in a vilifying manner

vil·i·pend \ˈviləˌpend\ *vb* -ED/-ING/-S [ME *vilipenden*, fr. MF *vilipender*, fr. ML *vilipendere*, fr. L *vilis* cheap, base, vile + *pendere* to weigh, estimate — more at PENDANT] *vt* **1 :** to hold or treat as of small worth or account **:** CONTEMN ⟨that petulant volatility which . . . ~*s* the conversation and advice of seniors —Sir Walter Scott⟩ **2 :** to speak of slightingly or disparagingly **:** express a low opinion of **:** DEPRECIATE ⟨a censorious critic might ~ it . . . as want of imagination —Frederick Pollock⟩ **~** *vi* **:** to be disparaging or depreciatory

vil·i·ty \ˈviləd·ē\ *n* -ES [ME *vilite*, fr. MF *vilité*, fr. L *vilitat-, vilitas* cheapness, baseness, vileness, fr. *vilis* cheap, base, vile + *-itat-, -itas* -ity — more at VILE] **1** *archaic* **:** VILENESS, BASENESS **2** *obs* **:** lowness of estate or value

vill \ˈvil\ *n* -S [AF *vill, vile*, fr. OF *ville, vile* farm, village — more at VILLAGE] **1 :** a division of a hundred for purposes of administration and taxation in English feudal law orig. equivalent to a manor and superseded by the parish **:** TOWNSHIP **2 :** VILLAGE

vill *abbr* village

vil·la \ˈvilə\ *n* -S [It, fr. L, country house, country estate; akin to L *vicus* row of houses, village — more at VICINITY] **1 :** a country estate: **a :** a pretentious rural or suburban residence with extensive grounds maintained as a pleasurable retreat from city life by a person of wealth **b** *pl also* **vil·lae** \-iˌlē\ [L] **:** an agricultural estate of Roman or early medieval times **2** *Brit* **:** a detached or semidetached urban residence with yard and garden space

vil·la·dom \-lədəm\ *n* -S [*villa* + *-dom*] *Brit* **:** the world constituted by villas and their occupants **:** SUBURBIA

vil·lage \ˈvilij, -lēj\ *n* -S *often attrib* [ME, fr. MF, fr. OF, fr. *ville, vile* farm, village (fr. L *villa* country house, country estate, village) + *-age*] **1 a :** a unit of compact settlement varying in size but usu. larger than a hamlet and smaller than a town and distinguished from surrounding rural territory **:** a small cluster of houses and other buildings (as stores and churches) forming a unit distinct from a surrounding rural area **b** (1) **:** one incorporated and given definite boundaries and powers by law **:** a minor municipality ⟨the distinction between cities and ~*s* is not one of size and population, but rather one of powers —F.A.Ogg & P.O.Ray⟩ (2) **:** an incorporated municipal unit in some states (as New York) having a separate status and some independent powers although still constituting part of the parent town ⟨a thickly settled area in a town, faced with some problems of living close together, may be incorporated into a ~ —*Our State & Local Gov't of N. Y.*⟩ (3) **:** an incorporated municipal unit in a Canadian province varying in population but usu. smaller than a town **c :** a unit of settlement having or held to have the status of a village but differing from the traditional village in some important respect: as (1) **:** one having a large population ⟨Spanish agricultural ~*s* of 10,000 or more inhabitants⟩ (2) **:** one constituting a unit in a predominantly urban rather than rural territory **2 a :** the citizens or inhabitants of a village ⟨the entire ~ turned out to welcome him⟩ **b :** the qualified voters of a village ⟨the ~ elects a council of five members⟩ **c :** the governing officials of a village acting on behalf of the village as a corporation or of the whole body of inhabitants ⟨the ~ purchased land for a new school⟩ **3 :** something (as an aggregation of burrows) resembling or suggesting a village ⟨a prairie dog ~⟩ **4 a :** a territorial area having the status of a village esp. as a unit of local government ⟨paved streets in the ~ but not in the rest of the town⟩ **b :** a section or district of a larger municipality (as a city) having characteristics that set it apart as an individual unit resembling a village ⟨Greenwich *Village* in New York⟩ **5 :** a relatively small group of people organized chiefly in families that constitutes a distinct social unit and usu. forms a community **6 :** any of various groups of residential and related buildings; *specif* **:** an institution (as for children requiring special care) providing residence in small groups occupying separate cottages

village cart *n* **:** CART 3b

village economy *n* **:** a stage in economic history following that in which agriculture is the principal pursuit and having for its characteristic features the village, barter trading, and little division of labor

vil·lage·less \-jləs\ *adj* **:** having no village

vil·lage·ous \-jəs\ *adj* **:** of or relating to a village or villagers

vil·lag·er \-jə(r)\ *n* -S **:** an inhabitant or resident of a village

vil·lage·ry \-jrē\ *n* -ES [*village* + *-ery*] **:** VILLAGES

vil·lagey *or* **vil·lagy** \-jē\ *adj* **:** resembling or suggesting a village (as in size, appearance, or habits)

vil·lag·ism \-ˌjizəm\ *n* -S **:** a word, form, or expression characteristic of village or rural speech as contrasted with urban

¹vil·lain \ˈvilən\ *n* -S [ME *vilein, vilain*, fr. MF, fr. ML *villanus*, fr. L *villa* country house, country estate, village + *-anus* -an — more at VILLA] **1 :** VILLEIN **2 :** a person of uncouth mind and manners **:** BOOR **3 :** a person of depraved and malevolent character devoted to base or evil acts **:** one who deliberately plots and does serious harm to others **4 :** a character in a story or play who opposes the hero **5 :** a person or thing blamed for a particular evil or difficulty ⟨the ~ of the Government's case . . . is the paper's advertising director —*Time*⟩ ⟨ozone, a form of oxygen, has been previously reported as a chief and elusive ~ in the . . . smog problem —*N.Y.Times*⟩

syn SCOUNDREL, BLACKGUARD, KNAVE, RASCAL, ROGUE, SCAMP, RAPSCALLION, MISCREANT: these words as here considered all describe low, mean, and reprehensible characters. VILLAIN describes one utterly given to crime, evil, and baseness ⟨are not made *villains* by the commission of a crime, but were *villains* before they committed it —John Ruskin⟩ SCOUNDREL may suggest blended worthlessness, meanness, and unscrupulousness ⟨a crew of pirates . . . will elect a boatswain to order them about and a captain to lead them and navigate the ship, though the one may be the most insufferable bully and the other the most tyrannical *scoundrel* on board —G.B.Shaw⟩ BLACKGUARD may suggest inveterate depravity; sometimes it is used as the antithesis of *gentleman* ⟨you must employ either *blackguards* or gentlemen, or, best of all, *blackguards* commanded by gentlemen, to do butcher's work with efficiency and dispatch —Rudyard Kipling⟩ KNAVE may suggest sly trickery and deceit ⟨cheating *knaves* gathered at the taverns⟩ ⟨more fool than *knave*⟩ RASCAL may suggest base dishonesty ⟨your true *rascal* is today your only true citizen of the world. He plunders all nations without pride in one or prejudice against another —Eric Linklater⟩ ROGUE may suggest the blended roughness and wiliness of a vagabond ⟨sturdy *rogues* taking to the roads as highwaymen⟩ SCAMP may describe one given to artful cheating, clever robbery, or interesting escapades ⟨a *scamp* who had pinched pennies out of the teacups of the poor by various shenanigans, who was distributing his largess to divert attention from his rascality —W.A.White⟩ RAPSCALLION may refer to an ill-dressed rogue or rascal rarely successful ⟨the *rapscallions* of the river, the Black Gangs —Meridel Le Sueur⟩ MISCREANT may refer to a singularly conscienceless villain ⟨a sordid glamour about imprisonment which makes the young *miscreant* feel important; he has the inverted satisfaction of being treated like a grown-up gangster —*Times Lit. Supp.*⟩

²villain \"\ *adj* [ME *vilein, vilain*, fr. MF, fr. *vilein, vilain*, n.] **:** of, being, or befitting a villain: **a :** of a base or depraved character **:** WICKED, DASTARDLY **b :** of low or common birth or origin

villainage *var of* VILLENAGE

vil·lain·ess \ˈvilənəs\ *n* -ES [*¹villain* + *-ess*] **:** a female villain

vil·lain·ize \-lə,nīz\ *vb* -ED/-ING/-S [*¹villain* + *-ize*] *vt* **:** VILIFY **~** *vi* **:** to play the role of a villain

¹vil·lain·ous \ˈvilənəs\ *adj* [ME *villenouse*, fr. MF *vileneus*, fr. *vilein, villain* + *-eus* -ous] **1 :** befitting a villain **:** proceeding from or revealing great depravity ⟨a ~ assault⟩ **2 :** having the character of a villain **:** DEPRAVED ⟨the ~ foe⟩ **3 :** highly objectionable **:** MEAN, BAD, WRETCHED, VILE, DETESTABLE ⟨~ weather⟩ ⟨a ~ jargon⟩ **syn** see VICIOUS

²villainous \"\ *adv* **:** VILLAINOUSLY ⟨apes with foreheads ~ low —Shak.⟩

vil·lain·ous·ly *adv* **:** in a villainous manner ⟨did the difficult, ~ fatiguing job —James Cameron⟩

vil·lain·ous·ness *n* -ES **:** the quality or state of being villainous **:** VILLAINY

vil·lainy \-nē, -ni\ *n* -ES [ME *vileinie, vilainie, vilenie*, fr. OF, fr. *vilein, vilain* villain, villein + *-ie* -y — more at VILLAIN] **1 a :** villainous action or conduct ⟨his master crime, a singular piece of atrocious ~ —George Borrow⟩ **b :** the quality or state of being villainous **:** extreme depravity or wickedness ⟨the ~ of a seducer⟩ ⟨a power of ~ walking in the world —J.M. Synge⟩ **2 :** a villainous act **:** a deed of an evil or objectionable character ⟨is not a brutal revelation of fact often a scoundrelly ~ —Cecil Sprigge⟩

vil·lan \ˈvilən\ *n* -S [ML *villanus* — more at VILLAIN] **:** VILLEIN

vi·llan·ci·co \ˌvēlyənˈthē(ˌ)kō\ *n* -S [Sp, fr. obs. Sp *villán* peasant, villein, fr. ML *villanus* — more at VILLAIN] **1 :** a Spanish part-song resembling the madrigal **2 :** a cantata or anthem sung in the churches

vil·la·nel·la \ˌviləˈnelə\ *n, pl* **villanel·le** \-elē\ [It, fr. *villano* rustic laborer, peasant, fr. ML *villanus*] **1 :** a 16th century Italian part-song unaccompanied and in free form and clownish and often parodistic in nature in sharp contrast to the sophistication of the contemporary madrigal **2 :** an instrumental piece in the style of a rustic dance

vil·la·nelle \ˌviləˈnel\ *n* -S [F, fr. It *villanella*] **:** a chiefly French poem having typically five tercets and a quatrain with the second lines having one rhyme and the remaining lines another and with the first and third lines of the first tercet repeated in alternation as the last line of the succeeding tercets and together as the closing couplet of the quatrain — compare VIRELAY

vil·la·no·va \ˌviləˈnōvə, ˌvēl-\ *adj, usu cap* [fr. *Villanova*, town in northeastern Italy] **:** VILLANOVAN

¹vil·la·no·van \-vən\ *adj, usu cap* [*Villanova*, town in northeastern Italy, its type station + E *-an*] **:** of or relating to an early Iron Age culture of northern Italy characterized by lake dwellings and urn burials in well tombs

²villanovan \"\ *n* -S *usu cap* **:** a member of the Villanovan people

vil·la·ri effect \vəˈlärē-\ *n, usu cap V* [after E. *Villari*, 19th cent. Ital. physicist] **:** change of magnetization as a result of longitudinal stress

villas *pl of* VILLA

vil·lat·ic \viˈlad·ik\ *adj* [L *villaticus*, fr. *villa* country house, country estate, village + *-aticus* (fr. *-atus* -ate + *-icus* -ic) — more at VILLA] **:** of or relating to a villa or a village **:** RURAL ⟨tame ~ fowl —John Milton⟩

vil·leg·gia·tu·ra \vəˌlejəˈtùrə\ *also* **vil·le·gia·ture** \vəˌlāzhəˈtü(ə)r\ *n* -S [*villeggiatura* fr. It, fr. *villeggiato* (past part. of *villeggiare* to reside in a country villa, fr. *villa*) + *-ura* -ure; *villegiature* fr. F *villégiature*, fr. It *villeggiatura* — more at VILLA] **1 :** residence in the country for a holiday **:** a country holiday ⟨go into ~ at the farm —W.J.Locke⟩ **2 :** a place that is suitable for a holiday from the city **:** rural or suburban retreat

vil·lein \ˈvilən, -iˌlān, viˈlān\ *n* -S [ME *vilein, vilain* — more at VILLAIN] **1 :** a free common villager or village peasant of any of the feudal classes lower in rank than the thane **2 :** a free peasant of a feudal class lower than a sokeman and higher in rank than the cotters and bordars and colliberts having property rights in both real and personal property and not adscript to the soil **3 :** an unfree peasant that is a slave as regards his feudal lord but free in his legal relations with respect to all others, that has no rights against the lord except that of protection from being maimed or killed, and that is subject to be sold by the lord or removed from his lands at will

vil·lein·hold \-nˌhōld\ *n* -S [*villein* + *-hold* (as in *freehold*)] **:** a tenement held by villein socage

villein socage *n* **:** a tenure of land held by a tenant villein owing by custom a duty to render to the feudal lord fixed and definite services of a base and servile nature

vil·len·age *also* **vil·lein·age** *or* **vil·lain·age** \-nij\ *n* -S [ME *vilenage*, fr. MF, fr. OF, fr. *vilein, vilain* villein + *-age* — more at VILLAIN] **1 :** tenure on the terms by which a villein held of his feudal lord **:** tenure at the will of the lord by villein services **2 :** the status of a villein

vi·lliaum·ite \vēˈyōˌmīt\ *n* -S [F *villiaumite*, fr. *Villiaume*, 20th cent. French explorer in Africa + F *-ite*] **:** a mineral (NaF) consisting of a sodium fluoride and occurring in small carmine to colorless isometric crystals (sp. gr. 2.8)

vil·li·cus \ˈviləkəs\ *n, pl* **vil·li·ci** \-ləˌsī\ [L *vilicus, villicus*, fr. *villa* country house, country estate + *-icus* -ic — more at VILLA] **1 :** the steward and overseer of a large farm or of farmlands in Roman and early medieval times **2 :** a member of a privileged class of feudal landless tillers holding a farm of a landlord for a part of the harvest or for a fixed fee

vil·lif·er·ous \(ˈ)viˈlif(ə)rəs\ *adj* [NL *villus* + E *-iferous*] **:** VILLOUS 1a

vil·li·form \ˈviləˌfȯrm\ *adj* [ISV *vill-* (fr. NL *villus*) + *-iform*] **:** having the form or appearance of villi **:** resembling the pile of velvet; *often* **:** resembling bristles in a brush ⟨a fish with ~ teeth⟩

vil·li·no \viˈlē(ˌ)nō\ *n, pl* **villi·ni** \-ēnē\ [It, dim. of *villa* — more at VILLA] **:** a residence for a single household separated from other houses by a yard **:** a detached house

vil·li·pla·cen·tal \ˌviləpləˈsentᵊl\ *adj* [NL *Villiplacentalia*] **:** of or relating to the Villiplacentalia

vil·li·plac·en·ta·lia \ˌviləˌplasᵊnˈtālēə\ *n pl, cap* [NL, fr. *villus* + *-i-* + *Placentalia*] **:** mammals having a nondeciduate villous placenta and comprising the cetaceans, sirenians, and ungulates

vil·lose \ˈviˌlōs, ˌ-ˈ-\ *adj* [L *villosus* hairy, shaggy — more at VILLOUS] **:** VILLOUS

vil·los·i·ty \viˈläsəd·ē\ *n* -ES [*villose* + *-ity*] **1 :** the state of being villous **2 a :** VILLUS **b :** a villous patch or area **3 :** a coating of long slender hairs

vil·lo·ta \viˈlōtə\ *n, pl* **villo·te** \-ˌtā\ [It *villotta*, fr. *villa* villa, village — more at VILLA] **:** a folk dance song of the 16th century that is homophonic in style and of northern Italian origin

vil·lous \ˈviləs\ *adj* [ME, fr. L *villosus* rough, shaggy, fr. *villus* shaggy hair, tuft of hair + *-osus* -ous — more at VELVET] **1 a :** covered or furnished with villi ⟨two ~ normal human ova⟩ **b :** of the character of a villus ⟨a ~ filament⟩ **2 :** having soft long hairs ⟨leaves ~ underneath⟩ — compare PUBESCENT — **vil·lous·ly** *adv*

vills *pl of* VILL

vil·lus \ˈviləs\ *n, pl* **vil·li** \-iˌlī\ [NL, fr. L, shaggy hair, tuft of hair — more at VELVET] **1 :** a small slender vascular process: as **a :** one of the minute fingerlike processes which more or less thickly cover and give a velvety appearance to the surface of the mucous membrane of the small intestine and serve in the absorption of nutriment and of which each has a central blindly ending lacteal surrounded by blood capillaries and covered with epithelium **b :** one of the branching processes of the surface of the chorion of the developing egg or blastodermic vesicle of most mammals that are restricted to particular areas or diffusely arranged and over parts of the surface become vascular and help to form the placenta **2 :** TROPHONEMA

vil·na \ˈvilnə\ *or* **vil·no** \-l(ˌ)nō\ *adj, usu cap* [fr. *Vilna, Vilno* (Vilnyus), Lithuania] **:** VILNYUS

vil·ny·us *or* **vil·ni·us** \ˈvilnēəs\ *adj, usu cap* [fr. *Vilnyus, Vilnius*, Lithuania] **:** of or from Vilnyus, the capital of Lithuania **:** of the kind or style prevalent in Vilnyus

vily *pl of* VILA

vim \ˈvim\ *n* -S [L, accus. of *vis* strength; akin to Gk *is* strength, Skt *vayas* strength, OE *wāth* wandering, pursuit, hunt, *wǣthan* to wander, hunt, OHG *weida* fodder, pasture, catch, *weidōn* to seek fodder, hunt, ON *veithr* catch, *veitha* to hunt, Gk *hiesthai* to hurry, Lith *vyti* to pursue, hunt, Skt *veti* he goes, advances] **:** robust energy and enthusiasm **:** VITALITY, ZIP ⟨the ~ . . . generally absent from more civilized gatherings —R.H. Croll⟩ ⟨woke up full of ~ and optimism⟩ **syn** see VIGOR

vi·ma·na \vəˈmänə\ *n* -S [Skt *vimāna*, lit., measuring out, traversing, fr. *vimāti* he measures, fr. *vi* apart + *māti* he measures — more at WITH, MEASURE] **:** a pyramidal tower built over the central shrine of a temple in India — compare GOPURA, SHIKARA

vim·i·nar·ia \ˌviməˈna(a)rēə\ *n, cap* [NL, fr. L *vimin-, vimen* withe + NL *-aria*] **:** a genus of Australian leafless shrubs (family Leguminosae) that resemble the brooms and have small orange-yellow flowers with a broad vexillum and connate keel petals and a one-seeded pod — see SWAMP OAK

vi·min·e·ous \vəˈminēəs\ *adj* [L *vimineus*, fr. *vimin-, vimen* pliant twig, withe + *-eus* -eous; akin to L *viēre* to plait — more at WITHY] **1** *obs* **:** woven of pliant twigs ⟨a ~ texture like a birdcage —Richard Tomlinson⟩ **2 :** of or producing long slender twigs or shoots ⟨a shrub of ~ habit⟩

vim·pa \ˈvimpə\ *n* -S [ML, fr. OIt *vimpa, glimpla*, fr. OF *guimple, wimple* veil, pennant, wimple — more at GUIMPE] **:** a veil of silk worn over the shoulders and hands of acolytes carrying the crosier and the miter in Roman Catholic pontifical services — compare HUMERAL VEIL

vi·na \ˈvēnə\ *also* **bi·na** \ˈbē-\ *n* -S [Skt & Hindi; Hindi *bīṇā*, fr. Skt *vīṇā*] **:** a musical instrument of India having usu. four strings and a long bamboo fingerboard with movable frets and a gourd resonator at each end

vi·na·ceous \(ˈ)vīˈnāshəs\ *adj* [L *vinaceus* of wine, fr. *vinum* wine + *-aceus* -aceous — more at WINE] **1 :** of the color wine **2 :** of the color wine red

vin·age \ˈvīnij\ *n* -S [F, fr. *vin* wine + *-age* — more at VINEGAR] **:** the adding of alcohol to wine

vi·na·gron \ˌvēnəˈgrōn\ *n* -S [MexSp *vinagrón* — more at VINEGARROON] **:** VINEGARROON

¹vin·ai·grette \ˌvinəˈgret, *usu* -ed·+V\ *n* -S [F, fr. *vinaigre* vinegar + *-ette* — more at VINEGAR] **1** [so called fr. its resemblance to vehicles used by French vinegar merchants] **:** a small 2-wheeled vehicle designed to be drawn or pushed ⟨sat in a ~, but the donkey refused to budge —O.S.J.Gogarty⟩ **2 :** VINAIGRETTE SAUCE **3 :** a small ornamental box or bottle that has a perforated top and is used for holding an aromatic preparation (as smelling salts)

²vinaigrette \ˌ==ˈ=\ *adj* : made or served with vinaigrette sauce ⟨~ salad dressing⟩ ⟨asparagus ~⟩

vinaigrette sauce *n* : a sauce made typically of vinegar, oil, onions, parsley, and herbs and used esp. on cold meats or fish

¹vi·nal \ˈvīnᵊl\ *adj* [L *vinalis*, fr. *vinum* wine + *-alis* -al] : of or from wine : VINOUS

²vinal \"\ *n* -s [poly*vin*yl *al*cohol] : any of various synthetic textile fibers that are long-chain polymers composed of at least 50 percent by weight of vinyl alcohol units —CH_2CHOH— and at least 85 percent by weight of vinyl alcohol units together with various vinyl acetal units

vi·nasse \vəˈnas\ *n* -s [F, fr. L *vinacea*, fem. of *vinaceus* vinaceous] : a residual liquid remaining from the fermentation and distillation of alcoholic liquors

vin·a·ya \ˈvinəyə\ *n* -s *usu cap* [Skt, discipline, lit., leading apart, separating, fr. *vi* apart, asunder + *nayati* he leads — more at WITH] : a code of monastic disciplinary rules in Buddhism

vin·ca \ˈviŋkə\ *n, cap* [NL, short for L *pervinca* periwinkle — more at PERIWINKLE] : a genus of often prostrate woody herbs (family Apocynaceae) comprising the Old World periwinkles and having solitary axillary blue, red, or white flowers with a plumose stigma

¹vin·cen·tian \vinˈsenchən\ *n* -s *usu cap* [Saint *Vincent* de Paul †1660 Fr. Roman Catholic priest + E *-an*, n. suffix] **1** : a member of a Roman Catholic society of priests founded in 1625 by St. Vincent de Paul and devoted to conducting missions and clerical seminaries — called also *Lazarist* **2** : SISTER OF CHARITY

²vincentian \(ˈ)=ˈ==\ *adj, usu cap* [Saint *Vincent* de Paul †1660 + E *-an*, adj. suffix] **1** : of, relating to, or founded by St. Vincent de Paul **2** : of or relating to the Vincentians

vin·cent's angina \ˈvin(t)sənts-\ *n, usu cap V* [after Jean Hyacinthe *Vincent* †1950 Fr. bacteriologist] : Vincent's infection of the tonsils, pharynx, and throat — called also *trench mouth*

vincent's infection *also* **vincent's stomatitis** *n, usu cap V* [after Jean H. *Vincent* †1950 Fr. bacteriologist] : infection of the respiratory tract and mouth by the fusiform bacillus often in association with a spirochete (*Borrelia vincentii*) producing destructive ulceration esp. of the mucous membranes of the cheeks, gums, and throat

vin·ce·tox·i·cum \ˌvin(t)səˈtäksəkəm\ *n, cap* [NL, fr. L *vincere* to conquer + *toxicum* poison; fr. the former belief that it was a counterpoison — more at TOXIC] : a large genus of chiefly tropical American vines (family Asclepiadaceae) having cordate leaves and large purple or greenish cymose flowers with the corolla rotate and 5-parted and an entire or lobed crown — see NEGRO VINE

vin·chu·ca \vinˈchükə\ *n* -s [Sp, fr. Quechua *wihchuykuk*] : any of several bugs of the genus *Triatoma* (esp. *T. infestans*)

vin·ci·ble \ˈvin(t)səbəl\ *adj* [L *vincibilis*, fr. *vincere* to conquer + *-ibilis* -ible — more at VICTOR] **1** : capable of being overcome or subdued : SURMOUNTABLE ⟨powerful governments showing signs of being ~⟩ ⟨our boys were plenty ~ in the . . . track events —*New Yorker*⟩ **2** : being within an individual's control and therefore involving moral responsibility — used esp. of lack of knowledge about theological concepts ⟨~ ignorance⟩

vin·cu·lum \ˈviŋkyələm\ *n pl* **vinculums** \-mz\ *or* **vincu·la** \-lə\ [L, fr. *vincire* to bind, tie — more at VETCH] **1** : a unifying bond : LINK, TIE ⟨the strong ~ between the candidate and his supporters⟩ **2** : a uniting band or bundle of fibers (as a commissure uniting the two main tendons of the foot in a bird) : FRENUM **3** : a straight horizontal mark in mathematics placed over two or more members of a compound quantity and equivalent to parentheses or brackets about them (as in $a-\overline{b-c}=a-[b-c]$)

vin·di·ca·ble \ˈvindəkəbəl, -dēk-\ *adj* [L *vindicare* + E *-able*] : capable of being vindicated : JUSTIFIABLE ⟨think every work of God ~ —S.J.Pratt⟩

vin·di·cate \ˈvindəˌkāt, *usu* -ād.+V\ *vt* -ED/-ING/-S [L *vindicatus*, past part. of *vindicare* to lay claim to, set free, avenge, fr. *vindic-, vindex* claimant, protector, avenger, fr. a prehistoric compound whose first constituent is of unknown origin and whose second constituent is the same as L *-dic-, -dex* (fr. *dicere* to determine, say) — more at DICTION] **1** *obs* : to set free : DELIVER ⟨~ ourselves into perfect liberty —Edmund Burke⟩ **2** : to take vengeance for : AVENGE ⟨~ the laws which have been breached —W.E.Jackson b. 1919⟩ **3 a** : to free from any question of error, dishonor, guilt, or negligence : EXONERATE, ABSOLVE ⟨the . . . politicians were *vindicated* on all counts —R.H.Rovere⟩ ⟨~ his official honor —Dumas Malone⟩ **b** (1) : to show to be true, reasonable, just, or acceptable against denial, disbelief, or criticism : PROVE, CONFIRM, SUBSTANTIATE ⟨many of his insights have been *vindicated* —G.C.Sellery⟩ ⟨efforts . . . to ~ their position as gentlefolk —Edmund Wilson⟩ ⟨the right . . . has been *vindicated* by the Supreme Court —R.J.Slavin⟩ (2) : to provide justification or defense for : JUSTIFY ⟨his negative attitude ~*s* resentment⟩ **c** : to protect from attack or encroachment : PRESERVE, DEFEND ⟨~ the glory of his name against all competition —John Milton⟩ **4** : to lay claim to : maintain a right to : ASSERT ⟨no one can ~ to himself . . . exclusive prerogative —*U.S. Code*⟩ ⟨~ their right to a place in the university —Walter Moberly⟩ **syn** see EXCULPATE, MAINTAIN

vin·di·ca·tion \ˌ==ˈkāshən\ *n* -s [L *vindication-, vindicatio*, fr. *vindicatus* (past part.) + *-ion-, -io* -ion] **1 a** : an act or instance of vindicating: as (1) : EXONERATION ⟨the ~ of a man falsely convicted of murder —*Current Biog.*⟩ (2) : JUSTIFICATION, DEFENSE ⟨undertook a successful ~ of democratic principles⟩ ⟨called on to say something in ~ of his behavior —Jane Austen⟩ (3) : SUBSTANTIATION, SUPPORT ⟨considered the event to be a ~ of the law of chance⟩ **b** : the state or condition of being vindicated ⟨sought ~ for being unjustly charged with subversion⟩ **2** : a means of gaining exoneration, justification, or support ⟨used his unhappy childhood as a ~ of his crimes⟩ ⟨discern a new ~ for poetry . . . and religion as revealers of reality —W.L.Sullivan⟩

vin·di·ca·tive \ˈvindəˌkād·iv, -ndəkəl, -ndēkəl, (ˈ)vinˈdikəl, |t|, |ēv *also* |əv\ *adj* [ML *vindicativus*, fr. L *vindicatus* (past part. of *vindicare*) + *-ivus* -ive] **1** *obs* : VINDICTIVE, VENGEFUL ⟨more ~ than jealous love —Shak.⟩ **2** *archaic* : of or related to punishment or discipline : PUNITIVE ⟨~ power . . . belongs not to the church —George Carleton⟩

vin·di·ca·tor \ˈvindəˌkād·ə(r), -ātə-\ *n* -s [LL, fr. L *vindicatus* + *-or*] : one that vindicates

vin·di·ca·to·ry \ˈvindəkəˌtōrē, -dēk-, (ˈ)vinˈdikə, -tȯr-, -ri\ *adj* **1** : providing vindication : JUSTIFICATORY ⟨writing urgent ~ letters . . . on his behalf —George Eliot⟩ **2** : providing punishment : PUNITIVE, RETRIBUTIVE ⟨~ justice⟩ **3** : providing sanctions esp. in law

vin·dic·tive \(ˈ)vinˈdiktiv, -tēv *also* -təv\ *adj* [L *vindicta* revenge, vindication (fr. *vindicare* to defend, avenge) + E *-ive*] **1 a** (1) : having a bitterly vengeful character : disposed to seek revenge ⟨a ~ man will look for occasions of resentment —James Martineau⟩ (2) : intended for or involving revenge ⟨punishments . . . essentially ~ in their nature —M.R.Cohen⟩ **b** : characterized by an intent to cause unpleasantness, damage, or pain : NASTY, VICIOUS, SPITEFUL ⟨letters . . . with rather ~ comments upon the people —Martha T. Stephenson⟩ ⟨a priggish and even ~ poem —Cyril Connolly⟩ **2** : intended for or involving retribution : PUNITIVE ⟨a ~ purpose, — a purpose to punish you for your suspicion —William Cowper⟩

syn REVENGEFUL, VENGEFUL: VINDICTIVE applies to a desire to see another suffer or a disposition to revenge oneself for real or imagined wrong or slight, sometimes with implacable malevolence, sometimes with spiteful malice ⟨his dark, handsome, aquiline features were convulsed into a spasm of *vindictive* hatred, which had set his dead face in a terribly fiendish expression —A. Conan Doyle⟩ ⟨the Muses are *vindictive* virgins, and avenge themselves without mercy on those who weary of their charms —L.P.Smith⟩ REVENGEFUL and VENGEFUL suggest truculent readiness to take vengeance on the part of one provoked ⟨the sorrow through the villages spread by triumphant cruelties of *vengeful* military force and punishments without remorse —William Wordsworth⟩ ⟨to some *vengeful* people the treaty seemed too easy upon Germany; to many liberals it seemed too harsh —Allan Nevins & H.S.Commager⟩ ⟨*revengeful* Nature grudged him the crops which she granted to more liberal husbandmen —W.M. Thackeray⟩

vindictive damages *n pl* : PUNITIVE DAMAGES

vin·dic·tive·ly \-təvlē, -li\ *adv* : in a vindictive manner ⟨~ plotted against his superiors⟩

vin·dic·tive·ness \-tivnəs, -tēv *also* -təv-\ *n* -ES : the quality or state of being vindictive ⟨a refusal that suggested . . . puritanical ~ —Alan Gregg⟩

¹vine \ˈvīn\ *n* -s *often attrib* [ME, fr. OF *vine, vigne*, fr. L *vinea* vine, vineyard, fr. fem. of *vineus* of wine, fr. *vinum* wine + *-eus* -eous — more at WINE] **1 a** : GRAPE 2 **b** : a plant having a woody or herbaceous stem that is too slender, flexible, or weak to hold itself erect and that supports itself in nature by climbing over an object (as a wall, fence, or trellis) or other plants by tendrils or by twining or that extends itself horizontally by running along the ground ⟨honeysuckle ~⟩ ⟨cucumber ~⟩ **c** : any of various lax sprawling herbaceous plants (as a tomato or potato plant) that lack modification for climbing — not used technically **2** *archaic* : VINEA

²vine \"\ *vb* -ED/-ING/-S *vi* : to form a vine : grow in the manner of a vine ⟨the grapes began to ~ soon after planting⟩ ⟨morning glories *vining* up the corn —J.H.Stuart⟩ ~ *vt* : to harvest (as peas) by means of a mechanical viner

vin·ea \ˈvinēə\ *n, pl* **vine·ae** \-ēˌē\ [L, vine, vinea] : a shedlike structure used in ancient Rome to protect besiegers

vin·e·al \ˈvinēəl\ *adj* [L *vinealis*, fr. *vinea* vine + *-alis* -al] **1** : of or relating to grapes or grapevines ⟨~ plantations —Sir Thomas Browne⟩ **2** : of or relating to wine ⟨importing of ~ spirits⟩

vine beetle *n* : any of several beetles injurious to the leaves, branches, or roots of the grapevine — compare GRAPE LEAFHOPPER, GRAPE ROOTWORM, SPOTTED PELIDNOTA

vine black *n* : a vegetable black pigment made by charring vine twigs, the lees of wine, old wine casks, or similar materials — compare FRANKFORT BLACK

vine borer *n* **1** : any of several beetles whose larvae bore in the wood or pith of the grapevine: as **a** : a small beetle (*Xylobiops basilaris*) whose larva bores in the stems **b** : a small reddish brown weevil (*Ampeloglypter sesostris*) that produces galls on the branches — see WOUND GALL **2** : a clearwing moth (*Memythrus polistiformis*) whose larva bores often destructively in the roots of the grapevine

vine cactus *n* : OCOTILLO 1

vine chafer *n* **1** : ROSE CHAFER **2** : SPOTTED PELIDNOTA

vined \ˈvīnd\ *adj* [in sense 1, fr. past part. of ²*vine*; in sense 2, fr. ¹*vine* + *-ed*] **1** : separated from the shells ⟨~ peas⟩ **2** : covered with vines ⟨a little ~ cottage⟩

vinedresser \ˈ=ˌ==\ *n* : one that cultivates and prunes grapevines

vine forester *n* : any of several moths of the genus *Alypia* having larvae that feed on the leaves of the grapevine

vine fretter *n* : a plant louse (esp. *Phylloxera vitifoliae*) that injures the grapevine — called also *vine louse*

¹vin·e·gar \ˈvinigə(r), -nēg-\ *n* -s *often attrib* [ME *vinegre*, fr. OF *vinaigre*, lit., sour wine, fr. *vin* wine (fr. L *vinum*) + *aigre* sharp, sour — more at WINE, EAGER] **1** : a sour liquid used as a condiment or a preservative that is obtained by acetic fermentation of dilute alcoholic liquids (as fermented cider, malt beer, or wine) or of dilute distilled alcohol and is often seasoned esp. with herbs ⟨tarragon ~⟩ **2** : disagreeableness of speech, disposition, or attitude : SOURNESS ⟨the smile couldn't disguise the ~ in her voice⟩ **3** : a pharmaceutical solution of the active principles of drugs in dilute acetic acid usu. prepared by maceration ⟨aromatic ~⟩ — see VINEGAR OF OPIUM **4** : vigorous strength and spirits : VIM ⟨just a kid, full of ~ —Eddie Krell⟩

²vinegar \"\ *vt* -ED/-ING/-S : to treat with vinegar : apply vinegar to ⟨proceeded to ~ the forehead . . . of the spinster aunt —Charles Dickens⟩

vinegar eel *also* **vinegar worm** *n* : a minute nematode worm (*Turbatrix aceti*) often found in great numbers in vinegar, sour paste, and other acid fermenting vegetable substances

vinegar fly *n* : any of various fruit flies (esp. *Drosophila melanogaster*) that often become pests by breeding in imperfectly sealed preserves and in pickles

vin·e·gar·ish \-rish, -rēsh\ *adj* : sour or sullen in disposition, speech, or manner : given to caustic comment : ACIDULOUS, WASPISH ⟨a ~, aggressive-mannered woman —*Wall Street Jour.*⟩

vinegar maker *n* : VINEGARROON

vinegar mother *n* : ⁴MOTHER 2

vinegar of lead : GOULARD'S EXTRACT

vinegar of opium : a solution of opium in diluted acetic acid — called also *black drop*

vinegar pie *n* : a pie consisting of a flour-thickened filling of water, vinegar, and butter sweetened with brown sugar and baked in a pastry shell

vin·e·gar·roon \ˌvinigəˈrün, -nēg-, -ˈrōn\ *n* -s [MexSp *vinagrón*, aug. of Sp *vinagre* vinegar, fr. OSp, fr. OF *vinaigre* — more at VINEGAR] : a large whip scorpion (*Mastigoproctus giganteus*) of the southern U. S. and Mexico that emits a vinegary odor when disturbed and is inaccurately held to be very venomous

vinegar rot *n* : a soft rot of sweet potatoes caused by any of several fungi of the genus *Rhizopus*

vinegar tree *n* : a sumac with acid berries sometimes used to intensify the sourness of vinegar; *esp* : STAGHORN SUMAC

vinegarweed \ˈ====ˌ=\ *n* : a Californian mint (*Trichostema lanceolatum*) that has light blue flowers and is a common bee plant

vin·e·gary \ˈvinig(ə)rē, -nēg-, -ri\ *adj* **1** : resembling vinegar esp. in taste : TART, SOUR ⟨munched bread and dark, ~ . . . olives —*New Yorker*⟩ **2 a** : having a disagreeable, bitter, or coldly severe character or manner : ACERBIC, CRABBED, ASTRINGENT ⟨a ~ unpleasant person —W.H.Wright⟩ ⟨gave him a thin ~ greeting —G.W.Brace⟩ **b** : easily moved to irascibility : PEPPERY, CHOLERIC ⟨~ but lovable old village practitioner —*Newsweek*⟩

vine hawk moth *n* : any of several hawk moths (esp. *Pholus achmeon* and *Ampelophaga myron*) whose larvae feed on grape leaves

vine hopper *n* : GRAPE LEAFHOPPER

vi·ne·i·ty \vəˈnēəd·ē\ *n* -ES [L *vineus* of wine + E *-ity* — more at VINE] : the quality or state of being wine ⟨the ~ of the eucharistic wine⟩

vineland \ˈ=ˌ=\ *n* : land adapted esp. to the cultivation of vines ⟨rich ~*s* producing grapes of fine quality⟩

vine leaf folder *or* **vine leaf roller** *n* : GRAPE LEAF FOLDER

vine leek *n* : a Eurasian plant (*Allium ampeloprasum*) that is probably the ancestor of the leek

vine·let \ˈvīnlət\ *n* : a young undeveloped vine

vine louse *or* **vine pest** *n* : VINE FRETTER

vine maple *n* **1** : a maple (*Acer circinatum*) of northwestern No. America having often prostrate stems that root freely and form dense thickets **2** : CANADA MOONSEED

vine mesquite *n* : a wiry stoloniferous perennial grass (*Panicum obtusum*) that grows esp. in sandy soil and along watercourses of the western U. S. and Mexico

vine mite *n* : a mite (*Tenuipalpus californicus*) that damages lemons and grapes

vine moth *n* : any of several moths whose larvae feed on grapevine

vine peach *n* : MANGO MELON

vin·er \ˈvīnə(r)\ *n* -s **1** : a machine in which fresh peas are separated from the pods and vines **2** : a mechanical pea harvester

vin·ery \ˈvīnərē\ *n* -ES : an area or building in which vines are grown ⟨grape ~⟩ ⟨pea ~⟩

vines *pl of* VINE, *pres 3d sing of* VINE

vine sawfly *n* : a small black sawfly (*Erythraspides pygmaea*) whose larva feeds on the leaves of the grapevine

vine scale *n* : any of several scales that attack grapevines: as **a** : a brown No. American unarmored scale (*Pulvinaria vitis*) that deposits its eggs in a cottony mass **b** : GRAPE SCALE

vine slug *n* : the black larva of the vine sawfly

vine sorrel *n* : SORREL VINE

vinestock \ˈ=ˌ=\ *n* : the main stem of a vine

vinet *n* -s [ME *vinnet*, fr. MF *vignete* — more at VIGNETTE] *obs* : VIGNETTE 1

vine weevil *n* : any of various weevils feeding on grape and often other plants; *esp* : BLACK VINE WEEVIL — compare VINE BORER 1b

vine wilt *n* : a stem rot of sweet potatoes that is caused by either of two fungi (*Fusarium batatatis* and *F. hyperoxysporum*)

vine·yard \ˈvinyə(r)d *sometimes* -nˌyärd *or* -yäd\ *n* [ME *vineyard, vineyerd*, fr. ¹*vine* + *yard, yerd* yard] **1** : a field of grapevines ⟨apple and peach orchards . . . mingle with farms and ~*s* —*Amer. Guide Series: Va.*⟩ **2** : an area or category of physical or mental occupation ⟨a . . . minister whose ~ was in the slums —*Brit. Books of the Month*⟩ ⟨beginning his labors in the ~ of gossip —*Time*⟩

vine·yard·ist \-dəst\ *n* -s : one who owns or cultivates a vineyard

vineyard plow *n* : a moldboard plow with a relatively small bottom used for plowing in orchards and vineyards

vingt-et-un \ˌvantāˈən, ˌvaⁿtāˈəⁿ\ *n* -s [F, lit., twenty-one (number)] : ³TWENTY-ONE 5

vingt-un \(ˈ)van-ˈtən, (ˈ)vaⁿˈtəⁿ\ *n* -s [by contr.] : VINGT-ET-UN

vin·ha·ti·co \vēnˈyäd·əˌkō\ *n* -s [Pg, prob. fr. *vinha* vineyard, fr. L *vinea* — more at VINE] **1 a** : any of several So. American leguminous timber trees of the genera *Plathymenia* and *Pithecolobium* **b** : the yellowish wood of any of these trees **2 a** : an ornamental tree (*Persea indica*) of the Azores and the Canary islands **b** : the coarse dark-colored wood of this tree

vi·nic \ˈvīnik, ˈvin-, -nēk\ *adj* [ISV *vin-* (fr. L *vinum* wine) + *-ic* — more at WINE] : of, relating to, or derived from wine or alcohol ⟨~ ether⟩ ⟨enchant the intellect . . . in a ~ drowsiness —J.P.Bishop⟩

vini·cul·tur·al \ˌvinəˈkəlch(ə)rəl\ *adj* [*viniculture* + *-al*] : VITICULTURAL

vini·cul·tur·al·ist \-rələst\ *n* : a person engaged in viticulture ⟨wines selected by . . . ~*s* and tasters —Roger Angell⟩

vini·cul·ture \ˈ==ˌkəlchə(r)\ *n* [ISV *vini-* (fr. L *vinum* wine) + *culture*] : VITICULTURE

¹vi·nif·era \(ˈ)vīˈnif(ə)rə\ *adj* [NL (specific epithet of *Vitis vinifera*), fr. L *vinifer* wine-producing] : of, relating to, or derived from a common European grape (*Vitis vinifera*) that is the chief source of Old World wine grapes and table grapes ⟨Delaware grapes contain both labrusca and ~ blood⟩ ⟨several new ~ hybrids⟩ ⟨a seedless ~ grape⟩

²vinifera \"\ *n* -s : a vinifera grape

vi·nif·er·ous \-rəs\ *adj* [L *vinifer*, fr. *vinum* wine + *-ifer* -iferous] **1** : yielding or grown for the production of wine ⟨the grape is the chief ~ fruit⟩ **2** [NL *vinifera* + E *-ous*] : VINIFERA

vin·i·fi·ca·tion \ˌvinəfəˈkāshən\ *n* -s [F, fr. *vin* wine + *-i-* + *-fication* — more at VINEGAR] : the conversion of a fruit juice or other saccharine solution into alcohol by fermentation

vining *pres part of* VINE

vi·no \ˈvē(ˌ)nō\ *n* -s [It & Sp, fr. L *vinum*] : WINE

vi·nos·i·ty \vīˈnäsəd·ē, -ətē, -i\ *n* -ES [LL *vinositas*, fr. L *vinosus* of wine + *-itas* -ity] : the characteristic body, flavor, and color of a wine ⟨similar in ~, . . . but with a distinctive bouquet —A.L.Simon⟩

vi·nous \ˈvīnəs\ *adj* [L *vinosus*, fr. *vinum* wine + *-osus* -ose] **1 a** : of, relating to, or having the characteristics of wine ⟨villages redolent with ~ aroma —Richard Ford⟩ ⟨~ and amorous verse —Douglas Bush⟩ ⟨~ liquid⟩ **b** : made with or containing wine ⟨~ medications⟩ **2** : caused by or resulting from drinking wine : showing the effects of the use of wine ⟨the hubbub of ~ political fervor —William Black⟩ ⟨~ bloodshot eyes⟩ **3** *of a bird* : VINACEOUS — **vi·nous·ly** *adv*

vin·quish \ˈviŋkwish\ *n* -ES [alter. of *avanquish*] *Scot* : ¹PINE 3

vin ro·sé \ˌvaⁿrōˈzā\ *n, pl* **vins rosés** \"\ [F, rosy wine] : WILD CHERRY 3

¹vint \ˈvint\ *vt* -ED/-ING/-S [prob. back-formation fr. *vintage*] : to make (wine) from fruit ⟨cherry-wine ~*ed* in the . . . forest —O.E.Schniebs⟩

²vint \"\ *n* -s [Russ, prob. fr. Yiddish, lit., wind, fr. MHG *wint*, fr. OHG — more at WIND] : a card game resembling whist and similar to auction bridge in its bidding that has every trick scored and on a failed bid has the declarer score as usual while the adversaries score 100 times the value for their tricks — called also *Russian whist*

vin·ta \ˈventə\ *n* -s [PhilSp] : a dugout canoe with double outriggers used in the Philippines — compare BANCA, BAROTO

¹vin·tage \ˈvintij, -tēj\ *n* -s [ME, alter. (influenced by *vineter, vintener* vintner) of *vindage, vendage*, fr. MF *vendenge, vendeigne*, fr. L *vindemia*, fr. *vinum* wine, grapes + *demere* to take off, fr. *de-* + *emere* to take — more at WINE, REDEEM] **1 a** (1) : the yield of grapes or wine from a vineyard during a single season ⟨never did . . . the vines yield a more luxuriant ~ —Mary W. Shelley⟩ ⟨half bottles . . . of the 1947 ~ —*New Yorker*⟩ (2) : WINE ⟨the ~ flowed freely during the reception⟩ (3) *or* **vintage wine** : a wine of a particular type, region, and year and usu. of superior quality that is dated and allowed to mature ⟨several ordinary wines and a bottle of ~⟩ ⟨sampled every ~ and kickshaw of the gourmet's art —S.J.Perelman⟩ **b** : a collection of persons or things that are contemporaneous with each other and share similar or identical characteristics : CROP ⟨the book is not of this season's ~ —Muna Lee⟩ ⟨was of the ~ of comfortably well-off intellectuals —Janet Flanner⟩ **2 a** : the activity or process of harvesting and pressing grapes, fermenting the juice, and caring for the new wine ⟨nearly time for the annual ~⟩ **b** : the season when this activity or process takes place ⟨the ~ . . . is a time of gaiety and . . . hard work —P.M.Wagner⟩ **3 a** : a period of origin or manufacture ⟨term of Edwardian ~ —*N.Y. Times Mag.*⟩ ⟨a small coupé of rather ancient ~ —Leslie Charteris⟩ **b** : length of existence : MATURITY, AGE ⟨preserved . . . shark's fins of twenty years' ~ —Eve Langley⟩ ⟨many of us, of a certain ~, have been forced to think back —John Mason Brown⟩

²vintage \"\ *vb* -ED/-ING/-S *vt* : to harvest (grapes) for making wine ⟨if . . . a first growth is *vintaged* a little too late —H.J. Newman⟩ ~ *vi* : to engage in the harvesting of grapes ⟨illustrations . . . of a winged Eros *vintaging* —Nelson Glueck⟩

³vintage \"\ *adj* **1 a** (1) : of or relating to a vintage ⟨prepared for the ~ activities in the vineyards⟩ (2) : unblended and dated with the year of vintage ⟨a ~ wine⟩ — compare NON-VINTAGE **b** : having a fine mellowed character ⟨drink a health in ~ vodka⟩ ⟨turning leaves make fall a ~ season⟩ **c** : of old, recognized, and enduring interest, importance, or quality : CLASSIC, VENERABLE ⟨~ comedy from the silent era —Arthur Knight⟩ ⟨collectors who . . . cherish ~ automobiles —Beverly Kelley⟩ ⟨an album of ~ tunes —Wilder Hobson⟩ **2 a** : marked by an advanced age : dating from the past : OLD, ARCHAIC ⟨a ~ actress but still thin and chic —Janet Flanner⟩ ⟨failing to answer seventy-two ~ traffic tickets —Robert Rice⟩ **b** : not fashionable or up-to-date : OLD-FASHIONED, OUTMODED ⟨~ plays of no merit whatsoever —Wolcott Gibbs⟩ ⟨a rumpled tweed suit of ~ cut —Jacob Hay⟩ **3** : of the best and most characteristic : having the typical and most admirable characteristics — used with a proper noun ⟨~ Shaw: a wise and winning comedy, beautifully played —*Time*⟩ ⟨seemed to be fine . . . but not absolutely first-rate ~ Old Vic —Mollie Panter-Downes⟩

vintage port *n* : a port wine that has a fruitier flavor and heavier body and is deeper red than either ruby or tawny port

vin·tag·er \-jə(r)\ *n* -s : one that takes part in a vintage ⟨green grapes . . . the ~*s* ought not to gather —Philip Miller⟩

vintage year *n* **1** : a year in which a vintage wine is produced ⟨the date of the *vintage year* is marked on the bottle⟩ **2** : a year of outstanding distinction or success ⟨not a *vintage year* in English scholarship —C.J.Sisson⟩ ⟨proved a *vintage year* from the radio engineer's point of view —*Wireless Engineer*⟩

vinted *past of* VINT

vin·tem \vēⁿˈtāⁿ\ *n* -s [Pg *vintem*, fr. *vinte* twenty, fr. L *viginti* — more at VICENARY] : an old Portuguese coin orig. of silver and later bronze and worth 20 reals

vinting *pres part of* VINT

vint·ner \ˈvintnə(r)\ *n* -s [ME *vineter, vintener*, fr. OF *vinetier*, fr. ML *vinetarius*, fr. L *vinetum* vineyard (fr. *vinum* wine, grapes) + *-arius* -ary] **1** : a person who sells wine : a wine merchant **2** : a person who makes wine ⟨collected wine-

making tips from leading amateur and professional ~s —*Packer*〉
vints *pres 3d sing of* VINT, *pl of* VINT
viny \'vīnē, -ni\ *adj* **1 :** of, relating to, or resembling vines **:** covered with or abounding in vines 〈~ low-lying plants〉 〈~ hillsides and forests〉 **2 :** having notably long vigorous prostrate stems 〈a ~ but very productive sweet potato〉
vi·nyl \'vīnᵊl *sometimes* 'vin-\ *n* -s *often attrib* [ISV *vin-* (fr. L *vinum* wine) + *-yl*] **1 :** a univalent radical $CH_2=CH$— derived from ethylene by removal of one hydrogen atom **2 :** a polymer of a vinyl compound or product made from one: as **a :** VINYL RESIN **b :** VINYL PLASTIC
vinyl acetal *n* **:** POLYVINYL ACETAL
vinyl acetate *n* **:** a flammable polymerizable liquid ester $CH_3COOCH=CH_2$ with a sharp odor that is prepared by catalytic addition of acetic acid to acetylene and that is used chiefly for the production of vinyl resins and in making other vinyl esters by reaction with other acids — see POLYVINYL ACETATE
vi·nyl·acetylene \¦==+\ *n* [*vinyl* + *acetylene*] **:** a sweet-smelling gaseous or low-boiling liquid unsaturated hydrocarbon $CH_2=CHC\equiv CH$ formed by dimerization of acetylene as an intermediate in making chloroprene and neoprene; 1-buten-3-yne
vinyl alcohol *n* **:** an unstable compound $CH_2=CHOH$ known only in the form of its polymers or derivatives (as vinyl acetate or vinyl chloride) because attempts to prepare it yield its tautomer acetaldehyde — see POLYVINYL ALCOHOL
vi·nyl·ate \'vīnᵊl,āt *sometimes* 'vin-\ *vt* -ED/-ING/-S [back-formation fr. *vinylation*] **:** to subject to vinylation
vi·nyl·a·tion \,==ˈāshən\ *n* -s [*vinyl* + *-ation*] **:** the introduction of the vinyl radical into a compound usu. by catalytic addition of the compound to acetylene 〈~ of alcohols yields vinyl ethers〉
vi·nyl·benzene \¦vīnᵊl+\ *n* [ISV *vinyl* + *benzene*] **:** STYRENE 1a
vinyl butyral *n* **:** POLYVINYL BUTYRAL
vinyl chloride *n* **:** a flammable gaseous compound $CH_2=CHCl$ with an ethereal odor prepared by catalytic addition of hydrogen chloride to acetylene or by pyrolysis of ethylene dichloride and used chiefly for making vinyl resins **:** chloroethylene — see POLYVINYL CHLORIDE
vinyl compound *n* **:** a compound containing the vinyl radical esp. in halides, esters, and ethers; *broadly* **:** any of the class of compounds including styrene and its derivatives and acrylic compounds — compare POLYVINYL
vinyl cyanide *n* **:** ACRYLONITRILE
vi·nyl·ene \'vīnᵊl,ēn *sometimes* 'vin-\ *n* -s [ISV *vinyl* + *-ene*] **:** a bivalent radical $—CH=CH—$ derived from ethylene by removal of one hydrogen atom from each carbon atom
vinyl ether *n* **1 :** a volatile flammable liquid unsaturated ether $(CH_2=CH)_2O$ that is made by removal of hydrogen and chlorine from dichloroethyl ether, that polymerizes on standing unless protected by an antioxidant, and that is used as an inhalation anesthetic for short operative procedures **2 :** an ether in which one of the radicals united to oxygen is vinyl 〈polymers of *vinyl ethers*〉
vinyl formal *n* **:** POLYVINYL FORMAL
vi·nyl·i·dene \vī'nilə,dēn\ *n* -s [ISV *vinyl* + *-idene*] **:** a bivalent radical $CH_2=C<$ derived from ethylene by removal of two hydrogen atoms from one carbon atom
vinylidene chloride *n* **:** a low-boiling flammable liquid compound $CH_2=CCl_2$ prepared usu. from trichloroethane and used in making saran by polymerization; 1,1-dichloro-ethylene — see POLYVINYLIDENE CHLORIDE
vinylidene dinitrile *or* **vinylidene cyanide** *n* **:** a compound $CH_2=C(CN)_2$ made from acetic acid and hydrogen cyanide and used chiefly in making nytril fibers
vinylidene resin *or* **vinylidene plastic** *n* **:** any of a group of tough thermoplastic resins or plastics formed by polymerization or copolymerization of a vinylidene compound (as vinylidene chloride with or without vinyl chloride or acrylonitrile) and used esp. for filaments, films, screens, and molded articles — compare POLYVINYLIDENE CHLORIDE, SARAN, VINYL RESIN
Vi·nyl·ite \'vīnᵊl,īt *sometimes* 'vin-\ *trademark* — used for any of a series of vinyl resins
vi·nyl·og \-,ȯg\ *n* -s [*vinyl* + *-log*] **:** a member of a vinylogous series
vi·nyl·o·gous \vī'niləgəs\ *adj* [*vinylog* + *-ous*] **:** of a related chemical type but differing in having one or more vinylene bridges between functional atoms in an organic molecule 〈acetaldehyde and crotonaldehyde are ~ compounds〉
vinyl plastic *n* **:** any of a group of tough durable plastics based on vinyl resins often compounded with other substances (as plasticizers, pigments, fillers, stabilizers, or lubricants) and used esp. in the form of films and sheeting, coatings, tile and flooring, foams, sound records, and other molded and extruded products
vi·nyl·pyridine \¦vīnᵊl+\ *n* [*vinyl* + *pyridine*] **:** any of three liquid isomeric bases $CH_2=CHC_5H_4N$ synthesized in various ways and used to introduce basic sites in polymer chains by copolymerizing with other vinyl-containing monomers (as acrylonitrile or styrene)
vi·nyl·pyrrolidone \"+\ *n* [*vinyl* + *pyrrolidone*] **:** a liquid compound $CH_2=CHC_4H_6NO$ made by condensation of acetylene and pyrrolidone and used in the manufacture of polyvinylpyrrolidone and in various copolymerizations — called also *N-vinylpyrrolidone*
vinyl resin *n* **1 :** any of a large group of thermoplastic resinous materials containing the recurring group $—CH_2CHX—$ and consisting essentially of polymers or copolymers of vinyl compounds (as vinyl chloride or vinyl acetate) and sometimes including polyvinylidene compounds — compare POLYVINYL ACETAL, POLYVINYL ACETATE, POLYVINYL ALCOHOL, POLYVINYL CHLORIDE **2 :** VINYL PLASTIC
vinyl sulfone *n* **:** a liquid compound $(CH_2=CH)_2SO_2$ some of whose derivatives are used as fiber-reactive dyes
vinyl-type polymerization *n* **:** addition polymerization of vinyl compounds or related unsaturated compounds (as vinylidene chloride)
vin·yon \'vin,yän\ *n* -s [fr. *Vinyon*, a trademark] **1 :** any of various synthetic textile fibers in filament or staple form that are long-chain polymers composed of at least 85 percent by weight of vinyl chloride units $—CH_2CHCl—$ often together with vinyl acetate units, that show good strength wet or dry, but that have a low softening temperature and can be easily molded **2 :** yarn or fabric made from vinyon fiber and used esp. for industrial filter cloth, fishing lines and nets, and clothing
¹viol *obs var of* VIAL
²vi·ol \'vī(ə)l *sometimes* -ī(,)ōl\ *n* -s [MF *viole* viol, viola, fr. OProv *viola, viula* viol, prob. fr. ML *vitula* fiddle — more at FIDDLE] **1 :** a bowed stringed musical instrument chiefly of the 16th and 17th centuries made with a relatively deep body and flat back and sloping shoulders, usu. six strings tuned in fourths, a fretted fingerboard, and a low-arched bridge, made in treble, alto, tenor, and bass sizes, and played in a vertical position resting on or between the knees of the player — see CONTRABASS, TREBLE VIOL, VIOLA DA BRACCIO, VIOLA DA GAMBA **2 :** a labial pipe-organ stop with string tone
³vi·ol \'vī(ə)l\ *n* -s [origin unknown] *archaic* **:** a large rope used esp. in weighing anchor
viol- *comb form* [ISV, fr. NL *Viola*] **:** pansy 〈*viol*aniline〉
viol *abbr* [L *violaceus*] purple
¹vi·o·la \vē'ōlə *sometimes* vī'-\ *n* -s [It & Sp, viol, viola, fr. OProv *viola, viula* viol] **1 :** a musical instrument of the violin family that is intermediate in size and compass between the violin and the violoncello, is tuned a fifth lower than the violin with its open string pitches being c, g, d′, a′, and has a somber tone quality when played on its lower strings but a more strident sound on its A string **2 :** a player of the viola **3 :** a string-toned labial pipe-organ stop of 8-foot or 4-foot pitch
²vi·o·la \vī'ōlə, 'vīələ\ *n* [NL, fr. L, violet — more at VIOLET] **1** *cap* **:** a very large genus of acaulescent or leafy-stemmed herbs or undershrubs (family Violaceae) having alternate stipulate leaves and both conspicuous petaliferous mostly vernal flowers and cleistogamous flowers borne on peduncles or stolons and sometimes concealed underground, the former with purple, yellow, or white petals often marked or variegated and with the corolla irregular and often spurred and the sepals eared at the base and the latter without petals, self-fertilized in the bud, and very fruitful — see PANSY, SWEET VIOLET, VIOLET, WILD PANSY **2** -s **:** any plant of the genus *Viola; esp* **:** any of numerous cultivated and sometimes naturalized hybrids orig. developed by crossing the garden pansy and the tufted pansy and having flowers intermediate in size between the garden pansy and the wild pansy
vi·o·la al·ta \vē,ōlə'altə\ *n, pl* **viola altas** [It, tall viola] **:** a large orchestral viola
viola bas·tar·da \-bä'stärdə\ *n, pl* **viola bastardas** [It, bastard viol] **1 :** a viola da gamba tuned and played according to the lute tablature **2 :** ²LIRA 3
vi·o·la·bil·i·ty \,vīələ'biləd·ē\ *n* **:** the quality or state of being violable
vi·o·la·ble \'vīələbəl\ *adj* [L *violabilis*, fr. *violare* to violate + *-abilis* -able — more at VIOLATE] **:** capable of being or likely to be violated 〈~ national boundaries〉 — **vi·o·la·ble·ness** *n* -ES — **vi·o·la·bly** \-blē, -li\ *adv*
vi·o·la·ce·ae \,vīə'lāsē,ē\ *n pl, cap* [NL, fr. *Viola*, type genus + *-aceae*] **:** a family of herbs, shrubs, and trees (order Hypericales) having pentamerous mostly irregular flowers and a one-celled ovary containing three parietal placentae
vi·o·la·ceous \¦==¦lāshəs\ *adj* [L *violaceus*, fr. *viola* violet + *-aceus* -aceous] **1 :** of the color violet **2** [NL *Violaceae* + E *-ous*] **:** of or relating to the family Violaceae — **vi·o·la·ceous·ly** *adv*
viola clef *n* **:** ALTO CLEF
vi·o·la da brac·cio \vē,ōlədə'brä(,)chō\ *n, pl* **vi·o·le da braccio** \-(,)lād-\ [It, arm viol] **:** a viol having approximately the range of the modern viola
viola da gam·ba \-də'gämbə, -'gam-, -'gȧm-, -'gaam-\ *n, pl* **viole da gamba** [It, leg viol] **1 :** a bass member of the viol family having a range approximating the cello and popular esp. in the 17th century **2 :** a string-toned pipe-organ stop of 8-foot pitch
viola d'a·mo·re \-də'mōrā\ *n, pl* **viole d'amore** [It, viol of love] **1 :** a tenor viol having usu. seven gut strings with seven or more wire strings passing under the fingerboard and sounding sympathetically as the first are played and producing a sweet tone **2 :** a soft string-toned pipe-organ stop of 8-foot or 4-foot pitch
viola da spal·la \-də'spälə\ *n, pl* **viole da spalla** [It, shoulder viol] **:** a cello carried in processions by a shoulder strap
viola di bor·do·ne \-dēbȯr'dōnā\ *n, pl* **viole di bordone** [It, bass viol] **:** a large viola d'amore
vi·o·lan \'vīə,lan\ *or* **vi·o·lane** \-,lān\ *n* -s [G *violan*, fr. L *viola* violet — more at VIOLET] **:** a diopside of a fine blue or violet color
vi·o·lan·in \,vīə'lanən\ *n* -s [ISV *viol-* + anthocy*anin*] **:** an anthocyanin that is obtained from the pansy as the bluish violet crystalline chloride $C_{36}H_{37}O_{18}Cl$ and yields on hydrolysis delphinidin, *para*-hydroxy-cinnamic acid, and glucosyl-rhamnose
vi·o·lan·throne \,vīə'lan,thrōn\ *n* [ISV *viol-* + *anthrone*] **:** a vat dye — see DYE table I (under *Vat Blue 20*)
viola pom·po·sa \vē,ōləpäm'pōsə\ *n, pl* **viole pompo·se** \-(,)läpäm'pō(,)sā\ [It, pompous viol] **1 :** an obsolete large viola with five strings **2 :** a string-toned pipe-organ stop usu. of 8-foot pitch
vi·o·la·rite \vī'ōlə,rīt\ *n* -s [L *violar*is of violet (fr. *viola* violet + *-aris* -ar) + E *-ite*; fr. its color] **:** a mineral Ni_2FeS_4 consisting of a sulfide of nickel and iron that is isomorphous with linnaeite, siegenite, carrollite, and polydymite
violas *pl of* VIOLA
¹vi·o·late \'vīə,lāt, *usu* -ād·+V\ *vt* -ED/-ING/-S [ME *violaten*, fr. L *violatus*, past part. of *violare* to treat with violence, injure, violate; akin to L *vis* strength — more at VIM] **1 :** to fail to keep **:** BREAK, DISREGARD 〈~ the law〉 **2 :** to do harm to the person or esp. the chastity of; *specif* **:** to commit rape on 〈~ a woman〉 **3 a :** to fail to show the requisite respect for **:** treat or handle in a disrespectful or high-handed manner **:** PROFANE, DESECRATE 〈~ a shrine〉 〈~ personal liberty〉 **b** *obs* **:** to damage or destroy esp. by violence **4 :** to interfere with by interruption or disturbance 〈~ an individual's privacy〉
²violate \"\ *adj* [L *violatus*, past part. of *violare*] *archaic* **:** VIOLATED — **vi·o·late·ly** *adv, archaic*
vi·o·lat·er \-ād·ə(r), -ātə-\ *n* -s [¹*violate* + *-er*] **:** VIOLATOR
vi·o·la·tion \,vīə'lāshən\ *n* -s [ME *violacion*, fr. L *violation-, violatio*, fr. *violatus* (past part.) + *-ion-, -io* -ion] **:** the act or action of violating or the quality or state of being violated: as **a :** an infringement or transgression 〈a ~ of law〉 〈~ of promises〉; *specif* **:** an infringement of the rules in sports that is less serious than a foul and that usu. involves technicalities of play (as a rules infraction in basketball for which the ball is awarded to the opponents out of bounds) **b :** an act of irreverence **:** DESECRATION, PROFANATION 〈~ of a church〉 **c :** INTERRUPTION, DISTURBANCE 〈~ of civil order〉 〈~ of the peace〉 **d :** RAVISHMENT, RAPE 〈the ~ of civilian population〉 **syn** *see* BREACH
vi·o·la·tion·al \¦==¦lāshənᵊl, -shnəl\ *adj* **:** of or relating to violation
vi·o·la·tive \'vīə,lād·iv, -lət-, |t|, |ēv *also* |əv\ *adj* **:** violating or tending to violate 〈~ gestures〉 〈~ of the principles of liberty〉
vi·o·la·tor \'vīə,lād·ə(r), -ātə-\ *n* -s [ME, ravisher, fr. L, violator, fr. *violatus* (past part. of *violare* to violate) + *-or*] **:** one that commits a violation
vi·o·la·xanthin \vī¦ōlə, ¦vīələ+\ *n* [NL *Viola* + E *xanthin*] **:** an orange to red crystalline carotenoid pigment $C_{40}H_{56}O_4$ obtained from yellow pansies and many other plants **:** zeaxanthin di-epoxide
vi·ole d'orchestre \vē'ōldō(r)'kestr(ᵊ), -t(rə)\ *n, pl* **violes d'orchestre** [F, orchestra viol] **:** an imitative string-toned pipe-organ stop of small scale and incisive quality
vi·o·lence \'vīələn(t)s *sometimes* 'vīl-\ *n* -s [ME, fr. OF, fr. L *violentia*, fr. *violentus* violent + *-ia* -y] **1 a :** exertion of any physical force so as to injure or abuse (as in warfare or in effecting an entrance into a house) **b :** an instance of violent treatment or procedure **2 :** injury in the form of revoking, repudiation, distortion, infringement, or irreverence to a thing, notion, or quality fitly valued or observed 〈no ~ has been done to expert military opinion —Sir Winston Churchill〉 〈did unconscious ~ to the instincts of the mystic —V.L.Parrington〉 **3 a :** intense, turbulent, or furious action, force, or feeling often destructive 〈the ~ of a volcanic eruption —R.W. Livingstone〉 〈hurled himself around the corner . . . with almost drunken ~ —Liam O'Flaherty〉 **b :** vehement feeling or expression **:** FERVOR, PASSION, FURY 〈the ~ of a fluent orator whose temper ran away with him —V.A.Froude〉 〈~ such as the normally placid New York art critics seldom resort to —R. M.Coates〉 **c :** an instance or show of such action or feeling **:** a tendency to violent action 〈the mounting ~s of the Whig rabble against their Tory neighbors —Margaret Evans〉 **d :** clashing, jarring, discordant, or abrupt quality 〈certain freaks and ~s in Mr. Palgrave's criticism —Matthew Arnold〉 〈the ~ of the contrasting colors〉 **4 :** undue alteration of wording or sense (as in editing or interpreting a text) **syn** *see* FORCE
¹vi·o·lent \-nt\ *adj* [ME, fr. MF, fr. L *violentus*; akin to L *violare* to violate — more at VIOLATE] **1 :** characterized by extreme force 〈a ~ storm〉 **:** marked by abnormally sudden physical activity and intensity 〈a ~ attack〉 **2 :** furious or vehement to the point of being improper, unjust, or illegal 〈lay ~ hands on an individual〉 〈a ~ denunciation〉 **3 :** extremely or intensely vivid or loud 〈~ colors〉 〈~ noise〉 **:** unusually intense 〈~ pain〉 **:** unnaturally strong 〈~ passion〉 **4 :** produced or effected by force **:** UNNATURAL 〈a ~ death〉 〈come to a ~ end〉 **5 :** tending to distort or misrepresent 〈a ~ interpretation〉 **6 :** extremely excited **:** emotionally aroused 〈become ~ after an insult〉 — **vi·o·lent·ly** *adv*
²violent *vi, obs* **:** to be violent or act violently **~** *vt, obs* **:** to constrain by or as if by violence
vi·o·lent·ness *n* -ES **:** the quality or state of being violent
violent profits *n pl* **:** rents or profits of an estate in Scots law obtained by a tenant wrongfully holding over after warning and recoverable in a process of removing at double the actual rate for urban land and at the highest possible yield for rural land
vi·o·les·cent \¦vīə¦lesᵊnt\ *adj* [L *viola* violet + E *-escent*] **:** tending to a violet color
vi·ole sor·dine \vē'ōlsȯr'dēn\ *n, pl* **viole sordines** [prob. modif. of F *viole sourdine* muted viol] **:** a soft string-toned pipe-organ stop imitating a muted violin
¹vi·o·let \'vīələt *sometimes* 'vīl-; *usu* -əd·+V\ *n* -s [ME, fr. MF *violete*, dim. of *viole* violet, fr. L *viola*, of non-IE origin; akin to the source of Gk *ion* violet] **1 a :** a plant of the genus *Viola; esp* **:** one of the small-flowered forms as distinguished from the typically larger-flowered violas and pansies **b :** any of several plants (as a dogtooth violet) of genera other than *Viola* **2 a :** any of a group of colors that resemble those of violets (sense 1) and are of reddish blue hue, low lightness, and medium saturation **b :** a reddish blue hue that is evoked in the normal observer under normal conditions by radiant energy of wavelength 420 millimicrons **3 :** cloth or clothing of the color violet **4 :** a pigment or dye that imparts a violet color **5 :** any of numerous small violet-colored butterflies of the family Lycaenidae **6 :** an overly fastidious, modest, or retiring person 〈a shrinking ~〉 〈a blushing ~〉
²violet \"\ *vt* **violetted; violetted; violetting; violets :** to make violet-hued
³vi·o·let \'vīə,let\ *n* -s [It *violetta* — more at VIOLETTE] **:** ¹VIOLETTE; *specif* **:** VIOLA D'AMORE
violet aphid *n* **:** a plant louse (*Neotoxoptera violae*) that feeds on violets
violet-bloom \'(=)=,=\ *n* **:** BITTERSWEET 2a
violet carmine *n* **:** a dark reddish purple that is bluer and deeper than royal purple (sense 1), redder, stronger, and slightly lighter than average plum (sense 6a), and redder and less strong than imperial (sense 10)
violet-ear \'=(=)=,=\ *n* **:** a tropical hummingbird of the genus *Colibri* having violet or bluish purple ear tufts
violet family *n* **:** VIOLACEAE
violet-green swallow *n* **:** a common swallow (*Tachycineta thalassina lepida*) of western No. America that is violet green above and that has white ear coverts, rump patches, and lower side
violet iris *n* **:** a dwarf iris (*Iris verna*) of eastern No. America with purplish blue flowers
vi·o·let·ish \'vīələd·ish\ *adj* **:** somewhat of the color violet
violet midge *n* **:** a cecidomyiid fly (*Contarinia violicola*) the larva of which feeds on violets in the eastern U.S.
violet parme *n, often cap P* **:** PARMA VIOLET 2a
violet ray *n* **1 :** an ultraviolet ray — not used technically **2 :** a high-frequency electric discharge from the outer surface of a one-electrode vacuum tube having violet-colored fluorescence and often used in therapeutic treatments
violet root rot *n* **:** a root rot (as of alfalfa, asparagus, and potato) caused by an imperfect fungus (*Rhizoctonia crocorum*) and characterized by a purplish growth of mycelium on the basal parts of the shoot and roots
violet scab *n* **:** a disease of violets and esp. of the sweet violet caused by a fungus (*Sphaceloma violae*) and characterized by brownish warty outgrowths on the leaves which become brittle and crack very easily when handled
violet shift *n* **:** the Doppler effect of recession **:** a shift of the spectrum toward shorter wavelengths
violet snail *or* **violet shell** *n* **:** a mollusk of the genus *Janthina*
¹vi·o·lette \¦vīə¦let\ *n* -s [It *violetta*, fr. *viola* viol, viola + *-etta* -ette (fr. F *-ette*)] **:** a small viol
²violette \"\ *n* -s [F, violet, violette, fr. MF *violete* — more at VIOLET] **:** a carved ornament resembling or suggesting a violet
violet tip *n* **:** an American butterfly (*Polygonia interrogationis*) the wings of which are mottled with various shades of red and brown and have violet tips
violet wood *n* **1 :** any of several hard purplish or reddish woods; *esp* **:** KINGWOOD **2 :** a tree that yields violet wood **3 :** PURPLEHEART
violet wood sorrel *n* **:** a perennial herb (*Oxalis violacea*) of the eastern U. S. with palmately compound usu. sensitive leaves and rose-purple or rarely white flowers
vi·o·lety \'vīələd·ē\ *adj* **:** resembling or suggesting a violet color or violets 〈a ~ odor〉 〈a ~ color〉 〈a ~ sky〉
¹vi·o·lin \,vīə'lin *sometimes* 'vīə,lin *or* -ələn\ *n* -s [It *violino*, dim. of *viola* viol, viola, fr. OProv *viola, viula* viol — more at VIOL] **1 a :** a bowed stringed musical instrument having four strings tuned at intervals of a fifth and a range from G below middle C to the fourth C above or higher which is distinguished from the viol in having a shallower body, shoulders at right angles with the neck, and a more curved bridge and is capable of a richer, more powerful, and more varied tone **b :** an 8-foot labial pipe-organ stop having a tone like a violin **2 :** a violin player 〈first ~ of an orchestra〉
²violin \"\ *vi* -ED/-ING/-S **:** to play the violin
vi·o·li·na \,vēə'lēnə\ *n* -s [alter. of ¹*violin*] **:** a string-toned pipe-organ stop of 4-foot pitch
violin clef *n* **:** G CLEF
violin diapason *n* **:** a metal labial pipe-organ stop of 8-foot pitch with a combination of diapason and string-toned quality

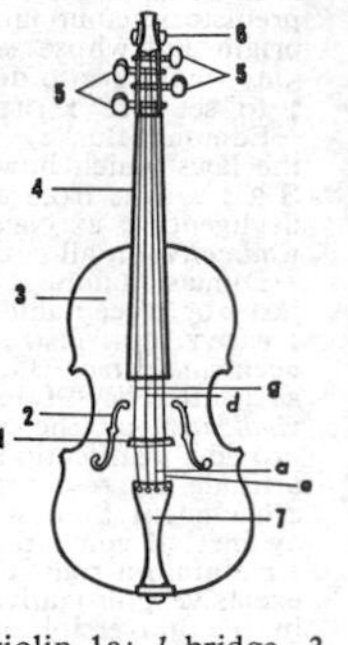

violin 1a: *1* bridge, *2* sound hole, *3* soundboard, *4* fingerboard, *5* pegs, *6* scroll, *7* string holder, *g* G string, *d* D string, *a* A string, *e* E string

vi·o·line \'vīə,lēn, -ələn\ *n* -s [F, fr. NL *Viola* + F *-ine*] **:** a moderate to strong violet
violine pink *n* **:** a moderate purplish red that is bluer and deeper than average rose, bluer and paler than magenta rose or average fuchsia rose, deeper than mallow, and bluer, lighter, and stronger than solferino
vi·o·lin·ette \¦vīələ¦net\ *n* -s [¹*violin* + *-ette*] **:** VIOLINO PICCOLO
vi·o·lin·ist \,vīə'linəst *sometimes* 'vīə,lin- *or* -ələn-\ *n* -s [It *violinista*, fr. *violino* violin + *-ista* -ist] **:** one who plays the violin
vi·o·lin·is·tic \¦vīələ¦nistik\ *adj* **:** relating to the violin and violin playing; *specif* **:** particularly suited to playing on the violin — **vi·o·lin·is·ti·cal·ly** \-tək(ə)lē\ *adv*
vi·o·li·no \,vēə'lē(,)nō\ *n* -s [It] **:** VIOLIN
violino pic·co·lo \-'pēkə,lō\ *n, pl* **violino piccolos** [It, little violin] **:** a small violin made with the same proportions as the ordinary violin and usu. tuned a third higher
¹vi·ol·ist \'vīələst\ *n* -s [²*viol* + *-ist*] **:** one who plays the viol
²vi·o·list \vē'ōləst *sometimes* vī'-\ *n* -s [¹*viola* + *-ist*] **:** one who plays the viola
violle standard \'vyȯl-\ *or* **violle** *n* -s *usu cap V* [after Jules *Violle* †1923 Fr. physicist] **:** a photometric unit that is the luminous intensity of a square centimeter of platinum at the temperature of solidification and equals about 20 candles
vi·o·lon \'vīələn, 'vēəl-, -,län\ *n* -s [MF, aug. of *viole* viol, viola — more at VIOL] **:** VIOLIN
vi·o·lon·cel·list \,vīələn'cheləst, ,vēəl-, -,län-\ *n* **:** CELLIST
vi·o·lon·cel·lo \-e(,)lō\ *n* [It, dim. of *violone*] **1 :** a bass violin that is the modern form of the viola da gamba with four strings tuned an octave lower than the viola and with a pitch compass of C to e″, that is held vertically on the floor between the player's knees while in a sitting position, and that when played produces a sonorous and expressive quality **2 :** a labial pipe-organ stop of similar quality
violoncello pic·co·lo \-'pēkə,lō\ *n* [It, little violoncello] **:** a small violoncello having the same shape and tuning
vi·o·lo·ne \,vēə'lōnā\ *n* -s [It, aug. of *viola* viol, viola — more at VIOLIN] **1 :** a viol of contrabass size and range **2 :** CONTRE BASSE
vi·o·lot·ta \,vēə'läd·ə\ *n* -s [It *viola* + *-otta* (aug. suffix)] **:** a violin having a range extending to a fourth below the range of the viola
viols *pl of* VIOL
vi·o·lu·ric acid \¦vīə¦lurik-\ *n* [ISV *viol*et + barbit*uric*] **:** a crystalline monobasic acid $HON(CONH)_2CO$ that is made from nitrous acid and barbituric acid or from hydroxylamine and alloxan, that tautomerizes in water from the isonitroso

form to the violet nitroso form, and that forms characteristic colored salts; 5-isonitroso-barbituric acid

vi·o·my·cin \ˌvīə'mīsᵊn\ *n* -s [*violet* + *-mycin;* fr. the color of the soil mold] **:** a basic polypeptide antibiotic produced by a soil actinomycete (as *Streptomyces puniceus*) and administered intramuscularly in the form of its sulfate in the treatment of tuberculosis esp. in combination with other drugs

vi·or·na \vī'ȯrnə\ *n, cap* [NL, fr. F *viorne* clematis, fr. L *viburnum* wayfaring tree] *in some classifications* **:** a genus of chiefly No. American vines or erect herbs (family Ranunculaceae) that have mostly solitary flowers with erect sepals and stamens and are usu. included in the genus *Clematis*

vi·os·ter·ol \vī'ästəˌrōl, -rōl\ *n* -s [ultra*violet* + *sterol*] **:** vitamin D_2 esp. when dissolved in an edible vegetable oil for use chiefly in infant nutrition

VIP \ˌvēˌī'pē\ *n* -s [*very important person*] **:** a person of considerable influence or prestige; *esp* **:** a high official receiving special privileges

vi·per \'vīpə(r)\ *n* -s [MF *vipere,* fr. L *vipera* adder, snake, perh. fr. *vivi-* + *-pera* (fr. *parere* to give birth to, produce); fr. an old belief that it is viviparous — more at PARE] **1 a :** a common European venomous snake (*Vipera berus*) that attains a length of two feet, varies in color from red, brown, or gray with dark markings to black, occurs across Eurasia from England to Sakhalin, and that is rarely fatal to man; *broadly* **:** any snake of the venomous Old World family Viperidae and sometimes of the closely related Crotalidae **b :** a venomous or reputedly venomous snake **2 :** a dangerous, malignant, or treacherous person ⟨they forgot that this helpless, shapeless mass of humanity . . . was a ~ they must crush —Liam O'Flaherty⟩

vi·pera \'vīpərə\ *n, cap* [NL, fr. L, viper] **:** a genus of Old World snakes that is the type of the family Viperidae

vi·per·an \'vīpərən\ *adj* [*viper* + *-an*] **:** VIPERINE

viperfish \'⸗⸗,⸗\ *n* **:** a fish of the family Gonostomatidae or of the related family Chauliodontidae

vi·pe·ri·an \(')vī'pirēən\ *adj* [*viper* + *-ian*] **:** VIPERINE

¹vi·per·id \'vīpərəd\ *adj* [NL *Viperidae*] **:** of or relating to the Viperidae

²viperid \"\ *n* -s **:** a snake of the family Viperidae

vi·per·i·dae \vī'perəˌdē\ *n pl, cap* [NL, fr. *Vipera,* type genus + *-idae*] **:** a widely distributed family comprising sluggish heavy-bodied Old World venomous snakes that are characterized by large tubular venom-conducting fangs erected by rotation of the movable premaxillary bone — see VIPER; compare CROTALIDAE

vi·per·i·form \'vīpərəˌfȯrm\ *adj* [*viper* + *-iform*] **:** resembling a viper

vi·per·ine \'vīpərən, -əˌrīn\ *adj* [L *viperinus,* fr. *vipera* viper + *-inus* -ine] **:** of, relating to, or resembling a viper **:** VENOMOUS

viperine snake *n* **1** *also* **viperine :** a snake of the family Viperidae **2 :** a small harmless snake (*Natrix viperinus*) colored much like the viper and found in southern Europe and northern Africa

vi·per·ish \'vīpərish\ *adj* [*viper* + *-ish*] **:** spitefully vituperative **:** VENOMOUS ⟨a fierce ~ tongue on occasion —Peggy Bennett⟩ — **vi·per·ish·ly** *adv*

viperlike \'⸗⸗,⸗\ *adj* [*viper* + *like*] **:** behaving like a viper

vi·per·ling \-ə(r)liŋ\ *n* -s [*viper* + *-ling*] **:** a young viper

vi·per·ous \'vīp(ə)rəs\ *adj* [*viper* + *-ous*] **1 :** of, relating to, or composed of vipers **2 a :** characteristic of a viper **:** deliberately treacherous **:** MALIGNANT, VENOMOUS ⟨~ treachery⟩ **b :** possessing qualities attributed to a viper ⟨a ~ murderer⟩

vi·per·ous·ly *adv* **:** in a viperous manner

viper's bugloss *n* **:** BLUEWEED 1

viper's-grass \'⸗⸗,⸗\ *n, pl* **viper's-grasses :** a perennial herb (*Scorzonera hispanica*) with narrow entire leaves, solitary heads of yellow flowers, and long white carrot-shaped roots that are eaten in Spain and elsewhere

viper wine *n* **:** a medicated wine containing a decoction from vipers formerly believed to restore vital powers

vip·i·on·i·dae \ˌvipē'änəˌdē\ *n pl, cap* [NL, fr. *Vipion-, Vipio,* type genus (fr. L, a small crane) + *-idae;* fr. their long legs] **:** a family of small ichneumon flies that is often included in Braconidae and includes forms which as larvae are parasites of various lepidopterous, hymenopterous, coleopterous, and dipterous insects

VIPs *pl of* VIP

vir *abbr* [L *viridis*] green

vi·rag·i·nous \və'rajənəs\ *adj* [L *viragin-, virago* virago + E *-ous*] **:** of, relating to, or characteristic of a virago

vi·ra·go \və'rä(ˌ)gō, -rā(-, -rä(- *also* 'virəˌgō\ *n, pl* **viragoes** *or* **viragos** [L *viragin-, virago* manlike heroic woman, fr. *vir* man, male — more at VIRILE] **1 :** a loud overbearing woman **:** SHREW, TERMAGANT **2 :** a woman of great stature, strength, and courage **:** one possessing supposedly masculine qualities of body and mind

vi·ral \'vīrəl\ *adj* [NL *virus* + ISV *-al*] **:** of or belonging to a virus **:** caused by a virus **:** concerned with or involving viruses — **vi·ral·ly** \-rəlē\ *adv*

vi·ra·les \vī'rä(ˌ)lēz\ *n pl, cap* [NL, fr. *virus* + *-ales*] **:** an order of parasitic plants consisting of the viruses and comprising three suborders — see PHAGINEAE, PHYTOPHAGINEAE, ZOOPHAGINEAE

viral hepatitis *n* **1 :** INFECTIOUS HEPATITIS **2 :** SERUM HEPATITIS

vi·ra·ma \və'rämə\ *n* -s [Skt *virāma,* lit., cessation, stop, fr. *viramati* he ceases, pauses, fr. *vi-* apart, asunder + *ramate* he stands still, rests — more at WITH, RIM] **:** a mark added to a consonant sign in Devanagari and related alphabets to indicate that the consonant sign stands only for a consonant and not for a combination of consonant plus following vowel

vir·e·lay *also* **vir·e·lai** \'virəˌlā\ *n* -s [ME, fr. MF *virelai,* alter. (influenced by *lai* lay) of OF *vireli,* prob. fr. the meaningless refrain *vireli*] **1 a :** an old French verse form having a refrain and composed wholly in two rhymes **b :** a verse form composed of stanzas indeterminate in length and number but usu. repeating one of the two rhymes of the first stanza in the second, the new rhyme of the second stanza in the third, until the last stanza where the unrepeated rhyme of the first stanza takes the place of a new rhyme — compare VILLANELLE **2 :** an old song or poem esp. with a refrain or an intricate or monotonous rhyme scheme

vire·ment \'virmäⁿ\ *n* -s [F, fr. MF, act of turning, fr. *virer* to turn + *-ment* — more at ENVIRON] **:** an administrative transfer of budgetary funds

vi·re·mia *also* **vi·rae·mia** \vī'rēmēə\ *n* -s [NL, fr. *virus* + *-emia*] **:** the presence of a virus in the blood of a host — **vi·re·mic** \(')vīˌrēmik\ *adj*

vi·rent \'vīrənt\ *adj* [L, fr. *virent-, virens* pres. part. of *virēre* to be green] **1 :** not withered **:** FRESH **2 :** green in color

vir·eo \'virēˌō\ *n* [L *vireon-, vireo,* a small bird, perh. the greenfinch, fr. *virēre* to be green] **1** -s **:** any of various small birds of the family Vireonidae — see RED-EYED VIREO, SOLITARY VIREO **2** *cap* [NL, fr. L] **:** a genus of vireos that is the type of the family Vireonidae

vir·e·on·i·dae \ˌvirē'änəˌdē\ *n pl, cap* [NL, fr. *Vireon-, Vireo,* type genus + *-idae*] **:** a family of small insectivorous American passerine birds that are plainly but delicately colored chiefly in olivaceous and grayish shades, that are sweet singers, and that usu. build pensile nests

¹vir·e·o·nine \'virēəˌnīn, -ˌnən\ *adj* [L *vireon-, vireo* vireo + E *-ine*] **:** of or relating to the vireos

²vireonine \"\ *n* -s **:** VIREO 1

vires *pl of* VIS

vi·res·cence \və'resᵊn(t)s, vī'-\ *n* -s [fr. *virescent,* after such pairs as E *intelligent: intelligence*] **:** the state or condition of becoming green: as **a :** such a condition due to the development of chloroplasts in organs (as petals) normally white or colored **b** *Austral* **:** BIG BUD

vi·res·cent \-nt\ *adj* [L *virescent-, virescens,* pres. part. of *virescere* to become green, incho. of *virēre* to be green] **:** beginning to be green **:** slightly green **:** developing or displaying virescence **:** GREENISH

virescent gold *n, often cap V&G* **:** an organic pigment — see DYE table I (under *Pigment Green 10*)

virg *abbr* [L *virgo*] virgin

vir·ga \'vərgə\ *n* -s [NL, fr. L, branch, rod, streak in the sky suggesting rain] **:** trailing wisps of precipitation falling from the base of a cloud but evaporating before reaching the ground

¹vir·gate \'vər|gət, 'vəl, 'vəil, |ˌgāt, *usu* -d·+V\ *n* -s [ML *virgata,* fr. *virga,* a land measure, fr. L, rod] **:** any of various old English units of land area equal to one quarter of a hide or one quarter of an acre

²virgate \"\ *adj* [NL *virgatus,* fr. L, made of twigs, striped, fr. *virga* branch, twig, rod, streak + *-atus* -ate — more at WHISK] **1 a :** having the form of a rod **:** shaped like a wand **b :** bearing many small twigs **2 :** slender and slightly toothed — used of the trophi of various rotifers

³vir·gate \ˌgāt\ *vi* -ED/-ING/-S [back-formation fr. *virgation*] **:** to branch in diverging lines

vir·gat·er \'vərˌgād·ər\ *n* -s [¹*virgate* + *-er*] **:** a holder of a virgate

vir·ga·tion \ˌvər'gāshən\ *n* -s [L *virga* branch + E *-ation*] **:** a branching arrangement of fault lines

vir·gil·ia \(ˌ)vər'jilēə, və'-, vā'-, vəi'-\ *n* [NL, fr. LL *Virgilius* (alter. of *Vergilius* — Publius Vergilius Maro †19 B.C. Roman poet) + NL *-ia*] **1** *cap* **:** a genus of southern African trees (family Leguminosae) having pinnate leaves and rose-purple flowers succeeded by a coriaceous 2-valved pod **2** -s **:** any of several trees related to or formerly included in the genus *Virgilia:* as **a :** YELLOWWOOD 1a **b :** KENTUCKY COFFEE TREE

¹virgilian *usu cap, var of* VERGILIAN

²vir·gil·i·an \(ˌ)vər'jilēən, və'-, vā'-, vəi'-\ *adj, usu cap* [*Virgil,* town of southeastern Kansas + E *-ian*] **:** of, relating to, or constituting a subdivision of the Pennsylvanian — see GEOLOGIC TIME table

¹vir·gin \'vərjən, 'vāj-, 'vəij-\ *n* -s [ME, fr. OF *virgine,* fr. L *virgin-, virgo* young woman, maiden, virgin, perh. fr. *virga* green branch, twig — more at WHISK] **1 a :** an unmarried or chaste woman noted in the early Christian Church for her piety and steadfast service to her faith and accorded by virtue of these qualities a special place among the members of the Christian community **b :** an unmarried woman devoted to a deity in a celibate life of service within a religious temple ⟨the Inca ~*s* of the Sun⟩ **2 a :** a usu. young woman noted for purity and chastity **b :** a young unmarried woman **3 :** a person who has not had sexual intercourse **4** *usu cap* **:** VIRGO **5 :** a picture of a madonna **6 :** a female animal that has never copulated

²virgin \"\ *adj* [ME, fr. ¹*virgin*] **1 :** free of impurity or stain **:** not defiled **:** UNSULLIED ⟨all their branches laden with soft . . . ~ snow —Willa Cather⟩ **2 :** being a virgin **:** CHASTE **3 :** made up of virgins ⟨watched his graceful maid as mid the ~ train she strayed —R.W.Emerson⟩ **4 :** of, relating to, characteristic of, or befitting a virgin **:** indicating modesty **:** MODEST ⟨was permitted no greater magnificence than a Greek robe of ~ white —Elinor Wylie⟩ **5 a :** not yet disturbed or made use of **:** FRESH, NEW, UNSPOILED, UNTAPPED ⟨a ~ wilderness of jagged mountains, deep ravines, and swift watercourses —*Amer. Guide Series: Oregon*⟩ **:** not altered by human activity **:** free from artificial alteration ⟨a ~ forest⟩ ⟨~ unplowed turf⟩ **b :** not previously treated or handled **:** not reclaimed or reworked: as (1) **:** of or relating to chemical wood pulp that has not previously been used (2) **:** never treated with dyes or bleaches ⟨~ hair⟩ **6 a** (1) **:** being made use of for the first time ⟨observed that the candles were not ~: both had been burned —Elizabeth Bowen⟩ (2) **:** processed or worked for the first time — see VIRGIN WOOL **b :** INITIAL, FIRST ⟨liked the idea of guicing my ~ steps on the hard road of letters —W.S. Maugham⟩ **7 a** *of a chemical element* **:** occurring naturally uncombined **:** NATIVE ⟨~ sulfur⟩ **b** *of a vegetable oil* **:** obtained from the first light pressing esp. of olives or walnuts in the cold **8 :** produced directly from ore or by primary smelting — used of metal to distinguish it from scrap or from metal obtained by remelting used material **9 :** never captured **:** UNSUBDUED — usu. used of a fortress **10 :** as yet without contact ⟨the second team, ~ to harness —Owen Wister⟩ ⟨absolutely ~ towards such experience —Walter Pater⟩ **syn** see YOUTHFUL

¹vir·gin·al \-nᵊl\ *adj* [ME, fr. MF or L; MF *virginal,* fr. L *virginalis,* fr. *virgin-, virgo* virgin + *-alis* -al] **1 :** of, relating to, or characteristic of a virgin or virginity **2 :** continuing in or maintaining a state of chastity **:** possessing the purity attributed to a virgin **3 :** essentially pure **:** PRISTINE, UNSULLIED, UNTOUCHED ⟨nor is there anything more ~ than the shimmer of young foliage —L.P.Smith⟩ **syn** see YOUTHFUL

²virginal \"\ *n* -s [prob. fr. L *virginalis* of or relating to a virgin; perh. fr. its being played by young girls] **:** a small rectangular spinet having no legs and having only one wire to a note, popular in the 16th and 17th centuries — often used in pl. ⟨plays upon the ~*s*⟩ ⟨a pair of ~*s*⟩

³virginal \"\ *vi, obs* **:** to tap with the fingers as if on a virginal

⁴virginal \"\ *n* -s *usu cap* [ML, fr. L *virginale,* neut. of *virginalis* of a virgin] **:** a book of the offices of the Virgin Mary

vir·gin·al·ist \-ᵊləst\ *n* -s [²*virginal* + *-ist*] **:** one who plays a virginal

vir·gin·al·ly \-ᵊlē\ *adv* [¹*virginal* + *-ly*] **:** in a virginal manner

virginal membrane *n* **:** HYMEN

virgin birth *n* **1 :** birth from a virgin **2** *sometimes cap V&B* **:** the theological doctrine that Jesus was miraculously begotten of God and born of a virgin mother — compare IMMACULATE CONCEPTION

virgin-born \'⸗⸗,⸗\ *adj* **:** PARTHENOGENETIC

virgin bower *n* **:** VIRGIN'S BOWER

virgin cork *n* **:** cork that is taken from young cork oaks and consists of epidermis, cortical tissue, and periderm

virgin dip *n* **:** the resin obtained during the first year a tree is tapped for turpentine

virgin forest *n* **:** OLD GROWTH 1

virgin honey *n* **:** honey that flows freely from the uncapped comb at ordinary temperature and is produced usu. by a young colony

¹vir·gin·ia \və(r)'jinyə, -nēə\ *adj, usu cap* [fr. *Virginia,* eastern state of the U.S., fr. L *virgin-, virgo* virgin; fr. Queen Elizabeth I's familiar appellation "the Virgin Queen"] **:** of or from the state of Virginia ⟨a *Virginia* plantation⟩ **:** of the kind or style prevalent in Virginia **:** VIRGINIAN

²virginia \"\ *n* -s *usu cap* **:** VIRGINIA TOBACCO

virginia cedar *n, usu cap V* **:** RED CEDAR 1a

virginia cowslip *or* **virginia bluebell** *n, usu cap V* **:** a smooth erect herb (*Mertensia virginica*) of eastern No. America having entire leaves and showy blue flowers that are pink in bud

virginia creeper *n, usu cap V* **:** a common No. American tendril-climbing vine (*Parthenocissus quinquefolia*) having palmately 5-foliolate or 7-foliolate leaves and bluish black berries — called also *American ivy, woodbine*

virginia creeper leafhopper *n, usu cap V* **:** a jassid bug (*Erythroneura ziczac*) that is highly destructive to Virginia creeper in parts of the U.S.

virginia crownbeard *n, usu cap V* **:** a tall perennial herb (*Verbesina virginica*) of the eastern U.S. with alternate leaves and paniculate heads of white flowers

virginia deer *n, usu cap V* **:** WHITE-TAILED DEER — used esp. of forms found in the eastern U.S.

virginia dogwood *n, usu cap V* **:** FLOWERING DOGWOOD

virginia false gromwell *n, usu cap V* **:** a false gromwell (*Onosmodium virginianum*)

virginia fence *or* **virginia rail fence** *n, usu cap V* **:** WORM FENCE

virginia goatsbeard *n, usu cap V* **:** a small pale green herb (*Cynthia virginica*) of the family Compositae with yellow flower heads

virginia goat's rue *n, usu cap V* **:** CATGUT 3a

virginia grape fern *n, usu cap V* **:** a rattlesnake fern (*Botrychium virginianum*)

virginia ham *n, usu cap V* **:** a flat lean hickory-smoked ham with dark red meat esp. from a peanut-fed hog

virginia knotweed *n, usu cap V* **:** an erect herb (*Polygonum virginiana*) of the family Polygonaceae of eastern No. America with ovate pointed leaves and spikes of small greenish or rose-colored flowers

virginia mallow *n, usu cap V* **:** a perennial herb (*Sida hermaphrodita*) that is native to the southeastern U.S. and has white flowers and leaves like those of the maple

¹vir·gin·ian \və(r)'jinyən, -inēən\ *n* -s *cap* [*Virginia,* eastern state of the U.S. + E *-an*] **:** a native or resident of the state of Virginia

²virginian \"\ *adj, usu cap* [*Virginia,* state of U.S. + E *-an*] **:** of, relating to, or characteristic of Virginia or Virginians

virginian creeper *n, usu cap V* **:** VIRGINIA CREEPER

virginia nightingale *n, usu cap V* **:** CARDINAL 5

virginian stock *n, usu cap V* **:** an erect branching annual cruciferous herb (*Malcolmia maritima*) sometimes cultivated for its loose racemes of white, pink, red, or lilac flowers

virginia opossum *n, usu cap V* **:** the common opossum (*Didelphis virginiana*) of No. America

virginia oyster *n, usu cap V* **:** the common edible oyster of the Atlantic coast of No. America

virginia pine *n, usu cap V* **1 :** LONGLEAF PINE **2 :** LOBLOLLY PINE 1 **3 :** a scrub pine (*Pinus virginiana*)

virginia poke *n, usu cap V* **1 :** a pokeweed (*Phytolacca americana*) **2 :** AMERICAN HELLEBORE 1

virginia quail *n, usu cap V* **:** BOBWHITE

virginia rail *n, usu cap V* **:** an American long-billed rail (*Rallus limicola*) resembling the king rail in color but scarcely larger than the sora

virginia reel *n, usu cap V* **:** an American longways danced usu. by from four to eight couples in which the head and foot couples perform a series of figures and all in turn participate in swinging with the head couple who then go to the foot permitting the dance to continue until each couple has taken part in the figures; *also* **:** the music for the dance

virginia sarsaparilla *n, usu cap V* **:** WILD SARSAPARILLA 1

virginia silk *n, usu cap V* **:** a common milkweed (*Asclepias syriaca*) of eastern No. America

virginia snakeroot *also* **virginia serpentaria** *or* **virginia serpentary** *n, usu cap V* **:** a birthwort (*Aristolochia serpentaria*) of the eastern U.S. with oblong leaves cordate at the base and a solitary basal very irregular flower

virginia stickseed *or* **virginia mouse-ear** *n, usu cap V* **:** a biennial No. American herb (*Lappula virginiana*) with broad oval leaves and prickly-barbed fruit

virginia stock *n, usu cap V* **:** VIRGINIAN STOCK

virginia strawberry *n, usu cap V* **:** a No. American herb (*Fragaria virginiana*) having white flowers and sweet scarlet fruit and being one of the plants used in developing the garden strawberry

virginia sumac *n, usu cap V* **:** STAGHORN SUMAC

virginia thorn *n, usu cap V* **:** WASHINGTON THORN

virginia thyme *n, usu cap V* **:** a fragrant perennial herb (*Pycnanthemum virginianum*) of eastern No. America with opposite linear lanceolate leaves and tiny close heads of flowers in a terminal cluster

virginia tobacco *n, usu cap V* **1 :** tobacco grown in colonial No. America and shipped from Virginia ports **2 a :** tobacco grown east of the Appalachian mountains and flue-cured **b :** any of various fire-cured, sun-cured, or air-cured tobaccos of the eastern U.S. — distinguished from *burley*

virginia wake-robin *n, usu cap V* **:** GREEN ARROW ARUM

virginia waterleaf *n, usu cap V* **:** a showy perennial herb (*Hydrophyllum virginianum*) with white flowers and foliage that is sometimes used as greens in the southeastern U.S. — called also *Shawnee salad, shawny*

virginia willow *also* **virginia tea** *n, usu cap V* **:** a No. American shrub (*Itea virginica*) with simple alternate leaves and small white flowers in simple racemes

virginia winterberry *n, usu cap V* **:** BLACK ALDER 1

virginia yellow pine *n, usu cap V* **:** SHORTLEAF PINE 1

virgin islander *n, cap V&I* [*Virgin Islands,* group of islands in the West Indies + E *-er*] **1 :** a native or inhabitant of the British Virgin Islands **2 :** a native or inhabitant of the Virgin Islands of the U.S.

vir·gin·i·ty \və(r)'jinəd·ē, -nətē, -i\ *n* -ES [ME *virginite,* fr. OF *virginité,* fr. L *virginitat-, virginitas* maidenhood, virginity, fr. *virgin-, virgo* virgin + *-itat-, -itas* -ity] **1 :** the quality or state of being chaste; *often* **:** the physical attributes distinguishing a virgin **2 :** the unmarried life **:** CELIBACY, SPINSTERHOOD **3 :** the quality or state of being fresh or new

vir·gin·i·um \və(r)'jinēəm\ *n* -s [NL, fr. *Virginia,* state of the U.S. + NL *-ium*] **:** chemical element 87 — superseded by *francium*

virgin moth *n* **:** WHITE MILLER 1b

vir·gin·o·ge·nia \ˌvərjənō'jēnēə\ *n, pl* **virginogeni·ae** \-nēˌē\ [NL, fr. L *virgin-, virgo* maiden + NL *-o-* + *-genia* (fr. Gk *-genēs* -gen)] **:** VIRGINOPARA — **vir·gin·o·gen·ic** \¦⸗⸗⸗¦jenik\ *adj*

vir·gi·nop·a·ra \ˌvərjə'näpərə\ *n, pl* **virginopa·rae** \-pəˌrē\ [NL, fr. L *virgin-, virgo* virgin + NL *-o-* + *-para*] **:** one of the polymorphic types of some plant lice; *specif* **:** an apterous parthenogenetic female derived from a parthenogenetic parent — **vir·gi·nop·a·rous** \¦⸗⸗¦näpərəs\ *adj*

virgin parchment *n* **:** fine parchment made from the skins of newborn lambs and kids

virgin rosin *n* **:** pale yellow rosin made from the first turpentine that exudes after a tree is boxed

virgins *pl of* VIRGIN

virgin's bower *n* **:** a plant of the genus *Clematis* esp. when small-flowered and climbing: as **a :** the European traveler's-joy **b :** a common clematis (*C. virginiana*) of eastern No. America that sprawls and scrambles over other plants and bears numerous panicles of small creamy white flowers **c :** a rather similar clematis (*C. ligusticifolia*) of the western U.S. with distinctively fragrant flowers

virgin's milk *n, often cap V* **:** a former cosmetic consisting either of the tincture of benzoin or some balsam or of lead subacetate precipitated by addition of water

virgin soil *n* **:** soil that has never been cultivated

virgin spawn *n* **:** mushroom spawn made by mixing the fresh spores directly with the nutritive material making up the bricks

virgin widow *n* **:** one widowed before the consummation of her marriage

virgin wool *n* **1 :** raw wool sheared from live sheep; *specif* **:** wool that has not been worked into yarn or cloth **2 :** WOOL 2a(2)

vir·go \'vər(ˌ)gō, 'vā(-, 'vəi(-\ *n* -s *usu cap* [L *virgin-, virgo* virgin] **:** the sixth sign of the zodiac — see SIGN table, ZODIAC illustration

vir·gu·la \'vərgyələ\ *n* -s [NL, fr. L, small rod — more at VIRGULE] **1 :** the axial support of various graptolites **2 :** a bilobate secretory reservoir in various cercariae — **vir·gu·lar** \-lər\ *adj*

vir·gu·lar·ia \ˌvərgyə'la(a)rēə\ *n, cap* [NL, fr. L *virgula* small rod + NL *-aria;* fr. the rodlike rachis] **:** a genus (the type of the family Virgulariidae) of pennatulaceans having a long rodlike rachis enclosing a slender round or square calcareous axis and having polyps that are arranged in transverse rows or clusters on short fleshy transverse processes borne on each side of the rachis for nearly its whole length

¹vir·gu·lar·i·an \¦⸗⸗¦la(a)rēən\ *adj* [NL *Virgularia* + E *-an*] **:** of or relating to the genus *Virgularia* or family Virgulariidae

²virgularian \"\ *n* -s **:** a virgularian pennatulacean

vir·gu·late \'vərgyələt, -yəˌlāt\ *adj* [L *virgulatus* striped, fr. *virgula* small rod, small stripe + *-atus* -ate] **:** having a shape resembling a rod

vir·gule \'vərˌgyül, 'vā,-, 'vəiˌ-\ *n* -s [F, fr. L *virgula* small rod, small stripe, obelus, dim. of *virga* branch, rod, stripe — more at WHISK] **1 a :** a short usu. slanting stroke or mark used in medieval manuscripts: as (1) **:** the earliest form of a comma usu. used to indicate a caesura (2) **:** an indication of a division of a word at the end of a line **b :** DIAGONAL 4 **2 :** a form of timepiece escapement that somewhat resembles the verge but has a comma-shaped projection from the balance staff serving as its pallet

vir·i·al \'virēəl\ *n* -s [G, fr. L *vires,* pl., strength, power + G *-ial;* akin to L *vis* strength, force, violence — more at VIM] **:** half the product of the stress due to the attraction or repulsion between two particles in space times the distance between them or in the case of more than two particles half the sum of such products taken for the entire system

virial coefficient *n* **:** one of the coefficients in a series of terms involving inverse powers of specific volume whose sum represents the product of specific volume by pressure for a pure gas ⟨useful form of the equation of state of a real gas is $pv = A + \frac{B}{v} + \frac{C}{v^2} + \ldots$, where A, B, C, etc. are functions of the temperature and are called the *virial coefficients* —F.W.Sears⟩

vi·ri·ci·dal \ˌvīrə'sīdᵊl\ *adj* [*viricide* + *-al*] **:** of or relating to a viricide **:** acting destructively on viruses

vi·ri·cide \'⸗⸗ˌsīd\ *n* -s [NL *virus* + E *-i-* + *-cide* (killer)]

: a physical or chemical agent that destroys or inactivates viruses

vir·id \'virə̇d\ *adj* [L *viridis* green — more at VERDANT] **:** vividly green **:** VERDANT ⟨the ~ brilliance of the grass —Mary McCarthy⟩ ⟨distant peaks, ~ vistas, nearby trees and bushes —Joseph Hergesheimer⟩

vir·i·dans \'virə,danz\ *adj* [NL, fr. L *viridant-, viridans,* pres. part. of *viridare* to make green, fr. *viridis* green] **:** ALPHA 3

vir·i·des·cent \¦virə¦desᵊnt\ *adj* [L *viridis* green + E *-escent*] **:** slightly green **:** GREENISH

vi·rid·i·an *also* **ve·rid·i·an** \və̇'ridēən\ *n* -s [L *viridis* + E *-ian*] **1 :** GUIGNET'S GREEN **2** *or* **viridian green :** a strong green that is bluer and duller than average mintleaf (sense 1) or primitive green — called also *chrome green, emeraude, French Veronese green, Veronese green*

vir·i·dig·e·nous \¦virə¦dijənəs\ *adj* [L *viridis* green + E *-genous*] **:** producing greenness

vir·i·din \'virədə̇n\ *n* -s [NL *viride* (specific epithet of *Trichoderma viride*) (fr. L, neut. of *viridis* green) + E *-in*] **:** a crystalline fungistatic antibiotic $C_{19}H_{16}O_6$ produced by a fungus (*Trichoderma viride*)

vir·i·dine green \'virə,dēn-, -,də̇n-\ *n* [obs. *viridine* chlorophyll, a green dye, fr. L *viridis* green] **:** a light yellow green that is greener and stronger than glass green and greener and lighter than sky green

viridine yellow *n* [obs. *viridine*] **:** a strong yellow green that is greener, lighter, and stronger than parrot green and greener than lovebird

vi·rid·i·ty \və̇'ridəd·ē\ *n* -ES [ME *viridite,* fr. MF *viridité,* fr. L *viriditat-, viriditas,* fr. *viridis* green + *-itat-, -itas* -ity — more at VERDANT] **1 :** the quality or state of being green **:** the color of grass or foliage **2 :** the quality or state of being or of appearing to be young, fresh, and innocent

vir·ile \'virə̇l, *chiefly Brit* -i,rīl\ *adj* [MF or L; MF *viril,* fr. L *virilis,* fr. *vir* man, adult male + *-ilis* -ile; akin to OE & OHG *wer* man, husband, ON *verr,* Goth *wair,* Skt *vīra* man, hero, and prob. to L *vis* strength — more at VIM] **1 a :** having the nature, properties, or qualities of an adult male **b :** characteristic of developed manhood; *specif* **:** capable of functioning as a male in copulation **2 :** characterized by energy and drive considered typically male ⟨existence of a ~ and ever stronger free society in our country —J.E.Allen⟩ ⟨described the inhabitants as an alert ~ efficient people —P.E.James⟩ **3 :** characteristically belonging to or associated with men **:** MASCULINE ⟨considered caps the only ~ form of headgear for a fellow —A.J.Liebling⟩ ⟨frowned around a ~ pipe —Berton Roueché⟩ **4 :** marked by unusual strength and vigor **:** DECISIVE, FORCEFUL ⟨talked with the ~ diction of a Yankee —Margaret Long⟩ ⟨translated into ~ tense American verse —Dudley Fitts⟩ **syn** see MALE

virile member *n* [trans. of L *membrum virile*] **:** PENIS

vir·i·les·cence \,virə'lesᵊn(t)s\ *n* -s [*virile* + *-escence*] **:** the acquiring of characters more or less like those of the male often by a barren or old female — **vir·i·les·cent** \¦==¦lesᵊnt\ *adj*

vi·ril·ia \vī'rilēə\ *n pl* [L, fr. neut. pl. of *virilis* virile] **:** the male genitals

vir·il·ism \'virə̇,lizəm\ *n* -s [ISV *virile* + *-ism*] **1 :** precocious development of secondary masculine characters in the male **2 :** the appearance of secondary male characters in the female

vi·ril·i·ty \və̇'riləd·ē, -ətē, -i\ *n* -ES [L *virilitat-, virilitas,* fr. *virilis* virile + *-itat-, -itas* -ity] **:** the quality or state of being virile: as **a :** the period of developed manhood — compare MULIEBRITY **b :** the capacity to function in copulation **c :** action attributed to masculine strength and drive ⟨to play soccer requires stamina and ~⟩ **d :** a vigorous often dynamic force ⟨literature has lost standards and discipline and at the same time ~ —Irving Babbitt⟩ ⟨industrial ~ in no way mars its gracious and orderly appearance —*Amer. Guide Series: Vt.*⟩

vir·il·iza·tion \,virə̇lə̇'zāshən\ *n* -s **:** the condition of being or process of becoming virilized

vir·il·ize \'virə̇,līz\ *vt* -ED/-ING/-S [*virile* + *-ize*] **:** to cause or produce virilism in

viri·local \¦virə+\ *adj* [L *vir* man + E -i- + *local*] **:** PATRILOCAL — **viri·locally** \"+\ *adv*

virl \'vərl\ *n* -s [ME *virole, virell, verelle* — more at FERRULE] *Scot* **:** FERRULE 1a

1**vi·roid** \'vī,rȯid\ *n* -s [NL *virus* + E *-oid,* n. suffix] **:** a hypothetical viruslike symbiont favorable to the host but tending to mutate to the virus form

2**viroid** \"\ *adj* [NL *virus* + E *-oid,* adj. suffix] **1 :** caused by a virus ⟨~ pneumonia⟩ **2 :** of or relating to viroids

vir·o·la \'virələ\ *n, cap* [NL] **:** a genus of chiefly So. American forest trees (family Myristicaceae) which yield pale to reddish brown wood — see BANAK, UCUUBA

vi·ro·log·i·cal \¦vīrə¦läjə̇kəl, -jēk-\ *or* **vi·ro·log·ic** \-jə̇k, -jēk\ *adj* **:** of or relating to virology — **vi·ro·log·i·cal·ly** \-k(ə)lē\ *adv*

vi·rol·o·gist \vī'räləjə̇st\ *n* -s **:** a specialist in virology

vi·rol·o·gy \-jē, -ji\ *n* -ES [ISV *viro-* (fr. NL *virus*) + *-logy*] **:** a branch of science that deals with viruses

1**vi·rose** \'vī,rōs, ='=\ *adj* [L *virosus* poisonous, fr. *virus* poison + *-osus* -ous — more at VIRUS] **1 :** having or suggestive of a poisonous quality **2 :** FETID, MALODOROUS

2**virose** \"\ *n* -s [F or G, fr. NL *virosis*] **:** VIROSIS

vi·ro·sis \vī'rōsə̇s\ *n, pl* **viro·ses** \-ō,sēz\ [NL, fr. *virus* + *-osis*] **:** infection with or disease caused by a virus

vi·rous \'vīrəs\ *adj* [NL *virus* + E *-ous*] **:** caused by a virus

vir·tu *or* **ver·tu** \,vər'tü, vā'-, ,vəi'-, '=,=, vir'-, viə'-\ *n* -s [It *virtù* & obs. It *vertù,* lit., virtue, strength, fr. L *virtut-, virtus* — more at VIRTUE] **1 :** a love of or a taste for curios or objets d'art **2 :** productions of art esp. of a curious or antique nature **:** OBJETS D'ART **3 a :** an artistic quality **b :** a study of the fine arts

vir·tu·al \'vərch(ə)wəl, 'vāch-, 'vəich-, -chəl\ *adj* [ME, fr. ML *virtualis,* fr. L *virtus* strength, virtue + *-alis* -al — more at VIRTUE] **1** *obs* **:** of, relating to, or possessing a power of acting without the agency of matter **2 :** notably effective **3 :** being functionally or effectively but not formally of its kind ⟨a ~ certainty⟩ ⟨the ~ abdication of parents from their role as educators —Dorothy Barclay⟩

virtual displacement *n* **:** an infinitesimal displacement of any point of a mechanical system that may or may not take place but that is compatible with the constraints of the system

virtual focus *n* **1 :** a point from which divergent rays (as of light) seem to emanate but do not actually do so (as in the image of a point source seen in a plane mirror) **2 :** a point toward which convergent rays are directed but which being intercepted they do not reach

virtual height *n* **:** the effective height of a layer of ionized gas in the atmosphere by which radio waves are reflected around the earth's curvature

virtual image *n* **:** an image (as seen in a plane mirror) formed of virtual foci

vir·tu·al·ism \-,lizəm\ *n* -s *sometimes cap* **:** the theological doctrine attributed to John Calvin and other Reformers that though the eucharistic elements remain unchanged in the Lord's Supper the spiritual body, blood, and benefits of Jesus Christ are conveyed through them

vir·tu·al·i·ty \,vərchə'waləd·ē\ *n* -ES **1 :** the essential nature **:** ESSENCE ⟨the relation between the actuality of the present moment and the *virtualities* of the subsisting past —Milic Capek⟩ **2 :** potential existence **:** POTENTIALITY, EFFICACY

vir·tu·al·ly \'vərch(ə)wəlē, 'vāch-, 'vəich-, -chəl-, -li\ *adv* [ME, fr. *virtual* + *-ly*] **1** *obs* **:** in essence **:** not merely formally **2 :** almost entirely **:** for all practical purposes ⟨unnoticed and ~ unknown —Philip Brady⟩ ⟨was ~ penniless —C.C.Cregan⟩

virtual pitch *n* **:** the distance a propeller would have to advance in one revolution so that there might be no thrust

vir·tue \'vər(,)chü, 'vā(-, 'vəi(-, *chiefly in southern U.S.* -,chə\ *n* -s [ME *vertu, virtu,* fr. OF, fr. L *virtut-, virtus* strength, manliness, virtue, fr. *vir* man — more at VIRILE] **1 a :** moral practice or action **:** conformity to a standard of right (as divine law or the highest good) **:** moral excellence **:** integrity of character **:** uprightness of conduct **:** RECTITUDE, MORALITY ⟨~ is not to be considered in the light of mere innocence, or abstaining from harm, but as the exertion of our faculties in doing good —Joseph Butler⟩ ⟨~ is its own reward⟩: as (1) **:** wisdom based on a knowledge of the good that makes one act in accordance with the good (2) **:** a habit involving the choice of excellence in conduct with the excellence being realized in a mean between excess and defect **b :** a particular moral excellence ⟨the very ~ of compassion —Shak.⟩ — see CARDINAL VIRTUE, NATURAL VIRTUE, THEOLOGICAL VIRTUE **2 a** *archaic* **:** supernatural power or influence exerted by a divine being **b virtues** *pl, usu cap* **:** an order of angels in various medieval descriptions of celestial hierarchies **3 :** a particular beneficial quality or efficacy in something ⟨a large spring of unusually fine water . . . credited with unusual ~*s* —*Amer. Guide Series: Maine*⟩ ⟨certain herbs have greater ~ when they are picked at midnight —Robert Graves⟩ **4 :** manly strength or courage **:** VALOR **5 :** a characteristic, quality, or trait known or felt to be excellent **:** MERIT, VALUE, WORTH ⟨unquestioned faith in the ~ of the cause he served —C.L. Becker⟩ ⟨the house is a graceful structure, built simply when simplicity was not considered a ~ —*Amer. Guide Series: Minn.*⟩ **6 :** an active quality or power whether of physical or of moral nature **:** the capacity or power adequate to the production of a given effect **:** ENERGY, POTENCY, STRENGTH ⟨the ~ to hold up her head and look the Square in the face —Arnold Bennett⟩ ⟨the rare ~ of being able to face up to any storm without hesitation —M.S.Handler⟩ **7 :** an ability or accomplishment **8 :** CHASTITY, PURITY; *esp* **:** the chastity of a woman ⟨the same grim jealousy it shows toward the ~ of its young women —*Newsweek*⟩ **syn** see EXCELLENCE — **by virtue of** *or* **in virtue of** *prep* **:** through the force of **:** by authority of ⟨the crossing could succeed only *by virtue of* its boldness —P.W.Thompson⟩ ⟨when technicians . . . assert their authority, it is *in virtue of* their experience —A.L.Guérard⟩

vir·tue·less \'==lə̇s\ *adj* [ME *virtules, vertules,* fr. *virtu, vertu* virtue + *-les* -less] **1 :** devoid of excellence or worth **2 :** lacking in moral goodness — **vir·tue·less·ness** *n* -ES

vir·tu·o·sa \,vərchə'wōsə, ,vāch-, ,vəich-, -ōzə\ *n, pl* **virtuo·se** \-sā, -zā\ *or* **virtuosas** [It, fem. of *virtuoso*] **:** a female virtuoso

vir·tu·ose \¦==¦wōs\ *adj* [It *virtuoso*] **:** VIRTUOSIC

vir·tu·osic \-¦wäsik\ *adj* [1*virtuoso* + *-ic*] **:** relating to or characteristic of a virtuoso ⟨a vehicle for the display of a ~ performer and his instrument —Robert Evett⟩

vir·tu·os·i·ty \,=='wäsəd·ē, -sətē, -i\ *n* -ES [1*virtuoso* + *-ity*] **1 :** an often dilettantish interest esp. in one of the fine arts or its products **2 a** (1) **:** great technical skill in the practice of the fine arts and esp. in the performance of music ⟨performed with ~ on the piano⟩ (2) **:** technical brilliance of performance without accompanying artistic insight ⟨a period of technical ~ without serious purpose —M.D.Geismar⟩ **b :** technical skill as manifested in the artistic product ⟨struck by the ease and ~ of the writing —Arnold Bennett⟩

1**vir·tu·o·so** \-'wō(,)sō, -)zō\ *n, pl* **virtuosos** \-)sōz, -)zōz\ *or* **virtuo·si** \-'wōsē, -ōzē\ [It, fr. *virtuoso,* adj., virtuous, learned, skilled, fr. LL *virtuosus* virtuous — more at VIRTUOUS] **1 :** one interested in the pursuit of knowledge **:** an experimenter or investigator esp. in the arts and sciences **:** SAVANT ⟨*virtuosi* collected shells, rocks, fossils —C.W.Shumaker⟩ ⟨Christian *virtuosi* who wished to unite the new science and religion against the threat of . . . atheistic mechanism —J.I.Cope⟩ **2 :** one devoted to virtu **:** one skilled in or having a taste for the fine arts **:** a collector or ardent admirer of curios or objects of art **3 :** one who excels in the technique of an art; *esp* **:** a musical performer (as on the violin or the piano) **syn** see EXPERT

2**virtuoso** \¦==¦=(,)=\ *adj* **:** of, relating to, or characteristic of a virtuoso **:** having the manner or style of a virtuoso ⟨does not compose for the orchestra in an obviously ~ way —Neville Cardus⟩

vir·tu·ous \'vərchəwəs, 'vāch-, 'vəich-\ *adj* [ME *virtuous, vertuous,* fr. MF *virtueus, vertueus,* fr. LL *virtuosus,* fr. *virtus* strength, virtue + *-osus* -ous — more at VIRTUE] **1** *obs* **:** displaying valor **:** BRAVE, VALIANT **2 :** capable of bringing forth a powerful effect **:** having potent usu. beneficial qualities **:** EFFICACIOUS **3 :** having or exhibiting virtue **:** acting in a just way and in accordance with moral laws **:** devoid of wickedness ⟨a ~ man⟩ **4 :** characterized by virtue **:** morally excellent **:** RIGHTEOUS ⟨~ indignation is a powerful stimulant but a dangerous diet —G.B.Shaw⟩ ⟨his eyes wild with ~ anger —Joseph Conrad⟩ **5 :** CHASTE, PURE ⟨would have known all about those young girls . . . whether they were still ~, what books they read —Aldous Huxley⟩ **syn** see MORAL

vir·tu·ous·ly *adv* [ME *virtuously, vertuously,* fr. *virtuous, vertuous* + *-ly*] **:** in a virtuous manner

vir·tu·ous·ness *n* -ES [ME *virtuousnesse, vertuousnesse,* fr. *virtuous, vertuous* + *-nesse* -ness] **:** the quality or state of being virtuous

virtus *pl of* VIRTU

vi·ru \vē'rü\ *adj, usu cap* [fr. the *Virú* valley, northwestern Peru] **:** GALLINAZO

vi·ru·ci·dal \¦vīrə¦sīdᵊl\ *adj* [NL *virus* + E *-cidal*] **:** tending to kill viruses **:** acting as a virucide

vi·ru·cide \'==,sīd\ *n* -s [NL *virus* + E *-cide*] **:** an agent that kills viruses

vir·u·lence \'vir(y)ələn(t)s\ *or* **vir·u·len·cy** \-nsē, -si\ *n, pl* **virulences** *or* **virulencies** [LL *virulentia* stench, infection, fr. L *virulentus* + *-ia* -y] **1 :** extreme bitterness or malignity of temper **:** RANCOR ⟨old age added ~ to her tongue —Harrison Smith⟩ **2 :** the quality or property of being virulent (as an infection) **:** VENOMOUSNESS, MALIGNANCY **3 :** the relative capacity of a microorganism to overcome the body defenses of the host — distinguished from *infectivity*

vir·u·lent \-nt\ *adj* [ME, fr. L *virulentus,* fr. *virus* slimy liquid, poison, stench — more at VIRUS] **1 :** characterized by rapid course, severity, and malignancy — used esp. of a disease or infection **2 :** extremely poisonous or venomous **:** DEADLY, NOXIOUS ⟨those mosquitoes must have been particularly ~ —*Farmer's Weekly* (*So. Africa*)⟩ **3 :** bitter in enmity **:** full of malicious hatred **:** MALIGNANT ⟨~ hostility . . . thwarted him at every turn —Allen Nevins & H.S.Commager⟩ **4 :** objectionably and sometimes intolerably harsh or strong ⟨the zeal for culture was equally ~ —T.S.Eliot⟩ ⟨wearing a *virulent*-purple bathrobe —Harold Brodkey⟩ ⟨a Mexican port stilled with plague . . . beneath the ~ sun —Sinclair Lewis⟩ **5 :** exhibiting virulence **:** able to overcome or break down the defensive mechanism of the host

vir·u·lent·ly *adv* **:** in a virulent manner ⟨laws ever more ~ isolationist —*President's Commission on Immigration & Naturalization*⟩

vir·u·lif·er·ous \¦vir(y)ə¦lif(ə)rəs\ *adj* [*virulence* + *-iferous*] **:** containing, producing, or conveying an agent of infection (as a bacterium, virus)

vi·rus \'vīrəs\ *n* -ES [L, slimy liquid, poison, stench; akin to OE *wāse* mire, marsh, OFris *wase* mud, ON *veisa* swamp, Gk *ios* poison, Skt *veṣati* it flows away, *viṣa* poison] **1** *archaic* **:** venom emitted by a poisonous animal **2** [NL, fr. L] **a :** the causative agent of an infectious disease **:** DISEASE GERM **b :** FILTERABLE VIRUS; *specif* **:** any of a large group of submicroscopic infective agents that are regarded either as the smallest microorganisms or extremely complex molecules and are composed typically of a protein coat surrounding an RNA or DNA core of genetic material, that are capable of growth and multiplication only in living cells, and that cause various important diseases in man, animals, or plants (as mumps, rabies, or tobacco mosaic) — see BACTERIOPHAGE, FIXED VIRUS, STREET VIRUS **c :** VIRUS DISEASE 1 ⟨has recovered from a ~ which confined her to her home —*Springfield* (*Mass.*) *Daily News*⟩ **3 :** a morbid corrupting quality in intellectual or moral conditions **:** something that poisons the mind or soul ⟨these particular officials affect the public service with an undemocratic ~ —Taylor Cole⟩ ⟨the force of this ~ of prejudice —V.S. Waters⟩ **4** [NL, fr. L] **:** an antigenic but not infective material (as vaccine lymph) obtainable from a case of an infectious disease **syn** see MICROORGANISM, POISON

virus abortion *n* **:** abortion in mares caused by a virus possibly identical with that of equine influenza

vi·rus·ci·dal \¦vīrə¦sīdᵊl\ *adj* [NL *virus* + E *-cidal*] **:** VIRUCIDAL

vi·rus·cide \'==,sīd\ *n* -s [NL *virus* + E *-cide*] **:** VIRUCIDE

virus disease *n* **1 :** a disease caused by a filterable virus (as leaf roll, foot-and-mouth disease, poliomyelitis, the common cold, influenza) **2 :** VIROSIS

viruslike \'==,=\ *adj* [NL *virus* + E *like*] **:** resembling or similar to a virus

virus pneumonia *n* **:** PRIMARY ATYPICAL PNEUMONIA

vi·rus·tat·ic \¦vīrə¦stad·ik\ *adj* [NL *virus* + E *static*] **:** tending to check the growth of viruses

virus x *n, sometimes cap V & usu cap X* **1 :** any of various viruses that are imperfectly identified **2** *or* **virus x disease :** a disease caused by a virus X

1**vis** *or* **viss** \'vis\ *n, pl* **vis** *or* **viss** [Tamil *vīsai* & Telugu *vīse*] **:** an old unit of weight used in Burma and southern India equal to 3.65 pounds; *also* **:** a modern Burmese unit equal to 3.60 pounds

2**vis** \"\ *n, pl* **vi·res** \'vī,rēz\ [L — more at VIM] **:** FORCE, POWER

3**vis** \'vē\ *n, pl* **vis** \"\ [by shortening] *archaic* **:** VIS-À-VIS 2

vis *abbr* **1** viscosity **2** *often cap* viscount **3** visibility; visible **4** visiting **5** visual

1**vi·sa** \'vēzə *sometimes* -ēsə\ *n* -s [F, fr. L, neut. pl. of *visus,* past part. of *vidēre* to see] **1 :** an endorsement made on a passport by the proper authorities (as of the country the bearer wishes to enter) denoting that it has been examined and that the bearer is permitted to proceed **2 :** a signature of formal approval by a superior upon a document requiring approval as to form or content

2**visa** \"\ *vt* **visaed** \-zəd,-səd\ **visaed** \"\ **visaing** \-zəiŋ, -sə-\ **visas 1 :** to give a visa to (a passport) ⟨provide themselves with passports and . . . have them ~*ed* by the consular officers —A.E.Aspinall⟩ **2 :** to give official approval to **:** RATIFY ⟨a list of topics and speakers must be presented and ~*ed* in advance of every meeting —*Nation*⟩

vis·age \'viz|ij, |ēj *sometimes* -is\ *n* -s [ME, fr. OF, fr. *vis* face (fr. L *visus* sight, vision, fr. *visus,* past part. of *vidēre* to see) + *-age* — more at WIT] **1 a :** the front part of the human head ⟨black hair . . . generally, rather handsome ~ —Charles Dickens⟩ **b :** the corresponding part of the head of a lower animal ⟨the pebble-smooth ~ of a tortoise —*Books of the Month*⟩ **2 a :** a cast of features that express emotion or character **:** expression of countenance ⟨a monstrous little man . . . with the ~ of a thief —Jean Stafford⟩ ⟨puts on a smiling ~ for the occasion⟩ **b :** APPEARANCE, LOOK, ASPECT ⟨the grimy, gloomy ~ of the mining town⟩ **3 :** visible surface — used esp. of the sun or moon ⟨fair moon . . . stoop thy pale ~ through an amber cloud —John Milton⟩ **4** *obs* **:** outward show **:** SEMBLANCE ⟨others . . . trimmed in forms and ~*s* of duty keep yet their hearts attending on themselves —Shak.⟩ **syn** see FACE

vis·aged \-jd\ *adj* [ME, fr. *visage* + *-ed*] **:** having a visage of a specified kind ⟨he was dour, dark ~, built like the base of an oak tree —Liam O'Flaherty⟩

vi·sam·min \və̇'samə̇n\ *n* -s [*vis* (prob. abbr. for *viscosity*) + *Ammi* + *-in*] **:** KHELLIN

vi·sar·ga \və̇'särgə\ *n* -s [Skt, lit., discharge, fr. *vi* asunder + *sarga* action of letting go, fr. *sṛjati* he lets go — more at WITH] **1 :** a Sanskrit postvocalic sound or group of sounds produced by keeping the vocal organs above the glottis in the same position as for the preceding vowel and continuing to expel air from the lungs but not vibrating the vocal cords **2 :** a sign used in writing Sanskrit to represent the visarga sound or sounds — see ALPHABET table

vis a ter·go \,visə'tər(,)gō\ *n, pl* **vires a tergo** [L] **:** a force acting from behind ⟨the *vis a tergo* imparted by the heart and transmitted through the arteries —*Science*⟩

1**vis-à-vis** \¦vēzə¦vē, -zä¦-\ *n, pl* **vis-à-vis** \"\ [F, lit., face to face] **1 :** one that is face-to-face with, opposite to, or paired with another: as **a :** one that faces another (as in a folk dance or a parlor game) ⟨each member can ask his *vis-à-vis* in the other team any question —K.M.Willey⟩ **b :** a partner at a social function **:** ESCORT, DATE ⟨invited . . . to be his *vis-à-vis* at a house party —Jean Stafford⟩ ⟨her *vis-à-vis* was a handsome, balding man —Wolcott Gibbs⟩ **c :** one holding an equal or parallel position **:** COUNTERPART 3b, OPPOSITE NUMBER 1 ⟨a field representative conferring with his *vis-à-vis* in the home office⟩ ⟨going across to talk with his American *vis-à-vis* —Frederick Simpich †1950⟩ **2 :** a carriage in which persons sit face to face **3 :** TÊTE-À-TÊTE

2**vis-à-vis** \"\ *prep* [F] **1 :** face-to-face with **:** OPPOSITE ⟨dining *vis-à-vis* his rival⟩ **2 :** in relation to **:** over against **:** TOWARD ⟨man's pride *vis-à-vis* the gods —Robert Gordis⟩ **3 :** in comparison with **:** as compared with ⟨traditional logic *vis-à-vis* dialectic —G.L.Kline⟩ ⟨the House, jealous of its powers *vis-à-vis* the Senate —A.J.Liebling⟩

3**vis-à-vis** \"\ *adv* [F] **:** in company **:** FACE-TO-FACE, TOGETHER ⟨found themselves *vis-à-vis* for the first time⟩

vi·sa·yan \və̇'sī(y)ən\ *usu cap, var of* BISAYAN

vis·breaking \'vis+,-\ *n* [*vis* (abbr. of *viscosity*) + *breaking*] **:** VISCOSITY BREAKING

visc *abbr* **1** viscosity **2** *often cap* viscount; viscountess

visc- *or* **visco-** *comb form* [ME, fr. L, fr. *viscum* mistletoe, birdlime — more at VISCOUS] **1 :** viscous **:** viscosity ⟨*visco*gen⟩ ⟨*visco*scope⟩ **2 :** viscous and ⟨*visco*elastic⟩

Vis·ca \'viskə\ *trademark* — used for an artificial straw made by spinning viscose in a flat filament capable of being braided, woven, or knitted and used esp. for women's hats

vis·cac·cia \vi'skakshēə\ [NL, fr. AmerSp *vizcacha*] **1** *syn of* LAGIDIUM **2** *syn of* LAGOSTOMUS

viscacha *or* **viscache** *var of* VIZCACHA

vis·car·ia \vi'ska(a)rēə\ *n* [NL, fr. *visc-* + *-aria*] *cap, in some classifications* **:** a genus of alpine or boreal plants with viscous stems and foliage that are usu. included in the genus *Lychnis*

viscer- *or* **visceri-** *or* **viscero-** *comb form* [LL, fr. L *viscera*] **1 :** visceral **:** viscera ⟨*viscer*algia⟩ ⟨*viscero*ptosis⟩ ⟨*viscero*genic⟩ **2 :** visceral and ⟨*visceri*pericardial⟩

viscera *pl of* VISCUS

vis·cer·al \'visərəl\ *adj* [LL *visceralis* intestinal, inguinal, fr. L *viscera* + *-alis* -al] **1 :** felt in the viscera **:** PHYSICAL, BODILY ⟨the ~ sensation of being catapulted down a roller coaster —Gilbert Seldes⟩ ⟨intense ~ delight —F.L.Allen⟩ **2 :** felt in the inner being **:** deep down **:** INNER ⟨his liberalism . . . is seldom ~ —H.J.Bresler⟩ ⟨had the . . . ~ conviction that he was at home —R.L.Mittenbuhler⟩ **3 :** of, relating to, or marked by instinctive or appetitive drives **:** not intellectual **:** NONRATIONAL, UNREASONING ⟨the conflict . . . between enlightened conservatives and the more ~ types —Rolfe Humphries⟩ **4 :** dealing with crude or elemental emotions **:** RAW, EARTHY ⟨as emotionally naked and relentlessly ~ a play as our theater has seen —Henry Hewes⟩ **5 :** of, relating to, or located on or among the viscera **:** SPLANCHNIC — compare PARIETAL 1a

visceral arch *n* **1 :** one of a series of bony or cartilaginous inverted arches that develop in the walls of the mouth cavity and pharynx of a vertebrate embryo and consist typically of a curved segmented bar or rod on each side meeting its fellow of the opposite side at the ventral end either directly or with the intervention of a median piece — compare BRANCHIAL ARCH, HYOID BONE, MANDIBULAR ARCH **2 :** one of the visceral arches together with the structures surrounding and supported by it

visceral bar *n* **:** one of various cartilaginous rods forming the skeletal frame of the visceral or branchial arches in rays and sharks and in the embryos of higher vertebrates

visceral cleft *n* **:** one of the clefts that occur on each side of the neck region between successive visceral arches in vertebrates and that may or may not extend through from the exterior to the cavity of the mouth and pharynx — compare BRANCHIAL CLEFT, SPIRACLE 3c

visceral ganglion *n* **:** either of a pair of ganglia in most mollusks that may lie close to or be fused with the pleural ganglia or may lie much farther back and are connected with the pleural ganglia by pleurovisceral connectives

visceral leishmaniasis *n* **:** KALA AZAR

visceral loop *n* **:** a loop that is formed in most mollusks by the visceral ganglia with their commissure and the pleurovisceral connectives and that gives off branches to the gill, osphradium, parts of the mantle, and various viscera

vis·cer·al·ly \-rəlē\ *adv* **:** in a visceral manner **:** UNREASONINGLY ⟨thought ~, with his heart and bowels instead of his brain —Malcolm Cowley⟩

visceral nerve *n* **:** a nerve supplying viscera; *specif* **:** any of the nerves forming the visceral loop of a mollusk

visceral nervous system *n* **:** SYMPATHETIC NERVOUS SYSTEM

vis·cer·ate \'visə,rāt\ *vt* -ED/-ING/-S [by alter.] *archaic* **:** EVISCERATE

vis·ceri·pericardial \¦visərə+\ *adj* [*viscer-* + *pericardial*] : of, relating to, or constituting the body cavity of a cephalopod mollusk that is incompletely divided into an upper cavity containing the heart and a lower one containing the viscera

vis·cero·cranium \¦visə(,)rō+\ *n* [NL, fr. *viscer-* + *cranium*] : SPLANCHNOCRANIUM

vis·cer·o·gen·ic \¦visərə¦jenik\ *adj* [*viscer-* + *-genic*] : arising within the body ⟨the common ~ desires for food, rest, sex, and safety⟩

vis·cero·inhibitory \¦visə(,)rō+\ *adj* [*viscer-* + *inhibitory*] : inhibiting functional activity of the viscera ⟨~ nerves⟩

vis·cero·motor \"+\ *adj* [*viscer-* + *motor*] : causing or concerned in the functional activity of the viscera ⟨~ nerves⟩

vis·cero·parietal \"+\ *adj* [*viscer-* + *parietal*] : of, relating to, or constituting the visceral ganglia of bivalve mollusks generally situated in contact with the posterior adductor muscles

vis·cer·op·to·sis \,visəräp'tōsəs\ *n* [NL, fr. *viscer-* + *ptosis*] : downward displacement of the abdominal viscera

vis·cer·op·tot·ic \¦===¦täd·ik\ *adj* [fr. NL *visceroptosis*, after such pairs as NL *neurosis*: E *neurotic*] : of, relating to, or affected by visceroptosis ⟨~ patients⟩

vis·cer·o·to·nia \,visərə'tōnēə\ *n* -S [NL, fr. *viscer-* + *-tonia*] : a pattern of temperament that is typical of the endomorphic individual, is marked by predominance of social over intellectual or physical factors, and exhibits conviviality, tolerance, complacency, and love of food — compare CEREBROTONIA, SOMATOTONIA

[1]**vis·cer·o·ton·ic** \¦===¦tänik\ *adj* [NL *viscerotonia* + E *-ic*] : exhibiting viscerotonia

[2]**viscerotonic** \"\ *n* -S : a viscerotonic individual : a typical endomorph

vis·cer·o·trop·ic \¦visərə·¦träpik\ *adj* [*viscer-* + *-tropic*] : turning towards or having an affinity for the viscera — used esp. of a virus

vis·cer·ot·ro·pism \,visə'rä·trə,pizəm\ *n* : the quality or state of being viscerotropic

vis·cer·ous \'visərəs\ *adj* [L *viscera* + E *-ous*] : VISCERAL

vis·cid \'visəd\ *adj* [LL *viscidus*, fr. L *viscum* mistletoe, birdlime — more at VISCOUS] **1 a** : having an adhesive quality : GLUEY, STICKY ⟨~ with resin⟩ **b** : having a glutinous consistency : VISCOUS ⟨a ~ scum⟩ **2** : covered with a sticky layer ⟨~ leaves⟩

vis·cid·i·ty \vi'sidəd·ē\ *n* -ES **1** : the quality or state of being viscid : STICKINESS **2** : viscid matter

viscidly *adv* : in a viscid manner

vis·cin \'visᵊn\ *n* -S [F, fr. *visc-* + *-in*] : a clear viscous tasteless substance from the mucilaginous sap of the mistletoe or holly — compare BIRDLIME, VISCUM

visco- — see VISC-

vis·co·elastic \¦viskō+\ *adj* [*visc-* + *elastic*] : having both viscous and elastic properties in appreciable degree ⟨~ cold tar⟩ ⟨~ asphalt⟩

vis·co·lize \'viskə,līz\ *vt* -ED/-ING/-S [back-formation fr. *Viscolizer*] : HOMOGENIZE

Vis·co·liz·er \-zə(r)\ *trademark* — used for a machine similar to a homogenizer but usu. operating at a lower pressure and having smaller openings

vis·com·e·ter \vi'skämədə(r)\ *n* [*visc-* + *-meter*] : an instrument with which to measure viscosity

vis·co·met·ric \¦viskə¦me·trik\ *adj* [*visc-* + *-metric*] : of, relating to, or ascertained by a viscometer or viscometry ⟨~ readings⟩

vis·co·met·ri·cal·ly \-rək(ə)lē\ *adv* [*viscometric* + *-ally* (as in *metrically*)] : in a viscometric manner : by means of a viscometer

vis·com·e·try \vi'skämə·trē\ *n* -ES [*visc-* + *-metry*] : measurement of viscosity

vis·co·scope \'viskə,skōp\ *n* [*visc-* + *-scope*] : an instrument for estimating viscosity

[1]**vis·cose** \'vi,skōs\ *adj* [ME, fr. LL *viscosus* viscous] **1** : VISCOUS ⟨a ~ solution⟩ **2** [[2]*viscose*] : of, relating to, or made from viscose ⟨~ yarn⟩

[2]**viscose** \"\ *n* -S **1** : a viscous sticky golden-brown solution consisting essentially of cellulose xanthate in sodium hydroxide that after ripening from one to several days is usu. extruded through spinnerets or dies and coagulated by means of a bath containing sulfuric acid and salts to form filaments, staple fibers, or films of regenerated cellulose — see CELLOPHANE, VISCOSE RAYON **2** : VISCOSE RAYON

viscose rayon *n* **1** : rayon fiber made from viscose in filament or staple form **2** : rayon yarn or fabric made from viscose rayon fiber

vis·co·sim·e·ter \,viskə'simədə(r)\ *n* [ISV *viscosity* + *-meter*] : VISCOMETER

vis·cos·i·met·ric \vi¦skäsə¦me·trik\ *adj* [*viscosity* + *-metric*] : VISCOMETRIC

vis·cos·i·met·ri·cal·ly \-rək(ə)lē\ *adv* : VISCOMETRICALLY

vis·co·sim·e·try \,viskə'simə·trē\ *n* -ES [ISV *viscosity* + *-metry*] : VISCOMETRY

vis·cos·i·ty \vi'skäsəd·ē, -ətē, -i\ *n* -ES [ME *viscosite*, fr. MF *viscosité*, fr. ML *viscositat-*, *viscositas*, fr. LL *viscosus* viscous + L *-itat-*, *-itas* -ity] **1 a** : the quality or state of being viscous; *specif* : the physical property of a fluid or semifluid that enables it to develop and maintain a certain amount of shearing stress dependent upon the velocity of flow and then to offer continued resistance to flow — compare COEFFICIENT OF KINEMATIC VISCOSITY, FLUIDITY **b** : COEFFICIENT OF VISCOSITY **c** : the capability possessed by a solid of yielding continually under shearing stress **2** : a viscous substance or mass

viscosity breaking *n* : a process of lowering the viscosity esp. of heavy straight-run residues in petroleum refining by mild cracking

viscosity index *n* : an arbitrary number assigned as a measure of the constancy of the viscosity of a lubricating oil with change of temperature such that a high index indicates that the viscosity changes little with temperature

vis·count \'vī,kaůnt\ *n* [ME *viscounte*, fr. MF *visconte*, *vicomte*, fr. ML *vicecomit-*, *vicecomes*, fr. LL *vice-* vice- + *comit-*, *comes* count — more at COUNT] **1** : an officer acting as the representative of a count in the administration of a district; *specif* : a sheriff or high sheriff in England **2** : a member of the fourth grade of the peerage in Great Britain ranking below an earl and above a baron

vis·count·cy \-tsē\ *n* -ES [*viscount* + *-cy*] : the rank or dignity of a viscount

vis·count·ess \-təs\ *n* [ME *viscountesse*, fr. *viscounte* viscount + *-esse* -ess] **1** : the wife or widow of a viscount **2** : a woman who holds in her own right the rank of viscount

vis·county \-tē\ *n* [*viscount* + *-y*] **1** : the territory or jurisdiction of a viscount **2** : VISCOUNTCY

vis·cous \'viskəs\ *adj* [ME *viscouse*, fr. LL *viscosus* full of birdlime, sticky, viscous, fr. L *viscus*, *viscum* mistletoe, birdlime made from berries of mistletoe + *-osus* -ose; akin to Gk *ixos* mistletoe, birdlime, Russ *vishnya* cherry, OHG *wīhsila* mahaleb cherry and perh. to OE *wāse* mire, marsh — more at VIRUS] **1 a** : having a ropy or glutinous consistency and the quality of sticking or adhering : VISCID, GELATINOUS, GLUEY **b** : having the physical property of viscosity ⟨diesel fuels are more ~ than gasoline —*Principles of Automotive Vehicles*⟩ **2** : suggestive of a gluey substance or mass esp. in lacking easy movement or fluidity ⟨the ~ flow of her prose could not cloy a public that feasted on its bright sweetness —J.D.Hart⟩ ⟨~ prose —Edmund Wilson⟩

vis·cous·ly *adv* : in a viscous manner ⟨few districts in which traffic flows as ~ as in midtown New York —*Harper's*⟩

vis·cous·ness *n* -ES *archaic* : VISCOSITY

vis·cum \'viskəm\ *n* [NL, fr. L, mistletoe, birdlime] **1** *cap* : a genus of Old World semiparasitic plants (family Loranthaceae) distinguished by the clustered axillary bracteate flowers with adnate anthers — see MISTLETOE **2** -S : birdlime made from the berries of the European mistletoe — compare VISCIN

vis·cu·ous \'viskyəwəs\ *adj* [L *viscum* + E *-ous*] *archaic* : VISCOUS

vis·cus \'viskəs\ *n*, *pl* **vis·cera** \'visərə\ [L] **1** : an internal organ of the body; *esp* : one (as the heart, liver, or intestine) located in the great cavity of the trunk proper **2** *viscera pl* : inner or interior matter or contents ⟨the magazine's *viscera* were arranged in an unusually agreeable order —*New Republic*⟩ ⟨getting at the *viscera* of the old sofa⟩

[1]**vise** \'vīs\ *n* -S [MF *vis*, *viz* something winding, winding stairway, screw, fr. L *vitis* vine — more at WITHY] : any of various tools having two jaws for holding work (as in saw filing) that close usu. by a screw, lever, or cam — see SWIVEL VISE, UNIVERSAL VISE

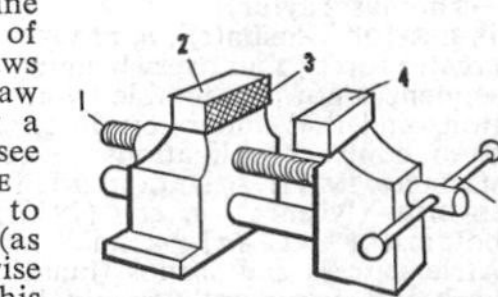

vise: *1* screw, *2* fixed jaw, *3* jaw plate, *4* movable jaw, *5* handle

[2]**vise** \"\ *vt* -ED/-ING/-S : to hold, force, or squeeze (as work) with or as if with a vise ⟨has a cigar butt *vised* in his teeth —James Stephens⟩

[3]**vi·sé** \'vē,zā, ='=\ *vt* **viséd** *also* **viséed**; **viséd** *also* **viséed**; **viséing**; **visés** [F, past part. of *viser* to put a visa to, examine a visa, fr. *visa* — more at VISA] : VISA

[4]**visé** \"\ *n* -S [F, past part.] : VISA

vise cap *n* : one of the two guards of soft material (as copper) fitting over the jaws of a metalworker's vise

vise coupling *n* : WEDGE COUPLING

vi·sé·ite \vē'zā,īt\ *n* -S [F, fr. *Visé*, town in Belgium, its locality + F *-ite*] : a mineral $Ca_5Al_{10}(PO_4)_6(SiO_4)_3(OH)_{10}\cdot 20\text{–}25H_2O$ consisting of a hydrous hydroxide phosphate and silicate of aluminum and calcium

viselike \'=,=\ *adj* : acting like a vise ⟨a ~ grip⟩

vise·man \'vīsmən\ *n*, *pl* **visemen** **1** : a man who works at a vise **2** : an alcohol distillery worker who with a wrench screws plugs and tops on tanks in which gas is held under pressure

vish·nu \'vish(,)nü\ *adj*, *usu cap* [fr. *Vishnu's* Temple, area on the Colorado river] : of, relating to, or constituting a division of the Archeozoic — see GEOLOGIC TIME table

vish·nu·ism \-ü,izəm\ *n* -S *usu cap* [*Vishnu*, second god of the Hindu triad of deities (fr. Skt *Viṣṇu*) + E *-ism*] : VAISHNAVISM

vish·nu·ite \-ü,īt\ *n* -S *usu cap* [*Vishnu* + E *-ite*] : a worshiper of Vishnu : VAISHNAVA

vis·i·bil·i·ty \,vizə'biləd·ē, -lətē, -i\ *n* -ES [LL *visibilitas*, fr. L *visibilis* visible + *-itas* -ity] **1** : the quality or state of being visible ⟨the ~ of a navigational light⟩ ⟨the need for improving the ~ of bicycles at night⟩ ⟨stage action with maximum ~ —Irving Kolodin⟩ **2** *archaic* **a** : something visible ⟨modelled . . . into a Shape, a *Visibility* —Thomas Carlyle⟩ **b** : something worth seeing : a notable sight ⟨have seen all the *visibilities* of Paris —Samuel Johnson⟩ **3 a** : the degree or extent to which something is visible (as by the degree of clearness of the atmosphere); *specif* : the mean greatest distance prevailing over the range of more than half of the horizon at which a large object (as a building or ship) may be seen and identified depending upon its size, distance from the observer, the contrast between it and surrounding objects, glare, transparency and illumination of the atmosphere between the object and the observer, and the condition of the observer's eye unaided by special optical devices ⟨~ up to five miles⟩ ⟨dust storms . . . reducing ~ to a few yards —Keith Ellis⟩ **b** : capability of being readily noticed ⟨advertising . . . that has the greatest ~ —*Publishers' Weekly*⟩ **c** : capability of being distinguished as belonging to a racial, religious, or social group on the basis of either physical or cultural characteristics **d** : capability of affording an unobstructed view ⟨a new car with improved front and rear ~⟩ ⟨an airplane with good ~ in the nose⟩ **4** : a measure of the ability of radiant energy to evoke visual sensation : the luminous efficiency of light of a specified wavelength expressed in lumens per watt or usu. as a percentage of its maximum value of about 680 lumens per watt at the green wavelength 5500 angstroms ⟨the ~ of yellow sodium light is about 76 percent⟩

visibility curve *n* : a curve expressing the values of visibility as a function of wavelength — compare VISIBILITY 4

visibility meter *n* : an instrument for measuring visibility

[1]**vis·i·ble** \'vizəbəl\ *adj* [ME, fr. MF or L; MF *visible*, fr. L *visibilis*, fr. *visus* (past part. of *vidēre* to see) + *-ibilis* -ible — more at WIT] **1 a** : capable of being seen : perceptible by vision ⟨~ light⟩ ⟨a ~ object⟩ ⟨a clearly ~ stain⟩ ⟨a ship barely ~ on the horizon⟩ ⟨a cupola ~ at night for miles —*Amer. Guide Series: Minn.*⟩ **b** : seen on earth : TEMPORAL ⟨the ~ church⟩ — compare CHURCH VISIBLE **c** : seen above ground : not subterranean ⟨lagoons with no ~ outlets⟩ **d** : tangibly present : AVAILABLE ⟨the total of ~ wheat as of this date⟩ **e** : of or relating to tangible exports and imports ⟨the ~ items in the balance of payments⟩ **f** : easily seen : impressive to the view ⟨colored slides . . . are both highly ~ and dramatic —J.K.Blake⟩ **g** : CONSPICUOUS ⟨his highly ~ neckties —Robert Rice⟩ **h** : possessing cultural visibility ⟨dietary habits may make the foreigner highly ~ in American culture⟩ **2** : capable of being perceived mentally : DISCOVERABLE, RECOGNIZABLE ⟨serves no ~ purpose⟩ ⟨had no ~ means of support⟩ ⟨the ~ facts of a man's environment —H.O. Taylor⟩ ⟨employees look for . . . a ~ path for advancement —A.S.Igleheart⟩ **3** : willing to receive visitors ⟨was ~ only to her most intimate friends⟩ **4** : devised in such a way that a particular part or a record made is always in full view or can be readily seen or referred to ⟨a ~ index⟩ ⟨a ~ ledger⟩

[2]**visible** \"\ *n* -S **1** : something visible ⟨preference for ~*s* . . . in teaching —I.A.Richards⟩; *specif* : the wavelength range of electromagnetic radiation that is perceptible to the human eye — used with *the;* see LIGHT 1c **2** : a biological mutation determinable by inspection — compare LETHAL 2a

visible church *n* : CHURCH VISIBLE

visible horizon *n* : APPARENT HORIZON

vis·i·ble·ness *n* -ES : VISIBILITY

visible spectrum *n* : the part of the electromagnetic spectrum to which the human eye is sensitive extending from a wavelength of about 3800 angstroms for violet light to about 7600 angstroms for red light

visible speech *n* **1** : a system of phonetic symbols that is intended to represent the positions of the vocal organs in producing speech sounds **2** : a method in which electronic equipment is used for making a spectrographic analysis so that speech is reproduced either as a continuous pattern on a fluorescent screen or as a permanent record on a spectrogram

visible supply *n* : the total of what is known to be available (as of stocks of grain in elevators and on the way to market)

vis·i·bly \'vizəblē, -li\ *adv* [ME *visibely*, fr. *visible* + *-ly*] : in a visible manner : OBVIOUSLY, NOTICEABLY ⟨the waters were ~ diminishing —Rex Ingamells⟩ ⟨the audience was ~ transported —Virgil Thomson⟩

vis·i·goth \'vizə,gäth, -,gȯth *sometimes* -isə,-\ *n*, *cap* [LL *Visigothi*, pl., of Gmc origin; prob. fr. a Gothic compound whose first constituent is akin to Goth *iusiza* better, OIr *fīu* worthy, Gk *eus* good, brave, Skt *vasu* good and whose second constituent is the same as the source of LL *Gothi* Goths — more at GOTH] : a member of the western division of the Goths that invaded the Roman empire beginning in the 4th century and later established kingdoms between the Loire and Gibraltar — called also *West Goth;* compare OSTROGOTH

[1]**vis·i·goth·ic** \¦==¦gäthik, -gȯth-, -thēk\ *adj*, *usu cap* **1** : of or relating to the Visigoths **2** : of or relating to an early medieval Spanish writing developed from the Roman cursive

[2]**visigothic** \"\ *n*, *usu cap* : a Visigothic script

vis·ile \'vi,zīl\ *n* -S [L *visus* (past part. of *vidēre* to see) + E *-ile* (as in *audile*)] : VISUALIZER

vis in·er·ti·ae \-ə'nərshē,ē\ *n*, *pl* **vires inertiae** [NL, lit., force of inertia] : INERTIA 1a

[1]**vi·sion** \'vizhən\ *n* -S [ME *visioun*, fr. OF *vision*, fr. L *vision-*, *visio*, fr. *visus* (past part. of *vidēre* to see) + *-ion-*, *-io* -ion — more at WIT] **1 a** : something seen otherwise than by the ordinary sight : an imaginary, supernatural, or prophetic sight beheld in sleep or ecstasy; *esp* : one that conveys a revelation ⟨a ~ of the night, when deep sleep falleth upon men —Job 33:15 (AV)⟩ **b** : a writing (as a poem) purporting to represent something beheld in a revelatory dream, trance, or ecstasy — compare DREAM VISION ⟨the masterpieces of the Middle Ages . . . the story cycle and the allegorical ~ —Boris Ford⟩ **c** : a vivid concept or object of imaginative contemplation ⟨brought ~*s* of wealth to be gained in silk culture —*Amer. Guide Series: Del.*⟩ **d** : the apparition of a person (as in a dream) : PHANTOM ⟨thus the ~ spoke —John Dryden⟩ **e** : a visual image without corporeal presence; *esp* : a manifestation to the senses of something immaterial (as a spiritual being or state) ⟨the baseless fabric of this ~ —Shak.⟩ ⟨look, not at ~*s*, but at realities —Edith Wharton⟩ **2 a** : the act or power of perceiving mental images (as those formed by the imagination) ⟨a listlessness of ~ behind a veneer of technical virtuosity —G.A.Wagner⟩ **b** (1) : a mode or way of seeing ⟨trying to express his ~ in terms of recognizable subject matter —*Times Lit. Supp.*⟩ ⟨every ~ of the world implies some sort of philosophy —Walter Lippmann⟩ (2) : unusual discernment or foresight ⟨a man of ~⟩ ⟨planning that combines realism with ~ —*advt*⟩ **c** : direct mystical awareness of the supernatural usu. in visible form ⟨a spirit and a *Vision* . . . beyond all that the mortal and perishing nature can produce —William Blake⟩ **3 a** : the act or power of seeing : visual sensation or the capacity for it : SIGHT ⟨the ~ of the audience comprised the speakers and actors of the play —Harley Granville-Barker⟩ ⟨cast out from God and blessed ~ —John Milton⟩ **b** : the special sense that is concerned with the perception and distinguishing of the qualities of an object (as color, luminosity, shape and size) constituting its appearance, that is mediated by the rods and cones of the retina stimulated by light projected from the object through the lens of the eye, and that is conducted centrally by the optic nerves and is coordinated esp. by centers in the lateral geniculate bodies and the occipital portion of the cerebral cortex **4 a** : something seen : an object of sight ⟨this glorious ~ of manly strength and beauty —G.B.Shaw⟩ **b** : something seen of such charm as to seem imaginary ⟨she was a ~ in that dress⟩ **c** : a momentary sight : GLIMPSE ⟨had caught a ~ of her, of something eager, cleverly active —J.D. Beresford⟩ **5** : a figure of speech by which something present to the imagination (as a person or scene) is represented as actually before the eyes (as in Tennyson's "I see the wealthy miller yet, his double chin, his portly size") — compare APOSTROPHE 1 **6** : a small motion-picture scene photographed by double exposure within a larger one usu. to indicate the thought of an actor at a particular moment — compare DISSOLVE **syn** see FANCY

[2]**vision** \"\ *vt* -ED/-ING/-S **1** : to make evident to the sight : show forth : DISPLAY ⟨the anger of God apparently ~*ed* . . . unto thee in the knitting of my brows —Thomas Nash⟩ **2** : to see in or as if in a vision : IMAGINE, ENVISION ⟨~*ed* the tiny town as the future metropolis —*Amer. Guide Series: Oregon*⟩ ⟨~*ed* a life of failure stretching before me —David Fairchild⟩

vi·sion·al \-nᵊl\ *adj* **1** : of, relating to, or of the nature of a vision ⟨gave a ~ interpretation to the biblical episode⟩ **2** : based upon or seen in a vision : UNREAL, IMAGINARY ⟨a ~ apparition⟩ — **vi·sion·al·ly** \-ᵊlē, -ᵊli\ *adv*

vi·sion·ar·i·ness \'vizhə,nerēnəs\ *n* -ES : the quality or state of being visionary

[1]**vi·sion·ary** \-rē, -ri\ *adj* **1 a** : capable of seeing visions : disposed or likely to see visions ⟨a ~ prophet⟩ ⟨people call you ~ . . . you see things before they happen —S.M.Crothers⟩ **b** : disposed to indulgence in reverie or fancy : full of imaginative conceptions : apt to accept and act on fancies as if realities : DREAMY, IMPRACTICAL ⟨one ~ explorer . . . devoted a season to gold digging —*Amer. Guide Series: Mass.*⟩ ⟨~ and sentimental persons —Willa Cather⟩ ⟨~ in expecting . . . enough popular support —E.S.Morgan⟩ **2 a** : having the nature of a vision : beheld or existing in a vision or dream : ILLUSORY, PHANTOM ⟨beheld . . . through so dim a medium that she looked ~ —Nathaniel Hawthorne⟩ ⟨clutched at some ~ object in the air —Thomas DeQuincey⟩ **b** : having no basis or justification in reality : incapable of being realized or achieved : UTOPIAN ⟨a ~ scheme⟩ ⟨discussions of monorail systems seemed academic, if not ~ —*Fortune*⟩ **c** : existing only in the imagination : UNREAL ⟨those who hazard a real blessing for some ~ good —*Encore*⟩ **3** : of, relating to, or characterized by vision or by visions ⟨able to endow a rapid sketch of some trees seen by a roadside with . . . ~ power —Stuart Preston⟩ ⟨the ~ hour —James Thomson †1748⟩ **syn** see IMAGINARY

[2]**visionary** \"\ *n* -ES **1** : a person who sees visions : SEER ⟨too clever to place any faith in the dreams of *visionaries* . . . knew all the priestcraft and fakery of his kind —Bruce Nelson⟩ **2** : one that relies or tends to rely on dreams and fancies or on imaginary or ideal conceptions or projects having little basis in reality : an impractical person : DREAMER, ENTHUSIAST ⟨ridiculed as a ~ when he first proposed the plan⟩ ⟨realized what a hopeless ~ he was —*Cosmopolitan*⟩

visioned *adj* [partly fr. [1]*vision* + *-ed* & partly fr. past part. of [2]*vision*] **1** : seen in a vision ⟨a ~ face⟩ **2 a** : produced by or experienced in a vision ⟨~ moods⟩ ⟨~ agony⟩ **b** : marked by visions ⟨a ~ sleep⟩ **3** : endowed with vision : INSPIRED ⟨a ~ experimenter⟩

visioning *n* -S [fr. gerund of [2]*vision*] : the act or an instance of seeing visions ⟨such ~*s* . . . produced much of the world's misery —Bruce Marshall⟩

vi·sion·ist \'vizhənəst\ *n* -S : VISIONARY 1

vi·sion·less \-nləs\ *adj* **1** : SIGHTLESS, BLIND ⟨~ eyes⟩ **2** : lacking vision or inspiration : UNINSPIRED ⟨a ~ leader⟩

vision quest *n* : a solitary vigil by an adolescent American Indian boy to seek spiritual power and learn through a vision the identity of his usu. animal or bird guardian spirit

visions *pl of* VISION, *pres 3d sing of* VISION

[1]**vis·it** \'vizət, *usu* -əd·+V\ *vb* **visited** \-zəd·əd, -z(ə)təd\ **visited**; **visiting** \-zəd·iŋ, -z(ə)tiŋ\ **visits** [ME *visiten*, fr. OF *visiter*, fr. L *visitare* to go to see, visit, freq. of *visere* to look at, go to see, fr. *vidēre* to see — more at WIT] *vt* **1 a** *archaic* : to come to or upon as a spiritual help : COMFORT — used of the deity ⟨~ us with Thy salvation —Charles Wesley⟩ **b** (1) : to bring trouble or harm to : AFFLICT — usu. used with *with* ⟨~*ed* his people with distempers —Tobias Smollett⟩ (2) : INFLICT, IMPOSE — usu. used with *on* or *upon* ⟨~*ed* his wrath upon them⟩ ⟨~*ed* everlasting grief on many people because of a few rash words —T.B.Costain⟩ ⟨the court ~*s* all costs on them —H.J.Laski⟩ **c** (1) : to take vengeance for : AVENGE ⟨~ the sins of the fathers upon the children⟩ (2) *obs* : to move vengefully against : come at ⟨ere the king dismiss his power, he means to ~ us —Shak.⟩ (3) : to exact retribution for : PUNISH ⟨now will he . . . ~ their sins —Hos 8:13 (AV)⟩ ⟨the legislature ~*ed* the action with censure⟩ **d** : to present itself to or come over momentarily ⟨~*ed* by a strange notion⟩ ⟨the surprise which ~*ed* me when I saw the blood —R.P.Warren⟩ **2 a** : to go to see and care for as a charitable work : minister to ⟨~*ing* the sick of the parish⟩ **b** (1) : to go to attend (a patient) — used esp. of a physician (2) : to go to see (as a physician or dentist) for professional service **3 a** : to make a social call upon ⟨~*ed* friends in the early evening⟩ **b** : to reside with temporarily as a guest : stay with ⟨~*ed* a colleague for a week at his summer home⟩ **c** : to have sexual relations with **d** : to frequent temporarily ⟨many migratory birds ~ these shores annually⟩ **4 a** : to go to see or sojourn at (a place) for a particular purpose (as for business, pleasure, or sight-seeing) ⟨what local points of interest they should ~ —Dana Burnet⟩ ⟨a medicinal spring . . . frequently ~*ed* by invalids —*Amer. Guide Series: N. H.*⟩ **b** : to go to (a place of business) on an errand ⟨enough time to ~ the stores before dinner⟩ **5 a** *obs* : to come to observe or test the spiritual state of — used of the deity ⟨God often descends to ~ men unseen —John Milton⟩ **b** : to go or come officially to oversee or correct the operation of : INSPECT ⟨a bishop ~*ing* his diocese⟩ ⟨a congressional committee ~*ing* a military base⟩ ⟨a department head ~*ing* classrooms⟩ **c** *archaic* : to make an official examination of (as baggage or a ship and its cargo) : SEARCH ~ *vi* **1** *obs* : to make an official inspection **2 a** : to make a call ⟨spends most of her afternoons ~*ing*⟩ **b** : to stay as a guest ⟨~*s* here for a month in every year⟩ **3** : to carry on casual conversation : CHAT ⟨let's sit here and ~ together for a while⟩ ⟨~*ing* with a neighbor on the telephone⟩ **4** : to progress around the set with a figure in square dancing

[2]**visit** \"\ *n* -S **1 a** : a short stay (as for sociability or friendship) that is usu. longer than a social call ⟨make a ~⟩ ⟨a ~ with friends⟩ ⟨pay a ~⟩ ⟨return a ~⟩ ⟨suburban housewives spending their afternoons in ~*s* and card playing⟩ **b** : a brief residence as a guest ⟨a weekend ~ with friends⟩ **c** : an extended but temporary stay : SOJOURN ⟨his annual summer ~*s* abroad⟩ **2 a** : a journey to and stay or short sojourn at a place for a particular purpose ⟨a ~ to a museum⟩ ⟨a ship's ~ to a port⟩ ⟨a ~ to a neighboring town⟩ ⟨an educational ~ to a

steel mill⟩ ⟨~s to points of historical interest⟩ **b :** a brief stop on an errand or for a business purpose ⟨telephoned between ~s to the stores⟩ ⟨a salesman's ~ to a firm⟩ ⟨repeated ~s to theatrical agencies⟩ **3 a** (1) **:** a professional call (as of a physician to treat a patient) ⟨paid the doctor for three home ~s⟩ (2) **:** a pastoral call by a clergyman on a parishioner ⟨met the minister returning from his afternoon ~s⟩ **b :** a call upon a professional man (as a physician or dentist) for consultation or treatment ⟨urged to make regular ~s to his dentist⟩ **4 :** an official call or tour (as for supervision or inspection) **:** VISITATION ⟨a ~ by a national officer to the local chapter of a fraternal order⟩ ⟨a committee of trustees on a ~ to a university⟩ **5 :** an official examination or search (as of goods or cargo); *specif* **:** the act of a naval officer of one state in boarding a neutral merchant vessel of another state in the exercise of the right of search

vis·it·able \ˈvizəd·əbəl, -z(ə)təb-\ *adj* **1 :** subject to visitation or inspection ⟨an institution maintained by the church and ~ by the bishop⟩ **2 :** accessible for visiting **:** OPEN ⟨a museum ~ only at certain hours⟩ ⟨the ~ countries of the globe —Raymond Walters b. 1912⟩ **3 :** socially eligible to receive visits ⟨became known to all the ~ people here —William Cowper⟩

vis·i·tan·dine \ˌvizəˈtandən, -ˌdēn\ *n* -s *usu cap* [F, fr. L *visitandum* (gerund of *visitare* to visit) + F *-ine*] **:** NUN OF THE VISITATION

¹vis·i·tant \ˈvizəd·ənt, -z(ə)tənt *also* -zətᵊnt\ *n* -s [L *visitant-, visitans*, pres. part. of *visitare* to visit] **:** one that visits: **a :** one that comes for a short or temporary stay **:** VISITOR, GUEST ⟨a frequent ~ at the rectory⟩ ⟨a ~ from the outside world —Clarice Short⟩; *esp* **:** one thought to come from a spirit world ⟨a ghostly ~⟩ ⟨heavenly ~s⟩ **b :** one that visits a place of religious or sightseeing interest **:** PILGRIM, TOURIST ⟨collected a small fee from ~s to the cathedral⟩ **c :** something (as a bodily or mental state) that comes to or over a person for a time ⟨that mood of sadness . . . my frequent ~ —George Eliot⟩ **d :** a bird that is not resident in a given region at all seasons but that appears there at regular or irregular intervals for a limited period ⟨a winter ~⟩

²visitant \"\ *adj* [L *visitant-, visitans*] **:** coming as or appearing in the character of a visitor **:** VISITING ⟨a devil ~ —Daniel Defoe⟩

vis·i·ta·tion \ˌvizəˈtāshən\ *n* -s [ME *visitacioun*, fr. MF *visitation*, fr. L *visitation-, visitatio*, fr. *visitatus* (past part. of *visitare* to visit) + *-ion-, -io* -ion — more at VISIT] **1 a :** an official visit of a superior or superintending officer to an institution (as a corporation, college, church) to inspect the manner in which it is conducted and see that its laws and regulations are observed and executed ⟨the ~ of a diocese by a bishop⟩ **b** (1) **:** a personal inquiry by a visiting officer of arms in Great Britain at different times into the rights of the people within his heraldic province to bear arms (2) **:** a documentary record of such an inquiry **c :** VISIT 5 **2 a :** a special dispensation of divine favor or wrath ⟨my Celestial Patroness who deigns her nightly ~ unimplored —John Milton⟩; *esp* **:** retributive calamity **:** divine judgment ⟨a ~ of the plague for the people's sins⟩ **b :** an unusual event likened to a special dispensation; *esp* **:** a severe trial **:** AFFLICTION ⟨suffered one ~ after another of disease and famine⟩ **3 a :** a visit to a place of interest (as on a sightseeing or educational tour) **b :** a visit for a charitable purpose ⟨a ~ of the sick⟩ **c** (1) **:** a pastoral call or official visit by a Protestant minister (2) **:** an official visit by one or more laymen on church business **d** *archaic* **:** a social call **4 :** resort to a place by animals (as birds or mammals) at an unusual time or in unusual numbers **5 :** a passing influence (as of something intangible or supernatural) **:** VISITING ⟨gentle ~s of calm thought —P.B.Shelley⟩
syn see TRIAL

vis·i·ta·tor \ˈ==ˌtād·ə(r)\ *n* -s [LL, fr. L *visitatus* (past part.) + *-or*] **:** an official visitor or examiner in the Roman Catholic Church ⟨the ~ visits all the monasteries in succession⟩

vis·i·ta·to·ri·al \ˌvizəd·əˈtōrēəl, -ətə-, -tȯr-\ *adj* [ML *visitatorius* visitatorial (fr. L *visitatus* + *-orius* -ory) + E *-al*] **:** of or relating to visitation or to a judicial visitor or superintendent ⟨~ authority⟩ ⟨~ jurisdiction⟩

vi·site \vēˈzēt\ *n* -s [F, lit., visit, fr. *visiter* to visit] **:** a cape or short cloak formerly worn by women in summer — compare ³POLKA

visited *past of* VISIT

visiter *var of* VISITOR

¹visiting *n* -s [ME, fr. gerund of *visiten* to visit — more at VISIT] **:** a fleeting influence (as from a spiritual source) ⟨no compunctious ~s of Nature shake my fell purpose —Shak.⟩

²visiting *adj* [fr. past part. of ¹*visit*] **:** giving professional or technical service or advice in the home and for short periods rather than by the day or week ⟨a ~ housekeeper⟩

visiting book *n* **:** a book containing a record of visits received, made, and to be made

visiting card *n* **:** a small card bearing the name and sometimes the address of a person or married couple for presentation (as when visiting or calling) — called also *calling card*

visiting couple *n* **:** the couple that momentarily is progressing around the set in square dancing

visiting day *n* **:** a day for receiving callers

visiting fireman *n* **1 :** a usu. important or influential visitor (as a high official from the headquarters of an organization or a general on a tour of inspection) whom it is desirable or expedient to show about or entertain impressively ⟨for an aspiring politician . . . a fine place to throw parties for *visiting firemen* and local bigwigs —Clare B. Luce⟩ **2 :** a visitor to a city (as a convention delegate) who goes out on the town and spends freely ⟨girls who will show your visitors what most *visiting firemen* want to see —Hal White⟩

visiting list *n* **:** a list of persons whom one visits socially

visiting nurse *n* **:** a nurse employed by a hospital or social-service agency to visit sick persons or perform other public health services in a community

visiting patrol *n* **:** a patrol that visits elements of its own command and those of adjacent units (as in an outpost) to maintain liaison

visiting professor *n* **:** a professor invited to join a college or university faculty for a limited time (as a half year or an academic year)

visiting teacher *n* **1 :** an educational officer employed by a public school system to go into the homes of pupils in order to effect cooperation between school and family, assist in the solving of social or emotional problems due to home environment, instruct sick or handicapped pupils unable to attend school, or enforce attendance regulations **2 :** a social worker whose duty is dealing with behavior problems among school children

visiting ticket *n, archaic* **:** VISITING CARD

vis·i·tor *also* **vis·it·er** \ˈvizəd·ə(r), -z(ə)tə-\ *n* -s [ME *visitour, visiter*, fr. MF *visiteur*, fr. OF *visiter* to visit + *-eur* -or — more at VISIT] **:** one that visits: **a :** a superior or a person lawfully appointed for the purpose who makes formal visits of inspection or supervision **b** (1) **:** a member of a board of overseers of an academic institution **:** TRUSTEE (2) *Brit* **:** a person of high rank or eminence serving as the highest authority and court of last appeal for a university ⟨if the fellows could not find a clear majority . . . for one candidate, it was left for the ~ to appoint —C.P.Snow⟩ **c :** one that makes charitable visits ⟨took a job as ~ to Boston's poor —J.S.Redding⟩; *esp* **:** a social worker assigned to visit clients in their homes **d :** one that makes social visits **:** CALLER, GUEST ⟨a warm welcome for ~s⟩ ⟨had no ~s all day⟩ **e :** one that goes to or stays at a place for a particular purpose (as business or sightseeing) **:** TOURIST, TRAVELER ⟨~s to a city for a convention⟩ ⟨~s at a vacation resort⟩ **f :** VISITANT d

vis·i·to·ri·al \ˌvizəˈtōrēəl, -tȯr-\ *adj* **:** VISITATORIAL; *specif* **:** of or relating to the visiting rights of one parent when custody of a child is awarded to the other

visitors' book *n* **:** a book or register for the signatures and often comments of visitors (as to a museum, a restaurant, or an exposition)

vis·i·tress \ˈvizə·trəs\ *n* -ES [*visitor* + *-ess*] *archaic* **:** a female visitor; *esp* **:** one who makes visits for social-service work

visits *pres 3d sing of* VISIT

vi·sive \ˈvīsiv\ *adj* [ML *visivus*, fr. L *visus* sight, vision + *-ivus* -ive — more at VISAGE] **1** *archaic* **:** of, relating to, or serving for vision ⟨the ~ sense —George Berkeley⟩ **2** *archaic* **:** capable of seeing or of being seen ⟨gives vision to ~ natures —Thomas Taylor⟩

vis ma·jor \-ˈmājə(r)\ *n, pl* **vires ma·jo·res** \-məˈjōˌrēz\ [L, greater force] **:** an overwhelming force of nature that has consequences not preventable by any due and reasonable precautions and that under certain circumstances is held to exempt from contract obligations — compare ACT OF GOD, FORCE MAJEURE, INEVITABLE ACCIDENT, UNAVOIDABLE CASUALTY

vis·mia \ˈvismēə\ *n, cap* [NL, fr. *Visme*, 18th cent. Port. botanist + NL *-ia*] **:** a small genus of tropical American or African trees and shrubs (family Guttiferae) with a resinous bark and usu. woolly terminal or axillary panicles of white, yellow, or brownish flowers

visne \ˈvēn(ē)\ *n* -s [ME, fr. MF *visné* neighborhood, fr. *visin, veisin* neighbor, fr. L *vicinus* — more at VICINITY] **1** *archaic* **:** VICINAGE; *esp* **:** the place (as the county) of a crime from which the jury is called **2** *archaic* **:** a jury of the visne

vis·no·my \ˈviznəmē\ *n* -ES [alter. of ME *phisnomye, phisonomie* physiognomy — more at PHYSIOGNOMY] *archaic* **:** PHYSIOGNOMY 2a

vi·son \ˈvīsᵊn\ *also* **vison weasel** *n* -s [F *vison*, fr. MF, a marten, perh. of Gmc origin; akin to OHG *wisula* weasel — more at WEASEL] **:** the American mink

vi·sor *also* **vi·zor** \ˈvīzə(r)\ *n* -s [ME *viser*, fr. AF, fr. OF *visiere*, fr. *vis* face + *-iere* -er — more at VISAGE] **1 :** the front piece of a helmet usu. containing openings for seeing and breathing; *esp* **:** an upper piece lifting or opening to show the face **2 a :** a mask for the face **:** VIZARD ⟨have worn a ~ and could tell a whispering tale in a fair lady's ear —Shak.⟩ **b :** something that disguises an evil purpose **:** outward semblance **:** MASK ⟨once sure of his ground, he dropped the ~⟩ **c** *obs* **:** FACE, COUNTENANCE ⟨give me a case to put my visage in: a visor for a ~ —Shak.⟩ **3 a :** a projecting front brim on a cap or hat for shading the eyes **:** PEAK **b** (1) **:** EYESHADE (2) **:** a projecting forepiece on an automobile windshield to protect the eyes from glare **c** (1) **:** an overhang (as for a window) to give shade (2) **:** a small inclined canvas or metal awning around a ship's pilothouse **d :** FACE GUARD **4 :** SUPERCILIARY RIDGE

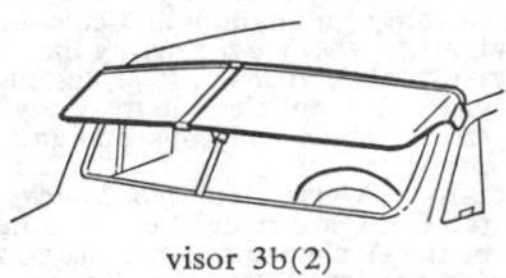
visor 3b(2)

vi·sored *also* **vi·zored** \-(r)d\ *adj* [ME *visered*, fr. *viser* visor + *-ed*] **1 :** covered or masked with a visor **:** DISGUISED ⟨~ falsehood and base forgery —John Milton⟩ **2 :** equipped with a visor ⟨a ~ helmet⟩ ⟨from under the ~ cap his glance was sharp —Kay Boyle⟩

vi·sor·less \-(r)ləs\ *adj* **:** having no visor

vis·pe·red \ˈvespəˌred\ *or* **vis·pa·rad** \-rad\ *n* -s [Av *vīspē ratavō* all the lords] **:** one of the supplementary ritual texts included in the Avestan sacred writings

viss *var of* VIS

vis·ta \ˈvistə\ *n* -s [It, sight, view, fr. *visto* (past part. of *vedere* to see), fr. L *vidēre*, fr. L *visus* (past part. of *vidēre* to see) + It *-to*, past part. suffix (fr. L *-tus*)] **1 a :** a more or less distant view through or along an avenue or opening (as between rows of trees) **:** PROSPECT ⟨garden . . . noted for its long ~s of formal beds between lines of evergreens —*Amer. Guide Series: Md.*⟩ ⟨a ~ opened among the dancers —Rebecca West⟩ **b :** an extended view afforded by an architectural feature (as a corridor or opening in walls) ⟨galleries extended into ~s by mirrors⟩ ⟨~s of stone passages with numbered doors —Christopher Isherwood⟩ **2 :** an extensive mental view (as over a stretch of time or a series of events) **:** a prospect opening out to thought ⟨before us an infinite ~ of human improvement —*Times Lit. Supp.*⟩ ⟨leading her memories down forgotten ~s —B.A.Williams⟩

vista dome *n* **:** DOME 4g(1)

vis·taed \-təd\ *adj* **1 :** affording or made to form a vista ⟨the ~ galleries . . . of this palace —Ruth Davidson⟩ **2 :** seen in or as if in a vista ⟨up ~ hopes I sped —F.J.Thompson⟩

vis·to \ˈvi(ˌ)stō\ *archaic var of* VISTA

¹vi·su·al \ˈvizh(ə)wəl, -zhəl\ *adj* [ME, fr. LL *visualis*, fr. L *visus* sight, vision (fr. *visus*, past part. of *vidēre* to see) + *-alis* -al — more at WIT] **1 :** of, relating to, or used in vision **:** serving as the instrument of seeing ⟨the ~ nerve⟩ ⟨the ~ sense⟩ **2 :** attained or maintained by sight ⟨~ impressions⟩ ⟨~ knowledge⟩ ⟨a language with which he had only a ~ acquaintance —H.J.Laski⟩ ⟨in the heavy growth . . . impossible to keep ~ contact —H.D.Skidmore⟩ **3 :** OPTICAL ⟨the ~ focus of a lens distinguished from the actinic focus⟩ **4 :** capable of being seen **:** VISIBLE ⟨~ objects⟩ ⟨a ~ equivalent for feelings which enrich experience —Michael Kitson⟩ **5 :** producing mental images **:** VIVID ⟨his narratives are stirringly ~ —John Mason Brown⟩ **6 :** done or executed with the aid of direct sight and without assistance (as from instruments or radar) ⟨~ flying⟩ ⟨~ bombing⟩ ⟨~ navigation⟩ **7 :** of, relating to, or constituting a means of instruction (as a map, chart, model, perspective drawing, or documentary film) that appeals to the sense of sight ⟨~ aid⟩ ⟨~ education⟩ ⟨~ lesson⟩ — compare AUDIO-VISUAL

²visual \"\ *n* -s **1** *archaic* **:** VISUAL RAY **2 :** VISUALIZER **3 :** a roughly sketched advertising layout — compare COMPREHENSIVE **4 visuals** *pl* **:** the picture images as distinguished from the sounds of a motion picture film ⟨a master film maker . . . knows how to keep his action taut, his ~s alive —Arthur Knight⟩

visual acuity *n* **:** the relative ability of the visual organ to resolve detail that is a function of sensitivity of a particular retina to light together with the minimum separable and the minimum visible characteristic of the optical system of that eye, that is usu. expressed as the reciprocal of the minimum angular separation in minutes of two lines just resolvable as separate, and that forms in the average human eye an angle of one minute

visual angle *n* **:** the angle formed by two rays of light or two straight lines drawn from the extreme points of a viewed object to the visual point of the eye

visual aphasia *n* **:** aphasia in which a person is unable to comprehend written words previously understood

visual area *n* **:** a sensory area of the occipital lobe of the cerebral cortex receiving afferent projection fibers concerned with the sense of sight

visual-auditory \ˌ=(=)=ˌ==ˌ==\ *adj* **:** AUDIO-VISUAL

visual-aural radio range *or* **visual-aural range** *n* **:** a radio aid to air navigation by which a pilot determines if he is on course by either an appropriate aural signal, a meter reading, or both

visual axis *n* **:** LINE OF VISION

visual binary *n* **:** a double star in which the components may be distinguished separately in a telescope of sufficient resolving power — compare BINARY STAR

visual communication *n* **:** any system of signaling in which the signals are received by the eye (as by lamps, wigwag, semaphore, pyrotechnics, or panels)

visual control *n* **:** a remote supervisory control system in which code signals in the form of electric impulses are sent out by a dispatcher and return signals are received through the medium of colored lights

visual field *n* **1 :** the entire expanse of space visible at a given instant without moving the eyes — called also *field of vision* **2 :** the visual content of a person's mind at a given instant

vi·su·al·ist \ˈvizhələst, -zh(ə)wəl-\ *n* -s **:** VISUALIZER

vi·su·al·i·ty \ˌvizhəˈwaləd·ē\ *n* -ES **1 :** the quality or state of being visual or visible **:** VISIBILITY **2 :** a mental image or picture **:** VIEW, GLIMPSE

vi·su·al·iz·able \ˈvizhəˌlīzəbəl, -zh(ə)wə-, ˌ=(=)=ˈ===\ *adj* **:** capable of being visualized

vi·su·al·iza·tion \ˌvizhələˈzāshən, -zh(ə)wəl-, -ˌlīˈ-\ *n* -s [ISV *visualize* + *-ation*] **1 :** the act or power of forming mentally visual images of objects not present to the eye ⟨aware of his uncanny gift of ~ —G.D.Brown⟩ **2 :** the act or process of putting into or interpreting in visual terms or in visible form ⟨means of ~, such as scale models . . . colored slides —J.L. Sert⟩ **3 a :** the process of exposing an organ to view by surgery ⟨~ of the gallbladder by a paramedian incision⟩ **b :** the process of making a viscus visible by injection of a radiopaque substance followed by roentgenography ⟨~ of the renal calyces by intravenous pyelography⟩ **4 :** a modern dance deriving its patterns entirely from movement equivalents of musical phrases and qualities

vi·su·al·ize \ˈvizhəˌlīz, -zh(ə)wə-\ *vb* -ED/-ING/-s *vt* **1 :** to make visual or visible **:** PICTURE; *esp* **:** to see a mental image of (something not before the eye) **:** picture mentally **:** IMAGE, IMAGINE ⟨~ a scene in all its concreteness —Herbert Read⟩ ⟨*visualized* atomic scientists as bearded old men⟩ **2 a :** to conceive definitely (as something abstract) **:** ENVISAGE ⟨~ a scheme⟩ ⟨*visualizing* anatomy as a living subject⟩ ⟨did not ~ a third alternative —E.H.Erikson⟩ **b :** FORESEE ⟨had not *visualized* such an attack⟩ **3 :** to make (an organ) visible by surgical or roentgenographic visualization ~ *vi* **1 :** to form a visual mental image of something not present before the eye at the time ⟨had the power of *visualizing* in minute detail⟩ **2 :** to become visible — used esp. of an internal bodily organ or condition ⟨the worm *visualized* through a bronchoscope —E.C. Faust⟩

vi·su·al·iz·er \-zə(r)\ *n* -s **1 :** one whose mental imagery is prevailingly visual — compare AUDILE, MOTILE **2 :** VIEWER **3 :** one that lays out advertising for a company preferring to have the work done by a newspaper or periodical or by an advertising firm rather than by its own advertising department

visual line *n* **:** LINE OF VISION

vi·su·al·ly \ˈvizhəlē, -zh(ə)wəl-, -li\ *adv* **:** in a visual manner: as **a :** with regard to vision ⟨gifted ~ to . . . an unusual degree —Osbert Sitwell⟩ **b :** by visual means ⟨the high points of his career . . . were all ~ recorded —R.W.Murray⟩

visual magnitude *n* **:** the brightness of a celestial body determined by eye estimation with or without optical aid or by other instrumentation equivalent to the eye in spectral sensitivity

visual plane *n* **:** a plane passing through the point of sight; *specif* **:** the plane in which the visual axes of the two eyes lie in binocular vision

visual point *n* **:** the point taken as the position of the eye in calculations of optical instruments; *specif* **:** the optical center of the cornea-lens system as backed by the vitreous humor

visual purple *n* **:** a photosensitive red or purple pigment in the retinal rods of various vertebrates; *esp* **:** RHODOPSIN — compare PORPHYROPSIN

visual ray *also* **visual beam** *n* **:** a ray from any point of the object field to the eye; *specif* **:** any ray that on its way to the retina passes through the visual point

visuals *pl of* VISUAL

visual telescope *n* **:** a refractor whose objective is designed to be achromatic in the yellow-green region of the spectrum where the human eye has its highest sensitivity

vis vi·va \-ˈvīvə\ *n, pl* **vires vi·vae** \-ī,vē\ [NL, living force] **:** the force of a moving body calculated as the product of its mass and the square of its velocity **:** twice the kinetic energy

vit *abbr* **1** vitamin **2** vitreous **3** vitrified

vi·ta \ˈvīd·ə, ˈwēˌtä\ *n, pl* **vi·tae** \-ˌīˌtē, -ēˌtī\ [L, lit., life — more at VITAL] **:** a brief autobiographical sketch (as in a thesis for a doctorate)

Vi·ta \ˈvīd·ə\ *trademark* — used for glass that does not obstruct ultraviolet rays

vi·ta·ce·ae \vīˈtāsēˌē\ *n pl, cap* [NL, fr. *Vitis*, type genus + *-aceae*] *cap* **:** a family of woody or herbaceous vines (order Rhamnales) having simple, palmate, or pinnate leaves, usu. tendril-bearing stems, and small greenish clustered flowers succeeded by a several-seeded berry — see CISSUS, PARTHENOCISSUS, VITIS — **vi·ta·ceous** \(ˈ)vīˈtāshəs\ *adj*

vi·tal \ˈvīd·ᵊl, -ītᵊl\ *adj* [ME, fr. MF, fr. L *vitalis* of life, fr. *vita* life + *-alis* -al; akin to L *vivere* to live — more at QUICK] **1 a :** existing as a manifestation of life ⟨~ powers⟩ ⟨recognizing no mystic ~ force⟩ **b :** concerned with or necessary to the maintenance of life ⟨blood and other ~ fluids⟩ ⟨the loss of ~ heat in shock⟩; *esp* **:** performing an essential role in the living body ⟨~ organs⟩ ⟨wounded in a ~ spot⟩ **2 a :** having or characterized by life **:** ANIMATE ⟨a ~ being⟩ **b :** full of life and vigor **:** ENERGETIC, ANIMATED ⟨spirits that live throughout, ~ in every part —John Milton⟩ ⟨this whole ~ world⟩ **3 :** characteristic of life or living beings **:** inhering in the living or organic ⟨~ activities⟩ ⟨expending ~ energies⟩ **4 a :** concerned with or affecting life esp. in some fundamental manner: as (1) **:** tending to renew or refresh the living **:** INVIGORATING ⟨warmed by the ~ rays of heaven's sun⟩ (2) **:** destructive to life **:** FATAL, MORTAL ⟨a ~ wound⟩ **b :** of the utmost importance **:** essential to the continued existence, vigor, efficiency, independence, or value of something expressed or implied ⟨a ~ point to the argument⟩ ⟨matters ~ to the national security⟩; *often* **:** taking priority in consideration over other factors or elements ⟨it is ~ to know what he plans⟩ **5** *obs* **:** capable of living **:** VIABLE **6 :** recording the chief data relating to lives ⟨~ records⟩ — see VITAL STATISTICS **7 :** of, relating to, or constituting the staining of living tissues (as by injecting a dye into a living animal) **syn** see ESSENTIAL

vital air *n, archaic* **:** OXYGEN

vital capacity *n* **:** the breathing capacity of the lungs expressed as the number of cubic inches or cubic centimeters of air that can be forcibly exhaled after a full inspiration

vital dye *n* **:** a dye or stain capable of penetrating living cells or tissues and not inducing immediate evident degenerative changes — called also *vital stain*

vital force *n* **:** ÉLAN VITAL

vital function *n* **:** a function of the body (as the circulation of the blood, respiration, or digestion) on which life is directly dependent

vital index *n* **:** the ratio of births to deaths in a human population at any given time

vi·tal·ism \ˈvīd·ᵊlˌizəm, -ītᵊl-\ *n* -s [*vital* + *-ism*] **1 :** a doctrine that the functions of a living organism are due to a vital principle (as an élan vital or entelechy) distinct from physicochemical forces — compare MECHANISM, ORGANICISM **2 :** a doctrine that the processes of life are not explicable by the laws of physics and chemistry alone and that life is in some part self-determining instead of mechanistically determined — compare ORGANICISM, ORTHOGENESIS

vi·tal·ist \-ləst\ *n* -s [*vitalism* + *-ist*] **:** a believer in vitalism

vi·tal·is·tic \ˌ==ˈistik\ *or* **vi·tal·ist** \ˈ==ˌəst\ *adj* **:** of, relating to, or characteristic of vitalism or vitalists — **vi·tal·is·ti·cal·ly** \ˌ==ˈistək(ə)lē\ *adv*

vi·tal·i·ty \vīˈtaləd·ē, -lətē, -i\ *n* -ES [L *vitalitat-, vitalitas*, fr. *vitalis* of life + *-itat-, -itas* -ity — more at VITAL] **1 a :** the peculiarity distinguishing the living from the nonliving and acting as if a specific force or principle — compare ÉLAN VITAL **b :** capacity to live and develop ⟨the ~ of a seed⟩; *also* **:** physical or mental vigor esp. when highly developed ⟨a man of great ~⟩ **2 a :** power of enduring or continuing **:** capacity for survival ⟨the ~ of an idiom⟩ **b :** lively and animated character **:** VIGOR ⟨the ~ of his reasoning⟩ ⟨inspired his helpers with a new ~⟩ **3 :** a manifestation or embodiment of vital force

vi·tal·iza·tion \ˌvīd·ᵊləˈzāshən, -ītᵊl-, -ᵊlˌīˈz-\ *n* -s **:** the quality or state of being vitalized

vi·tal·ize \ˈ==ˌīz\ *vb* -ED/-ING/-s *see -ize in Explan Notes* [ˈ*vital* + *-ize*] *vt* **1 :** to endow with vitality **:** give life or animation to **:** make vigorous or active ⟨~ the patriotism of a people⟩ **2 :** to portray (as in writing or painting) with lifelike effect ~ *vi* **:** to give life or animation

syn ENERGIZE, ACTIVATE: VITALIZE signifies to arouse, usu. something more or less inert or lifeless, to vital activity, often by communicating an impetus or force, or to impart significance or interest to (something) or make one aware of its inherent significance or interest, usu. suggesting a vigor, freshness, or health in the effect ⟨a force which can *vitalize* or destroy men —C.W.Cunnington⟩ ⟨a power of description that *vitalizes* his words —*Christian Science Monitor*⟩ ENERGIZE implies an arousing to activity by an imparting of force, heat, or any power that increases capacity for activity, esp. work, or an acting with a vitality presumably induced by such power ⟨oats are, without doubt, the best *energizing* food for horses —Henry Wynmalen⟩ ⟨storage batteries *energize* railroad block-signal circuits —J.A. Orsino & T.C.Lynes⟩ ACTIVATE stresses an arousing to activity by the influence of an external agent, esp. in imparting or arousing a beneficial or integrating activity ⟨breaks contact with the photoelectric cell and *activates* an alarm —Alan Hynd⟩ ⟨the report has done much to crystallize and *activate* official and private opinion —Walter White⟩

vi·tal·iz·er \-zə(r)\ *n* -s **:** one that vitalizes

Vi·tal·li·um \vīˈtalēəm\ *trademark* — used for a cobalt-chromium alloy of platinum-white color used esp. for cast dentures, prostheses, and industrial castings

vi·tal·ly \ˈvīdᵊlē, -ītᵊl-, -ᵊli\ *adv* **:** in a vital manner or to a vital degree ⟨~ interested in solving the problem⟩ **:** so as to be vital; *broadly* **:** NOTABLY, EXTREMELY, VERY

vi·tal·ness \-ᵊlnəs\ *n* -ES **:** the quality or state of being vital

vital principle *n* **:** a hypothetical force to which the functions and qualities peculiar to living matter are sometimes ascribed

vital red *n* **:** a disazo acid dye used as a biological stain and in the determination of the volume of blood in the body

vital revolution *n* **:** a marked historical change in the rate of reproduction in a society characterized by the achievement of a stable equilibrium of low death and birth rates

vi·tals \ˈvīdᵊlz, -ītᵊlz\ *n pl* [*vital;* trans. of L *vitalia*] **1 :** organs (as the heart, liver, lungs, and brain) that are most necessary for life **2 :** the parts essential for continued existence, health, or soundness ⟨the ~ of a state⟩ ⟨the ~ of a motor⟩

vital space *n* **:** LEBENSRAUM

vital spirits *n pl* **:** a product held to be derived from the natural spirits by commingling in the heart with respiratory air and to convey heat and life to the body by way of the arteries

vital stain *n* **:** VITAL DYE

vital statistics *n pl* **1 :** statistics relating to births, deaths, marriages, health, and disease — compare DEMOGRAPHY **2 :** facts (as physical dimensions or quantities) considered to be interesting or important ⟨the *vital statistics* of book publishing as an industry have long been inadequate —*Publishers' Weekly*⟩ ⟨her *vital statistics* are 34-24-36⟩

vi·ta·mer \ˈvīd·əmə(r)\ *n* -S [*vitamin* + *isomer*] **:** any of two or more compounds that relieve a particular vitamin deficiency ⟨a D ~⟩ ⟨biotin ~*s*⟩ — **vi·ta·mer·ic** \¦==¦merik\ *adj*

vi·ta·min *also* **vi·ta·mine** \ˈvīd·əmən, -ītəm-\ *n* -S *often attrib* [ISV *vit-* (fr. L *vita* life) + *amine;* prob. orig. formed in G; fr. the former belief that such substances were amines — more at VITAL] **:** any of various organic substances that individually or collectively are as far as is known essential to the nutrition of vertebrates, some invertebrates, many microorganisms, but prob. not most higher plants, that act typically in minute amounts in the regulation of various metabolic processes but do not provide energy or serve as building units, that are present in small amounts in various natural foodstuffs and are sometimes produced within the body (as by the action of intestinal bacteria in the rat) but are not ordinarily synthesized or stored in quantity in the human body, that may be detected as deficient in a particular organism by specific symptoms which can be relieved by administration of the appropriate vitamin, and that are commonly classified according to their water or fat solubility, their physiologic effects, or their chemical structure — see ANTIVITAMIN, AVITAMINOSIS, PROVITAMIN; compare AUXIN, GROWTH FACTOR

vitamin A \ˌ==məˈnā\ *n* **:** any of several fat-soluble vitamins or a mixture of two or more of them whose lack in the animal body causes keratinization of epithelial tissues (as in the eye with resulting nyctalopia and xerophthalmia): as **a** *also* **vitamin A_1** \ˌ==mə¦nā¦wən\ **:** a pale yellow crystalline highly unsaturated alicyclic alcohol $C_{20}H_{29}OH$ that occurs free or in the form of esters usu. along with smaller amounts of a cis isomer in animal products (as egg yolk, milk, and butter) and esp. in marine fish-liver oils (as of cod, halibut, and shark), that is synthesized biologically from carotene and other carotenoids and commercially, and that is used in various forms in medicine and nutrition (as in fortifying margarine and other foods and in supplementing animal feeds); all-*trans*-vitamin A — see IODOPSIN, RETINENE a, RHODOPSIN **b** *or* **vitamin A_2 :** a yellow viscous liquid alicyclic alcohol $C_{20}H_{27}OH$ that contains one more double bond in the molecule than vitamin A_1 and is less active biologically in mammals and that occurs esp. in the liver oil of freshwater fish — see PORPHYROPSIN, RETINENE b

vitamin B *n* **1 :** VITAMIN B COMPLEX **2 :** any of numerous members of the vitamin B complex: as **a** *or* **vitamin B_1 :** THIAMINE **b** *or* **vitamin B_2 :** RIBOFLAVIN **c** *or* **vitamin B_6 :** any or all of the three closely related compounds pyridoxine, pyridoxal, and pyridoxamine that occur widely in combined form (as in liver, cereals, royal bee jelly, and yeast), that prevent rat acrodynia and are considered generally essential in the nutrition of vertebrates including man, and that are interconvertible in mammals and birds but vary in their activity as growth factors for microorganisms; *esp* **:** PYRIDOXINE **d** *or* **vitamin B_{12}** (1) **:** a red crystalline complex cobalt-containing cyano antianemic compound $C_{63}H_{90}CoN_{14}O_{14}P$ that is in part related chemically to porphin and is in part a nucleotide, that occurs in most animal products and esp. liver, kidney, and various seafoods but is usu. obtained commercially by bacterial fermentation, that is essential for normal blood formation, neural function, and growth and maintenance in man, various lower animals, and many microorganisms, and that is used chiefly in the treatment of pernicious anemia and other macrocytic anemias and of neuropathies and as a growth factor esp. for hogs and poultry — called also *antianemic factor, cyanocobalamin;* see ANIMAL PROTEIN FACTOR, EXTRINSIC FACTOR (2) **:** any or all of various compounds having similar biological activity to vitamin B_{12} but differing chemically in containing hydroxyl or other group in place of the cyano group and readily interconvertible with vitamin B_{12} **:** COBALAMIN; *broadly* **:** any of various related compounds differing from vitamin B_{12} in other respects (as in biological activity for higher animals and in the chemical composition of the nucleotide portion of the molecule) and formed in many cases by bacterial fermentation **e** *or* **vitamin B_c :** FOLIC ACID 1 **f** *or* **vitamin B_T :** CARNITINE

vitamin B complex \-ˈbē,kăm,pleks\ *n* **:** a group of water-soluble vitamins that are found esp. in yeast, the germ of cereals, nuts, eggs, liver, meats, fish, and vegetables, that in addition to those given vitamin B names usu. include *para*-aminobenzoic acid, biotin, carnitine, choline, folic acid, *meso*-inositol, nicotinic acid or nicotinamide, and pantothenic acid, that in a few cases function as coenzymes, and that in some cases are growth factors for bacteria and are formed by bacterial action in the intestinal tract of various animals

vitamin C *n* **:** the antiscorbutic vitamin **:** ASCORBIC ACID 1

vitamin D *n* **:** any or all of several fat-soluble antirachitic vitamins that are related chemically to the steroids, that are essential for normal bone and tooth structure, and that occur esp. in the liver oils of various fishes, in egg yolk, and in milk or are produced by activation of sterols (as by ultraviolet irradiation of individual sterols or of foods containing them): as **a** *or* **vitamin D_2 :** a crystalline unsaturated alcohol $C_{28}H_{43}OH$ that is usu. prepared by irradiation of ergosterol and is used as a dietary supplement in human and animal nutrition (as in fortified milk or butter) and medicinally in the treatment and control of rickets, osteomalacia, and other hypocalcemic disorders — called also *calciferol, ergocalciferol;* compare VIOSTEROL **b** *or* **vitamin D_3 :** a crystalline unsaturated alcohol $C_{27}H_{43}OH$ that is the predominating form of vitamin D in most fish-liver oils and is formed in the skin of animals on exposure to sunlight or ultra-violet rays and is usu. made commercially by irradiation of dehydrocholesterol and that is used similarly to vitamin D_2 but is preferred for addition to poultry feeds because of its greater activity — called also *cholecalciferol* **c** *or* **vitamin D_4 :** a crystalline alcohol $C_{28}H_{45}OH$ isomeric with dihydrotachysterol and obtained by irradiation of a dihydro derivative of ergosterol

vitamine *var of* VITAMIN

vitamin E *n* **:** any or all of a group of fat-soluble vitamins that consist of the tocopherols, are essential in the nutrition of various animals (as some rodents, ruminant mammals, and poultry) in which their absence is associated with infertility, muscular dystrophy, or abnormalities in the vascular system, are found esp. in the leaves of many plants and in oils from seed germs, and are used chiefly in supplementing animal feeds and as antioxidants in foods and pharmaceutical preparations; *esp* **:** TOCOPHEROL a

vi·ta·mined \ˈ==mənd\ *adj* [*vitamin* + *-ed*] **:** full of or as if full of vitamins; *also* **:** vigorously and robustly healthy

vitamin G *n* **:** RIBOFLAVIN

vitamin H *n* **:** BIOTIN

vi·ta·min·ize \ˈvīd·əmə,nīz, -ītə-\ *vt* -ED/-ING/-S *see -ize in Explan Notes* [*vitamin* + *-ize*] **1 :** to provide with an optimum or a superior allotment of vitamins; *esp* **:** to introduce supplementary vitamins into (a foodstuff) **2 :** to make vigorous as if by the feeding of vitamins ⟨such ideas ~ his writings⟩

vitamin K *n* [Dan *koagulation* coagulation, fr. L *coagulation-, coagulatio*] **1 :** either of two naturally occurring fat-soluble vitamins that are essential for the clotting of blood because of their role in the production of prothrombin in the liver and that are used in preventing and treating hypoprothrombinemia and hemorrhage: **a** *or* **vitamin K_1 :** a yellow oily disubstituted naphthoquinone $CH_3(C_{20}H_{39})C_{10}H_4O_2$ that is obtained esp. from alfalfa or made synthetically (as from phytol and methylnaphthoquinone or their derivatives) and that has a fast, potent, and prolonged biological effect, is effective orally, and is useful esp. in treating hypoprothrombinemia induced by anticoagulant drugs; 2-methyl-3-phytyl-1,4-naphthoquinone — called also *phylloquinone, phytonadione* **b** *or* **vitamin K_2 :** a pale yellow crystalline disubstituted naphthoquinone $CH_3(C_{30}H_{49})C_{10}H_4O_2$ that is obtained esp. from putrefied fish meal and is synthesized by various bacteria (as in the intestines of man and higher animals) and that is much more unsaturated than vitamin K_1 and slightly less active biologically **2 :** any of several synthetic compounds that are closely related chemically to vitamins K_1 and K_2 but are simpler in structure and that have similar biological activity but except for menadione are less active than the natural vitamins: as **a** *or* **vitamin K_3 :** MENADIONE **b** *or* **vitamin K_4 :** a hydroquinone derivative $CH_3C_{10}H_5(OH)_2$ formed from menadione by hydrogenation and used in the form of its crystalline diacetate or the water-soluble crystalline sodium salt of its diphosphate; 2-methyl-1,4-naphthalene-diol **c** *or* **vitamin K_5 :** a water-soluble crystalline compound $CH_3C_{10}H_5(OH)NH_2$·HCl that inhibits the growth of various microorganisms and is useful esp. as a food preservative; 4-amino-2-methyl-1-naphthol hydrochloride **d** *or* **vitamin K_6 :** a toxic water-soluble crystalline compound $CH_3C_{10}H_5(NH_2)_2$·2HCl; 2-methyl-1,4-naphthalene-diamine dihydrochloride

vitamin M *n* **:** FOLIC ACID 1

vi·ta·min·ol·o·gy \ˌvīd·əməˈnäləjē\ *n* -ES [ISV *vitamin* + *-logy*] **:** a branch of knowledge dealing with vitamins, their nature, action, and use

vitamin P *n* [partly fr. *paprika;* partly fr. *permeability*] **:** a substance that is obtained from citrus fruits and esp. their peel and from some paprikas and is held to decrease capillary fragility and permeability in various animals but is not a vitamin **:** BIOFLAVONOID — see CITRIN

vitamin PP \ˌ===,pēˈpē\ *n* [*pellagra-preventive*] **:** a pellagra-preventive vitamin (as nicotinamide or nicotinic acid)

vi·ta·scope \ˈvīd·ə,skōp\ *n* [L *vita* life + E *-scope* — more at VITAL] **:** an early motion-picture projector — **vi·ta·scop·ic** \¦==¦skäpik\ *adj*

vite \ˈvēt\ *adv* [F, fr. MF, fr. *vite* rapid, swift, fr. OF *viste*] **:** QUICKLY, LIVELY — used chiefly as a direction in music

vi·tebsk \ˈvē,tepsk, -ebzk,-ebsk, vəˈt-\ *adj, usu cap* [fr. *Vitebsk*, city of northeast White Russia, U.S.S.R.] **:** of or from the city of Vitebsk, U.S.S.R. **:** of the kind or style prevalent in Vitebsk

vitel *abbr* vitellus

vitell- *or* **vitello-** *comb form* [L *vitellus*] **1 :** yolk **:** vitellus ⟨*vitell*in⟩ ⟨*vitello*genesis⟩ **2 :** vitelline and ⟨*vitello*intestinal⟩

vitel·lar·i·um \ˌvīd·əˈla(a)rēəm, ˌvid-·\ *n, pl* **vitellar·ia** \-ēə\ [NL, fr. *vitell-* + *-arium*] **1 :** a modified part of the ovary that in many flatworms and rotifers produces yolk-filled cells serving to nourish the true eggs — distinguished from *germarium* **2 :** the part of an insect ovariole in which the egg cells grow to mature size

vitel·lary \ˈvīd·ᵊl,erē, ˈvid-·; vīˈtelərē, vəˈt-\ *adj* [L *vitellus* + E *-ary*] **:** VITELLINE

vitel·lig·e·nous \¦vīd·ᵊl¦ijənəs, ¦vid-·\ *adj* [L *vitellus* + *-i-* + E *-genous*] **:** producing yolk ⟨~ cells in the ovaries which supply nutriment to the developing ova of many insects⟩

vi·tel·lin \vīˈtelən, vəˈt-\ *n* -S [ISV *vitell-* + *-in*] **:** a phosphoprotein constituting the principal protein in egg yolk and containing lecithin as often prepared — called also *ovovitellin*

vi·tel·line \-lən, -,lēn, -,līn\ *adj* [ME, fr. MF *vitellin*, fr. ML *vitellinus*, fr. L *vitellus* + *-inus* -ine] **1 :** resembling the yolk of an egg esp. in yellow color **2 :** of, relating to, or producing yolk

vitelline artery *n* **:** an artery that arises in a vertebrate embryo from the aorta or one of the aortic trunks of the embryo, is distributed by numerous branches over the yolk sac, and is usu. paired — compare VITELLINE VEIN

vitelline duct *n* **:** the duct by which the yolk sac or umbilical vesicle remains connected with the alimentary tract of the vertebrate embryo

vitelline gland *n* **:** VITELLARIUM

vitelline membrane *n* **:** a membrane enclosing the egg proper and corresponding to the cell wall of an ordinary cell; *esp* **:** a membrane separated from the surface of the egg in many invertebrates immediately the egg is fertilized, thus preventing other spermatozoa from entering

vitelline vein *n* **:** one of the veins in a vertebrate embryo that return the blood from the yolk sac to the heart or later to the portal vein and in mammals have their function of bringing nutriment to the embryo superseded early by that of the umbilical vein

vi·tel·lo·gene \vīˈtelə,jēn, vəˈt-\ *or* **vi·tel·lo·gen** \-jən, -,jen\ *n* -S [*vitell-* + *-gen*] **:** VITELLARIUM

vi·tel·lo·genesis \(,)vī,telə, vəˌt-+\ *n* [NL, fr. *vitell-* + *genesis*] **:** yolk formation

vitel·log·e·nous \¦vīd·ᵊl¦äjənəs, ¦vid-·\ *adj* [*vitell-* + *-genous*] **:** VITELLIGENOUS

vi·tel·lo·intestinal \ vīˌte(,)lō, vəˌt-+\ *adj* [*vitell-* + *intestinal*] **:** of, relating to, or connecting the intestine and yolk sac

vi·tel·lo·phag \vīˈtelə,fag, vəˈt-\ *also* **vi·tel·lo·phage** \-fāj\ *n* -S [*vitell-* + *-phage*] **:** any of the cleavage cells or nuclei in a centrolecithal egg that do not participate in embryo formation but remain in and function in the assimilation of the yolk

vi·tel·lus \vīˈteləs, vəˈt-\ *n* -ES [L, lit., little calf — more at VEAL] **:** the yolk of egg; *broadly* **:** the egg cell proper including the yolk but excluding any albuminous or membranous envelopes

vi·tex \ˈvī,teks\ *n* [NL *Vitic-, Vitex*, fr. L, chaste tree — more at WITHY] **1** *cap* **:** a large genus of chiefly tropical shrubs and trees (family Verbenaceae) having divided leaves and forking cymes of small flowers with a short tube and bilabiate limb — see AGNUS CASTUS, PURIRI **2** -ES **:** any plant of the genus *Vitex*

viti- *comb form* [L, fr. *vitis*] **:** vine ⟨*viti*culture⟩

¹vi·ti·ate \ˈvishēət\ *adj* [ME, fr. L *vitiatus*, past part. of *vitiare* to vitiate] **:** VITIATED

²vi·ti·ate \ˈvishē,āt, *usu* -ād· +V\ *vb* -ED/-ING/-S [L *vitiatus*, past part. of *vitiare* to vitiate, fr. *vitium* fault, vice — more at WITH] *vt* **1 :** to make incomplete, faulty, or defective **:** injure the substance or quality of **:** IMPAIR, CONTAMINATE, SPOIL, CORRUPT ⟨exaggeration ~*s* a style of writing⟩ ⟨the fox . . . ~*s* his line of scent with the gas fumes on the macadam highways —George Heinold⟩ **2 a :** to debase in moral or aesthetic standards **:** DEPRAVE, PERVERT ⟨*vitiated* by luxury⟩ ⟨*vitiating* the public taste⟩ **b** *obs* **:** to violate the chastity of **3 :** to make ineffective either wholly or in part **:** destroy the validity or force of (as of an instrument or transaction) **:** INVALIDATE; ⟨fraud ~*s* a contract⟩ **4 :** to make (air) impure by or as if by the accumulation of the products of respiration ~ *vi* **:** to become vitiated; *also* **:** to cause vitiation **syn** see DEBASE

vi·ti·a·tion \ˌvishēˈāshən\ *n* -S [L *vitiation-, vitiatio*, fr. *vitiatus* + *-ion-, -io* -ion] **1 :** the quality or state of being vitiated ⟨the air in the room showed marked ~⟩ **2 :** the act of vitiating ⟨protesting his ~ of the agreement⟩

vi·ti·a·tor \ˈ==,ād·ə(r), -,ātə-\ *n* -S [L, fr. *vitiatus* + *-or*] **:** one that vitiates

viti·ce·tum \ˌvid·əˈsēd·əm, ˌvīd-·\ *n, pl* **vitice·ta** \-ēd·ə\ *also* **viticetums** [irreg. (influenced by L *vitic-, vitex* chaste tree) fr. L *vitis* vine + *-etum* — more at WITHY] **:** a growth or plantation of vines, esp. grapevines

viti·cul·tur·al \¦vid·ə¦kəlch(ə)rəl, ¦vīd-·\ *adj* **:** of, relating to, or used in viticulture

viti·cul·ture \ˈ==,chə(r) *also* ,==ˈ==\ *n* [*viti-* + *culture*] **1 :** the cultivation of vines **:** grape growing **2 :** a branch of agricultural science concerned with the culture and production of grapes esp. for wine and market

viti·cul·tur·ist \¦==¦kəlch(ə)rəst\ *n* **:** a practicer of viticulture **:** a producer of grapes or vineyards

vit·i·lig·i·nous \¦vid·ᵊl¦ijənəs\ *adj* [NL *vitiligin-, vitiligo* + E *-ous*] **:** of, relating to, or characterized by vitiligo

vit·i·li·go \ˌ==ˈī(,)gō\ *n* -S [NL *vitiligin-, vitiligo*, fr. L, tetter; prob. akin to L *vitium* fault, blemish, vice — more at WITH] **:** a skin abnormality characterized by loss of pigment in areas of various shapes and sizes and by producing white patches surrounded by heavily pigmented borders — compare LEUKODERMA

vit·i·li·goid \¦==¦ī,gȯid\ *adj* [NL *vitiligo* + E *-oid*] **:** resembling vitiligo

vi·ti·os·i·ty \ˌvishēˈäsəd·ē\ *n* -ES [L *vitiositat-, vitiositas*, fr. *vitiosus* faulty, vicious + *-itat-, -itas* -ity — more at VICIOUS] **1 a** *obs* **:** DEFECT **b** *archaic* **:** DEFECTIVENESS **2** *archaic* **:** VICIOUSNESS, DEPRAVITY

vi·tious \ˈvishəs\ *archaic var of* VICIOUS

vi·tis \ˈvīd·əs\ *n, cap* [NL, fr. L, vine — more at WITHY] **:** a large genus (the type of the family Vitaceae) of woody vines having simple often lobed leaves and small polygamously dioecious flowers with the petals united in a cap that falls away entire from the hypogynous disk — see GRAPE 2

vitr- *or* **vitro-** *comb form* [L *vitrum* glass — more at WOAD] **:** glass **:** glassy ⟨*vitro*phyre⟩ ⟨de*vitr*ify⟩

vi·trailed \vəˈtrīd, ˈvi·trəld\ *adj* [F *vitrail* leaded glass window (fr. MF *vitral*, fr. *vitre* pane of glass, fr. L *vitrum* glass) + E *-ed*] **:** fitted with stained glass

vi·trail·list \vəˈtrīəst, ˈvi·trələst\ *n* -S [F *vitrail* + E *-ist*] **:** a maker or designer of work in stained glass

vit·rain \ˈvi·,trān\ *n* -S [*vitr-* + *-ain* (as in *fusain*)] **:** a constituent of banded bituminous coal that has a vitreous or glossy fracture — compare CLARAIN, DURAIN, FUSAIN

vi·trel·la \vəˈtrelə\ *n, pl* **vitrel·lae** \-e(,)lē\ [NL, fr. L *vitrum* glass + NL *-ella* — more at WOAD] **:** RETINOPHORE

vit·reo·dentine \¦vi·trē(,)ō+\ *n* [L *vitreus* vitreous + E *-o-* + *dentine*] **:** a dentine characterized by extreme hardness

¹vit·re·ous \ˈvi·trēəs\ *adj* [L *vitreus*, fr. *vitrum* glass — more at WOAD] **1 :** of, relating to, derived from, or consisting of glass **2 a :** resembling glass (as in color, composition, brittleness, or luster) **:** GLASSY ⟨~ rocks⟩ **b** *of a fired clay body* **:** having extremely low porosity because of the presence of a glassy phase **3 :** of, relating to, or constituting the vitreous humor of the eye ⟨the ~ chamber⟩ **4 :** of the color glass green — **vit·re·ous·ly** *adv* — **vit·re·ous·ness** *n* -ES

²vitreous \"\ *n* -ES **:** VITREOUS HUMOR

vitreous aggregate *n* **:** a brilliantly lustrous aggregate made with materials and by processes similar to those of the glass industry and used in the surface layer of ornamental concrete

vitreous china *n* **:** a hard-fired ceramic ware that has a dense, vitrified, but opaque body and is used esp. for plumbing fixtures

vitreous enamel *n* **:** a fired-on opaque glassy coating on steel or other metals — called also *porcelain enamel*

vitreous fusion *n* **:** gradual fusion (as of glass) not showing a sharp melting point

vitreous humor *also* **vitreous body** *n* **:** the clear colorless transparent jelly that fills the eyeball posterior to the lens, is enclosed by a delicate hyaloid membrane, and in the adult is nearly homogeneous but in the fetus is pervaded by fibers with minute nuclei at their points of junction

vitreous silica *n* **:** a chemically stable and refractory glass made of silica alone and when prepared from quartz marked by great transparency to light as well as to ultraviolet and infrared radiation — called also *fused quartz, quartz glass*

vi·tres·cence \vəˈtresᵊn(t)s\ *n* -S [fr. *vitrescent*, after such pairs as E *adolescent: adolescence*] **:** the quality or state of being or becoming vitreous

vi·tres·cent \-nt\ *adj* [*vitr-* + *-escent*] **:** capable of being formed into glass **:** tending to become glassy

vi·tres·ci·ble \vəˈtresəbəl\ *adj* [*vitrescent* + *-ible*] **:** VITRIFIABLE

vit·ric \ˈvi·trik\ *adj* [L *vitrum* glass + E *-ic* — more at WOAD] **:** having the nature or quality of glass **:** resembling glass — distinguished from *ceramic*

vit·ri·fac·tion \¦vi·trə¦fakshən\ *n* -S [*vitrify* + *-faction*] **:** VITRIFICATION

vit·ri·fi·able \ˈvi·trə,fīəbəl, ,==ˈ===\ *adj* **:** of a kind that can be vitrified ⟨~ colors⟩

vit·ri·fi·ca·tion \ˌvi·trəfəˈkāshən\ *n* -S [*vitrify* + *-fication*] **1 :** an act or instance or the process of vitrifying **2 a :** the condition of being vitrified **b :** a vitrified body

vitrified fort *n* **:** ancient masonry remains apparently of defensive works found esp. in Scotland, Ireland, France, and Germany and characterized by siliceous stones converted into a hard glassy material by the action of fire

vit·ri·form \ˈvi·trə,fȯrm\ *adj* [*vitr-* + *-iform*] **:** having the form or appearance of glass **:** GLASSY

vit·ri·fy \ˈvi·trə,fī\ *vb* -ED/-ING/-ES [F *vitrifier*, fr. MF, fr. L *vitrum* glass + MF *-ifier* -ify — more at WOAD] *vt* **:** to change into glass or a glassy substance by heat and fusion **:** make vitreous; *esp* **:** to produce in (a ceramic ware) enough glassy phase or close crystallization by high firing to make nonporous ~ *vi* **:** to undergo vitrification **:** become vitreous

vi·tri·na \vəˈtrīnə, -rēnə\ *n* [NL, fr. L *vitrum* glass + NL *-ina*] **1** *cap* **:** a genus of land snails (order Pulmonata) having a very thin translucent spiral shell with a large aperture **2** -S **:** VITREOUS HUMOR

vi·trine \vəˈtrēn\ *n* -S [F, fr. *vitre* pane of glass, fr. OF, fr. L *vitrum* glass] **:** a glass showcase for display (as of fine wares or specimens)

vit·ri·nite \ˈvi·trə,nīt\ *n* -S [*vitrin-* (fr. *vitrain*) + *-ite*] **:** the principal maceral of bright coal

¹vit·ri·ol \ˈvi·trēəl, *chiefly in substand speech* -rəl\ *n* -S [ME, fr. MF, fr. ML *vitriolum*, fr. LL *vitreolum*, neut. of *vitreolus* glassy, fr. L *vitreus* vitreous] **1 a :** a sulfate of any of various metals (as copper, iron, zinc); *esp* **:** a hydrate (as the heptahydrate) of such a sulfate having a glassy appearance or luster **b :** OIL OF VITRIOL **c** *obs* **:** any of various salts not sulfates ⟨~ de luna is silver nitrate⟩ **2 :** something felt to resemble vitriol esp. in caustic quality; *esp* **:** virulence of feeling or of speech

²vitriol \"\ *vt* -ED/-ING/-S **:** to expose to the action of vitriol; *esp* **:** to dip (as metal) in dilute sulfuric acid

vit·ri·o·lat·ed \ˈvi·trēə,lād·əd\ *adj* [fr. past part. of obs. E *vitriolate* to convert into or subject to the action of vitriol, fr. E ¹*vitriol* + *-ate*] **:** converted into a vitriol or other sulfate **:** subjected to the action of sulfuric acid

vitriolated tartar *n* **:** POTASSIUM SULFATE a

vit·ri·ol·ic \¦vi·trē¦älik, -lēk, *chiefly in substand speech* vəˈträ-\ *adj* [¹*vitriol* + *-ic*] **1 :** of or relating to vitriol **:** derived from or resembling vitriol ⟨a ~ liquid⟩ **2 :** marked by a caustic biting quality **:** VIRULENT ⟨a ~ denunciation⟩

vitriolic acid *n, archaic* **:** SULFURIC ACID; *esp* **:** OIL OF VITRIOL

vit·ri·ol·ized \ˈvi·trēə,līzd\ *adj* [fr. past part. of obs. E *vitriolize* to subject to the action of vitriol, fr. E ¹*vitriol* + *-ize*] **:** subjected to the action of vitriol and esp. oil of vitriol

vitriol stone *n* **:** a hard crystalline mass that consists chiefly of ferric sulfate and aluminum sulfate, is obtained by exposing pyritic schist to the atmosphere for some years, lixiviating the mass, and evaporating, and is used in manufacturing fuming sulfuric acid

vitro- — see VITR-

vit·ro·basalt \¦vi·(,)trō+\ *n* [*vitr-* + *basalt*] **:** BASALT GLASS

vitro-clarain \"+\ *n* [*vitr-* + *clarain*] **:** ANTHRAXYLON

vi·tro·clas·tic \¦vi·trə¦klastik\ *adj* [*vitr-* + *-clastic*] **:** of, relating to, or characterized by glassy rock fragments ⟨a ~ tuff⟩

vi·tro di tri·na \¦vi·(,)trōdə·ˈtrēnə\ *n* [It *vetro di trina*, lit., lace glass] **:** a Venetian glass or glassware in which white threads are embedded in transparent glass with a lacelike or netted effect

Vit·ro·lite \ˈvi·trə,līt\ *trademark* — used for a thick homogeneous opaque structural glass used esp. for ornamental finish on surfaces exposed to the weather

vit·ro·phyre \ˈvi·trə,fī(ə)r\ *n* -S [ISV *vitr-* + *-phyre;* orig. formed as G *vitrophyr*] **:** porphyritic glassy rock — **vit·ro·phyr·ic** \¦==¦fī(ə)rik\ *adj*

vit·ro·type \ˈvi·trə,tīp\ *n* [*vitr-* + *type*] **:** a photograph on glass or ceramic ware produced orig. about 1860 by a collodion process and burned into the surface

vi·tru·vi·an \vəˈtrüvēən\ *adj, usu cap* [Marcus *Vitruvius*

Pollio, 1st cent. B.C. Roman architect and engineer + E *-an*] **:** of, relating to, or being in the architectural style of Marcus Vitruvius Pollio

vitruvian scroll *n, usu cap V* **:** a scroll of convolved undulations used esp. in friezes of the composite order

Vitruvian scroll

vit·ry \ˈvi·trē\ *n* [F *vitré,* fr. *Vitré,* manufacturing and commercial town of northwest France] *archaic* **:** a light durable canvas

vit·ta \ˈvid·ə\ *n, pl* **vit·tae** \ˈvi,tē, -,tī\ *also* **vittas** [NL, fr. L, fillet, headband; akin to L *viēre* to twist, plait — more at WIRE] **1 a :** one of the oil tubes in the fruits of plants of the family Umbelliferae occurring commonly in the grooves between the ridges and affording by their number and position important diagnostic characters **b :** one of the internal septa in some diatoms (as of the genus *Tabellaria*) **2 :** STRIPE, STREAK

vit·ta·din·ia \,vid·əˈdinēə\ *n, cap* [NL, fr. C. *Vittadini* †1865 Ital. physician and botanist + NL *-ia*] **:** a small genus of composite herbs and subshrubs chiefly of the southern hemisphere that are sometimes cultivated for their flower heads which have yellow disks and white or blue ray florets

vit·tar·ia \vəˈta(a)rēə\ *n, cap* [NL, fr. L *vitta* fillet + NL *-aria* — more at VITTA] **:** a genus of tropical epiphytic ferns (family Polypodiaceae) having narrow grasslike fronds and linear marginal sori in continuous lines — see GRASS FERN, RIBBON FERN

vit·tate \ˈvi,tāt\ *adj* [L *vittatus* having a fillet, fr. *vitta* fillet + *-atus* -ate] **1 :** bearing or containing vittae **2 :** striped longitudinally

vit·tle *n* -s [ME *vitaille* — more at VICTUAL] **:** VICTUAL

vit·u·line \ˈvichə,līn, -,lən\ *adj* [L *vitulinus,* fr. *vitulus* calf + *-inus* -ine — more at VEAL] **:** of, relating to, or like a calf or veal

vi·tu·per·ate \vīˈtüpə,rāt, və|, |·ˈtyü\ *vb* -ED/-ING/-S [L *vituperatus,* past part. of *vituperare* to vituperate, fr. *vitium* fault, blemish, vice + *-perare* (fr. *parare* to prepare, make) — more at WITH, PARE] *vt* **:** to abuse in words **:** censure severely or abusively **:** BERATE ~ *vi* **:** to use abusive language **:** give vent to abusive utterances **syn** see SCOLD

vi·tu·per·a·tion \(,)vī,tüpəˈrāshən, və|, |·,tyü-\ *n* -S [ME, fr. MF, fr. L *vituperation-, vituperatio,* fr. *vituperatus* + *-ion-, -io* -ion] **:** an act or instance of vituperating **:** sustained and bitter railing and condemnation **:** vituperative utterance ⟨something ugly, sly, knowing, and triumphant that was far more evil than . . . any open ~ of abuse —Thomas Wolfe⟩ **syn** see ABUSE

vi·tu·per·a·tive \-ˈ-pə,rad·iv, -p(ə)rə|, |t|, |ēv *also* |əv\ *adj* [LL *vituperativus,* fr. L *vituperatus* + *-ivus* -ive] **:** uttering or given to censure **:** containing or characterized by wordy abuse **:** SCOLDING, ABUSIVE, RAILING — **vi·tu·per·a·tive·ly** \|əvlē, -li\ *adv*

vi·tu·per·a·tor \-pə,rād·ə(r), -ātə-\ *n* -S [L, fr. *vituperatus* + *-or*] **:** one that vituperates

vi·tu·per·a·to·ry \-p(ə)rə,tōrē, -tȯ|, |ri\ *adj* [L *vituperatus* + E *-ory*] **:** VITUPERATIVE

vi·tu·per·ous \vīˈtüp(ə)rəs, və|, |·ˈtyü-\ *adj* [MF *vitupereux,* fr. ML *vituperosus,* alter. of *vituperiosus*] **:** VITUPERATIVE

vi·u·va \vēˈüvə\ *n* -S [Pg *viúva,* lit., widow, fr. L *vidua* — more at WIDOW] **:** a California rockfish (*Sebastodes ovalis*) of a reddish olivaceous color with small black spots on the dorsal fins, sides, and back

viv *abbr* vivace

¹vi·va \ˈvē|və, |(,)vä, |(,)vä\ *interj* [It, long live, fr. 3d pers. sing. pres. subj. of *vivere* to live, fr. L — more at QUICK] — used to express good will or approval

²vi·va \ˈvīvə\ *n* -S *Brit* **:** ³VIVA VOCE

vi·va·ce \vēˈvä(,)chā, -,chē\ *adv (or adj)* [It, vivacious, fr. L *vivac-, vivax*] **:** in a brisk spirited manner — used as a direction in music

vi·va·cious \vəˈvāshəs, vī-\ *adj* [L *vivac-, vivax* long-lived, vivacious (fr. *vivere* to live) + E *-ious* — more at QUICK] **1** *archaic* **:** having vigorous powers of life **:** tenacious of life **:** LONG-LIVED ⟨the faith of Christianity is far more ~ than any mere ravishment of the imagination —Isaac Taylor⟩ **2 :** lively in temper or conduct **:** SPRIGHTLY ⟨in contrast to the dour, lethargic . . . orang, the chimpanzee is highly active, ~ —Weston La Barre⟩ ⟨a strong ~ strain, a bright noonday song, full of health and assurance —John Burroughs⟩ **syn** see LIVELY

vi·va·cious·ly *adv* **:** in a vivacious manner **:** with vivacity ⟨the texture of the stuff has sparkle; whatever he means to convey at the time is being ~ put —C.E.Montague⟩

vi·va·cious·ness *n* -ES **:** the quality or state of being vivacious **:** VIVACITY

vi·va·cis·si·mo \,vēvəˈchēsə,mō\ *adv (or adj)* [It, fr. *vivace* vivacious + *-issimo,* superlative suffix (fr. L *-issimus*)] **:** in a very lively or vivacious manner — used as a direction in music

vi·vac·i·ty \vəˈvasəd·ē, vī-, -sətē, -i\ *n* -ES [ME *vivacite,* fr. L *vivacitat-, vivacitas,* fr. *vivac-, vivax* + *-itat-, -itas* -ity] **1 :** the quality or state of being vivacious: **a** *obs* **:** vital force **:** natural vigor **b :** tenacity of life **:** LONGEVITY **c :** ANIMATION, LIVELINESS, SPRIGHTLINESS ⟨from languor she passed to the lightest ~; her temper became merry and wild —Elinor Wylie⟩ **d** *of a color* **:** BRILLIANCE **2 :** a vivacious act or expression

vi·va·men·te \,vēvəˈmentē\ *adv* [It, lively, quickly, fr. *vivo,* adj., alive, lively, quick — more at VIVO] **:** QUICKLY — used as a direction in music

vi·van·dier \,vē,vändˈyā\ *n* -S [MF, irreg. (influence of L *vivere* to live) fr. *viande* viand + *-ier* — more at VIAND] **:** a sutler for a French or some other Continental army

vi·van·dière \-ˈye(ə)r\ *n* -S [F, fem. of *vivandier*] **:** a woman formerly accompanying troops to sell provisions and liquor to the soldiers **:** a female sutler

vi·var·i·um \vīˈvereəm, -ˈva(a)r-,-ˈvār-\ *n, pl* **vivar·ia** \-ēə\ *or* **vivariums** [L, fr. *vivus* alive + *-arium* -ary — more at QUICK] **1** *archaic* **:** a place in which living animals are kept for food; *esp* **:** a fish pond or pool **2 :** an enclosure usu. of limited size with glass sides arranged for keeping or raising and observing animals or plants indoors; *esp* **:** one for terrestrial or partly terrestrial animals — called also *terrarium;* compare AQUARIUM, WARDIAN CASE

vi·va·ry \ˈvīvərē\ *n* -ES [L *vivarium*] **:** VIVARIUM

vi·vat \ˈvī,vat, ˈvē,vat, ˈvē,vät\ *interj* [L, long live, 3d pers. sing. pres. subj. of *vivere* to live — more at QUICK] **:** ¹VIVA

¹vi·va vo·ce \,vīvəˈvō(,)sē, -si\ *adv* [ML, lit., with the living voice] **:** by word of mouth **:** ORALLY ⟨gave an account *viva voce*⟩

²viva voce \"\ *adj* **:** expressed or conducted by word of mouth **:** ORAL ⟨*viva voce* voting⟩ ⟨a *viva voce* examination⟩

³viva voce \"\ *n, pl* **viva voces :** an examination conducted viva voce **:** oral examination

vi·vax \ˈvī,vaks\ *n* -ES [NL (specific epithet of *Plasmodium vivax*), fr. L, long-lived, vivacious — more at VIVACIOUS] **:** the tertian malaria parasite (*Plasmodium vivax*)

vivax malaria *n* **:** malaria caused by a malaria parasite (*Plasmodium vivax*) and marked by recurrence of paroxysms at 48-hour intervals — called also *tertian;* compare FALCIPARUM MALARIA

vive \ˈvēv\ *adj* [MF *vif* (fem. *vive*), fr. L *vivus* alive — more at QUICK] **1** *chiefly Scot* **a :** LIVELY, BRISK **b :** having active properties **:** FORCIBLE **2** *chiefly Scot* **a :** LIFELIKE **b :** VIVID **c :** distinctly perceived — **vive·ly** *adv, chiefly Scot*

vi·ver·ra \vīˈverə, vəˈv-\ *n, cap* [NL, fr. L, ferret; akin to OE *āc-weorna* squirrel, OHG *eihhurno, eihhorno,* ON *īkorni,* Lith *vaiverė,* *voverė* squirrel, *vaiveris* male polecat, male marten, Czech *veverka* squirrel] **:** a genus (the type of the family Viverridae) of civets comprising the common large civet (*V. zibetha*) of India and southeastern Asia

viver·ric·u·la \,vīvəˈrikyələ, ,viv-\ *n, cap* [NL, dim. of *Viverra*] **:** a genus of civets including the common small civet (*V. indica* syn. *V. malaccensis*) of southeastern Asia

¹vi·ver·rid \vīˈverəd, vəˈv-\ *adj* [NL *Viverridae*] **:** of or relating to the Viverridae

²viverrid \"\ *n* -S **:** a mammal of the family Viverridae

vi·ver·ri·dae \-rə,dē\ *n pl, cap* [NL, fr. *Viverra,* type genus + *-idae*] **:** a large family of somewhat catlike carnivorous mammals that are widely distributed in the warmer parts of the Old World, are rarely larger than a domestic cat but long, slender, and weasellike in build with short legs, rounded feet, and more or less retractile claws, and include civets, palm civets, genets, mongooses, and related forms

vi·ver·ri·form \-rə,fȯrm\ *adj* [NL *Viverra* + E *-iform*] **:** resembling or having the structure of a viverrid

vi·ver·rine \-,rīn, -rən\ *adj* [NL *viverrinus,* fr. *Viverra* + L *-inus* -ine] **:** of, relating to, or resembling the Viverridae

viverrine cat *n* **:** FISHING CAT

viverrine otter *n* **:** MAMPALON

vi·vers \ˈvēvərz\ *n pl* [MF *vivres,* pl. of *vivre* food, victual, fr. *vivre* to live, fr. L *vivere* — more at QUICK] *chiefly Scot* **:** VICTUALS, FOOD

vi·veur \(ˈ)vēˈvər(·)\ *n* -S [F, fr. *vivre* to live + *-eur* -or] **:** one who indulges freely or with habitual excess in the pleasures of life

vivi- *comb form* [MF, fr. L, fr. *vivus* — more at QUICK] **:** alive **:** living ⟨vividialysis⟩ ⟨viviperfuse⟩ ⟨vivisection⟩

viv·i·an·ite \ˈvivēə,nīt\ *n* -S [G *vivianit,* fr. J. G. *Vivian,* 19th cent. Eng. mineralogist + G *-it* -ite] **:** a mineral $Fe_3(PO_4)_2.8H_2O$ consisting of a hydrous ferrous phosphate that has limited isomorphism with annabergite, erythrite, and koettigite, is colorless when unaltered or blue to green when unaltered but grows darker on exposure, and occurs in monoclinic crystals or fibrous, massive, and earthy (hardness 1.5–2; sp. gr., 2.58–2.68)

viv·id \ˈvivəd\ *adj* -ER/-EST [L *vividus,* fr. *vivere* to live — more at QUICK] **1 :** having the appearance of vigorous life or freshness **:** ANIMATED, SPIRITED, FRESH, LIVELY ⟨figures so ~ that they seemed to breathe and speak before us —L.P. Smith⟩ ⟨an exuberant ~ young girl⟩ **2** *of a color* **:** very strong **:** very high in chroma ⟨the whole plant, turning red, is ~ against the alkali —*Amer. Guide Series: Nev.*⟩ **3 :** producing a strong or clear impression on the senses **:** SHARP, KEEN, INTENSE ⟨a ~ sensation of pain⟩ ⟨the first ~ notes of the bugle⟩; *specif* **:** producing or tending to produce distinct and lifelike mental images ⟨a ~ description⟩ **4 :** acting with distinctness and force **:** ACTIVE — used esp. of a mental faculty ⟨a ~ imagination⟩ ⟨thanks to her ~ eye, she re-creates fourteenth century England with broad strokes —Nardi Campion⟩ ⟨~ emotions⟩ — **viv·id·ly** *adv* — **viv·id·ness** *n* -ES

vi·vid·i·ty \vəˈvidəd·ē\ *n* -ES **:** VIVIDNESS

vi·vif·ic \(ˈ)vīˈvifik\ *adj* [L *vivificus,* fr. *vivi-* + *-ficus* -fic] **:** VIVIFYING, REVIVING, ENLIVENING

vi·vif·i·cate \vīˈvifə,kāt\ *vt* -ED/-ING/-S [ME *vivificaten,* fr. LL *vivificatus,* past part. of *vivificare,* fr. L *vivificus*] **:** to give life to **:** ANIMATE, REVIVE, VIVIFY ⟨God ~s and actuates the whole world —Henry More⟩

viv·i·fi·ca·tion \,vivəfəˈkāshən\ *n* -S [LL *vivification-, vivificatio,* fr. *vivificatus* + L *-ion-, -io* -ion] **:** the act of vivifying or state of being vivified **:** restoration of life **:** REVIVAL

viv·i·fi·er \ˈvivə,fī(ə)r, -īə\ *n* -S **:** one that vivifies

viv·i·fy \ˈvivə,fī\ *vb* -ED/-ING/-ES [MF *vivifier,* fr. LL *vivificare*] *vt* **1 :** to endue with life **:** QUICKEN, ANIMATE **2 :** to make vivid **:** make sharper, clearer, or brighter ⟨in the mood when the imagination intensely *vivifies* everything —George Meredith⟩ ~ *vi* **1 :** to impart life **2 :** to become alive **syn** see QUICKEN

¹vi·vip·a·ra \vīˈvipərə\ [NL, fr. fem. of L *viviparus* viviparous] *syn of* VIVIPARUS

²vivipara \"\ *n* -S **:** a mollusk of the genus *Viviparus* or the family Viviparidae

¹vi·vip·a·rid \-rəd\ *adj* [NL *Viviparidae* family of snails, fr. *Viviparus,* type genus + *-idae*] **:** of or relating to the genus *Viviparus* or the family Viviparidae

²viviparid \"\ *n* -S **:** a snail of the genus *Viviparus* or the family Viviparidae

vi·vip·a·rism \-,rizəm\ *n* -S [ISV *viviparous* + *-ism*] **:** viviparous reproduction

vivi·par·i·ty \,vīvəˈparəd·ē, ,viv-\ *n* -ES [ISV *viviparous* + *-ity*] **:** the quality or state of being viviparous

vi·vip·a·rous \(ˈ)vīˈvip(ə)rəs\ *adj* [L *viviparus,* fr. *vivi-* + *-parus* -parous] **1 :** producing living young instead of eggs from within the body in the manner of nearly all mammals, many reptiles, and a few fishes — compare LARVIPAROUS, OVIPAROUS, OVOVIVIPAROUS **2 :** germinating while still attached to the parent plant ⟨the ~ seed of the mangrove⟩ — **vi·vip·a·rous·ly** *adv* — **vi·vip·a·rous·ness** *n* -ES

viviparous perch *n* **:** SURF FISH

vi·vip·a·rus \-p(ə)rəs\ *n, cap* [NL, fr. L, adj., viviparous] **:** a widely distributed genus (the type of the cosmopolitan family Viviparidae of the suborder Taenioglossa) of freshwater snails that have a turbinate operculate shell which is usu. greenish and more or less banded with brown and that are born alive and with a well-developed shell

vi·vip·a·ry \-pərē\ *n* -ES [ISV *viviparous* + *-y*] **1 :** the development of vegetative shoots upon or among the reproductive organs of a plant (as in the proliferous flower clusters of some agaves or the growth of bulblets in the flower cluster of an onion) **2 :** VIVIPARITY

vivi·perfuse \,vivə+\ *vt* [*vivi-* + *perfuse*] **:** to perfuse (as an organ of the body) during life — **vivi·perfusion** \"+\ *n*

viv·i·sect \ˈvivə,sekt, ,==ˈ=\ *vb* -ED/-ING/-S [back-formation fr. *vivisection*] *vt* **:** to perform vivisection on **:** dissect alive ~ *vi* **:** to practice vivisection

viv·i·sect·ible \ˌ==ˈsektəbəl\ *adj* **:** that can be vivisected

viv·i·sec·tion \ˌ==ˈsekshən\ *n* [*vivi-* + *section*] **1 :** the cutting of or operation on a living animal usu. for physiological or pathological investigation; *broadly* **:** any form of animal experimentation esp. if considered to cause distress to the subject **2 :** subjection to minute or pitiless examination or criticism — **viv·i·sec·tion·al** \-shənᵊl, -shnəl\ *adj* — **viv·i·sec·tion·al·ly** \-lē, -əlē\ *adv*

viv·i·sec·tion·ist \ˌ==ˈseksh(ə)nəst\ *n* -S **:** a practitioner or advocate of vivisection **:** VIVISECTOR

viv·i·sec·tor \-tə(r)\ *n* -S **:** one that vivisects

vivi·sepulture \,vivə+\ *n* [*vivi-* + *sepulture*] **:** the act or practice of burying alive

vi·vo \ˈvē(,)vō\ *adv (or adj)* [It, alive, lively, quick, fr. L *vivus* alive — more at QUICK] **:** VIVACE — used as a direction in music

vi·vres \ˈvēvə(r)z, *F* vēvr(ᵊ) *or* vēv(rə)\ *n pl* [F — more at VIVERS] **:** FOODSTUFF, PROVISIONS

vi·vum va·di·um \ˌvīvəmˈvādēəm\ *n* [L] **:** LIVING PLEDGE

¹vix·en \ˈviksən\ *n* -S [fr. (assumed) ME (southern dial.) *vixen,* alter. of ME *fixen,* fr. OE *fyxe* (oblique cases *fyxan*), fem. of *fox*] **1 :** a female fox **2 :** a shrewish ill-tempered woman

²vixen \"\ *adj* **:** VIXENISH

vix·en·ish \-sənish\ *adj* **:** resembling a vixen **:** ILL-TEMPERED, SHREWISH — **vix·en·ish·ly** *adv* — **vix·en·ish·ness** *n* -ES

viz \ˈnamlē, -li; ˈviz; vəˈdelə,set, -,sət; vəˈdālə,ket, wēˈd-\ *abbr* [L *videlicet*] namely

¹viz·ard \ˈvizə(r)d\ *n* -S [alter. (influenced by *-ard*) of earlier *viser,* fr. ME, visor, mask — more at VISOR] **1 :** a mask for disguise or protection **2 :** DISGUISE, GUISE **3** *obs* **:** a prostitute wearing a mask in public

²vizard \"\ *vt* -ED/-ING/-S **:** to hide or disguise with or as if with a mask

vizard mask *n* **1** *archaic* **:** a mask for hiding the face **2** *archaic* **:** a person wearing such a mask; *specif* **:** PROSTITUTE

viz·ca·cha *or* **vis·ca·cha** \viˈskächə\ *or* **vis·ca·che** \-chē\ *also* **bis·ca·cha** \bi-\ *n* -S [Sp *vizcacha,* fr. Quechua *wiskácha*] **:** any of several So. American burrowing rodents closely related to the chinchilla — see MOUNTAIN VIZCACHA

viz·ca·che·ra \,viˌskäˈcherə\ *n* -S [AmerSp, fr. Sp *vizcacha*] **:** a group of burrows of the plains vizcacha — compare PRAIRIE DOG TOWN

viz·ca·chon \ˌviˌskäˈchōn, -chōn\ *n* -S [AmerSp *vizcachón,* aug. of *vizcacha*] **:** PLAINS VIZCACHA

vi·zier \vəˈzi(ə)r, -ˈziə *sometimes* ˈvizēə(r)\ *also* **vi·zir** \vəˈzi(ə)r, -ˈziə\ *n* -S [Turk *vezir,* fr. Ar *wazīr,* fr. *wazara* to bear a burden] **:** a high executive officer of various Muslim countries (as of the former Turkish empire) **:** a minister or councilor of state — compare GRAND VIZIER

vi·zier·ate \vəˈzirət, -ˈzi,rāt *sometimes* ˈvizēə,rāt; *usu* |d·+V\ *n* -S **1 :** the office, dignity, or authority of a vizier **2 :** the term of office of a vizier

vi·zier·ial \vəˈzirēəl\ *adj* **:** of, relating to, or issued by a vizier

vi·zier·ship \vəˈzi(ə)r,ship, -ˈziə,sh- *sometimes* ˈvizēə(r),sh-\ *n* **:** VIZIERATE

viznaga *var of* BISNAGA

vizor *var of* VISOR

vizs·la \ˈvizhlə\ *n* [fr. *Vizsla,* town in Hungary] **1** *usu cap* **:** a Hungarian breed of hunting dog resembling the Weimaraner but having a rich deep red coat and brown eyes **2** -S *sometimes cap* **:** a dog of the Vizsla breed

¹vizy *or* **viz·zy** \ˈvizi, ˈvēzi\ *vb* [ME *visien, vesien,* fr. MF *viser,* fr. (assumed) VL *visare,* intens. of L *vidēre* to see — more at WIT] *vt, Scot* **:** to look at closely **:** EXAMINE ~ *vi, Scot* **:** to take aim

²vizy *or* **vizzy** \"\ *n* **1** *Scot* **:** AIM 2 **2** *Scot* **:** a careful look

vl *abbr* violin

VL *abbr, often not cap* [L *varia lectio*] variant reading

vla *abbr* viola

VLA *abbr* very low altitude

vlach \ˈvläk, -lak\ *n* -S *cap* [Czech, Slovak, or Bulg, of Gmc origin; akin to OHG *Walah, Walh* Celt, Roman, OE *Wealh* Celt, Welshman — more at WELSH] **:** a member of a people scattered through southeastern Europe originating in the early middle ages prob. in the Balkans, speaking a Romanian dialect, and including chiefly mountain herdsmen (as in northwestern Greece) — called also *Wallach, Wallachian*

vlad·i·vos·tok \ˌvladəvəˈstäk, -dəˈväˌs-, -ˈstȯk, ,==ˈvä,stäk, *stress in Russian* ===ˈ\ *adj, usu cap* [fr. *Vladivostok,* U.S.S.R.] **:** of or from the city of Vladivostok, U.S.S.R. **:** of the kind or style prevalent in Vladivostok

vlei *also* **vlaie** *or* **vly** *in sense 1* ˈf|lā *or* ˈv| *or* |lī *or Afrik* ˈfləi, *in sense 2* ˈvlī *or* ˈflī\ *n* -S [in sense 1, fr. Afrik *vlei* meadow, valley, vlei, fr. MD *valeye* valley, field, fr. OF *valee;* in sense 2, fr. obs. D dial. (Hudson valley) *vlei,* fr. MD *valeye* — more at VALLEY] **1** *also* **vley** *southern Africa* **:** a marshy depression in which water collects in the wet season **:** a temporary lake **:** PAN **2** *North* **:** MARSH

vlei rat *n* **:** a southern African murid rodent (*Otomys irroratus*) that has long shaggy grizzled pelage, broad ears, and a short scaly tail and is often destructive to young conifers

vlem·inckx' solution \ˈvlemiŋ(k)s-\ *also* **vleminckx' lotion** *n, usu cap V* [after Jean F. *Vleminckx* †1876 Belg. physician] **:** an orange-colored solution containing calcium sulfides made by boiling a mixture of hydrated lime and sublimed sulfur in water and applied externally in the treatment of acne and other skin diseases

v-letter \ˈ=,==\ *n, usu cap V* **:** a letter sent by or prepared for V-mail

VLF *abbr, often not cap* very low frequency

VLR *abbr* very long range

vm *abbr* voltmeter

¹v-mail \ˈ=,=\ *n, usu cap V* [*V* abbr. for *victory* (in the World War II slogan *V for victory*)] **:** a system of mail transmission in which a letter written on a letter sheet is reproduced on photographic microfilm and forwarded in this form to be enlarged on photographic paper for delivery; *also* **:** mail or a letter prepared for or sent by this method of transmission

²v-mail \"\ *vt, usu cap V* **:** to send by V-mail

VMT *abbr* very many thanks

vn *abbr* violin

VN *abbr* **1** *often not cap* verb neuter **2** visiting nurse

v neck *n, cap V* **:** a V-shaped neck of a garment

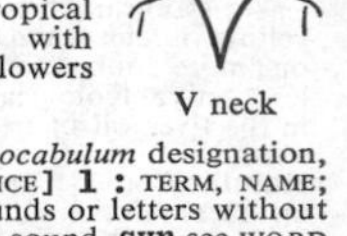
V neck

vo *abbr* verso

VO *abbr* **1** verbal order **2** very old

vo-ag \(ˈ)vōˌag, -a(a)g, -aig\ *adj* [*vo*cational *ag*riculture] **:** of or relating to vocational agriculture ⟨a *vo-ag* instructor⟩

vo·and·ze·ia \ˌvō,an(d)ˈzēyə\ *n, cap* [NL, fr. Malagasy *voandzou*] **:** a genus of tropical creeping herbs (family Leguminosae) with trifoliolate leaves and small axillary flowers

voc *abbr* **1** vocational **2** vocative

vocab *abbr* vocabulary

¹vo·ca·ble \ˈvōkəbəl\ *n* -S [MF, fr. L *vocabulum* designation, name, fr. *vocare* to call — more at VOICE] **1 :** TERM, NAME; *specif* **:** a word composed of various sounds or letters without regard to its meaning **2 :** an individual sound **syn** see WORD

²vocable \"\ *adj* [L *vocare* to call + E *-able*] **1 :** that may be voiced or uttered aloud **2 :** capable of utterance — **vo·ca·bly** \-blē, -li\ *adv*

vo·cab·u·lar \vōˈkabyələ(r), vəˈk-\ *adj* [L *vocabulum* + E *-ar*] **:** of or relating to words or phraseology **:** VERBAL ⟨a developing science frequently inherits its first ~ wardrobe from older relatives —G.L.Jepsen⟩

vo·cab·u·lary \=ˈ==,lerē, -ri\ *n* -ES *often attrib* [MF *vocabulaire,* prob. fr. ML *vocabularium,* fr. neut. of *vocabularius* vocabular, fr. L *vocabulum* designation, name + *-arius* -ary] **1 :** a list or collection of words or of words and phrases usu. alphabetically arranged and explained or defined; *specif* **:** a list in a foreign language textbook of the words and phrases taught or used ⟨study the ~ at the end of each chapter⟩ **:** LEXICON **2 :** a sum or stock of words employed by a language, group, individual, or work, or in relation to a subject **:** scope of language ⟨Latin contributions to the ~ of English⟩ ⟨words peculiar to the educationists' ~⟩ ⟨estimates his English speaking ~ at from 25,000 to 30,000 words —*Current Biog.*⟩ ⟨the ~ of nostalgia⟩ ⟨color *vocabularies* we acquire in the course of . . . experiences with colored objects —F.A.Geldard⟩ **3 :** a set or list of nonverbal symbols (as shorthand signs, sign language positions, marine alphabet flag signals) **4 :** a set of expressive forms used in an art **:** the range of elements composing a formal medium of artistic creation ⟨the Georgian and Federal styles . . . both used the classical ~ of columns, pilasters, pediments —H.S.Morrison⟩ ⟨the complex rhythms and brilliant effects . . . are the natural means of a man who has immense vitality and an enormous musical ~ —*New Yorker*⟩; *specif* **:** the code of set movements that form the basis of expression for a dance composer and his art product ⟨a rigid dance ~ based on five fundamental positions —*Newsweek*⟩ ⟨a considerable difference between ballet, which has a set ~ of movements, and modern dance, which . . . finds its pattern as it goes along —Philip Hamburger⟩ **5 :** a range of means by which one can apprehend experiences or express ideas or feelings ⟨dancing is but a part of her ~ of expression⟩ ⟨by face, gesture, and exquisite movement, she is, by turn, the playful child, the joyful maiden, and the awakened woman —*Newsweek*⟩

vocabulary entry *n* **:** a word (as the noun *book*), hyphened or open compound (as the verb *book-match* or the noun *book review*), word element (as the affix *pro-*), abbreviation (as *agt*), verbalized symbol (as *Na*), or term (as *man in the street*) entered alphabetically in a dictionary for the purpose of definition or identification or expressly included as an inflectional form (as the noun *books* or the verbs *booked* and *saw*) or as a derived form (as the noun *godlessness* or the adverb *globally*) or related phrase (as *one for the book*) run on at its base word and usu. set in a type (as boldface or small capitals) readily distinguishable from that of the running text which defines, explains, or identifies the entry

vocabulary test *n* **:** a test for knowledge (as of meaning or use) of a selected list of words that is often used as part of an intelligence test

¹vo·cal \ˈvōkəl\ *adj* [ME, fr. L *vocalis,* fr. *voc-, vox* voice + *-alis* -al — more at VOICE] **1 a :** uttered by the voice (as in speech or song) **:** ORAL ⟨silent and ~ prayers⟩ ⟨by gestures or ~ communication⟩ **b :** consisting of or characterized by tone produced in the larynx **:** uttered with voice rather than breath **:** VOICED, SONANT, INTONATED **2 a :** relating to, composed or arranged for, or sung by the human voice with or without accompaniment ⟨~ music⟩ ⟨~ technique⟩ — compare INSTRUMENTAL **b :** of or devoted to singing ⟨a recital of ~ students⟩ ⟨organized a ~ group to sing his compositions⟩ **3 :** VOCALIC **4 a :** having or exercising the power of producing voice, speech, or sound ⟨all ~ beings hymned their equal God —Alexander Pope⟩ ⟨our harps, no longer ~ now —Charles Wesley⟩ ⟨the brook ~, with here and there a silence —Alfred Tennyson⟩ **b :** expressive as if by speech ⟨not that she made a fuss, but her back was most extraordinarily ~ —Willa Cather⟩ **c :** full of the sound of voices **:** RESOUNDING ⟨forests, ~ with the songs of many birds —*Amer. Guide Series: Wash.*⟩ **d :** given to expressing oneself freely or insistently **:** OUTSPOKEN ⟨the islanders are, by nature, highly ~, and quite a few have reputations . . . as street-corner orators —*New Yorker*⟩ ⟨~ in support of his party's candidate⟩ ⟨one way of proving that you are a good security risk is to be ~ and aggressive about your patriotism —H.S.Commager⟩ **e :** formulated and expressed in words ⟨make ~ the aspiration of decent Americans for a just and lasting peace—Bruce Bliven b. 1889⟩ ⟨the demand for special-training courses has not yet become ~ —H.P.Hammond⟩ **5 :** of, relating to, or resembling the voice ⟨~ dysfunction due to a throat infection⟩ ⟨~ tone⟩ ⟨the organ had been . . . the vehicle of sacred music because of the sustained and ~ character of its tone —A.E.Wier⟩ **6 :** concerned with the production of voice ⟨the ~ tract⟩

syn ARTICULATE, FLUENT, ELOQUENT, VOLUBLE, GLIB: VOCAL applies to freely speaking out, usu. forcefully, insistently, or emphatically ⟨our most *vocal* theologians — one might almost say, most vociferous — are either at the humanist left or the neoorthodox right —W.L.Sperry⟩ ⟨this instantaneous indignation of the most impulsive and *vocal* of men —H.L.Mencken⟩ ARTICULATE may suggest exact, distinct, or fluent and unmistakable expression in words ⟨the deepest intuitions of a race are deposited in its art; no criticism can make these wholly *articulate* —Laurence Binyon⟩ ⟨perhaps the most *articulate* and effective champion of human freedom in post-Waterloo Europe —P.G.Trueblood⟩ FLUENT suggests, sometimes depreciatively, a facile, copious flow of words ⟨rage was making him *fluent;* the words came easily, in a rush —Aldous Huxley⟩ ⟨not a *fluent* talker. He seemed to express himself with difficulty —W.S.Maugham⟩ ELOQUENT may suggest easy expressive delivery of fervent, moving, or persuasive language ⟨the *eloquent* arguments delivered about the wording of each phrase of the Constitution⟩ VOLUBLE suggests fast utterance, sometimes inspired by protest or enthusiastic interest, that is hard to stop ⟨a *voluble* person, but at last the flow of words stopped —Ellen Glasgow⟩ ⟨she was *voluble*, however, on the subject of divine punishment, and it was with difficulty that Vance stemmed her oracular stream of words —W.H.Wright⟩ GLIB suggests ready facile utterance unembarrassed by the speaker's lack of depth, knowledge, wisdom, sincerity, or honesty ⟨in some colonies any *glib*-tongued man with a pleasing personality could induce men to enlist under him as captain —Allan Nevins & H.S.Commager⟩ ⟨a suspect who is a *glib* talker, who runs wild with his tongue and apparently gives out with all sorts of information —Lou Richter⟩

²**vocal** \"\ *n* -s **1 :** a vocal sound **2 :** a musical composition for or performance by the human voice with or without accompaniment **:** SONG ⟨arranges his own ~*s*⟩ ⟨puts down his horn and takes the ~*s* —Wilder Hobson⟩ — compare INSTRUMENTAL

vocal chink *n* **:** GLOTTIS

vocal cords *also* **vocal bands** *n pl* **:** either of two pairs of folds of mucous membrane that project into the cavity of the larynx and have free edges extending dorsoventrally toward the middle line: **a :** FALSE VOCAL CORDS **b** *or* **vocal folds :** TRUE VOCAL CORDS

¹**vo·cal·ic** \vō'kalik, və'-, -lēk\ *adj* [prob. fr. (assumed) NL *vocalicus*, fr. L *vocalis* vowel (fr. fem. of *vocalis* sounding, sonorous, vocal) + *-icus* -ic] **1 :** marked by or consisting of vowels ⟨the Gaelic language being uncommonly ~ —Sir Walter Scott⟩ **2 a :** being or functioning as a vowel ⟨~ and consonantal sounds⟩ **b :** of, relating to, or associated with a vowel ⟨a ~ sign⟩ ⟨the ~ ablaut⟩ **3 :** having the character or some of the characteristics of a vowel sound ⟨the ~ nature of *r* —John Peile⟩ **4 :** characterized by vowel change ⟨~ preterits⟩ — **vo·cal·i·cal·ly** *adv*

²**vocalic** \"\ *n* -s **:** a vowel sound or phoneme or a diphthong or triphthong that functions as the peak of syllables **:** a syllabic nucleus

vocalic harmony *n* **:** VOWEL HARMONY

vo·ca·lise \,vōkə'lēz, ˈ==,=\ *n, pl* **vocalises** \-z(əz)\ [F, fr. *vocaliser* to vocalize] **1 :** an exercise for singers, commonly using vowels or Italian syllables designed to develop vocal beauty or agility — compare SOLFÈGE **2 :** a vocalized melody or passage without words ⟨long and haunting series of unaccompanied Oriental ~*s* —Edward Sackville-West & Desmond Shawe-Taylor⟩

vo·cal·ism \'vōkə,lizəm\ *n* -s [ISV ¹*vocal* + *-ism*] **1 :** the exercise of the vocal organs in song or speech **:** VOCALIZATION **2 :** vocal art or technique **:** SINGING ⟨mistresses of ~ and . . . intelligent interpreters of songs —Virgil Thomson⟩ ⟨singing with fervor and appeal and accomplishing her best ~ of the season —*N.Y.Times*⟩ **3 a :** the vowel system (as of a language or dialect) ⟨a ~ richer than that of Greek —André Martinet⟩ — compare CONSONANTISM **b :** the vowel or sequence of vowels or quality peculiar to the vowel of a word, syllable, or group of related words

vo·cal·ist \-ləst\ *n* -s **:** a vocal artist **:** SINGER ⟨trumpeter and ~ in a jazz band⟩

vo·cal·i·ty \vō'kaləd·ē, -ətē, -i\ *n* -ES **1 :** possession or exercise of vocal powers ⟨the orator accompanied his fine ~ with a series of six gestures —S.H.Adams⟩ **2 :** the quality or state of being vocal; *specif* **:** the quality or state of being voiced or vocalic ⟨simple tones do have vowel quality, and ~ should be added to the list of tonal dimensions —R.S.Woodworth⟩

vo·cal·iza·tion \,vōkələ'zāshən, -ə,lī'z-\ *n* -s [ISV *vocalize* + *-ation*] **1 :** the act or process of vocalizing: as **a :** utterance with the voice ⟨among the anthropoids, ~ seems . . . to serve social purposes —Weston La Barre⟩ **b :** the change of a consonant to a vowel ⟨the ~ of *g* in Old English *plegere* to *y* in *player*⟩ **2 a :** a reading with the vowels supplied sometimes conjecturally of a word orig. written (as in Hebrew or Arabic) with only consonants **:** a vocalized form of a word in a consonantal text ⟨prefers *Yahweh* to *Jehovah* as the ~ of the Hebrew tetragrammaton *Yhwh*⟩ **b :** the insertion of vowels (as in reading or writing script customarily written only with consonants) ⟨the first step toward the ~ of the text had appeared in the use of . . . vowel letters —W.A.Jeffery⟩ **c :** a manner or system of vocalizing ⟨fix the Hebrew ~ . . . in consonance with the traditional pronunciation —William Chomsky⟩ **3 :** an instance or product of vocalizing

vo·cal·ize \ˈ==,līz\ *vb* -ED/-ING/-S *see -ize in Explan Notes* [in sense 1, prob. fr. F *vocaliser*, fr. *vocal*, adj. (fr. L *vocalis*) + *-iser* -ize; in other senses, ISV ¹*vocal* + *-ize*] *vt* **1 :** to give voice to **:** execute vocally **:** UTTER; *specif* **:** SING **2 a :** to make voiced rather than voiceless **:** VOICE **b :** to convert (as from a consonant) to a vowel ⟨*w* . . . after consonants became *vocalized* to *u* —Joseph Wright⟩ **3 :** to furnish (as a consonantal Hebrew or Arabic text) with vowels or vowel points or signs ⟨the Akkadian texts . . . ~ *spl* with *a; sapl-* —C.H. Gordon⟩ ⟨if it is necessary to indicate in your shorthand notes that a longhand abbreviation is to be used, write a fully *vocalized* outline —*Pitman Shorthand*⟩ **~** *vi* **1 :** to utter vocal sounds ⟨the gorilla is just as likely to thump upon the upper chest . . . as he is to ~ —Weston La Barre⟩ **2 :** SING; *specif* **:** to sing without words (as in practicing vowel sounds) ⟨with the spirituals she started singing words . . . instead of *vocalizing* —Virgil Thomson⟩

vo·cal·iz·er \-zə(r)\ *n* -s **:** one that vocalizes

vo·cal·ly \'vōkəlē, -li\ *adv* **1 :** in a vocal manner ⟨protested long and ~⟩ **2 :** as regards voice ⟨visually and ~ appealing⟩

vo·cal·ness *n* -ES **:** the quality or state of being vocal

vocal process *n* **:** the anterior angle of an arytenoid cartilage to which the true vocal cords of the corresponding side are attached

vocal qualifier *n* **:** VOICE QUALIFIER

vocals *pl of* VOCAL

vocal sac *also* **vocal pouch** *n* **:** one of a pair of inflatable resonating sacs in the mouth of various frogs; *also* **:** the unpaired sac in the true toads of the genus *Bufo*

vo·ca·tion \vō'kāshən\ *n* -s [ME *vocacioun*, fr. LL *vocation-, vocatio*, fr. L, summons, bidding, invitation, fr. *vocatus* (past part. of *vocare* to call) + *-ion-, -io* -ion — more at VOICE] **1 a :** a summons from God to an individual or group to undertake the obligations and perform the duties of a particular task or function in life **:** a divine call to a place of service to others in accordance with the divine plan ⟨does not the sense of divine ~ . . . need to be reintroduced as motivation into the profession of teaching —Gordon Poteat⟩; *specif* **:** a divine call to a religious career (as the priesthood or monastic life) as shown by one's fitness, natural inclinations, and often a conviction of divine summons ⟨resolve not to leave the seminary until someone in authority . . . tells him he has no ~ —J.H.Wilson⟩ **b :** the divine act by which an individual is invited or brought to accept salvation through the gospel — compare EFFECTUAL CALLING ⟨I press towards the mark, to the prize of the supernal ~ of God in Christ Jesus —Phil 3:14 (DV)⟩ **c :** an official invitation to a particular ecclesiastical office; *esp* **:** CALL 2d(1) **2 a** (1) **:** a task or function to which one is called by God ⟨the asceticism of the Middle Ages . . . regarded the religious calling as the only true ~ —E.G.Homrighausen⟩ ⟨getting married is an answer to an invitation from God; and . . . marriage is a ~ —M.J.Huber⟩ (2) **:** the responsibility of an individual or group to serve the divine purposes in every condition, work, or relationship of life **:** one's obligations and responsibilities (as to others) under God ⟨~ involves the total orientation of a man's life and work in terms of his ultimate sense of mission —R.F.West⟩ ⟨domination of physical nature is part of the ~ of man —*New Scholasticism*⟩ **b :** the work in which a person is regularly employed usu. for pay **:** line of work **:** OCCUPATION ⟨~; carpenter⟩ ⟨soon made art his ~, although he had intended to follow it only as a sideline —*Americas*⟩ ⟨those who are philosophers by ~ will . . . leave it to the amateur philosophizing of scientists and men of letters —R.B.Perry⟩ — opposed to *avocation* **c :** the special function of an individual or group within a larger order (as society) **:** ROLE ⟨being a husband and father is only one of many ~*s* of a married man —Margaret Deland⟩ **:** TASK ⟨it is not the ~ of the philosopher . . . to devise and furnish formulae that will define what are in all cases reasonable decisions —F.L.Will⟩ **3** *archaic* **:** the position in life in which God has placed a person **:** ESTATE, STATION ⟨walk worthy of the ~ wherewith ye are called, with all lowliness and . . . long suffering —Eph 4:1 (AV)⟩ **4 :** the membership of a particular occupational group **:** the persons engaged in a field of business, profession, or trade ⟨the ~ of politics contains probably more than its share of brave and conscientious men —John Lodge⟩ **5 :** a strong inclination toward a particular type of work or course of action ⟨moved by a deep messianic ~ —John Bright b. 1908⟩ ⟨though an earnest devotee, she felt no ~ for the cloister —Francis Parkman⟩ ⟨one who is not a dissenter by ~ —M.W.Straight⟩ ⟨a personage whom I might describe minutely, but I feel no ~ for the task —Charlotte Brontë⟩ **6 :** an entry into preparation for the priesthood or a religious order ⟨all religious communities, he said, are praying and hoping for ~*s* . . . to staff educational, charitable and other institutions —H.C.Bezou⟩

vo·ca·tion·al \(ˈ)=ˈkāshən³l, -shnəl\ *adj* **1 a :** of, relating to, or concerned with a vocation **b :** pursued as a vocation ⟨~ experience⟩ **2 :** of, relating to, or being in training in a specific skill or trade usu. with a view to gainful employment soon after completion of the course ⟨~ school⟩ ⟨~ guidance⟩

vocational agriculture *n* **:** agriculture as taught in high schools in the U.S.

vocational bureau *or* **vocational office** *n* **:** a placement service

vocational education *n* **:** training for a specific occupation in agriculture, trade, or industry through a combination of theoretical teaching and practical experience provided by many high schools in their commercial and technical divisions, and by special institutions of collegiate standing (as a college of agriculture, a school of engineering, or a technical institute)

vo·ca·tion·al·ism \=ˈ=shən³l,izəm, -shnə,li-\ *n* -s **:** emphasis on vocational training in education

vo·ca·tion·al·ist \-shən³ləst, -shnəl-\ *n* -s **:** an adherent or advocate of vocationalism

vo·ca·tion·al·ize \-shən³l,īz, -shnə,līz\ *vt* -ED/-ING/-S **:** to make vocational

vo·ca·tion·al·ly \(ˈ)=ˈ=shən³lē, -shnəlē, -li\ *adv* **1 :** with respect to a vocation ⟨~ valuable experience⟩ **2 :** in a vocational manner ⟨~ oriented curricula⟩

vocational psychology *n* **:** the application of psychological principles to the problems of vocational choice, selection, and training

¹**voc·a·tive** \'väkəd·iv, -ətiv\ *adj* [ME *vocatif*, fr. MF, fr. L *vocativus*, fr. *vocatus* (past part. of *vocare* to call) + *-ivus* -ive — more at VOICE] **1 a :** of, relating to, or being a grammatical case marking the one addressed — used esp. in the grammar of languages that have relatively full inflection ⟨Latin *Domine* in *miserere, Domine* "have mercy, O Lord" is in the ~ case⟩ ⟨a ~ ending⟩ **b** *of a word or word group* **:** marking the one addressed even when this relation is not marked by an inflectional element ⟨*mother* in "mother, come here", *beautiful* in "hello, beautiful", and *my beloved* in "be assured, my beloved, that I will come" are ~ expressions⟩ **2 :** characterized by fluent address toward others **:** VOLUBLE, GARRULOUS — **voc·a·tive·ly** \-əd·əvlē, -ətəv-, -li\ *adv*

²**vocative** \"\ *n* -s **1 :** the vocative case of a language **2 :** a form in the vocative case

vo·ce pi·ena \,vō(,)chāpē'enə\ *adv (or adj)* [It] **:** with full voice — used as a direction in music

voce ve·la·ta \-və'läd·ə\ *adv (or adj)* [It] **:** with veiled voice — used as a direction in music

vo·chys·ia \vō'kizh(ē)ə, -izēə, -is-\ *n, cap* [NL, irreg. fr. Galibi *vochy*, a tree of the genus Vochysia + NL *-ia*] **:** a genus (the type of the family Vochysiaceae) of tropical American trees and shrubs having showy fragrant flowers with a single stamen — see COPAIYÉ WOOD

vo·chys·i·a·ce·ae \=,==ˈāsē,ē\ *n pl, cap* [NL, fr. *Vochysia*, type genus + *-aceae*] **:** a family of tropical American trees and shrubs (order Geraniales) having large irregular flowers often with a single petal or stamen and a 3-angled capsular fruit — **vo·chys·i·a·ceous** \=,==ˈāshəs\ *adj*

vo·cif·er·ance \vō'sifərən(t)s, və'-\ *n* -s **:** VOCIFERATION, VOCIFEROUSNESS

vo·cif·er·ant \-nt\ *adj* [L *vociferant-, vociferans*, pres. part. of *vociferari* to cry out] **:** crying out noisily **:** CLAMOROUS, VOCIFEROUS

vo·cif·er·ate \-ə,rāt, *usu* -ād·+V\ *vb* -ED/-ING/-S [L *vociferatus*, past part. of *vociferari* to cry out, vociferate, fr. *voc-, vox* voice + *-ferari* (fr. *ferre* to carry) — more at VOICE, BEAR] *vi* **:** to cry out with quick noisy insistent vehemence ⟨purists have long *vociferated* against *mad* in the meaning "angry" —Thomas Pyles⟩ **~** *vt* **:** to utter with a loud voice **:** shout out ⟨an atmosphere of shrieks and moans; prayers *vociferated* like blasphemies —Joseph Conrad⟩ **syn** see ROAR

vo·cif·er·a·tion \=ˌ==ˈrāshən\ *n* -s [ME *vociferacion*, fr. MF *vociferation*, fr. L *vociferation-, vociferatio*, fr. *vociferatus* (past part.) + *-ion-, -io* -ion] **:** the act of vociferating **:** OUTCRY, CLAMOR ⟨the perpetual ~ of inflammatory opinion by all sorts of periodicals —George Sampson⟩

vo·cif·er·a·tor \=ˈ==,rād·ə(r)\ *n* -s **:** one that vociferates

vo·cif·er·ous \(ˈ)vō;sif(ə)rəs, və'-\ *adj* [LL *vocifer* (fr. L *vociferari*) + E *-ous*] **:** marked by or given to ready vehement insistent outcry ⟨adult newsboys hawk their papers and racing forms like sideshow barkers . . . a ~ performance —*Amer. Guide Series: Fla.*⟩ ⟨the Northern press and people were ~ for action —S.E.Morison & H.S.Commager⟩

syn CLAMOROUS, BOISTEROUS, OBSTREPEROUS, STRIDENT, BLATANT: VOCIFEROUS suggests ready, insistent, or vehement loud outcry ⟨the first California booster, the founder of a long line of *vociferous* enthusiasts whose clamor has resounded throughout the land —Herbert Asbury⟩ CLAMOROUS may add to VOCIFEROUS notions of sustained din or confused turbulence often in demand or protest ⟨the district had been *clamorous* with trucks arriving, backing in and out . . . the drivers bawling and cursing —Peggy Bacon⟩ ⟨the Federalists fairly overwhelmed the silent majority with *clamorous* argument —V.L. Parrington⟩ BOISTEROUS suggests unrestrained noise and noisy activity occasioned by rowdy high spirits or disdain or defiance of authority ⟨from the distant halls the *boisterous* revelry floated in broken bursts of faint-heard din and tumult —J.K. Jerome⟩ ⟨wild and *boisterous* factory girls —George Sampson⟩ OBSTREPEROUS suggests noisy, truculent unruliness in activity directed against control or authority ⟨disrespectful of Parliamentary decorum, they are so *obstreperous* that sittings sometimes have to be suspended to stop their hubbub —Janet Flanner⟩ STRIDENT suggests an insistent continuing harsh grating, jangling, or other unpleasant noise ⟨*strident* tones⟩ ⟨a *strident* electric gong kept ringing above the noise of the crowd —Louis Bromfield⟩ BLATANT, orig. suggesting an angry bellowing, now indicates any loud or vulgar obtrusiveness ⟨a *blatant* child . . . thoughtless, headstrong, jealous, and filled with a tinsel courage —Stephen Crane⟩ ⟨every dictator in history has been a notorious exhibitionist, tub-thumper, and *blatant* publicity hound —J.D.Voelker⟩

vo·cif·er·ous·ly *adv* **:** in a vociferous manner ⟨the young chirped ~ as I approached the nest —John Burroughs⟩

vo·cif·er·ous·ness *n* -ES **:** the quality or state of being vociferous

vo·cod·er \(ˈ)vō;kōdə(r)\ *n* [*voice coder*] **:** an electronic mechanism that reduces speech signals to slowly varying signals which can be transmitted over communication systems of limited frequency band width incapable of transmitting the original speech signals and that then can reconstruct a fair approximation to the original speech signals

vo·coid \'vō,kȯid\ *n* -s [*vocal* + *-oid*] **:** a vowel or vowel glide completely devoid of oral friction ⟨consider certain weak ~*s* as constituting nonsignificant transition sounds —K.L.Pike⟩

vo·der \'vōdə(r)\ *n* -s [*voice operation demonstrator*] **:** an electronic device that is capable of producing a recognizable approximation of speech

vod·ka \'vädkə *also* 'vȯd-\ *n* -s [Russ, fr. *voda* water; akin to Skt *udan* water — more at WATER] **:** a colorless and unaged liquor of neutral spirits distilled from a mash (as of rye or wheat) and treated so as to be without distinctive aroma or taste

vo·dun *also* **vo·doun** \vō'dün\ *n* -s [Haitian Creole *vodou, vodun*, of African origin; akin to Fon *vodū* spirit — more at VOODOO] **:** VOODOOISM 1

voe \'vō\ *n* -s [of Scand origin; akin to Norw *vaag* bay, inlet, ON *vāgr* creek, bay; akin to OE *wǣg* wave, sea, OHG *wāg* wave, sea, ON *vega* to move — more at WEIGH] **:** an inlet or narrow bay of the Orkney and Shetland islands

voet·gang·er \'füt,gäŋər\ *n* -s [Afrik, lit., pedestrian, fr. MD, fr. *voet* foot + *ganger* walker, fr. *ganc* act of going, walk; akin to OE *fōt* foot and to OHG *gang* act of going — more at FOOT, GANG] **:** the immature wingless young of a southern African locust (*Locustana pardalina*) which migrate in huge devastating swarms

¹**vo·ë·tian** \(ˈ)vō;ēshən\ *adj, usu cap* [Gysbertus *Voëtius* (Latinized name of Gisbert Voët) †1676 Dutch theologian + E *-an*] **:** of or relating to Voëtius the Calvinist opponent of Arminianism, Cocceianism, and Cartesianism

²**voëtian** \"\ *n* -s *usu cap* **:** a follower of Voëtius

voeu \'v|ə, |ər(·),|ə, F|œ\ *n, pl* **voeux** \|ə(z), |ərz, |ər(·), |ə(z), |œ\ [F *vœu* vow, wish, fr. OF *vou* — more at VOW] **:** a proposal or recommendation made by a country to an international body or conference

vo·ges-pros·kauer reaction \;fōgə;sprä,skau̇(ə)r-\ *or* **voges-proskauer test** *n, usu cap V&P* [after Otto *Voges* and Bernhard *Proskauer*, 19th cent. Ger. physicians] **:** a method for detecting the presence of acetyl methyl carbinol in a bacterial broth culture by adding a concentrated solution of sodium hydroxide whereupon the presence of the substance is indicated by a red color

vo·gie \'vōgi\ *adj* [origin unknown] **1** *Scot* **:** PROUD, VAIN **2** *Scot* **:** ELATED, MERRY

vo·glite \'vō,glīt\ *n* -s [G *voglit*, fr. J. F. *Vogl*, 19th cent. Ger. mineralogist + G *-it* -ite] **:** a mineral $Ca_2CuU(CO_3)_5.6H_2O$ consisting of a green hydrous carbonate of uranium, calcium, and copper

¹**vogue** \'vōg\ *n* -s [MF, action of rowing, course, fashion, vogue, fr. OIt *voga*, fr. *vogare* to row, sail; akin to OSp *bogar* to row, sail, OPg & OProv *vogar*] **1** *archaic* **:** the leading place in popularity or acceptance **2 a :** popular acceptation or favor **:** POPULARITY ⟨scheme for economic regeneration . . . enjoyed a great ~ a few years ago —H.P.Fairchild⟩ ⟨its ~ has gradually spread among the lovers of books —William McFee⟩ ⟨the slender, undeveloped figure then very much in ~ —Willa Cather⟩ **b :** a period of popularity ⟨in spite of the recent ~ of the Marxist theory —John Dewey⟩ **3 :** something or someone in fashion at a particular time ⟨strange genius . . . now taking posthumous revenge by making himself a ~ —Brand Blanshard⟩ ⟨when the bicycle ~ engulfed the country —Alfred Lief⟩ ⟨plaids were the ~ that season⟩ **4** *obs* **a :** general trend, current, or temper **b :** general character **syn** see FASHION

²**vogue** \"\ *adj* **:** being currently or temporarily in vogue **:** FASHIONABLE ⟨~ words and current cant —J.M.Barzun⟩

vogu·ish *also* **vogue·ish** \'vōgish, -gēsh\ *adj* **1 :** FASHIONABLE, SMART ⟨~ suit⟩ **2 :** suddenly or temporarily very popular ⟨their ~ meanings show a considerable extension of the earlier technical meanings of these terms —Thomas Pyles⟩

vo·gul \'vōgül\ *n, pl* **vogul** *or* **voguls** *cap* [Russ, fr. Ostyak *Uogal'*] **1 a :** a hunting and herding people of the northern Ural mountains akin to the Votyaks and Magyars and forming an autonomous district of the Soviet Union — called also *Mansi* **b :** a member of such people **2 :** the Finno-Ugric language of the Vogul people — see URALIC LANGUAGES table

¹**voice** \'vȯis\ *n* -s [ME *voice, vois*, fr. OF *vois, voiz*, fr. L *voc-, vox;* akin to L *vocare* to call, OHG *giwahanen* to mention, remember, *giwaht* mention, fame, ON *vāttr* witness, *vātta* to witness, affirm, Gk *epos* word, *opa* (acc.) voice, Skt *vāk* voice, *vakti* he says] **1 a :** sound produced by vertebrates by means of lungs, larynx or syrinx, and various buccal structures ⟨the chorused ~*s* of the birds⟩; *esp* **:** sound so produced by human beings (as in speaking, singing, crying, or shouting) **b** (1) **:** the musical sound produced by the vocal cords and resonated by the various cavities of head and throat and differing chiefly from voice in speaking in the greater prolongation of vowel sounds on definite pitches (2) **:** the power or ability to produce musical tones ⟨have a ~⟩ ⟨train the ~⟩ (3) **:** SINGER ⟨the great ~*s* of an age⟩ (4) *also* **voice part :** one of the melodic parts in a vocal or instrumental composition ⟨the bass ~ of a fugue⟩ (5) **:** condition of the vocal organs with respect to the production of esp. musical tones ⟨be in good ~⟩ (6) **:** the use of the voice in singing, acting, public speaking ⟨study ~⟩ ⟨classes in ~⟩ **c :** expiration of air with the vocal cords drawn close so as to vibrate audibly (as in uttering vowels and such consonant sounds as \v\ or \z\) — compare BREATH 7, VOICELESS, WHISPER **d :** the organs by which uttered sound is produced ⟨strained her ~ with coughing⟩ **e :** the faculty or power of utterance **:** SPEECH ⟨fear took away his ~⟩ **2 a :** characteristic sound produced by animals using other than vocal mechanisms (as stridulation) ⟨cheerful ~ of the cricket⟩ **b :** a sound resembling or suggesting vocal utterance ⟨distant ~ of a waterfall⟩ ⟨silvery ~*s* of bells⟩ ⟨hoarse ~ of a foghorn⟩ ⟨wailing ~*s* of sirens⟩ **3 :** something resembling human speech in being an instrument or medium of expression ⟨majestic ~ of the law⟩ ⟨~ of conservatism⟩ **4 a :** wish, choice, or opinion openly or formally expressed ⟨policy adopted despite many dissenting ~*s*⟩ **b :** the right to express a wish, choice, or opinion **:** SAY, SUFFRAGE ⟨every member of the family had a ~ in making the plan⟩ **5** *obs* **:** RUMOR, FAME **6 :** one that speaks **:** one that warns, urges, prompts, or commands ⟨guided by an inner ~⟩ ⟨ancestral ~*s* prophesying war —S.T.Coleridge⟩ ⟨~ of doom⟩ ⟨saw visions and heard ~*s*⟩ **7 :** distinction of form or a particular system of inflections of a verb to indicate the relation of the subject of the verb to the action which the verb expresses — see ACTIVE, MIDDLE, PASSIVE — **with one voice** *adv* **:** UNANIMOUSLY

²**voice** \"\ *vb* -ED/-ING/-S [ME *voicen, voisen*, fr. *voice, vois* voice] *vt* **1 a :** to give utterance to **:** UTTER ⟨a chance to ~ his objections⟩ ⟨has *voiced* the sentiments of the whole group⟩ **b** *obs* **:** REPORT, RUMOR **2** *obs* **:** to appoint by or as if by voting **:** ELECT **3 :** to adjust for producing the proper musical sounds **:** regulate the tone of ⟨to ~ the pipes of an organ⟩ **4 :** to utter with sonant or vocal tone produced by vibration of the vocal cords **:** pronounce with voice ⟨the vowels and such consonants as \b\, \v\, \j\ are *voiced* in contrast with \p\, \f\, \ch\⟩ **~** *vi* **:** to pronounce a sound with voice **syn** see EXPRESS

voice box *n* **:** LARYNX

voicecast \ˈ=,=\ *n* [¹*voice* + *-cast* (as in *broadcast*)] **:** radio broadcast of the speaking voice

voice coil *n* **:** a coil in an electro-acoustic instrument (as a microphone or a loudspeaker) that carries the audio frequency currents corresponding to the sound waves

voiced \'vȯist\ *adj* [in sense 1, fr. ¹*voice* + *-ed;* in sense 2, fr. past part. of ²*voice*] **1 a :** furnished with a voice or with a specified voice — used often in combination ⟨soft-*voiced*⟩ **b :** expressed by the voice ⟨a frequently ~ opinion⟩ **2 :** uttered with vocal cord vibration ⟨~ consonant⟩ — **voiced·ness** \'vȯisədnəs, -stnəs\ *n* -ES

voiced t *n* **:** a *t* or *tt* that is in some contexts articulated by many speakers of English as a flap rather than as a stop and is accompanied by voice with absence or reduction of the distinction commonly heard in other dialects (as Southern British) between pairs like *latter* and *ladder*, *hearty* and *hardy*, *leader* and *liter*, *let on* and *led on*, *metal* and *medal*

voice·ful \ˈvȯisfəl\ *adj* **:** having a voice or vocal quality **:** having a loud voice or many voices ⟨busy, ~ world —Odell Shepard⟩ — **voice·ful·ness** *n* -ES

voice glottis *n* **:** CORD GLOTTIS

voice key *n* **:** an electric key arranged to be opened or closed by speaking against it and used for measuring speech reaction time

voice leading *n* **:** the progression of the individual parts or voices in a vocal or instrumental composition

voice·less \ˈvȯisləs\ *adj* **1 :** having no voice, utterance, or vote **:** SILENT, MUTE, DUMB ⟨because native labor was ~ and constrained —C.W. de Kiewiet⟩ **2 :** uttered or pronounced without voice **:** not voiced **:** SURD ⟨~ fricative⟩ ⟨~ glide⟩ — **voice·less·ly** *adv* — **voice·less·ness** *n* -ES

voice part *n* **:** VOICE 1b(4)

voice pipe *or* **voice tube** *n* **:** SPEAKING TUBE

voice qualifier *n* **:** one of the manners of speaking (as whining, chuckling, loud tone of voice, rasp, general high pitch) that may accompany the articulation of the vowels and consonants of an utterance and convey a meaning of social relationship and emotion

voic·er \ˈvȯisə(r)\ *n* -S **:** one that voices; *specif* **:** one that voices organ pipes

voices *pl of* VOICE, *pres 3d sing of* VOICE

voice vote *n* **:** a parliamentary vote taken by calling for ayes and noes and estimating which response is stronger instead of by individual ballot or roll call — compare RISING VOTE, DIVISION 17

voicing *n* -S [fr. gerund of ²*voice*] **1 a :** final regulation of the pitch and tone of the pipes of an organ **b :** the tone resulting from such regulation **2 :** adjustment of the hardness of the felts of a piano for securing the desired quality and evenness of all the tones

¹**void** \ˈvȯid\ *adj* [ME *void, voide*, fr. OF *voide, vuide*, fr. (assumed) VL *vocitus*, fr. (assumed) VL *vocuus* empty, fr. L *vacuus* — more at VACUUM] **1 :** containing nothing ⟨the earth was without form, and ~ —Gen 1:2(AV)⟩ **2 :** unoccupied with work or business **:** IDLE, LEISURE ⟨~ hours⟩ **3 a :** having no holder or occupant **:** UNOCCUPIED, VACANT ⟨~ bishopric⟩ **b :** not occupied by inhabitants or buildings **:** DESERTED **4 a :** being without **:** WANTING, DEVOID — used with *of* ⟨~ of common sense⟩ ⟨~ of malice⟩ ⟨a bridge hand ~ of spades⟩ **b** *of a category, class, or suit* **:** having no members or examples ⟨bid a ~ suit as a slam signal⟩ **5** *obs* **:** wanting good qualities **:** FOOLISH, WORTHLESS ⟨idol ~ and vain —Alexander Pope⟩ **6 :** not producing any effect **:** VAIN, USELESS ⟨dull and ~ as a work of art —C.E.Montague⟩ **7 a :** of no legal force or effect and so incapable of confirmation or ratification **:** NULL ⟨declare a marriage ~⟩ ⟨~ ballot⟩ **b :** VOIDABLE **syn** see EMPTY

²**void** \"\ *n* -S **1 a :** empty or unfilled space **:** EMPTINESS, VACANCY, VACUUM ⟨gazing out into the ~⟩ ⟨wandering about in a ~⟩ **b :** a space not filled by anything solid **:** OPENING, GAP ⟨air-filled ~*s* of the soil⟩ ⟨alternation of solid and ~ that is characteristic of the Japanese house —Lewis Mumford⟩ **2 :** the quality or state of being without or free from something **:** LACK, ABSENCE, WANT ⟨loneliness that was one with the cruel ~ of the prairie sky —Walter O'Meara⟩ **3 :** a feeling of want or hollowness (as from unsatisfied desire) **4 :** SUNYATA 1 **5 :** absence of any card of a particular suit in a hand as orig. dealt ⟨partner has a ~ in spades⟩

³**void** \"\ *vb* -ED/-ING/-S [ME *voiden*, fr. MF *voidier, vuidier*, fr. OF, fr. (assumed) VL *vocitare*, fr. *vocuus* empty] *vt* **1 a :** to make empty or vacant **:** CLEAR ⟨press gallery has been ~*ed* of the customary bulky desks —*Springfield (Mass.) Union*⟩ **b :** VACATE, LEAVE ⟨~ the room⟩ **2 :** to cast out **:** DISCHARGE, EMIT ⟨~ excrement⟩ **3** *obs* **:** EXPEL, DISMISS **4 :** to cause to be of no validity or effect **:** NULLIFY, ANNUL ⟨~ a deed⟩ ⟨~ a pension⟩ ⟨~ an insurance policy⟩ ⟨~ a contract⟩ **5** *archaic* **:** AVOID, SHUN, EVADE, PREVENT ~ *vi* **1** *archaic* **:** to go out or away **:** DEPART **2 :** to eliminate solid or liquid waste from the body

void·able \-dəbəl\ *adj* [ME, fr. *voiden* to void + *-able*] **:** capable of being voided; *specif* **:** capable of being adjudged void, invalid, and of no force ⟨a ~ contract . . . may be set aside usually at the option of one party —S.B.Ackerman⟩ — **void·able·ness** *n* -ES

void·ance \-dən(t)s\ *n* -S [ME *voidaunce*, fr. MF *voidance vuidance*, fr. OF, fr. *voidier, vuidier* to void + *-ance*] **1 :** the act of voiding, emptying, ejecting, evacuating, casting away, or removing **2** *of a benefice* **:** the condition of being without an incumbent

void·ed \ˈvȯidəd\ *adj* **1 :** having a void or opening **2 :** having the inner part cut away or left vacant with a narrow border left at the sides and the tincture of the field seen in the vacant space — compare GAMMADION illustration

void·ee \ˈvȯidē\ *n* -S [ME *voidee, voide*, fr. MF *voidée, vuidé*, past part. of *voider, voidier* to void, fr. OF] **:** a serving of wine with comfits or spices after a feast and just before the departure or withdrawal of the company

void end *n* **:** an end in lawn bowls in which neither side scores a cast

void·er \ˈvȯidə(r)\ *n* -S [ME, fr. *voiden* to void + *-er*] **1 :** one that empties, vacates, or annuls **2** *dial* **a :** a tray or basket for clearing away (as a meal); *sometimes* **:** a basket for household articles (as clothes) **b :** a servant whose business is to clear away a table after a meal **3 a** *obs* **:** ARBOR, SCREEN **b :** a contrivance usu. of chain mail for covering any part of the body of an armored knight not protected by plate armor **4 :** a heraldic bearing identical with or narrower than a flasque

voiding *n* -S [ME, fr. gerund of *voiden* to void] **:** something that is voided: **a voidings** *pl* **:** EXCREMENT, DUNG **b** *obs* **:** scraps of food from a table

voiding knife *n, obs* **:** a scraper used in gathering fragments of food from the table to put them into a tray or basket

void·ness *n* -ES [ME *voidenes*, fr. *voide* void + *-nes* -ness — more at VOID] **:** the quality or state of being void **:** NULLITY

void-solid ratio *n* **:** the proportion of wall surface pierced by windows and doors

voile \ˈvȯil, *esp before pause or consonant* -ȯiəl, *F* ˈvwȧl\ *n* -S [F, veil, fr. L *vela*, neut. pl. of *velum* curtain, veil] **:** a fine soft sheer fabric with a clear finish made from various fibers in open plain weave and used in solid colors and printed or woven designs for women's summer clothing or curtains

voi·lier \vwȧˈlyā\ *n* -S [F, lit., sailor, sailmaker, fr. *voile* sail (fr. L *vela*, neut. pl. of *velum* sail) + *-ier* -er] **:** SAILFISH

voir dire \ˌvwärˈdi(ə)r\ *n* [AF, fr. OF, to say the truth, fr. *voir* true, truth (fr. L *verum*, fr. neut. of *verus* true) + *dire* to say, fr. L *dicere* — more at VERY, DICTION] **:** a preliminary examination to determine the competency of a witness or juror

voi·ture \vwȧˈtü(ə)r, -ä'tyü-, -üə, -äˈchü-; ˈvwächə(r)\ *n* -S [F, fr. L *vectura* vehicle — more at VECTURIST] **1** *obs* **:** means of travel **:** CONVEYANCE **2 a :** a light carriage **b :** a light open automobile **3 :** a local constituent unit of the Forty-and-Eight division of the American Legion

voi·tu·rette \ˌvwächəˈret\ *n* -S [F, fr. *voiture* + *-ette*] **:** a small usu. two-seater automobile

voivod, voivode *var of* VAIVODE

voivode·ship *also* **voi·vod·ship** \ˈvoi,vōd,ship\ *n* -S **:** one of the provinces of Poland

voix cé·leste \ˌvwäsāˈlest\ *n, pl* **voix célestes** [F, lit., heavenly voice] **:** a labial organ stop of 8-foot pitch with its characteristic soft tremulous tone produced either by the stop being used with another stop of slightly different pitch or by its being composed of two or three ranks of pipes tuned sharp or flat with each other

vol \ˈväl\ *n* -S [F, flight, fr. *voler* to fly, fr. MF — more at VOLLEY] **:** a heraldic charge consisting of two wings displayed and conjoined

vol *abbr* **1** volcanic; volcano **2** volume **3** volunteer

vola \ˈvōlə\ *n* -S [L — more at WALE] **:** the palm of the hand or sole of the foot

vo·la·dor \ˌvōləˈdȯ(ə)r\ *n* -S [Sp, flying fish, lit., flyer, fr. LL *volator*, fr. L *volatus* (past part. of *volare* to fly) + *-or*] **1 :** any of various flying fishes (as *Cypselurus californicus* of California and *Exocoetus mesogaster* and *C. bahaiensis* of the West Indies) **2 :** a widely distributed flying gurnard (*Dactylopterus volitans*) of the Atlantic ocean **3 :** any of various sailfishes (as *Istiophorus volador* of Florida and *I. americanus* of the Gulf Stream)

vo·la·do·ra \-ˈdōrə\ *n* -S [Sp, fem. of *volador* flying fish] **:** any of several small So. American characin fishes of some importance in mosquito control

vo·lage \vōˈlazh\ *adj* [ME, fr. MF, fr. L *volaticus* flying, volatile, fickle, fr. *volatus* (past part. of *volare* to fly) + *-icus* -ic] **:** FLIGHTY, GIDDY, FICKLE, FLEETING

¹**vo·lant** \ˈvōlənt\ *adj* [MF, fr. L *volant-, volans*, pres. part. of *volare* to fly — more at VOLATILE] **1 :** having the wings extended as if in flight — used of a heraldic bird usu. as viewed from the side or an angle or of a heraldic insect usu. as viewed from the back **2 a :** passing through the air upon or as if upon wings **:** FLYING **b** *obs* **:** passing from place to place **:** CURRENT **3 :** QUICK, NIMBLE **4 :** capable of flying **:** VOLITANT

²**volant** \"\ *n* -S [F, fr. *volant* flying] **:** ⁴FLOUNCE

¹**vo·lan·te** \vōˈläntā\ *adj* [It, lit., flying, fr. L *volant-, volans*, pres. part. of *volare* to fly] **:** moving with light rapidity — used as a direction in music

²**volante** \"\ *n* -S [Sp, lit., flying, fr. L *volant-, volans*, pres. part. of *volare* to fly — more at VOLATILE] **:** a 2-wheeled carriage formerly much used in Cuba, made with the axle behind the body, and driven by a rider on the horse

volante

volant piece *n* **:** an adjustable piece of medieval armor for guarding the throat in a joust

vo·la·pié \ˌvōləpēˈā\ *n* -S [Sp, lit., foot flight, fr. *volar* to fly (fr. L *volare*) + *pie* foot, fr. L *ped-, pes* foot — more at FOOT] **:** a method of killing a bull in which the matador advances head on toward the bull and lunges in over the horns to drive the blade between the shoulders

vo·la·pük \ˈvōləˌpük, ˈväl-, -puk\ *n* -S *usu cap* [Volapük, lit. world speech, fr. *vol* world (modif. of E *world*) + *pük* speech, modif. of E *speak*] **:** an artificial international language based largely on English but built upon some root words from German, French, and Latin

¹**vo·lar** \ˈvōlə(r)\ *adj* [L *vola* palm of the hand, sole of the foot + E *-ar*] **:** relating to the palm of the hand or sole of the foot; *specif* **:** located on the same side as the palm of the hand ⟨the ~ surface of the forearm —R.S.Woodworth⟩

²**volar** \"\ *adj* [L *volare* to fly + E *-ar*] **:** relating to or used in flight

vo·la·ry \ˈvōlərē, ˈväl-, -ri\ *n* -ES [L *volare* to fly + E *-ary*] **1 :** a large birdcage **:** AVIARY **2 :** the birds in an aviary **:** a flight or flock of birds

vo·la·ta \vōˈlädə\ *n* -S [It, fr. *volare* to fly, fr. L] **:** a rapid series of musical notes (as a roulade)

¹**vol·a·tile** \ˈvälədᵊl, -ətᵊl *sometimes* -ə(ˌ)til, *chiefly Brit* -əˌtīl\ *n* -S [ME *volatil*, fr. OF, backformation fr. *volatille, volatilie* group of birds, fr. ML *volatilia*, fr. neut. pl. of L *volatilis* winged, volatile] **1 :** a winged animal **:** BIRD, WILDFOWL **2 :** a volatile substance ⟨coffee ~*s*⟩

²**volatile** \"\ *adj* [F, fr. L *volatilis*, fr. *volatus* (past part. of *volare* to fly) + *-ilis* -ile; prob. akin to Skt *garuda*, a mythical bird, *garut* wing of a bird] **1 :** passing through the air on wings **:** having the power to fly **:** FLYING; *also* **:** moving about as if by flight **2 :** easily passing off by evaporation **:** readily vaporizable at a relatively low temperature ⟨~ matter⟩ ⟨~ solvents⟩ **3 a :** AIRY, LIGHTHEARTED, LIVELY ⟨people think that I am ~ because I dance and go to the movies —Ellen Glasgow⟩ ⟨had a ~ mind and was furiously interested in Indians and geography —Bernard De Voto⟩ **b :** easily aroused or moved **:** easily affected by circumstances ⟨these things annoyed and irritated, even drove her ~ temper to a distraction —Ellis St. Joseph⟩ ⟨if, as mortals, they are violent and ~, it is because their emotions are near the surface —John Mason Brown⟩ ⟨the developments which even my ~ suspicions hadn't allowed me to foresee —Ralph Ellison⟩ **c :** tending to burst forth or erupt into violent action **:** EXPLOSIVE ⟨faced with a highly ~ social situation . . . with the problem of reconciliation in this city of forty-eight different ethnic groups —Jean Burden⟩ ⟨world government . . . could halt rigidly and abruptly whatever danger of war might proceed out of the highly ~ competition for military supremacy between the two —Norman Cousins⟩ **4 a :** characterized by quick or unexpected changes **:** not steady or predictable **:** CHANGEABLE, FICKLE ⟨as giddy and ~ as ever —Jonathan Swift⟩ ⟨the most ~ of men, and what is true today may be quite false before the winter snows . . . have melted —Bruce Bliven b. 1889⟩ ⟨in the midst of an area whose politics are explosively ~ —E.A.Kehr⟩ ⟨this ~ element of reader preference —*Printers' Ink*⟩ **b :** subject to or characterized by wide price fluctuations ⟨~ markets⟩ ⟨~ common stocks⟩ **5 :** difficult to capture or hold permanently **:** EVANESCENT, TRANSITORY ⟨so ~ an essence that he escaped definition —Elinor Wylie⟩ ⟨what we actually traffic in are living ideas; the books are only containers for a more ~ commodity —*Publishers' Weekly*⟩ **syn** see ELASTIC

volatile liniment *n* [so called fr. the ready evaporation of ammonia] **:** a liniment composed of ammonia water and a fixed oil (as sesame, olive, or sweet almond)

vol·a·tile·ness *n* -ES **:** the quality or state of being volatile **:** VOLATILITY

volatile oil *n* **:** an oil that vaporizes readily; *specif* **:** ESSENTIAL OIL — distinguished from *fixed oil*

volatile salt *n* **1 :** AMMONIUM CARBONATE c **2 :** SAL VOLATILE 2

vol·a·til·i·ty \ˌväləˈtiləd-ē, -ilətē, -i\ *n* -ES **:** the quality or state of being volatile ⟨high ~ in gasoline is an advantage in the starting of cold engines —H.L.Williams⟩

vol·a·til·iz·able \ˈvälədᵊlˌīzəbəl, ˌ==ˈ===\ *adj* [ISV *volatilize* + *-able*] **:** capable of being volatilized

vol·a·til·iza·tion \ˌvälədᵊləˈzāshən, -lətᵊl-, -ᵊlˌī-\ *n* -S [prob. fr. (assumed) NL *volatilization-, volatilizatio*, fr. *volatilizare* to volatilize + L *-ation-, -atio* -ation] **1 :** the act or process of volatilizing **2 :** the state of being volatilized

vol·a·til·ize \ˈvälədᵊlˌīz, -ətᵊl-\ *vb* -ED/-ING/-S [prob. fr. (assumed) NL *volatilizare*, fr. L *volatilis* volatile + LL *-izare* -ize] *vt* **:** to make volatile **:** cause to exhale or evaporate **:** cause to pass off in vapor ~ *vi* **:** to become volatile **:** pass off in vapor

vol·a·tize \ˈvälə,tīz\ *vb* -ED/-ING/-S [²*volatile* + *-ize*] **:** VOLATILIZE

vol-au-vent \ˌvōlōˈväⁿ, ˌväl-\ *n* -S [F, lit., flight in the wind] **:** a large patty shell filled with a ragout of meat, fowl, game, or fish

vol·borth·ite \ˈväl,bȯrˌthīt\ *n* -S [F *volborthite*, fr. Alexander von *Volborth* †1876 Russian paleontologist + F *-ite*] **:** a mineral $Cu_3(VO_4)_2.3H_2O$ consisting of a hydrous vanadate of copper and occurring in small green or yellow 6-sided tabular crystals or in globular forms

volc *abbr* volcanic; volcano

vol·can \ˈvälkən\ *n* -S [Sp *volcán*, fr. Pg *volcão*, fr. L *Volcanus, Vulcanus*, Roman god of fire] **:** VOLCANO

¹**vol·can·ic** \(ˈ)välˈkanik, -nēk *sometimes* -ˈkān-\ *adj* [F *volcanique*, fr. *volcan* volcano (fr. It *volcano, vulcano*) + *-ique* -ic — more at VOLCANO] **1 a :** of or relating to a volcano ⟨~ activity⟩ ⟨~ steam⟩ **b :** characterized by or composed of volcanoes ⟨a ~ region⟩ ⟨a ~ chain⟩ ⟨a ~ range⟩ **c :** produced, influenced, or changed by a volcano or by volcanic agencies **:** made of materials from volcanoes ⟨a ~ mountain⟩ **2 :** resembling a volcano esp. in explosive violence or latent explosive violence **:** characteristic of a volcano **:** VIOLENT, VOLATILE ⟨blurting out a few ~ words, and then relapsing —Thomas Wolfe⟩ ⟨long-oppressed ~ emotions erupt, old family feuds flare up —Vicki Baum⟩ ⟨this ~ tempest of a man, fierce, merciless to the flesh —H.O.Taylor⟩ ⟨the ~ tremors that now convulse civilization —Sumner Welles⟩ ⟨major adjustments of one kind or another are essential to stabilize that politically ~ region —Vera M. Dean⟩ — **vol·can·i·cal·ly** \-nək(ə)lē, -nēk-, -li\ *adv*

²**volcanic** \"\ *n* -S **:** a volcanic rock

volcanic ash *or* **volcanic ashes** *n* **:** ASH 1c

volcanic bomb *n* **:** BOMB 4

volcanic cloud *n* **:** a convoluted rolling mass of partly condensed water vapor and dust that is generally highly charged with electricity and that overhangs a volcano during eruption

volcanic cone *n* **:** a conical mountain or hillock built up of cinders, tuff, breccia, and lava by volcanic eruptions

volcanic dust *n* **:** fine particles of rock powder that are blown out from a volcano and that may remain suspended in the atmosphere for long periods producing red sunsets and climatic modifications thousands of miles away

volcanic foci *n pl* **:** the subterranean centers of volcanic action

volcanic glass *n* **:** natural glass produced by the cooling of molten lava too rapidly to permit crystallization

vol·ca·nic·i·ty \ˌvälkəˈnisəd-ē\ *n* -ES [F *volcanicité*, fr. *volcanique* volcanic + *-ité* -ity] **:** VOLCANISM ⟨results of ~⟩

volcanic mud *n* **:** mud that is formed by the mixture with water of volcanic ash or of other fragmental products of volcanic explosions and that is often initially hot and may flow much like a lava stream

volcanic neck *n* **:** a column of igneous rock that is formed by congelation of lava or the consolidation of volcanic breccia in the conduit of a volcano and that may later be left standing above the adjacent country by the removal of surrounding rocks by erosion

volcanic rock *n* **:** an igneous rock (as basalt or obsidian) solidified on or near the surface — compare EFFUSIVE 3

volcanic water *n* **:** water of volcanic origin or deriving its heat and chemical activity from volcanic sources or volcanism

volcanic wind *n* **:** a wind associated with a volcanic outburst and due to the eruption or to convection currents over hot lava

vol·can·ism \ˈvälkəˌnizəm\ *n* -S [ISV *volcano* + *-ism*] **:** volcanic power or action **:** the quality or state of being volcanic ⟨~ includes all phenomena connected with the movement of heated material from the interior to or toward the surface of the earth —P.G.Worcester⟩ ⟨the craters on the moon appear to have been formed by meteoritic impact rather than ~ —*Jour. of Geol.*⟩

vol·can·ist \-nəst\ *n* -S [F *volcaniste*, fr. *volcan* volcano + *-iste* -ist] **1 :** one who specializes in the study of volcanic phenomena **2 :** PLUTONIST

vol·can·ize \-ˌnīz\ *vt* -ED/-ING/-S **:** to subject to or cause to undergo and be affected by volcanic heat

vol·ca·no \välˈkā(ˌ)nō\ *n, pl* **volcanoes** *or* **volcanos** [It *volcano, vulcano*, fr. L *Volcanus, Vulcanus*, Roman god of fire and metalworking represented in Greco-Roman myth as the blacksmith of the gods forging thunderbolts on Mount Etna and other volcanoes] **1 a :** a vent in the earth's crust from which molten or hot rock and steam issue **b :** a more or less conical hill or mountain composed wholly or in part of the material ejected from such a vent and often having a depression or crater at its top **2 :** something suggestive of a volcano esp. in suppressed force or violence of outbursts ⟨~*es* of gunfire erupted —Kenneth Roberts⟩ ⟨chief of foreign correspondents who can only guess which ~ of international antipathies will erupt next —F.L.Mott⟩ ⟨the muttering ~ of . . . politics shot forth a shower of sparks which all but extinguished the life of his father —Barbara Henderson⟩

vol·ca·no·log·ic \ˌvälkənᵊlˈäjik\ *or* **vol·ca·no·log·i·cal** \-jəkəl\ *adj* **:** of or relating to volcanology

vol·ca·nol·o·gist \ˌvälkəˈnäləjəst\ *n* -S **:** a geophysicist who specializes in volcanology

vol·ca·nol·o·gy \-jē, -ji\ *n* -ES [*volcano* + *-logy*] **:** a branch of science that deals with volcanic phenomena

volcans *pl of* VOLCAN

¹**vole** \ˈvōl\ *n* -S [F, prob. fr. *voler* to fly, fr. MF — more at VOLLEY] **:** GRAND SLAM 1a — **go the vole :** to risk all for great gains; *also* **:** to try everything ⟨he has *gone the vole* — has been soldier, ballad singer, traveling tinker, and is now a beggar —Sir Walter Scott⟩

²**vole** \"\ *n* -S [earlier *vole mouse*, fr. *vole* (of Scand origin) + *mouse*; akin to Norw *voll* meadow, field, ON *vǫllr* — more at WOLD] **:** any of various rodents of the chiefly palaearctic genus *Microtus* that are closely related to the lemmings and muskrats but in general resemble murid mice or rats, typically have a stout body, rather blunt nose, short tail, and short ears, inhabit both moist meadows and dry uplands, and do much damage to crops; *also* **:** any of various other rodents of the family Cricetidae — compare LEMMING MOUSE, RED-BACKED MOUSE, WATER VOLE

American vole

³**vo·lé** \vōˈlā\ *adj* [F, past part. of *voler* to fly] *of a ballet step* **:** executed with the greatest possible elevation

vole bacillus *n* [²*vole*; fr. its having been first described as causing tuberculosis in the wild vole *Microtus agrestis*] **:** a morphologically and culturally distinct strain of the tubercle bacillus that is serologically indistinguishable from the human and bovine strains and that has been used to immunize individuals against the latter strains

vo·le·mic \vōˈlēmik\ *adj* [*volume* + *-emia* + *-ic*] **:** of, relating to, or concerned with the volume of circulating blood or plasma ⟨gelatin and dextrin are used as ~ expanders⟩ — often used in combination ⟨normo*volemic*⟩ ⟨hypo*volemic*⟩

vo·lem·i·tol \vōˈleməˌtȯl, -tōl\ *n* -S [ISV *volem-* (fr. NL *volemus* — specific epithet of *Lactarius volemus* — fr. L *volemum*, a pear) + *-itol*] **:** a slightly sweet crystalline heptahydroxy alcohol $C_7H_9(OH)_7$ found esp. in a mushroom (*Lactarius volemus*)

vo·lent \ˈvōlənt\ *adj* [L *volent-, volens*, pres. part. of *velle* to will, wish — more at WILL] **:** exercising volition

vol·ery \ˈvälərē, -ri\ *n* -ES [modif. (influenced by *-ery*) of F *volière* volary, fr. *voler* to fly + *-ière* -er] **:** VOLARY

vo·let \(ˈ)vōˈlā\ *n* -S [F, lit., kerchief, small veil, fr. *voler* to fly] **:** either of the folding side compartments or wings of a triptych

vol·go·grad \ˈvälgəˌgrad, ˈvōl-, ˈvȯl-\ *adj, usu cap* [fr. *Volgograd*, city in southeastern U.S.S.R.] **:** STALINGRAD

vol·hard method \ˈfōl,härt-\ *n, usu cap V* [after Jakob *Volhard* †1910 Ger. chemist] **:** a method for the determination of chlorine, bromine, and iodine in the form of halides by precipitating them with excess silver nitrate and titrating the excess with a thiocyanate solution

vol·i·tant \ˈväləd-ənt, -lətənt *also* -lətᵊnt\ *adj* [L *volitant-, volitans*, pres. part. of *volitare* to fly about, flutter] **:** able to fly **:** FLYING; *also* **:** moving about

vol·i·tate \ˈväləˌtāt\ *vi* -ED/-ING/-S [L *volitatus*, past part. of *volitare* to fly about] **:** to flutter or fly hither and thither

vol·i·ta·tion \ˌ==ˈtāshən\ *n* -S [LL *volitation-, volitatio*, fr. L *volitatus* (past part. of *volitare* to fly about, flutter, freq. of *volare* to fly) + *-ion-, -io* -ion — more at VOLATILE] **:** the act or power of flying — **vol·i·ta·tion·al** \ˌ==ˈtāshənᵊl\ *adj*

vo·li·tion \vōˈlishən\ *n* -S [F, fr. ML *volition-, volitio*, fr. L *vol-* (stem of *velle* to will, wish) + *-ition-, -itio* (as in L *position-, positio* position) — more at WILL] **1 :** the act of willing or choosing **:** the act of deciding (as on a course of action or an end to be striven for) **:** the exercise of the will ⟨followed my father of my own ~ —C.H.Marshall⟩ ⟨our children do not seek school of their own ~ nor do they remain there willingly —C.H.Grandgent⟩ ⟨without my ~ . . . I have become involved in something malignant —C.B.Kelland⟩ **2 :** the termination of an act or exercise of choosing or willing **:** a state of decision or choice **3 :** the power of willing or determining **:** WILL ⟨she marshaled her ~, all her self-control and strength, to shout —Arnold Bennett⟩ ⟨the exercise of their ~ we construe as revolt —George Meredith⟩ ⟨orders his people not as automatons, but as characters moved by their own ~ —P.E. More⟩

vo·li·tion·al \-shənᵊl, -shnəl\ *adj* **:** of, relating to, or of the nature of volition **:** possessing or exercising volition — **vo·li·tion·al·ly** \-shənᵊlē, -shnəlē, -i\ *adv*

vo·li·tion·less *adj* **:** having no volition **:** lacking volition

¹vol·i·tive \ˈväləd·iv, -ətiv\ *adj* [ML *volitivus*, fr. L *vol-* (stem of *velle* to will) + *-itivus* (as in L *positivus* positive)] **1 :** of or relating to the will **:** originating in the will **:** having the power to will **2 :** expressing a wish or permission ⟨the Latin ~ subjunctive with *ut*⟩

²volitive \"\ *n* -s **:** a volitive verb form

vol·i·to·ri·al \¦välə¦tōrēəl\ *adj* [NL *volitor* bird able to fly (fr. L *volitare* to fly about + *-or*) + E *-ial*] **:** able to fly **:** FLYING

völ·ker·wanderung \ˈfəlkə(r),vändə,rün\ *n, pl* **völkerwan·derung·en** \-ŋən\ [G (trans. of L *migratio gentium*), fr. *völker* nations (pl. of *volk* people, nation, fr. OHG *folc*) + *wanderung* wandering, migration, fr. MHG *wanderunge*, fr. *wandern* to wander + *-unge* -ing (fr. OHG *-unga*) — more at FOLK, WANDER] **:** the migration of nations; *esp* **:** the movement into southern and western Europe of the Teutonic peoples, Huns, and Slavs from the 2d century A.D. to about the 11th century reaching the peak in the 5th and 6th centuries and closing with the settling of Norsemen in England and France

volk·mann's canal \ˈfōlkmənz-, ˈvō-\ *n, usu cap V* [after Alfred W. *Volkmann* †1877 Ger. physiologist] **:** one of many nutrient canals transmitting blood vessels from the periosteum into the bone but not forming the center of a Haversian system

volks·deut·scher \ˈfōlks,dȯichə(r)\ *n, pl* **volksdeut·sche** \-chə\ *usu cap* [G, fr. *volks* (gen. of *volk* people, nation) + *deutscher*, n., German, fr. *deutsch*, adj., German, fr. OHG *diutisc* — more at DUTCH] **:** a person of German ethnic origin long settled in a central or east European country, repatriated for political reasons by the Nazi regime, and expelled into West Germany after World II

volks·lied \ˈfōlk,slēt\ *n, pl* **volkslie·der** \-ēdə(r)\ *usu cap* [G, fr. *volks* (gen. of *volk* people) + *lied* song — more at LIED] **:** a folk song — compare LIED

volks·raad \ˈfōlks,rät\ *n* -s *usu cap* [Afrik, fr. D *volks* (gen. of *volk* people, fr. MD *volc, follc*) + *raad* council; akin to OHG *folc* people — more at FOLK, RAAD] **:** PARLIAMENT, LEGISLATURE: as **a :** the legislative assembly of the So. African Republic before it became the Transvaal province of the Union of So. Africa **b :** the legislative assembly of the Orange Free State before it became a province of the Union of So. Africa **c :** the legislative assembly of the Dutch East Indies

¹vol·ley \ˈvälē, -li\ *n, pl* **volleys** *also* **vollies** [MF *volee* flight, volley, fr. *voler* to fly, fr. L *volare* — more at VOLATILE] **1 a :** a flight of missiles (as arrows or bullets) **:** the simultaneous or nearly simultaneous discharge of a number of missile weapons (as muskets or rifles) ⟨some companies being able to attain three ~*s* per minute —R.K.Sprague⟩ ⟨both were killed by a British ~ a few minutes later —*Amer. Guide Series: Md.*⟩ **b :** one round per gun in an artillery battery fired as soon as each gun is ready without regard to the order of firing **c :** a mining blast consisting of a number of holes fired simultaneously **d** (1) **:** the flight of the ball in tennis or the course of the ball before striking the ground ⟨a ball hit on the ~⟩; *also* **:** a return of the ball before it touches the ground (2) **:** FULL TOSS (3) **:** a kick of the ball in soccer before it rebounds (4) **:** the exchange of the shuttlecock in badminton following the serve **2 a :** a burst or emission of many things at once ⟨every push of the pole against the loose mud of the bottom brought forth ~*s* of bubbles —C.S.Forester⟩ ⟨writing ~*s* of letters —G.B.Shaw⟩ ⟨broke into a ~ of curses —R.H.Davis⟩ **b :** a burst of simultaneous or immediately sequential nerve impulses passing to an end organ, synapse, or center ⟨two distinct ~*s* occur in each heart cycle —Albert Hemingway⟩ **c :** a short response (as *Amen*) said in unison by Salvationists — **at the volley** *or* **on the volley** *adv* (*or adj*) **1 :** at random **:** in passing **2 :** in flight — used of a ball in sports

²volley \"\ *vb* **volleyed** *also* **vollied; volleyed** *also* **vollied; volleying; volleys** *also* **vollies** *vt* **1 a :** to discharge in or as if in a volley **b :** to utter rapidly and vehemently ⟨driver then ~*ed* a string of curses —Marcia Davenport⟩ ⟨she ~*ed* him a string of questions —Maurice Hewlett⟩ **2 :** to propel (an object of play) while in the air and before touching the ground: as **a :** to hit (a tennis ball) on the volley **b :** to kick (a soccer ball) before a rebound ~ *vi* **1 a :** to become discharged in or as if in a volley **b :** to make a volley ⟨their eyes, diminished in mirth, twinkled at each other . . . as if wit had ~*ed* between them —G.D.Brown⟩; *specif* **:** to volley an object of play (as in tennis) **2 :** to make loud sounds continuously or repeatedly ⟨a trickle of water ~*ed* loudly on the tarpaulin —C.S.Forester⟩

volleyball \ˈ=,=\ *n* **:** a game played on a rectangular court

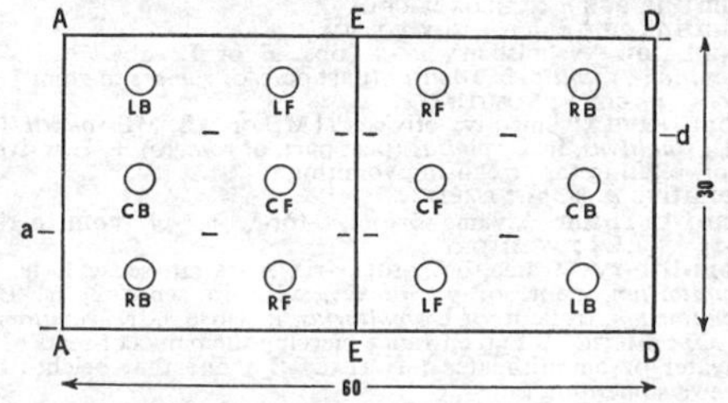

volleyball court: end lines, *AA, DD;* sidelines, *AD, AD;* net, *EE;* serving area, *Aa,* Dd; left back, *LB;* center back, *CB;* right back, *RB;* left forward, *LF;* center forward, *CF;* right forward, *RF*

not exceeding 60 feet in length by 30 feet in width usu. by teams having six players to a side by volleying a large inflated ball with the hands over a net 8 feet high; *also* **:** the ball for use in this game

vol·ley·er \-lēə(r), -liə(r)\ *n* -s **:** one that volleys (as in tennis)

volley fire *n* **1 :** artillery fire in which the pieces included in the command fire the specified number of rounds as rapidly as is consistent with accuracy and without regard to the other pieces **2 :** infantry fire in which the unit fires simultaneously at the word of command

volof *usu cap, var of* WOLOF

¹vol·plane \ˈväl,plān\ *n* [F *vol plané*, fr. *vol* flight (fr. *voler* to fly) + *plané*, past part. of *planer* to glide, soar — more at PLANE] **:** a glide in an airplane

²volplane \"\ *vi* **1 a :** to glide in an airplane **b :** GLIDE 3 **2 :** to sail or coast through the air in the manner of an airplane that glides ⟨these small creatures ~ from tree to tree with the assistance of a membrane joining fore and hind legs —R.T. Littlejohns⟩

vol·sci \ˈväl,sī\ *n pl, usu cap* [L] **:** a people of ancient Italy dwelling between the Latins and Samnites and becoming part of the Roman republic about 373 B.C.

¹vol·sci·an \ˈvälshən\ *n* -s *usu cap* [L *Volsci* + E *-an*] **1 :** a member of the Volsci **2 :** the Italic language of the Volsci

²volscian \"\ *adj, usu cap* **:** of or relating to the Volsci or their language

vol·sel·la \välˈselə\ *n* -s [NL, fr. L, tweezers] **:** VULSELLUM

volsellum \-ləm\ *n, pl* **volsella** \-lə\ [NL, alter. of L *vulsella* tweezers, fr. *vellere* to pluck, pull — more at VULNERABLE] **:** VULSELLUM

vol·stead·ian \(ˈ)väl¦stedēən, (ˈ)vōl-, (ˈ)vȯl-\ *adj, usu cap* [*Volstead* Act, congressional act passed October 28, 1919 to enforce prohibition (after Andrew J. *Volstead* †1947 Am. legislator and author of the Volstead Act) + E *-an*] **:** of or relating to prohibition ⟨~ days⟩ ⟨~ restrictions⟩

vol·stead·ism \ˈ=,ste,dizəm\ *n* -s *usu cap* [*Volstead* Act + E *-ism*] **:** the doctrine of or adherence to prohibition

¹volt \ˈvōlt\ *n* -s [F *volte*, fr. It *volta* turn, volt, fr. *voltare* to turn, fr. (assumed) VL *volvitare*, freq. of L *volvere* to roll — more at VOLUBLE] **1 a :** a tread or gait in which a horse going sideways makes a turn round a center **b :** a circle traced by a horse in this movement **c :** the ground marked for the volt **2 :** a leaping movement in fencing to avoid a thrust

²volt \"\ *n* -s [after Alessandro *Volta* †1827 Ital. physicist] **1 :** the practical mks unit of electrical potential difference and electromotive force that is equal to the difference of potential between two points in a conducting wire carrying a constant current of one ampere when the power dissipated between these two points is equal to one watt, that is equivalent to the potential difference across a resistance of one ohm when one ampere is flowing through it, and that is taken as the standard in the U. S. **2 :** a unit of electrical potential difference and electromotive force equal to 1.00034 volts and formerly taken as the standard in the U. S. — called also *international volt*

vol·ta \ˈvōltə, ˈväl- *or* **vol·te** \-tā\ *n, pl* **volte** [*volta* fr. It. turn, lavolta, fr. *voltare* to turn; *volte* fr. F, fr. It *volta*] **:** LAVOLTA

vol·ta effect \ˈvōltə-, ˈvältə-\ *n, usu cap V* [after Alessandro *Volta* †1827 Ital. physicist] **:** the difference of potential observable between two dissimilar metals when placed in contact with one metal becoming positive and the other negative — called also *contact potential*

volt·age \ˈvōltij, -tēj\ *n* -s [ISV ²*volt* + *-age*] **1 :** electric potential or potential difference expressed in volts **2 :** intensity of feeling **:** EFFECTIVENESS, POWER ⟨the ~ of his verse is praised —J.L.Sweeney⟩ ⟨by slow degrees the author raises the ~ of her story —John Barkham⟩ ⟨she was shocked by the ~ of his rapacious tone —Peggy Bennett⟩

voltage amplification *n* **:** the ratio of the alternating voltage produced at the output terminals of an amplifier to the alternating voltage impressed at the input terminals

voltage divider *n* **:** a resistor or series of resistors that is provided with taps at certain points and that is used to provide various potential differences from a single power source — called also *potential divider*

voltage multiplier *n* **:** an accelerator in which particles (as protons) are propelled by means of high voltages produced by capacitors in series with each capacitor charged to a higher potential than the preceding one

voltage regulator *n* **:** a transformer having its primary winding in shunt and its secondary winding in series with an alternating-current circuit the voltage of which may be regulated by varying the voltage ratio of transformation

¹vol·ta·ic \(ˈ)väl¦tāik, (ˈ)vōl-, -āēk\ *adj* [Alessandro *Volta* †1827 Ital. physicist + E *-ic*] **:** of, relating to, or producing direct electric current by chemical action (as in a battery) **:** GALVANIC ⟨~ cell⟩

²vol·ta·ic \välˈtāik\ *n, usu cap* [upper *Volta* river valley in Ghana and Upper *Volta*, West Africa + E *-ic*] **:** GUR

³voltaic \(ˈ)=¦==\ *adj, usu cap* [Upper *Volta*, West Africa + E *-ic*] **1 a :** of, relating to, or characteristic of Upper Volta **b :** of, relating to, or characteristic of the people of Upper Volta **2 :** of, relating to, or characteristic of the Gur language

voltaic couple *n* **:** a pair of substances usu. but not necessarily metals capable of acting together as an electric source when dipped in an electrolyte

voltaic pile *n* **:** ⁵PILE 6a

¹vol·tair·e·an *or* **vol·tair·i·an** \=ˈta(a)rēən, -ˈter-\ *n, usu cap* [*Voltaire* (F. M. Arouet) †1778 Fr. writer + E *-an*, n. suffix] **:** a follower of Voltaire or an advocate of Voltairianism

²voltairean *or* **voltairian** \(ˈ)=¦===\ *adj, usu cap* [*Voltaire* + E *-an*, adj. suffix] **:** of, relating to, or typical of Voltaire

vol·taire chair \(ˈ)vōl¦ta(a)|(ə)r-, (ˈ)vōl-, -te|, |ə *also* (ˈ)väl-\ *n, usu cap V* [prob. after *Voltaire* †1778 Fr. writer] **:** an armchair with a low seat and a high back

vol·tair·i·an·ism \=ˈ=rēə,nizəm\ *n* -s *usu cap* [*Voltaire* †1778 Fr. writer + E *-ianism* (as in *trinitarianism*)] **:** the theories or practices of Voltaire characterized by a skeptical but deistic religious attitude, opposition to intolerance, and castigation of bigotry

vol·ta·ism \ˈvältə,izəm\ *n* -s [ISV ¹*voltaic* + *-ism*] **:** GALVANISM 1

vol·ta·ite \ˈvältə,īt\ *n* -s [It *voltaita*, fr. Alessandro *Volta* †1827 Ital. physicist + It *-ita* -ite] **:** a mineral $(K,Fe)_3Fe(SO_4)_3.4H_2O$ or $HK_2Fe_4(Fe,Al)_3(SO_4)_{10}.13H_2O$ consisting of a hydrous sulfate of potassium and iron

vol·tam·e·ter \välˈtaməd·ə(r), vōl-, -mətə-\ *n* [ISV ¹*voltaic* + *-meter*] **:** an apparatus for measuring the quantity of electricity passed through a conductor by the amount of electrolysis produced (as by measuring the gases generated from acidulated water or by weighing the silver deposited from a solution of silver nitrate) — **vol·ta·met·ric** \¦väItə¦me·trik, ¦vōl-, -rēk\ *adj*

volt-ammeter \ˈ=ˈ=,==\ *n* **:** an instrument for indicating one or more ranges of volts and amperes by changing terminal connections

volt-ampere \ˈ=ˈ=,=\ *n* **:** a unit of electric measurement that is equal to the product of a volt and an ampere and that for direct current constitutes a measure of power equivalent to a watt and for alternating current a measure of apparent power

volta's pile *n, usu cap V* [after Alessandro *Volta* †1827 Ital. physicist] **:** ⁵PILE 6a

volt box *n* **:** a resistance box provided with taps, usu. used with a potentiometer for measuring potentials beyond the range of that instrument, and so constructed that by means of the taps a definite fraction (as 1/10 or 1/100) of the potential applied to the volt box is made available for potentiometer measurement

¹volte *var of* VOLTA

²volte \ˈvält, ˈvōlt\ *n* -s [F — more at VOLT] **:** ¹VOLT 1

¹volte-face \-t(ə)¦fäs\ *n* [F, fr. It *voltafaccia*, fr. *volta* turn + *faccia* face, fr. (assumed) VL *facia* — more at VOLT, FACE] **:** a change of front **:** a facing about **:** ABOUT-FACE, REVERSAL ⟨he performed a *volte-face* and attacked his former associates —S.F.Mason⟩ ⟨a *volte-face* in American economic policy —*Foreign Affairs*⟩ ⟨a last-minute *volte-face* against the spearhead of his own clan — the ultramodernists —*Canadian Art*⟩ ⟨not that an instant *volte-face* took place . . . in politics, manners, and customs —R.A.Hall b. 1911⟩

²volte-face \"\ *vi* **:** to perform a volte-face **:** face about

vol·ti·geur \,vältəˈzhər\ *n* -s [F, lit., leaper, fr. *voltiger* to leap, vault (fr. It *volteggiare*, freq. of *voltare* to turn) + *-eur* -or — more at VOLT] **:** a member of any of various French organizations of light infantry; *often* **:** a sharpshooter in the French army

vol·tin·ism \ˈvōltᵊn,izəm\ *n* -s [*voltine* (as in *bivoltine*) + *-ism*] **:** the frequency or number of annual broods (as of insects) — compare POLYVOLTINE, UNIVOLTINE

vol·ti su·bi·to \ˈvōltēˈsübēd·(,)ō\ [It, lit., turn quickly] **:** turn the page quickly — used as a direction in music; abbr. *v.s.*

volt·me·ter \ˈvōlt,mēd·ə(r), -ētə-\ *n* [ISV ²*volt* + *-meter*] **:** an instrument (as a galvanometer) for measuring in volts the differences of potential between different points of an electrical circuit

vol·to·li·za·tion \,vältələˈzāshən\ *n* -s **:** the process of voltolizing

vol·to·lize \ˈvältə,līz\ *vt* -ED/-ING/-S [²*volt* + *-ol* + *-ize*] **:** to subject (as an oil) to an electric discharge

volts *pl of* VOLT

voltz·ite \ˈvält,sīt\ *n* -s [G *voltzit*, fr. Philippe L. *Voltz* †1840 Fr. mining engineer + G *-it* -ite] **:** a mineral Zn_5OS_4 consisting of a zinc oxysulfide and occurring in implanted spherical globules of a yellowish or reddish color

vol·u·bil·i·ty \,välyəˈbiləd·ē, -ilətē, -i\ *n* -ES [L *volubilitas*, fr. *volubilis* voluble + *-itas* -ity] **:** the quality or state of being voluble ⟨from her ~ of tongue seemed likely to stretch the discourse to an interminable length —Henry Fielding⟩

vol·u·ble \ˈvälyəbəl\ *adj* [MF or L; MF *voluble*, fr. L *volubilis*, fr. L *volvere* to roll, turn, revolve + *-bilis* capable of being acted upon; akin to Gk *eilyein* to roll, wrap, fold, Goth *-walwjan* to roll, OE *walwian*, *wealwian*, OHG *wellan* to roll, OSlav *valiti* to roll, trundle, Skt *valati* he turns; basic meaning: turning, rolling] **1 a :** easily rolling or turning **:** easily set in motion **:** apt to roll **:** ROTATING, REVOLVING **b :** having the power or habit of twining ⟨a ~ plant stem⟩ **2 :** CHANGEABLE, UNSTABLE, FICKLE **3 :** characterized by ease and smoothness of utterance **:** characterized by ready or rapid speech **:** GLIB, FLUENT ⟨seemed ~, prone to speech as I had never seen him before —Jack London⟩ ⟨that he, who once had been so ~, should have become almost inarticulate —Ellen Glasgow⟩ **syn** see TALKATIVE, VOCAL

vol·u·ble·ness *n* -ES **:** VOLUBILITY

vol·u·bly \-blē, -li\ *adv* **:** in a voluble manner **:** GLIBLY ⟨a boiling pot of enthusiasms and animosities, which he pours out ~, skillfully, and eloquently —Brand Blanshard⟩

vol·u·crine \ˈvälyə,krīn, -əkrən\ *adj* [L *volucris* flying creature, bird (akin to L *volare* to fly) + E *-ine* — more at VOLATILE] **:** of or relating to birds

¹vol·ume \ˈvälyəm *also* -l(,)yüm\ *n* -s [ME *volum, volume*, fr. MF, fr. L *volumen* roll of writing, book, volume, fr. *volvere* to roll — more at VOLUBLE] **1 :** a written document (as on parchment) rolled up on a short staff for keeping and unrolled for reading **:** SCROLL **2 a :** a collection of printed sheets bound together whether constituting a single work ⟨a ~ of memoirs⟩, a part of a work ⟨the first ~ of a long biography⟩, or a part in a related series of works ⟨the ~ of Victorian poetry in the series of English poetry⟩ **:** BOOK; *esp* **:** the part of an extended work bound up together in one cover — compare BROCHURE, PAMPHLET, TOME **b :** an arbitrary number of issues of a periodical or the issues printed within a set time (as a year) ⟨each issue of a magazine bears a ~ number and an issue number which are assigned by the publisher and continue in regular sequence from Volume 1, No. 1. —*Theory & Practice of Bookbinding*⟩ **c :** ALBUM 1c ⟨the Russian basso, has done a ~ of lieder —*Harper's*⟩ **3 a :** something that may be studied and interpreted like a book ⟨the ~ of nature⟩ **b :** something having a rounded or swelling form suggestive of a scroll **:** COIL, CONVOLUTION, TURN ⟨imbedded in the ~*s* of her hair —J.F. Cooper⟩ ⟨feminine attributes of even greater value than the curves and ~*s* of the female body —Frank Budgen⟩ **4 :** space occupied or enclosed by cubic units (as inches, feet, quarts, pecks, bushels, gallons) **:** COMPASS, CAPACITY ⟨the ~ of a container⟩; *specif* **:** the number of cubes each with an edge one unit long that can be fitted exactly into a solid (as some rectangular parallelepipeds) when it can be fitted in such a manner or a number that is equally acceptable as a measure of the solid (as a sphere or cone) when it cannot be fitted in this manner

VOLUME FORMULAS

FIGURE	FORMULA	MEANING OF LETTERS
cube	$V=a^3$	a=one of the dimensions
rectangular prism	$V=abc$	a=length; b=width; c=depth
pyramid	$V=\frac{Ah}{3}$	A=area of base; h=height
cylinder	$V=\pi r^2h$	π=3.1416; r=radius of the base; h=height
cone	$V=\frac{\pi r^2h}{3}$	π=3.1416; r=radius of the base; h=height
sphere	$V=\frac{4\pi r^3}{3}$	π=3.1416; r=radius

5 a : AMOUNT, BULK, MASS, QUANTITY ⟨as a composer he produced a considerable ~ of church music —J.T.Howard⟩ ⟨the ~ of employment rose —Oscar Handlin⟩ ⟨the flow of income to individuals was of record dollar ~ —Milton Gilbert⟩ ⟨a large ~ of unclassified technological data has been published —R.A.Tybout⟩ ⟨overwhelmed by the ~ and violence of his dispatches —Pierre Frédérix⟩ ⟨a sales ~ of . . . a million dollars on his books —*Current Biog.*⟩ ⟨shelled clams are bought by the count or by ~ —Marjorie M. Heseltine & Ula M. Dow⟩; *often* **:** a considerable quantity ⟨profits are made by selling ~ at market price —*Wall Street Jour.*⟩ ⟨chance that the snow will fall in ~, and soon —J.M.Vander Voort⟩ ⟨pouring forth a ~ of amiable absurdities —Victoria Sackville-West⟩ **b :** the amount of a substance that occupies a particular volume ⟨one ~ of the material which has been collected is added to 9 ~*s* of normal saline —F.J.Hamilton⟩ ⟨water on electrolysis gives 2 ~*s* of hydrogen to one of oxygen⟩ **c :** the number of vehicles or pedestrians that pass a given point during a specified period of time ⟨the ~ of traffic⟩ **d** (1) **:** a shaped or defined mass in a sculpture or an architectural structure (2) **:** the representation of mass or three-dimensional shape in a drawing or painting **6 a :** the degree of loudness or the intensity of a sound ⟨by the last chorus the ~ of sound was overwhelming —Agnes S. Turnbull⟩ ⟨a desire for ever greater ~ overtook musicians and instrument-makers —Robert Donington⟩; *also* **:** LOUDNESS ⟨a singer who could look pathetic and who had ~ —Jo Sullivan⟩ **b :** the magnitude of an audio frequency wave in an electric circuit **7 :** a characteristic of auditory sensations such that high tones seem small and sharp while low tones appear to fill much space **syn** see SIZE

²volume \"\ *adj* **:** of, dealing with, or involving large quantities ⟨~ production of airplanes⟩ ⟨~ sales of books⟩

³volume \"\ *vb* -ED/-ING/-S *vi* **:** to roll or rise in volume ⟨her dress *volumed* —George Meredith⟩ ⟨a drift of pale, *voluming* smoke arose from the sawdust pile —J.G.Cozzens⟩ ⟨the blood cry went up and *volumed* in a discordant chorus —J.F.Dobie⟩ ~ *vt* **1 :** to collect or gather in or as if in a volume **2 :** to send or give out in volume

volume color *n* **:** BULKY COLOR

vol·umed \-md\ *adj* **1 :** having the form of a roll **:** occurring in rounded masses ⟨~ mist⟩ **2 :** having bulk **:** MASSIVE, GREAT **3 :** having such or so many volumes — used in combination ⟨a three-*volumed* history⟩

volume displacement *n* **:** displacement of a fluid expressed in terms of volume as distinguished from displacement expressed in terms of mass

vol·u·me·nom·e·ter \,välyəmēˈnäməd·ə(r)\ *n* [ISV *volumeno-* (fr. NL *volumen* volume, fr. L, book) + *-meter*] **:** an instrument for measuring the volume and indirectly the specific gravity of a body (as a solid) by means of the difference in pressure caused by its presence and absence in a closed air space — **vol·u·me·nom·e·try** \-ˈnämə·trē\ *n* -ES

volume resistance *n* **:** the electrical resistance of a body to current passing through its bodily substance irrespective of any surface leakage

volume table *n* **:** a tabulated statement of the yield of trees upon the basis of various measurements of diameter and height

vo·lu·me·ter \vəˈlüməd·ə(r), -mətə- *also* vəlˈyü- *or* välˈyü-; ˈvälyə,mēd·ə(r), -ētə-\ *n* [ISV, blend of ¹*volume* and *-meter*] **:** an instrument for measuring volumes (as of gases or liquids) directly or (as of solids) by displacement of a liquid

vol·u·met·ric \¦välyə¦me·trik, -rēk\ *also* **vol·u·met·ri·cal** \-rəkəl, -rēk-\ *adj* [ISV, blend of ¹*volume* and *metric*] **:** of or relating to the measurement of volume — **vol·u·met·ri·cal·ly** \-rək(ə)lē, -rēk-,-li\ *adv*

volumetric analysis *n* **1 :** quantitative analysis by the use of definite volumes of standard solutions of reagents **2 :** analysis (as by the eudiometer) of gases by volume

volumetric flask *n* **:** a graduated flask for use in volumetric analysis

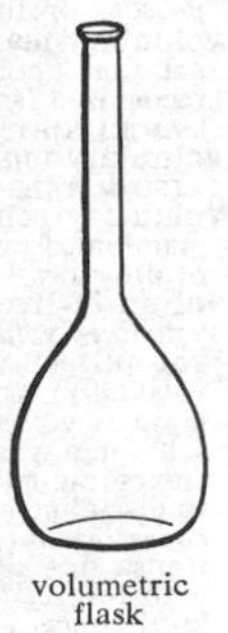

volumetric flask

volumetric solution *n* **:** a standard solution for use in volumetric analysis

vol·u·mette \¦välyə¦met\ *n* -s [¹*volume* + *-ette*] **:** a small volume ⟨a ~ of poems⟩

volume unit *n* **:** a unit equal to a decibel for specifying the power level of a signal in audio equipment above a value of 1 milliwatt in a 500 ohm circuit

vo·lu·mi·nal \vəˈlümənᵊl\ *adj* [L *volumin-*, *volumen* + E *-al*] **:** of or relating to volume

vo·lu·mi·nos·i·ty \və,lüməˈnäsəd·ē\ *n* -ES **:** the quality or state of being voluminous; *also* **:** an instance of this

vo·lu·mi·nous \vəˈlümənəs *also* vəlˈyü-\ *adj* [LL *voluminosus* full of folds, fr. L *volumin-*, *volumen* roll of writing, book + *-osus* -ose — more at VOLUME] **1 :** of or relating to volume **2 :** winding or full of windings **:** consisting of many folds, coils, or convolutions **3 a :** having or marked by great volume **:** BULKY, LARGE, SWELLING ⟨her extremely fair hair very ~ and noticeable —F.M.Ford⟩ ⟨a ~ Negress held him by the hand —P.L.Fermor⟩ ⟨in song, where a more ~ output of air is customary —C.H.Grandgent⟩ ⟨his chin sunk in a billow of his ~ white shirt front —Haldane Macfall⟩; *specif* **:** FULL ⟨a ~ nightgown of outing flannel —Adria Langley⟩ ⟨coats are ~ but hang in nice straight lines —Lois Long⟩ **b :** seeming to fill a large indefinite space ⟨critic who described her voice as "fresher, freer, and firmer . . . more under control and more ~ at the full" —*Current Biog.*⟩ **c :** NUMEROUS ⟨it is more work to keep track of ~ pink slips than to spend occasional checks —Joanne Wheeler⟩ **4 a :** filling or capable of filling a large volume or several volumes ⟨a ~ correspondence⟩ ⟨~ evidence⟩ ⟨~ notes⟩ ⟨a ~ report⟩ **b :** consisting of or containing many volumes ⟨a ~ publication⟩ **c :** writing or speaking much or at great length ⟨a ~ and energetic writer of letters, memoranda, and diaries —J.T.Flexner⟩ — **vo·lu·mi·nous·ly** *adv* — **vo·lu·mi·nous·ness** *n* -ES

voluntaries *pl of* VOLUNTARY

vol·un·tar·i·ly \ˌvälənˌterəlē, -rəli\ *adv* [ME, fr. [1]*voluntary* + *-ly*] **:** in a voluntary manner **:** of one's own free will **:** SPONTANEOUSLY

vol·un·tar·i·ness \ˈ==ˌterēnəs, -rin-\ *n* -ES **:** the quality or state of being voluntary **:** SPONTANEOUSNESS; *specif* **:** the quality or state of being free in the exercise of one's will

vol·un·ta·rism \ˈväləntəˌrizəm\ *n* -S [[1]*voluntary* + *-ism*] **:** the principle or system of supporting or doing something by voluntary action or of relying upon voluntary action ⟨the essence of democracy is, of course, ~ as opposed to coercion —M.A. Tuve⟩: as **a :** a theory that conceives will to be the dominant factor in experience or in the constitution of the world — compare FICHTEANISM, INTELLECTUALISM, SCHOPENHAUERISM, SCOTISM **b (1) :** the principle of supporting a religious system and its institutions by voluntary association and effort rather than by state aid or patronage **(2) :** insistence upon this principle as alone consistent with true religious freedom **c :** a principle calling for development of union labor relations with employers by free choice of the workers and without outside influence, assistance, or interference; *also* **:** the principle of free collective bargaining without governmental imposition of terms — **vol·un·ta·rist** \-ˌrəst\ *n* -S — **vol·un·ta·ris·tic** \ˌ===ˈristik, -stēk\ *adj*

[1]**vol·un·tary** \ˈvälənˌterē, -ri\ *adj* [ME, fr. L *voluntarius*, fr. *voluntas* will, choice (fr. *vol-*, stem of *velle* to will, wish) + *-arius* -ary — more at WILL] **1 a :** proceeding from the will **:** produced in or by an act of choice ⟨~ action⟩ **b :** performed, made, or given of one's own free will ⟨a ~ task⟩ ⟨~ services⟩ ⟨~ contributions⟩ ⟨~ efforts⟩ **c** *obs* **:** READY, WILLING **d :** done by design or intention **:** not accidental **:** INTENTIONAL, INTENDED ⟨~ manslaughter⟩ **e :** acting of oneself **:** not constrained, impelled, or influenced by another **:** SPONTANEOUS, FREE ⟨~ worker⟩ ⟨~ or forced labor⟩ **f** *obs* **:** growing spontaneously **g :** acting or done of one's own free will without valuable consideration **:** acting or done without any present legal obligation to do the thing done or any such obligation that can accrue from the existing state of affairs **2 :** of or relating to the will **:** subject to or regulated by the will ⟨~ behavior⟩ ⟨~ control⟩ ⟨~ motions⟩ **3 :** able to will ⟨man is a ~ agent⟩ **4 a :** provided or supported by voluntary action or support ⟨the hospital is a ~ one with 400 beds —*Science*⟩ ⟨the importance of ~ societies in a democracy⟩ **b :** of or relating to voluntarism ⟨sell blanket insurance policies covering medical, dental, and hospital care to the public on a ~ basis —*Current Biog.*⟩

syn VOLUNTARY, INTENTIONAL, DELIBERATE, WILLFUL, and WILLING can agree in meaning done, made, brought about, and so on, of one's own free will. VOLUNTARY implies freedom from any compulsion that could constrain one's choice; often it suggests merely spontaneity, or, in contrast with *involuntary*, stresses the control of the will ⟨a *voluntary* confession of guilt⟩ ⟨a *voluntary* taking of life⟩ ⟨*voluntary* muscle movements⟩ INTENTIONAL contrasts with *accidental* and *inadvertent* in specifying an intention and purpose ⟨an *intentional* insult⟩ ⟨any injury to bystanders at an auto race cannot be considered *intentional*⟩ DELIBERATE carries the idea of full knowledge or full consciousness of the nature of an intended action ⟨a *deliberate* lie⟩ ⟨*deliberate* acts of vandalism⟩ ⟨an organized and *deliberate* attack — carefully planned and calculated —*N.Y. Times*⟩ WILLFUL adds to DELIBERATE the idea of a refusal to be advised or directed in any way and an obstinate determination to act despite all wiser opposing forces or considerations ⟨a *willful* disobedience⟩ ⟨a gigantic glorification of vice and crime, a *willful* inversion of all normal ethical standards —Joseph Frank⟩ WILLING implies such qualities as agreeableness or openmindedness that make one ready or eager to accede to others' wishes or effect an end pleasing to them ⟨my most *willing* activity is listening to my secretary —O. W. Holmes †1935⟩ ⟨no aspect of the world of science to which we cannot find *willing* and thrilling guidance —G.I.Schwartz⟩

[2]**voluntary** \"\ *adv* [ME, fr. [1]*voluntary*] **:** VOLUNTARILY

[3]**voluntary** \"\ *n* -ES [[1]*voluntary*] **1 a :** a piece of music performed extempore and often improvised usu. serving as a prelude to a set performance **b :** a usu. pipe-organ solo played before, during, or after a religious service and sometimes extemporized **2 :** something done, made, or given voluntarily **:** a voluntary action or piece of work **:** a voluntary contribution **3 :** one who engages in an affair of his own free will **:** VOLUNTEER **4 :** one who advocates voluntarism **5 :** a fall of a horseback rider for which there is insufficient cause

voluntary affidavit *or* **voluntary oath** *n* **1 :** an affidavit or oath not required by law **:** one made in an extrajudicial matter **2 :** an affidavit or oath taken before one not authorized to administer it

voluntary association *n* **:** an unincorporated group associated for some specific purpose — used chiefly of commercial or financial associations

voluntary bankruptcy *n* **:** a bankruptcy declared upon petition of the bankrupt

voluntary chain *n* **:** a voluntary association of independent retailers in a given line of business (as groceries or drugs) for collective action in buying, advertising, and other phases of management

voluntary conveyance *n* **:** a conveyance without valuable consideration

voluntary escape *n* **:** the escape of a prisoner without prison breach and with the custodian's consent — contrasted with *negligent escape*

voluntary hospital *n* **1 :** a hospital that is operated under individual, partnership, or corporation control and provides mainly semiprivate and private care **2** *Brit* **:** a hospital that is supported by voluntary contributions

voluntary improvement *n* **:** an improvement on land serving merely for adornment of the property

vol·un·tary·ism \ˈvälənˌterēˌizəm\ *n* -S **:** VOLUNTARISM ⟨~ in cultural affairs is an American way which is not defunct —Leland Hazard⟩ — **vol·un·tary·ist** \-ēəst\ *n* -S

voluntary jurisdiction *n* **1 :** jurisdiction in cases not admitting of contentious litigation **2 :** jurisdiction acquired over a person only by virtue of his consent as opposed to compulsory jurisdiction that may be exercised against his will

voluntary manslaughter *n* **:** manslaughter resulting from an act done upon a sudden heat or passion due to provocation recognized as adequate in law — compare INVOLUNTARY MANSLAUGHTER

voluntary muscle *n* **:** muscle under voluntary control **:** STRIATED MUSCLE

voluntary school *n* **:** a usu. denominational English school maintained by a voluntary body and administered by a board of directors — see AIDED SCHOOL, CONTROLLED SCHOOL

vol·un·ta·tive \ˈvälənˌtādiv\ *adj* [ML *voluntativus*, fr. L *voluntat-, voluntas* will, choice + *-ivus* -ive] **:** VOLUNTARY

[1]**vol·un·teer** \ˌvälənˈti(ə)r, -iə\ *n* -S [obs. F *voluntaire* (now *volontaire*), fr. *voluntaire*, adj., voluntary, fr. L *voluntarius* — more at VOLUNTARY] **1 :** one who enters into or offers himself for any service of his own free will: as **a :** one who enters into military service voluntarily but who is then subject to discipline and regulations like other soldiers — opposed to *conscript* **b (1) :** one who renders a service or takes part in a transaction while having no legal interest, duty, or authority with respect to it **:** an intruder in a transaction who has no legal concern or interest to advance or to protect (as where one renders a service without any express or implied agreement for compensation or seeks to become the servant of another without his assent or pays the debt of a stranger) **(2) :** one who receives a conveyance or transfer of property without giving valuable consideration **:** a gratuitous grantee or transferee **:** DONEE **2 :** a volunteer plant ⟨oats may persist as a ~ for several years⟩ **3** *usu cap* **:** an officer or member of the Volunteers of America organized in 1896 along military lines for evangelistic and philanthropic work

[2]**volunteer** \"\ *adj* **1 :** of or relating to a volunteer **:** consisting of volunteers **:** VOLUNTARY ⟨a ~ fire department⟩ ⟨~ advice⟩ ⟨~ work⟩ **2 :** growing spontaneously without direct human control or supervision ⟨in some areas there is still an adequate ~ crop of game; in others management is essential⟩; *esp* **:** growing without cultivation from seeds lost from a previous crop ⟨a stand of ~ wheat⟩

[3]**volunteer** \"\ *vb* -ED/-ING/-S *vt* **:** to offer or bestow voluntarily or without solicitation or compulsion ⟨~ his services⟩ ⟨~ help⟩ ⟨~ information⟩ ⟨~ a donation⟩ ~ *vi* **1 :** to enter into or offer oneself for any service of one's own free will without solicitation or compulsion **:** OFFER ⟨~ in an undertaking⟩ ⟨~ for the army⟩ **2 :** to grow spontaneously **:** form a volunteer crop or stand ⟨many clovers perpetuate themselves indefinitely by ~*ing*⟩

[1]**vo·lup·tu·ary** \vəˈləpchəˌwerē, -ri\ *adj* [LL *voluptuarius*, alter. of L *voluptarius*, fr. *voluptas* pleasure + *-arius* -ary] **:** VOLUPTUOUS, LUXURIOUS ⟨when words are turned to purely ~ uses and divorced from rational purpose, the result is not a real advance but rather the beginning of decadence —Irving Babbitt⟩

[2]**voluptuary** \"\ *n* -ES [modif. (influenced by LL *voluptuarius*, adj.) of L *voluptarius* voluptuous person, fr. *voluptarius*, adj., voluptuous] **:** a voluptuous person **:** one who makes luxury and the gratification of sensual appetites his chief care **:** SENSUALIST ⟨a comprehensiveness of outlook unknown both to the ~ and to the ascetic —Bertrand Russell⟩

vo·lup·tu·ate \-ˌwāt\ *vi* -ED/-ING/-S [*voluptu*ous + *-ate*] **:** LUXURIATE ⟨second largest sugar producing country in the world, *voluptuated* in crazy wealth —John Gunther⟩

vo·lup·tu·os·i·ty \=ˌ==ˈwäsəd·ē\ *n* -ES [ME *voluptuosite*, fr. ML *voluptuositas*, fr. L *voluptuosus* voluptuous + *-itas* -ity] **:** VOLUPTUOUSNESS

vo·lup·tu·ous \vəˈləpchəwəs, -chəs\ *adj* [ME, fr. L *voluptuosus*, fr. *voluptas* pleasure, delight + *-osus* -ose; akin to L *volup* agreeably, pleasurably, Gk *elpis* hope, expectation, L *velle* to will, wish — more at WILL] **1 a :** full of delight or pleasure esp. to the senses **:** ministering to, relating to, inclining to, or arising from sensuous or sensual gratification **:** LUXURIOUS, SENSUOUS ⟨music arose with its ~ swell —Lord Byron⟩ ⟨the kind of sleep which you can feel yourself enjoying with an almost ~ pleasure —Louis Bromfield⟩ ⟨the riotous decor, the ~ ceiling, the flowering dazzle of the chandelier —Claudia Cassidy⟩ ⟨the ~ contortions of dancers —Lewis Mumford⟩ ⟨~ narratives of the far-away South Seas —C.R.Anderson⟩ ⟨anchorites in their cells are at times tormented by ~ visions —Rebecca West⟩ **b :** suggesting sensual pleasure by fullness and beauty of form ⟨she was startlingly good-looking, of ~ build —Ngaio Marsh⟩ **2 :** given to or spent in enjoyments of luxury, pleasure, or sensual gratifications ⟨depiction of the ~ life —J.D.Hart⟩ ⟨a long and ~ holiday —Edmund Wilson⟩ **syn** see SENSUOUS

vo·lup·tu·ous·ly *adj* [ME, fr. *voluptuous* + *-ly*] **:** in a voluptuous manner ⟨sniffed the scent ~ —James Reynolds⟩ ⟨relatively slim-lipped and less ~ curved —*Time*⟩

vo·lup·tu·ous·ness *n* -ES **:** the quality of being voluptuous ⟨her outlines had lost the ~ which had once made them such an asset —Leslie Charteris⟩

vo·lu·ta \vəˈlüd·ə, -ütə *also* vəlˈyü-\ *n* [L] **1** -S *obs* **:** VOLUTE **2** *cap* [NL, fr. L] **:** the type genus of Volutidae — see VOLUTE 3

vol·u·ta·tion \ˌvälyəˈtāshən\ *n* -S [L *volutation-, volutatio*, fr. *volutatus* (past part. of *volutare* to roll about, wallow, freq. of *volvere* to roll) + *-ion-, -io* -ion] **:** the action of rolling or wallowing

[1]**vo·lute** \vəˈlüt *also* vəlˈyüt, *usu* -üd.+V\ *n* -S [L *voluta*, fem. of *volutus*, past part. of *volvere* to roll, turn — more at VOLUBLE] **1 :** a spiral or scroll-shaped form ⟨locks of hair were curled in little flat ~*s* —Herman Goodman⟩ ⟨the bright overturning ~ of a wave —Henry Beston⟩ **2 :** an object or part having a spiral or scroll-shaped form: as **a :** a spiral scroll-shaped ornament that forms the chief feature of the Ionic capital and that also appears in the Corinthian and Composite capitals **b :** the ornamental scroll-shaped bottom end of a stair rail on top of the newel **c :** a turn of a spiral shell **d :** the spiral casing surrounding the impeller of a volute pump; *also* **:** VOLUTE PUMP **3 :** any of numerous marine gastropod mollusks of *Voluta* and related genera of the family Volutidae whose shell is usu. rather thick, has a short spire, wide aperture, conspicuous columellar folds, and usu. is inoperculate — compare MUSIC SHELL

[2]**volute** \"\ *adj* **1 :** having a spiral or scroll-shaped form **:** rolled up **:** VOLUTED ⟨a ~ ornament⟩ ⟨a ~ termination of a stair rail⟩ **2 :** having a part of spiral form or operating with a rotary action — used esp. of machinery

vo·lut·ed \-üd·əd\ *adj* **:** having a spiral scroll **:** scroll-shaped

vo·lu·tel·la \ˌvälyəˈtelə\ *n, cap* [NL, fr. L *voluta* spiral scroll + *-ella*] **:** a genus of imperfect fungi (family Tuberculariaceae) characterized by setose sporodochia and unicellular ovoid to oblong conidia — see DRY ROT 2b

volute pump *n* **:** a centrifugal pump with a spiral casing

volute spring *n* **:** a spring formed of a conically spiral coil of plate, rod, or wire that is extended or extensible in the direction of the axis of the coil in which direction its elastic force is exerted

vo·lu·ti·dae \vəˈlüd·əˌdē\ *n pl, cap* [NL, fr. *Voluta*, type genus + *-idae*] **:** a family of gastropods (division Rachiglossa) comprising the volutes

vol·u·tin \ˈvälyəd·ən, -ətən\ *n* -S [G, fr. *volut-* (fr. NL *volutans* — specific epithet of the bacterium *Spirillum volutans* in which volutin was first found — fr. L, rolling, tumbling, pres. part. of *volutare* to roll about, wallow) + *-in* (as in *chromatin*) — more at VOLUTATION] **:** a basophilic substance that is probably a nucleic acid compound and that is widely distributed as granules in the cytoplasm or vacuoles of microorganisms

vo·lu·tion \vəˈlüshən\ *n* -S [L *volutus* (past part. of *volvere* to roll) + E *-ion*] **1 :** a rolling or revolving motion **2 :** a spiral turn **:** TWIST, CONVOLUTION **3 :** a whorl of a spiral shell **:** VOLUTE

[1]**vol·u·toid** \ˈvälyəˌtȯid\ *adj* [NL *Voluta* + E *-oid*] **:** resembling or related to the Volutidae

[2]**volutoid** \"\ *n* -S **:** a volutoid gastropod

vol·va \ˈvälvə\ *n* -S [NL, fr. L *volva, vulva* covering, integument, womb — more at VULVA] **:** a membranous bulbous sac or cup that surrounds the base of the stipe in many gill fungi (as of the genus *Amanita*) and is formed by the rupture of the universal veil — compare VELUM

vol·var·ia \välˈva(a)rēə\ *n, cap* [NL, fr. *volva* + *-aria*] **:** a genus of agarics having pink spores and a distinct volva and including a fungus (*Volvaria bombycina*) that is parasitic on various trees

vol·vate \ˈvälvət, -lˌvāt\ *adj* [NL *volva* + E *-ate*] **:** provided with or characterized by a volva

volve *vt* -ED/-ING/-S [L *volvere* to roll, turn over] *obs* **:** CONSIDER

vol·velle *also* **vol·vell** \ˈvälˌvel\ *n* -S [ME *volvelle*, prob. fr. ML *volvella*, fr. L *volvere* to roll, turn + *-ella*] **:** an old contrivance for ascertaining the time of the rising and setting of the moon and sun and the time of high and low tide consisting of one or more movable circles with pointers and figures of the moon and sun which are placed upon several graduated and figured circles drawn on the leaf of a book

vol·vo·ca·ce·ae \ˌvälvəˈkāsēˌē\ *n pl, cap* [NL, fr. *Volvoc-, Volvox*, type genus + *-aceae*] **:** a family of unicellular or colonial biflagellate free-swimming flagellates that are usu. held to be green algae of the class Chlorophyceae — see VOLVOX; compare PHYTOMONADINA — **vol·vo·ca·ceous** \ˌ==ˈkāshəs\ *adj* — **vol·vo·cine** \ˈ==ˌsīn, -sən\ *adj*

vol·vo·ca·les \ˌ==ˈkā(ˌ)lēz\ *n pl, cap* [NL, fr. *Volvoc-, Volvox* + *-ales*] **:** an order of chiefly freshwater green algae (class Chlorophyceae) that are solitary or colonial usu. with a strictly fixed number of cells in the colony — compare HETEROCAPSALES, VOLVOCACEAE

vol·voc·i·dae \välˈväsəˌdē\ *n pl, cap* [NL, fr. *Volvoc-, Volvox*, type genus + *-idae*] **:** a family of flagellates (order Phytomonadina) more or less equivalent to the Volvocaceae

vol·vox \ˈvälˌväks\ *n, cap* [NL, fr. L *volvere* to roll — more at VOLUBLE] **:** a genus of minute pale green flagellates that occur in spherical colonies about one fiftieth of an inch in diameter, that are propelled through water by means of minute colorless flagella which rotate the colony about an axis so that one end is constantly anterior, and that are treated as green algae and the type of the family Volvocaceae or as plantlike flagellates and the type of the family Volvocidae

vol·vu·lus \ˈvälvyələs\ *n* -ES [NL, fr. L *volvere* to roll, turn] **:** a twisting of the intestine upon itself that causes obstruction — compare ILEUS

volyer *var of* FOLLYER

[1]**vom·ba·tid** \ˈvämbəd·əd, -ətəd\ *adj* [NL *Vombatidae*] **:** of or relating to the Vombatidae

[2]**vombatid** \"\ *n* -S **:** a marsupial of the family Vombatidae **:** WOMBAT

vom·bat·i·dae \vämˈbad·əˌdē\ *n pl, cap* [NL, fr. *Vombatus*, type genus + *-idae*] **:** a family of marsupials including the wombats

vom·ba·tus \vämˈbäd·əs, -bād·əs\ *n, cap* [NL, modif. of E *wombat*] **:** a genus of mammals comprising the common Australian and Tasmanian wombats and being the type of the family Vombatidae

vo·mer \ˈvōmə(r)\ *n* -S [NL, fr. L, plowshare — more at WEDGE] **1 a :** a bone of the skull of most vertebrates that is situated below the ethmoid region, that develops from lateral halves which remain separate in some animals, that in man forms a vertical plate pointed in front and expanding at the upper back part into lateral wings, and that constitutes part of the nasal septum **b :** a corresponding bone in teleost fishes that forms the front part of the roof of the mouth and often bears teeth **2 :** PYGOSTYLE

vomer·ine \ˈvōməˌrīn, ˈväm-, -ˌrən\ *adj* [NL *vomer* + E *-ine*] **:** of or relating to the vomer

vomerine cartilage *n* **:** JACOBSON'S CARTILAGE

vomero- *comb form* [NL *vomer*] **:** vomerine and ⟨*vomero*palatine⟩

vom·ero·nasal \ˌväməˌrō+\ *adj* [*vomero-* + *nasal*] **:** of or relating to the vomer and the nasal region and esp. to Jacobson's organ or Jacobson's cartilage

vom·ero·palatine \"+\ *n* [*vomero-* + *palatine*] **:** a bone in the roof of the mouth of ganoid fishes and some amphibians formed by the fusion of the vomer and the palatine bones

vom·i·cine \ˈväməˌsēn, -sən\ *n* -S [NL *vomica* (in *nux-vomica*, specific epithet of the nux vomica tree *Strychnos nux-vomica*) + ISV *-ine*] **1 :** BRUCINE **2 :** a crystalline alkaloid $C_{22}H_{24}N_2O_4$ occurring with brucine and strychnine

[1]**vom·it** \ˈvämət, *usu* -əd.+V\ *n* -S [ME *vomet, vomit, vomite*, fr. MF *vomite, vomit*, fr. L *vomitus*, fr. *vomitus*, past part. of *vomere* to vomit; akin to ON *vāma* sickness, nausea, Norw *vimla* to be sick, be nauseous, Gk *emein* to vomit, Skt *vamiti, vamoti* he vomits] **1 a :** an act or instance of disgorging the contents of the stomach through the mouth **b :** the disgorged contents of the stomach **c :** a disease characterized by vomiting — compare BLACK VOMIT **2** *archaic* **:** a pharmaceutical preparation that causes vomiting **:** EMETIC **3 a :** a disgusting or contemptible person or thing ⟨must not think that nausea and ~ are the ultimate realities of our time —Lewis Mumford⟩ **b :** a violent discharge **:** BELCH, GUSH ⟨an enemy craft hit by a torpedo, breaking in two . . . as the ~ of flame and spray subsides —Alfred Stanford⟩

[2]**vomit** \"\ *vb* -ED/-ING/-S [ME *vomiten*, fr. L *vomitare*, fr. *vomitus*, past part. of *vomere* to vomit] *vi* **1 :** to bring up the contents of the stomach ⟨the baby who eats too long or too much will tend to regurgitate, or ~ —Morris Fishbein⟩ **2 :** to spew forth **:** BELCH, GUSH ⟨great clouds of steam ~*ing* from their exhausts —Nevil Shute⟩ **3** *archaic* **:** to cause vomiting ⟨emetic tartar, when introduced into the jugular vein, will ~ in one or two minutes —J.M.Good⟩ ~ *vt* **1 a :** to disgorge (the contents of the stomach) through the mouth **:** RETCH ⟨the Lord spoke to the fish, and it ~*ed* out Jonah upon the dry land —Jonah 2:10 (RSV)⟩ **b :** to cast out in a repulsive or vituperative manner ⟨~*s* him out penniless and friendless . . . to renew his criminal career —Maury Maverick⟩ ⟨his own epitaph is here ~*ed* forth in . . . corrosive aphorisms —R.W.Speaight⟩ **2 :** to eject violently or abundantly **:** SPEW, SPOUT ⟨roar and fume and ~ sparks —C.G.D.Roberts⟩ **3** *archaic* **:** to cause to vomit ⟨he is ~*ing* and purging his patients with herbs —George Catlin⟩

vom·it·er \-əd·ə(r), -ətə-\ *n* -S **1 :** one that vomits **2** *obs* **:** EMETIC

vomiting *n* -S [ME, fr. gerund of *vomiten* to vomit] **:** an act or instance of disgorging the contents of the stomach through the mouth — called also *emesis*

vomiting center *n* **:** a nerve center in the medulla oblongata concerned in the act of vomiting

vomiting gas *n* **:** CHLOROPICRIN

vomiting nut *n, obs* **:** NUX VOMICA

vo·mi·tion \vəˈmishən\ *n* -S [obs. F or L; obs. F, fr. L *vomition-, vomitio*, fr. *vomitus* (past part. of *vomere* to vomit) + *-ion-, -io* -ion] **:** VOMITING

[1]**vom·i·tive** \ˈvämədˌiv, -ətiv\ *adj* [MF or ML; MF *vomitif*, fr. ML *vomitivus*, fr. L *vomitus* (past part. of *vomere*) + *-ivus* -ive] **:** of, relating to, or causing vomiting

[2]**vomitive** *n* -S *obs* **:** EMETIC

vom·i·to·ri·um \ˌväməˈtōrēəm, -tȯr-\ *n, pl* **vomito·ria** \-rēə\ [LL] **:** VOMITORY

[1]**vom·i·to·ry** \ˈväməˌtōrē, -tȯr-, -ri\ *n* -ES [in sense 1, fr. L *vomitorium*, neut. of *vomitorius*, adj.; in sense 2, fr. LL *vomitorium*, fr. neut. of L *vomitorius*; in sense 3, fr. [2]*vomitory*] **1** *obs* **:** EMETIC **2 :** an entrance piercing the banks of seats of a theater or amphitheater **:** PORTAL **3 :** one that belches or spews something out

[2]**vomitory** \"\ *adj* [L *vomitorius*, fr. *vomitus* (past part. of *vomere* to vomit) + *-orius* -ory — more at VOMIT] *archaic* **:** VOMITIVE

vom·i·tous \-məd·əs, -mətəs\ *adj* [[1]*vomit* + *-ous*] **:** VOMITIVE — **vom·i·tous·ly** *adv*

vom·i·tu·ri·tion \ˌvämachəˈrishən\ *n* -S [[2]*vomit* + *-urition* (as in *micturition*)] **:** repeated ineffectual attempts at vomiting **:** RETCHING

vom·i·tus \ˈvämədəs, -ətəs\ *n* -ES [L — more at VOMIT] **:** VOMIT 1b

von baer's law \välnˈba(a)(ə)rz-, fəl, vəl, -be(ə)rz-\ *n, usu cap B* [after Karl E. *von Baer* †1876 Estonian embryologist] **:** a principle in biology: the development of an organism proceeds from the general to the special and embryos belonging to various classes closely resemble one another in their earlier stages but diverge more and more as development proceeds — compare RECAPITULATION THEORY

von behr trout \-ˈbe(ə)r-\ *n, usu cap B* [prob. fr. the name *von Behr*] **:** a European brown trout (*Salmo trutta*)

v-1 *also* **v-one** \ˈvēˈwən\ *n* -S *usu cap V* [*v-1* fr. G, symbol for *V-eins* V-one; *v-one* part trans. of G *V-eins*, abbr. for *vergeltungswaffe eins*, lit., reprisal weapon (No.) one] **:** ROBOT BOMB

von grae·fe's sign \välnˈgrāfəz-, fəl, vəl\ *n, usu cap G* [after Albrecht *von Graefe* †1870 Ger. ophthalmologist] **:** the failure of the upper eyelid to follow promptly and smoothly the downward movement of the eyeball that is seen in exophthalmic goiter

von mo·na·kow's tract \-ˈmōnəˌkōfs-\ *n, usu cap M* [after Konstantin *von Monakow* †1930 Russ. neurologist] **:** a rubrospinal tract

von pir·quet's test \-(ˈ)pirˈkāz-\ *n, usu cap P* **:** PIRQUET TEST

von reck·ling·hau·sen's disease \-ˈrekliŋˌhaùzənz-\ *n, usu cap R* [after Friedrich D. *von Recklinghausen* †1910 Ger. pathologist] **:** NEUROFIBROMATOSIS

[1]**voo·doo** *also* **vou·dou** \ˈvü(ˌ)dü *sometimes* ˌ=ˈ=\ *n* -S *often attrib* [LaF *voudou*, of African origin; akin to Fon *vodũ* spirit, Ewe *voˈdu*[3] tutelary deity, demon] **1 :** VOODOOISM **2 a :** one who deals in spells and necromancy **:** SORCERER **b (1) :** a sorcerer's spell **:** HEX, JINX ⟨put a ~ on an enemy⟩ **(2) :** a hexed object **:** CHARM

[2]**voodoo** \"\ *vt* -ED/-ING/-S **:** to bewitch by or as if by means of voodoo **:** HEX

voo·doo·ism *also* **vou·dou·ism** \ˈ=ˌ=ˌizəm\ *n* -S **1 :** a religion originating in Africa as a form of ancestor worship, practiced chiefly by Negroes of Haiti and to some extent other West Indian islands and the U.S., and characterized by propitiatory rites and use of the trance as a means of communicating with animistic deities — called also *vodun*; compare OBEAH **2 :** the practice of black magic **:** CONJURING, WITCHCRAFT

voo·doo·ist \-əst\ *n* -S **1 :** an adherent or practitioner of voodooism ⟨from the animists' viewpoint, it is not contradictory for a ~ in Haiti to regard himself as a good Roman

Catholic —E.A.Nida⟩ **2 :** SORCERER, VOODOO — **voo·doo·is·tic** \¦=,=¦istik\ *adj*

voor·trek·ker \'fōr,trekə(r)\ *n* -S *often cap* [Afrik, fr. *voor* before, in front (fr. MD *vore*) + *trekker* emigrant, fr. *trek* to pull, move, emigrate + *-er*; akin to OHG *fora* before — more at FORE, TREK] **:** a So. African pioneer; *esp* **:** one of the Boers who took part in the trek from Cape Colony to the Transvaal in 1834–37

VOP *abbr, often not cap* valued as in original policy

VOR *abbr* very high-frequency omnirange

-vo·ra \v(ə)rə\ *n pl comb form* [NL, fr. L, neut. pl. of *-vorus* -vorous] **:** ones that eat (something specified) ⟨Insecti*vora*⟩

vo·ra·cious \vō'rāshəs, və'r-\ *adj* [L *vorac-, vorax* voracious (fr. *vorare* to devour) + E *-ious*; akin to OHG *querdar* bait, ON *krās* dainty, tidbit, L *gurges* whirlpool, Gk *bora* food, meat, *bibrōskein* to devour, Skt *girati* he swallows] **1 :** having a huge appetite **:** GREEDY, RAVENOUS ⟨the most ~ and demanding of the breakfast-food public — the kiddies —Bennett Cerf⟩ ⟨because so many normal joys had been denied him he was all the more ~ for pleasure —Mary Webb⟩ **2 :** excessively eager **:** AVID, INSATIABLE ⟨a ~ appetite⟩ ⟨his ~ love of life —*Time*⟩ ⟨the ~ reading odysseys of your childhood —J.H.Burns⟩

syn VORACIOUS, GLUTTONOUS, RAVENOUS, RAVENING, and RAPACIOUS agree in meaning excessively greedy. VORACIOUS implies a gorging with anything that satisfies an excessive appetite ⟨a *voracious* shark decimating a school of fish⟩ ⟨pay taxes to *voracious* governments —W.F.Hambly⟩ ⟨a *voracious* reader of poetry —Elinor Wylie⟩ GLUTTONOUS emphasizes greediness and delight in excessive eating ⟨his *gluttonous* appetite for food, praise, pleasure —A.L.Guérard⟩ ⟨his sickness was inflamed by a *gluttonous* debauch —J.R.Green⟩ ⟨*gluttonous* for jewels —John Gunther⟩ RAVENOUS implies abnormally great hunger and suggests violent, grasping methods of dealing with food or whatever satisfies the hunger ⟨a child with a *ravenous* desire for candy⟩ ⟨this fish is remarkably *ravenous;* nothing living that he can seize upon escapes his jaws —William Bartram⟩ ⟨mad hungers that grew more *ravenous* as he fed them —Oscar Wilde⟩ RAVENING comes closer to RAPACIOUS in suggesting a violent, predatory seizing for oneself ⟨the hordes of *ravening* ants —William Beebe⟩ ⟨stood off the other *ravening* creditors —R.L.Taylor⟩ ⟨the jaeger, a *rapacious* tyrant, plays a role as villainous as that of the sparrow hawk and the prairie falcon farther inland —*Amer. Guide Series: Wash.*⟩ ⟨a *rapacious* divorcee on the prowl —Helen Howe⟩ ⟨a mind *rapacious* for all knowledge⟩

vo·ra·cious·ly *adv* **:** in a voracious manner **:** AVIDLY, GREEDILY

vo·ra·cious·ness *n* -ES *archaic* **:** VORACITY

vo·rac·i·ty \vō'rasəd-ē, və'r-, -sətē, -i\ *n* -ES [MF *voracité*, fr. L *voracitat-, voracitas*, fr. *vorac-, vorax* voracious + *-itat-, -itas* -ity] **:** the quality or state of being voracious

vo·ra·go \və'rā,gō\ *n* -ES [L, fr. *vorare* to devour — more at VORACIOUS] **:** an engulfing chasm **:** ABYSS

vo·rant \'vōrənt, 'vȯr-\ *adj* [L *vorant-, vorans*, pres. part. of *vorare* to devour] *heraldry* **:** shown in the act of devouring ⟨a serpent crowned ~ a child —Iain Moncreiffe⟩

vorce cell \'vō(ə)rs, -ō(ə)rs, -ōəs, -ō(ə)s-\ *n, usu cap V* [after Lafayette Denton *Vorce* †1953 Am. chemical engineer] **:** a cylindrical cell that has graphite anodes and a steel cathode with an asbestos diaphragm and that is used for making sodium hydroxide and chlorine by electrolysis of sodium chloride

-vore \,vō(ə)r, ,vȯ(ə)r, ,vōə, ,vō(ə)\ *n comb form* -S [F, fr. *-vore* -vorous, fr. L *-vorus*] **:** one that eats (something specified)

vor·hand \'fōr,hänt\ *n* [G, fr. *vor* fore, before (fr. OHG *fora*) + *hand*, fr. OHG *hant* — more at FORE, HAND] **:** FOREHAND 6

vor·la·ge \-,lägə\ *n* -S [G, lit., forward position, fr. *vor* fore, before + *lage* position, fr. OHG *lāga*; akin to OHG *ligen* to lie — more at LIE] **:** the position of a skier leaning forward from the ankles usu. without lifting the heels from the skis

vor·mela \vȯr'mēlə\ *n, cap* [NL] **:** a genus of carnivorous mammals (family Mustelidae) comprising the tiger weasels and sometimes treated as a subgenus of *Mustela*

vo·ro·nezh \və'rōnish\ *adj, usu cap* [fr. *Voronezh*, U.S.S.R.] **:** of or from the city of Voronezh, U.S.S.R. **:** of the kind or style prevalent in Voronezh

-vo·rous \v(ə)rəs\ *adj comb form* [L *-vorus*, fr. *vorare* to devour — more at VORACIOUS] **:** eating **:** feeding on ⟨carni*vorous*⟩ ⟨pisci*vorous*⟩

vor·spiel \'fōr,shpēl\ *n* [G, fr. *vor* before, fore + *spiel* play, performance, fr. OHG *spil* — more at SPIEL] **:** a musical prelude or overture

vor·tex \'vȯr¦,teks, -ō(ə)\ *n, pl* **vorti·ces** \d·ə,sēz\ *also* **vortex·es** \¦,teksəz\ [NL, fr. L *vertex, vortex* whirl, whirlpool — more at VERTEX] **1 a :** a supposed collection of particles of very subtle matter endowed with a rapid rotary motion around an axis which is also the axis of a sun or a planet **b :** something resembling such rapid rotary motion ⟨look forward to a time when human beings shall have sloughed off the body and become *vortices* of thought —*Harper's*⟩ **2 :** a region within a body of fluid in which the fluid elements have an angular velocity **3** [L] **a** (1) **:** a rapidly spiraling column of air **:** TORNADO, WHIRLWIND; *esp* **:** the eye of a cyclone (2) **:** a rapidly spinning current of water **:** MAELSTROM, WHIRLPOOL (3) **:** an eddying current in the slipstream of an airplane **b** (1) **:** something that resembles a whirlwind or whirlpool **:** SWIRL, WHIRL ⟨the hellish ~ of battle —*Time*⟩ ⟨such a ~ of accepted invitations . . . makes me positively dizzy —Siegfried Sassoon⟩ ⟨created a ~ of speculation wherever she passed —V.L.Parrington⟩ (2) **:** a turbulent center ⟨became the howling ~ of an alarmed hospital —Earle Birney⟩ ⟨politically and commercially it has become the ~ of eastern South Jersey —*Amer. Guide Series: N.J.*⟩ (3) **:** a situation or predicament into which one is irresistibly drawn ⟨the conflict . . . drew into its ~ the best energies of a generation —*Amer. Guide Series: Va.*⟩ ⟨was sucked into the ~ of the . . . scandal —G.H.Genzmer⟩ (4) **:** the spiral arrangement of the muscular fibers at the apex of the heart

vor·ti·cal \'vȯ(r)d·¦əkəl, -(t¦, ¦ēk-\ *adj* [L *vortic-, vortex* + E *-al*] **:** of, relating to, or resembling a vortex **:** SWIRLING — **vor·ti·cal·ly** \-k(ə)lē, -li\ *adv*

vortical motion *n* **:** motion of a fluid (as at the boundary between two layers flowing in opposite directions) in which each individual particle rotates about its own axis — called also *rotational motion*

vor·ti·cel·la \,vȯrd·ə'selə\ *n* [NL, fr. L *vortic-, vortex* + NL *-ella*] **1** *cap* **:** a genus (the type of the family Vorticellidae) of stalked bell-shaped peritrichous ciliates with a marginal row of strong cilia about the oral disk **2** *pl* **vorticel·lae** \-e,lē\ *or* **vorticellas :** any ciliate of the genus *Vorticella* or of the family Vorticellidae

¹vor·ti·cel·lid \¦=¦selə̇d\ *adj* [NL *Vorticellidae*] **:** of or relating to the Vorticellidae

²vorticellid \"\ *n* -S **:** VORTICELLA 2

vor·ti·cel·li·dae \,=='selə,dē\ *n pl, cap* [NL, fr. *Vorticella*, type genus + *-idae*] **:** a family of marine or freshwater free-living or ectocommensal ciliates — see VORTICELLA

vor·ti·cism \'vȯ(r)d·ə,sizəm\ *n* -S [L *vortic-, vortex* + E *-ism*] **:** an offshoot of futurism flourishing in England in the second decade of the 20th century and designed to relate all art forms directly to the machine and modern industrial civilization

vor·ti·cist \-əsə̇st\ *n* -S **:** an advocate or practitioner of vorticism

vor·tic·i·ty \vȯ(r)'tisəd·ē\ *n* -ES [L *vortic-, vortex* + E *-ity*] **1 :** the state of a fluid in vortical motion **2 :** twice the angular velocity of a small element of fluid around which there is circulation

vor·ti·cose \'vȯ(r)d·ə,kōs\ *adj* [L *vorticosus, verticosus*, fr. *vortic-, vertic-, vortex* vortex + *-osus* -ose] **:** VORTICAL — **vor·ti·cose·ly** *adv*

vor·tig·i·nous \(')vȯ(r)¦tijənəs\ *adj* [L *vortigin-, vortigo, vertigin-, vertigo* action of whirling + E *-ous* — more at VERTIGO] **1** *archaic* **:** VORTICAL **2** *archaic* **:** moving in a series of eddies **:** SWIRLING

vos·gi·an *also* **vos·ge·an** \'vōzhēən\ *adj, usu cap* [F *Vosgien*, fr. *Vosges* mountains, northeastern France + F *-ien* -ian] **:** of or relating to the Vosges mountains

vot·able \'vōd·əbəl\ *adj* **1 :** eligible to vote ⟨a ~ citizen⟩ **2 :** capable of being voted upon or decided by vote

vo·tal \'vōd·ᵊl\ *adj* [L *votum* vow, wish + E *-al* — more at VOW] *archaic* **:** VOTIVE

vo·ta·ress \'vōd·ərə̇s, -tə-\ *n* -ES [*votary* + *-ess*] **:** a female votary

vo·ta·rist \-rə̇st\ *n* -S [*votary* + *-ist*] **:** VOTARY

vo·ta·ry \-rē, -ri\ *n* -ES [L *votum* vow + E *-ary* — more at VOW] **1** *archaic* **a :** one pledged by solemn vows to a religious life **:** MONK, NUN ⟨monasteries of *votaries* under special . . . rules —John Owen⟩ **b :** a sworn adherent ⟨the *votaries* . . . that are vow-fellows with this virtuous duke —Shak.⟩ **2 a :** an ardent enthusiast **:** ADDICT, DEVOTEE ⟨it was a paper for the home . . . and the female sex became its faithful *votaries* —John Buchan⟩ ⟨gaming tables, thronged all night by the *votaries* of chance —Bayard Taylor⟩ **b :** a devoted admirer **:** DISCIPLE, FAN ⟨this volume . . . records the scattered yet absorbing talk of master and ~ —Gene Baro⟩ **3 a :** an adherent of a pagan deity ⟨cultivate the goodwill of the gods, and so . . . induce them to bestow their benefits on their *votaries* —E.O.James⟩ **b :** a devout or zealous worshiper ⟨a temple indifferent to the plight of . . . *votaries* below —Charlton Agburn⟩ **c :** a dedicated believer **:** staunch advocate ⟨each religious dogma has its *votaries*⟩ ⟨affluent *votaries* of the status quo —Hodding Carter⟩

¹vote \'vōt, *usu* -ōd·+V\ *n* -S [ME (Sc), fr. L *votum* vow, wish — more at VOW] **1 a :** a usu. formal expression of opinion or will in response to a proposed decision; *esp* **:** one given as an indication of approval or disapproval of a proposal, motion, or candidate for office ⟨proposal was rejected by 5 ~*s* in favor, 51 against, with two abstentions —*U.N.Bull.*⟩ ⟨4000 write-in ~*s* for another candidate —H.H.Martin⟩ — see CASTING VOTE **b :** the total number of such expressions of opinion made known at a single time (as at an election) ⟨to increase its ~ the party must appeal to the farmers⟩ ⟨their aggregate popular ~ in that region fell below 1200 —H.R.Penniman⟩ ⟨polled a large ~⟩ **c :** an expression of opinion or preference that is held to resemble a vote ⟨the consumer, by his ~*s* when he buys or fails to buy, is the ultimate sovereign in a free economy —Eugene Staley⟩ ⟨deserves a ~ of thanks for his hard work⟩ **d :** BALLOT 1 ⟨members . . . who cast their ~ into a single urn —E.S.Stavelay⟩ **2 :** the collective opinion or verdict of a body of persons expressed by voting ⟨the legislative ~ on any issue thus tends to represent . . . the balance of power among the contending groups —Earl Latham⟩ ⟨refused to take a ~ on the question⟩ ⟨chosen by the ~ of the people of the city⟩ **3 :** the right to cast a vote ⟨every member of the community . . . should have a ~ in electing those delegates —William Blackstone⟩; *specif* **:** the right of suffrage **:** FRANCHISE ⟨the 19th Amendment gave American women the ~ in national elections⟩ **4 a :** the act or process of voting ⟨the question came to a ~⟩ ⟨elect judges by popular ~ —F.A.Ogg & P.O.Ray⟩ ⟨put a question to the ~⟩ **b :** a method of voting ⟨roll-call ~⟩ **5** *obs* **a :** a prayer of intercession **:** ENTREATY, PETITION ⟨the heavens consent . . . in answer to the public ~*s* —Ben Jonson⟩ **b :** an earnest desire **:** WISH ⟨the glory of God, is to be the alpha and omega of all our ~*s* and desires —Robert Sanderson⟩ **6** *obs* **:** BELIEF, REPORT ⟨by common ~, reputed the greatest empire in the Orient —Thomas Herbert⟩ **7 :** a decision passed by or carried in an assembly as the result of voting **:** a formal expression of a wish, will, or choice (as in regard to a proposed measure) voted by a meeting ⟨giving the ~*s* of Parliament the authority of laws —Alexander Mudie⟩ — compare CENSURE 6, CONFIDENCE 6d **8 a :** a person who is merely an embodiment of the right to vote ⟨from a patriot of distinguish'd note have . . . purg'd me to a simple ~ —Alexander Pope⟩ **b :** VOTER ⟨took up his challenge in the name of the 39,000 stay-at-home ~*s* —J.J.Chapman⟩ **9 a :** a number of voters or potential voters constituting a group usu. with some common and identifying characteristics ⟨appeals to the Polish ~⟩ **b :** the collective opinion expressed through voting of such a group ⟨elections in which the independent ~ has obviously tipped the balance —John Lodge⟩; *esp* **:** the electoral support of such a group ⟨Democrats need to worry about losing the Negro ~ —Samuel Lubell⟩ **10** *chiefly Brit* **a :** a proposition to be voted upon; *esp* **:** a legislative money item ⟨nearly two hundred ~*s*, covering all branches of administrative expenditure . . . comprise the estimates —T.E.May⟩ **b :** APPROPRIATION ⟨prisons had to be equipped and staff paid out of the annual ~*s* for the naval services —Olive Anderson⟩ **11** *often cap* **:** a daily record of proceedings in the House of Commons — usu. used in pl. ⟨no motion for the issue of a new writ shall be made without previous notice . . . in the ~*s* —T.E.May⟩

²vote \"\ *vb* -ED/-ING/-S *vi* **1 :** to express one's views in response to a poll ⟨~ by a show of hands⟩; *esp* **:** to exercise a political franchise ⟨was interested in politics long before he was old enough to ~⟩ **2 :** to express an opinion ⟨*voted* by acts ranging from sullenness to suicide against the regime —D.W. Treadgold⟩ **~** *vt* **1 a :** to choose or endorse by vote **:** ELECT, RATIFY ⟨~ a straight party ticket⟩ ⟨the resolution was *voted* by a two-thirds majority⟩ — often used with *in* ⟨~ *in* the whole slate of officers⟩ **b :** to decide the disposition of by vote ⟨one British colony after another . . . was *voting* itself into an American state —Dorothy C. Fisher⟩ ⟨a small membership meeting . . . *voted* the organization out of existence —*Newsweek*⟩ **c :** to defeat by vote ⟨~ down a motion⟩ ⟨~ an incumbent out of office⟩ **d :** to authorize by vote ⟨~ an appropriation⟩ ⟨*voted* an adequate force for the expedition — S.J.Buck⟩ ⟨*voted* the president special emergency powers⟩ **2 a :** to adjudge by general agreement **:** DECLARE ⟨got talking who was the cleverest man . . . and we *voted* it was you — Frances H. Eliot⟩ **b :** to offer as a suggestion **:** MOVE, PROPOSE ⟨I ~ we anchor out here —C.S.Forester⟩ **3 a :** to cause to vote in a given way **:** control the franchise of ⟨mobilize small armies of cheap laborers . . . to be *voted* at the polls for a consideration —C.G.Bowers⟩ ⟨build up a bloc of . . . states which could be *voted* as a unit —*Newsweek*⟩ **b :** to cause to be cast for or against a proposal in accordance with the wishes of the owner ⟨nearly all the . . . stockholders mail proxies to me so I can ~ them at the meetings —Erle Stanley Gardner⟩

vo·teen \vō'tēn\ *n* -S [prob. alter. of *devotee*] *Irish* **:** an uncommonly devout person **:** religious zealot

vote·less \'vōtlə̇s\ *adj* **:** having no vote; *esp* **:** denied the political franchise

vot·er \'vōdə(r), -ōtə-\ *n* -S **1 :** one that votes **2 :** one having the legal right to vote

¹voting *n* -S [fr. gerund of ²*vote*] **:** the act or process of casting a vote esp. in a political election

²voting *adj* [fr. pres. part. of ²*vote*] **1 :** of, relating to, or used in conducting a poll ⟨~ precinct⟩ ⟨~ machine⟩ **2 :** entitling one to vote ⟨~ age⟩ ⟨~ stock⟩

voting trust *n* **:** an arrangement transferring the voting rights of shares in a corporation from stockholders to trustees for a specified period

vo·tive \'vōd·¦iv, -ōt¦, ¦ēv *also* ¦əv\ *adj* [L *votivus*, fr. *votum* vow + *-ivus* -ive] **1 a :** offered or erected in fulfillment of a vow and often in gratitude for deliverance from distress ⟨a hundred ~ tapers burning in receptacles of ruby glass —Herman Smith⟩ ⟨~ gifts from women desiring offspring —Heinrich Zimmer⟩ ⟨on this green bank . . . we set today a ~ stone; that memory may their deed redeem —R.W.Emerson⟩ **b :** undertaken or performed in fulfillment of a vow ⟨a ~ pilgrimage⟩ **2 :** consisting of or expressing a vow, wish, or desire ⟨a ~ prayer or benediction —Robert Sanderson⟩

votive dance *n* **:** a ritual dance performed or sponsored by an individual in fulfillment of a vow to a supernatural being

votive mass *n, often cap M* **:** a mass celebrated in place of the mass appointed for the day except when that takes precedence due to festal rank or identity of intention and offered in special devotion (as in honor of a saint or the angels) or applied for the benefit of a particular purpose (as peace or the spread of the faith) or person (as an invalid) **:** a mass provided in the missal for a special intention, occasion, or devotion: **a :** one of a strict class that must be said on a certain day including masses (as a mass of the Blessed Virgin on Saturdays or a requiem on All Souls' Day) prescribed in the rubrics of the missal, solemn masses ordered by the pope or ordinary for grave occasions (as the election of a bishop or a time of war), masses of the forty hours devotion, and nuptial and some requiem masses **b :** one (as for the private intention of a donor) that may be said at the discretion of the priest

votive office *n* **:** an office of special devotion formerly permitted in the Roman Catholic Church to be celebrated in place of the office appointed for the day unless the festal rank of the day prevented

vo·tress \'vō·trə̇s\ *n* -ES [by alter.] *archaic* **:** VOTARESS

vo·ty·ak *or* **vo·ti·ak** \'vōd·ē,ak\ *n, pl* **votyak** *or* **votiak** *also* **votyaks** *or* **votiaks** *cap* [Russ *Votyak* member of the Votyaks, fr. *Vot'* Votyak people, fr. Cheremis *ǒdə*, fr. Votyak *Udmurt* Votyak man] **1 a :** a Finno-Ugrian people of the Udmurt Republic in eastern Soviet Russia, Europe — called also *Udmurt* **b :** a member of such people **2 :** the Finnic language of the Votyak people

vou *abbr* voucher

vou·a·ca·poua \,vüəkə'püə\ [NL, fr. Galibi *wakápu* angelim] *syn of* ANDIRA

¹vouch \'vau̇ch\ *vb* -ED/-ING/-ES [ME *vochen, vouchen*, fr. MF *vocher, voucher*, fr. L *vocare* to call, summon, fr. *voc-, vox* voice — more at VOICE] *vt* **1 :** to summon (a vouchee) into court to warrant or defend a title — used esp. in the phrase *vouch to warranty;* compare VOUCH IN **2** *archaic* **a :** AVOUCH 2, 3 ⟨to ~ this, is no proof —Shak.⟩ ⟨be glad to have found this ~*ed* by better authority —Henry Hallam⟩ **b :** to bear witness **:** TESTIFY ⟨the Prior . . . will ~ for me that they are more than half heathen —Sir Walter Scott⟩ **c :** to serve as a sponsor for ⟨want no patrons for to ~ my books —Thomas Pecke⟩ **3** *archaic* **a :** to cite as authority or supporting evidence ⟨~ every man's experience to warrant this truth —Cunelgus Bonde⟩ **b :** to refer to or quote in support of an opinion or statement ⟨~ examples out of the ancient histories —Thomas Danett⟩ ⟨for the truth of this I ~ the mathematicians —William Wollaston⟩ **4 a :** to give tangible support to **:** PROVE, SUBSTANTIATE ⟨~*ed* his words by his deeds —Isaac D'Israeli⟩ **b** (1) **:** to verify (a business transaction) by examining documentary evidence (2) **:** to attest the necessity of (a payment) **5** *archaic* **:** VOUCHSAFE ⟨means ~*ed* heretofore to some —P.J.Bailey⟩ **~** *vi* **1 :** to give a guarantee **:** become surety ⟨good friends who are willing to ~ for you and give you the old buildup —W.J.Reilly⟩ ⟨no observer can ~ for his own unconscious, and the personality of a field worker inevitably influences his results —Ralph Linton⟩ **2 a :** to supply supporting evidence or testimony ⟨who is going to assemble it and ~ for the names cited —*Saturday Rev.*⟩ ⟨a young man . . . whose very countenance may ~ for your being amiable —Jane Austen⟩ **b :** to give personal assurance ⟨what I didn't see and hear for myself I got from good report and I can ~ for the truth of it —H.E. Giles⟩ ⟨~*ed* for it with his most eloquent oaths —George Meredith⟩

²vouch *n* -ES *obs* **:** a positive assertion **:** ALLEGATION, DECLARATION ⟨my ~ against you . . . will so your accusation overweigh —Shak.⟩

vouch·ee \(')vau̇¦chē\ *n* -S [ME, fr. *vouchen* to vouch + *-ee*] **1 :** one called into court to warrant or defend a title in a common recovery **2** *archaic* **:** one cited as an authority or sponsor ⟨some respectable names are occasionally attached as ~*s* —*Fraser's Mag.*⟩ **3 :** one for whom another vouches

¹vouch·er \'vau̇chə(r)\ *n* -S [MF *vocher, voucher* to vouch] **1 :** an act of summoning one into court to warrant or defend a title or to undertake the defense of a case in which he is ultimately liable to the person sued **2 a :** a piece of supporting evidence **:** PROOF ⟨destruction of the ~*s* of the cruise . . . the logbooks, the meteorological registers, the surveys, and the journals —E.K.Kane⟩ **b :** a documentary record of a business transaction ⟨canceled checks are often called ~*s* because they offer proof of payment —G.G.Munn⟩ **c :** a written affidavit or authorization **:** CERTIFICATE, CREDENTIAL ⟨servicemen traveling on free ~*s* —S.P.B.Mais⟩

²voucher \"\ *vt* **vouchered; vouchered; vouchering** \-ch(ə)riŋ\ **vouchers 1 :** to establish the authenticity of **:** CERTIFY, VERIFY ⟨every invoice or bill received must be ~*ed* —H.S.Noble⟩ **2 :** to prepare a voucher for ⟨coded, abstracted, indexed, inspected, noted and ~*ed* through 288 separate steps —*Time*⟩ — **vouch·er·able** \-ch(ə)rəbəl\ *adj*

³voucher \"\ *n* -S [¹*vouch* + *-er*] **1** *obs* **:** VOUCHEE 1 **2** *archaic* **a :** one that corroborates **:** AUTHORITY ⟨sayings of the Fathers, whom he quotes as his ~*s* —Jonathan Edwards⟩ **b :** one that sponsors or guarantees **:** SURETY ⟨notwithstanding you are these people's ~, this appears but a scheme —Elizabeth Inchbald⟩ **3 :** a tangible proof **:** EVIDENCE, WITNESS ⟨Indian fighters with ~*s* . . . dangling from their belts —J.F.Dobie⟩

voucher check *n* [¹*voucher*] **:** a check carrying a notation of the invoices or items covered either on its face or on a detachable stub

voucher clerk *n* **1 :** one who makes out vouchers payable and records authorized disbursements in a voucher register **2 :** one who prorates the cost of lost or damaged goods among the railroads over which they were carried

voucher payable *n* **:** ACCOUNT PAYABLE

voucher register *n* **:** a book of original entry for vouchers

voucher system *n* **:** a system of accounting in which a voucher (as for an account payable) is prepared usu. with supporting documents attached for each transaction or a series of transactions affecting a single account and when approved is entered in a voucher register

vouch in *vt* **:** to call into court to defend a lawsuit against another and to be made liable to pay in whole or in part any judgment secured for the plaintiff ⟨a defendant *vouches in* his own liability insurance company to defend a negligence case against him⟩

vouch·safe \(,)vau̇ch'sāf\ *vt* -ED/-ING/-S [ME *vouchen sauf*, fr. *vouchen* to vouch + *sauf* safe — more at VOUCH, SAFE] **1 a :** to furnish often in a gracious or condescending manner **:** ACCORD, SUPPLY ⟨asked no questions . . . *vouchsafed* no information —I.V.Morris⟩ ⟨occasionally a true poet is *vouchsafed* to the world —Rumer Godden⟩ ⟨some of the information *vouchsafed* by colleagues was only imperfectly grasped by him —R.A. Fowkes⟩ ⟨discipline that only a systematic and formal study of language . . . can ~ —H.R.Warfel⟩ **b :** to choose to give by way of reply ⟨know little more . . . than what he has *vouchsafed* in occasional interviews —T.H.White b. 1915⟩ **2 :** to grant as a privilege **:** ALLOW, PERMIT ⟨settle terms for evacuating their 1500 wounded, as *vouchsafed* by the Communists at Geneva —*Time*⟩ ⟨we are seldom *vouchsafed* a glance behind this barrier —J.K.Galbraith⟩ **3 a :** to grant as a special favor **:** CONDESCEND, DEIGN ⟨~, O Lord, to keep us this day without sin —*Bk. of Com. Prayer*⟩ **b** *obs* **:** to accept graciously ⟨~ good morrow from a feeble tongue —Shak.⟩ **syn** see GRANT

vouch·safe·ment \-mənt\ *n* -S *archaic* **:** an act or instance of vouchsafing **:** BOON, CONCESSION ⟨a merciful ~ from God to mankind —Thomas Amory⟩ ⟨the sovereign ~ of mercy to some —R.W.Hamilton⟩

voudou *var of* VOODOO

vouge \'vüzh\ *n* -S [F, fr. ML *vidubium* scythe, of Celt origin; akin to Bret *gwif* two-tined fork, W *gwyddif* scythe] **:** a long-handled pike of the late medieval period resembling a halberd

vous·soir \(')vü¦swär\ *n* -S [F, fr. (assumed) VL *volsorium*, fr. *volsus* (alter. of L *volutus*, past part. of *volvere* to roll, turn) + L *-orium* -ory — more at VOLUBLE] **:** one of the tapering or wedge-shaped pieces forming an arch or vault — compare INTRADOS, KEYSTONE, SPRINGER

vou·vray \vü'vrā\ *n* -S *usu cap* [F, fr. *Vouvray*, village in Loire dept., France, where it is produced] **:** a still or sparkling white wine from the Touraine district in the Loire valley of France

¹vow \'vau̇\ *n* -S [ME *vowe, vow, vou*, fr. OF *vo, vou, vowe*, fr. L *votum*, fr. neut. of *votus*, past part. of *vovēre* to vow; akin to Gk *euchesthai* to pray, vow, Skt *ohate* he praises] **1 a :** a solemn promise **:** PLEDGE ⟨make a ~ to give up smoking⟩; *specif* **:** OATH ⟨makes ~ . . . nevermore to give the assay of arms against your Majesty —Shak.⟩ **b :** a promise of constancy and esp. of marital fidelity ⟨exchange marriage ~*s*⟩ **2 a** *obs* **:** a votive offering ⟨the vast treasures of the abbey . . . crucifixes, and ~*s*, crowns and reliquaries —Thomas Gray⟩ **b :** a promise of dedication to the monastic life — compare SIMPLE VOW, SOLEMN VOW **3 :** an earnest wish or declaration **:** PRAYER ⟨it is customary for a song of lamentation to close with a ~ of gratitude and praise —E.A.Leslie⟩

²vow \"\ *vb* -ED/-ING/-S [ME *vowen, vouen*, fr. OF *vower, vouer*, fr. *vo, vowe, vou*, n.] *vt* **1 a :** to promise solemnly **:** SWEAR ⟨~*ed* never to leave each other —*Amer. Guide Series: Texas*⟩ ⟨leaders ~ . . . filibuster won't derail program —*Wall Street Jour.*⟩ ⟨when a man ~*s* a vow to the Lord . . . he shall not break his word —Num 30:2(RSV)〉 **b :** to resolve to bring about **:** PLEDGE 〈with rhetorical swagger . . . *~ing* the death of an aristocrat —F.J.Mather〉 **2 :** to dedicate to a specified pursuit or service **:** CONSECRATE 〈creatures of the Devil, *~ed* to idolatry —Nevil Shute〉 〈virgins *~ed* to Heaven —Alfred Austin〉 〈his country . . . was *~ed* to other quests than that of the Holy Grail —Clifton Fadiman〉 **~** *vi* **:** to make a solemn promise 〈the hall was all in tumult — some *~ing*, and some protesting —Alfred Tennyson〉

3**vow** \"\ *vb* -ED/-ING/-S [ME *vowen*, short for *avowen* — more at AVOW] **:** AVOW, DECLARE 〈I ~ there's a heap of stars out tonight —Elizabeth M. Roberts〉

4**vow** \"\ *interj* [(*I*)*vow* (avow)] *chiefly Scot* — used to express an emphatic degree (as of surprise or admiration) 〈it's long since I saw you, and ~! ye're grown gaudy and grand —William Nicholson〉

vowed *adj* [fr. past part. of 2*vow*] **1 :** bound by or as if by a vow **:** PLEDGED, SWORN **2** *archaic* **:** VOTIVE 1b

1**vow·el** \'vau̇(ə)l\ *n* -S *often attrib* [ME, fr. MF *vouel, voieue*, fr. L *vocalis*, fr. fem. of *vocalis* sounding, sonorous — more at VOCAL] **1 :** one of a class of speech sounds (as of the *o* of English *hot*, the *i* of English *give*, the *u* of English *put*, or the *ü* of German *fünf* "five") in the articulation of which the oral part of the breath channel is not blocked and is not constricted enough to cause audible friction; *broadly* **:** the one most prominent sound in a syllable — compare CONSONANT **2 :** a letter or other symbol representing a vowel 〈a Hebrew manuscript without *~s*〉 — usu. used in English of *a, e, i, o, u,* and sometimes *y*

2**vowel** \"\ *vt* **voweled** *or* **vowelled; voweled** *or* **vowelled; voweling** *or* **vowelling; vowels 1 :** to furnish with vowel signs, points, or letters 〈distinguish the pointed or *~ed* from the unpointed text of the Old Testament —J.F.McCurdy〉 **2 :** to pay with an IOU

vowel declension *n* **:** a declension characterized by the addition of case endings to a stem that ends in a vowel

vowel harmony *n* **:** a structural feature of some languages (as Finnish and Turkish) whereby the vowels of the language are divided into two or more classes and affixed morphemes have vowels that vary so as to belong to the same class as that of the morpheme to which they are affixed

voweling *or* **vowelling** *n* -S [fr. gerund of 2*vowel*] **:** VOCALISM 3b

vow·el·ize \'vau̇ə,līz\ *vt* -ED/-ING/-S **1 :** to produce or cause by means of vowels **2 :** to make vocalic **3 :** 2VOWEL 1

vow·el·less \'==ləs\ *adj* **:** having no vowels

1**vowellike** \'==,=\ *adj* [1*vowel* + *like*] **:** resembling a vowel esp. in sonority and freedom from obstruction in utterance 〈\l\, \m\, \n\, \ŋ\, \r\, \w\, and \y\ are ~〉

2**vowellike** \"\ *n* **:** a vowellike sound

vowel point *also* **vowel mark** *n* **:** a mark placed below or otherwise adjacent to a consonant in some languages (as Hebrew) and representing the vowel sound that precedes or follows the consonant sound

vowel rhyme *n* **:** ASSONANCE 2b

vowel sign *n* **1 :** VOWEL POINT **2 :** a shorthand symbol for a vowel

vowel system *n* **:** the system of vowels, vowel sounds, or vowel indications of a language or of a group of related languages

vowel triangle *n* **:** a triangular or a trapezoidal or trapeziform figure on which vowels are charted according to the position of the part of the tongue that is highest in their articulation

vow·ely *or* **vow·el·ly** \'vau̇(ə)lē, -li\ *adj* **:** full of or marked by vowels

vow·er \'vau̇(ə)r, -au̇ə\ *n* -S [2*vow* + *-er*] **:** one that vows

vox an·ge·li·ca \,väk,san'jeləkə\ *n, pl* **vox angelicas** [NL, lit., angelic voice] **1 :** VOIX CÉLESTE **2 :** any of various labial and reed pipe-organ stops having a notably refined quality of tone

vox hu·ma·na \,väks,hyü'mänə, -mānə\ *n, pl* **vox humanas** [NL, lit., human voice] **:** a reed pipe-organ stop of usu. 8-foot pitch made to give a sound imitative of the human voice and usu. employing a tremolant

vox po·pu·li \-'päpyə,lī\ *n, pl* **vox populis** [L, lit., voice of the people] **:** popular sentiment 〈*vox populi* was whooping it up in the galleries . . . and making no impression upon the massed delegates below —S.H.Adams〉

1**voy·age** \'vȯi(-i)j, 'vȯiēj, 'vȯ(i)yij, -yēj\ *n* -S [ME *veyage, vayage, voyage*, fr. OF *veiage, vayage, voiage*, fr. LL *viaticum*, fr. L, traveling money, provisions for a journey, fr. neut. of *viaticus* of a journey, fr. *viatus* (past part. of *viare* to travel, fr. *via* way) + *-icus* -ic — more at VIA] **1 a :** an act or instance of traveling **:** EXCURSION, TOUR 〈the glee club . . . Christmas trip, a ~ taken annually to advertise the institution —*Scribner's*〉 〈spent the last fortnight in *~s* through furniture shops —H.J. Laski〉 **b :** something that resembles a trip 〈a couple from London, bound . . . on the ~ of matrimony —Tobias Smollett〉 **2** *obs* **a :** a military expedition 〈the Simeonites' second ~ against the Amalekites —Thomas Fuller〉 **b :** a private venture 〈if he should intend this ~ toward my wife, I would turn her loose to him —Shak.〉 **3 a :** a journey by water **:** CRUISE 〈with a fair sea ~, and a fair land journey —Charles Dickens〉 〈icebergs . . . breaking loose for their long ~ to obliteration —Valter Schytt〉 **b :** a journey through air or space 〈the first human balloon ~ —Charles Dimont〉 〈the earth in its annual ~ round the sun —R.S.Ball〉 〈a rocket ~ to the moon〉 **4 :** an account of a journey and esp. of an exploratory trip by sea 〈Canto XXVI, the ~ of Ulysses —T.S.Eliot〉 **5 a :** an expedition undertaken for the collection at sea of a commercial cargo for disposal usu. on return to the home port 〈a whaling ~〉 **b** (1) **:** the proceeds of such a nautical enterprise 〈share a ~〉 (2) **:** a crew member's share of such proceeds 〈said . . . he was willing to bet his whole ~ that the ship had overrun her reckoning —H.A.Chippendale〉

2**voyage** \"\ *vb* -ED/-ING/-S *vi* **:** to take a trip **:** TRAVEL 〈~ up the seaway aboard the royal yacht —*Newsweek*〉 〈novelists have *voyaged* in imagination from planet to planet in rockets —Waldemar Kaempffert〉 **~** *vt* **:** SAIL, TRAVERSE 〈~ the briny deep〉 〈in a year, Americans *voyaged* 18,059,000,000 scheduled air-passenger-miles —*Time*〉

voyage charter party *n* **:** a charter party whereby the owner of a ship agrees to transport on his ship with his crew and master in control of the navigation a full shipload of cargo owned or furnished by another person

voyage policy *n* **:** a marine insurance policy covering only a stated voyage

voy·ag·er *pronunc at* VOYAGE + ə(r)\ *n* -S **:** one that voyages **:** TRAVELER

voy·a·geur \,vwäyä'zhər(·), ¦vȯi(y)ä-, ¦vȯyä-; ¦vȯi·i¦jər(·), ¦vȯ(i)yi¦-\ *n* -S [CanF, fr. F, traveler, voyager, fr. *voyager* to travel (fr. *voyage*, n.) + *-eur* -or] **:** a man employed by a fur company to transport goods and men to and from remote stations in the Northwest principally by boat 〈bateaux of the French-Canadian *~s*, laden with bales of furs, shot its rapids and paddled its smooth waters —*Amer. Guide Series: Oregon*〉

voy·eur \(')vwä¦yər(·), (')vȯi¦y-\ *n* -S [F, lit., one who sees, fr. MF, fr. *voir* to see (fr. L *vidēre*) + *-eur* -or — more at WIT] **1 :** one whose sexual desire is concentrated upon seeing sex organs and sexual acts — called also *peeping tom* **2 :** an unduly prying observer usu. in search of sordid or scandalous sights 〈a sordid sideshow for political *~s* —A.M.Schlesinger b.1917〉

voy·eur·ism \-ə,rizəm\ *n* -S **:** the tendencies, act, or looking of a voyeur 〈~ into neighboring apartment houses —John Lardner〉 — compare EXHIBITIONISM

voy·eur·is·tic \¦=,=¦ristik\ *adj* **:** of, relating to, or having the characteristics of a voyeur 〈~ drives〉 — **voy·eur·is·ti·cal·ly** \-tək(ə)lē\ *adv*

VP *abbr* **1** vapor pressure **2** variable pitch **3** *often not cap* various pagings **4** *often not cap* various places **5** *often not cap* verb passive **6** verb phrase **7** vest pocket **8** vice-president **9** voting pool **10** vulnerable point

v-particle \'=,===\ *n, cap V* [so called fr. the shape of its track in a cloud chamber] **:** a charged or uncharged elementary short-lived particle produced by collisions of very high energy particles with nuclei

VPM *abbr, often not cap* **1** vibrations per minute **2** volts per mil

VPP *abbr* value payable by post

VPS *abbr, often not cap* vibrations per second

VR *abbr* **1** *often not cap* variant reading **2** *often not cap* verb reflexive **3** vicar rural **4** vocal resonance **5** voltage regulator; voltage relay **6** vulcanized rubber

vrack \'vrak\ *Scot var of* WRACK

vraic \'vrāk\ *n* -S [F dial. (Channel islands), alter. of F *varec* — more at VAREC] **1 :** seaweed found in the Channel islands where it is collected and burned for manure **2 :** the fertilizer obtained in the Channel islands by burning vraic

vraick·ing \-kiŋ, -kēŋ\ *n* -S **:** the gathering of vraic

vrba·ite \'vərbə,īt\ *n* -S [G *vrbait*, fr. Karel *Vrba* †1922 Bohemian mineralogist + G *-it* -ite] **:** a mineral $TlAs_2SbS_5$ consisting of a sulfide of thallium, arsenic, and antimony and occurring in small gray-black to dark-red orthorhombic crystals

vrbl *abbr* variable

vred·en·burg·ite \'vredᵊn,bər,gīt\ *n* -S [*Vredenburg*, Alabama + E *-ite*] **1 :** a mineral consisting of an oriented intergrowth of jacobsite and hausmannite — called also *beta-vredenburgite* **2 :** a homogeneous mineral $(Mn,Fe)_3O_4$ that has the same composition as beta-vredenburgite, is stable at high temperature, and in rare instances is preserved in a metastable state at ordinary temperature — called also *alpha-vredenburgite*

vrg *abbr* veering

vrie·sia \'vrēzh(ē)ə, -zēə\ *n* [NL, fr. W. H. de *Vriese* †1862 Dutch botanist + NL *-ia*] **1** *cap* **:** a genus of chiefly epiphytic herbs (family Bromeliaceae) having densely rosetted leaves, free petals, and basal scales on the inner sides of the petals **2** -S **:** any plant of the genus *Vriesia*

1**vrille** \'vril\ *n* -S [F, lit., tendril, fr. OF *veille*, fr. L *viticula*, dim. of *vitis* vine — more at WITHY] **:** the nose-first spinning descent of an airplane deliberately induced as a maneuver

2**vrille** \"\ *vi* -ED/-ING/-S [F *vriller*, fr. *vrille*] **:** to execute a vrille

v roof *n, cap V* **:** GABLE ROOF, PEAKED ROOF

vrouw *or* **vrow** \'vr¦au̇, 'fr¦, ¦ō\ *n* -S [D *vrouw* & Afrik *vrou* woman, married woman, wife, fr. MD *vrouwe* lady, woman — more at FROW] **1 :** a Dutch or Afrikaner woman **2 :** MISTRESS — usu. used preceding the name of a Dutch or Afrikaner married woman

vs *abbr* **1** verse **2** versus

VS *abbr* **1** vertical stripes **2** veterinary surgeon **3** vibration seconds **4** *often not cap* [L *vide supra*] see above **5** visible supply **6** visual signaling **7** *often not cap* [It] volti subito **8** volumetric solution

v's *or* **vs** *pl of* v

vsb *abbr* visible

vsby *abbr* visibility

v-shaped \'=¦=\ *adj, cap V* **:** having the general shape of the letter V or resembling a V in cross section

v-shaped comb *n, cap V* **:** a comb of some domestic fowl with two hornlike sections forming a V — see LA FLÈCHE

v sign *n, cap V* [*v* abbr. for *victory*] **:** a sign made by raising the index and middle fingers in a V and used as a victory salute (as by the allied nations during World War II), a gesture of approval, or an okay

V sign

vsn *abbr* vision

vss *abbr* **1** verses **2** versions

v-stern \'=,=\ *n, cap V* **:** a square stern with the transom inclined from the vertical

VSW *abbr* very short wave

VT *abbr* **1** vacuum tube **2** variable time **3** *often not cap* verb transitive **4** voice tube

vt *abbr* voting

v tail *cap V, var of* VEE TAIL

VTC *abbr* voting trust certificate; voting trust company

vt fuze \'vē'tē-\ *n, usu cap V&T* [variable *time fuze*] **:** PROXIMITY FUZE

v thread *cap V, also* **vee thread** *n* **:** a screw thread having a thread angle of 60 degrees with the bisector of the angle being perpendicular to the axis of the thread and the crests and roots of the threads being lines formed by the intersections of the sides

VTO *abbr* vertical takeoff

VTR *abbr* video tape recorder

VTVM *abbr* vacuum tube voltmeter

v-2 *also* **v-two** \'vē'tü\ *n* -S *usu cap V* [*v-2* fr. G, symbol for *V-zwei* V-two; *v-two* part trans. of G *V-zwei*, abbr. for *vergeltungswaffe zwei*, lit., reprisal weapon (No.) two] **:** a rocket-propelled bomb of German invention that ascends to an altitude of over 60 miles and descends at a speed far greater than that of sound

v-type engine \'=,=-\ *n, cap V* **:** an internal-combustion engine in which two sets of cylinders are arranged side by side in two planes making an angle with each other so that a cross section perpendicular to the shaft would be V-shaped

VU *abbr* volume unit

vug *or* **vugg** *or* **vugh** \'vəg, 'vu̇g\ *n* -S [Corn. dial. *vooga, fouga* underground chamber, fr. L *fovea* small pit] **:** a small unfilled cavity in a lode or in rock usu. lined with a crystalline layer of different composition from the surrounding rock

vug·gy \'vəgē, 'vu̇gē\ *adj* **:** of or relating to a vug

vu·gu·sa \və'güsə\ *n, pl* **vugusa** *or* **vugusas** *usu cap* **1 :** a Bantu-speaking people of western Kenya — see BANTU KAVIRONDO **2 :** a member of the Vugusa people

vul·can \'vəlkən\ *n* -S *often cap* [in sense 1, fr. It *vulcano, volcano*; in other senses, after *Vulcan*, ancient Roman god of fire and metalworking — more at VOLCANO] **1** *obs* **:** VOLCANO **2 :** a worker in metals; *esp* **:** BLACKSMITH **3** *obs* **:** FIRE

vulcan fast pigment *n, usu cap V&F* **:** any of several organic pigments — see DYE table I (under *Pigment Orange, Pigment Red, Pigment Yellow*)

vul·ca·ni·an *also* **vul·ca·ne·an** \,vəl¦kānēən\ *adj* [L *Vulcanius* of Vulcan (fr. *Vulcanus* Vulcan) + E *-an*] **1** *usu cap* **:** of, relating to, or associated with the ancient god Vulcan or to working in iron or other metals **2 a :** VOLCANIC **b :** of or relating to a volcanic eruption in which highly viscous or solid lava is blown into fragments and dust

vul·can·ic \,vəl¦kanik\ *adj, often cap* **:** VULCANIAN

vul·can·ic·i·ty \,vəlkə'nisəd·ē\ *n* -ES **:** VOLCANICITY

vul·can·ism \'vəlkə,nizəm\ *n* -S **:** VOLCANISM

vul·can·ist \-.nəst\ *n* -S [*Vulcan*, god of fire and metalworking + E *-ist*] **:** VOLCANIST

vul·can·ite \-,nīt\ *n* -S [*vulcan* + *-ite*] **:** a hard vulcanized rubber **:** EBONITE, HARD RUBBER

vul·can·i·zate \'vəlkənə,zāt, -ə,nī,zāt, *usu* -ād·+V\ *n* -S [*vulcanize* + *-ate*] **:** a vulcanized product

vul·can·iza·tion \,==nə'zāshən, -,nī'z-\ *n* -S [ISV *vulcanize* + *-ation*] **1 :** the act or process of treating crude rubber, synthetic rubber, or other plastic rubberlike material with a chemical (as sulfur or a compound of sulfur) to decrease its plasticity, tackiness, and sensitivity to heat and cold and to give it useful properties (as elasticity, strength, and stability) — see ACCELERATOR, COLD CURE, OPEN CURE **2 :** the act or process of treating (as for hardening) various materials in any of various ways — compare VULCANIZED FIBER, VULCANIZED OIL

vul·can·ize \'==,nīz\ *vb* -ED/-ING/-S *see -ize in Explan Notes* [ISV *vulcan* + *-ize*] *vt* **:** to subject to the process of vulcanization **~** *vi* **:** to undergo vulcanization

vulcanized fiber *n* [fr. *Vulcanized Fibre*, a trademark] **:** a tough substance that is made both in hard grades with the consistency of horn and in softer flexible grades by treating cellulose (as paper from rags) usu. with a solution of zinc chloride or sulfuric acid and compressing it and that is used chiefly for luggage and for electrical and mechanical applications

vulcanized oil *n* **:** any of various brown or white elastic materials made from unsaturated fatty oils (as rape oil or linseed oil) by heating with sulfur or by reaction with sulfur monochloride and used chiefly in compounding rubber and in coatings

vul·can·iz·er \'vəlkə,nīzə(r)\ *n* -S **:** one that vulcanizes: as **a :** one that cures tires by vulcanization **b :** one that makes a bakelite matrix and from it prepares a vulcanized rubber printing plate — compare STEREOTYPER **a c :** an apparatus in which rubber is vulcanized

vulcano *obs var of* VOLCANO

vul·can·o·log·i·cal \,vəlkənə¦läjəkəl\ *adj* **:** VOLCANOLOGIC

vul·can·ol·o·gist \,==¦näləjəst\ *n* -S **:** VOLCANOLOGIST

vul·can·ol·o·gy \-jē, -ji\ *n* -ES [ISV *vulcan* + *-o-* + *-logy*] **:** VOLCANOLOGY

1**vul·gar** \'vəlgə(r)\ *adj, sometimes* -ER/-EST [ME, fr. L *vulgaris, volgaris* of the mob, of the common people, common, vulgar, fr. *vulgus, volgus* mob, common people + *-aris* -ar; akin to W *gwala* sufficiency, enough, Bret *awalc'h* enough, Toch B *walke* long, Skt *varga* group, body of men, and perh. to Gk *eilein* to press, squeeze] **1 a :** generally used, applied, or accepted **:** found in ordinary practice 〈the ~ course of events〉 **b :** usual or customary in sense or interpretation **:** having the common or recognized meaning **:** taken in the ordinary way 〈they reject the ~ conception of miracle —W.R.Inge〉 **2 :** of or relating to common speech **:** VERNACULAR 〈it is quite possible for a language which is no longer the language of ~ communication to remain the language of scholarship for generations and even for centuries —Norbert Wiener〉 〈the ~ languages of Europe〉 **3 a :** of or relating to the common people **:** belonging to the rank and file of a community or group or to an undistinguished or indistinguishable mass **:** PLEBEIAN 〈keep their knowledge to themselves, safe from the ~ herd —R.A. Hall b.1911〉 〈vegetarianism is a diet for heroes and saints, not for ~ persons —G.B.Shaw〉 **b :** widely known **:** generally current **:** PUBLIC 〈followed the ~ opinion of the day〉 〈must inevitably be . . . a history of ~ errors —J.H.Sledd〉 **c :** usual, typical, or ordinary in kind **:** of the common sort 〈paints the objects themselves in all their ~ everydayness —Roger Fry〉 〈conceal the details of a commonplace ~ death —James Joyce〉 **d** *obs* (1) **:** not developed or refined beyond the ordinary **:** having the qualities or understanding of common people (2) **:** generally comprehensible **:** intelligible to the average mind **4 a :** lacking in cultivation, perception, or taste **:** COARSE, ILL-BRED, ILL-MANNERED, RUDE 〈an essentially ~ mind, incapable of any real finesse or delicacy —H.J.Laski〉 〈thought the farm hands who ate so greedily were ~ —Sherwood Anderson〉 〈had quitted the ways of ~ men, without light to guide him on a better way —Thomas Hardy〉 **b :** falling short of an artificial gentility or veneer **:** regarded as common by overrefined, precious, or affected persons 〈she must neither move nor speak like other women, because it would be ~ —George Savile〉 **c :** morally crude, undeveloped, or unregenerate **:** SELF-CENTERED, SELF-SEEKING, SELF-AGGRANDIZING, GROSS 〈no ~ ambition, no morbid lust for material gain at the expense of others, had led us to the field —Sir Winston Churchill〉 **d :** ostentatious, elaborate, or excessive esp. in expenditure or display **:** lacking simplicity, moderation, or propriety **:** PRETENTIOUS, VAIN 〈saw so many ~ abuses of money as I grew older that I developed a positive disdain for the ostentatious symbols of wealth —Elsa Maxwell〉 **5 a :** marked by coarseness of speech or expression **:** crude or offensive in language **:** EARTHY **b :** lewd, obscene, or profane in expression or behavior **:** INDECENT, INDELICATE 〈names too ~ to put into print —H.A.Chippendale〉 **6 :** marked by lack of discrimination, coherence, or selection **:** shaped by no unifying viewpoint or conception **:** flashy, congested, or extravagant in execution or performance 〈the ~ . . . concept of spectacle rather than selective art —Roger Burlingame〉 〈a luridly spectacular, aggressively tawdry, affirmatively ~ novelist of the fourth class —James Gray〉 **7 :** dominated or prevailingly colored by the material concerns or business of life **:** not relieved by graces, manners, or arts 〈becoming by giant strides more urban, more commercial and more ~ —*Times Lit. Supp.*〉 **syn** see COARSE, COMMON

2**vulgar** \"\ *n* -S [ME, fr. *vulgar*, adj.] **1** *obs* **:** VERNACULAR **2 :** a vulgar or common person

vul·gare \,vəl'ga(a)rē, -gārē\ *adj* [NL (specific epithet of *Triticum vulgare*, a species of wheat), fr. L, neut. of *vulgaris* common — more at VULGAR] **:** of or relating to common wheat

vulgar era *n* **:** CHRISTIAN ERA

vulgar establishment *n* **:** the average interval of time that occurs between the moon's upper transit and the first high water following the transit and that is taken at the time of the full moon or new moon — called also *common establishment, establishment of the port*

vulgar fraction *n* **:** COMMON FRACTION

1**vul·gar·i·an** \,vəl¦gerēən, -ga(a)r-, -gār-\ *adj* [L *vulgarius* common, vulgar (fr. *vulgus* mob, common people + *-arius* -ary) + E *-an* — more at VULGAR] **:** of, relating to, or characteristic of a vulgar person **:** marked by vulgarity **:** COARSE, LOW

2**vulgarian** \"\ *n* -S **:** a vulgar person 〈a juicy old ~ full of loving guile —Stanley Kauffmann〉

vul·gar·ism \'vəlgə,rizəm\ *n* -S [1*vulgar* + *-ism*] **1 a :** a word or expression originated or used chiefly by illiterate persons **:** a substandard use **:** BARBARISM, SOLECISM 〈"he ain't got no sense" is traditionally regarded as a ~〉 **b :** a lewd, profane, or coarse word or phrase **:** OBSCENITY **2 :** VULGARITY 〈there is an inherent contradiction between art and ~ —Herbert Read〉

vul·gar·i·ty \,vəl'garəd·ē, -ətē, -i, *also* -ger-\ *n* -ES [LL *vulgaritas*, fr. L *vulgaris* common, vulgar + *-itas* -ity — more at VULGAR] **1** *obs* **a :** the common people **b :** the run-of-mill average of a class **2** *obs* **:** the quality or state of being widely diffused **3** *obs* **:** the quality or state of being usual or ordinary **:** COMMONNESS **4 a :** the quality or state of being vulgar 〈the ~ of a picture-postcard scene —Winthrop Sargeant〉 〈would never stoop to the ~ of boasting how frequently he has been right —John Mason Brown〉 **b :** something vulgar (as an act or display) 〈some of the elegances were astounding *vulgarities* — for instance, seating a chimpanzee at a formal dinner —Gene Baro〉

vul·gar·iza·tion \,vəlgərə'zāshən, -ə,rī'z-\ *n* -S **1 :** a making widely familiar **:** POPULARIZATION 〈the book is unpretentious — a sensible piece of ~ —*New Republic*〉 〈a work of ~ marked by scholarly accuracy —Kemp Malone〉 **2 :** COARSENING, DEBASEMENT 〈a general ~ of taste and feeling —August Heckscher〉

vul·gar·ize \'==,rīz\ *vb* -ED/-ING/-S *see -ize in Explan Notes* [1*vulgar* + *-ize*] *vi* **:** to behave in a vulgar manner **~** *vt* **1 :** to spread widely **:** diffuse generally **:** POPULARIZE **2 :** to make vulgar **:** COARSEN 〈written and repeated brutalities hit the mind more deeply and ~ the spirit more grossly than those that we see in real life —J.C.Powys〉

vul·gar·iz·er \-zə(r)\ *n* -S **:** one that vulgarizes

vulgar latin *n, cap V&L* **:** the nonclassical Latin of ancient Rome including both the speech of plebeians and the informal daily speech of educated Romans that is scantily recorded in literature but attested by inscriptions and established by comparative evidence as the chief source of the Romance languages

vulgar law *n* **:** law arising in the time of the Roman Empire from sources (as foreigners in the provinces) other than the Roman law or applicable in places or provinces not under the Roman law

vul·gar·ly *adv* [ME, fr. *vulgar*, adj. + *-ly*] **:** in a vulgar manner

vul·gar·ness *n* -ES *archaic* **:** VULGARITY

vulgar purgation *n* [so called fr. its not having been sanctioned by the church] **:** purgation by combat or by ordeal by fire or water — compare CANONICAL PURGATION

vulgar substitution *n* [trans. of LL *substitutio vulgaris*] **:** SUBSTITUTION 1a(1)

vul·gate \'vəl,gāt, -,gət, *usu* -d·+V\ *n* -S [ML *Vulgata*, fr. LL *vulgata* (*editio*) Septuagint, Latin translation of the Septuagint, fr. L *vulgata* (fem. of *vulgatus* ordinary, common, general, fr. past part. of *vulgare* to make known, publish, fr. *vulgus* mob, common people) + *editio* edition — more at VULGAR] **1** *usu cap* **:** an edition or copy of the Latin Bible authorized and used by the Roman Catholic Church **2 :** any commonly accepted text or reading of an author's work **3 a :** common or informal speech 〈a remarkable ear for the ~ —M.D.Geismar〉 **b :** substandard or illiterate speech

1**vul·gus** \'vəlgəs\ *n* -ES [L — more at VULGAR] **:** the common people

2**vulgus** \"\ *n* -ES [prob. alter. of obs. E *vulgars* English sentences to translate into Latin, fr. pl. of E 2*vulgar*] **:** a short composition in Latin verse formerly common as an exercise in some English public schools

vulned \'vəlnd\ *adj* [L *vulnus* wound + E *-ed*] *heraldry* **:** WOUNDED

vul·ner·a·bil·i·ty \,vəln(ə)rə'biləd·ē, -lətē, -i\ *n* **:** the quality or state of being vulnerable

vul·ner·a·ble \'vəlnər(ə)bəl, -nrəb-\ *adj* [LL *vulnerabilis*, fr.

L *vulnerare* to wound (fr. *vulner-, vulnus* wound) + *-abilis* -able; akin to Goth *wilwan* to rob, *wulwa* robbery, MLG *wlete* wound, L *vellere* to pluck, pull, Gk (Homeric) *oulē* wound, Per *valāna, vālāna* wound, Hitt *ualḫmi* I battle] **1 :** capable of being wounded **:** defenseless against injury ⟨the problem of protecting the ~ human body —Lionel Whitby⟩ **2 :** open to attack or damage **:** readily countered **:** inviting obvious retort, ridicule, or obloquy **:** ASSAILABLE ⟨a scientific statement is a ~ statement —M.G.Joos⟩ ⟨weren't charged with anything perverse, simply with some affairs with women that made them ~ to the new Puritans —W.H.Hale⟩ ⟨the man who can read commercial documents . . . is far less ~ to fraud —Jerome Ellison⟩ **3 :** exposed to capture **:** likely to be reduced by military assault ⟨a particularly ~ outpost —*N.Y. Herald Tribune*⟩ **4 :** liable to increased penalties but entitled to increased bonuses after winning a game of contract bridge

vul·ner·a·ble·ness *n* -ES **:** VULNERABILITY

vul·ner·a·bly \ˈvəlnər(ə)blē, -nrəb-, -li\ *adv* **:** in a vulnerable manner

¹vul·ner·ary \ˈvəlnəˌrerē, -ri\ *adj* [L *vulnerarius*, fr. *vulner-, vulnus* wound + *-arius* -ary] **1 :** promoting the healing of wounds **:** CURATIVE, SANATIVE ⟨a ~ herb⟩ ⟨a ~ application⟩ **2 :** WOUNDING

²vulnerary \"\ *n* -ES **:** a vulnerary remedy

vul·pe·ci·dal *or* **vul·pi·ci·dal** \ˌvəlpəˈsīdᵊl\ *adj* **:** of, relating to, or committing vulpecide

vul·pe·cide *or* **vul·pi·cide** \ˈ==ˌsīd\ *n* -S [*vulpecide* irreg. fr. L *vulpes* fox + E *-cide; vulpicide* fr. L *vulpes* fox + E *-i-* + *-cide*] **1 :** a person killing a fox by means other than those of hunting with hounds **2 :** the killing of a fox by means other than those of hunting with hounds

vul·pec·u·la \ˌvəlˈpekyələ\ [NL, fr. L, small fox, a small shark, dim. of *vulpes* fox, a shark] *syn of* ALOPIAS

vul·pe·cu·li·dae \ˌvəlpəˈkyüləˌdē\ [NL, fr. *Vulpecula* + *-idae*] *syn of* ALOPIIDAE

vul·pes \ˈvəlˌpēz\ *n, cap* [NL, fr. L, fox — more at VULPINE] **:** a genus of mammals (family Canidae) including the common red fox and closely related animals — see FOX 1; compare FENNEC, GRAY FOX

vul·pine \ˈvəlˌpīn, -ˌpən\ *adj* [L *vulpinus*, fr. *vulpes* fox + *-inus* -ine; akin to Gk *alōpēx* fox, Arm *aluēs* fox, Skt *lopāśa* jackal, fox, Lith *vilpišys* wildcat] **1 :** of, relating to, or resembling a fox **2 :** marked by slyness or predatoriness **:** CRAFTY ⟨believed the mildest house agent grew ~ at sight of them —Audrey Barker⟩

vulpine opossum *or* **vulpine phalanger** *n* **:** a common Australian opossum (*Trichosurus vulpecula*) that is gray above fading to yellowish on the underparts

vul·pin·ic acid \ˌvəlˈpinik-\ *or* **vul·pic acid** \ˈvəlpik-\ *n* [*vulpinic* ISV *vulpin-* (fr. NL *vulpina* — specific epithet of *Cetraria vulpina* —, fr. fem. of L *vulpinus* vulpine) + *-ic; vulpic* fr. NL *vulpina* + E *-ic*] **:** a yellow crystalline compound $C_{19}H_{14}O_5$ occurring in various lichens (as *Cetraria vulpina*) and also made synthetically **:** the methyl ester of pulvinic acid

vul·pi·nite \ˈvəlpəˌnīt\ *n* -S [G *vulpinit*, fr. *Vulpino*, Lombardy, Italy + G *-it* -ite] **:** a mineral consisting of a scaly granular grayish white variety of anhydrite

vul·sel·la \ˌvəlˈselə\ *n* -S [NL, fr. L, tweezers] **:** VULSELLUM

vul·sel·lum \-ləm\ *n, pl* **vulsel·la** \-lə\ [NL, alter. of L *vulsella* tweezers, fr. *vellere* to pluck, pull — more at VULNERABLE] **:** a surgical forceps with serrated, clawed, or hooked blades

vul·tur \ˈvəltər\ *n, cap* [NL, fr. L, vulture] **:** a formerly comprehensive genus of vultures that is usu. restricted to the Andean condor

¹vul·ture \ˈvəlchə(r)\ *n* -S [ME, fr. L *vultur;* prob. akin to L *vellere* to pull, pluck — more at VULNERABLE] **1 :** any of various large raptorial birds of temperate and tropical regions that are related to the hawks, eagles, and falcons but have weaker claws and the head usu. naked, that subsist chiefly or entirely on carrion, and that constitute the families Aegypiidae and Cathartidae and include some of the largest birds of flight — see BLACK VULTURE, CONDOR, EGYPTIAN VULTURE, KING VULTURE, LAMMERGEIER, TURKEY BUZZARD **2 :** someone or something likened to a vulture: as **a :** an emotion or passion that preys on the mind or body **b :** a rapacious or predatory person or one pursuing vile or base objects ⟨shyster lawyers, crooked photographers and assorted ~s circling a big cash settlement —*Time*⟩ ⟨a ~ of an old woman who preyed on her lodgers and boarders⟩

vulture

²vulture \"\ *vt* **vultured; vultured; vulturing** \-ch(ə)riŋ\ **vultures :** to make prey or loot of **:** SNATCH, SWIPE ⟨had *vultured* the library's reference and guidebooks —*Newsweek*⟩

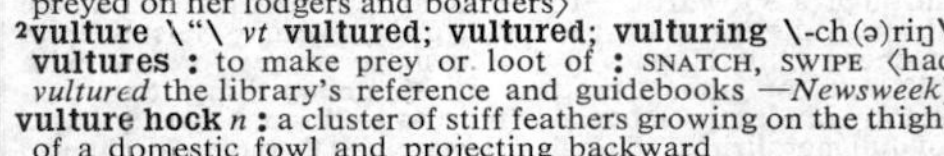

vulture hock *n* **:** a cluster of stiff feathers growing on the thighs of a domestic fowl and projecting backward

vulture–hocked \ˈ==ˌhäkt\ *adj* **:** having vulture hocks

vulture–like \ˈ==ˌ=\ *adj* **:** resembling a vulture

vulture raven *n* **:** either of two large ravens of eastern Africa belonging to the genus *Corvultur* and having a thick arched bill

vul·tur·ine \ˈvəlchəˌrīn, -ˌrən\ *adj* [L *vulturinus*, fr. *vultur* + *-inus* -ine] **1 a :** of or relating to the vultures **b :** characteristic of a vulture ⟨a ~ taste for offal⟩ **2 :** marked by a vile rapacity **:** PREDATORY ⟨~ congressmen —John Brooks⟩ ⟨this ~ essay —E.J.Kahn⟩

vulturine eagle *n* **:** an eagle (*Aquila verreauxii*), of southern Africa having the lower back and rump white and the rest of the plumage black

vulturine guinea fowl *n* **:** a large long-tailed guinea fowl (*Acryllium vulturinum*) of eastern Africa with a naked head and lanceolate blue, black, and white feathers on the neck, breast, and shoulders, a back mostly black spotted with white, and a bluish abdomen that becomes purple on the sides

vulturine sea eagle *n* **:** EAGLE VULTURE

vul·tur·ish \ˈvəlchərish, -rēsh\ *adj* **:** VULTUROUS

vul·tur·ous \-rəs\ *adj* **:** resembling a vulture esp. in rapacity or scavenging habits ⟨~ expectancy⟩

vulv- *or* **vulvo-** *comb form* [NL *vulva*] **1 :** vulva ⟨*vulvitis*⟩ **2 :** vulvar and ⟨*vulvovaginal*⟩

vul·va \ˈvəlvə\ *n* -S [NL, fr. L *vulva, volva* covering, integument, womb; akin to Skt *ulva, ulba* vulva, womb, placenta, L *volvere* to roll, turn — more at VOLUBLE] **1 a :** the external parts of the female genital organs **b :** the opening between the projecting parts of the external organs **2 :** the orifice of the oviduct of an insect or other invertebrate

vul·val \-vəl\ *adj* [*vulv-* + *-al*] **:** VULVAR

vul·var \-və(r)\ *adj* [*vulv-* + *-ar*] **:** of or relating to the vulva

vul·vate \-ˌvāt, -ˌvət, *usu* -d·+V\ *adj* [*vulv-* + *-ate*] **:** VULVAR, VULVIFORM

vul·vi·form \ˈvəlvəˌfȯrm\ *adj* [*vulv-* + *-iform*] **1 :** having an oval shape with a middle cleft and projecting lips **2 :** suggesting a cleft with projecting edges — used of plant forms

vul·vi·tis \ˌvəlˈvīdəs\ *n* -ES [NL, fr. *vulv-* + *-itis*] **:** inflammation of the vulva

vul·vo·vaginitis \ˌvəlvə+\ *n* [NL, fr. *vulv-* + *vaginitis*] **:** coincident inflammation of the vulva and vagina

vum \ˈvəm\ *vi* [prob. alter. of ³*vow*] *dial* **:** AVOW, SWEAR ⟨I ~, I'd soon put harness on myself as worry along with that lazy mule —Elizabeth M. Roberts⟩

vv *abbr* **1** *often cap both Vs* [L *venerabiles*] venerables **2** verbs **3** verses **4** violins **5** volumes

VV *abbr, often not cap* vice versa

v–value \ˈ=ˌ=(ˌ)=\ *n, usu cap 1st V* **:** the reciprocal of the dispersive power of an optical medium

VW *abbr* **1** very worshipful **2** vessel wall

vy *abbr* very

vying *pres part of* VIE

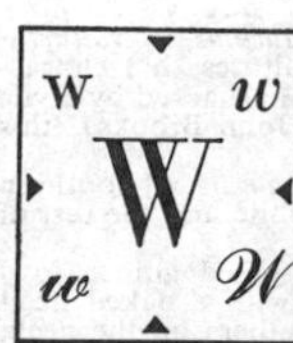

1w \'dəbəl(,)yü, -lyə; *in rapid speech also* -b(ə)yə *or* -byē\ *n, pl* **w's** *or* **ws** *often cap, often attrib* **1 a :** the 23d letter of the English alphabet **b :** an instance of this letter printed, written, or otherwise represented **c :** a speech counterpart of orthographic *w* (as *w* in *woo, watt, sway,* or German *wasser*) **2 :** a printer's type, a stamp, or some other instrument for reproducing the letter *w* **3 :** someone or something arbitrarily or conveniently designated *w* esp. as the 22d or when j is used for the 10th the 23d in order or class **4 :** something having the shape of the letter W

2w *abbr, often cap* **1** wall **2** wanting **3** war **4** warden **5** warehouse; warehousing **6** warm **7** waste **8** water **9** watt **10** weather **11** week **12** weight **13** west; western **14** wet **15** whip **16** white **17** wicket **18** wide **19** widow **20** width **21** wife **22** wind **23** wire **24** with **25** won **26** wood **27** word **28** work **29** wrong

3w *symbol, cap* **1** energy **2** [G *wolfram*] tungsten

1wa \'wä\ *Scot & dial Eng var of* WOE

2wa \"\ *Scot & dial Eng var of* WAY

3wa \"\ *n, pl* **wa** *or* **was** *usu cap* **1 a :** a people in the Wa States of northeastern Burma and adjoining parts of Yunnan province, China who have never been subdued by the Burmese or the Chinese, have preserved ancient cultural traits (as head hunting and the erection of megalithic monuments), are excellent agriculturists in mountain farming, and in the Wild Wa area do not wear clothes — called also *Kawa* **b :** a member of such people **2 :** the Mon-Khmer language of the Wa people

WA *abbr* **1** warm air **2** with average

wa' \'wȯ, 'wä\ *Scot var of* WALL

1waac \'wak\ *n* -s *usu cap* [*W*omen's *A*rmy *A*uxiliary *C*orps] **:** a member of the Women's Army Auxiliary Corps formed in England during World War I

2waac \"\ *n* -s *usu cap* [*W*omen's *A*rmy *A*uxiliary *C*orps] **:** a member of the Women's Army Auxiliary Corps formed in the U.S. during World War II — compare WAC

waaf \'waf\ *n* -s *usu cap* [*W*omen's *A*uxiliary *A*ir *F*orce] **:** a member of the Women's Auxiliary Air Force formed as an auxiliary of the British Royal Air Force during World War II

waahoo *var of* WAHOO

wab \'wab\ *Scot & dial Eng var of* WEB

wabanaki *usu cap, var of* ABNAKI

1wabble *var of* WOBBLE

2wab·ble \'wäbəl\ *n* -s [alter. of *5warble*] **:** the larva of a botfly (*Bogeria emasculator*) that infests squirrels and destroys their testes

wab·by \'wäbē\ *or* **whab·by** \'(h)w-\ *n* -ES [origin unknown] **:** RED-THROATED LOON

wa·be·no \wȯ'bē(,)nō\ *n* -s [Ojibwa *wâbanow*, lit., I am a sorcerer] **:** an Ojibwa shaman

wab·ster \'wabztə(r), -bst-\ *Scot & dial Eng var of* WEBSTER

wab·ur *also* **wab·ber** \'wäbə(r)\ *n* -s [Ar *wabr*, fr. *wabar* to be hairy] **:** SYRIAN HYRAX

wac \'wak\ *n* -s *usu cap* [*W*omen's *A*rmy *C*orps] **:** a member of the Women's Army Corps established in the U.S. during World War II as successor to the Women's Army Auxiliary Corps — compare 2WAAC

wac·ca·maw \'wäkə,mȯ\ *n, pl* **waccamaw** *or* **waccamaws** *usu cap* **1 :** a Siouan people of the Waccamaw river valley in eastern So. Carolina **2 :** a member of the Waccamaw people

wach·na \'wäknə\ *or* **wachna cod** *n* -s [Russ *vakhnya*] **:** a cod (*Eleginus nawaga*) of Alaska and Kamchatka

wack \'wak\ *or* **whack** \'(h)wak\ *n* -s [prob. back-formation fr. *wacky*] *slang* **:** a wacky person **:** CRACKPOT, SCREWBALL

wacke \'wakə\ *n* -s [G, fr. MHG, large stone, fr. OHG *waggo*] **:** GRAYWACKE

wack·en·ro·der solution \'väkən,rōdə(r)-\ *n, usu cap W* [prob. after H. W. F. *Wackenroder* †1854 Ger. chemist and apothecary] **:** a solution containing colloidal sulfur and polythionic acids obtained by passing hydrogen sulfide into a saturated aqueous solution of sulfur dioxide

wack·i·ly \'wakəlē, -li\ *adv* **:** in a wacky manner

wack·i·ness \-kēnəs, -kin-\ *n* -ES **:** the quality or state of being wacky

wacky \-kē, -ki\ *or* **whacky** \'(h)w-\ *also* **wack·ey** *or* **wack·ie** \'w-\ *adj* **wackier** *or* **whackier**; **wackiest** *or* **whackiest** [perh. fr. E dial. *whacky* fool, fr. *whack*-head fool, lit., one who has been whacked on the head + E *-y*] **:** eccentric or irrational esp. in an amusing, absurd, or fantastic manner ⟨his somewhat ~ philosophy pervades the family life —E.E. Calkins⟩ ⟨that explanation was just as ~ as many others —R.M.Blough⟩; *broadly* **:** CRAZY, INSANE ⟨if she kept on with such illogical ideas . . . she would end up as ~ as the other patients —Nancy Hale⟩

wa·co \'wā(,)kō\ *n, pl* **waco** *or* **wacos** *usu cap* [fr. Caddoan *Wehiko* Mexico; fr. their frequent fighting with the Mexicans] **1 :** a Caddo people of Oklahoma and Texas **2 :** a member of the Waco people

1wad \'wad, 'wäd\ *n* -s [ME(Sc), alter. of E *wed*] *Scots law* **:** PLEDGE — **in wad :** PLEDGED

2wad \'wäd *also* 'wȯd\ *n* -s [origin unknown] **1 a :** a usu. small mass, bundle, or tuft ⟨always has with him a ~ of photos —Walter Sullivan⟩ ⟨little ~s of mutton —Katherine Mansfield⟩ ⟨spread ~s of marmalade —Anthony Powell⟩ ⟨a glowing ~ of fireflies along the ground —William Goyen⟩ **b :** a soft mass (as of a loose fibrous material) variously used (as to stop an aperture, pad a garment, or hold grease around an axle) ⟨replaced cotton ~s in vials with a foamed polystyrene plug —*Modern Packaging*⟩ **c** (1) **:** a relatively soft plug used to retain a charge of powder, to keep the powder and shot close, or to avoid windage esp. in a muzzle-loading cannon or gun (2) **:** a disk of felt or paper used to separate the components of a shotgun cartridge or to retain the powder in a blank cartridge — see CARTRIDGE illustration **d :** a piece of clay used in ceramics for various purposes; *specif* **:** a strip of moist clay laid around the rim of a sagger to form a bed for a superimposed sagger in the kiln **e :** a small mass of a chewing substance ⟨a ~ of tobacco⟩ ⟨a ~ of gum⟩ **2 a :** a considerable amount ⟨bought himself a big ~ of radio time —R.P.Warren⟩ ⟨a whopping ~ of surpluses —*Sydney (Australia) Bull.*⟩ — often used in pl. ⟨has been getting ~s of publicity —*New Yorker*⟩ **b :** the amount which one is capable of expending — usu. used with *shoot* ⟨going to shoot our whole ~ at the carrier —E.L.Beach⟩ **3 a :** a roll of paper money ⟨produced a ~ of dirty notes —T.H.Barnardo⟩ ⟨a ~ on your hip that would choke a coal chute —Raymond Chandler⟩ **b :** a supply of money ⟨bet his ~ on a race⟩ **c :** a large amount of money ⟨idea of making a ~ and setting the folks up in style —Hiram Haydn⟩ ⟨quite a ~, close on two thousand dollars —Nevil Shute⟩

3wad \"\ *vt* **wadded; wadded; wadding; wads 1 :** to form into a wad or into wadding ⟨~ tow⟩; *esp* **:** to roll or crush into a tight wad ⟨they *wadded* their paper napkins into small, round balls —Grace Metalious⟩ ⟨handed the driver a *wadded* bill —Lillian Ross⟩ — often used with *up* ⟨took off my shirt, *wadded* it up —Herbert Passin⟩ **2 a :** to insert or crowd a wad into ⟨~ a gun⟩ **b :** to hold in by a wad ⟨~ a bullet in a gun⟩ **3 :** to stuff or line with some soft substance (as cotton) **:** PAD ⟨long blue gowns over *wadded* coats and trousers —Nora Waln⟩ ⟨let up rowing to ~ the oarlocks so they wouldn't make a noise —H.L.Davis⟩; *broadly* **:** to pack tightly ⟨families . . . were *wadded* closely into the available space —Julian Dana⟩

4wad \'wad, 'wäd\ *n* -s [prob. of Scand origin; akin to ON *vathr* fishing line, measuring line] *dial Eng* **:** LINE; *esp* **:** one marked in land surveying

5wad \", *in sense 2* 'wäd *also* 'wȯd\ *n* -s [origin unknown] **1** *dial Eng* **:** GRAPHITE, BLACK LEAD **2 :** an amorphous dull brown or black mineral substance that occurs usu. in low places, consists chiefly of oxides of manganese with varying amounts of other minerals (as copper, cobalt, and silica) and water, is commonly very soft but sometimes hard and compact, and is used in making chlorine and as a pigment **:** BOG MANGANESE — called also *black ocher;* compare BAUXITE, LIMONITE

6wad \'wäd, ,wəd\ *Scot & dial Eng var of* WOULD

wad·able *or* **wade·able** \'wādəbəl\ *adj* **:** capable of being waded ⟨a ~ stream⟩

wadcutter \'=,==\ *n* [*2wad* + *cutter*] **:** a cylindrical bullet having a flat top instead of a pointed or rounded nose or a truncated version of one of the latter

wad·der \'wädə(r) *also* 'wȯd-\ *n* -s **:** one that wads

1wad·ding \-diŋ\ *n* -s [*2wad* + *-ing*] **1 a :** wads or material for making wads **b :** a soft mass or sheet of short loose fibers used for stuffing or padding (as quilts, costumes, upholstery, or packages) **c** (1) **:** a soft absorbent paper used in hospitals and as sanitary napkins (2) **:** a loosely formed crepe paper used for packing **2** *or* **wadding thread :** a stuffer thread

2wad·ding \'wadin\ *Scot var of* WEDDING

1wad·dle \'wäd³l *also* 'wȯd-\ *vi* **waddled; waddled; waddling** \-d(³)liŋ\ **waddles** [freq. of *1wade*] **1 :** to walk with short steps swinging the forepart of the body from side to side ⟨ducks *waddling* to water⟩ ⟨*waddling* around with a fat man's strut —W.A.White⟩ **2 :** to move clumsily in a manner suggesting a waddle ⟨a bulldozer *waddled* up —M.O.Williams⟩ ⟨watched the steamer ~ out into the river —R.J.White⟩

2waddle \"\ *n* -s **:** the act of waddling **:** an awkward clumsy swaying gait **:** TODDLE

wad·dling·ly *adv* [*waddling* (pres. part. of *1waddle*) + *-ly*] **:** in a waddling manner

wad·dly \-d(³)lē\ *adj* **:** having or suggesting a waddle ⟨a ~ person⟩ ⟨watching the small form . . . disappear with its curious ~ walk —John Dos Passos⟩

1wad·dy \'wädē, -di *also* 'wȯd-\ *n* -ES [native name in Australia, perh. modif. of E *2wood*] **1 :** a straight tapered throwing-stick used in hunting and war by aborigines esp. of Australia **2 :** a piece of wood **:** STICK, PEG, WALKING STICK

2waddy \"\ *vt* -ED/-ING/-ES *Austral* **:** to attack or beat with a waddy

3waddy *or* **wad·die** \"\ *n, pl* **waddies** [origin unknown] **1** *West* **:** COWBOY 3 **2** *West* **:** RUSTLER C

4waddy *var of* WADI

1wade \'wād\ *vb* -ED/-ING/-S [ME *waden*, fr. OE *wadan;* akin to OHG *watan* to go, wade, ON *vatha* to go through, wade, L *vadere* to go, OE *wæd* ford, ON *vath*, L *vadum*] *vi* **1** *obs* **:** GO, PASS, PENETRATE **2 :** to step in or through a medium (as water, mud, or sand) that offers more resistance than air ⟨*waded* through a snowdrift —F.V.W.Mason⟩ ⟨burros came *wading* through the corral dust —F.B.Gipson⟩ ⟨*wading* waist-deep in bushes —A.W.Hughes⟩ **3 :** to move or get forward with difficulty or labor **:** proceed slowly among things that constantly hinder or embarrass ⟨have to ~ through twenty pages of dull moralizing —Douglas Stewart⟩ ⟨~ through slaughter to a throne —Thomas Gray⟩ **4 :** to set to work or attack with determination or vigor — used with *in* or *into* ⟨obtained some textbooks and *waded* in⟩ ⟨~ into the morning's mail⟩ ⟨*waded* into his opponent with his bare fists⟩ ⟨*waded* into the reputations of our national heroes —C.V.Woodward⟩ **~** *vt* **:** to pass or cross by wading ⟨~ a stream⟩ ⟨~ mud⟩

2wade \"\ *n* -s **:** an act of wading ⟨go for a ~ in the brook⟩

wadeable *var of* WADABLE

wade·ite \'wā,dīt\ *n* -s [Arthur *Wade* †1951 Eng. geologist + E *-ite*] **:** a mineral $K_2CaZr(SiO_3)_4$ consisting of a silicate of potassium, calcium, and zirconium

wad·er \'wādə(r)\ *n* -s **1 :** one that wades **2 :** WADING BIRD **3 a :** WADING BOOT **b :** a waterproof garment that consists of trousers sometimes reaching to the armpits, has attached socks or waterproof boots or shoes, and is worn (as by anglers or duck hunters) over the regular clothing — often used in pl. ⟨a pair of ~s⟩

wader 3b

wadge \'waj\ *n* -s [alter. of *1wedge*] **1** *Brit* **:** BUNCH, BUNDLE ⟨the ~ of letters was in his hands —Elizabeth Bowen⟩ **2** *Brit* **:** SLAB, WEDGE ⟨twisting a biscuit deep into the thick ~ of yogurt —G.A.Wagner⟩

wad hook *n* [*2wad*] *archaic* **:** WORMER 2

wa·di *also* **wa·dy** *or* **wad·dy** \'wädē, -di\ *or* **oued** \'wed\ *n, pl* **wadis** *also* **wadies** *or* **waddies** *or* **oueds** [Ar *wādiy*] **1 :** the bed or valley of a stream in arid regions of southwestern Asia and northern Africa that is usu. dry except during the rainy season and that often forms an oasis **:** GULLY, RAVINE, WASH **2 a :** a shallow usu. sharply defined depression in a desert region of poorly developed drainage in southwestern Asia and northern Africa

wading bird *n* [*wading* (pres. part. of *1wade*) + *bird*] **:** any of many long-legged birds including the shorebirds (as sandpipers and snipe) and the inland water birds (as cranes and herons) that wade in water in search of food

wading boot *n* [*wading* (gerund of *wade*) + *boot*] **:** a high waterproof boot worn esp. by fishermen; *esp* **:** HIP BOOT

wading pool *n* **:** a shallow pool of portable or permanent construction used (as in a park) by children for wading

wa·djak man \'wä,jäk-, 'wä,dyäk-\ *n, usu cap W* [fr. *Wadjak*, locality in Java where the skulls were discovered] **:** an extinct large-headed man of primitive proto-Australoid type known from two Javanese skulls that is often set apart as a species (*Homo wadjakensis*) but is probably a primitive form of modern man (*Homo sapiens*) intermediate between Solo man and the modern Australian natives

wad·mal *or* **wad·mol** *or* **wad·mel** \'wädməl\ *n* -s [ME *wadmoll, wadmale*, fr. ON *vathmāl*, lit., standard cloth, fr. *vāth* cloth, clothing + *māl* measure — more at WEED, MEAL] **:** a coarse rough woolen fabric formerly used in the British Isles and Scandinavia for protective coverings and warm clothing

wad·na \'wädnə\ [*6wad* + *na*] *Scot & dial Eng* **:** would not

wads *pl of* WAD, *pres 3d sing of* WAD

1wad·set \'wad,set, 'wäd-\ *vt* [Sc, alter. of ME *wedsetten* to pledge, fr. *1wed* + *setten* to set] *Scots law* **:** MORTGAGE, PLEDGE

2wadset \"\ *n* -s [Sc, alter. of ME *wedset* mortgage, fr. *wedsetten* to pledge] *Scots law* **:** MORTGAGE, PLEDGE, PAWN; *esp* **:** a mortgage of real estate given by a borrower to a lender formerly transferring possession only but later the legal title

wad·set·ter \-tər\ *n* [*1wadset* + *-er*] **1** *Scot* **:** MORTGAGOR **2** *Scot* **:** MORTGAGEE

WAE *abbr* when actually employed

wae·suck \'wā,sək\ *or* **wae·sucks** \-ks\ *interj* [Sc *wae* woe (fr. ME *wa*) + *suck*, *sucks*, alter. of E *sake, sakes* — more at WOE] *Scot* — used to express grief or pity

waf \'waf\ *n* -s *usu cap* [*W*omen in the *A*ir *F*orce] **:** a member of the women's component of the U. S. Air Force formed after World War II

WAF *abbr, often not cap* with all faults

1wa·fer \'wāfə(r)\ *n* -s [ME *wafre, wafer*, fr. ONF *waufre*, of Gmc origin; akin to MD *wafel, wafer* waffle — more at WAFFLE] **1 a :** a thin crisp cake or cracker **b :** a thin cake or piece of bread usu. unleavened, circular, and stamped with a cross or sacred monogram that is used in a religious service esp. in the celebration of the Eucharist in high liturgical churches — compare ALTAR BREAD **2 :** an adhesive disk of dried paste made of flour mixed with gum or of gelatin, isinglass, or similar material with added coloring matter and used as a seal (as for letters or the attaching of papers) **3** *or* **wafer capsule :** CACHET 3 **4 :** a thin disk or ring resembling a wafer and variously used (as for a valve, diaphragm, or tumbler in a lock)

2wafer \"\ *vt* -ED/-ING/-S **:** to seal, close, or fasten with a wafer

wafer ash *n* **:** HOP TREE

wafer bread *n* **1 :** eucharistic bread in the form of wafers **2 :** corn bread baked in thin sheets esp. by southwestern Indians

wafer iron *n* [ME *wafer iren*, fr. *1wafer* + *iren* iron] **:** a long-handled pair of iron tongs molded with a design that is impressed upon the wafer batter in baking

wafer sheet *n* **:** a very thin sheet of baked dough used in pharmacy for making small envelopes or cachets

wafer-thin \'==;'=\ *adj* **:** PAPER-THIN ⟨holding a *wafer-thin* majority on the executive board —J.C.Cort⟩

1waff \'waf\ *vb* -ED/-ING/-S [ME (northern) *waffen*, alter. of ME *waven* to wave] *chiefly Scot* **:** WAVE, FLUTTER, WAG, FLAP

2waff \"\ *n* -s **1** *chiefly Scot* **:** a waving motion **:** FLAPPING **2** *chiefly Scot* **:** PUFF, GUST, WHIFF, ODOR **3** *chiefly Scot* **:** GLIMPSE **4** *chiefly Scot* **:** WRAITH

3waff \"\ *adj* [alter. of *2waif*] *Scot* **:** WORTHLESS, DISREPUTABLE, LOWBORN, PALTRY — **waff·ness** *n* -ES

waff·ie \-fi\ *n* -s [*3waff* + *-ie*] *Scot* **:** VAGRANT, VAGABOND

1waf·fle \'wäfəl, 'wȯf-\ *n* -s [D *wafel*, fr. MD *wafel, wafer;* akin to MLG *wafel* waffle, OHG *waba* honeycomb, *weban* to weave — more at WEAVE] **1 :** a crisp cake made of pancake batter baked in a waffle iron ⟨had ~s for supper⟩ **2 :** WAFER 1a

2waffle \"\ *also* **waf·fled** \-ld\ *adj* **:** having an indented latticed pattern or form

3waffle \"\ *vi* **waffled; waffled; waffling** \-f(ə)liŋ\ **waffles** [freq. of obs. *waff* to yelp, of imit. origin] **:** to talk foolishly **:** BLATHER ⟨art writers can ~ on without saying anything that matters —*Times Lit. Supp.*⟩

waffle cloth *n* [*2waffle*] **:** HONEYCOMB 3b(2)

waffle ingot *n* **:** an ingot of aluminum about three inches square and a quarter of an inch thick

waffle iron *n* [*1waffle*] **:** a utensil for cooking waffles that consists of two metal parts hinged together so as to shut upon each other and impress square, round, or oval surface projections on the waffle in baking

waffle iron

waffle piqué *n* [*2waffle*] **:** a fine cotton usu. printed honeycomb cloth

waffle weave *n* **:** HONEYCOMB 3b(1)

wafs *pl of* WAF

1waft \'wäft, 'waft, 'waa(ə)ft, 'waift, 'wäft *also* 'wȯft\ *vb* -ED/-ING/-S [fr. (assumed) ME *waughten* to guard, convoy (whence ME *waughter* wafter, convoy), fr. MD or MLG *wachten* to watch, guard; akin to OE *wæccan* to watch — more at WAKE] *vt* **1** *obs* **:** to act as convoy to **:** sail in company with (as for protection) **2** [prob. alter. of *1waff*] *obs* **:** to signal to (as by waving the hand) **:** BECKON ⟨who ~s us yonder —Shak.⟩ **3** *archaic* **:** to convey by water **:** transport across a body of water ⟨~ me safely cross the Channel —Shak.⟩ **4 :** to cause to move or go lightly by or as if by the impulse of wind or waves **:** to bear along on or as if on a buoyant medium ⟨a light hot gust of wind ~*ed* the clouds towards other slopes —Anna Seghers⟩ ⟨the aroma of coffee was ~*ed* in —Ellen Glasgow⟩ ⟨milkweed is already ~*ing* silky down across the bog grass —D.C. Peattie⟩ ⟨he ~*ed* the subject aside with the smoke from his cigar —Marguerite Steen⟩ **~** *vi* **:** to become moved or pass on or as if on a buoyant medium ⟨scent of oregano ~s from their doors —Franc Shor⟩ ⟨light classical tunes ~ from amplifiers —C.M.Barss⟩ ⟨the waiter . . . nodded and ~*ed off* —Peter De Vries⟩

2waft \"\ *n* -s **1 :** something (as an odor) that is wafted **:** something fleeting **:** something that lingers lightly **:** WHIFF ⟨stale ~ of an exotic perfume —C.D.Lewis⟩ ⟨a ~ of carbolic acid was borne on a warm gust of wind —Cyril Connolly⟩ ⟨fragmentary ~s of village gossip floated in at the windows —Richard Church⟩ **2 :** a wafting movement **:** PUFF, GUST ⟨every ~ of the air —H.W.Longfellow⟩ ⟨expresses every whim and ~ of his time —*John o' London's Weekly*⟩ **3 :** the act of wafting; *esp* **:** a signal made by waving something (as a flag) in the air **4** *or* **weft** \'weft\ **a :** a pennant or a stopped or knotted flag used to signal or sometimes to show the direction of the wind to the steersman **b :** the knot in such a flag

3waft \'waft\ *Scot var of* WEFT

waft·age *pronunc at* 1WAFT + ij\ *n* -s [*1waft* + *-age*] **:** the act of wafting or state of being wafted **:** passage or conveyance on or through a buoyant medium; *broadly* **:** CONVEYANCE, CARRIAGE ⟨boats prepared for ~ to and fro —Michael Drayton⟩

waft·er \"+ə(r)\ *n* -s [ME *waughter* convoy, commander of a convoy, fr. (assumed) ME *waughten* to guard, convoy + ME *-er* — more at WAFT] **1 :** one that wafts; *specif* **:** a revolving disk or fan for a blower **2** *obs* **:** a transport or passenger boat or its master; *also* **:** a warship serving as a convoy to such a boat

waf·ture \'wäfchə(r), 'waf-\ *n* -s [*1waft* + *-ure*] **1 :** the act of wafting or waving **:** a wavelike motion **:** WAFT, BECKONING **2 :** something wafted or conveyed by or as if by a breeze or the waves of the sea

1wag \'wag, -aa(ə)g, -aig\ *vb* **wagged; wagged; wagging; wags** [ME *waggen;* akin to ON *vagga* cradle, Sw *vagga* to rock, MHG *wacken* to totter; akin to OE *wagian* to move, swing, totter, OHG *wagōn* to move, surge, ON *vaga* to wag; akin to OE *wegan* to move — more at WAY] *vi* **1 :** to be in action or motion **:** MOVE, STIR ⟨see . . . how the world ~s —Shak.⟩ **2 :** to move to and fro or up and down esp. repeatedly and with a quick or jerky motion **:** OSCILLATE, SWITCH, WAGGLE, WAVE, WIGWAG **3 :** to keep moving in chatter or gossip ⟨his tongue ~s incessantly⟩ ⟨beards *wagged* throughout the scientific world —Webb Garrison⟩ ⟨heads *wagged* for a time —Louis Bromfield⟩ ⟨his lips were still *wagging* —*Time*⟩ **4 a** *archaic* **:** to move from a place **:** pack off **:** DEPART ⟨~ to town⟩ **b** *archaic* **:** to wander from place to place **:** TRAVEL **c** *slang* **:** to play truant from school ⟨the school we both attended — when not *wagging* it —*Sydney (Australia) Bull.*⟩ **5 a :** to move with a wagging or wobbling motion **:** WADDLE ⟨a dog *wagging* down the street⟩ **b** *of an animal* **:** to wag the tail ⟨a pack of dogs — they fawned, they *wagged*, they growled —Helen Howe⟩ **~** *vt* **1 a** *archaic* **:** MOVE, STIR, BUDGE **b** *dial* **:** to carry or haul with difficulty **:** LUG ⟨~ groceries home in a cart⟩ ⟨a small child . . . compelled to ~ her baby brother around with her —Theodore Garrison⟩ **2 a :** to swing to and fro or up and down esp. repeatedly and with a quick or jerky motion **:** SHAKE, SWITCH, WAVE ⟨ducks . . . nonchalantly *wagging* their tails —Edmund Wilson⟩ ⟨formation leaders have telegraphed their dive attacks by *wagging* their wings before coming in —Keith Ayling⟩ ⟨naval vessels . . . would be *wagging* and hoisting flags and blinking lights at one another —Gavin Douglas⟩; *specif* **:** to nod (the head) or shake (a finger) at (as in assent or mild reproof) ⟨don't ~ your finger at me⟩ **b :** to move (as the head) animatedly in conversation ⟨a scandalous event that set the villagers to *wagging* their tongues⟩ ⟨a theory for philosophers to ~ their heads over —Henry Bordeaux⟩ **3 :** to strongly influence or exert control over (a related thing) out of proportion to size or true importance ⟨the tail ~s the dog⟩ ⟨instances . . . in which the choirs are *wagging* the church —Maurice Thompson⟩

2wag \"\ *n* -s **:** an act of wagging **:** NOD ⟨a ~ of the head⟩

3wag \"\ *n* -s [prob. short for obs. *waghalter* gallows bird, fr. *1wag* + *halter*] **1** *obs* **a :** a mischievous boy **b :** a young man **:** CHAP **2 :** one full of sport and humor **:** WIT, JESTER, JOKER ⟨we wink at ~s when they offend —John Dryden⟩ ⟨many of the most celebrated ~s of history —E.J.Kahn⟩

wag *abbr* wagon; wagoner

wa·gang *or* **wa'·gang** \'wä,gaŋ\ *or* **wa·gang·ing** \-ŋin\ *or* **wa·gaun** \-,gȯn\ *n* -s [*wagang, wa'gang* fr. *2wa* + *gang* (act of going); *waganging* fr. *2wa* + *ganging*, gerund of *gang* (to go); *wagaun* fr. *2wa* + Sc *gaun*, gerund of *go*] *Scot* **:** DEPARTURE, LEAVE-TAKING, DEATH

wag-at-the-wall *var of* WAG-ON-THE-WALL

1wage \'wāj\ *vb* -ED/-ING/-S [ME *wagen* to pledge, give as security, engage, employ, fr. ONF *wagier*, fr. *wage* pledge] *vt* **1** *dial* **:** to put upon wages **:** ENGAGE, HIRE, EMPLOY ⟨won't be able to ~ them, like you ~ hands, at sixteen shillings a month —John Masefield⟩ **2 :** to bind oneself to **:** agree to abide the event of ⟨~ trial by battle⟩ — compare WAGER OF LAW **3 :** to engage in (as a contest) as if by previous gage or pledge **:** carry on actions that constitute or promote ⟨~ war⟩ ⟨~ a campaign⟩ ⟨~ a battle⟩ ⟨~ a filibuster⟩ ⟨farmers still ~ a losing fight with poor, stony land —*Amer. Guide Series: Conn.*⟩ ⟨an intense game of bridge that had been *waged* en route —*N.Y.Times*⟩ ⟨we are now *waging* peace —J.F.Dulles⟩ **4** *obs* **:** to let out for hire or reward **:** hire out **5** [by alter.] **:** WEDGE *vt* 6 **~** *vi* **:** to be in process of occurring ⟨the riot *waged* for several hours —*Amer. Guide Series: Md.*⟩ ⟨controversy ~s even more fiercely —O. Elfrida Saunders⟩

2wage \"\ *n* -s *often attrib* [ME, pledge, security, wage, fr. ONF, of Gmc origin; akin to Goth *wadi* pledge — more at WED] **1 a :** a pledge or payment of usu. monetary remuneration by an employer esp. for labor or services usu. according to contract and on an hourly, daily, or piecework basis and often including bonuses, commissions, and amounts paid by the employer for insurance, pension, hospitalization, and other benefits; *esp* **:** such remuneration paid to a skilled or unskilled laborer ⟨pelt . . . would bring about fifty dollars which wasn't a bad ~ for their two days' work —Robert Lund⟩ ⟨the starting ~ was $17.50 a month —J.L.Marshall⟩ ⟨~ freeze⟩ ⟨~ scale⟩

— often used in pl. but sometimes sing. in constr. ⟨a freeman makes himself a servant to another by selling him for a certain time the service he undertakes to do in exchange for ~s he is to receive —John Locke⟩ ⟨work by the day at lower ~s —*Current Biog.*⟩; see LIVING WAGE, MINIMUM WAGE; compare SALARY **b wages** *pl but sing or pl in constr* **:** the share of the annual product or national dividend that is the return to labor as distinct from the remuneration received by capital or land — compare INTEREST, PROFIT, RENT **2 :** RECOMPENSE, REQUITAL, REWARD — usu. used in pl. but sing. or pl. in constr.; used chiefly with *of* ⟨for the ~s of sin is death —Rom 6:23 (RSV)⟩ ⟨loving falsehood, ignorant of the ~s of uprightness —E.J. Goodspeed⟩ ⟨the gods give thee fair ~ and dues of death —A.C.Swinburne⟩

syn WAGE *or* WAGES, SALARY, STIPEND, FEE, PAY, HIRE, and EMOLUMENT can all mean the price paid someone for his labor or services. WAGE or WAGES applies chiefly to an amount paid daily or weekly esp. for chiefly physical labor ⟨earn a day's *wage*⟩ ⟨receives his *wages* in cash once a week⟩ SALARY and STIPEND usu. apply to a fixed compensation commonly paid at longer intervals than wages and usu. for services that require training or special ability, STIPEND often applying specially to the pay of a teacher, magistrate, or clergyman or to money received as from a scholarship or pension, and usu. implying a relatively small sum ⟨an executive's *salary*⟩ ⟨the *salary* of a white-collar worker⟩ ⟨a minister's *stipend* often includes the use of a house⟩ ⟨a modest *stipend* from a retirement policy⟩ FEE applies to the price asked or paid for the services of a physician, lawyer, artist, or other professional ⟨a lawyer's *fee*⟩ ⟨a *fee* for professional services⟩ ⟨pays its authors and illustrators very reasonable *fees* —Lilo Linke⟩ PAY is usu. the equivalent of WAGES, SALARY, or STIPEND ⟨a teacher's *pay*⟩ ⟨a porter's *pay*⟩ ⟨the *pay* scale of workers or executives⟩ ⟨a clergyman's *pay*⟩ HIRE is archaic in the sense of WAGES but occurs sometimes in the sense of *rental fee* ⟨lends his pen for small *hires* —George Meredith⟩ ⟨the films can be had at a reasonable *hire* charge —*Paper & Print*⟩ EMOLUMENT is bookish except in the plural when it often means the rewards, usu. other than pay, of one's work or office ⟨wages include *emoluments* of value, like pension and insurance benefits, which may accrue to employees out of their employment relationship —C.W.Boyce⟩ ⟨old institutions whose prestige, influence and *emoluments* of power depend upon the preservation of the old order —John Dewey⟩ ⟨salary £550 with no *emoluments* —*Farmer & Stock-Breeder*⟩ ⟨on observing women kissing the veteran Franklin, he asked if that was one of the *emoluments* of his office —C.G.Bowers⟩

wage bill *n* **:** the total amount paid in wages by a business establishment or industry usu. figured on an annual basis

wage board *n* **:** a board established by law to investigate wage rates

wage bracket *n* **:** a stipulated wage rate varying from a low limit to a high limit for a particular purpose

waged *adj* [ME, fr. past part. of *wagen* to engage, employ — more at WAGE] **:** receiving wages **:** HIRED ⟨large plots of ground at economic rents, and decently ~ people paying them —John Galsworthy⟩

wage dividend *n* **:** payment of a share of profits in a profit-sharing plan to employees in relation to dividends paid to stockholders and in relation to the proportionate earnings of each employee

wage earner *n* **:** one that works for wages or salary

wage-fund theory *or* **wages-fund theory** *n* **:** a theory in economics: there is at any one time a rigid capital fund available for wage payments, and increases in wage rates to any groups will only redistribute wage payments, not increase the aggregate of wages paid — compare IRON LAW OF WAGES, SUBSISTENCE THEORY

wage home *n* **:** a foster home in which children must earn their board by working

wag·el \ˈwagəl\ *or* **wagel gull** *var of* WAGGEL

wage·less \ˈwājləs\ *adj* **:** having no wages **:** UNPAID ⟨a ~ menial —Holbrook Jackson⟩ — **wage·less·ness** *n* -ES

wage level *n* **:** the approximate position of wages at any given time in any occupation or trade or esp. in industry at large

¹wa·ger \ˈwājə(r)\ *n* -S [ME *wageour, wager* pledge, bet, prize, fr. AF *wageure*, fr. ONF *wagier* to pledge + *-ure* — more at WAGE] **1 a :** something (as a sum of money) that is risked on an uncertain event **:** BET, STAKE, PRIZE ⟨laid a ~ of five dollars on the race⟩ **b :** an act of betting; *specif* **:** WAGERING CONTRACT ⟨the outcome may be sufficiently in doubt to make a true ~ possible —Oswald Jacoby⟩ **c :** something on which bets are laid **:** the subject of a bet **:** GAMBLE ⟨do a stunt as a ~⟩ **2** *archaic* **:** an act of giving a pledge to take and abide by the result of some action: as **a :** TRIAL BY BATTLE **b :** WAGER OF LAW

²wager \"\ *vb* **wagered; wagered; wagering** \-j(ə)riŋ\ **wagers** *vt* **:** to hazard on the issue of a contest or on a question that is to be decided or on a casualty **:** RISK, VENTURE; *specif* **:** to lay as a gamble ⟨~ five dollars on a horse⟩ ~ *vi* **:** to make a bet **:** lay a wager

³wa·ger \"\ *n* -S **:** one that wages **:** one that engages in a contest or competition **:** COMPETITOR ⟨the great numbers of these fish show that they are successful ~s of life —William Beebe⟩

wage rate *n* **:** the amount of base wage paid to a worker per unit of time (as per hour or day) or per unit of output if on piecework

wage reopening *n* **:** the contractual right of a union or management to seek a change in wage rates at some specified time during the life of the contract

wa·ger·er \ˈwājərə(r)\ *n* -S **:** one that wagers **:** BETTOR

wagering *adj* [fr. gerund of ²*wager*] **:** relating to the act of one who wagers **:** BETTING

wagering contract *n* **:** a contract by which a promisor agrees that upon the occurrence of an uncertain event or condition he will render a performance for which there is no agreed consideration exchanged, and under which the promisee or the beneficiary of the contract is not made whole for any loss caused by such occurrence (as in options, insurance contracts, trading in futures, or betting contracts)

wager of battle [trans. of ML *vadiatio duelli*] **:** TRIAL BY BATTLE ⟨defiant men, accepting the *wager of battle* —D.D.Martin⟩

wager of law [trans. of ML *vadiatio legis*] **:** the act of a party having the negative in an action in early English law in giving a pledge or in binding himself to resort to and abide the event of an attempt to prove his case by the oath of himself and the required number of compurgators

wager policy *n* **:** a marine insurance policy covering property in which the insured does not possess an insurable interest capable of legal proof

wages *pres 3d sing of* WAGE, *pl of* WAGE

wage scale *n* **1 :** a schedule of rates of wages paid for related tasks **2 :** the level of wages paid by an individual employer

wages council *n* **:** TRADE BOARD

wage slave *n* **:** one whose toil for wages is tantamount to slavery

wage structure *n* **:** the schedule of wage differentials among jobs in a plant, industry, or country

wage system *n* **:** an industrial system in which free laborers are hired by capitalists to do a large part of the productive work of society as contrasted with slavery or serfdom on the one hand and small proprietorship on the other

wageworker \ˈ≈,≈≈\ *n* **:** WAGE EARNER

wagged *past of* WAG

wag·gel \ˈwagəl\ *or* **waggel gull** *n* [origin unknown] *Brit* **:** a black-backed gull in immature plumage

wag·ger \ˈwagə(r)\ *n* -S **:** one that wags

wag·gery \ˈwagərē, ˈwaag-, ˈwaig-, -ri\ *n* -ES [²*wag* + *-ery*] **1 :** the manner or action of a wag **:** mischievous merriment **:** PLEASANTRY, JOCULARITY, WAGGISHNESS ⟨witches of the conventional sort are an easy target for ~ —*Times Lit. Supp.*⟩ ⟨fair sample of early wartime radio ~ —*Coronet*⟩ **2 :** a bit of foolery **:** JEST; *esp* **:** PRACTICAL JOKE ⟨man given to little *waggeries* —Anthony Trollope⟩

wagging *pres part of* WAG

wag·gish \-gish, -gēsh\ *adj* [²*wag* + *-ish*] **1 :** resembling or characteristic of a wag **:** sportively or good-humoredly mischievous or roguish **:** FROLICSOME ⟨a company of ~ boys —Roger L'Estrange⟩ ⟨a ~ disposition⟩ **2 :** done or made in waggery or for sport **:** SPORTIVE, HUMOROUS ⟨a ~ trick⟩ — **wag·gish·ly** *adv* — **wag·gish·ness** *n* -ES

¹wag·gle \ˈwagəl, ˈwaig-\ *vb* **waggled; waggled; waggling** \-g(ə)liŋ\ **waggles** [freq. of ¹*wag*] *vt* **1 :** to move back and forth or up and down esp. repeatedly and with a jerky or undulating movement **:** WAG ⟨a bird ~s his tail⟩ ⟨*waggled* his forefinger in the air⟩ ⟨the pilot *waggled* his wings as a signal —F.B.Colton⟩ ⟨we grown-ups ~ our heads when we greet a baby —Benjamin Spock⟩ ⟨clenched a big fist and *waggled* it experimentally —L.C.Douglas⟩ **2 :** to impart a waggle to (a golf club) ~ *vi* **1 :** to move back and forth or up and down esp. repeatedly and with a jerky or undulating movement **:** WAG, WOBBLE ⟨boats were gently *waggling* at their moorings —Sylvia T. Warner⟩ ⟨prancing firmly, her flowered muslin bustle *waggling* as she went —F. Tennyson Jesse⟩ **2 :** to move with a pronounced swinging motion (as of the hips) **:** WADDLE ⟨teaching a maid to ~ provocatively —*New Yorker*⟩

²waggle \"\ *n* -S **:** an instance of waggling **:** a jerky motion back and forth or up and down **:** WOBBLE ⟨reminds them with a ~ of one gnarled finger —Fulton Oursler⟩; *specif* **:** a preliminary swinging of a golf club head back and forth over the ball in preparing to start the stroke

wag·gly \-g(ə)lē, -li\ *adj* [¹*waggle* + *-y*] **1 :** having a wavering or wobbly course ⟨a ~ path⟩ **2 :** characterized by a waggling movement ⟨a ~ dog⟩

wag·gon \ˈwagən\ *chiefly Brit var of* WAGON

wag·gy \ˈwagē\ *adj* -ER/-EST [¹*wag* + *-y*] **:** having a tendency to wag **:** given to wagging ⟨hounds with ~ tails⟩

wagh *var of* WAUGH

waging *pres part of* WAGE

wag·ner·esque \ˌvägnəˈresk\ *adj, usu cap* [Richard *Wagner* †1883 + E *-esque*] **:** resembling or suggesting in style and treatment the work of Wagner

¹wag·ne·ri·an \(ˈ)väg¦nirēən, -¦nēr-\ *adj, usu cap* [Richard *Wagner* †1883 Ger. tone poet, composer, and writer on music + E *-ian*] **1 :** relating to, characterized by, or resembling the theories or style of Wagner **2 :** belonging to, characteristic of, or suggestive of the operas of Wagner ⟨a *Wagnerian* singer⟩ ⟨misty, *Wagnerian* mountains —G.A.Wagner⟩ ⟨thunderstorms . . . capable of truly *Wagnerian* effects —Andrew Hamilton & Chandler Harris⟩

²wagnerian \"\ *n* -S *usu cap* [Richard *Wagner* †1883 + E *-ian*] **:** an admirer of the musical theories and style of Wagner

wag·ne·ri·an·ism \väg¦nirēə,nizəm, -ˈnēr-\ *n* -S *usu cap* [²*wagnerian* + *-ism*] **:** WAGNERISM

wag·ner·ism \ˈvägnə,rizəm\ *n* -S *usu cap* [Richard *Wagner* †1883 + E *-ism*] **1 :** Wagner's theory and practice in the composition of opera **2 :** the influence of the work of Wagner in the world of music

¹wag·ner·ite \ˈvägnə,rīt, ˈwag-\ *n* -S [G *wagnerit*, fr. F. M. von *Wagner* †1851 Ger. mining engineer + G *-it* -ite] **:** a mineral $Mg_2(PO_4)F$ consisting of a magnesium fluorophosphate and occurring in yellow monoclinic crystals and also in massive forms

²wag·ner·ite \ˈvägnə,rīt\ *n* -S *usu cap* [Richard *Wagner* †1883 + E *-ite*] **:** an adherent of Wagnerism **:** WAGNERIAN

wag·ner rearrangement \ˈvägnə(r)-\ *or* **wag·ner-meer·wein rearrangement** \-ˈmer,vīn-\ *n, usu cap W&M* [after Georg *Wagner* 19th cent. Russ. chemist] **:** a reaction that is applicable esp. to organic compounds containing a neopentyl or similar grouping, that is thought to proceed by way of a carbonium ion, and that involves change of the carbon skeleton (as from pinene to bornyl chloride by hydrogen chloride, from neopentyl iodide to *tert*-amyl acetate by silver acetate, or from methyl-*tert*-butyl-carbinol to tetramethyl-ethylene by acids) — compare PINACOLONE

wag·ner tuba \ˈvägnə(r)-\ *n, usu cap W* [after Richard *Wagner* †1883 Ger. composer] **:** a brass wind musical instrument between a French horn and a tuba in construction and timbre designed by Wagner and called for in his scores

¹wag·on \ˈwagən, ˈwaig- *sometimes* ˈwaag- *or* -gᵊŋ\ *n* -S *often attrib* [earlier *wagan, wagen, waghen*, fr. D *wagen*, fr. MD — more at WAIN] **1 a :** a heavy four-wheel usu. uncovered vehicle designed esp. for transporting bulky commodities and drawn orig. by animals ⟨ox ~⟩ but now often by a motor vehicle (as a tractor) ⟨freight ~⟩ ⟨farm ~⟩ ⟨~ road⟩ — see COVERED WAGON; compare CART, DRAY, VAN, WAIN **b :** a similar but lighter typically horse-drawn vehicle for transporting goods or passengers — see SPRING WAGON **c :** a four-wheeled cart, trailer, or powered vehicle for hauling men (as a fire-fighting squad, a police detail, or prisoners) or equipment ⟨hose ~⟩ ⟨searchlight ~⟩ ⟨sheriff's ~⟩; *specif* **:** PATROL WAGON ⟨call the ~⟩ **2** *Brit* **:** a vehicle for transporting goods on a railway corresponding in general to the American freight car but usu. of much smaller capacity — compare ³VAN 2 **3 :** a cart, trailer, motortruck, or small wheeled cabin used (as on the street or by a traveling show) esp. to dispense foods or other articles ⟨hot dog ~⟩ ⟨ice-cream ~⟩ ⟨popcorn ~⟩ ⟨ticket ~⟩ ⟨book ~⟩ **4 :** COASTER WAGON **5 :** a tool used by goldbeaters and others to cut and trim gold leaf and formed like a miniature sledge with runners of malacca reed that form the cutting edges **6 :** DINNER WAGON ⟨the waiter appeared . . . with his ~ of hors d'oeuvres —Gwethalyn Graham⟩ **7 :** a delivery truck ⟨bread ~⟩ ⟨milk ~⟩ **8 :** STATION WAGON **9 :** a low sliding or rolling platform used for the quick shifting of scenes on a theater stage — see WAGON STAGE **10 :** a large earth-moving trailer with a dump body — **off the wagon** *adv (or adj)* **:** no longer under pledge or resolution to abstain from alcoholic beverages — **on the wagon** *adv (or adj)* **:** under pledge or resolution to abstain from alcoholic beverages ⟨I do drink . . . but I'm *on the wagon* just now —Dan Wickenden⟩

wagon 1a

²wagon \"\ *vb* -ED/-ING/-S *vi* **:** to travel or transport goods by wagon ⟨like ~*ing* on smooth, silent wheels across a roadless prairie —S.H.Adams⟩ ~ *vt* **:** to transport (goods) by wagon

wag·on·age \-gənij\ *n* -S [¹*wagon* + *-age*] **1** *archaic* **:** transportation by wagon **2** *archaic* **:** money paid for carriage or conveyance in a wagon

wagon boss *n* **1 :** a man in charge of a wagon train **2** *West* **:** a man in charge of a roundup

wagon box *also* **wagon bed** *n* **:** the body of a wagon

wagon breast *n* **:** a breast in a coal mine into which wagons can be taken

wagon ceiling *n* **:** BARREL CEILING

¹wag·on·er \-gənə(r)\ *n* -S [¹*wagon* + *-er*] **:** one that hauls heavy loads in a wagon **:** the driver of a wagon

²wagoner \"\ *n* -S [after Lucas J. *Waghenaer*, 16th cent. Du. cartographer] *archaic* **:** a book of nautical charts

wag·on·ette \ˌ≈gə¦net\ *n* -S [¹*wagon* + *-ette*] **:** a light wagon having two facing seats along the sides back of a transverse seat in front and designed to carry six or more

wagonette

wag·on·ful \ˈ≈≈,fu̇l\ *n* -S [¹*wagon* + *-ful*] **:** WAGONLOAD

wagon-head \ˈ≈≈,≈\ *or* **wag·on-head·ed** \ˈ≈≈,≈≈\ *adj* [¹*wagon* + *head* or *headed*] **:** barrel-vaulted ⟨*wagon-head* ceiling⟩

wagon jobber *or* **wagon distributor** *n* **:** a wholesaler or jobber who services retailers with merchandise (as grocery specialties) carried on a truck and thus combines selling with delivery

wa·gon-lit \ˈvagōⁿˈlē\ *n, pl* **wagons-lits** *or* **wagon-lits** \-ē(z)\ [F, fr. *wagon* railroad car (fr. E ¹*wagon*) + *lit* bed, fr. L *lectus* — more at LIE] **1 :** a railroad sleeping car esp. of continental Europe having beds in separate compartments **2 :** a compartment or accommodation in a wagon-lit ⟨had engaged a *wagon-lit* —*Spectator*⟩

wagonload \ˈ≈≈,≈\ *n* **:** the quantity that a wagon contains ⟨~s of people⟩ ⟨a ~ of hay⟩

wagonmaker \ˈ≈≈,≈≈\ *n* **:** one that makes wagons

wag·on·man \ˈ≈≈mən\ *n, pl* **wagonmen 1 :** ¹WAGONER **2 :** FOOTMAN 2d

wagon master *n* **:** a person in charge of one or more wagons esp. for transporting freight

wagon roof *n* **:** BARREL ROOF

wagons *pl of* WAGON, *pres 3d sing of* WAGON

wagon seat *n* **:** a settee usu. in the form of a double chair with slat back and turned posts and used orig. both in the house and in the market wagon

wagon seat

wagon sheet *n* **:** a sheet of canvas used esp. to cover a wagon or a truck bed

wagonsmith \ˈ≈≈,≈\ *n* [¹*wagon* + *smith*] **:** one who builds and repairs wagons and carts

wagon soldier *n, slang* **:** ARTILLERYMAN

wagon stage *n* **1 :** WAGON 9 **2 :** a theater stage equipped with wagons for the quick shifting of scenes

wagon table *n* **:** DINNER WAGON

wag-on-the-wall \ˈ≈≈≈ˈ≈\ *or* **wag-on-the-wall clock** \ˈ≈≈≈ˈ≈-\ *also* **wag-at-the-wall** \ˈ≈≈≈ˈ≈\ *n* **:** a wall clock with pendulum and weights exposed

wagon top *n* **:** the enlarged rear part of the shell of a locomotive boiler over the furnace

wagon train *n* **:** a group of wagons (as of settlers or of supplies for a column of troops) traveling overland

wagon vault *n* **:** BARREL VAULT

wagonway \ˈ≈≈,≈\ *n, archaic* **:** TRAMROAD

wagon wheel *n* **:** MILL

wagonwright \ˈ≈≈,≈\ *n* **:** WAINWRIGHT

wagonyard \ˈ≈≈,≈\ *n* **:** an enclosure where wagoners can put up their wagons and teams

wags *pres 3d sing of* WAG, *pl of* WAG

wagtail \ˈ≈,≈\ *n* [¹*wag* + *tail*] **1 :** any of numerous chiefly Old World birds (family Motacillidae) related to the pipits and having a trim slender body and a very long tail that they habitually jerk up and down — see PIED WAGTAIL, YELLOW WAGTAIL **2 :** a bird resembling a wagtail (as an American water thrush or an Australian fantail); *esp* **:** WILLIE WAGTAIL

wagtail flycatcher *n* **:** PIED WAGTAIL

¹wah \ˈwä\ *n* -S [fr. native name in Nepal, of imit. origin] **:** PANDA

²wah *var of* WAUGH

wah·ha·bi *or* **wa·ha·bi** \wəˈhäbē, wäˈ-, -bi\ *n* -S [Ar *wahhābīy*, fr. Muḥammad b. ʽAbd al-*Wahhāb* (Abdul-Wahhab) †1787 Arab religious reformer] **1** *cap* **:** a puritanical Muslim sect founded in Arabia in the 18th century by the reformer Muhammad ibn-Abdul Wahhab and revived by Ibn Saʽud in the 20th century **2** *usu cap* **:** a member of the Wahhabi sect

wah·ha·bism *or* **wa·ha·bism** \-ˈhä,bizəm\ *n* -S *cap* [*wahhabi* + *-ism*] **:** the doctrines or practice of the Wahhabi

wah·ha·bite *or* **wa·ha·bite** \-,bīt\ *n* -S *usu cap* [*wahhabi* + *-ite*] **:** WAHHABI 2

wa·hi·ne \wäˈhēnā\ *n* -S [Maori & Hawaiian] **:** a Polynesian woman ⟨the Maori ~ had always fought side by side with her man —*Times Hist. of the War*⟩

wah·len·ber·gia \,wälənˈbərjēə\ *n, cap* [NL, fr. Göran *Wahlenberg* †1851 Swed. botanist + NL *-ia*] **:** a genus of perennial herbs (family Campanulaceae) chiefly of the southern hemisphere that differs from the closely related genus *Campanula* in the loculicidal capsule

¹wa·hoo \ˈwä¦hü\ *also* **wha·hoo** \ˈ(h)w-\ *n* -S [Creek *ûhawhu* cork elm] **:** any of various American trees or shrubs: as **a :** ROCK ELM 1a **b :** WINGED ELM **c :** CASCARA BUCKTHORN **d :** BASSWOOD 1 **e :** UMBRELLA TREE 1

²wahoo *or* **waa·hoo** \"\ *n* -S [Dakota *wāhu*, lit., arrowwood] **:** either of two No. American spindle trees: **a :** a shrub or small shrubby tree (*Euonymus atropurpureus*) having purple capsules which in dehiscence expose the scarlet-ariled seeds and a root bark with cathartic properties — called also *burning bush* **b :** STRAWBERRY BUSH 1a

³wahoo \"\ *n* -S [origin unknown] **:** a large vigorous mackerel (*Acanthocybium solanderi*) that is bluish black above fading to gray or silvery below, is cosmopolitan in warm seas, and is highly esteemed for sport and food

⁴wahoo \"\ *interj, chiefly West* — used to express exuberance or enthusiasm or to attract attention

wah·pe·ku·te \ˈwäpə,küd·ē\ *n, pl* **wahpekute** *or* **wahpekutes** *usu cap* **1 :** a portion of the eastern forest group of the Dakota people **2 :** a member of the Wahpekute division of the Dakota people

wah·pe·ton \ˈwȯpətən\ *n, pl* **wahpeton** *or* **wahpetons** *usu cap* **1 :** a portion of the eastern forest group of the Dakota people **2 :** a member of the Wahpeton division of the Dakota people

wah-wah *var of* WOU-WOU

wai·a·ta \ˈwīəd·ə\ *n* -S [Maori] **:** a Maori song usu. commemorative of some important event ⟨sung at tribal gatherings⟩

wai·cu·ri \wīˈkürē\ *n, pl* **waicuri** *or* **waicuris** *usu cap* **1 a :** an Indian people of southern Baja California in Mexico **b :** a member of such people **2 :** a language of the Waicuri people

waidner-burgess standard \¦wīdnər¦bərjəs-\ *n, usu cap W&B* [after Charles W. *Waidner* †1922 and George K. *Burgess* †1932 Am. physicists] **:** a unit of luminous intensity equal to the luminous intensity of one square centimeter of ideal blackbody at the freezing point of platinum or to 60 candles

¹waif \ˈwāf\ *n* -S [ME, fr. ONF, adj., lost, unclaimed, prob. of Scand origin; akin to ON *veif* flapping or waving thing, *veifa* to wave — more at WIPE] **1 a** (1) **:** a piece of property (as something washed up by the sea or a stray animal) whose owner cannot be found — often used in the expression *waifs and strays* (2) **:** the right (as of the lord of the manor in medieval law) to such property **b waifs** *pl* **:** stolen goods thrown away by a thief in his flight claimable by the king or by the lord of the manor if the king has granted him franchise of waif but recoverable by the owner if he prosecutes the thief to conviction **2 a :** something found without an owner; *esp* **:** something that comes along by chance **:** a stray bit ⟨a ~ of travel lore from the mysterious Orient —J.L.Lowes⟩ **b :** a stray person or animal (as a homeless child or a lost sheep) **:** VAGRANT ⟨street ~s . . . were fed —*N. Y. Times*⟩ ⟨a lonely ~ of a cat —Richard Lockridge⟩

²waif \"\ *adj* **1** *chiefly Scot* **:** VAGRANT **2** *chiefly Scot* **:** CIRCULATING, CURRENT — used of a report or rumor ⟨heard a ~ word . . . that you were a hard man to drive —R.L.Stevenson⟩

³waif \"\ *n* -S [prob. of Scand origin; akin to ON *veif* waving thing] **1 :** a small flag or other device set to mark the position and establish prior right to the floating body of a harpooned whale **2 :** WAFT 4

⁴waif \"\ *vt* -ED/-ING/-S **:** to mark or signal the position of (as a harpooned whale) with a waif

wai·il·at·pu·an \(ˌ)wī¦ilət¦püən\ *or* **wai·lat·pu·an** \ˌwīlə-\ *n, pl* **waiilatpuan** *or* **waiilatpuans** *or* **wailatpuan** *or* **wailatpuans** *usu cap* [Cayuse *Wayúletpu* Cayuse men + E *-an*] **1 a :** an American Indian people of northern Oregon comprising the Cayuse and the Molala **b :** a member of such people **2 :** a language family consisting of the languages of the Cayuse and the Molala peoples

¹wail \ˈwāl, *esp before pause or consonant* -āəl\ *vb* -ED/-ING/-S [ME *wailen, weilen*, of Scand origin; akin to ON *væla, vāla* to wail; akin to ON *vei* woe — more at WOE] *vi* **1 :** to express sorrow audibly **:** make mournful outcry **:** LAMENT, WEEP ⟨a child ~*ing* for his mother⟩ **2 :** to make a sound resembling or suggestive of a mournful cry ⟨deep in the grass . . . the curlew ~*ed* —Eve Langley⟩ **3 :** to express dissatisfaction plaintively **:** COMPLAIN ⟨stop ~*ing* about our divisions and emphasize our unity —W.E.Barton⟩ ~ *vt, archaic* **:** to grieve over **:** BEWAIL ⟨~ her wretched fate —William Morris⟩

²wail \"\ *n* -S [ME, fr. *wailen*] **1 :** the act, process, or practice of wailing **:** loud lamentation **:** KEEN ⟨there was weeping and ~ from young and old —Tom Taylor⟩ **2 a :** a usu. prolonged cry or sound expressing grief or pain ⟨a long broken ~ of pain —Scott Fitzgerald⟩ **b :** a sound suggestive of wailing ⟨the ~ of an air-raid siren⟩ **c :** a querulous expression of grievance **:** COMPLAINT ⟨their ~s penetrated the official dom —*N. Y. Times*⟩

wai·la·ki \ˈwīləkē\ *n, pl* **wailaki** *or* **wailakis** *usu cap* [Wintun *wailaka*, lit., northern language] **1 a :** an Athapaskan people of the Eel river basin in northwestern California **b :** a member of such people **2 :** a dialect of the Kato language spoken by the Wailaki people

wail·er \ˈwālə(r)\ *n* -s **:** one that wails; *specif* **:** a professional mourner

wail·ful \ˈ=fəl\ *adj* **1 :** expressing grief or pain **:** SORROWFUL, MOURNFUL ⟨tangle her desires with ~ sonnets —*Shak.*⟩ **2 :** uttering a sound suggestive of mourning or wailing ⟨the ~ bagpipes⟩ ⟨the ~ sough of the wind through the trees⟩ — **wail·ful·ly** \-fəlē, -li\ *adv*

wail·ing·ly *adv* **:** in a wailing manner

wailing wall *n* [fr. the *Wailing Wall*, ancient wall on Mt. Zion, Jerusalem that is held by Jews to be the remains of the Temple destroyed by the Romans in A.D. 70 and at which they traditionally bewail their loss and seek consolation] **:** a source of comfort and consolation in misfortune ⟨a soldier making the chaplain's office his *wailing wall*⟩

wain \ˈwān\ *n* -s [ME, fr. OE *wægn, wæn;* akin to MD *wagen* wagon, cart, OHG *wagan*, ON *vagn* wagon, cart, OE *wegan* to move, carry, *weg* way — more at WAY] **1 :** a usu. large and heavy vehicle for farm use **:** WAGON, CART ⟨a hay ~ on a meadow —Wolfgang Born⟩ **2** *archaic* **:** CHARIOT

wain·age \-nij\ *n* -s [ONF *waaignage*, fr. *waaignier* to till, earn, gain (of Gmc origin) + *-age;* akin to OHG *weidanōn* to hunt, search for food — more at GAIN] **:** implements of feudal husbandry

wain·man \ˈ=mən\ *n, pl* **wainmen** [ME, fr. ¹*wain* + *man*] **:** ¹WAGONER

¹**wain·scot** \ˈwānzkə|t, -nsk- *also* -nz,kä| *or* -nz,kō| *or* -n,skä| *or* -n,skō|; *usu* |d·+V; *also chiefly Brit* ˈwen-\ *n* -s [ME, fr. MD *wagenschot*, prob. fr. *wagen* wagon, cart + *schot* shot, crossbar, wooden partition; akin to OE *scot* shot — more at WAIN, SHOT] **1 a** *Brit* **:** a fine grade of oak imported for woodwork **b** (1) **:** a wooden lining of an interior wall usu. paneled (2) **:** a lining of an interior wall irrespective of material ⟨a tile ~⟩ **c :** the lower three or four feet of an interior wall when finished differently from the remainder of the wall (as with wood panels, tile, or marble slabs) **2 :** any of various European and American noctuid moths belonging to the genera *Leucania* and *Cirphis* that are reddish or yellowish and are streaked or lined with black and white and that in the larval stage are army worms

²**wainscot** \"\ *vt* **wainscoted** *also* **wainscotted; wainscoted** *also* **wainscotted; wainscoting** \-ōd·iŋ, |t|, |ēŋ *also* -əd *or* -äl\ *also* **wainscotting** \-ə|, -ä|\ **wainscots** \-ōts *also* -äts *or* -ōts\ **:** to line (as a wall) with or as if with boards or paneling ⟨~ a hall⟩ ⟨~*ed* with looking glass —Joseph Addison⟩

³**wainscot** \"\ *adj* **1 :** made of wainscot ⟨a ~ door⟩ **2 :** resembling or suggestive of wainscot (as in hardness or color) ⟨a ~ face⟩ **3** *or* **wainscoted :** provided with or lined with a wainscot or with paneling of any sort ⟨a ~ wall⟩ ⟨a ~ seat⟩

wainscot chair *n* **:** a very early Colonial heavy oak chair of framed construction with solid panels in back and seat and sometimes turned posts and carved back

wainscot chair

wain·scot·ing *also* **wain·scot·ting** \-ōd·iŋ, |t|, |ēŋ *also* -əd *or* -äl\ *n* -s [fr. gerund of ²*wainscot*] **1 :** the material used to wainscot a house **2 :** WAINSCOT 1b, 1c, PANELING

wainscot oak *n* **:** ¹TURKEY OAK

wainwright \ˈ=,=\ *n* [OE *wægnwyrhta*, fr. *wægn* wagon + *wyrhta* worker, maker — more at WAIN, WRIGHT] **:** a maker and repairer of wagons

wair *Scot var of* ⁶WARE

waist \ˈwāst\ *n* -s [ME *wast, waste*, fr. (assumed) OE *wæst* growth; akin to OE *wæstm* growth, increase, ON *vöxtr*, Goth *wahstus* growth, increase, OE *weaxan* to grow, increase — more at WAX] **1 a :** the part of the human body immediately below the ribs or thorax **:** the small part of the body between the thorax and hips **b :** the greatly constricted basal part of the abdomen of some insects (as various wasps and flies) **2 :** the part of something that corresponds in position to or in some way resembles the human waist **:** the middle or central part esp. when narrower or less thick than the ends ⟨the ~ of a boiler⟩ ⟨the ~ of a saddle⟩ ⟨the ~ of a violin⟩ ⟨the narrow ~ of a peninsula⟩: as **a :** the part of a vessel's deck between the poop and forecastle **:** the middle part of a sailing vessel between foremast and mainmast **b :** the smallest part of a shoe or last between the ball and instep **c** (1) **:** the narrow after-portion of the fuselage of an airplane (2) **:** the middle section of the fuselage of a bomber **3** *obs* **:** a belt for the waist **:** GIRDLE **4 a :** a garment or the part of a garment covering the body from the neck to the waistline or just below: (1) **:** the upper part of a woman's dress (2) **:** BLOUSE (3) **:** a child's undergarment to which other garments may be buttoned **b :** WAISTLINE

waist anchor *n* **:** SHEET ANCHOR

waist·band \ˈwās(t)+,-\ *n* **:** a band or sash worn around the waist; *specif* **:** a fitted band forming the top edge of trousers, shorts, breeches, or skirt or the lower edge of a sweater, blouse, or jacket

waist board *n* **:** temporary planking in the waist and esp. in the gangway of a ship to protect against seas

waist boat *n* **:** a boat carried in the waist of a whaling vessel on the port side and usu. commanded by the second mate

waistcloth \ˈ=,=\ *n* **1 a waistcloths** *pl* **:** cloths hung about a ship's waist as adornment or as a screen for the men when in action **b :** HAMMOCK CLOTH **2 :** LOINCLOTH

waist·coat \ˈweskə|t, ˈwā,skō|, ˈwāst,kō|, *usu* |d·+V\ *n* **1 :** an ornamental garment worn under a doublet, pulled through at the slashes, and sometimes showing at the neck and cuffs **2 a** *chiefly Brit* **:** a short sleeveless collarless coat for men worn under a jacket **:** VEST **b :** a garment of similar design ⟨a life-saving ~⟩ **3 a** *obs* **:** a woman's garment resembling a man's vest and worn to show underneath a gown **b :** such a short coat worn by a woman as an outer garment **4** *archaic* **a :** a man's undershirt **b :** a woman's camisole

waist·coat·ed \-kə|d·əd, -kō|, |təd\ *adj* **:** having or wearing a waistcoat ⟨a ~ gentleman⟩

waist-deep \ˈ=ˈ=\ *adj* **1 :** rising to the waist **:** WAIST-HIGH ⟨the water was only *waist-deep* at one end of the pool⟩ **2 :** sunk to the waist ⟨stood *waist-deep* in the surf⟩

waist·ed \ˈwāstəd\ *adj* **1 :** having a waist of a specified kind — usu. used in combination ⟨long-*waisted*⟩ ⟨wasp-*waisted*⟩ **2 :** shaped like a waist

waist·er \ˈwāstə(r)\ *n* -s **:** a usu. green or broken-down seaman stationed in the waist of a ship (as a whaling vessel)

waist-high \ˈ=ˈ=\ *adj* **1 :** reaching to or being at the level of the waist ⟨*waist-high* waves⟩ ⟨the batter let a good *waist-high* ball go by⟩ **2 :** reaching only a middle level in quality **:** MEDIOCRE ⟨a *waist-high* culture⟩

waist·less \ˈwāstləs\ *adj* **:** having no waist **:** UNSHAPELY

waistline \ˈ=,=\ *n* **1 :** an arbitrary line encircling the narrowest part of the waist; *specif* **:** the part of a garment that covers this natural line of the waist and that may be above or below it as fashion dictates **2 :** body circumference at the waist or belly **:** GIRTH ⟨dieting to reduce the ~⟩

waist sheet *n* **:** a vertical steel plate that secures the waist of a locomotive boiler to the frames of the locomotive allowing at the same time a small amount of expansion and contraction — compare BELLY BRACE

¹**wait** \ˈwāt, *usu* -ād·+V\ *vb* -ED/-ING/-S [ME *waiten*, fr. ONF *waitier* to watch, of Gmc origin; akin to OHG *wahta* watch, guard, *wahhēn, wahhōn* to watch, be awake — more at WAKE] *vt* **1 a :** to stay in place or remain inactive in expectation of **:** stay for **:** AWAIT ⟨~*ed* his turn to play⟩ ⟨horses . . . ~*ing* their riders —L.C.Douglas⟩ ⟨~*ed* their coming with dignity —Elizabeth Middleton⟩ **b** (1) **:** to hold back in expectation of **:** delay in hope of **:** defer until ⟨~ a favorable opportunity⟩ ⟨~*ed* a better day —*Century Mag.*⟩ ⟨~*ed* her chance —Amelia Walden⟩ (2) **:** to delay in hope of a favorable change in or cessation of ⟨*wait* out the stock market⟩ ⟨*wait* out a storm⟩ **2** *archaic* **:** to accompany with ceremony or respect **:** attend on **:** ESCORT ⟨bids him ~ her to her sacred dome —Alexander Pope⟩ **3** *archaic* **:** to be ready or available for ⟨tea and coffee ~ your pleasure in the drawing room —R.S.Surtees⟩ **4 :** to delay serving (a meal) **:** put off **:** HOLD, KEEP ⟨~*ed* dinner for the latecomers to arrive⟩ **5 :** to serve the eaters sitting at ⟨earned a few dollars ~*ing* table —Ralph Ellison⟩ **~** *vi* **1 a :** to remain stationary in readiness or expectation ⟨sat and ~*ed* for the man in charge⟩ ⟨~*ing* in line for hours⟩ ⟨kept us ~*ing* in the rain⟩ **b** *obs* **:** to remain hopeful and trusting ⟨truly my soul *waiteth* upon God —Ps 62:1 (AV)⟩ **c** (1) **:** to linger expectantly at or near a place **:** hang around ⟨~*ing* around hoping to see a celebrity⟩ (2) *of a hawk* **:** to circle above the hunter till the game is sprung **d :** to pause or halt for another to catch up ⟨~*ed* up for me . . . and we went along side by side —Helen Eustis⟩ **e** *South & Midland* **:** to stay expectantly for another to speak or act ⟨come on, we're ~*ing* on you⟩ **f :** to delay going to bed ⟨~*ed* up to see a late show on television⟩ **2 a :** to look forward expectantly ⟨~*ing* to see his rival lose⟩ ⟨~*ing* for the shell to explode⟩ **b :** to hold back expectantly **:** delay until the proper condition has come about ⟨~*ing* for his chance to strike⟩ ⟨a land where wealth ~*ed* on a lot of hard work —J.H.Plumb⟩ ⟨~*ed* till the war's end to get married⟩ **c :** to hold back in a competition (as a race) with the expectation of closing strong to win in the final stage ⟨~*ed* off, well behind the leaders, until the last lap⟩ **3 a** *archaic* (1) **:** to be in readiness to serve or execute orders ⟨they also serve who only stand and ~ —John Milton⟩ (2) **:** to act as an attendant ⟨maids of honor to ~ upon the queen —*Amer. Guide Series: Md.*⟩ (3) *South & Midland* **:** to attend a bride or groom at a wedding ceremony **b :** to supply the wants of another **:** SERVE ⟨~*ed* on her children hand and foot⟩ **c :** to serve at meals **:** be a waiter ⟨specialized either in ~*ing* or in cookery —G.V.Selsey⟩ — usu. used in the phrases *wait at table* or *wait on table* ⟨as a student he ~*ed* at table for two years⟩ ⟨~*s* on tables when the restaurant is crowded⟩ **d :** to serve a customer or client (as in a shop) ⟨looked around for a salesgirl to ~ on her⟩ **e :** to serve as escort ⟨~*ed* upon the visiting dignitaries to their lodgings⟩ **4 :** to make a formal call ⟨a delegation ~*ed* on the commissioners —Meridel LeSueur⟩ **5 a :** to be ready and available ⟨a letter ~*ing* for you on the table⟩ ⟨slippers ~*ed* by the bed —Mary Cable⟩ ⟨ideas . . . ~*ing* for discovery —A.N.Whitehead⟩ **b :** to remain temporarily neglected ⟨your letter has ~*ed* longer than they often do —O.W.Holmes †1935⟩ **c :** to remain unrealized for a time ⟨the establishment of large purses ~*ed* until the seventies —*Amer. Guide Series: N.Y.*⟩ **6** *Brit* **:** PARK 1 **syn** see STAY — **in waiting :** in attendance (as at a royal court) — usu. used in combination ⟨lord-*in-waiting*⟩ ⟨ladies-*in-waiting*⟩

²**wait** \"\ *n* -s [ME *waite* watchman, watchman who sounds watch, public musician, watch, wait, fr. ONF, watchman, watch, of Gmc origin; akin to OHG *wahta* watch, guard] **1 a :** one of a band of public musicians in England employed usu. by a city to play for processions or at official or public entertainments ⟨the ~ who played the bagpipes —*London Calling*⟩ **b** (1) **:** one of a group of street or rustic serenaders who play or sing at night for small gratuities esp. around the Christmas season (2) **:** a piece of music provided by these musicians **c :** SHAWM; *esp* **:** one played by the town musicians of England **2 a :** a position from which a person in concealment can watch usu. with intent to attack or surprise **:** AMBUSH — used chiefly in the expression *lie in wait* ⟨thieves lying in ~ around the bend of the road⟩ **b :** a condition or attitude of watchfulness and expectancy ⟨anchored in ~ for early morning fishing —Fred Zimmer⟩ **3 a :** an act of waiting ⟨endless ~*s* that make up a soldier's life —Dixon Wecter⟩ **b :** a period of waiting **:** DELAY, INTERVAL ⟨a long ~ in line⟩ ⟨a week's ~ before delivery⟩; *specif* **:** a break or pause (as between the acts) in a theatrical performance **:** INTERMISSION ⟨run off the program without ~*s*⟩

wait-a-bit \ˈ===,=\ *n* [trans. of Afrik *wacht-en-bitje*] **:** any of several plants bearing thorns or stiff hooked appendages that catch and tear the clothing: as **a :** NEW ZEALAND BRAMBLE **b :** GREENBRIER **c :** any of various hawthorns **d** *southern Africa* **:** any of various acacias and mimosas **e :** GRAPPLE PLANT **f :** PRICKLY ASH **g** *West Indies* **:** COCKSPUR 2b

wait-awhile \ˈ==,=\ *n* -s **1 :** an Australian wattle tree (*Acacia colletioides*) that makes an impenetrable thicket **2 :** WAIT-A-BIT

waited *past of* WAIT

wait·er \ˈwād·ə(r), -ātə-\ *n* -s [ME, fr. *waiten* to wait + *-er*] **1 a** *archaic* **:** one that watches (as at a city gate) **:** WATCHMAN, GUARD **b** *Brit* **:** a customs official — compare LANDWAITER **2 :** one that waits or attends upon another: as **a** *obs* **:** a lord-in-waiting or lady-in-waiting **b** *dial South* **:** an attendant of the bride or groom at a wedding **c** *archaic* **:** MANSERVANT **d :** WAITING MAID **e :** a uniformed official attendant on the London stock exchange **f :** a man who waits on table (as in a hotel or restaurant) — compare COUNTERMAN **3 :** a vessel or tray on which something (as a breakfast or tea service) is carried **:** SALVER ⟨bringing a ~ laden with all he could desire —B.A.Williams⟩

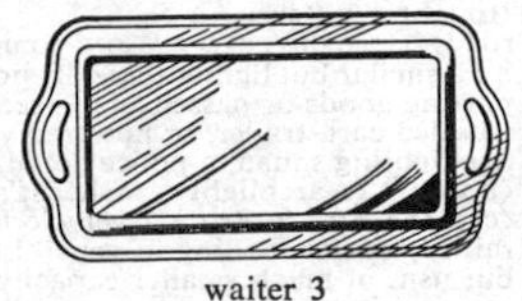

waiter 3

wait·er·ing \ˈwād·əriŋ, -ātər-, -ä·tr-, -rēŋ\ *n* -s **:** service or employment as a waiter ⟨worked at ~ in the evenings⟩

waiting *pres part of* WAIT

waiting game *n* **:** a strategy (as in a game) in which one or more participants withhold action for the time being in the hope of having a favorable opportunity for more effective action at a later period

waiting list *also* **wait list** *n* **:** a list or roster of those waiting (as for a professional or business opportunity, for election to a club, or appointment to a position) ⟨placed on the *waiting list* by the college admissions committee⟩ ⟨a long *wait list* for tourist class accommodations⟩

waiting maid *or* **waiting woman** *n* **:** a maid or woman who waits on another as a personal servant

waiting man *n* **:** a man who waits on another as a personal servant; *esp* **:** VALET

waiting move *n* **:** COUP DE REPOS

waiting period *n* **:** a stated period in various forms of insurance (as accident and health, workmen's compensation and unemployment or idleness insurance) after the beginning of disability during which no benefits are paid

waiting room *n* **:** a room for the use of persons waiting (as at a railroad station or in the office suite of a professional man or official)

waiting table *n* **:** SERVING TABLE

wait·ress \ˈwā·trəs\ *n* -ES [*waiter* + *-ess*] **:** a girl or woman who waits on table (as in a hotel or restaurant) — compare COUNTERGIRL

waits *pres 3d sing of* WAIT, *pl of* WAIT

waive \ˈwāv\ *vt* -ED/-ING/-S [ME *weiven*, fr. ONF *weyver*, fr. *waif* lost, unclaimed — more at WAIF] **1 :** to declare (as a woman failing to defend an accusation) outside the benefit and protection of feudal law **2 a** *archaic* **:** to give up (as a position, custom, or intention) **:** FORSAKE ⟨*waived* his intention of landing on that island, and steered for Ternate —James Mill⟩ **b** *obs* **:** to withdraw (as a motion) formally **3 :** to throw away (stolen goods) **:** ABANDON — compare ¹WAIF 1b **4** *archaic* **:** to shunt aside (as a danger or duty) **:** EVADE, DECLINE ⟨the most effectual mode of . . . *waiving* all discussions —Sir Walter Scott⟩ ⟨'tis still the wiser way to ~ contention with superior sway —Alexander Pope⟩ **5** *obs* **:** to neglect to take advantage of **:** DISREGARD **6 a :** to relinquish voluntarily (as a legal right) ⟨~ a jury trial⟩ ⟨~ fulfillment of certain onerous provisions of a contract⟩ **b :** to refrain from pressing or enforcing (as a claim or rule) **:** dispense with **:** FORGO ⟨~ a portion of the tax due⟩ ⟨~*s* his opposition to the bill⟩ ⟨~ the customary formalities⟩ ⟨*waived* the club rules to admit him⟩ **7 :** to put off from immediate consideration **:** DEFER, POSTPONE ⟨*waiving* this theory for the present, let us resume the inquiry —John Marshall⟩ **8 :** to dismiss (as a person or thought) with or as if with a wave of the hand ⟨evils . . . are not magically *waived* out of existence —John Dewey⟩ ⟨~ the whole business aside —O.S.J.Gogarty⟩ ⟨said "no" and *waived* them off —E.L.Masters⟩ **syn** see RELINQUISH

waiv·er \ˈwāvə(r)\ *n* -s [AF *weyver*, fr. ONF *weyver* to abandon, waive (taken as a n.)] **1 :** the act of waiving or intentionally relinquishing or abandoning a known right, claim, or privilege ⟨the defendant's ~ of a jury trial⟩ ⟨a ~ of the privilege of immunity from prosecution⟩ ⟨a ~ of a contract provision⟩; *specif* **:** the relinquishment by a team of one professional baseball league of the right to buy the contract of a player at a stipulated price before he can go to a club of any other league ⟨asked for ~*s* on him and he left the big leagues for good —Christopher Mathewson⟩ **2 :** the document or legal instrument evidencing an act of waiving ⟨signed a ~ of immunity⟩

waiver of premium : a clause in an insurance policy providing continued coverage without payment of premiums under stated circumstances

wai·wai \ˈwī,wī\ *also* **woy·a·wai** *or* **woy·a·way** \ˈwȯiə,wī\ *n, pl* **waiwai** *or* **waiwais** *usu cap* **1 a :** a Cariban people of the borderlands of Brazil, British Guiana, and Surinam **b :** a member of such people **2 :** the language of the Waiwai people

wajang *var of* WAYANG

wa·ka \ˈwäkə\ *n* -s [Maori] **:** CANOE; *broadly* **:** a Maori seagoing craft

wa·kan \wäˈkän\ *or* **wa·kan·da** \-ndə\ *or* **wa·kon** \wäˈkän\ *or* **wa·kon·da** \-ndə\ *n* -s [Siouan] **:** a supernatural force similar to mana believed by the Sioux to pervade animate and inanimate objects in varying degrees sometimes giving them extraordinary powers and usu. assumed to be the cause of extraordinary happenings ⟨the eagle has ~, because it can soar higher than any other bird and for a longer time —W.D. Wallis⟩

wa·kash·an \wäˈkashən\ *or* **wa·kash** \-ˈkash\ *n, pl* **wakashan** *or* **wakashans** *or* **wakash** *or* **wakashes** *usu cap* [*wakash* fr. Nootka *waukash* good; *wakashan* fr. *Wakash* + E *-an*] **1 :** a language family of British Columbia and Washington comprising Kwakiutl and Bellabella as the two main branches and Nootka **2 a :** a Wakashan-speaking people **b :** a member of any such people

wa·ka·ya·ma \ˌwäkəˈyämə\ *adj, usu cap* [fr. *Wakayama*, Japan] **:** of or from the city of Wakayama, Japan **:** of the kind or style prevalent in Wakayama

¹**wake** \ˈwāk\ *vb* **waked** \ˈwākt\ *or* **woke** \ˈwōk\ **waked** *or* **wok·en** \ˈwōkən\ *or* **woke; waking; wakes** [ME *waken* (past *wok, wook*, past part. *waken*), fr. OE *wacan* to wake, be born (past *wōc*, past part. *wacen*) and ME *waken, wakien* (past & past part. *waked*), fr. OE *wacian* to watch, be awake (past *wacode*, past part. *wacod*); akin to OE *wæccan* to watch, be awake, OHG *wahhēn, wahhōn*, ON *vaka*, Goth *wakan;* akin to OE *weccan* to rouse, stir, waken, OHG *wecchan*, ON *vekja*, Goth us*wakjan* to rouse, waken, L *vegēre* to rouse, excite, be active, Skt *vāja* strength, speed, vigor, contest, prize] *vi* **1 a :** to be or continue awake **:** refrain from sleep ⟨usually asleep, and in our *waking* hours always held back —Sir Winston Churchill⟩ **b** *obs* **:** to work all night **:** stay awake engaged in activity **c :** to remain awake on watch or guard esp. over a sick person or a corpse **d** *obs* **:** to stay up late in revelry ⟨the king doth ~ tonight, and takes his rouse —*Shak.*⟩ **2 a :** to become roused from sleep **:** stop sleeping **:** AWAKE ⟨soon *woke* refreshed —Eudora Welty⟩ ⟨ruffled his hair as if he had just *woken* —Audrey Barker⟩ — often used with *up* ⟨I *waked* up at 3 o'clock in the morning —Joyce Cary⟩ ⟨the boy had *waked* from dreams —Ralph Robin⟩ **b :** to become stirred from a dormant, torpid, or inactive state ⟨*woke* out of his trance —O.S.J.Gogarty⟩ ⟨the old feelings had *woken* —Rumer Godden⟩ — often used with *up* ⟨on national holidays . . . the little place ~*s* up —Tom Marvel⟩ **c :** to enter into a new state of awareness or consciousness **:** become free from misconception or illusion ⟨has *woken* up and . . . rescinded its previous resolution —*Cape Town (So. Africa) Monitor*⟩ — usu. used with *to* ⟨social scientists have *waked* to the story's importance —Roger Burlingame⟩ ⟨*woke* up to the fact that this was a delusion —*Atlantic*⟩ **~** *vt* **1 :** to stand watch over (as a dead body) **:** hold a wake over ⟨will be *waked* at the church rectory —*Springfield (Mass.) Union*⟩ ⟨*waked* the departed term most gloriously over eggs, pie, and cider —W.G.Hammond⟩ **2 a :** to rouse from sleep **:** AWAKEN ⟨was *woken* by raucous bird cries —A.H.Barton⟩ — often used with *up* ⟨a young physicist *woke* up his wife —Laura Fermi⟩ ⟨is partly *waked* up . . . by the crying of one of his children —Edmund Wilson⟩ ⟨snakes are *woken* up by heat —T.H.White b. 1906⟩ **b :** to bring to motion, action, or life **:** STIR, EXCITE ⟨an offense against himself which *woke* his terrible wrath —H.E.Scudder⟩ ⟨his tears *woken* and then held back —H.E.Bates⟩ ⟨*woke* up latent possibilities —Norman Douglas⟩ **c :** to arouse conciousness or interest in **:** ALERT ⟨what ~*s* him up is the horrified refusal of his future wife to be kissed —Anthony Quinton⟩ — usu. used with *to* ⟨*woke* the publishers to the fact that there was an enormous . . . audience —Harrison Smith⟩ **d** (1) *archaic* **:** to break the silence of ⟨no wind *waked* the wood —C.K.D. Patmore⟩ (2) **:** to cause (an echo) to resound ⟨his great laugh *woke* distant echoes in the forest —Irving Bacheller⟩

²**wake** \"\ *n* -s [ME, fr. *waken, wakien* to wake] **1 :** the state of being awake **:** a condition of sleeplessness ⟨making such difference twixt ~ and sleep —*Shak.*⟩ **2** [trans. of ML *vigilia;* fr. the early church custom of preceding certain festivals by services lasting through the night] **a** (1) **:** an annual English parish festival formerly held in commemoration of the church's patron saint either on the saint's day or on a selected Sunday (2) **:** a vigil of fasting and prayer formerly held on the night prior to a wake or other feast day **b :** a period of festivities usu. including a fair or market orig. connected with the wake of an English parish church — usu. used in pl. but sing. or pl. in constr. ⟨fairs, markets, folk dancing and all kinds of amusements characterize *Wakes* Week celebration —Dorothy G. Spicer⟩ **c** *Brit* **:** an annual holiday or vacation from work — usu. used in pl. but sing. or pl. in constr. ⟨the ~*s* . . . had closed the workshops —*Manchester Examiner*⟩ **3 a :** a watch held over the body of a dead person prior to burial and sometimes accompanied by festivity ⟨when the boys gather to hold a ~ . . . they'll have to bring their own drinking —F.B.Gipson⟩ ⟨mourn their dead with the primitive wails of a Corsican ~ —Marguerite Yourcenar⟩ **b :** a gathering or party marking a change of circumstance likened to a wake ⟨the bridal ~ that the villagers gave —*Christian Science Monitor*⟩ ⟨a few old friends . . . hold a brief ~ over old days —J.R. Allan⟩

³**wake** \"\ *adj* [ME, by shortening] **:** AWAKE ⟨whose struggle is to keep the world of ~ men from their sleep world —E.J. Fitzgerald⟩

⁴**wake** \"\ *n* -s [of Scand origin; akin to ON *vǫk* hole, opening in the ice, Sw *vak*, Dan *vaage;* akin to MD *wak* damp, wet — more at HUMOR] **1 :** the track left by a ship or other body in the water ⟨the ~ of a ship showing green and white —Stewart Beach⟩ ⟨beaver ~*s* glistening under the moonlight —R.M. Ormes⟩; *broadly* **:** a turbulent condition of the air or other fluid left behind by a body moving through it ⟨the ~ of an airplane wing⟩ **2 :** the path of light left or apparently left by a moving luminous body or its reflection ⟨staring out over the water at the figure receding beyond the moon's ~ —R.O. Bowen⟩ **3 :** the visible or otherwise detectable trace of a body moving on land ⟨a big red truck passes . . . and a billowing ~ of dust floats toward the house —Helen Upshaw⟩ — **in the wake of 1 a :** in the immediate rear of ⟨when alighting from the train, unless . . . others are getting out *in your wake* —Agnes M. Miall⟩ ⟨*in the wake of* trappers and solitary riflemen came land-hungry settlers —*Amer. Guide Series: Ind.*⟩ ⟨we scrambled *in the wake of* their powerful, barging bodies —Christopher Isherwood⟩ **b :** in the slot or path behind an opening (as in a canvas covering) through which something (as a mast) protrudes **2 :** in the path or territory passed over by ⟨the floods began to recede leaving swamps *in their wake* —V.W.Turner⟩ ⟨sacked and burned as they went, leaving scarcely a cabin *in their wake* —*Amer. Guide Series: La.*⟩ **3 :** as a result of **:** as a consequence of ⟨responsibilities which follow *in the wake of* war —F.D.Roosevelt⟩ ⟨mass immigration . . . brought *in its wake* grave problems of public health and poor relief —*Amer. Guide Series: N.Y.*⟩

wake·ful \ˈwākfəl\ *adj* **1 :** WATCHFUL, VIGILANT **2 :** not sleeping or able to sleep **:** SLEEPLESS, RESTLESS ⟨books for night reading when ~ —Agnes M. Miall⟩ — **wake·ful·ly** \-fəlē, -li\ *adv* — **wake·ful·ness** \-lnəs\ *n* -ES

wake gain *n* : an increase in the propeller thrust of a ship due to the forward motion of the wake

wake·less \'wākləs\ *adj, of sleep* : SOUND, UNBROKEN

wak·en \'wākən\ *vb* **wakened; wakened; wakening** \-k(ə)niŋ\ **wakens** [ME *waknen, wakenen,* fr. OE *wæcnan, wæcnian;* akin to ON *vakna* to awaken, Goth ga*waknan;* derivative fr. the root of E 1*wake*] *vi* **1** : to become active, aware, or animated ⟨a vigorous artist's shaping spirit may chance to ~ —Warren Beck⟩ ⟨~ to the point about seven minutes after —H.J.Laski⟩ **2** : to cease to sleep : AWAKE ⟨had ~*ed* and heard the lion —Ernest Hemingway⟩ — often used with *up* ⟨pleasant to ~ up in that bed —Willa Cather⟩ ~ *vt* **1** : to stir or rouse out of sleep : WAKE ⟨~*ed* at 5:30 by reveille —*Harper's*⟩ **2** : to excite into life, activity, or awareness ⟨stained glass in churches always ~*ed* some strange fancy in his mind —T.B.Costain⟩ ⟨~ the reader's sympathy for the man or woman involved —C.B.Tinker⟩ — often used with *up* ⟨~*s* up . . . government agencies to the wanton waste —*Canadian Forum*⟩ **syn** see STIR

wak·en·er \-k(ə)nə(r)\ *n* -S : one that causes to waken

wak·en·ing \-k(ə)niŋ, -nēŋ\ *n* -S [ME, fr. gerund of *wakenen* to waken] **1** : AWAKENING **2** *Scots law* : revival of an action or of the process for it

wak·er \'wākə(r)\ *n* -S [ME, fr. *waken* to wake + *-er*] **1** : WAKENER **2** : one that is wakened

wake·rife \'wā,krīf\ *adj* [ME (Sc) *walkryfe,* fr. *walk* awake (fr. *walken, waken* to wake, fr. OE *wacan*) + *ryfe* rife, fr. OE *rȳfe* — more at WAKE, RIFE] *Scot* : WAKEFUL, WATCHFUL, ALERT

wake-robin \'=,==\ *n* [prob. fr. 1*wake* + *robin*] **1** *Brit* **a** : a plant of the genus *Arum; esp* : CUCKOOPINT **b** : SPOTTED ORCHIS **2 a** : any of various American plants of the genus *Trillium* **b** : ARROW ARUM **c** : an American plant of the genus *Arisaema; esp* : JACK-IN-THE-PULPIT **3** : any of several tropical American plants of the genera *Anthurium* and *Philodendron*

wakes *pres 3d sing of* WAKE, *pl of* WAKE

1**wake-up** \'=,=\ *n* -S [fr. *wake up,* v.] : FLICKER

2**wake-up** \"\ *n* -S [fr. *wake up,* v.] *Austral* : a person on the alert : one not likely to be fooled

wakf *var of* WAQF

wak·hi \wäk'hē\ *n, pl* **wakhi** *or* **wakhis** *usu cap* **1** : an Indo-European people of Alpine type on the northern slope of the Hindu Kush **2** : a member of the Wakhi people

waking *pres part of* WAKE

wakon *or* **wakonda** *var of* WAKAN

wa·kore \wä'kōr\ *n, pl* **wakore** *or* **wakores** *usu cap* [Songhai] : SARAKOLLE

wal *abbr* walnut

WAL *abbr, often not cap* wider all lengths

walach *cap, var of* WALLACH

walachian *usu cap, var of* WALLACHIAN

wa·la·pai *also* **hua·la·pai** \'wälə,pī\ *or* **hual·pai** \-l,-\ *n, pl* **walapai** *or* **walapais** *also* **hualapai** *or* **hualapais** *or* **hualpai** *or* **hualpais** *usu cap* [Yuman *Xawálapáiya,* lit., pine tree people] **1 a** : an Indian people of the central Colorado river valley, Arizona **b** : a member of such people **2** : a Yuman language of the Walapai people

wal·chia \'walkēə, 'wȯl-\ *n, cap* [NL, fr. Johann E. I. *Walch* †1778 Ger. mineralogist + NL *-ia*] : a genus of pinaceous fossil trees that resemble araucarias, are characteristic of the Permian but range through the Triassic, and have short triangular spirally arranged falcate leaves and ovate cones with persistent ovate scales

wal·den inversion \'wȯldən-\ *n, usu cap W* [after Paul *Walden* †1957 Latvian organic chemist] : an inversion of configuration of one optically active compound into another that may or may not lead to a change in the direction of optical rotation and that may be of either of two general types: **a** : inversion involving two reactions in which an optically active compound is changed to another by substitution at its asymmetric center and then regenerated (as *dextro*-alanine is changed to *levo*-bromo-propionic acid by nitrosyl bromide and then to *levo*-alanine by ammonia) but as the optical isomer of the original compound **b** : inversion involving one reaction of an optically active compound at its asymmetric center with resulting configurational change from D to L or vice versa regardless of change in optical rotation (as from levorotatory L-bromo-propionic acid to levorotatory D-alanine by ammonia but not from dextrorotatory L-alanine to levorotatory L-bromo-propionic acid because no inversion of configuration occurs although optical inversion does)

wal·den·ses \wäl'den(t),sēz, wȯl-\ *or* **val·den·ses** \val-\ *n pl, usu cap* [ME *Waldensis,* fr. ML *Waldenses, Valdenses,* fr. Peter *Waldo* (or *Valdo*) *fl* 12th cent. A.D. Fr. heretic] : a body of Christians arising in southern France in the 12th century, adopting Calvinist doctrines in the 16th century, suffering severe persecution until recent times, and now living chiefly in Piedmont — called also *Vaudois*

1**wal·den·si·an** \(')=¦den(t)sēən\ *adj, usu cap* [*Waldenses* + E *-an*] : of, relating to, or constituting the Waldenses

2**waldensian** \"\ *n* -S *usu cap* : one of the Waldenses

wal·dey·er's plasma cell \'väl,dī(ə)rz-\ *n, usu cap W* [after Heinrich W. G. von *Waldeyer*-Hartz †1921 Ger. anatomist] : a coarsely granular connective tissue cell found esp. in the neighborhood of blood vessels

waldeyer's tonsillar ring *n, usu cap W* [after Heinrich von *Waldeyer*-Hartz] : a partial ring of tonsillar or adenoid tissue formed by the two palatine tonsils, the pharyngeal tonsil, and the lingual tonsil

waldeyer's vascular layer *n, usu cap W* [after Heinrich von *Waldeyer*-Hartz] : the vascular layer of the ovary

waldeyer's zonal layer *n, usu cap W* [after Heinrich von *Waldeyer*-Hartz] : LISSAUER'S TRACT

wald·flöte \'vält,flōtə\ *n* -S *usu cap* [G, lit., forest flute, fr. *wald* forest (fr. OHG) + *flöte* flute, fr. MF *flaute* — more at WOLD, FLUTE] : WALDFLUTE

wald·flute \'wȯld,flüt, 'vält,-\ *n* [part trans. of G *waldflöte*] : a soft pipe-organ flute stop of 8-foot and 4-foot pitch

wald·hei·mia \wȯld'hīmēə\ *n, cap* [NL, fr. G. F. von *Waldheim* †1853 Ger. paleontologist + NL *-ia*] : a genus of brachiopods closely resembling *Terebratula* but having longer brachial loops and including many fossil forms and a few that still exist in the deep sea

wald·horn \'wȯld,hȯrn, 'vält,-\ *n* [G, fr. MHG *walthorn,* lit., forest horn, fr. *walt* forest (fr. OHG *wald*) + *horn,* fr. OHG — more at HORN] **1** : the old valveless hunting horn : NATURAL HORN — compare FRENCH HORN **2** : a pipe-organ reed stop with a tone like that of a natural horn

wald·meister \'wȯld,mīstə(r), 'vält-\ *n* -S [G, lit., forest master, forest officer, fr. MHG *waltmeister,* fr. *walt* forest + *meister* master, fr. OHG *meistar,* fr. L *magister* — more at MASTER] : SWEET WOODRUFF

wal·dorf salad \'wȯl,dȯrf-, -dȯ(ə)f-\ *n, usu cap W* [fr. *Waldorf*-Astoria Hotel, N.Y. City] : a salad made typically of diced apples, celery, and nuts and dressed with mayonnaise

wald·stein·ia \wȯld'stīnēə\ *n, cap* [NL, fr. Franz A. von *Waldstein* †1823 Austrian botanist + NL *-ia*] : a genus of perennial herbs (family Rosaceae) of the north temperate zone resembling strawberries but having yellow flowers that have terminal styles and few carpels and are seated on a short hairy receptacle — see BARREN STRAWBERRY

1**wale** \'wāl, *esp before pause or consonant* -āəl\ *n* -S [ME, fr. OE *walu;* akin to ON *valr* round, L *vola* hollow of the hand or foot, palm, sole, *volvere* to roll — more at VOLUBLE] **1 a** : a streak or ridge made on the skin esp. by the stroke of a whip : WEAL, WELT **b** : a narrow raised surface : RIDGE ⟨plowing the stubble into ~*s* —John Masefield⟩ **2 a** : one of a number of strakes usu. made of extra thick and strong planks in the sides of a wooden ship : 3BEND 2b — usu. used in pl.; see MAIN WALES **b** *obs* : GUNWALE **3 a** (1) : one of a series of even ribs in the warp or weft of a fabric or sometimes on the diagonal (2) : a lengthwise row of loops in a knitted fabric — compare COURSE **b** : the texture esp. of a fabric **4** *or* **whale** \'(h)w-\ : a horizontal constructional member made of a strong material (as timber or steel) and used for bracing vertical members (as the sheeting of a trench) **5** : one of the two ridges on the outside of a horse collar between which the hame lies **6** : a course of weaving in basketmaking consisting of three or four rods worked alternately one after and over the other to form a binding ⟨a firmly woven ~ round the base is necessary to keep a good shape —Katherine S. Woods⟩ — see BASKET illustration

2**wale** \"\ *vt* -ED/-ING/-S **1** : to mark (as the skin) with welts **2 a** : to wattle (as the web of a gabion) esp. with more than two rods at once **b** : to furnish (as a basket) with wales **3** : to fasten or brace with a constructional wale

3**wale** \"\ *n* [ME (Sc & northern dial.) *wale, wal,* fr. ON *val* choice; akin to OHG *wala* choice, *wellen* to choose, ON *velja,* Goth *waljan* to choose, *wiljan* to wish — more at WILL] **1** *dial Brit* : the act of choosing : opportunity for choosing : CHOICE **2** *dial Brit* : the best one, ones, part, or kind : PICK ⟨scones, the ~ o' food —Robert Burns⟩

4**wale** \"\ *vb* -ED/-ING/-S [ME (Sc & northern dial.) *walen,* fr. *wale, wal* choice] *dial Brit* : CHOOSE

waled \¦wā(ə)ld\ *adj, of a fabric* : having wales esp. of a specified kind — often used in combination ⟨a blouse of wide-*waled* white piqué —Lois Long⟩

walee *var of* WALI

wale knot *n* [by alter.] : WALL KNOT

walepiece \'=,=\ *n* **1** : 1WALE 4 **2** : a horizontal piece esp. of timber attached to a structure (as a pier) to ward off dangerous impact

1**wal·er** \'wālə(r)\ *n* -S *often cap* [New So. *Wales,* Australia + E *-er*] : a horse from New So. Wales : a rather large rugged saddle horse of mixed ancestry exported in quantity from Australia to British India for military use during the 19th century

2**waler** \"\ *or* **whal·er** \'(h)w-\ *n* -S [1*wale or whale* + *-er*] : 1WALE 4

wales \'wālz, *esp before pause or consonant* -āəlz\ *adj, usu cap* [fr. *Wales,* peninsula on western part of the island of Great Britain] : of or from Wales : of the kind or style prevalent in Wales : WELSH

walhalla *usu cap, var of* VALHALLA

1**wa·li** *also* **wa·lee** \'wälē\ *n* -S [Ar *walīy* (pl. *wulāt*)] **1** : an Arab provincial governor **2** : VALI 1

2**wali** \"\ *n* -S [Ar *walīy* (pl. *awliyā'*), lit., benefactor, guardian] : a Muslim saint

wal·ie \'wāli\ *var of* WALLY

wal·ing \'wāliŋ\ *n* -S [1*wale* + *-ing*] **1** : the constructional wales used for bracing vertical members (as the sheeting of a trench) **2** : 1WALE 4

wa·lise \wə'lēs\ *Scot var of* VALISE

1**walk** \'wȯk\ *vb* -ED/-ING/-S [ME *walken* (past *welk,* past part. *walke*), fr. OE *wealcan* to roll, toss (past *weolc,* past part. *wealcen*) and ME *walkien* (past *walkede,* past part. *walked*), fr. OE *wealcian* to roll up, muffle up; akin to MD *walken* to knead, beat, press, full, OHG *walchan,* ON *vālka* to roll, L *valgus* bowlegged, Skt *valgati* he hops, jumps] *vi* **1 a** *obs* : to move onward or about : JOURNEY, ROAM, WANDER **b** (1) *of a spirit* : to move about in visible or otherwise perceptible form : APPEAR ⟨the time when . . . spirits ~ and ghosts break up their graves —Shak.⟩ (2) : to persist or recur hauntingly in the memory ⟨a figure who will ~ in our imagination long after the book has been put down —E.A.Weeks⟩ **c** *obs* : CIRCULATE, SPREAD **d** *archaic* : to be in motion **e** *obs, of the tongue* : to move incessantly : WAG **f** *of a ship* : to make headway **2 a** : to move along on foot : advance by steps ⟨we would ~ on . . . to the next camp —E.E.Shipton⟩ ⟨the millions of cattle that ~*ed* to Kansas —M.C.Boatright⟩ **b** (1) : to come or go on foot without hesitation or without ceremony — usu. used with a following adverb or preposition ⟨don't knock; just ~ in⟩ ⟨she'd ~*ed* in on the family —Mary Deasy⟩ ⟨the workmen ~*ed* off their jobs⟩ ⟨the two committee members who felt offended got up and ~*ed* out of the meeting⟩ (2) : to come or go as if proceeding on foot promptly or without deliberation — usu. used with a following adverb or preposition ⟨a government so weak as to tempt neighboring countries to ~ in and take over⟩ ⟨not seeing where the attorney's questions were leading, the witness ~*ed* right into his trap⟩ ⟨a figure worthy of the Periclean Age had ~*ed* into our epoch —Lucien Price⟩ **c** (1) : to go on foot for exercise or pleasure : go for a walk : take a walk ⟨made it his habit to ~ around the block ten times before breakfast⟩ ⟨went ~*ing* in the park⟩ (2) *Brit* : to engage in courtship esp. by going for walks — used with *out, together, out together,* or a prepositional phrase introduced by *with,* or with *out* followed by a prepositional phrase introduced by *with* ⟨she is ~*ing* out with a garage mechanic⟩ ⟨he is ~*ing* out with our maid⟩ ⟨they start ~*ing* out, they get engaged, and finally they get married —Richard Harrison⟩ ⟨a woman . . . who consents to ~ with you —Thomas Hardy⟩ **d** (1) *of a quadruped* : to go on foot at a gait in which there are always at least two feet on the ground — compare 2WALK 9b (2) : to ride an animal at such a gait ⟨the horsemen galloped the first half mile and ~*ed* the rest of the way⟩ **e** *of a biped* : to go on foot without lifting one foot clear of the ground before the other touches the ground ⟨part of the time we ~*ed* and part of the time we ran⟩ **3 a** *obs* : to go away : LEAVE **b** : to leave in consequence of being dismissed **4** [trans. of LL *ambulare,* trans. of Heb *hōlēkh*] **a** : to pursue a course of action or way of life : conduct oneself : BEHAVE ⟨~ warily⟩ ⟨~ in darkness —Jn 8:12(AV)⟩ ⟨everyone who has ~*ed* in sadness because his destiny has not fitted his aspirations —W.H.White⟩ **b** : to be or act in association : continue in union : ASSOCIATE ⟨~ humbly with thy God —Mic 6:8(AV)⟩ ⟨the British and American peoples will . . . ~ together side by side in majesty, in justice, and in peace —Sir Winston Churchill⟩ ⟨loved to ~ with a minority —W.A.White⟩ **5** : to move about on foot while sleeping ⟨almost every adult sleepwalker has a history of having ~*ed* as a child —*This Week Mag.*⟩ — usu. used with *in one's sleep* ⟨people who ~ in their sleep⟩ **6** : to move or progress slowly as if at a walk instead of a run **7** : to go to first base as the result of a base on balls **8** *of an inanimate object* **a** : to move in a manner that is suggestive of walking ⟨so as not to wobble the ladder and make the poles ~ —*Training Manual for Auxiliary Firemen*⟩ **b** : to stand with an appearance of moving in a particular direction in consequence of having or consisting of similar members repeated at regular intervals suggestive of strides ⟨the long . . . dock that ~*ed* across the mud flats of the bay —F.G.Slaughter⟩ ⟨the transmission towers ~*ed* down a slope —D.S.Boyer⟩ ~ *vt* **1 a** : to pass on foot or as if on foot through, along, over, or upon : TRAVERSE, PERAMBULATE ⟨~ the avenue⟩ ⟨~ a tightrope⟩ ⟨had to ~ the floor with the baby almost an hour before he got it to sleep⟩ ⟨evil forces that ~ the world —C.T.Lanham⟩ ⟨the ghost . . . ~*s* the corridors every night —J.P.Marquand⟩ **b** : to perform or accomplish by going on foot ⟨~ guard⟩ **2 a** : to cause (an animal) to go on foot by leading, riding, or driving esp. at a walking pace ⟨a rider ~*ing* his horse⟩ ⟨~*ing* a dog on a leash⟩ ⟨steers that were ~*ed* to market⟩ **b** : to cause to move by walking ⟨formerly when the airship had to be pulled to the ground and ~*ed* into its hangar —*No. Amer. Rev.*⟩ ⟨~*ed* his bicycle up the hill⟩; *specif* : to haul (as an anchor) by walking round the capstan **c** : to carry while walking ⟨who had once ~*ed* the mails down the beaches —Marjory S. Douglas⟩ **3** : to follow on foot as for the purpose of measuring or surveying ⟨~ a boundary⟩ **4 a** : to accompany on foot : walk with : take for a walk ⟨we'll ~ you to the bus stop⟩ **b** : to compel to walk (as by a command or by support and propulsion) ⟨they ~*ed* you into jail —Karl Shapiro⟩ ⟨it may be necessary to pick the patient up, ~ him about, and stimulate him in other ways in order to keep him awake —Morris Fishbein⟩ **5** *obs* : to be present at : ATTEND ⟨~ the exchange⟩ **6** : to bring to a specified condition by walking ⟨~ someone off his feet⟩ ⟨~*ed* the entire afternoon away —Sherwood Anderson⟩ **7** : to move (an object or objects) in a manner suggestive of walking ⟨she ~*ed* a spinning wheel into the house, making it use first one and then the other of its own spindling legs to achieve progression rather than lifting it by main force —C.E.Craddock⟩ ⟨warships were ~*ing* a barrage up and down the beach —Ira Wolfert⟩ ⟨he ~*ed* his . . . fingers along the couch back —Wallace Stegner⟩ **8 a** : to perform (a dance) at a walking pace ⟨~ a quadrille⟩ **b** : to go through (a play or acting part) perfunctorily as in an early stage of rehearsal **9 a** *chiefly Brit* : to put or keep (a young foxhound or other puppy) at walk **b** : to put or keep (a gamecock stag) in a walk **10** : to pursue as a course of action or way of life ⟨as you ~ your mystic way —W.S.Gilbert⟩ ⟨would have to ~ a careful course —Thomas Sugrue⟩ **11 a** : to give a base on balls to **b** : to cause (a run) to be scored by giving a batter a base on balls with the bases full — sometimes used with *in* ⟨~*ed* in the winning run⟩ — **walk around 1** : to consider from many different points of view ⟨we *walked around* the problem for two hours —H.J. Laski⟩ **2** : to treat with caution ⟨critics *walk around* it gently —J.C.Trewin⟩ — **walk away from 1** : to outrun or get the better of without difficulty **2** : to survive (an accident) with little or no injury — **walk away with 1** : to win or take by outdoing one's competitors without difficulty ⟨*walked away with* first prize⟩ ⟨expects to *walk away with* the nomination⟩ **2** : to take over unexpectedly from someone else : 2STEAL 1g ⟨a new actor in a minor role amost *walked away with* the picture⟩ — **walk into 1 a** : ATTACK **b** : to reprimand harshly : criticize severely **2 a** : to eat or drink greedily ⟨*walked* right *into* the beer and pretzels⟩ **b** : to use up rapidly — **walk off with 1 a** : to steal and take away ⟨a sneak thief who *walked off with* $35,000 —*N.Y.Times*⟩ **b** : to take over unexpectedly from someone else : 2STEAL 1g ⟨a bit player who *walked off with* the show⟩ **2** : to win or gain esp. by outdoing one's competitors without difficulty ⟨after mortgaging off their costs . . . they were able to *walk off with* $2,084,823 in profits —*Time*⟩ ⟨thirty-four stories which have *walked off with* first prizes —James Kelly⟩ — **walk one's chalks** [prob. fr. the military practice of making a soldier walk along a chalked line to prove that he is sober] *slang* : to leave quickly and unceremoniously : DECAMP — **walk over** *also* **walk all over** : to disregard the wishes or feelings of : treat badly ⟨in those days the histrionic possibilities of young children were unsuspected by the parents and schoolmasters who *walked over* them —H. G.Wells⟩ — **walk over the course 1** *of a racehorse* : to go over a course at a walk so as to be judged the winner of a race in which there is no other starter : walk over **2** : to win an easy victory — **walk spanish** *usu cap S* **1** : to be lifted up by the collar and the seat of the trousers and made to walk on tiptoe **2** : to leave in consequence of being dismissed, expelled, or discharged ⟨if in his presence we had dared talk Greek we should certainly have *walked Spanish* —Joseph Jefferson⟩ **3** : to force (a person) to walk Spanish — **walk the chalk line** *or* **walk the chalk mark** *or* **walk chalk** *also* **walk a chalk line** : to behave in a strictly disciplined or obedient way : conduct oneself without deviation from propriety — **walk the floor** : to pace back and forth in a room because of pain or esp. worry — **walk the hospitals** *also* **walk the hospital** *or* **walk the wards** : to make the rounds of hospital wards in the study or practice of medicine or surgery — **walk the plank 1** : to be compelled esp. by pirates to walk along a plank sticking out over the side of a ship until one falls into the sea **2** : to vacate an office or position under compulsion — **walk the streets** : to walk around on the streets as a prostitute looking for customers — **walk through 1** : to go through (a play, scene, or acting part) perfunctorily as in an early stage of rehearsal ⟨she merely *walked through* the part, mumbling her lines —*Time*⟩ **2** : to deal with or carry out perfunctorily ⟨there is a tendency for students to consider such tests a mere matter of routine and to just *walk through* them —*Quarterly Jour. of Speech*⟩

2**walk** \"\ *n* -S [ME, fr. *walken* to walk] **1 a** : an act or instance of going on foot esp. for exercise or pleasure ⟨go for a ~⟩ ⟨take a ~⟩ ⟨fond of long ~*s*⟩ **b** *obs* : PEREGRINATION, TRAVEL **2 a** : accustomed place of walking : HAUNT **b** *obs* : place or area of movement of an object or objects : RANGE, COURSE **3** : a place designed for walking: **a** (1) : a passage (as a portico or aisle) for walking in a church or other public building : AMBULATORY (2) : a balustraded roof area or a railed platform above the roof of a dwelling house : WIDOW'S WALK **b** (1) : a path specially arranged or paved for walking ⟨a graveled ~ in a garden⟩ (2) **walks** *pl, obs* : PLEASURE GROUNDS ⟨he hath left you all his ~*s,* his private arbors and new-planted orchards —Shak.⟩ (3) : SIDEWALK **c** (1) : AVENUE 3b (2) : a public avenue for promenading : PROMENADE **d** : ROPE WALK **4** : a place or area of land in which animals feed and exercise with minimal restraint: **a** (1) : a pen to keep poultry in : fowl run (2) : a place where a young gamecock is kept for exercise and experience away from other male birds **b** : land serving as pasture esp. for sheep **c** *chiefly Brit* : a farm or cottage to which a kennel-bred foxhound or other puppy is sent to develop and to become accustomed to livestock ⟨sending out foxhound puppies to ~ —E.G.W.W.Harrison⟩ ⟨hound puppies are out at ~ —C.E.Hare⟩ **d** : the entire range of a territorial animal **5** : an area that constitutes a section of a park or esp. forest and is under the charge of a ranger that patrols it **6** : distance to be walked ⟨living within a short ~ of one's place of employment⟩ ⟨a quarter mile ~ from here⟩; *esp* : distance as measured in time required by a walker to cover ⟨within ten minutes' ~⟩ **7** *Brit* : a ceremonial procession **8 a** : manner of living : CONDUCT, BEHAVIOR **b** *obs* : a course of action in a particular set of circumstances **9 a** : the gait of a biped in which the feet are lifted alternately with one foot not being lifted clear of the ground before the other touches the ground ⟨he started at a ~ but soon broke into a run⟩ **b** : the gait of a quadruped in which there are always at least two feet on the ground; *specif* : a slow flat-footed four-beat gait of a horse in which the feet strike the ground in the sequence near hind, near fore, off hind, off fore at such a rate that there are always at least two feet on the ground **c** : an extremely low rate of speed ⟨shortage of raw materials slowed production down to a ~⟩ **10 a** : a suitable course or route to walk for exercise or pleasure ⟨there are delightful ~*s* in almost every direction from here⟩ **b** : a route regularly traversed by a person in the performance of a particular activity (as patrolling, begging, or the delivery of mail or commodities) ⟨the postmen's rounds are known as ~*s,* though the postmen may use motor-vans or pedal cycles —W.D.Sharp⟩ **11** : characteristic manner of walking ⟨his ~ is just like his father's⟩ **12 a** : social or economic status ⟨persons from every ~, including members of various royal families —*N.Y.Times*⟩ — used esp. in the phrase *walk of life* ⟨from all ~*s* of life including even the nobility —Roy Lewis & Angus Maude⟩ **b** (1) : range or sphere of action : FIELD, PROVINCE ⟨distinguished figures in science, politics, and affairs, . . . and particularly in the ~ of letters —Richard Gottheil⟩ ⟨had a duty to go into the higher ~ of the House of Commons —H.J.Laski⟩ (2) : VOCATION — used esp. in the phrase *walk of life* ⟨whatever your ~ of life — actor, journalist, musician, psychiatrist, politician —J.B. Boothroyd⟩ **13** : ASSOCIATION 1 ⟨a closer ~ with God —William Cowper⟩ **14** : a West Indian plantation of trees arranged in rows with wide spaces between them ⟨the Spaniards left behind them well-established cacao ~*s* . . . in Jamaica —A.E.Aspinall⟩ **15** : onward course or journey ⟨a deliberate ~ down the road to moral ruin —M.B.Ridgway⟩ **16** : DEPARTURE, WALKOUT — used esp. in the phrase *take a walk* **17** : a trial of speed in walking over a course : walking race **18** : BASE ON BALLS **19** : an intermittent creeping motion of equipment from a desired fixed position because of vibration or tilting — **in a walk** *adv* : with little effort : without enough competition or resistance to require much exertion ⟨won *in a walk*⟩

3**walk** \"\ *vt* -ED/-ING/-S [ME *walken,* fr. MD, to knead, press, full — more at 1WALK] *Brit* : 5FULL

walk·able \-kəbəl\ *adj* **1** : suitable or fit for walking ⟨a ~ path⟩ ⟨~ countryside⟩ ⟨~ shoes⟩ **2** : capable of being traversed by walking ⟨a ~ distance⟩

walkabout \'==,=\ *n* -S [fr. the phrase *walk about*] *chiefly Austral* **1 a** : a short period of wandering bush life engaged in by an Australian aborigine as an occasional interruption of regular work **b** : a similar period of wandering life engaged in by a nonwhite native of a southwest Pacific island **2** : a walking tour : walking trip

walkabout disease *or* **walking disease** *n* : a disease of horses marked by cirrhosis of the liver, severe nervous symptoms, and continuous aimless walking and usu. believed to be caused by eating poisonous vegetation — compare WINTON DISEASE

walk-around \'==,=\ *n* -S [fr. the phrase *walk around*] **1** *or* **walk-round** \'=,=\ **a** : a number in a blackface minstrel show in which all the performers dance around the stage one at a time often with each one doing his specialty on coming to the center of the stage; *broadly* : a dance number in which the entire company of performers moves in a circle **b** : the music for such a number ⟨his minstrel leader asked him to compose a new *walk-around* . . . for use the next day —*Time*⟩ **2** : a circus

act in which a clown or group of clowns walk all the way around the arena performing as they go
walk-around bottle *or* **walk-around oxygen bottle** *also* **walk-around oxygen unit** *or* **walk-around** *n* -s : a portable container of oxygen for use in high-altitude flying when moving around in the airplane or as an emergency supply if the airplane's oxygen system fails
walk·a·thon \ˈwȯkə,thän\ *n* -s [²walk + marathon] **1** : a dance marathon **2** : a walking marathon
walkaway \ˈ⸗⸗,⸗\ *n* -s [fr. *walk away*, v.] **1** : a race in which the winner finishes at a slow pace because he has outdistanced all other competitors **2** : an easily won contest **3** : a thing easily accomplished **4** : a person that escapes from prison on foot
walk back *vi* : to ease back the fall of a hoisting-tackle while keeping it in hand
walk clerk *n, Brit* : a bank messenger or clerk that presents bills and checks to other banks for collection
walk down *vt* **1** : to overcome the effect of (a poison) by walking **2** : to wear down in walking : walk longer or farther than ⟨I could *walk down* most of the boys —Mrs. Humphry Ward⟩ **3** *West* : to capture (wild horses) by forcing to keep on the move until exhausted and then maneuvering into an enclosure
walked *past of* WALK
¹**walk·er** \ˈwȯkə(r)\ *n* -s [ME *walkere*, fr. OE *wealcere*, fr. *wealcan* to roll, toss + -*ere* -er — more at WALK] *dial Brit* : ¹FULLER 1
²**walker** \"\ *n* -s [ME, fr. *walken* to walk + -*er* — more at WALK] **1** : one that walks: as **a** *obs* : FORESTER, GAMEKEEPER **b** : one that conducts himself in a specified way ⟨disorderly ∼*s*⟩ **c** : a competitor in a walking race **d** : a cursorial insect; *esp* : a stick insect or other member of the Phasmatodea **e** : a peddler going on foot **f** : a bird that walks instead of hopping **g** : one that patrols or supervises on foot **h** : a hunter that walks up game **i** : an ambulatory patient **2** : something used in walking: as **a walkers** *pl, obs* : FEET **b** : a framework usu. of metal and cloth mounted on wheels or casters and designed to support a child learning to walk ⟨the baby . . . may be strolling around unassisted or in a ∼ —H.R.Litchfield & L.H.Dembo⟩ — called also *go-cart, baby walker* **c** : an apparatus with wheels or gliders, handgrips, and often adjustable crutches that is used by invalids and the handicapped in learning to walk again **d** : a walking shoe

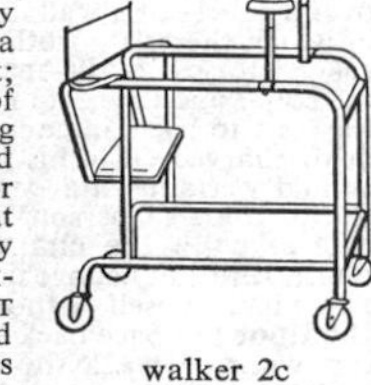

walker 2c

³**walker** \"\ *or* **walker hound** *n* -s *usu cap W* [after John W. *Walker*, 19th cent. Am. sportsman who helped develop the strain] : an American foxhound of a strain developed by crossing English foxhounds with several highly regarded American strains
walker-on \ˈ⸗⸗ˈ⸗\ *n, pl* **walkers-on** : one that plays a walk-on
walk·ie \ˈwȯkē\ *n* -s [¹walk + -ie] : a lift truck of platform or forklift type operated by a person on foot
walkie-lookie \ˌwȯkēˈlu̇kē\ *n* -s : a complete portable one-man television camera
walkie-talkie *also* **walky-talky** \ˌwȯkēˈtȯkē\ *n, pl* **walkie-talkies** *also* **walky-talkies** : a compact battery-operated radio transmitting and receiving set that is carried on a person's back to provide two-way communication
¹**walk-in** \ˈ⸗,⸗\ *adj* [fr. the phrase *walk in*] **1 a** : large enough to be walked into ⟨*walk-in* closet⟩ ⟨*walk-in* refrigerator⟩ **b** : arranged so as to be entered directly rather than through a lobby ⟨*walk-in* apartment⟩ **2** : being a person that walks in ⟨for treating *walk-in* neurotics rather than locked-in psychotics —*Time*⟩ : of or connected with persons that walk in ⟨sales are attributed to *walk-in* trade, rather than to any particular promotion —*Retailing Daily*⟩
²**walk-in** \"\ *n* -s **1** : a walk-in refrigerator or cold storage room **2** : an easy election victory
¹**walking** *n* -s [ME, fr. gerund of *walken* to walk — more at WALK] **1 a** : the action of one that walks ⟨does more ∼ than he used to⟩ ⟨∼ is good exercise⟩ **b** : movement of an inanimate object in a manner suggestive of such action **2** : kind of behavior ⟨wary ∼⟩ **3** : a journey made on foot **4** : the condition of a surface (as of a path or walk) for one that is traversing it on foot ⟨the ∼ is slippery⟩ **5** : manner in which one walks
²**walking** *adj* [in sense 1, fr. ME, fr. pres. part. of *walken* to walk; in senses 2 & 3, fr. ME, fr. gerund of *walken* to walk; in other senses, fr. pres. part. of ¹walk] **1** : that walks: as **a** : going around in human form ⟨a ∼ encyclopedia⟩ ⟨a ∼ advertisement for her boss's fashion departments —Rollie Abrahams⟩ **b** : going around from place to place as a regular practice esp. in carrying out the tasks of an occupation or office **c** : able to walk in spite of a sickness or injury : ¹AMBULATORY 4a ⟨inspected troops in their foxholes and talked to ∼ wounded —*Springfield (Mass.) Union*⟩ **2 a** : used for or in walking ⟨∼ shoes⟩ : suitable for walking ⟨London is such a wonderful ∼ town —Richard Joseph⟩ **b** : characterized by, connected with, or consisting of the action of walking ⟨a ∼ tour⟩ **3** : of, relating to, or appropriate to a person being dismissed **4** : that moves or appears to move in a manner suggestive of walking: as **a** *of a plant* : propagating itself (as by stolons or rhizomes) in a manner suggestive of strides ⟨∼ orchid⟩ **b** : that swings or rocks back and forth ⟨∼ beam⟩ **c** *of a livestock brand* : having stylized feet — see BRAND illustration **5** *of a disease* **a** : characterized by the affected individual's retention of ability to stay out of bed and walk around ⟨∼ pneumonia⟩ **b** : characterized by abnormal or excessive walking **6** : guided or operated by a man on foot ⟨∼ cultivator⟩ ⟨∼ plow⟩
walking bass *n* : an evenly accented repeated bass figure often in short octaves used esp. in piano blues — compare BOOGIE-WOOGIE
walking beam *n* : an oscillating lever that pivots on a central axis and serves for transmitting power in such a way as to produce a reciprocating or reversible motion — called also *working beam*
walking-beam \ˈ⸗⸗,⸗\ *vi* -ED/-ING/-S *West, of a horse* : to leap in bucking so as to land alternately on front and hind feet
walking boat *or* **walking scow** *n* : a scow that is moved by lowering and lifting of spuds and is used esp. for laying pipe in swift rivers
walking boss *n* : FOREMAN
walking cast *n* : a cast that is worn on a patient's leg and has a stirrup with a heel or other supporting device embedded in the plaster to facilitate walking
walking crane *n* : a light crane traveling on an overhead channel iron and a single rail vertically beneath this in the floor
walking delegate *n* : a business representative of a labor union appointed to visit members and their places of employment, to secure the enforcement of union rules and agreements, and at times to represent the union in dealing with employers : BUSINESS AGENT
walking disease *var of* WALKABOUT DISEASE
walking fern *n* [so called fr. the fact that it seems to move from place to place due to its forming identical new plants from the elongate tips of its fronds] : a fern of the genus *Camptosorus* (esp. *C. rhizophyllus*)
walking fish *n* : any of various fishes that are able to conserve oxygen so that they can survive for a considerable time out of water: as **a** : SNAKEHEAD 3 **b** : any of several tropical catfishes (as of the genus *Doras* or *Clarias*) **c** : MUDSKIPPER **d** : CLIMBING PERCH
walking gentleman *n* : an actor engaged for parts of little importance where impressive appearance is desired
walking heel *n* **1** : a heel that is somewhat lower and broader than a Cuban heel and is used on women's shoes **2** : a heel embedded in a walking cast
walking horse *n, sometimes cap W&H* : TENNESSEE WALKING HORSE
walking lady *n* : the female counterpart of a walking gentleman
walking leaf *n* **1** : WALKING FERN **2** : LEAF INSECT
walking leg *also* **walking foot** *n* : an appendage of an arthropod adapted for walking
walking line *n* : an imaginary line upon which the widths of the treads of a stair are set out generally about 18 inches from the inside of the handrail
walking-out \ˈ⸗⸗ˈ⸗\ *adj* [fr. pres. part. of the phrase *walk out*] *chiefly Brit* : prescribed or intended for a soldier on pass ⟨*walking-out* uniform⟩
walking papers *also* **walking orders** *n pl* : an order to leave : DISMISSAL, DISCHARGE ⟨his boss and his fiancée gave him his *walking papers* on the same day⟩
walking part *n* : WALK-ON
walking rapier *or* **walking sword** *n* : a very light sword formerly worn as part of a gentleman's civilian costume
walking staff *n* : a stick held in the hand and used for support in walking
walking step *n* : a simple dance step that when executed with alternate feet results in a rhythmic walk — see ONE-STEP
walking stick *n* **1** : a stick held in the hand and used for support in walking or esp. as a fashionable and often ornamental accessory for a man taking a walk **2** *usu* **walkingstick** \ˈ⸗⸗,⸗\ : STICK INSECT; *esp* : a phasmid insect (*Diapheromera femorata*) common in parts of the U.S.
walking-stick palm \ˈ⸗⸗,⸗-\ *n* : a slender Australian pinnate-leaved palm (*Bacularia monostachya*) whose stems are used for walking sticks
walking straw *n* : STICK INSECT; *esp* : a large Australian phasmid insect (*Palophus titan*) that reaches a length of 10 inches
walking ticket *n* : WALKING PAPERS
walking tyrant *n* : a stout-legged crested tyrant flycatcher (*Machetornis rixosa*) of So. America
walk-in-walk-out \ˈ⸗ˈ⸗ˈ⸗ˈ⸗\ *adj, chiefly Austral* : characterized by or consisting of the sale of a piece of real property as a completely going concern without removal of any removable property (as furniture or livestock) that is on it at the time
walk·ist \ˈwȯkəst\ *n* -s [¹walk + -ist] : ²WALKER 1c
¹**walk-mill** \ˈ⸗,⸗\ *n* [ME *walkmil, walkemilne*, prob. part trans. of MD *walkemole*, fr. *walken* to knead, full + *mole, molen* mill; akin to OHG *muli, mulin* mill — more at WALK, MILL] *dial Brit* : FULLING MILL
²**walk-mill** \"\ *n* [¹walk] : a mill powered by one or more persons or animals walking
walk off *vt* : to rid oneself of by walking ⟨*walking off* a cramp in my leg —Mary R. Rinehart⟩ ⟨started home in a mood of discouragement but soon *walked it off*⟩ : rid oneself of the effects of by walking ⟨better *walk* some of this food *off* —Evelyn Barkins⟩
walk on *vi* [fr. the phrase *walk on*] : to play a walk-on
walk-on \ˈ⸗,⸗\ *n* -s **1** : a small usu. nonspeaking part in a dramatic production — compare ³BIT 3f **2** : one that plays a walk-on
walk out *vi* **1** : to go on strike ⟨members of sympathetic . . . unions also *walked out* —*Current Biog.*⟩ **2** : to walk with long steps **3** : to take oneself out as an expression of disapproval ⟨at one meeting the United States delegate *walked out* in protest —*Current Biog.*⟩ — often used with *of* ⟨members who *walked out* of the assembly —*New Statesman & Nation*⟩ — **walk out on** : to leave abruptly : leave before the completion of a performance or process ⟨has even been known to *walk out on* the writhing of some of the screen's most celebrated heavy emoters —*New Republic*⟩ : leave in the lurch ⟨*walked out on* his wife and children⟩ : ABANDON ⟨thinking of *walking out on* the practice of law and starting a business⟩
walkout \ˈ⸗,⸗\ *n* -s [*walk out*] **1 a** : ²STRIKE 7a **b** : an informal or unauthorized strike **2 a** : the action of leaving a meeting or organization as an expression of disapproval ⟨recriminations, ∼*s*, border clashes . . . may accompany the United Nations consideration of this question —L.E.Browne⟩ **b** : continued absence from the meetings of an organization as an expression of disapproval ⟨a new effort last week to end Russia's ∼ and the U.N. stalemate —*Time*⟩ **3 a** : a prospective customer that leaves a store without making a purchase **b** : the departure of a prospective customer from a store without making a purchase
walk over *vi, of a racehorse* : to go over a course at a walk so as to be judged the winner of a race in which there is no other starter
walkover \ˈ⸗,⸗⸗\ *n* -s [*walk over*] **1 a** (1) : a horse race with only one starter (2) : a horse race in which the starters all belong to the same interests or individuals **b** : the action or an instance of walking over on the part of a racehorse ⟨in the case of a purse, the consent of the stewards is necessary to dispense with a ∼ —N. Y. State Racing Commission⟩ **2 a** : a one-sided contest : easy or uncontested victory **b** : something easily accomplished **3** : a synchronized swimming stunt which is executed from either a front or back layout position and in which the trunk is brought to a vertical position with the head down and the legs are raised successively in an arc above the water and meet as the body surfaces in the opposite layout position from the start
walk-round *var of* WALK-AROUND
walks *pres 3d sing of* WALK, *pl of* WALK
walks·man \ˈwȯksmən\ *n, pl* **walksmen** [*walk's* (gen. of ²*walk*) + *man*] *Brit* : one that patrols waterworks or waterways on foot for purposes of inspection and maintenance
walk-through \ˈ⸗,⸗\ *n* -s [fr. *walk through*, v.] **1** : a perfunctory performance of a play, scene, or acting part as in an early stage of rehearsal **2** : a television rehearsal in which the actors go through all stage business without cameras **3** : a tunnel for pedestrians
walk-trot \ˈ⸗ˈ⸗\ *adj, of a horse* : THREE-GAITED
walk up *vt* **1** : to cause (a game bird or mammal) to rise or break cover by approaching on foot ⟨spend a September day *walking up* partridges —J.R.Beddington⟩ — compare DRIVE 8b **2** : to raise (a stage flat) to a vertical position by lifting and pushing up from beneath starting with the upper edge while someone else holds the lower edge in place with his foot — compare ²FOOT 9 ∼ *vi, dial* : to walk faster
¹**walk-up** \ˈ⸗,⸗\ *adj* [fr. the phrase *walk up*] **1** : located above the ground floor in a building with no elevator ⟨a *walk-up* apartment⟩ **2** : consisting of several stories and having no elevator ⟨no *walk-up* tenement, unless fireproof, should exceed six stories in height —J.G.Hill⟩
²**walk-up** \"\ *n* -s **1** : a building of several stories with no elevator; *esp* : a walk-up apartment house ⟨lived on the top floor of a five-flight *walk-up* —Viña Delmar⟩ **2 a** : an apartment located above the ground floor in a building with no elevator ⟨his apartment, a one-room *walk-up* —Truman Capote⟩ **b** : a place of business reached by walking up one or more flights of stairs **3** : a trapshooting game in which several traps are hidden at intervals on either side of a path along which the shooter is to walk and each trap is sprung without warning as the shooter approaches it
walkway \ˈ⸗,⸗\ *n* : a passageway used or intended for walking: as **a** : SIDEWALK **b** : a path for pedestrians esp. in a garden or park ⟨box hedges mark the ∼*s* —J.B.Cabell⟩ **c** : a passageway in a place of employment (as a factory or restaurant) designed to be walked on by the employees in the performance of their duties ⟨accident prevention by making floors and ∼*s* safe —R.H.Lansburgh⟩ **d** : a walk connecting the entrance door of a house with a sidewalk, street, or road ⟨each of the houses had a graveled ∼ . . . leading down to the highway —Earl Hamner⟩
walkyrie *usu cap, var of* VALKYRIE
walky-talky *var of* WALKIE-TALKIE
¹**wall** \ˈwȯl\ *n* -s [ME, fr. OE *weall* rampart, wall; akin to OS *wal* rampart, MHG *wall*; all fr. a prehistoric WGmc word borrowed fr. L *vallum* rampart set with palisades, wall, fr. *vallus* stake, palisade; akin to Skt *vala* beam, pole, Goth *walus* stick, staff, ON *vǫlr* round stick, *valr* round, L *volvere* to roll — more at VOLUBLE] **1 a** (1) : a high thick masonry structure forming an enclosure chiefly for defense against invasion ⟨hurled stones and spears at the attackers from the ∼⟩ — usu. used in pl. ⟨citizens ran to defend the ∼*s* of the city⟩ (2) : a masonry fence around a garden, park, or estate ⟨the ∼ of the villa follows the road for miles⟩ **b** : a rampart of considerable height and thickness and usu. great length serving as a fortification (as on a border between territories or countries) ⟨the great Chinese ∼ extended for more than 1500 miles⟩ **c** : a structure that serves to hold back pressure (as of water or sliding earth) — see RETAINING WALL, SEAWALL **2** : a vertical architectural member used to define and divide space ⟨a continuously curving ∼ gives the building its shape⟩; *esp* : one of the sides of a room or building that connects the floor and ceiling or foundation and roof ⟨the inside ∼*s* are all movable —*London Calling*⟩ ⟨the house has a glass ∼ facing the garden⟩ — see CAVITY WALL, FACED WALL, NONBEARING PARTITION, PARTY WALL, STORAGE WALL **3** : the side of a footpath next to buildings ⟨the passenger who takes the ∼ brushes the dim glass with his sleeve —Charles Dickens⟩ **4 a** : an extreme or desperate position — usu. used in the phrase *to the wall* ⟨schools whose teachers . . . were driven to the ∼ financially —Dixon Wecter⟩ ⟨pushing them to the ∼ in the competitive struggle —T.W.Arnold⟩ **b** : a state of defeat, failure, or ruin — usu. used in the phrase *to the wall* ⟨let the weakest go to the ∼ —*Art & Industry*⟩ ⟨since the war, several . . . magazines have gone to the ∼ —P.W.Crowcroft⟩ **5 walls** *pl* : a physical, intellectual, or spiritual area of influence ⟨evident to those outside our academic ∼*s* —J.B.Conant⟩ **6 a** : the external layer of structural material surrounding an object ⟨surgical instruments for penetrating the ∼ of the body⟩ ⟨muscle ∼⟩ — often used in pl. ⟨staves form the ∼*s* of a barrel⟩ ⟨stomach ∼*s*⟩ **b** (1) : one of the surfaces of country rock lying adjacent to a vein, ore deposit, or coal seam (2) : one of the surfaces of a geological fault zone — see FOOTWALL, HANGING WALL **7 a** (1) : something resembling a wall in appearance ⟨a towering mountain ∼⟩ ⟨a ∼ of water, 75 feet high, . . . rushed upon the city —*Amer. Guide Series: Pa.*⟩ ⟨a stream flowing between the valley ∼*s*⟩ (2) : something that resembles a wall in function esp. by establishing limits or providing defense ⟨a sovereign state would be outside the American tariff ∼*s* —S.F.Bemis⟩ ⟨two men hurt on the football team's forward ∼⟩ ⟨going through the enemy's ∼ in linear formation —Tom Wintringham⟩ **b** : something immaterial or intangible that acts as a barrier to communication, understanding, or accomplishment ⟨the ∼ of reserve the old man had built around himself —Ben Riker⟩ ⟨break down the ∼ of condescension —Charles Angoff⟩ ⟨unable to break through the ∼ of employer resistance —Frank O'Leary⟩ **8** : the arrangement of tiles previous to the drawing of hands in a Mah-Jongg game
²**wall** \"\ *vt* -ED/-ING/-S [ME *wallen*, fr. *wall*, n.] **1 a** : to provide or cover with a wall ⟨to keep out street noises . . . the house was ∼*ed* on that facade —*Current Biog.*⟩ **b** : to surround or confine with or as if with walls : hem in — usu. used with *in* ⟨planning to ∼ in the garden for privacy⟩ ⟨a lake ∼*ed* in by snow-covered peaks⟩ ⟨was ∼*ed* in by authority —W.P. Webb⟩ **c** : to separate or shut out by means of or as if by means of a wall : PARTITION — usu. used with *off* ⟨∼*ed* off half the house to make two apartments⟩ ⟨∼*ed* off their world . . . from the rest of human society —H.S.Truman⟩ **d** : to border or form a boundary on in the manner of a wall : BOUND ⟨tall chestnut trees ∼ the broad avenue⟩ **2 a** : to shut behind a wall : seal within or as if within walls : IMMURE, INCARCERATE — usu. used with *up* ⟨had ∼*ed* the monster up within the tomb —E.A.Poe⟩ ⟨compelled . . . to spend their time ∼*ing* up this danger —Lillian Smith⟩ **b** : to seal up (an opening) with or as if with a wall ⟨∼*ed* up the crevice —Oliver La Farge⟩ **3** : to cover the walls of (a room) with something ⟨this study is ∼*ed* with books —Lucien Price⟩ **syn** see ENCLOSE
³**wall** \"\ *adj* : of or relating to a wall : beside, attached to, or growing on a wall ⟨∼ cabinets⟩ ⟨a ∼ clock⟩ ⟨∼ plants⟩
⁴**wall** \"\ *vb* -ED/-ING/-S [ME (Sc) *wawlen*, prob. fr. ME *wawil-* (in *wawil-eghed* walleyed) — more at WALLEYED] *vt* : to roll (one's eyes) in or as if in expression of emotion ⟨mooning about, . . . playacting and ∼*ing* her eyes —Frances G. Patton⟩ ∼ *vi, of the eyes* : to roll in a dramatic manner ⟨big eyes would ∼ up to the ceiling with a look of fear in them —Carson McCullers⟩
⁵**wall** \"\ *n* -s : WALL KNOT
wal·la·ba \ˈwäləbə *also* ˈwȯl-\ *n* -s [Arawak] : any of several trees of the genus *Eperua*; *esp* : a valuable timber tree (*E. falcata*) of the Guianas and northern Brazil having pinnate leaves, clusters of red flowers, and reddish brown very durable wood that is used for palings and shingles
wal·la·by \ˈwäləbē, -bi *also* ˈwȯl-\ *n, pl* **wallabies** *also* **wallaby** [fr. *wolabā*, native name in New So. Wales, Australia] **1** : any of various small and medium-sized kangaroos of *Macropus* and several related genera that are more brightly colored and much smaller than the typical kangaroos — see NAIL-TAILED WALLABY, PADEMELON, ROCK WALLABY **2** : the fur of a wallaby
wallaby acacia *n* : a shrubby Australian wattle (*Acacia rigens*) having linear terete phyllodes with short often recurved points
wallaby bush *n* : an evergreen shrub (*Beyeria viscosa*) of the family Euphorbiaceae that has small heathlike leaves and chiefly axillary flowers and is found in Australia and Tasmania
wallaby ear *n* : a virus disease of Indian corn that is characterized by a dwarfing of the whole plant and an accentuating of its green color and by small swellings on the secondary veins of the underside of top leaves in young plants which enlarge from tip to base of the leaf blade
wallaby grass *n* : any of various Australasian grasses of the genus *Danthonia*
wal·lace's line \ˈwäləsəz-, ˈwȯləsəz-\ *also* **wallace line** *n, usu cap W* [after Alfred Russel *Wallace* †1913 Eng. naturalist] : a hypothetical boundary separating the characteristic Asiatic fauna and flora from that of Australasia, marking the common boundary of the Oriental and Australian biogeographic regions, and usu. passing between Bali and Lombok, between Celebes and Borneo or to the east of Celebes, and to the east of the Philippines — see WEBER'S LINE
wal·lach *or* **wal·ach** \ˈwälək *also* ˈwȯl-\ *n* -s *cap* [G *Wallache, Walache*, of Slav origin; akin to Czech *Vlach* — more at VLACH] : VLACH
¹**wal·la·chi·an** *or* **wa·la·chi·an** \wäˈlākēən, wə·- -ˈlak- *also* wȯ·-\ *n* -s *cap* [*Wallachia, Walachia*, former principality now part of Romania + E -*an*] **1 a** : a native or inhabitant of Wallachia **b** : Romanian as spoken in Wallachia **2** : VLACH
²**wallachian** *or* **walachian** \"\ *adj, usu cap* **1** : of, relating to, or characteristic of Wallachia **2** : of, relating to, or characteristic of the Wallachians
wallachian sheep *n, usu cap W* : one of a breed of domestic sheep of southeastern Europe and western Asia that have very long upright spirally twisted horns and are used for the production of wool, meat, and milk
wal·la·go \ˈwälə,gō\ *n* -s [NL, fr. native name in Bengal] : a large freshwater catfish (*Wallago attu*) of southeastern Asia
wal·lah *also* **wal·la** \ˈwälə *also* ˈwȯlə\ *n* -s [Hindi -*wālā*, -*wal* man, one who is in charge, fr. Skt *pāla* protector; akin to Skt *pāti* he protects — more at FUR] **1** : a person who is associated with a particular type of work or who performs a specific duty or service — usu. used in combination ⟨fancies himself a home workshop ∼ —A.C.Spectorsky⟩ ⟨the book ∼ was an itinerant peddler —George Orwell⟩ **2** : a person who holds an important position in an organization or in a particular situation — usu. used in combination ⟨keep . . . these professional staff ∼*s* off my neck —William Chamberlain⟩ ⟨appointed head ∼ in charge of dinner tonight —Robert Carson⟩
wall anchor *n* : BEAM ANCHOR
wall and crown *n* : a single wall knot with a crown
wall arcade *n* : an ornamental arcade built against or as part of a wall
wal·la·roo \ˌwäləˈrü *also* ˌwȯl-\ *n* -s [fr. *wolarū*, native name in New So. Wales, Australia] : EURO
wal·la·sey \ˈwäləsē *also* ˈwȯl-\ *adj, usu cap* [fr. *Wallasey*, England] : of or from the county borough of Wallasey, England : of the kind or style prevalent in Wallasey
wal·la·wal·la \ˈwäləˈwälə *also* ˈwȯləˈwȯlə\ *n, pl* **wallawalla** *or* **wallawallas** *usu cap* [Shahaptian, lit., little river, dim. of *wana* river] **1 a** : a Shahaptian people of southeastern Washington and northeastern Oregon **b** : a member of such people **2** : a Shahaptian language of the Wallawalla people
walla-walla \"\ *n* -s [Hindi *walwalā*, *walwala* tumult, uproar, noise] : an unintelligible sound produced by many people talking at once ⟨no noise, no coolies making *walla-walla* —Virginia A. Oakes⟩
wall barley *n* : a European annual grass (*Hordeum murinum*) that resembles the related barley but occurs as a weed in waste ground esp. along roadsides and hedgerows
wall bed *n* : RECESS BED
wall bee *n* : MASON BEE

wallboard \'=,=\ *n* **:** a structural boarding of any of various materials (as wood pulp, gypsum, plastic) made in large rigid sheets and used esp. for sheathing interior walls and ceilings — compare PLASTERBOARD, PLYWOOD

wall box *n* **:** a frame set in a wall to receive a pillow block or bearing for a shaft passing through the wall

wall clamp *n* **:** a clamp for holding walls or parts of a double wall together

wall creeper *n* **:** a small bird (*Tichodroma muraria*) of the family Certhiidae that is mostly gray, black, and white with a crimson wing patch, inhabits cliffs in the mountains of southern Asia, Europe, and northern Africa, and frequents the walls of towns during migration

wall cress *n* **:** any of several low-growing or mat-forming cresses that are often cultivated in rock gardens or allowed to spread over walls: as **a :** a rock cress of the genus *Arabis* **b :** MOUSE-EAR CRESS **c :** AUBRIETIA 2

walled plain *n* **:** a large crater on the surface of the moon having a broad nearly level floor

walled toe *var of* WALL TOE

wall·er \'wȯlə(r)\ *n* -s [ME *wallare*, fr. *wallen* to wall + *-are* -er] **:** one that builds or repairs walls

wal·le·ri·an degeneration \wä'lirēən-, wȯ'lirēən-\ *n, usu cap W* [*wallerian* fr. Augustus V. *Waller* †1870 Eng. physiologist + E *-an*] **:** a degeneration of nerve fibers that follows injury or disease and progresses from the seat of injury along the axon away from the nerve cell body while the part between the seat of injury and the nerve cell body remains intact

wal·let \'wälət, 'wȯl-, *usu* -əd+V\ *n* -s [ME *walet*] **1 a :** a bag for carrying miscellaneous articles (as personal belongings) while traveling ⟨without a crust in my ~, as beggars usually have —Harriet Martineau⟩ ⟨grew so weary . . . he drew from his ~ a share of the pearls —J.F.Dobie⟩ — compare KNAPSACK **1 2 :** any of various folding pocketbooks: as **a :** BILLFOLD 1 **b :** a pocketbook that contains compartments for change, photographs, cards, and keys and often has a snap or zipper fastener **c :** a pocketbook that is large enough to accommodate unfolded foreign currency or personal papers (as a passport or checkbook)

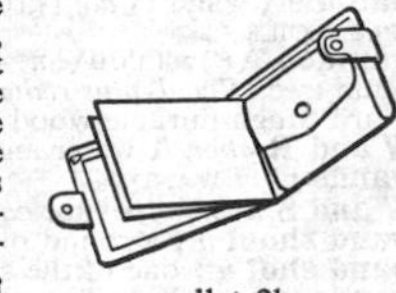
wallet 2b

wall·ette \(')wȯ¦let\ *n* -s [¹*wall* + *-ette*] **:** a low thin miniature wall (as for ornamental or experimental purposes)

wall·eye \'wȯ,lī\ *n* [back-formation fr. *walleyed*] **1 a :** an eye (as of a horse) having a light gray or bluish white iris **b :** an eye having an opaque white cornea **c :** an eye that turns outward showing more than a normal amount of white **2 a :** LEUCOMA **b :** strabismus in which the eye turns outward — called also *exotropia*; compare CROSS-EYE 1 **3 walleyes** *pl* **:** eyes affected with divergent strabismus **4** *or* **walleyed pike** *also* **walleye pike :** a large vigorous American freshwater food and sport fish (*Stizostedion vitreum*) that has large prominent eyes and is related to the perches but more closely resembles the true pike in appearance and behavior

wall-eyed \-īd\ *adj* [by folk etymology (influence of ¹*wall*) fr. ME *wawil-eghed*, part trans. of ON *vagl-eygr* walleyed, fr. *vagl* beam, roost, beam in the eye + *eygr, eygthr* eyed; akin to ON *vega* to move, carry, lift — more at WEIGH] **1 a :** having very light gray or whitish eyes ⟨a ~ horse⟩ **b :** having the eyes directed outward **:** affected with a divergent squint ⟨the operation turned him from cross-eyed to ~⟩ **2 :** affected with leucoma **3 :** marked by a wild irrational staring of the eyes ⟨flailed away in ~ fear —*Time*⟩ ⟨had a ~ fit —Ross Santee⟩ **4 :** having an oblique uncertain appearance or character ⟨~ . . . foreign policy —*New Yorker*⟩

walleye pollack *n* **:** a food fish (*Theragra chalcogramma*) of the northern Pacific related to and closely resembling the pollack

wall fern *n* **:** a low-growing mat-forming fern (*Polypodium vulgare*) that grows esp. in the crevices of rocks and is often cultivated as an ornamental

wallflower \'=,=\ *n* **1 :** any of several Old World herbaceous or subshrubby perennial cruciferous plants (genus *Cheiranthus*); *esp* **:** a hardy erect herb (*C. cheiri*) that is widely cultivated for its showy very fragrant usu. yellow or brownish yellow single or double flowers which appear early in the spring **2 :** a plant of the genus *Erysimum* (as the wormseed mustard or prairie rocket) **3 :** a person who from shyness or unpopularity remains on the sidelines of a social activity (as a dance) ⟨a ~ who never wants to meet people⟩ ⟨men were scarce, and ~s wore their peculiar pathetic expression —John Galsworthy⟩ **4** *or* **wallflower brown :** a dark red to moderate reddish brown that is yellower than garnet brown — called also *burnt russet, Cuba, palissandre* **5 :** an Australian desert shrub (*Gastrolobium grandiflorum*)

wallflower 1

wall fruit *n* **:** fruit borne by trees trained against a wall

wall garden *n* **:** a garden consisting of plants set in soil in the crevices between the rocks of a wall

wall gecko *n* **:** any of several harmless Old World geckos that feed on insects and have suckers on the feet for clinging to a surface (as a wall)

wall germander *n* **:** an often shrubby European perennial germander (*Teucrium chamaedrys*) that has red-purple or bright rose flowers with red and white spots and is used as a border plant

wall grass *n* **:** a common stonecrop (*Sedum acre*)

wall green *n* **:** a moderate to strong bluish green

wall hanging *n* **:** a drapery or tapestry hung against a wall for decoration

wall hawkweed *n* **:** a European hawkweed (*Hieracium murorum*) with mostly basal leaves and yellow flower heads on glandular stalks that often grows on walls

wall·ing \'wȯliŋ\ *n* -s [ME, fr. *wall* + *-ing*] **1 :** WALL ⟨a ~ of stone or sods rises to a height of five or six feet —C.D.Forde⟩ **2 :** material for walls

walling crib *n* **:** a heavy timber or cast-iron ring built into the wall of a mine shaft to support the lining

wall ink *n* **:** a brooklime (*Veronica beccabunga*) that is native to Europe but established in northeastern No. America

wall knot *n* **:** an overhand or double knot that is crowned or double-crowned and made by interweaving the unlaid strands at the end of a rope

wall-less \'wȯlləs\ *adj* **:** lacking walls ⟨its *wall-less* ground floor is open to the winds —*Bookman*⟩

wall lettuce *n* **:** a European wild lettuce (*Lactuca muralis*) with coarse foliage and yellow flowers in loose clusters

wall link *n* **:** WALKING FERN

wall lizard *n* **:** a common lizard (*Lacerta muralis*) of southern Europe, Asia Minor, and northern Africa that frequents houses and lives in the chinks and crevices of walls

wall·man \'wȯlmən\ *n, pl* **wallmen :** a wrecker who uses a wrecking bar and other hand tools to demolish the roofs and walls of buildings

wall knot

wall newspaper *n* **:** an often handwritten or typed newssheet that is usu. posted on a bulletin board or wall ⟨*wall newspapers* found in every shop, office, and farm —Alex Inkeles⟩

wal·lon \wälō"\ *usu cap, archaic var of* WALLOON

¹**wal·loon** \wä'lün, wə'- *also* wȯ'-\ *adj, usu cap* [MF *Wallon*, adj. & n., of Gmc origin; prob. akin to OHG *Walah, Walh* Celt, Roman, OE *Wealh* Celt, Welshman — more at WELSH] **1 :** of, relating to, or characteristic of the Walloons **2 :** of, relating to, or written or spoken in the French dialect of the Walloons

²**walloon** \"\ *n* -s *cap* [MF *Wallon*] **1 :** a member of a chiefly Celtic people of southern Belgium (as Hainaut, Namur, Liège, and Luxembourg), Brabant, and adjacent parts of France — compare FLEMING, BELGIAN **2 :** a French dialect of the Walloons

³**walloon** \"\ *n* -s [prob. fr. ¹*walloon*] **:** TOBACCO MOSAIC

¹**wal·lop** \'wäləp *also* 'wȯl-\ *n* -s [ME *wallop, walop*, fr. ONF *walop*, fr. *waloper* to gallop] **1** *obs* **:** GALLOP **2** *obs* **:** a bubbling motion and sound (as of a boiling substance) ⟨let it only boil five or six ~s —George Hartman⟩ **3** *chiefly Brit* **:** a noisy clumsy movement of the body ⟨a sagging sack of flesh . . . he went in with a ~ —Adrian Bell⟩ **4 a :** a powerful blow **:** ²PUNCH 2 ⟨got a hard ~ in the mouth —*Baltimore (Md.) Sun*⟩ ⟨the ~s from the wind made you feel tired —Greville Texidor⟩ **b :** something resembling a wallop esp. in sudden jarring force ⟨the sight of him hit my dried-up soul a ~ —*N. Y. Herald Tribune*⟩ ⟨woodwinds . . . underlined by an explosive percussive ~ —Aaron Copland⟩ **c :** the ability (as of a boxer) to hit hard ⟨has a terrific ~ in his left hand⟩ **5 a :** effective physical, emotional, or psychological force or influence **:** IMPACT ⟨the ~ from an atomic bomb —*N. Y. Times*⟩ ⟨full page advertising . . . carries a tremendous sales ~ —*Playthings*⟩ ⟨a movie with a dramatic ~⟩ ⟨cannot pack the political ~ needed to swing Congress —*New Republic*⟩ **b :** a pleasant or exciting emotional response **:** THRILL, KICK ⟨the kids . . . get a big ~ out of it —Robert Wilder⟩ **6** *Brit* **:** ¹BEER ⟨was a great one for ~ and darts with the villagers in the local —Angus Wilson⟩

²**wallop** \"\ *vb* -ED/-ING/-S [ME *walopen*, fr. ONF *waloper*] *vi* **1** *obs* **:** GALLOP **2 a :** to move with reckless or disorganized haste **:** advance in a headlong rush ⟨a fat spaniel dog . . . ~*ed* along the deck —D.C.Russell⟩ ⟨ships . . . were ~*ing* across the Atlantic freighted with more cigars —Aldous Huxley⟩ **b** (1) **:** to move violently and often noisily about **:** WALLOW ⟨sea-beasts who roared and rolled and ~*ed* —Rudyard Kipling⟩ ⟨the very cows joined in . . . ~*ing*, tail lashing —Virginia Woolf⟩ (2) **:** to progress in a lurching ungainly manner **:** FLOUNDER ⟨watched the old car ~ down the rutted lane⟩ **3 :** to boil with a loud bubbling noise ⟨an immense pot . . . surging and ~*ing* with some kind of savory stew —Nathaniel Hawthorne⟩ **4** *chiefly Scot* **:** to flap about **:** FLUTTER, FLOP ⟨keep his nether garments from ~*ing* behind him —Peter McNeill⟩ ~ *vt* **1 a :** to thrash soundly (as with the hands or fists) **:** BEAT, POUND, LAMBASTE ⟨always doing the wrong thing and being ~*ed* for it —Ruth Park⟩ ⟨~*ed* the living daylights out of his attacker⟩ **b :** to gain a decisive victory over **:** beat by a wide margin **:** TROUNCE ⟨~*ed* him in the first match they played —Jack Barnaby⟩ ⟨~*ed* the champions 10 to 3 yesterday —*Springfield (Mass.) Republican*⟩ **2 a :** to hit with great force **:** SOCK, SLUG ⟨unfortunately . . . it was a gendarme I had ~*ed* —H.A.Chippendale⟩ **b** (1) **:** to send (as a baseball) a long distance by a solid hit ⟨~*ed* the ball against the facade of the third deck —*N. Y. Times*⟩ (2) **:** to get (as a run in baseball) by batting well ⟨~*ed* 16 home runs last season⟩ **3 :** to scrub (kitchen utensils) clean ⟨by night he ~*ed* pots and pans in a hotel kitchen —R.M. Yoder⟩ **4 :** to move (as material for shipment) by hand ⟨togged like the rest of the gang . . . he ~*s* sacks of sugar, coal, assorted cargo —*Time*⟩

wal·lop·er \-pə(r)\ *n* -s **:** one that wallops

¹**walloping** *adj* [fr. pres. part. of ²*wallop*] **1 :** outstandingly large in size or degree **:** WHOPPING ⟨accumulate a ~ collection of institutional freaks —*New Yorker*⟩ ⟨able to get a ~ promotion —A.C.Spectorsky⟩ **2 :** exceptionally fine or impressive **:** SMASHING ⟨a ~ new production —Douglas Watt⟩ ⟨the men in the blue-trimmed white . . . won their last race by a ~ twelve lengths —*Newsweek*⟩

²**walloping** *adv* **:** TERRIFICALLY, SPANKING ⟨going to have a ~ big gas bill —*Lippincott's Mag.*⟩ ⟨a ~ dirty great big umbrella —Richard Llewellyn⟩

¹**wal·low** \'wä(,)lō, \|lə *also* 'wȯ\|; \|ləw *or* \|lō+V\ *vb* -ED/-ING/-S [ME *walwen, walowen*, fr. OE *wealwian* — more at VOLUBLE] *vi* **1 a :** to roll or move oneself about in an indolent ungainly manner **:** sprawl luxuriously ⟨took films of hippos as they ~*ed* in a mudhole⟩ ⟨too tired to do anything but ~ in a hot tub⟩ **b :** to toss oneself about helplessly or frantically ⟨lay on the ground . . . ~*ing* and pitching and screaming —F.B.Gipson⟩ **c** (1) *of a ship* **:** to pitch and roll in rough water ⟨the boats were ~*ing* in the waves . . . likely to be swamped —J.G.Gilkey⟩ (2) **:** to sail esp. with a heavy rolling motion ⟨~*ed* through a quarter mile of whitecaps —Franc Shor⟩ ⟨fleets . . . that ~ up and down the British coasts —*Lamp*⟩ **d :** to move in an awkward, lurching, and disorganized manner ⟨dawn found the convoy ~*ing* around —Nathaniel Benchley⟩ **e** *of an airplane* **:** to lurch and wobble (as from shifting air currents) ⟨altitudes . . . at which fighters perform sluggishly, ~, lose control —H.W.Baldwin⟩ **2 :** to billow forth **:** SURGE, ROLL ⟨fat polysyllables . . . ~*ed* off his tongue —J.T.Farrell⟩ ⟨the launch heaved on a . . . slowly ~*ing* sea —Aldous Huxley⟩ **3 :** to devote oneself entirely or as if entirely **:** become obsessed (as with a particular mode of behavior or area of interest) — usu. used with *in* ⟨publicly ~*ed* in his infamies —Merle Miller⟩ ⟨the tendency to ~ in national self-absorption —Max Ascoli⟩ ⟨our gripes editor literally ~*s* in gripes —*Jewelers' Circular-Keystone*⟩; *esp* **:** to take unrestrained or excessive pleasure **:** REVEL — usu. used with *in* ⟨enjoyed sitting . . . and ~*ing* in the sensual melodies —Osbert Sitwell⟩ **4 a :** to become abundantly supplied **:** LUXURIATE — usu. used with *in* ⟨nauseating baby talk in which some . . . books ~ —Margaret F. Kieran⟩ ⟨a family that ~*s* in money⟩ **b :** to indulge oneself habitually and immoderately — usu. used with *in* ⟨film stars who ~ in luxury⟩ **5 :** to become helpless or ineffectual **:** lose the ability to function naturally or efficiently ⟨the economic catastrophe in which they were . . . ~*ing* —J.P.O'Donnell⟩ ⟨left to ~ in its ignorance —Lennox Robinson⟩ ~ *vt* **:** to roll (something) about ⟨~*ing* these problems around in his mind —F.B.Gipson⟩

syn WELTER, FLOUNDER, GROVEL: WALLOW implies a movement of rolling to and fro, as of a ship in the trough of a wave or an animal in mire ⟨wind and sea had risen, and the little *Torakina* was rearing, plunging and *wallowing* as she took up the strain of her tow —R.S.Porteous⟩ ⟨a jeep came *wallowing* through the mud —Norman Mailer⟩ ⟨was *wallowing* in self-abasement —*Times Lit. Supp.*⟩ WELTER sometimes implies wallowing but more often implies a rolling or tossing helplessly, as at the mercy of a storm ⟨the lifeboat and its passengers *weltered* in the sea for over a week⟩ ⟨the mass of the people were *weltering* in shocking poverty whilst a handful of owners wallowed in millions —G.B.Shaw⟩ FLOUNDER stresses a helpless stumbling or struggling in an effort to make progress ⟨crews *floundering* through the wet black muck —Marjory S. Douglas⟩ ⟨her feet grew heavier with each step and she *floundered* among the hollows like an old, awkward fish —Audrey Barker⟩ ⟨many writers have *floundered* in one medium of speech while in another they have moved with ease —H.O.Taylor⟩ GROVEL implies a crawling or wriggling close to the ground, as in abject fear, self-abasement, or complete degradation ⟨fluttered to the ground and *groveled* on the sand in what appeared to be a kind of frenzy —E.A.Armstrong⟩ ⟨one moment he towered in imagination, the next he *groveled* in fear —G.D.Brown⟩ ⟨a mean, timeserving little man, *groveling* odiously before the wealthy people in the district who patronize his shop —Peter Forster⟩

²**wallow** \"\ *n* -s **1 :** an act or instance of wallowing ⟨the apogee of earthly reward, a luxurious ~ in glamour —R.L. Taylor⟩ **2 a** (1) **:** an area that is wet and muddy or filled with dust and is used by animals for wallowing ⟨the rhino, huge and gray in the brush, almost white from the dried mud of the ~ —Ernest Hemingway⟩ ⟨elephants using the shallow stream bed for a ~⟩ (2) **:** a depression in the ground formed by the wallowing of animals ⟨great herds left the landscape pitted with ~*s*⟩ — see BEAR WALLOW, BUFFALO WALLOW, HOG WALLOW **b** (1) **:** a declivity or area that is often filled with water or mud and resembles an animal wallow — compare MUDHOLE 1, SWALE 2 ⟨black ~*s* . . . where cars or wagons had been bogged down —L.C.Stevens⟩ ⟨an open field that was often a ~ of mud —Joseph Wechsberg⟩ (2) **:** KOMMETJE **3 :** a state or condition of degradation or degeneracy ⟨the awful ~ that circumstance has plunged him into —John McCarten⟩

³**wallow** \"\ *vi* [ME *weolewen, wallowen*, fr. OE *wealwian*; akin to MLG *welen* to wither, MD *welken* to welk — more at WELK] *Scot* **:** FADE, WITHER

wal·low·er \|ləwə(r), |lōə(r)\ *n* -s [¹*wallow* + *-er*] **:** one that wallows

wallowish *adj* [obs. E dial. *wallow* tasteless, insipid (fr. ME *walhwe, walh*) + E *-ish* — more at WAUGH] **:** FLAT, INSIPID ⟨give a taste and edge . . . to that dull and ~ flatness —Philemon Holland⟩

wall painting *n* **:** FRESCO 1

¹**wallpaper** \'=,==\ *n* **:** decorative paper used to cover the walls of a room ⟨hid the plain white walls with hideous flowered ~⟩

²**wallpaper** \"\ *vt* **:** to provide the walls of (as a room) with wallpaper ~ *vi* **:** to put wallpaper on a wall

wall pellitory *n* **:** a European herb (*Parietaria officinalis*) that has diuretic properties and grows on walls

wall pepper *n* **:** a stonecrop (*Sedum acre*)

wall-piece \'=,=\ *n* **:** a cannon mounted on a wall or a rail of a ship ⟨two large *wall-pieces* . . . loaded . . . with musket balls —*Naval Chronicle*⟩

wall plate *n* [ME *walplate*] **1 :** PLATE 5a(1) — see ROOF illustration **2 :** one of the main side timbers of a mine shaft — compare END PLATE **3 :** SWITCH PLATE

wall plug *n* **:** an electric receptacle having its face flush with or recessed in a wall

wall pressure *n* **:** the pressure exerted on the contents of a plant cell by the cell wall that is equal in force and opposite in direction to the turgor pressure

wall reaction *n* **:** a reaction that is localized on the walls of the containing vessel and is often catalyzed by contact with the walls

wall rock *n* **:** a rock through which a fault or vein runs **:** the country rock next to a fault, vein, or ore deposit

wall rocket *n* **:** any of several plants of the genus *Diplotaxis* found often in quarries and on old walls; *esp* **:** a European weed (*D. tenuifolia*) with rather large yellow flowers that is adventive in No. America

wall rue *or* **wall rue spleenwort** *n* **:** a small delicate spleenwort (*Asplenium rutamuraria*) found on a steep slope (as a wall or cliff) in Eurasia and No. America

walls *pl of* WALL, *pres 3d sing of* WALL

wall speedwell *n* **:** CORN SPEEDWELL

wall street *n, usu cap W&S* [fr. *Wall Street*, street in lower Manhattan, N. Y. City, on and near which are concentrated the Stock Exchange and other exchanges and financial houses] **:** the influential financial interests of the U. S. economy

wall street·er \-,strēd·ə(r)\ *n, usu cap W&S* [*Wall Street*, N. Y. City + E *-er*] **:** a person who is involved in Wall Street ⟨*Wall Streeters* agreed that heavy speculation . . . made the sell-off inevitable —*Newsweek*⟩

wall tent *n* **:** a tent with four perpendicular cloth walls

wall toe *also* **walled toe** *n* **:** a toe of a shoe having the vamp stitched to the top edge of the vertical stiffened sides in the style of a moccasin

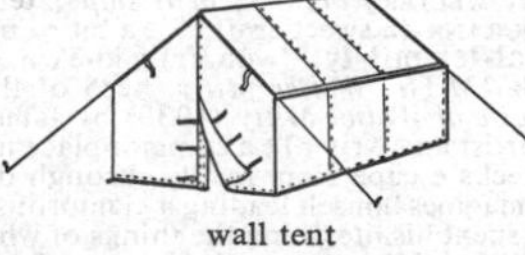
wall tent

wall tree *n* **:** a tree (as a fruit tree) trained against a wall

wall wasp *n* **:** any of several solitary wasps of the genus *Odynerus* that make their nests in the crevices of walls

wallwort \'=,=\ *n* [alter. (influenced by ¹*wall*) of earlier *walwort* danewort, fr. ME *walwort, walwurt*, fr. OE *wealhwyrt*, lit., foreign herb, fr. *Wealh* Welshman, foreigner + *wyrt* herb, root; prob. fr. the belief that it grew where Welsh blood was spilled — more at WELSH, WORT] **:** any of several Welsh plants that grow on or in walls: as **a :** DANEWORT **b :** WALL PELLITORY **c :** a stonecrop (*Sedum acre*) **d :** WALL RUE

wal·ly \'wālī\ *adj* [prob. fr. ³*wale* + *-y*] *Scot* **:** FINE, SPLENDID, STURDY

wal·ly·drai·gle \'wāli,drāgəl\ *n* -s [origin unknown] *Scot* **:** a feeble, undergrown, or slovenly creature

¹**walm** *n* -s [ME, bubbling of water, fr. OE *wælm, wielm* action of boiling or bubbling; akin to OHG *walm* action of boiling, OE *weallan, wyllan* to bubble, well — more at WELL] *obs* **:** WALLOP 2

²**walm** \'wäm\ *vi* [ME *walmen*, fr. *walm*, n.] *archaic* **:** to well up (as water) **:** gush forth ⟨waters spring and ~ out of the inner parts of the earth —Stephen Batman⟩

wal·nut \'wȯl(,)nət, *usu* -əd+V\ *n* [ME *walnot*, fr. OE *wealhhnutu*, lit., foreign nut, fr. *Wealh* Welshman, foreigner + *hnutu* nut — more at WELSH, NUT] **1 a :** an edible nut produced by a tree of the genus *Juglans*; *esp* **:** ENGLISH WALNUT 2 **b** *or* **walnut tree** [ME *walnotetre, walnot tree*] **:** a tree bearing this nut — see TREE illustration **c :** the wood of a walnut tree; *esp* **:** BLACK WALNUT **2 :** any of several trees of genera other than *Juglans*: as **a :** ACAPU **b :** AFRICAN WALNUT **c :** BLACK POISON **3** *chiefly NewEng* **:** HICKORY NUT **4 :** a moderate reddish brown that is the color of the heartwood of the black walnut — distinguished from *walnut brown*

walnut aphid *n* **:** a plant louse (*Chromaphis juglandicola*) that is destructive to walnuts esp. in California

walnut blight *n* **:** a disease of the English walnut caused by a bacterium (*Xanthomonas juglandis*) and characterized by black dead spots on the young fruits, leaves, and shoots

walnut borer *n* **1 :** a blue-winged longicorn beetle (*Gaurotes cyanipennis*) whose larva bores into the wood of the black walnut **2 :** any of several ambrosia beetles (esp. *Anisandrus pyri* or *A. dispar*) that bore under the bark or in the wood of the black walnut

walnut brown *n* **:** a light yellowish brown that is redder, lighter, and stronger than khaki, paler and slightly yellower than cinnamon, slightly redder and lighter than manila, and stronger and slightly redder and lighter than fallow and is the color of the shell of the English walnut — distinguished from *walnut*; called also *taffy*

walnut casebearer *n* **:** a small phycitid moth (*Mineola palliolella*) whose larva lives in a portable case on the walnut

walnut caterpillar *n* **:** the hairy gregarious caterpillar of a walnut moth (*Datana integerrima*)

walnut curculio *n* **:** WALNUT WEEVIL

walnut family *n* **:** JUGLANDACEAE

walnut husk fly *n* **:** any of several trypetid flies (esp. *Rhagoletis completa* and *R. suavis*) whose larvae live in the husks of black and other walnuts

walnut moth *n* **:** any of several moths whose larvae eat the foliage of the walnut: as **a :** REGAL MOTH **b :** IMPERIAL MOTH **c :** LUNA MOTH **d :** any of several red underwings of the genus *Catocala* **e :** a dagger moth (*Acronicta americana*) found also on the maple **f :** any of three arctiid moths of the genus *Halisidota* (*H. caryae, H. tesselaris, H. maculata*) **g :** a moth (*Datana integerrima*) whose larva feeds on and often defoliates walnut, hickory, birch, oak, chestnut, linden, and apple

walnut oil *n* **:** a very pale fatty oil that does not turn yellow, that is obtained from English walnuts, and that is used in foods, artists' colors, paints, and soap

walnut scale *n* **:** a round scale (*Aspidiotus juglans-regiae*) that infests the English walnut

walnut shell *n* **1 :** the shell or half shell of a walnut **2 :** a very light boat ⟨nursed our *walnut shell* tenderly over their crests —Erskine Childers⟩

walnut spanworm *n* **:** a worm that is the larva of a geometrid moth (*Conoides plumogeraria*) and that sometimes defoliates the English walnut in California

walnut sphinx *n* **:** a large brown and gray sphinx (*Cressonia juglandis*) whose larva feeds on the leaves of the black walnut and hickory

walnut weevil *n* **:** any of several weevils (as *Conotrachelus juglandis*) that feed on the foliage and fruit of walnuts

walnut worm *n* **:** a caterpillar that is the larva of a walnut moth

wal·pi *also* **hual·pi** \'wälpē\ *n, pl* **walpi** *or* **walpis** *also* **hualpi** *or* **hualpis** *usu cap* **1 :** a Shoshonean people occupying a pueblo in northeastern Arizona **2 :** a member of the Walpi people

¹**wal·pol·ian** *also* **wal·pol·ean** \(')wȯl¦pōlēən *sometimes* (')wäl¦-\ *adj, usu cap* [Horace *Walpole* †1797 Eng. man of letters + E *-an*] **1 :** of, relating to, or having the characteristics of Horace Walpole or his writings ⟨a *Walpolian* letter writer⟩ **2** [Robert *Walpole* †1745 Eng. statesman + E *-an*] **:** of, relating to, or having the characteristics of Robert

Walpole or his political policies ⟨turned them into sound *Walpolean* Whigs —J.H.Plumb⟩

[2]**walpolian** \"\ *n* -s *usu cap* [Horace *Walpole* †1797 + E *-an*, n. suffix] **:** an admirer or student of the writings of Horace Walpole ⟨ardent *Walpolians* and collectors of private press issues —*Saturday Rev.*⟩

wal·pur·gis night \väl'pu̇rgəs-, -ü(ə)gəs-; val'pərjəs-, wäl-, wȯl-, -pə̄l, -pəil, |gəs-\ *or* **wal·pur·gis·nacht** \väl'pu̇rgə-,snäkt, -ü(ə)g-\ *n* -s *usu cap W&N* [*walpurgis night* part trans. of G *walpurgisnacht*, fr. *Walpurgis* St. Walburga †A.D. 777 Eng. saint whose feast day falls on May Day + G *nacht* night, fr. OHG *naht* — more at NIGHT] **1 :** the evening preceding May Day **:** the evening of April 30 believed esp. during medieval and Renaissance times to be an occasion when witches celebrate a sabbat **2 :** something (as an event or situation) having an orgiastic or nightmarish character ⟨the big, wicked party that should be the . . . *Walpurgis Night* of his book —*New Republic*⟩ ⟨the relationship . . . became a protracted *Walpurgisnacht* —George Stevens⟩

wal·pur·gite \wäl'pər,jīt, wȯl-, -,gīt\ *n* -s [G *walpurgin* (fr. *Walpurgis*, vein in mine at Schneeberg, central Germany + G *-in* -ine) + E *-ite*] **:** a mineral $Bi_4(UO_2)(AsO_4)_2O_4.3H_2O(?)$ consisting of a hydrous bismuth uranium arsenate and oxide occurring in thin yellow crystals

wal·rus \'wȯlrəs, 'wäl-\ *n, pl* **walrus** *or* **walruses** [D *walrus, walros*, of Scand origin; akin to Dan & Norw *hvalros* walrus, ON *rosmhvalr* walrus, *hvalr* whale — more at WHALE] **1 :** either of two large marine mammals (family Odobenidae) that may exceed a ton in weight and are hunted for the tough heavy hide, the ivory tusks, the oil yielded by the blubber, and locally for the flesh: **a :** a mammal (*Odobenus rosmarus*) of the northwestern Atlantic and Arctic oceans — called also *Atlantic walrus* **b :** a mammal (*O. divergens*) of the Bering sea and the Arctic coasts of Alaska and Siberia that is sometimes held to be a variety of the Atlantic walrus — called also *Pacific walrus* **2 :** the hide of the walrus used esp. for covering buffing wheels or split and tanned and used for luggage leather

walrus bird *n* [so called fr. its puffing out of its breast like a walrus] **:** PECTORAL SANDPIPER

walrus moustache *n* **:** a heavy often shaggy moustache with drooping ends resembling the moustache of a walrus ⟨an old man with a dirty yellow *walrus moustache* —Anthony West⟩

wal·sall \'wȯl,sȯl\ *adj, usu cap* [fr. *Walsall*, England] **:** of or from the county borough of Walsall, England **:** of the kind or style prevalent in Walsall

walt \'wȯlt\ *adj* [obs. E dial. *walt* to overturn, tumble, totter, fr. ME *walten*; akin to OE *wealtan, wæltan* to turn, roll — more at WELTER] *archaic, of a ship* **:** tending to list **:** UNSTEADY, [9]CRANK ⟨a sweet craft, . . . a bit ~ perhaps —S.H.Adams⟩

wal·ter mit·ty \'wȯltə(r)'mid·ē\ *n, pl* **walter mittys** *usu cap W&M* [fr. *Walter Mitty*, hero of the short story *The Secret Life of Walter Mitty* (1939) by James G. Thurber *b*1894 Am. artist and writer] **:** a commonplace unadventurous person who seeks escape from reality through daydreaming and typically imagines himself leading a glamorous life and becoming famous ⟨spent his life doing the things of which the world's wistful . . . *Walter Mittys* can only dream —James Gray⟩

walter's pine *n, usu cap W* [after Thomas *Walter*, 18th cent. Eng. naturalist] **:** SPRUCE PINE 1a

wal·tham·stow \'wȯltham,stō\ *adj, usu cap* [fr. *Walthamstow*, England] **:** of or from the municipal borough of Walthamstow, England **:** of the kind or style prevalent in Walthamstow

wal·ther·ite \'vältə,rīt\ *n* -s [G *waltherit*, perh. fr. *Walther*, a 19th cent. Austrian mining official + G *-it* -ite] **:** a mineral consisting of an ill-defined carbonate of bismuth having green to brownish green doubly terminated prismatic crystals

wal·ther's canal \'vältə(r)z-\ *or* **walther's duct** *n, usu cap W* [after Augustin Friedrich *Walther* †1746 Ger. anatomist] **:** any of several small inconstant efferent ducts of the sublingual gland opening into the mouth

[1]**wal·to·ni·an** \wȯl'tōnēən\ *n* -s *usu cap* [Izaak *Walton* †1683 Eng. biographer and author + E *-an*, n. suffix] **:** a follower of Izaak Walton or his writings; *esp* **:** ANGLER ⟨fish that any *Waltonian* might well stare at —John Coulter⟩

[2]**waltonian** \(')=¦===\ *adj, usu cap* [Izaak *Walton* †1683 + E *-an*, adj. suffix] **:** of, relating to, or reflecting the characteristics of Izaak Walton or his writings on angling ⟨sporting facilities include trout fishing in *Waltonian* streams —*London Calling*⟩

walty \'wȯltē\ *adj* [*walt* + *-y*] *of a ship* **:** tending to list **:** [9]CRANK

[1]**waltz** \'wȯlts *also* -ls\ *n* -ES [G *walzer*, fr. *walzen* to roll, revolve, dance, fr. OHG *walzan* to turn, roll — more at WELTER] **1 :** a round dance in ¾ time with a strong accent on the first beat of the measure that is characterized by one step to the beat typically executed with a constant gyrating motion at a moderately fast tempo — see [3]BOSTON 1 **2 a :** the music for dancing a waltz **b :** an instrumental, orchestral, or vocal composition in ¾ time intended chiefly for concert performance

[2]**waltz** \"\ *vb* -ED/-ING/-ES [G *walzen*] *vi* **1 :** to dance a waltz ⟨tried to ~ for the first time in years⟩ **2 a :** to move about in a lively whimsical often aimless manner ⟨think they can just ~ in and out of the house all day⟩ ⟨don't like strangers ~*ing* around up here —John Hersey⟩ **b :** to move along in an excited, noisy, or attention-seeking manner **:** FLOUNCE ⟨saw the jolly bunch come ~*ing* in for eats —Sinclair Lewis⟩ ⟨~*ed* out to the ladies' room to talk and smoke —Catherine Hubbell⟩ **3 a :** to advance easily and successfully **:** proceed without a hitch **:** BREEZE — usu. used with *through* ⟨you'll ~ through most European customs —T.H.Fielding⟩ ⟨~*ed* through the big games —*Christian Science Monitor*⟩ **b :** to approach boldly — used with *up* ⟨can't just ~ up and introduce ourselves⟩ ~ *vt* **1 :** to lead (a partner) in a waltz **:** dance a waltz with ⟨~*ed* her around the room at a dizzying clip⟩ **2 a :** to lead (as a person) in a hasty, determined, and unceremonious manner **:** MARCH ⟨grabbed the child's arm and ~*ed* him upstairs⟩ ⟨~*ed* him through many phases of religiosity —Clemence Dane⟩ **b :** CARRY, LUG ⟨had to ~ this package all over town⟩ — **waltz matilda** *usu cap M* [*matilda* fr. the feminine name *Matilda*; prob. fr. the manner in which the swagman carried his swag and fr. the fact that he never parted with it and considered himself married to it] *Austral* **:** to travel around on foot esp. carrying a pack or swag — **waltz off with :** to win (as a prize) esp. by beating one's opponents easily ⟨*waltzed off with* several honors in this category —Lois Long⟩

[3]**waltz** \"\ *adj* [[1]*waltz*] **:** of, relating to, or having the characteristics of a waltz ⟨~ step⟩ ⟨~ tune⟩

waltz·er \-sə(r)\ *n* -s **:** one that waltzes

waltzing mouse *n* **:** a mouse of a genetic variant or a breed believed to have originated in Japan and characterized by an inability to progress in a straight line and a tendency to whirl about in small circles

waltz jump *n* **:** THREE JUMP

waltz swing *n* **:** a common square-dance swing danced clockwise right side to right side with the gentleman's right hand at the lady's back, his left hand holding her right, and her left hand on his shoulder

waly \'wālī\ *interj* [prob. contr. of [1]*wellaway*] *chiefly Scot* — used to express sorrow

WAM *abbr, often not cap* words a minute

wa·ma·ra \'wämərə\ *n* -s [Arawak] **1 :** a tree (*Swartzia tomentosa*) of British Guiana **2 :** the very hard purplish black wood of the wamara that has a straight fine uniform grain and is used for various purposes but sparingly because of the difficulty of working it

wam·ben·ger \'wam,beŋgə(r)\ *n* -s [origin unknown] **:** a widely distributed Australian pouched mouse (*Phascogale penicillata*)

[1]**wam·ble** \'wämbəl, 'wam- *also* 'wȯm-\ *vb* **wambled; wambled; wambling** \-b(ə)liŋ\ **wambles** [ME *wamlen*; akin to Dan *vamle* to become nauseated, L *vomere* to vomit — more at VOMIT] *vi* **1 a :** to feel nausea **b** *of a stomach* **:** ROLL **2 :** to move unsteadily or with a weaving or rolling motion ⟨a *wambling* conversation⟩ ⟨a story that ~*s* on and on⟩ ~ *vt* **:** to turn over and over **:** SPIN, REVOLVE

[2]**wamble** \"\ *n* -s **1 :** a rumbling or disturbance of the stomach **2 :** an irregular gait or movement **:** a reeling or staggering gait

wamble–cropped *also* **wamble–cropt** \'==,kräpt\ *adj* [[2]*wamble* + *crop* (stomach) + *-ed*] *dial* **:** having a rumbling stomach; *also* **:** SICKLY

wam·bli·ness \-blēnəs\ *n* -ES **:** the quality or state of being wambly

wambling *adj* [fr. pres. part. of [1]*wamble*] **1 :** REELING, TOTTERING ⟨a ~ gait⟩ **2 :** WEAK, INEFFECTIVE ⟨a ~ teacher⟩ — **wam·bling·ly** *adv*

wam·bly \-blē, -li\ *adj* -ER/-EST [[2]*wamble* + *-y*] *dial* **:** FAINT, SQUEAMISH; *also* **:** SHAKY

wame \'wām\ *n* -s [ME, alter. of *wamb* — more at WOMB] *chiefly Scot* **:** BELLY

wam·pa·no·ag \,wämpə'nō,ag *also* ,wȯm-\ *n, pl* **wampanoag** *or* **wampanoags** *usu cap* [Natick *Wampan-ohke*, lit., eastern land, fr. *wampan* white, light, of the dawn + *ohke* land, earth] **1 :** an Indian people of Rhode Island east of Narragansett Bay and neighboring parts of Massachusetts **2 :** a member of the Wampanoag people

[1]**wam·pee** \wäm'pē *also* wȯm-\ *n* -s [of Algonquian origin; akin to Natick *wampan*, *wómpi* white, Shawnee *wapa*] **1** *South* **:** PICKERELWEED 1 **2** *South* **:** ARROW ARUM

[2]**wampee** *also* **wam·pi** \"\ *n* -s [Chin (Pek) *huang*[2] *-p'i*[2], fr. *huang*[2] yellow + *p'i*[2] skin] **:** an Asiatic tree (*Clausena lansium*) of the family Rutaceae cultivated in Hawaii; *also* **:** its fruit which is about the size of a large grape and which has a hard rind

wam·pish \'wampish\ *vb* -ED/-ING/-ES [origin unknown] *Scot* **:** FLUCTUATE, SWING

wam·pum \'wämpəm *also* 'wȯmp-\ *n* -s [short for *wampumpeag*, fr. Narraganset *wampompeag*, fr. *wampan* white + *api* string + *-ag*, pl. suffix] **1 :** beads made of shells polished and strung together in strands, belts, or sashes and used by the No. American Indians as money, ceremonial pledges, and ornaments **2** *slang* **:** MONEY

wampum belt *n* **:** a belt of varicolored wampum arranged in patterns and used as a mnemonic device or ceremonially esp. in the ratification of treaties — compare WAR BELT

wam·pum·peag \-pəm,pēg\ *n* -s [Narraganset *wampompeag* — more at WAMPUM] **:** WAMPUM; *esp* **:** wampum made of the less valuable white rather than dark purple or black shell beads

wampum snake *n* **:** any of several brightly marked American snakes (as the horned viper or hoop snake)

wam·pus \'wämpəs *also* 'wȯm-\ *n* -ES [prob. short for *catawampus*] *dial* **:** a strange, objectionable, or monstrous person or thing

wa·mus *or* **wam·mus** \'wȯməs, 'wäm-\ *or* **war·mus** \'wȯrm-\ *n* -ES [D *wambuis, wammes*, fr. MD *wambeis*, fr. OF *wambeisun*, aug. of *wambeis, gambais* doublet, of Gmc origin; akin to OHG *wamba* belly — more at WOMB] *dial* **:** a warm work jacket made usu. in a belted cardigan style and of sturdy knitted or woven fabric

[1]**wan** \'wän *also* 'wȯn\ *adj* **wanner; wannest** [ME, fr. OE *wann, wan* dark, gloomy, livid] **1** *archaic* **:** DARK, DUSKY **:** lead-colored ⟨~ water⟩ **2 a :** suggesting poor health **:** SICKLY, PALLID ⟨a ~ complexion⟩ **b :** lacking human vitality **:** FEEBLE ⟨a ~ personality⟩ **3 a :** DIM, LUSTERLESS ⟨~ stars⟩ **b :** barely perceptible **:** FAINT ⟨a ~ light⟩ **4 :** showing little effort **:** LANGUID ⟨a ~ laugh⟩ **5 :** tending toward or suggestive of failure or incompetence **:** INEFFECTUAL ⟨~ efforts⟩

[2]**wan** \"\ *vb* **wanned; wanned; wanning; wans** *vi* **:** to grow or become pale or sickly ~ *vt* **:** to make wan **:** cause to appear pale or sickly

[3]**wan** \"\ *n* -s **:** PALENESS, PALLOR

[4]**wan** \'wän *also* 'wȯn\ *dial var of* ONE

wan·chancy \wän'chan(t)sē\ *adj* [Sc *wanchance* misfortune (fr. *wan-* deficient, mis- — fr. ME — + *chance*) + *-y* — more at WANTON] *chiefly Scot* **:** ILL-FATED, MISCHIEVOUS ⟨the ~ bullet maun have weakened his chest —John Buchan⟩; *also* **:** UNCANNY, WEIRD

wand \'wänd *also* 'wȯnd\ *n* -s [ME *wond, wande*, fr. ON *vǫndr*; akin to Goth *wandus* rod, OE *windan* to wind, twist — more at WIND] **1** *archaic* **:** a slender often flexible pole used as a pointer, goad, or whip or for fishing or measuring **2 a :** a slender wooden or metal staff carried (as by a verger, beadle, or sheriff) often in advance of a dignitary in a procession **:** VERGE **b** *Scots law* **:** a baton or staff that with the blazon constitutes the insignia of a messenger of a court that must be shown in executing a caption **3 a :** a slender rod often carried by fairies or other beings associated with magic or the supernatural **b :** a slender flexible rod used by conjurers and magicians **4 a :** a peeled stick stuck up as a mark for archers in England **b :** a slat 6 feet by 2 inches used in the U.S. as a target in archery and stood at 100 yards for men and at 60 for women **5 a :** a light rod of wood or metal used in calisthenic exercises or mass gymnastic displays **b :** the rigid tube between the hose and nozzle of a vacuum cleaner

wand bearer *n* **:** a verger in some English cathedrals

[1]**wan·der** \'wändə(r) *also* 'wȯn-\ *vb* **wandered; wandered; wandering** \-d(ə)riŋ\ **wanders** [ME *wandren, wanderen*, fr. OE *wandrian*; akin to MD & MLG *wanderen* to wander, MHG *wandern*, OE *windan* to turn, wind, twist — more at WIND] *vi* **1 a :** to move about without a fixed course, aim, or goal ⟨~ about the world⟩ **b :** to go idly about for pleasure or relaxation ⟨a crowd ~*ing* on a village green⟩ **2 a :** to travel esp. slowly by a devious or indirect route **:** take a roundabout or leisurely course ⟨cattle ~*ing* toward pasture⟩ **b :** to take a slow winding course **:** MEANDER ⟨a ~*ing* stream⟩ **3 a :** to deviate (as from a path or course) **:** STRAY ⟨~ from a trail⟩ **b :** to go astray morally **:** ERR ⟨~ from proper conduct⟩ **4 :** to depart from normal mental status **:** lose touch with everyday rational conduct **:** become harmlessly irrational ⟨old men with ~*ing* minds⟩ **5 :** to pass esp. without plan from one to another **:** CIRCULATE ⟨a ~*ing* rumor⟩ ~ *vt* **:** to roam over ⟨~ woodlands⟩

[2]**wander** \"\ *n* -s **:** the act or action of wandering **:** RAMBLE, STROLL ⟨out for a ~ in the countryside⟩

wan·der·er \-dərə(r)\ *n* -s **:** one that wanders: as **a** *cap* **:** a Scottish Covenanter during the time of persecution **b** (1) **:** a brown and black American butterfly (*Feniseca tarquinius*) of the family Lycaenidae whose larva feeds on woolly aphids of the genus *Schizoneura* esp. on the alder blight; *also* **:** a monarch or other butterfly of the genus *Danaus* (2) **:** WANDERING SPIDER

[1]**wandering** *n* -s [ME, fr. gerund of *wanderen* to wander] **1 :** a going or traveling about from place to place esp. pointlessly or leisurely — often used in pl. **2 :** movement away from the proper, normal, or usual course — often used in pl. **3 :** mental deviation usu. of a harmless nature — often used in pl.

[2]**wandering** *adj* [ME, fr. pres. part. of *wanderen* to wander] **:** characterized by aimless, slow, or pointless movement: as **a :** WINDING, MEANDERING ⟨a ~ course⟩ **b :** not keeping a rational or sensible course **:** VAGRANT, ERRANT **c :** NOMADIC ⟨~ tribes⟩ **d** *of a plant* **:** having long runners or tendrils **:** TRAILING **e :** FLOATING ⟨~ kidney⟩

wandering albatross *n* [[2]*wandering*] **:** a large black-winged white albatross (*Diomedea exulans*) widely distributed in southern oceans

wandering ant *n* **:** ARMY ANT

wandering cell *n* **:** an amoeboid phagocyte: as **a :** an actively motile reticuloendothelial cell of the tissues **b :** LEUKOCYTE

wandering dune *n* **:** a dune slowly shifted by the wind because it has not sufficient vegetation to anchor it

wandering jenny *n* **:** MONEYWORT

wandering jew *n, usu cap J* [after the *Wandering Jew*, legendary figure condemned to wander the earth until the second coming of Christ for having mocked at Him on His way to the crucifixion] **1 :** any of several plants of the genera *Zebrina* and *Tradescantia*; *esp* **:** either of two trailing or creeping cultivated plants (*Zebrina pendula* and *Tradescantia fluminensis*) **2** *dial Brit* **a :** STRAWBERRY GERANIUM **b :** KENILWORTH IVY

wan·der·ing·ly *adv* **:** in a wandering manner

wandering milkweed *n* **:** SPREADING DOGBANE

wan·der·ing·ness *n* -ES **:** the quality or state of being wandering, errant, aimless, or pointless

wandering of the poles [[1]*wandering*] **:** the change in position of the terrestrial poles within an area not over 40 feet in diameter caused by slight more or less cyclic shifts of the body of the earth on its rotational axis and resulting in the variation of latitude

wandering rash *n* [[2]*wandering*] **:** GEOGRAPHIC TONGUE

wandering sailor *also* **wandering sally** *n* **:** MONEYWORT

wandering spider *n* **:** a spider that wanders about in search of its prey rather than trapping it with a fixed web

wandering star *n* **:** any of the seven planets of ancient astronomy

wandering tattler *n* **:** either of two shorebirds (*Heteroscelus incanus* and *H. brevipes*) summering on the coasts and interior of Alaska and Siberia and wintering in many Pacific islands and being similar in form and size to the yellowlegs although the color of their upperparts is a uniform slaty gray

wan·der·lust \'wändə(r),ləst *also* 'wȯn-\ *n* [G, fr. *wandern* to wander (fr. MHG) + *lust* desire, pleasure, fr. OHG — more at WANDER, LUST] **:** strong or unconquerable longing for or impulse toward wandering or traveling — **wan·der·lust·er** \-tə(r)\ *n* — **wan·der·lust·ful** \-tfəl\ *adj*

wan·der·oo \¦wändə¦rü *also* ¦wȯn-\ *n* -s [Sinhalese *vanduru*, pl. of *vandurā*, fr. Skt *vānara* monkey — more at BANDAR] **1 :** PURPLE-FACED LANGUR **2 :** LION-TAILED MACAQUE

wanders *pres 3d sing of* WANDER, *pl of* WANDER

wander termite *n* **:** any of various termites that forage in the open and do not like the majority remain in the shelter of their nests and galleries

wanderyear \'==,=\ *n* [trans. of G *wanderjahr*] **:** a year of wandering or traveling esp. before settling down to one's trade or profession

W and F *abbr* water and feed

wandflower \'=,==\ *n* [*wand* + *flower*] **1 :** a plant or flower of the genus *Sparaxis*; *esp* **:** a showy often cultivated plant (*S. tricolor*) with tawny yellow often purple-spotted flowers **2 :** GALAX 2

W and I *abbr* weighing and inspection

wan·dle \'wandᵊl\ *adj* [prob. irreg. fr. *wand*] *chiefly Scot* **:** SUPPLE, AGILE

wan·doo \(')wän¦dü\ *n* -s [native name in Australia] **:** a gum tree (*Eucalyptus redunca*) of western Australia yielding a hard tough durable wood and a tanning extract

W and R *abbr* **1** water and rail **2** welfare and recreation

wands *pl of* WAND

W and S *abbr, often not cap* whiskey and soda

wand shoot *n* **:** a round of 36 arrows shot at a wand

wand shot *n* **:** one of the shots of a wand shoot

wands·man \'wän(d)zmən *also* 'wȯn-\ *n, pl* **wandsmen** [*wand's* (gen. of *wand*) + *man*] **:** WAND BEARER

[1]**wane** \'wān\ *vi* -ED/-ING/-S [ME *wanien, wanen*, fr. OE *wanian*; akin to OHG *wanōn* to wane, ON *vana* to lessen; all fr. a prehistoric Gmc adj. represented by OE & OHG *wan* wanting, deficient, absent, ON *vanr*, Goth *wans*; akin to L *vanus* empty, vain, Gk *eunis* bereft, lacking, Skt *ūna* wanting, deficient, and perh. to L *vacare* to be empty, *vacuus* empty] **1 :** to decrease in size or extent **:** DWINDLE: as **a :** to diminish in phase or intensity — used of the moon and other satellites and inferior planets; opposed to *wax*; see MOON illustration **b :** to become less in brilliance or power **:** grow dim — used of light or color **c :** to flow out **:** EBB — used of water or the tide **2 :** to fall esp. gradually from power, prosperity, or influence **:** DECAY, DECLINE ⟨a *waning* political party⟩

[2]**wane** \"\ *n* -s [ME, fr. *wanen* to wane] **1 a :** the act or action of decreasing or of diminishing ⟨strength on the ~⟩ **b :** the period or time of decreasing or diminishing ⟨the ~ of colors of a sunset⟩ **2 :** the act, time, or phenomenon of decreasing in phase or intensity; *specif* **:** the period from full phase of the moon to the new moon **3** [ME, defect, shortage, fr. OE *wana*; akin to OE *wan* deficient — more at [1]WANE] **:** an edge or corner defect in lumber characterized by the presence of bark or by lack of wood — compare WANEY 2

waney *or* **wany** \-nē\ *adj* **wanier; waniest** [[2]*wane* + *-y*] **1 :** waning or diminished in some parts **2** *of sawed timber* **:** cut so near the outside of the log that there is no square edge

wang \'wäŋ\ *n* -s [Chin (Pek) *wang*[2] king, prince] **:** a Chinese ruler before the 3d century B.C. or a Chinese prince of high rank after the 3d century B.C.

wan·ga *or* **ouan·ga** \'waŋgə\ *n* -s [Haitian Creole *ouanga*, of Bantu origin; akin to Kimbundu *wanga* witchcraft, Tshiluba *bwanga* charm, fetish] **:** voodoo sorcery; *also* **:** a voodooistic charm or spell

wan·gen·steen apparatus \'waŋgən,stēn-\ *also* **wangensteen appliance** *n, usu cap W* [after Owen H. *Wangensteen* *b*1898] **:** the apparatus used in Wangensteen suction

wangensteen suction *n, usu cap W* [after Owen H. *Wangensteen* *b*1898 Am. surgeon] **:** a method of draining fluid or secretions from body cavities (as the stomach) by means of an apparatus that operates on negative pressure

[1]**wan·gle** \'waŋgəl, -aiŋ-\ *vb* **wangled; wangled; wangling** \-g(ə)liŋ\ **wangles** [perh. alter. of [1]*waggle*] *vi* **1 :** to extricate oneself (as from a crowd or difficulty) **:** WIGGLE **2 :** to resort to trickery, makeshift, or devious methods ⟨*wangling* to forestall ultimate payment of a debt⟩ ~ *vt* **1 :** SHAKE, WIGGLE **2 :** to adjust or manipulate for personal or fraudulent ends **:** FAKE ⟨~ accounts⟩ **3 :** to make or get by or as if by wriggling ⟨~ one's way through a crowd⟩ **:** FINAGLE ⟨~ an invitation to a party⟩; *also* **:** to persuade or convince by cunning or devious methods ⟨~ a person into loaning money⟩

[2]**wangle** \"\ *n* -s **:** the act of wangling; *also* **:** something procured by wangling

wan·gler \-g(ə)lə(r)\ *n* -s **:** one that wangles

wan·hap \'wän,hap\ *n* [Sc *wan-* deficient, mis- (fr. ME) + *hap* — more at WANTON] *Scot* **:** MISFORTUNE, MISHAP

wan·hap·py \(')=¦hapi\ *adj* [Sc *wan-* + *happy*] *Scot* **:** UNFORTUNATE

wan·hsi·en \'wänshē'en\ *adj, usu cap* [fr. *Wanhsien*, city of south central China] **:** of or from the city of Wanhsien, China **:** of the kind or style prevalent in Wanhsien

wan·i·gan *or* **wannigan** \'wälnəgən, |nēg- *also* 'wȯl\ *or* **wan·gan** *or* **wan·gun** \|ŋg-\ *n* -s [of Algonquian origin; akin to Abnaki *waniigan* trap, lit., that into which something strays] **1 :** a chest for supplies **2 :** a shelter for sleeping, eating, storage, or office space often mounted on wheels or crawler treads and towed by tractor or mounted on a raft or boat **3 :** debts incurred by lumbermen at a company store

waning *pres part of* WANE

wan·ion \'wänyən\ *n* -s [fr. the obs. phrase *in the waniand* unluckily, lit., in the waning (moon), fr. ME, fr. *waniand*, northern pres. part. of *wanien* to wane] *archaic* **:** PLAGUE, VENGEANCE — used in the phrase *with a wanion*

wan·ka·pin \'wäŋkə,pin\ *n* -s [Ojibwa *wankipin*, lit., crooked root] **:** WATER CHINQUAPIN

wan·kle \'waŋkəl\ *adj* [ME *wankel, wankill*, fr. OE *wancol*; akin to OHG *wanchal* unsteady, *wankōn* to stagger, sway — more at WINK] **1** *chiefly dial* **:** UNSTEADY, UNSTABLE; *also* **:** FICKLE, IRRESOLUTE **2** *chiefly dial* **:** SICKLY, FEEBLE

wan·ky \'waŋkē\ *adj* -ER/-EST [alter. of *wankle*] *dial* **:** WEAK, FEEBLE

wan·ly *adv* [ME *wanliche*, fr. [1]*wan* + *-liche* -ly] **:** in a feeble, pale, sickly, or languid manner

wanned *past of* WAN

wan·ne–eick·el \'vänə'īkəl\ *adj, usu cap W&E* [fr. *Wanne-Eickel*, industrial city of western Germany] **:** of or from the city of Wanne-Eickel, Germany **:** of the kind or style prevalent in Wanne-Eickel

wanner *comparative of* WAN

wan·ness \'wännəs *also* 'wȯn-\ *n* -ES [ME *wannesse*, fr. [1]*wan* + *-nesse* -ness] **:** the quality or state of being wan

wannest *superlative of* WAN

wanning *pres part of* WAN

wans *pres 3d sing of* WAN, *pl of* WAN

[1]**want** \'wänt\ *n* -s [ME *wont, wonte*, fr. OE *wand, wond*; prob. akin to OE *windan* to turn, wind — more at WIND] *dial Brit* **:** a European mole (*Talpa europaeus*)

[2]**want** \'wȯnt, 'wänt; *want to is often* 'wȯn(t)ə *or* 'wän(t)ə\ *vb* -ED/-ING/-S [ME *wanten*, fr. ON *vanta*; akin to ON *vanr* wanting, deficient — more at WANE] *vt* **1 :** to fail to possess the required or usual amount of **:** LACK ⟨~ strength to walk⟩ **:** be deficient in ⟨~ courtesy⟩ **2 a** (1) **:** to desire without reservation **:** wish earnestly — used with the infinitive ⟨~*ing* to rise in the world⟩ ⟨~*s* to be home⟩ (2) **:** to feel a profound yearning for **:** CRAVE ⟨~ relaxation⟩ **b :** to be inclined to **:** LIKE ⟨call it what you ~, the judge said it was murder⟩ **3** *dial* **:** to dispense with **:** do without **4 :** to have need of **:** REQUIRE ⟨this motor ~*s* the attention of a good mechanic⟩ **5 :** to suffer from the lack of ⟨thousands ~*ing* food and shelter⟩ **6 :** to be under obligation **:** OUGHT, SHOULD — used

with the infinitive ⟨you ~ to act decently in all situations⟩ **7 :** to wish or demand the presence of ⟨the boss ~*s* you in the front office⟩ **:** wish to speak to or see ⟨the teacher ~*s* you⟩ **8 :** to hunt or seek for apprehension ⟨~*ed* for war crimes⟩ ~ *vi* **1 a** *archaic* **:** to be lacking or nonexistent **:** fail to be present, available, or forthcoming **b :** to be deficient or short ⟨it ~*s* three minutes to twelve⟩ **2 :** to be in need (as of food or shelter) **:** be needy or destitute ⟨the family would never allow their children to ~⟩ **3 :** to have or feel need **:** LONG — usu. used with *for* and sometimes *of* ⟨never ~*s* for friends⟩ **4 a :** to be necessary or needed ⟨it ~*s* no extended examination . . . to reveal the egregious character of the supposition —C.I.Lewis⟩ **b :** to become required **:** become morally demanded ⟨it ~*s* all our efforts to succeed⟩ **5 :** to desire earnestly to come or go — used with a directional adverb ⟨the visitor ~*s* in⟩ ⟨the dog ~*s* out⟩ **syn** see DESIRE, LACK

³want \'wȯnt, 'wänt\ *n* -s [ME, fr. *wanten* to want] **1 a :** the quality or state of lacking ⟨~ of common sense⟩ or failing to possess a required or usual amount ⟨a loss incurred by his ~ of two points⟩ **b :** dire need (as of the necessities of life) **:** DESTITUTION ⟨a nation living in ~⟩ **2 a :** something needed or desired ⟨sufficient means to satisfy his moderate ~*s*⟩ **b :** something wished for or wanted ⟨his ~*s* are rarely satisfied⟩ **c :** a feeling of lacking something coupled with the desire or need for it **3 :** personal defect **:** FAULT ⟨whatever his ~*s*, he has always been honest⟩ **syn** see ABSENCE

want ad *n* **:** an advertisement in the classified section of a newspaper stating that something is wanted (as an employee, employment, or a specified article)

want·age \-tij\ *n* -s [²*want* + *-age*] **:** amount wanting **:** SHORTAGE

wantage rod *n* **:** a graduated rod used as a gage of wantage in the contents of a cask or barrel

wanted circular *n* [*wanted* past part. of ²*want;* fr. the use of the word as a heading for the circular] **:** a circular that bears the picture and description of a person charged with a crime and identifies the police seeking his arrest

want·er \-tə(r)\ *n* -s **1 :** one that wants or is in need **2** *dial* **:** one wanting a spouse; *esp* **:** BACHELOR

wanthill \'wänt,hil\ *n* [ME *wonthill*, fr. *wont* want, mole + *hill*] *dial Brit* **:** MOLEHILL

¹wanting *adj* [fr. pres. part. of ²*want*] **1 :** not present **:** not being in evidence **:** ABSENT ⟨seed plants are totally ~ there —R.E.Coker⟩ **2 a :** not being up to standards or expectations ⟨I cannot feel that even the programs I find ~ are all of low quality —Gilbert Seldes⟩ **b :** lacking in natural or required ability or capacity **:** DEFICIENT ⟨a candidate tested and found ~⟩ ⟨~ in common sense⟩ **c** *chiefly dial* **:** mentally defective ⟨"What does Amen mean?" was always asked of the youngest Todd child, who was, poor boy, ~ —Margaret Deland⟩ **3** *obs* **:** being in need **:** DESTITUTE

²wanting *prep* [fr. pres. part. of ²*want*] **1 :** not with **:** WITHOUT ⟨a book ~ a cover⟩ **2 :** LESS, MINUS ⟨a month ~ two days⟩

want·less \'≈ləs\ *adj* **:** being without want or desire

want·less·ness *n* -ES [*wantless* + *-ness*] **:** the quality or state of being without want or desire

want list *n* **:** a list compiled (as by a hobbyist or the curator of a collection) that indicates specific items lacking and needed and that is circulated among dealers and retailers

¹wan·ton \'wȯnt°n, 'wän-, -tən\ *adj* [ME, fr. *wan-* deficient, wrong, mis- (fr. OE, fr. *wan* wanting, deficient) + *towen*, past part. of *teen* to draw, train, discipline, fr. OE *tēon* — more at WANE, TOW] **1** *archaic* **:** lacking discipline **:** not susceptible to control **:** UNRULY **2 :** excessively merry or gay **:** FROLICSOME ⟨a ~ party⟩ ⟨~ holidays⟩ **3 :** UNCHASTE, LEWD, LUSTFUL ⟨~ books⟩; *also* **:** SENSUAL **4** *obs* **:** given to self-indulgence and the enjoyment of luxury **:** VOLUPTUOUS **5 a :** marked by or manifesting heedless disregard of justice or of the rights, safety, and feelings of others **:** brutally insolent **:** MERCILESS, INHUMANE ⟨~ victors⟩ ⟨~ cruelty⟩ ⟨~ exercise of power⟩ **b :** having no just foundation or real provocation **:** willfully malicious ⟨a ~ attack⟩ ⟨~ insults⟩ ⟨~ prejudice⟩ **6 :** being without check or limitation **:** UNRESTRAINED: as **a :** luxuriantly rank ⟨~ vegetation⟩ **b :** unduly lavish **:** EXTRAVAGANT, PRODIGAL ⟨~ imagination⟩ ⟨~ speech⟩

²wanton \"\ *n* -s **1 :** a pampered or overindulged individual; *esp* **:** a spoiled child **2 :** an excessively playful or frolicsome child or animal **3 :** a person given over to luxurious self-enjoyment **:** TRIFLER ⟨play the ~⟩ **4 :** a lewd or lascivious person

³wanton \"\ *vb* -ED/-ING/-S *vi* **1 :** to engage in amorous play **:** DALLY **2 :** to indulge in a continuous carefree or voluptuous mode of living **:** play the voluptuary **3 :** to wallow in unrestrained brutality and cruelty **4 :** to be or become excessively free or extravagant (as in growth, expression, or conduct) **:** LUXURIATE **5 :** to spend time trifling ~ *vt* **:** to pass or waste wantonly or in wantonness ⟨~ money away⟩

wan·ton·er \"+ə(r)\ *n* -s [¹*wanton* + *-er*] **:** one that wantons **:** WANTON

wan·ton·ly *adv* [ME, fr. ¹*wanton* + *-ly*] **:** in a wanton manner ⟨~ wasting time⟩ ⟨animals ~ killed for sport⟩ ⟨~ disrespectful of personal liberty⟩

wan·ton·ness \-t°n(n)əs, -tən(-\ *n* -ES [ME *wantonnes*, fr. ¹*wanton* + *-nes* -ness] **1 :** the quality or state of being wanton ⟨ideas characterized chiefly by their sheer ~⟩ ⟨the ~ of jungle growth⟩ ⟨negligence amounting to ~⟩ **2 :** an instance or example of wanton action

wants *pres 3d sing of* WANT, *pl of* WANT

wantwit \'≈,≈\ *n* [ME, fr. *wanten* to want + *wit*] **:** a person wanting wit **:** FOOL

wan·ty \'wänti\ *n* -ES [ME *wayntе, wanteye*, prob. fr. *wame, wamb* belly + *tey, tye* tie — more at WAME, WOMB, TIE] *dial Brit* **:** GIRTH, SURCINGLE; *also* **:** a leather tie

wany *var of* WANEY

wanze \'wänz\ *vb* -ED/-ING/-S [ME *wansen*, fr. OE *wansian*, fr. *wan* wanting, deficient — more at WANE] *archaic* **:** WANE, DECREASE

¹wap \'wap, 'wäp\ *vi* **wapped; wapped; wapping; waps** [ME *wappen*, prob. of imit. origin] **1** *dial* **:** to pull or throw roughly **2** *dial* **:** BEAT, STRIKE **3** *dial* **:** to blow in gusts

²wap \"\ *n* -s [ME, fr. *wappen* to throw, strike, blow in gusts] **1** *dial* **:** BLOW, KNOCK **2** *Scot* **a :** BLAST, STORM **b :** FIGHT

³wap \"\ *vt* **wapped; wapped; wapping; waps** [ME *wappen*, of unknown origin] *dial* **:** to fold up **:** BIND, WRAP

⁴wap \"\ *n* -s **1** *dial* **:** a wrapping (as a turn of string around a rope or other string) **2** *dial* **:** a bundle or truss of straw

wap·a·too \'wäpə,tü\ *or* **wapata** *or* **wapato** *or* **wappato** *n* -s [Chinook jargon *wapatoo*, fr. Cree *wāpatowa* white mushroom] **:** either of two plants of the genus *Sagittaria* (*S. latifolia* and *S. cuneata*) having edible tubers

wap·en·take \'wapən,tāk, 'wäp- *also* 'wȯp-\ *n* -s [ME, fr. OE *wǣpentæc*, fr. ON *vāpnatak* act of grasping weapons, fr. *vāpna* (gen. pl. of *vāpn* weapon) + *tak* act of grasping, fr. *taka* to take; prob. fr. the brandishing of weapons as an expression of approval when the chief of the wapentake entered upon his office — more at WEAPON, TAKE] **1 :** a subdivision of some English shires (as Leicestershire, Lincolnshire, Northamptonshire, Nottinghamshire, and Yorkshire) corresponding to a hundred **2 :** the court or court bailiff of a wapentake

wa·pi·si·a·na \,wə,pēsē'änə\ *or* **wa·pi·sha·na** \,wäpē'shänə\ *n, pl* **wapisiana** *or* **wapisianas** *or* **wapishana** *or* **wapishanas** *usu cap* **1 a :** an Arawakan people of southern Surinam and adjacent parts of Brazil **b :** a member of such people **2 :** the language of the Wapisiana people

wa·pi·ti \'wäpəd·ē, -ətē, -i *also* 'wȯp-\ *n, pl* **wapiti** *or* **wapitis** [of Algonquian origin; akin to Cree *wapitew* white, whitish, Shawnee *wapiti;* fr. its white rump and tail] **1 :** a North American deer (*Cervus canadensis* and related forms) that is similar to the European red deer but considerably larger, has antlers with a long heavy beam with brow antler, bay antler, royal antler, surroyal tine, and forked terminal tines but no palmations or cuplike crown, a light reddish buff body becoming a dark brown on the head and limbs and blackish on the belly, and a short tail and large rump patch of buffy white, and that is nearly extinct over most of the U.S. — called also *elk* **2 :** an eastern Asiatic red deer (*Cervus elaphus xanthopygus*) related to the wapiti — called also *Altai wapiti*

wap·pen·schaw·ing \'wapən,shȯ·iŋ\ *or* **wap·pen·schaw** \-,shȯ\ *n* -s [ME (northern dial.) *wapynschawyng*, fr. *wapen* weapon (fr. ON *vāpn*) + *schawing*, gerund of *schawen* to show, fr. OE *scēawian* to look, look at — more at WEAPON, SHOW] **:** an exhibition of arms according to individual rank formerly made at various seasons in each district of Scotland

wap·per-jawed \¦wäpə(r)¦jȯd\ *adj* [origin unknown] **:** having a crooked, undershot, or wry jaw

wap·pin·ger \'wäpinjə(r)\ *n, pl* **wappinger** *or* **wappingers** *usu cap* [of Algonquian origin; akin to Natick *Wampan-ohke*, lit., eastern land — more at WAMPANOAG] **1 :** an Indian people living between the lower Hudson and Connecticut rivers **2 :** a member of the Wappinger people

wap·po \'wä(,)pō\ *n, pl* **wappo** *or* **wappos** *usu cap* [AmerSp *guapo* brave, fr. Sp, showy, good-looking] **1 a :** an Indian people of northwestern California **b :** a member of such people **2 :** a Yukian language of the Wappo people

waqf *or* **wakf** \'wəkf\ *n* -s [Ar *waqf*] **1 :** an Islamic endowment of property to be held in trust and used for a charitable or religious purpose **2 :** a Muslim religious or charitable foundation created by an endowed trust fund

¹war \'wȯ(ə)r, 'wȯ(ə)\ *n* -s *often attrib* [ME *werre, warre*, fr. ONF *werre*, of Gmc origin; akin to OHG *werra* confusion, strife; akin to OHG *werran* to confuse, L *verrere* to sweep, and perh. to Gk *erhein* to go, go to ruin] **1 a** (1) **:** a state of usu. open and declared armed hostile conflict between political units (as states or nations) ⟨~ cannot exist between two countries unless each of them has its own government —E.D. Dickinson⟩ — see CIVIL WAR, COLD WAR, LIMITED WAR; compare BATTLE, RIOT (2) **:** a period of armed conflict between political units ⟨the neighboring countries fought a ~ over the disputed territory⟩ — sometimes used in pl. ⟨gone off to the ~*s*⟩; *also* **:** STATE OF WAR 2 (3) **:** STATE OF WAR 1b ⟨hostilities were officially ended . . . though . . . the ~ was not yet officially over —F.A.Ogg & P.O.Ray⟩ **b** *archaic* **:** an engagement in a war **:** BATTLE **c :** the art, activity, profession, or science of military operations **:** the methods and principle of warfare **d** (1) *obs* **:** weapons and equipment for war (2) *archaic* **:** soldiers armed and equipped for war **e :** a conflict carried on by one or a few of the normal means of war or one field of military activity distinguished from other activities in a war ⟨a naval ~ for control of trade routes⟩ ⟨integrating the conduct of the ground and air ~*s*⟩ **2 a :** a state of hostility, conflict, opposition, or antagonism between mental, physical, social, or other forces ⟨these factions were more at ~ than were the two real political parties —Roy Lewis & Angus Maude⟩ ⟨the children would in all probability fare better in peace with one parent than in ~ with two —E.F.Melson⟩ ⟨making ~ on the periodic invasion of insects —Emery Neff⟩ ⟨his innate gentleness at ~ with his fierce sense of power —Robert Payne⟩ **b :** a struggle of any degree of intensity carried on between opposing forces (as desires, social groups, or physical forces) in a particular field or by a particular means or for a particular goal ⟨a ~ against want and destitution and economic demoralization —F.D. Roosevelt⟩ ⟨price ~⟩ ⟨a ~ of scurrilous pamphlets —V.L. Parrington⟩ ⟨a personal ~ against engulfment in the provincial pattern of conformity —Henry Cavendish⟩ ⟨class ~⟩ **3 :** a card game for children in which the cards are turned up one by one, the highest takes the others, and a tie occasions a situation in which the next turn decides; *also* **:** the situation occasioned by a tie in the game of war

²war \"\ *vi* **warred; warred; warring; wars** [ME *werrien, werren, warren*, fr. *werre* war] **1 :** to make or wage war **:** carry on armed hostilities ⟨nations . . . *warred* repeatedly against their victims and against one another —H.R.Isaacs⟩ **2 :** to be in active or vigorous conflict or contention esp. during an extended period ⟨the desire for life *warred* with his fear and hate of it —Douglas Stewart⟩ ⟨landowners and squatters *warred* for years over clouded titles —Julian Dana⟩ **syn** see CONTEND

³war \'wȧr\ *adv* (*or adj*) [ME *werre, war*, fr. ON *verri*, adj., *verr*, adv. — more at WORSE] *chiefly Scot* **:** WORSE

⁴war \"\ *vt* **warred; warred; warring; wars** [ME *warren*, fr. ³*war*] *Scot* **:** WORST, OVERCOME

⁵war \'wȧr\ *dial past of* BE

war *abbr* warrant

wa·ra·bi \'wȯrəbē, wə'räbē\ *n* -s [Jap] **:** a brake (*Pteridium aquilinum*) whose young fronds are eaten in Japan

wa·ral *or* **wor·ral** *or* **wor·rel** \'wȯrəl\ *n* -s [Ar *waral*] **:** an African monitor (*Varanus niloticus*) that is semiaquatic, attains a length of five feet, and lives chiefly on fish and on crocodile eggs

wa·ran·gal \'wərəngəl\ *adj, usu cap* [*Warangal*, city of south central India] **:** of or from the city of Warangal, India **:** of the kind or style prevalent in Warangal

war·a·tah *or* **war·ra·tau** \¦wȯrə¦tō, -tä\ *n* -s [native name in Australia] **:** an Australian plant of the genus *Telopea* (as *T. speciosissima* and *T. oreades*) with heads of showy crimson flowers

war baby *n* [¹*war*] **1 :** a child born or conceived during a war; *esp* **:** an illegitimate child born in wartime of a serviceman **2 :** an industry or product developed or greatly expanded because of wartime needs ⟨out of the electronic tube . . . has come one particularly tough little . . . *war baby* —*Fortune*⟩ **3 :** a stock or security whose value is greatly enhanced because of a state of war

war bag *or* **war sack** *n* [¹*war;* fr. its being orig. used by soldiers] **:** a gunny sack, duffle bag, or other container in which a cowboy keeps his personal possessions

war belt *n* **:** a wampum belt used either to transmit a declaration of war or to summon allies in case of war

warbird \'≈,≈\ *n* **1 :** a military airplane; *also* **:** a crew member of a military airplane **2** *dial* **:** SCARLET TANAGER

¹war·ble \'wȯrbəl, 'wȯ(ə)b-, *NewEng & N. Y. City often* 'wäb-\ *n* -s [in sense 1, fr. ME *werble*, fr. ONF, of Gmc origin; akin to MHG *wirbel* whirl, tuning peg, OHG *wirbil* whirlwind — more at WHIRL; in other senses, fr. ³*warble*] **1 a :** AIR, TUNE, MELODY; *esp* **:** a joyful song **:** CAROL **b :** a melodious succession of low and pleasing sounds ⟨a canary's ~⟩ **c :** a musical trill **2 :** the action of warbling **3 :** the art or manner of singing with trills, runs, or quavers **4 :** a tone that is produced electronically usu. by an oscillator and is varied in frequency cyclically over a fixed range

²warble \"\ *vi* [ME *warbellen*] *of a hawk* **:** to bring together or cross wings upon the back

³warble \"\ *vb* -ED/-ING/-S [ONF *werbler*, fr. *werble* air, modulation, warble] *vi* **1 a :** to sing in a trilling manner or with many turns and variations **:** sing softly and quaveringly or with rapid modulations in pitch **b** *archaic* **:** to give forth the low murmuring sound of a running brook **:** BABBLE **c :** to make or emit sounds with turns, variations, and rapid modulations in pitch ⟨the bluebird *warbled*, the robin called —John Burroughs⟩ **2 :** to become uttered, sounded, or produced with trills, quavers, and rapid modulations in pitch **3 :** SING ~ *vt* **1 :** to sing or utter in a trilling or quavering manner **:** render with turns, runs, or rapid modulations **:** TRILL ⟨moan and ~ the latest cowboy songs —D.B.Davis⟩ **2 :** to express by or as if by warbling **:** utter musically ⟨boys to ~ the praises of God —Norman Douglas⟩

⁴warble \"\ *vi* [origin unknown] *obs* **:** SHAKE, VIBRATE

⁵warble \"\ *n* -s [perh. of Scand origin; akin to obs. Sw *varbulde* boil, fr. *var* pus + *bulde* swelling; akin to OE *wearr* callosity, *weart* wart and to OE *blāwan* to blow — more at WART, BLOW] **1 :** a swelling under the hide esp. of the back of cattle, horses, and various other mammals caused by the maggot of a botfly or warble fly **2 :** the maggot of a warble fly

war·bled \-bəld\ *adj* [⁵*warble* + *-ed*] **:** infested with warbles — used of an animal or hide

warble fly *n* [⁵*warble*] **:** any of various dipterous flies (as an ox warble fly) of the family Oestridae that lay eggs on the feet and legs of cattle and other mammals whence they are licked off and hatch in the mouth or esophagus and burrow through the tissues to the skin and beneath it to the back of the animal where they live until ready to pupate and cause warbles

war·bler \-bl(ə)r\ *n* -s [³*warble* + *-er*] **1 :** one that warbles **:** SINGER, SONGSTER **2 a :** any of numerous small Old World singing birds of the family Sylviidae many of which are noted songsters and are related more closely to the thrushes with which they are often associated as a subfamily than to the American warblers and are represented in the U.S. only by the kinglets and gnatcatchers — see BLACKCAP, BLUETHROAT, REED WARBLER, SEDGE WARBLER, WHITETHROAT **b :** any of numerous small brightly colored American songbirds that constitute the family Parulidae, are insectivorous, highly migratory, and chiefly arboreal, and have a song which is generally weak and unmusical but very characteristic for each species — called also *wood warbler* — see BLACK-THROATED BLUE WARBLER, CHESTNUT-SIDED WARBLER, WATER THRUSH, YELLOWTHROAT, YELLOW WARBLER; compare CHAT, REDSTART **c :** any of numerous small Australasian birds esp. of the genera *Malurus* and *Gerygone* (family Muscicapidae) **3 :** a twirl or flourish to embellish a bagpipe melody

warbler green *n* **:** a light olive color that is greener and deeper than citrine, redder and deeper than grape green, and redder than old moss green — called also *romantic green*

warbling vireo *n* [*warbling* (pres. part. of ³*warble*) + *vireo*] **:** a vireo (*Vireo gilvus*) of temperate No. America having a grayish green back and whitish underparts

war·bly \-b(ə)lē\ *adj* -ER/-EST [³*warble* + *-y*] **:** marked by warbling **:** QUAVERY ⟨hoarse tuneless and ~ voices —Peggy Bennett⟩

warbonnet \'≈,≈≈\ *n* [¹*war*] **:** a ceremonial headdress of some of the Plains Indians that consists of a cap with an extension down the back and is decorated with feathers of the golden eagle

war bride *n* **1 :** a woman who marries a serviceman ordered into active service in time of war **2 :** a woman who marries a serviceman esp. of a foreign nation met during wartime

war·burg \'wȯr,bərg\ *adj, usu cap* [fr. Otto H. *Warburg* †1938 Ger. physiologist] **:** of, relating to, or of the kind introduced, described, or devised by the German general physiologist Otto Warburg ⟨*Warburg* flasks⟩ ⟨a *Warburg* respirometer⟩

warburg apparatus *n, usu cap W* **:** a complex respirometer consisting of a battery of constant-volume manometer-flask units with a mechanically agitated constant-temperature bath and used esp. in the study of cellular respiration and metabolism or fermentation and other enzymatic reactions

warburg's tincture *n, usu cap W* [after Carl *Warburg* 19th cent. Austrian physician] **:** a liquid preparation containing quinine, aloes, rhubarb, angelica seed, elecampane, saffron, fennel, and other ingredients formerly used as an antiperiodic and invented by Dr. Carl Warburg

warburg's yellow enzyme *n, usu cap W* [after Otto *Warburg* †1970] **:** YELLOW ENZYME a

war captain *or* **war chief** *n* **:** an American Indian chief who is the military leader of his group or tribe

war chest *n* **:** a fund accumulated to finance a war; *broadly* **:** a fund earmarked for a specific purpose, action, or campaign ⟨a *war chest* with which to finance its drive to unionize the steel industry —*N.Y.Times*⟩

war clause *n* **:** a clause included in some life insurance policies issued during wartime that limits the insurer's liability to a return of premiums if the insured dies as a result of war or while serving in the military or naval services outside the home area

war cloud *n* **:** an ominous sign of war **:** a threat of or a situation that threatens war

war club *n* **:** a club used by warriors; *esp* **:** a club-shaped implement used as a weapon by American Indians — compare THROWING-STICK 2

war correspondent *n* **:** a correspondent employed to report news concerning the conduct of a war and esp. of events at the scene of battle

warcraft \'≈,≈\ *n* **1 :** the art of war **:** knowledge and skill in the conduct of military operations **2** *pl* **warcraft :** a military or naval ship or plane

war crime *n* **:** a crime (as genocide, maltreatment of prisoners, or any atrocity) committed during or in connection with war — usu. used in pl.

war cry *n* **1 :** a cry used by a body of fighters in war to encourage each other or to disconcert or terrify the enemy — compare REBEL YELL **2 :** a catchword, phrase, or slogan used to rally people to a group or cause or to emphasize or epitomize a program

¹ward \'wȯ(ə)rd, 'wȯ(ə)d\ *n* -s *often attrib* [ME, fr. OE *weard* (fem.); akin to OHG *warta* act of watching, OE *weard* (masc.) watchman, keeper, guard, OHG *wart*, ON *vörthr*, Goth *daurwards* doorkeeper, OE *warian* to beware, guard — more at WARE] **1 a :** the action or process of guarding **:** WATCH, GUARD, KEEPING, PROTECTION, CARE — used esp. in the phrase *watch and ward* **b :** WARDSHIP **c :** CASTLE-GUARD **d :** WARDHOLDING **2 a :** a group acting as guards **:** GUARD, WATCH **b** *obs* **:** GARRISON **3 :** the state of being under guard or in guardianship; *esp* **:** confinement under guard **:** CUSTODY ⟨put them in ~ in the house of the captain of the guard —Gen 40:3 (AV)⟩ **4 :** a place that is guarded or arranged for one in ward: as **a :** the inner court of a castle or fortress **b** (1) *obs* **:** JAIL, PRISON (2) **:** a division (as a cell, block, or wing) of a prison **c** *Scot* **:** an enclosure for cattle **d** (1) **:** a large room in a hospital where a number of patients are accommodated ⟨a 4-bed ~⟩ ⟨a 12-bed ~⟩ (2) **:** a division in a hospital for the care of patients suffering the same disease ⟨a diabetic ~⟩ ⟨an isolation ~⟩ **5 :** any of various administrative divisions: as **a :** a division, district, or quarter of a town or esp. a city for representative, executive, or magisterial purposes that is often merely or chiefly a division for election purposes and as such is in the larger cities often subdivided into precincts **b :** a division of the English counties of Cumberland and Northumberland and of some Scottish counties corresponding to a hundred **c :** the Mormon local congregation having auxiliary organizations (as Sunday schools and relief societies) and one or more quorums of each office of the Aaronic priesthood **d :** an electoral district in the state of Louisiana **6 :** a projecting ridge of metal in a lock casing or keyhole permitting only the insertion of a key with a corresponding notch; *also* **:** a corresponding notch in a bit of a key **7 :** a person who is under guard, protection, or surveillance: as **a :** a minor who is subject to wardship **b** *obs* **:** an orphan who is underage **c** (1) **:** a person who by reason of minority, lunacy, or other incapacity is under the protection of a court either directly or through a guardian appointed by the court — called also *ward of court;* see WARD IN CHANCERY (2) **:** the condition or status of a ward **d :** a person or sometimes a state, territory, or body of persons under the protection or tutelage of a person, public agency, or government ⟨the Indians who were ~*s* of the United States⟩ **8 a :** a means of defense **:** PROTECTION ⟨this staff is ~ against the darts —Henry Treece⟩ **b** *obs* **:** a guarding or defensive motion or position in fencing

²ward \"\ *vb* -ED/-ING/-S [ME *warden*, fr. OE *weardian;* akin to OHG *wartēn* to observe, watch, take care, ON *vartha* to guard; all fr. a prehistoric WGmc-NGmc verb akin to OE *weard* watchman, guard] *vt* **1 :** to keep watch over **:** keep in safety or custody **:** serve as guard, guardian, or protector for ⟨a warden's business is to ~ the people who are put in his charge —Phil Stong⟩ ⟨the bald mountains that ~ the Cap Rock —Margaret Cousins⟩ **2 a :** to fend off (~ a blow or weapon) **:** PARRY — usu. used with *off* ⟨shields his face with one arm . . . to ~ off a blow —Inez Karma & Gilbert Millstein⟩ **b :** to turn aside (something threatening or harmful) **:** DEFLECT — usu. used with *off* ⟨a magic charm to ~ off evil —M.J. Herskovits⟩ ⟨our nation has ~*ed* off all enemies —D.D. Eisenhower⟩ ~ *vi* **1** *archaic* **:** to fight defensively with a sword, shield, or other weapon **:** parry blows **2** *obs* **:** to take care **:** BEWARE **syn** see PREVENT

¹-ward \-wə(r)d\ *also* **-wards** \-dz\ *adj suffix* [-*ward* fr. ME, fr. OE *-weard;* akin to OHG *-wart, -wert* -ward, ON *-verthr*, Goth *-wairths*, L *vertere* to turn — more at WORTH; *-wards* fr. *-wards*, adv. suffix] **1 :** that moves, tends, faces, or is directed toward ⟨migration city*ward* —V.D.Reed⟩ ⟨the door on the river*ward* side —D.C.Peattie⟩ ⟨advances land*wards* from the . . . coast —W.G.East⟩ ⟨hat with the crown up*ward* —William Cowper⟩ **2 :** that occurs or is situated in the direction of ⟨sunrise to right, sunset left*ward* —George Meredith⟩

²-ward \"\ *or* **-wards** \"\ *adv suffix* [-*ward* fr. ME, fr. OE *-weard*, adj. suffix; *-wards* fr. ME, fr. OE *-weardes*, gen. sing. neut. of *-weard*, adj. suffix] **1 :** in a (specified) spatial or temporal direction ⟨signals beamed up*ward* from the ground —F.B.Colton⟩ ⟨the war has gone north*ward* —H.L.Matthews⟩ ⟨after*ward* vigilantism broke loose —V.H.Jensen⟩ ⟨the coastal plain . . . is confined land*wards* by . . . mountains —W.G. East⟩ **2 :** toward a (specified) point, position, or area ⟨bent earth*ward* by a thousand gales —Norman Douglas⟩ ⟨equator*ward* from this latitude —*Science*⟩

ward·able \'wȯ(r)dəbəl\ *adj* [¹*ward* + *-able*] **:** liable to castle-guard

war dance *n* **1 :** a dance usu. representing war in pantomime that is performed by primitive peoples as preparation for battle or in celebration of victory **2 :** an American Indian dance consisting of vigorous sideward bouncing steps for a mixed round or toe-heel steps for a male solo that is used as a ceremonial dance or show dance **3 :** vigorous jumping about suggestive of an Indian war dance

ward bed *n* **1 :** bed, board, and medical and nursing care in a hospital ward **2 :** care of a patient at expense of the hospital in return for providing an opportunity for clinical study ⟨admitted to a *ward bed* because he was of interest to the doctors⟩

war debt *n* **:** a debt contracted by a state in order to carry on and pay for a war

ward·ed \'wȯrdəd, 'wȯ(ə)d-\ *adj* [¹*ward* + *-ed*] **:** provided with a ward ⟨~ lock⟩ ⟨~ key⟩

ward eight *n* [prob. fr. *Ward Eight*, municipal division of Boston, Mass., where it originated] **:** a mixed drink consisting of whiskey, lemon juice, and grenadine often served with crushed ice and a little soda water in a tall glass and garnished with a maraschino cherry and slice of orange

war democrat *n, usu cap W&D* **:** a member of the Democratic party in the border or northern states of the U.S. who favored the prosecution of the Civil War

war·den \'wȯrdᵊn, 'wȯ(ə)d-\ *n* -s [ME *wardein*, fr. ONF, fr. *warder* to ward, guard, of Gmc origin; akin to OHG *wartēn* to watch, take care — more at WARD] **1 :** one having care or charge of something **:** GUARDIAN, KEEPER **2 :** a person invested with power to govern or control **:** a chief executive officer: as **a :** REGENT 2 **b :** a member of the governing body of a guild and esp. of a livery company of the City of London **c :** an officer in charge of a port or market **d :** the governor of a town, district, or fortress **e :** the chief executive of a borough in Connecticut **f :** the head of a county council in Quebec and the Maritime Provinces **3 a :** an official charged with special supervisory duties or with the enforcement of specified laws or regulations ⟨a game ~⟩ ⟨air raid ~⟩ — see FIRE WARDEN **b :** an official in charge of the operation of a prison **c :** any of various officials of the British crown or royal household having designated administrative duties ⟨~ of the mint⟩ **d** (1) **:** an official in charge of a polling place (2) **:** an officer who formerly presided at meetings of a ward **4 a :** CHURCHWARDEN 2 **b :** any of various British college officials whose duties range from those of a dean to those of a head of residence **c :** either of two officials in a symbolic lodge whose duty is to assist the worshipful master — called also respectively *junior warden, senior warden* **5 :** GATEKEEPER, PORTER

war·den·cy \-nsē\ *n* -ES [*warden* + *-cy*] **:** WARDENSHIP

warden of the peace [trans. of AF *gardeins de la pees*] **:** CONSERVATOR OF THE PEACE

war·den·ship \-n,ship\ *n* [ME, fr. *wardein* warden + *-ship*] **:** the office, jurisdiction, or powers of a warden

¹**ward·er** \'wȯrdər, 'wȯ(ə)də(r\ *n* -s [ME, fr. AF *wardere*, fr. *warde* act of guarding (of Gmc origin; akin to OHG *warta* act of watching) + *-ere* -er — more at WARD] **1 a :** one that keeps guard esp. at a tower, gate, or door **:** WATCHMAN, PORTER **b :** an officer of a secret society who is stationed near the door inside a lodge room during a meeting — compare SENTINEL 3 **2** *Brit* **a :** WARDEN; *esp* **:** CARETAKER, CUSTODIAN **b :** a prison guard

²**warder** \"\ *n* -s [ME, perh. fr. *warden* to ward + *-er*] **:** a truncheon or staff used by a king or commander in chief to signal orders

war·der·ship \-,ship\ *n* [¹*warder* + *-ship*] **:** the office, position, or function of a warder

ward heeler *n* **:** HEELER 4

ward hill \'wȯrd¦-, 'wȯ(ə)d-\ *n* [alter. of earlier E dial. *wart hill*, fr. *wart* beacon (prob. fr. ON *vartha* beacon) + *hill*; akin to OHG *warta* act of watching — more at WARD] *dial Brit* **:** BEACON 1

wardholding \'≠,≠≠\ *n* **:** tenure by military service orig. at the need of a feudal lord

ward·ian case \¦wȯ(r)dēən-\ *n, usu cap W* [Nathaniel B. *Ward* †1868 Eng. botanist, its inventor + E *-ian*] **1 :** a portable case made with glass sides and top and metal, earthen, or wooden base and used in growing or transporting living plants in soil or in pots **2 :** GLASS GARDEN

ward in chancery : a ward under the care of a chancery court

¹**warding** *n* -s [ME, fr. gerund of ²*ward*] *Scot* **:** confinement in prison

²**warding** *n* -s [¹*ward* + *-ing*] **:** the making of warded keys

warding file *n* **:** a thin file used chiefly for cutting wards in keys

ward·ite \'wȯr,dīt\ *n* -s [Henry A. *Ward* †1906 Am. naturalist + E *-ite*] **:** a mineral $Na_4CaAl_{12}(PO_4)_8(OH)_{18}.6H_2O$ consisting of a hydrous basic sodium, calcium, and aluminum phosphate and occurring in green concretionary masses (hardness 5, sp. gr. 2.8)

ward leon·ard system \'wȯrd'lenərd-\ *n, usu cap W&L* [after Harry *Ward Leonard* †1915 Am. electrical engineer & inventor] **:** a regenerative electrical system by which variations in motor speeds for all loads carried by a motor are obtained without rheostatic losses in the main circuit

ward·less \'wȯrdləs\ *adj* **:** having no ward ⟨a ~ key⟩

ward meetinghouse *n* **:** a Mormon center of worship for a ward that is roughly equivalent to a parish church

ward·mote \'wȯ(ə)d,mōt\ *n* -s [ME, fr. ¹*ward* + *mot, mote* moot] *Brit* **:** an assembly of the citizens of a ward; *specif* **:** a meeting usu. sitting as a court that is held in each ward of the City of London and has supervision of matters relating to the watch, police, and weights and measures

ward of court : WARD 7c(1)

war dog *n* **1 :** a dog trained to serve on the battlefield **2 a :** a thoroughly experienced soldier **b :** one who demands or threatens war

war·dour street \'wȯ(r)də(r)-\ *adj, usu cap W&S* [fr. *Wardour Street*, London, England, formerly center of the antique and spurious antique trade] **:** falsely imitative of archaic forms ⟨*Wardour Street* English⟩

ward·ress \'wȯrdrəs, -ȯ(ə)d-\ *n* -ES [¹*warder* + *-ess*] **:** a female warder in a prison

ward·robe \'wȯr,drōb, -ȯ(ə)d-\ *n* [ME *warderobe*, fr. ONF *warderoube*, fr. *warder* to guard (of Gmc origin; akin to OHG *wartēn* to watch, take care) + *roube* booty, robe, of Gmc origin; akin to OHG *roub* booty — more at WARD, ROBE] **1 a :** a room or closet where clothes are kept or stored **:** DRESSING ROOM, CLOTHES CLOSET **b :** a room in a theater where costumes and properties are kept, repaired, and cared for **c :** CLOTHESPRESS 1 **d** (1) **:** WARDROBE TRUNK (2) **:** WARDROBE CASE **2 a :** the collection of wearing apparel and accessories in the possession of one person, family, or institution or for one season, activity, or occupation ⟨his summer ~⟩ ⟨a new ~ for a trip abroad⟩ **b :** a number or collection of one article of dress suitable for various occasions ⟨a topper completed his ~ of hats⟩ **3 :** the department of a royal or noble household given the care of wearing apparel, jewels, and personal articles

wardrobe bed *n* **:** a folding bed serving as a wardrobe when closed

wardrobe case *n* **1 :** a large suitcase having some features (as hangers and compartments) of a wardrobe trunk **2 :** WARDROBE TRUNK

wardrobe trunk *n* **:** an upright trunk in which garments may be hung and other articles packed in separate compartments

wardroom \'≠,≠\ *n* [¹*ward* + *room*] **1 a :** the space in a warship allotted for living quarters to the commissioned officers excepting the captain; *specif* **:** the messroom assigned to these officers **b :** the officers dining in a wardroom **2** *Brit* **:** GUARDROOM

wardrobe trunk

war drum *n* **:** a drum beaten as a summons to war or as an accompaniment to marching or fighting

wards *pl of* WARD, *pres 3d sing of* WARD

-wards — see -WARD

ward school *n* **:** a common school administered by a city ward

ward·ship \'wȯrd,ship, -ȯ(ə)d-\ *n* [ME, fr. ¹*ward* + *-ship*] **1 a :** the office of a guardian or keeper **:** care and protection of a ward **:** the right of guardianship **:** GUARDIANSHIP **b :** the feudal right to the custody of the body of an infant heir of a tenant by knight's service or military sergeanty, by socage, or by copyhold and to the custody of the ward's property orig. with the right of the lord to dispose of the ward in marriage and to retain the rents and profits of his land subject to the ward's right to suitable support and that in guardianship by socage terminated when the ward reached 14 years of age and by military sergeanty at 21; *also* **:** a similar right of wardship under Scots feudal law **2 :** the state of being under a guardian

ward sister *n* **:** a British registered nurse who is in charge of a ward in a hospital

wards·man \'wȯ(ə)dzmən\ *n, pl* **wardsmen** [*wards* (gen. of ¹*ward*) + *man*] *Brit* **:** an inmate or guard in charge of a ward in a prison workhouse

wardwalk *n* **:** a periodical round of the wards of a hospital by a member of the medical staff for observation of patients and for clinical instruction — usu. used in pl.

wardwite \'≠,≠\ *n* [ME, fr. OE *weardwite*, fr. *weard* ward + *wite*] **:** a fine paid by a tenant to his lord for failure to furnish castle-guard

¹**ware** \'wa(a)|(ə)r, 'we|, |ə\ *n* -s [ME, fr. OE *wār*; akin to Fris *wier* seaweed, OE *wīr* wire — more at WIRE] *dial Brit* **:** SEAWEED

²**ware** \"\ *adj* [ME *war, ware*, fr. OE *wær* — more at WARY] **1 :** AWARE, COGNIZANT, CONSCIOUS ⟨was ~ of black looks cast at me —Mary Webb⟩ **2** *archaic* **:** WARY, VIGILANT, HEEDFUL

³**ware** \"\ *vt* -ED/-ING/-S [ME *waren*, fr. OE *warian*; akin to OHG *biwarōn* to keep, protect, ON *vara* to be aware; all fr. a WGmc-NGmc verb derived fr. the adjective represented by OE *wær* aware, cautious — more at WARY] **:** to take heed of **:** beware of **:** AVOID, SHUN — used chiefly as a command to hunting animals ⟨~ chase⟩ ⟨~ rabbit⟩ ⟨~ wheat⟩

⁴**ware** \"\ *n* -s [ME, fr. OE *waru*; akin to MHG *ware* ware, ON *vara* and prob. to OE *wær* aware, cautious, prudent — more at WARY] **1 a :** manufactured articles, products of art or craft, or farm produce offered for sale **:** articles of merchandise **:** GOODS, COMMODITIES ⟨the peddler unpacked his ~⟩ **b :** an item offered for sale **:** an article of merchandise ⟨a favorite ~ is a Bible —Henry Lee⟩ ⟨buses, trucks, diesel engines and other heavy ~*s* —Mitchell Gordon⟩ ⟨fruit-vendors who exposed their ~*s* of brightest hues on the pavement —Norman Douglas⟩ **2 :** goods, commodities, manufactures, or produce of a specific class or kind ⟨coopers' ~⟩ ⟨household ~⟩ ⟨mahogany ~⟩ — usu. used in combination ⟨hard*ware*⟩ ⟨silver*ware*⟩ ⟨tin*ware*⟩ ⟨glass*ware*⟩ ⟨table*ware*⟩: as **a** *Brit* **:** potatoes of marketable size and suitable for table use **b :** FABRICS, CLOTH **c** *obs* **:** LIVESTOCK **d :** pottery, dishes, or other items of fired clay ⟨~ which comes from the kiln cracked —Daniel Rhodes⟩ ⟨a yellow ~ with mottle glaze —*Amer. Guide Series: Md.*⟩ **3 :** an intangible item (as a service or a literary product) that is a marketable commodity ⟨an information officer . . . is under constant pressure to provide more ~*s* —Herbert Agar⟩ ⟨the ~*s* of legitimate show business —*Amer. Guide Series: N.Y. City*⟩ ⟨nothing so quenches the enthusiasm of the teacher as a too-utilitarian view of his ~*s* —Lyle Owen⟩ **4 :** a group of pottery types classified by archaeologists according to characteristics of temper and hardness, type of paste, or similar surface treatment rather than by shape or decoration

⁵**ware** \"\ *n* -s [ME, fr. ON *vār* — more at VERNAL] *Scot* **:** the spring season

⁶**ware** \"\ *vt* [ME *waren*, fr. ON *verja* to clothe, invest, spend — more at WEAR] *Scot* **1 :** SPEND, EXPEND **2 :** SQUANDER, WASTE

war eagle *n* [so called fr. the use of its feathers in war bonnets by the Plains Indians] **:** GOLDEN EAGLE

ware goose *n* [¹*ware*; fr. its feeding on seaweed] *Brit* **:** BRANT

wa·re·hou \¦wärə¦hō, -hau̇\ *n* -s [Maori] **:** a purple and silver sea bream (*Seriola brama*) widely distributed off southern and eastern Australia and New Zealand and esteemed as food

¹**warehouse** \'≠,hau̇s\ *n* [ME *warehous*, fr. ⁴*ware* + *hous* house] **1 :** a structure or room for the storage of merchandise or commodities: **a :** a wholesale establishment of the service type in which large inventories are carried **b :** a wholesale establishment operated by a chain store organization **c :** a place for the storing of surplus or reserve stocks of merchandise by a retail store **d :** a public institution for the storing of goods for others **2** *Brit* **:** RETAIL STORE

²**ware·house** \-au̇z, -au̇s\ *vt* **1 :** to deposit, store, or secure in a warehouse; *specif, Brit* **:** to allow (imported goods) to be deposited in a public or bonded warehouse or in the government or customhouse stores without duty pending payment of duty and consumption in the home market or reexport free from duty **2 :** to put or hold in safekeeping **:** STORE **3 :** to hold a shipment beyond the free time permitted a consignee to obtain or take delivery of his goods

warehouse bond *n* **:** a bond for the safe custody and redelivery of stored goods upon surrender of the warehouse receipt

ware·house·man \'≠,hau̇smən, -au̇zm-, -au̇,sman, -au̇z,man, -ma(ə)n\ *n, pl* **warehousemen 1 :** one who manages or works in a warehouse; *specif* **:** one who acts as a temporary custodian of goods or merchandise stored in his warehouse for a fee **2** *Brit* **:** a wholesale merchant **3 :** a pottery worker who inspects, sorts, and stamps bisque

ware·hous·er \-au̇zə(r)\ *n* [¹*warehouse* + *-er*] **:** WAREHOUSEMAN 1

warehouse receipt *n* **:** a receipt that constitutes a document of title and is issued by a warehouseman engaged in the business of storage for hire

warehouse-to-warehouse insurance *n* **:** marine insurance that covers a cargo through the various stages of transportation, processing, and warehousing from the time it leaves the warehouse of the consignor until it reaches that of the consignee

wareroom \'≠,≠\ *n* **:** a room in which goods are exhibited for sale

wares *pl of* WARE, *pres 3d sing of* WARE

war·fa \'wärfə\ *n* -s [origin unknown] *dial* **:** swayback of lambs

war·fare \'wȯr,fa(a)(ə)r, -fe|, 'wȯ(ə),f. . .|ə\ *n* [ME, military expedition, warfare, fr. *warre*, war + *fare*] **1 :** military operations between enemies **:** armed contest **:** HOSTILITIES, WAR; *broadly* **:** activity undertaken by a political unit (as a state or nation) to weaken or destroy another ⟨diplomatic ~⟩ ⟨economic ~⟩ ⟨psychological ~⟩ **2 :** the process of struggle between competing entities **:** CONFLICT ⟨high hills whose owners wage unceasing ~ with drought —*Amer. Guide Series: Texas*⟩ **3 :** Salvationist evangelical activity

war·fa·rin \'wȯ(r)fərən\ *n* -s [*W*isconsin *A*lumni *R*esearch *F*oundation (its patentee) + coum*arin*] **:** a crystalline compound $C_{19}H_{16}O_4$ that is made by condensation of hydroxycoumarin and benzylidene-acetone, that exerts a biological effect like that of dicoumarol, and that is used as a rodenticide and in medicine as an anticoagulant

war·far·ing \'wȯ(r),fa(a)riŋ, -fer-, -rēŋ\ *n* -s [fr. gerund of obs. E *warfare* to wage war, fr. *warfare*, n.] **:** WARFARE

war feast *n* **:** a victory feast esp. of No. American Indians

war footing *n* **:** the condition of being prepared to undertake or maintain war

war game *n* [trans. of G *kriegspiel*] **1 :** a simulated battle or campaign designed to test concepts rather than the skill of forces or fitness of troops or equipment and usu. conducted in conferences by officers acting as the opposing staffs — compare COMMAND POST EXERCISE, FIELD EXERCISE, MANEUVER **2 :** a two-sided umpired training maneuver with actual elements of the armed forces participating

war gas *n* **:** a gas (sense 5) for use in warfare — compare LACRIMATOR, NERVE GAS, STERNUTATOR, VESICANT

war hammer *n* **:** a weapon having a heavy head usu. with one blunt and one spiked extremity; *esp* **:** one with a long handle for infantry used in medieval warfare esp. for breaking armor

war hatchet *n* **:** a hatchet or tomahawk used by American Indians during war or symbolically in declaring war or peace

war hawk *n* **:** one who clamors for war; *esp* **:** one of a group of American congressmen favoring war with Britain around 1812 primarily in order to annex Canada

warhead \'≠,≠\ *n* **:** the section of a torpedo or other missile containing the explosive, chemical, or incendiary charge and the means of setting it off

war-horse \'≠,≠\ *n* **1 :** a horse used in war; *esp* **:** a powerful horse for military service **:** CHARGER **2 :** a veteran soldier or public person (as a politician) **:** an old campaigner, leader, or partisan who has had a stormy but successful career **3 :** a work of art (as a musical composition, a ballet, or a play) that because of much repetition as part of the standard repertory has become extremely hackneyed ⟨a symphonic *war-horse*⟩ ⟨a *war-horse* of the concert stage⟩

wa·ri \'wä'rē, 'wärē\ *n* -s [fr. native name in western Africa] **:** MANCALA

warier *comparative of* WARY

wariest *superlative of* WARY

war·i·ly \'wa(a)rəlē, 'wer-,'war-, -li\ *adv* [*wary* + *-ly*] **:** in a wary manner **:** CAUTIOUSLY

war·i·ness \-rēnəs, -rin-\ *n* -ES **:** the quality or state of being wary **:** WATCHFULNESS, CAUTION

waring *pres part of* WARE

wa·ring·in \wə'riŋən\ *n* -s [Jav] **:** a common fig (*Ficus benjamina*) of India that resembles the banyan, is often cultivated for ornament, and has inedible fruit

war·i·son \'warəsən\ *n* -s [prob. a misunderstanding by Sir Walter Scott in the *Lay of the Last Minstrel* (1805) of *waryson* in "minstrels, play up for your waryson" in the "Battle of Otterbourne", which is fr. ME *warison* reward, fr. ONF, defense, possessions, fr. *warir* to protect, provide, of Gmc origin; akin to OHG *werien* to defend — more at WEIR] **:** a bugle call to attack

war kite *n* **:** a large kite formerly used to lift a man into the air for military or meteorological observation

wark·loom *or* **wark·lume** \'wär,klüm\ *n* [alter. of earlier *workloom*, fr. ME, fr. *work* + *lome, loom* loom] *Scot* **:** TOOL, IMPLEMENT

war·less \'wȯrləs, -ȯ(ə)l-\ *adj* **:** free from war — **war·less·ly** *adv* — **war·less·ness** *n* -ES

war·li \'wȯrlē\ *n, pl* **warli** *or* **warlis** *usu cap* **1 :** a people of India inhabiting the region north of Bombay **2 :** a member of the Warli people

warlike \'≠,≠\ *adj* [ME *werlik*, fr. *werre* war + *lik* like] **1** *obs* **:** ready for war **:** equipped to fight **2 :** fit for, disposed to, or fond of war **:** BELLICOSE ⟨~ savages⟩ ⟨a ~ disposition⟩ **3 :** of, relating to, concerned with, or useful in war **:** MILITARY, MARTIAL ⟨accused him of supplying the enemy with ~ stores —*Times Lit. Supp.*⟩ **4 :** befitting or characteristic of war or a soldier ⟨~ fury⟩

war·ling \'wärliŋ, 'wȯr- *n* -s [prob. fr. ¹*war* + *-ling*; word coined to contrast with *darling*] **:** a person detested or disliked

war·lock \'wȯr,läk\ *n* -s [ME *warloghe, warlach*, fr. OE *wǣrloga* one that breaks faith, scoundrel, the Devil, fr. *wǣr* faith, troth + *-loga* (fr. *lēogan* to lie, belie, betray) — more at VERY, LIE] **1 :** one given to black magic **:** SORCERER, WIZARD **2 :** CONJUROR

war·lock·ry \'wärləkri\ *n* [*warlock* + *-ry*] *Scot* **:** SORCERY

warlord \'≠,≠\ *n* **1 :** a supreme military leader **2 :** a military commander exercising civil power seized or maintained by force usu. purely from self-interest and usu. over a limited region with or without recognition of a central government, sometimes having effective control over the central government or administration, and sometimes obtaining de facto or de jure recognition of foreign powers

war·lord·ism \'≠,lȯ(r),dizəm\ *n* -s **:** the policies or practices of a warlord

¹**warm** \'wȯ(ə)rm, 'wȯ(ə)m\ *adj* -ER/-EST [ME, fr. OE *wearm*; akin to OHG *warm* warm, ON *varmr*, L *formus* warm, Gk *thermos* hot, Skt *gharma* heat, OPruss *gorme*] **1 a** (1) **:** having or manifesting heat esp. to a moderate or pleasurable degree; *usu* **:** not quite hot ⟨the ~, almost the hot carriage —William Sansom⟩ ⟨so ~ and balmy that the windows were flung open —W.M.Thackeray⟩ (2) **:** perceptibly above bodily temperature without being painful or harmful ⟨a ~ bath⟩ ⟨~ soup⟩ **b :** having the heat naturally appropriate to a living warm-blooded animal ⟨the body was still ~⟩ **c :** sending or giving out heat usu. to a comfortable or beneficial degree **:** producing sensations of heat ⟨a ~ radiator⟩ ⟨the sunshine was ~⟩ **d :** conserving or tending to maintain or preserve heat and esp. a satisfactory degree of heat ⟨~ insulation⟩ ⟨a ~ sweater⟩ **e** (1) **:** marked by or conducive to sensations of heat brought about by strenuous exertion that when resulting from sport or pleasurable exertion are often accompanied by a glow of well-being ⟨~ after playing tennis⟩ ⟨a ~ climb⟩ (2) **:** limber and ready for action after preliminary exercise ⟨rewrite the memorized piece until you feel your hand is ~ —C.I.Blanchard & C.E.Zoubek⟩ **2 a :** comfortably established or settled **:** secure and comfortable ⟨a ~ existence in his old age⟩ **b** *Brit* **:** being in comfortable financial circumstances **:** RICH, WELL-TO-DO **3 a :** marked by strong feeling, passion, or enthusiasm **:** ARDENT, ZEALOUS ⟨being . . . of a ~ and impetuous nature, responded to their affection with quite a tropical ardor —W.M. Thackeray⟩ ⟨expostulated in ~ terms —T.B.Macaulay⟩ **b :** marked by brisk excitement, lively exchanges, sharp disagreement, hot temper, or anger **:** not smooth, mild, soothing, or placating ⟨that political campaign, which was a ~ and bitter one —P.B.Kyne⟩ ⟨continual ~ controversy and occasional litigation —R.I.McDavid⟩ **4 a** (1) **:** readily showing or reacting to love, affection, fondness, appreciative pleasure, or gratitude **:** often demonstratively genial, cordial, sympathetic, or affectionate ⟨his seemingly rough exterior covered a ~ heart —D.E.Smith⟩ ⟨~ with the love of mankind —H.O. Taylor⟩ ⟨a wave of genial friendliness flowed from the ~ silly hearts of Britons —Rose Macaulay⟩ (2) **:** accompanied by, giving rise to, or giving the impression of a feeling of love, tenderness, gratitude, well-being, or pleasure ⟨his eyes . . . met hers with clear, frank, ~ regard —Zane Grey⟩ ⟨the ~ sense of community life —Andrew Phelan⟩ ⟨a rich ~ voice⟩ ⟨revived ~ memories of pleasant times⟩ **b** (1) **:** marked by sexual desire or passion **:** LEWD, LECHEROUS ⟨another lascivious mother and a ~ daughter —Elizabeth Hardwick⟩ (2) **:** emphasizing or exploiting sexual imagery or incidents ⟨difficult to see why this book should have been suppressed before the war; there are no ~ passages —Graham Greene⟩ **5 :** accompanied or marked by extreme danger, duress, or pain ⟨met with such a ~ reception that he fled —*Amer. Guide Series: Md.*⟩ **6 a :** newly made **:** still strong **:** FRESH ⟨a ~ scent⟩ **b :** near to a goal, object, or solution sought ⟨indicative words . . . show the searcher when he is getting ~ —A.J.Ayer⟩ **7 :** having the color or tone of something (as fire or the sun) that imparts heat; *specif* **:** of a hue in the range yellow through orange to red **syn** see TENDER

²**warm** \"\ *vb* -ED/-ING/-S [ME *warmen* to make warm, become warm; partly fr. OE *wyrman* to make warm; akin to OHG *warmen, wermen* to make warm, ON *verma*, Goth *warmjan*; partly fr. OE *wearmian* to become warm; akin to OHG *warmēn* to become warm; all fr. prehistoric Gmc verbs derived fr. an adjective represented by OE *wearm* warm] *vt* **1 a :** to make warm **:** communicate a degree of heat to **:** supply or furnish warmth to ⟨in front of the fireplace ~*ing* himself —Laura Krey⟩ ⟨the sun ~*ing* the morning air⟩ ⟨~ the baby's milk⟩ **b :** to provide with a means of maintaining heat ⟨of wine red brocade, ~*ed* with an inner lining of grey squirrel fur —Nora Waln⟩ **2 a :** to infuse with or with the appearance of love, friendship, well-being, or pleasure ⟨a fine expression of personal faith ~*s* the heart of the hearer —William James⟩ ⟨~*ed* by the sense of renewed solidarity with his group —Thomas Munro⟩ ⟨a voice . . . ~*ed* . . . by fits of genial, deep chuckling —Osbert Sitwell⟩ ⟨a barrel of home brew . . . ~*ed* things up —Roderick Finlayson⟩ **b :** to fill with anger, zeal, hatred, or passion ⟨the sense of urgency increasingly ~*s* the words of the man —Waldo Frank⟩ **c :** to impart life, color, or zest to ⟨the blood that ~*s* an English yeoman —A.E.Housman⟩ ⟨the walls were ~*ed* and adorned with tapestry —G.M.Trevelyan⟩ ⟨lime juice, which the gentlemen ~*ed* with a little brandy —Rachel Henning⟩ **3 :** to open (a house) by an entertainment **:** give a housewarming in or for **4 a** (1) **:** to reheat (cooked food) for eating — often used with *over* ⟨bitter coffee ~*ed* over from the night before —George Bradshaw⟩ (2) **:** to prepare (a meal) by reheating leftovers — often used with *over* **b :** to revive or reuse esp. in a situation where vigor, cogency, or significance is no longer present ⟨~*ing* old feuds for the sake of politics —Dixon Wecter⟩ — usu. used with *over* ⟨his illustrative examples are almost invariably ~*ed* over from other writings —S.L.A.Marshall⟩ **5 :** to make ready for operation or performance by preliminary exercise or operation ⟨sparks shot down toward the water as a turret gunner ~*ed* his guns

—Howard Hunt⟩ ⟨men ~*ing* their boat motors —G.S.Perry⟩ — often used with *up* ⟨begin each practice period by ~*ing* up your hand —C.I.Blanchard & C.E.Zoubek⟩ **~** *vi* **1 :** to become warm or warmer in temperature **:** become moderately heated **:** grow warm ⟨the earth may be gradually ~*ing* —A.E. Benfield⟩ ⟨June ~*ed* into July —Josephine Johnson⟩ — sometimes used with *up* ⟨once the milk is in the can it cools down or ~*s* up very slowly —*Farmer's Weekly (So. Africa)*⟩ **2 a :** to become ardent or interested **:** grow sympathetic, angry, fervent, or impassioned ⟨gaining confidence and ~*ing* to his task —John Buchan⟩ ⟨many people can only ~ up at a party —Vance Packard⟩ ⟨whose whole face ~*ed* as she talked —Robert Friedman⟩ ⟨his desire for revenge ~*ed* easily into madness —John Erskine †1951⟩ **b :** to become filled with affection, love, friendship, or kindliness — used with *to* or *toward* ⟨always ~*ed* toward anyone who praised his kids —Ross Annett⟩ **3 :** to experience feelings of well-being, success, pleasure, or happiness **:** BASK ⟨we ~ with pleasure at mere mention of their names —Ralph Ellison⟩ **4 :** to become ready for operation or performance by preliminary activity or gradual increase in speed or activity ⟨the radio ~*ed* and music came on —William George⟩ — usu. used with *up* ⟨planes on deck ready to ~ up and take off —K.M.Dodson⟩ — **warm the bench :** to serve as a substitute on an athletic team **:** be a bench warmer ⟨patiently *warmed the bench* while his teammates played —Margery Miller⟩

³warm \"\ *adv, often* -ER/-EST [ME *warme,* fr. OE *wearme,* fr. *wearm* warm, adj.] **:** WARMLY — usu. used in combination ⟨*warm*-clad⟩ ⟨*warm*-tinted⟩

⁴warm \"\ *n* -S **1 a** [ME, fr. ¹*warm*] *dial* **:** WARMTH, HEAT **b** [²*warm*] *dial* **:** the act of warming or state of being warmed **2** [¹*warm*] **:** BRITISH WARM

war·man \'wȯrmən\ *n, pl* **warmen** [ME *werman,* fr. *werre* war + *man*] **:** WARRIOR, SOLDIER

warm blood *n* **:** a warm-blooded animal (as a bird or mammal)

warm-blooded \'ˌ=ˌ=\ *adj* **1 :** having warm blood; *specif* **:** having a relatively high and constant body temperature (as a bird or mammal) usu. considerably above that of the surrounding medium **:** HOMOIOTHERMIC **2 :** fervent or ardent in temper or spirit **:** liable to rapid changes or great extremes in temperament — **warm-blood·ed·ness** *n* -ES

warmed *past of* WARM

warmed-over \'ˌ=ˌ=\ *adj* [*warmed* (past part. of ²*warm*) + *over*] **1 :** REHEATED ⟨*warmed-over* cabbage⟩ **2 :** introduced or examined again without new life or interest **:** not fresh **:** STALE ⟨*warmed-over* plays of the commercial theater —Marc Connelly⟩ ⟨most printed lectures are skimpy *warmed-over* tidbits —Carleton Beals⟩

warmed-up \'ˌ=ˌ\ *adj* **1 :** WARMED-OVER 1 **2 :** SHORT-FED

warm·er \'wȯrmər, 'wȯ(ə)mə(r\ *n* -S **1 :** one that warms: as **a :** a workman who heats pipes, rivets, rubber, or other items **b :** a worker who kneads dried devulcanized scrap rubber with pigments between the rolls of a warming mill to form homogeneous lumps for further refining — called also *reclaimer* **c :** a device for warming or keeping warm — usu. used with a qualifying term ⟨foot ~⟩ ⟨vegetable ~⟩ **2 :** FOULING SHOT

warmest *superlative of* WARM

warm front *n* **:** the forward boundary of a warm air mass moving to replace a retreating cold air mass — see FRONT illustration

warm·ful \'=fəl\ *adj* [⁴*warm* + *-ful*] **:** full of or affording warmth

warmhearted \'ˌ=ˌ=\ *adj* [¹*warm* + *hearted*] **:** marked by or indicative of ready affection, generosity, cordiality, sympathy, or compassion ⟨a ~ welcome to the stranger⟩ **syn** see TENDER

warm·heart·ed·ness *n* **:** the quality or state of being warmhearted

warm house *n* **:** HOTHOUSE 4

warm-in boy \'=ˌ=-\ *n* [²*warm*] **:** one who reheats glassware in a furnace and passes it to the next worker for further processing

warming *n* -S [fr. gerund of ²*warm*] **:** THRASHING, TROUNCING

warming house *n* **:** CALEFACTORY

warming pad *n* **:** a body or bed warmer operated electrically or chemically

warming pan *n* **1 :** a long-handled covered pan filled with live coals used to warm a bed **2 :** one who fills temporarily a position or office intended for another **:** LOCUM TENENS

warming pan

warming-up \'=ˌ=ˌ\ *adj* [fr. gerund of *warm up*] **:** of, relating to, consisting of, or used for a warm-up ⟨*warming-up* period⟩ ⟨*warming-up* jacket⟩

war·min·ster broom \'wȯ(r),minz|tə(r)-, -n(t)s|\ *n, usu cap W* [fr. *Warminster,* urban district of Wiltshire, England] **:** a European hybrid broom (*Cytisus praecox*) that has sulphur-yellow flowers densely packed along slender branches and is used as an ornamental

warm·ish \'wȯrmish\ *adj* **:** somewhat warm

warm·ly *adv* [¹*warm* + *-ly*] **1 :** in a manner that causes or maintains warmth ⟨the sun shone ~⟩ ⟨~ wrapped against the cold⟩ **2 :** in a manner characterized or accompanied by warmth of emotion **:** FERVENTLY, ZEALOUSLY, AFFECTIONATELY ⟨audiences received her ~ —Alan Tomkins⟩ ⟨waxed ~ indignant —S.P.B.Mais⟩ **3 :** in a courageous, hostile, aggressive, or violent manner ⟨~ pursued the enemy —Robert Rogers⟩

warm·ness *n* -ES [ME, fr. OE *wearmnes,* fr. *wearm* warm + *-nes* -ness] **:** WARMTH

warmonger \'ˌ=ˌ=\ *n* [¹*war* + *monger*] **1** *obs* **:** MERCENARY **2 :** one who stirs up war **:** JINGO

warmongering \'ˌ=ˌ(=)=\ *n* [¹*war* + *mongering*] **:** the acts or practices of a warmonger

war·mouth \'wȯr,mau̇th\ *also* **warmouth bass** *or* **warmouth perch** *n* -S [origin unknown] **:** a freshwater sunfish (*Chaenobryttus coronarius*) of the eastern U. S. chiefly west or south of the Alleghenies

warms *pres 3d sing of* WARM, *pl of* WARM

warm sea *n* **:** WARM WATER

warm sector *n* **:** the region of warm air bounded by the cold front and a warm front of a cyclone

warm sepia *n* **:** COCONUT 4

warm spot *n* **1 :** a cutaneous sensory end organ that is stimulated by an increase of temperature in its immediate environment **2 :** a point or region that is a seat of affection or love ⟨had a *warm spot* in his heart for his childhood sweetheart⟩

warm spring apache *n, usu cap W&S&A* [*warm spring,* trans. of Sp *Ojo Caliente,* name of village in north central New Mexico] **1 :** an American Indian people constituting a subdivision of the Gileños **2 :** a member of the Warm Spring Apache people

warmth \'wȯ(ə)rm(p)th, 'wȯ(ə)m-\ *n* -S [ME *wermth;* akin to MHG *wermede* warmth, OE *wearm* warm — more at WARM] **1 :** the quality or state of being warm in temperature **:** gentle heat ⟨the ~ of the sun⟩ ⟨a snug, cosy ~ enveloped him —O.E. Rölvaag⟩ **2 :** the quality or state of being warm in feeling **:** emotional intensity (as passion, enthusiasm, irritation, anger, or love) ⟨the ~ of his reception⟩ ⟨in the ~ of debate⟩ **3 :** a glowing effect such as is produced by the use of warm colors

warmth·less \-ləs\ *adj* **:** lacking warmth — **warmth·less·ness** *n* -ES

warm up *vi* [²*warm* + *up*] **1 :** to engage in exercise or practice esp. immediately before entering a game or contest in order to limber up the muscles, work up speed, or get in condition ⟨the pitcher was *warming up* with an overhand delivery —Dan Polier⟩ **2 :** to approach a state of or become characterized by violence, conflict, or danger ⟨as the campaign *warmed up* . . . hired assassins had been brought in —H.H.Martin⟩

warm-up \'=ˌ=\ *n* -S [*warm up*] **1 :** a period of practice or a series of exercises designed to loosen the muscles and increase the circulation of an athlete prior to competition **2 :** the running of an engine, radio, or other device prior to operation for the purpose of bringing the working parts and the lubricant to efficient operating temperature **3 :** entertainment provided before a live radio or television audience to make it responsive to the show **4 :** practice or preparation preliminary to an important event or procedure

warm-up suit *n* **:** SWEAT SUIT

warmus *var of* WAMUS

warm water *n* **:** an ocean or sea not in the arctic or antarctic regions

warmwater \'ˌ=ˌ=\ *adj* [*warm water*] **:** of, relating to, or occurring in warm water ⟨a ~ port⟩ ⟨~ fisheries⟩

warn \'wȯ(ə)rn, 'wȯ(ə)n\ *vb* -ED/-ING/-S [ME *warnen,* fr. OE *warnian* to take heed, warn; akin to OHG *warnōn* to take heed, OE *wær* aware, wary — more at WARY] *vt* **1 a :** to put on guard **:** give notice, information, or intimation to beforehand esp. of approaching or probable danger or evil ⟨by . . . the display of a red lamp they managed to ~ the driver —O.S. Nock⟩ ⟨~*ed* them about the quicksand⟩ — sometimes used with *off* ⟨young folks are ~*ed* off —Theodore Dreiser⟩ **b :** ADMONISH, REPREHEND, COUNSEL ⟨~*ed* me not to be too eager —*London Calling*⟩ ⟨against such idiocy we are ~*ed* by an adage —W.F.Hambly⟩ **c :** to notify or apprise esp. in advance **:** call to one's attention **:** make aware **:** INFORM ⟨must ~ you that they're only my opinions —Richard Joseph⟩ ⟨the mounting heat of June ~*ed* us that the exposition would close its doors —Agnes Repplier⟩ **2 :** to notify, summon, or dismiss by authority **:** bid to go or leave **:** COMMAND ⟨a corporal called . . . to ~ him for Driving School immediately —Earle Birney⟩ ⟨heroes . . . ~*ed* so imperiously out of her modern living room —Virginia Woolf⟩ **3 :** to prohibit from advancing, trespassing, or remaining by a warning gesture, notice, order, or device ⟨lighthouses were built to ~ sailors off the rocky . . . coast —*Amer. Guide Series: Oregon*⟩ ⟨~*ed* away an English vessel —D.E.Clark⟩ ⟨had been in the garden but an armed Partisan appeared and ~*ed* her inside —Milton Bracker⟩ **4 :** to relate or report as a warning, intimation, caution, or admonishment ⟨the commission could only ~ that chaos and war would result —R.C.Pollock⟩ **~** *vi* **1 :** to give a warning ⟨their titles . . . ~ of a meaning which goes behind story, people, even setting —E.K.Brown⟩ ⟨he ~*s* against . . . a fatal illusion —A.L.Locke⟩ **2** *dial Brit, of a clock* **:** to strike a specified hour or to make sounds preparatory to striking

syn CAUTION, FOREWARN: WARN is a general term lacking specific connotation and varying in meaning from simple appraisal of something, with or without any possible dangers, to truculent threats of personal violence ⟨the introductory music *warns* us that another enjoyable evening of television is about to commence —*advt*⟩ ⟨I *warn* him that the sword I wear shall pink his lily-scented cassock through and through, next time I catch him underneath your eaves —Robert Browning⟩ CAUTION may suggest a more formal, mild, well-meaning admonition, esp. against imprudence, carelessness, or folly ⟨*cautions* his readers against the common error of looking to antiquity for knowledge —H.T.Buckle⟩ FOREWARN is likely to be used in more specific situations and to imply warning of coming danger given in time to permit prudent defense and safeguarding ⟨very likely the parson had reason for being mad . . . there was a suggestiveness in the names of the acts which would have *forewarned* anybody —Margaret Deland⟩

warn·er \'wȯrnər, 'wȯ(ə)nə(r\ *n* -S **:** one that warns

war neurosis *n* **:** a neurosis (as hysteria or anxiety) occurring in soldiers during war and attributable in large measure to their war experiences — compare COMBAT FATIGUE

¹warning *n* -S [ME, fr. OE *warnung,* fr. *warnian* to warn + *-ung* -ing] **1 a :** the action of one that warns **:** the action or fact of putting one on his guard by intimating danger, evil consequences, or penalties from an act or course of conduct ⟨give ~⟩ ⟨without ~ she began to beat him on the head —Sherwood Anderson⟩ **b :** the fact or state of being warned ⟨he had ~ of his illness⟩ **2 :** something that warns or serves to warn: as **a :** ADMONITION **b :** an example or case having a deterrent effect ⟨his life will be a ~ to others⟩ **c :** CALLING, SUMMONS; *also* **:** a summoning bell or other signal **d :** a notice from one or the other of two parties to a business relation (as of landlord and tenant) that it will be terminated at a certain time **e :** a notice advising a student that his academic or social record is unsatisfactory **f :** a notice, bulletin, or signal that serves to caution of the approach of danger ⟨hurricane ~⟩ ⟨air raid ~⟩; *esp* **:** STORM WARNING **3 :** the partial unlocking of a striking mechanism of a clock accompanied by a sound intimating that the clock is about to strike

²warning \"\ *adj* [partly fr. ¹*warning;* partly fr. pres. part. of *warn*] **:** serving as an alarm, signal, summons, or admonition **:** announcing something imminent or impending or the presence of danger ⟨~ bell⟩ ⟨~ shot⟩ ⟨~ examples of the old vices —J.G.Frazer⟩ — **warn·ing·ly** *adv*

warning coloration *n* **:** an arrangement of colors possessed by an animal otherwise defended that serves to make it conspicuous and thus warn a possible enemy against an attack — compare APOSEMATIC

warning net *n* **:** an integrated system of communications that warns of the approach or movement of hostile or aggressive military forces and esp. of hostile military airplanes

warning piece *n* **:** WARNING; *esp* **:** a deterrent example

warn off *vt, Brit* **:** RULE OFF

war note *n, archaic* **:** an instrumental summons to battle

warns *pres 3d sing of* WARN

warn't \'wȯ(ə)nt, 'wänt *sometimes* 'wənt\ [⁵*war* + *-n't*] **1** *dial* **:** WASN'T **2** *dial* **:** WEREN'T

war of nerves : psychological tactics of assailing the morale of an opponent by broadcasting propaganda, spreading rumors through secret agents or neutral channels, or otherwise creating mental confusion and indecision

wa·ro·pen \wə'rōpən\ *n, pl* **waropen** *or* **waropens** *usu cap* **1 a :** a people inhabiting the coastal area of Geelvink Bay, Netherlands New Guinea **b :** a member of such people **2 :** the Austronesian language of the Waropen people

¹warp \'wȯ(ə)rp, 'wȯ(ə)p\ *n* -S *often attrib* [ME, fr. OE *wearp;* akin to OHG *warf* warp, ON *varp* throw, cast, *verpa* to throw, cast — more at ²WARP] **1 a** (1) **:** a series or sheet of parallel yarns or threads set up for textile processing; *specif* **:** a series of yarns extended lengthwise in a loom thereby forming the lengthwise threads of a woven fabric and usu. twisted tighter than the filling yarns and sized for protection during the weaving in of the filling threads (2) **:** one of the threads of a warp (3) **:** a fabric classified according to its warp rather than its filling (*warp*-faced) (4) **:** the cords that form the carcass of a pneumatic tire **b :** the basic foundation or material of a structure or entity ⟨the homemade myth that was the ~ of his work —Babette Deutsch⟩ ⟨the ~ of the economic structure is agriculture —*Amer. Guide Series: N. C.*⟩ **2 :** a rope attached at one end to an anchor, post, or other fixed object and used to haul a ship or boat toward the object **3** *dial Brit* **:** a unit of count for fish or oysters equal to 4 or sometimes 3 or 2 ⟨six ~ of herring⟩ **4 a** (1) **:** sediment deposited by water (as when alluvial soil is formed) (2) **:** sediment developed or disturbed in situ by congeliturbation (3) **:** a bed or layer of deposited sediment **b :** a slight flexure of strata **5** [²*warp*] **a** (1) **:** the state or fact of being out of true in plane or line; *also* **:** an instance of warping (as a twist, bend, or crook) — used esp. of improperly seasoned wood ⟨a ~ in a door panel⟩ (2) **:** a variation from a true or plane surface; *esp* **:** one caused by warping of lumber (3) **:** the amount a surface warps or an allowance made for warping ⟨the ~ of a board⟩ **b :** a mental twist or aberration **:** a perverse or abnormal way of thinking, judging, or acting ⟨the ~ of battle might remain in him a long time —Dixon Wecter⟩

²warp \"\ *vb* -ED/-ING/-S [ME *warpen,* fr. OE *weorpan* to throw, cast; akin to OHG *werfan* to throw, cast, ON *verpa,* Goth *wairpan,* Gk *rhembein* to whirl] *vt* **1 a :** to turn or twist out of shape ⟨trees ~*ed* by the wind⟩ ⟨the occasional ~*ing* of logic and possibility —D.R.Weimer⟩; *esp* **:** to twist or bend out of a flat plane by or as if by contraction, curving, drying, dampness, or heat ⟨the hot sun ~*ed* the cabin's walls⟩ **b :** to give a mental twist to **:** make perverse or biased **:** cause to judge, choose, or act wrongly ⟨their minds are ~*ed* with suspicion —T.B.Costain⟩ ⟨characters ~*ed* in infancy and intelligence stunted at school —Bertrand Russell⟩ ⟨a few men at the top, whose thinking is ~*ed* by dogma —Elmer Davis⟩ **:** cause to turn aside from a chosen or correct ethical, religious, or intellectual choice or path **:** lead astray **:** PERVERT ⟨aroused judgment easily becomes ~*ed* —Dorothy Sayers⟩ ⟨the social lies that ~ us from the living truth —Alfred Tennyson⟩ **c :** to falsify, misinterpret, or give a false coloring to by wresting or twisting **:** DISTORT ⟨histories . . . are too often ~*ed* by an unfortunate bias —W.R.Inge⟩ ⟨other forms of political activity, which . . . badly ~ the meaning of elections —Elmo Roper & Louis Harris⟩ **d :** to deflect from a course **:** cause to veer ⟨long-term profit trends of the publicly regulated industries are ~*ed* from time to time by legislation —Julius Grodinsky⟩ **e :** to change the form of (a wing) by twisting esp. to provide lateral control **f :** to flex slightly (as by differential vertical movements in the earth's crust) **2** [ME *warpen,* fr. ¹*warp*] **a :** to wind (yarns) on a warp beam **:** arrange (yarns) so as to form a warp **b** *obs* **:** FABRICATE, DEVISE **c :** WEAVE, INTERLACE **3** [¹*warp*] **:** to move (as a ship) by hauling on a warp attached to a fixed object (as a buoy or anchor) ⟨as each ship was loaded . . . another vessel would be ~*ed* into the vacancy at the dock —L.C.Douglas⟩ ⟨with practiced maneuvers the boats were ~*ed* alongside —Luis Marden⟩ **4** *Brit* **:** to cast (young) prematurely — used of a domestic animal **5** [¹*warp*] **a :** to let the tide or other water in upon (low-lying land) for fertilizing by a deposit of warp **b :** to fill up (as a channel) with warp **:** CHOKE **~** *vi* **1 a :** to become twisted out of shape by or as if by contraction or shrinkage **:** become twisted or bent out of a flat plane ⟨the lock walls of some early canals . . . were of wood, and . . . began to bulge and ~ almost as soon as completed —A.F.Harlow⟩ **b** (1) **:** to become biased **:** alter a choice, opinion, or liking under influence ⟨he never ~*ed* from the path of common sense —Timothy Dwight⟩ (2) **:** to have a bias or perverse inclination or attraction **2 a** (1) *of a ship* **:** to become moved by warping ⟨help carriers ~ into dock —*Nat'l Geographic*⟩ (2) **:** to warp a ship **:** move a ship by a warp **b :** to progress slowly or circuitously or with effort as if being warped **c** *archaic* **:** to whirl or glide in the air ⟨a pitchy cloud of locusts, ~*ing* on the eastern wind —John Milton⟩ **3 :** to wind yarn off bobbins for forming the warp **:** wind a warp on a warp beam **syn** see DEFORM

warp·age \-pij\ *n* -S [²*warp* + *-age*] **:** the action, process, or result of warping

war paint *n* **1 :** paint put on the face and other parts of the body by American Indians as a token of going to war **2 :** full, ceremonial, or official dress **:** REGALIA, FINERY **3 :** MAKEUP 4a

warp and woof *n* **:** WARP 1b ⟨the vigorous Anglo-Saxon base had become the *warp and woof* of English speech —H.R. Warfel⟩

war party *n* **1 :** a group of No. American Indians on the warpath **2 :** a political party advocating or upholding a war **:** a jingoist political group

warpath \'=ˌ=\ *n* [¹*war* + *path*] **1 a :** the route taken by a party of American Indians going on a warlike expedition or to war **b :** the expedition itself or the ensuing state of war **2 :** a hostile course of action or frame of mind

warp beam *n* **:** a double-flanged roll on which warp is wound for a loom

warp·er \'wȯrpər, 'wȯ(ə)pə(r\ *n* -S **:** one that warps: as **a :** a worker who prepares yarn for a warp by winding it in sheet form onto a beam or in rope form into a ball — compare BEAMER 1b **b :** a machine used for this work

warp-face \'=ˌ=\ *adj, of a fabric* **:** having the face formed by warp threads

warping *n* -S [ME, fr. gerund of ²*warp*] **1 :** the preparation of a warp for a loom **2 :** a wound thread attaching a fly to a fishhook

warping bank *n* **:** a bank of earth raised round a field to retain water used in warping

warping board *also* **warping bar** *n* **:** a board with pegs to separate yarn groups used by many hand weavers in preparation of their warps — called also *bartree*

warping bridge *n* **:** DOCKING BRIDGE

warp knit *n* **:** a warp-knitted fabric

warp-knitted \'=ˌ=ˌ=\ *adj* **:** produced by warp knitting

warp knitting *n* **:** machine knitting made on a machine that takes yarn from a warp beam and produces fabric with lengthwise threads — compare WEFT KNITTING

warp land *n* **:** land fertilized by warp

warplane \'=ˌ=\ *n* [¹*war* + *plane*] **:** a military airplane; *esp* **:** one designed for combat purposes

war·ple \'wärpəl\ *vb* [perh. freq. of ²*warp*] *Scot* **:** TWIST, INTERTWINE, WRIGGLE

warple way *or* **warple road** \"\ *n* [origin unknown] *dial Eng* **:** BRIDLE PATH

war post *also* **war pole** *n* **:** a post sometimes painted red around which American Indians dance and into which they strike their tomahawks in connection with ceremonies of war

war potential *n* **:** the economic capabilities of a nation to wage war

war power *n* **:** the power to make war; *specif* **:** an extraordinary power exercised usu. by the executive branch of a government in the prosecution of a war and involving an extension (as by legislation or judicial interpretation) of powers constitutionally belonging to the government in peacetime

warp-pile \'=ˌ=\ *adj, of a fabric* **:** having a pile formed by extra warp threads

warp print *n* **:** a fabric with shadowy indistinct patterns produced by printing the warp threads before weaving

warps *pl of* WARP, *pres 3d sing of* WARP

war·ra·gal *or* **war·ri·gal** \'wȯrəgəl\ *n* -S [fr. native name in Australia] **1** *Austral* **:** DINGO **2** *Austral* **:** a wild horse

war·ran·dice \'wärəndəs\ *n* -S [ME, fr. AF *warandise,* alter. of ONF *warantise* guarantee — more at WARRANTISE] **:** an obligation or clause by which a grantor binds himself that the right conveyed will be effectual under Scots law **:** WARRANTY

¹war·rant \'wȯrənt, 'wär-\ *n* -S [ME *warant, warrant* protector, protection, warrant, fr. ONF *warant,* modif. (influenced by *warir* to protect, preserve, of Gmc origin; akin to OHG *werien* to defend) of a Gmc noun represented by OHG *werēnto* guarantor, fr. pres. part. of *werēn* to warrant; akin to OHG *wāra* bond, trust, care — more at WEIR, VERY] **1 a** (1) **:** sanction furnished by or as if by law or a superior **:** AUTHORIZATION ⟨have the ~ of old friendship —W.B.Yeats⟩; *also* **:** the evidence for or a token of authorization ⟨the prophet may deliver his burden with no ~ but the awful "thus saith the Lord" —M.R.Cohen⟩ (2) **:** something that serves as a pledge, guarantee, or insurance **:** VOUCHER, PLEDGE, SECURITY ⟨his worth is ~ for his welcome hither —Shak.⟩ **b** (1) **:** something serving as a reason or ground for a belief, opinion, or action **:** JUSTIFICATION, RIGHT, FOUNDATION ⟨these two developments . . . give ~ in saying that the meetings mark the beginning of something new —Dean Acheson⟩ ⟨had heard people speak slightingly — perhaps without ~ — of his business ability —A.W.Long⟩ (2) **:** something serving as confirmation or proof ⟨their obviously increasing sophistication in matters of theory and method is a ~ of prodigious effort —W.W.Taylor⟩ **2 a :** a commission or document giving authority to do something **:** an act, instrument, or obligation by which one person authorizes another to do something which he has not otherwise a right to do and thus secures him from loss or damage; *specif* **:** a writing that authorizes a person to pay or deliver to another and the other to receive money or other consideration ⟨a ~ on a city treasurer⟩ **b** (1) **:** a precept or writ issued by a competent officer or magistrate authorizing an officer to make an arrest, a seizure, or a search or to do other acts incident to the administration of justice ⟨a ~ of attachment⟩ — see BENCH WARRANT, SEARCH WARRANT (2) **:** a magistrate's summons in a petty or summary proceeding in Virginia; *also* **:** a proceeding so begun (3) **:** a call for a town meeting stating the matters to be acted upon at the meeting **c :** an official certificate of appointment issued to an officer of lower rank than a commissioned officer — see WARRANT OFFICER **d** *Brit* **:** a receipt given to a person who has deposited goods in a warehouse by assignment of which the title to the goods is transferred **e** (1) **:** a short-term obligation of a municipality or other governmental body issued in anticipation of revenue (2) **:** an instrument issued by a corporation giving to the holder the right to subscribe to the capital stock of the corporation at a fixed price either for a limited period or perpetually **3 :** WARRANT OFFICER **4 :** a declaration of royal or other official determination ⟨precedence is determined by royal ~⟩ — **of warrant** *obs* **:** JUSTIFIED, WARRANTED — **out of warrant** *obs* **:** UNWARRANTED

²warrant \"\ *vt* -ED/-ING/-S [ME *waranten,* fr. ONF *warantir,* fr. *warant* protector, protection, warrant] **1** *obs* **:** PROTECT

2 a : to declare or maintain with little or no fear of being contradicted or belied **:** be certain **:** be sure that ⟨I ~ he'll be with us when he's wanted —A.B.Paterson⟩ **b :** to assure (a person) of the truth of what is said **:** tell with assurance or positiveness **3 a :** to guarantee to a person good title to and undisturbed possession of (as an estate) **:** secure (an estate granted) to a grantee **:** ASSURE 5c **b :** to provide a guarantee of the security of (as title to property sold) usu. by an express covenant in the deed of conveyance **c :** to guarantee (as a fact or a statement of fact) to be at present or at a future time as represented ⟨the author hereby ~*s* . . . that the said work is an original work —John Gloag⟩ **d :** to guarantee (as goods sold) esp. in respect of the quality or quantity specified ⟨~*ed* against faulty workmanship or material for a period of ninety days after purchase —*advt*⟩ **4 :** to guarantee security or immunity to **:** give assurance against harm, loss, or damage **:** SECURE ⟨I'll ~ him from drowning —Shak.⟩ **5 :** to give authority or power to for doing or forbearing to do something **:** give warrant or sanction to **:** AUTHORIZE ⟨the law ~*s* this procedure⟩ **6 a :** to give proof of the authenticity or truth of **:** ATTEST ⟨his belief that metaphysics gives better ~*ed* knowledge than science —Sidney Hook⟩ **b :** to give assurance of the nature of or for the undertaking of **:** GUARANTEE ⟨a pill ~*ed* to cure measles, toothache, and rupture —C.E.Montague⟩ ⟨the most eloquent preacher, ~*ed* to produce a new religion every Sunday evening —W.L. Alden⟩ **7 :** to serve as or give sufficient ground or reason for **:** require or permit as a consequence **:** JUSTIFY ⟨sufficiently distinct to ~ a name of its own —Jacquetta & Christopher Hawkes⟩ ⟨the deposits contain too high a percentage of sulphur to ~ development —George Wythe⟩ ⟨theologians whose stature ~*ed* inclusion —R.P.Ramsey⟩ **syn** see ASSERT

war·rant·able \-ntəbəl\ *adj* **1 :** capable of being warranted **:** JUSTIFIABLE ⟨a ~ outlay⟩ **2** *of a stag* **:** old enough to be hunted — **war·rant·able·ness** \-bəlnəs\ *n* -ES — **war·rant·ably** \-blē,-bli\ *adv*

war·rant·ee \ˌ≈rən¦tē\ *n* -S [²*warrant* + *-ee*] **:** the person to whom a warranty is made

war·rant·er \ˈ≈rəntə(r)\ *n* -S [²*warrant* + *-er*] **:** WARRANTOR

war·ran·tise *or* **war·ran·tize** \-n.ˌtīz\ *n* -S [ME *warantise, warantize,* fr. ONF *warantise,* fr. *warantir* to warrant] **1** *archaic* **:** WARRANT, GUARANTEE **2** *obs* **:** PERMISSION

warrantize *vt* -ED/-ING/-S [ME *warantizen,* fr. *warantise*] *obs* **:** WARRANT, GUARANTEE

war·rant·less \ˈwȯrəntləs, ˈwär-\ *adj* **:** UNWARRANTED ⟨~ accusations⟩

warrant of arrest : a warrant authorizing and commanding the arrest of a specific thing or person designated by name or by description ⟨a John Doe *warrant of arrest*⟩

warrant of attorney : written authority given by a person empowering another to transact business for him; *specif* **:** written authority given by a client to his attorney to appear for him in court and to allow judgment to pass against him esp. in connection with a note or bond accompanied by a defeasance

warrant officer *n* **:** an officer in the army, navy, air force, or marine corps occupying a grade between that of commissioned officer and noncommissioned officer

war·ran·tor \ˌ≈rən¦tȯ(ə)r, -ō(ə), ˈ≈rəntə(r)\ *n* -S [²*warrant* + *-or*] **:** one that warrants or gives a warranty

warrants *pl of* WARRANT, *pres 3d sing of* WARRANT

war·ran·ty \ˈwȯrəntē, ˈwär-, -ti\ *n* -ES [ME *warantie,* fr. ONF, fr. fem. of *waranti,* past part. of *warantir* to warrant] **1 a** (1) **:** the undertaking or obligation of a feudal lord to defend his vassal tenant in the possession of the land held of him as lord, whether orig. received by the lord by commendation or not or to give the tenant lands of equal value (2) **:** a real covenant binding the grantor of an estate of freehold and his heirs to warrant and defend the title and in case of eviction by title paramount to yield other lands of equal value in recompense — see SPECIAL WARRANTY **b :** a collateral undertaking that a fact regarding the subject of a contract is or will be as it is expressly or impliedly declared or promised to be and although breach of such an undertaking does not void the contract it does make the warrantor liable for damages **c :** a statement expressly or impliedly made in an insurance policy by the insured that a fact relating to the subject of insurance or the risk exists or will exist or that some related act has been done or will be done and that must be literally true or fulfilled if the policy is not to become void — distinguished from *representation* **2 :** something that authorizes, sanctions, supports, or justifies **:** a justificatory mandate or precept **:** substantiating evidence, proof, or assurance **:** WARRANT, AUTHORIZATION ⟨a glib fluency is no ~ of genuine talent —A.T.Weaver⟩ ⟨by what ~ has he assumed such powers⟩ **3 :** a usu. written guarantee of the integrity of a product and the good faith of the maker given to the purchaser and generally specifying that the maker will for a period of time be responsible for the repair or replacement of defective parts and will sometimes also provide periodic servicing ⟨a one-year ~ on a television set⟩

warranty deed *n* **:** a deed containing a covenant of warranty; *esp* **:** one certifying that the covenantor has a good title in fee simple free and clear of all liens and encumbrances and that the covenantor will defend against the claims of all persons

waratau *var of* WARATAH

war·rau \wəˈraů\ *n, pl* **warrau** *or* **warraus** *usu cap* **1 a :** a people of Venezuela and British Guiana **b :** a member of such people **2 :** the language of the Warrau people

war·rau·an \-aůən\ *n* -S *usu cap* [*warrau* + *-an*] **:** the language family of which Warrau is the only member

warred *past of* WAR

war·ree \wäˈrē, ˈwä(ˌ)rē\ *n* -S [Miskito *ŭári,* prob. fr. Sp *jabalí* wild boar — more at JABALI] **:** WHITE-LIPPED PECCARY

war·ren \ˈwȯrən, ˈwär-\ *n* -S [ME *wareine, warenne,* fr. ONF *warenne,* prob. of Gmc origin; akin to OHG *werien* to defend, protect — more at WEIR] **1** *Brit* **a :** a place privileged by prescription or grant from the king for keeping any of various animals (as hares, conies, partridges, or pheasants) **b :** a privilege by royal grant or prescription of hunting in a warren and taking wild animals **2 a :** an area esp. of uncultivated ground for the breeding of rabbits; *also* **:** a place abounding in rabbits **b :** the rabbits inhabiting a warren **3 a :** a tenement or a district as crowded and as full of life as a rabbit warren **:** a densely populated dwelling, slum, or quarter **b :** a maze of narrow winding streets or passages

¹**war·ren·er** \-nə(r)\ *n* -S [ME *warenner,* fr. ONF *warennier,* fr. *warenne* warren + *-ier* -er] **1 :** a keeper of a warren **:** GAMEKEEPER **2 :** one that maintains a rabbit warren

²**war·re·ner** \"\ *n* -S [Tasmanian *warrenah* turbo] **:** any of several small top shells of the southern coast of Australia and Tasmania

war·ren girder *or* **warren truss** \¦wȯrən-, ¦wär\ *n, usu cap W* [after Russell *Warren* †1860 Am. architect] **:** a truss consisting of upper and lower members connected by members arranged in the form of a series of isosceles triangles

Warren girder

warrigal *var of* WARRAGAL

warring *pres part of* WAR

war·rior \ˈwȯryə̇r, ˈwȯ(ə)yə(r, ˈwȯrē| *also* ˈwärē| *sometimes* ˈwäry|\ *n* -S *often attrib* [ME *werreour, werriour,* fr. ONF *werreieur,* fr. *werreier* to make war (fr. *werre* war) + *-eur* -or — more at WAR] **1 a :** a man engaged or experienced in warfare and esp. in primitive warfare or the close combat typical of ancient or medieval times ⟨the wagon train was attacked by Indian ~*s*⟩; *broadly* **:** a person of demonstrated courage, fortitude, zeal, or pugnacity **b :** an advocate of war **:** JINGO ⟨preventative ~⟩ **2 :** a So. American hummingbird of the genus *Oxypogon* having a helmetlike crest

warrior ant *n* **:** SANGUINARY ANT

warrior bush *n* **:** CURRANT BUSH 2

war·rior·ess \|ərəs\ *n* -ES [*warrior* + *-ess*] **:** a female warrior

war·rior·ship \|ə(r),ship\ *n* [*warrior* + *-ship*] **:** the practices, occupation, or status of a warrior

war risk insurance *n* **1 :** term insurance written by the U.S. government for members of the military and naval forces **2 :** insurance that protects against loss due to acts of war

war road *n* **:** WARPATH 1a

war room *n* **:** a room at a military headquarters where situation maps are maintained

warrtd *abbr* warranted

wars *pl of* WAR, *pres 3d sing of* WAR

war sack *var of* WAR BAG

¹**war·saw** \ˈwȯr(ˌ)sȯ, ˈwȯ(ə)(ˌ)-\ *adj, usu cap* [fr. *Warsaw,* capital of Poland] **:** of or from Warsaw, the capital of Poland **:** of the kind or style prevalent in Warsaw

²**warsaw** \"\ *or* **warsaw grouper** *n* -S [modif. of AmerSp *guasa*] **:** a large grouper: as **a :** BLACK GROUPER **b :** SPOTTED JEWFISH

war service chevron *n* **:** a small chevron worn on the lower part of the sleeve of a military uniform to indicate that the wearer has seen service in a former war

warship \ˈ≈ˌ≈\ *n* **:** a government ship employed for war purposes; *esp* **:** one armed for combat — called also *war vessel*

¹**war·sle** *or* **wars·tle** \ˈwä(r)səl\ *vb* -ED/-ING/-S [ME *werstelen, warstelen,* alter. of *wrestlen, wrastlen* — more at WRESTLE] *Scot* **:** WRESTLE, STRUGGLE, FLOUNDER

²**warsle** *or* **warstle** \"\ *n* -S *Scot* **:** a wrestling bout **:** TUSSLE

war song *n* **:** a song relating to war; *esp* **:** a song accompanying an Amerindian war dance that incites military ardor

warst \ˈwärst\ *dial var of* WORST

wart \ˈwȯ(ə)r|t, ˈwȯ(ə)|, *usu* |d.+V\ *n* -S [ME *werte, wart,* fr. OE *wearte;* akin to OHG *warza* wart, ON *varta,* L *verruca* wart, Skt *varṣman* height, top, surface] **1 a :** a horny projection on the skin usu. of the extremities produced by proliferation of the skin papillae and caused by a virus — called also *verruca vulgaris* **b :** any of numerous verrucous skin lesions **2 :** an excrescence or protuberance more or less resembling a true wart; *specif* **:** a glandular excrescence or hardened protuberance on a plant (as in potato wart) **3 a :** someone or something suggestive of a wart esp. in smallness or obnoxiousness ⟨a misplaced ~ of real estate that nearly everybody wanted cut down —N.M.Clark⟩ **b** *Brit* (1) **:** a junior midshipman (2) **:** a young subaltern

war-tax stamp *also* **war stamp** *n* **:** a postage stamp used to raise war revenue instead of to pay postage

wart cress *n* **:** SWINE CRESS

wart disease *n* **:** POTATO WART

wart·ed \ˈwȯrd·əd, ˈwȯ(ə)|, |təd\ *adj* [*wart* + *-ed*] **:** having warts **:** VERRUCOSE

wartflower \ˈ≈ˌ≈\ *n* **:** CELANDINE 1

wart grass *or* **wart spurge** *n* **:** SUN SPURGE

warthog \ˈ≈ˌ≈\ *n* **:** an African wild hog of the genus *Phacochoerus* (esp. *P. aethiopicus* of southern Africa or *P. africanus* of northeastern Africa) having two pairs of rough warty excrescences on the face and large protruding tusks

warthog of southern Africa

wartime \ˈ≈ˌ≈\ *n, often attrib* **:** a period during which a war is in progress ⟨the economies of ~⟩ ⟨~ shortages⟩ ⟨~ rationing⟩

wart·less \ˈwȯrtləs, ˈwȯ(ə)t-\ *adj* **:** having no warts **:** free from warts

wartlike \ˈ≈ˌ≈\ *adj* **:** resembling a wart

war trail *n* **:** WARPATH 1a

wart snake *n* **:** any of several nonvenomous East Indian snakes constituting the family Acrochordidae, being covered with wartlike tubercles or spinose scales, and usu. lacking cephalic plates and ventral scutes

wartweed \ˈ≈ˌ≈\ *n, dial Eng* **:** any of several plants thought to cure warts: as **a :** SUN SPURGE **b :** DEVIL'S MILK 1 **c :** CELANDINE 1 **d :** NIPPLEWORT

wartwort \ˈ≈ˌ≈\ *n* [ME, fr. *wart* + *wort*] **1 :** a lichen of *Verrucaria* or a related genus having a warty thallus **2 :** WARTWEED

warty \ˈwȯr|d·|ē, ˈwȯ(ə)|, |t|, |i\ *adj* -ER/-EST [ME, fr. *wart* + *-y*] **1 :** having warts or wartlike protuberances **:** full of warts **:** covered with warts **:** VERRUCOSE ⟨a ~ leaf⟩ **2 :** of the nature of or resembling a wart **:** WARTLIKE ⟨formation of ~cutaneous nodules —D.T.Smith⟩

war vessel *n* **:** WARSHIP

war-weariness \ˈ≈ˌ≈≈≈\ *n* **:** a state of disillusion or depression felt toward the end of or immediately after a protracted war

war-weary \ˈ≈ˌ≈≈\ *adj* **1 :** affected by war-weariness **:** tired of or depressed by war **2 :** of, relating to, or being a combat plane so worn or damaged as to be beyond repair and consigned to be scrapped, cannibalized, or used for target practice

war whoop *n* **:** a war cry esp. of American Indians

war·wick·ite \ˈwȯr(w)iˌkīt, ˈwäri,-\ *n* -S [*Warwick,* village of southeastern N.Y. + E *-ite*] **:** a mineral (Mg, Fe)$_3$Ti(BO$_4$)$_3$ consisting of a borate of titanium, iron, and magnesium and occurring in brown to black orthorhombic prisms (hardness 3–4, sp. gr. 3.4)

war·wick·shire *or* **warwick** \ˈwȯr|ik,shi(ə)r, ˈwär|, -|ēk-, -shiə, -ˌshə(r), *US also* ˈwȯ(r)w|\ *adj, usu cap* [fr. *Warwickshire, Warwick,* county of central England] **:** of or from the county of Warwick, England **:** of the kind or style prevalent in Warwick

¹**war·wolf** \ˈwär,≈, ˈwȯr-\ *archaic var of* WEREWOLF

²**war·wolf** \ˈwȯr,≈\ *n, pl* **warwolves** [¹*war* + *wolf;* trans. of ML *lupus belli*] **:** a medieval siege engine for throwing stones and other missiles

warworn \ˈ≈ˌ≈\ *adj* [*war* + *worn*] **:** showing the effects of war or military service **:** ruined, ravaged, or laid waste by war

wary \ˈwa(a)|rē, ˈwe|, ˈwā|, |ri\ *adj* -ER/-EST [²*ware* (fr. ME *war, ware,* fr. OE *wær* aware, wary) + *-y;* akin to OHG *giwar* aware, attentive, ON *varr* aware, wary, Goth *wars,* L *verērī* to fear, Gk *horan* to see, *-oros* watcher, *ōra* care] **1 :** marked by keen caution, cunning, and watchful prudence in detecting and escaping danger ⟨these figures were ~ in their movements and perfectly silent of foot —Joseph Conrad⟩ ⟨a subtle diplomacy and ~ tactics —Arnold Bennett⟩ **2 :** PROVIDENT, ECONOMICAL **syn** see CAUTIOUS

war zone *n* **1 :** a zone in which belligerents are conducting hostile operations during a war **2 :** a designated area esp. on the high seas within which rights of neutrals are not respected by a belligerent nation in time of war

¹**was** [ME (1st & 3d sing. past indic.), fr. OE (1st & 3d sing. past indic. of *wesan* to be); akin to OFris *wesa* to be, *was* was, OHG *wesan* to be, *was* was, ON *vera* to be, *var* was, Goth *wisan* to be, *was* was, Skt *vasati* he lives, dwells, stays, and prob. to L *Vesta* goddess of the hearth, Gk *hestia* hearth, home, goddess of the hearth; basic meaning: to live, stay] *past 1st & 3d sing of* BE, *dial & archaic past 2d sing of* BE, *substand & archaic past pl of* BE, *substand & archaic past subjunctive of* BE

²**was** \ˈwəz, ˈwäz *also* ˈwȯz\ *n* -ES [ME, fr. ¹*was*] **:** something that was **:** PAST

³**was** *pl of* WA

wa·sa·bi \ˈwäsəbē\ *n* -S [Jap] **1 :** an Asiatic herb (*Eutrema wasabi*) of the family Cruciferae **2 :** the thick greenish root of wasabi that is grated in Japan like horseradish and eaten with fish and other food

was·co \ˈwä(ˌ)skō\ *n, pl* **wasco** *or* **wascos** *or* **wascoes** *usu cap* [Wasco *wasq'o* cup, small bowl; fr. a cup-shaped rock near their main village always full of water] **1 a :** an Indian people of northern Oregon **b :** a member of such people **2 :** a dialect of Upper Chinook

wase \ˈwāz\ *n* -S [ME; akin to MLG *wase* bundle of sticks, pad to support a burden on the head, MSw *vasi* bundle of straw] **1** *chiefly dial* **:** a wisp or bundle of hay or straw **2** *chiefly dial* **:** a pad (as of straw) to support a burden on the head

¹**wash** \ˈwȯsh, ˈwäsh, ˈwōish, ÷ ˈwȯ(ə)rsh *or* ˈwärsh\ *vb* **washed** \-sht\ **washed** *or archaic* **wash·en** \-shən\ **washing; washes** [ME *waschen, wasshen, washen,* fr. OE *wascan, wæscan, waxan;* akin to OHG *waskan* to wash, ON *vaska,* OE *wæter* water — more at WATER] *vt* **1 a :** to cleanse by the action of water or other liquid **:** dip, rub, or scrub in or with a liquid for the purpose of cleansing ⟨~ clothes⟩ ⟨~ your hands and face⟩ ⟨~ the baby⟩ **b :** to remove (as dirt or coloring) by rubbing or drenching with water or other liquid ⟨~ the stain out of the shirt⟩ ⟨~ the mud off the car⟩ **2 a :** to cleanse the body or esp. the hands and face of with water ⟨~*ed* himself thoroughly before sitting down to eat⟩ **b :** to free from ceremonial or moral defilement by cleansing with water or something likened to it in action or effect **:** cleanse or purify spiritually ⟨~ me thoroughly from my iniquity —Ps 51:2 (RSV)⟩ ⟨a quiet that ~*es* your mind clean —Wynford Vaughan-Thomas⟩ **c :** to purge away **:** OBLITERATE — usu. used with *away* ⟨my sins, which were many, are all ~*ed* away —R.H.McDaniel⟩ **d :** to cleanse (as the face or fur) by licking or by rubbing with the paw usu. moistened with saliva — used esp. of cats **3 a :** to bathe or moisten (a bodily part or injury) with a liquid ⟨~ the wound with water⟩ ⟨~ the eyes with a mild antiseptic solution⟩ **b :** to wet with tears ⟨tidings to ~ the eyes of kings —Shak.⟩ **c** (1) **:** to wet thoroughly **:** DRENCH, SATURATE ⟨roses ~*ed* with dew —John Milton⟩ (2) **:** to overspread with light **:** BATHE, SUFFUSE ⟨the sunlight ~*ing* their branches —James Still⟩ ⟨a late moon had come up and the barnyard was ~*ed* with moonlight —Sherwood Anderson⟩ **d** *archaic* **:** to occupy (oneself) in the action or sport of bathing ⟨he went but forth to ~ him in the Hellespont, and being taken with the cramp, was drowned —Shak.⟩ **e :** to pass water over or through esp. so as to carry off material from the surface or interior **4 a :** to touch in flowing **:** flow along the border of **:** dash or overflow against or over **:** LAVE ⟨the countries whose shores are ~*ed* by its waves —*Irish Digest*⟩ **b :** to flow through and supply water to ⟨a fine camping site, ~*ed* by a mountain stream⟩ **5 a :** to move, carry, or deposit by or as if by the force of water in motion ⟨the mill, bridge, dam, and several houses were ~*ed* away in a flood —*Amer. Guide Series: Md.*⟩ ⟨sediment ~*ed* down from the upper lakes —*Amer. Guide Series: Mich.*⟩ ⟨a wave of liberal reform ~*ed* the Indian peones back onto their lands —Green Peyton⟩ **b :** to cause to be in a specified place or condition by or as if by the thrust or sweep of water ⟨sometimes a whole school of pilot whales is trapped in shoal water and ~*ed* ashore —*Amer. Guide Series: N.C.*⟩ ⟨was ~*ed* overboard and drowned —W.A.Ganoe⟩ **6 a :** to wear away by the action of water **:** ERODE ⟨the dirt road had been ~*ed* by heavy rains⟩ **b :** to form (a break or opening) by the action of water ⟨the top speed a boat could make without ~*ing* a break in the berm —Edward Stanley⟩ **7 a :** to subject (as earth, gravel, or crushed ore) to the action of water to separate the valuable material from the worthless or less valuable ⟨the most successful method of ~*ing* sand for gold —Mary S. Broome⟩ — compare ³LEACH 1a, LIXIVIATE **b :** to separate (particles) from ore or other substance by agitation with or in water **c :** to remove something from as if by the action of water ⟨the words tending to be ~*ed* of all specific meaning —H. P. Van Dusen⟩ **d** (1) **:** to pass through a bath of some liquid to carry off impurities or soluble components (2) **:** to pass (a gas or gaseous mixture) through or over a liquid for the purpose of purifying it esp. by removing soluble components — see ²SCRUB 2a **e :** to bleach (a carpet or rug) by a chemical process **8 a :** to cover or daub lightly with an application of a liquid (as whitewash or varnish) **b :** to cover with a thin or watery coat of color **:** tint lightly and thinly ⟨the moors are ~*ed* with purple of the wild cranberries —Mary H. Vorse⟩ ⟨an architect's dream in palest grays ~*ed* with mauve —Claudia Cassidy⟩ **c :** to depict or paint by a broad sweep of thin or watery color with a brush — often used with *in* ⟨a few loosely *washed*-in ink blots —W.S. Baldinger⟩ **d :** to overspread (as an animal's throat) with an outer flush or tint of another color **e :** to overlay with a thin coat of metal by deposit from a solution ⟨steel ~*ed* with silver⟩ **9** *dial Eng* **:** to launder clothes for **10 :** to cause to swirl ⟨picked up his glass and ~*ed* the brandy about in its deep base —Helen Howe⟩ **11 :** to shuffle (playing cards) preparatory to dealing; *esp* **:** to shuffle for dealing by another **12 :** to dephosphorize (molten pig iron) by adding substances containing iron oxide and sometimes manganese oxide ~ *vi* **1 :** to cleanse oneself or a part of one's body with water ⟨~*es* before each meal⟩ **2 a :** to become worn away by the action of water **:** become eroded ⟨the harrowed land ~*ed* —Russell Lord⟩ — often used with *away* **b :** to become lost, impaired, or worn away as if by erosion — usu. used with *away* ⟨their social and their cultural identity ~*ed* away after some centuries —A.L.Kroeber⟩ **3 :** to clean something by rubbing or dipping it in water **:** perform the operation of cleansing in water ⟨told . . . she should be at home minding women's work, she answered there were plenty to spin and ~ —R.L.Stevenson⟩ **4 a :** to be carried or floated along on water **:** DRIFT ⟨huge cakes of ice ~*ing* along the side⟩ **b :** to pour, sweep, or flow in a stream or current ⟨feeling the wind ~ pleasantly against his face —Norman Mailer⟩ ⟨successive waves of pioneers ~*ing* westward —Green Peyton⟩ **5 :** to serve as a cleansing agent ⟨this soap ~*es* thoroughly⟩ **6 a :** to undergo without damage the operation of being laundered ⟨this material doesn't ~ well⟩ **b** (1) **:** to undergo successfully submission to a test or process of proof **:** bear investigation ⟨his story sounds good, but it won't ~⟩ ⟨an interesting theory that won't ~⟩ (2) **:** to inspire belief **:** gain acceptance ⟨that yarn didn't ~ with him —P.E.Lehman⟩ **7 a** *of a wave* **:** BREAK ⟨has a delightful location on the eastern shore, with slow waves ~*ing* almost at the base of its single street —*Amer. Guide Series: Vt.*⟩ **b :** to move with a lapping or splashing sound ⟨heard the ripple ~*ing* in the reeds —Alfred Tennyson⟩ **c :** to shuffle a deck of cards ⟨it's my turn to ~⟩ **8 :** to make a wash sale — **wash one's dirty linen in public :** to carry on or discuss personal, domestic, or private quarrels or scandals in public ⟨advised the members of his party not to *wash their dirty linen in public*⟩ — **wash one's hands of :** to disclaim or renounce interest in, responsibility for, or further connection with ⟨resigned and *washed his hands of* the whole mess⟩

²**wash** \"\ *n* -ES [ME *wasche,* fr. *waschen* to wash] **1 a** (1) **:** the process or work of washing clothing or household linen ⟨did a full day's ~⟩ **:** the process of being washed ⟨his shirts shrank in the ~⟩ (2) **:** an accumulation of articles (as of clothing) set apart for washing or in process of being washed ⟨a string of ~ hung drying in the hall —Eugene Kinkead⟩ ⟨the family ~⟩ ⟨the week's ~⟩ **b :** the act of washing **:** a cleansing or wetting with water ⟨the car needs a good ~⟩ **c :** a washing of oneself esp. of one's face and hands ⟨recorded all the things which he was supposed to do — the two hot ~*es* and the two cold ~*es* a day —Pierre Burton⟩ ⟨rolled up his sleeves and gave himself a quick ~⟩ **2 a** (1) **:** the surging action or attack of waves ⟨exposed to the ~ of waves at their base —P.E.James⟩ (2) **:** SURGE ⟨her novel comes as a great ~ of fresh air —Sylvia Stallings⟩ **b :** erosion by action of waves **c :** the sound of water breaking against or over a surface ⟨heard the ~ of waves upon rocks —Nevil Shute⟩ **3 a :** a piece of ground washed by the action of a sea or river or sometimes covered and sometimes left dry **:** the shallowest part of a river, estuary, or arm of the sea **b :** BOG, FEN, MARSH **c** (1) **:** a shallow body of water (2) **:** a shallow creek **d** *West* **:** the dry bed of an intermittent stream often at the bottom of a canyon — called also *dry wash* **4 a :** waste liquid (as from a bath) **b** *chiefly dial* **:** stale urine formerly used in washing clothes, soapmaking, and dyeing **c :** SLOP, SWILL **d :** worthless dregs **:** REFUSE **5** *dial chiefly Eng* **:** a dry measure of varying capacity for oysters and whelks **6 a** (1) **:** an insipid or wishy-washy beverage ⟨still felt refreshed and stimulated, after a few swallows of this ~ —Emily Hahn⟩ (2) **:** vapid writing or speech **b** (1) **:** fermented wort from which spirit is distilled — called also *distillers' beer* (2) **:** a mixture of dunder, molasses, water, and scummings used in the West Indies for distillation **7 a :** a wide sweep or splash esp. of color made by or as if by a long stroke with a coarse brush ⟨the leaves had not turned, but there was a gold ~ over everything —Anne G. Winslow⟩ ⟨a magnificent full-grown male with the rich, almost golden-yellow ~ over the belly —Thomas Barbour⟩ **b** (1) **:** a thin coat of paint (as watercolor) ⟨the pencil and ~ studies pinned to the walls —C.D.Lewis⟩ (2) **:** WASH DRAWING (3) **:** a flat tone used for pictorial clarity in architectural drawings **c :** a liquid mixture of slight consistency used for coating a wall or other surface thinly ⟨the cottages are still thatched with straw, and the walls are gay with the old pink ~ —*advt*⟩ **d :** a thin coat of metal laid on something for beauty or preservation or deposited on a metal for counterfeiting a precious metal **8 a :** LOTION 2 ⟨a good ~ for festering or cankered wounds and sores —Emily Holt⟩ **b :** a liquid cosmetic,

dentifrice, or hairdressing ⟨perfumed alcoholic ~*es* have had a vogue —Herman Goodman⟩ **c :** a mixture of ingredients (as beaten egg and water or milk) used by bakers for giving a glaze to baked goods **9 a :** material transported or deposited by water: as (1) **:** loose or eroded surface material of the earth (as gravel and other rock debris) transported and deposited by running water **:** ALLUVIUM, SILT; *esp* **:** coarse alluvium (2) **:** ALLUVIAL FAN (3) **:** a mound of detritus spreading in fan-shaped corrugated slopes below a gash in a cliff **b :** the action of run-off water in wearing away soil (as in gullying or sheet erosion) **:** the eroding of soil by rain wash **10 :** an underground den esp. of a bear **11 :** soil yielding precious metal or gems under washing **12 a :** the backward current or disturbed water caused by some action or movement (as of oars or a steamer's screw or paddles) **:** a surge set up by and trailing after some moving object or process (as a ship, storm, or tidal wave) esp. as dissipated in force or transmitted to a distance from the center of the disturbance ⟨was left swaying like a small boat in the ~ of a millionaire's yacht —Maurice Cranston⟩ **b :** a similar disturbance or wavelike agitation in the air set up by the passage of a storm center or rushing object (as an airplane) **c :** a disturbance in the air produced by the passage of an airfoil or propeller ⟨the ~ from the prop tugged at the loose ends of his scarf —Howard Hunt⟩ **d :** the dissipated current or force in the trail of an intellectual or social movement **:** EDDY ⟨hard to know how much . . . is solid accomplishment that will last, and how much is the ~ of a wave of opinion —A.L.Kroeber⟩ ⟨traveled there in the ~ of the war —J.R.Walsh⟩ **13 :** WASH SALE **14 a :** the upper surface of a member or material when given a slope to shed water **:** WEATHERING **b :** a structure or receptacle shaped so as to receive and carry off water

³wash \"\ *adj* [¹*wash*] **:** capable of being washed without injury **:** WASHABLE ⟨~ fabrics⟩ ⟨a ~ dress⟩ ⟨~ goods⟩

⁴wash *adj* [perh. alter. (influenced by ²*wash*) of *wearish*] *obs* **:** WASHY, WEAK ⟨their bodies of so weak and ~ a temper —Francis Beaumont & John Fletcher⟩

wa·sha \ˈwäshə\ *n, pl* **washa** *or* **washas** *usu cap* **1 :** a Chitimachan people of southeastern Louisiana **2 :** a member of the Washa people

wash·abil·i·ty \ˌwȯshəˈbilәd-ē, ˌwäsh-, ˌwȯish-\ *n* **:** the quality or state of being washable

¹wash·able \ˈwȯshәbәl, ˈwäsh-, ˈwȯish-, ÷ ˈwȯrsh- *or* ˈwärsh-\ *adj* **1 :** capable of being washed without suffering damage or loss of color ⟨a ~ dress⟩ **2 :** soluble in water ⟨~ ointment bases —*Amer. Druggist*⟩ ⟨~ ink⟩

²washable \"\ *n* -S **:** a fabric or garment that may be washed without injury or change

wash and wear *adj* **:** of, relating to, or constituting a fabric or garment not needing to be ironed after washing

washaway \ˈ=,=ˌ=\ *n* -S [fr. the phrase *wash away*, fr. ¹*wash* + *away*] *Brit* **:** WASHOUT

wash ball *n* **:** a ball of toilet soap

wash barrel *n* **:** a barrel in which split mackerel are washed with salt water to extract the blood before salting

washbasin \ˈ=,==\ *n* **:** WASHBOWL

washboard \ˈ=,=\ *n, often attrib* **1 :** a broad thin plank fixed along a gunwale or set on the sill of a lower deck port to keep out the sea — called also *washstrake, wasteboard* **2 :** BASEBOARD **3 a :** a corrugated rectangular surface (as of zinc or glass) in a wooden frame on which clothes are rubbed in washing **b :** a road or pavement so worn by traffic as to be corrugated transversely **c :** a corrugated surface (as of glass or wood)

washboard 3a

washboiler \ˈ=,==\ *n* **:** a large metal vessel used for boiling clothes

wash boring *n* **:** a boring system by which material loosened by a bit is borne to the surface in the annular space between the bit and casing by water forced down through the pipe bearing the bit

wash bottle *n* **:** a bottle or flask provided with one bent tube passing through the stopper for directing a stream of water on anything to be washed or rinsed and with means for forcing (as by blowing into a second tube passing through the stopper or by squeezing if the bottle is flexible) the water through the tube

washbowl \ˈ=,=\ *n* **:** a large bowl for water to wash one's hands and face — called also *washbasin*

wash·brew \ˈwȯsh,brü, ˈwäsh-\ *n, dial Eng* **:** oatmeal boiled until gelatinous **:** FLUMMERY 1a

wash brush *n* **:** a large brush for applying a wash

wash bulkhead *n* **:** a bulkhead in a ballast tank to prevent excessive movement of liquid in the tank

washcloth \ˈ=,=\ *n* **:** a cloth used for washing one's face and body

wash–colored \ˈ=,==\ *adj* **:** colored as if with a wash or water-color

washday \ˈ=,=\ *n* **:** a day regularly set aside (as once a week) for washing clothes (as of a family or institution) ⟨on the evening of the second ~ —Flora Thompson⟩

wash dirt *n* **:** earth washed or to be washed for gold **:** WASHING STUFF

wash·dish \ˈ=,=, *in sense 2* ˈwash,- *or* ˈwäsh,-\ *n* **1 :** WASHBOWL **2** [so called fr. the motion of its tail resembling the motion of one washing dishes] *dial Eng* **:** PIED WAGTAIL

wash down *vt* **1 :** to move or carry downward by action of water or other liquid; *specif* **:** to facilitate the passage of (food) down the gullet with accompanying swallows of liquid ⟨bolted a hot dog and *washed* it *down* with soda⟩ **2 :** to wash the whole length or extent of ⟨*washed down* and scrubbed out with disinfectant, making sure that no corners or grooves . . . are missed out —Henry Wynmalen⟩

washdown \ˈ=,=\ *adj* [*wash down*] **:** constructed with provision for washing contents downward ⟨a ~ water closet⟩

wash drawing *n* **:** water-color painting in or chiefly in washes esp. in black, white, and gray tones only

washed *past of* WASH

washed–curd cheese \ˈ=,=-\ *n* [*washed*, past part. of ¹*wash*] **:** cheddar cheese in which the curd is washed before being pressed into forms to remove a portion of the whey, lactose, and soluble milk salts and produce a soft body with open texture

washed metal *n* **:** iron treated so as to remove most of the silicon and phosphorus and not too much of the carbon

washed–out \ˈ=ˈ=\ *adj* [fr. past part. of *wash out*] **1 a :** faded in color **:** lacking in brightness or vividness ⟨a very pale, *washed-out* blue —Eden Phillpotts⟩ **b** *of a photographic print* **:** lacking detail in highlights **2 :** depleted in vigor or animation **:** played out **:** EXHAUSTED ⟨worked from seven in the morning until noon, and I was limp, *washed-out* —Richard Wright⟩ **3 :** ERODED ⟨coal workings line the route in this hilly, *washed-out* section —*Amer. Guide Series: Pa.*⟩

washed sale *n* **:** WASH SALE

washed–up \ˈ=ˈ=\ *adj* [fr. past part. of *wash up*] **1 :** ready for the discard **:** done for **:** played out ⟨as far as he's concerned, you're a *washed-up* nobody —Albert Morgan⟩ **2** *usu* **washed up :** at the end of an association or activity **:** ready to call it quits **:** THROUGH ⟨he was completely *washed up* with his wife . . . he never visited her —Morton Faber⟩ ⟨I'm *washed up* with the rackets —Allan Bruce⟩

washen *archaic past part of* WASH

¹wash·er \ˈwȯshə(r), ˈwäsh-, ˈwȯish-, ÷ ˈwȯrsh- *or* ˈwärsh-\ *n* -S [ME *wassher*, fr. *washen* to wash + *-er*] **1 a :** a person who washes; *specif* **:** a worker who cleans by washing (as clothes, animals, or materials or products in processes of preparation, manufacture, or maintenance) **b :** a machine for washing something: as (1) **:** a device for removing dirt and soluble impurities from pulp and paper stock (2) **:** WASHING MACHINE (3) **:** an apparatus or device for washing photographic materials to remove soluble chemical products (as produced by development or fixing) (4) **:** an apparatus in which gases are washed **:** SCRUBBER c ⟨rotary ~*s*⟩ **2** [ME; fr. the motion of its tail resembling the motion of one washing clothes or dishes] *dial Eng* **:** PIED WAGTAIL **3 :** any of various flat thin rings or perforated plates (as of metal or leather) used in joints or assemblies to insure tightness, prevent leakage, or relieve friction — see LOCK WASHER, SPRING WASHER **4** [so called fr. its habit of washing its food before eating] **:** RACCOON

²washer \"\ *vt* -ED/-ING/-S **:** to furnish with a washer

wash·er·less \-(r)ləs\ *adj* **:** not having a washer

wash·er·man \ˈ=ˌmən\ *n, pl* **washermen 1 :** a man who works at washing clothes esp. for hire **:** LAUNDRYMAN **2 :** one who operates a machine that washes: as **a :** a papermaker who washes cooked rags or wood pulp **b :** one who washes devulcanized scrap rubber to remove sodium hydroxide solution

washer–up \ˈ=ˈ=\ *n, pl* **washers–up** *Brit* **:** DISHWASHER

washerwife \ˈ==,=\ *n, Scot* **:** WASHERWOMAN

washerwoman \ˈ==,==\ *n, pl* **washerwomen 1 :** LAUNDRESS; *esp* **:** one who takes in washing **2** [so called fr. the resemblance of the up-and-down motion of its tail to the motion of a woman scrubbing clothes] *dial Eng* **:** PIED WAGTAIL

wash·ery \ˈwȯshərē, ˈwäsh-, ˈwȯish-\ *n* -ES [¹*wash* + *-ery*] **:** a place at which material (as wool, ore, coal, or crushed stone) is freed from impurities or dust by washing

washes *pres 3d sing of* WASH, *pl of* WASH

washfast \ˈ=,=\ *adj* **:** resistant to fading or discoloration by washing ⟨a ~ blouse⟩ — **wash·fast·ness** *n*

washfountain \ˈ=,==\ *n* **:** a large circular washbowl set in the floor and supplied with running water from a central spray to permit simultaneous use by a number of people

wash gravel *n* **:** gravel washed to extract gold

wash–hand \ˈ=,=\ *adj, Brit* **:** designed for use in washing the hands or for holding utensils for such purpose ⟨a *wash-hand* basin⟩ ⟨a *wash-hand* stand⟩

washhouse \ˈ=,=\ *n* **:** a house or building used or equipped for washing; *esp* **:** one for washing clothes **:** LAUNDRY

washier *comparative of* WASHY

washiest *superlative of* WASHY

washin \ˈ=,=\ *n* -S [¹*wash* (flow, stream) + *in*] **:** a permanent twist or warp of an airplane wing such that the tip section has a larger angle of attack than the root section

wash·i·ness \ˈwȯshēnəs, ˈwäsh-, ˈwȯish-\ *n* -ES **:** the quality or state of being washy

washing *n* -S [ME *wasching*, fr. gerund of *waschen* to wash] **1 :** the act or action of one that cleanses with water ⟨gave himself a good ~⟩ ⟨gave the clothes a thorough ~⟩ **2 washings** *pl* **a :** liquid that has been used to wash something **b** (1) **:** metal (as gold dust) obtained by washing (2) **:** a place or soil yielding metal or gems under washing **c :** material collected by the washing of a bodily cavity ⟨sinus ~*s*⟩ ⟨throat ~*s*⟩ **3 a :** the action of waves or running water **:** the erosion or removal of material by running water **b washings** *pl* **:** material abraded or transported by the action of water **4 a :** the operation of bathing, drenching, or coating with a liquid (as in mining ore) **b :** the act or process of applying a thin coat of paint (as watercolor) **c :** the dipping of fruits (as apples, pears, or plums) in a dilute solution of hydrochloric acid followed by rinsing in water as a means of removing spray residues that might be toxic to humans **5 :** a thin covering or coat ⟨a ~ of silver⟩ **6 :** clothes or other articles washed or to be washed esp. at one time **:** WASH ⟨the ~ was hanging in the back garden —J.I. Jones⟩ **7 :** the execution of a wash sale

washing bottle *n* **1 :** WASH BOTTLE **2 :** a bottle for use in washing gases by passing them through liquid contained in it

washing engine *n* **:** a device much like a beater in which rags are washed by a stream of water and also reduced to threads and fibers

washing machine *n* **:** a machine for washing; *specif* **:** a usu. power-driven machine for washing clothes and household linen

washing powder *n* **:** a powder for washing (as a soap powder or a powder containing a synthetic detergent and alkaline builder)

washing soda *n* **:** SODIUM CARBONATE a(3)

washing stuff *n* **:** an earthy deposit containing gold that may be extracted by washing

wash·ing·ton \ˈwȯshiŋtən, ˈwäsh-, ˈwȯish-, -shēŋ- *sometimes* -shənt-, ÷ ˈwȯrsh- *or* ˈwärsh-\ *adj, usu cap* **1** [fr. *Washington*, capital city of U.S., after George *Washington* †1799 first president of the U.S.] **:** of or from the city of Washington, D.C. ⟨a *Washington* legislator⟩ **:** of the kind or style prevalent in Washington **:** WASHINGTONIAN **2** *or* **washington state** *usu cap W & often cap S* [fr. *Washington*, northwestern state of U.S., after George *Washington* †1799] **:** of or from the state of Washington ⟨*Washington* apples⟩ **:** of the kind or style prevalent in Washington **:** WASHINGTONIAN

washington clam *n, usu cap W* **:** a butter clam (*Saxidomus nuttallii*)

washington grass *n, usu cap W & often cap G* **:** a water shield (*Cabomba caroliniana*)

washington handpress *n, usu cap W* [after George *Washington* †1799] **:** a hand-operated printing press perfected about 1829

¹wash·ing·to·nia \ˌ==ˈtōnēə\ *n, cap* [NL, fr. George *Washington* †1799 + NL *-ia*] **:** a genus of massive fan palms of California and adjacent Mexico having large plicate leaves cut nearly to the middle and often bearing filaments on their margins and a smooth trunk bearing a large shaggy mass of persistent dead leaf remains

²washingtonia \"\ [NL, fr. George *Washington* †1799 + NL *-ia*] *syn of* OSMORHIZA

³washingtonia \"\ [NL, fr. George *Washington* †1799 + NL *-ia*] *syn of* SEQUOIA

¹wash·ing·to·ni·an \ˌ==ˈtōnēən\ *adj, usu cap* **1** [George *Washington* †1799 first president of the United States + E *-an*] **:** of, relating to, or characteristic of George Washington **2** [*Washington*, capital city of U.S.A., or northwestern state of U.S.A. + E *-an*] **a :** of, relating to, or characteristic of Washington, D.C., or the state of Washington **b :** of, relating to, or characteristic of the people of Washington, D.C., or the state of Washington

²washingtonian \"\ *n* -S **1** *cap* **:** a native or resident of Washington, D.C., or the state of Washington **2** *usu cap* [*Washington* Temperance Society, founded 1840 + E *-an*] **:** a member of the Washington Temperance Society

wash·ing·to·ni·ana \ˌ==ˌtōnēˈanə, -ˈänə, -ˈānə *also* -ˈānə\ *n pl, usu cap* [George *Washington* †1799 + E *-ana*] **:** material (as papers, books, letters, or relics) relating to George Washington

washington lily *n, usu cap W* **:** a large white-flowered lily (*Lilium washingtonianum*) of the Pacific coast of the U.S. that is widely cultivated for ornament

washington palm *n, usu cap W* **:** a large fan palm (*Washingtonia filifera*) with many slender filaments hanging from its leaf margins — called also *California fan palm*

washington pie *n, usu cap W* [after George *Washington* †1799] **:** cake layers put together with a jam or jelly filling

washington plant *n, usu cap W* **:** FANWORT

washington post *n, usu cap W&P* **:** an American ballroom dance of the end of the 19th century

washington's birthday *n, usu cap W&B* [after George *Washington* †1799 first president of the United States] **1 :** February 22 formerly observed as a legal holiday in most of the states of the U.S. **2 :** the third Monday in February observed as a legal holiday in most states of the U.S. — called also *Presidents' Day*

washington thorn *n, usu cap W* [fr. *Washington*, D.C., capital city of the U.S.] **:** a hawthorn (*Crataegus phaenopyrum*) of eastern No. America that is often cultivated for its bright red fruit and showy autumn foliage

wash·i·ta \ˈwäsh,ətȯ\ *adj, usu cap* [fr. Fort *Washita*, Texas] **:** of or relating to a subdivision of the Comanchean — see GEOLOGIC TIME table

washita stone *n* [fr. *Washita* (*Ouachita*) river, southwest Arkansas] **:** a porous variety of novaculite used esp. for sharpening woodworking tools

washland \ˈ=,=\ *n* **:** land or a stretch of land washed periodically by an overflowing stream

washleather \ˈ=,==\ *n* **1 :** a soft leather usu. made of split sheepskin dressed with oil in imitation of chamois **2** *chiefly Brit* **:** a piece of washleather or soft cloth used for dusting or cleaning **:** CHAMOIS ⟨was flicking over the radiator with a ~ —Nicholas Monsarrat⟩

wash·man \ˈ=mən\ *n, pl* **washmen 1 a :** a man who washes clothes **b :** a textile worker who scours cloth during manufacturing **2 :** a man who applies wash (as in tinplate making)

wash mill *n* **:** any of several machines for washing clay, hides, or materials for cement

wash–mouth \ˈwȯsh,mau̇th\ *n, dial Eng* **:** BLABBERMOUTH

washo \ˈwä(,)shō\ *n, pl* **washo** *or* **washos** *usu cap* **1 a :** an Indian people of the vicinity of Lake Tahoe, California and Nevada **b :** a member of such people **2 :** a Washoan language of the Washo people **3 :** WASHOAN

wa·sho·an \wäˈshōən\ *n* -S *usu cap* [*Washo* + *-an*] **:** a language family of the Hokan stock comprising the Washo language

wash·oe process \ˈwä(,)shō-\ *n, usu cap W* [fr. *Washoe* county, northwest Nevada] **:** a process of treating silver ores by grinding in pans or tubs with the addition of mercury and sometimes of chemicals (as blue vitriol and salt)

wash–off relief \ˈ=,=-\ *n* **:** an image in relief in color photography produced by hardening the exposed portions of a usu. gelatinous colloid layer and washing off the unhardened portions (as with hot water)

wash oil *n* **:** oil (as straw oil) used in scrubbing esp. coke-oven gas for absorbing light oil and recovering benzene and other aromatic compounds

wash out *vt* **1 :** to wash free of some extraneous substance (as dirt, soap, chemicals) **2 a :** to drain of color in laundering ⟨this fabric is *washed out*⟩ **b :** to deplete of strength or vitality **:** EXHAUST ⟨after his recent illness, he is *washed out* for the time being⟩ **c :** to cancel out **:** OFFSET ⟨have *washed out* the effect of government reduction of its debt by the creation of bank deposits —T.O.Waage⟩ **d :** to eliminate as useless or unsatisfactory **:** DISCARD, REJECT; *specif* **:** to dismiss (a student or candidate) as failing to qualify **3 a :** to destroy or render useless by the force or action of water ⟨the storm *washed out* the bridge⟩ ⟨the heavy rains *washed out* the road⟩ **b :** to rain out ⟨the second game of the doubleheader was *washed out* by a sudden downpour⟩ **~** *vi* **1 :** to become depleted of color or vitality **:** FADE ⟨technicolor makeup . . . *washes out* on TV —*Newsweek*⟩ **2 :** to fail to meet requirements or measure up to a standard; *specif* **:** to fail in a course of training ⟨*wash out* of flight school⟩ **3 :** WASH 2a

washout \ˈ=,=\ *n* -S [*wash out*] **1 a :** a channel cut by erosion in one sedimentary deposit and filled with the material of a younger deposit **b :** the washing out or away of earth esp. in the bed of a road or railroad by rain or a freshet; *also* **:** a place where the earth is washed away ⟨traffic was delayed by a ~ after the storm⟩ **c :** WASH 3d **2 :** the act or process of washing or flushing out a container or pipe; *also* **:** a plumbing device for such process **3 a :** one that fails to measure up to expectations or requirements **:** a total loss **:** FAILURE, FLOP ⟨the first really hopeful idea he had reached had proved a ~ —F.W. Crofts⟩ ⟨the failures, the drunks, the ~*s*, the fellows running away from themselves —Hugh MacLennan⟩ ⟨the day was a ~⟩ **b :** a person (as a flying cadet or college student) who has been failed out of a course of training or study **c :** the act or fact of failing (as in a course of training or study) **4 :** a permanent twist or warp of an airplane wing such that the tip section has a smaller angle of attack than the root section **5 :** an emergency signal given by hand or lantern to stop a railroad train

wash plain *n* **:** ALLUVIAL PLAIN

wash plate *n* **:** any of several plates fitted in a ship's bottom to prevent surging of bilge water when the ship is rolling or pitching **:** BAFFLE

wash port *n* **:** FREEING PORT

washpot \ˈ=,=\ *n* **:** a pot for washing: as **a :** a large metal pot used outdoors for boiling clothes over an open fire ⟨playing out there in the yard . . . around an old fire-blackened ~ —F. B. Gipson⟩ **b :** a pot containing melted tin into which the plates are dipped to be coated in tinplate manufacturing

wash primer *n* **:** a primer of low nonvolatile content and special adhesive and protective properties for coating metal

washrack \ˈ=,=\ *n* **:** WASHSTAND 2

washrag \ˈ=,=\ *n* **:** a piece of cloth used in washing; *specif* **:** WASHCLOTH

washroom \ˈ=,=\ *n* **1 :** a room (as in a restaurant or public building) equipped with washing and toilet facilities **:** LAVATORY 3a **2 :** a room in a dyeing plant in which fabrics are washed

wash sale *n* **:** a prearranged fictitious sale of securities with no real change of ownership that is made to influence the market or to establish a loss for tax purposes

washstand \ˈ=,=\ *n* **1 a :** a piece of furniture combining features of a table and cupboard and used to hold articles (as a pitcher, basin, or towel) for washing the hands and face **b :** a washbowl (as of porcelain) permanently set in place (as on a wall) and attached to water and drainpipes **2 :** a place (as in a garage) having water and drainage facilities for the washing of vehicles

washstrake \ˈ=,=\ *n* -S **:** WASHBOARD 1

wash·tail \ˈwȯsh,-, ˈwäsh,-\ *n* [so called fr. the up-and-down motion of its tail] *dial Eng* **:** PIED WAGTAIL

washtray \ˈ=,=\ *n* **:** LAUNDRY TRAY

washtrough \ˈ=,=\ *n* **:** a trough used for washing; *specif* **:** BUDDLE

washtub \ˈ=,=\ *n* **:** a tub in which clothes or other items are washed

wash up *vi* **1 :** to wash one's face and hands **2** *Brit* **:** to wash the dishes after a meal ⟨went straight to the sink where his wife was *washing up* —D.H.Lawrence⟩ **~** *vt* **1 :** to get rid of by washing ⟨*wash up* the spilled milk⟩ **2 :** EXHAUST, FINISH ⟨guess we've *washed up* that subject —Philip Barry⟩ ⟨a setback that *washed* him *up* as a heavyweight contender⟩

washup \ˈ=,=\ *n* -S [*wash up*] **1 a :** the act or process of washing clean ⟨thorough ~*s*, sterilization of cleaned surfaces —*Experiment Station Record*⟩ ⟨presses get frequent ~*s* else their product would be lousy beyond description —P.R.Russell⟩ **b :** the act or process of washing ore **2 :** a place for washing

wash·way \ˈwȯsh,-, ˈwäsh,-\ *n, dial Eng* **:** a place on a roadway covered by running water

washwheel \ˈ=,=\ *n* **:** a smooth or flanged rotating cylinder in which clothes or other fabrics are washed

washwoman \ˈ=,==\ *n, pl* **washwomen :** WASHERWOMAN

washwork \ˈ=,=\ *n* **:** WASH DRAWING

washy \ˈwȯshē, ˈwäsh-, ˈwȯish-, -shi, ÷ ˈwȯrsh- *or* ˈwärsh-\ *adj* -ER/-EST [²*wash* + *-y*] **1 a** *obs* **:** being full of moisture **:** WATERY ⟨they . . . on the ~ ooze deep channels wore —John Milton⟩ **b :** easily eroding or washing out or away ⟨a ~ bank⟩ ⟨a ~ hillside⟩ **2 a :** lacking in substance or strength **:** DILUTED, THIN, WATERY ⟨~ tea⟩ **b :** deficient in brightness or richness of color **:** PALLID ⟨these strong earth colors attack the frail pink of the cherry blossoms . . . and leave it looking ~ and dirty —Anthony West⟩ ⟨a ~ pink or red with too much blue in it —E.H.M.Cox⟩ **c :** lacking in vigor, individuality, or definiteness ⟨keeping one foot in a sort of ~ respectability —Compton Mackenzie⟩ **3** *obs* **:** lacking in moral stamina or strength of character **:** FRIVOLOUS, LOOSE **4 a** *of a domestic animal* **:** lacking in condition and in firmness of flesh **:** having a tendency to scour or sweat profusely on slight exertion ⟨a ~ steer⟩ ⟨a ~ horse⟩ **b :** tending to produce flabbiness or scouring in animals ⟨~ grass⟩ ⟨~ feed⟩

was·n't \ˈwəzᵊn(t), ˈwäz- *also* ˈwȯz-; *in rapid speech* ˈwədᵊn(t); *dial* ˈwänt\ [by contr.] **:** was not

¹wasp \ˈwäsp, ˈwȯsp\ *n* -S [ME *waspe*, fr. OE *wæps, wæfs, wæsp*; akin to OHG *wafsa, wefsa* wasp, Lith *vapsa* gadfly, L *vespa* wasp, OE *wefan* to weave — more at WEAVE] **1 a :** any of numerous winged hymenopterous insects that generally have a slender smooth body with the abdomen attached by a narrow stalk, well-developed wings, biting mouthparts, and in the females and workers a more or less formidable sting, that belong to many different families and include forms of social as well as of solitary habits, and that are largely carnivorous and often provision their nests with caterpillars, insects, or spiders killed or paralyzed by stinging for their larvae to feed on — compare SPHECOIDEA, VESPOIDEA; DIGGER WASP, HORNET, YELLOW JACKET; BEE **b :** any of various hymenopterous insects (as a chalcid fly or ichneumon fly) having larvae that are parasitic esp. on other insect larvae **2 a :** a waspish person **b :** something that stings or infuriates

wasp

²wasp \"\ *n* -S *usu cap* [*W*omen's *A*ir Force *S*ervice *P*ilots] **:** a member of the Women's Air Force Service Pilots of the U.S. Army air forces disbanded in December 1944

wasp ant *n* : VELVET ANT

wasp bee *n* : CUCKOO BEE

wasp beetle *n* : a black-and-yellow longicorn beetle resembling a wasp

wasp fly *n* **1** : any of various syrphus flies that resemble wasps **2** : THICKHEADED FLY

wasp·i·ly \-pəlē\ *adv* [*waspy* + *-ly*] : WASPISHLY

wasp·ish \-pish, -pēsh\ *adj* [¹*wasp* + *-ish*] **1 a** : resembling a wasp in behavior; *esp* : easily irritated : quick to take offence : SNAPPISH, TESTY ⟨witty and ~ and said whatever came into his head about his colleagues —Frank O'Connor⟩ ⟨his answers were crisp, though he could become ~ when annoyed —H.F. & Katharine Pringle⟩ **b** : marked by irritability or petulance ⟨the fourth-raters who use a staff captain's armlet as an excuse for ~ display of minor power —Fred Majdalany⟩ **2** : resembling a wasp in form; *esp* : slightly built ⟨the grim, black spars and ~ hull of a small man-of-war craft —Herman Melville⟩ **syn** see IRRITABLE

wasp·ish·ly *adv* : in a waspish manner

wasp·ish·ness *n* -ES : the quality or state of being waspish

wasp·ling \-pliŋ\ *n* -S [¹*wasp* + *-ling*] : the larva of a social wasp

wasp's nest *n* : HORNET'S NEST

wasp spider *n* : a spider that resembles a wasp in form

wasp waist *n* : a very slender waist; *specif* : a woman's tightly laced waistline

waspy \-pē, -pi\ *adj* -ER/-EST [¹*wasp* + *-y*] **1** : resembling a wasp : WASPISH ⟨a fierce, ~ little animal —F.B.Gipson⟩ **2** : full of wasps

¹**was·sail** \ˈwäsəl, |,sāl *also* ˈwȯl *sometimes* ˈwa|; ˌˈsāl, *esp before pause or consonant* -əl\ *n* -S [ME *wæs hæil, washail,* fr. ON *ves heill* be in good health, fr. *ves* (imper. sing. of *vera* to be) + *heill* healthy — more at WAS, WHOLE] **1** : an early English toast to someone's health or good luck made when offering him a cup of wine or drinking to him — compare DRINK HAIL **2** : a liquor formerly drunk in England on festive occasions (as at Christmas and Twelfth Night) and made of ale or wine flavored with spices and other ingredients (as sugar, toast, roasted apples) **3** : riotous drinking : REVELRY ⟨became a place of ~ and fellowship —Julian Dana⟩ ⟨a certain seediness in the morning after such ~ —Paul de Kruif⟩ **4** *archaic* **a** : a festive or drinking song or glee **b** : a carol sung by wassailers

²**wassail** \"\ *vb* -ED/-ING/-S [ME *wesseylen,* fr. *washail* wassail] *vi* **1** : to hold a wassail : CAROUSE **2** *dial Eng* : to sing carols from house to house usu. at Christmas time ~ *vt* : to drink to the health or thriving of ⟨ceremonies of . . . ~*ing* fruit trees, caroling from house to house —Dorothy G. Spicer⟩

wassail bowl *n* **1** : a bowl used for the mixing and serving of wassail **2** : WASSAIL 2

wassail cup *n* : WASSAIL BOWL

was·sail·er \-lə(r)\ *n* -S [²*wassail* + *-er*] **1** : one that carouses : REVELER ⟨some ~s want to linger on until the small hours —John Kobler⟩ **2** *archaic* : one who goes about singing carols

was·sail·ry \-lrī\ *n* -ES [¹*wassail* + *-ry*] : REVELRY

was·ser·mann \ˈwäsə(r)mən, ˈvä-\ *n* -S *usu cap* : WASSERMANN TEST

wassermann reaction *n, usu cap W* [after August von *Wassermann* †1925 Ger. bacteriologist] : a complement-fixing reaction occurring with the serum of syphilitic patients and used as a test for syphilis, being ordinarily made by heating the patient's serum to destroy complement, mixing it with a fortified alcoholic extract of beef heart that is a nonspecific but effective antigen, and adding this mixture to a mixture of washed red blood corpuscles (as of sheep) and a serum (as of rabbit) containing a specific hemolysin for them after which the serum from a syphilitic patient combines with the antigen from the beef heart and absorbs the available complement so that there is no hemolysis while a serum that is not syphilitic causes no reaction in the first mixture and leaves complement free to cause hemolysis when the second mixture is added

wassermann test *n, usu cap W* : a test for the detection of syphilitic infection using the Wassermann reaction

was·sie \ˈwäsē\ *n* -S [origin unknown] : a large cleavage of a crystal (as an octahedron divided in two) split for cutting

wast [alter. (influenced by *was,* 1st & 3d sing. past indic., & *art,* 2d sing. pres. indic.) of ME *were* — more at WERE] *archaic past 2d sing of* BE

wast·able \ˈwāstəbəl\ *adj* [ME, fr. *wasten* to waste + *-able*] : subject to waste

wast·age \-tij, -tēj\ *n* -S [²*waste* + *-age*] **1 a** : loss, decrease, or destruction of something (as by use, decay, erosion, leakage) ⟨the fill is . . . largely the product of mass ~ from nearby hillsides —*Jour. of Geol.*⟩ ⟨the eggs and larvae . . . are subject to tremendous ~ as a result of the activities of carnivores —W.H. Dowdeswell⟩ **b** : losses that occur in a herd of cattle from any cause (as death, disease, or sale) — usu. expressed as a percentage of the number of cattle in the herd **2** *Scot* : a waste or desert place : waste ground **3** : wasteful spending or use of something : loss through wastefulness ⟨man's ~ of the earth's resources —*Brit. Bk. News*⟩ ⟨these delays, these ~s of effort and money —Eric Ambler⟩ **4** : something produced by wasting ⟨chips of flint, chert, and other stone — the ~ of implement making —*Amer. Guide Series: Mich.*⟩

¹**waste** \ˈwāst\ *n* -S [ME *waste, wast;* in sense 1, fr. ONF *wast,* fr. *wast,* adj., wild, desolate, waste, fr. L *vastus* unoccupied, desolate, waste; akin to OE *wēste* desolate, waste, OHG *wuosti,* L *vanus* empty, vain; in other senses, fr. ME *wasten* to waste — more at WANE] **1 a** (1) : an uninhabited or sparsely settled region : WILDERNESS ⟨this ~ of mud; water, and monotonous vegetation —Wilfred Thesiger⟩ ⟨the trackless ~s of the pine hills —Adria Langley⟩ (2) : barren land worthless for cultivation and more or less bare of vegetation : DESERT ⟨a sandy ~ of several square miles that was once forest and later farm lands —*Amer. Guide Series: Mich.*⟩ (3) : a desolate and cheerless region or place; *specif* : a place made barren or forbidding by human agency ⟨a quiet countryside was converted by the ironmasters into one of the ugliest ~s ever created by man —L.D.Stamp⟩ (4) : something arid, deserted, or forbidding ⟨so was his life become a hopeless ~ —B.A. Williams⟩ **b** : uncultivated land; *specif* : land subject to the right of common **c** (1) : a broad and empty expanse (as of water or air) ⟨outposts staring over the seething Atlantic ~s —Marjory S. Douglas⟩ (2) : an endless stretch (as of time) ⟨all those who have died throughout the long ~s of time —J.S. Bradford⟩ ⟨one o'clock, and then another long, long ~ of quarters —Rumer Godden⟩ **d** : a disused part of a coal mine **2 a** : the act or action of wasting : useless or profitless consumption or expenditure : loss without equivalent gain ⟨this present era of efficiency ought . . . to avoid the ~ of ability —C.H.Grandgent⟩ ⟨~ of time⟩ ⟨~ of money⟩ **b** : an instance of wasting ⟨thought it was an economic ~ to have a car sitting in the garage all day long —M.M.Musselman⟩ **3 a** : loss through breaking down of bodily tissue **b** : gradual loss or decrease by use, wear, or decay **c** *chiefly dial* : a bodily consumption by disease **4 a** : damaged, defective, or superfluous material produced during or left over from a manufacturing process or industrial operation : material not usable for the ordinary or main purpose of manufacture: as (1) : material rejected during a textile manufacturing process and either recovered for reworking (as yarn) or used usu. for wiping dirt and oil from hands and machinery (2) : SCRAP (3) : fluid (as steam) allowed to escape without being utilized (4) : worthless material removed in mining or digging operations (5) : a soft absorbent material that when saturated with oil and packed in a journal of a railroad car equipped with solid bearings serves to lubricate the journal **b** : refuse from places of human or animal habitation: as (1) : GARBAGE, RUBBISH ⟨no receptacle for ~ may be washed in a pond, lake, or stream —*Amer. Guide Series: N.H.*⟩ (2) **wastes** *pl* : EXCREMENT, ORDURE ⟨the proper disposal, or lack of disposal here, of human ~s —*Orient Bk. World*⟩ ⟨barnyard ~s⟩ (3) : SEWAGE **c** : material derived by mechanical and chemical weathering and moved down sloping surfaces or carried by streams to the sea ⟨as rock ~ continues to stream away from every part of the area in turn, valleys are widened —Arthur Holmes⟩ **5 a** : destruction or injury done to property (as houses, woods, or land) by a temporary or life tenant to the prejudice of the heir or of him in reversion or remainder — see PERMISSIVE WASTE **b** : destruction, ruin, or devastation caused by some disaster (as war, fire, or flood) ⟨give edge unto the swords that make such ~ —Shak.⟩ **6** *obs* : CONSUMPTION, USE ⟨have the expense and ~ of his revenues —Shak.⟩ **7** : WASTE PIPE **8** *archaic* : OVERABUNDANCE, PROFUSION **syn** see REFUSE — **go to waste** *or* **run to waste** : to flow off as superfluous or waste liquid : become wasted or lost without producing any good or achieving any purpose

²**waste** \"\ *vb* -ED/-ING/-S [ME *wasten,* fr. ONF *waster,* fr. L *vastare* to lay waste, ravage, fr. *vastus* desolate, waste] *vt* **1** : to lay waste : bring to ruin : DEVASTATE ⟨shown how the Union preserved the States from *wasting* and destroying one another —Van Wyck Brooks⟩ **2** : to cause to shrink in physical bulk or strength : cause to become consumed or weakened : EMACIATE, ENFEEBLE ⟨the emaciated and battered figure of that poet whom desire, disease, and prison *wasted* —F.J. Mather⟩ **3 a** : to wear away or impair gradually : diminish by constant loss : use up : CONSUME ⟨the broad gray summit is barren and desolate-looking . . . *wasted* by ages of gnawing storms —John Muir †1914⟩ ⟨the aboriginal population had been *wasted* by the epidemics of the eighteenth century —W. C.Massey⟩ **b** *archaic* : SPEND, USE ⟨companions that do converse and ~ the time together —Shak.⟩ **c** : to dispose of as waste ⟨the dirty water is drained off from the top and *wasted* into a sewer —V.M.Ehlers & E.W.Steel⟩ **4 a** : to spend or use needlessly, carelessly, or without valuable result : consume or employ to no purpose : SQUANDER ⟨~ money⟩ ⟨~ time⟩ ⟨~ effort⟩ ⟨~ sympathy⟩ **b** : to leave unrecognized or unappreciated ⟨an actor *wasted* on an inattentive audience⟩ ⟨a pun *wasted* on his students⟩ ⟨full many a flower is born to blush unseen and ~ its sweetness on the desert air —Thomas Gray⟩ **c** : to allow to be used inefficiently or become dissipated or lost ⟨heat *wasted* in the process⟩ **d** : to let pass without taking advantage of ⟨~ a golden opportunity⟩ **5** *obs* : IMPOVERISH ⟨have *wasted* myself out of my means —Shak.⟩ ~ *vi* **1 a** : to lose weight, strength, or vitality : become gradually feebler — often used with *away* ⟨women and children . . . *wasting* away in the mills —V.L.Parrington⟩ **b** *of a jockey* : to exercise in order to lose weight ⟨had little difficulty in making eight stone, but . . . took rides at 7 st. 4 lb. and under, and *wasted* hard to make it —Richard Lane⟩ **2 a** : to become diminished in bulk or substance : become worn away by degrees ⟨still remaining, but gradually *wasting* from the surface rock on which they were carved —*Amer. Guide Series: Oregon*⟩ **b** : to become consumed : become used up ⟨allowed our natural riches to ~ with startling rapidity —*U. S. Code*⟩ **3** : ELAPSE, PASS ⟨time ~s too fast —Laurence Sterne⟩ **4** : to spend money or consume property extravagantly or improvidently ⟨~ not, want not⟩ **5** : to run off as waste ⟨allowing water to ~ when it reaches a certain elevation —*Water & Sewage Control Engineering*⟩ ⟨~s back into the sea through short rivers —Roscoe Fleming⟩

syn SQUANDER, DISSIPATE, FRITTER, CONSUME: WASTE implies ill-considered or thoughtless expenditure, fruitless and sometimes prodigal, without fit return or valuable result ⟨what a tremendous amount of energy is *wasted* in hauling, lifting, and spinning unnecessarily heavy masses of metal —Waldemar Kaempffert⟩ ⟨the windows were thickly frosted over, so that . . . art in dressing them was quite *wasted* —Arnold Bennett⟩ SQUANDER applies to silly, reckless, profuse expenditure likely to impoverish ⟨*squanders* in reckless gambling and debauchery —C.C.Walcutt⟩ ⟨*squandering* your early enthusiasm in futile attempt to excite the world about your ideas and your plans —W.J.Reilly⟩ DISSIPATE may suggest extravagant scattering or dispersion through indulgence or folly to the point of exhaustion ⟨doubtless his great and varied mental powers were *dissipated* by desultory labors, and by his inability to concentrate on a single task —Merle Curti⟩ ⟨unable to weather the storms of Reconstruction, its endowment *dissipated* in worthless securities, the institution was closed —*Amer. Guide Series: N.C.*⟩ FRITTER implies gradual dissipation of resources by piecemeal expenditure by bits, usu. on foolish trifles ⟨*fritter* away a fortune on petty vices⟩ ⟨the cathode was slowly *frittered* away, its substance becoming encrusted on the walls and other parts of the tube —K.K.Darrow⟩ CONSUME may refer to any wasteful devouring or destroying ⟨tuberculosis that *consumed* her at the age of thirty-four —Harry Levin⟩ ⟨for some cities are desolated by ruin, others *consumed* by the sword —G.G. Coulton⟩ **syn** see in addition RAVAGE

— **waste one** : to purposely pitch a bad ball to a batter in a baseball game ⟨was ahead of the hitter and decided to *waste one* in the hope of getting him to swing⟩ — **waste one's breath** : to speak without result : accomplish nothing by speaking

³**waste** \"\ *adj* [ME *waste, wast,* fr. ONF *wast* — more at ¹WASTE] **1 a** (1) : wild and uninhabited : not supporting or incapable of supporting a living community : BARREN, DESOLATE ⟨~ places⟩ (2) : ARID, DISMAL, EMPTY ⟨the ~ realms of nonexistence —L.P.Smith⟩ **b** : not used for pasture or crops : UNCULTIVATED, UNPRODUCTIVE ⟨a small piece of ~ land which the farmers could readily spare —R.P.T.Coffin⟩ **2** : being in a ruined or uncultivated condition : DEVASTATED ⟨arrives at a large city, burnt and ~ —*Publ's Mod. Lang. Assoc. of Amer.*⟩ ⟨a bombing that laid ~ the city⟩ ⟨for lack of manpower, large areas lie ~⟩ **3** *archaic* : UNOCCUPIED, VACANT ⟨a large ~ barn, which had survived the farmhouse to which it had once belonged —Sir Walter Scott⟩ **4** [¹*waste*] **a** : thrown away or aside as worthless, defective, or of no further use during or at the end of a process : REFUSE ⟨~ steam⟩ ⟨~ material⟩ **b** : allowed to escape unused ⟨~ power⟩ **c** : excreted by an animal body ⟨~ matter⟩ **5** [¹*waste*] : serving to conduct or hold refuse material; *specif* : carrying off, providing for, or regulating the outflow of superfluous water ⟨a ~ cock⟩ ⟨a ~ drain⟩ ⟨a ~ spout⟩

waste bank *n* : a bank made of earth excavated during the digging of a ditch and laid parallel to it

¹**wastebasket** \ˈ-,-\ *n* [³*waste* + *basket*] : a basket for disposing of unwanted odds and ends esp. wastepaper — called also *scrap basket*

²**wastebasket** \"\ *vt* : to put into a wastebasket

wastebin \ˈ-,-\ *n* : TRASH CAN

wasteboard \ˈ-,-\ *n* : WASHBOARD

waste bowl *n* : a small bowl forming part of a tea service and used for waste tea or tea leaves

wasted *adj* [ME, fr. past part. of *wasten* to waste] **1** : laid waste : RAVAGED ⟨did fix mine eye upon the ~ building —Shak.⟩ **2** : impaired in strength or health : made weak or thin (as from disease or hunger) : EMACIATED ⟨kept life in his ~ frame not by hope but only by a grim ancient concentration —R.O.Bowen⟩ **3** *obs* : ELAPSED ⟨the chronicle of ~ time —Shak.⟩ **4** : unprofitably used, made, or expended : SQUANDERED ⟨~ effort⟩ ⟨a ~ trip⟩ ⟨~ money⟩

waste·ful \ˈwāstfəl\ *adj* [ME, fr. ¹*waste* + *-ful*] **1** *archaic* : serving to lay waste : causing devastation : DESTRUCTIVE ⟨when ~ war shall statues overturn —Shak.⟩ **2 a** : expending or tending to expend something valuable in a useless or extravagant manner : given to or marked by waste : LAVISH, PRODIGAL ⟨incompetent, ~, and corrupt . . . squandered money in bucketfuls —Allan Nevins & H.S.Commager⟩ ⟨in the same ~ spirit, they had cooked . . . three times more than we could eat —R.L.Stevenson⟩ **b** : causing needless loss or expenditure — used with *of* ⟨a defective boiler that is ~ of fuel⟩ **c** *archaic* : causing loss of bodily strength or weight ⟨lacking the burthen of lean and ~ learnings —Shak.⟩ **3** *archaic* : DESOLATE, UNINHABITED ⟨in wilderness and ~ deserts strayed —Edmund Spenser⟩ — **waste·ful·ly** \-fəlē, -li\ *adv* — **waste·ful·ness** *n* -ES

waste gate *n* **1** : a gate by which superfluous water (as of a reservoir) is discharged **2** : a device for controlling the pressure in the nozzle box of a turbosupercharger by discharging into the free atmosphere a portion of the exhaust gases that would otherwise pass through the turbine wheel : BLAST GATE

waste heat *n* : heat rejected or escaping from furnaces of various types (as coke ovens, cement kilns, or steel furnaces) after it has served its primary purpose

waste-heat boiler *n* : a steam boiler in which waste heat is used to evaporate water into steam

wasteland \ˈ-,-\ *n* **1** : barren or uncultivated land : WASTE **2** : a devastated place or area ⟨a ~ of burned houses and barns —A.E.Stevenson b. 1900⟩ ⟨a ~ of ruins and rubble —Robert Shaplen⟩ **3** : something (as an era, a way of life) that is emotionally or spiritually arid, barren, and desolate ⟨a ~ of futility and emptiness —J.W.Aldridge⟩ ⟨a ~ of vulgarity, platitude, and dulled perception —Anthony West⟩

was·tel bread \ˈwästᵊl-\ *or* **wastel cake** *n* [ME *wastel breed,* fr. *wastel* wastel bread (fr. ONF, fr. the Gmc source of OF *gastel* cake) + *breed* bread — more at GATEAU, BREAD] : bread formerly made of very fine flour; *also* : a cake or loaf of such bread

waste leaf *n* **1** : either of two protective extra blank leaves tipped on as the first and last leaves of a book and torn off when endpapers are affixed — called also *smut sheet* **2** : ENDPAPER

waste·less \ˈwāstləs\ *adj* [¹*waste* + *-less*] : incapable of being used up : INEXHAUSTIBLE ⟨a ~ source of energy⟩

waste·man \-tmən\ *n, pl* **wastemen** : a worker who removes waste: as **a** : one who collects and disposes of waste that accumulates during a manufacturing process **b** : a mine worker who keeps working areas and passageways free of refuse and repairs brattices — called also *jerry man*

waste mold *n* : a sculptor's mold that cannot be removed from the cast without being destroyed — compare PIECE MOLD

waste·ness \ˈwās(t)nəs\ *n* -ES [ME *wastnesse,* fr. ³*waste* + *-nesse* -ness] : the quality or state of being waste : a desolate state or condition ⟨a day of trouble and distress, a day of ~ and desolation —Zeph 1:15 (AV)⟩

waste nut *n* : an internally threaded floor flange for a pipe (as for waste)

waste of assets : DEVASTAVIT 1

wastepaper \ˈ-,-\ *n* **1 a** : paper discarded as superfluous or not fit for a particular use but usu. regarded as valuable raw material in some processes (as the manufacture of paperboard) **b** : worthless paper ⟨invested in fraudulent stocks that are just so much ~⟩ **2** *usu* **waste paper** : ENDPAPER

waste nut

wastepile \ˈ-,-\ *n* : TALON 3a

waste pipe *n* : a pipe for carrying off superfluous fluid : an escape pipe; *specif* : an outlet pipe for carrying off liquid waste (as from a washbowl, bathtub, or sink)

waste product *n* **1** : debris resulting from a process (as of manufacture) that is of no further use to the system producing it ⟨the *waste products* of one industry may be the raw materials of another⟩ **2** : material (as feces, urine, or desquamated cells) discharged from or stored in an inert form in a living body as a by-product of its vital activities ⟨animal *waste products* fill much of the nitrogen demand of plants⟩

¹**wast·er** \ˈwāstə(r)\ *n* -S [ME, fr. *wasten* to waste + *-er*] **1 a** (1) : one that spends or consumes extravagantly : PRODIGAL, SPENDTHRIFT, SQUANDERER ⟨a ~ who had run through a large fortune⟩ (2) : a dissolute person : GOOD-FOR-NOTHING, WASTREL ⟨a handsome face, though you didn't need to look twice to see that it was the face of a ~ —*Strand Mag.*⟩ **b** : one that uses wastefully or causes or permits waste ⟨a speaker who is a great ~ of words⟩ ⟨a procedure that is a ~ of time⟩ **c** (1) : one that lays waste or ruins : DESOLATER, DESTROYER, DEVASTATOR ⟨the ruin of youth, the ~ of fortunes, the destroyer of families —Lafcadio Hearn⟩ ⟨have created the ~ to destroy —Isa 54:16 (AV)⟩ (2) *archaic* : one of a class of thieves of 14th century England **2 a** : an animal (as a lamb that fails to fatten or a bird rejected for breeding) of inferior quality **b** : something that is useless or defective : an imperfect or inferior manufactured article or object **3** : a jockey who works with specified success or lack of success to take off weight ⟨a bad ~ who can't make the weight⟩

²**waster** \"\ *n* -S [ME, of unknown origin] *archaic* : a wooden sword or cudgel used in fencing or singlestick

³**waster** \"\ *n* -S [alter. (influenced by *leister*) of ME *waspere,* fr. *wa-* (of unknown origin) + *spere* spear] *Scot* : LEISTER

wast·er·ful \-(r)fəl\ *adj* [fr. obs. *waster* to be a waster, waste (fr. ¹*waster*) + *-ful*] *Scot* : WASTEFUL

wastery *var of* WASTRY

wastes *pl of* WASTE, *pres 3d sing of* WASTE

wastethrift \ˈ-,-\ *n* [²*waste* + *thrift* (savings)] : SPENDTHRIFT

wastetime \ˈ-,-\ *n* [²*waste* + *time*] *archaic* : PASTIME

waste-wax process *n* : CIRE PERDUE

wasteway \ˈ-,-\ *n* : a channel for carrying off superfluous water

wasteweir \ˈ-,-\ *n* : a weir for the escape of superfluous water

wasteyard \ˈ-,-\ *n* : a yard for storing refuse

¹**wasting** *adj* [ME, fr. pres. part. of *wasten* to waste] **1** : serving or acting to lay waste : DEVASTATING ⟨see the cities and the towns defaced by ~ ruin —Shak.⟩ **2** : undergoing gradual loss, diminution, or decay ⟨a ~ fortune⟩ ⟨a ~ muscle⟩ ⟨sands and clays brought from the ~ Andes by the great rivers —P.E.James⟩ **3** : causing decay or loss of strength ⟨hectic elements producing ~ fevers in the blood of society —*Times Lit. Supp.*⟩ — **wast·ing·ly** *adv* — **wast·ing·ness** *n* -ES

²**wasting** *n* -S [ME, fr. gerund of *wasten* to waste] **1** *archaic* : the act or action of devastating : DESOLATION ⟨violence shall no more be heard in thy land, ~ nor destruction within thy borders —Isa 60:18 (AV)⟩ **2** : wasteful use or expenditure ⟨the ~ of money⟩ **3 a** : the process or condition of wasting away : gradual loss of strength or substance : ATROPHY ⟨results in sores, ~, and eventually death —J.F.M.Middleton⟩ **b** (1) : gradual consumption or wearing away ⟨things Grecian grandeur with the rude ~ of old time —John Keats⟩ (2) : MASS-WASTING **c** : the process of exercising or training to lose weight

wasting asset *n* : property (as mines or lumber tracts) subject to depletion

wasting disease *n* : cobalt deficiency disease of sheep and cattle — compare ¹PINE 3

wasting palsy *or* **wasting paralysis** *n* : CREEPING PARALYSIS

¹**was·trel** \ˈwāstrəl *sometimes* ˈwäs-\ *n* -S [²*waste* + *-rel* (as in *scoundrel*)] **1** *dial Eng* : a piece of waste land beside a road **2 a** : something rejected or discarded as useless or imperfect ⟨~s from the workshops of neolithic peoples —A.H.Keane⟩ ⟨in the first thinning only the ~s and dead trees are removed —John Simpson⟩ **b** : an emaciated and unhealthy animal **3 a** : GOOD-FOR-NOTHING, PROFLIGATE ⟨was regarded as essentially a ~ and, given the opportunity, a Grade A guttersnipe —Stanley Walker⟩ **b** : VAGABOND, WAIF ⟨the girlish ~ who had drifted into the house —*Harper's*⟩ **4** : one that wastes : SPENDTHRIFT, WASTER ⟨a spendthrift and ~ of the world's stored energy —W.P.Webb⟩

²**wastrel** \"\ *adj* **1** : rejected as defective : WORTHLESS **2** : wasting or going to waste : SPENDTHRIFT ⟨the end of his now ~ ways —Maristan Chapman⟩

¹**wast·rife** \ˈwā,strīf\ *adj* [¹*waste* + *rife*] *Scot* : WASTEFUL

²**wastrife** \"\ *n* -S *Scot* : WASTEFULNESS

wast·ry *also* **waste·ry** *or* **wast·rie** \ˈwāstri\ *n* [²*waste* + *-ry, -ery*] *Scot* : PRODIGALITY, WASTE

wasty \ˈwāstē\ *adj* -ER/-EST [¹*waste* + *-y*] **1** *archaic* : WASTEFUL **2** : containing or yielding much waste ⟨~ wool⟩ **3** *of livestock* : excessively fat

¹**wat** \ˈwat\ *Scot var of* WET

²**wat** \ˈwät\ *n* -S *often cap* [ME, prob. fr. *Wat,* nickname for *Walter*] *archaic* : HARE

³**wat** \"\ *n* -S [Siamese, fr. Skt *vāṭa* enclosed ground] : a Buddhist temple or monastery in Thailand

wa·tap \wäˈtäp\ *also* **wa·ta·pe** *or* **wat·ta·pe** \-pē\ *n* -S [CanF *watap,* fr. Algonquin] : a thread made of the stringy roots of any of various coniferous trees and used by American Indians esp. for sewing together strips of birch bark in canoes

¹**watch** \ˈwäch *also* ˈwȯch\ *vb* -ED/-ING/-ES [ME *wacchen,* fr. OE *wæccan;* akin to OE *wacian* to wake — more at WAKE] *vi* **1 a** : to keep vigil as a devotional exercise ⟨taught me how to ~ and pray —Philip Doddridge⟩ **b** : to be awake : to be or continue without sleep : WAKE ⟨could you not ~ one hour —Mk 14:37 (RSV)⟩ **c** : to remain awake during the night in attendance on a sick person ⟨~*ed* by his bedside until morning⟩ **2 a** : to be on one's guard or on the lookout : be attentive or vigilant ⟨~ jealously for any infringements of their rights —W.G.Hardy⟩ **b** : to keep guard : act as guard ⟨told him to ~ outside and see that no one entered⟩ **3 a** : to

keep someone or something under close observation ⟨seemed to feel her eyes on me all the time . . . ~ing, prying, judging —T.B.Costain⟩ **b** : to observe as a spectator : look on ⟨the nation ~ed while stocks rose to staggering heights —*Amer. Guide Series: Minn.*⟩ **4** *of an otter* : to retire into a lair to rest **5** : to serve on a ship's watch **6** *of a buoy* : to float properly in its place **7** : to remain unfolded or unclosed — used of a flower **8** : to look with expectation : be expectant : WAIT ⟨~ed for the signal⟩ ⟨~ed for the train⟩ ~ *vt* **1** : to keep under guard ⟨protected by a pair of high fences ~ed by armed guards —*Lamp*⟩ **2 a** : to observe closely in order to check on action or change : keep tabs on ⟨says he's positive they're being ~ed by the police —Mary Deasy⟩ ⟨every eye was fixed aloft, ~ing the masts, which were expected every moment to go over the side —Frederick Marryat⟩ **b** : to look at : OBSERVE ⟨~ a bus approaching you —Bertrand Russell⟩ ⟨sat very still and ~ed him —Raymond Chandler⟩ **c** : to be a spectator at : look on at ⟨people have a hard time getting to ~ afternoon entertainment in this age —John Lardner⟩ ⟨~ a ball game⟩ **3 a** : to take care of : TEND ⟨~ed the baby while her mother shopped⟩ **b** : to attend to : OVERSEE ⟨will ~ their plane reservations and their weight, their hotel bookings and their manners —Harry Gordon⟩ **c** : to be careful of ⟨as a performer I'd have to rest, ~ my diet —Barbara B. Jamison⟩ **d** : to make sure ⟨~ that he doesn't fall⟩ **4** : to keep (a hawk) from sleep for the purpose of tiring and taming ⟨my lord shall never rest, I'll ~ him tame —Shak.⟩ **5** : to be on the alert for : be ready to take advantage of or use : wait for : BIDE ⟨an adversary of no common prowess was ~ing his time —T.B. Macaulay⟩ ⟨~ed his opportunity⟩ **6** : to keep in touch with : remain aware of or informed about ⟨no one who has ~ed the course of history during the last generation can have felt doubt of its tendency —Henry Adams⟩ **7** *Brit* : to provide with watchmen : POLICE **syn** see SEE — **watch it** : look out : be careful ⟨you got live ammunition there . . . *watch it* —Wirt Williams⟩ — **watch one's step** : to proceed with extreme care : act or talk warily ⟨the columnist dealing largely with news always has to *watch his step* if he is to avoid distortion —F.L.Mott⟩ — **watch over** : to have charge of : care for : SUPERINTEND ⟨*watches over* the safety of perhaps 250 landings and takeoffs a day —Ivor Jones⟩

²watch \"\ *n* -ES [ME *wacche*, fr. OE *wæcce*, fr. *wæccan*, v.] **1 a** : the act of keeping awake for the purpose of guarding, protecting, or attending : sleepless vigilance ⟨kept ~ by his bed —Robert Browning⟩ **b** *obs* : the state of being awake : SLEEPLESSNESS, WAKEFULNESS ⟨fell into a sadness, then into a fast, thence to a ~ —Shak.⟩ **c** : a wake over a dead body **d** : a state of alert and continuous attention to some situation, course of events, or danger ⟨in a position to keep a close ~ over events —R.P.Brooks⟩ ⟨wide open were the gates and no ~ kept —Alfred Tennyson⟩ **e** : close observation over someone : SURVEILLANCE ⟨kept a careful ~ over the prisoner⟩ ⟨kept a close ~ over his son⟩ **2 a** : any of the definite divisions of the night made by ancient peoples **b** : one of the indeterminate wakeful intervals marking the passage of night — usu. used in pl. ⟨the silent ~es of the night⟩ **3 a** : one that watches : LOOKOUT, WATCHMAN ⟨a yell from the bow ~ —Vincent McHugh⟩ **b** *archaic* : the office or function of a sentinel or guard ⟨as I did stand my ~ upon the hill —Shak.⟩ **c** *obs* : the cry of a watchman or sentinel ⟨his sentinel, the wolf, whose howl's his ~ —Shak.⟩ **4** : a person or group of persons charged with the duty or function of protecting life or property or preserving the peace: as **a** : a body of soldiers or sentinels making up the guard of a camp or town ⟨some of the ~ came into the city —Mt 28:11 (AV)⟩ **b** : a watchman or body of watchmen formerly assigned to patrol the streets of a town at night, announce the hours, and act as police ⟨they fight! I will go call the ~ —Shak.⟩ **c** *usu cap* : a company of irregular Highland troops ⟨the Black *Watch*⟩ **5** : a flock of nightingales **6 a** (1) : a portion of time during which a part of a ship's company is required to be on deck ready for duty — see AFTERNOON WATCH, DOGWATCH, FIRST WATCH, FORENOON WATCH, MIDWATCH, MORNING WATCH (2) : the part of a ship's company required to be on duty during a particular watch ⟨one by one, junior members of the ~ reported that they had been properly relieved —K.M.Dodson⟩ — see PORT WATCH, STARBOARD WATCH (3) : a sailor's assigned duty period ⟨everything was peaceful during his ~⟩ **b** : a period of duty : SHIFT ⟨was the duty sergeant on the 4 P.M. to midnight ~ for four years —*Springfield (Mass.) Union*⟩ **7 a** : a portable timepiece that has a movement driven in any of several ways (as by a spring or a battery) and is designed to be worn (as on the wrist) or carried in the pocket — compare CLOCK **b** *obs* : the dial of a clock **c** : the going train in a striking clock **d** : a ship's chronometer **8** : a place of observation : a lookout station ⟨three of us were catfooting up a shallow draft to our ~es —Ed Shearer⟩ — **on the watch** : on the alert

³watch \"\ *adj* **1** : used while or for watching : qualified to watch : used or serving as a lookout ⟨a ~ mastiff⟩ **2** : of, belonging to, or used by a watchman or watcher ⟨a ~ pole⟩

watch·able \-chəbəl\ *adj* : worth watching ⟨her manner . . . totally unselfconscious and yet so ~ for its own sake —Lucien Price⟩

watch and ward *or* **watching and warding** *n* [ME *wacche and warde*] **1** : the act of keeping guard : continuous unbroken vigilance and guard ⟨a handful of men kept *watch and ward* against the Iroquois —Francis Parkman⟩ **2 a** : service as a watchman or sentinel required from a feudal tenant — compare BURGAGE 2 **b** : service as a watchman specified as one of the chief duties of a constable

watch and watch *n* : the regular alternation in being on and off watch of the two watches into which a ship's crew is usu. divided

watchband \'⸗,⸗\ *n* : the bracelet or strap of a wristwatch

watch bell *n* [ME *wacche belle*, fr. *wacche* watch + *belle* bell — more at WATCH, BELL] : BELL 3a

watch bill *n* : a list of a ship's company divided into watches

watchboat \'⸗,⸗\ *n* : a boat engaged in patrolling

watch box *n* **1** : SENTRY BOX **2** : a shelter for a person (as a watchman or policeman) on watch

watch candle *n* : a slow-burning candle used (as by those who watch by the sick or deceased) during night watches or at a shrine

watch cap *n* : a knitted close-fitting navy blue cap worn esp. by enlisted men in the U. S. Navy in cold or stormy weather

watchcase \'⸗,⸗\ *n* **1** *obs* : SENTRY BOX **2 a** : the outside metal covering of the works of a watch **b** : a case for holding a watch

watch chain *n* : a usu. precious metal chain fastened to the pendant of a pocket watch — see ALBERT

watch charm *n* : a small ornament designed to dangle from a watch chain

watch clock *n* : WATCHMAN'S CLOCK

watch coat *also* **watch cloak** *n* : a warm overcoat worn esp. by sailors and soldiers on watch in cold or stormy weather

watchcry \'⸗,⸗\ *n* **1** : the cry of a watchman making his rounds **2** : a word or phrase briefly embodying the guiding principle of a party or movement and used as a slogan : WATCHWORD

watch crystal *n* : a concavo-convex glass covering the dial of a watch — called also *watch glass*

watch desk *n* : a desk in a fire station at which a fireman is on duty at all times

¹watchdog \'⸗,⸗\ *n*, *often attrib* [²*watch* + *dog*] **1** : a dog kept to guard against trespassers or thieves **2** : one that guards against loss, waste, theft, or undesirable practices ⟨should deal with its responsibilities in this matter as a ~ on behalf of the nation as a whole —Stephen King-Hall⟩

²watchdog \"\ *vt* : to act as a watchdog for ⟨opposed tax funds for television as part of its role of *watchdogging* the public purse —Richard Lewis⟩

watched *past of* WATCH

watch·er \'wächə(r) *also* 'wȯch-\ *n* -s : one that watches: as **a** : one that sits up or continues awake at night ⟨get on your nightgown, lest occasion call us, and show us to be ~s —Shak.⟩ **b** : one that keeps awake for the purpose of guarding : WATCHMAN ⟨the tapes and the lights instantly alert round-the-clock ~s when a criminal has run afoul of an electric or electronic snare —Alan Hynd⟩ **c** : ANGEL 1b **d** (1) : one that keeps watch beside a dead person (2) : one that attends a sick person at night **e** : OBSERVER, VIEWER ⟨an intense ~ of the scene —Elizabeth M. Roberts⟩ ⟨the sky ~s tell us of the birth and death of stars —*Scientific American Reader*⟩ **f** : a representative of a party or candidate who is stationed at the polls on an election day to watch the conduct of officials and voters **g** : one that is employed to watch equipment to see that a manufacturing or other process is carried out correctly: as (1) : one that runs an embroidering machine (2) : a textile worker who watches the fixing of colors on printed cloth **h** : one that tests the gas content of petroleum tanks before cleaners enter them

watches *pres 3d sing of* WATCH, *pl of* WATCH

watch·et \'wächət *also* 'wȯch-\ *n* -s [ME *wachet*, fr. ONF] **1** *or* **watchet blue** : a light blue color ⟨her dressing gown of *watchet blue* —Llewelyn Powys⟩ **2** *archaic* **a** : a light blue cloth **b** : a light blue angler's fly

watcheye \'⸗,⸗\ *n* : WALLEYE 1; *esp* : a walleye of a dog

watch face *n* : the dial of a watch

watch fire *n* : a fire lighted at night as a signal or for the use of a guard

watch fob *n* : ³FOB 2

watch·ful \'wächfəl *also* 'wȯch-\ *adj* **1** *archaic* **a** : not able or accustomed to sleep or rest : WAKEFUL ⟨to thee I do commend my ~ soul —Shak.⟩ **b** : causing sleeplessness ⟨~ cares —Shak.⟩ **c** : spent in wakefulness : SLEEPLESS ⟨twenty ~, weary, tedious nights —Shak.⟩ **2** : marked by vigilance ⟨there was a ~ dignity in the room —J.P.Marquand⟩ **3** *archaic* : requiring vigilance **4** : carefully observant or attentive : full of vigilance : being on the watch ⟨an instructed and ~ physician might well hope to cure you —Nathaniel Hawthorne⟩ ⟨has been equally ~ to assure scope for the states upon which the Union rests —Felix Frankfurter⟩ ⟨~ against attack⟩

syn VIGILANT, WIDE-AWAKE, ALERT: WATCHFUL is a general term indicating being on the lookout, often for danger, adverse developments, or opportunity ⟨glanced aside with a *watchful* air, just as a hound may often be seen to take sidelong note of some suspicious object —Nathaniel Hawthorne⟩ ⟨*watchful* of wind, water, and every movement of his opponents, he lost no chance to gain an inch —G.H.Genzmer⟩ VIGILANT suggests unremitting, keen, often wary watchfulness ⟨the *vigilant* eye of the Town Watch —*Amer. Guide Series: Mass.*⟩ ⟨eternally *vigilant* against attempts to check the expression of opinions that we loathe —O.W.Holmes †1935⟩ WIDE-AWAKE may stress keen awareness of relevant developments and situations ⟨was *wide-awake* now, and practical, ready to cope with the truth, whatever it was —Kathleen Freeman⟩ ALERT suggests careful watchfulness and ready promptness in apprehending danger or coping with difficulty or seizing opportunity ⟨standing silent and *alert*, like a sentinel on duty, in some dark corner —J.G.Frazer⟩ ⟨the auction conducts the sales . . . and is *alert* to expand the market outlet —*Amer. Guide Series: N.H.*⟩

watch·ful·ly \-fəlē, -li\ *adv* : in a watchful manner ⟨paused, and the room was ~ silent —J.P.Marquand⟩

watch·ful·ness *n* -ES : the quality or state of being watchful

watchful waiting *n* : a policy of taking no immediate action with respect to a situation or course of events but of following its development intently

watch glass *n* **1** : WATCH CRYSTAL **2 a** : a usu. glass dish similar to a watch crystal in shape but made in various sizes **b** : SYRACUSE WATCH GLASS

watch gun *n* : a gun sometimes fired on shipboard at 8 p.m. when the first watch begins

watch hand *n* : the hour hand or the minute hand of a watch

watchhouse \'⸗,⸗\ *n* [ME *wache howsse*] **1** : a house in which a guard is placed **2** : a place where persons under temporary arrest are kept : POLICE STATION

watching *pres part of* WATCH

watching and warding *var of* WATCH AND WARD

watching brief *n* **1** : a retainer of a lawyer merely to watch proceedings for one not a party to them **2** : a commission to observe proceedings (as of a legislative body) for persons who may be concerned in them

watchkeeper \'⸗,⸗⸗\ *n* : one who serves in a ship's watch; *specif* : one (as a quartermaster or radio operator) having special duties requiring a separate routine of watchkeeping from that of the port and starboard watches

watchkeeping \'⸗,⸗⸗\ *n* : the duty or function of keeping watch

watch key *n* : a square-holed key that is used to wind some watches

watch·less \'wächləs *also* 'wȯch-\ *adj* **1** : not watching : lacking in vigilance ⟨a ~ soldier⟩ **2** : having no watch or watchman : UNGUARDED ⟨a ~ fortress⟩ **3** : not divided into watches : not marked by wakefulness ⟨a ~ night⟩ — **watch·less·ness** *n* -ES

watch light *n* : a light that is used by watchers or by a watchman

watch line *n* : a fire hose left attached to a hydrant for a time as a precautionary measure after fire apparatus has been withdrawn from the scene of a fire

watchmaker \'⸗,⸗⸗\ *n* : one that makes or repairs watches or clocks

watchmaking \'⸗,⸗⸗\ *n* : the work or occupation of a watchmaker

watch·man \'⸗mən\ *n*, *pl* **watchmen** [ME *waccheman*, fr. *wacche* watch + *man*] **1** : one who keeps watch : GUARD, SENTINEL: as **a** : one formerly assigned to guard the streets of a city by night **b** : one who is employed to stand watch over or to patrol property for the purpose of protecting it against theft, fire, or other damage **c** : one who keeps guard at a particular place to warn persons of imminent danger **d** : a fireman on duty at a watch desk **2** : ⁵FLAG 3b

watchman beetle *n* : a European dorbeetle

watch·man·ly *adj* : belonging to or suitable for a watchman

watchman's clock *n* : a telltale clock for watchmen; *esp* : one in which a single clock contains the apparatus for recording the times of visiting several stations

watchman's rattle *n* : ²RATTLE 2b

watch mark *n* : a mark formerly worn (as in the U. S. Navy) on the right or the left sleeve to indicate the wearer's watch as the starboard or the port watch

watchmate \'⸗,⸗\ *n* : a man on duty in the same watch with another

watch meeting *n* : a watch-night service

watch night *n* **1** : a devotional exercise lasting until after midnight and held orig. each month by Wesleyan Methodists and later by them and others on New Year's Eve **2** *usu cap W&N* : the last night of the year

watch officer *n* : a naval officer or petty officer who stands a watch — compare OFFICER OF THE DECK

watch out *vi* : to be vigilant : look out — often used with *for* ⟨had better *watch out* for himself, or one day he would be sorry —Robert Westerby⟩

watchout \'⸗,⸗\ *n* -s [*watch out*] : LOOKOUT 3 ⟨kept an increasing ~ for city and state corruption —*Time*⟩

watch paper *n* : an ornamental packing formerly placed inside a watchcase and made of paper fancifully cut or printed and sometimes bearing the maker's or repairer's name

watch pocket *n* : ³FOB 1

watch rate *n* : a tax rate for meeting the expense of a municipal watch

watch room *n* **1** : a room for watchmen **2** : a continuously attended room in a fire station in which alarms are received

watch screw thread *n* : a screw thread sometimes used in American watches and having a V profile with a 45-degree included angle for nickel and brass and a 60-degree included angle for steel

watch seal *n* : a seal or a trinket in imitation of a seal worn attached to a watch chain

watch spring *n* : one of the several springs in a watch; *specif* : MAINSPRING

watch stander *n* : a member of a ship's company standing watch

watch stuffer *n*, *slang* : one who palms off poor or worthless watches as good ones

watch stuffing *n*, *slang* : the practice of a watch stuffer

watch tackle *n* : a light 2-sheave tackle commonly used as a luff upon luff by the watch on shipboard for jobs (as the handling of yardarms) that usu. require all hands — called also *handy-billy*, *jigger*

watchtower \'⸗,⸗\ *n* **1 a** : a tower on which a sentinel is or may be placed : LOOKOUT **b** : an observation point ⟨from this somewhat unpromising ~ . . . surveyed English life —*Quarterly Rev.*⟩ **2** *archaic* : LIGHTHOUSE **3** : a turret-shaped projection of the cephalothorax of a spider supporting an eye

watch train *n* : the time train of a watch

watchwoman \'⸗,⸗⸗\ *n*, *pl* **watchwomen** : a woman who watches or serves as a guard

watchword \'⸗,⸗\ *n* [ME *waccheword*, fr. *wacche* watch + *word*] **1 a** : a secret word that is used as a signal permitting a person to pass a guard : PASSWORD ⟨stealthy guests have secret ~s, private entrances —Robert Browning⟩ **b** : a word or phrase used as a sign of recognition among members of the same society, class, or group **2** *archaic* : a prearranged signal for attack or other action **3** *archaic* : a watchman's call **4 a** : a word or motto that embodies a principle or guide to action of an individual or group : SLOGAN ⟨the ~ of the conservative is "order" —H.N.Maclean⟩ ⟨"death rather than crime", such is the good man's ~ —W.E.Channing⟩ **b** : a guiding principle ⟨make cost reduction through production efficiency your ~ —*Successful Farming*⟩

watchwork \'⸗,⸗\ *n* : the wheelwork of a watch; *also* : a similar small wheelwork — compare CLOCKWORK

wate \'wāt\ *chiefly Scot var of* ²WOT

¹wa·ter \'wȯd|ə(r), 'wä|, |tə(r)\ *n* -s *often attrib* [ME, fr. OE *wæter*; akin to OHG *wazzar* water, ON *vatn*, Goth *wato* water, L *unda* wave, Gk *hydōr* water, Skt *udan*] **1 a** : the liquid that descends from the clouds as rain, forms streams, lakes, and seas, issues from the ground in springs, and is a major constituent of all living matter and that when pure consists of an oxide of hydrogen H_2O or $(H_2O)_x$ in the proportion of 2 atoms of hydrogen to one atom of oxygen and is an odorless, tasteless, very slightly compressible liquid which appears bluish in thick layers, freezes at 0° C and boils at 100° C, has a maximum density at 4° C and a high specific heat, contains very small equal concentrations of hydrogen ions and hydroxide ions, reacts neutrally, and constitutes a poor conductor of electricity, a good ionizing agent, and a good solvent — compare HEAVY WATER, ICE, STEAM, WATER VAPOR **b** (1) : a natural mineral water — usu. used in pl. ⟨drank the ~s for rheumatism⟩ (2) *archaic* : a place (as a spa) purveying such waters for remedial purposes : WATERING PLACE **2** : a particular quantity or mass of water: as **a** : a portion of water to drink ⟨brought her ~ in a silver cup⟩ **b** (1) **waters** *pl* : the water occupying or flowing in a particular bed ⟨the limpid ~s of a mountain brook⟩ (2) *chiefly Brit* : a body of still fresh water : LAKE, POND, POOL (3) *chiefly Scot* : STREAM, RIVER; *also* : land abutting a stream : the bank of a stream **c** : a portion of water for a particular use — usu. used in pl. ⟨wash the greens in three ~s⟩ **d** : a quantity or depth of water adequate for some purpose (as navigation) ⟨a boat drawing three feet of ~⟩ ⟨there is ~ for trout⟩ **e** **waters** *pl* (1) : a band of seawater abutting on the land of a particular sovereignty and under the control of that sovereignty : the marine territorial waters of a state ⟨an invasion of British ~s⟩ (2) : the sea of a particular part of the earth ⟨the fleet was in eastern ~s⟩ **f** : a water supply ⟨threatened to turn off the ~⟩ ⟨our ~ was from springs⟩ **3** : a means of transport on water or travel or transportation by such ⟨we went by ~⟩ ⟨they came by air but sent their heavy baggage by ~⟩ **4** : the level of water at a particular state of the tide : TIDE ⟨waiting for low ~⟩ ⟨high ~ was at six o'clock⟩ **5** : any of various liquid preparations containing or resembling water: as **a** (1) : a liquid (as a pharmaceutical or cosmetic preparation) prepared (as by solution or infusion) with water — compare FLORIDA WATER, LAVENDER WATER, TOILET WATER (2) : a watery solution of a gaseous or readily volatile substance — compare AMMONIA WATER, CAMPHOR WATER **b** *archaic* : a distilled fluid (as an essence); *esp* : a distilled alcoholic liquor **c** *obs* : a strong acid; *esp* : NITRIC ACID **6** : a liquid (as a secretion, effusion, or humor) formed in or circulating in a living body: as **a** : TEARS ⟨a blow that brought the ~ to his eyes⟩ **b** : URINE ⟨passed a bloody ~⟩ **c** : a plant juice or other plant fluid; *esp* : COCONUT MILK **d** : SALIVA ⟨the smell of fresh bread brought the ~ to his mouth⟩ **e** : AMNIOTIC FLUID ⟨a dry birth with little ~⟩ — usu. used with *the* and in pl. ⟨after the ~s broke the labor was brief⟩ **7 a** : the limpidity and luster of a precious stone and esp. a diamond ⟨a diamond of the first ~ is perfectly clear and transparent⟩ — compare RIVER 3 **b** : an indicated and usu. exceptional degree of some quality (as excellence or villainy) ⟨a fool of the purest ~⟩ **c** : a wavy lustrous pattern (as of a textile or metal surface) ⟨a shimmering ~ played along the supple blade⟩ **8** : WATERCOLOR; *esp* : a picture done in watercolor **9 a** : capital stock not representing assets of the issuing company and not backed by earning power **b** : fictitious or exaggerated asset entries (as for goodwill or other intangibles or for mining claims or other speculative or undeveloped assets) that give a stock an unrealistic book value — **above water** *adv* : out of difficulty or embarrassment ⟨an island that still depends on smuggling to keep the economy *above water* —David Butwin⟩ — **in smooth water** : progressing without impediment — **on the water** *or* **upon the water** : enroute aboard or in a ship at sea

²water \"\ *vb* -ED/-ING/-s [ME *wateren*, fr. OE *wæterian*, fr. *wæter*, n.] *vt* **1** : to wet or supply with water or watery fluid : moisten, sprinkle, or soak with water : overflow with water : IRRIGATE ⟨~ flowers⟩ ⟨rain ~ing the soil⟩ ⟨with tears ~ing the ground —John Milton⟩ **2** : to supply (as an army or ship) with water for drink : cause or allow to drink : give drink to or lead to a stream of water or other drinking place ⟨~ cattle and horses⟩ **3** : to supply water to (as through the soil) ⟨land or vegetation ~ed by the Missouri⟩ : supply (as a boiler or engine) with water **4** *archaic* : to embrace within a surrounding or protecting stream, moat, or body of water ⟨a city ~ed about⟩ **5** : to treat with or as if with water: as **a** *obs* : to soak in water (as for softening, macerating, or freshening) **b** : to sprinkle or drench so as to impregnate with water or a solution **c** : to impart a lustrous appearance and wavy pattern to (cloth) by calendering **d** : to spray or sprinkle (as a roadway) with water to lay dust **e** : to flood (as a ship in a lock) with water at the base for lifting **6 a** : to make dilute by or as if by the addition of water ⟨~ing the wine to make it last⟩ — sometimes used with *down* **b** : to reduce by addition or change usu. so as to weaken in force or efficacy : temper or soften in pungency, vigor, or positiveness — usu. used with *down* ⟨~ed down his remarks⟩ ⟨took care to ~ his radicalism down in public⟩ **c** (1) : to cause (oysters) to swell by soaking in water (2) : to cause (livestock) to put on specious weight by salting and watering heavily before marketing **d** : to add to the aggregate par value of (stock or other securities) without a corresponding addition to the assets represented by the security ~ *vi* **1** : to form or secrete water or watery matter: as **a** : to produce or shed tears ⟨eyes ~ing from the smoke⟩ **b** : to secrete or become filled with saliva usu. in anticipation of food ⟨mouths ~ed as we waited for dinner⟩ **2** : to get or take water: as **a** : to take on a supply of water ⟨the boat docked to ~⟩ **b** : to drink water : take a drink of water — usu. used of lower animals ⟨lions ~ing at dusk⟩

water adder *n* [ME] **1** : WATER MOCCASIN **2** : a common harmless American water snake (*Natrix sipedon*)

wa·ter·age \-ərij\ *n* -s [¹*water* + *-age*] *Brit* : transportation (as of goods) by water; *also* : money paid for such transportation

water agrimony *n* **1** : BUR MARIGOLD **2** : HEMP AGRIMONY

water antelope *n* : WATERBUCK

water arum *n* : a bog herb (*Calla palustris*) with a long creeping rhizome and reddish berries

water ash *n* **1** : any of several No. American ashes (as *Fraxinus nigra* and *F. pauciflora*); *specif* : a tree (*F. caroliniana*) of river swamps of the southern U. S. **2** : BOX ELDER

water avens *n* : an erect perennial herb (*Geum rivale*) of the north temperate zone with pinnate leaves and few nodding purple flowers

water back *n* **1** : a cistern used in brewing for storing hot or cold water **2 a** : a reservoir at the back of a wood or coal range for heating and storing water **b** : a system of tubes often enclosed in a solid casting, placed in the firebox of a wood or coal range on the side opposite the oven for heating water, and connected with a storage tank separate from the range

water bag *n* **1 :** a bag for holding water; *esp* **:** one designed to keep water cool for drinking by evaporation through a slightly porous surface **2 a :** the reticulum of a camel or a closely related animal **b :** the fetal membranes enclosing the amniotic fluid — used esp. of domestic animals **c :** a pouch filled with serous fluid; *also* **:** any of several abnormalities of domestic animals characterized by such a pouch

water·bail·age \ˈ==,bālij\ *n* -S **:** a duty imposed on goods transported by water

water bailiff *n* [ME] **1** *obs* **:** an English customs officer required to search ships **2 :** any of various former British officials having specified jurisdiction over the water: as **a :** an official superseded in 1771 having jurisdiction over fishing on the Thames **b :** an official in the Isle of Man having jurisdiction over fishery and some maritime jurisdiction prior to 1885 **c :** a police officer on a river employed esp. for the prevention of poaching

water balance *n* **:** the ratio representing the difference between water assimilated into the body and that lost from the body (as in urine, feces, and sweat) and being under average conditions approximately equal to unity

water ballast *n* **:** water in specially constructed compartments (as of a ship or balloon) to serve as ballast

water ballet *n* **:** a synchronized sequence of evolutions performed by a group of swimmers — compare AQUACADE, SYNCHRONIZED SWIMMING

water bar *n* **1 :** a ridge made across a hill road to divert rain water to one side **2 :** a bar inserted in a joint (as between the wood and stone sills of a window) to prevent passage of water **3 :** a tubular bar built into a fire grate as the heating unit of a system of hot water pipes

water bath *n* **1 :** a bath composed of or using water **2 :** a vessel containing usu. heated water over or in which something (as food) in a separate container is processed — called also *bain-marie;* compare STEAM TABLE

water bear *n* **1 :** POLAR BEAR **2 :** TARDIGRADE

water-bearer \ˈ==,==\ *n* [ME *waterberere,* fr. *water* + *berere* bearer] **:** a carrier of water for drinking or domestic use from a well or other source

water-bearing \ˈ==,==\ *adj* **:** yielding or holding water **:** laden with percolating water **:** permeable by water ⟨*water-bearing* strata⟩

water bed *n* **:** a soil or rock layer that is laden with water or through which water percolates; *sometimes* **:** a swampy surface area

water beech *n* **:** AMERICAN HORNBEAM

water beetle *n* **:** any of numerous oval flattened usu. black or dark-colored lustrous aquatic beetles that belong to Dytiscidae and several other families (as Haliplidae, Gyrinidae, and Hydrophilidae) and that swim with great agility by means of their fringed hind legs which act together as oars

water beetle

water bellows *n pl* **:** TROMPE

water-belly \ˈ==,==\ *n* **:** ascites of domestic mammals or birds

water betony *n* **:** a Eurasian plant (*Scrophularia aquatica*) of moist places with paniculate greenish purple flowers

water bewitched *n, dial Eng* **:** drink (as tea or grog) much diluted; *also* **:** a flat or insipid compound

water-bind \ˈ==,=\ *vt* **:** to consolidate (as road-building material) with water

water birch *n* **:** any of several American birches growing typically in moist places: as **a :** RIVER BIRCH **b :** WESTERN PAPER BIRCH

water bird *n* [ME] **:** an aquatic bird **:** a swimming or wading bird — compare WATERFOWL

water biscuit *n* **1 :** a cracker made of flour and water sometimes with added salt and fat **2 :** any of various hemispherical or discoid masses produced in fresh water both now and in remote geological times by various blue-green algae

water bitternut *n* **:** WATER HICKORY

waterblink \ˈ==,=\ *n* **:** WATER SKY

water blinks *n pl but sing or pl in constr* **:** BLINKS

water blister *n* **1 :** a blister with a clear watery content that is not purulent or sanguineous — compare BLOOD BLISTER **2 a :** a local injury to a plant caused by sunlight converging through a drop of water or a bubble in glass **b :** a disease of pineapples caused by a fungus (*Ceratostomella paradoxa*) and characterized by soft watery lesions on the fruit

water blob *n, dial Eng* **:** any of various aquatic or marsh plants: as **a :** a marsh marigold (*Caltha palustris*) **b :** WHITE WATER LILY

water bloom *n* **1 :** the accumulation of algae and esp. of various blue-green algae at or near the surface of a body of water often occurring suddenly and in large quantities and causing discoloration or forming a definite scum **2 a :** a scum that is formed by water bloom **b :** an algae causing water bloom

water blue *n, often cap W&B* **1 :** SOLUBLE BLUE 1 **2 :** BREMEN BLUE 1

water boa *n* **:** ANACONDA 2

water boat *n* **:** a boat carrying fresh water to ships

water boot *n* **:** a watertight boot for wear in water

waterborne \ˈ==,=\ *adj* **1 :** floated or floating upon the water **:** supported by water so as not to sink or to touch bottom **2 a :** conveyed by water and esp. by boat (~ traffic) **b :** transmitted by water and esp. by drinking water (~ diseases)

waterbosh \ˈ==,=\ *n* **:** ¹BOSH 2

water bottle *n* **:** a container (as of leather, rubber, or glass) for carrying or holding water; *specif* **:** a specially constructed vessel that is used for collecting samples of water at any desired depth

water bottom *n* **1 a :** the space between the outer and inner bottom plating in a ship used to carry water ballast **b :** a similar space in a petroleum storage tank **2 :** land underlying water

water bouget *n* **1 :** a leather bag formerly used (as by a soldier) for carrying water and handled suspended one at each end of a pole or yoke **2** *or* **water budget :** a conventionalized representation of a pair of water bougets used as a heraldic charge

water bouget 2

water bough *n* [ME *water bow,* fr. *water* + *bow, bough* bough — more at BOUGH] *dial chiefly Eng* **:** an overshadowed shoot from a tree trunk — compare WATER SPROUT

water-bound \ˈ==,=\ *adj* **1 :** restrained from going by flooding waters **2 :** consolidated or held together by water; *esp* **:** thoroughly soaked at the time of laying so that a natural cement formed from water and stone dust unites the particles — used of a macadam road surface

water bow *n* **:** RAINBOW

water box *n* **1 :** a box-shaped receptacle (as in a steam condenser) for holding water **2 :** WATER GLASS 3

water boy *n* **:** one who keeps a group (as of laborers or football players) supplied with drinking water

waterbrain \ˈ==,=\ *n* **:** GID

water brake *n* **:** a brake working by water pressure; *esp* **:** a locomotive brake that admits water to the locomotive cylinders and offers resistance to the movement of the pistons while descending a grade

water brash *n* **:** combined excessive salivation and acid regurgitation

water-break *n* **1 :** a place in a brook where the surface of the water is broken by irregularities on the bottom **2 :** a structure (as a breakwater) for deflecting or breaking the force of moving water

water breaker *n* **:** a cask for holding water used esp. for drinking water aboard ship

water breather *n* **:** an animal that obtains its respiratory oxygen from water usu. by means of gills

water bridge *n* **:** a bridge wall forming a water space at the back of the furnace of a steam boiler system

wa·ter·broo \ˈwȯtər,brü, ˈwät-\ *n, Scot* **:** WATER GRUEL

wa·ter·brose \-,brōz\ *n* **:** a Scots brose of meal and water

water brush *n* **1 :** GROUNDSEL BUSH **2 :** a brush with long soft bristles used esp. for dampening the mane and tail and washing the feet and legs of a horse

water bubbler *n* **:** DRINKING FOUNTAIN

waterbuck \ˈ==,=\ *n* [trans. of Afrik *waterbok*] **:** any of various antelopes that commonly frequent streams or wet lands: as **a :** either of two large coarse-haired reddish brown to grayish brown antelopes (*Kobus ellipsiprymnus* and *K. defassa*) of eastern Africa that are competent swimmers **b :** any of several kobs **c :** REEDBUCK

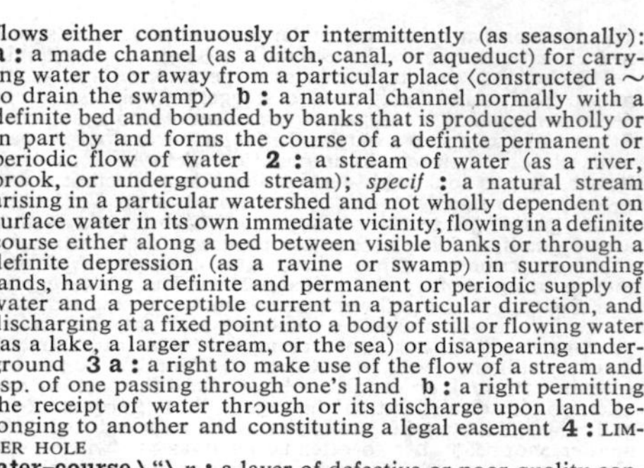

waterbuck

water buffalo *n* **:** an Asiatic buffalo (*Bubalus bubalis* or *Bos bubalis*) that is often domesticated — called also *water ox;* compare ANOA, CARABAO

water bug *n* **:** any of various insects or other small arthropods that frequent water: as **a :** CROTON BUG **b :** any of numerous aquatic bugs esp. of the family Belostomatidae that have long fringed hind legs which act like oars **c** *or* **water boatman :** BOAT BUG **d :** WATER SCORPION

water bugle *n* **:** a bugleweed (*Lycopus virginicus*)

wa·ter·bury *R* ˈwȯ|d·ə(r),berē, ˈwä|, |tə(r)-, -ri *sometimes* -,bər-; -*R* -ə,ber- *sometimes* -,bər-\ *adj, usu cap* [fr. *Waterbury,* Conn.] **:** of or from the city of Waterbury, Conn. ⟨the *Waterbury* brass industry⟩ **:** of the kind or style prevalent in Waterbury

water-bus \ˈ==,=\ *n* **:** a small boat engaged in the transport of passengers over a regular local route on inland waters in a manner comparable to a bus on land

waterbush \ˈ==,=\ *n* **:** a hardy fast-growing Australian boobyalla (*Myoporum montanum*) that grows esp. along watercourses in dry sandy regions and is often cultivated for shelter belts or hedging

water butt *n* **1 :** a large cask set up on end to contain water and esp. to store rainwater **2 :** a receptacle for water (as for a fountain or lavatory)

water buttercup *n* **1 :** an aquatic plant of the genus *Ranunculus* **2 :** a marsh marigold (*Caltha palustris*)

water cabbage *n* **1 :** a white water lily (*Nymphaea odorata*) **2 :** WATER LETTUCE

water call *n* **:** a trumpet or bugle call summoning mounted troops to water their horses

water caltrop *n* **1 :** WATER CHESTNUT **2 :** either of two pondweeds (*Potamogeton crispus* and *P. densus*)

water carpet *n* **:** GOLDEN SAXIFRAGE

water carriage *n* **1 a :** transportation or conveyance (as of persons or goods) by water **b :** disposal (as of sewage) by means of flowing water **2 :** means or facilities of conveyance by water **3** *dial chiefly Eng* **:** a canal or ditch for draining water

water carrier *n* **1 :** a carrier of goods or people using the sea or waterways in transportation **2 a :** a man or beast that carries or distributes water (as to domestic establishments or troops) **b :** a tank, pipe, or channel for conveying water **c :** a rain cloud

wa·ter·cast·er \ˈ==,kastə(r)\ *n, archaic* **:** a person claiming to diagnose a disease by inspection of a sample of urine

water cat *n* **:** NAIR

water cavy *n* **:** CAPYBARA

water celery *n* **1 :** CURSED CROWFOOT **2 :** TAPE GRASS

water cell *n* **:** a cell containing water; *esp* **:** one of the chambers in which water is stored in a camel's stomach

water-cement ratio *n* **:** the ratio of mixing water to cement in a concrete expressed by volume or by weight or as the number of gallons of water per bag of cement

water centipede *n* **:** HELLGRAMMITE

water channel *n* **:** a channel (as a ditch along a highway) for directing the course of water

waterchat \ˈ==,=\ *n* **1 :** any of numerous So. American tyrant flycatchers of *Fluvicola* and related genera **2 :** a thrush of the genus *Enicurus* (family Turdidae) **:** FORKTAIL

water chestnut *n* **1 a :** a plant of the genus *Trapa* (esp. *T. natans* and *T. bicornis*) **b :** the edible nutlike spiny-angled fruit of a water chestnut **2 a :** a Chinese sedge (*Eleocharis tuberosa*) **b :** the edible tuber of this sedge

water chevrotain *n* **:** a western African chevrotain (*Hyemoschus aquaticus*) that has a larger body and shorter legs than the related kanchils and napus — called also *water deer*

water chicken *n* **:** FLORIDA GALLINULE

water chickweed *n* **1 :** BLINKS **2 :** a water starwort (*Callitriche palustris*)

water chinquapin *n* **:** an American lotus (*Nelumbo lutea*); *also* **:** its edible nutlike seed that has the flavor of a chinquapin

water chute *n* **:** a chute usu. with flowing water that is equipped with boats which slide down into a pool or lake

water civet *n* **:** a tropical African semiaquatic fish-eating civet (*Osbornictis piscivora*) somewhat resembling the otters in habits

water-clear \ˈ==ˈ=\ *adj* **:** perfectly transparent and nearly or wholly colorless ⟨a *water-clear* crystal⟩ ⟨*water-clear* honey⟩

water clock *n* **:** an instrument designed to measure time by the fall or flow of a quantity of water

water clock

water closet *n* **1 a :** a closet, compartment, or room for defecation and excretion into a hopper fitted with a device for flushing away with water **:** BATHROOM **b :** the hopper and its accessories **2** *dial* **:** PRIVY

waterclover \ˈ==,==\ *n* **:** CLOVER FERN

water cock *n* **:** a large gallinule (*Gallicrex cinerea*) of southeastern Asia and the East Indies of which in the breeding season the male is black and has a fleshy red caruncle on the top of its head

water colly *n, dial Brit* **:** WATER OUZEL

watercolor \ˈ==,==\ *n, often attrib* **1 :** a paint of which the liquid is a water dispersion of the binding material (as glue, casein, or a gum) and which is prepared in the form of solid dry cakes or in a semifluid or pasty state in tubes or pans **2 :** the art or method of painting with watercolors **3 :** a picture or design executed in watercolors ⟨an exhibition of ~s⟩

watercolored \ˈ==,==\ *adj* **1 :** of the color of water **:** PELLUCID **2 :** painted in watercolors

watercolorist \ˈ==,==\ *n* **:** one who paints in watercolors

watercolor pencil *n* **:** a pencil with colored lead that when wet flows and blends like watercolor

water column *n* **1 :** WATER GAGE; *also* **:** the column of water in the gage **2 a :** a vertical pipe with valves and spout for delivering water to a locomotive tender **b :** a device that is connected to the back boiler head of a locomotive and bears the water glass, the gauge cocks, and usu. a lighting element

water company *n* **1 :** an organization engaged in the supplying of water for industrial and domestic purposes (as to an urban area) **2 :** a unit of a fire department primarily concerned with and equipped for the purpose of controlling fire by means of water

water-consolidated \ˈ===ˈ==,==\ *adj* **:** WATER-BOUND 2

water-cool \ˈ==ˈ=\ *vt* **:** to cool by means of water and esp. circulating water (as in a water jacket) ⟨*water-cooling* the engine⟩

water-cooled transformer \ˈ==,=-\ *n* **:** an oil-filled transformer in which the oil is cooled by circulating water

water cooler *n* **1 :** a tank in which water is cooled by circulation round coils containing cold liquid (as brine) **2 :** a tank containing artificially cooled drinking water

water core *n* **1 :** a hollow core through which water circulates in a founding mold and which is used (as in casting a cannon) for cooling the interior of a casting more rapidly than the outside while the metal is solidifying **2 a :** a physiological disease of fruits (as apples) in which parts of the inner tissues esp. close to the core become water-soaked, hard, and glassy **b :** a similar disease of turnips caused by boron deficiency

water couch *n* **1** *chiefly Africa* **:** any of several paspalums: as **a :** JOINT GRASS 1 **b :** DITCH MILLET **2** *Austral* **:** a dropseed (*Sporobolus virginicus*) of New World origin that is a salt-tolerant shore and marsh grass useful as a soil stabilizer and good for grazing

watercourse \ˈ==,=\ *n* **1 :** a channel through which water flows either continuously or intermittently (as seasonally): **a :** a made channel (as a ditch, canal, or aqueduct) for carrying water to or away from a particular place ⟨constructed a ~ to drain the swamp⟩ **b :** a natural channel normally with a definite bed and bounded by banks that is produced wholly or in part by and forms the course of a definite permanent or periodic flow of water **2 :** a stream of water (as a river, brook, or underground stream); *specif* **:** a natural stream arising in a particular watershed and not wholly dependent on surface water in its own immediate vicinity, flowing in a definite course either along a bed between visible banks or through a definite depression (as a ravine or swamp) in surrounding lands, having a definite and permanent or periodic supply of water and a perceptible current in a particular direction, and discharging at a fixed point into a body of still or flowing water (as a lake, a larger stream, or the sea) or disappearing underground **3 a :** a right to make use of the flow of a stream and esp. of one passing through one's land **b :** a right permitting the receipt of water through or its discharge upon land belonging to another and constituting a legal easement **4 :** LIMBER HOLE

water-course \ˈ"\ *n* **:** a layer of defective or poor-quality concrete (as in a wall) caused by the accumulation of excess mixing water and fine material at the surface of a pour

water cow *n* **1 :** a female water buffalo **2 :** SEA COW

water crack *n* **1 :** a crack in steel that is larger than a check and that is produced during the process of hardening **2 :** a fine crack in plaster that results from excess water or from the application of the succeeding coats too soon after the first coat

water cracker *n* **:** WATER BISCUIT

watercraft \ˈ==,=\ *n* **1 :** skill in managing boats or in other aquatic activities **2 a :** SHIP, BOAT **b :** equipment for water transport **:** VESSELS

water crake *n* **1 :** WATER OUZEL **2 :** SPOTTED CRAKE **3** *dial Eng* **:** a water rail (*Rallus aquaticus*)

water crane *n* **1 :** a gooseneck apparatus to supply (as to the tender of a locomotive) water from an elevated tank **2 :** a hydraulic crane

water creeper *n* **:** any of numerous widely distributed small but broad flat leathery bugs (family Naucoridae) that are actively predacious in and about freshwater

watercress \ˈ==,=\ *n* [ME *watercresse,* fr. *water* + *cresse* cress — more at CRESS] **1 :** any of several water-loving cresses (family Cruciferae): as **a :** a perennial cress (*Nasturtium officinale*) that grows chiefly in springs or running water and has creeping or floating freely rooting stems and roundish somewhat fleshy pungent leaves which are used in salads and sometimes as a potherb **b :** MARSH CRESS **c :** AMERICAN WATERCRESS **2 :** CRESS GREEN

water crow *n* [ME *water crowe*] **1** *dial Brit* **a :** WATER OUZEL **b :** a European coot (*Fulica atria*) **2 :** SNAKEBIRD 1

water crowfoot *n, pl* **water crowfoots :** an aquatic crowfoot or buttercup: as **a :** a white-flowered herb (*Ranunculus aquatilis*) used in England as food for cattle **b :** YELLOW WATER CROWFOOT

watercup \ˈ==,=\ *n* **1 :** MARSH PENNYWORT **2 :** TRUMPET 3d(2) **3 :** PITCHER PLANT a

water cure *n* **1 :** HYDROPATHY, HYDROTHERAPY **2 :** a torture consisting of forcing a person to drink large quantities of water in a short time

water curtain *n* **:** a sheet of water usu. formed from above (as at the proscenium arch of a theater or in a mine) esp. as a screen to prevent spread of fire

water cut *n* **:** a cut taken by a machine tool when a supply of water is kept on the cutting surface and marked usu. by the production of a bright smooth finish

water cycle *n* [*cycle* fr. *-cycle* (as in *bicycle*)] **:** any of various more or less experimental watercraft propelled by treadles after the manner of a bicycle

water damage insurance *n* **:** insurance against loss that is due to direct damage by rain or leakage of plumbing but not by flood

water deer *n* **1 :** a small Chinese deer (*Hydropotes inermis*) lacking antlers in both sexes and having the upper canines enlarged into tusks in the male **2 :** WATER CHEVROTAIN

water devil *n* **1 :** the rapacious larva of a water beetle of the genus *Dytiscus* — called also *water tiger* **2 :** HELLGRAMMITE

water diviner *n* **:** a dowser for water

water dock *n* [ME *waterdokke,* fr. *water* + *dokke, dock, docke* dock — more at DOCK] **1 :** any of several docks growing in wet places: as **a :** a coarse erect European perennial dock herb (*Rumex hydrolapathum*) with a much-branched inflorescence **b :** a very similar dock (*R. orbiculatus*) of eastern No. America **2 :** GOLDEN CLUB

waterdoe \ˈ==,=\ *n* **:** a female waterbuck

water dog *n* [ME *waterdogge,* fr. *water* + *dogge* dog — more at DOG] **1 :** a dog (as a retriever or water spaniel) experienced and strong as a swimmer or trained to retrieve waterfowl **2 a** *dial* **:** OTTER **b :** any of several large salamanders: as (1) **:** MUD PUPPY; *esp* **:** HELLBENDER (2) **:** GIANT NEWT **3 :** a person (as a skilled sailor or swimmer) who is quite at ease on or in the water **4 :** a small cloud that is held to indicate the approach of rain

water dragon *n* **1 :** a large Australian lizard (*Physignathus lesueurii*) that frequents water and is reported to make an uncanny sound by means of inflated cheek pouches **2 a :** a marsh marigold (*Caltha palustris*) **b :** LIZARD'S-TAIL

water-drinking \ˈ==,==\ *adj* **1 :** favoring or habituated to the drinking of water and esp. the waters of mineral springs **2 :** favoring water as a beverage as opposed to alcoholic liquor

waterdrop \ˈ==,=\ *n* **:** a drop or dropping of water: as **a :** RAINDROP **b :** TEARDROP

water dropwort *n* **1 :** a plant of the genus *Oenanthe*; *esp* **:** a European poisonous herb (*O. crocata*) having tuberous roots, a yellow juice that stains the skin, yellow flowers, and foliage resembling that of celery — compare WATER FENNEL **2 :** a leafless herb (*Oxypolis canbyi*) of the southeastern U. S. with hollow leaflike stems and slender compound umbels of tiny white flowers

water drum *n* **:** a drum having the body partly immersed in water or partly filled with water

water dust *n* **:** particles of water composing clouds or fog

water eagle *n* **:** OSPREY

watered *past of* WATER

watered-down \ˈ==,=ˈ=\ *adj* [fr. past part. of *water down,* v.] **:** made weak as if by the addition of water **:** attenuated or lessened in force or value by watering ⟨turned in a *watered-down* report⟩

watered-silk \ˈ==ˈ=\ *adj* **:** having a pattern like that of silk subjected to watering ⟨the flame grain which gives wood a *watered-silk* appearance⟩

water elephant *n* **:** HIPPOPOTAMUS

water elm *n* **:** any of several trees of the family Ulmaceae that prefer or thrive in a moist environment: as **a :** AMERICAN ELM **b :** WINGED ELM **c :** CEDAR ELM **d :** PLANER TREE **e :** a common Eurasian elm (*Ulmus laevis*) that closely resembles American elm **f :** a tall spreading Japanese tree (*Zelkova serrata*) sometimes cultivated as an ornamental

water engine *n* **1 a :** FIRE ENGINE **b :** an engine used to pump up water (as from a well) **2 :** an engine for applying water power; *also* **:** a hydraulic engine

water equivalent *n* **:** the product of the mass of a body by its specific heat equal numerically to the mass of water that is equivalent in thermal capacity to the body in question

wa·ter·er \ˈwȯ|d·ərə(r), ˈwä|, |tər-\ *n* -S **:** one that waters (as crops, soil, coal, or roadways): as **a :** a person who obtains or supplies drinking water ⟨helping out as a ~ of horses and cleaner of stables⟩ **b :** a device used for supplying water to livestock and esp. poultry and often equipped with an automatic float valve

water eryngo *n* **:** a button snakeroot (*Eryngium aquaticum*)

¹waterfall \ˈ==,=\ *n* [ME, fr. *water* + *fall*] **1 a :** a perpendicular or very steep descent of the water of a stream **:** CASCADE, CATARACT, FALL **b** *obs* **:** a riffle or rapid in a swift stream **2 :** a falling away of the ground such as to cause drainage of water **3 :** something felt to resemble a waterfall: as **a :** a cascade of cloth **b :** a fall of waved hair

²waterfall \ˈ"\ *adj* **:** arranged like a waterfall ⟨a ~ arrangement of the drums of a 3-drum hoist in which the axis of the

center drum is higher than that of one end drum and lower than that of the other end drum); *esp* **:** curving smoothly from horizontal to perpendicular ⟨a ~ edge on a chair seat⟩
water-fast \'≈,≈\ *adj* **1** *chiefly Scot* **:** WATERTIGHT **2 :** not leachable by water ⟨a *water-fast* dye⟩
water feather *or* **water featherfoil** *n* **:** a featherfoil (*Hottonia inflata*)
water feeder *or* **water feed** *n* **:** a device or pipe for supplying water (as in a boiler or tank)
water fence *n* **1 :** a stream or ditch that forms a boundary (as of a field) **2 :** a fence (as between fields) extending out into a margining body of water so that grazing animals may not pass by water from one plot to another
water fennel *n* **1 :** WATER DROPWORT 1; *esp* **:** a European poisonous herb (*Oenanthe aquatica*) with fibrous roots **2 :** WATER STARWORT
water-fennel oil *n* **:** an essential oil containing phellandrene and phellandral obtained from a water fennel (*Oenanthe aquatica*)
water fern *n* **1 :** a fern ally of the families Salviniaceae or Marsileaceae **2 :** a fern of the genus *Osmunda* (esp. *O. regalis*) **3 :** FLOATING FERN 1
waterfinder \'≈,≈≈\ *n* **:** one that is occupied in finding sources of water supply; *esp* **:** a water dowser
water finish *n* **:** a very high finish given to paper or board by applying water as it passes the calender stack — compare DRY FINISH — **water-finished** \'≈,≈'≈\ *adj*
water fire *n* **:** a European acrid aquatic weed (*Bergia ammannioides*) of the family Elatinaceae
wa·ter·fit \'wätər,fit\ *or* **wa·ter·foot** \-fu̇t\ *n* [¹*water* + *fit* (Sc var of *foot*) or *foot*] *Scot* **:** a river mouth
water flag *n* **1 :** YELLOW IRIS **2 :** a common blue flag (*Iris versicolor*)
water flaxseed *n* **:** GREAT DUCKWEED
water flea *n* **:** any of various small active dark or brightly colored aquatic entomostracan crustaceans (as of the genera *Cyclops* and *Daphnia*)
waterflood \'≈,≈\ *n* [ME, fr. OE *wæterflōd* fr. *wæter* water + *flōd* flood — more at WATER, FLOOD] **1 :** a sweeping flood of water **2 :** the act of flooding (as an oilwell) with water
water flow *n* **:** a flow or flowing of water; *also* **:** the amount of water flowing (as past a valve) per unit of time
water flower *n* [ME *water flour*, fr. *water* + *flour* flower — more at FLOWER] **:** WATER BLOOM — usu. used in pl.
water fly *n* **1 :** STONE FLY **2 :** a fly (as a dragonfly) habitually found over or by the water
water fog *n* **:** a fine spray or fog formed by sending one high-pressure stream of water against another in the tip of a nozzle and used esp. for checking combustion by its immediate transformation into steam
wa·ter·ford \'wȯd|d·ə(r)fə(r)d, 'wä|, |tə(r)f-\ *adj, usu cap* [fr. *Waterford*, Ireland] **1 :** of or from the county borough of Waterford, Ireland **:** of the kind or style prevalent in Waterford **2 :** of or from County Waterford, Ireland **:** of the kind or style prevalent in County Waterford
waterfowl \'≈,≈\ *n* [ME *water foul*, fr. *water* + *foul* fowl — more at FOWL] **1 :** a bird that frequents the water or lives about rivers or lakes or on or near the sea; *esp* **:** a swimming bird **2 waterfowl** *pl* **:** the swimming game birds as distinguished from upland game birds and shorebirds
water foxtail *n* **:** MARSH FOXTAIL
water frame *n* **:** a primitive power spinning machine driven by waterpower
water fringe *n* **:** FLOATING HEART
waterfront \'≈,≈\ *n, often attrib* **1 :** land, land with buildings, or a section of a town fronting or abutting on a body of water ⟨tenements along the ~⟩ **2 :** WATER BACK 2b
water frontage *n* **:** frontage abutting on water
water funk *n* **:** a fearful shrinking from water and esp. from entering the water; *also* **:** a person afflicted with a fear of water
water furrow *n* [ME *water forowe*, fr. OE *wæterfurh*, fr. *wæter* water + *furh* furrow — more at WATER, FURROW] **:** a furrow for conducting or diverting water
water-furrow \'≈,≈(,)≈\ *vt* [*water furrow*] **:** to make water furrows in **:** drain or irrigate by water furrows
water gage *n* **1 :** an instrument for measuring the depth or quantity of water or for indicating the height of its surface esp. in a steam boiler **2 :** an instrument for measuring a moderate air pressure hydrostatically (as in a ventilating system) **3 :** water pressure expressed in inches of height
water gain *n* **:** water that bleeds from concrete as it is placed into forms and compacted, accumulates at the surface of the concrete, and usu. increases in amount as the concrete fills more and more of the form
water gall *n* **1** *obs* **:** a spot of low boggy land **2** *chiefly dial* **:** a watery or rainy look in the sky usu. accompanying a rainbow; *also* **:** a secondary or broken rainbow **3 :** JELLYFISH
water gang *n* [ME, fr. *water* + *gang*] *chiefly Scot* **:** a water or stream channel esp. when constructed artificially (as for land drainage or irrigation)
water gap *n* **:** a pass in a mountain ridge through which a stream runs
water garden *n* **1 :** a garden in which aquatic plants predominate **2 :** a garden built about a stream or pool as a central feature
water gas *n* **:** a poisonous flammable gaseous mixture made principally of carbon monoxide and hydrogen with small amounts of methane, carbon dioxide, and nitrogen and usu. by blowing air and then steam over red-hot coke or coal, used esp. formerly as a fuel (as in welding) and after carbureting as an illuminant but chiefly as a source of hydrogen and as a synthesis gas — see BLUE GAS, CARBURETED WATER GAS
water-gas tar *n* **:** tar formed in making carbureted water gas and used chiefly in tar road materials
¹water gate *n* [ME *watergate*, fr. *water* + *gate* (way)] *chiefly Scot* **:** a natural channel for water **:** WATERCOURSE
²water gate *n* [ME *watergate*, fr. *water* + *gat*, *gate* gate (opening)] **1 :** a gate (as of private grounds or a building) giving access to a body of water **2 :** a gateway or sluice for the passage of water; *also* **:** a gate or valve controlling the flow of water **:** FLOODGATE — compare GATE VALVE **3 :** a passageway for passage of traffic by water
water germander *n* **:** a soft hairy perennial European mint (*Teucrium scordium*) having chiefly axillary rose-pink to purple flowers and found in marshy places
water-gild \'≈,≈\ *vt* **1 :** to gild (a metallic surface) by coating thinly with gold amalgam and then volatilizing the mercury by heat **2 :** to electroplate with a thin gold film by simple immersion
water gillyflower *n* **:** a featherfoil (*Hottonia inflata*) with spongy inflated flower stalks — called also *water violet*
water gladiole *n* **:** FLOWERING RUSH
water gland *n* **:** a group of cells situated immediately below a hydathode and serving to regulate the excretion of water
water glass *n* **1 :** WATER CLOCK, CLEPSYDRA **2 :** a glass vessel for holding water: as **a :** a drinking glass **:** TUMBLER **b :** a container for growing a flowering bulb (as a hyacinth) in water **c** *archaic* **:** a finger bowl of glass **3 :** an instrument consisting of an open box or tube with a glass bottom used for examining objects in or under the water (as upon the sea bottom in shallow places) **4 a :** a water-soluble substance consisting of sodium silicate $Na_2O.xSiO_2$ of varying composition that is found in commerce as a glassy mass, a stony powder, or a viscous syrupy liquid dissolved in water that is used chiefly as a cement and adhesive, as a builder for soaps and synthetic detergents, as a protective coating and fireproofing agent in papermaking and in the textile industry, in making artificial stone, and in preserving eggs — called also *soluble glass* **b :** a similar substance consisting of potassium silicate — called also *potash water glass* **5 :** WATER GAGE 1
water-glass painting *n* **:** STEREOCHROMY
water gnat *n, Brit* **:** MARSH TREADER
water goggles *n pl but sing or pl in constr* **:** a marsh marigold (*Caltha palustris*)
water gold *n* **:** a liquid amalgam of gold
water grain *n* **:** a grain imparted to leather by hand-treating it while wet with a cork-covered board
water grampus *n, dial* **:** HELLGRAMMITE
water grass *n* **1 :** any of various grasses or grasslike plants that thrive in wet places: as **a :** DALLIS GRASS **b** *dial Eng* **:** VELVET GRASS **c** *dial Eng* **:** HORSETAIL **d :** BARNYARD GRASS **2** *dial Brit* **:** WATERCRESS
water grate *n* **:** a furnace grate with hollow water-cooled bars
water green *n* **:** a pale to grayish yellow green that is yellower and stronger than ingenue
water-ground \'≈,≈\ *adj* **:** ground between millstones by means of water power ⟨*water-ground* meal⟩
water gruel *n* [ME *water grewel*, fr. *water* + *grewel* gruel — more at GRUEL] **:** a thin gruel made chiefly with water
water guard *n* **:** a guard whose duty is to police a harbor or river; *also* **:** a body of customs officers detailed to watch ships (as to prevent smuggling)
water guinea *or* **water guinea hen** *n* **:** AMERICAN COOT
water gum *n* **1 :** any of several Australian trees that grow near water; *esp* **:** a small to medium-sized tree (*Tristania laurina*) that yields a tough strong close-grained pinkish wood sometimes used for tool handles and mallets **2 :** BLACK GUM 2
water gun *n* **:** WATER PISTOL
water hair grass *n* **:** BROOK GRASS
water hammer *n* **1 :** a vessel (as a tube) partly filled with water, exhausted of air, and hermetically sealed so that when reversed or shaken the water strikes in solid mass with a sound like that of a hammer **2 :** a concussion or sound of concussion of moving water against the sides of a containing pipe or vessel on a sudden stoppage of flow; *esp* **:** such a concussion or sound made by water in a steam pipe **3 :** the act or process of water-hammering
¹water-hammer \'≈,≈≈\ *vi* [*water hammer*] *of water* **:** to strike with a hammering sound against the walls of a sealed containing vessel from which the air has been removed
²water-hammer \"\ *adj* [*water hammer*] **:** of or relating to a water hammer; *esp* **:** characterized by a sharp but quickly fading impact ⟨a *water-hammer* pulse⟩ — compare CORRIGAN PULSE
water hare *n* **:** SWAMP RABBIT
water haul *n* **1 :** a haul of a net that catches no fish **2 :** a fruitless effort; *often* **:** a trip or call wasted because of failure to meet or see a person intended
water hawthorn *n* **:** CAPE PONDWEED
waterhead \'≈,≈\ *n* **1 :** the source or headwater of a stream **2 :** a dammed up body of water (as for supplying a garden or mill); *also* **:** the height or quantity so retained **3 a :** a large head; *esp* **:** HYDROCEPHALUS **b** *chiefly dial* **:** one with an excessively large head and usu. subnormal intelligence
water heater *n* **1 :** an apparatus for heating and usu. storing hot water (as for domestic use) **2 :** a hot water heating system
water hemisphere *n* **:** the geographical hemisphere having a maximum surface of water
water hemlock *n* **1 a :** a tall erect Eurasiatic perennial herb (*Cicuta virosa*) that is locally abundant in marshy areas or along streams and is highly poisonous **b :** any of several other plants of the genus *Cicuta* (as the American spotted cowbane) **2 :** either of two water dropworts (*Oenanthe crocata* and *O. aquatica*) — compare WATER FENNEL
water hemp *n* **1 :** a plant of the genus *Acnida* **2 :** HEMP AGRIMONY
water hen *n* **:** any of various birds of the family Rallidae (as a coot); as **a :** GALLINULE **b :** AMERICAN COOT **c :** any of several Australian birds of the genus *Tribonyx*
water hickory *n* **:** a hickory (*Carya aquatica*) of the southern U. S. having many narrow leaflets and rather bitter nuts — called also *bitter pecan, water bitternut*
water hog *n* **1 :** CAPYBARA **2 :** BUSHPIG
water hole *n* **1 :** a natural hole or hollow containing water: as **a :** one in the dry bed of an intermittent river **b :** a spring in a desert **c :** a small pool, pond, or lake **2 :** a hole in a surface of ice
water holly *n* **:** an Oregon grape (*Mahonia nervosa*)
water horehound *n* **:** a mint of the genus *Lycopus; esp* **:** BUGLEWEED
water horizon *n* **:** a stratum or layer of porous rock that will yield water to a well
water horse *n* [ME, fr. *water* + *hors*, *horse* horse — more at HORSE] **1** *obs* **:** HIPPOPOTAMUS **2 :** a fabulous water spirit resembling a horse **:** HIPPOCAMPUS, KELPIE
water horsetail *n* **1 :** STONEWORT **2 :** an aquatic horsetail (as *Equisetum fleuratile*)
water house *n* **:** a building in which a head of water forced up (as from a well) is retained in a reservoir for conveyance by pipes
wa·ter·house-frid·er·ich·sen syndrome \'wȯd|d·ə(r),hau̇-'sfrid(ə)riksən-, 'wä|, |tə(r)-\ *n, usu cap W&F* [after Sir Herbert *Waterhouse* †1931 Brit. physician and Carl *Friderichsen* b1886 Dan. physician] **:** acute and severe meningococcemia with hemorrhage into the adrenal glands
waterhouse stop *n, usu cap W* [after Major J. *Waterhouse*, 19th cent. Brit. photochemist] **:** any one of a set of thin metal plates that each have a round or specially shaped hole corresponding to a particular photographic lens aperture and are inserted as required into a slot in the barrel of a lens esp. for use in photoengraving
water hyacinth *n* **:** a tropical floating aquatic plant (*Eichhornia crassipes*) having spikes of large blue flowers and roundish leaves and being troublesome in clogging waterways esp. in the southern U. S.
water hyssop *n* **:** any of several plants of the genus *Bacopa; esp* **:** the small widely distributed creeping herb (*B. monniera*) that is used locally in India as an aperient and diuretic
water ice *n* **1 :** a frozen dessert consisting of water, sugar, and flavoring — compare SHERBET 2 **2 :** massive ice formed by the downward freezing of water
wa·ter·ie \'wȯd|d·ərē, 'wä|, |tə-, -ri\ *n* -s [¹*water* + *-ie*] **:** WAGTAIL; *esp* **:** PIED WAGTAIL
waterier *comparative of* WATERY
wateriest *superlative of* WATERY
wa·ter·i·ly \-rəlē\ *adv* **:** with watery exudation **:** in a watery way
water-inch \'≈'≈\ *n* **:** the discharge from a circular sharp-edged orifice one inch in diameter with a head of one line above the top edge that is commonly estimated at 14 pints per minute and that constitutes an old unit of hydraulic measure
wa·ter·i·ness \'wȯd|d·ərēnəs, 'wä|, |tər-, -rin-\ *n* -ES [ME *watrinesse*, fr. *watery, watry* watery + *-nesse* -ness] **1** *obs* **a :** watery matter in a substance **b :** watery secretion **2 :** the condition of being watery ⟨the ~ of Venice⟩: as **a :** the condition of being too thin, sodden, or insipid because of the presence of excessive water ⟨a soup tasteless because of ~⟩ ⟨the ~ of blood once supposed to affect malaria victims⟩ **b :** the condition of lacking solid substance as if diluted with water ⟨a flimsy composition with a deadly ~ of style⟩
¹watering *n* -s [ME, fr. OE *wæterung*, fr. *wæterian* to water + *-ung* -ing — more at WATER] **1 :** the act or action of one that waters; *also* **:** an instance of such **2** *chiefly dial* **:** a source or supply of water (as for irrigation or cattle) **3 :** a ditch for drainage; *also* **:** marshland with such ditches **4 :** a moiré appearance (as of a textile or metal)
²watering *adj* [ME, fr. pres. part. of *wateren* to water — more at WATER] **:** used in watering, serving to water, or providing with or yielding water ⟨a ~ bucket⟩ ⟨~ eyes⟩ ⟨a ~ resort⟩
watering cart *n* **:** a cart equipped to carry water (as for sprinkling roads or irrigating fields)
wateringhole \'≈≈≈,≈\ *n* **:** WATER HOLE 1
watering house *n, Brit* **:** a public house providing water for horses and refreshments for coachmen and travelers
watering place *n* [ME] **1 :** a place where animals come to drink; *also* **:** a place (as a pool or container of running water) where livestock may be taken to drink **2 :** a place where water supplies (as for a ship or caravan) may be obtained **3 :** a health or recreational resort featuring marine or fresh-water activities
watering pot *n* **1** *or* **watering can :** a vessel usu. in the form of a can with a spout having a perforated nozzle that is used to sprinkle water (as on plants or clothes) **2 :** WATERING-POT SHELL
watering-pot shell \'≈≈≈,≈-\ *n* **:** any of several marine bivalve mollusks (genus *Brechites*) having small valves consolidated with a capacious calcareous tube which encases the entire animal and is closed at the anterior end by a convex disk perforated by many pores like the nozzle of a watering pot; *also* **:** the shell of such a mollusk
watering slip *n* **:** an incline built into a river to give firm footing to cattle or horses led there to drink
watering trough *n* **1 :** a drinking trough for livestock **2 :** TRACK PAN
water injection *n* **:** introduction of water to an internal-combustion engine to enhance combustion power for quick take-off or bursts in speed
water-in-oil \'≈≈'≈\ *adj* **:** consisting of water dispersed in oil — distinguished from *oil-in-water* ⟨*water-in-oil* emulsions⟩
wa·ter·ish \'wȯd|d·ərish, 'wä|, |tər-, -rēsh\ *adj* **1 a :** resembling water esp. in appearance or consistency ⟨a ~ discharge⟩ **b :** lacking in intensity **:** PALE ⟨muddy yellows and ~ blues⟩ ⟨~ moonlight⟩ **2 a :** full of water or watery liquid **:** DILUTE, THIN, SLOPPY ⟨~ wine⟩ ⟨a ~ gruel⟩ **b :** lacking in substance or savor **:** FLAT, FLAVORLESS, INSIPID **3 a :** somewhat watery **:** containing water or water vapor ⟨a ~ sky⟩ ⟨~ land requiring drainage⟩ **b :** marked by considerable wetness ⟨a ~ season⟩ — **wa·ter·ish·ness** *n* -ES
water ivy *n* **:** a European water crowfoot (*Ranunculus hederaceum*) with white flowers and ivy-shaped leaves that is naturalized in eastern No. America
water jacket *n* **:** an outer casing which holds water or through which water circulates to cool the interior; *specif* **:** the enclosed space surrounding the cylinder block of an internal-combustion engine and containing the cooling liquid
water-jacket \'≈,≈≈\ *vt* [*water jacket*] **:** to provide with a water jacket
water-jet \'≈,≈\ *adj* **:** operated or driven by a jet of water
water joint *n* **:** a joint in a stone pavement that is slightly raised to prevent water from settling therein
water jump *n* **:** an obstacle (as in a steeplechase) consisting of a pool, stream, or ditch of water
water kelpie *n* **:** KELPIE
water knot *n* **:** a knot made with interlocking halfknots and used esp. to join the ends of fishlines
water-laid \'≈,≈\ *adj* **1** *of cordage* **a :** having a left-hand twist **b :** CABLE-LAID **2 :** deposited in or by water **:** SEDIMENTARY
wa·ter·land·er \'wȯd|d·ə(r),landə(r), 'wä|, |tə(r),-\ *n* -S *usu cap* [D, lit., inhabitant of Waterland, fr. *Waterland*, district in northern Holland, Netherlands + D *-er*] **:** one of a liberal body of Dutch Mennonites separated from the conservative Mennonites after 1555 and later reunited with the liberalized older body
wa·ter·land·ian \,≈≈'landēən\ *n, usu cap* [*Waterland* + E *-an*] **:** WATERLANDER
water lane *n* **1 :** a lane with a stream flowing alongside **2 a :** a narrow open passageway through water (as amid weeds, ice, or shipping) **b :** LANE 3a
waterleaf \'≈,≈\ *n, pl* **waterleafs 1 :** a plant of the genus *Hydrophyllum* **2** *pl also* **waterleaves :** a completely unsized paper (as blotting paper)
water leaf *n* **:** an ornament prob. representing an ivy leaf and found in Greek art
waterleaf family *n* **:** HYDROPHYLLACEAE
water leg *n* **:** a downward extension of a steam boiler in the form of a narrow space between vertical plates often nearly surrounding the furnace and ashpit and supporting the boiler
water lemon *n* **1 :** JAMAICA HONEYSUCKLE **2 :** SWEET CALABASH
water lens *n* **:** a lens whose refracting medium is water contained in a suitably shaped vessel of transparent material
water lentil *n* **:** LESSER DUCKWEED — usu. used in pl.
wa·ter·less \'wȯd|d·ə(r)ləs, 'wä|, |tə(r)-\ *adj* [ME *waterles*, fr. OE *wæterlēas*, fr. *wæter* water + *-lēas* -less] **1 :** destitute of or deficient in water **:** DRY ⟨a ~ well⟩ ⟨had to cross 100 miles of ~ country⟩ **2 :** not requiring water (as for cooling or cooking); *often* **:** AIR-COOLED — **wa·ter·less·ly** *adv* — **wa·ter·less·ness** *n* -ES
waterless cooker *n* **1 :** any of various containers usu. with a very thick bottom and a close cover in which food can be cooked without burning in juices released in cooking or in very little water **2 :** PRESSURE COOKER
water lettuce *n* **:** a common tropical floating plant (*Pistia stratiotes*) forming a rosette of spongy wedge-shaped leaves — called also *water cabbage*
water level *n* **1 :** an instrument to show the level by means of the surface of water in a trough or in the legs of a U-tube **2 :** a slightly inclined level (as in a mine) for draining **3 :** the surface of still water: as **a :** the level assumed by the surface of a particular body or column of water **b :** the waterline of a vessel **c :** WATER TABLE 3
water lily *n* **1 :** a plant or flower of the family Nymphaeaceae — see LOTUS, SPATTERDOCK **2 :** any of various aquatic plants with more or less showy flowers: as **a :** FLOATING HEART **b :** WATER HYACINTH **3 :** ZYGADENE

water lily

water-lily family *n* **:** NYMPHAEACEAE
water-lily tree *n* **:** a mountain magnolia (*Magnolia fraseri*)
water-lily tulip *n* **:** a tulip (*Tulipa kaufmanniana*) of Central Asia and Asia Minor having recurved brightly colored petals and being used as an ornamental
water lime *n* **1 :** HYDRAULIC LIME **2 :** a limestone from which hydraulic lime may be made
waterline \'≈,≈\ *n* **1 a :** any of several lines that are marked upon the outside of a ship and correspond with the surface of the water when it is afloat on an even keel — see SHIP illustration **b :** any of various lines of a ship, model, or plan parallel with the surface of the water at various heights from the keel **2 :** SHORELINE **3 a :** the level represented by the uppermost limit of ground wholly saturated with water **:** the level of the water in soil **:** WATER TABLE **b :** the desired or actual level of water (as in a boiler or tank) **4 :** a line of stain marking a former passage or upper level of water ⟨the flood left a ~ on housefronts and fences⟩ ⟨~s from old leaks⟩ **5 :** a line (as of piping or hose) for carrying water
waterline model *n* **:** a ship model formed of boards shaped according to the waterlines in the plans and laid upon each other to form a solid model
water lizard *n* **1 :** MONITOR LIZARD **2 :** any of various mostly large salamanders (as a mud puppy or water dog)
water lobelia *n* **:** an erect perennial aquatic herb (*Lobelia dortmanna*) of Europe and No. America with submerged spongy leaves and an emersed raceme of blue flowers
waterlocked \'≈,≈\ *adj* **:** nearly surrounded by water ⟨a ~ tongue of land⟩
water locust *n* **:** a honey locust (*Gleditsia aquatica*) growing in swamps and bottomlands of the southern U. S., producing short oval pods, and having dark heavy wood that takes a good polish
wa·ter·log \'≈≈,lȯg *also* -,läg\ *vb* [back-formation fr. *waterlogged*] *vt* **1 :** to make (as a boat) unmanageable by flooding — used of the sea or a leak **2 :** to deprive (as floating timber) of buoyancy by saturation with water **3 :** to saturate (as soil) with water; *esp* **:** to cause the water table of (soil) to rise high enough to expel normal soil gases and interfere with plant growth or cultivation **4 :** to cause to deteriorate or to become unmanageable or unserviceable as if by saturation with excess of water ⟨whenever I've got *waterlogged* with study —W.S. Maugham⟩ ⟨an unbalanced capital structure may ~ the strongest company⟩ ~ *vi* **:** to become sodden, inert, or unmanageable by or as if by excessive saturation with water
wa·ter·logged \-gd\ *adj* [¹*water* + *log*, n. + *-ed*] **1 :** subjected to waterlogging ⟨a ~ boat⟩ ⟨~ timbers⟩ **2 :** EDEMATOUS
wa·ter·loo \¦wȯd|d·ə(r)¦lü, ¦wä|, |tə-\ *n* -S *sometimes cap* [fr. *Waterloo*, Belgium, scene of Napoleon's defeat (1815)] **:** a decisive or disastrous defeat or reverse
water loop *n* **:** an unintended uncontrollable violent turn of a seaplane moving on the water at high speed
water louse *n* **:** an aquatic isopod
water lung *n* **:** the respiratory tree of a holothurian
water main *n* **:** a pipe or conduit for conveying water (as from a reservoir)
water mallow *n* **:** a rose mallow (*Hibiscus moscheutos*)

wa·ter·man \'≈≈mən\ *n, pl* **watermen** [ME, fr. *water* + *man*] **1 :** one that works or lives on or is skilled in the ways of water or watercraft: as **a :** a boatman who plies for hire usu. on inland waters or harbors **b :** a person who makes his living from the water (as by fishing, crabbing, or oystering) **c :** a sprite or demon inhabiting the water **:** MERMAN **d :** a person skilled in boating esp. as a sport; *often* **:** OARSMAN **2 :** one employed in connection with the distributing or supplying of water: as **a :** a worker who releases water through valves or sluices (as in waterworks or for irrigation) **b :** a worker who waters roads (as in a mine) **c** *Brit* **:** an attendant (as on a cabstand) who supplies water to the horses **d :** a worker who quenches coke with water for removal from the oven **e :** a worker who brings billet molds to filling temperature by spraying with hot or cold water **f :** an auto worker who puts water into radiators before cars are driven from the assembly line **3 :** a worker who bales into cars water that has collected in a mine for hauling to the surface or who pumps such water to the surface

wa·ter·man·ship \-n,ship\ *n* **:** the business, skill, or art of a waterman: as **a :** expertness or technique in the handling of a boat and esp. in rowing; *often* **:** skill in managing an oar in water as distinguished from techniques (as of handling the body) involved in the stroke **b :** expertness or technique in the handling of oneself (as in swimming) in the water **:** personal aquatic skill or understanding

waterman's knot *n* **:** FISHERMAN'S KNOT

water maple *n* **:** any of several maples that prefer or thrive in damp locations: as **a :** RED MAPLE **b :** a silver maple (*Acer saccharinum*)

water marigold *n* **:** a No. American aquatic herb (*Megalodonta beckii*) of the family Compositae having finely dissected leaves and heads of yellow flowers

1watermark \'≈,≈\ *n* [1*water* + *mark*] **1 :** a mark indicating the height to which water has risen or at which it has stood or is expected to stand **:** WATERLINE; *esp* **:** TIDEMARK **2 :** a marking in paper resulting from differences in thickness usu. produced by pressure of a projecting design in the mold or on the dandy roll and visible when the paper is held up to the light; *also* **:** the design or the metal pattern producing the marking — compare IMPRESSED WATERMARK

2watermark \"\ *vt* **1 a :** to mark (paper) with a watermark **b :** to impress (a given design) as a watermark **2 :** to determine the watermark on (a stamp) usu. for philatelic purposes

watermark detector *n* **:** a device for determining the watermark on a stamp

watermark disease *n* **:** a disease of willows and esp. the cricket-bat willow (*Salix alba caerulea*) in England in which a bacterium (*Erwinia salicis*) invades the vessels and causes wilting and browning of the leaves and a brown watery stain of the wood

watermaster \'≈,≈≈\ *n* **:** one in charge of the distribution of irrigation water from a main canal

water meadow *n* **:** a meadow or piece of low flat land capable of being kept in fertility by being overflowed from some adjoining stream

watermeal \'≈≈,≈\ *n* **:** any of various minute aquatic plants of the genus *Wolffia*

water measure *n* [ME *water mesure*, fr. *water* + *mesure* measure — more at MEASURE] **:** an old English system of capacity measure used for articles shipped by water and based on a bushel defined by statute in 1494 as equal to five pecks Winchester measure and in 1701 as equal to a heaped Winchester bushel

water measurer *n* **:** any of several aquatic insects; *esp* **:** WATER STRIDER

wa·ter·mel·on \'wȯd|ə(r),melən, 'wäl, |tə(r)-, *dial* -,milyən\ *n* **1 a :** a large oblong or roundish fruit having a hard green or white rind that is often striped or variegated and a pink, yellowish, or red pulp that contains a copious sweet watery juice and many seeds **b :** a vine (*Citrullus vulgaris*) that bears watermelons and is native to tropical Africa but widely cultivated **2 :** a deep pink to moderate red that is yellower and stronger than laurel pink and very slightly yellower and stronger than rose dorée **3 :** a skipjack (*Katsuwonus pelamis*)

watermelon begonia *n* **:** a peperomia (*Peperomia sandersi*) used as a greenhouse plant or houseplant and having silvery striped foliage

water meter *n* **:** an instrument for recording the quantity of water passing through a particular outlet

water milfoil *n* **:** an aquatic plant of the genus *Myriophyllum*

water-milfoil family *n* **:** HALORAGACEAE

water mill *n* [ME *water mille*, fr. *water* + *mille* mill — more at MILL] **:** a mill whose machinery is moved by water

water-millet \'≈≈,≈≈\ *n* **:** a tall aquatic perennial grass (*Zizaniopsis miliacea*) of the southern U. S. having long leaves and narrow terminal panicles of flowers

water mint *n* **:** any of several mints that thrive in wet places: as **a :** a European mint (*Mentha aquatica*) sometimes having a perfume resembling that of bergamot and naturalized locally in eastern No. America **b :** a closely related tall hairy mint (*M. longifolia*) of similar distribution

water mite *n* **:** a mite of the group Hydrachnellae; *esp* **:** a free-living freshwater mite of the family Hydrachnidae — called also *water spider, water tick*

water moccasin *n* **1 :** a venomous pit viper (*Agkistrodon piscivorus*) of the southern U. S. that is closely related to the copperhead, is olive or brownish above, paler on the sides, and indistinctly barred with black, has the young much brighter and reddish brown barred with dark brown edged with white, and is semiaquatic and abundant in marshes and abandoned rice ditches where it feeds chiefly on fish and amphibians **2 :** WATER SNAKE a — not used technically

water mold *n* **:** an aquatic fungus; *esp* **:** a mold of the order Saprolegniales

water mole *n* **1 :** DESMAN **2 :** PLATYPUS

water monitor *n* **:** a very large lizard (*Varanus salvator*) of India that frequents the borders of streams, swims actively, and may become five or six feet long; *broadly* **:** any of various aquatic monitors

water monkey *n* **:** a jar or bottle (as of porous earthenware) in which water is cooled by evaporation

water moss *n* **1 :** an aquatic plant (as various algae or liverworts) that suggests a moss in appearance or habit of growth **2 :** a moss of the genus *Fontinalis* (esp. *F. antipyretica*)

water moth *n* **1 :** any of numerous small pyralidid moths (as members of the genera *Nymphula* and *Elophila*) having larvae that live beneath the surface of fresh waters usu. in cases; *esp* **:** a moth of the genus *Acentropus* **2 :** CADDIS FLY

water motor *n* **:** a prime mover driven by water; *specif* **:** a small waterwheel driven by water from a street main

water mouse *n* [ME *watermowse*, fr. *water* + *mous, mowse* mouse — more at MOUSE] **:** any of several relatively small and somewhat aquatic rodents: as **a :** BEAVER RAT **b :** WATER VOLE

water mouth *n, Scot* **:** a river mouth

water navelwort *n* **1 :** a common water milfoil (*Myriophyllum spicatum*) of the north temperate zone **2 :** a marsh pennywort (*Hydrocotyle umbellata*) that is widely distributed in the New World and in Africa

water nerveroot *n* **:** SWAMP MILKWEED

water net *n* **:** a freshwater alga of the genus *Hydrodictyon*

water newt *n* **:** an aquatic salamander **:** TRITON

water nixie *n* **:** a female water sprite

water nut *n* **1 :** WATER CHESTNUT **2 :** WATER CHINQUAPIN

water nymph *n* [ME *water nimphe*, fr. *water* + *nimphe* nymph — more at NYMPH] **1 :** a goddess (as one of the naiads, Nereids, or Oceanids) of classical mythology associated with a body of water **2 a :** a common white water lily (*Nymphaea odorata*); *broadly* **:** a plant or flower of the genus *Nymphaea* **b :** a plant of the genus *Naias* **3 :** DRAGONFLY

water oak *n* **1 :** any of numerous American oaks that thrive in wet soils (as the pin oak, laurel oak, or willow oak) **:** SWAMP OAK; *esp* **:** POSSUM OAK **2** *Austral* **a :** BOTTLEBRUSH 1a(1) **b :** CASUARINA 2

water oat *n* **:** WILD RICE 1a — often used in pl. with sing. or pl. constr.

water of ayr *or* **water-of-ayr stone** *n, usu cap A* [fr. *Water of Ayr*, river in Scotland] **:** AYR STONE

water of constitution : water so combined in a molecule that it cannot be removed without disrupting the entire molecule — distinguished from *water of hydration*

water of crystallization : water of hydration that is present in many crystallized substances and that is usu. essential for maintenance of a particular crystal structure (as in Glauber's salt)

water of dehydration : water of hydration set free by chemical changes

water of hydration : water that is chemically combined with a substance to form a hydrate and can be expelled (as by heating) without essentially altering the composition of the substance — distinguished from *water of constitution*

water of life [ME *water of lif*, trans. of LL *aqua vitae* (as in Rev 22:1), trans. of Gk *hydōr zōēs*] **1 :** something that gives spiritual refreshment or eternal life **2** [trans. of ML *aqua vitae*] **:** a strong distilled alcoholic drink (as brandy or whiskey)

water of plasticity : water added to dry clay to make it plastic (as for use by a potter)

water-oleander \'≈≈¦≈≈≈\ *n* **:** SWAMP LOOSESTRIFE

wa·ter·ol·o·ger \,wȯd|ə'räləjə(r), ,wäl, |tə'-\ *n* -s [1*water* + *-o-* + *-loger* (fr. *-logy* + *-er*)] *archaic* **:** WATERCASTER

water on the brain : HYDROCEPHALUS

water on the knee : an accumulation of inflammatory exudate in the knee joint often following an injury

water opal *n* **:** HYALITE

water opossum *n* **:** YAPOK

water ordeal *n* **:** an ordeal (as of plunging a bare arm into boiling water) in which water is the testing agent and in which innocence or guilt is held to be proved (as by the condition of the arm) **:** an ordeal of casting an accused person bound hand and foot into a river or pond in which sinking or floating is taken as evidence respectively of innocence or guilt

water organ *n* **:** HYDRAULUS

water ouzel *n* **:** any of several birds of the genus *Cinclus* (esp. *C. cinclus* and *C. mexicanus*) that are related to the thrushes and that are not web-footed but dive into swift mountain streams and walk on the bottom in search of food — called also *dipper*

water over the dam : something that is beyond recall or reconsideration

water ox *n* **:** WATER BUFFALO

water pad·da \-'padə\ *n* [Afrik *waterpadda*, fr. *water* (fr. MD) + *padda* toad, frog, fr. MD *padde* toad; akin to OE *wæter* water and to MLG *padde, pedde* toad — more at WATER, PADDOCK] **:** a southern African burrowing terrestrial toad (*Breviceps gibbosus*)

water paint *n* **:** paint in which water is the volatile portion of the vehicle

water parsley *n* **:** any of several bog or aquatic plants of the family Umbelliferae (as a water parsnip or wild celery)

water parsnip *n* **:** a plant of the genus *Sium*

water parting *n* **:** a summit or boundary line separating the drainage districts of two streams or coasts **:** DIVIDE — compare WATERSHED

water partridge *n* **:** RUDDY DUCK

water pennywort *n* **:** MARSH PENNYWORT

water pepper *n* **:** a widely distributed annual smartweed (*Polygonum hydropiper*) of moist soils having greenish flowers and extremely acrid peppery juice and formerly used in medicine for its irritant and stimulant properties

water persicaria *n* **:** an aquatic herb (*Polygonum amphibium*) of Europe and No. America with floating leaves and emersed dense racemes of pinkish flowers

water pewit *n* **:** PHOEBE

water pheasant *n* **1 :** MERGANSER: **a :** GOOSANDER **b :** HOODED MERGANSER **c :** AMERICAN MERGANSER **2 :** PHEASANT-TAILED JACANA

wa·ter·phone \'≈≈,fōn\ *n* [1*water* + *-phone*] **:** HYDROPHONE

water pick *n* **:** a small conical metal or plastic water container having a pointed base and a rubber cap with an opening through which the stem of a flower can be inserted and used in making floral designs and arrangements usu. on a foundation of plastic

water pig *n* **1 :** CAPYBARA **2 :** GOURAMI

water pilot *n* **:** a water snake (*Natrix taxispilota*) chiefly of the southeastern U.S.

water pimpernel *n* **1 :** BROOKWEED **2 :** SCARLET PIMPERNEL

water pine *n* **:** a Chinese evergreen tree (*Glyptostrobus pensilis*) that grows in wet places and is commonly planted around the edges of rice fields

water pipe *n* [ME *waterpipe*, fr. *water* + *pipe*] **1 :** a pipe for conveying water **2 :** a smoking device used chiefly in the Orient, made of a bowl mounted on a vessel of water, often provided with a long flexible tube terminating in a mouthpiece, and so arranged that the smoke is drawn from the bowl through the water where it is cooled and up the tube to the mouth — compare HOOKAH, HUBBLE-BUBBLE 1, NARGILEH

water pipit *n* **:** a widely distributed pipit (*Anthus spinoletta*) of the northern hemisphere; *esp* **:** a bird of a common American race (*A. s. rubescens*)

water pistol *n* **:** a toy pistol designed to throw a jet of liquid — called also *water gun*

water plane *n* **1 :** an airplane equipped to land on water **:** SEAPLANE **2 :** the plane of a given waterline of a ship

water plant *n* **:** a plant growing in water **:** AQUATIC, HYDROPHYTE

water plantain *n* **:** a plant of the genus *Alisma*

water-plantain family *n* **:** ALISMATACEAE

water-plantain spearwort *n* **:** a No. American aquatic crowfoot (*Ranunculus ambigens*) that roots freely at the lower nodes and has chiefly narrow acuminate leaves

water platter *n* **:** VICTORIA 2b

water plug *n* **:** FIREPLUG

water pocket *n* **:** a pocket (as in rock) where water may gather; *esp* **:** a water hole in the bed of an intermittent stream occurring typically as a bowl at the foot of a cliff over which the stream leaps when in the flood stage

water point *n* **:** POINT 6f

water polo *n* **:** a goal game played in a swimming pool by teams of seven swimmers with a ball resembling a soccer ball

water poplar *n* **:** any of several poplars that thrive in wet areas: as **a :** a cottonwood (*Populus deltoides*) **b :** BLACK POPLAR

water poppy *n* **:** a Brazilian aquatic herb (*Hydrocleis nymphoides*) cultivated for its yellow flowers that resemble poppies

water pore *n* **1 :** a pore by which the water tubes of various invertebrates open externally **2 :** HYDATHODE

waterpot \'≈≈,≈\ *n* [ME *waterpot, waterpott*, fr. *water* + *pot, pott* pot — more at POT] **1 :** a vessel for holding or conveying water **2 :** WATERING POT

waterpower \'≈≈,≈≈\ *n* **1 a :** the power of water employed to move machinery **b :** a fall of water suitable for such use **2 :** a water privilege for a mill

waterpower engineering *n* **:** a branch of civil engineering that deals with the construction of works to develop waterpower

water press *n* **:** HYDRAULIC PRESS

water pressure *n* **:** pressure exerted by water **:** hydraulic pressure **:** HYDROSTATIC PRESSURE

water primrose *n* **:** PRIMROSE WILLOW

water privilege *n* **:** the right to use water esp. as a source of mechanical power; *also* **:** a place (as a mill site) where water is or may be so used

1waterproof \¦≈≈¦≈\ *adj* [1*water* + *proof*] **:** impervious to water: as **a :** covered or treated with a material (as a solution of rubber) to prevent permeation by water **b :** relating to or characterizing a machine or structure so constructed that a stream of water may be directed on it under specified conditions without the water entering — **wa·ter·proof·ness** *n* -ES

2waterproof \"\ *n* **1 :** a waterproof fabric **2** *chiefly Brit* **:** RAINCOAT

3waterproof \"\ *vt* **:** to make waterproof

wa·ter·proof·er \"+ə(r)\ *n* **:** one that waterproofs something (as roofs or fabrics): as **a :** a worker who waterproofs something manually or mechanically **b :** a waterproofing material (as for roofs)

waterproofing *n* **1 :** the act or process of making something waterproof **2 :** the condition of being made waterproof **3 :** something (as a treatment or coating) capable of imparting waterproofness

waterproof watch *n* **:** a wristwatch whose movement is enclosed in a case in which the openings for the winding and cover are sealed with gaskets and able to withstand pressures equal to several fathoms of submersion

water pump *n* **:** a pump for raising or circulating water

water puppy *n* **:** MUD PUPPY

water purslane *also* **water puslen** *n* **1 :** MARSH PURSLANE **2 :** a submerged aquatic or mud herb (*Peplis diandra*) of the family Lythraceae that occurs in the central U. S. and Mexico

waterquake \'≈≈,≈\ *n* **:** a disturbance of water by seismic action

water rabbit *n* **:** SWAMP RABBIT

water race *n* **:** 1RACE 2c

water radish *n* **:** YELLOW CRESS b; *esp* **:** a coarse perennial stoloniferous herb (*Rorippa amphibia*) that is widely distributed in the northern hemisphere

water rail *n* **1 :** any of numerous rails of the genus *Rallus* (esp. *R. aquaticus*) **2** *dial Eng* **:** MOORHEN 2

water-rake \'≈≈,≈\ *vt* **:** to harvest (cranberries) by flooding the bog and then scooping up the floating berries with a special rake

water ram *n* **:** HYDRAULIC RAM

water rat *n* **1 :** a rodent that frequents water: as **a :** a vole of the genus *Arvicola*; *esp* **:** a common large British vole (*A. amphibius*) **b :** BROWN RAT; *broadly* **:** an amphibious rodent of the genus *Rattus* **c :** MUSKRAT; *esp* **:** ROUND-TAILED MUSKRAT **d :** any of various Australasian rodents of *Hydromys* or a related genus **:** BEAVER RAT **e :** any of several moderate-sized southern African rats (genus *Dasymys*) with long silky fur and scaly tails that commonly inhabit reedbeds **2 :** a waterfront loafer or petty thief

water rate *n* **1** *or* **water rent :** a rate or tax for supply of water **2 :** the amount of water in the form of condensed steam used by a turbine or engine for a given rate of energy output

water rattler *also* **water rattle** *n* **:** DIAMONDBACK RATTLESNAKE

water-repellent \¦≈≈¦≈≈\ *adj* **:** having a surface that repels water; *esp* **:** treated with a finish that is resistant but not impervious to penetration by water

water requirement *n* **:** the ratio of the weight of water absorbed during the growth of a plant to the dry matter produced often expressed as the number of grams of water taken up per gram of dry weight of plant product

water reserve *n* **:** a tract of land (as in parts of Australia) reserved for feeding streams that are utilized for water supply

water-resistant \¦≈≈¦≈≈\ *adj* **:** resistant to but not wholly proof against the action or entry of water ⟨a *water-resistant* watchcase⟩

water-ret \'≈≈,≈\ *vt* **:** to ret (as flax) with water

water rheostat *n* **:** a rheostat used for dissipating large amounts of electrical energy and made of a vessel (as a tank) that contains water often with added sodium carbonate and usu. has one fixed electrode and one movable electrode

water rice *n* **:** WILD RICE 1a

water right *n* **:** a right to the use of water (as for irrigation) either orig. acquired by appropriation and perfected by beneficial use or derived through ownership of riparian land and in the U.S. if acquired by appropriation resting either in the company making the diversion or in the individual to whose land it is delivered depending upon the statutes and court decisions of the state concerned — compare LITTORAL RIGHT, RIPARIAN RIGHT

water ring *n* **:** a continuous sloping ring or groove cut in the rock around the wall of a mine shaft to catch and divert seepage

water robin *n* **:** a leaden gray Asiatic thrush (*Rhyacornis fuliginosa* or *Phoenicurus fuliginosa*) that frequents running water

water roll *n* **:** a melodious liquid trill in the song of a canary

water-rolled \'≈≈,≈\ *adj* **:** worn round or smooth through being rolled by water ⟨*water-rolled* gravel⟩

water rot *n* **1 :** WATER SPOT **2 :** PINK ROT 1

water-rot \'≈≈,≈\ *vt* [by folk etymology] **:** WATER-RET

waterrug *n, obs* **:** a shaggy or rough-coated water dog

water rush *n* **:** SOFT RUSH

waters *pl of* WATER, *pres 3d sing of* WATER

water sail *n* **:** a small sail sometimes set under a lower studding sail or under a spanker boom and extended nearly to the water

water sallow *n* **:** GRAY WILLOW 2

water sapphire *n* **:** a deep blue iolite sometimes used as a gem — called also *saphir d'eau*

wa·ter·scape \'≈≈,skāp\ *n* -s [1*water* + *-scape*] **:** a water or sea view **:** SEASCAPE

water scavenger beetle *n* **:** a water beetle of the family Hydrophilidae

water scorpion *n* **:** any of numerous aquatic bugs constituting the family Nepidae and having the front legs fitted for seizing and holding prey and the end of the abdomen prolonged by a long breathing tube formed of two appressed grooved bristles — called also *water bug*

water seal *n* **:** a seal formed by water to prevent the passage of gas

water set *n* [1*water* + *set*, past part. of *set*] **:** a trap set under water usu. to avoid human scent on the trap or to drown a trapped animal so that its struggles will not injure the fur or allow escape

water shamrock *n* **:** BUCKBEAN

watershed \'≈≈,≈\ *n* [prob. trans. of G *wasserscheide*] **1 :** WATER PARTING **2 :** a region or area bounded peripherally by a water parting and draining ultimately to a particular watercourse or body of water **:** the catchment area or drainage basin from which the waters of a stream or stream system are drawn **3 :** something (as a sloping contour or member) introduced into a structure primarily to shed or throw off water ⟨a narrow ~ over a car window⟩ **4 :** a crucial or dividing point, line, or factor ⟨his achievement would rank as a ~ in recent European history —*Newsweek*⟩ ⟨without crossing the ~ of war —H.L. Stimson⟩ ⟨the ~ moments of history —C.H.Sykes⟩

water shield *n* **1 :** an aquatic plant (*Brasenia schreberi*) with floating leaves olive green above and red below and all underwater parts covered with a thick layer of jellylike slime — called also *water target* **2 :** FANWORT; *esp* **:** a common aquatic plant (*Cabomba caroliniana*) of eastern No. America with oblong to obovate often basally notched floating leaves and white yellow-spotted flowers

water-shield family *n* **:** CABOMBACEAE

watershoot \'≈≈,≈\ *n* **1 :** SUCKER, WATER SPROUT **2 a** *obs* **:** water draining off a piece of land **b :** a trough or channel for discharging water (as from a downspout) **c** *also* **watershot** \'≈≈,≈\ **:** DRIP 4

water shrew *n* **:** any of numerous semiaquatic shrews usu. living adjacent to swift-flowing streams and having hind feet that are typically fringed with long stiff hairs and are sometimes partially webbed: as **a :** a widely distributed Old World shrew (*Neomys fodiens*) **b :** any of several shrews (genus *Chimarrogale*) of Japan, Borneo, and Sumatra **c :** any of several web-footed shrews (genus *Nectogale*) of Tibetan uplands **d :** a common No. American shrew (*Sorex palustris*)

1waterside \'≈≈,≈\ *n* [ME, fr. *water* + *side*] **:** the land (as the seaside or a riverside) bordering a body of water

2waterside \"\ *adj* **1 :** of, relating to, or located on the waterside ⟨~ trees⟩ **2 :** employed along the waterside ⟨~ workers⟩; *also* **:** of or relating to the workers along the waterside ⟨a ~ strike⟩

wa·ter·sid·er \"+ə(r)\ *n* -s *Austral* **:** LONGSHOREMAN

water silk *n* **:** an alga of the genus *Spirogyra*

water silvering *n* **:** silvering done with silver amalgam

water skegs *n pl but sing or pl in constr* **:** a common yellow iris (*Iris pseudacorus*)

water ski *n* **:** a ski that is broader and shorter than a snow ski and that planes over the water when the skier is towed by a speedboat

water-ski \'≈≈,≈\ *vi* [*water ski*] **:** to plane over water on water skis esp. as a sport

waterskin \'≈≈,≈\ *n* **:** a container of skin to hold water

water skipper *or* **water skater** *n* **:** WATER STRIDER

water sky *n* **:** dull neutral-colored sky near the horizon caused by the reflection of the color of the sea and so indicating open water when seen over an ice-covered sea — compare BLINK

water slater *n* **:** a freshwater isopod of *Asellus* or related genus

water slide *n* **:** a flume for use esp. in logging

water smartweed *n* **:** any of various mostly perennial smartweeds (*Polygonum punctatum*) having lanceolate to lance-oblong leaves with a short petiole gradually broadened at the base

watersmeet \ˈ≈,≈\ *n* **:** a meeting place of two rivers ⟨each of these torrents ran down a gorge of its own, the one on the east, the other on the west of the ~ —Hilaire Belloc⟩

water smoke *n* **1 :** mist or foggy vapor rising from the surface of a body of water **2 :** the moisture that rises in the firing of clayware in the form of vapor from the green brick as it is undergoing heating

water–smoke \ˈ≈,≈\ *vt* **:** to drive off the moisture in (as green brick) in the preliminary stage of burning by means of a slow fire

water snake *n* **:** any of numerous snakes frequenting or inhabiting freshwaters and feeding largely on aquatic animals: as **a :** any of various snakes constituting a cosmopolitan genus (*Natrix*), being common in the eastern U. S. and sometimes a pest in fish hatcheries and rearing pools, and reaching a length of four feet **b :** an eastern Asian or Australian snake of the family Homalopsidae with valvular nostrils and often a compressed tail **c :** WART SNAKE

water snowflake *n* **:** an Asiatic floating plant (*Nymphoides indicum*) often cultivated for its starlike white flowers

water–soak \ˈ≈,≈\ *vt* **:** to soak in water **:** fill the interstices of with water ~ *vi* **:** to become soaked with water ⟨a fabric that does not *water-soak* easily⟩

water soldier *n* **1 :** a European aquatic plant (*Stratiotes aloides*) of the family Hydrocharitaceae with bayonet-shaped leaves that are submerged in the vegetative stage and float in the flowering stage **2 :** a water lettuce (*Pistia stratiotes*)

water–soluble \ˈ≈¦≈≈≈\ *adj* **:** soluble in water ⟨*water-soluble* vitamin B⟩ — compare SPIRIT-SOLUBLE

water spaniel *n* **:** a rather large spaniel that has a heavy curly coat and is adapted esp. for retrieving waterfowl — see IRISH WATER SPANIEL

water speedwell *n* **:** any of several speedwells; *esp* **:** an aquatic herb (*Veronica anagallis-aquatica*) found in wet places in Eurasia and America

water spider *n* **1 a** *or* **water spinner :** an aquatic European spider (*Argyroneta aquatica*) that constructs beneath the surface of the water a bell-shaped structure of silk which is open beneath and filled with air carried down by the spider in the form of small bubbles **b :** any of various spiders that habitually live on or about the water; *esp* **:** a large American spider (*Dolomedes sexpunctatus*) that runs rapidly on the surface of water **2 :** WATER MITE

water spike *n* **:** any of several plants of the genera *Potamogeton* or *Hydrostachys*

watersplash \ˈ≈,≈\ *n* **:** a shallow ford in a stream

water spot *n* **:** any of several diseases of fruits characterized by water-soaked lesions; *esp* **:** a physiological disorder of citrus fruits which occurs during the rainy season and in which the air spaces under the epidermis of the rind become filled with liquid

waterspout \ˈ≈,≈\ *n* [ME *water spoute*, fr. *water* + *spoute* spout — more at SPOUT] **1 a :** a pipe, duct, or orifice from which water is spouted or through which it is carried (as from a roof gutter to a cistern) — compare DOWNSPOUT **b :** water spouting out from or as if from a waterspout **2 :** a slender funnel-shaped or tubular column of rapidly rotating cloud-filled wind usu. extending from the underside of a cumulus or cumulonimbus cloud down to a cloud of spray torn up by the whirling winds from the surface of an ocean or lake, being either straight and vertical or inclined and tortuous as it moves along, and consisting largely of water **3 :** a torrential burst of rain **:** rainfall of the nature or intensity of a cloudburst **syn** see WIND

water sprite *n* **1 :** a sprite held to inhabit or haunt the water **:** WATER NYMPH — compare KELPIE, NAIAD, NEREID, NIX **2 :** FLOATING FERN 1

water sprout *n* **1 :** an extremely vigorous but usu. unproductive shoot originating from an adventitious or a latent bud on the trunk or a main limb of a tree (as a fruit tree) — compare WATER SUCKER **2 :** WATER SUCKER

water spruce *n* **:** BLACK SPRUCE 1

water stain *n* **:** a wood stain in which water is the solvent or dispersion medium

water stair *n* **:** a stairway leading to the water (as at a boat landing) — often used in pl. but sing. or pl. in constr.

water star grass *n* **:** a grassy-leaved No. American aquatic herb (*Heteranthera dubia*) with yellow star-shaped blossoms

water starwort *n* **:** a plant of the genus *Callitriche*

wa·ter·stead \ˈwätə(r),sted, ˈwȯtə-\ *n, dial Eng* **:** the bed of a stream

water stoma *n* **:** HYDATHODE

waterstone \ˈ≈,≈\ *n* **:** a whetstone or grindstone used with water rather than oil

water stop *n* **1 :** a device or construction designed to bar the passage of water **2 :** a place (as on a stage road) where water is regularly available

water strider *n* **1 :** any of various long-legged bugs that constitute the family Gerridae and move about on the surface of fresh waters or more rarely on the ocean — called also *water skipper* **2 :** a bug of the family Veliidae

water string *n* **:** the final string of casing or pipe set to exclude water from the producing formation of an oil or gas well

water–struck brick \ˈ≈,≈-\ *n* **:** brick made by slop-molding — compare SAND-STRUCK BRICK

water sucker *n* **:** a vigorous shoot originating from a bud at the base of or on the root of a plant (as the banana) — compare WATER SPROUT 1

water supply *n* **:** source, means, or process of supplying water (as for a community) usu. including reservoirs, tunnels, and pipelines and often the watershed from which the water is ultimately drawn

water–supply engineering *n* **:** a branch of civil engineering dealing with the development and maintenance of water supplies

water swallow *n* **1 :** WATER WAGTAIL **2** *dial Eng* **:** SINK 5

water system *n* **1 :** a river with its tributaries **2 :** WATER SUPPLY

water tabby *n* **:** a tabby fabric with a watered finish

water table *n* [ME] **1 :** a stringcourse or similar member when projecting so as to throw off water; *esp* **:** the first table above the ground at the top of a foundation and beginning of the upper wall **2 :** a gutter on the side of a road to carry off water **3 :** the upper limit of the portion of the ground wholly saturated with water whether very near the surface or many feet below it — called also *groundwater level*

water tabling *n* **:** architectural water tables (as of a building)

water target *n* **:** WATER SHIELD 1

water taxi *n* **:** a boat functioning (as about a harbor) as a taxi

water telescope *n* **1 :** WATER GLASS 3 **2 :** a telescope devised for looking into a body of water

water tender *n* **1 a :** a workman who attends to the condition of the water in steam boilers **b :** a petty officer (as in the U. S. Navy) in charge in a fireroom and responsible esp. for proper supplying of water to the boilers and adjustment of burners **2 :** a truck equipped with a water tank and used esp. in fire fighting

water thermometer *n* **:** a thermometer filled with water instead of mercury and used esp. for ascertaining the precise temperature at which water is most dense

water thief *n* **1** *obs* **:** PIRATE **2 :** a valve with multiple connections that permits bleeding a large line through several subordinate lines

water thrush *n* **1 :** any of several No. American warblers of the genus *Seiurus* usu. living in the vicinity of streams and having plumage that is olivaceous above and streaked below **2 :** a European water ouzel (*Cinclus cinclus*) **3** *dial Eng* **:** PIED WAGTAIL

water thyme *n* **:** a waterweed (*Elodea canadensis*)

water tick *n* **:** WATER MITE

water tiger *n* **:** WATER DEVIL 1

watertight \ˈ≈¦≈\ *adj* [ME *water thicht*, fr. *water* + *thicht, thight, tight* tight — more at TIGHT] **1 :** of such precision of construction or fit as to be impermeable to water except when under sufficient pressure to produce structural discontinuity by rupture ⟨a ~ flashing⟩ ⟨~ joints⟩ **2 :** so devised (as in planning or phrasing) as to leave no possibility of misconstruction or evasion ⟨a ~ lease⟩ ⟨the precautions taken against cheating were ~ —A.G.N.Flew⟩ ⟨has created a ~ and very real world of his own —C.J.Rolo⟩ — **wa·ter·tight·ness** *n*

watertight compartment *n* **:** a compartment (as in a ship) having watertight doors by which it can be entirely separated from the rest of the structure of which it is a part

water tower *n* **:** a tower or standpipe serving as a reservoir to deliver water at a required head; *specif* **:** a fire apparatus having a vertical pipe that can be extended to various heights and supplied with water under high pressure (as by several motor pumpers) and used to deliver water at heights unattainable by the ordinary apparatus

water treader *n* **:** a bug of the family Mesoveliidae usu. found at the edges of ponds but sometimes on the surface of the water

water tree *n* **:** any of several chiefly tropical plants with fluids that may be used as an emergency source of drinking water: as **a :** a large Ceylonese pitcher plant (*Nepenthes distillatoria*) **b :** an African woody vine (*Tetracera potatoria*) that yields abundant watery sap when a large stem is cut **c :** any of several chiefly arborescent Australian plants (as of the family Proteaceae) that yield a watery sap when the bark or roots are cut; *esp* **:** a needle wood (*Hakea leucoptera*) that stores water in its thickened roots

water trefoil *n* **:** BUCKBEAN

water tube *n* **:** a tube for passing or holding water: as **a :** a tube in some steam boilers in which water circulates and steam is generated **b :** a tube of a system of tubular excretory organs in many invertebrates that have external openings and that are held to be analogous in function to the kidneys of vertebrates

watertube boiler \ˈ≈,≈-\ *n* **:** a steam boiler in which water to be heated circulates in tubes exposed to fire and enveloped by hot gases — compare FIRE-TUBE BOILER

water tunnel *n* **:** a device for the study or testing of the flow about bodies in which water is the mobile fluid — compare WIND TUNNEL

water tupelo *n* **:** TUPELO GUM

water turbine *n* **:** a turbine in which the actuating fluid is water

water turkey *n* **:** a New World snakebird (*Anhinga anhinga*)

water tuyere *n* **:** a water-jacketed tuyere

water twist *n* **:** an eddy or whirlpool in a stream

water uintjie *n* **:** CAPE PONDWEED

water vacuole *n* **:** a vacuole containing watery fluid; *esp* **:** CONTRACTILE VACUOLE

water vapor *n* **:** water in a vaporous form esp. when below boiling temperature and diffused (as in the atmosphere) — compare STEAM

water varnish *n* **:** a varnish in which water is the solvent and water-soluble gums are the nonvolatile ingredients

water–vascular \ˈ≈¦≈≈≈\ *adj* **:** of, relating to, or made up of vessels that in many invertebrates contain a watery fluid — see WATER-VASCULAR SYSTEM

water–vascular system *n* **:** a system of vessels in echinoderms containing a watery fluid that is analogous to blood, is used for the movement of tentacles and tube feet, and may also function in excretion and respiration

water velvet *n* **:** a plant of the genus *Azolla*

water vine *n* **1 :** any of several Asiatic climbing plants (genus *Phytocrene*) of the family Icacinaceae with stems that yield a copious and refreshing watery sap **2 :** WATER TREE b

water violet *n* **:** WATER GILLYFLOWER

water viper *n* **:** WATER MOCCASIN 1

water vole *n* **:** a vole that frequents water: as **a :** WATER RAT 1a **b :** a western No. American vole (*Microtus richardsoni*)

water wagon *n* **:** a wagon used (as with troops on the march) to carry water — **on the water wagon** *adv (or adj)* **:** on the wagon

water wagtail *n* **1 :** WAGTAIL; *esp* **:** PIED WAGTAIL **2 :** WATER THRUSH 1

waterwall \ˈ≈,≈\ *n* [ME *waterwal*, fr. *water* + *wal* wall — more at WALL] **1 :** a wall built beside or around a body of water **2 :** an arrangement of pipes carrying water and so grouped as to form a protective wall between a fire (as in a boiler) and the lining of a furnace

water wally *n* **:** a woody herb or low shrub (*Baccharis glutinosa*) ranging from the southwestern U. S. to western So. America and used locally for thatching and in making brooms — called also *batamote*

water wand *n* **:** a device screwed onto the end of a garden hose to reduce the pressure of the water without decreasing the volume

wa·ter·ward \ˈ≈wə(r)d\ *also* **wa·ter·wards** \-dz\ *adv* **:** toward water or a particular body of water ⟨cattle turning ~⟩

water–washed \ˈ≈,≈\ *adj* **:** washed or swept with water; *esp* **:** washed by the waves of the sea

water wave *n* **1 :** a gravity wave on water **2 :** a method or style of setting hair by dampening with water and forming into waves

water–waved \ˈ≈,≈\ *adj* **1 :** marked with a pattern or striping suggesting a wave of water **2** *of hair* **:** set in a water wave

waterway \ˈ≈,≈\ *n* [ME *waterwey*, fr. OE *wæterweg*, fr. *wæter* water + *weg* way — more at WATER, WAY] **1 :** a way or channel by which water may pass or escape; *often* **:** a made and often grassed channel that is provided to carry storm water away from a point where it is likely to cause erosion **2 a :** the outer planking of a deck of a ship which is much heavier than the rest of the deck and of which the inboard edge is grooved to form a passage for water to the scuppers; *also* **:** the passage so formed — see SHIP illustration **b :** passage in a steel ship formed by angle irons and the deck stringer **3 a :** breadth of water available for passage (as of boats) **:** FAIRWAY 1a ⟨the ~ of a canal⟩ **b :** a way or route for traffic by water **:** a navigable body or course of water ⟨the Great Lakes provide a ~ to the heart of the continent⟩ **4 :** the open passage area in a cock or valve

waterweed \ˈ≈,≈\ *n* **:** any of several floating or submerged aquatic plants: as **a :** an American plant (*Elodea canadensis*) that has elongate branching stems and small opposite or verticillate leaves and is naturalized in parts of Europe; *broadly* **:** any plant of the genus *Elodea* **b :** a California primrose willow (*Jussiaea californica*)

water weevil *n* **:** RICE WATER WEEVIL

waterwheel \ˈ≈,≈\ *n* [ME *waterwhele*, fr. *water* + *whele* wheel — more at WHEEL] **1 :** a wheel made to rotate by direct action of water: as **a :** a vertical wheel on a horizontal shaft moved at a comparatively low velocity by the action or weight of the water on or in floats or buckets on its rim — see BREAST WHEEL, OVERSHOT WHEEL, PONCELET WHEEL **b :** a turbine operated by water **2 :** a wheel (as a noria) for raising water **3 :** the paddle wheel of a steamship **4 :** a synchronized swimming stunt which is executed with the body lying on the side and in which the knees are drawn toward the chest and the body is propelled in a circle by alternate pedaling movements of the legs and feet

water whip *n* **:** a gun-tackle purchase hooked to a yard (as of a ship) and used in hoisting in moderate weights

water–white \ˈ≈,≈\ *adj* **:** approaching water in colorlessness and clarity ⟨*water-white* honey from fireweed⟩

water white oak *n* **:** an overcup oak (*Quercus lyrata*)

water willow *n* **1 :** any of several plants that thrive in wet areas and are felt to resemble willows: as **a** (1) **:** PURPLE LOOSESTRIFE (2) **:** SWAMP LOOSESTRIFE **b :** FIREWEED b **c :** a plant of the genus *Justicia*; *esp* **:** a No. American rhizomatous plant (*J. americana*) that has slender elongated leaves and dense capitate to ellipsoidal inflorescences with pale violet or white flowers **2 :** any of several willows that thrive in wet areas

water wing *n* **1 water wings** *pl* **:** a pneumatic device to give support to the body of a person swimming or learning to swim ⟨disgusted Londoners discovered that their car was as useful to them as *water-wings* in a desert —Mollie Panter-Downes⟩ **2 :** a wall forming a wing to the abutment of a bridge or pier and extending laterally along the shore on either side as a protection from the current

waterwise \ˈ≈,≈\ *adv* **:** in the manner of water ⟨flowing ~⟩

water witch *n* **1 :** a witch reputed to live in or haunt a body of water **2 a :** DABCHICK **b** *dial Eng* **:** STORM PETREL **3 a** *or* **water witcher :** a dowser for water **b :** any of various devices for determining usu. electrically the presence of water (as in a tank or underground)

water witching *n* **:** the act of dowsing for water

waterwood \ˈ≈,≈\ *n* **1 :** a West Indian tree (*Chimarrhis cymosa*) of the family Rubiaceae with greenish white flowers **2 :** a Central American mangrove (*Cassipourea elliptica*) with hairy white flowers **3 :** a southern African tree (*Syzygium cordatum*) of the family Myrtaceae having light easily worked wood that is used for flooring and joinery

waterwork \ˈ≈,≈\ *n* [ME *waterwerk*, fr. *water* + *werk, wurk, work* work — more at WORK] **1 :** something (as a tank, dock, canal lock, levee, or seawall) built in, for, or as a protection against water **2 :** a mechanism, contrivance, or set of equipment for handling water: as **a :** an ornamental or spectacular display of water mechanically produced **:** FOUNTAIN, CASCADE — usu. used in pl. **b** (1) *obs* **:** a mechanical contrivance for raising and distributing water (2) **waterworks** *pl* **:** the whole system of reservoirs, channels, mains, and pumping and purifying equipment by which a water supply is obtained and distributed to consumers; *also* **:** a pumping or purifying station of such a system **c waterworks** *pl* (1) **:** the channels by which sap or other vital fluid is handled in the living body ⟨the complex ~s of a tree⟩ (2) *slang* **:** KIDNEYS **3 waterworks** *pl* **:** tears or the shedding of tears

waterworker \ˈ≈,≈≈\ *n* **:** one who works along the waterside, in the waterworks of a city, or in trenching to make drains for carrying water

waterworn \ˈ≈,≈\ *adj* **:** worn, smoothed, or polished by the action of water

waterwort \ˈ≈,≈\ *n* [ME, fr. OE *wæterwyrt*, fr. *wæter* water + *wyrt* wort — more at WATER, WORT] **1 :** a plant of the family Elatinaceae **2 :** a plant of the family Philydraceae **3 :** MAIDENHAIR SPLEENWORT

waterworthy \ˈ≈,≈≈\ *adj* **:** SEAWORTHY

wa·tery \ˈwȯd|ə̇rē, ˈwä|, |tə-, -ri\ *adj, sometimes* -ER/-EST [ME, fr. OE *wæterig*, fr. *wæter* water + *-ig* -y] **1 a :** consisting of or filled with water ⟨fish within their ~ residence —John Milton⟩ ⟨a ~ grave⟩ **b :** containing, sodden with, or yielding water ⟨a ~ stratum⟩ ⟨~ skies⟩ **:** WET, BOGGY ⟨a ~ northland soil⟩ **c :** made of or prepared with water or sometimes with a watery liquid ⟨~ vapors⟩ ⟨a ~ solution⟩ **d :** exuding or infiltrated with a watery liquid ⟨the ~ vesicles of ivy poisoning⟩: as (1) **:** full of lacrimal secretion ⟨with ~ eyes⟩ (2) *obs, of the mouth* **:** WATERING **2 :** felt to resemble water: as **a :** having the fluidity of water **:** lacking or depleted in viscosity **:** THIN ⟨the ~ blood of anemia⟩ ⟨a ~ liquid⟩ **b** (1) **:** deficient in color or intensity as if diluted with water **:** PALE ⟨a ~ blue⟩ ⟨~ sunlight⟩ (2) **:** exhibiting weakness and vapidity **:** PALLID, WISHY-WASHY ⟨a ~ style in writing⟩ **c** (1) **:** lacking in substance and deficient in savor ⟨a ~ soup⟩ (2) **:** having a soft soggy texture ⟨stale ~ vegetables⟩ ⟨a well-flavored fish but inclined to be ~⟩ **3 :** of, relating to, or connected with water ⟨a ~ deity⟩: as **a** *archaic* **:** living or growing in water **:** AQUATIC **b** *of a sign of the zodiac* **:** having a cold and moist complexion

water yarrow *n* **:** a featherfoil (*Hottonia inflata*)

watery hide disease *n* **:** yellow fat disease of mink

watery rot *n* **:** PINK ROT 1

wath \ˈwath\ *n* -s [ME, of Scand origin; akin to ON *vath* ford; akin to OE *wæd* ford, OHG *wat* ford, OHG *watan* to wade — more at WADE] *chiefly dial* **:** ¹FORD 1

wa·ther \ˈwäthə(r)\ *chiefly Irish var of* WATER

wats *pl of* WAT

wat·so·nia \wätˈsōnēə *also* wȯt-\ *n* [NL, fr. Sir William *Watson* †1787 Eng. botanist + NL *-ia*] **1** *cap* **:** a genus of southern African herbs (family Iridaceae) that resemble gladioli, are often cultivated for ornament, and have showy spikes of nearly regular and mostly red or white flowers and chiefly basal leaves **2** -s **:** any plant or flower of the genus *Watsonia*

wat·so·ni·an \(ˈ)≈¦sōnēən\ *adj, usu cap* [John B. *Watson* †1958 Amer. psychologist + E *-ian*] **:** of or relating to the behavioristic theories of the psychologist Watson

wat·so·ni·us \≈ˈsōnēəs\ *n, cap* [NL, after Dr. *Watson*, 20th cent. Nigerian physician] **:** a genus of conical digenetic trematodes (related to *Paramphistomum*) that are parasitic in the intestine of African primates rarely including man

watt \ˈwät *also* ˈwȯ|, *usu* |d.+V\ *n* -s [after James *Watt* †1819 Scot. mechanical engineer and inventor] **1 :** the absolute mks unit of power equal to one absolute joule per second and taken as the standard in the U. S. **:** 1⁄746 horsepower **2 :** a unit of power equal to about 1.00017 watts — called also *international watt*

watt·age \|d·ij, |tij, -ēj\ *n* -s **:** amount of power expressed in watts

wattape *var of* WATAP

watt current *n* **:** the component of the current in an alternating circuit that is in phase with the electromotive force

¹**wat·teau** \(ˈ)wä¦tō, *also* (ˈ)wȯ¦-\ *adj, usu cap* [after Jean Antoine *Watteau* †1721 Fr. painter] **1 :** of or relating to the painter Watteau **2** *of women's dress* **:** of the kind or style represented in Watteau's painting: as **a :** having back pleats falling loosely from the neckline to the hem **b** *of a hat* **:** shallow-crowned and having a wide brim turned up at the back to hold flower trimmings

²**watteau** \"\ *n, pl* **watteaux** \"\ *often cap* **:** a Watteau hat

watt·er \ˈwä|d·ə(r), |tə- *also* ˈwȯ|\ *n* -s [*watt* + *-er*] **:** one (as a light bulb or a radio station) having a specified wattage — usu. used in combination ⟨you'll need at least a 60 ~ in that lamp⟩ ⟨the station was a 250 ~⟩

watte·ville·ite \ˈwätvi,līt\ *n* -s *usu cap* [G *wattevillit*, fr. Baron Oscar de *Watteville*, 19th cent. Frenchman + G *-it* -ite] **:** a mineral $Na_2Ca(SO_4)_2.4H_2O$(?) that is a hydrous sulfate of sodium and calcium and occurs as aggregates of minute hairlike crystals

watt–hour \ˈ≈¦≈\ *n* **:** a unit of work or energy equivalent to the power of one watt operating for one hour and equal to about 2655 foot-pounds

watt–hour meter *n* **:** a device to record electric energy usu. in kilowatt-hours **:** an integrating wattmeter

¹**wat·tle** \ˈwäd·ᵊl, |tᵊl *also* ˈwȯ|\ *n* -s [ME *wattel*, fr. OE *watel, watol, watul*; akin to OE *wætla* & *wethel* bandage, OHG *wadal*] **1 a :** a fabrication of rods or poles interwoven with slender branches, withes, or reeds and used esp. formerly in building construction ⟨the walls were of ~ and covered with moss—R.L. Stevenson⟩ **b :** material (as rods, branches, and reeds) for such construction **c** *dial Eng* **:** STICK, STAVE, WAND **d** *dial Eng* **:** HURDLE 1a **e wattles** *pl* **:** poles laid on a roof to support thatch **2 :** a fleshy dependent process usu. about the head or neck of an animal: as **a :** a naked, fleshy, usu. wrinkled, and highly colored process of the skin hanging from the chin or throat of a bird or reptile — see COCK illustration **b** (1) *dial Eng* **:** a flap of loose hanging flesh on either side of the throat of some swine (2) **:** loose flesh hanging from the human jaw ⟨a ~ of flesh dangled from his jawbone —T.W.Duncan⟩ **c :** a barbel of a fish **d :** a livestock identification mark in which the skin on the dewlap or other part of the body is slit **3** *Austral* **a** (1) *archaic* **:** a tree yielding slender poles suitable for wattle; *esp* **:** a small slender swamp tree (*Callicoma serratifolia*) of the family Cunoniaceae (2) **:** a tree or shrub of the genus *Acacia* — see BLACK WATTLE, GOLDEN WATTLE, SILVER WATTLE **b :** WATTLE BARK

²**wattle** \"\ *vt* **wattled; wattled; wattling** \|d·ᵊliŋ, |t(ᵊ)l-\ **wattles** [ME *watlen*, fr. *wattel*, n.] **1 :** to form or build of or with wattle ⟨soon *wattled* the sides and thatched the roof of a snug little camp⟩ **2 a :** to form into wattle **:** interlace (as withes) to form wattle **b :** to unite or make solid and continuous by interweaving light flexible material (as withes or osiers) ⟨*wattling* the stakes into a firm palisade⟩ **3 :** to enclose (as sheep) with or as if with wattle **:** ENFOLD

³**wattle** \"\ *n* -s [ME (Sc) *wattell*, of Scand origin; akin to Norw dial. *veitla, veitsla, veitsle* entertainment, party, ON *veizla* gift, entertainment, feast, fr. *veita* to grant, give, give a feast; akin to OHG *weizen* to show, prove, *wizzan* to know — more at WIT] **:** annual entertainment formerly provided the foud in the Orkney and Shetland islands; *also* **:** tax paid in commutation of this service

wattle and daub *n* **:** framework of woven rods and twigs covered and plastered with clay and used in building construction ⟨a rough stable of *wattle and daub*⟩

wattle bark *n* **:** an astringent bark derived from various Australian acacias and used in tanning

wattlebird \ˈ≈,≈\ *n* **1 :** any of several Australasian honey eaters of the genus *Anthochaera* having fleshy pendulous ear wattles: as **a :** a common largely grayish brown Australian bird (*A. carunculata*) with white shaft stripes on the feathers of the upperparts and a white tail tip **b** : a closely related and somewhat similar Tasmanian bird (*A. paradoxa*) **2** : WATTLE CROW

wattle crow *n* : either of two long-tailed slaty gray corvine birds (*Callaeas cinerea* and *C. wilsoni*) of New Zealand having a brightly colored subcircular fleshy wattle on each side of the base of the lower mandible

wattled *adj* **1 a** : furnished with pendent fleshy processes ⟨a ~ goat⟩ : having enlarged wattles ⟨a ~ honey eater⟩ **b** : depicted with wattles of a specified color ⟨a cock's head ~ argent⟩ **2 a** : made or strengthened with wattle ⟨a ~ terrace⟩ ⟨~ walls⟩ **b** : formed for temporary use from hurdles of wattle ⟨a ~ sheepfold⟩ **3** : interlaced into or as if into wattle ⟨~ reeds⟩

wattle day *n, usu cap W&D* : August 1 or September 1 according to the forwardness of the flowering of the wattle in each state constituting a general holiday in Australia dedicated to the encouragement of the arts

wattled bird of paradise : a bird of paradise (*Paradigalla carunculata*) having an erect yellowish wattle in front of each eye and a bluish pendent one at each angle of the mouth

wattled crow *n* **1** : WATTLEBIRD 1 **2** : WATTLE CROW

wattled honey eater *n* : WATTLEBIRD 1

wattled plover *or* **wattled lapwing** *n* : any of various plovers of the warmer parts of the Old World that resemble the lapwings but have about the face and esp. between the eye and the bill variously colored fleshy wattles and are usu. placed in a distinct subfamily of Charadriidae

wattled stare *or* **wattled starling** *n* : SADDLEBACK 2d

wattle extract *n* : a vegetable tanning material made from wattle bark

wattle gum *n* : gum arabic obtained from wattles (as *Acacia pycnantha*) in the form of reddish tears or lumps — compare AUSTRALIAN GUM

watt·less component \ˈ=ləs-\ *n* [*wattless* fr. *watt* + *-less*] : REACTIVE COMPONENT

wattless power *n* : REACTIVE VOLT-AMPERES

wattless volt-amperes *n pl* : the product of the reactive component of current by voltage or of the reactive component of voltage by current

wattle turkey *n* : the Australian brush turkey

wattlework \ˈ=₌,=\ *n* : coarse wickerwork : WATTLE 1a

wattling *pres part of* WATTLE

watt·meter \ˈ=,mēd·ə(r), -ētə-\ *n* [ISV *watt* + *-meter*] **1** : an instrument for measuring electric power in watts **2** : WATT-HOUR METER

watt-second \ˈ=ˈ=₌\ *n* : JOULE

wa·tu·si *also* **wa·tus·si** \wäˈtüsē, -si\ *or* **wa·tut·si** \-ütˈs-\ *n pl, usu cap* : TUSI

wau·co·bi·an \wȯˈkōbēən\ *adj, usu cap* [*Waucoba* mountains, range in eastern Calif. + E *-an*] : of or relating to a subdivision of the American Cambrian — see GEOLOGIC TIME table

¹**waugh** \ˈwȯf\ *adj* [prob. fr. ME *walh, walhwe,* fr. OE *wealg;* akin to OE *wlæc, wlacu* lukewarm — more at WELKIN] **1** *chiefly Scot* : INSIPID, NAUSEOUS, STALE **2** *chiefly Scot* : FAINT, WEAK

²**waugh** *also* **wagh** *or* **wah** \ˈwȯ, ˈwä\ *interj* [imit. of a child's cry] — used to express anger, disgust, or grief

¹**waught** \ˈwäkt\ *vb* -ED/-ING/-S [origin unknown] *chiefly Scot* : to drink deep : QUAFF

²**waught** \"\ *n* -S *chiefly Scot* : a copious draft

wauk \ˈwȯk\ *Scot var of* WAKE

wau·ke \ˈwaùkä\ *n* -S [Hawaiian] *Hawaii* : PAPER MULBERRY

wau·ke·gan juniper \wȯˈkēgən-\ *n, usu cap W* [fr. *Waukegan,* city in northeastern Illinois] : a creeping juniper (*Juniperus horizontalis douglasi*) having long branches and blue-green leaves that turn purplish in winter

wauk·en \ˈwȯkən\ *Scot var of* WAKEN

wauk·rife \ˈwȯ,krīf\ *chiefly Scot var of* WAKERIFE

waul \ˈwȯl\ *var of* WAWL

waulk \ˈwȯk\ *Scot var of* ³WALK

waur \ˈwär\ *Scot var of* ³WAR, ⁴WAR

¹**wave** \ˈwāv\ *vb* -ED/-ING/-S [ME *waven,* fr. OE *wafian* to wave with the hands; akin to OE *wǣfre* wavering, restless — more at WAVER] *vi* **1 a** : to flutter in a breeze ⟨*waving* battle streamers⟩ : float, play, or shake in an air current : move up and down or to and fro : FLAP **b** *obs* : to bob on or as if on the surface of the water : toss or fluctuate in water or air **2** *archaic* : to waver irresolutely between conflicting courses of action or opinion : HESITATE, VACILLATE **3** : to motion with the hands or with something held in them in signal, greeting, or salute ⟨continued to ~ to him until the train disappeared in the distance⟩ **4 a** *of water* : to move in waves, fluctuations, or undulations : HEAVE **b** *of a crowd* : to move in a restless, irregular, or fluctuating way likened to that of sea waves **5** : to become moved or brandished to and fro ⟨handkerchiefs *waved* as the president rode by⟩ ⟨his sword *waved* and flashed⟩ **6** *obs* : to bend from side to side : move sinuously **7** : to move before the wind with a wavelike motion and appearance ⟨field of *waving* grain⟩ **8** : to follow a curving line or take a wavy form : UNDULATE ⟨seen from a distance, its outline curves and *~s* in a Romanesque tracery⟩ ~ *vt* **1** : to swing (something) back and forth; *esp* : to lift up (a sacrifice) and move back and forth before the altar in consecration ⟨take the breast of the ram of Aaron's ordination and ~ it for a wave offering before the Lord —Exod 29:26 (RSV)⟩ **2** : to impart a curving or undulating shape or design to : decorate with a wavy surface, edge, or outline ⟨*waved* her hair and manicured her nails⟩ **3 a** : to motion to (someone) to go in an indicated direction or to stop : FLAG, SIGNAL ⟨*waved* down an approaching motorist to ask for help⟩ ⟨looked at my identification card and then *waved* me on⟩ **b** : to gesture with (as the arm) in greeting or farewell, in celebration of someone's triumph, or in homage to an honored person : make a sweeping, circling, or twirling movement with ⟨*waved* hats and handkerchiefs in welcome to their returning hero⟩ **c** : to indicate by a sweep of hand or arm : SIGNIFY ⟨*waved* farewell from the ship's rail⟩ ⟨*waved* dismissal as he turned and left⟩ ⟨the officer *waved* acknowledgement —Wirt Williams⟩ **4** : to flap (the wings) in or as if in flight **5** : BRANDISH, FLOURISH, SHAKE ⟨*waved* a loaded pistol menacingly⟩ **6** : to blow (something) to and fro : FLUTTER ⟨the troops plodded by and a desultory breeze *waved* their banners from time to time⟩ **7** *archaic* : to move (the head) up and down : BOB **8** : to toss (as a blossom) in the breeze ⟨trees *waved* leafy heads⟩ **syn** see SWING

²**wave** \"\ *n* -S **1 a** : a ridge or swell on the surface of a liquid (as of the sea) having normally a forward motion distinct from the oscillatory motion of the particles that successively compose it : a minute ridge that is largely dependent on surface tension : a ridge of larger size that is dependent on the force of gravity : an undulation that is dependent on the friction between wind and water — compare BREAKER, RIPPLE **b** : a body of water **2 a** : a shape or outline having successive curves like those of ocean waves : one of the crests of such a form or a crest with its adjacent trough **b** : a natural waviness of the hair or a dressing intended to simulate it — compare MARCEL, PERMANENT WAVE **c** : an undulating line or streak (as in glass, steel, or textiles) or a pattern formed by such lines **3** : something likened to an ocean wave as stormy or unsettling: as **a** : a surge of sensation or emotion ⟨a ~ of nausea⟩ ⟨a ~ of anger⟩ ⟨a ~ of tenderness⟩ **b** : one of the troubles or vicissitudes of life or fortune **c** : a tide of opinion or sentiment carrying many with it : a movement sweeping large numbers in a common direction : CONTAGION **d** : a peak or climax of intensity : the moment of greatest activity or strongest feeling ⟨a ~ of enthusiasm⟩ **4** : a sweep of hand or arm or of some object held in the hand used as a signal, greeting, or other indication **5** : a long ridge of ground rounded into the shape of an ocean wave **6** : a rolling or undulatory movement or one of a series of such movements passing along a surface or through the air **7** : a movement likened to that of an ocean wave: as **a** : a tide, advance, or surge of settlers : one of a succession of influxes of people migrating into a region **b** (1) : a large group of animals of one kind ⟨the final ~ of migrating ducks⟩ (2) : a sudden rapid increase in an animal population or its effects ⟨a very severe fly-strike ~ followed the moist summer⟩ **c** : a line of attacking or advancing troops, landing craft, combat vehicles, or aircraft ⟨it was D company; our second ~ —H.G.Wells⟩ **8** : a disturbance or variation that transfers itself and energy progressively from point to point in a medium or in space in such a way that each particle or element influences the adjacent ones and that may be in the form of an elastic deformation or of a variation of level or pressure, of electric or magnetic intensity, of electric potential, or of temperature — see LONGITUDINAL WAVE, TRANSVERSE WAVE **9** : a change in temperature or a period of hot or cold weather — compare COLD WAVE, HOT WAVE **10** : EARTH WAVE 1 **11** : RADIO WAVE **12** : an undulating or jagged line constituting a graphic representation (as of heart action in an electrocardiogram, brain waves in an electroencephalogram, an earthquake in a seismogram, or a varying electric current in an oscilloscope)

³**wave** \"\ *archaic var of* WAIVE

⁴**wave** \"\ *n* -S *usu cap* [*W*omen *A*ccepted for *V*olunteer *E*mergency Service] **1** : a member of the Women's Reserve of the U. S. Navy formed during World War II **2** : a woman serving in the U. S. Navy

wave analyzer *n* : a harmonic analyzer applied to wave-form-curve analysis

wave antenna *n* : a radio antenna of great length with special circuit arrangements permitting utilization of the antenna's directional properties

wave band *n* **1** : a range of radio-wave frequencies assigned to a particular type of broadcasting (as television or FM) **2** : ¹CHANNEL 1i

wave base *n* : the depth in a body of water (as a lake or sea) at which wave motion becomes inappreciable

wave-built \ˈ=,=\ *adj* : built up by the action of lake or sea waves and their concomitant currents ⟨a *wave-built* beach⟩

wave-built terrace *n* : a terrace built up of loosened material at the edge of a wave-cut terrace

wave changer *n* : a device in a radio transmitting set for effecting a rapid change from one frequency to another

wave-cut \ˈ=,=\ *adj* : cut away by the action of waves of a lake or sea and their concomitant currents

wave-cut terrace *n* : a shallow-water shelf inclining gently away from the base of an eroded sea cliff

waved *adj* [partly fr. ²*wave* + *-ed,* partly fr. past part. of ¹*wave*] : having a wavelike form or outline: as **a** : UNDULATING, INDENTED, CURVING ⟨the ~ cutting edge of a bread knife⟩ **b** *of cloth* : having wavelike lines of color : WATERED **c** : moved or swung to and fro

wave equation *n* **1** : a partial differential equation of the second order whose solutions describe wave phenomena (as the transverse vibrations of a stretched string) **2** : SCHRÖDINGER EQUATION

wave filter *n* : ¹FILTER 3

wave form *n* : a curve that represents the condition of a wave-propagating medium at a given instant and is usu. a graph in rectangular coordinates whose abscissas represent distances along the direction of propagation and whose ordinates represent the corresponding values of the propagated variation or disturbance — called also *wave shape*

wave front *n* **1** : a surface composed at any instant of all the points just reached by a vibrational disturbance in its propagation through a medium **2** : a surface so drawn as to pass through those parts of a wave where the distortion or displacement of the medium through which the wave passes is everywhere the same

wave function *n* : a solution of the wave equation

wave guide *n* : a metal pipe of circular or rectangular cross section or a dielectric cylinder of such dimensions that it will propagate electromagnetic waves of a given frequency used for channeling ultrahigh-frequency waves in radio and television transmission because of the low loss by attenuation and radiation

wave height *n* : the vertical distance between the trough of a wave and the following crest

wavelength \ˈ=,=\ *n* : the distance in the line of advance of a wave from any one point to the next point at which at the same instant there is the same phase ⟨if *N* is the frequency of the waves and λ their ~, their velocity of advance is the product *N*λ⟩

wave·less \ˈwāvləs\ *adj* : having no waves : CALM, SMOOTH, UNRUFFLED

wave·less·ly *adv* : in a waveless manner

wave·let \ˈwāvlət\ *n* -S **1** : a little wave : RIPPLE **2** : one of the elementary waves each with a point source of which any advancing wave front is the envelope — see HUYGENS' PRINCIPLE

wavelike \ˈ=,=\ *adj (or adv)* : having the form, movement, or other characteristics of a wave : resembling a wave in manner of propagation

wave line *n* : WAVEMARK

wa·vell·ite \ˈwāvə,līt\ *n* -S [William *Wavell* †1829 Eng. physician + E *-ite*] : a mineral $Al_3(PO_4)_2(OH)_3.5H_2O$ consisting of a hydrous basic aluminum phosphate and occurring usu. in hemispherical radiated aggregates varying from white to yellow, green, or black

wavemark \ˈ=,=\ *n* [²*wave* + *mark*] **1** : a very small ridge of sand made by a wave when it advances upon a low sandy beach and marking the limit of advance **2** : one of many undulations on the bedding surfaces of a sedimentary rock due to wave action during the period of deposition — compare RIPPLE MARK

wave-mechanical \ˈ=+ˈ=₌=\ *adj* : of or relating to wave mechanics

wave mechanics *n pl but sing or pl in constr* : a theory of matter holding that elementary particles (as electrons, protons, neutrons) have wave properties and seeking a mathematical interpretation of the structure of matter on the basis of these properties

wave·me·ter \ˈwāv,mēd·ə(r)\ *n* [²*wave* + *-meter*] : a device to measure the wavelength or the frequency of an electromagnetic or radio signal

wave molding *n* : a molding with a profile that suggests one or more breaking waves — compare VITRUVIAN SCROLL

wave moth *n* : any of many small geometrid moths of *Sterrha* and related genera having wavy markings on the wings

wave motion *n* : the motion of the particles of a medium in mechanically propagated waves (as water waves or sound waves)

wave motor *n* : a prime mover engine actuated by waves of water

wave number *n* : the number of waves per centimeter of light of a given wavelength : the reciprocal of the wavelength ⟨spectroscopists frequently specify a wave by the *wave number* —R.E.Lapp & H.L.Andrews⟩

wave-off \ˈ=,=\ *n* -S [fr. the phrase *wave off*] : a visible signal given by an officer on the deck of an aircraft carrier to the pilot of an approaching airplane usu. indicating that his approach is unsatisfactory for a successful landing, and that he must circle the carrier and make a new approach — compare LANDING SIGNAL OFFICER

wave offering *n* : a sacrificial offering elevated and swung to and fro in ancient Jewish religious ceremony and afterwards reserved for the personal use of the priestly families

wave of oscillation : a wave in which the particles of water move in closed vertical orbits

wave of the future : a line of historical development prob. sure to shape or dominate the future : a movement representing a trend that will inevitably prevail or forces that will certainly triumph

wave of translation : a wave in which the particles of water move forward in the direction of wave propagation

wave packet *n* : a pulse (as an electromagnetic pulse) that is the resultant of a number of wave trains of differing wavelengths and speed and has a definite group velocity

wave pattern *n* : an undulating line that often appears in primitive ornament (as in the decoration of pottery)

wave plate *n* **1** : HALF-WAVE PLATE **2** : QUARTER-WAVE PLATE

¹**wa·ver** \ˈwāvə(r)\ *vi* **wavered; wavered; wavering** \-v(ə)riŋ\ **wavers** [ME *waveren;* akin to MHG *wabern* to waver, OE *wǣfre* wavering, restless, ON *vafra* to hover about, OE *wefan* to weave — more at WEAVE] **1 a** : to vacillate irresolutely between options or attractions : hesitate undecided at a choice : fluctuate in opinion, allegiance, or direction : act inconstant or uncertain : VARY ⟨*~s* between easy tolerance and a bigotry which would have made the Puritans squirm —Green Peyton⟩ ⟨*~ed* between sympathy and superiority —Mary Austin⟩ ⟨*~s* between writing an adult fairy tale, a slick romance, and a social satire —Martin Levin⟩ **b** : to change, alternate, or shift between objects, conditions, uses, or otherwise ⟨a mood that *~ed* between uncertain cheer and blackest gloom⟩ **2 a** : to weave or sway unsteadily to and fro : move back and forth : REEL, TOTTER ⟨*~ed* back and forth a little as he spoke —Irwin Shaw⟩ ⟨on this point of view the character stands, *~s,* or falls —F.J.Hoffman⟩ **b** : to move in an unsteady or uncontrolled manner : FLUTTER, QUIVER ⟨the feather *~ed* to the floor —Elinor Wylie⟩ ⟨a thin grey stinking smoke *~ed* up —Claud Cockburn⟩ ⟨it *~ed* as he raised it and fired —Sherwood Anderson⟩ **c** : to approach or withdraw in an undecided or hesitant manner ⟨they both hesitated, and, as it were, *~ed* uncertainly towards each other —Arnold Bennett⟩ **d** : to follow a changing or random line : move in a purposeless way or as if impelled by chance influences ⟨the story *~s* and loses some of its . . . effectiveness —Edmund Fuller⟩ **3 a** : to move with a shifting or uncertain gaze : turn uneasily, timidly, or weakly one way and another ⟨his glance *~ed* like that of a cornered animal⟩ **b** : to give an unsteady sound : QUAVER, SHAKE ⟨her voice *~ed* with strain⟩ **c** : to evince uncertainty or vagueness of mind (as in great perplexity or shock) : WANDER ⟨his wits at last *~ed* from the prolonged and intense horror⟩ **4 a** : to fluctuate in brightness : FLICKER, GLIMMER ⟨the candle flames *~ed* —Margaret A. Barnes⟩ ⟨the thin blue light *~ed* and vanished and *~ed* again —Ellen Glasgow⟩ **b** : to move with the indistinctness or uncertainty of a shadow ⟨the silhouette of a moving cat *~ed* across the moonlight —Scott Fitzgerald⟩ ⟨before my face *~ed* an incense cloud the like of which I had never smelt —Elinor Wylie⟩ **5** : to falter in battle : hesitate as if about to give way : CHECK ⟨the line *~ed* and broke —John Buchan⟩ **syn** see HESITATE, SWING

²**waver** \"\ *n* -S [earlier *waiver,* prob. fr. *waive* + *-er*] *dial Eng* : a young tree left uncut during timber clearing

³**wav·er** \"\ *n* -S [¹*wave* + *-er*] : one that waves: as **a** : one that swings something to and fro ⟨they are *~s* of flags and shouters of slogans⟩ **b** : a vibrating roller that smooths and distributes ink on the inking table of a printing press **c** (1) : a hairdresser who does waving (2) : a device (as an iron) for waving hair

⁴**wa·ver** \"\ *n* -S [¹*waver*] : an act of wavering, quivering, or fluttering

wa·ver·er \ˈwāvərə(r)\ *n* -S : one that wavers; *esp* : a vacillating or indecisive person

wa·ver·ing·ly *adv* : in a wavering manner

wa·very \-v(ə)rē\ *adj* : WAVERING

waves *pres 3d sing of* WAVE, *pl of* WAVE

wave set *n* : a somewhat viscous solution with which hair is wet before setting in order to make the waves or curls last

wave shape *n* : WAVE FORM

wave·son \ˈwāvsən\ *n* [²*wave* + *-son* (as in AF *floteson* flotsam) — more at FLOTSAM] : goods that after shipwreck appear floating on the sea : FLOTSAM

wave surface *n* **1** : WAVE FRONT **2** : a combination of wave fronts developed simultaneously from a single center (as of light in uniaxial and biaxial crystals) ⟨the *wave surface* for a uniaxial doubly refracting substance consists of a sphere enclosing or enclosed by an ellipsoid of revolution⟩

wave system *n* : a system of traffic regulation in which the signals on a street or highway change progressively permitting traffic to proceed at a uniform predetermined speed without stopping

wave theory *n* **1** : UNDULATORY THEORY **2** [trans. of G *wellentheorie*] : a theory in linguistics: branches develop from a parent language (as Indo-European) by waves of linguistic change with the result that adjacent branches have more features in common than those that are widely separated — compare FAMILY-TREE THEORY

wave train *n* : a succession of similar waves at equal intervals

wave trap *n* : a tuned radio circuit used to improve the selectivity of radio apparatus or to eliminate interference

wave variable *n* : a quantity (as the pressure in sound-wave propagation) whose periodic variations are primarily responsible for the propagation of a wave

wave velocity *n* : PHASE VELOCITY

wave wheel *n* **1** : a rope pulley with a groove of wavy outline to increase the grip on the rope **2** : a wheel with wavy outline used as a cam to give a reciprocating movement

wave winding *n* : an armature winding in which the coils are laid in two layers and follow each other on the surface of the armature in the form of waves with the coils being so connected in series that there are only two paths for the flow of current whatever the number of poles in the machine — called also *series winding;* compare LAP WINDING, RING WINDING

wave-worn \ˈ=,=\ *adj* : showing attrition from waves

wa·vey *also* **wa·vy** \ˈwāvē\ *n, pl* **waveys** *or* **wavies** [of Algonquian origin; akin to Ojibwa *wêwe* goose, Cree *wehwew*] : SNOW GOOSE

wav·i·ly \ˈwāvəlē, -li\ *adv* : in a wavy manner

wav·i·ness \-vēnəs, -vin-\ *n* -ES : the quality or state of being wavy

waving *pres part of* WAVE

wav·ing·ly *adv* : in a waving manner

wavy \ˈwāvē, -vi\ *adj* -ER/-EST **1** : rising or swelling in waves : abounding in waves ⟨a ~ lake⟩ **2** : playing or moving to and fro with an undulating motion : FLUCTUATING, WAVERING ⟨a ~ flame⟩ **3** : having a wavelike form or outline : CURVING, ROLLING ⟨~ terrain⟩ **4** : UNDULATE **5** : having transverse lines or bars curving in a manner suggesting a succession of waves — compare BARRY-WAVY

¹**waw** \ˈwȯ\ *n* -S [ME *wawe, waghe;* akin to OE *wagian* to move, swing — more at WAG] *archaic* : WAVE

²**waw** \"\ *vi* -ED/-ING/-S [imit.] *chiefly Scot* : to utter the characteristic cry of a cat

³**waw** \"\ *n* -S *chiefly Scot* : the cry of a cat

⁴**waw** *or* **vav** \ˈväv, ˈvȯv\ *n* -S [Heb *wāw,* lit., hook] **1** : the sixth letter of the Hebrew alphabet — symbol ו; see ALPHABET table **2** : the letter corresponding to Hebrew waw in the Phoenician or in any of various other Semitic alphabets

wa·was·keesh \wəˈwä,skēsh\ *n* -ES [prob. fr. Ojibwa *wâwâshkeshi* deer] : WAPITI 1

wawl \ˈwȯl\ *vi* -ED/-ING/-S [imit. of an infant's cry] *chiefly Scot* : WAIL, HOWL, SQUALL

¹**wax** \ˈwaks\ *n* -ES *often attrib* [ME *wax, wex,* fr. OE *weax;* akin to OHG *wahs* wax, ON *vax,* Lith *vaškas* wax, and prob. to OHG *wiohha* lint, wick — more at WICK] **1 a** : a substance that is secreted by bees by special glands on the underside of the abdomen, deposited as thin scales, and used after mastication and mixture with the secretion of the salivary glands for constructing the honeycomb, that is then glossy and hard but plastic when warm, insoluble in water but partly soluble in boiling alcohol and in ether, and miscible with oils and fats, and that is a mixture consisting of the palmitate of myricyl alcohol and other higher esters, free cerotic acid, and hydrocarbons — called also *beeswax* **b** : BEESWAX 2 **2** : any of various natural or synthetic substances resembling beeswax in physical properties or chemical composition or both and used chiefly in candles, in coatings (as for paper), and in polishing materials: as **a** : any of a class of substances (as carnauba wax, spermaceti, Chinese wax) of plant or animal origin that differ from fats in being less greasy, harder, and more brittle and in containing principally esters of higher fatty acids and higher monohydroxy alcohols instead of glycerol, free higher acids and alcohols, and saturated hydrocarbons — see VEGETABLE WAX, WAX INSECT **b** : a solid substance (as ozokerite or paraffin wax) of mineral origin consisting usu. of higher hydrocarbons : MINERAL WAX **c** : a pliable or liquid composition that may or may not contain wax and is used esp. in uniting surfaces, excluding air, making patterns or impressions, or producing a waxlike polished surface ⟨etching ~⟩ ⟨dental *~es*⟩ ⟨floor *~es*⟩ **d** : a resinous preparation used by shoemakers for rubbing thread **3** : something likened to wax as soft, impressionable, or readily molded ⟨thy noble shape is but a form of ~, digressing from the valor of a man —Shak.⟩ **4** : SEALING WAX **5** *or* **wax white** : a pale to grayish greenish yellow **6** : a waxlike product secreted by plants **7** : CERUMEN **8** : a substance secreted by some scales that is similar to beeswax — see WAX INSECT **9** : a phonograph recording

²**wax** \"\ *vt* -ED/-ING/-ES [ME *waxen, wexen,* fr. *wax, wex* wax] **1** : to treat, polish, or rub with wax ⟨~ a floor⟩ ⟨~ a thread⟩ **2** : to stiffen with wax ⟨~ a mustache⟩ **3** : to record on

phonograph records ⟨a vibrato-cluttered duet . . . ~*ed* 23 years ago —*Time*⟩

³**wax** \"\ *vi* **waxed; waxed** \-st\ *or archaic* **wax·en** \-sən\ **waxing; waxes** [ME *waxen, wexen*, fr. OE *weaxan*, akin to OHG *wahsan* to increase, grow, ON *vaxa*, Goth *wahsjan*, Gk *auxanein*, L *augēre* — more at EKE, v.] **1 a :** to increase in size, numbers, strength, prosperity, or intensity **:** grow larger, fuller, stronger, or more numerous ⟨mankind, let us hope, will dwindle and die more contented than it ever was when it ~*ed* and struggled —George Santayana⟩ **b :** to grow in volume or duration (as a swelling river or days lengthening in spring) **c :** to grow and develop as an animal or a person does in maturing **d :** to gain in importance or power ⟨the culmination of the Progressive movement which had been ~*ing* since before the turn of the century —J.A.Huston⟩ **e :** to grow more active or conspicuous **:** gain in vigor ⟨rancor ~*ed* among them⟩ **2 :** to increase in phase or intensity — used chiefly of the moon, other satellites, and inferior planets; opposed to *wane;* see MOON illustration **3 :** to assume a specified characteristic, quality, or state **:** BECOME ⟨~*ed* indignant editorially —*America*⟩ ⟨ate enormously and ~*ed* fatter —Edna Ferber⟩

⁴**wax** \"\ *n* -ES [ME, fr. *waxen* to increase, grow] **1 :** INCREASE, GROWTH ⟨pileated woodpeckers . . . are on the ~ now and are expected to continue so —Christopher Rand⟩ **2 :** the increase in phase or intensity of the moon from new to full or of some other satellite or planet

⁵**wax** \"\ *n* -ES [perh. fr. ³*wax*] **:** a fit of temper **:** RAGE ⟨had been in a ~ at its loss —John Buchan⟩

⁶**wax** \"\ *vt* -ED/-ING/-ES [prob. fr. ²*wax*] **:** to get the better of **:** beat soundly or badly (as in a game)

wax bean *n* **:** any of various kidney beans that have the pods creamy yellow to bright yellow when suitably matured for use as snap beans — compare GREEN BEAN

wax begonia *n* **:** a cultivated fibrous-rooted begonia derived from the species begonia (*Begonia semperflorens*)

wax·berry \'waks- — *see* BERRY\ *n* **1 :** the wax-covered fruit of the wax myrtle; *also* **:** WAX MYRTLE **2 :** SNOWBERRY 1

waxberry cornel *n* **:** RED OSIER 2

waxbill \'ˌ=ˌ=\ *n* **:** any of numerous Old World birds of the family Ploceidae having white, pink, or reddish bills of a waxy appearance; *esp* **:** any of various birds of the genus *Estrilda* commonly kept as cage birds

wax–billed \'ˌ=ˌ=\ *adj* **:** having a bill suggesting sealing wax in color — used of a bird

waxbird \'ˌ=ˌ=\ *n* **:** WAXWING

wax brown *n* **:** BEESWAX 3

waxbush \'ˌ=ˌ=\ *n* **:** WAXWEED

wax–chandler \'ˌ=ˌ==\ *n* [ME *wax chandeler*] **:** a chandler dealing in wax candles

wax cloth *n* **1 :** a fabric waterproofed with wax or paraffin **2 :** OILCLOTH

wax creeper *n, southern Africa* **:** either of two vines of the family Asclepiadaceae: **a :** a plant (*Microloma tenuifolia*) **b :** WAX PLANT 2

wax distillate *n* **:** PARAFFIN DISTILLATE

wax dolls *n pl but sing or pl in constr* **:** a common fumitory (*Fumaria officinalis*)

waxed *past of* WAX

waxed end *or* **wax end** *n* **:** a thread formed of a number of filaments rubbed with shoemaker's wax, usu. pointed with a bristle, and used in sewing leather in which holes have been made (as in shoemaking)

waxed paper *or* **wax paper** *n* **:** paper coated or otherwise treated with wax to make it waterproof and greaseproof and used esp. as a wrapping

¹**waxen** *archaic past part of* ³WAX

²**wax·en** \'waksən\ *adj* [ME, fr. ¹*wax* + *-en*] **1 :** made of wax ⟨a ~ record —*Congressional Record*⟩ ⟨~ tapers⟩ **2 :** covered with wax ⟨an ancient ~ writing tablet⟩ **3 :** resembling wax in pliability or impressionability ⟨men have marble, women ~, minds —Shak.⟩ **4 a :** having the smooth bloodless appearance of wax **:** seeming to lack vitality or animation **:** PALLID ⟨the poor face with the same awful, ~ pallor —Bram Stoker⟩ **b :** having a lustrous smoothness **5 :** of the color wax

waxen chatterer *n* **:** BOHEMIAN WAXWING

wax engraving *n* **:** a process for preparing letterpress printing surfaces in which the design is cut or formed in a thin wax coating on a metal plate that is then electrotyped or in which hand-cut additions or corrections are made in a regular wax electrotype mold before deposition of the shell

wax·er \'waksə(r)\ *n* -S **:** one whose work is applying or polishing with wax: as **a :** one that waxes furniture or automobiles **b :** an operator of a machine for waxing the sprocket holes of motion-picture film to ease passage of the film through the projector **c :** one that puts protective wax on the plain parts of glass articles to protect them while designs are etched **d :** an operator of a machine for waxing yarn to increase its strength

wax·er·man \-(r)mən\ *n, pl* **waxermen :** an operator of a machine for coating paper with a waterproofing wax

waxes *pl of* WAX, *pres 3d sing of* WAX

wax extractor *n* **:** a device or machine for extracting and rendering beeswax from the empty honeycomb by applying heat

waxflower \'ˌ=ˌ=\ *n* **1 :** a climbing plant (*Stephanotis floribunda*) of Madagascar often cultivated in the greenhouse for its fragrant white flowers **2 :** an epiphytic tree (*Clusia insignis*) of British Guiana **3 :** INDIAN PIPE **4 :** SPOTTED WINTERGREEN

wax gland *n* **:** a gland (as in the honeybee and some scales) that secretes wax

wax gourd *n* **1 :** a tropical Asiatic twining plant (*Benincasa hispida*) **2 :** the edible fruit of the wax gourd resembling a pumpkin and having a waxy pulverulent coat

wax hair *n* **:** wax secreted by some psyllids or coccids and extruded as a filament through the opening of the wax gland

wax·haw \'waks,hȯ\ *n, pl* **waxhaw** *or* **waxhaws** *usu cap* **1 :** an extinct Siouan people of north central So. Carolina and south central No. Carolina **2 :** a member of the Waxhaw people

waxier *comparative of* WAXY

waxiest *superlative of* WAXY

wax·i·ly \'waksəlē\ *adv* **:** in a waxy manner

wax·i·ness \-sēnəs\ *n* -ES **:** the quality or state of being waxy

waxing *n* -S [ME, fr. gerund of *waxen* to treat with wax — more at WAX] **1 :** the act of applying wax (as in polishing) **2 a :** the making of a phonograph record **b :** a phonograph record ⟨orchestral ~*s*⟩

wax insect *n* **1 :** any of several scales of the family Coccidae that secrete a wax from their bodies; *esp* **:** a Chinese scale (*Ericerus pe-la*) that yields much of the commercial Chinese wax **2 :** any of several homopterous insects of the family Fulgoridae that secrete a wax used by the Chinese (as for candles)

wax jack *n* **:** an 18th century silver desk accessory with a central spindle and a very long wax taper coiled about it like a rope with its lighted end held in a socket and used to melt sealing wax

wax jack

wax light *n* **:** a wax candle **:** TAPER

waxlike \'ˌ=ˌ=\ *adj* **:** resembling wax

waxmallow \'ˌ=ˌ(ˌ)=\ *n* [¹*wax* + *mallow*] **:** any of various plants (genus *Malvaviscus*) of the family Malvaceae having drooping flowers like those of the hibiscus

wax·man \'waksmən\ *n, pl* **waxmen :** a worker who removes from the filters wax that accumulates during the pressing of paraffin distillate

wax moth *n* **1 :** BEE MOTH **2 :** a moth (*Achroia grisella*) smaller than the bee moth but similar in appearance and habits — called also *lesser wax moth*

wax myrtle *n* **:** any of several shrubs or trees of the genus *Myrica; esp* **:** a shrub (*M. cerifera*) of eastern No. America having aromatic foliage and small hard berries with a thick coating of white wax that is used for candles — called also *bay myrtle, puckerbush;* see BAYBERRY 2

wax painting *n* **:** encaustic painting

wax palm *n* **:** any of several palms that yield wax: as **a :** a pinnate-leaved palm (*Ceroxylon andicolum*) of the Andes on the stem of which is produced a resinous wax which is mixed with tallow to make candles **b :** CARNAUBA 1

wax paper *var of* WAXED PAPER

wax pine *n* **:** a tree of the genus *Agathis*

wax plant *n* **1 :** INDIAN PIPE **2 :** a cultivated twiner (*Hoya carnosa*) of Australia with glossy succulent leaves and umbels of pink and white star-shaped flowers **3 :** any of several begonias with shining foliage **4 :** WAX MYRTLE

wax pocket *n* **:** one of the cavities on the ventral abdominal surface into which wax is secreted by a honeybee

waxpod bean \'ˌ=ˌ=-\ *n* **:** WAX BEAN

wax privet *n* **:** JAPANESE PRIVET b

wax process *n* **:** a method of making a foundry pattern in wax and using this pattern either as the master pattern or as a pattern for making the master pattern in white metal

wax red *n* **:** COPPER 5a

wax scale *n* **1 :** a scale that secretes wax — see FLORIDA WAX SCALE **2 :** one of the small flakes of wax secreted in a wax pocket of a honeybee

wax spray *n* **:** a spray or dip of melted paraffin, paraffin emulsion, or a similar material applied to plants in leaf to reduce transpiration after transplanting, to dormant shrubs (as roses) to prevent drying when on display or out of the ground for some other reason, and to cut flowers and root vegetables to prevent wilting

wax stone *n* **:** a lump of mixed earthy matter and mineral boiled in copper vats to separate the wax in the production of ozocerite

wax tablet *n* **:** a writing tablet of wood or bone covered with wax and written on with a style in ancient Roman and medieval times

wax tailings *n pl* **:** a dark-colored residue of former methods of petroleum distillation containing amorphous wax and formerly used in cracking and in waterproofing compositions

wax tree *n* **:** a tree yielding wax: as **a :** JAPANESE WAX TREE **b :** an arborescent evergreen privet (*Ligustrum lucidum*) of eastern Asia that is wholly glabrous, has dark green lustrous leaves and terminal panicles of white flowers, and is sometimes used in mild regions as a street tree **c :** a Chinese ash (*Fraxinus chinensis*) that is commonly encrusted with white wax by a wax insect (*Ericerus pe-la*) and is a major source of Chinese wax **d :** WAX MYRTLE

waxweed \'ˌ=ˌ=\ *n* **:** a small purple-flowered herb (*Cuphea petiolata*) of eastern No. America having a viscid pubescence

wax white *n* **:** ¹WAX 5

waxwing \'ˌ=ˌ=\ *n* **:** any of several American and Eurasian passerine birds of the genus *Bombycilla* that are chiefly brown with a showy crest and velvety plumage and secondaries that have small red waxlike tips — see BOHEMIAN WAXWING, CEDAR WAXWING; BIRD illustration

waxwork \'ˌ=ˌ=\ *n* **1 a :** an effigy in wax usu. representing a person ⟨she sat so still that she might have been a ~ —Agatha Christie⟩ **b waxworks** *pl but sing or pl in constr* **:** an exhibition of wax effigies ⟨visited a ~*s*⟩ **2 :** BITTERSWEET 2b

wax worm *n* **:** a worm that is the larva of the bee moth

¹**waxy** \'waksē, -si\ *adj* -ER/-EST **1 a :** made of or resembling wax ⟨round and shiny as a ~ pippin —C.G.Glover⟩ **b :** soft or readily shaped like wax **:** IMPRESSIONABLE **c :** having the smoothness, luster, or whiteness of wax ⟨his thin face had a ~ pallor —Kenneth Roberts⟩ **d :** having a surface covered with wax or having the appearance of such a surface ⟨a ~ leaf⟩ **2 :** affected with amyloid degeneration

²**waxy** \"\ *adj* -ER/-EST [⁵*wax* + *-y*] **:** ANGRY, VEXED ⟨never does say very much unless he's downright ~ —Samuel Butler †1902⟩ ⟨it's quilts my wife gets ~ about —Bruce Marshall⟩

waxy cast *n* **:** a dense highly refractile urinary cast

waxy corn *or* **waxy maize** *n* **:** an Indian corn with grains that have a waxy appearance when cut, that contain only branched-chain starch, and that are used esp. for desserts and adhesives and as a replacement for tapioca

waxy degeneration *n* **:** AMYLOIDOSIS

wax yellow *n* **:** a moderate yellow that is darker than colonial yellow and deeper than mustard yellow

waxy flexibility *n* **:** a condition in which a patient's limbs retain any position into which they are manipulated by another person and which occurs esp. in catatonic schizophrenia

¹**way** \'wā\ *n* -S [ME *way, wey*, fr. OE *weg;* akin to OHG *weg* way, ON *vegr*, Goth *wigs* way, OE *wegan* to move, L *vehere* to carry, Gk *ochein* to carry, *ochos* carriage, Skt *vahati* he carries, pulls] **1 a :** a thoroughfare used or designed for traveling or transportation from place to place **:** PATH, ROAD, STREET ⟨rough uneven ~*s* —Shak.⟩ ⟨the garagemen across the ~ —William Faulkner⟩ ⟨expressways or limited access ~*s* of the best modern type —S.J.Williams⟩ ⟨the Appian *Way*⟩ **b :** a band of light in the night sky resembling a road **c :** an opening for passing through ⟨this door is the only ~ into the room⟩ **d :** the roadway of a railroad ⟨permanent ~⟩ **2 :** that along which one passes to reach some place **:** the track traveled by a person or thing in his or its progress or passage **:** the course of travel from one place to another **:** ROUTE ⟨asked the ~ to the museum⟩ ⟨pupils will find their own ~ to school —*Deerfield (Wisc.) Independent*⟩ ⟨the ~ of a ship in the midst of the sea —Prov 30:19 (AV)⟩ ⟨in the streets the unfortunate foot traveler still picked his ~ through the muck —J.W.Krutch⟩ ⟨take a flashlight to light your ~ to the barn⟩ ⟨going your ~ and will be glad to give you a lift⟩ **3 a :** a nonspatial course (as a series of actions or sequence of events) leading in a stated or implied direction or toward a stated or implied objective ⟨cleared the ~ for a more purely rational interpretation of the world —M.F.A.Montagu⟩ ⟨smooth the ~ for statehood —*Current Biog.*⟩ ⟨his entering upon the ~ of salvation —Catherine Rau⟩ ⟨point the ~ to the discovery of new facts —F.A.Geldard⟩ **b** (1) **:** a course of action ⟨my best ~ is to creep under his gaberdine —Shak.⟩ ⟨take the easy ~ out⟩ (2) *obs* **:** the best or most desirable course of action ⟨it is our ~, if we will keep in favor with the King, to be her men and wear her livery —Shak.⟩ (3) **:** the opportunity, capability, or fact of doing as one pleases ⟨had made up his mind, and in the end he had his ~ —Ellen Glasgow⟩ ⟨for any one group to get its ~ —T.V.Smith⟩ ⟨gets the heroine alone in a bedroom and . . . has his ~ with her —*Time*⟩ ⟨time has its ~ with you —Vachel Lindsay⟩ **c :** a possible decision, action, or outcome **:** POSSIBILITY ⟨no ~ but this — killing myself, to die upon a kiss —Shak.⟩ ⟨there were no two ~*s* about it — this was the rudest, surliest, most ill-mannered town on the face of the earth —Hamilton Basso⟩ **4 a :** the mode in which something is done or happens **:** MANNER, METHOD, STYLE ⟨win him over to our ~ of thinking —A.J.Ayer⟩ ⟨societies whose ~ of life seemed so different from that of our own people —Edward Sapir⟩ ⟨manipulate ideas in an original ~ —Vance Packard⟩ ⟨her ~ of doing her hair⟩ ⟨these two books, each admirable in its ~ —*Geog. Jour.*⟩ ⟨one's character is defined by the ~ in which the rules are embodied in one's behavior —Margaret Mead⟩ — often used as the principal word in an adverbial phrase with no preposition ⟨the people who think this ~ —D.W.Brogan⟩ ⟨learn the full meaning of independence the hard ~ —Augusta Baker⟩; often used with and modified by an adjective clause containing no relative pronoun or other introductory word ⟨insight into the ~ the mind actually works —C.I.Glicksberg⟩ ⟨that's the ~ things go⟩ ⟨so that's the ~ you do it⟩ **b :** ASPECT, FEATURE, RESPECT, POINT — used as the principal word in an adverbial phrase with *in* as introductory preposition ⟨people who can in no ~ be classed as criminals —D.W.Maurer & V.H.Vogel⟩ or sometimes with no preposition ⟨one student who is outstanding in scholarship, another who is outstanding in athletic ability, and a third who is outstanding both ~*s*⟩ **c :** the condition of being or acting on a specified scale — used in phrases with *in a* and an adjective ⟨real estate, a field of activity which he had entered in a small ~ —T.H.Jack⟩ ⟨the United States entered the international investment market in a substantial ~ —Frank Parker⟩ **d :** the usual or characteristic state of affairs — used with *with* ⟨he is very censorious, but then that is the ~ with reformed scoundrels⟩ ⟨as is the ~ with dreams, I took it to be a sort of personal and private message or communication —Walter de la Mare⟩ **e :** mode of existence as shown esp. by status, occupation, traits, or qualities **:** manner of occurrence — used with *the, this,* or *that* in phrases that contain no preposition and that stand in predicative or modifying relation to the verb *be* or a few other verbs ⟨so attentive to other women that I have heard his wife ask him a dozen times not to be that ~⟩ ⟨it's too bad we can't offer you a job, but that's just the ~ things are⟩ ⟨what everyone wants to know about the president is how he got this ~ —G.W.Martin⟩ ⟨they themselves are flabby and smug, but they want to stay that ~ —*Time*⟩ ⟨business has been good and we're doing everything we can to keep it that ~ —*Item*⟩ ⟨well, Your Honor, it was this ~⟩ **5 a** (1) **:** a characteristic or habitual manner of acting ⟨justify the ~*s* of God to men —John Milton⟩ ⟨ignorant zealot though he was . . . he turned many from evil ~*s* —H.E.Starr⟩ ⟨it was the white man's ~ to assert himself in any landscape, to change it —Willa Cather⟩ ⟨knew nothing of the ~*s* of seafaring men —L.C.Douglas⟩ ⟨description of the ~*s* of nesting gannets —E.A.Armstrong⟩ (2) **:** an individual peculiarity **:** personal trait **:** IDIOSYNCRASY ⟨that's just his ~ and you shouldn't let it bother you⟩ ⟨a good fellow when you get used to his ~*s*⟩ (3) **:** an ingratiating or otherwise effective mode of behavior ⟨he has such a ~ with him that he makes lots of friends wherever he goes⟩ ⟨keen to show . . . what a ~ he had with him in this matter of tracking down seams —Gwyn Thomas⟩ (4) **:** a recognized practice, tendency, or quality ⟨great actresses have a ~ of scoring some of their most resounding successes in plays which are far from great —Peter Forster⟩ ⟨what seems impossible has a ~ of suddenly coming to you —Denis Johnston⟩ (5) **:** an endearing trick of behavior ⟨greatly captivated by the ~*s* of his host's children⟩ (6) **:** ability to get along well or to perform well ⟨his ~ with women and his extravagant habits made him many friends and much trouble —W.P.Webb⟩ ⟨had a ~ with animals —Oden Meeker⟩ ⟨has always had a ~ with metals —*Time*⟩ **b :** a regular continued course or mode of life, action, or existence ⟨thanks to their isolation these people go their own ~ in many things —Samuel Van Valkenburg & Ellsworth Huntington⟩ ⟨as the American ~ is made better known to the world —V.G.F. Reynolds⟩ ⟨came up against them in the ~ of business —Stuart Piggott⟩ **c** (1) **:** a course or mode of life set forth in terms of a standard to be maintained or of gradual difficult progress toward excellence in motivation and action usu. under religious sanctions **:** body of ethical practice esp. as taught by a religion ⟨not in one great Oriental religion only, the *Way* became a symbol of man's onward struggle and upward striving, of a journey towards a state of personal goodness and individual happiness —E.R.Pike⟩ ⟨the ~ to Christ⟩ (2) *often cap* **:** the Christian religion ⟨that if he found any belonging to the *Way*, men or women, he might bring them bound to Jerusalem —Acts 9:2 (RSV)⟩ **6 :** the length of a course traversed or to be traversed in space, time, range of possibilities, or progress toward a stated or implied objective **:** DISTANCE ⟨a house a little ~ out of town —Calvin Kentfield⟩ ⟨let me go back a little ~ and give you some background to this basic premise of our foreign policy —Dean Acheson⟩ ⟨transcended but a little ~ the region of commonplace —Thomas Carlyle⟩ ⟨not as capable as his brother by a long ~⟩ ⟨at a cost estimated all the ~ from one to two million dollars⟩ ⟨has come a long ~ in his knowledge of international geography —Gordon Walker⟩ ⟨this proposal should go a long ~ towards meeting another criticism —*Economist*⟩ **7 a :** movement or progress along a spatial or other course ⟨led the ~ into the heart of Chile's southern frontier —P.E.James⟩ ⟨led the ~ to unanimity —Beverly Smith⟩ ⟨held his ~ in spite of all obstacles⟩ ⟨forced his ~ through the crowd⟩ ⟨working his ~ through college⟩; *specif* **:** advancement in one's career ⟨when he had his ~ still to make —Osbert Sitwell⟩ **b :** an advance or progression accompanied by a specified action — used as the object of a verb that serves only to indicate what action accompanies the advance ⟨a white cat purring its ~ gracefully among the wine cups at a feast —Agnes Repplier⟩ ⟨barbarians who cough their ~ through concerts —Justina Hill⟩ **8 :** a method of attaining or accomplishing something **:** MEANS ⟨this delicious easy ~ of getting additional iron and calcium —*advt*⟩ ⟨a ~ to make a living —S.H.Adams⟩ ⟨~*s* of helping the aged to live out their declining years —A.W.Hummel⟩ ⟨the attack was made, not in the ~ of storm —T.B.Macaulay⟩ — sometimes used as the principal word in an adverbial phrase with no preposition ⟨thought he could win the game that ~⟩ **9 a :** a direction of motion, facing, pointing, or nonspatial advance or tendency — often used as the principal word in an adverbial or adjectival phrase with no preposition ⟨is coming this ~⟩ ⟨turn your head the other ~⟩ ⟨shift his expectation one ~ or another —Margaret Mead⟩ ⟨the money was divided three ~*s*⟩ ⟨with no glance . . . her ~ —Amy Lowell⟩ ⟨how its decision can go any other ~ —*Commonweal*⟩ ⟨either there is a valid contract or there is not; you cannot have it both ~*s*⟩ ⟨an honest answer one ~ or the other —M.R.Cohen⟩ ⟨hard to make a very conclusive case either ~ —Bruce Payne⟩ ⟨sometimes a noun is derived from a verb and sometimes it is the other ~ around⟩ **b :** a part of a town, city, country, or the world **:** LOCALITY, DISTRICT, NEIGHBORHOOD, VICINITY — used with a preceding possessive adjective or place-name which in turn is sometimes preceded by a preposition ⟨great explosions coming from Dunkirk ~ —P.W.Thompson⟩ or by no directional word at all ⟨had just rented a tidy-sized farm Shorwell ~ —J.B.Priestley⟩ but most frequently by a directional adverb ⟨the weather has been good out our ~⟩ ⟨that little old college down Cambridge ~ —Jean Stafford⟩ **c** (1) **:** a direction with reference to the lie of a natural growth (as hair or feathers) ⟨stroking the cat's fur the wrong ~⟩ (2) **:** ¹GRAIN 6d ⟨cut cloth the ~ of the goods instead of on the bias⟩ **d** (1) **:** one of the lines terminating at a hydraulic or other valve — often used in attributive noun compounds with a numeral as first constituent ⟨a four-*way* valve⟩ (2) **:** one of the operating positions of an electric switch — used in attributive noun compounds with a numeral as first constituent ⟨a three-*way* switch⟩ **e :** participating party **:** PARTICIPANT — used in attributive noun compounds with a numeral as first constituent ⟨a three-*way* discussion⟩ **10 a :** condition esp. with regard to health, prosperity, or future prospects ⟨if the people cannot depend upon the promises of their president they are in a bad ~ —J.P.Warburg⟩ ⟨been very ill this week . . . and though now in a ~ to be well, am like to be confined some days longer —Thomas Gray⟩ ⟨the state was in a fair ~ to get a new instrument of government —*Nation*⟩ ⟨would have put himself in a fair ~ of getting shot —Charles Dickens⟩ ⟨put him in the ~ of another chance —Hamilton Basso⟩ ⟨if anyone were in the ~ of getting information —F.Tennyson Jesse⟩ **b** *Brit* **:** a state of mind; *esp* **:** a condition of abnormal nervous tension or excitement ⟨she was quite in a ~ —Arnold Bennett⟩ **11 a :** room to advance, pass, or progress **:** opportunity to proceed ⟨give ~⟩ ⟨make ~⟩ **b :** freedom of action or opportunity ⟨let me have ~ . . . to find this practice out —Shak.⟩ **c :** a place or position to be occupied by someone else or something else — used as object of *make* ⟨several one-family houses torn down to make ~ for an apartment house⟩ **12 :** scope or range of observation, experience, or possible acquisition ⟨intrigues with low women that fell in my ~ —Benjamin Franklin⟩ **13 a ways** *pl but sometimes sing in constr* **:** an inclined structure usu. of timber upon which a ship is built or upon which a ship is supported in launching ⟨the ~*s* are either of yellow or pitch pine —A.C.Holms⟩ ⟨owned three steamboats, . . . a marine ~*s*, and several landing fleets —Frederick Way⟩ ⟨all American flag shipping, afloat or on the ~*s* —*N. Y. Herald Tribune*⟩ — compare BILGE WAYS, DOGSHORE, GROUND WAYS, SLIDING WAYS **b ways** *pl* **:** the longitudinal guides or guiding surfaces on the bed of a machine (as a planer or lathe) along which a table or carriage moves **c :** a structure or member of a set of structures designed to guide the movement of an object along a strictly determined path ⟨stainless steel weatherstripping . . . serves as sash ~ for both upper and lower sash —*Sweet's Catalog Service*⟩ **14 :** a group with common features **:** CATEGORY, KIND, DESCRIPTION — usu. used in a prepositional phrase introduced by *in* ⟨has little in the ~ of financial resources —L.M. Chamberlain⟩ ⟨everything you need in the ~ of vitamins —Gregor Felsen⟩ ⟨have picked up one or two gems in the antique ~ —H.J.Laski⟩ ⟨in ~ of compensation, he was allowed a pension —James Mill⟩ **15 a :** the motion or speed of a ship or boat through the water ⟨a ship on starting gathers ~⟩ ⟨when actually moving through the water, a vessel has ~ on her; if moving too fast she is said to have too much ~ on

—*Manual of Seamanship*⟩ **b :** the motion or speed of something or someone traveling otherwise than through water ⟨the pavement was on a slight incline, the perambulator had a little ~ on it, and the whole force of the wind behind —J.D. Beresford⟩ **16 :** a line of business or of professional activity **17 :** RIGHT-OF-WAY 1,2 **18** *dial Brit* **:** REASON, CAUSE **19** *usu cap* **:** a Navaho ceremonial rite that consists largely of chants and dances and is performed for protection against various ill effects and assurance of general well-being and good fortune ⟨Red Ant *Way*⟩ ⟨Mountain Top *Way*⟩

syn WAY, ROUTE, COURSE, PASSAGE, PASS, ARTERY mean, in common, a track or path traversed in going from one place to another. WAY is general and inclusive of any track or path, often figurative, specif. signifying a road in combinations or special phrases ⟨rail*way*⟩ ⟨high*way*⟩ ⟨the only other village was one day's mule trip farther into the interior, but the *way* was so steep and slippery in places that we walked almost as much as we rode —C.B.Hitchcock⟩ ⟨the water continues its *way* down the valley for 5 kilometers —N.R.Heiden⟩ ⟨the *way* was now open for the final act —W.C.Ford⟩ ROUTE signifies a way, often circuitous, followed with regularity by a person or animal or laid out to be followed as by a tourist or army ⟨a paper *route*⟩ ⟨a milk truck following a morning delivery *route*⟩ ⟨the dog team trails and canoe *routes* of trader, trapper and missionary in the bush country —W.J.Granberg⟩ ⟨a much traveled main *route* from Boston to Albany⟩ COURSE is often interchangeable with ROUTE but more often implies a path followed by or as if by a stream, star, or other moving natural object impelled by or in a path determined by natural forces ⟨the *course* of a river⟩ ⟨a meteor's *course*⟩ ⟨a ship's *course*⟩ ⟨the *course* of the seasons⟩ or a predetermined or more or less compulsory way or route followed in human activities or enterprises ⟨a *course* of study for an academic degree⟩ ⟨a golf *course*⟩ ⟨a race*course*⟩ PASSAGE stresses a crossing over or a passing through, often designating the thing passed through, usu. something narrow where transit might be restricted ⟨a rough *passage* to America by boat⟩ ⟨a narrow *passage* from kitchen to basement⟩ ⟨restrict the *passage* into the stomach⟩ PASS usu. designates a passage through or over something that presents an obstacle (as a mountain or river) ⟨a narrow *pass* over the Alps⟩ ⟨a shallow ford constituted the only *pass* across the river⟩ ARTERY is applied to one of the great continuous traffic channels (as a great central rail route, river, or highway) from which branch off smaller or shorter channels ⟨the Congo river would remain the main traffic *artery* —G.G.Weigend⟩ ⟨the main *artery* between Buffalo and Niagara Falls —*Retailing Daily*⟩ ⟨the need for improvement of main *arteries* interconnecting cities and for express highways in cities —*Britannica Bk. of the Yr.*⟩ **syn** see in addition METHOD

— **all the way** *also* **the whole way** *adv* **1 :** as far as possible ⟨a resolute attempt to go *the whole way* in the direction of complete analysis —A.N.Whitehead⟩ **2 :** from the beginning to the end or to this point ⟨it has been New Hampshire, New Hampshire with me *all the way* —Robert Frost⟩ ⟨stays in the game *all the way* —J.W.Rouse⟩ **3 :** so far as complete agreement or compliance ⟨can't go *the whole way* with the book —Louis Kronenberger⟩ ⟨went *all the way* for Moscow —*Time*⟩ **4 :** so far as not to stop short of sexual intercourse ⟨she went *all the way* with him⟩ — **by way of** *prep* **1 :** by the agency of **:** through the medium of ⟨master workmen may receive instructions *by way of* drafts, models, frames —B.G.Gerbier⟩ **2 :** as an instance or example of **:** for the purpose of ⟨*by way of* illustration⟩ **3 :** by the route that passes through **:** VIA ⟨drove home *by way of* the mountains⟩ **4 a :** in the habit of — used with a following gerund ⟨was *by way of* being particular about his appearance —Cicely F. Smith⟩ **b :** in the state of — used with a following gerund ⟨is *by way of* doing better work now than formerly⟩ — **each way** *Brit, of a bet on a racehorse* **:** to win or to place — **go out of one's way :** to take special pains **:** act with or as if with a deliberate purpose ⟨*went out of his way* to stimulate consumption while retaining strict curbs on investment —*New Statesman & Nation*⟩ ⟨could have deceived only those who *went out of their way* to be deceived —R.D.Altick⟩ — **go the way of :** to pass out of existence or into a declining state like ⟨is Christian civilization *going the way of* the Roman Empire —*Time*⟩ — **have everything one's own way** *or* **have it all one's own way :** to carry out one's plans without effective opposition ⟨the victorious invaders *had everything their own way*⟩ — **hold way** *or* **keep way** *obs* **:** to keep pace — **in a big way :** emphatically so **:** THOROUGHLY, ENTHUSIASTICALLY — **in a way** *adv* **1** *also* **in a kind of way** *or* **in a sort of way :** within limits **:** with reservations ⟨I like the new arrangement, *in a way*⟩ **2 :** from one point of view ⟨*in a way*, elementary schooling is more important than secondary schooling⟩ — **in one's way** *also* **in the way 1 :** on or along one's path, road, or course **:** in a position to be encountered by one ⟨an opportunity had been put *in my way* —Ellen Glasgow⟩ **2** *obs* **:** while traveling or proceeding **:** in the course of one's journey **3 :** in such a position as to obstruct or hinder **:** constituting an obstruction, obstacle, or encumbrance ⟨trees were unhesitatingly cut down if they were *in the way* —David Fairchild⟩ ⟨knowledge unused is like dead lumber, constantly *in our way* —T.V.Smith⟩ ⟨let a mere fact stand *in the way* of a good idea —Arthur Knight⟩ **4** *in the way, Brit* **:** at hand **:** within reach **:** PRESENT ⟨I was not *in the way* at first, and knew nothing of it —Jane Austen⟩ **5** *obs* **:** constituting or involving a gain on one's part ⟨it might have been thousands *in my way* had I continued my business —Mathew Bishop⟩ — **make the best of one's way** *Brit* **:** to go as quickly as possible — **one's way around** *also* **one's way about 1 :** the details and procedures with which familiarity is needed ⟨soon learned *his way around*⟩ ⟨knows *his way about*⟩ **2 :** the modes of behavior needed for successful functioning in ⟨knew *his way around* Washington⟩ — **on the way** *or* **on one's way :** moving along one's course **:** in progress **:** COMING, GOING, ADVANCING — **out of the way** *or* **out of one's way 1 a :** out of or outside of the proper course of action **:** in the wrong **:** out of place **b :** WRONG, AMISS, IMPROPER ⟨oblivious of having said anything *out of the way* —Gilbert Parker⟩ **2 a :** off the beaten track **:** hard to reach or find **:** in or to a secluded place **:** some distance away **b :** UNUSUAL, REMARKABLE ⟨met nothing more *out of the way* than a cow eating and an old man walking —Virginia Woolf⟩ **3 :** off the course one is following or intends to follow ⟨this town is fifty miles *out of his way*⟩ ⟨such a digression would take us too far *out of our way*⟩ **4 a :** in or into such a position as not to obstruct ⟨I'll move my car *out of your way* so that you can pull out of the driveway⟩ **:** in or into a condition of having been already dealt with or accomplished ⟨after the months of preparatory work are *out of the way* —*Amer. Fabrics*⟩ **b :** in or into such a position as not to be run over or collided with ⟨before your father backs the car out of the garage, get your doll *out of the way*⟩ **:** out of the path of a dangerous advance ⟨get *out of the way* of the train⟩ ⟨*out of* harm's *way*⟩ **5** *out of one's way, Brit* **:** outside one's field of activity or interest **:** not in one's line **6** *obs* **:** not in the usual or proper place **:** LOST, MISLAID **7** *out of one's way, obs* **:** constituting or involving a loss on one's part ⟨it may be ten pounds *out of my way* to be turned out of my work —John Nelson⟩ — **the way 1** *Irish* **:** in such a way that ⟨they soldered the bottom of a tin dish to the top of his skull *the way* you could hear his brains ticking inside —James Stephens⟩ **2** *Irish* **:** in order that ⟨it's only letting on you are to be lonesome, *the way* you'd get around me now —J.M. Synge⟩ **3 :** in view of the manner in which ⟨you'd think we were millionaires, *the way* we have to finance this department —Dorothy Sayers⟩ — **the way of all flesh 1** *also* **the way of all the earth :** the course or passage from life to death ⟨the days of David drew nigh that he should die, and he charged his son Solomon, saying: I am going *the way of all flesh* —3 Kings 2:1–2 (DV)⟩ ⟨this day I am going *the way of all the earth* —Jos 23:14 (AV)⟩ **2 :** the common experience of all mankind — **under way** *adv* **1** *of a ship or boat* **a :** in motion through the water **b :** not at anchor **:** not made fast to the shore **:** not aground **2 :** in motion along a course **:** in progress **:** on the way

²**way** *vt* -ED/-ING/-S *obs* **:** to break or train (a horse) to the road

³**way** \ˈwā\ *adj* **:** of, connected with, or constituting an intermediate point on the route from one place to another

⁴**way** \ˈ"\ *adv* [ME, short for *away, on way* — more at AWAY] **1** *chiefly dial* **:** ¹AWAY 2 ⟨go ~⟩ **2 a :** ¹AWAY 7 ⟨sleeves that dangle ~ below the tips of the fingers —Lois Long⟩ ⟨forging ~ ahead in education —J.T.Farrell⟩ **b** *chiefly dial* **:** all the way **:** ²CLEAR c ⟨pull the switch ~ back⟩ **c** *dial* **:** EXTREMELY ⟨till ~ late in the morning —Mary S. Watts⟩ — **from way back 1 :** from an out-of-the-way rural locality **2 :** from a time far in the past **:** of long standing ⟨friends *from way back*⟩ **3 :** of the most thoroughgoing or expert kind ⟨a deadbeat *from way back*⟩ ⟨an artist *from way back* —Mark Twain⟩

⁵**way** \ˈ"\ *v imper* [prob. alter. of *whoa*] *dial Brit* — used as a command to a team or draft animal to stop

-way \ˌwā\ *adv suffix* [ME, fr. ¹*way*] **:** in (such) a way, course, direction, or manner ⟨broad*way*⟩ ⟨lyra*way*⟩

way and structures *n pl* **:** the fixed facilities of a railroad including the track and structures needed for its operation

wa·yang *also* **wa·jang** \ˈwäˌyäŋ\ *n* -S [Jav *wayang*, lit., shadow] **:** an Indonesian and esp. Javanese dramatic representation of mythological events in a puppet shadow play or by human dancers

¹**wayback** \ˈ≈,≈\ *adj* [fr. the phrase (*from*) *way back*] **:** of, relating to, or situated in the backcountry

²**wayback** \ˈ"\ *n, dial* **:** RUSTIC, YOKEL

waybeam \ˈ≈,≈\ *n* **:** a beam supporting a way; *specif* **:** either of two longitudinal beams resting on transverse girders and supporting the rails of a road crossing a bridge

way bennet *or* **way bent** *n* **:** WALL BARLEY

¹**waybill** \ˈ≈,≈\ *n* [¹*way* + *bill*] **1 :** a list of passengers in a public vehicle **2 :** an itinerary prepared for a traveler **3 :** a document that is prepared by the carrier (as a railroad company) transporting a shipment of goods, that contains such information as the nature of the shipment, the name of its consignor and consignee, its origin, route, destination, and the charges paid, and that serves as a means of identification, a guide for routing, and a basis for freight accounting and almost all other carrier records and statistics

²**waybill** \ˈ"\ *vt* -ED/-ING/-S **:** to enter in a waybill **:** send accompanied by a waybill

way-bit *n* [alter. (influenced by ¹*way*) of northern dial. phrase *wee bit* little] *obs* **:** a little distance

way·bread \ˈwāˌbred\ *n* [ME *weybrede*, fr. OE *wegbrǣde*; akin to MD *wegebrede* broad-leaved plantain, OHG *wegabreita*; all fr. a prehistoric WGmc compound whose first constituent is represented by OE *weg* way and whose second constituent is akin to OE *brād* broad; fr. its broad leaves and the fact that it frequently grows by the wayside — more at WAY, BROAD] *Brit* **:** BROAD-LEAVED PLANTAIN 1

way car *n* **1 :** ¹CABOOSE 3 **2 :** a freight car used to transport less-than-carload shipments to way stations

way chain *n, Brit* **:** a clog or brake for the wheel of a vehicle

¹**wayed** \ˈwād\ *adj* [ME, fr. ¹*way* + *-ed*] **:** having such a way or such or so many ways — used in combination ⟨wide-*wayed*⟩

²**wayed** *past of* WAY

¹**way·fare** \ˈwāˌfa(a)(ə)r, -ˌfe(|, |ə\ *n* [ME, fr. ¹*way* + *fare*, n.] **1** *archaic* **:** an act or course of journeying **2** *obs* **:** money or provisions for a journey

²**wayfare** \ˈ"\ *vi* -ED/-ING/-S **:** JOURNEY, TRAVEL

way·far·er \-ˌfa(a)rə(r), -ˌfer-\ *n* -S [ME *weyfarere*, fr. *wey* way + *-farere* traveler, fr. *faren* to go, travel + *-ere* -er — more at FARE] **1 :** a traveler esp. on foot **2 :** a transient patron of an inn or hotel

way·far·ing \-riŋ, -rēŋ\ *adj* [ME *wayfaringe*, alter. (influenced by *-inge* ³-ing) of *wayfarende*, fr. OE *wegfarende*, fr. *weg* way + *farende*, pres. part. of *faran* to go — more at WAY, FARE] **:** traveling esp. on foot **:** being on a journey **:** PASSING

wayfaring tree *n* **1 :** a Eurasian shrub (*Viburnum lantana*) that has large ovate leaves and dense cymes of small white flowers and is common along waysides **2 :** HOBBLEBUSH

way freight *n* **1 :** freight for a way station **2 :** a freight train stopping to put off goods at way stations

waygang \ˈ≈,≈\ *n* [⁴*way* + *gang*, n.] *Scot* **:** the act of leaving **:** DEPARTURE

¹**waygate** *n* [⁴*way* + *gate* (journey, way)] *obs* **:** the act of leaving **:** DEPARTURE

²**waygate** \ˈ≈,≈\ *n* [¹*way* + *gate* (journey, way)] *Brit* **:** PATH, PASSAGEWAY

¹**waygoing** \ˈ≈,≈≈\ *n* [⁴*way* + *going*] *chiefly Scot* **:** the act of leaving **:** DEPARTURE

²**waygoing** \ˈ"\ *adj* **1** *chiefly Scot* **:** going away **:** DEPARTING **2** *Brit* **:** of or relating to one that goes away

waygoing crop *n* **:** AWAY-GOING CROP

way·goose \ˈwāˌgüs\ *n, pl* **waygooses** [origin unknown] *dial Eng* **:** WAYZGOOSE

waying *pres part of* WAY

waylay \(ˈ)≈ˈ≈\ *vt* **waylaid; waylaid; waylaying; waylays** [¹*way* + *lay*] **1 a :** to lie in wait for **:** attack from ambush ⟨another band . . . waiting there to ~ him —S.H.Adams⟩ ⟨many a family coach was *waylaid* and its occupants robbed —F.W.Burgess⟩ **b :** to take possession of (something in transit) from or as if from ambush **:** INTERCEPT **c :** to stop (someone) for the purpose of conversation ⟨on the way out a group of seniors *waylaid* the president and asked if something couldn't be done about one of the boys who could not graduate —Josephine Y. Case⟩ **d :** to defeat or overwhelm as if by a surprise attack ⟨the 1930's, when social need once more *waylaid* the masses of Americans —Louis Filler⟩ ⟨I am *waylaid* by beauty —Edna S. V. Millay⟩ **2 :** to beset (as a passageway) with a force capable of attacking whoever approaches **3** *obs* **:** to check the course of **:** OBSTRUCT, BLOCK

wayleave \ˈ≈,≈\ *n* [ME *wayleve*, fr. ¹*way* + *leve* leave] **1 :** an easement consisting of permission to cross land or of a right-of-way across land **2** *or* **wayleave rent :** the rent paid for a wayleave

way·less \ˈwāləs\ *adj* [ME *wayles, weyles*, fr. OE *weglēas*, fr. *weg* way + *-lēas* -less] **:** having no road or path

way mail *n* **1 :** mail picked up or left off at a way station **2 :** mail given to a mail carrier en route from one post office to another

waymaker \ˈ≈,≈≈\ *n* [ME *way maker*] **1 :** one that makes a road; *specif* **:** an English royal official of the 16th and early 17th centuries with the duty of keeping the highways in good repair **2** *obs* **:** PRECURSOR

way·man \ˈwāmən\ *n, pl* **waymen 1 :** a railroad laborer employed in laying or keeping in repair the tracks **2 :** a shipwright that prepares and lays launching ways

waymark \ˈ≈,≈\ *n* **:** an object serving as a guide to someone traveling

way·ment \ˈwāmənt\ *vi* -ED/-ING/-S [ME *waymenten*, fr. ONF *waimenter*, fr. *wai*, interj., woe (of Gmc origin; akin to Goth *wai*, interj., woe) + OF *menter* (as in *lamenter* to lament) — more at WOE, LAMENT] *archaic* **:** LAMENT, GRIEVE

way-off \ˈ≈ˈ≈\ *adj* [fr. the adverbial phrase *way off*] *dial* **:** FAR-OFF 1

way of necessity : a right-of-way that arises from necessity (as when one buys land accessible only over other lands of the vendor) and terminates when the necessity ceases

way of the cross *usu cap W&C* **1 :** STATIONS OF THE CROSS **2 :** the course taken in visiting in succession the stations of the cross

way of the wine : the left-to-right direction in which wine is passed at table

way passenger *n* **:** a passenger getting on or off at a way station or other intermediate point on a line of travel

way point *n* **:** an intermediate point on a route or line of travel; *esp* **:** WAY STATION

waypost \ˈ≈,≈\ *n* **:** GUIDEPOST 1

wayrod \ˈ≈,≈\ *n* [¹*way* + *rod*] **:** the carriage rod of a typewriter

¹**ways** *pl of* WAY, *pres 3d sing of* WAY

²**ways** \ˈwāz\ *n pl but sing in constr* [ME *wayes*, fr. *wayes*, gen. of *way*] **1 :** WAY 9a ⟨come a little nearer this ~ —Shak.⟩ **2 :** WAY 6 ⟨a long ~ from home⟩ ⟨went a good ~⟩

-ways \ˌwāz\ *adv suffix* [ME *-ways, -weys*, fr. *ways, weyes, wayes*, gen. of *way, wey* way — more at WAY] **:** in (such) a way, course, direction, or manner ⟨side*ways*⟩ ⟨bar*ways*⟩

ways and means *n pl* [ME *weys and menes, weyes and meanes*] **1 :** methods and resources for accomplishing something and esp. for defraying expenses **2 a** *often cap W&M* **:** methods and resources for raising the necessary revenues for the expenses of a political unit (as a nation or state) **b** *often cap W&M* **:** a legislative committee concerned with this function ⟨the chairman of Ways and Means was formerly appointed at the beginning of a new Parliament —T.E.May⟩ ⟨the *Ways and Means* made its first formal proposals on tax legislation for the current session of Congress —*N.Y.Times*⟩

¹**way shaft** *n, Brit* **:** ¹WINZE

²**way shaft** *n* [alter. of *weighshaft*] **:** ¹ROCKSHAFT

¹**wayside** \ˈ≈,≈\ *n* [ME] **:** the side of a road or path **:** land adjacent to a road or path ⟨cornfields along the ~⟩ ⟨many former advocates of this policy have fallen by the ~⟩

²**wayside** \ˈ"\ *adj* **:** of, connected with, or situated at the side of a road or path ⟨~ flowers⟩; *specif* **:** situated adjacent to a highway so as to be accessible to motorists ⟨~ restaurants⟩

wayside cross *n* **:** a cross set up along a road or path as a place for the devotions of passersby

wayside pulpit *n* **:** an outdoor bulletin board used by a church for posting pointed and provocative messages before passersby

way station *n* **:** an intermediate station between principal stations on a line of travel esp. on a railroad **:** local station

way-stop \ˈ≈,≈\ *n* **:** an intermediate stop on a line of travel

waythorn \ˈ≈,≈\ *n* **:** a common buckthorn (*Rhamnus cathartica*) of Eurasia

way traffic *n* **:** traffic involving way stations **:** local traffic

way train *n* **:** a train that stops at way stations **:** accommodation train for passengers

way·ward \ˈwāwə(r)d\ *adj* [ME *wayward, weyward*, short for *awayward, aweyward* turned away, fr. *away, awey*, adv., away + *-ward* — more at AWAY] **1 :** characterized by extreme willfulness and by determination to follow one's own capricious, wanton, or depraved inclinations to the point of being ungovernable ⟨the ~ child who persists in wandering away —A.R.Mead⟩ ⟨the glamorous sin . . . associated with what is known as ~ passion —*Tomorrow*⟩ ⟨the ~ power of the emotionally excited masses —Vernon Mallinson⟩ **2 :** following no clear principle or law **:** UNPREDICTABLE, ERRATIC ⟨there was no room in that precision for the eccentricity, the ~ act —Graham Greene⟩ **3 :** opposite to what is desired or expected **:** UNTOWARD, VEXING ⟨~ fate⟩ **syn** see CONTRARY

wayward child *or* **wayward minor** *n* **:** a child having a status arbitrarily defined by statute in some states, usu. being under a stated age, habitually associating with vicious or immoral persons, or growing up in circumstances likely to cause him to commit crimes or be willfully disobedient of parental or other lawful authority and therefore become subject to custodial care and protection for his own welfare — compare JUVENILE DELINQUENT, STUBBORN CHILD

waywarden \ˈ≈,≈≈\ *n* [¹*way* + *warden*] **1 :** a supervisor of highways esp. as an elected member of a board **2** *Brit* **:** one that maintains the trenches of a sewage disposal plant

way·ward·ly *adv* [ME *weywardly*, fr. *weyward* wayward + *-ly*] **:** in a wayward manner

way·ward·ness *n* -ES [ME *weywardnesse*, fr. *weyward* wayward + *-nesse* -ness] **:** the quality or state of being wayward

way-wise \ˈ≈,≈\ *adj* **1** *of a horse* **:** well broken esp. for use on the road or on a racetrack **2** *dial* **:** EXPERIENCED

way·wis·er \ˈwāˌwīzə(r)\ *n* -S [part trans. of D *wegwijzer* guide, signpost, waywiser, lit., one that shows the way, fr. *weg* way + *wijzer* one that shows, fr. MD *wiser*, fr. *wisen* to show; akin to MD *wijs* wise, OE *wīs* — more at WISE] **:** an instrument (as an odometer or pedometer) for measuring the distance traversed by a walker, vehicle, or ship

way·wode \ˈwāˌwōd\ *n* -S [by alter.] **:** VAIVODE

wayworn \ˈ≈,≈\ *adj* **:** wearied by traveling

waywort \ˈ≈,≈\ *n* [ME *waywurt*, fr. ¹*way* + *wurt* wort; fr. its prevalence along roads] **:** ¹SCARLET PIMPERNEL

wayz·goose \ˈwāzˌgüs\ *n, pl* **wayzgooses** [alter. of *waygoose*] **:** a printers' annual outing or entertainment

¹**wa·zir** \wəˈzi(ə)r\ *n* -S [Ar *wazīr* — more at VIZIER] **:** VIZIER

²**wazir** \ˈ"\ *or* **wa·ziri** \-ˈirē\ *n, pl* **wazir** *or* **wazirs** *or* **waziri** *or* **waziris** *usu cap* **:** a member of a Pathan people inhabiting Waziristan in northwestern West Pakistan

wb *abbr* weber

WB *abbr* **1** wallboard **2** warehouse book **3** *often not cap* water ballast **4** water board **5** waybill **6** weather bureau **7** westbound **8** wet bulb **9** wheelbase

WBC *abbr* white blood cells; white blood count

WBS *abbr, often not cap* without benefit of salvage

WC *abbr* **1** water closet **2** west central **3** will call **4** without charge **5** wood casing **6** working capital

w chromosome *n, usu cap W* **:** a sex chromosome of the kind distinctively characteristic of the female in organisms (as moths) in which the female has two kinds of sex chromosomes — compare Z CHROMOSOME

wd *abbr* **1** weed **2** wind **3** window **4** wood **5** word **6** would **7** wound

WD *abbr* **1** war damage **2** war department **3** works department

wdg *abbr* **1** winding **2** wording

wdr *abbr* wider

wdt *abbr* width

¹**we** \(ˈ)wē, ˌwi, *before* "'re" *or* "are" *usu* (ˌ)wi\ *pron, pl in constr* [ME, fr. OE *wē*; akin to OHG *wir* we, ON *vēr*, Goth *weis*, Skt *vayam*] **1 a :** I and the rest of a group that includes me **:** you and I **:** you and I and another or others **:** I and another or others not including you — used as a nominative pronoun of the first person plural as the subject of a verb ⟨~ live here⟩ ⟨~ the people of the United States . . . do ordain and establish this constitution —*U.S.Constitution*⟩ or in the predicate after a copulative verb ⟨it is ~ who are the virtuous ones —Vance Packard⟩ or in comparisons after *than* or *as* when the first term in the comparison is a subject ⟨you know as much about it as ~⟩ or in some absolute constructions ⟨ignorant, you say? ~?⟩ or after *but* in a compound subject ⟨none but ~ may say this⟩; used archaically as subject of an immediately preceding verb to introduce a request or proposal made by the speaker or writer to the group that includes himself where the current construction in ordinary present-day English consists of *let us* or *let's* followed by the verb ⟨prepare ~ for our marriage —Shak.⟩; see OUR, US; compare I, OURS **b :** people in general including the speaker or writer ⟨when ~ mind labor, then only, *we're* too old —Robert Browning⟩ **2 :** ²I 1 — used by kings and other sovereigns ⟨our sometime sister, now our queen, . . . have ~ . . . taken to wife —Shak.⟩; used by editors and other writers to keep an impersonal character or to avoid the egotistical sound of a repeated *I* **3 a** *dial chiefly Eng* **:** US — used emphatically as object of a verb or preposition ⟨to poor ~ thine enmity's most capital —Shak.⟩ ⟨the likes of ~⟩ **b** *chiefly substand* **:** US — used in a compound object or in apposition with a following noun ⟨he disturbed those in the dining room, those in the hall, and even ~ who had retired upstairs⟩ ⟨as to ~ men —Fanny Burney⟩ **4 :** YOU — used coaxingly (as to a child) ⟨~ don't want to wake Daddy, do ~⟩ or encouragingly (as to a patient) ⟨how are ~ feeling this morning⟩ or in sarcasm ⟨aren't ~ getting a little impudent⟩

²**we** \ˈwē\ *n* -S **:** a group that is consciously felt as such by its members ⟨the crowd is like a community in that it can be any size, the difference being that the *We* precedes the I —Howard Griffin⟩

¹**wea** \ˈweə\ *dial var of* WOE

²**wea** \ˈwēə\ *n, pl* **wea** *or* **weas** *usu cap* **1 a :** an Indian people of Indiana associated with the Miami **b :** a member of such people **2 :** the language of the Wea people

wea *abbr* weather

we-adar *usu cap W&A, var of* VEADAR

¹**weak** \ˈwēk\ *adj* -ER/-EST [ME *waike, weike, weke*, fr. ON *veikr*; akin to OE *wāc* pliant, soft, weak, OHG *weih* yielding, soft, OE *wīcan* to yield, give way, OHG *wīhhan*, ON *vīkja* to move, turn, recede — more at WEEK] **1 :** lacking strength **:** not strong: as **a :** deficient in strength of body ⟨~ with hunger⟩ ⟨sick man welcomed him as eagerly as his ~ state permitted —Charles Reade⟩ **b :** not able to sustain or exert much weight, pressure, or strain **:** having small capability of exerting or resisting force ⟨~ rope⟩ ⟨~ joint in a chair⟩ ⟨red planet possesses only a ~ gravity —J.G.Vaeth⟩ ⟨~ ignition spark⟩ **c :** not able to resist external force or withstand attack **:** easily subdued or overcome ⟨even if the ~ witness tells the truth he is a slender reed —L.P.Stryker⟩ **d :** readily subject to failure, collapse, or breakdown ⟨~ heart⟩ ⟨~ nerves⟩ **2 a :** mentally or intellectually deficient **:** lacking judgment or discernment ⟨a superstition imposing only on ~ intellects⟩ **b :** not having full conviction **:** not firmly decided **:** WAVERING, VACILLATING ⟨realize how ~ the love of truth is in the majority —W.R.

Inge⟩ **c :** resulting from or indicating lack of judgment, discernment, or firmness **:** UNWISE, FOOLISH ⟨not generosity but mere ~ indulgence⟩ **d :** not able to withstand temptation or persuasion **:** easily impressed or swayed ⟨~ virtue⟩ ⟨~ determination⟩ ⟨men are so ~ and women so unscrupulous —W.S.Maugham⟩ **3 :** not having power to convince **:** not supported by force of truth or logic ⟨~ argument⟩ ⟨~ case at law⟩ **4 a :** lacking in power to perform properly a function or office ⟨~ eyes⟩ ⟨~ sense of direction⟩ **b :** lacking skill or proficiency ⟨a good fielder but a ~ batter⟩ ⟨special tutoring for the ~*er* students⟩ **c :** showing or indicating a lack of skill or aptitude ⟨mathematics was his ~*est* subject⟩ ⟨his penetration of human psychology and his creation of character is ~ —R.A.Hall b. 1911⟩ **d :** wanting in vigor of expression or artistic effect ⟨~ line⟩ ⟨~ retort⟩ ⟨a painfully ~ story apparently meant to be fantasy —Raymond Walters b. 1912⟩ **5 :** lacking force of utterance or sound **:** not sonorous **:** FAINT ⟨sick man spoke in a ~ voice⟩ ⟨~ protest⟩ **6 a :** not thoroughly or abundantly impregnated with the usual or required ingredients **:** DILUTE ⟨~ coffee⟩ ⟨~ acid solution⟩ **b :** lacking normal intensity or potency ⟨~ colors⟩ ⟨~ strain of virus⟩ ⟨~ winter sunlight⟩ **c :** lacking contrast **:** THIN ⟨~ photographic negative⟩ **d** *of flour* **:** made from a soft wheat and containing a relatively low percentage of gluten and lacking cohesiveness — opposed to *strong* **7 a :** not having or exerting authority or political power ⟨~ king⟩ ⟨~ government⟩ **b :** not equal to the need or emergency **:** INEFFECTIVE, IMPOTENT ⟨~ attempts at resistance⟩ ⟨~ measures to control crime⟩ **8 a** *of a verb* **:** belonging to a conjugation that forms the past tense and past participle by adding the suffix *-ed* or *-d* or *-t* (as *dash, dashed; grate, grated; deal, dealt*) **:** REGULAR — opposed to *strong* **b** *of a noun or adjective declension* **:** having the less full case inflection characteristic of Proto-Germanic stems in *-n* (as Old English *oxa, oxan;* German *ochs, ochsen*) — opposed to *strong* **c :** of or relating to a class of Hebrew or Syriac consonants or to a verb having one or more such consonants in the root **9 a :** bearing the minimal degree of stress occurring in the language **:** LIGHT ⟨~ syllable⟩ ⟨~ stress⟩ **b :** having little or no stress and obscured vowel sound **:** UNEMPHATIC — used of monosyllabic pronouns, prepositions, auxiliaries ⟨*would* is often heard in its ~ form *'d*⟩ **10 :** tending toward a lower price ⟨wheat is ~⟩ ⟨a ~ market⟩ **11 :** having only a slight degree of ionization in solution — used of acids and bases; opposed to *strong*

syn WEAK, FEEBLE, FRAIL, FRAGILE, INFIRM, and DECREPIT mean, in common, not strong enough to bear strain or pressure or stand up under difficulty or effort. WEAK, of wider application than all the rest and interchangeable with any of them, implies deficiency, inferiority, or impairment of strength, power, skill, control, or influence ⟨a sick and *weak* old man⟩ ⟨a *weak* rung of a ladder⟩ ⟨Antonius was *weak* and vicious, and Catiline could mould him as he pleased —J.A.Froude⟩ ⟨a *weak*, timid face —Sherwood Anderson⟩ ⟨to say that one part of a painting, drama, or novel is too *weak*, means that some related part is too strong —John Dewey⟩ ⟨a *weak* excuse⟩ ⟨a *weak* police department⟩ FEEBLE suggests extreme pitiable weakness, usu. of persons or their acts or utterances ⟨a *feeble* old man⟩ ⟨a *feeble* attempt to resist oppression⟩ ⟨a *feeble* cough⟩ ⟨a *feeble* excuse⟩ ⟨a *feeble* imagination⟩ FRAIL, implying physical weakness, suggests rather a natural delicacy or slightness of constitution than an impairment of strength ⟨seemed rather *frail*, for there was a delicate pallor on his high, intelligent forehead and there was an invalid's languor in his whole attitude —Jean Stafford⟩ ⟨begins to lose the rather *frail* grasp she has on reality — *New Yorker*⟩ ⟨beauty, that *frailest* and most elusive of concepts —W.H.Auden⟩ FRAGILE, frequently interchangeable with FRAIL, stresses the idea of extremely easy destructibility ⟨a tall *fragile* vase⟩ ⟨the spirit of a little boy is a *fragile* thing and not to be pushed around beyond endurance —Christine Govan⟩ ⟨a wild deer, *fragile* and untamed —Elinor Wylie⟩ INFIRM implies loss especially of physical strength, and a consequent instability or unsoundness, often implying illness or old age ⟨the present king, *infirm* both in body and mind —A.T.Mahan⟩ ⟨mighty in reasoning but *infirm* in moral feeling —W.L.Sullivan⟩ ⟨an old man too *infirm* to go out in wet weather⟩ ⟨lack of direction in the main plan, *infirm* judgments, and cowardly estimates — Maurice Bowra⟩ DECREPIT applies to things or persons worn out or broken down by use or age ⟨grown so *decrepit* and feeble with old age as to threaten demise altogether —W.M. Thackeray⟩ ⟨a *decrepit* ramshackle building⟩ ⟨our own civilization appears to be growing *decrepit* and ready to fall — Bertrand Russell⟩ ⟨government that replaced the *decrepit* monarchy and corrupt dictatorship —Oscar Handlin⟩

²weak \"\ *n* -s **:** the thinnest most flexible portion of a foil blade **:** the foremost one third of the blade

³weak \"\ *vb* -ED/-ING/-S [ME *waiken, weiken,* fr. *waike, weike* weak] *archaic* **:** WEAKEN

weak·en \'wēkən\ *vb* **weakened; weakened; weakening** \-k(ə)niŋ\ **weakens** [¹*weak* + *-en*] *vt* **1 :** to make weak **:** lessen the strength of **:** ENFEEBLE ⟨disease ~s the body⟩ ⟨fatigue ~*ed* his grip⟩ ⟨wetting ~s paper⟩ ⟨floodwaters ~*ed* the foundations of the bridge⟩ ⟨doubts ~*ed* his resolve⟩ ⟨hypotheses which . . . rather than affirm purely mechanistic interpretations of nature —J.W.Krutch⟩ **2 :** to reduce in intensity or effectiveness ⟨milk ~*ed* one half to two thirds with plain boiled water —Morris Fishbein⟩ ~ *vi* **1 :** to become weak ⟨steadily ~*ing* storm⟩ **:** lose strength or spirit or determination **:** become less firm or resolute ⟨the Middle West was ~*ing* in its allegiance to the Democratic party —*Amer. Guide Series: Ind.*⟩ **2 :** to change from a complex to a simple sound (as from a diphthong to a long vowel) **:** change from a strong to a weak sound **:** change from an open to a close vowel

syn WEAKEN, ENFEEBLE, DEBILITATE, UNDERMINE, SAP, CRIPPLE, DISABLE can mean, in common, to lose or cause to lose strength, vigor, or energy. WEAKEN, the most general of the group, signifies the loss of physical strength, soundness, or stability, or, in extension, of quality, intensity, or effective power ⟨*weakened* by failing health —C.H.Lincoln⟩ ⟨the days and nights of dissipation had *weakened* and depressed him — Louis Bromfield⟩ ⟨has left rural churches *weakened* in numbers and financial resources —*Amer. Guide Series: N.Y.*⟩ ⟨the spirit of adventure is not stimulated but *weakened* by poverty —M.R.Cohen⟩ ENFEEBLE implies a more obvious condition, usu. suggesting a helplessness or feebleness or forcelessness ⟨despite an *enfeebled* body, the mental faculties . . . can remain intact to the very end of life —*Current Biog.*⟩ ⟨can excessive reading actually *enfeeble* one's thinking apparatus —A.N. Whitehead⟩ ⟨the years had not *enfeebled* his acting —E.H. Collis⟩ DEBILITATE suggests a less marked, usu. more temporary, impairment of strength or vitality ⟨ivy *debilitates* trees, disintegrates mortar in walls and dislodges roof tiles —F.D. Smith & Barbara Wilcox⟩ ⟨avoid embroilments which *debilitate* our strength —*Current Biog.*⟩ ⟨the fears and the rages that *debilitate* —H.A.Overstreet⟩ UNDERMINE and SAP suggest a weakening by the effects of some surreptitious or insidious force, often carrying the idea of a draining of strength or a slow caving in or breaking down ⟨the members of his family *undermined* by dissipation, crime and madness —*Times Lit. Supp.*⟩ ⟨the emotions which would have *undermined* and demoralized him had he not sworn beforehand to abjure that —Marcia Davenport⟩ ⟨a gradual oxidation of the rubber thread which *undermines* the quality of the rubber —Albert Thompson & Sigfrid Bick⟩ CRIPPLE, meaning basically to maim or mutilate, suggests a serious impairment of force or effect similar to if not greater than that caused by a loss of a limb to a person ⟨the brain-injury victims, *i.e.*, those who have been *crippled* by such things as blows, encephalitis, or a sustained high fever in infancy —*Time*⟩ ⟨a heavy winter snowfall *cripples* transportation —Corey Ford⟩ DISABLE implies any force that makes unfit or which incapacitates, especially suddenly ⟨*disabled* for field work by an accident which resulted in the loss of his right leg —C.W.Mitman⟩ ⟨*disabled* the car so it wouldn't run —W.W.Haines⟩ ⟨an indifferent memory *disabled* him from mastering the Indian languages —Francis Parkman⟩

weak·en·er \-k(ə)nə(r)\ *n* -s **:** one that weakens

weaker *comparative of* WEAK

weaker sex *n* **:** WOMANKIND

weaker vessel *n* [so called fr. the metaphor in 1 Pet 3:7 (AV)] **:** WOMAN

weakest *superlative of* WEAK

weak feints *or* **weak faints** *n pl* **:** the last runnings in the distillation of alcoholic liquor (as whiskey)

weakfish \'ˌ=ˌ=\ *n* [obs. D *weekvis,* fr. *week* soft, tender, weak (fr. MD *weec*) + *vis* fish (fr. MD *visch, vis*); fr. its tender flesh; akin to OE *wāc* soft and to OE *fisc* fish — more at WEAK, FISH] **1 :** any of several marine food fishes (genus *Cynoscion*); *esp* **:** a common sport and market fish (*C. regalis*) of the eastern coast of the U. S. from Cape Cod to Florida — see SPOTTED WEAKFISH **2 :** ²MAIGRE 1

weak grade *n* **:** a member of an ablaut series (as a low or a neutral vowel) occurring in a syllable bearing reduced stress

weakhanded \'ˌ=ˌ=ˌ=\ *adj* **1 a :** having weak hands **b :** DISPIRITED **2 :** having an insufficient number of employees **:** SHORTHANDED

weak-headed \'ˌ=ˌ=ˌ=\ *adj* **:** having a weak head: as **a :** liable to dizziness **:** easily affected by drinking **b :** wanting in strength of mind or purpose **:** WEAK-MINDED **c :** having a feeble intellect — **weak-head·ed·ly** *adv* — **weak-head·edness** *n* -ES

weakhearted \'ˌ=ˌ=ˌ=\ *adj* [¹*weak* + *hearted*] **:** of little courage **:** FAINTHEARTED ⟨the ~ liberals have left us and we are ready to build —Henry Wallace⟩ — **weak·heart·ed·ly** *adv* — **weak·heart·ed·ness** *n*

weaking *pres part of* WEAK

weak·ish \'wēkish\ *adj* **:** somewhat weak ⟨~ tea⟩ ⟨~ market⟩ — **weak·ish·ly** *adv* — **weak·ish·ness** *n* -ES

weak-kneed \'ˌ=ˌ=\ *adj* **:** easily yielding **:** lacking will power or resolution **:** IRRESOLUTE ⟨role of the dissenter is not for the *weak-kneed* —B.F.Wright⟩ — **weak-kneed·ly** *adv* — **weak-kneed·ness** *n* -ES

weak·li·ness \'wēklēnəs\ *n* -ES **:** the quality or state of being weakly **:** PUNINESS

¹weak·ling \'wēkliŋ, -lēŋ\ *n* -s [¹*weak* + *-ling*] **:** one that is weak in body or character or mind ⟨football, of course . . . the dream of every male ~ —Dorothy Witton⟩ ⟨greedy and often half-witted and half-alive ~s who will do anything for cigars, champagne, motorcars —G.B.Shaw⟩

²weakling \"\ *adj* **:** lacking strength or fortitude ⟨~ government that permits such a mess to fester —Don Porter⟩

¹weak·ly *adv* -ER/-EST [ME *weikly, wekely,* fr. *weike, weke* weak + *-ly,* adv. suffix] **:** in a weak manner ⟨~ agreed to a compromise⟩ **:** to a weak degree **:** FEEBLY, SLIGHTLY ⟨painting and drawing were ~ developed —Clark Wissler⟩

²weak·ly *adj* -ER/-EST [¹*weak* + *-ly,* adj. suffix] **:** not strong or robust **:** FEEBLE, WEAK ⟨~ infant⟩ **:** SICKLY, PUNY ⟨~ plant⟩

weak mayor *n* **:** a mayor in a mayor-council method of municipal government whose powers of policy-making and administration are by charter in large degree subordinate to the council — compare COUNCIL-MANAGER PLAN, STRONG MAYOR

weak-minded \'ˌ=ˌ=ˌ=\ *adj* **:** having or indicating a weak mind **:** FOOLISH ⟨thinks I'm *weak-minded* because I play golf —W.H. Wright⟩; *sometimes* **:** FEEBLEMINDED — **weak-mind·ed·ly** *adv* — **weak-mind·ed·ness** *n*

weak neck *n* **:** a physiological disease of sorghum characterized by breaking of the stalk below the head

weak·ness *n* -ES [ME *waikenes, weikenes,* fr. *waike, weike* weak + *-nes* -ness] **1 :** the quality or state of being weak **:** want of strength **:** lack of vigor ⟨it was a month after his illness before he recovered from his ~⟩; *also* **:** an instance or a period of feebleness or vacillation ⟨agreed in a moment of ~ to become chairman⟩ **2 :** something that is a mark of lack of strength or resolution **:** FAULT, DEFECT ⟨admitting frankly the possession of vices and ~*es* that all of us have and few of us care to acknowledge —H.L.Mencken⟩ **3 :** an object of special desire, concern, or fondness ⟨~ for salted peanuts⟩ ⟨the thirteenth century had a ~ for the word *speculum* —H.O.Taylor⟩

weaks *pl of* WEAK, *pres 3d sing of* WEAK

weak side *n* **1 :** the side or aspect of a person's character or disposition through which he is most easily influenced esp. for the worse **2 :** the side of a football formation having the smaller number of players

weak sister *n* **:** a member of a group who needs aid **:** an element or factor that is weak and ineffective as compared with others in the group ⟨weed out the *weak sisters* among the salesmen⟩ ⟨a subject introduced into the curriculum for the benefit of the *weaker sisters* —Kemp Malone⟩

weaky \'wēki\ *adj* [¹*weak* + *-y*] *dial Eng* **:** WET, DAMP

¹weal \'wēl, *esp before pause or consonant* 'wēəl\ *n* -s [ME *wele, weale,* fr. OE *wela,* akin to OS *welo* weal, OE *wel* well — more at WELL, adv.] **1** *obs* **:** WEALTH, RICHES **2 :** a sound, healthy, or prosperous state **:** WELL-BEING, PROSPERITY, HAPPINESS, WELFARE — used chiefly in the phrase *weal or woe* ⟨power of determining the ~ or woe of the people —J.G. Frazer⟩ **3** *obs* **:** BODY POLITIC, COMMONWEAL ⟨the special watchmen of our English ~ —Shak.⟩

²weal \"\ *vt* -ED/-ING/-S [alter. (influenced by *wheal*) of *wale*] **:** to raise weals on (as with a whip) **:** WALE

³weal \"\ *n* -s [alter. (influenced by *wheal*) of *wale*] **:** a stripe or raised line made by a stroke (as of a whip) on the skin **:** WALE

weald \'wēld, *esp before pause or consonant* 'wēəld\ *n* -s [fr. the *Weald,* wooded district in Kent, Surrey, & Sussex counties, southeast England, alter. (influenced by OE *weald*) of ME *Weeld* the Weald, fr. OE *weald* wood, forest — more at WOLD] **1 :** a heavily wooded area **:** FOREST ⟨*Weald* of Kent⟩ **2 :** a wild or uncultivated usu. upland region **:** WOLD ⟨by glimmering waste and ~ —Alfred Tennyson⟩

wealpublic *n* [ME *weale publique,* fr. *weale* weal + *publique* public, adj.; trans. of L *bonum publicum*] **1** *obs* **:** the public good **2** *obs* **:** COMMONWEALTH

wealth \'welth *also* -ltth\ *n* -s [ME *welthe,* fr. *wele* weal] **1** *obs* **:** WEAL, WELFARE, GOOD, HAPPINESS ⟨let no man seek his own, but every man another's ~ —1 Cor 10:24 (AV)⟩ **2 :** large possessions **:** abundance of things that are objects of human desire **:** abundance of worldly estate **:** AFFLUENCE, RICHES **3 :** abundant supply **:** large accumulation ⟨piles up a great ~ of detail to show —Ruth Moore⟩ ⟨~ of original documents⟩ **:** PROFUSION ⟨~ of curly black hair⟩ ⟨described with a ~ of examples⟩ **4 a :** all property that has a money value or an exchangeable value ⟨money, ~, possessions, and particularly the accumulation, retention, and use of them, are the distinguishing mark of the middle classes —Ray Lewis & Angus Maude⟩ ⟨slaves . . . were a ~ to be squandered without limit to make more ~ —Marjory S. Douglas⟩ **b :** all material objects that have economic utility; *esp* **:** the stock of useful goods having economic value in existence at any one time ⟨national ~⟩

wealth·i·ly \-thəlē, -li\ *adv* [*wealthy* + *-ly*] **:** with riches **:** with material success **:** in a wealthy manner

wealth·i·ness \-thēnəs, -thin-\ *n* -ES **:** the quality or state of being wealthy **:** RICHNESS, OPULENCE

wealth·less \-thləs\ *adj* [*wealth* + *-less*] **:** having no money or property

wealthy \-thē, -thi\ *adj* -ER/-EST [ME *welthy,* fr. *welthe* wealth + *-y*] **1** *obs* **:** enjoying a condition of well-being **:** physically well cared for **2 :** having wealth **:** having large possessions of lands, goods, money, or securities **:** OPULENT, AFFLUENT ⟨school for the sons of ~ families⟩ **3 :** characterized by abundance **:** AMPLE, FULL, ABUNDANT ⟨flowers and fruits of a land ~ in both —Douglas Carruthers⟩ **syn** see RICH

¹wean \'wēn\ *vt* -ED/-ING/-S [ME *wenen,* fr. OE *wenian* to accustom, wean; akin to OHG *giwennen* to accustom, ON *venja,* OE *wunian* to dwell, be used to — more at WONT] **1 :** to accustom (a child or other young animal) to loss of mother's milk **:** cause to cease to depend on the mother for nourishment; *also* **:** to accustom (young animals) to get along without some special comfort ⟨~ chicks from the hover⟩ **2 :** to detach or alienate the affections of from some object of desire **:** reconcile to the deprivation or loss of something ⟨the troubles of age were intended . . . to ~ us gradually from our fondness of life —Jonathan Swift⟩ ⟨low prices of movies may have ~*ed* large sections of the public away from the legitimate theater —Donald Messenger⟩ ⟨~*ed* my young soul from yearning after thine —Emily Brontë⟩ **syn** see ESTRANGE

²wean \"\ *n* -s [contr. of *wee ane* wee one, fr. *wee* + *ane*] *dial Brit* **:** INFANT, CHILD

weaned·ness \'wēnədnəs, -ēn(d)nəs\ *n* -ES [*weaned* (past part. of ¹*wean*) + *-ness*] **:** the quality or state of being weaned; *esp* **:** detachment from worldly things

wean·el \'wēnᵊl\ *n* -s [ME *weynelle,* fr. *wenen, weynen* to wean] *dial Eng* **:** WEANLING

wean·er \'wēnə(r)\ *n* -s **1 :** one that weans; *specif* **:** a device for preventing animals that are being weaned from suckling **2 :** a young animal weaned from its mother: as **a** *chiefly Austral* **:** a lamb between weaning and its first shearing or up to the appearance of the first two permanent teeth **b :** a weaned calf **c :** a weaned pig

wean·ie \'wēni\ *n* -s [¹*wean* + *-ie*] *Scot* **:** BABY

¹wean·ling \'wēnliŋ, -lēŋ\ *n* -s [¹*wean* + *-ling*] **:** a child or animal newly weaned

²weanling \"\ *adj* **:** recently weaned; *also* **:** of or relating to a weanling

wean·ly \'wēnli\ *adj* [²*wean* + *-ly*] **:** CHILDISH, FEEBLE

wean·yer \'wēnyə(r)\ *n* -s [irreg. fr. ¹*wean* + *-er*] *dial Eng* **:** WEANLING

¹weap·on \'wepən, *dial* 'wēp-\ *n* -s [ME *wepen, wepne,* fr. OE *wǣpen;* akin to OHG *wāffan* weapon, ON *vāpn,* Goth *wepna* (pl.) weapons] **1 :** an instrument of offensive or defensive combat **:** something to fight with **:** something (as a club, sword, gun, or grenade) used in destroying, defeating, or physically injuring an enemy ⟨the rifle is the basic infantry ~ —M.M.Johnson⟩ **2 :** an animal's claw, teeth, talon, spur, or beak used as a means of attack; *esp* **:** the spur of a gamecock **3 :** a means of contending against another ⟨has codes of honor, rules, beliefs, and other ~s to protect him on the trail —Donn Byrne⟩ ⟨a politician who uses character assassination as a political ~ —Croswell Bowen⟩ ⟨sarcasm was his favorite ~⟩

syn WEAPON and ARM indicate something used in combat as an instrument or means of attack or defense. WEAPON applies to anything used or usable in injuring, destroying, or defeating an enemy or opponent. ARM, usu. in the plural, signifies an instrument or object designed for or used in fighting ⟨a large yearly appropriation for *arms*⟩ but is often restricted to the class of weapons wielded by the hand and arm (as swords, pistols, or rifles)

²weapon \"\ *vt* -ED/-ING/-S [ME *wepnen,* fr. OE *wǣpnian,* fr. *wǣpen* weapon] **:** ARM ⟨a folk in a cold climate . . . crudely ~*ed* —*Time*⟩

¹weap·on·eer \ˌwepəˈni(ə)r\ *n* -s [¹*weapon* + *-eer*] **:** one who activates an atomic bomb into readiness for release upon a target

²weaponeer \"\ *vi* -ED/-ING/-S **:** to engage in developing and perfecting military weapons ⟨caught up with or surpassed us in the matter of atomic ~*ing* —Philip Wylie⟩

weap·on·less \'wepənləs\ *adj* [ME *wepneles,* fr. OE *wǣpenlēas,* fr. *wǣpen* weapon + *-lēas* -less] **:** lacking weapons **:** UNARMED

weap·on·ry \-nrē\ *n* -ES [¹*weapon* + *-ry*] **1 :** aggregate of weapons ⟨jellyfish . . . are equipped with ingenious ~ —*Newsweek*⟩ **2 :** the science of designing and making weapons ⟨approaching era of nuclear ~ —Russell Baker⟩

weapon salve *n* **:** a salve believed to cure a wound by being applied to the weapon that made the wound

weapons carrier *n* **:** a light truck designed to carry machine guns or mortars and their crews

weap·on·shaw·ing \'wepən,shȯ·iŋ\ *or* **weap·on·shaw** \-,shȯ\ *or* **weap·on·show·ing** \-,shōiŋ\ *or* **weap·on·show** \-,shō\ *dial var of* WAPPENSCHAWING

weaponsmith \'ˌ=ˌ=ˌ=\ *n* **:** a maker of weapons

¹wear \'wa(a)(ə)r, 'weǀ, ǀə\ *vb* **wore** \'wō(ə)r, 'wȯ(ə)r, -ōə, -ō(ə)\ **worn** \'wō(ə)rn, 'wȯ(ə)rn, -ōən, -ō(ə)n\ *or substand* **wore; wearing; wears** [ME *weren,* fr. OE *werian* to clothe, put on, wear; akin to OHG *werien* to clothe, ON *verja* to clothe, invest, spend, Goth *wasjan* to clothe, L *vestis* clothing, garment, Gk *hennynai* to clothe, *esthēs* clothing, Skt *vaste* he puts on, wears] *vt* **1 :** to bear or have upon the person ⟨*wore* a coat⟩ ⟨~ a riding habit⟩ **:** to have attached to the body or part of it or to the clothing ⟨*wore* a ring on her left hand⟩ ⟨~ a necklace⟩ ⟨*wore* a badge on his lapel⟩ ⟨*wore* a red ribbon in her hair⟩ **2 a :** to use habitually for clothing or adornment ⟨~s a toupee⟩ ⟨~s size eleven shoes⟩ ⟨still ~*ing* black for her husband⟩ **b :** to carry on or as if on the person ⟨~ a sword⟩ ⟨~ a cane⟩ ⟨~s the stamp of suffering on his face⟩ ⟨these sixty years he ~s lightly —I.A.Gordon⟩ **3 a :** to hold the rank or dignity or position signified by (an ornament) ⟨~ the royal crown⟩ ⟨~ the palm⟩ ⟨born to ~ the purple⟩ **b :** to have or show an appearance of ⟨*wore* a happy smile⟩ ⟨his face *wore* its usual solemn expression⟩ ⟨if malice and vanity ~ the coat of philanthropy —R.W.Emerson⟩ **c :** to show or fly (a flag or colors) on a ship **4 a :** to cause to deteriorate by use ⟨gave away suits she had scarcely *worn*⟩ **b :** to impair or diminish by use or attrition **:** consume or waste gradually ⟨age had *worn* and sharpened the fine features —Virginia Woolf⟩ — used often with *away* ⟨letters on the stone had been *worn* away by weathering⟩ or *down* ⟨mountains *worn* down to low hills⟩ or *off* ⟨silver plating *worn* off here and there⟩ or *through* ⟨coat *worn* through at the elbows⟩ **5 :** to cause or produce gradually by friction or attrition ⟨~ a channel in the rock⟩ ⟨~ a hole in the rug⟩ **6 :** to exhaust or lessen the strength of **:** WEARY, FATIGUE ⟨the strain of the war had been ~*ing* them —Lucien Price⟩ **7** *archaic* **:** to let (time) go by **:** PASS, SPEND **8 :** to cause (a ship) to go about by putting the helm up instead of down as in tacking so that the vessel's stern is presented to the wind ~ *vi* **1 a :** to endure use **:** last under use or the passage of time ⟨this coat material should ~ for years⟩ **b :** to retain quality or vitality ⟨attempt to find out how certain orchestral works are . . . ~*ing* —Deems Taylor⟩ **2 :** to diminish or decay through use ⟨heels of his boots were ~*ing* unevenly⟩ **:** suffer damage or extinction by use or by passage of time **:** PASS — used usu. with *away, off, on, out* ⟨his patience began to ~ away⟩ ⟨waiting for the effect of the drug to ~ off⟩ ⟨it grew colder as the day *wore* on⟩ **3 :** to grow or become by or as if by attrition or use — used with some adjectives ⟨his stock of money began to ~ very low —Sir Walter Scott⟩ ⟨felt his temper ~*ing* thin and ready to snap⟩ ⟨hair ~*ing* thin on top⟩ **4** *Scot* **:** PROCEED, PROGRESS **5** *of a ship* **:** to go about by turning the stern to the wind — compare TACK 1b — **wear blue** *of a car or train* **:** to display a blue flag or blue light to indicate the undergoing of inspection or repair **:** be delayed by car trouble — **wear green** *of a train* **:** to display green flags to indicate that another section of the same train follows — **wear on :** IRRITATE, RUB, FRAY ⟨silence and darkness of the grove were ~*ing on* him, eroding his courage —Norman Mailer⟩ — **wear stripes** [fr. the traditional striped uniform worn by prisoners] **:** to serve in prison — **wear the trousers** *or* **wear the pants :** to have the controlling authority in a household — **wear the willow :** to be in mourning

²wear \"\ *n* -s [ME *were,* fr. *weren* to wear] **1 :** the act of wearing or state of being worn **:** USE ⟨clothes for everyday ~⟩ ⟨a 5-year-old ox will have all his teeth in *wear* —*Animal Management*⟩ ⟨discarded after years of hard ~⟩ **2 a :** clothing or an article of clothing usu. of a particular kind or fashionable style; *esp* **:** clothing worn for a special occasion or popular during a specific period ⟨examples of beautiful 16th century glove ~⟩ ⟨motley's the only ~ —Shak.⟩ — often used in combination ⟨fashions in neck*wear*⟩ ⟨fabric expressly for travel*wear* —*Women's Wear Daily*⟩ **b :** FASHION, VOGUE ⟨realizes that the flowers from his garden may not always be the ~ —H.S.Canby⟩ **3 :** wearing quality **:** durability under use ⟨shown 2 to 2½ times the ~ life of comparable gauges . . . of all silk hose —W.E.Shinn⟩ **4 :** the result of wearing or use **:** diminution or impairment due to use ⟨better cornering and reduced tire ~ on turns —*Annual Report General Motors Corp.*⟩ ⟨*wear*-resistant surface⟩

³wear \'wi(ə)r\ *vt* -ED/-ING/-S [ME *weren* to defend, protect, fr. OE *werian* — more at WEIR] *Scot & dial Eng* **:** to collect and drive (as sheep) into an enclosure

wear·abil·i·ty \ˌwa(a)rəˈbiləd·ē, ˌwer-\ *n* [¹*wearable* + *-ity*] **:** capacity or suitability for wear; *esp* **:** durability under wear

¹wear·able \'wa(a)rəbəl, 'wer-\ *adj* [¹*wear* + *-able*] **:** capable of being worn **:** suitable to be worn ⟨~ hearing aid⟩

²wearable \"\ *n* -s **:** GARMENT — used usu. in pl. ⟨soft dressmaker lines are found in all feminine ~s these days —*Westinghouse Mag.*⟩ ⟨summer ~s⟩

wear and tear *n* **:** the loss or injury to which something is subjected by or in the course of use; *esp* **:** normal depreciation

wear down *vt* **:** to weary and overcome by persistent resistance

or pressure ⟨monitoring ten panels of instruments . . . for hours at a stretch can *wear* a man *down* —Richard Thruelsen⟩
wear·er \'wa(ə)r(ə)r\ *n* -s [ME *werer,* fr. *weren* to wear + *-er*] **:** one that wears or carries something as a covering or accessory of the body ⟨~ of a cloak⟩ ⟨the crown and its ~⟩
wea·ri·able \'wirēəbəl, 'wēr-\ *adj* **:** capable of being wearied **:** easily wearied — **wea·ri·a·ble·ness** *n* -ES
wearied *adj* [fr. past part. of ³*weary*] **:** FATIGUED, EXHAUSTED ⟨ills of mind . . . which oppress the ~ brain of the thinker —J.W.Krutch⟩ — **wea·ried·ly** *adv* — **wea·ried·ness** *n* -ES
wearier *comparative of* WEARY
wearies *pres 3d sing of* WEARY, *pl of* WEARY
weariest *superlative of* WEARY
wea·ri·ful \'wirēfəl, 'wēr-, -rif-\ *adj* [ME *weriful,* fr. *werien* to weary + *-ful*] **1 :** causing weariness **:** wearying to the patience or endurance **:** TEDIOUS, VEXATIOUS ⟨~ delay —John Buchan⟩ **2 :** full of weariness **:** WEARIED — **wea·ri·ful·ly** \-f(ə)lē\ *adv* — **wea·ri·ful·ness** *n* -ES
wea·ri·less \-rēləs, -ril-\ *adj* [ME *weriles,* fr. *werien* to weary + *-les* -less] **:** TIRELESS, UNWEARIABLE — **wea·ri·less·ly** *adv*
wea·ri·ly \-rəlē, -li\ *adv* **:** in a weary manner ⟨~ threw myself on the bed in my clothes —Mary W. Shelley⟩
wear-in \'=,=\ *n* -s **:** BREAK-IN 1, 3
wea·ri·ness \'wirēnəs, 'wēr-, -rin-\ *n* -ES [ME *werinesse,* fr. OE *wērignes,* fr. *wērig* weary + *-nes* -ness] **1 :** the quality or state of being weary **:** FATIGUE, TIREDNESS ⟨ready to drop from ~⟩ **2 :** tedium or ennui resulting from monotony or satiation ⟨when she turned into the house, she knew to ~ what she should find awaiting her —Ellen Glasgow⟩
¹**wearing** *n* -s [ME *wering,* fr. gerund of *weren* to wear] *obs* **:** CLOTHES, GARMENTS ⟨give me my nightly ~, and adieu —Shak.⟩
²**wearing** *adj* [ME *wering,* fr. gerund of *weren* to wear] **:** intended for wearing on the person ⟨~ apparel⟩
³**wearing** *adj* [fr. pres. part. of ¹*wear*] **1 :** causing or inflicting wear **:** FATIGUING, EXHAUSTING ⟨~ journey⟩ **2 :** subjected to wear ⟨~ surface of a tooth⟩
wearing course *n* **:** the surface layer of a pavement that takes the wear of traffic
wear·ing·ly *adv* **:** in a wearing manner **:** FATIGUINGLY
wear iron *or* **wear plate** *n* [²*wear*] **:** an iron plate to take wear: as **a :** CRAMP IRON **b** *Brit* **:** TIE PLATE 3
wear·ish \'wirish\ *adj* [ME *werische*] **1** *dial* **a :** TASTELESS, INSIPID **b :** SICKLY, WITHERED **c :** SQUEAMISH **2** *dial* **:** being raw and cold ⟨~ mist⟩
wea·ri·some \'wirēsəm, 'wēr-, -ris-\ *adj* [ME *werisom,* fr. *werien* to weary + *-som* -some] **:** causing weariness **:** TIRESOME, TEDIOUS ⟨other people's dreams are so dreadfully ~ —Walter de la Mare⟩ ⟨ski tows . . . eliminating ~ climbing to the top of the trails —*Amer. Guide Series: N.H.*⟩ — **wea·ri·some·ly** *adv* — **wea·ri·some·ness** *n* -ES
wear off *vi* **:** to diminish gradually in effect **:** pass away ⟨it's late and the liquor begins to *wear off* —John Steinbeck⟩ ⟨they must be unhappy when the novelty *wears off* —Glenway Wescott⟩
wear out *vb* [ME *weren out,* fr. *weren* to wear + *out*] *vt* **1 :** to make useless esp. by long or hard usage ⟨*wore out* four pairs of gloves shaking 6000 hands —Jane Muskie⟩ **2 :** HARASS, TIRE, EXHAUST ⟨economic sections are so detailed . . . that they *wear out* the reader —R.V.Harlow⟩ ⟨hope you're not going to *wear* yourself *out* waiting on him —Ellen Glasgow⟩ **3 :** ERASE, EFFACE **4 :** to endure through **:** OUTLAST ⟨*wear out* a storm⟩ **5 :** to consume (as time) tediously ⟨*wear out* idle days⟩ **6** *dial* **:** BEAT, WHIP ⟨things mama used to say she'd *wear* us *out* for saying —Lillian Smith⟩ ~ *vi* **:** to become useless from long or excessive wear or use ⟨when a field is *wearing out,* the corn growing shorter and bearing fewer ears —Merran McCulloch⟩
wear-out \'=,=\ *n* -s [*wear out*] **:** depreciation through wear ⟨the rapidity of *wear-out* of a piece of machinery⟩
wearproof \'=;=\ *adj* [²*wear* + *proof*] **:** resistant to wear ⟨~ tool⟩
wears *pl of* WEAR, *pres 3d sing of* WEAR
¹**wea·ry** \'wirē, 'wēr-, -ri\ *adj* -ER/-EST [ME *wery,* fr. OE *wērig;* akin to OS *wōrig* weary, OHG *wuorag* intoxicated, OE *wōrian* to wander, totter, ON *ōrar* (pl.) fits of madness, Gk *hōrakian* to faint] **1 a :** having the strength much impaired by toil or exertion **:** worn out in respect to strength, endurance, vigor ⟨followed by troops of ~, dirty children —Irving Bacheller⟩ ⟨~ wings that rise and fall all day long —Edna S. V. Millay⟩ **b :** having lost freshness or virtue or usefulness ⟨if another leftover is some ~ noodles —R.P.Smith⟩ ⟨programs on television have degenerated into ~, predictable repetitions of each other —Edwin O'Connor⟩ **2 :** expressing or characteristic of weariness ⟨~, disillusioned note of futility in our life —J.C. Powys⟩ ⟨a ~ sound that was not a sigh nor a groan —Charles Dickens⟩ **3 :** having one's patience, tolerance, or pleasure exhausted **:** impatient of the continuance or recurrence of something — used with *of* ⟨councils grew ~ of reiterating a demand which could not be enforced —R.W.Southern⟩ ⟨~ to death of this eight years profitless war —Harold Nicolson⟩ **4 :** exhausted by suffering or sorrow **:** mentally or spiritually fatigued **:** SAD ⟨effete, ~, burnt-out revolutionists —H.F. Mooney⟩ ⟨a world grown ~ with fear —Robert Payne⟩ **5 :** causing weariness of body or spirit ⟨ahead of them lay many ~ miles of desert sand —G.F.Hudson⟩ **:** TIRESOME, TEDIOUS ⟨bacon, beans, and bread make a ~ meal three times a day —Allan Seager⟩ **6** *Scot & dial Eng* **a :** SICKLY, PUNY, WEAK **b :** WRETCHED, GRIEVOUS, UNFORTUNATE, DISASTROUS
²**weary** \"\ *adv* -ER/-EST **:** WEARILY, WEARYINGLY
³**weary** \"\ *vb* -ED/-ING/-ES [ME *werien,* fr. OE *wērigian, wērgian,* fr. *wērig* weary] *vi* **1 :** to become weary **:** TIRE ⟨tendency to ~ of burdens —Dean Acheson⟩ **2 :** to become exhausted in patience, tolerance, or liking ⟨telling stories when they *wearied* of cards and games —A.B.Paterson⟩ ⟨people ~ of old lies —Stuart Chase⟩ **3 :** to wait wearily **:** long or pine in expectation ⟨paced up and down . . . ~*ing* for the boat to get around —William Black⟩ ⟨~*ing* in spiritual wastes of sand and thorns —C.E.Montague⟩ **4 :** to bring on weariness **:** become monotonous or boring **:** PALL ~ *vt* **1 :** to reduce or exhaust the physical strength or endurance of **:** FATIGUE ⟨think out a solution without ~*ing* the body by needless movement —James Hewitt⟩ **2 :** to make mentally or spiritually weary **:** exhaust the patience or tolerance of ⟨exceeds and *wearies* credibility —John Mason Brown⟩ ⟨anxieties that lined his forehead and *wearied* his mind —Lennox Robinson⟩ — often used with *out* ⟨paternal affection was not yet *wearied* out —T.B.Macaulay⟩
syn see TIRE
⁴**weary** \'wiri\ *n* -ES [prob. fr. ¹*wary*] *Scot* **:** CURSE, PLAGUE — used in mild imprecation ⟨oh, ~ on the wars —Sir Walter Scott⟩
wearying *adj* [fr. pres. part. of ³*weary*] **:** that wearies ⟨find the life of the cafes more congenial than the ~ tensions of the casino —A.G.N.Flew⟩ — **wea·ry·ing·ly** *adv*
weary out *vt* **:** to pass or spend (time) in monotony, tedium, or longing ⟨*wearied out* the lonely days⟩
weary willie *n, usu cap both Ws* [¹*weary* + *Willie,* nickname for *William*] **:** one who avoids or dislikes work ⟨a general truancy by the *Weary Willies,* leaving the work-gluttons to do their share and do it better —*Manchester Guardian Weekly*⟩; *specif* **:** TRAMP ⟨the railroad had helped to create the *Weary Willie* —S.H.Holbrook⟩
weas *pl of* WEA
wea·sand *or* **wea·zand** *also* **we·sand** \'wēz°nd, 'wiz°n(d)\ *n* -s [ME *wesand,* fr. (assumed) OE *wǣsend* gullet; akin to OE *wāsend* gullet, OFris *wāsande* windpipe, OHG *weisunt* windpipe, gullet] **1 a** *archaic* **:** GULLET, ESOPHAGUS **b :** the musculature associated with the gullet and the windpipe **:** THROAT ⟨cut his ~ with thy knife —Shak.⟩ **2** *archaic* **:** WINDPIPE, TRACHEA
wease-allan \wē'zalən\ *dial var of* WEESE-ALLAN
¹**wea·sel** \'wēzəl\ *n, pl* **weasels** *also* **weasel** [ME *wesele,* fr. OE *weosule, wesle;* akin to OHG *wisula* weasel, OSw *visla,* L *virus* slimy liquid, poison, stench, and prob. to Skt *visra* musty, smelling of raw meat — more at VIRUS] **1 a :** any of various small slender-bodied carnivorous mammals (genus *Mustela*) that are related to the minks and polecats, are very active, bold, and bloodthirsty, kill many small birds and mammals and esp. great numbers of mice, rats, and other vermin, and have a mostly reddish brown coat with white or yellowish underparts which in the northern forms turns white in winter and a black-tipped tail — see BONAPARTE'S WEASEL, ERMINE, LEAST WEASEL, LONG-TAILED WEASEL, YELLOW WEASEL **b :** any of various mammals felt to resemble the true weasels in appearance or habits — usu. used in combination **c :** the fur or pelt of any of these animals **2** *usu cap* **:** a South Carolinian — used as a nickname **3 :** a person like a weasel in furtiveness, elusiveness, cunning, treachery **:** SNEAK **4 :** WEASEL WORD **5 :** a light personnel and cargo carrier self-propelled on wide rubber-padded semiflexible tracks and built either as a land vehicle capable of traveling over snow or ice or sand or as an amphibious vehicle with baffle plates on the tracks capable also of traversing swamps and rivers
²**weasel** \"\ *vi* **weaseled; weaseled; weaseling** \-z(ə)liŋ\ **weasels** [*weasel word*] **1 :** to use weasel words **:** EQUIVOCATE ⟨uneasy and evasive liar who ~*ed* and retreated when his credibility was questioned —*New Republic*⟩ **2 :** to escape from or evade a situation or obligation — often used with *out* ⟨the way men will ~ out of their missteps —Jean Stafford⟩
weasel cat *n* **:** LINSANG
weasel coot *or* **weasel duck** *n* **:** a female or young male of the smew
weasel-faced \'==,=\ *adj* **:** having a thin sharp face like that of a weasel
weasel family *n* **:** MUSTELIDAE
weaselfish \'==,=\ *n* **:** ROCKLING 1
weasel-headed armadillo \'==,==-\ *n* **:** PELUDO
weasel lemur *n* **:** a small active lemur (*Lepilemur mustelinus*) that is reddish brown above, grayish brown below, and white on the throat — called also *nattock*
weasellike \'==,=\ *adj* **:** resembling a weasel in form or behavior ⟨~ head⟩ ⟨~ agility⟩
wea·sel·ly \'wēz(ə)lē\ *adj* [¹*weasel* + *-ly*] **:** resembling or suggesting a weasel esp. in appearance ⟨weak-chinned ~ face⟩
weaselsnout \'==,=\ *n* [¹*weasel* + *snout*] **:** a yellow-flowered European dead nettle (*Lamium luteum*)
weasel spider *n* **:** an arachnid of the order Solpugida
weasel word *n* [¹*weasel* + *word;* fr. the weasel's reputed habit of sucking the contents out of an egg white leaving the shell superficially intact] **:** a word that destroys the force of a statement by equivocal qualification ⟨I have couched my comments . . . in the most innocuous of *weasel words* —Richard Joseph⟩ **:** a word used in order to evade or retreat from a direct or forthright statement or position ⟨*weasel words* are the adman's way of crossing his finger behind his back when he makes a somewhat elastic statement —Robert Littell⟩
weasel-worded \'==;wərdəd\ *adj* [*weasel word* + *-ed*] **:** containing weasel words **:** phrased with deliberate ambiguity **:** lacking forthrightness
wea·ser \'wēzə(r)\ *also* **weaser sheldrake** *n* -s [origin unknown] **:** the American merganser
wea·son \'wēz°n\ *Scot var of* WEASAND
¹**weath·er** \'weth̲ə(r)\ *n* -s [ME *weder,* fr. OE; akin to OHG *wetar* weather, ON *vethr,* OSlav *vetrŭ* wind, and perh. to Skt *vāta* wind — more at WIND] **1 :** state of the atmosphere at a definite time and place with respect to heat or cold, wetness or dryness, calm or storm, clearness or cloudiness **:** meteorological condition **2 a :** a particular kind of atmospheric state **:** one of the possible or known states of the atmosphere — used chiefly in pl. ⟨good hat for all ~*s*⟩ ⟨in most ~*s* the sheep and cattle . . . could be driven to the capital —G.M.Trevelyan⟩ **b :** a condition or vicissitude of life or fortune ⟨changes in our own country's moral ~ —E.R.May⟩ ⟨dark ~ of fatality and grim resolution —Thomas Wolfe⟩ **3 :** disagreeable atmospheric conditions: as **a :** RAIN, STORM ⟨we are expecting some ~⟩ ⟨because of tide and brewing ~ —P.A.Zahl⟩ **b** *obs* **:** a shower of rain or snow **c** *obs* **:** SKY **d :** cold air and dampness ⟨clothing to keep out the ~⟩ **4 a :** the direction from which the wind is blowing **:** WINDWARD **b :** the windward side **5 :** the angle that the sail of a windmill makes with its plane of revolution **6** [³*weather*] **:** WEATHERING **7** [²*weather*] **:** the portion of siding or shingles that is exposed rather than hidden by overlap ⟨a ~ of four inches⟩ — **under the weather 1 :** somewhat ill **2 :** somewhat drunk
²**weather** \"\ *adj* **:** being toward the direction from which the wind blows **:** WINDWARD ⟨~ beam⟩ ⟨~ braces⟩ — opposed to *lee*
³**weather** \"\ *vb* **weathered; weathered; weathering** \-th̲(ə)riŋ\ **weathers** [ME *wederen, wetheren,* fr. *weder* weather] *vt* **1 :** to expose to the open air **:** subject to the action of the elements **2 a :** to sail or pass to the windward of ⟨~ a cape⟩ **b :** to make headway against (a storm or hard blow) **3 :** to bear up against and come safely through (a storm or a threatening or dangerous time) ⟨now we have ~*ed* another war —*Lancet*⟩ **4 a :** to slope (as a roof) so as to shed water **b :** to set (the sails of a windmill) so they will be adjusted to the wind **5 :** to tether (a hawk) unhooded in the open air **6 :** to make unable to move because of bad weather — used usu. with *in* ⟨wouldn't want to get ~*ed* in among those high passes —F.V.W.Mason⟩ ~ *vi* **1 :** to undergo or endure the action of the elements **:** wear away, disintegrate, discolor, or deteriorate under atmospheric influences ⟨shingles had ~*ed* to a silvery gray⟩ — often used with *away* ⟨where the softer rock has ~*ed* away into soil⟩ **2 :** to last under use or exposure or passage of time ⟨some paints ~ better than others⟩ **3** *dial* **:** STORM — **weather along :** to make headway in adverse weather — **weather on** *or* **weather upon :** to gain the advantage of by sailing to windward of
weath·er·abil·i·ty \,weth̲ərə'bilədē\ *n* [³*weather* + *-ability*] **:** capability of withstanding weather ⟨~ of a plastic⟩
weather-beaten \'==,==\ *also* **weather-beat** \'==,=\ *adj* [¹*weather*] **1 :** beaten by severe weather **:** worn or damaged by exposure to the weather **2 :** toughened, tanned, or bronzed by the weather ⟨*weather-beaten* face⟩
¹**weatherboard** \'==,=\ *n* **1 :** CLAPBOARD, SIDING **2 :** the weather side of a ship
²**weatherboard** \"\ *vt* **:** to nail boards upon (a roof or wall) so as to lap one over another to exclude and shed rain
weatherboard·ing \" +iŋ\ *n* [¹*weatherboard* + *-ing*] **:** CLAPBOARDS, SIDING
weather-bound \'==,=\ *adj* **:** kept in port or at anchor or from travel or sport by bad weather — called also *weather-fast*
weather bow *n* [²*weather*] **:** the side of the bow toward the wind
weather box *n* [¹*weather*] **:** WEATHER HOUSE
weather breeder *n* **:** a fine day often of unusual calmness and clearness that precedes stormy weather
weather bureau *n* **:** an organization engaged in the collection of weather reports as a basis for weather predictions, storm warnings, and the compiling of statistical records
weather-burned \'==,=\ *adj* [¹*weather* + *burned,* past part. of *burn*] **:** browned by sun and wind
weather cast *n* **:** a weather forecast
weather caster *n* [*weather cast* + *-er*] **:** a weather forecaster
weather chart *n* **:** WEATHER MAP
weather cloth *n* **:** a tarpaulin used to shield men on watch on the deck or bridge of a ship from rain or wind
¹**weathercock** \'==,=\ *n* [ME *wedercoc,* fr. *weder* weather + *cok, coc* cock] **1 a :** a vane often in the figure of a cock mounted so as to turn freely with the wind and show its direction **b :** a person or thing that changes readily or often **:** one who veers with every change of current opinion ⟨~*s* before the prevailing winds of doctrine —*Scribner's*⟩ **2 :** JEWELWEED a

weathercock 1a

²**weathercock** \"\ *vt* **1 :** to supply with a weathercock ⟨~ a steeple⟩ **2 :** to serve as a weathercock for ⟨~ the forces of revolution⟩ ~ *vi* **:** to behave like a weathercock; *specif, of an airplane* **:** to turn into the wind
weather contact *n* **:** an electrical contact due to poor insulation during wet weather
weather cross *n* **:** a leakage between wires due to wet weather
weather cycle *n* **:** periodic recurrence of some feature of the weather
weather deck *n* **:** a deck having no overhead protection from the weather — see DECK illustration
weather door *n* **1 :** an opening in a louver **2 :** TRAPDOOR 2 **3 :** STORM DOOR
weathered *adj* [fr. past part. of ³*weather*] **1 :** seasoned by exposure to the weather **2 a :** altered in color, texture, composition, or form by exposure to the weather ⟨~ rock⟩ **b** *of woodwork* **:** artificially given the appearance caused by weathering **3 :** made sloping so as to throw off water ⟨~ windowsill⟩ — see JOINT illustration
weathered oak *n* **1 :** FUMED OAK **2 :** LEAFMOLD
weath·er·er \'weth̲(ə)rə(r)\ *n* -s **:** one that weathers
weather eye *n* **1 :** an eye quick to observe coming changes in the weather ⟨the old-timer with his *weather eye* proves to be nearer the mark than we are with all our paraphernalia —G.H. T. Kimble⟩ **2 :** constant and shrewd watchfulness and alertness ⟨the chief in order to preserve his dynasty had always to keep a *weather eye* on these rising families —Ralph Linton⟩
weather-fast \'==,=\ *adj* **:** WEATHER-BOUND
weatherfish \'==,=\ *n* **:** any of several European and Asiatic loaches (genus *Misgurnus*) that burrow in mud at the bottom of streams and ponds but are supposed to become restless and swim about during thunderstorms — compare DOJO
weather flag *n* **:** a flag used to indicate the weather expected in from 12 to 36 hours
weather gall *n* **:** SUN DOG
weather gauge *n* [²*weather*] **1 :** the position of a sailing ship to the windward of another that gives an advantage in maneuvering **2 :** a superior position **:** ADVANTAGE ⟨got the *weather gauge* on him now⟩
weather-gauge \'==,=\ *vt* [*weather gauge*] **:** to keep the weather gauge of
weathergaw \'==,=\ *Scot var of* WEATHER GALL
weatherglass \'==,=\ *n* [¹*weather*] **1** *obs* **:** THERMOMETER **2 :** a simple instrument for showing changes in atmospheric pressure by the changing level of liquid in a spout connected with a closed reservoir; *broadly* **:** BAROMETER
weathergleam \'==,=\ *n, chiefly Scot* **:** clear or light sky near the horizon
weather-going tide \'==,==-\ *n* [²*weather*] **:** a tide running against the wind
weatherhead \'==,=\ *n* [¹*weather*] *dial Eng* **:** SECONDARY RAINBOW
weath·er·headed \'weth̲ə(r),-\ *adj* [*weather-* (prob. alter. of ¹*wether*) + *headed*] *archaic* **:** FOOLISH
weather helm *n* [²*weather*] **1 :** a tendency of a sailing vessel to come up into the wind ⟨catboats . . . generally carry very heavy *weather helms* —H.A.Calahan⟩ **2 :** the condition of the helm when put or held slightly toward the weather side

weatherglass 2

weather house *n* [¹*weather*] **:** a toy house that indicates changes in atmospheric humidity by the appearance or retirement of toy images moved by varying tension of a gut string — called also *weather box*
weatherier *comparative of* WEATHERY
weatheriest *superlative of* WEATHERY
weathering *n* -s [fr. gerund of ³*weather*] **1 :** exposure of a hawk to the weather **2 :** the action of the elements in altering the color, texture, composition, or form of exposed objects; *specif* **:** the physical disintegration and chemical decomposition of earth materials at or near the earth's surface **3 :** slope given to a surface (as of a sill) to throw off water
weather joint *n* **:** a masonry joint in which the mortar is recessed at the top with the trowel while the mortar is still green
weath·er·li·ness \'weth̲ə(r)lēnəs, -lin-\ *n* -ES **:** the quality of being weatherly
weath·er·ly *adj* [¹*weather* + *-ly*] **:** able to sail close to the wind with little leeway ⟨do not know how ~ the ship will be . . . how well she will go to windward —Alan Villiers⟩
weathermaker \'==,==\ *n* **:** a weather prophet
weatherman \'==,=\ *n, pl* **weathermen :** one who gives out reports and forecasts of the weather **:** METEOROLOGIST
weather map *n* **:** a synoptic chart showing the principal meteorological elements (as temperature, pressure, precipitation, wind direction and speed, air masses, fronts) at a given hour and over an extended region — called also *weather chart*
weather molding *n* **1 :** DRIP 4 **2 :** ASTRAGAL 1a
weath·er·most \'weth̲ə(r),mōst\ *adj* [²*weather* + *-most*] **:** farthest to windward
weather observer *n* [¹*weather*] **:** one whose duty is the systematic observation, measurement, and reporting of meteorological conditions
weath·er·ol·o·gy \,weth̲ə'räləjē\ *n* -ES [¹*weather* + *-o-* + *-logy*] **:** METEOROLOGY
Weath·er-Om·e·ter \-'ämədə(r)\ *trademark* — used for a machine for testing the ability of paints and coatings to withstand weather
weather out *vi* [³*weather*] **:** to become exposed as surrounding softer rock disintegrates ⟨strata were pushed into folds that have now *weathered out* into long east-west ridges —*Amer. Guide Series: Ark.*⟩
weather plant *n* [¹*weather*] **:** a plant whose leaves are sensitive to atmospheric influences and are thus supposed to indicate weather changes; *specif* **:** INDIAN LICORICE
¹**weatherproof** \'==;=\ *adj* **:** able to withstand exposure to weather without damage or loss of function ⟨~ coat⟩ ⟨~ electric wiring⟩ — **weath·er·proof·ness** *n*
²**weatherproof** \"\ *vt* **:** to make weatherproof ⟨~ a cabin⟩
weather report *n* **:** a systematic statement of the existing and usu. the predicted meteorological conditions over a particular area
weathers *pl of* WEATHER, *pres 3d sing of* WEATHER
weather sheet *n* [²*weather*] **:** a rope that extends the windward corner of a square sail
weather ship *n* [¹*weather*] **:** a ship that goes to sea specifically to obtain weather observations for use by meteorologists
weather shore *n* [²*weather*] **:** a shore lying to the windward ⟨ships hug a *weather shore* to get a lee, but they give a lee shore a wide berth —Gavin Douglas⟩
weather side *n* **:** the side (as of a ship) to windward **:** the side exposed to weather
weather signal *n* [¹*weather*] **:** a visual signal (as a flag or lights) giving information about predicted temperature, rain or snow, or wind direction — compare STORM SIGNAL
weather slating *n* **:** slate used on side walls of a building
weather stain *n* **:** discoloration caused by exposure to the weather ⟨walls with the *weather stains* of centuries⟩
weather-stained \'==,=\ *adj* [¹*weather* + *stained*] **:** discolored by exposure to the weather ⟨*weather-stained* statue⟩
weather station *n* **:** a station for taking, recording, and reporting meteorological observations
weather strip *also* **weather stripping** *n* **:** a strip of material to cover the joint of a door or window and the sill, casing, or threshold so as to exclude rain, snow, and cold air
weather-strip \'==,=\ *vt* [*weather strip*] **:** to apply weather strip to
weather table *n* **:** WATER TABLE 1
weather tide *n* [²*weather*] **:** a tide setting against the wind
weathertight \'==;=\ *adj* [¹*weather* + *tight*] **:** proof against wind and rain ⟨~ storage bin⟩ — **weath·er·tight·ness** *n*
weather tile *n* **:** any of a series of tiles covering a wall and overlapped like shingles
weather vane *n* **:** VANE 1a
weath·er·ward \'weth̲ə(r)wə(r)d\ *adv* [¹*weather* + *-ward*] **:** toward the wind or the weather side ⟨the ~ wall of every building —Tom Hopkinson⟩
weather wheel *n* [²*weather*] **:** the position of responsibility at the weather side of the helm of a ship when two or more helmsmen are stationed at the wheel — compare LEE WHEEL
weather-wise \'==,=\ *adj* [ME *wederwise,* fr. *weder* weather + *wise*] **1 :** skillful in forecasting the changes of the weather **2 :** skillful in forecasting changes in opinion or feeling ⟨a *weather-wise* politician⟩
weatherworn \'==,=\ *adj* **:** worn by exposure to the weather ⟨white slab, on which the letters were faint and ~ —Ruth Suckow⟩
weath·ery \'weth̲(ə)rē\ *adj* -ER/-EST [¹*weather* + *-y*] **1 :** changeable like the weather **2 :** impaired in quality by unseasonable rains ⟨~ tea⟩

weat·ings \ˈwētiŋz\ *n pl* [prob. fr. *wheat* + *-ing*] *Brit* : MIDDLINGS 1b

¹weave \ˈwēv\ *vb* **wove** \ˈwōv\ *or* **weaved; wo·ven** \ˈwōvən\ *or* **weaved; weaving; weaves** [ME *weven,* fr. OE *wefan;* akin to OHG *weban* to weave, ON *vefa,* Gk *hyphos* web, *hyphainein* to weave, Skt *ubhnāti* he laces up, covers over, *ūrṇavābhi* spider] *vt* **1 a :** to form (cloth) by interlacing strands (as of yarn); *specif* **:** to make (cloth) on a loom by interlacing warp and filling threads **b :** to interlace (as threads) into a cloth ⟨~ wool into tweeds⟩ **c :** to join, mend, or embroider (woven or knitted fabric) with stitches that match or imitate those of the article **d :** to make (as a basket or wreath) by intertwining rushes, twigs, or flowers ⟨~ a chair seat⟩ ⟨~ a garland⟩ ⟨the girls . . . ~ crowns of snowdrops, violets, and other flowers —J.G.Frazer⟩ **2 :** SPIN — used chiefly of spiders and some insects **3 :** to twist together or interlace esp. to form a texture, fabric, or design **:** ENTWINE ⟨~ osiers into baskets⟩ ⟨~ the holly round the Christmas hearth —Alfred Tennyson⟩ **4 a :** to produce by elaborately combining available materials or elements **:** CONTRIVE ⟨~ a plot⟩ ⟨enchantments that you *wove* —G.B.Shaw⟩ — often used with *about* or *around* ⟨~ a new romance about the fallen hopes —V.L.Parrington⟩ ⟨~ around it a story of violence and intrigue —John Brooks⟩ **b :** to bring together and interrelate so as to form a coherent whole **:** JOIN, UNITE — usu. used with *into* or *together* ⟨had *woven* episodes from many sources into a single narrative⟩ ⟨richly ~s together varied aspects of experience —*New Republic*⟩ **c :** to introduce as an appropriate element **:** work in — usu. used with *in* or *into* ⟨*weaving* in an exciting subplot —Chad Walsh⟩ ⟨*wove* into their songs the theme of jubilee —W.F.Hambly⟩ **5** *Scot* **:** KNIT **6 :** to direct (as the body) in a winding or zigzag course esp. to avoid obstacles ⟨going about the crowd and *weaving* her person in and out —Thomas DeQuincey⟩ ~ *vi* **1 :** to work at weaving **:** make cloth **2** *of an insect* **:** to spin a web or cocoon **3 :** to move in a devious, winding, or zigzag course turning or twisting in and out esp. to avoid obstacles ⟨~s down the ice with the puck⟩ ⟨*weaved* in and out through the traffic⟩ ⟨*weaving* through opposing tacklers for a 20-yard gain⟩ ⟨among them ran the children, playing, *weaving* in and out —Irwin Shaw⟩ **4 a :** to move across and back repeatedly **:** SHUTTLE ⟨can ~ back and forth between periods of time at his will —Bernard DeVoto⟩ **b :** to spread a weld by moving the electrode back and forth across the line of travel in arc welding

²weave \ˈ"\ *n* -s **1 :** something woven; *esp* **:** woven cloth **:** FABRIC **2 :** any of the patterns or methods for interlacing the threads of woven fabrics — see PLAIN WEAVE, SATIN WEAVE, TWILL WEAVE **3 :** a slow lateral motion of the projected image on a motion-picture screen

³weave \ˈ"\ *vb* -ED/-ING/-S [ME *weven* to move to and fro, wave, signal; akin to ON *veifa* to wave — more at WIFE] *vt, obs* **:** to signal to (a ship or its passengers) by waving ~ *vi* **1 a :** to move unsteadily or waveringly from side to side **:** SWAY ⟨a tree *weaving* before it falls⟩ ⟨his knees buckle slightly as he ~s on his feet —Wayne Hughes⟩ ⟨was *weaving* and had trouble finding the keyhole —Polly Adler⟩ ⟨his eyes close, his head ~s, and the music . . . starts —*Time*⟩ **b** (1) **:** to move from side to side incessantly and restlessly **:** ROCK, OSCILLATE ⟨the preacher . . . *weaving* first to one side of the platform and then the other —Mark Twain⟩ (2) *of a horse* **:** to sway and shift weight nervously — compare WEAVING ⟨the horse that bucks . . . ~s —*Amer. Guide Series: Nev.*⟩ **c :** to lurch or stagger from side to side while moving forward **:** REEL, CAREEN ⟨*weaving* down the sidewalk was a trio of drunken sailors —*Boston Herald*⟩ **2 :** to work one's way toward or away from a boxing opponent while eluding his blows with swaying, turning, and slipping movements of the body ⟨a middleweight . . . fast, shifty, hard-hitting, *weaving* in with short, savage punches —Gene Tunney⟩

¹weav·er \-və(r)\ *n* -s [ME *wever,* fr. *weven* to weave + *-er*] **1 :** one that works at weaving: as **a :** one that weaves textiles on hand or automatic looms **b :** one that mends garments by reweaving **c :** one that weaves baskets (as of rattan or cane) **d :** INTERLACER 2 **2 :** a reed or splint that is woven (as in basketry) over and under the staves **3 :** WEAVERBIRD

²weaver *var of* WEEVER

weaverbird \ˈ≈,≈\ *n* **:** any of numerous Asiatic, East Indian, and African birds of the family Ploceidae that resemble finches in general appearance but have ten instead of nine primaries and that vary widely in habits and coloration but are mostly characterized by their construction of elaborate nests of interlaced grass and other vegetation which are chiefly either pensile with an entrance at the bottom or on the side or large, dome-shaped, and inhabited by many pairs of birds — see AVADAVAT, JAVA SPARROW, SOCIABLE WEAVERBIRD, WHYDAH

weaver finch *n* **:** WEAVERBIRD

weavers broom *n* [*weaver's* (gen. of ¹*weaver*) + *broom;* fr. its use in weaving baskets] **:** SPANISH BROOM 1

weaver shell *n* **:** SHUTTLE SHELL

weaver's knot *or* **weaver's hitch** *n* **:** SHEET BEND

weavers'-shuttle \ˈ≈≈,≈≈\ *n* **:** EGG COWRY

weaves *pres 3d sing of* WEAVE, *pl of* WEAVE

weave shed *n* **:** a room or building housing looms

weaving *n* -s [ME *weving,* fr. gerund of *weven* to weave] **1 a :** the process of forming cloth usu. on a loom by the interlacing of threads, yarns, or other strands **b :** the business of making cloth **2 :** a debilitating vice of nervous stabled horses consisting of rhythmic swaying back and forth while shifting the weight from one side to the other **3 :** the action of a vehicle that alternately diverges from and merges into traffic flows moving in the same direction, shifting from one lane to another, and repeatedly crossing the paths of other vehicles

weazand *var of* WEASAND

wea·zen \ˈwēzᵊn\ *vb* -ED/-ING/-S [alter. of *wizen*] **:** SHRINK

wea·zened \-ᵊnd\ *also* **wea·zen** \-ᵊn\ *adj* [alter. of *wizened, wizen*] **:** WIZENED

weazen-faced \ˈ≈≈,≈\ *adj* **:** having a wizened face

¹web \ˈweb\ *n* -s *often attrib* [ME, fr. OE; akin to OHG *weppi* web, ON *vefr,* OE *wefan* to weave — more at WEAVE] **1 a :** a fabric as it is being woven on a loom or as it appears when removed from a loom ⟨a ~ of lace⟩ **b** *archaic* **:** a garment made of such a fabric **c :** the filmlike sheet of fibers delivered by various textile machines esp. on a card ⟨~s of fibers are produced in a wide sheet⟩ ⟨carded ~s of nylon⟩ **d :** WARP ⟨~ and woof⟩ **2 a :** COBWEB 1 ⟨the spider spins its ~⟩ ⟨the ~s of the silkworm⟩ ⟨the crossed ~s are attached to the frame of the surveyor's telescope⟩ **b :** SNARE, ENTANGLEMENT ⟨enmeshed in the ~ of conflict and fear —William Peden⟩ ⟨the most intricate ~ of espionage and intrigue that any modern state has endured —R.H.Jackson⟩ **3 :** a tissue or membrane of an animal or plant: as **a :** the membrane uniting fingers or toes either at their bases (as in man) or for a greater part of their length (as in many water birds and amphibians) — see GOOSE illustration **b :** the tissue between the larger veins of a leaf esp. of tobacco **4 :** WEBBING 2 **5** *archaic* **:** a thin film growing over or covering the eye **6 a :** a thin metal sheet, plate, or strip **b :** the vertical plate or portion connecting the upper and lower flanges or parts of a girder or rail — see T RAIL illustration **c :** the arm of a crank **7 a :** an intricate structure resembling or suggestive of something woven **:** MAZE ⟨the ~ of little wrinkles that radiated from the corners of her eyes —Hamilton Basso⟩ ⟨silvery birches spread a fragile ~ of loveliness over the highway —*Amer. Guide Series: Maine*⟩ ⟨a ~ of railroad tracks —*Amer. Guide Series: Fla.*⟩ **b :** a complex arrangement, pattern, or development ⟨the stuff of our lives is . . . a tangled ~ —Havelock Ellis⟩ ⟨this intricate ~ of social relations —Ralph Pieris⟩ ⟨the economy . . . has become a closely woven ~ —Roger Burlingame⟩ ⟨the close ~ of history —Herbert Agar⟩ **8 :** the series of barbs implanted on each side of the shaft of a feather **:** VANE, VEXILLUM **9 a :** a continuous sheet of paper manufactured or undergoing the process of manufacture on a paper machine **b :** a reel of such paper for use in a rotary printing press **10 :** a thin portion of material or a partition molded into hollow tile or other earthenware product to strengthen it **11 :** the portion of a ribbed vault between the ribs **12 :** SNOWSHOE ⟨would . . . get out their ~s and snowshoe down —Helen Rich⟩ **13 :** a radio or television network ⟨news analysts are . . . covered by the ~'s contract restrict private comment —Saul Carson⟩ ⟨the ~ was made up of member stations of the . . . Intercollegiate Broadcasting System —*Newsweek*⟩

²web \ˈ"\ *vb* **webbed; webbed; webbing; webs** [in sense 1, fr. ME *webben,* fr. OE *webbian* to weave, devise; akin to ON *vefja* to wind, wrap, MHG *weben* to weave, OE ¹*web;* in other senses, fr. ¹*web*] *vt* **1** *archaic* **:** to weave (a cloth or fabric) with a loom **2 a :** to weave a web upon ⟨spiders ~ the grasses⟩ **b :** to cover with a web or network ⟨roads *webbed* the forest land, connecting outlying farms . . . with the towns —*Amer. Guide Series: Tenn.*⟩ **3 :** ENTANGLE, ENSNARE ⟨the spider ~s a fly⟩ ~ *vi* **:** to construct or form a web ⟨the electrical cables which *webbed* everywhere —Fred Bradna & Hartzell Spence⟩ ⟨it was so cold . . . the hairs in his nostrils *webbed* into instant ice —Wallace Stegner⟩

webbed \ˈwebd\ *adj* [¹*web* + *-ed*] **:** provided with a web: as **a :** having the toes or fingers united by a web ⟨the ~ feet of aquatic fowls⟩ **b :** COBWEBBED

web·bing \ˈwebiŋ, -bēŋ\ *n* -s [¹*web* + *-ing*] **1 a :** a narrow woven or braided fabric of textile fibers with or without rubber or other elastomer **b :** a strong narrow fabric closely woven of plied yarns that is designed for bearing weight and is used esp. for straps, harness, or upholstery **c :** a strap or girth of a hand printing press **2 :** a webbed state (as of the toes of a bird); *also* **:** the membranous web involved **3 :** a finish defect consisting of intersecting cracks and ridges formed usu. when a varnish or other coating expands on the surface it covers **:** ALLIGATORING

webbing clothes moth *also* **webbing moth** *n* **:** a clothes moth (*Tineola bisselliella*) whose larva attacks carpets, tapestry, and other woolen goods and forms a web in which it lives

web blight *n* **:** a disease of beans and other crop plants caused by a fungus (*Pellicularia filomentosa*) and characterized by a mycelial growth on or around water-soaked spots on stems, leaves, and pods

web·by \ˈwebē\ *adj* -ER/-EST [¹*web* + *-y*] **:** of, relating to, or consisting of a web ⟨long ~ hair hung down over their emaciated faces —Jack Belden⟩

we·be·los \ˈwebə,lōz\ *n, pl* **webelos** [fr. the phrase *we'll be loyal scouts*] **:** a cub scout of the fifth rank who is at least 10½ years old and is preparing for entrance into boy scouting

weber \ˈwebə(r), ˈvāb-,ˈwēb-\ *n* -s [after Wilhelm E. *Weber* †1891 Ger. physicist] **:** the practical mks unit of magnetic flux equal to that flux which in linking a circuit of one turn produces in it an electromotive force of one volt as the flux is reduced to zero at a uniform rate of one ampere per second **:** 10^8 maxwells

weber-fechner law \-ˈfek|nə(r)-, -k|\ *n, usu cap W&F* [after Ernst H. *Weber* †1878 Ger. physiologist & anatomist, & Gustav T. *Fechner* †1887 Ger. psychologist] **:** an approximately accurate generalization in psychology: the intensity of a sensation is proportional to the logarithm of the intensity of the stimulus causing it — called also *Fechner's law*

we·be·ri·an \weˈbirēən, vāˈ-,wēˈ-\ *adj, usu cap* [Max *Weber* †1920 Ger. sociologist and political economist + E *-ian*] **:** of or relating to the socioeconomic theories of Max Weber

weberian apparatus *n, usu cap W* [Ernst H. *Weber* †1878 + E *-an*] **:** the entire set of structures including the Weberian ossicles and their ligaments by which the air bladder of some fishes is connected to the ear

weberian ossicle *n, usu cap W* **:** one of the series of small bones that extends from the dorsal wall of the air bladder to the region of the ear in fishes (order Ostariophysi)

weber·ite \ˈwebə,rīt, ˈvāb-,ˈwēb-\ *n* -s [Dan *weberit,* fr. Theobald *Weber,* 19th cent. Dan. industrialist + Dan *-it* -ite] **:** a mineral Na_2MgAlF_7 consisting of a fluoride of sodium, magnesium, and aluminum

weber's corpuscle *or* **weber's pouch** *n, usu cap W* [after Moritz I. *Weber* †1875 Ger. anatomist] **:** PROSTATIC UTRICLE

weber's law *n, usu cap W* [after Ernst H. *Weber* †1878] **:** an approximately accurate generalization in psychology: the smallest change in the intensity of a stimulus capable of being perceived is proportional to the intensity of the original stimulus

weber's line *n, usu cap W* [after Max *Weber* †1937 Ger. zoologist] **:** a hypothetical boundary lying approximately along the Australo-Papuan Shelf and being sometimes preferred to Wallace's line as the common boundary of the Oriental and Australian biogeographic regions

web-fed \ˈ≈ˈ≈\ *adj* **:** designed to print a continuous roll of paper ⟨*web-fed* rotary newspaper press⟩ — compare SHEET-FED

webfoot *in sense 1* ˈ≈,≈, *in senses 2 & 3* ˈ≈,≈\ *n, pl* **webfeet** [¹*web* + *foot*] **1 :** a foot having webbed toes **2 :** a bird or other animal having webbed feet **3** *also* **web·foot·er** \-ˈfu̇d-ə(r)\ *usu cap* **:** OREGONIAN — used as a nickname

web-footed \ˈ≈ˈ≈\ *adj* [¹*web* + *footed*] **:** having webbed feet

web-footed shrew *n* **:** WATER SHREW

web frame *n* **:** a frame of heavy scantling used in ship construction and made by riveting a wide plate to a frame and stiffening the plate by riveting two reverse frames to its inner edge

web-glazed \ˈ≈ˈ≈\ *adj* **:** glazed in a calender having alternate rolls of polished iron and compressed cotton or paper

web glazing *n* **:** the glazing or finishing of paper in web form

web lead *n* **:** sheet lead

web·less \ˈwebləs\ *adj* **:** having no webs

weblike \ˈ≈,≈\ *adj* **:** similar to or suggestive of a web

web member *n* **:** one of the several members joining the top and bottom chords of a truss or lattice girder

web plate *n* **:** a plate connecting the flanges of a plate girder or a built-up steel column

web press *n* **:** a press that prints a web or continuous roll or reel of paper

web printing *n* **:** the action or the process of printing on a web press

web rot *n* **:** a rot of the tobacco leaf affecting chiefly the tissue between the main veins

webs *pl of* WEB, *pres 3d sing of* WEB

web saw *n* **:** a saw stretched in a frame

web spinner *n* **:** an insect that spins a web: as **a :** any of various small slender campodeiform insects with biting mouthparts that constitute the order Embiodea and live in silken tunnels that they spin **b :** WEBWORM

web·ster \ˈwebztə(r), -bst-\ *n* -s [ME, fr. OE *webbestre* female weaver, fr. *webbian* to weave, devise + *-estre* -ster — more at WEB, v.] *archaic* **:** WEAVER

web·ste·ri·an \(ˈ)webzˈtirēən, -bˈst-, -tēr-\ *adj, usu cap* **1** [Daniel *Webster* †1852 Am. lawyer & statesman + E *-ian*] **:** of, relating to, or characteristic of the statesman Daniel Webster **2** [Noah *Webster* †1843 Am. lexicographer & author + E *-ian*] **:** of, relating to, or characteristic of the lexicographer Noah Webster or his dictionary

web-winged \ˈ≈ˈwiŋd\ *adj* [¹*web* + *winged*] **:** having wings formed by membranes extended between digits

webworm \ˈ≈,≈\ *n* **:** any of various caterpillars that are more or less gregarious and spin large webs in which they live

wechs·ler-belle·vue test \ˌwekslə(r)ˈbel,vyü-\ *n, usu cap W&B* [after David *Wechsler* †1981 Am. psychologist and *Bellevue* Psychiatric Hospital] **:** a test of general intelligence and coordination involving both verbal and performance tests

¹wed \ˈwed\ *n* -s [ME, fr. OE *wedd* pledge, agreement, security; akin to OHG *wetti* pledge, ON *veth,* Goth *wadi,* L *vad-, vas* bail, security] **1** *dial Brit* **:** a person or thing given or deposited as a pledge **2** *dial Brit* **:** STAKE, WAGER

²wed \ˈ"\ *vb* **wedded** *also* **wed; wedded** *also* **wed; wedding; weds** [ME *wedden* to engage, pledge, marry, fr. OE *weddian;* akin to MHG *wetten* to pledge, ON *vethja* to wager, Goth *gawadjon* to espouse, marry, OE *wedd* pledge] *vt* **1 :** to take for wife or husband by a formal ceremony **:** MARRY ⟨bring me to your mother's house and there I will ~ you —Padraic Colum⟩ ⟨with this ring I thee ~ —*Bk. of Com. Prayer*⟩ **2 :** to join or bind in marriage ⟨he was *wedded* on July 12 —Francis Hackett⟩ ⟨the book gives the name of the minister who ~ them⟩ **3** *dial Brit* **:** ENGAGE, PLEDGE, WAGER **4 a :** to unite or join firmly as if by the affections or bond of marriage ⟨has ~ himself to the traditions of his people⟩ ⟨soon she too was . . . *wedded* to the place —S.T.Williamson⟩ ⟨was ~ to misfortune at birth⟩ **b :** to place in close or intimate association ⟨the far distant day when coal was *wedded* to iron —G.M. Trevelyan⟩ ⟨has invested millions of dollars to ~ farm and factory in continuous cycles of production —*Current Biog.*⟩ ⟨the English pantomime . . . ~s music hall and the fairy tale —Henry Hewes⟩ **5** *archaic* **:** to lend support to (as a cause) **:** ESPOUSE ~ *vi* **:** to enter into matrimony ⟨she ~ while still very young⟩

wedded *also* **wed** *adj* [*wedded* fr. ME, fr. OE *geweddod,* fr. past part. of *weddian* to wed; *wed* fr. ME *wedde,* fr. past part. of *wedden* to wed] **1 :** joined in marriage **:** MARRIED ⟨wilt thou have this woman to thy ~ wife —*Bk. of Com. Prayer*⟩ ⟨the ~ pair leave the church⟩ **2 :** of or relating to marriage or persons married ⟨no greater blessing . . . than pure ~ love —M.J.Huber⟩ ⟨forsaking his sole existence for the ~ life⟩ ⟨~ bliss⟩ **3 a :** devotedly or firmly attached or joined as if by marriage ⟨that kind of mellow wisdom . . . not ~ to private dogmas —H.J.Laski⟩ ⟨attract voters not ~ to either of the two major parties —*Times Lit. Supp.*⟩ ⟨a good boy, *wed* to peace and study —Carl Sandburg⟩ ⟨gaiety . . . ~ to melancholy —John Mason Brown⟩ **b :** existing in close or intimate association ⟨form and subject matter are ~ from the beginning —Edward Sapir⟩ ⟨austerity and discipline ~ to labor and endurance —W.C.Dickinson⟩ ⟨the gramophone ~ to the thin sweet singing of the olive leaves in the evening wind —John Galsworthy⟩

wed·dell·ite \wəˈde,līt, ˈwedᵊl,īt\ *n* -s [*Weddell* sea, arm of southern Atlantic ocean in Antarctica + E *-ite*] **:** a mineral $CaC_2O_4.2H_2O$ consisting of hydrous oxalate of calcium that is polymorphous with whewellite and is found as tiny isolated crystals in mud at the bottom of the Weddell sea, Antarctica

wed·dell seal \wəˈdel-, ˈwedᵊl-\ *n, usu cap W* [after James *Weddell* †1834 Eng. navigator] **:** a large brown antarctic seal (*Leptonychotes weddelli*) valued for its flesh and blubber

wed·der \ˈwedə(r)\ *n* -s [ME *weder* — more at WETHER] *Brit* **:** WETHER 2

wed·ding \ˈwediŋ, -dēŋ\ *n* -s [ME, fr. OE *weddung,* fr. *weddian* to wed + *-ung* -ing] **1 a :** the marriage ceremony usu. with its accompanying festivities **:** NUPTIALS, ESPOUSAL ⟨sending out invitations to the ~⟩ **b :** a wedding anniversary or its celebration — usu. used in combination ⟨golden ~⟩ **2 :** an act, process, or instance of joining or uniting in close association often of opposed or disparate elements ⟨the result was a ~ of the delicate and the rough —D.S.Stewart⟩ ⟨has not yet achieved the ~ of the serious and the popular —Harold Rogers⟩ ⟨this production is a happy ~ of taste, talent, and technique —Lila Glaser⟩ **3 :** a strong fine-textured smooth dull writing paper suitable for engraved wedding invitations

wedding cake *n* **:** a cake made for a wedding: as **a :** a dark unleavened fruited cake usu. elaborately decorated **b :** a light fruited cake or a white butter cake usu. heavily frosted and decorated

wedding day *n* **1 :** the day of a wedding **2 :** the anniversary of a wedding day

wed·ding·er \ˈwediŋə(r)\ *n* -s [*wedding* + *-er*] *dial Brit* **:** one present at a wedding esp. as a guest

wedding flight *n* **:** NUPTIAL FLIGHT

wedding march *n* **:** a march of slow tempo and stately character composed or played to accompany the bridal procession

wedding ring *n* [ME, fr. *wedding* + *ring*] **:** a ring often consisting of a plain gold or platinum band given by the groom to the bride during the wedding service; *also* **:** a similar ring given by the bride to the groom in a double-ring service

¹wedge \ˈwej\ *n* -s [ME *wegge,* fr. OE *wecg;* akin to OHG *weggi, wecki* wedge, ON *veggr,* Lith *vagis* wedge, peg, and prob. to L *vomis, vomer* plowshare, Gk *ophnis*] **1 :** a piece of material (as wood or metal) tapering to a thin edge used for splitting wood or rocks, for raising heavy bodies, and by being driven into a space between objects for tightening ⟨drove the ~ into the log with a maul⟩ **2 a :** a lump or mass of something solid ⟨ate ~s of brown bread dipped in coffee —Kay Boyle⟩ ⟨fine, well-aged Herkimer county cheddar . . . is sold in ~s —*New Yorker*⟩ ⟨a thick ~ of estuarine clay was laid down over the earlier valley peats —J.N.Jennings & Joyce Lambert⟩ **b** *obs* **:** a gold or silver ingot **3 a :** something (as a device, policy, or action) causing a breach or separation ⟨time . . . to unite this country instead of attempting to drive a ~ between any segments of our population —Earl Bunting⟩ ⟨slavery . . . had driven a ~ between the North and the South —Oscar Handlin⟩ ⟨driving a ~ of sardonic laughter and comment into the wall of prejudice —V.P.Hass⟩ **b :** something used to initiate an extended action or development ⟨looked upon the union . . . as a growing ~ in the fight to end discrimination —*Current Biog.*⟩ ⟨bill is merely another ~ to pry billions out of the American exchequer —J.S.Lawrence⟩ ⟨the officers' fraternity . . . was taken as the entering ~ of military despotism —Dixon Wecter⟩ ⟨the thin end of the improving ~ has come in —John Russell b. 1872⟩ **4 :** something shaped like or suggestive of a wedge: as **a :** an array of troops or tanks drawn up or moving in the form of a wedge ⟨the armored ~ drove forward to make openings in the enemy line⟩ **b :** a formation of flying wild fowl ⟨the high ~ and honk of birds flying south —Meridel LeSueur⟩ **c :** a section of land narrowing to a point ⟨a small ~ of an island —Iain Hamilton⟩ ⟨a ~ of green forest juts out into the field⟩ **d :** VOUSSOIR **e** (1) **:** the wedge-shaped stroke in cuneiform characters ⟨cuneiform . . . is at first sight only a meaningless jumble of ~s —S.L.Caiger⟩ (2) **:** HAČEK **f :** a wedge-shaped region of high barometric pressure **g** (1) **:** WEDGE HEEL (2) **:** a shoe that has a wedge heel **h :** an iron golf club that has a broad low-angled face for giving maximum loft from sand traps and from deep rough **:** a heavy niblick **i :** a piece of optical glass or crystal (as in a compensator or a photometer) having a progressive variation in thickness or absorption density from one side to the other **5 :** the type of cutting and piercing machinery formerly classed as a mechanical power **6 :** a piece of bone removed (as from a foot) to correct deformity or malposition ⟨a ~ resection⟩

wedge 1

²wedge \ˈ"\ *vb* -ED/-ING/-S [ME *weggen,* fr. *wegge* wedge] *vt* **1 :** to fasten or tighten by driving or forcing in a wedge ⟨~s the pegs in tightly⟩ ⟨the carpenter ~s up the post under the beam⟩ ⟨the builder ~s the wooden partition to the overhead construction⟩ **2 :** to force or drive (an object) into something where it is tightly held **:** SQUEEZE ⟨the flood ~s debris into the crotches of the trees⟩ ⟨was *wedged* in between his two bedfellows, both of whom were aggressively large —T.B.Costain⟩ ⟨the houses . . . appear to be *wedged* in the rocky hillside —*Amer. Guide Series: Md.*⟩ ⟨seeking to ~ an advancing force between the enemy's strongpoints⟩ **3 :** to separate or force apart with or as if with a wedge ⟨the axman ~s open the log for finer splitting⟩ ⟨seeks to ~ apart his enemies, to divide and conquer⟩ **4 :** to cram or pack into a small or restricted space **:** CROWD ⟨thousands of homes had been *wedged* into the tiny valley⟩ ⟨Sunday driving ~s the cars together on miles of congested highways⟩ **5 :** to overthrow or direct the fall of (a tree) by driving wedges into the kerf made by the sawyer **6 :** to cut (clay) into wedge-shaped masses and work by dashing together to expel air bubbles ~ *vi* **:** to become tight or fixed by or as if by being wedged ⟨hold the wood properly so that the saw will not ~⟩ — **wedge one's way :** to push or move in or forward in the manner of a wedge ⟨~s his way into the crowd⟩ ⟨*wedged* its way into the national market —*Advertising Age*⟩

wedgebill \ˈ≈,≈\ *n* [¹*wedge* + *bill*] **1 :** an Australian crested bird (*Sphenostoma cristatum*) that has a wedge-shaped bill and is related to the bellbird (*Oreoica gutturalis*) **2 :** a So. American hummingbird (*Schistes geoffroyi*) having a very thick tapered bill

wedge bone *n* **:** a small unpaired bone or nodule that often occurs between the centra of the cervical vertebrae of lizards

wedge clamp *n* **:** a clamp with one end contacting the work below its surface and the other end butting against a crosspiece so that the tightening of a bolt passing through its center causes the clamp to wedge the work in position

wedge coupling *n* **:** a shaft coupling that grips with an action similar to that of a wedge

wedged \ˈwejd\ *adj* [¹*wedge* + *-ed*] **:** shaped like a wedge ⟨~ cuneiform characters⟩ ⟨the ~ formation of flying geese⟩

wedge disks *n pl* **:** disks usu. rotating and arranged in sets of two wedging a member between their surfaces
wedge furnace \'wej-\ *n, usu cap W* [after Utley *Wedge*, its inventor] **:** a mechanical shaft furnace for roasting ore that has several hearths one above the other and rabbles attached to a central revolving shaft
wedge gage *n* **:** a wedge with a graduated edge to measure the width of a space into which it is thrust
wedge gear *n* **:** a friction gear wheel with wedge-shaped circumferential grooves
wedge graft *n* **:** CLEFT GRAFT
wedge heel *n* **:** a heel extending from the back of the shoe to the front of the shank and having a tread formed by an extension of the sole — called also *wedge*
wedge micrometer *n* **:** a sensitive wedge gage
wedge of emersion *or* **wedge of immersion :** the wedge-shaped volume of a ship that emerges from the water or is immerged when the ship is inclined or heeled

wedge heel

wedge out *vi* **:** to become progressively thinner or narrower to the point of disappearance ⟨the reservoir bed *wedges out* toward the east⟩
wedge photometer *n* **:** an instrument for comparing stellar brightnesses on the basis of the calibrated progressive absorption of a neutral-density optical wedge or wedge of glass
wedg·er \'wejə(r)\ *n* -s [²*wedge* + *-er*] **:** a shoe worker who sets a wedge between the outsole and upper at the shank to form a spring heel — called also *springer*
wedge shell *n* [¹*wedge*] **:** a marine bivalve mollusk of the family Donacidae; *also* **:** its wedge-shaped shell
wedge spectrogram *n* **:** a photograph obtained with a wedge spectrograph
wedge spectrograph *n* **:** a spectrograph in which the light is modulated by an optical wedge
wedge-tailed \'≈,≈\ *adj* **:** having a tail that has the middle pair of feathers longest with the rest successively and decidedly shorter and all more or less attenuate
wedge-tailed dove *or* **wedge-tailed pigeon** *n* **:** any of various Asiatic pigeons of the genus *Treron*
wedge-tailed eagle *n* **:** an Australian eagle (*Uroaëtus audax*) that destroys lambs and young kangaroo — called also *eagle-hawk*
wedge-tailed gull *n* **:** ROSS'S GULL
wedge-tailed shearwater *n* **:** a shearwater (*Puffinus pacificus*) of the Pacific and Indian oceans
wedge verse *n* **:** rhopalic verse
wedgework \'≈,≈\ *n* **:** the action of frost, roots, and other forces in disintegrating rocks as if by the insertion of a wedge; *also* **:** the results of such action
Wedg·ies \'wejēz, -jiz\ *trademark* — used for shoes having a wedge heel
wedging *n* -s [fr. gerund of ²*wedge*] **:** the act or process of one that wedges; *specif* **:** the springing out or dislodging of ice or rock by frost acting as a wedge ⟨frost ~ . . . is common at high altitudes wherever suitably jointed rocks and water are exposed to a great daily range of temperatures —R.F.Flint⟩
wedging crib *or* **wedging curb** *n* **:** a curb of close-fitting planks behind which wedges are driven in to make a watertight packing between the tubbing in a shaft and the rock walls
Wedg·wood \'wej,wu̇d\ *trademark* — used for a pottery (as bone china, jasperware, or queensware)
wedgwood blue *n, often cap W* [fr. *Wedgwood*, a trademark; from a typical color of Wedgwood ware] **1 :** a variable color averaging a pale blue that is redder, stronger, and slightly lighter than average powder blue, redder and lighter than Sistine, lighter, stronger, and slightly redder than average cadet gray, and redder, lighter, and stronger than old blue **2 :** either of two colors averaging a grayish purplish blue — see DARK WEDGWOOD
wedgwood green *n, often cap W* **:** a grayish yellow green that is yellower, lighter, and slightly less strong than average sage green, stronger, slightly yellower, and lighter than mermaid, yellower, lighter, and stronger than palmetto, and yellower and deeper than celadon
wedgy \'wejē, -ji\ *adj* -ER/-EST [¹*wedge* + *-y*] **:** resembling a wedge in shape
wed·lock \'wed,läk\ *n* -s [ME *wedlac, wedlok*, fr. OE *wedlāc*, fr. *wedd* pledge + *-lāc*, suffix denoting activity, prob. fr. *lāc* warlike activity, play — more at WED, LAKE (amusement)] **1** *obs* **:** the marriage bond or contract **2 a :** the state of being married **:** MARRIAGE, MATRIMONY ⟨where love cannot be, there can be left of ~ nothing but the empty husk —John Milton⟩ **b** *archaic* **:** a marital union **:** a wedded life **3** *obs* **:** WIFE — **out of wedlock** *adv* **:** with the natural parents not legally married to each other
wednes·day \'wenzdē, -di *also* -(,)dā\ *n* -s *usu cap* [ME *wodnesday, wednesday*, fr. OE *wōdnesdæg*; akin to OFris *wênsdei* Wednesday, ON *ōthinsdagr*; all fr. a prehistoric WGmc-NGmc compound formed from components represented by OE *Wōden*, the chief god of the Germanic peoples, identified with the Roman Mercury, and OE *dæg* day; trans. of L *Mercurii dies*, lit., day of Mercury (the Roman god of commerce and the planet Mercury) — more at DAY] **:** the fourth day of the week **:** the day following Tuesday
wednes·days \-ēz,-iz,-āz\ *adv, usu cap* **:** on Wednesday repeatedly **:** on any Wednesday
weds *pl of* WED, *pres 3d sing of* WED
¹**wee** \'wē\ *n* -s [ME *wei, we*, fr. OE *wǣge* weight, wey — more at WEIGH, n.] *chiefly Scot* **:** a little bit **:** short time ⟨bide a ~⟩
²**wee** \"\ *adj, sometimes* **we·er** \'wē(ə)r, 'wi|, |ə\ *sometimes* **we·est** \'wēəst\ [ME *we*, fr. *we*, n., wee] **1 :** very small **:** LITTLE, YOUNG ⟨a ~ tot of about five⟩ **2 :** very early ⟨awakened in the ~ hours of the morning⟩ **syn** see SMALL
³**wee** \"\ *interj* [imit.] — used to simulate the squeal of a pig
¹**weed** \'wēd\ *n* -s [ME *wed, weed*, fr. OE *wēod* herb, grass, weed; akin to OS *wiod* weed, MD *wiet*, OHG *wiota* fern] **1 a** (1) **:** an introduced plant growing in ground that is or has been in cultivation usu. to the detriment of the crop or to the disfigurement of the place **:** an economically useless plant **:** a plant of unsightly appearance; *esp* **:** one of wild or rank growth (2) **:** a tree or shrub of low economic value that tends to grow freely and by its presence to exclude or retard more valuable plants ⟨gray birch is a common ~ species in much of New England⟩ (3) **:** a form of vegetable life of exuberant growth and injurious effect (as various molds or bacteria frequently contaminating cultures) (4) **:** a forb in rangeland **b :** wild growth usu. in the nature of rank grass or undergrowth ⟨the land must be cleared of ~ —Emil Lengyel⟩ **2 :** a marine or freshwater plant **:** SEAWEED **3 :** an obnoxious growth, thing, or person ⟨militarism is a tough ~ to kill —F.S. Oliver⟩ **4 a :** TOBACCO; *esp* **:** tobacco prepared for use (as a cigar or cigarette) ⟨made the students promise to shun both ~ and wine —*Time*⟩ **b** *slang* **:** MARIJUANA **5 a :** something of little value; *specif* **:** an animal of poor conformation, lacking in stamina, and unfit to breed from **b :** an animal that is detrimental esp. in preoccupying habitats that might otherwise harbor more desirable forms ⟨carp forms one of the worst ~ species in some areas⟩ or in damaging the habitat value of the land on which they live ⟨uncontrolled deer herds may become serious ~s⟩
²**weed** \"\ *vb* -ED/-ING/-S [ME *weden*, fr. OE *wēodian*; akin to OS *wiodōn* to weed, MD *wieden*, OE *wēod* weed] *vi* **:** to remove weeds or something harmful ~ *vt* **1 a :** to free from noxious plants **:** clear of weeds ⟨~ a garden⟩ **b** (1) **:** to free from something that is hurtful or offensive (2) **:** to diminish by removing the less desirable portions of **:** CULL ⟨before beginning to classify and catalog an old library, ~ the collection —Susan Akers⟩ ⟨~ a stable of horses⟩ **2 a :** to remove on account of being a weed ⟨~ crabgrass from the lawn⟩ **b :** to remove on account of being harmful or superfluous **:** get rid of — often used with *out* ⟨~ out impractical schemes not worth further appraisal —R.P.Cooke⟩
³**weed** \"\ *n* -s [ME *wede*, fr. OE *wǣd, gewǣde*; akin to OS *wād, giwādi* clothing, OHG *wāt, giwāti*, ON *vāth* cloth, clothing, Lith *austi* to weave] **1 a :** an article of clothing **:** GARMENT; *esp* **:** one that is indicative of a person's occupation, situation, or position — often used in pl. **b :** something that resembles an outer garment **:** FLESH **2 :** an article or style of dress usu. black worn as a sign of mourning: as **a :** a widow's black veils — usu. used in pl. ⟨she had abandoned the cocoon of crape but still wore ~s —Arnold Bennett⟩ **b :** a band of crape or heavy black cloth worn on a man's hat as a sign of mourning — usu. used in pl. ⟨a coachman and a footman both with ~s on their hats —Kate D. Wiggin⟩
⁴**weed** \"\ *n* -s [by shortening fr. obs. Sc *wedenonfa'* ague, lit., attack of madness, fr. OE *wēde, wēden-* mad, frenzied + Sc *onfa'* attack, fr. ME *onfall*, fr. OE *onfeall*, fr. *on* + *feall* fall; akin to OE *wōd* mad — more at WOOD, ON, FALL] **1 :** a sudden illness or relapse often attended with fever **2 a :** lymphangitis in the horse accompanied by fever and marked by swelling of the legs **b :** mastitis esp. of sheep
weed·age \-dij\ *n* -s [¹*weed* + *-age*] **:** WEEDS
weed burner *n* **:** a device for burning or flaming weeds esp. along railroad tracks usu. consisting of large torches fired by petroleum fuels
weed·ed \'wēdəd\ *adj* [in sense 1, fr. past part. of ²*weed*; in sense 2, fr. ¹*weed* + *-ed*] **1 :** cleared of weeds **2 :** having many weeds **:** WEEDY
weed·er \'wēdə(r)\ *n* -s **:** one that weeds: as **a :** one of various devices for freeing an area (as a garden) from weeds **b :** one whose work is weeding (as farm or garden crops, lawns, flower beds)

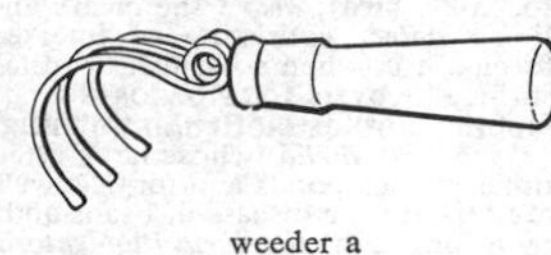
weeder a

weed·ery \-dərē\ *n* -ES [¹*weed* + *-ery*] **:** WEEDS; *also* **:** a place full of weeds
weed fallow *n* **:** fallow land where weeds are permitted to grow
weedhook \'≈,≈\ *n* [ME *wedehoke*, fr. OE *wēodhōc*, fr. *wēod* weed + *hōc* hook] **:** a hook to cut weeds; *specif* **:** a curved steel rod attached by one end to a plow beam and extending to the front and side of the plow bottom for bending over weeds so that they are completely buried in a furrow bottom by the furrow slice
weed·i·cide \'wēdə,sīd\ *n* -s [¹*weed* + *-i-* + *-cide*] **:** HERBICIDE
weed killer *n* **:** HERBICIDE
weed·less \'wēdləs\ *adj* **1 :** free from weeds ⟨a ~ garden⟩ **2 :** made in such a manner as not to catch in or become clogged by weeds
weed species *n* **:** a species having the potentiality for over-populating an area and upsetting its normal biological balance
weed tree *n* **:** a tree of a kind having little or no commercial value ⟨the poplar is a *weed tree* in some coniferous forests⟩
¹**weedy** \'wēdē, -di\ *adj* -ER/-EST [ME, fr. ¹*weed* + *-y*] **1 :** abounding with weeds ⟨a ~ garden⟩ **2 a :** of, relating to, or consisting of weeds **b :** resembling a weed esp. in respect to rank growth or ready propagation in cultivated places ⟨a plant of ~ habit⟩ **3 :** noticeably lean and scrawny **:** LANKY ⟨light carriage with its pair of ~, young horses —Joseph Hergesheimer⟩ ⟨he was ~; on his pale thin face was the look of delicate health —Oliver LaFarge⟩
²**weedy** \"\ *adj* [³*weed* + *-y*] **:** dressed in mourning ⟨she was as ~ as in the early days of her mourning —Charles Dickens⟩
wee folk *n pl* **:** FAIRIES
wee frees \-'frēz\ *n pl, usu cap W&F* [fr. *Wee Free (Kirk)*, nickname applied to minority of the Free Church of Scotland] **:** members of the Free Church of Scotland formed of a minority of the original Free Church of Scotland who refused to enter into a merger in 1900 with the United Presbyterian Church to form the United Free Church of Scotland
week \'wēk\ *n* -s [ME *weke, wike, wolk*, fr. OE *wice, wicu, wucu*; akin to OHG *wehha, wohha* week, *wehsal* change, turn, ON *vika* week, Goth *wiko* order, turn, L *vicis* change, turn, ON *vīkja* to move, turn, OE *wīr* wire — more at WIRE] **1 a :** one of a series of seven-day cycles used in various calendars but esp. in the Jewish and Gregorian calendars and in the old Julian calendar from the time of Constantine **b** (1) **:** a week beginning with a specified day or containing a specified holiday ⟨the ~ of the 18th⟩ ⟨Easter ~⟩ ⟨Christmas ~⟩ (2) **:** a week appointed for public recognition of some cause ⟨Better Speech *Week*⟩ ⟨Fire Prevention *Week*⟩ **2 a :** any seven consecutive days **b :** a series of regular working, business, or school days during each seven-day period **c :** one of the four periods into which in accounting a month is often divided in reporting gross earnings with the first three containing seven days each and the fourth including the rest of the month **d :** a regularly recurring calendrical cycle of days unrelated to astronomical phenomena usu. smaller than a month ⟨spends a native ~ of four days —M.J.Herskovits⟩ **3 a :** a week ago from a specified day ⟨it was Sunday ~ when he came⟩ ⟨she was here this day ~⟩ ⟨last Sunday ~⟩ **b :** a week from a specified day ⟨the game will be played on Saturday ~⟩ ⟨next Sunday ~⟩ ⟨school begins a ~ today⟩
week·day \'≈,dā\ *n, often attrib* [ME *wolkday*, fr. OE *wicdæg* day of the week, fr. *wice, wicu* week + *dæg* day] **:** a day of the week except Sunday or sometimes except Saturday and Sunday **:** WORKING DAY
week·days \-āz\ *adv* **:** on weekdays repeatedly **:** on any weekday ⟨gets up early ~⟩
¹**week·end** \'wē;kend\ *n* **:** the end of the week **:** the period between the close of one working or business or school week and the beginning of the next (as from Friday evening to Monday morning or from Saturday evening to Tuesday morning)
²**weekend** \"\ *vi* **:** to spend the weekend ⟨~*ed* with friends⟩
weekend bag *or* **weekend case** *or* **week·end·er** \'wē-;kendə(r)\ *n* **:** a traveling bag of a size to carry clothing and personal articles for a weekend trip
week·end·er \'wē;kendə(r)\ *n* -s [²*weekend* + *-er*] **1 :** one that vacations for a weekend ⟨~s in the country . . . who prefer nature to neon —*New Yorker*⟩ **2 :** one that comes to visit for a weekend
week·ends \-n(d)z\ *adv* **:** on weekends repeatedly **:** on any weekend ⟨sleeps late ~⟩
¹**week·ly** \'wēklē, -li\ *adv* [ME *wikely*, fr. *wike* week + *-ly*] **:** every week **:** once a week **:** by the week
²**weekly** \"\ *adj* [*week* + *-ly*] **1 :** occurring, appearing, or being made, done, or acted upon every week or once a week **2 :** reckoned by the week ⟨a ~ rate of pay⟩ ⟨a ~ rental⟩
³**weekly** \"\ *n* -ES **:** a weekly newspaper or periodical
week·night \'≈,≈\ *n* **:** a weekday night
week·nights \'≈,nīts\ *adv* **:** on weeknights repeatedly **:** on any weeknight ⟨gets six hours' sleep ~⟩
week of prayer : a week beginning with the first Sunday in January each year instituted in 1846 by the Evangelical Alliance and observed by various Protestants throughout the world
week work *n* **1 :** the weekly service of labor due from a villein or unfree tenant to his feudal lord usu. amounting to 2 or 3 days but 4 or 5 in summer **2 :** work for which one is employed by the week
¹**weel** \'wē(ə)l\ *n* -s [ME *wel, wele*, fr. OE *wǣl* eddy, pool; akin to MD *wael* pool, OLF *wāl* abyss, OHG *wuolen* to stir up, rumple, Skt *vālati* he turns — more at VOLUBLE] *dial Eng & Scot* **:** a deep still pool; *also* **:** WHIRLPOOL
²**weel** \"\ *n* -s [ME *wyle, wele*, fr. OE *wile-* (fr. *wilige* basket) — more at WILLY] **1 a :** a wickerwork or slotted trap for fish, esp. eels **b :** a conventionalized heraldic representation of such a trap **2 :** a basket esp. for fish
³**weel** \"\ *dial Eng & Scot var of* ⁴WELL
weem \'wēm\ *n* -s [ScGael *uaim, uaimh*] *Scot* **:** a natural or artificial cavern or pit; *esp* **:** one used as a place of habitation
ween \'wēn\ *vt* -ED/-ING/-S [ME *wenen*, fr. OE *wēnan*; akin to OHG *wānen* to ween, ON *væna* to hope, Goth *wenjan*, Skt *vanati* he wishes — more at WISH] **1** *archaic* **:** BELIEVE, CONCEIVE, IMAGINE, SUPPOSE **2** *archaic* **:** EXPECT, PURPOSE
weenie *var of* WIENIE
wee·ny \'wēnē\ *also* **ween·sy** \-n(t)sē\ *adj, sometimes* -ER/-EST [²*wee* + *tiny*] **:** exceptionally tiny **syn** see SMALL
¹**weep** \'wēp\ *vb* **wept** \'wept\ **wept; weeping; weeps** [ME *wepen*, fr. OE *wēpan*; akin to OHG *wuofjan* to weep, ON *œpa* to cry, scream, Goth *wopjan* to cry out, OSlav *vabiti* to call to, summon] *vt* **1 :** to express deep sorrow for usu. by shedding tears **:** BEWAIL, LAMENT ⟨the poet stayed to ~ the rose's fading —Katherine Hoskins⟩ **2 a :** to pour forth (tears) from the eyes ⟨*wept* tears of joy⟩ **b** *obs* **:** to shed drop by drop ⟨my heart ~s blood in anguish —Ben Jonson⟩ **3 a :** to spend in weeping — used with *away* ⟨into some low cave to crawl and there . . . ~ my life away —Alfred Tennyson⟩ **b :** to bring (oneself) to a specified condition by shedding tears ⟨finally *wept* herself to sleep⟩ **4 :** to utter or express while shedding tears ⟨~*ing* his welcomes forth —Shak.⟩ **5 :** to exude (as sap or serous fluid) slowly **:** OOZE ~ *vi* **1 :** to reveal an extreme inner emotion by a visual display esp. of lamentation and crying **:** express grief or other passion by shedding tears ⟨they *wept* together in silence —H.W.Longfellow⟩ **2 a :** to drop water **:** DRIP ⟨a sadder day had not been seen; even the clouds *wept*⟩ **b :** to flow or run in drops ⟨the blood ~s from my heart —Shak.⟩ **c :** to leak in trickles ⟨the bulkhead's buckling . . . and she's beginning to ~ down the joints —F.W.Crofts⟩ **3 :** to droop over **:** BEND ⟨the willow ~s⟩ **4 a :** to discharge a serous fluid ⟨~*ing* burned areas⟩ **b** *of the stem of a plant* **:** to exude water under pressure **:** BLEED **5 :** to form beads of liquid on the surface ⟨baked meringue is sometimes seen to ~⟩ — **weep one's heart out :** to cry long and exhaustingly
²**weep** \"\ *n* -s **1 :** weeping or a fit of weeping ⟨there was a scene — a ~ or two —Rudyard Kipling⟩ — often used in pl. **2 :** an exudation of moisture **:** LEAK
³**weep** \"\ *n* -s [imit.] **:** LAPWING
weep·er \'wēpə(r)\ *n* -s [ME *weper*, fr. *wepen* to weep + *-er*] **1 a :** one that weeps **:** one that sheds tears **b :** a professional mourner **2 :** a small statue of a figure in mourning frequently found in medieval tomb sculpture **3 :** a badge of mourning in the 18th and 19th centuries: as **a :** a white band worn as a cuff or on a cuff **b :** a man's long black hatband **c :** a widow's black veil — usu. used in pl. **4 :** CAPUCHIN 3 **5 :** a penitent who in the early church stood in the atrium begging the prayers of those who entered **6 :** a streamer of moss hanging from a tree **7 a :** WEEP HOLE **b :** SPARGE PIPE **8 :** long and flowing side-whiskers
weep hole *n* **:** a hole in a retaining wall, canal paving, or other structure to drain off accumulated water which might otherwise induce inordinate pressure back of or under the structure
weeping *adj* [ME *weping*, fr. pres. part. of *wepen* to weep] **1 :** accompanied by tears **:** TEARFUL ⟨~ gratitude⟩ **2 :** expressing or showing emotion by shedding tears ⟨held the ~ girl in his arms⟩ **3 :** exuding liquid in drops or very slowly **:** surcharged with moisture **:** OOZING ⟨pustular ~ folliculitis⟩ **4 :** RAINY, DRIPPING ⟨a ~ day⟩ **5 :** having slender pendent branches — used esp. of a tree
weeping cross *n* [trans. of ML *crux lacrimans*] **:** a cross erected on or by the highway esp. for the devotions of penitents
weeping cypress *n* **:** a tree (*Cupressus penebris*) with graceful drooping branches used as an ornamental in cemeteries and conservatories
weeping golden bell *or* **weeping forsythia** *n* **:** a Chinese shrub (*Forsythia suspensa*) with pendulous branches and yellow flowers
weeping honey locust *n* **:** a tree that is a variety (*Gleditsia triacanthos bujoti*) of the common honey locust characterized by pendulous branchlets
weeping lantana *n* **:** TRAILING LANTANA
weeping love grass *n* **:** a perennial southern African grass (*Eragrostis curvula*) introduced into the U. S. esp. for erosion control
weep·ing·ly *adv* [ME *wepingly*, fr. *weping* weeping + *-ly*] **:** in a weeping manner
weeping monkey *n* **:** CAPUCHIN 3
weeping mountain ash *n* **:** a variety (*Sorbus aucuparia pendula*) of the mountain ash of Eurasia with long pendulous branches
weeping myall *n* **:** an Australian acacia (*Acacia pendula*) with pendulous branches and very hard heavy durable dark brown or purplish wood
weeping oak *n* **1 :** CALIFORNIA WHITE OAK **2 :** an oak that is a variety (*Quercus robur pendula*) of the English oak characterized by pendulous branches
weeping pea tree *n* **:** a tree that is a horticultural variety (*Caragana arborescens pendula*) of a common Asiatic pea tree and has showy yellow flowers and pendulous branches
weeping red cedar *n* **:** a juniper that is a variety (*Juniperus virginiana pendula*) of the common red cedar characterized by pendulous branchlets
weeping rock *n* **:** a porous rock from which water oozes
weeping spring *n* **:** a spring that discharges water slowly
weeping spruce *n* **:** a tall spruce (*Picea breweriana*) of California and Oregon with slender pendulous branches and soft, heavy, and close-grained wood — called also *Brewer's spruce*
weeping willow *n* **:** an Asiatic willow (*Salix babylonica*) that is familiar in general cultivation from which it often escapes, has branches that droop perpendicularly, and occurs in several varieties
weeps *pres 3d sing of* WEEP, *pl of* WEEP
weepy \'wēpē, -pi\ *adj* -ER/-EST [¹*weep* + *-y*] **1 :** oozing moisture **:** SEEPY **2 :** tending to be tearful **:** verging on tears ⟨a ~ old lady —S.V.Benét⟩
weer *comparative of* WEE
weese-allan *or* **weese-allen** \wē'zalən\ *n* [origin unknown] *Scot* **:** PARASITIC JAEGER
wee·shy *also* **wee·shie** \'wēshē\ *adj* [prob. fr. ²*wee*] *Irish* **:** TINY, WEENY
weest *superlative of* WEE
¹**weet** \'wēt\ *vb* -ED/-ING/-S [ME *weten*, alter. of *witen* — more at WIT] *archaic* **:** KNOW ⟨I bind on pain of punishment the world to ~ we stand up peerless —Shak.⟩
²**weet** \"\ *Scot var of* WET
weet·less \-ləs\ *adj* [¹*weet* + *-less*] **:** UNWITTING
weet-weet \'wēt-,wēt\ *n* -s [imit.] **1** *dial Eng* **:** the common European sandpiper **2** *dial* **:** SPOTTED SANDPIPER
weety \'wēti\ *adj* [²*weet* + *-y*] *Scot* **:** RAINY
wee·ver \'wēvə(r)\ *also* **weever fish** *or* **weaver** *n* -s [ONF *wivre* viper — more at WYVERN] **:** any of several edible marine fishes of the family Trachinidae that have a broad spinose head with the eyes looking upward and a long dorsal fin supported by many strong sharp venomous spines that cause painful wounds: as **a :** a British weever (*Trachinus draco*) that becomes a foot long — called also *greater weever* **b :** a British weever (*T. vipera*) that is about half as large — called also *lesser weever*
wee·vil \'wēvəl *sometimes* -(,)vil\ *n* -s [ME *wivil, wevel*, fr. OE *wifel*; akin to OHG *wibil* beetle, ON *tordyfill* dung beetle, Lith *vabalas* beetle, OE *wafian* to wave — more at WAVE] **:** any of numerous snout beetles (group Rhynchophora) in which the head is elongated and usu. curved downward to form a snout bearing the jaws at the tip, the antennae are usu. geniculate, and the covering of the body is rough and hard and which although of small size may be very injurious as the larvae of some live in nuts, fruit, and grain and eat out the interior while the larvae of others bore under the bark and into the pith of trees and other plants — see BOLL WEEVIL, PEA WEEVIL, SEED WEEVIL, STRAWBERRY CROWN BORER

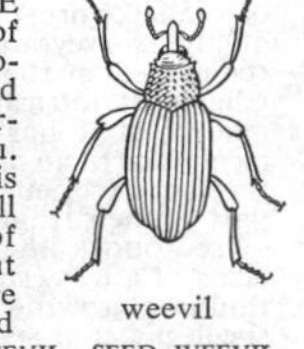
weevil

wee·viled *or* **wee·villed** \-ld\ *adj* [*weevil* + *-ed*] **:** WEEVILY
wee·vily *or* **wee·vil·ly** \-v(ə)lē, -li\ *adj* **:** infested with weevils
¹**wee-wee** \'wē,wē\ *vi* **wee-weed; wee-weeing; wee-wees** [baby talk] **:** URINATE — not often in polite use
²**wee-wee** \"\ *n* -s **:** URINE — not often in polite use
weeze \'wēz\ *vi* -ED/-ING/-S [ME *wesen*, fr. OE *wēsan*, fr. *wōs* juice, sap — more at SHUTUR SOWAR] *Scot & dial Eng* **:** OOZE
WEF *abbr, often not cap* with effect from
¹**weft** \'weft\ *n* -s [ME, fr. OE; akin to ON *veptr* weft, OE *wefan* to weave — more at WEAVE] **1 a :** the thread or yarn that crosses the warp and extends from selvage to selvage of a cloth **:** the thread carried by the shuttle **:** a filling thread **:** WOOF, PICK **b :** yarn used for this purpose **2 :** WEB, FABRIC; *also* **:** an article of woven fabric ⟨let thy ~ be of one woof and warp —Elizabeth B. Browning⟩ **3 :** a thin layer esp. of cloud, mist, or smoke **4 :** filling for baskets or mats; *also* **:** the fabric made with them **5 :** a thin feltlike layer of interlacing hyphae **6 :** a switch used by beginners for practice training in hairdressing techniques
²**weft** \"\ *vi* -ED/-ING/-S **:** to form or weave a weft

[3]**weft** \"\ *n* -s [by alter.] *archaic* : WAIF
[4]**weft** *var of* WAFT
weft fork *n* [[1]*weft*] : FILLING FORK
weft-knit \ˈ⸗,⸗\ *or* **weft-knitted** \ˈ⸗;⸗⸗\ *adj* : made by weft knitting ⟨most sweaters, bathing suits . . . are made of *weft-knit* fabrics —G.A.Urlaub⟩
weft knitting *n* : knitting in which each row of loops is formed by a crosswise thread made chiefly on circular or flat machines — compare WARP KNITTING
weftwise \ˈ⸗,⸗\ *adj* [[1]*weft* + *-wise*] : of or relating to the weft : running across the warp : CROSSWISE ⟨a ~ design⟩
we·ge·ner hypothesis \ˈvāgənə(r)-\ *n, usu cap W* [after Alfred L. *Wegener* †1930 Ger. geophysicist] : a hypothesis in geology: the existing continents were orig. one land area of which portions have separated and since Carboniferous time have slowly drifted apart moving on a plastic substratum
we-group \ˈwē,⸗\ *n* [*we* + *group*] : INGROUP
wehr·lite \ˈwər,līt, ˈver-\ *n* -s [F, fr. A. *Wehrle* †1835 Austrian mining commissioner + F *-ite*] : a mineral approximately Bi_2Te_3 consisting of a native alloy of bismuth and tellurium
wehr·macht \ˈver,mä|kt, ˈveə,m-, -mä|, |kt\ *n* -s *usu cap* [G, fr. *wehr* defense (fr. OHG *werī*) + *macht* force, might, fr. OHG *maht* — more at WEIR, MIGHT] : the armed forces esp. of Germany from 1935 to 1945
wei·bull·ite \ˈwī,bu̇,līt\ *n* -s [Sw *weibullit*, fr. Kristian Oskar M. *Weibull* †1923 Swed. mineralogist + Sw *-it* -ite] : a mineral PbBi(S,Se) consisting of seleniferous sulfide of lead and bismuth and occurring usu. in massive prismatic to fibrous aggregates
weid \ˈwēd\ *Scot & Irish var of* [4]WEED
wei·ge·la \wīˈjēlə, -ˈgē-, ˈwījələ, ˈwīgələ\ *n* [NL, fr. Christian E. *Weigel* †1831 Ger. physician] **1** *cap* : a genus of showy shrubs (family Caprifoliaceae) sometimes esp. formerly included in the genus *Diervilla* but distinguished by having the corolla not 2-lipped **2** -s : any shrub of the genus *Weigela* (esp. *W. florida*)
wei·ge·lia \wīˈjēlēə, -ˈgēl-\ *n* -s [NL, fr. Christian E. *Weigel* †1831 + NL *-ia*] **1** : WEIGELA 2 **2** : a moderate red that is yellower and paler than cerise, claret (sense 3a), or average strawberry (sense 2a) and paler than Turkey red
wei·gert's method \ˈvīgə(r)ts-\ *n, usu cap W* [after Karl *Weigert* †1905 Ger. pathologist] : a method of tracing the course of medullated nerve fibers by hardening the tissues in a solution of potassium dichromate and staining the sections for myelin sheaths
[1]**weigh** \ˈwā\ *vb* -ED/-ING/-S [ME *weyen, weghen*, fr. OE *wegan* to move, carry, weigh; akin to OHG *wegan* to move, carry, weigh, ON *vega* to move, carry, weigh, Goth *gawigan* to move, shake, L *vehere* to carry — more at WAY] *vt* **1** : to examine by a balance : ascertain the heaviness of ⟨~ myself on a bathroom scales⟩ ⟨a thinking brain capable of ~*ing* stars or atoms —L.C.Eiseley⟩ — often used with *up* ⟨when cotton was picked and ~*ed* up —Lillian Smith⟩ **2** *obs* : ESTEEM, REGARD **3 a** : OUTWEIGH ⟨a clean windscreen . . . could ~ the balance between life or death on the roads —Priscilla Hughes⟩ — often used with *down* **b** : COUNTERBALANCE ⟨better placed than some to ~ the particular criticisms against the general indictment —Barbara Ward⟩ — sometimes used with *off* ⟨the two commands must be ~*ed* off the one against the other —J.C.Swaim⟩ **c** : to make heavy : WEIGHT ⟨sewing silk, ~*ed* with fillers to lend luster —A.A. Stonehill⟩ ⟨sack of meal slung over his shoulder and ~*ing* him forward —E.L.Thomas⟩ — often used with *down* ⟨his style is ~*ed* down with localisms —*Americas*⟩ ⟨she ~*ed* down her repertory with these plays —Frances Frenaye⟩ **4** : to consider or examine for the purpose of forming an opinion or coming to a conclusion : consider carefully esp. by balancing one quality, aspect, or thing against another in order to make a choice, decision, or judgment : EVALUATE, PONDER ⟨in philosophy, the fact, the theory, the alternatives, and the ideal are ~*ed* together —A.N.Whitehead⟩ ⟨grand jury is currently ~*ing* indictments —*Newsweek*⟩ ⟨no tedious ~*ing* of pros and cons —*Irish Digest*⟩ ⟨experts are already ~*ing* the significance of the move —*Nation*⟩ — often used with *up* ⟨~*ing* up several propositions —*Farmer's Weekly (So. Africa)*⟩ ⟨accustomed to ~ up situations and make decisions quickly —*Times Rev. of Industry*⟩ **5 a** : to heave up (an anchor) preparatory to sailing **b** *archaic* : HEAVE, HOIST, RAISE **6** : to measure or portion out (a definite quantity of a commodity or substance) on or as if on a scales — often used with *out* or *up* ⟨~ out equal portions⟩ **7** : to hold or balance in the hand for or as if estimating the weight ⟨~*ed* a stone, then threw it⟩ **8** : to determine the force in pounds that will draw (a bow) the length of the appropriate arrow **9** : to determine the pressure required to pull (the trigger of a firearm) ~ *vi* **1 a** : to have weight : be heavy : have a specified weight ⟨he ~*s* 200 pounds⟩ ⟨a sirloin steak ~*ing* six pounds —Jane Nickerson⟩ **b** : to register a weight (as on a scales) — used with *in* or *out* and *at* ⟨a largemouth bass that ~*ed* in at better than fourteen pounds —Horace Sutton⟩ ⟨the hog ~*ed* out at 225 pounds after butchering⟩ — compare WEIGH IN, WEIGH OUT **2** : to be considered as important : have weight in the intellectual balance : carry weight : COUNT, MILITATE, TELL ⟨such recommendations will ~ in the candidate's favor⟩ ⟨those pieces of evidence will ~ heavily against him⟩ ⟨for the purposes of an editor of poetry stylistic evidence is evidence that must ~ —*Times Lit. Supp.*⟩ ⟨arguments which . . . would be likely to ~ with other conscientious parents —Bertrand Russell⟩ **3 a** : to press down with or as if with a heavy weight ⟨have one's gun ~*ing* on one's arm —T.H.White b. 1906⟩ ⟨extension of his erudition (which never ~*s*) to other literatures —A.T.MacAllister⟩ ⟨taxes ~ heavily on the incentive to save —A.E.Buck⟩ **b** : to be a source of doubt, indecision, worry, or regret : have a saddening or disheartening effect ⟨shook their heads sadly . . . as though the recollection of the interview ~*ed* heavily —R.H. Davis⟩ — usu. used with *on* or *upon* ⟨the responsibility for her decision ~*ed* on her —Laura Krey⟩ ⟨their insecurity ~*s* upon them and causes much bitterness —L.S.B.Leakey⟩ **4** : to weigh anchor ⟨the fleet ~*ed* and proceeded to the anchorage —S.E.Morison⟩ **5 a** : to weigh in ⟨finished third in a 2500-meter hurdle race . . . and went in to ~ —Ernest Hemingway⟩ **b** : to weigh out ⟨the jockeys ~*ed* out at once⟩ **syn** see BURDEN, CONSIDER, DEPRESS — **weigh anchor 1** : to hoist a boat's anchor **2** : to make ready to start — **weigh one's words** : to choose or use one's words deliberately
[2]**weigh** \"\ *n* -s [ME *weye, weighe*, fr. OE *wǣge* weight, wey; akin to OHG *wāga* weight, scale, ON *vāg* weight, scale, OE *wegan* to move, carry, weigh] **1** *dial Eng* : WEY **2** : WEIGHING ⟨cheating the miners on the ~ —James Higgins⟩ ⟨recommendations as to ~*s*, qualities, and grades —*Jour. of Home Economics*⟩
[3]**weigh** \"\ *n* -s [alter. of *way*] : WAY — used in the phrase *under weigh* as a variant of *under way* ⟨the ship's captain . . . immediately got under ~ —Deneys Reitz⟩ ⟨studies under ~ will show . . . the meaning of different scores —*Science*⟩ ⟨a political reaction which was already visibly under ~ —George Orwell⟩
weigh·able \ˈwāəbəl\ *adj* [ME *weiable*, fr. *weien, weyen* to weigh + *-able*] : capable of being weighed
weigh·age \ˈwāij\ *n* -s [[1]*weigh* + *-age*] *Brit* : a duty or toll paid for weighing merchandise
weighbar \ˈ⸗,⸗\ *or* **weighbar shaft** *n* [[1]*weigh* + *bar*] *Brit* : ROCKSHAFT; *esp* : one in a radial gear
weighbeam \ˈ⸗,⸗\ *n* [[1]*weigh* + *beam*] : a large steelyard
weighbridge \ˈ⸗,⸗\ *n* [[1]*weigh* + *bridge*] : a platform scale flush with the roadway (as for weighing vehicles, cattle, or coal)
weigh down *vt* [ME *weghen down*] **1** : to cause to bend down or sink : OVERBURDEN ⟨branches *weighed down* with fruit⟩ ⟨faculty members . . . already *weighed down* with heavy teaching loads —*Educational & Psychological Measurement*⟩ ⟨the term, being so *weighed down* with false meaning —M.F.A. Montagu⟩ **2** : OPPRESS, DEPRESS ⟨a melancholy damp . . . to *weigh* thy spirits *down* —John Milton⟩ ⟨a black depression *weighed* me *down* —Kenneth Roberts⟩
weighed *adj* [fr. past part. of [1]*weigh*] : TESTED, TRIED, EXPERIENCED, BALANCED ⟨~ judgments⟩
weigh·er \ˈwāə(r), ˈwe(ə)r, ˈweə\ *n* -s [ME *weyer*, fr. *weyen* to weigh + *-er* — more at [1]WEIGH] : one that weighs: as **a** : one that weighs materials or products for purposes of verification, adjustment, or record **b** : a customs inspector who determines and records the weight of merchandise **c** : a worker who weighs out ingredients for a given product
weighhouse \ˈ⸗,⸗\ *n* [ME *weyhous*, fr. *weyen* to weigh + *hous* house] : a building at or within which goods are weighed
weigh in *vi* **1 a** : to have oneself or one's possessions (as baggage) weighed (as before an airplane flight) **b** *of a boxer or wrestler* : to have oneself weighed by a medical examiner on the day of a fight **c** *of a jockey* : to have oneself weighed with saddle and weights at the finish of a race — compare WEIGH OUT **2** : to enter as a participant, contributor, or mediator ⟨a bystander *weighed in* to stop the fight⟩ ⟨with a battle of quick wits to be fought in front of 500 people nature *weighs in* with an increased dose of adrenalin —D.E.Morris⟩ ~ *vt* **1** : to take the weight of esp. before an airplane flight or as a test of qualification before a contest (as a boxing match) **2** : to take the weight of (a jockey) after a race — compare WEIGH OUT
weigh-in \ˈ⸗,⸗\ *n* -s [*weigh in*] : an instance of weighing in a contestant : the act of weighing in contestants ⟨the official *weigh-in* usually takes place about noon —Nat Fleischer⟩
weighing *n* -s [ME *weying*, fr. gerund of *weyen* to weigh] **1 a** : the act of one that weighs ⟨weights for the more precise ~*s* in physical and chemical laboratories —T.W.Lashof & L.B.Macurdy⟩ **b** : a quantity weighed as one lot **2** *Brit* : the settling or subsiding of a mine roof
weighing machine *n* : [1]SCALE 2c
weigh larry *n* : [4]LARRY 2
weighlock \ˈ⸗,⸗\ *n* [[1]*weigh* + *lock*] : a lock (as on a canal) in which boats are weighed and their tonnage is settled
weigh·man \ˈwāmən\ *n, pl* **weighmen** [[1]*weigh* + *man*] : a man whose work is weighing articles or goods : WEIGHER
weighmaster \ˈ⸗,⸗⸗\ *n* [[1]*weigh* + *master*] : a company employee or licensed public official who verifies the weight of loads (as of coal, ore, or grain)
weigh·ment \ˈwāmənt\ *n* -s : an act of weighing ⟨sensitivity permits ~*s* to fractions of a gram —*advt*⟩
weigh out *vi, of a jockey* : to have oneself weighed with saddle and weights before the start of a race — compare WEIGH IN 1c ~ *vt* : to take the weight of (a jockey) before the start of a race as a test of qualification — compare WEIGH IN 2
weigh-out \ˈ⸗,⸗\ *n* -s [*weigh out*] : the weighing out of a jockey
weighs *pres 3d sing of* WEIGH, *pl of* WEIGH
weigh scale *n* [ME *weyscale*, fr. *weyen* to weigh + *scale*] **1** : SCALEPAN **2 weigh scales** *pl* : a pair of scales
weighshaft \ˈ⸗,⸗\ *n* [[1]*weigh* + *shaft*] : ROCKSHAFT
[1]**weight** \ˈwāt, *usu* -ād.+V\ *n* -s [ME *weght, wight*, fr. OE *wiht*; akin to MHG *gewiht* weight, ON *vætt* weight, OE *wegan* to weigh — more at WEIGH] **1 a** : the often specified amount that a thing weighs : quantity of heaviness ⟨a basketball player with a playing ~ of 215 pounds⟩ ⟨two hundred and fifty pounds is considered the most desirable ~ for butchering . . . hogs —F.J.Haskin⟩ ⟨a diamond of five carats ~⟩ ⟨gross ~⟩ ⟨net ~⟩ — see LEGAL WEIGHT **b** (1) : the standard or established amount that a given thing should weigh — see SHORT WEIGHT (2) : one of the classes into which contestants in a sports event (as a boxing or wrestling match) or other contest are divided according to their body weight ⟨preliminary bouts in several ~*s*⟩ ⟨learnt when to stand and fight at his own ~ —H.A.Sinclair⟩ — see FEATHERWEIGHT; compare CATCHWEIGHT (3) : the poundage including that of the jockey, equipment, and any added lead that is necessary to make up the total required to be carried by a horse in a handicap race according to its rated ability (4) : BASIS WEIGHT **2 a** : a quantity or thing weighing a fixed and usu. specified amount ⟨equal ~ of water and air⟩ ⟨the necessary ~ of cold water is placed in a large steam-jacketed cooking kettle —*Bindery Glues*⟩ **b** : a heavy object (as a ball of metal) that is thrown, put, or lifted as an athletic game or exercise — compare HAMMER 4, SHOT 2b **c** : one of the iron disks used in playing the game of shuffleboard **3 a** : a unit of weight or mass ⟨table of ~*s*⟩ — see MEASURE table, METRIC SYSTEM table **b** : a piece of metal, glass, wood, or other material having an exact specified weight for use in weighing other articles (as in a scale) **c** *dial* : a customary local unit for a particular commodity **d** : a system of related units of weight ⟨avoirdupois ~⟩ ⟨troy ~⟩ **e** *Austral* : PENNYWEIGHT **4 a** : a ponderous mass : something heavy : LOAD ⟨a heavy ~ to carry so far⟩ **b** : a heavy contrivance or object to hold or press something down or to counterbalance: as (1) : a piece of lead or other relatively heavy material attached to a fishing line to cause it to sink (2) : PAPERWEIGHT ⟨a collection of very good-looking ~*s* —*New Yorker*⟩ (3) : a piece of lead sewed into a hem (as of a coat or curtain) to keep it hanging straight ⟨drapery ~⟩ (4) : a heavy metal object used to drive a clock **c** : the heaviness of overlying material (as rock over a mine shaft) **d** : CORPULENCE ⟨had grown portly with the years, but carried his ~ well —F.J.Mather⟩ **5 a** : BURDEN, PRESSURE ⟨could force a rescue by sheer ~ of numbers —T.B.Costain⟩ ⟨hangs like some guilty ~ of dark, unfathomed remembrances upon my energies —Thomas De Quincey⟩ ⟨never thought her poor brain could stand the ~ of such a secret —Kathleen Freeman⟩ ⟨the ~ of sky and stone seemed to slow the pace of the Sunday walkers —Kay Boyle⟩ **b** : PONDEROUSNESS ⟨empire fell to pieces of its own ~, largely because it had never been able to build any system of government except a simple tyranny —C.S. Forester⟩ **6 a** : relative heaviness : ponderability regarded as a property of matter ⟨~ is a quality of material substances⟩ **b** : the force with which a body is attracted toward the earth or a celestial body by gravitation and which is a quantity dependent on the place where it is determined : the product of the mass of a body by the local gravitational acceleration expressed in any of the units (as pound, ounce, newton, or dyne) by which force is measured **7 a** : the relatively great importance or authority accorded something ⟨had a great reputation in the parish for sober living and ~ in business —Mary Deasy⟩ ⟨discussion of the merits and demerits of toll roads produced a debate of considerable ~ —*N.Y. Times*⟩ **b** : measurable influence esp. in determining the acts of others ⟨throw one's ~ behind a candidate⟩ ⟨the professor had a lot of ~ to throw around the campus —Bennett Cerf⟩ **c** : power to influence the judgment ⟨their opinions always carried ~ —A.W.Long⟩ ⟨gives some ~ to his assertion that the act was sudden and unpremeditated —E.L.Pearson⟩ ⟨these replies lend ~ to the generally-expressed view —*Wall Street Jour.*⟩ **8** : something acting with heavy or overpowering force ⟨principles and rules . . . have petrified with the accumulated ~ of precedent on precedent —B.N.Cardozo⟩ ⟨futile to think of escape from the ~ of global responsibilities —Oscar Handlin⟩ ⟨having first justified with a ~ of scholarship my unscholarly assumption —F.R.Leavis⟩ **9** : the pull required to draw a bow to the full extent and measured in pounds **10** : the quality (as lightness or heaviness) that makes a fabric or garment suitable or adaptable for a particular use or season — often used in combination ⟨dress-*weight*⟩ **11** : ATOMIC WEIGHT **12** : the degree of thickness of the strokes of a type character **13** : stress value, quantity, or general sonority in individual sounds, syllables, and units of rhythmic structure in verse **14 a** : a relative value assigned to an item in a group or series under consideration ⟨the use of some system of ~*s* for differences in skills is difficult —W.E.Moore⟩ ⟨few data are available on the relative ~ of various emotions —J.E.Anderson⟩ ⟨if you have five problems . . . allot your time proportionately unless a ~ is given —W.F.Crum⟩ ⟨the most useful direct source was given a ~ of ten, the second most useful, a ~ of nine —Saul Herner⟩ **b** (1) : the frequency of an item in a frequency distribution (2) : a number assigned to express the relative importance of such an item (3) : the factor by which the value of such an item is multiplied in forming the weighted average of the values of the various items **syn** see IMPORTANCE, INFLUENCE
[2]**weight** \"\ *vt* -ED/-ING/-S **1 a** : to load or make heavy with or as if with a weight ⟨~ the head of a golf club with lead⟩ ⟨sat next to a dame who was ~*ed* with jewels —H.J.Laski⟩ ⟨never had he dreamed that words could be so ~*ed* with unfamiliar meaning —Christine Weston⟩ — often used with *down* ⟨a coarse net is thrown over the roof and ~*ed* down —L.D.Stamp⟩ **b** : to increase in heaviness by adding an inferior ingredient ⟨tea that has been ~*ed*⟩ **c** : to make (yarn or cloth) heavier by adding any of various substances (as sizing, clay, or flock); *esp* : to pass (silk) through baths of tin salts **d** : to make thicker ⟨with the camera lens, type can be reduced, enlarged, ~*ed*, slanted —*Book Production*⟩ **2** : to oppress with a burden (as sorrow, dejection, or discouragement) — often used with *down* ⟨was ~*ed* down with many cares⟩ **3 a** : WEIGH 1 ⟨test tubes and crucibles . . . and scales that ~*ed* your signature —Thomas Wood †1950⟩ **b** : to feel the weight of : HEFT ⟨~ a stone⟩ **4 a** : to assign a value expressing the relative importance of (a thing) as the result of a measurement or judgment **b** : to attach factors indicative of their relative frequency or importance (to the various items of a frequency distribution) ⟨the prices thus obtained were ~*ed* according to the net sales of each type of store —*Experiment Station Record*⟩ **5** : to arrange, bias, or incline in a particular direction by manipulation ⟨the tax structure . . . which was ~*ed* so heavily in favor of the upper classes —A.S.Link⟩ ⟨legislatures create vested and sentimental interests which ~ national policy in the direction of patchwork rather than mosaic —H.D.Lasswell⟩ **6** : to assign a handicap weight to (a racehorse) **7** : to shift the burden of weight upon ⟨~ the inside ski⟩ **syn** see BURDEN
[3]**weight** \"\ *n* -s [ME *wheit, wehit, weght*, akin to OE *wiht* weight — more at [1]WEIGHT] : a leather-covered hoop like a sieve but without holes used for winnowing grain
weight·age \ˈwād·ij\ *n* -s [[2]*weight* + *-age*] : the assignment of a quota (as of members of a legislature) to a particular segment of the population as a special favor or concession in a proportion above that allowable on a strictly numerical basis
weight agreement *n* : an arrangement between shippers and carriers that allows the use of estimated weight of shipment components in obtaining freight charges and total weight
weight box *or* **weight pocket** *n* : a channel in a window frame in which the sash weights move up and down
weight boy *n* : a textile worker who weighs yarn and distributes it to winders
weight cloth *n* : a saddlecloth into which flat lead pieces are fitted when a jockey's weight is less than the amount his horse must carry
weighted *adj* [fr. past part. of [2]*weight*] **1** : made heavy or weighty : LOADED ⟨~ silk⟩ **2 a** : relatively evaluated or adjusted ⟨a system of ~, proportionate voting —*Current Biog.*⟩ **b** : having a statistical weight attached ⟨construct a ~ aggregative index number —F.E.Croxton & D.J.Cowden⟩ — **weight·ed·ly** *adv* — **weight·ed·ness** *n* -ES
weighted average *or* **weighted mean** *n* : an average of the values of a set of items to each of which is accorded a weight indicative of its frequency or relative importance
weighted value *n* : the product of the value of an item of a frequency distribution by its weight
weight·er \ˈwād·ə(r)\ *n* -s : one that weights; *specif* : a textile worker who increases the weight of yarns or fabrics by adding substances by chemical or mechanical methods
weight font *n* : type packaged in an assortment and quantity sufficient to fill a job case and sold by weight
weight for age : a weight apportioned to a racehorse according to its age irrespective of any other penalties or allowances
weight·i·ly \ˈwād·ᵊlē, -ātᵊl, |ōl|, |i\ *adv* : in a weighty manner ⟨the speech was weighty in substance and ~ delivered —J.A. Froude⟩ ⟨moved slowly and ~ —Mary R. Rinehart⟩
weight·i·ness \|ēnəs, |in-\ *n* -ES : the quality or state of being weighty
[1]**weighting** *n* -s [fr. gerund of [2]*weight*] **1 a** : the act of one who weights ⟨some of the author's ~*s* might be disputed —Walter Millis⟩ **b** : something used as a weight **2** *or* **weighting allowance** *Brit* : a salary differential to compensate for a difference in living costs ⟨given a London ~⟩
[2]**weighting** *Brit var of* WEIGHING 2
weight in hand : the actual weight of an archery bow
weight·less \ˈwātləs\ *adj* **1** : having no weight **2** : having little or no perceptible weight ⟨floating freely in a ~ condition, at the same velocity as the spaceship —*Current Biog.*⟩ ⟨a baby bat . . . fluffy and ~ as a moth —Frederic Prokosch⟩ ⟨jackets made of a ~ polyester fabric⟩ — **weight·less·ly** *adv* — **weight·less·ness** *n* -ES
weight lifter *n* : one that competes in or exercises by means of weight lifting
weight lifting *n* : a sport in which barbells are lifted competitively or as an exercise — compare CLEAN AND JERK, PRESS 9a, SNATCH
weight man *n* : an athlete who competes in one or more field events (as the hammer throw, shot put, discus throw, or javelin throw)
weight of metal : the total weight of the projectiles that can be fired from a single gun in a given time or of those that can be fired simultaneously from an assemblage of guns
weight of wind : the wind pressure measured in inches of water that is supplied to a pipe-organ stop or group of stops
Weight·om·e·ter \wād·ˈäməd·ə(r)\ *trademark* — used for an automatic weighing device
weights *pl of* WEIGHT, *pres 3d sing of* WEIGHT
weighty \ˈwād·ē, -ātē, |i\ *adj* -ER/-EST [ME, fr. [1]*weight* + *-y*] **1 a** : having much importance or consequence : MOMENTOUS ⟨let me have your advice in a ~ affair —Jonathan Swift⟩ ⟨a ~ problem⟩ **b** : expressing or characterized by seriousness or gravity : EARNEST, SOLEMN ⟨a ~ plea⟩ ⟨looked upon me with a ~ countenance —William Penn⟩ ⟨a rather ~ pause —Louis Auchincloss⟩ ⟨a ~, consequential, humorless manner —Kingsley Amis⟩ **2 a** : weighing a considerable amount ⟨a ~ load⟩ ⟨several loads of extremely ~ cattle —*Chicago Daily Drovers Jour.*⟩ ⟨put the ~ parcel back into the woman's arms —G.G. Carter⟩ **b** : of large size : CORPULENT ⟨a ~ man⟩ **c** : falling or pressing heavily ⟨a ~ blow⟩ **d** : heavy in proportion to its bulk : of high specific gravity ⟨a ~ metal⟩ **3** : hard to be borne : BURDENSOME, GRIEVOUS, ONEROUS ⟨a ~ evil⟩ **4** *obs* : of standard weight ⟨contract to be paid in ~ money —John Locke⟩ **5** : having much force, influence, or authority : POWERFUL, TELLING ⟨is pretty clear that no book in the 18th century made quite so ~ or so wide an impact —H.J.Laski⟩ **syn** see HEAVY
wei·hai·wei \ˈwāˈhīˈwī\ *adj, usu cap* [fr. *Weihaiwei*, China] : of or from the city of Weihaiwei, China : of the kind or style prevalent in Weihaiwei
weil-fe·lix reaction \ˈvī(ə)lˈfāliks-\ *or* **weil-felix test** *n, usu cap W&F* [after Edmund *Weil* †1922 and Arthur *Felix* †1956 Austrian physicians] : an agglutination test for various rickettsial infections (as typhus fever and scrub typhus) using particular strains of bacteria of the genus *Proteus* that have antigens in common with the rickettsias to be identified
weil's disease \ˈvī(ə)lz-, ˈwī(ə)lz-\ *n, usu cap W* [after Adolf *Weil* †1916 Ger. physician] : a leptospirosis that is characterized by chills, fever, muscle pain, and hepatitis manifested by more or less severe jaundice and that is caused by a spirochete (*Leptospira icterohaemorrhagiae*)
wei·mar·an·er \ˈvīmə,ränə(r), ˈwī-, -,rän-, -,ran-, ,⸗⸗ˈ⸗⸗\ *n* [G, fr. *Weimar*, city in central Germany where the breed was developed] **1** *usu cap* : a German breed of large gray, short-haired sporting dogs with pendulous ears and cropped tail **2** -s *often cap* : a dog of the Weimaraner breed
[1]**wei·mar·i·an** \vīˈma(ə)rēən, wī-\ *adj, usu cap* [*Weimar*, Germany + E *-an*] **1** : of, relating to, or characteristic of Weimar, Germany **2** : of, relating to, or characteristic of the residents of Weimar, Germany
[2]**weimarian** \"\ *n* -s *cap* : a native or resident of Weimar, Germany
weiner *var of* WIENER
wein·man·nia \wīnˈmanēə\ *n, cap* [NL, fr. J. W. *Weinmann*, 18th cent. Ger. apothecary + NL *-ia*] : a large genus of shrubs and trees (family Cunoniaceae) that are found chiefly in the southern hemisphere and have opposite mostly simple leaves, racemose flowers, a free ovary, and 2-celled 2-valved capsules — see TENIO
wein·schenk·ite \ˈvīn,sheŋ,kīt\ *n* -s [G *weinschenkit*, fr. Ernst H. O. K. *Weinschenk* †1921 Ger. petrographer + G *-it* -ite] : a mineral $(Er,Y)PO_4.2H_2O$ consisting of a hydrous phosphate of rare earths and occurring in white rounded aggregates and radiating masses
[1]**weir** \ˈwi(ə)r, ˈwa(ə)r, ˈwe|, |(ə)\ *n* -s [ME *were*, fr. OE *wer*; akin to OHG *werī* defense, ON *ver* fishing place, OE *werian* to defend, protect, hinder, OHG *werien, werren* to defend, ON

verja, Goth *warjan* to defend, L *aperire* to open, *operire* to close, cover, Gk *erysthai* to protect, guard, Skt *vṛṇoti* he covers, envelops, holds back, surrounds] **1 :** a fence or enclosure (as of stakes, brushwood, or netting) set in a stream, tideway, or inlet of the sea for taking fish **:** FISHGARTH ⟨eel ~⟩ ⟨herring ~⟩ **2 a :** a dam in a stream to raise the water level or divert its flow — see LEAPING WEIR **b :** a notch in a levee or other barrier across or bordering a stream to regulate the flow of water (as in time of flood) — see WASTEWEIR **3** *dial Eng* **:** a bank or levee built to hold a river in its bed or to direct it into a new bed **4 :** a device (as a notch in a dam) for determining the quantity of water flowing over it from measurements of the depth of water over the crest or sill and known dimensions of the device — see CIPOLLETTI WEIR

2weir \"\ *vt* -ED/-ING/-S **:** to put a weir in or on ⟨~ a river⟩

3weir \'wi(ə)r\ *Scot var of* WAR

weir basin *n* **:** a wide approach to the upstream side of an irrigation weir constructed so as to reduce to a minimum the effect of the momentum of the approaching water on the flow over the weir

weir box *n* **:** a wooden or concrete box oblong in shape and open at both ends which is set lengthwise in a canal and in which a weir for the measurement of irrigation water is set crosswise

1weird \'wi(ə)rd, -i(ə)d\ *n* -S [ME *wierd, werd, wird,* fr. OE *wyrd;* akin to OHG *wurt* fate, ON *urthr* weird, fate, OE *weorthan* to become — more at WORTH] **1 a :** FATE, DESTINY, LOT, FORTUNE; *esp* **:** ill fortune **:** a disastrous destiny **b** *usu cap* **:** 1FATE 3, NORN **2 a :** SOOTHSAYER **b :** SPELL, CHARM **c :** a supernatural tale **3 :** PROPHECY, PREDICTION

2weird \"\ *vt* -ED/-ING/-S [ME (Sc) *weirden, werden,* fr. *wierd, werd* fate] **1** *Scot* **:** to assign to a certain fate **:** DESTINE **2** *Scot* **:** to foretell or assign as a fate **:** PREDICT

3weird \"\ *adj* -ER/-EST [ME (Sc) *werd,* fr. *werd,* n., fate] **1** *archaic* **:** of, relating to, or dealing with fate or the Fates **2 a :** of or relating to witchcraft or to the supernatural **:** caused by or suggesting magical influence ⟨Spanish horses, which appeared as ~ centaurs to the amazed Indians —R.W. Murray⟩ ⟨~ stories of the supernatural, rousing terror and pity —Frank Monaghan⟩ **b :** UNEARTHLY, MYSTERIOUS ⟨a ~ desert of congealed lava —Tom Marvel⟩ ⟨around the sun appears the ~, pearly corona seen on earth only during total eclipses —Waldemar Kaempffert⟩ ⟨the ~, ringing voices of veeries —W.P.Smith⟩ **3 :** curious in nature or appearance **:** of strange or extraordinary character **:** ODD, UNUSUAL, FANTASTIC ⟨some trick of the moonlight, some ~ effect of shadow —Bram Stoker⟩ ⟨in this section grow many ~ varieties of cactus —*Amer. Guide Series: Texas*⟩ ⟨~ prophets popped up everywhere —G.W.Johnson⟩ ⟨some of his statements on local and state politics are a bit ~ —G.E.Mowry⟩

syn WEIRD, EERIE, and UNCANNY agree in the sense of fearfully or mysteriously strange or fantastic. WEIRD applies in one sense to something unearthly or preternaturally mysterious; in another sense, to something strangely or absurdly queer ⟨something a trifle *weird* about leaving the little man alone among those dead servants —G.K.Chesterton⟩ ⟨a touch of the *weird* or ghostly —P.E.More⟩ ⟨a procession of *weird* characters: sorcerers, syndics, half-wits, adolescent girls in pregnancy, hermaphrodites —Richard Plant⟩ ⟨preaching a *weird* interpretation of the Scriptures —*Amer. Guide Series: Ind.*⟩ EERIE suggests an uneasy, often fearful premonition that malign powers or influences are at work ⟨some *eerie* moments among the corpses —*Times Lit. Supp.*⟩ ⟨the flutes keep up an *eerie* wail —Horace Sutton⟩ ⟨the poem has an *eerie* quality, like that of dream or of neurosis —Yvor Winters⟩ ⟨the spruce trees and rocks loomed out of the fog in *eerie,* blurred shapes —Jean Potter⟩ UNCANNY suggests in one sense uncomfortable strangeness or mysteriousness; in another more common sense, merely beyond ordinary powers to comprehend or as though supernatural ⟨some *uncanny* apparition in a graveyard⟩ ⟨the machines operate with *uncanny* precision at high speeds —*Envelope*⟩ ⟨the natives display *uncanny* proficiency in detecting the whereabouts of fish —Bill Beatty⟩

weird·ie *or* **weirdy** \-dē\ *n, pl* **weirdies** *slang* **:** one that is extraordinarily strange, eccentric, or unnatural ⟨filmland's horrific *weirdies* —*Newsweek*⟩

weird·less \-dləs\ *adj, chiefly Scot* **1 :** ILL-FATED **2 :** IMPROVIDENT — **weird·less·ness** *n* -ES *chiefly Scot*

weirdlike \'ₛ,ₛ\ *adj* **:** WEIRD

weird·li·ness \-dlēnəs\ *n* -ES *chiefly Scot* **:** the quality or state of being weirdly

1weird·ly *adj* -ER/-EST [1*weird* + *-ly*] **1** *Scot* **:** PROSPEROUS, FORTUNATE **2** *chiefly Scot* **:** of or relating to the supernatural **:** GHOSTLY

2weirdly *adv* [3*weird* + *-ly*] **:** in a weird manner ⟨the ~ beautiful moonlight —Joseph Furphy⟩

weird·ness *n* -ES **:** the quality or state of being weird

weird sister *n, usu cap W&S* [ME *werd sister*] **:** 1FATE 3, NORN

weiring *n* -S [fr. gerund of 2*weir*] **1 :** the building of a weir (as in a stream for catching fish) **2 :** material for building a weir

weir·less \'ₛləs\ *adj* **:** lacking a weir **:** not provided with weirs

weirs *pl of* WEIR, *pres 3d sing of* WEIR

weir vine *n* [1*weir*] **:** a tuberous-rooted morning glory (*Ipomoea calobra*) that is an aggressive weed and reputed to be responsible for livestock poisoning in parts of Australia

weis·bach·ite \'wīs,bä,kīt\ *n* -S [G *weisbachit,* fr. Julius A. *Weisbach* †1901 Ger. mineralogist + G *-it* -ite] **:** a variety of anglesite containing barium

weisenheimer *var of* WISENHEIMER

1weis·man·ni·an \vī'smänēən, wī'sman-\ *adj, usu cap* [August *Weismann* †1914 Ger. biologist + E *-an,* adj. suffix] **:** of or relating to the theories or teachings of Weismann

2weismannian \"\ *n* -S *usu cap* [August *Weismann* + E *-an,* n. suffix] **:** an adherent of Weismann

weis·mann·ism \'vī,smä,nizəm, 'wīsmə,n-\ *n* -S *usu cap* [August *Weismann* †1914 + E *-ism*] **:** the theories of heredity and development proposed by August Weismann; *esp* **:** the concepts of continuity of the germ plasm and dichotomy of germ and soma with their correlates of germinal transmission of hereditary qualities and absence of inheritance of acquired characters

weiss beer \'wīs-, 'vīs-\ *n* [G *weissbier,* lit., white beer] **:** a light-colored highly effervescent beer made from unboiled wheat-malt worts with top-fermentation yeast

weiss·ite \'wī,sīt\ *n* -S [Louis *Weiss,* 20th cent. Am. mine owner + E *-ite*] **:** a mineral Cu_5Te_3 consisting of a massive bluish black copper telluride

weiss·nicht·wo \'vī,snik(t)'vō\ *n* -S *usu cap* [fr. *Weissnichtwo,* imaginary city in the satirical work *Sartor Resartus* (1833–34) by Thomas Carlyle †1881 Scot. essayist and historian, fr. G *weiss nicht wo* (I) know not where] **:** an indefinite, unknown, or imaginary place

weit·spek·an \'wit,spekən\ *n* -S *usu cap* [Yurok *Weitspekw,* a Yurok village + E *-an*] **:** a language family of the Ritwan stock comprising only Yurok

we·jack \'wē,jak\ *n* -S [of Algonquian origin; akin to Ojibwa *otchig* fisher, Cree *otchek;* perh. influenced by Ojibwa *wajashk* muskrat] **1 :** FISHER 2 **2 :** WOODCHUCK

we·ka \'wekə\ *n* -S [Maori] **:** any of several flightless New Zealand rails (genus *Gallirallus,* syn. *Ocydromus*) of thievish disposition having short wings each with a spur used in fighting — called also *Maori hen, wood hen*

welch *var of* WELSH

welch bacillus \'welch-, -lsh-\ *n, usu cap W* [after William Henry *Welch* †1934 Am. pathologist] **:** a clostridium (*Clostridium perfringens*) that causes gas gangrene

welchman *var of* WELSHMAN

welch plug *n* [prob. fr. the name *Welch*] **:** a plug for sealing an unused end of an oil passage drilled through a hollow crankshaft, crank arm, or crankpin

1wel·come \'welkəm, 'weůk-\ *interj* [ME, alter. (influenced by *wel* well) of *wilcume,* fr. OE *wilcuma, wilcume,* fr. *wilcuma* desirable guest; akin to OHG *willicomo* desirable guest; prob. both fr. a prehistoric WGmc compound whose constituents are represented by OE *will, willa* will, wish and OE *cuma* guest; akin to OE *cuman* to come — more at WELL, WILL, COME] — used to express a greeting of pleasure or goodwill or a cordial salutation to a guest or newcomer upon his arrival

2welcome \"\ *vt* -ED/-ING/-S [ME *welcomen,* alter. (influenced by *wel* well) of *wilcumen,* fr. OE *wilcumian,* fr. *wilcuma,* interj., welcome & *wilcuma,* n., desirable guest] **1 :** to greet (as a visitor) with courtesy or cordiality **:** receive hospitably and gladly **:** give a friendly reception to **:** make welcome ⟨ran . . . to ~ them at the door —J.C.Powys⟩ ⟨they *welcomed* the travelers home⟩ **2 :** to greet or receive with something esp. of an unpleasant nature ⟨they *welcomed* the intruder with a hail of bullets⟩ **3 a :** to greet heartily or joyfully ⟨*welcomed* his arrival from abroad⟩ **b :** to greet with pleasure the coming or occurrence of **:** accept with an expression of pleasure ⟨no mariner . . . ~*s* rough water —S.E.Morison⟩ ⟨those who deplore and those who ~ the change —John Strachey⟩ ⟨the society ~*s* applications from interested persons⟩

3welcome \"\ *adj* [ME, alter. (influenced by *wel* well) of *wilcume* desirable guest, fr. OE *wilcuma*] **1 :** received gladly into one's presence or companionship **:** admitted willingly to the company, house, or entertainment **:** highly acceptable as a visitor or companion ⟨a ~ guest⟩ ⟨visitors are always ~ here⟩ **2 :** giving pleasure **:** highly acceptable, agreeable, or pleasing **:** received with gladness or delight esp. in response to a need or desire ⟨revivals offered ~ interludes in pioneer life —*Amer. Guide Series: Minn.*⟩ ⟨the sight of the island was right ~ —Herman Melville⟩ ⟨providing an easy and ~ solution of an . . . awkward problem —W.L.Sperry⟩ **3 :** freely or willingly permitted **:** cordially invited ⟨he was ~ to come and go —W.M. Thackeray⟩ **4** — used in the phrase, "You're welcome" as a reply to an expression of thanks **syn** see PLEASANT

4welcome \"\ *n* -S **1 a :** a cordial, kindly, pleasant, or hearty greeting or reception given to one (as a guest, newcomer, or stranger) usu. upon arrival ⟨to thee and thy company I bid a hearty ~ —Shak.⟩ ⟨a packed house . . . roared a three-minute ~ —*Current Biog.*⟩ ⟨the ~ he received justified his visit —A.R.Forde⟩ **b :** a greeting or reception resembling such an act of welcoming but having a different nature usu. of a specified kind ⟨our men gave the enemy a hot ~ —Bill Alcine⟩ ⟨the delegation received a rather cool ~⟩ **2 :** the action of welcoming or of saluting or treating as welcome **:** hearty or hospitable reception (as of a stranger or guest) ⟨bore the means of goodly ~, flesh and wine —Alfred Tennyson⟩

welcome home *n* [fr. the phrase *welcome home*] **1 :** a reception usu. of a cordial nature provided to celebrate the return home of a person ⟨invited me to a supper for my *welcome home* —Philemon Holland⟩ **2 :** an expression of welcome made at a person's homecoming ⟨the *welcome home* which rang from every spire and steeple —*London Daily Telegraph*⟩

wel·come·ly *adv* **1 :** with a feeling or expression of welcome **:** with joy, pleasure, or hospitality **:** GLADLY ⟨I have been very kindly and ~ entertained —Thomas Chalmers⟩ **2 :** in a manner so as to produce welcome, gratification, or pleasure ⟨the conductor's ~ brisk tempo —Robert Lawrence⟩ ⟨the picture is ~ modest in all that it attempts —Brendan Gill⟩

welcome mat *n* **:** something held to resemble a mat placed before a door as a symbol of hospitality and pleasant reception ⟨rolled out the *welcome mat* for the visiting dignitaries⟩

wel·come·ness *n* -ES *archaic* **:** the quality or state of being welcome

wel·com·er \-mə(r)\ *n* -S **:** one that welcomes ⟨a crowd of ~*s* awaited the incoming train⟩ ⟨the traditional ~ of the outcast, America —J.R.Krueger⟩

1weld \'weld\ *also* **woald** *or* **wold** *or* **would** \'wōld\ *n* -S [ME *welde, wold;* akin to MLG *wolde* weld, MD *woude*] **1 :** DYER'S ROCKET **2 :** a yellow dye that is obtained from weld and contains luteolin as its chief coloring **3 :** ACACIA 5

2weld \'weld\ *vb* -ED/-ING/-S [alter. (influenced by *welled,* past part. of *well* to boil, rise, well) of obs. E *well* to weld, fr. ME *wellen* to boil, well, weld — more at WELL] *vi* **:** to become or be capable of being welded **:** undergo junction by welding ⟨iron ~*s* easily⟩ ⟨the parts ~*ed* together perfectly⟩ ~ *vt* **1 a :** to unite or consolidate (as metallic parts) by heating to a plastic or fluid state the surfaces of the parts to be joined and then allowing the metals to flow together with or without the addition of other molten metal or by hammering or compressing with or without previous softening by heat — compare GAS WELDING **b :** to unite (plastics) in a similar manner by heating **c :** to produce or repair (as an article) by this method ⟨~*ed* pipe⟩ ⟨~*ed* the crack in the tube⟩ **d :** to produce or create as if by such a process ⟨~ a political party out of . . . divisive elements —Gladwin Hill⟩ ⟨solidarity ~*ed* out of emergency —Amy Loveman⟩ ⟨West ~*s* reply to Soviet —Carlyle Morgan⟩ **2 :** to unite closely or intimately **:** join closely or inseparably **:** form into or as if into a single unit ⟨her gratitude ~*ed* her to him forever —Harrison Smith⟩ ⟨~ the warring Gaelic and English elements into a Norman-Irish nation —Brian Fitzgerald⟩ **3 :** to cause (tissues) to form a seal by adhesion

3weld \"\ *n* -S **1 :** a welded joint **:** the junction of a welded piece — see ARC WELD, BUTT WELD, CAULK WELD, CLEFT WELD, MASH WELD, PLUG WELD, RIPPLE WELD, RIVET WELD, SCARF-WELD, SEAM WELD **2 :** the union of metals by welding **:** the state or condition of being welded **3 :** the adhesion of tissues to form a seal ⟨a natural ~ formed by the healing together of artery and vein⟩

4weld \"\ *adj* [3*weld*] **:** WELDABLE; *specif* **:** made without complete fusion ⟨~ iron⟩ ⟨~ steel⟩

weld·abil·i·ty \,weldə'bilәd·ē\ *n* -ES **:** the quality, state, or property of being weldable **:** the capacity to undergo welding ⟨the chief factors governing ~ of aluminum —E.G.West⟩ ⟨tables on ~ of materials —W.A.Stanley⟩

weld·able \'weldəbəl\ *adj* **:** capable of being welded

welded tuff *n* **:** a tuff deposit sufficiently thick and hot at the time of emplacement that the fragments soften and coalesce to form a rock which simulates rhyolite or obsidian

weld·er \'weldə(r)\ *n* -S **:** one that welds: as **a :** one whose work is welding **b :** a machine used in welding

welder's helmet *n* **:** a helmet used in arc welding that shields the front of the head, has a protective lens for the eyes, and is fitted with a headgear on which it can usu. be tilted up out of the way

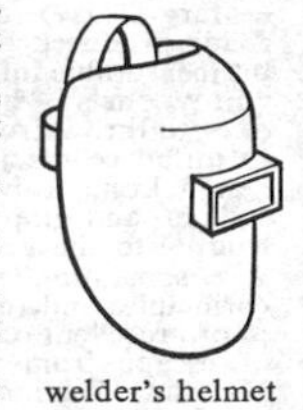
welder's helmet

welding *n* -S [fr. gerund of 2*weld*] **:** the action or process of making or joining with a weld

welding blowpipe *or* **welding torch** *n* **:** a blowpipe used in fusion welding

welding powder *n* **:** a powder used as a flux in welding

welding rod *n* **:** a rod or heavy wire that melts and thus supplies metal in fusion welding

weld·less \'weldləs\ *adj* **:** having no welds **:** made without a weld ⟨~ chain⟩ ⟨~ steel tubes⟩

weld·ment \-dmənt\ *n* -S **:** a unit formed by welding together an assembly of pieces ⟨the gear housings . . . are made of steel castings and ~*s* —Carl Himmelright⟩

weld metal *n* **:** the part of the metal of a welded joint that has been fused in its formation

wel·don process \'weldən-\ *n, usu cap W* [after Walter *Weldon* †1885 Eng. chemist] **:** a process used formerly for the recovery of manganese dioxide in making chlorine from hydrochloric acid in a stoneware still by adding lime to the still liquor and oxidizing with air to precipitate a mud containing calcium manganite and yielding chlorine when recirculated and treated with hydrochloric acid

wel·dor \'weldə(r)\ *n* -S [2*weld* + *-or*] **:** one whose work is welding **:** one skilled in welding **:** WELDER a

weld screw *n* **:** a screw that has a flat offset head and can be made captive by spot welding

1wel·fare \'wel,fa(a)(ə)r, -,fe|, |ə\ *n* -S [ME, fr. the phrase *wel faren* to fare well, fr. OE *wel faran,* fr. *wel* well + *faran* to fare — more at WELL, FARE] **1 a :** the state of faring or doing well **:** thriving or successful progress in life **:** a state characterized esp. by good fortune, happiness, well-being, or prosperity ⟨we can use the knowledge . . . for the future ~ of humanity —H.S.Truman⟩ ⟨a generous mother who sincerely seeks her child's ~ —H.M.Parshley⟩ ⟨increasing production has made ~ for all seem . . . possible —A.J.Toynbee⟩ — opposed to *illfare* **b :** the state or condition (as of a person or enterprise) in regard to well-being; *esp* **:** one's condition in regard to health, happiness, or prosperity ⟨the effects of climate upon the ~ . . . of man —D.H.K.Lee⟩ ⟨guilty of gross negligence of the ~ of his workers —T.P.Whitney⟩ **c :** the sum of individual utilities **:** a social optimum **2 :** WELFARE WORK ⟨helped to make music a recognized part of industrial ~ —Kenneth Baynes⟩ **3 :** RELIEF 2a

2welfare \"\ *adj* **:** of, relating to, or concerned with welfare and esp. with improvement of the welfare of social groups (as children, workers, or underprivileged or disabled persons) ⟨~ agencies⟩ ⟨~ services⟩ ⟨private ~ foundations⟩

welfare capitalism *n* **:** capitalism characterized by a concern for the welfare of various social groupings (as workers) expressed usu. through social-security programs, collective-bargaining agreements, state industrial codes, and other guarantees against insecurity

welfare economics *n* **:** a branch of economics dealing with human welfare, the defining of wealth, and the establishment of guides for social policy aiming at the maximization of total individual utilities

welfare factor *n* **:** any factor (as availability of food or shelter) that tends to stimulate population growth — compare DECIMATING FACTOR

welfare fund *n* **:** a fund usu. established by an employer from which benefits are paid to employees in time of sickness or other specified occasion and commonly set up in response to union pressure and as a contractual obligation

welfare state *n* **1 :** a social system based upon the assumption by a political state of primary responsibility for the individual and social welfare of its citizens usu. by the enactment of specific public policies (as health and unemployment insurance, minimum wages and prices, and subsidies to agriculture, housing, and other segments of the economy) and their implementation directly by governmental agencies **2 :** a political unit (as a nation or state) characterized by the operation of the system of the welfare state

welfare stat·er \-'stād·ə(r)\ *n* **:** one that believes in or advocates a welfare state

welfare statism *n* **:** a belief in or the advocacy or practice of policies associated with or designed to bring about a welfare state

welfare work *n* **1 :** organized efforts by a community, organization, or individual for the social betterment and general improvement in the welfare of a group in society (as underprivileged or disabled persons) **2 :** the provision of fringe benefits (as group insurance and pension plans, medical services, and educational and recreational activities) by a corporation as a labor policy esp. during the first quarter of the 20th century

wel·far·ism \'wel,fa(ə),rizəm, -,fe,r-\ *n* -S **:** the complex of policies, attitudes, and beliefs associated with welfare statism ⟨the bias of the Administration toward ~ —Jules Abels⟩ ⟨part of the same structure of ~ is government support of farm products prices —*Wall Street Jour.*⟩

welk \'welk\ *vi* -ED/-ING/-S [ME *welken,* prob. fr. MD; akin to OHG *irwelkēn* to welk, *irwelhēn* to become soft, *wolkan* cloud] **1** *dial chiefly Eng* **:** to lose freshness or greenness **:** dry up **:** FADE, WILT, WITHER **2** *obs* **:** to become less (as in power or brightness) **:** WANE

wel·kin \'welkən\ *n* -S [ME *welkin, welkne, wolkne* cloud, welkin, fr. OE *wolcen;* akin to OS & OHG *wolkan* cloud, *welk* moist, gentle, faded, OE *wlæc, wlacu* lukewarm, OIr *folc* flood of water, OSlav *vlaga* moisture] **1 :** the vault of heaven **:** FIRMAMENT, SKY ⟨fearsome storm-god . . . with his great ~ shuddering voice —Weston La Barre⟩ ⟨a chorus . . . that made the very ~ ring —Thomas Barbour⟩ **2 :** the celestial regions as the abode of God or the gods **:** the heavens **3 :** the upper atmosphere **:** the air in which clouds float ⟨the Air Force, as the custodian of our ~ —*New Yorker*⟩ ⟨scattered songsters probe the ~ —Jack Lusby⟩

1well \'wel\ *n* -S [ME *welle,* fr. OE (northern & Midland dial.) *welle;* akin to OHG *wella* wave, ON *vella* boiling heat, OE *weallan* to bubble, boil — more at 3WELL] **1 a :** an issue of water from the earth **:** a spring rising to the surface of the earth and forming a pool or rivulet **:** a pool fed by a spring ⟨the ~ flows in a pure and abundant stream from the granite rock —J.M.Jephson & L.A.Reeve⟩ **b :** a spring of water traditionally held to be of miraculous origin or to have supernatural healing or magical powers and often associated with a particular saint ⟨St. Gulval's *Well* . . . was famous for its prophetic properties —W.C.Meller⟩ **c (1) :** MINERAL SPRING **(2) wells** *pl* **:** a place where mineral springs are located and where invalids often resort **:** WATERING PLACE 3, SPA — used chiefly in place names ⟨Tunbridge *Wells*⟩ **d** *chiefly Scot* **:** a fountain fed by a spring **e (1) :** something resembling a spring (as in flowing or being used for drinking) ⟨start the ~*s* of plenty bubbling . . . with British gold —J.P.Fitzpatrick⟩ **(2) :** an origin from which something springs or arises **:** a source of supply **:** FOUNTAIN, WELLSPRING ⟨the ~*s* of his loquacity were dried up —C.S.Forester⟩ ⟨the native ~ of English in our young —J.M.Barzun⟩ **(3) :** a dangerous eddy **:** WHIRLPOOL — used esp. of eddies near the northern coast of Scotland **2 :** a pit or hole sunk (as by digging, boring, or drilling) into the earth to such a depth as to reach a supply of water, generally having a cylindrical form, and often walled with stone, bricks, or tubbing to prevent the earth from caving in **3 :** a part of a boat or other craft resembling a well: as **a :** a vertical enclosure in the middle of a ship's hold that reaches from the bottom to the lower deck and that contains and is designed to protect from damage and facilitate the inspection of the pumps — called also *pump well* **b :** a compartment in the hold of a fishing boat that is tight at the sides but has holes in the bottom to let in water to keep fish alive **c (1) :** a vertical passage into which a propeller may be drawn up or from which a periscope may be raised **(2) :** a hollow compartment recessed in an airplane wing or fuselage into which a unit (as a wing flap or landing gear wheel) retracts **d :** an enclosure in a ship's bottom into which water drains and is then pumped out; *esp* **:** the space between two tanks or sections of the double bottom or between either and a bulkhead **e :** a vertical passage in the bow of some old-style monitors in which the anchor is stowed **f :** the part of the main deck between the raised forecastle and the poop of a well-decked ship **4 :** a shaft or pit dug or bored in the earth: as **a :** one used for the storage of ice **b :** a shaft or excavation in the earth made in military mining from which run branches or galleries **c :** a shaft or hole sunk to obtain oil, brine, or gas ⟨an oil ~⟩ ⟨salt ~*s*⟩ **d :** RELIEF WELL **e (1) :** a pit or hole in the ground reaching to hardpan or bedrock **(2) :** a hollow cylinder of reinforced concrete, steel, timber, or masonry built in such a hole as a support for a bridge or building **f :** a tile stack for drainage **5 :** a part of a building or similar structure resembling a well: as **a :** an open space extending vertically through floors of a structure (as a stairwell or elevator shaft) ⟨a spiral stairway with an open ~ extending through three stories —*Amer. Guide Series: Md.*⟩ **b :** the space in an English law court set off immediately in front of the judge's bench and usu. occupied by solicitors **c :** an open shaft formed by surrounding walls and extending vertically through the floors of a structure to provide light and air to interior areas **d :** the place in a lecture hall, legislative chamber, or similar large assembly room where the speaker is located and around which the seats rise in tiers or on a slope **:** the area between the rostrum or stage and the first row of seats **:** PIT **6 :** a heraldic bearing representing the part of the wall of a well aboveground **7 :** a vessel or space having a construction or shape that suggests a well for water: as **a :** a space or receptacle resembling a box located in the body of a vehicle and used for luggage **b :** a deep drawer or hollow interior area used as a receptacle in a piece of furniture (as a desk or bureau) ⟨pine cupboard . . . having hinged cover over a ~ —*Parke-Bernet Galleries Cat.*⟩ ⟨a ~ with a compartmented interior⟩ **c :** the lower part of a furnace into which the molten metal runs **d :** a small receptacle in a larger vessel or unit ⟨the ~ in a jar of paste⟩ ⟨the ~ of a fountain pen⟩ ⟨this bent pipe had a bowl which retained the objectionable moisture in its ~ —*Irish Digest*⟩ ⟨lubricating oil ~*s* located in a planer bed⟩ — see INKWELL **e (1) :** an indentation or cavity in a surface ⟨tree ~*s*⟩ ⟨cellar window ~*s*⟩ **(2) :** one of the tiny depressed spots incised or etched in a gravure plate and holding the ink when the surface of the plate is wiped clean before a sheet is printed **(3) :** the dark center of a diamond cut too thick **8 a :** something resembling a well in being damp, cool, deep, or dark ⟨a great ~ of a cupboard⟩ ⟨make your room a cool ~ of dusk —Claudia Cassidy⟩ **b :** something resembling a well in constituting a deep vertical hole ⟨the ~ in a glacier⟩ ⟨poked ~*s* in the biscuit to hold the molasses —Eudora Welty⟩ ⟨a stove ~⟩ **c :** something held to resemble a well in constituting a deep reservoir from which one may draw ⟨a great ~ of friendship and respect for . . . the United States —R.M.Nixon⟩ ⟨the inner ~ of strength into which the peasant woman . . . must repeatedly dip —Lucy Crockett⟩ **9 a :** a pronounced minimum of a variable in physics ⟨energy ~⟩ ⟨potential ~⟩ **b :** a region in which such minimum occurs **10 :** STILLING BASIN **11 :** [1]FOUNTAIN 4 **12 :** a small leather cup fixed to or suspended from an archer's belt to hold the tips of arrows thrust thereunder

[2]**well** \"\ *adj* [ME *welle*, fr. *welle*, n.] **1 :** of, relating to, or having the characteristics of a well ⟨utilized the ~ principle in construction⟩ ⟨a ~ cover⟩ ⟨~ rope⟩ ⟨~ shape⟩ **2 :** used in connection with a well ⟨a ~ sweep⟩ ⟨~ drill⟩ **3 :** designed so as to have a part that is held to resemble a well ⟨~ railroad cars⟩ ⟨the ~ type of saddle⟩ ⟨~ slides⟩ **4 :** having a wellhole ⟨a ~ staircase⟩ ⟨~ stairs⟩

[3]**well** \"\ *vb* -ED/-ING/-S [ME *wellen*, fr. OE (northern & Midland dial.) *wellan* to cause to well; akin to MHG *wellen* to cause to well, ON *vella;* causative fr. the root of OE *weallan* to bubble, boil, OHG *wallan*, ON *vella* to well over, boil, L *volvere* to roll — more at VOLUBLE] *vi* **1 :** to rise to the surface in a copious stream and then usu. flow forth ⟨a clear small stream . . . ~*ed* from a rock hard by —G.P.R.James⟩ ⟨tears ~*ed* up in her eyes⟩ ⟨a spring . . . ~*ed* out of the rock into a stone basin —Willa Cather⟩ **2 :** to rise to the surface like a flood of liquid **:** spring up and often pour forth ⟨anger ~*ed* in his stomach like bile —Hugh MacLennan⟩ — often used with *up* ⟨great pity ~*ed* up from his generous heart —Rafael Sabatini⟩ ⟨an immense yearning for security ~*ed* up through the land —Oscar Handlin⟩ **~** *vt* **:** to pour forth from the depths ⟨some classic fountain . . . ~*ed* its pure waters in a sacred shade —Washington Irving⟩

[4]**well** \"\ *adv* **bet·ter** \'bed·ə(r), -etə-\ **best** \'best\ [ME *wel*, fr. OE; akin to OHG *wela*, *wola* well, ON *vel*, Goth *waila* well, OE *wyllan* to wish — more at WILL] **1 a :** in a good or proper manner **:** in accordance with a high standard of morality **:** in a way that is morally good **:** JUSTLY, RIGHTLY ⟨it is . . . doing ~ that entitles us to heaven —William Burkitt⟩ **b :** satisfactorily with respect to conduct or action ⟨worked ~ under difficult conditions⟩ ⟨the inability . . . of these children to do ~ in advanced academic areas —J.B.Conant⟩ **2 a :** in a manner that constitutes good treatment or confers a benefit **:** CONSIDERATELY, GENEROUSLY, KINDLY ⟨wished them ~⟩ ⟨spoke ~ of your idea⟩ **b :** in a kindly or friendly manner **:** with friendly words **:** with favor or welcome ⟨was ~ received at court⟩ ⟨her first novel was ~ received by the critics⟩ **3 a :** with skill or aptitude **:** in a skillful or expert manner **:** EXCELLENTLY, EXPERTLY ⟨sing ~⟩ ⟨paints ~⟩ ⟨a wonderful story, ~ written and sensitive —Peter Blake⟩ **b :** SATISFACTORILY ⟨plan has worked ~⟩ **c :** with good appearance or effect **:** ELEGANTLY ⟨carried himself ~⟩ **4 :** with careful or close attention **:** ATTENTIVELY ⟨watch ~ what I do⟩ **5 :** to a high point or degree ⟨they got on ~ together⟩ ⟨~ deserved the honor⟩ ⟨she did not seem so ~ pleased⟩ ⟨the legendary lore which I love so ~ —Sir Walter Scott⟩ ⟨you will be ~ rewarded by a visit —Dana Burnet⟩ — often used in combination ⟨a *well*-equipped kitchen⟩ ⟨*well*-populated areas⟩ **6 :** to the full degree or extent **:** FULLY, QUITE ⟨~ aware of the difficulties⟩ ⟨~ worth the price⟩ ⟨~ out of sight⟩ ⟨~ past the appropriate age⟩ ⟨arrived before dinner had ~ begun⟩ ⟨~ able to take care of himself⟩ **7 a :** in a way appropriate to the facts or circumstances **:** FITTINGLY, PROPERLY, RIGHTLY ⟨as the author ~ says⟩ ⟨a large box will answer the need almost equally ~⟩ **b :** in a prudent manner **:** SENSIBLY — used with *do* ⟨reasonable people . . . will do ~ to demand better evidence —M.R.Cohen⟩ ⟨do ~ to examine the grounds for this adverse opinion —I.A.Richards⟩ **8 :** in accordance with the occasion or circumstances **:** as a natural result or consequence **:** with propriety or good reason **:** NATURALLY, PROPERLY ⟨I cannot ~ refuse⟩ ⟨this decision may ~ be questioned⟩ ⟨took pride, as ~ she might, in her hair —Samuel Richardson⟩ ⟨old residents . . . speak of it with considerable affection, as ~ they might —John De Meyer⟩ **9 a :** in such manner as is desirable or pleasing **:** as one could wish **:** without harm or accident **:** FAVORABLY, FORTUNATELY, HAPPILY, PROSPEROUSLY, SUCCESSFULLY ⟨everything went ~ that morning⟩ ⟨piano and violin do not mix too ~ even in chamber music —P.H.Lang⟩ **b :** with success from a material point of view **:** ADVANTAGEOUSLY, PROPERLY ⟨he married ~⟩ ⟨he hadn't made a fortune . . . but he'd done fairly ~ —Frank Sargeson⟩ **10 a :** without trouble or difficulty **:** EASILY, READILY ⟨nor were the refugees such as a country can ~ spare —T.B.Macaulay⟩ ⟨appearing to know more of that abode of evil than she ~ could —H.S.Scott⟩ ⟨no transcript can ~ be found which does not differ from its prototype in some small points —F.H.A.Scrivener⟩ **b :** in all likelihood **:** INDEED ⟨a basic conflict that may ~ last for the balance of this century —J.B.Conant⟩ ⟨maintenance of the high level of expenditures . . . might ~ have a disastrous effect —D.W.Mitchell⟩ **11 :** in a state of prosperity, plenty, or comfort **:** in a prosperous or affluent manner ⟨he lives ~⟩ **12 :** in a thorough manner **:** to an extent approaching completeness ⟨after being ~ dried with a sponge⟩ **13 a :** without doubt, uncertainty, or question **:** CLEARLY, DEFINITELY ⟨~ remembered the stirring appeal⟩ ⟨~ knew the penalty⟩ **b :** CLOSELY, FAMILIARLY, INTIMATELY ⟨must know their own country ~ —*London Calling*⟩ **c :** in exact outlines **:** CLEARLY, DEFINITELY ⟨the tree stood out ~ against the horizon⟩ ⟨remembered ~ the incident he mentioned⟩ **14 :** with spirit and courage **:** BRAVELY, GALLANTLY ⟨fought ~ against overwhelming odds⟩ **15 :** with equanimity or good nature **:** without resentment ⟨reported that he took the disappointment ~⟩ **16 :** to a considerable extent **:** more than a little **:** CONSIDERABLY, FAR ⟨grows in hot, moist regions ~ into the temperate zone —G.S.Brady⟩ ⟨a population of ~ over a million people —L.D.Stamp⟩ ⟨~ north of the island —George Bradshaw⟩ **17 :** ENOUGH, SUFFICIENTLY — used in giving nautical commands (as concerning hoisting or lowering or bracing yards) — **as well** *adv* [ME *as wel*] **1 :** in addition **:** ALSO, TOO ⟨resists not only DDT but other well-known insecticides *as well* —H.J.Clausen⟩ ⟨worked as a shipwright in . . . Singapore, where he was an armament officer *as well* —*Current Biog.*⟩ **2 :** to the same extent or degree **:** as much ⟨the court . . . is open *as well* to the humblest as to the mightiest —*Adoptive Rite Ritual*⟩ ⟨our churchmen have become wealthy *as well* by the gifts of pious persons as by . . . bribes —Sir Walter Scott⟩ **3 a :** with equivalent or comparable effect ⟨my devotion might *as well* have been offered to . . . a statue in a museum —W.B.Yeats⟩ **b :** to a slight or possible advantage ⟨might just *as well* become reconciled to the fact that you're going to have trouble —Richard Joseph⟩ — **as well as** *adv* [ME *as wel as*] **:** and not only **:** and in addition ⟨is skillful *as well as* strong⟩ ⟨introduced the use of the gnomon . . . *as well as* made the first map —Benjamin Farrington⟩

[5]**well** \", *dial* 'wal\ *interj* [ME *wel*, fr. OE, fr. *wel*, adv.] **1** — used to express satisfaction with what has been said or done **2 a** — used to express assent or resignation **b** — used to express surprise and expostulation and often reduplicated **3** — used to indicate resumption of a thread of discourse or to introduce a remark

[6]**well** \'wel\ *adj* [ME *wel*, fr. *wel*, adv.] **1 a :** being in good standing or estimation **:** being on good terms **:** being in favor ⟨of great importance to us . . . to be ~ with the French government —H.J.Temple⟩ **b** *archaic* **:** being on terms of intimacy or familiarity ⟨all our set were ~ with some fine woman or other —B.H.Malkin⟩ **c :** pleased or satisfied with oneself ⟨being extremely ~ with himself —Agnes Bennett⟩ **2 :** being a cause for satisfaction or approval **:** SATISFACTORY, PLEASING ⟨saw . . . that all was not ~ with him —Washington Irving⟩ ⟨all's ~ that ends well⟩ **3 a :** being in a state of affluence or prosperity **:** WELL-OFF ⟨he must be very ~ in the world —B.H. Malkin⟩ — see WELL-TO-DO **b :** being in satisfactory condition or circumstances ⟨he will not change while he is as ~ where he is⟩ **4 :** being in accordance with advantage **:** deserving to be recommended **:** ADVISABLE, DESIRABLE ⟨it is not ~ to anger him⟩ ⟨it might be ~ for you to review the four basic steps —W.J.Reilly⟩ — sometimes used with *as* ⟨if you stay . . . it is as *well* to bring plenty of provisions —G.W.Murray⟩ **5 a :** being in health **:** sound in body and mind **:** free of or recovered from sickness, infirmity, disease, or ailment **:** HEALTHY ⟨a ~ man⟩ ⟨he looks ~⟩ **b** (1) **:** CURED ⟨the rheumatism . . . is now near quite ~ —Jonathan Swift⟩ (2) **:** being in a good or sound condition ⟨his health . . . is still pretty ~ —Oliver Goldsmith⟩ **6 :** pleasing or satisfactory in appearance ⟨looked very ~ when he was dressed —Ellery Queen⟩ ⟨the polished floor looks ~ —Herbert Spencer⟩ **7** *archaic* **:** good in quality or character ⟨it is really very ~ for a novel —Jane Austen⟩ **8 :** being a cause for thankfulness **:** lucky and gratifying **:** FORTUNATE ⟨it is ~ that this has happened⟩ — **all very well :** proper under the circumstances ⟨it is *all very well* . . . to advise the French in the columns of the *New York Times* —Frank Gorrell⟩ — **very well** — used to signify agreement, approval, or understanding of instructions — **well and good** — used to signify acceptance (as of a situation or decision) ⟨if that's the case, *well and good* — we can proceed accordingly⟩ **syn** see HEALTHY

[7]**well** \'wel\ *n, pl* **well :** a well person **:** one sound in health — usu. used collectively ⟨prevent the ~ from becoming infected⟩

[8]**well** \"\ *n* -S [ME *wel*, fr. *wel*, adv., well] *obs* **:** WELL-BEING ⟨restore you to your wonted ~ —Edmund Spenser⟩

[9]**well** \"\ *n* -S [[4]*well*] *chiefly Brit* **:** WELL ENOUGH ⟨when best to operate and when to leave ~ alone —Harvey Graham⟩ ⟨content to let ~ alone and to maintain . . . a defensive policy —C.E.Robinson⟩

well·a·day \'welə¦dā\ *n or interj* [by alter.] **:** WELLAWAY

well-advised \¦==¦=\ *adj* [ME *wel avised*, fr. *wel* well + *avised* advised] **1 :** acting with wisdom, wise counsel, or proper deliberation **:** PRUDENT ⟨he would be *well-advised* to heed this advice⟩ **2 :** resulting from, based upon, or showing careful deliberation or wise counsel ⟨a *well-advised* silence⟩ ⟨*well-advised* plans⟩

well-affected \¦==¦==\ *adj* **:** favorably disposed or inclined (as toward a person or a political authority)

well-and-tree platter \'=='=-\ *n* **:** a platter having a depressed design of a trunk and branches through which meat juices flow into a large depression at one end

well-and-tree platter

well-appointed \¦==¦==\ *adj* **:** having good and complete equipment **:** properly fitted out ⟨a most comfortable and *well-appointed* residence —O.F.Morshead⟩

[1]**well·a·way** \'welə¦wā\ *interj* [ME *welaway*, *weleaway*, alter. (influenced by *wel* well and *away*) of *weilawei*, fr. OE *weilāwei*, lit., woe! lo! woe!, alter. (influenced by ON *vei* woe) of *wālāwā*, fr. *wā* woe + *lā* lo + *wā* woe — more at WELL, WOE] — used to express sorrow or lamentation

[2]**wellaway** \"\ *n* -S [ME *welaway*, fr. *welaway*, interj.] **:** LAMENT ⟨whispering her sad ~ —Thomas Woolner⟩

well·a·wins \-winz\ *Scot var of* WELLAWAY

well-being \'=¦==\ *n* **:** the state or condition of being well **:** a condition characterized by happiness, health, or prosperity **:** moral or physical welfare ⟨the elders were responsible . . . for the spiritual *well-being* of the people —V.L.Parrington⟩ ⟨achieved a degree of economic *well-being* —*Amer. Guide Series: N.Y.*⟩ ⟨a threat to the *well-being* of the republic —Lewis Nordyke⟩ ⟨an increased sense of *well-being*⟩ — opposed to *ill-being*

[1]**well-beloved** \¦==¦=(=)\ *adj* [ME *welbeloved*, fr. *wel* well + *beloved*] **1 :** sincerely and deeply loved ⟨my *well-beloved* wife⟩ **2 :** sincerely respected — used in various ceremonial forms of address

[2]**well-beloved** \"\ *n* [ME *welbeloved*, fr. *welbeloved*, adj.] **:** a well-beloved person **:** a dearly loved one

well-beseen *adj* [ME *wel besein*, fr. *wel* well + *besein*, *beseen*, past part. of *beseen* to see, regard, favor — more at BESEE] *obs* **:** having or making a good appearance

well boat *n* **:** a boat having a well in which fish or lobsters can be kept alive

wellborn \'=¦=\ *adj* [ME *well born*, fr. OE *wel-boren*, fr. *wel* well + *boren* born] **1 a :** born of a family of good, noble, or high standing ⟨a rich and ~ husband —Clement Greenberg⟩ **b :** having the characteristics of an offspring of such birth; *esp* **:** gentle and courteous in manner **2 :** born of parents genetically fitted for the production of sound offspring

well-breathed \'=¦=\ *adj* [ME *wel brethed*, fr. *wel* well + *brethed* breathed] **:** having good breathing capacity **:** strong or sound of wind ⟨on thy *well-breath'd* horse keep with thy hounds —Shak.⟩

well-bred \'=¦=\ *adj* **1 a :** belonging to a good family and properly brought up **:** having good breeding ⟨a gentleman *well-bred* and of good name —Shak.⟩ **b :** displaying good breeding **:** refined in manners **:** courteous in speech and behavior **:** CULTIVATED, REFINED ⟨a young man too *well-bred* to admit how bored he was —Mary Austin⟩ ⟨a happy and *well-bred* community —T.C.Roughley⟩ **2 :** of good breed **:** having a good pedigree ⟨*well-bred* swine⟩ ⟨*well-bred* horses⟩

well car *n* **:** a railroad flatcar having a depression or opening in the center of the deck for handling oversize loads that would not on regular flat cars come within overhead clearance limitations — called also *well-hole car*

well casing *n* **1 :** the tubular boring or drilling apparatus used in sinking a well and esp. an oil well **2 :** the tubular lining of a bored or drilled well

well-child clinic *n* **:** a clinic devoted to the proper care of and the prevention of diseases in small children (as by instructions and inoculations)

well-closed \'=¦=\ *adj* **:** of uniform formation — used of paper; contrasted with *wild*

well-conditioned \¦==¦==\ *adj* [ME *wele condicionde*, fr. *wele*, *wel* well + *condicionde*, *condiciouned* conditioned] **1 :** characterized by proper disposition, morals, or behavior **:** RIGHT-MINDED **2 :** having a good physical condition **:** HEALTHY, SOUND ⟨a *well-conditioned* animal⟩

well cress *n* [ME *welle-carse*, fr. OE *wyllecærse*, fr. *wylle*, *welle* well + *cærse* cress — more at WELL (spring), CRESS] **:** WATERCRESS 1a

well-day \'=¦=\ *n* **:** a day characterized by one's freedom from sickness ⟨the victim of a slight, ramshackly physique . . . never knowing a *well-day* —V.L.Parrington⟩; *specif* **:** one free from attacks of a recurrent disorder ⟨repeated cold and hot fits . . . with one or more *well-days* between them —Michael Underwood⟩

well deck *n* [[1]*well*] **:** a space on the weather deck of a ship lying at a lower level between a raised forecastle or poop and the bridge superstructure

well-decked \'=,dekt\ *adj* **:** having a well deck ⟨a *well-decked* ship⟩

well decker *n* **:** a well-decked ship

well-disposed \¦==¦=\ *adj* [ME *weldisposed*, fr. *wel* well + *disposed*] **:** having a good disposition; *esp* **:** disposed to be friendly, favorable, or sympathetic

well-done \'=¦=\ *adj* [ME] **1 :** rightly or properly performed **:** skillfully executed ⟨a *well-done* job⟩ **2 :** cooked thoroughly **:** cooked until the center is brownish-gray ⟨a *well-done* roast⟩ ⟨ordered a steak *well-done*⟩

well drain *n* **1 :** a well or pit for draining wet land **2 :** a drain discharging into a well

well-drain \'=,=\ *vt* [*well drain*] **:** to drain (land) by well drains from which the water is pumped out

well-dressing \'=,==\ *n* **:** an ancient custom in rural areas in England of adorning local wells with floral decorations usu. as part of a religious service in thanksgiving for an abundant supply of pure water

welled \'weld\ *adj* [[1]*well* + *-ed*] **:** having or constructed with a well ⟨a ~ fishing boat⟩ ⟨a plate with a ~ center⟩

well enough *n* [fr. the phrase *well enough*] **:** an existing fairly satisfactory condition ⟨I should have let *well enough* alone —Louis Auchincloss⟩ ⟨unable to leave *well enough* alone⟩

wel·ler·ism \'welə,rizəm\ *n* -S *usu cap* [Sam *Weller*, witty servant of Mr. Pickwick in the story *Pickwick Papers* (1836–37) by Charles Dickens †1870 Eng. novelist] **:** an expression of comparison comprising a usu. well-known quotation followed by a facetious sequel (as "every one to his own taste," said the old woman as she kissed the cow)

well-favored \'=¦==\ *adj* [ME *wel favoured*, fr. *wel* well + *favoured*, past part. of *favouren* to favor — more at FAVOR] **:** having a fine or attractive appearance **:** pleasing to the eye **:** GOOD-LOOKING, HANDSOME ⟨Rachel was beautiful and *well-favored* —Gen 29:17 (AV)⟩ our Southern women are *well-favored* —Lillian Hellman⟩ — **well-fa·vored·ness** *n* -ES

well-fixed \'=¦=\ *adj* **:** having plenty of money or property **:** WELL-TO-DO, PROSPEROUS ⟨being a *well-fixed* boy in a poor neighborhood had its disadvantages —*Time*⟩

well-found \'=¦=\ *adj* **1** *archaic* **:** tried and found to be well or good **:** COMMENDABLE **2 :** fully furnished **:** properly equipped ⟨a *well-found* ship⟩

well-founded \'=¦==\ *adj* **1 :** constructed on a solid or firm foundation ⟨a *well-founded* building⟩ **2 :** having a firm foundation in fact **:** based on excellent reasoning, information, judgment, or grounds ⟨hope your fears are not *well-founded* —Allen Upward⟩ ⟨a doctrine . . . *well-founded* in principle —Richard Olney⟩

well grass *n, Scot* **:** WATERCRESS

well-groomed \'=¦=\ *adj* **1 :** well dressed and scrupulously neat ⟨*well-groomed* men⟩ **2** *of a horse* **:** carefully tended and curried **3 :** well cared for **:** made neat, tidy, and attractive down to the smallest details ⟨a *well-groomed* lawn⟩

well-grounded \'=¦==\ *adj* **:** WELL-FOUNDED

well-grown \'=¦=\ *adj* **:** having attained a satisfactory growth or development; *esp* **:** having almost reached maximum physical growth

well-hained \'=¦hānd\ *adj, chiefly Scot* **:** well or carefully preserved ⟨some buxom widow or *well-hained* spinster —John Galt⟩

well-handled \'=¦==\ *adj* [ME *wel handeled*, fr. *wel* well + *handeled*, past part. of *handelen* to handle — more at HANDLE] **1 :** being or having been managed or administered efficiently ⟨a *well-handled* fund⟩ **2 :** having been handled a great deal ⟨*well-handled* goods on a store counter⟩

wellhead \'=,=\ *n* [ME *welleheved*, fr. *welle* well + *heved* head — more at WELL (spring), HEAD] **1 :** the place where a spring emerges from the ground **:** the source from which a stream flows ⟨traveled . . . among the ~*s* of wild rivers —R.L. Stevenson⟩ **2 :** the principal source **:** FOUNTAINHEAD ⟨from the ~ of pure science flow fertilizing streams which serve industry —Benjamin Farrington⟩ **3 a :** the top of a well ⟨Federal price control of natural gas at the ~ —Gene Smith⟩ **b :** a structure built over the top of a well ⟨an authentic Roman ~⟩

well-heeled \'=¦=\ *adj* **:** having plenty of money **:** WELL-FIXED ⟨well-dressed, *well-heeled* and well-mannered clientele —Richard Thruelsen⟩ ⟨an expert lobby every whit as influential and *well-heeled* as the China lobby —*Atlantic*⟩

wellhole \'=,=\ *n* **1 :** the hole, pit, or shaft of a well **2 a :** the open space in a floor or through a series of floors for the accommodation of a staircase **b :** the open space about which the stairs of a winding or circular staircase turn **3 :** a cavity for movement of a counterbalance or similar mechanical device

well-hole car *n* **:** WELL CAR

well house *n* [ME *welhous*, fr. *welle* well + *hous* house] **:** a covered structure (as a house or room) built around the top of a well

well-hung \'=¦=\ *adj* **1 :** hung skillfully and therefore working readily and freely **:** fluent in speech **:** GLIB ⟨a *well-hung* tongue⟩ **2 :** attached or suspended so as to hang well ⟨a *well-hung* skirt⟩ **3 :** hung long enough to acquire the proper flavor — used chiefly of game

welling *pres part of* WELL

[1]**wel·ling·ton** \'weliŋtən\ *or* **wellington boot** *n* -S *usu cap W* [after Arthur Wellesley, 1st Duke of *Wellington* †1852 Brit. general and statesman] **1 :** a leather boot having a loose top with the front usu. coming above the knee **2 :** HALF WELLINGTON **3 :** a high rubber boot often reaching to the knee

[2]**wellington** \"\ *adj, usu cap* [fr. *Wellington*, New Zealand] **1 :** of or from Wellington, the capital of New Zealand **:** of the kind or style prevalent in Wellington **2 :** of or from the provincial district of Wellington, New Zealand **:** of the kind or style prevalent in Wellington provincial district

wel·ling·to·nia \,weliŋ'tōnēə\ [NL, fr. 1st Duke of *Wellington* †1852 + NL *-ia*] *syn of* SEQUOIA

wel·ling·to·ni·an \¦==¦tōnēən\ *adj, usu cap* [1st Duke of *Wellington* †1852 + E *-an*] **:** of, relating to, or having the characteristics of the Duke of Wellington

well-knit \'=¦=\ *adj* [ME *wele knitte*, fr. *wele*, *wel* well + *knitte* knit, past part. of *knitten* to knit — more at KNIT] **:** firmly knit; *esp* **:** firmly and strongly constructed, compacted, or framed ⟨a *well-knit* athlete⟩ ⟨a *well-knit* argument⟩ ⟨a *well-knit* composition⟩ ⟨*well-knit* communities⟩

well-known \'=¦=\ *adj* [ME *well knowen*, fr. [4]*well* + *knowen* known] **:** fully known: as **a :** widely known **:** generally acknowledged **:** known to many ⟨one of their most *well-known* physical peculiarities —C.D.Forde⟩ ⟨a *well-known* drama critic⟩ ⟨dined at a *well-known* restaurant⟩ **b :** closely, intimately, or thoroughly known ⟨a *well-known* voice reached her ears —Fanny Burney⟩

well-liking \'=¦==\ *adj* [ME *wel liking*, fr. *wel* well + *liking*, pres. part. of *liken* to like — more at LIKE] **:** being in good condition **:** having a good appearance **:** HEALTHY, THRIVING ⟨the righteous . . . shall be fat and *well-liking* —*Bk. of Com. Prayer*⟩

well log *n* **:** [1]LOG 3b(3)

well-looked \'=¦=\ *adj, chiefly Scot* **:** GOOD-LOOKING ⟨she must have been beautiful and is still *well-looked* —J.G. Lockhart⟩

well-made play \'=,=-\ *n* **:** a play constructed according to a predetermined pattern and aiming at neatness of plot and theatrical effectiveness but often being mechanical and stereotyped

well-mannered \'=¦==\ *adj* **:** having or displaying good manners **:** showing good taste **:** properly behaved **:** COURTEOUS, POLITE, WELL-BRED 1b ⟨*well-mannered* folk of comfortable means —Robert Shaplen⟩ ⟨a soundly constructed cabinet of *well-mannered* contemporary design —*advt*⟩ ⟨a *well-mannered* colt⟩

well-mean·er \'='mēnə(r)\ *n* **:** a well-meaning person **:** one whose intentions are good ⟨*well-meaners* think no harm —John Dryden⟩

well-meaning \'=¦==\ *adj* [ME *wel-mening*, fr. *wel* well + *mening*, pres. part. of *menen* to intend — more at MEAN] **:** having or motivated by good intentions but often producing unwelcome results through inefficiency or lack of wisdom ⟨the son's *well-meaning* efforts threw a singular chill upon the father's admirers —W.S.Maugham⟩ ⟨a rather stupid, *well-meaning* mother —*N.Y. Herald Tribune Bk. Rev.*⟩

well·ness *n* -ES **:** the quality or state of being in good health

well-nigh \'=¦=\ *adv* [ME *welneih*, *wel-neh*, fr. *wel* well + *neih*, *neh* nigh] **:** very nearly **:** ALMOST ⟨the resulting recording is *well-nigh* perfect —Thomas Heinitz⟩ ⟨the right of any senator to speak out at *well-nigh* any time —Lindsay Rogers⟩ ⟨for *well-nigh* a quarter of a century —*Blackwood's*⟩

well-off \'=¦=\ *adj* **1 :** being in good condition **:** situated in favorable circumstances **:** fortunately situated ⟨he doesn't know when he's *well-off* —H.A.Smith⟩ **2 :** well provided **:** having no lack — used esp. with *for* ⟨we are very *well-off* now for outdoor labor —Rachel Henning⟩ **3 :** WELL-TO-DO ⟨died so *well-off* that he was able to leave each of his eight children one million dollars —Green Peyton⟩

well over *vi* **:** OVERFLOW ⟨his heart *welled over* with joy —D.C. Murray⟩

well point *n* **:** a hollow pointed rod with a perforated intake driven into an excavation to lower the water table by pumping and thus minimize flooding during construction

well-read \'=¦=\ *adj* **:** characterized by extensive reading **:** well informed or deeply versed through reading ⟨our high respect for a *well-read* man —R.W.Emerson⟩ — often used with *in* ⟨a person *well-read* in medieval history⟩

well-ribbed-up \'=,='=\ *adj* **:** WELL-SPRUNG

well rig *also* **well rigging** *n* **:** the apparatus used in boring and finishing a well

wells *pl of* WELL, *pres 3d sing of* WELL

well-set \'=¦=\ *adj* [ME *wel sett*, fr. *wel* well + *sett* set] **1 :** properly or skillfully set : well or firmly established **2 :** strongly built : firmly knit ⟨the sailor short but *well-set* —Alexander Hamilton †1732⟩

well-set-up \'=,=¦=\ *adj* : well formed, framed, or fashioned ⟨a handsome *well-set-up* blond young man —Dorothy C. Fisher⟩

well shrimp *n* : any of various usu. blind and white crustaceans living in subterranean waters and wells

wells·ian \'welzēən\ *adj, usu cap* [Herbert G. *Wells* †1946 Eng. novelist, sociological writer and historian + E *-an*] : of, relating to, or characteristic of H. G. Wells or his writings ⟨a pseudo-mystical . . . utopia on the *Wellsian* plan —Allen Tate⟩

wells·ite \'wel,zīt\ *n* -s [Horace L. *Wells* †1924 Am. chemist + E *-ite*] : a mineral $(Ba,Ca,K_2)Al_2Si_3O_{10}.3H_2O$ of the phillipsite group consisting of a silicate of aluminum, calcium, barium, and potassium

well smack *n* : ⁶SMACK b

well-spoken \'=¦=\ *adj* [ME *wel spoken*, fr. *wel* well + *spoken*] **1 :** speaking well, kindly, or fittingly : courteous and refined in speech ⟨found these people gentle, pious, and *well-spoken* —Willa Cather⟩ ⟨a knight *well-spoken* —Shak.⟩ **2 :** spoken with propriety ⟨*well-spoken* words⟩

wellspring \'=,=\ *n* [ME *welle spring*, fr. OE *wyllspring*, *welspring*, fr. *wylle*, *welle* well + *spring*] **1 :** a source of continual supply or emanation ⟨our colleges . . . are ~*s* of humanistic and scientific learning —A.W.Griswold⟩ ⟨understanding is a ~ of life unto him that hath it; but the instruction of fools is folly —Prov 16:22 (AV)⟩ **2 :** FOUNTAINHEAD 1 ⟨water . . . drawn recently from a ~ —J.D.Chambers⟩

well-sprung \'=¦=\ *adj* : rounded rather than lank or flattened — used of the rib cage or body contour of a domestic animal or bird

wellstrand \'=,=\ *n* -s [ME *welle strond*, fr. *welle* well + *strond* strand] *Scot* : a stream flowing from a spring

well sweep *n* : SWEEP 1a

well-tempered \'=¦==\ *adj* [ME *wel temperit*, fr. *wel* well + *temperit* tempered] **1 a** *obs* : properly constituted physically ⟨a strong *well-tempered* stomach —Algernon Sydney⟩ **b :** having a good or equable disposition; *esp* : GOOD-NATURED ⟨a discreet and *well-tempered* officer —George Grote⟩ **2 :** treated so as to develop the desired degree of hardness and elasticity ⟨*well-tempered* steel⟩ ⟨a *well-tempered* sword blade⟩ **3 :** mixed to the proper consistency — used esp. of mortar and clay

well-thought-of \'=¦=,=\ *adj* : being of good repute : REPUTABLE ⟨a *well-thought-of* young man⟩

well-thought-out \'=,=¦=\ *adj* : logically considered : well and carefully reasoned ⟨moved according to a *well-thought-out* plan —Edita Morris⟩ ⟨another *well-thought-out* bit of wisdom —S.H.Adams⟩

well-timbered \'=¦==\ *adj* **1 a :** well braced or strengthened by timbers ⟨a *well-timbered* house⟩ ⟨a *well-timbered* mine⟩ **b :** strongly made or put together : having a good structure or constitution ⟨a *well-timbered* horse⟩ **2 :** having a good quantity of growing timber ⟨a *well-timbered* tract of land⟩

well-timed \'=¦=\ *adj* **1 a :** happening or coming at an opportune moment : done at a suitable, convenient, or good time : TIMELY ⟨*well-timed* political reforms⟩ **b :** actuated at the proper moment or in regular time ⟨*well-timed* oars⟩ **2 :** trained or adjusted to keep proper time ⟨a *well-timed* crew⟩ ⟨a *well-timed* chronometer⟩ **syn** see SEASONABLE

¹**well-to-do** \¦==¦=\ *adj* [fr. the phrase *to do well*] **1 :** having more than adequate material and esp. financial resources : having plenty of money or a comfortable income : being in easy or affluent circumstances : PROSPEROUS, WELL-OFF ⟨a fashionable and *well-to-do* family —*Hearst's*⟩ ⟨*well-to-do* but not with one of the great fortunes —John Buchan⟩ **2 :** indicating or having the characteristics of prosperity ⟨the house had a *well-to-do* look⟩ ⟨a *well-to-do* suburb with pronounced intellectual interests —Jane Cobb⟩

²**well-to-do** \"\ *n pl* : well-to-do persons — usu. used with *the* ⟨only the *well-to-do* could afford to patronize them —Foster Hailey⟩ ⟨favored as a resort by the *well-to-do* —*Amer. Guide Series: Mich.*⟩

well-to-live \¦==¦=\ *adj* [fr. the phrase *to live well*] *chiefly dial* : WELL-TO-DO

well tomb *n* : a tomb having a well or shaft for an entrance

well-to-pass \¦==¦=\ *adj* [fr. the phrase *to pass well*] *Scot* : WELL-TO-DO

well trap *n* : a trap (as in a sewer or drainpipe) holding water and checking the escape of foul air and odors

well-turned \'=¦=\ *adj* **1 :** symmetrically shaped or rounded : well formed : SHAPELY ⟨her *well-turned* form⟩ ⟨a *well-turned* ankle⟩ **2 :** concisely and appropriately expressed ⟨a *well-turned* phrase⟩ ⟨a *well-turned* compliment⟩ **3 :** expertly rounded or turned ⟨a *well-turned* arch⟩ ⟨*well-turned* columns⟩

well-willed \'=¦=\ *adj* [ME] *chiefly Scot* : favorably, kindly, or generously disposed

well-willer \'=¦==\ *n* [ME] **1 :** one bearing goodwill : one disposed to be kind or friendly : WELL-WISHER **2** *obs* : AMATEUR 1 ⟨so much a *well-willer* to the satire that he spares no man —John Dryden⟩

well-willing \'=¦==\ *adj* [ME] *archaic* : favorably or kindly disposed : BENEVOLENT, LOYAL ⟨ruggedly faithful and *well-willing* to their friends —R.L.Stevenson⟩

well-wish \'=,=\ *n* : a good or kindly wish ⟨tendered hurried *well-wishes* —Linton Wells⟩

well-wisher \'=¦==\ *n* : one that wishes well to another ⟨*well-wishers* made contributions toward her musical education —*Current Biog.*⟩ ⟨he knows the park service has many *well-wishers* —R.M.Yoder⟩

well-wishing \'=¦==\ *n* : the act of one who wishes well to another ⟨much hand-shaking and *well-wishing* —J.R.Harris⟩

well-worn \'=¦=\ *adj* **1 a :** having been much used or worn ⟨*well-worn* shoes⟩ **b :** made stale or threadbare by use : TRITE, COMMONPLACE ⟨a *well-worn* quotation⟩ ⟨a *well-worn* theme⟩ **2 :** worn well or properly ⟨*well-worn* honors⟩

welly \'welī\ *adv* [by contr.] *dial Eng* : WELL-NIGH ⟨~ thirty miles off —George Eliot⟩

wels \'welz\ *n* -ES [G, fr. MHG; akin to OPruss *kalis* sheatfish] : SHEATFISH

Wels·bach \'welz,bak, -bäk\ *trademark* — used for a burner for producing gaslight by the combustion of a mixture of air and gas or vapor to heat to incandescence a gas mantle or for the mantle used with such a burner

¹**welsh** *or* **welch** \'welsh, -lch\ *adj, usu cap* [ME *walisch, welisch*, fr. OE (northern & Midland dial.) *wælisc*, *welisc* Celtic, Welsh, foreign, fr. OE *Walh*, *Wealh* Celt, Welshman, foreigner (of Celtic origin; akin to the source of L *Volcae*, a Celtic people of southeastern Gaul) + *-isc* -ish] **1 a :** of, relating to, or characteristic of Wales **b :** of, relating to, or characteristic of the Welsh people **2 :** of, relating to, or characteristic of the Welsh language

²**welsh** *or* **welch** \"\ *n* [ME *Walsche*, *Welsse*, fr. *walisch*, *welisch*, adj.] **1** *pl in constr, cap* : the natives or inhabitants of Wales descended from romanized Britons **2** -ES *cap* : a Celtic language of the Welsh people possessing an extensive and actively growing literature and used as the language of education in some communities in Wales — see INDO-EUROPEAN LANGUAGES table **3** -ES *usu cap* : WELSH PONY **4** *or* **welsh black a** *usu cap W&B* : a Welsh breed of large black dual-purpose cattle **b** -ES *usu cap W & often cap B* : an animal of this breed **5 a** *usu cap* : a Welsh breed of long-bodied lop-eared swine of good bacon type **b** -ES *or* **welsh pig** *usu cap W & often cap P* : an animal of this breed

³**welsh** *or* **welch** \"\ *vi* -ED/-ING/-ES [prob. fr. ¹*welsh*] **1 :** to cheat by avoiding payment of bets ⟨~*ed* on a daily-double payoff⟩ **2 :** to avoid dishonorably the fulfillment of an obligation ⟨~ on its contract with the government for slum clearance —*New Republic*⟩

welsh cob *n* **1** *usu cap W&C* : a breed of medium-sized cobby horses with a high stylish action developed by interbreeding Welsh ponies with larger horses (as hackneys or thoroughbreds) **2** *usu cap W & often cap C* : a horse of the Welsh Cob breed

welsh cor·gi \-'kȯrgē\ *n, pl* **welsh corgis** *usu cap W* : a short-legged long-backed dog with foxy head belonging to either of two Welsh varieties — see CARDIGAN, PEMBROKE

welsh drake *n, usu cap W* : GADWALL

welsh dresser *also* **welsh cupboard** *n, usu cap W* : a cabinet (as for a dining room) with open shelves above a table surface and drawers and often closed cupboards below

Welsh dresser

welsh·er *or* **welch·er** \'welshə(r), -lch-\ *n* -s : one that welshes

welsh groin *n, usu cap W* : an underpitch groin

welsh harp *n, usu cap W* : a large triple harp with two rows of strings tuned diatonically in unison and the third row supplying the chromatic sharps and flats

welsh main *n, usu cap W* : a cockfight in which a number of cocks are paired, the winners again paired, and so on until there is but a single survivor

welsh·man *or* **welch·man** \-smən\ *n, pl* **welshmen** *or* **welchmen** [ME *Walsheman*, *wellisseman*, fr. OE *Wilisc man*, fr. *wilisc*, *wielisc* Welsh + *man*] **1** *cap* : a native or inhabitant of Wales : one of the Welsh **2** *South* : BLACK BASS; *esp* : SMALLMOUTH BLACK BASS

welsh mortgage *n, usu cap W* : an obsolete mortgage in which the mortgagee may keep the rents and profits of the estate in satisfaction of interest but cannot enforce payment of the principal and the mortgagor can redeem at any time by payment of the principal — compare LIVING PLEDGE

welsh mountain *n, usu cap W&M* : a breed of small white horned upland sheep of good mutton conformation native to Wales

welsh mountain pony *n, usu cap W&M* : a small sturdy pony native to the mountains of Wales and seldom exceeding 12 hands in height

welsh mountain sheep *n, usu cap W&M* : a sheep of the Welsh Mountain breed

welsh·ness *n* -ES *usu cap* : the quality or state of being Welsh : Welsh character

welsh onion *n, usu cap W* : an Asiatic onion (*Allium fistulosum*) with tufted glabrous foliage and slender bulbs that is sometimes cultivated for its leaves which are used in seasoning and its bulbs which are used as early green onions

welsh pony *n, usu cap W* : any of several stocky sturdy ponies of Welsh origin; *specif* : WELSH MOUNTAIN PONY

welsh poppy *n, usu cap W* : a widely cultivated western European plant (*Meconopsis cambrica*) of the family Papaveraceae with showy pale-yellow pedunculate flowers

welsh process *n, usu cap W* : a process in which ore (as copper ore) is smelted to matte that is then changed to metallic copper by alternate roasting and smelting in reverberatories and which is mostly superseded by Bessemer converting

welsh rabbit *n, usu cap W* [¹*rabbit* 1] : melted and often seasoned cheese sometimes mixed with ale or beer and poured over toasted bread or crackers

welsh rarebit *n, usu cap W* [by alter.] : WELSH RABBIT

welsh runt *n, usu cap W* : one of the Welsh breed of cattle

welsh·ry *or* **welsh·ery** \'welsh(ə)rē, -lch-\ *n* -ES *usu cap* : a district or quarter (as of a town or city) populated by the Welsh

welsh springer spaniel *n* **1** *usu cap W & both Ss* : a Welsh breed of red and white or orange and white small-eared springer spaniels somewhat smaller and more active than the English springer **2** *usu cap W & often cap both Ss* : a dog of the Welsh Springer Spaniel breed

welsh terrier *n, usu cap W&T* **1 :** a breed of wiry-coated terriers resembling airedales but smaller and developed in Wales for hunting otter, fox, and badger **2** *usu cap W & often cap T* : a dog of the Welsh Terrier breed

welsh vault *n, usu cap W* : an underpitch vault — see VAULT illustration

welshwoman \'=,==\ *n, pl* **welshwomen** *cap* [ME *Walsshwoman*, fr. *walssh*, *welisch* Welsh + *woman*] : a woman native or inhabitant of Wales

¹**welt** \'welt\ *vb* -ED/-ING/-S [ME *welten*, of Scand origin; akin to ON *velta* to roll, turn over — more at WELTER] *chiefly dial* : OVERTURN

²**welt** \"\ *n* -s [ME *welte*, *walte*; perh. akin to ME *welten* to overturn] **1 a :** a strip of leather or other material inserted in a shoe between the edges of the sole and upper through which the sole and upper are stitched or stapled together — see GOODYEAR WELT, STORM WELT **b :** a strip of material (as leather) used to ornament the upper of a shoe **2 a :** a doubled edge, strip, insert, or seam sewn (as on a garment) for ornament or reinforcement: as (1) : a folded-back edge of a straw or felt hat brim (2) : an applied edge along the front of a vest or the top of a pocket (3) : WELTING 1b **b :** the top strip or hem of heavier yarn in machine-knit stockings **3 a :** an elongated raised area on a surface : a raised stripe or band : RIDGE **b :** a raised area, ridge, or seam on the body surface (as from scarring or a blow) **c** *dial* : a heavy or damaging blow ⟨hit him a ~ with a club⟩ **4 a :** a strip of wood fastened over a flush seam or joint or an angle to strengthen it **b :** a strip riveted or otherwise fastened upon the edges of plates that form a butt joint in steam boilers and sheet-steel work

³**welt** \"\ *vb* -ED/-ING/-S [ME *walten*, fr. *welte*, *walte* welt] *vt* **1 :** to furnish with a welt; *specif* : to stitch a welt on (a shoe) **2 a :** to raise a welt on the skin of **b :** to hit hard **3** *Brit* : to join (two pipes) by lapping the metal at the ends one over the other and pressing the lapped portion together ~ *vi* : to become marked with welts

⁴**welt** \"\ *dial Eng var of* ²WILT

welt·an·schau·ung \'velt'än,shau̇əŋ, -au̇·(,)u̇ŋ\ *n, pl* **weltanschauungs** \-ŋz\ *or* **welt·an·schau·ung·en** \-ŋən\ *often cap* [G, lit., world view, fr. *welt* world (alter. of OHG *weralt*, *worold*) + *anschauung* view, fr. MHG *anschouwunge* contemplation, observation, fr. *an-* (fr. OHG *ana-*, fr. *ana*, adv. & prep., on, at) + *schouwunge* look, sight, fr. *schouwen* to look at, see (fr. OHG *scouwōn*) + *-unge* -ing (fr. OHG *-unga*) — more at WORLD, ON, SHOW] **1 :** a conception of the course of events in and of the purpose of the world as a whole forming a philosophical view or apprehension of the universe : the idea embodied in a cosmology : outlook on the world — called also *world view* **2 :** philosophy of life : IDEOLOGY **3 :** the cosmologic conception of society and its institutions held by its members

welted thistle *n* : a European biennial thistle (*Carduus crispus*) that is introduced in No. America and has the flower heads in crowded clusters at the ends of spiny-winged branches

¹**wel·ter** \'weltə(r)\ *vb* **weltered; weltered; weltering** \-t(ə)riŋ\ **welters** [ME *welteren*; akin to MD *welteren* to roll, wrap, MHG *welzeren* to turn, roll, OE *weltan*, *wæltan*, OHG *walzan*, ON *velta* to roll, turn over, Goth *waltjan* to roll, L *volvere* — more at VOLUBLE] *vi* **1 a :** to twist or roll one's body (as of a hog in mire) : WRITHE, TOSS, TUMBLE **b :** to rise and fall or toss about in or with waves ⟨survivors . . . ~*ed* in the sea for four days —*Time*⟩ **2 :** to become deeply sunk, soaked, or involved ⟨score technical successes, even if their backers ~ in red ink —Gilbert Gabriel⟩ **3** *dial* : to move unsteadily : REEL, STAGGER **4 :** to be in a state of turmoil ⟨cabs, carriages and crosstown cars all ~*ing* together —Brander Matthews⟩ ~ *vt, obs* : to cause to roll or overturn **syn** see WALLOW

²**welter** \"\ *n* -s **1 :** a state of wild disorder : TURMOIL ⟨the long rollers . . . crash in a ~ of foam —*Amer. Guide Series: Calif.*⟩ ⟨the ~ of anarchy, murder, civil war, bankruptcy, pestilence, and famine —*London Times*⟩ : RIOT ⟨with a ~ of color in its own formal flower beds —Alan Edwards⟩ **2 :** a chaotic mass or jumble ⟨a ~ of flailing hoofs and sods of turf —James Reynolds⟩ ⟨an atrocious road . . . that was a ~ of mud in the winter —Walter Macken⟩ ⟨this section is . . . a bewildering ~ of classical, Arabian, scholastic, and magical ideas —Harvey Graham⟩

³**welter** \"\ *vt* -ED/-ING/-S [prob. fr. *welt* (alter. of *welk*) + *-er* (as in *wither*)] : WITHER, WILT

⁴**welter** \"\ *n* -s [prob. fr. ²*welt* + *-er*] : WELTERWEIGHT 1,3 ⟨boxed with top-line pro ~*s* and soon they were paying him for working out —Lester Bromberg⟩

⁵**welter** \"\ *adj* : of, relating to, or being a race in which welterweights are carried

⁶**welt·er** \"\ *n* -s [³*welt* + *-er*] : one that welts; *specif* : a worker who forms or fastens welts on shoes, hosiery, leather goods, or straw-hat brims

welter-out \'=='=\ *n* : a rander who trims shoe welts

welterweight \'==,=\ *n* [⁴*welter* + *weight*] **1 :** a heavyweight horseman **2 :** a weight of 28 pounds sometimes imposed in a horse race (as a steeplechase or hurdle race) in addition to weight for age **3 :** a boxer or wrestler of a weight class heavier than a lightweight and lighter than a middleweight: as **a :** a professional boxer weighing more than 135 but not over 147 pounds **b :** an intercollegiate boxer weighing more than 135 but not over 145 pounds

welting *n* -s [fr. gerund of ³*welt*] **1 a :** the welts sewed or otherwise attached (as to a garment) for strengthening or decoration **b :** trimming made of a cotton cord covered with a bias strip of fabric and used in seams or along edges of slipcovers, bedspreads, or upholstery **c :** material for welts **2 :** a beating such as might raise welts

welt·po·li·tik \'velt,pōlə'tēk\ *n* -s [G, fr. *welt* world (alter. of OHG *weralt*, *worold*) + *politik* politics, fr. F *politique*, fr. MF, fr. *politique*, adj., political — more at WORLD, POLITIC] : participation in the discussion and decision of international problems : international politics

welts *pres 3d sing of* WELT, *pl of* WELT

welt·schmerz \'velt,shmerts\ *n* -ES *often cap* [G, lit., world pain, fr. *welt* world + *schmerz* pain, fr. OHG *smerzo* — more at SMART (n.)] **1 :** mental depression or apathy caused by comparison of the actual state of the world with an ideal state : sentimental pessimism **2 :** a mood of sentimental sadness

welt seam *or* **welted seam** *n* **1 :** a seam with cord welting inserted **2 :** a flat thickened seam stitched first on the wrong side and then on the right side

welt seam 2

welt shoe *n* : a shoe or boot constructed with a welt that is united to the upper lining and insole lip without stitching inside the shoe and then attached to the outsole

wel·witsch·ia \wel'wichēə\ *n, cap* [NL, fr. Friedrich *Welwitsch* †1872 Austrian botanist + NL *-ia*] : a monotypic genus of desert plants (family Gnetaceae) of southwestern Africa characterized by a trunk less than a foot high but often six feet in circumference, two persistent leaves that grow at the base and die at the apex, and cone-shaped inflorescences

wem \'wem\ *n* -s [ME, alter. (influenced by *wemmen* to stain, fr. OE *wemman*, fr. *wamm* spot, stain) of OE *wamm* spot, stain; akin to OS *wam* evil, crime, ON *vamm* blemish, Goth *wamm* spot and perh. to ON *vāma* sickness, nausea — more at VOMIT] **1** *archaic* : a moral stain **2** *chiefly dial* : a flaw or stain in something material **3** *archaic* : a bodily spot or scar

wem·bley \'wemblē, -li\ *adj, usu cap* [fr. *Wembley*, England] : of or from the municipal borough of Wembley, England : of the kind or style prevalent in Wembley

¹**wen** \'wen\ *n* -s [ME *wenn*, *wenne*, fr. OE *wenn*; akin to MLG *wene* wen, Dan dial. *vann* and prob. to OE *wund* wound — more at WOUND] **1 :** a cyst formed by obstruction to the excretion of material from a sebaceous gland and filled with sebaceous material : SEBACEOUS CYST **2 :** an abnormal growth protruding from a surface : EXCRESCENCE

²**wen** \"\ *n* -s [OE] : a rune adopted into the Old English alphabet having the value of Modern English *w* and after the 13th century being entirely replaced by that letter

we·natch·ee *or* **we·natchi** \wə'nachē\ *n, pl* **wenatchee** *or* **wenatchees** *or* **wenatchi** *or* **wenatchis** *usu cap* **1 a :** an Indian people of north central Washington **b :** a member of such people **2 :** a dialect of the Salishan language of Columbia

¹**wench** \'wench\ *n* -ES [ME *wenche*, short for *wenchel* child, fr. OE *wencel*; akin to OHG *wanchal* unsteady, *wankōn* to stagger, totter, flicker — more at WINK] **1 a :** a young woman : GIRL ⟨good girl . . . you were the best-dressed ~ in the room —Sinclair Lewis⟩ **b** *chiefly dial* : a female child **c :** a female servant : MAID **2 :** a lewd woman **3 :** a girl or woman of a socially low class ⟨known as a female impersonator, and introduced the Negro ~ characterization to minstrelsy —C.F. Wittke⟩

²**wench** \"\ *vi* -ED/-ING/-ES : to consort with lewd women; *esp* : to practice fornication

wench·er \-chə(r)\ *n* -s : one that wenches

wen·chow \'wən¦jō\ *adj, usu cap* [fr. *Wenchow*, China] : of or from the city of Wenchow, China : of the kind or style prevalent in Wenchow

¹**wend** \'wend\ *vb* -ED/-ING/-S [ME *wenden*, fr. OE *wendan*; akin to OHG *wenten* to turn, wend, ON *venda*, Goth *wandjan*; causative fr. the root of E *wind* (to turn)] *vi* **1** *obs* : to occur in the course of events : come about **2** *obs* : to turn from one direction, position, condition, or form to another **3** *obs* : to go or pass away : DEPART, END **4 :** to direct one's course : go one's way : PROCEED, TRAVEL ⟨through the fields and the woods and over the walls I have ~*ed* —Robert Frost⟩ ~ *vt* **1** *obs* : to change the direction, position, or character of **2** *archaic* : to turn (a ship's head) in tacking **3** *obs* : to cause (oneself) to go : BETAKE **4 :** to proceed on (one's way) : go on : DIRECT ⟨leisurely the governor and his associates ~*ed* their way . . . up the valley —J.E.Winston⟩

²**wend** \"\ *n* -s *cap* [G *Wende*, fr. OHG *Winida*; akin to OE *Winedas*, pl., Wends, ON *Vindir*] **1 :** a member of a Slavic people occupying eastern Germany to the Baltic sea during the early medieval period and now surviving along the middle and upper Spree river **2 :** WENDISH

wendigo *var of* WINDIGO

¹**wend·ish** \'wendish, -dēsh\ *adj, usu cap* [G *wendisch*, fr. *Wende* Wend + *-isch* -ish] : of or relating to the Wends or their language

²**wendish** \"\ *n* -ES *cap* : the West Slavic language of the Wends

w-engine *n, cap W* : an internal-combustion engine in which three sets of cylinders are arranged side by side in three planes making angles so that a cross section perpendicular to the shaft would have the general shape of the letter W

wen-li \'wən'lē\ *n* -s [Chin (Pek) *wên² li³*, fr. *wên²* literature + *li³* style] : the archaic style of classical Chinese literary composition having many complex rules and prevailing until the literary revolution of 1917 : a literary style of Chinese as distinguished from colloquial style — compare PAI-HUA

wen·lock \'wen,läk\ *n, usu cap* [fr. *Wenlock*, borough of Shropshire, England] : a subdivision of the Upper Silurian in Great Britain

wen·lock·i·an \(')wen¦läkēən\ *adj, usu cap* [*Wenlock*, England + E *-an*] : of or relating to a subdivision of the European Silurian — see GEOLOGIC TIME table

wen·nel \'wenᵊl\ *dial var of* WEANEL

wen·ny \'wenē, -ni\ *adj* -ER/-EST [¹*wen* + *-y*] **1 :** having the character of a wen : resembling a wen **2 :** afflicted with wens

wen·ro \'wen,rō\ *or* **wen·roh·ro·non** \,=,='rō,nän\ *n* -s *usu cap* : ERIE

wens *pl of* WEN

wens·ley·dale \'wenzlē,dāl\ *n* -s *usu cap* [fr. *Wensleydale*, locality in Yorkshire, England] **1 a :** a white cheese eaten fresh before curing **b :** a pale soft cheese blue-veined after curing **2 :** a hornless long-wooled mutton type sheep of an English breed developed by intercrossing Leicesters and native Yorkshire sheep

¹**went** \'went\ [ME, past & past part. of *wenden* to turn, go — more at WEND] *past or substand past part of* GO

²**went** \"\ *n* -s [ME, fr. *wenden*; influenced by ME *went*, past of *wenden* & by OE *wend* course, fr. *wendan* to wend — more at WEND] **1** *Brit* : a traveled way : ROAD, LANE, ALLEY, PASSAGE; *specif* : CROSSROAD ⟨the finger post at the centre of a four ~ way —*Architect & Building News*⟩ **2** *obs* : a turn of events

wen·tle·trap \'wentᵊl,trap\ *n* [D *wenteltrap* winding stair, fr. MD *wendeltrappe*, fr. *wendel* turning, winding (fr. *wenden* to turn) + *trappe* step, stairs; akin to OE *wendan* to turn, wend — more at WEND, TRAP] **1 :** any of numerous graceful usu. white spirally coiled and tapering gastropod mollusk shells that have longitudinal ridges surrounding the whorls, are favorites with collectors, and include one form formerly commanding very high prices — called also *staircase shell* **2 :** any of various mollusks (family Epitoniidae) of which the shell is a wentletrap

wen-yen \'wən'yen\ *n* -s [Chin (Pek) *wên²-yen²*, fr. *wên²* literature + *yen²* language] **:** written Chinese of or conforming to the complex style used in classical literature **:** classical Chinese — compare PAI-HUA

wen·zel \'ven(t)səl\ *n* -s [G, lit., servant, knave, fr. *Wenzel* Czech, fr. *Wenzeslaus* Wenceslas, after *Wenzeslaus* St. Wenceslas †A.D.935 Duke of Bohemia and patron saint of Czechoslovakia] **:** JACK 1c(1)

wept *past of* WEEP

wer *also* **were** \'wər, 'we(ə)r, 'wi(ə)r\ *n* -s [OE *wer* man, husband, wergild — more at VIRILE] **:** WERGILD

were [ME *were* (2d sing. past indic. and 1st, 2d, & 3d sing. past subj.), *weren* (past pl. indic. & subj.), fr. OE *wǣre* (2d sing. past indic. and 1st, 2d, & 3d sing. past subj. of *wesan* to be), *wǣron* (past pl. indic. of *wesan*), *wǣren* (past pl. subj. of *wesan*); akin to OFris *wēre* were (2d sing. past indic. of *wesa* to be), OHG *wāri* (2d sing. past indic. of *wesan* to be) — more at WAS] *past 2d sing & pl, past subjunctive, dial past 1st & 3d sing of* BE

weren't *R* ¦wər(-ə)nt, *-R* ¦wənt *or* ¦wərənt *sometimes* ¦wə̄nt; *archaic or Brit* ¦wa(ə)|(ə)rnt *or* ¦we| *or* |rənt *or* |ənt\ [by contr.] **:** were not

were·wolf *also* **wer·wolf** \'wi(ə)r,wu̇lf, 'wər-, 'we(ə)r-, 'wiə,w-, 'wə̄,w-, 'weə,w-\ *n, pl* **were·wolves** \-lvz\ [ME, fr. OE *werewulf, werwulf*; akin to MD *weerwolf*, OHG *werwolf*; all fr. a prehistoric WGmc compound whose constituents are represented by OE *wer* man and OE *wulf* wolf — more at WOLF] **1 :** a person transformed temporarily or permanently into a wolf or capable of assuming a wolf's form **:** LYCANTHROPE **2 :** a person whose cunning savagery suggests that of a werewolf

werf \'verf\ *n* -s [Afrik, lit., shipyard, fr. MD — more at WHARF] *southern Africa* **:** the space around homestead and outbuildings **:** FARMYARD

wer·gild *or* **wer·geld** *also* **were·gild** \'wər,gild, 'we(ə)r-, 'wi(ə)r-\ *n* -s [ME, fr. OE; akin to MD *weergelt*, OHG *wergelt* wergild; all fr. a prehistoric WGmc compound whose constituents are represented by OE *wer* man and OE *gild, geld* payment — more at VIRILE, GELD (tax)] **:** the value set in Anglo-Saxon and Germanic law upon the life of a man in accordance with a fixed scale increasing from the churl to the king and paid as compensation to the kindred or lord of a slain person or as a fine for some serious crime — compare BLOOD FEUD, BLOODWITE, ERIC

we·ri \'wārē\ *n* -s [Maori] **:** AWETO

werl·hof's disease \'ver(ə)l,hōfs-\ *n, usu cap W* [after Paul G. *Werlhof* †1767 Ger. physician] **:** PURPURA HEMORRHAGICA

¹**wer·ne·ri·an** \,wər¦nirēən, (')ver-\ *adj, usu cap* [Abraham G. *Werner* †1817 Ger. geologist and mineralogist + E *-an*] **1 :** of or relating to A.G.Werner who classified minerals according to their external characters and advocated the theory that the strata of the earth's crust were formed by depositions from water **2 :** of or according to the Wernerian system or theory **:** NEPTUNIAN

²**wernerian** \"\ *n* -s *usu cap* **:** a supporter of the Wernerian theory **:** NEPTUNIST

wer·ner·ite \'wərnə,rīt\ *n* -s [F, fr. A.G.*Werner* †1817 + F *-ite*] **:** SCAPOLITE

wer·nick·e's area \'vernəkəz-, -kēz-\ *n, usu cap W* **:** the part of the superior temporal convolution that houses Wernicke's center

wernicke's center *n, usu cap W* [after Karl *Wernicke* †1905 Ger. neurologist] **:** the auditory word center located in the posterior part of the superior temporal convolution

wernicke's convolution *or* **wernicke's gyrus** *n, usu cap W* [after Karl *Wernicke* †1905] **:** the superior temporal convolution

wernicke's prism *n* [prob. after F. Alexander *Wernicke* †1915 Ger. mathematician and physicist] **:** a direct prism for projection

wer·o·wance \'werə,wan(t)s\ *n* -s [Delaware (Virginia dial.) *wirowántēsu*, lit., he is rich, fr. *wiro* to be rich] **:** an Indian chief of Virginia or Maryland; *broadly* **:** a No. American Indian chief

wersh \'wersh\ *Scot var of* WEARISH

werst *var of* VERST

wert [alter. (influenced by *art*, 2d sing. pres. indic.) of ME *were* — more at WERE] *archaic past 2d sing & archaic past subjunctive 2d sing of* BE

wer·the·ri·an *also* **wer·te·ri·an** \(')ver¦tirēən\ *adj, usu cap* [*Werther*, romantic hero of the love story *Die Leiden des Jungen Werthers* The Sorrows of Werther (1774) by Johann Wolfgang von Goethe †1832 Ger. poet + E *-an*] **:** resembling or characteristic of Werther; *esp* **:** morbidly sentimental

wer·ther·ism \'verdə,rizəm\ *n* -s *usu cap* [*Werther* + E *-ism*] **:** the quality or state of being Wertherian

wes *pl of* WE

we·sak \'we,sāk\ *n* -s *usu cap* [Sinhalese, Baisakh (month of the Hindu year), fr. Skt *Vaiśākha*] **:** the Buddhist New Year festival celebrating the birthday of the Buddha at the May full moon

wesand *var of* WEASAND

we'se \'wēz\ [by contr. & alter. fr. *we is*] *dial* **:** we are

wes·kit \'weskət, *usu* -əd·+V\ *n* -s [alter. of *waistcoat*] **:** VEST 2a, 2b

¹**wes·ley·an** \'wesləən, 'wez-\ *adj, usu cap* [John *Wesley* †1791 and his brother Charles *Wesley* †1788 Eng. theologians + E *-an*] **:** of, relating to, or characteristic of John or Charles Wesley or Wesleyanism

²**wesleyan** \"\ *n* -s *usu cap* **:** METHODIST; *esp* **:** an adherent of Wesleyanism

wes·ley·an·ism \-ēə,nizəm\ *also* **wes·ley·ism** \-ē,izəm\ *n* -s *cap* [*wesleyanism* fr. ¹*wesleyan* + *-ism*, *wesleyism* fr. John *Wesley* †1791 + E *-ism*] **:** METHODISM 1; *specif* **:** the system of Arminian Methodism taught by John Wesley — compare CALVINISM

wesleyan methodist *n, usu cap W&M* **:** a Protestant Christian dedicated to the principles of evangelical Christianity taught by John Wesley; *specif* **:** a member of any of various bodies of Methodists (as the Wesleyan Methodists of Great Britain, the Wesleyan Methodist Church of America, the Irish Wesleyan Methodist Church, the Wesleyan Methodist Connection, the Wesleyan Methodist Church in Canada, or the Wesleyan Methodist Association)

we·sort \'wē,sȯrt\ *n, usu cap* [prob. fr. *we sort* (i.e., our sort)] **:** one of a group of people of mixed white, Indian, and Negro ancestry living in southern Maryland

wes·sel \'wesəl\ *adv* [irreg. fr. *west*] *Scot* **:** WESTWARD

wes·sel·ton \-tən, -tᵊn\ *n* -s [fr. *Wesselton*, one of the Kimberley mines, Kimberley, So. Africa] **:** a high-grade diamond ranking below a river

wes·sex·man \'wesəksmən\ *n, pl* **wessexmen** *cap* [*Wessex*, section of southern England + E *-man*] **:** a native or inhabitant of Wessex

wessex saddleback *n* [fr. *Wessex*, England, where it was orig. bred] **1** *usu cap W&S* **:** an old British breed of medium-sized black white-belted swine perhaps not distinct from the American Hampshire **2** -s *usu cap W & often cap S* **:** an animal of the Wessex saddleback breed

¹**west** \'west\ *adv* [ME, fr. OE; akin to OHG *westar* to the west, ON *vestr* and prob. to L *vesper, vespera* evening, Gk *hesperos*] **1 :** to, toward, or in the west **:** WESTWARD **2 :** to the realm of the departed beyond the sunset — used in the phrase *to go west* ⟨realized what awaited her if I 'went ~' —*Time*⟩ ⟨what had seemed a promising line of research had gone ~ —F.W.Crofts⟩

²**west** \"\ *adj* [ME, fr. OE *west-*, fr. *west*, adv.] **1 a :** situated toward or at the west ⟨the ~ meadow⟩ ⟨the ~ side of the house **b** [ME, fr. OE *westan-*, fr. *westan*, adv.; akin to OHG *westana* from the west, ON *vestan*; derivative fr. the root of E ¹*west*] **:** coming from the west ⟨a ~ wind⟩ **2 :** situated in the opposite direction from the altar of a church **:** lying in that part of the church directly opposite the chancel

³**west** \"\ *n* -s [ME, fr. *west*, adv.] **1 a :** the general direction of sunset **:** the direction toward the left of one facing north **b :** the part of the sky in which celestial bodies set; *specif* **:** the place on the horizon where the sun sets when it is near one of the equinoxes **c :** the cardinal point directly opposite to east — abbr. *W*; see COMPASS CARD **d :** the point of the horizon having an azimuth or bearing of 270° and marking one intersection of the horizon and the celestial equator **:** the direction of the sky's daily apparent rotation **:** the direction opposite to that of the earth's rotation and its revolution around the sun **2** *usu cap* **a :** regions or countries lying to the west of a specified or implied point of orientation (as in the U. S. the states lying in general west of the Mississippi river); *specif* **:** the noncommunist countries of Europe and America ⟨held discussions on disarmament proposals put forward by the *West*⟩ **b :** something (as people, culture, or institutions) characteristic of the West ⟨a book such as this makes for closer understanding between the East and the *West* for the insight it gives into the Chinese mind —*Times Lit. Supp.*⟩ ⟨accused the *West* of plotting a new war —*Sat. Eve. Post*⟩ ⟨the old *West* of gun-toting marshals and Pony Express⟩ **3 :** the west wind **4** *often cap* **a :** the one of four positions at 90-degree intervals that lies toward the west **b :** a person (as a bridge player) occupying such a position in the course of a specific activity

⁴**west** \"\ *vi* -ED/-ING/-S [ME *westen*, fr. *west*, adv.] **:** to move or veer toward the west

⁵**west** \"\ *n* -s [origin unknown] *dial Eng* **:** ⁴STY

westabout \'⸗,⸗\ *adv (or adj)* [²*west* + *about*] **:** about in tacking so as to head west; *broadly* **:** toward the west **:** WESTWARD

¹**west african** *adj, usu cap W&A* [*West Africa* + E *-an*] **1 :** of, relating to, or characteristic of West Africa — usu. used specif. of the part of Africa lying to the north of the Gulf of Guinea and often excluding Morocco, northern Algeria, and Tunisia **2 :** of, relating to, or characteristic of the West Africans

²**west african** *n, cap W&A* **:** a native or inhabitant of West Africa — usu. used specif. of the Negro peoples of the part of Africa lying to the north of the Gulf of Guinea

west african oil palm *n, usu cap W&A* **:** AFRICAN OIL PALM

west african pidgin *n, usu cap W&A* **:** an English-based pidgin language in use in various areas in West Africa, particularly the Cameroons

west aramaic *n, cap W&A* **:** WESTERN ARAMAIC

west-atlantic \¦⸗⸗¦⸗⸗\ *n, cap W&A* **:** a branch of the Niger-Congo family of languages including Wolof, Serer, Balante, Limba, Temne, Kissi, and Gola which are spoken in West Africa from Senegal to Liberia and Fulani which has spread eastward from Senegal to the Cameroons

westbound \'⸗,⸗\ *adj* [¹*west* + *bound*] **:** traveling or headed in a westerly direction; *broadly* **:** headed west or south — used of freight cars in railroad accounting

¹**west by north :** a compass point that is one point north of due west **:** N 78° 45′ W — abbr. *WbN, W by N*; see COMPASS CARD

²**west by north** *adv (or adj)* **1 :** toward west by north **2 :** from west by north

¹**west by south :** a compass point that is one point south of due west **:** S 78° 45′ W — abbr. *WbS, W by S*; see COMPASS CARD

²**west by south** *adv (or adj)* **1 :** toward west by south **2 :** from west by south

west coast hemlock *n* **:** WESTERN HEMLOCK

¹**west·er** \'westə(r)\ *vi* [ME *westren*, fr. ¹*west* + *-ren* (as in *clatren* to clatter)] **1 :** to move westward ⟨began his ~*ing* in 1678 —Bernard De Voto⟩ — used esp. of a celestial body in its course ⟨a ~*ing* sun shone through the rose window —*N.Y. Times*⟩ **2 :** to turn, veer, or shift to the west

²**wester** \"\ *n* -s [²*west* + *-er*] **1 :** a strong west wind ⟨the ~ came as steady as the trades —John Masefield⟩ **2 :** a storm with west winds

west·er·li·ness \-lēnəs, -lin-\ *n* -ES **:** the situation of being westerly

west·er·ling \'westərliŋ, -təl-, -tᵊl-\ *n* -s [obs. E *wester* western + E *-ling*] *archaic* **:** WESTERNER

¹**west·er·ly** \'westə(r)lē, -li; *-R* -təl- *sometimes* -tᵊl-\ *adj* [obs. E *wester* western (fr. ME, fr. OE *westra* more towards the west, fr. *west*, adv. + *-ra* -er) + E *-ly*] **1 :** situated or directed toward the west **:** WESTERN ⟨a ~ suburb⟩ ⟨wended their way in a ~ direction up the valley —J.E.Winston⟩ **2 :** blowing from the west ⟨a ~ breeze⟩

²**westerly** \"\ *adv* **1 :** from the west ⟨the wind blew ~⟩ **2 :** toward the west ⟨we began to steer away ~ —Daniel Defoe⟩

³**westerly** \"\ *n* -ES **:** a wind blowing from the west ⟨the prevailing *westerlies* of the temperate zones⟩

west·er·most \'westə(r),mōst, *esp Brit also* -,məst\ *adj* [obs. E *wester* western + E *most*] **:** WESTERNMOST

¹**west·ern** \'westə(r)n, *-R also* -tᵊn\ *adj* [ME *westeren, westerne*, fr. OE *westerne*; akin to OHG *westrōni* western, ON *vestrœnn*, derivative fr. the root of E ¹*west*] **1** *often cap* **:** of, relating to, originating or dwelling in, or characteristic of a region conventionally designated West: as **a :** steeped in or stemming from the Greco-Roman traditions of the Occident rather than those of Islam, India, or the Far East ⟨the *Western* tradition began to take distinctive shape with the mingling of Greco-Roman and Hebraic-Christian elements in the later days of the Roman Empire —J.A.Corry⟩ ⟨in the nineteenth century, the adoption of . . . superior *Western* technology appeared to Far Eastern statesmen to be a legitimate risk as well as an imperative necessity —A.J.Toynbee⟩ ⟨barriers, between a ~ eye and the beauty of a Chinese vase —J.A.Macy⟩ **b :** of or relating to the noncommunist countries of Europe and America ⟨~ emphasis on individualism⟩ ⟨American tendency to consult with the *Western* powers on what is good for Asia, instead of first consulting with the Asian nations themselves —Mochtar Lubis⟩ **c** (1) **:** of or relating to the American West ⟨~ settlers⟩ ⟨~ plains⟩ ⟨~ cattle ranches⟩ ⟨the ~ grosbeak closely resembles the rose-breasted grosbeak except in plumage⟩ (2) **:** of or relating to folk music characteristic of the American West ⟨favorite hillbilly — or, if you prefer, ~ — crooner —*Ochiltree* (*Texas*) *County Herald*⟩ (3) **:** of or relating to a literary western ⟨resorts to every typical *Western* element: the fugitive bandit, the sheriff in pursuit, the girl, the gun play, and the great outdoors —Delmore Schwartz⟩ **2 a :** situated in or lying toward the west ⟨around the ~ and southern sides of the track are grandstands —*Amer. Guide Series: Ind.*⟩ ⟨islands in the ~ half of the archipelago⟩ **b :** coming from the west — used chiefly of the wind ⟨a ~ gale⟩ **c** (1) **:** going toward or facing the west ⟨the ~ voyage of Columbus⟩ ⟨a room with a ~ exposure⟩ (2) **:** corresponding to the westering course of the sun **:** DECLINING ⟨we . . . on the ~ side of life —H.W.Longfellow⟩ **3** *usu cap* **:** of or relating to the Roman Catholic and Protestant segment of Christianity ⟨*Western* liturgies⟩ — compare EASTERN ORTHODOX

²**western** \"\ *n* -s **1** *often cap* **:** WESTERNER **2 a :** one that is produced in or characteristic of a western region and esp. the western U. S. ⟨ewes in this experiment were two-year-old ~*s* —W.C.Coffey⟩ ⟨in felt hats ranchers prefer broad-brimmed ~*s*⟩ **b :** GENERAL AMERICAN **c :** WESTERN SANDWICH **3** *often cap* **:** a story of frontier life ⟨historical novels also rank high, and so do murder mysteries and *Westerns* —Bruce Bliven b. 1889⟩ ⟨a traditional *Western* in a novel Australian setting —*Films in Review*⟩; *specif* **:** a play (as a moving picture or a radio or television play) dealing usu. with life in the western U.S. during the latter half of the 19th century ⟨rattling good ~ about the first cattle drive over the Chisholm Trail —*Time*⟩ ⟨~*s*, those simple . . . sagas of manly men and womanly women —Virginia Graham⟩

western aramaic *n, cap W&A* **:** the subgroup of Aramaic languages used in Syria and Palestine and by people from this area including the language of the Aramaic portions of the Bible and of the Targums

western arborvitae *n* **:** CANOE CEDAR

western australia *adj, usu cap W&A* [fr. *Western Australia*, state in Australia] **:** of or from the state of Western Australia **:** of the kind or style prevalent in Western Australia **:** WESTERN AUSTRALIAN

¹**western australian** *adj, usu cap W&A* **1 :** of, relating to, or characteristic of Western Australia **:** WESTRALIAN **2 :** of, relating to, or characteristic of the Western Australians **:** WESTRALIAN

²**western australian** *n, cap W&A* **:** a native or inhabitant of Western Australia **:** WESTRALIAN

western azalea *n* **:** a deciduous shrub (*Rhododendron occidentale*) of the Coast range of No. America having usu. white flowers

western baboon *n* **:** a common baboon (*Papio papio*) of the Guinea coast of Africa

western balsam *n* **:** LOWLAND FIR

western bezoar *n, usu cap W* **:** a bezoar consisting chiefly of calcium phosphate found in the Peruvian llama

western birch *n* **:** WESTERN PAPER BIRCH

western black pine *n* **1 :** JEFFREY PINE **2 :** the wood of the Jeffrey pine

western blight *n* **:** WESTERN TOMATO BLIGHT

western bluebird *n* **:** a bluebird (*Sialia mexicana occidentalis*) of western No. America that is typically more purplish than the eastern form and has a patch of chestnut on the back

western brome grass *n* **:** a perennial grass (*Bromus marginatus*) of western No. America valued as a range grass

western buckeye *n* **:** a shrub (*Aesculus arguta*) of the central U. S. sometimes cultivated for its palmately compound leaves and dense racemes of yellow flowers

western catalpa *n* **:** a large often cultivated tree (*Catalpa speciosa*) having purple-streaked paniculate flowers and long thick podlike fruits — called also *cigar tree, hardy catalpa*; compare INDIAN BEAN 1

western cedar *n* **1** *or* **western juniper a :** a timber tree (*Juniperus occidentalis*) of the Pacific coast of the U. S. often of shrubby growth in the mountains **b :** the wood of the western cedar tree **2 :** CANOE CEDAR

western chicken flea *n* **:** a rather large flea (*Ceratophyllus niger*) that breeds in hen droppings and feeds as an adult on various birds and mammals including man

western chimpanzee *n* **:** a chimpanzee of Sierra Leone that is sometimes considered a separate race (*Pan troglodytes verus*)

western chokecherry *n* **:** a chokecherry (*Padus demissa*) of the western U. S.

western church *n, usu cap W & often cap C* **1 :** the churches of the West and esp. of western Europe and the Americas **:** Western Christianity **2 :** one of the churches of Western Christianity (as the church of the Latin Patriarchate)

western coffee *n* **:** CASCARA BUCKTHORN

western crab apple *n* **:** IOWA CRAB

western daisy *n* **:** an herb (*Astranthium integrifolia*) of the central U. S. that has violet flowers and a branched stem, resembles and is closely related to the common English daisy, and is often included in the genus *Bellis*

western diamond rattlesnake *or* **western diamondback** *n* **:** a large and notably venomous rattlesnake (*Crotalus atrox*) of dry areas of the southwestern U. S. and adjacent Mexico with a predominantly grayish to buffy ground, large light-margined rhomboid to diamond-shaped blotches on the back, and a black and white ringed tail

western dogwood *n* **:** PACIFIC DOGWOOD

western dropwort *n* **:** a medicinal herb (*Gillenia trifoliata*) used by American Indians

western duck sickness *n* **:** DUCK SICKNESS

west·ern·er *R* 'westə(r)nər, *-R* -tənə(r *also* -tᵊnə(r\ *n* -s *usu cap* **1 a :** a native or inhabitant of a western region ⟨*Westerners* from French West and Equatorial Africa —Michael Barbour⟩; *esp* **:** a native or inhabitant of the western U. S. ⟨the nasal twang of a *Westerner*⟩ **b :** a native or inhabitant of an occidental country ⟨*Westerners* do not understand Asiatics —H.B.Acton⟩ **c :** a supporter of the ideals and policies of the noncommunist countries of Europe and America ⟨many ~*s* mistakenly supposed that because the Soviet mind was politically mutilated it could not achieve much in science and technology —E.K.Lindley⟩ **2 a :** an adherent or advocate of western beliefs and practices ⟨a *Westerner* who wants to grapple with this subject, must try, for a few minutes, to slip out of his native Western skin and look . . . through the eyes of the great non-Western majority of mankind —A.J.Toynbee⟩ **b :** a member of the 19th-century Russian intelligentsia advocating the adoption of western European institutions or culture — compare SLAVOPHILISM

western fir *n* **1 a :** DOUGLAS FIR **b :** any of several western No. American trees of the genus *Abies* **2 :** the wood of a western fir

western frame *n* **:** PLATFORM FRAME

western framing *n* [so called fr. its use in the western U. S.] **:** a method of building construction in which the supporting studs extend from the top of each tier of joists to the underside of the tier next above so that each floor is independently framed

western grape rootworm *n* **:** a grape rootworm (*Adoxus obscurus*)

western grape skeletonizer *n* **:** a small zygaenid moth (*Harrisina brillians*) whose larva is an important pest of grape in California

western grebe *n* **:** a large grebe (*Aechmophorus occidentalis*) of western No. America

western hemisphere *n* **:** the vertical half of the earth that lies chiefly to the west of the Atlantic ocean and includes No. and So. America and minor land masses

western hemlock *n* **:** a commercially important timber tree (*Tsuga heterophylla*) ranging from Alaska to California and having leaves that are of uniform width throughout and lack prominent pale stomatic lines beneath — called also *Pacific hemlock, west coast hemlock*; compare EASTERN HEMLOCK

western hindi *n, cap W&H* **:** a group of Indic dialects of northern India

west·ern·ism \-,nizəm\ *n* -s *often cap* **1 a :** a locution or pronunciation characteristic of a western region and esp. of the western U. S. **b :** an attitude or trait characteristic of a westerner **2 a :** a western institution or concept ⟨the Japanese took over the forms of ~, including a constitution and a parliament —Nathaniel Peffer⟩ **b :** adherence to or advocacy of western traditions and techniques

west·ern·iza·tion \,⸗⸗nə'zāshən, -,nī'z-\ *n* -s *often cap* **:** conversion to or adoption of western traditions or techniques ⟨~ and industrialization of primarily agricultural nations⟩

west·ern·ize \'⸗⸗,nīz\ *vb* -ED/-ING/-S *see -ize in Explan Notes, sometimes cap, vt* **1 :** to imbue with qualities native to or associated with a western region and esp. the western U. S. **2 :** OCCIDENTALIZE ⟨was *Westernizing* his subjects by force, like any good Eastern autocrat —A.L.Kroeber⟩ ~ *vi* **:** to become occidentalized ⟨wish to ~ even while ridding themselves of Western rule —A.G.Meyer⟩

western kingbird *n* **:** ARKANSAS KINGBIRD

western larch *n* **1** *or* **western tamarack :** an important timber tree (*Larix occidentalis*) of western No. America with pale green sharply pointed leaves and oblong cones — called also *Oregon larch* **2 :** the wood of the western larch

west·ern·ly *adj* **:** WESTERLY

western meadowlark *n* **:** a meadowlark (*Sturnella neglecta*) of western No. America

west·ern·most \'⸗⸗,mōst, *esp Brit also* -,məst\ *adj* **:** farthest to the west **:** most western

western mountain ash *n* **:** an ash (*Sorbus sitchensis*) of the Pacific coast of No. America — called also *mountain ash*

western mugwort *n* **:** PRAIRIE SAGE

western palm warbler *n* **:** a warbler (*Dendroica palmarum*) of central Canada and the Mississippi valley having yellowish underparts and a chestnut crown when adult

western paper birch *n* **:** a birch (*Betula fontinalis*) of western No. America resembling the paper birch of the northeastern U. S. but with brownish bark — called also *mountain birch, swamp birch, western birch*

western paradise *n, usu cap W&P* **:** PURE LAND

western peach borer *n* **:** a borer that attacks peach and other stone fruit trees in western No. America and is considered a variety (*graefi*) of the eastern peach tree borer

western peony *n* **:** an herbaceous perennial (*Paeonia brownii*) native to western U. S., but cultivated elsewhere for its brownish red flowers

western pine *n* **:** PONDEROSA PINE

western pine beetle *n* **:** a destructive bark beetle (*Dendroctonus brevicomis*) attacking various pines in the western U. S.

western pitch pine *n* **:** PONDEROSA PINE

western plum *n* **:** SIERRA PLUM

western poppy *n* **:** a showy Californian annual herb (*Papaver californicum*) with flowers having striking red petals that are green at the base

western ragweed *n* **:** a coarse perennial ragweed (*Ambrosia psilostachya*) that resembles common ragweed but has perennial creeping roots — called also *perennial ragweed*

western red cedar *n* **1 a :** ROCKY MOUNTAIN JUNIPER **b :** the wood of Rocky Mountain juniper **2 a :** CANOE CEDAR **b :** the wood of the canoe cedar **3 :** WESTERN CEDAR 1

western red lily *n* **:** a slender erect herb (*Lilium umbellatum*) of the prairies of central No. America having narrow mostly alternate leaves and erect orange-red flowers spotted toward the base

western redtail *n* **:** a red-tailed hawk (*Buteo borealis calurus*) of western No. America

western ring-necked snake *n* **:** a small innocuous No. American snake (*Storeria occipitomaculata*) that is dark gray or brown above and on the undersurface white anteriorly and reddish posteriorly — called also *red-bellied snake*

western roll *n, usu cap W* **:** a technique of high jumping in which the leg farthest from the bar lifts first, the jumper's side is to the bar as the body passes over it, and a three-point landing is made on the take-off leg and both hands — compare EASTERN ROLL, SCISSORS

western rust *n* **:** a rust of the raspberry caused by a fungus (*Phragmidium imitans*)

western rye *or* **western rye grass** *n, usu cap W* **:** SLENDER WHEAT GRASS

western saddle *n, often cap W* **:** STOCK SADDLE

western sage *n* **:** either of two plants of the western U. S.: **a :** PRAIRIE SAGE **b :** an herb (*Artemisia ludoviciana*) that resembles prairie sage

western sa·moa \-sə'mōə\ *adj, usu cap W&S* [fr. *Western Samoa,* country in South Pacific ocean] **:** of or from the country of Western Samoa **:** of the kind or style prevalent in Western Samoa

western sand cherry *n* **:** a dwarf ornamental shrub (*Prunus besseyi*) of the western U. S. with elliptic leaves and large sweet edible fruit

western sandpiper *n* **:** a small sandpiper (*Ereunetes mauri*) very closely related to the semipalmated sandpiper which it chiefly replaces in western No. America but frequently occurring also along the Atlantic coast

western sandwich *n* **:** a sandwich of which the filling usu. is a beaten egg cooked with minced ham and onion — called also *Denver sandwich, western*

western sneezeweed *n* **:** a rather rank perennial herb (*Helenium hoopesii*) of the western U. S. having yellow flowers, being poisonous to stock, and causing spewing sickness in sheep

western spruce *n* **:** SITKA SPRUCE

western sudanic *n, usu cap W&S* **:** a language family of West Africa to which were added the Bantu and Adamawa-Eastern languages to form the Niger-Congo family

western sugar maple *n* **:** a forest tree (*Acer grandidentatum*) of western No. America having the leaves hairy underneath and the lobes usu. toothed — called also *bigtooth maple*

western tanager *n* **:** a tanager (*Piranga ludoviciana*) of western No. America the male of which is black, yellow, and orange-red

western tent caterpillar *n* **:** a caterpillar that is the larva of a lasiocampid moth (*Malacosoma pluviale*) and that feeds on cherry, apple, and other trees in western U. S. and Canada

western tomato blight *or* **western yellow blight** *n* **:** a disease of the tomato that is common west of the Rocky mountains and is caused by the curly top virus of sugar beets and transmitted by the beet leafhopper but produces entirely different effects from typical curly top (as yellowing of foliage sometimes with some purple coloration, premature ripening of the fruit, or rigidity of the foliage)

western wallflower *n* **1 :** a prairie rocket (*Erysimum asperum*) chiefly of the western U. S. having orange-yellow flowers **2 :** SPREADING DOGBANE

western wheatgrass *n* **1 :** a valuable forage grass (*Agropyron smithii*) of the western U. S. **2 :** BLUESTEM 1a

western white fir *n* **:** LOWLAND FIR

western white pine *n* **1 :** a white pine (*Pinus monticola*) with stout blue-green leaves 2 to 4 inches long and long-stalked cones 5 to 12 inches long **2 :** PONDEROSA PINE 1 **3 :** LIMBER PINE

western X-disease *n* **:** a disease of peaches and cherries caused by a form or strain of the X-disease virus found in northwestern U. S. and adjacent Canada

western yellow pine *n* **:** PONDEROSA PINE

western yew *n* **:** PACIFIC YEW

westers *pres 3d sing of* WESTER, *pl of* WESTER

west germanic *n, usu cap W&G* **:** a subdivision of the Germanic languages including English, Frisian, Dutch, and German

west goth *n, cap W&G* **:** VISIGOTH

west ham *adj, usu cap W&H* [fr. *West Ham,* southeastern England] **:** of or from the county borough of West Ham, England **:** of the kind or style prevalent in West Ham

west highland *n, usu cap W&H* [fr. *West Highlands,* western part of the Highlands of Scotland] **:** a breed of small very hardy beef cattle from the Highlands of Scotland having thick shaggy hair varying from dun to brindle or black and long curved horns set widely apart

west highland white terrier *n, usu cap 1st W&H* **:** a small white dog of a breed developed in Scotland to dig out small quarry that has a hard uncurled outer coat about 2½ inches long, a soft undercoat, a medium-width head with powerful jaws and sharp-pointed small ears, a compact body, short and muscular forelegs and hind legs, and a tail about five or six inches long

west indiaman *n, usu cap W&I* [*West India* + E *man*] **:** a sailing ship formerly running to the West Indies and the east coast of America and usu. much smaller than East Indiamen

¹west indian *adj, usu cap W&I* [*West India* (former name of the *West Indies,* group of islands enclosing the Caribbean sea) + E *-an,* adj. suffix] **:** of, relating to, or characteristic of the West Indies or its people

²west indian *n, cap W&I* [*West India* + E *-an,* n. suffix] **:** a native or inhabitant of the West Indies

west indian arrowroot *n, usu cap W&I* **:** INDIAN ARROWROOT 1b

west indian birch *n, usu cap W&I* **:** GUMBO LIMBO 1

west indian boxwood *n, usu cap W&I* **:** ZAPATERO 2b

west indian cane weevil *n, usu cap 1st W&I* **:** a tropical American snout beetle (*Metamasius hemipterus*) that is destructive to sugarcane esp. in the West Indies

west indian cherry *n, usu cap W&I* **:** BARBADOS CHERRY 1

west indian ebony *n, usu cap W&I* **:** COCUSWOOD

west indian fruit fly *n, usu cap W&I* **:** a small fly (*Anastrepha mombinpraeoptans*) of the family Trypetidae whose larvae develop in citrus and other fruits in tropical America

west indian gherkin *n, usu cap W&I* **:** GHERKIN 1

west indian ivy *n, usu cap W & 1st I* **:** a climbing plant of the genus *Marcgravia*

west-indian-ivy family *n, usu cap W & 1st I* **:** MARCGRAVIACEAE

west indian locust *n, usu cap W&I* **:** a tropical American tree (*Hymenaea courbaril*) yielding hard brown wood used for building and having bijugate leaves, white flowers, and woody pods containing an edible pulp

west indian mahogany *n, usu cap W&I* **:** a mahogany (*Swietenia mahogani*); *also* **:** MAHOGANY 1a(1)

west indian peach scale *n, usu cap W&I* **:** a widely distributed polyphagous scale insect (*Aulacaspis pentagona*) that is esp. destructive to peach and mulberry and occurs generally in tropical and subtropical regions

west indian sandalwood *n, usu cap W&I* **:** a Jamaica rosewood (*Amyris balsamifera*)

west indian satinwood *n, usu cap W&I* **:** SATINWOOD 2a(1)

west indian tea *n, usu cap W&I* **:** a goatweed (*Capraria biflora*) the leaves of which are sometimes used in the West Indies for tea

west indian yellowwood *n, usu cap W&I* **:** HERCULES'-CLUB 1a

west india seal *n, usu cap W&I* **:** a large earless seal (*Monachus tropicalis*) of the West Indies that is nearly extinct

west indies *adj, usu cap W&I* [fr. *West Indies,* group of islands between North and South America enclosing the Caribbean sea; fr. the belief of Columbus that it was a new route to India] **:** of or from the West Indies group of islands **:** of the kind or style prevalent in the West Indies **:** WEST INDIAN

west·ing \'westiŋ\ *n* -s [in sense 1, fr. ¹*west* + *-ing;* in sense 2, fr. gerund of ⁴*west*] **1 :** difference in longitude to the west from the last preceding point of reckoning **2 :** westerly progress **:** a going westward ⟨trade winds . . . would blow me across on my ~ as they had blown Columbus —Alan Villiers⟩

west·land \'westlənd\ *adj, usu cap* [fr. *Westland,* New Zealand] **:** of or from the provincial district of Westland, New Zealand **:** of the kind or style prevalent in Westland provincial district

westland pine *n, usu cap W* [fr. *Westland,* New Zealand] **:** SILVER PINE 4

west·lin \'westlən\ *or* **west·ling** \", -liŋ\ *adj* [*westlin* alter. of *westland,* fr. ²*west* + *land; westling* alter. (influenced by *-ing*) of *westlin*] *Scot* **:** WESTERLY ⟨when the fringe was red on the ~ hill —James Hogg⟩

west·lins \-nz\ *or* **west·lings** \-nz, -ŋz\ *adv* [³*west* + *-lins* (alter. of *-lings*) or *-lings*] *Scot* **:** to the west

west lo·thi·an \-'lōthēən, -thyən\ *adj, usu cap W&L* [fr. *West Lothian,* Scotland] **:** of or from the county of West Lothian, Scotland **:** of the kind or style prevalent in West Lothian

west·meath \(')wes(t)¦mēth\ *adj, usu cap* [fr. *Westmeath,* Ireland] **:** of or from county Westmeath, Ireland **:** of the kind or style prevalent in county Westmeath

west·min·ster chimes \'wes(t),minztə(r)-, -n(t)stə(r)-, *substand* (')=¦minəstə(r)-\ *n, usu cap W* [fr. *Westminster,* section of London in which the House of Parliament is located] **:** clock chimes on four bells or gongs fashioned after the tune of the chimes on the House of Parliament clock in London

west·mor·land \'wes(t)mə(r)lənd, *U S also* (')=¦mōrl- *or* (')=¦mórl- *or* (')=¦mōəl- *or* (')=¦mó(ə)l-\ *adj, usu cap* [fr. *Westmorland,* England] **:** of or from the county of Westmorland, England **:** of the kind or style prevalent in Westmorland

west·most \'wes(t)mōst, *esp Brit also* -,məst\ *adj* [alter. (influenced by ¹*most*) of ME *westmest,* fr. OE, superl. of *west,* adv.] **:** WESTERNMOST ⟨the appeal of our ~ land is in its . . . terrain, climate —Aubrey Drury⟩

west·ness \'wes(t)nəs\ *n* -ES **:** the quality or state of being west

¹west-northwest \(¦)=¦=¦=\ *adv (or adj)* [ME *west-north-west*] **1 :** toward west-northwest **2 :** from west-northwest

²west-northwest \"\ *n* **:** a compass point that is two points north of due west **:** N 67°30′ W — abbr. *WNW;* see COMPASS CARD

Wes·ton \'westən\ *trademark* — used for a voltaic cell used as a standard of electromotive force

west·phal balance \'wes(t),fōl-\ *n, usu cap W* [prob. after Wilhelm H. *Westphal,* 20th cent. Ger. physicist] **:** a balance having the buoyancy of a float balanced by sliding weights that is used for determining specific gravity (as of liquids or mineral fragments) — called also *Mohr balance*

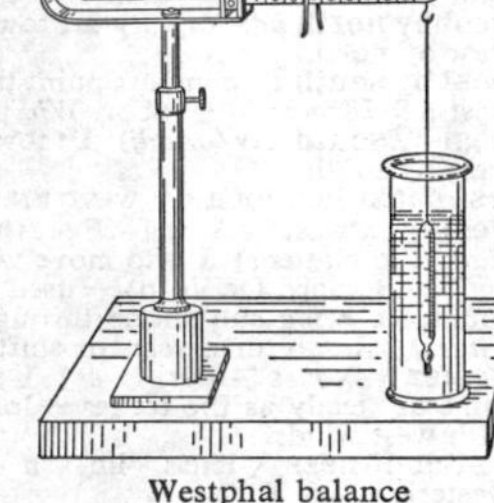

Westphal balance

¹west·pha·lian \(')wes(t)-¦fālyən, -lēən\ *adj, usu cap* [*Westphalia,* former province of Prussia + E *-an*] **1 a :** of, relating to, or characteristic of Westphalia or Westphalians **b :** of, relating to, or characteristic of the Westphalian dialect **2 :** of or relating to a subdivision of the Upper Carboniferous — see GEOLOGIC TIME table

²westphalian \"\ *n* -s *cap* **:** a native or inhabitant of Westphalia

westphalian ham *n, usu cap W* **:** a ham of distinctive flavor produced by smoking with juniper brush

west point *n, often cap W&P* [fr. *West Point,* U. S. military academy at West Point, N. Y.] **:** a grayish blue that is redder and paler than electric, duller and very slightly redder than copenhagen, and duller and very slightly greener than Gobelin

¹wes·tra·lian \(')we¦strālyən *sometimes* -lēən\ *adj, usu cap* [*Westralia* (contr. of *Western Australia*) + E *-an*] **:** of, relating to, or characteristic of Western Australia or its inhabitants

²westralian \"\ *n* -s *cap* **:** a native or inhabitant of Western Australia

westralian jewfish *n, usu cap W* **:** JEWFISH 2a

wests *pl of* WEST, *pres 3d sing of* WEST

west saxon *n, cap W&S* [ME] **1 :** a native or inhabitant of the West Saxon kingdom **2 :** a dialect of Old English **:** the chief literary dialect in pre-Conquest England

west semitic *n, cap W&S* **:** the Semitic languages other than Akkadian

¹west-southwest \(¦)=¦=¦=\ *adv (or adj)* [ME *west southwest*] **1 :** toward west-southwest **2 :** from west-southwest

²west-southwest \"\ *n* **:** a compass point that is two points south of due west **:** S 67°30′ W — abbr. *WSW;* see COMPASS CARD

west virginia *adj, usu cap W&V* [fr. *West Virginia,* state in the east central U. S., fr. ²*west* + *Virginia,* eastern state of which West Virginia was a part until the American Civil War] **:** of or from the state of West Virginia ⟨*West Virginia* coal⟩ **:** of the kind or style prevalent in West Virginia **:** WEST VIRGINIAN

¹west virginian *adj, usu cap W&V* [*West Virginia* + E *-an*] **:** of, relating to, or characteristic of West Virginia or West Virginians

²west virginian *n, cap W&V* **:** a native or resident of West Virginia

¹west·ward \'westwə(r)d\ *adv (or adj)* [ME, fr. OE *westweard,* fr. ¹*west* + *-weard* -ward] **:** toward the west ⟨the pioneers trekked ~⟩

²westward \"\ *n* **:** westward direction or part ⟨the Rockies lie to the ~⟩

west·ward·ly *adv (or adj)* **:** in a westward direction

west·wards \-dz\ *adv* [³*west* + *-wards*] **:** WESTWARD ⟨walked swiftly ~ through the twilight —Michael Arlen⟩

¹wet \'wet, *usu* -ed.+V\ *vb* **wet** *or* **wetted; wet** *or* **wetted; wetting; wets** [ME *weten,* fr. OE *wǣtan,* fr. *wǣt,* adj., wet] *vt* **1 :** to make wet **:** soak or moisten with water or other liquid **:** dip in a liquid ⟨sand *wetted* by the waves —G.W.Murray⟩ ⟨~ his pencil and got ready to write —Josephine Pinckney⟩ **2 :** to suffuse (the eyes) with tears **:** dampen (something) with tears **:** fall on and moisten (something) **3 :** to take a drink or treat to a drink in celebration or honor of ⟨~ a bargain⟩ ⟨~ a commission in the army⟩ **4 :** to soak (grain) in malting **5 :** to urinate in or on ⟨~ the bed⟩ **6 :** to make (tea) by pouring boiling water on the leaves ⟨I ~ a cup of tea —Bryan MacMahon⟩ **~** *vi* **1 :** to become wet **2 :** URINATE — **wet one's whistle :** to take a drink ⟨'tis a hot day and I think our friends will need to *wet their whistles* before long —*Boys' Life*⟩ — **wet the other eye :** to take another drink of liquor ⟨moisten your clay, *wet the other eye* —Charles Dickens⟩

²wet \"\ *adj* **wetter; wettest** [ME *wet, wete, wette,* partly fr. past part. of *weten* to wet & partly fr. OE *wǣt* wet; akin to OFris *wēt* wet, ON *vātr* wet, *vatn* water — more at WATER] **1 a :** consisting of, containing, covered with, or soaked with water or some other liquid **:** having water or other liquid on the surface or penetrating beyond it **:** MOIST ⟨~ tears⟩ ⟨the ~ sea⟩ ⟨a ~ floor⟩ ⟨~ fields⟩ ⟨got his clothes ~ when he fell in the water⟩ ⟨a rag ~ with oil⟩ ⟨cheeks ~ with happy tears⟩ **b :** moistened by dipping in or sprinkling with water or other liquid ⟨it had been raining and the newspaper at the door was ~⟩ ⟨grass ~ with dew⟩ **c** *of natural gas* **:** containing appreciable quantities of gasoline or other readily condensable hydrocarbons **2 :** RAINY: as **a :** having frequent rains ⟨the ~ season⟩ **b :** promising rain ⟨a ~ sky⟩ **c :** laden with or bearing moisture or vapor **:** HUMID ⟨a ~ wind⟩ **d :** accompanied by rain ⟨the city gave us a ~ welcome⟩ **3 :** still moist enough to smudge or smear ⟨the signature was still ~⟩ ⟨~ paint⟩ **4 :** not processed, dried, or reduced **:** remaining in or near the natural state of a freshly caught fish **5 a :** devoted to, associated with, or used for drinking or conviviality ⟨have a ~ night —W.M.Thackeray⟩ **b :** addicted to drink **c :** showing some degree of intoxication **:** DRUNK, SOUSED **d :** consisting of alcoholic liquor ⟨~ cargo⟩ **e :** trading in alcoholic liquor ⟨a ~ canteen⟩ **f :** permitting the manufacture and sale of alcoholic liquor **:** not prohibiting traffic in intoxicants ⟨a ~ county⟩ **g :** committed to or advocating a policy of permitting such traffic or opposed to its prohibition ⟨a ~ candidate⟩ ⟨a ~ platform⟩ **6 :** preserved, bottled, or put up in liquid (as fruit in syrup or a zoological specimen in alcohol) **7 :** lax in the observances of one's sect — used chiefly of a Friend **8 :** employing or done by means of or in the presence of water or other liquid ⟨~ extraction of copper⟩ ⟨a ~ process⟩ — compare DRY 3b **9** *of a boat* **:** tending to take water or spray over the bows or sides **10 :** perversely wrong **:** away off **:** wide of the mark **:** MISGUIDED ⟨he's all ~⟩ **11 a :** designed to contain liquids **:** TIGHT ⟨a ~ cask⟩ ⟨~ barrel⟩ **b :** of or having reference to such containers ⟨~ coopering⟩ ⟨a ~ cooper⟩ **12 :** giving milk **:** LACTATING ⟨a ~ cow⟩ **13 :** SLOW 5e **14 :** grown in wet or damp soil ⟨a ~ crop⟩ **15** *of stolen livestock* **:** smuggled across a river by fording **16 :** soiled with one's own urine — used chiefly of a baby **17 :** not accepted as a good fellow or a regular guy **18 :** sloppily sentimental ⟨touches of silliness which might so easily have been merely ~ —Kingsley Amis⟩

syn DAMP, DANK, MOIST, HUMID: WET is a general term describing either something with an outer layer covered with water or other liquid or something soaked throughout more or less thoroughly ⟨a *wet* sidewalk⟩ ⟨drying her *wet* hands⟩ ⟨*wet* clothes⟩ ⟨a *wet* sponge⟩ DAMP may suggest slight or moderate wetness, sometimes unpleasant, permeating, or dispiriting, sometimes useful ⟨the chill and the vapor taken together told a poor tale of the island. It was plainly a *damp,* feverish, unhealthy spot —R.L.Stevenson⟩ ⟨the rain poured down with quiet persistency. Everything in the boat was *damp* and clammy —J.K.Jerome⟩ ⟨sheets should be *damp* when ironed⟩ DANK is almost never without the notion of sickly, disagreeable, or penetrating dampness ⟨*dank* with the marshy moisture of many low grounds —Charles Dickens⟩ ⟨passed his hand across his forehead. It was *dank* with clammy sweat —Oscar Wilde⟩ ⟨from the jungle a *dank* sulphurous breeze exuded —Norman Mailer⟩ MOIST suggests a moderate or slight wetness, enough to keep a thing from being described as dry ⟨the *moist* forehead of a sick man⟩ ⟨the depths of the valley, where the air was *moist* and cool —C.B.Nordhoff & J.N.Hall⟩ HUMID usu. applies to moisture in the air ⟨the *humid* prairie heat, so nourishing to wheat and corn, so exhausting to human beings —Willa Cather⟩

³wet \"\ *n* -s [ME *wet, wete,* fr. OE *wǣt, wǣta,* fr. *wǣt,* adj., wet] **1 :** WATER, WETNESS, MOISTURE ⟨gleaming and trembling drops of ~ —Marjory S. Douglas⟩ ⟨carefully wringing the ~ out —W.H.Hudson †1922⟩ **2 a :** rainy weather **:** RAIN, RAINSTORM ⟨stay out all night in the ~ —H.L.Davis⟩ **b** *chiefly Austral* **:** the rainy season ⟨had begun shearing, but were sorely hindered by the ~ —Rachel Henning⟩ **3 a** *chiefly Brit* **:** a drink of alcoholic liquor ⟨cross over to the ale tent for your ~ —A.J.Liebling⟩ **b :** an advocate of a policy of permitting the sale of intoxicating liquors — opposed to *dry* ⟨the drys lied to make prohibition look good; the ~s lied to make it look bad —G.W.Johnson⟩

we·ta \'wād·ə\ *n* -s [Maori] **:** any of various large wingless long-horned insects (family Stenopelmatidae) of New Zealand; *esp* **:** a large clumsy insect (*Deinacrida heteracantha*) measuring four inches in length

wet-and-dry-bulb thermometer \¦==¦=¦=-\ *n* **:** PSYCHROMETER

wetback \'=,=\ *n* [²*wet* + *back*] **:** a Mexican who enters the U.S. illegally (as by wading or swimming the Rio Grande) ⟨~s . . . willing to work for nothing if a rancher would conceal them —Irving Shulman⟩ — compare BRACERO

wet bargain *n* **:** DUTCH BARGAIN

wetbird \'=,=\ *n* [so called fr. the belief that its cry foretells rain] *dial Eng* **:** CHAFFINCH

wet blanket *n* **1 :** a blanket soaked in water (as for quenching a fire) **2 :** someone or something that quenches or dampens enthusiasm or pleasure ⟨a woman who cannot laugh is a *wet blanket* —W.M.Thackeray⟩

wet-blanket \'=¦==\ *vt* [*wet blanket*] **:** to quench or dampen with or as if with a wet blanket **:** DISCOURAGE, DEPRESS

wet-bulb temperature \'=¦=-\ *n* **:** temperature indicated by a wet-bulb thermometer that is lower than the actual temperature of the air — compare PSYCHROMETER

wet-bulb thermometer *n* **:** the thermometer with moistened bulb in a psychrometer

wet butt *n* **:** a softening and discoloration of tobacco caused by freezing before curing is complete

wet cell *n* **:** a voltaic cell in which the electrolyte is a liquid

wet-clean \'=¦=\ *vt* **:** to clean by means of water

wet cleaning *n* **:** cleaning in which water is used

wet dock *n* **:** a dock where the water is shut in and kept at a given level to facilitate the loading and unloading of ships

wet dog *n* **:** a tobacco leaf with undesirable odor and color

wet down *vt* **:** to dampen by sprinkling with water

wet dream *n* **:** an erotic dream culminating in orgasm and in the male accompanied by nocturnal emission

wet end *n* **:** the part of a paper machine between the point where the stock is fed in and the driers

wet·fast·ness \'=¦=s(t)nəs\ *n* **:** resistance to change on wetting — used esp. of a dye

wet feet *n* **:** the condition of plants growing with excessive water at their roots

wet fly *n* **:** any of various artificial flies intended to be presented to fish below the surface of the water

wet fog *n* **:** fog that wets objects exposed to it

wet goods *n pl* **:** liquid goods in casks or bottles (as paints, oils, beer, or spirits); *esp* **:** intoxicating liquors

wet-grind \'=¦=\ *vt* **:** to grind under a coolant liquid

weth·er \'wethə(r)\ *n* -s [ME *wether, weder,* fr. OE *wether;* akin to OHG *widar* ram, ON *vethr* ram, Goth *withrus* lamb, L *vitulus* calf, *vetus* old, Gk *etos* year, Skt *vatsa* calf, *vatsara* year; basic meaning: yearling] **1** *obs* **:** a male sheep **:** RAM **2 :** a male sheep castrated before sexual maturity usu. when only a few weeks old and before the development of secondary sex characters — compare BELLWETHER **3 :** a male goat castrated when young

wetherhog \'==,=\ *n* [*wether* + *hog*] *dial Brit* **:** a wether of the second season

¹wetland \'=,=\ *n* [²*wet* + *land*] **:** land containing much soil moisture (as swamp or bog) — usu. used in pl. ⟨discussed the effect of dwindling ~s on ducks and geese —R.R.Camp⟩

²wetland \"\ *adj, of a plant* **:** growing or thriving in wetlands

wet lap *n* **:** a sheet of pulp removed from a wet machine

wet·ly *adv* **:** in a wet manner

wet machine *or* **wet press** *n* **:** a papermaking machine that forms slush pulp into heavy sheets by pressing out enough water so that the sheet may be cut from the roll and folded into laps — called also *decker*

wet milking *n* **:** the milking of a cow or other animal with the hands and teats wet (as with milk) often resulting in udder infections in cattle

wet mill *n* **:** a sawmill at which logs are sorted in water

wet milling *n* **:** a process of milling (as of corn) involving preliminary soaking in water or other liquid

wet mix *n* **:** the mixture obtained when water is added to cement, sand, and coarse aggregate

wet mop *n* **:** a mop for swabbing floors with water

wet mop

wet-my-lip \'=(,)=,=\ *n* [imit. of its note] *dial Eng* **:** QUAIL 1a(1)

wet·ness *n* -ES [ME *wetnes,* fr. OE *wǣtnes,* fr. *wǣt* wet + *-nes* -ness — more at WET] **1 a :** the quality or state of being wet **b :** something wet (as a wet spot) **2 :** WETNESS FRACTION

wetness fraction *n* **:** a fraction expressing the ratio of the weight of free water particles to that of the whole in a quantity of wet steam

wet nurse *n* **:** one that cares for and suckles young not her own

wet-nurse \'=¦=\ *vt* [*wet nurse*] **1 :** to care for and suckle as a wet nurse **2 :** to devote unremitting or excessive care to **:** tend sedulously ⟨not up to the court to *wet-nurse* the schools —J.J.Parker⟩

wet off *vt* **:** to detach (blown glass) from a blowpipe or prepare for fracture at some other point by touching with a tool often wet with water

wet out *vt* **:** to wet thoroughly; *specif* **:** to make (textiles) more

absorbent by treating with a wetting agent prior to dyeing or bleaching
wet pan *n* **:** a machine used for grinding and blending clays and consisting of a circular iron pan in which heavy wheels or rollers revolve
wet-pipe system \'=,=-\ *n* **:** a sprinkler system in which the pipes contain water under pressure even when not in use
wet plate *n* **:** an iodized collodion-coated photographic glass plate exposed while wet after sensitizing in a silver nitrate solution — compare COLLODION PROCESS
wet-plate process \'=,=-\ *n* **:** an early collodion process
wet pleurisy *n* **:** pleurisy with effusion of exudate into the pleural cavity
wet pox *n* **:** FOWL POX b
wet-process machine \'=,=,=-\ *n* **:** a machine for cleaning apples and pears of spray residues by means of washes, sprays, and dips of either acid or alkaline solutions
wetproof \'=,=\ *adj* **:** WATERPROOF
wet pulp *n* **:** paper pulp from a wet machine usu. containing 50 to 65 percent of water
wet return *n* **:** a pipeline in a steam heating system for returning water of condensation to the boiler that being located below the waterline of the boiler can contain only water rather than the steam mixed with water which a return pipe located above the waterline may contain
wet rot *n* **1 :** a soft rot in which the decayed tissues are markedly watery **2 :** decay of timber by fungi that attack wood having high moisture content
wets *pres 3d sing of* WET, *pl of* WET
wet-salt \'=,=\ *vt* **:** to treat (hides) with wet salt — compare DRY-SALT
wet-shod \'=,=\ *adj* [ME] *dial* **:** having one's shoes or feet wet
wet smack *n, slang* **:** a social misfit **:** a dull or obnoxious person
wet steam *n* **:** steam composed of water vapor mixed with droplets of liquid water — compare DRY STEAM
wet strength *n* **:** the tensile strength of paper when wet
wet suit *n* **:** a close-fitting suit made of material (as sponge rubber) that water will go through but that retains body heat and worn (as by a water skier or skin diver) esp. in cold water
wet·ta·bil·i·ty \,wed·ə'biləd·ē, ,wetə'bilətē, -i\ *n* **:** the quality or state of being wettable or the degree to which something can be wet
wet·ta·ble \'wed·əbəl, -etə-\ *adj* **:** capable of being wetted; *specif* **:** having the ability (as after the addition of a wetting agent) of being wetted by or readily mixing with water or other liquid — used of insoluble substances ⟨DDT supplied as a ~ powder may be suspended in water —*Introduction to Agric. Biochem.*⟩
wettable sulfur *n* **:** finely divided sulfur to which a wetting agent has been added for use in agricultural sprays
wetted *past of* WET
wetted surface *n* **:** the surface of a ship's hull in contact with the water under specified conditions
wet·ter \'wed·ə(r), -etə-\ *n* -s **:** one that wets: as **a :** a workman who wets the work in various manufacturing processes **b :** WETTING AGENT
wetter-off \'==,=\ *n, pl* **wetters-off** [fr. *wet off,* v.] *Brit* **:** CRACKER-OFF
wetter-out \'==,=\ *n, pl* **wetters-out :** a worker who wets out textiles
wettest *superlative of* WET
wetting *pres part of* WET
wetting agent *or* **wetting-out agent** \'==,=-\ *n* **:** any of numerous water-soluble or liquid usu. synthetic organic substances that promote spreading of a liquid on a surface or penetration into a material esp. by their oriented adsorption on the surfaces in such a way that the wetting liquid is no longer repelled and that are used in mixing solids with liquids, in spreading liquids on surfaces, and as penetrants (as in the textile industry or in spraying with insecticides or fungicides) **:** a surface-active agent having higher wetting power than detergent or other powers
wet·tish \'wed·|ish, -et|, |ēsh\ *adj* **:** somewhat wet **:** MOIST
wet wash *n* **:** laundry returned damp and unironed
wet-waxed \'=,=\ *adj, of waxed paper* **:** so made that much of the wax remains on the surface as a nearly continuous film — compare DRY-WAXED
wet well *n* **:** FISH WELL
wet wind *n* **:** any one of the winds at any given place that are most frequently followed by rain or snow
wetwood \'=,=\ *n* **:** wood having a water-soaked or translucent appearance because of abnormally high water content sometimes due to bacteria and sometimes to physiological factors
wex·ford \'weksfə(r)d\ *adj, usu cap* [fr. *Wexford,* Ireland] **:** of or from County Wexford, Ireland **:** of the kind or style prevalent in County Wexford
wey \'wā\ *n* -s [ME, fr. OE *wǣge* weight, wey — more at WEIGH (n.)] **:** any of various old units of weight used locally in the British Isles esp. for cheese, wool, and salt; *also* **:** a Scotch and Irish unit of capacity (as for coal or grain) equal to 41.28 bushels
wey·mouth pine \'wāməth-\ *n, usu cap W* [after Thomas Thynne †1714 first Viscount of *Weymouth*] **:** WHITE PINE 1a
WF *abbr* **1** water finish **2** wing forward **3** wrong font
wg *abbr* wing
WG *abbr* **1** weight guaranteed **2** wire gauge
wgt *abbr* weight
wh *abbr* **1** which **2** white
WH *abbr* **1** water heater **2** *often not cap* watt-hour
wha \(')(h)wȧ, -wa\ *Scot & dial Eng var of* WHO
whaap *var of* WHAUP
whabby *var of* WABBY
[1]**whack** \'hwak *also* 'wak\ *vb* -ED/-ING/-S [prob. of imit. origin] *vt* **1 a :** to strike with a smart or resounding blow ⟨~ his desk with a schoolmaster's ruler that serves him as a gavel —Janet Flanner⟩ ⟨~ the ball into left field⟩ ⟨~ the little boy for talking back⟩ **b :** to cut with or as if with a whack **:** CHOP ⟨ran down and captured turkey gobblers and ~*ed* off their heads —C.T.Jackson⟩ ⟨the house ~*ed* $63.8 million from the proposed . . . budget —*New Republic*⟩ **c :** to take vigorous action against ⟨the French police . . . have ~*ed* some of the smartest bars in town with gigantic fines —Janet Flanner⟩ **2 :** to put, get, or make by vigorous or hurried action — often used with *up* or *out* ⟨before their homes were finished, the busy colonists had ~*ed up* . . . a sort of meeting place and school —S.H.Holbrook⟩ ⟨~*ed* up half a million signatures to its petition against the bill —Mollie Panter-Downes⟩ **3 a :** to work as a driver of (oxen or mules) **:** DRIVE **b :** to drive to greater speed or activity — usu. used with *up* **4** *chiefly Brit* **:** to get the better of **:** DEFEAT ⟨if you are ~*ed* today, you may win tomorrow —Winnie Barber⟩ **~** *vi* **:** to strike something with a smart or resounding blow ⟨wanted to dawdle . . . and ~ at things with a switch —Marcia Davenport⟩
[2]**whack** \"\ *n* -s **1 a :** a smart or resounding blow ⟨gave the rioter a ~ on the head with his nightstick⟩; *also* **:** the sound of or as if of such a blow ⟨heard the ~ of the speedboat on the waves⟩ **b :** a vigorous attack ⟨takes a good ~ at false living and false gods —Virgilia Peterson⟩ **2 a :** PORTION, SHARE, ALLOWANCE ⟨a European calamity fund . . . into which every country would pay its ~ —Mollie Panter-Downes⟩ **b** *chiefly Brit* **:** the statutory daily minimum ration of food and drink allowed a merchant seaman ⟨we lived on our bare ~ —Albert Sonnichsen⟩ **3** *Midland* **:** AGREEMENT, BARGAIN, DEAL **4 :** CONDITION, STATE ⟨the tycoon is in fine ~ —John Hay †1905⟩ **5 a :** an opportunity or attempt to do something **:** CHANCE ⟨having first ~ at original-cast album privileges —J.M.Conly⟩ **:** TRY ⟨some horsebreaker had already taken a ~ at these ponies and hadn't done a very cute job —F.B.Gipson⟩ **b :** a single action or occasion **:** STROKE, TIME ⟨made several style changes with one ~⟩ ⟨borrow fifty dollars all at one ~ —G.S.Perry⟩ — **out of whack 1 :** out of order or shape ⟨threw his back *out of whack* doing a tango —*Time*⟩ ⟨everything was completely *out of whack,* none of the joints fitted —Norman Mailer⟩ ⟨repairing everything that got *out of whack* —Joseph Mitchell⟩ **2 :** out of accord ⟨parts washing is *out of whack* with their other production methods —*Automotive Industries*⟩
[3]**whack** *var of* WACK
whacked *adj* [fr. past part. of [1]*whack*] *Brit* **:** EXHAUSTED
whack·er \-kə(r)\ *n* -s **1 :** one that whacks: as **a :** the driver of a team of oxen or mules **:** DROVER **b :** CAR KNOCKER **2 :** something uncommonly large; *specif* **:** a great lie
[1]**whack·ing** \-kiŋ, -kēŋ\ *adj* [fr. pres. part. of [1]*whack*] **:** very large **:** WHOPPING ⟨swept . . . into power with a ~ parliamentary majority —J.W.Vandercook⟩
[2]**whacking** \"\ *adv* **:** VERY, EXTREMELY ⟨a ~ big diamond⟩ ⟨a ~ good story⟩
whack up *vt* [[2]*whack*] **:** to divide into shares ⟨a tidy $3,000,000 profit which they *whacked up* among themselves —*Time*⟩
whack-up \'=,=\ *n* -s [*whack up*] **:** the act of whacking up; *specif* **:** the division of the loot of a robbery
whacky *var of* WACKY
whae \(')(h)wā\ *Scot & dial Eng var of* WHO
whahoo *var of* WAHOO
whai·sle *or* **whai·zle** \'(h)wāzəl\ *Scot var of* WHEEZLE
wha·ka·pa·pa \,(h)wäkə'päpə, 'fäk-\ *n* -s [Maori] **:** a Maori genealogy
[1]**whale** \'hwāl, *esp before pause or consonant* -āəl; *also* 'wā-\ *n, pl* **whale** *or* **whales** *often attrib* [ME, fr. OE *hwæl;* akin to OHG *hwal* whale, ON *hvalr,* and prob. to L *squalus,* a sea fish] **1 :** an aquatic mammal of the order Cetacea that superficially resembles a large fish and is valued commercially for whale oil, for the flesh which is used as human food and in animal feeds and fertilizers, and formerly for baleen; *esp* **:** one of the larger members of this group — compare DOLPHIN, PORPOISE; see TOOTHED WHALE, WHALEBONE WHALE, ZEUGLODON **2 a :** a person or thing with an extraordinary appetite or keenness ⟨a ~ for work⟩ ⟨the great ship — an insatiable ~ that ate men and gold —James Dugan⟩ **b :** a person or thing impressive in size or qualities or superlatively good of kind ⟨not impressed by the pronouncements of the scientific ~*s*⟩ ⟨a ~ of a difference⟩ ⟨a ~ of a story⟩ — often used intensively in the phrase *a whale of a* ⟨borrowed a ~ of a lot of money⟩ ⟨a ~ of a good time⟩

sperm whale

[2]**whale** \"\ *vi* -ED/-ING/-S **:** to engage in whale fishing
[3]**whale** \"\ *vb* -ED/-ING/-S [origin unknown] *vt* **1 :** LASH, THRASH ⟨~ a boy for lying⟩ **2 :** to strike or hit vigorously ⟨~ the ball for a home run⟩ **3 :** to bring by thrashing or striking ⟨~ the dust out of the carpets⟩ **4 :** to defeat soundly ⟨*whaled* their rivals 20 to 0⟩ **~** *vi* **:** to perform an action with great vigor; *esp* **:** to make a vigorous attack on a person or thing — often used with *away* ⟨uses his daily column to ~ away at his pet peeves⟩
[4]**whale** *var of* WALE
whaleback \'=,=\ *n* [[1]*whale* + *back*] **1 :** something (as a hill or wave) shaped like the back of a whale **2 a :** TURTLEBACK c **b :** a steamship having sides curving in towards the ends, a spoon bow, and a very convex upper deck formerly used (as for carrying grain or ore) on the Great Lakes
whale-backed \'=,=\ *also* **whaleback** \'=,=\ *adj* **:** shaped like or resembling a whale's back
whaleback roof *n* **:** RAINBOW ROOF
whale barnacle *n* **:** any of several barnacles of *Coronula* and related genera that are parasitic on whales
whalebird \'=,=\ *n* **:** any of several gregarious seabirds that follow whaling ships to feed on oil and offal; *esp* **:** a petrel of the genus *Prion* of southern oceans having a peculiar broad lamellate bill
whaleboat \'=,=\ *n* **1 :** a long narrow rowboat made with a bold sheer, both ends sharp and raking, a lean afterbody, and no deadwood, often steered with an oar, and formerly used by whalemen for hunting whales **2 :** a long narrow flat-floored rowboat or motorboat that is sharp and rounded at both ends in the manner of the original whaleboats, that is fitted with buoyancy tanks, and that is often carried by warships and merchant ships
whalebone \'=,=\ *n* -s *often attrib* [[1]*whale* + *bone*] **1 :** BALEEN **2 :** an article made of baleen (as a strip used to stiffen a corset or dress)
whalebone tree *n* **:** a medium-sized tree (*Pseudomorus brunoniana*) of the family Moraceae of Norfolk island and Australia having yellow close-grained hard wood
whalebone whale *n* **:** any of various usu. large whales having in the adult plates of baleen dependent from the upper jaw instead of teeth, frequenting chiefly colder regions, and constituting the suborder Mysticeti — see FINBACK, GRAY WHALE, HUMPBACK, RIGHT WHALE, RORQUAL; compare TOOTHED WHALE
whale catcher *also* **whale chaser** *n* **:** a sturdy fast quick-turning steel ship about 135 feet in length equipped with a harpoon gun in the bow and used for hunting whales as one of a fleet attached to a factory ship
whale factory ship *n* **:** a large ship designed to take aboard and obtain oil and other products from whales
whale feed *or* **whale food** *n* **:** BRIT 2
whale fin *n* **:** BALEEN
whale finger *n* **:** ERYSIPELOID
whale fisher *or* **whale fisherman** *n* **:** WHALER 1
whale fishery *n* **1** *or* **whale fishing :** the occupation of taking whales **2 :** a region where whales are pursued
whalehead \'=,=\ *or* **whale-headed stork** \'=,==-\ *n* **:** SHOEBILL
whalehide \'=,=\ *n* **:** a parchmentized wet strength kraft paper
whale iron *n* **:** HARPOON
whalelike \'=,=\ *adj* **:** resembling a whale or that of a whale
whale line *also* **whale rope** *n* **1 :** a strong solidly made 3-strand manila rope about six inches in diameter used in whaling as a harpoon line or towline **2** *slang* **:** a cowboy's manila lariat
whale louse *n* **1 :** any of several degenerate amphipod crustaceans (genus *Cyamus*) parasitic on cetaceans **2 :** WHALE BARNACLE
whale·man \'=mən\ *n, pl* **whalemen 1 :** a man employed on a whaling ship **2 :** a whaling ship
whale oil *n* **:** a water-white to brown oil obtained from the blubber of whales and used in tempering steel, in dressing leather, after hydrogenation in making margarine and soap, as a lubricant, and formerly as an illuminant — called also *train oil*
[1]**whal·er** \'hwālə(r) *also* 'wāl-\ *n* -s [[1]*whale* + *-er*] **1 :** a person or ship employed in the whale fishery **:** WHALEMAN **2 :** WHALEBOAT 2 **3** *also* **whaler shark :** any of several moderate to large size sharks (genus *Carcharhinus*) common along shore and in estuaries about Australia, New Guinea, and New Zealand **4** *Austral* **:** a strolling bushman **:** SWAGMAN, SUNDOWNER; *esp* **:** a swagman who keeps near some large river ascending on one bank and descending on the other
[2]**whaler** \"\ *n* -s [[3]*whale* + *-er*] **1 :** one that whales **2 :** something extraordinary (as in size) **:** WHOPPER
[3]**whaler** *var of* WALER
whal·ery \'hwālərē *also* 'wāl-\ *n* -ES [[1]*whale* + *-ery*] **1 :** WHALE FISHERY 1 **2 :** a shore station or factory ship where whales are taken for the extraction of oil and other products
whales *pl of* WHALE, *pres 3d sing of* WHALE
whale shark *n* **:** a harmless shark (*Rhincodon typus*) found in all tropical waters, reaching a length of 45 feet, having very small teeth, and feeding on small fish and other animals strained out of the water by its fine-set gill rakers
whaleship \'=,=\ *n* **:** a ship used in whaling **:** WHALER
whale's-tongue \'=,=\ *n, pl* **whale's-tongues :** a marine worm of the genus *Balanoglossus*
whale sucker *n* **:** a remora (*Remilegia australis*) of the Pacific ocean
[1]**whaling** *n* -s [fr. gerund of [2]*whale*] **:** the occupation of catching and rendering whales
[2]**whaling** *n* -s [fr. gerund of [3]*whale*] **:** THRASHING, BEATING
[3]**whaling** *adj* [fr. pres. part. of [3]*whale*] **:** WHACKING ⟨a ~ price to pay⟩
[4]**whaling** *adv* **:** VERY, EXTREMELY ⟨a ~ big family⟩
whaling gun *n* [[1]*whaling*] **:** a gun or other device for discharging a projectile (as a harpoon or bomb) at a whale
whaling master *n* **1 :** a captain of a whaling vessel **2 :** a man in charge of a whaling station
whaling port *n* **:** a port where many whalers are owned or registered
whally \'(h)wȯlē\ *adj* [prob. alter. of *walleyed*] **:** having the iris of light color **:** WALLEYED
whalp \'(h)walp\ *Scot & dial var of* WHELP
[1]**wham** \'hwam, -aa(ə)m *also* 'wa-\ *n* -s [imit.] **1 :** the loud sound of a hard impact or explosion ⟨startled by the harsh ~ of a gun going off —R.M.Randall⟩ **2 :** a solid blow ⟨shook the table with an emphatic ~ of his fist⟩
[2]**wham** \"\ *vb* **whammed; whammed; whamming; whams** *vt* **:** to propel, strike, or beat forcibly or so as to produce a loud impact ⟨~ two shots into the man —Charles Askins b. 1907⟩ ⟨~ the culprit with her broom⟩ ⟨~ a bass drum⟩ **~** *vi* **:** to make a wham **:** hit or explode with a loud or heavy impact ⟨shells from the battleships were *whamming* over our heads —Ernie Pyle⟩ ⟨skids and ~*s* against a stone wall⟩
[3]**wham** \"\ *or* **wham·mo** \-,mō\ *adv* [*wham* fr. [1]*wham; whammo* fr. [1]*wham* + *-o*] **:** with violent abruptness ⟨quietly fishing when ~ — I got a strike⟩ ⟨you're sitting around talking and ~ something starts —Norman Mailer⟩
whame \'(h)wām\ *n* -s [origin unknown] **:** GADFLY
wham·mel *or* **wham·mle** \'(h)waməl\ *dial var of* WHEMMEL
wham·my \'hwamē *also* 'wamē *or* -mi\ *n* -ES [prob. fr. [1]*wham* + *-y*] **1 :** something used to bring good or bad luck **:** a magical practice, gesture, or object **2 :** a supernatural power bringing bad luck to a person **:** a magical curse or spell **:** JINX, HEX ⟨put the ~ on a player by talking about his success⟩ **3 :** a potent force or attack; *specif* **:** a paralyzing or lethal blow
whamp \'(h)wȧmp\ *n* -s [origin unknown] *dial Eng* **:** WASP
wham·ple \'(h)wampəl\ *n* -s [origin unknown] *Scot* **:** BLOW, STROKE
whan \(')(h)wȧn, (')(h)wan\ *dial var of* WHEN
[1]**whang** \'hwaŋ, 'hwaiŋ *also* 'wa-\ *n* -s [alter. of ME *thwang* thong — more at THONG] **1** *dial* **a :** THONG **b** *or* **whang leather :** RAWHIDE **2 :** an act or instance of whanging: **a :** BLOW, WHACK **b** *Brit* **:** a large piece or slice **:** CHUNK **3 :** PENIS — often considered vulgar
[2]**whang** \"\ *vb* -ED/-ING/-S *vt* **1 a** *dial* **:** FLOG, BEAT, THRASH **b :** to propel or strike with force ⟨~ the ball up against the left-field fence —*Springfield (Mass.) Republican*⟩ ⟨stopped so suddenly his head ~*ed* the dashboard⟩ **2** *chiefly Scot* **:** to chop off or up **~** *vi* **1 :** to strike or beat with force or violence ⟨riveters were still ~*ing* away at the bulkheads —James Dugan⟩ **2 :** to attack vigorously ⟨~*ed* away in the Gazette — . . . clamoring for a primary system —W.A.White⟩ ⟨~ away at arithmetic and spelling until . . . I could quit school —C.T.Jackson⟩
[3]**whang** \"\ *n* -s [imit.] **:** a loud sharp vibrant or resonant sound ⟨the ~ of hammers⟩
[4]**whang** \"\ *vb* -ED/-ING/-S *vi* **:** to make a whang ⟨the cymbals ~ —Vachel Lindsay⟩ ⟨the racket smacked, the sheep gut ~*ed* and the white ball came steaming across —R.P.Warren⟩ **~** *vt* **:** to strike with a whang **:** make a whang with ⟨~ a guitar⟩
whang·doo·dle \(')(h)waŋ'düd³l, -waiŋ-\ *n* [origin unknown] **1 a :** an imaginary creature of undefined character **b :** one that whangs; *esp* **:** a person that vigorously assails objects of his dislike **2 :** stuff and nonsense **:** POPPYCOCK, FRIPPERY **3 whangdoodles** *pl* **:** ROODLES
whang·ee *also* **whang·hee** \(')(h)waŋ'gē\ *n* -s [prob. fr. Chin (Pek) *huang²-li²* fr. *huang²* yellow + *li²* bamboo cane] **1 :** any of several Chinese bamboos of the genus *Phyllostachys* **2 :** a walking stick or riding cane of whangee
whang up *vt* **:** to make in a hasty manner
whap *var of* WHOP
wha·pu·ku \'h(w)ä,pükə, 'wä-\ *n* -s [Maori] **:** a large edible marine fish (*Polyprion oxygeneios*) of New Zealand waters that is closely related to or perhaps identical with the stone-bass
whar \(')(h)wär, (')(h)wá(r\ *dial var of* WHERE
wha·re \'(h)wärä, 'fä-\ *n* -s [Maori] **1 :** a Maori hut or house **2** *NewZeal* **:** a temporary or roughly built hut in the bush
[1]**wharf** \'(h)wȯ(ə)r|f, -ō(ə)|\ *n, pl* **wharves** \|vz\ *also* **wharfs** *often attrib* [ME *wherf, wharf,* fr. OE *hwearf* turn, exchange, crowd, bank, wharf; akin to MD *werf* shipyard, OHG *hwarb* turn, ON *hvarf* circle, crowd, OE *hweorfan* to turn, move around, OHG *hwerban,* ON *hverfa,* Goth *hwairban,* Gk *karpos* wrist; basic meaning: turn] **1 :** a structure of timber, masonry, cement, earth, or other material built along or at an angle from the shore of navigable waters (as a harbor or river) and made with a sometimes partially covered platform so that vessels may lie close alongside to receive and discharge cargo and passengers; *specif* **:** a structure of open rather than filled construction extending parallel to the shoreline **2** *obs* **:** the bank of a river or the shore of the sea
syn WHARF, DOCK, PIER, QUAY, SLIP, BERTH, JETTY, and LEVEE signify a structure used by boats and ships for taking on or landing cargo or passengers. WHARF, prob. the oldest of the terms applies to any structure projecting from the shore that permits boats or ships to lie alongside for loading or unloading ⟨a ship maneuvering slowly up to the *wharf*⟩ ⟨the townsfolk rush to the *wharves* to welcome with cheers and banners the precious cargo of food —*Life*⟩ ⟨at the foot of this street . . . a rude *wharf* of logs was chained together and moored —*Amer. Guide Series: Vt.*⟩ ⟨a boy sitting on the edge of the *wharf,* his feet dangling in the water⟩ DOCK is usu. interchangeable with WHARF but can be restricted to signify an enclosed basin which permits the entrance of a vessel for loading or unloading or which, with floodgates and a method of exhausting water, can be used for building or repairing ships ⟨a summer lake cottage with a short *dock* for canoes and rowboats⟩ ⟨a *dock* on Occoquan Creek —*Amer. Guide Series: Va.*⟩ ⟨the New York *docks*⟩ ⟨bring a ship into *dock* for repairs⟩ PIER is interchangeable with DOCK or WHARF esp. a large or long one shooting out quite a distance into a body of water ⟨a sloping earthen *pier* for the launching of boats —G.S.Perry⟩ ⟨a fishing dragger unloading its catch at a *pier* —Don Smith⟩ ⟨pulled the canoe up on the *pier* to empty it⟩ ⟨the New York harbor *piers*⟩ QUAY usu. refers to an artificial embankment lying along or projecting from a shore and mainly used for loading or unloading; the term normally applies to wharves or piers characteristic of small places ⟨so she, also, got into the small boat; and together they went in to the *quay,* and got ashore —William Black⟩ ⟨a *quay* is a docking facility at which ships lie parallel to the shoreline —*N.Y. Times*⟩ SLIP applies to a sloping ramp usu. constructed or used where the shore is high and shore water shallow ⟨on the *slip* a thick water hose was connected from a hydrant to the ship —Vernon Pizer⟩ ⟨rolling barrels down a *slip* into the ship's hold⟩ BERTH and less commonly SLIP (in a second sense) apply to the space between two piers or wharves which gives room for a ship when anchored or not in use, although SLIP is more common for such a space construed for ferryboat landings or boardings ⟨about to sail from her *berth* at the foot of Fifth Street —*Ships and the Sea*⟩ ⟨a deep-chested liner rears through the thin haze, easing her way to a Hudson river *berth* —*Amer. Guide Series: N.Y. City*⟩ ⟨transatlantic liners in adjoining *slips* down at the docks⟩ ⟨a series of steamship piers and ferry *slips*⟩ JETTY although commonly applied to a structure serving as a breakwater for a harbor applies also to a small pier of timbers, usu. not very substantial ⟨the harbor, from 30 to 60 feet deep, is protected by white marble *jetties* —*Amer. Guide Series: Fla.*⟩ ⟨fishermen . . . take their accustomed places on the wharves and *jetties* for the summer sport of gawking —Anthony Anable⟩ ⟨a *jetty* is usu. built so that it lies parallel with the direction of the tidal stream, and at such *jetties* ships should always berth against the stream —*Manual of Seamanship*⟩ LEVEE applies to an embankment for confining or restricting floodwaters but in the South and West, where a levee is often used for landing, the term is often the equivalent of QUAY ⟨build emergency *levees* to control a dangerously rising river⟩ ⟨down by the river's borders the new *levees* proclaim the grandsons' plans for a resurrected river traffic —*Amer. Guide Series: Minn.*⟩
[2]**wharf** \"\ *vb* -ED/-ING/-S *vt* **1** *obs* **:** to guard or secure by a firm wall of timber or stone constructed like a wharf **2 :** to furnish with a wharf **3 :** to place upon a wharf **:** bring to a wharf **~** *vi* **:** DOCK
wharf·age \-fij\ *n* -s [ME, fr. [1]*wharf* + *-age*] **1 a :** the provision or the use of a wharf **b :** the handling or stowing of goods on a wharf **2 a :** the charge for the use of a wharf for freight handling or ship dockage **b :** a charge assessed for

handling incoming or outgoing cargo on a wharf **3 :** the wharf accommodations of a place **:** WHARVES

wharf boat *n* **:** a boat moored and used for a wharf at a bank of a river or in a like situation where the height of the water is so variable that a fixed wharf is impracticable

wharf borer *n* **:** a small wood boring beetle (*Nacerda melanura*) of the family Oedemeridae that is destructive to piling and wood under wharves, buildings near the water, and sometimes telegraph poles

wharf crab *n* **:** a small pink crab (*Pachygrapsus gracilis*) common on piles along the tropical American Atlantic coast

wharfe·dale \'(h)wȯ(r)f,dāl\ *n* -s *usu cap* [fr. *Wharfedale*, district of western Yorkshire, England; fr. the manufacture of such presses in the district] *Brit* **:** STOP-CYLINDER PRESS

wharf fish *n* **:** CUNNER b

wharf·ie \'(h)wȯ(r)fē\ *n* -s [¹*wharf* + -*ie*] *Austral* **:** STEVEDORE, LONGSHOREMAN

wharf·ing \'(h)wȯ(r)fiŋ, -fēŋ\ *n* -s [¹*wharf* + -*ing*] **1 a :** something serving as a wharf **b :** the materials of a wharf **c :** the wharves of a harbor **2 :** the facing of seawalls and embankments with sheet piling secured by ties

wharf·in·ger \-fənjə(r)\ *n* -s [irreg. fr. *wharfage* + -*er*] **1 :** a person or company operating a marine terminal with facilities for the berthing of ships and the loading, unloading, and storage of goods **:** the operator or manager of a commercial wharf; *specif* **:** one in charge of the handling of freight at a wharf who assigns the workers and facilities needed for the loading and unloading, storage, or removal of goods **2** *Brit* **:** the representative of a shipowner or charterer who receives goods at a wharf and checks the amount and condition of goods received, loaded, and unloaded

wharf·less \'₌lə̇s\ *adj* **:** having no wharf

wharf·man \-mən\ *n, pl* **wharfmen :** DOCKMAN

wharfmaster \'₌,₌\ *n* **:** the manager of a wharf (as of a municipality) **:** WHARFINGER

wharf monkey *n* **:** a terrestrial isopod of the genus *Ligia* common about wharves along the coasts of most warm countries

wharf rat *n* **1 :** BROWN RAT **2 :** a person who loafs or sometimes lives around wharves sometimes with intent to steal from ships or warehouses

wharfs *pres 3d sing of* WHARF, *pl of* WHARF

wharf spike *n* **:** DOCK SPIKE

¹**wharl** \'(h)wärl, -wȧl\ *n* -s [imit.] **:** a guttural pronunciation of the letter *r* **:** BURR

²**wharl** *var of* WHORL

wharn·cliffe meeting \¦(h)wȯ(r)n,klif-\ *n, usu cap W* [after Edward Mackenzie, 1st Earl of *Wharncliffe* †1899 Brit. railway chairman] **:** a meeting of the proprietors or members of a British company convened as required by a standing order of parliament to approve a bill to be presented to parliament conferring powers on the company

whar·ton's duct \'(h)wȯ(r)t³nz-\ *n, usu cap W* [after Thomas *Wharton* †1673 Eng. physician and anatomist] **:** the duct of the submaxillary gland that opens into the mouth on a papilla at the side of the frenum of the tongue

wharton's jelly *n, usu cap W* **:** a soft connective tissue that occurs in the umbilical cord and consists of large stellate fibroblasts and a few wandering cells and macrophages embedded in a homogeneous jellylike intercellular substance

wharve \'(h)wȯ(ə)rv, -ō(ə)v\ *n* -s [ME *wherve*, fr. OE *hweorfa*; akin to OHG *hwerbo* turn, whirl, hinge, OE *hweorfan* to turn — more at WHARF] **:** WHORL 1

wharves *pl of* WHARF

whase \(¦)(h)wäz, -wȯz, -wāz\ *chiefly Scot var of* WHOSE

¹**what** \(¦)(h)wə̇t, (¦)(h)wät *also* (¦)(h)wȯt\ *pron* [ME, fr. OE *hwæt*, neut. of *hwā* who; akin to OHG *hwaz*, neut. interr. pron., ON *hvat*, Goth *hwa* — more at WHO] **1 a** (1) — used in direct or indirect questions as an interrogative pronoun expressing inquiry about the identity of an object or matter ⟨~ is this⟩ ⟨~ did you say⟩ ⟨~ are those things on the table⟩ ⟨~ happened after that⟩ ⟨tell me ~ you are looking for⟩ ⟨I wonder ~ his motives were⟩ ⟨he knows ~ he should do⟩ ⟨he knows ~ to do⟩ ⟨he's looking for something, but I don't know ~⟩ ⟨the controversy . . . centers largely on . . . who advocated ~ —*Christian Science Monitor*⟩; often used by itself esp. to ask for repetition of an utterance not properly heard or understood or to indicate that the speaker has heard someone addressing him and is ready to listen to whatever the one addressing him wishes to say; often used in connection with another word or words to ask for repetition of the particular part of an utterance that has not been properly heard or understood ⟨found ~⟩ (2) **:** a person or thing of how much value or consequence — used in rhetorical questions ⟨~ is man, that thou art mindful of him —Ps 8:4 (AV)⟩ ⟨~'s Hecuba to him, . . . that he should weep for her —Shak.⟩ ⟨~ is home without a mother —Septimus Winner⟩ **b** (1) *archaic* **:** ¹WHO 1 — used predicatively in direct or indirect questions as an interrogative pronoun expressing inquiry about the identity of a person ⟨is it but thought so? ~ are they that think it —Shak.⟩ ⟨lo ~ is he . . . is it not Lancelot —Alfred Tennyson⟩ (2) — used predicatively in direct or indirect questions as an interrogative pronoun expressing inquiry about the character, occupation, position, or role of a person ⟨~ do you think I am, a fool⟩ ⟨ask him ~ he wants to be when he grows up⟩ ⟨you are the villain and she is the heroine, but ~ is he⟩ **c :** how much ⟨~ do people generally tip —Richard Joseph⟩ ⟨to know ~ of any great man survives —Irwin Edman⟩ **d** (1) — used as an exclamation expressing surprise or excitement and frequently introducing a question ⟨~, no breakfast⟩ (2) *chiefly dial* — used to call someone or to engage someone's attention in order to say something to him ⟨~, Diggory? You are having a lonely walk —Thomas Hardy⟩; often followed by *ho* ⟨~, ho! slave —Shak.⟩ **e :** one or ones of what sort — used predicatively ⟨~ is she, that all our swains commend her —Shak.⟩ ⟨you know ~ he is about anything disagreeable — how he simply ignores its existence —Richard Bagot⟩ ⟨you know not ~ temptation is —Robert Browning⟩ **f :** how noteworthy a thing — used interjectionally ⟨~ has God wrought —Num 23:23 (RSV)⟩ **g :** SOMETHING — used in a few more or less fixed expressions directing attention to a suggestion or statement that the speaker is about to make ⟨I'll tell you ~⟩ ⟨tell you ~⟩ ⟨do you know ~⟩ ⟨know ~⟩ **h** — used after *or* at the end of a question to express inquiry about the possibilities not included in the immediately preceding word or series of words ⟨is it a freak, or ~⟩ ⟨is it a reptile, an amphibian, or ~⟩ ⟨is it raining, or snowing, or ~⟩ **i** *chiefly Brit* — used esp. at the end of an utterance as a tag that is essentially meaningless but has the appearance of inviting agreement or disagreement with the statement just made ⟨a clever play, ~⟩ **2** *chiefly substand* — used as a function word to introduce a restrictive or nonrestrictive relative clause and to serve as a substitute within that clause for the substantive modified by that clause ⟨the guy ~ says 'taint so —*Amer. Songbag*⟩ ⟨the newspaper placard, ~ had kicked itself loose from one corner —Richard Llewellyn⟩; compare ⁴THAT 1, ²WHICH 3, ¹WHO 3 **3 a :** that which **:** those which **:** those things that **:** those who or whom **:** the one or ones that ⟨the wind was . . . blowing in a direction opposite to ~ would carry the sparks to the lumber —W.L. Moore †1927⟩ ⟨any imposts or duties on imports or exports, except ~ may be absolutely necessary for executing its inspection laws —*U. S. Constitution*⟩ ⟨attributed it to the folly of ~ he conceived to be irresponsible demagogues —Robert White⟩ ⟨has no income but ~ he gets from his writings⟩ ⟨have no children but ~ you see here⟩ — sometimes used parenthetically or at the beginning of a sentence in reference to a clause or phrase that is yet to come or is not yet complete ⟨but, ~ more amazed him, his wife had willingly accompanied their flight —John Dryden⟩ ⟨the number of summonses jumped . . . at a rate of close to 200,000 a year. *What*'s more, the magistrates . . . give stiffened fines —G.S.Perry⟩ ⟨he brought also, ~ is rarer than depth of moralism, an art finely rounded —Carl Van Doren⟩; compare ²WHICH 3 **b :** as much as **:** as many as ⟨the individual soul . . . must struggle alone, with ~ of courage it can command —Bertrand Russell⟩ ⟨there are 34 candidates on the squad, nearly triple ~ reported for competition three years ago —*Springfield (Mass.) Union*⟩ **c :** the kind that **:** the same as ⟨the speech was very much ~ everyone expected⟩ ⟨a sleepy little town that is just ~ it was forty years ago⟩ **:** equal to that which ⟨countries whose economic strength is not ~ it was⟩ **4 a :** ¹WHATEVER 1a ⟨come ~ may⟩ ⟨say ~ you will⟩ **b** *obs* **:** WHOEVER 1 ⟨~ in the world he is that names me traitor, villain-like he lies —Shak.⟩ — **no matter what :** regardless of anything else ⟨wait there till I come back, *no matter what*⟩ — **what about 1 :** what is to be said about **:** what is the situation with respect to ⟨*what about* a house, and schools for the children —J.G.Gilkey⟩ **2 :** how about ⟨*what about* coming with us⟩ ⟨*what about* doing it yourself⟩ — **what an if** *or* **what and if** *archaic* **:** what if — **what else 1 :** anything else **:** unspecified other things ⟨with promise of his sister, and *what else* —Shak.⟩ **2 :** CERTAINLY **:** yes indeed — used after a statement to emphasize it or by itself as an emphatic affirmative reply to a question — **what for 1** *chiefly dial* **:** what kind of — used either inseparably or with a verb and its subject between *what* and *for* ⟨*what* is he *for* a fool —Shak.⟩; used with an immediately following object of *for* usu. consisting of a singular count noun with indefinite article ⟨*what for* an apple is that⟩, a plural count noun with no article ⟨*what for* horses are those⟩, or a mass noun with no article ⟨*what for* tobacco are you smoking⟩ **2 :** for what purpose **:** for what reason **:** WHY — usu. used with the other words of a question between *what* and *for* ⟨*what* did you do that *for*⟩ except when used alone; used inseparably at the beginning of a question in some dialects ⟨*what for* did you do that⟩ **3 :** punishment esp. by blows or by a sharp reprimand ⟨puts his little boy across his knee and gives him *what for* —Rebecca West⟩ ⟨gave him *what for* in violent Spanish —*New Yorker*⟩ ⟨Mama certainly gave Papa the *what for* —Marquis James⟩ **:** rough treatment inflicted esp. on an offender ⟨went away to give the . . . generals *what for* —J.T. Winterich⟩ **:** severe pain ⟨my corn's a-giving me *what for* —A.E.Coppard⟩ — **what have you :** WHATNOT 1a ⟨novels, plays, short stories, travelogues, and *what have you* —Haldeen Braddy⟩ ⟨sell it, broadcast it, set it to music, or *what have you* —Margaret Nicholson⟩ ⟨barbarous or medieval or *what have you* —S.M.Kuhn⟩ — **what if :** what will or would be the result if ⟨*what if* it be a poison —Shak.⟩ **:** what does it matter if ⟨he won't object, and anyway, *what if* he does⟩ — **what it takes :** the ability, qualities, or resources needed for success or for the attainment of a particular goal ⟨he certainly has more of *what it takes* than anybody else of his generation —Edmund Wilson⟩ ⟨those who have *what it takes* to solve the problems in an environment —W.J.Reilly⟩ — **what of 1 :** what is to be said about **:** what is the situation with respect to ⟨watchman, *what of* the night —Isa 21:11 (RSV)⟩ **2 :** what importance can be assigned to ⟨all this is so; but *what of* this, my lord —Shak.⟩ — **what's o'clock** *Brit* **:** what time is it **:** what time it is — **what's what** *or* **what is what** *or* **what was what :** the true state of things ⟨exploration of *what's what* with the American businessman —*advt*⟩ ⟨all the . . . millionaire paper-mill women knew *what was what* when it came to fashion —Edna Ferber⟩ — **what's with** *slang* **:** what is the reason for **:** what is wrong with — **what though 1** *obs* **:** what does that matter ⟨I keep but three men and a boy . . . but *what though?* yet I live like a poor gentleman born —Shak.⟩ **2 :** what does or would it matter if **:** even granting or supposing that ⟨*what though* the rose have prickles, yet 'tis plucked —Shak.⟩ ⟨*what though* the field be lost? all is not lost —John Milton⟩

²**what** \"\ *adv* [ME, fr. OE *hwæt*, fr. *hwæt*, neut. interr. pron.] **1** *obs* **:** WHY ⟨~ should I stay —Shak.⟩ **2 :** HOW **:** in what respect **:** how much ⟨~ does it matter⟩ **3 a :** PARTLY — used two or more times in the same sentence to introduce a pair or series of prepositional phrases in parallel construction ⟨~ with the war, ~ with the sweat, ~ with the gallows, and ~ with poverty, I am custom-shrunk —Shak.⟩ ⟨~ through banks, and ~ through policemen, the concern has dwindled to nothing —Thomas DeQuincey⟩ **b** — used to introduce a prepositional phrase that expresses cause and has more than one object ⟨~ for poisons, conspiracies, and assassinations . . . there was no going there by day —Laurence Sterne⟩; used principally before phrases beginning with *with* ⟨~ with the drought and a strike in the mine, life is hard —*Time*⟩

³**what** \"\ *adj* [ME, fr. ¹*what*] **1 a** (1) — used in direct or indirect questions as an interrogative adjective expressing inquiry about the identity or nature of a person, object, or matter ⟨~ minerals do we export⟩ ⟨~ news have you had from him⟩ ⟨~ arrangements have been made⟩ ⟨declaring ~ officer shall then act as president —*U.S. Constitution*⟩ ⟨the debate . . . as to who made ~ blunder —C.B.Randall b. 1891⟩ (2) **:** how much ⟨finally got it written — with ~ effort, and ~ joy, only the amateur writer knows —Elmer Davis⟩ **b** (1) **:** how remarkable for good or bad qualities **:** how surprising **:** how great **:** how small — used esp. in exclamatory utterances and in dependent clauses of like nature ⟨~ a county for marine wonders —R.M.Lockley⟩ ⟨~ a suggestion⟩ ⟨with ~ relief this priggish load of nonsense falls from our shoulders —Sean O'Faolain⟩ ⟨you can imagine ~ a struggle we had⟩ ⟨~ a chance⟩ ⟨~ fools these mortals be —Shak.⟩; usu. followed by *a* or *an* when the following noun is a singular count noun (2) — used esp. in exclamatory utterances and in dependent clauses of like nature before a combination of a descriptive adjective and its noun and serving to intensify the meaning of the adjective ⟨~ a charming girl⟩ ⟨remembering ~ great disappointment he had felt⟩ ⟨~ partial judges are our love and hate —John Dryden⟩; usu. followed by *a* or *an* when the noun is a singular count noun **2 a** (1) **:** ²WHATEVER 1a ⟨serve ~ master you like⟩ ⟨invent ~ excuses you please⟩ (2) **:** ANY ⟨she wore not upon her person any female ornament of ~ kind soever —Sir Walter Scott⟩ **b :** the . . . that **:** such . . . as **:** as much . . . as **:** as many . . . as ⟨the rescue ship came back with ~ survivors had been found⟩ ⟨to restrain ~ power either the devil or any earthly enemy hath to work us woe —John Milton⟩ ⟨~ time we had left was spent on fruitless errands —Bruce Mason⟩ — **what countryman :** a native or inhabitant of what country — used in direct or indirect questions — **what price 1 :** what is the value of ⟨*what price* glory —Laurence Stallings & Maxwell Anderson⟩ **2 :** what is the situation with respect to **:** what do you think of **:** how about — **what time :** at the time that **:** WHEN, WHILE ⟨*what time* I am afraid, I will trust in thee —Ps 56:3 (AV)⟩ ⟨they kept their powerful jaws wide open, *what time* a bird hopped about . . . picking food from between the teeth —*Times Lit. Supp.*⟩ — **what way 1** *dial chiefly Brit* **:** HOW ⟨*what way* was he drowned —J.M. Synge⟩ **2** *Scot* **:** WHY

⁴**what** \'₌\ *n* -s [ME, fr. ¹*what*] **1 a** *obs* **:** STUFF, MATTER, SUBSTANCE ⟨such homely ~ as serves the simple clown —Edmund Spenser⟩ **b :** THING, OBJECT **2 a :** the thing or things involved or meant or referred to **:** the identity or nature of something ⟨the ~ and how of jazz —P.V.R.Key⟩ **b :** all that may be known or stated about an individual thing **:** the complex of qualities that constitute the character of a thing — compare ⁶THAT 2

⁵**what** \(¦)₌\ *conj* [¹*what*] *substand* — used esp. after *than* as a function word introducing a clause ⟨she can run better than ~ I can —W.S.Maugham⟩

whatabouts \'₌₌,₌\ *also* **whatabout** \'₌₌,₌\ *n, pl* **whatabouts** [¹*what* + *about, abouts* (as in *whereabouts*)] **:** the things with which one is busied

what-do-you-call-it *or* **what-do-you-call-them** *also* **what-do-you-call-her** *or* **what-do-you-call-him** \(h)wäldə,₌₌, -wə-,-wō-, ¦tdə-\ *n* -s **:** a thing or person that the speaker cannot (as from not knowing or from forgetting) or does not wish to name ⟨hand me one of those little *what-do-you-call-thems*⟩

what-e'er \₌'₌\ *pron* [by contr.] **:** WHATEVER

¹**whatever** \(')₌'₌₌\ *pron* [ME, fr. ¹*what* + *ever*] **1 a :** anything that **:** everything that ⟨take ~ you want⟩ ⟨~ Earth, all-bearing mother, yields —John Milton⟩ **b :** no matter what ⟨seeing only his faults, and seeing them as unforgivable in his case ~ they may be elsewhere —C.H.Sykes⟩ ⟨~ the cause, this animosity grew deeper and deeper —E.V.Burkholder⟩ **c :** anything at all **:** any of various other things that might also be mentioned **:** what not ⟨any appliance — stove, lantern, or ~ — that is fueled by gasoline —*New Yorker*⟩ ⟨until you find your buffalo or rhinoceros or ~ —Alan Moorehead⟩ ⟨a marriage contract — whether it is monogamous or polygamous or ~ —Weston La Barre⟩ ⟨workers constantly walk in . . . arguing, complaining, or ~ —*Time*⟩ **d :** something similar but hard to identify or classify with certainty ⟨had lain abed some days with the measles or ~ —Mary Austin⟩ ⟨wouldn't have had a moustache when a small boy or ~ —Henry James †1916⟩ **2 :** ¹WHAT 1a(1) — used in questions expressing astonishment or perplexity ⟨~ do you mean by that⟩

²**whatever** \"\ *adj* [ME, fr. ³*what* + *ever*] **1 a :** any . . . that **:** all . . . that ⟨and buy peace . . . on ~ terms could be obtained —C.S.Forester⟩ ⟨have provided most of the backbone for ~ musical tradition we have —Virgil Thomson⟩ **b :** no matter what ⟨by ~ circumstances he had been led to a hatred of the slave power and a heightened devotion to the Union, the change was one which in a measure transformed him —W.J. Ghent⟩ **2 a :** any . . . at all ⟨men and women of ~ scholastic training or none at all —Alvin Johnson⟩ **b :** being in existence **:** of any kind at all — used for emphasis after the substantive it modifies ⟨any language ~ —W.D.Preston⟩ ⟨no damage ~ —A.T.Weaver⟩ ⟨the most entrancing young girl ~ —Carl Van Doren⟩

³**whatever** \"\ *adv* [²*what* + *ever*] **:** in any case ⟨but how far could I trust them, and in what way were they different from the trustees? *Whatever*, I was committed; I'd learn in the process of working with them, I thought —Ralph Ellison⟩

what-is-it \₌'₌₌\ *or* **what·sis** \'(h)wätsə̇s, -wət-,-wȯt-\ *or* **what·sit** \-tsə̇t\ *n* [*what-is-it* fr. the expression *what is it; whatsis* perh. alter. of the expression *what's this; whatsit* perh. fr the expression *what's it*] **:** a thing of unspecified, nondescript, or mysterious character ⟨took a little *what-is-it* out of the toolbox and used it to fix the lamp⟩

whatlike \'₌,₌\ *adj* [¹*what* + *like*] *dial* **:** of what sort or kind — used as an indefinite relative

What·man \'(h)wätmən, -wȯt-\ *trademark* — used for drawing papers or boards of high quality

what·ness *n* -ES [¹*what* + -*ness*] **:** the what of a thing; *esp* **:** QUIDDITY

whatnot \'₌,₌\ *n* -s [fr. the query *what not?*, fr. ¹*what* + *not*] **1 a :** any of various other things that might also be mentioned ⟨electric refrigerators, washing machines, radios, television sets, or ~ —F.L. Allen⟩ ⟨stockbrokers, solicitors, auctioneers, ~ —John Galsworthy⟩ ⟨every aspect — historical, geographical, and ~ — of tea —Mollie Panter-Downes⟩ ⟨some other thing (intuitionism or ~) —J.H.Muirhead⟩ ⟨beaches, parks . . . harbors, and a lot of less worthy government ~s may benefit —Hale Champion⟩ **b :** a nondescript person or thing ⟨the biggest souvenir of all the gimmicks and ~s . . . a huge globe —*Springfield (Mass.) Republican*⟩ **c :** MISCELLANY ⟨a straggling army of human ~ (adventurers, scientists, convict laborers) —*Time*⟩ **2 :** a light open set of shelves for bric-a-brac

whatnot 2

whatreck \(')₌'₌\ *adv* [fr. the query *what reck?*, fr. ³*what* + obs. *reck* care, heed, fr. *reck*, vb.] *Scot* **:** NOTWITHSTANDING

whats *pl of* WHAT

what's \(¦)(h)wäts, (¦)(h)wəts *also* (¦)(h)wȯts\ [¹*what* + 's] **1 :** what is ⟨*what's* his name⟩ **2 :** what has ⟨*what's* he done⟩ **3 :** what does ⟨*what's* he want⟩

what's its name *or* **what's their name** *or* **what's her name** *or* **what's his name** *n* **:** WHAT-DO-YOU-CALL-IT

whatso \'₌,₌\ *pron or adj* [ME, fr. ¹*what* + *so*] **:** WHATEVER

what·so·e'er \¦₌sō¦we(ə)r, ¦₌sō¦e(ə)r, -a(ə)(ə)r, -eə, -a(ə)ə\ *pron* [by contr.] **:** WHATSOEVER

¹**what·so·ev·er** \¦₌sō¦wevə(r), -sō¦ev-\ *pron* [ME, fr. *whatso* + *ever*] **:** ¹WHATEVER 1a, 1b ⟨wife that ailed, do ~ he would —Robert Browning⟩

²**whatsoever** \"\ *adj* **:** ²WHATEVER ⟨~ things are true . . . think on these things —Phil 4:8 (AV)⟩; *esp* **:** of any kind soever ⟨exercise exclusive legislation in all cases ~ over such district —*U. S. Constitution*⟩

what·som·ever \¦₌sə¦mevə(r)\ *also* **what·som·dev·er** \-səm¦de-\ *adj or pron* [ME *whatsomever*, fr. *what sum* whatever (fr. ¹*what* + ME — northern dial. — *sum*, rel. adv., as, of Scand origin; akin to ON *sem* as, OE *same* — in *swā same* so as, likewise) + *ever* — more at SAME] *dial* **:** WHATSOEVER

what·ten *or* **whatn** *also* **what·en** \'(h)wät³n, -wə- *also* -wȯ-\ *or* **what·na** \-tnə\ *adj* [ME (northern dial.) *whatkin*, fr. ³*what* + *kin* kindred, kind of — more at KIN] **1** *dial* **:** what kind of **2** *dial* **:** WHAT

what with *prep* [²*what*] **:** on account of ⟨*what with* summertime it was still broad daylight when, around half past eight, I entered the big living room —Valentine Williams⟩

what-you-call-it *or* **what-you-call-them** *also* **what-you-call-her** *or* **what-you-call-him** \'(h)wächə,₌₌, -wəch-, -wȯch-, -chē,₌₌\ *n* -s **:** WHAT-DO-YOU-CALL-IT ⟨supposed to go to church on *what-you-call-it* Sunday⟩

what-you-may-call-it *or* **what-you-may-call-them** *also* **what-you-may-call-her** *or* **what-you-may-call-him** \-chəmə,₌₌, -chēm-\ *n* -s **:** WHAT-DO-YOU-CALL-IT ⟨decided that the *what-you-may-call-it* was a boat rather than a car⟩ ⟨went to *what-you-may-call-her's* house⟩

what·you·may·jig·ger \-mə,jigə(r)\ *n* [*what-you-may-*call-it + E dial. thingumajigger, alter. of *thingumajig*] **:** THINGUMBOB, WHAT-DO-YOU-CALL-IT

whau \'(h)waů, 'faů\ *n* -s [Maori] **1 :** a New Zealand tree (*Entelea arborescens*) of the family Tiliaceae **2 :** the very light wood of the whau used esp. for making floats for native fishing nets

¹**whaup** \'(h)wäp, -wȯp\ *n, pl* **whaup** *also* **whaups** [imit.] *Scot & dial Eng* **:** a European curlew (*Numenius arquata*) — called also *great whaup*

²**whaup** \"\ *n* -s [alter. of ²*whoop*] *Scot & dial Eng* **:** OUTCRY, FUSS

whaur \(¦)hwȯr, (¦)hwȧr\ *Scot & Irish var of* WHERE

¹**wheal** \'hwēl, *esp before pause or consonant* -ēəl; *also* 'wē-\ *vt* -ED/-ING/-S [alter. (influenced by obs. E *wheal* to suppurate, come to a head, fr. ME *whelen*, fr. OE *hwelian*; perh. akin to Latvian *kvēle* inflammation) of *wale*] **:** to make or cause wheals upon ⟨now am ~*ed*, one wide wound all of me —Robert Browning⟩

²**wheal** \"\ *n* -s [alter. (influenced by obs. E *wheal* pustule, fr. ME *whele*; akin to OE *hwelian* to suppurate) of *wale*] **:** a sudden elevation on the skin surface: **a :** a ridge or mark raised on the skin by or as if by a stroke of a whip **:** WALE, WEAL, WELT ⟨his back covered with ~s from the lashing⟩ **b :** the transient lump occurring at the site of injection of a solution before the solution is normally dispersed **c :** a steep-sided elevation with a rounded or flat top that is often accompanied by itching or burning and forms the characteristic lesion of urticaria

whealing *n* -s **:** the act or process of developing or being marked by wheals

whealworm \'₌,₌\ *n* [obs. E *wheal* pustule + *worm*] **:** CHIGGER 2

wheat \'hwēt *also* 'wēt, *usu* -ēd-+V\ *n* -s *often attrib* [ME *whete*, fr. OE *hwǣte*; akin to OHG *weizzi* wheat, ON *hveiti*, Goth *hwaiteis* wheat, *hweits* white — more at WHITE] **1 :** a cereal grain that yields a fine white flour, is the chief breadstuff of temperate climates, is used also in alimentary pastes, and is important in animal feeds esp. as bran or middlings — see WHOLE WHEAT FLOUR **2 :** any of various grasses that constitute the genus *Triticum*, are characterized by wide climatic adaptability, and are cultivated in most temperate areas for the wheat they yield and on a major commercial scale esp. in Europe, No. America, and Australia; *esp* **:** an annual cereal grass (*T. aestivum* syn. *T. vulgare*) that is known only as a cultigen and has a long dense 4-sided spike of which each spikelet contains two, three, or sometimes more white to dark-red kernels that separate readily from the chaff in threshing — called also *common wheat*; see CLUB WHEAT, DURUM WHEAT, EINKORN, EMMER, POLISH WHEAT, SPELT **3 a wheats** *pl*, *Brit* **:** wheat plants ⟨the ~s are not doing well⟩ **b :** a crop or kind of wheat ⟨tried a new Canadian ~ this year⟩ ⟨the ~ in the northern states⟩ **4 :** a variable color averaging a light yellow that is less strong and very slightly lighter than average maize, redder

wheat: *1* beardless, *2* bearded

and less strong than popcorn, and redder and duller than jasmine

wheat and rye nematode *n* : WHEATWORM

wheat aphid *or* **wheat aphis** *n* : any of several plant lice of the family Aphididae (as the grain aphid *Macrosiphum granarium* and *Rhopalosiphum prunifoliae*) that suck the sap of growing wheat — called also *wheat louse, wheat plant louse*

wheat beetle *n* **a** : SAW-TOOTHED GRAIN BEETLE **b** : DRUGSTORE BEETLE

wheat belt *n* : an agricultural region in which more land is devoted to the production of wheat than to any other one crop ⟨off with his plane and his combines on his annual swing northward through the *wheat belt* —E.L.Howe⟩

wheatbird \ˈ=,=\ *n* : HORNED LARK

wheat bread *n* : a bread made of a combination of white and whole wheat flours as distinguished from bread made entirely of whole wheat flour or white flour

wheat bug *n* : a true bug (as *Miris tritici* or a related species) that damages wheat

wheat bulb fly *n* : the adult of the wheat bulb worm

wheat bulb worm *n* : the larva of a small fly (as *Meromyza americana* in No. America or *Hylemyia coarctata* in Europe) that infests the stalk of wheat

wheat cake *n* : a griddle cake made of wheat flour

wheat chafer *n* : a beetle (as *Anisoplia austriaca* in parts of Europe) that feeds on growing wheat

wheat cutworm *n* : a lepidopterous larva (as the fall army worm and several true cutworms) that cuts off the stalk of wheat at the base

wheat duck *n* : BALDPATE 2

[1]**wheatear** \ˈ=,=\ *n* [ME *whete ere*, fr. *whete* wheat + *ere* ear (of grain) — more at EAR] : an ear or spike of wheat

[2]**wheatear** \"\ *n* [back-formation fr. *wheatears*, prob. by folk etymology or euphemism fr. *white arse*] : a small bird (*Oenanthe oenanthe*) of northern Europe, Asia, and Alaska that is related to the stonechat and whinchat, that in the male has a bluish gray back, buffy breast, white rump and belly, blackish wings, and a black line through the eye, and that inhabits chiefly rocky places

wheatear cockle *n* [[1]*wheatear*] : WHEATWORM

wheat eel *or* **wheat eelworm** *n* : WHEATWORM

[1]**wheat·en** \ˈhwēt[ə]n *also* ˈwē-\ *adj* [ME *wheten*, fr. OE *hwǣten*, fr. *hwǣte* wheat + *-en* — more at WHEAT] : of, relating to, or made of wheat ⟨~ bread⟩ ⟨~ straw⟩

[2]**wheaten** \"\ *n* -s : the color of wheat; *specif* : a pale yellow or fawn characteristic of certain breeds of dogs

wheat fly *n* **1** : WHEAT MIDGE **2** : WHEAT GALLFLY **3** : HESSIAN FLY **4** : any of several flies of the genus *Oscinis* (as *O. soror*) whose larvae live in the stems of wheat

wheat gallfly *n* : the imago of the jointworm

wheat germ *n* : the embryo or germ of the wheat kernel separated in milling flour and used in food products as a source of vitamins

wheat-germ oil *n* : a yellow unsaturated fatty oil obtained from wheat germ and containing vitamin E

wheatgrass \ˈ=,=\ *n* : a grass of the genus *Agropyron*: as **a** : BEARDED WHEATGRASS **b** : WESTERN WHEATGRASS **c** : COUCH GRASS

wheathead armyworm *n* : a worm that is the larva of a noctuid moth (*Faronta diffusa*) and is destructive to the heads of timothy, wheat, and other grasses

wheat jointworm *n* : a jointworm (*Harmolita tritici*) that attacks wheat and sometimes other cereal grasses

wheatland \ˈ=,=\ *n* : land sown or suitable for sowing with wheat

wheatland plow *n* : ONE-WAY

wheat·less \ˈ=lə̇s\ *adj* : having no wheat

wheat louse *n* : WHEAT APHID

wheat maggot *n* : a maggot that is the larva of a wheat fly and esp. of a wheat midge

wheatmeal \ˈ=,=\ *n* [ME *whetemele*, fr. OE *hwǣtemelu*, fr. *hwǣte* wheat + *melu* meal — more at MEAL (flour)] *chiefly Brit* : a pure unbleached meal obtained by grinding the entire unadulterated wheat berries

wheat midge *n* **1** : a small two-winged fly (*Sitodiplosis mosellana*) that is destructive to growing wheat both in Europe and America **2** : HESSIAN FLY

wheat mite *n* : FLOUR MITE

wheat mosaic *or* **wheat rosette** *n* : a virus disease of wheat characterized by either a light yellowish green or a dark bluish green mottling and streaking

wheat moth *n* : a moth (as a grain moth, Mediterranean flour moth, or meal moth) whose larvae devour the grains of wheat chiefly after it is harvested — compare ANGOUMOIS GRAIN MOTH

wheat pest *n* : a small midge (*Oscinis frit*) that does great damage to wheat in Europe

wheat pit *n* : a market or exchange where wheat stocks are bought and sold

wheat plant louse *n* : WHEAT APHID

wheat poisoning *n* : grass tetany affecting cattle grazing on wheat

wheat rust *n* **1** : any of three destructive diseases of wheat caused by rust fungi: as **a** : stem rust of wheat that may attack leaf sheathes, leaves, and spike, as well as the culm of the plant **b** : orange leaf rust of wheat **c** : stripe rust of wheat **2** : a rust fungus (as *Puccinia graminis*) that attacks wheat

wheats *pl of* WHEAT

wheat sawfly *n* **1** : WHEAT STEM SAWFLY **2** : any of several small American sawflies of the genus *Dolerus* (as *D. collaris* and *D. arvensis*) whose larvae injure the stems or heads of wheat **3** : a sawfly (*Pachynematus extensicornis*) whose larvae feed on the blades of wheat and other grasses

wheat scab *n* : a destructive disease of wheat caused by fungi of the genera *Fusarium* and *Gibberella* and characterized by bleached blighted heads and kernels with a scabby appearance from the tufted mycelia outgrowths — compare HEAD BLIGHT

wheat smut *n* : a smut of wheat (as bunt)

wheat stem maggot *n* : a maggot that is the larva of a small pale yellow black-striped fly (*Meromyza americana*) of the family Chloropidae and that bores in the stems of wheat and other cereals

wheat stem rust *n* : WHEAT RUST 1a

wheat stem sawfly *n* **1** : a No. American sawfly (*Cephus cinctus*) having larvae that bore in the stems of wheat and other small grains causing great loss of crop **2** : EUROPEAN WHEAT STEM SAWFLY

wheat·stone bridge \ˈ(h)wēt,stōn-, *chiefly Brit* -,stən-\ *n, usu cap W* [after Sir Charles *Wheatstone* †1875 Eng. physicist] : a bridge for measuring electrical resistances consisting of a conductor joining two branches of a circuit

wheatstone cipher *n, usu cap W* [after Sir Charles *Wheatstone*] : a progressive-alphabet cipher in which the next alphabet is used whenever the plaintext letter does not stand later in the plain component than the preceding plaintext letter

wheatstone transmitter *n, usu cap W* [after Sir Charles *Wheatstone*] : an automatic telegraph transmitter using a perforated tape engaging with one end of a marking rod or lever the other end of which opens and closes the circuit

wheat strawworm *n* : a worm that is the larva of a small chalcid wasp (*Harmolita grandis*) and that is highly destructive to wheat and other grasses

wheat take-all *n* : TAKE-ALL

wheat thief *n* **1** : GROMWELL **2** : [3]CHESS

wheat thrips *n* : any of numerous thrips that infest wheat and damage the grain: as **a** : FLOWER THRIPS **b** : GRAIN THRIPS **c** : GRASS THRIPS

wheat weevil *n* **1** : GRAIN WEEVIL **2** : the rice weevil when found in wheat **3** : WHEAT THRIPS

wheatworm \ˈ=,=\ *n* : a small nematode worm (*Anguina tritici*) that is parasitic on wheat, oats, and other grasses, that invades the plant at the leaf axil as a larva where it induces stunting and distortion of leaves, and that subsequently passes to the inflorescence and causes the seeds to be replaced by galls in which the larva matures and produces a new generation of larvae to be distributed in the soil when the gall is shed and decays — called also *wheat eel*

whee \ˈhwē *also* ˈwē\ *interj* [origin unknown] — used to express delight or general exuberance

[1]**whee·dle** \ˈhwēd[ə]l *also* ˈwē-\ *vb* **wheedled; wheedled; wheedling** \-d(ə)liŋ\ **wheedles** [origin unknown] *vt* **1 a** : to influence or inveigle by soft words or flattery : COAX, CAJOLE ⟨how she *wheedled* him —W.S.Gilbert⟩ ⟨many of whom had to be *wheedled* . . . and coddled for weeks before they could be persuaded —*N.Y.Times*⟩ **b** : to allure, draw, or induce by wheedling — usu. used with *into* ⟨~s me into feeling fond of her in spite of myself —G.B.Shaw⟩ ⟨no hucksters to ~ you into buying souvenirs —Frederick Nebel⟩ ⟨had threatened and *wheedled* hundreds of heathens into Christianity —Vicki Baum⟩ **2 a** : to gain or get away by wheedling ⟨the first move of any politician . . . was to ~ the editorial backing of some newspaper —W.A.Swanberg⟩ — usu. used with *from* or *out of* ⟨~s a couple of dollars house money from him —H.H.Reichard⟩ ⟨*wheedled* consent from them —C.V.Little⟩ ⟨have scrounged and begged . . . in an effort to ~ money out of the American public —A.J.Daley⟩ ⟨young herons . . . ~ a meal out of mother after fledging —*Nat'l Geographic*⟩ **b** : to get or take something from by wheedling — usu. used with *out of* ⟨had *wheedled* the . . . woman out of her geraniums —Mary Austin⟩ ⟨~ you out of a horse —J.B.Cabell⟩ **~** *vi* : to use soft words or flattery ⟨when he chose to ~, was hard to resist —John Buchan⟩ — **wheedle one's way** : to move or advance toward an objective by wheedling ⟨*wheedle their way* into a soft berth where 50 men do the work of 10 —Frank O'Leary⟩ ⟨*wheedled his way* onto the stage —*Time*⟩ ⟨responsible officials have often been able to circumvent extremist popular opinions and to *wheedle their way* towards moderation and good sense —Walter Lippmann⟩

[2]**wheedle** \"\ *n* -s : an act or instance of wheedling

whee·dling·ly *adv* : in a wheedling manner : with wheedling

[1]**wheel** \ˈhwēl, *esp before pause or consonant* -ēəl; *also* ˈwē-\ *n* -s *often attrib* [ME *whel, wheel, whele*, fr. OE *hweogol, hweohl, hwēol*; akin to OFris *hwēl* wheel, MD *wiel*, MLG *wēl*, ON *hvēl, hjōl* wheel, L *colere* to cultivate, inhabit, Gk *kyklos* ring, circle, cycle, wheel, *pelesthai* to be, become, *telos* end, OSlav *kolo* wheel, Skt *cakra* wheel, *carati* he moves, goes; basic meaning: to bend, turn] **1 a** : a circular frame of metal, wood, or other hard material that may be solid, partly solid, or spoked and that has a hub at the center for attachment to or suspension from an axle on which it may revolve and bear a load esp. along the ground **b** : such a circular framework often with cogs or teeth on the rim used to transmit or modify force and motion in machinery or a mechanical contrivance **2** : a wheel designed for a specific purpose, a structure resembling a wheel, or a contrivance or apparatus having a wheel as its principal part: as **a** : a chiefly medieval instrument of torture resembling a cartwheel and designed for stretching, disjointing, or otherwise mutilating a victim **b** : POTTER'S WHEEL **c** : SPINNING WHEEL **d** : STEERING WHEEL **e** : a screw propeller on a boat **f** : BICYCLE 1 **g** : any of many revolving disks or drums (as a wheel of fortune, lottery wheel, or a roulette wheel) used as gambling paraphernalia **3 a** : the imaginary wheel symbolizing fate or chance that personified fortune is said to turn ⟨so much often depends on the turn of fortune's ~⟩ **b** : a recurring course, development, or action : ROUND, CYCLE ⟨reach back through all those turns of the ~ of time —Marcia Davenport⟩ ⟨the ~ of events is brought full circle in four farm seasons —Robert Hazel⟩ ⟨by . . . World War II the ~ of history had made a full turn —R.M.Upton⟩ **4** : something resembling a wheel in shape or motion: as **a** : a usu. symbolic circular design in ancient art having radii suggesting spokes **b** : CARTWHEEL 1a **c** : a round flat cheese ⟨a ~ of mild cheddar —Leslie Waller⟩ **d** : a circular design in needlework with radiating bars resembling a cartwheel or a spider's web **e** : one of the revolving concentric spheres to which the planets and fixed stars are attached in the Ptolemaic astronomical system **f** : a firework that rotates while burning — compare PINWHEEL **5** : a movement similar to that of a wheel: as **a** : a curving or circular movement ⟨the dizzying ~ of the dance⟩ ⟨the graceful ~ of the gulls over the harbor⟩ **b** : a rotation or turn usu. about an axis or center; *specif* : a turning movement of troops or ships in line in which the units preserve alignment and relative positions as they change direction by pivoting on a unit at the end of the line or upon an imaginary point beyond it ⟨eventually the great movement out of the beachhead would be by an enormous left ~, bringing our front onto the line of the Seine —D.D.Eisenhower⟩ **6 a** : a moving or essential part of something resembling a machine ⟨the ~s of social progress have turned but slowly —Gilbert Parker⟩ ⟨the ~s of government⟩ ⟨making sure that the library ~s turn easily —H.M.Lydenberg⟩ **b** (1) : a directing or controlling force or person ⟨in this complex world there are ~s within driving forces without⟩ ⟨a big financial ~ in her company . . . is serving as a dollar-a-year man in Washington —John McCarten⟩ (2) : a political leader usu. in a party organization ⟨got a firm promise of financial help from several Tammany ~s —W.A.Swanberg⟩ **7** : the refrain or burden of a song — compare [4]BOB 4 **8 a** : a string or circuit of theaters or places of entertainment ⟨lifted her from a burlesque ~ and made her a star —William Du Bois⟩ ⟨Oklahoma City and Tulsa are on wrestling ~s and boxing circuits —*Amer. Guide Series: Okla.*⟩ **b** : a sports league ⟨treasurer of her league and tops the ~ in averages —*Woman Bowler*⟩

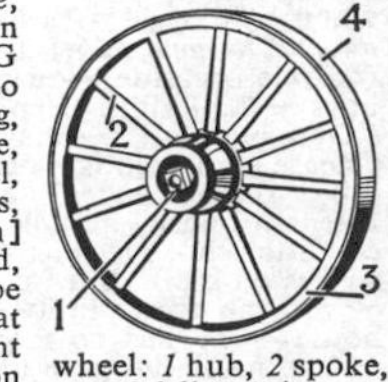
wheel: *1* hub, *2* spoke, *3* felly, *4* tire

[2]**wheel** \"\ *vb* -ED/-ING/-S [ME *whelen*, fr. *whel, wheel, whele* wheel, n.] *vi* **1 a** : to move or turn like a wheel on or as if on an axis : REVOLVE ⟨always showing the same face to the earth, the moon does not ~ on its own center⟩ **b** (1) : to become giddy ⟨the head ~s in the sudden fast turns⟩ (2) : SWAY, REEL ⟨an inebriate ~s down the street⟩ **2** : to turn about a pivot (as in marching) while maintaining a straight or unbroken front ⟨the soldiers ~ed in platoons —Van Wyck Brooks⟩ ⟨the battalion would have ~ed to the flank and cut off the Germans from . . . escape —Walter Bernstein⟩ **3 a** : to turn and face toward a different direction often in sudden fashion ⟨~ed and entered the monastery —Gilbert Parker⟩ ⟨~ed round in his chair with his eyes wide upon her —E.T.Thurston⟩ ⟨the commander ~ed about and walked briskly aft —L.C.Douglas⟩ **b** : to alter or reverse one's opinion or course of action ⟨her mind will ~ around to the other extreme —Liam O'Flaherty⟩ **4** : to move or go in a circuit or spiral : CIRCLE ⟨a flock of . . . pigeons ~s over the curving roofs —James Cameron⟩ ⟨the sun ~ed over the sky —John Steinbeck⟩ ⟨the earth will ~ around its orbit —Waldemar Kaempffert⟩ ⟨the plane ~s off to the west⟩ **5** : to extend in a circle or curve ⟨across valleys where young cotton ~ed slowly in fanlike rows —William Faulkner⟩ ⟨the shadows ~ across the snow⟩ **6** : to drive or go on or as if on wheels or in a vehicle with wheels ⟨she ~ed to the door —Nelson Algren⟩ ⟨the hack ~ed more slowly as the driver puzzled out addresses —T.W.Duncan⟩ ⟨climbs on his bicycle and ~s down the road⟩ **7** : to make with a wheel a series of small indentations along the upper edge of the heel of a shoe **~** *vt* **1** : to cause to turn or revolve on or as if on a certain axis : ROTATE ⟨reloaded and ~ed the cylinders to make certain they were turning free and fast —S.H.Holbrook⟩ **2 a** : to convey or move on or as if on wheels or in a wheeled vehicle ⟨she is carried down and ~ed everywhere —Arnold Bennett⟩ ⟨an authentic hospital patient was ~ed in —R.M.Yoder⟩ ⟨so much American writing on education is ~ed remorselessly out again and even embellished —Brand Blanshard⟩ **b** : to draw or push on wheels ⟨~ed his big guns into action —*Current Biog.*⟩ ⟨he was ~ing the bicycle which Dougal had ridden —John Buchan⟩ **c** : to drive or operate (a vehicle) often at high speed ⟨~ing trucks along cement highways with sleepy eyes —Julian Dana⟩ ⟨taxicab drivers ~ their vehicles through the streets with gay abandon —*Geog. School Bull.*⟩ ⟨was ~ing a passenger train towards Knoxville —H.G.Monroe⟩ **3** : to cause (a rank or body of troops) to turn on a pivot in uniform alignment ⟨the officer ~s the company around the flank⟩ **4** : to make or perform in a circle, spiral, or curve ⟨where the beetle ~s his droning flight —Thomas Gray⟩ **5** : to turn (a person or animal) in or toward a different direction ⟨bewilderment ~ed her round —Michael Arlen⟩ ⟨~ed my horse and cantered off —Eve Langley⟩ ⟨~ed her horse about —Clara Morris⟩ **6 a** : to dress (a skin) on a wheel : FLUFF **b** : PINWHEEL **7** : to indent (the upper edge of the heel of a shoe) with a corrugated wheel **8** : to convey or transmit (electric power) through or over transmission lines ⟨the refusal of the . . . company, which owns the power lines that run from the dam to their farms, to ~ government power —*New Republic*⟩ **syn** see TURN — **wheel and deal** : to take the part of a leader or wheel and to take charge of affairs or arrangements ⟨showed the town how an absolute dictator *wheels and deals* —*Newsweek*⟩

wheel·age \-lij\ *n* -s [[1]*wheel* + *-age*] : a tax or toll on the passage of wheeled vehicles

wheel alignment *n* : the alignment or adjustment of the front wheel suspension and steering mechanism of an automotive vehicle

wheel and axle *n* : a mechanical device consisting of a grooved wheel turned by a cord or chain with a rigidly attached axle (as for winding up a weight) together with the supporting standards — see SIMPLE MACHINE

wheel animal *or* **wheel animalcule** *also* **wheel bearer** *n* : ROTIFER

wheel–back \ˈ=,=\ *n* : a chair back having a splat or spindles cut out, carved, or arranged so as to represent a wheel

wheel barometer *n* : a siphon barometer that is equipped with a float from which a cord passes over a pulley and moves an index

[1]**wheelbarrow** \ˈ=,=(,)=\ *n* [ME *whelbarewe*, fr. *whel* wheel + *barewe* barrow — more at BARROW (cart)] **1** : a small vehicle with handles and one or more wheels for carrying small loads; *esp* : a vehicle with a single wheel suspended between the ends of two shafts that support a boxlike body and serve as handles at the rear — compare BARROW, HANDBARROW **2** : an exercise in which a person walks on his hands with his legs supported in an inclined position by another who holds his legs in the manner of the handles of a wheelbarrow ⟨the children play ~ at the party⟩

[2]**wheelbarrow** \"\ *vt* -ED/-ING/-S : to convey or transport in a wheelbarrow

wheel·bar·row·er \-rəwə(r)\ *n* : one that conveys loads in a wheelbarrow

wheelbarrow sprayer *n* : a small sprayer consisting usu. of a pressure tank, a spray receptacle, and a hose and nozzle suspended and moved on the frame of a wheelbarrow

wheelbase \ˈ=,=\ *n* **1** : the figure enclosed by lines through the points of contact of the wheels of a vehicle with the surface or rails on which they run; *esp* : the length of this figure measured in the direction of motion of the vehicle **2** : the distance in inches between the front and rear axles of an automotive vehicle or between the centers of the points of contact of the front and rear wheels with the ground

wheelbox \ˈ=,=\ *n* : a box or casing containing the steering gear of a ship and supporting the wheel

wheel bug *n* : a large No. American reduviid bug (*Arilus cristatus*) with a high serrated crest on its prothorax that sucks the blood of other insects

wheel chain *n* : a chain used as a wheel rope on a ship

wheelchair \ˈ=,=\ *n* : a chair mounted on wheels and usu. propelled by the occupant by means of hand rims attached to the two large side wheels — compare BATH CHAIR

wheelchair

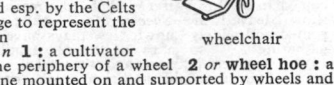

wheel chock *n* : a wedge-shaped wooden block or metal structure placed in front of the wheels of an airplane to prevent its motion on the ground

wheel control *n* : the control of an airplane by the wheel of the control column; *also* : CONTROL COLUMN

wheel cross *n* : an ancient 4-spoked wheel design used esp. by the Celts in the Bronze Age to represent the chariot of the sun

wheel cultivator *n* **1** : a cultivator with blades on the periphery of a wheel **2** *or* **wheel hoe** : a cultivating machine mounted on and supported by wheels and often pushed by hand

wheeled \ˈhwē(ə)ld *also* ˈwē-\ *adj* [[1]*wheel* + *-ed*] **1** : furnished or equipped with wheels ⟨~ vehicles⟩ ⟨a ~ plough⟩ **2** : moving or functioning by means of wheels ⟨~ traffic⟩

wheel·er \-ēlə(r)\ *n* -s [ME *wheler*, fr. *whel* wheel + *-er*] **1** : a maker of wheels **2** : one that wheels: as **a** : a worker who trucks loads of materials or products by hand (as at a factory, construction project, or mine) : PUSHER **b** : one that turns so as to face in a different direction; *specif* : a fighting cock that maneuvers by pretending to run away and then suddenly turning to attack his pursuing opponent **c** : WHEEL SCRAPER **3** : a horse or other draft animal pulling in the position nearest the front wheels of a wagon ⟨with our big team as ~s —Emma Yates⟩ **4** : a vehicle (as a truck or locomotive) having wheels ⟨a big eight ~ of a mighty fame —Carl Sandburg⟩ **5** : one of the granite paving blocks laid contiguous to the curb esp. on grades to carry heavy wheel loads **6** : one that indents shoes with a wheel ⟨welt ~⟩

wheel excavator *n* : a power-driven wheel-supported machine used for excavating trenches for tile drains — compare BACKHOE

wheel governor *n* : a common type of shaft governor arranged inside the rim of a wheel

wheelhorse \ˈ=,=\ *n* **1 a** : a horse that in a hitch of four or more horses pulls a vehicle in a position nearest the front wheels **b** : a horse that is a strong and willing worker **2** : a steady and effective worker or adherent esp. in a political party or body ⟨had been a useful ~ pushing through legislation desired by the administration —R.D.Leigh⟩ ⟨the day-to-day work of the union is carried on by a few ~s who are willing to put in the necessary time —L.G.Reynolds⟩

wheelhouse \ˈ=,=\ *n* : a structure housing a wheel: as **a** : PILOTHOUSE **b** : PADDLE BOX

wheeling *n* -s [ME *wheling*, fr. gerund of *whelen* to wheel — more at WHEEL] **1** : the act or process of one that wheels **2** : the condition of a road relative to passage on wheels ⟨reports good ~ over the new turnpike⟩ **3** : an ornamental line made on the sole or heel of a shoe by means of a corrugated wheel

wheel lathe *n* : a lathe designed esp. for turning locomotive and railroad car wheels

wheel·less \ˈ(h)wē(ə)llə̇s\ *adj* **1** : having no wheels ⟨dragging a ~ stoneboat⟩ **2** : lacking wheeled vehicles ⟨criminals, degenerates, the genuinely low types . . . are entirely missing in ~ societies —J.W.Vandercook⟩

wheel load *n* : the part of the load of a vehicle that is carried by a single wheel and transmitted by it to a road surface or a track

wheel lock *n* : an obsolete gunlock in which sparks are struck from a flint or a piece of iron pyrites by a revolving wheel; *also* : a gun equipped with such a gunlock

wheel·man \ˈ=mən\ *n, pl* **wheelmen** **1** : one who tends or manages a wheel: as **a** : HELMSMAN **b** : the driver of an automobile ⟨you had to have a ~ to drive the getaway car and . . . an extra gunman —*Police Gazette*⟩ **2** : CYCLIST

wheel map *n* : a medieval map made in the shape of a disk with Jerusalem usu. at the center

wheel money *n* : a wheel-shaped metal object of the Bronze Age regarded by some as money and by others as a symbol of the sun

wheel of fortune **1** : WHEEL 3a **2** : a gambling device consisting of a revolving wheel with sections indicating chances taken or bets placed

wheel of life : the endless series of transmigratory cycles of birth, death, and rebirth esp. in Buddhism : the process of samsara resembling a wheel

wheel ore *n* : the mineral bournonite esp. when occurring in wheel-shaped twin crystals

wheel organ *n* : the corona of a rotifer

wheel plate *n* : QUADRANT PLATE

wheel plow *n* : a plow mounted on wheels

wheelrace \ˈ=,=\ *n* : the place in which a waterwheel is set

wheel report *n* : a listing of cars comprising a train as it enters or leaves a yard on which the conductor records all setoffs and pickups en route

wheel rod *n* : a length of metal rod taking the place of a portion of a wheel chain or wheel rope

wheel rope *n* **:** a rope on a ship leading from the axis or barrel of a steering wheel or from a steering engine to the tiller for moving the rudder

wheels *pl of* WHEEL, *pres 3d sing of* WHEEL

wheel scraper *n* **:** a road or earth scraper mounted on wheels

wheels·man \ˈ(h)wē(ə)lzmən\ *n, pl* **wheelsmen :** one who handles or steers with a wheel; *esp* **:** HELMSMAN

wheelspin \ˈ⸗ˌ⸗\ *n* **:** the rotation of the wheels of a wheeled vehicle with little or no traction

wheel tracery *n* **:** tracery (as in a wheel window) radiating from a center like the spokes of a wheel

wheel trap *n* **:** a fish trap used esp. in Alaska consisting of a wheel revolved by the current and provided with scoops for taking fish and a receptacle in which the scoops deposit them

wheel tree *n* **1 :** PADDLEWOOD **2 :** an Australian tree (*Stenocarpus sinuatus*) of the family Proteaceae that is widely cultivated as a shade tree and for its circular clusters of showy bright red to orange scarlet flowers

wheel trolley *n* **:** a grooved rotating wheel attached to the end of the trolley pole of an electric railway car or bus for making constant rolling contact with the trolley wire

wheel watch *n* **:** a watch or tour of duty at the wheel of a ship ⟨standing a long *wheel watch* in the slow hours of the night⟩

wheel well *n* **:** a recessed compartment on the underside of an airplane for the reception of a wheel of a retractable landing gear

wheel window *n* **:** a circular window having radiating mullions like the spokes of a wheel — compare ROSE WINDOW, WHEEL TRACERY

wheelwork \ˈ⸗ˌ⸗\ *n* **:** wheels in gear and their connected parts in a mechanism

wheelwright \ˈ⸗ˌ⸗\ *n* [ME *whelwright*, fr. *whel* wheel + *wright*] **:** a man whose occupation is to make or repair wheels and wheeled vehicles; *specif* **:** an automobile serviceman who repairs or adjusts wheels

wheely \ˈhwēlē *also* ˈwē- *or* -li\ *adj* **:** of or relating to a wheel or a circular form or movement

1wheen \ˈ(h)wēn\ *adj* [ME (Sc) *quheyne*, fr. OE *hwǣne*, *hwēne*, adv., somewhat, a little, instr. of *hwōn* little] *dial Brit* **:** not many **:** FEW ⟨get a ~ biscuits for the beasts —J.J.Bell⟩

2wheen \ˮ\ *n* -s [ME (Sc) *quheyne*, fr. OE *hwǣne, hwēne*, adv., somewhat, a little] *dial Brit* **:** a considerable number **:** a fair amount ⟨for quite a ~ of years —*Irish Digest*⟩ ⟨mix in a ~ of common life for novelty and variation —Joseph Macleod⟩

whee·ple \ˈ(h)wēpəl\ *vb* -ED/-ING/-S [imit.] *vi, dial Brit* **:** to utter a prolonged whistle or shrill cry ⟨a curlew ~*s*⟩ **~** *vt, dial Brit* **:** to give forth (a shrill cry or whistle) **:** WHISTLE ⟨he sometimes *wheepled* a tune of his own making —G.D.Brown⟩

1wheeze \ˈhwēz *also* ˈwēz\ *vb* -ED/-ING/-S [ME *whesen*, prob. of Scand origin; akin to ON *hvæsa* to hiss; akin to OE *hwǣst* action of blowing, L *queri* to complain, Skt *śvasiti* he breathes, snorts, sighs] *vi* **1 :** to breathe with difficulty with a usu. audible sibilant or whistling sound ⟨went to every doctor and still he coughed and still he *wheezed* —N.R.Nash⟩ ⟨I *wheezed* asthmatically with my face in the ground —A.R.Matthews⟩ **2 :** to make a sound resembling that of wheezing esp. while moving ⟨the old car jerked and *wheezed* over the country road⟩ ⟨they heard a bullet ~ about their heads —J.H.Stuart⟩ **~** *vt* **:** to utter with a sound of wheezing ⟨the ancient organ ~*s* out its tune⟩

2wheeze \ˮ\ *n* -s **1 a :** a sibilant whistling sound caused by difficult or obstructed respiration ⟨unmoving except for the heavy ~ of his breath —Herbert Gold⟩ ⟨a history of ~ is . . . significant in any patient presenting a mass in the chest —*Jour. Amer. Med. Assoc.*⟩ **b :** a sound similar to a wheeze ⟨the ability to diagnose accurately a ~ under a hood . . . on the highway —W.C.Oursler⟩ **2 a** (1) **:** a stage joke told by a comedian or clown ⟨if a ~ clicks at a matinee and an evening show I leave it in —*Success Mag.*⟩ (2) **:** such a joke oft repeated and widely known ⟨few plays have ever succeeded in gathering . . . so many of the old familiar ~*s* —*Nation*⟩ (3) **:** a practical joke **:** TRICK ⟨thought it was just a ~ of the purser to turn us all out bright and early —Thomas Wood †1950⟩ **b :** a trite saying or proverb ⟨the ancient ~ that Hollywood buys good stories about bad girls and makes them into bad stories about good girls —R.L.Blakesley⟩ ⟨the ~ that in life you get exactly what you give —T.H.Fielding⟩

wheez·i·ly \-zəlē, -li\ *adv* **:** in a wheezy manner

wheez·i·ness \-zēnəs, -zin-\ *n* -ES **:** the quality or state of being wheezy

wheez·ing·ly *adv* **:** with a wheeze ⟨the asthmatic speaks ~⟩

whee·zle \ˈhwēzəl *also* ˈwē-\ *vi* -ED/-ING/-S [freq. of 1*wheeze*] *dial Brit* **:** WHEEZE

wheezy \-zē, -zi\ *adj* -ER/-EST **1 :** inclined to wheeze **:** afflicted with wheezing ⟨fat, stiff-jointed, ~ veterans —Robert Graves⟩ **2 :** making or having a wheezing sound ⟨the ~ music of a Gramophone —W.S.Maugham⟩ ⟨owns a ~ old car —F.L.Allen⟩

whe·kau \ˈ(h)weˌkau̇, ˈfe-\ *n* -s [Maori] **:** LAUGHING OWL

1whelk \ˈhw|elk, |eu̇k *also* ˈw|\ *n* -s [ME *wilke, welke, whelke*, fr. OE *weoloc, wioloc;* akin to MD *willoc, wilc, welc* whelk, ON *vil* intestines, L *volvere* to turn — more at VOLUBLE] **1 :** any of numerous large marine gastropod mollusks of the family Buccinidae: as **a :** a snail of the genus *Buccinum; esp* **:** a large elongated snail (*B. undatum*) of both coasts of the Atlantic that is much used as food in Europe **b :** any of various No. American mollusks of the genus *Busycon* **:** WINKLE 2 — see RED WHELK **2 :** any of various mollusks of families other than Buccinidae that resemble whelks — usu. used with a qualifying term; compare DOG WHELK

2whelk \ˮ\ *vi* -ED/-ING/-S **:** to obtain or gather whelks

3whelk \ˮ\ *n* -s [ME *whelke*, fr. OE *hwylca*, fr. *hwelian* to suppurate, come to a head — more at WHEAL] **1 :** PAPULE, PUSTULE **2 :** WELT, WALE, WHEAL

1whelked \-kt\ *adj* [1*whelk* + *-ed*] **:** formed like a whelk shell **:** TWISTED, CONVOLUTED ⟨~ horns⟩

2whelked \ˮ\ *adj* [3*whelk* + *-ed*] *archaic* **:** having whelks or ridges on the flesh

whelk tingle *n* [1*whelk*] **:** DOG WHELK

whelm \ˈhw|elm, |eu̇m *also* ˈw|\ *vb* -ED/-ING/-S [ME *whelmen*, perh. alter. (influenced by *helmen* to helm) of *whelven* to turn upside down — more at HELM, WHELVE] *vt* **1 a** *dial Eng* **:** to turn (as a dish or vessel) upside down usu. to cover something **b :** to throw or place (an object) upon something so as to engulf or crush it ⟨~*s* his hat down over his eyes⟩ **2 a :** to cover or engulf completely usu. so as to wreck or destroy **:** BURY, SUBMERGE ⟨sand all around them, about to creep up on them and ~ them —Mary H. Vorse⟩ ⟨the avalanche ~*s* the mountain village in tons of snow⟩ **b :** to engulf or overcome in the manner of a storm or flood with usu. disastrous effect ⟨winter darkness ~*s* the woods⟩ ⟨long afterwards ~*ed* in some European convulsion —G.M.Trevelyan⟩ ⟨booming money . . . so fast that the problem was how to get rid of it before it ~*ed* you into suffocation —William Faulkner⟩ **c :** to overcome in thought or feeling **:** OVERWHELM ⟨had been so ~*ed* in astonishment that they had not lifted a finger to aid their chief —C.E.Craddock⟩ ⟨drawn into overmastering passion, ~*ed* with a rush of joy and triumph —G.A.Wagner⟩ ⟨gathering around to ~ him with arguments⟩ **~** *vi* **:** to pass or go over something so as to bury or submerge ⟨the river ~*ed* —Kenneth Rexroth⟩ ⟨the battle lines ~*ed* and divided —C.P.Aiken⟩ **syn** see OVERPOWER

1whelp \ˈhw|elp, |eu̇p *also* ˈw|\ *n* -s [ME, fr. OE *hwelp;* akin to OS *hwelp* whelp, OHG *hwelf, welf*, ON *hvelpr* whelp, and perh. to OE *hwelan* to war, rage, *hlōwan* to low — more at LOW] **1 a :** one of the young of various carnivorous mammals (as the wolf, otter, or fox) ⟨the tracks of the mother wolverine and three full-size ~*s* —*Fur-Fish-Game*⟩; *specif* **:** one of the young of a dog **b :** a young boy or girl ⟨the older folk would be huddled together . . . praying for their wayward ~*s* —L.C. Douglas⟩ **2 a :** an ill-considered or despised person ⟨that awkward ~ with his money bags —Joseph Addison⟩ **b** *obs* **:** the offspring of such a person or being ⟨the devil's ~*s*⟩ **c :** PUP 2 ⟨the young ~ had learned his lesson —Edna Ferber⟩ **3 a :** any of the longitudinal ribs or ridges on the barrel of a capstan or windlass — usu. used in pl. ⟨the ~*s* of a windlass⟩ **b :** SPROCKET 2a **4** *Brit* **:** a medium-sized auxiliary warship first constructed in the early 17th century **5** *usu cap* **:** TENNESSEAN — used as a nickname

2whelp \ˮ\ *vb* -ED/-ING/-S [ME *whelpen*, fr. *whelp*, n.] *vt* **1 :** to bring forth **:** give birth to — used esp. of the female dog ⟨the bitch ~*s* her young⟩ **2** *archaic* **:** to bring forth as if by giving birth ⟨~*s* a pack of lies⟩ **~** *vi* **:** to bring forth young ⟨where they crawl out on the ice to ~ —O.F.Backer⟩

3whelp \ˮ\ *n* -s [alter. of *welt*] *dial* **:** WELT, WALE ⟨rubbed the mare and showed me a ~ on her left flank —T.H.Phillips⟩

whelp·less \ˈ⸗ˌləs\ *adj* **:** having no whelps; *esp* **:** bereft of whelps

whelve \ˈ(h)welv, -weu̇v\ *vt* -ED/-ING/-S [ME *whelven*, fr. OE *gehwielfan, gehwelfan* to arch, bend over; akin to OHG *welben* to vault, arch — more at GULF] *dial Eng* **:** to turn (as a dish or vessel) upside down usu. to cover something

1whem·mel *or* **whem·mle** \ˈ(h)weməl\ *vb* -ED/-ING/-S [alter. of *whelm*] *vt, Scot* **:** OVERTURN, UPSET **~** *vi, Scot* **:** to stumble or become overturned

2whemmel *or* **whemmle** \ˮ\ *n* -s *Scot* **:** CONFUSION, OVERTHROW

1when \(ˌ)hwen, (ˌ)wen, ˌ(h)wən\ *adv* [ME *when, whan*, fr. OE *hwenne, hwanne;* akin to OFris *hwenne* when, OHG *hwenne, hwanne*, Goth *hwan* when, how, OE *hwā* who — more at WHO] **1 a :** at what time **:** in what period **:** how long ago ⟨asked him ~ it happened⟩ **:** how soon **:** after how long a lapse of time ⟨~ will he return⟩ **b :** in what circumstances ⟨~ shall we three meet again —Shak.⟩ **2 :** at which time **:** and then **:** WHEREUPON ⟨the tree will eventually die of old age and fall down ~ the problem solves itself —F.D.Smith & Barbara Wilcox⟩ **3 :** at, in, or during which ⟨a generation ~ medical science has . . . prolonged the span of life —*N.Y. Times*⟩ **4 :** ENOUGH ⟨say ~⟩ **5 :** at a former time; *esp* **:** at a less prosperous time ⟨his old associates . . . brag fondly of having known him ~ —Vance Packard⟩

2when \ˮ\ *conj* [ME *when, whan*, fr. OE *hwenne, hwanne*, fr. *hwenne, hwanne*, adv.] **1 a :** at or during the time that **:** WHILE ⟨on one occasion, ~ a boy, I went fishing with three other boys —W.J.Reilly⟩ ⟨I could not say "Amen!" ~ they did say "God bless us!" —Shak.⟩ **b :** just after the moment that ⟨please stop writing ~ the bell rings⟩ ⟨went back to his old job ~ the war ended⟩ **c :** at any and every time that ⟨~ he listens to music, he falls asleep⟩ **2 :** in the event that **:** on condition that **:** IF ⟨the batter is out ~ he bunts foul with two strikes on him⟩ **3 a :** considering that ⟨why use water at all ~ you can drown in it —Stuart Chase⟩ ⟨how can he buy the house ~ he has no money⟩ **b :** in spite of the fact that **:** ALTHOUGH ⟨he gave up politics ~ he might have made a great career in it⟩

3when \ˮ\ *pron* [1*when*] **:** what or which time ⟨in 1934, since ~ he has been working at landscapes and portraits —*Horizon*⟩

4when \ˈhwen *also* ˈwen\ *n* -s [1*when*] **:** the time in which something is done or comes about ⟨piecing together the story of my visit there — the ~ and the why of it —W.B.Mowery⟩ ⟨remembering exactly the who, ~, what and how of any occasion —J.M.Barzun⟩

when·as \(ˈ)(h)weˈnaz, ˌ(h|wəˈ-\ *conj* [ME (Sc) *when as*, fr. ME 1*when* + *as*] **1** *archaic* **:** at the or any time when **:** WHILE ⟨~ in silks my Julia goes —Robert Herrick †1674⟩ **2** *archaic* **:** for the reason that **:** AS **3** *obs* **:** ALTHOUGH, WHEREAS ⟨cried "All hail!" ~ he meant all harm —Shak.⟩

1whence \ˈhwen(t)s *also* ˈwe-\ *adv* [ME *whennes, whannes*, fr. *whenne, whanne* whence (fr. OE *hwanon, hwanone*) + *-s*, gen. sing. noun ending functioning adverbially; akin to OS *hwanan* whence, OHG *hwanān, hwanana* whence, OE *hwā* who — more at WHO, -S] **1 a :** from what place ⟨are the pigments imported and, if so, ~ —*Notes & Queries on Anthropology*⟩ — often used with *from* ⟨asks from ~ these lines come —*N.Y. Times Bk. Rev.*⟩ **b :** from what source, origin, antecedent, or cause ⟨~ do these questionings well up —S.C.Pepper⟩ — often used with *from* ⟨from ~ could this possibility issue —F.S.Haserot⟩ **2 :** from or out of which place, source, or cause ⟨a native of Europe, ~ it was introduced into many parts of the world —Jane Nickerson⟩ ⟨sketches the lawless society ~ the ballads sprang —DeLancey Ferguson⟩ — often used with *from* **3 :** upon which ground **:** by reason of or in consequence of which fact or circumstance **:** WHEREFORE ⟨came a whacking header onto my arms and nose and nothing broke — ~ I infer that my bones are not yet chalky —O.W. Holmes †1935⟩

2whence \ˮ\ *n* -s **:** a place or source from which someone or something springs **:** ANTECEDENT ⟨deals only with the momentary what, neglecting the ~ —J.P.M.Somerville⟩

whenceforth \(ˈ)⸗ˈ⸗\ *adv, archaic* **:** WHENCE ⟨another house, ~ his flame . . . shines stark —A.D.Ficke⟩

whenceforward \(ˈ)⸗ˈ⸗⸗\ *adv* **:** from which time or place onward

1whencesoever \ˈ⸗⸗ˈ⸗⸗\ *conj* **:** from any or every place from which **:** no matter from what place

2whencesoever \ˮ\ *adv* **:** from what place soever **:** from what cause or source soever

whencever \(ˈ)⸗ˈ⸗⸗\ *conj* [1*whence* + *ever*] **:** WHENCESOEVER

1when·ev·er \(h)weˈnevə(r), (h)wəˈ-\ *conj* [ME *when ever*, fr. 2*when* + *ever*] **1 :** at any or all times that **:** in any or every instance in which ⟨~ he leaves the house, he always takes his umbrella⟩ **2** *chiefly Scot* **:** as soon as ⟨~ he entered my room, he rushed at me . . . and shed tears of delight over our romantic meeting after twenty years —Harry Lauder⟩

2whenever \ˮ\ *adv* **1 :** at whatever time **:** no matter when ⟨welcomes originality ~ shown⟩ **2** *usu* **when ever :** WHEN — used in questions expressing surprise or bewilderment ⟨*when ever* did I make such a promise⟩

when–issued \⸗ˈ⸗(ˌ)⸗\ *adj* [fr. the phrase *when issued*] **:** of, relating to, or constituting a securities contract on which settlement is not required until the securities are ready for delivery

when·ness \ˈhwennəs *also* ˈwe-\ *n* -ES **:** position or relation in time

whenso \ˈhwen(ˌ)sō\ *conj* [ME *when so*, fr. 1*when* + *so*] *archaic* **:** WHENSOEVER

1when·so·ev·er \ˈhwensəˈwevə(r), -sōˈe- *also* ˈwen-\ *conj* [ME, fr. *when so* + *ever*] **:** at what time soever **:** at whatever time **:** WHENEVER ⟨ye have the poor with you always, and ~ ye will ye may do them good —Mk 14:7 (AV)⟩

2whensoever *adv, obs* **:** at any time whatever ⟨if his fitness speaks, mine is ready; now or ~ —Shak.⟩

when·som·ev·er \-səˈme-\ *adv or conj* [ME, alter. (influenced by *-som-* as in *whatsomever*) of *whensoever*] *chiefly dial* **:** WHENSOEVER

1where \(ˈ)hw|e(ə)r, (ˈ)w|, |eə *sometimes* |a(a)(ə)r *or* |a(a)ə; *when completely unstressed often* (h)wə(r); *more often under secondary than primary stress* (h)wər(·) *or* (h)wə̄\ *adv* [ME *where, wher*, fr. OE *hwǣr;* akin to OHG *hwār* where, ON *hvar*, Goth *hwar* where, Skt *kar*hi when, OE *hwā* who — more at WHO] **1 a** (1) **:** at or in what place ⟨~ do you think you are⟩ ⟨asked him ~ he lived⟩ ⟨~'*s* the fire⟩ (2) **:** in what situation, position, or circumstances **:** at what point ⟨~, precisely, should a man's crusading zeal abate —Lucien Price⟩ ⟨~ else numerically are you going to draw the line —Weston La Barre⟩ (3) **:** in what respect or particular ⟨does not hesitate, as he looks back, to admit ~ he was wrong —*Times Lit. Supp.*⟩ **b :** to what or which place **:** in what or which direction **:** to what goal or result **:** WHITHER ⟨~ are you rushing⟩ ⟨doesn't know ~ he is heading⟩ **c :** from what place or source ⟨~ did he get such an absurd idea⟩ **2** *archaic* **:** HERE, THERE — used to call attention to something or indicate direction of movement ⟨but soft, behold! lo, ~ it comes again —Shak.⟩ **3 :** at which part, stage, or passage ⟨I forget ~ we were reading⟩

2where \ˮ\ *conj* [ME *where, wher*, fr. OE *hwǣr*, fr. *hwǣr*, adv.] **1 a :** at or in the place in which ⟨~ you lodge I will lodge —Ruth 1:16 (RSV)⟩ **b :** to the place at, in, or to which ⟨~ you go I will go —Ruth 1:16 (RSV)⟩ **:** a place at, in, or to which ⟨couldn't see well from ~ he was sitting⟩ **c :** at the part, stage, or passage at which ⟨toward the end of the book, ~ the author tells of the heroine's return home⟩ **2 :** WHEREVER ⟨removed all restrictions on his movements and permitted him to go ~ he wished⟩ **3 :** at or in which place ⟨the room ~ he was working⟩ ⟨the store ~ she bought her clothes⟩ **4 :** WHEREAS ⟨~ she was fascinated by people he shows here only a laboriously sophisticated amusement —Anthony Quinton⟩ **5 a :** under conditions in which **:** in circumstances in which ⟨it is unfortunately necessary to determine this ~ the custody of the children is involved —Louis Auchincloss⟩ **b :** in the respect in which ⟨~ others are weak, he is strong⟩ **c :** so far as **:** to the extent that ⟨the prospects . . . were truly and literally hopeless, ~ England was concerned —Sacheverell Sitwell⟩ **d :** of such a sort that ⟨limited definition to such explanations of the meaning of a symbol as asserted the equivalence of two expressions; ~ the defining expression had to contain more symbols than the defined expression —R.G.F.Robinson⟩

3where \ˮ\ *n* -s [ME *where, wher*, fr. *where, wher*, adv.] **:** LOCATION, PLACE; *esp* **:** the place in which something mentioned is or occurs ⟨discussed the ~ and how of the accident⟩

4where \ˮ\ *pron* [1*where*] **:** what or which place ⟨~ did you come from⟩

1where·abouts \ˈ⸗əˌbau̇ts, ˌ⸗⸗ˈ⸗\ *also* **where·about** \-t\ *adv* [*whereabouts* fr. ME *wheraboutes*, fr. ME *wher aboute* + *-s*, gen. sing. noun ending functioning adverbially; *whereabout* fr. ME *wher aboute*, fr. *wher* where + *aboute, about* about — more at -S] **1 :** about where **:** near what place ⟨to know at the outset ~ the line will be drawn —F.W.Maitland⟩ **2** *obs* **:** at what work **:** on what business or errand ⟨I must not have you henceforth question me whither I go, nor reason *whereabout* —Shak.⟩

2whereabouts \ˮ\ *n pl but sing or pl in constr*, *also* **whereabout :** the place or general locality where a person or thing is ⟨had for long been determined to discover the *whereabout* of the gold country —*Times Lit. Supp.*⟩ ⟨his ~ was known only to his personal staff —*Fortune*⟩ ⟨his ~ are kept secret —*Manchester Guardian Weekly*⟩

whereafter \(ˈ)⸗ˈ⸗⸗\ *adv* [ME *wherafter*, fr. *wher* where + *after*] **:** after which ⟨dissolve the starch glaze, ~ the chintzes become dull fuzzy cotton —*For Instance*⟩

whereanent \ˈ⸗⸗ˈ⸗\ *adv* [1*where* + *anent*] *chiefly Scot* **:** concerning which

1whereas \(ˈ)⸗ˈ⸗\ *conj* [ME *where as*, fr. 1*where* + *as*] **1** *archaic* **:** WHERE ⟨home she came, ~ her mother blind sat in eternal night —Edmund Spenser⟩ **2 :** considering that **:** in view of the fact that **:** SINCE — usu. used to introduce a preamble (as to a law or contract) that is the basis of a following declaration, affirmation, command, or request **3 a :** when in fact **:** while on the contrary **:** the case being in truth that — used to introduce a statement in opposition or contrast to a preceding or sometimes following statement ⟨was spending practically all of his time on the inside dealing with things, ~ his yearnings were to deal more with people —W.J.Reilly⟩ **b :** ALTHOUGH ⟨seeing I have once begun, I will speak to my Lord, ~ I am dust and ashes —Gen 18:27 (NCE)⟩ ⟨~ it is quite dangerous to draw conclusions . . . one cannot avoid being struck with some gross changes —Abram Kardiner⟩ **c :** at the same time that **:** WHILE ⟨its isolation favored the development of a unified and distinctive culture, ~ its nearness to the European continent was a guarantee against a too sharp differentiation from western civilization —Kemp Malone⟩

2whereas \ˮ\ *n* -ES **1 :** an introductory statement of a formal or legal document **:** PREAMBLE ⟨learned his way through ~*es* at . . . law school —Roland Gelatt⟩ **2 :** a conditional or qualifying statement ⟨dilutes it with various discreet ~*es* —H.L.Mencken⟩

whereat \(ˈ)⸗ˈ⸗\ *adv* [ME *whare at*, fr. *whare, where, wher* where + *at*] **1 :** at or toward which ⟨an icy tea party, ~ the girl was present, unexplained, unaccounted for, and ignored —Maurice Hewlett⟩ **2 :** in consequence of which **:** on which account **:** WHEREUPON ⟨~ the seeker after precision may wax angry or sarcastic —H.A.Overstreet⟩

where away *adv* **1 :** in what direction — usu. used aboard ship as a question in response to a call from a lookout that something (as land) has been sighted **2** *usu* **whereaway** \ˈ⸗⸗ˌ⸗\ *chiefly dial* **:** WHEREABOUTS

whereby \(ˈ)⸗ˈ⸗\ *adv* [ME *wherby*, fr. *where, wher* where + *by*] **1 a :** by or through which **:** by the help of which **:** in accordance with which ⟨the means ~ such an end is effected —Norman Friedman⟩ ⟨the old logic of judgment, ~ discipline meant salvation —D.R.Meyer⟩ **b** *archaic* **:** near or along which ⟨the throne ~ she fell —Alfred Tennyson⟩ **2** *obs* **:** by what **:** HOW ⟨~ shall I know this —Lk 1:18 (AV)⟩ **3 a :** as a result of which **:** in consequence of which ⟨a respite, four days' grace, ~ she told her story to the world —Robert Browning⟩ **b** *chiefly dial* **:** WHEREUPON ⟨~ thou didst desire to eat some, ~ I told thee they were ill for a green wound —Shak.⟩

wherefor \(ˈ)⸗ˈ⸗\ *adv* [ME *wherfor, wherfore* for which, for what reason, fr. *where, wher* where + *for, fore* for] **:** for which ⟨a mistake the responsibility ~ is his alone⟩

1where·fore \R ˈhw|erˌfō(ə)r, -fȯ(ə)r *also* ˈw| *sometimes* |a(a)rˌ- *or* -ˌfər; -R |eəˌfōə, -fȯ(ə) *sometimes* |a(a)əˌ- *or* -ˌfə, +V ˮ *or* -fō(ə)r *or* -fȯ(ə)r *or* -ˌfər\ *adv* [ME *wherfor, wherfore* for which, for what reason] **1 :** for what reason **:** for what end or object ⟨~ do I assume these royalties —John Milton⟩ **2** *archaic* **:** in consequence of which **:** WHY

2wherefore *also* **where·for** \ˮ\ *conj* [ME *wherfor, wherfore*, fr. *wherfor, wherfore*, adv.] **:** for that reason **:** and in consequence of that fact or consideration **:** SO ⟨the Lord . . . rested the seventh day; ~ the Lord blessed the sabbath day —Exod 20:11 (AV)⟩

3wherefore \ˮ\ *n* -s [1*wherefore*] **:** an answer or statement giving an explanation **:** CAUSE, REASON ⟨they say every why hath a ~ —Shak.⟩ ⟨totally in the dark as to the whys and ~*s* of her sister's moods —Mrs. Humphry Ward⟩

wherefrom \(ˈ)⸗ˈ⸗\ *adv* **:** from which ⟨exhibitions of materials in use ~ one could obtain objective information —*Internat'l Council for Building Documentation*⟩

wherein \(ˈ)⸗ˈ⸗\ *adv* [ME *wherin*, fr. *where, wher* where + *in*] **1 :** in what **:** in what particular or regard ⟨~ consists the peculiarity in the connotation of a relative name —J.S.Mill⟩ **2 a :** in which **:** WHERE ⟨citizens of the United States and of the State ~ they reside —*U. S. Constitution*⟩ **b :** in the course of or during which ⟨a period ~ he took no active part in politics⟩ **3 :** in regard to which ⟨a controversy ~ he took a prominent part⟩ **4** *obs* **:** in whatever regard ⟨~ our entertainment shall shame us we will be justified in our loves —Shak.⟩

whereinsoever \ˈ⸗(ˌ)⸗⸗ˈ⸗⸗\ *adv* **:** in whatever matter, respect, or action

where·into \(ˈ)⸗+\ *adv* **:** into which ⟨the brook ~ he loved to look —R.W.Emerson⟩

where·ness *n* -ES **:** the quality or state of being in a particular place **:** position or presence in a definable place ⟨where was the ~ of a dreamer —Ross Lockridge⟩

whereof \(ˈ)⸗ˈ⸗ *sometimes* -ˈäf\ *adv* [ME *wherof*, fr. *where wher* where + *of*] **1 :** of what ⟨knows ~ he speaks —H.U. Ribalow⟩ ⟨~ are you made, that millions of strange shadows on you tend —Shak.⟩ **2 a :** of which ⟨modernized old houses, ~ even the new ones are often as classically beautiful as ever —*Yankee*⟩ ⟨punishment for crime ~ the party shall have been duly convicted —*U. S. Constitution*⟩ **:** of whom ⟨the very earliest poets ~ there is record —J.C.Powys⟩ **b** *archaic* **:** with or by which ⟨wine ~ his sire . . . was poisoned —Christopher Marlowe⟩

whereon \(ˈ)⸗ˈ⸗\ *adv* [ME *wheron*, fr. *where, wher* where + *on*] **1** *archaic* **:** on what ⟨~ do you look —Shak.⟩ **2 a :** on which ⟨conducted ranches ~ to grow supplies for sale —P.A. Rollins⟩ ⟨that day . . . ~ he says I shall yield up my crown —Shak.⟩ **b :** to, toward, or upon which ⟨the things ~ he cast his eyes —R.W.Emerson⟩ **c :** in the course of which **:** in connection with which ⟨installed a service between New York and San Francisco, ~ the planes flew only by daylight —A.F. Harlow⟩ **d :** following which **:** WHEREUPON ⟨~ the people answered with a shout —Robert Browning⟩

whereout \(ˈ)⸗ˈ⸗\ *adv* [ME *wherout*, fr. *where, wher* where + *out*] *archaic* **:** out of which **:** WHENCE

whereover \(ˈ)⸗ˈ⸗⸗\ *adv* [ME *wherover*, fr. *where, wher* where + *over*] **:** over which ⟨~ richest leaves have lain —Mark Van Doren⟩

wheres *pl of* WHERE

whereso \ˈ⸗(ˌ)⸗\ *conj* [ME *wher so*, fr. *where, wher*, adv., where + *so*] *archaic* **:** WHERESOEVER

1where·so·ev·er \ˈhwersəˈwevə(r), -sōˈe- *also* ˈwer-\ *conj* [ME *whersoever*, fr. *wher so* + *ever*] *archaic* **:** in, to, or from whatever place

2wheresoever *adv, obs* **:** in any place whatever

where·som·ev·er \-səˈme-\ *conj* [ME *whersomever, whersumever*, fr. ME (northern dial.) *wher sum* wherever (fr. ME *where, wher* where + ME — northern dial. — *sum,* rel. adv., as) + ME *ever* — more at WHATSOMEVER] *chiefly dial* : WHERESOEVER

wherethrough \(ˈ)=ˈ=\ *conj* [ME *wherthrough,* fr. *where, wher* where + *through*] **1 a :** through which : from one side to another of which ⟨foliage ~ the sun shot sudden showers of light —Robert Nichols⟩ **b :** during which ⟨seven long years of lack ~ he hath not ceased to seek for thee —Edwin Arnold⟩ **2 :** because of which : on account of which ⟨is in control of clocks, ~ it calls the tune —David Morton⟩

whereto \(ˈ)=ˈ=\ *adv* [ME *wherto,* fr. *where, wher* where + *to*] **1 :** to what : to what place, purpose, or end ⟨~ tends all this —Shak.⟩ **2 :** to which ⟨the present species, ~ the latter term would perhaps be more appropriate —James Stevenson-Hamilton⟩

whereunder \(ˈ)=ˈ=\ *conj* [ME *wherunder,* fr. *where, wher* where + *under*] : under which ⟨trees ~ the animals may find shelter —Henry Wynmalen⟩

where·until \(ˌ)=+\ *adv, chiefly dial* : WHERETO

where·unto \"+\ *adv* [ME *wherunto,* fr. *where, wher* where + *unto*] : WHERETO

whereup \(ˈ)=ˈ=\ *conj* : up which

whereupon \ˈ==,=, ˌ==ˈ=\ *adv* [ME *wherupon,* fr. *where, wher* where + *upon*] **1 a** *obs* : for what reason : WHEREFORE ⟨hath sent to know . . . ~ you conjure from the breast of civil peace such bold hostility —Shak.⟩ **b** *archaic* : upon what ⟨~ are the foundations thereof fastened —Job 38:6 (AV)⟩ **2 :** upon which : on the top or surface of which ⟨a point of rock ~ a pale-colored village balanced itself —Elizabeth Bowen⟩ **3 a** *obs* : by reason of which ⟨~ I command thee to open thy affair —Shak.⟩ **b** *archaic* : upon which as ground or support ⟨~ Saint Ambrose makes a comment with much fruit —Robert Browning⟩ **4 :** closely following and in consequence of which ⟨has to banish his wicked foster brothers . . . ~ they become pirates —G.B.Saul⟩ **5** *obs* : concerning which ⟨this remedy, ~ we are now present here together —Shak.⟩ **6** *archaic* : to, toward, or on which ⟨that ~ they set their minds —Ezek 24:25 (AV)⟩

¹**wher·ev·er** \(h)weˈrevə(r), (h)wəˈ-\ *adv* [ME *wher ever,* fr. *where, wher,* adv., where + *ever*] **1 :** where in the world — used in questions expressing astonishment or bewilderment ⟨~ did you get that hat⟩ **2 :** at, in, or to any or every place in or to which ⟨he goes ~ needed⟩ : in every instance or circumstance in which ⟨help is given ~ needed⟩ **3 :** anywhere at all ⟨explore northward or ~ by sea —Bernard De Voto⟩

²**wherever** \"\ *conj* [ME *wher ever,* fr. *where, wher,* adv., where + *ever*] : at, in, or to any or all places that : in any circumstance in which ⟨~ he goes, he is welcomed with open arms⟩ ⟨~ it is possible, he tries to help out⟩

¹**wherewith** \(ˈ)=ˈ=\ *adv* [ME *wherwith,* fr. *where, wher* where + *with*] **1** *archaic* : with what ⟨if the salt have lost his savor, ~ shall it be salted —Mt 5:13 (AV)⟩ **2 a :** with which : by means of which ⟨no metal tools ~ to break ground —Russell Lord⟩ ⟨the pleasant rites ~ the pagan Teutons had celebrated the victory of the sun —Will Durant⟩ **b** *archaic* : by reason of which : on account of which ⟨dreamed dreams, ~ his spirit was troubled —Dan 2:1 (AV)⟩ **3** *archaic* : WHEREAT, WHEREUPON ⟨close to her ear touching the melody; ~ disturbed, she uttered a soft moan —John Keats⟩

²**wherewith** \"\ *pron* [ME *wherwith,* fr. *wherwith,* adv.] : that with or by which — used with an infinitive ⟨had not ~ to feed himself⟩

³**wherewith** \"\ *n* -S : WHEREWITHAL

¹**where·with·al** \ˈ=wȧ,thȯl, -,thȯl, ˌ==ˈ=\ *adv* [¹*where* + *withal*] **1** *archaic* : WHEREWITH 1 ⟨take no thought, saying . . . ~ shall we be clothed —Mt 6:31 (AV)⟩ **2 :** out of or by means of which ⟨the material ~ to have evolved this elegant creature, man —Weston La Barre⟩

²**wherewithal** \"\ *pron* : WHEREWITH ⟨buying lots of old iron at sales, in the hope of finding therein ~ to patch up his dilapidated machines —Adrian Bell⟩

³**wherewithal** \ˈ=,=\ *n* -S [²*wherewithal*] : means or resources for purchasing or doing something ⟨must present to the courts the ~ to create a framework of liberty under law —Herbert Feinstein⟩; *specif* : financial resources : MONEY ⟨had to keep raising his budget and rushing out to find more ~ —*New Yorker*⟩

¹**wher·ret** \ˈ(h)wərət\ *n* -S [imit.] *chiefly dial* : a cuff on the face or ear : BOX, SLAP

²**wherret** \"\ *vt* -ED/-ING/-S *chiefly dial* : to give a cuff or blow to

³**wherret** *or* **wherrit** \"\ *vt* -ED/-ING/-S [perh. alter. of *worrit*] *dial* : TEASE, WORRY

wher·ry \ˈhwerē, -ri *also* ˈwe-\ *n* -ES [ME *whery*] **1 :** any of various light boats: as **a :** a long light rowboat made sharp at both ends and used to transport passengers on rivers and about harbors **b :** a narrow open racing or exercise boat rowed by one person with sculls **c :** a small square-sterned rowboat pulled by a single pair of oars **2 :** a large light barge, lighter, or fishing boat varying in type in different parts of Great Britain; *specif* : a broad-beamed light-draft cargo or passenger boat with sharp stem and stern, little freeboard, and usu. a single gaff sail without a boom — called also *Norfolk wherry*

wher·ry·ite \-rē,īt\ *n* -S [Edgar T. *Wherry* b1885 Am. mineralogist + E *-ite*] : a mineral $Pb_4Cu(CO_3)(SO_4)_2(OH,Cl)_2O(?)$ consisting of a basic carbonate and sulfate of lead and copper and sometimes containing chlorine

wher·ry·man \ˈ==mən\ *n, pl* **wherrymen 1** *chiefly Brit* : one who works on a wherry or who rows passengers in a wherry for hire **2 :** WATER STRIDER

¹**whet** \ˈhwet *also* ˈwet; *usu* -ed·+V\ *vt* **whetted; whetted; whetting; whets** [ME *whetten,* fr. OE *hwettan;* akin to OHG *wezzen* to whet, ON *hvetja* to whet, incite, Goth *gahwatjan* to incite; causative fr. the adj. represented by OE *hwæt* bold, vigorous, OHG *waz* sharp, ON *hvatr* bold, vigorous; prob. akin to L *triquetrus* three-cornered] **1 a :** to sharpen (as a tool edge) by rubbing on or with something (as a stone) : HONE ⟨~ a scythe⟩ ⟨~ a knife⟩ ⟨an axe *whetted* to a razor edge⟩ **b :** to rub vigorously together as if sharpening ⟨*whetted* his hands . . . to get them warm —J.H.Stuart⟩ **2** *archaic* : urge on : INCITE, AROUSE ⟨I will ~ on the king —Shak.⟩ **3 :** to make keen or more acute (as a faculty or desire) : STIMULATE, EXCITE ⟨~ the appetite⟩ ⟨curiosity . . . *whetted* rather than satisfied —G.N.Ray⟩ ⟨~*s* the emotions to bullfight sharpness —H.W.Young⟩ — **whet one's whistle** *archaic* : WET ONE'S WHISTLE

²**whet** \"\ *n* -S **1** *dial* **a :** a spell of work between two whettings of the scythe : TURN **b :** TIME, WHILE ⟨I'll bear it this ~ —Charlotte Brontë⟩ ⟨stood talking a long ~⟩ **2 :** something that sharpens or makes keen (as desire or appetite): **a :** GOAD, INCITEMENT ⟨gave a ~ to his revenge⟩ **b :** APPETIZER ⟨gives our wish for blue a ~ —Robert Frost⟩; *esp* : a drink of liquor : APERITIF ⟨the beery breath of a ~ . . . taken as he came along —Charles Dickens⟩

¹**wheth·er** \ˌ(h)weth̲ə(r) *also* (ˌ)(h)wəth̲-\ *pron* [ME, fr. OE *hwæther, hwether;* akin to OHG *hwedar* which of two, ON *hvārr,* Goth *hwathar,* L *uter,* Gk *poteros,* Skt *katara;* all fr. a prehistoric IE compound pronoun formed from the root of the pronoun represented by Skt *ka* who by the addition of a comparative suffix *-ter-* — more at WHO] **1** *archaic* : which one of the two : ²WHICH 1a ⟨~ of them twain did the will of his father —Mt 21:31 (AV)⟩ ⟨might get a great deal or a little, we did not know ~ —Daniel Defoe⟩ **2** *archaic* : whichever one of the two : ¹WHICHEVER ⟨put it into . . . glasses or pots, ~ you have —Eliza Moxon⟩

²**whether** \"\ *adj* [ME, fr. OE *hwæther, hwether,* fr. *hwæther, hwether,* pron.] **1** *obs* : being which one of the two : ¹WHICH 1a ⟨the dispute ~ life is to be preferred, the active or the contemplative —Henry Dodwell⟩ **2** *obs* : being whichever one of the two : ²WHICHEVER

³**whether** \"\ *conj* [ME, fr. OE *hwæther, hwether,* fr. *hwæther, hwether,* pron.] **1 —** used as a function word followed usu. by correlative *or* or by *or whether* to indicate (1) until the early 19th century a direct question involving alternatives ⟨~ does doubting consist in embracing the affirmative or negative side of a question —George Berkeley⟩; (2) an indirect question involving alternatives ⟨hard to decide ~ he should agree or ~ he should raise certain objections⟩ ⟨the question as to ~ a man is really the best judge of his own life work or not —T.H. Savory⟩ ⟨compelled to doubt ~ universal schooling will suffice to curb our evil instincts —A.L.Guérard⟩; (3) alternative conditions or possibilities ⟨a material form, ~ animate or inanimate —J.G.Frazer⟩ ⟨I was of two minds ~ to go or stay —Helen Eustis⟩ ⟨passing judgment on ~ or not a given school was performing satisfactorily —J.B.Conant⟩ ⟨see me no more, ~ he be dead or no —Shak.⟩ ⟨the undergraduate, ~ he be a concentrator in the sciences, the humanities, or the social sciences —*General Education in a Free Society*⟩ **2 :** EITHER — used with correlative *or* ⟨aimed to win ~ by hook or crook⟩ ⟨seated him next to her ~ by accident or design⟩ **3** *obs* : WHEREVER, IF ⟨charity never faileth: but ~ there be prophecies, they shall fail —1 Cor 13:8 (AV)⟩

⁴**wheth·er** \ˈhwet̲h̲ə(r) *also* ˈw| *or* |ət̲h̲-\ *n* -S : a choice between alternatives ⟨considering all the whys and ~*s* of the matter⟩

whether or no *also* **whether or not** *adv* : in any case : WILLY-NILLY ⟨I will go *whether or no*⟩ ⟨obliged to take the stranger by the hand *whether or not* and show him civilities —Mark Twain⟩

whetrock \ˈ=,=\ *n, South* : WHETSTONE

whet slate *n* : a variety of slate used for sharpening cutting instruments

whetstone \ˈ=,=\ *n* [ME *whetston,* fr. OE *hwetstān,* fr. *hwettan* to whet + *stān* stone] **1 :** a natural or artificial stone for whetting edge tools ⟨a blade sharpened on a well-oiled ~⟩ **2 :** something that sharpens, makes keen, or stimulates ⟨as the wit or the appetite⟩ ⟨the dullness of the fool is the ~ of the wits —Shak.⟩

whetted *past of* WHET

whet·ten \-etᵊn\ *vt* -ED/-ING/-S [irreg. fr. ¹*whet* + *-en,* v. suffix] : WHET

whet·ter \-ed·ə(r)\ *n* -S : one that whets ⟨a ~ of scythes⟩ ⟨a ~ of the appetite⟩

whetting *pres part of* WHET

¹**whew** \ˈ(h)wü, ˈhyü\ *vi* -ED/-ING/-S [ME *whewen,* of imit. origin] **1 :** to make a whistling noise : WHISTLE ⟨the soft ~*ing* of the cranes flying overhead —Lawrence Durrell⟩ **2 :** to utter an exclamatory whew ⟨he ~*ed* with relief when they all got safely over —J.T.Farrell⟩ **3** *dial* : to move quickly : bustle about

²**whew** \", *as an exclamation a whistling sound consisting typically of* k *followed by voiceless* ü *or of voiceless* ue *preceded by a rounding of the lips & followed by voiceless* ü\ *n* -S **1 :** a whistling sound ⟨the ~ of the plover⟩ ⟨the ~ of lead still singing in their ears —Thomas Carlyle⟩ **2 :** a sound like a half-formed whistle uttered as an exclamation ⟨gave a long ~ when he realized the size of the job⟩ — used interjectionally chiefly to express amazement, discomfort, or relief ⟨~! never have I seen such flying feet —Arnold Bennett⟩ ⟨~, it's hot here⟩ ⟨~, that was a close call⟩

whew duck *n, dial Brit* : WIDGEON 1a(1)

whew·ell·ite \ˈhyüə,līt\ *n* -S [William *Whewell* †1866 Eng. philosopher + E *-ite*] : a mineral $CaC_2O_4.H_2O$ consisting of calcium oxalate occurring in colorless or white monoclinic crystals polymorphous with weddellite

whew·er \ˈ(h)wüə(r), ˈhyü-\ *n* -S [⁵*whew* + *-er*] *dial Eng* : WIDGEON 1a

whewl \ˈ(h)wül\ *vi* -ED/-ING/-S [imit.] *dial Eng* : to cry complainingly : WHINE, HOWL

¹**whey** \ˈhwā *also* ˈwā\ *n* -S [ME, fr. OE *hwæg;* akin to MD *wey* whey, *hoy* whey, MLG *hoie,* and perh. to L *caseus* cheese — more at CHEESE] : the serum or watery part of milk containing sugar, minerals, and lactalbumin that is separated from the thicker or more coagulable part or curd esp. in the process of making cheese

²**whey** \"\ *vb* -ED/-ING/-S *vt* : to cause whey to separate from (milk or buttermilk) ~ *vi* : to separate in the form of whey

³**whey** \"\ *adj* **1 :** of or relating to whey ⟨~ powder⟩ ⟨~ butter⟩ **2 :** resembling whey (as in consistency or color) : WATERY, PALE ⟨a sprig . . . with a ~ face and a satchel —Sir Walter Scott⟩

whey·ey \-āē\ *adj* [¹*whey* + *-y*] : consisting of, containing, or resembling whey : WHEYISH

whey-face \ˈ=,=\ *n* : a person having a pale face (as from fear) : WEAKLING ⟨thou lily-liver'd boy . . . *whey-face* —Shak.⟩

whey-faced \ˈ=,=\ *adj* : having a face suggestive of whey : PALE, PALLID ⟨straggled . . . in little processions, *whey-faced,* thin, ragged —Jan Struther⟩

whey·ish \-āish\ *adj* : somewhat like whey — **whey·ish·ness** *n* -ES

whf *abbr* wharf

whfg *abbr* wharfage

whge *abbr* wharfage

¹**which** \(ˌ)hwich, (ˌ)wich\ *adj* [ME, which, of what kind, fr. OE *hwilc;* akin to OHG *wilīh* which, of what kind, OSw *hvilkin* of what kind, Goth *hwileiks;* all fr. a prehistoric Gmc compound whose first constituent is akin to OE *hwā* who and whose second constituent is represented by OE *gelīc* like — more at WHO, LIKE] **1 a :** being what one or ones out of a group — used as an interrogative adjective in direct or indirect questions ⟨~ tie should I wear with this shirt⟩ ⟨deciding ~ candidate he is going to vote for⟩ ⟨kept a record of ~ employees took their vacations in July and ~ ones in August⟩ **b** *obs* : ³WHAT 1a (1) ⟨from ~ lord to ~ lady —Shak.⟩ **2 :** ²WHICHEVER ⟨it will not fit, turn it ~ way you like⟩ **3 —** used as a function word to introduce a nonrestrictive relative clause and to modify a noun in that clause and to refer together with that noun to a word or word group in a preceding clause or to an entire preceding clause or sentence or longer unit of discourse ⟨that a new currency should be made ready for any possible emergency, ~ currency would . . . be available for immediate use —Jack Bennett⟩ ⟨the word occurs as a Yiddish loan in German, ~ language might thus have been the medium of transmission —Thomas Pyles⟩ ⟨a licensed practitioner of medicine of the state of Tennessee, ~ practitioner must also sign the prescription —*Bull. of Meharry Med. Coll.*⟩ ⟨that this city is a rebellious city . . . : for ~ cause was this city destroyed —Ezra 4:15 (AV)⟩ ⟨Abraham had two sons, the one by a bondmaid, the other by a free woman. But he who was of the bondwoman was born after the flesh; but he of the free woman was by promise. *Which* things are an allegory —Gal 4:22–4 (AV)⟩; sometimes used archaically with preceding *the* ⟨I am appointed a preacher, and an apostle, and a teacher of the Gentiles. For the ~ cause I also suffer these things —2 Tim 1:11–12 (AV)⟩

²**which** \"\ *pron* [ME, fr. OE *hwilc,* fr. *hwilc,* adj., which, of what kind] **1 a :** what one or ones out of a group — used as an interrogative pronoun in direct or indirect questions ⟨~ of those houses do you live in⟩ ⟨~ of you want tea and ~ want lemonade⟩ ⟨he asked ~ he should take⟩ ⟨he is down at the lake swimming or canoeing, I don't know ~⟩ **b :** ¹WHAT 1a(1) — used as recently as the 17th century in questions of regular syntactical form containing a verb with a subject that may or may not be *which* itself ⟨I have many ill qualities. *Which* is one —Shak.⟩; used dialectally by itself to ask for repetition of an utterance not properly heard or understood; sometimes used in informal speech in connection with other words to ask for repetition or explanation of the particular part of an utterance that has not been properly heard or understood ⟨he said he wanted a ~⟩ **2 :** ¹WHICHEVER ⟨take ~ you like⟩ **3 —** used as a function word to introduce a restrictive or nonrestrictive relative clause and to serve as a substitute within that clause for the substantive modified by that clause; used in any grammatical relation within the relative clause except that of a possessive; used esp. in reference to animals, inanimate objects, groups, or ideas ⟨fish ~ are dangerous at some particular time of the year —Margaret Mead⟩ ⟨grapefruit juice . . . sweetened to improve its palatability for the rats, ~ would not otherwise drink it —Henry Hicks⟩ ⟨the bonds ~ represent the debt —G.B.Robinson⟩ ⟨the kind of . . . church ~ you would expect a decent body of merchants to erect —Douglas Goldring⟩ ⟨a generation ~ had been taught . . . to appreciate the beauty of simplicity —Bernard Groom⟩ ⟨they form the Samnite tribes, ~ settled south and southeast of Rome —Ernst Pulgram⟩ ⟨some of the difficulties ~ must be guarded against —*Eastman Kodak Monthly Abstract Bull.*⟩ ⟨new problems arose, the investigation of ~ would necessitate additional material —Robert Balk⟩; used freely in reference to persons as recently as the 17th century ⟨our Father ~ art in heaven —Mt 6:9 (AV)⟩, and still occas. so used ⟨a human ~ . . . would unhesitatingly sacrifice a score of opossums for a real scientific need —William Beebe⟩ ⟨think of the children ~ are threatened —H.R.Hays⟩ but usu. with some implication of emphasis on the function or role of the person rather than on the person himself ⟨the Republican presidential electors ~ we had chosen at the state convention —W.A.White⟩ ⟨chiefly they wanted husbands, ~ they got easily —Lynn White⟩; used by speakers on all educational levels and by many reputable writers, though disapproved by some grammarians, in reference to an idea expressed by a word or group of words that is not necessarily a noun or noun phrase ⟨the attitude is . . . that failure to publish is tantamount to suppression, ~ of course it isn't —R.H.Rovere⟩ or in reference to a clause or sentence ⟨in August of that year he resigned that post, after ~ he engaged in ranching —*Current Biog.*⟩ ⟨I have forgotten them now. *Which* makes no difference —W.A.White⟩; sometimes used parenthetically in reference to a clause that is yet to come or is not yet complete ⟨yours is the earth and everything that's in it, and — ~ is more — you'll be a man —Rudyard Kipling⟩ ⟨the demonstrated — ~ was indeed the truth — that the days of capitalism were numbered —Christopher Hollis⟩; used regularly to introduce a restrictive relative clause having as its antecedent the demonstrative pronoun *that* ⟨ultimate truth still remains in that outside world of that ~ is —Weston La Barre⟩; sometimes used archaically with preceding *the* ⟨this time of long silence, of reverie, in the ~ . . . his eyes were placidly shut —Maurice Hewlett⟩; sometimes used after *so* or *such* with the implication that the action or state expressed in the clause introduced by *which* is a real or appropriate consequence of what is expressed by the phrase containing *so* or *such* ⟨there is not any argument so absurd, ~ is not daily received —Jeremy Bentham⟩ ⟨there rooted betwixt them then such an affection ~ cannot choose but branch now —Shak.⟩; sometimes used dialectally with a following personal pronoun or possessive adjective referring to the same antecedent ⟨she had a big something under her arm ~ I couldn't make out what it was —Helen Eustis⟩ ⟨the man ~ his head was cut off —*Western Folklore*⟩; occasionally used dialectally as a word that merely introduces a clause or sentence and has no reference to any expressed or implied antecedent ⟨~ we had a small game —Bret Harte⟩; compare ⁴THAT 1, WHO, WHOSE, ¹WHAT 3a — **which is which** *or* **which was which :** what is or was the distinct and esp. nameable identity of each member of a group — used as a direct or indirect question ⟨those two fellows are the Jones brothers, John and William, but *which is which*⟩ ⟨so many kings of France named Louis that I can hardly remember *which was which*⟩

whichaway \ˈ==,=\ *dial var of* WHICHWAY

¹**which·ev·er** \(h)wiˈchevə(r)\ *pron* [ME *which ever,* fr. ²*which* + *ever*] : whatever one or ones out of a group : no matter which one or ones ⟨would like to speak to your father or your mother, ~ is at home⟩ ⟨take two of the four elective subjects, ~ you prefer⟩ ⟨enter law or some other profession, but ~ you choose, put your whole heart into it⟩

²**whichever** \"\ *adj* : being whatever one or ones out of a group : no matter which ⟨walk . . . back to ~ chair he happened to be using at the time —Grace Metalious⟩ ⟨a general reserve fund out of which additional advertising money could be drawn to back ~ books need it —*Publishers' Weekly*⟩ ⟨its soothing . . . effect will be the same ~ way you take it —*Punch*⟩

¹**which·so·ev·er** \ˌhwichsəˈwevə(r), -sōˈe- *also* ˌwi-\ *pron* [ME, *which so* whichever (fr. ²*which* + *so*) + *ever*] : WHICHEVER

²**whichsoever** \"\ *adj* : WHICHEVER

whichway *also* **whichways** \ˈ=,=\ *adv* **1** *dial* : WHERE ⟨~ is he⟩ **2 :** EVERY WHICH WAY ⟨leaving her towel and brush and comb lying ~ —W.D.Edmonds⟩

¹**whick·er** \ˈhwikə(r) *also* ˈwi- *also* **wick·er** \ˈwi-\ *vi* -ED/-ING/-S [imit.] : NEIGH, WHINNY ⟨horses . . . pawed, and ~*ed* —John Masefield⟩

²**whicker** \"\ *n* -S : NEIGH, WHINNY

¹**whid** \ˈ(h)wid\ *n* -S [origin unknown] **1** *Brit* : WORD **2** *Scot* : LIE

²**whid** \"\ *n* -S [perh. of Scand origin; akin to ON *hvitha* squall of wind — more at WHITHER] *Scot* : a silent rapid motion

³**whid** \"\ *vi, Scot* : to move nimbly and silently

whidah *var of* WHYDAH

whiel·don ware \ˈ(h)wēldən-\ *n, usu cap 1st W* [after Thomas Whieldon †1795 Eng. potter] : a fine English ceramic ware produced by Thomas Whieldon (1719–95) at his Staffordshire pottery and often characterized by marbleized and tortoise-shell effects

¹**whiff** \ˈhwif *also* ˈwif\ *n* -S [imit.] **1 a** (1) : a quick puff or slight gust of air ⟨the wind came in ~*s* —Wallace Stegner⟩ (2) : a puff, gust, or wave of odor ⟨wafted a feline ~ —David Walker⟩ (3) : a puff or small cloud of vapor, gas, or liquid in the air ⟨a ~ of smoke hangs over a sleeping volcano —Richard Church⟩ ⟨~*s* of spray from the fountain —Lawrence Durrell⟩ **b** (1) : an inhalation of odor, smoke, gas, or vapor ⟨she went off at the first ~ of ether —O.S.J.Gogarty⟩ (2) *obs* : a drink or sip of liquor **c :** a slight puffing or whistling sound ⟨the almost inaudible ~ of his spread wings —Saul Bellow⟩ **2 :** a slight trace or sample : INTIMATION, HINT ⟨his unerring detection of the faintest ~ of sentiment —H.J.Muller⟩ ⟨there is more than a ~ of propaganda —Richard Mallett⟩

²**whiff** \"\ *vb* -ED/-ING/-S *vi* **1 :** to move with or as if with a puff of air; *also* : to make or produce a puffing or whistling sound **2 :** to emit whiffs : PUFF **3 :** to inhale an odor : engage in sniffing **4 :** FAN 4 ~ *vt* **1 a :** to carry or convey by or as if by a whiff : BLOW ⟨the storm . . . ~*ed* smoke and ashes into their faces —Isak Dinesen⟩ **b :** to expel or puff out in a whiff : EXHALE **c :** SMOKE 3a **2 :** to cause (a batter) to fan in baseball or softball : strike out

³**whiff** \"\ *n* -S [origin unknown] : any of several flatfishes related to the turbot; *esp* : a small European fish (*Lepidorhombus megastoma*)

whif·fet \ˈhwifət *also* ˈwi-\ *n* -S [prob. alter. of *whippet*] **1 :** a very small dog **2 :** a small, young, or unimportant person : WHIPPERSNAPPER

¹**whif·fle** \ˈhwifəl *also* ˈwi-\ *vb* **whiffled; whiffled; whiffling** \-f(ə)liŋ\ **whiffles** [prob. fr. ²*whiff* + *-le*] *vi* **1 a** *of the wind* : to blow unsteadily or in gusts **b** (1) : FLICKER, FLUTTER (2) : to change from one course or opinion to another as if blown by the wind : be fickle : VACILLATE **2 a :** to emit or produce a light whistling or puffing sound **b :** to flourish a sword in sword dancing so as to produce a whistling sound ~ *vt* **1 :** to blow, disperse, emit, or expel with or as if with a whiff **2 :** to flourish (a sword) in sword dancing so as to produce a whiffling sound

²**whiffle** \"\ *n* -S : the action, motion, or sound of whiffling

¹**whif·fler** \ˈ(h)wif(ə)lə(r)\ *n* -S [alter. of earlier *wifler,* fr. obs. E *wifle* battle-ax (fr. ME, fr. OE *wifel* dart, javelin) + E *-er;* akin to ON *veifa* to wave — more at WIFE] *Brit* : one that clears the way for a procession

²**whif·fler** \ˈhwif(ə)lə(r) *also* ˈwi-\ *n* -S [¹*whiffle* + *-er*] **1 :** one that frequently changes his opinion or course **2 :** one that uses shifts and evasions in argument

whif·fle·tree \ˈhwifəl(ˌ)trē, -ˌtri *also* ˈwi-\ *or* **whip·ple·tree** \-ipəl-\ *n* [*whiffletree* alter. of *whippletree,* fr. *whipple-* (perh. irreg. fr. *whip*) + *tree*] : the pivoted swinging bar to which the traces of a harness are fastened and by which a vehicle or implement is drawn — called also *singletree, swingletree;* compare DOUBLETREE

¹**whig** \ˈ(h)wig\ *n* -S [origin unknown] *Scot* : any of various elements or products of milk; *esp* : WHEY

²**whig** \ˈhwig *also* ˈwig\ *n* -S *usu cap* [short for *whiggamore*] **1 :** a Presbyterian or Covenanter in Scotland in the 17th century — compare TRUE BLUE **2 :** one favoring the exclusion in 1679–80 of the Duke of York from the line of succession to the British throne principally because of his Roman Catholicism — usu. used disparagingly; opposed to *Tory* **3 :** a member or supporter of the Whig party in British politics **4 :** an American favoring colonial interests and esp. independence from Great Britain during the American Revolution — opposed to *Tory* **5 :** a member or supporter of the Whig party in American politics

³**whig** \"\ *adj, usu cap* **1 :** of, relating to, or characterized by Whiggery: as **a :** of, relating to, or constituting one of the two major British political groups of the 18th and early 19th cen-

turies arising from the Roundheads and associated chiefly at first with support of the Hanoverians but later with efforts to limit the royal authority and increase parliamentary power and with preference for Dissenters rather than the established Anglican church — compare CONSERVATIVE 2b(1), KING'S FRIENDS, LIBERAL 5d(1), RADICAL 3c(1), TORY a **b :** of, relating to, or constituting a major 19th century American political party arising about 1834 from the National Republicans and other groups opposed to the Jacksonian Democrats and associated chiefly with manufacturing, commercial, and financial interests, a protective tariff, a national government public works program, and opposition to a strong presidency until succeeded about 1854 by the Republican party **2 :** favoring, belonging to, or composed of members of a Whig party or group ⟨*Whig* candidates⟩ ⟨*Whig* platform⟩

⁴whig \'(h)wig\ *vi* **whigged; whigged; whigging; whigs** [perh. fr. ²*whig*] *Scot* **:** to move steadily on **:** jog along

whig·ga·more \'(h)wigə,mō(ə)r\ *n* -s *usu cap* [perh. irreg. fr. obs. E dial. *whig* yokel, rustic, perh. fr. E ¹*whig*] **1 :** a member of a band composed largely of inhabitants of the southwestern part of Scotland that in 1648 marched to Edinburgh to oppose the king, Duke of Hamilton, and court party **2 :** ²WHIG 1

whig·gery \'hwigərē, -ri *also* 'wi-\ *n* -ES *usu cap* **1 :** the principles, policies, and practices of or associated with Whigs ⟨American Liberalism . . . smacks more of eighteenth-century *Whiggery* —*Manchester Guardian Weekly*⟩ **2 :** a Whig party or its members ⟨sympathize with the low-churchmen of *Whiggery* —D.P.French⟩

whig·gi·fy \-gə,fī\ *vt* -ED/-ING/-ES *sometimes cap* **:** to make Whig **:** influence by Whig principles or policies

whig·gish \-gish, -gēsh\ *adj, sometimes cap* **:** of, relating to, or having the characteristics of a Whig **:** inclined toward Whiggery ⟨~ principles⟩

whig·gish·ly *adv, often cap* **:** in a whiggish manner ⟨persons . . . ~ inclined —Narcissus Luttrell⟩

whig·gism *or* **whig·ism** \'hwi,gizəm *also* 'wi,-\ *n* -s *usu cap* **:** WHIGGERY 1

whig·ling \-,gliŋ\ *n* -s *usu cap* **:** a petty Whig

whig·ma·lee·rie *also* **whig·ma·lee·ry** \hwigmə'lirē, -ri *also* ,wig-\ *n, pl* **whigmaleeries** [origin unknown] **1 :** WHIM, VAGARY, FANCY ⟨shy fellow full of caprice and ~ —*Life*⟩ **2 :** an odd or fanciful contrivance **:** GIMCRACK, NOTION ⟨producing gadgets, gimmicks, fizgigs, and ~s for Latin-American consumption —Alva Johnston⟩

¹while \'hwīl, *esp before pause or consonant* -īəl; *also* 'wī-\ *n* -s [ME *whil, while,* fr. OE *hwīl;* akin to OHG *hwīla* time, while, ON *hvīla* bed, Goth *hweila* time, while, L *quies* rest, quiet, OSlav *pokojĭ* rest] **1 a :** a period of time **:** TIME ⟨any critic may after a ~ exhaust his interest in a subject —C.W.Shumaker⟩ ⟨takes us quite a ~ to find out —Sean O'Faolain⟩ **b :** the time during which an action takes place or a condition exists ⟨looking here and there and calling his name, though I knew all the ~ it was too late —Mary Webb⟩ ⟨went to her herb garden for her seasonings . . . and thus preserved the health of her family, the ~ she saved her purse —Van Wyck Brooks⟩ **c :** the time at which an event takes place **:** a time marked by the occurrence of an action or a condition **:** OCCASION ⟨one ~, it seems, he trapped in the . . . mountains —J.F.Dobie⟩ ⟨were ~s when I was terrible bored —John Buchan⟩ **d :** a relatively short period of time **:** a brief time ⟨if you've been reading this book for over an hour, you'd better put it aside for a ~ —W.J.Reilly⟩ ⟨went away and came back again in a ~ —Pearl Buck⟩ **e :** the period of time needed (as for the performance of an action) ⟨a breathing ~ —Shak.⟩ **f** *archaic* **:** a time marked by bad conditions ⟨God help the ~ —Shak.⟩ **2 :** the time and effort used (as in the performance of an action) **:** TROUBLE, EXERTION ⟨aesthetic matters are important, and . . . it is worth the ~ of a healthy male to take them seriously —H.L.Mencken⟩ ⟨knew all the right people too because it was worth their ~ to know him —J.P.Marquand⟩

²while \"\ *conj* [ME *whil, while,* fr. *whil, while,* n.] **1 a :** during the time that ⟨instructed and encouraged the boy ~ he made an almost incredible . . . record of precocity —Alexander Cowie⟩ ⟨were killed ~ attempting a burglary —A.F.Harlow⟩ **b :** until the end of the time that **:** as long as ⟨~ there's life there's hope⟩ **c :** during which time **:** and during the same time **:** and meanwhile ⟨hurried to get ready ~ the others just sat⟩ **2** *archaic* **:** UNTIL ⟨~ hunger make you eat —Christopher Marlowe⟩ **3 a :** at the same time that on the contrary **:** when on the other hand **:** WHEREAS ⟨for many people a line of ten words requires perhaps eight fixations, ~ a good reader can grasp half a line as a unit —Russell Cosper & Barriss Mills⟩ ⟨~ her book shows the uneven hand of a novice at writing, it frequently stops the reader by its poetic simplicity —Rose Feld⟩ **b :** in spite of the fact that **:** ALTHOUGH ⟨~ the evidence he has obtained may be said to fit the theory, the importance of some of it is questionable —*Notes & Queries*⟩ ⟨~ a magnificent organizer of espionage, he was a poor observer himself —Allen Upward⟩ **4 :** at the same time that in a similar manner **:** when correspondingly **:** and also ⟨~ the book will be welcomed by scholars, it will make an immediate appeal to the general reader —*Brit. Bk. News*⟩ ⟨wild grapes grow in profusion along the sides of back roads, ~ blackberries and wild raspberries are common —*Amer. Guide Series: N.H.*⟩

³while \"\ *prep* [ME *whil,* fr. *whil, while,* n.] *archaic* **:** UNTIL ⟨~ then, God be with you —Shak.⟩

⁴while \"\ *vb* -ED/-ING/-s [¹*while*] *vt* **:** to cause to pass esp. without boredom or in a pleasant manner — usu. used with *away* ⟨*whiled* away the tedium of debate by drawing caricatures —Dumas Malone⟩ ⟨may ~ away the time tootling on his recorder —*Newsweek*⟩ **~** *vi, archaic* **:** to pass tediously — **whil·er** \-lə(r)\ *n* -s

whileas \(')⸗'⸗\ *conj, archaic* **:** WHILE

whilere \(')⸗'⸗\ *adv* [ME *whileer,* fr. OE *hwīle ǣr,* fr. *hwīle* formerly, once (fr. *hwīle,* accus. of *hwīl* time, while) + *ǣr* early, earlier — more at ERE] *archaic* **:** a while ago **:** some time before

¹whiles \'hwī(ə)lz *also* 'wī-\ *conj* [ME, fr. *whil, while,* conj., while + -*es,* gen. sing. ending of nouns (functioning adverbially) — more at -s] **1** *archaic* **:** WHILE 1 **2** *obs* **:** UNTIL ⟨he shall conceal it ~ you are willing it shall come to note —Shak.⟩ **3** *obs* **:** WHILE 3a

²whiles \"\ *n* [ME, fr. -*whiles* (as in *otherwhiles*) — more at OTHERWHILE] *archaic* **:** WHILE 1a, 1b, 1c, 1d

³whiles \"\ *adv* [ME(Sc) *quhilis* at times, formerly, fr. ME(Sc) *quhile,* ME *while* at times, formerly (fr. OE *hwīle* formerly, once) + ME(Sc) -*is,* ME -*es,* gen. sing. ending of nouns (functioning adverbially)] *chiefly Scot* **:** at times **:** from time to time **:** SOMETIMES ⟨we read your things in the paper, and we ~ read about you —John Buchan⟩

whil·ie *also* **whiley** \'(h)wīli\ *n* [¹*while* + -*ie*] *Scot* **:** a little while

¹whilk \'(h)wilk\ *chiefly Scot var of* WHICH

²whilk \"\ *archaic var of* WHELK

whil·kut \'hwīl,küt *also* 'wī-\ *n, pl* **whilkut** *or* **whilkuts** *usu cap* **1 :** an Athapaskan people of the Mad river valley in northwestern California **2 :** a member of the Whilkut people

whil·la·bal·loo \'(h)wiləbə,lü\ *Scot & Irish var of* HULLABALOO

whil·la·loo *also* **whil·la·luh** *or* **whil·li·lew** \'(h)wilə,lü\ *n* [IrGael *uile liūgh*] *dial Brit* **:** HULLABALOO

whil·li·kers \'(h)wilikə(r)z, -lēk-\ *or* **whil·li·kins** \-kənz\ *interj* [origin unknown] **:** ⁶GEE

whil·ly \'(h)wili\ *vt* [prob. irreg. fr. ¹*whillywha*] *Scot* **:** CAJOLE, WHEEDLE, GULL

¹whil·ly·wha *also* **whil·ly·whaw** \'(h)wili,(h)wȯ\ *n* -s [origin unknown] **1** *Scot* **:** a deceitful flatterer **2** *chiefly Scot* **:** a coaxing deceitful speech — usu. used in pl.

²whillywha \"\ *vt, Scot* **:** to dupe by flattering **:** WHEEDLE, CAJOLE **~** *vi, Scot* **:** to talk in a coaxing manner

¹whi·lom \'hwīləm *also* 'wī-\ *adv* [ME, formerly, at times, fr. OE *hwīlum* at times, dat. pl. of *hwīl* time, while — more at WHILE] *archaic* **:** at a time in the past **:** FORMERLY, ONCE

²whilom \"\ *adj* [ME, fr. *whilom,* adv.] **:** having been at an earlier time **:** FORMER ⟨the poor gentleman had grievous treatment at the hands of his ~ friends —Agnes Repplier⟩

¹whilst \'hwī(ə)lst *also* 'wī-\ *conj* [ME *whilest,* alter. of ¹*whiles*] **1** *chiefly Brit* **:** WHILE 1, 3, 4 **2** *archaic* **:** UNTIL

²whilst \"\ *n* [ME (northern dial.) *quilest,* fr. ME (northern dial.) *quilest,* ME *whilest,* conj.] *archaic* **:** WHILE

¹whim \'hwim *also* 'wim\ *n* -s [short for *whim-wham*] **1** *archaic* **:** a fanciful or fantastic device, object, or creation **2 :** a capricious or eccentric idea, notion, or vagary usu. occurring suddenly or spontaneously **:** CAPRICE, FANCY ⟨every royal master had ~s of his own — antiquated prejudices, family ties, fragments of knowledge to which he attached exaggerated importance —A.J.P.Taylor⟩ ⟨the ~ struck him to become an army flier —Green Peyton⟩ ⟨a defense of reason against unreason, conviction against ~, knowledge against mere shifting mood-of-the-moment —Alan Devoe⟩ ⟨~s of nature⟩ ⟨~s of fate⟩ **3 a** *or* **whim gin** *also* **whin** \-in\ **:** a hoisting device esp. for raising ore or water from mines consisting of a large vertical drum on which a rope is wound with one or more radiating arms or beams to which a horse may be yoked — called also *whimsy* **b** *Austral* **:** a large jinker

²whim \"\ *vt* **whimmed; whimmed; whimming; whims :** to desire fancifully or capriciously

whim·brel *or* **wimbrel** \'(h)wimbrəl\ *n* -s [perh. imit.] **:** a European curlew (*Numenius phaeopus*) related and similar to the Hudsonian curlew of America

whim gin *n* **:** WHIM 3a

¹whim·per \'hwimpə(r) *also* 'wi-\ *vb* **whimpered; whimpered; whimpering** \-p(ə)riŋ\ **whimpers** [imit.] *vi* **1 a :** to make a low whining plaintive or broken sound ⟨had seen the old general ~ like a whipped dog —F.M.Ford⟩ **b :** to complain or protest with or in the manner of a whimper **:** WAIL, WHINE ⟨always coming around to ~ over his troubles⟩ ⟨knocking on the door to ~ for admission⟩ **2 :** to make a low plaintive murmuring sound ⟨the wind ~s in the aspens⟩ ⟨the tiny brook ~s softly through the stones and mosses⟩ **~** *vt* **:** to utter with or in a whimper ⟨they neither bray nor ~ nihilism; they prefer to fight —Charles Lee⟩ ⟨were forever ~*ing* that God had hidden his face from them —L.C.Douglas⟩

²whimper \"\ *n* -s **1 :** a low whining broken cry **:** a low peevish sound expressive of complaint or grief ⟨the baby continued to cry, but its cries . . . were little more than troubled ~s —Roark Bradford⟩ ⟨when the pack had been taken over half a dozen fields, there came a ~ and then a lifting chorus —E.J. Oates⟩ ⟨the moaning ~ of the tenor saxophone⟩ **2 :** a petulant or puling complaint or protest ⟨without even a ~ of protest from party headquarters —*Time*⟩ ⟨the old ~ of sterility that comes up in every decade —*New Statesman & Nation*⟩

whim·per·ing·ly *adv* [*whimpering* (pres. part. of ¹*whimper*) + -*ly*] **:** in a whimpering manner **:** with whimpering

whim·si·cal \'hwimzəkəl, -zēk- *also* 'wi-\ *adj* [¹*whimsy* + -*ical*] **1 :** full of, actuated by, or exhibiting whims **:** CAPRICIOUS, NOTIONAL, FANCIFUL ⟨although so sedate, she was also ~ and freakish —Virginia Woolf⟩ ⟨hard to tell when he was really peevish or merely ~ —W.L.Howard⟩ **2 a :** resulting from or determined or characterized by whim or caprice ⟨a glint of provocative, ~ fun in his blue eyes —Monica Pearson⟩ ⟨~ notions which indicate that reason is out of touch with the real —Marjorie Harris⟩ ⟨~, precarious, unlikely ventures —Audrey Barker⟩ ⟨~ evaluations of justice and equity . . . based on a purely social concept —*Current Biog.*⟩ ⟨many of these ~ creations seem to suffer from too much striving to be different —Betty Pepis⟩ **b :** subject to erratic behavior or unpredictable change **:** UNCERTAIN ⟨one cotton mill and a ~ power plant —Virginia A. Oakes⟩ ⟨a ~ market fluctuating according to world conditions⟩ ⟨the ~ moods of the Alpine sun —Claudia Cassidy⟩ — **whim·si·cal·ly** \-zək(ə)lē, -zēk-, -li\ *adv* — **whim·si·cal·ness** *n* -ES

whim·si·cal·i·ty \,hwimzə'kalədē, -lətē, -i *also* ,wi- *n* -ES **:** the quality or state of being whimsical **:** WHIMSICALNESS ⟨to liberate a small nation simply because one approves of it is mere ~ —Robert Lynd⟩

whim·sied \'hwimzēd, -zid *also* 'wim-\ *adj* **:** filled with whimsies **:** WHIMSICAL

¹whim·sy *or* **whim·sey** \-zē, -zi\ *n, pl* **whimsies** *or* **whimseys** [irreg. fr. *whim-wham*] **1 :** WHIM, CAPRICE, VAGARY ⟨applies the results of scientific knowledge . . . to satisfy material human needs and *whimsies* —I.I.Rabi⟩ ⟨our peculiar *whimseys,* prejudices, or intellectual limitations —M.R.Cohen⟩ ⟨carved by the ~ of ancient glaciers —*Christian Science Monitor*⟩ **2 :** a fanciful or fantastic device, object, or creation esp. in writing, art, or decoration ⟨can mix realism with an agreeable touch of poetry and fantasy that never degenerates into ~ —*Times Lit. Supp.*⟩ ⟨tells himself that myth is mere ~ having no relevance to human life —Richard Chase⟩ ⟨Victorian ~ returned . . . and glitter and embroidery replaced the lack of fabric trimming —*Fashion Digest*⟩ **3 :** WHIM 3a

²whimsy *or* **whimsey** \"\ *adj* **:** WHIMSICAL

whim·sy-wham·sy \-'(h)wamzē\ *n* -ES [redupl. of ¹*whimsy*] **:** WHIM-WHAM ⟨gremlins are . . . supposed to cause trouble such as engine failure in airplanes, a curious piece of *whimsy-whamsy* —Henry Alexander⟩ ⟨the theme of displaced war orphans . . . becomes here, in spite of shrewd descriptive touches, plain *whimsy-whamsy* —Sarah Campion⟩

whim-wham \'hwim,(h)wam, -aam *also* 'wi-\ *n* [origin unknown] **1 :** a whimsical object or device esp. of ornament or dress **:** TRIFLE, TRINKET ⟨a beret and a raffish tweed *whim-wham* —S.J.Perelman⟩ ⟨among the 16 *whim-whams* missing: . . . a pair of earrings —*Time*⟩ **2 :** NOTION, FANCY, WHIM ⟨these papers on society and its *whim-whams* or fads —E.W. Morse⟩ ⟨relish for personalities, gossips, *whim-whams* —S.T. Williams⟩ **3 whim-whams** *also* **wim-wams** *pl* **:** JIMJAMS, JITTERS ⟨took barbiturates to kill the *whim-whams* —G.V. Jones⟩ ⟨that job would have given me the *whim-whams* for a month —Howard Greig⟩

¹whin \'hwin *also* 'win\ *n* -s [ME (northern dial.) *quin,* of unknown origin] **:** a particularly hard rock; *esp* **:** one that on weathering cumbers the ground with large fragments **:** WHINSTONE

²whin \"\ *n* -s [ME *whynne,* of Scand origin; akin to Sw *ven* bent grass, Norw *kvein* bent grass, Sw dial. *hven* swamp — more at OBSCENE] **1 :** FURZE **2 :** WOODWAXEN

³whin *var of* WHIM

whin·berry \'⸗-\ — *see* BERRY\ *n* [alter. (influenced by ²*whin*) of earlier *winberry,* fr. ME *wynneberie,* fr. OE *wīnberige* whortleberry, grape — more at WINEBERRY] *dial Eng* **:** WHORTLEBERRY 1

whinchat \'⸗,⸗\ *n* [²*whin* + *chat*] **:** a small European saxicoline bird (*Saxicola rubetra*) that is mottled brown and buff above and buff below with white markings on the wings and above and below the eyes and that is usu. found in grassy meadows

whin·dle \'(h)wind³l\ *vi* [freq. of ¹*whine*] *dial chiefly Eng* **:** WHINE, WHIMPER

¹whine \'hwīn *also* 'wīn\ *vb* -ED/-ING/-S [ME *whinen,* fr. OE *hwīnan* to whiz; akin to ON *hvīna* to whiz and perh. to OSlav *svistati* to hiss] *vi* **1 a :** to utter a high-pitched plaintive or distressed cry ⟨hearing the dog ~ at the door⟩ ⟨tossing and turning, the child ~s in its sleep⟩ **b :** to make a sound similar to such a cry ⟨the saws buzz and ~ —*Amer. Guide Series: Maine*⟩ ⟨sirens *whined* loud and clear —*Springfield (Mass.) Union*⟩ ⟨car starters ~ and trucks . . . rattle out —Marjory S. Douglas⟩ **c :** to move or proceed with the sound of a whine ⟨mosquitoes *whined* through the dark —Josephine Johnson⟩ ⟨the bullet *whined* over the heads of the boys —S.H.Holbrook⟩ ⟨a taxi *whined* through the streets —Walter Sorell & Denver Lindley⟩ ⟨the wind . . . *whined* and moaned through the rigging —Kenneth Roberts⟩ **2 :** to utter a complaint or lament with or as if with a whine ⟨is not a man to ~ and complain; he has too much spirit —Jane Austen⟩ ⟨~ about . . . her troubles —E.A.Weeks⟩ ⟨the counteraction of the doctrine of love when that pules and ~s —R.W.Emerson⟩ **~** *vt* **:** to utter or express with or as if with a whine ⟨the prisoner ~s his innocence⟩ ⟨~ the song in nasal tones⟩ ⟨~ their troubles to the world⟩

²whine \"\ *n* -s **1 a :** a prolonged high-pitched cry usu. expressive of distress or pain ⟨weak, premature babies will cry with a low feeble ~ . . . like the mewing of a cat —Morris Fishbein⟩ ⟨the strange uncontrollable ~ of a man weeping —Graham Greene⟩ — compare WHIMPER **b :** a sound resembling such a cry ⟨the ~ of the wind and the hiss of the sleety snow —F.V.W. Mason⟩ ⟨the ~ of the saw biting into a log —*Amer. Guide Series: Ark.*⟩ ⟨the ~ and whistle of bombs —Peter Ustinov⟩ ⟨the high-pitched ~ of the engines —*London Calling*⟩ ⟨the ~ of the Hawaiian boy's guitar —Frances McFadden⟩ **2 :** a complaint or lament uttered with or as if with a whine ⟨wearied by the unremitting ~ of her special pleading —Dwight MacDonald⟩ ⟨if your letter is a gripe or ~, it will be brushed off —H.D.Scott⟩ ⟨the self-pitying ~ of most contemporary fiction —Selden Rodman⟩

whin·er \-nə(r)\ *n* -s **:** one that whines

whing \'hwiŋ *also* 'wiŋ\ *n* -s [imit.] **:** a sharp high-pitched ringing sound ⟨came the sustained ~ of a bullet that ricocheted somewhere near —Donald Stokes⟩ — sometimes used interjectionally

whing-ding \'(h)wiŋ,diŋ\ *var of* WINGDING

whinge \'(h)winj\ *vi* **whinged; whinged; whingeing** *also* **whinging; whinges** [fr. (assumed) ME (northern dial.) *whingen,* fr. OE *hwinsian;* akin to OHG *winsōn* to moan; derivative fr. the root of E ¹*whine*] *dial Brit* **:** WHINE, WHIMPER

whing·er \'(h)wiŋ(g)ə(r), -injə-\ *n* -s [by alter.] *chiefly Scot* **:** WHINYARD

whin·i·ness \'hwīnēnəs, -nin- *also* 'wī-\ *n* -ES **:** the quality or state of being whiny **:** QUERULOUSNESS

whin·ing·ly *adv* [*whining* (pres. part. of ¹*whine*) + -*ly*] **:** in a whining tone or manner ⟨the boards creaked ~ beneath their feet —Donn Byrne⟩

whin·ner \'hwinə(r) *also* 'wi-\ *vi* [freq. of ¹*whine*] **1** *dial* **:** to whine feebly **2** *dial* **:** WHINNY, WHICKER

whin·nock \'(h)winək\ *vi* [prob. irreg. fr. ¹*whine*] *dial Eng* **:** WHIMPER

¹whin·ny \'hwinē, -ni *also* 'wi-\ *adj* [ME *whynny,* fr. *whynne* whin + -*y*] *archaic* **:** abounding in gorse or furze

²whinny \"\ *vb* -ED/-ING/-ES [perh. irreg. fr. ¹*whine*] *vi* **:** to neigh esp. in a low or gentle fashion **:** WHICKER ⟨the white mares . . . *whinnied* and shook their bells —William Saroyan⟩ ⟨she was stepping high and *whinnied* to her old teammates of the wagon —Hervey Allen⟩ **~** *vt* **:** to utter with or as if with a whinny ⟨the horses ~ their greeting from the stalls⟩

³whinny \"\ *n* -ES **1 :** NEIGH, WHICKER ⟨a low ~ told her in what stall her horse would be —Elizabeth M. Roberts⟩ **2 :** a sound resembling a whinny **:** WHINE ⟨gave a kind of ~ between hysteria and indignation —Katherine A. Porter⟩ ⟨a clatter of machinery and the piercing ~ of old valves —John Cheever⟩

whins *pl of* WHIN

whinstone \'⸗,⸗\ *n* [¹*whin* + *stone*] **:** basaltic rock **:** TRAP; *also* **:** any of various other dark resistant rocks (as chert)

whiny *or* **whiney** \'hwīnē, -ni *also* 'wī-\ *adj* **whinier; whiniest :** WHINING, QUERULOUS ⟨people get rude and ~ and exacting when they are exhausted —Peggy Durdin⟩

whin·yard \'hwinyə(r)d *also* 'wi-\ *n* [ME *whyneherd, whyneard*] **:** a short sword

¹whip \'hw|ip *also* 'w|; *dial* |ùp *or* |əp\ *vb* **whipped; whipped; whipping; whips** [ME *wippen, whippen;* akin to MLG & MD *wippen* to move up and down, sway, swing, MHG *wipfen* to jump, leap, OE *wīpian* to wipe — more at WIPE] *vt* **1 a :** to take, pull, snatch, jerk or otherwise move very quickly and forcefully — usu. used with *out* ⟨*whipped* out his gun —Green Peyton⟩ ⟨*whipped* out an old tattered leather wallet —Irwin Shaw⟩ **b :** to throw or project with great speed ⟨*whipped* a fast ball across⟩ ⟨saw a rocket *whipped* into space —John Lardner⟩ **2 a :** to strike with a lash, rod, whip, or other slender lithe implement ⟨*whipped* Macleod across the face with his cane —Ian Finlay⟩ **:** to punish by beating **:** FLOG ⟨*whipped* for witchcraft —*Amer. Guide Series: Conn.*⟩; *broadly* **:** SPANK ⟨a tired child should never be *whipped*⟩ **b :** to drive with a whip **:** make go by or as if by using a whip **:** force or urge on ⟨*whipped* up the old mare —E.T.Thurston⟩ ⟨have to ~ themselves to their work —Ira Wolfert⟩ **c :** to make or bring out by or as if by striking with a whip ⟨the wind *whipped* tears in her eyes⟩ **d :** to strike as a lash does ⟨a brisk breeze *whipped* the surface of the river —C.S.Forester⟩ **3 a :** to bind or wrap (as a fishing rod) with twine or other small cord in order to protect and strengthen ⟨~ a rope⟩ **b :** to bind (a rope end) with sail twine or other small stuff in order to prevent fraying or unlaying **4 a :** to punish esp. with stinging words **:** make suffer **:** ABUSE ⟨they would ~ me with their fine wits —Shak.⟩ **b :** CONFOUND ⟨~ me such honest knaves —Shak.⟩ **5 :** to seam or hem with shallow overcasting stitches (as on gloves, napkins, lace) **6 :** to thoroughly overcome **:** DEFEAT ⟨they never knew when they were *whipped* —L.C.Douglas⟩ ⟨the crew is not out to ~ a rival boat —Frederick Way⟩ **7 :** to stir up **:** AROUSE, INCITE — usu. used with *up* ⟨deliberately trying to ~ up a new emotion —Ellen Glasgow⟩ ⟨*whipped* up his interest in radical causes —Ishbel Ross⟩ **8 :** to make or compose in or as if in an extemporaneous manner **:** produce in a hurry — usu. used with *up* ⟨a sketch . . . an artist might ~ up but not the actual blueprint —*N.Y.Times*⟩ **9 :** to fish (water) with rod, line, and artificial lure with a motion like that employed in using a whip **10 :** to beat (as eggs) usu. with a whisk, fork, or other instrument to increase volume by incorporation of air into the material ⟨*whipping* plastic⟩ **11 :** to gather together or hold together for united action in the manner of a party whip **~** *vi* **1 :** to move nimbly **:** start, turn, go or pass quickly or suddenly **:** WHISK ⟨*whipped* around the corner⟩ ⟨*whipping* through the supper dishes —C.B.Davis⟩ **2 :** to thrash about flexibly in the manner of a whiplash **:** SWISH ⟨a flag on shore is *whipping* out from its staff —H.A.Calahan⟩ **3 :** to fish by whipping the water — **whip into shape :** to bring forcefully to a desired state or condition ⟨could have been *whipped into shape* at a fraction of the cost of government study —C.B. Rawson⟩ — **whip the devil around the stump :** to effect by indirect means or by subterfuge what cannot be accomplished directly ⟨it was characteristic . . . that he could *whip the devil around the stump* yet really give him a whipping —G.W.Johnson⟩

²whip \"\ *n* -s [ME *wippe, whippe,* fr. *wippen, whippen,* v.] **1 a :** an instrument consisting usu. of a handle and lash forming a flexible rod that is used for whipping — see HORSEWHIP, RIDING WHIP

whip 4b

b : something that resembles or acts as a whip ⟨the wind had a ~ in it —J.B.Clayton⟩ ⟨more violent in their wielding of the ~ of scorn —F.B.Millett⟩ ⟨he will never be a ~ for any cause —Jean Burden⟩ **2 :** a stroke or cut with or as if with a whip ⟨a quick ~ of the eyes and he passed —D.M.Davin⟩ **3 a :** a plant (as a fruit tree) having one season's growth from the time of budding or grafting and usu. forming a simple unbranched shoot **b :** a tall slender tree unlikely to develop into a desirable crop tree and harmful to its neighbors by its swaying **4 a :** a dessert made by whipping a portion of the ingredients (as cream, whites of eggs, ice cream, or gelatine) **b :** a kitchen utensil made of braided or coiled wire or perforated metal with a handle and used in whipping cream, whites of eggs, or other materials **5 :** one of the arms of a windmill on which the sails are spread **6 a :** SINGLE WHIP **b :** DOUBLE WHIP **7 :** one that handles a whip: as **a :** a driver of horses **:** COACHMAN ⟨a noted ~ in those days of the stagecoach —H.C.Barnabee⟩ **b :** WHIPPER-IN 1 **8 :** an extra yarn in figure weaving not belonging to either warp or filling **9 a :** a member of a legislative body appointed by his political party to act as a liaison between the leaders and the other members of the party primarily to enforce party discipline and to secure the attendance of party members at important sessions esp. for voting **b** *sometimes cap* **:** a document received by a member of the British House of Commons from his political party that ~ recites the business to be taken in the following week —Herbert Morrison⟩ **10 :** WHIP-ROUND **11 a :** a whipping motion **:** a thrashing about ⟨the ~ of a snapped cable⟩ **b :** the transverse vibration of the muzzle end of long guns **c :** an unstable motion back and forth in a mechanical part (as a loose bearing) **12 :** the quality of being flexible **:** FLEXIBILITY, GIVE ⟨knobby canes with the ~ of whalebone and the toughness of steel —*Irish Digest*⟩ ⟨a racket frame that has too much ~ —Jack Kramer⟩ **13 :** any of various pieces that operate with a quick vibratory motion (as a spring in an electrical device for making a circuit or a rocking lever actuated by the prolong in a piano action) **14 :** an amusement device of cars which circle with sudden jerks **15 :** a short vertical antenna usu. used in mobile radio equipment consisting of a rod or streamlined stub similar in general appearance to a horsewhip

whipbird \'⸗,⸗\ *n* **:** COACHWHIP BIRD

whipcord \'⸗,⸗\ *n, often attrib* [ME *wippecord, whippecord,* fr. *wippe, whippe* whip + *cord*] **1 a :** a thin tough cord made of braided or twisted hemp or catgut often used for whips and whiplashes **b :** a twilled cloth made usu. of hard-twisted cotton or worsted yarns with fine diagonal cords or ribs on the face and used chiefly for sportswear, uniforms, and upholstery **2 :** either of two marine brown algae having very long slender flexible fronds: **a :** a seaweed (*Chorda filum*) of the order Laminariales **b :** a smaller seaweed (*Chordaria flagelliformis*) of the order Chordariales

whipcrack \'≈,≈\ *n* **:** the cracking of a whip; *also* **:** a sound resembling the crack of a whip ⟨the hollow rising hum of skis . . . ended in the tiny furious ~s of flapping pants as the jumper became airborne —*Newsweek*⟩

whip-cracker \'≈,≈≈\ *n* **:** one that cracks a whip **:** one whose position enables him to exact authority

whip crane *n* **:** a simple form of crane on the principle of the wheel and axle

whip eel *n* **:** an eel of the family Moringuidae

whip-ended \'≈,≈≈\ *adj, of an archery bow* **:** bending too much near the ends

whip graft *n* **1** *or* **whip and tongue graft :** a plant graft made by interlocking a small tongue and notch in the obliquely cut base of the scion with corresponding cuts in the stock — called also *tongue graft;* see GRAFT illustration **2 :** SPLICE GRAFT

whip grass *n* **:** an American nut rush (*Scleria triglomerata*) with stout angled stems and flat leaves

whip hand *n* **1 :** the hand holding the whip in driving **2 :** positive control **:** ADVANTAGE ⟨have been negotiating as if they had the *whip hand* —*N.Y.Times*⟩

whip hoist *n* **:** SINGLE WHIP

whip kick *n* **:** BREASTSTROKE KICK

¹whiplash \'≈,≈\ *n* [²*whip* + *lash*] **1 a :** the lash of a whip ⟨the lion trainer's ~ —E.B.White⟩ **b :** something resembling or thought to resemble a blow from a whip ⟨the ~ of fear or panic —R.S.Banay⟩ ⟨the ~ of inflation —E.O.Hauser⟩ **2 :** a flagellum having a long rigid basal portion and a short thin lash — compare FLIMMER, TINSEL

²whiplash \"\ *vt* **:** to flay with or as if with a whip ⟨~*ed* by that determination that distinguished him —B.P.Thomas⟩

whiplash injury *n* **:** injury of the cervical spine and cerebral concussion occurring in an automobile collision which causes forceful flexion or extension of the neck and violent oscillation of the head forward and backward or backward and forward

whiplike \'≈,≈\ *adj* **:** resembling a whip ⟨the ~ tail of the stingray⟩

whipmaster \'≈,≈≈\ *n* **:** one that uses a whip **:** one that exerts power and control

whip·pa·ree *also* **whip·pe·ree** \,hwipə'rē *also* ,wi-\ *n* -s [alter. of *whip ray*] **:** STINGRAY

whipped *adj* [fr. past part. of ¹*whip*] **1 :** subjected to whipping **2 :** beaten until light and frothy ⟨~ cream⟩ **3 :** beaten with or as if with a whip **:** BROKEN, DEFEATED ⟨the men . . . had the ~ look of vagabonds —Kenneth Roberts⟩

whip·per \'hwipə(r) *also* 'wi-\ *n* -s **:** one that whips

whipper-in \'≈≈'≈\ *n, pl* **whippers-in** [*whip in,* v. + *-er*] **1 a :** a huntsman's assistant who whips in the hounds **b :** one whose position is analogous to a huntsman's assistant **2 :** WHIP 9 **3 :** the last horse in a race

whip·per·snap·per \'hwipə(r),snapə(r) *also* 'wi-\ *n* [alter. (influenced by *whip*) of *snippersnapper*] **:** a diminutive, insignificant, or presumptuous person

whippertail \'≈≈,≈\ *n, NewEng* **:** a common smooth dogfish (*Mustelus canis*) of the western Atlantic

whip·pet \'hwipət *also* 'wi-; *usu* -əd·+V\ *n* -s [prob. fr. ¹*whip* (to move nimbly) + *-et*] **1 a** *obs* **:** a small dog **b :** a small swift slender dog of greyhound type developed in the north of England from a cross between the Italian greyhound and a terrier **2** *also* **whippet tank :** a small tank used in World War I by the Allied armies

whip·pi·ness \'hwipēnəs *also* 'wi-\ *n* -ES **:** the quality or state of being whippy

whipping *n* -s [fr. gerund of ¹*whip*] **1 :** the act of one that whips: as **a :** a severe beating or chastisement ⟨took the ~ without a murmur⟩ **b :** stitching with small overcasting stitches **c :** fishing in water with rod, line, and artificial lures **2 :** material used to whip or bind: as **a :** small stuff with which a rope end is whipped; *also* **:** the finished lashing or binding as opposed to the material it is made of **b :** pitched twine that binds together the head and shaft of a golf club **c :** SERVING 3

whipping 2a

whipping boy *n* **1 :** a boy formerly educated with a prince and punished in his stead **2 :** SCAPEGOAT ⟨the favorite *whipping boy* of French letters, the French middle class —*Time*⟩

whipping cream *n* **:** cream suitable for whipping containing not less than 30 percent and as much as 36 percent of butterfat — compare COFFEE CREAM

whipping post *n* **:** a post formerly usu. in public to which offenders are tied to be legally whipped

whipping tom *n, usu cap T* [*Tom* fr. *Tom,* nickname for *Thomas*] **:** one conspicuous for whipping others

whipping top *or* **whip top** *n* **:** a top that is spun by whipping

whippletree *var of* WHIFFLETREE

whip·poor·will \,(h)wipə(r)ˈwil *also* -i(p)(,)pu̇r¦w- *or* -u̇ə¦w-\ *n* -s [imit.] **1 :** a nocturnal goatsucker (*Caprimulgus vociferus*) of the eastern U.S. and Canada that is related to the European nightjar, that is seldom seen although its call is often heard at nightfall or just before dawn, that is spotted, barred, and vermiculated with black, brown, and buffy, and that has the terminal half of the outer tail feathers white and a crescent in the throat which is white in the male and buffy in the female **2** *NewEng* **:** a moccasin flower (*Cypripedium acaule*)

whippoorwill's-shoe \'≈≈,≈'≈\ *n, pl* **whippoorwill's-shoes 1 :** an American plant of the genus *Cypripedium* **2** *also* **whippoorwill's-boot** \'≈≈,≈'≈\ *pl* **whippoorwill's-boots :** a pitcher plant (*Sarracenia purpurea*)

whip purchase *n* **:** WHIP CRANE

whip·py \'hwipē *also* 'wi-\ *adj* -ER/-EST [²*whip* + *-y*] **1 :** of, relating to, or resembling a whip **2 :** unusually resilient **:** SPRINGY ⟨a very ~ fly rod —J.D.Bates⟩

whip ray *n* **:** STINGRAY

whip roll *n* **:** a roll or bar above the warp beam and behind the reed over which the warp threads pass in the process of weaving

whip-round \'≈,≈\ *n* -s [fr. the phrase *whip round*] *chiefly Brit* **:** a collection of money made usu. for a benevolent purpose ⟨we'll have a *whip-round* and . . . make up for what was in your purse —*Strand Mag.*⟩

whips *pres 3d sing of* WHIP, *pl of* WHIP

¹whipsaw \'≈,≈\ *n* [²*whip* + *saw*] **1 :** a narrow pit saw tapering from butt to point, having hook teeth, and averaging from 5 to 7½ feet in length for use by one or two men **2 :** a two-man crosscut saw

²whipsaw \"\ *vt* **1 :** to saw with a whipsaw **:** cut as if with a whipsaw **2 :** to cheat or victimize (an opponent) esp. at poker by collusion of two players only one of whom can win but both of whom raise so as to increase the size of the pot **3 :** to use more favorable terms gained (as in one company) as the precedent or leverage to win equal or greater concessions from (as a related company)

whip scorpion *n* **:** an arachnid of the order Pedipalpida

whip shot *n* **:** a method of throwing dice so that one or both dice will not change vertical position while in the air or spinning along a surface but will come to rest with the same number topmost as when they left the shooter's hand

whip snake *n* **:** any of various slender snakes: as **a :** a long bright-green harmless tree snake (*Philodryas viridissimus*) of So. America — called also *emerald whip snake* **b :** COACHWHIP SNAKE **c :** a snake of a boigid genus (*Dryophis*) of Asia having a long leaflike head **d :** any of several small Australian snakes (genera *Demansia* and *Denisonia*) that are venomous but not deadly

whipsocket \'≈,≈≈\ *n* **1 :** the whipstock into which a lash is fitted **2 :** a socket into which the butt end of a whip is inserted when the whip is not in use

whip stall *n* **:** a maneuver in which an airplane is put into a steeper climbing attitude than it is able to maintain and is held in this attitude until the speed is reduced to the stalling speed causing it to whip sharply into a steep nose down attitude that is maintained until flying speed is regained

whip·ster \'hwipstə(r) *also* 'wi-\ *n* -s [¹*whip* + *-ster*] **1 :** WHIPPERSNAPPER **2 :** one that uses a whip

¹whipstitch \'≈,≈\ *vt* [¹*whip* + *stitch,* n.] **1 :** WHIP 5 **2 :** OVERCAST 3a

²whipstitch \"\ *n* **1 :** a shallow overcasting stitch **2 :** a small interval of time **:** INSTANT, MINUTE

whipstock \'≈,≈\ *n* **1 :** the handle of a whip **2 :** a long wedge dropped into or placed in a petroleum well to deflect the drill to one side of some obstruction

whiptail \'≈,≈\ *n* **1 :** a whip-tailed animal: as **a :** WHIP SCORPION **b :** a long-tailed skua **c :** a lizard of the genus *Cnemidophorus* **d** *or* **whip-tailed shark :** THRESHER 2 **e :** a relatively large bluish-gray wallaby (*Macropus parryi*) with a long slender tail that occurs in mountain forests of Queensland and New South Wales and is readily tamed **f :** GRENADIER **2 :** a disease of cauliflower that is very prevalent on acid soils, is caused by malnutrition and in some cases by molybdenum deficiency, and is characterized by narrowed ruffled leaves with irregular edges sometimes reduced nearly to the midrib **3** *usu* **whip tail :** a slender tail tapering from the base towards the tip

whip-tailed *also* **whiptail** \'≈,≈\ *adj* **:** having a tail like a whiplash

whip-tailed lizard *n* **:** WHIPTAIL 1c

whip-tailed ray *n* **:** STINGRAY

whip-tailed scorpion *n* **:** WHIP SCORPION

whip thread *or* **whip yarn** *n* **:** a secondary warp thread twisted around another warp thread to make the fabric firmer and used esp. in lappet weaving

whip-tom-kelly \'≈≈'≈≈\ *n* [imit.] **:** any of various vireos (as the black-whiskered vireo)

whip-tongue \'≈,≈\ *n* **:** a wild madder (*Galium mollugo*)

whip top *var of* WHIPPING TOP

whipworm \'≈,≈\ *n* [so called fr. its shape] **:** a parasitic nematode worm (as the human whipworm [*Trichuris trichiura*]) of the family Trichuridae characterized by a body that is thickened posteriorly and is very long and slender anteriorly

¹whir *also* **whirr** *R* 'wh¦ər *also* 'w¦, + *vowel* ¦ər·; ¦ə̄, + *suffixal vowel* ¦ər· *also* ¦ər, + *vowel in a following word* ¦ər· *or* ¦ə *also* ¦ər\ *vb* **whirred; whirred; whirring; whirs** [ME (Sc) *quirren,* prob. of Scand origin; akin to Dan *hvirre* to whirl, whir, ON *hverfa* to turn around — more at WHARF] *vi* **1 :** to fly, revolve, or move rapidly with the sound of a whir ⟨grouse and ptarmigan *whirred* across the uplands —*Amer. Guide Series: Wash.*⟩ ⟨the small electric fan . . . *whirred* with a monotonous drone —Erskine Caldwell⟩ ⟨the breezes ~ through the trees —Gladwin Hill⟩ ⟨telephone *whirred* —Claud Cockburn⟩ ~ *vt* **:** to move or carry rapidly with the sound of whirring ⟨had been *whirring* the dial of the telephone —Erle Stanley Gardner⟩ ⟨the car ~*s* him away into the night⟩

²whir *also* **whirr** \"\ *n* -s [ME (Sc) *quirre,* fr. *quirren,* v.] **:** a continuous fluttering or generally vibratory sound made by something in rapid motion ⟨the hunter may delight in the ~ of the ruffed grouse —*Amer. Guide Series: N.H.*⟩ ⟨the strident ~ of the big locusts —Willa Cather⟩ ⟨the ~ of wheels and spinning tops —K.K.Darrow⟩ ⟨the ~ of spinning propellers —*Amer. Guide Series: Conn.*⟩

¹whirl \'hw¦ərl *also* 'w¦, *esp before pause or consonant* ¦ər·əl; ¦ə̄l, ¦əil\ *vb* -ED/-ING/-S [ME *whirlen,* prob. of Scand origin; akin to ON *hvirfla* to whirl; akin to MD *wirvel, wervel, warvel* bolt for closing a door, hinge, whirlwind, *wervelen* to turn, OHG *wirbil* whirlwind, ON *hvirfill* circle, ring, crown of the head, *hverfa* to turn around — more at WHARF] *vi* **1 a :** to move or turn in a circle or similar curve **:** CIRCLE ⟨his sister ~*s* round and round on the carousel —H.N.Maclean⟩ ⟨our sun and the stars near it are ~*ing* in roughly circular orbits —B.J. Bok⟩ **b :** to move circularly in various or random directions esp. with force or speed ⟨the wind . . . ~*ed* round her in eddies and spirals —J.C.Powys⟩ ⟨the dancers ~ about the room⟩ ⟨his thoughts were ~*ing* wildly —Morley Callaghan⟩ ⟨separated by a wide gulf in which ~*ed* the nothingnesses of training and temperament —S.E.White⟩ **2 a :** to turn on or around an axis like a wheel **:** SPIN, REVOLVE, ROTATE ⟨the potter's wheel ~*s* at its work⟩ ⟨the eddies of the flooding river ~ menacingly⟩ **b :** to turn abruptly around or aside **:** WHEEL ⟨~*ed* about to the door —Liam O'Flaherty⟩ ⟨the tiger saw the movement and ~*ed* to face me —Edison Marshall⟩ ⟨strode away 20 paces, ~*ed* suddenly, and blazed away —C.B.Davis⟩ **c :** to turn around while bent considerably out of true through the effect of centrifugal force **3 :** to pass, move, or go quickly **:** SPEED, RUSH ⟨the landlady ~*ed* down the hallway —J.B. Clayton⟩ ⟨the carriages used to ~ by the house⟩ ⟨the General Court ~*ed* into special session —J.R.Aswell & E.J.Michelson⟩ **4 :** to become giddy or dizzy **:** REEL ⟨all of a sudden my head ~*ed,* and the lights went out and I fell —Dorothy Baker⟩ ~ *vt* **1 :** to drive, impel, or convey with or as if with a rotary motion ⟨cottonwoods . . . snapped off and were ~*ed* away —*Amer. Guide Series: Tenn.*⟩ ⟨the pair jumped into a car and were ~*ed* away —S.H.Adams⟩ ⟨has been ~*ed* . . . to the height of fame —T.H.White b.1915⟩ **2 a :** to cause to turn usu. rapidly on or around an axis **:** ROTATE ⟨the catapult officer ~*ed* one finger above his head —J.A.Michener⟩ ⟨subjects will be ~*ed* at speed approaching 1000 miles an hour —*All Hands*⟩ ⟨~*ed* the helpless characters around while war or peace was being decided —Henri Peyre⟩ **b :** to cause to turn abruptly around or aside ⟨caught a swift purple gaze of eyes as she ~*ed* her head —Zane Grey⟩ **3** *obs* **:** to throw or hurl violently with a revolving motion ⟨a sling to ~ stones⟩ **4** *archaic* **:** to cause to become giddy ⟨the sight of the vast canyon ~*s* his brain⟩ **5 :** TWIST 5 **syn** see TURN

²whirl \"\ *n* -s [ME *whirle,* fr. *whirlen,* v.] **1 :** WHORL 1 **2 a :** a rapid rotating or circling movement **:** SPIN, GYRATION ⟨the ~ of the buzz saw —*Amer. Guide Series: La.*⟩ ⟨gave the crank a ~ —John Hermann⟩ ⟨snatched up a black net scarf . . . and with a sudden ~ draped herself —Winifred Bambrick⟩ ⟨guide vanes add ~ to the working fluid —E.L.Hunsaker & W.A.Stoner⟩ **b :** something undergoing such a movement **:** VORTEX, EDDY ⟨the ~*s* of the pool⟩ ⟨tropical cyclones are small cyclonic ~*s* —Sverre Petterssen⟩ **3 a :** a confused tumult **:** COMMOTION, BUSTLE ⟨had plunged into a ~ of work —Will Irwin⟩ ⟨a ~ of people riding or walking to the market place —*Lamp*⟩ ⟨we avoided the gay social ~ . . . because we wanted something more solid from life —Gráinne Andrews⟩ **b :** a confused or disturbed mental state **:** TURMOIL ⟨passed his days in a ~ of febrile excitement —Emily Skeel⟩ ⟨that these distinguished men were calling upon me quite set me in a ~ —David Fairchild⟩ ⟨in a ~ all the time —Arnold Bennett⟩ **4 :** rapid, intense, or impelled movement **:** RUSH ⟨the ~ of vehicles fills the streets⟩ ⟨a ten-day ~ through allied capitals —*N.Y.Times*⟩ ⟨had forgotten his lunch and returned in a ~ to get it —Agnes S. Turnbull⟩ **5 :** a whorl of parts on a plant or animal **:** VERTICIL **6 :** a hook or reel of a rope winch by which the strands of a rope are twisted; *also* **:** the winch to which the hook or reel is attached **7 :** an experimental or brief attempt **:** TRY ⟨there had been her own veto of a career as a fashion designer after a trial ~ —*Current Biog.*⟩ ⟨took a ~ at the intellectual life —Kay Rogers⟩ ⟨pleaded with us to give whale steak a ~ —*New Yorker*⟩

whirlabout \'≈≈,≈\ *n* -s [fr. *whirl about,* v.] **:** the act or process of whirling about ⟨amid a ~ of colored carnival lights —Samuel Yellen⟩

whirlbat *n* [alter. (influenced by ¹*whirl*) of *hurlbat*] *obs* **:** ³CESTUS

whirlblast \'≈,≈\ *n* **:** WHIRLWIND, HURRICANE

whirlbone \'≈,≈\ *n* [ME *whirlebon,* fr. *whirlen* to whirl + *bon* bone — more at BONE] **1** *dial Eng* **:** HUCKLEBONE 1 **2** *dial Eng* **:** PATELLA

whirl drill *n* **:** a hand drill consisting of a spindle with a small heavy flywheel near the drill end turned by two twisted strings attached to the other end of the spindle and to the ends of a transverse piece that slides on the spindle

whirl·er \-lə(r)\ *n* -s **:** one that whirls: as **a :** DERVISH 2 **b :** a circular appliance capable of being rotated by hand used by potters for finishing wares **c :** a whirling table for coating photographic plates **d :** a machine for putting a sensitized coating on the printing plate in offset lithography **e :** a hook for twisting hemp into rope yarn

whirl·ey crane \-lē-\ *or* **whirley** *n* -s [*whirley* alter. of ¹*whirly*] **:** a crane free to rotate 360 degrees in picking up and depositing its load

whirl·i·cote \'hwərlə,kōt *also* 'wər-\ *n* -s [prob. alter. of ME *whirlecole,* fr. *whirlen* to whirl + *-cole* (origin unknown)] **:** a heavy and luxurious carriage **:** COACH

whirlier *comparative of* WHIRLY

whirlies *pl of* WHIRLY

whirliest *superlative of* WHIRLY

¹whirl·i·gig \'hw¦ərlə,gig, ¦ə̄l-, ¦əil- *also* 'w¦\ *n* [ME *whirlegigge,* fr. *whirlen* to whirl + *gigge* top — more at GIG] **1 :** a child's toy having a whirling or spinning motion **2 :** a mechanical apparatus having a whirling or rotary movement: as **a :** a medieval instrument for punishing petty offenders consisting of a wooden cage for whirling around an offender at high speed **b :** MERRY-GO-ROUND **3 :** something that continuously whirls, moves, or changes: as **a** *obs* **:** a fanciful trifle or notion **b :** a circling or repetition of time or events **:** WHEEL ⟨their best work outlines the ~ of taste —Douglas Bush⟩ ⟨the ~ of fortune —J.D.Hart⟩ **c** *archaic* **:** a flighty unstable person **4 :** WHIRLIGIG BEETLE

²whirligig \"\ *vi* **:** to whirl like a whirligig **:** SPIN, TURN

whirligig beetle *n* **:** any of numerous beetles of the family Gyrinidae that have a firm oval usu. dark body with a bronzy luster and that live mostly on the surface of water where they move swiftly about in curves

whirling *pres part of* WHIRL

whirling dervish *n* **:** DERVISH 1

whirl·ing·ly *adv* **:** with a whirling movement

whirling table *n* **:** any of various apparatus for producing rapid rotary and usu. horizontal motion (as to demonstrate a law in physics or to coat plates evenly in photography)

whirl plate *n* **:** a disk inserted in a sprayer nozzle with holes designed to impart a whirling action to the spray

¹whirlpool \'≈,≈\ *n* [²*whirl* + *pool*] **1 a :** water moving rapidly in a circle so as to produce a depression or cavity in the center into which floating objects may be drawn **:** EDDY, VORTEX — compare MAELSTROM **b :** a body of water having a more or less circular motion caused by its flowing in an irregular channel or by the meeting of opposing currents **c :** WHIRLPOOL BATH **2 a :** a confused tumult and bustle **:** WHIRL ⟨walking down the gangway into a furious human ~ of customs, passport regulations, and bellowing loudspeakers —Wynford Vaughan-Thomas⟩ ⟨the turbulent ~ of pioneer politics —*Amer. Guide Series: Minn.*⟩ **b :** a magnetic or impelling force by which something is or may be pulled under or engulfed ⟨refusing to be drawn into this ~ of intrigue —A.D.White⟩ ⟨under their stagnant respectability are ~*s* of evil and passion —Laurent LeSage⟩ ⟨a seething ~ of competition and intrigue in which everyone is . . . unscrupulous —David Cecil⟩ **3 :** GURGES

²whirlpool \"\ *vi* **:** to eddy or spin around like a whirlpool ⟨the feather . . . ~*ed* down —Gerald Durrell⟩

whirlpool bath *n* **:** a therapeutic bath in which a whirling churning stream of hot water is forcibly directed against a part of the body

whirlpuff \'≈,≈\ *n* [ME *whirle puff,* fr. *whirlen* to whirl + *puff, puf, puffe* puff — more at PUFF] *dial Eng* **:** a whirling gust or blast of wind

whirls *pres 3d sing of* WHIRL, *pl of* WHIRL

whirl·wig \'hwərl,wig *also* 'wə-\ *n* [blend of *whirligig* and *earwig*] **:** WHIRLIGIG BEETLE

¹whirlwind \'≈,≈\ *n, often attrib* [ME *whirlwind, whirlewind,* fr. *whirlen* to whirl + *wind*] **1 a :** a small rotating windstorm of limited or localized extent marked by an inward and upward spiral motion of the lower air that is followed by an outward and upward spiral motion and usu. a progressive motion at all levels **:** a vortex of air — see DUST DEVIL ⟨little ~*s* twisted and died across the prairie —Edwin Granberry⟩ ⟨a small ~ . . . knocked two men off their feet and whisked away paper cartons and other debris —*Springfield (Mass.) Daily News*⟩ **b :** TORNADO 2a **2 a :** a confused rush or tumultuous procession of events or developments **:** WHIRL ⟨lived in a ~ of examiner's meetings, visits on business . . . innumerable callers, some political jobs —H.J.Laski⟩ ⟨~ of our departure —David Fairchild⟩ ⟨the ~ of child stardom —Joanna Spencer⟩ **b :** a destructive force or agency ⟨the storm has been sown, and the ~ must be reaped —Gilbert Parker⟩ ⟨farmers are reaping another golden crop of corn, and Republicans are reaping a political ~ —W.M.Blair⟩ **syn** see WIND

²whirlwind \"\ *vi* **:** to move like a whirlwind ⟨is ~*ing* through the states on his campaign⟩

¹whirly \'hw¦ərlē, ¦ə̄l-, ¦əil-, -li *also* 'w¦\ *adj* -ER/-EST [¹*whirl* + *-y*] **:** marked by or exhibiting a rotary or whirling motion

²whirly \"\ *n* -ES **:** a small whirlwind

whirlybird \'≈≈,≈\ *n* **:** HELICOPTER

whirr *var of* WHIR

whir·ra \'(h)wirə\ *var of* WIRRA

whirred *past of* WHIR

whirring *pres part of* WHIR

whir·ry \'(h)wəri\ *vb* **whirried; whirried; whirrying; whirries** [perh. blend of ¹*whir* and *hurry*] *vt, Scot* **:** to convey quickly ~ *vi, Scot* **:** HURRY

whirs *pres 3d sing of* WHIR, *pl of* WHIR

whir·tle \'hwərd·ᵊl *also* 'wə-\ *n* -s [ME *wirtil*] **:** a perforated steel die through which wires or tubes are drawn

¹whish \'hwish *also* 'wi-\ *vb* -ED/-ING/-ES [imit.] *vt* **:** to urge on or cause to move with a whish ⟨heard them ~*ing* up the sheep —Joseph Hocking⟩ ⟨heard him ~ the match across his pants —Helen Rich⟩ ~ *vi* **1 :** to make a sibilant sound **:** move with a whish ⟨a starter ~*ed,* and an engine took hold —G.R. Stewart⟩ ⟨water ~*es* past the prow⟩ **2 :** to move fast **:** WHIZ ⟨trees ~ past the train windows⟩ ⟨~*es* in with a roar and bursts in the street —Ernest Hemingway⟩

²whish \"\ *n* -ES **:** a rushing sound **:** SWISH — used interjectionally to convey an impression of rapid movement ⟨touched a match to the skyrocket and ~ it was off⟩

³whish \'(h)wish\ *vb* -ED/-ING/-ES [imit.] *dial Brit* **:** SHUSH — often used in the imperative to enjoin silence

¹whisht \'(h)wisht\ *n* -s [imit.] *chiefly Scot & Irish* **:** HUSH, SILENCE ⟨the ~ of death upon his face —Louise Garnett⟩ — often used interjectionally to enjoin silence ⟨~ now . . . I hear people again coming by the stream —J.M.Synge⟩

²whisht \"\ *chiefly Scot & Irish var of* ³WHISH

¹whisk \'hwisk *also* 'wi-\ *n* -s [ME *wisk, wisk,* prob. of Scand origin; akin to ON *visk* wisp; akin to OE *wiscian* to plait, gran*wisc* awn, OHG *wisc* wisp, L *viscus* entrails, *virga* branch, twig, rod, Skt *veṣka* noose, *vēṣa* costume; basic meaning: to turn] **1 a :** a quick light brushing or whipping motion **:** FLICK, SWISH ⟨as the tear dripped slowly down . . . caught it with a neat little ~ of her tongue —Katherine Mansfield⟩ ⟨could . . . hear the ~ and slither of tails —James Schuyler⟩ **b :** a swift passage ⟨the line's four-times-a-week ~ from London to home (two hours) —Horace Sutton⟩ **2 :** something used as or resembling a whip or brush: as **a :** a hairlike insect appendage — used esp. of the setae of the Plectoptera **b :** a small usu. wire kitchen implement used for hand beating of food (as eggs, cream, or potatoes) — compare WHIP 4b **c** (1) **:** a flexible bunch (as of twigs, feathers, or straw) attached to a handle for use as a brush — compare FEATHER DUSTER, FLY WHISK (2) **:** WHISK BROOM **d :** TUFT, WISP ⟨wind . . . skiffing the ~ of her frock —Bruce Marshall⟩ **e :** the tail of an angler's fly **3 :** a wide ornamental collar of fine fabric and lace usu. supported at the back and worn in the early 17th century **4 :** a plant part (as a panicle of broomcorn) used in making brushes

²whisk \"\ *vb* -ED/-ING/-S [ME (Sc) *quhisken,* of Scand origin; akin to ON *viska* to wipe, whisk; akin to OE *wiscian* to plait — more at ¹WHISK] *vi* **1 :** to move nimbly and quickly **:** FRISK, POP ⟨gray bodies ~ up and down the hickory trunks —Marjorie K. Rawlings⟩ ⟨porters . . . bowed and ~*ed* about him —Frederick Way⟩ **2 :** to travel swiftly **:** ZIP ⟨the Broadway Limited . . . ~*ed* through like a comet —*True*⟩ ~ *vt* **1 a :** to impart brisk or rapid motion to **:** FLICK, WHIP ⟨seeing him ~ his eloquent tail —E.S.McCartney⟩ ⟨showed both sides, draped it over her left hand, ~*ed* away the cloth —Martin Gardner⟩ ⟨machine picks up threads . . . and ~*s* them into a detachable aluminum hopper for ready disposal —*Steel*⟩ **b :** to transport swiftly **:** HURRY, SPEED ⟨dreams of rocket ships that will ~ him across the Atlantic between breakfast and luncheon —Waldemar Kaempffert⟩ ⟨too soon . . . their mother would ~ them off to bed —Flora Thompson⟩ ⟨an endless belt ~*s* the shopper's groceries . . . out to pickup stations —J.N.Wallace⟩ **2 :** to mix or fluff up by or as if by beating with a whisk ⟨~*ing* a mixture in a yellow bowl —Kathryn Grondahl⟩ ⟨wind . . . ~*ed* and matted the flakes into huge grey discs —O.E.Rölvaag⟩ **3 :** to brush or wipe off lightly ⟨~ crumbs from the table⟩ ⟨can be ~*ed* clean with a damp cloth —*advt*⟩

³whisk \"\ *interj* — used to convey an impression of sudden swift motion ⟨he's going to taste it, when ~! it's gone —Hugh Walpole⟩

⁴whisk \"\ *n* -s [perh. fr. ¹*whisk*] *dial* **:** WHIST

whisk broom *n* **:** a small broom with a short handle used esp. as a clothes brush or for light cleaning chores

¹whisk·er \'hwiskə(r) *also* 'wi-\ *n* -s [²*whisk* + *-er*] **1 a :** a hair of the beard — usu. used in pl. ⟨had a two days' growth of thick, grizzled ~*s* —Danforth Ross⟩ **b whiskers** *pl* (1) *archaic* **:** MOUSTACHE (2) **:** the part of the beard growing on the sides of the face or on the chin; *esp* **:** SIDE-WHISKERS **c :** HAIRBREADTH ⟨temperatures hovered a ~ below freezing —*Springfield (Mass.) Daily News*⟩ **2 a :** one of the long projecting hairs or bristles growing near the mouth of an animal (as a cat or bird) **b :** an antenna or feeler esp. of an insect **c whiskers** *pl* **:** an abundant grayish white growth of a mold (genus *Mucor* and related fungi) on food (as bread or meat) consisting of superficial hyphae **3** *or* **whisker boom :** an outrigger extending on each side of the bowsprit to spread the jib and flying jib guys — usu. used in pl.; see SHIP illustration **4 :** a hairy shred or filament likened to a whisker: as **a :** CAT WHISKER **b :** HAIRLINE 2c(4) — usu. used in pl.

whisk broom

²whisker \"\ *vt* -ED/-ING/-S **1 :** to furnish with whiskers ⟨a ~*ed* jersey with rabbit's hair content —*Women's Wear Daily*⟩ **2 :** to remove the splinters from (a gun stock)

whisk·er·age \-kərij\ *n* -s [¹*whisker* + *-age*] **:** style of wearing the whiskers ⟨changes had come about in . . . facial ~ —Thomas Wolfe⟩

whisk·ered \-kə(r)d\ *adj* [¹*whisker* + *-ed*] **:** having or wearing whiskers

whiskered auklet *n* **:** an auklet (*Aethia pygmaea*) having filamentous white feathers on the sides of the head

whiskered bat *n* **:** a small bat (*Myotis mystacinus*) of Europe and Asia having a fringe of long hairs on its upper lip

whiskered tern *n* **:** a common tern (*Chlidonias hybrida*) of the warmer parts of the Old World having a broad white stripe at the corner of the mouth

whisker jumper *n* **:** a stay leading from the end of a whisker boom to secure it to the cutwater — usu. used in pl.; see SHIP illustration

whisker pole *n* **:** a light boom with jaws at one end that fit around the mast and a point at the other end that goes through the clew of the jib to wing it out when running before the wind

whisk·ery \-kərē\ *adj* **:** having or resembling whiskers ⟨a ~ chin⟩ ⟨this yarn has ~ roots —Colin Simpson⟩

¹whis·key *or* **whis·ky** \'hwiskē, -ki *also* 'wi-\ *n, pl* **whiskeys** *or* **whiskies** *often attrib* [IrGael *uisce beathadh* & ScGael *uisge beatha*, lit., water of life, fr. OIr *uisce* water + *bethad*, gen. of *bethu* life; akin to Gk *hydōr* water and to Gk *bios* life, mode of life — more at WATER, QUICK] **1 :** a distilled alcoholic liquor that is made from fermented mash of grain (as rye, corn, barley, or wheat) or potatoes and usu. contains from 40 percent to 50 percent of alcohol — compare BLENDED WHISKEY, BOURBON 4, SCOTCH WHISKY **2 :** a drink of whiskey ⟨takes an occasional ~⟩

²whiskey *or* **whisky** \"\ *n, pl* **whiskeys** *or* **whiskies** [²*whisk* + *-y*] **:** a gig with a small body that resembles a chair and is suspended on leather braces attached to springs — compare DENNET

³whiskey \"\ *usu cap* — a communications code word for the letter *w*

whiskey poker *n* [¹*whiskey*] **:** draw poker in which an extra hand is dealt facedown and may be taken entire by the first player who then if he has not passed discards his original hand faceup for exchange individually or entire by each following player until one of the players knocks, the drawing ends, and the hands are shown to determine the winner

whiskey sour *n* **1 :** a cocktail usu. made of whiskey, bitters, sugar, and varying proportions of lemon juice shaken up in cracked ice and served with a fruit garnish (as orange or maraschino cherry) **2 :** a slender usu. footed glass for serving a whiskey sour

whis·kin \'hwiskən\ *n* -s [origin unknown] *archaic* **:** a shallow drinking bowl

whisking *pres part of* WHISK

whisks *pl of* WHISK, *pres 3d sing of* WHISK

whisky cherry *n* **:** BLACK CHERRY 2

whisky jack *n* [alter. of obs. *whisky john*, fr. Cree *wiskatjān*] **:** CANADA JAY

whisp *var of* WISP

whiskey sour 2

¹whis·per \'hwispə(r) *also* 'wi-\ *vb* **whispered; whispered; whispering** \-p(ə)riŋ\ **whispers** [ME *whisperen*, fr. OE *hwisprian*; akin to OHG *hwispalōn* to whisper, ON *hviskra* to whisper, *hvina* to whiz — more at WHINE] *vi* **1 :** to speak softly with little or no vibration of the vocal cords esp. with the aim of preserving secrecy ⟨everybody ~*ing* and then stopping when he came in —Mary Barrett⟩ **2 :** to make a sibilant sound that resembles whispering ⟨the flames ~*ed;* the kettle hummed —Ellen Glasgow⟩ ⟨a breeze ~*s* through the pines⟩ ~ *vt* **1 a :** to address in a whisper ⟨I'd ~ her, and take her for a midnight stroll —Padraic Colum⟩ **b :** to influence or impel by whispering ⟨a voice . . . ~*s* me on —E.R.B.Lytton⟩ **2 a :** to report or suggest confidentially ⟨the ~*ed* reason behind much of the opposition —*Newsweek*⟩ ⟨no evil lurked in . . . their hearts to ~ doubts concerning the goodness of life —V.L.Parrington⟩ **b :** to utter or communicate in or as if in a whisper ⟨they sat closely together as she ~*ed* some of her pleasantest memories —T.B.Costain⟩ ⟨he ~*ed* . . . "the coast is clear" —Archie Binns⟩

²whisper \"\ *n* -s **1 a :** an act or instance of whispering ⟨~*s* so fierce they could be heard all over the house —Peggy Bennett⟩; *specif* **:** speech in which vibration of the vocal cords is replaced by a fricative sound made by the breath in the whisper glottis while the cord glottis is closed **b :** a sibilant sound that resembles whispered speech **:** SUSURRUS ⟨a smoldering log settled with a ~ on the hearth —Ngaio Marsh⟩ **2 a :** a whispered rumor or suggestion ⟨never been a ~ of anything crooked about them —F.W.Crofts⟩ **b :** a confidential report or communication **3 :** a barely discernible quantity **:** HINT, TRACE ⟨hardly a ~ of concern has been voiced —Eric Sevareid⟩ ⟨a ~ of the perfume she used —C.O.Gorham⟩

whis·per·er \-pərə(r)\ *n* -s **1 :** one that whispers; *specif* **:** RUMORMONGER **2 :** a horse trainer who soothes unmanageable mounts by whispering to them

whisper glottis *n* [fr. its use in the production of whisper] **:** the opening between the arytenoid cartilages as distinguished from that between the vocal cords proper — compare CORD GLOTTIS

¹whispering *n* -s [ME, fr. OE *hwisprung*, fr. *hwisprian* to whisper + *-ung* -ing] **1 a :** whispered speech ⟨~ caused by laryngitis⟩ **b :** GOSSIP, RUMOR ⟨foul ~*s* are abroad —Shak.⟩ **2 :** a sibilant sound **:** WHISPER ⟨flitting shapes and tiny ~*s* —Marjory S. Douglas⟩

²whispering *adj* [fr. pres. part. of ¹*whisper*] **1 :** making a sibilant sound **:** SUSURRANT ⟨music in a quick and ~ rhythm —Archibald MacLeish⟩ **2 a :** told in or confined to a whisper ⟨a ~ tale⟩ ⟨a ~ voice⟩ **b :** communicating in whispers ⟨~ lovers⟩ **c :** spreading confidential and esp. derogatory reports ⟨~ tongues can poison truth —S.T.Coleridge⟩ — **whis·per·ing·ly** *adv*

whispering bells *n pl but sing or pl in constr* [²*whispering*] **:** CALIFORNIA YELLOW BELLS

whispering campaign *n* [¹*whispering*] **:** the systematic dissemination by word of mouth of derogatory rumors or charges esp. against a candidate for public office ⟨his opponents had hinted in his career by a *whispering campaign* —Willa Cather⟩

whispering gallery *or* **whispering dome** *n* **:** a gallery or dome so constructed that sounds produced in the area are concentrated in another by reflection from the walls so that feeble sounds are audible at an extraordinary distance

whis·per·ous \'hwisp(ə)rəs *also* 'wi-\ *adj* [²*whisper* + *-ous*] **:** WHISPERY — **whis·per·ous·ly** *adv*

whis·pery \-rē, -ri\ *adj* [²*whisper* + *-y*] **1 :** resembling a whisper ⟨stopped his breathing . . . to be able to hear any sound, however small and ~ —W.V.T.Clark⟩ **2 :** full of whispers ⟨a swamp is a ~ place —Edward Kimbrough⟩

¹whist \'(h)wist\ *dial Brit var of* ³WHISH

²whist \'hwist *also* 'wi-\ *adj* [ME, fr. ¹*whist*] **:** QUIET, SILENT ⟨the winds are ~ —J.R.Drake⟩

³whist \"\ *n* -s [alter. (perh. influenced by ¹*whist* — fr. the silence observed during play) of earlier *whisk*, prob. fr. ²*whisk;* fr. whisking up the tricks] **:** a card game for four players in two partnerships that is played with a pack of 52 cards dealt one at a time of which the last card belongs to the dealer and is turned to determine trump for the hand and that scores one point for each trick in excess of six and sometimes additional points for the ace, king, queen, and jack of trumps — see LONG WHIST, SHORT WHIST; compare ⁴BRIDGE

whist drive *n, Brit* **:** a progressive whist party

whist family *n* **:** a group of card games including whist and games from which it developed or which are based on it — compare BRIDGE

¹whis·tle \'hwisəl *also* 'wi-\ *n* -s *often attrib* [in sense 1, fr. ME, fr. OE *hwistle;* akin to OE *hwistlian* to whistle; in other senses, fr. ME, fr. *whistlen* to whistle] **1 a :** a small wind instrument in which sound is produced by the forcible passage of breath through a slit in a short tube (as of wood or metal) ⟨willow ~⟩ ⟨police ~⟩ — compare FIPPLE FLUTE **b :** a device through which air or steam is forced into a cavity or against a thin edge to produce a shrill whistling sound ⟨boat ~⟩ ⟨factory ~⟩ **2 a :** a shrill clear sound produced by forcing breath out or air in through the puckered lips ⟨her figure . . . inspires admiring ~*s* —*Time*⟩ **b :** the sound produced by a whistle ⟨the ~ of a distant train⟩ **c :** a signal (as a warning or summons) given by or as if by whistling ⟨all his followers . . . were ready at his ~ —T.B.Macaulay⟩ **3 :** a sound that resembles a whistle ⟨a ~ of wings —William Beebe⟩ ⟨the whine and ~ of bombs —Peter Ustinov⟩; *specif* **:** the shrill clear note of a bird or other animal ⟨the ~ of a cardinal⟩ ⟨the ~ of a marmot⟩

²whistle \"\ *vb* **whistled; whistled; whistling** \-s(ə)liŋ\ **whistles** [ME *whistlen*, fr. OE *hwistlian;* akin to ON *hvīsla* to whisper, *hvīna* to whiz — more at WHINE] *vi* **1 a :** to utter a shrill clear sound by blowing or drawing air through the pursed lips ⟨sat up and *whistled* with surprise —T.B.Costain⟩ **b :** to utter a shrill note or call resembling a whistle ⟨the dove ~*s* and the pigeons coo —Louise Bogan⟩ **c :** to make a shrill clear sound esp. due to rapid movement ⟨wind *whistled* among the cornices —Louis Bromfield⟩ ⟨bullets began to ~ among the branches —Stephen Crane⟩ **d :** to blow or sound a whistle **2 a :** to signal by or as if by whistling ⟨the referee ~*s* and play is resumed⟩ **b :** to issue an order or summons by or as if by whistling ⟨~ to a dog⟩ ⟨~ for a taxi⟩; *specif* **:** to demand without result ⟨never returned the book he borrowed so next time he wants one he can just ~⟩ ⟨did a sloppy job so he can ~ for his money⟩ **3 :** SQUEAL 2a ~ *vt* **1 a :** to signal or summon by or as if by whistling ⟨*whistled* the chief engineer to give her all he could —H.A.Chippendale⟩ — often used with *up* ⟨persuaded . . . to put off *whistling* up the law —William Brandon⟩ ⟨~ up hypothetical vectors . . . to explain the facts for them —*Amer. Naturalist*⟩ **b :** to dismiss by or as if by whistling ⟨told him he might . . . ~ me off, save himself, and I would say no word of blame —Mary Johnston⟩ ⟨that . . . historical happening cannot be *whistled* away —*Times Lit. Supp.*⟩ **c :** to impel or influence by whistling ⟨*whistled* himself out of the scrub and back onto the road —Stetson Kennedy⟩ **2 a :** to utter or express in a whistle ⟨~ a tune⟩ ⟨a group of reclining soldiery *whistled* appreciation each time they passed —Margery Sharp⟩ ⟨quail ~ about us their spontaneous cries —Wallace Stevens⟩ **b :** to send or drive with a whistle ⟨~ a shot or two over his head —Alan Le May⟩ ⟨broke off a switch and *whistled* it angrily through the air —D.C.Peattie⟩ **3** *obs* **:** to disclose confidentially **:** WHISPER ⟨they dare speak felony, ~ treason —John Taylor⟩ — **whistle in the dark :** to keep up one's courage by or as if by whistling ⟨a series of optimistic statements and much *whistling in the dark* —Rupert Emerson⟩

whis·tle·able \-ləbəl\ *adj* **:** capable of being whistled ⟨a ~ tune⟩

whistle duck *n* **:** AMERICAN GOLDENEYE

whistle–pig \'==,=\ *n, chiefly Midland* **:** WOODCHUCK

whistle post *n* **:** a marker alongside a railroad track designating a point at which trains are to whistle (as for a station or crossing)

whistle punk *n* **:** a lumberjack who operates the signal wire running to a donkey engine whistle

whis·tler \'hwis(ə)lə(r) *also* 'wi-\ *n* -s [ME, fr. OE *hwistlere*, fr. *hwistlian* to whistle + *-ere* -er] **1 :** one that whistles: as **a :** a player on the fife, flute, or pipe **b** (1) **:** any of various Australian and Polynesian birds (as of the genus *Pachycephala*) that are related to the shrikes and have a whistling call — called also *thickhead* (2) **:** AMERICAN GOLDENEYE **c :** a large mountain marmot (*Marmota caligata*) of northwestern No. America of a hoary color with blackish head and feet **d :** a broken-winded horse **e :** a rising and falling noise heard on radio resulting from an electrical disturbance caused by a lightning discharge **2 :** one that evokes whistles of admiration ⟨it was a ~ of a story . . . while it lasted —*Newsweek*⟩

whis·tle·ri·an \(')(h)wi¦slirēən\ *adj, usu cap* [James A. M. *Whistler* †1903 Am. painter and etcher + E *-ian*] **:** of, relating to, or having the characteristics of the painter Whistler or his work

¹whistle–stop \'==,=\ *n* **1 a :** a small station at which trains stop only on signal **:** FLAG STOP **b :** a small community **:** TANK TOWN ⟨posters that brought in the yokels from fifty miles around every *whistle-stop* we played —Bennett Cerf⟩ **2 :** a brief personal appearance esp. by a political candidate usu. on the rear platform of a train during the course of a tour ⟨allowing people to savor his personality (which is the real purpose of a *whistle-stop*) while thawing them out with an anecdote —John Mason Brown⟩ **3 :** an insignificant or routine way station ⟨Gander, that global *whistle-stop* in the midst of Newfoundland's immense forests —*Friends Intelligencer*⟩ ⟨life is a *whistle-stop* between eternities —Rosa Marinoni⟩

²whistle–stop \"\ *vi* **1 :** to make a tour (as a campaign swing) pausing at all way stations ⟨*whistle-stop* across the country⟩ **2 :** to make personal appearances or speeches at whistle-stops ⟨*whistle-stopping* eastward through Utah in behalf of the . . . Democratic ticket —I.W.Russell⟩

whistlewing \'==,=\ *n* **:** AMERICAN GOLDENEYE

whistlewood \'==,=\ *n* **:** a tree with an easily separable bark used for making whistles: as **a :** STRIPED MAPLE **b :** BASSWOOD 1 **c :** WILLOW **d :** ALDER **e :** SYCAMORE 2 **f :** ROWAN TREE

¹whistling *n* -s [ME, fr. OE *hwistlung*, fr. *hwistlian* to whistle + *-ung* -ing] **1 a :** an act or instance of emitting whistles ⟨by repeated ~ and the display of a red lamp they managed to warn the driver —O.S.Nock⟩ ⟨myna birds kept up an impudent cackling and ~ —John Dos Passos⟩ **b :** WHISTLE ⟨the ~ of the wind⟩ **2 :** ROARING 2

²whistling *adj* [ME, fr. pres. part. of *whistlen* to whistle] **:** equipped with or making the sound of a whistle ⟨~ teakettle⟩ ⟨came in to land in a ~ sideslip —*Sydney (Australia) Bull.*⟩ — **whis·tling·ly** *adv*

whistling arrow *n* [²*whistling*] **:** an arrow with a perforated head that whistles in flight

whistling buoy *n* **:** a buoy that makes a whistling sound due to the action of waves and usu. marks a shoal or channel entrance — see BUOY illustration

whistling dick *n* **:** an Australian shrike thrush (*Colluricincla harmonica*)

whistling duck *n* **1 :** GOLDENEYE **2 :** TREE DUCK **3 :** AMERICAN SCOTER

whistling eagle *or* **whistling kite** *n* **:** a small Australian fishing kite (*Haliastur sphenurus*) related to the Brahminy kite — called also *whistling hawk*

whistling frog *n* **:** a small So. American terrestrial frog (*Leptodactylus ocellatus*) whose call is a clear whistle

whistling hawk *n* **1 :** WHISTLING EAGLE **2 :** CHANTING FALCON

whistling jar *n* **:** an ancient Peruvian clay bottle often in the form of a bird or animal with two apertures so arranged that when a liquid is poured from one the inrushing air produces a whistling sound in the other

whistling marmot *n* **:** WHISTLER 1c

whistling moth *n* **:** an Australian moth (*Hecatesia fenestrata*) of the family Agaristidae that in the male has a ribbed membranous area on the fore wing which produces whistling noise in flight

whistling plover *n* **1 :** GOLDEN PLOVER **2 :** BLACK-BELLIED PLOVER

whistling snipe *n* **:** WOODCOCK 1a(2)

whistling swan *n* **1 :** a wild swan (*Olor columbianus*) with a soft musical note formerly widely distributed in No. America and still breeding in some numbers in Alaska and northwestern Canada and migrating to and wintering in the U.S. chiefly in the southern Atlantic states **2 :** WHOOPER SWAN

whistling teal *n* **:** TREE DUCK

whistling thrush *n* **:** any of several thrushes of the genus *Myophonus* of Asia and the East Indies that are generally black glossed with blue, have a patch of bright blue on each shoulder, and have a loud clear whistle

whis·tly \'hwis(ə)lē *also* 'wi-\ *adj* [¹*whistle* + *-y*] **:** resembling a whistle

¹whit \'hwit *also* 'wi-; *usu* -id·+V\ *chiefly dial var of* WHITE

²whit \"\ *n* -s [alter. of ME *wight, wiht* creature, thing, bit — more at WIGHT] **:** the smallest part or particle imaginable **:** BIT, JOT, IOTA ⟨cared not a ~⟩ ⟨so shall I no ~ be behind in duty —Shak.⟩

³whit \"\ *adj, usu cap* [*Whit*sunday] **:** WHITSUN

⁴whit \"\ *interj* [imit.] — used to simulate the chirp of a bird or a quick dull sound (as of a bullet striking)

¹white \'hwīt *also* 'wīt; *usu* -īd·+V\ *adj* -ER/-EST [ME *white, whit*, fr. OE *hwīt;* akin to OHG *hwīz, wīz* white, ON *hvítr*, Goth *hweits*, Skt *śiśvinde* it has become white, *śveta* white] **1 a :** free from color **:** quite colorless and transparent **b** (1) **:** of a color like that of new snow or clean milk **:** having the color of good bond paper or the traditional lily; *specif* **:** of the color white ⟨well-bleached linen is perfectly ~⟩ ⟨~ roses⟩ (2) *of light* **:** having some energy in nearly every part of the visible spectrum **c :** light or pallid in color: as (1) **:** having the natural color largely abstracted through use or age **:** WHITENED, GRAYED ⟨the ~ hairs of old age⟩ ⟨a dress ~ from many washings⟩; *often* **:** shown to be aged by whitened hair ⟨this ~ old man⟩ (2) **:** light yellow or amber in color ⟨a ~ table wine⟩ (3) **:** deficient in color **:** ASHEN, WAN ⟨lips ~ with fear⟩ (4) **:** lustrous pale gray **:** SILVERY ⟨cheap tableware of some ~ alloy⟩; *also* **:** made of silver (5) *of cordage* **:** not darkened by an impregnation of tar (6) *of an organism or one of its parts* **:** deficient in pigmentation **:** ALBINO, ALBINOTIC **2 a** *of a human being* (1) *archaic* **:** having lightly pigmented skin, hair, and eyes **:** fair-complexioned **:** BLONDE (2) *sometimes cap* **:** belonging to a racial group or subdivision of a racial group characterized by reduced skin pigmentation, typically represented by the European Caucasoids, and usu. specif. distinguished from persons belonging to groups marked by black, brown, yellow, or red skin coloration (3) **:** being of white ancestry either wholly unmixed with Negro blood or having an admixture of Negro blood less than that specified in various statutes of some states of the U.S. **b :** of, relating to, or consisting of white and esp. Caucasoid people ⟨~ races⟩ ⟨~ Australia⟩ ⟨~ schools⟩ **c :** marked by upright fairness **:** straightforward and kindly **:** square-dealing ⟨a ~ man if ever there was one⟩ **3 :** free from spot or blemish: as **a :** free from moral stain or impurity **:** outstandingly righteous **:** INNOCENT ⟨a ~ spirit⟩ ⟨seeing everything as spiritually black or ~⟩ **b :** unmarked by writing or printing ⟨balancing the ~ spaces on the sheet⟩ **c :** not marked by or connected with malignant influences or intent **:** not intended to cause harm ⟨a ~ lie⟩ ⟨~ magic⟩ **d :** burnished or polished until shining bright and free from spot or mar ⟨clad in ~ armor⟩ **e :** notably pleasing or auspicious **:** FAVORABLE, FORTUNATE **4 :** clothed or covered with something white: as **a** (1) **:** wearing or habited in white ⟨~ friars⟩; *also* **:** of, relating to, or being a religious order (as the Carmelite) of which the garb is white ⟨a ~ abbey⟩ (2) **:** wearing white armor ⟨a ~ knight⟩ **b :** covered with snow **:** SNOWY ⟨the ~ hills of a northern winter⟩; *also* **:** marked by the presence of snow ⟨a long ~ winter⟩ ⟨hoping for a ~ Christmas⟩ **c :** made white by some covering deposit ⟨floors ~ with dust⟩ **5** *obs* **a :** designed to make a good impression **:** superficially pleasing or plausible **:** SPECIOUS **b :** regarded with especial favor **:** FAVORITE **6 a** *archaic* (1) *of a grain crop* **:** becoming lighter colored in ripening (2) *of soil* **:** suited to the growing of white crops **b :** that is whitened in the course of processing or purifying ⟨~ soap⟩ ⟨a fine ~ flour⟩ **7 a** (1) **:** heated to the point of whiteness — see WHITE HEAT (2) **:** characteristic of a white heat ⟨metal heated to a ~ glow⟩ **b :** notably ardent **:** violently heated **:** PASSIONATE ⟨a ~ fury⟩ **8** [so used fr. the white flag of the Bourbons] **a :** being or acting in opposition to a radical or revolutionary policy or doctrine **:** ultraconservative or reactionary in outlook and action ⟨a ~ faction in French politics⟩ — compare RED 7a **b :** instigated or carried out by reactionary forces usu. as a counterrevolutionary measure ⟨a ~ terror⟩ ⟨a ~ purge⟩ **9 :** not featuring open warfare and the shedding of blood but involving oblique methods ⟨a ~ war of propaganda and bribery⟩ **10 :** of, relating to, or constituting a musical tone quality characterized by a controlled pure sound, a lack of warmth and color, and a lack of resonance

²white \"\ *adv* -ER/-EST **:** in a fair upright manner **:** DECENTLY, WHITELY ⟨treated us ~⟩

³white \"\ *n* -s [ME *white, whit*, fr. OE *hwīt*, fr. *hwīt*, adj.] **1 a :** the neutral or achromatic object color of greatest lightness **:** the lightest gray **:** the achromatic color bearing the least resemblance to black **b :** the one of the six psychologically primary colors that is characteristically perceived to belong to objects which reflect diffusely nearly all incident energy throughout the visible spectrum **c :** any of several object colors of very low or zero saturation and high or very high lightness; *esp* **:** a very light gray **2 a :** a white-colored part of something (as meat or wood): as (1) **:** a clear semifluid mass of albuminous material surrounding the yolk of an egg — see EGG illustration (2) **:** the white part of the ball of the eye surrounding the transparent cornea (3) **whites** *pl* **:** blank spaces in a printed picture or design; *also* **:** the corresponding parts of a plate or mold (4) **:** the light-colored pieces in a two-handed board game; *also* **:** the player by whom or the side of the board from which these are played (5) **whites** *pl* **:** wing feathers of the male ostrich **b :** a white spot: as (1) *archaic* **:** a white target (2) **:** the fifth or outermost circle of an archery target; *also* **:** a shot that hits it (3) **:** a light-colored mark shot at in rovers (4) **:** a mark pinned on a butt **3 :** one that is or approaches the color white: as **a** (1) **:** white clothing ⟨the bride was dressed in ~⟩ (2) **whites** *pl* **:** a white costume of a usu. specified kind ⟨naval personnel in summer ~*s*⟩ ⟨tennis ~*s*⟩ **b :** white cloth **c :** WHITE WINE **d** (1) **:** a white mammal (as a horse or a hog) — compare CHESTER WHITE, YORKSHIRE (2) **:** any of numerous butterflies of *Pieris* and related genera in which the color is usu. white ⟨the cabbage butterfly is often known as the cabbage ~⟩ **e :** a white pigment (as zinc oxide) **f :** a white-colored product (as white flour, pins, or sugar) — usu. used in pl. **4** *archaic* **:** SILVER; *esp* **:** a silver coin **5 whites** *pl* **:** LEUKORRHEA **6** *often cap* **:** a person with a white skin **:** a member of the Caucasoid division of mankind **7** *often cap* **a :** a member of a white party esp. in European politics; *esp* **:** one of the Bianchi **b :** a person of ultraconservative political outlook **:** REACTIONARY — **in the white 1** *of a skin* **:** limed but not yet tanned **2** *of woodwork* **:** dressed and smoothed but not yet painted or varnished

⁴white \"\ *vt* -ED/-ING/-S [ME *whiten*, fr. ¹*white*] **:** WHITEN

⁵white \"\ *vb* -ED/-ING/-S [alter. of obs. *thwite*, fr. ME *thwiten* — more at WHITTLE] *Brit* **:** CUT, WHITTLE

whiteacre \'=,==\ *n* **:** a particular piece of land esp. in distinction from blackacre — used as an arbitrary name

white adder's–mouth \-'==,=\ *n* **:** a small No. American terrestrial orchid (*Malaxis brachypoda*) with a single leaf and a spike of greenish white flowers

white adder's–tongue *n* **:** a white-flowered dogtooth violet (*Erythronium albidum*) found in mountainous woods of eastern No. America — called also *white clintonia*

white admiral *n* **:** any of several butterflies of the genus

Limenitis having white bands on the wings; *esp* : BANDED PURPLE — compare RED ADMIRAL
white agaric *n* : PURGING AGARIC
white alder *n* **1 a** : any of several native alders (as *Alnus rhombifolia*) of western No. America **b** : GRAY ALDER **2** : any shrub or tree of the genus *Clethra* **3** : a southern African tree (*Platylophus trifoliatus*) of the family Cunoniaceae **4** : PRIVET ANDROMEDA **5** : a winterberry (*Ilex verticillata*)
white-alder family *n* : CLETHRACEAE
white alert *n* : the all-clear signal after an alert; *also* : the period of return to normalcy following an alert — compare BLUE ALERT, RED ALERT, YELLOW ALERT
white alkali *n* **1** : a mixture of salts (as sodium sulfate, magnesium sulfate, and sodium chloride) forming a white crust on some alkali soils **2** : refined soda ash
white ant *n* : TERMITE
white-ant \ˈ=ˌ=\ *vt* -ED/-ING/-S [*white ant*] : to wreck or take over surreptitiously as if by the boring of termites : undermine by underhanded means ⟨the popular front was *white-anted* by a Communist minority⟩
white antimony *n* : VALENTINITE
white apple *n* : GROUNDNUT 2a
white apple leafhopper *n* : a cicadellid insect (*Typhlocyba pomaria*) that infests apples in parts of the U.S. and Canada
white arsenic *n* : ARSENIC TRIOXIDE
white ash *n* **1 a** (1) : an American ash (*Fraxinus americana*) having leaves pale green or silvery white below — see TREE illustration (2) : the hard brownish wood of white ash used for tools, furniture, and interior finishings **b** : GREEN ASH **c** : FRINGE TREE **d** : any of several Australian eucalypts (esp. *Eucalyptus coriacea*, *E. fraxinoides*, or *E. globulus*) **e** : WHITE ALDER 2 **2** : OAR 1a
white-ash \ˈ=ˈ=\ *adj* [*white ash*] : made of the wood of white ash
white ash herb *n* : GOUTWEED
white asp *or* **white aspen** *n* : WHITE POPLAR 1a
white avens *n* : a bennet (*Geum virginianum*)
white bachelor's-button *n* : WHITE CAMPION a
whiteback \ˈ=ˌ=\ *n* : CANVASBACK
white-backed skunk \ˈ=ˌ=-\ *n* : HOG-NOSED SKUNK
white bacon *n, South & Midland* : BACON 3
whitebait \ˈ=ˌ=\ *n* [ˈ*white* + *bait*] **1** : the young of several European herrings and esp. of the common herring (*Clupea harengus*) or of the sprat (*C. sprattus*) **2** : any of various small fishes likened to the European whitebait and used as food: as **a** : ICEFISH a **b** : the young of various fishes of the genus *Galaxias* and of several salmonid fishes (genus *Retropinna*) that appear in large schools in New Zealand rivers and lakes **c** : any of various smelts (family Osmeridae) of the coast of California **d** : any of numerous silversides (family Atherinidae) **e** : any of various anchovies of both fresh and salt water in the U.S.
white baker *n, Brit* : SPOTTED FLYCATCHER
white ball *n* : CUE BALL 2
white ballet *n* [trans. of F *ballet blanc*] : BALLET BLANC
white balsam *n* **1** : either of two firs of western America: **a** : WHITE FIR 1a(1) **b** : ALPINE FIR **2** : BALSAM OF PERU **3** : a balsamweed (*Gnaphalium obtusifolium*)
white baneberry *also* **white bead** *n* : a white-fruited baneberry (as *Actaea alba* of No. America) — called also *white cohosh*
whitebark \ˈ=ˌ=\ *n* **1** : any of several American trees (as the white poplar or whitebark pine) with pale or whitish bark **2** *Austral* : a blueberry ash (*Elaeocarpus cyaneus*)
whitebark pine *also* **whitebarked pine** \ˈ=ˌ=-\ *n* : a pine (*Pinus albicaulis*) of the western U.S. having thin pale brown or creamy white bark and soft brittle wood
white bass *n* **1** : a No. American freshwater food fish (*Lepibema chrysops*) that is abundant in the region of the Great Lakes and upper Mississippi and very similar to the yellow bass but shorter and more compressed **2** : WHITE PERCH 1
white basswood *n* : an American basswood (*Tilia heterophylla*) of the Allegheny region
white bay *n* **1** : RED BAY **2** : SWEET BAY 2
white·beam \ˈ=ˌbēm\ *n* [ˈ*white* + -*beam* (as in *quickbeam*)] : a European ornamental tree (*Sorbus aria* or *Pyrus aria*) having leaves with a white-tomentose undersurface, corymbose white flowers, and red fruits
white bean *n* : an Australian tree (*Ailanthus imberbiflora*) with up to 50 leaflets in each pinnate leaf and a thin fruit in the form of a pod
white bear *n* **1** : GRIZZLY BEAR **2** : POLAR BEAR
whitebeard \ˈ=ˌ=\ *n* [ME *whiteberd*, fr. ˈ*white* + *berd* beard] : an old man : GRAYBEARD
white bedstraw *n* : WILD MADDER 2a
white beech *n* **1** : AMERICAN BEECH **2** *dial Eng* : HOP HORNBEAM **3** : QUEENSLAND BEECH
white beet *n* : CHARD
white-bellied nuthatch \ˈ=ˌ==-\ *n* : WHITE-BREASTED NUTHATCH
white-bellied seal *n* : MONK SEAL
white-bellied swallow *n* : a widely distributed No. American swallow (*Iridoprocne bicolor*) that nests in holes in trees and is iridescent greenish blue above and pure white below
whitebelly \ˈ=ˌ==\ *n* : any of several birds with wholly or partly white underparts: as **a** : BALDPATE 2 **b** : PRAIRIE CHICKEN 1 **c** : SHARP-TAILED GROUSE **d** : a pigeon (*Leptotila jamaicensis*) common in Jamaica
white ben *n* [ˈ*white* + obs. *behen, ben* bladder campion, fr. NL *behen*] : BLADDER CAMPION 1
white bent *also* **white bent grass** *n* **1** : a redtop (*Agrostis alba*) **2** : MATGRASS 1b
white·berry \ˈ=- — *see* BERRY\ *n* : WHITE BANEBERRY
whitebill \ˈ=ˌ=\ *n* **1 a** : AMERICAN COOT **b** : SLATE-COLORED JUNCO **2** : a West Indian sardine (*Harengula macrophthalmus*)
white birch *n* **1** : either of two European birches with white or ash-colored bark: **a** : a birch (*Betula pendula*) with smooth twigs and markedly drooping branches **b** : a birch (*B. pubescens*) with pubescent twigs and somewhat drooping branches **2** : either of two No. American birches with predominantly white bark: **a** : PAPER BIRCH **b** : AMERICAN GRAY BIRCH
whitebird \ˈ=ˌ=\ *n, Brit* : SPOTTED FLYCATCHER
white bird's-eye *n* : either of two common stitchworts (*Stellaria media* and *S. holostea*)
white biskop *n* : a biskop (*Sparodon durbanensis* or *Sparus durbanensis*) that is usu. somewhat smaller than the black biskop, is silvery with grayish fins and somewhat bluish above, and has the two middle upper teeth large and protruding
white blast *n* : injury to plants caused by the feeding of insects (as the onion thrips) and characterized by a fading and shriveling of the tissues
white blister *n* : WHITE RUST
white blood cell *n* : a blood cell that does not contain hemoglobin : LEUKOCYTE
white-blooded \ˈ=ˈ==\ *adj* : having blood that is not reddened by hemoglobin; *often* : ANEMIC
white·blow \ˈhwīt,blō *also* ˈwī-\ *n* [fr. earlier *whiteblowe grass*, fr. obs. *whiteblowe* whitlow (alter. of ME *whitflowe*) + *grass* — more at WHITLOW] : WHITLOW GRASS a
white bomb·way *also* **white bomb·we** \-ˈbäm(ˌ)(b)wā\ *or* **white bom·be** \-m(ˌ)bā\ *n* [origin unknown] : an Indian timber tree (*Terminalia procera*) having lustrous light brown wood with slight dark streaks
white bone *n, often cap W&B* **1** : a lower class Lolo; *esp* : a free descendant of Chinese captives — distinguished from *black bone* **2** : a Kazak noble descended from a medieval Khan — distinguished from *black bone*
white book *n* [ME *whit boke*, fr. *whit* white + *boke, book* book] : an official report of government affairs bound in white — compare WHITE PAPER
whitebottle \ˈ=ˌ==\ *n* **1** : BLADDER CAMPION 1 **2** : DAISY 1b
white box *n* : any of several Australian eucalypts having white or light-colored bark
white·boy \ˈ=ˌbȯi\ *n* **1** *archaic* : a favored person : PET **2** *usu cap* [so called fr. their wearing white shirts outside their other clothes as a means of recognition on their night raids] : one of an agrarian association formed among the Irish peasants in 1761 esp. to redress their grievances against their landlords and to resist collection of tithes
white·boy·ism \-ȯi,izəm\ *n* -S *usu cap* : the principles or conduct of the Whiteboys
white brant *n* : LESSER SNOW GOOSE
white brass *n* : an inferior brass containing more than 49 percent zinc
white bread *n* [ME *whitbred*, fr. *whit* white + *breed* bread] : bread made from white and esp. bleached flour — compare WHOLE WHEAT FLOUR
white break *n* : a virus disease of the gladiolus characterized by gray or yellowish specking or streaking resembling thrips injury and by striking white blotchery of colored flowers
white-breasted nuthatch \ˈ=ˌ==-\ *n* : a common nuthatch (*Sitta carolinensis carolinensis*) of America east of the Rocky mountains that has a black head, largely bluish gray upper parts, and the underbody mostly white
white bronze *n* : a very light colored bronze having large proportion of tin in its composition
white broom *n* : a low European shrub (*Cytisus albus*) with trifoliolate leaves and yellowish white flowers
white brush *n* : a low shrub (*Lippia ligustrina*) of the southwestern U.S. and adjacent Mexico having fragrant white racemose flowers that yield much honey
white bryony *n* : either of two European bryonies (*Bryonia alba* and *B. dioica*)
white bud *n* : a zinc deficiency disease of Indian corn characterized by light yellow streaking and white necrotic spotting in the young emerging leaves
white buffalo *n* **1** : MOUNTAIN GOAT 1 **2** *or* **white buffalo fish** : SMALLMOUTH BUFFALO
white bur-sage *n* : a low whitish brittle-twigged somewhat spiny shrub (*Franseria dumosa*) of the southwestern U.S. that is a locally important browse plant esp. for sheep and goats
white bush *n* **1** *Brit* : a white-flowered hawthorn **2** : a sweet pepperbush (*Clethra alnifolia*) **3** : PRIVET ANDROMEDA
white buttercup *n* : GRASS-OF-PARNASSUS
white butterfly *n, chiefly Brit* : WHITE 3d(2)
white buttonwood *n* **1** : WHITE MANGROVE 1 **2** : a plane (*Platanus occidentalis*) of eastern No. America having the lobes of the leaves shallow and broader than long
white cake *n* : a butter cake in which the whites but not the yolks of eggs are used
white camas *n* : a camas (*Zigadenus glaucus*) chiefly of eastern U.S. having a creamy white perianth that is suffused with green, bronze, or purple
white campion *n* : any of several white-flowered herbs: as **a** : a viscid-pubescent European herb (*Lychnis alba*) with fragrant flowers — called also *white cockle* **b** : STARRY CAMPION **c** : SNOWY CAMPION
white cankerroot *or* **white cankerweed** *n* : a rattlesnake root (*Prenanthes alba*)
white·cap \ˈ=ˌkap\ *n* **1 a** : the male of the European redstart **b** *Brit* : WHITETHROAT 1 **c** : TREE SPARROW 1 **2** : a wave crest breaking into white foam **3 a** : HORSE MUSHROOM **b** : HARDHACK 1 **4 a** : one who wears a white cap **b** *also* **white·cap·per** *usu cap* \-pə(r)\ : a member of a group using a white cap as an identifying badge; *esp* : one of a self-appointed vigilance committee attempting by lynch-law methods to drive away or coerce persons obnoxious to it
white carp *n* : CARPSUCKER
white cast iron *n* : WHITE IRON 2
white cat *or* **white catfish** *n* : any of several No. American freshwater catfishes (genus *Ictalurus*); *esp* : a catfish (*I. catus*) that is native to coastal streams of the eastern and southern U.S. and introduced in California and Nevada, is pale olive to bluish above and silvery below, and reaches a length of two feet
white cedar *n* **1** : any of various No. American trees: as **a** (1) : SOUTHERN WHITE CEDAR (2) : the soft wood of the southern white cedar largely used for shingles, boats, woodenware, and posts **b** : PORT ORFORD CEDAR **c** : MACNAB CYPRESS **d** : CALIFORNIA JUNIPER **e** : CANOE CEDAR **f** : INCENSE CEDAR **g** : a common arborvitae (*Thuja occidentalis*) — see TREE illustration **2 a** : a timber tree (*Protium altissimum*) of Guiana **b** : its fragrant wood used esp. for cabinetwork and canoes **3** *Austral* : CHINABERRY 2; *also* : its wood **4** : any of several So. American trees of the genus *Tabebuia*
white cell *n* : WHITE BLOOD CELL
white cement *n* : a portland cement made from raw materials very low in the iron compounds that give the gray color to the usual portland cement
white chamomile *n* : a common chamomile (*Anthemis nobilis*)
white·chap·el cart \ˈhwīt,chapəl- *also* ˈwī-\ *or* **whitechapel** *n* -S *usu cap W* [fr. *Whitechapel*, district of eastern London, England] : a light 2-wheeled spring cart used esp. for family or light delivery service
white charlock *n* : JOINTED CHARLOCK
white-cheeked goose \ˈ=ˌ=-\ *n* : a goose that constitutes a variety (*Branta canadensis occidentalis*) of the Canada goose and has the white head patch divided by a black band under the throat so as to form two cheek patches
white-cheeked pintail *n* : BAHAMA DUCK
white cherry *n* : COACHWOOD 1b
white chestnut oak *n* : CHESTNUT OAK
white-chinned petrel \ˈ=ˌ=-\ *n* : a large petrel (*Procellaria aequinoctialis*) of southern oceans that is all black except for a white mark on the chin and often extended on to the face
white chip *n* **1** : a white-colored poker chip that is usu. the least valuable chip **2** : a token or sum of insignificant worth — compare BLUE CHIP
white chub *n* : SPOTTAIL SHINER
white cinnamon *n* **1** : WINTER'S BARK **2** : CANELLA 3
white clematis *n* : any of several clematises; *esp* : a white-flowered clematis (*Clematis ligusticifolium*) of western No. America
white clergy *n* : the Russian Orthodox secular clergy — distinguished from *black clergy*
white clintonia *n* : WHITE ADDER'S-TONGUE
white cloud mountain fish *also* **white cloud** *n* : a very small Chinese freshwater fish (*Tanichthys albonubes*) that is brilliantly striped in gold and blue with the caudal fin red and tipped with white in the male and is often kept in the tropical aquarium
white clover *n* : a clover with white flowers: as **a** : WHITE DUTCH CLOVER **b** : WHITE SWEET CLOVER
white coal *n* **1 a** : WATERPOWER **b** : ELECTRICITY **2** : TASMANITE
whitecoat \ˈ=ˌ=\ *n* **1** : a very young hair seal and esp. a harp seal **2** : the soft pliable white woolly skin of the whitecoat
white coat *n* : the finishing coat in plastering
white cockle *n* : WHITE CAMPION a
white cohosh *n* : WHITE BANEBERRY
white-collar \ˈ=ˈ==\ *adj* **1** : belonging or relating to a population segment or class made up of salaried employees (as teachers, sales persons, office workers, civil servants) whose duties permit the wearing of street clothes and call for well-groomed appearance — compare BLUE-COLLAR **2** : of, relating to, characteristic of, or restricted to individuals of the white-collar segment or of a corresponding socioeconomic level ⟨*white-collar* housing⟩ ⟨*white-collar* crime⟩
whitecomb \ˈ=ˌ=\ *n* : favus of fowls that is marked by proliferation of grayish white crumbly crusts about the comb, earlobes, and wattles and sometimes progresses to the feathered surfaces where loss of feathers and cuplike encrusted lesions may follow
white commissure *n* : the ventral commissure of the spinal cord
white coolwort *n* : FALSE MITERWORT
white copperas *n* **1** : GOSLARITE **2** : COQUIMBITE
white coral *n* : a graceful branched coral (*Amphihelia oculata*) native to the Mediterranean
whitecorn \ˈ=ˌ=\ *n, dial Brit* : a small grain (as wheat, barley, or oats) that becomes light-colored as it ripens
white cornel *n* : FLOWERING DOGWOOD
white corpuscle *n* : LEUKOCYTE
white count *n* [*white* (*corpuscle*) + *count*] : the count or the total number of the leukocytes in blood usu. stated as the number in one cubic millimeter
white crab *n* **1** : GHOST CRAB **2** : GREAT LAND CRAB
white crappie *n* : a crappie (*Pomoxis annularis*) that is typically smaller and more silvery than the black crappie, highly esteemed as a panfish, and often used for stocking small ponds — called also *white perch*
white-crested touraco \ˈ=ˌ==-\ *n* : a southern African touraco (*Tauraco corythaix*)
white cricket *n* : TREE CRICKET
white croaker *n* : either of two fishes found along the California coast: **a** : KINGFISH 1a(2) **b** : QUEENFISH a
white crop *n* : a crop of grain (as wheat, rye, barley, or oats) that loses its green color or becomes white in ripening as distinguished from a green crop or a root crop
white-cross diatom *n* : a diatom of a genus (*Stauroneis*) related to *Navicula* with longitudinal and transverse bands that form a cross
white crow *n, Africa* : an Old World vulture (*Neophron percnopterus*)
white-crowned pigeon \ˈ=ˌ=-\ *n* : a large chiefly slate-colored pigeon (*Columba leucocephala*) of Florida and the West Indies having the head white above
white-crowned sparrow *n* : a sparrow (*Zonotrichia leucophrys*) of northern and western No. America that is related to the white-throated sparrow and has the head striped with white and black
whitecup \ˈ=ˌ=\ *n* : a prostrate woody Argentine herb (*Nierembergia rivularis*) with white or rarely blue-tinged or rose-tinged tubular flowers
white curlew *n* : WHITE IBIS
white currant *n* : any of various white-fruited garden currants derived from a natural species (*Ribes sativum*)
white cutch *n* : GAMBIER
white cypress *n* **1** : a bald cypress (*Taxodium distichum*) **2** : WHITE CYPRESS PINE
white cypress pine *n* : an Australian evergreen timber tree (*Callitris glauca*) yielding a pale fragrant insect-resistant timber
whited *adj* [ME, fr. past part. of *whiten* to white] **1** : covered with white or whiting; *esp* : WHITEWASHED **2** : made white : WHITENED, BLEACHED
white daisy *n* : DAISY 1b
white dammar *n* : PINEY DAMMAR
white damp *n* : a poisonous gas encountered in coal mines and made up chiefly of carbon monoxide
white dead nettle *n* : a European dead nettle (*Lamium album*) with white flowers
white deal *n, Brit* : NORWAY SPRUCE; *also* : its wood
white death shark *n* : GREAT WHITE SHARK
white diarrhea *n* : any of several diseases of birds or mammals marked by passage of pale or whitish diarrheic stools: as **a** : pullorum disease esp. in young birds **b** : WHITE SCOURS **c** : coccidiosis of chickens
white dock *n* : a perennial No. American dock (*Rumex mexicanus*) with pale-green leaves like those of a willow
white dogwood *n* **1** : any of several white-flowered shrubs or trees of the genus *Cornus* (as flowering dogwood) **2** *Brit* : GUELDER ROSE
whited sepulcher *n* [so called fr. the simile applied by Jesus to the scribes and Pharisees, Mt 23:27 (AV)] : a person inwardly corrupt or wicked but outwardly or professedly virtuous or holy : HYPOCRITE
white dutch clover *also* **white dutch** *n, usu cap D* : a Eurasian clover (*Trifolium repens*) that has long stalked leaves and round heads of white or pink-tinged flowers and is a common ingredient of lawn and pasture grass-seed mixtures and an important honey plant — compare WHITE SWEET CLOVER, SHAMROCK
white dwarf *n* : a whitish star of high surface temperature and very low intrinsic brightness usu. with a mass about comparable to that of the sun but of such small dimensions that its average density is enormous
white-ear \ˈ=ˌ=\ *n* [alter. of (assumed) ME *whit-ers*, fr. *whit* white + *ers* rump — more at ASS] : ²WHEATEAR
white eardrops *n pl but sing or pl in constr* : DUTCHMAN'S-BREECHES
white-eared hummingbird \ˈ=ˌ=-\ *n* : a hummingbird of the genus *Hylocharis* (as *H. leucotis* of Central America or *H. xantusii* of Lower California)
white earth *n* **1** : a siliceous earth from eastern Bavaria used as a substrate for organic pigments for paints **2** : an impure silica
white elephant *n* **1** : an albinic Indian elephant of which more or less of the usual dark pigment is absent from the skin giving it a pale color and which is rare and sometimes venerated in India, Ceylon, Siam, and Burma **2 a** : a property requiring much care and expense and yielding little profit **b** : an object (as a gadget or trinket) that is no longer esteemed by its owner though not without value to others ⟨conducted a *white elephant* sale to help the church⟩ **3** : a badge or emblem showing the figure of a white elephant
white elm *n* **1** : AMERICAN ELM **2** : ROCK ELM 1
white ensign *n* : the British naval ensign
white-eye \ˈ=ˌ=\ *n* **1 a** : SILVEREYE **b** : WHITE-EYED VIREO **c** : WHITE-EYED DUCK a **2 a** : HADDOCK **b** : WALLEYE 4
white-eyed coot \ˈ=ˌ=-\ *n* : WHITE-WINGED SCOTER
white-eyed duck *also* **white-eyed pochard** *n* : either of two pochards having males with the irises of the eyes white: **a** : a widely distributed Old World duck (*Aythya nyroca*) **b** : an Australian duck (*Aythya australis*) — called also *hardhead*
white-eyed tit *n* : SILVEREYE
white-eyed towhee *n* : a towhee (*Pipilo erythrophthalmus alleni*) of Florida
white-eyed vireo *n* : a vireo (*Vireo griseus*) of the eastern U.S. with a greenish olive back, white underparts, and a yellow ring around the white eye
white-eyelid monkey *n* : MANGABEY
whiteface \ˈ=ˌ=\ *n* **1** : a white-faced animal; *specif* : HEREFORD **2 a** : BALDPATE 2; *also* : BLUE-WINGED TEAL **b** : any of several Australian passerine birds of the genus *Aphelocephala* that resemble tits **3 a** : dead-white facial makeup **b** : a performer (as a clown) wearing whiteface
white-faced \ˈ=ˈ=\ *adj* **1 a** : having a wan pale face **b** : having the face white in whole or in part — used esp. of animals in which other parts of the body, hair, or plumage are dark **2** : having a white facing : white-fronted ⟨a *white-faced* storefront⟩ ⟨a *white-faced* hem⟩
white-faced duck *or* **white-faced teal** *n* : BLUE-WINGED TEAL
white-faced glossy ibis *n* : a glossy ibis (*Plegadis guarauna*) occurring from the southwestern U.S. southward through much of So. America and having reddish lores and usu. white feathers about the base of the bill
white-faced hornet *n* : a large American hornet (*Vespula maculata*) predominantly dull black with striking white markings on head, thorax, and abdomen — called also *bald-faced hornet*
white father *n, usu cap W&F* [so called fr. his customarily dressing in white] : a member of the Society of African Missioners founded about 1868 by the Abbé Lavigerie
white feather *n* [so called fr. the superstition that a white feather in the plumage of a gamecock is an indication that he is a poor fighter] : a mark or symbol of cowardice — used chiefly in the phrase *show the white feather*
white fiber *n* **1** : a medullated nerve fiber **2** : one of the inelastic fibers of typical connective tissue
white fibrous tissue *n* : typical connective tissue in which white fibers predominate as distinguished from elastic tissue
white·field·ian \(ˈ)hw|it;fēldēən, |it *also* (ˈ)w|\ *also* **white·field·ite** \ˈ=ˌfēl,dīt\ *n* -S *usu cap* [George *Whitefield* †1770 Eng. evangelist and founder of Calvinistic Methodists + E -*ian*, -*ite*] : an adherent or follower of the evangelist George Whitefield
white fig *n* : PURPLE FIG
white finch *n, dial Eng* : CHAFFINCH
white fir *n* **1 a** : any of several firs of western America: as (1) : a tree (*Abies concolor*) with a narrow erect crown, pale foliage, and soft wood that is used for lumber — called also *California white fir, Colorado fir* (2) : LOWLAND FIR (3) : AMABILIS FIR (4) : ALPINE FIR **b** : the wood of a white fir **2** *Brit* : NORWAY SPRUCE; *also* : its wood **3** : a Chinese evergreen tree (*Cupressus funebris*) with gracefully drooping branches

1whitefish \'⸗,⸗\ *n, pl* **whitefish** *or* **whitefishes** [ME *whitfish,* fr. *whit* white + *fish*] **1 a :** any of various food fishes (family Salmonidae) esp. of the genus *Coregonus* that resemble the salmon and trout in having an adipose dorsal fin but have a smaller and nearly or quite toothless mouth and that inhabit clear lakes and streams of No. America, Europe, and Asia — see LAKE WHITEFISH, MENOMINEE WHITEFISH, ROCKY MOUNTAIN WHITEFISH; compare CISCO, HOUTING, LAKE HERRING **b :** any of various fishes (as a menhaden, a young bluefish, or a whiting) in some respect felt to resemble the true whitefishes **c** *Brit* **:** any of various market fishes (as cod, sole, halibut) with white flesh that is not oily **d :** BELUGA **2 :** the flesh of a whitefish esp. as an article of food

2whitefish \"\ *vi* **:** to fish for whitefish — **whitefisher** \'⸗,⸗⸗\ *n* — **whitefishery** \'⸗,⸗(⸗)⸗\ *n*

white flag *n* **1 :** a flag or something used as a flag of plain white that in all civilized armies is recognized as a flag of truce and as a token of surrender when displayed over a place, position, or body of men **2 :** a token of weakness or yielding

white flesh·er \-'fleshə(r)\ *n* [*white flesh* (fr. 1*white* + *flesh*) + *-er*] *dial* **:** RUFFED GROUSE

white flux *n* **:** a flux consisting chiefly of potassium carbonate and obtained as a white or grayish mass by the deflagration of tartar with an equal or larger amount of saltpeter

whitefly *n* **:** any of numerous small injurious homopterous insects constituting the family Aleyrodidae, being related to the scales, and being usu. covered with a white or gray powder — see CITRUS WHITEFLY, GREENHOUSE WHITEFLY

whitefoot \'⸗,⸗\ *n, pl* **whitefeet** *see sense 3* **1 :** a white mark on a horse's foot between the fetlock and the coffin; *also* **:** a horse having such a mark **2** *usu cap* **:** one of a secret society replacing the Whiteboys in Ireland about 1832 **3** *pl* **whitefoots :** WHITE-FOOTED MOUSE

white-footed mouse \'⸗,⸗⸗-\ *n* **:** any of numerous No. American mice of the genus *Peromyscus; esp* **:** a common woodland mouse (*P. leucopus*) of the eastern U.S.

white fox *n* **:** ARCTIC FOX

white friar *n, often cap W&F* [ME *white frere,* fr. 1*white* + *frere* friar; fr. his white habit] **:** a Carmelite monk

white fringe *n* **:** FRINGE TREE

white-fringed beetle *also* **white-fringed weevil** \'⸗,⸗-\ *n* **:** a flightless beetle (*Pantomorus leucoloma* or *Graphognathus leucoloma*) native to So. America but recently introduced into Australia and the southeastern U.S. where it is a pest of cultivated plants

white fringed orchid *or* **white fringed orchis** *n* **:** a bog orchid (*Habenaria albiflora*) of eastern No. America with sheathing leaves and a spike of pure-white fringed flowers

white fringe fungus *n* **:** a fungous parasite (*Fusarium aleyrodis*) of the white fly

white fritillary *n* **:** a California bulbous herb (*Fritillaria liliacea*) with white and sometimes green-veined flowers

whitefront \'⸗,⸗\ *n* **:** WHITE-FRONTED GOOSE

white-fronted capuchin \'⸗,⸗⸗-\ *n* **:** a So. American monkey (*Cebus albifrons*) of a reddish brown color with white face, forehead, shoulders, and breast

white-fronted goose *n* **:** a large widely distributed grayish brown goose (*Anser albifrons*) of northern Europe and No. America with a white forehead and black, white, and gray underparts — see TULE GOOSE

white-fronted lemur *n* **:** a lemur (*Lemur albifrons*) of Madagascar having a white forehead

white-fronted owl *n* **:** SAW-WHET OWL

white frost *n* **:** FROST 1c(1)

white fungus *or* **white fungus disease** *n* **1 :** a disease of fishes caused by a fungus (*Saprolegnia ferox*) and characterized by a white coating of hyphae esp. on peripheral parts (as fins) **2 :** a disease of insects caused by a fungus of the genus *Beauveria* — compare CALCINO

white gall *n* **:** an oak apple collected after the escape of its gall wasp and lighter in color and poorer in tannin than a green gall

white game *n* **:** ptarmigan in winter plumage

white gasoline *or* **white gas** *n* **:** gasoline containing no tetraethyl lead

white gentian *n* **:** FEVERROOT

white ginger *n* **1 :** the rootstock of ginger dried and scraped — called also *African ginger, cochin ginger;* distinguished from *black ginger* **2 :** a large Indian herb (*Hedychium coronarium*) that is widely cultivated in warm regions for its showy white fragrant flowers

white goat *n* **:** MOUNTAIN GOAT 1

white gold *n* **1 :** a pale alloy of gold that somewhat resembles silver or platinum and usu. contains nickel with or without other alloying metals (as tin, zinc, or copper) **2 :** a natural resource (as sugar or cotton) that is white or becomes white in processing

white goldenrod *n* **:** SILVERROD 2

white goods *n pl* **1 a :** white fabrics esp. of cotton or linen **b :** articles (as sheets, towels, tablecloths, or curtains) orig. or typically made of white cloth **2 :** major household and esp. electric appliances (as washers, stoves, or refrigerators) that are typically finished in white enamel

white goose *n* **:** SNOW GOOSE

white goosefoot *n* **:** LAMB'S-QUARTERS 1

white gourd melon *also* **white gourd** *n* **:** WAX GOURD 2

white grama *n* **:** a grass (*Leersia virginica*) found in moist places in the eastern U.S.

white granite *n* **:** a ceramic ware like or identical with ironstone china

white grass *n* **1 :** VELVET GRASS **2 :** WHITE GRAMA

white grease *n* **:** lard considered unfit for human consumption and used industrially — compare YELLOW GREASE

white grouse *n* **1 :** PTARMIGAN **2 :** SHARP-TAILED GROUSE

white grub *n* **:** a grub that is the larva of a June beetle or other related beetle and that feeds on the roots of grasses and other plants

white grunt *n* **:** a common grunt (*Haemulon plumieri*) of Florida and the West Indies that is typically striped with blue and a brassy yellow

white guard *n, sometimes cap W&G* [from the *White Guard,* anti-Communist force organized in Finland in 1918] **:** a reactionary or counterrevolutionary force or party

white guillemot *n* **:** BLACK GUILLEMOT — used esp. when it is in winter plumage

white gum *n* **:** any of numerous Australian eucalypts (as *Eucalyptus viminalis, E. haemastoma, E. gunnii, E. coriacea*) having notably pale bark

white gyrfalcon *n* **:** a gyrfalcon (*Falco rusticolus candicans*) of northern No. America that is predominantly white with slaty or brownish gray barring or spotting on the upper parts

white-haired \'⸗¦⸗\ *adj* [ME *white-harid,* fr. 1*white* + *hered, harid* haired] **1 :** having white hair or covered with white hairs ⟨a *white-haired* plant⟩ **2 :** FAIR-HAIRED 2

white hake *n* **:** a hake (*Urophycis tenuis*) that is a leading food fish along the New England coast and southward

white·hall \'hwīt,hȯl *also* 'wī-\ *adj, usu cap* [fr. *Whitehall,* thoroughfare of Westminster metropolitan borough, London, England, lined with chief offices of the British government] **:** of or relating to Whitehall esp. as symbolizing the British government or its policies ⟨a *Whitehall* statement⟩

whitehanded \'⸗¦⸗\ *adj* **1 a :** having white hands **b :** having white paws **2 :** having or keeping the hands free from evil acts; *broadly* **:** PURE, UNSTAINED, UNSULLIED

whitehanded gibbon *n* **:** LAR

white-hard \'⸗¦⸗\ *adj* **:** quite dry but unfired — used of clay or clay ware

white harvest *n* **:** a harvest when the ground is white from hoarfrost **:** a late harvest

white hat *n, slang* **:** an enlisted man in the U.S. Navy

white hawk *n, Irish* **:** a male hen harrier

whitehead \'⸗,⸗\ *n* **1 :** any of various birds with more or less white about the head: as **a :** BLUE GOOSE **b :** SURF SCOTER **c :** a small New Zealand bird (*Mohoua ochrocephala albicilla*) that resembles a warbler **d :** a domestic pigeon of a breed distinguished by a white head **2 :** MILIUM 3 **3 :** any of several diseases of grasses characterized by bleaching of the heads: as **a :** such a condition in oats due to stem injury by maggots or thrips **b whiteheads** *pl but sing or pl in constr* **:** TAKE-ALL

white-headed \'⸗¦⸗⸗\ *adj* **1 a :** having the head white **b** (1) **:** having white hair (2) **:** having very light hair **2 :** highly favored **:** FORTUNATE ⟨the *white-headed* boy . . . of the new generation —Van Wyck Brooks⟩

white-headed eagle *n* **:** BALD EAGLE

white-headed fungus *or* **white-headed scale fungus** *n* **:** a fungus (*Podonectria coccicola*) that is parasitic on scales and esp. the purple scale and the Glover scale

white-headed goose *n* **:** BLUE GOOSE

white-headed gull *n* **:** HEERMANN'S GULL

white-headed harpy *n, Brit* **:** MARSH HARRIER

white-headed stilt *n* **:** a stilt (*Himantopus leucocephalus* or *H. himantopus leucocephalus*) that is predominantly white with black wings and markings on nape and mantle and that is widely distributed in the southwestern Pacific including Australia and New Zealand — see KAKI

white-headed tern *n* **:** a So. American tern (*Sterna trudeaui*) that has the top of the head white and without a black crest

white-headed woodpecker *n* **:** a woodpecker (*Dendrocopos albolarvatus*) of the Sierra Nevada and Cascade ranges that is predominantly black with a white wing patch, white head and neck, and a red patch just above the nape

1white·head·ian \(')hwīt¦hedēən *also* (')wī-\ *adj, usu cap* [Alfred North *Whitehead* †1947 Eng. mathematician and philosopher + E *-ian*] **:** of, relating to, or typical of Alfred North Whitehead or his organismic or process philosophy

2whiteheadian \"\ *n -s usu cap* **:** a follower of A. N. Whitehead

white heart *n* **1 white hearts** *pl but sing or pl in constr* **:** DUTCHMAN'S-BREECHES **2 :** SQUIRREL CORN

white-heart hickory *n* **:** MOCKERNUT

white heat *n* **1 :** a temperature (as for copper and iron from 1500° to 1600° C) higher than red heat at which a body becomes brightly incandescent so as to appear white **2 :** a state of intense mental or physical strain, emotion, or activity ⟨his anger was at *white heat*⟩ ⟨the campaign was at a *white heat*⟩

white heath aster *n* **:** HEATH ASTER

white heel splitter *n* **:** a large No. American freshwater mussel (*Lasmigona complanata*) with a sharp alate process behind the umbones

white heifer disease *n* **:** a congenital abnormality of the reproductive organs of heifers resulting in sterility and occurring chiefly in white or nearly white animals of the Shorthorn breed

white hellebore *n* **1 :** an herb of the genus *Veratrum* (as the European *V. album* or the American *V. viride*) — called also *false hellebore* **2 :** the roots or rhizomes of a white hellebore

white heron *n* **1 :** GREAT WHITE HERON **2 :** SNOWY EGRET

white hickory *n* **1 :** any of several hickories (as the shagbark or mockernut) **2 :** the firm whitish sapwood of a hickory

white holland *n, usu cap W&H* **:** a medium-sized pure-white domestic turkey of a variety possibly derived as a sport from the Bronze

white holly *n* **:** a common American holly (*Ilex opaca*)

white honeyflower *n* **:** LOCUST 3a(2)

white honeysuckle *n* **1 :** SWAMP AZALEA **2** *dial Eng* **:** WHITE CLOVER **3 :** HONEYSUCKLE 2b

white hoolet *n, dial Eng* **:** BARN OWL

white hope *n* **1** *slang* **:** a white contender for a pugilistic championship held by a colored person **2 :** one of which much is expected; *esp* **:** a person undertaking a difficult task

white horde *n, usu cap W&H* **:** a Mongolian people powerful in Russia in the 14th century — compare GOLDEN HORDE

white horehound *n* **:** HOREHOUND 1a

white horse *n* **1 :** WHITECAP 2 **2 :** a large mass of tough sinewy oilless substance lying in the head of a sperm whale just above the upper jaw and extending in streaks into the junk above it **3 :** any of several suckers; *esp* **:** a common sucker (*Catostomus commersoni*)

white·horse \'hwīt,hȯ(ə)rs *also* 'wī-\ *adj, usu cap* [fr. *Whitehorse,* town of southern Yukon, Canada] **:** of or from Whitehorse, the capital of Yukon Territory, Canada **:** of the kind or style prevalent in Whitehorse

white horse nettle *n* **:** TROMPILLO

white-hot \'⸗¦⸗\ *adj* **:** being at or radiating white heat; *esp* **:** ardently zealous or fervid

white house *adj, usu cap W&H* [fr. the *White House,* mansion in Washington, D.C. assigned to the use of the president of the United States] **:** of or relating to the White House esp. as symbolizing the presidency or its policies ⟨the *White House* staff⟩

white hun *n, usu cap W&H* **:** EPHTHALITE

white hunter *n* **:** a white man who is expert in jungle lore and usu. serves as guide and professional hunter to an African safari

white ibis *n* **1 :** an ibis (*Eudocimus albus*) of tropical America and the southern U.S. having white plumage with the wings tipped with black **2 :** an Asiatic ibis (*Threskiornis melanocephala*) having the plumage chiefly white and the bare skin of head and neck blue-black

white ice *n* **:** coarsely granular porous ice (as of a glacier) that is usu. formed by compaction of snow and appears white to the eye **:** NÉVÉ — compare BLACK ICE, BLUE ICE

white indian *n, usu cap W&I* **:** an American Indian of light or partially albino complexion: as **a :** a Cuna of Panama **b :** MENOMINI

white indian hemp *n, usu cap I* **:** SWAMP MILKWEED

white ipecac *or* **white ipecacuanha** *n* **1 :** IPECAC SPURGE **2 a :** a Brazilian plant (*Ionidium ipecacuanha*) of the family Violaceae **b :** the root of this plant which has the properties of ipecac

white iron *n* **1 :** iron in thin sheets coated with tin **:** TINPLATE **2 :** a hard silvery-white pig iron or cast iron having its carbon content almost entirely in combined form

white ironbark *n* **:** any of several Australian eucalypts (esp. *Eucalyptus paniculata* and *E. leucoxylon*) with pale bark and light-colored very hard wood used esp. in bridges and buildings and for railroad ties

white iron pyrites *n pl but sing or pl in constr* **:** MARCASITE 1b

white ironwood *n* **1 a :** a timber tree (*Hypelate trifoliata*) of the family Sapindaceae that occurs in Florida and the West Indies and has edible berries **b :** the hard wood of this tree that is used in shipbuilding and for wheel spokes, tool handles, and similar items and that resembles mahogany — called also *Madeira wood* **2 a :** a southern African timber tree (*Toddalia lanceolata*) of the family Rutaceae **b :** the dark tough elastic hard wood of this tree

white jade *n* **:** ALABASTER 2

white kalmuck *n, usu cap W&K* **:** an Altaic Tartar

white kite *n, Irish* **:** a male hen harrier

white label *n* [so called fr. its bearing a hand-written or typed white label in contrast to the printed label used on trade records] **:** one of the first group of phonograph records pressed from a recording usu. for executive, artist, and reviewer opinion

white lady *n* **:** a cocktail consisting of gin, Cointreau liqueur, lemon juice, and often white of egg shaken with cracked ice and strained before serving

white lady's-slipper *or* **white lady-slipper** *n* **:** a No. American lady's slipper (*Cypripedium candidum*) having greenish white flowers striped purplish within

white lake bass *n* **:** WHITE BASS

white land crab *n* **:** GREAT LAND CRAB

white lark *n, dial Eng* **:** SNOW BUNTING

white latten *n* **:** TINPLATE

white lauan *n* **:** a light-colored lauan; *esp* **:** a grayish red wood obtained from a Philippine tree (*Pentacme contorta*) of the family Dipterocarpaceae and often used as a substitute for mahogany

white laurel *n* **1 :** SWEET BAY 2 **2 :** a shrub (*Rhododendron occidentalis*) of the Pacific coast of the U.S. with yellow⸗blotched flowers

white lead *n* [ME *white led,* fr. 1*white* + *leed, led* lead] **:** any of several poisonous white pigments containing lead: as **a :** a pigment consisting of basic lead carbonate of variable composition and physical properties that is usu. produced from metallic lead or litharge, acetic acid, moisture, and carbon dioxide by various processes (as the Dutch process, Carter process, or chamber process) and marketed as a heavy powder or as a paste in linseed oil, that has good hiding power esp. in the case of the finer particle sizes and forms tough flexible films tending to chalk and darkening by reaction with hydrogen sulfide in industrial atmospheres, and that is now used chiefly in exterior paints often in mixtures with other white pigments — called also *basic carbonate white lead, ceruse;* see FLAKE WHITE, KREMNITZ WHITE **b :** a pigment that consists essentially of a mixture of equimolar ratios of normal lead sulfate and monobasic lead sulfate and is used in mixtures with other pigments in exterior paints — called also *basic sulfate white lead;* compare SUBLIMED WHITE LEAD **c :** a pigment consisting either of a basic lead silicate approximately $Pb_3(OH)_2SiO_3$ or of a surface layer of monobasic lead silicate and monobasic lead sulfate on a core of silica — called also *basic silicate white lead*

white lead ore *n* **:** CERUSSITE

white leaf *n* **1 :** WHITE POPLAR 1a **2 :** tragacanth consisting of thin translucent pieces of horny texture

white leather *n* **1 :** leather prepared with alum and salt **:** tawed leather **2 :** the ligamentum nuchae of a quadruped

white-leaved sage \'⸗,⸗-\ *n* **:** PURPLE SAGE 1

white leg *n* **:** MILK LEG 1

white leghorn *n, often cap W&L* **:** a pure white domestic fowl of outstanding egg-producing ability constituting a variety of the Leghorn breed

white lettuce *n* **:** RATTLESNAKE ROOT a

white light *n* **1 :** light that has the same spectral energy distribution as unobstructed noon sunlight and is approximately the same as that of a blackbody radiator at 6000° C **2 :** light that to the normal eye matches the color of noon sunlight although it may have a different spectral energy distribution

white lightning *n* **:** MOONSHINE 3

1white lime *n* **:** pure lime

2white lime *or* **white linden** *n* **:** any of several lindens or basswoods with leaves white or whitish beneath

white line *n* [trans. of NL *linea alba*] **:** a band or edge of something white: as **a** (1) **:** LINEA ALBA (2) **:** the tendinous arch of the pelvic fascia (3) **:** the cross section of the leafy layer of a horse's hoof where the periphery of the sole unites with the lower border of the wall and bars of the hoof **b :** a blank line in a printed text **c :** untarred rope or other cordage **d :** a line or part of a metal cut or engraving that prints white by reason of having the design cut away and the background left high; *also* **:** the technique of producing such effects **e :** a stripe painted on a road and used to guide traffic

white-line \'⸗,⸗\ *vt* [*white line*] **:** to mark with a white line

white-lined sphinx \'⸗,⸗-\ *n* **:** an American sphinx moth (*Celerio lineata*) whose larvae eat the leaves of cotton, apple, grape, currant, and many other plants, whose fore wings are olive brown with a longitudinal buff stripe and with most of the veins lined with white, and whose hind wings are black with a central reddish band

white linn *n* **:** WHITE LIME

white-lipped \'⸗¦⸗\ *adj* **:** having white lips

white-lipped peccary \'⸗,⸗-\ *n* **:** a peccary (*Tayassu pecari*) that is larger than the collared peccary and predominantly blackish with whitish cheeks

white-lipped snake *n* **:** an Australian elapid snake (*Denisonia coronoides*) that is related to the copperhead but not esp. dangerous, is brown to olive above shading to creamy white or salmon pink ventrally, and has the upper lip usu. white and bounded by a black streak and sometimes a yellow collar about the neck

white liquor *n* **:** the cooking liquor prepared from recovered alkali in the sulfate and soda processes

white list *n* **:** a list of approved or favored items: as **a :** a list of business concerns that are worthy of patronage by reason of compliance with usu. specified conditions (as in regard to treatment of employees) **b :** a list of cultural or amusement items (as plays or books) approved (as in respect to moral worth or orthodoxy) **c :** a list of actual or potential employees who are desirable for employment — compare BLACKLIST

white-list \'⸗,⸗\ *vt* [*white list*] **:** to include on a white list

white-livered \'⸗¦⸗⸗\ *adj* [1*white* + *livered;* fr. the former belief that the choleric temperament depends on the body's producing large quantities of yellow bile] **:** deficient in vigor and courage **:** COWARDLY, PUSILLANIMOUS ⟨a *white-livered* backslider⟩ ⟨born *white-livered*⟩

white liverwort *n* **:** GRASS-OF-PARNASSUS

white locoweed *also* **white loco** *n* **:** a perennial herb (*Oxytropis lambertii*) of the western U.S. that is very poisonous to stock and has linear to elliptic or oblong leaves and elongate flower clusters

white locust *n* **:** LOCUST 3a

white lotion *n* **1 :** a fluid astringent preparation made of lead acetate, zinc sulfate, and water and used largely in veterinary practice for wounds, scratches, or suppurations **2 :** a preparation made of sulfurated potash instead of lead acetate and used in dermatologic practice for various skin diseases

white louse *or* **white louse scale** *n* **:** a scale (*Unaspis citri*) that is esp. destructive to citrus in Australia

white lupine *n* **:** a Eurasian white-flowered lupine (*Lupinus albus*) widely cultivated for forage and erosion control

1white·ly *adv* [ME *whitly,* fr. *whit* white + *-ly,* adv. suffix] **:** so as to show or appear white **:** with an effect of whiteness ⟨reflect light ~ like clouds or snow —*Time*⟩

2white·ly *adj* [ME *whitly,* fr. *whit* white + *-ly,* adj. suffix] *chiefly Scot* **:** light in color **:** WHITISH, PALE

white mahogany *n* **1 a :** a pale or light-colored mahogany **b :** PRIMAVERA 2 **2 a :** an Australian eucalypt (*Eucalyptus triantha* or *E. acmenoides*) that yields a pale strong straight⸗grained wood used esp. for railway ties and posts **b :** the wood of this tree

white maire *n* **:** a small New Zealand tree (*Olea lanceolata*) with slender opposite leaves and small apetalous flowers followed by red pulpy drupes

white mallow *n* **1 :** MARSHMALLOW 1 **2 :** ALKALI MALLOW

white mangrove *n* **1 :** a small shrub to moderately large tree (*Laguncularia racemosa*) of the family Combretaceae that grows in brackish waters along the seacoasts of western Africa and tropical America, has flowers with fine small petals and a persistent top-shaped calyx, and is locally important as a source of tannins **2 :** a small or medium-sized tree (*Avicennia officinalis*) growing in brackish water esp. along the shores of the southwestern Pacific, having leaves white beneath, and yielding hard pale lumber and usable quantities of tannin; *broadly* **:** any of several mangroves of the genus *Avicennia*

white man's burden *n* [fr. "The White Man's Burden" (1899), poem by Rudyard Kipling †1936 Eng. writer] **:** the supposed duty of the white peoples to manage the affairs of the undeveloped colored races

white·man's foot \'⸗,manz-\ *n* **:** BROAD-LEAVED PLANTAIN

white mapau *n* **:** either of two New Zealand trees: **a :** a small often shrubby tree (*Carpodetus serratus*) with panicles of small white flowers followed by shining black capsules **b :** TARATA

white maple *n* **1 a :** any of several maples having pale bark: as (1) **:** SILVER MAPLE (2) **:** OREGON MAPLE (3) **:** RED MAPLE **b :** WHITE MAPAU **2 :** the clear pale sapwood of a sugar maple (*Acer saccharum*)

white mariposa *n* **:** a California perennial herb (*Calochortus venustus*) with typically white red-blotched flowers

white-marked tussock moth \'⸗,⸗-\ *n* **:** a tussock moth (*Hemerocampa leucostigma*) having larvae that sometimes defoliate various shade and fruit trees

white marlin *n* **:** a sport fish (*Makaira albida*) of the Atlantic ocean that is blue above and silvery below and seldom attains a weight of 100 pounds — compare BLUE MARLIN

white matter *n* **:** neural tissue esp. of the brain and spinal cord that consists largely of medullated nerve fibers, has a whitish color, and typically underlies the cortical gray matter or is gathered into central tracts and peripheral nerves

white meat *n* [ME *whit-mete,* fr. *whit* white + *mete* meat] **1** *archaic* **:** food (as butter or cheese) derived from milk **:** dairy products **2 a** (1) **:** a meat (as veal or pork) that is light in color esp. when cooked — compare RED MEAT (2) **:** meat of those portions (as breast and wings) of a table fowl that are nearly white when cooked — compare DARK MEAT **b** *South* **:** fat salt pork **:** FATBACK **3** *slang* **:** ACTRESS

white-meat tuna *n* [*white meat*] **:** ALBACORE; *also* **:** the canned flesh of this fish

white melilot *n* **:** WHITE SWEET CLOVER

white merganser *n, dial Eng* **:** a smew (*Mergus albellus*)

white metal *n* **1 :** any of several lead-base or tin-base bearing

metals **2 :** any of several white alloys (as pewter or britannia) **3 :** copper matte having virtually all the iron removed and containing therefore about 80 percent copper and 20 percent sulfur
white mica *n* **:** MUSCOVITE
white miller *n* **1 a :** CASEMAKING CLOTHES MOTH **b :** a common American arctiid moth (*Diacrisia virginica*) that is pure white with a few small black spots — compare WOOLLY BEAR **2 :** an artificial angling fly with white wings and hackle, white silk body, and silver ribbing and tag
white mineral oil *n* **:** LIQUID PETROLATUM
white mineral primer *n* **:** a white pigment consisting of calcium carbonate
white mint *n* **:** a peppermint with light-green stems and foliage that is cultivated chiefly in Europe — compare BLACK MINT
white mold *n* **1 :** COTTONY ROT **2 :** any of several diseases of plants that resemble cottony rot and are caused by fungi esp. of the genus *Ramularia* or *Erostrotheca*
white monk *n, often cap W&M* [ME, fr. *white* + *monk;* fr. the color of his habit] **:** a Cistercian monk
white moss *n* **:** a pale grayish or whitish moss (genus *Leucobryum*) growing chiefly in open damp woodlands and forming rounded masses like large pincushions; *esp* **:** a common moss (*L. glaucum*) of eastern No. America
white mountain apache *n, usu cap W&M&A* [fr. *White Mountain* (Sierra Blanca Peak) in southern New Mexico] **:** a division of the San Carlos Apache
white mountain ash *n* [[1]*white* + *mountain ash*] **:** an Australian mountain ash (*Eucalyptus fraxinoides*) that has rough bark on the lower trunk and yields a lumber very similar to that of the European or American ashes
white mountain butterfly *n, usu cap W&M* [fr. *White Mountains,* mountains of the Appalachian range in northern New Hampshire] **:** a delicate brownish butterfly (*Oeneis melissa semidea*) of the family Satyridae found near the peaks of the White mountains
white mouse *n* **:** an albino house mouse
white mulberry *n* **:** an Asiatic mulberry tree (*Morus alba*) with white to light or dull red fruits that is the favored tree for feeding silkworms and is widespread in cultivation and as an escape — compare BLACK MULBERRY
white mule *n* [so called fr. its lack of color and fr. its powerful kick] **:** MOONSHINE 3
white mullein *n* **:** a densely hairy Eurasian herb (*Verbascum lychnitis*) with racemose white flowers that is naturalized in No. America
white mullet *n* **1 :** a silvery mullet (*Mugil curema*) of the Atlantic and Pacific coasts **2 :** any of several silvery suckers of the genus *Moxostoma* (family Catostomidae); *esp* **:** a fish (*M. papillosum*) of the coastal streams from the Dismal swamp southward
white mundic *n* **:** ARSENOPYRITE
white muscle disease *n* **1 :** STIFF-LAMB DISEASE **2 :** a disease of calves similar to or identical with stiff-lamb disease
white mustard *n* **:** a Eurasian mustard (*Brassica hirta*) with rough-hairy foliage, a long-beaked hispid pod, and pale yellow seeds that yield mustard and mustard oil — compare BLACK MUSTARD
whit·en \ˈhwīt[ə]n *also* ˈwī-\ *vb* **whitened; whitened; whitening** \-t(ə)niŋ\ **whitens** [ME *whitenen,* fr. [1]*white* white + *-nen* -en] *vt* **1 :** to make white or whiter in any way (as by bleaching or blanching or by whitewashing) ⟨~ cloth⟩ **2 :** to give an often specious appearance of purity, guiltlessness, or propriety to **3 :** to deposit a white film of silver on (a metal) by simple immersion ~ *vi* **:** to grow white **:** turn or become white ⟨the hair ~s with age⟩ ⟨the sea ~s with foam⟩ **syn** see PALLIATE
white-necked raven \ˈ⸗ˌ⸗-\ *n* **:** a raven (*Corvus cryptoleucus*) of the southwestern U.S. having the neck feathers white at the base but black at the tips
whitened *adj* [fr. past part. of *whiten*] **:** made white; *esp* **:** given an artificial or specious whiteness (as by bleaching or glossing over)
white negro *n, usu cap N* **1 :** a light-complexioned Negro (as a mulatto) **2 :** an albinotic Negro
whit·en·er \-t(ə)nə(r)\ *n* -S **:** one that whitens: as **a :** an agent (as a bleach) used to impart whiteness to something **b :** a worker whose occupation involves whitening something or applying a whitener to something **c :** a worker who removes a thin layer from hides to remove imperfections or to expose superior leather
white·ness *n* -ES [ME *whitenes,* fr. OE *hwītnes,* fr. *hwīt* white + *-nes* -ness — more at WHITE] **1 :** the quality or state of being white: as **a** (1) **:** white color (2) **:** degree of resemblance to white color **b :** lack of ruddy warmth in the complexion **:** dull pallor (as from terror, grief, or illness) **:** PALENESS **c :** freedom from stain or blemish **:** PURITY, CLEANNESS **2 :** white substance
white night *n* [trans. of F *nuit blanche*] **:** a sleepless night
[1]**whitening** *n* -S [fr. gerund of *whiten*] **1 :** the act or process of making or becoming white **2 :** something that is used to make white **:** WHITING **3 :** the operation of shaving leather on the flesh side to even its thickness
[2]**whitening** *adj* [fr. pres. part. of *whiten*] **1 :** serving to whiten or active in whitening ⟨a ~ compound⟩ ⟨the ~ action of a bleach⟩ **2 :** tending to whiten **:** gradually becoming white ⟨whitening ~ bones⟩
whitening stone *n* **:** a sharpening and polishing stone used esp. by cutlers; *also* **:** a finishing grindstone of fine texture
white noise *n* [so called fr. the analogy of its composition to that of white light] **:** a heterogeneous mixture of sound waves (as thermal noise) extending over a wide frequency range
white-nosed guenon *or* **white-nosed monkey** \ˈ⸗ˌ⸗-\ *n* **:** a monkey (*Cercopithecus nictitans*) of western central Africa marked with a white blotch on the muzzle
white note *n* **:** an open-faced musical note (as a 𝅗𝅥 or 𝅝)
white nun *n* **:** SMEW
white nun orchid *or* **white nun** *n* **:** a very showy tropical American orchid (*Lycaste skinneri*) bearing solitary predominantly white flowers that are often suffused with rose or marked with rosy crimson
white oak *n* **1 :** any of numerous Old World and American oaks having 6 to 8 stamens in each floret, acorns that mature in one year and have the inner surface of the shell smooth, the acorn cup covered with woody scales, and leaf veins that never extend beyond the margin of the leaf: as **a** (1) **:** DURMAST (2) **:** ENGLISH OAK **b :** a large slow-growing long-lived oak (*Quercus alba*) of the eastern U.S. having leaves with usu. 7 deep rounded entire lobes, moderately large acorns, and stout spreading branches that form a broad open head and yielding a moderately heavy wood that is very hard and strong and esp. durable when exposed (as by contact with soil) to damp — see TREE illustration **c :** any of various other American oaks (as the bur oak or the basket oak) felt to resemble the eastern white oak **2 :** wood or lumber obtained from white oak trees
white oakum *n* **:** oakum from untarred rope
white of egg *n, pl* **whites of egg** *or* **whites of eggs :** WHITE 2a(1)
white of the eye : WHITE 2a(2)
white oil *n* **:** any of various colorless odorless tasteless mineral oils prepared from a high-boiling petroleum distillate (as by treating with sulfuric acid, neutralizing, washing, and filtering hot through activated carbon or clay) and used as lubricants for textile and food machinery and in medicine and pharmaceutical preparations
white opal *n* **:** an opal with a predominantly light-colored body
white out *vt* [[4]*white* + *out*] **:** to widen the spacing and esp. the interlinear spacing in (printed matter) by or as if by inserting leads
whiteout \ˈ⸗ˌ⸗\ *n* -S [[4]*white* + *out*] **:** a surface weather condition in an arctic area in which no object casts a shadow, the horizon cannot be seen, and only dark objects are discernible and which is caused by heavy cloud cover over a snow surface so that light coming through the clouds is essentially equal to the light reflected off the snow
white owl *n* **1 a :** SNOWY OWL **b :** BARN OWL **2** *dial* **:** a chamber pot
white paper *n* **1 :** a government report on any subject; *esp* **:** an English publication that is usu. less extensive than a blue book **2 :** a detailed or authoritative report ⟨the network prepared a *white paper* on farm problems⟩ — compare WHITE BOOK
white pareira *also* **white pareira brava** *n* **:** a white or yellowish starchy root that is obtained from a tropical American woody vine (*Abuta rufescens*) and has properties similar to true pareira — compare YELLOW PAREIRA
white partridge *n* **:** PTARMIGAN
white pear *n* **:** either of two southern African timber trees: **a :** a tree (*Pterocelastrus rostratus*) of the family Celastraceae yielding a hardwood used esp. in wagons **b :** a tree (*Apodytes dimidiata*) of the family Icacinaceae yielding a good construction timber
white pelican *n* **:** a very large American pelican (*Pelecanus erythrorhynchos*) that is predominantly white with black wing feathers; *also* **:** any of several similar Old World pelicans (esp. *P. onocrotalus*)
white pepper *n* **:** pepper ground after the outer husk has been removed
white peppermint *n* **1 :** an Australian eucalypt (*Eucalyptus stuartiana*) with a spreading crown and pendulous branches **2 :** WHITE MINT
white perch *n* **1 :** a small anadromous sea bass (*Morone americana*) that is dark green above and silvery below, is found along the coast and in coastal streams of the eastern U.S., and is closely related to the yellow bass **2 :** FRESHWATER DRUM **3 :** a pile perch or related fish of California **4 :** WHITE CRAPPIE
white petroleum jelly *or* **white petrolatum** *n* **:** PETROLATUM b
white phosphorus *n* **:** the element phosphorus in its white or yellowish allotropic form — called also *yellow phosphorus*
white pickle *or* **white-pickle mosaic** *n* **:** a cucumber mosaic in which the fruit becomes pale-colored
white pigweed *n* **:** LAMB'S-QUARTERS 1
white pine *n* **1 a :** a tall-growing pine (*Pinus strobus*) of eastern No. America having smooth bark, long-stalked green cones, leaves in clusters of five, and young shoots with tufts of hair below the insertion of the leaf bundles — called also *American white pine, eastern white pine;* see TREE illustration **b :** any of several other evergreen trees felt to resemble the white pine esp. in having leaves in bundles of five: as (1) **:** SUGAR PINE (2) **:** WESTERN WHITE PINE (3) **:** LIMBER PINE (4) **:** LODGEPOLE PINE (5) **:** WHITEBARK PINE (6) **:** ENGLEMANN SPRUCE **c :** the wood of a white pine and esp. of the eastern white pine which is much used in building construction **2 a** *Austral* (1) **:** any of several camphorwoods (esp. *Callitris robusta*) (2) **:** SHE-PINE (3) **:** COLONIAL PINE **b** *NewZeal* **:** KAHIKATEA
white pine aphid *n* [*white pine*] **:** a plant louse (*Cinara strobi*) that feeds on twigs and branches of white pine in the eastern U.S.
white pine blister rust *also* **white-pine rust** *n* **:** a disease of 5-leaved pine (as Swiss pine or various No. American white pines) that is prob. of Asiatic origin but widely established in Europe and No. America, is caused by a rust fungus (*Cronartium ribicola*) with a complex life cycle requiring a plant of the genus *Ribes* (as a currant or gooseberry) as alternate host, and is marked by destructive invasion of the bark and underlying tissues with swelling and girdling of the infected branch or tree leading to death of the parts above the lesion — compare FELT RUST
white pine resin *n* **:** SANDARAC 3b
white pine weevil *n* **:** a small elongated brownish weevil (*Pissodes strobi*) that feeds in and destroys the new shoots of white pine and Norway spruce and sometimes of other pines and spruces
white pitch *n* **:** a turpentine oleoresin obtained in Europe chiefly from the Scotch pine or the cluster pine, purified by melting with water and straining, and frequently substituted for Burgundy pitch — compare GALIPOT
white plague *n* **:** tuberculosis of the lungs
white plantain *n* **1 :** a pussytoes (*Antennaria plantaginifolia*) **2 :** a rattlesnake plantain (*Goodyera repens*)
white pointer *n, Austral* **:** GREAT WHITE SHARK
white pond lily *n* **:** any of several white-flowered water lilies; *esp* **:** a common No. American water lily (*Nymphaea odorata*) with very fragrant white flowers and rhizomes sometimes used as an astringent
white popinac *n* **:** a small evergreen tropical American leguminous tree (*Leucaena glauca*) that is sometimes cultivated in warm regions for its showy globose heads of white flowers and is widely naturalized in tropical regions
white poplar *n* **1 a :** a Eurasian poplar (*Populus alba*) that is widely cultivated and naturalized in the U.S. and has whitish bark and leaves with a white-tomentose lower surface **b :** an aspen (*Populus tremuloides*) of the U.S. with small leaves and long petioles **2 :** the wood of a tulip tree (*Liriodendron tulipifera*)
white port *n* **:** a heavy-bodied straw-colored dessert wine
white potato *n* **:** POTATO 2a(2)
white prairie clover *n* **:** a prairie clover (*Petalostemon candidum*) of central No. America with terminal spikes of white-petaled flowers
white precipitate *n* **:** either of two mercury-ammonia compounds: **a :** AMMONIATED MERCURY **b :** a crystalline compound $Hg(NH_3)_2Cl_2$ usu. obtained by adding a solution of mercuric chloride to a hot solution of ammonia and ammonium chloride — called also *fusible white precipitate*
white primary *n* **:** a party primary in a southern state open to white voters only ⟨Supreme Court . . . decisions which outlawed the *white primary* —*New Republic*⟩
whiteprint \ˈ⸗ˌ⸗\ *n* **:** a diazotype in which the graphic image appears in black or a color on a white background; *also* **:** a process used for making such prints
white puccoon *n* **:** BLOODROOT 1
white pudding *n* **:** any of several light-colored sausages: as **a :** a mixture of meat (as heart, lungs, liver, or muscle) ground with beef suet or pork fat, mixed with bread crumbs, herbs, onion, and spices, stuffed into sausage casings, and fried or broiled fresh **b :** a mixture of chopped pork fat and oatmeal seasoned with onion, salt, and pepper, stuffed into sausage casings, and cooked fresh
white purslane *n* **:** FLOWERING SPURGE
white pyrite *n* **:** MARCASITE
white quebracho *n* **:** QUEBRACHO 1a
whiter *comparative of* WHITE
white rainbow *n* **:** a bow or arc of light formed by refraction and reflection from drops of water (as of a cloud of fog) too minute to give distinctly the concentric bands of color of the typical rainbow
white rat *n* **:** a rat of an albino strain of the Norway rat that is used extensively as a laboratory animal in biological experimentation
white ratany *n* **:** CHACATE
white rattlesnake *n* **:** a rattlesnake (*Crotalus mitchellii*) of the desert regions of the southwestern U.S. that is light yellowish gray with small brown spots
white rent *n* [ME *white rente,* fr. [1]*white* + *rente* rent] **:** rent reserved or payable in silver — opposed to *black rent;* compare ALBA FIRMA
white rhinoceros *n* **:** a large African rhinoceros (*Ceratotherium simus*) that is a light slaty gray and rare over most of its former range
white ribbon *n* **:** the distinctive badge of various organizations for the promotion of sexual purity or temperance
white robin *n* **:** WHITE CAMPION a
white robin snipe *n* **:** a knot when in fall plumage
white rock *n, usu cap W&R* [[1]*white* + (*Plymouth*) *rock*] **1 :** a white domestic fowl of the Plymouth Rock breed **2 :** any heavy-bodied white domestic fowl as distinguished from a white leghorn or a colored fowl — used esp. in the live poultry market
whiteroot \ˈ⸗ˌ⸗\ *n* **:** BUTTERFLY WEED 1
white rot *n* **1 :** any of several plants (as marsh pennywort and butterwort) formerly held to produce rot in sheep **2 a :** a disease of grapes caused by an imperfect fungus (*Coniothyrium diplodiella*) that produces white or grayish brown-bordered spots on young shoots and fruit **b :** any of several wood rots of various trees caused chiefly by fungi of the genus *Fomes* **c :** a fungous rot of onions, garlic, shallots, and related plants caused by a fungus (*Sclerotinia cepivorum*) and characterized by production of abundant white mycelium **3 :** a watery spoiled condition of eggs in which the white is mixed with the yolk; *also* **:** an egg so spoiled
whiterump \ˈ⸗ˌ⸗\ *n* [[1]*white* + *rump*] **1 :** HUDSONIAN GODWIT **2** *Brit* **:** WHEATEAR
white-rumped sandpiper \ˈ⸗ˌ⸗-\ *n* **:** a common small migratory sandpiper (*Erolia fuscicollis*) of eastern No. America that breeds in the arctic and winters in southern So. America and that is streaked buff and grayish brown with a conspicuous white rump
white-rumped shrike *n* **:** a western No. American shrike (*Lanius ludovicianus excubitorides*) that is largely gray above and plain white on the underparts
white russian *n, usu cap W&R* [*White Russia,* region of western U.S.S.R. + E *-an*] **:** BELORUSSIAN
white rust *n* **1 :** any of various fungous diseases of plants caused by fungi of the genus *Albugo* and characterized by a white powdery mass of conidia exposed by the rupture at maturity of sori produced just beneath the epidermis of the host **2 :** a fungus of the genus *Albugo*
whites *pl of* WHITE, *pres 3d sing of* WHITE
white sage *n* **:** any of several shrubs of western America having canescent or hoary foliage: as **a :** a low shrub (*Ramona polystachya*) of the western U.S. and adjacent Mexico **b :** a common sagebrush (*Artemisia ludoviciana*) **c :** WINTER FAT **d :** CHAMISO **e :** a California aromatic shrubby herb (*Salvia apiana*) that is a good source of honey
white sale *n* **:** a sale of white goods
white salmon *n* **1 :** SILVER SALMON **2 :** a large squawfish (*Ptychocheilus lucius*) of the Colorado river basin that reaches a length of five feet **3 :** YELLOWTAIL a **4 :** INCONNU
white sandbox *n* **:** a young or second-growth sandbox tree with white wood — compare YELLOW SANDBOX
white sanicle *n* **:** WHITE SNAKEROOT
white sapota *also* **white sapote** *n* **:** a Mexican and Central American tree (*Casimiroa edulis*) cultivated for its round pulpy edible fruit, styptic leaves, and narcotic seeds
white sapphire *n* **:** clear or colorless corundum
white sauce *n* **:** a sauce in which the thickening agent (as flour) has not been browned, which consists essentially of milk, cream, or stock with flour and seasoning, and which forms the basis for various sauces ⟨mushroom sauce made with a basic *white sauce*⟩ — see VELOUTÉ
white scale *n* **:** any of various white or pale scales: as **a :** an oleander scale (*Aspidiotus hederae*) **b :** COTTONY-CUSHION SCALE **c :** ROSE SCALE
white scour *n* **:** an infectious diarrhea of calves and sometimes lambs found shortly after birth, marked by profuse yellowish-white discharges, with great dullness, prostration, sunken eyes, retracted belly, hurried breathing, and a subnormal temperature, and caused usu. by coliform bacteria — usu. used in pl.
white sea bass *n* **:** a large croaker (*Cynoscion nobilis*) of the Pacific coast of No. America that is bluish gray above and silvery below, is closely related to the Atlantic weakfishes, and is an important sport and food fish
white senega *n* **1 :** SENEGA ROOT **2 :** SENEGA 2b
white shad *n* **:** a shad (*Alosa sapidissima*)
white shark *n* **:** GREAT WHITE SHARK
white sheep *n* **1 :** DALL SHEEP **2 :** a normal well-behaved individual among a group of discreditable individuals — compare BLACK SHEEP
white shellac *n* **:** a shellac prepared by bleaching orange shellac
white shirt *n, South* **:** REDHEADED WOODPECKER
white shrimp *n* **:** LAKE SHRIMP
whiteside \ˈ⸗ˌ⸗\ *n, dial Eng* **:** GOLDENEYE
white-sided dolphin \ˈ⸗ˌ⸗-\ *n* **:** a spectacled dolphin (*Lagenorhynchus acutus*) of the northern Atlantic
white-sided duck *n* **:** TUFTED DUCK 1
white silk-cotton tree *n* **:** an East Indian tree (*Cochlospermum religiosum*) that yields a gum and has seed pods which yield a fiber — compare BASSORA GUM, KUMBI
white siris *n* **1 a :** a tree (*Albizzia procera*) of India and eastward to the Philippines having a bark used locally as a source of fish poisons and yielding a wood somewhat resembling walnut and resistant to termite attack **b :** a rather large chiefly tropical Australian tree (*Ailanthus imberbiflora*) having a very light soft straight-grained wood often used for toys and boxes **2 :** the wood of a white siris
white sister *n, usu cap W&S* **:** a member of a religious congregation founded by the Abbé Lavigerie as an auxiliary to the White Fathers
white slave *n* **1 :** a woman or girl held unwillingly for purposes of commercial prostitution **2 :** a woman or girl who is transported knowingly in interstate or foreign commerce or in territory subject to federal jurisdiction for purposes of prostitution or debauchery or for other immoral purpose or practice with the intention of inducing, enticing, or compelling her to such purpose or practice and without regard to whether her consent is given
white slaver *n* **:** one engaged in white slave traffic **:** a procurer of white slaves
white slavery *n* **:** enforced prostitution
[1]**whitesmith** \ˈ⸗ˌ⸗\ *n* [[1]*white* + *smith*] **1 :** one who works in tinned or galvanized iron or white iron **:** TINSMITH **2 :** a worker in iron who finishes or polishes the work — sometimes distinguished from *blacksmith*
[2]**whitesmith** \″\ *vi* **:** to work as a whitesmith
white smut *n* **1 :** a plant disease caused by a fungus of the genus *Entyloma* and characterized by light-colored leaf spots formed by the sori and covered with aerial conidia that give them a white powdery appearance **2 :** a fungus of the genus *Entyloma*
white snail *n* **1 :** ROMAN SNAIL **2 :** a European snail (*Helix pisana*) introduced into California where it is a serious pest of citrus plants
white snakeroot *n* **:** a No. American herb (*Eupatorium rugosum*) bearing flat-topped clusters of small white flower heads and being a cause of trembles and milksickness — called also *white sanicle*
white snipe *n* **1** *chiefly Midland* **:** SANDERLING **2** *West* **:** AVOCET
white snowbird *n* **:** SNOW BUNTING
white soapwort *n* **:** RED CAMPION
white sock *n, pl* **white sox :** BLACKFLY — usu. used in pl.
white soft paraffin *n* **:** PETROLATUM b
white sour *n* **1 :** a treatment (as of cotton) with dilute hydrochloric or sulfuric acid to complete the bleaching process and cleanse the fabric **2 :** the bath or solution used in the white sour
white speck *n* **:** FROGEYE a(1)
white spine *or* **white-spine cucumber** *n* **:** any of various cucumbers that bear rather large fruits with pointed white tubercles and are esp. suitable for forcing and slicing
white spirit *n* **:** PETROLEUM SPIRIT — often used in pl.
white spot *n* **1 :** any of several diseases of plants marked by light-colored lesions: as **a :** a disease of alfalfa characterized by spotting and yellowing of the foliage and caused by an unbalanced water supply (as from heavy rainfall following a drought) **b :** HEAT CANKER **c :** a disease of turnips caused by a fungus (*Cercosporella brassicae*) **2 :** ICH — usu. used in pl.
white spruce *n* **1 :** any of several spruces: as **a :** a No. American spruce (*Picea glauca*) with short blue-green leaves and slender cones **b :** ENGELMANN SPRUCE **2 :** the wood of a white spruce; *esp* **:** the light pale tough straight-grained wood of the common white spruce (*Picea glauca*) which is used for construction and as a source of paper pulp
white squall *n* **:** a sudden gust of wind or furious blow that is reputed to come up without being marked in its approach otherwise than by whitecaps or white broken water on the surface of the sea — compare BLACK SQUALL
white squill *n* **:** a commercial squill in which the bulb scales are white or yellowish and which is obtained esp. in Malta — compare RED SQUILL
whitest *superlative of* WHITE
white staff *n* **1 a :** a white wand or staff that is a symbol of office of several officials (as of the British government or royal household) **b :** an office of which a white staff is a symbol **2** *also* **white staff officer :** an official who carries a white staff
white star *n* **1 :** a star of spectral type *A* or *F* having a moderate surface temperature and a white or yellowish color

2 a : an annual morning glory (*Ipomoea lacunosa*) of the southern U. S. with star-shaped leaves and small white or purplish flowers **b :** a bellflower (*Campanula carpatica alba*) with white flowers
white steenbras *n* **:** a southern African sea bream (*Pagellus lithognathus*) — compare RED STEENBRAS
white–stem filaree *n* **:** MUSK CLOVER
white stem pine *n* **:** WHITEBARK PINE
white's thrush *n, usu cap W* [after Gilbert *White* †1793 Eng. clergyman and naturalist] **:** a ground thrush (*Zoothera dauma aurea*) of eastern Asia that rarely straggles to Europe
white stock *n* **:** soup stock made from veal or chicken without colored seasonings and often used in white sauce
white stone *n* **:** a clear colorless imitation gem (as a rhinestone) that simulates the diamond
white stopper *n* **:** any of several trees of the genus *Calyptranthes; esp* **:** a common West Indian tree (*C. pallens*) with light gray bark, shining leaves, and small paniculate flowers
white stork *n* **:** a large white stork (*Ciconia ciconia*) with red bill and legs and black flight feathers that is the common stork of Europe
white streak *n* **:** a virus disease of narcissus characterized by dark green narrow streaks on leaves and flower stems that after flowering turn whitish gray or yellowish
white stringybark *n* **:** an Australian stringybark (*Eucalyptus eugenioides*) with white wood
white stuff *n* **1 :** a composition of whiting and glue used by gilders to cover frames before gilding **2** *slang* **:** any of several addictive drugs usu. taken by injection
white stumpnose *n* **:** a southern African sea bream (*Rhabdosargus tricuspidens*) that closely resembles the common silver bream but is usu. much smaller and is an important sport and market fish — compare RED STUMPNOSE
white sturgeon *n* **:** a sturgeon (*Acipenser transmontanus*) of the Pacific coast of No. America that is the largest freshwater fish of No. America, may become 11 feet long and weigh over half a ton, and is marketed in large numbers
white substance of schwann *usu cap 2d S* [after Theodor *Schwann* †1882 Ger. naturalist, anatomist, & physiologist] **:** MYELIN
white sucker *n* **1 :** a common sucker (*Catostomus commersonii*) **2 :** any of various redhorses **3 :** CARPSUCKER
white sugar *n* [ME *white sugre,* fr. ¹*white* + *sugre* sugar] **:** sugar that in bulk appears white; *esp* **:** GRANULATED SUGAR
white sunday *n, usu cap W&S* [by alter. (influenced by the etymology of *Whitsunday*)] **:** WHITSUNDAY
white supremacist *n* [*white supremacy* + *-ist*] **:** an advocate of or believer in white supremacy ⟨*white supremacists* . . . devise new methods to disenfranchise Negroes —*New Republic*⟩
white supremacy *n* **1 :** the supremacy of white persons over all other racial groups **2 :** a doctrine based on a belief in the inherent superiority of the white race over the Negro race and the correlative necessity for the subordination of Negroes to whites in all relationships; *esp* **:** one that seeks to perpetuate such alleged superiority by restricting political, economic, and social powers and opportunities to white persons ⟨resentment among the colored peoples of the world against the arrogance of *white supremacy* —Frances Witherspoon⟩
white surf fish *n* **:** any of several surf fishes of the California coast that are white or dull silvery in color
white swallowwort *n* **:** a European twining vine (*Cynanchum vincetoxicum*) whose root has been used as an emetic, cathartic, and diuretic
white swamp gum *n* **:** CIDER GUM
white swamp honeysuckle *n* **:** SWAMP AZALEA
white sweet clover *n* **:** a white-flowered usu. tall-growing and biennial sweet clover (*Melilotus alba*) that is a valuable honey plant — called also *white melilot;* compare HUBAM CLOVER
white sycamore *n* **1 :** a bushy-headed Australian tree (*Cryptocarya obovata*) with the leaves pale on the undersurface **2 :** a showy tree (*Polyscias elegans*) of the family Araliaceae that is sometimes cultivated for ornament
whitetail \ˈ⸗,⸗\ *n* **:** any of various animals with white about the tail: as **a :** WHITE-TAILED DEER **b** *dial Eng* **:** WHEATEAR **c :** an Ecuadorian hummingbird (*Urochroa bougueri*) with a partially white tail
white–tailed deer \ˈ⸗,⸗-\ *n* **:** an American deer of the genus *Odocoileus* (*O. virginianus*) that occurs from southern Canada south to northeastern Brazil and Peru and is characterized by a rather long tail white on the undersurface and graceful forward-arching antlers with upright basal snags
white–tailed eagle *n* **1 :** BALD EAGLE **2** *Brit* **:** WHITE-TAILED SEA EAGLE
white–tailed emerald *n* **:** either of two greenish Central American hummingbirds of the genus *Elvira*
white–tailed gnu *n* **:** a very dark gnu (*Connochaetes gnou*) having a partially white tail and being formerly abundant in southern Africa but now restricted to game preserves — called also *black wildebeest*
white–tailed hawk *n* **:** a large hawk (*Buteo albicaudatus*) ranging from Texas to So. America and having the underparts, rump, and tail predominantly white
white–tailed jackrabbit *n* **:** a jackrabbit (*Lepus townsendi*) of the northern great plains that has a white tail and commonly becomes wholly white in winter
white–tailed kite *n* **:** a kite (*Elanus leucurus majusculus*) of warm and tropical America that is largely gray above with black wing coverts and white head, breast, tail, and underparts
white–tailed mongoose *n* **:** a mongoose of the genus *Ichneumia* (*I. albicauda*) distinguished by its white tail
white–tailed ptarmigan *n* **:** a rather small ptarmigan (*Lagopus leucurus*) of mountainous regions from Alaska to New Mexico that becomes pure white in winter
white–tailed sea eagle *n* **:** a bulky long-winged sea eagle (*Haliaeetus albicilla*) that is distinguished by a short white wedge-shaped tail
white–tailed tropic bird *n* **:** a tropic bird (*Phaëthon lepturus*) that has a yellow bill and white tail
white tamarind *n* **1 :** a timber tree (*Acacia glomerosa*) of Mexico and Central America **2 :** the hard heavy tough elastic straight-grained nearly white wood of the white tamarind that is used esp. for floors, joinery, and tool handles
white tassel flower *n* **:** a prairie clover (*Petalostemon candidus*) with silky spikes of white flowers — called also *white tassels*
white tassels *n pl but sing or pl in constr* **:** WHITE TASSEL FLOWER
white tea tree *n* **1 :** an Australian tea tree (*Melaleuca leucadendron*) with white bark **2 :** a New Zealand tea tree (*Leptospermum ericoides*) with heathlike foliage
white tern *n* **:** FAIRY TERN a
white thistle *n* **:** PRICKLY POPPY
whitethorn \ˈ⸗,⸗\ *n* [ME *white thorn,* fr. *white* + *thorn*] **1 a :** a hawthorn (*Crataegus oxycantha*) **b :** SCARLET HAW **2 :** any of several acacias that have peeling bark which gives the trunk a whitish appearance **3 :** a whitish-barked shrub (*Ceanothus incana*) of the coastal mountains of the western U. S. that has often spinose branchlets, leaves whitish beneath, and small white flowers in panicles
white thread *n* **:** a bark disease of rubber trees (genus *Hevea*) and cacao caused by a basidiomycete (*Cyphella heveae*) and characterized by the appearance of white strands of mycelium on the tapped surfaces of the trees
whitethroat \ˈ⸗,⸗\ *n* **1 :** an Old World warbler (*Sylvia communis*) with a white throat, pale gray cap, rusty upperparts, and pale pinkish buff underparts — called also *greater whitethroat* **2 :** WHITE-THROATED SPARROW
white–throated sparrow \ˈ⸗,⸗⸗-\ *n* **:** a common brown sparrow (*Zonotrichia albicollis*) of eastern No. America having a striped crown and a large white patch on the throat
white–throated thickhead *n* **:** THUNDERBIRD 1
white tie *n* **1 :** the white bow tie worn with men's formal evening dress — compare BLACK TIE **2 :** formal evening dress for men ⟨an affair requiring *white tie*⟩
whitetip \ˈ⸗,⸗\ *n* **:** a hummingbird of the genus *Urosticte* with white-tipped tail feathers
white tip *n* **1 :** a disease of leeks esp. in Britain caused by a fungus (*Phytophthora porri*) and characterized by yellowing and dieback of the leaf tips which finally turn white **2 :** any of several diseases of cereal grasses (as maize) and other crop plants caused by mineral deficiencies and resembling fungous white tip in symptoms **3 :** a disease of rice caused by a nematode (*Aphelenchoides oryzae*) and characterized by whitening of the leaf tips
whitetip clover *n* **:** a clover (*Trifolium variegatum*) having flowers purple but often with a white tip
white titi *n* **:** TITI 1b
white–toothed shrew \ˈ⸗,⸗-\ *n* **:** any of various shrews of *Crocidura* or related genera having white teeth — compare RED-TOOTHED SHREW
whitetop \ˈ⸗,⸗\ *n* **1 a** (1) **:** a redtop (*Agrostis alba*) (2) **:** a grass (*Fluminea festucacea*) of northwestern No. America that is an important source of food for wild birds (3) *also* **white topped grass :** any of several grasses of the genus *Danthonia* **b :** FLEABANE **c :** any of several Australian eucalypts; *esp* **:** a widely distributed blackbutt (*Eucalyptus pilularis*) **d :** HOARY CRESS **2 :** a covered wagon with a white top
white–topped aster \ˈ⸗,⸗-\ *n* **:** a plant of the genus *Sericocarpus*
white trash *n* **:** POOR WHITES
white trefoil *n* **:** WHITE DUTCH CLOVER
white trout *n* **1 :** SAND SQUETEAGUE **2 a** *dial Eng* **:** a young sea trout **b :** SUNAPEE TROUT
white trumpet lily *n* **:** a lily (*Lilium longiflorum*) with very fragrant long funnel-formed pure white flowers borne singly or in pairs
whitevein \ˈ⸗,⸗\ *n* **:** a disease of tobacco manifesting itself in the veins of the leaves which become white during curing — often used in pl. but sing. in constr.
white vervain *also* **white verbena** *n* **:** a common American vervain (*Verbena urticaefolia*) with narrow spikes of white flowers
white vitriol *n* **:** zinc sulfate heptahydrate
white wagtail *n, chiefly Brit* **:** PIED WAGTAIL
¹**whitewall** \ˈ⸗,⸗\ *n* [¹*white* + *wall;* fr. its white underparts] *dial Eng* **:** SPOTTED FLYCATCHER
²**whitewall** \ˈ"\ *or* **whitewall tire** *n* [¹*white* + *wall*] **:** an automobile tire having a white sidewall
white walnut *n* **1 a** (1) **:** BUTTERNUT 1b (2) **:** an American hickory; *esp* **:** SHAGBARK HICKORY 1 **b :** the light-colored wood of one of these trees often as specif. distinguished from black walnut **2** *Austral* **:** WHITE SYCAMORE 1
whiteware \ˈ⸗,⸗\ *n* [¹*white* + *ware*] **:** a class of ceramic products that include porcelain, china, pottery, earthenware, stoneware, and vitreous tile, are usu. but not necessarily white, and consist typically of clays, feldspar, potter's flint, and whiting
¹**whitewash** \ˈ⸗,⸗\ *vb* [³*white* + *wash,* v.] *vt* **1 :** to wash, treat, or cover with white liquid composition; *esp* **:** to whiten with whitewash **2 :** to give a speciously pure or fair appearance to: as **a :** to gloss over or cover up (as vices or crimes) **b :** to exonerate or clear (as a person) of charges by means of a superficial or perfunctory investigation or examination or through artful or biased presentation of data **c** *Brit* (1) **:** to legally clear (a bankrupt) of liabilities (2) **:** to free a bankrupt from (debt) by a legal process **3 :** to hold (an opponent) scoreless in a game or contest **:** shut out **4 :** to cause a permanent efflorescent scum to form on (brick) usu. by careless drying, too rapid an application of heat in a kiln, or the use of a clay containing soluble sulfates ~ *vi* **1 :** to whitewash something or someone **2 :** to become whitewashed **:** take whitewash ⟨the wall ~*es* very easily⟩ **syn** see PALLIATE
²**whitewash** \ˈ"\ *n* **1 :** a liquid composition that imparts a white coating to a surface: as **a :** a liquid (as a skin bleach) for whitening the skin **b :** a composition (as of lime and water or whiting, size, and water) for whitening structural surfaces (as of plaster, masonry, or wood) **c :** bird excrement esp. when appearing as a chalky coating on or about a nest or perching site **2 a :** an act or instance of glossing over (as a vice or a reputation) or of clearing a bankrupt; *often* **:** a production or activity (as a book, an article, a verdict, a report, or an investigation) that whitewashes somebody or something **b :** a defeat in a contest in which the loser fails to score **3 :** an efflorescence on the surface of a brick
whitewasher \ˈ⸗,⸗⸗\ *n* **:** one that whitewashes; *esp* **:** one who puts on whitewash
white water *n* **1 a :** frothy water (as in breakers, rapids, or waterfalls) **:** QUICKWATER **b :** sea water appearing light in color over a sandy bottom **2 :** water that has been separated in a paper mill from pulp or paper stock and carries short fibers, fillers, and soluble materials — compare SAVE-ALL
white–water \ˈ⸗,⸗⸗\ *vi, of a whale* **:** to beat the water with the flukes
white water crowfoot *n* [¹*white* + *water crowfoot*] **:** a white-flowered water crowfoot
white water lily *n* [¹*white* + *water lily*] **:** a white-flowered water lily of the genus *Nymphaea* (esp. *N. odorata*) as distinguished from the yellow water lilies of the genus *Nymphaea*
white wavey *n* **:** LESSER SNOW GOOSE
white wax *n* **:** any of various waxes that are naturally white or are rendered so by bleaching: as **a :** BEESWAX 2b — used esp. in pharmacy **b :** CHINESE WAX
white wax scale *n* **:** a scale (*Ceroplastes destructor*) that is a pest on citrus in parts of Australia
white way *n* [*great white way*] **:** a brilliantly lighted street or avenue esp. in a city's business or theater district
white weasel *n* **:** ERMINE 1
whiteweed \ˈ⸗,⸗\ *n* **:** any of various weeds with a white or whitish flower: as **a :** DAISY 1b **b :** HOARY CRESS **c :** DAISY FLEABANE
white whale *n* **:** BELUGA 2
white wheat *n* **:** a wheat with white or pale yellow kernels that are usu. soft and suitable for pastry flour — compare SOFT WHEAT
white widgeon *n, dial Eng* **:** SMEW
white wild indigo *n* **:** a white-flowered plant of the genus *Baptisia*
white willow *n* **1 :** a large willow (*Salix alba*) of Eurasia and northern Africa that is often cultivated and has silky pubescent leaves, gray bark, and light soft tough wood — called also *Huntingdon willow* **2 :** any of several American willows having canescent leaves
white wine *n* [ME *white win,* fr. ¹*white* + *win* wine] **:** a wine ranging in color from faintly yellow (as champagne) to amber (as sherry) that is produced from light-colored grapes or from dark grapes fermented without the pulp, skins, and seeds — compare RED WINE, ROSÉ
whitewing \ˈ⸗,⸗\ *n* **1 a** *Brit* **:** CHAFFINCH **b :** WHITE-WINGED SCOTER **c :** a white-winged dove (*Zenaida asiatica*) found in Jamaica **2 :** a person and esp. a street sweeper wearing a white uniform
white–winged \ˈ⸗ˈ⸗\ *adj* **:** having wings that are white or marked with white
white–winged blackbird *n* **:** LARK BUNTING
white–winged black tern *n* **:** a widely distributed but predominantly Eurasian black tern (*Chlidonias leucopterus*) with conspicuous white shoulder patches and tail
white–winged chough *n* **:** a black Australian corvine bird (*Corcorax melanorhamphus*) that is black with white wing patches
white–winged crossbill *n* **:** a crossbill (*Loxia leucoptera*) of northern No. America with two white wing bars in both sexes
white–winged dove *n* **:** a wild pigeon (*Zenaida asiatica*) of the southern U. S. and southward
white–winged junco *n* **:** a rather large western junco (*Junco aikeni*) that is light gray above and has two white bars on each wing
white–winged scoter *also* **white–winged coot** *n* **:** a large and very common American scoter (*Melanitta deglandi*) that is closely related to the velvet scoter of Europe and has a white speculum of the wing and in the adult male a white spot under the eye
white witch *n* **:** a witch who practices white magic **:** a beneficent witch
white wolf *n* **:** a large wolf (*Canis lupus tundrarum*) of arctic No. America
whitewood \ˈ⸗,⸗\ *n* **1 :** any of various trees that have light-colored or almost white wood: as **a :** BASSWOOD 1a **b :** COTTONWOOD 1 **c :** TULIP TREE **d** (1) **:** either of two trees (*Tabebuia leucoxylon* and *T. pentaphylla*) that are found in the West Indies (2) **:** either of two lauraceous trees (*Ocotea leucoxylon* and *Nectandra antillana*) of the same region **e :** CANELLA 3 **f** (1) **:** a tree (*Atalaya hemiglauca*) of the family Sapindaceae that is found in Australia (2) **:** a cheesewood (*Pittosporum bicolor*) of the same region **g** *Brit* (1) **:** LINDEN (2) **:** WAYFARING TREE (3) **:** NORWAY SPRUCE **2 a :** the wood of a whitewood; *esp* **:** the pale yellowish or brownish soft wood of the tulip tree that is used chiefly for woodenware and interior finishings and in boatbuilding **b :** SAPWOOD **3 :** a rather small tropical American tree (*Drypetes diversifolia*) of the family Euphorbiaceae with milky white bark and ivory white fruits
whitewood bark *n* **:** CANELLA ALBA
white wood sorrel *n* [¹*white* + *wood sorrel*] **:** a white-flowered wood sorrel (as *Oxalis acetosella*)
white work *n* **:** needlework done in white on a white fabric
whiteworm \ˈ⸗,⸗\ *n* **:** WHITE GRUB
white worm *n* **:** an enchytraeid worm used as food for aquarium fish — compare ENCHYTRAE
white wreath aster *n* **:** a No. American herb (*Aster multiflorus*) with a profusion of small white flower heads
whitey *var of* WHITY
white yam *n* **:** a yam (*Dioscorea alata*) that is widely cultivated throughout Australasia and Polynesia for its large roots which have a fine white flesh and are eaten baked or boiled or cooked with coconut milk
white yolk *n* **:** a light yellow yolk that forms thin layers and alternates with yellow yolk in the yolk mass of a bird's egg
whitey wood *n* **:** MAHOE 3
whit·field's ointment \ˈhwit,fēldz- *also* ˈwi-\ *also* **whitfield ointment** \-d-\ *n, usu cap W* [after Arthur *Whitfield* †1947 Eng. dermatologist] **:** an ointment that contains benzoic acid and salicylic acid and is used for its keratolytic effect in treating ringworm and other fungal skin diseases
¹**whith·er** \ˈhwithə(r) *also* ˈwi-\ *adv* [ME *whider, whider,* fr. OE *hwider,* fr. *hwi-* (akin to L *quis* who) + *-der* (as in *hider* hither) — more at WHO, HITHER] **1 :** to what place — used interrogatively ⟨~ went the whistling winds⟩ **2 :** to what or which place — used relatively ⟨we came unto the land ~ thou sentest us —Num 13:27 (AV)⟩ **3 :** to what point, degree, end, conclusion, or design **:** WHEREUNTO, WHERETO — used interrogatively or relatively in a sense not physical ⟨~ will this abuse drive him⟩ ⟨nor have I . . . ~ to appeal —John Milton⟩
²**whither** \ˈ"\ *conj* [ME *whither, whider,* fr. OE *hwider,* fr. *hwider,* adv.] **:** to the place at, in, or to which **:** WHERE ⟨whence I departed, ~ I return —Robert Browning⟩
³**whither** \ˈ"\ *vb* -ED/-ING/-S [ME (Sc) *quhediren, quhethiren, quhidderen,* of Scand origin; akin to Norw dial. *kvidra* to move rapidly to and fro, ON *hvitha* squall of wind, OE *hwitha, hwithu* air, breeze, *hwinan* to make a whizzing sound — more at WHINE] *vi, chiefly Scot* **:** HURRY, RUSH, WHIZ, BLUSTER ~ *vt, chiefly Scot* **:** to throw violently **:** HURL, SHAKE
⁴**whither** \ˈ"\ *n* -S [ME (Sc) *quhidder,* fr. *quhidderen* to *witinc,* fr. *wit* white + *-inc* -ing; akin to OE *hwīt* white and to blow) *chiefly Scot* **:** HURRY, RUSH
whitherso \ˈ⸗⸗,⸗\ *adv* [ME, fr. ¹*whither* + *so*] *archaic* **:** WHITHERSOEVER
whithersoever \ˈ⸗⸗(,)⸗ˈ⸗⸗\ *adv* [ME, fr. ¹*whither* + *so* + *ever*] **:** to whatever place **:** to what place soever **:** WHERESOEVER ⟨I will go ~ you lead⟩
whitherto *adv* [¹*whither* + *to*] *obs* **:** WHITHER
whith·er·ward \-(r)wə(r)d\ *also* **whith·er·wards** \-dz\ *adv* [ME *whitherward, whiderwardes,* fr. *whither, whider* whither + *-ward, -wardes, -ward, -wards*] **:** in what direction **:** toward what or which place **:** toward the place that ⟨knowing not ~ to turn for aid⟩
¹**whit·ing** \ˈhwīd·iŋ, -ītˌ, |ēŋ *also* ˈwī-\ *n* -S [ME, fr. MD *witinc,* fr. *wīt* white + *-inc* -ing; akin to OE *hwīt* white and to OE *-ing* — more at WHITE, -ING] **:** any of various marine food fishes: as **a** (1) **:** a common European fish (*Merlangus merlangus*) of the family Gadidae (2) **:** SILVER HAKE; *broadly* **:** a fish of the genus *Merluccius* **b :** any of several No. American sciaenid fishes (genus *Menticirrhus*) — see CORBINA 1, KING WHITING, NORTHERN WHITING, SILVER WHITING **c** *Austral* (1) **:** a fish of the genus *Sillago* (2) **:** a kelpfish of the genus *Odax*
²**whiting** \ˈ"\ *n* -S [ME, fr. gerund of *whiten* to white] **1** *archaic* **:** the act or process of making white (as by whitewashing or bleaching) **2 :** calcium carbonate prepared as powder by grinding chalk, limestone, or a synthetic product (as precipitated calcium carbonate) and used as a pigment and extender, in putty, and in rubber compounding and paper coating
whiting time *n* [²*whiting*] *obs* **:** the time for bleaching clothes
¹**whit·ish** \ˈhwīd·ish, -ītˌ, |ēsh *also* ˈwī-\ *adj* [ME, fr. ¹*white* + *-ish*] **1 :** somewhat white **:** approaching white **2** *of a color* **:** of a light tint **:** PALE, DILUTE
²**whitish** \ˈ"\ *n* -ES **:** a whitish color
whit·ish·ness *n* -ES **:** the quality or state of being whitish
whit·leather \ˈhwit,- *also* ˈwit,-\ *n* [ME *whitlether,* fr. *whit* white + *lether* leather] **:** WHITE LEATHER
whit·ley council \ˈhwitlē- *also* ˈwi-\ *n, usu cap W&C* [after John H. *Whitley* †1935 Eng. labor expert] **:** one of the permanent voluntary boards in various English industries that are representative of both capital and labor and are organized to settle wages, hours, and other matters of dispute
whit·ling \ˈhwitliŋ *also* ˈwit-\ *n* -S [¹*whit* + *-ling*] **:** SEA TROUT; *esp* **:** a large sea trout
whit·lock·ite \ˈhwit,lä,kīt *also* ˈwi-\ *n* -S [Herbert P. *Whitlock* †1948 Am. mineralogist + E *-ite*] **:** a rare mineral $Ca_3(PO_4)_2$ consisting of calcium phosphate in hexagonal crystals
whit·low \ˈhwit(,)lō *also* ˈwi-\ *n* -S [ME *whitflawe, whitflowe, whitlowe,* prob. fr. *whit* white + *flawe* flaw] **:** ³FELON 1
whitlow grass *n* **:** any of several inconspicuous herbs formerly thought to cure whitlow: as **a :** an annual weed (*Draba verna*) of Europe and No. America with a rosette of basal leaves and tiny flowers succeeded by oblong pods — called also *shadflower* **b :** a small Old World saxifrage (*Saxifraga tridactylites*) **c :** WHITLOWWORT
whitlowwort \ˈ⸗⸗,⸗\ *n* [*whitlow* + *wort;* fr. its being supposed to cure whitlow] **:** a plant of the genus *Paronychia*
whit·man·ese \ˌhwitmə¦nēz, -ēs *also* ˌwi-\ *n* -S *usu cap* [Walt *Whitman* †1892 Am. poet + E *-ese*] **:** language or expression of the kind characteristic of the poet Walt Whitman
whit·man·esque \-¦nesk\ *or* **whit·ma·ni·an** \hwitˈmānēən *also* wi-\ *adj, usu cap* [Walt *Whitman* †1892 + E *-esque* or *-ian*] **:** of, relating to, or resembling Whitman or his literary style
whit·ma·ni·ac \⸗ˈmānē,ak\ *n, usu cap* [blend of *Whitman* and *maniac*] **:** an enthusiast about the poet Whitman
whit·mon·day \ˈ⸗ˈ⸗(,)⸗\ *n, usu cap* [³*whit* + *monday*] **:** the day after Whitsunday observed as a legal holiday in England, Wales, and Ireland
whitney *var of* WITNEY
whit·rack \ˈ(h)wit,rak\ *or* **whit·rick** \-,rik\ *var of* WHITTRET
whit·ster \ˈhwitstə(r) *also* ˈwi-\ *n* -S [ME, fr. *whiten* to white + *-ster*] **:** a linen bleacher
¹**whit·sun** \ˈhwitsən *also* ˈwi-\ *adj, usu cap* [ME *whitson,* fr. *whitsonday* Whitsunday] **:** of, relating to, or observed on Whitsunday or at Whitsuntide ⟨*Whitsun* eve⟩ ⟨*Whitsun* plays⟩
²**whitsun** \ˈ"\ *n* -S *usu cap* [by shortening] **:** WHITSUNTIDE
whitsun ale *n, usu cap W* **:** a church-ale formerly held at Whitsuntide
whit·sun·day \ˈhwit¦səndē, -di, -tsən,dā\ *n, usu cap* [ME *whitesunnedei, witsonday,* fr. OE *hwīta sunnandæg,* lit., white Sunday, fr. *hwīt* white + *sunnandæg* Sunday; prob. fr. the custom of wearing white robes by the newly-baptized, who were numerous at this season] **1 :** PENTECOST 2 **2 :** the 15th day of May that is under Scots law the usual day for the removal of tenants of both burgh and rural tenements
whitsun farthings *n pl, usu cap W* **:** offerings formerly made to the parish priest or to the mother church at Pentecost
whitsun monday *n, usu cap W&M* **:** WHITMONDAY
whitsun term *n, usu cap W* **:** the third term of the academic year at a Scottish university beginning in mid-April and lasting for 9 or 10 weeks
whit·sun·tide \ˈ⸗⸗,tīd\ *n, usu cap* [ME *whitsontide,* fr. *whitson* whitsun + *tide*] **:** the week beginning with Whitsunday and esp. the first three days of this week **:** the season of Pentecost
whitsun tuesday *n, usu cap W&T* [¹*whitsun* + *tuesday*] **:** WHIT-TUESDAY
whit·taw·er \ˈhwi,tȯ(ə)r *also* ˈwi-\ *also* **whit·taw** \-ȯ\ *n* -S

[ME *whittawer*, fr. *whit*lether whitleather + *tawer*] **1** *archaic* **:** one who processes skins by tawing (as to form rawhide) **2** *chiefly dial* **:** a harness maker **:** SADDLER

whit·ten \ˈ(h)witᵊn\ *or* **whitten tree** *n* -s [fr. (assumed) ME *whitten tree*, fr. OE *hwītingtrēow*, fr. *hwīt* white + *-ing* + *trēow* tree] *dial Eng* **:** any of several trees or shrubs: as **a :** GUELDER-ROSE **b :** WAYFARING TREE **c :** ROWAN TREE

whit·ter·ick \ˈ(h)witərik\ *n* -s [prob. imit.] *dial Brit* **:** a European curlew (*Numenius arquata*)

whit·tie-what·tie \ˈ(h)witi,(h)wäti\ *n* -s [prob. redupl. of ¹*what*] *Scot* **:** vague or frivolous talk **:** indecisive or evasive conduct **:** PRETEXT

¹**whit·tle** \ˈhwid·ᵊl, -itᵊl *also* ˈwi-\ *n* -s [ME *whitel*, fr. OE *hwītel*; akin to ON *hvītill* white bed cover, OE *hwīt* white] **1** *archaic* **:** a covering (as a cloak, shawl, or blanket) of heavy fabric **2** *chiefly dial* **:** a flannel (as a petticoat or band) for a baby

²**whittle** \"\ *n* -s [ME *whittel*, alter. of *thwitel*, fr. *thwiten* to cut down, whittle, fr. OE *thwītan*; akin to ON *thveita* to hew, hurl, and perh. to Lith *tvyskinti* to strike sharply] **1 :** KNIFE; *esp* **:** a large strong sheath or clasp knife **2** *dial Brit* **:** WHETSTONE, STEEL

³**whittle** \"\ *vb* **whittled; whittled; whittling** \-d·ᵊliŋ, -t(ᵊ)liŋ\ **whittles** *vt* **1 a :** to pare or cut off chips from the surface of (wood) with a knife **:** cut or shape (as a piece of wood) by so paring or cutting ⟨~ a stick⟩ **b :** to form by whittling ⟨*whittled* a whip from limber ash⟩ — often used with *out* ⟨*whittling* out clothespins while he talked⟩ **2 :** to reduce, diminish, remove, or destroy gradually as if by cutting off bits with a knife **:** PARE ⟨a new line designed to ~ the waist⟩ — usu. used with an adverb (as *away, down, off, up*) ⟨~ down expenses⟩ ⟨~ away a fortune⟩ **3** *obs* **:** to whet the spirits of by drink **:** ply with liquor **:** make inebriated **~** *vi* **1 :** to cut or shape a piece of wood by slowly paring it with a knife **2 :** to wear oneself or another out with worrying or fretting

⁴**whit·tle** \ˈ(h)witᵊl\ *n* -s [by alter.] *chiefly Scot* **:** WHITLOW

whit·tler \ˈhwid·ᵊlə(r), -it(ᵊ)l- *also* ˈwi-\ *n* -s **:** one that whittles

whittling *n* -s [fr. gerund of ³*whittle*] **:** a piece cut away in whittling **:** CHIP, SHAVING

whit·tret \ˈ(h)witrət\ *n* -s [ME *whitrat*, fr. *whit* white + *rat*] *chiefly Scot* **:** WEASEL

whit-tuesday \ˈ;ˈ;(,);\ *n, usu cap W&T* [³*whit* + *tuesday*] **:** the day after Whitmonday

whit week *n, usu cap 1st W & sometimes cap 2d W* [³*whit*] **:** WHITSUNTIDE

whit·worth's quick return \ˈhwit,wərths- *also* ˈwi-\ *n, usu cap W* [after Sir Joseph *Whitworth* †1887 Eng. mechanical engineer and inventor] **:** a quick return in which the follower is a bar rotating or oscillating about one end and carrying a sliding driving sleeve or block rotated uniformly in a circle eccentric to the bar's motion

Whitworth's quick return: *a* follower, *b* sleeve

whitworth thread *n* [after Sir Joseph *Whitworth* †1887] **:** a screw thread with V-shaped cut used chiefly in Britain for screws of larger sizes

whity *or* **whitey** \ˈhwīd·|ē, -īt|, |i *also* ˈwī-\ *adj* [¹*white* + *-y*] **:** WHITISH — usu. used in combination ⟨a dull ~ gray⟩ ⟨~ yellow hair⟩

¹**whiz** *or* **whizz** \ˈhwiz *also* ˈwiz\ *vb* **whizzed; whizzed; whizzing; whizzes** [imit.] *vi* **:** to hum, whir, or hiss like a speeding object (as an arrow or ball) passing through air **:** fly or move swiftly with a hissing or buzzing sound **~** *vt* **:** to cause to whiz: as **a :** to project with sufficient speed to produce a whiz **b :** to rotate very rapidly; *specif* **:** to treat (as grain or sugar) in a whizzer

²**whiz** *or* **whizz** \"\ *n, pl* **whizzes 1 a :** a hissing, buzzing, or whirring sound ⟨the air filled with a ~ from passing traffic⟩ **b :** a movement or passage of something accompanied by such a sound ⟨following the ~ of the bee with her eye⟩; *sometimes* **:** a fast trip ⟨took a ~ to the shore⟩ **2 :** an arrangement or agreement felt to be satisfactory **:** BARGAIN, DEAL

³**whiz** *or* **whizz** \"\ *adv* [²*whiz*] **:** with a whiz

⁴**whiz** \"\ *n, pl* **whizzes** [prob. alter. (influenced by ¹*whiz*) of *wiz*] **:** a person notably qualified or able usu. in a specified field of interest **:** WIZARD 3 ⟨a ~ at mathematics⟩

whizbang *or* **whizzbang** \ˈ;,;\ *n* [²*whiz* + *bang*] **1 a :** a whizzing ending in a bang **b :** one that speeds usu. noisily to a climax **:** WHIZ **2 a :** a small shell of such high velocity that the sound it makes in passing through the air is almost simultaneous with its explosion **b :** a firecracker or similar firework resembling such a shell **c :** a robot bomb

whiz-bang \ˈ;ˈ;\ *adj* **:** EXCELLENT, EXPERT, NOTABLE ⟨a *whiz-bang* technician⟩

whizgig \ˈ;,;\ *n* [¹*whiz* + *gig*] **:** something (as a toy) that whirls with a whizzing sound

whiz·zer \ˈhwizə(r) *also* ˈwi-\ *n* -s **1 :** one that whizzes: as **a :** BULL-ROARER **b :** a centrifugal machine for drying something (as grain, sugar, nitrated cotton) **:** HYDROEXTRACTOR; *also* **:** its attendant **2 :** something notable of its kind: as **a :** an outstandingly attractive or able person **:** WHIZ; *esp* **:** a showily beautiful person **b :** a shrewd, slick, or mischievous trick ⟨the ~ they pulled on us⟩

whizzing *adj* [fr. pres. part. of ¹*whiz*] **:** that whizzes — **whizzing·ly** *adv*

whizzing stick *n* **:** BULL-ROARER

whiz·zle \ˈhwizəl *also* ˈwi-\ *vb* -ED/-ING/-S [¹*whiz* + *-le*] *vi* **:** WHIZ; *esp* **:** make a whizzing sound **~** *vt* **:** to get by stealth or cunning

whl *abbr* wheel

whm *abbr* weighmaster

¹**who** \(ˈ)hü, ˌü\ *pron* [ME, fr. OE *hwā*; akin to OHG *hwer*, interrog. pron., who, OSw *hvar*, Goth *hwas*, L *quis*, interrog. pron., who, *qui*, rel. pron., who, Gk *tis*, interrog. pron., who, Skt *ka*] **1 :** what person or persons **:** which person or persons — used as an interrogative pronoun in direct or indirect questions and serving to ask for specification ⟨~ were appointed to serve on the committee⟩ ⟨tell me ~ was elected president⟩ or to ask for identification ⟨~ is that at the door⟩ ⟨find out ~ they are⟩ or to question someone's character, status, authority, or antecedents ⟨~ are you to give orders to us⟩ or to represent a personal name not properly heard or understood ⟨Mrs. ~⟩ or to introduce a rhetorical question implying the answer *no one* or *nobody* ⟨~ cares⟩ ⟨~ wouldn't⟩ ⟨by the cut of my clothes, the pattern of my shoes and ~ knows what unconscious attributes, he recognized me as an American —Saul Bellow⟩; used by speakers on all educational levels and by many reputable writers, though disapproved by some grammarians, as the object of a verb or a following preposition ⟨~ did I see but a Spanish lady —Padraic Colum⟩ ⟨~ do you think I got a letter from —Walt Whitman⟩ ⟨do not know ~ the message is from —G.K.Chesterton⟩ or less frequently as the object of a preceding preposition ⟨between ~ —Shak.⟩ ⟨stolen from ~ —Ruth Park⟩; compare WHAT, WHOM, WHOSE **2 a :** any person or persons that **:** WHOEVER — used with or without a correlative substantive in a following main clause ⟨~ tells me true, though in his tale lie death —Shak.⟩ ⟨~ seeks, and will not take when once 'tis offered, shall never find it more —Shak.⟩ ⟨his almost obsessional anxiety for personal sincerity, suffer ~ may —Sean O'Faolain⟩; used without criticism as the subject of the clause that it introduces; used by speakers on all educational levels and by many reputable writers, though disapproved by some grammarians, as the object of a verb in the clause that it introduces ⟨I serve ~ I like —*Irish Digest*⟩; compare WHAT, WHOM **b** *archaic* (1) **:** the particular person or persons that **:** he, she, or those that ⟨a fair wrought car . . . : ~ stood therein did seem of great renown —John Keats⟩ (2) *pl in constr* **:** some persons that — used after *there* ⟨if there be ~ convulsively insist upon it —Walt Whitman⟩ **3 —** used as a function word to introduce a restrictive or nonrestrictive relative clause and to serve as a substitute within that clause for the substantive modified by that clause; used esp. in reference to persons ⟨any reader ~ wishes to join with me in this argument —J.E.Baker⟩ ⟨novelists ~ write . . . as they must —Malcolm Cowley⟩ ⟨my father, ~ was a lawyer⟩ but also in reference to groups ⟨Congress, ~ can always speak more precisely —C.P.Curtis⟩ ⟨a generation ~ had known nothing but war —R.B.West⟩ ⟨the English firms ~ opened branches in New York —Hellmut Lehmann-Haupt⟩ or in reference to animals ⟨these were a pair of owls, ~ . . . showed little sign of alarm —Nathaniel Hawthorne⟩ ⟨one of those dogs ~ . . . fawn all over tramps —Nigel Balchin⟩ or in reference to inanimate objects esp. with the implication that the object is felt to have personality ⟨dolls of an older age bracket, ~ are supposed to provide a little girl with a feeling of having a younger sister —*New Yorker*⟩ or with the implication that the reference is really to a person or persons possessing or producing or operating the object ⟨a number of deep southern accents ~ assert that they have been immensely impressed —Blake Clark⟩ ⟨a late legendary accretion, contradicted by earlier sources ~ maintain a Davidic ancestry —F.M.Cross⟩ ⟨the plaintive woodwinds ~ opened the passage —Marcia Davenport⟩; sometimes used after *such* with the implication that the action or state expressed in the clause introduced by *who* is a real or appropriate consequence of what is expressed by *such* or by the phrase containing *such* ⟨such ~ . . . no beauty lack —Shak.⟩; used universally and without criticism as the subject of the clause that it introduces; used by speakers on all educational levels and by many reputable writers, though disapproved by some grammarians, as the object of a verb in the clause that it introduces ⟨old peasants . . . ~, if isolated from their surroundings, one would expect to see in a village church —John Berger⟩ or less frequently as the object of a preceding or following preposition in the clause that it introduces ⟨of ~ I know nothing —Raymond Paton⟩; compare ⁴THAT 1, WHICH, WHOM, WHOSE — **as who** *archaic* **:** as one that **:** as if someone ⟨he nods at us, *as who* should say, "I'll be even with you" —Shak.⟩ ⟨she recoiled — *as who* finds thorns where she sought flowers —Robert Browning⟩ ⟨such speech . . . was probably . . . a mere freak of the tongue . . . *as who* should go to a masked ball in guise of Mephistopheles —John Morley⟩ — **as who should say** *archaic* **:** so to speak ⟨I would build large — in fine embossed vaults and painted arches, *as who should say* —Henry James †1916⟩ — **who is who** *or* **who's who** *or* **who was who :** the identity of or the noteworthy facts about each of a number of persons ⟨lived in this town long enough to know *who's who*⟩ ⟨before I had learned *who was who*⟩

²**who** \ˈhü\ *n* -s **:** the person or persons involved or meant or referred to ⟨I shall ask the next banana peddler the ~ and the why of it —Carl Sandburg⟩

whoa \ˈ(h)wō, ˈhō\ *also* **wo** *or* **woa** \ˈwō\ *v imper* [ME *whoo, who*] — a command to a draft animal to stand still — compare GIDDAP

who·dunit \(ˈ)hüˈdənət, *usu* -əd·+V\ *n* -s [fr. the substandard expression *who done it*] **:** a detective story or a mystery story presented as a novel, a play, or a motion picture ⟨the tautness of a fine ~ —*Newsweek*⟩

who·ev·er \hüˈevə(r)\ *pron* [ME *who ever*, fr. ¹*who* + *ever*] **1 :** whatever person **:** any person at all that **:** no matter who — used in any grammatical relation except that of a possessive ⟨sells . . . eggs to ~ has the money to buy —J.R.Chamberlain⟩ ⟨~ he picks has to have the stature of a collaborator, not a subordinate —*Time*⟩ ⟨~ she weds, she never descends below the rank to which she was born —Agnes M. Miall⟩ ⟨he is a good man himself, ~ his friends are⟩ ⟨that is not true, ~ you heard it from⟩ **2 :** ¹WHO 1 — used in questions expressing astonishment or perplexity ⟨~ can that be⟩

¹**whole** \ˈhōl, *dial* ˈhəl *or with a vowel approaching* ə\ *adj* [ME *hool* healthy, unhurt, entire, fr. OE *hāl*; akin to OHG *heil* healthy, unhurt, ON *heill*, Goth *hails* healthy, well, W *coel* omen, OSlav *cělŭ* healthy, unhurt] **1 a** (1) **:** free of wound or injury **:** UNHURT ⟨thousands . . . who have been killed or wounded . . . might still be alive and ~ —Patrick McMahon⟩ (2) **:** recovered from a wound or injury **:** RESTORED (3) **:** HEALED ⟨here, with one balm for many fevers found, ~ of an ancient evil, I sleep sound —A.E.Housman⟩ **b :** free of defect, damage, or impairment **:** INTACT, UNBROKEN, UNMARRED ⟨anxious lest they were broken and thus make an evil omen, but they were ~ —Pearl Buck⟩ **c :** physically sound and healthy **:** free of disease or deformity ⟨they that are ~ need not a physician —Lk 5:31 (AV)⟩ **2 a :** having all its proper parts or components **:** lacking nothing that belongs to it **:** diminished or reduced in no way **:** ENTIRE ⟨have given a ~ philosophy of history interpreted through these factors —P.A.Sorokin⟩ ⟨brings on a ~ symphony of hammerings and hissings —R.M. Hodesh⟩ ⟨a quorum for the purpose shall consist of two thirds of the ~ number of senators —*U.S.Constitution*⟩ **b :** containing all its natural constituents, components, or elements **:** deprived of nothing by refining, processing, or separation **:** UNMODIFIED ⟨~ blood⟩ ⟨~ milk⟩ **3 a :** constituting the total sum or undiminished entirety of **:** INTEGRAL ⟨engineering feats . . . that have severed ~ continental land masses —M.J. Herskovits⟩ ⟨give their ~ time to the study of patients —*Official Register of Harvard Univ.*⟩ ⟨a ~ two miles of the riverbank had been acquired by the city —Leslie Charteris⟩ **b :** each of or all of the ⟨lost money the ~ 10 days⟩ ⟨took part in the ~ series of battles⟩ **c** *chiefly Scot* **:** constituting the entire number or the totality of — usu. used with *the* or a possessive pronoun **4 a :** constituting an undivided unit **:** UNBROKEN, UNCUT ⟨~ nuts⟩ ⟨a ~ roast suckling pig⟩ **b :** directed to one end **:** completely focused or channeled **:** not scattered or dispersed **:** CONCENTRATED, UNDISTRACTED ⟨gave it his ~ attention⟩ ⟨put his ~ soul into the performance⟩ **5 :** seemingly complete or total ⟨the ~ aim of present strategy is to deter aggression —Denis Healey⟩ **:** very great ⟨felt a ~ lot better for the news⟩ **:** very many **:** EXTENSIVE ⟨~ farms were overrun⟩ **:** LARGE, TREMENDOUS **6 :** constituting a person in his full nature, development, or relations: as **a :** involving mind, body, and emotions ⟨the ~ child — physical, emotional, social — is now considered in planning his remedial work —*College English*⟩ ⟨the spiritual life is or should be a harmonious development of the ~ man —W.R.Inge⟩ **b :** involving moral, social, economic and all other activities and relationships ⟨the central focus of education is the student . . . this is the ~ student in all his relationships and adjustments —D.D.Feder⟩

syn ENTIRE, TOTAL, ALL, GROSS: WHOLE may imply that nothing, or nothing salient, has been left out, omitted, ignored, depreciated, alloyed, or taken away ⟨devoting his *whole* energy to the task⟩ ⟨he of the *whole* party might be supposed untouched by the passion of death —Thomas De Quincey⟩ ⟨throughout his *whole* career he was keenly alive to the course of political events —W.C.Ford⟩ ENTIRE may suggest a being completed, finished, or perfected ⟨my strength is unimpaired, my mind is *entire* —O.S.J.Gogarty⟩ ⟨always the *entire* person, never the mere teacher, who spoke —C.N. Greenough⟩ TOTAL may imply that all possible items or constituents have been counted, weighed, reckoned, or considered ⟨the Soviet threat is *total;* it affects every form of human endeavor —H.S.Truman⟩ ⟨open our homes and our community life to these visitors from abroad so that they can see how we live in our *total* social environment —D.J.Shank⟩ ALL, followed by *the* or by a possessive or demonstrative pronoun sometimes equals WHOLE ⟨*all* the city was in an uproar⟩ ⟨*all* the cake was eaten⟩ or sometimes ENTIRE ⟨*all* their development⟩ ⟨*all* their attention focused on the scene⟩ or sometimes TOTAL ⟨*all* his savings⟩ GROSS adds the indication that no deductions, as for costs, taxes, and replacement funds, have been made ⟨his *gross* salary was a thousand a month, but various taxes made large inroads in this⟩ ⟨the foregoing figures are *gross*, rather than net dividends —*Yrbk. of Railroad Information*⟩ — **out of whole cloth :** out of pure fabrication **:** without basis ⟨a tissue of lies made up *out of whole cloth* —*Current History*⟩

²**whole** \"\ *adv* [ME *hoole*, fr. *hool*, adj., healthy, unhurt, entire — more at ¹WHOLE] **:** ENTIRELY, ALTOGETHER — used in combination chiefly in contrast to *half* ⟨laying a half-dirty cloth upon a *whole*-dirty deal table —Sir Walter Scott⟩

³**whole** \"\ *n* -s [ME *hool*, fr. *hool*, adj.] **1 :** a complete amount or sum **:** a number, aggregate, or totality lacking no part, member, or element **:** an unreduced or unimpaired entirety ⟨the ~ of our creative literature . . . has this law of nature behind it —Herbert Agar⟩ ⟨the ~ of their relationship passed before him —Hamilton Basso⟩ **2 :** something constituting a complex unity **:** a coherent system or organization of parts fitting or working together as one ⟨built its "A" mill, incorporating parts of earlier buildings, and unifying the ~ by a new facade —*Amer. Guide Series: Minn.*⟩ ⟨a musical design can be discovered in particular scenes, and in his more perfect plays as ~s —T.S.Eliot⟩ **syn** see SUM — **on the whole** *adv* **1 :** in view of all the circumstances or conditions **:** all things considered ⟨*on the whole* it seemed best to cut the visit short⟩ **2** *archaic* **:** at the end **:** in conclusion **:** FINALLY **3 :** in general **:** in most instances **:** despite some exceptions **:** TYPICALLY ⟨fathers *on the whole* listed three times as many favorable as unfavorable reactions to having children —C.B.Palmer b. 1910⟩

whole binding *n* **:** FULL BINDING

whole blood *n* [ME *hole blode*, fr. *hole, hool* entire, whole + *blode, blood* blood] **1 :** descent from the same two parents rather than only one — used esp. in the phrase *brothers* (*or sisters*) *of the whole blood;* compare HALF BLOOD **2 :** FULL BLOOD

whole-bound \ˈ;ˈ;\ *adj* **:** FULL-BOUND

whole cannon *n* **:** a 16th and 17th century cannon throwing a projectile weighing from 70 to 120 pounds — compare DEMICANNON

whole-colored \ˈ;,;;\ *adj, chiefly Brit* **:** being all of one color **:** CONCOLOROUS

whole culverin *n* **:** a 16th and 17th century culverin throwing a ball of from 40 to 60 pounds — compare DEMICULVERIN

whole deal *n* **:** a deal board 1¼ inches thick — compare SLIT DEAL

whole-footed *adj* [ME *hole-foted*, fr. *hole, hool* entire, whole + *foted* footed] *obs* **:** having the feet whole (as a solid-hoofed animal or a web-footed bird)

whole gale *n* **:** wind having a speed of 55 to 63 miles per hour — see BEAUFORT SCALE table

wholehearted \ˈ;ˈ;;\ *adj* **:** undivided in purpose, enthusiasm, or will **:** HEARTY, ZESTFUL ⟨~ cooperation⟩ ⟨~ effort⟩ **syn** see SINCERE

whole·heart·ed·ly *adv* **:** in a wholehearted manner

whole·heart·ed·ness *n* **:** the quality or state of being wholehearted

whole hog *n* **:** the whole way or farthest limit **:** ALL ⟨they are the "*whole hog* or none" variety —H.L.Ickes⟩ — used esp. in the phrase *go the whole hog* ⟨went the *whole hog* and named a name —*Time*⟩ ⟨go *whole hog* for knitwear —*New Yorker*⟩ ⟨you might as well go the *whole hog* and line all the dales and lakes with factories —S.P.B.Mais⟩

whole-hog·ger \-ˈhȯgə(r), -ˈhäg-\ *n* **:** one that supports or promotes something without reservation, qualification, or hesitation **:** one that goes the limit or the whole hog ⟨a *whole-hogger* for economy in every constituency except his own —*Irish Statesman*⟩

¹**whole-length** \ˈ;ˈ;\ *adj* **1 :** carried to the full or natural extent **:** not curtailed or abbreviated **:** UNABRIDGED ⟨a *whole-length* analysis⟩ **2 :** having, accommodating, or representing the full height of the human figure **:** not proportionately reduced or foreshortened ⟨a *whole-length* mirror⟩ ⟨a *whole-length* portrait⟩ ⟨a *whole-length* statue⟩

²**whole-length** \ˈ;,;\ *n* **:** a whole-length picture or statue ⟨on the walls were framed *whole-lengths* of a number of 19th century authors⟩ — compare HALF-LENGTH

whole life insurance *n* [*whole life* (fr. ¹*whole* + *life*) + *insurance*] **:** ORDINARY LIFE INSURANCE

wholely *var of* WHOLLY

whole meal *n* **1 :** WHOLE-WHEAT FLOUR **2** *Brit* **:** WHEATMEAL

whole·ness *n* -ES [ME *hoolnesse*, fr. *hool* entire, whole + *-nesse* -ness] **:** the quality or state of being whole **:** an unreduced or unbroken completeness or totality **:** a hale vigor or soundness **:** INTEGRITY

whole note *n* **:** a musical note equal in value to four quarter notes or two half notes — called also *semibreve;* see NOTE illustration

whole number *n* **:** INTEGER

whole plate *n, chiefly Brit* **:** a photographic plate or film 6½x8½ inches in size

whole rest *n* **:** a musical rest corresponding in value to a whole note

wholes *pl of* WHOLE

whole-sail \ˈ;,;\ *adj* **:** being a breeze or wind that permits use of full sail or of nearly full sail **:** not requiring taking in of light sails

¹**whole·sale** \ˈhōl,sāl\ *n* [ME *holesale*, fr. *hole, hool* entire, whole + *sale*] **1 :** the sale of goods or commodities in quantity usu. for resale (as by a retail merchant) **2 :** a large scale or indiscriminate transaction or maneuver — used esp. in the phrase *by wholesale* ⟨killed off the pests by ~⟩

²**wholesale** \"\ *adj* **1 :** of, relating to, or engaged in the sale of goods or commodities in quantity for resale ⟨a ~ grocer⟩ ⟨a ~ lot of store fixtures⟩ ⟨~ failures increased by 36 percent —Eric Sevareid⟩ **2 :** performed on a large scale **:** handling or affecting large numbers or quantities **:** EXTENSIVE, MASSIVE ⟨~ blackmail and extortion amounting to millions —A.L. Vogelback⟩ ⟨~ character assassination —R.L.Roy⟩ ⟨the ~ intrusion of the neon-lit world of mass entertainment — film, radio, jazz — has also left its mark —M.J.Lasky⟩ ⟨a ~ attack upon those who teach English in our colleges —J.D.Adams⟩ **3 :** marked by failure of discrimination, selection, or discretion **:** made, applied, or carried out so as to affect large numbers in the same way without regard to the merits of individual instances ⟨the ~ character of this answer prevents critical examination and discrimination of the particular facts involved in the actual problem —John Dewey⟩

³**wholesale** \"\ *adv* [²*wholesale*] **:** in a wholesale manner ⟨although wartime experience yielded valuable lessons, it cannot be applied ~ to peace —*Economist*⟩

⁴**wholesale** \"\ *vb* -ED/-ING/-S [¹*wholesale*] *vi* **:** to sell at wholesale ⟨averaged a straight $50 markup when he *wholesaled* to the bootlegger —*Motor Trend*⟩ ⟨small plastic novelties that ~ at $2 a hundred⟩ **~** *vt* **:** to sell (something) at wholesale ⟨it was *wholesaling* education in diluted form —Dwayne Orton⟩

wholesale life insurance *n* [²*wholesale* + *life insurance*] **:** life insurance covering a smaller group of employees than the minimum required for a group life insurance policy

whole·sal·er \-ālə(r)\ *n* -s [¹*wholesale* + *-er*] **:** a merchant middleman who sells chiefly to retailers, other merchants, or industrial, institutional, and commercial users mainly for resale or business use — called also *jobber*

whole snipe *n* **:** a common snipe (*Capella gallinago*) of Europe and parts of Asia and Africa — compare GREAT SNIPE, JACKSNIPE

whole·some \ˈhōlsəm *also* -lts-\ *adj, often* -ER/-EST [ME *holsom, hoolsom*, fr. *hol, hool* healthy, entire, whole + *-som* -some] **1 :** promoting health or well-being of mind or spirit **:** tending to moral soundness or vigor **:** corrective or sanative in effect **:** BENEFICIAL, SALUTARY ⟨passes through the ~ ordeal of the royal presence, and issues from it free from all taint —W.M.Thackeray⟩ ⟨brought these difficult situations into the ~ light of world public opinion —Huntington Gilchrist⟩ **2 a :** promoting health of body **:** health-giving **:** SALUBRIOUS ⟨perhaps because our sedative airs are more ~ for those who suffer from high blood pressure —Rebecca West⟩ **b :** tending to restore health **:** CURATIVE, REMEDIAL ⟨prescribe a ~ regimen for the convalescents⟩ **3 a :** sound in body, mind, or morals **:** not sickly, morbid, or diseased **:** HEALTHY ⟨the ~ gush of natural feeling —Nathaniel Hawthorne⟩ ⟨she may be described as plain in appearance, but with a ~ air —C.G.Bowers⟩ **b :** having the simple health or vigor of normal domesticity ⟨~ as the smell of homemade bread just out of the oven —Pamela Taylor⟩ ⟨~ family life⟩ **4 a** *obs* **:** SEAWORTHY **b** *archaic* **:** safely navigable — used of the sea **5 a :** having the value of a needed warning **:** based on well-grounded fear **:** CAUTIONARY, PRUDENT ⟨lived in a ~ dread of her tempers —T.B. Costain⟩ ⟨had too ~ an awareness of the logical difficulties —Benjamin Farrington⟩ **b :** SAFE ⟨it wouldn't be ~ for you to go down there —Mark Twain⟩ **syn** see HEALTHFUL, HEALTHY

whole·some·ly *adv* [ME *holsomliche*, fr. *holsom* wholesome + *-liche* -ly] **:** in a wholesome manner

whole·some·ness *n* -ES [ME *holsomnesse*, fr. *holsom* wholesome + *-nesse* -ness] **:** the quality or state of being wholesome

whole-souled \ˈ;ˈ;\ *adj* **:** moved by ardent enthusiasm or single-minded devotion or attachment **:** WHOLEHEARTED ⟨has demonstrated a *whole-souled* allegiance to the democratic world —B.C.Limb⟩ ⟨men whose dedication to their country was *whole-souled* —Eric Sevareid⟩ **syn** see SINCERE

whole step *or* **whole tone** *n* **:** a musical interval comprising two half steps (as C–D or F♯–G♯)
whole stuff *n* **:** STUFF 2c
whole-time \'=;=\ *adj* **:** FULL-TIME ⟨never possible to maintain a *whole-time* company —Gabriel Fallon⟩
whole-tone scale *n* **:** a musical scale progressing by whole steps
whole vamp *n* **:** a one-piece shoe upper seamed at the back above the heel
whole wheat *adj* **:** made of ground entire wheat berries
whole wheat flour *n* **:** flour that is ground from the whole grain and contains all the constituents of the wheat kernels
who·lism \'hō,lizəm\ *n* -s [by alter. (influenced by ³*whole*)] **:** HOLISM
who·lis·tic \(')hō¦listik\ *adj* [by alter. (influenced by ³*whole*)] **:** HOLISTIC
whol·ly *also* **whole·ly** \'hōl(l)ē, |i, *when emphatic also* 'hōl|l\ *adv* [ME *hoolly,* fr. *hool* entire, whole + *-ly*] **1 :** to the full or entire extent **:** without diminution or reduction **:** ALTOGETHER, COMPLETELY, TOTALLY ⟨the land is used ~ for crops —P.E. James⟩ **2 :** to the exclusion of other things **:** SOLELY ⟨in order to devote himself ~ to this work he resigned —G.F.Smythe⟩ ⟨much prefer to be ~ agriculturalists —L.S.B.Leakey⟩
whom \(')hüm, ,üm\ *pron, objective case of* WHO [ME, fr. OE *hwām,* dat. of *hwā* who — more at WHO] **1 :** ¹WHO 1 — sometimes used as object of a verb or a following preposition ⟨~ shall I send —Isa 6:8 (AV)⟩ ⟨my question was ~ were all the Christmas signals for —W.T.Scott⟩ or more frequently as the object of a preceding preposition ⟨never send to know for ~ the bell tolls —John Donne⟩ though now often considered stilted esp. in oral use; occas. used as predicate nominative with a copulative verb esp. in the vicinity of a preposition or a verb of which it might mistakenly be considered the object ⟨~ say ye that I am —Mt 16:15 (AV)⟩ ⟨regardless of ~ his friends may be⟩ **2 a :** ¹WHO 2a — used as object of a verb or preposition ⟨~ he strikes his crooked tushes slay —Shak.⟩ ⟨I will . . . be gracious to ~ I will be gracious —Exod 33:19 (AV)⟩ ⟨ask ~ you will⟩ **b** *archaic* **:** ¹WHO 2b — used as object of a verb or preposition ⟨how can I curse ~ God has not cursed —Num 23:8 (RSV)⟩ ⟨there are to ~ my satire seems too bold —Alexander Pope⟩ **3 :** ¹WHO 3 — used as the object of a verb or a preceding preposition ⟨those ~ oppression had goaded to rebellion —T.B.Macaulay⟩ ⟨the universities, by ~ he was abundantly honored —J.A.Pollard⟩ ⟨his pet toad ~ he fed regularly —Osbert Sitwell⟩ ⟨these moral types, ~ all recognize —V.S.Pritchett⟩ or less frequently as the object of a following preposition ⟨the man ~ you addressed the letter to⟩; sometimes used as the subject of the clause that it introduces esp. in the vicinity of a verb of which it might mistakenly be considered the object ⟨a . . . recruit ~ he hoped would prove to be a crack salesman —Bennett Cerf⟩ ⟨people . . . ~ you never thought would sympathize —Shea Murphy⟩
whom·ev·er \hü'mevə(r)\ *pron, objective case of* WHOEVER [ME *whom ever,* fr. *whom* + *ever*] **:** WHOEVER 1 — used as object of a verb or preposition ⟨so that she could help ~ she married —Lillian Ross⟩ ⟨~ this alleged autobiography . . . is about, it is a real life —*Springfield (Mass.) City Library Bull.*⟩; sometimes used as the subject of a verb or as predicate nominative with a copulative verb esp. after a preposition or a verb of which it might mistakenly be considered the object ⟨simple possession of the note would be enough to insure the future of ~ held it —Arthur Knight⟩ ⟨I go out to talk to ~ it is —*Guatemala News*⟩ ⟨he attacked ~ disagreed with him⟩
¹**whomp** \'hw|ämp *also* 'w| *or* |ȯmp\ *or* **whoomp** \|ümp\ *n* -s [imit.] **:** a loud slap, crash, or crunch ⟨an alert beaver slaps his heavy flat tail with a tremendous ~ on the surface of the water —Alan Devoe⟩ ⟨could hear the occasional ~ of their guns echoing across the hills —William English⟩
²**whomp** \"\ *vb* -ED/-ING/-S *vi* **:** BANG, SLAP ⟨bombs ~*ed* down —*advt*⟩ ~ *vt* **1 :** BANG, SLAP **2 :** to defeat overwhelmingly **:** TROUNCE ⟨~*ed* their arch-rival in the season's climactic football game⟩
whomp up *vt* **1 :** to stir up **:** AROUSE ⟨*whomp up* interest in the unveiling of new models —*Time*⟩ **2 :** to knock together **:** cook up ⟨have a syndicate call you up and ask you to *whomp up* something special for them —Mel Lazarus⟩ ⟨*whomped up* a story, mailed it, and sat back to await a check —*New Orleans (La.) Times-Picayune*⟩
whom·so \'hüm,sō\ [ME *whom so,* fr. *whom* + *so*] *objective case of* WHOSO
whom·so·ev·er \,hümsə'wevə(r), -sō'e-\ [ME, fr. *whom so* + *ever*] *objective case of* WHOSOEVER
¹**whoo** \'hwü *also* 'wü\ *interj* [origin unknown] — used to express sudden excitement, astonishment, or relief
²**whoo** \'hü\ *n* -s [imit.] **:** the cry of an owl
¹**whoof** \'hwu̇f *also* 'wu̇f\ *n* -s [imit.] **:** a deep snorting sound (as made by a four-footed animal)
²**whoof** \"\ *vb* -ED/-ING/-S *vi* **:** to utter a whoof **:** SNORT ~ *vt* **:** SNORT, BLOW
¹**whoop** \'h|üp, 'hw| *also* 'w| *or* |u̇p; *with reference to coughing* 'h|üp, |u̇p *also* 'hw| *sometimes* 'w|\ *vb* -ED/-ING/-S [ME *whopen,* alter. of *hopen, houpen,* fr. MF *houpper,* of imit. origin] *vi* **1 :** to utter a whoop in expression of eagerness, enthusiasm, or enjoyment **:** SHOUT, HALLOO ⟨made a man want to cry and ~ all at the same time —Laura Krey⟩ **2 :** to utter the cry of an owl **:** HOOT **3 :** to give the spasmodic cough of whooping cough **4 :** to roar support **:** express vociferous endorsement ⟨was ~*ing* for leftist candidates⟩ **5 a :** to go with a roar **:** move with a loud noise of the vehicle or with a shouting of the occupants ⟨a noisy gang, squashed into five cars and a taxi, were ~*ing* through the quieter squares —Dorothy Sayers⟩ ⟨the Western express . . . ~s out through the suburbs —Lawrence Constable⟩ **b :** to be rushed through by acclamation or with noisy support ⟨the bill ~*ed* through both houses⟩ **c :** to blow noisily ⟨a stiff west wind was ~*ing* in off the prairies —F.B.Gipson⟩ ~ *vt* **1 a :** to utter, cheer on, or express with a whoop **:** urge or press clamorously ⟨~*ed* us in to wash for lunch —William DuBois⟩ ⟨machine men crowded on his bandwagon, ~*ed* him into office —William Manchester⟩ ⟨~*ed* a welcome⟩ **b :** to rush through or adopt with noisy enthusiasm ⟨it ~*ed* through on a voice vote a stopgap foreign aid appropriation bill —*Current Biog.*⟩ **2 a :** to arouse sentiment for **:** agitate in behalf of **:** BOOM ⟨the literary reviews for five or six years past have been ~*ing* up all sorts of palpable quacks —H.L.Mencken⟩ **b :** to stir up **:** EXCITE ⟨~*s* up a selling boom —Wallace Stegner⟩ **3 :** BOOST, RAISE ⟨the tip ~*ed* the price up to 80 times the prewar quotation —Sylvia F. Porter⟩ ⟨so if I was fool enough to never ~ the ante I'd get the credit for lying anyway —Sinclair Lewis⟩ — **whoop it up 1 :** to celebrate riotously or noisily **:** CAROUSE ⟨a bunch of the boys were *whooping it up* in the Malamute saloon —R.W.Service⟩ ⟨mobs of drunken men were *whooping it up* —S.H.Holbrook⟩ **2 :** to stir up enthusiasm **:** beat the drum ⟨tried to *whoop it up* again afterwards in the Senate —*New Republic*⟩ ⟨*whooping it up* for tribal self-government —Oliver La Farge⟩
²**whoop** \"\ *n* -s [ME *whope* (used interjectionally), alter. of *houp,* fr. *hopen, houpen,* v.] **1 a :** a sound expressive of eagerness, exuberance, or jubilation ⟨goes out on the town with a ~ and a holler —John McCarten⟩ — often used interjectionally **b :** the shout of men in battle or pursuit **:** WAR CRY ⟨with ~ and halloo, like a troop of Don Cossacks —Washington Irving⟩ **c :** a shout of hunters (as at the kill) **2 :** the cry of an owl **:** HOOT **3 :** the crowing intake of breath following a paroxysm in whooping cough **4 :** a variation of hide-and-seek **5 :** the smallest bit **:** HOOT, DAMN ⟨didn't give a ~⟩ ⟨not worth a ~⟩
³**whoop** \'hüp\ *n* -s [alter. of ⁴*hoop*] **:** HOOPOE
whoop-de-do *or* **whoop-de-doo** \'h|üpdē,dü, 'hw| *also* 'w| *or* |u̇p-\ *n* -s [prob. irreg. fr. ²*whoop*] **1 :** hilarious partying **:** roistering conviviality **:** HIGH JINKS ⟨there is dancing in the streets, music, singing and general *whoop-de-do* —Al Colby⟩ **2 :** an organized public affair or activity of any of various kinds: as **a :** a lively social function or party **b :** the spectacle of political contest, oratory, and maneuver ⟨political *whoop-de-do*⟩ **c :** the doings contrived to attract attention to a commercial promotion **:** a publicity stunt or campaign ⟨enlisted every means of publicity in the *whoop-de-do* of launching a new car⟩ **3 :** agitated public discussion or debate **:** a stir of opinion ⟨a lot of foolish *whoop-de-do* in England when it was announced that an American was going to portray royalty in this film —John McCarten⟩
¹**whoop·ee** \'hw|ü(,)pē, |ü(- '=;= *also* 'w| *sometimes* 'h|\ *or* **hoop·ee** \'h|\ *interj* [irreg. fr. ²*whoop*] — used to express exuberant delight
²**whoopee** *or* **hoopee** \'=(,)=\ *n* -s **1 :** the feverish alcohol-and-sex partying first widely conspicuous during the U.S. prohibition era — often used in the phrase *make whoopee* ⟨accused her of making ~ while he was locked up, and of being unfaithful to him —Edmund Wilson⟩ **2 :** any boisterous convivial fun ⟨college-boy ~ —*Amer. Guide Series: Md.*⟩
whoop·er \'h|üpə(r), 'hw| *also* 'w| *or* |u̇p\ *n* -s **1 :** one that whoops **2 :** WHOOPING CRANE
whooper swan \'==-\ *also* **hoop·er** \'h|\ *or* **hooper swan** *n* -s **:** a common Old World swan (*Olor cygnus*)
whooping cough *n* **:** an infectious inflammation of the air passages with a convulsive spasmodic cough sometimes followed by a crowing intake of breath — called also *pertussis*
whooping crane *n* **:** a large white nearly extinct No. American crane (*Grus americana*) noted for its loud whoop
whooping swan *n* **:** WHOOPER SWAN
whoop·la \'h|ü,plä, 'hw| *also* 'w| *or* |u̇,-\ *n* -s [alter. (influenced by ²*whoop*) of *hoopla*] **1 :** a noisy commotion **:** TO-DO ⟨newspaper ~ about the new champion⟩ ⟨the whole ~ is making readers expect too much —Theodore Pratt⟩ **2 :** boisterous merrymaking **:** SHINDIG, WHOOPEE ⟨throw ~ or stay out all night —Calder Willingham⟩
whoops *like* OOPS\ *interj* [irreg. fr. ²*whoop*] — used to express mild apology, surprise, or dismay
whoop-up \'=,=\ *n* -s [fr. the verb phrase *whoop up*] **:** a rousing affair **:** WHOOP-DE-DO
whoos *pl of* WHOO
¹**whoosh** \'hw|üsh *also* 'w| *or* -u̇sh\ *or* **woosh** \'w|\ *vb* -ED/-ING/-ES [imit.] *vi* **:** to rush past or gush out **:** move explosively **:** HISS ⟨an occasional car ~*ed* by on the road —Hollis Alpert⟩ ⟨black oil ~*ed* up as the drill broke through⟩ ~ *vt* **:** to move (someone or something) with an explosive or sibilant rush or gush **:** operate or carry on a current of air or other fluid ⟨~*ed* the doors open —Raymond Chandler⟩ ⟨its rotors ~ the dust or chemicals or seed exactly where the farmer wants them —F.J.Taylor⟩
²**whoosh** \"\ *n* -ES **:** a swift or explosive rush **:** GUSH, HISS ⟨a branch load of snow slipped to the ground with a faint ~ —Oliver La Farge⟩ ⟨a ~ of air so powerful that roofs were lifted from their homes —Dean Jennings⟩ ⟨with a ~ the fire took hold —John Onslow⟩
whoo·sis \'hüzəs\ *or* **whoo·sy** \-zē\ *n, pl* **whoosises** *or* **whoosies** [*whoosis* perh. alter. of the expression *who's this; whoosy* perh. alter. of the expression *who's he*] **:** someone or something whose name one does not know or cannot recall **:** an indefinite or unspecified person or thing or one that is representative or typical ⟨don't print Senator *Whoosis'* blow-off yesterday —F.L.Mott⟩ ⟨the choke will be a ~ on the dash —F.C.Othman⟩
¹**whop** *also* **whap** \'hw|äp *also* 'w| *or* |ȯp\ *or* **wop** \'w|\ *vt* **whopped; whopped; whopping; whops** [ME *whappen,* alter. of *wappen* to throw, strike, blow in gusts — more at WAP] **1 :** to pull or whip out **2 a :** to belabor heavily **:** BEAT, STRIKE, THRASH ⟨feel like somebody just *whopped* me in the belly with a sledgehammer —Budd Schulberg⟩ **b :** to defeat totally **:** OVERCOME, VANQUISH ⟨*whopped* a highly touted football eleven⟩
²**whop** \"\ *or* **wop** \"\ *n* -s [ME *whapp,* alter. of *wap* — more at WAP] **:** a heavy blow **:** THUD, THUMP — often used interjectionally
whop·per \-pə(r)\ *n* -s [¹*whop* + *-er*] **1 :** something unusually large or otherwise extreme or extravagant of its kind ⟨returned with an armful of harmonicas, ranging in length from one inch to a ~ of over two feet —*New Yorker*⟩ ⟨spent a thousand dollars on a ~ of a black velvet backdrop —R.L. Taylor⟩ **2 :** an extravagant or monstrous lie ⟨droning ~*s* into the telephone and unloading misrepresented stocks —A.W. Baum⟩
¹**whopping** *adj* [fr. pres. part. of ¹*whop*] **:** extremely large **:** EXTRAORDINARY, EXTRAVAGANT, OUTRAGEOUS ⟨netted a ~ buffalo —G.S.Perry⟩ ⟨distills a good deal of sardonic fun from the ~ errors of the nation's oracles —C.J.Rolo⟩
²**whopping** *adv* **:** EXTREMELY, IMMENSELY, VERY ⟨they all got ~ drunk —Jim Rearden⟩ ⟨a ~ big cruise ship —*New Yorker*⟩
³**whopping** *n* -s [fr. gerund of ¹*whop*] **:** a heavy pounding or beating
whor·age \'hōrij, 'hȯr-\ *n* -s **:** WHORE
¹**whore** \'hō(ə)r, 'hȯ(ə)r, -ōə, -ȯ(ə), *chiefly euphemistic* 'hu̇(ə)r *or* -ü(ə)r\ *n* -s [ME *hore, hoore,* fr. OE *hōre;* akin to OHG *huora* whore, ON *hōra* whore, *hōrr* adulterer, Goth *hors* adulterer, L *carus* dear — more at CHARITY] **1 :** a woman who practices unlawful sexual commerce; *esp* **:** one who prostitutes her body for hire **:** HARLOT, PROSTITUTE **2 :** one regarded as actuated by corrupt, unworthy, or idolatrous motives ⟨our own 20th-century species of literary ~ —H.J.Kaplan⟩
²**whore** \"\ *vb* -ED/-ING/-S *vi* **1 a :** to have unlawful sexual intercourse with a whore **b :** to play the whore **:** act as a prostitute **2 :** to pursue a faithless, unworthy, or idolatrous desire ⟨go a *whoring* after their gods —Exod 34:15 (AV)⟩ ⟨the great depression has not sent them *whoring* after planned economy —E.A.Mowrer⟩ ~ *vt, obs* **:** to corrupt by lewd intercourse **:** DEBAUCH ⟨he that hath kill'd my king, and *whored* my mother —Shak.⟩
whore·dom \-dəm\ *n* -s [ME *hordom,* fr. ON *hōrdōmr* adultery, fr. *hōrr* adulterer + *-dōmr* -dom] **1 a :** the conduct or practices of a whore **:** bawdy behavior **:** HARLOTRY, PROSTITUTION **b :** the practice of consorting with whores **:** illicit intercourse with whores **c :** unlawful sexual indulgence **:** FORNICATION, LEWDNESS, UNCHASTITY **2 :** faithless, unworthy, or idolatrous practices or pursuits **:** DISLOYALTY ⟨philosophers and pupils alike were pulled along in the stream of ~ and sin —Maurice Samuel⟩
whorehouse \'=,=\ *n* [ME *horehous,* fr. *hore* whore + *hous* house] **:** BROTHEL
whoremaster \'=,==\ *n* **:** a man consorting with whores or given to lechery **:** FORNICATOR
whoremonger \'=,==\ *n, archaic* **:** WHOREMASTER
whorer *n* -s *obs* **:** WHOREMASTER
whore's bird *n* **:** BASTARD
whore·son \'hōrsᵊn, 'hȯr- -ōəs-, -ō(ə)s-\ *n, often attrib* [ME *horesone,* fr. *hore* whore + *sone* son] **1 :** BASTARD **2 :** a coarse fellow — used as a generalized term of abuse
whor·ish \'hōrish, 'hȯr-, -rēsh\ *adj* **1 :** of or resembling a whore **:** LEWD **2** *obs* **:** DISLOYAL, IDOLATROUS, UNFAITHFUL
¹**whorl** \'hw|ō(ə)rl, |ərl, *esp before pause or consonant* -rəl; |ō(ə)l, |əl, |əil *also* 'w|\ *also* **wharl** \|är(ə)l\ *n* -s [ME *whorle, wharle, whorwhil, wharwyl,* prob. alter. of *whirle, wherle, wherwill* whorl of a spindle, whirl — more at WHIRL] **1 :** a drumlike section on the lower part of a spindle in spinning or weaving machinery serving as a pulley for the tape drive that rotates the spindle **2 :** an arrangement of two or more anatomical parts or organs of one kind in a circle around the same point on an axis ⟨a ~ of leaves⟩ ⟨a ~ of flowers⟩ **3 a :** something that whirls, coils, or spirals or whose form suggests such movement ⟨~*s* of rising chimney smoke⟩ ⟨a first grade school paper of Spencerian push-ups and ~*s* —William Humphrey⟩ **b :** a circular or spiral shape; *esp* **:** one used as a design motive (as in furniture) **4 :** one of the turns of a univalve shell **5 :** a terra-cotta disk that suggests a whorl, is found in ruins of ancient cities in Asia Minor, Africa, Italy, and India, and is supposed by some to have been used on spindles **6 :** a fingerprint in which the central papillary ridges turn through at least one complete circle — see FINGERPRINT illustration
²**whorl** \"\ *vb* -ED/-ING/-S *vt* **:** to arrange or form in coiled or spiral shapes ⟨the ~*ed* grain of his hair —Crary Moore⟩ **:** arrange in a whorl ~ *vi* **:** to turn with a spinning or spiral motion **:** SWIRL, WHIRL ⟨watching the . . . billowing snow as it ~*ed* down —Jean Stafford⟩ ⟨hung over the banister until the blood ~*ed* in her eyes —Nancy Cardozo⟩
whorled \-ld\ *adj* [¹*whorl* + *-ed*] **:** having or arranged in whorls; *esp* **:** VERTICILLATE ⟨~ leaves⟩
whorled aster *n* **:** a No. American perennial herb (*Aster acuminatus*) with apparently whorled leaves and showy white flowers
whorled loosestrife *n* **:** a common No. American yellow-flowered herb (*Lysimachia quadrifolia*) with whorls of four or five leaves
whorled mallow *n* **:** CURLED MALLOW
whorled milkweed *n* **:** either of two No. American milkweeds with narrow leaves and greenish white flowers: **a :** an herb (*Asclepias verticillata*) mostly of the eastern states **b :** an herb (*A. galioides*) of the Great Plains region
whorled pogonia *or* **whorled snakemouth** *n* **:** a No. American green-flowered terrestrial orchid (*Isotria verticillata*) with a whorl of five leaves
whorled rosinweed *n* **:** a tall perennial herb (*Silphium trifoliatum*) of the eastern U.S. with yellow flowers and leaves in whorls of three
whorlflower \'=,=\ *n* **:** a Eurasian herb of the genus *Morina* (family Dipsacaceae) with flowers in dense whorls
whorl foot *n* **:** SCROLL FOOT
whorl grass *n* **:** BROOK GRASS
whorly \-lē\ *adj* [¹*whorl* + *-y*] **:** WHORLED
whorlywort \'==,=\ *n* **:** CULVER'S ROOT
whort \'hw|ərt, |ət, |əit *also* 'w|; *usu* |d·+V\ *or* **whor·tle** \|d·ᵊl, |t'l\ *or* **wort** \'w|\ *n* -s [*whort* alter. of E dial. *hurt,* short for E *hurtleberry; whortle* short for *whortleberry; wort* alter. of *whort*] **1 :** WHORTLEBERRY 1a **2 :** BEARBERRY 1
whor·tle·berry \'=-- — *see* BERRY\ *n* [alter. of *hurtleberry*] **1 a :** a sweet edible European blueberry that is purplish black with a glaucous bloom **b :** a low-growing erect rhizomatous shrub (*Vaccinium myrtillus*) whose fruit is a whortleberry **2 a :** HUCKLEBERRY 1a **b :** BLUEBERRY 1
whos *pl of* WHO
¹**whose** [ME *whos* (gen. of ¹*who,* ¹*what*), alter. (influenced by ¹*who*) of *whas, whes,* fr. OE *hwæs,* gen. of *hwā* who, *hwæt* what — more at WHO, WHAT] *obs possessive of* ¹WHO *and* ¹WHAT
²**whose** \(')hüz *sometimes* ,üz\ *adj* [ME *whos,* gen. of ¹*who,* ¹*what*] **1 :** of what person or persons: **a :** of or belonging to what person or persons as possessor or possessors **:** due to what person or persons **:** inherent in what person or persons **:** associated or connected with what person or persons ⟨~ gorgeous vesture heaps the ground —Robert Browning⟩ ⟨inquire ~ son the stripling is —1 Sam 17:56 (RSV)⟩ — compare ¹WHO 1 **b :** of or relating to what person or persons as author or authors, doer or doers, giver or givers, or agent or agents **:** effected by what person or persons **:** experienced by what person or persons as subject ⟨~ plays are greater than Shakespeare's⟩ ⟨so many people have helped me that I don't know ~ help has been most valuable⟩ — compare ¹WHO 1 **c :** of or relating to what person or persons as object of an action **:** experienced by what person or persons as object ⟨in ~ honor was the monument erected⟩ ⟨asking ~ promotion would be in the best interests of the company⟩ — compare ¹WHO 1 **2 a :** of whom: (1) **:** of or belonging to whom as possessor or possessors **:** due to whom **:** inherent in whom **:** associated or connected with whom ⟨a man ~ shoes do not fit⟩ ⟨an organization ~ members . . . exercise influence in every continent —Denis Healey⟩ ⟨a chicken ~ head has been cut off —Nancy Mitford⟩ — used as a possessive adjective corresponding in meaning to the relative pronoun *who;* compare ¹WHO 3 (2) **:** of or relating to whom as author or authors, doer or doers, giver or givers, or agent or agents **:** effected by whom **:** experienced by whom as subject ⟨the law courts, ~ decisions were important —F.L.Mott⟩ — used as a possessive adjective corresponding in meaning to the relative pronoun *who;* compare ¹WHO 3 (3) **:** of or relating to whom as object of an action **:** experienced by whom as object ⟨that maid ~ sudden sight hath thralled my wounded eye —Shak.⟩ ⟨these puissant legions, ~ exile hath emptied heaven —John Milton⟩ — used as a possessive adjective corresponding in meaning to the relative pronoun *who;* compare ¹WHO 3 **b :** of which: (1) **:** of or belonging to which as possessor or possessors **:** inherent in which **:** associated or connected with which ⟨inventor of simple clothes ~ elegance derives from her hand-finished detail —Lois Long⟩ ⟨a sentence ~ grammatical subject is a demonstrative pronoun —R.E.Gahringer⟩ — used as a possessive adjective corresponding in meaning to the relative pronoun *which;* compare ²WHICH 3 (2) **:** of or relating to which as agent or agents **:** effected by which **:** resulting from which ⟨the current thought . . . to ~ influences he was subject —L.P.Smith⟩ ⟨a simple legal monopoly ~ reward to the inventor would be primarily in royalties —Robert Reuben⟩ — used as a possessive adjective corresponding in meaning to the relative pronoun *which;* compare ²WHICH 3 (3) **:** of or relating to which as object of an action **:** undergone by which as object ⟨the first poem ~ publication he ever sanctioned —J.W.Krutch⟩ ⟨logical techniques ~ extravagant use is known to give rise to . . . paradoxes —C.G.Hempel⟩ — used as a possessive adjective corresponding in meaning to the relative pronoun *which;* compare ²WHICH 3 **3 a :** of any person or persons that **:** of whomever ⟨~ hatred is covered by deceit, his wickedness shall be showed before the whole congregation —Prov 26:26 (AV)⟩ ⟨ask ~ advice you please⟩ — compare ¹WHO 2a **b** *archaic* **:** the particular person or persons of whom **:** he, she, or those of whom ⟨"Happy," I said, "~ home is here" —R.W.Emerson⟩ — compare ¹WHO 2b(1)
³**whose** \"\ *pron, sing or pl in constr* [ME *whos,* gen. of ¹*who,* ¹*what*] **:** whose one or whose ones — used without a following noun as a pronoun equivalent in meaning to the adjective *whose* ⟨~ shall those things be, which thou hast provided —Lk 12:20 (AV)⟩ ⟨tell me ~ it was —Shak.⟩ ⟨God, ~ I am, and whom I serve —Acts 27:23 (AV)⟩
¹**whosesoever** \¦=;=;=\ *adj* [²*whose* + *soever*] **:** ¹WHOSEVER ⟨~ sins ye remit —Jn 20:23 (AV)⟩
²**whosesoever** \"\ *pron* **:** ²WHOSEVER
¹**whos·ever** \(')hü¦zevə(r)\ *adj* [²*whose* + *ever*] **:** of, belonging to, or relating to whomever ⟨~ hat this is, I wish he would come and claim it⟩
²**whosever** \"\ *pron* **:** whosever one or whosever ones — used without a following noun as a pronoun equivalent in meaning to the adjective *whosever* ⟨~ these gloves are, I wish he would come and claim them⟩
who·so \'hü(,)sō\ *pron* [ME *who so,* fr. *who* + *so*] **:** WHOEVER
who·so·ev·er \,hüsə'wevə(r), -sō'e-\ *pron* [ME, fr. *who so* + *ever*] **:** whatever person **:** any person whatever that **:** WHOEVER
whosomever *pron* [ME *whosumever, whasumever,* fr. ME (northern dial.) *wha sum* whoever (fr. ME — northern dial. — *wha* who — fr. OE *hwā* — + ME — northern dial. — *sum,* rel. adv., as) + ME *ever* — more at WHATSOMEVER] *obs* **:** WHOEVER
who's who \'hüz-\ *n, often cap both Ws* [fr. the expression *who is who, who's who*] **1 :** any of various compilations containing brief biographical sketches of distinguished or prominent persons in a geographical area or a professional or other group ⟨a list of officers and members . . . and a *who's who* of cartographers —*Geog. Rev.*⟩ **2 :** the leaders of a community or group **:** those exercising influence or power **:** ELITE ⟨the event will draw . . . the *who's who* of the film capital —*Los Angeles (Calif.) Examiner*⟩
WHP *abbr, often not cap* water horsepower
whr *abbr* whether
whs *abbr* warehouse
whse *abbr* warehouse
whsle *abbr* wholesale
whsmn *abbr* warehouseman
whsng *abbr* warehousing
wht *abbr* white
whuff \'hwəf *also* 'wəf\ *or* **whuf·fle** \-fəl\ *vb* -ED/-ING/-S [imit.] **:** to blow noisily
whump \'hwəmp *also* 'wə-\ *vi* -ED/-ING/-S [imit.] **:** BANG, THUMP
whurl \'hwərl\ *vi* -ED/-ING/-S [imit.] *archaic* **:** to make any of various throaty sounds (as a roar, snarl, or purr)
whvs *abbr* wharves
¹**why** \(')(h)wī\ *adv* [ME, fr. OE *hwȳ, hwī;* akin to ON *hvī* why; both fr. a prehistoric NGmc-WGmc instrumental case form of the pronoun represented by OE *hwæt* what — more at WHAT] **1 :** for what cause, reason, or purpose **:** on what account **:** to what end **:** WHEREFORE — used to introduce a question in direct or indirect discourse ⟨~ must you make difficulties⟩ ⟨asked ~ the work had been stopped⟩ **2 a :** for which **:** on account of which — used chiefly with *reason* to introduce a relative clause ⟨the reason ~ his conclusion seemed plausible —R.J. Butler⟩ **b :** for what reason or cause **:** on account of what —

used without an expressed antecedent to introduce a relative clause ⟨I don't know ~ he left town⟩ — **for why** *dial* : BECAUSE, WHY

²**why** \'hwī *also* 'wī\ *n* -s [ME, fr. *why*, adv.] **1** : the reason or cause of something ⟨a surging symphonic commentary on the ~ of man's being —William Peden⟩ ⟨statistical studies solve the problems of where and when; for the hows and ~s we must generally use other techniques —G.W.Brainerd⟩ **2** : a baffling problem : ENIGMA ⟨all the great ~s of life —H.G. Wells⟩

³**why** \'wī *also* 'hwī\ *interj* [¹*why*] — used to indicate a pause or the resumption after a pause in expression ⟨if America splits the infinitive, ~, the infinitive is split, and no rule will mend it —A.L.Guérard⟩

whyd·ah *or* **whid·ah** \'hwidə *also* 'wi-\ *n* -s [alter. (influenced by *Whydah*, *Ouidah*, town in southern Dahomey where such birds are found) of *widow* (in *widow bird*)] : any of various African weaverbirds which are mostly black with white or buffy markings, which are often kept as cage birds, and of which the males although no larger than a canary have drooping tail feathers often a foot in length during the breeding season — compare PARADISE WEAVER

why·ev·er \hwī'evə(r) *also* wī-\ *adv* : for whatever reason : WHY

why·for \'hwī,- *also* 'wī,-\ *n* -s [E dial. *whyfor*, adv., why, fr. E ¹*why* + *for*] : REASON, WHEREFORE ⟨provided the ~s of the programs themselves —Arthur Krock⟩

why-not *n* [fr. the expression *why not*] *obs* : a return challenge demanding what bars an action or negates an assertion — **at a why-not** *obs* : at a disadvantage

whyo \'hwī(,)ō *also* 'wī-\ *n* -s [fr. *oh-why-oh-why-oh*, signal cry of a former New York City gang] : a member of a gang of holdup men

WI *abbr* **1** *often not cap* when issued **2** wrought iron

wi' \(')wi\ *Scot & dial var of* WITH

WIA *abbr* wounded in action

wibbly-wobbly \;wib(ə)lē;=(=)=\ *adj* [by redupl.] : WOBBLY

wich *or* **wych** \'wich, 'wīch\ *n* -ES [ME *witz*, fr. OE *wīch*, *wīc*, fr. *-wīch*, *-wīc* -wich (suffix of place-names, as in *Northwich*, *Middlewich*, districts of England associated with salt manufacturing), fr. *wīc* dwelling place, village, town — more at WICK (farm)] *dial Eng* : SALT PIT

¹**wich·i·ta** \'wichə,tò\ *n, pl* **wichita** *or* **wichitas** *usu cap* **1 a** : a Caddo people or confederacy of peoples ranging between the Arkansas river in Kansas and central Texas **b** : a member of such people **2** : the language of the Wichita people

²**wichita** \"\ *adj, usu cap* [fr. *Wichita*, Kansas] : of or from the city of Wichita, Kansas : of the kind or style prevalent in Wichita

wich·i·tan \-ō(ə)n\ *n* -s *cap* [*Wichita*, city in south central Kansas or *Wichita* Falls, city in northern Texas + E *-an*] : a native or resident of Wichita, Kansas, or Wichita Falls, Texas

wi·chu·rai·ana \wə,chürə'anə, -rə'ya-, -ānə\ *also* **wi·chu·ra** \wə'chürə\ *or* **wichura rose** *n* -s [*wichuraiana* fr. NL (specific epithet of *Rosa wichuraiana*), fr. M. E. *Wichura* †1866 Ger. lawyer and botanist + NL *-iana*, *-ana*, fr. L, fem. of *-ianus*, *-anus* -an; *wichura* fr. M. E. *Wichura*] : an Asiatic rose (*Rosa wichuraiana*) which has prostrate creeping stems and from which several rambler roses have been developed

¹**wick** \'wik\ *n* -s [ME *wicke*, *wike*, *weke*, fr. OE *wēoce*; akin to OHG *wiohha* lint, wick, OIr *figim* I weave, OE *wōcie* noose, Skt *vāgurā* net, noose; basic meaning: to weave, web] **1 a** : a bundle of fibers or a loosely twisted, braided, or woven cord, tape, or tube usu. of soft spun cotton threads that by capillary attraction draws up to be burned a steady supply of the oil in lamps or the melted tallow or wax in candles **b** : a strip of material (as gauze or strands of catgut) placed in a wound to serve as a drain **2** : WICKING

²**wick** \"\ *n* -s [ME *wik* dwelling place, village, town, farm, fr. OE *wīc*; akin to OFris *wīk* dwelling place, town, OHG *wīch*; all fr. a prehistoric WGmc word borrowed fr. L *vicus* village — more at VICINITY] *dial Eng* : FARMSTEAD; *specif* : a dairy farm or house

³**wick** \"\ *n* -s [ME *wik*, fr. ON *vik*; akin to ON *vīkja* to move, turn] *archaic* : CORNER, ANGLE; *esp* : a corner of the eye or mouth

⁴**wick** \'wik, 'wīk\ *n* -s [ON *vīk*; akin to OE *wīc* bay, creek, MLG *wīk* bay, creek, ON *vīkja* to move, turn — more at WEEK] *chiefly Scot* : a small inlet : CREEK

⁵**wick** \'wik\ *vb* -ED/-ING/-S [origin unknown] *vt* : to make an inwick upon (another stone) in curling ~ *vi* : INWICK — **wick a bore** : to make a shot through a wick or narrow port in curling

⁶**wick** \"\ *n* -s **1** : a narrow port or passageway in the course in curling that is flanked by the stones of previous players **2** : INWICK

⁷**wick** \"\ *dial Eng var of* ¹QUICK

⁸**wick** \"\ *dial Brit var of* WEEK

wickape *var of* WICOPY

wick·a·wee \'wikə,wē\ *n*-s [perh. of Algonquian origin; akin to Natick *wequai* light] : an Indian paintbrush (*Castilleja coccinea*)

¹**wick·ed** \'wikəd\ *adj* -ER/-EST [ME, alter. (influenced by *-ed*) of *wicke* wicked] **1** : evil in character, behavior, tendency, or influence : being or acting contrary to moral or divine law : SINFUL, BAD ⟨a ~ ruler⟩ ⟨the ~ stepmother⟩ ⟨a ~ deed⟩ ⟨a ~ intent⟩ ⟨a ~ book⟩ ⟨a ~ law⟩ ⟨so simple and trustful . . . it would be ~ to hurt her —Mary Webb⟩ **2 a** : having a bad disposition : INTRACTABLE, VICIOUS — used esp. of an animal ⟨a ~ horse⟩ **b** : inclined to mischief; *esp* : playfully or engagingly mischievous : ROGUISH ⟨smiling . . . at the ~, witty little girl —Jean Stafford⟩ **c** : open to censure : WRONG, REPREHENSIBLE ⟨however ~ it may be to try to shock the public —Clive Bell⟩ **d** : verging on the indecent : IMPROPER, RISQUÉ ⟨sing ~ lyrics in the corners of the bar —Horace Sutton⟩ **e** : showing or expressing ill will : MALEVOLENT, MALICIOUS ⟨a ~ look⟩ ⟨a woman with a ~ tongue in her head⟩ ⟨a ~ anecdote⟩ ⟨a cauldron of ~ gossip —L.P.Smith⟩ **3 a** (1) : disgustingly unpleasant; *esp* : offensive to the smell or taste : VILE ⟨a gas with a ~ odor⟩ (2) *archaic* : poor in quality ⟨they talk ~ French —Horace Walpole⟩ **b** *archaic* : POISONOUS, NOXIOUS ⟨~ dew . . . from unwholesome fen —Shak.⟩ **c** : causing or likely to cause harm : DANGEROUS ⟨a ~ storm⟩ ⟨the ~ horns of a bull⟩ **d** : difficult to pass through or over : almost impassable or impenetrable ⟨find their way over the ~ roads —C.G.Bowers⟩ ⟨the ~ sort of scrub jungle —Edison Marshall⟩ **e** : causing discomfort or distress : SEVERE ⟨suffering through ~ winter weather⟩ ⟨a ~ headache⟩ **f** : causing annoyance : TROUBLESOME, VEXATIOUS ⟨a ~ growth of weeds⟩ **4 a** : going beyond reasonable limits : OUTRAGEOUS, TERRIBLE ⟨had a ~ fire loss⟩ ⟨a ~ shame⟩ ⟨charged ~ prices⟩ ⟨a ~ examination⟩ ⟨was game to take a ~ amount of punishment —Althea Gibson⟩ **b** (1) : showing impressive or formidable skill : EXCELLENT ⟨plays a ~ game of bridge⟩ ⟨dances a ~ Charleston —*Bookman*⟩ (2) : difficult to cope with or to compete against ⟨a ~ drive⟩ **syn** see BAD

²**wicked** \"\ *n, pl* **wicked** [ME, fr. ¹*wicked*] : a wicked person — usu. used in pl. with *the* ⟨the ~ are made to suffer —*Publishers' Weekly*⟩

³**wicked** \"\ *adv* [ME, fr. ¹*wicked*] *chiefly dial* : WICKEDLY

⁴**wicked** \'wikt\ *adj* [¹*wick* + *-ed*] : having a wick — used chiefly in combination ⟨a two-*wicked* lamp⟩

wick·ed·ly *adv* [ME, fr. ¹*wicked* + *-ly*] : in a wicked manner: as **a** : EVILLY, INIQUITOUSLY ⟨~ ruined a trusting partner⟩ **b** : OFFENSIVELY, HORRIBLY ⟨this book is ~ superficial —*Times Lit. Supp.*⟩ **c** : VICIOUSLY, FIERCELY ⟨~ repressive of important civil liberties —*New Statesman & Nation*⟩ **d** : MALICIOUSLY ⟨this gay little book . . . is ~ witty —Regina J. Woody⟩ ⟨the most ~ amusing epigrams ever coined —Stephen Williams⟩

wick·ed·ness *n* -ES [ME, fr. ¹*wicked* + *-ness*] **1 a** : the quality or state of being wicked : EVIL, SINFULNESS ⟨policies of almost unmitigated ~ —Alfred Cobban⟩ **b** : wicked character or conduct : VICE ⟨though the bars are closed . . . ~ goes on —Green Peyton⟩ **2** : something wicked : a wicked action ⟨rushed off to some of her ~es —Joseph Conrad⟩

wick·en \'wikən\ *var of* WIGGEN

¹**wick·er** \'wikə(r)\ *n* -s [ME *wiker*, of Scand origin; akin to Sw dial. *vikker* willow, Sw *vika* to bend, ON *vīkja* to move, turn — more at WEEK] **1** : a small pliant twig or osier : a rod for plaiting basketwork : WITHE **2 a** : WICKERWORK **b** : something made of wicker (as a basket)

²**wicker** \"\ *adj* : made or consisting of wicker : incased in wickerwork ⟨a ~ basket⟩ ⟨a ~ chair⟩ ⟨a ~ flask⟩

³**wicker** \"\ *vt* -ED/-ING/-S : to incase or cover (as a bottle or chair) with wickerwork

⁴**wicker** *var of* WHICKER

wickerwork \'==,=\ *n, often attrib* : work consisting of a texture of osiers, twigs, or rods : BASKETRY ⟨a huge figure of ~⟩ ⟨~ cages⟩

wick·et \'wikət, *usu* -əd·+V\ *n* -s [ME *wiket*, fr. ONF, of Gmc origin; akin to MD *wiket*, *winket* wicket, *wiken* to yield, give way, OE *wīcan* — more at WEAK] **1** : a small gate or door; *esp* : one forming part of or placed near a larger gate or door **2** : an opening that resembles a window; *esp* : a grilled or grated window (as at a ticket office, cashier's or teller's desk) **3 a** : a small gate for emptying the chamber of a canal lock or regulating the amount of water passing through a channel (as to a waterwheel) **b** : the entrance door to a kiln **c** : any gate of a shutter dam **d** : a very wide stall or heading used with very wide pillars in the wicketwork system of coal mining in North Wales **4 a** : either of the two frameworks at which the ball is bowled in cricket consisting of three stumps stuck close together in the ground and surmounted with two bails placed end to end in grooves on the top **b** : STUMP 7a **c** : a rectangular area of a cricket field with a long dimension of 22 yards bounded by the two bowling creases and a width of 10 feet — called also *pitch* ⟨a fast ~⟩ ⟨a bowler's ~⟩ **d** (1) : the period of play from the commencement of a batsman's innings to his dismissal ⟨the fifth ~ added only 17 runs⟩ (2) : the part of this period when two batsmen are together ⟨a profitable first-*wicket* partnership⟩ **e** : one innings by a batsman that is not completed or not begun ⟨a team wins by 4 ~s when with two not-out players batting and 3 men yet to go in it surpasses the opposing team's total score⟩ **f** : dismissal of a batsman ⟨the bowler worked hard for his ~s⟩ ⟨the bowler captured 7 ~s in one innings⟩ **5** : an arch or hoop in croquet — **on a bad wicket** : in a weak or unfavorable position ⟨forced to fight a by-election *on a bad wicket* —Sir Winston Churchill⟩ — **on a good wicket** : in a strong or favorable position ⟨the organized interests are *on a* fairly *good wicket* as regards their share in the national income —A.J. Brüwer⟩

wicket dam *n* : SHUTTER DAM

wicket door *or* **wicket gate** *n* : WICKET 1

wicketkeep \'==,=\ *n* [by shortening] : WICKETKEEPER

wicketkeeper \'==,==\ *n* : a fieldsman in cricket wearing gloves and pads who stands behind the striker's wicket and whose chief duties are to catch, stump, or run out the batsman and to prevent byes — see CRICKET illustration

wicketwork \'==,=\ *n* : a bord-and-pillar system of coal mining

wick·ing \'wikiŋ, -kēŋ\ *n* -s [¹*wick* + *-ing*] : material used for wicks

wick·i·up \'wikē,əp\ *n* -s [Sac, Fox & Kickapoo *wikiyap* house, dwelling, hut] **1** : a hut used by the nomadic Indians of the arid regions of the western and southwestern U. S. that is typically elliptical in form and has a rough frame covered with reed mats or grass or brushwood — compare LODGE 8a **2** : any rude temporary shelter or hut

wickiup 1

wick·liff·ian \(')wi¦klifēən\ *or* **wick·liff·ite** \'wiklə,fīt\ *n* -s [John *Wickliffe* (Wycliffe) †1384 Eng. religious reformer and theologian + E *-an* or *-ite*] *usu cap* : LOLLARD 2

wick·low \'wi,klō\ *adj, usu cap* [fr. County *Wicklow*, Ireland] : of or from County Wicklow, Ireland : of the kind or style prevalent in County Wicklow

wicks *pl of* WICK, *pres 3d sing of* WICK

wick·up \'wi,kəp\ *n* -s [Cree *wikupiy*] : WICOPY

wicky \'wikē, -ki\ *n* -ES [prob. alter. (influenced by *-y*) of ²*quicken*] **1** *chiefly South* : any of various low-growing laurels (genus *Kalmia*); *esp* : SHEEP LAUREL **2** *dial Eng* : ROWAN TREE 1

wic·o·py *or* **wick·a·pe** \'wikəpē\ *n, pl* **wicopies** *or* **wickapes** [Cree *wikupiy* inner bark of basswood] **1** : LEATHERWOOD 1a **2** : a basswood (*Tilia glabra*) **3** : WILLOW HERB 1

¹**wid** \'wid\ *Scot var of* WOOD

²**wid** \(')wid\ *dial var of* WITH

wid *abbr* widow; widower

wi·dal's reaction *or* **wi·dal reaction** \wē¦dal(z)-, vē¦, -däl(z)-\ *n, usu cap W* [after Fernand *Widal* †1929 Fr. physician] : a specific reaction consisting in agglutination of typhoid bacilli or other salmonellas when mixed with serum from a patient having typhoid fever or other salmonella infection and constituting a test for the disease

widal's test *or* **widal test** *n, usu cap W* [after F. *Widal*] : a test for detecting typhoid fever and other salmonella infections using the Widal reaction

wid·der \'widə(r)\ *dial var of* WIDOW

wid·der·shins \'widə(r),shinz\ *or* **with·er·shins** \'withə(-\ *adv* [*widdershins* fr. MLG *weddersinnes*, fr. MHG *widersinnes*, fr. *widersinnen* to go back, go against, fr. *wider* back, against, again (fr. OHG *widar*) + *sinnen* to travel, go, fr. OHG *sinnan* (akin to OHG *sind* journey, road); *withershins* alter. (influenced by obs. E *wither-*, prefix, fr. OE, against, counter, fr. *wither*, adv.) of *widdershins* — more at WITH, SEND] : in a left-handed or contrary direction : CONTRARILY, COUNTERCLOCKWISE — used esp. of ritual circumambulation; compare DEASIL ⟨turned to his right, knowing that it is unlucky to walk about a church ~ —Dorothy Sayers⟩

¹**wid·di·fow** *also* **wid·di·fu** \'widi,fü\ *adj* [¹*widdy* + *fow*, *fu'*] *Scot* : fit for the gallows : RASCALLY

²**widdifow** *also* **widdifu'** \"\ *n* -s *Scot* : GALLOWS BIRD, RASCAL

¹**wid·dle** \'wid°l\ *vi* -ED/-ING/-S [short for earlier *widdle-waddle*, redupl. of *waddle*] **1** *chiefly dial* : WRIGGLE **2** *chiefly dial* : WADDLE

²**widdle** \"\ *n* -s **1** *chiefly dial* : STRUGGLE **2** *chiefly dial* : WRIGGLE

wid·drim \'widrəm\ *also* **wid·den·dream** \'wid°n,drēm\ *n* -s [OE *wōddrēam*, fr. *wōd* mad + *drēam* joy, noise — more at VATIC, DREAM] *chiefly Scot* : mental excitement or confusion : a mad fit : FURY

¹**wid·dy** \'widi\ *n* -ES [ME (Sc) *widdy*, *wedde*, *wethy*, fr. *wethy*, *withie* withy, fr. OE *withig* willow, withy — more at WITHY] **1** *Scot & dial Eng* : a rope made of osiers or similar twigs : WITHY **2** *Scot & dial Eng* : a hangman's noose : HALTER

²**wid·dy** \-dē, -di\ *dial var of* WIDOW

¹**wide** \'wīd\ *adj* -ER/-EST [ME *wid*, *wide*, fr. OE *wīd*; akin to OHG *wīt* wide, large, ON *vīthr*; prob. all fr. a prehistoric WGmc-NGmc compound formed from components represented by OE *with* against, towards, opposite and Goth *iddja* he went — more at WITH, ISSUE] **1 a** : having or covering great extent : SPACIOUS, VAST ⟨the whole ~ world⟩ ⟨~ seas⟩ ⟨~ cottonfields⟩ ⟨a ~ agricultural and dairying area —*Amer. Guide Series: Mich.*⟩ **b** : extending over, reaching, or affecting a vast area : far-spreading : EXTENSIVE ⟨large windows . . . commanded a ~ sweep of the far ravine slopes —Victor Canning⟩ ⟨a painter of ~ reputation⟩ ⟨~ publicity⟩ ⟨satisfy your *widest* ambition —William Osler⟩ **c** : extending throughout or covering a specified area or scope — often used in combination ⟨city-*wide*⟩ ⟨nation*wide*⟩ ⟨a world*wide* problem⟩ ⟨industry-*wide* bargaining⟩ **d** : having a large scope or range : covering, including, or allowing great variety or breadth : not limited : COMPREHENSIVE, ALL-INCLUSIVE ⟨a ~ assortment⟩ ⟨~ experience⟩ ⟨insurance with ~ coverage⟩ ⟨historical works addressed to a very ~ public —G.M.Trevelyan⟩ ⟨far too ~ a query to be dealt with —Guy Eden⟩ **e** : marked by breadth and tolerance : not limited or constrained by parochialism or prejudice : LIBERAL, BROAD ⟨the utmost desire to be ~ and impartial —John Galsworthy⟩ ⟨a statesman of ~ views⟩ **f** : AMPLE, ROOMY ⟨a national taste for ~ trousers⟩ **2 a** : having extension from side to side of a specified dimension ⟨3 feet ~⟩ ⟨a mile-*wide* lake⟩ ⟨a trail one man ~⟩ ⟨piled in tiers 4 cans ~⟩ **b** : having much distance or extent between the sides : large in breadth relative to its length or to others of its kind : not narrow : BROAD ⟨a ~ road⟩ ⟨a ~ arch⟩ ⟨the *widest* part of a river⟩ ⟨a horse with a ~ muzzle⟩ ⟨brawny girls, ~ as they were tall —Truman Capote⟩ **c** : opened, expanded, or stretched apart to the fullest extent ⟨~ nostrils⟩ ⟨stared with ~ eyes⟩ — often used postpositively ⟨greeted him with arms ~⟩ **d** : ³LAX **4** **3 a** : extending a considerable distance between limits ⟨~ variations in ability among students⟩ ⟨the ~ difference in their stations in life —T.B.Costain⟩ **b** : having or showing a great difference or fluctuation between the highest and lowest levels (as of prices quoted or bid and asked on an exchange) ⟨a ~ drop in hog prices⟩ ⟨a need to provide for *wider* operating margins in a business⟩ **c** (1) *archaic* : distant from a specified place — used with *of* ⟨thirty miles ~ of the place appointed —Jonathan Swift⟩ (2) *archaic* : different or divergent from something specified — used with *of* ⟨examine whose notions are *widest* of the common road —George Berkeley⟩ (3) : straying or deviating from something specified — used with *of* ⟨far ~ of reality —Lucien Price⟩ (4) *obs* : missing the truth : WRONG, INCORRECT ⟨she was a little ~ there —Elkanah Settle⟩ (5) *obs* : mentally unsound : DELIRIOUS ⟨still, still far ~ —Shak.⟩ (6) : far off the intended course : away from the point aimed at ⟨a ~ arrow⟩ ⟨pitched four ~ balls⟩ ⟨a ~ shot⟩ — used often in the expression *wide of the mark* ⟨nothing could be more ludicrously ~ of the mark —F.R.Leavis⟩ **4** *of an animal ration* : relatively rich in carbohydrate as compared with protein — compare NARROW **5** *slang Brit* **a** : WIDE-AWAKE, SOPHISTICATED **b** : characterized by clever but ethically questionable behavior : SHARP ⟨a good fellow so long as you watched out for yourself . . . a ~ man —Robert Westerby⟩ **syn** see BROAD

²**wide** \"\ *adv* -ER/-EST [ME, fr. OE *wīde*, fr. *wīd*, adj., wide] **1 a** : over a great distance or extent : FAR, WIDELY ⟨wandered ~ through many lands⟩ — used often in the phrase *far and wide* ⟨searched far and ~⟩ **b** : over a specified distance, area, or extent ⟨expanded the business country-*wide* within a few years⟩ **2 a** : so as to leave much space or distance between ⟨told to stand with legs *wider* apart⟩ **b** : so as to move apart or away ⟨shaking ~ thy yellow hair —P.B.Shelley⟩ **c** : so as to pass at or clear by a considerable distance ⟨ran ~ around left end for a 10-yard gain⟩ **3** : to the fullest extent : COMPLETELY ⟨opened her eyes ~⟩ ⟨spread the map ~⟩ — often used as an intensive with *open* ⟨a *wide*-open window⟩ ⟨the *wide*-open spaces⟩ ⟨a locomotive running with the throttle ~ open⟩ ⟨left himself ~ open to criticism⟩ **4 a** : so as to pass to the side of or away from the intended course or miss the aim or objective : ASTRAY ⟨the bullet went ~⟩ ⟨drove ~ of the green on the short sixth hole⟩ **b** *chiefly dial* : at a considerable distance : FAR — often used with *of* ⟨lying . . . ~ of all other forts —George Washington⟩

³**wide** \"\ *or* **wide ball** *n* -s : a bowled ball in cricket that is delivered so high or wide of the wicket as to be out of the striker's reach, that does not count in the over unless hit, and that counts one run unless otherwise scored from — compare EXTRA 1c

wide-angle \'=¦==\ *adj* **1** : having or covering an angle of view wider than the ordinary — used esp. of lenses of shorter than normal focal length **2** : having, involving the use of, or relating to a wide-angle lens ⟨*wide-angle* camera⟩ ⟨*wide-angle* photography⟩

¹**wide-awake** \¦==¦=\ *adj* : fully awake : not drowsy or dull : KNOWING, KEEN, ALERT ⟨he was tired, exhausted, and yet *wide-awake* —Vicky Baum⟩ ⟨listened with *wide-awake* interest —A.C.Whitehead⟩ ⟨a *wide-awake* town⟩ **syn** see WATCHFUL

²**wide-awake** \"\ *n* -s **1** *also* **wide-awake hat** : a low-crowned and wide-brimmed soft felt hat worn chiefly by men **2** *usu cap* : a member of any of the companies of young men in the presidential campaign of 1860 favoring the Republican candidate and wearing uniforms including a wide-awake hat **3** [prob. imit. of its cry] **a** : SOOTY TERN **b** : any of several terns resembling the sooty tern

wide-awake·ness \-nəs\ *n* -ES : the quality or state of being wide-awake : ALERTNESS, LIVELINESS ⟨saw signs of a new *wide-awakeness* in the company personnel⟩

wide-eyed \'=¦=\ *adj* **1** : having the eyes widely open ⟨lay *wide-eyed*, staring . . . at the flickering lights —Zane Grey⟩ **2** : struck with wonder or astonishment : AMAZED ⟨watched *wide-eyed* as the handlers drew the reptiles from their containers —*Amer. Guide Series: Texas*⟩ **3** : marked by unsophisticated or uncritical acceptance or admiration : NAÏVE ⟨*wide-eyed*, idol-worshiping theatergoers —Leslie Rees⟩ ⟨*wide-eyed* innocence⟩ ⟨a *wide-eyed* belief in the goodness of everybody⟩

wide-flung \'=¦=\ *adj* : FAR-FLUNG

wide gage *n* : BROAD GAGE

wide·ly *adv* : in a wide manner: as **a** : over a wide space or extent : EXTENSIVELY ⟨traveled ~⟩ **b** : over a wide range : BROADLY ⟨a ~ representative selection of recent books⟩ **c** : with a great distance between : FAR, GREATLY ⟨~ separated outposts⟩ ⟨~ varying concepts⟩ **d** : to a great extent or degree ⟨departed ~ from his prepared address⟩

widemouthed \'=¦=\ *adj* **1** : having a wide mouth ⟨a ~ person⟩ ⟨a ~ bottle⟩ **2 a** : uttered with wide open mouth : LOUD, RESOUNDING ⟨~ blasphemy⟩ **b** : DEVOURING, GREEDY ⟨~ time⟩

wid·en \'wīd°n\ *vb* **widened; widened; widening** \-d(°)niŋ\ **widens** [¹*wide* + *-en*] *vt* **1** : to increase the width of : BROADEN ⟨~ a road⟩ ⟨the breach between the former friends⟩ **2** : to enlarge the scope or extend the range of : EXPAND ⟨~*ing* . . . the domain of freedom —Stephen Duggan⟩ ~ *vi* **1** : to grow or become wide or wider ⟨a river ~*ing* at a bend⟩ ⟨my nostrils ~ to the smell —Amy Lowell⟩ **2** : to increase in extent or scope ⟨his interests ~*ed* in college⟩ ⟨a vocabulary that ~*ed* from use —W.A.White⟩

wid·en·er \-d(°)nə(r)\ *n* -s : one that widens: as **a** : BROACH 5 **b** : REAMER a(1)

wide·ness *n* -ES [ME *widnesse*, fr. OE *wīdnes*, fr. *wīd* wide + *-nes* -ness — more at WIDE] : the quality or state of being wide : BREADTH, WIDTH

wider *comparative of* WIDE

wide-ranging \'=¦==\ *adj* : covering a wide range : extensive in scope : COMPREHENSIVE ⟨a list of *wide-ranging* topics⟩ ⟨*wide-ranging* studies⟩

wide-screen \'=¦=\ *adj* : of or relating to a projected picture whose aspect ratio is substantially greater than 1.33:1 ⟨*wide-screen* presentation⟩ ⟨the *wide-screen* process⟩

wide-spectrum \'=¦==\ *adj, of a medicinal substance* : BROAD-SPECTRUM

widespread \'=¦=\ *adj* **1** : widely extended or spread out ⟨~ wings⟩ ⟨~ horns⟩ ⟨a ~ layer of yellow gravel —*Amer. Guide Series: Tenn.*⟩ **2** : widely circulated or diffused : generally prevalent ⟨a ~ doctrine⟩ ⟨~ dissatisfaction⟩

wide-spreading \'=¦==\ *adj* **1** : stretching or extending far ⟨*wide-spreading* plains⟩ ⟨*wide-spreading* shade⟩ **2** : spreading over or affecting a wide area : FAR-REACHING ⟨*wide-spreading* disease⟩

widest *superlative of* WIDE

wide-watered \'=¦==\ *adj* : having a wide expanse of water: as **a** : bordering the sea ⟨some *wide-watered* shore —John Milton⟩ **b** : traversed by wide streams ⟨*wide-watered* fen —Alexander Pope⟩

widework \'=,=\ *n* : a bord-and-pillar system of coal mining in which the very narrow pillars left to support the roof are not recovered

wid·geon *also* **wi·geon** \'wijən\ *n, pl* **widgeon** *or* **widgeons** *also* **wigeon** *or* **wigeons** [origin unknown] **1 a** : any of several freshwater ducks of the genus *Mareca* that are between the teal and the mallard in size: as (1) : an Old World duck (*M. penelope*) that has in the male a pale buff crown, chestnut head and neck, grayish lavender breast, and white belly (2) : BALDPATE 2 (3) : a duck (*M. sibilatrix*) of southern So. America that has the entire head nearly white **b** *chiefly dial* : any of various ducks of other genera: as (1) : SAND WIDGEON (2) : SEA WIDGEON **2** *obs* : a foolish fellow : SIMPLETON, GOOSE

widgeon coot *n* : RUDDY DUCK

widgeon grass *n* **1** : EELGRASS 1 **2** : TASSEL GRASS

wid·get \'wijət, *usu* -əd·+V\ *n* -s [alter. of *gadget*] **1** : a usu. small device, contrivance, or mechanical part (as a fitting or attachment) : GADGET ⟨the manufacture of anything from four-motor bombers to . . . ~s —R.T.Frankenstein⟩; *specif* : a small cylindrical container for carrying messages (as of stock exchange transactions) through pneumatic tubes **2 :** an unnamed article considered for purposes of hypothetical example as the typical product of a company ⟨allowing the manufacturer to deduct the fair market value of the ~*s* —*Harvard Law Rev.*⟩

wid·ish \ˈwīdish, -dēsh\ *adj* [¹*wide* + *-ish*] **:** somewhat wide ⟨~ shoulders⟩ ⟨a ~ collection⟩

wid·man·staet·ten figures \ˈwidmən,s\|tetᵊn-, ˈvitmən,s(h)\|\ *also* **wid·man·staet·ti·an figures** \¦==¦s(h)ted·ēən-\ *n pl, usu cap W* [*widmanstaetten* after Aloys B. *Widmannstätten* †1849 Austrian mineralogist; *widmanstaettian* fr. Aloys B. *Widmannstätten* + E *-an*] **:** figures that appear on etched meteoric iron and exhibit its crystalline structure

¹**wid·ow** \ˈwi(,)dō, -,də; -,dəw, -,dō+V\ *n* -s [ME *widewe, widwe,* fr. OE *widewe, wuduwe;* akin to OHG *wituwa, witawa* widow, Goth *widuwo,* L *vidua* widow, *-videre* to separate, Gk *ēitheos* unmarried youth, Skt *vidhavā* widow, *vidhura* separated from, *vindhate* he lacks] **1 a :** a woman who has lost her husband by death and has not since remarried — often used as if a title before a woman's marriage name ⟨the ~ Jones⟩ ⟨a tavern kept by ~ Smith⟩ **b :** a particular woman identified as having survived her husband and often as having thereby acquired legal rights that are not lost by subsequent remarriage by her though they may sometimes be lost by decree, statute, or construction (as on account of the survivor's desertion or adultery) **c** *dial Brit* **:** WIDOWER **d :** a woman whose husband deserts her or spends much time (as in a sports activity) away from her **:** GRASS WIDOW 2 — usu. used with a qualifying word ⟨poker ~⟩ ⟨fishing ~⟩ ⟨club ~⟩; compare GOLF WIDOW **2 :** one of a special class of women in the early Christian church serving as deaconesses in the performance of works of charity and in some liturgical offices (as the baptism of women) **3 :** an extra hand or part of a hand of cards that is dealt face down and usu. placed at the disposal of the highest bidder — see KITTY, SKAT **4 a :** a short line ending a paragraph and appearing at the top of a printed page or column **b :** a short line at the foot of a page or column

²**widow** \"\ *vt* -ED/-ING/-S **1 :** to cause to become a widow **:** bereave (a person) of a spouse ⟨women ~*ed* by the war⟩ ⟨he hath ~*ed* and unchilded many a one —Shak.⟩ **2 :** to survive as the widow of ⟨let me be married to three kings . . . and ~ them all —Shak.⟩ **3 :** to deprive of something greatly loved or needed **:** make desolate — usu. used with *of* ⟨the ~*ed* isle —John Dryden⟩ ⟨tank supporters . . . ~*ed* of tanks —A.J. Liebling⟩

widow-bench \ˈ=(,)=,=\ *n* **:** the portion besides her jointure allowed to a widow from her deceased husband's estate in English law — compare FREE BENCH

widow bewitched *n, chiefly dial* **:** a woman separated from her husband **:** GRASS WIDOW 2

widow bird *or* **widow finch** *n* [so called fr. its dark plumage and long black tail feathers like a widow's veil] **:** WHYDAH

widow duck *n* **:** a West Indian tree duck (*Dendrocygna viduata*)

wid·ow·er \ˈwidəwə(r), -dōə-\ *n* -s [ME *widewer,* fr. *widewe* widow + *-er*] **1 :** a man who has lost his wife by death and has not married again **2 :** a particular man identified as having survived his wife and often as having thereby acquired legal rights that are not lost by subsequent remarriage by him though they may sometimes be lost by decree, statute, or construction (as on account of the survivor's desertion or adultery)

wid·ow·ered \-ə(r)d\ *adj* **:** made a widower ⟨his ~ father —William Humphrey⟩

wid·ow·er·hood \-ə(r),hu̇d\ *n* **1 :** the quality or state of being a widower **2 :** the period during which a man remains a widower

widowhead *n* [ME *widewehed,* fr. *widewe* widow + *-hed* -hood (akin to ME *-hod, -had* -hood)] *obs* **:** WIDOWHOOD

wid·ow·hood \ˈ=(,)=,hu̇d\ *n* [ME *widewehod, widewehad,* fr. *widewe* widow + *-hod, -had* -hood — more at WIDOW] **1 :** the quality or state of being a widow ⟨destined to an early ~⟩ **2 :** the period during which a person remains a widow ⟨married again after a brief ~⟩

widow lady *n, chiefly dial* **:** WIDOW

wid·ow·ly *adj* **:** of, relating to, or befitting a widow ⟨~ grief⟩

widow-maker \ˈ=(,)=,==\ *n* **:** something dangerous to a worker's life or health; *specif* **:** a loose limb hanging in or falling from a tree in logging

wid·ow·man \-,mən\ *n, pl* **widowmen** *chiefly dial* **:** WIDOWER

widow monkey *n* **:** a So. American titi (*Callicebus torquatus*) that is black except for dull whitish arms, neck, and face and a ring of pure white around the face

widow right *n* **:** a widow's right (as dower, quarantine, or statutory share) in her deceased husband's estate

widows *pl of* WIDOW, *pres 3d sing of* WIDOW

widow's chamber *n* **:** the bedchamber apparel and furniture passing to the widow of a freeman of London by a custom formerly recognized in English law

widow's-cross \ˈ=(,)=ˈ=\ *n, pl* **widow's-crosses :** an evergreen fleshy-leaved herb (*Sedum pulchellum*) of the eastern U.S. often cultivated for its rosy purple showy flowers

widow's frill *n* **:** STARRY CAMPION

widow's mite *n* [so called fr. the widow who cast two mites (a farthing) into the Temple treasury (Mark 12:42)] **:** a small contribution that is willingly given and is all one can afford ⟨gave his *widow's mite* to the cause⟩

widow's peak *n* [so called fr. the former belief that it is an omen of early widowhood] **:** PEAK 8

widow's quarantine *n* **:** QUARANTINE 1

widow's-tears \ˈ=(,)=ˈ=\ *n pl but sing or pl in constr* **:** SPIDERWORT 1a

widow's walk *n* [so called fr. its use by the wives of seamen] **1 :** a railed observation platform built above the roof of a coastal dwelling for an unobstructed outlook to sea — called also *captain's walk* **2 :** a balustraded roof area

widow's walk

widow woman *n, chiefly dial* **:** WIDOW

width \ˈwidth, -itth, *chiefly substand* -ith\ *n, pl* **widths** \"s, -idts, -it(t)s\ [¹*wide* + *-th*] **1 :** a distance from side to side **:** measure taken at right angles to length **:** BREADTH ⟨the ~ of a ribbon⟩ ⟨the ~ of a printed letter⟩ ⟨carpeting available in several ~*s*⟩ ⟨traveled across the ~ of the country⟩ **2 a :** largeness or greatness in extent **:** SPACIOUSNESS, SCOPE, RANGE ⟨gives you no idea of the ~ and the depth of his knowledge —K.C.Wheare⟩ ⟨the ~ of his invective —H.J.Laski⟩ **b :** FULLNESS, AMPLITUDE ⟨give ~ to a sleeve⟩ **c :** freedom from narrowness, constraint, or limitation **:** COMPREHENSIVENESS, LIBERALITY ⟨a ~ of view⟩ ⟨concerned to give medical education a greater cultural ~ —Walter Moberly⟩ **3 :** a measured and cut piece of material ⟨a ~ of calico⟩ ⟨a ~ of board⟩ **4 :** girth at the widest part — used of a shoe last and usu. given by a letter designating a standard size ⟨wears an E ~ shoe⟩

widthways \ˈ=,=\ *adv* **:** WIDTHWISE

widthwise \ˈ=,=\ *adv* **:** in the direction of the width **:** LATITUDINALLY ⟨trimmings placed ~ —*Women's Wear Daily*⟩

wie·de·mann effect \ˈvēdə,män-, ˈwēdəmən-\ *n, usu cap W* [after Gustav H. *Wiedemann* †1899 Ger. physicist] **:** twisting of a ferromagnetic rod due to the joint action of a longitudinal current in the rod and a longitudinal magnetic field — compare MAGNETOSTRICTION

wiedemann-franz law \-ˈfrän(t)s-, -ˈfran(t)s-\ *n, usu cap W&F* [after Gustav H. *Wiedemann* †1899 and Rudolph *Franz* †1902 Ger. physicists] **:** a statement in physics: at a given temperature the ratio of the thermal to the electrical conductivity has nearly the same value for most metals and approximately is proportional to the absolute temperature of the metal

wiegela *syn of* WEIGELA

wield \ˈwēld, *esp before pause or consonant* -ēəld\ *vt* -ED/-ING/-S [ME *welden* to have power over, control, fr. OE *wieldan;* akin to OHG *waltan* to rule, ON *valda* to rule, wield, Goth *waldan* to rule, dominate, OIr *flaith* power, rule, L *valēre* to be strong, be well, be worth, Lith *veldėti* to rule, Toch B *walo* king] **1** *chiefly dial* **:** to deal successfully with **:** MANAGE ⟨weighty work, which he cannot ~ by himself —Thomas Fuller⟩ **2 :** to use (as a tool or instrument) esp. with full command or power **:** HANDLE, MANIPULATE, CONTROL ⟨~ a broom⟩ ⟨~ a paintbrush⟩ ⟨~*ed* a pen with clerkly precision —T.B.Costain⟩ ⟨~*ed* the two languages with facility⟩ **3 a :** to show or exert one's power or authority by means of **:** GOVERN, RUN ⟨those who ~*ed* the bureaucratic machine —Hugh Seton-Watson⟩ **b :** to exercise (as power, authority, sovereignty) **:** EMPLOY ⟨~ influence⟩ ⟨a highly centralized executive ~*ing* absolute power —Aldous Huxley⟩ **4** *obs* **:** EXPRESS ⟨I love you more than word can ~ the matter —Shak.⟩ **syn** see HANDLE

wield·er \-də(r)\ *n* -s **:** one that wields (as a weapon or implement)

wieldy \-dē, -di\ *adj* **1 :** capable of wielding **:** STRONG ⟨entrusted to ~ hands —Anthony Harris⟩ **2 :** capable of being wielded **:** MANAGEABLE ⟨is a large but ~ book —*New Republic*⟩

wien bridge \ˈvēn-, ˈwēn-\ *n, usu cap W* [after Max *Wien* †1938 Ger. physicist] **:** a bridge for measuring or comparing capacitances — compare BRIDGE 6

wie·ner *or* **wei·ner** \ˈwēnə(r)\ *n* -s [*wiener* short for *wienerwurst; weiner* alter. of *wiener*] **:** FRANKFURTER

wie·ner schnit·zel \ˈvēnə(r),shnitsəl, ˈwēnə(r),sn-\ *n, usu cap W* [G, lit., Vienna cutlet] **:** a thin breaded veal cutlet served with a garnish (as lemon wedges, capers, or a fried egg)

wie·ner·wurst \ˈwēnə(r),= — *last syllable as at* LIVERWURST\ *n* [G, fr. *Wiener* of Vienna (fr. *Wien* Vienna) + *wurst* sausage, fr. OHG — more at WURST] **1 :** VIENNA SAUSAGE **2 :** FRANKFURTER

wie·nie *or* **wee·nie** \ˈwēnē, ˈwinē, -ni\ *n* -s [*wienie* fr. *wiener* + *-ie; weenie* alter. of *wienie*] *slang* **:** WIENER

wien's displacement law \ˈvēnz-, ˈwēnz-\ *n, usu cap W* [after Wilhelm *Wien* †1928 Ger. physicist] **:** a statement in physics: the wavelength of thermal radiation most copiously emitted by a blackbody is inversely proportional to the absolute temperature of the body

wies·ba·den \ˈvēs,bädᵊn, ˈvis-\ *adj, usu cap* [fr. *Wiesbaden,* Germany] **:** of or from the city of Wiesbaden, Germany **:** of the kind or style prevalent in Wiesbaden

wie·sen·bo·den \ˈvēzᵊn,bōdᵊn\ *n* -s [G, meadow soil, fr. *wiesen* (pl. of *wiese* meadow, fr. OHG *wisa*) + *boden* ground, soil, fr. OHG *bodam* bottom; akin to OE *wāse* mud, mire — more at OOZE, BOTTOM] **:** any of an intrazonal group of dark brown to black meadow soils rich in organic matter with gray underlayers developed through poor drainage in humid or subhumid grassy or sedgy regions

¹**wife** \ˈwīf\ *n, pl* **wives** \-īvz\ [ME *wif,* fr. OE *wīf;* akin to OHG *wīb* woman, wife, ON *vīf* woman; perh. akin to ON *veipr* head covering — more at WIPE] **1 a** *dial* **:** WOMAN — compare OLD WIFE **b :** a woman acting in a specified capacity — used in combination: as (1) **:** one who sells something **:** VENDER ⟨a fish*wife*⟩ ⟨an oyster*wife*⟩ (2) **:** one who has charge of something **:** KEEPER ⟨hen*wife*⟩ (3) **:** a woman worker ⟨washer*wife*⟩ ⟨hostler*wife*⟩ **2 a :** a married woman ⟨a ~ can take credit for the good in her husband —Lenard Kaufman⟩ **b :** a woman who on the basis of her tribal or societal institutions is married ⟨in sororal polygyny when a man married the eldest daughter each of her sisters became his ~ also⟩ **3 :** the female of a pair of mated animals ⟨a new ~ for the gander is introduced into the pen⟩

²**wife** \"\ *vb* -ED/-ING/-S [ME *wifen,* fr. *wif* wife] **:** WIVE

wife·hood \ˈwīf,hu̇d\ *n* [ME *wifhod, wifhode,* fr. OE *wīfhād* womanhood, fr. *wīf* woman, wife + *-hād* -hood] **:** the quality or state of being a wife ⟨achieved the status of ~⟩

wife·less \-ləs\ *adj* [ME *wifles,* fr. OE *wīflēas,* fr. *wīf* wife + *-lēas* -less] **:** having no wife ⟨the only ~ man in the group of old classmates⟩

¹**wifelike** \ˈ=,=\ *adv* **:** in a wifely manner ⟨laid, ~, her hand in one of his —Alfred Tennyson⟩

²**wifelike** \"\ *adj* **:** WIFELY

wife·li·ness \ˈwīflēnəs, -lin-\ *n* -ES **:** the quality or state of being wifely ⟨vague piecemeal efforts at ~ —Martha Gellhorn⟩

wife·ly *adj* [ME *wifly,* fr. OE *wīflic,* fr. *wīf* wife + *-līc* -ly] **1 :** of, relating to, or befitting a wife ⟨~ virtues⟩ ⟨~ duty⟩ ⟨a ~ act⟩ **2 :** having the character or look of a wife ⟨stout and ~, in her chaste cambric nightgown —Ellen Glasgow⟩

wife's equity \ˈwīfs- *sometimes* -īvz-\ *n* **:** the equitable right or claim of a married woman prior to the married women's separate property acts as against her husband or his assignees or creditors to a reasonable provision (as by way of settlement) out of her choses in action or out of any property of hers under the jurisdiction of the court of chancery for the support of herself and her children

wif·ey *or* **wif·ie** \ˈwīfē, -fi\ *n* **:** WIFE — not often in formal use

wif·ish \-fish, -fēsh\ *adj* **:** WIFELY

¹**wig** \ˈwig\ *n* -s [ME *wigge,* fr. MLG, wedge, wedge-shaped cake; akin to MD *wegge* wedge, OHG *weggi, wecki* — more at WEDGE] *Brit* **:** a bun flavored with spices and caraway seeds

²**wig** \"\ *n* -s [short for ¹*periwig*] **1 a :** a manufactured covering of hair for the head usu. made of human hair that is woven or attached to a piece of net or a skullcap and worn as a cover for baldness or thin hair or as part of theatrical costume, official or professional dress, or fashionable attire ⟨London barristers wearing ~*s*⟩ ⟨the elaborately curled and powdered ~*s* of the 18th century⟩ — see PERUKE **b :** TOUPEE 2 **2 a :** a person wearing a wig (as a judge or lawyer) **b :** DIGNITARY, BIGWIG **3 :** an act of wigging **:** REBUKE **4 a :** the coarse fur on the shoulders of a large male hooded seal **b :** a male fur seal — **wigs on the green :** a bitter dispute **:** FUSS, CLASH ⟨feared . . . *wigs on the green* at the annual stockholders' meeting —*Time*⟩

³**wig** \"\ *vt* **wigged; wigged; wigging; wigs 1 :** to supply with a wig **2 :** to scold severely **:** CENSURE, REBUKE ⟨*wigged* me for being there the other night —*Delineator*⟩ **syn** see SCOLD

wig·an \ˈwigən\ *n* -s [fr. *Wigan,* Lancashire, England, where it was orig. manufactured] **:** a plain-weave cotton fabric with a stiff finish used for interlining (as tailored coats or jackets)

wig block *n* **:** a round-topped block for making, dressing, or holding a wig

wigeon *var of* WIDGEON

wigged \¦wigd\ *adj* **:** wearing a wig ⟨the judge, all ~ and robed⟩

wig·gen *or* **wig·gin** \ˈwigən\ *n* -s [alter. of ²*quicken*] *dial* **:** ROWAN TREE 1

wig·ger \-gə(r)\ *n* -s **:** WIGMAKER

wig·gery \-gərē, -ri\ *n* -ES **1 :** the use of wigs ⟨preferred ~ to baldness —Anthony Trollope⟩ **2 :** a business dealing in wigs ⟨a visit to a nearby theatrical ~ —P.G.Wodehouse⟩

wig·ging \-giŋ, -gēŋ\ *n* -s [²*wig* + *-ing*] **1 :** severe censure from one in authority **:** DRESSING DOWN, SCOLDING ⟨the ~ I received from my editor —C.A.Lejeune⟩ **2** *Austral* **a :** the removal of wool from around the eyes of sheep to prevent obstruction of vision **b :** wool so removed — usu. used in pl. ⟨~*s* . . . mixed with good-quality lambs' wool —R.G. Montgomery⟩

¹**wig·gle** \ˈwigəl\ *vb* **wiggled; wiggled; wiggling** \-g(ə)liŋ\ **wiggles** [ME *wiglen, wigelen,* of LG or D origin; akin to MLG *wiggelen* to totter, reel, MFlem *wigelen* to totter, reel, rock, MD *wiege* cradle; akin to OHG *wiga* cradle, OE *wegan* to move — more at WAY] *vi* **1 :** to move back and forth or up and down with quick jerky or shaking motions **:** JIGGLE, OSCILLATE ⟨a compass needle *wiggling* crazily⟩ ⟨the screen . . . image ~*s* —M.C.Faught⟩ ⟨high heels that make a woman ~ . . . when she walks —Wolcott Gibbs⟩ **2 :** to proceed with twisting and turning movements **:** WRIGGLE, WORM ⟨~ through a crowd⟩ ⟨has an unimaginable gift of *wiggling* in wherever he wants to —O.W.Holmes †1935⟩ ~ *vt* **:** to cause to wiggle ⟨*wiggled* his eyebrows —John Fountain⟩ ⟨found his toe and *wiggled* it —Winifred Bambrick⟩

²**wiggle** \"\ *n* -s **1 :** the motion of one that wiggles ⟨she was all smiles . . . and ~*s* coming down the broad stairs —Calvin Kentfield⟩ **2 :** shellfish or fish in cream sauce with peas ⟨shrimp ~⟩ — **get a wiggle on** *slang* **:** hurry up **:** HUSTLE ⟨better *get a wiggle on* or we'll be late⟩

wiggle nail *n* **:** CORRUGATED FASTENER

wig·gler \-g(ə)lə(r)\ *n* -s [¹*wiggle* + *-er*] **1 :** one that wiggles **2 :** the larva or pupa of the mosquito — called also *wriggler* **3 :** a tool for positioning work centers accurately by exaggerating deviations

wiggle-tail \ˈ==,=\ *n* **1 :** WIGGLER **2** *dial* **:** TADPOLE

wiggle-tail cultivator *n* **:** a riding row-crop cultivator designed to permit easy control of the cultivator gangs in the cultivation of crooked rows

¹**wiggle-waggle** \¦==¦==\ *adj* [redupl. of ¹*wiggle*] **:** INDECISIVE, VACILLATING ⟨has gone *wiggle-waggle* and cannot be persuaded to be categorical —Lionel Hale⟩

²**wiggle-waggle** \"\ *vi* [redupl. of ¹*wiggle*] **:** to move jerkily back and forth **:** wiggle and waggle from one thing to another **:** VACILLATE ⟨*wiggle-waggles* between appeals for charity and responsible state action —*Nation*⟩

³**wiggle-waggle** \"\ *or* **wiggle-woggle** \¦==¦==\ *n* **:** something (as an amusement park contrivance) that wiggle-waggles ⟨flips flaps, switchbacks, *wiggle-woggles* —Rose Macaulay⟩

wig·gly \ˈwig(ə)lē, -li\ *adj* **-ER/-EST** *also* **wiggly-waggly** \¦=(=)=¦=(=)=\ *adj* **:** tending to wiggle **:** WIGGLING, WRIGGLY ⟨follow a ~ course⟩ ⟨~ lines⟩ ⟨~ worms⟩

wig·gy \ˈwigē\ *adj* -ER/-EST [¹*wig* + *-y*] **1 :** marked by excessive gravity and formality **:** POMPOUS ⟨a dried up, ~ . . . little scandalmonger —Richard Dehan⟩ **2 :** BEWIGGED

¹**wight** \ˈwīt, *usu* -īd·+V\ *n* -s [ME *wight, wiht* creature, thing, fr. OE *wiht;* akin to OHG *wiht* creature, thing, ON *vættr* creature, being, Goth *waihts* thing, OSlav *veštĭ*] **1 :** a living being **:** CREATURE, MAN ⟨no patriarch he . . . but a withered, anxious, crabbed ~ —Compton Mackenzie⟩ ⟨yonder a maid and her ~ —Thomas Hardy⟩ ⟨one of those benighted ~*s* —Norman Cousins⟩ ⟨any luckless ~ . . . who gets his wife in bad with her boss —G.W.Johnson⟩ **2** *archaic* **:** a preternatural being (as a fairy or witch) ⟨protection against uncouth ~*s* —William Morris⟩

²**wight** \"\ *adj* [ME *wight, wiht,* of Scand origin; akin to ON *vīgr* skilled in fighting, in fighting condition (neut. *vīgt*), *vīg* fight — more at VICTOR] **1** *archaic* **:** VALIANT, STALWART **2** *dial* **a :** STRONG **b :** SWIFT

³**wight** \"\ *or* **wight·ly** *adv* [*wight* fr. ME, fr. *wight, wiht* strong, swift; *wightly* fr. ME, fr. *wight, wiht* strong, swift + *-ly*] *dial* **1 :** STRONGLY **2 :** SWIFTLY

wig·less \ˈwigləs\ *adj* **:** having or wearing no wig ⟨tumbles headlong and ~ to the floor —Agnes Repplier⟩

wigmaker \ˈ=,==\ *n* **:** one that makes or deals in wigs

wigs *pl of* WIG, *pres 3d sing of* WIG

wig·town·shire \ˈwigtən,shi(ə)r, -,taun-\ *or* **wigtown** *adj, usu cap* [fr. *Wigtownshire* or *Wigtown,* Scotland] **:** of or from the county of Wigtown, Scotland **:** of the kind or style prevalent in Wigtown

¹**wig·wag** \ˈwi,gwag, -aa(ə)g, -aig\ *vb* [E dial. *wig* to move, shake (prob. back-formation fr. E ¹*wiggle*) + E ¹*wag*] *vi* **1 :** to signal by waving a flag or portable light according to a code in which movements to the right and left are the elements of the code alphabet and a movement to the front indicates the end (as of a word or message) **2 :** to make a signal (as with the hand or arm) ⟨~*s* through the window of his office —*advt*⟩ ~ *vt* **1 :** to signal (as a message) by wigwagging ⟨the mariner *wigwagged* the necessary directions —*Amer. Guide Series: Conn.*⟩ **2 :** to cause to wigwag ⟨*wigwagged* the white flags —*Blue Bk.*⟩

²**wigwag** \"\ *n, often attrib* **1 a :** the art or practice of wigwagging ⟨no wireless reports . . . and the papers got their news by ~ —Harland Manchester⟩ ⟨the ~ system⟩ **b :** a wigwagged message **2 :** a polishing device used by watchmakers and clockmakers in which the polisher has a back-and-forth motion

wigwag signal *n* **:** a signal at a railway grade crossing that indicates the approach of a train by the horizontal swinging of a disk

wig·wam \ˈwi,gwäm *also* -gwȯm\ *n* -s [Abnaki & Massachuset *wīkwām,* lit., their dwelling] **1 a :** a hut of the Indians of the region of the Great Lakes and eastward having typically an arched top and consisting of a framework of poles overlaid with bark, rush mats, or hides — compare LODGE 8a **b :** a roughly similar hut ⟨a rough ~ fashioned of fir boughs —F.V. W.Mason⟩ **2 :** a large building serving as the headquarters or meeting place (as convention hall) of a U.S. political organization (as the convention hall of the Republican Party in 1860 or any of the successive buildings housing the Tammany Society of New York) **3 :** a moderate brown that is yellower, lighter, and stronger than chestnut brown, auburn, bay, or tobacco and redder, lighter, and stronger than coffee

wigwam

wiik·ite \ˈvē,kīt\ *n* -s [Sw *wiikit,* fr. F. J. *Wiik* †1909 Finnish mineralogist + Sw *-it* -ite] **:** a mineral consisting probably of a mixture of samarskite, betafite, and perhaps allanite and occurring in pegmatite in Impilakhti parish on Lake Ladoga, Finland

wijs method \ˈvīs-\ *n, usu cap W* [after Jacob J. Alexander *Wijs* †1942 Dutch analytical chemist] **:** a method for determining the iodine number (as of an oil or fat) that consists in adding a solution of iodine monochloride in glacial acetic acid and estimating the excess of unused halogen by titration with sodium thiosulfate

wi·ke·no \wəˈkā(,)nō\ *n, pl* **wikeno** *or* **wikenos** *usu cap* **1 :** a Bellabella people of British Columbia **2 :** a member of the Wikeno people

wi·ki·wi·ki \¦wēkē¦wēkē\ *adv* [Hawaiian] *Hawaii* **:** QUICKLY, FAST

wik·stroe·mia \wikˈstrōmēə, -rēm-\ *n, cap* [NL, fr. J. E. *Wikström* †1856 Swed. botanist + NL *-ia*] **:** a genus of chiefly Asiatic shrubs (family Thymelaeaceae) including some (as *W. canescens*) with bark that yields a fiber used in making paper and cloth

wil·bur·ite \ˈwilbə,rīt\ *n* -s *usu cap* [John *Wilbur* †1856 Am. Quaker preacher + E *-ite*] **:** a member of the Religious Society of Friends (Conservative) formed in the U. S. in 1845 as a protest on behalf of Inner Light against the doctrine of the Gurneyites

wil·co \ˈwil(,)kō\ *interj* [short for the phrase *will comply*] — used esp. in radio and signaling to indicate that a message received will be complied with

¹**wild** \ˈwīld, *esp before pause or consonant* ˈwīəld\ *adj* -ER/-EST [ME *wilde,* fr. OE; akin to OHG *wildi* wild, ON *villr* wild, gone astray, bewildered, Goth *wiltheis* wild, W *gwyllt,* Corn *guyls*] **1 a** (1) **:** living in a state of nature **:** inhabiting natural haunts (as the forest or open field) **:** not tamed or domesticated ⟨a ~ ox⟩ ⟨~ duck⟩ (2) **:** being one of a kind not ordinarily subjected to domestication ⟨the tame ~ goose finally flew away⟩ — compare FERAL (3) **:** SHY 1a **b** (1) **:** growing or produced without the aid and care of man **:** not cultivated **:** brought forth by unassisted nature or by animals not domesticated **:** NATIVE ⟨~ furs⟩ ⟨the closest ~ relative of cultivated corn —P.C.Mangelsdorf⟩ ⟨~ honey⟩ (2) **:** related to or resembling a corresponding cultivated or domesticated organism — used in vernacular names of plants and animals; see WILD OAT, WILD ONION **c :** not living near or associated with man — used esp. of a mosquito that does not breed near human habitations in distinction from one that habitually does so **d :** of or belonging to organisms in a state of nature **:** typical of undomesticated animals or uncultivated plants ⟨the ~ state⟩ ⟨~ nature⟩ **2 a :** not inhabited or cultivated ⟨the only profit in ~ land was to clear and plant it with one's own hands or to sell it —*Amer. Guide Series: N.Y.*⟩ **b :** not being or appearing amenable to human habitation or cultivation **:** ROUGH, WASTE, DESOLATE ⟨becomes much ~*er* as the trees give place to bare granite crags —S.P.B.Mais⟩ **3 a** (1) **:** not subjected to restraint or regulation **:** UNCONTROLLED, INORDINATE, UNGOVERNED ⟨mobs are ~, unpredictable, vicious, and insanely cruel when aroused —P.I.Wellman⟩ ⟨the ~ frenzy of religious camp meetings —J.T.Adams⟩ ⟨a piano played with a ~ exuberance —Louis Bromfield⟩ (2) **:** abandoned to or overcome by passion, desire, or emotion ⟨the frenzied old man, ~ with hatred and insane with baffled desire —W.M. Thackeray⟩ ⟨~ with grief⟩; *also* **:** passionately eager, enthusiastic, desirous, or angry ⟨he was ~ to own a toy train —J.C.Furnas⟩ ⟨his sponsors . . . are ~ about him as a salesman —Howard Taubman⟩ ⟨boys ~ for the venture —Marjory S. Douglas⟩ ⟨straining and ~ to take to the air —Kay Boyle⟩ ⟨was ~ at people talking, and upsetting him —Sheila Kaye-Smith⟩ (3) **:** not amenable to control, restraint, or domestication **:** UNRULY, UNGOVERNABLE, RECKLESS ⟨bars and bowling alleys full of ~ youths breezily and brutally telling each other off —Robert Lowry⟩ ⟨a rabble of ~ country lads —W.B.

Yeats⟩ ⟨the zebra is too ~ to be used as a draft animal⟩ ⟨a ~ mop of hair —Irwin Shaw⟩ (4) *of a ship* **:** hard to steer or tending to yaw from the course (5) **:** not capped **:** not brought into controlled or regulated production — used of an oil or gas well **b :** marked by turbulent violent agitation **:** ROUGH, TEMPESTUOUS, STORMY ⟨the sea against the west coast was ~ with storm —Ernesta D. Barlow⟩ ⟨it's a ~ night . . . to be out in the rain —J.M.Synge⟩ **c :** LICENTIOUS, DISSOLUTE **d :** exceeding normal or conventional bounds in thought, design, conception, execution, or nature **:** EXTRAVAGANT, FANTASTIC, VISIONARY ⟨overmatched in lush, easy wealth the ~*est* dreams of fantasy —T.H.White b. 1915⟩ ⟨remonstrating against the ~ project —H.E.Scudder⟩ ⟨~ beliefs about the origin of these fishes —J.L.B.Smith⟩ ⟨the ~*est* complexity ever added to the steam engine —George Zabriskie⟩ ⟨a ~ array of bathhouses, dance halls, freak shows, fun houses —*Amer. Guide Series: N.Y. City*⟩ ⟨a necktie of ~ colors and pattern⟩ **e** (1) **:** become destructive or ferocious through escape from normal restraints ⟨~ cells forming a tumor⟩ ⟨a dog gone ~⟩ (2) **:** escaped from or beyond human control ⟨the brakes gave out and . . . not even a fool would ride a ~ truck . . . with an overload of logs —Hugh Fosburgh⟩ — compare WILDFIRE **f** (1) **:** characteristic or indicative of strong or overwhelming passion, desire, or emotion ⟨looked at me with a ~ stare of agony —Walter O'Meara⟩ ⟨a ~ gleam of delight in his eyes —*Irish Digest*⟩ ⟨taken his ~ words in earnest —George Meredith⟩ (2) **:** characterized or marked by the presence or activity of unruly, intemperate, abandoned, or impassioned persons ⟨a ~ 5-hour street battle —*Current History*⟩ ⟨a ~, frontier town —*Amer. Guide Series: Texas*⟩ ⟨found dead on a beach, apparently following a ~ party —M.S.Forbes⟩ **4 a :** not acculturated to an advanced civilization **:** RUDE, UNCIVILIZED, BARBARIC ⟨~ natives⟩ ⟨~ practices⟩ **b :** not yielding to a governmental authority **:** SAVAGE, INTRACTABLE, REBELLIOUS ⟨~ border tribes⟩ **c :** resembling a barbarian or a wild animal **:** BRUTALIZED ⟨dirty, ~, and degraded as only the worst slaves of antiquity had been —Lewis Mumford⟩ **5 :** characteristic of, appropriate to, or expressive of wilderness, wildlife, or people in a simple or uncivilized society or environment ⟨~ and rugged grandeur —Elinor Wylie⟩ ⟨~ love of freedom —Meridel Le Sueur⟩ ⟨in the brush a soft persuasive cooing . . . subtle and ~ and unobtrusive —John Burroughs⟩ **6 a :** deviating from a natural or expected course, goal, or practice **:** acting, appearing, or being manifested in an unexpected, undesired, or unpredictable manner **:** RANDOM, ERRATIC ⟨impulsive grammar and ~ spelling —C. W. Cunnington⟩ ⟨giving a ~ guess, I suggested that the model was one twelfth the size of the ordinary chair —S.P.B. Mais⟩ ⟨~ price fluctuations —W.R.Langdon⟩ ⟨swing across traffic in a ~ circle —Green Peyton⟩ **b :** not accounted for by known theories ⟨afterimages . . . although perhaps not strictly hallucinations might be alleged as ~ sense-data —R.J. Hirst⟩ **7 :** great in extent, size, quantity, or intensity **:** EXTREME, PRODIGIOUS ⟨~ and precarious leaps —D.L.Busk⟩ ⟨a ~ headache that did not leave her for days —Louis Bromfield⟩ ⟨the world's ~*est* religious fanatics —Isaac Deutscher⟩ **8** *of a playing card* **:** having a denomination determined by the will of the holder — compare DEUCES WILD, JOKER **9** *of paper* **:** loose and irregular in formation so as to appear mottled when looked through — contrasted with *well-closed*

²**wild** \"\ *n* -s **1 :** a region or tract that is sparsely inhabited or uncultivated **:** WILDERNESS ⟨the ruthless life of the ~ —James Stevenson-Hamilton⟩ ⟨settlers had to cross this Indian-infested ~ —*Amer. Guide Series: Texas*⟩ ⟨living in the ~*s* of Africa hunting crocodiles —*Publishers' Weekly*⟩ **2 :** a wild, free, or natural life or existence ⟨corn in the ~ may well have been a plant with low survival value —P.C.Mangelsdorf⟩

³**wild** \"\ *adv* **1 :** WILDLY ⟨~ shy about seeing any of her own people —Mary Deasy⟩ **2 :** without regulation or control **:** UNCONTROLLEDLY ⟨given over to violence, society is an engine running ~ —F.H.Giddings⟩

wild alder *n* **:** GOUTWEED

wild alfalfa *n* **1 :** SWEET CLOVER **2 :** a yellow-flowered Eurasian medic (*Medicago falcata*) **3 :** a scurfy pea (*Psoralea tenuiflora floribunda*) **4 :** DEERWEED

wild allspice *n* **:** SPICEBUSH

wild almond *n* **1 :** a southern African tree (*Brabejum stellatifolium*) of the family Proteaceae; *also* **:** its edible seed sometimes used in place of coffee **2 :** JAVA ALMOND **3 :** any of various trees of the genus *Prunus* (esp. *P. fasciculata*)

wild and woolly *adj* **:** marked by boisterous and untamed ways of living and by lack of polish and refinement ⟨the *wild and woolly* West of the American plains and mesas —B.S.Mason⟩

wild angelica *n* **:** a European herb (*Angelica sylvestris*) with compound leaves and white flowers that is adventive on Cape Breton island

wild apple *n* **1 :** an apple that grows wild: as **a :** OREGON CRAB APPLE **b :** SIBERIAN CRAB **2 :** the fruit of the native cranberry

wild arum *n* **:** CUCKOOPINT

wild ash *n* **:** AMERICAN MOUNTAIN ASH

wild ass *n* **:** any of several plain-colored or nearly plain-colored equine mammals (as the kiang or onager) of Asia and northeast Africa that are related to and resemble the domesticated ass

wild balsam *n* **:** JEWELWEED b

wild balsam apple *n* **:** WILD CUCUMBER c

wild banana *n* **:** a banana (as *Musa glauca* or *M. davyae*) that grows wild

wild barley *n* **:** any of various grasses of the genus *Hordeum* that are not commonly cultivated for grain: as **a :** WALL BARLEY **b :** a biennial or perennial No. American weedy grass (*H. jubatum*) with bristly awns and glumes that may injure the mouths of grazing animals

wild basil *n* **:** an aromatic herb (*Satureia vulgaris*) that is widely distributed in the U.S., Europe, and Asia and that has capitate clusters of small pink-and-white flowers

wild bean *n* **:** any of various wild plants of the family Leguminosae; *esp* **:** any of various plants of the genera *Phaseolus*, *Apios*, and *Strophostyles*

wild bee *n* **:** any of numerous undomesticated social bees; *also* **:** the honeybee when escaped from domestication

wild beet *n* **1 :** PIGWEED a **2 :** a perennial evening primrose (*Oenothera fruticosa*) of the eastern and central U.S. that is sometimes used as a potherb

wild begonia *n* **:** a dock (*Rumex venosus*) with broad rose-colored veiny wings on the fruit — called also *wild hydrangea*

wild bergamot *n* **:** MONARDA 2; *esp* **:** a fragrant No. American herb (*Monarda fistulosa*) having a terminal capitate cluster of rather large pink or purple flowers

wild black cherry *n* **:** BLACK CHERRY 2

wild black currant *n* **:** any of several uncultivated black-fruited currants; esp. **:** an unarmed No. American shrub (*Ribes americanum*) with racemose greenish yellow flowers and black smooth fruit — called also *flowering currant*

wild bleeding heart *n* **:** a weak glaucous herb (*Dicentra eximia*) of the eastern U.S. that has finely divided leaves and is often cultivated for its rose-pink short-spurred showy flowers

wild bluegrass *n* **:** any of several forage grasses of the genus *Poa* (esp. *P. sandbergii*) found in prairie regions of No. America

wild blue phlox *n* **:** a showy No. American herb (*Phlox divaricata*) often cultivated for its profusion of tubular blue faintly fragrant flowers — called also *wild sweet William*

wild boar *n* **:** a wild hog (*Sus scrofa*) of continental Europe, southwestern Asia, and northern Africa from which most domestic swine have been derived and which has coarse and grizzled hair and the tusks or canines of both jaws often much enlarged; *broadly* **:** any of various related wild hogs of southeastern Asia

wild·bore \ˈwī(ə)ld,bō(ə)r\ *n* -s [origin unknown] **:** a formerly popular durable woolen dress fabric

wild brier *n* **:** an uncultivated species of brier: as **a :** DOG ROSE **b :** SWEETBRIER

wild buckwheat *n* **1 :** BLACK BINDWEED 1 **2 :** a low-growing shrub of the genus *Eriogonum* (esp. *E. fasciculatum*)

wild bugloss *n* **:** BUGLOSS 4

wild burnet *n* **:** a burnet (*Sanguisorba canadensis*) of No. America

wild cabbage *n* **1 :** a plant that is the wild original of the cultivated cabbage and is common near the seacoast in various parts of Europe **2 :** a succulent herb (*Caulanthus crassicaulis*) of the family Cruciferae that is native to the western U.S. and has edible foliage

wild calla *n* **1 :** an arrow arum (*Peltandra sagittaefolia*) of the southern U. S. **2 :** WATER ARUM

wild canary *n* **1 :** GOLDFINCH 3 **2 :** YELLOW WARBLER 1a

wild caraway *n* **1 :** either of two Indian plantains (*Cacalia suaveolens* and *C. atriplicifolia*) **2 :** YAMP

wild carrot *n* **:** a Eurasian weed (*Daucus carota*) that is prob. the original of the cultivated carrot, is widely naturalized as a weed, and has an acrid and unpleasantly flavored root — called also *lace flower, Queen Anne's lace*

¹**wildcat** \ˈ⸗,⸗\ *n* -s *see sense 1b* [ME *wilde cat*, fr. *wilde* wild + *cat*] **1 a :** either of two cats that somewhat resemble the domestic tabby cat in color and pattern but are usu. somewhat heavier in build and that are usu. held to be among the ancestors of the domestic cat: (1) **:** EUROPEAN WILDCAT (2) **:** KAFFIR CAT **b** *or pl* **wildcat :** any of various small or medium-sized cats (as the jungle cat, the lynx, or the ocelot) **c :** a feral domestic cat **2 :** a savage quick-tempered hard-fighting person **3 a :** wildcat currency **b :** a wildcat oil or gas well **c :** a wildcat strike **4 :** a drum or wheel on a windlass having in its circumference a deep groove with projections that engage the links of a chain cable as it passes and thus regulate the speed of the cable **:** CABLE WHEEL — called also *cable holder*

²**wildcat** \"\ *adj* **1 a** (1) **:** financially irresponsible or unreliable ⟨~ banks⟩ ⟨worthless stock in a ~ mine⟩ (2) **:** issued by a financially irresponsible banking establishment ⟨~ currency⟩ **b :** operating or being produced or carried on outside the bounds of standard, recognized, or legitimate business practices ⟨~ breweries⟩ ⟨~ stock speculation⟩ ⟨~ promoters⟩ ⟨a ~ airline⟩ **c :** of, relating to, concerned with, or being an oil or gas well drilled in territory not known to be productive ⟨there may be oil but drilling for it would be strictly a ~ operation —*Newsweek*⟩ ⟨~ wells⟩ ⟨~ drilling⟩ **d :** initiated by a group of workers without formal union approval or in violation of a contract ⟨~ strike⟩ ⟨~ work stoppage⟩ **2 a :** *of a cartridge* **:** having a bullet of a standard commercial caliber but using an expanded case or a case designed for a bullet of a greater caliber but necked down for the smaller bullet **b** *of a rifle* **:** using wildcat cartridges

³**wildcat** \"\ *vi* **wildcatted; wildcatted; wildcatting; wildcats 1 :** to prospect and drill an experimental oil or gas well or sometimes a mine shaft in territory not known to be productive **2 :** to engage in wildcat speculations, operations, or enterprises **3 :** to run a railroad locomotive and tender

wild·cat·ter \"+ə(r)\ *n* -s [³*wildcat* + *-er*] **1 :** one that drills wells in the hope of finding oil in territory not known to be an oil field **2 :** one that promotes unsafe and unreliable enterprises; *esp* **:** one that sells stock in enterprises of this kind **3** [*wildcat (cartridge)* + *-er*] **:** one that designs, builds, or fires wildcat cartridges and rifles as a hobby

wild celandine *n* **:** JEWELWEED

wild celery *n* **:** TAPE GRASS

wild cherry *n* **1 :** an uncultivated cherry tree or its fruit: as **a :** BIRD CHERRY **b :** PIN CHERRY **c :** BLACK CHERRY 2 **2 :** a tropical American shrub (*Rhacoma crossopetalum*) of the family Celastraceae; *also* **:** the edible red fruit of this shrub **3 :** a dark red to purplish red that is stronger and slightly lighter than plum violet, stronger and slightly darker than neutral red, and much stronger than sultana — called also *vin rosé*

wild chervil *n* **1 :** a coarse erect biennial herb (*Anthriscus sylvestris*) of the family Umbelliferae that is widely distributed in the Old World and an introduced weed in eastern No. America **2 :** HONEWORT b

wild chestnut *n* **1 a :** a proteaceous shrub (*Brabejum stellatifolia*) of southern Africa **b :** the nut of this plant containing a kernel that is edible when roasted **2 :** a southern African tree (*Calodendron capense*) of the family Rutaceae with panicles of handsome white flowers for which it is sometimes cultivated; *also* **:** its edible black seed **3 :** a Philippine tree (*Castanopsis philippinensis*) related to the true chestnut; *also* **:** the seed of this tree

wild cinnamon *n* **1 :** a tree (*Canella winterana*) of Florida and the West Indies with white bark and small flowers in terminal cymes **2** *or* **wild clove :** BAYBERRY 1a

wild clary *n* **:** WILD SAGE 1

wild coffee *n* **1 :** FEVERROOT **2 :** CASCARA BUCKTHORN **3 :** a plant of the genus *Psychotria*

wild columbine *n* **:** COLUMBINE 1a

wild comfrey *n* **:** either of two perennial herbs (*Cynoglossum virginianum* and *C. boreale*) of the eastern U. S. having large bristly leaves and small blue flowers

wild corn *n* **:** a clintonia (*Clintonia umbellulata*)

wild cotton *n* **1 :** COTTON GRASS **2 a :** a shrubby herb (*Gossypium thurberi*) of southern Arizona and Mexico **b :** any of various cultivated cottons that have escaped and established themselves in subtropical or tropical areas **3 :** any of several plants of the genera *Abutilon* and *Hibiscus* (esp. *H. moscheutos*) **4** *Austral* **:** any of various milkweeds; *esp* **:** either of two milkweeds (*Asclepias fruticosa* and *A. physocarpa*) that have been introduced into Australia from So. Africa and are poisonous to cattle

wild cranesbill *n* **:** any of several wild geraniums (esp. *Geranium maculatum* and *G. dissectum*)

wild crocus *n* **:** PASQUEFLOWER

wild cucumber *n* **:** any of various vines related to or felt to resemble the cucumber: as **a :** SQUIRTING CUCUMBER **b :** STAR CUCUMBER **c :** a No. American vine (*Echinocystis lobata*) with greenish spiny fruit — called also *wild balsam apple*

wild currant *n* **:** any of several plants of the genus *Ribes* that produce fruit resembling cultivated currants

wild date *n* **1 :** a Spanish bayonet (*Yucca mohavensis*) of southern California with edible fruit used by the Indians **2 :** an Indian date (*Phoenix sylvestris*) that is grown for ornament and has gray-green leaves

wild dilly *n* **:** ⁴DILLY 2

wild dog *n* **:** any of various undomesticated mammals of the family Canidae (as the dingo, the African hunting dog, or the dhole) that are felt to resemble domestic dogs esp. as distinguished from jackals or wolves

wild dove *n* **:** MOURNING DOVE

wild duck *n* **:** an undomesticated duck; *esp* **:** MALLARD

wil·de·beest \ˈwildə,bēst *sometimes* ˈvi-\ *n, pl* **wildebeests** \-ts\ *also* **wildebeest** \-t\ *or* **wildebees·te** \-tə\ [Afrik *wildebees* (pl. *wildebeeste*), fr. *wild, wilde* wild (fr. MD *wilt, wilde*; akin to OE *wilde* wild) + *bees* beast, ox, fr. MD *beeste* beast, animal, fr. OF *beste* — more at WILD, BEAST] **:** GNU

wil·de dagga \ˈwildə-\ *n* [Afrik, fr. *wild, wilde* wild + *dagga*] **:** DAGGA 2

wild elder *n* **:** BRISTLY SARSAPARILLA

wild emmer *n* **:** WILD WHEAT 1

¹**wilder** *comparative of* WILD

²**wil·der** \ˈwildə(r)\ *vb* -ED/-ING/-S [prob. irreg. fr. *wilderness*] *vt* **1** *archaic* **:** to lead astray **2** *archaic* **:** BEWILDER, PERPLEX ~ *vi, archaic* **:** STRAY, WANDER

wil·der·ment \-(r)mənt\ *n* [*wilder* + *-ment*] *archaic* **:** BEWILDERMENT

wil·der·muth's auricle \ˈvildə(r),müts-\ *or* **wildermuth's ear** *n, usu cap W* [after Hermann A. *Wildermuth* †1907 Ger. neurologist] **:** an ear in which the antihelix is large and the helix bent downward

wil·der·ness \ˈwildə(r)nə̇s\ *n* -ES [ME *wildernesse*, fr. *wildern, wildren* wild, savage (fr. OE *wilddēoren* of or like wild beasts, fr. *wilddēor, wildēor*, alter. — influenced by *dēor* beast — of assumed OE *wildor* wild beast — whence OE *wildru*, pl., wild beasts; akin to OE *wilde* untamed, wild) + *-nesse* -ness — more at WILD, DEER] **1 a** (1) **:** a tract of land or a region (as a forest or a wide barren plain) uncultivated and uninhabited by human beings **:** WILD, WASTE (2) **:** an empty or pathless area or region ⟨in remote ~*es* of space groups of nebulae are found —G.W.Gray b. 1886⟩ (3) **:** a part of a garden devoted to wild growth **b :** something likened to a wilderness in barrenness, confusion, or dangerousness ⟨the ~ in the mind, the desert wastes in the heart —Anne M. Lindbergh⟩ ⟨a ~ of tumbledown shacks and gasworks —T.D.Durrance⟩ ⟨a ~ of sociological theory —H.J.Muller⟩ ⟨such a ~ of black hair that he appeared to be wearing a shako —*New Yorker*⟩ **2** *obs* **:** WILDNESS **3 :** a confusing multitude or mass **:** a great number or quantity ⟨I would not have given it for a ~ of monkeys —Shak.⟩

wilderness area *n* **:** an area (as of national forest land) set aside by government for preservation of natural conditions for scientific or recreational purposes

wildest *superlative of* WILD

wild-eyed \ˈ⸗,⸗\ *adj* **1 :** appearing or being furious or raving ⟨a *wild-eyed* and frantic young man, pale, dishevelled, and palpitating, burst into the room —A. Conan Doyle⟩ **2 :** consisting of or favoring extreme political or social measures **:** RADICAL, VISIONARY ⟨a *wild-eyed* internationalist dream of a world state —A.H.Vandenberg †1951⟩ ⟨*wild-eyed* reformers and rubble theorists —Gordon Merrick⟩

wild fig *n* **1 :** CAPRIFIG **2 :** any of several wild plants of the genus *Ficus* native to Florida (as *F. aurea*) **3 :** a West Indies tree (*Clusia flava*) or its fig-shaped fruit

wildfire \ˈ⸗,⸗\ *n* [ME *wilde fire*, fr. *wilde* wild + *fire*] **1 :** a sweeping and destructive conflagration **2 a :** a flammable composition very hard to quench when kindled **:** GREEK FIRE **b :** something resembling or suggesting wildfire in unquenchable intensity or inclusiveness in action ⟨spread through the crowd like ~⟩ **3 :** the ignis fatuus or a similar phosphorescent appearance **4 :** HEAT LIGHTNING **5 :** a destructive disease of tobacco caused by a bacterium (*Pseudomonus tabaci*) and characterized by small brown spots usu. surrounded with broad yellowish halos that enlarge quickly, turn tan or dark brown, dry or rot, and fall out — compare BLACKFIRE

wild flag *n* **1 :** an Australian plant of the genus *Patersonia* (family Iridaceae); *also* **:** its showy blue or purple flower **2 :** SWEET FLAG

wild flax *n* **1 :** GOLD OF PLEASURE **2 :** any of several wild plants of the genus *Linum* (esp. *L. lewissi*)

wild flower *n* **:** the flower of a wild or uncultivated plant; *also* **:** the plant bearing such a flower

wild forget-me-not *n* **:** any of several wild flowers (as a bluet) with blossoms suggestive of forget-me-nots

wild four-o'clock *n* **:** a common umbrellawort (*Mirabilis nyctaginea*) of the central and southern U. S.

wildfowl \ˈ⸗,⸗\ *n* [ME *wilde foul*, fr. *wilde* wild + *foul* fowl] **:** GAME BIRD; *esp* **:** a game waterfowl (as a wild duck or Canada goose)

wildfowl·er \"+ə(r)\ *n* [*wildfowl* + *-er*] **:** one that engages in wildfowling

wildfowl·ing \"+iŋ\ *n* -s [*wildfowl* + *-ing*] **:** the hunting of wildfowl as a sport or occupation

wild foxglove *n* **1 :** DOWNY FALSE FOXGLOVE **2 :** a plant of the genus *Penstemon*

wild fuchsia *n* **:** a California perennial (*Zauschneria californica*) that is related to the fuchsias and sometimes cultivated for its showy scarlet flowers

wild garden *n* **:** a garden in which colonies of hardy wild and garden plants are naturalized in positions where they will appear to be growing naturally

wild garlic *n* **:** any of several usu. pungent weedy plants of the genus *Allium*; *esp* **:** CROW GARLIC

wild gasoline *or* **wild gas** *n* **:** gasoline that is too volatile for commercial use; *esp* **:** natural gasoline that has not been stabilized

wild geranium *n* **:** any of several plants of the family Geraniaceae: as **a :** CRANESBILL; *esp* **:** SPOTTED CRANESBILL **b :** STORKSBILL 1

wild ginger *n* **1 :** a tropical Old World aromatic plant (*Zingiber zerumbet*) related to and resembling common ginger **2 a :** a No. American perennial herb (*Asarum canadense*) with kidney-shaped to cordate leaves, purplish brown flowers, and a pungent creeping rhizome — called also *black snakeroot, Canada ginger* **b :** any of various other plants of the genus *Asarum* — see HEARTLEAF **3 :** an Australian perennial plant (*Alpinia coerulea*) related to the common ginger

wild goose *n, pl* **wild geese** [ME *wilde gos*, fr. OE *wilde gōs*, fr. *wilde* wild + *gōs* goose] **1 :** an undomesticated goose: as **a** *Eng* **:** GREYLAG **b :** CANADA GOOSE **2 :** an Irish Jacobite who left Ireland after the abdication of James II and served in the French army; *broadly* **:** an expatriate Irishman

wild gooseberry *n* **1 :** any of several plants of the genus *Ribes*; *esp* **:** a common No. American spiny shrub (*R. cynosbati*) with racemose green flowers and bitter bristly green fruit **2 :** the fruit of a wild gooseberry

wild-goose chase *n* [so called fr. the characteristic flight of wild geese in a group spaced at intervals behind a leader that sets the course] **1** *obs* **:** a cross-country ride in which the leading horseman can set the course for all contestants so long as he can hold the lead **2 :** a pursuit after something unattainable **:** a futile pursuit or chase

wild-goose plum *n* **1 :** either of two wild plums (*Prunus hortulana* and *P. munsoniana*) of the central and south central U.S. that have reddish to yellow fruits and have given rise to several cultivated plums **2 :** any of various cultivated plums that are or are thought to be derived from the native wild-goose plums

wild gourd *n* **:** PRAIRIE GOURD

wild grape *n* **1 :** a grape growing in nature; *often* **:** a species grape (as a fox grape) **2 :** a southern African vine (*Rhoicissus capensis*) of the family Vitaceae with kidney-shaped leaves and yellow green to black fruit in loose bunches

wild guelder rose *n* **:** CRANBERRY BUSH 2

wild hazel *n* **1 :** an American hazel (*Corylus americana*) **2 :** JOJOBA

wild hedgebur *n* **:** CLEAVERS

wild heliotrope *n* **:** any of various plants of the genus *Phacelia* having blue or purple flowers

wild hemp *n* **1 :** HEMP AGRIMONY **2 :** GREAT RAGWEED **3 :** a hemp nettle (*Galeopsis tetrahit*)

wild hip·po \-ˈhi(,)pō\ *n* -s [¹*wild* + *hippo*, alter. of *ipecac*] **1 :** IPECAC SPURGE **2 :** FLOWERING SPURGE

wild hoarhound *n* **:** any of several bonesets (as *Eupatorium rotundifolium* or *E. verbenaefolium*)

wild holly *n* **:** MOUNTAIN HOLLY 1

wild hollyhock *n* **:** any of several mallows (esp. of the genera *Callirhoë*, *Sidalcea*, and *Sphaeralcea*) resembling the common hollyhock

wild honeysuckle *n* **1 :** PINXTER FLOWER **2 :** SCARLET GAURA **3 :** any of several shrubs of the genus *Lonicera* (esp. *L. dioica*) that grow wild

wild hop *n* **:** VIRGIN'S BOWER b

wild horse *n* [ME *wilde hors*, fr. OE, fr. *wilde* wild + *hors* horse] **1 :** an undomesticated horse (as Przhevalski's horse) **2 :** a feral domestic horse

wild hyacinth *n* **1 :** a No. American bulbous plant (*Camassia scilloides*) with linear basal leaves and white racemose flowers **2 :** WOOD HYACINTH **3 :** BRODIAEA 2

wild hydrangea *n* **1 :** a No. American shrub (*Hydrangea arborescens*) having white flowers and being cultivated for ornament **2 :** WILD BEGONIA

wild hyssop *n* **:** BLUE VERVAIN

wild indigo *n* **1 :** a plant of the genus *Baptisia*: as **a :** INDIGO BROOM **b :** BLUE FALSE INDIGO **2 :** BASTARD INDIGO 2

¹**wild·ing** \ˈwīldiŋ, -dēŋ\ *n* -s [¹*wild* + *-ing*] **1 a** (1) **:** a wild or uncultivated plant of natural origin and growth; *usu* **:** a wild apple or crab apple (2) **:** the fruit of a wilding **b :** a cultivated plant sprung up spontaneously **:** ESCAPE **2 :** a wild animal

²**wilding** \"\ *adj* **:** not tame **:** not domesticated or cultivated **:** WILD ⟨~ bee —W.C.Bryant⟩

wild ipecac *n* **1 :** IPECAC SPURGE **2 :** FEVERROOT

wild iris *n* **:** BLUE FLAG

wild irishman *n, usu cap I, NewZeal* **:** TUMATAKURU

wild·ish \ˈwīldish, -dēsh\ *adj* **:** somewhat wild — **wild·ish·ness** *n* -ES

wild ivy *n* **:** an Australian woody vine (*Platylobium triangulare*) of the family Leguminosae having leaves suggesting those of English ivy, yellow flowers, and broad flat pods and being often cultivated

wild jalap *n* **1 :** MAYAPPLE 1 **2 :** MAN-OF-THE-EARTH

wild job's tears *n pl but sing or pl in constr, usu cap J* **:** VIRGINIA FALSE GROMWELL

wild kale *n* **1 :** CHARLOCK **2 :** WILD RADISH

wild land *n* **:** land that is uncultivated or unfit for cultivation **:** WASTELAND, DESERT

wild leek *n* **:** either of two perennial herbs of the genus *Allium:* **a :** a coarse Old World herb (*A. ampeloprasum*) that is widely naturalized, has a large bulb with papery outer coats, and bears a tall stalk of whitish or greenish purple-tinged flowers **b :** a No. American herb (*A. tricoccum*) with a slender bulb, fleshy leaves, and whitish flowers

wild lemon *n* **1 :** MAYAPPLE 1 **2 a :** any of several Australian shrubs (as *P. oleifolia*) of the genus *Plectronia* (family Rubiaceae) **b :** a caper (*Capparis nobilis*) **3** *NewZeal* **:** TARATA

wild lettuce *n* **1 a :** a weedy lettuce that is an escape from a cultivated strain **b :** any of several native wild plants of the genus *Lactuca:* as (1) **:** PRICKLY LETTUCE (2) **:** a blue lettuce (*L. pulchella*) (3) **:** a tall No. American herb (*L. canadensis*) that resembles prickly lettuce but lacks spines **2 :** FALSE WINTERGREEN

wild licorice *also* **wild liquorice** *n* **1 :** a No. American herb (*Glycyrrhiza lepidota*) that is closely related to the true licorice and has a root with similar properties — called also *American licorice* **2 :** INDIAN LICORICE **3 :** any of several plants with sweetish roots: as **a :** either of two bedstraws (*Galium circaezans* and *G. lanceolatum*) **b :** an Australian germander (*Teucrium corymbosum*) **4 :** BUTTONBUSH

wildlife \ˈ=,=\ *n, often attrib* [¹*wild* + *life*] **:** living things that are neither human nor domesticated; *esp* **:** the mammals, birds, and fishes that are hunted by man for sport or food — compare GAME

wild lilac *n* **:** a shrub of the genus *Ceanothus*

wild lily of the valley 1 : FALSE LILY OF THE VALLEY **2 :** WHITE ADDER'S-TONGUE **3 :** either of two wintergreens of the genus *Pyrola:* **a :** a plant (*P. elliptica*) with oblong leaves and white to pinkish flowers that is prob. native to Japan but widely distributed in No. America **b :** a plant (*P. rotundifolia*) with rounded leaves and very fragrant creamy white flowers that is widely distributed in northerly parts of both Old and New Worlds; *esp* **:** FALSE WINTERGREEN

wild lime *n* **1 :** MOUNTAIN PLUM **2 :** COLIMA **3 :** OGEECHEE LIME

wild·ling \ˈwī(ə)l(d)liŋ, -(d)lēŋ\ *n* -S [¹*wild* + *-ling*] **1 :** a wild flower, plant, or seedling **2 :** a wild animal

wild lupine *n* **:** an erect herb (*Lupinus perennis*) of eastern and central No. America with palmately compound leaves and showy racemose blue flowers — called also *Indian beet, old-maid's-bonnet*

wild·ly \ˈwī(ə)l(d)lē, -(d)li\ *adv* [ME *wildely*, fr. *wilde* wild + *-ly*] **:** in a wild manner

wild madder *n* **1 :** MADDER 1, 2 **2 :** either of two bedstraws: **a :** a Eurasiatic herb (*Galium mollugo*) that has ample panicles of small white flowers and is naturalized in eastern No. America — called also *infant's-breath, white bedstraw* **b :** an American herb (*G. tinctorium*) with terminal flowers in clusters of two or three

wild man *n* **1 a :** an uncivilized man **:** SAVAGE **b :** a man of fierce and ungovernable character **c :** a man holding radical political views **2** *also* **wild man of the woods :** ORANGUTAN

wild mandrake *n* **1 :** an enchanter's nightshade (*Circaea lutetiana*) **2 :** MAYAPPLE 1

wild mango *n* **:** an African tree (*Irvingia gabonensis*) of the family Simaroubaceae with an edible yellow fruit that somewhat resembles the mango but is valued esp. for its oil-rich seed and a hard heavy greenish wood that is exceptionally resistant to termite attack — see DIKA 2a, DIKA BREAD

wild mangosteen *n* **1 :** SANTOL **2 :** the fruit of the santol

wild marigold *n* **1 :** POT MARIGOLD **2 :** PINEAPPLE WEED

wild marjoram *n* **:** a Eurasian perennial herb (*Origanum vulgare*) with the spikes of flowers clustered in panicles — compare SWEET MARJORAM

wild masterwort *n* **:** GOUTWEED

wild millet *n* **:** any of various grasses related to or felt to resemble millet: as **a :** a foxtail of the genus *Setaria* **b :** BARNYARD GRASS; *broadly* **:** any of several grasses (as shama millet) of the genus *Echinochloa*

wild mint *n* **:** a wild plant of the family Labiatae; *specif* **:** PENNYROYAL

wild monkshood *n* **:** a perennial No. American herb (*Aconitum uncinatum*) having leaves divided only to the base and the inflorescence being a loose panicle and flowers with a hooded erect sepal

wild morning glory *n* **1 :** HEDGE BINDWEED **2 :** FIELD BINDWEED

wild musk *n* **:** ALFILARIA

wild mustard *n* **:** any of several plants of the family Cruciferae; *esp* **:** CHARLOCK

wild·ness \ˈwī(ə)l(d)nəs\ *n* -ES [ME *wildenesse*, fr. *wilde* wild + *-nesse* -ness] **1 :** WILDERNESS **2 :** the quality or state of being wild

wild nutmeg *n* **:** MACASSAR NUTMEG

wild oat *n* **1 a :** a wild grass of the genus *Avena:* as (1) **:** a European annual weed (*A. fatua*) that is common in meadows and pastures (2) **:** WILD RED OAT **b :** TALL OAT GRASS **c :** a plant of the genus *Uvularia* **2 wild oats** *pl* **a :** offenses and indiscretions ascribed to youthful exuberance **b :** male premarital promiscuity — usu. used in the phrase *sow one's wild oats*

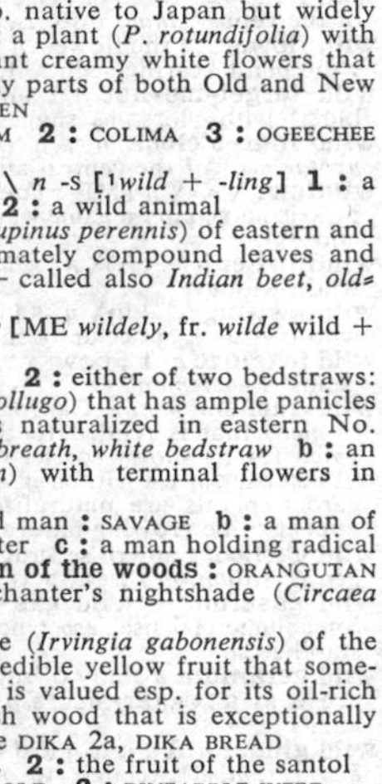

wild oat 1a (1): *1* whole plant, *2* panicle, *3* single spikelet, *4* lemma

wild oat grass *n* **1 :** WILD OAT 1 **2 :** YELLOW OAT GRASS **3 :** a grass of the genus *Danthonia*

wild–oat kicker *n* **:** a grain cleaner in which the sieve is so constructed that the kernels come to an angle in the throat which they cannot pass through and are kicked backward in the direction of the throw of the sieve and eventually discharged from the machine

wild oleander *n* **:** SWAMP LOOSESTRIFE

wild olive *n* **1 :** OLEASTER 2 **2 :** any of various trees that resemble the olive or have fruits resembling its fruit: as **a :** TUPELO 1 **b :** SILVER BELL **c :** DEVILWOOD **d :** MASTIC BULLY **e :** OLEASTER 1; *also* **:** any of several related shrubs and trees **f :** JAVA ALMOND **g :** MOUNTAIN PLUM **h** (1) **:** an Indian tree (*Elaeocarpus serratus*) with a lightweight streaked grayish wood (2) **:** a tree (*Putranjiva roxburghii*) of the family Euphorbiaceae of southeastern Asia with leaves and fruits used in folk medicine

wild onion *n* **1 :** any of several plants of the genus *Allium:* as **a :** NODDING ONION **b :** CROW GARLIC **2** *West* **:** DEATH CAMAS **3 :** a bulbless fleshy-leaved Australian plant (*Breebine semibarbata*) of the family Liliaceae

wild opium *n* **1 :** WILD LETTUCE 1b(3) **2 :** PRICKLY LETTUCE

wild orange *n* **1 :** TRIFOLIATE ORANGE **2** *South* **:** CHERRY LAUREL 2 **3** *Austral* **:** WILD LEMON 2a **4 :** a West Indian tree (*Drypetes glauca*) of the family Euphorbiaceae **5 :** HERCULES'-CLUB 1a

wild orange lily *n* **:** WOOD LILY 1b

wild pansy *n* **:** a common and long-cultivated European herb (*Viola tricolor*) which has rounded basal leaves and pinnately parted stem leaves and short-spurred flowers that are prevailingly blue or purple mixed with white and yellow and from which most of the common garden pansies are derived — called also *heartsease, Johnny-jump-up*

wild parsley *n* **:** any of numerous wild plants of the family Umbelliferae with finely divided foliage resembling that of parsley; *esp* **:** CORN PARSLEY

wild parsnip *n* **:** the wild original form of the cultivated parsnip growing as a weed in both Europe and America and having an acrid and bitter root

wild passionflower *n* **:** MAYPOP

wild pea *n* **:** any of several usu. vining plants of the family Leguminosae and esp. of the genera *Lathyrus, Vicia,* or *Strophostyles*

wild peach *n* **1 :** any of various trees or shrubs of the genus *Prunus* (esp. *P. andersonii*) **2** *South* **:** CHERRY LAUREL 2 **3 :** an African tree of the genus *Kiggelaria* (family Flacourteaceae)

wild peanut *n* **:** HOG PEANUT

wild pear *n* **1 :** an uncultivated shrub or tree of the genus *Pyrus* **2 :** a So. American timber tree (*Clethra tinifolia*) that resembles the pear tree in habit and foliage

wild pennyroyal *n* **:** any of several low-growing aromatic herbs of the family Labiatae (esp. of the genera *Mentha* and *Satureia*)

wild pepper *n* **1 :** a tropical Old World shrub (*Vitex trifolia*) with pleasantly aromatic foliage and seeds that are used in folk medicine **2** *dial Eng* **:** YARROW **3 :** JACK-IN-THE-PULPIT **4 :** PAINTED TRILLIUM

wild peppergrass *n* **:** PEPPERGRASS 1

wild petunia *n* **:** a plant of the genus *Ruellia*

wild pig *n* **:** PECCARY

wild pigeon *n* **:** an undomesticated pigeon: as **a :** ROCK PIGEON **b :** PASSENGER PIGEON

wild pine *n* **1 :** SCOTCH PINE **2 :** any of various West Indian plants of the family Bromeliaceae; *esp* **:** PINGUIN

wild pineapple *n* **1 :** PINGUIN **2 :** either of two plants of the genus *Ananas* (*A. bracteata* and *A. magdalenae*)

wild pink *n* **1 a :** an American catchfly of the genus *Silene; esp* **:** a catchfly (*S. caroliniana*) of the eastern U. S. having pale-pink or whitish flowers **b :** any of several pinks (as the Deptford pink) growing wild **2 :** an orchid (*Arethusa bulbosa*) with sepals and petals arching over the column and typically magenta pink

wild pitch *n* **:** a baseball pitch that cannot be caught or controlled by the catcher with ordinary effort and that enables a base runner to advance

wild plantain *n* **:** a tropical American plant (*Heliconia caribaea*) resembling the banana but having brilliant orange flowers with scarlet sheaths and leaves that are used in the West Indies as coverings for packages

wild plum *n* **1 :** an uncultivated plum; *esp* **:** one of a species (as *Prunus domestica* or *P. americana*) that is closely related to or a source of the cultivated plums **2 :** WILD PRUNE **3 :** BLACK APPLE

wild portulaca *n* **:** a purslane (*Portulaca oleracea*)

wild potato *n* **1 :** MAN-OF-THE-EARTH 1 **2 :** a tropical American plant (*Ipomoea fastigiata*) sometimes held to be the source of the sweet potato **3 :** WAPATOO **4 :** a spring beauty (*Claytonia virginica*)

wild prune *n* **:** a southern African tree (*Pappea capensis*) having hard wood used for furniture; *also* **:** the edible red fruit of the wild prune resembling that of the cherry

wild pumpkin *n* **:** PRAIRIE GOURD

wild quinine *n* **:** AMERICAN FEVERFEW

wild radish *or* **wild rape** *n* **:** any of several plants of the genus *Raphanus; esp* **:** JOINTED CHARLOCK

wild raisin *n* **1 :** SHEEPBERRY 1 **2 :** WITHE ROD

wild red cherry *n* **:** PIN CHERRY

wild red currant *n* **1 :** a straggling or reclining shrub (*Ribes triste*) with branches often rooting and purplish to smoke-colored flowers **2 :** a red-fruited southern African shrub or tree of the genus *Rhus* (esp. *R. laevegata*)

wild red oat *n* **:** an oat (*Avena sterilis*) of the Mediterranean region sometimes held to be the progenitor of the modern cultivated oat

wild red raspberry *n* **:** RED RASPBERRY 1a, 1b; *also* **:** its fruit

wild rhubarb *n* **:** CANAIGRE

wild rice *n* **1 a :** a tall aquatic No. American perennial grass (*Zizania aquatica*) with panicles bearing pistillate flowers above and staminate below and grain that is used for food formerly esp. by the Indians and now also gathered and marketed **b :** an Asiatic grass (*Z. latifolia*) resembling No. American wild rice **2 :** SHAMA MILLET

wild rocket *n* **1 :** a spider flower (*Cleome serrulata*) **2 :** HEDGE MUSTARD

wild rose *n* **1 :** any of various roses growing wild: as **a :** SWEETBRIER **b :** SWAMP ROSE **2 :** a dark pink that is bluer and deeper than dusty coral and stronger and slightly lighter than colonial rose

wild rosemary *n* **1 :** BOG ROSEMARY **2 :** MARSH TEA **3 :** a small Australian shrub (*Cassinia laevis*) of the family Compositae

wild rubber *n* **:** rubber derived from uncultivated trees and esp. from a Brazilian tree (*Hevea brasiliensis*) as distinguished from that derived from plantation trees — compare PARA RUBBER

wild rye *n* **:** any of several grasses of the genus *Elymus*

wild sage *n* **1 :** a Eurasian sage (*Salvia verbenaca*) that is naturalized in No. America and has blue flowers and foliage resembling that of the verbena — called also *vervain sage, wild clary* **2 :** SAGEBRUSH **3 :** RED SAGE

wild sago *n* **:** COONTIE

wild sapodilla *n* **:** ⁴DILLY 2

wild sarsaparilla *n* **1 :** a common No. American perennial herb (*Aralia nudicaulis*) having long-stalked basal ternate leaves with pinnately 3- to 5-foliolate divisions, greenish flowers borne usu. in three simple umbels, and aromatic roots used as a substitute for sarsaparilla **2 :** a catbrier (*Smilax glauca*)

wild senna *n* **:** any of various plants of the genus *Cassia; esp* **:** a No. American perennial herb (*C. marilandica*) the leaves of which are used medicinally in the same manner as the official senna

wild sensitive plant *n* **:** any of several herbs of the genus *Cassia* **:** SENSITIVE PEA

wild service tree *also* **wild service** *n* **:** SERVICE TREE 1b

wild sheep *n* **:** an undomesticated sheep (as the argali, the mouflon, or the bighorn)

wild silk *n* **:** silk furnished by wild silkworms — compare TUSSAH

wild silkworm *n* **:** any of various chiefly Asiatic silkworms which have not been domesticated (as the tussah, yamamai, pernyi, and ailanthus silkworms) and whose silk is commercially valuable

wild snakeroot *n* **:** GROUND IVY 1

wild snapdragon *n* **:** a toadflax (*Linaria vulgaris*)

wild snowball *n* **:** NEW JERSEY TEA

wild spikenard *n* **1 :** FALSE SPIKENARD **2 :** WILD SARSAPARILLA 1

wild spinach *n* **:** any of several plants of the genus *Chenopodium* (as *C. album* and *C. bonus-henricus*) sometimes used as substitutes for spinach

wild stonecrop *n* **:** a succulent herb (*Sedum ternatum*) of rocky woods in the eastern U.S. that is often cultivated for its cymose white flowers

wild strawberry *n* **1 :** an uncultivated plant of the genus *Fragaria:* as **a :** a European plant (*F. vesca*) naturalized or native in No. America having luscious red or rarely white fruit and being one of the species used in breeding the common garden strawberry **b :** VIRGINIA STRAWBERRY **c :** CHILEAN STRAWBERRY **2 :** the fruit of a wild strawberry plant

wild succory *n* **:** CHICORY

wild sunflower *n* **1 :** any of several uncultivated plants of the genus *Helianthus* **2 :** ELECAMPANE

wild swan *n* **:** any swan except the tamed mute swan; *esp* **:** WHOOPER SWAN

wild sweet pea *n* **:** CATGUT 3a

wild sweet potato *n* **1 :** MAN-OF-THE-EARTH 1 **2 :** SAND VINE

wild sweet william *n, often cap 2d W* **1 :** a phlox (*Phlox maculata*) of the eastern U.S. often cultivated for its blue or purple flowers **2 :** WILD BLUE PHLOX **3 :** a soapwort (*Saponaria officinalis*)

wild tamarind *n* **:** any of several West Indian trees (as *Lysiloma bahamensis* and species of *Pithecolobium*) that resemble the tamarind

wild tansy *n* **1 :** RAGWEED 2a **2 :** YARROW

wild tare *n* **:** any of several vetches; *esp* **:** NARROW-LEAVED VETCH

wild teasel *n* **:** a Eurasian herb (*Dipsacus sylvestris*) that resembles fuller's teasel and is naturalized in the U.S.

wild thyme *n* **:** a perennial thyme (*Thymus serpyllum*) that is common on banks and hillsides in Europe and naturalized in the U.S. and spreads by creeping stems — called also *creeping thyme*

wild tobacco *n* **1 :** any of several plants of the genus *Nicotiana:* as **a :** a shrubby poisonous So. American herb (*N. glauca*) widely naturalized — called also *marijuana, tree tobacco* **b :** an herb (*N. rustica*) of eastern No. America formerly cultivated by the Indians **2 :** a tropical shrub (*Solanum verbascifolium*) with white flowers and yellow fruit **3 :** a tropical American herb (*Pluchea odorata*) with aromatic foliage and pink flowers **4 :** INDIAN TOBACCO 1

wild tomato *n* **1 :** BLOODBERRY **2 :** HORSENETTLE; *also* **:** a related weed (*Solanum triflorum*) with deeply pinnatifid leaves and green berries

wild tonguegrass *n* **:** PEPPERGRASS 1

wild tulip *n* **1 a :** a native European tulip (*Tulipa sylvestris*) **b** *dial Eng* **:** GUINEA-HEN FLOWER **2 :** MARIPOSA LILY

wild turnip *n* **1 a :** any of several plants of the genus *Brassica; esp* **:** RUTABAGA **b :** WILD RADISH **2 :** JACK-IN-THE-PULPIT **3 :** BREADROOT 1

wild type *n* **:** the typical form of an organism as ordinarily encountered in nature in contrast to natural or laboratory mutant individuals

wild valerian *n* **:** GARDEN HELIOTROPE 1

wild vanilla *n* **:** a perennial herb (*Trilisa odoratissima*) of the southeastern U.S. with leaves having the fragrance of vanilla and being sometimes mixed with tobacco to give aroma

wild vetch *n* **1 :** PRAIRIE BIRD'S-FOOT TREFOIL **2 :** TUFTED VETCH

wild vine *n* **:** a vine that grows wild: as **a :** BRYONY 1 **b :** BLACK BRYONY **c :** FOX GRAPE

wild wall *n* **:** a flat on a motion picture or television set that can be quickly and silently removed during shooting

wild west *also* **wild western** *adj, often cap 1st W & usu cap 2d W* [fr. *Wild West*, name applied to the western U.S. in its frontier period] **:** of, relating to, or concerned with the western U.S. in its frontier and lawless period ⟨*wild West* magazine⟩

wild wheat *n* **:** a wheat (*Triticum dicoccum dicoccoides*) that occurs wild in Palestine, is sometimes held to be the prototype of cultivated wheat, and has a brittle rachis with the joints separating at maturity and stiff glumes holding the kernels very tightly — called also *wild emmer*

wildwind \ˈ=,=\ *n* **:** HURRICANE

wild winterpea *n* **:** SINGLETARY PEA

wild wisteria *n* **:** GROUNDNUT 2a

wildwood \ˈ=,=\ *n* **:** a wood unaltered or unfrequented by man

wild woodbine *n* **1 :** VIRGINIA CREEPER **2 :** YELLOW JESSAMINE 2

wild yam *n* **1 :** any of various uncultivated plants of the genus *Dioscorea* (as *D. paniculata* of eastern No. America) **2 :** NATIVE POTATO 1

wild yeast *n* **:** any of various yeasts occurring naturally in the air or on surfaces esp. of fruits as distinguished from those selected and artificially cultured (as for use in brewing or baking)

wild yellow lily *n* **:** MEADOW LILY

¹wile \ˈwīl, *esp before pause or consonant* ˈwīəl\ *n* -S [ME *wil*, fr. (assumed) ONF, prob. of Gmc origin; akin to OE *wigle* divination, sorcery — more at WITCH] **1 :** a trick or stratagem intended to ensnare or deceive **:** a sly artifice; *also* **:** a beguiling or playful trick ⟨television advertising in America has simply adapted old ~*s* to new forms of expression —E.S.Turner⟩ **2 :** TRICKERY, DECEITFULNESS, GUILE **syn** see TRICK

²wile \"\ *vt* -ED/-ING/-S [ME *wilen*, fr. *wil* wile] **1 :** to lure by or as if by a magic spell **:** ENTICE, BEGUILE, ALLURE ⟨his sermons would ~ the birds from the trees —John Buchan⟩ **2** [perh. alter. (influenced in meaning by L *decipere diem*, lit., to cheat the time, F *tromper le temps*) of *while*] **:** to pass or spend pleasurably **:** WHILE — often used with *away* ⟨~ away the long days —Virginia Woolf⟩

wile·ly \ˈwī(ə)llē\ *adj* [¹*wile* + *-ly*] **:** WILY

wil·fley table \ˈwilflē-\ *n, usu cap W* [after *Wilfley*, its inventor] **:** a sand table that separates heavy mineral particles from lighter gangue by means of longitudinal riffles impeding the downward flow and a horizontal reciprocating motion carrying the heavy particles off the end of the table — compare SHAKING TABLE

wilful *var of* WILLFUL

wil·ga \ˈwilgə\ *n* -S [fr. native name in New South Wales] **:** an Australian plant of the genus *Geijera* (family Rutaceae); *esp* **:** a tree (*G. parviflora*) with aromatic hard wood and foliage resembling that of a willow

wil·ger \ˈwilgə(r)\ *n* -S [ME *wilghe* willow — more at WILLOW] **:** OSIER 1a

wil·helms·ha·ven \ˈvil,helmz,hävən\ *adj, usu cap* [fr. *Wilhelmshaven*, seaport of northwest Germany] **:** of or from the city of Wilhelmshaven, Germany **:** of the kind or style prevalent in Wilhelmshaven

wilier *comparative of* WILY

wiliest *superlative of* WILY

wil·i·ly \ˈwīləlē, -əli\ *adv* **:** in a wily manner **:** SLYLY

wil·i·ness \-īlēnəs, -lin-\ *n* -ES **:** the quality or state of being wily

wi·li·wi·li \ˈwēlēˈwēlē\ *n* -S [Hawaiian] **:** any of several coral trees of the islands of the Pacific ocean having light soft wood which is often used for the outriggers of canoes; *esp* **:** a Hawaiian tree (*Erythrina sandwicensis*) with brilliant orange-red or sometimes yellow flowers

wilk \ˈwilk\ *archaic var of* WHELK

wil·ke·ite \ˈwilkē,īt\ *n* -S [R. M. *Wilke*, 20th cent. Am. mineral collector + E *-ite*] **:** a mineral consisting of an hydroxylapatite in which phosphorous is partly replaced by carbon, sulfur, silicon, or a combination thereof — compare APATITE

¹will \ˌwəl, ˌ(ə)l, (ˌ)wil\ *vb, past* **would** \ˌwəd, ˌ(ə)d, (ˌ)wu̇d\ *or archaic 2d sing* **wouldst** \ˌwə|dzt, (ˌ)wu̇|, |dst, |tst\ *or* **would·est** \ˈwu̇dəst\ *pres sing & pl* **will** *or archaic 2d sing* **wilt** \ˌwəlt, (ˌ)wilt\ [ME *wille, will, wil* wish, wishes, desire, desires, intend, intends (1st & 3d sing. pres. indic., past *wolde, wold*, infin. *willen*), fr. OE *wile, wille* (past *wolde*, infin. *wyllan*); akin to OHG *willu* wish, *wili* wishes, will (infin. *wellen, wollen*), ON *vilja* wish, will, *vill* wishes, will (infin. *vilja*), *velja* to choose, Goth *wiljau* wish, will, *wili* wishes, will (infin. *wiljan*), *waljan* to choose, L *velle* to wish, Gk (Doric) *lēn*, Skt *vṛṇoti* he chooses, likes] *vt* **:** to be inclined to **:** CHOOSE ⟨call it what you ~⟩ — often used in the form *would* with an object clause ⟨*would* that I were young again⟩ ⟨I *would* to heaven I had never seen him⟩ ~ *verbal auxiliary* **1 —** used to express desire, choice, willingness, consent, or in negative constructions refusal ⟨the immortal gods ~ have no part in this affair —John Buchan⟩ ⟨perverse set of facial muscles that ~ not, like those of other people, interpret the language of his soul —Emily Brontë⟩ ⟨how long ~ we put up with the . . . refusal of refrigerators to fit —*Pencil Points*⟩ ⟨could find no one who *would* take the job⟩ ⟨if we ~ all do our best, we shall succeed⟩ ⟨~ you please stop that racket⟩ **2 —** used to express frequent, customary, or habitual action or natural tendency or disposition ⟨has a quick temper and ~ get angry over nothing⟩ ⟨*would* fall asleep reading his newspaper⟩ ⟨~ sit for hours watching the sea⟩ ⟨~ work one day and loaf the next⟩ **3 a —** used to express simple futurity ⟨much like a delayed action bomb that ~ not explode for half a generation —C.P.Taft⟩ ⟨cherish the belief that some day a perfect society ~ banish evil —Crane Brinton⟩ ⟨tomorrow morning I ~ wake up in this first-class hotel suite —Tennessee Williams⟩ ⟨have not employed it and probably never ~ —R.W.Bliss⟩ ⟨some other time we ~ say what it was —*Notes & Queries*⟩ ⟨list . . . ~ be sent as usual for a stamped and addressed envelope —May L. Becker⟩ ⟨cannot foresee what ~ happen, but a study of past changes may give us an idea as to what may happen —C.E.P. Brooks⟩ ⟨problem of corruption and morality ~ remain very real and earnest —Estes Kefauver⟩ **b —** used to express simple action or intention without conscious reference to future time ⟨quite a famous view . . . a good many people ~ stop and take pictures of it —G.W.Brace⟩ ⟨we ~ now illustrate the procedure in detail —Z.S.Harris⟩ ⟨I ~ give you two propositions for the year 1778: a little learning was a dangerous thing, and so was being an American —A.W.Griswold⟩ **4 —** used to express capability or sufficiency ⟨square pegs ~ not fit in round holes⟩ ⟨this ~ do if there is nothing better⟩ ⟨back seat ~ hold three passengers⟩ ⟨might go for a tramp somewhere. My finances ~ just run to it —John Buchan⟩ ⟨this ~ serve to illustrate the kind of problem —F.N.Robinson⟩ ⟨found that his old rubbers *would* not go over his new shoes⟩ ⟨three yards of cloth ~ make a skirt and jacket⟩ **5** — used to express probability or recognition and often equivalent to the simple verb ⟨that ~ be the milkman at the back door⟩ ⟨this house with the green shutters ~ be theirs⟩ ⟨she *would* have been about twenty when she married⟩ ⟨discover a plant growing and clinging close to the rocks. This ~ be the walking fern or walking leaf —Anne Dorrance⟩ ⟨glass that hides the pendulum ~ often display a fine example of primitive painting —Ellwood Kirby⟩ **6 a** — used to express determination, insistence, persistence, or willfulness ⟨I have made up my mind to go and go I ~⟩ ⟨for some perverse reason he ~ put his worst foot forward⟩ ⟨had what the doctors ~ call influenza, as though there were only one form of it —Lord Dunsany⟩ ⟨police are excellent fellows, but . . . they ~ hare off after motive, which is a matter for psychologists —Dorothy Sayers⟩ **b** — used to express inevitability ⟨accidents ~ happen⟩ ⟨what ~ be, ~ be⟩ ⟨murder ~ out⟩ **7** — used to express a command, exhortation, or injunction ⟨you ~ do as I say, at once⟩ ⟨color arrangements ~ be as prescribed in instructions issued by the Commanding General —*Army Regulations & Ordinances*⟩ ⟨proposing . . . that all disputes . . . ~ be referred to an impartial tribunal —T.F. Reynolds⟩ ⟨with his petition the applicant ~ produce the evidence on which he relies —F.J.Grant⟩ **~ *vi* 1 :** have a wish or desire : be inclined or disposed : be pleased ⟨Lord, if thou *wilt*, thou canst make me clean —Mt 8:2 (AV)⟩ ⟨for better, for worse, and whether we ~ or no —*advt*⟩ ⟨factors for which man is responsible and which he can control or change if he ~ —L.A.White⟩ **2** *archaic* : will go ⟨thither ~ I then —Sir Walter Scott⟩ — **if you will :** if you wish to call it that ⟨a kind of preoccupation, or obsession *if you will* —Louis Auchincloss⟩ — **will I, nill I** *or* **will he, nill he** *or* **will ye, nill ye :** whether I, he, or you will it or not : WILLY-NILLY

²**will** \ˈwil\ *n* -s [ME *wille, will, wile, wil*, fr. OE *willa, will*; akin to OHG *willo, willio* will, ON *vili, vil*, Goth *wilja* will, *wiljan* to wish — more at ¹WILL] **1 :** DESIRE, WISH; *esp* **:** a desire to act in a particular way: **a :** DISPOSITION, INCLINATION, LIKING ⟨my poverty, but not my ~, consents —Shak.⟩ ⟨not, sir, from want of ~, for she is docile and obedient —W.H. Hudson †1922⟩ ⟨primary determinant is the claims of the parties, their desires and ~*s* —Samuel Alexander⟩ ⟨responsible artist has no ~ to confuse emotion and thinking —René Wellek & Austin Warren⟩; *often* : desire or inclination to act in a particular way in contrast to means or ability ⟨had a strong ~ to succeed but little capacity⟩ ⟨where there's a ~ there's a way⟩ ⟨perceived that granted the ~ they could link their abilities to the new world —*Times Lit. Supp.*⟩ ⟨with the best ~ in the world . . . could not live forever —Max Peacock⟩ ⟨proof of their capacity and ~ to watch and warn and purge —B.N.Cardozo⟩ **b :** fleshly or carnal desire : APPETITE, PASSION ⟨a fear of hunger and death, and a ~ for food and springtime and life —Emma Hawkridge⟩ ⟨his own ~ stirred to the woman —Dan Jacobson⟩ **c :** CHOICE, DETERMINATION, INTENTION ⟨a universe as devoid of ~ and purpose as man, deterministically viewed, appears to be —F.B.Millett⟩ ⟨too much disposed to make the empire a thing of plan and ~ —H.G. Wells⟩ ⟨impels you to do things against your reasoned ~ and intentions —Rose Macaulay⟩ **2 a :** something wished for or desired; *esp* : a choice or determination of one having authority, discretion, or power ⟨thy ~ be done —Mt 6:10 (AV)⟩ ⟨he holds him with his glittering eye . . . the mariner hath his ~ —S.T.Coleridge⟩ ⟨failed to accomplish his ~⟩ ⟨determined to have his ~ of them⟩ ⟨will do it . . . if it is God's ~ that it should be done —Gilbert Parker⟩ ⟨the means at his disposal for making his ~ known by the written word —R.W.Southern⟩ ⟨let him be apprehended and learn our awful ~ —W.S.Gilbert⟩ ⟨man's attempt to impose his own ~ on things —Norman Goodall⟩ **b** (1) *archaic* : an expression of a desire or a determination : REQUEST, COMMAND, DECREE (2) [fr. the phrase *our will is* which introduces it] **:** the part of a summons or other signet letter that expresses its will or command **3 :** the act or process or the felt or known experience of willing: **a :** the act of choosing or determining : settlement of mental uncertainty or indecision : choice or decision of a mental issue : VOLITION 2 **b :** the total conscious process involved in effecting a decision **c :** action directed esp. toward a goal clearly known in advance and requiring effort to overcome obstacles or contrary desires — compare CONATION **4 a :** a mental power or a disposition or the sum of mental powers or dispositions manifested in such operations and functions as wishing, choosing, desiring, intending ⟨the precise relation between the activities of human ~*s* and other forms of activity in the natural world is a highly speculative problem —H.H.Williams⟩: as (1) *Scholasticism* **:** the faculty of the soul coordinate with the intellect that determines rational choices in accordance with what the intellect has determined as good or bad; *also* **:** a choice determined by the will esp. as distinguished from instinctive or purely natural desires (2) **:** a faculty of the mind that is usu. coordinate with thought and feeling and determines action and esp. moral action in accordance with ideals, principles, and facts ⟨the moral ~, controlled by consciousness of duty that transcends sense and experience —John Dewey⟩ (3) **:** the combined rational and irrational, conscious and unconscious forces within a person that determine his choices and actions ⟨the ~ . . . is a collective term for all the impulses to motion or action —G.S.Morris⟩; *also* : the rational conscious forces or the irrational unconscious forces separately ⟨what people want when they talk about freedom . . . is the idea that the conscious ~ is the master of their destiny —John Hospers⟩ (4) **:** a disposition to act according to particular principles or to conform in conduct and thought to general or ideal ends ⟨the ~ to believe⟩ ⟨the ~ to agree⟩ ⟨pathetically preserve the ~ to conquer, even when life no longer presents them with anything worth winning —Lawrence Binyon⟩ ⟨like all the young ladies of fiction in her period, she had cultivated the ~ to faint —S.M.Crothers⟩ — compare GOOD WILL, ILL WILL **b :** the collective desire, intention, or determination of a group or of mankind either when all are agreed or as determined by an interplay and elimination of divergent and conflicting wishes ⟨the ~ of the people⟩ ⟨give expression to a national ~ —W.J.Shepard⟩ ⟨the law cannot be more important than the local ~ to have this law —Spencer Parratt⟩ ⟨yielded to what was clearly the popular ~ —Lindsay Rogers⟩ **c** *often cap* : a transcendent reality of which individual wills are particular and partial manifestations **5 :** power coupled with desire or intention: **a :** power to control, determine, or dispose : arbitrary disposal ⟨deliver me not over unto the ~ of mine enemies —Ps 27:12 (AV)⟩ ⟨victims of a despot's ~⟩ ⟨the nameless chief whose ~ raised this stupendous fortress —Jacquetta & Christopher Hawkes⟩ ⟨the serf did not know today what he would have to do tomorrow — he was at the ~ of another —R.W.Southern⟩ **b :** power of controlling one's own actions or emotions : SELF-CONTROL, SELF-DIRECTION ⟨a man of iron ~⟩ ⟨faltering man . . . advanced a step or two by his own ~ —Thomas Hardy⟩ ⟨wife who was just my shadow without any character or ~ of her own —Havelock Ellis⟩ ⟨his ~, so long lying fallow, was overborne by her determination —Joseph Conrad⟩ ⟨the sudden collapse of her ~ when the strangers enter her house —Bernard De Voto⟩ **c :** the power of choosing and of acting in accordance with choice ⟨an indomitable ~ that knew but one course — to break as much new land as possible each day —O.E.Rölvaag⟩ ⟨science, which gave us this dread power . . . does not show us how to prevent its baleful use. Only in the ~ of mankind lies the answer —B.M.Baruch⟩ **6 :** a legal declaration of a person's mind as to the manner in which he would have his property or estate disposed of after his death; *esp* **:** a written instrument legally executed by which a man makes disposition of his estate to take effect after his death — see NUNCUPATIVE WILL; compare DEED, TESTAMENT — **against one's will :** in opposition to one's own inclination or to another's wish or intention ⟨was practicing the violin, as usual *against his will*⟩ ⟨father disowned her for marrying *against his will*⟩ — **at will** *adv* **:** as one wishes : as or when it pleases or suits oneself ⟨dreamer apparently moves about *at will* in the past, as well as in the present —Weston La Barre⟩ ⟨blues sweep up from below, driving the school to the surface, there feeding upon them *at will* —L.K.Parritt⟩ ⟨mounted . . . on bases that could be rotated *at will* —*Military Rev.*⟩ **:** subject to one's discretion or pleasure : at one's disposal ⟨where person enters land by permission of owner for an indefinite period, and without reservation of rent, he is tenant *at will* by implication —*North Eastern Reporter*⟩ — **of one's own will** *or* **of one's own free will :** of one's own accord : VOLUNTARILY — **one's own sweet will :** one's own wish or intention ⟨disposing of it in the fullness of time at *his own sweet will* —Edward Sapir⟩ — **with a will** *adv* **:** with willingness and zeal : EARNESTLY, ENERGETICALLY, HEARTILY ⟨went to work *with a will* to qualify himself —H.E. Scudder⟩

³**will** \"\ *vb* -ED/-ING/-S [ME *willen*, fr. OE *willian*, fr. *willa* will] *vt* **1** *archaic* **:** to long for : DESIRE, WISH **2 a :** to order or direct by a will or testament ⟨~*ed* that his property be divided equally among his children⟩ **b** (1) **:** to dispose of or give by a will : BEQUEATH, DEVISE ⟨~*ed* his entire estate to his wife⟩ ⟨~*ed* his property away from his own family⟩ (2) **:** to hand down or transmit as if by a will or testament ⟨the abundant beauty he ~*ed* to the world —*Time*⟩ ⟨these things are literally in our blood and in our bones . . . ~*ed* to us genetically —Weston La Barre⟩ **3 :** to determine by the will (as to do something or that something shall be done or shall come about): as **a** (1) **:** to decide or decide upon by an act of choice or volition ⟨fully aware that he lives in an age of conformity, he is proud that his conformity is ~*ed* —Leo Marx⟩ ⟨the assumption . . . that institutions are rational and ~*ed* —H.J.Muller⟩ ⟨American people . . . have ~*ed* that all of their sons and daughters shall be educated to the limit of their capacity —*English Language Arts*⟩ ⟨efforts of the business man can never be successful unless the community ~*s* it so —Roy Lewis & Angus Maude⟩ (2) **:** DECREE, ORDAIN ⟨if Providence so ~*s* it⟩ (3) **:** INTEND, PURPOSE ⟨~*ed* more mischief than they durst —A.E.Housman⟩ ⟨can adjust a few screws, then go away entirely, knowing that his precise work will be finished for him exactly as he ~*ed* it —Roger Burlingame⟩ ⟨believe that whatever is ~*ed* can be achieved if only you invent the right machines —Norman Podhoretz⟩ **b** (1) **:** to attempt to cause or bring about by exercise of the will ⟨haunted by the thought that he had ~*ed* her death⟩ ⟨all humans desire objects and ~ their attainment —Samuel Alexander⟩ ⟨a positive nihilist, an intellectual force ~*ing* destruction —T.S.Eliot⟩ ⟨author ~*s* a meaning into a passage that cannot sustain it —Charles Jackson⟩ (2) **:** to bring about by power of the will ⟨the more accurate understanding of disease . . . that some of it is psychological, even to the extent that it is ~*ed* by the patient —H.A.Overstreet⟩ ⟨a last despairing attempt to ~ the kind of life he wanted into existence —D.H.Lawrence⟩ ⟨entranced, he tried . . . to ~ the vision to remain —Olive Johnson⟩ ⟨~*ed* his countenance back to composure —J.H.Wheelwright⟩ **c :** to influence or control (as another person) by exercise of one's will (as through hypnotism) **4** *archaic* **:** COMMAND, ENJOIN, ORDER **~ *vi* 1 :** to exercise the will ⟨striving might be bearable were there a highest good, to which, by ~*ing*, I could attain —Josiah Royce⟩ ⟨would no longer have to go on ~*ing* against her —F.M.Ford⟩ **2 :** DESIRE, WISH: as **a :** DECIDE, DETERMINE, DECREE ⟨king nominated as he ~*ed* to bishopric and abbacy —Hilaire Belloc⟩ ⟨the right . . . to dispose of his labor and capital as he ~*ed* —C.A.Cooke⟩ **b :** CHOOSE, ELECT, PREFER ⟨watching the . . . donkeys and mules which wandered as they ~*ed* —Nicholas Monsarrat⟩ ⟨trees that have grown where they ~*ed* out of the jumble —Martin Flavin⟩

syn WILL, BEQUEATH, DEVISE, LEAVE, and LEGATE can mean to give a part or the whole of one's possessions to another by a last will and testament. WILL implies the provision or the existence of a last will and testament ⟨*will* your property to your children⟩ ⟨*will* a sum of money to a charitable institution⟩ BEQUEATH is much used in wills by the testator and in legal, historical, and literary use, often implying no more than a proved intention ⟨*bequeath* to each of my sons an equal division of all I own⟩ ⟨*bequeathed* to the organization his personal fortune and the entire income from his real estate⟩ BEQUEATH in legal use is commonly distinguished from DEVISE by implying a gift of personalty rather than a gift of realty ⟨*devised* his library, his public and private papers and letters, as well as the stately "Mount Vernon" with its surrounding 4,000 acres —G.W.Goble⟩ LEAVE is the usual unspecific term for any of the preceding terms ⟨at his death the man *left* his small independent income to his brother⟩ ⟨*leave* a legacy to the town⟩ LEGATE is the same as BEQUEATH except in always implying a formal will ⟨my library of manuscripts I *legate* to my alma mater⟩

⁴**will** \"\ *adv* (*or adj*) [ME, fr. ON *villr* wild, gone astray — more at WILD] **1** *dial* **:** out of the way : ASTRAY **2** *dial* **:** at a loss

⁵**will** \"\ *vi* [ME *willen*, fr. ON *villask*, reflex. of *villa* to bewilder, fr. *villr* wild, bewildered, gone astray] *dial* **:** to become lost : go astray : WANDER

will·able \-ləbəl\ *adj* [³*will* + *-able*] **:** capable of being willed or wished : that may be determined by will

wil·lam·ette mite \wəˈlamət\ *n, usu cap W* [fr. *Willamette* river valley, northwest Oregon] **:** a plant-feeding mite (*Tetranychus willamettei*) that is a serious pest on raspberries in parts of the U.S. and Canada

will-call \ˈ=,=\ *n* [fr. the phrase (*the purchaser*) *will call*] **1 :** a retail sale in which something is reserved by a deposit with full payment to be made when the merchandise is called for at a later date **2 :** LAYAWAY 2

willed \ˈwild\ *adj* [ME, fr. ²*will* + *-ed*] **1 :** having a will esp. of a specified kind — used chiefly in combination ⟨strong-*willed*⟩ ⟨weak-*willed*⟩ **2** *archaic* **:** DISPOSED, INCLINED — **willed·ness** \ˈwil(d)nəs\ *n* -ES

wil·lem·ite \ˈwilə,mīt\ *n* -S [G *willemit*, fr. *Willem* (William) I †1843 king of the Netherlands + G *-it* -ite] **:** a mineral Zn_2SiO_4 consisting of zinc silicate, occurring in hexagonal prisms and in massive or granular forms, and varying in color from white or greenish yellow to green, reddish, and brown

will·er \ˈwilə(r)\ *n* -S [³*will* + *-er*] **:** one that wills; *esp* **:** one that wields an influence (as in hypnotism) by means of the will

willes·den \ˈwilzdən\ *adj, usu cap* [fr. *Willesden*, municipal borough of southeast England] **:** of or from the municipal borough of Willesden, England **:** of the kind or style prevalent in Willesden

willesden paper *n, usu cap W* **:** paper waterproofed by the Willesden process

willesden process *n, usu cap W* [so called fr. its original use in paper manufacturing at Willesden, England] **:** a process for waterproofing cellulose material (as paper, canvas, or rope) by passing it through Schweizer's reagent and drying to give a green varnished surface

wil·let \ˈwilət, *usu* -əd·+V\ *n, pl* **willet** [imit.] **:** a large shore bird (*Catoptrophorus semipalmatus*) of the eastern and Gulf coasts and the central parts of No. America having summer plumage barred and mottled with blackish patches and in winter the upperparts plain brownish gray, the breast pale gray, and the belly white

¹**wil·ley** \ˈwilē\ *n* -S [alter. of ¹*willy*] **:** WILLOW 3a

²**willey** \"\ *vt* **willeyed; willeyed; willeying; willeys :** to process (as cotton) with a willey : WILLOW

wil·ley·er \-ēə(r)\ *n* -S [²*willey* + *-er*] **1 :** WILLOWER 1 **2 :** WILLOW 3a

will·ful *or* **wil·ful** \ˈwilfəl\ *adj* [ME *wilful*, fr. (assumed) OE *wilful* willing (whence OE *wilfullice* willfully), fr. OE *wil* will + *-ful*] **1 :** governed by will without yielding to reason or without regard to reason : obstinately or perversely self-willed ⟨devil took possession . . . I became obstinate and ~ —L.N. Chambers⟩ ⟨seemed ~ as children, believing that the wish justified the act —C.B.Nordhoff & J.N.Hall⟩ ⟨the moral passions are even more ~ and imperious and impatient than the self-seeking passions —Lionel Trilling⟩ **:** STUBBORN ⟨possibly a few ~ people might deny that Vermont is the most beautiful state —Bernard DeVoto⟩ **2 :** done deliberately : not accidental or without purpose : INTENTIONAL, SELF-DETERMINED ⟨a ~ injury⟩ ⟨~ murder⟩ ⟨~ distortion of the facts⟩ ⟨alleged ~ failure to register —*Current Biog.*⟩ **3** *obs* **:** ready or disposed to comply : WILLING **4** *obs* **:** done of one's own free will : not compulsory **syn** see UNRULY, VOLUNTARY

will·ful·ly *or* **wil·ful·ly** \-fəlē, -li\ *adv* [ME *wilfully*, fr. OE *wilfullice*, fr. (assumed) OE *wilful* + OE *-lice* -ly] **:** in a willful manner

will·ful·ness *or* **wil·ful·ness** *n* -ES [ME *wilfulnesse*, fr. *wilful* + *-nesse* -ness] **:** the quality or state of being willful

will·ge·rodt-kin·dler reaction \ˈvilgə,rōtˈkindlə(r)-\ *n, usu cap W&K* [after Conrad *Willgerodt*, 19th cent. Ger. chemist, and K. H. J. *Kindler* b1891 Ger. chemist] **:** a modified Willgerodt reaction in which the ketone is heated with sulfur and a dry amine in an open apparatus provided the amine (as morpholine) is sufficiently high boiling

willgerodt reaction *n, usu cap W* **:** a reaction usu. of an aryl alkyl ketone $ArCO(CH_2)_nH$ (as acetophenone) with an aqueous solution of yellow ammonium polysulfide in a heated sealed tube to yield an amide $Ar(CH_2)_{n-1}CONH_2$ (as alpha-phenyl-acetamide) substituted terminally by aryl

¹**wil·liam** \ˈwilyəm\ *n* -S *often cap* [fr. *bill*, after *Bill* (nickname for *William*): *William*, given name] **:** a piece of paper money : BILL ⟨a ten-dollar ~⟩

²**william** \"\ *usu cap* — a communications code word for the letter *w*

william and mary *n, usu cap W&M* [after *William* III †1702 and *Mary* II †1694 joint sovereigns of England] **:** a style of English furniture popular from about 1689 to the early 18th century that shows Dutch influence and is characterized by the use of walnut, grained veneers, trumpet legs, needlepoint upholstery, and teardrop brasses

wil·liam·ite \-yə,mīt\ *n* -S *usu cap* [*William* III †1702 prince of Orange & King of England + E *-ite*] **:** a partisan of William of Orange

wil·liams·ite \ˈwilyəm,zīt\ *n* -S [L. W. *Williams*, 19th cent. Am. mineral collector + E *-ite*] **:** a mineral consisting of a green variety of serpentine used for decorative purposes

wil·liam·so·nia \,wilyəmˈsōnēə\ *n, cap* [NL, fr. William C. *Williamson* †1895 Eng. naturalist + NL *-ia*] **:** a genus (the type of the family Williamsoniaceae) of fossil cycads having slender more or less branched stems and conspicuous bracts or scales associated with the fructification and occurring in rocks from the Upper Triassic to Middle Cretaceous in both the New and Old Worlds

wil·liam·son's blue \ˈwilyəmsənz-\ *or* **williamson's violet** *n, usu cap W* [after Alexander W. *Williamson* †1904 Eng. chemist] **:** any of several iron blue pigments

williamson synthesis *n, usu cap W* [after Alexander W. *Williamson* †1904] **:** a method of synthesizing ethers by reaction of a sodium alkoxide with a halogen derivative of a hydrocarbon (as an alkyl halide) ⟨ethyl cellulose is made by the *Williamson synthesis*⟩

wil·lie \ˈwilē\ *n* -S [prob. fr. way*bill*, after *Bill* (nickname for *William*): *Willie*, nickname for *William*] **:** a waybill for a loaded railroad car

willie-boy \ˈ=,=,=\ *n, often cap W* [*Willie* (nickname for *William*) + E *boy*] *slang* **:** a dandified or effeminate young fellow

willied *past of* WILLY

wil·lie gow \ˈwiliˈgü\ *n* [*Willie* (nickname for *William*) + Sc *gow*, alter. of *gull*] *dial chiefly Scot* **:** HERRING GULL

willie haw·kie \-ˈhȯki\ *n* [*Willie* (nickname for *William*) + E dial. (Ir) *hawkie* grebe, of unknown origin] *Irish* **:** LITTLE GREBE

¹**willies** *pl of* WILLY, *pres 3d sing of* WILLY

²**wil·lies** \ˈwilēz, -liz\ *n pl* [origin unknown] **:** a fit of nervousness or of acute mental uneasiness or discomfort : CREEPS, HEEBIE-JEEBIES — used with *the* ⟨gives his mother the ~ by walking across on the handrails —John Sack⟩ ⟨always get the ~ when I see them sparks flying around —Maxwell Griffith⟩ ⟨keeping people fresh after they're dead. Give you the ~ —Ngaio Marsh⟩

willie wagtail *n* [*Willie* (nickname for *William*) + *wagtail*] **1** *Scot* **:** PIED WAGTAIL **2 :** a common, conspicuous, and very tame black-and-white wagtail (*Rhipidura leucophrys*) of Australia, New Guinea, and the Solomon islands

wil·lie-waught \ˈwili,wäkt\ *n* -S [by incorrect division fr. *guidwillie waught* in *Auld Lang Syne* by Robert Burns †1796 Scot. poet] **:** a deep draft (as of ale)

¹**will·ing** \ˈwiliŋ, -lēŋ\ *n* -S [ME, fr. OE *willung*, fr. *willian* to will + *-ung* -ing] *archaic* **:** DESIRE, LONGING

²**willing** \"\ *adj, sometimes* -ER/-EST [ME, fr. pres. part. of *willen* to be willing — more at ¹WILL] **1 :** inclined or favorably disposed in mind : READY ⟨felt ~ rather to starve at sea than to confront such perils —R.L.Stevenson⟩ ⟨are ~ to prefer the better when the best is unattainable —M.R.Cohen⟩ ⟨must be ~ to be educated —Vera M. Dean⟩ ⟨~ and eager to help⟩ ⟨mothers are now ~, even anxious, to take their children to the nurses —Margaret Biddle⟩ **2 :** ready or prompt to act or to respond : not slow, lazy, or reluctant ⟨that instinct which makes each sex . . . the ~ slave of the other —Richard Jefferies⟩ ⟨~ workers⟩ ⟨a ~ horse⟩ ⟨turn a ~ ear to popular protests —V.L.Parrington⟩ ⟨where ears are ~, talk tends to be loud and long —Aldous Huxley⟩ ⟨a ~ source of information —Paul Moor⟩ ⟨wind . . . increased in strength, urging on the too ~ waves —*Harper's*⟩ **3** *archaic* **:** DESIROUS, WISHFUL **4** *obs* **:** DELIBERATE, INTENTIONAL **5 :** done or borne or given or accepted of choice or without reluctance : VOLUNTARY ⟨a ~ sacrifice⟩ ⟨~ obedience⟩ **6** [fr. pres. part. of ³*will*] **:** of or relating to the will or power of choosing : VOLITIONAL ⟨the ~ faculty⟩ **7** *Austral* **:** STRENUOUS ⟨a bit ~, but not too bad —G.H.Johnston⟩ **syn** see VOLUNTARY

³**willing** \"\ *adv, archaic* **:** WILLINGLY

willinghearted \ˈ=,=ˈ=\ *adj* [²*willing* + *hearted*] **:** heartily willing or disposed

will·ing·hood \ˈwiliŋ,hu̇d\ *n* [²*willing* + *-hood*] **:** WILLINGNESS

will·ing·ly *adv* [ME, fr. ²*willing* + *-ly*] **:** in a willing manner

will·ing·ness *n* -ES **:** the quality or state of being willing

will-in-the-wisp *obs var of* WILL-O'-THE-WISP

wil·lis's artery \ˈwiləsəz-\ *n, usu cap W* [after Thomas *Willis* †1675 Eng. anatomist and physician] **:** COMMUNICATING ARTERY

willis's circle *n, usu cap W* [after Thomas Willis †1675] **:** CIRCLE OF WILLIS

willis's cords *or* **willis's trabeculae** *n pl, usu cap W* [after Thomas *Willis* †1675] **:** slender fibers crossing the venous sinuses of the dura mater esp. at the lower extremity of the superior sagittal sinus

willis system *n, usu cap W* [after Robert *Willis* †1875 Eng. mechanician] **:** a system of using for the generating circle of cycloidal teeth a circle equal in radius to a pinion having twelve teeth of the given pitch

wil·li·waw *or* **wil·ly·waw** \ˈwilē,wȯ\ *or* **wul·li·wa** \ˈwəl-\ *n* -S [origin unknown] **1 a :** a sudden violent gust of cold land air common along mountainous coasts of high latitudes **b :** any sudden violent wind **2 :** a violent commotion or agitation : STORM, TEMPEST ⟨kicking up a great ~ of dust —*Time*⟩

will-less \ˈwilləs\ *adj* [³*will* + *-less*] **:** involving no exercise of the will : INVOLUNTARY ⟨blind *will-less* obedience⟩ **:** having no will : not exercising the will ⟨how circumstances . . . ensnared him and would have made *will-less* a far more intransigent character —Harvey Breit⟩ ⟨thinks human beings are as *will-less* as rats in a trap —J.T.Farrell⟩ ⟨baffled, unknowingly powerful, utterly *will-less* —*New Republic*⟩ — **will-less·ly** *adv* — **will-less·ness** *n* -ES

wil·lock \ˈwilək\ *n* -S [*Will* (nickname for *William*) + *-ock*] *chiefly Brit* **:** any of several birds of the family Alcidae: **a :** GUILLEMOT **b :** PUFFIN **c :** RAZORBILL 1

will-o'-the-wisp \ˈwiləthəˈwisp\ *also* **will-of-the-wisp** \-ləfth-\ *n* [*Will* (nickname for *William*) + *of* + *the* + *wisp*] **1 :** IGNIS FATUUS **2 :** a delusive goal ⟨followed the *will-o'-the-wisp* of universal disarmament —G.F.Eliot⟩ — **will-o'-the-wisp·ish** \-pish\ *adj*

¹**wil·low** \ˈwi(,)lō, -lə; -ləw *or* -lō+V\ *n* -S *often attrib* [ME *wilghe, welew, wilowe*, fr. OE *welig*; akin to MD, MLG, & MHG *wilge* willow, Gk *helikē*, and perh. to Gk *helissein* to wind — more at HELENIUM] **1 a :** a tree or shrub of the genus *Salix* many of which are of economic importance as sources of wood, osiers, or bark useful for tanning and a few of which (as the white willow and weeping willow) are ornamental shade trees **b :** any of several other plants more or less like a willow — compare DESERT WILLOW, WILGA, WILLOW HERB **2 :** something derived from a willow tree: as **a :** OSIER 2 **b :** a sprig or garland of willow (as of weeping willow) worn as a symbol of lost love ⟨twenty years time, when you're wearing the ~, you'll be sorry you went about outgrowing everybody in such a hurry —Margaret Kennedy⟩ **c :** an object made of willow wood; *esp* **:** CRICKET BAT **3** [alter. of ¹*willy*] **a :** a textile machine in which cotton or wool is opened and cleaned by a

spiked drum revolving in a box studded internally with spikes — called also *willower, willy* **b :** DUSTER 1b

2willow \"\ *vt* -ED/-ING/-S **1 :** to open and clean (textile fibers) with a willow **2 :** to put (raw material for making paper pulp) through a duster

willow acacia *n* **:** either of two Australian shrubby acacias (*Acacia saligna* and *A. salicina*) having showy yellow flower heads and phyllodia that resemble willow leaves

willow aphid *n* **:** any of several plant lice that feed on willows; *esp* **:** an aphid (*Pterochlorus salignus*) occurring in Africa, Asia, Europe, and No. America

willow beauty *n* **:** a European geometrid moth (*Selidosema gemmaria*)

willow beetle *n* **:** any of several leaf beetles that feed on the leaves of willows; *also* **:** any beetle that bores in the wood

willowbiter \'==,==\ *n, Brit* **:** either of two titmice: **a :** BLUE TIT **b :** MARSH TIT

willow blight *n* **:** either of two fungous diseases of willow: **a :** WILLOW SCAB **b :** BLACK CANKER 1b

willow borer *n* **1 :** any of several small bronzy longicorn beetles of the genus *Agrilus* that bore in the sapwood of the willow tree and often kill it: as **a :** a beetle (*A. politus*) **b :** a beetle (*A. anxius*) that infests also poplars and birches **2 :** POPLAR BORER **3 :** a European weevil (*Cryptorhynchus lapathi*) introduced and destructive to willows in the eastern U.S.

willow cat *or* **willow catfish** *n* **:** a large yellowish unspotted catfish (*Ictalurus anguilla*) of the lower Mississippi valley — called also *Fulton cat*

willow chafer *n* **1 :** GOLDSMITH BEETLE b **2 :** any of several beetles related to the goldsmith beetle

willow cottonwood *n* **:** a narrow-leaved cottonwood (*Populus angustifolia*) of western No. America

wil·lowed \'wilōd\ *adj* [1*willow* + *-ed*] **:** edged with or abounding in willows ⟨elm-lined roads and ~ backwaters —Elizabeth Pennell⟩

wil·low·er \'wiləwə(r), -lōə(r)\ *n* -S [2*willow* + *-er*] **1 :** a textile worker who operates a willow **2 :** WILLOW 3a

willow family *n* **:** SALICACEAE

willow fly *n* **:** any of various greenish European stone flies of the genus *Chloroperla*

willow gall *also* **willow apple** *n* **:** any of various galls on willow leaves or shoots; *esp* **:** PINECONE WILLOW GALL

willow goldfinch *n* **:** a goldfinch (*Spinus tristis salicamans*) of the Pacific coast

willow grain *n* **:** a surface finish produced on leather by boarding

willow green *n* **:** a variable color averaging a light olive that is greener, lighter, and stronger than citrine, greener and deeper than grape green, and greener, lighter, and stronger than old moss green

willow herb *n* **1 :** a plant of the genus *Epilobium; esp* **:** FIREWEED b — see HAIRY WILLOW HERB **2 a :** PURPLE LOOSESTRIFE **b :** SWAMP LOOSESTRIFE

willow lark *n, dial Eng* **:** SEDGE WARBLER

willow leaf beetle *n* **:** any of various often destructive cerambycoid beetles that feed esp. on the leaves of willows: as **a** (1) **:** a beetle (*Lina scripta*) that often defoliates and kills willows and poplars (2) **:** a beetle (*Pyrrhalta decora*) of similar habits **b :** a beetle (*Phyllodecta vitellinae*)

willow–leaved jasmine \'==,=-\ *n* **:** a So. American shrub (*Cestrum parqui*) often cultivated for its greenish yellow fragrant flowers

willowlike \'==,=\ *adj* [1*willow* + *like*] **:** resembling or characteristic of a willow **:** WILLOWY

willow louse *n* **:** a plant louse that infests the willow; *esp* **:** an aphid (*Clavigerus salicis*) common in the U.S.

willow moth *n* **:** any of numerous moths whose larvae infest the willow tree; *esp* **:** either of two dagger moths (*Acronicta oblinita* and *A. americana*)

willow myrtle *n* **:** an Australian shrub or tree (*Agonis flexuosa*) of the family Myrtaceae with willowlike leaves and showy white flowers in axillary heads

willow oak *n* **:** any of several oaks with lanceolate leaves: as **a** (1) **:** an oak (*Quercus phellos*) of the eastern U.S. with linear entire leaves (2) **:** the soft but strong and heavy light-brown wood of this tree that is sometimes used in construction **b :** LAUREL OAK 1a

willow pattern *n* **:** a design used in decorating willowware

willow poplar *n* **:** BLACK POPLAR 1

willow ptarmigan *or* **willow grouse** *n* **:** a ptarmigan (*Lagopus lagopus*) that is circumpolar in distribution

willows *pl of* WILLOW, *pres 3d sing of* WILLOW

willow sawfly *n* **:** any of numerous sawflies that infest the willow: as **a :** a large American sawfly (*Cimbex americana*) whose larva is pale greenish with a black dorsal stripe **b :** a steel-blue sawfly (*Dolerus arvensis*) or a related smaller brownish fly (*D. bicolor*) **c :** a black sawfly (*Nematus ventralis*) whose yellow-spotted blackish larva infests also the wild cherry

willow sawfly a

willow scab *n* **:** a disease of willow trees caused by a fungus (*Fusicladium saliciperdum*) and characterized by rapid killing of leaves and canker and dieback of young shoots — called also *willow blight*

willow shoot *n* **1 :** a shoot or branch of a willow **2 :** one of the abnormal slender willowlike shoots produced by peach trees affected with yellows — compare PEACH YELLOWS

willow slug *n* **:** a slug that is the larva of a willow sawfly

willow slug caterpillar *n* **:** a caterpillar that is the spinose larva of a moth (*Euclea delphinii*) and that feeds on willow, oak, pear, and other deciduous trees

willow thrush *n* **:** a thrush (*Hylocichla fuscescens salicicola*) closely related to the veery

willow tit *n* **:** BLACK-CAPPED CHICKADEE

willow tree *n* [ME *wilowe tree*, fr. *wilowe* willow + *tree*] **1 :** a tree of the genus *Salix* **2 :** an Australian tree or shrub of the genus *Pittosporum*

willow warbler *also* **willow sparrow** *n* **:** any of several Old World warblers of the genus *Phylloscopus; esp* **:** a small songbird (*P. trochilus*) common in Europe that is delicate greenish above and white below — compare KENNICOTT'S WILLOW WARBLER

willowware \'==,=\ *n* **:** blue-and-white dinnerware decorated with a story-telling design featuring a large willow tree by a little bridge introduced into England from China in the late 18th century and widely copied in Europe and America usu. in blue but sometimes also in red

willowware platter

willowweed \'==,=\ *n* **1 :** a European loosestrife (*Lysimachia vulgaris*) — called also *willowwort* **2** *dial Eng* **:** any of various narrow-leaved plants of the genus *Polygonum* **3 :** WILLOW HERB

willow–wielder \'==,==\ *n* **:** one that wields a willow; *esp* **:** a cricket batsman

willowworm \'==,=\ *n* **:** a worm that is the larva of a willow moth or willow sawfly

willow wren *n* **1 :** WILLOW WARBLER **2 :** CHIFFCHAFF

wil·lowy \'wiləw|ē, -lō|, |i\ *adj* [*willow* + *-y*] **1 :** WILLOWED **2 :** resembling a willow **:** gracefully tall and slender **:** DELICATE, SUPPLE ⟨a sheath that belongs only on ~ women —*New Yorker*⟩

willpower \'=,==\ *n* **:** WILL 5b

wills *pl of* WILL, *pres 3d sing of* WILL

will·some \'wilsəm\ *adj* [ME *wilsom*, fr. 2*will* + *-som* -some] *archaic* **:** WILLFUL

will to power [trans. of G *wille zur macht*] **1 :** the drive of the Nietzschean superman to perfect and transcend the self through the possession and exercise of creative power ⟨the *will to power* . . . is as far from a lust for domination as it is from the pursuit of pleasure for its own sake —*Times Lit. Supp.*⟩ **2 :** a conscious or unconscious desire to exercise authority over others ⟨populations enslaved by a dictator's *will to power*⟩

wil·lugh·beia \,wilə'bēə\ *n, cap* [NL, after Francis *Willughby* †1672 Eng. naturalist] **:** a genus of often climbing shrubs (family Apocynaceae) having small flowers with a one-celled ovary and a pulpy indehiscent fruit

will–wil·let \'wil'wilət\ *n* [imit.] *chiefly South* **:** WILLET

will–with–the–wisp \'wilwithə'wisp\ *n* [*Will* (nickname for *William*) + *with* + *the* + *wisp*] *archaic* **:** WILL-O'-THE-WISP

1wil·ly \'wilē, -li\ *n* -ES [fr. (assumed) ME, fr. OE *wiliga, wilige;* akin to OE *welig* willow — more at WILLOW] **1** *dial Eng* **a :** a large wicker basket **b :** a wicker fish trap **2 :** WILLOW 3a

2willy \"\ *vt* **willied; willied; willying; willies :** WILLOW 1

wil·ly–muf·ty \'wili,məfti\ *n* [*willy* (alter. of 1*willow*) + E dial. *mufty*, a kind of warbler, irreg. fr. *muff*] *dial Eng* **:** WILLOW WARBLER

wil·ly–nil·ly \'wilē'nilē, -li. .li\ *adv* (*or adj*) [alter. of *will I nill I* or *will he nill he* or *will ye nill ye*] **:** by compulsion **:** without regard to individual inclination **:** HELPLESSLY, INEVITABLY ⟨let the world drift *willy-nilly* towards disaster —C.P.Romulo⟩ ⟨animals . . . forced together *willy-nilly* by the action of wind, tidal currents, or waves —W.C.Allee⟩ ⟨*willy-nilly*, the situations in which we use words —I.A.Richards⟩

willy–wagtail \'==',=,=\ *n* [*Willy* (nickname for *William*) + *wagtail*] **:** WILLIE WAGTAIL

willywaw *var of* WILLIWAW

wil·ly–wick·et \'wili,wikət\ *n* [imit.] *dial Brit* **:** a common Eurasian sandpiper (*Tringa hypoleucos*) that is dark olive brown above and has largely white underparts

wil·ly–wil·ly \'wilē,wilē\ *n, pl* **willy–willies** [prob. fr. native name in Australia] *Austral* **:** TROPICAL CYCLONE

wil·ming·ton \'wilmiŋtən\ *adj, usu cap* [fr. *Wilmington*, commercial and industrial city of northern Delaware] **:** of or from the city of Wilmington, Del. ⟨*Wilmington* schools⟩ **:** of the kind or style prevalent in Wilmington

wil·ming·to·ni·an \,wilmiŋ'tōnēən\ *n* -S *cap* [*Wilmington*, Del. + E *-ian*] **:** a native or resident of Wilmington, Delaware

wilms's tumor \'vilmzəz-\ *n, usu cap W* [after Max *Wilms* †1918 Ger. surgeon] **:** a sarcoma of rapid development affecting the kidney chiefly of children and made up of embryonal elements

wil·na \'vilnə\ *or* **wil·no** \-l(,)nō\ *adj, usu cap* [*Wilna* fr. G, Vilnyus, capital of Lithuania; *Wilno* fr. Pol, Vilnyus] **:** VILNYUS

wil·son chamber \'wilsən-\ *n, usu cap W* [after C. T. R. *Wilson* †1959 Scot. physicist] **:** CLOUD CHAMBER

wil·so·ni·an \wil'sōnēən\ *adj, usu cap* [Woodrow *Wilson* †1924 28th president of the U.S. + E *-an*] **:** of, relating to, or characteristic of Woodrow Wilson ⟨affirm the *Wilsonian* principle of the right of national self-determination for all peoples —E.E.Schaftschneider⟩

wil·son·ism \'wilsə,nizəm\ *also* **wil·so·ni·an·ism** \wil'sōnēə,n-\ *n*, -S *usu cap* [*wilsonism* fr. Woodrow *Wilson* †1924 + E *-ism; wilsonianism* fr. *wilsonian* + *-ism*] **:** principles or practices advocated by Woodrow Wilson

wilson's petrel *n, usu cap W* [after Alexander *Wilson* †1813 Am. ornithologist] **:** a petrel (*Oceanites oceanicus*) that breeds in the southern hemisphere but is common in the north Atlantic in summer

wilson's phalarope *n, usu cap W* [after Alexander *Wilson*] **:** a phalarope (*Steganopus tricolor*) breeding on the northern Great Plains in Canada

wilson's plover *n, usu cap W* **:** a ring plover (*Charadrius wilsonia*) of the coast of the U.S., Central America, and So. America

wilson's snipe *n, usu cap W* **:** an American snipe (*Capella gallinago delicata*)

wilson's tern *n, usu cap W* **:** a widely-distributed medium-sized tern (*Sterna hirundo*) with a white deeply forked tail, red black-tipped bill, and orange red feet

wilson's thrush *n, usu cap W* **:** VEERY

wilson's warbler *or* **wilson's blackcap** *n, usu cap W* **:** a small fly-catching warbler (*Wilsonia pusilla*) of eastern and northern No. America that is bright yellow with a black crown — called also *blackcap*

1wilt *archaic pres 2d sing of* WILL

2wilt \'wilt\ *vb* -ED/-ING/-S [alter. of *welk*] *vi* **1 a :** to lose turgor as a result of water loss ⟨the plants ~*ed* under the hot sun⟩ **b :** to become limp **:** SAG, COLLAPSE ⟨the parachute . . . starting to ~ as its great circumference swayed over and touched the paving —J.G.Cozzens⟩ **2 a :** to break down or give way **:** become dispirited **:** FLAG, SUCCUMB ⟨~*ed* before his opponent's barrage of hard drives —John Rendel⟩ ⟨nor did I ever see the nation droop and ~ as we saw it wither under the panic of 1907 —W.A.White⟩ **b :** to lose vitality **:** EBB, FADE ⟨almost laughable the way the bluster ~*ed* out of him —Ross Annett⟩ ⟨the romance . . . blossomed for six or seven months and then ~*ed*—Saxe Commins⟩ ~ *vt* **:** to cause to wilt; *esp* **:** to make (salad greens) limp by marinating in hot grease **syn** see DROOP

3wilt \"\ *n* -S **1 :** an act or instance of wilting or the state of being wilted ⟨feels a distinct ~ of enthusiasm —*Time*⟩ ⟨the train ride . . . brought him to his painting in an advanced state of August ~—Lucien Price⟩ **2** *also* **wilt disease a :** a disease of plants characterized by loss of turgidity esp. in leaf tissues, by subsequent drooping, and often by shriveling and caused by the activities of insects, viruses, fungi, and bacteria (as by actually obstructing the water-carrying vessels or by producing substances toxic to them) and by abnormal physiological or soil conditions — see FUSARIUM WILT, VERTICILLIOSIS **b :** a highly infectious often fatal disease of various caterpillars caused by a filterable virus which develops mainly in the nuclei of the cells in the insect's body, causes the viscera to liquefy, and aids greatly in reducing the abundance of many noxious insects (as the gypsy moth)

wilting *n* -S [fr. gerund of 2*wilt*] **:** a condition of decreased turgidity in the cells of a plant — see INCIPIENT WILTING, PERMANENT WILTING, TEMPORARY WILTING

wilting coefficient *also* **wilting point** *n* **:** the level of soil moisture at which water becomes unavailable to plants and permanent wilting ensues **:** ECHARD

wilting range *n* **:** the range of soil-moisture percentages throughout which permanent wilting occurs **:** the range between the wilting coefficient and ultimate complete permanent wilting or even death of the plant

1wil·ton \'wilt°n\ *also* -tən\ *n* -S *usu cap* [fr. *Wilton*, municipal borough of southern England] **:** a carpet woven with loops like the Brussels carpet but differing from it in being heavier, having a velvet cut pile, being generally of better materials, and having designs adapted from Oriental patterns

2wilton \"\ *adj, usu cap* [fr. *Wilton* farm, near Grahamstown, southern Union of South Africa] **:** of, relating to, or constituting a Mesolithic culture of southern Africa characterized by cave dwellings, rock shelters, and rock paintings

1wilt·shire \'wilt,shi(ə)r, -,shiə, -,shə(r)\ *adj, usu cap* [fr. *Wiltshire*, county of southern England] **:** of or from Wiltshire, England **:** of the kind or style prevalent in Wiltshire

2wiltshire \"\ *or* **wiltshire horn** *n, usu cap W&H* **:** an old English breed of pure-white sheep with long spirally curved horns and a long arched head

3wiltshire \"\ *or* **wiltshire cheese** *n, usu cap W* **:** an English cheese similar to derby

wiltshire bacon *n, usu cap W* **:** bacon from a Wiltshire side

wiltshire side *n, usu cap W* **:** half of a lean hog carcass with foreleg cut off at or above the knee joint and hind leg cut off at or above the hock joint used fresh or after removal of large bones cured and smoked in one piece

wily \'wīlē, -li\ *adj* -ER/-EST [ME, fr. *wil* wile + *-y*] **1 :** full of guile **:** CRAFTY ⟨too ~ a villain to remain in a place where he knows he will be searched for —C.B.Nordhoff & J.N.Hall⟩ ⟨led us by devious routes along precipitous trails . . . to film the ~ sheep —A.M.Bailey⟩ **2 :** showing artful cunning **:** CLEVER, SUBTLE ⟨it was ~ of her to wear a green stone . . . that intensified the green of her eyes —Frances Towers⟩ **syn** see SLY

wim·ber·ry \'wim- — *see* BERRY\ *var of* WHINBERRY

1wim·ble \'wimbəl\ *n* -S [ME, fr. AF, fr. MD *wimmel* auger; akin to MLG *wimmel* auger] **1 :** any of various instruments for boring holes: as **a :** GIMLET **b :** a brace whose head and handle both are used in turning **c** (1) **:** an auger for boring in earth (2) **:** a scoop for clearing out boreholes in mines **2 :** an instrument for twisting ropes

2wimble \"\ *vb* **wimbled; wimbled; wimbling** \-b(ə)liŋ\ **wimbles** [ME *wimblen*, fr. *wimble*, n.] *vt* **1** *archaic* **:** to bore with or as if with a wimble **2 :** to twist (as rope) with a wimble ~ *vi, archaic* **:** BORE, PENETRATE

3wimble \"\ *adj* [origin unknown] *archaic* **:** ACTIVE, SPRIGHTLY

wimbrel *var of* WHIMBREL

WIMC *abbr, often not cap* whom it may concern

wim·ick *or* **wim·mick** \'wimik\ *vi* -ED/-ING/-S [imit.] *dial Eng* **:** CRY, WHIMPER

wim·mera rye grass \'wimərə-\ *n, usu cap W* [fr. *Wimmera*, Australia] *Austral* **:** a Mediterranean grass (*Lolium subulatum*) grown in Australia for forage

1wim·ple \'wimpəl\ *n* -S [ME *wimpel*, fr. OE; akin to OS *wimpal* veil, banner, MD *wimpel* veil, banner, wimple, OE *wīpian* to wipe — more at WIPE] **1 :** a cloth covering for the neck and the sides of the face that is pinned to the hair, a band, or a hat and worn esp. by women in the late medieval period and by nuns **2** *Scot* **a :** a crafty turn **:** TWIST **b :** CURVE, BEND **3** *Brit* **:** RIPPLE

wimple 1

2wimple \"\ *vb* **wimpled; wimpled; wimpling** \-p(ə)liŋ\ **wimples** [ME *wimplen*, fr. *wimpel*, n.] *vt* **1 :** to cover with or as if with a wimple **:** VEIL, WRAP **2 :** to cause to ripple ⟨a warm south wind *wimpled* her fields of golden grain —Cy Warman⟩ ~ *vi* **1 :** to fall or lie in folds **2** *chiefly Scot* **:** to follow a curving course (as of a stream) **:** MEANDER, TWIST, WIND **3 :** RIPPLE ⟨over the little brook which *wimpled* along below towered an arch —J.R.Lowell⟩ ⟨a third voice came *wimpling* and warbling —Virginia Woolf⟩

wimpled *adj, obs* **:** BLINDFOLDED ⟨this ~, whining, purblind, wayward boy —Shak.⟩

wims·hurst machine \'wimz,hərst-\ *n, usu cap W* [after James *Wimshurst* †1903 Eng. engineer] **:** an electric machine of the induction type having two closely parallel glass plates revolving in opposite directions and bearing a set of metal carriers corresponding pairs of which on the two plates act momentarily as small electrophorus elements and usu. being provided with Leyden jars for storing the accumulated charges

wim–wams *var of* WHIM-WHAMS

1win \'win\ *vb* **won** \'wən\ **won; winning; wins** [ME *winnen*, fr. OE *winnan* to struggle, fight, toil; akin to OHG *winnan* to struggle, fight, ON *vinna* to work, avail, conquer, win, Goth *winnan* to suffer, L *vener-, venus* love, sexual desire, *venerari* to venerate, Skt *vanati, vanoti* he desires, loves, Hitt *u̯en-, u̯ent-* to copulate; basic meaning: to strive] *vi* **1 :** to gain the victory in a contest **:** overcome an opponent **:** PREVAIL, SUCCEED ⟨struck for higher wages and *won* —*Amer. Guide Series: N.Y.*⟩ — often used with *out* as an intensive ⟨in most mature adults these counterforces of course ~ out —Fredric Wertham⟩ **2 a :** to succeed esp. by effort in arriving at a place or a state **:** succeed in getting **:** GET ⟨beasts that had *won* to the high ground —J.R. Fethney⟩ ⟨making a great effort . . . he might ~ back to cool sanity —*Hearst's*⟩ ⟨the production *won* through finally owing to the sincerity of the two leading actors —T.C.Worsley⟩ **b** *chiefly Scot* **:** to work up the ability **:** MANAGE, CONTRIVE **3 a** *archaic* **:** to obtain an advantage **:** be in a superior position **:** be master or conqueror — used with *upon, on*, or *of* ⟨have seen . . . the firm soil ~ of the watery main —Shak.⟩ **b :** to gain favor or influence — used with *upon* or *on* ⟨~*s* upon me hourly —S.T.Coleridge⟩ ~ *vt* **1 :** to get possession of by or as if by effort **:** GAIN, OBTAIN, SECURE ⟨made as many as 300 tenement-house calls a week and *won* an intimate knowledge of the poor man —Jerome Ellison⟩ ⟨*won* master's degrees in education and philosophy —*Newsweek*⟩ ⟨*winning* his way up —Charles Dickens⟩ ⟨regiments which *won* fame —H.L.Merillat⟩ ⟨*won* the support of influential friends —C.G.Woodson⟩ **2 a :** to conquer in or as if in battle and take into possession ⟨the individual foot soldier who alone is able to ~ and hold ground —D.W.Mitchell⟩ ⟨the riflemen goes up on land *won* from the desert and the sea —Geoffrey Godsell⟩ **b** *obs* **:** to defeat (a person) in a fight **:** BEAT **c :** to be the victor in ⟨just as we *won* the war, so we can ~ the peace —Helen Douglas⟩ ⟨sought means to ~ the election —W.C.Ford⟩ **3 :** to obtain in return for work **:** EARN ⟨the several ways in which men have *won* their livelihood —W.G.V.Balchin & Norman Pye⟩ **4 a :** to gain in or as if in competition ⟨~*s* a prize⟩ ⟨*won* a senate seat —Carol L. Thompson⟩ ⟨*won* several battle stars . . . and a commendation ribbon —*Current Biog.*⟩ ⟨*won* his point easily⟩ **b** *obs* **:** to gain (as time or space) so as to have an advantage ⟨your way is shorter . . . you'll ~ two days upon me —Shak.⟩ **c :** to take (a trick) in a card game **5 a :** to influence so as to gain the favor of **:** make friendly or favorable to oneself or to one's cause ⟨a mellow charm that ~*s* the listener in unassuming ways —Harold Rogers⟩ ⟨*won* the hearts of his military staff —F.L. Paxson⟩ ⟨makes the neutral reader wonder whether it is aimed to ~ him for the communist or the fascist state —C.D.Lewis⟩ ⟨~ back to active church membership many who had lost contact —E.C.Helmreich⟩ — often used with *over* ⟨resort to argument in order to ~ him over to our way of thinking —A.J. Ayer⟩; *specif* **:** to induce (another) to accept oneself in marriage ⟨his deformity prevents him from *winning* the woman he loves —F.E.Coenen⟩ **b** *archaic* **:** PERSUADE, ENTICE ⟨the man whom music ~*s* to stay nigh —Alexander Pope⟩ **6 a** *chiefly dial* **:** HARVEST, GATHER **b** (1) **:** to obtain (as ore, coal, clay) from a mine or pit (2) **:** to prepare (as a vein or bed) for regular mining esp. by making shafts, gangways, and levels (3) **:** to recover (as metal) from ore **7 :** to reach esp. by effort ⟨were worsted in the field, but many lived to ~ the great cave —H.R.Haggard⟩ **syn** see GET

2win \"\ *n* -S **1 :** an act or instance of winning esp. in a game or contest **:** VICTORY ⟨had all their ~*s* in cycling and swimming —*News from New Zealand*⟩; *specif* **:** first place at the finish of a horse race — compare PLACE, SHOW **2 :** something that is won (as in a game or contest) **:** GAIN, PROFIT, TAKE, WINNING

3win \"\ *vi* **winned; winned; winning; wins** [ME *winen;* akin to OE *wunian* to reside, live — more at WONT] *dial Brit* **:** RESIDE, LIVE

4win \"\ *vt* [prob. fr. 1*win*] *dial Brit* **:** to dry (as hay) by exposure to the air or heat

1wince \'win(t)s\ *vi* -ED/-ING/-S [ME *wenchen, winchen, winsen*, fr. (assumed) ONF *wencier, wenchier*, of Gmc origin like OF *guenchier* to turn aside, swerve; akin to OHG *wankōn* to totter, waver, ON *vakka* to stray, wander about, OE *wancol* unsteady, *wincian* to blink, close one's eyes — more at WINK] **1** *archaic* **:** to kick restively from pain or impatience ⟨a fly . . . may sting a stately horse and make him ~ —Samuel Johnson⟩ **2 :** to shrink back involuntarily (as from pain) **:** draw back or contract in an attempt to avoid pain **:** FLINCH ⟨sharp stinging flurries of snow that made you ~ and gasp —John Connell⟩ ⟨her eyes *winced* with the glare of the sun —Waldo Frank⟩ ⟨took a pleasure in saying things that made his wife ~ —Rudyard Kipling⟩ **syn** see RECOIL

2wince \"\ *n* -S **1** *archaic* **:** KICK **2 :** an act or instance of involuntarily drawing back or contracting esp. in reaction to pain ⟨took the cruel blow without ~ or cry —A. Conan Doyle⟩ ⟨thought with an unpleasant ~ of the money that he had already spent —Gabrielle Long⟩

3wince \"\ *Brit var of* 1WINCH 1b, 3

1winc·er \-sə(r)\ *n* -S [ME *wynsare*, fr. *winsen* to wince + *-are* -er] **:** one that winces; *specif, archaic* **:** KICKER

2wincer \"\ *Brit var of* WINCHER

win·cey \'win(t)sē\ *or* **win·sey** \-nzē\ *n* -S [alter. (influenced by the *w* of *linsey-woolsey*) of *linsey*] **:** a plain or twilled fabric with wool weft and cotton or linen warp that is used esp. for warm shirts, skirts, and pajamas

win·cey·ette \,win(t)sē¦et\ *n* -S **:** a British flannelette of cotton napped on both sides and used esp. for underwear, pajamas, and house dresses

1winch \'winch\ *n* -ES [ME *winche*, fr. OE *wince;* akin to OE *wincian* to close one's eyes, blink — more at WINK] **1 a** *obs* **:** ROLLER, REEL **b :** a roller placed between two dyeing vats in such a way that the fabric placed over the roller can be shifted from one vat to the other **2** : any of various machines or instruments for hauling or pulling: as **a** : a powerful machine having one or more barrels or drums on which to coil a rope, cable, or chain for hauling or hoisting : WINDLASS **b** *Brit* : a reel for a fishing rod **c** : any of various textile machines having a roller for moving fabric through a vat during finishing and dyeing processes **3** : a crank with a handle for giving motion to a revolving part of a machine

²winch \"\ *vt* -ED/-ING/-ES **1** : to hoist or haul with or as if with a winch **2** : to put into a dyeing vat by means of a winch

³winch \"\ *archaic var of* ¹WINCE

winch·er \-chə(r)\ *n* -S : one who operates a winch : WINCHMAN

win·ches·ter bushel \'win,chestə(r)-, -nchəs-\ *n, usu cap W* [after *Winchester*, England] : a unit of dry capacity equal to 2150.42 cubic inches or the volume of a cylinder 18½ inches in internal diameter and 8 inches deep

winchester goose *n, usu cap W* [fr. *Winchester*, England; fr. the fact that in the 16th cent. the brothels of Southwark were under the jurisdiction of the bishop of Winchester] **1** *obs* : a venereal disease causing a swelling in the groin **2** *obs* : a person infected with a venereal disease: *specif* : PROSTITUTE

winchester measure *n, usu cap W* [fr. *Winchester*, England] : an old English series of measures orig. made standard at Winchester, England

winch·man \'winchmən\ *n, pl* **winchmen** : one who runs a winch; *specif* : a worker who moves heavy objects (as machinery, ship's cargo, fishing nets, or logs) by means of a winch

winc·ing·ly *adv* : in a wincing manner

¹wind \'wind, *chiefly poetic* 'wīnd\ *n* -S *often attrib* [ME *wind, winde*, fr. OE *wind*; akin to OHG *wint* wind, ON *vindr*, Goth *winds*, L *ventus*; all fr. a prehistoric IE participial stem fr. the root represented by OE *wāwan* to blow, OHG *wāen*, Goth *waian*, Gk *aēnai*, Skt *vāti* it blows, *vāta* wind] **1 a** : a natural movement of air of any velocity; *esp* : air in natural motion parallel to the surface of the earth ⟨a light ~ had come up⟩ ⟨the ~*s* devastated the city⟩ — compare CURRENT **b** : an artificially produced movement of air ⟨felt the ~ of a bullet as it passed his temple —C.B.Kelland⟩ **2 a** : a destructive force or influence ⟨the ~ of war had swept his home away —Stuart Cloete⟩ ⟨sow the ~ and reap the whirlwind⟩ **b** : a force or agency that carries along or influences ⟨withstood the ~*s* of popular opinion —Felix Frankfurter⟩ ⟨the bracing ~*s* of human sympathy and understanding —J.D.Adams⟩ **c** : TENDENCY, TREND ⟨quick perception of the way campus ~*s* were blowing —Arnold Nicholson⟩ ⟨too much impressed by current theological ~*s* —I.G.Whitchurch⟩ **3 a** (1) : the air that is inhaled and exhaled by the lungs : BREATH ⟨leaned there on the cable, catching his ~ —Wright Morris⟩ ⟨smote him with brutal violence in the stomach, knocking the ~ out of him —Dorothy Sayers⟩ (2) : power of respiration : ability to breathe properly ⟨established his own studio for the businessman anxious about his weight and his ~ —D.G. Villard⟩ ⟨~ and leg muscles —*Athletic Jour.*⟩ (3) : the pit of the stomach where a blow may paralyze the diaphragm and cause temporary loss of breath : SOLAR PLEXUS ⟨hit a small boy in the ~ to see him double up —W.B.Yeats⟩ **b** : breath used in speaking ⟨wrote . . . in sonorous and rolling sentences in which one can still hear the ~ of his oratory —Marjory S. Douglas⟩ **4** : gas generated in the stomach or the intestines **5 a** : compressed air or gas ⟨was considered a little balmy when he seriously proposed stopping a train with ~ —W.J. Reilly⟩ **b** *archaic* : AIR ⟨the sword itself must be wrapped up close . . . that it taketh no ~ —Francis Bacon⟩ **6** : something that is insubstantial: as **a** : mere talk : idle words ⟨talks about erasing the border by a march on the North. This is mere ~. There will be no march —J.V.Kelleher⟩ **b** : NOTHING, NOTHINGNESS ⟨theories based on ~⟩ **c** : vain self-satisfaction ⟨all puffed up with ~⟩ **7 a** : air carrying a scent (as of a hunter or game) ⟨a great number of deer . . . entirely ignorant of anything amiss till after they passed me and received my ~ —Ed Shearer⟩ **b** *archaic* : exposure to the public : CURRENCY — used with *get* or *take* ⟨the project had taken ~ and created a general sensation —W.H.Prescott⟩ **c** : slight information esp. about something intended to be kept secret : INTIMATION ⟨the unhappy reporters who by this time had got ~ of something and turned up in battalions —Dorothy Sayers⟩ ⟨caught ~ of this situation —Richard Hellman⟩ **8 a** : air used for producing musical tone: as (1) : breath passed through the vocal organs in singing (2) : breath used to blow a wind instrument (3) : the compressed air used to produce sound on an organ **b** (1) : musical wind instruments esp. as distinguished from strings and percussion ⟨music for strings and for ~ —D.W.Stevens⟩ ⟨the triplets played by the ~*s* —Max Rudolf⟩ ⟨a good deal of ~ detail is lost —Edward Sackville-West & Desmond Shawe-Taylor⟩ (2) **winds** *pl* : the players of wind instruments esp. in an orchestra **9 a** : a direction from which the wind may blow : a point of the compass; *esp* : one of the cardinal points ⟨come from the four ~*s*, O breath, and breathe upon these slain —Ezek 37:9 (RSV)⟩ **b** : the direction from which the wind is blowing — used esp. with regard to a sailing ship's course **10** : a condition of oblivion, ineffectualness, or waste — usu. used in pl. ⟨cast the facts of royal history to the ~*s* and invented his own essential drama —Leslie Rees⟩ ⟨went through deep snow, all anxiety thrown to the four ~*s* —D.B.MacMillan⟩ **11** : MONEY ⟨came to me this morning to raise the ~ —Anthony Trollope⟩ **12** : a state of intoxication (I'm not in the ~ at all events, for you see I'm perfectly sober —Frederick Marryat) — compare SHEET IN THE WIND **13** : a big fuss : DISTURBANCE ⟨raised the ~ over the inferior merchandise⟩ **14 a** : a state of fear — used with *up* ⟨deathtraps, hard to fly, easy to crash . . . good pilots had their ~ up about the planes —H.H.Arnold & I.C. Eaker⟩ ⟨you put the ~ up me —Richard Llewellyn⟩ **b** : a state of nervous irritable excitement — used with *up* ⟨got their ~ up about the neighbors' new fence⟩

syn BREEZE, GALE, HURRICANE, GUST, BLAST, SQUALL, ZEPHYR, WHIRLWIND, CYCLONE, TYPHOON, TORNADO, WATERSPOUT, TWISTER: WIND is a general term applicable to air in any sort of natural motion ⟨light western *winds*⟩ ⟨*winds* of gale force⟩ BREEZE is applicable to a relatively light but fresh wind with moderate velocity, often to a pleasing wind ⟨not a steady, strong *breeze* like the trade winds of the low latitudes, but a boisterous stormy wind —P.E.James⟩ ⟨enjoying the brisk *breeze* that blew about his yellow hair —William Black⟩ GALE indicates a high wind, one between a breeze and a hurricane, sometimes of destructive force ⟨not an inch of shelter anywhere in a *gale*, and the salt rain driven by the wind penetrates the thickest coat —Richard Jefferies⟩ HURRICANE indicates a wind of maximum velocity and consequent destructive violence ⟨towns and villages wrecked by the *hurricane*⟩ GUST indicates a sudden short wind, usu. more severe than a puff, often accompanied by rain ⟨a great *gust* of wind shook the windows of the house —J.C.Powys⟩ BLAST may indicate a sudden wind with severe driving force ⟨a copse of dark firs swayed uneasily under the heavy *blasts* of the gathering storm —F.V.W.Mason⟩ SQUALL refers to any sudden violent gust, esp. to a sea gust with driving force ⟨continuous and violent *squalls* nearly wrecked the craft —Alexander Klemin⟩ ZEPHYR indicates a light gentle delicate wind, one that would not disturb halcyon weather ⟨soft the *zephyr* blows —Thomas Gray⟩ WHIRLWIND may apply to any swirling wind; technically it indicates a rotating windstorm with the lower air spiraling inward and upward ⟨the *whirlwind* came fast. I could see the tops of the trees writhing and twisting —John Onslow⟩ CYCLONE often indicates a rotating system of very high destructive winds about a moving center of low pressure ⟨*cyclones* like those that lift roofs off houses in Kansas —Waldemar Kaempffert⟩ TYPHOON is used in reference to cyclones in Asian Pacific waters ⟨*typhoons* in Joseph Conrad's novels⟩ TORNADO refers to a swirling wind accompanied by a funnel-shaped cloud moving with a force so violent that it cannot be measured accurately ⟨Kansas takes to the cyclone cellar when a *tornado* sweeps by and sucks wells dry —Waldemar Kaempffert⟩ WATERSPOUT indicates a funnel-shaped or tubular column of wind enclosing a quantity of water. TWISTER is a general informal term for any swirling wind like a tornado or waterspout ⟨the first *twisters* hit in the early evening —*Time*⟩ ⟨when a *twister* had come at home, all the windows in Mr. Dannenbaum's house had been blown out —Jean Stafford⟩

—**between wind and water 1** : near the waterline of a ship : in the part of a side of a ship that rises above and falls below the surface of the water esp. with reference to damage **2** : at a serious or dangerous point — **by the wind** *or* **on a wind** *or* **on the wind** : close to the wind — **down the wind** *archaic* : toward, to, or in a state of decay — **have in the wind** : to be on the scent of — **have the wind of 1** : to be on the side from which the wind is blowing with respect to : be to windward of **2** : to be on the scent of **3** : to have a superior position to : have at a disadvantage — **in the wind** *adv (or adj)* : about to happen : ASTIR, AFOOT, UP ⟨something was *in the wind*⟩ ⟨other projects than a new building were *in the wind* —Ben Riker⟩ — **near the wind 1** : close to the wind : CLOSE-HAULED **2** : close to a point of danger : near the permissible limit ⟨one of his racy tales, heavily spiced with native argot and sailing perilously *near the wind* —Edward Lockspeiser⟩ — **off the wind** : away from the direction from which the wind is blowing : sailing free — **under the wind 1** : on the side away from the direction from which the wind is blowing : to leeward **2** : in a place that is protected from the wind : under the lee

²wind \'wind\ *vb* -ED/-ING/-S [ME *winden*, fr. ¹*wind*] *vt* **1** : to smell the scent of : follow by the scent ⟨an otter could ~ a fish at 40 furlongs —C.E.Hare⟩ **2** : to expose to the air or wind : dry by exposing to air **3** *dial chiefly Brit* : WINNOW **4** : to take the breath away from : make short of breath ⟨her hoof hit my side and ~*ed* me —Adrian Bell⟩ ⟨until acclimated, a person becomes ~*ed* from exertion —Bob Koonce⟩ **5** : to regulate the wind supply of (an organ pipe) **6** : to rest (as a horse) in order to allow the breath to be recovered ~ *vi* **1** : to scent game : sniff in the air as if catching the scent of game — used of an animal and esp. of a dog **2** *dial* : to pause for breath

³wind \'wīnd, 'wind\ *vb* **winded** \-dəd\ *or* **wound** \'waund\ **winded** *or* **wound; winding; winds** [¹*wind* (but often altered in pronunciation & conjugation by influence of ⁴*wind*)] *vt* **1** : to cause (as a horn) to sound by blowing esp. with the breath : BLOW ⟨little fishing boats ~ their conchs —Mary H. Vorse⟩ **2** : to sound (as a call or note) on or as if on a horn ⟨*wound* a rousing call —R.L.Stevenson⟩ ~ *vi* : to produce a sound on or as if on a horn

⁴wind \'wīnd\ *vb* **wound** \'waund\ *also* **winded; wound** *also* **winded; winding; winds** [ME *winden*, fr. OE *windan* to turn, twist, move with speed or force, brandish; akin to OHG *wintan* to wind, ON *vinda*, Goth *biwindan* to wind around, wrap, *uswindan* to plait, Umbrian *ohavendu* let him turn aside, Arm *gind* ring; basic meaning: twist] *vi* **1** *obs* **a** (1) : to move with speed or force : RUSH, SPRING (2) : PASS **b** : GO, PROCEED ⟨~ away, be gone I say —Shak.⟩ **2** *archaic* : WRIGGLE, SQUIRM, WRITHE **3** : to bend out of a flat plane : WARP **4 a** *obs* : to move in a curve ⟨a creature that I teach to fight, to ~, to stop, to run directly on —Shak.⟩ **b** : to have a curving course or shape : extend in curves ⟨a small road that *wound* up through pines —G.W.Brace⟩ ⟨the staircase *wound* round this hall —Margaret Deland⟩ ⟨a cave which ~*s* far into the cliff —A.A.Grace⟩ **c** : to move on a curving esp. sinuous course ⟨the river ~*s* down through rugged terrain⟩ ⟨a long caravan of cars *wound* through the streets —*Phoenix Flame*⟩ ⟨within the lines of these universal qualities ~ the divergencies of medieval thought —H.O.Taylor⟩ **5 a** : to move so as to encircle ⟨loose tapes which ~ around the baby's limbs —Morris Fishbein⟩ **b** : to exhibit the defective gait of winding **6 a** : to change the direction toward which the prow is headed : turn when lying at anchor **b** : to lie with the prow headed toward a designated point of the compass **7** *of a horse* : to turn or veer to the left : HAW ~ *vt* **1 a** *obs* : to make by or as if by twisting, plaiting, or weaving : WEAVE **b** : to bring into a close relationship as if by weaving or wrapping : ENTANGLE, INVOLVE, ENMESH ⟨the greatest crises of life steal on us imperceptibly and have sometimes . . . *wound* us in their consequences before we know —William Black⟩ — often used with *up* ⟨compassion . . . is intricately *wound* up with the doctrine of right living —Edmond Taylor⟩ **c** : to introduce sinuously or stealthily : INSINUATE ⟨the impulse to know . . . ~*s* itself into every action —H.O.Taylor⟩ **d** *obs* : to put (as money) into circulation : CIRCULATE **2** *archaic* : to hold in the hand and use : WIELD, HANDLE **3 a** : to encircle or cover with something pliable : bind with or as if with loops of string or layers of cloth ⟨*wound* the top with a new piece of string⟩ ⟨the women were *wound* up in fishtailed skirts —G.H.Reed b. 1887⟩ ⟨sleep thou, and I will ~ thee in my arms —Shak.⟩ **b** (1) : to turn completely or repeatedly esp. about an object with which contact is made : COIL, TWINE, WRAP ⟨*wound* a heavy scarf around his neck⟩ ⟨devised a way of ~*ing* silk on a spool —*Amer. Guide Series: N.J.*⟩ (2) : to remove by unwinding : UNWIND — used with *off* or *from* ⟨*wound* all the thread off the bobbin⟩ **c** (1) : to hoist or haul (as coal from a pit) by means of a rope, cable, or chain that is pulled by machinery — often used with *up* ⟨~ up a bucket from a well —Adrian Bell⟩ (2) : to move (a ship) by hauling (as on a capstan) **d** (1) : to tighten the spring of in order to start or keep running ⟨four hours of moderate light ~ the clock completely —*Jewelers' Circular-Keystone*⟩ — often used with *up* ⟨*wound up* the toy soldiers⟩ (2) *obs* : to make tighter (as the strings of a musical instrument) : TIGHTEN, TUNE — often used with *up* (3) : to move with a crank : CRANK ⟨*wound* down the window on the right hand side of the car —J.M.Cain⟩ **e** : to raise to a high level (as of excitement, tension, or preparedness) — usu. used with *up* ⟨get so easily *wound* up . . . about these things that we could go on and on —W.F.Hambly⟩ **4 a** : to cause to move in a curving line : cause to follow a curving course or path ⟨processions . . . *wound* themselves about the town in circles —Julian Dana⟩ **b** (1) *archaic* : to turn the course or direction of; *esp* : to turn or lead (a person) as one wishes ⟨can ~ the proud earl to his will —Sir Walter Scott⟩ (2) *obs* : ATTRACT, LURE, ENTICE **c** (1) : to cause (as a ship) to change direction : TURN (2) : to turn (as a ship) end for end **d** : to traverse on a curving course ⟨~*s* the wood —John Dryden⟩ **e** (1) : to effect by or as if by curving ⟨*wound* his way up the tree —Willa Cather⟩ ⟨the forest through which the river ~*s* its course —Alexander MacDonald⟩ (2) : to follow the curving course of ⟨enabled travelers to reach the Mississippi without ~*ing* the endless curves of the Arkansas —*Amer. Guide Series: Ark.*⟩ **f** : to turn (a horse) to the left

syn TWIST, TWINE, ENTWINE, COIL, CURL, WREATHE agree with WIND in referring either to a circular, spiral, or writhing motion or to a curved and bent outline or shape; WIND esp. emphasizes action or motion, orig. an even-paced, repeated turning about a fixed point, now frequently a rambling or climbing in serpentine curves over an extended area ⟨*wind* thread or tape on a reel⟩ ⟨the road *winds* along the river⟩ TWIST orig. and basically is to turn two threads about each other; it retains the suggestion of revolving within a narrow compass or of an outline having many small kinks rather than describing large loops or curves ⟨the train *wound* around the mountain⟩ ⟨the dancer *twisted* slowly about herself⟩ ⟨a *winding* river⟩ ⟨a *winding* staircase⟩ TWINE orig. is close to TWIST but does not have the connotation of tortuousness; it suggests something long and supple draped in spirals or loops about a solid body ⟨the symbol of a serpent *twined* round a staff⟩ ⟨vines *twining* about a tree may kill it⟩ ENTWINE is orig. an intensive form of TWINE; it may suggest merely a complete twining about or an inextricable entanglement. COIL, CURL, and WREATHE place less emphasis on the action or motion of bending than on the resulting shape; COIL means to roll, wind, or spin in rings or spirals ⟨she wore her hair *coiled* on top of her head⟩ ⟨the waters in the maelstrom *coiled* and hissed⟩ CURL refers to the appearance made by a body of greater length than thickness in bending from its full extension into a shape suggesting a coil of hair, or by a flat surface in rippling and creasing ⟨smoke *curling* in the blue air⟩ ⟨*curling* waves tossed against the shore⟩ ⟨lips *curled* in derision⟩ WREATHE may suggest creasing or crinkling ⟨*wreathed* in smiles⟩ or the assumption of a wreathy appearance ⟨mists of night *wreathe* up from meadows —Walter de la Mare⟩

⁵wind \'wīnd\ *n* -S **1** : a mechanism (as a winch) for winding **2** : an act or instance of winding: as **a** (1) : the condition of being warped or twisted ⟨took the board out of ~⟩ (2) : the amount of warp **b** : an act or instance of hoisting or pulling by a mechanism that winds (as a winch) **c** : an act or instance of tightening the spring of a mechanism (as a watch or clock) **d** : COIL, TWIST, TURN **e** : a particular method of winding ⟨a very open ~ is used on the size tube . . . to minimize thread to thread adhesion —V.A.Schiffer⟩

wind·age \'windij, -dēj\ *n* -S [¹*wind* + *-age*] **1 a** : the space between the projectile of a smoothbore gun and the surface of the bore **b** : the difference between the diameter of the bore of a muzzle-loading rifled cannon and that of the projectile cylinder **2 a** : the amount of sight deflection necessary to compensate for wind displacement so as to aim a gun accurately **b** (1) : the influence of the wind in deflecting the course of a projectile (2) : the amount of deflection due to the wind **3 a** : the disturbance of the air caused by a passing object (as a projectile) **b** : air friction against a rapidly moving esp. rotating object (as a flywheel or the armature of a dynamo) **4** : the surface exposed (as by a ship) to the wind

wind angle *n* : the angle between the true course of an airplane and the direction of the wind

windbag \'=,=\ *n* [ME *wind bagge*, fr. ¹*wind* + *bagge* bag] **1** : a bag of wind or air; *specif* : the bag of a bagpipe **2** : a loquacious usu. pompous person who has little to say : one who talks volubly to little effect

wind·bag·gery \"+ərē\ *n* -ES [*windbag* + *-ery*] : pompous meaningless talk

wind band *n* **1** : a band of wind instruments; *esp* : a military band **2** : the wind instruments of an orchestra : WINDS

wind beam *n* [ME *windbeme*, fr. ¹*wind* + *beem, beme* beam; fr. its function as a wind-brace] : COLLAR BEAM

windbeaten \'=,==\ *adj* [¹*wind* + *beaten*, past part. of *beat*] : beaten by or as if by the wind

wind-bell \'=,=\ *n* **1** : a cluster of small pieces of glass or metal tied loosely together in such a way that they tinkle when blown by the wind ⟨the bell-like tinkle of glass *wind-bells* suspended along the corridor —Herman Smith⟩ **2** : a bell that is light enough to be moved and sounded by the wind

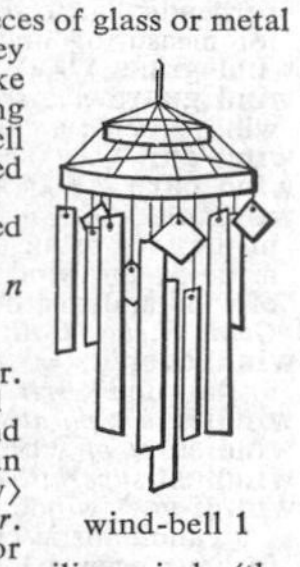

wind-bell 1

wind belt *n* : a belt or row of trees planted to serve as a windbreak : SHELTERBELT

wind·berry \'win(d)- — *see* BERRY\ *n* : MOUNTAIN CRANBERRY

wind bill *n, Scot* : ACCOMMODATION BILL

windblow \'=,=\ *n* [prob. back-formation fr. *windblown*] : a deposit of windblown sand

windblown \'=,=\ *adj* **1** : blown by the wind ⟨the summits . . . are so ~ that they can scarcely be called skiable —C.M.Dudley⟩ ⟨masses of sandstone and ~ sands —*Jour. of Geol.*⟩; *specif* : having a permanent set or character of growth determined by the prevailing winds ⟨the ~ trees along the coast⟩ **2** : cut so that the ends turn outward and to the front as if blown by a wind from behind ⟨the ~ bob of the flapper —Lois Long⟩

wind-borne \'=,=\ *adj* : carried by the wind ⟨*wind-borne* sand —*Plane Talk*⟩ ⟨*wind-borne* soil deposits —*Amer. Guide Series: Wash.*⟩

windbound \'=,=\ *adj* **1** : prevented from sailing by a contrary or a high wind ⟨the crews of schooners ~ under the lee of the island —*Amer. Guide Series: Mich.*⟩ **2** : held back as if by an unfavorable wind

wind box *n* **1** : a receptacle from which a blast of air is supplied (as to the tuyeres of a cupola, blast furnace, or forge) **2** : WIND-CHEST

wind-brace \'=,=\ *n* : a brace (as a strut) to strengthen a frame or structure against the wind

wind bracing *n* **1** : the act or process of bracing a frame against winds **2** : WIND-BRACES

windbreak \'=,=\ *n* **1** : something that breaks the force of the wind: as **a** : rowed or clumped trees or shrubs that give protection against the wind esp. to buildings and nearby gardens and orchards — compare SHELTERBELT **b** : a rough temporary wall for protection against the wind **2** : the breaking of trees by the wind

windbreaker \'=,==\ *n* [¹*wind* + *breaker*] : something that breaks the wind : WINDBREAK

Windbreaker \"\ *trademark* — used for an outer jacket made of wind-resistant material

wind-broken \'=,==\ *adj, of a horse* : having the power of breathing impaired by the rupture, dilatation, or running together of air cells of the lungs so that while the inspiration is by one effort, the expiration is by two : affected with pulmonary emphysema or with heaves

windburn *n* **1** : injury caused by excessive wind on foliage or thin bark **2** : an irritated condition of the skin that is analogous to sunburn and caused by exposure to the wind

windburned \'=,=\ *adj* [¹*wind* + *burned*, past part. of *burn*] : burned by the wind : showing the effects of windburn ⟨~ arms⟩

wind catcher *n* : WIND SCOOP

windcharger \'=,==\ *n* : a generator driven by a windmill and used to charge storage batteries

windcheater \'=,==\ *n, chiefly Brit* : an outer jacket of wind-resistant material

wind-chest \'=,=\ *n* : a reservoir for supplying air under pressure to the pipes or reeds of an organ

wind chill *n* : the cooling effect of moving air on a body expressed as the amount of heat lost per unit area per unit of time and taking into account both temperature and wind speed

wind cloud *n* : a cloud accompanied or followed by considerable wind

wind colic *n* **1** *archaic* : intestinal colic **2** : BLOAT 2b : BLOAT COLIC ⟨a horse with *wind colic*⟩

wind cone *n* : WIND SOCK

wind conveyor *n* : CONVEYER 2a(9)

wind cripple *n* : a tree stunted or injured by the wind

wind direction *n* : the direction from which the wind blows

winddog \'=,=\ *n* : SUN DOG

wind drift *n* : the drift of the wind; *specif* : the average direction of the wind over a period of time

¹winded \'windəd\ *adj* [ME, fr. ¹*wind* + *-ed*] : having wind or breath of a designated kind — usu. used in combination ⟨long-*winded*⟩

²winded *adj* [fr. past part. of ²*wind*] : having lost one's breath esp. from exertion : short of breath ⟨both boys were thoroughly ~ at the end of the race⟩

wind egg *n* [¹*wind*; fr. the former belief that such eggs were the result of conception by the wind] : an unimpregnated, addled, or imperfect egg; *esp* : an egg with a soft noncalcareous shell

wind engine *n* : an engine that gets its motive power from the wind (as a windmill or the rotor of a rotor ship)

¹wind·er \'wīndə(r)\ *n* -S [⁴*wind* + *-er*] : one that winds: as **a** (1) : a worker who winds yarn or thread (2) : a textile worker who operates a machine for winding yarn from one package to another — called also *redrawer, swifter* (3) : ²TUBER d (4) : an operator of a machine for forming strips of paper into spiral tubing for use in making containers or covers **b** *obs* (1) : TENDRIL (2) : a twining plant **c** (1) : WINCH (2) : REEL, SPOOL (3) : any of various textile machines for winding thread and yarn on or off bobbins, reels, spools, or cones (4) : a machine used in papermaking that winds into rolls the slit and trimmed paper coming from the reels **d** : a key for winding a mechanism (as a clock) **e** : a step that is wider at one end than at the other (as in a spiral staircase) — compare FLIER

²wind·er \'wīndə(r), 'win-\ *n* -S [³*wind* + *-er*] : one that winds a horn or other wind instrument

³wind·er \'wində(r)\ *n* -S [²*wind* + *-er*] : something that takes the breath away: as **a** : a hard blow with the fist **b** : a fast run

wind erosion *n* : the erosion and dispersal of topsoil by the wind esp. in dust storms

windfall \'=,=\ *n, often attrib* [ME, fr. ¹*wind* + *fall*] **1 a** : something that is blown down by the wind: as (1) : a tree knocked down by the wind (2) : fruit blown off a tree **b** : an instance of being blown down by the wind ⟨excessive ~ in the residual stands —W.N.Sparhawk⟩ **c** : a tract where the trees have been blown down by the wind **2** : an unexpected or sudden gain or advantage ⟨the decline in Atlantic fares may enable me to steal over one day if I get a ~ —H.J.Laski⟩ ⟨detectives questioning neighbors . . . soon found themselves with a ~ of leads —E.D.Radin⟩ ⟨all the ~ money received by housing promoters —Alvin Shuster⟩

windfallen \'=,==\ *adj* [¹*wind* + *fallen*] **:** blown down by the wind

wind-fertilization \'=,==(,)='==\ *n* **:** ANEMOPHILY

wind-fertilized \'='==,=\ *adj* [¹*wind* + *fertilized*, past part. of *fertilize*] **:** ANEMOPHILOUS

windfirm \'=,=\ *adj* **:** firm enough to withstand strong wind ⟨one of the most ~ of trees —*Scientific American*⟩

windfish \'=,=\ *n* **1 :** a fallfish (*Semotilus corporalis*) of northeastern No. America **2 :** GOLDEN SHINER

windflaw \'=,=\ *n* **:** a gust of wind **:** FLAW

windflower \'=,=\ *n* **1 :** ANEMONE 1 **2 :** RUE ANEMONE

wind-force \'=,=\ *n* **1 :** a definite number (as 5 or 7) on an arbitrary wind scale — compare BEAUFORT SCALE **2 :** the pressure exerted by a wind

wind furnace *n* **:** a natural-draft furnace

windgall \'=,=\ *n* **1 :** a soft tumor or synovial swelling on a horse's leg in the region of the fetlock joint **2 :** SUN DOG

wind-galled \"+d\ *adj* [*windgall* + *-ed*] **:** affected with windgall

wind gap *n* **:** a notch in the crest of a mountain ridge **:** a pass that is not occupied by a stream — called also *air gap, wind valley*

wind gauge *n* **1 :** an instrument used (as in target firing) to determine and sometimes record the force and direction of the wind **:** ANEMOMETER **2 :** a graduated scale on the rear sight of a small-arms rifle by which the sight can be adjusted to correct the deviation of the bullet due to a wind component perpendicular to the line of fire **3 :** a device on a pipe organ for measuring and indicating the amount of wind pressure

wind-grass \'=,=\ *n* **1 :** SILKY BENT GRASS **2 :** ROUGH BENT

wind guard *n* **:** something that gives protection against the wind; *specif* **:** a chimney cowl

wind-gun \'=,=\ *n, archaic* **:** AIR RIFLE 1

wind harp *n* **:** AEOLIAN HARP

windhole \'=,=\ *n* **1 :** a ventilating shaft in a mine **2 :** a hole in the foot of an organ pipe for admitting wind **3 :** a hole made by the wind ⟨sandstone formations tooled by centuries of wind and weather, pockmarked with ~*s* and caves —*Amer. Guide Series: Calif.*⟩

windhover \'=,==\ *n* [¹*wind* + *hover*, v.; fr. its habit of hovering in the wind] *Brit* **:** KESTREL

windier *comparative of* WINDY

windies *pl of* WINDY

windiest *superlative of* WINDY

win·di·go \'wində,gō\ *also* **wen·di·go** \'wen-\ *n* -s [Ojibwa] **:** a cannibalistic creature of Algonquian mythology believed to have been a lost hunter forced by hunger to eat human flesh and thereafter to have become a crazed man-eating ogre roaming the forest

wind·i·ly \'windəlē, -li\ *adv* **:** in a windy manner

wind indicator *n* **:** a large weathercock mounted on the ground at airports to indicate the direction of the wind

wind·i·ness \-dēnəs, -din-\ *n* -ES [ME *windinesse*, fr. ¹*windy* + *-nesse* -ness] **:** the quality or state of being windy: as **a :** FLATULENCE **b :** lack of substance **:** VERBOSITY, POMPOSITY ⟨showed up the ~ of their arguments, the sublime folly of their attempts —Virginia Woolf⟩ **c :** the presence of wind in the atmosphere ⟨average hourly velocity is considered a good index of ~ —*New Yorker*⟩ **d :** BREATHINESS

¹**wind·ing** \'wīndiŋ, -dēŋ\ *n* -s [ME, fr. OE *windung*, something twined or plaited, a hurdle, fr. *windan* to wind + *-ung* -ing] **1 a** (1) **:** the material (as wire or rope) that is wound or coiled about an object (as an armature) (2) **:** a single turn of the wound material **b** *chiefly dial* **:** a pliable rod **:** WITHY **2 a :** the action of coiling, twining, or twisting a pliable material about an object or about itself ⟨the ~ of thread on a spool⟩ ⟨silk ~⟩ **b :** the manner of winding pliable material about an object — see SERIES WINDING, SHUNT WINDING **3 a :** a curved or sinuous course, passage, or line ⟨knows all the ~*s* of the cave —A.A.Grace⟩ **b** (1) **:** movement or progress in a curve or a series of curves ⟨following the ~*s* of the creek until it led us far back into the hills —Mary S. Broome⟩ (2) **:** a sinuous movement in conduct or thought **:** a devious or tortuous way or method — usu. used in pl. ⟨all the ~*s* of this sordid intrigue —J.W.Beach⟩ **4 a :** the act or action of hoisting or pulling by means of a mechanism that winds (as a winch) **b :** the act or action of tightening a spring or other mechanism (as in a clock or watch) by turning a key, stem, or screw **5 :** the state, quality, or fact of being twisted or warped out of a plane ⟨drove wooden piles that would stay out of ~⟩ **6 :** a defective gait of a horse in which one foreleg is twisted in front of and around the other

²**winding** \"\ *adj* [fr. present participle of ⁴*wind*] **1 :** marked by winding: as **a :** having a pronounced curve ⟨the rough ~ stairs of the medieval fortress —Claudia Cassidy⟩; *esp* **:** SPIRAL **b :** having a course that winds ⟨a ~ road⟩ **c :** DIGRESSIVE, RAMBLING ⟨the conclusion of the long and ~ stories —Sir Walter Scott⟩ **2** *obs* **:** TRICKY, DECEITFUL, WILY **3 :** STAGGERING, REELING ⟨a kick that sent him ~ —G.S.Perry⟩ — **wind·ing·ly** *adv* — **wind·ing·ness** *n* -ES

winding engine *n* **:** a hoisting engine **:** HOIST

winding frame *n* **:** WINDER c(3)

winding pendant *n* **:** a pendant secured around a masthead into an eye at the lower end of which a winding tackle hooks

winding pinion *n* **:** a small steel wheel in the winding mechanism of a watch with both radial and perpendicular teeth through which the winding stem fits

winding rack *n* **:** a toothed sector or bar activated by a plunger in the case that winds up the repeating mechanism in a repeating watch

winding-sheet \'==,=\ *n* [ME *winding shete*, fr. ¹*winding* + *shete* sheet] **1 :** a sheet in which a corpse is wrapped **:** SHROUD **2 :** a sheetlike formation of tallow or wax around a guttered candle that is an omen of death or calamity

winding strips *or* **winding sticks** *n pl* **:** two equal short straightedges with parallel edges placed transversely on a surface to test its trueness

winding tackle *n* **:** a tackle consisting of a fixed triple block and a double or triple movable block hooked to a winding pendant for hoisting heavy articles in or out of a ship

wind instrument *n* [¹*wind*] **:** a musical instrument sounded by wind and esp. by the breath

wind·jam \'win(d),jam, -aam\ *vi* [back-formation fr. *windjammer*] *slang* **:** to talk excessively **:** talk a great deal without saying anything of substance

wind·jam·mer \-mə(r)\ *n* -s [¹*wind* + *jam*, v. + *-er*] **1** *slang* **:** a wind instrument player: as **a :** a brass player in a circus band **b :** an army bugler or trumpeter **2** *slang* **:** a very talkative person **:** WINDBAG **3 a :** SAILING SHIP **b :** a member of the crew of a sailing ship

wind·lace \'windləs\ *archaic var of* WINDLASS

¹**wind·lass** \'windləs\ *n* -ES [ME *wynlase, wyndelas, wyndlas*, alter. (prob. influenced by ME *windlen*, freq. of *winden* to wind) of *wyndas*, fr. ON *vindáss*, fr. *vinda* to wind + *āss* pole, beam] **1 :** any of various machines for hoisting or hauling: as **a :** a horizontal barrel supported in vertical standards and turned by a crank with a handle so that the hoisting rope is wound around the barrel — see DIFFERENTIAL WINDLASS **b :** a horizontal barrel with whelps turned by handspikes inserted in radial holes near each end and formerly used to raise the anchor — compare CAPSTAN **c :** a powerful steam or electric winch having a horizontal or a vertical shaft and two drums that is used to raise the anchor and is mounted on the forecastlehead **d :** a winch used in agriculture that has a vertical drum and is operated by a tractor **2 :** a small winch formerly used to bend a crossbow

windlass

²**windlass** \"\ *vt* -ED/-ING/-ES **:** to hoist or haul with or as if with a windlass

³**windlass** *n* -ES [alter. (influenced by ⁴*wind*) of ME *wanlas*] **1** *obs* **:** a roundabout way taken to intercept game in hunting **:** a roundabout movement **2** *obs* **:** a circuitous method **:** ARTIFICE, MANEUVER

wind·lass·er \-sə(r)\ *n* -s [¹*windlass* + *-er*] **:** an operator of a windlass

¹**win·dle** \'win(d)ᵊl\ *n* -s [ME, fr. OE *windel* basket, fr. *windan* to wind, twist, plait — more at WIND] **:** a locally varying measure (as for wheat) used in northern England and Scotland

²**windle** \"\ *n* [perh. fr. ¹*wind*] *dial Eng* **:** REDWING 1

win·dles \'windᵊlz\ *n pl but sing or pl in constr* [E dial. *windle*, short for *windlestraw*] **:** a ribgrass (*Plantago lanceolata*)

wind·less \'windləs\ *adj* [ME *windles*, fr. ¹*wind* + *-les* -less] **:** marked by absence of wind ⟨a ~ day⟩ — **wind·less·ly** *adv* — **wind·less·ness** *n* -ES

win·dle·straw \'win(d)ᵊl,strȯ\ *also* **win·dle·strae** \-rā\ *n* -s [fr. (assumed) ME *windlestraw, windelstree*, fr. OE *windelstrēaw*, fr. *windel* basket + *strēaw* straw — more at WINDLE, STRAW] **1** *Brit* **:** a dry thin stalk of grass **2** *Brit* **:** any of various grasses with an elongated stalk **3** *chiefly Scot* **:** something that is weak, light, or insubstantial; *specif* **:** a thin or weak person **4 :** WHITETHROAT 1

win·dlin \'windlən\ *or* **win·dling** \-lən, -liŋ\ *n* -s [perh. fr. gerund of obs. *windle* to wind, fr. ME *windlen* — more at WINDLASS] *chiefly Scot* **:** a bundle of hay or straw

wind load *n* [¹*wind*] **:** the load on a structure due to the action of wind

wind machine *n* **1 :** a machine for creating an artificial wind: as **a :** a machine for creating a blast of air on a theatrical stage **b :** a large fan used to circulate air in an orchard to prevent frost damage **2 :** a device used for imitating the sound of the wind (as in a theater)

wind mantle *n* **:** WINDBREAK 1a — used chiefly in forestry

¹**windmill** \'=,=\ *n* [ME *windmulle*, fr. ¹*wind* + *mille, mulle* mill] **1 a :** a mill operated by the wind usu. acting on oblique vanes or sails which radiate from a horizontal shaft — compare SMOCK MILL **b :** any of various similar mechanisms: (1) **:** a wind-driven water pump (2) **:** a wind-driven electric generator **c :** the wind-driven wheel of a mill operated by the wind or of a similar mechanism **2 :** something that resembles or suggests a windmill: as **a :** PINWHEEL 2a **b** *slang* **:** HELICOPTER **c :** a prostrate annual plant (*Allionia incarnata*) of the Colorado and Mohave deserts that has viscid stems and white to rose flowers in groups of three **3 a** *obs* **:** a fanciful scheme or plan **b** [so called fr. the episode in *Don Quixote* by Miguel de Cervantes Saavedra †1616 Span. writer, in which the hero attacks windmills under the illusion that they are giants] **:** an imaginary wrong, evil, or opponent — used esp. in the phrase *to tilt at windmills*

modern windmill 1a

²**windmill** \"\ *vt* **:** to cause to move like a windmill ⟨~*ed* his arms —John & Ward Hawkins⟩ ~ *vi* **:** to move like a windmill ⟨the other soldier hit him . . . they were ~*ing* into each other without doing any damage —Thomas Williams⟩; *specif* **:** to rotate from the force of the air when the engine is not operating ⟨the propeller . . . will ~ and crank the engine —F.H.Colvin⟩

windmill·er \"+ə(r)\ *n* [¹*windmill* + *-er*] **:** the operator of a windmill

windmill grass *n* **:** any of various grasses of the genus *Chloris*; *esp* **:** an Australian grass (*C. truncata*) having numerous long spikes disposed like the vanes of a windmill

windmill palm *n* **:** a hemp palm (*Trachycarpus excelsa*)

windmill pink *n* **:** a European catchfly (*Silene gallica*) with hairy foliage and small white racemose flowers that is widely naturalized in No. America

wind motor *n* **:** WINDMILL 1b

wind music *n* **:** music written for or produced by wind instruments

win·dore \'win,dō(ə)r\ *n* -s [alter. (influenced by *door*) of ¹*window*] *archaic* **:** WINDOW

¹**win·dow** \'win(,)dō, -,də; -,dəw *or* -,dō + V; *dial* 'windər *or* -dē *or* -di\ *n* -s *often attrib* [ME *windowe*, fr. ON *vindauga*, fr. *vindr* wind, air + *auga* eye — more at WIND, EYE] **1 a** (1) **:** an opening in a wall of a building or a side of a vehicle to admit light usu. through a transparent or translucent material (as glass), usu. to permit vision through the wall or side, and often to admit air (2) **:** an opening in a partition or a wall through which business is carried on (as by a bank teller or a ticket agent) **b :** a space behind a window; *esp* **:** a space behind a glass window that is used for display esp. of merchandise **c** (1) **:** the casement, sash with its fittings, or other framework that closes a window opening (2) **:** WINDOWPANE ⟨the ball broke a ~⟩ **2 :** a means of entrance (as to the mind); *esp* **:** a means of obtaining information or maintaining contact ⟨dedicated himself to the task of keeping his country a ~ on the West —Charles Hodges⟩ **3 a :** any of various openings resembling or suggestive of a window: as (1) **:** a small opening through which it is possible to see **:** SLOT (2) **:** a small opening in an anatomical structure **:** FENESTRA (3) **:** FENSTER (4) **:** a transparent panel (as in an envelope, paper bag, or carton) (5) **:** a transparent plate (as in the front of a diving helmet) **b :** EYE ⟨a pair of indigo ~*s* —*N.Y.Sun*⟩ **c :** a small polished facet on the surface of a rough gemstone that permits inspection of the interior **4 :** strips of foil or metal-coated paper dropped from airplanes to interfere with an enemy's radar detection by creating spurious images — called also *chaff* **5 :** a hairless patch on a pelt or fur

²**window** \"\ *vt* -ED/-ING/-S **1** *obs* **:** to place in a window **2 :** to provide with or as if with windows

window back *n* **:** the inside face of the piece of wall between the windowsill and the floor esp. when ceiled

window band *n* **:** RIBBON WINDOWS

window bar *n* **1 :** a wood or metal division between the panes of a window **2 :** a bar for fastening a window or a shutter **3 :** a bar for preventing passage through a window

window bay *n* **:** BAY WINDOW

window board *n* **:** a board used in a window as a part of the ledge or frame or as a shutter

window bole *n, chiefly Scot* **:** a small opening in a wall to let in light and air usu. closed with a wooden shutter

window box *n* **1 :** one of the hollows in the sides of a window frame for the weights that counterbalance a lifting sash **2 :** a box designed to hold soil for growing plants on a windowsill or at the level of the sill

window card *n* **:** a descriptive advertising card used in a retail store window

window decoration *n* **:** a decoration for a window; *esp* **:** material used to trim a retail store window

window display *n* **:** a display of goods in a window designed to attract customers

window-dress \'==,dres\ *vt* [back-formation fr. *window dresser*] **:** to make appear more attractive or more favorable ⟨may be necessary to *window-dress* . . . an offering of bonds —*Scientific American*⟩

window dresser *n* [¹*window* + *dresser*] **1 :** one that arranges merchandise and decorations in a show window — called also *window trimmer* **2 :** one that distorts facts or puts up a front in order to make a favorable impression ⟨value him as one of the greatest *window dressers* of their party and defenders of its misdeeds —*Nation*⟩

window dressing *n* [¹*window* + *dressing*] **1** *Brit* **:** the wooden or stone trim of a window **2 :** the arrangement of merchandise and decorations in a show window esp. of a retail store **3 a** (1) **:** the act or practice of making a false or misleading statement of facts (as of financial condition or a political situation) or of putting up a front in order to make a better impression ⟨too much *window dressing* by companies which hire . . . a half-dozen Negroes just to prove for the record that they do not discriminate —Elmo Roper⟩ (2) **:** the making of adjustments (as in bank statements) that are within the limits of acceptable practice to improve the appearance of a financial position **b :** something that improves the external appearance (as of an organization or an action) and helps to make a better impression **:** FRONT, FACADE, COVER-UP ⟨letting big business run the show with labor representation on his staff only as *window dressing* —*Wall Street Jour.*⟩ ⟨the sententious piety is merely *window dressing*, a means of passing off spicy stories —A.E.Rodway⟩

windowed *adj* [¹*window* + *-ed*] **1 :** having windows **2 :** having ornamental openings **3 :** filled with holes **:** RAGGED

windowed plant *also* **window plant** *n* **:** any of several plants esp. of *Mesembryanthemum* or the related genus *Fenestraria* having transparent triangular areas in their leaves

window-efficiency ratio *n* **:** DAYLIGHT FACTOR

window envelope *n* **:** an envelope having a transparent panel through which the address on the enclosure is visible

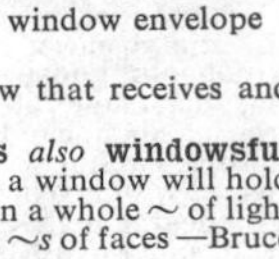
window envelope

window fixture *n* **:** a piece of furniture or a form used in dressing a store window

window fly *n* **:** any of several small black flies of the family Scenopinidae that are often found on windows; *esp* **:** a fly (*Scenopinus fenestralis*) whose larvae feed on the larvae of the clothes moth

window frame *n* **:** the frame of a window that receives and holds the sashes or casements

win·dow·ful \'==,fu̇l\ *n, pl* **windowfuls** *also* **windowsful** [¹*window* + *-ful*] **:** as much or as many as a window will hold or allow to pass through or be visible ⟨let in a whole ~ of light —*Commonweal*⟩ ⟨a full train . . . piled with ~*s* of faces —Bruce Marshall⟩

window gardening *n* **:** the growing of ornamentals in receptacles placed in the windows of the home

window glass *n* **:** sheet glass made in shapes suitable for windows

window head *n* **:** the upper transverse member of a window

win·dow·less \'==ləs\ *adj* **:** having no window — **win·dow·less·ness** *n* -ES

windowlight \'==,=\ *n* **:** WINDOWPANE 1

win·dow·man \'==mən\ *n, pl* **windowmen :** a man in charge of a window (as in a ticket office or a bank)

window martin *or* **window swallow** *n* **:** MARTIN 1

window mirror *n* **:** a small mirror placed outside a window (as of an automobile) and adjusted to reflect objects within a desired area

window-money \'==,==\ *n, archaic* **:** WINDOW-TAX

window oyster *or* **window shell** *n* **:** WINDOWPANE OYSTER

windowpane \'==,=\ *n* **1 :** a pane in a window **2 :** a thin spotted American flounder (*Lophopsetta maculata*) remarkable for its translucency

windowpane oyster *or* **windowpane shell** *n* **:** a mollusk of the genus *Placuna* that is esp. common in the Philippines and has a large flat somewhat pearly paper-thin shell used for thousands of years esp. by the Chinese as a substitute for glass

windows *pl of* WINDOW, *pres 3d sing of* WINDOW

window screen *n* **1 :** a screen usu. of wire mesh designed to fit into a window frame and keep out insects when the window is open **2 :** an ornament (as a grille, lattice, or piece of stained glass) used to fill a window opening

window seat *n* **:** a seat at a window: as **a :** a seat built into a window recess **b :** an upholstered stool with arms designed to fit into a window recess

window shade *n* **:** SHADE 7g

window-shop \'==,=\ *vi* **:** to look at the displays in store windows without going inside the stores to make purchases

window-shopper \'==,==\ *n* **:** one that window-shops

windowshut \'==,=\ *n, archaic* **:** WINDOW SHUTTER

window shutter *n* **:** a shutter for a window

windowsill \'==,=\ *n* **:** the sill of a window; *specif* **:** the horizontal member at the bottom of a window opening

window stop *n* **:** a narrow strip that holds a window sash in position in a window frame

window-tax \'==,=\ *n* **:** a tax formerly levied in England on all windows and openings for light in houses in cities and towns

window trim *n* **1 :** WINDOW DECORATION **2 :** the moldings covering the jambs and head of a window

window trimmer *n* **:** WINDOW DRESSER 1

win·dowy \'windəwē\ *adj* [¹*window* + *-y*] **:** having many windows or openings

windpipe \'=,=\ *n* **:** the passage for the breath from the larynx to the lungs **:** TRACHEA

wind-pollinated \'='==,==\ *adj* [¹*wind* + *pollinated*, past part. of *pollinate*] **:** pollinated by wind-borne pollen

wind poppy *n* **:** a California wild poppy (*Papaver heterophyllum* or *Meconopis heterophylla*) with variable pinnate or pinnately divided leaves and bright brick-red flowers with a dark blotch at the base of each petal

wind power *n* **:** mechanical power derived from winds

windproof \'=,=\ *adj* **:** proof against the wind ⟨a ~ jacket⟩

wind-puff \'=,=\ *n* **1 :** puffing of the skin about a wound caused by air that has entered (as after the caponizing of a cockerel) **2 :** WINDGALL 1

wind pump *n* **:** a pump moved by a windmill

wind resistance *n* **:** the resistance that still air offers to movement esp. of a vehicle

wind ripple *n* **:** one of many wavelike undulations produced on the surface of sand by wind and occas. found in rocks of aeolian origin

windroad \'=,=\ *n* **:** AIRWAY 1

wind-rode \'=,=\ *adj* [¹*wind* + *rode*, chiefly dial. past part. of *ride*] **:** caused to ride with head to the wind practically unaffected by tide or current — used of a ship at anchor with wind and tide approximately opposed; opposed to *tide-rode*

windroot \'=,=\ *n* **:** BUTTERFLY WEED 1

wind rose *n* **1 a :** a European poppy (*Papaver argemone*) adventive in No. America having red dark-eyed flowers **b :** a purple-flowered perennial southern European herb (*Roemeria hybrida*) of the family Papaveraceae **c :** PRICKLY POPPY **d :** CORN POPPY **2** [G *windrose* compass card, lit., rose of winds, fr. *wind* (fr. OHG *wint*) + *rose* (fr. L *rosa*) — more at WIND, ROSE] **a :** a diagram showing for one place the relative frequency or frequency and strength of winds from different directions **b :** a diagram showing the average occurrence of other meteorological phenomena (as rain and sunshine) with winds from different directions

¹**wind·row** \'win(d),rō\ *also* **win·row** \'win,rō\ *n* [¹*wind* + *row*] **1 a** (1) **:** a row of hay raked up to dry before being rolled or pitched into cocks (2) **:** a similar row (as of grain) for drying **b :** a row heaped up by or as if by the wind ⟨powdery new snow . . . cut sharp in ~*s* —Brooks Atkinson⟩ ⟨the tides heap the western beaches with ~*s* of shells —Marjory S. Douglas⟩ **c** (1) **:** a long low ridge of road-making material that has been scraped to the side of a road (2) **:** BANK, RIDGE, HEAP ⟨these rock ~*s*, piled up as fields are cleared of stones, hold water on the land —Quentin Keynes⟩ ⟨beneath the wagons lay ~*s* of slumbering men —T.W.Duncan⟩ **2 :** a furrow in which sugarcane stalks are laid in order to obtain a new crop of cane from the eyes of the stalks or to protect the stalks from frost

²**windrow** \"\ *also* **winrow** \"\ *vt* -ED/-ING/-S **:** to put into windrows

wind·row·er \-ōə(r)\ *n* -s [²*windrow* + *-er*] **1 :** a curved finger device attached to the rear of the cutter bar of a mowing machine to windrow the swath **2 :** SIDE-DELIVERY RAKE **3 :** SWATHER **4 :** a sugarcane cutter that drops the cut cane into large rows

winds *pl of* WIND, *pres 3d sing of* WIND

windsail \'=,=\ *n* **1 :** the sail of a windmill **2 :** a wide tube or funnel of canvas used to carry air for ventilation into the lower compartments of a ship

wind scale *n* **:** a series of numbers or words corresponding to various ranges of wind speeds for indicating the force of the wind — see BEAUFORT SCALE

wind scoop *n* **:** a scoop-shaped device attached to an air port of a ship to direct outside air inside the ship — called also *wind catcher*

wind scorpion *n* [trans. of Ar *'aqrab al-rīh*; fr. its extreme agility] **:** an arachnid of the order Solpugida

windscreen \'=,=\ *n* **1 :** a screen that protects against the wind **2** *Brit* **:** an automobile windshield

wind shake *n* **1 :** a shake in timber attributed to high winds ⟨pine free from knots, *wind shakes*, and other defects —*U.S. Daily*⟩ **2 :** a defective condition marked by wind shakes

wind-shaken \'=,==\ *adj* **1 :** shaken by the wind **2 :** affected by wind shake

wind sheet *n* **:** the current of air that strikes the upper lip of a flue pipe in an organ
wind shelf *n* **:** SMOKE SHELF
windshield \'⸗,⸗\ *n* **1 :** a shield that protects against the wind: as **a** (1) **:** a transparent screen (as of glass) that protects the occupants of a vehicle from the wind; *esp* **:** a transparent glass screen that forms the upper front of the passenger compartment of an automobile (2) **:** a metal screen to prevent the wind from blowing on a flame **b :** a tight cuff inside the sleeve of a coat or jacket to keep the wind out **2 :** a cap of light metal placed over the head of a projectile to streamline it
windshield wing *n* **:** an adjustable glass piece attached to the side of the windshield of an automotive vehicle
windshield wiper *n* **:** a device usu. in the form of a rubber squeegee attached to an oscillating arm for wiping the windshield of an automobile or other vehicle
wind-shift line *n* **:** SQUALL LINE
windship \'⸗,⸗\ *n* **:** SAILING SHIP
wind-shock \'⸗,⸗\ *n, archaic* **:** WIND SHAKE 1
windslab \'⸗,⸗\ *n* **:** a crust or mass of snow packed tightly by the wind
wind slash *n* **:** WINDFALL 1c
wind sock *also* **wind sleeve** *n* **:** a truncated cloth cone that is open at both ends and mounted in an elevated position with the large end held open by a rigid ring in a vertical plane so that the cone is free to rotate about a vertical axis to indicate the direction of the wind — called also *wind cone*
¹wind·sor \'winzə(r)\ *adj, usu cap* [fr. *Windsor,* municipal borough of southern England and seat of Windsor Castle, principal residence of England's sovereigns] **1 :** of or from the town of Windsor, England **2 :** of or originating with the household of Windsor Castle
²windsor \"\ *or* **windsor soap** *n* -s *usu cap W* **:** a scented usu. brown soap
³windsor \"\ *adj, usu cap* [fr. *Windsor,* city of southeast Ontario, Canada] **:** of or from the city of Windsor, Ont. **:** of the kind or style prevalent in Windsor
⁴windsor \"\ *adj, usu cap* [*Windsor chair*] **:** made in the style of a Windsor chair ⟨a *Windsor* settee⟩
windsor bean *also* **windsor** *n* -s *usu cap W* [¹*windsor*] **:** BROAD BEAN
windsor blue *n, often cap W* **:** a grayish purplish blue that is redder and paler than average delft and redder, lighter, and stronger than average navy blue
windsor chair *also* **windsor** *n* -s *usu cap W* [¹*windsor*] **:** a wooden chair of stick construction having a spindle back, turned raking legs, and usu. a saddle seat
windsor green *n, often cap W* **:** LIGHT CHROME GREEN
windsor knot *n, usu cap W* **:** a knot used for tying four-in-hand ties that is wider than the usual four-in-hand knot
windsor tan *n, often cap W* **:** a brownish orange that is redder and duller than leather, less strong, slightly yellower, and lighter than spice, slightly yellower and lighter than prairie brown, and slightly redder and darker than Titian, amber brown, or gold pheasant
windsor tie *n, usu cap W* **:** a broad necktie usu. tied in a loose bow

Windsor side chair

wind-splitter \'⸗,⸗⸗\ *n* **:** a streamlined train of the early 20th century
wind sprint *n* **:** a sprint performed as a training exercise to develop the wind
wind stack *n* **:** a stack of straw made by a wind stacker
wind stacker *n* **:** an apparatus using an air current generated by a fan to stack straw from a threshing machine
wind·ster \'wīn(d)ztə(r), -n(t)st-\ *n* -s [⁴*wind* + *-ster*] *archaic* **:** a person who winds thread or yarn
wind stop *n* [¹*wind*] **1 :** the part of a window frame that covers the joint between the movable sash or casement and the hanging stile **2 :** WEATHER STRIP
windstorm \'⸗,⸗\ *n* **:** a storm characterized by high wind with little or no precipitation
windsucker \'⸗,⸗⸗\ *n* [¹*wind* + *sucker*] **:** a horse that has the habit of wind sucking
wind sucking *n* [¹*wind* + *sucking,* gerund of *suck*] **:** a bad habit of horses which is related to, often associated with, and similar in effect to crib-biting and in which an affected animal presses the nose against or grasps with the teeth the manger or other object, arches the neck, and swallows or goes through the motions of swallowing quantities of air
windswept \'⸗,⸗\ *adj* [¹*wind* + *swept,* past part. of *sweep*] **:** swept by or as if by wind
wind-swift \'⸗,⸗\ *adj* **:** swift as the wind
wind tee *n* **:** a large weather vane shaped like an airplane or a horizontal letter T located on or near a landing field to indicate wind direction to airplane pilots — called also *landing T*
windthrow \'⸗,⸗\ *n* **:** the uprooting and overthrowing of trees by the wind
wind-throw \"\ *vt* [*windthrow*] **:** to uproot and overthrow (a tree) in the wind ⟨a celebrated walnut which was *wind-thrown* . . . some years back —Colin Gibson⟩
wind thrush *n, dial Eng* **:** REDWING 1
windtight \'⸗,⸗\ *adj* **:** AIRTIGHT 1
wind-trunk \'⸗,⸗\ *n* **:** the duct by which compressed air passes from the bellows to the wind-chest of a pipe organ
wind tunnel *n* **:** a tunnellike passage through which air is blown at a known velocity to determine the effects of wind pressure on an object (as an airplane part or model or a guided missile) placed in the passage — compare WATER TUNNEL
wind up *vb* [⁴*wind* + *up*] *vt* **1** *archaic* **:** to bring together (as a speech) in a final summarizing statement **:** sum up **2 :** to bring to a conclusion **:** END ⟨*wound up* their 27th annual convention here with high praise for the . . . hospitality and cooperation —Benjamin Welles⟩ ⟨a final chapter for the woman golfer *winds up* an unusually helpful manual —*Times Lit. Supp.*⟩ **3 a :** to put in order for the purpose of bringing to an end ⟨the companies are *winding up* their business affairs by retiring their capital stock and paying dividends —*Monsanto Mag.*⟩ ⟨top strategists wished they could *wind up* this session of Congress —*Newsweek*⟩ **b :** to put in order for the purpose of disposal and transferring title **:** SETTLE ⟨an estate is to be *wound up* —*Farmer's Weekly (So. Africa)*⟩ **~** *vi* **1 a :** to come to a conclusion **:** END ⟨*wound up* with a glorification of the resistance movement —A.H.Vandenberg †1951⟩ **b :** to arrive in a place, situation, or condition at the end or as a result (as of a course of action) **:** end up ⟨almost all check crooks *wind up* in jail —Joseph Nolan⟩ ⟨though they started as simple farmers they *wound up* as millionaires —W.P.Webb⟩ **2 a :** to give a preliminary swing to the arm (as before pitching a baseball) **b :** to make preparations **:** work up preliminary momentum **:** get ready ⟨disc jockey . . . *winding up* for an affirmation about snow tires —C.W.Morton⟩
¹windup \'⸗,⸗\ *n* -s [*wind up*] **1 a :** the act of bringing to an end ⟨the ~ of certain paper formalities next month —*Wall Street Jour.*⟩ ⟨no ~ report but an introduction —Meyer Levin⟩ **b :** a concluding act or part **:** END, FINISH, SETTLEMENT ⟨a very good ~ to a successful evening —Agnes M. Miall⟩ **2 :** a preliminary swing of the arm (as before pitching a baseball)
²windup \"\ *adj* [⁴*wind* + *up*] **:** having a part designed for winding up; *esp* **:** having a spring that is wound up by hand for operation ⟨~ toys⟩
wind valley *n* [¹*wind*] **:** WIND GAP
wind vane *n* **1 :** the sail of a windmill **2 :** VANE 1a
¹wind·ward \'win(d)wə(r)d, *esp nautical* -ndə(r)d\ *adj* [¹*wind* + *-ward*] **1 a :** moving toward the direction from which the wind is blowing **:** sailing against the wind ⟨a ~ tide⟩ **b :** situated toward the direction from which the wind is blowing ⟨the side the wind reaches first is the ~ . . . side —Gavin Douglas⟩ — opposed to *leeward* **2 :** WEATHERLY — **wind·ward·ness** *n* -ES
²windward \"\ *n* -s **:** the side or direction from which the wind is blowing ⟨to sail to ~ . . . sail about 45° away from the direction of the wind, then change the direction —H.A.Calahan⟩ — opposed to *leeward* — **to windward** *adv* **:** into or in an advantageous position
wind·ward·ly *adj* [²*windward* + *-ly*] **:** WINDWARD 1b, 2
wind·ward·most \-d,mōst\ *adj* [¹*windward* + *-most* (as in *foremost*)] *archaic* **:** most windward
windway \'⸗,⸗\ *n* **:** a passage for air: as **a :** an airway (as for ventilation) in a mine **b :** the narrow slit between the languet and lower lip of an organ flue pipe through which the air current is directed against the upper lip
windwheel \'⸗,⸗\ *n* **:** a wheel rotated by the wind to drive a mechanism (as a windmill)
wind-wing \'⸗,⸗\ *n* **1 :** WINDSHIELD WING **2 :** a small panel in an automobile window that can be turned outward for ventilation
¹windy \'windē, -di\ *adj* -ER/-EST [ME, fr. OE *windig,* fr. ¹*wind* + *-ig* -y] **1 a :** marked by considerable movement of air: as (1) **:** regularly blown on or through by the wind ⟨a ~ headland running out to the gray northern sea —Andrew Lang⟩ ⟨a tottering structure with vast ~ rooms —Sally Carrighar⟩ (2) **:** marked by strong wind ⟨~ gusts of hail —Mary Austin⟩ ⟨got soaked in a ~ downpour⟩ (3) **:** marked by the presence of more wind than usual ⟨a ~ day⟩ (4) **:** swayed by the wind **:** moving to and fro in the wind ⟨the rank ~ grass of this prairie —Sinclair Lewis⟩ **b** (1) **:** resembling or suggestive of the wind in or as if in physical quality **:** VIOLENT, STORMY (2) *obs* **:** CHANGEABLE, INCONSTANT **c :** producing or controlling wind **2 a :** FLATULENT 2 ⟨an empty ~ stomach —J.M. Synge⟩ **b :** FLATULENT 3 ⟨~ buns —Edith C. Rivett⟩ **3 a :** marked by inflated often pretentious verbosity **:** characterized by long-windedness and lack of substance **:** VERBOSE, BOMBASTIC ⟨~ after-dinner eulogies —J.D.Hart⟩ ⟨a ~ politician⟩ **b :** lacking content or substance **:** EMPTY, INSUBSTANTIAL, FLIMSY ⟨this ~ study promoted the increasing emptiness of philosophy —H.O.Taylor⟩ **4 a** *archaic* **:** productive of pride or conceit **b** *chiefly Scot* **:** PROUD, CONCEITED **5 :** played by means of wind; *esp* **:** played on a wind instrument ⟨a larghetto non troppo with responses by the oboes, clarinets, flutes, and bassoons that was a ~ delight —Janet Flanner⟩ **6 :** BREATHY **7** *chiefly Brit* **:** FRIGHTENED, FEARFUL, NERVOUS — **on the windy side :** out of reach **:** SAFE, CLEAR ⟨still you keep o' th' *windy side* of the law —Shak.⟩
²windy \"\ *n* -ES **1** *slang* **:** an exaggerated story **:** a tall tale **2** *slang* **:** BLUFF, HOAX
windy city *adj, usu cap W&C* [fr. *the Windy City,* nickname for Chicago] *slang* **:** of or relating to the city of Chicago, Ill. ⟨*Windy City* politicos⟩
¹wine \'wīn\ *n* -s *often attrib* [ME *win,* fr. OE *wīn;* akin to OHG *wīn* wine, ON *vīn,* Goth *wein;* all fr. a prehistoric Gmc word borrowed fr. L *vinum* wine, of non-IE origin; akin to the source of Gk *oinos* wine, Arm *gini*] **1 a :** the fermented juice of the grape containing varying percentages of alcohol and having a composition and character that depends chiefly upon the grapes used and the climate and soil of the area in which they are grown — see APPETIZER WINE, DESSERT WINE, FORTIFIED WINE, SPARKLING WINE, TABLE WINE; RED WINE, ROSÉ, WHITE WINE; GENERIC WINE, VARIETAL WINE; HIGH WINE, LOW WINE **b :** a wine, mixture of water and wine, or wine substitute (as grape juice) used in Christian communion services **:** SACRAMENTAL WINE **c :** a pharmaceutical preparation using fined wine as a vehicle ⟨~ of iron⟩ **2 :** the usu. fermented juice of various agricultural products (as peaches, oranges, blackberries) used as a beverage **3 :** something resembling wine esp. in an ability to invigorate, intoxicate, or spread a feeling of well-being ⟨his was the sparkling ~ of speech —*Manchester Guardian Weekly*⟩ ⟨tasted the ~ of audience approbation —*Western Speech*⟩ ⟨could catch . . . the ~ of a high, clean air —Emerson Hough⟩ **4 :** WINEGLASS 1 ⟨shearing off . . . ~s to their proper height —Percival Marson⟩ **5** *Brit* **:** a social gathering in an English university at which wine is served ⟨when I go out to a ~ I always bring my own straws —W.W.Reade⟩ **6 :** a variable color averaging a dark red that is yellower and duller than cranberry, yellower, less strong, and very slightly lighter than average garnet, and bluer and duller than pomegranate
²wine \"\ *vb* -ED/-ING/-S *vt* **:** to treat to wine **:** provide with wine ⟨at a dinner ⟨would ~ and dine the . . . members of Congress —*American*⟩ **~** *vi* **:** to drink wine esp. with a dinner ⟨*wined* and dined with the leading citizens of each country during his tour of Europe⟩
wineberry \'⸗- — *see* BERRY\ *n* [ME *winberi, winberie* grape, wineberry, fr. OE *winberige* grape, fr. *wīn* wine + *berige, berie* berry — more at BERRY] **1 :** a raspberry (*Rubus phoenicolasius*) of China and Japan grown for ornament and for the small red acid fruits half enclosed in the hairy calyx **2 :** MAKOMAKO 1
wine-cask borer \'⸗,⸗-\ *n* **:** any of several ambrosia beetles that make burrows in the wood of wine casks
wine cellar *n* **:** a room used for storing wines
wine cooler *n* **:** a vessel or container in which wine is cooled or kept cool; *specif* **:** a metal-lined wooden container on castered legs often with a lid used esp. in the 18th and early 19th centuries for cooling wine ⟨a Baltimore Hepplewhite mahogany inlaid *wine cooler* —*advt*⟩
wine-cup \'⸗,⸗\ *n* **:** FRINGED POPPY MALLOW
wine dregs *n pl* **:** DREGS OF WINE
wine ferment *n* **:** WINE YEAST
wine fly *n* **:** a fly (as the vinegar fly) found about wine vats
wine gallon *n* **:** an old English unit of capacity for wine equal to the volume of a cylinder seven inches in diameter and six inches high and equivalent to the standard U. S. gallon

wine cooler

¹wineglass \'⸗,⸗\ *n* **1 :** a drinking glass that is used for serving wine and has a foot and stem and a variously shaped cup holding from four to six ounces **2 :** a unit of measure that is used in mixing drinks and is equal to four ounces
²wineglass \"\ *adj* **:** having the shape of a wineglass ⟨lawns . . . covered with ~ elms and willows —Van Wyck Brooks⟩
wine grape *n* **:** a grape used in making wine; *esp* **:** a European grape (*Vitis vinifera*)
winegrower \'⸗,⸗⸗\ *n* **:** one that cultivates a vineyard and makes wine from the grapes
wine growing *n* **:** the occupation or industry of cultivating vineyards and producing wine
winehouse \'⸗,⸗\ *n* **:** WINESHOP ⟨each political party . . . has its own hotel and ~ in town —Joseph Wechsberg⟩
wine jar *n* **:** TUN SHELL 2
wine lees *n pl* [ME *win lies,* fr. *win* wine + *lies,* pl. of *lie* lee — more at LEE] **:** DREGS OF WINE
wine·less \'⸗ləs\ *adj* **:** lacking wine ⟨a ~ banquet⟩
wine of ipecac : a solution of an alcoholic extract of ipecac in sherry wine or diluted alcohol
wine of opium : a solution of opium in aromatized sherry or diluted alcohol having the strength of ordinary laudanum
wine palm *n* **:** any of several palms (as the coquito and the macaw palm) whose sap is used to make palm wine — compare TODDY PALM
wine plant *n* **:** a common garden rhubarb (*Rheum rhaponticum*)
winepress \'⸗,⸗\ *n* **:** a vat in which juice is expressed from grapes by treading or by means of a plunger
wine purple *n* **:** a moderate purplish red that is bluer and deeper than average rose or violine pink and bluer than magenta rose
wine red *n* **:** the variable color of red wine averaging a dark red that is stronger and slightly yellower and lighter than average wine, yellower and duller than cranberry, and yellower, lighter, and stronger than average garnet
win·ery \'wīn(ə)rē, -ri\ *n* -ES **:** a building or plant where wine is made
wines *pl of* WINE, *pres 3d sing of* WINE
wineshop \'⸗,⸗\ *n* **:** a café or tavern that specializes in serving wine
wineskin \'⸗,⸗\ *n* **:** a bag made from almost the entire skin of an animal and used for holding wine — compare BOTTLE 1b
wine stone *n* **:** ¹ARGOL
wine taster *n* **1 :** one that tests wine by tasting **2 :** a small flat bowl used to hold a sample of wine being tested
wine thrush *n* [so called fr. its color] *dial Eng* **:** REDWING 1
winey *var of* WINY
wine yeast *n* **:** a yeast (esp. *Saccharomyces cerevisiae*) that induces alcoholic fermentation in grape juice — called also *wine ferment*
wine yellow *n* **:** a pale to grayish yellow that is greener and less strong than Naples yellow or cream buff
¹wing \'wiŋ\ *n* -s *often attrib* [ME *winge, wenge,* of Scand origin; akin to Dan & Sw *vinge* wing, ON *vængr;* akin to OE *wāwan* to blow, OHG *wāhen, wāen,* OSw *vīa,* Goth *waian* to blow, Skt *vāti* it blows — more at WIND] **1 a :** an organ of aerial flight **:** one of the movable feathered or membranous paired appendages by means of which an animal (as a bird, bat, or insect) is able to fly; *also* **:** such an appendage even though rudimentary if possessed by an animal belonging to a group characterized by the power of flight — see ³BAT, BIRD 2a, PTERODACTYL **b :** any of various organic structures (as of the flying fish, flying frog, or flying lemur) providing means of limited flight **c :** one of the broad thin anterior lobes of the foot of a pteropod **d :** the shoulder of a hare or rabbit **2 :** an appendage or part likened to a wing in shape, appearance, or position: as **a :** a device (as for swimming) attached to the shoulders **b :** a shoulder ornament or knot; *esp* **:** a projecting piece attached at the shoulder edge of a 17th century gown or doublet **c** (1) **:** a vane of an arrow (2) **:** the part of a footing forming a side of the splice on an arrow **d :** ALA ⟨the ~ of the nose⟩; *esp* **:** any of the four winglike processes of the sphenoid **e :** a curving lock of hair ⟨has two ~s of pure white in her black hair —Frances Crane⟩ **f :** the arc-shaped piece on a pair of wing compasses or dividers that permits the legs to be fixed at a desired angle **g :** the outside corner of the share of a moldboard plow **h :** a turned-back or extended edge on an article of clothing — see WING COLLAR **i :** a sidepiece at the top of an armchair **j :** a projecting part on one side of a fishnet or at the entry of a trap or corral **k :** either of the parts of a double door or screen **l** (1) **:** a foliaceous, membranous, or woody expansion on a plant (as along the sides of various stems and petioles, of samaras, or of some capsules) (2) **:** either of the two lateral petals of a papilionaceous flower **m :** WING RAIL **n** *Brit* **:** a curved fender for a vehicle; *also* **:** a projecting sidepiece of a dashboard or carriage top **o :** either or any of two or more projections serving as guides (as on a check valve) or as stops (as on a gudgeon) to prevent turning in the socket **3 a :** one of the vanes of a windmill **b :** one of the floats of a waterwheel **c :** SAIL **d :** one of the airfoils that develop a major part of the lift which supports a heavier-than-air airplane **4 a :** a means of flight or rapid progress ⟨fear lent ~s to inspiration —*Time*⟩ **b :** the special attribute of a divine messenger ⟨know that ~s have brushed us⟩ or an angelic nature ⟨seems almost to have sprouted ~s lately⟩ **5 a :** the act or manner of flying **:** FLIGHT ⟨dog required to . . . exhibit steadiness to ~ and shot —W.F.Brown b. 1903⟩ ⟨crow makes ~ to the rooky wood —Shak.⟩ **b :** strength of flight **:** ability to fly **6 a :** ARM; *esp* **:** a throwing or pitching arm **b :** throwing ability **7 a :** the part of the hold or orlop deck of a ship that is nearest the sides **b :** the outboard ends of a ship's bridge **c :** a platform or an overhanging portion of the deck of a ship projecting forward and abaft the paddle box of a side-wheel steamer and supporting the box and protecting the wheel **d :** an addition at the end of a dam but not necessarily in line with it **:** WING WALL **e :** WING JAM **8 :** a side or outlying region or district ⟨no stone in the whole of that ~ of Pakistan suitable for . . . road metalling —D.G.Bridson⟩ **9 :** a part or feature of a building projecting from and subordinate to the main or central part; *broadly* **:** any section of a building ⟨surgical ~ of a hospital⟩ **10 a :** one of the pieces of scenery at the side of the stage **b wings** *pl* **:** the area at the side of the stage out of sight ⟨performers waiting in the ~s for their cues⟩ **11 a :** a division of an army or fleet on either side of a main central body **b :** either member of a body of troops that is divided into two parts **c :** either side or outer extremity of a chess board **d :** one of the positions or players on either side of a center position or of the central lengthwise line of the field, court, or rink in a team sport; *esp* **:** such a position or player on the forward line of a team **12 a :** either of two opposing groups within an organization or society **:** FACTION **b :** a section of an organized body (as a political party or legislative chamber) representing a group or faction holding distinct opinions or policies — compare LEFT WING, RIGHT WING **13 :** a unit of military airplanes: **a :** a unit of an echelon of the U. S. Air Force higher than a group and lower than an air division composed of a headquarters and usu. four groups **b :** two or more squadrons of naval airplanes not carrier based ⟨heavy attack ~⟩ ⟨patrol ~⟩ **14 :** a tap dance step characterized by a sideward slide and retrieve of one foot; *also* **:** a waltz step similarly executed — **on the wing 1 :** in flight **:** FLYING **2 :** in motion **:** TRAVELING ⟨*on the wing* gathering material for his novels —James Reynolds⟩ — **on wings** *adv* **:** as if flying **:** LIGHTHEARTEDLY — **take wing :** to begin flight **:** depart swiftly **:** fly away — **under one's wing :** under one's protection **:** in one's charge or care
²wing \"\ *vb* -ED/-ING/-S *vt* **1** *obs* **a :** to carve (a bird) for serving **b :** to pluck the wings from (as an insect) **2 a :** to fit with wings ⟨sailcloth that ~*ed* the clipper ships —*Women's Wear Daily*⟩ **b :** to attach feathers to (an arrow) **:** FLETCH ⟨he himself who had ~*ed* the arrow of his fate —C.S.Forester⟩ **3 :** to enable to fly or move swiftly **:** give speed to ⟨fear ~*ed* his feet⟩ **4** *archaic* **:** to supply with pieces or divisions at the side **:** FLANK **5 a :** to wound in the wing **:** disable the wing of ⟨~ a flying duck⟩ **:** bring down by shooting **b :** to hit or wound (as with a bullet) without killing ⟨~*ed* by a sniper⟩ **6 :** to pass through in flight **:** traverse with or as if with wings ⟨the blue deep thou *wingest* —P.B.Shelley⟩ **7 :** to effect or achieve by flying ⟨~*ing* our way out to India —Dillon Sipley⟩ **8 :** to send off swiftly **:** let fly **:** DISPATCH ⟨would start to ~ punches —A.J.Liebling⟩ **9 :** to shift (weights) in a ship to near the sides in order to lengthen the period of roll — used usu. with *out* ⟨~ out ballast⟩ **10 :** to set (a sail) to catch a following wind — used with *out* ⟨jibs are ~*ed* out by means of a whisker pole —G.W.Elder & Ernest Ratsey⟩ **11** *dial* **:** to brush or sweep with or as if with a wing **~** *vi* **1 :** to go with or as if with wings **:** FLY, SAIL ⟨swallows ~*ing* southward⟩ ⟨watch the racing fleets ~ up to the start —E.A.Weeks⟩ **2** *of a horse* **:** to swing one or more of the legs out from the body
wing and wing *adv* **:** with sails boomed out on both sides ⟨running *wing and wing* before the wind⟩
wingback \'⸗,⸗\ *n* **:** a football back whose position on offense is outside of the offensive end; *also* **:** the position of a player so stationed
wing back formation *n* **:** an offensive formation in football in which a back is placed just behind or slightly beyond and to the rear of an end
¹wing band *n* **1 :** WING BAR 1 **2 :** a metal clip placed in the wing of a domestic fowl for purposes of identification
²wing band *vt* **:** to mark (a bird) with a wing band
wing bar *n* **1 :** a line of contrasting color across the middle of a bird's wing made by markings on the wing coverts — see COCK illustration **2 :** a sandbar which partially crosses the entrance to a bay or mouth of a river
wing bay *n* **:** SPECULUM 5
wingbeat \'⸗,⸗\ *n* **:** a stroke of a bird's wings in flying
wing bolt *n* **:** a bolt having a head like a wing nut
wing bow *n* **:** the lesser coverts of the shoulder or bend of a bird's wing when distinctively colored — used esp. of poultry; see GOOSE illustration
wing car *n* **:** a car suspended off the center line of an airship — called also *sidecar*
wing case *n* **:** ELYTRON 1
wing cell *n* **1 :** one of the areas bounded by veins in an insect's wing **2 :** CELL 3c
wing chair *or* **winged chair** *n* **:** an upholstered armchair with high solid back and sides turned at such an angle that they provide a rest for the head and protection from drafts — called also *draft chair, lug chair*

wing chair

wing collar *n* **1 :** a man's stand-up collar having the upper corners turned down to form wings and worn esp. for formal dress **2 :** a woman's folding or spreading collar with pointed corners

wing commander *n* **:** an officer (as in the British Royal Air Force) equivalent in rank to a lieutenant-colonel in the army

wing compass *n* **:** a carpenter's compass having a metal arc and binding screw for setting at the desired degree of opening

wing cover *n* **:** ELYTRON 1

wing covert *n* **:** one of the coverts of the wing quills — see BIRD illustration

wing dam *n* **:** PIER DAM

wing-dam \'ˌ=ˌ=\ *vt* [*wing dam*] **:** to provide (as a river) with a wing dam

wing deck *n* **:** WING 7c

wing·ding \'wiŋ,diŋ\ *n* -s [origin unknown] **1** *slang* **a :** a nervous seizure or attack induced by narcotics **b :** a pretended fainting fit or illness **c :** a fit of rage **:** TANTRUM **d :** SPREE **2 a :** a wild or lively or lavish party **b** *slang* **:** a social affair ⟨a series of proms and ~*s* his frat was giving —Frank Sullivan⟩

wing dividers *n pl* **:** a pair of dividers that resemble a wing compass

winged \ˌwiŋd *or except in sense 1a(2)* 'wiŋəd\ *adj* [ME, fr. *winge* wing + *-ed*] **1 a** (1) **:** having wings ⟨~ seed⟩ ⟨~ mirror⟩ ⟨~ statue of Mercury⟩ (2) **:** having wings of a specified character — usu. used in combination ⟨strong-*winged*⟩ ⟨white-*winged*⟩ ⟨double-*winged* hospital building⟩ **b :** using wings in flight **:** capable of flight ⟨~ insect⟩ ⟨all ~ creatures⟩ **2 a :** soaring with or as if with wings **:** LOFTY, ELEVATED ⟨free, passionate, ~ love — Sinclair Lewis⟩ **b :** SWIFT, RAPID ⟨the ~ days flew on —Winston Churchill⟩ ⟨~ gossip of the town —A.W.Long⟩

winged disk *n* **:** SUN DISK

winged elm *or* **wing elm** *n* **:** a No. American elm (*Ulmus alata*) having twigs and young branches with prominent corky projections

winged everlasting *n* **:** an Australian herb (*Ammobium alatum*) with white woolly foliage and winged stems

wing·ed·ly \'wiŋədlē\ *adv* **:** on or as if on the wing **:** LIGHTLY, SWIFTLY, EXALTEDLY

wing·ed·ness *n* -ES **:** the quality or state of having wings

winged pea *n* **:** a European annual herb (*Lotus tetragonolobus*) having a 4-winged edible pod

winged pigweed *n* **:** a bushy annual weed (*Cycloloma atriplicifolium*) of the family Chenopodiaceae of central No. America having the flowers greenish and the fruiting calyx horizontally winged

winged spindle tree *or* **winged euonymus** *n* **:** a shrub or small tree (*Euonymus alatus*) of China and Japan that has winged branches and is used as an ornamental

winged thistle *n* **:** an annual thistle (*Carduus tenuiflorus*) of New Zealand where it has become a troublesome weed because of its prolific seeding

winged yam *n* **:** WHITE YAM

wing·er \'wiŋə(r)\ *n* -s [¹*wing* + *-er*] **1 :** a cask stowed in the wing of a ship **2 :** a player in a wing position in football, soccer, rugby, hockey; *esp* **:** BREAKAWAY 6

wing feather *n* **:** one of the feathers of a bird's wing; *esp* **:** one of the flight feathers

wingfish \'ˌ=ˌ=\ *n* **:** a sea robin having large pectoral fins like wings

wing flap *n* **:** a hinged or pivoted and sometimes extensible portion of an airplane wing used to increase the lift and drag for making landings at reduced speeds

wing-footed \'ˌ=ˌ==\ *adj* **1 :** having winged feet **:** SWIFT, FLEET ⟨*wing-footed* messenger⟩ **2 :** having the anterior lobes of the foot so modified as to form a pair of winglike swimming organs — used of the pteropod mollusks

wing forward *n* **:** a position or player on the wing of a forward line in a team game (as soccer, rugby, or hockey); *esp* **:** BREAKAWAY 6

wing game *n, Brit* **:** GAME BIRDS — distinguished from *ground game*

wing gap *n* **:** GAP 4a(1)

wing half *or* **wing halfback** *n* **:** the right or left halfback in hockey or soccer or rugby

wingier *comparative of* WINGY

wingiest *superlative of* WINGY

winging *pres part of* WING

wing jam *n* **:** a jam of logs that slants upstream until the upper end rests against the shore

wing key *n* **:** BIT KEY

wing·less \'ˌ=ləs\ *adj* **1 :** having no wings ⟨~ insect⟩ **2 a :** incapable of flight ⟨~ bird⟩ **b :** slow-moving **:** PEDESTRIAN ⟨~ verse⟩ — **wing·less·ness** *n* -ES

wing·let \-lət\ *n* -s **1 :** a very small wing **2 :** BASTARD WING

winglike \'ˌ=ˌ=\ *adj* **:** resembling a wing in form or lateral position

wing loading *or* **wing load** *n* **:** the gross weight of an airplane fully loaded divided by the area of the supporting surface

wing louse *n* **:** a biting louse (*Lipeurus caponis*) that occurs on the wing feathers of poultry

wing·man \'ˌ=mən\ *n, pl* **wingmen :** a pilot that flies behind and outside the leader of a flying formation so as to furnish support or protection; *also* **:** the plane flown in this position

wing mite *n* **:** a feather mite (*Pterolichus obtusus*) that is parasitic on poultry

wing net *n* **:** a fishing stake net with side extensions

wing nut *n* **1 :** a nut with wings affording a grip for the thumb and finger **2 :** a tree of the genus *Pterocarya*

wing nut 1

wingover \'ˌ=ˌ==\ *n* -s [fr. the phrase *wing over*] **:** a flight maneuver in which a plane is put into a climbing turn until nearly stalled after which the nose is allowed to fall while the turn is continued until normal flight is attained in a direction opposite to that in which the maneuver was entered

wing pad *n* **:** the undeveloped wings of the active pupa of an insect

wing passage *n* **:** a passageway in a ship below the main deck next to a side

wing petal *n* **:** WING 2 l (2)

wingpiece \'ˌ=ˌ=\ *n* **:** a piece of scenery slid in from the wings

wing plow *n* **:** a snowplow with side extensions

wing quill *n* **:** one of the flight feathers of a bird's wing

wing rail *n* **:** either of the two outside rails of a railroad frog of which both are rigid in a rigid frog and one is hinged in a spring rail frog

wing roll *n* **:** rotation of an airplane on its longitudinal axis

wings \'wiŋz\ *n pl* **:** insignia consisting of an outspread pair of stylized bird's wings which with various superimposed devices are awarded usu. on completion of prescribed training (as to a qualified pilot, bombardier, gunner, navigator, observer, flight surgeon, or other crew member or a balloon pilot in the armed services) — called also *aviation badge*

wing scout *n* **:** a senior girl scout who is a member of a troop specializing in aviation

wing sheath *n* **:** ELYTRON

wing shell *n* **1** *obs* **:** ELYTRON **2 a :** any of various marine bivalves of the family Pteriidae and esp. the genus *Pteria* in which the hinge border projects like a wing **b :** a shell of the genus *Strombus* **c :** a pteropod shell **d :** a piddock shell

wing shooting *n* **:** the act or practice of shooting at game birds in flight or at flying targets

wing shot *n* **1 :** a shot at a flying bird or target **2 :** one skilled in wing shooting

wing skid *n* **:** a skid attached to an airplane wing near the tip to protect the wing from contact with the ground

wing slot *n* **:** an adjustable opening between either the leading edge of an aileron and the rest of a wing or the leading edge of a wing and a cap fitting over it

wing snail *n* **:** PTEROPOD

wingspan \'ˌ=ˌ=\ *n* [¹*wing* + *span*] **:** the length of an airplane wing measured between outermost tips regardless of intervening elements

wingspread \'ˌ=ˌ=\ *n* **:** the spread of the wings **:** WINGSPAN; *specif* **:** the extreme measurement between the tips or outer margins of the wings (as of a bird or insect) when fully extended or expanded

wingstem \'ˌ=ˌ=\ *n* [¹*wing* + *stem*] **1 :** GOLDEN IRONWEED **2 :** CROWNBEARD

wing three-quarter *n* **:** a rugby player positioned at either end of the three-quarter line; *also* **:** the position of such a player

wing tie *n* **:** a bow tie with flaring ends

wing tip *n* **1 :** a toecap having a point extending back toward the throat of the shoe and curving sides extending toward the shank **2 :** a shoe having a wing tip

wing-tip flare \'ˌ=ˌ=ˌ=\ *n* **:** an electrically operated light attached to the tips of airplane wings

wing-tip float *n* **:** a small float on the underside of a tip of the lower wing of a seaplane

wing top *n* **:** a wing-shaped metal top that fits on a Bunsen burner and gives a broad flat flame

wing tract *n* **:** the tract bearing the wing feathers including the primaries, secondaries, and wing coverts — compare PTERYLOSIS

wing transom *n* **:** the upper and outer transom of the stern frame of a ship

wing truss *n* **:** the structural frame comprising struts, wires or tie rods, and spars by which the wing loads of an airplane are transmitted to the fuselage

wing valve *n* **:** a check valve provided with wings to guide the valve to its seat

wing wale *n* **:** WING 7c

wing wall *n* **:** a subordinate lateral wall (as an abutment) or an oblique retaining wall (as of a bridge approach)

wingy \'wiŋē, -iŋi\ *adj* -ER/-EST **1 :** having wings **:** RAPID, SWIFT **2 :** soaring with or as if with wings **:** LOFTY **3 :** resembling or suggesting a wing in shape or position **:** WINGLIKE ⟨~ sleeves⟩

winier *comparative of* WINY

winiest *superlative of* WINY

wining *pres part of* WINE

win·ish \'wīnish\ *adj* [¹*wine* + *-ish*] **:** of, relating to, characteristic of, or resembling wine

¹**wink** \'wiŋk\ *vb* -ED/-ING/-S [ME *winken*, fr. OE *wincian*; akin to MD *winken* to stagger, wink, OHG *winchan* to stagger, wink, *wankōn* to stagger, totter, flicker, ON *vakka* to stray, hover, Lith *vengti* to avoid, Skt *vañgati* he limps — more at PREVARICATE] *vi* **1 a :** to close one's eyes ⟨kept my eyes shut . . . I ~*ed* as close as ever I could —Sir Walter Scott⟩ **b** *obs* **:** to take a nap **:** SLEEP **2 a :** to give a glance or sign with the eyes ⟨saw her mother ~ at her across the room and knew she would have to leave⟩ **b :** to shut one eye briefly in a teasing or jocular manner ⟨never did any harm to ~ at a pretty girl⟩ ⟨grinned and ~*ed* knowingly⟩ **3 :** to close and open the eyelids quickly and involuntarily ⟨staring at each other as if a bet were depending on the first man who ~*ed* —George Eliot⟩ **4 :** to avoid seeing or noting something as if by closing the eyes **:** CONNIVE — usu. used with *at* ⟨have ~*ed* at his frequent absences from school —George Sampson⟩ ⟨stubbornly refused to ~ at a violation of the law —Oscar Handlin⟩ **5 :** to gleam or flash fitfully or intermittently **:** FLICKER, TWINKLE ⟨at twilight, when the little fires ~ in the mountain dusk —E.W. Smith⟩ ⟨the house windows are ~*ing* with yellow lamplight —Phil Stong⟩ ⟨copper pans ~ on the walls —Katherine Mansfield⟩ **6 a :** to terminate suddenly **:** come to an end — usu. used with *out* ⟨when his employment . . . ~*ed* out he had bought a one-way ticket —Ellery Sedgwick⟩ ⟨the spark of enterprise has by no means ~*ed* out in this young generation —Dixon Wecter⟩ **b :** to stop shining — usu. used with *out* ⟨the lights ~*ed* out along the bridge —Elizabeth Enright⟩ **7 :** to signal a message with a light ⟨the destroyer was ~*ing* urgently —Vincent McHugh⟩ **~** *vt* **1 :** to cause to open and shut ⟨~*ed* his eyelids once or twice and squared his jaw —Donn Byrne⟩ **2 :** to affect or influence by or as if by blinking the eyes ⟨replied, shaking her head, ~*ing* back the tears —Frank Norris⟩ **3 :** to signal with (a light) esp. by blinking ⟨~*ing* their flashlights hopefully —M.W.Childs⟩ **4 :** to disregard or ignore intentionally ⟨there was no ~*ing* the matter: these two were enemies —Georgiana Pentlarge⟩

²**wink** \"\ *n* -s [ME, fr. *winken* to wink] **1 a :** a closing of the eyelids in or as if in sleep **:** a brief period of sleep **:** NAP ⟨sleep was one ~ —George Meredith⟩ ⟨I didn't get a ~ on the night —Hall Caine⟩ **b** *obs* **:** DEATH ⟨give mine enemy a lasting ~ —Shak.⟩ **2 a :** a glance or sign with or as if with the eyes usu. of admonition, command, direction, or invitation ⟨the bloke . . . tipped him the ~ —Richard Llewellyn⟩ ⟨had the ~ from Moscow —*New Republic*⟩ **b :** an act of winking; *esp* **:** the brief shutting of one eye ⟨a ~ of his eye and a twist of his head soon gave me to know I had nothing to dread —Clement Moore⟩ **3 a :** the time required to close and open an eye **:** an exceedingly brief period **:** INSTANT ⟨quick as a ~⟩ ⟨he was gone in a ~⟩ **b :** the smallest possible amount ⟨so dark, we couldn't see a ~⟩ ⟨an average of a ~ over 10 p.c. for the eighteen years —*Sydney (Australia) Bull.*⟩ **4 :** a quick closing and opening of the eyelids **:** BLINK ⟨several ~*s* brushed the tears away⟩ ⟨the eyelid . . . is likely to give a small reflex ~ to any sudden stimulus —R.S.Woodworth⟩ **5 :** an intermittent gleam **:** FLASH, SPARKLE ⟨the planes were little silver ~*s* way out to the west —Joseph Dever⟩ ⟨saw the ~ at her bow and thought she was signaling —Vincent McHugh⟩

³**wink** \"\ *n* -s [by shortening] *Brit* **:** ²PERIWINKLE

⁴**wink** \"\ *n* -s [short for *tiddledywink*] **:** a small disk used in the game tiddledywinks — called also *tiddledywink*

wink·er \-kə(r)\ *n* -s **:** one that winks: as **a :** a horse's blinder **:** BLINKER **b :** EYE ⟨just keep your ~*s* glued to me —*Metropolitan Mag.*⟩; *also* **:** EYELASH ⟨rolled his left eyelid up with careful fingers and . . . found the ~ —P.D.Boles⟩ **c :** CONCUSSION BELLOWS

winking cartilage *n* **:** the nictitating membrane when cartilaginous (as in a horse and various other mammals)

wink·ing·ly *adv* **:** in a winking manner

winking muscle *n* **:** the orbicularis of the eye that by its contraction draws the eyelids together

¹**win·kle** \'wiŋkəl\ *n* -s [short for *periwinkle*] **1 :** ²PERIWINKLE **2 :** any of various whelks esp. of the genus *Busycon* that destroy large numbers of oysters and clams by drilling their shells and rasping away their flesh

²**winkle** \"\ *vt* -ED/-ING/-S **:** to displace, extract, or evict from a position — usu. used with *out* ⟨failed to ~ out those two or three machine guns which were firing through some concealed opening —Peter Rainier⟩ ⟨the first year of nursing training ~*s* out most of the unsuitable subjects —Cormac Swan⟩

³**winkle** \"\ *vi* -ED/-ING/-S [¹*wink* + *-le*] **:** TWINKLE

winn \'win\ *chiefly Scot var of* ²WIND 3

win·na \ˌwinə\ [alter. (influenced by ¹*na*) of ME *winnot*, contr. of *will not*] *Scot* **:** will not

win·nable \'winəbəl\ *adj* **:** able to be won ⟨the war is not militarily ~ —Thomas Griffith⟩

win·nard \'winə(r)d\ *n* -s [prob. by shortening & alter. fr. G dial. *weingartdrossel* winnard, lit., vineyard thrush, fr. G *weingarten* vineyard (fr. MHG *wīngarte*, fr. *wīn* wine — fr. OHG — + *garte* garden, fr. OHG *garto*) + *drossel* thrush, fr. OHG *droscala* — more at WINE, YARD, THRUSH] *dial Eng* **:** the European redwing

win·ne·ba·go \ˌwinə'bā,gō\ *n, pl* **winnebago** *or* **winnebagos** *or* **winnebagoes** *usu cap* **1 a :** a Siouan people in eastern Wisconsin south of Green Bay **b :** a member of such people **2 :** the language of the Winnebago people

winned *past of* WIN

win·ner \'winə(r)\ *n* -s [ME, fr. *winnen* to win + *-er* — more at WIN] **:** one that wins: as **a :** one that is or will become successful esp. through praiseworthy ability and hard work **b :** a victor esp. in games and sports **c :** one that brings victory **d :** one that wins admiration ⟨a real ~ is her day costume —Lois Long⟩ **e :** FACEMAN **f :** a card that wins a trick or may be expected to win a trick **:** PLAYING TRICK

winner's circle *n* **:** an enclosure near a racetrack where the winning horse and jockey are brought for photographs and awards

win·nie \'winē, -ni\ *n* -s *usu cap* [*winner* + *-ie*] **:** any of several bronze statuettes awarded annually by a professional group for fashion design

¹**win·ning** \'winiŋ, -nēŋ\ *n* -s [ME, fr. gerund of *winnen* to win] **1 :** the act of one that wins **:** ACQUISITION, VICTORY ⟨the ~ of the peace —Norman Foerster⟩ **2 a :** a captured territory **:** CONQUEST ⟨the Antonine ~*s* . . . rose in revolt against the overstretched-out garrison —Jacquetta & Christopher Hawkes⟩ **3 :** the gaining esp. of a following or another's allegiance or trust ⟨the ~ of the people to his political beliefs⟩ **4 :** something one wins; *esp* **:** the money won by success in a competition **:** GAIN, PROFIT — usu. used in pl. ⟨gave . . . total ~*s* as $6119 —*Current Biog.*⟩ **5 a :** a shaft or pit opening made to win coal **b** (1) **:** a portion of a coal bed ready for mining (2) **:** a more or less isolated section of a mine

²**winning** \"\ *adj* [fr. pres. part. of ¹*win*] **1 a :** of, relating to, or used for or in the act of winning ⟨before a country is ready to relinquish any ~ weapons it must have more than words to reassure it —B.M.Baruch⟩ **b :** successful in competition ⟨a ~ team⟩ **2 :** adapted to win favor **:** ATTRACTIVE, CAPTIVATING, CHARMING ⟨an engaging modesty and a ~ sense of humor —R.M.Lovett⟩ ⟨a ~ rather than forceful personality —F.H.Ristine⟩ **syn** see SWEET

winning gallery *n* **:** a netted opening which is below the side penthouse, which is farthest from the dedans, and into which a played ball is counted as winning in court tennis

winning hazard *n* **:** a hazard in pool that pockets the object ball

win·ning·ly *adv* **:** in a winning manner ⟨smiled ~ —S.E. White⟩ ⟨the familiar theme is ~ presented —Caroline Tunstall⟩

win·ning·ness *n* -ES **:** the quality or state of being winning ⟨conscious of his charm, of the ~ of his personal style —Lionel Trilling⟩

winning opening *n* **:** the dedans, grille, or winning gallery of a court-tennis court

win·ni·nish *also* **win·no·nish** *n, pl* **win·ni·nish** *also* **win·no·nish** \ˌwinə'nish\ [Montagnais *wananish*, dim. of *wanans* salmon] **:** OUANANICHE

win·ni·peg \'winə,peg\ *adj, usu cap* [fr. *Winnipeg*, Manitoba] **:** of or from Winnipeg, the capital of Manitoba **:** of the kind or style prevalent in Winnipeg

win·ni·peg·ger \-gə(r)\ *n* -s *cap* [*Winnipeg* + E *-er*] **:** a native or resident of Winnipeg, Manitoba

¹**win·nock** \'winək\ *n* -s [ME (Sc) *windok*, *windowe* — more at WINDOW] *Scot* **:** WINDOW ⟨the doors and ~*s* rattle —Robert Burns⟩

²**winnock** \"\ *var of* WHINNOCK

¹**win·now** \'wi(,)nō, -,nə, *often* -ˌəw+V\ *vb* -ED/-ING/-S [ME *winewen*, *windewen*, fr. OE *windwian* to fan, winnow; akin to OHG *wintōn* to fan, winnow, Goth *diswinthjan*, L *ventilare* to fan, winnow, *vannus* winnowing fan, *ventus* wind — more at WIND] *vt* **1 a** (1) **:** to separate and drive off (as chaff) by subjection to wind or a current of air (2) **:** to get rid of (as that which is undesirable or unwanted) **:** take out **:** DELETE, REMOVE — often used with *out* ⟨~ out certain inaccuracies —Stanley Walker⟩ **b :** to analyze and assort to obtain the most desirable **:** SELECT, SEPARATE, SIFT ⟨~*ed* out facts and probabilities from prejudices —William Vogt⟩ ⟨an old hand at ~*ing* what is true and significant —Oscar Lewis⟩ **2 a :** to treat (as grain) by exposure to wind or a current of air so that waste matter is eliminated ⟨when the grain was flailed they ~*ed* it —Pearl Buck⟩ **b :** to treat in a manner resembling this **:** free of useless, unwanted, or baser components ⟨~ the immense number of applications —W.H.Hale⟩ ⟨the lack of discipline and the failure to ~ her material —Dachine Rainer⟩ **3 :** to beat with or as if with wings **:** make a way through by flying ⟨geese ~*ing* the purple dusk⟩ **4 :** to blow on **:** FAN ⟨the wind ~*ing* his thin white hair —*Time*⟩ **~** *vi* **1 a :** to separate chaff from grain by fanning **b :** to separate the desirable from the undesirable by careful perusing ⟨appointed an editor to ~ through the day's diplomatic dispatches and produce a daily news file —W.M.Healy⟩ **2 :** to move or pass on a course with or as if with wings ⟨the petrel . . . came ~*ing* in from afar on the sea —D.L.Sharp⟩ **3 :** to blow in gusts

²**winnow** \"\ *n* -s **1 :** a device for winnowing **2 :** the act of winnowing **:** a motion resembling that of winnowing

win·now·er \-,nəwə(r)\ *n* -s [ME *winewer*, fr. *winewen* to winnow + *-er*] **:** one that winnows; *esp* **:** a winnowing machine

winnowing basket *or* **winnowing-fan** \'ˌ==ˌ=ˌ=\ *n* **1 :** a device for winnowing grain **2 :** a representation of a winnowing basket used as a heraldic design

wi·no \'wī,nō\ *n* -s [¹*wine* + *-o*] **:** one who is chronically addicted to drinking wine

winrace \'ˌ=ˌ=\ *n* [fr. the phrase *win* (the) *race*] **:** the fastest time made by the winning horse in a public trotting race

winrow *var of* WINDROW

wins *pres 3d sing of* WIN, *pl of* WIN

winsey *var of* WINCEY

wins·low's foramen \'winz,lōz-\ *n, usu cap W* [after Jacques B. *Winslow* †1760 Fr. anatomist] **:** EPIPLOIC FORAMEN

wins·low system \'winz,lō-\ *n, usu cap W* [after Thomas Newby *Winslow* †1942 Am. lawyer, mathematician, and bridge expert] **:** a method of bidding at contract bridge based upon valuation of an ace as 1½ probable tricks, king 1, queen ½, and jack ¼ and on the principle that the lowest-ranking four-card suit regardless of its high-card content should be bid first

win·some \'win(t)səm\ *adj, sometimes* -ER/-EST [ME *wonsom*, *wunsum*, fr. OE *wynsum*, fr. *wynn* joy, pleasure (akin to OS *wunnia* joy, pleasure, OHG *wunna*, *wunnī*) + *-sum* -some; akin to L *venus* love — more at WIN] **1 :** causing joy or pleasure **:** AGREEABLE, PLEASANT, WINNING ⟨~ tableaux of old-fashioned literary days —J.D.Hart⟩ ⟨the wide-eyed and ~ lass —*Current Biog.*⟩ **2 :** very lighthearted **:** CHEERFUL, GAY ⟨misled by ill example and a ~ nature —Francis Jeffrey⟩ **syn** see SWEET

win·some·ly *adv* **:** in a winsome manner

win·some·ness *n* -ES **:** the quality or state of being winsome ⟨the calculating ~ of a man who is spoiled by the ladies —Kenneth Roberts⟩

¹**win·ter** \'wintə(r)\ *n* -s *often attrib* [ME, fr. OE; akin to OHG *wintar*, ON *vetr*, Goth *wintrus*, and prob. to OE *wæter* water — more at WATER] **1 a :** the season between autumn and spring reckoned astronomically as extending from the December solstice to the March equinox **b :** the season comprising the months of December, January, and February **c** *Brit* **:** the season comprising the months of November, December, and January **d :** the colder half of the year — contrasted with *summer* **e :** the rainy season in the tropics **f :** the season reckoned astronomically in the southern hemisphere as extending from the June solstice to the September equinox **2 :** YEAR ⟨happened many ~*s* ago⟩; *esp* **:** one of the years of one's life ⟨a man of 70 ~*s*⟩ **3 :** a period felt to resemble winter esp. in being marked by dreariness, lack of activity, adversity, or decay **4** [*winter yellowlegs*] *chiefly NewEng* **:** GREATER YELLOWLEGS

²**winter** \"\ *vb* **wintered; wintered; wintering** \-ntəriŋ, -n·triŋ\ **winters** [ME *wintren*, fr. ¹*winter*] *vi* **1 :** to pass the winter ⟨~ in the city⟩ ⟨bears ~*ing* in a rocky den⟩ **2 :** to feed or find food during the winter — used with *on* ⟨small birds ~*ing* on the seeds of weeds and grasses⟩ **~** *vt* **1 :** to keep, feed, or manage during the winter ⟨~ young cattle on straw⟩ **2 :** to affect like winter **:** give a wintery aspect to **3 :** WINTERIZE

win·tera \'wintərə\ *n, cap* [NL, after John *Wynter* (or *Winter*), 16th cent. Brit. naval officer] **:** the type genus of the family Winteraceae

win·ter·a·ce·ae \ˌ==ˌ='rāsē,ē\ *n pl, cap* [NL, fr. *Wintera*, type genus + *-aceae*] **:** a small family of chiefly tropical shrubs and trees (order Ranales) characterized by alternate aromatic pellucid-dotted leaves without stipules and rather small usu. cymose or fasciculate flowers with a single whorl of carpels and sometimes included in Magnoliaceae

winter aconite *n* **:** a small Old World perennial herb (*Eranthis hyemalis*) often cultivated for its bright yellow flowers which often are produced before the snow is off the ground

winter annual *n* **:** a plant that germinates in autumn, lives through the winter, and produces seed and dies in the following season

winter apple *n* **:** a late-ripening apple that keeps well in winter

winter band *n* **:** the annulus of a fish scale

winter barley *n* **:** barley that is sown in the fall and ripens during the following spring or summer

winter beer *n* **:** SCHENK BEER

winterberry \'ˌ=ˌ= — *see* BERRY\ *n* **:** any of various American plants of the genus *Ilex* having bright red berries persistent through the winter: as **a :** BLACK ALDER 1 **b :** SMOOTH WINTERBERRY

winter bird *n* **:** any of several birds seen chiefly in winter; *esp* **:** ATLANTIC KITTIWAKE
winterbloom \ˈ==,=\ *n* **1 :** WITCH HAZEL 2a **2 :** AZALEA
winter bonnet *n, dial Brit* **:** a European gull (*Larus canus*)
winterbound \ˈ==,=\ *adj* **:** restrained (as from a favored sport or other outdoor activity) by winter
winterbourne \ˈ==,=\ *n* **:** a stream that flows only or chiefly in winter
winter bud *n* **1 :** STATOBLAST **2 :** the dormant much condensed shoot of a woody plant enclosed in protective scales or covering that enable it to survive the winter
winter bunting *n* **:** SNOW BUNTING
winter cabbage *n* **:** any of various cabbages that will survive the winter in the open in mild regions (as the southern U.S.); *esp* **:** SAVOY 1
winter cauliflower *n* **:** BROCCOLI 1
winter cherry *n* **1 a :** CHINESE LANTERN PLANT **b :** the fruit of this plant **2 :** BALLOON VINE **3 :** JERUSALEM CHERRY
winter chip bird *n* **:** TREE SPARROW 2
winter-clad \¦==¦=\ *adj* **:** clothed suitably for winter
winter count *n* **:** a calendar or year record of the No. American Indians involving pictographic accounts of events and serving as tribal chronicles
winter crane fly *n* **:** a fly of the family Trichoceratidae often appearing in swarms during fall, winter, and spring
wintercreeper \ˈ==,==\ *n* **:** an evergreen shrubby, trailing, or climbing euonymus (*Euonymus fortunei*) that is widely cultivated as an ornamental in several horticultural varieties differing chiefly in habit or in form or color of leaves
winter cress *n* [prob. trans. of D *winterkers*] **:** any of several Eurasian yellow-flowered cresses constituting the genus *Barbarea* and sometimes cultivated for winter salad
winter crookneck *n* **:** any of several crooknecks that are winter squashes of the pumpkin group, are noted for their keeping qualities, and usu. have smooth variously striped rinds — compare SUMMER CROOKNECK
winter crop *n* **:** a crop (as of oats) fall-sown for growth during the winter and maturing in the spring
winter daffodil *n* **:** an autumn-blooming perennial herb (*Sternbergia lutea*) of the Mediterranean region having solitary yellow flowers and being often grown as an ornamental
winter duck *n* **1** *Brit* **:** PINTAIL 1a **2 :** OLD SQUAW
wintered *adj* [fr. past part. of ²*winter*] **:** subjected to the action of wintery conditions **:** chilled or altered by exposure to winter
winter egg *n* **:** a thick-shelled usu. sexually produced egg of many and esp. freshwater invertebrates that lives through the winter and hatches in the spring — compare SUMMER EGG
win·ter·er \ˈwintərə(r), -n·trə(r)\ *n* -S **:** one that winters: as **a :** a winter resident or visitor ⟨the southern ~*s*⟩ ⟨some birds are coastal ~*s*⟩ **b** *archaic* **:** an animal taken in charge through a winter **c :** a fur trader's employee formerly remaining in Indian country throughout the winter
winter-fallow \¦==¦==\ *vt* [¹*winter* + *fallow*, v.] **:** to fallow in the winter
winter fallow *n* [¹*winter* + *fallow*, n.] **:** ground fallowed in winter
winter fat *n* **:** a tomentose shrub (*Eurotia lanata*) of the family Chenopodiaceae that is common in parts of the southwestern U.S. and yields valuable forage to stock — called also *white sage, winter sage*
¹**winterfeed** \¦==¦=\ *vb* [¹*winter* + *feed*, v.] *vt* **1 :** to provide (as cattle) with feed to supplement or replace pasturage during the winter **2 :** to feed out (as grain) to livestock during the winter **~** *vi* **:** to winterfeed grain or livestock ⟨had to ~ because of the heavy storms⟩
²**winterfeed** \"\ *n* [¹*winter* + *feed*, n.] **:** livestock feed for winter use ⟨~ for 50 head⟩
winter flounder *n* **:** a rusty brown often red-spotted flounder (*Pseudopleuronectes americanus*) of northeastern No. America that is an important market fish esp. in winter
winter garden *n* **:** a garden maintained in winter whether outdoors or in a conservatory
winter golf *n* **:** golf played under special rules that permit a player to improve the lie of his ball when on the fairway
winter grape *n* **:** CHICKEN GRAPE
winter grass *n* **:** any of several grasses that provide winter grazing or forage
win·ter·green \ˈwintə(r),grēn\ *n* [trans. of D *wintergroen*] **1 :** a plant of the genus *Pyrola; esp* **:** a plant (*P. minor*) of northern latitudes that has small round basal evergreen leaves — see SHINLEAF **2 a :** any of various plants of the genus *Gaultheria; esp* **:** a low evergreen No. American herb (*G. procumbens*) with white bell-shaped flowers followed by spicy red berries and shining aromatic leaves that yield a useful oil — see CHECKERBERRY, WINTERGREEN OIL **b :** the flavor of wintergreen oil; *also* **:** something (as a lozenge) flavored with this oil **3 :** PIPSISSEWA **4 :** a dark yellowish green that is duller and slightly greener than holly green (sense 1), greener, lighter, and stronger than deep chrome green, greener and duller than golf green, and greener and slightly lighter than average hunter green — compare WINTER GREEN
winter green *n* [¹*winter* + *green*] **:** a moderate yellowish green that is deeper than tarragon, yellower and duller than malachite green, and yellower and deeper than verdigris — compare WINTERGREEN
wintergreen barberry *n* **:** a Chinese evergreen shrub (*Berberis julianae*) that is used as an ornamental and has glabrous branchlets, 3-parted spines, acute spiny-toothed leaves, and black fruit
wintergreen family *n* **:** PYROLACEAE
wintergreen oil *n* **1 :** a colorless, yellowish, or reddish aromatic essential oil obtained from macerated leaves of wintergreen, composed principally of methyl salicylate, and used similarly — called also *gaultheria oil;* compare BIRCH OIL 2 **2 :** METHYL SALICYLATE
winter gull *n, Brit* **:** a common European gull (*Larus canus*) — called also *winter mew*
winter-habited \¦==¦habədəd\ *adj* **:** having growth of such a character as to require a period of cold weather to mature and produce seed — used esp. of a winter wheat; compare SPRING-HABITED
winter hail *n* **:** hail consisting of small pellets of ice that are frozen raindrops from nimbus clouds — compare SUMMER HAIL
winterhain \ˈ==¦=\ *vi* -ED/-ING/-S *dial Brit* **:** to let pasture lie without cattle in winter esp. in order to take off a crop of hay in the spring
winterhardiness \¦==¦===\ *n* **:** the quality or state of being winter-hardy
winter-hardy \¦==¦==\ *adj* **:** hardy in respect to winter conditions; *esp* **:** able to withstand much cold ⟨*winter-hardy* chrysanthemums⟩
winter hawk *n* **:** RED-SHOULDERED HAWK
winter hazel *n* **:** any of several Asiatic deciduous shrubs or small trees (genus *Corylopsis*) that are closely related to the witch hazels and are sometimes cultivated for their yellow flowers which appear in nodding racemes subtended by large bracts before the unfolding of the leaves — called also *flowering hazel*
winter heath *or* **winter heather** *n* **:** SPRING HEATH
winter heliotrope *n* **:** a European sweet coltsfoot (*Petasites fragrans*) with lilac flower heads
winter honeysuckle *n* **:** a widely cultivated half-evergreen Chinese shrub (*Lonicera fragrantissima*) with stiff leathery leaves and very fragrant creamy-white flowers borne in winter or early spring and followed by red fruits
winter huckleberry *n* **:** FARKLEBERRY
winterier *comparative of* WINTERY
winteriest *superlative of* WINTERY
wintering *pres part of* WINTER
winter injury *n* **:** injury to plants (as woody plants) occurring in winter and caused usu. directly by low temperatures, by lack of water, or by the effect of winter winds
win·ter·ish \ˈwintərish, -n·trish\ *adj* [¹*winter* + *-ish*] **:** suitable to winter **:** suggestive of winter **:** somewhat wintry — **win·ter·ish·ly** *adv*
winter itch *n* **:** an itching disorder affecting some persons in winter esp. in a dry climate
win·ter·iza·tion \ˌwintərəˈzāshən, -ə,rīˈz-\ *n* -S **1 :** the quality or state of being winterized **2 :** the act or process of winterizing
win·ter·ize \ˈ==,rīz\ *vt* -ED/-ING/-S [¹*winter* + *-ize*] **:** to make ready for winter or winter use and esp. resistant or proof against the freezing temperature, wind, and snow of winter: as **a :** to treat (a fatty oil) by cooling so that a solid portion is precipitated and then filtering **:** DESTEARINATE **b :** to make (as an automobile) ready or safe for use in freezing weather with deicers, special lubricants, antifreeze, and similar equipment **c :** to outfit (as a weapon) with protective coverings or equipment against freezing weather
winter jasmine *n* **:** a trailing Chinese shrub (*Jasminum nudiflorum*) that is often used as an ornamental and has green stems and bright yellow flowers
winter-kill \ˈ==¦=\ *vt* **:** to cause the death of (as plants) by exposure to winter conditions **~** *vi* **:** to die as a result of exposure to winter conditions and esp. to conditions of unusual severity ⟨the wheat *winter-killed* badly during the dry open winter⟩
winterkill \"\ *n* [*winter-kill*] **:** mortality resulting from severe winter conditions (as of fish by smothering in an ice-covered shallow lake)
winter leaf *n* **:** SEDGE 3
win·ter·less \ˈ== ləs\ *adj* **:** free from winter **:** not characterized by wintery conditions (as of weather)
winter lettuce *n* **:** ENDIVE
winterlong \¦==¦=\ *adj* [ME, fr. ¹*winter* + *long*] **:** excessively or tiresomely long
win·ter·ly *adj* [¹*winter* + *-ly*] **:** of or resembling winter **:** occurring in winter **:** suitable to winter **:** WINTRY, CHEERLESS
winter melon *n* **:** a muskmelon (*Cucumis melo inodorus*) having a smooth rind and a sweet white or greenish flesh that lacks a musky aroma
winter mew *n, Brit* **:** WINTER GULL
winter midge *n* **:** any of various flies that sometimes appear in numbers or in swarms in winter; *esp* **:** WINTER CRANE FLY
winter moth *n* **:** any of several geometrid moths (as *Operophtera brumata* or *Erannis tiliaria*) in which the females are often wingless
winter oats *n pl but sing or pl in constr* **:** any of various oats that are sown in the fall and harvested early the following summer
winter oil *n* **:** oil prepared so as not to solidify or become cloudy in moderately cold weather: as **a :** cottonseed oil deprived of the stearin **b :** a relatively thin lubricating oil
winter onion *n* **:** any of several garden onions that persist from year to year, usu. form small bulbs, and are used chiefly for early salad onions
winter pause *n* **:** a more or less prolonged period occurring in winter between successive cycles of the egg-laying of a domestic fowl
winterpea \ˈ==,=\ *n* **:** a peavine (*Lathyrus hirsutus*) with densely silky pods that is native to the Mediterranean region but introduced into the U.S. as a green manure or winter forage crop
winter pear *n* **:** a late-ripening pear that keeps well in winter
winter plum *n* **:** PERSIMMON 1a; *also* **:** the fruit of this tree
winter-proud \¦==¦=\ *adj, chiefly Brit* **:** prematurely grown or luxuriant — used of a fall-sown crop
winter purslane *n* **1 :** an Indian lettuce (*Montia perfoliata*) **2 :** PURSLANE SPEEDWELL
winter quarters *n pl but sing or pl in constr* **:** a winter residence or station (as of a military unit or a circus)
winter radish *n* **:** any of various cultivated radishes (as the daikons) mostly of oriental origin that have large compact firm-fleshed roots which may be kept through much of the winter
winter rape *n* **:** ²RAPE 2
winter rose *n* **1 :** CHRISTMAS ROSE **2 :** any of various late-blooming roses of the hybrid perpetual type
winter rye *n* **:** any of various ryes that are sown in the fall and harvested early in the following summer
winters *pl of* WINTER, *pres 3d sing of* WINTER
winter sage *n* **:** WINTER FAT
winter savory *n* **:** a perennial savory (*Satureia montana*) that is an erect subshrub with coriaceous lanceolate-linear leaves and pink or white flowers and that has been cultivated for its foliage which has a flavor of thyme
winter's bark *n, often cap W* [after John *Wynter* (or *Winter*), 16th cent. Brit. naval officer] **1 :** an aromatic bark with tonic and stimulant properties **2 :** an evergreen tree (*Drimys winteri*) found from Mexico southward throughout So. America and yielding winter's bark and a light soft straight-grained brown wood that somewhat resembles and is used similarly to basswood
winter sheldrake *n* **:** GOOSANDER
winter skate *n* **:** a skate (*Raja diaphanes*) of the Atlantic coast of the U.S. closely resembling the little skate but of a lighter color and somewhat larger size
winter sleep *n* **:** HIBERNATION
winter snipe *n* **:** an American red-backed sandpiper (*Erolia alpina pacifica*)
winter solstice *n* **1 :** the point in the sky occupied by the sun on or about December 22d when winter begins in the northern hemisphere **:** the December solstice **2 :** the time at which the sun reaches the December solstice for dwellers in the northern hemisphere or the June solstice for those in the southern hemisphere
winter spore *n* **:** a resting spore that serves to carry a plant over the winter — compare SUMMER SPORE
winter squash *n* **:** any of various squashes derived from a natural species (*Cucurbita maxima*) or pumpkins from a species (*C. moschata*) that are used chiefly as table vegetables when fully mature and are capable of withstanding storage for several months — compare SUMMER SQUASH
winter sucker *n* **:** SPOTTED SUCKER 1
winter sunscald *n* **:** sunscald of woody plants occurring in winter and caused by freezing of areas of bark and the underlying tissues esp. on the sun-exposed side which is exposed to wide daily temperature variation
winter sweet *n* **1 a :** WILD MARJORAM **b :** CRETAN DITTANY **2 :** JAPAN ALLSPICE **3 :** an ornamental African shrub or small tree (*Acocanthera spectabilis*) of the family Apocynaceae growing in warm countries and having thick leathery leaves, white or pink flowers, and globose purplish black fruit
winter sweet pea *n* **:** DARLING PEA
winter teal *n* **:** GREENWING
winter tick *n* **:** an ixodid tick (*Dermacentor albipictus*) that is actively parasitic during the winter months on domestic and big-game animals in parts of western U.S. and Canada
wintertide \ˈ==,=\ *n* [ME, fr. OE *wintertīd*, fr. ¹*winter* + *tīd* — more at TIDE] **:** the season of winter **:** WINTERTIME
wintertime \ˈ==,=\ *n* [ME, fr. ¹*winter* + *time*] **:** the period when wintry weather prevails **:** WINTER
winter vetch *n* **:** HAIRY VETCH
winter wagtail *n* **:** GRAY WAGTAIL
win·ter·ward \ˈ== ,wə(r)d\ *also* **win·ter·wards** \-dz\ *adv* [¹*winter* + *-ward*, *-wards*] **:** in the direction of winter
winterweed \ˈ==,=\ *n* **:** a weedy plant that remains green during winter: as **a :** a common chickweed (*Stellaria media*) **b :** IVY-LEAVED SPEEDWELL
winter wheat *n* **:** a wheat that is sown in autumn and ripens the following spring or summer
winter wren *n* **:** a very small wren (*Troglodytes troglodytes hiemalis*) of the coniferous forests of the northern U.S. and Canada that migrates southward in winter, is dark cinnamon brown barred with black, and is the American representative of the common European wren
winter yellowlegs *n pl but sing or pl in constr* **:** GREATER YELLOWLEGS
win through *vi* **:** to survive difficulties and reach a desired or satisfactory end ⟨his strong constitution *won through* to recovery⟩ ⟨only the greatest efforts would allow them to *win through* to the headwaters of the river⟩
win·tle \ˈwintᵊl\ *vi* [perh. fr. Flem *windtelen* to roll, reel; akin to MD *wentelen* to roll] *Scot* **:** STAGGER, REEL, WRIGGLE, ROLL
win to *vi, chiefly Scot* **:** to begin to eat **:** fall to
win·ton disease \ˈwintᵊn-, -tən-\ *n, usu cap W* [prob. fr. *Winton*, town in southern South Island, New Zealand] **:** cirrhosis of the liver in horses and cattle resulting from the chronic poisoning by toxic constituents of ragworts and other noxious plants eaten in the pasturage — compare WALKABOUT DISEASE
win·tri·ly \ˈwin·trəlē, -li\ *adv* **:** in a wintry manner **:** so as to be wintry
win·tri·ness \-trēnəs, -trin-\ *n* -ES **:** the quality or state of being wintry
win·try \-trē, -ri\ *or* **win·tery** \-ntərē, -n·trē, -ri\ *adj* -ER/-EST [*winter* + *-y*] **1** *archaic* **:** of, relating to, occurring in, or suitable to winter **2 :** resembling or characteristic of winter **:** HIEMAL, COLD, STORMY ⟨was subjected to severe ~ weather⟩ **3 a :** subjected to the action of winter **:** weathered by winter ⟨brown ~ grasses⟩ **b :** seeming as if affected by winter **:** AGED, WHITE, CHILLING, CHEERLESS ⟨a ~ smile⟩
win·tun \(ˈ)win·¦tün\ *or* **win·tu** \-ü\ *n, pl* **wintun** *or* **wintuns** *or* **wintu** *or* **wintus** *usu cap* [Wintun, people] **1 a :** an Indian people of the Sacramento valley, California **b :** a member of such people **2 :** a Copehan language of the Wintun people **3 :** COPEHAN 1
winy *or* **winey** \ˈwīnē, -ni\ *adj* **winier; winiest** [ME *wyny*, fr. *win, wyn* wine + *-y*] **1 a :** having the taste or qualities of wine **:** resembling wine **:** VINOUS ⟨grapes of a ~ taste⟩ ⟨a ~ color⟩ **b** *of the air* **:** crisply fresh and fragrant ⟨~ autumn skies⟩ **2 :** influenced or affected by wine or spirits **:** DRUNKEN
¹**winze** \ˈwinz\ *n* -S [alter. of earlier *winds*, prob. fr. *winds*, pl. of ⁵*wind*] **:** a vertical or steeply inclined opening or passageway driven to connect one mine working place with another at a lower level
²**winze** \"\ *n* [Flem or D *wensch* wish, fr. MD, fr. *wenschen* to wish; akin to OHG *wunsken* to wish — more at WISH] *Scot* **:** CURSE
¹**wipe** \ˈwīp\ *vb* -ED/-ING/-S [ME *wipen*, fr. OE *wīpian;* akin to OHG *wīfan* to swing, wind around, *weif* bandage, ON *veipr* head covering, Goth *weipan* to crown, *wipja* crown, L *vibrare* to vibrate, Skt *vepate* he trembles, it vibrates] *vt* **1 a :** to rub with or as if with something soft for cleaning or drying ⟨*wiped* his nose with his handkerchief⟩ ⟨~ the enamel with a damp cloth⟩ **b :** to clean or dry by rubbing ⟨~ your shoes before going in⟩ — usu. used with *on* ⟨*wiped* his hands on the grass⟩ **c :** to draw, pass, or move for or as if for rubbing or cleaning ⟨*wiped* his hand across his forehead⟩ ⟨*wiping* a soft cloth back and forth over the waxed surface⟩ **2 a :** to remove by or as if by rubbing ⟨~ the tears off⟩ ⟨*wiping* off the spilled oil⟩ ⟨*wiped* the smudge away with his hand⟩ ⟨~ out what you have written⟩ **b :** to completely expunge **:** OBLITERATE, ABOLISH, CANCEL ⟨his heroic end *wiped* his foolish life from human memory⟩: as (1) **:** to cause to cease to exist **:** ANNIHILATE — usu. used with *out* ⟨the enemy *wiped* out the defending force⟩ (2) **:** to terminate by or as if by payment — usu. used with *off* or *out* ⟨received money to ~ off most of his debts⟩ ⟨past dishonor *wiped* out by valiant deeds⟩ (3) **:** to exhaust (a margin) on an exchange — used with *out* ⟨the fall in prices *wiped* out his margin⟩ **3 a** *chiefly dial* **:** to punish either with physical violence or stern censure; *usu* **:** STRIKE, BEAT, DRUB **b** *obs* **:** CHEAT, DEFRAUD, TRICK **4 a :** to spread in a thin and rather uniform layer by or as if by wiping ⟨~ a coating of heavy grease over all exposed surfaces⟩ **b :** to form (a joint between lead pipes) by applying solder in repeated increments that are individually spread and shaped with greased cloth pads **~** *vi* **:** to make a motion of or like that of wiping something ⟨she *wiped* vigorously but the stain remained⟩ **syn** see EXTERMINATE — **wipe one's boots on :** to treat with indignity **:** withhold respect from — **wipe one's eye 1 :** to get in ahead of one; *esp* **:** to shoot game another has aimed at **2 :** to take the conceit out of one — **wipe the floor with** *or* **wipe the ground with :** to defeat decisively
²**wipe** \"\ *n* -S **1 a** (1) **:** BLOW, STRIKE, SWIPE (2) *obs* **:** a mark from or as if from a blow **b :** a harsh sarcastic remark **:** GIBE, JEER **2 :** an act or instance of wiping ⟨give the table a ~ with your cloth⟩ **3 a** *slang* **:** HANDKERCHIEF **b :** WIPER a(3) **c :** a small surgical sponge (as of gauze or cellulose) **4** *or* **wipe off :** a transitional effect during a projected picture whereby one scene progressively replaces another as a boundary line moves across vertically, horizontally, or in some special pattern
wipe break *or* **wipe breaker** *n* **:** an electrical interrupter consisting essentially of one or more wipers revolving against contact pieces
wipe joint *n* **:** a wiped plumbing joint
wip·er \ˈwīpə(r)\ *n* -S **:** one that wipes: **a** (1) **:** something (as a towel or sponge) used for wiping (2) *slang* **:** HANDKERCHIEF (3) **:** a projecting tooth, tumbler, eccentric, tappet, or cam on a rotating or oscillating piece used esp. for raising a stamper, the helve of a power hammer, or other part intended to fall by its own weight (4) *or* **wiper ring :** RING OILER (5) **:** a rod or an attachment to hold a rag for wiping out the bore of the barrel of a firearm (6) **:** a moving contact for making connections with the terminals of an electrical device (as a rheostat) — compare ³BRUSH 3a **b** (1) **:** a roundhouse employee who cleans locomotives (2) **:** a worker who removes dirt and grease from machinery (as in a shop or engine room) (3) **:** a worker who with an asbestos pad wipes surplus aluminum from the sealed joints of glass bricks
wiper shaft *n* **:** a shaft carrying a wiper or a wiper wheel on machinery
wiper wheel *n* **:** a wheel (as in a trip hammer) with wipers on its rim
wipe up *vt* **:** to make clean by or as if by wiping **:** MOP UP, DEFEAT, DESTROY
wiping contact *n* [*wiping* (gerund of ¹*wipe*) + *contact*] **:** an electric contact made by wiping or rubbing one surface on another
wiping rod *n* **:** WIPER a(5)
wir \(ˈ)wir\ *adj* [by alter.] *Scot & dial Eng* **:** OUR
wir·able \ˈwīrəbəl\ *adj* **:** capable of being wired
¹**wire** \ˈwī(ə)r, -īə\ *n* -S *often attrib* [ME, fr. OE *wīr;* akin to ON *vīravirki* wirework, filigree, OHG *wiara* fine gold, L *viēre* to twist together, plait, Gk *iris* rainbow; basic meaning: bend, turn] **1 a :** metal in the form of a usu. very flexible thread or slender rod **b :** a thread or rod of such material — compare CORD 3b **2 :** the strings of a musical instrument; *broadly* **:** STRINGED INSTRUMENT **3 a :** WIREWORK; *esp* **:** WOVEN WIRE ⟨screen ~⟩ **b :** the meshwork of parallel or woven wire on which the wet web of paper forms and is drained **4 :** a wire-like thing (as a thin plant stem or a hair); *specif* **:** BINE, STOLON 1a ⟨hop ~*s*⟩ ⟨strawberry ~*s*⟩ **5** *usu* **wires** *pl* **a :** a system of wires used to operate the puppets in a puppet show **b :** the network of hidden influences controlling the action of a person or organization ⟨pull the ~*s* for office⟩ **6 a :** a line of wire for conducting electrical current — compare CORD 3b **b** (1) **:** a telegraph wire or cable (2) **:** a telegraph system ⟨send a message by ~⟩ ⟨the ~*s* of Europe were hot with telegrams —C.E. Black & E.C.Helmreich⟩ (3) **:** TELEGRAM, CABLEGRAM ⟨send a ~⟩ ⟨~ news⟩ **c :** a telephone wire or system ⟨heard a familiar voice over the ~⟩ ⟨as soon as she could get that man off the ~ —F.M.Ford⟩ **7 :** a metal snare (as for rabbits) **8** *Scot* **:** KNITTING NEEDLE **9** *slang* **:** PICKPOCKET; *esp* **:** the member of a pickpocket team who picks the victim's pocket **10 :** fencing or a fence of barbed wire ⟨a horse cut by ~⟩ ⟨behind the ~ of a prison stockade⟩; *also* **:** a barbed wire entanglement (as on a battlefield) **11 :** WIRE ROPE **12 :** a wire-haired dog **13 :** a wire strung high between the winning posts between which the horses pass at the finish of a race ⟨finished a dismal last at the ~ —F.M.Blunk⟩; *broadly* **:** the finish line of a race ⟨as the campaign goes down to the ~ —Elmo Roper & Louis Harris⟩ **14 :** a wire on which acrobats perform ⟨~ act⟩ ⟨~ walker⟩ — see HIGH WIRE, SLACK WIRE, TIGHTWIRE **15 a :** a long rod or strip of metal with a smooth or cutting edge used in the formation of looped or cut pile in carpet weaving **b :** the fineness of carpets measured by the number of rows of tufts per inch **16 :** metal thread or rod used in surgery to suture soft tissue or transfix fractured bone — compare TANTALUM GAUZE **17 :** information surreptitiously or privately exchanged between gamblers (as by a signal) **18 :** magnetic recording wire — **under the wire** *adv (or adj)* **1 :** at the finish line ⟨the third horse *under the wire*⟩ **2 :** before a deadline **:** at the last moment ⟨pay one's taxes just *under the wire*⟩ — **under wire :** fenced with barbed wire ⟨six sections *under wire*⟩
²**wire** \"\ *vb* -ED/-ING/-S [ME *wiren*, fr. ¹*wire*] *vt* **1 :** to provide with wire **:** use wire on for any purpose **:** string, stiffen, or connect with wire ⟨~ corks in bottles⟩ ⟨~ a skeleton⟩ ⟨~ beads⟩ ⟨~ a fence⟩ ⟨~ a hat⟩ ⟨~ a house for electricity⟩ ⟨~ electric lights together⟩ **2 :** to snare by means of a wire ⟨~ a rabbit⟩ **3 :** to send or send word to by telegraph ⟨~ me the

news⟩ **4 :** to place (a croquet ball) behind the wire of an arch thus preventing a successful shot **~** *vi* **:** to send a telegraphic message ⟨~ home for money⟩
wire agency *n* **:** WIRE SERVICE
wirebar \ˈ=ˌ=\ *n* **:** a cast bar of metal ready for making into wire
wirebird \ˈ=ˌ=\ *n* [so called fr. the wire grass in which it lives] **:** a plover (*Charadrius sanctaehelenae*) of the island of St. Helena
wire bridge *n* **:** a bridge suspended from wire cables
wire brush *n* **:** ³BRUSH 1b
wire cloth *n* **:** a fabric of woven metallic wire (as for strainers)
wire coat *n* **:** a coat (as of various dogs) of extremely wiry and dense outer hair
wire copy *n* **:** copy sent to a newspaper, periodical, or news broadcast by a wire service
wire–cut \ˈ=ˈ=\ *adj* **:** cut or shaped by or as if by a taut wire ⟨*wire-cut* brick⟩ ⟨*wire-cut* tile⟩ — compare MOLDED BRICK 1
wire cutter *n* **:** a worker or appliance employed in cutting wire
wired *adj* [ME, fr. past part. of *wiren* to wire] **1 :** reinforced by wire (as for strength or stiffness) **2 :** furnished with wires (as for electricity or telephone connections) **3 :** bound with wire ⟨a ~ container⟩ **4 :** having a wirework netting or fence ⟨a ~ enclosure for chickens⟩ **5 :** back to back (sense 2)
wired music *n* **:** a sound reproducing system using a central disc reproducing system and telephone-line connections to many loudspeakers located in customers' factories, shops, and offices
wired radio *or* **wired wireless** *also* **wire radio** *n* **:** a system for distributing radio programs over wire lines or by means other than the usual method of transmitting the signals through space
wire drag *n* **:** a wire usu. several thousand feet in length, maintained horizontally at any desired depth by means of attached weights, buoyed at intervals, towed by a power boat at each end, and used to locate submerged obstructions projecting above the depth at which it is set
wiredraw \ˈ=ˌ=\ *vt* [back-formation fr. *wiredrawer*] **1 a :** to draw or stretch forcibly **:** ELONGATE, DISTORT, WREST ⟨my sense has been *wiredrawn* into blasphemy —John Dryden⟩ **b :** to draw or spin out to great length, tenuity, or overrefinement **:** ATTENUATE **2 :** to draw (metal) into wire
wiredrawer \ˈ=ˌ=(=)\ *n* [ME, fr. ¹*wire* + *drawer*] **:** one that draws metal into wire
wiredrawing *n* [fr. gerund of *wiredraw*] **:** the act, process, or occupation of drawing metal into wire
wiredrawn \ˈ=ˈ=\ *adj* [fr. past part. of *wiredraw*] **:** drawn out long and fine like wire **:** excessively minute and fine ⟨~ comparisons —Virginia Woolf⟩ ⟨~ theories⟩
wire edge *n* **1 :** the thin wirelike thread of metal sometimes formed on the edge of a tool (as a chisel or razor) in attempting to sharpen it **2 :** an edge on a coin forming a high thin border around the design
wire–feed \ˈ=ˈ=\ *adj* [¹*wire* + *feed*, n.] *of a machine tool* **:** having apparatus for maintaining a feed of wire
wire gauge *n* **1 :** a gauge esp. for measuring the diameter of wire or the thickness of sheet metal often consisting of a metal plate with a series of notches of various widths in its edge **2 :** any of various systems consisting of a series of standard sizes used in describing the diameter of wire or the thickness of sheet metal **3 :** any of the designated sizes in a wire gauge system

wire gauge

wire gauze *n* **:** a gauzelike weave of fine wires **:** an esp. fine wire cloth — compare TANTALUM GAUZE
wire glass *also* **wired glass** *n* **:** glass with wire netting embedded in it during manufacture to reduce the probability of its shattering when cracked by shock or by heat — called also *safety glass*
wire grass *n* **:** any of various grasses having wiry culms or leaves: as **a :** a European slender-stemmed meadow grass (*Poa compressa*) widely naturalized in the U.S. and Canada — called also *Canada bluegrass* **b :** YARD GRASS **c :** BERMUDA GRASS **d :** any of several grasses of the genus *Aristida* **e :** any of several grasses of the genus *Sporobolus* **f :** NIMBLE WILL **g :** LITTLE BLUESTEM **h :** BROOMROOT
wire grub *n* **:** WIREWORM
wire gun *n* **:** WIRE-WOUND GUN
wirehair \ˈ=ˌ=\ *n* **:** a wirehaired fox terrier
wirehaired \ˈ=ˈ=\ *adj* **:** having a stiff wiry outer coat of hair — used esp. of a dog
wirehaired pointing griffon *n* **:** a large bird dog originating in Europe and having a harsh wiry coat, a long skull, a square muzzle, and a definite moustache and eyebrows
wirehaired terrier *n* **:** a wirehaired fox terrier
wire house *n* **:** a brokerage firm connected with its branch offices and correspondents by private leased telephone or telegraph wires
wire lath *n* **:** a plaster base consisting of wire netting
¹**wire·less** \ˈ=ləs\ *adj* **1 :** having no wire or wires **2** *chiefly Brit* **:** of or relating to radiotelegraphy, radiotelephony, or radio
²**wireless** \"\ *n* -ES **1 a :** RADIOTELEGRAPH ⟨~ message⟩ **b** *or* **wireless telephony :** RADIOTELEPHONY ⟨~ operator⟩ **c** *chiefly Brit* **:** RADIO ⟨turn on the ~⟩ ⟨heard on the ~⟩ ⟨~ set⟩ ⟨state-controlled ~⟩ **2 :** a moderate blue that is greener and duller than average copen or Dresden blue and paler and slightly redder than azurite blue
³**wireless** \"\ *vb* -ED/-ING/-ES [²*wireless*] **:** RADIO ⟨the lightship ~*ed* a warning to vessels in the vicinity —*Amer. Guide Series: N.C.*⟩
wireless compass *n, chiefly Brit* **:** RADIO COMPASS, DIRECTION FINDER
wire·less·ly *adv* [¹*wireless* + *-ly*] **:** by a means not employing wires **:** by means of radio
wire·less·ness *n* -ES **:** the quality or state of being wireless
wireless telegraphy *also* **wireless telegraph** *n* **:** RADIOTELEGRAPH
wireless telephone *n* **:** RADIOPHONE 2
wirelike \ˈ=ˌ=\ *adj* **:** resembling a wire esp. in thinness and flexibility **:** WIRY ⟨~ plant stems⟩
wire line *n* **1 :** a line using wire; *esp* **:** a telegraph or telephone line **2 :** CHAIN LINE
wire·man \ˈ=mən\ *n, pl* **wiremen** [¹*wire* + *man*] **1 a :** LINEMAN 2 **b :** one who installs and repairs electric wiring (as in buildings, mines, automobiles, railroad cars, or telegraphic apparatus) **c :** a maintenance electrician who keeps electrical equipment (as motors, switches, or switchboards) in running condition **2 :** an operator of a machine for bending sheet-metal stamping over a wire to form a finished edge
wire mark *n* **:** the impression made on the bottom side of a paper web by the surface contour of the wire — compare WATERMARK 2
wire micrometer *n* **:** FILAR MICROMETER
wire money *n* **:** money consisting of larins
wire nail *n* **:** a nail made of wire; *specif* **:** any one of several nails made of wire and designed for special uses — see BOX NAIL, FINISHING NAIL; compare CUT NAIL
wire netting *n* **:** a texture of woven wire coarser than wire gauze
wirephoto \ˈ=ˈ=(ˌ)=\ *vt* [*Wirephoto*] **:** to transmit (a picture) by electrical signals over wire lines
Wirephoto \"\ *trademark* — used for a photograph transmitted by electrical signals over telephone wires
wire plant *n* **:** a woody almost leafless New Zealand vine (*Muehlenbeckia complexa*) rampant in California as an introduced plant — called also *maidenhair-vine, wire vine*
wire–pull \ˈ=ˌ=\ *vi* [back-formation fr. *wire-puller*] **:** to pull wires ⟨knows how to *wire-pull* and intrigue —P.L.Ford⟩
wire–puller \ˈ=ˌ==\ *n* [¹*wire* + *puller*] **:** one that uses secret or underhand means to influence the acts of a person or organization ⟨a hardheaded practical *wire-puller*, unyieldingly jealous of his career —John Gunther⟩
wire–pulling *n* -S [¹*wire* + *pulling*, gerund of *pull*] **:** the use of means to influence secretly the acts of a person or organization ⟨economic power or political *wire-pulling* —S.E.Morison⟩ ⟨can be done but it needs a week of *wire-pulling* and persuasion —Enid Bagnold⟩
wir·er \ˈwīrə(r)\ *n* -S **:** one that wires or uses wire **:** WIREMAN; *esp* **:** a trapper who uses a wire trap
wire radio *var of* WIRED RADIO
wire–record \ˈ==ˌ=\ *vt* [back-formation fr. *wire recorder*] **:** to make a wire recording of ⟨*wire-record* an interview⟩
wire recorder *n* [¹*wire* + *recorder*] **:** a magnetic recorder using magnetic wire
wire recording *n* [¹*wire* + *recording*] **:** magnetic recording on magnetic wire; *also* **:** the recording made by this process
wire reducer *n* **:** a heavy curved wire used in the seed cups of grain drills to cut down the rate of planting of small seeds
wire rod *n* **:** a metal rod from which wire is drawn
wire room *n* [so called fr. its being provided with apparatus for the receipt of race results by wire] **:** a room or establishment where bookmaking is carried on under cover of legitimate business
wire rope *n* **:** a rope formed wholly or chiefly of wires — compare CABLE, FLAT ROPE, FLATTENED STRAND ROPE, HAND ROPE 2, STEEL-CLAD ROPE, TRANSMISSION ROPE
wire ropeway *or* **wire tramway** *n* **:** a ropeway using a wire cable
wire rush *n* **:** any of various plants with wiry stems; *esp* **:** a slender rushlike New Zealand herb (*Hypolaena lateriflora*) of the family Restionaceae that has scaly leaves and often grows in dense mats
wires *pl of* WIRE, *pres 3d sing of* WIRE
wire saw *n* **:** HELICOIDAL SAW
wire service *n* **:** a news agency that sends out syndicated news copy by wire to subscribing newspapers, periodicals, or news broadcasters
wire–shafted \ˈ=ˈ==\ *adj* **1 :** having all or part of the shaft without webs ⟨*wire-shafted* feather⟩ **2** *of a bird* **:** having wire-shafted feathers
wire side *n* **1** *of handmade paper* **:** the side of the sheet in contact with the mold during manufacture — called also *right side* **2** *of machine-made paper* **:** the side of the sheet in contact with the wire during manufacture — called also *wrong side;* compare FELT SIDE
wire silver *n* **:** native silver in the form of wires or threads
wiresmith \ˈ=ˌ=\ *n* **:** one who makes wire esp. by the old method of hammering up strips of metal
wire solder *n* **:** solder in the form of wire
wire stem *n* **:** a disease of cabbage, cauliflower, and related plants that is caused by a fungus (*Pellicularia filamentosa*) and is similar to damping-off but attacks older seedlings and produces a constricted wiry stem
wire stitch *n* **1 :** SADDLE STITCH **2 :** SIDE STITCH
wire–strain gauge \ˈ=ˌ=-\ *n* **:** a device that consists of a fine wire firmly bonded to thin paper and that when attached to an object subjected to stress indicates minute changes in strain by corresponding changes in electrical resistance of the wire as it is likewise elongated
wire stretcher *n* **:** a device used (as in fencing) to pull wire taut
wire tack *n* **:** a tack machine-fabricated from wire stock
wiretail \ˈ=ˌ=\ *n, West* **:** RUDDY DUCK
wire–tailed \ˈ=ˈ=\ *adj* **:** having wire-shafted tail quills
wire–tailed bird of paradise : TWELVE-WIRED BIRD OF PARADISE
¹**wiretap** \ˈ=ˌ=\ *vb* [back-formation fr. *wiretapper*] *vi* **:** to tap a telephone or telegraph wire to get messages, information, or evidence **~** *vt* **:** to obtain (information) by tapping a wire
²**wiretap** \"\ *n* **1 :** the act or an instance of wiretapping ⟨transcripts of ~s made by the police department —*N.Y. Times*⟩ **2 :** a device for wiretapping ⟨had used a ~ in this detection —*Current Biog.*⟩
³**wiretap** \"\ *adj* **:** obtained by or involving wiretapping ⟨~ evidence⟩ ⟨a ~ scandal⟩
wiretapper \ˈ=ˌ==\ *n* [¹*wire* + *tapper*] **1 :** one that taps telephone or telegraph wires to get messages, information, or evidence **2 :** a swindler who professes to have information obtained by tapping wires
wire–toothed leather \ˈ=ˈ=-\ *n* **:** leather set or studded with wire teeth and used esp. for covering the cylinders of carding machines
wire twist *n* **:** a combination of welded and twisted wires used in making the barrels of some shotguns
wire vine *n* **:** WIRE PLANT
wireway \ˈ=ˌ=\ *n* **1 :** a conduit for wires; *esp* **:** one to conceal electric wires in a building while rendering them permanently accessible **2 :** a cash or parcel railway having wire tracks **3 :** WIRE ROPEWAY
wireweed \ˈ=ˌ=\ *n* **:** KNOTGRASS 1
wire wheel *n* **1 :** a rotary wire brush (as for cleaning metalwork) **2 :** a wheel (as for motorcars) with spokes of wire

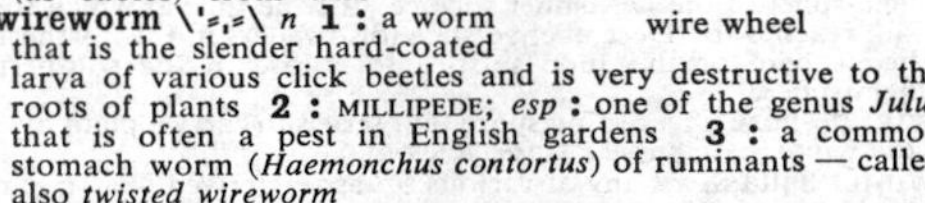
wire wheel

wirework \ˈ=ˌ=\ *n* **1 :** work of wires; *esp* **:** openwork made of wire **:** WIRE NETTING **2 :** walking on wires esp. by acrobats
wireworker \ˈ=ˌ==\ *n* [¹*wire* + *worker*] **:** one that makes things (as cables) from wire
wireworm \ˈ=ˌ=\ *n* **1 :** a worm that is the slender hard-coated larva of various click beetles and is very destructive to the roots of plants **2 :** MILLIPEDE; *esp* **:** one of the genus *Julus* that is often a pest in English gardens **3 :** a common stomach worm (*Haemonchus contortus*) of ruminants — called also *twisted wireworm*
wire–wound gun \ˈ=ˈ=-\ *n* **:** a gun in the construction of which an inner tube either entire or in segments is wound with wire under tension to insure greater soundness and uniformity of resistance and in which hoops and jackets are sometimes shrunk on the tube over the wire — compare DAMASCUS BARREL
wir·i·ly \ˈwīrəlē, -li\ *adv* **:** in a wiry manner
wir·i·ness \-rēnəs, -rin-\ *n* -ES **:** the quality or state of being wiry
wiring *n* -S [fr. gerund of ²*wire*] **1 :** the act, practice, or an instance of providing or using wire **2 :** a system of wires **:** WIREWORK; *esp* **:** an arrangement of wires used for electric distribution (as in a building) **3 :** the process of mounting with wire in taxidermy
wiring diagram *n* **:** a line drawing showing how the electrical connections of a device are made
wiring die *n* **:** one of a set of shaping dies consisting of a matrix and a punch for curling sheet metal around a wire to form a rim (as of a tinware utensil) or for making a similar rim without the wire
wiring press *n* **:** a shaping press for curling sheet metal around a wire to form a rim (as of a tinware utensil) or for making a similar rim without the wire — see WIRING DIE
wirk \ˈwərk\ *Scot var of* WORK
wirl \ˈwərl\ *or* **wirl·ing** \-lən, -liŋ\ *n* -S [origin unknown] *Scot & dial Eng* **:** a stunted or puny creature
wirr \ˈwər\ *n or vb* [imit.] *Scot* **:** GROWL
wir·ra \ˈwirə\ *interj* [*oh wirra*, fr. IrGael *a Muire*, lit., O Mary] *Irish* — usu. used to express lament, grief, or concern
wir·rah \ˈwirə\ *n* -S [fr. native name in Australia] **:** an Australian spotted food fish (*Acanthistius serratus*) of the family Serranidae
wir·ri·cow \ˈwərə,kü\ *var of* WORRICOW
wiry *also* **wirey** \ˈwīrē, -ri\ *adj* **wirier; wiriest** [¹*wire* + *-y*] **1 a :** made or consisting of wire ⟨a ~ cage⟩ **b :** resembling wire in form and flexibility ⟨crown of ~ gray curls —Anne Parrish⟩ ⟨~ grass⟩ **c** (1) *of sound* **:** produced by or suggestive of the vibration of wire ⟨her ~, plaintive voice —Marcia Davenport⟩ ⟨beyond a ~ cheeping, has no song —D.C. Peattie⟩ (2) *in sound reproduction* **:** characterized by excessive accentuation of higher-pitched tones **2** *of the pulse* **:** small but tense **3 :** characterized by a lean supple vigorous physique **:** SINEWY ⟨the ~ figure of a long-distance runner —*Phoenix Flame*⟩ ⟨chariots drawn by the ~ little British ponies —A.C.Whitehead⟩
wis \ˈwis\ *vb* [by incorrect division fr. *iwis* (understood as *I wis*, with *wis* incorrectly supposed to be an archaic pres. indic. of ¹*wit*)] *archaic* **:** KNOW
wis·con·sin \wəˈskän(t)sən\ *adj, usu cap* [fr. *Wisconsin*, northern state of U.S., of Algonquian origin; prob. akin to Ojibwa *wishkonsing* place of the beaver] **1 :** of or from the state of Wisconsin ⟨*Wisconsin* dairy products⟩ **:** of the kind or style prevalent in Wisconsin **2 :** belonging to the fourth glacial stage during the glacial epoch in No. America
wis·con·sin·ite \-sə,nīt\ *n* -S *cap* [*Wisconsin*, state of U.S. + E *-ite*] **:** a native or resident of the state of Wisconsin
wisconsin weeping willow *n, usu cap 1st W* **:** a hybrid willow (*Salix blanda*) derived from a cross between the weeping willow and the crack willow
wisconsin white pine *n, usu cap 1st W* **1 :** a common white pine (*Pinus strobus*) **2 :** the wood of the Wisconsin white pine tree
wis·dom \ˈwizdəm\ *n* -S [ME, fr. OE *wīsdōm*, fr. *wīs* wise + *-dōm* -dom] **1** *usu cap* **:** the effectual mediating principle or personification of God's will in the creation of the world **:** LOGOS **2 a** (1) **:** accumulated information **:** philosophic or scientific learning **:** KNOWLEDGE ⟨all the ~ of the ages . . . available at negligible cost to all of us within the covers of books —Bennett Cerf⟩ (2) **:** accumulated lore or instinctive adaptation ⟨a heritage of animal ~ built up through many generations of . . . fighting for existence —J.T.McNish⟩ **b :** the intelligent application of learning **:** ability to discern inner qualities and essential relationships **:** INSIGHT, SAGACITY ⟨a long book, illuminated not only with learning but with ~ —Gerald Bullett⟩ ⟨~ grows out of the temper and heart of a man as well as out of his intellect —James Bryce⟩ — compare VIRTUE **c :** good sense **:** JUDGMENT, PRUDENCE ⟨faced with a vote of no confidence . . . had the ~ to resign —B.K.Sandwell⟩ **d** *obs* **:** SANITY ⟨pray heaven his ~ be not tainted —Shak.⟩ **3 a** *archaic* **:** an embodiment of wisdom **:** APHORISM **b :** a wise attitude or course of action ⟨the English aristocracy showed a statesmanlike readiness to admit newcomers . . . a ~ which marked them off from the pedigree-ridden and politically frivolous aristocracies of Europe —D.W.Brogan⟩ **c** *archaic, often cap* **:** a person of superior intellectual attainments ⟨many of the best ~s of our nation —Gervase Markham⟩ — often used as a title or mode of address ⟨can your ~ possibly entertain a wish to converse with me —Sir Walter Scott⟩ **4 :** the teachings of the ancient wise men (as of Babylon, Egypt, or Palestine) relating to the art of living and sometimes to philosophical problems concerning the universe, man, or God and forming a class of literature represented in the Hebrew books of Job, Proverbs, Ecclesiastes, Ecclesiasticus, and the Wisdom of Solomon **syn** see SENSE
wisdom tooth *n* [trans. of NL *dentes sapientiae* (pl.), lit. teeth of wisdom; fr. their not usually being cut until the late teens] **:** the last tooth of the full set on each half of each jaw in man
¹**wise** \ˈwīz\ *n* -S [ME, fr. OE *wīse* manner, melody; akin to OHG *wīsa* manner, style, tune, ON *vīsa* stanza, ōthru*vīs* otherwise, Gk *eidos* appearance, form, kind, *idein* to see — more at WIT] **:** MANNER, WAY ⟨the house differed in no ~ from its neighbors —Maurice Samuel⟩ — often used in combination ⟨like*wise*⟩ ⟨other*wise*⟩
²**wise** \"\ *adj* -ER/-EST [ME *wise, wis, wys*, fr. OE *wīs* wise, knowing; akin to OHG *wīs* wise, ON *vīss*, Goth un*weis* unknowing, OE *witan* to know — more at WIT] **1 a** (1) **:** characterized by wisdom **:** SAGE, SAGACIOUS ⟨the ~ man and teacher of the tribe —Nancy K. Hosking⟩ ⟨men may be ~ . . . though their fund of knowledge is small —S.H.Slichter⟩ (2) **:** all-wise ⟨which the ~ powers deny us for our good —Shak.⟩ **b** (1) **:** well informed or instructed **:** KNOWLEDGEABLE ⟨a portion of reading quite indispensable to a ~ man —R.W.Emerson⟩ ⟨grew up . . . ~ in plants, wild animals, and the habits of their own goats and sheep —T.E.Lawrence⟩ (2) **:** showing instinctive wisdom ⟨these dogs are bred . . . as rugged individuals each ~ in his own nose —D.C.Peattie⟩ **c :** exercising sound judgment **:** JUDICIOUS, PRUDENT ⟨conservation and ~ use of resources can make a wealthy people in a lonely land —H.W.Odum⟩ ⟨~ handling of a situation⟩ ⟨a ~ investment⟩ **2** *archaic* **:** mentally sound **:** SANE **3 a :** evidencing or hinting at the possession of inside information **:** KNOWING ⟨when questioned about the incident he looked ~ but refused to talk⟩ ⟨the ~ money was ten to one⟩ **b :** possessed of inside information **:** ALERT ⟨unless they're ~ to the slow, steady creep of the tide, they'll be in up to their hubcaps before they realize it —J.W.Noble⟩ ⟨able to sneak it in without the MPs getting ~ —James Jones⟩ ⟨old timers put him ~ to the tricks of cardsharpers⟩ **c :** shrewdly resourceful **:** CRAFTY, SMART **4** *archaic* **:** skilled in magic or divination **5 :** INSOLENT, SMART-ALECKY, FRESH ⟨a bunch of ~ kids throwing snowballs at buses⟩
syn SAGE, SAPIENT, JUDICIOUS, PRUDENT, SENSIBLE, SANE: WISE indicates discernment based not only on factual knowledge but on judgment and insight ⟨*wise* men . . . anticipate possible difficulties, and decide beforehand what they will do if occasions arise —J.A.Froude⟩ ⟨she was also *wise* beyond her years, and she knew that when he no longer needed her advice he would dispense with her —Harrison Smith⟩ SAGE is used interchangeably with WISE but may also suggest venerability ⟨the *sage* enchanter Merlin's subtle schemes —William Wordsworth⟩ ⟨her *sage* plan to make the family feel her worth, and to conquer the members of it one by one —George Meredith⟩ SAPIENT may imply a canny shrewdness rather than profound wisdom ⟨the *sapient* leader who shall bring order out of the wild misrule —V.L.Parrington⟩ ⟨a *sapient*, instructed, shrewdly ascertaining ignorance —Walter Pater⟩ JUDICIOUS suggests judgment that is fair, level-headed, sound, and wise ⟨it is not *judicious*, unbiased, academic; it is passionate, biased and provocative —H.L.Matthews⟩ ⟨with *judicious* officers the most unruly seamen can at sea be kept in some sort of subjection —Herman Melville⟩ PRUDENT suggests exercise of the restraint of sound practical wisdom and discretion to avoid anything rash or ill-advised ⟨too *prudent* to say or hint anything which could create a suspicion in her colleague's breast —Anthony Trollope⟩ ⟨in the pursuit of pleasure, as in the purchase of securities, the *prudent* Southern gentleman has always preferred safety to hazard —Ellen Glasgow⟩ SENSIBLE describes action according to good sense and accustomed rationality ⟨let us, like *sensible* men, choose the lesser evil —John Strachey⟩ ⟨any *sensible* doctor when stricken by disease distrusts his own introspective diagnosis and calls in a colleague —C.K.Ogden & I.A.Richards⟩ SANE, usu. contrasted with *insane*, indicates mental soundness, rationality, and level-headedness without wild quirks or deep derangements ⟨I am no lunatic in a mad fit, but a *sane* man fighting for his soul —Bram Stoker⟩ ⟨praise all their wares in terms so extravagant that a *sane* buyer is instantly steeled against believing even that percentage of these praises which may perhaps be true —C.E.Montague⟩
³**wise** \"\ *n, pl* **wise** [ME, fr. OE *wīsa*, fr. *wīs* wise] **:** WISE MAN, SAGE — usu. used in pl. ⟨a word to the ~ is sufficient⟩ ⟨books . . . by the ~ of other days —V.L.Parrington⟩
⁴**wise** \"\ *adv* [ME, fr. ²*wise*] *archaic* **:** WISELY
⁵**wise** \"\ *vb* -ED/-ING/-S [²*wise*] *vt* **:** to supply with information **:** make wise ⟨I'll ~ you. You've been bilked —*McClure's*⟩ — usu. used with *up* ⟨think their talent will flower magically if they are *wised* up to a few tricks of the trade —Jan Peerce⟩ **~** *vi* **:** to become informed or knowledgeable **:** get hep **:** LEARN — used with *up* ⟨you can ~ up on details . . . by reading a booklet —*Kiplinger Washington Letter*⟩ ⟨people are *wising* up . . . to the fact that they have been deprived of a lot of good music —*Wall Street Jour.*⟩
⁶**wise** \"\ *vt* -ED/-ING/-S [ME *wisen*, fr. OE *wīsian;* akin to OHG *wīsen* to show the way, ON *vīsa*, Goth fulla*weisjan* to persuade; all fr. a prehistoric Gmc adj. represented by OE *wīs* wise, knowing] **1** *chiefly Scot* **a :** to show (a person) the way **:** DIRECT, GUIDE **b :** ADVISE, PERSUADE ⟨took me by the hand, and *wised* me to go back —John Galt⟩ **2** *chiefly Scot* **:** to divert or impel in a given direction **:** SEND, TURN ⟨fish rushed . . . before him, as he quietly *wised* them shoreward —J.K.Hunter⟩
-wise \ˌwīz\ *adv comb form* [ME, fr. OE *-wīsan*, fr. *wīse* manner — more at ¹WISE] **1 a :** in the manner of ⟨crab*wise*⟩ ⟨fan*wise*⟩ **b :** in the position or direction of ⟨end*wise*⟩ ⟨slant*wise*⟩ ⟨clock*wise*⟩ **2 :** with regard to **:** in respect of ⟨style*wise*⟩
wise·acre \ˈwī,zākə(r)\ *n* -S [MD *wijssegger* soothsayer, modif. (influenced by MD *segger* sayer, fr. *seggen* to say + *-er;* akin to OE *secgan* to say) of OHG *wīzzago* prophet; akin to OE *witega* wise man, prophet, *witan* to observe, see to, re-

proach — more at SAY, WITE] **1 :** one who represents himself as well-informed or clever **:** KNOW-IT-ALL, SMART ALECK ⟨has now demonstrated that this subterranean reservoir, which ~*s* contended was fed by a flowing underground stream, can be emptied and caused to remain empty —D.D.Martin⟩ **2 :** WISE MAN, SAGE — usu. used disparagingly ⟨some of the saws of the old rural ~*s* —A.O.D.Claxton⟩

¹wisecrack \'ˌ,ˌ\ *n* [²*wise* + *crack*] **:** a clever remark or rejoinder **:** QUIP, WITTICISM ⟨always trying to banish tension and worry with a quip or a ~ —C.W.M.Hart⟩ ⟨essays . . . interspersed with sardonic ~*s* in which supposedly lofty ideals are mercilessly derided —*Times Lit. Supp.*⟩ **syn** see JOKE

²wisecrack \"\ *vi* **:** to make a wisecrack ⟨is humorous and can ~ on occasions —Walter Pach⟩ ~ *vt* **:** to say by way of a wisecrack **:** QUIP

wise·crack·er \-kə(r)\ *n* [²*wisecrack* + *-er*] **:** one that makes wisecracks **:** SMART ALECK

wise guy *n* **:** a cocky conceited fellow **:** KNOW-IT-ALL, WISEACRE ⟨the *wise guy* who was going to show . . . headquarters how to run a battle —R.M.Ingersoll⟩ ⟨talks like a *wise guy* —Delmore Schwartz⟩

wisehead \'ˌ,ˌ\ *n* **:** WISEACRE

wisehearted \'ˌ¦ˌˌ\ *adj* [²*wise* + *hearted*] **:** of an understanding disposition **:** DISCERNING ⟨a ~ observer would have guessed at once the reason for her tears⟩

wiselike \'ˌ,ˌ\ *adj* [²*wise* + *like*] *chiefly Scot* **:** of a rational or suitable nature **:** SENSIBLE, BECOMING

wise·ling \'wīzliŋ, -lēŋ\ *n* -S [²*wise* + *-ling*] *archaic* **:** WISEACRE, WITLING

wise·ly *adv, sometimes* -ER/-EST [ME, fr. OE *wīslīce*, fr. *wīs* wise + *-līce* -ly] **:** in a wise manner **:** DISCERNINGLY, PRUDENTLY

wise man *n* [ME, fr. OE *wīs man*, fr. *wīs* wise + *man*] **:** a man of unusual learning, judgment, or insight often serving as a counselor **:** SAGE; *specif* **:** a member of a scholarly class esp. in Palestine during the biblical period distinguished from both priest and prophet as a thinker versed in general ethical and religious questions and fostering instruction of religious truths with a practical import and a distinctive emphasis on the role of wisdom in the conduct of daily life — compare WISDOM 4

wise·ness *n* -ES [ME *wisnesse*, fr. *wis, wise* wise + *-nesse* -ness] **:** the quality or state of being wise **:** WISDOM

wis·en·heim·er *or* **weis·en·heim·er** \'wīzᵊn,hīmə(r)\ *n* -S [²*wise* + G *-enheimer* (as in G family names such as *Guggenheimer, Oppenheimer*)] **:** one who has the air of knowing all about something or everything **:** WISEACRE ⟨emerges from comparative obscurity to national prominence — much to the . . . chagrin of the ~*s* —Arthur Godfrey⟩

wi·sent \'vē,zent\ *n* -S [G, fr. OHG *wisunt* — more at BISON] **:** a European bison (*Bison bonasus*) — called also *aurochs*

wiser *comparative of* WISE

wises *pl of* WISE, *pres 3d sing of* WISE

wisest *superlative of* WISE

wisewoman \'ˌ,ˌˌ\ *n, pl* **wisewomen** [ME, fr. ²*wise* + *woman*] **1 :** a woman versed in charms, conjuring, or fortune-telling **:** SEERESS, WITCH **2 :** MIDWIFE

¹wish \'wi|sh, *dial* 'wü| *or* |sht\ *vb* -ED/-ING/-ES [ME *wisshen*, fr. OE *wȳscan*; akin to OHG *wunsken* to wish, ON *œskja*, Skt *vāñchati* he wishes, *vanati, vanoti* he loves, desires — more at WIN] *vt* **1 a :** to have a desire for **:** WANT, CRAVE ⟨the best friend a man could ~⟩ ⟨they want to be led, and they ~ to remain free – Alexis de Tocqueville⟩ **b :** to yearn for (something unattainable) ⟨I ~ I were young again⟩ ⟨about this time of year I begin to ~ that some one would invent a bathing suit that could be worn to work —*Nation's Business*⟩ **c** *archaic* **:** to hope against hope ⟨I ~ I suffer no prejudice by it —Philip Henry⟩ **2 a :** to invoke upon ⟨~ the team success⟩ — often used in formulas of greeting ⟨~ him good night⟩ **b :** to harbor a specified feeling for ⟨very sincerely ~ him happy —Jane Austen⟩ ⟨embarrassed by her parents' solicitude and ~*ed* them miles away⟩ **c** *dial* **:** to invoke evil on by witchcraft **:** CONJURE ⟨when he hears that he has been ~*ed*, he . . . takes to his bed at once —E.B.Tylor⟩ **3 a :** to give form to (a wish) ⟨~ a wish⟩ **b :** to express a wish for ⟨the Persians did not ~ a strong ruler —William Clark⟩ ⟨students who ~ help in planning their courses⟩ **c :** to request in the form of a wish **:** ORDER ⟨my mother ~*es* you to get the car ready⟩ ⟨when a visitor . . . ~*es* a license to operate a rented car —Bert Pierce⟩ ⟨do you ~ cream or lemon in your tea⟩ **4 a :** to have the intention of **:** PROPOSE ⟨the point I ~ to make⟩ ⟨if men really ~ to be good, they will become good —J.B. Mozley⟩ **b :** to look forward to **:** ANTICIPATE ⟨at length the day so long ~*ed* and expected came —Clara Reeve⟩ **c** *archaic* **:** to speak favorably of **:** RECOMMEND ⟨I was ~*ed* to your worship, by a gentleman —Ben Jonson⟩ ⟨an acquaintance . . . had ~*ed* her to that place —Sir Walter Scott⟩ **d :** to confer (something unwanted) upon someone **:** FOIST ⟨at the annual meeting the job of secretary was ~*ed* on me —F.S.Blanchard⟩ ⟨a friend ~*ed* a small blue mule on me —E.A.Mills⟩ ~ *vi* **1 :** to have a desire **:** WANT, LONG ⟨~ for a puppy⟩ ⟨~ for the courage to stand up to a bully⟩ ⟨as enthralling a pastime as anybody . . . could ~ for —*New Yorker*⟩ **2 :** to make a wish ⟨~ on a falling star⟩ **syn** see DESIRE

²wish \"\ *n* -ES [ME *wisshe*, fr. *wisshen* to wish] **1 a :** an act or instance of wishing **:** unfulfilled desire **:** LONGING, WANT ⟨if ~*es* were horses, beggars would ride⟩ ⟨religion is built not of ~*es* but of will —W.L.Sullivan⟩ **b :** an object of desire **:** GOAL ⟨our only ~ was to reach some inhabited place and get something to eat —Heinrich Harrer⟩ **2 a :** an expressed desire **:** indirect mandate **:** WILL ⟨discharge their functions . . . in full accord with the popular ~ —*London Calling*⟩ **b :** a request couched in terms of wishing ⟨cross your fingers and make a ~⟩ ⟨out of deference to his parents' ~*es* —E.S.Bates⟩ **3 a :** an expression of good will ⟨take from my mouth, the ~ of happy years —Shak.⟩ ⟨when you see him, give him my best ~*es*⟩ **b** *archaic* **:** an invocation of evil **:** MALEDICTION ⟨this was my ~: be thou (quoth I) accurst —Shak.⟩

wisha \'wishə\ *interj* [IrGael *ō* oh + *muise* indeed] *chiefly Irish* — used as an intensive or to express surprise

wishbone \'ˌ,ˌ\ *n* [so called fr. the superstition that when two persons pull it apart the one getting the longer fragment will have his wish granted] **1** *or* **wishing bone :** a furcula in front of the breastbone in a bird consisting chiefly of the two clavicles ankylosed at their median or lower end and usu. movably articulated with both the scapula and coracoid at the other end and often having at the median point of union a process that is large and flattened in the domestic fowl **2 :** something that resembles the wishbone of a bird: as **a :** an automobile suspension **b :** a crossarm for electric wires on poles

wishbone bush *n* **:** any of various plants of the genus *Mirabilis*; *esp* **:** a California four-o'clock (*Mirabilis laevis*) with red flowers

wishbone flower *n* **:** TORENIA 2

wish·er \-shə(r)\ *n* -S **:** one that wishes ⟨~*s* were ever fools —Shak.⟩

wish·ful \'ˌfəl\ *adj* [²*wish* + *-ful*] **1** *obs* **:** fulfilling a wish **:** ATTRACTIVE, DESIRABLE ⟨having so ~ an opportunity . . . I could not but send you this friendly salute —James Howell⟩ **2 a :** expressive of a wish **:** HOPEFUL, LONGING ⟨looked at the toys with ~ eyes⟩ ⟨the performance of ~ magical exercises —Frederica de Laguna⟩ **b :** having a wish **:** EAGER, DESIROUS ⟨~ to have your cake and eat it —P.B.Kyne⟩ **3 :** based on wishes rather than reality ⟨the ~, ideal America of the American myth —Joseph Frank⟩ ⟨indulged . . . in ~ dreams of an easy peace —Hans Kohn⟩ — **wish·ful·ly** \-fəlē, -li\ *adv*

wish fulfillment *n* **:** the gratification of a desire esp. as gained symbolically (as in dreams, daydreams, symptomatic acts, or other symptoms)

wish·ful·ness *n* -ES **:** the quality or state of being wishful

wishful thinker *n* **:** one that indulges in wishful thinking

wishful thinking *n* **1 :** illusory attribution of actuality to what one wishes to be or become true and discovery of justifications for what one wants to believe through unconscious motivation in order to avoid facing painful or unpleasant facts **2 :** AUTISM, WISH FULFILLMENT

¹wishing *n* -S [ME *wisshing*, fr. gerund of *wisshen* to wish] **:** an act or instance of wishing ⟨~ won't pay the rent⟩

²wishing *adj* [fr. pres. part. of ¹*wish*] **1** *archaic* **:** WISHFUL ⟨returned to cheer his ~ tenant's sight —Allan Ramsay †1758⟩ **2** [¹*wishing*] **:** regarded as having the power to grant wishes ⟨~ cap⟩ ⟨~ well⟩

wish·ly *adv* [prob. alter. (influenced by ¹*wish*) of *wistly*] *archaic* **:** INTENTLY, WISHFULLY

wish·osk·an \wə'shäskən\ *n* -S *usu cap* **:** a language family of the Ritwan stock comprising only Wiyot

wish·ram \'wi,shram\ *n, pl* **wishram** *or* **wishrams** *usu cap* **1 a :** an Indian people of Klickitat county in the southern part of the state of Washington **b :** a member of such people **2 :** a dialect of Upper Chinook

wisht \'wisht\ *adj* [prob. fr. past part. of E dial. *wish* to invoke evil upon, bewitch] *dial Brit* **:** DISMAL, EERIE

wish-wash \'wish,wȯsh, -,wäsh, -,wȯish, *chiefly in substand speech* -,wȯrsh *or* -,wärsh\ *n* [redupl. of ²*wash*] **1 :** a weak thin drink **2 :** insipid talk or writing **:** CLAPTRAP, TWADDLE ⟨forget all the *wish-wash* about neoromanticism —Louis MacNeice⟩

wishy-washily \¦wishē¦wȯshəlē, -ishi¦|, |wäsh-, |wȯish-, -li, *chiefly in substand speech* |wȯrsh- *or* |wärsh-\ *adv* **:** in a wishy-washy manner **:** INSIPIDLY

wishy-washiness \-shēnəs, -shin-\ *n* **:** the quality or state of being wishy-washy **:** INSIPIDITY

wishy-washy \-shē, -shi\ *adj* [redupl. of *washy*] **1 :** lacking in strength or flavor **:** WEAK, INSIPID ⟨their *wishy-washy*, watery wine —Andrew Balfour⟩ **2 :** lacking in character or determination **:** VAPID, NAMBY-PAMBY ⟨pale, *wishy-washy* eyes —Jack London⟩ ⟨dim, *wishy-washy* pseudo-Impressionism —R.M.Coates⟩ ⟨a *wishy-washy* neutralist platform —*Time*⟩ **syn** see INSIPID

wising *pres part of* WISE

wis·ket \'wiskət, *usu* -əd·+V\ *n* -S [E dial., small twig, basket, prob. of Scand origin; akin to ON *visk* wisp — more at WHISK] *dial Eng* **:** BASKET; *esp* **:** a straw provender basket

wis·li·ze·nus's cottonwood \¦vislət¦sānəsəz-\ *n, usu cap W* [after Frederick A. *Wislizenus* †1889 Am. physician and explorer born in Germany] **:** a poplar (*Populus wislizenii*) of the southwestern U.S. that is often planted as a shade tree in arid regions and has large yellowish green leaves — called also *Wiz·le·zen's poplar* \'vislə,zänz-\

wislizenus oak *n, usu cap W* [after Frederick A. *Wislizenus* †1889] **:** a live oak (*Quercus wislizenii*)

¹wisp \'wisp\ *also* **whisp** \'hwisp *also* 'wisp\ *n* -S [ME *wisp, wips*; perh. akin to OE *wīpian* to wipe — more at WIPE] **1 a :** a small handful (as of hay or straw) **b :** something that resembles a wisp: as (1) **:** a tenuous strip or fragment ⟨a ~ of chiffon⟩ ⟨roughly-chinked log-cabins . . . stood in a ~ of open —S.V.Benét⟩ ⟨strange ~*s* of psychological jargon —*Times Lit. Supp.*⟩ (2) **:** a filamentous streak ⟨a ~ of smoke or cloud⟩ ⟨~*s* of mist floated like trails of luminous dust —Joseph Conrad⟩ (3) **:** something frail or fleeting ⟨a delicate little ~ of an old lady —*Century Mag.*⟩ ⟨a mere ~ of a smile —L.C.Douglas⟩ (4) **:** WILL-O'-THE-WISP **c :** a flock of birds (as snipe) **2** *chiefly Brit* **a :** a pad of twisted or plaited hay or straw for grooming the coat of an animal **b :** a twisted wreath or wad (as of straw or hemp) used as a buffer **c :** a thick twist of hay or straw used as a torch

²wisp \"\ *vb* -ED/-ING/-S *vt* **1** *chiefly Brit* **a :** to rub down or massage (as a horse) with a wisp **b :** CRUMPLE, TWIST **2 :** to make or cover with wisps ⟨a cigarette ~*ing* smoke at the corner of his mouth —Raymond Chandler⟩ ⟨the sky all ~*ed* with mist —W.F.Wray⟩ ~ *vi* **:** to emerge or drift in wisps ⟨a thread of smoke ~*ing* out of the funnel —William Wertenbaker⟩ ⟨her hair began to ~ into her eyes —Mary Manning⟩

wisp·i·ly \-pəlē, -li\ *adv* **:** in a wispy manner

wisp·i·ness \-pēnəs, -pin-\ *n* -ES **:** the quality or state of being wispy

wisp·ish \-pish, -pēsh\ *adj* [¹*wisp* + *-ish*] **:** resembling a wisp **:** INSUBSTANTIAL, WISPY

wispy \-pē, -pi\ *adj* -ER/-EST [¹*wisp* + *-y*] **:** consisting of, resembling, or characterized by wisps **:** FRAIL, NEBULOUS ⟨hair . . . drawn carelessly at the back into a ~ bun —Fred Majdalany⟩ ⟨a ~ little fellow with small hands and feet —Edmund Wilson⟩ ⟨have only a few, ~ memories of my existence prior to our moving there —Marc Connelly⟩

wis·sel \'wisəl\ *n* -S [ME, exchange, fr. MD; akin to OHG *wehsal* change, turn, ON *gjafavīxl* exchange of gifts — more at WEEK] **1** *chiefly Scot* **:** CHANGE 6b **2** *chiefly Scot* **:** RETRIBUTION — used esp. in the phrase *get the wissel of one's groat*

¹wist *past of* WIT

²wist \'wist\ *n* -S [ML *wista*, prob. fr. OE *wist* food, sustenance; akin to OHG *wist* food, sustenance, ON *vist*] **:** an old Sussex unit of land area estimated as equal to 16 or 18 acres or in Anglo-Saxon times to 60 acres

³wist \"\ *vt* -ED/-ING/-S [alter. (influenced by ¹*wist*) of *wis*] *archaic* **:** KNOW ⟨it . . . took at last a certain shape I ~ —S.T. Coleridge⟩

wis·tar·berg glass \'wistər,bərg-\ *n, usu cap W* [fr. *Wistarberg*, name of the glassworks where it was produced, fr. Caspar *Wistar* †1752 + G *berg* mountain, fr. OHG — more at BARROW] **:** glass made in southern New Jersey in the 18th century

wis·tar glass \'wistə(r)-\ *n, use cap W* [after Caspar *Wistar* †1752 Am. glass manufacturer] **:** WISTARBERG GLASS

wis·tar·ia \wə'stirēə, -tēr- *also* -ter- *or* -ta(a)r- *or* -tär-\ *n* -S [NL, alter. (influenced by the name *Wistar*) of *Wisteria*] **1 :** WISTERIA 2 **2 a :** a pale purple that is redder and paler than average lavender, bluer and lighter than phlox pink, and bluer, lighter, and stronger than flossflower blue **b :** a light violet that is redder, less strong, and slightly darker than average bright periwinkle — called also *wistaria violet*

wistaria blue *n* **:** a light purplish blue that is redder and deeper than lupine and darker and slightly redder than average periwinkle

wistaria violet *n* **:** WISTARIA 2b

wis·te·ria \-tirēə, -tēr-\ *n* [NL, fr. Caspar *Wistar* †1818 Am. physician + NL *-ia*] **1** *cap* **:** a genus of chiefly Asiatic mostly woody vines (family Leguminosae) several members of which are grown for ornament and which have pinnately-compound leaves and showy blue, white, purple, or rose pealike flowers in long drooping racemes that are succeeded by long flattened pods **2** -S **:** any plant or flower of the genus *Wisteria*: as **a :** CHINESE WISTARIA **b :** JAPANESE WISTARIA

wist·ful \'wistfəl\ *adj* [fr. *wistly* + *-ful*; in senses 2 & 3 influenced in meaning by ²*wish*] **1** *obs* **:** INTENT **2 a :** full of timorous longing or unfulfilled desire **:** MELANCHOLY, YEARNING ⟨those ~ little ads which the lovelorn . . . place in the classified columns —E.B.White⟩ ⟨the ~ gaze of the explorer has turned upward to the clouds —Waldemar Kaempffert⟩ **b :** inspiring wistfulness **:** reminiscently evocative ⟨the ~ fragility of all new feeling —Marcia Davenport⟩ ⟨deserted buildings above which ~ flags fly bravely —George Haines⟩ **3 :** musingly sad **:** PENSIVE, MOURNFUL ⟨the sensitive and ~ response of a poet to the gentler phase of beauty —*Amer. Guide Series: Minn.*⟩ ⟨would fix her eyes on the distance in dreary contemplation, and her mind would follow her eyes, in a vacant and ~ regard —G.D.Brown⟩ — **wist·ful·ly** \-fəlē, -li\ *adv*

wist·ful·ness *n* -ES **:** the quality or state of being wistful ⟨his eyes already had the exile's ~ —Mollie Panter-Downes⟩

wis·ti·ti \'wistətē\ *also* **wis·tit** \-stət\ *or* **ouis·ti·ti** \'wistətē\ *n* -S [F *ouistiti*, of imit. origin] **:** MARMOSET; *esp* **:** a marmoset (*Callithrix jacchus*)

wist·less \'wistləs\ *adj* [fr. *wistful*, after such pairs as *heedful: heedless*] *archaic* **:** HEEDLESS

wistly *adv* [prob. fr. ¹*whist* + *-ly*] *obs* **:** INTENTLY, WISTFULLY

¹wit \'wit, *usu* -id·+V\ *vb, past* **wist** \'wist\ *past part* **wist**; *pres part* **witting**; *pres 1st & 3d sing* **wot** \'wät, *usu* -äd·+V\ [ME *witen* (1st & 3d sing. pres. *wot, wat*, pres. pl. *witen*, past *wiste*, past part. *witen, wist*), fr. OE *witan* (1st & 3d sing. pres. *wāt*, pres. pl. *witon*, past *wiste, wisse*, past part. *witen*); akin to OHG *wizzan* to know (1st & 3d sing. pres. *weiz*, past *westa, wessa*, past part. *giwizzan*), ON *vita* (1st & 3d sing. pres. *veit*, past *vissa*, past part. *vitathr*), Goth *witan* to know (1st sing. pres. *wait*, past *wissa*), L *vidēre* to see, Gk *eidenai* to know, *oida* I know, *idein* to see, Skt *veda* I know, he knows, *vidyā* knowledge; basic meaning: to see] *vt* **1 a** *archaic* **:** to be aware of **:** KNOW ⟨little *witting* that so soon shadows would close in upon them —J.M.Barrie⟩ — used in imperative to convey positive assurance ⟨please you ~: the epitaph is . . . writ —Shak.⟩ **b** *chiefly Midland* **:** THINK, SUPPOSE ⟨they are too bold and crafty, I ~ —Horace Kephart⟩ **2** *obs* **:** to find out **:** DISCOVER, LEARN ⟨stood afar off, to ~ what would be done to him —Exod 2:4 (AV)⟩ ~ *vi* **1** *archaic* **:** to be aware **:** KNOW ⟨we ~ well of many things that we would never prove —Adeline Whitney⟩ **2** *archaic* **:** to become informed

²wit \"\ *n* -S [ME, fr. OE; akin to OHG *wizzi* knowledge, understanding, wit, ON *vit*, Goth *-witi* knowledge, OE *witan* to know — more at ¹WIT] **1 a :** MIND, MEMORY ⟨cannot put himself inside the ~ of the slow Neanderthal —Emma Hawkridge⟩ **b :** reasoning power **:** INTELLIGENCE ⟨the moron who hasn't the ~ to hold a job —F.L.Allen⟩ **c** *obs* **:** mechanical skill **:** INVENTIVENESS ⟨the enemy was oftener overcome . . . by the architect's ~ —James Leoni⟩ **2 a :** SENSE 2a — often used in pl. ⟨thou hast more of the wild goose in one of thy ~*s*, than I am sure I have in my whole five —Shak.⟩ **b** (1) **:** mental soundness **:** SANITY ⟨you have lost your ~, or you would never say such a thing —Humayun Kabir⟩ — often used in pl. ⟨scared me out of my ~*s* —A.J.Russell⟩ (2) **:** mental capability **:** pragmatic resourcefulness **:** INGENUITY ⟨has enough shrewd ~ to handle any situation —John Erskine †1951⟩ — often used in pl. ⟨wrested submission from nature by their determination and ~*s* —John DeMeyer⟩ ⟨was at her ~*s'* end —Edith Sitwell⟩ **3 a :** astuteness of perception or judgment **:** ACUMEN, WISDOM ⟨the ~ that gives sharp decisions on matters of high policy —Constance Foley⟩ ⟨if love is a thorn, they show no ~ who foolishly hug and foster it —W.S.Gilbert⟩ **b :** creative imagination **:** intellectual brilliance or subtlety ⟨skill in improvising fugues is a matter of ~ and inclination rather than an exhibition of facility in execution —A.E.Wier⟩ ⟨poems . . . where an atmosphere of ~ and elegance assures poignancy of meaning —R.P.Blackmur⟩; *specif* **:** the ability to discover amusing analogies between apparently unrelated things and to express them cleverly ⟨follow the metaphysical school of writers of ~ —Stephen Spender⟩ **c** (1) **:** a talent for banter or persiflage (2) **:** REPARTEE, SATIRE ⟨brevity is the soul of ~⟩ ⟨~ has been made a weapon of political dispute —G.F. Sensabaugh⟩ **4 a :** a man of superior intellectual attainments **:** THINKER, BRAIN ⟨nimble and versatile Athenian ~*s* trained to preternatural acuteness by the debates of the law courts and the Assembly —G.L.Dickinson⟩ **b :** an imaginatively perceptive and articulate individual esp. skilled in banter or persiflage

syn HUMOR, IRONY, SARCASM, SATIRE, REPARTEE: WIT implies intellectual brilliance and quickness in perception combined with a gift for expressing ideas in an entertaining, often laughter provoking, pointed way, usu. connoting the unexpected or apt turn of phrase or idea and often suggesting a certain brittle unfeelingness ⟨portrayed feminine character with an extraordinary *wit* and insight —John Erskine †1951⟩ ⟨a speech as full of *wit* and brilliance as any he had ever made —Stewart Cockburn⟩ ⟨had a playful *wit* which was sometimes very biting —Gertrude Stein⟩ HUMOR in this comparison can signify a disposition to see the ludicrous, comical, ridiculous, or absurd or to give it expression or can apply to the expression itself, often suggesting a generalness or a greater kindliness or sympathy with human failings than does WIT ⟨a man of great *humor*, full of jokes and laughter⟩ ⟨was always saved by her crisp sense of *humor*, her shrewd and mischievous wit —Havelock Ellis⟩ ⟨parliamentary *humor* is not remarkable for its subtlety. It is broad rather than deep. It is *humor*, not wit —E.H.Collis⟩ ⟨the modern sense of *humor* is the quiet enjoyment and implicit expression of the fun of things —Louis Cazamian⟩ ⟨a *humor* that grows from a deep understanding of human foibles and fortitudes, a humor of compassionate knowledge as well as of situation —Katherine G. Jackson⟩ IRONY applies chiefly to a way of speaking or writing in which the meaning intended is contrary to that expressed on the surface ⟨beset with confusion and humiliation he said in blunt *irony*, "I am certainly enjoying myself"⟩ but in a more literary or dramatic sense it implies a deeper perception of the discrepancies implicit in life and character or applies to the actual discrepancies (as between appearance and reality, what is promised and what fulfilled, what is intended and what achieved, what seemingly should be and what actually is), applying frequently to a situation in which what results is the direct, often tragic, opposite of what was desired, intended, or worked for ⟨the dramatic *irony* of the play in which the hero intent upon the greatest good he knows achieves by his very pursuit of it destruction and death⟩ ⟨the patient had sought violent death, but, with the usual *irony* of life, it was the doctor whom sudden death overcame —Havelock Ellis⟩ ⟨the *irony* of Fielding's life that at the moment of his success he lost his happiness —*Time*⟩ ⟨an *irony* of nature that our teeth, which decay so painfully while we live, stop decaying at our death, and outlast all the rest of us —Leonard Woolley⟩ SARCASM applies chiefly to a type of humor intended to cut or wound, often employing ridicule or bitter irony ⟨the satire has become in some instances *sarcasm* — and heavy sarcasm at that —John Woodburn⟩ SATIRE can apply to any criticism or censure relying on exposure, often by irony and often subtle, of the ridiculous or absurd qualities of something ⟨Jonson's drama is only incidentally *satire*, because it is only incidentally a criticism upon the actual world —T.S.Eliot⟩ ⟨*satire*, which holds up to ridicule conduct, beliefs, or institutions disapproved of by the author, may be seriously corrective in purpose, and in such case is intermediate between pure comedy and social drama —K.T.Rowe⟩ ⟨one whose conversation dealt a good deal in *satire* and jokes at someone else's expense⟩ REPARTEE, sometimes still applied to a witty or clever retort, applies chiefly to the power or the art of replying quickly and with wit, humor, or, infrequently, sarcasm ⟨half a dozen smart *repartees* were possible —Aldous Huxley⟩ ⟨she has a clever, coherent way of making her points, and is concise in reply if questioned, quick at *repartee* if heckled —Rose Macaulay⟩ **syn** see in addition MIND

wi·tan \'wi,tän\ *n pl* [OE, pl. of *wita* sage, advisor; akin to OHG *wizzo* sage, Goth *-wita* one who knows, *witan* to know — more at ¹WIT] **1 :** members of the king's advisory council in Anglo-Saxon England **2 :** WITENAGEMOT

¹witch \'wich\ *n* -ES [ME *wyche*, fr. OE *wice, wic*; prob. akin to OE *wīcan* to yield, give way — more at WEAK] **:** any of several trees having pliant branches

²witch \"\ *n* -ES [ME *wicche*, fr. OE *wicca*, masc., wizard & *wicce*, fem., witch; akin to OE *wiccian* to practice witchcraft, MHG *wicken* to bewitch, to divine, OE *wīgle* divination, *wīglian* to divine, *wīg* idol, image, ON *vē* temple — more at VICTIM] **1 a** *dial Brit* **:** WIZARD, SORCERER **b** (1) **:** a woman practicing the black arts **:** SORCERESS ⟨Halloween ~ on a broomstick⟩ ⟨heard of one old ~ changing herself into a pigeon —John Rhys⟩ (2) **:** an ugly old woman **:** CRONE, HAG ⟨a skinny old ~ with a face like a meat ax and a voice like a buzz saw —Helen Eustis⟩ **c** (1) **:** one supposed to possess supernatural powers esp. by compact with the devil or a familiar (2) **:** a magic spell **:** HEX ⟨it's my idea . . . he put the ~*es* on it —Helen Rich⟩ **d** *or* **witch·er** \-chə(r)\ -S **:** DOWSER **2 :** one that bewitches ⟨the quaint ~ memory —P.B.Shelley⟩; *specif* **:** a particularly charming or alluring woman **3 a** (1) **:** STORM PETREL (2) **:** GREBE (3) *or* **witch bird :** ANI **b** *also* **witch flounder :** a small-mouth blackish or brownish deepwater flounder (*Glyptocephalus cynoglossus*) of the north Atlantic that is of some importance as a food fish **c :** WITCH MOTH

³witch \"\ *adj* **:** of, relating to, or used against witches ⟨~ cult⟩ ⟨~ doors used to ward off evil spirits⟩

⁴witch \"\ *vb* -ED/-ING/-ES [ME *wicchen*, fr. OE *wiccian* to practice witchcraft] *vt* **1 :** BEWITCH **2 :** DOWSE

witch alder *n* [¹*witch*] **:** FOTHERGILLA 2

witch ball *n* **:** a hollow sphere of plain or striated glass hung in cottage windows in the 18th century to ward off evil spirits but later often posed on top of a vase or suspended by a cord (as from the mantelpiece or rafters) for decorative effect

witch cake *n* **:** a cake made by a witch for working magic or for use in testing one accused of witchcraft

witchcraft \'ˌ,ˌ\ *n* [ME *wicchecraft*, fr. OE *wiccecrǣft*, fr. *wicca, wicce* wizard, witch + *crǣft* craft] **1 a :** an act or instance of employing sorcery esp. with malevolent intent **:** a magical rite or technique ⟨in practicing ~, the witch . . . secured an article of the proposed victim's clothing —J.J. Honigmann⟩ **b :** the exercise of supernatural powers **:** alleged intercourse with the devil or with a familiar **2 a :** an irresistible influence or fascination **:** CHARM, ENCHANTMENT ⟨he hath a ~ over the king in's tongue —Shak.⟩ ⟨the ~ of harmonic sound —R.W.Emerson⟩ **syn** see MAGIC

witch doctor *n* **1 :** a professional worker of magic in a primitive society occupying a tribal position similar to that of a shaman or medicine man who by the use of spells, charms, herbal remedies, and incantations seeks to cure illness, detect witches, and counteract malevolent magical influences — called also *witchman* **2 :** one employing techniques or mumbo jumbo like those of a witch doctor ⟨a clairvoyant or *witch doctor* of some kind —Osbert Sitwell⟩ ⟨political *witch doctors*⟩ ⟨*witch doctors* of modern business . . . exorcising the demon of pessimism —C.W.Ferguson⟩

witch doctress *n* **:** a female witch doctor

witch elm *var of* WYCH ELM

witch·en \ˈwichən\ *n* -S [short for *witchen elm*, fr. *witchen*, adj. (fr. ¹*witch* + *-en*) + *elm*] **1** *archaic* **:** WYCH ELM **2 :** a rowan tree (*Sorbus aucuparia*)

witch·ery \-ch(ə)rē, -ri\ *n* -ES **1 a :** the practice of witchcraft **:** SORCERY ⟨an old crone accused of ~⟩ **b :** an act or instance of witching — usu. used in pl. ⟨a woman infamous for sortileges and *witcheries* —Sir Walter Scott⟩ **2 :** an irresistible fascination **:** CHARM, SPELL ⟨lovingly . . . dallies with the ~ of the old learning —P.E.More⟩ **syn** see MAGIC

witch·es' brew *or* **witch·es' broth** *also* **witch's brew** \ˈwichəz-\ *n* **:** a fearsome mixture **:** a confused condition ⟨a fantastic *witches' brew* of contradictions —*Newsweek*⟩

witches'-broom \ˈ⸗⸗ˌ⸗\ *or* **witch broom** *n* **:** an abnormal tufted growth of small branches on a tree or shrub caused by fungi, viruses, mistletoes, insect injury, or physiological disturbances — called also *hexenbesen, staghead*

witches'-butter \ˈ⸗⸗ˌ⸗⸗\ *n* **1 :** any of various gelatinous blue-green algae esp. of the genus *Nostoc* **2 :** a yellow jelly fungus (*Tremella lutescens*)

witches' cauldron *n* **:** an unholy combination or set of circumstances **:** a turbid or menacing situation ⟨let us look into this *witches' cauldron* — the battle of Germany —J.F.C. Fuller⟩

witches'-horse \ˈ⸗⸗ˌ⸗\ *n* **:** STICK INSECT

witches' milk *n* **1 :** MARE'S TAIL 2a **2** *or* **witch's milk :** secretion from the mammary glands of the newborn of both sexes presumably due to placental permeability to the lactation-producing hormones of the mother

witches' money-bags *n* **:** an orpine (*Sedum telephium*)

witches' sabbath *n, often cap W&S* **:** SABBAT

witches' stirrup *or* **witches' bridle** *n* **:** a tangle in a horse's mane

witches'-thimble \ˈ⸗⸗ˌ⸗⸗\ *n, dial Eng* **:** any of several European plants: as **a :** a harebell (*Campanula rotundifolia*) **b :** SEA CAMPION **c :** a foxglove (*Digitalis purpurea*) **d :** a bluebottle (*Centaurea cyanus*)

witch·et·ty grub \ˈwichəd·ē, -chətē, -i\ *or* **witchetty** *n* -ES [*witchetty* native name in Australia] **:** any of various large white grubs that are larvae esp. of moths of the genus *Cossus*, frequent the roots of Australian acacia, are relished by the aborigines, and form the chief food of the marsupial mole

witchfinder \ˈ⸗ˌ⸗⸗\ *n* **:** a detector of witches; *specif* **:** a 17th century investigator charged with hunting down and obtaining evidence against supposed witches

witch fire *n* **:** SAINT ELMO'S FIRE

witch flounder *n* **:** WITCH 3b

witchgrass \ˈ⸗ˌ⸗\ *n* **1** [prob. alter. of *quitch grass*] **:** COUCH GRASS 1a **2** [²*witch* + *grass*] **:** any of several grasses of the genus *Panicum*; *esp* **:** a No. American panic grass (*P. capillare*) with slender brushy panicles that is often a weed on cultivated land — called also *tumble grass*

witch hazel \ˈwich,hāzəl, ˈwi,chā-, ⸗ˈ⸗⸗\ *n* [¹*witch*] **1 a :** WYCH ELM **b :** HORNBEAM 1a **c :** ROWAN TREE 1 **2 a :** a tree or shrub of the genus *Hamamelis*: as (1) **:** a common shrub (*Hamamelis virginiana*) of eastern No. America having leaves like those of the hazel and small yellow flowers that appear after the leaves have fallen (2) **:** VERNAL WITCH HAZEL **b :** an alcoholic solution of a distillate of the bark of a witch hazel (*H. virginiana*) widely used as a remedy for bruises and sprains and as a mildly astringent lotion

witch-hazel family *n* **:** HAMAMELIDACEAE

witch hob·ble \-ˈhäbəl\ *or* **witch hop·ple** \-ˈhäpəl\ *n* [¹*witch*] **1 :** HOBBLEBUSH **2 :** CRANBERRY BUSH 2

witch·hood \ˈ⸗,hu̇d\ *n* **:** the state of being a witch

witch-hunt \ˈ⸗,⸗\ *n* **1 :** a searching out and persecution of persons accused of witchcraft **2 :** an investigation of or campaign against dissenters (as political opponents) conducted on the pretext of protecting the public welfare and resulting in public persecution and defamation of character ⟨*witch-hunts* for reds in faculties —Laird Bell⟩ ⟨a fascist *witch-hunt* against all those who dare to question Russian policies —Alexander Baird⟩ — **witch-hunter** \ˈ⸗,⸗⸗\ *n*

witch-hunting \ˈ⸗,⸗⸗\ *n* **:** the act or process of carrying on a witch-hunt ⟨various forms of hysteria such as *witch-hunting* and a search for scapegoats —N.J.Padelford⟩ — compare RED-BAITING

¹**witch·ing** \ˈwichiŋ, -chēŋ\ *n* -S [ME *wicching*, fr. OE *wiccung*, fr. *wiccian* to practice witchcraft + *-ung* -ing — more at WITCH] **:** the practice of witchcraft **:** SORCERY

²**witching** \"\ *adj* [fr. pres. part. of obs. E *witch* to practice witchcraft, fr. ME *wicchen*, fr. OE *wiccian*] **1 :** of, relating to, or suitable for sorcery or supernatural occurrences ⟨'tis now the very ~ time of night, when churchyards yawn —Shak.⟩ ⟨the ~ light of a fen fire —O.E.Rölvaag⟩ **2** [fr. pres. part. of ⁴*witch*] **:** BEWITCHING, FASCINATING ⟨a terrain which nature has adorned with ~ beauty —Raymond Moley⟩ — **witch·ing·ly** *adv*

witching stick *n* **:** DOWSING ROD

witch light *n* **:** SAINT ELMO'S FIRE

witchlike \ˈ⸗,⸗\ *adj* **:** having the gnarled appearance or evil character associated with witches ⟨elderbushes and hawthorns, all old, crabbed and ~ —H.E.Bates⟩

witch·man \ˈ⸗mən\ *n, pl* **witchmen :** WITCH DOCTOR

witch-mark \ˈ⸗,⸗\ *n* **:** a mark on the body supposedly identifying or caused by a witch

witch moth *n* **:** any of various noctuid moths some of which are large and which belong to *Erebus* and related genera; *specif* **:** BLACK WITCH

witch's brew *var of* WITCHES' BREW

witch's pouch *n* **:** SHEPHERD'S PURSE

witch stick *n* **:** DOWSING ROD

witchweed \ˈ⸗,⸗\ *n* [²*witch* + *weed*] **:** any of a genus (*Striga*, family Scrophulariaceae) of hemiparasitic herbs with red or yellow irregular flowers; *esp* **:** one (*S. lutea*) that parasitizes corn in the southeastern U. S.

witchwoman \ˈ⸗,⸗⸗\ *n, pl* **witchwomen :** a female witch doctor

witchwood \ˈ⸗,⸗\ *n* [¹*witch* + *wood*] **1** *dial Eng* **a :** WYCH ELM **b :** ROWAN TREE 1 **c :** a spindle tree (*Euonymus europaeus*) **2 :** AMERICAN MOUNTAIN ASH **3 :** MARRON GLACÉ

witchy \ˈwichē, -chi\ *adj* -ER/-EST **1 :** resembling or characteristic of a witch **:** MALEVOLENT, WITCHLIKE ⟨a terrible little woman, a little ~ moron —Peggy Bennett⟩ **2 :** produced by or suggestive of witchcraft ⟨~ little houses . . . straight from a child's book of fairy tales —William Sansom⟩ ⟨there was a round moon . . . and the yard was full of a white ~ radiance —C.G.D.Roberts⟩

wit-cracker *n, obs* **:** one who makes wisecracks

¹**wite** \ˈwīt, *usu* -īd·+V\ *n* -S [ME, fr. OE *wīte*; akin to OHG *wīzi* fine, punishment, ON *vīti* fine, punishment, OE *wītan* to look after, blame] **1 a :** a penal fine for serious crimes payable under early English law to the king or other authority having jurisdiction — see BLOODWITE **b :** an exemption from payment of such a fine **2** *chiefly Scot* **:** responsibility for a fault or misfortune ⟨now it's done . . . and who's to bear the ~ of it —R.L.Stevenson⟩

²**wite** \"\ *vt* [ME *witen*, fr. OE *wītan* to see to, look after, reproach, blame; akin to OS *wītan* to blame, OHG *wīzan* to blame, punish, ON *vīta* to fine, OE *witan* to be aware, know — more at WIT, v.] *chiefly Scot* **:** to impute blame to **:** CENSURE

wi·te·na·ge·mot *or* **wi·te·na·ge·mote** \ˌwitˀnəgəˈmōt, ˌwitˀn-ˈägə,m-\ *n* -S [OE *witena gemōt*, fr. *witena* (gen. pl. of *wita* sage, advisor) + *gemōt* gemot — more at WITAN, GEMOT] **:** an Anglo-Saxon council of perhaps 100 nobles, prelates, and influential officials convened from time to time to advise the king on administrative and judicial matters — called also *witan*; compare GEMOT, MOOT 1a

wit·gat·boom \ˈwit,gat\ *or* **wit·gat** \-,büm\ *n* -S [*witgat* fr. Afrik, short for *witgatboom*, lit., white hole tree, fr. MD *wit* white + *gat* hole, opening + *boom* tree; akin to OE *hwīt* white, *gæt* opening, *bēam* tree — more at WHITE, GATE, BEAM] **:** a So. African shrub or tree (*Boscia albitrunca*) of the family Capparidaceae having white hard close-grained wood and roots that are roasted as a coffee substitute

¹**with** \(ˌ)wi|th, |th, ˌwə|\ *prep* [ME, fr. OE, prep. & adv., against, opposite, toward, with; akin to OE *wither* against, OS *with, withar* against, with, OHG *widar* against, back, again, ON *vith, vithr* against, with, Goth *withra* against, OSlav *vŭtorŭ* other, second, Skt *vi* apart, asunder, *vitaram* farther and perh. to L *vitium* fault, vice; basic meaning: apart, divided] **1 a :** in opposition to **:** AGAINST ⟨fought bitterly ~ his partner⟩ ⟨had had a constant tussle ~ insomnia —Lucien Price⟩ **b :** away from **:** so as to be separated or detached from ⟨broke ~ his family and left home⟩ ⟨refused adamantly to part ~ any of his most cherished possessions⟩ **2 a :** alongside of **:** near to **:** ⟨the boat was running close in ~ the land⟩ **b :** in a line or on a course paralleling the direction or movement of ⟨~ the grain⟩ ⟨~ the wind⟩ **c :** in the same direction as the course or motion of **:** favorable to ⟨the wind was ~ the boat⟩ ⟨the tide is ~ us⟩ **3 a** — used as a function word to indicate one to whom a communication or statement is made ⟨a grave mistake to go into long explanations ~ such a person —W.J.Reilly⟩ **b** *archaic* **:** in the mind or will of **:** WITHIN ⟨consider ~ yourselves, to bring in . . . a lion among ladies is a most dreadful thing —Shak.⟩ **4 a** — used as a function word to indicate one that shares in an action, transaction, or arrangement ⟨we who have worked ~ them day and night —J.K. Blake⟩ ⟨three quarters of its annual business . . . is now done ~ Americans —E.O.Hauser⟩ ⟨a salon . . . brought off in an academic town ~ young men and women on cookies and hot chocolate —Lucien Price⟩ **b** — used as a function word to indicate the object of attention, behavior, or feeling ⟨their satisfaction ~ the institution —E.P.Vonderhaar⟩ ⟨get tough ~ him⟩ ⟨angry ~ her⟩ ⟨in love ~ her⟩ **c :** in respect to **:** so far as concerns ⟨on friendly terms ~ all nations⟩ ⟨expressed agreement ~ his views⟩ ⟨seemed to be all right ~ her whether we bought or not —G.P.Musselman⟩ **d** — used to indicate the object of an adverbial expression of imperative force ⟨off ~ his head⟩ ⟨away ~ him⟩ **e :** as the doer, giver, or victim of ⟨charged ~ murder⟩ ⟨threatened ~ tuberculosis⟩ **f :** OVER, UPON ⟨no longer has any influence ~ him⟩ **g :** in the performance, operation, or use of ⟨prospering ~ their dairy industry —C.B.Hitchcock⟩ ⟨the trouble ~ this machine⟩ ⟨something went wrong ~ the radio⟩ **5 a** — used as a function word to indicate the object of a statement of comparison, equality, or sameness ⟨this house is identical ~ the one you have just seen⟩ ⟨on equal terms ~ the other applicants⟩ **b** — used as a function word to express agreement or concurrence ⟨if we accept this evidence we must conclude, ~ him, that the painting is a forgery⟩ ⟨oar flashing ~ oar⟩ **c :** on the side of **:** willing to give aid or support to **:** FOR ⟨if he's trying to cut down accidents, I'm ~ him⟩ ⟨the election will show whether the people are ~ him in this new policy⟩ **d :** as well as **:** not inferior to ⟨can pitch ~ the best of them⟩ **6 a :** in the judgment or estimation of ⟨he stood well ~ his fellow classmates⟩ **b :** in or according to the experience or practice of ⟨~ many of us, our ideas seem to fall by the wayside —W.J.Reilly⟩ ⟨~ the surrealists . . . the ideal is nothing else than the material world reflected by the human mind —Herbert Read⟩ ⟨an accustomed action ~ her, to seem thus washing her hands —Shak.⟩ **c :** after the manner, judgment, or practice of **:** LIKE ⟨suffer ~ Job⟩ **7 a** (1) *archaic* **:** by the direct act of ⟨here is himself, marred, as you see, ~ traitors —Shak.⟩ (2) *obs* **:** born of or procreated by ⟨she speaks, and 'tis such sense that my sense breeds ~ it —Shak.⟩ **b :** by means of **:** by the use or agency of **:** THROUGH ⟨the plot is unfolded almost entirely ~ the camera rather than ~ words —*Time*⟩ ⟨one of the nicest ways to say "Merry Christmas" is ~ a gift you've created yourself —*Item*⟩ ⟨just got in ~ the bus —Alasdair Carmichael⟩ **c :** by the presence, addition, or contiguity of ⟨bordered front and back ~ boxwood hedges —*Amer. Guide Series: Pa.*⟩ ⟨an attic filled ~ junk⟩ ⟨an atmosphere permeated ~ suspicion⟩ **d :** as a result of **:** in consequence of **:** because of ⟨pale ~ anger⟩ ⟨had woken up, about 1 o'clock, ~ a fellow blowing his horn —Dorothy Sayers⟩ ⟨was rosy ~ breasting the hill —Maurice Hewlett⟩ **8 a** — used as a function word to indicate manner of action ⟨ran ~ effort⟩ ⟨spoke ~ ease⟩ **b** — used as a function word to indicate a related or supplementary fact or circumstance ⟨stark silence ~ no recognition whatsoever is the common reception —W.J.Reilly⟩ ⟨morning sessions are largely case problems, ~ guest speakers in the afternoon —C.F.Craig⟩ ⟨remains essentially unchanged, ~ many old houses now largely owned by summer residents —*Amer. Guide Series: N.H.*⟩ **c** — used as a function word to indicate an emotional or mental state accompanying a specified action ⟨~ purity and holiness will I pass my life and practice my art —*Hippocratic Oath*⟩ ⟨looked on ~ horror⟩ **d** — used as a function word to indicate a circumstance accompanying or a result attendant on a specified action ⟨looking out over the water ~ his chin supported on his hands —E.G.O'Neill⟩ ⟨told us about it ~ detail —W.A.White⟩ ⟨escaped ~ a brief imprisonment when less affluent agitators were hanged —*Amer. Guide Series: N.C.*⟩ ⟨attacked ~ great loss of life⟩ **e** — used as a function word to indicate connection or relationship in idea, state, or action ⟨taking one day ~ another⟩ ⟨~ such speed, caution was impossible⟩ **9 a :** immediately consequent upon — used before a demonstrative pronoun ⟨~ this she seizeth on his sweating palm —Shak.⟩ **b :** at the moment or time of ⟨is up ~ the dawn⟩ **:** on the occurrence of or as a result of the occurrence of ⟨~ whose death the scepter passed into other hands —Kemp Malone⟩ ⟨~ the outbreak of the Civil War he returned North —T.S.Palmer⟩ **c** — used as a function word to indicate a person or thing that serves as a point of departure or conclusion ⟨we will begin ~ you⟩ ⟨ended the lecture ~ this quotation⟩ **d :** at the same time as **:** at the time a specified action or event is performed or experienced by ⟨men who were born just before or ~ the century —Manès Sperber⟩ ⟨the captain went down ~ his ship⟩ **e :** in the course of ⟨~ time the amount of fossil fuels remaining approaches zero —W.P.Webb⟩ **f :** in proportion to ⟨the pressure varies ~ the depth⟩ **10 a** — used as a function word to indicate addition or supplement ⟨his own funds, ~ the money he borrowed, enabled him to gain control of the business⟩ **b :** inclusive of ⟨it costs five dollars, ~ the tax⟩ **c** *archaic* — used as a function word to invoke evil or misfortune ⟨show your knave's visage, ~ a pox to you —Shak.⟩ **d** — used as a function word to indicate something given, received, or taken for granted ⟨~ your leave⟩ ⟨~ your permission⟩ **e** — used as a function word to introduce a refrain (as of a poem or song) ⟨~ hey, ho, the wind and the rain —Shak.⟩ **f** — used as a function word to indicate combination or mixture of ingredients ⟨blend melted chocolate ~ the batter⟩ ⟨heat milk ~ honey⟩ **g :** joined to **:** placed, arranged, or grouped in the same space, combination, package, or getup as ⟨put the bill away ~ the others⟩ ⟨ordered onion ~ his hamburger⟩ ⟨wore a cloth cap ~ his sport shirt⟩ **h** — used as a function word to introduce an expression of gratitude, regard, or affection esp. in a message or letter ⟨we return your contribution ~ thanks⟩ ⟨~ the compliments of the author⟩ **11 a** — used as a function word to indicate accompaniment or companionship ⟨a man of sorrows and acquainted ~ grief —Isa 53:3 (AV)⟩ **b :** at the home of **:** VISITING ⟨her mother is ~ her for the summer⟩ **:** in attendance on **:** SEEING ⟨the doctor is ~ him now⟩ **c :** in the company of **:** as companion of ⟨went to the theater ~ his wife⟩ ⟨his long friendship ~ his rival for the position⟩ **d :** present to ⟨this hot spell has been ~ us for a week⟩ ⟨peace be ~ you⟩ **e :** as part of **:** having membership or participation in ⟨seven hundred and one men who graduated from Harvard ~ the class of 1904 —F.D. Roosevelt⟩ ⟨goes along ~ the crowd⟩ ⟨has been ~ the firm for twenty years⟩ **12 a :** in the care, guidance, or possession of ⟨left the money ~ his mother⟩ ⟨carried his prejudices abroad ~ him⟩ ⟨the children went to the fair ~ their teacher⟩ **b :** having the possession, keeping, or guidance of **:** having, holding, or wearing ⟨came ~ good news⟩ ⟨a bride ~ a large fortune⟩ ⟨a diplomat ~ important missions —G.C. Sellery⟩ ⟨marched in ~ their uniforms of scarlet and gold —P.D.Whitney⟩ **c :** characterized or distinguished by ⟨a man ~ a hot temper⟩ ⟨a woman ~ a sharp tongue⟩ ⟨a knife ~ a dull blade⟩ **d :** by reason of having, containing, or giving forth ⟨it was pouring ~ rain —Archibald Marshall⟩ ⟨the air is sharp ~ frost —Corey Ford⟩ **e** — used as a function word to indicate one that possesses a specified attribute ⟨has a pleasing way ~ her⟩ **f** — used as a function word to indicate an object or source of concern or puzzlement ⟨what's ~ him⟩ ⟨what's ~ liberalism today —Eric Goldman & Mary Paull⟩ **13 a :** allowing for **:** in spite of **:** NOTWITHSTANDING ⟨a really tip-top man, ~ all his wrongheadedness —H.J.Laski⟩ **b :** except at the cost or loss of ⟨cannot do this ~ impunity⟩ ⟨cannot attain this ~ honor⟩ **c** — used as a function word to indicate a qualification or proviso ⟨accepted the offer ~ certain conditions⟩ **d :** except for ⟨finds that, ~ one group of omissions and one important addition, they reflect that curriculum —Gilbert Highet⟩ — **with it** *slang* **:** on the beam ⟨wake up and get *with it*⟩ — **with the sun** *adv* **:** in the direction of the sun's motion as it appears to one facing south in the northern hemisphere **:** CLOCKWISE — opposed to *against the sun*

²**with** \ˈwith, -th\ *adv* **:** so as to have something present or added ⟨I'll have my hamburger ~⟩

³**with** *also* **withe** \ˈwith\ *n, pl* **withes** [alter. of *width*] **:** one of the partitions between the flues in a chimney

¹**with·al** \wəˈthȯl, -thȯl\ *adv* [ME *withal, withall*, fr. *with*, prep., + *al, all* all — more at WITH, ALL] **1 :** together with this **:** in addition **:** BESIDES ⟨he was a supporter of all constructive work and ~ an excellent business man —A.W.Long⟩ **2** *archaic* **:** THEREWITH ⟨if he do bleed, I'll gild the faces of the grooms ~ —Shak.⟩ **3 :** on the other hand **:** for all that **:** NEVERTHELESS ⟨incessantly badgering, cajoling and driving, but a gentleman ~ —Anthony Leviero⟩ ⟨her voice was hoarse and rough but had an appealing warmth ~ —Peter Abrahams⟩

²**withal** \"\ *prep* [ME *withall*, fr. *withall*, adv.] *archaic* **:** WITH — used postpositively with a relative or interrogative pronoun as object ⟨tell you who time ambles ~ —Shak.⟩

wi·tha·nia \wəˈthānēə\ *n, cap* [NL, fr. *withan* (of unknown origin) + NL *-ia*] **:** a small genus of Old World tropical shrubs (family Solanaceae) having woolly leaves and clustered bell-shaped flowers with an enlarged fruiting calyx and including one plant (*W. coagulans*) used in the East Indies as a substitute for rennet in making cheese

with·draw \wəthˈdrȯ, with-\ *vb* [ME *withdrawen*, fr. ¹*with* + *drawen* to pull, draw — more at DRAW] *vt* **1 a :** to take back or away (something bestowed or possessed) ⟨*withdrew* his acceptance of the invitation —*Current Biog.*⟩ ⟨~*s* her awareness and love from the one person . . . who most deserves her awareness and love —Lionel Trilling⟩ **b :** to remove from use or cultivation ⟨lands *withdrawn* from commercial use —*Amer. Guide Series: Wash.*⟩ **2 a :** to remove or draw out from a place or position ⟨~ strip slowly from water —*Monsanto Mag.*⟩ ⟨from his dispatch case . . . *withdrew* a document —*Time*⟩ **b :** to turn away (as the eyes) from an object of attention ⟨*withdrew* his eyes from the scene⟩ ⟨*withdrew* his glance⟩ **c :** to remove (money) from a place of deposit or investment **d** (1) **:** to draw back or aside (as a curtain or veil) (2) **:** to draw back (as a bolt) from a fastening **3 a** *archaic* **:** to disengage or remove (oneself) from a place, position, office, or situation ⟨~ yourselves and leave us here alone —Shak.⟩ **b :** to draw away or turn aside from some activity or interest **:** DISTRACT, DIVERT ⟨even so grave an undertaking could not wholly ~ her from more congenial pursuits —Walter Bagehot⟩ **c :** to cause to return or retire from a place or activity ⟨*withdrew* his son from the school⟩ ⟨*withdrew* the troops from the attack⟩ **d :** to dismiss (a juror) from a jury **4 a :** to eliminate from consideration or set outside of a category or group ⟨*withdrew* his name from the list of nominees⟩ ⟨had *withdrawn* one dogma after another from the domain of pure reason —G.G.Coulton⟩ **b :** to abandon the prosecution of **:** cease to proceed with ⟨~ its objections to the . . . agreements —*Current Biog.*⟩ **c** (1) **:** to make a retraction of (an assertion or expression) **:** take back **:** RECALL, UNSAY ⟨demanded that the speaker ~ the word *fraudulent*⟩ (2) **:** to recall or remove (a motion) from consideration under parliamentary procedure ~ *vi* **1 a :** to move back or away from a place, position, group, or person **:** RETIRE ⟨the dancers ~ to a clear space at the farther end of the banqueting-hall —Lafcadio Hearn⟩ ⟨was forced more and more to ~ from the gaieties of the capital —Martha T. Stephenson⟩ **b :** to draw back from a battlefield or area of conflict **:** RETREAT ⟨must either maintain ourselves there in force or ~ —*Atlantic*⟩ **2 a :** to remove oneself from participation or activity in something ⟨*withdrew* from the church of her family —*Amer. Guide Series: Tenn.*⟩ ⟨*withdrew* from newspaper work to devote his full time to writing —*Atlantic Bull.*⟩ **b :** to resign from or cease attendance at a school or course of study ⟨*withdrew* after a year or so without taking a degree —*Current Biog.*⟩ **c :** to become socially or emotionally detached ⟨her mother . . . had *withdrawn* farther and farther into herself —Ethel Wilson⟩ **3 :** to recall a motion from consideration under parliamentary procedure **syn** see GO

with·draw·able \-ȯəbəl\ *adj* **:** capable of being withdrawn

with·draw·al \-ȯ(ə)l\ *n* -S **1 a :** retreat or retirement esp. into a more secluded or less exposed place or position ⟨sought national security in ~ from areas of conflict —A.O.Wolfers⟩ ⟨their furtive glances, odd silences, and sudden ~s into family jocularity and isolation —Virginia Woolf⟩ **b :** an operation by which a military force disengages from the enemy **c** (1) **:** social or emotional detachment ⟨this immense power of ~, this concentration upon the things of the spirit —Agnes Repplier⟩ (2) **:** a pathological retreat from objective reality (as in some schizophrenic states) **2 :** RETRACTION, REVOCATION ⟨insisted upon a ~ of the statement and a public apology⟩ **3 :** the act of drawing someone or something back from or out of a place or position ⟨the commission of the League of Nations which supervised the ~ of foreigners —*Times Lit. Supp.*⟩ **4 a :** the act of taking back or away something that has been granted or possessed ⟨the ~ of storage privileges —*Amer. Guide Series: Minn.*⟩ ⟨the ~ of esteem or love —Abram Kardiner⟩ **b :** removal from a place of deposit or investment ⟨made several large ~s from the bank within the space of a week⟩ **c :** the discontinuance of administration or use of a drug ⟨discomfort resulting from ~ of the opiate⟩ ⟨the ~ effects of barbiturates⟩ **d :** COITUS INTERRUPTUS

withdrawal symptom *n* **:** one of a group of symptoms (as nausea, sweating, or depression) produced in a person by deprivation of an addicting drug

with·draw·er \-ȯ(ə)r, -ȯə\ *n* [ME, fr. *withdrawen* to withdraw + *-er*] **:** one that withdraws

withdrawing *adj* [fr. pres. part. of *withdraw*] **:** that withdraws; *specif* **:** RECEDING, RETIRING ⟨a sharp face that was sour and ~ —J.A.Michener⟩ — **with·draw·ing·ness** *n* -ES

withdrawing room *n* [*withdrawing* fr. gerund of *withdraw*] **:** a room for retirement from another room (as a dining room) **:** DRAWING ROOM

with·draw·ment \-mənt\ *n* -S **:** WITHDRAWAL

with·drawn \-ȯn\ *adj* [fr. past part. of *withdraw*] **1 :** removed from immediate contact or easy approach **:** ISOLATED, SECLUDED ⟨during the long windswept winters is a lonely, ~ community —*Amer. Guide Series: Mich.*⟩ ⟨led cramped, ~ lives —Gordon Merrick⟩ **2 :** socially detached and unresponsive **:** INTROVERTED ⟨there is nothing ~ or coldly impersonal about him —Nancy Ross⟩ — **with·drawn·ness** \-ȯnnəs\ *n* -ES

¹**withe** \ˈwith *also* -ith *or* -īth, *dial* ˈhwith\ *n* -S [ME, fr. OE *withthe* — more at WITHY] **1 a :** a band consisting of a twig twisted **b :** a slender flexible branch or twig (as of osier) used as a band or rope **:** WITHY **c :** a slender twig ⟨the young man imagines that he can fight his way through the world with a ~ of sorrel wood —Donn Byrne⟩ ⟨a small ~ of a man —Peter De Vries⟩ **2 a :** a tropical American weedy herb (*Heliotropium fruticosum*) whose stems are used in Jamaica for making baskets **b :** WITHE ROD **3** *also* **wythe** \"\ **a :** a boom iron; *specif* **:** the boom iron that secures the flying jib boom **b :** a metal ring or band on a mast or other spar **4** *or* **wythe** \"\ **:** TIER 2d

²**withe** \"\ *vt* -ED/-ING/-S [ME *withen*, fr. ¹*withe*] **1** *archaic* **:** to wind or twist like a withe **2 a :** to bind or fasten with a withe **b :** to snare (deer) with a noose of withes

³**withe** *var of* WITH

with·en \ˈwithən, ˈwīth-\ *n* -S [ME, prob. short for *withen-tre* willow tree, fr. *withen*, adj. (prob. fr. ¹*withy* + *-en*) + *tre* tree] *archaic* **:** WILLOW

¹**with·er** \ˈwithə(r)\ *vb* **withered; withered; withering**

\-th(ə)riŋ\ withers [ME *widderen, widren;* prob. akin to ME *wederen* to weather — more at WEATHER] *vi* **1 :** to become dry and sapless **:** shrivel up ⟨crops ~*ed* and crumbled to dust —*Amer. Guide Series: Texas*⟩ **2 :** to lose bodily moisture **:** become dried up **:** waste away in body ⟨seeming to contract, to ~ before their shocked eyes, with his cheeks and the hollows behind his ears all sunken in —Angus Mowat⟩ **3 :** to lose vitality, force, or freshness **:** DECAY, DECLINE, FADE ⟨the tariffs and prohibitions which caused industries to flourish or ~ —*Times Lit. Supp.*⟩ — often used with *away* **~** *vt* **1 a :** to cause (as a plant) to dry up **:** SHRIVEL ⟨the cold winds blew from the east, ~*ing* grass and plants and trees —Kathleen Freeman⟩ **b :** to subject (tea leaves) to a drying process **c :** to check the growth of (germinating barley) on the malting floor in brewing **2 :** to cause to shrink, wrinkle, or decay ⟨age cannot ~ her —Shak.⟩ **3 a :** to cause to lose freshness, vitality, or force ⟨control will ~ science by destroying its precious essence of originality and spontaneity —R.P.Patterson⟩ **b :** to make speechless or incapable of action **:** PARALYZE, STUN ⟨~*ed* him with a look —Dorothy Sayers⟩ ⟨before she could ~ him for his impertinence, he swept her on to the floor in a waltz —Anthony Glyn⟩

²wither \"\ *n* -s **:** the process of withering tea leaves ⟨black, well twisted leaf denotes a good ~ —W.A.Ukers⟩

withered *adj* [fr. past part. of ¹*wither*] **:** shriveled and shrunken from drying **:** WIZENED ⟨a lanky scarecrow of a man with ~ face and lantern jaws —W.F.Starkie⟩ ⟨leaning heavily on ~ phrases —Kevin Desmond⟩ — **with·ered·ness** *n* -ES

withered leaf *n* **:** FEUILLE MORTE

withered rose *n* **:** a grayish red to moderate reddish brown

with·er·er \-th(ə)rə(r)\ *n* -s **:** one that withers

withering *adj* **1 :** acting or serving to cut down or destroy **:** ANNIHILATING, DEVASTATING ⟨guns mounted on railway cars opened a ~ fire —Alexander Forbes⟩ ⟨to compliments inflated I've a ~ reply —W.S.Gilbert⟩ **2 :** used for drying or curing ⟨~ floor⟩ — **with·er·ing·ly** *adv*

with·er·ite \'withə,rīt\ *n* -s [G *witherit,* irreg. fr. William *Withering* †1799 Eng. physician + G *-it* -ite] **:** a mineral $BaCO_3$ consisting of a native barium carbonate isostructural with aragonite and occurring as orthorhombic white or gray six-sided twin crystals and also in columnar or granular masses (hardness 3–3.75, sp. gr. 4.27–4.35)

with·er·nam \'withə(r),näm\ *n* -s [ME, fr. AF, fr. OE *wither* against + *nām* seizure, fr. *niman* to take — more at WITH, NIMBLE] **1 :** the action of taking by way of reprisal **:** a second or reciprocal distress of other goods in lieu of goods taken by a first distress and eloigned **2 :** a writ used in connection with the action of replevin that issues to a defendant in replevin when he has obtained judgment for a return of the chattels replevied and fails to obtain them on the writ of return and that authorizes the taking of other goods of the same value — called also *capias in withernam, writ of reprisal*

withe rod *n* [¹*withe*] **:** either of two No. American viburnums (*Viburnum cassinoides* and *V. nudum*) with tough slender shoots like those of an osier and flat heads of white or creamy flowers

with·ers \'withə(r)z\ *n pl* [prob. fr. obs. E *wither-* (prefix), against, in resistance of, counter (fr. OE, fr. *wither,* adv., against) + E *-s,* n. pl. suffix; fr. the withers being the parts which resist the pull in drawing a load] **1** *also* **wither a :** the ridge between the shoulder bones of a horse — see HORSE illustration **b :** the part between the shoulder bones at the base of the neck in various animals (as the deer, ox, or sheep) **2 :** FEELINGS, SENSIBILITIES ⟨our ~ are unwrung —Shak.⟩ ⟨try to wring your ~ with a story of attempted suicide —Richard Blaker⟩

withershins *var of* WIDDERSHINS

withertip \'==,=\ *n* [¹*wither* + *tip*] **:** a blighting of terminal shoots or of the tips of leaves esp. characteristic of various anthracnoses of citrus plants — compare CITRUS ANTHRACNOSE, LIME ANTHRACNOSE

withertop \'==,=\ *n* [¹*wither* + *top*] **:** a calcium deficiency disease of flax characterized by loss of turgidity of the stem near its apex and subsequent death of the tip

withes *pl of* WITHE, *pres 3d sing of* WITHE

withewood \'=,=\ *n* [¹*withe* + *wood*] **:** WITHE ROD

with·hold \wəth'hōld, with'h-\ *vb* **with·held** \-'held\ **with·held** \"\ *or archaic* **with·hold·en** \-'hōldən\ **withholding; withholds** [ME *withholden,* fr. ¹*with* + *holden* to hold — more at HOLD] *vt* **1 :** to hold back **:** keep from action **:** CHECK, RESTRAIN ⟨frequent bursts of grief . . . obliged her, at intervals, to ~ her pen —Jane Austen⟩ **2 :** to desist or refrain from granting, giving, or allowing **:** keep in one's possession or control **:** keep back ⟨distribute among the youngsters all blankets and provisions and gear, ~*ing* for myself only a canteen —Hodding Carter⟩ ⟨~ permission⟩ **3** *obs* **:** to keep prisoner **:** DETAIN ⟨she perforce ~*s* the loved boy —Shak.⟩ **~** *vi* **:** FORBEAR, REFRAIN ⟨a police traffic commission *withheld* from banning them —John Robbins⟩ **syn** see KEEP

with·hold·er \-də(r)\ *n* **:** one that withholds

with·hold·ing \-diŋ, -dēŋ\ *n* [ME *withholding,* fr. gerund of *withholden* to withhold] **:** the act or procedure of deducting a tax payment from income at the source

withholding tax *n* **:** a deduction levied as a tax upon income (as salaries, wages, fees, or dividends) at the source

withier *comparative of* WITHY

withiest *superlative of* WITHY

¹with·in \wə'thin, -thin\ *adv* [ME *withinne, withinnen,* fr. OE *withinnan,* fr. *with,* prep. + *innan,* adv. & prep., in, inwardly, within, fr. *in,* prep. — more at WITH, IN] **1 a :** on the inside or on the inner side **:** INTERNALLY, INSIDE ⟨had plastered the walls and whitewashed them ~ and without —Ellen Glasgow⟩ **b :** inside the body **:** underneath the skin ⟨a man whose blood is warm ~ —Shak.⟩ **c :** HEREIN ⟨the person ~ named⟩ **2 :** inside the bounds of a place or region ⟨but whom they fear'd without, they found ~ —John Dryden⟩ ⟨traitors ~, as well as exiles without —George Grote⟩ **3 a :** in or into a building **:** INDOORS ⟨rooms for rent, inquire ~⟩ **b :** in an inner room or enclosure ⟨presenting action which must be shown ~ (as in a curtained study or bedroom) —Leslie Hotson⟩ **c :** behind the scenes — used in stage directions ⟨one calls ~ —Shak.⟩ **d :** at home ⟨not being ~ when he called —Jane Austen⟩ **4 :** in one's inner thought, disposition, or character **:** INWARDLY ⟨an air of aloofness about him . . . he lived ~ —H.A. McHugh⟩ ⟨outwardly calm but raging ~⟩

²within \"\ *prep* [ME *withinne, withinnen,* fr. OE *withinnan,* fr. *with,* prep., + *innan,* adv. & prep.] **1** — used as a function word to indicate enclosure or containment: as **a :** in the inner being of ⟨build up a state of tension ~ themselves —Vance Packard⟩ ⟨his heart sank ~ him⟩ **b** (1) **:** in the inner or interior part of **:** INSIDE OF ⟨the water is stored ~ the soil —W.P.Webb⟩ ⟨the spirit of adventure being strong ~ me —H.A.Chippendale⟩ (2) **:** in the limits or compass of **:** not beyond ⟨research conducted ~ university grounds —J.B. Conant⟩ ⟨~ the country⟩ ⟨~ the company⟩ **c :** enclosed or confined by ⟨~ the walls⟩ ⟨~ the doors⟩ **d :** forming a section of **:** included in ⟨a continent ~ a continent —Allan Murray⟩ ⟨a musical ~ a musical —*Time*⟩ **e** *archaic* **:** on the further side of **:** approached by means of **2 a** (1) **:** not longer in time than **:** before the end or since the beginning of ⟨~ four years he had become superintendent —*Current Biog.*⟩ ⟨troops would be withdrawn . . . ~ two years after the end of the war —F.W.D.Deakin⟩ (2) *obs* **:** during the course of **:** at any time during ⟨died ~ the year of our redemption four hundred twenty-six —Shak.⟩ **b** (1) **:** not exceeding in quantity or degree ⟨lived ~ his income⟩ (2) — used as a function word to indicate a specified difference or margin of error ⟨came ~ two percentage points of a perfect mark⟩ ⟨guessed her weight to ~ two pounds⟩ **c :** not farther in length or distance than **:** nearer than ⟨took pictures ~ feet of stampeding elephants, ~ inches of the fangs of deadly snakes —H.C.Adamson⟩ ⟨~ one short flight of a cuckoo from this home —John Galsworthy⟩ **d** (1) **:** not going outside the scope or influence of **:** subject to ⟨societies have to operate ~ the possibilities and limitations of their particular historical situation —Erich Fromm⟩ ⟨the producer must indeed work ~ conditions set by consumers' demand —G.D.H.Cole⟩ (2) — used as a function word to indicate accessibility to some action, effort, or means of perception ⟨~ reach⟩ ⟨~ sight⟩ ⟨~ hearing⟩ (3) **:** not beyond the capacity or power of ⟨indulge in indoor and outdoor sports ~ their physical capabilities —J.A.Brussel⟩ ⟨the hunter will usually gallop well ~ himself —Henry Wynmalen⟩ **3 a :** to the inside of **:** INTO ⟨sunk the sea ~ the earth —Shak.⟩ ⟨escaped, however, and fled ~ the British lines —*Amer. Guide Series: N. H.*⟩ **b** *archaic* **:** in or into the midst or keeping of ⟨take every object by the hand, and lead it ~ me —Walt Whitman⟩ **c** (1) — used as a function word to indicate self-containment or independence ⟨the world to which they belonged . . . was strictly circumscribed and complete ~ itself —Laurence Binyon⟩ (2) **:** with respect to **:** so far as concerns ⟨things good ~ themselves but beyond the possibility of accomplishment —W.J.Humphreys⟩ **d** *obs* **:** in the control of ⟨good madam, keep yourself ~ yourself —Shak.⟩

³within \"\ *adj* **:** lying or to be found inside **:** ENCLOSED, INCLUDED ⟨the ~ complaint⟩ ⟨the ~ indictment⟩

⁴within \"\ *n* -s **:** an inner or enclosed place or space ⟨the ~ of the stand always has an air of coziness —John McNulty⟩

withindoors \=¦=¦=\ *adv* [fr. the phrase *within doors*] **:** INDOORS

withing *pres part of* WITHE

¹with·in·side \wə¦thin¦sīd, -th-\ *also* **with·in·sides** \-dz\ *adv* [*withinside* fr. *within* + *side* (as in *inside*); *withinsides* fr. *withinside* + *-s*] **1** *archaic* **:** on the inner side **2 a :** on the inside ⟨perceived almost immediately ~ the missing turbot —Hugh McCrae⟩ **b :** INDOORS ⟨sat ~ tailor-wise and busily stitching —R.L.Stevenson⟩

²withinside \"\ *prep, archaic* **:** INSIDE ⟨has put certain whim-whams ~ the glass —Thomas Gray⟩

with·ness *n* -ES [¹*with* + *-ness*] **:** the state or fact of being close to or connected with someone or something **:** close association or proximity ⟨two people with each other in ~ —Truman Capote⟩

¹with·out \wə'thau̇t, -thau̇t, *usu* -d.+V\ *prep* [ME *withoute, withouten,* fr. OE *withūtan,* fr. *with,* prep. + *ūtan,* adv., outside, fr. *ūt* cut — more at WITH, OUT] **1 a :** at, to, or on the outside of **:** exterior to ⟨had to stand ~ the door —F.L.Packard⟩ ⟨had placed themselves ~ the church —Valentine Ughet & Eleanor Davis⟩ ⟨solidarity and goodwill within and ~ the clan —W.W. Howells⟩ **b :** out of the range of ⟨today, it is a goal, not ~ our immediate grasp, but attainable —S.J.Holbel⟩ **c :** BEYOND, PAST ⟨just ~ the trees —William Bartram⟩ **2 :** not derived from or connected with **:** external to ⟨light in me, light ~ me, everywhere change —Robert Browning⟩ **3 a :** not using or being subjected to ⟨spent the evening ~ conversation⟩ ⟨worked ~ coercion⟩ **b :** exempt or free from ⟨~ end⟩ ⟨~ fail⟩ ⟨~ fear⟩ **4 a :** not accompanied by or associated with **:** separated from ⟨smoke ~ fire⟩ ⟨taste ~ extravagance⟩ ⟨music ~ tears⟩ **b :** suffering the deprivation or absence of **:** not having **:** LACKING ⟨~ money or resources⟩ ⟨~ a roof over his head⟩ **c :** lacking the company or companionship of ⟨could not live ~ her⟩ **5 a :** not securing or receiving ⟨was fired ~ explanation⟩ ⟨was welcomed back ~ reproaches⟩ **b :** not admitting of ⟨a condition ~ remedy⟩ **c** — used as a function word to indicate the absence or neglect of an action ⟨people who look ~ seeing, listen ~ hearing, read ~ understanding, and act ~ thinking —*Phoenix Flame*⟩

²without \"\ *adv* [ME *withoute, withouten,* fr. OE *withūtan,* fr. *with,* prep. + *ūtan,* adv.] **1 :** on the outside **:** EXTERNALLY ⟨the church, a decent enough fourteenth-century . . . structure ~ —Osbert Lancaster⟩ **2 a :** outside of a particular place; *specif* **:** outside of the house **:** OUTDOORS ⟨an afternoon which was dismal ~ and within —Lucien Price⟩ **b :** outside of a class, community, or membership **3 :** in outward action, circumstance, or being **:** OUTWARDLY ⟨whether ~ or within, never . . . flagging in energy or zest —Emily Skeel⟩ ⟨within be fed, ~ be rich no more —Shak.⟩ **4 :** with a lack of something **:** so as to be deprived ⟨his parents were poor, and he learned to do ~⟩ ⟨go ~⟩

³without \"\ *n* -s **:** an outer place or region ⟨from the far ~ to the deep within —James Stephens⟩ ⟨a disintegration from within, aided no doubt by the allied victory, but not imposed from ~ —C.E.Black & E.C.Helmreich⟩

⁴without \"\ *conj* [ME *withoute,* fr. *withoute,* prep.] *chiefly dial* **:** EXCEPT, UNLESS ⟨not ~ the prince be willing —Shak.⟩ ⟨you don't know about me ~ you have read a book —Mark Twain⟩

withoutdoor *adj* [fr. *withoutdoor,* adv.] *obs* **:** OUTDOOR, EXTERIOR ⟨praise her but for this, her ~ form —Shak.⟩

withoutdoors *also* **withoutdoor** \=¦=¦=\ *adv* [fr. the phrase *without doors, without door*] **1 :** OUTDOORS ⟨the candles alight in the room . . . made all things ~ loom strange —Thomas Hardy⟩ **2** *usu* **without doors :** outside of a group, community, or deliberative body ⟨in arguing the case before the generality of voters *without doors* a more cautious approach was necessary —V.L.Parrington⟩

with·out·en \wə'thau̇tᵊn, -thau̇-\ *prep* [alter. (influenced by ¹*outen*) of *without*] *chiefly dial* **:** WITHOUT ⟨come to this country ~ a cent —Elizabeth M. Roberts⟩

without prejudice *adv* (*or adj*) **:** without injury to or detraction from one's own rights or claims or any cause of action or defense asserted

¹with·out·side \wə¦thau̇t¦sīd, -th-\ *adv* [*without* + *side* (as in *outside*)] **1** *archaic* **:** on the outer part or surface **2** *archaic* **:** OUTDOORS

²withoutside \"\ *prep, archaic* **:** OUTSIDE

with prejudice *adv* (*or adj*) **:** final and binding with the effect of res judicata

with·stand \wəth'stand, with-, -aa(ə)nd\ *vt* [ME *withstanden, withstonden,* fr. OE *withstandan,* fr. ¹*with* + *standan* to stand — more at STAND] **1 a :** to stand up against **:** offer opposition to **:** RESIST; *esp* **:** to make a successful stand against ⟨the first vertebrate I have ever known to ~ the army ants —William Beebe⟩ ⟨capable of ~*ing* a prolonged infantry siege —*Amer. Guide Series: Pa.*⟩ ⟨having *withstood* the pressure of her parents —Rose Macaulay⟩ **b :** to be proof against the pressure, impact, or effect of **:** be unaffected by ⟨looks well built to ~ work and worry —R.M.Yoder⟩ ⟨~ the drying up during the summer of the shallow ponds where it frequently lives —W.H.Dowdeswell⟩ **c :** to resist yielding to the attraction or influence of **:** FORBEAR ⟨the questionable capacity of most men, including himself, to ~ temptation —Laura Krey⟩ **2** *archaic* **:** to stop or obstruct the course of **:** stand in the way of **~** *vi* **:** to make resistance **:** OPPOSE, RESIST ⟨was firm, *withstood,* refused —Robert Browning⟩ **syn** see CONTEST

with·stand·er \-də(r)\ *n* [ME *withstonder,* fr. *withstonden* to withstand + *-er*] **:** one that withstands

with·stand·ing·ness *n* -ES **:** power or inclination to withstand

with·stay \wəth'stā, with-\ *vt* [¹*with* + *stay*] **:** to delay or hinder the course or coming of **:** WITHSTAND

with·wind \'wi,thwīnd\ *n* [ME *withewinde,* fr. OE *withewinde, withowinde,* fr. *withe-, witho-* (prob. akin to *withthe* withe) + *winde,* prob. fr. *windan* to turn — more at WIND] **:** BINDWEED

¹withy \'withē, -thē\ *n* -ES [ME, fr. OE *wīthig;* akin to OE *withthe* withe, OHG *wīda* willow, ON *vīthr* willow, *vith* withy, Goth *kunawida* chain, L *vitis* vine, *vitex* chaste tree, Gk *oisos* chaste tree, *itea* willow, *in-, is* tendon, sinew, muscle, OSlav *viti* to turn, wind, L *viēre* to twist together, plait — more at WIRE] **1 :** WILLOW; *esp* **:** OSIER 1 **2 a :** a flexible slender twig or branch (as of osier); *esp* **:** one used for binding **b :** a loop or hoop formed with a withy

²withy \'withē *also* -ithē *or* -īthē, *dial* 'hwithē\ *adj* -ER/-EST [¹*withe* + *-y*] **:** like a withy **:** flexible and tough; *specif* **:** AGILE, WIRY ⟨as ~ as a rattlesnake —W.R.Waterman⟩

withywind \'==,=\ *n* [alter. (influenced by ¹*withy*) of *withwind*] **:** BINDWEED

wit·less \'witləs\ *adj* [ME *witles,* fr. OE *witlēas,* fr. ²*wit* + *-lēas* -less] **1 :** destitute of understanding **:** wanting intelligence, wisdom, or good sense **:** lacking or not guided by judgment **:** FOOLISH, HEEDLESS, ILL-JUDGED ⟨interrupted by some ~ coxcombs⟩ ⟨~ obstinacy⟩ **2 :** mentally deranged **:** out of one's wits **:** INSANE, MAD **3 a :** deficient in mental capacity **:** having undeveloped or impaired intellectual power **:** lacking in intelligence **:** dull-witted **:** STUPID **b :** incapable of understanding or apprehending something ⟨~ to discern true values⟩ **4 :** lacking knowledge, awareness, or consciousness of something ⟨~ of the storm his words excite —Peter Crook⟩ **5 :** destitute of wit ⟨a matter-of-fact speech entirely ~⟩

wit·less·ly *adv* **:** in a witless manner **:** FOOLISHLY, STUPIDLY

wit·less·ness *n* -ES **:** the quality or state of being witless **:** FOLLY, SENSELESSNESS, STUPIDITY ⟨the oratory . . . broke new ground in oppressiveness and ~ —R.H.Rovere⟩

wit·ling \'witliŋ\ *n* -s [²*wit* + *-ling*] **:** a person of little wit or understanding **:** a pretender to wit **:** one given to smart sayings inferior in wit ⟨ye newspaper ~*s!* ye pert scribbling folks! —Oliver Goldsmith⟩

wit·loof \'wit,lōf\ *or* **witloof chicory** *n* -s [D dial. *witloof* chicory, lit., white foliage, fr. D *wit* white (fr. MD) + *loof* foliage, fr. MD, leaf; akin to OE *hwīt* white and *lēaf* leaf — more at WHITE, LEAF] **:** CHICORY 1; *also* **:** its crown of foliage as a salad green **:** ENDIVE 2

¹wit·ness \'witnəs\ *n* -ES [ME *witnesse,* fr. OE *witnes* knowledge, testimony, witness, fr. *wit,* n. + *-nes* -ness — more at WIT] **1 a** (1) **:** attestation of a fact or an event **:** EVIDENCE, TESTIMONY (2) *obs* **:** attestation or evidence provided by a person in court **b :** such testimony by signature or oath **2 :** one that gives evidence regarding matters of fact under inquiry; *specif* **:** one who testifies or is legally qualified to testify in a cause or to give evidence before a judicial tribunal or similar inquiry ⟨no person . . . shall be compelled in any criminal case to be a ~ against himself —*U.S.Constitution*⟩ ⟨one of the oil industry's most persuasive ~*es* before congressional committees —*Current Biog.*⟩ **3 a :** one who is called on to be present at a transaction so as to be able to testify to its having taken place (as one who witnesses a will, deed, or marriage); *specif* **:** one who sees the execution of an instrument and subscribes to confirm its authenticity by his testimony ⟨no ~ . . . can take any benefit under any testamentary document which is witnessed by him —Edward Jenks⟩ **b** *obs* **:** a sponsor or godparent at baptism **4 a :** one that is cognizant of something by direct experience **:** one who beholds or otherwise has personal knowledge of something ⟨a ~, though hardly . . . an actor, in these scenes —J.H.Newman⟩ ⟨standing there, I was ~ of a little incident —A.T.Quiller-Couch⟩ ⟨the clock also was a ~ to the success of the evening —Viola Meynell⟩ — see EARWITNESS, EYEWITNESS **b :** one, often God, who is invoked as cognizant of a fact and offered as one's surety — usu. used in asseverations ⟨though, God's my ~, there's no spite in me —Charles Kingsley⟩ **c :** one who by action or word gives testimony of fidelity to Christ and the Christian faith ⟨you may feel the call to be a ~ for Jesus —Rex Ingamells⟩ **5 a :** something that serves as or furnishes evidence or proof **:** an evidential mark, sign, or token ⟨prehistoric peoples left behind material ~*es* to their cultures —Brewton Berry⟩ ⟨the party's press . . . is likewise ~ to its weakened state —J.G.Colton⟩ **b :** something that serves as an evidential example offered in substantiation of a statement — used to introduce a name or instance ⟨the universities are showing the way, ~ their contribution to winning the war —Walter Moberly⟩ ⟨our grammar — ~ our verb system — is a marvel of flexibility —Charlton Laird⟩ — sometimes used with *as* ⟨outlaws have always been romanticized . . . as ~ Jesse James —*Ballad Book*⟩ **c :** a manuscript or an early version of a manuscript that in textual criticism constitutes evidence of authority for a text — usu. used in pl. ⟨few of these ~*es* contain the complete New Testament —I.M. Price⟩ **d :** public testimony by word or deed to one's religious faith ⟨live a life of Christian ~ alongside Communism —F.T. Cartwright⟩ ⟨the church . . . is not to abdicate its Christian ~ to government and secular society —K.D.Miller⟩ **6 :** PROOF 5b **7** *usu cap* **:** a member of Jehovah's Witnesses — **bear one witness :** to give evidence in corroboration of one's action or assertion **:** serve as a witness of one's action — **bear witness :** to furnish or constitute proof esp. by oral or written testimony ⟨great structures which *bear witness* to the prestige of the leaders —*Irish Digest*⟩ ⟨you will *bear witness* that I have done so⟩ — **with a witness** *archaic* **:** with clear evidence **:** without a doubt **:** to a great degree **:** with a vengeance **:** EFFECTUALLY, UNMISTAKABLY ⟨this, I confess, is haste *with a witness* —Robert South⟩

²witness \"\ *vb* -ED/-ING/-ES [ME *witnessen,* fr. *witnesse* witness] *vt* **1 :** to furnish evidence or proof such as to establish **:** give testimony to **:** provide oral or written evidence of **:** bear witness to **:** testify to **:** ATTEST ⟨early writers ~ the antiquity of the custom⟩ ⟨ready to ~ that the handwriting is that of the defendant⟩ **2 :** to act as legal witness of: as **a** *obs* **:** to give formal or sworn evidence of (as in court) ⟨you said you saw one here in court could ~ it —Shak.⟩ **b :** to see the execution of (as an instrument) and subscribe for the purpose of establishing authenticity **:** attest formally by signature **:** sign as a witness of the execution of (as a signature or writing) ⟨~ a will⟩ **c :** to be formally present as a witness of (as a transaction or the execution of a convict) **3 :** to give or constitute evidence of **:** furnish proof of **:** serve as a token or sign showing **:** BETOKEN, EVINCE ⟨your actions ~ your guilt⟩ ⟨our wounds ~ the ferocity of the attack made upon us⟩ **4 :** to establish by sworn or attested evidence contained therein **:** furnish formally attested evidence of — used of a document ⟨this indenture further ~*es* that injury to stock amounts to two hundred dollars⟩ **5 a** *obs* **:** to show or evidence by one's behavior ⟨he roll'd his eyes that ~*ed* huge dismay —Alexander Pope⟩ **b :** to bear witness to (as an object of allegiance or devotion) by speech or conduct **:** show evidence of by one's behavior ⟨more effectively to ~ Christ in our daily lives⟩ **6 :** to see or know by reason of personal presence **:** have direct cognizance of **:** observe with one's own eyes or ears **:** be present as an observer at **:** experience by personal observation — used esp. of something of a formal nature or of more than ordinary significance ⟨the inauguration . . . is said to have been ~*ed* by ten million persons —F.L.Mott⟩ ⟨the accident was ~*ed* by many fishermen —Norman Douglas⟩ **7 :** to constitute the scene of **:** form part of the setting of **:** be associated with ⟨this village ~*ed* . . . the last stand of the mule-drawn streetcar —*Amer. Guide Series: La.*⟩ ⟨the French Revolution ~*ed* some . . . bloody massacres —Alfred Cobban⟩ ⟨the postwar period has ~*ed* a number of developments in exchange rate practices —R.F.Mikesell⟩ **~** *vi* **1 :** to bear witness **:** give evidence **:** TESTIFY — usu. used with *to* or *against* ⟨hoping that they might ~ to the truth of his doctrine —J.L.Teller⟩ ⟨in these ways we ~ against our professed faiths —J.F.Dulles⟩ **2 :** to make known to others (as by speech or conduct) the religious experience one has undergone or the religious truths in which one believes **:** bear witness to one's religious convictions

³witness \"\ *adj* [ME *witnesse,* fr. *witnesse,* n., witness] **1 :** of, relating to, or used by a witness ⟨~ room⟩ ⟨~ fee⟩ **2 :** serving as a landmark or survey reference point ⟨~ tree⟩ ⟨~ stake⟩ — compare WITNESS CORNER

wit·ness·able \-səbəl\ *adj* **:** capable of being witnessed ⟨the workings of one mind are not ~ by other observers —Gilbert Ryle⟩

witness-box \'==,=\ *n, chiefly Brit* **:** an enclosure in which a witness sits or stands while testifying in court ⟨entered the *witness-box* —*Contemporary Rev.*⟩

witness corner *n* **:** a post or monument used esp. by surveyors as a reference point for the location of an inaccessible corner

witnessed *adj* [fr. past part. of ²*witness*] **:** attested by a witness; *specif* **:** attested by a disinterested broker — used of a securities transaction for the account of a broker who is in default on a contract made on the floor to deliver or accept delivery of such securities ⟨a ~ purchase⟩ ⟨a ~ sale⟩

wit·ness·er \-sə(r)\ *n* -s [ME, fr. *witnessen* to witness + *-er*] *archaic* **:** one that witnesses **:** WITNESS

witnesses *pl of* WITNESS, *pres 3d sing of* WITNESS

witness stand *n* **:** a usu. raised platform where a witness sits or stands while testifying in court or before an investigating committee ⟨chose to take the *witness stand* in her own defense —W.C.Mathes⟩ ⟨put upon the *witness stand* at a congressional hearing —Upton Sinclair⟩

wit·ney *or* **whit·ney** \'(h)witnē, -ni\ *n* -s [*Witney,* town in Oxfordshire, England where it was orig. manufactured] **1 :** a heavy woolen cloth used esp. for blankets **2 :** a soft woolen overcoating with a napped surface similar to chinchilla

wi·to·to *also* **ui·to·to** \wə'tōd·(,)ō\ *n, pl* **witoto** *or* **witotos** *also* **uitoto** *or* **uitotos** *usu cap* **1 a :** a people of southeastern Colombia **b :** a member of such people **2 :** the language of the Witotoan people of uncertain relationship — **wi·to·to·an** *or* **ui·to·to·an** \-ōd·əwən\ *adj, usu cap*

wits *pl of* WIT

wit·te·boom \'vid·ə,büm\ *n, pl* **witteboom** [Afrik, prob. fr. MD *witboom* white poplar, lit., white tree, fr. *wit* white + *boom* tree; akin to OE *hwīt* white and *bēam* tree — more at WHITE, BEAM] *southern Africa* **:** SILVER TREE 1

wit·ted \'wid·əd, -itəd\ *adj* [ME, fr. ²*wit* + *-ed*] **:** having wit or understanding — usu. used in combination ⟨a dull-*witted* adaptation of the . . . classic —Philip Hamburger⟩ ⟨make the keenest-*witted* man . . . little better than a blunderer —Allen Upward⟩ — **wit·ted·ness** *n* -ES

¹wit·ter \ˈwid·ə(r), -itə-\ *n* -s [obs. E *witter* sign, mark, token, prob. back-formation fr. E *wittering*] **:** the tee aimed at in curling

²witter \"\ *n* -s [origin unknown] *chiefly Scot* **:** BARB

wit·ter·ing \ˈwitərən, -riŋ\ *n* -s [ME (Sc) *wittering, witering,* fr. gerund of *witteren, witeren* to clarify, inform, teach, of Scand origin; akin to ON *vitra* to manifest, reveal, *vitr* wise, *vita* to know — more at WIT] *chiefly Scot* **:** a piece of information (as a sign, token, or hint)

¹witt·gen·stein·ian \ˌvitgənˌs(h)tīnēən\ *adj, usu cap* [Ludwig *Wittgenstein* †1951 Austrian philosopher + E *-an*] **:** of, relating to, or having the characteristics of the philosopher Ludwig Wittgenstein or his methods of linguistic analysis

²wittgensteinian \"\ *n* -s *usu cap* **:** a follower of Wittgenstein or an advocate of his analytical methods in philosophy

wit·ti·chen·ite \ˈwid·ə̇kəˌnīt\ *n* -s [G *wittichenit,* fr. *Wittichen,* Baden, Germany, its locality + G *-it* -ite] **:** a mineral Cu_3BiS_3 consisting of a tin-white to steel-gray copper bismuth sulfide and usu. occurring in massive form

wit·ti·cism \ˈwid·əˌsizəm, -itə-\ *n* -s [*witty* + *-cism* (as in *criticism*)] **1** *archaic* **:** a mean, sarcastic, or contemptible gibe **:** JEER **2 :** a witty saying, sentence, or phrase **:** a clever or amusing expression **:** a piece of wit **syn** see JOKE

wit·ti·cize \-ˌsīz\ *vi* -ED/-ING/-S [fr. *witticism,* after E *criticism: criticize*] **:** to express oneself wittily or indulge in witticisms

wit·ti·ly \ˈwid·ᵊlē, -it|, |ᵊli, |əl-\ *adv* [ME *wittiliche,* fr. *witty* + *-liche* -ly] **:** in a witty manner ⟨the doctor reasons very ~ but not convincingly —James Boswell⟩ ⟨so ~ satirical that the House rocked with laughter —*Amer. Guide Series: Minn.*⟩

wit·ti·ness \|ēnə̇s, |in-\ *n* -ES **:** the quality or state of being witty ⟨the ~ of his remarks⟩

¹wit·ting \ˈwid·iŋ, -itiŋ, -ēŋ\ *n* -s [ME, fr. gerund of *witen* to know — more at WIT] **1** *chiefly dial* **:** knowledge or awareness of something **:** COGNIZANCE **2** *chiefly dial* **:** information obtained or communicated **:** INTELLIGENCE, NEWS, TIDINGS

²witting \"\ *adj* [fr. pres. part. of ¹*wit*] **1 a :** cognizant or aware of something **:** CONSCIOUS ⟨came to make you ~ of the same —F.S.Ellis⟩ **b :** consciously being or doing something specified ⟨a ~ tool of the Communists⟩ **2 :** done with the knowledge of the doer **:** performed or acted consciously, deliberately, or knowingly **:** INTENTIONAL ⟨~ lies and all sorts of hypocrisy —H.B.Alexander⟩ ⟨this process of ~ repression —W.H.R.Rivers⟩

wit·ting·ly *adv* **:** with knowledge or awareness of what one is doing **:** by design **:** CONSCIOUSLY, DELIBERATELY, INTENTIONALLY, KNOWINGLY ⟨never ~ wishing to do hurt to anyone —Bruce Marshall⟩ ⟨had ~ exceeded his authority —R.G. Usher⟩

witt·ite \ˈwiˌtīt\ *n* -s [Sw *wittit,* fr. T. *Witt,* 20th cent. mining engineer + Sw *-it* -ite] **:** a mineral $Pb_5Bi_6(S,Se)_{14}$ consisting of a sulfide and selenide of lead and bismuth

¹wit·tol \ˈwid·ᵊl, -itᵊl\ *n* -s [earlier *wit-wal,* fr. ME *wetewold,* fr. *weten, witen* to be aware, know + *-wold* (as in *cokewold* cuckold) — more at WIT] **1** *archaic* **:** a man who is aware of and submits to his wife's infidelity **:** a tame or contented cuckold **2 :** a half-witted person **:** one having little sense or perception **:** FOOL

²wittol \"\ *n* -s [perh. alter. of *whitetail*] *dial Eng* **:** WHEATEAR

wit·ty \ˈwid·|ē, -it|, |i\ *adj, usu* -ER/-EST [ME, fr. OE *wittig,* fr. ²*wit* + *-ig* -y] **1 a** *chiefly dial* **:** having good mental capacity **:** CLEVER, INTELLIGENT **b** *obs* **:** possessed of cunning or craftiness esp. in intrigue **:** WILY **2 a :** evincing or requiring good mental capacity **:** clever in conception **:** ingenious or subtle in expression ⟨fallacies . . . concealed in florid, ~ or involved discourses —John Locke⟩ ⟨architecture as elaborate and costly as it was ingenious and ~ —John Summerson⟩ ⟨the costumes are sumptuous and ~ —Virgil Thomson⟩ **b** *obs* **:** skillfully contrived for an evil purpose **:** ingeniously and cunningly devised ⟨the most ~ and exquisite torments —John Scott †1695⟩ **3 :** marked by or full of wit **:** amusingly or cleverly novel (as in expression or point of view) **:** smartly facetious or jocular ⟨one of the *wittiest* books in English —Irving Howe⟩ ⟨makes a number of wise and ~ comments —S.K.Padover⟩ **4 a :** possessing wit **:** quick or ready in the perception or expression of amusing points of view and of intellectually entertaining congruities and incongruities **:** brightly or cleverly facetious ⟨unpredictably ~, eloquent, and satirical in his sermons —G. H. Genzmer⟩ ⟨seeks to establish the picture of ~ and adroit parliamentarian —*N.Y.Times*⟩ **b** *obs* **:** sharply critical **:** SARCASTIC ⟨so unmercifully ~ upon the women —Joseph Addison⟩

syn HUMOROUS, FACETIOUS, JOCULAR, JOCOSE: WITTY suggests cleverness, quickness, and sparkle of mind esp. in repartee, sometimes caustic ⟨the *witty* treatment of beauty as a coin that shines by being kept current —Cleanth Brooks⟩ ⟨she was clever, *witty,* brilliant, and sparkling beyond most of her kind —Rudyard Kipling⟩ ⟨everybody was being exquisitely *witty* at their expense —Roy Lewis & Angus Maude⟩ HUMOROUS is generic, applying to anything that provokes laughter, usu. genial ⟨broad smiles broke out on the faces of the friends. Sometimes, they thought, life was very, very *humorous* —John Steinbeck⟩ ⟨physicists have a little *humorous* puzzle which asks: How can you prove that the temperature of Hell is uniform —Warren Weaver⟩ ⟨wizened *humorous* physiognomy long ago earned him the nickname of Prune-face —J.A. Coleman⟩ FACETIOUS usu. applies to clumsy or inappropriate jesting or somewhat derogatorily to attempts at wittiness or humorousness that please their maker more than others ⟨scowl at all *facetious* remarks at his expense⟩ ⟨used to be merely *facetious* as often as he was funny —*N.Y. Herald Tribune Bk. Rev.*⟩ JOCULAR can mean playfully humorous but usu. implies a fondness for joking, suggesting strongly a temperamental desire to keep others amused ⟨in these careless days he was always gleeful and *jocular,* even as afterwards his entire saintly life was glad with an invincible gaiety of spirit —H.O. Taylor⟩ ⟨the watercolor lesson enlivened by the *jocular* conversation of the kindly, humorous old man was always great fun —Joseph Conrad⟩ JOCOSE is close to FACETIOUS though less derogatory, suggesting a habitual waggishness or sportiveness ⟨sometimes composed something gay and even *jocose* —J.N. Forkel⟩ ⟨considered it a laughable affair, and was continually bobbing his head out the galley door to make *jocose* remarks —Jack London⟩ ⟨colonies of tiny shingled shacks, each labeled clearly with its sentimental or *jocose* name —F.L.Allen⟩

wit·wall \ˈwiˌtwȯl\ *n* -s [obs. E, golden oriole, fr. obs. G *witwal, wittewal* (now *widewal, wiedewal*), fr. MHG *witewal, wittewal,* fr. *wite* wood (fr. OHG *witu*) + *-wal* (of unknown origin) — more at WOOD] *dial Brit* **:** the European great spotted woodpecker

wive \ˈwīv\ *vb* -ED/-ING/-S [ME *wiven,* fr. OE *wīfian,* fr. *wīf* woman, wife — more at WIFE] *vi* **:** to marry a woman **:** take a wife **:** get married ~ *vt* **1 :** to marry to a wife **:** provide with a wife **:** obtain a wife for **2 :** to take for a wife **:** take to wife **:** make one's wife **3 :** to become the wife of ⟨any drab would suffice to ~ such pitiful adventurers —J.R.Lowell⟩

wivern *or* **wiver** *var of* WYVERN

wives *pl of* WIFE

wi·yot \ˈwīˌyät\ *n, pl* **wiyot** *or* **wiyots** *usu cap* **1 a :** a Ritwan people of the coast of northern California **b :** a member of such people **2 :** the language of the Wiyot people

wiz \ˈwiz\ *n* -ES [by shortening] **:** WIZARD 3

¹wiz·ard \ˈwizə(r)d\ *n* -s [ME *wysard,* fr. *wys* wise + *-ard* — more at WISE] **1** *archaic* **:** a man of wisdom and knowledge **:** SAGE, WISE MAN **2 :** one devoted to the black art **:** one skilled in the knowledge and practice of the occult arts **:** a man who practices witchcraft **:** MAGICIAN, SORCERER **3 :** one endowed with exceptional skill or able to achieve something held to be impossible **:** a genius or prodigy esp. in a particular field of endeavor ⟨one of the early production ~*s* of Hollywood —*New Yorker*⟩ ⟨he is the math ~ of the class —F.G.Jennings⟩ ⟨a financial ~⟩ **4 :** WITCH DOCTOR, MEDICINE MAN **syn** see EXPERT

²wizard \"\ *adj* **1 :** possessed of the powers or characteristics of a wizard **:** being a wizard **:** having magical influence or power ⟨the ~ eye of the fire —P.E.More⟩ **2 :** of, relating to, or associated with wizardry **:** MAGICAL, BEWITCHED, CHARMED, ENCHANTED ⟨~ wands⟩ **3** *chiefly Brit* **:** superlative in design, appearance, or performance **:** worthy of the highest praise **:** EXCELLENT, EXTRAORDINARY ⟨she was a ~ dancer —Paul Gallico⟩ ⟨this cake is ~ —Elizabeth Goudge⟩

³wizard \"\ *vb* -ED/-ING/-S *vi* **:** to practice wizardry or magic art ~ *vt* **:** to transport by or as if by wizardry ⟨we were ~*ed* . . . to what looked like rangeland —A.H.Brown⟩

wiz·ard·ly *adj* **:** of or relating to a wizard **:** resembling, befitting, or having the characteristics of a wizard **:** WEIRD ⟨a ~ creature⟩ ⟨~ powers⟩

wiz·ard·ry \ˈwizə(r)drē, -ri\ *n* -ES **1 :** the art or practices of a wizard **:** magic skill **:** SORCERY, WITCHCRAFT **2 a :** something held to resemble the art of a wizard **:** a seemingly magical transforming power or influence ⟨proved his ~ as a vote-getter —Beverly Smith⟩ ⟨employs electronic ~ to track down stray communications signals —W.E.Laidlaw⟩ ⟨the ~ of science⟩ **b :** great skill or cleverness in an activity ⟨the ~ of his legal maneuvering⟩ **syn** see MAGIC

¹wizen \ˈwizᵊn, ˈwēz-\ *vb* **wizened; wizened; wizening** \-z(ᵊ)niŋ\ **wizens** [ME *wisenen,* fr. OE *wisnian, weosnian;* akin to OHG *wesanēn* to wither, ON *visna* to wither, L *viescere* to shrivel, wither, Lith *vysti* to wither, L *viēre* to twist together — more at WIRE] **:** to dry up **:** WITHER, SHRIVEL

²wizen \"\ *adj* [back-formation fr. *wizened*] **:** WIZENED ⟨his face would be wrinkled and ~ —Oscar Wilde⟩ ⟨growing thin and ~ in a solitary prison —W.S.Gilbert⟩

wiz·ened \-nd\ *adj* [fr. past part. of ¹*wizen*] **:** being dried up and shrunken **:** SHRIVELED, WITHERED ⟨~ trees at timberline —Alicita & Warren Hamilton⟩ ⟨~ apples⟩ ⟨the scars gave him a ~ and drawn appearance —F.L.Paxson⟩

wiz·zled \ˈwizəld\ *adj* [¹*wizen* + *-led* (as in *shrivelled, wrinkled*)] **:** being wizened and shriveled — usu. used with *up* ⟨a little old woman with a ~ up face —*Knickerbocker*⟩

wk *abbr* **1** weak **2** week **3** *sometimes cap* well-known **4** work **5** wreck

wkg *abbr* working

wkly *abbr* weekly

wkr *abbr* **1** worker **2** wrecker

WL *abbr* **1** waterline **2** wavelength

wldr *abbr* welder

wm *abbr, sometimes cap* wattmeter

WM *abbr* **1** watermark **2** white metal

wmk *abbr* watermark

wmkd *abbr* watermarked

wn *abbr* winch

wnd *abbr* wind

wng *abbr* warning

WNP *abbr* wire nonpayment

WNW *abbr* west-northwest

¹wo \ˈwō\ *archaic var of* WOE

²wo *or* **woa** *var of* WHOA

WO *abbr* **1** wait order **2** walkover **3** war office **4** warrant officer **5** water-in-oil **6** wireless operator **7** *often not cap* without

¹woad \ˈwōd\ *n* -s [ME *wod, wood,* fr. OE *wād;* akin to MD *wede* woad, OHG *weit* woad, L *vitrum* woad, glass (fr. its color), Gk *isatis* woad] **1 :** a plant of the genus *Isatis; esp* **:** a European biennial herb (*I. tinctoria*) formerly grown for the blue coloring matter yielded by its leaves **2 :** a blue dye prepared esp. formerly from the leaves of woad and containing indigo (sense 1b) as its essential constituent **3 :** a dark blue that is slightly paler than the color marine corps, paler than Japan blue, and redder and duller than Peking blue

²woad \"\ *vt* -ED/-ING/-S [ME *wooden,* fr. *wood, wod* woad] **:** to dye or treat with woad

woad·er \-d·ə(r)\ *n* -s [ME *woder,* fr. *wod* woad + *-er*] **:** WOADMAN

woad·man \-dmən\ *n, pl* **woadmen :** one who dyes with woad

woad vat *n* **:** a vat containing woad for reducing natural indigo by fermentation

woad·wax·en \ˈwōdˌwaksən\ *also* **woad·wax** \-ˌwaks\ *n, pl* **woadwaxens** *also* **woadwaxes** [*woadwaxen* alter. (influenced by ¹*woad*) of *woodwaxen; woadwax* alter. (influenced by ¹*woad*) of *woodwax*] **:** WOODWAXEN

woald *var of* WELD

wob \ˈwäb\ *Scot & dial Eng var of* WEB

WOB *abbr, often not cap* washed overboard

wob·be·gong \ˈwäbēˌgäŋ\ *n* -s [native name in New So. Wales] *Austral* **:** CARPET SHARK

¹wob·ble *also* **wab·ble** \ˈwäbəl *also* ˈwȯb-\ *vb* **wobbled; wobbled; wobbling** \-b(ə)liŋ\ **wobbles** [prob. fr. LG *wabbeln* to wobble; akin to MHG *wabelen* to waver, ON *vafla* to hover about, OE *wǣfre* wavering, restless — more at WAVER] *vi* **1 a :** to move or move along with an irregular rocking or staggering motion **:** move or swing unsteadily and clumsily backward and forward or from side to side **:** vary from a true course by tilting unsteadily from side to side ⟨ducks go *wobbling* by in two straight lines —Norman MacCaig⟩ ⟨the baby's head *wobbled* safely to rest on her shoulder —Margaret A. Barnes⟩ ⟨saw an open car ahead of her ~ to the side of the road, one of its tires flat —*New Yorker*⟩ **b :** to shake unsteadily **:** TREMBLE, QUAVER ⟨a *wobbling* chin⟩ ⟨his voice *wobbled*⟩ **2** *dial Eng* **:** to boil vigorously **3 :** to waver or vacillate between different courses of action, policies, or parties **:** show indecision ⟨his first play . . . *wobbled* between melodrama and passionate tragedy —Sheldon Cheney⟩ ~ *vt* **:** to cause to move with a wobbling or lurching motion from side to side ⟨most airplanes plunge straight, others ~ their wings as they dive —Wolfgang Langewiesche⟩

²wobble *also* **wabble** \"\ *n* -s **1 a :** a hobbling or rocking unequal motion (as of a wheel unevenly hung) **:** a staggering to and fro **:** a wobbling gait ⟨a rotational ~ of the earth's axis in space —S.F.Mason⟩ **b :** an uncertainly directed movement **:** FLUCTUATION ⟨a faint ~ of doubt —Robert Lynd⟩ ⟨the sort of serious ~ that accompanies maladjustments between political and economic development —Colin Legum⟩ **c :** an intermittent variation (as in volume of sound) **:** QUAVER ⟨a ~ in the sound of a phonograph record⟩ ⟨a vocal ~⟩ **2 wobbles** *pl but usu sing in constr* **:** a disease of horses that is marked by degenerative changes in the spinal cord and nerves resulting in ataxia chiefly of the hind legs and that in Australia has been reported to result from feeding on various palms but in the U.S. is held to be a recessive hereditary trait

wobble plate *n* **:** SWASH PLATE

wobble pump *n* **:** an auxiliary hand pump used to supply fuel to the carburetor of an airplane engine when the power-driven pump fails or for forcing fuel from an extra tank

wob·bler *also* **wab·bler** \-b(ə)lə(r)\ *n* -s **:** one that wobbles: as **a :** an elliptic cutterhead placed on a shaft at such an angle as to correspond with an oblique section of a right circular cylinder **b :** either of the grooved ends more or less resembling either a 3-lobed or 4-lobed gear wheel in cross section that project beyond the housings in a rolling mill and transmit power to a roll from the junction boxes **c :** a fishing lure of the spoon type that wobbles when drawn through the water

wobble saw *n* **:** DRUNKEN SAW

wob·bli·ness *also* **wab·bli·ness** \-b(ə)lēnə̇s\ *n* -ES **:** the state of being wobbly

wobbling *also* **wabbling** *adj* **:** that wobbles, permits a vacillating motion, or operates with such motion — **wob·bling·ly** *also* **wab·bling·ly** *adv*

wobbling disk *n* **:** SWASH PLATE

wobbling of the pole 1 : the slow gyration of the earth's axis in space as a result of lunisolar precession **2 :** NUTATION 2 **3 :** the wandering of the poles

¹wob·bly *also* **wab·bly** \-b(ə)lē, -li *or* **wob·ble·dy** \-bəldē, -di\ *adj* -ER/-EST [*wobbledy* fr. *wobbled* (past part. of *wobble*) + *-y*] **1 :** inclined to shake, sway, or quaver unsteadily **:** wavering or trembling uncertainly (as from wear or fatigue) **:** SHAKY ⟨a ~ chair⟩ ⟨a ~ government⟩ ⟨felt a little ~ when he saw all the people —R.C.Wood⟩ ⟨~ handwriting⟩ **2 :** given to vacillation or inclined to vacillate **:** FLUCTUATING, IRRESOLUTE, UNCERTAIN, DOUBTFUL ⟨after a very ~ introduction, he writes with vigor and clarity —*New Statesman & Nation*⟩ ⟨sound way of bolstering ~ foreign economies —*Time*⟩ ⟨the statistics were a bit ~ — good round figures not exempt from the suspicion of exaggeration —G.B.Munson⟩

²wobbly \"\ *n* -ES *usu cap* [origin unknown] **:** a member of the Industrial Workers of the World ⟨life was real and . . . earnest for the *Wobblies* of yesteryear —John Cournos⟩

wob·bu·la·tor \ˈwäbyəˌlād·ə(r)\ *n* -s [¹*wobble* + *-ulator* (as in *modulator*)] **:** a testing device for radio sets in which the frequency is varied periodically and automatically over a predetermined range

WOC \ˌdəbəl(ˌ)yüˌōˈsē, -lyə,ō-\ *n* -s [*WOC, abbr.*] **:** one serving as a dollar-a-year man esp. in the U.S. government

WOC *abbr, often not cap* without compensation

wod *dial var of* WOULD

wodge \ˈwäj\ *n* -s [prob. alter. of *wedge*] *Brit* **:** a bulky bulging object **:** MASS, LUMP ⟨mopped up the mess with a special ~ of blotting paper —Margery Allingham⟩ ⟨an enormous ~ of English press cuttings —Richard Aldington⟩

¹woe \ˈwō\ *interj* [ME *wo, wa,* fr. OE *wā;* akin to OHG *wē* interj. used to express grief, ON *vei,* Goth *wai,* L *vae*] — used to express grief, regret, or distress

²woe \"\ *adj* [ME *wo,* fr. *wo, wa,* interj.] *dial* **:** WOEFUL, SORROWFUL, GRIEVED, MISERABLE, MELANCHOLY ⟨she waxed wondrous ~ —Edmund Spenser⟩

³woe \"\ *n* -s [ME *wo,* fr. *wo, wa,* interj.] **1 a :** a miserable or sorrowful state **:** a condition of deep suffering from misfortune, affliction, or grief **:** DISTRESS ⟨a scene of ~⟩ ⟨a tale of ~⟩ ⟨for weal or ~⟩ ⟨want and ~⟩ — often used in denunciation or in exclamations of sorrow ⟨~ to me! For I am lost —Isa 6:5 (RSV)⟩ **b :** CALAMITY, MISFORTUNE, TROUBLE — usu. used in pl. ⟨economic ~*s*⟩ ⟨papers and magazines are always full of their gripes, squawks, and ~*s* —E.L.Jones⟩ **2 :** CURSE, ANATHEMA ⟨this ~ came out of Christ's mouth —Samuel Rutherford⟩ **syn** see SORROW

woe·be·gone \ˈwōbēˌgȯn, -bə̇ˌ- *also* -ˌgän\ *adj* [ME *wo begon,* fr. *wo,* n., woe + *begon,* past part. of *begon* to go about, beset, fr. OE *begān,* fr. *be-* + *gān* to go — more at GO] **1** *archaic* **:** beset or overwhelmed with woe **:** immersed in grief or sorrow **:** WOEFUL ⟨so ~ was he with pains of love —Edward Fairfax⟩ **2 a :** exhibiting a condition of suffering, great woe, sorrow, or misery ⟨their ~ faces⟩ ⟨a grimy ~ expression —Israel Zangwill⟩ **b :** dismal-looking **:** DESOLATE, DILAPIDATED ⟨a ~ village⟩ **syn** see DOWNCAST

woe·be·gone·ness \-nnə̇s\ *n* **:** the quality or state of being woebegone

woe·ful *also* **wo·ful** \ˈwōfəl\ *adj, sometimes* **woefuller;** *sometimes* **woefullest** [ME *woful, waful,* fr. *wo, wa,* n., woe + *-ful*] **1 :** full of woe **:** distressed with grief or calamity **:** SAD, SORROWFUL, AFFLICTED, WRETCHED ⟨two ~ young people —Walter de la Mare⟩ ⟨a ~ sight⟩ ⟨bade us farewell with ~ prophecies —*Springfield (Mass.) Union*⟩ **2 :** involving, bringing, or relating to woe ⟨~ want⟩ ⟨O ~ day! O day of woe! —Ambrose Philips⟩ **3 :** CALAMITOUS, LAMENTABLE, DEPLORABLE ⟨the notes . . . are in part ~ nonsense —Herbert Weinstock⟩ ⟨a ~ lack of balance —A.L.Scott⟩

woe·ful·ly *also* **wo·ful·ly** \-f(ə)lē, -li\ *adv* [ME *wofully,* fr. *woful* + *-ly*] **:** in a woeful manner **:** MOURNFULLY, WRETCHEDLY, DEPLORABLY ⟨these reports were ~ inadequate —Vera M. Dean⟩ ⟨fine performances lavished on ~ thin material —Arthur Knight⟩

woe·ful·ness *also* **wo·ful·ness** *n* -ES **:** the quality or state of being woeful

woeh·ler·ite *or* **wöh·ler·ite** \ˈvōləˌrīt\ *n* -s [G *wöhlerit,* fr. Friedrich *Wöhler* †1882 Ger. chemist + G *-it* -ite] **:** a mineral $NaCa_2(Zr,Cb)Si_2O_8(O,OH,F)$ consisting of a basic silicate of zirconium, calcium, sodium, niobium, and other minerals in yellow or brown prismatic crystals

woevine \ˈ=ˌ=\ *n* [³*woe* + *vine*] **:** DODDER LAUREL

wof·fler \ˈwäflə(r)\ *n* -s [prob. fr. E dial. *woffle* to glide along quickly (prob. freq. of *woft* to waft, alter. of E *waft*) + E *-er*] *Brit* **:** REPAIRER

woft \ˈwäft\ *Scot var of* WEFT

¹wog \ˈwäg\ *Scot var of* WAG

²wog \"\ *n* -s *sometimes cap* [prob. short for *golliwog*] **1 :** a native of a Middle or Far Eastern country — usu. used disparagingly **2 :** a usu. dark-skinned foreigner — usu. used disparagingly

³wog \"\ *n* -s [prob. short for *polliwog*] *chiefly Austral* **:** a pathogenic microorganism ⟨the oxygen in the air immediately kills the ~*s* that have caused the trouble —*Sydney (Australia) Bull.*⟩; *broadly* **:** an injurious or repugnant organism ⟨spiders, centipedes, beetles, and innumerable other ~*s* —I.L.Idriess⟩

WOG *abbr, often not cap* with other goods

wog·gle \ˈwägəl *also* ˈwȯg-\ *vb* **woggled; woggled; woggling** \-g(ə)liŋ\ **woggles** [alter. (influenced by ¹*wobble*) of ¹*waggle*] **:** WAGGLE

wohl degradation *or* **wohl reaction** \ˈvōl-\ *n, usu cap W* [after Alfred *Wohl fl* 1920 Ger. chemist] **:** a sequence of reactions for converting an aldose sugar to one containing one carbon atom less (as galactose to lyxose) by forming the oxime of the original aldose and next the corresponding acetylated nitrile and finally removing hydrogen and cyanogen in the form of hydrogen cyanide by means of ammoniacal silver hydroxide

wöh·ler's law \ˈvōlə(r)z-\ *n, usu cap W* [after Friedrich *Wöhler* †1882 Ger. chemist] **:** a law of strength of materials: the breaking strength of a material decreases with repetition of the strain and with the range of the strain variations

wohl·fahr·tia \vōlˈfärd·ēə\ *n* [NL, perh. modif. (influenced by G *wohlfahrt* welfare) of Peter *Wolfart* †1726 Ger. medical writer + NL *-ia*] **1** *cap* **:** a genus of larviparous sarcophagid flies that commonly deposit their larvae in wounds or on the intact skin of man and domestic animals causing severe cutaneous myiasis **2** -s **:** any fly of the genus *Wohlfahrtia*

wohl·will process \ˈvōlˌvil-\ *n, usu cap W* [after Emil *Wohlwill* †1912 Ger. inventor] **:** an electrolytic process for refining gold using a hydrochloric-acid electrolyte

woi·lie \ˈwȯilē\ *n* -s [native name in Western Australia] **:** a rat kangaroo (*Bettongia penicillata*) of temperate Australia

woi·wode \ˈwȯiˌwōd\ *n* [alter. of *voivode,* fr. Russ *voevoda* — more at VAIVODE] VAIVODE

WOJG *abbr* warrant officer junior grade

wo·kas \ˈwōkəs\ *n* -ES [Klamath *wókas* seed of the wokas] **1 :** a western American spatterdock (*Nuphar polysepalum*) **2 :** the dried and roasted seeds of the wokas used as food among the Klamath Indians

woke *past of* WAKE

woken *past part of* WAKE

wo·kowi \wōˈkōwē\ *n* -s [Comanche] **:** MESCAL 1

WOL *abbr* wharf owner's liability

¹wold \ˈwōld\ *n* -s [ME *wald, wold,* fr. OE *weald, wald* wood, forest; akin to OHG *wald* forest, ON *vǫllr* field, meadow, and perh. to OE *wilde* untamed, wild — more at WILD] **1 :** an upland plain **:** a region without woods ⟨between the forests were open ~*s* —Charles Kingsley⟩ ⟨deeds of hill and ~ —Robert Browning⟩ ⟨midday hush in many wilds and ~*s* —Norman Douglas⟩ **2 :** an open hilly or rolling region ⟨the Yorkshire ~*s*⟩

²wold *var of* WELD

wold mouse *n, Brit* **:** VOLE

wolds·man \ˈwōldzmən\ *n, pl* **woldsmen :** one who dwells on a wold or in a region of wolds

¹wolf \ˈwu̇lf\ *n, pl* **wolves** *see sense 1* \-lvz\ *often attrib* [ME, fr. OE *wulf;* akin to OHG *wolf,* ON *ūlfr,* Goth *wulfs,* L *lupus,* Gk *lykos,* Skt *vṛka*] **1** *pl also* **wolf 1 a :** any of various large predatory mammals of the genus *Canis* that resemble the related dogs, are destructive to game and livestock, and may rarely attack man esp. when several animals have gathered in a pack; *esp* **:** any of various forms of a species (*C. lupus*) which was once almost universally present in the

wolf

northern hemisphere and of which the common European form (*C. l. lupus*) is yellowish or brownish gray with rather coarse fur, erect pointed ears, and a bushy tail — see COYOTE, DIRE WOLF, GRAY WOLF, JAPANESE WOLF, RED WOLF **b** : the fur of a wolf **c** : TASMANIAN WOLF **d** : EGYPTIAN JACKAL **2 a** (1) : a fierce, rapacious, or destructive person (2) : a relentless crafty person (3) : a clever experienced trader (as in securities) — compare LAMB 3c (4) : a man forward, direct, and zealous in amatory attentions to women : MASHER (5) *slang* : an active homosexual **b** (1) : a corrupting or destructive agency ⟨boys and girls now being thrown to the *wolves* of paternal ignorance, social neglect, and youthful impulses —P.L.Boynton⟩ (2) : dire poverty : FAMINE, STARVATION — used with *door* ⟨keep the ~ from the door⟩ ⟨the ~ is at the door⟩ (3) : a voracious appetite ⟨deaden the gnawing ~ within —Elizabeth C. Gaskell⟩ **c** [trans. of ML *lupus*] *archaic* : an eating ulcer or cancer **d** (1) : a grub that is the larva of various small beetles or moths and that infests granaries (2) : the maggot of a warble fly **3** [G; fr. the howling sound] **a** (1) : dissonance in some chords on organs, pianos, or other instruments with fixed tones tuned by unequal temperament (2) : an instance of such dissonance **b** : a harshness due to faulty vibration in various tones in a bowed instrument **4** : a cub scout of the second rank who is at least eight years old — **wolf in sheep's clothing** : one who cloaks a hostile intention with a friendly manner

[2]**wolf** \"\ *vb* -ED/-ING/-S *vt* : to eat greedily : devour ravenously ⟨~*ed* two large plates of the stew —D.G.Gerahty⟩ ⟨~*ing* every volume on social and economic matters he could lay his hands on —*Time*⟩ ⟨sustained high-speed driving ~*s* up a lot more gas than ordinary commuter travel —P.W. Kearney⟩ ~ *vi* **1** : to hunt for wolves **2** : to philander aggressively

wol·fach·ite \'vōl,fäk,īt\ *n* -S [G *wolfachit*, fr. *Wolfach*, Baden, Germany + G *-it* -ite] : a silver-white or tin-white mineral Ni(As,Sb)S consisting of nickel sulfide, arsenide, and antimonide

wolf·berry \'wu̇lf- — *see* BERRY\ *n* [*wolf* + *berry*] **1** : a western American shrub (*Symphoricarpos occidentalis*) sometimes cultivated for its white berries **2** : MOUNTAIN CRANBERRY **3** : BITTERSWEET 2a **4** : any of various plants of the genus *Lycium*; *esp* : MATRIMONY VINE

wolf call *n* : a whistle, howl, or other sound by a male expressing approval or admiration of a girl's or woman's appearance

wolf·camp \'wu̇lf,kamp\ *adj*, *usu cap* [fr. *Wolfcamp*, locality near Leonard Mountain, western Texas] : of or relating to a subdivision of the American Permian — see GEOLOGIC TIME table

wolf child *n* : a child popularly believed to have been suckled and reared by wolves or other wild animals

wolf cub *n*, *Brit* : a boy who is a member of a division of the Boy Scouts for boys from 8 to 11 years old — compare CUB SCOUT

wolf dog *n* **1** : any of various large dogs (as the Irish wolfhound) formerly kept for hunting wolves **2** : the offspring of a cross between a wolf and a domestic dog **3** : a dog resembling or thought to resemble a wolf irrespective of its actual breeding

wolf eel *n* : a long slender wolffish (*Anarhichthys ocellatus*) occurring along the coast from Alaska to southern California

wolfe·ite \'wu̇l,fīt\ *n* -S [Caleb Wroe *Wolfe* *b*1908 Am. crystallographer + E *-ite*] : a mineral $(Fe,Mn)_2(PO_4)(OH)$ that consists of basic iron phosphate and is isomorphous with triploidite and isostructural with sarkinite

wolf·er \'wu̇lfə(r)\ *n* -S [[2]*wolf* + *-er*] **1** : one that hunts wolves usu. for their pelts **2** : one that wolfs food or drink

wolf·fia \'wu̇lfēə, 'vȯl-\ *n*, *cap* [NL, fr. Johann F. *Wolff* †1806 Ger. physician and botanist + NL *-ia*] : a genus of widely distributed floating aquatic plants (family Lemnaceae) that are the smallest flowering plants known, consist merely of a minute ovoid or globose leafless thallus producing the flowers from clefts or grooves, and are distinguished from members of the genus *Lemna* by the one-celled anthers and by the absence of roots

[1]**wolff·ian** *also* **wolf·ian** \-ēən\ *adj*, *usu cap* [Christian von *Wolff* (*Wolf*) †1754 Ger. philosopher + E *-an*] : of or relating to Christian Wolff or his rationalistic philosophy

[2]**wolffian** \"\ *adj*, *often cap* [Kaspar Friedrich *Wolff* †1794 Ger. anatomist and embryologist + E *-an*] : discovered or first described by Kaspar Friedrich Wolff

wolffian body *n*, *often cap W* [[2]*wolffian*] : MESONEPHROS

wolffian duct *n*, *often cap W* [[2]*wolffian*] : MESONEPHRIC DUCT

wolffian ridge *n*, *often cap W* [[2]*wolffian*] **1** : a longitudinal ridge on either side of the trunk in some vertebrate embryos (as of the chick) from which the limb buds arise **2** : a slight ridge on either side of the midline in vertebrate embryos giving rise to the mesonephros

wolffian tubule *n*, *often cap W* [[2]*wolffian*] : a mesonephric tubule

wolffish \'⸗,⸗\ *n* [[1]*wolf* + *fish*] : any of several large marine blennies notable for their strong teeth and ferocity: as **a** : a blenny (*Anarhichas lupus*) of the north Atlantic that is brownish or bluish gray with from 9 to 12 dark crossbars, has a tough scaleless skin from which fine leather is made, and reaches a length of 4 to 6 feet **b** : a similar fish (*A. orientalis*) of the north Pacific that is plain brown in color — see WOLF EEL

wolff-kish·ner reaction \'wu̇lf'kishnə(r)-\ *n*, *usu cap W&K* [after Ludwig *Wolff* *fl*1914 and N. *Kishner* *fl*1914 Ger. chemists] : an indirect reduction of an aldehyde or ketone to the corresponding hydrocarbon by heating the hydrazone or semicarbazone derivative with an alcoholic solution of sodium ethoxide or with solid potassium hydroxide

wolf grape *n* **1** : BITTERSWEET 2a **2** : CHICKEN GRAPE

wolf herring *n* : a large greatly elongated voracious clupeoid fish (*Chirocentrus dorab* or possibly related species) that has long powerful fangs, is widely distributed along tropical Indo-Pacific shores, and is in some areas esteemed as food though fierce and dangerous to handle

wolf·hound \'wu̇lf,hau̇nd, -l,fau̇-\ *n* : any of several large dogs used now or orig. in hunting the wolf and other large animals — compare BORZOI, IRISH WOLFHOUND

wolf·ian \'wu̇lfēən, 'vȯl-\ *adj*, *often cap* [Friedrich August *Wolf* †1824 Ger. classical philologist and Homeric critic] : of or relating to Friedrich August Wolf

wolfier *comparative of* WOLFY

wolfiest *superlative of* WOLFY

wolfing *pres part of* WOLF

wolf-in-the-tail \'⸗⸗⸗\ *n* : nonspecific debility of cattle — compare HOLLOW HORN

wolf·ish \'wu̇lfish, -fēsh\ *adj* [[1]*wolf* + *-ish*] : of or characteristic of a wolf : having the qualities or form of a wolf : WOLFLIKE; *esp* : FEROCIOUS, RAVENOUS ⟨the smell of such fare would prove no irresistible temptation to ~ nostrils —C.G.D.Roberts⟩ ⟨a ~ wind had begun to clamor at the doors —Archibald Rutledge⟩ ⟨~ pursuit of pleasure —G.K.Chesterton⟩

wolf·ish·ly *adv* : in a wolfish manner : RAVENOUSLY ⟨eyed our food ~ —Virginia D. Dawson & Betty D. Wilson⟩

wolf·ish·ness *n* -ES : the quality or state of being wolfish

wolflike \'⸗,⸗\ *adj* : resembling, suggestive of, or having the characteristics of a wolf

wolf·ling \'wu̇lfliŋ\ *n* -S [ME *wulfling*, fr. *wulf* wolf + *-ling*] : a little or young wolf

wolf note *n* : WOLF 3

wolf number \'wu̇lf-, 'vȯlf-\ *n*, *usu cap W* [after Rudolf *Wolf* †1893 Swiss astronomer] : SUNSPOT NUMBER

wolf pack *n* [intended as trans. of G *rudel* flock, herd, pack (in *rudeltaktik* wolf-pack tactics, *rudelsystem* wolf-pack system)] **1 a** : a tactical unit of two or more submarines that make a coordinated attack on shipping **b** : a group of two or more fighter planes making a coordinated attack **2** : a roving gang of roughneck teen-agers

wolf·ram \'wu̇lfrəm, 'vȯl-\ *n* -S [G, alter. (influenced by *wolf* wolf) of *wolffram*, *wolform*, *volfram*, of unknown origin] **1** : TUNGSTEN — symbol *W*; see ELEMENT table **2** : WOLFRAMITE

wolfram- *or* **wolframo-** *comb form* [ISV *wolfram*] : TUNGST- ⟨*wolframic*⟩ ⟨*wolframo*phosphate⟩

wolf·ram·ate \-rə,māt\ *n* -S [ISV *wolfram-* + *-ate*] : TUNGSTATE

wolf·ram·ic \wu̇l'framik\ *adj* [*wolfram-* + *-ic*] : TUNGSTIC

wolframic acid *n* : TUNGSTIC ACID

wolf·ra·mine \'wu̇lfrə,mēn, -,mən\ *n* -S [*wolfram-* + *-ine*] : TUNGSTITE

wolf·ra·min·i·um \,wu̇lfrə'minēəm\ *n* -S [NL, fr. *wolfram-* + *-inium* (as in *aluminium*)] : a light aluminum alloy similar to romanium

wolf·ram·ite \-rə,mīt, *usu* -īd.+V\ *n* -S [G *wolframit*, fr. *wolfram-* + *-it* -ite] : a mineral $(Fe,Mn)WO_4$ that consists of an iron manganese tungstate of a usu. brownish or grayish black color and submetallic luster, is isomorphous with and intermediate between huebnerite and ferberite, occurs in monoclinic crystals commonly twinned so as to imitate orthorhombic tabular forms and in granular or columnar masses, shows a highly perfect cleavage, and is used as a source of tungsten and tungsten compounds (hardness 5–5.5, sp. gr. 7.1–7.5) — called also *wolfram*

wolfram lamp *n* : TUNGSTEN LAMP

wolfram ocher *n* : TUNGSTITE

wolfs *pres 3d sing of* WOLF

wolfs·bane \'wu̇lfs,bān\ *n* [*wolfs* (gen. of *wolf*) + *bane*; trans. of NL *lycoctonum*, lit., wolf-killing] **1** : ACONITE 1; *esp* : a highly variable yellow-flowered Eurasian herb (*Aconitum lycoctonum*) with a somewhat fibrous rootstock and broadly lobed leaves — compare MONKSHOOD **2** : WINTER ACONITE

wolf's-head \'⸗,⸗\ *n* [ME *wolfesheved*, fr. OE *wulfesheāfod*, interj. used in wolf-hunting and in pursuing an outlaw, lit., head of a wolf, fr. *wulfes* (gen. of *wulf* wolf) + *hēafod* head — more at WOLF, HEAD] **1** *archaic* : OUTLAW **2** *archaic* : OUTLAWRY

wolfskin \'⸗,⸗\ *n*, *often attrib* **1** : the skin of a wolf **2** : a garment or blanket made of this skin

wolf's-milk \'⸗,⸗\ *n*, *pl* **wolf's-milks** [so called fr. its acrid milky juice] : SPURGE: as **a** : LEAFY SPURGE **b** : SUN SPURGE

wolf's moss *n* [prob. so called fr. its having been used to poison wolves] : a yellow lichen (*Letharia vulpina*) of arctic and alpine regions sometimes used for a dye

wolf snake *n* : any of various harmless colubrid snakes having elongated teeth: as **a** : CAPE WOLF SNAKE **b** : any of a genus (*Lycodon*) of active arboreal nocturnal snakes widespread in southeastern Asia

wolf's peach *n*, *archaic* : TOMATO

wolf spider *n* : any of various active wandering ground spiders belonging to the family Lycosidae — see TARANTULA

wolf teeth *n pl* : the ratchet and crown wheels that mesh on curved tooth flanks and similarly relieved tooth backs in a fine pocket watch

wolf tone *n* : WOLF 3

wolf tooth *also* **wolf's tooth** *n* **1** : a small vestigial first premolar that is sometimes present in a horse on each side in front of the normal grinders and that is regularly found in some fossil members of the family Equidae **2** : NEEDLE TOOTH **3** : a protruding incisor (as in a guinea pig or rabbit)

wolf tree *n* : a forest tree whose size and position cause it to prevent the growth of many small and potentially more valuable trees around it by usurping their space, light, and nourishment

wolf vault *n* : a vault in gymnastics in which one leg is in squat position and the other is extended to its own side as the body passes over the apparatus

wolf whistle *n* : a wolf call consisting of a 2-toned whistle

wolf willow *n* : BUFFALO BERRY

wolfy \'wu̇lfē\ *adj* -ER/-EST : resembling a wolf (as in fierceness)

wol·las·ton doublet \'wu̇ləstən-\ *n*, *usu cap W* [after William H. *Wollaston* †1828] : a magnifying glass made of two plano-convex lenses and designed to correct spherical and chromatic aberration

wol·las·ton·ite \-tə,nīt\ *n* -S [William H. *Wollaston* †1828 Eng. chemist and physicist + E *-ite*] : a triclinic mineral $CaSiO_3$ of a white to gray, red, yellow, or brown color consisting of native calcium metasilicate occurring usu. in cleavable masses and sometimes in tabular twinned crystals (hardness 4.5–5, sp. gr. 2.8–2.9) — called also *tabular spar*

wollaston prism *n*, *usu cap W* [after William H. *Wollaston* †1828] : a double-image compound prism producing two divergent beams of light plane-polarized at right angles to each other and consisting of two equal right-angled prisms of Iceland spar or quartz cemented along their long faces and so cut that in one the light passes along the optic axis and in the other at right angles to that axis

wollaston wire *n*, *usu cap W* [after William H. *Wollaston* †1828] : a very fine usu. platinum wire used for cross hairs in telescope eyepieces

wol·lo·mai \'wälə,mī\ *n* -S [native name in New So. Wales] : SNAPPER 3c

wo·lof \'wō,läf\ *also* **jo·lof** \'yō-\ *or* **vo·lof** \'vō-\ *n* -S *usu cap* **1 a** : a people of the western Sudan near the mouth of the Senegal and Gambia rivers who are among the most deeply pigmented of Africans **b** : a member of such people **2 a** : a West-Atlantic language of the Wolof people **b** : a trade language in Senegal

wolve \'wu̇lv\ *vi* -ED/-ING/-S [fr. [1]*wolf*, after such pairs as E *half*: *halve*, v.] **1** : WOLF **2** *of a pipe organ* : to produce a sound like the howl of a wolf (as from failure of air supply)

wol·ve·boon \'vȯlvə,bün\ *n* -S [Afrik, lit., wolf bean, irreg. fr. MD *wolf* + *boon*, *bone* bean; akin to OE *wulf* wolf and OHG *bōna* bean — more at WOLF, BEAN] : a small southern African tree or shrub (*Toxicodendrum capensis*) of the family Euphorbiaceae with very poisonous foliage

wolv·er \'wu̇lvə(r)\ *n* -S [*wolve* + *-er*] **1** : one that behaves like a wolf **2** : one that hunts wolves

wol·ver·hamp·ton \'wu̇lvə(r),ham(p)tən\ *adj*, *usu cap* [fr. *Wolverhampton*, England] : of or from the county borough of Wolverhampton, England : of the kind or style prevalent in Wolverhampton

wol·ver·ine *also* **wol·ver·ene** \,wu̇lvə'rēn\ *n* -S *see sense 1* [alter. of earlier *wolvering*, prob. irreg. fr. *wolv-* (as in *wolves*, *wolvish*) + *-ing*, n. suffix] **1** *pl also* **wolverine a** : a northern No. American carnivorous mammal (*Gulo luscus*) of the family Mustelidae that resembles and is often considered conspecific with the glutton of Europe, is blackish with a pale forehead and a light band on each side of the body, and is noted for its thievishness, strength, and cunning — called also *carcajou* **b** : the fur of the wolverine **2** *usu cap* : MICHIGANDER — used as a nickname

wolves *pl of* WOLF

wolv·ish \'wu̇lvish\ *adj* [ME, fr. *wolves* + *-ish*] *archaic* : WOLFISH

[1]**wom·an** \'wu̇mən *sometimes esp in the South* 'wōm- *or* 'wəm-\ *n*, *pl* **wom·en** \'wimən\ [ME *woman*, *wumman*, *wimman*, *wimmon*, *wifmon*, fr. OE *wīfmon*, *wīfman*, fr. *wīf* woman, wife + *mon*, *man* man — more at WIFE, MAN] **1 a** (1) : a female human being — distinguished from *man* ⟨the *women* gardened and cooked while the men hunted and fished⟩ (2) : an adult female human being — distinguished from *girl* ⟨the *women* and girls formed a glee club⟩ (3) : a female human being as such and without regard to any special status (as of birth, position, or office) ⟨she is a queen but she is also a ~⟩ (4) : a female human being of a class or character lower than that normally considered a lady **b** : a female human being belonging to a particular and usu. specified category (as by birth, residence, or membership) ⟨a ~ of affairs⟩ ⟨several Christian *women*⟩ — usu. used in combination ⟨char*woman*⟩ ⟨washer*women*⟩; compare MAN 2b **c** (1) *chiefly dial* : WIFE (2) : MISTRESS 6a (3) *women*, *pl* : human females as partners in sexual intercourse or irregularities ⟨refrained from *women* during Lent⟩ **d** (1) : one possessing in high degree the qualities considered distinctive of womanhood (as gentleness, affection, and domesticity or on the other hand fickleness, superficiality, and folly) (2) : womanly character or quality : WOMANLINESS **2** : the female part of the human race : female human beings esp. when viewed as a natural kind or personified as an individual : WOMANKIND ⟨~ is the glory of all created existence —Samuel Richardson⟩ **3** : a human female that serves or is subordinate to another ⟨expect the ~ to come in to clean the rugs⟩; *esp* : one that is the personal maid of another

[2]**woman** \"\ *adj* [ME, fr. *woman*, n.] **1** : of, belonging to, or characteristic of a woman : WOMANLY ⟨~ talk⟩ ⟨~ clothes⟩ **2** : FEMALE ⟨a ~ doctor⟩ ⟨~ students⟩ ⟨memorable ~ characters of world literature —*Tomorrow*⟩

[3]**woman** \"\ *vt* -ED/-ING/-S [[1]*woman*] **1** : to make into a woman or the likeness of a woman **2** *obs* : to make effeminate **3** *obs* : to associate (one) with a woman ⟨to have him see me ~*ed* —Shak.⟩ **4** : to furnish or staff with women

woman chaser *n* : PHILANDERER

woman-child \'⸗⸗,⸗\ *n*, *archaic* : a female infant

womanfolk \'⸗⸗,⸗\ *n*, *pl* **womenfolk** *also* **womanfolk** *or* **womenfolks** [[2]*woman* + *folk*] **1** *chiefly dial* : WOMAN **2** *womenfolk also womanfolk or womenfolks pl* : the women of a group (as a family or community) ⟨get the *womenfolk* off to the hills —E.M.Forster⟩

wom·an·ful·ly \-nfəlē\ *adv* [[1]*woman* + *-fully* (as in *manfully*)] : with womanly constancy or spirit

woman-grown \'⸗⸗'⸗\ *adj* : grown to womanhood

woman hater *n* : MISOGYNIST

wom·an·head \-n,hed\ *n* [ME *womanhede*, fr. [1]*woman* + *-hede* -hood (akin to ME *-hod*, *-had* -hood)] *archaic* : WOMANHOOD

wom·an·hood \-n,hu̇d\ *n* [ME *womanhod*, fr. [1]*woman* + *-hod* -hood] **1** : the state of being a woman : the distinguishing character or qualities of a woman or of womankind **2** : WOMEN, WOMANKIND ⟨the ~ of a nation⟩

wom·an·house \'wu̇mən,hüs\ *n* [[2]*woman* + *house*] *Scot* : LAUNDRY

wom·an·ish \'wu̇mənish *sometimes esp in the South* 'wōm- *or* 'wəm-\ *adj* [ME, fr. [1]*woman* + *-ish*] **1** *archaic* : of or belonging to women : done by women ⟨~ work⟩ **2** : characteristic of a woman : suitable to or resembling a woman : FEMININE ⟨love her for the sake of her gentle and ~ ways —A.W.Kinglake⟩ ⟨nothing ~ in the room except a full-length mirror —Raymond Chandler⟩ **3** : unsuitable to a man or to a strong character of either sex : not strong or virile ⟨hence, ~ fears, traitors to love and duty —S.T.Coleridge⟩ ⟨disdaining all the ~ peace talk about them —James Cameron⟩ ⟨womanly, yet quite unlike the ~ women —George Meredith⟩ **syn** see FEMALE

wom·an·ish·ly *adv* : in a womanish manner

wom·an·ish·ness *n* -ES : the quality or state of being womanish

wom·an·i·ty \wu̇'manəd·ē\ *n* -ES : the nature of women : normal womanhood : WOMANLINESS

wom·an·ize \'wu̇mə,nīz *sometimes esp South* 'wōm- *or* 'wəm-\ *vb* -ED/-ING/-S *vt* : to make effeminate ~ *vi* **1** *archaic* : to become effeminate **2** : to pursue or associate illicitly with women

wom·an·iz·er \-zə(r)\ *n* -S : a man who pursues or associates illicitly with women ⟨men who had been terrific ~*s* —Polly Adler⟩

womankind \'⸗⸗,⸗\ *n* [ME *woman kinde*, fr. [1]*woman* + *kinde* kind] **1** : the females of the human race : WOMEN ⟨~ with her tools of magic, the broom and mop —Nathaniel Hawthorne⟩ **2** : the women members of a family, household, or community ⟨businessmen and their ~ —S.P.Sherman⟩ **3** *archaic* : a female person

wom·an·less \-nləs\ *adj* : without a woman : having no women ⟨~ men⟩

[1]**womanlike** \'⸗⸗,⸗\ *adj* [ME, fr. [1]*woman* + *like*, adj.] : resembling or characteristic of a woman : having qualities natural to or peculiar to women: as **a** *of a woman* : manifesting characteristic feminine foibles ⟨a ~ lack of promptness⟩ **b** *of a man* : WOMANISH ⟨ashamed at being surprised in a ~ expression of sorrow —Sir Walter Scott⟩ **syn** see FEMALE

[2]**womanlike** \"\ *adv* [ME, fr. [1]*woman* + *like*, adv.] : WOMANLY

wom·an·li·ness \-nlēnəs, -lin-\ *n* -ES : the quality of being womanly

[1]**wom·an·ly** *adj*, *often* -ER/-EST [ME *wommanlich*, fr. *womman* woman + *-lich* -ly, adj. suffix] **1** : marked by qualities characteristic of a woman; *esp* : marked by qualities becoming a well-balanced adult woman ⟨~ manners⟩ ⟨~ advice⟩ **2** : possessed of the character or behavior befitting a grown woman : no longer childish or girlish : becoming to a grown woman ⟨little girl . . . wearing a ~ sort of bonnet much too large for her —Charles Dickens⟩ **3** : characteristic of, belonging to, or suitable to women : conforming to or motivated by a woman's nature and attitudes rather than a man's ⟨convinced that drawing was a waste of time, if not downright ~, like painting on China —Kenneth Roberts⟩ ⟨her usual ~ volubility —Anthony Trollope⟩ **syn** see FEMALE

[2]**wom·an·ly** *adv* [ME *wommanliche*, fr. *womman* woman + *-liche* -ly, adv. suffix] : in a womanly or distinctively feminine manner

wom·an·ness \-mən(n)əs\ *n* -ES : WOMANLINESS

woman of letters 1 : a learned woman **2** : a literary woman

woman of the bedchamber : one of a group of ladies of noble family attendant on a British queen or princess and ranking below those bearing the title *lady of the bedchamber* but having similar duties — called also *bedchamber woman*

woman of the house : LADY OF THE HOUSE

woman of the street *or* **woman of the streets** : PROSTITUTE, STREETWALKER

woman of the town : PROSTITUTE, WHORE

woman of the world 1 : a sophisticated or worldly woman **2** : a woman of the world of fashion or high life

woman-post \'⸗⸗,⸗\ *n*, *archaic* : a female messenger

womanpower \'⸗⸗,⸗⸗\ *n* : power available from or supplied by the effort of women ⟨mobilization of ~ reserves —Fritz Sternberg⟩ ⟨the Navy called for ~ to take over administrative and desk work —Walter Karig⟩

womans *pres 3d sing of* WOMAN

woman's man *n* : LADIES' MAN

woman's rights *n pl* : the legal, political, and social rights of women : FEMINISM 2

woman's-tongue tree \'⸗⸗,⸗-\ *or* **woman's tongue** *n* [so called fr. the clatter of its dry pods when ripe] : LEBBEK

woman suffrage *n* : the suffrage possessed and exercised by women — compare MANHOOD SUFFRAGE, UNIVERSAL SUFFRAGE

woman-suffragist \'⸗⸗'⸗⸗⸗\ *n*, *pl* **woman-suffragists** *or* **women-suffragists** : an advocate of woman suffrage

[1]**womb** \'wüm\ *n* -S [ME *wombe*, *wambe*, *wamb*, fr. OE *wamb*, *womb*; akin to OHG *wamba* belly, ON *vömb* belly, womb, Goth *wamba* belly] **1** *obs* : BELLY **2 a** : UTERUS ⟨transgressors from the ~ —William Cowper⟩ ⟨the lamb . . . leaves the ~ —*New Zealand Jour. of Agric.*⟩ ⟨each adult female fly carries over 50 living larvae in her ~ —*Farm Management*⟩ **b** : CRADLE 1b ⟨from the ~ to the tomb⟩ **3 a** : a cavity or space like a womb in containing and enveloping ⟨the soul remembers the primal silence, the ~ of Night —C.I.Glicksberg⟩ **b** : a place or space where something is generated or produced ⟨the snow . . . would have been shed off around the sides, and piled down into the glacier ~*s* —John Muir †1914⟩ **c** : a period of gestation : circumstances providing the protection and nurture necessary for birth or early development ⟨the Church, a survival from the dying society, became the ~ from which in due course the new one was born —A.J.Toynbee⟩ ⟨prepared themselves to leave the ~ of government protection —S.T. Kimball⟩ ⟨the embryonic State would strangle in its ~ —Tom Marvel⟩

[2]**womb** \"\ *vt* -ED/-ING/-S : to enclose in or as if in a womb ⟨a new era was born . . . ~*ed* in war's destruction —*Time*⟩

wom·bat \'wäm,bat *also* 'wȯm-, *usu* -ad.+V\ *n* -S [native name in New So. Wales] **1 a** : any of several sturdily built Australian marsupials (family Vombatidae) having stocky bodies, short legs, and rudimentary tails, and in general resembling small bears — see HAIRY-NOSED WOMBAT **b** : the fur of the wombat **2** : KOALA 2

wombat

wombed \'wümd\ *adj* [ME, fr. *wombe* womb + *-ed*] : having a womb

wom·ble \'wäməl\ *dial var of* WAMBLE

womby \'wümē\ *adj* -ER/-EST [[1]*womb* + *-y*] *archaic* : HOLLOW

women *pl of* WOMAN

womenfolk *or* **womenfolks** *pl of* **womanfolk**

womenkind \ˈ⸗,⸗\ *n* [ME *womenkinde*, fr. *women* + *kinde* kind] **:** WOMANKIND 1, 2 ⟨a special place was set apart for the ~ to come and pray —Elizabeth Montizambert⟩ ⟨the tasks ~ had to perform —*New Zealand Home Jour.*⟩
women's room *n* **:** LADIES' ROOM
womens.wear *or* **women's wear** \ˈ⸗⸗,⸗\ *n* **1** *usu women's wear* **:** clothing for women **2 :** a fabric (as worsted) suitable for women's clothing
wom·mera *also* **wom·era** *or* **wom·er·ah** \ˈwämərə *also* ˈwȯm-\ *or* **woom·er·ah** \ˈwüm-\ *n* -s [native name in New So. Wales] **:** THROWING-STICK; *specif* **:** one used by Australian aborigines
womp \ˈwämp\ *n* -s [imit. of the sound of a small explosion (as of an electric bulb)] **:** an abrupt increase in the illumination of a television screen resulting from an abrupt increase in signal strength
[1]**won** \ˈwən\ *vi* **wonned; wonned; wonning; wons** [ME *wonen, wunen*, fr. OE *wunian* — more at WONT] *archaic* **:** DWELL, ABIDE ⟨the wild beast, where he ~*s* in forest wild —John Milton⟩
[2]**won** [ME *wan, won* (past) & *wonnen* (past part.), fr. OE *wann, wonn* (past) & *gewunnen* (past part.)] *past of* WIN
[3]**won** \ˈwən\ *dial var of* ONE
[1]**won·der** \ˈwəndə(r)\ *n* -s [ME *wonder, wunder*, fr. OE *wundor*; akin to OHG *wuntar* wonder, ON *undr*] **1 :** a cause of astonishment or surprise **:** something that excites wonder **:** MARVEL ⟨fingers and toes are apparent ~*s* to the little baby —C.S.Kilby⟩: as **a :** a fact or circumstance giving occasion to be surprised ⟨it's a ~ he wasn't killed⟩ ⟨no ~ he left after being insulted so⟩ ⟨the ~ is that he was nominated at all —J.A. Huston⟩ ⟨small ~ that all this extraordinary activity . . . would have exhausted his vitality —H.W.Wiley⟩ **b :** an extraordinary deed or occurrence attributed to supernatural agency **:** MIRACLE ⟨performed among you . . . with signs and ~*s* and mighty works —2 Cor 12:12 (RSV)⟩ **c :** something extraordinarily effective **:** a marvelous result or achievement ⟨a new hairdo that did ~*s* for her looks⟩ ⟨free individuals working together . . . can accomplish ~*s* —J.C.Penney⟩ **d :** a person or thing that excites amazed admiration ⟨a secretary who is a ~ of efficiency⟩ ⟨the pyramids and other ~*s* of the ancient world⟩ **2 :** the quality of exciting amazed admiration ⟨the beauty and ~ of some of these lovely melodies —Warwick Braithwaite⟩ ⟨the glories of His righteousness and ~*s* of His love —Isaac Watts⟩ **3 a :** a state of fascinated or questioning attention before what strikes one as strange beyond understanding **:** an attitude or feeling of amazed admiration or nascent, perplexed, or bewildered curiosity aroused by the extraordinary and unaccountable **:** a sense of mystery **:** MARVELING ⟨stood struck with wide-eyed ~ before the colossal statue⟩ ⟨two impulses in man: one is to accept and take for granted; the other is to look with inquiry and ~ —J.E.Park⟩ ⟨looked at each other in silent ~ —G.D.Brown⟩ **b :** a feeling of doubt or uncertainty **:** a curious concern ⟨your ~ as to what will become of your shares when the banks are nationalized —G.B.Shaw⟩ **4** *obs* **:** great esteem **:** ADMIRATION **5 :** a twisted cruller

syn MARVEL, PRODIGY, MIRACLE, PHENOMENON: WONDER usu. designates what excites surprise, astonishment, or amazement typically by its perfection, greatness, or inexplicableness ⟨the *wonders* of Creation —L.P.Smith⟩ ⟨she is a *wonder* at her job —R.E.Roberts⟩ ⟨a *wonder* how many wild animals survive⟩ MARVEL usu. designates what excites surprise or astonishment by its extraordinariness, strangeness, or curiousness ⟨the endurance of the inequalities of life by the poor is the *marvel* of human society —J.A.Froude⟩ ⟨their hypocrisy is a perpetual *marvel* to me —W.M.Thackeray⟩ ⟨the *marvel* of the play is the bewildering rapid chaotic action —T.S.Eliot⟩ ⟨a *marvel* on the flying trapeze⟩ PRODIGY designates what makes one marvel because of its oddness or unusualness, esp. in degree of skill, endurance, size, or accomplishment ⟨a *prodigy* of wastefulness, corruption, ignorance, and indolence —T.B.Macaulay⟩ ⟨performed *prodigies* in transporting to France a gigantic army —G.W.Johnson⟩ ⟨women performing *prodigies* of endurance, bravery, and hope —*Newsweek*⟩ ⟨the Shoshones feared . . . this *prodigy*, the first white man they had ever seen —A.J. Toynbee⟩ ⟨a land of *prodigies:* mountains, precipices, cataracts, dead craters, snowy ascents, vertiginous cliffs —*Amer. Guide Series: Calif.*⟩ MIRACLE applies to something very unusual, esp. so contrary to normal expectations that it seems to surpass human comprehension and often approaches the supernatural ⟨their conversations are *miracles* of studied, stilted eloquence —B.R.Redman⟩ ⟨the ears of an owl are a very *miracle* of sensitiveness —C.G.D.Roberts⟩ ⟨studied constantly long hours that were a *miracle* of concentration —Adria Langley⟩ ⟨the *miracle* which we call genius —J.L. Lowes⟩ PHENOMENON, implying something exceptional or extraordinary, sometimes, in informal application to persons, suggests the eccentric or odd ⟨it did snow considerably in Vermont that July, a natural *phenomenon* that gave Thompson a tremendous reputation —*Amer. Guide Series: Vt.*⟩ ⟨the captain — a *phenomenon* during prohibition because he was honest —J.F.Dinneen⟩ ⟨an American *phenomenon*, a self-taught mechanical genius —Don Wharton⟩ ⟨your nephew Caligula is a *phenomenon*. He's treacherous, cowardly, lustful, vain, deceitful, and he'll play some very dirty tricks on you before he's done —Robert Graves⟩ ⟨in a group of extroverts the introvert will be considered something of a *phenomenon*⟩
— **for a wonder** *adv* **:** in the way of an extraordinary circumstance esp. in view of the past **:** SURPRISINGLY ⟨the children, *for a wonder*, kept still long enough for her to hear⟩ — **to a wonder** *archaic* **:** to an astonishing extent ⟨she was ugly *to a wonder* —William Cowper⟩
[2]**wonder** \"\ *adj* **1 :** of an extraordinary character **:** being such as excites amazed admiration **:** WONDERFUL, MARVELOUS ⟨a family of chemicals . . . of such exciting potency that the popular name for them is "~ hormones" —D.C.Cooley⟩ ⟨~ fibers and miracle finishes⟩ **2 :** of or relating to things that excite amazed admiration ⟨a ~ city⟩ ⟨a ~ book⟩ ⟨the Elizabethan ~ age of adventure —*Spectator*⟩ **3 :** having or manifesting magical power ⟨wore a ~ bag around his neck⟩
[3]**wonder** \"\ *adv, archaic* **:** WONDERFULLY, AMAZINGLY, EXCEEDINGLY, VERY ⟨delicate ~ white crystals —*Westminster Gazette*⟩
[4]**wonder** \"\ *vb* **wondered; wondered; wondering** \-d(ə)riŋ\ **wonders** [ME *wondren, wundren*, fr. OE *wundrian*; akin to OHG *wuntarōn* to wonder, ON *undra* to wonder, OE *wundor* wonder] *vi* **1 a :** to be in a state of rapt or questioning attention toward the extraordinary or mysterious **:** feel or become struck with wonder **:** MARVEL ⟨~*ed* at the delicacy of form and color —W.B.Yeats⟩ ⟨though no . . . rapturous insight troubled her childlike soul, yet she could ~ and gaze —A.J.Munby⟩ **b :** to feel or become struck with surprise ⟨couldn't help ~*ing* at the size of the servings⟩ ⟨~*ed* to see them all standing there waiting⟩ ⟨shouldn't ~ if he came after all⟩ ⟨I ~ . . . that he keeps that reminder of his sufferings by him —Charles Dickens⟩ **2 :** to wish to know something **:** feel curiosity or doubt **:** query in the mind ⟨~*ed* as to the feasibility of the plan⟩ ⟨said he had found it but you couldn't help ~*ing*⟩ ⟨looks up in the dictionary words he ~*s* about⟩ ~ *vt* **1 :** to be curious or in doubt about **:** wish to know ⟨~*ed* why they came⟩ ⟨~ if it will rain⟩ ⟨on whom, one ~*s*, do these expensive weeklies live —Aldous Huxley⟩ **:** ask or puzzle in one's mind about ⟨~*ed* what he should do⟩ **2** *archaic* **:** to look upon with often admiring wonder ⟨I felt all, loved all, ~*ed* all —Charles Lamb⟩ **3** *dial* **:** to cause to wonder — usu. used in the phrase *it wonders me* **4 :** to make an occasion for wonder — usu. used in the phrase *to be wondered* ⟨it is little to be ~*ed* that her students idolized her⟩
won·der·berry \ˈ⸗⸗- — *see* BERRY\ *n* **1 :** the edible fruit of the black nightshade — called also *sunberry* **2 :** BLACK NIGHTSHADE
won·der·boom \ˈvändə(r),büm\ *n* -s [Afrik, lit., wonder tree, fr. MD, fr. *wonder* + *boom* tree; akin to OE *wundor* wonder and OHG *boum* tree — more at WONDER, BEAM] **:** a fig (*Ficus pretoriae*) with fruits borne in the leaf axils of the terminal branchlets that is widely distributed in tropical and subtropical Africa
wonder boy *n* **:** a very popular or successful person
wonder child *n* **:** a child prodigy
wonder drug *n* **:** MIRACLE DRUG
won·der·er \ˈwəndərə(r)\ *n* -s **:** one that wonders
[1]**won·der·ful** \-də(r)fəl\ *adj, sometimes* **wonderfuller;** *sometimes* **wonderfullest** [ME, fr. OE *wundorful*, fr. *wundor* wonder + *-ful*] **1 a :** exciting wonder **:** MARVELOUS, SURPRISING, STRANGE, ASTONISHING ⟨a feast ~ to behold⟩ **b** *obs* **:** MIRACULOUS **2 :** unusually good, interesting, amusing, lovely **:** ADMIRABLE — used as a generalized term of approval ⟨in love with a ~ girl⟩ ⟨having a ~ time⟩ — **won·der·ful·ness** *n* -ES
[2]**wonderful** \"\ *adv* [ME, fr. [1]*wonderful*] *dial* **:** WONDERFULLY ⟨gets ~ excited —Adrian Bell⟩
won·der·ful·ly \-f(ə)lē, -li\ *adv* [ME *wonderfulliche*, fr. [1]*wonderful* + *-liche* -ly] **1 :** in such a way or to such an extent as to excite wonder **:** MARVELOUSLY, AMAZINGLY ⟨a ~ beautiful sunset⟩ ⟨had worked ~ for years⟩ **2 :** EXCEEDINGLY, VERY ⟨not very imaginative but ~ pleasing —George Saintsbury⟩
won·der·ing·ly *adv* **:** in a wondering manner ⟨looked ~ at the skyscrapers⟩
won·der·land \ˈwəndə(r),land, -laa(ə)nd, -,lənd\ *n* **1 :** a fairylike imaginary realm **2 :** a place (as one containing extraordinary natural features) that excites admiration or wonder ⟨a scenic ~⟩
won·der·less \-(r)ləs\ *adj* **:** having no wonder
won·der·ment \-(r)mənt\ *n* -s **1 :** a state or feeling of wonder **:** ASTONISHMENT, SURPRISE ⟨saw with ~ that her fingers were trembling —Walter Macken⟩ **2 :** something exciting wonder **:** a cause of or occasion for wonder; *also* **:** something that evokes admiring wonder **3 :** the quality of being wonderful or marvelous **4 :** an exclamation or other utterance expressive of wonder **5 :** curiosity about something **:** WONDERING ⟨their ~ about the outcome⟩
wondermonger \ˈ⸗⸗,⸗⸗\ *n* [[1]*wonder* + *monger*] **:** a person who tells of or exploits strange or freakish things
won·der·some \-(r)səm\ *adj, dial Brit* **:** WONDERFUL
wonderwork \ˈ⸗⸗,⸗\ *n* **1 :** WONDER 1b **2 :** something that excites amazed admiration
wonder-worker \ˈ⸗⸗,⸗⸗\ *n* **:** one that performs wonders
wonderworld \ˈ⸗⸗,⸗\ *n* **:** WONDERLAND
[1]**won·drous** \ˈwəndrəs\ *adj* [alter. (influenced by *-ous*) of ME *wonders*, adj., wondrous, fr. gen. of [1]*wonder*] **:** exciting wonder or surprise **:** WONDERFUL, ASTONISHING, MARVELOUS ⟨a ~ fairy tale⟩ ⟨colors and shades changed in slow, ~ transformation —Zane Grey⟩ ⟨~ new ways to kill bacteria —Vance Packard⟩ — **won·drous·ly** *adv* — **won·drous·ness** *n* -ES
[2]**wondrous** \"\ *adv, archaic* **:** WONDERFULLY ⟨grew ~ cold —S.T.Coleridge⟩
wone *archaic var of* WON
wong *n* -s [ME, fr. OE *wong, wang;* akin to OHG *-wang* field, ON *vangr* garden, field, Goth *wangs*] *obs* **:** FIELD, MEADOW
wonga-wonga \ˈwäŋəˈwäŋə\ *or* **wonga** \ˈwäŋə\ *n* -s [native names in New So. Wales] **1 a :** an Australian woody vine (*Pandorea pandorana*) with loose panicles of yellowish white flowers **b** *Austral* **:** a narrow-leaved cattail (*Typha angustifolia*) **2 :** a very large Australian pigeon (*Leucosarcia melanoleuca*) with very white flesh
wong·shy \ˈwäŋˈshē\ *n* -ES [Chin (Pek) *huang[2]-chih[1]* yellow gardenia] **1 :** an Asian tree (*Gardenia grandiflora*) **2 :** a yellow dye containing crocin derived from the pods of the wongshy
wo-ni \ˈwōˈnē\ *n, pl* **wo-ni** *or* **wo-nis** *usu cap* **1 :** a Nosu people of southern Yunnan province of China subject to the Chinese **2 :** a member of the Wo-ni people
won·ing *or* **won·ning** \ˈwəniŋ\ *n* -s [ME, fr. OE *wunung*, fr. *wunian* to dwell + *-ung* -ing — more at WONT] *dial* **:** DWELLING
won·ky \ˈwäŋkē\ *adj* [alter. of *wanky*] **1** *Brit* **:** UNSTEADY, SHAKY ⟨the bridge stands . . . though one of the arches is ~ —*Manchester Guardian Weekly*⟩ **2** *Brit* **:** AWRY, WRONG ⟨hoped that nothing had gone ~ with the dinner —P.G. Wodehouse⟩
won·na \ˈwənə\ [by contr.] *dial Brit* **:** will not
wonne *var of* [2]WON
wonned *past of* WON
wonning *pres part of* WON
wons *pres 3d sing of* WON, *pl of* WON
[1]**wont** \ˈwȯnt, ˈwōnt *sometimes* ˈwänt *or* ˈwənt\ *adj* [ME *wont, woned*, fr. past part. of *wonen, wunen* to dwell, be used to, fr. OE *wunian;* akin to OHG *wonēn* to dwell, remain, be used to, ON *una* to dwell, be content, Goth *-wunan* to be content, Skt *vanati* he loves — more at WIN] **:** ACCUSTOMED, USED — used predicatively ⟨slept longer than he was ~⟩ and usu. followed by *to* and an infinitive ⟨assumed an air of great gravity, as he was ~ to do when about to perpetrate a joke —O.S.J. Gogarty⟩; *also* **:** INCLINED, APT ⟨fresh, intimate, and revealing as letters are ~ to be —Gladys Wrigley⟩
[2]**wont** \"\ *n* -s [ME, fr. past part. of *wonen* to be used to] **:** CUSTOM, HABIT, USE, USAGE ⟨life is an affair of use and ~ and persists substantially unchanged —Walter Moberly⟩ ⟨far more serious and thoughtful than was her ~ —William Black⟩
syn see HABIT
[3]**wont** \"\ *vb* **wont; wont** *or* **wonted; wonting; wonts** [ME *wunten*, prob. fr. *wunt, wont*, past part. of *wunen, wonen* to be used to] *vt* **:** ACCUSTOM, HABITUATE ⟨~ ourselves with their strange aspect —R.W.Emerson⟩ ~ *vi* **:** to have the habit or custom of doing something — usu. followed by *to* and an infinitive ⟨the merry pipe, that ~ to cheer the harvesting —Robert Bridges †1930⟩
won't \ˈwōnt *also* ˈwənt *sometimes* ˈwünt\ [by contr.] **:** will not
wont·ed \ˈwȯntəd, ˈwōn- *sometimes* ˈwän- *or* ˈwən-\ *adj* [ME, prob. fr. [2]*wont* + *-ed*] **:** ACCUSTOMED, CUSTOMARY, ⟨maintained his ~ courtesy⟩ **syn** see USUAL
wont·ed·ly *adv* **:** CUSTOMARILY, USUALLY
wont·ed·ness *n* -ES **:** the condition of being habituated to a thing, person, or practice
wont·less \-tləs\ *adj, archaic* **:** UNACCUSTOMED, UNWONTED
won ton \ˈwänˈtän\ *n, pl* **won tons** [Chin (Cant) *wan t'an*] **:** filled pockets of noodle dough boiled in and eaten with soup
[1]**woo** \ˈwü\ *vb* -ED/-ING/-S [ME *wowen*, fr. OE *wōgian;* perh. akin to L *vovēre* to vow — more at VOW] *vt* **1 :** to solicit in love **:** sue for the affection of and usu. marriage with **:** COURT ⟨could ~ her and win her —Theodor Reik⟩ **2 :** to solicit or entreat esp. with ingratiating importunity **:** beseech solicitously ⟨the young author trying to ~ his reader, via heavy humor —Frances Keene⟩ **3 :** to seek to gain or bring about **:** act in such a way as to tend to bring about ⟨feels entitled to all the dollars it can ~ from the public —Jerome Ellison⟩ **4 :** to tend to bring about unintentionally ⟨~*ing* defeat —Florence Converse⟩ ~ *vi* **1 :** to court a woman **:** make love **2 :** to make pleading solicitation or invitation
[2]**woo** \"\ *n* -s **:** LOVE — used esp. in the phrase *pitch woo*
[3]**woo** \"\ *vi* -ED/-ING/-S [origin unknown] **:** MAH-JONGG
[1]**wood** \ˈwüd, ˈwōd, ˈwůd\ *adj* [ME *wod*, fr. OE *wōd* mad — more at VATIC] **1** *archaic* **:** INSANE, MAD **2** *archaic* **:** ENRAGED, VIOLENT
[2]**wood** \ˈwůd\ *n* -s [ME *wode, wude*, fr. OE *wudu, widu;* akin to OHG *witu* wood, ON *vithr* tree, wood, OIr *fid* tree] **1 a** (1) **:** a dense growth of trees usu. greater in extent than a grove and smaller than a forest ⟨out in the ~ —J. G.Frazer⟩ — often used in pl. but sing. or pl. in constr. ⟨would take our children into a nearby ~*s* —Herbert Gold⟩

woods, 5d: *1* driver, *2* brassie, *3* spoon, 4 cleek

(2) **:** growing trees found in natural groves ⟨gentle risings covered with ~ —Thomas Gray⟩ **b :** a tract of land on which stand growing trees **:** WOODLAND **c** *archaic* **:** FOREST 6a **2 :** the hard fibrous substance that makes up the greater part of the stems and branches of trees or shrubs beneath the bark, is found to a limited extent in herbaceous plants, and consists technically of the aggregated xylem elements intersected in many plants with the rays **3 a :** the trunks or large branches of trees sawed or otherwise prepared for commercial use **:** TIMBER, LUMBER — see HARDWOOD, SOFTWOOD **b :** trees or branches cut or sawed for use in a fire **:** FIREWOOD **4 :** a form or condition of wood substance or timber; *esp* **:** the wood of a particular kind of tree ⟨some ~*s* warp easily⟩ **5 :** something made of wood: as **a :** a part (as a handle or shaft) made of wood **b :** a wooden cask or keg ⟨draft beer from the ~ —B.M.Brown⟩ **c :** BOWL 1b **d :** a golf club (as a driver, brassie, or spoon) having a massive head (as of wood, metal, or composition material) and used esp. to drive the ball from the tee — compare IRON **e :** pins in a bowling alley; *esp* **:** pins that have been knocked down **6 :** the fundamental substance of a person's character (of what ~ a minister is made —Benjamin Disraeli) **7 :** ALMOND 6a **8 :** a wood shot in golf — **out of the wood** *Brit* **:** out of the woods — **out of the woods :** escaped from a situation of perplexity, anxiety, peril, or difficulty **:** safe after hazard ⟨after rallying from the . . . attack, the patient believed he was *out of the woods* —S.H. Adams⟩
[3]**wood** \"\ *adj* **1 :** made of wood **:** WOODEN **2 :** suitable or used for or engaged in cutting or otherwise working with wood **3** *or* **woods** \-dz\ **:** living or growing in woods
[4]**wood** \"\ *vb* -ED/ING/-S *vt* **1 :** to supply or load with wood esp. for fuel ⟨~*ing* the stove —Jan Burroway⟩ **2 :** to cover with a growth of trees **:** plant with trees **3 :** to surround (the jack) with bowls in the game of bowls ~ *vi* **:** to gather or take on wood — often used with *up*
wood agate *n* **:** agate formed by petrifaction of wood
wood alcohol *n* **:** METHANOL — distinguished from *grain alcohol*
wood alloy *n* **:** a mixture of wood and other substances (as urea or resin) often in layers that have been subjected to heat and pressure producing density, hardness, and stability in excess of the wood itself — compare COMPREG
wood almond *n* **:** the oily edible seed of a West Indian woody vine (*Hippocratea comosa*); *also* **:** the plant itself
wood anemone *n* **:** any of several spring-flowering plants of the genus *Anemone* with tuberous roots, a single whorl of leaves, and solitary white flowers: as **a :** a common anemone (*A. quinquefolia*) of eastern No. America with solitary often pink-tinged white flowers **b :** a European anemone (*A. nemorosa*) that is common in deciduous woodlands
wood ant *n* **1 a :** a large widely distributed ant (*Formica rufa*) or a related American ant (*F. exsectoides*) that lives in woods and builds large nests **b :** CARPENTER ANT **2 :** TERMITE
wood apple *n* **1 :** a small tree (*Limoina acidissima* or *Feronia elephantum*) of the family Rutaceae of southeastern Asia that yields a hard heavy durable yellowish wood and is often cultivated for its acid hard-rinded fruit which is used as a food and together with the leaves in folk medicine **2 :** the fruit of the wood apple
wood-apple *n* **:** a gum obtained from the wood apple and used like gum arabic
wood aster *n* **:** any of several asters of eastern No. America usu. growing in woods (esp. *Aster cordifolius, A. macrophyllus,* and *A. divaricatus*)
wood avens *n* **:** a European avens (*Geum urbanum*) with bright yellow flowers that is adventive in the northeastern U. S.
wood baboon *n* **:** [6]DRILL
woodbark \ˈ⸗,⸗\ *n* **:** a grayish yellowish brown that is stronger than deer, lighter and stronger than acorn, and lighter, stronger, and slightly yellower than olive wood — called also *blondine, sable*
wood bass *n* **:** GREEN SUNFISH
wood bedstraw *n* **:** a European perennial herb (*Galium sylvaticum*) with narrow leaves in groups of six or eight and open panicles of tiny white flowers that is naturalized in the eastern U. S. — called also *Scotch mist*
wood betony *n* **1 :** a common betony (*Stachys betonica*) **2 :** a lousewort (*Pedicularis canadensis*) of eastern No. America with pinnately parted leaves and irregular red or yellowish flowers in bracted spikes
woodbin \ˈ⸗,⸗\ *n* **:** a bin for holding firewood
woodbine \ˈ⸗,⸗\ *also* **woodbind** \ˈ⸗,⸗\ *n* [ME *wodebinde*, fr. OE *wudubinde*, fr. *wudu* wood + *-binde* (fr. *bindan* to tie, bind); fr. its winding about trees — more at WOOD, BIND] **1 :** any of several honeysuckles; *esp* **:** a European twining shrub (*Lonicera periclymenum*) **2 :** VIRGINIA CREEPER **3 :** YELLOW JESSAMINE 2 **4 :** HEDGE BINDWEED 1
woodbine green *n* **:** a moderate yellow green to olive green that is yellower and stronger than art green — called also *peridot*
wood bison *n* **1** *also* **wood buffalo :** a bison that is a variety (*Bison bison athabascae*) of the American bison and is restricted to wooded regions of northern Alberta, Canada **2 :** WOODLAND BISON
wood block *n* **1 :** a solid block of wood usu. with plane faces **2 :** WOODCUT **3 :** BLOCK 1g
wood-block \ˈ⸗,⸗\ *adj* [*wood block*] **:** made of, done with, or printed from wood blocks ⟨*wood-block* printing⟩ ⟨*wood-block* prints⟩
wood borer *n* **1 :** a grub that is the wood-boring larva of any of numerous beetles (as a click beetle, longicorn beetle, buprestid, or weevil) — compare APPLE TREE BORER **2 :** a borer (as the peach tree borer) that is the larva of any of various lepidopterous insects and esp. of a clearwing moth or a goat moth **3 :** a borer that is the larva of a horntail (family Siricidae) **4 :** any of several bivalve mollusks (as the teredos and members of the genus *Xylophaga*) that bore in wood **5 :** any of several small crustaceans (as the gribble) that bore in wood
wood-boring \ˈ⸗;⸗⸗\ *adj* **:** excavating galleries in wood in feeding or in constructing a nest ⟨*wood-boring* worms had eaten many of . . . the boxes —David Masters⟩
woodbound \ˈ⸗;⸗\ *adj* **1 :** bound with wood **2 a :** having trees or hedges as obstructions to agriculture **b :** surrounded by woodland
woodbox \ˈ⸗,⸗\ *n* **:** WOODBIN
wood brick *n* **:** wood of the size and shape of a brick inserted in brickwork to supply a hold for the attachment of finishings
wood brown *n* **:** ALMOND 6a
wood bud *n* **:** a plant bud that produces a shoot or branch — compare FLOWER BUD
woodburning \ˈ⸗,⸗⸗\ *n* **:** the art or process of burning a design usu. on wood or leather esp. with an electrically heated tool
wood·bury·type \ˈwůd,berē,tīp, -,bər-\ *n* [Walter Bentley *Woodbury* †1885 Eng. photographer and inventor + E *type*] **:** a process in which a gelatin relief produced by photographic methods and hardened is powerfully pressed on a plate of soft metal to produce an intaglio impression that upon inking may be used to print pictures directly; *also* **:** a print thus made
wood-carver \ˈ⸗,⸗⸗\ *n* **:** a person whose occupation is wood carving
wood carving *n* **:** the art of fashioning or ornamenting objects of wood by cutting with a sharp implement held in the hand; *also* **:** an object of wood so fashioned or ornamented
wood charcoal *n* **:** charcoal prepared from wood **:** CARBO LIGNI
woodchat \ˈ⸗,⸗\ *n* **1 :** any of several Asian birds of the family Turdidae and the genus *Erithacus* the males of which are mostly bright blue marked with red or rufous beneath **2** *or* **woodchat shrike :** a European shrike (*Lanius senator*) whose males have the head and nape rufous red and the back, wings, and tail black varied with white
woodchopper \ˈ⸗,⸗⸗\ *n* **:** one engaged in chopping wood and esp. chopping down trees
[1]**wood·chuck** \ˈwůd,chək\ *n* -s [by folk etymology fr. Ojibwa *otchig* fisher, marten, or Cree *otcheck*] **1 :** a thickset marmot (*Marmota monax*) of the northeastern U.S. and Canada with a chiefly grizzled reddish brown color — called also *groundhog* **2 :** any of various marmots of mountainous parts of western No. America that are related to the eastern woodchuck

woodchuck 1

[2]**woodchuck** \"\ *n* -s [[1]*wood* + *chuck* (to pat, jerk)] **:** RED-HEADED WOODPECKER
wood coal *n* **1 :** CHARCOAL **2 :** LIGNITE
woodcock \ˈ⸗,⸗\ *n, pl* **woodcocks** *or* **woodcock** [ME *wodecok*, fr. OE *wuducocc*, fr. *wudu* wood + *cocc* cock — more at WOOD, COCK] **1 a** (1) **:** an Old World limicoline bird (*Scolopax rusticola*) that ranges from the British Isles to Japan, migrates south-

ward, and has large eyes, a long bill very sensitive at the tip used in probing the ground for earthworms, and a variously mottled black, chestnut, gray, and buff color (2) : a smaller related American bird (*Philohela minor*) that is distinguished by having the three outer primaries shortened and conspicuously narrowed instead of the first only as in the European woodcock, that frequents woodlands, and that is prized as a game bird **b** : PILEATED WOODPECKER **2** [so called fr. the ease with which the woodcock is taken in a snare] *archaic* : a gullible person : SIMPLETON **3** *or* **woodcock soil** : a soil consisting of clay and gravel **4** *or* **woodcock shell** : the shell of any of various mollusks of the genus *Murex* having a very long canal

woodcock snipe *n* **1** *Brit* : GREAT SNIPE **2** : WOODCOCK 1a(2)

wood cooker *n* : VATMAN b

wood copper *n* : a fibrous olivenite

wood crab *n* : an amphibious crab (*Sesarma cinereum*) that resembles the related fiddler crabs and lives on or about wharves or sometimes in mangrove swamps along the Atlantic coast of tropical America

woodcraft \ˈ=,=\ *n* **1** : skill and practice in anything relating to the woods and esp. in maintaining oneself and making one's way, in hunting or trapping, or in tracking and studying wildlife **2** : skill in shaping or constructing articles from wood

wood cree *n, usu cap W&C* [trans. of Cree *Sakawithiniwuk*, lit., people of the woods] **1** : an Algonquian people formerly inhabiting the northeastern portion of the Cree territory — compare PLAINS CREE **2** : a member of the Wood Cree people

woodcreeper \ˈ=,==\ *n* : WOODHEWER 1

woodcut \ˈ=,=\ *n* **1 a** : the process or technique of cutting a design on wood usu. with the grain or sometimes on metal for use as a letterpress printing surface — compare WOOD ENGRAVING **b** : a print so produced **2** : a letterpress printing surface consisting of a wooden block with a usu. pictorial design cut with the grain

woodcutter \ˈ=,==\ *n* **1** : a person who cuts wood **2** : one that produces woodcuts

¹woodcutting \ˈ=,==\ *n* **1** : WOODCUT **2** : the action or occupation of cutting wood or timber

²woodcutting \ˈ=ˌ==\ *adj* **1** : of or relating to woodcuts or making woodcuts **2** : engaged in or designed or used for cutting wood ⟨a ~ circular saw⟩

wood dove *n* [ME *wode dowe*] : WOOD PIGEON; *esp* : STOCK DOVE

wood drake *n* : the male of the wood duck

wood duck *n* **1** : a showy American duck (*Aix sponsa*) which nests in hollow trees and the male of which has a large crest and plumage varied with green, purple, black, white, and chestnut — called also *summer duck, wood widgeon* **2** : HOODED MERGANSER **3** : an Australian goose (*Chenonetta jubata*) having elongated deep brown feathers on the rear part of the neck

¹wooded *past of* WOOD

²wood·ed \ˈwu̇dəd\ *adj* : covered with growing trees

wood·en \ˈwu̇dᵊn\ *adj, sometimes* -ER/-EST **1 a** : made or consisting wholly or sometimes partly of wood ⟨~ houses⟩ ⟨~ box⟩ **b** *obs* : engaged in or concerned with the preparation of wood **c** : resembling or producing a sound characteristic of a struck hollow wooden object ⟨the ~ sound of numskulls being soundly hit —Edith Sitwell⟩ **2 a** : resembling wood in stiffness and lack of resilience ⟨the hands are also . . . ~, not only hard, but lifeless —C.W.H.Johnson⟩ ⟨wooden-faced country people —William Faulkner⟩ ⟨a ~ military posture⟩ ⟨a ~ and inflexible policy —W.M.Dacey⟩ **b** : lacking in ease, grace, charm, liveliness, lifelikeness, interest, or zest : AWKWARD, CLUMSY, DRY, LIFELESS, DULL ⟨hear the ~ dialogue —Shak.⟩ ⟨cooperation . . . has frequently been reluctant and ~ —Woodrow Wyatt⟩ ⟨party debates are ~ and tedious formalities —Christopher Hollis⟩ ⟨a ~ and perfunctory pedagogue —John Dewey⟩ ⟨book is ~ and insensitive —George Nobbe⟩ **3** : WOODED **syn** see STIFF

wooden brick *n* : WOOD BRICK

wood engraver *n* : an engraver on wood; *esp* : one that makes wood engravings **2** : ENGRAVER BEETLE

wood engraving *n* **1 a** : the art or process of cutting a design upon wood and esp. upon the end grain of wood for use as a letterpress printing surface — compare WOODCUT 1a **b** : a wooden letterpress printing surface bearing a usu. pictorial design produced by wood engraving **2** : a design printed from a wood engraving

woodenhead \ˈ==,=\ *n* : BLOCKHEAD

wooden-headed \ˈ==ˈ==\ *adj* : STUPID, DULL, UNINTELLIGENT

wooden horse *n* **1** *archaic* : SHIP **2** : a ridged or studded wooden device which soldiers formerly were condemned to sit astride as a military punishment

wooden indian *n, usu cap I* : a standing wooden image of an American Indian brave used esp. formerly for advertising before a cigar store

wood·en·ly *adv* : in a wooden manner

wood·en·ness \-ᵊn(n)əs\ *n* -ES : the quality or state of being wooden

wooden nickel *n* **1** : a wooden commemorative or souvenir token having the value of a five-cent piece **2** *or* **wooden nutmeg** : something utterly worthless accepted as a gift or purchased by a gullible person

wooden pear *n* : NATIVE PEAR

wooden shoe *n* : SABOT 1a

wooden spoon *n* **1** : a spoon made of wood presented orig. at Cambridge University to the man ranking lowest among those taking honors in the mathematical tripos and at other colleges and universities to other selected recipients **2** : the recipient of a wooden spoon

wooden Indian

wooden tongue *n* : actinobacillosis or actinomycosis of cattle esp. when chiefly affecting the tongue

wooden walls *n pl* [trans. of Gk *xylinon teichos*, sing.] : warships used as coastal defense

woodenware \ˈ==,=\ *n* : articles made of wood for table, kitchen, and other domestic use ⟨salad bowls and other ~⟩

wood·eny \ˈwu̇dᵊnē, -ᵊni\ *adj* [*wooden* + *-y*] : WOODEN

wood·er \ˈwu̇də(r)\ *n* -S : a person that cuts or gathers wood esp. for fuel

wood fern *n* : any of various ferns of the genus *Dryopteris*

wood fiber *n* **1** : XYLEM FIBER **2** : wood reduced to fine shreds

wood-fibered plaster \ˈ=ˌ==-\ *n* : a gypsum plaster containing shredded wood fiber to reduce the weight and to improve its sound-absorbing properties

wood filler *n* : a composition of silica and oil or varnish to fill the pores of open-grained wood (as oak) before varnishing

woodfish \ˈ=,=\ *n* : SILVERFISH 2

wood float *n* : FLOAT 5a

wood flour *n* : finely powdered wood or sawdust used chiefly as an adsorbent in dynamite and as a filler in plastics and linoleum — called also *wood meal*

wood flower *n* : WOOD ROSE 1

wood fretter *n* : an animal that in the adult or larval stage bores in the wood or beneath the bark of trees : WOOD BORER

wood fringe *n* : CLIMBING FUMITORY

wood frog *n* **1** : a common eastern No. American frog (*Rana sylvatica*) that lives chiefly in moist woods and woodland pools and is drab or yellowish brown with a black stripe on each side of the head **2** : a brightly colored western No. American frog (*Rana aurora*) of similar habitats to the eastern wood frog

wood gas *n* : gas obtained by the destructive distillation of wood, composed chiefly of hydrogen, carbon monoxide, carbon dioxide, and methane, and used as a fuel and illuminant

wood·gate rust \ˈwu̇d,gāt-\ *n* [fr. *Woodgate*, Oneida County, N.Y.] : a disease of the Scotch pine caused by a rust fungus of the genus *Cronartium* that forms galls upon twigs and branches

wood gatherer *n, usu cap W&G* : the second of four ranks attained by camp fire girls — compare FIRE MAKER, TORCH BEARER, TRAIL SEEKER

woodgeld \ˈ=,=\ *n* [ME *wodegeld*, fr. *wode* wood + *geld* tax, fr. OE *gield, geld* — more at GELD] : money paid in feudal times for the privilege of gathering or cutting wood in a forest; *also* : immunity from this payment granted by the king

wood grass *n* **1** : an American perennial grass (*Sorghastrum nutans*) that is valued for hay and has long flat leaves and large plumelike panicles **2** : KNOTROOT GRASS

wood groundsel *n* : a European annual herb (*Senecio sylvaticus*) that is widely naturalized as a weed in No. America and has pinnatifid leaves and small yellow flower heads in corymbs

wood grouse *n* **1** *Brit* : CAPERCAILLIE **2** : SPRUCE GROUSE

woodgrub \ˈ=,=\ *n* : a grub that is the larva of any of numerous wood-boring insects

wood gum *n* : XYLAN

wood hen *n* [ME *wodehen*, fr. *wode* wood + *hen*] **1** : WOODCOCK 1a(2) **2** : WEKA

woodhewer \ˈ=,==\ *n* **1** : any of numerous So. and Central American birds (family Dendrocolaptidae) that have a curved bill and stiffened tail feathers and climb and feed like woodpeckers — called also *tree creeper* **2** : WOODPECKER

wood hoopoe *n* : a bird of the genus *Phoeniculus*

woodhorse \ˈ=,=\ *n* : WALKING STICK 2

wood horsetail *n* : a common herb (*Equisetum sylvaticum*) of the north temperate zone with drooping whorls of usu. forked branches

wood·house·ite \ˈwu̇d,hau̇,sīt\ *n* -S [Charles D. *Woodhouse* *b*1888 Am. mineralogist + E *-ite*] : a mineral $CaAl_3(PO_4)(SO_4)(OH)_6$ of the beudantite group consisting of a basic sulfate and phosphate of aluminum and calcium isomorphous with svanbergite, hinsdalite, corkite, and beudantite

wood hyacinth *n* : a European squill (*Scilla nonscripta*) having a scape bearing a raceme of drooping blue, purple, white, or sometimes pink bell-shaped flowers — called also *harebell*

wood ibis *n* **1** : a large wading bird (*Mycteria americana*) of the family Ciconiidae that frequents wooded swamps of So. and Central America and the southern U. S., has the bill heavy at the base and the head and upper neck naked in the adult, and is white with tail and primaries black **2** : any of various Old World birds of the genus *Ibis* — called also *wood stork*

woodier *comparative of* WOODY

woodies *pl of* WOODY

woodiest *superlative of* WOODY

wood·i·ness \ˈwu̇dēnəs, -din-\ *n* -ES **1** : the quality, state, or condition of being woody **2** : a virus disease of passion fruit esp. troublesome in Australia and characterized by woody tissue in the fruit and gradual decline of the vines

¹wooding *pres part of* WOOD

²wood·ing \ˈwu̇diŋ, -dən\ *n* [¹*wood* + *-ing*] *Scot* : GROVE, WOOD

wood jack *n* : a pucellas having prongs tipped with wood

woodkern \ˈ=,=\ *n* [¹*wood* + *kern* (soldier)] : an Irish robber or outlaw frequenting a forest

woodknife \ˈ=,=\ *n* [ME *wodeknif*, fr. *wode* wood + *knif* knife] *archaic* : DIRK, DAGGER

¹wood·land \ˈ=lənd, -,land, -,laa(ə)nd\ *n* [ME *wodeland*, fr. OE *wudulond*, fr. *wudu* wood + *lond* land — more at WOOD, LAND] **1 a** : land covered with woody vegetation : TIMBERLAND, FOREST **b** : a plot of wooded land managed or used in conjunction with a farm **2** *or* **woodland green** : a moderate olive green that is greener and darker than holly green (sense 2) and greener and slightly deeper than Lincoln green

²woodland \"\ *adj* [ME *wodeland*, fr. *wodeland*, n.] **1 a** : of, relating to, or occurring in woodland ⟨a shady ~ path⟩ ⟨~ streams⟩ **b** : growing or living in woodland ⟨~ herbs⟩ ⟨~ birds⟩ **c** : constituting or made up of woodland ⟨large ~ areas⟩ **2** *usu cap* : of or belonging to a cultural pattern extending over midwestern, eastern, and northeastern U. S. and Canada beginning about 500 B.C. and in some areas extending into historic times characterized by flexed burials, side-notched and stemmed projectile points made from cores, grooved axes, and pottery usu. with a grit temper and in globular forms with conical or truncated base and no handles

woodland bison *n* : a bison that is an eastern variety (*Bison bison pennsylvanicus*) of the American bison and is prob. extinct as a pure race

woodland brown *n* : a dark grayish brown that is slightly yellower than average chocolate brown and slightly yellower and less strong than African brown

woodland caribou *n* : any of several rather large caribou of wooded regions including one formerly abundant in much of the northern U. S. but now nearly exterminated

wood·land·er \ˈwu̇dləndə(r)\ *n* -S : an inhabitant of woodland

woodland rose *n* : MUSCADE

woodland star *n* : a plant of the genus *Lithophragma* of the family Saxifragaceae; *esp* : a California perennial herb (*L. affinis*) cultivated for its racemose white flowers

wood lark *n* [ME *wodelarke*, fr. *wode* wood + *larke* lark] : a small European lark (*Lullula arborea*) that utters its notes while on the wing

wood laurel *n* **1** : SPURGE LAUREL 1 **2** : MOUNTAIN LAUREL 1

wood·less \ˈwu̇dləs\ *adj* : having no wood; *esp* : TREELESS

wood lily *n* [ME *wode lilie*] **1 a** : LILY OF THE VALLEY **b** : a red-flowered lily (*Lilium philadelphicum*) of the eastern U. S. — called also *red lily* **c** : a plant of the genus *Trillium* **2** : a wintergreen (*Pyrola minor*) **3** : an Australian orchid (*Dendrobium speciosum*) with creamy fragrant flowers

wood lock *n* : a piece of wood fitted between a gudgeon and a pintle to keep a rudder from rising

woodlore \ˈ=,=\ *n* : WOODCRAFT 1

woodlot \ˈ=,=\ *n* : a relatively restricted area devoted to the growing of forest trees ⟨a farm ~⟩

wood louse *n* **1** : a terrestrial isopod crustacean (suborder Oniscoidea) that has a flattened elliptical body often capable of being rolled into a ball and seven pairs of walking legs, is commonly dull brown or gray, usu. lives under stones or bark, and may damage the roots of young trees — called also *pill bug, slater, sow bug*; compare SEA LOUSE **2** : any of several small wingless insects of the order Corrodentia that live under bark, in the crevices of walls, and among old books and papers — compare BOOK LOUSE, DEATHWATCH **3** : TERMITE

wood·man \ˈwu̇dmən\ *n, pl* **woodmen** [ME *wodeman*, fr. *wode* wood + *man*] **1 a** : WOODSMAN **b** : one who cuts wood esp. for fuel **2** *usu cap* [fr. Modern *Woodmen* of America, society founded at Lyons, Iowa in 1883 and *Woodmen* of the World, society founded at Omaha, Nebraska in 1890] : a member of either of two fraternal and beneficiary societies

wood meadow grass *n* : a slender European grass of shady places (*Poa nemoralis*) of some agricultural value

wood meal *n* : WOOD FLOUR

wood mint *n* : either of two No. American herbs of the genus *Blephilia* (*B. hirsuta* and *B. ciliata*)

wood mite *n* : any of numerous mites (family Oribatidae) that are free-living usu. in moss or under stones in wooded or shady areas

woodmonger \ˈ=,==\ *n* [ME *wodemonger*, fr. *wode* wood + *monger*] : a dealer in wood

wood·mote \ˈwu̇d,mōt\ *n* -S [¹*wood* + *-mote* (as in *gemote*)] : a former minor English forest court with cognizance of trespasses in a forest

wood moth *n* : a moth with a larva that bores in wood: as **a** : any of various moths of the family Cossidae **b** : any of various dull heavy-bodied moths of the family Zeuzeridae; *esp* : an Australian moth (*Xyleutes boisduvali*) with narrow brownish wings heavily covered with gray scales and having a span of up to 10 inches in the larger female, a large cylindrical abdomen, and a 6 to 7 inch larva that bores in various eucalypts and is considered a delicacy by the aborigines

wood mouse *n* : a mouse inhabiting wooded regions: as **a** : a European mouse (*Apodemus sylvaticus*) **b** : any of several American white-footed mice (*Peromyscus*) **c** : RED-BACKED MOUSE

wood·ness *n* -ES [ME *wodnesse, wodnes*, fr. OE *wōdnes*, fr. *wōd* mad + *-nes* -ness — more at VATIC] **1** *archaic* : INSANITY, MADNESS **2** *archaic* : RAGE, FURY

wood nettle *n* : an American perennial herb (*Laportea canadensis*) found in rich woods and provided with stinging hairs

woodnote \ˈ=,=\ *n* : a sound or call (as of a bird) natural in a wood

wood nymph *n* **1** : a nymph living in woods — called also *dryad* **2 a** : any of several showy moths of the genus *Euthisanotia* with bright-colored larvae some of which (as *E. grata* and *E. unio*) feed on leaves of the grapevine **b** : any of several satyrid butterflies (as a grayling) **c** : any of several So. American hummingbirds of the genus *Thalurania* the males of which are bright blue or green and blue

wood oil *n* **1** : any of various oils derived from wood: as **a** : GURJUN BALSAM **b** : an oil (as pine oil) obtained by the destructive distillation of wood **2** : TUNG OIL

wood oil tree *n* : TUNG TREE

wood-oil-tree family *n* : DIPTEROCARPACEAE

wood opal *n* : wood petrified with opal

wood owl *n* **1** : an owl living in trees; *esp* : an owl of the genus *Strix* (as the European tawny owl and American barred owl) **2** *Brit* : LONG-EARED OWL

wood paper *n* : paper made from wood pulp

wood parenchyma *n* : the vertical and usu. axially arranged parenchyma of the xylem that is believed to function chiefly in carbohydrate storage — compare PHLOEM PARENCHYMA, RAY PARENCHYMA

wood partridge *n* **1** : any of several small partridges of Java, Sumatra, Borneo, and neighboring regions belonging to the genera *Caloperdix, Rollulus*, and *Melanoperdix* **2** : SPRUCE GROUSE

wood pea *n* : FLAT PEA 1

woodpecker \ˈ=,==\ *n* : any of numerous birds of the family Picidae that have zygodactyl feet, stiff spiny tail feathers used in climbing or resting on tree trunks, a usu. extensile tongue, a very hard bill used to drill the bark or wood of trees for insect food or to excavate nesting cavities, and generally parti-colored usu. strongly contrasted black, white, brown, green, yellow, orange, and red plumage in varying proportions — see CALIFORNIA WOODPECKER, DOWNY WOODPECKER, FLICKER, GREAT SPOTTED WOODPECKER, GREEN WOODPECKER, HAIRY WOODPECKER, IMPERIAL WOODPECKER, IVORY-BILLED WOODPECKER, PICULET, PILEATED WOODPECKER, REDHEADED WOODPECKER, SAPSUCKER, THREE-TOED WOODPECKER, WRYNECK

wood pewee *n* : a small tyrant flycatcher (*Contopus virens*) of eastern No. America that is dark olive-gray on the back, grayish olive on the breast and sides, and yellowish white on the belly and that has a very plaintive note resembling the syllables *pee-a-wee; also* : a related bird (*C. sordidulus*) that inhabits western No. America

wood pigeon *n* **1** : RINGDOVE 1; *also* : any of various related Asiatic pigeons **2** : BAND-TAILED PIGEON **3** : a large purple and white pigeon (*Hemiphaga novaeseelandiae*) of New Zealand **4** : STOCK DOVE

woodpile \ˈ=,=\ *n* : a pile of wood (as firewood)

wood pimpernel *n* : a European loosestrife (*Lysimachia nemorum*) with nearly prostrate stems and yellow flowers

wood pink *n* : a caespitose European herb (*Dianthus sylvestris*) that is used as an ornamental and has odorless purple flowers

wood pocket *n* : a virus disease of citrus and esp. lemons characterized by breaks or defects on the bark beneath which the wood is discolored

wood poppy *n* : CELANDINE POPPY

woodprint \ˈ=,=\ *n* : WOODCUT

wood pulp *n* : pulp from softwood or hardwood that is made either mechanically or by a chemical process and that is used in making paper, rayon, and other cellulose derivatives — compare GROUNDWOOD, SODA PULP, SULFATE PROCESS, SULFITE PULP

wood pussy *n* : SKUNK

wood quail *n* **1** : WOOD PARTRIDGE 1 **2** : any of numerous heavy-billed forest-dwelling tropical American birds of the genus *Odontophorus* resembling partridges

wood-queest \ˈ=,=\ *or* **wood-quest** \ˈ=,kwest\ *n, dial Eng* : RINGDOVE

wood rabbit *n* : COTTONTAIL

woodrack car \ˈ=,=-\ *n* : a flat car with attached ends and sometimes sides for hauling wood and usu. pulpwood loaded transversely

wood rail *n* : a forest-dwelling rail; *esp* : a member of the tropical American genus *Aramides*

woodranger \ˈ=,==\ *n* : RANGER 4a

wood rat *n* : any of numerous native voles of *Neotoma* and related genera (family Cricetidae) of the southern U. S. and western No. America having soft fur light gray to ocherous above and white below, well-furred tails, and large ears — compare PACK RAT

wood ray *n* : XYLEM RAY

woodreed \ˈ=,=\ *n* **1** : any of several tall perennial grasses (genus *Cinna*) chiefly of moist woodlands — compare INDIAN REED **2** : BUSHGRASS

woodreeve \ˈ=,=\ *n, Brit* : an overseer of a forest

wood robin *n* **1** : any of several muscicapine New Zealand birds of the genus *Petroica* that are grayish black and white or pure white and are good songsters **2** : WOOD THRUSH 1

wood rose *n* **1 a** : the corrugated often flowerlike woody scar left upon the host when a mistletoe is wrenched from its support — called also *wood flower* **b** : a shrub rose (*Rosa gymnocarpa*) of the California coastal area having long straight prickles, red flowers, and pear-shaped or globose fruit with deciduous calyx lobes **2** : a light grayish brown to reddish brown that is darker and slightly less strong than sandstone — called also *sorghum brown*

wood rosin *n* : rosin obtained from the stumps or other dead wood of pine trees (as longleaf pine) by solvent extraction along with the volatile turpentine or after removal of the turpentine by steam distillation

wood·ruff \ˈwu̇(,)drəf\ *n* -S [ME *woderofe, woderove*, fr. OE *wuduroƒe*, fr. *wudu* wood + *-rofe* (perh. akin to ON *rōfa* hard part of a tail, MLG *röve* turnip) — more at WOOD, RAPE (herb)] : a plant of the genus *Asperula*: as **a** : SWEET WOODRUFF **b** : DYER'S WOODRUFF

woodruff key *n, usu cap W* [prob. fr. the name *Woodruff*] : a shaft key made in the form of a segment of a disk and used with shafts not more than 2½ inches in diameter

wood rush *n* : a plant of the genus *Luzula* (as *L. campestris*) growing chiefly in woodlands and having the leaf sheaths open and the capsule few-seeded

¹woods *pl of* WOOD, *pres 3d sing of* WOOD

²woods *var of* WOOD

wood sage *n* **1** : a European germander (*Teucrium scorodonia*) with one-sided racemes of yellow flowers that is naturalized in No. America **2** : AMERICAN GERMANDER

wood's alloy *or* **wood's metal** *n, usu cap W* [after B. *Wood*, 20th cent. Am. metallurgist] : a fusible alloy containing about 50 percent bismuth with lead, tin, and cadmium that melts at about 160° F

wood sandpiper *n* : an Old World shorebird (*Tringa glareola*) related to the green sandpiper and the American solitary sandpiper

woods colt *n* **1** : a horse that is the offspring of a chance mating **2** : BASTARD

wood screw *n* : a pointed metal screw formed with a sharp thread of comparatively coarse pitch for insertion in wood

woodsere \ˈ=,=\ *n* -S [¹*wood* + *sere*, adj.] : CUCKOO SPIT 1

wood shamrock *n* : a wood sorrel (*Oxalis montana*)

¹woodshed \ˈ=,=\ *n* : a shed for storing wood and esp. firewood

²woodshed \"\ *vi* **woodshedded; woodshedded; woodshedding; woodsheds** [fr. E slang *woodshed*, n., an arduous rehearsal esp. for a radio program, fr. E ¹*woodshed*; fr. woodsheds being formerly used in administering sound parental thrashings] : to practice on a musical instrument

wood sheldrake *n* : HOODED MERGANSER

woodshop \ˈ=,=\ *n* : a shop in which woodworking is carried on

wood shot *n* **1** : a golf shot played with a wood **2** : a shot in a racket game in which the ball or shuttlecock is stroked with any of the wooden parts of the racket rather than the strings

wood shrike *n* : either of two tropical Asiatic birds (genus *Tephrodornis*) related to the minivets but superficially resembling shrikes in the shape of the bill and their gray, black, and white plumage

wood·sia \ˈwu̇dzēə\ *n, cap* [NL, fr. Joseph *Woods* †1864 Eng. botanist + NL *-ia*] : a genus of small or medium-sized rock-inhabiting ferns (family Polypodiaceae) of temperate or cold regions having pinnate or bipinnate fronds, round sori, and wholly inferior roundish or stellate indusia

woodside \ˈ=,=\ *n* [ME *wood side, wode side*] : the margin of or country bordering on a wood

woodskin \"\ *n* [*wood* + *skin*] : bark from which canoes are made; *also* : a canoe made of bark ⟨~s of the Indians had passed up and down and left no trace —William Beebe⟩

wood slave *n* : a small gecko (*Sphaerodactylus argus* or a related species) of Jamaica

wood's light \ˈwu̇dz-\ *n, usu cap W* [after Robert W. *Wood*

†1955 Am. physicist] **:** ultraviolet obtained from a suitable source (as an arc) by means of a special filter and used to reveal the presence of fluorescent minerals, to detect counterfeit currency and forgeries of documents or paintings, and in the diagnosis of various forms of tinea

woods·man \'wu̇dzmən\ *n, pl* **woodsmen 1 :** one who lives in or frequents a forest **:** an expert in the arts and skills of living or travelling in the woods **2 :** one who works in the woods; *specif* **:** a foreman in charge of the felling of trees and removal of logs

woodsmoke \'=,=\ *n* **:** smoke produced by burning wood

wood snail *n* **:** a European edible snail (*Helix nemoralis*)

wood snipe *n* **:** WOODCOCK 1a(2)

wood sorrel *n* **1 a :** a plant of the genus *Oxalis*; *esp* **:** a white-flowered to reddish flowered stemless herb (*O. montana*) with trifoliate leaves that is sometimes considered to be the original shamrock **b :** any of several yellow-flowered plants of the related genus *Xanthoxalis* **2 :** SHEEP SORREL 1 **3 :** a West Indian begonia (*Begonia acutifolia*)

wood-sorrel family *n* **:** OXALIDACEAE

woods phlox *n* **:** SOAPWORT 1

wood spirit *n* **:** METHANOL; *esp* **:** crude methanol obtained as a distillate from wood — sometimes used in pl.

wood·spite \'=,spīt\ *n* -S [alter. of earlier *wood-speight*, *woodspecht*, fr. ¹*wood* + *speight*, *specht* green woodpecker, fr. ME *specht*, prob. fr. MD, woodpecker; akin to OHG *speh*, *speht* woodpecker — more at PIE] **:** GREEN WOODPECKER

wood spurge *n* **1 :** a European spurge (*Euphorbia amygdaloides*) with greenish yellow terminal flower clusters **2 :** a No. American spurge (*Euphorbia commutata*) resembling the European wood spurge

woods run *n* **:** the average run of logs of all sizes and grades as they come from the forest

wood star *n* **:** any of several small chiefly So. American hummingbirds (as of the genera *Chaetocercus* and *Acestrura*)

woodstone \'=,=\ *n* **:** petrified wood

wood stork *n* **:** WOOD IBIS; *esp* **:** an Old World wood ibis

wood strawberry *n* **:** any of several wild strawberries; *esp* **:** a European herb (*Fragaria vesca*)

wood sugar *n* **1 :** xylose obtained from plant sources **2 :** a mixture of pentose and hexose sugars obtained by the hydrolysis of pentosans and cellulose of wood

wood swallow *n* **:** any of several Australasian and Asiatic passerine birds (as of the genus *Artamus*) related to the shrikes but resembling swallows — called also *swallow shrike*

¹**woodsy** \'wu̇dzē, -zi\ *adj* -ER/-EST [*woods* + *-y*, adj. suffix] **:** of, relating to, characteristic of, suggestive of, or of the nature of woods ⟨look for trillium and violets in ~, shady spots —*Girl Scout Handbk.*⟩ ⟨pine walled and smelling fresh and ~ —Adria Langley⟩

²**woodsy** \"\ *n* -ES [*woods* + *-y*, n. suffix] **:** BACKWOODSMAN 1

wood tar *n* **:** tar obtained by the destructive distillation of wood either as a deposit from pyroligneous acid or as a residue from the distillation of the acid or of wood turpentine and used in the crude state as fuel or for preserving rope and wood and for caulking or fractionated to yield creosote, oils, and pitch — compare PINE TAR

wood-tar creosote *n* **:** CREOSOTE 1

wood-tar pitch *n* **:** PITCH 1b

wood thrush *n* **1 :** a large thrush (*Hylocichla mustelina*) of eastern No. America that is rusty brown on the head and back becoming olivaceous on the rump and tail, has the under parts white marked with large tear-shaped spots, frequents woods and thickets, and is noted for its loud clear song **2 :** MISTLE THRUSH **3 :** SONG THRUSH 1

wood tick *n* **:** any of several ixodid ticks whose young cling to bushes but fasten on the body of an animal touching them often producing troublesome sores; *esp* **:** AMERICAN DOG TICK

wood tin *n* **:** cassiterite occurring in fibrous form

wood tortoise *or* **wood terrapin** *or* **wood turtle** *n* **:** a common No. American tortoise (*Clemmys insculpta*) the shell of which is marked with strong grooves and ridges like sculptured figures

woodturner \'=,==\ *n* **:** one whose occupation is wood turning

wood turning *n* **:** the art or process of fashioning wooden pieces or blocks into various forms and shapes by means of a lathe

wood turpentine *n* **:** turpentine oil obtained from pine and other resinous woods by steam distillation, destructive distillation, or extraction with solvents; *esp* **:** TURPENTINE 2b

wood-vamp \'=,=\ *n* **:** DECUMARY

wood vetch *also* **wood vetchling** *n* **1 :** a European vetch (*Vicia sylvatica*) sometimes planted for forage **2 :** a slender perennial vetch (*Vicia caroliniana*) growing chiefly in rich open woodland in eastern and central No. America

wood vinegar *n* **1 :** PYROLIGNEOUS ACID **2 :** imitation vinegar consisting essentially of dilute acetic acid colored with caramel

wood violet *n* **1 a :** HEDGE VIOLET **b :** BIRD'S-FOOT VIOLET **2 :** a deep purple that is bluer and stronger than hyacinth violet, bluer and deeper than petunia violet, and bluer, lighter, and stronger than imperial purple (sense 2)

wood·wall *or* **wood·wale** \'wu̇,d(w)ȯl, -,dwəl, -,dᵊl\ *n* -S [ME *wodewale* golden oriole, fr. or akin to MD *wedewale*; akin to MHG *witewal* golden oriole — more at WITWALL] *Brit* **:** GREEN WOODPECKER

wood want *n* **:** a thinness or wane on the edge of a barrel stave

wood warbler *n* **1 :** an American warbler esp. of the genus *Dendroica* — compare BAY-BREASTED WARBLER, BLACK-POLL WARBLER, BLACK-THROATED GREEN WARBLER, CAPE MAY WARBLER, CHESTNUT-SIDED WARBLER, MYRTLE WARBLER, PINE WARBLER, PRAIRIE WARBLER, YELLOW WARBLER **2 :** a European warbler (*Phylloscopus sibilatrix*)

¹**wood·ward** \'wu̇,dwȯrd\ *n* -S [ME *wodeward*, fr. OE *wuduweard*, fr. *wudu* wood + *weard* ward] **:** an English forest officer charged with guarding a wood

²**wood·ward** \-dwə(r)d\ *adv* [¹*wood* + *-ward*] **:** toward a wood

wood·war·dia \wu̇'dwȯrdēə\ *n, cap* [NL, fr. Thomas J. *Woodward* †1820 Eng. botanist + NL *-ia*] **:** a genus of chain ferns (family Polypodiaceae) having linear lanceolate pinnae and sori in rows

wood·ward·ite \'wu̇dwə(r),dīt\ *n* [Samuel P. *Woodward* †1865 Eng. naturalist + E *-ite*] **:** a mineral $Cu_4Al_2(SO_4)(OH)_{12}.2\text{-}4H_2O$ consisting of a hydrous basic sulfate of copper and aluminum found in greenish blue to turquoise-blue botryoidal concretions orig. in Cornwall

woodware \'=,=\ *n* **:** WOODENWARE

wood wasp *n* **1 :** HORNTAIL **2 :** a European wasp (*Vespa sylvestris*) that builds its nest in trees **3 :** any of various solitary wasps that excavate galleries in decaying wood

wood·wax·en \'wu̇,dwaksən\ *also* **woodwax** \'=,=\ *n, pl* **woodwaxens** *also* **woodwaxes** [ME *wodewexen*, alter. of OE *wuduweaxe*, fr. *wudu* wood + *-weaxe* (prob. fr. *weaxan* to grow) — more at WOOD, WAX] **:** a yellow-flowered Eurasian shrub (*Genista tinctoria*) common as a weed in England, adventive in No. America, and sometimes cultivated for ornament — called also *dyer's-broom, dyeweed, greenweed, greenwood, whin, woadwaxen*

wood widgeon *n* **:** WOOD DUCK 1

¹**wood·wind** \'wu̇,dwind\ *or* **woodwind instrument** *n* **1 :** one of a group of orchestral or band wind instruments comprised of flutes, clarinets, oboes, bassoons, and sometimes saxophones **2 woodwinds** *pl* **:** the woodwind section of a band or orchestra

²**woodwind** \"\ *adj* **:** of, relating to, or resembling a woodwind instrument, a performer on a woodwind instrument, or the music performed on woodwinds ⟨~ quintet⟩

wood-wool \'=,=\ *n* **:** fine wood shavings or prepared wood fibers used for surgical dressings, as a substitute for hair in plaster, and as a packing and insulating material

woodwork \'=,=\ *n* **1 :** work made of wood ⟨war called for an immense production of all kinds of ~ — furniture for barracks and huts, ammunition cases, vehicles, rifle-stocks —Gordon Russell⟩; *esp* **:** interior fittings (as moldings or stairways) of wood ⟨richly carved ~ with fruits and garlands frames the fireplace —H.S.Morrison⟩ — compare MILLWORK **2 :** work (as carpentry or joinery) done in or with wood

woodworker \'=,==\ *n* **1 a :** a person who works in wood (as a carpenter, joiner, or cabinetmaker) **b :** MILLMAN 2 **c :** a worker who makes wooden tools, forms, templates, dies, and other items used in the construction of aircraft parts **2 :** a woodworking machine for various kinds of work consisting of a planer and circular saw and having attachments for dadoing, routing, boring, mortising, and other operations

¹**woodworking** \'=,==\ *adj* **:** of, relating to, engaged in, or used for working or shaping things of wood

²**woodworking** \"\ *n* **:** the act, process, or occupation of working with wood **:** CARPENTRY, JOINERY, TURNERY

woodworm \'=,=\ *n* **:** a worm that is the larva of a wood borer

wood wren *n* **1 :** WOOD WARBLER **2 :** WILLOW WARBLER

woodwright \'=,=\ *n* **:** WOODWORKER

¹**woody** \'wu̇dē, -di\ *adj* -ER/-EST [ME *woddy*, *wody*, fr. *wode* wood + *-y*] **1 a :** abounding or overgrown with woods ⟨a ~ land⟩ **b** *obs* **:** of or relating to woods **:** SYLVAN **2 a :** of or containing wood or wood fibers **:** consisting mainly of hard lignified tissues ⟨a perennial herb with a ~ crown⟩ **b :** having woody parts ⟨a ~ perennial⟩ **3 :** characteristic of or resembling wood ⟨a ~ taste⟩

²**woody** \'wədi, 'wüdi\ *n* -ES *Scot* **:** WITHY 2

woodyard \'=,=\ *n* **:** a yard for storing or sawing wood

woody aster *n* **:** a woody herb (*Aster xylorrhiza*) of the western U.S. that is very poisonous to sheep

woody fiber *n* **1 :** XYLEM **2 :** a wood fiber

woody nightshade *n* **:** BITTERSWEET 2a

woody pear *n* **:** NATIVE PEAR

woody tongue *n* **:** WOODEN TONGUE

wooed *past of* WOO

woo·er \'wüə(r), 'wu̇(ə)r, 'wu̇ə\ *n* -S [ME *wowere*, fr. OE *wōgere*, fr. *wōgian* to woo + *-ere* -er — more at WOO] **:** one that woos **:** SUITOR, LOVER

¹**woof** \'wu̇f, 'wüf\ *n* -S [alter. (influenced by *weave* and *warp*) of earlier *ofe*, fr. ME *oof*, fr. OE *ōwef*, fr. *ō-* (fr. *on*) + *wefan* to weave — more at WEAVE] **1 a :** a filling thread or yarn in weaving **:** WEFT **b :** thread for or as if for the woof **c :** woven fabric; *also* **:** the texture of such a fabric **2 :** a basic or essential element or material ⟨the ~ of his chorus . . . is an infectious Negro song —Lazare Saminsky⟩ ⟨the warp is twelve fugues and the ~ twelve interludes —*Saturday Rev.*⟩

²**woof** \"\ *vt* -ED/-ING/-S **:** to weave in the manner of a woof crossing a warp

³**woof** \'wu̇f\ *n* -S [imit.] **1 :** a low gruff sound typically produced by a dog as a suppressed bark **2 :** a low note emitted by sound reproducing equipment — contrasted with *tweet*

⁴**woof** \"\ *vi* -ED/-ING/-S **:** to make the sound of a woof ⟨the bull . . . ~*ed* through wide nostrils —Ernest Hemingway⟩

woof·er \'wu̇fə(r)\ *n* -S **:** a loudspeaker that is usu. larger than a tweeter, is responsive only to the lower acoustic frequencies, and is used for reproducing sounds of low pitch

wooing *pres part of* WOO

woo·ing·ly *adv* **:** ATTRACTIVELY, ALLURINGLY

¹**wool** \'wu̇l\ *n* -S *often attrib* [ME *wolle*, *wulle*, fr. OE *wull*; akin to OHG *wolla* wool, ON *ull*, Goth *wulla* wool, L *vellus* fleece, *lana* wool, *lanugo* down, Gk *lēnos* wool, Skt *ūrṇā*] **1 :** the soft wavy or curly hypertrophied undercoat of various hairy mammals made up of fibers consisting of linear aggregates of keratin molecules within a matrix that are distinguished from typical hairs by their covering of minute projecting scales to which the felting property of the fiber is due, saturated in its natural state with fatty and other materials (as suint, yolk), and esp. developed by selective breeding in the domesticated sheep where it more or less completely replaces the primitive double coat — see BLOOD 7, FLEECE 1a, 1b, SPINNING COUNT **2 a** (1) **:** a textile fiber produced from raw wool that is characterized by absorbency, insulation, resiliency, a tendency to shrink in hot water, and ability to take and hold dyes well and that may be spun into woolen or worsted yarn or used for felt, flock, or stuffing (2) **:** textile fiber from the fleece of the sheep or lamb or from the hair of the Angora or Kashmir goat, camel, alpaca, llama, or vicuna used for the first time in the making of a finished product — used as a label on products; called also *virgin wool*; compare REPROCESSED, REUSED **b :** a yarn spun from such wool for weaving, knitting, or crocheting **c :** a product of wool; *esp* **:** a woven fabric or garment of such fabric **3 :** something resembling or suggesting wool in texture or appearance **:** a flocculent substance or mass: as **a :** a dense felted pubescence on the surface of plants **:** TOMENTUM **b :** a material formed (as by shredding or melting and blowing) into a filamentous mass — usu. used in combination; see LEAD WOOL, MINERAL WOOL, STEEL WOOL **c :** short thick often crisp curly hair on a human head **d :** the thick furry or hairy coat of some insects (as hairy caterpillars) **e :** the flocculent waxy secretion of some scales **4 :** something that conceals the truth or impedes understanding ⟨the cozy generalizations . . . were part of the same ~ of self-deception —Norman Cousins⟩ — usu. used in the phrase *pull the wool over one's eyes* ⟨taken for several hundred dollars by a sharper who pulled the ~ over his eyes⟩ **5 :** WOOL SPONGE — **all wool and a yard wide :** marked by superior quality, genuineness, or ingenuousness — **in one's wool :** persistently annoying **:** in one's hair — **in the wool** *Austral, of a sheep* **:** ready for shearing

²**wool** \"\ *vt* -ED/-ING/-S **1 :** to pull or tousle the hair of **2 :** to treat roughly **:** rough up **:** tussle with **:** BEAT

woolball \'=,=\ *n* **:** a hair ball of a sheep

wool-blind \'=¦=\ *adj, of a sheep* **:** having wool that is grown over the eyes and interferes with vision

wool blindness *n* **:** impaired vision in woolly-faced sheep due to wool covering the eyes

wool card *n* **:** a machine with bent wire teeth for carding wool — **wool carder** *n* — **wool carding** *n*

wool classer *n, Austral* **:** WOOL GRADER

wool classing *n, Austral* **:** WOOL GRADING

wool clip *n* **:** the annual crop of wool ⟨the Australian *wool clip*⟩

wool comb *n* **:** a machine for laying wool fibers in parallel relationship and dropping out fibers shorter than a predetermined length

wool comber *n* **:** one that combs wool

woold \'wüld\ *vt* -ED/-ING/-S [obs. D *woelde*, past part. (taken as verb) of *woelen* to woold, fr. MD, to toss, twist, woold; akin to OHG *wuolen* to stir up, rumple — more at WEEL] **:** to wind or wrap a rope or chain round (as a mast or yard sprung or made of two or more pieces) at a fish or scarf for strengthening

woold·er \-də(r)\ *n* -S [alter. (influenced by *woold*) of earlier *woller*, prob. fr. obs. D *woelen* to woold + E *-er*] **1 :** a stick used (as in woolding) to tighten a rope at a knot **2** *or* **woolder stick :** one of the handles of the ropemaking top formed by a wooden pin passing through it

woolding *n* -S [alter. (influenced by *woold*) of earlier *wooling*, fr. ME *wolinge*, *woling*, prob. fr. MD, action of binding, woolding, fr. *woelen*, *wolen* to twist, woold] **:** a rope or chain used in woolding

wool-dyed \'=¦=\ *adj* **:** DYED-IN-THE-WOOL

wool eating *n* **:** a gnawing of wool esp. where stained with urine or feces that occurs esp. in stabled sheep and is prob. a form of pica

wooled \¦wu̇ld\ *adj* **1 :** having wool of a specified quality — often used in combination ⟨a long-*wooled* sheep⟩ **2 :** bearing wool **:** UNSHORN ⟨the price advantage of ~ lambs⟩

¹**wool·en** *or* **wool·len** \'wu̇lən\ *adj* [ME *wollen*, fr. OE *wullen*, fr. *wull* wool + *-en*] **1 :** made of wool ⟨~ goods⟩; *specif* **:** of, being, or made from a soft fuzzy loosely twisted yarn that is spun from short wool fibers separated by carding and is used esp. for knitting and for napped and bulky fabrics — compare WORSTED **2** *obs* **:** wearing coarse woolen due to poverty or penance **3 :** of or concerned with the manufacture, commercial handling, or sale of woolen products ⟨a ~ mill⟩ ⟨~ workers⟩

²**woolen** *or* **woollen** \"\ *n* -S [ME *wollen*, fr. *wollen*, adj.] **1 :** a fabric made of wool; *specif* **:** any of various loosely woven fabrics made of woolen yarns usu. having a fuzzy or napped face and used esp. for clothing and blankets ⟨tweed is a popular ~⟩ **2 :** garments of woolen fabric — usu. used in pl. **3 :** woolen yarn

wool·er \-lə(r)\ *n* -S [¹*wool* + *-er*] **:** an animal (as an Angora rabbit) bred or kept for its wool

woo·lert \'wülə(r)t\ *n* -S [prob. alter. of E dial. *owlard* barn owl, fr. E *owl* + *-ard*] *dial Eng* **:** BARN OWL

wool extract *n* **:** EXTRACT WOOL

wool fast blue *n, often cap W&F&B* **:** any of several acid dyes — see DYE table I (under *Acid Blue 59* and *102*)

wool fat *n* **:** wool grease esp. after refining **:** LANOLIN

woolfell \'=,=\ *n* [ME *wolle felle*, fr. *wolle* wool + *felle*, *fel* fell] *Brit* **:** a skin from which the wool has not been sheared or pulled

woolf engine \'wu̇lf-\ *n, usu cap W* [after Arthur *Woolf* †1837 Eng. mining engineer] **1 :** the first practical compound engine **2 :** a compound engine having no receiver

wool-gather \'=,==\ *vi* [back-formation fr. *woolgathering*] **:** to indulge in woolgathering — **woolgatherer** \'=,===\ *n*

woolgathering \'=,=(=)=\ *n* **1 :** the act of gathering wool shed from the sheep in tufts and found caught on bushes **2 :** the act of indulging in vagrant fancies **:** foolish or purposeless thinking or imagining

wool grade *n* **:** one of the recognized standard categories into which wool is divided, based chiefly on fineness of fiber — compare BLOOD 7, SPINNING COUNT

wool grader *n* **:** one that grades or classes fleeces

wool grading *n* **:** the separation of whole fleeces according to quality, condition, soundness, and color into lots similar in character and value

wool grass *n* **1 :** an American sedge (*Scirpus cyperinus*) with numerous clustered woolly spikelets **2 :** RAVENNA GRASS

wool grease *n* **:** a fatty slightly sticky water-insoluble wax that coats the surface of the fibers of sheep's wool, consists chiefly of esters of higher alcohols (as cholesterol and lanosterol) with various fatty acids, is extracted with organic solvents or by scouring with soap or detergents, and is used esp. in the dressing of leather and furs, in lubricating greases, slushing compounds, and printing inks, and as a source of lanolin — called also *degras, wool fat, wool wax*

wool green S *n, usu cap W&G* **:** an acid dye — see DYE table I (under *Acid Green 50*)

woolgrower \'=,==\ *n, chiefly Brit* **:** one that raises sheep for the production of wool

wool-hat \'=,=\ *n* **1 :** a broad-brimmed hat of coarse wool felt **2** *also* **woolhatter** \'=,==\ [*woolhatter* fr. *wool-hat* + *-er*] **:** a small farmer in the South (as in Georgia)

woolhead \'=,=\ *n* **:** BUFFLEHEAD

woolier *comparative of* WOOLY

woolies *pl of* WOOLY

wooliest *superlative of* WOOLY

wooling *pres part of* WOOL

woolled \¦wu̇ld\ *chiefly Brit var of* WOOLED

woollen *var of* WOOLEN

wool·len·ize \'wu̇lə,nīz\ *vt* -ED/-ING/-S **:** to give (vegetable fiber) the appearance of wool by chemical treatment

woollike \'=,=\ *adj* **:** resembling wool in texture or appearance

wool·li·ness \'wu̇lēnəs, -lin-\ *n* -ES **:** the quality or state of being woolly

¹**wool·ly** *also* **wooly** \'wu̇lē, -li\ *adj* **woollier** *also* **woolier; woolliest** *also* **wooliest** [¹*wool* + *-y*, adj. suffix] **1 a :** of, relating to, or bearing wool ⟨a besmocked yokel . . . with his ~ flock —*N. Y. Herald Tribune Bk. Rev.*⟩ **:** having the character of wool ⟨although these animals are true sheep, their coat is hairy and not ~ —*Natural History*⟩ **b :** characteristic of wool ⟨the ~ smell of wet mittens —Merle Crowell⟩ **2 :** resembling wool or that of wool ⟨a ~ fog⟩ ⟨a ~ beard⟩ **3 a :** thickly covered with long hair or fuzz ⟨~ cloth coats⟩ ⟨a child's ~ bunny⟩; *specif* **:** LANATE **b** *of lumber* **:** that dresses with a stringy or fuzzy surface ⟨alder is inclined to be ~ and should be sanded —Andrew Wood & Thomas Linn⟩ **4 :** wanting in clearness, definiteness, or sharpness of outline **:** CONFUSED, BLURRY ⟨substitute clear and distinct ideas for vague and ~ ones —F.R.Cowell⟩ ⟨~ thinking⟩ ⟨the guides confessed that they were somewhat ~ on dates —*Time*⟩ **:** INDISTINCT ⟨the ~ sound of a worn record⟩ ⟨~ lithographs from old plates⟩ **5 :** marked by a sometimes violent lack of order or restraint; *typically* **:** having the rough virility of the West in frontier times

²**wool·ly** *also* **wool·ie** *or* **wooly** \'wu̇lē, -li\ *n, pl* **woollies** *or* **woolies** [¹*wool* + *-y* or *-ie*, n. suffix] **1 :** a garment made from wool: as **a** *chiefly Brit* **:** a woolen sweater **b :** underclothing of knitted wool — usu. used in pl. **2** *West & Austral* **:** SHEEP

³**wool·ly** *or* **wooly** \'wu̇lē, -li\ *n, pl* **woollies** *or* **woolies** [by shortening & alter.] **:** WILLIWAW

woolly alder aphid *n* **:** a plant louse (*Prociphilus tessellatus*) that feeds on the alder and secretes a white woolly substance

woolly ant *n* **:** VELVET ANT

woolly aphid *n* **:** any of several plant lice of the genus *Eriosoma* that are covered with a dense coat of white filaments somewhat resembling fine wool or cotton; *esp* **:** WOOLLY APPLE APHID — called also *woolly plant louse*

woolly apple aphid *n* **:** a cosmopolitan dull reddish woolly aphid (*Eriosoma lanigerum*) that is primarily a bark feeder attacking both aerial parts and roots of apple and other trees — called also *American blight*

woolly bear *also* **woolly bear caterpillar** *n* **:** any of various rather large very hairy caterpillars that are usu. larvae of moths of the family Arctiidae, feed on plants and include some destructive pests (as the salt-marsh caterpillar) — see YELLOW WOOLLY BEAR

woolly beard grass *n* [so called fr. the silky hairs on the spikes] **:** a grass of the genus *Erianthus*

woolly beech aphid *n* **:** a widely distributed plant louse (*Phyllaphis fagi*) that feeds on various beeches

woolly buckeye *n* **:** a small tree or shrub (*Aesculus discolor*) of the southern U. S. often cultivated for its red and yellow flowers and its tomentose leaves

woolly buckthorn *n* **:** FALSE BUCKTHORN

woolly butt *n* **1 :** any of several eucalypts having woolly trunks: as **a :** an Australian eucalypt (*Eucalyptus longifolia*) having hard wood used for many purposes and bark that is fibrous on old trees **b :** WOOLLY GUM **2 :** BASTARD MAHOGANY 1a(1)

woolly croton *n* **:** HOGWORT

woolly finger *n* **:** any of several grasses of the genus *Digitaria*; *esp* **:** a southern African grass (*D. pentzii*) introduced into the U. S. (as for pasture)

woolly fleece *n* **:** CIRROCUMULUS

woolly foot *or* **woolly foot grama** *n* [so called fr. its woolly base] **:** a valuable grazing grass (*Bouteloua eriopoda*) found in arid regions of the U. S. and adjacent Mexico

woolly gum *n* **:** a blackbutt (*Eucalyptus pilularis*)

woolly head *n, South* **:** an impenetrable thicket of rhododendron or mountain laurel

woolly-headed \'=(=)¦=\ *adj* **1 :** having hair resembling wool **2 :** marked by vague or confused perception or thinking

woolly hedge nettle *n* **:** LAMB'S EARS

woolly knot *n* **:** a crown-gall tumor from which many fine roots are formed — compare HAIRY ROOT

woolly lemur *or* **woolly avahi** *n* **:** a small long-tailed woolly-haired lemur (*Lichanotus laniger* or *Avahi laniger*) of Madagascar closely related to the larger indri

woolly lip fern *n* **:** a small No. American fern (*Cheilanthes lanosa*) having stipes and lower frond surfaces densely woolly

woolly locoweed *also* **woolly loco** *n* **:** a perennial herb (*Astragalus mollissimus*) of the western U. S. having compound leaves and dense spikes of violet-purple flowers and foliage that is poisonous to cattle

woolly mammoth *n* **:** a heavy-coated mammoth (*Mammuthus primigenius*) common in the colder portions of the northern hemisphere and known not only from fossil remains but also from the drawings of palaeolithic man and from entire cadavers unearthed from frozen Siberian tundras — called also *northern mammoth*

woolly manzanita *n* **:** a tomentose California shrub (*Arctostaphylos tomentosus*) that is common in the chaparral and has white or pink flowers and brownish red fruit

woolly monkey *n* **1 :** any of several large prehensile-tailed monkeys (genus *Lagothrix*) of the Amazon basin **2 :** WOOLLY SPIDER MONKEY

woolly opossum *n* **:** an opossum of the genus *Philander* having no well-developed pouch and carrying the young on the mother's back

woolly painted cup *n* **:** a white woolly somewhat shrubby California herb (*Castilleja foliolosa*) with greenish yellow flowers

woolly pink *n* **:** CORN COCKLE

woolly plant louse *n* **:** WOOLLY APHID

wool·ly-pod \'==,=\ *n* **:** any of several plants of the genus *Astragalus* that have pubescent seed pods
woollypod vetch \'==,=-\ *n* **:** a European vetch (*Vicia dasycarpa*) naturalized in the U. S. and used for forage
woolly py·rol \-'pī,rōl, -rōl\ *n* [*pyrol* fr. NL *Pyrola*] **:** URD
woolly rhinoceros *n* **:** an extinct 2-horned rhinoceros (*Opsiceros antiquitatis* or *Rhinoceros antiquitatis*) inhabiting the arctic regions during the Pleistocene, having a dense coat of woolly hair, and being found frozen in the ice of Siberia with the flesh and hair well preserved
woolly root *n* **:** HAIRY ROOT
woolly spider monkey *n* **:** any of several Brazilian spider monkeys (genus *Brachyteles*) characterized by stocky build, rounded head, and finely woolly fur
woolly thistle *n* **1 :** COTTON THISTLE **2 :** a thistle (*Cirsium flodmanii*) of western No. America with white woolly leaves
woolly whitefly *n* **:** a whitefly (*Aleurothrixus floccosus*) widespread in the warmer countries of the New World and injurious to citrus fruits, guavas and other trees
woolly wolf *n* **:** CHANCO
woolly worm *n* **1 :** a sawfly larva that covers itself with a white woolly secretion **2 :** WOOLLY BEAR 1
wool maggot *n* **:** the larva of a blowfly (as *Phormia regina*) that causes strike in sheep
wool·man \'wu̇lmən\ *n, pl* **woolmen** [ME *wolleman*, fr. *wolle* wool + *man*] **:** a dealer in wool
wool moth *n* **:** CLOTHES MOTH
wool·ner's tubercle \'wu̇lnə(r)z-\ *or* **woolner's point** *or* **woolner's tip** *n, usu cap W* [after Thomas *Woolner* †1892 Eng. sculptor and poet] **:** DARWIN'S TUBERCLE
wool oil *n* **1 :** any oil used for oiling wool before spinning **2 a :** an oily substance in wool fiber that makes the fiber soft and pliable **b :** an oil obtained (as by distillation with steam) from wool grease
woolpack \'=,=\ *n* [ME *wolpak, wullepak*, fr. *wolle, wulle* wool + *pak* pack] **1 a :** a wrapper of canvas or other strong fabric into which fleeces are packed for shipment **b :** the complete package of wool and wrapper **2 :** something resembling or suggesting a woolpack; *esp* **:** a rounded cumulus cloud springing from a horizontal base
woolrock \'=,=\ *n* **:** a finely fibrous woollike rock material manufactured from limestone and other rocks
wool rot *n* **:** RAIN ROT
wools *pl of* WOOL, *pres 3d sing of* WOOL
woolsack \'=,=\ *n* [ME *wollesak*, fr. *wolle* wool + *sak* sack] **1 :** a sack for wool **2** [so called fr. its being made of a large square bag of wool without back or arms and covered with cloth] **a :** a rectangular divan that is the official seat of the Lord Chancellor in the House of Lords **b :** the office of Lord Chancellor **3 :** an official seat in the House of Lords for one of the judges of the High Court of Justice **4 :** the office of a judge
wool scour *n, Austral* **:** a place for scouring wool
wool scourer *n* **:** an operator of a machine for scouring raw wool
wool·sey \'wu̇lzē, -zi\ *n* -S [by shortening] **:** LINSEY-WOOLSEY
woolshed \'=,=\ *n* **:** a building or range of buildings (as on an Australian sheep station) in which sheep are sheared and wool is prepared for market
woolskin \'=,=\ *n* [ME *wolle skin*] **:** a sheepskin having the wool still on it
woolsorter \'=,==\ *n* **:** one that sorts wool according to grade specifications
woolsorter's disease *n* **:** pulmonary anthrax that is an occupational hazard due to inhalation of bacterial spores (*Bacillus anthracis*) from contaminated wool or other hair
woolsower \'=,==\ *n* **:** a multicellular gall on the white oak made by a gallfly (*Andricus seminator*) in which each cell is covered by a coating of woolly filaments
wool sponge *n* **:** a soft-fibered durable commercial sponge; *esp* **:** a sponge (*Hippiospongia lachne*) occurring in the Gulf of Mexico, the Caribbean sea, and off the southeastern coast of Florida
wool stapler *n* **:** one that deals in wool; *esp* **:** one that buys raw wool and sorts it before selling to a manufacturer
wool table *n* **:** a strong table with various devices for collecting and bundling loose wool for marketing
wool·ton pie \'wu̇ltən-\ *n, usu cap W* [after Frederick James Marquis, 1st Baron *Woolton* †1964 Eng. businessman] **:** a vegetable pie
wool top *n* [ME *wolletoppe*, fr. *wolle* wool + *toppe* top] **:** TOP 2c(1)
wool tree *n* **:** a tree of the genus *Ceiba; esp* **:** CEIBA 2a
wool twine *n* **:** a twine (as of paper, jute) for bundling wool
wool·ward \'wu̇lwə(r)d\ *adv* [ME *wolleward, wellewerd*, prob. fr. (assumed) OE *wullwerd*, fr. OE *wull* wool + *-werd* wearing, fr. stem of *werian* to wear — more at WOOL, WEAR] *archaic* **:** with woolen next to the skin (as in penance)
wool waste *n* **:** WASTE 4a(1)
wool wax *n* **:** WOOL GREASE
woolweed \'=,=\ *n* **:** PIPEWORT
woolwheel \'=,=\ *n* **:** a hand and foot operated spinning wheel for spinning wool
woolwork \'=,=\ *n* **:** needlework (as embroidery on canvas or knitting) made with wool
wooly *var of* WOOLLY
woomera *or* **woomerah** *var of* WOMMERA
woon *also* **wun** \'wün\ *n* -S [Burmese *wun*] **:** a governor or other administrative officer in Burma
woops *like* OOPS\ *interj* [by alter.] **:** OOPS
woos *pres 3d sing of* WOO, *pl of* WOO
woosh *var of* WHOOSH
wootz \'wüts\ *or* **wootz steel** *n* -ES [prob. alter. of *wook*, fr. Kanarese *ukku* steel] **:** a steel made anciently in India by crude methods in small crucibles according to the oldest known process for making fused steel
wooz·i·ly \'wüzəlē, 'wüz-, -li\ *adv* **:** in a woozy manner
wooz·i·ness \-zēnəs, -zin-\ *n* -ES **:** the quality or state of being woozy
woozy \-zē, -zi\ *adj* [prob. alter. of *oozy*] **1 :** BEFUDDLED ⟨still ~ from the narcotics which eased the pain —*Time*⟩ ⟨pseudo-mystical doctrine which he finds impracticable and ~ —A.J. Nock⟩ **2 :** affected with dizziness, mild nausea, or weakness **:** SICK ⟨she came out nicely, but I felt ~ in the stomach —B.T. Guyton⟩ **3 :** resembling an alcoholic hallucination or euphoria or something experienced in one ⟨a way of making life look delightfully ~ —*Time*⟩ **4 :** VAGUE, BLURRY, WOOLLY ⟨~ sentimentality⟩
¹wop *var of* WHOP
²wop \'wäp\ *n* -S *sometimes cap* [It (Sicilian & Neapolitan dial.) *guappo* bold, handsome, bully, dandy, fr. Sp *guapo*] **:** ITALIAN — usu. used disparagingly
¹wopse \'wäps\ *dial var of* WASP
²wopse \"\ *vt* -ED/-ING/-S [origin unknown] *dial* **:** to heap, wrap, or tangle in a disorderly way
³wopse \"\ *n* -S *dial* **:** a disorderly mass **:** HEAP, MESS, TANGLE
wopsy \-sē\ *adj* **:** marked by disorder **:** IRREGULAR ⟨if your top-knot is very indifferent and ~, take intensive hair treatments —*Delineator*⟩
wor *abbr, often cap* worshipful
¹worces·ter \'wu̇stə(r)\ *adj, usu cap* [*Worcester*, city in west central England] **1 :** of or from the city of Worcester, England **:** of the kind or style prevalent in Worcester **2** [*Worcestershire, Worcester*, county in west central England] **:** WORCESTERSHIRE **3** [*Worcester*, city in central Massachusetts] **:** of or from the city of Worcester, Mass. ⟨*Worcester* factories⟩ **:** of the kind or style prevalent in Worcester
²worcester \"\ *n* -S *usu cap* **:** WORCESTER CHINA
worcester china *or* **worcester porcelain** *n, usu cap W* **:** a soft paste porcelain made at Worcester, England, since 1751
¹worces·ter·shire \-,shi(ə)r, -,shiə, -shə(r)\ *adj, usu cap* [*Worcestershire*, county in west central England] **:** of or from Worcestershire, England **:** of the kind or style prevalent in Worcestershire
²worcestershire \"\ *n* -S *usu cap* **:** WORCESTERSHIRE SAUCE
worcestershire sauce *or* **worcester sauce** *n, usu cap W* **:** a pungent sauce of soy, vinegar, and many other ingredients orig. made in Worcester, England
¹word \'wərd, 'wəd, 'wəid\ *n* -S *often attrib* [ME, fr. OE; akin to OHG *wort* word, ON *orth*, Goth *waurd*, L *verbum* word, Gk *eirein* to say, *rhēma* word, *rhētōr* orator, Lith *vardas* name] **1 a :** something that is said **:** UTTERANCE, STATEMENT ⟨my father loved you; he said he did, and with his deed did crown his ~ —Shak.⟩ ⟨not a ~ about his plans⟩ ⟨said a ~ to his employer on behalf of a friend who was looking for work⟩ **b words** *pl* (1) **:** TALK, DISCOURSE, SPEECH, LANGUAGE ⟨putting one's feelings into ~*s*⟩ ⟨wonderful beyond ~*s*⟩ (2) **:** the text of a vocal musical composition ⟨trivial ~*s* set to splendid music⟩ **c** (1) **:** a short conversation ⟨would like to have a ~ with you⟩ (2) **:** a short remark ⟨a ~ of advice⟩ **2 a** (1) **:** a speech sound or series of speech sounds that symbolizes and communicates a meaning without being divisible into smaller units capable of independent use **:** linguistic form that is a minimum free form ⟨the order of the ~*s* in a phrase⟩ ⟨the meaning of a ~⟩ (2) **:** the entire set of linguistic forms produced by combining a single base with various inflectional elements (as affixes) without change in the part of speech ⟨*man, man's, men,* and *men's* are different forms of one ~⟩ — see PARADIGM **b :** a written or printed character or combination of characters representing a spoken word; *esp* **:** any segment of written or printed discourse ordinarily appearing between spaces or between a space and a punctuation mark ⟨average number of ~*s* to a line⟩ **c :** CODE GROUP **d :** a combination of electrical or magnetic impulses conveying a quantum of information in communication and computer work **3 :** ORDER, COMMAND, INSTRUCTION ⟨don't move till I give the ~⟩ ⟨his ~ is law⟩ **4** *or* **word of god** *usu cap W & cap G* **a :** the divine Wisdom esp. as finding manifestation in the world and man and above all in Jesus Christ **:** LOGOS; *specif* **:** the second person of the Trinity ⟨the Logos is both the reason and the *Word of God* —W.F.Howard⟩ ⟨Christ is the *Word* become flesh —J.A.Mackay⟩ **b :** the gospel message **:** ¹GOSPEL 1; *also* **:** the content, communication, and effectual implementation of the gospel in the lives of men ⟨the Bible contains the *Word of God* to man —L.A.Weigle⟩ ⟨preach the *Word* in the mountains of eastern Tennessee —H.L.Mencken⟩ **c :** a self-revelation from God to men **:** God's disclosure of himself to men; *also* **:** the expressed or manifested mind and will of God ⟨God's *Word* was one of the most general terms used by Israel for revelation —G.E.Wright⟩ **d :** God's creative and redemptive activity esp. as manifested in the creation and preservation of the world and in acts of salvation in the lives of men ⟨by the *Word of God* heavens existed long ago —2 Pet 3:5 (RSV)⟩ ⟨upholding the universe by his *Word* of power —Heb 1:3 (RSV)⟩ ⟨for the *Word of God* is living and active, sharper than any two-edged sword —Heb 4:12 (RSV)⟩ **e :** a holy book **:** canon or collection of sacred scriptures divinely inspired by God ⟨will be readings from the *Words of God* — the Torah, the Bible, the Koran —Edris Rice-Wray⟩ **5 a :** NEWS, REPORT, ACCOUNT, MESSAGE, INFORMATION — used in the singular and often with no article ⟨brought ~ that a financial backer of the expedition . . . had died —*Amer. Guide Series: Maine*⟩ ⟨sent ~ . . . that he planned to attend —*N.Y. Times*⟩ ⟨in Washington when the ~ came of a great defeat at Bull Run⟩ **b :** common talk or report **:** RUMOR — used in the singular and often with no article ⟨~ of the prowess of the twelve-year-old got about —*Current Biog.*⟩ ⟨the ~ has gone about that there will be no prosecution —Tom Fitzsimmons⟩ **6 :** the act of speaking or of making verbal communication of any kind ⟨loyal in ~ and deed⟩ **:** product of such an act ⟨what people learn from the written ~⟩ **7 a :** SAYING, PROVERB, MAXIM **b :** a motto esp. in heraldry **8 a** (1) **:** PROMISE ⟨I give you my ~⟩ ⟨kept her ~⟩ ⟨as good as his ~⟩ (2) **:** the honor involved in the keeping of a promise ⟨pledged himself on his ~ to be present⟩ **b :** an assertion implying the authority or truthfulness of the person making it ⟨not that I doubt your ~⟩ ⟨take my ~ for it⟩ ⟨has the doctor's ~ for it that no operation is needed⟩ **9 :** a quarrelsome utterance or conversation ⟨one ~ led to another⟩ — usu. used in pl. ⟨some ~*s* between him and his father⟩ ⟨he and his friend had ~*s* and parted⟩ and sometimes with an adjective modifier ⟨some hard ~*s* passed between them⟩ **10 a :** a verbal signal **:** PASSWORD, WATCHWORD **b :** the most appropriate term to indicate what kind of action is required or prevalent — used in the predicate after *the* ⟨in dealing with difficult children, patience is the ~⟩ **c :** the most appropriate term to express the idea intended — used in the predicate after *the* ⟨mediocre is not the ~ for his performance; it was incredibly bad⟩
syn WORD, VOCABLE, and TERM can mean any letter or combination of letters or any sound or combination of sounds capable of being pronounced and expressing an idea that is by tradition or common consent associated with the letters or the sounds. WORD applies to a letter or combination of letters or a sound or a combination of sounds that forms an indivisible whole constituting one of the ultimate units of a language; VOCABLE throws emphasis upon a word as pronounced or spelled rather than as a unit of meaning ⟨a flat denial of poetic possibilities, in the case of any *vocable*, is liable to disastrous refutation —J.L.Lowes⟩ ⟨accustomed to songs in which the words are often merely convenient *vocables* with the melody usually more important than the text —Evelyn H. Scholl⟩ TERM applies both to words and to phrases that express a whole idea and form one of the units of expression in a language, applying esp. to units with a more or less precise technical use or meaning ⟨the *term* communism is used today to describe both a political philosophy and its translation into reality —H.W.Gatzke⟩ ⟨"the most important woman in Finland" is a *term* which has been applied —*Current Biog.*⟩ ⟨all professions are likely to develop innumerable *terms* that constitute an almost private jargon
— at a word *adv* **1 :** at a single word of command, request, or suggestion **2 :** in short **:** to sum up **:** CONCISELY **— good word 1 :** a favorable statement ⟨say a *good word* for him⟩ **2 :** good news ⟨spreading the *good word*⟩ ⟨hello, there; what's the *good word*⟩ **— in a word** *also* **in one word :** in short **:** to sum up **— in so many words 1 :** in exactly those terms ⟨implied that such actions were criminal but did not say so *in so many words*⟩ **2 :** in plain forthright language ⟨*in so many words*, she wasn't fit to be seen —Jean Stafford⟩ **— my word** — used to express surprise ⟨*my word*, what a nasty look she gave you⟩ **— of few words :** not inclined to say more than necessary **:** LACONIC ⟨a man *of few words*⟩ **— of many words :** TALKATIVE, VERBOSE **— of one's word :** that can be relied on to keep a promise — used only after *man* or *woman* ⟨a man *of his word*⟩ ⟨a woman *of her word*⟩ **— upon my word** *also* **on my word :** with my assurance **:** ASSUREDLY, INDEED ⟨*upon my word*, I never heard of such a thing⟩ **— words of one syllable :** plain forthright language ⟨he had had a bit too much; in *words of one syllable*, he is drunk⟩
²word \"\ *vb* -ED/-ING/-S [ME *worden*, fr. *word*, n. — more at ¹WORD] *vi, archaic* **:** to use words **:** SPEAK **~** *vt* **1 :** to utter or recite as spoken words **2** *obs* **:** to ply with words **3 :** to express in words **:** PHRASE ⟨a strongly *~ed* message⟩ **4** *obs* **:** to bring into some condition by talking ⟨be *~ed* to death —James Howell⟩ **— word it** *obs* **:** to bandy words **:** DISPUTE
word accent *var of* WORD STRESS
word·age \-dij, -dēj\ *n* -S **1 a :** WORDS ⟨keeps the music programs tied together with ~ —Saul Carson⟩ **b :** VERBIAGE 1 ⟨all the lobby and meeting-room ~ produced only these skimpy results —*Newsweek*⟩ **2 :** the number or quantity of words ⟨six long stories, ranging in ~ from 17,000 to 35,000 —Anthony Boucher⟩ **3 :** the use or choice of words **:** WORDING 2 ⟨signs of youth and inexperience in the ~, some of which is at random —*N. Y. Herald Tribune Bk. Rev.*⟩
word association *n* **:** free association in which a word serves as the stimulus object
word association test *n* **:** a method for exploring the content of the mind wherein the subject is required to respond to a stimulus word with the first word he thinks of or with one of a specified class of words
word-blind \'=,=\ *adj* **:** afflicted with word blindness
word blindness *n* **:** a condition in which a person is no longer able to recognize the words that he sees **:** ALEXIA
wordbook \'=,=\ *n* **1 :** a book containing a collection of words **:** VOCABULARY, DICTIONARY, LEXICON **2 :** LIBRETTO
word-bound \'=,=\ *adj* **:** lacking in fluency **:** taciturn because of limited vocabulary or unwillingness to talk
word-building \'=,==\ *n* **:** the act or process of forming words: **a :** WORD-FORMATION **b :** the act or process of spelling out words (as in a contest) with the use of only those letters found in a particular word or phrase
word-catcher \'=,==\ *n* **1 :** one that cavils at words **2 :** one that collects words and their different senses **:** LEXICOGRAPHER — used disparagingly
word-catching \'=,==\ *n* -S **:** concern with minute points of wording
word class *n* **:** a linguistic form class whose members are words; *esp* **:** PART OF SPEECH 1
word-deaf \'=,=\ *adj* **:** afflicted with word deafness
word deafness *n* **:** loss or lack of the ability to recognize words that are heard
word·er \'wərdər\ *n* -S **1** *obs* **:** a verbose person **2 :** one that puts something into words
word family *n* **:** a group of cognate words esp. within a single language ⟨the *word family* to which English *write, rewrite writer*, and *writ* belong⟩
word field *n* **:** FIELD 8c
word-formation \'==*'*=\ *n* **:** the formation of words in a language by the processes of derivation and composition
word for word *adv* [ME] **:** in the exact words **:** VERBATIM, LITERALLY, EXACTLY ⟨repeated the message *word for word*⟩
word-for-word \'=='=\ *adj* [*word for word*] **:** being in or following the exact words ⟨a *word-for-word* translation⟩ **:** VERBATIM ⟨the *word-for-word* transmission of legends —George Grey⟩
word game *n* **:** a game in which players compete in forming, thinking of, or guessing words according to a set of rules
word-hoard \'=,=\ *n* [trans. of OE *wordhord*] **:** a supply of words **:** VOCABULARY ⟨given to much free and easy unlocking of his *word-hoard* —G.K.Anderson⟩
word·ie \'wərdi\ *n* -S [¹*word* + *-ie*] *Scot* **:** a mere word **:** WORD
wordier *comparative of* WORDY
wordiest *superlative of* WORDY
word·i·ly \'wərd[ə]lē, 'wəd|, 'wəid|, |əl|, |i\ *adv* **:** in a wordy manner
word·i·ness \-dēnəs, -din-\ *n* -ES **:** the quality or state of being wordy
wording *n* -S [fr. gerund of ²*word*] **1 :** the act of talking or of uttering as words **2 :** the act or manner of expressing in words **:** PHRASING, PHRASEOLOGY ⟨mystical writing where the ~ takes on poetic quality —Thomas Munro⟩
word·ish \-dish\ *adj* **1** *obs* **:** made up of or having to do with words **:** VERBAL **2** *obs* **:** containing more words than necessary **:** VERBOSE, WORDY **— wordishly** *adv, obs* **— wordishness** *n* -ES *obs*
wor·dle \'wərd[ə]l\ *n* -S [alter. of ME *wirtil* whirtle] **:** any of several pivoted pieces forming the throat of an adjustable die used in drawing wire or lead pipe
word·less \'wərdləs, 'wəd-, 'wəid-\ *adj* [ME *wordles*, fr. ¹*word* + *-les* -less] **1 :** not expressed or not expressible in words ⟨choking exasperation and ~ shame —Thomas Wolfe⟩ **:** involving no use of words ⟨~ intercourse with rude nature —John Burroughs⟩ **2 a :** saying nothing **:** SILENT, SPEECHLESS ⟨he stood helpless — ~ even —Lew Wallace⟩ **b :** lacking ability or inclination to express oneself freely in words **:** INARTICULATE, TACITURN ⟨a calm, ~ man —W.A.White⟩ **3 :** not consisting of or accompanied by words ⟨with a ~ squeak —P.G.Wodehouse⟩ ⟨the ~ language of architecture —E.M. Bridge⟩ ⟨~ music⟩ **— word·less·ly** *adv* **— word·less·ness** *n* -ES
word-lore \'=,=\ *n* **:** study of or information about words ⟨a modest book on *word-lore* —Ernest Weekley⟩
word-magic \'=,==\ *n* **:** magic involving the use of words in a manner determined by a belief that the very act of uttering a word summons or directly affects the person or thing that the word refers to
word-man \'=,=\ *n, pl* **word-men :** one that is skilled in the use of words
wordmonger \'=,==\ *n* **:** a dealer in words: as **a :** one that uses words for show or without enough regard for meaning **b :** a writer by profession
word-mongering \'=,=(=)=\ *n* **:** the use of empty or bombastic words ⟨mere *word-mongering* divorced from actual life —Forrest Morgan⟩
word-mongery \'=,məŋg(ə)rē, -mäŋ-\ *n* -ES [¹*word* + *-mongery* (as in *ironmongery*)] **:** WORD-MONGERING
word-music \'=,==\ *n* **:** the musical quality of spoken language or of written language designed to be spoken (as in a play)
word of god *usu cap W & cap G* **:** WORD 4
word of honor : a promise or engagement made with or confirmed by a pledge of one's honor for its fulfillment
word of mouth : oral communication ⟨news spread by *word of mouth*⟩
word-of-mouth \'=='=\ *adj* [*word of mouth*] **:** orally communicated **:** involving or consisting of oral communication ⟨*word-of-mouth* advertising⟩
word order *n* **:** the order or arrangement of words in a phrase, clause, or sentence
word-paint \'=,=\ *vt* [back-formation fr. *word-painter* & *word-painting*] **:** to depict graphically in words
word-painter \'=,==\ *n* **:** a writer of vivid or graphic descriptive power
word-painting \'=,==\ *n* **1 :** WORD PICTURE **2 :** the action of depicting something graphically in words
word-perfect \'='==\ *adj* **:** being in the state of having completely and accurately memorized something consisting of words ⟨an actor may become *word-perfect* in his part —C.S. Myers⟩
word picture *n* **:** a graphic or vivid description in words
wordplay \'=,=\ *n* **1 :** verbal wit based on the peculiarities of words and esp. on the various meanings expressed by a single word or by two or more words of like sound ⟨a pun is a form of ~⟩ **2 :** an instance of wordplay
words *pl of* WORD, *pres 3d sing of* WORD
word salad *n* **:** a jumble of extremely incoherent speech as sometimes observed in schizophrenia
word-sign \'=,=\ *n* **:** a visual or tactile symbol or group of symbols representing a word: as **a :** a single character used to represent a word in a regular system of writing **:** LOGOGRAM ⟨the *word-signs* used in Egyptian hieroglyphic writing⟩ **b :** a stroke or simple character used in shorthand as a brief way of representing a word of frequent occurrence or a derivative of such a word **c :** a braille character of one cell or two cells that can stand for a whole word
word-slinger \'=,==\ *n* **:** a professional writer; *esp* **:** a hack writer
wordsmith \'=,=\ *n* **:** a craftsman or artist whose medium is words
words of administration : the words spoken by the officiating clergyman in administering the Communion elements to the people
words of institution : the portion of a Christian Communion service based on the words of Mk 14:22–24 and used as the warrant from Jesus Christ for the continued celebration of the Eucharist
words of limitation : the words in a deed or will that describe the nature and extent of the estate granted or devised
words of procreation : the words necessary in conveying a fee in tail to indicate to whose children the conveyed estate is to be entailed
word-spinning \'=,==\ *n* **:** the action or process of expressing oneself in words in a showy or esp. verbose manner
word square *n* **1 :** ACROSTIC 3 **2 word squares** *pl but sing in constr* **:** a game in which each player tries to fill letters as they are called one at a time into a block of squares to form words horizontally and vertically
word·ster \'wərdztə(r), -dst-\ *n* -S **:** one that is adept in the use of words esp. in an empty or bombastic manner
word-stock \'=,=\ *n* **:** the vocabulary of a language, dialect, or idiolect
word stress *or* **word accent** *n* **:** the manner in which stresses are distributed on the syllables of a word — compare SENTENCE STRESS
¹words·worth·ian \,wərdz'wərthēən\ *n* -S *usu cap* [William *Wordsworth* †1850 Eng. poet + E *-an*, n. suffix] **1 :** a follower, imitator, or admirer of the poet Wordsworth **2 :** a student of or authority on Wordsworth or his works
²wordsworthian \'=;'===\ *adj, usu cap* [William *Wordsworth* + E *-an*, adj. suffix] **:** of, resembling, belonging to, or charac-

teristic of the poet Wordsworth or his poetry — **words·worth·ian·ism** \ˌ═'══ə,nizəm\ *n* -s *usu cap*

word value *n* : the effectiveness of a word to express the exact shade of meaning desired and to fit into the rhythmical structure of a phrase or sentence

[1]**wordy** \'wərdē, 'wȯd-, 'wəid-, -di\ *adj* -ER/-EST [ME, fr. OE *wordig*, fr. [1]*word* + *-ig* -y] **1** : using or containing many words : VERBOSE ⟨a ~ and insolent braggart —Sir Walter Scott⟩ ⟨finding ~ fault with the conditions under which he lives —Agnes Repplier⟩ **2** : of, belonging to, or consisting of words : VERBAL ⟨~ war⟩

syn WORDY, VERBOSE, PROLIX, DIFFUSE, and REDUNDANT can all mean using or marked by the use of more, usu. far more, words than are necessary to express the thought. WORDY suggests garrulousness when applied to what is spoken ⟨the newspapers of the day . . . printed long *wordy* editorials —Marjory S. Douglas⟩ ⟨proceedings, which were long and disorderly, were delayed by *wordy* disputes —F.H.Underhill⟩ ⟨a senile and *wordy* character⟩ VERBOSE suggests overabundance of words as a literary or rhetorical fault ⟨slow, *verbose*, and ineffective instructional methods —R. E. De Kieffer⟩ ⟨not diffuse, but they are *verbose* in the exact sense of that term; they are too luxurious in words —H.S.Canby⟩ PROLIX implies so much attention to minute detail as to extend the matter beyond all due bounds, strongly implying tediousness ⟨his style is . . . excessively long-winded and *prolix* —R.A.Hall b. 1911⟩ ⟨the style is forceful, repetitive and *prolix* —Cyril Connolly⟩ DIFFUSE implies lack of compactness and sense of point, suggesting a wordy ranging over a subject ⟨this is a sprawling, formless, *diffuse*, and unselective book —Orville Prescott⟩ ⟨fear . . . that I was getting too *diffuse*; but now I am glad that I went into detail from the first —Bram Stoker⟩ REDUNDANT applies to something superfluous, to repetitious and unnecessary words or phrases, or to a speaker or writer whose style is marked by them, usu. habitually ⟨she had been, like nearly all very young writers, superfluous of phrase, *redundant* —Rose Macaulay⟩ ⟨a wordy, *redundant*, cliché-ridden style⟩ ⟨a most *redundant* after-dinner speaker⟩

[2]**wordy** \'wərdi\ *chiefly Scot var of* WORTHY

wore [ME (Sc) *wour* (past)] *past or substand past part of* WEAR

wore-out \'═'═\ *substand var of* WORN-OUT

[1]**work** \'wərk, 'wōk, 'wəik\ *n* -s [ME *werk, work*, fr. OE *werc, weorc, worc*; akin to OHG *werc, werah* work, ON *verk*, Gk *ergon* work, *erdein, rhezein* to do, make sacrifice, Av *vərəzyeiti* he works] **1** : activity in which one exerts strength or faculties to do or perform: **a** : sustained physical or mental effort valued as it overcomes obstacles and achieves an objective or result ⟨the hours of busiest ~ and closest application —W.C. Brownell⟩ — contrasted with *play* **b** : the labor, task, or duty that affords one his accustomed means of livelihood ⟨six days shalt thou labor and do all thy ~ —Exod 20:9 (AV)⟩ ⟨the ~ of a permanent secretary is worth £3,000 a year —Virginia Woolf⟩ **c** : strenuous activity marked by the presence of difficulty and exertion and absence of pleasure ⟨sculling against a swift current is ~ —Richard Jefferies⟩ **d** : occasional or temporary activity toward a desired end : CHORE ⟨the ~ of putting up storm windows⟩ **e** : a specific task, duty, function, or assignment often being a part or phase of some larger activity ⟨the handler's ~ is to put the goods on the siding but not to load the car⟩ **2 a** : energy expended by natural phenomena ⟨these boulder deposits are the ~ of glaciers⟩ **b** : the result of such energy ⟨sand dunes are the ~ of sea and wind⟩ **c** : the transference of energy that is produced by the motion of the point of application of a force (as when a compressed spring in a toy gun by its expansion and loss of potential energy gives kinetic energy to a bullet or when the falling weight of a pile driver drives in a pile) and is measured by multiplying the force and the displacement of its point of application in the line of action — see ERG, JOULE, KILOGRAM-METER **3 a** : something that results from a particular manner or method of working, operating, or devising ⟨tracked down by careful police ~⟩ ⟨sonata with intricate passage ~ for the right hand⟩ ⟨telecast was notable for the flexibility of the camera ~ —Irene Kuhn⟩ **b** : something that results from the use or fashioning of a particular material ⟨silver ~ of earlier artists⟩ ⟨fine porcelain ~ in many styles⟩ or employment of a particular technique ⟨boxes adorned with elaborate filigree ~⟩ **c** : NEEDLEWORK, FANCYWORK **4 a** : a fortified structure (as a fort, earthen barricade, trench) **b works** *pl* : structures in engineering (as docks, bridges, or embankments) or mining (as shafts or tunnels) **5 works** *pl but sing or pl in constr* : a place where industrial labor is carried on : PLANT, FACTORY ⟨cement ~s⟩ ⟨chemical ~s⟩ ⟨start in the office rather than in the ~s —Roy Lewis & Angus Maude⟩ **6 works** *pl* : the working or moving parts of a mechanism ⟨cleaning the ~s of a clock⟩ **7 a** *dial Eng* : DISTURBANCE, BOTHER, TO-DO, TROUBLE **b** : froth or foam caused by fermentation **8 a** : something produced or accomplished by effort, exertion, or exercise of skill ⟨this book is the ~ of many hands⟩ **b** : something produced by the exercise of creative talent or expenditure of creative effort : artistic production ⟨literary, scientific, and artistic ~s, including writings, musical, dramatic, and cinematographic works, and paintings, engravings, and sculpture —*Universal Copyright Convention*⟩ **c** : the act or process of working a degree — used in Masonic and some other ritualistic orders ⟨made the ~ up-to-date, brisk, with only one 45-minute degree —C.W. Ferguson⟩ **9 works** *pl* : performance of moral or religious acts ⟨faith by itself if it has no ~s, is dead —Jas 2:17 (RSV)⟩ ⟨salvation by ~s⟩ ⟨performance of all the ~s prescribed by the law —E.F.Scott⟩ **10 a** : effective operation : EFFECT, RESULT ⟨wait for time to do its healing ~⟩ ⟨loathed war and all its ~s —V.L.Parrington⟩ **b** : manner of working : WORKMANSHIP, MANAGEMENT, EXECUTION ⟨better tools make for better ~⟩ **11 a** : the material or piece of material that is operated upon at any stage in the process of manufacture ⟨the ~ was put under the drop hammer and quickly pounded into shape for the next operation⟩ **b** : ore before it is dressed **12** : BREAK 4c(6) **13 works** *pl* **a** : everything possessed or available ⟨I had the ~s, the bottom half of the menu, from grapefruit to rice pudding —Saul Bellow⟩ ⟨builders are including complete kitchens . . . and buyers want the ~s —*Kiplinger Washington Letter*⟩ ⟨the whole ~s, rod, reel, tackle box, went overboard⟩ **b** : subjection to drastic treatment : unsparing or ruthless handling : all possible abuse including murder — usu. used with *get* ⟨get the ~s⟩ or *give* ⟨gave him the ~s⟩ **14** *slang* : dice designed for cheating

syn OCCUPATION, EMPLOYMENT, BUSINESS, PURSUIT, CALLING: WORK is the general term with less specific connotation and wider application than others in this series; it may or may not suggest laborious, burdensome, onerous expenditure of energy ⟨the *work* of a ditchdigger⟩ ⟨a miner's *work* is difficult⟩ OCCUPATION may indicate the trade, craft, vocation, or profession which one has chosen and prepared himself for and which one is apt usu. to follow ⟨allowed to choose his *occupation* —W.R.Inge⟩ or whatever occupies one's time and energies, quite purposefully as a means of livelihood or less so as an avocation or interest ⟨a generation still in the process of discovering its own identity and desperately engaged in that *occupation* —R.B.West⟩ EMPLOYMENT is likely to center attention on an employer-employee relationship and imply an agreement or contract about wages or working conditions ⟨resumed his *employment* with the Smith Plumbing Company, plumbing being his occupation⟩ or may indicate merely that at which one employs himself, without suggestions of work ⟨their chief *employment* is to talk of what they once were and of what they may yet be —T.B.Macaulay⟩ BUSINESS suggests work of a commercial or mercantile nature and is likely to be limited to situations of authority unless the question of a rightful or suitable assumption of a role or function is concerned ⟨his *business* is selling insurance and my work as clerk in his office is not very hard⟩ BUSINESS in situations not involving means of livelihood may be used in reference to financial transactions or to necessary and burdensome tasks but hardly to avocations ⟨the messy *business* of infant feeding —*New Yorker*⟩ PURSUIT may suggest either a vocation or an avocation followed with zeal or resolution ⟨lost all soul or sensation, but for this one *pursuit* —Mary W. Shelley⟩ ⟨the law, being a profession, was accounted a more gentlemanly *pursuit* than business —Edith Wharton⟩ CALLING may indicate a profession or vocation to which one has been called by some inspiration or intuition ⟨that luckiest of fairy-gifts, a *calling*, an industry, something that she loved to do —L.P.Smith⟩ or may indicate the simplest craft or trade ⟨in his shepherd's *calling* he was prompt —William Wordsworth⟩

syn LABOR, TOIL, TRAVAIL, GRIND, DRUDGERY: WORK is a very general word usable in a variety of contexts; LABOR differs from WORK in often being limited to purposive, necessary expenditure of effort, usu. of a fatiguing or onerous nature ⟨*labor* is doing what we must; leisure is doing what we like —G.B. Shaw⟩ ⟨any activity becomes *work* when it is directed by accomplishment of a definite material result, and it is *labor* only as the activities are onerous, undergone as mere means by which to secure a result —John Dewey⟩ TOIL indicates fatiguing prolonged work ⟨the labor of sifting, combining, constructing, expunging, correcting, testing: this frightful *toil* is as much critical as creative —T.S.Eliot⟩ TRAVAIL is likely to stress painfulness, difficulty, or struggle in work ⟨the sentimentalist escapes the stern *travail* of thought —J.L.Lowes⟩ ⟨I must admit the doubt in view of the *travail* that I suffered —B.N.Cardozo⟩ GRIND suggests dreary monotonous repetition of burdensome or taxing work ⟨nothing left for my mother to do but to take in student boarders. This she did until every child was out of college — a long hard *grind* —A.W.Long⟩ DRUDGERY applies to continuing dull, menial, irksome work ⟨*drudgery* can be cut down. Most men have had to dig for their lives since Adam, but this is now avoidable —Francis Hackett⟩ ⟨the act of scrupulous revision (endless pruning and trimming for the sake of a sound and flexible prose style) that provides the writer's best solace even while it makes *drudgery* —Ellen Glasgow⟩

— **at work 1** : engaged in working (as at one's occupation) **2** : OPERATING, FUNCTIONING ⟨stronger pressures that have been *at work* on the national character —W.C.Dickinson⟩ ⟨evidence of a fine culture *at work* even in the lowliest carpenter —*Amer. Guide Series: N.H.*⟩ — **in the works** : in process of preparation or development or completion ⟨a plan of reorganization is reported to be now *in the works*⟩ — **in work 1** : in process of being done ⟨company . . . has three films *in work* right now —Kirk Douglas⟩ **2** *of a horse* : in training — **make short work of** : to deal with or dispose of quickly or summarily — **out of work** : without regular employment : JOBLESS

[2]**work** \"\ *adj* **1** : suitable or styled for wear while working ⟨~ clothes⟩ ⟨~ shoes⟩ **2** : used for work ⟨~ elephant⟩

[3]**work** \"\ *vb* **worked** \-kt\ *or* **wrought** \'rȯt, *usu* -ȯd.+V\ **worked** *or* **wrought; working; works** [ME *worchen, worken, werken* (past *wroughte, wroghte*, past part. *wrought, wroght*), fr. OE *wyrcan, wircan* (past *worhte*, past part. *geworht*); akin to OHG *wurchen, wirchen* to work (past *worhta*, past part. *giworht*), ON *yrkja* (past *orti*, past part. *yrt, ort*), Goth *waurkian* (past *waurhta*), OE *weorc* work — more at [1]WORK] *vt* **1** : to bring to pass : EFFECT ⟨~ havoc⟩ ⟨~ miracles⟩ ⟨had meant to ~ her own will on the interior of the house —Arnold Bennett⟩ **2 a** : to fashion or create by expending labor or exertion upon : FORGE, SHAPE ⟨~ flint into tools⟩ **b** : to make or decorate with needlework; *esp* : EMBROIDER ⟨the buttonholes of the dress were ~*ed* in a contrasting color⟩ ⟨~*ed* a floral design in wool and silk on the shawl⟩ **3 a** : to prepare for use by stirring or kneading ⟨~ the putty into the right consistency⟩ **b** : to bring into a desired form by a gradual process of cutting, hammering, scraping, pressing, stretching ⟨~ cold steel⟩ **4** : to set or keep in motion, operation, or activity ⟨~ cattle in a roundup⟩ : cause to operate or produce ⟨a pump ~*ed* by hand⟩ ⟨~ a quarry⟩ ⟨~ farmland⟩ **5** : to work out (a problem) : SOLVE ⟨~ difficult calculations in his head⟩ **6 a** : to cause to toil or labor ⟨~*ed* his horses nearly to death⟩ : get work out of : cause to perform ⟨~ dogs in a circus act⟩ **b** : to make use of ⟨~*ed* her charm and looks to get her way⟩ : EXPLOIT **c** : to control or guide the operation of ⟨all the yard switches are ~*ed* from a central tower⟩ **7** : to carry on an operation through or in or along ⟨the salesman ~*ed* both sides of the street⟩ ⟨fisherman ~*ed* the stream from the bridge down to the pool⟩ **8** : to pay for with labor or service ⟨~ out a fine⟩ ⟨~ off a debt⟩ ⟨~*ed* his way through college⟩ **9 a** : to get (oneself or an object) into or out of a condition or position by gradual stages ⟨~*ed* himself out of his bonds and called the police⟩ ⟨~*ed* himself into a position of leadership⟩ ⟨patiently ~*ing* the boulder out of the hole⟩ ⟨swinging his arms to ~ the stiffness out of his shoulders⟩ **b** : CONTRIVE, ARRANGE — used chiefly with *it* ⟨we can ~ it so that you can take your vacation⟩ **10 a** *archaic* : to influence by acting upon : LEAD, INDUCE ⟨I have been ~*ing* him to abandon her —Sir Walter Scott⟩ **b** : to practice trickery or cajolery or some devious procedure on for some end ⟨~*ed* the management for a free ticket⟩ **c** : EXCITE, PROVOKE ⟨~*ed* himself into a rage⟩ **11** : to work off (sense 2) **12** : to bud or graft (plants) — usu. used with *on* ⟨apples ~*ed* on seedling stocks are often esp. vigorous⟩ **13** : to sort (mail) by place of destination **14** : to manipulate (a bait or lure) for fish with maximum effectiveness in a natural manner **15** : to go through the ceremonies of (a degree) — used in Masonic and some other ritualistic orders ~ *vi* **1 a** : to exert oneself physically or mentally esp. in sustained effort for a purpose or under compulsion or necessity — contrasted with *play* **b** : to perform or carry through a task requiring sustained effort or continuous repeated operations ⟨~*ed* for hours clearing up the yard⟩ ⟨~*ing* away at his algebra⟩ ⟨~*ing* all day over a hot stove⟩ ⟨~*ing* on his book for years⟩ **c** : to perform work or fulfill duties regularly for wages or salary ⟨he ~s at plumbing⟩ ⟨~s in an insurance office⟩ ⟨~s for an oil company⟩ ⟨obliged to ~ for a living⟩ **2 a** *archaic* : ACT, BEHAVE **b** *obs* : CONTRIVE, ARRANGE **3** : to function or operate according to plan or design ⟨the mechanism was heavy and awkward but it ~*ed*⟩ ⟨hinges ~ better with oil⟩ **4** : to exert an influence or tendency ⟨developments which ~ for increasing the significance of the net income figure —*Jour. of Accountancy*⟩ **5** : to produce a desired effect or result : SUCCEED ⟨all things ~ together for good to them that love God —Rom 8:28 (AV)⟩ — often used with *out* ⟨hoped the plan would ~ out⟩ **6 a** : to make way slowly and with difficulty : move or progress laboriously or with sustained effort ⟨~*ed* up from office boy to president⟩ **b** : to sail to windward **7** : to permit of being worked : react in a specified way to being worked ⟨this wood ~s easily⟩ **8 a** : to be in agitation or restless motion ⟨the sea ~s high —Shak.⟩ **b** : FERMENT 1 — used esp. of a liquid or yeast **c** : to move slightly in relation to another part — used of parts (as of a ship's frame or plates) normally rigidly connected ⟨~*ed* in a seaway . . . and leaked —Alan Villiers⟩ **d** : to move in an undesigned direction due to imperfect fitting ⟨the shaft ~s in its bearing⟩ **e** *of rock* : to undergo slow moving, heaving, sinking, or sliding **f** : to get into a specified condition by slow or imperceptible movements ⟨the knot ~*ed* loose⟩ ⟨plug ~*ed* out of the pipe⟩ ⟨his jacket had ~*ed* up at the back of his neck⟩ **9** : to work a degree — used in Masonic and some other ritualistic orders

syn see ACT — **work at** : to be engaged or employed in : PRACTICE ⟨trained as a carpenter but seldom *works at* it⟩ ⟨less attractive girls must *work* harder *at* being popular —Lester David⟩ — **work double tides** : to perform the labor of two days in one — **work even** : to continue a knitting pattern without any alteration — **work into** : to force, urge, or insinuate into ⟨*worked* his foot *into* the boot⟩ ⟨*work* new courses *into* the curriculum⟩ — **work on 1** : AFFECT ⟨poetry *works on* the mind of the reader — not directly but by indirection —C.I.Glicksberg⟩ ⟨*worked on* his sympathies to get a loan⟩ **2** : to strive to influence or persuade ⟨noble hero . . . is *worked on* and betrayed by devilish Italian cunning —F.R. Leavis⟩ ⟨sent a high-priced lobby to *work on* the legislature —Beverly Smith⟩ — **work one's way** : to advance slowly against resistance or obstruction ⟨*worked his way* to the center of the jostling crowd⟩ ⟨*worked his way* cautiously down the cliff⟩ — **work the oracle** *Brit* : to gain something or succeed by scheming or wire pulling; *specif* : to raise money by doubtful ways — **work upon** : to have effect upon : operate on : PERSUADE, INFLUENCE ⟨so *worked upon* her adopted father with his threats —Max Peacock⟩ — **work water** *of a boiler* : FOAM, PRIME

work·abil·i·ty \ˌwərkə'bilədē, ˌwōk-, ˌwəik-, -lətē, -i\ *n* : the quality or state of being workable

work·able \'wərkəbəl, 'wōk-, 'wəik-\ *adj* **1** : capable of being worked ⟨~ plastic⟩ ⟨~ vein of coal⟩ ⟨~ lumber⟩ **2** : capable of being put into successful operation : PRACTICABLE, FEASIBLE ⟨finding a ~ program for disarmament —C.E.Egan⟩ — **work·able·ness** *n* -ES

work·a·day \-kə,dā\ *adj* [alter. of earlier *workyday*, fr. obs. *workyday* workday (n.), fr. ME *werkeday*, irreg. fr. *werk* work + *day*] **1** : relating to or suited for working days ⟨~ clothes⟩ **2** : EVERYDAY, PROSAIC, ORDINARY ⟨invested ~ things and people with romance and fantasy —Margaret Rutherford⟩

work and back *n* : SHEETWORK 1

work-and-back \'══'═\ *adv (or adj)* [*work and back*] : SHEETWISE

work and tumble *or* **work and flop** *vb* : to print by the work-and-tumble method

work-and-tumble \'══'══\ *or* **work-and-flop** \'══'═\ *adv (or adj)* : with all the pages of a signature imposed in one form so that when the sheet is printed, turned over side for side, backed, and cut two complete copies result

work and turn *vb* : to print by the work-and-turn method

work-and-turn \'══'═\ *adv (or adj)* : with all the pages of a signature imposed in one form so that when the sheet is printed, turned over end for end, backed, and cut two complete copies result

work and twist *or* **work and whirl** *vb* : to print by the work-and-twist method

work-and-twist *or* **work-and-whirl** \'══'═\ *adj* : involving a method whereby a sheet is printed twice on the same side from a two-up form by reversing the sheet when feeding the second time so that the part already printed by the first section of the form will be printed by the second section and vice versa

work·away \'═ə,wā\ *n* [[3]*work* + *a* + *way*] : a person who works his passage on a ship

workbag \'═,═\ *n* : a bag for holding implements or materials for work; *esp* : a bag for holding needlework

workbank \'═,═\ *n* : [3]BANK 3b

workbasket \'═,══\ *n* : a basket for needlework

workbench \'═,═\ *n* : a strong heavy waist-high table on which the work esp. of mechanics, machinists, and carpenters is performed

workboard \'═,═\ *n* : a board providing support and surface for manual work

workboat \'═,═\ *n* : a boat used for work purposes (as commercial fishing, harbor and waterway maintenance, ferrying supplies and machinery) rather than for sport or for passenger or naval service

workbook \'═,═\ *n* **1** : a book outlining a suggested course of study in some subject or field **2** : a book or pamphlet setting forth rules governing the manner or method of work **3** : a book in which is recorded work done or planned **4** : a student's individual exercise or practice book consisting of a progressive series of problems to be solved directly on the pages and often supplementing the use of a textbook

workbox \'═,═\ *n* : a box for holding instruments and materials esp. for needlework

work-brittle \'═,══\ *adj* [[1]*work* + *brittle*] *dial* : INDUSTRIOUS

work camp *n* : a camp for workers: as **a** : PRISON CAMP 1 **b** : a short-term group project in which individuals from one or more religious organizations volunteer their labor for the purpose of helping others in need; *also* : the group of workers of such a project

work car *n* : a railroad car used in the construction and maintenance of track

work curve *n* : a graphic record of the amount done in each successive part of a prolonged period of work — compare FATIGUE CURVE

[1]**workday** \'═,═\ *n* [ME *werkday*, fr. *werk* work + *day*] **1** : a day on which work is performed as distinguished from Sunday or a holiday : WORKING DAY **2 a** : the period of time in a day during which work is performed **b** : the number of hours determined by law, custom, or agreement during which a workman hired at a stated wage must work to be entitled to a day's pay

[2]**workday** \"\ *adj* : WORKADAY

work-dog \'═,═\ *n* : WORKING DOG

worked *adj* [fr. past part. of [3]*work*] : that has been subjected to some process of development, treatment, or manufacture ⟨cottons that have a ~ look and discourage need for any elaboration —*Women's Wear Daily*⟩ ⟨newly ~ field⟩ ⟨wall of ~ stone⟩

worked lumber *n* : lumber that has been matched or lapped or patterned or molded

worked up *adj* [fr. past part. of *work up*] : emotionally aroused : EXCITED, ANGRY ⟨was quite *worked up* and said they had been very anxious for our safety —A.F.Ellis⟩

work·er \'wərkər; 'wōkə(r, 'wəik-\ *n* -s [ME *worcher, werker*, fr. *worchen, werken* to work + *-er*] **1** : DOER, CREATOR ⟨~ of miracles⟩ ⟨~ of magic spells⟩ **2 a** : LABORER, TOILER ⟨~s in the Lord's vineyard⟩ ⟨migratory ~s in the orchards⟩ **b** : one who is employed esp. at manual or industrial labor for a wage ⟨rate increases for all the ~s in the steel industry⟩ **c** : one who works in a particular field ⟨~s in cancer research⟩ or industry or with a particular material — often used in combination **d** : a member of the working class ⟨party of ~s and small farmers⟩ **3** : one of the neuter usu. sterile individuals of the social ants, bees, and termites — see ANT illustration, HONEYBEE illustration **4 a** : a 2-handled scraping knife used in dressing leather **b** : a bobbin that moves across the pillow forming the pattern in bobbin lace — compare HANGER 5 **c** : any of various small rollers or cylinders in a textile machine (as a fearnought or carder) that has wire teeth set at such an angle as to draw the fiber bodily away from the large cylinder — compare STRIPPER 5 **5** *or* **worker plate** : a usu. electrotype plate from which printing is done — compare CASTER 1b **6 a** : one who works for a political party or party machine esp. to get out the vote **b** : SOCIAL WORKER **7** : WORKING FIRE

worker cell *n* : any of the smaller cells of a honeycomb in which larvae of worker bees are reared

worker comb *n* : the portion of honeycomb composed of worker cells

worker major *n* [*worker* + *major*, adj.] : MAXIM 4

worker minor *n* [*worker* + *minor*, adj.] : MINIM 6

worker-priest \'══'═\ *n* : a French Roman Catholic priest who for missionary purposes spends part of each weekday as a worker in a secular job

work farm *n* : a farm on which minor offenders are confined and put to work

workfellow \'═,═(,)═\ *n* [[1]*work* + *fellow*] : one engaged in the same work with another : companion in work

workfolk *or* **workfolks** \'═,═\ *n pl* : working people; *esp* : farm workers

work force *n* **1** : the workers engaged in a specific activity ⟨the factory's *work force*⟩ **2** : the number of workers potentially assignable for any purpose ⟨yearly additions to the nation's *work force*⟩

work·ful \'wərkfəl\ *adj, archaic* : DILIGENT, INDUSTRIOUS

work function *n* : the energy that is needed for a particle to come from the interior of a medium and break through the surface — used esp. of the photoelectric and thermionic emission of electrons from metals

workgirl \'═,═\ *n* : a girl employed for wages in manual labor esp. in industry

workhand \'═,═\ *n* : a person employed (as on a farm or in a factory or shop) by some one else

work harden *vt* [[1]*work*] : to harden and strengthen (metal) by cold-working

work hardness *n* : hardness of a metal induced by cold-working

workhead \'═,═\ *n* : a head (as of a lath) that holds the work

workhorse \'═,═\ *n* **1** : a horse used chiefly for labor as distinguished from driving, riding, or racing **2 a** : a person who undertakes arduous labor **b** : a markedly useful or durable vehicle, craft, or machine ⟨helicopter today . . . is the ~ of the air —W.O.Murphy⟩ **3** : SAWHORSE, TRESTLE 1a

workhouse \'═,═\ *n* [ME *werkhous*, fr. OE *weorchūs*, fr. *weorc* work + *hūs* house] **1** *obs* : WORKSHOP, FACTORY **2** *Brit* : a house in which able-bodied poor are maintained at public expense and compelled to labor **3** : a house of correction in which minor offenders are confined and put to work

work in *vt* [[3]*work*] **1** : to insert or cause to penetrate by repeated or continued effort ⟨spread on the ointment and *work* it *in* thoroughly with the fingers⟩ **2** : to interpose or insinuate gradually or unobtrusively ⟨*work in* a few topical jokes⟩ : add as an ingredient or so as to be an integral part : INTERWEAVE, INTERMINGLE

[1]**working** *adj* [fr. gerund of [3]*work*] **1 :** adequate to permit work to be done : sufficient in strength or numbers to accomplish results ⟨the party has a ~ majority in the senate⟩ ⟨~ knowledge of at least one other modern language —B.B.Thomas⟩ **2 :** assumed or adopted to permit or facilitate further work or activity ⟨a ~ draft of a peace treaty was submitted for discussion⟩ ⟨necessity for ~ agreements with her neighboring states on interstate construction projects —*Amer. Guide Series: N.J.*⟩

[2]**working** *n* -s [fr. gerund of [3]*work*] : an excavation or group of excavations made in mining, quarrying, or tunneling — used chiefly in pl. ⟨the ~s extended for miles underground⟩

working asset *n* [[1]*working*] : an asset other than a capital asset

working ball *n* [*working* (pres. part. of [3]*work*) + *ball*] : a bowling ball having sufficient spin to scatter the pins upon impact

working barrel *n* : the cylinder of a deep-well or mine pump

working beam *n* : WALKING BEAM

working capital *n* [[1]*working*] **1 :** capital currently used in business operations; *specif* : the excess of current assets over current liabilities **2 :** all capital of a business except that invested in capital assets

working card *n* [*working*, gerund of [3]*work*] : UNION CARD 1

working circle *n* : an area of forest from which a sustained yield of timber and by-products is planned

working class *n* [*working*, pres. part. of [3]*work*] : the class of people who are employed for wages usu. in manual labor; *also* : the social class, grade, or stratum made up of these workers

working-class \'=,=,=\ *adj* [*working class*] : relating to, deriving from, or suitable to the class of wage workers ⟨*working-class* attitude⟩ ⟨*working-class* virtues⟩ ⟨*working-class* solidarity⟩

working day *n* [*working*, gerund of [3]*work*] **1 :** a day when work is normally done as distinguished from Sundays and legal holidays **2 :** WORKDAY 2

working-day \'=,=,=\ *adj* [*working day*] : relating to or characteristic of working days : WORKADAY ⟨how full of briers is this *working-day* world —Shak.⟩

working dog *n* : a dog suited by size, breeding, or training for useful labor (as draft, sled, or herding work) as distinguished from one suited primarily for pet, show, or sporting use

working drawing *n* : a scale drawing of an object to be made or structure to be built intended for direct use by the workman — compare DETAIL DRAWING

working face *n* **1 :** FACE 10a **2 :** the surface (as of a block of stone or wood) to be operated upon or measured from ⟨measure the desired thickness from the *working face*⟩

working fire *n* : a fire requiring considerable work to extinguish : a bad fire

working fit *n* [[1]*working*] : SNUG FIT

working fluid *n* [*working*, pres. part. of [3]*work*] : a fluid working substance

working gauge *n* [*working*, gerund of [3]*work*] : a gauge used in testing work in the process of manufacture

working hole *n* : a hole in the side of a glass furnace through which molten glass is drawn off

working hunter *n* : a horse in a competitive event judged according to the pace, manners, way of going, and jumping style without regard to conformation

working hypothesis *n* [[1]*working*] : a hypothesis adopted as a guide to experiment or investigation or as a basis of action

working load *n* [*working*, gerund of [3]*work*] : the maximum load that a rope or structural member or machine is designed to bear

work·ing·man \'=,=,man, -,maa(ə)n\ *n, pl* **workingmen** [*working* (pres. part. of [3]*work*) + *man*] : one who works for wages usu. at manual labor : one of the working class as distinguished from the professional and business classes

working model *n* : a model of an actual or proposed machine that can do on a small scale the work which the machine itself does or is expected to do ⟨a *working model* of a freight locomotive⟩

working order *n* : a condition of a machine in which it functions according to its nature and purpose ⟨put a watch in good *working order*⟩

working paper *n* [*working*, gerund of [3]*work*] **1 a :** a paper on which tentative figures, memoranda, data, or analyses of accounts are set down during the conduct of a survey (as an audit) of a business **b :** a tentative statement prepared to serve as a basis for discussion or negotiation **2 working papers** *pl* **:** official documents legalizing the employment of a minor ⟨before being employed the boy had to produce his *working papers*⟩

working party *n* **1 :** a body of servicemen detailed to perform an assigned task beyond their ordinary duties **2** *Brit* **:** a committee created to investigate a problem ⟨report of the *working party* on the employment of blind persons —*Brit. Information Services*⟩

working pattern *n* : a pattern made from a master pattern and used in the making of the mold in which the required part is cast

working pit *n* : a mine shaft in which ore is hoisted and workmen are carried

working rod *n* : PUNTY

workings *pl of* WORKING

working sail *n* [*working*, pres. part. of [3]*work*] : one of the sails normally used in all weathers as distinguished from light sails added for light winds

working stress *n* [*working*, gerund of [3]*work*] : the stress to which material may be safely subjected in the course of ordinary use

working substance *n* [*working*, pres. part. of [3]*work*] : a usu. fluid substance that through changes of temperature, volume, and pressure is the means of carrying out thermodynamic processes or cycles (as in a heat engine or a refrigerating machine)

workingwoman \'=,=,=\ *n, pl* **workingwomen** **1 :** a woman who is gainfully employed **2 :** the wife of a workingman

work in process : work in any of the stages through which it passes in being made into a finished product out of raw material

work in progress : work with which an artist or writer is engaged but which is not completed or approaching completion

work lead *n* : LEAD BULLION

work·less \'=ləs\ *adj* [[1]*work* + *-less*] **1** *obs* **:** not accomplishing any work or effect : not functioning **2** *obs* **:** not carried out in practice **3 :** being without work or out of work : UNEMPLOYED, JOBLESS — **work·less·ness** *n* -ES

work load *n* **1 :** the amount of work or of working time expected from or assigned to an employee **2 :** the total amount of work to be performed by a department or other group of workers in a period of time ⟨weekly *work load*⟩

work·man \'=mən\ *n, pl* **workmen** [ME *werkman*, fr. OE *weorcman*, fr. *weorc* work + *man*] **1 :** WORKINGMAN **2 a :** a skilled laborer : ARTISAN, CRAFTSMAN ⟨certain more or less educated *workmen* rough of speech and manner —W.B.Yeats⟩ **3 :** one who creates or fashions esp. with skill and expertness ⟨untiring *workmen*, they have spared no pains to produce a poetry finer than that of any other country —Amy Lowell⟩

workmanlike \'=,=,=\ *adj* [ME *werkmanlike*, fr. *werkman* workman + *like*] : worthy of a good workman : well performed : SKILLFUL ⟨the book is a ~ job, with chronology, bibliography, and index —Louise S. Bechtel⟩ ⟨~ vocalization of a difficult part —Irving Kolodin⟩

[1]**work·man·ly** *adv* [ME *warkmanly*, fr. *werkman*, *warkman* workman + *-ly*, adv. suffix] *archaic* : in a skillful manner ⟨so the blood and tears are drawn —Shak.⟩

[2]**work·man·ly** *adj* [*workman* + *-ly*, adj. suffix] : WORKMANLIKE

work·man·ship \'=,=,ship\ *n* [ME *werkmanschipe*, fr. *werkman* workman + *-schipe* -ship] **1 :** the art or skill of a workman : the execution or manner of making or doing something : CRAFTSMANSHIP; *also* : the quality imparted to a thing in the process of making : the character given to a work by the art or skill of the workman ⟨a vase of exquisite ~⟩ **2 :** something that is effected, made, or produced : MANUFACTURE, WORK; *esp* : something made by manual labor ⟨such roofs . . . are splendid pieces of ~ —Richard Jefferies⟩

workmaster \'=,=,=\ *n* : a master workman

workmate \'=,=\ *n, chiefly Brit* : a fellow worker

workmen's compensation insurance *n* : insurance against statutory damages (as provided by a workmen's compensation act) arising from injury to employees while in the employ of the insured employer

work of art 1 : a product of one of the fine arts; *esp* : a painting or sculpture of high artistic quality **2 :** an act or thing giving high aesthetic satisfaction to the beholder or auditor : something that has value or gives pleasure apart from its practical effect or usefulness ⟨take a detached view of their own lives and look upon them rather as *works of art* —André Maurois⟩

work off *vt* [[3]*work*] **1 :** to dispose of or get rid of by work or activity ⟨*work off* a debt⟩ ⟨pick a fight to *work off* a grudge⟩ : finish up ⟨when current defense contracts are *worked off* —*Time*⟩ **2 :** to print in final form for delivery or further processing : run off ⟨*work off* a poster⟩ ⟨*work off* a job⟩ **3 :** to palm off : pass off ⟨tried to *work off* the poem as his own⟩

work out *vt* **1 :** to effect by labor and exertion ⟨*work out* your own salvation —Phil 2:12 (AV)⟩ ⟨each novel's leading character *works out* his destiny —Otis Fellows⟩ **2 a :** to solve (as a problem) by a process of reasoning or calculation **b :** to devise, arrange, or achieve esp. by resolving difficulties or conflicts ⟨a better route was *worked out* —G.R.Stewart⟩ ⟨*work out* a plan of complete reconstruction —S.P.B.Mais⟩ ⟨*worked out* a compromise agreement that ended the dispute⟩ **c :** DEVELOP, ELABORATE ⟨whole sonata . . . was deeply felt and finely *worked out* —*N.Y.Times*⟩ ⟨though the final situation is not *worked out* with psychological profundity —Leslie Rees⟩ **3 :** to discharge fully (as a debt) by labor instead of money payment ⟨servants who had *worked out* their terms of servitude —R.A.Billington⟩ **4 :** to exhaust (as a mine or vein) by working ~ *vi* **1 a :** to prove effective or practicable or suitable ⟨if the plan *works out* satisfactorily⟩ **b :** to amount to a total or calculated figure : come to a figure — used with *at* ⟨this rate *works out* at an increase of 88°F for every mile . . . towards the center of the earth —W.E.Swinton⟩ **2 :** to go through a training or practice session esp. in an athletic specialty ⟨*works out* daily with sparring partners⟩ **3 :** to work outside the home as hired help : hire out

workout \'=,=\ *n* -s [*work out*] **1 :** a practice game, bout, or run : an exercise designed to test one's fitness or to increase one's fitness esp. for athletic competition ⟨daily ~s with barbells⟩ **2 :** a test or trial for determining ability or capacity or suitability ⟨in the production of dangerous war materials . . . automation has had its most complete ~ —Robert Bendiner⟩

work-out \'=,=\ *adj* [*work out*] *of a market* : not characterized by firm bids and offers

work over *vt* [[3]*work*] **1 :** to subject to thorough examination or study or treatment ⟨shelf stock would get thoroughly *worked over* as shoppers sought out packages with the latest dates —*Modern Packaging*⟩ ⟨spent some time in *working over* the available books —A.T.Weaver⟩ ⟨*working over* not only the edge and point but the entire surface of their artifacts —A.L.Kroeber⟩ **2 a :** to do over : REWORK ⟨saved the play by *working* the first act *over*⟩ ⟨*worked over* the old furniture⟩ **b :** to revise or alter radically or systematically ⟨the frontier . . . had *worked* them *over* inside —W.P.Webb⟩ **3 a :** to beat up or manhandle esp. with deliberate thoroughness ⟨none of them hesitated to *work* a man *over* for shifting a little out of line or talking —R.O.Bowen⟩ ⟨*working* them *over* with sabers, billies, and gun butts —*Time*⟩ **b :** to pick the pockets of **c :** to subject to thorough or systematic artillery fire, bombing, or strafing ⟨destroyers had *worked over* the point with their five-inch guns —Bill Alcine⟩

workpeople \'=,=,=\ *n pl* [[1]*work* + *people*] *chiefly Brit* : WORKERS, EMPLOYEES

work permit *n* : an authorization to work on a given job issued by a union to a nonmember

workpiece \'=,=\ *n* : a piece of work in process of manufacture

workplace \'=,=\ *n* : a place (as a shop or factory) where work is done

work print *n* : a completely edited motion-picture print used as a guide in cutting the original negative from which the final production prints will be made

work relief *n* : relief of the unemployed through wages paid for jobs provided by the government on public works

workroom \'=,=\ *n* : a room used esp. for manual work

works *pl of* WORK, *pres 3d sing of* WORK

works council *n* : a body or committee formed by an employer among workers within his organization for the discussion of problems of industrial relations

work sheet *n* **1 a :** a sheet that is used in making preliminary plans, auxiliary computations, notes, or comments as a guide in doing some piece of work **b :** a specially prepared sheet, pamphlet, or booklet containing data of assistance in planning and accomplishing some piece of work **c :** a working paper used by an accountant to assemble figures for financial statements of a business; *specif* : a sheet with a sufficient number of columns to provide for entering the trial balance, adjusting entries, profit and loss, and balance sheet items **2 a :** a sheet of paper on which are printed exercises and problems to be solved by a student **b :** a leaf or page in a workbook **3 :** JOB TICKET 1

workshop \'=,=\ *n* **1 a :** a small establishment where manufacturing or craftwork is carried on by a proprietor with or without helpers and often without power machinery — compare FACTORY, MACHINE SHOP **b :** a place or a method of literary or artistic creation ⟨not what the composer tells us about his ~ but what he is able to convey . . . through his finished work alone —Eric Blom⟩ **2 a :** a course or seminar emphasizing free discussion, exchange of ideas, demonstration of methods, and practical application of skills and principles given mainly for adults already employed in the field esp. of the social sciences and the practical and fine arts ⟨summer ~ in short-story writing⟩ ⟨choreographers' ~⟩ **b :** LABORATORY 1b

work-shy \'=,=\ *adj* [[1]*work* + *shy*] : disinclined or unwilling to work : LAZY

works manager *n* : an official in a manufacturing company who is usu. the head of the production departments

work song *n* : a song sung in rhythm with work — compare CHANTEY

work spreading *n* [[1]*work* + *spreading*, gerund of *spread*] : a method of reducing unemployment by the arrangement of work and working hours of employees so as to spread the available work among the largest practicable number of workers

workstand \'=,=\ *n* [[2]*work* + *stand*] : WORKTABLE

workstock \'=,=\ *n* : farm livestock (as horses and mules) kept for labor rather than for production of a marketable product

work stone *n* : an inclined grooved stone or iron plate to conduct molten lead from the hearth in a lead smelting furnace to the metal pot

work stoppage *n* : concerted cessation of work by a group of employees usu. more spontaneous and less serious than a predetermined and organized strike

work-stopper \'=,=,=\ *n, chiefly Austral* : a labor organizer who induces workmen to strike in order to obtain their objectives

work-study program *n* : a high school or college student's program so planned as to allow for work experience

worktable \'=,=,=\ *n* : a table for holding working materials and implements; *esp* : a small table with drawers and other conveniences for needlework

work ticket *n* **1 :** JOB TICKET 1 **2 :** JOB ORDER

work train *n* : a train for transporting men and materials for construction, repairs, or maintenance of a railroad

work up *vb* [[3]*work*] *vt* **1 :** to stir up : ROUSE, EXCITE ⟨*work up* indignation against the murderers —C.H.Sykes⟩ : summon up ⟨the novelist can *work up* sufficient interest in them to record their minor and pathetic self-deceptions —Dachine Rainer⟩ ⟨*work up* a sweat in a gymnasium⟩ **2 :** DEVELOP, ELABORATE ⟨to have *worked up* a scheme to the point where it is necessary to have outside capital —Mary Austin⟩ ⟨*work up* some strong emotional scenes —Henry Hewes⟩ ⟨*work up* a comedy act⟩ **3 :** to keep (a crew) at work upon needless jobs for punishment ~ *vi* **1 :** to rise gradually and steadily in intensity or emotional tone ⟨story develops . . . and *works up* to a brilliant conclusion —*Sydney (Australia) Bull.*⟩ ⟨afternoon thunderstorm beginning to *work up* —G.R.Stewart⟩ **2 :** to improve in efficiency ⟨the fleet . . . has been gradually *working up* as it steams eastward —H.W.Baldwin⟩ **3 :** to rise to the printing surface — used of a space, lead, or other part of a form not intended to print

work-up \'=,=\ *n* -s [*work up*] **1 :** an unintended mark upon a printed sheet caused by the rising in the chase of a space, lead, or piece of furniture while the job is on the press or the form is being molded for plating **2 :** the laboratory, X-ray, and other procedures involved in the diagnostic study of a patient with regard to his symptoms or complaints ⟨cardiac *work-up*⟩ ⟨entered the hospital for a gastric *work-up*⟩

workweek \'=,=\ *n* [[1]*work* + *week*] : the hours or days of work in a calendar week ⟨40-hour ~⟩ ⟨a 5-day ~⟩

workwoman \'=,=,=\ *n, pl* **workwomen** : a woman who works : a female worker

[1]**world** \'wərld, *esp before pause or consonant* -rəld; 'wə̄ld\ *n* -s [ME *weorld*, *world*, fr. OE *weoruld*, *woruld*, *worold* human existence, this world, age; akin to OHG *weralt*, *worolt* age, world, ON *veröld*; all fr. a prehistoric WGmc-NGmc compound whose first constituent is represented by OE *wer* man and whose second constituent is akin to OE *yldo* age, *ald* old — more at VIRILE, OLD] **1 a :** the earthly state of human existence : this present life **b :** a future state of existence : the life after death — usu. used with a qualifier ⟨a better ~ where he expected to meet all . . . who had gone before him —Van Wyck Brooks⟩ ⟨the next ~⟩ **2 a :** the earth with all its inhabitants and all things upon it ⟨a Great Spirit who rules the ~ —F.J.Haskin⟩ ⟨a voyage around the ~⟩ **b :** something (as a sphere or whole) held to resemble or suggest the world **3 :** individual experience of or concern with life on earth : the sum of the affairs which affect the individual : course of life : CAREER ⟨I hope the ~ goes well with you⟩ **4 :** all the inhabitants of the earth : the whole of mankind : the human race : human society ⟨the whole ~ was redeemed by Christ —H.P. Liddon⟩ **5 :** the concerns of the earth and its affairs as distinguished from heaven : the pursuits and interests of this life as distinguished from the life to come : the present existence and its interests : temporal or mundane affairs ⟨I too love the earth and hate the ~ —George Santayana⟩ **6 :** secular affairs or interests as distinguished from religious or clerical **7 :** the earth and the heavens : the entire universe as an orderly system : the system of created things **8 :** a part of the universe constituting a distinct entity and usu. possessing one or more peculiar and identifying characteristics ⟨the lower ~⟩ — see NETHERWORLD, UNDERWORLD **9 :** the section of mankind engrossed in the concerns or pleasures of this present life and as a result often held to constitute the ungodly part of mankind : worldly persons **10 a :** a particular division, section, or generation of the inhabitants of the earth distinguished by living together at the same place or at the same time **b** (1) **:** a more or less definite class or division of persons distinguished by some usu. specified characteristic (as interests or occupation) ⟨insistence upon a more complete devotion from the performing and listening ~s —J.N.Burk⟩ (2) **:** the sphere, domain, region, or realm of the interests of a particular group of persons ⟨my experiences in the academic ~ —Hans Meyerhoff⟩ ⟨the ~ of American history⟩ **11 :** human society : the scene of the customs, practices, and interests of men as social beings : public or social affairs and occupations : social or business life, manners, and usages ⟨voices which we hear in solitude . . . grow faint and inaudible as we enter into the ~ —R.W.Emerson⟩ **12 :** a period or age of human history having certain peculiar and identifying characteristics ⟨the ~ of the 19th century⟩ **13 :** a part, division, or section of the earth together with its inhabitants and concerns that is a separate independent unit : a division of the globe with its inhabitants : a part of the globe as known or contemplated at a particular period or by a particular people — see NEW WORLD, OLD WORLD **14 :** the sphere or scene of one's life and action : the area of one's interests and activities : the realm in which one moves or lives ⟨among the friends of his three ~s, the intellectuals, the . . . family circle, and the farmers —H.S. Canby⟩ **15 :** an indefinitely great multitude or quantity : a large number : an infinite or vast amount ⟨there were ~s of cattle in Texas —E.C.Abbott & Helena Smith⟩ ⟨you will find a ~ of delight in some of the lovely pieces —*Irish Digest*⟩ — sometimes used adverbially with *a* or in pl. ⟨a ~ too wide⟩ ⟨his vernacular was ~s away from her formal art —Carl Van Doren⟩ **16 a :** the whole body of living persons : people in general : society at large : PUBLIC **b :** the people of a particular district or area in general : local society **17 :** WORLD'S PEOPLE **18 :** a group of beings or things having certain characteristics in common and held to constitute a whole **19 :** one of the grand divisions or primary groups of natural objects : KINGDOM 6 ⟨animal ~⟩ ⟨inorganic ~⟩ **20 :** a planet or other celestial body; *esp* : one that is inhabited and the scene of interests analogous to those of earth dwellers **21 :** an area of the hand or fingers held by palmists to represent mind in the case of the upper division or material matters in the case of the middle division or sensual or base qualities in the case of the lower division: **a :** an area of a finger constituted by a phalanx or of the thumb constituted by a phalanx or the Mount of Venus ⟨the three ~s of palmistry apply just as much to the thumb as to any of the fingers —W.G.Benham⟩ **b :** a division of the hand constituted by the fingers or by the area between the base of the fingers and the middle of the palm or by the area between the middle of the palm and the wrist — **against the world :** against all opposition : in the face of all mankind — **for worlds :** for all the wealth in the world : on any account — usu. used in the negative ⟨I wouldn't stand in his way *for worlds* —W.S.Gilbert⟩ — **in the world :** among innumerable possibilities : EVER — used as an intensive ⟨where *in the world* did you go⟩ ⟨what *in the world* is it⟩ — **out of this world :** of the highest quality : remarkably fine : of extraordinary excellence : MAGNIFICENT, SUPERB ⟨her voice is simply *out of this world*⟩ ⟨genuine Belgian cooking that is *out of this world* —T.H. Fielding⟩

[2]**world** \"\ *adj* **1 :** of or relating to the world ⟨a ~ hypothesis⟩ ⟨a ~ championship⟩ **2 a :** extending or found throughout the world : UNIVERSAL, WORLDWIDE ⟨~ affairs⟩ ⟨~ problems⟩ ⟨a ~ language⟩ ⟨~ culture⟩ **b :** involving or applying to the whole world ⟨~ government⟩ ⟨a ~ state⟩ ⟨~ politics⟩ **c :** known and usu. renowned throughout the world ⟨~ figures⟩ ⟨a ~ artist⟩

world-beater \'=,=,=\ *n* : one that does or is able to excel all others of its kind (as in quality or performance) : CHAMPION ⟨a very good artist without being a *world-beater* —*Sydney (Australia) Bull.*⟩ ⟨a story . . . that is a *world-beater*, bar none —*Blue Bk.*⟩

world communion sunday *n, usu cap W&C&S* : the first Sunday in October on which ecumenical Christians around the world celebrate Holy Communion as an expression of their Christian unity

world day of prayer *usu cap W&D&P* : the first Friday in Lent observed by ecumenical Christians around the world as a day of worship and prayer for missions

world federalism *n* **1 :** federalism on a worldwide basis **2** *usu cap* **a :** the principles and policies of the World Federalists **b :** the body or movement composed of World Federalists

[1]**world federalist** *adj, usu cap W&F* : of, relating to, or associated with World Federalism ⟨*World Federalist* principles⟩

[2]**world federalist** *n* **1 :** an adherent or advocate of world federalism **2** *usu cap* **:** a member of a movement arising after World War II advocating the formation of a federal union of the nations of the world with limited but positive governmental powers

world·ful \-d,fu̇l\ *n, pl* **worldfuls** [[1]*world* + *-ful*] : as much or as many as would fill a world ⟨a whole ~ of light and joy —William Black⟩

world ground *n* : the underlying basis of reality

world·ing \-diŋ\ *n* -s [alter. (influenced by [2]*-ing*) of *worldling*] : WORLDLING

world island *n, usu cap W & I* : the landmass consisting of Europe, Asia, and Africa ⟨who rules the *World Island* commands the world —H.J.Mackinder⟩ — used chiefly in geopolitics; compare HEARTLAND

world·let \-dlə̇t\ *n* -s [[1]*world* + *-let*] : a little world

world·li·ness \-dlēnə̇s, -lin-\ *n* -ES [ME *worldlynesse*, fr. *worldly* + *-nesse* -ness] : the quality or state of being worldly : a disposition or tendency to emphasize the things of the world rather than those of the spirit : devotion to or love of worldly affairs usu. accompanied by neglect of religious duties or spiritual needs

world·ling \-dliŋ, -lēŋ\ *n* -s [1*world* + *-ling*] **1 :** a person engrossed in the concerns of this present world : one devoted to this world and its interests, pleasures, and enjoyments : a worldly or worldly-minded person ⟨among ~*s* unlikely to be offended by a whiff of the smoking room —J.B.Boothroyd⟩ **2 :** a citizen or inhabitant of the world : EARTHLING 1 ⟨the new element where . . . the pressure would kill a ~ in a few seconds —J.E.Belliveau⟩

world·ly \'wər(ə)l(d)lē, 'wə̄l(d)-, -(d)li\ *adj, sometimes* -ER/-EST [ME, fr. OE *woruldlic*, fr. *woruld* world + *-lic* -ly] **1 :** of or relating to this world : associated with the earthly existence of man : earthly rather than heavenly or spiritual ⟨concentration upon ~ goods and ~ advancement —Lewis Mumford⟩ ⟨the ~ kind of charm one associates with cabaret singers —Henry Hewes⟩ ⟨~ fame⟩ **2** *archaic* **:** of, relating to, or associated with the earth or its inhabitants : EARTHLY 1a ⟨~ creatures⟩ **3 :** interested in or concerned with the enjoyments of this present existence : devoted to the world and its pursuits : characterized by interest in and concentration on practical and immediate affairs and concerns (as success, gain, pleasure, or self-esteem) and indifference to matters spiritual ⟨the most ~ of the eighteenth-century ecclesiastics —Hilaire Belloc⟩ ⟨the fashionable talk of her ~ rival —W.M.Thackeray⟩ **4 :** WORLDLY-WISE **syn** see EARTHLY

worldly-minded \¦==¦==\ *adj* **:** devoted to or engrossed in worldly interests : having one's thoughts or interests set upon things of this world ⟨one society is genuinely pious, another *worldly-minded* —H.L.Kroeber⟩ — **worldly-minded·ness** *n*

worldly-wise \¦==¦=\ *adj* [ME, fr. *worldly* in a worldly manner (fr. *worldly*, adj.) + *wise*] **:** wise as to things and ways of this world

worldly wise·man \-'wīz,man, -,mən\ *n, often cap both Ws* [*worldly-wise* + *man*] **:** one wise in the ways of the world ⟨a *worldly wiseman* among idealists —R.M.Lovett⟩

world power *n* [trans. of G *weltmacht*] **:** a political unit (as a nation or state) powerful enough to affect the entire world by its influence or actions — compare GREAT POWER

world premiere *n* **:** the first regular performance (as of a theatrical production) anywhere

worlds *pl of* WORLD

world's end *n* **:** the end or most distant part of the world : the remotest regions of the earth — compare THULE

world series *n* **1 :** a series of baseball games played in the fall of each year between the pennant winners of the major leagues to decide the professional championship of the U.S. **2 :** a championship contest resembling the world series ⟨the *world series* of dogdom⟩

world's fair *n* **:** an international exposition usu. featuring exhibits and participants from all over the world ⟨the sort of temporary structure you see at a *world's fair* —E.B.White⟩

world's fair plant *n, usu cap W&F* [so called fr. its use as a garden decoration at the Chicago World's Fair of 1893] **:** SUMMER CYPRESS

world-shaking \'=,==\ *adj* **:** sufficiently important to affect decisively the entire world : EARTHSHAKING ⟨the contest . . . was no *world-shaking* affair —G.C.Sellery⟩

world soul *n* **:** a spiritual being having the same relation to the world as a whole that the soul has to the individual being : an animating spirit or creative principle of the universe related to the world as the human soul is to the body : an intelligent animating, indwelling principle of the cosmos held to be its organizing or integrating cause or its source of motion — compare ABSOLUTE 2a(1), ATMAN, NOUS 1a

world's people *n pl* **:** persons who are not members of one's own religious group — used chiefly by the Friends and the Shakers

world spirit *n* **1 :** the animating spirit of the universe : WORLD SOUL **2 :** 2GOD b(1), b(2), b(3)

world's record *n* **:** a record officially recognized as the best established anywhere in the world ⟨set a new *world's record* for the 100-yard dash⟩

world's wonder *n* **:** SOAPWORT 1

world view *n* [trans. of G *weltanschauung*] **:** WELTANSCHAUUNG ⟨the ceremonial cycle . . . reflects and reaffirms the Hopi *world view* —Laura Thompson⟩ ⟨each individual has his own experiences and out of them forms his *world view* —J.L. Myres⟩

world war *n* **:** a war involving most of the nations or a preponderant portion of the territory of the earth

1world·ward \'wər(ə)ldwərd\ *adv* [1*world* + *-ward*] **:** in the direction of or toward the world ⟨went ~ from the island —Bayard Taylor⟩

2worldward \"\ *adj* **:** directed toward or facing the world ⟨~ conduct⟩

world-weariness \'=,===\ *n* **:** the quality or state of being world-weary

world-weary \'=,==\ *adj* **:** weary of the world or wearied by the life of the world; *esp* **:** bored by overindulgence in material pleasures ⟨a *world-weary* young man⟩ ⟨our *world-weary* generation⟩

worldwide \'=¦=\ *adj* **:** extended or extending throughout the entire world ⟨movement toward ~ unity in the churches —Liston Pope⟩ ⟨a ~ empire⟩ ⟨~ disarmament⟩

world-wise \'=,=\ *adj* **:** WORLDLY-WISE ⟨a statesman . . . experienced and *world-wise* —*Fortnightly Rev.*⟩

world without end *adv* [ME *world withouten end*, fr. *world* + *withouten* without + *end*] **:** as if in a state of existence having no end : ETERNALLY, FOREVER ⟨as it was in the beginning, is now, and ever shall be, *world without end* —*Bk. of Com. Prayer*⟩

1world-without-end \'==,='=\ *adj* **:** lasting for all time : EVERLASTING, ETERNAL, PERPETUAL ⟨a time . . . too short to make a *world-without-end* bargain in —Shak.⟩

2world-without-end \"\ *n* **:** a state of existence having no end : ETERNITY, PERPETUITY

1worm \'wərm, 'wə̄m, 'wəim\ *n* -s *often attrib* [ME, fr. OE *wyrm* serpent, dragon, worm; akin to OHG *wurm* serpent, dragon, worm, ON *ormr*, Goth *waurms* serpent, L *vermis* worm, Gk *rhomos* woodworm] **1 a :** EARTHWORM; *broadly* **:** an annelid worm **b :** any of numerous relatively small more or less elongated usu. naked and soft-bodied animals resembling an earthworm: as (1) **:** a member of the old group Vermes (2) **:** an insect larva; *esp* **:** one that is a destructive grub, caterpillar, or maggot (3) **:** SHIPWORM (4) **:** BLINDWORM **2 a :** a human being resembling a worm or reptile as an object of contempt, loathing, or pity : WRETCH ⟨made me feel a ~ for my ignorance —H.J.Laski⟩ ⟨who, like the ~*s* they are, hide under the rock of the Fifth Amendment —*Phoenix Flame*⟩ **b :** something that inwardly torments or devours in a manner suggestive of the gnawing, boring, or working of a worm ⟨the ~ of care . . . gives her no rest —Padraic Fallon⟩ ⟨the ~ of conscience gnaws incessantly⟩ **c** *obs* **:** an impulse, perversity, or marked irrationality of mind **3** *archaic* **:** SNAKE, SERPENT, DRAGON **4 a :** a disorder caused by the presence of parasitic worms in the body and esp. in the intestines : HELMINTHIASIS — usu. used in pl. **b** *Scot* **:** TOOTHACHE **5 a :** LYTTA **b :** VERMIS **6 :** something (as a mechanical device) spiral or vermiculate in form or appearance: as **a :** a double corkscrew on the end of a rammer for extracting a wad or ball from a muzzle-loading gun **b :** the thread of a screw **c :** a short revolving screw whose threads gear with the teeth of a worm wheel or a rack — compare WORM THREAD **d** (1) **:** a tube or pipe twisted into coils; *also* **:** a system of such coiled tube or pipe (2) **:** a spiral condensing tube used in distilling **e** (1) **:** ARCHIMEDES' SCREW (2) **:** a conveyor working on the principle of such a screw **7 :** something resembling or suggestive of an earthworm ⟨far away . . . a miniature ~ of train rolled tinily along the embankment —Bruce Marshall⟩ ⟨in some line regiments a black ~ in the gold lace . . . denotes a perpetual mourning for some famous general —*N.Y.Times*⟩

2worm \"\ *vb* -ED/-ING/-S *vi* **1 :** to hunt or dig for worms ⟨birds and children are ~*ing* on the lawn after the rain⟩ **2 a :** to move, go, or proceed sinuously in or as if in the manner of a worm ⟨~*ed* through the snow and peered over a snow-covered rock beside the roadway —F.V.W.Mason⟩ ⟨we ~*ed* into the . . . office —Vincent McHugh⟩ ⟨the preposterous irrelevancy which ~*ed* through his mind —Marcia Davenport⟩ **b** (1) **:** to proceed or make one's way insidiously or deviously often with harmful intent or effect — usu. used with *into* ⟨spies ~ into important positions⟩ ⟨plans to ~ into his teacher's favor⟩ ⟨they have ~*ed* into the government and the labor movement —*Newsweek*⟩ (2) **:** to evade or escape in indirect or subtle fashion : WRIGGLE — usu. used with *out of* ⟨hopes to ~ out of his difficulties⟩ ⟨will do wrong and then try to ~ out of his punishment if he can⟩ **3 :** to lay a small line or yarn in the interstices between the strands of a larger rope in order to make an even surface before parceling and serving **4 :** to fish with worm as bait ~ *vt* **1 :** to cut the lytta from under the tongue of (a dog) to prevent madness **2 :** to make a screw thread on ⟨a machine that ~*s* screws⟩ **3 :** to cause to be eaten by worms ⟨a ~*ed* tree stump⟩ ⟨finds that his winter suit has been badly ~*ed*⟩ ⟨the old beams are firm and have not been ~*ed*⟩ **4 :** to remove or clear out worms from ⟨the dog has been ~*ed*⟩ **5 a :** to cause to move or proceed in or as if in the manner of a worm ⟨solid rock into which the drill had ~*ed* its long tongue —Thomas Wood †1950⟩ ⟨~ his big brown hand into his trousers pocket —J.N.Hall⟩ ⟨the queue ~*ed* itself on a little —Jan Struther⟩ ⟨~*ed* the strip deep into the American public consciousness —Coulton Waugh⟩ **b :** to insinuate or introduce (oneself) by devious or subtle means — usu. used with *into* ⟨seeks to ~ himself into a commanding position⟩ ⟨the group is ~*ing* itself into public favor⟩ **6 :** to wind rope or yarn spirally round and between the strands of (as a cable) before serving ⟨~ rope⟩ **7 a :** to obtain or extract by artful or insidious questioning ⟨determined not to let them ~ the secret from him⟩ — usu. used with *out of* ⟨~*ed* this information out of the prisoner —Shipley Thomas⟩ ⟨had ~*ed* out of them what they had been doing —Oscar Wilde⟩ **b :** to procure or acquire by pleading, asking, or persuading ⟨is trying to ~ a pension from the government⟩ — usu. used with *out of* ⟨is expected in time to ~ all the money out of him⟩ ⟨is ~*ing* permission out of his parent⟩ **8 :** to clean or draw a wad or cartridge from (a muzzle-loading firearm) with a wormer

worm bark *n* **1 :** the bark of the cabbage bark sometimes used in medicine as a vermifuge — compare SURINAM CABBAGE TREE **2 :** CABBAGE BARK

wormcast \'=,=\ *n* **1 :** a cylindrical mass of earth voided by an earthworm **2 :** the fossil trail of a worm

worm conveyor *n* **:** CONVEYER 2a(8)

worm drive *n* **:** a drive or propulsion gear comprising a worm engaged with a driver gear usu. at right angles

worm-eaten \'=,==\ *adj* [ME *worm-eten*, fr. 1*worm* + *eten*, past part. of *eten* to eat] **1 a :** eaten or burrowed by worms ⟨*worm-eaten* timber⟩ **b :** resembling something filled with wormholes : PITTED ⟨the material has a *worm-eaten* appearance⟩ **2 :** WORN-OUT, ANTIQUATED, DECAYED ⟨attempting new projects with *worm-eaten* methods⟩ ⟨wanted to update the *worm-eaten* regulations⟩

worm-eating warbler \'=,==-\ *n* [1*worm* + *eating*, pres. part. of *eat*] **:** a warbler (*Helmitheros vermivorus*) of the eastern U.S. of chiefly terrestrial habits that is olivaceous above and creamy below with black and buffy stripes on the crown

worm eel *n* **:** any of numerous small wormlike burrowing tropical eels (family Echelidae) in some respects resembling the large conger eels

worm·er \'wərmər\ *n* -s **1 :** one that worms; *specif* **:** a drug or medicine used to remove or clear out worms (as from dogs or poultry) **2 a :** a double corkscrew on the end of a rammer for extracting a wad or cartridge from a muzzle-loading gun **b :** a rammer with such a screw

worm fence *n* **:** a zigzag fence with each section consisting of usu. six to eight rails that interlock with the rails of adjacent sections and are supported by crossed poles — called also *snake fence, Virginia fence*

worm gear *n* **1 :** WORM WHEEL **2 :** a gear of a worm and a worm wheel working together

worm gear 2

worm grass *n* **1 :** PINKROOT **2 :** a European white-flowered stonecrop (*Sedum album*)

wormhole \'=,=\ *n* **:** the burrow of a worm; *esp* **:** a minute hole in wood, cloth, or paper made by a worm or larva

wor·mi·an bone \'wȯ(r)mēən-\ *n, usu cap W* [NL *wormianus* of Worm, fr. Ole *Worm* †1654 Dan. physician + L *-ianus* -ian] **:** a small irregular plate of bone interposed in a suture between large cranial bones

wormier *comparative of* WORMY

wormiest *superlative of* WORMY

worming *n* -S [fr. gerund of 2*worm*] **1 :** the action of one that worms **2 :** small stuff used to worm a rope or cable

worm·ish \'wərmish\ *adj* [1*worm* + *-ish*] **:** WORMLIKE

worm·less \-mlə̇s\ *adj* **:** free from or lacking worms

wormlike \'=,=\ *adj* **:** resembling or suggestive of a worm : VERMIFORM

worm·ling \-mliŋ\ *n* -S [1*worm* + *-ling*] **1 :** a small worm **2 :** WRETCH ⟨the poor ~*s* of the earth⟩

worm lion *n* **:** any of various flies (genus *Vermileo*) of the family Rhagionidae having larvae that excavate pits in the sand like those of the ant lion

worm lizard *n* **:** a wormlike limbless lizard of the genus *Amphisbaena*

worm moss *n* **:** CORSICAN MOSS

worm-nest \'=,=\ *n* **:** a swelling or nodule in the brisket or flank of cattle containing worms of the genus *Onchocerca*

worm out *vt* [2*worm* + *out*] **1 :** to push or force out by subtle pressure or undermining ⟨is trying to *worm* his partner *out* of the business⟩ **2 :** to dispossess or take from by subtle or deceptive means ⟨his associates hope to *worm* him *out* of his inheritance⟩

worm powder *n* [1*worm*] **:** an anthelmintic powder

wormroot \'=,=\ *n* **:** PINKROOT

worms *pl of* WORM, *pres 3d sing of* WORM

wormseed \'=,=\ *n* [ME *wyrmsed*, fr. *wyrm, worm* worm + *sed* seed] **1 :** any of various plants whose seeds possess anthelmintic properties: as **a :** any of several ragweeds (as *Artemisia santonica* and *A. pauciflora*) **b :** MEXICAN TEA **2 a :** the fruit of the Mexican tea **b :** SANTONICA 2; *also* **:** LEVANT WORMSEED 1

wormseed mustard *n* **:** a slender yellow-flowered mustard (*Erysimum cheiranthoides*) that is often troublesome as a weed and has seed formerly reputed to be anthelmintic

wormseed oil *n* **:** either of two essential oils: **a :** LEVANT WORMSEED OIL **b :** CHENOPODIUM OIL

worm's-eye view \'=,=-\ *n* **:** a view as if by a worm from below or the underside ⟨from both the bird's-eye view of the executive and the *worm's-eye view* of the employee, she has been familiar with industrial problems —*Current Biog.*⟩

worm shell *n* **:** a shell of *Vermetus* or a related genus

worm snake *n* **:** any of various small harmless burrowing snakes of wormlike appearance: as **a :** THUNDER SNAKE 2 **b :** BLIND SNAKE

worm thread *n* **:** a form of screw thread suitable for the worms of worm gearing

worm trail *n* **:** any of various markings in fossiliferous rocks made by the passage of extinct worms

worm tube *n* **1 :** the membranous shell-like tube made by many marine worms; *also* **:** such a tube when fossilized **2 :** WORM 6d(2)

wormweed \'=,=\ *n* **:** PINKROOT

worm wheel *n* **:** a toothed wheel gearing with the threads of a worm

worm-wheel hob thread *n* **:** the thread form on hobs used for cutting worm-wheel teeth or worm threads

worm wire *n* **:** FISH TAPE

wormwood \'=,=\ *n* [ME *wormwode*, alter. (influenced by 1*worm* & *wode* wood) of *wermode*, fr. OE *wermōd* wormwood, absinthe; akin to OHG *wermuota* wormwood] **1 :** a plant of the genus *Artemisia; esp* **:** a European woody herb (*A. absinthium*) of a bitter slightly aromatic taste used chiefly in making absinthe **2 :** something bitter, galling, or grievous : BITTERNESS ⟨the gall and ~ of being a cripple —Dixon Wecter⟩ ⟨it was ~ for him to accept charity⟩

wormwood oil *n* **:** a dark green to brown bitter narcotic essential oil obtained from the leaves and tops of a wormwood (*Artemisia absinthium*) and used as a flavoring agent in liqueurs and esp. formerly in medicine as a tonic and anthelmintic — called also *absinthe oil*

wormwood sage *n* **:** a perennial white or tawny tomentose sagebrush (*Artemisia frigida*) with a stout woody crown, small leaves twice or thrice ternately divided, and flower heads with many long hairs between the flowers

wormy \'wərmē, 'wə̄m-, 'wəim-, -mi\ *adj* -ER/-EST [ME, fr. 1*worm* + *-y*] **1 :** attacked or burrowed by worms ⟨~ wood⟩ ⟨a ~ apple⟩ **2 :** infested or afflicted with worms ⟨~ fish⟩ ⟨a ~ dog⟩ **3 :** full of or abounding in worms ⟨the ~ soil⟩ ⟨a ~ grave⟩ **4 :** resembling or suggestive of the appearance, habits, or condition of a worm ⟨~ lengths of licorice candy⟩ ⟨all the ~ expressions indicative of bad conscience, false modesty, and genteelism —J.M.Barzun⟩

wormy halibut *n* **:** Pacific halibut infected with a myxosporidian protozoan (*Unicapsula muscularis*) that invades the muscle fibers and forms long swollen cysts which make the flesh unsuitable for table use

worn [ME] *past part of* WEAR

worn-down \'=¦=\ *adj* **1 :** showing the effect of wear ⟨a *worn-down* pair of shoes⟩ ⟨the *worn-down* riverbed⟩ ⟨a *worn-down* estate⟩ **2 :** nervously exhausted or fatigued ⟨a *worn-down* woman weary of eternal housework⟩ ⟨a *worn-down* and enfeebled old man⟩

worn·ness \'wōrnnə̇s, 'wȯr-\ *n* -ES **:** the quality or state of being worn ⟨overhead rehearsal lights . . . drained the color from the scenery and accentuated its wrinkled ~ —Truman Capote⟩

worn-out \'=¦=\ *adj* [fr. past part. of *wear out*] **1 :** used, damaged, or worn to the extent of being nearly or completely useless or unserviceable : DILAPIDATED ⟨an old *worn-out* suit⟩ ⟨a *worn-out* automobile⟩ **2 :** entirely spent or exhausted in strength, energy, or vitality : DISSIPATED, DEPLETED ⟨fertilizer was applied to *worn-out* soils —P.E.James⟩ ⟨buying *worn-out* horses and cattle⟩ **3 :** being out of fashion or use : STALE, TRITE, HACKNEYED ⟨a recurrence of *worn-out* adjectives makes much of his work monotonous —Roland Mathias⟩ ⟨the poet is betrayed by clichés and *worn-out* figures of speech —Burges Johnson⟩ — **worn-out·ness** *n* -ES

wo·ro·ni·na·ce·ae \wə,rōnə'nāsē,ē\ *n pl, cap* [NL, fr. *Woronina*, genus of fungi (fr. Michael S. *Woronin* †1903 Russ. mycologist) + *-aceae*] *in some classifications* **:** a family of simple fungi (order Chytridiales) distinguished from others of the order by biflagellate zoospores

worral *or* **worrel** *var of* WARAL

wor·ri·cow \'wəri,kü\ *n* [1*worry* + *cow* (goblin)] *Scot* **:** BUGABOO, HOBGOBLIN; *specif* **:** DEVIL

worried *adj* [fr. past part. of 1*worry*] **1 :** mentally troubled or concerned : DISTRESSED ⟨they were perplexed, vexed and ~ —Ernie Pyle⟩ **2 :** marked or accompanied by worry ⟨a ~ frown⟩ ⟨made one last ~ check of their patients —J.P.O'Neill⟩ ⟨gave one of his ~ mornings to a . . . scouting of proposed contracts —J.G.Cozzens⟩ — **wor·ried·ly** \'wər·¦ə̇dlē, 'wə·r¦, ¦ēd-, -li\ *adv*

wor·ri·er \¦ēə(r)\ *n* -S **:** one that worries

wor·ri·less \¦ələ̇s\ *adj* [2*worry* + *-less*] **:** free from care or worries

wor·ri·ment \¦ēmənt, ¦im-\ *n* -S [1*worry* + *-ment*] **:** an act or instance of worrying; *also* **:** TROUBLE, WORRY ⟨when the news spread . . . there was ~, fear, anger —A.S.Romer⟩ ⟨my lameness . . . was another ~ —Hamlin Garland⟩

wor·ri·some \¦ēsəm, ¦is-\ *adj* [*worry* + *-some*] **1 :** causing distress or worry ⟨there arises . . . a particularly ~ predicament —P.B.Rice⟩ ⟨the most ~ job on the flight deck —Richard Thruelson⟩ ⟨nothing more ~ than strong enemy probing patrols —E.J.Kahn⟩ **2 :** inclined to worry or fret ⟨she will be efficiently ~ about his sore throats, headaches —H.A. Overstreet⟩ ⟨the conviction of my more ~ friends that the two extremes . . . will join forces to destroy the democratic system —T.N.Stern⟩ — **wor·ri·some·ly** *adv*

1wor·rit \'wərə̇t\ *vb* -ED/-ING/-S [alter. of 1*worry*] *vt, dial Eng* **:** VEX, DISTRESS, WORRY ~ *vi, dial Eng* **:** to become worried or show anxiety or concern

2worrit \"\ *n* -S *dial Eng* **:** a worried condition; *also* **:** WORRY, TROUBLE

1wor·ry \'wər·¦ē, 'wə·r¦, ¦i\ *vb* -ED/-ING/-ES [ME *wirien, werien, worien* to strangle, worry with the teeth, fr. OE *wyrgan* to strangle; akin to OHG *wurgen* to strangle, ON *virgill* halter, Lith *veržti* to constrict, press, OE *wringan* to wring] *vt* **1** *dial Brit* **:** CHOKE, STRANGLE **2 a :** to harass by tearing, biting, or snapping esp. at the throat ⟨wolves ~ the sheep⟩ ⟨the dog is ~*ing* a bone⟩ **b :** to bite at or upon ⟨*worried* his lower lip with his teeth —Jack Dillon⟩ ⟨pounced on a hangnail and *worried* it with her teeth —Edna Ferber⟩ **c :** to touch, poke, or disturb (something) repeatedly ⟨*worried* his breakfast rather than ate it —Charles Dickens⟩ ⟨snores that seemed to ~ the back of her nose —Richard Llewellyn⟩ ⟨was ~*ing* the pattern of the carpet with his toes⟩ ⟨is learning to ~ the sword of his opponent⟩ **d :** to change the position of, convey, or adjust usu. in a specified place by repeated pushing, hauling, or moving back and forth ⟨Lucas *worried* off the cap —John Updike⟩ — often used with *into* ⟨we inched a log to the bank . . . and *worried* it into the stream —Kenneth Roberts⟩ ⟨the heavy implement had to be lifted . . ., *worried* into position, bolted into place —*Time*⟩ **3 a :** to assail with rough or aggressive attack or treatment : HARASS, TORMENT ⟨it was unseemly to the last degree that the disciples . . . should ~ and vex each other with injurious treatment —William Cowper⟩ ⟨the artillery *worries* the enemy with intermittent shelling⟩ ⟨a ghost will ~ him to the grave —Ernest Beaglehole⟩ **b :** to subject to persistent or nagging attention or effort ⟨France's government amended and *worried* the agreement right up to the last moment —*Time*⟩ ⟨no other play in which Shakespeare *worries* a word like that —William Empson⟩ ⟨opinions long since discussed and *worried* to the bone —*Current History*⟩ — often used with *out* ⟨will ~ out the meaning of a pamphlet . . . beyond his capacity —J.A.R.Pimlott⟩ ⟨professors . . . are apt to ~ all the light and joy out of knowledge —M.B.Smith⟩ ⟨hotels were ~*ing* out ways to increase services —P.J.C.Friedlander⟩ **c :** to plague or beset with requests or demands : IMPORTUNE ⟨needled and nudged and *worried* him till . . . he consented —Ellery Sedgwick⟩ ⟨the child *worries* its parents with questions⟩ — often used with *out* ⟨teacher . . . began to ~ the life out of me to complete it —David Fairchild⟩ **4 :** to afflict with mental distress or agitation : make anxious : FRET, TROUBLE ⟨a routine task which permits their minds to wander and . . . doesn't ~ them at night —W.J.Reilly⟩ ⟨his careful repetitions, his imaginative shortcuts . . . ~ the academic mind —Margery Bailey⟩ ⟨what's ~*ing* you —Robert Keable⟩ ~ *vi* **1** *dial Brit* **:** to become choked or strangled : CHOKE **2 :** to move, proceed, or progress by unceasing or difficult effort : STRUGGLE ⟨the ancient car *worries* up the hill⟩ — usu. used with *along* or *through* ⟨*worried* along six months trying to support a large . . . family —Scott Fitzgerald⟩ ⟨one must ~ through the work of the week⟩ **3 :** to feel or experience concern, disquietude, or anxiety : FRET ⟨if her uncle had been troubled . . . a few years more served only to show how uselessly he had *worried* —Stark Young⟩ ⟨although sheep and goats do not ~ as we do, they can . . . be brought into states of chronic unrelieved tension —H.S.Liddell⟩ — often used with *about* or *over* ⟨began to ~ about venturing so far from home in the new car —M.M.Musselman⟩ ⟨pay . . . a good travel agent and let him ~ about this sort of detail —Richard Joseph⟩ ⟨*worried* over her husband's health —Ruth P. Randall⟩

syn ANNOY, FRET, HARASS, HARRY, NAG, PLAGUE, PESTER, BOTHER, TEASE, TANTALIZE: WORRY suggests continued menacing, attacking, or disturbing to drive a quarry or enemy to despair, rashness, submission, or defeat ⟨a policy of *worrying* the enemy⟩ ⟨took on the mighty galleons like terriers *worrying* bulls —Nora Stirling & Ruth Knight⟩ ⟨*worried* into his grave by the leaden-faced likeness of a British spy whom he had hanged —*Amer. Guide Series: N.Y.*⟩ ANNOY may refer to continued molesting, intruding, interfering with, hectoring, or otherwise bedeviling until the victim is angered or discomposed ⟨one or more dogs that will locate the lion . . . and are almost certain to *annoy* the wounded beast into disclosing himself sooner or later —James Stevenson-Hamilton⟩ FRET may suggest a rancorous eating or gnawing at or a continuing vexing that leaves one no peace ⟨that hidden bond which at other moments galled and *fretted* him so as to mingle irritation with the very sunshine —George Eliot⟩ ⟨*fretting* their team into skittishness and then pretending to be terror-stricken —H.L.Davis⟩ HARASS may apply to continual attacks, persecutions, or exactions that fray, exhaust, or distract ⟨*harassed* by the depredations of British raiders —*Amer. Guide Series: Conn.*⟩ ⟨the new government was *harassed* by internal controversies and by assassinations, disorders, and insurrections —J.F.Bell⟩ HARRY may suggest more directly oppressive persecution than HARASS ⟨had been *harrying* the main pirate fleets about the coast of Cuba —Marjory S. Douglas⟩ ⟨*harrying* Southern sympathizers by arbitrary arrests —*Encyc. Americana*⟩ NAG indicates an annoying or discomposing by persistent rebuke or reminder about shortcomings ⟨the only one who *nagged* him and tried to get him to behave himself —Delmore Schwartz⟩ ⟨let her children's minds alone. She did not pry into their thoughts or *nag* them —Willa Cather⟩ PLAGUE applies to tormenting affliction of painful disease or something likened to it ⟨the gastric disturbance which has been *plaguing* him for years —*Newsweek*⟩ ⟨the civil war which has *plagued* the republic since its inception —*Americana Annual*⟩ ⟨horse thieves were the worst nuisance, next to Indians; and they would go on *plaguing* Texas for thirty years —Green Peyton⟩ PESTER may suggest constant annoyance by or like that by vermin or children ⟨*pestered* with incredible swarms of flies, fleas, and bugs —Tobias Smollett⟩ ⟨*pester* the president with urgencies which perhaps no other man in Washington would have ventured —S.H.Adams⟩ BOTHER indicates vexatious troubling, often continued, that interferes with composure, serenity, or concentration ⟨*bothered* by incompetence in many places, ignorance in others and downright double-dealing in still others —F.V.W.Mason⟩ ⟨*bothered* with a lot of phone calls asking you to this luncheon and that meeting —W.H.Whyte⟩ TEASE applies to the annoyance of either repeated importunities or vexing railleries ⟨I say you cannot go and I will not be *teased* about it —Pearl Buck⟩ TANTALIZE suggests awakening expectation and withholding or frustrating satisfaction ⟨a young dancer, holding aloft in one arm an infant whom she *tantalizes* with a bunch of grapes held high in the other hand —*Amer. Guide Series: Mass.*⟩ ⟨low islands swung over the horizon and *tantalized* us with the belief that they were mainland —Farley Mowat⟩ **syn** see in addition ANNOY

[2]**worry** \"\ *n* -ES **1 a :** mental distress or agitation resulting from concern usu. for something impending or anticipated **:** ANXIETY ⟨got on better with my work, being free of ~ —Mary Webb⟩ ⟨hours of . . . careful thought, new administrative problems, ~ —Bruce Payne⟩ ⟨was in a state of ~ because of fear for the loss of her commercial eminence —A.F.Harlow⟩ **b :** an instance or occurrence of such distress or agitation ⟨after a while . . . my mind comes out of the ~ and I start thinking straight —Bant Singer⟩ ⟨is in a great ~ about her school grades⟩ **c :** a cause of worry **:** TROUBLE, DIFFICULTY, COMPLICATION ⟨has another serious ~ about the boys, their tendency to steal⟩ ⟨a bother and a ~ . . . is the London traffic —Richard Joseph⟩ ⟨his biggest ~ is transportation⟩ — often used in pl. ⟨was also in better health and spirits . . . fairly free from *worries* —Havelock Ellis⟩ ⟨wearied him . . . with household *worries* —Haldane Macfall⟩ ⟨few are without financial *worries*⟩ **d :** a state of unease and irritability in quadruped mammals resulting from exposure to biting arthropods (as flies or ticks); *also* **:** an organism causing such worry **2 :** the act or process of seizing an animal with the teeth and shaking it so as to kill or injure it ⟨the corpse of the otter was thrown to the hounds . . . in the ~ —Eric Bennett⟩ **syn** see CARE

wor·ry·ing·ly *adv* [*worrying* (pres. part. of [1]*worry*) + *-ly*] **:** in a worrying manner **:** with worry

worry line *n*, *usu cap W* **:** a line on the palm that intersects the Lifeline or a fine line rising from the Lifeline and is usu. held by palmists to indicate an impediment to a person's career

worrywart \'==,=\ *n* **:** one who is inclined to expect the worst or worry unduly **:** PESSIMIST, FUSSBUDGET ⟨you're a ~ and . . . get yourself into a sweat about things that can't be helped or haven't happened and probably never shall happen —*Chatelaine*⟩

[1]**worse** \'wərs, 'wə̄s, 'wəis\ *adj*, *comparative of* BAD *or of* ILL [ME *werse, wurse, worse*, fr. OE *wiersa, wyrsa;* akin to OHG *wirsiro* worse, ON *verri*, Goth *wairsiza;* comparative (with the suffix represented by OE *-ra*) of a root perh. represented by OHG *werran* to confuse — more at WAR, -ER] **1 :** of inferior or deteriorated quality, value, or material condition ⟨the swampy land he bought appears ~ than the rocky land he sold⟩ ⟨his shoes are rather the ~ for wear⟩ ⟨the monuments were . . . in a state the ~ for an earthquake —Douglas Carruthers⟩ ⟨his house . . . was the ~ for the weather —H.M. Tomlinson⟩ **2 a :** more unfavorable, unpleasant, or unlucky **:** more painful or grievous **:** less agreeable or desirable ⟨the consequences of the second attempt are ~⟩ ⟨was not the artistic type . . . ~ luck —James Jones⟩ ⟨are questions of degree and . . . are none the ~ for it —E.N.Griswold⟩ ⟨if the facts indicate that the hero is inadequate, so much the ~ for the facts —G.W.Johnson⟩ **b :** more faulty, unsuitable, or incorrect **:** ill-conceived **:** UNATTRACTIVE, INAPPROPRIATE ⟨displays manners ~ than those of a boor⟩ ⟨the food is bad, the service ~⟩ ⟨would not convey the thought that an opinion is the ~ for being lightened by a smile —B.N.Cardozo⟩ **c :** less skillful or efficient **:** doing work more poorly ⟨~ than any carpenter I know⟩ **3 a :** bad, evil, ill, or corrupt in a greater degree **:** more reprehensible ⟨it may be no ~ to cheat than to steal⟩ ⟨breed ~ criminals out of men —Hodding Carter⟩ **b :** poorer in health or physical condition **:** more sick or infirm ⟨appears ~ since his accident⟩ ⟨decided to let the tooth get ~ —W.J. Reilly⟩ ⟨people have been kept awake for five or six days . . . without being any the ~ for it physically —Geoffrey Jefferson⟩

[2]**worse** \"\ *n* -S [ME, fr. OE *wyrse*, fr. neut. of *wyrsa*, adj.] **1 a :** something that is worse ⟨if he were not dead, ~ must have happened to him —Vicki Baum⟩ ⟨living in an atmosphere . . . full of boredom and sometimes of ~ —Louis Bromfield⟩ ⟨threatened excommunication and ~ —G.C.Sellery⟩ ⟨thought he was an atheist and ~ —Van Wyck Brooks⟩ **b :** a greater degree of ill or badness **:** the quality or state of being worse ⟨if ~ comes to worst⟩ ⟨had taken a turn for the ~ —Greer Williams⟩ ⟨whether the change was for the better or for the ~ —*Times Lit. Supp.*⟩ **2 :** a person of inferior or less virtuous character ⟨fear there will be a ~ come in his place —Shak.⟩ ⟨tossing the rascals out only to see their places taken by ~⟩

[3]**worse** \"\ *adv*, *comparative of* BAD *or of* ILL [ME *werse, wurse, worse*, fr. OE *wiers, wyrs;* akin to OHG *wirs* worse, ON *verr*, Goth *wairs;* all fr. the root represented by OE *wiersa*, adj., worse] **:** in a worse manner **:** to a worse extent or degree ⟨we sleep ~ in very hot weather —Geoffrey Jefferson⟩ ⟨this week the confusion . . . has become ~ confounded —*Economist*⟩ ⟨it is possible for a society to attain new peaks in its culture while many of its members are ~ off than before —A.L.Kroeber⟩ ⟨I write the better when laurel-crowned and the ~ for criticism —W.T.Scott⟩

[4]**worse** \"\ *vb* -ED/-ING/-S [[1]*worse*] *vt*, *archaic* **:** to make worse ~ *vi*, *archaic* **:** to become worse **:** WORSEN

worse·ment \-smənt\ *n* -S [[4]*worse* + *-ment*] **:** deterioration in the value or usefulness of a piece of real property caused by action taken by outside persons or interests without the consent of the owner of the property — compare BETTERMENT

wors·en \'wərsᵊn, 'wə̄s-, 'wəis-\ *vb* **worsened; worsened; worsening** \-s(ᵊ)niŋ\ **worsens** [ME *worsenen*, fr. [1]*worse* + *-nen -en*] *vt* **:** to make worse **:** cause to deteriorate **:** IMPAIR ⟨the unfortunate disputes . . . still further ~*ed* relations —Sir Winston Churchill⟩ ⟨revolution . . . actually ~*ed* their economic status —*New Republic*⟩ ⟨heavy storms ~*ed* the fuel shortage⟩ ~ *vi* **:** to become worse **:** DETERIORATE ⟨the lot of the slaves ~*ed* —W.L.Sperry⟩ ⟨international relations may suddenly ~⟩ ⟨the seas . . . were distinctly higher and the weather was obviously ~*ing* —Bill Redgrave⟩

worse·ness *n* -ES **:** the quality or state of being worse

worser *substand comparative of* BAD *or of* ILL

[1]**wor·ship** \'wərshəp, 'wə̄sh-, 'wəish-\ *n* [ME *worschipe, worshipe*, fr. OE *weorthscipe*, fr. *weorth* worthy + *-scipe* -ship — more at WORTH] **1 a** *archaic* **:** HONOR, REPUTE, CREDIT **b** *archaic* **:** DIGNITY, IMPORTANCE, RANK **c** *sometimes cap*, *chiefly Brit* **:** a person of standing or importance — used as a title or mode of address esp. for holders of various high offices ⟨his *Worship* the Sheriff —Max Peacock⟩ **2 :** the reverence or veneration tendered a divine being or supernatural power; *also* **:** an act, process, or instance of expressing such veneration by performing or taking part in religious exercises or ritual ⟨all ~ is an effort of the individual to realize . . . the real presence of the Divine —W.W.Comfort⟩ **3 :** a form or type of worship or religious practice with its creed and ritual ⟨foreigners had been thronging to Rome, bringing with them their foreign cults, and she had permitted these ~*s* —John Buchan⟩ ⟨members of the Handsome Lake ~ may greet each as brother and sister —F.W. Voget⟩ **4 :** respect, admiration, or devotion for an object of esteem ⟨it cannot be called love that a lad of twelve . . . felt for an exalted lady, his mistress: but it was ~ —W.M.Thackeray⟩ ⟨the ~ of the movie hero —J.M.Barzun⟩ ⟨the ~ of the machine —C.I.Glicksberg⟩ ⟨the materialism of America, its new sense of power, its old ~ of success —Irwin Edman⟩

[2]**worship** \"\ *vb* **worshiped** *or* **worshipped; worshiped** *or* **worshipped; worshiping** *or* **worshipping; worships** [ME *worschipen, worshipen*, fr. *worschipe* worship] *vt* **1 :** to honor or reverence as a divine being or supernatural power **:** VENERATE ⟨the Father, the Son, and Holy Spirit are uncreated and are to be ~*ed* together as one God —K.S.Latourette⟩ ⟨the emperor, . . . ~*ed* as a god, is to serve as an instrument —Vera M. Dean⟩ **2 :** to regard with respect, honor, or devotion **:** ADORE ⟨in the Renaissance men ~*ed* antiquity —Stephen Spender⟩ ⟨admire the poetry and ~ the memory of the poet —William Du Bois⟩ ⟨whom I . . . ~*ed* as only a young lover can —J.A.Rice⟩ ⟨in his calm, unexcited way, he ~*s* success —Rose Macaulay⟩ ⟨he had the wildness we all ~*ed* —Eudora Welty⟩ ~ *vi* **:** to perform or take part in worship or the act of worship ⟨asks why people ~ and gives three reasons —E.E.Aubrey⟩ ⟨the old wooden meeting house where he had ~*ed* for so long —Catherine D. Bowen⟩ ⟨content to ~ at the shrine of the respectable and the traditional —C.I.Glicksberg⟩ **syn** see REVERE

wor·ship·able \-pəbəl\ *adj* [[2]*worship* + *-able*] **:** WORSHIPFUL 3

wor·ship·er *or* **wor·ship·per** \-pə(r)\ *n* -S [ME *worschiper*, fr. *worschipen* to worship + *-er*] **:** one that worships

wor·ship·ful \-pfəl\ *adj* [ME *worschipful*, fr. *worschip* worship + *-ful*] **1 a** *archaic* **:** marked by a good quality or property **:** NOTABLE, DISTINGUISHED **b** *usu cap*, *chiefly Brit* — used as a formal title for various persons or groups of rank or distinction ⟨the *Worshipful* Company of Carpenters —E.E.Reynolds⟩ ⟨*Worshipful* Grand Masters and Wardens —C.W.Ferguson⟩; compare RIGHT WORSHIPFUL **2 :** rendering adoration or reverence **:** VENERATING, WORSHIPING ⟨litanies may express all kinds of ~ attitudes —M.H.Shepherd⟩ ⟨the feeling . . . was more than warm; it was ~ —M.M.Hunt⟩ ⟨a vast audience . . . attentive, but not ~ —Corra Harris⟩ **3 :** warranting worship or capable of being worshiped ⟨the giant ~ effigies . . . commanding the conquered palace squares —Alfred Frankfurter⟩ ⟨any disrespect shown to the ~ animal . . . had to be atoned for —J.G.Frazer⟩ — **wor·ship·ful·ly** \-fəlē, -li\ *adv* — **wor·ship·ful·ness** *n* -ES

wor·ship·ing·ly *or* **wor·ship·ping·ly** *adv* [*worshiping, worshipping* (pres. part. of [2]*worship*) + *-ly*] **:** in a worshiping or adoring manner ⟨regarding her ~⟩

wor·ship·less \-pləs\ *adj* **:** lacking worship or worshipers **:** UNWORSHIPED

[1]**worst** \'wərst, 'wə̄st, 'wəist\ *adj*, *superlative of* BAD *or of* ILL [ME *worste, werste*, fr. OE *wyrresta, wyrsta, wierresta, wersta;* akin to OHG *wirsisto* worst, ON *versta;* superlative (with the suffix represented by OE *-st, -est*) of the root found in OE *wiersa* worse — more at WORSE, -EST] **1 :** most bad, evil, ill, or corrupt **:** most reprehensible ⟨his ~ fault⟩ ⟨man's ~ sin⟩ ⟨the ~ villain⟩ ⟨cottages of the ~ landlords had at least fresher air than the overcrowded slums —G.B.Shaw⟩ **2 a :** most unfavorable, unpleasant, or unlucky **:** most painful or grievous **:** least agreeable or desirable ⟨the ~ fate that can befall any nation —Kemp Malone⟩ ⟨the periodic famines . . . lost their ~ terrors —G.M.Trevelyan⟩ ⟨this is their ~ problem —Darcy Ribeiro⟩ ⟨his ~ enemies . . . admitted that he had thrown out the grafters —R.E.Merriam⟩ ⟨the ~ part of the arctic winter —Brigitte Gerland⟩ ⟨the ~ kind of indigestion —C.S.Forester⟩ **b :** most unsuitable, faulty, unattractive, or ill-conceived ⟨has the ~ manners she ever saw⟩ ⟨usually chooses the ~ time to visit⟩ ⟨their latest decision is probably the ~ step they can take⟩ **c :** least skillful or efficient **:** doing work most poorly ⟨the ~ plumber you can hire⟩ ⟨the ~ sort of equipment for the job at hand⟩ **3 :** most wanting in quality, value, or material condition ⟨unaccountably choosing the ~ land of the tract⟩ ⟨his house is not the ~ for being built of secondhand lumber⟩ ⟨poor planning and equipment may well bring about the ~ results⟩ — **the worst way** *adv* **:** very much **:** as much as possible ⟨such men certainly did seem to need indoctrination *the worst way* —J.G.Cozzens⟩ ⟨wanted to be an opera singer *the worst way*⟩

[2]**worst** \"\ *n* -S [ME *worste, werste*, fr. *worste, werste*, adj.] **1 :** something that is worst: as **a :** something that is most reprehensible or morally objectionable ⟨can usually be expected to do and say the ~⟩ ⟨so pure of heart that his ~ is another man's good⟩ **b :** something that is most unfavorable, unpleasant, or unlucky **:** a state most painful or grievous or least desirable or agreeable ⟨may as well learn the ~⟩ ⟨prepare for the ~⟩ ⟨the great storm doing its ~⟩ ⟨in his sulk he can be seen at his ~⟩ ⟨the ~ is yet to come⟩ **c :** something that is most wanting in quality, value, or material condition ⟨can be counted on to choose the ~⟩ ⟨examples of the ~ and the best of the period's architecture —*Amer. Guide Series: Minn.*⟩ ⟨of all the faulty pieces of work he selected only a few of the ~⟩ **d :** the greatest degree of ill or badness ⟨if worse comes to ~⟩ **2 :** one who is most reprehensible or deficient in moral character or being ⟨the ~ of a vicious lot⟩ ⟨of all the dishonest politicians, he is the ~⟩

[3]**worst** \"\ *adv*, *superlative of* BAD *or of* ILL [ME *worst, werst*, fr. OE *wyrst, wyrrest, wierst*, superlative of *wyrs, wiers* worse] **:** to the most extreme degree of badness or inferiority **:** in a manner most bad, unpleasant, unfortunate, harmful ⟨the mining centers suffered ~ —George Farwell⟩ ⟨groups who need the subsidies ~ lose out —T.W.Arnold⟩ ⟨the ~ dressed person present⟩

[4]**worst** \"\ *vt* -ED/-ING/-S [[1]*worst*] **1** *chiefly archaic* **:** WORSEN **2 a :** to get the better of in a fight, conflict, or contest **:** DEFEAT, OVERTHROW ⟨one who had been personally ~*ed* in combat —A.C.Whitehead⟩ ⟨had been ~*ed* in his first encounter with partisan government —Tremaine McDowell⟩ ⟨the champion ~*s* all his opponents⟩ **b :** to defeat in a debate, argument, or suit **:** OUTDO, BEST ⟨could so easily ~ . . . his mother in the medium of words —E.K.Brown⟩ ⟨seeking to ~ his detractor in a court of law⟩

[1]**wor·sted** \'wu̇stəd, 'wərs-, 'wə̄s-, 'wəis-\ *n* -S [ME *worstede, worsted*, fr. *Worthstede, Worsted* (now *Worstead*), parish & village of Norfolk, England] **1** *or* **worsted yarn :** a smooth compact yarn spun with average to hard twist from long wool fibers that have been carded and combed and used esp. for firm napless fabrics, carpeting, or knitting wools **2 :** any of various closely woven fabrics (as gabardine and serge) made from worsted yarns usu. with a smooth napless face and used esp. for suitings and tailored garments

[2]**worsted** \"\ *adj* [ME, fr. [1]*worsted*] **1 :** made of worsted or worsted yarn ⟨~ suiting⟩ ⟨~ suit⟩ **2 :** of, relating to, or concerned with worsted or worsted products esp. in manufacture and commercial handling ⟨~ mill⟩

worsted card *n* **:** a wool card that produces lap for combing as distinguished from the woolen card that produces sliver for spinning

[1]**wort** \'wər|t, 'wȯ(ə)r|, 'wə̄|, 'wəi|, -ȯ(ə)|, *usu* |d·+V\ *n* -S [ME *wurt, wort, wert*, fr. OE *wyrt* herb, plant, root; akin to OHG *wurz* herb, plant, ON *urt* herb, Goth *waurts* root, L *radix*, Gk *rhiza* — more at ROOT] **1 a :** PLANT; *esp* **:** an herbaceous plant — usu. used in combination **b** *archaic* **:** POTHERB **2 worts** *pl*, *obs* **:** CABBAGES

[2]**wort** \"\ *n* -S [ME, fr. OE *wyrt;* akin to OS *wurtia* spice, MHG *würze* spice, brewer's wort, OE *wyrt* herb, plant, root — more at [1]WORT] **:** an infusion of malt consisting of a dilute solution of sugars that is fermented to form beer

[3]**wort** *var of* WHORT

[1]**worth** \'wərth, 'wə̄th, 'wəith\ *vi* -ED/-ING/-S [ME *worthen*, fr. OE *weorthan, wurthan;* akin to OHG *werdan* to become, ON *vertha*, Goth *wairthan*, L *vertere* to turn, Skt *vartate* it is turned, happens, Lith *versti* to turn, *virsti* to fall, become] *archaic* **:** to come to be **:** BECOME — usu. used in the phrase *woe worth* with a following noun or pronoun

[2]**worth** \"\ *adj* [ME, fr. OE *weorth* of (a specified) value, worthy; akin to OHG *werd* worth, worthy, ON *verthr*, Goth *wairths*, OE *wierthe* worth, worthy] **1** *archaic* **:** having monetary or material value ⟨my time or labor was little ~ —Daniel Defoe⟩ **2** *archaic* **:** exhibiting or marked by desirable or useful qualities **:** ESTIMABLE ⟨she is a woman more ~ than any man —Shak.⟩ ⟨whose life, whose thoughts were little ~ —Alfred Tennyson⟩

[3]**worth** \"\ *prep* [ME, fr. OE *weorth*, adj.] **1 a :** having the value of **:** equal in value to ⟨the horse is ~ $300⟩ ⟨grants in . . . the state were to be ~ millions in timber and iron —*Amer. Guide Series: Minn.*⟩ ⟨decide whether they are ~ the price asked —S.H.Adams⟩ ⟨the matter is not ~ a straw⟩ ⟨what's it ~⟩ **b :** having possessions or income equal to **:** equal in worth to **:** possessed of ⟨he is ~ at least $500,000⟩ ⟨was ~ a small fortune —Angus Macleod⟩ **2 :** furnishing an equivalent for **:** justifying the expenditure or exchange of ⟨are incentives ~ the effort —Bruce Payne⟩ ⟨doesn't think he's ~ a damn —Hamilton Basso⟩ **3 :** deserving of ⟨such books are ~ deliberate and thoughtful perusal —L.R.McColvin⟩ ⟨the scene is well ~ a visit —Ted Sumner⟩ ⟨ideals ~ fighting for⟩ ⟨the question of what emotions are ~ expressing —C.W.H.Johnson⟩ ⟨hardly ~ our attention⟩ **4 :** capable of ⟨ran for all he was ~⟩ — **worth one's salt :** worth one's salary or keep ⟨is so useless as to be hardly *worth his salt*⟩; *also* **:** having substantial or significant value or merit ⟨it isn't long before an author *worth his salt* can emerge with material for a best seller —Phyllis McGinley⟩

[4]**worth** \"\ *n* -S [ME, fr. OE *weorth;* akin to OHG *wert* value, price, worth, ON *verth*, Goth *wairth;* all fr. a prehistoric substantive use of the adjective represented by Goth *wairths* worth, worthy] **1 a :** monetary value ⟨mining operations of tremendous ~ —R.L.Taylor⟩ ⟨farmhouse and lands of little ~⟩ **b :** the equivalent of a specified amount or figure ⟨a penny's ~ of wine —E.O.Hauser⟩ ⟨$130 ~ of corn and alfalfa —Clyde Hostetter⟩ ⟨insuring that the government gets its money's ~ —T.W.Arnold⟩ ⟨an hour's ~ of hard labor⟩ **2 :** the usu. relative value of something measured or judged by its qualities or by the esteem with which it is regarded ⟨device that proved its ~ —C.L.Boltz⟩ ⟨collections of independent essays or chapters of varying ~ —F.N.Robinson⟩ ⟨the ultimate ~ of elaborate techniques —Howard M. Jones⟩ ⟨the ultimate test of true ~ is pleasure —G.L.Dickinson⟩ **3 a :** moral, intellectual, or personal value ⟨inspired by a sense of individual human ~ —George Woodcock⟩ ⟨the child . . . whose dignity and ~ are respected —Dorothy Barclay⟩ ⟨problem of aging is to retain a sense of ~ —George Lawton⟩ **b :** MERIT, EXCELLENCE ⟨most colleges offer scholarships on the basis of need and ~⟩ ⟨work at which they have proved their ~ and their competence —F.J.R.Rodd⟩ ⟨propensity is to build up reputations beyond their intrinsic ~ —*Atlantic*⟩ **4 :** the value of one's material possessions **:** WEALTH, RICHES ⟨his personal ~ is estimated at five million⟩ **syn** see VALUE

worth·ful \-thfəl\ *adj* [[4]*worth* + *-ful*] **1 :** full of worth or merit **:** HONORABLE, WORTHY ⟨a good and ~ man⟩ ⟨something which is superhuman . . . and supremely ~ —H.C.Smith⟩ **2 :** having value or worth **:** ESTEEMED, VALUABLE ⟨transmitting to the young that which they regard as ~ in their culture —J.L.Childs⟩ — **worth·ful·ness** *n* -ES

worthiest of blood *Brit* **:** most worthy of those of the same blood to succeed or inherit — usu. used with reference to males as opposed to females

wor·thi·ly \'wərt͟həlē\ *adv* [ME, fr. [1]*worthy* + *-ly*] **:** in a worthy manner **:** with worthiness

wor·thi·ness \-t͟hēnəs\ *n* -ES [ME *worthinesse*, fr. [1]*worthy* + *-nesse* -ness] **:** the quality or state of being worthy

worth·less \'wərthləs, 'wə̄th-, 'wəith-\ *adj* [[4]*worth* + *-less*] **1 a :** lacking value or material worth **:** VALUELESS ⟨finding the country flooded with ~ currency and black markets —*Current Biog.*⟩ ⟨insisted that the Sudan was a ~ desert —Herman Ausubel⟩ **b :** of no value, use, or profit **:** USELESS ⟨the stream took a bend back toward the ocean, and it would be ~ to follow it any longer —Norman Mailer⟩ ⟨their estimated costs of clothing may well be ~ unless the girls . . . pin them down to accuracy —J.A.Leavitt & C.O.Hanson⟩ ⟨such statistical knowledge may be ~ to many people⟩ **2 a :** lacking moral character **:** LOW, DESPICABLE ⟨deceived by a ~ woman⟩ ⟨ran off with a ~ laughing fellow who lived by gambling —Sinclair Lewis⟩ **b :** lacking merit or worth **:** UNPRODUCTIVE, INCOMPETENT ⟨its vast possessions . . . had been squandered by ~ abbots —H.O.Taylor⟩ ⟨so ~ that they had to plunder friends as well as foes —Charles Kingsley⟩ — **worth·less·ly** *adv* — **worth·less·ness** *n* -ES

worthwhile \'=;=\ *adj* [[2]*worth* + *while*, n.] **:** being worth the time spent **:** of sufficient value to repay the effort ⟨if any ~ results were to be achieved —H.L.Ickes⟩ ⟨a ~ trip for sightseers —Lucy Burnham⟩ ⟨make life a ~ experience —Y.H. Krikorian⟩ — **worth·while·ness** *n* -ES

[1]**wor·thy** \'wərt͟hē, 'wə̄t͟h-, 'wəit͟h-, -t͟hi\ *adj*, *usu* -ER/-EST [ME, fr. [4]*worth* + *-y*] **1 a :** having worth, value, or importance **:** GOOD, ESTIMABLE ⟨has become the ~ custom to hold a benefit performance —R.P.Cooke⟩ ⟨the results of moral rules are not always as ~ as the motives for adopting them —W.L.Miller⟩ ⟨great and ~ things —H.D.Thoreau⟩ ⟨became identified with many ~ causes —A.E.Wier⟩ **b :** marked by personal qualities warranting honor, respect, or esteem **:** HONORABLE, MERITORIOUS ⟨the tribunal was composed of ~ men . . . of eminent respectability and talents —J.L.Motley⟩ ⟨the father was a ~ burgher, innkeeper, and brewer —Dora Clark⟩ ⟨announcing . . . that his former wife was not a ~ woman —H.F.Coleru⟩ **2 a :** having sufficient worth, value, or importance **:** sufficiently good or estimable ⟨performing deeds ~ to be handed down in . . . legends —C.B.Nordhoff & J.N.Hall⟩ ⟨think of something ~ to say —William Saroyan⟩ — often used with *of* ⟨mere resort to defensive measures is not ~ of the American spirit —*New Republic*⟩ ⟨brings to basketball an intensity ~ of a loftier pursuit —Stanley Frank⟩ ⟨a cause ~ of the best endeavors —W.H.Allison⟩ **b :** possessing personal qualities of sufficient worth, respect, or esteem **:** sufficiently honorable or meritorious ⟨no student deemed ~, and chosen for admission, would be kept out by lack of funds —N.M.Pusey⟩ ⟨a ~ successor⟩ ⟨a ~ antagonist⟩ ⟨every man ~ to be called a man —Thomas De Quincey⟩ — often used with *of* ⟨~ of his hire⟩ ⟨are ~ of the great faith, the high hopes, we have placed in them —F.D.Roosevelt⟩ ⟨you might be . . . *worthier* of yourself —Charles Dickens⟩

[2]**worthy** \"\ *n* -ES [ME, fr. [1]*worthy*] **:** a person of eminence, distinction, or renown ⟨a great New England ~ —Van Wyck Brooks⟩ ⟨keep alive the memory of many *worthies* —Perry Miller⟩

[3]**worthy** \"\ *adv* [ME, fr. [1]*worthy*] **:** WORTHILY

[4]**worthy** *vt* -ED/-ING/-ES [ME *worthyen*, fr. [1]*worthy*] *obs* **:** to make worthy **:** EXALT, HONOR

worts *pl of* WORT

[1]**wot** *pres 1st & 3d sing of* WIT

[2]**wot** \'wät\ *vb* **wotted; wotted; wotting; wots** [ME *woten*, alter. (influenced by *wot*, 1st & 3d sing. of *witen*) of *witen* to know — more at WIT] *vt*, *dial chiefly Brit* **:** to have knowledge of **:** KNOW ~ *vi*, *dial chiefly Brit* **:** to have knowledge — often used with *of* ⟨perhaps other kingdoms that we ~ not of —D.C. Peattie⟩

[3]**wot** \"\ *substand var of* WHAT

wou·bit \'wü,bit\ *n* -S [ME *wolbode*, fr. *woll* wool + *-bode* (perh. akin to OE *budda* beetle)] *dial Brit* **:** a hairy caterpillar; *esp* **:** WOOLLY BEAR

wough \'wō, 'wȯ\ *n* -S [ME *wogh*, fr. OE *wōg, wāh;* akin to OFris *wāch* wall, OS *wēg*, L *vincire* to bind, lace — more at VETCH] **1** *dial Brit* **:** the wall or partition of a house **2** *Scot* **:** the wall rock beside a vein of lead

[1]**would** \ˌwəd, ˌ(ə)d, (ˈ)wu̇d\ [ME *wolde, wulde, wold*, fr. OE *wolde;* akin to OHG *wolta* wished, desired, ON *vilda*, Goth *wilda* — more at WILL] *past of* WILL **1 a** *archaic* **:** WISHED, DESIRED, INTENDED ⟨he ~ that they should go⟩ **b** *archaic* **:** wish for **:** WANT ⟨what ~ these people⟩ ⟨they ~ a word with us⟩ **c** (1) **:** strongly desire **:** WISH ⟨I ~ I had brought better news

—W.S.Gilbert〉 〈we ~ all were perfect —Edward Sapir〉 (2) — used in auxiliary function with *rather* or *sooner* to express preference between alternatives 〈his flock ~ rather let him starve than increase the living by one penny —Emily Brontë〉 〈he ~ sooner die than face them〉 **2 a** — used in auxiliary function to express wish, desire, or intent 〈the problem of him who ~ determine the . . . pattern of a language —*Internat'l Jour. of Amer. Linguistics*〉 〈~ unite the nations of America into a real system —C.R.Fish〉 **b** — used in auxiliary function to express willingness or preference 〈as ye ~ that men should do to you, do ye also to them likewise —Lk 6:31 (AV)〉 〈parents ~ have their children do well〉 **c** — used in auxiliary function to express plan or intention 〈promised that we ~ correct . . . mistakes —Virginia Prewett〉 〈deciding that they ~ visit as many friends as possible〉 **d** — used in auxiliary function in the negative to express refusal 〈contrary to advice he ~ not have an auxiliary engine in his boat〉 〈despite a good offer, he ~ have none of it〉 **e** — used in auxiliary function to express disposition or inclination 〈~ express the opinion that the . . . question has been practically settled —Norman Douglas〉 〈~ propose that all candidates be accepted〉 〈~ like to recommend a series of articles —R.C.Pooley〉 **f** — used in auxiliary function to express insistence or determination 〈regardless of warnings he ~ play with fire〉 〈the child ~ have its way〉 〈he ~ not be crossed〉 〈you might expect that he ~ not be deterred〉 **3** — used in auxiliary function to express custom or habitual action 〈we ~ meet every morning —O.S.J.Gogarty〉 〈the swagman ~ for long periods be without . . . female company —William Power〉 〈he ~ stand . . . blows without winking or shedding a tear —Emily Brontë〉 **4** — used in auxiliary function to express consent or choice 〈could be helped if he ~ only do his part〉 〈~ put it off indefinitely if he could〉 **5 a** — used in auxiliary function in the conclusion of a conditional sentence to express a contingency or possibility 〈if he were coming, he ~ be here now〉 〈had all the possibilities been ruled out, we ~ have had to accept all three —Z.S.Harris〉 〈~ have done it myself but for my temporary incapacitation —Sir Winston Churchill〉 **b** (1) — used in auxiliary function in the conclusion of a conditional sentence to express volition or intention 〈if I were a librarian, I ~ put this book in . . . my display —Pearl Buck〉 〈if we had thought that the institute was a school, we ~ never have come —*Time*〉 (2) — used in auxiliary function in a statement of advice or recommendation based on the implied condition *if I were you* 〈I ~ go today while the weather is pleasant〉 〈telling them he *wouldn't* take any such risk, he ordered them to go home〉 **c** — used in auxiliary function in a noun clause completing a statement of desire, request, or advice 〈we wish that he ~ go〉 〈the express desire of his parents was that he ~ finish school〉 〈prefer that she ~ not go again〉 **6 a** — used in auxiliary function to express futurity from a point of view in the past 〈kept on looking for . . . the money that ~ solve his problems —E.L.Acken〉 〈the lowness of his funds ~ presently compel his return —John Buchan〉 〈proposed a council . . . whereby peace ~ be preserved —F.L.Schuman〉 **b** — used in auxiliary function to express probability or presumption in past or present time 〈the hands of the watch show that it ~ be about five o'clock that it was submerged〉 〈no one, for example, could have predicted . . . whether or not his pistol ~ have missed fire —L.A.White〉 〈at this time of day the fire ~ have burned low —P.H.Newby〉 〈from his appearance he ~ be the one we are looking for〉 **7** : COULD 〈no stone ~ shatter that glass〉 〈the barrel ~ hold 20 gallons〉 **8** — used in auxiliary function to express a request with which voluntary compliance is expected 〈~ you please help us〉 **9** *obs* : ought to 〈that ~ be scanned —Shak.〉 **10** — used in auxiliary function to express doubt or uncertainty 〈the explanation . . . ~ seem to go deeper —F.H.Hartmann〉 〈for the survival of our society it ~ appear essential —Dorothy Barclay〉 〈the mechanics of transmitting the sound were perfect, I ~ say —Philip Hamburger〉 **11** : SHOULD 〈knew I ~ enjoy the trip〉 〈~ be glad to know the answer〉 〈feel that we ~ recognize them easily〉 〈if you ~ be interested, I could arrange an interview〉 〈it was ordered that he ~ go〉

²would \'wu̇d\ *n* -s : a conditional or undecided wish or intention 〈a life of inaction cluttered with ~s〉

³would *var of* WELD

¹would–be \'=,=\ *adj* [fr. the phrase *would be*] : desiring or professing to be : wishing to be reputed 〈good musicianship will enable a *would-be* conductor . . . to improve himself —Warwick Braithwaite〉 〈retaliatory power is one strong deterrent to a *would-be* aggressor —D.D.Eisenhower〉 — often used disparagingly 〈looked like what he was, a *would-be* fighter who . . . had nowhere to go —Hamilton Basso〉 〈turn lesson notes into *would-be* textbooks and go in vain the round of the publishers —James Britton〉

²would–be \"\ *n* -s : one who wishes to be or to be reputed something one is not — usu. used disparagingly 〈compelled to listen to has-beens and *would-bes* trying to put over bad plays —A.L.Burt〉 〈nothing but these *would-bes* in New York getups, drinking tea —Sinclair Lewis〉

would·ing \'wu̇diŋ\ *n* -s [fr. ¹*would*, after such pairs as ¹*will*: ¹*willing*] *archaic* : emotion of desire : INCLINATION

wouldn't \'wu̇dᵊnt\ [by contr.] : would not

wouldst *or* **wouldest** *archaic past 2d sing of* WILL

woulff bottle \'wu̇lf-\ *n, usu cap W* [alter. of *Woulfe bottle*, after Peter *Woulfe* †1803 Eng. chemist] : a bottle or jar with two or three necks used in washing or absorbing gases

¹wound \'wünd, *chiefly dial* 'wau̇nd\ *n* -s [ME *wunde, wound*, fr. OE *wund*; akin to OHG *wunta* wound, ON *und*] **1 a** : an injury to the body consisting of a laceration or breaking of the skin or mucous membrane usu. by a hard or sharp instrument forcefully driven or applied 〈has a deep festering knife ~ across the palm〉 〈the hollow-nosed bullet leaves a jagged ~〉 **b** (1) : an opening made in the skin or a membrane of the body incidental to a surgical operation or procedure (2) : a cut or slash made on a tree or plant 〈a metal receptacle to catch the sap that dripped from the ~ —Hamilton Basso〉 **2 a** : a mental or emotional hurt or blow to the pride, sensitivity, or reputation 〈lived . . . under the uneasy strain of avoiding ~s to their self-esteem —Oscar Handlin〉 〈inflicts ~s upon the human spirit which no surgery can heal —Virginia Woolf〉 〈in the hospital wards he was confronted with every type of psychiatric ~ —Don Wharton〉 **b** : a similar hurt or blow affecting a political body or a social group and usu. giving rise to resentments or animosities 〈wish that the bitter strike would leave no deep ~s —Mary K. Hammond〉 〈reopens the party's ~s by attacking the past leadership —R.L.Strout〉 〈the perfect way to heal many of the world's worst ~s —P.M.Mazur〉

syn TRAUMA, TRAUMATISM, LESION, BRUISE, CONTUSION: WOUND generally implies a significant injury inflicted by an outside agent (as a gun, knife, or fist) that breaks the skin and usu. the tissues beneath 〈a gunshot *wound*〉 〈the *wound* made by the surgeon's knife〉 TRAUMA designates physical injury or mental or emotional shock that leaves a lasting morbid or abnormal impression on the mind 〈a birth *trauma*〉 〈the *traumata* of war〉 〈discomfort, pain, and *trauma* to the middle ear —H.G.Armstrong〉 〈great social *traumas* like the French Revolution and the American Civil War —Alexander Heard〉 although sometimes it extends in meaning to designate the effects of a traumatic injury or a TRAUMATISM 〈the multiple symptoms of a *traumatism* — a fear of dirt or scum, a constant washing of the hands, much talk about impurity〉 LESION designates the effect on the tissues caused by a wound, trauma, or injury resulting from disease or degeneration, implying a pathological alteration in tissue or loss of function 〈tubercular *lesions* in the lungs〉 〈occasionally the so-called rheumatic *lesions* affect the joints, giving symptoms like those of growing pains —Morris Fishbein〉 〈some obscure sort of psychological *lesion* —Nathaniel Burt〉 BRUISE is the standard and CONTUSION the medical term for an injury ordinarily the result of impact that results in the disorganization of subcutaneous tissues with usu. no break in the skin but with black and blue discoloring 〈a *bruise* on the arm from a flying stone〉 〈a *contusion* on the hip from a fall on the ice〉

²wound \"\ *vb* -ED/-ING/-S [ME *wunden, wounden*, fr. OE *wundian*; akin to OHG *wuntōn* to wound, ON *undathr* wounded (part.), Goth *gawundondans* wounding (part. pl.); all fr. a prehistoric Gmc verb derived fr. the root of OE *wund* wound] *vt* **1 a** : to inflict a wound upon : CUT, STAB, PIERCE, LACERATE 〈using his knife to ~ and maim his opponent〉 〈flying shrapnel had ~*ed* several others〉 〈the bullet ~*ed* him in the shoulder〉 〈had been ~*ed* in the battle —E.K.Alden〉 **b** : to make a tear, breach, or opening in (something) in the manner of a wound 〈was sure he had mortally ~*ed* the submarine —Walter Karig〉 〈the trees are ~*ed* and the sap allowed to run out —G.S.Brady〉 〈the volcanic crust is ~*ed* by the upheaval〉 **2** : to hurt or damage as if by a wound : INJURE 〈had tried to ~ him by some cheap irony, sarcasm, or just plain rudeness —Bruce Mason〉 〈the ability to ~ the enemy through trade . . . by applications of the rule of contrabrand —F.L.Paxson〉 〈the 18th century . . . was so ~*ed* by the memories of the religious wars —Herbert Agar〉 **~** *vi* : to inflict a wound 〈intending only to ~, not to kill〉 〈critical remarks often ~ deeply〉

³wound [ME *wounden* (past pl. & past part.), fr. OE *wundon* (past pl.) & *gewunden* (past part.)] *past of* WIND

wound chevron *or* **wound stripe** *n* : a small gold chevron formerly worn on the lower part of the right sleeve of the U. S. army uniform to indicate that the wearer had been wounded in action

wound cork *n* : cork formed over the wounded surface of a tree or plant — compare PERIDERM

¹wounded *adj* [ME, fr. past part. of *wounden* to wound] : injured, hurt by, or suffering from a wound 〈nursing his ~ arm〉 〈does not wish to leave a ~ name behind him —E.C. Wagenknecht〉 〈seeking to salve her ~ feelings〉 〈the underbrush had to be cut away and ~ fields reopened —Russell Lord〉 〈had gone up with the 8th Army . . . working on ~ tanks —Irwin Shaw〉 — **wound·ed·ly** *adv*

²wounded *n, pl* **wounded** : one that is wounded — usu. used collectively 〈treatment of the ~〉

wound fungus *n* : a fungus that is a wound parasite

wound gall *n* : an elongated swollen or tuberous gall on the branches of the grapevine caused by a vine borer (*Ampeloglypter sesostris*) whose larvae inhabit the galls

wound hormone *n* : a substance (as traumatic acid) that promotes the healing of wounds in plants

wound·i·ly \'wündəlē, 'wau̇n-\ *adv* [²*woundy* + *-ly*] *chiefly archaic* : EXCESSIVELY, EXTREMELY 〈that gauntlet of yours is ~ heavy —J.H.Wheelwright〉

wound·ing·ly *adv* : in a wounding manner : HURTFULLY

wound·less \'wündləs\ *adj* **1** *obs* : INVULNERABLE 〈the ~ air —Shak.〉 **2** : free from wounds : UNWOUNDED

wound parasite *n* : a usu. weakly parasitic fungus that becomes established in a plant following damage by other agencies

wound rocket *n* [so called fr. its use in healing wounds] : YELLOW ROCKET

wound root *n* : a root originating in callus tissue near a cut or damaged surface as distinguished from a root arising from a normal meristematic region or from a primary root

wound–rotor motor \'=,==-\ *n* [*wound*, past part. of *wind*] : an induction motor with a rotor having a polyphase winding to permit secondary circuit adjustment not possible in the case of a squirrel-cage induction motor

¹wounds *pl of* WOUND, *pres 3d sing of* WOUND

²wounds \waündz\ *interj* [fr. the oath *by God's wounds*] *archaic* — used as an oath or strong affirmation

woundwort \'=,=\ *n* : any of various plants whose soft downy leaves have been used in the dressing of wounds: as **a** : KIDNEY VETCH **b** : a mint of the genus *Stachys* **c** : a comfrey (*Symphytum officinale*) **d** : HERCULES ALLHEAL

¹woundy \'wündē, 'wau̇n-\ *adv* [²*wounds* + *-y*] *dial chiefly Eng* : EXTREMELY, EXCESSIVELY

²woundy \"\ *adj* [²*wounds* + *-y*] *dial chiefly Eng* : very great : EXTREME

wou·ra·li \wü'rälē\ *or* **wou·ra·ri** \-ärē\ *n* -s [Macushi] : CURARE

wou–wou \'wau̇,wau̇\ *or* **wah–wah** \'wä,wä\ *n* -s [Sundanese *owa*] **1** : SILVER GIBBON **2** : AGILE GIBBON

¹wove [ME *wof, woof*, alter. of *waf*, fr. OE *wæf*] *past of* WEAVE

²wove \'wōv\ *adj* [*wove*, archaic past part. of ¹*weave*] *of paper* : made with a dandy roll covered with woven wire and therefore showing no laid lines

woven [ME, alter. of *weven, iweven*, fr. OE *wefen, gewefen*] *past part of* WEAVE

woven wire *n* : wire crossed and interlaced to form a network

¹wow \'wau̇\ *interj* — used as an exclamation of pleasure, surprise, or strong feeling

²wow \"\ *n* -s [¹*wow*] : a sensational hit : a striking success 〈a lively and entertaining story . . . should be a ~ on the screen —E.E.Calkins〉 〈was a ~ in the campus frolic —Robertson Davies〉 〈as a radio sportscaster . . . was called a ~ from the start —*Current Biog.*〉 〈a correct translation of these documents would be a ~ —*Nation*〉

³wow \"\ *vt* -ED/-ING/-S : to excite to enthusiastic admiration 〈~*ed* their audience with a knowing parody —Bennett Cerf〉 〈was ~*ing* the voters everywhere with his . . . political minstrelsy —*Time*〉 〈will borrow almost any idea which is currently ~*ing* the customers —Martin Mayer〉

⁴wow \"\ *vi* -ED/-ING/-S [imit.] *dial Brit* : HOWL, WAIL, MEW

⁵wow \"\ *n* -s [imit.] **1** *dial chiefly Brit* : BARK, WHINE, WAIL **2** : a distortion in reproduced sound consisting of a relatively slow rise and fall of pitch caused by variation of speed in the sound reproducing system (as in the record, film, tape, or motor); *also* : the variation in speed causing such a distortion — compare FLUTTER 4a

wowf \'wau̇f\ *adj* [origin unknown] *Scot* : WILD, CRAZED

wow·ser \'wau̇zə(r)\ *n* -s [origin unknown] *chiefly Austral* : one who is censoriously hostile to minor vices or disapproves of various forms of popular amusement (as Sunday sports) — used disparagingly of an obtrusively puritanical person 〈responsible for closed restaurants, limited movies . . . and a sanctimonious appearance of the streets are the ~s —J.M. Raleigh〉 〈both were denounced as equally obscene by the . . . ~s —H.L.Mencken〉

woyawai *or* **woyaway** *usu cap, var of* WAIWAI

WP *abbr* **1** wastepaper **2** water packed **3** *often not cap* waterproof; waterproofing **4** weather permitting **5** weatherproof **6** white phosphorus **7** wild pitch **8** wire payment **9** without prejudice **10** working point **11** working pressure

WPA *abbr* with particular average

WPC *abbr, often not cap* watts per candle

wpfl *abbr* worshipful

wpm *abbr* words per minute

wpn *abbr* weapon

WPP *abbr, often not cap* waterproof paper packing

wr *abbr* writing paper

WR *abbr* **1** wardroom **2** warehouse receipt **3** war risk **4** washroom **5** with rights

¹wrack *also* **rack** \'rak\ *n* -s [ME, fr. OE *wræc*; akin to OE *wrecan* to drive, drive out, punish — more at WREAK] **1** *archaic* **a** : PUNISHMENT; *also* : VENGEANCE **b** : vengeful or hostile attack or persecution **2 a** : disastrous and violent damage, defeat, or dislocation : RUIN, DOWNFALL, DESTRUCTION 〈times of ~ and misery —A.L.Kroeber〉 〈his few acres, heavily mortgaged and gone to ~ —Dixon Wecter〉 **b** *obs* : a cause of ruin **c** *dial* : something that has suffered wrack : something shattered or destroyed **d** : a vestigial remain of something destroyed 〈of the original simple scheme hardly a ~ remains —Nathan Isaacs〉

²wrack \"\ *n* -s [ME *wrak*, fr. MD; akin to OE *wræc* punishment, something driven by the sea] **1 a** : a wrecked ship **b** : a piece of wreckage 〈nosing his boat among ~ heaps to salvage piling that has come loose —R.J.Smith〉 **c** (1) : SHIPWRECK 2 (2) : SHIPWRECK 3 **d** *dial* : the violent destruction of a structure, machine, or vehicle **2 a** : marine vegetation (as eelgrass or various seaweeds); *esp* : KELP — compare SEA WRACK **b** : any of various dried seaweeds used for coarse cordage, stuffing, or other purposes **c** : vegetable rubbish collected on water, cast on the shore, or piled in a field : WEEDS

³wrack \"\ *vb* -ED/-ING/-S [ME *wracken*, fr. *wrak* shipwreck, wreckage] *vi, obs* : to become wrecked or ruined : undergo destruction **~** *vt* : to wreck beyond repair : utterly ruin : cause the destruction of 〈the wind may ~ a house that isn't adequately nailed —*Design for Homes*〉 **syn** see DESTROY

⁴wrack \"\ *vb* -ED/-ING/-S [by alter.] : ⁴RACK 〈a land ~*ed* by domestic fears and uncertainty —Mark Gayn〉 〈tend to ~ or distort the car frame —*Power*〉 〈~*ed* with scurvy —Stuart Keate〉 〈depth charges ~*ed* aft of them —R.O.Bowen〉

⁵wrack \"\ *n* -s [by alter.] : ³RACK

⁶wrack \"\ *n* -s [by alter.] : ¹RACK 2a

wrack·ful \-fəl\ *adj* : causing wrecks or wreckage : DESTRUCTIVE, INJURIOUS

wrack grass *n* [²*wrack*] : EELGRASS 1

wraith \'rāth\ *n, pl* **wraiths** \-ths *sometimes* -t͟hz\ [origin unknown] **1 a** : an apparition of a living person in his exact likeness seen usu. just before his death — compare DOPPELGÄNGER **b** : a visible apparition of a dead person : GHOST, SPECTER **2** : WATER SPRITE **3** : an insubstantial copy, remainder, or appearance of something : SHADOW 〈pale ~s of their formidable namesakes —*Times Lit. Supp.*〉 〈hits not the ~ of socialism but the flesh and blood of the farmers —M.W. Straight〉 **4** : a barely visible gaseous or vaporous column resembling a wraith 〈thin ~s of smoke curled up and lost themselves in the sky —E.A.McCourt〉

wrake *obs var of* ³WRACK *vt*

wran \'ran\ *dial Brit var of* WREN

wrang \"\ *dial var of* WRONG

wran·gle \'raŋgəl, -aiŋ-\ *vb* **wrangled; wrangled; wrangling** \-g(ə)liŋ\ **wrangles** [ME *wranglen*; akin to LG *wrangeln* to wrangle, *wrangen* to struggle, wrestle, ME *wringen* to wring, twist, wrest — more at WRING] *vi* **1** : to dispute angrily : quarrel peevishly and noisily : BRAWL, ALTERCATE, BICKER **2** : to engage in argument, dispute, or controversy 〈solemn conclaves dignifiedly *wrangled* over proper compounding of herbs or incense —L.C.Douglas〉 **~** *vt* **1 a** : to obtain by wrangling 〈started to ~ one or two scholarships . . . for gifted children —Gertrude Samuels〉 **b** : to influence or persuade by wrangling **c** : to waste or expend in wrangling 〈had been *wrangling* away their reserves —Bruce Marshall〉 **2 a** : to round up, corral, herd, and care for (as horses) : take charge of (a remuda) 〈*wrangling* cattle for a living〉 **b** : direct and oversee the activities of (guests at a dude ranch) 〈on the lookout for some handsome, easy-talking gent to ~ tenderfeet —F.B.Gipson〉

²wrangle \"\ *n* -s **1** : an angry, bitter, noisy, or prolonged dispute or quarrel 〈emerged victorious in nasty ~s with old guardists —*Newsweek*〉 **2** : the action or process of wrangling : angry disputation : CONTROVERSY 〈after an hour's ~, both of these disputes to go over until tomorrow —A.H.Vandenberg †1951〉 **syn** see QUARREL

wran·gler \-ŋg(ə)lə(r)\ *n* -s **1** : one that wrangles: **a** : an angry or bickering disputant **b** : a participant in an argument, debate, or controversy **c** *obs* : OPPONENT, ANTAGONIST **2** : one who obtains first class honors in the mathematical tripos at Cambridge University — see SENIOR WRANGLER **3** : HORSE WRANGLER; *broadly* : COWBOY

¹wrap \'rap, *dial* 'räp\ *vb* **wrapped** *also* **wrapt** \-pt\ **wrapped** *also* **wrapt; wrapping; wraps** [ME *wrappen*; prob. akin to Dan dial. *vravle* to twist together, wind, Gk *rhaptein* to sew, stitch together — more at RHAPSODY] *vt* **1 a** : to cover, envelop, or enclose esp. entirely or to a great extent within a covering (as a garment or cloth) esp. by winding or folding 〈let him ~ her shoulders in the white shawl —Marcia Davenport〉 — often used with *about, around*, or *up* 〈he was *wrapped* up in a blanket —Georg Meyers〉 **b** : to envelop (as with paper) and usu. secure (as with string) for protection or convenience in transportation or storage : enclose in a package, parcel, or bundle : do up — usu. used with *up* 〈the waitress ~s up your table-scraps in a napkin —Corey Ford〉 〈*wrapped* up in Christmas wrapping paper —*Crompton & Royton Chronicle*〉 **c** : to enclose wholly or partially by coiling, looping, grasping, or embracing 〈a store-bought watermelon *wrapped* in her arms —Eudora Welty〉 〈*wrapped* in chains —H.E.Rieseberg〉 **d** : to coil, fold, draw, or twine (as a string or cloth) esp. so as to envelop or encompass — usu. used with *about, around*, or *round* 〈~ a rubber band around the thread tight up against the nut —*Gadgets Annual*〉 〈~ a car around a pole —Mel Heimer〉 〈the cold rain *wrapped* his thin shirt and trousers round his body and legs —Marcia Davenport〉 〈lay down, *wrapping* the cloak about her —Louis Bromfield〉 **e** : to serve as a surrounding cover, envelope, wrapping, coil, loop, or band for 〈a white mink stole will ~ her —*Springfield (Mass.) Union*〉 **2** *obs* : to double or gather up in pliant folds so as to be more compact : FOLD 〈the napkin . . . *wrapped* together in a place by itself —Jn 20:7 (AV)〉 **3 a** : to envelop or enclose completely 〈the bluffs . . . *wrapped* in mist —*Amer. Guide Series: Tenn.*〉 〈dusk had *wrapped* the city —T.B.Costain〉 〈store was *wrapped* in flames —*N. Y. Herald Tribune*〉 **b** : to involve, encompass, suffuse, or surround with or in an aura, viewpoint, condition, feeling, or state 〈the sense of fate that *wrapped* his folktales —Van Wyck Brooks〉 〈the whole thing was *wrapped* in disgrace —Robert Reid〉 **c** : to engross the attention or interest of to the exclusion of anything else : completely involve mentally or emotionally 〈a boy and girl *wrapped* in a world of each other —Harold Griffin〉 〈walked along *wrapped* in my own thoughts —Carolyn Hannay〉 — usu. used with *up* 〈*wrapped* up in a ceremonial veneration of the past —Oscar Handlin〉 〈he was all *wrapped* up in his daughter —Erle Stanley Gardner〉 **4 a** : to conceal or obscure the nature of as if by enveloping or enfolding : hide by enveloping in something extraneous, irrelevant, vague, or verbose 〈its origin is *wrapped* in multiplied legends —*Amer. Guide Series: Ark.*〉 — often used with *up* 〈the book is overwritten and *wrapped* up in needless jargon —Sidney Hook〉 〈agriculturists and private utilities equally ~ up their selfish interests in states' rights language —C.H.Pritchett〉 **b** : VEIL, CONCEAL 〈clouds *wrapped* the peak from view〉 **5** : to enclose as if with a protective covering 〈*wrapped* in the authority of his office —*Newsweek*〉 〈have become impatient with those . . . who ~ themselves in the Constitution —*Episcopal Churchnews*〉 **6** : to add as a wrap — used with *round* or *around* 〈as inserts in the printed book, halftone illustrations may be . . . *wrapped* around a certain number of text pages —*Publisher to Author*〉 **7** : to enclose within a small compass — usu. used with *up* 〈a little brochure was designed to ~ up a selling message along with some more information —*Printers' Ink*〉 〈~s up two important driving conveniences . . . into one handy accessory —*Buick Mag.*〉 **~** *vi* **1 a** : to wind, coil, or twine so as to partially or completely encircle something 〈windshields have compound curves that ~ around —*Christian Science Monitor*〉 〈a vine ~s round the pillar〉 **b** : to become spread over a person or object as a covering 〈coats that ~ around —*advt*〉 **2** : to put on clothing : DRESS — usu. used with *up* 〈~ up warm, and we'll go —W. F. De Morgan〉 **3** : to be subject to covering, enclosing, or packaging — usu. used with *up* 〈the hydrogen bomb ~s up into a fairly small package —R.H.Rovere〉

²wrap \"\ *archaic var of* ³RAP

³wrap \", *dial* 'räp\ *n* -s [ME *wrappe*, fr. *wrappen* to cover, wrap] **1 a** (1) : a covering that encompasses something : WRAPPER, WRAPPING 〈put . . . into gaily drawn paper ~s —*Newsweek*〉 (2) : material for wraps 〈use of transparent film as a ~ for bundling packages —*Modern Packaging*〉 (3) : the process or product or a manner of wrapping 〈supervising the ~ of a great sheaf of tiger lilies —Christopher Morley〉 〈produces uniformly neat, tight ~s —*Fishing Gazette*〉 **b** : an article of clothing that may be wrapped round a person; *esp* : a garment (as a coat, jacket, or shawl) for outdoor wear as part of a costume or in cold or stormy weather **c** : a warm covering (as a blanket or shawl) used while traveling or sleeping **d** : a 4-page insert folded around text leaves of a book and sewed in — called also *wraparound* **2 a** : a single turn or convolution of something wound around an object 〈at the end of each strip I would make a couple of ~s with wire to hold the bark in place —W.D.Wallace〉 **b** : a unit of length in warping equivalent to 3000 yards **c** : a surface pattern or clock on men's hose made by knitting in extra yarns **3 wraps** *pl* **a** : RESTRAINT 〈was under ~s from the higher command —G.S.Patton〉 〈is unequivocal when she takes off the ~s —Edmund Fuller〉 **b** : SECRECY, CENSORSHIP 〈the plan was kept carefully under ~s until after the election —Don Pryor〉 〈airplane makers took the ~s off a brand-new jet engine —*New Orleans (La.) Times-Picayune*〉

wraparound \'==,=\ *n* -s [fr. *wrap around*, v.] **1** : a garment (as a dress, robe, skirt, or coat) made with a full-length opening and adjusted to the figure by wrapping around **2** : WRAP 1d **3** : an object that encircles or esp. curves and laps over another 〈~ windshield〉

wrap·page \'rapij, -pēj, *dial* 'räp-\ *n* -s **1** : something that wraps : an outer covering (as of a package); also : wrapping material 2 : WRAPPER 3

wrappedwork \ˈ≈,≈\ n [wrapped (past part. of ¹wrap) + work] : basketwork in which the weft is wrapped once around each warp in turn

¹wrap·per \ˈrapə(r), dial ˈräp-\ n -s [ME wrappere, fr. wrappen to wrap + -ere -er] 1 : that in which something is wrapped : a piece of material formed into a wrapping for a parcel, package, or article ⟨candy ~⟩ ⟨coin ~⟩ : as a : a tobacco leaf used for the outside covering of plugs, twists, and esp. cigars — compare BINDER, FILLER b (1) : JACKET 3f(1) (2) : the paper cover of a pamphlet or booklet or of a book not bound in boards — often used in pl. (3) : a paper wrapping around a finished book covering it entirely and usu. having sealed ends c : a sheet of paper for wrapping around but not completely enclosing a newspaper or magazine in the mail; also : such a sheet bearing an imprinted stamp esp. for mailing newspapers d : a sheet spread over unused furniture or merchandise in a store or warehouse as a protection against dust or fading 2 : one that wraps; esp : one whose work is wrapping articles usu. to protect, decorate, or facilitate handling or storing them 3 : an article of clothing designed to be worn wrapped around the body: as a : DRESSING GOWN ⟨in her ~ and nightgown —Louis Auchincloss⟩ ⟨a baby's ~ of pink flannel —Ellen Glasgow⟩ b : MOTHER HUBBARD c : SHAWL ⟨she had thrown a loose white ~ round her shoulders —Mabel Collins⟩ d dial Eng : a workman's apron, overall, or smock

²wrapper \ˈ"\ vt -ED/-ING/-S : to envelop in or provide with a wrapper — often used with up

wrap·per·ing \-pəriŋ, -rēŋ\ n -s [¹wrapper + -ing] 1 : coarse material used for wrapping 2 : a loose outer garment for outdoor wear

wrapping n -s [ME, fr. gerund of wrappen to wrap] 1 a : something used to wrap an object : WRAPPER, COVERING, WRAP ⟨tear the ~s from a parcel⟩ ⟨the natural man beneath the theological ~s —V.L.Parrington⟩ b : clothing or an article of clothing that swathes or envelops ⟨the little children help to take away the baby's ~s —Nora Waln⟩ 2 : the act or process in basketwork of passing the weft completely around each warp in turn

wrapping-gown \ˈ≈≈,≈\ n : NIGHTGOWN

wraprascal \ˈ≈,≈≈\ n [¹wrap + rascal] : a long loose overcoat worn esp. in the 18th century

wraps pres 3d sing of WRAP, pl of WRAP

wrapt past of WRAP

wrap up vt 1 a : to bring to an esp. successful conclusion : END, FINISH, CONCLUDE ⟨wrapped up the case to their own satisfaction —John Lardner⟩ ⟨ready to wrap up the truce —N.Y. Times⟩ b : to confirm or assure the success of (as something practically won, reached, or assured) ⟨wrapped up the fight in the seventh round —Globe & Mail⟩ 2 : to involve deeply ⟨indeed, the whole policy of a cabinet may be wrapped up in the tax proposals —F.A.Ogg & Harold Zink⟩ ⟨the success of America is all wrapped up in and almost completely dependent on the efforts of 160 million people —G.M.Humphrey⟩ 3 : to make a single comprehensive report from ⟨the stories of newsmen on the scene were . . . wrapped up under a Tokyo dateline —Bruce Westley⟩

wrap-up \ˈ≈,≈\ n -s [wrap up] : a summarizing news report ⟨in just a moment we'll give you the wrap-up —Harry Wismer⟩

wrasse \ˈras, -aa(ə)s, -ais\ n -s [Corn wragh, gwragh] : any of numerous elongate compressed but heavy-bodied usu. brilliantly colored marine fishes of the family Labridae that are related to the parrot fishes but have separate teeth in their jaws and conspicuous thick lips, that are common along rocky shores, and that include various important food fishes esp. of warm seas as well as some that are reputed poisonous — see BALLAN, DONCELLA, GREEN WRASSE, HOGFISH 1a

¹wrath \ˈrath, ˈrāth, ˈräth, chiefly Brit ˈrōth\ n -s [ME wrath, wrathe, wraththe, fr. OE wrǣththu, wrǣththo, fr. wrāth angry, wroth — more at WROTH] 1 : a strong enraged feeling expressed vehemently and accompanied by bitterness, malignancy, or condemnation ⟨the ~ of the workers and peasants was being roused to liquidate the national capitalists —Raja Hutheesing⟩ 2 : righteous indignation and condemnation esp. of a deity or sovereign; also : retribution inspired by righteous indignation : justified punishment ⟨threats of the ~ to come —Max Peacock⟩ 3 a archaic : a fit of anger : a moment or period of malignant or indignant feeling b : an act inspired by wrath 4 : intense force or raging violence usu. joined with a seeming malevolence ⟨the great ~ of summer's heat has enveloped the state —Rufus Jarman⟩ syn see ANGER

²wrath \ˈ"\ adj : WRATHFUL

wrath·ful \-fəl\ adj [ME, fr. ¹wrath + -ful] 1 : feeling wrath : vehemently incensed and condemnatory, bitter, or vindictive 2 : arising from, marked by, or indicative of wrath 3 : having a threatening, ominous, or violent appearance ⟨~ skies⟩ syn see ANGRY

wrath·ful·ly \-fəlē, -li\ adv [ME wrathfulliche, fr. wrathful + -liche -ly] : in a wrathful manner

wrath·ful·ness n -ES [ME wrathefulnesse, fr. wratheful, wrathful + -nesse -ness] : the quality or state of being wrathful

wrath·i·ly \-thəlē, -li\ adv : in a wrathy manner

wrathy \-thē, -thi\ adj -ER/-EST [¹wrath + -y] : WRATHFUL

wrawl \ˈrōl\ vi -ED/-ING/-S [ME wrawlen, of imit. origin] dial Brit : CRY, HOWL, MEWL

wrax·le \ˈraksəl\ vi wraxled; wraxled; wraxling \-s(ə)liŋ\ wraxles [ME wraxlen, fr. OE wraxlian, wræxlian; akin to OE wrǣstlian to wrestle — more at WRESTLE] dial : WRESTLE

¹wreak \ˈrēk\ vt -ED/-ING/-S [ME wreken, fr. OE wrecan to drive, drive out, punish, avenge; akin to MD wreken to punish, avenge, OHG rehhan to avenge, ON reka to drive, push, avenge, Goth wrikan to persecute, L urgēre to press, drive, urge, Lith vargti to suffer distress and perh. to Skt vrajati he goes, proceeds; basic meaning: push, drive] 1 a (1) archaic : to take vengeance for : inflict punishment in retribution for : AVENGE ⟨~ thy wrongs in battle line —Sir Walter Scott⟩ (2) archaic : to avenge an injury done to ⟨grant me some knight to . . . ~ me for my son —Alfred Tennyson⟩ b : to act so as to exact or inflict (vengeance or punishment) ⟨the woeful retribution Nature ~ed upon a life of indulgence —George Meredith⟩ ⟨~ vengeance on the disturbers of their rights —R.W.Southern⟩ 2 a : to give free play or course to (a drive or an esp. malevolent feeling) : find outlet for in action or expression : INDULGE, GRATIFY ⟨must ~ my anger somewhere —H.J.Laski⟩ ⟨during one of these explosions he ~s the fullness of his fury upon his wife —Michele Cantarella⟩ ⟨could ~ his hungry curiosity upon her —Arnold Bennett⟩ b : to express or release completely : EXPEND ⟨an agony quickly ~ed and exhausted —F.J.Mather⟩ ⟨~ing our energies upon reforms —B.N.Cardozo⟩ 3 : to bring about (harm) : CAUSE, INFLICT ⟨employed to ~ evil on personal enemies —Notes & Queries on Anthropology⟩ ⟨the terribly severe winter . . . ~ed havoc among the animals —Alexander Tewnion⟩

²wreak \ˈ"\ n -s [ME wreke, fr. wreken to punish, avenge, wreak] archaic : REVENGE, VENGEANCE

wreak·ful \-fəl\ adj : REVENGEFUL

¹wreath \ˈrēth\ n, pl wreaths \-thz, -ths\ [ME wrethe, fr. OE writha; akin to OE wrīthan to twist — more at WRITHE] 1 : something twisted or intertwined into an approximately circular or spiral shape ⟨the tight plaited ~ of hair above her soft shrunken face —Helen Shaw⟩: as a (1) : a coronet, band, or fillet of intertwined flowers or leaves worn or bestowed as a mark of honor or victory or symbol of esteem : GARLAND, CHAPLET ⟨laurel ~⟩ (2) : a representation of such a garland made in metal or stone as a decoration (3) : an arrangement of foliage or flowers with or without decorative accessories on a circular base (as of wire) ⟨Christmas ~⟩ ⟨funeral ~⟩ b : an heraldic representation of a band or roll encircling a helmet, supporting a crest, and usu. representing a twist of two cords of silk one of which is tinctured like the principal metal and the other like the principal color in the arms; also : CHAPLET 1b c : the tail of a boar d archaic : a winding motion or the product of a winding motion : a partial or complete twist or twisting about a circle e : a cluster of spiraling or intertwining tendrils f : one of the turns of a spiral or ringed structure : WHORL g : a rising and coiling stream of smoke or vapor h : the part of the string or handrail in a geometrical stair that twists around a curve 2 obs : CREASE, WRINKLE 3 : a drift or bank of snow

wreath 1a(3)

²wreath \ˈ"\ vb -ED/-ING/-S : WREATHE

wreathe \ˈrēth\ vb -ED/-ING/-S [partly fr. ME wrethen, writhen, past part. of writhen to writhe and partly fr. ¹wreath — more at WRITHE] vt 1 a : to cause to writhe : TWIST, CONTORT ⟨wreathing his hands —C.S.Forester⟩ b : to alter the configurations of (the face) so as to smile ⟨their faces wreathed with pleasant social smiles —Margaret A. Barnes⟩ 2 a : to shape into a wreath or something resembling a wreath ⟨daisies and buttercups wreathed into a garland⟩ b : INTERWEAVE ⟨wreathing violins ~ a delicate countermelody —E.J.Stringham⟩ c : to coil so as to encircle something ⟨wreathed his legs about his stool⟩ 3 : to encircle, adorn, or crown with or as if with a wreath ⟨a poet's brow wreathed with laurel⟩ ⟨a high-waisted skirt . . . is wreathed with a black suede belt —New Yorker⟩ ⟨clouds wreathed the tallest pinnacles —G.W.Long⟩ 4 obs : to cause to rotate by force : twist about : wrench or turn forcibly 5 Scot : to surround or burden with (a yoke) ~ vi 1 : to twist in coils : WRITHE ⟨like the cobras they travel with head raised, and the body sways with a . . . wreathing movement —C.H.Curran & Carl Kauffeld⟩ ⟨smoke wreathing slowly from his short pipe —E.L.Thomas⟩ 2 : to take on the shape of a wreath : to move or extend in circles or spirals syn see WIND

wreath·en \ˈrēthən\ adj [ME wrethen, fr. past part. of writhen to writhe] 1 archaic : made into a wreath : WREATHED 2 archaic : formed, united, or disposed by or as if by twining or interweaving : INTERLACED, INTERTWINED

wreath·er \-thə(r)\ n -s : one that wreathes

wreath goldenrod n : a No. American perennial herb (Solidago caesia) with alternate lanceolate leaves and interrupted axillary clusters of yellow flower heads

wreath·ing·ly adv : in a wreathing manner : SPIRALLY

wreath·less \ˈrēthləs\ adj : having no wreath

wreath·let \-lət\ n -s : a small wreath

wreath shell n : TURBAN SHELL

wreathy \ˈrēthē, ˈrēthē, -i\ adj 1 : having the form of a wreath : WREATHED, TWISTED, CURLED, SPIRAL 2 : constituting a wreath

¹wreck \ˈrek\ n -s [ME wrek, fr. AF wrek, wrec, warec, of Scand origin; akin to ON rek wreck, reka to drive, push — more at WREAK] 1 : something that is cast up on the land by the sea; specif : goods and other material cast upon the land by the sea after a shipwreck ⟨when flotsam, jetsam and lagan are thrown by the waves on land, they become ~ —F.D.Smith & Barbara Wilcox⟩ 2 dial Brit : WRACK 2 3 a : the destruction or injury of a vessel by being cast on shore or on rocks or by being disabled or sunk by the force of winds or waves or by other accident : SHIPWRECK; also : an instance of such destruction or foundering b : the action of wrecking or the fact or state of being wrecked : destruction, disorganization, or serious injury of something esp. by violence : the process of bringing or being brought to disaster ⟨tempted motorists to such high speeds that ~s were frequent —Amer. Guide Series: Ark.⟩ ⟨two points of view are left, after the ~ of the naive progress-myth —Herbert Agar⟩ 4 a : a hulk or the ruins of a wrecked or stranded ship : a ship dashed against rocks or land and broken or otherwise made useless; also : a dilapidated old ship beyond or near the end of service b : the disordered or broken remains of something that has been wrecked, demolished, or otherwise ruined ⟨saw the ~ of a great civilization . . . and nothing left except some ruins and rocks —F.D.Roosevelt⟩ ⟨are these rings, perhaps, the ~s of ancient novae —Waldemar Kaempffert⟩ ⟨in the ~ of the ancient literature it is not easy to illustrate as abundantly —Benjamin Farrington⟩; also : the physically or spiritually broken or decayed remains of a person ⟨seeing the ~ of the flamboyant figure, to offer him food and drink —E.V.Lucas⟩ ⟨a ~ of former talent —H.J.Laski⟩ c : something that has been wrecked or disabled : something shattered or in a state of ruin or dilapidation ⟨an equally prominent location to deposit the ~ of a car —G.R.Stewart⟩; also : a person or animal of broken constitution, health, or spirits ⟨such work killed many of them, or deformed them, or left them tubercular ~s —Stringfellow Barr⟩ ⟨this poor ~ of a gutless coward —Barnaby Conrad⟩

²wreck \ˈ"\ vb -ED/-ING/-S [ME wrekken, fr. wrek wreck] vt 1 : to cast ashore 2 a : to reduce to a ruinous state by violence : overthrow, shatter, or destroy by force : cause to crash or suffer ruin ⟨~ a train⟩ ⟨the cashier's errors ~ed the bank⟩ : break up completely : FRUSTRATE ⟨~ a political program⟩ ⟨ambition ~ed his marriage⟩ b : to destroy, disable, or seriously damage (as a ship) by driving against the shore or on rocks or by causing to become unseaworthy or to founder : SHIPWRECK c : to involve in a wreck : cause to suffer or to be lost by shipwreck : ruin, damage, or imperil by wreck ⟨~ed freight⟩ ⟨passengers ~ed on the coast⟩ d : to involve in irreparable disaster or ruin ⟨~ himself with dissipation⟩ ⟨~ their future happiness⟩ e : to bring to a condition of complete physical impairment or to an unsound condition ⟨~ his constitution⟩ 3 a obs : WREAK 1b b : WREAK 3 ⟨they ~ havoc with hives, smashing commercial hives into splinters —Wildlife in North Carolina⟩ 4 : to free (tar) of liquid accumulated on the surface ~ vi 1 : to suffer wreck : become wrecked ⟨when the car ~ed at 3:30 a.m. —Springfield (Mass.) Daily News⟩ 2 : to search out, remove, rob, salvage, or repair wreckage or a wreck syn see DESTROY

wreck·age \-kij, -kēj\ n -s [²wreck + -age] 1 : the act or process of wrecking or the state of being wrecked ⟨its mutilated statues surviving the ~ of centuries —Agnes Repplier⟩ ⟨tried for alleged espionage, ~, counterrevolution —N.S. Timasheff⟩ 2 a : something that has been wrecked : the remains of a wreck b : fragments of wreck or of a wreck c : broken, disrupted, and disordered parts or material from a wrecked building or structure 3 : wretched or degraded beings cast off by society

wreck·er \ˈrekə(r)\ n -s 1 : one that wrecks: as a : one that wrecks ships (as by false signals) esp. for plunder b : one whose work is the demolition and removal of buildings or structures and usu. the salvage of material c : one that disrupts or frustrates plans, processes, or progress ⟨counterrevolutionary ~s had wormed their way into the census bureau and doctored the figures —Edmund Stevens⟩ 2 a : one that searches for or works upon the wrecks of ships: as (1) : one that appropriates wreck washed ashore or visits a wreck for plunder (2) : one that is employed in saving a wrecked or abandoned ship or property or lives from a wrecked ship b (1) : a ship employed in searching for or salvaging wrecked ships (2) : a railroad train or car equipped to clear wreckage from tracks, repair damaged roadbed and trackage, set upright usable rolling stock, and remove damaged rolling stock (3) : an automotive vehicle with hoisting apparatus and mechanical equipment for towing wrecked or disabled automobiles, freeing automobiles stalled in snow or mud, or making minor repairs or adjustments at the roadside — called also tow car c : one that purchases or acquires junked automobiles and salvages parts and material d : an operator of a railroad or automotive wrecker

wreckfish \ˈ≈,≈\ n [¹wreck + fish; fr. its being often found with wreckage] : STONEBASS

wreck·ful \ˈ≈fəl\ adj, archaic : causing wreck : involving ruin : DESTRUCTIVE

¹wrecking n -s [fr. gerund of ²wreck] 1 a : the action of causing a shipwreck esp. to obtain plunder b : the action or process or an instance of causing ruin, destruction, or the complete frustration of an enterprise 2 [¹wreck + -ing] : the action or occupation of saving or salvaging wrecked ships, vehicles, structures, or cargoes

²wrecking adj : engaged, used, or adapted or equipped for use in wrecking or demolishing something or in salvaging shipwrecks or otherwise removing wrecks or recovering ships, railroad rolling stock, or automobiles from a wrecked or disabled condition ⟨~ crew⟩ ⟨~ car⟩

wrecking ball n : SKULL CRACKER

wrecking bar n : an iron bar with one end bent and split to form a claw for pulling nails and the other end slightly bent and chisel-shaped for prying

wrecking frog n : RERAILER

wreckling obs var of RECKLING

wrecks pl of WRECK, pres 3d sing of WRECK

wreck train n : a train equipped to clear tracks of debris or damaged equipment following a wreck or destruction by other means

¹wren \ˈren\ n -s [ME wrenne, fr. OE wrenna, wrænna; prob. akin to OHG rentilo wren, Icel rindill] 1 : any of numerous small more or less brown singing birds constituting the family Troglodytidae; esp : a very small European wren (Troglodytes troglodytes) of a dark brown color barred and mottled with black that has a short erect tail and is a good singer — see CACTUS WREN, CANYON WREN, CAROLINA WREN, HOUSE WREN, MARSH WREN, ROCK WREN, WINTER WREN 2 : any of numerous small singing birds more or less like the true wrens in size and habits; esp : any of various European warblers (as the reed wren, sedge warbler, willow wren, golden-crested kinglet, or ruby-crowned kinglet) 3 slang : a young woman : GIRL

²wren \ˈ"\ n -s usu cap [Women's Royal Naval Service] : a member of the Women's Royal Naval Service established as an auxiliary of the British Navy during World War I, reorganized during World War II, and subsequently incorporated into the regular navy

wren babbler n : any of numerous small timaliine birds of Napothera and several related genera common in southern Asia and the East Indies

wren-boy \ˈ≈,≈\ n, Brit : one of a party of masked or costumed male singers that goes from house to house on Boxing Day carrying a holly bush with a wren or bright bits of cloth attached and begging gifts

¹wrench \ˈrench\ vb -ED/-ING/-ES [ME wrenchen, fr. OE wrencan to twist, wrench; akin to OHG renken to twist, wrench, Lith rengtis to bend over heavily, twist oneself, L vergere to bend, incline, Skt varjati he bends, turns; basic meaning: turning, bending, twisting] vi 1 a : to make or seem to make a sudden, sharp, or violent turning or twisting motion ⟨of a sudden her heart ~ed —Scott Fitzgerald⟩ ⟨the trail teetered down into a gulch and ~ed up the other side —A.B.Guthrie⟩; also : to undergo a turning or twisting by an outer force b of a hare : to veer so as to approach at less than a right angle 2 : to perform the action of pulling or straining at something with an esp. violent twisting ⟨tighten the nuts by light ~ing —B.G.A. Skrotzki & W.A.Vopat⟩ ⟨suspense ~ing at the pit of his stomach —Marcia Davenport⟩ ~ vt 1 : to twist violently to one side or out of line, shape, or position ⟨the wind ~ed the stems double —Pearl Buck⟩ ⟨~ed his head around —F.V.W. Mason⟩ 2 : to injure or disable by a violent twisting or straining : SPRAIN ⟨every joint and every muscle was ~ed —R.O.Bowen⟩ 3 : to alter from an original, normal, or true significance, intention, situation, or function ⟨a readiness to ~ language in order to gain nervous immediacy —Irving Howe⟩ ⟨these, then, are the highlights of the essay ~ed from their context —L.W.Elder⟩; esp : DISTORT, PERVERT ⟨a distributive language . . . has been ~ed . . . to make it fit an alien grammar —Charlton Laird⟩ ⟨each object is ~ed from its original purpose and changed into a work of art —G.H. Hamilton⟩ 4 a : to pull, jerk, or tighten by a twisting motion or with violence ⟨~ed open the back door —Patrick Campbell⟩ b : to wrest or force by or as if by a violent wrench or sudden twist : snatch forcibly ⟨by a terrible effort ~ed the tightening fingers away —Oscar Wilde⟩ ⟨~ed the jacket from him with unnecessary violence —G.B.Shaw⟩ ⟨~ing every penny from the poor —Michael McLaverty⟩ ⟨custom ~ed from her a small, stiff bow —Elizabeth Bowen⟩ c : to violently alter the situations, surroundings, or characteristics of ⟨had to ~ themselves back to the dull reality of the apartment —Bernard Frizell⟩ ⟨~ed from their older tribal society and thrust into new ways of life —H.R.Isaacs⟩ 5 : to cause (a hare) to swerve in a wrench 6 : to cause to suffer emotional distress or mental anguish : RACK ⟨a kaleidoscope of heart-wrenching incidents —Newsweek⟩ 7 NewZeal : ROOT-PRUNE

syn WREST, WRING: WRENCH indicates a twisting or turning with considerable force, often with an abrupt tug or yank, so that the thing affected is twisted, distorted, or forced out of position; it may stress the violence of exertion in pulling or yanking ⟨carelessly wrenching the pipe until it bent⟩ ⟨a wrenching effect on the basic structural line —Sidney Hyman⟩ ⟨jerked and wrenched savagely at his bridle, stopping the hard-breathing animal with a furious pull near the colonel —Stephen Crane⟩ WREST commonly indicates a twisting or wrenching, sometimes with crude violence, sometimes with continuing deftness and dexterity, from another's possession into one's own ⟨through the efforts of bold and ambitious men who wrest the power from the lords —Frank Thilly⟩ ⟨while one group of Mississippi valley pioneers advanced into the Southwest to wrest Texas from its Mexican owners —R.A.Billington⟩ ⟨when we could wrest the initiative from our enemies —F.D. Roosevelt⟩ WRING indicates a compressive twisting together, often to express or extract ⟨wring out wet clothes⟩ ⟨more farm output, both of foodstuffs and raw materials, must be wrung from the hard-pressed peasants —H.R.Lieberman⟩ ⟨wringing more blackmail from this unwarlike nation —C.S.Forester⟩

²wrench \ˈ"\ n -ES 1 : an act of wrenching or an instance of being wrenched: as a : a violent twisting to one side or out of shape or a pull with or as if with twisting ⟨with an immense ~ . . . he shook the men from off his back —Liam O'Flaherty⟩ b (1) : a sharp twist or sudden jerk straining muscles or ligaments : SPRAIN (2) : an injury by twisting (as in a joint) c : an often distorting or perverting alteration from a normal pattern or original signification ⟨in . . . the famous speech . . . a curious ~ and change of tone occurs shortly before the ending —Margery Bailey⟩ d : a separation or other change in circumstances causing acute emotional distress ⟨the ~ it must have been for my wife to leave her infant son at home —O.S.J. Gogarty⟩ ⟨it would be more of a ~ . . . to change . . . than to continue in the old cumbersome habits —A.L.Kroeber⟩; also : a painful twinge of feeling or sometimes a temporary or permanent psychological alteration caused by separation, loss, or other emotionally or psychologically disturbing events ⟨does not require too much of a psychological ~ for a hardened soldier to get rid of one, two, or three, if he is not in a mood to take prisoners —Theodore Draper⟩ ⟨the ~ from my childish faith in my father as perfect and omniscient —G.B.Shaw⟩ 2 : a turn at an acute angle made by a coursed hare 3 : a hand tool that usu. consists of a bar or lever with adapted or adjustable jaws, lugs, or sockets either at the ends or between the ends and is used for holding, twisting, or turning a bolt, nut, screwhead, pipe or other object; also : a power tool for similar purposes 4 : a physical system consisting of a force and a couple in a plane perpendicular to the force 5 : something causing a total upset or breakdown — used in such phrases as throw a wrench into ⟨before he could land another job, hard luck threw a ~ into his plans —F.B.Gipson⟩

³wrench \ˈ"\ dial var of RINSE

wrenched \-cht\ adj [fr. past part. of ¹wrench] : of, relating to, or being an accent that for the sake of metrical conformity is forced from a normally stressed syllable to one that is normally unstressed ⟨the accent on land in "and whén he cáme to fár Scotlánd" is ~⟩ — compare HOVERING ACCENT

wrench·er \-chə(r)\ n -s : one that wrenches or works with a wrench

wrenches pres 3d sing of WRENCH, pl of WRENCH

wrench head n : a head for a bolt or screw shaped (as square or hexagonal) so as to be readily gripped between the jaws of a wrench

wrench·ing·ly adv : to a wrenching degree ⟨can pose for the wife a ~ tough dilemma —W.H.Whyte⟩

wren·let \ˈrenlət\ n -s : a little wren

wren·e·an or **wren·ni·an** \ˈrenēən\ adj, usu cap [Christopher Wren †1723 Eng. architect + E -an] : of, relating to, or having the characteristics of the architect Wren or his works

wrens pl of WREN

wren's flower n [prob. after Christopher Wren †1723] : HERB ROBERT

wren-tit \ˈ≈,≈\ n : a small brown California bird (Chamaea fasciata) resembling a wren and having soft plumage and a long tail and short rounded wings — see PALLID WREN-TIT

wren warbler n : any of several small Asiatic and African sylviid birds of the genus Prinia some of which construct nests similar to those of tailorbirds

[1]wrest \'rest\ *vb* -ED/-ING/-S [ME *wresten, wrasten,* fr. OE *wrǣstan* to turn, twist, wrest; akin to ON *reista* to twist, wring, bend, OE *wrīthan* to twist — more at WRITHE] *vt* **1 a :** to pull, force, or move by violent wringing or twisting movements ⟨the rumble of freight being ~*ed* ashore —Archie Binns⟩ **b** *obs* **:** to insert by forcible twisting or wrenching **2 :** to gain with difficulty by or as if by coercive force, violent action, or steady determined labor ⟨they ~ a narrow survival from their extreme environment —A.L.Kroeber⟩ ⟨a tragedy that ~*s* poetry from what is sordid and properly colloquial —John Gassner⟩ ⟨~ control of the government from the military —W.J.Coughlin⟩ **3 a :** to divert to an unintended, unnatural, or esp. improper use ⟨wrong of her to take life in her hands and try to ~ it to her own purpose —Agnes S. Turnbull⟩ ⟨the evidence . . . was violently ~*ed* to fit the narrowness of the theory —F.A. Pottle⟩ **b** (1) **:** to misinterpret or misapply (a law) intentionally ⟨~ the laws so as to make officers appear guilty of offenses —*Salvation Army Orders*⟩ (2) *obs* **:** to divert or prevent (as a legal proceeding) from a just action or decision ⟨thou shalt not ~ judgment —Deut 16:19 (AV)⟩ **c :** to deflect or change from a true or normal bearing, significance, or interpretation **:** DISTORT ⟨every day they ~ my words —Ps 56:5 (AV)⟩ **~** *vi, obs* **:** to force one's way with violent effort **syn** see WRENCH

[2]wrest \"\ *n* -S [ME *wrest, wrast,* fr. *wresten, wrasten* to wrest] **1 :** the action of wresting **:** WRENCH, TWIST **2 :** a key or wrench formerly used for turning wrest pins in a harp, piano, or other stringed musical instrument

[3]wrest \"\ *n* -S [alter. (influenced by [2]*wrest*) of obs. E dial. *rest, reest,* fr. ME *rest,* fr. OE *rēost*] **:** the curved surface of a plow moldboard

wrest block *n* **:** PIN BLOCK

wrest·er \'restə(r)\ *n* -S **:** one that wrests meanings **:** PERVERTER

[1]wres·tle \'resəl, ÷ 'ras-\ *vb* **wrestled; wrestled; wrestling** \-s(ə)liŋ\ **wrestles** [ME *wrestlen, wrastlen,* fr. OE *wrǣstlian,* freq. of *wrǣstan* to turn, twist, wrest — more at WREST] *vi* **1 a :** to contend by grappling with and striving to trip or throw down an opponent — see WRESTLING **b :** to combat or overcome an opposing tendency or force, an unworthy psychic drive, or an antagonistic person or group ⟨he *wrestled* with his soul for a long time —Nicolas Slonimsky⟩ ⟨*wrestling* all his life with a feeling that he must be two different people at the same time —Eleanor Harris⟩ ⟨the devilish and the divine ~ for this boy's soul —Lee Rogow⟩ ⟨had to ~ desperately for a living in a . . . more competitive economy —C.J.Rolo⟩ **c :** to engage in deep or serious thought, consideration, or debate ⟨the engineer who must ~ with mining, water-supply, or transportation problems —P.E.James⟩ ⟨brooding over and *wrestling* with ideas —M.R.Cohen⟩ ⟨*wrestling* with the difficulties of transforming the reality of experience into the autonomous reality of fiction —Carlos Lynes⟩ **d :** to engage in or as if in a violent or determined purposive struggle ⟨stevedores *wrestled* with their loads —Joseph Wechsberg⟩ ⟨a nest of ants *wrestling* and tugging at a handful of bread crumbs —Norman Mailer⟩ ⟨less painful to slip a check into an envelope than ~ with the Christmas crowds —*New Yorker*⟩ **e :** to pray earnestly ⟨God's Son was *wrestling* in an agony of prayer —W.F. Hambly⟩ **2 a :** to twist about **:** WRITHE, SQUIRM **b :** to proceed or attempt to proceed with labored or strenuous effort ⟨the icebreaker . . . could smash, slash, and ~ almost indefinitely through solid pack ice —R.E.Byrd⟩ **~** *vt* **1 a :** to engage in (a match, bout, or fall) in wrestling **b :** to wrestle with **:** seek to throw down in or as if in wrestling ⟨~ an alligator⟩ **2 :** to thrust or carry with an action or an effort like wrestling **:** move or force by or as if by wrestling ⟨*wrestled* cotton bales on the levee —H.A.Sinclair⟩ ⟨*wrestled* a kind of manhole from the top of one tank —*New Yorker*⟩ ⟨~ the car along gravelly roads —R.M.Hodesh⟩

syn TUSSLE, GRAPPLE, SCUFFLE: WRESTLE applies to a struggling for mastery by the use, mainly or solely, of dexterous holds with the hands, arms, or legs; figuratively, it may designate a laborious striving at close quarters for mastery ⟨the perfectionist's instinct for *wrestling* with a problem until he had shaped it to his mental image —Irving Kolodin⟩ ⟨the senate was *wrestling* with the definition of unfair practices —F.L.Paxson⟩ TUSSLE may suggest a lighter, less arduous contesting or coping with at close quarters ⟨in bed screaming, determined to run away, *tussling* with my mother and father —Richard Wright⟩ ⟨all major presidents have *tussled* with the Supreme Court —R.A.Billington⟩ GRAPPLE may center attention on coming to grips with and striving for a vantage hold calculated to gain one mastery ⟨*grappled* and fell with his man, and shot him with a pistol —C.S.Forester⟩ ⟨a serious intelligence that must *grapple* with realities and shape them to its will —V.L.Parrington⟩ SCUFFLE may apply to a short, haphazard, and not very serious contest involving confusion, scrambling, and noise ⟨*scuffled* together, their laughter hooting down the street —Gordon Webber⟩

[2]wrestle \"\ *n* -S **:** the action or an instance of wrestling ⟨after a lengthy ~, he succeeded in extracting a tooth —R.L.Taylor⟩ ⟨the metaphysical ~ with the question of what is reality —Robert Richman⟩; *specif* **:** a struggle between two persons to see which will throw the other down **:** a wrestling bout

wres·tler \-s(ə)lə(r)\ *n* -S [ME *wrestlere, wrastlere,* fr. OE *wrǣstlere,* fr. *wrǣstlian* to wrestle + *-ere* -er] **:** one that wrestles; *specif* **:** one that engages in the sport of wrestling

wrestling *n* -S [ME *wresteling, wrasteling,* fr. OE *wrǣstlung,* fr. *wrǣstlian* to wrestle + *-ung* -ing] **:** the act of one who wrestles; *specif* **:** the sport consisting of the hand-to-hand combat between two unarmed contestants who seek to throw each other — compare CATCH-AS-CATCH-CAN, GRECO-ROMAN WRESTLING, JUJITSU

wrest pin *n* **:** a pin in a stringed musical instrument (as a harp, piano) around which the ends of the strings are coiled and by which the instrument is tuned

wrest plank *n* **:** PIN BLOCK

wrests *pres 3d sing of* WREST, *pl of* WREST

wretch \'rech\ *n* -ES [ME *wrecche,* fr. OE *wrecca, wræcca* outcast, exile, stranger; akin to OS *wrekkio* outcast, stranger, OHG *reccho, reckio* banished man, outcast, OE *wrecan* to drive out, punish — more at WREAK] **1 a :** a miserable person **:** one profoundly unhappy or in great misfortune, poverty, or distress ⟨starving, spiritless ~*es* —F.V.W.Mason⟩ **b :** something (as a child or pet) in slight misfortune ⟨the poor darling ~ —P.L.Fermor⟩ **2 :** one sunk in vice or degradation **:** a base, despicable, or vile person **:** one who is wicked, cruel, or contemptible ⟨a malignant ~ will cut his own throat because he sees you give alms to the deserving —Edmund Burke⟩

wretch·ed \'rechəd\ *adj, usu* -ER/-EST [ME *wrecched,* fr. *wrecche* wretch + *-ed*] **1 :** deeply afflicted, dejected, or distressed from want, disease, or mental anguish **:** extremely unhappy or unfortunate ⟨the ~ wife of the innocent man thus doomed to die —Charles Dickens⟩ ⟨the most ~ of all the sufferers from medieval lack of cleanliness —Edwin Benson⟩ **2 a :** characterized by or tending to produce misery **:** SQUALID, DISMAL, FOUL ⟨living conditions are ~ because the soil is so poor and dry —Juan Comas⟩ ⟨~ houses along the tracks . . . so old that some of them had earthen floors —Morley Callaghan⟩ **b :** producing or being marked by discomfort or distress ⟨spend a ~ night on the floor —Archie Binns⟩ ⟨a ~ journey by stage —Elinor Wylie⟩ ⟨~ health⟩ **3 :** having a mean or contemptible nature or appearance: as **a :** BASE, VILE **b :** MEAGER, PALTRY, INSUFFICIENT ⟨his ~ store of a few dried beans —Pearl Buck⟩ **c :** marked by mistreatment, undernourishment, or overuse **:** SHABBY, OUTWORN, GAUNT ⟨the scrawniest, ~*est* horse I had ever seen —Peter Kalischer⟩ ⟨a ~ purple and black costume that was frayed and stained —Barnaby Conrad⟩ ⟨the most ~ set of animals that he could buy . . . mangy lions and panthers and sick bears —Robert Graves⟩ **d :** exhibiting very poor quality or ability **:** inexpert, crude, or scanting in execution ⟨the latter poem being so ~ by the standard of the former —Robert Fitzgerald⟩ ⟨the army's ~ supply system had blundered again —F.V.W.Mason⟩ ⟨coinage of this period is noted for its ~ workmanship —J.F.Lhotka⟩ **syn** see MISERABLE

wretch·ed·ly *adv* [ME *wrecchedliche,* fr. *wrecched* wretched + *-liche* -ly] **1 :** in a wretched manner **2 :** to a deplorable or distressing degree **:** LAMENTABLY

wretch·ed·ness *n* -ES [ME *wrecchednesse,* fr. *wrecched* wretched + *-nesse* -ness] **:** the quality or state of being wretched **:** distress or hardship that is caused esp. by deprivation or affliction

wretch·less \'≈ləs\ *adj* [by alter.] *obs* **:** RECKLESS

wretch·less·ness *n* -ES [by alter.] **1** *obs* **:** RECKLESSNESS **2 :** callous disregard

wrfg *abbr* wharfage

WRI *abbr* war risk insurance

wried *past of* WRY

wrier *comparative of* WRY

wriest *superlative of* WRY

[1]wrig·gle \'rigəl\ *vb* **wriggled; wriggled; wriggling** \-g(ə)liŋ\ **wriggles** [ME *wrigglen,* fr. or akin to MLG *wriggeln* to wriggle; akin to D *wriggelen* to jerk, squirm, Norw dial. *rigla* to totter, OE *wrigian* to turn, go — more at WRY] *vi* **1 :** to move the body or a bodily part to and fro with short writhing motions like a worm **:** SQUIRM, WRITHE ⟨*wriggled* uncomfortably in his chair —Israel Zangwill⟩ **2 :** to move or advance with short quick contortions or by twisting and turning **:** go sinuously **:** MEANDER ⟨*wriggled* up the narrow gap between the cliff and the ice —*Sydney (Australia) Bull.*⟩ ⟨the narrowest apertures were wide enough for him to ~ through —R.M. Lovett⟩ ⟨an alluvial river *wriggling* downhill —A.W.Baum⟩ **3 :** to extricate or insinuate oneself or reach a goal by subtle maneuvering, equivocation, or ingratiation ⟨careful to ~ out of final opinions stated in quotable form —John Mason Brown⟩ ⟨attempts to ~ free from the moral obligation —John Burke⟩ **~** *vt* **1 :** to cause to move in short quick contortions **:** bring or set in motion by twisting or turning ⟨dancing girls . . . *wriggled* their hips in sensuous contortions —Harrison Forman⟩ **2 :** to introduce, insinuate, or bring into a state or place by or as if by wriggling ⟨*wriggled* her little person out over their backs —F. Tennyson Jesse⟩ ⟨languages can ~ themselves . . . into another compartment in a fairly short span —A.L.Kroeber⟩ **3 :** to proceed upon (one's way) by wriggling ⟨using every handhold on the rock in front I *wriggled* . . . my way up —John Hunt & Edmund Hillary⟩

[2]wriggle \"\ *n* -S **1 :** the action of wriggling **:** a short or quick writhing motion or contortion **:** a flection of the body **2 :** a formation or marking of sinuous design **:** something having a sinuous course or appearance caused or as if caused by wriggling ⟨the wavy ledges that once served as handles . . . degenerated to mere decorative ~*s* —V.G.Childe⟩ ⟨a ~ of barbed wire . . . marks the line of schism —A.J.Liebling⟩ **3 :** EYEBROW 3

wrig·gler \-g(ə)lə(r)\ *n* -S **:** one that wriggles; *specif* **:** WIGGLER 2

wrig·gling·ly *adv* **:** in a wriggling manner

wrig·gly \-g(ə)lē, -li\ *adj* -ER/-EST [[1]*wriggle* + *-y*] **:** wriggling or tending to wriggle **:** SQUIRMING

wright \'rīt, *usu* -īd.+V\ *n* -S [ME *wright, wrighte,* fr. OE *wyrhta, wryhta* worker, maker, wright; akin to OFris *wrichta* worker, OHG *wurhto* worker, OE *weorc, worc* work — more at WORK] **:** a workman in wood **:** CARPENTER — usu. used in combination ⟨mill*wright*⟩ ⟨ship*wright*⟩

wright buckwheat \'rīt-\ *n, usu cap W* [after Charles *Wright* †1885 Am. botanical explorer] **:** a woody-stemmed perennial (*Eriogonum wrightii*) of the desert regions of southwestern No. America

wright lippia *n, usu cap W* [after Charles *Wright* †1885] **:** a spreading aromatic shrub (*Lippia wrightii*) of the deserts of California

wright's stain \'rīts-\ *n, usu cap W* [after James Homer *Wright* †1928 Am. pathologist] **:** a stain that is a modification of the Romanowsky stain and is much used in staining blood and blood-living parasites

[1]wring \'riŋ\ *vb* **wrung** \'rəŋ\ **wrung; wringing; wrings** [ME *wringen,* fr. OE *wringan;* akin to MD *wringen* to wring, OHG *ringan* to strain, wrestle, struggle — more at WORRY] *vt* **1 a :** to compress by squeezing or twisting esp. so as to make dry or to extract moisture or liquid ⟨~ the laundry dry⟩ ⟨~ berries for wine⟩ **b** *obs* **:** to subject to extortion or coercion **:** SQUEEZE, OPPRESS **2 a :** to extract or obtain by or as if by twisting and compressing ⟨humidity . . . is *wrung* out by the gallon —Jim Riggs⟩ **b :** to exact or acquire by violence or coercion, against resistance, or with difficulty ⟨had to ~ whatever we've had out of barren ground —Ellen Glasgow⟩ ⟨wealth . . . *wrung* from the work of others —Bruce Marshall⟩ ⟨~ trade concessions from local rulers —Stringfellow Barr⟩ ⟨a confession was *wrung* from him —Harry Silver⟩ **c :** to bring to a specified state by or as if by compressing and squeezing **:** DRAIN ⟨never one to let an issue pass until it has been *wrung* dry —Cabell Phillips⟩ ⟨her voice was *wrung* of its . . . richness —Virginia Woolf⟩ **3 a :** to twist with a forcible or violent wrenching motion **:** twist so as to strain or sprain ⟨~ his neck⟩ **:** to twist (as a face) into a distorted shape **:** CONTORT, SCREW ⟨a smile *wrung* his lips —Ellen Glasgow⟩ **b :** to twist together (clasped hands) as a sign of anguish, despair, or disapproval ⟨she *wrung* her hands in mock despair —Oscar Wilde⟩ ⟨~*ing* your hands and complaining about the poor preparation of the students —J.B.Conant⟩ **c :** to bend or twist out of position or course ⟨a gust of wind *wrung* the sailboat to the side⟩ **4 :** to place, position, or insert by a twisting or writhing movement ⟨two blocks are *wrung* side by side on an optical flat —C.E.Haven & A.G.Strang⟩ ⟨~ or tap them into the holes —H.D.Burghardt & Aaron Axelrod⟩ **5 :** to affect painfully by or as if by a pinching, squeezing, twisting, or contorting action **:** cause distress or anguish to **:** RACK, TORMENT, TORTURE ⟨bumping over the rutted roads *wrung* her stomach muscles —Adria Langley⟩ ⟨where the shoe ~*s* him⟩ ⟨the plight of these people is a human tragedy which ~*s* the heart —H.G.Rickover⟩ **6 :** to shake (a hand) vigorously, tightly, or heartily as a greeting or a sign of affection ⟨*wrung* his hand like a pump handle —*English Digest*⟩; *also* **:** to wring the hand of **7 :** WREATHE, COIL **~** *vi* **1 :** to twist and turn esp. in pain, discomfort, or anguish **:** SQUIRM, WRITHE ⟨~*s* at some distress —Shak.⟩ **2 :** to undergo pain or anguish **syn** see WRENCH

[2]wring \"\ *n* -S [ME, fr. *wringen* to wring] **:** the act or process of wringing

wringbolt \'≈,≈\ *n* [alter. of *ringbolt*] **:** an eyebolt with the end cut in a wood screw used in shipbuilding as a temporary plank fastening while the permanent fastenings are being driven

wring·er \'riŋə(r)\ *n* -S [[1]*wring* + *-er*] **1 :** a worker who removes excess moisture from articles (as textiles, clothing, tobacco leaves, or leather) by wringing between rollers or in a centrifugal extractor **2 :** a machine or device for pressing out liquid or moisture ⟨clothes ~⟩ ⟨mop ~⟩ **3 :** an event, experience, or process that causes pain, hardship, or exhaustion — used in the phrase *through the wringer* ⟨workers, who have already undergone two loyalty or security investigations . . . must go through the ~ a third time —Elmer Davis⟩

wringer 2

wringing-wet \¦≈¦≈\ *adj* **:** so wet that liquid may be wrung out

wring-off \'≈,≈\ *n* -S [fr. the phrase *wring off*] **:** the twisting or gnawing off of a caught body part (as a paw) by an animal intent on escaping a trap

wringstaff \'≈,≈\ *n, pl* **wringstaves** [*wring* (as in *wringbolt*) + *staff*] **:** a strong piece of wood used in the ring of a wringbolt

[1]wrin·kle \'riŋkəl\ *n* -S [ME, back-formation from *wrinkled* twisted, winding, prob. fr. OE *gewrinclod,* past part. of *gewrinclian* to wind, fr. *ge-* (perfective and collective prefix) + *-wrinclian* to wind; akin to OE *wrencan* to twist — more at CO-, WRENCH] **1 :** a small ridge, prominence, or furrow esp. when formed on a surface by the shrinking or contraction of a smooth substance **:** a slight fold **:** CORRUGATION, CREASE ⟨~*s* in cloth⟩: as **a :** a small crease or ridge in the skin esp. when due to age, care, or fatigue ⟨a wrinkled face, with the shiny skin all drawn into ~*s* —Arnold Bennett⟩; *also* **:** loose pendulous folds of skin on the forehead and cheeks of some dogs ⟨a bloodhound with excellent ~⟩ **b :** a ripple on the surface of a liquid **c :** a ridge or fold as a topographical configuration ⟨a slight ~ on the surface of the ice cap —P.E. Victor⟩ **2 a :** METHOD, TECHNIQUE, *also* **:** information about a method **:** SUGGESTION, HINT ⟨welcomed the ~ about ruling a fine line with a knife edge through carbon paper —*Publishers' Weekly*⟩ ⟨learning countless little ~*s* on how to care for clothes in winter —Theodora Stanwell-Fletcher⟩ **b :** an innovation in method, technique, or equipment **:** a change in customary procedure or attitude ⟨the sit-down strike, an obstructionist ~ imported from abroad —*Current History*⟩ ⟨a new ~ whereby the exhaust gases are used to spin small turbines geared direct to the propeller shaft —P.J.C. Friedlander⟩ **3 :** FAULT, BLEMISH ⟨undertook to defend the Church with all her ~*s* —V.G.Kiernan⟩

[2]wrinkle \"\ *vb* **wrinkled; wrinkled; wrinkling** \-k(ə)liŋ\ **wrinkles** *vi* **1 :** to be or become marked with or contracted into wrinkles **:** become puckered or shrink into furrows and ridges ⟨the corners of her eyes *wrinkling* with amusement —Morley Callaghan⟩ ⟨his stomach *wrinkled* up like an unpropped wall collapsing on its own foundations —Liam O'Flaherty⟩ **2 :** to move or become moved in slight furrows, waves, or coils ⟨his pajama jacket had *wrinkled* up to his chin —Alan Moorehead⟩ ⟨a single wave starts lightly and easily shoreward, *wrinkling* between reeds —Theodore Roethke⟩ **~** *vt* **1 :** to contract into furrows and prominences **:** make wrinkles in **:** CORRUGATE, CREASE, PUCKER ⟨a homemade pink voile dress . . . *wrinkled* as tissue paper —Eudora Welty⟩ ⟨young mountain belts, where . . . the earth has recently been *wrinkled* and cracked —Howel Williams⟩ **2 :** to form wrinkles in the integument of or surrounding ⟨~ her nose appreciatively —Elizabeth Goudge⟩ ⟨*wrinkling* up his face as though he had already forgotten —P.H.Newby⟩

[3]wrinkle \"\ *n* -S [by alter.] *dial* **:** WINKLE

wrin·kled·ness *n* -ES **:** the quality or state of being wrinkled

wrin·kle·less \'≈≈ləs\ *adj* **:** having no wrinkles **:** SMOOTH

wrinkle–lipped bat \'≈≈¦≈-\ *n* **:** any of various widely distributed chiefly tropical free-tailed bats (family Molossidae)

wrin·kly \'riŋk(ə)lē, -li\ *adj* -ER/-EST **:** having wrinkles **:** CORRUGATED, PUCKERED

wrisberg's cartilage *n, usu cap W* [after Heinrich A. *Wrisberg* †1808 Ger. anatomist] **:** CARTILAGE OF WRISBERG

wrisberg's ganglion *n, usu cap W* [after Heinrich A. *Wrisberg* †1808] **1 :** a small ganglion in the superficial cardiac plexus **2 :** GASSERIAN GANGLION

wrisberg's nerve *n, usu cap W* [after Heinrich A. *Wrisberg* †1808] **1 :** GLOSSOPALATINE NERVE **2 :** the medial brachial cutaneous nerve

wrist \'rist\ *n* -S *often attrib* [ME, fr. OE; akin to OFris *wrist, wirst* wrist, MHG *rist* wrist, ankle, ON *rist* instep, OE *wrǣstan* to turn, twist — more at WREST] **1 :** the joint or the region of the joint between the human hand and the arm or a corresponding part on a lower animal **:** CARPUS ⟨~ strap⟩ ⟨~ stroke⟩ **2 :** the part of a garment or glove covering the wrist

wrist·band \'ris(t),≈ *archaic chiefly Brit* 'riz,≈ *or* -,band\ *n* **1 :** the lower part of a sleeve covering the wrist and usu. being a cuff, ruffle, or band **2 :** something in the shape of a band encircling the wrist

wrist·bone \'ris(t)¦≈\ *n* **1 :** a carpal bone **2 :** the styloid process of the radius in man that forms a prominence on the outer side of the wrist above the thumb

wrist·drop \'ris(t),≈\ *n* **:** paralysis of the extensor muscles of the hand causing the hand to hang down at the wrist

wrist·er \'ristə(r)\ *n* -S **1 :** a warm knitted covering for the wrist **2 :** a machine operator who stitches the wristbands to gloves and mittens

wrist joint *n* **:** the articulation at the wrist

wrist·let \'ris(t)lət\ *n* -S **:** a band or strap encircling the wrist; *specif* **:** a close-fitting knitted band worn for warmth and attached to a sleeve, glove, or mitten

wristlet watch *n, Brit* **:** WRISTWATCH

wrist·lock \'rist,≈\ *n* **:** a wrestling hold in which one contestant is thrown or made helpless by a twisting grip on the wrist

wrist pin *n* **:** a stud or pin that forms a journal (as in a crosshead or trunk piston) for a connecting rod — see CROSSHEAD illustration

wrist play *n* **:** batting in cricket characterized by free movement of the wrists

wrist shot *n* **:** a short golf stroke played chiefly from the wrists and usu. with an iron

wrist·watch \'ris,twäch\ *n* **:** a small watch attached to a bracelet or strap to fasten about the wrist

wristwatch

wrist·work \'ris,twərk\ *n* **:** flexion of the wrist (as in stroking a ball); *esp* **:** WRIST PLAY

wristy \'ristē, -ti\ *adj* -ER/-EST **:** using wrist play

writ \'rit, *usu* -id.+V\ *n* -S [ME, fr. OE; akin to ON *rit* writing, writ, Goth *writs* stroke, letter — more at WRITE] **1 :** something that is written **:** writing or a written document — used esp. in the phrases *holy writ* and *sacred writ* **2 a :** a formal written document; *specif* **:** a legal instrument in epistolary form issued under seal in the name of the English monarch from Anglo-Saxon times to declare his grants, wishes, and commands — see ORIGINAL WRIT **b :** an order or mandatory process in writing issued under seal in the name of the sovereign or of a court or judicial officer from the proper authority commanding the person to whom it is directed to perform or refrain from performing an act specified therein: as (1) **:** one used in a particular legal action ⟨~ of account⟩ ⟨~ of aiel⟩ ⟨~ of covenant⟩ ⟨~ of detinue⟩ (2) **:** one used to enforce a right ⟨~ of dower⟩ ⟨~ of entry⟩ ⟨~ of possession⟩ (3) **:** one used to convey a command or put something (as a court decision) in force ⟨~ of execution⟩ — see WRIT OF PROHIBITION (4) **:** one used to redress a wrong ⟨~ of spoliation⟩ **c :** such a written order held to constitute a symbol of the power and authority of the issuer ⟨the mountain ranges . . . halted the reach of the royal ~ and the king's command —W.C.Dickinson⟩ — usu. used with *run* ⟨northern Zululand was a sort of Alsatia where the Queen's ~ did not run —Deneys Reitz⟩ ⟨peoples outside the United States where our laws do not govern and our ~ does not run —Dean Acheson⟩ **d :** a document issued usu. by the clerk of the crown in chancery directing the returning officer of a British parliamentary constituency to hold an election for a member of the House of Commons

writ·able \'rīd·əbəl, -ītə-\ *adj* [[1]*write* + *-able*] **:** capable of being put in writing **:** reducible to written form

writ·a·tive \'rīd·əd·iv\ *adj* [[1]*write* + *-ative*] **:** addicted to writing

[1]write \'rīt, *usu* -īd.+V\ *vb* **wrote** \'rōt, *usu* -ōd.+V\ *also dial* **writ** \'rit, *usu* -id.+V\ *or South* **writ·ten** \'rit°n\ **written** *also* **writ** *or dial* **wrote; writing; writes** [ME *writen,* fr. OE *wrītan* to scratch, draw, engrave, write; akin to OS *wrītan* to tear, wound, scratch, write, OHG *rīzan* to tear, ON *rīta* to write on parchment, Goth *writs* stroke, letter, Gk *rhinē* file, rasp, Skt *vraṇa* wound, tear, *vrhati* he tears, plucks; basic meaning: incision, tearing] *vt* **1 a** (1) **:** to draw or form by or as if by scoring or incising a surface ⟨creases . . . *written* by laughter —Monica Pearson⟩ (2) **:** to trace (a symbol or a meaningful combination of symbols) by carving or scoring **:** INSCRIBE ⟨a psalter *written* on wax —Eleanor Hull⟩ ⟨the engraver *wrote* the inscription composed for the trophy⟩ **b** (1) **:** to form or trace (a character or series of characters) on paper or other suitable material with a pen or pencil ⟨~ 7 instead of 9⟩ (2) **:** to form or record (a meaningful sign) by a series of written characters ⟨*wrote* 1000 words this afternoon —Arnold Bennett⟩ (3) **:** to spell in writing ⟨words *written* alike but pronounced differently⟩ **c :** to write significant or legible characters upon **:** cover, fill, or fill in by writing ⟨~ a check⟩ ⟨~ ten pages a day⟩ ⟨~ a postcard⟩ **d :** to form or produce (a legible character) in, upon, or by means of a suitable medium ⟨his name *written* in lights on the marquee⟩ ⟨an advertisement *written* by skywriting⟩ ⟨*wrote* the letter *A* on the frosted windowpane⟩ **e :** to produce (symbols or words) by machine ⟨by hitting combinations of keys, a child can ~ the letters he wants —Lois Henderson⟩ **f :** DICTATE 1 ⟨*wrote* the speech twice; the first time he forgot to put a disc in his dictation machine —Leonard Lyons⟩ **2 :** to put down esp. on paper in order to record, relate, or explain **:** set down in writing ⟨whose life has lately been *written* —Norman Douglas⟩ ⟨may have *written* these notes about that date —R.S.Whipple⟩ ⟨when a man ~s his wrongs —W.L.Sullivan⟩: as **a** : to draw up : DRAFT ⟨get a lawyer to ~ your will⟩ ⟨~ a more liberal program which might run into a presidential veto —John Bird⟩ **b** (1) : to compose in a literary form : be the author of : construct according to literary precepts ⟨more concerned to ~ an adventure story than to compile a careful geographical work —*Geog. Jour.*⟩ ⟨this middle eighteenth century *wrote* little literature —V.L.Parrington⟩ ⟨all the poetry that has ever been *written* —T.S.Eliot⟩ ⟨~ the libretto for an opera⟩ ⟨*wrote* a suitable epitaph —J.G.Colton⟩ (2) : to compose in musical form : be the composer of ⟨a commission to ~ an opera —H.T. & D.A.Schnittkind⟩ ⟨~ a string quartet⟩; *also* : to produce musical notation for ⟨the guitar is sounded an octave lower than *written*⟩ **c** : to set forth in written language : express in literary form : reveal, describe, treat of, or depict by means of words ⟨the great poet, in *writing* himself, writes his time —T.S.Eliot⟩ ⟨could not ~ a claim —John McNulty⟩ ⟨if I could ~ the beauty of your eyes —Shak.⟩ **d** (1) : to communicate a message by ⟨judged that at least one of every fifty residents . . . had *written* me a letter —Jane Woodfin⟩ (2) : to make known in writing ⟨*wrote* that he was leaving⟩ **e** : to use or exhibit (a specific script, language, or literary form or style) in writing ⟨blind people who ~ Braille —Lois Henderson⟩ ⟨~*s* French with ease⟩ ⟨~*s* a free and easy vernacular⟩ ⟨~ poetry⟩; *esp* : to make use of (an easy flowing script) ⟨taught to ~ cursive rather than to print⟩ **f** : to write contracts or orders for ⟨dealers began to get traffic and ~ business —William McNeill⟩ ⟨~ options on securities⟩; *esp* : UNDERWRITE ⟨~ life insurance⟩ **3** : to make a permanent impression of : mark indelibly ⟨a law of right conduct, *written* in our hearts —Herbert Agar⟩ ⟨history, adventure, and romance are *written* in the doorways and roof lines —*Amer. Guide Series: Del.*⟩ **4** : to communicate with in writing : write a message to ⟨he *wrote* them upon his arrival⟩ **5** : to style, call, sign, or exhibit in writing : set down : record to be something ⟨his desire to ~ himself M.A. on the title page —J.H.Sledd & G.J.Kolb⟩ **6** : to make necessary : ORDAIN, FATE ⟨so be it, it is *written* —D.C.Peattie⟩ **7** : to cause to appear evident or obvious : impress the stamp of ⟨the happiness and peace *written* on the faces of these people —G.P.Musselman⟩ ⟨his crafty caution *written* all over him —H.J.Laski⟩ **8** : to bring, force, effect, or cause the introduction or removal of by writing ⟨major achievements of the U. S. labor movements are *written* into collective bargaining contracts —V.G.Reuther⟩ ⟨has *written* the forlorn little working girl . . . into American fiction —Harry Hansen⟩ ⟨his love was *written* into his affectionate letters —Ruth P. Randall⟩ ⟨~ oneself into fame and fortune —Charles Lee⟩ **9** : to take part in or bring about (something worthy of recording) ⟨medical research in America today is *writing* one of the most heartwarming chapters in the story of mankind —*advt.*⟩ ⟨the Colorado river has been *writing* a record of history in the earth's crust —*Hot-Metal Magic*⟩ **10** READ 1i ~ *vi* **1 a** : to make significant characters or inscriptions by or as if by incising, scratching, engraving, or esp. penning ⟨*wrote* on stone tablets⟩; *also* : to permit or be adapted to writing ⟨this pen ~*s* well⟩ **b** : to form or produce letters, words, or sentences with a pen, pencil, or machine ⟨on the typewriter, having taught herself to ~ by position and touch —S.H.Adams⟩ **2** : to compose, communicate by, or send a letter ⟨*wrote* home in glowing terms of the land of their adoption —*Lutheran Quarterly*⟩ ⟨had *written* to some missionary society —W.B.Yeats⟩ **3 a** : to produce or be engaged in producing a poem, book, play, story, or article : give literary or journalistic form to a conception, plot, or happening ⟨*writing* on a second novel —J.K.Hutchens⟩ ⟨*wrote* to a simple and direct theme — human endurance —Leslie Rees⟩ ⟨*writing* despairingly of her husband's being drafted —Margaret Redfield⟩ **b** : to compose music ⟨~ in the sonata form⟩ ⟨~ for four voices⟩ **c** : to become regularly employed or occupied in writing: as (1) : to become engaged in journalism : do editorial work or reporting ⟨~*s* for the press⟩ (2) : to follow the profession of author or composer — **write home about** : to comment on at length and esp. in a favorable manner ⟨as a forest, it was nothing to *write home about* —Gerard Newton⟩ ⟨the entertainment at the embassy was something to *write home about*⟩ — **write one's own ticket** : to select a course of action or a position or salary entirely according to one's own wishes or desires ⟨allowed the scientists to *write their own tickets* for the kind of research setup they want —E.P.Snow⟩ — **writ large** *also* **written large** : written or manifested on an expanded scale or in a clearer or more prominent manner ⟨the results are *writ large* in the story of the war —J.P.Baxter b.1893⟩ ⟨the problems of modern totalitarianism are only our own problems *writ large* —*Times Lit. Supp.*⟩ — **writ small** : on a diminished scale ⟨personality is culture *writ small* —C.K.Kluckholn⟩

²write \"\ *n* -s : sharp clear typewritten lettering or impression ⟨clearness of ~⟩

write down *vt* **1** : to commit to writing : record in written form ⟨*write down* each letter as you receive it —*Boy Scout Handbk.*⟩ ⟨instruments . . . which automatically *write down* their impressions of temperature —Waldemar Kaempffert⟩ ⟨*writes* herself *down* as a United States citizen —*Current Biog.*⟩ **2** : to record, regard, or reveal as being ⟨not to be somewhat hilarious would be to *write* oneself *down* a bore —H.A. Overstreet⟩ **3 a** : to depreciate, disparage, or injure by writing ⟨has very properly *written down* his value as a straight novelist —*Times Lit. Supp.*⟩ **b** : to reduce in status, rank, or value ⟨the legal position of the service secretaries was therefore *written down* —T.K.Finletter⟩; *specif* : to reduce the book value of ⟨*write down* an asset⟩ **c** : to play down in writing ⟨each of the men's parts is deliberately *written down* to leave her role supreme —*Times Lit. Supp.*⟩ ~ *vi* : to write so as to appeal to a lower level of taste, comprehension, or intelligence : popularize or simplify unduly ⟨unnecessary *writing down* to the juvenile audience —Anthony Boucher⟩

write-down \ˈ=,=\ *n* -s [*write down*] : a deliberate reduction in the book value of an asset : the process of purposively reducing value

write in *vt* [ME *writen in*] **1 a** : to insert in a document, text, or other writing ⟨*write in* an amendment to a law⟩ **b** (1) : to insert (a name not listed on a ballot or voting machine) in an appropriate space by writing or use of a printed sticker (2) : to cast (a vote) in this manner **2** : to write to a center of activity or source of supply ⟨teachers are encouraged to *write in* their requests —James Britton⟩

write-in campaign \ˈ=,=-\ *n* : a political campaign carried on to encourage writing in a candidate's name

write-in vote *or* **write-in** *n* -s : a vote cast by writing in the name of a candidate ⟨received 10,000 *write-in votes* for governor⟩ ⟨a heavy *write-in vote* for his opponent⟩

write off *vt* **1 a** (1) : to reduce the estimated value of : DEPRECIATE ⟨the $50,000,000 item of "Good Will" . . . had been *written off* to a nominal $1 —*Woolworth's First 75 Years*⟩ (2) : to take off the books : CANCEL ⟨*write off* uncollectibles⟩ **b** : to derogate or deny the worth of : regard or concede to be lost, outmoded, exhausted, outworn, destroyed, or useless ⟨the lighter, translucent style was more or less *written off* —Israel Citkowitz⟩ ⟨*writing* its mission *off* as a complete failure —*Current History*⟩ **c** : DESTROY, KILL, END ⟨*written off* a pretty shabby kind of life by getting himself killed —Angus Mowat⟩ **2** : to write fluently, rapidly, or without hesitation ⟨set to work to learn what he had *written off* by heart —Nevil Shute⟩

write-off \ˈ=,=\ *n* -s **1 a** : an elimination from the books : CANCELLATION **b** : the act of eliminating from the books ⟨the *write-off* of uncollectibles⟩ **2 a** : a reduction in book value : DEPRECIATION ⟨a *write-off* for amortization⟩ **b** : the act of reducing book value

write out *vt* **1** : to put in writing ⟨*wrote out* the Greek alphabet —Joseph Gaer⟩; *esp* : to put into a full and complete written form : make a full record or statement of in writing ⟨the book in which he *wrote out* his plots —Peter Forster⟩ **2** : to exhaust the literary ability or resources of (oneself) by writing too much ⟨an American who had *written* himself *out* —Perry Miller⟩

writ·er \ˈrīd·ə(r), -ītə-\ *n* -s [ME *writere*, fr. OE *wrītere*, fr. *wrītan* to write + *-ere* -er — more at WRITE] **1** : one that practices writing as an occupation: as **a** (1) : one that writes books, articles, or other material for publication (2) : one that writes stories, scenarios, or advertising for motion pictures (3) : a composer of music **b** (1) : SCRIVENER, SCRIBE (2) : a clerk of the East India Company (3) : YEOMAN 1f **c** (1) : WRITER TO THE SIGNET (2) *Scot* : LAWYER, SOLICITOR; *also* : a lawyer's chief clerk **d** (1) : one that writes insurance (2) : one that accepts, records, and issues receipts for bets as agent of a numbers game **e** : one that transcribes or paints lettering for signs or ornaments **2 a** : one that writes or is able to write : PENMAN **b** : BRAILLEWRITER **3** : a person engaged in writing ⟨a number of agricultural economists, the ~ included —C.C.Mitchell⟩ ⟨eludes this ~'s memory —E.A. Lahey⟩

writer's cramp *also* **writer's palsy** *or* **writer's spasm** *n* : a painful spasmodic cramp of muscles of the hand or fingers brought on by excessive use in writing

writ·er·ship \ˈ==,ship\ *n* : the position or function of a writer in the East India Company

writer to the signet [ME] : a Scotch judicial officer responsible for preparing warrants, writs, and other documents and being orig. a clerk in the office of the secretary of state

writes *pres 3d sing of* WRITE, *pl of* WRITE

write up *vt* [ME (Sc) *writen up*] **1 a** : to write an account of : describe fully ⟨stuff on the early history of toleration . . . which, when *written up*, will . . . be quite new —H.J.Laski⟩ ⟨*wrote* him *up* on the front page —Irwin Deutscher⟩ **b** : to put into finished written form (as the raw material of a report or a piece of fiction) ⟨*write up* a story idea in the form of a one-act play⟩ ⟨*wrote up* his notes on the train⟩ **c** : to increase the interest or significance of (a piece of writing) by attractive language or presentation **2** : to bring up to date the writing of **3** : to set down an unduly high value for : increase the book value of ⟨*write up* an asset⟩ **4** : to write a summons for : prefer charges against ⟨cars found parked in the streets . . . will be *written up* —*Springfield (Mass.) Union*⟩

write-up \ˈ=,=\ *n* -s [*write up*] **1 a** : an esp. flattering written or printed official, literary, or journalistic account **b** : a written or printed account designed to emphasize or overstress the interest or significance of a topic **2 a** : an increase in the book value or alleged assets of a corporation **b** : the act of setting down an unduly high value

¹writhe \ˈrīth\ *vb* -ED/-ING/-S [ME *writhen*, fr. OE *wrīthan* to twist; akin to OHG *rīdan* to turn, twist, ON *rītha* to twist, writhe, OSw *vritha* to twist, Lith *riesti* to wind, roll, OE *wrigian* to turn, go — more at WRY] *vt* **1 a** : to twist into coils or folds **b** : to twist so as to distort, strain, break off, or cause pain : WRENCH, WRING **c** : to twist (the body or a bodily part) in pain **2** : INTERTWINE ⟨so *writhed* together that you can liken them only to a forest of snakes —Thomas Wood †1950⟩ ~ *vi* **1 a** : to move or proceed with twists and turns : wind in a sinuous fashion ⟨wreaths of windblown smoke . . . ~ in long spirals —Alice Duncan-Kemp⟩ ⟨the line *writhed* across the canvas —F.J.Mather⟩ ⟨a six-foot boa constrictor . . . *writhed* up a high-tension tower —*Time*⟩ **b** : to exhibit writhing markings : become covered with twists and contortions ⟨the canvas ~*s* with curves —F.J. Mather⟩ ⟨a black tonneau *writhing* with carvings —Earle Birney⟩ **2** : to become twisted, contorted, or wrested about in or as if in pain or struggling ⟨*writhed* and thrashed . . . in a sort of convulsion —C.G.D.Roberts⟩ ⟨the victim ~*s* and curls amid the stench of burning flesh —H.G.Armstrong⟩ ⟨dancing girls leaped and *writhed* and wriggled their hips —Harrison Forman⟩ **3** : to suffer keenly from something tormenting ⟨touched some hidden nerve of pride, and made her ~ in agony —G.D.Brown⟩ ⟨corrupt men in the machines ~ in the presence of his obvious integrity —Helen Fuller⟩

syn AGONIZE, SQUIRM, WRITHE mean to twist or turn, usu. continually, in physical or mental distress. WRITHE always suggests nervous or convulsive contortions; in application to physical distress it implies great pain; in application to mental distress, it implies a torturing sense of embarrassment, shame, bafflement, or frustration ⟨saw an owl rise with the tiny rabbit *writhing* in its claws —Willard Robertson⟩ ⟨a great human hulk *writhing* under the unutterable torments of mastery he cannot contend with —George Meredith⟩ ⟨the rest of one's being *writhes* helplessly under a double shame —J.C. Powys⟩ AGONIZE can suggest either severe pangs (as of torture or anguish) or the struggles of one straining violently for a particular end (as victory) ⟨finally recognizes the hopelessness of his marriage and clears out, upset and *agonized* over events —Chad Walsh⟩ ⟨the gray-minded people who cannot rejoice just as they cannot *agonize* —Edith Hamilton⟩ ⟨her tender, innocent *agonizings* for . . . the children's happiness —Agnes S. Turnbull⟩ SQUIRM implies wriggling or turning on a less dignified scale, suggesting great uneasiness rather than profound distress, as from shrinking or wincing under sarcasm or embarrassment ⟨*squirmed* like a little boy called on to explain himself before the principal —Dorothy Baker⟩ ⟨felt so embarrassed that I *squirmed* —Edita Morris⟩

²writhe \"\ *n* -s : an act or instance of writhing : CONTORTION, TWIST ⟨a more than ordinary ~ of the body —Aldous Huxley⟩

writh·en \ˈrithən\ *adj* [ME, fr. OE, fr. *gewrithen*, past part. of *wrīthan* to twist] **1** : INTERTWINED; *also* : COILED, LOOPED **2** : subjected to writhing : WRITHED, TWISTED, CONTORTED ⟨~ thorns and strange wild flowers —S.P.B.Mais⟩ ⟨lay ~ and gasping on the pavement —Arthur Morison⟩

writh·ing·ly \ˈrīthiŋlē\ *adv* : in a writhing manner : with or by twisting

wri·thled \ˈrithəld\ *adj* [¹*writhe* + *-led* (as in *wrinkled*)] *archaic* : WRINKLED, SHRIVELED

¹writing *n* -s [ME, fr. gerund of *writen* to write — more at WRITE] **1** : the act or process of one who writes ⟨with one ~, copies may be made —E.M.Robinson⟩: as **a** : the act or art of forming letters on stone, paper, wood, or other suitable medium to record the ideas which characters and words express or to communicate the ideas by visible signs : the use of characters to record in visible form words or sounds ⟨if ~ were not to be done on stone with a chisel but on wood or papyrus —Georg Steindorff & K.C.Seele⟩ ⟨~ on the air with the index finger . . . took the place of pad and pencil —Caroline Yale⟩; *specif* : HANDWRITING 1 **b** : the act or practice of literary, journalistic, or other composition in words ⟨engaged in the ~ of a novel⟩; *also* : the act or practice of musical composition ⟨his adroit ~ for the keyboard —Arthur Berger⟩ **2** : something written: as **a** : letters or characters formed on a surface that serve as visible signs of ideas, words, or symbols ⟨alphabetic ~⟩ ⟨cuneiform ~⟩ ⟨syllabic ~⟩ ⟨do you recognize the ~⟩ **b** : a letter, note, or notice used to communicate or record information **c** (1) : a written composition : a book, pamphlet, poem, article, or other literary production : PUBLICATION ⟨his biographies and ~*s* on medical subjects —*Current Biog.*⟩ ⟨a wide variety of ~*s* about literature —C.W. Shumaker⟩ ⟨his collected ~*s* in 10 volumes⟩ (2) : a musical composition (3) : a literary, artistic, or musical composition (as a novel or sculpture) that can be copyrighted **d** : INSCRIPTION **e** (1) : a written or printed paper or document (as a deed, contract, pleading in court) (2) : an impression of characters on paper or other substance by printing, photography, pencil, pen and ink, or other means **3** : a style or form of composition : a manner of literary or musical expression ⟨straightforward narrative interspersed with passages in baroque ~⟩ **4** : the occupation of a writer; *esp* : the profession of authorship — **writing on the wall** : HANDWRITING ON THE WALL

²writing *adj* **1** [¹*writing*] : of, relating to, or used in or for writing ⟨~ table⟩ ⟨~ pad⟩ **2** [fr. pres. part. of ¹*write*] : engaged in writing

writing arm *n* : the wooden arm of a tablet-arm chair widened to form a writing surface

writing bureau *n, Brit* : BUREAU 1a

writing chair *n* [ME *writing chare*] **1** : CORNER CHAIR **2** : TABLET-ARM CHAIR

writing desk *n* : a desk often with a sloping top for writing upon; *also* : a portable case containing writing materials for and having a surface for writing

writing arm on a Windsor chair

writing ink *n* : ink that is to be used with a pen and that may be permanent (as a blue-black ink) consisting essentially of a dispersion of gallic acid or tannin, ferrous sulfate, and often a blue dye in water or nonpermanent containing soluble dyes and including washable inks — compare INDIA INK 2

writing master *n* : an instructor in penmanship

writing paper *n* : paper intended for writing upon with ink that is usu. finished with a smooth surface and sized

writing school *n* : a school teaching mainly writing common till the end of the 18th century and found in frontier regions still later

writ of assistance **1** : a writ issued by a court of equity to a sheriff, marshal, or other law officer for the enforcement of an order or decree of the court; *esp* : one used to enforce an order for the possession of lands **2** : a writ issued to a sheriff or other officer to aid in the search for smuggled or otherwise uncustomed goods

writ of certiorari : CERTIORARI

writ of cla·re con·stat \-ˌkla(a)rēˈkänˌstat\ [*clare constat* fr. L, it is clearly established] : a writ in Scots law by which a superior confirms the heirship of a person claiming to be the next heir of the last tenant deceased — compare PRECEPT OF CLARE CONSTAT

writ of consultation : a writ by which a cause improperly removed by prohibition from one court to another is returned to the court from which it came — compare PROCEDENDO

writ of cosinage : a writ formerly used to recover possession of an estate in lands when a stranger has entered after the death of a lineal kinsman

writ of election : a writ to order the holding of an election; *specif* : one used to call a special election to fill a vacancy in an elective office ⟨when vacancies happen in the representation of any state . . . the executive authority of such state shall issue *writs of election* to fill such vacancies —*U.S.Constitution*⟩

writ of error : a writ that lies in a competent court after judgment in an action at law in a court of record directing the latter to examine the record or more commonly to remit the record to an appellate court in order that some alleged error in the proceedings or in the judgment of the court may be corrected if it exists ⟨appeal has now generally superseded the proceeding by *writ of error*⟩ — compare CORAM NOBIS

writ of extent : a writ formerly used to recover debts of record to the British crown and under which the lands, goods, and person of the debtor might all be seized to secure payment

writ of extent in aid : a writ of extent issued at the suit of a crown debtor against his debtor

writ of extent in chief : a writ of extent issued at the suit of the crown

writ of inquiry : a writ issued in an action at law where the defendant has suffered judgment to pass against him by default in order to ascertain and assess the plaintiff's damages where they cannot readily be ascertained by mere calculation

writ of privilege : a writ to deliver a privileged person from custody when arrested in a civil suit

writ of prohibition : a writ issued by a superior tribunal and directed to an inferior court commanding the latter to cease from the prosecution of a suit depending before it

writ of protection **1** : a writ issued out of the chancery to free an English subject absent overseas on royal service from most legal suits but usu. not charges of felony and in disuse since the 17th century **2** : a judicial writ issued to a person required to attend court (as party or juror) and intended to secure him from arrest in coming, staying, and returning

writ of recaption : a rarely used writ by which pending an action of replevin damages may be recovered for one whose goods being distrained for rent or service are distrained again for the same cause

writ of reprisal : WITHERNAM 2

writ of right **1** : an original writ used to protect a feudal tenant in the enjoyment of his freehold property by trial of the rights of the parties in the court of the manor **2** : a common law writ for restoring to its owner freehold property unjustly withheld

writ of right close : a writ of right used for tenants of the ancient demesne and directed to the bailiff of the manor commanding the lord to do right in his court

writ of right patent : a writ of right directed to the sheriff and used in behalf of a person claiming to hold land by free tenure of a mesne lord

writ of summons : a writ issued by the clerk of the crown on behalf of the British monarch summoning a lord spiritual or a lord temporal to attend parliament

writs *pl of* WRIT

written [ME *writen, written* (past part.), fr. OE *gewriten*] *past part & South past of* WRITE

wrizzled *adj* [alter. of *writhled*] *obs* : WRINKLED, SHRIVELED

wrm *abbr* wardroom

wrnt *abbr* warrant

WRO *abbr, often not cap* war risks only

wrocht \ˈräkt\ *Scot var of* WROUGHT

wro·claw \ˈvrōtˌsläf\ *adj, usu cap* [fr. *Wroclaw*, Poland] : of or from the city of Wroclaw, Poland : of the kind or style prevalent in Wroclaw

¹wrong \ˈrȯŋ *also* ˈräŋ\ *n* -s [ME *wrong, wrang*, fr. OE *wrang*, fr. (assumed) OE *wrang, adj.* — more at ²WRONG] **1** : an injurious, unfair, or unjust act : violation of the right ⟨set forth once again . . . so many were the ~*s* that were to be righted, the grievances to be redressed —Malcolm Muggeridge⟩ ⟨two ~*s* don't make a right⟩ **2** : something that is wrong, immoral, or unethical; *esp* : principles, practices, or conduct contrary to justice, goodness, or equity or to laws accepted as having divine or human sanction ⟨not to know right from ~⟩ ⟨the ~ is not all on one side⟩ **3** : action or conduct inflicting harm without due provocation or just cause : serious injury wantonly inflicted or undeservedly sustained : unjust or unmerited treatment ⟨have done so with a sense of ~ toward her —Gretchen Finletter⟩ ⟨see ~*s* on all sides⟩ ⟨roused by a sense of ~ to herself or others —Gilbert Parker⟩ **4** : the state, position, or fact of being or doing wrong ⟨was all-powerful and never in the ~ —F.M.Ford⟩: as **a** : the state of being mistaken or incorrect ⟨the election showed clearly how far in the ~ his predictions had been⟩ **b** : the state of being guilty of an unpardonable offense or of indefensible conduct or procedure ⟨thorough investigation proved him irreparably in the ~⟩ **5** *archaic* : physical harm or damage ⟨newts and blindworms do no ~, come not near our Fairy Queen —Shak.⟩ **6** : a violation of the legal rights of another : an invasion of right to the damage of the party who suffers it : TORT — see PRIVATE WRONG; compare PUBLIC WRONG

²wrong \"\ *adj, sometimes* **wrong·er** \-ŋə(r)\ *sometimes* **wrong·est** \-ŋəst\ [ME *wrong, wrang*, fr. (assumed) OE *wrang*, of Scand origin; akin to ON *rangr* awry, wrong, Dan & Norw *vrang*; akin to MD *wranc* sour, bitter, MHG *ranc* action of twisting, OE *wringan* to wring — more at WORRY] **1** : deviating from what is just and good : lacking in moral rectitude and integrity ⟨parsons . . . thought it would be ~ for them . . . to undertake combatant service —Rose Macaulay⟩ **2** : not according to the moral standard : not ethically right or just : SINFUL, IMMORAL ⟨~ principles of conduct⟩ ⟨some habits are not ~ but are unsocial⟩ ⟨those who hold that a lie is always ~ —Bertrand Russell⟩ **3** : not right or proper according to a specified or implied code, standard, or convention : at variance with what is generally acceptable or preferable ⟨packing off those who talked to the ~ people —R.S.Brown⟩ ⟨unfortunately was seen in all the ~ places⟩ **4** : not fitted or qualified for a particular intention or purpose : lacking suitability : INAPPROPRIATE ⟨the person in the ~ job who feels —W.J.Reilly⟩ ⟨it seemed that he had said the ~ thing —Max Peacock⟩ **5** : not agreeing with or conforming to facts : ERRONEOUS, INCORRECT ⟨gives his book a ~ date —DeLancey Ferguson⟩ ⟨the figures are correct but the sum is ~⟩ **6** : not up to the mark : not quite right : AMISS, UNSATISFACTORY ⟨there is something ~ about the way the story ends⟩ ⟨what's ~ with tea —Herbert Passin⟩ ⟨don't see anything ~ with it⟩ **7** : not in accordance with one's intent, end, needs, or expectations ⟨went up the ~ valley and lost several precious days —Heinrich Harrer⟩ ⟨took the ~ size container and ran out of water⟩ **8** : of, relating to, or constituting the side of something that is usu. held to be opposite to the principal one, that is the one naturally or by design turned down, inward, or away from one, and that is the least finished or polished ⟨the ~ side of the fabric⟩ ⟨pulled her pocket ~ side out —Margaret Deland⟩ ⟨using the ~ end of the brush —David Sylvester⟩ **9 :** of, relating to, or being the side that one disagrees with or disapproves of ⟨the intellectual exercise of arguing on the ~ side of a question⟩ **10 a :** least favorable, convenient, or safe : DISADVANTAGEOUS ⟨the ~ side of the railroad tracks —J.A. Morris b. 1904⟩ ⟨the tide was ~ for a landing —Carl Markwith⟩ **b :** contrary or opposite to that which is desirable, customary, or legitimate ⟨a broken-down old soldier on the ~ side of seventy —D.G.Gerahty⟩ ⟨got started on the ~ foot —Lee Greene⟩ ⟨driving on the ~ side of the white line —*Phoenix Flame*⟩ ⟨born on the ~ side of the blanket⟩ ⟨swallowed something the ~ way and almost choked⟩ **11 a :** acting, thinking, or judging in a manner at variance with truth or the facts : incorrect in opinion, judgment, or procedure : MISTAKEN ⟨the book . . . is often amusing, always arch and clever, and usually ~ —John Farrelly⟩ **b :** mentally unstable : INSANE ⟨he is ~ in the head⟩ **12 a :** betting that a dice shooter's next roll or series of rolls will lose **b :** due to lose on the next roll or series of rolls — used of a dice shooter ⟨ten bucks he's ~⟩

³wrong \"\ *adv* [ME *wrong, wrang,* fr. *wrong, wrang,* adj.] **1 :** in a way inconsistent with fact or truth : in a mistaken or erroneous manner : without accuracy : INCORRECTLY ⟨guessed ~⟩ ⟨did his homework all ~⟩ **2 :** without regard for what is proper or fitting : without propriety ⟨embarrassment made him act ~⟩ **3 :** in a manner not regarded as just or upright ⟨should be made to put right what he has done ~⟩ **4 a :** in a wrong direction : AMISS, ASTRAY ⟨the package sent ~ by the post office⟩ ⟨got lost because he turned ~ at the junction⟩ **b :** without regard for moral laws : on an evil or unvirtuous course ⟨a slum environment may cause a child to go ~⟩ **5 :** in an unsuccessful or unfortunate way ⟨what has gone ~ and what has led to the government's failure —J.G.Palfrey⟩ **6 :** out of working or proper functional order or condition ⟨the lock of one of them goes ~ —Charles Dickens⟩ ⟨his kidneys may go ~ —H.A.Overstreet⟩ **7 :** in a wrong position or relationship : in a false light ⟨don't get me ~ —T.V.Smith⟩

⁴wrong \"\ *vt* -ED/-ING/-S [ME *wrongen, wrangen,* fr. *wrong, wrang,* adj.] **1 a :** to do wrong to : treat with injustice : deprive of some right or withhold some act of justice from ⟨where we have ~*ed* the public trust, let there be no excuses —A.E.Stevenson b.1900⟩ **b :** to treat disrespectfully or dishonorably : VIOLATE ⟨the girl he had loved and married and ~*ed* —Zane Grey⟩ **2 :** to deprive wrongfully : DEFRAUD, DISPOSSESS — usu. used with *of* ⟨it would ~ the Indians out of their land —William Bartram⟩ **3** *archaic* **:** to mar the appearance or effect of : IMPAIR, SPOIL ⟨an indifferent good play but ~*ed* by the women . . . in their parts —Samuel Pepys⟩ **4 :** to impute a base motive to : dishonor or discredit esp. by false statement : MALIGN ⟨you ~ him; his interests are wider than that —Israel Zangwill⟩ **5 :** to harm physically : INJURE **6 :** BLANKET 3d

syn OPPRESS, PERSECUTE, AGGRIEVE: WRONG suggests injuring someone in some unjust way; for example, by depriving him of rightful property or his good name or by violating something he holds sacred ⟨he had *wronged* her; he had betrayed her; he had trampled her pride in the dust —Ellen Glasgow⟩ OPPRESS suggests causing someone to suffer by inhumanely laying a too heavy burden upon him ⟨no matter how high it raises prices, how much it controls supply or to what extent it *oppresses* the general consumer —C.A.Cooke⟩ ⟨*oppress* with excessive taxation⟩ PERSECUTE suggests relentlessly or unremittingly subjecting someone to annoyance or suffering ⟨*persecute* a child by constant criticism⟩ ⟨when true science was *persecuted* under the Roman tyrants, superstition and false philosophy flourished the more —*Encyc. Americana*⟩ AGGRIEVE suggests giving someone by an injustice (as a wrong or oppression) reason for protest ⟨the too familiar story of a sensitive child *aggrieved* by devilish adults —Elizabeth Janeway⟩ ⟨provisions should be made for recourse to the courts by parties who may be *aggrieved* by such orders —S.T.Powell⟩

wrongdoer \'=,==\ *n* [ME *wrong doer*] **1 :** one that does wrong; *esp* **:** a transgressor of moral laws **2 :** one who violates the legal right of another to his damage for which a legal remedy is available : one who commits a tort or trespass : one guilty of malfeasance : TORT-FEASOR, TRESPASSER

wrongdoing \'=,==\ *n* [ME *wrongedoing,* fr. ¹*wrong* + *doing,* n.] **1 :** evil behavior or action : transgression of moral or civil law **2 :** an instance of doing wrong

wronged *adj* [fr. past part. of ⁴*wrong*] **:** being injured unjustly : suffering a wrong : HARMED, VIOLATED

wrong·er \'rȯŋə(r) *also* 'räŋ-\ *n* -S [ME, fr. *wrongen* to wrong + *-er*] **1 :** one that wrongs or does wrong **2** *obs* **:** one that misuses : ABUSER

wrongest *superlative of* WRONG

wrong font *n* **:** a character in a piece of printing that is not of the same font as the other characters or does not match them in style or size or that is contrary to specification — abbr. *wf*

wrong·ful \'=fəl\ *adj* [ME, fr. ¹*wrong* + *-ful*] **1 :** full of wrong : INJURIOUS, UNJUST, UNFAIR ⟨a ~ act⟩ **2 :** not rightful esp. in law : having no legal sanction : UNLAWFUL, ILLEGITIMATE ⟨the ~ heir to a throne⟩ ⟨~ occupation of an estate⟩ — **wrong·ful·ly** \-f(ə)lē, -li\ *adv* — **wrong·ful·ness** \-fəlnəs\ *n* -ES

wrongful abstraction *n* **:** the unauthorized taking and removal by an employee of his employer's property in violation of instructions or the employer's legal rights resulting in loss or damage to the employer regardless of who may benefit therefrom

wrongful death *n* **:** the unjustified killing of another

wronghead \'=,=\ *n* [²*wrong* + *head*] **:** one that is wrongheaded

wrongheaded \'=,==\ *adj* **1 :** stubborn in adherence to wrong opinion or principles : obstinately wrong : PERVERSE ⟨too ~ to . . . abandon his original objective —Robert Graves⟩ **2 :** marked by perversity ⟨politics seem so complicated and so ~ —Felix Walter⟩ ⟨a quite ~ view of the poet —Douglas Bush⟩ — **wrong·head·ed·ly** *adv* — **wrong·head·ed·ness** *n* -ES

wronghearted \'=,==\ *adj* [²*wrong* + *hearted*] **:** wrong or perverse in feeling : UNJUST — **wrong·heart·ed·ness** *n*

wronging *pres part of* WRONG

wrong·ly *adv* [ME *wrongly, wrongliche,* fr. ²*wrong* + *-ly, -liche* -ly] **1 :** in an improper or inappropriate fashion or way ⟨the sort of story that ~ handled would make the most dreadful melodrama —*Sydney (Australia) Bull.*⟩ **2 :** without justice or fairness ⟨wouldst not play false and yet wouldst ~ win —Shak.⟩ **3 :** without accuracy : INCORRECTLY ⟨the police pass was ~ filled up —Arnold Bennett⟩ **4 :** in error : by mistake ⟨rightly or ~ these men had a different philosophy of education —C.S. Stine⟩

wrong·ness *n* -ES **:** the quality or state of being wrong: as **a :** the lack of correctness or suitability ⟨a fisherman can explain . . . the ~ of the weather or the bad water —*Wall Street Jour.*⟩ **b :** the lack of moral uprightness or justice ⟨those which judge the rightness or ~ of acts by their consequences —Lucius Garvin⟩

wrong·ous \'rȯŋəs *also* 'räŋ-\ *adj* [alter. (influenced by *-ous*) of earlier *wrongus, wrangus,* fr. ME *wrongwise, wrongwis wrangwis,* fr. *wrong, wrang,* adj., wrong + *wise, wis* wise — more at WRONG, WISE] **1 :** characterized by unfairness : INIQUITOUS, WRONGFUL **2 :** lacking propriety : UNFITTING **3 :** ILLEGAL, UNLAWFUL ⟨~ imprisonment⟩ — **wrong·ous·ly** *adv*

wrongs *pl of* WRONG, *pres 3d sing of* WRONG

wrong side *n* **1** *of handmade paper* **:** the side opposite the wire side **2** *of machine-made paper* **:** WIRE SIDE

wrong'un \'=ən\ *n* -S [contr. of *wrong one*] **:** GOOGLY

wron·ski·an \'(v)rä|nzkēən, -rȯ|, |nskēən\ *or* **wronskian determinant** *n* -S *usu cap W* [Józef Maria *Wroński* (Hoene-Wroński) †1853 Pol. mathematician and philosopher + E *-an*] **:** a mathematical determinant whose first row consists of *n* functions of *x* and whose following rows consist of the successive derivatives of these same functions with respect to *x*

wrop \'räp\ *dial var of* WRAP

wros·tle \'räsᵊl\ *dial Eng var of* WRESTLE

wrote [ME *wroot* (past), fr. OE *wrāt*] *past or dial past part of* WRITE

wroth \'rȯth *also* 'rōth *or* 'räth\ *adj* [ME *wroth, wrath,* fr. OE *wrāth;* akin to OS *wrēth* angry, OHG *reid* twisted, ON *reithr* angry, wroth, OE *wrīthan* to twist — more at WRITHE] **1 :** moved to intense anger : highly incensed : WRATHFUL ⟨but ~ as he was on his return, a short struggle . . . ended in a reconciliation —J.R.Green⟩ **2 :** being in wild commotion : TURBULENT ⟨the ~ sea's waves are edged with foam —Robert Browning⟩ **syn** see ANGRY

wroth·ful \'=fəl\ *adj* [obs. E *wroth* anger, wrath (fr. ME, fr. *wroth,* adj.) + E *-ful*] **:** filled with anger

wrothy \-thē\ *adj* -ER/-EST [*wroth* + *-y*] **:** WRATHFUL

wrought \'rȯt, *usu* -ȯd·+V\ *adj* [ME *wrought, wroght,* fr. *wrought, wroght* (past part. of *worchen, worken* to work), fr. OE *geworht* (past part. of *wyrcan* to work) — more at WORK] **1 :** CREATED, SHAPED ⟨and a young lad whose freckled face bore as . . . finely ~ features as one could wish to see —Sidney Lovett⟩ **2 a :** worked into shape by artistry or effort : FASHIONED, FORMED ⟨beautifully ~ garland of spring flowers⟩ **b :** fashioned with particular adherence to form or style ⟨this highly ~, artificial conversation, with its . . . high-piled metaphors —Virginia Woolf⟩ ⟨the most highly ~ and finished of English elegies —Marion Tucker⟩ **3 :** finished in an elaborate decorative style : EMBELLISHED, EMBROIDERED, ORNAMENTED ⟨the slippers were . . . curiously ~ with colored beads —William Black⟩ ⟨the screen was . . . ~ with a rather florid Louis Quatorze pattern —Oscar Wilde⟩ **4 :** processed for use : MANUFACTURED ⟨a gown of ~ silk⟩ **5 a :** beaten into shape by tools : shaped by a mechanical action (as rolling, forging, extrusion, or drawing) : HAMMERED — used of metals ⟨a bracelet of ~ silver⟩ ⟨a tray of ~ copper⟩ ⟨~ brass and bronze are less expensive than some other metals —A.H. Brownell⟩ **b :** produced by one of these methods ⟨searched the shops for ~ work⟩ **6 :** not crude or plain : FINISHED ⟨the ~ oaken beams —John Keats⟩ **7 :** deeply stirred : possessed of an excited state of mind : unduly stimulated ⟨when I am highly ~, I faint —W.S.Gilbert⟩ — often used with *up* ⟨let myself get ~ up over nothing —Ellen Glasgow⟩

wrought iron *n* **:** a commercial form of iron containing less than 0.3 percent and usu. less than 0.1 percent carbon and carrying also 1 or 2 percent of slag mechanically mixed with it and orig. made directly from ore (as in the Catalan forge) but subsequently by puddling — compare INGOT IRON

wrps *abbr* wrappings

wrt *abbr* wrought

wrung \'rəŋ\ *adj* [ME *wrungen,* fr. *wrungen* (past part. of *wringen* to wring), fr. OE *gewrungen* (past part. of *wringan* to wring) — more at WRING] **1 :** subjected to wringing : SQUEEZED **2 :** marked by suffering, grief, or pain : thoroughly distressed ⟨looked so ~ and shaken —H.L.Davis⟩

¹wry \'rī\ *vb* **wried; wried; wrying; wrys** [ME *wrien,* fr. OE *wrigian* to turn, incline, go; akin to OFris *wrigia* to bow, bend, MHG *rigel* kerchief wound around the head, OE *wrigels* covering, veil, L *ricula* small veil, *rica* headkerchief, veil, MLG *wrīch* twisted, cranky, Gk *rhoikos* crooked, Lith *rišti* to bind, tie, Av *urvisyeiti* he turns, revolves; basic meaning: turning, winding] *vi* **:** to make contortions : TWIST, WRITHE ~ *vt* **1** *obs* **:** to turn aside, away, or around : AVERT, DEFLECT **2 a :** to twist around : WRING **b :** to pull out of or as if out of proper shape : make awry **3 :** to contort in order to express emotion ⟨knows he is goin to die and ~*s* up his face —R.P. Warren⟩

²wry \"\ *adj* **wryer; wryest 1 a :** turned abnormally to one side ⟨~ neck⟩ ⟨~ mouth⟩ **b :** having a bent or twisted shape or condition : CONTORTED ⟨the tangle of ~ shadows thrown about the hut by a small flame —C.E.Montague⟩ **2 a :** twisted to express an emotion usu. of disgust or displeasure ⟨took another drink . . . making a ~ face —Erskine Caldwell⟩ **b :** made by a deliberate distortion of the facial muscles often to express irony or mockery ⟨at the door he turned with a ~ smile —Agnes S. Turnbull⟩ **3 :** marked by perversity : contrary to what is considered right : WRONGHEADED ⟨wondered how he had come to make such a ~ thing of his life —Elizabeth Taylor⟩ **4 a :** marked by a clever twist often with a hint of irony ⟨the ~ humor of the poem —W.L.Sperry⟩ ⟨with a ~ Scottish wit —*Time*⟩ **b :** grimly humorous often with a hint of bitterness ⟨a ~ pleasure to be . . . reminded of all that one is missing —Irwin Edman⟩ ⟨many seem to incline to the ~ view that taxes are here to stay —C.H.Greenewalt⟩ ⟨a chorus of ~ laughs —Lou Stoumen⟩

³wry \"\ *adv* [²*wry*] **:** AWRY

wrybill \'=,=\ *or* **wry-billed plover** *n* **:** a peculiar shorebird (*Anarhynchus frontalis*) of New Zealand that is related to the plovers and unique in having its bill sharply deflected to the right

wry-billed \'=,=\ *adj* **:** having the bill bent to one side

wry·ly *adv* **:** in a wry manner : with a caustic twist : DRYLY ⟨smiled rather ~ to himself —Louis Auchincloss⟩ ⟨a ~ humorous study of lower-middle-class life in a London suburb —*Time*⟩

wrymouth \'=,=\ *n* [²*wry* + *mouth*] **:** a large eellike blenny (*Cryptacanthodes maculatus*) of the northern Atlantic coast of No. America

wry-mouthed \'=,=\ *adj* **1 :** having a crooked or distorted mouth **2 :** twisted as if coming from a wry mouth : having a caustically bitter or humorous turn or twist ⟨plenty of thrilling incident and . . . *wry-mouthed* satire —R.E.Roberts⟩

wryneck \'=,=\ *n* [²*wry* + *neck*] **1 :** any of various woodpeckers (genus *Jynx*) that differ from the typical woodpeckers in having soft tail feathers and a peculiar manner of writhing the neck: as **a :** a common bird (*J. torquilla*) of Europe and Asia that is intimately variegated in black, brown, and buff **b :** a similar bird (*J. pectoralis*) of central and southern Africa **2 :** one that has a wry neck **3 :** TORTICOLLIS

wry·ness *n* -ES **:** the quality or state of being wry ⟨big in the way it treats human beings with a ~ born of compassion —Eric Goldman⟩

wrytail \'=,=\ *n* [²*wry* + *tail*] **:** a tail twisted to one side; *specif* **:** a genetic variation in domestic cattle in which the base of the tail is distorted and the tail partially turned to right or left

WS *abbr* **1** water-soluble **2** water supply **3** weather station **4** weather stripping **5** wetted surface **6** wingspread **7** writer to the signet

w's *or* **ws** *pl of* W

w-shaped \'==(,)=\ *adj, cap W* **:** having the shape of a capital W

WSW *abbr* west-southwest

wt *abbr* **1** warrant **2** weight **3** without

WT *abbr* **1** war tax **2** wartime **3** water tank **4** water tender **5** watertight **6** wireless telegraphy **7** wireless telephone; wireless telephony **8** *often not cap* with title

wth *abbr* width

wthr *abbr* weather

wtr *abbr* **1** waiter **2** winter **3** writer

wu \'wü\ *n* -S *usu cap* [Chin (Pek) *wu²*] **:** a group of Chinese dialects spoken in the lower Yangtze valley

wu·chang \'wü¦chäŋ\ *adj, usu cap* [fr. *Wuchang,* China] **:** of or from the city of Wuchang, China : of the kind or style prevalent in Wuchang

wuch·er·e·ria \,wükə'rirēə\ *n, cap* [NL, fr. O. *Wucherer,* 19th cent. Ger. physician + NL *-ia*] **:** a genus of filarial worms (family Dipetalonematidae) including the parasite (*W. bancrofti*) of tropical elephantiasis and a related worm (*W. malayi*)

wud \'wu̇d\ *adj* [alter. of ¹*wood*] *chiefly Scot* **:** INSANE, MAD

wud·dy \'wu̇dē\ *var of* WIDDY

wu·han \'wü¦hän\ *adj, usu cap* [fr. *Wuhan,* China] **:** of or from the city of Wuhan, China : of the kind or style prevalent in Wuhan

wu·hu \'wü¦hü\ *adj, usu cap* [fr. *Wuhu,* China] **:** of or from the city of Wuhu, China : of the kind or style prevalent in Wuhu

wu·lam·ba \wü'lämbə\ *n, pl* **wulamba** *or* **wulambas** *usu cap* **:** an Australian people of Arnhemland

wul·fen·ite \'wu̇lfə,nīt\ *n* -S [G *wulfenit,* fr. Franz Xaver von *Wulfen* †1805 Austrian mineralogist + G *-it* -ite] **:** a tetragonal mineral $PbMoO_4$ consisting of native lead molybdate that is isomorphous with stolzite and prob. with scheelite and powellite and that is bright orange-yellow to red, gray, green, or brown usu. in tabular crystals or in granular masses (hardness 2.75–3, sp. gr. 6.7–7.0) — called also *yellow lead ore*

wull \(ˈ)wəl\ *Scot var of* WILL

wulliwa *var of* WILLIWAW

wump \'wəmp\ *or* **wumph** \-m(p)f\ *n* -S [imit.] **:** a heavy sound caused esp. by a falling object ⟨with a dull *wumph* ice bridges we had used during the day would collapse overnight —John Hunt⟩

wun *var of* WOON

wun·der·kind \'vu̇ndə(r),kint, 'wən-\ *n, pl* **wunderkin·der** \-ində(r)\ *or* **wunderkinds** [G, fr. OHG *wunter* wonder (fr. OHG *wuntar*) + *kind* child, fr. OHG — more at WONDER, KIN] **:** a child prodigy : one that succeeds in a competitive or highly difficult field or profession at an early age ⟨naturally he is spoiled, being such a ~ —Eleanor Clark⟩ ⟨the ~ of advertising at 31⟩

wundt·i·an \'vu̇ntēən\ *adj, usu cap* [Wilhelm *Wundt* †1920 Ger. physiologist and psychologist + E *-an*] **:** of or relating to Wilhelm Wundt or his theories or investigations

wung-out \'wəŋ¦=\ *adj* [fr. the verbal phrase *wing out,* after such pairs of phrases as E *wring out: wrung out*] **:** having sails set wing and wing

wup *Scot var of* ²OOP

wup·per·tal \'vu̇pər,täl\ *adj, usu cap* [fr. *Wuppertal,* Germany] **:** of or from the city of Wuppertal, Germany : of the kind or style prevalent in Wuppertal

wur·ley \'wərlē\ *n, pl* **wurleys** *or* **wurlies** [native name in So. Australia] **1 :** a native Australian hut **2 :** the nest of the house-building rat of Australia

würm \'vu̇(ə)rm, 'wu̇(ə)rm, 'wərm, *Ger* 'vʏrm\ *n* -S *usu cap* [fr. *Würm,* lake in southern Germany] **:** the fourth and last stage of glaciation in Europe

würm·ian \-u̇rmēən, -ərm-,-ʏrm-\ *adj, usu cap* **:** of or relating to the Würm

wur·rung \'wərəŋ\ *n* -S [native name in Australia] **:** a nail-tailed wallaby (*Onychogalea lunata*) of southwestern and central Australia

wur·rup \-rəp\ *n* -S [native name in Australia] **:** a hare wallaby (*Lagorchestes hirsutus*) of the central and western parts of Australia

wurst *R* 'wərst, 'wu̇(ə)rst, *-R* 'wəst, 'wu̇əst, *R* + *-R* 'wu̇st *sometimes* 'wu̇sht\ *n* -S [G, fr. OHG; akin to MLG & MD *worst* — more at BRATWURST] **:** SAUSAGE 1a

wur·ster's salt \'wər|stərz-, 'wu̇(r)|, 'vu̇r|\ *n, usu cap W* [after C. *Wurster fl* 1805 Ger. chemist] **:** any of several deeply colored semiquinones formed by partial oxidation (as with bromine) of the conjugate acid of *para*-phenylenediamine or its *N*-alkyl derivatives: as **a** *or* **wurster's red** *or* **wurster's red salt :** a red product made fom N,N-dimethyl-*para*-phenylenediamine **b** *or* **wurster's blue** *or* **wurster's blue salt :** a blue product made from tetramethyl-*para*-phenylenediamine

wurtz column \'wə|rts-, 'wu̇|\ *or* **wurtz tube** *n, usu cap W* [after Charles A. *Wurtz* †1884 Fr. chemist] **:** a bulbed fractionating column for laboratory distillations

wurtz-fittig reaction *or* **wurtz-fittig synthesis** \'=ˈfid·ig-\ *n, usu cap W&F* [after Charles A. *Wurtz* †1884 Fr. chemist and Rudolf *Fittig* †1910 Ger. chemist] **:** a synthesis of aliphatic or usu. alkyl-substituted aromatic hydrocarbons (as toluene) from two molecules of organic halogen compound (as one molecule each of methyl bromide and bromo-benzene) and two atoms of sodium — compare FITTIG REACTION, WURTZ REACTION

wurtz·i·lite \'wərtsə,līt\ *n* -S [Henry *Wurtz* †1910 Am. mineralogist and chemist + connective *-i-* + *-lite*] **:** an asphalt similar to uintaite in composition

wurtz·ite \'wərt,sīt\ *n* -S [F, fr. Charles A. *Wurtz* †1884 Fr. chemist + F *-ite*] **:** a brownish black mineral ZnS that consists of zinc sulfide in hemimorphic hexagonal crystals or a fibrous state and that is polymorphous with sphalerite — **wurtz·it·ic** \(ˈ)wərt¦sid·ik\ *adj*

wurtz reaction *n, usu cap W* [after Charles A. *Wurtz* †1884] **:** a synthesis of aliphatic hydrocarbons (as butane) from two molecules of an alkyl halide (as ethyl iodide) and two atoms of sodium

wurzel *n* -S [by shortening] **:** MANGEL-WURZEL

wu·sih \'wü¦shē\ *adj, usu cap* [fr. *Wusih,* China] **:** of or from the city of Wusih, China : of the kind or style prevalent in Wusih

wüst·ite *also* **wust·ite** \'wu̇,stīt, 'vʏ,-\ *n* -S [G *wüstit,* fr. Ewald *Wüst fl* 1907 Ger. geologist + G *-it* -ite] **:** an artificial mineral FeO consisting of ferrous oxide

wusun *usu cap, var of* USUN

wuth·er \'wət͟hə(r)\ *vi* -ED/-ING/-S [alter. of ³*whither*] *dial Eng* **:** to blow with a dull roaring sound ⟨from time to time the wind ~*ed* in the chimney at his back —R.L.Stevenson & Lloyd Osbourne⟩

wu wei \'wü'wā\ *n* [Chin (Pek) *wu² wei²,* lit., not to act] **:** the practice advocated by Taoism of letting one's action follow the simple and spontaneous course of nature (as by keeping to a minimum governmental organization and regulation) rather than interfering with the harmonious working of universal law by imposing arbitrary and artificial forms : doing or making nothing except in conformity to the Tao

wu·wei \'wü¦wā\ *adj, usu cap* [fr. *Wuwei,* China] **:** of or from the city of Wuwei, China : of the kind or style prevalent in Wuwei

WVTR *abbr* water vapor transmission rate

WW *abbr* **1** warehouse warrant **2** water-white **3** waterworks **4** *often not cap* with warrants **5** world war

WWA *abbr* with the will annexed

wy·an·dot *also* **wy·an·dotte** \'wīən,dät\ *n, pl* **wyandot** *or* **wyandots** *also* **wyandotte** *or* **wyandottes** *usu cap* **1 a :** a subgroup of the Hurons **b :** a member of such people **2 :** the language of the Wyandot people

wy·an·dotte \-,dät\ *n* [prob. fr. *Wyandotte* Wyandot] **1** *usu cap* **:** an American breed of medium-sized domestic fowls that are derived largely from dark Brahmas and spangled Hamburgs, are in the typical variety white laced with black, and are bred in several color varieties **2** -S *often cap* **:** a bird of the Wyandotte breed

wych *var of* WICH

wych elm *or* **witch elm** \'wi,chelm, -ēu̇m, ='=\ *also* **wych hazel** \'wich,hāzəl, 'wi,chā-, ='==\ *n* [*wych* fr. ME *wyche* — more at WITCH (tree)] **1 :** a Eurasian elm (*Ulmus glabra*) that is common in England, Scotland, and Ireland and has shorter leafstalks but larger fruit than English elm **2 :** the wood of the wych elm

wyc·liff·ian *or* **wyc·lif·ian** \(ˈ)wi¦klifēən\ *adj, usu cap* [John *Wycliffe* (*Wyclif*) †1384 + E *-an*] **:** WYCLIFFITE

wyc·liff·ism *or* **wyc·lif·ism** \'wiklə,fizəm\ *n* -S *usu cap* [John *Wycliffe* (*Wyclif*) + E *-ism*] **:** the teachings or principles of John Wycliffe

wyc·liff·ist *or* **wyc·lif·ist** \-,fəst\ *n* -S *usu cap* [ME *Wiclifist,* fr. John *Wiclif* (Wycliffe, Wyclif) + E *-ist*] **:** LOLLARD 2

¹wyc·liff·ite *also* **wyc·lif·ite** \-,fīt\ *n* -S *usu cap* [John *Wycliffe* (*Wyclif*) †1384 Eng. religious reformer and theologian + E *-ite*] **:** LOLLARD 2

²wycliffite *also* **wyclifite** \"\ *adj, usu cap* **:** of or relating to John Wycliffe or his doctrines teaching that all secular and ecclesiastical authority is derived from God and is forfeited by one who is in mortal sin, that the doctrine of transubstantiation is false, and that monasticism is to be condemned

wyc·ombe chair \'wickəm-\ *n, usu cap W* [fr. High *Wycombe,* locality in Buckinghamshire, England, where it was extensively manufactured in the 19th century] **:** WINDSOR CHAIR

wyde \'wīd\ *Scot var of* WADE

wye *also* **wy** \'wī\ *n* -S **1 :** the letter Y **2 :** something resembling the letter Y in shape

wye level *n* **:** Y LEVEL

wy·e·thia \wī'ēthēə\ *n, cap* [NL, fr. Nathaniel J. *Wyeth* †1856 Am. explorer + NL *-ia*] **:** a genus of plants (family Compositae) that resemble sunflowers, are found esp. in the western U.S., and have pistillate fertile ray flowers

¹wyke·ham·ist \'wikəməst\ *n* -S *usu cap* [NL *Wykehamista,* fr. William of *Wykeham* (Wickham) †1404 Eng. prelate and statesman who founded Winchester College + L *-ista* -ist] **:** a student or graduate of Winchester College

²wykehamist \"\ *adj, usu cap* **:** of or belonging to Winchester College

wylie·coat \'wīli,kōt, 'wil-\ *n* [ME (Sc) *wyle cot,* fr. *wyle* (of unknown origin) + *cot, cote* coat — more at COAT] **1** *chiefly Scot* **:** a warm undergarment **2** *chiefly Scot* **:** PETTICOAT **3** *chiefly Scot* **:** a nightgown for a woman or child

wyn \'win\ *n* -S **:** ²WEN

¹wynd \'wīnd\ *n* -S [ME (Sc) *wynde,* prob. fr. *wynden* to proceed, go, turn, wind, fr. OE *windan* — more at WIND, v.] *chiefly Scot* : a very narrow street : ALLEY, CLOSE

²**wynd** \ˈwīn(d)\ *or* **wyne** \ˈwīn\ *v imper* [ME (Sc) *wynden* to proceed, go, turn] *chiefly Scot* : HAW

wyn·ker·nel \ˈwiŋkə(r),nel\ *n* [perh. alter. of ¹*win* + *kernel*] *dial Eng* : MOORHEN 1

wyn·yar·dia \wənˈyärdēə\ *n, cap* [NL, fr. *Wynyard*, town on northwestern coast of Tasmania + NL *-ia*] : a genus of Tasmanian Pliocene or Miocene primitive fossil phalangers sometimes regarded as ancestral to the modern Australian opossums

wy·o·ming \(ˈ)wīˈōmiŋ, -mēŋ\ *adj, usu cap* [fr. *Wyoming*, state in the western U.S., fr. *Wyoming* valley, eastern Pennsylvania, fr. Lenape *M'cheuwómink*, site prob. located in the Wyoming valley, lit., on the great plain] : of or from the state of Wyoming ⟨a *Wyoming* ranch⟩ : of the kind or style prevalent in Wyoming

wy·o·ming·ite \-,īt\ *n* -s *cap* [*Wyoming* state + E *-ite*] : a native or resident of the state of Wyoming

wyte *chiefly Scot var of* WITE

wythe *var of* WITHE

wy·vern *also* **wi·vern** \ˈwīvə(r)n\ *or* **wi·ver** \-və(r)\ *n* -s [ME *wyvere, guivere* viper, fr. ONF *wivre* & OF *guivre* viper, wyvern, modif. (influenced by OHG *wipera* adder, snake, fr. L *vipera*) of L *vipera* — more at VIPER] **1 a** : a fabulous animal usu. represented as a 2-legged winged creature resembling a dragon — compare COCKATRICE **b** : the heraldic representation of such a monster **2** : an image or figure made in the likeness of a wyvern

wyvern 1b

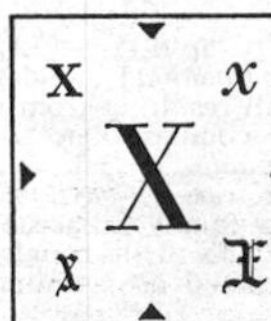

¹**x** \ˈeks\ *n, pl* **x's** *or* **xs** *or* **x'es** *or* **xes** \ˈeksəz\ *often cap, often attrib* **1 a** : the 24th letter of the English alphabet **b** : an instance of this letter printed, written, or otherwise represented **c** : a speech counterpart of orthographic *x* (as *x* in *xylophone, extra, next,* or *ox*) **2** : ten — see NUMBER table **3** : a printer's type, a stamp, or some other instrument for reproducing the letter *x* **4** : someone or something arbitrarily or conveniently designated *x*: as **a** : the 24th in order or class **b** : the 23d in order or class when j is not used **c** : the 21st in order or class when j, v, and w are not used **d** : the first in an order or class including x, y, and sometimes z **5 a** : UNKNOWN QUANTITY 1 ⟨find the value of *x* in the equation $x-4=3$⟩ **b** : an arbitrarily chosen value from the domain of a variable ⟨in the equation $y=x^2$, let $x=4$⟩ **c** : X-COORDINATE **6 a** : something (as a cross) having the shape of the letter X **b** : something (as a $10 bill) marked with an X **7** [so called fr. the use of the letter in crossing out mistakes in writing] : something (as a statement, answer, or result) that is wrong : MISTAKE, ERROR **8** *x's pl, often cap* : ATMOSPHERICS 1 **9** : the basic or monoploid number of chromosomes of a polyploid series : the number contained in a single genome — compare N

²**x** \ˈ"\ *vt* **x-ed** *also* **x'd** *or* **xed**; **x-ed** *also* **x'd** *or* **xed** \ˈekst\ **x-ing** *or* **x'ing** \ˈeksiŋ\ **x'es** *or* **xes** \ˈeksəz\ **1** : to mark with an *x* ⟨*x-ed* his ballot clearly⟩ **2** : to cancel or obliterate with or as if with a series of *x's* — usu. used with *out* ⟨*x-ing out* most of what he had written⟩

³**x** *abbr, often cap* **1** cross **2** ex **3** experimental **4** extra **5** xenon

⁴**x** *symbol* **1** unknown quantity **2 a** times : by **b** hybrid ⟨the license reads Dachshund *x*⟩ ⟨a tall willow (*Salix x blanda*) developed in cultivation⟩ : hybridity **c** out of ⟨a litter by a grade sire *x* a scrub dam⟩ **3** *cap* [fr. the Greek letter X] Christ : Christian **4** power of magnification **5** *cap* reactance **6** abscissa **7** crossed with **8** kiss **9** a playing card of low rank **10** *cap* chemical group — used esp. of a univalent anion or typically univalent negative radical (as halogen) in general formulas **11** the person in question — used esp. by an illiterate in place of a signature **12** the place in question — used on a map or picture **13** — used to indicate choice or approval (as on a ballot)

xan·ci·dae \ˈzaŋkə,dē, ˈzansə-\ *n pl, cap* [NL, fr. *Xancus*, type genus + *-idae*] : a family of gastropod mollusks (suborder Rachiglossa) comprising the oriental chank and related forms

xan·cus \ˈzaŋkəs\ *n, cap* [NL, perh. modif. of Skt *śaṅkha* conch — more at CONCH] : the type genus of the family Xancidae — compare CHANK SHELL

xanth- *or* **xantho-** *comb form* [NL, fr. Gk, fr. *xanthos*; perh. akin to OHG *hasan* gray — more at HARE] **1** : yellow ⟨*xanthoma*⟩ ⟨*xanthelasma*⟩ ⟨*xanthoderma*⟩ **2** : xanthic acid ⟨*xanthate*⟩ **3** : yellow or yellowish and ammoniacal — in names of salts of cobalt ⟨*xantho*cobaltic chloride⟩

xan·tha·mide \ˈzan(t)thə,mīd, zanˈtha,m-, -,məd\ *n* [*xanth-* + *amide*] : an amide $ROCSNH_2$ of a xanthic acid

¹**xan·thate** \ˈzan,thāt\ *n* -s [*xanth-* + *-ate*] : a compound that is a salt or ester of a xanthic acid and that is usu. colorless and soluble in the case of the alkali metal salts but yellow and insoluble in the case of the copper salts ⟨sodium ~⟩ ⟨potassium butyl ~ C_4H_9OCSSK⟩ — compare VISCOSE

²**xanthate** \ˈ"\ *vt* -ED/-ING/-s : to convert (as alkali cellulose) into a xanthate by reaction with carbon disulfide — compare SULFIDE

xan·tha·tion \zanˈthāshən\ *n* -s [*xanthate* + *-ion*] : the process of xanthating ⟨~ is a step in the manufacture of viscose⟩

xan·the·las·ma \,zan(t)thəˈlazmə\ *n* -s [NL, fr. *xanth-* + Gk *elasma* metal plate] : xanthoma of the eyelid

xan·thene \ˈzan,thēn\ *n* -s [*xanth-* + *-ene*] **1 a** : a white

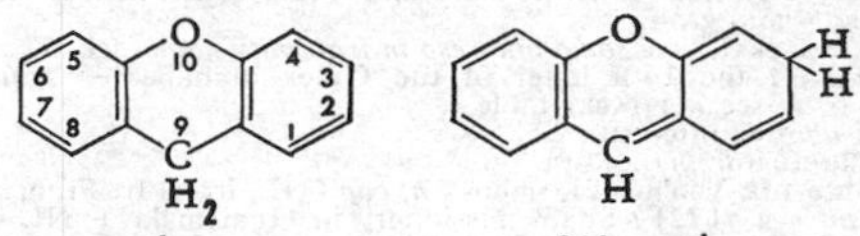

xanthene

crystalline heterocyclic compound $C_{13}H_{10}O$ obtained by reduction of xanthone — called also *9H-xanthene*; compare STRUCTURAL FORMULA **b** : an isomeric compound $C_{13}H_{10}O$ that is the parent of the colored forms of the xanthene dyes — called also *3H-xanthene* **2** : any of various derivatives of the two xanthenes; *esp* : XANTHENE DYE

xanthene dye *n* : any of a group of brilliant fluorescent yellow to pink to bluish red dyes characterized by the presence of the xanthene nucleus, known sometimes in colorless as well as colored forms, and used chiefly in dyeing textile fibers, in coloring paper, in producing fluorescent effects, and as organic pigments — see PHTHALEIN, RHODAMINE; compare TRIPHENYLMETHANE DYE

xan·the·nyl \ˈzan(t)thə,nil\ *or* **xan·thyl** \-thəl\ *n* -s [*xanthene* or ISV *xanth-* + *-yl*] : a univalent radical $C_{13}H_9O$ derived from xanthene

xan·thi·an \ˈzan(t)thēən\ *adj, usu cap* [*Xanthus* + E *-an*] : of or relating to the ancient town of Xanthus in Lycia in Asia Minor ⟨the *Xanthian* marbles⟩

xan·thic \ˈzan(t)thik\ *adj* [F *xanthique*, fr. *xanth-* + *-ique* -ic] **1 a** : of, relating to, or tending toward a yellow color **b** *of a flower* : colored with some tint of yellow — compare CYANIC 2 **2** : of or relating to xanthin or xanthine

xanthic acid *n* **1 a** : a colorless unstable oily thio acid C_2H_5OCSSH obtained in the form of its potassium salt by reaction of potassium ethoxide with carbon disulfide; *O*-ethyl dithiocarbonate **b** : any of a series of analogous unstable thio acids ROCSSH obtained in the form of their salts by reaction of alkoxides with carbon disulfide : an *O*-ester of dithio-carbonic acid ⟨methyl *xanthic acid* CH_3OCSSH⟩ **2** : a hypothetical thio acid HOCSSH whose *O*-esters are the xanthic acids : dithio-carbonic acid

xan·thi·dae \ˈzan(t)thə,dē\ *n pl, cap* [NL, fr. *Xanthus*, type genus (fr. Gk *xanthos* yellow) + *-idae*] : the largest family of crabs (superfamily Brachyrhyncha) comprising chiefly small littoral or shallow water marine crabs with oval carapaces armed with spines or lobes along the anterolateral margin and including the edible stone and coral crabs

xan·thid·i·um \zanˈthidēəm\ *n, cap* [NL, fr. *xanth-* + *-idium*] : a genus of deeply constricted spiny desmids (family Desmidiaceae) including some that are common plankton forms

xan·thin \ˈzan(t)thən\ *n* -s [ISV *xanth-* + *-in*] : a carotenoid pigment (as cryptoxanthin or zeaxanthin) soluble in alcohol

xan·thine \ˈzan,thēn, ˈzan(t)thən\ *n* -s [ISV *xanth-* + *-ine*; fr. its yellow residue when evaporated with nitric acid] **1** : a feebly basic crystalline nitrogenous compound $C_5H_4N_4O_2$ that is found esp. in animal tissue and in various plants, forms by hydrolysis of guanine, and yields uric acid on oxidation; 2,6-dihydroxypurine — compare HYPOXANTHINE **2** : any of various derivatives of xanthine — compare CAFFEINE, THEOBROMINE, THEOPHYLLINE

xanthine oxidase *n* : a crystallizable flavoprotein enzyme containing iron and molybdenum that promotes the oxidation esp. of hypoxanthine and xanthine to uric acid and of many aldehydes to acids and that is obtained usu. from milk or liver

xan·thip·pe \zanˈt(h)ipē\ *or* **xan·tip·pe** \-ˈti-\ *n* -s *usu cap* [after *Xanthippe*, wife of Socrates †399 B.C. Greek philosopher] : an ill-tempered woman : SHREW

xan·thism \ˈzan,thizəm\ *n* -s [*xanth-* + *-ism*] : coloring (as of the skin or pelt) marked by a predominance of yellow pigments

xan·thi·um \ˈzan(t)thēəm\ *n, cap* [NL, fr. Gk *xanthion*, a plant used to dye the hair yellow, fr. *xanthos* yellow] : a genus of coarse and rough or spiny herbs (family Compositae) having small heads of greenish flowers of which the pistillate enclosed in an involucre becomes a burr covered with hooked bristles — see COCKLEBUR

xantho- — see XANTH-

xan·tho·ceph·a·lus \,zan(t)thōˈsefələs\ *n, cap* [NL, fr. *xanth-* + *-cephalus*] : a genus of blackbirds comprising only the yellow-headed blackbird of western No. America

xan·thoc·er·as \zanˈthäsərəs\ *n, cap* [NL, fr. *xanth-* + *-ceras*] : a monotypic genus of Chinese shrubs (family Sapindaceae) that have pinnately compound leaves, racemose rather showy white flowers with red or yellow spots, and a fruit resembling the horse chestnut but without prickles

xan·thoch·roi \zanˈthäkrə,wī\ *n pl, sometimes cap* [NL, fr. *xanth-* + Gk *ōchroi*, nom. pl. masc. of *ōchros* pale, yellow] : caucasoids having light hair and fair skin — compare MELANOCHROI

xan·tho·chro·ic \ˌzan(t)thəˈkrōik\ *adj* [NL *xanthochroi* + E *-ic*] **1** : relating to or belonging to the xanthochroi **2** [NL *xanthochroia* + E *-ic*] : relating to or marked by xanthochroism

xan·thochroid \ˈzan(t)thə,krȯid, zanˈthä,k-\ *adj* [NL *xanthochroi* + E *-oid*] : XANTHOCHROIC 1

xan·thoch·ro·ism \zanˈthäkrə,wizəm\ *n* -s [NL *xanthochroia* yellow skin discoloration (fr. Gk *xanthochroos* xanthochroous + NL *-ia*) + E *-ism*] **1** : abnormal coloration of feathers (as in some parrots) in which yellow replaces the normal color **2** : a genetic variation in various vertebrates characterized by local or general absence of black and brown pigment with normal development of the red and golden pigments (as of skin or feathers) resulting in a yellow to reddish coloration

xan·tho·chro·mia \,zan(t)thəˈkrōmēə\ *n* -s [NL, fr. *xanth-* + *-chromia*] : yellowish discoloration (as of the skin or cerebrospinal fluid) — **xan·tho·chro·mic** \ˌ==ˈ=mik\ *adj*

xan·thoch·ro·ous \(ˈ)zanˈthäkrəwəs\ *adj* [Gk *xanthochroos*, fr. *xanth-* + *-chroos* -chroous] : having a yellowish skin and fair hair

xan·thoc·o·nite \zanˈthäkə,nīt\ *n* -s [G *xanthokon* xanthoconite (fr. *xanth-* + Gk *konis* dust) + E *-ite*; fr. the color of its streak powder — more at INCINERATE] : a cochineal-red to orange-yellow to brown mineral Ag_3AsS_3 consisting of a silver arsenic sulfide and occurring in tabular crystals and often flat rhombohedrons — compare PROUSTITE

xan·tho·derm \ˈzan(t)thə,dərm\ *n* -s [ISV *xanth-* + *-derm*] : a person with a yellow skin; *esp* : one belonging to a race characterized by yellow skin

xan·tho·der·ma \ˌ==ˈdərmə\ *n* -s [NL, fr. *xanth-* + *-derma*] : yellow color of the skin

xan·tho·gen \ˈzan(t)thəjən, -,jen\ *n* -s [ISV *xanth-* + *-gen*] : either of two univalent radicals: **a** : the radical C_2H_5OCSS— derived from xanthic acid (sense 1a) **b** : the radical HOCSS— derived from xanthic acid (sense 2)

xan·tho·gen·ate \ˈzan(t)thəjə,nāt, zanˈthäjə,n-\ *n* -s [ISV *xanthogen* + *-ate*] : XANTHATE

xan·tho·gen·ic acid \ˌ==ˈjenik-\ *n* [ISV *xanthogen* + *-ic*] : XANTHIC ACID 1

xan·tho·leucophore \ˌzan(t)(,)thō+\ *n* [*xanth-* + *leucophore*] : a leucophore (as of a frog) containing yellow pigment as well as guanine — compare XANTHOPHORE

xan·tho·ma \zanˈthōmə\ *n, pl* **xanthomas** \-məz\ *or* **xan·thoma·ta** \-məd·ə\ [NL, fr. *xanth-* + *-oma*] : a condition that is marked by the development (as on the eyelids, neck, or back) of irregular yellow patches or nodules on the skin and is seen in disturbances of cholesterol metabolism

xan·tho·ma·to·sis \(,)zan,thōməˈtōsəs\ *n, pl* **xanthomatoses** \-ō,sēz\ [NL, fr. *xanthomat-, xanthoma* + *-osis*] : a disturbance of cholesterol metabolism marked by an increase of cholesterol in the body with deposit of xanthomatous matter in the skin and other tissues sometimes in tumorous masses

xan·thoma·tous \(ˈ)zanˈthäməd·əs, -thōm-\ *adj* [NL *xanthomat-, xanthoma* + E *-ous*] : of, relating to, marked by, or characteristic of xanthoma or xanthomatosis

xan·tho·mel·a·noi \,zan(t)thōˈmelə,nȯi\ *n pl, sometimes cap* [NL, fr. *xanth-* + Gk *melanoi*, nom. pl. masc. of *melanos* black; akin to Gk *melas* black — more at MULLET] : xanthomelanous peoples

xan·tho·mel·a·nous \ˌ==ˈmelənəs\ *adj* [*xanth-* + *melanous*] : having olive or yellow skin and black hair

xan·thom·e·ter \zanˈthämәd·ə(r)\ *n* [*xanth-* + *-meter*] : a chromometer for use with sea or lake water

xan·thom·o·nad \zanˈthämə,nad\ *n* -s [NL *Xanthomonad-, Xanthomonas*] : a bacterium of the genus *Xanthomonas*

xan·thom·o·nas \-,nəs, -,nas\ *n, cap* [NL, fr. *xanth-* + *-monas*] : a large genus of bacteria (family Pseudomonadaceae) that are distinguished from members of the closely related *Pseudomonas* by production of yellow pigments insoluble in water and that include numerous plant pathogens some of which cause necrotic conditions

xan·thone \ˈzan,thōn\ *n* -s [ISV *xanth-* + *-one*] : a crystalline ketone $C_6H_4(CO)(O)C_6H_4$ that is the parent of several natural yellow pigments (as gentisin), that is usu. obtained by distilling phenyl salicylate, and that gives a yellow solution with pale blue fluorescence in sulfuric acid; xanthen-9-one

xan·tho·phore \ˈzan(t)thə,fō(ə)r\ *n* -s [*xanth-* + *-phore*] : a chromatophore containing a yellow pigment that is typically a carotinoid and occurring esp. in fishes and crustaceans

xan·tho·phy·ce·ae \ˌ==ˈfīsē,ē\ *n pl, cap* [NL, fr. *xanth-* + *-phyceae*] : a class of algae (division Chrysophyta) in which the green pigments of the chromatophores are partially masked by xanthophyll and reserves are commonly stored in the form of oil and which comprise the yellow-green algae

xan·tho·phyll \ˈ==,fil\ *n* -s [F *xanthophylle*, fr. *xanth-* + *-phylle* -phyll] **1** : LUTEIN 1 **2** : any of several neutral yellow carotenoid pigments that are found esp. in the flowers, fruits, or leaves of plants and that are oxygen derivatives (as carotenols or ketones) of the carotenes but differ from the carotenes by their preferential solubility in alcohol and by their insolubility in petroleum ether (~ esters) — **xan·tho·phyl·lic** \ˌ==ˈfilik\ *adj* — **xan·tho·phyl·lous** \-ləs\ *adj*

xan·tho·phyl·lite \ˌ==ˈfi,līt\ *n* [G *xanthophyllit*, fr. *xanth-* + *-phyll* + *-it* -ite; fr. its color and foliated structure] : SEYBERTITE

xan·tho·proteic reaction *or* **xanthoproteic test** \ˌzan(t)thə + ...-\ *n* [ISV *xanth-* + *proteic*] : the reaction of warm concentrated nitric acid with tyrosine or tyrosine-containing proteins (as in human skin) to form a yellow color that is intensified to orange-yellow by the addition of alkali

xan·thop·ter·in \zanˈthäptərən\ *n* -s [*xanth-* + *pter-* + *-in*] : a yellow crystalline amphoteric high-melting pigment $H_2NC_6HN_4(OH)_2$ that occurs esp. in the wings of yellow butterflies and also in the urine of mammals and that is convertible into leucopterin by oxidation and into folic acid by the action of various microorganisms; 2-amino-4,6-dihydroxy-pteridine

xan·tho·purpurin \ˌzan(t)(,)thō+\ *n* [ISV *xanth-* + *purpurin*] : PURPUROXANTHIN

xan·tho·rham·nin \,zan(t)thəˈramnən\ *n* -s [ISV *xanth-* + *rhamn-* + *-in*] : a yellow crystalline glycoside $C_{34}H_{42}O_{20}$ that occurs in Persian berries and yields rhamnetin and rhamninose on enzymatic hydrolysis

xan·tho·rhi·za *or* **xan·thor·rhi·za** \,zan(t)thəˈrīzə\ *n* -s [NL, fr. *xanth-* + *-rhiza*] : a plant of the genus *Zanthorhiza* : YELLOWROOT

xan·tho·ria \zanˈthōrēə\ *n, cap* [NL, irreg. fr. Gk *xanthos* yellow — more at XANTH-] : a genus of yellow or orange and foliaceous or arborescent lichens

xan·thor·rhoea \,zan(t)thəˈrēə\ *n* [NL, fr. *xanth-* + *-rrhea*; fr. the yellow gum it exudes] **1** *cap* : a genus of Australian plants (family Liliaceae) having a thick woody trunk or caudex that bears a cluster of stiff linear leaves and a dense terminal spike of small flowers — see GRASS TREE **2** -s : any plant of the genus *Xanthorrhoea*

xan·tho·siderite \ˌzan(t)(,)thō+\ *n* [G *xanthosiderit*, fr. *xanth-* + *siderit* siderite] : GOETHITE

xan·tho·sine \ˈzan(t)thə,sēn, -sən\ *n* -s [*xanth-* + *-sine* (as in *guanosine*)] : a crystalline nucleoside $C_{10}H_{12}N_4O_6$ that is formed by deamination of guanosine and yields xanthine and ribose on hydrolysis

xan·tho·sis \zanˈthōsəs\ *n, pl* **xantho·ses** \-ō,sēz\ [NL, fr. *xanth-* + *-osis*] **1** : yellow discoloration of the skin from abnormal causes **2** : a virus disease of the strawberry plant characterized by crinkling and curling, yellowing and dwarfing of the leaves, and stunting of the entire plant

xan·tho·so·ma \,zan(t)thəˈsōmə\ *n, cap* [NL, fr. *xanth-* + *-soma*] : a genus of tropical American aroids having hastate leaves, a shield-shaped style projecting beyond the ovary, and thick tubers — see YAUTIA

xan·tho·toxin \ˌzan(t)thə+\ *n* [ISV *xanth-* + *toxin*] : a crystalline lactone $C_{12}H_8O_4$ obtained esp. from the fruits of an African tree (*Zanthoxylum senegalense*) and used in conjunction with ultraviolet light in the treatment of vitiligo

xan·thot·ri·chous \(ˈ)zanˈthä·trəkəs\ *adj* [*xanth-* + *-trichous*] : having blonde or yellow hair

xan·thou·ra \zanˈthürə\ [NL, fr. *xanth-* + *-ura*] *syn of* CYANOCORAX

xan·thous \ˈzan(t)thəs\ *adj* [*xanth-* + *-ous*] **1** : having yellowish, red, auburn, or brown hair **2** : marked by yellow coloration ⟨a ~ tumor⟩

xan·thox·e·nite \zanˈthäksə,nīt\ *n* -s [*xanth-* + *xen-* + *-ite*] : a mineral $2Ca_2Fe(PO_4)_2(OH).3H_2O$ consisting of a basic hydrous calcium ferric phosphate and occurring in thin yellow monoclinic plates

xan·thox·y·la·ce·ae \(,)zan,thäksəˈlāsē,ē\ [NL, fr. *Xanthoxylum* + *-aceae*] *syn of* ZANTHOXYLACEAE

xan·thox·y·le·tin \-ˈlētᵊn\ *n* -s [*xanthoxyl-* (fr. NL *Xanthoxylum*) + *-et-* + *-in*] : a crystalline compound $C_{15}H_{14}O_4$ obtained from the bark of a prickly ash (*Zanthoxylum americanum*) — called also *xanthoxylin-N*

xan·thox·y·lin \zanˈthäksələn\ *n* -s [ISV *xanthoxyl-* (fr. NL *Xanthoxylum*) + *-in*] **1 a** : a crystalline phenolic ketone $C_{10}H_{12}O_4$ obtained from seeds of a shrubby Chinese tree (*Zanthoxylum piperitum*) **b** : any of several crystalline compounds obtained from the bark of other trees of the genus *Zanthoxylum*; *esp* : XANTHOXYLETIN **2** *or* **xanthoxylin extract** : a purified alcoholic extract of prickly-ash bark

¹**xan·thox·y·lum** \-ləm\ [NL, fr. *xanth-* + *-xylum*] *syn of* ZANTHOXYLUM

²**xanthoxylum** \ˈ"\ *var of* ZANTHOXYLUM

xanth·uren·ic acid \ˌzan(t)th(y)əˌrenik-\ *n* [*xanth-* + *-urenic* (as in *kynurenic*)] **:** a yellow crystalline phenolic acid $(HO)_2$-C_9H_4NCOOH closely related to kynurenic acid and excreted in the urine when tryptophan is added to the diet of experimental animals deficient in pyridoxine; 4,8-dihydroxy-quinaldic acid

xan·thy·drol \zanˈthīˌdrȯl, -rōl\ *n* [ISV *xanth-* + *hydrol*] **:** a crystalline secondary alcohol $C_6H_4(CHOH)(O)C_6H_4$ that is obtained by reduction of xanthone and is readily oxidized back to it, that forms salts with strong acids and with sulfuric acid gives a yellow solution with green fluorescence, and that is used esp. to characterize and determine urea by the formation of an insoluble product; xanthen-9-ol

xan·thyl \ˈzan(t)thəl\ *var of* XANTHENYL

xan·tu·si·idae \ˌzantəˈsīəˌdē\ *n pl, cap* [NL, fr. *Xantusia*, type genus (fr. János *Xántus* †1894 Hung. ornithologist + NL *-ia*) + *-idae*] **:** a small family of nocturnal carnivorous ovoviviparous terrestrial lizards of arid southwestern No. America

xan·tus's murrelet \ˈ(k)sänˌtüshəz-, ˈsh\ *n, usu cap X* [after János *Xántus* †1894] **:** a murrelet (*Endomychura hypoleucus*) of the California and Mexican coast that is slaty gray above and has white underparts and wing lining

xar·que \ˈshärkē, -kə\ *n* -s [Pg, fr. Sp *charque, charqui*] **:** CHARQUI

xat \ˈkät\ *n* -s [Haida] **:** a carved pole erected as a memorial to the dead by some Indians of western No. America

xa·ve·ri·an \zāˈvirēən, zaˈv-\ *adj, usu cap* [irreg. fr. St. Francis *Xavier* †1552 Span. Jesuit missionary + E *-an*] **:** of, relating to, or named after St. Francis Xavier

xaverian brother *n, usu cap X&B* **:** a member of a teaching congregation of lay brothers in the Roman Catholic Church founded in 1839 in Bruges

x-axis \ˈ=,==\ *n* **1 :** the axis of abscissas in a plane Cartesian coordinate system **2 :** one of the three axes in a three-dimensional rectangular coordinate system

x-body \ˈ=,==\ *n, usu cap X* **:** an amoeboid or amorphous inclusion body typical of some virus diseases of plants

XC *abbr* ex coupon

x-chair \ˈ=,=\ *n, usu cap X* **:** a usu. folding chair of ancient origin in which the legs cross to support the seat and are continuous with the arms

x chromosome *n, usu cap X* **:** a sex chromosome that carries factors for femaleness and usu. occurs paired in each female zygote and cell and single in each male zygote and cell — compare Y CHROMOSOME, Z CHROMOSOME

x-coordinate \ˈ==,=(=)=\ *n* **1 :** ABSCISSA **2 :** one of the three coordinates in a three-dimensional rectangular coordinate system

XD *abbr, often not cap* ex dividend

x'd *past of* X

x-disease \ˈ==,=\ *n, usu cap X* **:** any of various usu. virus diseases of obscure etiology and relationships: as **a :** a viral encephalitis of man first detected in Australia — called also *Australian X-disease* **b :** BLUE COMB **c :** HYPERKERATOSIS 2b **d :** a serious and widespread virus disease of peaches and related stone fruits characterized by yellowing and shot-holing of the leaves, early defoliation, and loss or mummification of the fruit — called also *yellow-red virosis*

Xe *symbol* xenon

xe·bec \ˈzēˌbek, zəˈbek\ *n* -s [prob. modif. (influenced by obs. Sp *xabeque* xebec — now *jabeque* — or Catal *xabec*, both fr. Ar *shabbāk*) of F *chebec*, fr. Ar *shabbāk*] **:** a Mediterranean sailing ship that has a long overhanging bow and stern, is usu. three-masted with a lateen rig, but often carries square sails on the foremast

x-ed *also* **xed** *past of* X

xe·ma \ˈzēmə\ *n, cap* [NL] **:** a monotypic genus of small black-headed gulls of arctic America having a slightly forked tail

xen- *or* **xeno-** *comb form* [LL, fr. Gk, fr. *xenos*] **1 :** guest **:** foreigner ⟨*xeno*mania⟩ **2 a :** strange **:** foreign ⟨*Xen*urus⟩ **b :** intrusive ⟨*xeno*lith⟩ **c :** HETER- ⟨*xeno*genesis⟩

xen·acan·thi \ˌzenəˈkanˌthī\ *n pl, cap* [NL, irreg. fr. *xen-* + Gk *akantha* spine — more at ACANTH-] *syn of* XENACANTHINI

¹xen·acan·thine \ˌzenəˈkan(t)thən, -anˌthīn\ *adj* [NL *Xenacanthini*] **:** of or relating to the Xenacanthini

²xenacanthine \ˈ"\ *n* -s [NL *Xenacanthini*] **:** a fish or fossil of the division Xenacanthini

xen·acan·thi·ni \ˌzenəˌkanˈthīˌnī, -ˈkan(t)thəˌnī\ *n pl, cap* [NL, fr. *xen-* + *acanth-* + *-ini*] *in some classifications* **:** a division of fossil elasmobranchs that is nearly equivalent to Ichthyotomi

xe·nar·chi \zəˈnärˌkī\ *n pl, cap* [NL, fr. *xen-* + Gk *archos* rectum, anus; akin to Gk *archein* to begin — more at ARCHI-] *in some classifications* **:** an order of fishes that comprises only the pirate perches and is usu. included in the order Salmopercae

xe·nar·thra \zəˈnärthrə\ *n pl, cap* [NL, fr. *xen-* + *arthra*, pl. of *arthron*] **:** a suborder or other division of Edentata comprising the American anteaters, armadillos, sloths, and usu. the extinct ground sloths — **xe·nar·thral** \-thrəl\ *or* **xe·nar·throus** \-thrəs\ *adj* — **xe·nar·thran** \-thrən\ *adj or n*

-xene \kˌsēn\ *n comb form* -s [F *-xène*, fr. Gk *-xenos* stranger, fr. *xenos*] **1 :** substance rarely associated with (such) a mineral ⟨anthraco*xene*⟩ **2 :** intrusive mineral of (such) a character ⟨leuco*xene*⟩ ⟨caco*xene*⟩

xe·nia \ˈzēnēə, -nyə\ *n* -s [NL, fr. Gk, hospitality, fr. *xenos* guest + *-ia* -y] **:** the effect of genes introduced by a male nucleus on structures (as endosperm or the fruit of a seed plant) other than the embryo; *also* **:** the effect of a gene capable of manifesting its dominant influence in the presence of two allelic genes — compare DOUBLE FERTILIZATION, METAXENIA

xe·nial \-nēəl, -nyəl\ *adj* [Gk *xenios* xenial (fr. *xenos* guest) + E *-al*] **:** of, relating to, or constituting hospitality or relations between host and guest and esp. among the ancient Greeks between persons of different cities ⟨~ relationship⟩ ⟨~ customs⟩

xe·nic·i·dae \zəˈnisəˌdē\ [NL, fr. *Xenicus*, genus of passerine birds (fr. Gk *xenikos* of a stranger or foreigner, fr. *xenos* guest, stranger + *-ikos* -ic) + *-idae*] *syn of* ACANTHISITTIDAE

xe·ni·um \ˈzēnēəm\ *n, pl* **xe·nia** \-nēə\ [L, fr. Gk *xenion*, fr. neut. of *xenios* of hospitality, xenial] **1 :** a present given among the ancient Greeks and Romans to a guest or stranger and esp. to a foreign ambassador **2** *xenia pl* **:** gifts sometimes given compulsorily to medieval rulers and churches

xen·o·ber·y·ces \ˌzenōˈberəˌsēz\ *n pl, cap* [NL, fr. *xen-* + *Beryces*, pl. of *Beryx*, genus of fishes] *in some classifications* **:** a small order of fishes related to and commonly included in Berycomorphi

xeno·biosis \ˌzenəˌbīˈōsəs\ *n, pl* **xenobio·ses** \-ōˌsēz\ [NL, fr. *xen-* + *-biosis*] **:** symbiosis in which members of two species of ants live together in the same nest but do not rear their young in common

xen·o·blast \ˈzenəˌblast\ *n* [*xen-* + *-blast*] **:** a crystal in metamorphic rock that is not bounded by its own faces but has its outlines impressed upon it by neighboring crystals — contrasted with *idioblast* — **xen·o·blas·tic** \ˌ==ˈblastik\ *adj*

xeno·cen·tric \ˌzenəˈsen·trik\ *adj* [*xen-* + *-centric*] **:** oriented toward or preferring a culture other than one's own

xe·noc·ra·te·an \ˌzeˌnäkrəˈtēən, zəˈn-\ *adj, usu cap* [*Xenocrates* †314 B.C. Greek Platonic philosopher + E *-an*] **:** XENOCRATIC

xen·o·crat·ic \ˌzenəˈkrad·ik\ *adj, usu cap* [*Xenocrates* †314 B.C. Greek Platonic philosopher + E *-ic*] **:** of or relating to the philosopher Xenocrates or to his doctrines in which he combined Pythagorean conceptions with Platonism

xeno·cryst \ˈzenəˌkrist\ *n* -s [*xen-* + *crystal*] **:** a crystal foreign to the rock in which it occurs — **xeno·crys·tic** \ˌ==ˈkristik\ *adj*

xeno·diagnosis \ˌzenō+\ *n* [NL, fr. *xen-* + *diagnosis*] **:** the detection of a parasite (as a blood parasite of man) by allowing a suitable intermediate host (as an insect) to consume supposedly infected material (as blood) and after an incubation period examining the intermediate host for the parasite ⟨doubtful cases of Chagas' disease confirmed by ~⟩

xeno·diagnostic \ˈ"+\ *adj* [ISV *xen-* + *diagnostic*] **:** of, relating to, or involving xenodiagnosis

xen·o·do·chei·on·ol·o·gy \ˌzenədəˌkīəˈnäləjē\ *n* -ES [Gk *xenodocheion* inn + E *-o-* + *-logy*] **:** the lore of hotels and inns

xen·o·do·che·um \ˌzenədəˈkēəm\ *n* -s [LL, fr. Gk *xenodocheion*, fr. *xenodochein* to entertain guests, fr. *xen-* + *dechesthai* to take, receive; akin to Gk *dokein* to seem good — more at DECENT] **:** an ancient Greek inn or hostel

xen·o·do·chi·um \-ˈkīəm\ *n, pl* **xenodo·chia** \-īə\ [LL, fr. Gk *xenodocheion* inn] **:** a medieval house for the care of the poor, strangers, pilgrims, or the sick

xe·nog·a·my \zəˈnägəmē\ *n* -ES [ISV *xen-* + *-gamy*] **:** fertilization by cross-pollination; *esp* **:** cross-pollination between flowers on different plants — compare GEITONOGAMY

xeno·genesis \ˌzenə+\ *n* [NL, fr. *xen-* + L *genesis*] **:** the fancied production of an organism altogether and permanently unlike the parent

xeno·glos·sy \ˈzenəˌgläsē, -lȯsē\ *n* -ES [ISV *xen-* + *gloss-* + *-y*] **:** purported use (as by a medium) while in a trance state of a language unknown to the individual under normal conditions

xeno·lith \ˈzenəˌlith\ *n* -s [*xen-* + *-lith*] **:** a fragment of a rock included in another rock — **xeno·lith·ic** \ˌ==ˈlithik\ *adj*

xeno·mania \ˌzenə+\ *n* [NL, fr. *xen-* + *mania*] **:** an inordinate attachment to foreign things (as customs, institutions, manners, fashions)

xe·no·mi \zəˈnōˌmī\ *n pl, cap* [NL, fr. *xen-* + Gk *ōmos* shoulder; fr. the distinct character of the pectoral arch — more at HUMERUS] *in some classifications* **:** an order of soft-rayed freshwater teleost fishes comprising the blackfish (*Dallia pectoralis*) and being commonly included usu. in the order Haplomi or among the Isospondyli

xeno·mor·pha \ˌzenəˈmȯrfə\ [NL, fr. *xen-* + *-morpha*] *syn of* TARDIGRADA 2

xeno·mor·phic \ˌ==ˈmȯrfik\ *adj* [*xen-* + *-morphic*] **:** ALLOTRIOMORPHIC

xenon \ˈzēˌnän, ˈzeˌnän\ *n* -s [Gk, neut. of *xenos* strange] **:** a heavy colorless inert gaseous element that occurs in air to the extent of about one part in 20 million by volume and in gases from hot springs, that is obtained along with krypton from liquid air, and that is used in thyratrons and specialized electric lamps — symbol *Xe*; see ELEMENT table

xen·o·pel·ti·dae \ˌzenəˈpeltəˌdē\ *n pl, cap* [NL, fr. *Xenopeltis*, type genus (fr. *xen-* + Gk *peltē* small shield) + *-idae* — more at PELTA] **:** a family of harmless terrestrial or burrowing snakes that is intermediate in many respects between the Boidae and Colubridae and includes solely the sunbeam snake

xe·noph·a·ne·an \zəˌnäfəˈnēən\ *adj, usu cap* [*Xenophanes*, 6th cent. B.C. Greek philosopher + E *-an*] **:** of or relating to the Eleatic philosopher Xenophanes or his doctrines noteworthy for their emphatic but perhaps pantheistic monotheism

xeno·phile \ˈzenəˌfīl\ *n* -s [ISV *xen-* + *-phile*] **:** one attracted to foreign things (as manners, styles, people) — **xe·noph·i·lous** \zeˈnäfələs, zəˈn-\ *adj*

xeno·phobe \ˈzenəˌfōb\ *n* -s [ISV *xen-* + *-phobe*] **:** one unduly fearful of what is foreign and esp. of people of foreign origin **:** a xenophobic person

xeno·pho·bia \ˌ==ˈfōbēə\ *n* [NL, fr. *xen-* + *phobia*] **:** fear and hatred of strangers or foreigners or of anything that is strange or foreign

xeno·phobic \ˌ==ˈfōbik *also* -ˈfäb-\ *adj* [NL *xenophobia* + E *-ic*] **:** of, relating to, or characterized by xenophobia ⟨~ responses⟩ ⟨a ~ person⟩

xen·o·phon·te·an \ˌzenəˈfäntēən, -ˌfänˈtē-\ *or* **xen·o·phon·ti·an** \-ˈfäntēən\ *or* **xen·o·phon·tine** \-ˈfänˌtīn, -äntᵊn\ *adj, usu cap* [Gk *Xenophōnt-, Xenophōn* Xenophon †355 B.C.? Greek historian and essayist + E *-an* or *-ine*] **:** of or relating to Xenophon

xe·noph·o·ra \zəˈnäfərə\ *n* [NL, fr. *xen-* + *-phora*] **1** *cap* **:** a genus of gastropod mollusks comprising the carrier snails (coextensive with the family Xenophoridae of the suborder Taenioglossa) **2** -s **:** any mollusk of the genus *Xenophora* — **xe·noph·o·ran** \-rən\ *adj*

xeno·pithe·cus \ˌzenəpəˈthēkəs, -ˈpithək-\ *n, cap* [NL, fr. *xen-* + *-pithecus*] **:** a genus of eastern African Lower Miocene apes known from imperfect fossil remains and possibly on the ancestral line of the orangutan

xeno·plas·tic \ˌzenəˈplastik\ *adj* [*xen-* + *-plastic*] **:** involving or occurring between distantly related individuals ⟨a successful ~ graft between plants of different genera is rare⟩ — **xeno·plas·ti·cal·ly** \-tək(ə)lē\ *adv*

xeno·pod·i·dae \ˌzenəˈpädəˌdē\ *n pl, cap* [NL, fr. *Xenopod-, Xenopus* + *-idae*] **:** a family of amphibians comprising *Xenopus* and a few related genera that are often included in the family Pipidae

xenopsyl·la \ˌzeˌnäpˈsilə, ˌzenəˈsilə\ *n, cap* [NL, fr. *xen-* + Gk *psylla* flea — more at PSYLLA] **:** a genus of fleas (family Pulicidae) including several (as the oriental rat flea) that are important as vectors of plague

xe·nop·te·ri \zəˈnäptəˌrī\ [NL, fr. *xen-* + Gk *pteron* wing — more at FEATHER] *syn of* XENOPTERYGII

xe·nop·te·ryg·ii \zəˌnäptəˈrijēˌī, (ˌ)zeˌn-\ *n pl, cap* [NL, fr. *xen-* + *-pterygii*] **:** an order of bony fishes that is coextensive with the family Gobiesocidae

xen·o·pus \ˈzenəpəs\ *n, cap* [NL, fr. *xen-* + *-pus*] **:** a genus that comprises African aquatic frogs having broad triangular heads, weak forelimbs, powerful, clawed hindlimbs, and no tongue or teeth and is sometimes made the type of a separate family but more often included among the Pipidae

xeno·rhyn·chus \ˌzenəˈriŋkəs\ *n, cap* [NL, fr. *xen-* + *-rhynchus*] **:** a genus of East Indian and Australian storks

xe·nos \ˈzēˌnäs\ *n, cap* [NL, fr. Gk *xenos* stranger, strange] **:** a genus of strepsipterons that are parasites of various wasps

xeno·sau·ri·dae \ˌzenəˈsȯrəˌdē\ *n pl, cap* [NL, fr. *Xenosaurus*, type genus (fr. *xen-* + *-saurus*) + *-idae*] **:** a monotypic family of slender-bodied Mexican lizards that is held to be intermediate between Iguanidae and Anguidae and comprises forms with the upper surface covered with minute granules and tubercles

xen·o·time \ˈzenəˌtīm\ *n* -s [F *xénotime*, irreg. (influence of *xén-* xen-) fr. Gk *kenos* empty, vain + *timē* honor; fr. the fact that it was wrongly thought at first to contain a new metal] **:** a mineral YPO_4 that is a phosphate of yttrium occurring in usu. brown or yellow tetragonal crystals and rolled grains and that often also contains thorium, erbium, cerium, or other elements (hardness 4–5, sp. gr. 4.45–4.56)

-xe·nous \ksənəs\ *adj comb form* [Gk *-xenos* stranger, fr. *xenos*] **:** host ⟨lipo*xenous*⟩

xe·nu·rus \zəˈn(y)u̇rəs\ [NL, fr. *xen-* + *-urus*] *syn of* CABASSOUS

-xe·ny \ksənē, -nī\ *n comb form* -ES [Gk *-xenos* + E *-y*] **:** (such) a host relationship ⟨lipo*xeny*⟩

xenyl \ˈzēnᵊl, ˈzen-\ *n* -s [ISV *xen-* + *-yl*] **:** a univalent radical $C_6H_5C_6H_4$- derived from biphenyl; biphenyl-yl

xer- *or* **xero-** *comb form* [LL, fr. Gk *xēr-, xēro-*, fr. *xēros* — more at SERENE] **1 a :** dry **:** arid ⟨*xer*ic⟩ **b :** dry place ⟨*xero*philous⟩ **2 :** using a dry process in the making of (such) a product ⟨*xero*graphy⟩ ⟨*xero*printing⟩

xe·ra·fin \ˌsherəˈfēⁿ, -ēn\ *also* **xe·ra·fim** *or* **xe·ra·phim** \-ēⁿ,-ēm\ *n* -s [Pg *xerafim*, fr. Ar *sharīfī*, fr. *sharīf* noble] **:** a silver coin current in Portuguese India before the 19th century and worth 300 to 360 reis

xe·ran·the·mum \zəˈran(t)thəməm\ *n* [NL, fr. *xer-* + *-anthemum*] **1** *cap* **:** a genus of annual densely tomentose herbs (family Compositae) native to southern Europe, containing one of the most widely cultivated everlastings (*X. annuum*), and having solitary chaffy or silvery flower heads with purplish tubular flowers **2** -s **:** any plant or flower of the genus *Xeranthemum*

xe·rarch \ˈziˌrärk, ˈzēˌr-\ *adj* [*xer-* + *-arch*] *of an ecological succession* **:** developing in a dry place — compare HYDRARCH, MESARCH

xe·ric \ˈsirik, ˈzēr-\ *adj* [*xer-* + *-ic*] **1** *of an environment* **:** low or deficient in moisture that is available for the support of plant life — compare HYDRIC, MESIC **2 :** of, relating to, or suited to a xeric environment **:** XEROPHYTIC — **xe·ri·cal·ly** \-k(ə)lē\ *adv*

xe·ro·cole \ˈzirəˌkōl\ *or* **xe·roc·o·lous** \zəˈräkələs\ *adj* [*xer-* + *-cole* or *-colous*] **:** XEROPHILOUS

xe·ro·der·ma \ˌzirəˈdərmə\ *n* -s [NL, fr. *xer-* + *-derma*] **:** a disease of the skin characterized by dryness and roughness and a fine scaly desquamation

xe·ro·gel \ˈzirəˌjel\ *n* [G, fr. *xer-* + *gel*] **:** a solid formed from a gel by drying with unhindered shrinkage — compare AEROGEL

xero·graph·ic \ˌzirəˈgrafik\ *adj* [ISV *xerography* + *-ic*] **:** of, relating to, used in, or prepared by xerography ⟨~ techniques⟩ ⟨a ~ print⟩

xe·rog·ra·phy \zəˈrägrəfē\ *n* -ES [ISV *xer-* + *-graphy*] **:** the formation of pictures or copies of graphic matter by the action of light on an electrically charged photoconductive insulating surface in which the latent image usu. is developed with powders that adhere only to the areas that remain electrically charged and in which the image formed by the powders sometimes is transferred to a sheet of paper

xe·ro·morph \ˈzirəˌmȯrf\ *n* [ISV *xer-* + *-morph*] **:** a plant with typical xerophytic morphology; *esp* **:** XEROPHYTE — **xe·ro·mor·phism** \-rˌbizəm\ *n* — **xe·ro·mor·phy** \-rfē\ *n* -ES

xe·ro·mor·phic \ˌ==ˈmȯrfik\ *also* **xe·ro·mor·phal** \-fəl\ *or* **xe·ro·mor·phous** \-fəs\ *adj* [*xeromorph* + *-ic* or *-al* or *-ous*] **1 :** of, relating to, or being a xeromorph **2** [*xer-* + *-morphic* or *morph-* + *-al* or *-morphous*] **:** of, relating to, or constituting climatic conditions favorable for the development of xerophilous vegetation

xe·roph·a·gy \zəˈräfəjē\ *also* **xe·ro·pha·gia** \ˌzirəˈfāj(ē)ə\ *n, pl* **xerophagies** *also* **xerophagias** [LL *xerophagia*, fr. Gk *xērophagia* eating of dry food, fr. *xērophagein* to eat dry food (fr. *xēros* dry + *phagein* to eat) + *-ia* -y — more at SERENE, BAKSHEESH] **:** the strictest Christian fast which is observed chiefly in the Eastern churches during Lent or esp. Holy Week and in which only bread, salt, water, and vegetables may be eaten and meat, fish, milk, cheese, butter, oil, wine, and all seasonings or spices are excluded

xe·ro·phile \ˈzirəˌfīl\ *or* **xe·ro·phil** \-ˌfil\ *n* -s [ISV *xer-* + *-phil*, n. comb form] **:** XEROPHYTE

xe·roph·i·lous \zəˈräfələs\ *or* **xe·ro·phile** \ˈzirəˌfīl\ *also* **xe·ro·phil·ic** \ˌzirəˈfilik\ *or* **xe·ro·phil** \ˈ==ˌfil\ *adj* [*xerophilous, xerophilic* fr. *xer-* + *-philous* or *-philic*; *xerophile, xerophil* ISV *xer-* + *-phil*, adj. comb form] **:** thriving in or tolerant or characteristic of an environment that is poor in available moisture ⟨a *xerophile* vegetation⟩ ⟨several ~ snails⟩ **:** adapted to life in the presence of minimal amounts of water ⟨*xerophilic* leaves⟩ — **xe·roph·i·ly** \zəˈräfəlē\ *n* -ES

xe·roph·o·bous \zəˈräfəbəs\ *adj* [*xer-* + *-phobous*] *of a plant* **:** having little capacity to resist drought

xe·roph·thal·mia \ˌziˌräfˈthalmēə, ˌzēˌr-, ÷ -äpˈth-\ *n* [LL, fr. Gk *xērophthalmia*, fr. *xēr-* xer- + *-ophthalmia*] **:** a dry thickened lusterless condition of the eyeball resulting from a severe systemic deficiency of vitamin A — compare KERATOMALACIA — **xe·roph·thal·mic** \ˌ==ˌ=ˈmik\ *adj*

xe·ro·phyl·lum \ˌzirəˈfiləm\ *n, cap* [NL, fr. *xer-* + *-phyllum*] **:** a small genus of tall No. American herbs (family Liliaceae) having thick woody rootstocks, simple stems with rough-edged linear leaves, and small white flowers in a dense terminal raceme — see SOUR GRASS, SQUAW GRASS

xe·ro·phyte \ˈzirəˌfīt\ *n* -s [*xer-* + *-phyte*] **:** a plant structurally adapted for life and growth with a limited water supply esp. by means of mechanisms (as epidermal thickening, waxy or resinous coats, or dense pubescence) that limit transpiration or that provide for the storage of water — used both of desert plants and of those occupying environments (as salt marshes or acid bogs) where water absorption is impeded by excess salts or acids in solution; compare HYDROPHYTE, MESOPHYTE

xe·ro·phyt·ic \ˌ==ˈfid·ik\ *adj* **:** of, relating to, typical of, or being a xerophyte **:** showing xeric adaptations ⟨~ vegetation⟩ ⟨~ structural adaptations⟩ ⟨a ~ life⟩ — **xe·ro·phyt·i·cal·ly** \-d·ək(ə)lē\ *adv*

xe·ro·phyt·ism \ˈ==ˌfīd·ˌizəm\ *n* -s **:** the quality or state of being xerophytic

xe·ro·phyt·iza·tion \ˌ==ˌfīd·əˈzāshən, -d·ˌīˈz-\ *n* -s [*xer-* + *phyt-* + *-ization*] **:** adaptation to more xeric conditions esp. as a factor in speciation

xe·ro·plas·tic \ˌzirōˈplastik\ *adj* [*xer-* + *-plastic*] **:** induced by or developing under the influence of a xeric environment

xe·ro·printing \ˈzirō, ˈzērō+,-\ *n* [*xer-* + *printing*] **:** an application of xerography to the mass production of graphic images in which the image plate is fixed to a cylinder and automatically charged and powdered for repeated electrostatic transfer of an image to machine-fed paper

xe·ro·radiograph \ˌzi(ˌ)rō, ˌzē(ˌ)rō+\ *n* [*xer-* + *radiograph*] **:** a radiograph made with the use of xerographic techniques to record the image — **xe·ro·radiographic** \ˈ"+\ *adj*

xe·ro·radiography \ˈ"+\ *n* [*xer-* + *radiography*] **:** radiography using xerographic techniques to record the image

xe·ro·sere \ˈzirəˌsi(ə)r\ *n* [*xer-* + *sere*] **:** the seral stages of a xerarch succession **:** a dry-land sere

xe·ro·sis \zəˈrōsəs\ *n, pl* **xero·ses** \-ōˌsēz\ [NL, fr. Gk *xērōsis*, fr. *xēr-* xer- + *-ōsis* -osis] **:** abnormal dryness of a body part or tissue (as the skin or conjunctiva)

xe·ro·sto·mia \ˌzirəˈstōmēə\ *n* -s [NL, fr. *xer-* + *-stomia*] **:** abnormal dryness of the mouth due to insufficient secretions

xe·ro·therm \ˈzirəˌthərm\ *n* [ISV *xer-* + *-therm*] **:** a plant that thrives in a hot dry environment

xe·ro·ther·mic \ˌ==ˈthərmik\ *adj* [*xer-* + *thermic*] **1 a :** being hot and dry **:** characterized by heat and dryness ⟨a ~ climate⟩ ⟨a prolonged postglacial ~ period⟩ **b :** concerned with or stressing the significance of xerothermic climate ⟨a ~ theory⟩ **2 :** adapted to or thriving in a xerothermic environment ⟨~ insects⟩

xe·rus \ˈzirəs\ *n, cap* [NL, fr. Gk *xēros* dry; fr. the texture of the fur] **:** a genus of coarse-haired long-tailed African ground squirrels that somewhat resemble prairie dogs in habits

x'es *or* **xes** *pl of* x, *pres 3d sing of* X

XF *abbr* extra fine

x factor *n* **:** a relevant but unidentified factor

xg *abbr* crossing

x height *n* **:** the distance between the top and bottom of a printed letter (as x, a, r, w) without an ascender or descender; *also* **:** the corresponding dimension in the type from which such letters are printed

xho·sa *also* **xo·sa** \ˈkōsə, ˈkȯ|, |zə\ *n, pl* **xhosa** \-ə\ *or* **xhosas** \-əz\ *or* **ama·xho·sa** \ˌämə+\ *or* **ama·xo·sa** *or* **ama·ko·sa** *also* **xosa** *or* **xosas** *usu cap* **1 a :** a Ngoni Bantu-speaking people of eastern Cape Province related to the Zulu **b :** a member of such people **2 :** a Bantu language of the Xhosa people closely related to Zulu and Swazi with which it forms the Ngoni group

xi \ˈzī, ˈksī, ˈksē *sometimes esp in fraternity names* ˈekˌsī\ *n* -s [Gk] **:** the 14th letter of the Greek alphabet — symbol Ξ or ξ; see ALPHABET table

XI *abbr* ex interest

xicaque *var of* JICAQUE

xi·me·nia \hə̇ˈmēnēə, -mān-\ *n, cap* [NL, irreg. fr. Francisco *Ximénez* †1721? Span. missionary in Guatemala + NL *-ia*] **:** a small genus of widely distributed tropical shrubs or trees (family Olacaceae) having alternate leaves, a persistent calyx, bearded petals, and drupaceous fruit — see FALSE SANDALWOOD, SOUR PLUM 2

xin·ca \ˈshiŋkə\ *n* -s *usu cap* **1 a :** an Indian people of southeastern Guatemala **b :** a member of such people **2 :** a Xincan language of the Xinca people

xin·can \-kən\ *n* -s *usu cap* [*Xinca* + E *-an*] **:** a language family of uncertain relationships comprising the Xinca language

x-ing *or* **x'ing** *pres part of* X

x-intercept \ˈ=,=,==\ *n* **:** the x-coordinate of the point where a line, curve, or surface intersects the x-axis

xiph- *or* **xiphi-** *or* **xipho-** *comb form* [NL, fr. Gk, fr. *xiphos*] **1 :** swordlike **:** sword-shaped ⟨*xipho*phyllous⟩ ⟨*xiphi*plastron⟩ **2 :** xiphoid and ⟨*xipho*costal⟩

xiph·i·as \ˈzifēəs\ *n* [NL, fr. L, swordfish, fr. Gk, *xiphias* sword] **1** *cap* **:** a genus (the type of the family Xiphiidae) of large scombroid fishes comprising the common swordfish **2** *pl* **xiphias :** SWORDFISH

xi·phid·io·cercaria \zəˌfidē(ˌ)ō+\ *n* [NL, fr. Gk *xiphidion* (dim. of *xiphos* sword) + NL *cercaria*] **:** a cercaria having a stylet in the oral sucker with which it actively penetrates the definitive host

xiphi·hu·mer·alis \ˌzifēˌhyümə'ralə̇s, -räl-,-räl-\ *n* [NL, fr. *xiph-* + *humeralis* humeral, fr. *humerus* + L *-alis* -al] **:** a muscle in some mammals that extends from the xiphoid cartilage to the proximal end of the humerus

xiph·i·oid \ˈzifēˌȯid\ *adj* [NL *Xiphias* + E *-oid*] **:** resembling or related to the genus *Xiphias*

xiphi·plastral \ˌzifə+\ *adj* [NL *xiphiplastron* + E *-al*] **:** of or relating to the xiphiplastron

xi·phi·plas·tron \"+\ *n, pl* **xiphiplastra** [NL, fr. *xiph-* + *plastron*] **:** the posterior and fourth lateral plate in the plastron of a turtle

xi·phi·ster·nal \"+\ *adj* [NL *xiphisternum* + E *-al*] **:** of or relating to the xiphisternum

xi·phi·ster·num \"+\ *n, pl* **xiphisterna** [NL, fr. *xiph-* + *sternum*] **1 :** the posterior segment of the sternum **:** XIPHOID PROCESS **2 :** XIPHIPLASTRON

xiph·is·ura \ˌzifəˈsu̇rə\ *or* **xiph·i·ura** \-fēˈ(y)u̇-\ *or* **xiph·ura** \zəˈf(y)u̇-\ [*xiphisura* fr. NL, alter. of *Xiphosura; xiphiura, xiphura* fr. NL, fr. *xiph-* + *-ura*] *syn of* XIPHOSURA

xiph·i·um iris \ˈzifēəm-\ *n, sometimes cap X* [*xiphium* fr. NL, fr. Gk *xiphion* corn flag, fr. *xiphos* sword] **:** SPANISH IRIS

xipho·costal \ˌzifō+\ *adj* [*xiph-* + *costal*] **:** of, relating to, or connecting the xiphoid process and the ribs

xiph·odon \ˈzifəˌdän\ *n, cap* [NL, fr. *xiph-* + *-odon*] **:** a genus of small two-toed artiodactyls (suborder Tylopoda) from the Eocene of Europe (the type of the family Xiphodontidae)

¹xi·phoid \ˈzīˌfȯid, ˈzi-\ *also* **xi·phoi·dal** \zīˈfȯidᵊl, zəˈf-\ *adj* [*xiphoid* fr. NL *xiphoides*, fr. Gk *xiphoeidēs*, fr. *xiphos* sword + *-oeidēs* -oid; *xiphoidal* fr. NL *xiphoides* + E *-al*] **1 :** shaped like a sword **:** ENSIFORM **2 :** of, relating to, or constituting the xiphisternum

²xiphoid \"\ *n* -s **:** XIPHISTERNUM, XIPHOID PROCESS

xiphoid bone *n* **:** a slender ossification in the nuchal ligament of some birds (as the cormorant)

xiphoid cartilage *n* **:** XIPHOID PROCESS 1

xiphoid process *n* **1 :** the posterior and lowest division of the sternum in man that is usu. more or less cartilaginous throughout life; *broadly* **:** XIPHISTERNUM **2 :** the tail of a king crab

xi·phop·a·gus \zəˈfäpəgəs\ *n* -ES [NL, fr. *xiph-* + *-pagus*] **:** an abnormality of animal twinning in which the twins are united at the xiphoid process — compare SIAMESE TWIN

xi·phoph·o·rus \zəˈfäfərəs\ *n, cap* [NL, fr. *xiph-* + *-phorus*] **:** a genus of topminnows (family Poeciliidae) comprising the swordtails

xi·pho·phyl·lous \ˌzifəˈfiləs\ *adj* [*xiph-* + *-phyllous*] **:** having sword-shaped leaves

xiph·o·su·ra \ˌzifəˈsu̇rə\ *n pl, cap* [NL, fr. Gk *xiphos* sword + NL *-ura*] **:** an order of arthropods comprising the king crabs and extinct related forms and usu. including only the two recent genera *Limulus* (syn. *Xiphosurus*) with representatives along the American coast of the Atlantic and *Tachypleus* with species along the Asiatic coast of the Pacific — **xiph·o·su·ran** \ˌ==ˈsu̇rən\ *adj or n* — **xiph·o·sure** \ˈ==ˌsu̇(ə)r\ *n* -s — **xiph·o·su·rous** \ˌ==ˈsu̇rəs\ *adj*

xiph·y·dri·idae \ˌzifəˈdrīəˌdē\ *n pl, cap* [NL, fr. *Xiphydria*, type genus (fr. Gk *xiphydrion*, a shell fish, fr. *xiphos* sword) + *-idae*] **:** a small family of horntails comprising the wood wasps and characterized by a thorax humped in front resembling a neck

x-irradiate \ˌ=ˈ===\ *vt, usu cap X* **:** to irradiate with X rays — **x-irradiation** \ˌ====ˈ==\ *n, usu cap X*

xis *pl of* XI

xl *abbr* **1** crystal **2** extra large

x line *n* **:** a horizontal line bounding the upper limit of the x height of a letter

x-man \ˈekˌsman\ *n, pl* **x-men :** a postal service employee who checks a railway car in mail service for possible lost or mislaid mail

xmas \ˈkrisməs *sometimes* ˈeksm-\ *n* -ES *usu cap* [*x* (symbol for *Christ*) + *-mas* (in *christmas*)] **:** CHRISTMAS

xn *abbr, often cap* Christian

XN *abbr* ex new

xnty *abbr, often cap* Christianity

XO *abbr* executive officer

xo·a·non \ˈzōəˌnän\ *n, pl* **xoa·na** \-ənə\ [Gk] **:** a primitive image of wood sometimes recalling in shape the block or tree-trunk from which it was cut

xo·no·tlite \ˈzōnəˌtlīt\ *n* -s [G *xonotlit*, fr. Tetala de *Xonotla*, village in Pueblo, Mexico, its locality + G *-it* -ite] **:** a mineral $5CaSiO_3 \cdot H_2O$ that is a hydrous calcium silicate

xosa *usu cap, var of* XHOSA

XP \ˈkīˈrō\ *symbol* [fr. the Greek letters XP] — used as a Christian symbol and monogram for *Christ*

x-protein \(ˈ)=+\ *n, often cap X* **:** a fraction of plasma protein held to be distinct from globulin, albumin, or fibrinogen or to be a complex of these possessing special properties by reason of its physical state — see CONGLUTININ

XQ *abbr* cross question

XR *abbr, often not cap* ex rights

x-radiate \ˈ=ˈ==ˌ=\ *vt, often cap X* **:** to expose (as a body part) to X-radiation

x-radiation \ˌ=ˌ==ˈ==\ *n, usu cap X* **1 :** exposure to X rays (as for therapeutic purposes) **:** IRRADIATION **2 :** radiation composed of X rays

x ray \ˈeksˌrā *also* ˈ=ˈ=\ *n, usu cap X* [¹*x*; trans. of G *x-strahl*] **1 :** any of the electromagnetic radiations having the nature of visible light but a wavelength approximately between 0.1 and 100 angstroms that is usu. produced by bombarding a metallic target with fast electrons in vacuum so that the spectrum of the radiation emitted consists of lines characteristic of the target material and that has the properties of ionizing a gas upon passage through it, of penetrating through various thicknesses of all solids, of producing secondary radiations by impinging on material bodies, and of acting on photographic films and plates and on fluorescent screens **:** a photon or a stream of photons produced by excitation of an atom by impact of a fast moving electron **2 :** a photograph obtained by the use of X rays

x-ray \"\ *vb, often cap X, vt* **:** to expose to the action of X rays **:** examine, treat, or photograph with X rays **:** IRRADIATE ~ *vi* **:** to employ X rays

xray \"\ *usu cap* — a communications code word for the letter *x*

x-ray absorbing glass *n* **:** glass that resists the penetration of X rays and gamma rays and ordinarily contains a high content of lead oxide

x-ray fish *n* **:** GLASSFISH

x-ray microscope *n, usu cap X* **:** an instrument in which X-ray diffraction patterns of crystals are translated into pictures showing the relative positions of the atoms in a crystal as if in a photomicrograph of very high magnification

x-ray photograph *or* **x-ray picture** *n, usu cap X* **:** a shadow picture made with X rays; *esp* **:** one revealing the internal structure of objects opaque to ordinary light — **x-ray photography** *n, usu cap X*

x-ray spectrograph *n, usu cap X* **:** a spectrograph for dispersing X rays and measuring their wavelengths

x-ray spectrometer *n, usu cap X* **:** a spectrometer for measuring the angles of diffraction of X rays produced by reflection from a crystal or for measuring X-ray spectra

x-ray spectrum *n, usu cap X* **:** the spectrum of an emission of X rays that is obtained by dispersion with either a crystal grating or a ruled grating

x-ray therapy *n, usu cap X* **:** ROENTGENOTHERAPY

x-ray tube *n, usu cap X* **:** a high-vacuum tube in which a concentrated stream of electrons from a thermionic cathode strikes a metal target and produces X rays from the side of the tube at right angles in a quantity and intensity that is controlled by the cathode temperature, with a wavelength and hardness that depends upon the voltage applied to the tube terminals, and with a spectral character determined by the material of the target

x's *or* **xs** *pl of* x

x-stool \ˈ=ˌ=\ *n, cap X* **:** the simplest and most ancient of stools supported on an X-shaped frame and often designed to fold — compare X-CHAIR

x-stretcher \ˈ=ˌ==\ *n, cap X* **:** a crossed stretcher for furniture

xt *abbr, often cap* Christian

xtal *abbr* crystal

xtian *abbr, often cap* Christian

xtra \ˈekstrə\ *usu cap* — a communications code word for the letter *x*

xtry *abbr* extraordinary

xty *abbr, often cap* Christianity

XU *abbr, often not cap* x unit

x unit *n, usu cap X* **:** a unit of wavelength that is used for X rays and gamma rays and that is equal to approximately 10^{-11} centimeters

xu·rel *like* JUREL\ *n* -s [modif. of Sp *jurel* — more at JUREL] **1 :** BIG-EYED SCAD **2 :** SAUREL

x virus *n, usu cap X* **1 :** a latent virus **2 :** latent virus disease in which symptoms are absent

XW *abbr, often not cap* ex warrant

xx-disease \(ˈ)ekˈseks-\ *n, usu cap both Xs* [so called fr. being of obscure etiology] **:** HYPERKERATOSIS 2b

xy·el·i·dae \zīˈeləˌdē\ *n pl, cap* [NL, fr. *Xyela*, type genus (fr. Gk *xyelē* curved knife, fr. *xyein* to scratch, scrape) + *-idae*] **:** a small family of primitive sawflies having larvae that feed on the foliage of trees

xyl- *or* **xylo-** *comb form* [L, fr. Gk, fr. *xylon;* perh. akin to Lith *šulas* pillar, post, OE *syl* — more at SILE] **1 a :** wood **:** woody ⟨*xylo*phone⟩ ⟨*xyl*oma⟩ **b :** xylem **2 a :** xylene ⟨*xyl*ic⟩ ⟨*xylo*quinone⟩ **b :** xylose ⟨*xyl*onic acid⟩ ⟨*xylo*ketose⟩ **3** *xylo-, usu ital* **:** having the stereochemical arrangement of atoms or groups found in xylose ⟨L-*xylo*-ascorbic acid⟩

xy·lan \ˈzīˌlan\ *n* -s [ISV *xyl-* + *-an*] **:** a pentosan that yields xylose on hydrolysis, that occurs in the cell walls of land plants, and that comprises up to one third of straw, corncobs, oat hulls, and cottonseed hulls and up to one quarter of wood

xy·lar·ia \zīˈla(a)rēə\ *n, cap* [NL, fr. *xyl-* + *-aria*] **:** the type genus of Xylariaceae comprising fungi with perithecia borne in the upper part of erect black corky or woody stromata — see BLACK ROOT ROT

xy·lar·i·a·ce·ae \(ˌ)zīˌla(a)rēˈāsēˌē\ *n pl, cap* [NL, fr. *Xylaria*, type genus + *-aceae*] **:** a family of ascomycetous fungi (order Sphaeriales) characterized by dark brown to black usu. nonseptate ascospores and conidia borne superficially on the stroma

xy·la·ry \ˈzīlərē\ *adj* [*xyl-* + *-ary*] **:** of, relating to, associated with, or constituting wood and esp. xylem ⟨wax does not seem to be secreted . . . in the ~ tissues of plants —*Economic Geology*⟩

xy·leb·o·rus \zīˈlebərəs\ *n, cap* [NL, fr. Gk *xyleboros* eating wood, fr. *xylē-* (fr. *xylon* wood) + *boros* gluttonous, fr. *bora* food, meat — more at VORACIOUS] **:** a large genus of small ambrosia beetles

xy·lem \ˈzīləm, -ˌlem\ *n* -s [G, fr. Gk *xylon* wood] **:** a complex tissue in the vascular system of higher plants consisting of vessels, tracheids, or both usu. together with wood fibers and parenchyma cells, functioning chiefly in conduction but also in support and storage, and typically constituting the woody element (as of a plant stem) — compare PHLOEM

xylem fiber *n* **:** any of various fibers located in or associated with xylem and typically having an angular cross-section and heavily lignified walls with prominent bordered pits — compare PHLOEM FIBER

xylem parenchyma *n* **:** WOOD PARENCHYMA

xylem ray *or* **xylary ray** *n* **:** a vascular ray or portion of a vascular ray that is located in xylem — called also *wood ray;* compare PHLOEM RAY

xy·lene \ˈzīˌlēn\ *n* -s [ISV *xyl-* + *-ene*] **1 :** any of three toxic flammable oily isomeric aromatic hydrocarbons $C_6H_4(CH_3)_2$ that are dimethyl homologues of benzene and are obtained from wood tar or commercially in mixtures of the three with ethylbenzene from light oils from coal tar or coke-oven gas or from petroleum distillates by processes for producing toluene: **a :** the ortho isomer used chiefly in making phthalic anhydride — called also *ortho-xylene, o-xylene* **b :** the para isomer used chiefly in making terephthalic acid — called also *para-xylene, p-xylene* **c :** the meta isomer occurring in the mixtures in larger amounts than the other components and used chiefly in making isophthalic acid and xylidines — called also *meta-xylene, m-xylene* **2 :** a commercial mixture containing xylenes and ethylbenzene used chiefly as a solvent, as a blending agent esp. in aviation gasoline, or in making xylidines

xylene light yellow *n, often cap X&L&Y* **:** an acid dye — see DYE table I (under *Acid Yellow 17*)

xylene musk *n* **:** MUSK XYLENE

xy·lene·sulfonic acid \ˌzīˌlēn+. . .-\ *n* [*xylene* + *sulfonic*] **:** any of six crystalline isomeric acids $(CH_3)_2C_6H_3SO_3H$ obtained by sulfonation of the xylenes but most readily of *ortho-* and *meta-*xylenes, which can thus be separated from *para*-xylene in the commercial mixture

xy·le·nol \ˈzīləˌnȯl, -ˌnōl\ *n* -s [ISV *xylene* + *-ol*] **:** any of six crystalline isomeric phenols $(CH_3)_2C_6H_3OH$ or a mixture of them derived from the xylenes, found in coal tar, and used chiefly as disinfectants and in making phenolic resins; dimethyl-phenol; *esp* **:** the meta or 3,5-isomer constituting the most abundant xylenol in coal tar — compare CHLOROXYLENOL

xy·le·nyl \-ˌnil\ *n* -s [*xylene* + *-yl*] **:** XYLYL

xy·leu·tes \zīˈlüdˌ(ˌ)ēz\ *n, cap* [NL, fr. Gk *xyleus* woodcutter, fr. *xyleuein* to cut wood, fr. *xylon* wood] **:** a genus of moths (family Zeuzeridae) comprising the wood moths of Australia and southeast Asia

xylia \ˈzīlēə, ˈzil-\ *n, cap* [NL, fr. *xyl-* + *-ia;* fr. the woody pod] **:** a genus of Asiatic trees (family Leguminosae) having globose heads of small greenish flowers succeeded by falcate compressed pods — see ACLE, PYINKADO

xy·lic acid \ˌzī¦lik-, ˈ¦zi¦\ *n* [ISV *xyl-* + *-ic*] **:** any of six isomeric crystalline carboxylic acids $(CH_3)_2C_6H_3COOH$ derived from xylene; dimethyl-benzoic acid

xyli·dine \ˈzīləˌdēn, ˈzil-, -ˌdᵊn\ *n* -s [ISV *xyl-* + *-idine*] **1 :** any of six toxic liquid or low-melting crystalline compounds $(CH_3)_2C_6H_3NH_2$ that are amino derivatives of the xylenes and are made from them by nitration and subsequent reduction and that are used chiefly as intermediates for azo dyes and in organic synthesis: as **a :** the asymmetric meta isomer constituting the major part of mixed xylidines; 2,4-dimethyl-aniline — called also *2,4-xylidine, meta-4-xylidine* **b :** the pale yellow crystalline para isomer; 2,5-dimethyl-aniline — called also *2,5-xylidine* **c :** the crystalline asymmetric ortho isomer used in synthesizing riboflavin; 3,4-dimethyl-aniline — called also *3,4-xylidine, ortho-4-xylidine* **2 :** a commercial mixture of xylidines produced from commercial xylene

xy·lin·de·in \zīˈlindēən\ *n* -s [F *xylindéine*, fr. *xyl-* + *inde* indigo + *-ine* — more at INDE BLUE] **:** a yellow to brown crystalline compound $C_{34}H_{26}O_{11}$ produced by a fungus (*Peziza aeruginosa*) in green-rotted wood that dyes wool and cotton green

xy·li·tol \ˈzīləˌtȯl, -tōl\ *n* -s [*xyl-* + *-itol*] **:** a sweet crystalline pentahydroxy alcohol $C_5H_7(OH)_5$ obtained by reduction of xylose

xylo- — see XYL-

xylo-ascorbic acid \ˌzī(ˌ)lō+. . .-\ *n* **:** ASCORBIC ACID 1

xy·lo·bal·sa·mum \ˌzīlōˈbȯlsəməm\ *n* [L, fr. Gk *xylobalsamon*, fr. *xyl-* + *balsamon* balsam tree, balsam — more at BALM] **:** the dried twigs or fragrant wood of a balm of Gilead (*Commiphora meccanensis*)

xy·loc·o·pa \zīˈläkəpə\ *n, cap* [NL, fr. Gk *xylokopos* woodcutter, fr. *xyl-* + *-kopos* (fr. *koptein* to cut off) — more at CAPON] **:** a genus of carpenter bees that is the type of the family Xylocopidae

xy·lo·cop·i·dae \ˌzīləˈkäpəˌdē\ *n pl, cap* [NL, fr. *Xylocopa*, type genus + *-idae*] **:** a family that comprises hairy stout usu. large chiefly tropical bees which excavate nest galleries in dry wood or pithy stems and that is sometimes made a subfamily of Apidae

xy·log·ly·phy \zīˈläglǝfē, ˈzīləˌglifē\ *n* -ES [*xyl-* + Gk *glyphē* carving, carved work + E *-y* — more at GLYPH] **:** artistic wood carving

xy·lo·graph \ˈzīlə graf, -rȧf\ *n* [back-formation fr. *xylography*] **:** an engraving on wood; *also* **:** an impression from such an engraving **:** a print made by xylography

xy·log·ra·pher \zīˈlägrəfə(r)\ *n* -s [*xylography* + *-er*] **:** one that practices or is skilled in xylography

xy·lo·graph·ic \ˌzīləˈgrafik\ *also* **xy·lo·graph·i·cal** \-fəkəl\ *adj* [*xylographic* fr. F *xylographique*, fr. *xylographie* + *-ique* -ic; *xylographical* fr. *xylography* + *-ical*] **:** of, relating to, or expressed in xylography — **xy·lo·graph·i·cal·ly** \-fək(ə)lē\ *adv*

xy·lo·graph·i·ca \ˌ==ˈ=fəkə\ *n pl* [NL, fr. neut. pl. of (assumed) NL *xylographicus* xylographic, fr. L *xyl-* + *graphicus* graphic] **:** BLOCK BOOKS

xy·log·ra·phy \zīˈlägrəfē\ *n* -ES [F *xylographie*, fr. *xyl-* + *-graphie* -graphy] **1 a :** WOOD ENGRAVING **b :** WOODCUT **2 :** the art of making prints from the natural wood grain **3 :** a method of printing in colors upon wood

xy·loid \ˈzīˌlȯid\ *adj* [ISV *xyl-* + *-oid*] **:** resembling wood **:** having the qualities or nature of wood **:** WOODY, LIGNEOUS

xy·lo·ketose \ˌzī(ˌ)lō+\ *n* [ISV *xyl-* + *ketose*] **:** XYLULOSE

xy·lol \ˈzīˌlōl, -ˌlȯl\ *n* -s [ISV *xyl-* + *-ol*] **:** XYLENE — used esp. of the commercial mixture

xy·lol·o·gy \zīˈläləjē\ *n* -ES [ISV *xyl-* + *-logy*] **:** a branch of dendrology dealing with the gross and the minute structure of wood

xy·lo·man·cy \ˈzīləˌman(t)sē\ *n* -ES [*xyl-* + *-mancy*] **:** divination by means of pieces of wood

xy·lom·e·ter \zīˈläməd·ə(r)\ *n* [ISV *xyl-* + *-meter*] **:** an instrument used to determine specific gravity of wood

-x·y·lon \ˌksəˌlän\ *n comb form* [NL, fr. Gk *xylon* — more at XYL-] **1 :** one having (such) wood — in generic names ⟨Haemato*xylon*⟩ **2 :** one living in (such)a relation to wood ⟨Hypo*xylon*⟩ **3 :** wood ⟨laurino*xylon*⟩

xy·lon·ic acid \(ˈ)zī¦länik-\ *n* [ISV *xyl-* + *-onic*] **:** an acid $C_4H_5(OH)_4COOH$ obtained as a syrup by oxidizing xylose

Xy·lo·nite \ˈzīləˌnīt\ *trademark* — used for a plastic

¹xy·loph·a·ga \zīˈläfəgə\ *n, cap* [NL, fr. *xyl-* + *-phaga*] **:** a genus of marine bivalve mollusks (family Pholadidae) that bore holes in wood

²xylophaga \"\ *n pl, cap* [NL, fr. *xyl-* + *-phaga*] **:** a group of insects that feed on or in wood; *esp* **:** a division of beetles

xy·lo·phag·i·dae \ˌzīləˈfajəˌdē\ *n pl, cap* [NL, fr. *Xylophagus*, type genus (fr. Gk *xylophagos* xylophagous) + *-idae*] **:** a family of dipterous flies whose predaceous larvae frequently live in decayed wood

xy·loph·a·gous \(ˈ)zīˈläfəgəs\ *adj* [Gk *xylophagos* wood-eating, fr. *xyl-* + *-phagos* -phagous] **:** feeding on or in wood — used esp. of insect larvae, crustaceans, and mollusks

xy·loph·i·lous \(ˈ)zīˈläfələs\ *adj* [*xyl-* + *-philous*] **:** attracted to wood **:** growing or living in or on wood ⟨~ fungi⟩ ⟨a ~ beetle⟩

xylo·phone \ˈzīləˌfōn *also* ˈzil-\ *n* [*xyl-* + *-phone*] **1 a :** a percussion musical instrument consisting of a series of wooden bars graduated in length to sound the musical scale, supported on belts of straw or felt, and sounded by striking with two small wooden hammers and comprising from 30 to 55 bars arranged in two rows and tuned chromatically with or without carefully tuned resonators **b :** an organ percussion stop of similar tone quality **2 :** an instrument to determine the elastic properties of woods

xylophone 1a

xylo·phon·ic \ˌ==¦fänik\ *adj* **:** relating to or sounding like a xylophone

xylo·phon·ist \ˈzīləˌfōnəst *also* ˈziləˌfōn- *sometimes* zīˈläfən- *or* zəˈläfən-\ *n* -s **:** a performer on the xylophone

xy·lo·pia \zīˈlōpēə\ *n, cap* [NL, prob. fr. *xyl-* + *-opia*] **:** a large genus of chiefly tropical American trees or shrubs (family Annonaceae) with coriaceous often distichous leaves, rather large flowers, aromatic berries, and usu. bitter wood — see EMBIRA, GUINEA PEPPER

xy·lo·porosis \ˌzīlə+\ *n* [NL, fr. *xyl-* + *porosis*] **:** a disease of citrus trees associated with lack of compatability between scion and stock and characterized by pits in the xylem

xy·lo·pyrography \"+\ *n* [*xyl-* + *pyrography*] **:** pyrography upon wood

xy·lo·quinone \"+\ *n* [ISV *xyl-* + *quinone*] **:** any of several yellow crystalline compounds $(CH_3)_2C_6H_2O_2$ obtained in general by oxidation of xylidines or xylenols; dimethyl-benzoquinone

xy·lose \ˈzīˌlōs *also* -ōz\ *n* -s [ISV *xyl-* + *-ose*] **:** a crystalline aldose sugar of the pentose class $C_5H_{10}O_5$ that is not fermentable with ordinary yeasts and that is found esp. as the D-form as a constituent of xylans and obtained therefrom by hydrolysis with acids — compare WOOD SUGAR

xy·lo·side \ˈzīləˌsīd-ˌsəd\ *n* -s [*xylose* + *-ide*] **:** a glycoside that yields xylose on hydrolysis

xy·los·ma \zīˈläzmə\ *n, cap* [NL, fr. *xyl-* + *-osma*] **:** a genus of American and Asiatic usu. evergreen trees and shrubs (family Flacourtiaceae) with axillary thorns and fine-textured woods

xy·lo·stro·ma \ˌzīlə¦strōmə\ *n, pl* **xylostroma·ta** \-məd·ə\ *also* **xylostromas** [NL, fr. *xyl-* + *stroma*] **:** the closely felted sterile mycelium of various wood-destroying fungi formerly believed to represent a distinct genus — **xy·lo·stro·ma·toid** \-məˌtȯid\ *adj*

xy·lo·tile \ˈzīləˌtīl\ *n* -s [G *xylotil*, fr. *xyl-* + Gk *tilos* something plucked, fr. *tillein* to pluck] **:** a mineral approximately $(Mg,Fe)_3Fe_2Si_7O_{20}.11H_2O$ that is a hydrous iron magnesium silicate, occurs in delicately fibrous forms, and is derived from alteration of asbestos or chrysolite

xy·lo·tom·ic \ˌzīlə¦tämik\ *or* **xy·lo·tom·i·cal** \-məkəl\ *adj* **:** of or relating to xylotomy

xy·lot·o·mist \-məst\ *n* -s **:** one skilled in xylotomy

xy·lot·o·mous \(ˈ)zīˈläd·əməs\ *adj* [*xyl-* + *-tomous*] **:** capable of boring or cutting wood — used of an insect

xy·lot·o·my \-mē\ *n* -ES [*xyl-* + *-tomy*] **:** the art of preparing sections of wood (as by means of a microtome) for microscopic examination

xy·lo·trya \ˌzīləˈtrīə\ *n, cap* [NL, fr. *xyl-* + Gk *tryein* to rub, wear out; akin to Gk *tribein* to rub, grind — more at THROW] **:** a genus of marine bivalves that is closely related to and often included in *Teredo* and comprises forms as destructive to timber

xy·lo·typographic \ˌzīlə+\ *adj* [*xyl-* + *typographic*] **:** of or relating to wooden type **:** printed from wooden type or from wood blocks — **xy·lo·typography** \"+\ *n*

xy·lu·lose \ˈzīl(y)əˌlōs *also* -ōz\ *n* -s [ISV *xyl-* + *-ulose* (as in *cellulose*)] **:** a ketose sugar $C_5H_{10}O_5$ of the pentose class that is formed from xylose by epimerization and from D-arabitol by bacterial oxidation, that like ribulose plays a role in carbohydrate metabolism, and that is found in the urine in cases of pentosuria; *threo-*pentulose

-x·y·lum \ˌksələm\ *n comb form* [NL, fr. Gk *xylon* — more at XYL-] **:** one having (such) wood — in generic names ⟨Erythro*xylum*⟩ ⟨Zantho*xylum*⟩

xy·lyl \ˈzīləl\ *n* -s [ISV *xyl-* + *-yl*] **:** any of several isomeric univalent radicals C_8H_9 derived from the three xylenes by removal of a hydrogen atom; *esp* **:** a radical of the formula $(CH_3)_2C_6H_3$—; dimethyl-phenyl — compare TOLYL

xy·lyl·ene \ˈzīləˌlēn\ *n* -s [ISV *xylyl* + *-ene*] **1 :** any of several isomeric bivalent radicals C_8H_8 derived from the three xylenes by removal of one hydrogen atom from each of two carbon atoms; *esp* **:** any of the three radicals having the formula $-CH_2C_6H_4CH_2-$; phenylene-di-methylene **2 :** a reactive hydrocarbon $CH_2{=}C_6H_4{=}CH_2$ that is formed by pyrolysis of *para*-xylene under low pressure followed by quick chilling in a solvent at −80° C and that polymerizes to an insoluble white mass at room temperature — called also *para-xylylene, p-xylylene*

xy·phoid \ˈzīˌfȯid, ˈzi-\ *adj or n* [by alter.] **:** XIPHOID

xyr·i·da·ce·ae \ˌzirəˈdāsēˌē\ *n pl, cap* [NL, fr. *Xyrid-, Xyris*, type genus + *-aceae*] **:** a family of herbs (order Xyridales) with basal equitant usu. distichous leaves and leafless scapes bearing flowers in dense heads in the axils of imbricated scales — see XYRIS — **xyr·i·da·ceous** \ˌ==¦dāshəs\ *adj*

xyr·i·da·les \ˌ==ˈdā(ˌ)lēz\ *n pl, cap* [NL, fr. *Xyrid-, Xyris* + *-ales*] **:** an order of monocotyledonous herbs having flowers mostly with regular corolla and compound superior ovary — see BROMELIACEAE, COMMELINACEAE, XYRIDACEAE

xy·ris \ˈzīrəs\ *n, cap* [NL, fr. L, an iris, fr. Gk] **:** a large genus (the type of the family Xyridaceae) of chiefly American marsh plants having mostly yellow flowers with three sepals of which the two lateral are small, keeled, and persistent and the other is membranous and spreading — see YELLOW-EYED GRASS

xyst \ˈzist\ *n* -s [L *xystus*] **:** XYSTUS

xys·tum \ˈzistəm\ *n, pl* **xys·ta** \-tə\ [L, fr. Gk *xyston*, fr. neut. of *xystos* scraped, polished, fr. *xyein* to scrape, polish] **:** XYSTUS

xys·tus \ˈzistəs\ *n, pl* **xys·ti** \-ˌstī, -ˌstē\ [L, fr. Gk *xystos*, fr. *xystos*, adj., scraped, polished; fr. its smooth floor] **:** a long and open portico used esp. by ancient Greeks or Romans for athletic exercises in wintry or stormy weather; *sometimes* **:** a walk lined with trees

¹y \ˈwī\ *n, pl* **y's** *or* **ys** \ˈwīz\ *often cap, often attrib* **1 a :** the 25th letter of the English alphabet **b :** an instance of this letter printed, written, or otherwise represented **c :** a speech counterpart of orthographic *y* (as *y* in *yard, my, city,* or Swedish *fyr*) **2 :** a printer's type, a stamp, or some other instrument for reproducing the letter *y* **3 :** someone or something arbitrarily or conveniently designated *y:* as **a :** the 25th in order or class **b :** the 24th in order or class when j is not used **c :** the 22d in order or class when j, v, and w are not used **d :** the second in order or class when x is made the first **4 :** something having the shape of the letter Y: as **a :** a forked holder to support the telescope of a leveling instrument or the axis of a theodolite **:** WYE **b :** a principal railroad track and two diverging branches arranged like the letter Y that with a cross track connecting the diverging branches are used in reversing engines or trains **c :** SIAMESE 4 **5 a :** UNKNOWN QUANTITY 1 **b :** Y-COORDINATE

²y \ˈ"\ *adj, cap* [abbr. of *Young* (as in *Young Men's Christian Association, Young Women's Christian Association, Young Men's and Young Women's Hebrew Association*)] **:** of or relating to the Young Men's Christian Association, the Young Women's Christian Association, or the Young Men's and Young Women's Hebrew Association

³y *abbr, often cap* **1** yard **2** year **3** yellow **4** yen **5** yeoman; yeomanry **6** younger; youngest **7** your

⁴y *symbol* **1** unknown quantity **2** an ordinate **3** *cap* admittance **4** *cap* yttrium

y- *prefix* [ME *y-, i-,* fr. OE *ge-,* perfective, associative, and collective prefix (often used to form perfective verbs whose past participles were subsequently made to function as the past participles of the corresponding simple verbs) — more at CO-] — used in a few esp. archaic past participles that have survived or have been revived from an earlier period of the language and occas. in other verb forms coined by analogy with such past participles ⟨*y*pointing⟩

¹-y *also* **-ey** \ē, i\ *adj suffix, usu* **-ier**; *usu* **-iest** [ME, fr. OE *-ig;* akin to OHG *-īg -y,* ON *-igr,* Goth *-eigs, -igs,* L *-icus,* Gk *-ikos,* Skt *-ika*] **1 a :** characterized by **:** full of — in adjectives formed from nouns ⟨blossom*y*⟩ ⟨dirt*y*⟩; in many words formed from a base word having final postconsonantal mute *e* and with omission of the *e* ⟨mir*y*⟩ ⟨mir*ey*⟩ ⟨spin*y*⟩ ⟨spin*ey*⟩; accompanied by doubling of the final consonant of the base word immediately after a short stressed vowel ⟨legg*y*⟩ ⟨mudd*y*⟩; in the form *-ey* regularly after a final *y* ⟨clay*ey*⟩ or vowel other than postconsonantal mute *e* ⟨mosquito*ey*⟩ ⟨glu*ey*⟩ sometimes with a change of *y* to *i* ⟨ski*ey*⟩ or where *-y* would duplicate another word ⟨hol*ey*⟩ **b :** having the character of **:** composed of — in adjectives formed from nouns ⟨ic*y*⟩ ⟨water*y*⟩ ⟨lac*y*⟩ ⟨wax*y*⟩ ⟨rant*y*⟩ **c :** characteristic of, resembling, or suggesting someone or something indicated **:** having some of the qualities of **:** that is like or like that of — in adjectives formed from nouns ⟨home*y*⟩ ⟨wintr*y*⟩ ⟨folks*y*⟩ ⟨garbag*y*⟩ ⟨win*y*⟩ often with a disparaging connotation ⟨gadget*y*⟩ ⟨milquetoast*y*⟩ ⟨schoolteacher*y*⟩ ⟨rabbit*y*⟩ ⟨Hollywood*y*⟩ ⟨bedroom*y*⟩ ⟨barn*y*⟩ ⟨stag*y*⟩ **d :** devoted to **:** addicted to **:** enthusiastic over — in adjectives formed from nouns ⟨hors*y*⟩ ⟨outdoors*y*⟩ ⟨ism*y*⟩ **2 a :** tending or inclined to — in adjectives formed from verbs ⟨cling*y*⟩ ⟨sleep*y*⟩ ⟨chatt*y*⟩ ⟨cri*ey*⟩ **b :** giving occasion for (specified) action ⟨tear*y*⟩ ⟨yumm*y*⟩ — usu. in adjectives formed from verbs ⟨munch*y*⟩ ⟨picnick*y*⟩ **c :** performing (specified) action or being in a (specified) mode of existence **:** -ING — in adjectives formed from verbs ⟨twinkl*y*⟩ ⟨curl*y*⟩ **3 a :** somewhat **:** rather **:** -ISH — in adjectives formed from adjectives ⟨purpl*y*⟩ ⟨sued*y*⟩ ⟨wooden*y*⟩ **b :** having (such) characteristics to a marked degree ⟨Scotch*y*⟩ ⟨Dutch*y*⟩ or in an affected or superficial way ⟨French*y*⟩ — in adjectives formed from adjectives

²-y \ˈ"\ *n suffix, pl* **-ies** [ME *-ie,* fr. OF, fr. L *-ia,* fr. Gk *-ia, -eia*] **1 :** state **:** condition **:** quality — chiefly in combining forms derived from French, Latin, or Greek ⟨-alg*y*⟩ ⟨-andr*y*⟩ ⟨-crac*y*⟩ ⟨-soph*y*⟩ ⟨-tom*y*⟩ **2 :** activity, place of business, or goods dealt with ⟨chandler*y*⟩ ⟨cooper*y*⟩ ⟨laundr*y*⟩ ⟨executr*y*⟩ **3 :** whole body or group ⟨soldier*y*⟩

³-y \ˈ"\ *n suffix, pl* **-ies** [ME *-ie,* fr. AF, fr. L *-ium*] **:** instance of a (specified) action ⟨expir*y*⟩ ⟨entreat*y*⟩ ⟨inquir*y*⟩

⁴-y — see -IE

y' \y(ə)\ *pron* [by contr.] **:** YOU ⟨*y'*know⟩ ⟨*y'*all⟩

ya *var of* YAH

ya·ba bark \ˈyäbə-\ *n* [*yaba* fr. AmerSp, prob. fr. Taino] **:** ANGELIM

¹yab·ber \ˈyabə(r)\ *also* **yabber-yabber** \ˌ≈≈ˈ≈≈\ *n* -S [prob. modif. (influenced by *jabber*) of *yabba,* native name in Australia] *Austral* **:** TALK, JABBER, LANGUAGE, CONVERSATION ⟨all ~ and chatter ceased around the campfires —Francis Birtles⟩

²yabber \ˈ"\ *vi* -ED/-ING/-S *Austral* **:** to indulge in yabber

³yabber \ˈ"\ *n* -S [by alter.] **:** YABBY

yab·bi \ˈyabē\ *n, pl* **yabbies** [native name in Tasmania] **:** TASMANIAN WOLF

yab·by *or* **yab·bie** \ˈyabē\ *n, pl* **yabbies** [native name in Gippsland] **:** a small burrowing crayfish (*Parachaeraps bicarinatus*) that is found in most creeks and water holes in Australia

ya·bim *or* **ja·bim** \ˈyäbəm\ *n, pl* **yabim** *or* **yabims** *or* **jabim** *or* **jabims** *usu cap* **1 a :** a Melanesian people of Morobe, Papua New Guinea **b :** a member of such people **2 :** the language of the Yabim people

ya·cal \ˈyäkäl\ *n* -S [Tag *yakál*] **1 :** any of several hard heavy durable yellowish brown woods obtained from trees of the family Dipterocarpaceae chiefly in the Philippines — compare LAUAN **2 :** a tree whose wood is a yacal

yac·a·re \ˈyakə͵rā, ≈≈ˈ≈\ *var of* JACARE

ya·ca·ta \ˈyäkəd·ə\ *n* -S [MexSp *yácata*] **:** a mound of earth in Mexico faced with stone without mortar and probably a habitation site

yac·ca \ˈyakə\ *n* -S [AmerSp *yaca,* fr. Taino] **1 :** any of several West Indian podocarps (as *Podocarpus coriacea* and *P. purdieana*) **2 :** the wood of a yacca

yacca gum *n* **:** ACAROID RESIN

¹yacht \ˈyät, *usu* -äd·+V\ *n* -S *often attrib* [earlier *yaught,* fr. obs. D *jaght* (now *jacht*), fr. MLG *jacht,* short for *jachtschiff, jageschiff* light sailing vessel, fast pirate ship, lit., hunting ship, fr. *jacht-, jage* hunt (fr. *jagen* to hunt, fr. OHG *jagōn*) + *schiff* ship, fr. OHG *skif;* akin to OFris *jagia* to hunt and perh. to Skt *yahu* restless, swift, strong — more at SHIP] **1 :** a sailing or power boat used for pleasure (as racing or cruising) and characteristically built for speed with a sharp prow and graceful lines: as **a :** any of various large racing and cruising sailboats (as of the international class) **b :** a steam-driven or motor-driven ship or large powerboat equipped often elegantly for pleasure cruising or private travel (as by a head of state) **2 :** a dice game played in numerous forms and under various names with 5 or 10 dice in which the object is to make certain combinations in a prescribed number of casts

²yacht \ˈ"\ *vi* -ED/-ING/-S **:** to race or cruise in a yacht ⟨the Spanish pretender now ~*s,* plays golf —*Current Biog.*⟩

yacht chair *n* **:** a light nonadjustable folding armchair for outdoor use

yacht club *n* **:** an association of yachtsmen organized to promote, organize, and regulate yachting (as racing)

yacht ensign *n* **:** a U. S. ensign resembling the national ensign but having the stars on the union replaced by a white foul anchor surrounded by 13 white stars in a circle and authorized by law to be flown on licensed yachts owned by citizens

yacht chair

yachting *n* -S [fr. gerund of ²*yacht*] **:** the action, fact, or pastime of racing or cruising in a yacht

yacht rope *n* **:** rope of the best quality usu. made from fine soft white Manila fibers

yachts·man \ˈyätsmən\ *n, pl* **yachtsmen** [*yachts* (gen. of ¹*yacht*) + *man*] **:** a person who owns or sails a yacht **:** one devoted to yachting

yachty \ˈyäd·ē\ *adj* **:** resembling or befitting a yacht

yack \ˈyak\ *var of* ²YAK, ³YAK

¹yad \ˈyad\ *or* **yade** \ˈyād\ *Scot var of* YAUD

²yad \ˈyäd\ *n* -S [Heb *yādh* hand] **:** a pointer tapering into the shape of a closed hand with extended index finger used as a guide for the reader of the scrolls of the Law in a synagogue

yae \ˈyā\ *adj* [alter. of *ae*] *chiefly Scot* **:** ONE

yaff \ˈyaf\ *vi* -ED/-ING/-S [imit.] *Scot* **:** BARK, YELP, YAP

yaf·fil \ˈyafəl\ *dial Eng var of* ¹YAFFLE

yaf·fin·gale \ˈyafən͵gāl *sometimes* -fiŋ͵g- *or* -fēŋ͵g-\ *n* -S [¹*yaffle* + *-ingale* (as in *nightingale*)] *dial Eng* **:** GREEN WOODPECKER

¹yaf·fle \ˈyafəl\ *or* **yaf·fler** \-f(ə)lə(r)\ *n* -S [*yaffle* imit. of the bird's laughing sound; *yaffler* fr. *yaffle* + *-er*] *dial* **:** GREEN WOODPECKER

²yaffle \ˈ"\ *vi* -ED/-ING/-S [*yaff* + *-le*] *dial Eng* **:** YAFF

³yaffle \ˈ"\ *n* -S [origin unknown] *dial* **:** ARMFUL

ya·ger \ˈyägə(r)\ *n* -S [modif. of G *jäger* — more at JAEGER] **1 :** JAEGER 1 **2 :** a rifle having a short barrel and large bore formerly used in the U. S.

yagi \ˈyägē, ˈyagē\ *n* -S [after Hidetsugu *Yagi* *b*1886 Jap. electrical engineer who developed it] **:** a highly directional and selective shortwave antenna consisting of a horizontal conductor of one or two dipoles connected with the receiver or transmitter and of a set of nearly equal insulated dipoles parallel to and on a level with the horizontal conductor

ya·gua \ˈyägwə\ *n* -S [AmerSp, fr. Taino] **1 :** a Puerto Rican palm (*Roystonea borinqueana*) that resembles the royal palm **2 :** the thick woody sheathing leaf base of the yagua palm

ya·gua·za \ˌyäˈgwäsə,-äzə\ *n* -S [AmerSp *yaguasa,* prob. fr. Taino] **:** a tree duck (*Dendrocygna arborea*) of the West Indies

¹yah *also* **ya** \ˈya\ *interj* [prob. imit. of the sound of retching] — used to express disgust, contempt, defiance, or derision

²yah *or* **jah** \ˈyä\ *n, cap* [Heb *Yāh*] **:** YAHWEH

yah·gan \ˈyägən\ *n, pl* **yahgan** *or* **yahgans** *usu cap* [*Yahga,* locality in Tierra del Fuego frequented by the Yahgans + E *-an*] **1 a :** a nomadic hunting and fishing people of Tierra del Fuego **b :** a member of such people **2 :** the language of the Yahgan people

ya·hi \ˈyähē\ *n, pl* **yahi** *or* **yahis** *usu cap* [Yahi, person] **1 a :** an extinct Indian people of the Pitt river valley in northern California **b :** a member of such people **2 :** a Yanan language of the Yahi people

ya·hoo \ˈyä͵hü, yä'hü, ˈyā͵hü, yə'hü\ *n* -S *often cap* [fr. *Yahoo,* one of an imaginary race of brutes having the form of men in *Gulliver's Travels* (1726) by Jonathan Swift †1745 Brit. satirist] **:** an uncouth or rowdy person ⟨novels in which all country people were mean-minded ~*s* —Russell Lord⟩

ya·hoo·ism \-ü͵izəm\ *n* -S *often cap* **:** behavior characteristic of a yahoo **:** ROWDYISM

yahr·zeit *also* **jahr·zeit** \ˈyär͵tsīt, ˈyȯr͵-\ *n* -S *often cap* [Yiddish *yartsayt, yortsayt,* fr. MHG *jārzīt* anniversary, lit., year's time, fr. *jār* year (fr. OHG) + *zīt* time, fr. OHG — more at YEAR, TIDE] **:** the anniversary of the death of a parent or near relative observed annually among Jews by the recital of the Kaddish and the lighting of a memorial candle or lamp

ya·hu \ˈyä͵hü\ *n, cap* [NL, transliteration of the Hebrew tetragrammaton *Yhwh* as some modern scholars believe it was pronounced before the Jews ceased to pronounce it about three centuries B.C.] **:** YAHWEH

yah·weh *also* **yah·veh** *or* **jah·weh** *or* **yah·veh** *or* **jah·ve** *or* **jah·we** *or* **yah·vè** *or* **yah·we** *or* **ja·vé** \ˈyä(͵)wā, ˈyä(-, -)v|, |e\ *n* -S *cap* [NL, fr. Heb *Yhwh*] **:** ²GOD — used as a scholarly transliteration of the Hebrew tetragrammaton; compare JEHOVAH, YAH, YHWH

yah·wism *also* **jah·vism** *or* **jah·wism** *or* **yah·vism** \-͵wizəm, -͵vi-\ *n* -S *cap* **1 :** the religion and worship of Yahweh — compare ELOHISM **2 a :** the religion of the Israelites **b :** the early preexilic phase of the Judaic religion

¹yah·wist *also* **jah·vist** *or* **jah·wist** *or* **yah·vist** \-͵wəst, -͵və-\ *n* -S *usu cap* **1 :** the author of the Yahwistic or J passages of the Old Testament which refer to God as *Yahweh* and which are believed to have emanated from Judah, the southern kingdom of the ancient Israelites — called also *Jehovist;* compare JEHOVAH **2 :** a worshiper of Yahweh

²yahwist \ˈ"\ *adj, usu cap* **:** YAHWISTIC

yah·wis·tic *also* **jah·vis·tic** *or* **jah·wis·tic** *or* **yah·vis·tic** \(ˈ)yä¦wistik, (ˈ)yä¦-, -¦vi-, -tēk\ *adj, usu cap* **1 :** characterized by the use of *Yahweh* as the name of God **:** written by the Yahwist — used of some parts of the Old Testament; **2 :** of, belonging to, or characteristic of the religion and worship of Yahweh ⟨the *Yahwistic* faith⟩ ⟨a *Yahwistic* rite⟩

yair \ˈya(a)|(ə)r, ˈye|, |ə, *Scot* ˈyār\ *n* -S [ME (Sc & northern dial.) *yare,* fr. OE *-gear* enclosure (as in *mylengear* mill enclosure); prob. akin to OE *geard* enclosure — more at YARD] *chiefly Scot* **:** an enclosure for catching salmon as the tide ebbs

ya·jé \yäˈhā\ *n* -S [AmerSp *yajé, yagé*] **:** a Brazilian plant (*Prestonia amazonica*) of the family Apocynaceae

¹yak \ˈyak\ *n, pl* **yaks** *also* **yak** [Tibetan *gyak*] **:** a large wild or domesticated ox (*Bos grunniens* syn. *Poephagus grunniens*) of Tibet and adjacent elevated parts of central Asia having short smooth hair on the back and long wavy hair on the breast, sides, legs, and tail, being in the wild blackish brown and up to about six feet high at the shoulder and 1200 pounds in weight but smaller and varying in color under domestication, and living as a beast of burden and source of flesh, milk, hide, and hair

yak

²yak \ˈ"\ *n* -S [prob. imit. of the sound of chattering teeth] **:** persistent or voluble talk **:** idle chatter **:** YAMMER

³yak \ˈ"\ *vi* **yakked; yakked; yakking; yaks :** to talk persistently **:** CHATTER, YAMMER ⟨*yakked* on endlessly about her operation⟩ ⟨the old man would ~ at us for not showing proper respect —Edward Newhouse⟩

⁴yak \ˈ", ˈyäk\ *n* -S [imit.] **1** *slang* **:** LAUGH ⟨the jokes that used to get snickers now get ~*s* —Douglas Anderson⟩ **2** *slang* **:** JOKE, GAG ⟨grinding out ~*s* for radio comedians —Robert Fontaine⟩

ya·ka \ˈyäkə\ *n, pl* **yaka** *or* **yakas** *usu cap* **:** a member of a Bantu people near the mouth of the Congo river widely known for their carved masks

yak·a·mik \ˈyakəmik\ *n* -S [modif. of Pg *jacamí,* fr. Tupi] **:** TRUMPETER 3a

ya·kan \ˈyäkən\ *n* -S *usu cap* **:** a member of a Moro people inhabiting the interior of Basilan Island, Philippines

¹yak·e·ty-yak *or* **yak·i·ty-yak** *also* **yack·e·ty-yack** \ˌyakəd·ē-ˈyak\ *n* -S [by redupl.] **:** ²YAK

²yakety-yak *or* **yakity-yak** *also* **yackety-yak** \ˈ"\ *vi* **:** ³YAK

yak·i·ma \ˈyakə͵mȯ, -͵mä\ *n, pl* **yakima** *or* **yakimas** *usu cap* **1 a :** a Shahaptian people or group of peoples of the lower Yakima river valley, south central Washington **b :** a member of such people **2 :** the language of the Yakima people

ya·kin \ˈyə'kēn, ˈyä͵k-\ *n* -S [native name in Assam] **:** TAKIN

yak·ka \ˈyakə\ *or* **yak·ker** \-kə(r)\ *n* -S [native name in Queensland] *Austral* **:** WORK, LABOR

yak·o·nan \ˈyakənən\ *n* -S *usu cap* **:** a language family of the Penutian stock in Oregon consisting of Alsea, Siuslaw, and Yaquina

yak·sha *also* **yak·sa** \ˈyəkshə\ *n* -S *often cap* [Skt *yakṣa*] **:** a local tutelary spirit or earth jinni of India regarded as a patron of wealth and fertility

ya·kut \yəˈküt\ *n, pl* **yakut** *or* **yakuts** *usu cap* **1 a :** a Turkic people of northeastern Siberia living mainly in the Lena river basin and practicing herding, crafts, and trading and in the south some agriculture **b :** a member of such people **2 :** the Turkic language of the Yakut people

yak·u·tat \ˈyakə͵tat\ *n, pl* **yakutat** *or* **yakutats** *usu cap* **1 :** a Tlingit people occupying the area about Yakutat Bay, Alaska **2 :** a member of the Yakutat people

yakutat bear *n, usu cap Y* [from *Yakutat* Bay, Alaska] **:** a large brown bear (*Ursus dalli*) of the vicinity of Yakutat Bay related to the Kodiak bear

yakutat hut *n, usu cap Y* [fr. *Yakutat* Bay, Alaska] **:** a square demountable temporary structure built of prefabricated wood panels

¹yak-yak \(ˈ)ya¦kyak\ *n* [by redupl.] **:** ²YAK

²yak-yak \ˈ"\ *vi* [by redupl.] **:** ³YAK

yale \ˈyāl, *esp before pause or consonant* -āəl\ *n* -S [ME *eale,* fr. L, an animal of Ethiopia] **:** a mythical beast resembling an antelope, having large erect tusks and long horns pointing in any direction at will, and sometimes being represented as a supporter for heraldic arms

yale

yale blue *n, often cap Y* [fr. *Yale* University, New Haven, Connecticut] **:** a deep blue that is lighter and stronger than royal (sense 8b), redder and paler than imperial blue, and redder and very slightly paler than Napoleon blue

y'all \ˈyȯl\ *pron* [by contr.] *chiefly South* **:** YOU-ALL

yam \ˈyam, -aa(ə)m\ *n* -S [earlier *inany, iname, nname,* fr. Pg *inhame* & Sp *ñame,* of West African origin; prob. akin to Fulani *nyami* to eat] **1 a :** the edible starchy tuberous root of various plants of the genus *Dioscorea* (as *D. sativa* or *D. alata*) that largely replaces the potato as a staple food in tropical climates and is cooked in the same way but has coarser flesh **b :** a plant of the genus *Dioscorea* (as *D. paniculata*) **c :** any of several similar plants — usu. used in combination ⟨round ~⟩ ⟨native ~⟩ **2 a** *Scot* **:** POTATO **b :** SWEET POTATO; *esp* **:** one with deep orange flesh that remains moist when baked

yama·craw \ˈyamə͵krȯ, ˈyam-\ *n* -S *usu cap* **:** YAMASEE

yam·a·mai \͵yaməˈmī\ *n* -S [Jap] **1 :** a large Japanese silkworm (*Antheraea yamamai*) whose larva feeds on the oak and furnishes excellent silk **2 :** silk produced by the yamamai

yam·a·nai \-ˈnī\ *n* -S [Burmese *yamanē*] **:** a Burmese tree (*Gmelina arborea*) the hard wood of which is used for making clogs

ya·ma·see *or* **ya·mas·see** \ˈyäməsē\ *or* **yem·as·see** \ˈyem-\ *n, pl* **yamasee** *or* **yamasees** *or* **yamassee** *or* **yamassees** *or* **yemassee** *or* **yemassees** *usu cap* **:** an Indian of a Muskogean people of the lower Savannah and the coast of Georgia driven to Florida after defeat by the whites in 1716 and finally incorporated with the Creeks and Seminoles

ya·ma·to \yäˈmä(͵)tō\ *n, pl* **yamato** *cap* [Jap] **:** a Japanese of the principal racial stock of Japan that is of ancient origin, has possibly Alpine characteristics, and is supposed to have entered Japan from the mainland in the protohistoric period — compare AINU

yam bean *n* **:** a tropical twining plant (*Pachyrhizus erosus*) with tuberous roots resembling turnips which are eaten raw as a salad or cooked and edible pods and seeds which yield rotenone and oils

yamel \ˈyäməl,ˈyam-\ *also* **yam·hill** \ˈyam͵hil\ *n, pl* **yamel** *or* **yamels** *also* **yamhill** *or* **yamhills** *usu cap* **1 :** a Kalapooian people of the Yamhill river valley, northwestern Oregon **2 :** a member of the Yamel people

ya·men \ˈyämən\ *n* -S [Chin (Pek) *ya²-men²*] **:** an establishment used by a Chinese government official or department for official business and often as a residence **:** HEADQUARTERS, OFFICE, COURT

yam family *n* **:** DIOSCOREACEAE

ya·mi \ˈyämē\ *n, pl* **yami** *or* **yamis** *usu cap* **1 a :** a Malaysian people inhabiting Hungtow Island, near southern Taiwan **b :** a member of such people **2 :** an Austronesian language of the Yami people

¹yam·mer \ˈyamə(r)\ *vb* **yammered; yammered; yammering** \-m(ə)riŋ\ **yammers** [alter. (influenced by G *jammern*) of ME *yomeren* to murmur, complain, be sad, fr. OE *gēomrian;* akin to OHG *jāmarōn* to complain, be sad, *jāmar* distress, misery — more at KATZENJAMMER] *vi* **1 a :** to utter repeated cries of distress or sorrow **:** WAIL, WHIMPER ⟨a child that kept ~*ing* till its mother came⟩ **b :** to utter persistent complaints **:** WHINE, GRUMBLE, SCOLD ⟨~*ed* at an umpire loudly enough to get himself tossed out of a game —*Time*⟩ **2 :** to talk persistently or volubly and often loudly ⟨~*ing* and gesticulating to each other about their . . . adventures —Frederick Mears⟩ ⟨caused the purists to ~ for censorship —D.W.Maurer⟩ ⟨~*s* away about the brotherhood of man —P.B.Kyne⟩ **3 :** to make a loud repetitive noise ⟨heard the diesels ~*ing* monotonously belowdecks⟩ ~ *vt* **:** to utter complainingly, insistently, or volubly

²yammer \ˈ"\ *n* -S **:** a yammering utterance or noise ⟨set up a petulant ~⟩ ⟨the ~ of a machine gun⟩

yamp \ˈyamp\ *or* **yam·pa** *also* **yam·pah** \-mpə\ *n* -S [of Shoshonean origin; akin to Shoshoni *yampa* yamp, Ute *yampä*] **:** either of two western No. American plants of the genus *Carum* (*C. gairdneri* and *C. kelloggii*) with fleshy edible roots — called also *squawroot;* see INDIAN POTATO; compare CARAWAY

yam·pee \ˈyampē\ *n* -S [perh. fr. *yampee* yamp] **:** CUSH-CUSH

yams *pl of* YAM

yam stick *n* **:** a hardwood stick three or four feet in length with edged or pointed ends used by the aboriginal women of Australia for digging (as roots or bulbs)

yam tree *n* **:** either of two black kurrajongs (*Sterculia diversifolia* and *S. quadrifida*)

¹yan \ˈyan\ *Scot & dial Eng var of* ONE

²yan \ˈyän\ *dial var of* YON

ya·na \ˈyänə\ *n, pl* **yana** *or* **yanas** *usu cap* [Yana, person] **1 a :** an extinct Indian people of the Pitt river valley of northern California **b :** a member of such people **2 :** a Yanan language of the Yana people

ya·na·co·na \͵yänəˈkōnə\ *n* -S [AmerSp, fr. Quechua *yanacuna,* pl. of *yana* servant, slave] **:** a Peruvian or Bolivian Indian serf or servant on an estate

ya·nan \ˈyänən\ *n* -S *usu cap* [*Yana* + E *-an*] **:** a language family of the Hokan stock comprising Yahi and Yana

yan·der \ˈyandə(r)\ *dial var of* YONDER

¹yang \ˈyäŋ, ˈyaŋ\ *n* -S [Chin (Pek) *yang²* bright, masculine principle] **:** the masculine and positive principle (as of activity, height, light, heat, or dryness) in nature that according to traditional Chinese cosmology combines and interacts with its opposite yin to produce everything that comes into existence

²yang \ˈyaŋ, -aiŋ\ *n* -S [imit.] **:** the cry of the wild goose **:** HONK

³yang \ˈ"\ *vi* -ED/-ING/-S **:** to make the natural honking cry of the wild goose

⁴yang \ˈyäŋ\ *n* -S [Thai *yāng*] **:** a Siamese gurjun (*Dipterocarpus tuberculatus*)

yang·chow \ˈyäŋ¦jō\ *adj, usu cap* [fr. *Yangchow,* China] **:** of or from the city of Yangchow, China **:** of the kind or style prevalent in Yangchow

yang·go·na \yäŋˈgōnə\ *or* **ya·qo·na** \yəˈkōnə\ *n* -S [Fijian *yanggona*] **:** KAVA

yang-kin \ˈyäŋˈkin\ *n* -S [Chin *yang²-k'in²,* prob. fr. *yang²* foreign + *ch'in²* lute, guitar] **:** a Chinese dulcimer

yang ko \ˈyäŋˈkō\ *n* [Chin (Pek) *yang¹-ko¹,* lit., rice song] **:** a Chinese dance and song of transplanting rice

yang shao \ˈ≈ˈshau̇\ *adj, usu cap Y&S* [Chin (Pek) *yang³-shao²*] **:** of or relating to a late Neolithic and Bronze Age culture of north China characterized by small settlements of circular pit houses, irrigation, loom weaving, and a fine painted pottery and in its late stage by metallurgy

yang·tao \ˈ≈ˈtau̇\ *n* -S [Chin (Pek) *yang²-t'ao²*] **:** CHINESE GOOSEBERRY

¹yank \ˈyaŋk, -aiŋk\ *n* -S *usu cap* [by shortening] **:** YANKEE

²yank \ˈ"\ *n* -S [origin unknown] **1** *Scot* **:** a sudden hard blow **2 :** a strong sudden pull **:** JERK ⟨grabbed the weed and gave it a ~ to uproot it⟩

[3]**yank** \"\ *vb* -ED/-ING/-S *vt* **1 :** to pull with a quick vigorous movement ⟨angrily ~*ed* the weed out by the roots⟩ **2 :** to cause to go in a rude or abrupt manner ⟨the offending copies were ~*ed* out of the school libraries —*Time*⟩ ⟨~*ed* before the school board to explain his statement⟩ **3 :** to take out or away in a quick vigorous or rudely abrupt manner ⟨have his tonsils ~*ed*⟩ ⟨he was ~*ed* in the sixth when he issued three walks —*N.Y. Times*⟩ ~ *vi* **:** to pull on something with a quick vigorous movement ⟨~*ed* at the door trying to open it⟩ ⟨the other man ~*ed* down on the halyard and the flags fell —Wirt Williams⟩ **syn** see JERK

yankapin *var of* YONCOPIN

[1]**yan·kee** \'yaŋkē, -aiŋ-\ *n* -S *usu cap* [origin unknown] **1 a :** a native or inhabitant of New England **b :** a New Englander descended from old New England stock; *specif* **:** one having qualities of character (as conservatism, thrift, pertinacity, or shrewdness) and often also of speech traditionally associated with inhabitants of New England **c :** a native or inhabitant of the northern States as distinguished from a Southerner **d :** a native or citizen of the U. S. **2 :** the English language as spoken or pronounced by Yankees; *esp* **:** New England dialect

[2]**yankee** \"\ *adj, usu cap* **1 :** of, relating to, or characteristic of the Yankees **2 :** having qualities (as shrewdness, reserve, or mechanical ingenuity) traditionally ascribed to New England Yankees

[3]**yankee** \"\ *usu cap* — a communications code word for the letter *y*

yankee corn *n, usu cap Y* **:** FLINT CORN

yan·kee·dom \'==,dəm\ *also* **yankee-doodle·dom** \¦==-'düdᵊldəm\ *n* -S *usu cap Y & D* **1 :** the realm of the Yankees **2 :** YANKEES

yankee-doodle \¦=='düdᵊl\ *n* -S *usu cap Y&D* [fr. *Yankee Doodle*, popular song during the American Revolutionary War] **:** YANKEE

yan·kee·fy \'==,fī\ *vt* -ED/-ING/-ES *usu cap* [[1]*yankee* + *-fy*] **:** to cause to become like a Yankee ⟨regarded by the natives as *Yankeefied* and foreign —Nell Lewis⟩

yan·kee·ism \-ē,izəm\ *n* -S *usu cap* **1 :** a Yankee idiom, word, or custom **2 :** Yankee characteristics or customs

yan·kee·ize \-,īz\ *vt* -ED/-ING/-S *usu cap* **:** YANKEEFY

yankeeland \'==,=\ *n, usu cap* **:** the region inhabited by Yankees ⟨youth of twenty years . . . with an air about him suspiciously redolent of *Yankeeland* —*Encore*⟩

yankee machine *n, usu cap Y* **:** a paper machine in which the web of paper is dried completely on a single large polished steam-heated cylinder

yank·ton \'yaŋktən, -aiŋ-\ *n, pl* **yankton** *or* **yanktons** *usu cap* [Dakota *ihanketonwan* end village] **1 :** one of the western prairie subdivisions of the Dakota people **2 :** a dialect of Dakota

yank·to·nai \,=tə'nā\ *n, pl* **yanktonai** *or* **yanktonais** *usu cap* [Dakota *ihanketonwanna* little end village] **:** one of the western prairie subdivisions of the Dakota people

yan·ni·gan \'yanə́gən, -anēg-\ *n* -S [perh. alter. of *young one*] **:** a member of a scrub team in baseball

yan·qui \'yäŋkē\ *n* -S *often cap* [Sp, fr. E [1]*yankee*] **:** a citizen of the U.S. as distinguished from a Latin American

yan·tra \'yən·trə\ *n* -S [Skt] **:** a geometrical diagram used like an icon in meditation upon or worship of a deity chiefly in tantric worship

[1]**yao** \'yau̇\ *n, pl* **yao** *or* **yaos** *usu cap* **1 a :** an aboriginal people inhabiting chiefly mountainous parts of southwestern China, northern Thailand, Laos, and Tonkin **b :** a member of such people **2 :** the language of the Yao people — see MIAO-YAO

[2]**yao** \"\ *n, pl* **yao** *or* **yaos** *usu cap* **1 a :** an African people living in the vicinity of Lake Nyasa, Central Africa **b :** a member of such people **2 :** a Bantu language of the Yao people

[1]**yap** \'yap\ *vb* **yapped; yapped; yapping; yaps** [imit.] *vi* **1 :** to bark snappishly **:** YELP ⟨followed by four little dogs who *yapped* at his heels⟩ **2 :** to talk in a shrill insistent often idle manner **:** CHATTER, SCOLD ⟨the local paper . . . had been *yapping* for years about the need for a swimming pool —G.S. Perry⟩ ⟨~ at him for staying away so long —Walter Karig⟩ ~ *vt* **:** to utter in a yappy manner **:** BARK

[2]**yap** \"\ *n* -S **1 a :** a snappish bark **:** YIP, YELP **b :** shrill insistent often idle talk **:** CHATTER, COMPLAINT **2 a :** an unsophisticated, ignorant, or uncouth person **:** BUMPKIN, GREENHORN **b :** a contemptible person **3** *slang* **:** MOUTH ⟨told him to shut his ~⟩ ⟨always shooting off his ~⟩

yap·ese \(')ya¦pēz, (')yä¦-, -pēs\ *n, pl* **yapese** *cap* [*Yap* island + E *-ese*] **:** a Micronesian native or inhabitant of Yap island in the Caroline Islands

yap·man \'yapmən, 'yäp-\ *n, pl* **yapmen** *cap* [*Yap* island + *man*] **:** YAPESE

ya·pock *or* **ya·pok** \yə'päk, 'yapək\ *n* -S [fr. *Oyapock* (*Oyapok*), river in northern So. America; fr. its presence in large numbers on the river's banks] **:** an aquatic opossum (*Chironectes minimus*) of So. America

yapon *or* **yapa** *var of* YAUPON

yapp binding \'yap-\ *also* **yapp** *n* -S [after *Yapp*, a 19th cent. Eng. bookseller] *Brit* **:** DIVINITY CIRCUIT BINDING

yap·per \'yapə(r)\ *n* -S [[1]*yap* + *-er*] **:** one that yaps ⟨a nation of ~*s* and listeners and movie watchers —H.A.Lincoln⟩

yap·ping·ly *adv* **:** in a yapping manner

yap·py \'yapē\ *adj* -ER/-EST [[1]*yap* + *-y*] **1 :** given to yapping ⟨affections were expended on ~ little beasts —*New Yorker*⟩ **2 :** resembling or characteristic of a yap

yaqona *var of* YANGGONA

ya·qui \'yäkē\ *n, pl* **yaqui** *or* **yaquis** *usu cap* **1 a :** a Taracahitian people of Sonora, Mexico **b :** a member of such people **2 :** the language of the Yaqui people

ya·quina \yə'kwēnə, -kwinə\ *n, pl* **yaquina** *or* **yaquinas** *usu cap* **1 a :** an Indian people of the Pacific coast of Oregon **b :** a member of such people **2 :** a Yakonan language of the Yaquina people

yar *var of* YARE

yar·age \'yarij, -rēj\ *n* -S [[1]*yare* + *-age*] *chiefly Brit* **:** HANDINESS, MANEUVERABILITY — used of a ship

yar·ak \'yarak\ *n* -S [Per *yārakī* power, strength] **:** good flying condition **:** FETTLE — used of a hawk or other bird used in hunting ⟨eagles . . . are difficult to get into ~ —Douglas Carruthers⟩

ya·ray \yə'rī\ *n* -S [AmerSp] **:** any of several slender Puerto Rican fan palms (esp. *Sabal causiarum*) the leaves of which are widely used in making hats

yarb \'yärb, 'yȧb\ *dial var of* HERB

yar·bor·ough \'yär(,)bərə, -,brə\ *n* -S *usu cap* [after Charles Anderson Worsley, 2d Earl of *Yarborough* †1897 Eng. nobleman who was said to have bet a thousand to one against the dealing of such a hand] **:** a hand in bridge or whist containing no card higher than a nine

[1]**yard** \'yärd, 'yȧd\ *n* -S [ME *yarde, yerde*, fr. OE *gierd, geard* rod, twig, measure, yard; akin to OHG *gart* stick, goad, ON *gaddr* goad, spike, Goth *gazds* goad, MIr *gat* willow twig, L *hasta* spear] **1 :** any of various units of measure: as **a** *dial Eng* **:** ROD, POLE, PERCH **b** *obs* **:** YARD OF LAND **c :** a unit of length equal in the U.S. to 0.9144 meter and in Great Britain to the distance at 62°F between two transverse marks on two gold plugs in a bronze bar kept at the Standards Office of the Board of Trade at Westminster — abbr *yd.*; see MEASURE table **d :** a unit of volume (as for sand or gravel) equal to a cubic yard **2** *archaic* **:** PENIS **3 a :** a great length or quantity ⟨his photographic memory enabled him to tuck away ~*s* of facts and quotations —R.B.Nye⟩ **b** *slang* **:** one hundred dollars **4 :** a long spar tapered toward the ends and set athwart a mast to support and spread the head of a square sail, lateen, or lugsail or to hoist signal flags **:** GAFF — compare [2]BOOM 1; see SHIP illustration

[2]**yard** \"\ *n* -S [ME *yard, yerd, yerde*, fr. OE *geard* enclosure, court, yard; akin to OHG *gart* enclosure, *garto* garden, ON *garthr* yard, Goth *gards* house, L *hortus* garden, Gk *chortos* farmyard, Skt *gṛiha* house, *harati* he takes; basic meaning: to gird, enclose] **1 a :** a small usu. walled and often paved vacant area open to the sky and adjacent to a building **:** COURT **b :** the grounds of a public building or group of buildings ⟨inn ~⟩; *specif* **:** CAMPUS 1 ⟨college ~⟩ **c :** a usu. high-walled open-air exercise area for prisoners ⟨prison ~⟩ **2 a :** the grounds immediately surrounding a house and usu. comprising lawn, shrubbery and other plantings, recreation and service areas ⟨front ~⟩ **b :** an area devoted to the cultivation of crops **:** GARDEN, FIELD **3 a** (1) **:** an enclosure for poultry or livestock ⟨chicken ~⟩ (2) **:** a group of beehives kept together and managed as a unit **b** (1) **:** an area set aside for a particular business or activity (2) **:** an assembly or storage area ⟨rows of snowplows in the city ~*s*⟩; *specif* **:** LANDING 2b **c :** a system of tracks and sidings usu. at a railroad terminal used for storage and maintenance of cars and making up trains **4 :** a locality in a forest where moose or deer herd in winter for feeding and protection ⟨moose ~⟩

[3]**yard** \"\ *adj* [ME, fr. [2]*yard*] **1 a :** of, relating to, or employed in the yard or garden surrounding a house ⟨~ light⟩ ⟨~ boy⟩ **b :** belonging to or stationed in a courtyard ⟨~ gate⟩ ⟨~ dog⟩ **2 :** of or from a run or enclosure for animals ⟨~ dung⟩ **3 :** attached to or employed by an establishment operating a yard ⟨~ patrol⟩ ⟨~ craft⟩ **4 :** of, relating to, or employed in a railroad yard ⟨~ clerk⟩ ⟨~ engine⟩ ⟨~ service⟩

[4]**yard** \"\ *vb* -ED/-ING/-S [[2]*yard*] *vt* **1 a :** to drive into or confine in a restricted area **:** HERD, PEN ⟨the sheep were ~*ed* at night —Rex Ingamells⟩ **b :** to confine to winter quarters ⟨when the deer are ~*ed* in deep snow —Hugh Fosburgh⟩ **2 :** to deliver to or store in a yard ⟨~ a freight car⟩; *esp* **:** to pile (logs) temporarily at a central point (as on a landing) ~ *vi* **:** to congregate in winter quarters ⟨mild winters, allowing deer to roam rather than ~ —*Wildlife Rev.*⟩ — often used with *up* ⟨show a tendency to ~ up near favorite feeding areas —Frank Dufresne⟩

[1]**yard·age** \-dij, -dēj\ *n* -S [[2]*yard* + *-age*] **1 :** the use of a livestock enclosure for animals in transit provided by a railroad at a station **2 :** a charge made by a railroad for the use of a livestock enclosure

[2]**yardage** \"\ *n* -S [[1]*yard* + *-age*] **1 :** the linear yards of advance made or cubic yards mined used as a basis for determining wages of coal miners **2 a :** an aggregate number of yards ⟨a large ~ of work-shirt chambrays —John Hoye⟩ ⟨the par and ~ of each of the ten golf courses — *N.Y.Herald Tribune*⟩ **b :** an amount expressed in yards: as (1) **:** an extent (as of cloth) measured in linear yards ⟨the dress floats out to an extravagant drift of ~ at the hem —*N.Y. Times*⟩ (2) **:** a distance covered in linear yards ⟨running plays that piled up ~ —*Time*⟩ (3) **:** an area covered in square yards ⟨increase plaster ~ by sizing dry walls⟩ (4) **:** a volume of material in cubic yards ⟨every great dam requires the moving of immense ~ —*Newsweek*⟩ **3 :** YARD GOODS ⟨they've been buying satin ~ . . . for a month now —Ray Bradbury⟩

yar·dang \'yär,däŋ\ *n* -S [Turk, abl. of *yar* steep bank, precipice] **:** a sharp-crested ridge carved by wind erosion from soft but coherent deposits (as clayey sand)

yardarm \'=,=\ *n* [[1]*yard* + *arm*] **:** either end of the yard of a square-rigged ship usu. including the outer quarter — see SHIP illustration

yardbird \'=,=\ *n* **1 :** a soldier assigned to a menial task (as policing an area) or restricted to a limited area as a disciplinary measure **2 :** an untrained or inept enlisted man ⟨the rank of ~ — one level below private — has never been officially recognized —*N.Y.Times*⟩ ⟨everyone from the company commander to the sorriest ~ —Burtt Evans⟩

yard boss *n* **1 :** a foreman who directs laborers in the yard of an industrial plant **2** *also* **yarder boss :** a logger who directs and assists chokermen, riggers, and other workmen in a yard where logs are stored

yard conductor *n* **:** a railroad employee who directs a switch engine crew in accordance with the yardmaster's instructions

yard donkey *n* **:** YARDER

yard·er \'yärdər, 'yȧdə(r\ *n* -S [[2]*yard* + *-er*] **:** a donkey engine that is used to haul logs from the stump to the skid road or to a landing

yard goods *n pl* **:** fabrics sold by the yard **:** PIECE GOODS

yard grass *n* **:** a coarse annual grass (*Eleusine indica*) that has flowers in fingerlike spikes and is widely distributed as a weed esp. in lawns

yarding *n* -S [fr. gerund of [4]*yard*] **1 :** the act or process of conveying something (as logs) to an enclosure, assembly point, or loading point **2** *chiefly Austral* **:** delivery or arrival of livestock at the market ⟨a heavy ~ of lambs⟩

yardland \'=,=\ *n* [ME *yerdlond*, fr. *yerde* yard (measure) + *lond* land] **:** VIRGATE

yard limit *n* **:** the point at which a line of track enters or leaves a railroad yard

yard-long bean \'=¦=-\ *n* **:** ASPARAGUS BEAN

yard lumber *n* **:** lumber intended for general building purposes that is of various shapes and sizes and is less than 5 inches thick

[1]**yard·man** \'yärdmən, 'yȧd-\ *n, pl* **yardmen** [[2]*yard* + *man*] **1 :** a man employed by the day to do such outdoor work as mowing lawns, shoveling snow, and washing automobiles **2 :** one who works in the yard of a commercial establishment; *esp* **:** one who supervises the handling of building materials in a lumberyard **3 :** a railroad man employed in yard service

[2]**yardman** \"\ *n, pl* **yardmen** [[1]*yard* + *man*] **:** a sailor assigned to the yards

yardmaster \'=,==\ *n* **:** the man in charge of operations in a railroad yard

yard of ale 1 : a slender horn-shaped glass about three feet tall usu. holding two or three pints **2 :** the amount contained in a yard of ale

yard of land [ME *yerde of londe*] **1 :** VIRGATE **2 :** a strip of land a rod wide; *esp* **:** one having an area of ¼ acre

yard rope *n* **:** a rope kept rove off at a masthead for sending the yard up or down

yards *pl of* YARD, *pres 3d sing of* YARD

yardstick \'=,=\ *n* **1 a :** a measuring stick three feet long usu. marked off in feet, inches, and fractions of inches **b :** a standard basis of calculation ⟨these distances were the ~*s* for measuring . . . extragalactic distances —Adolph Knopf⟩ **2 :** a test or standard applied in making a critical judgment **:** CRITERION, TOUCHSTONE ⟨development of atomic power by the Government as a ~ for measuring the costs of private producers —Don Pryor⟩ ⟨let the general good be our ~ on every great issue —D.D.Eisenhower⟩ ⟨the level of excellence achieved in the novel . . . provides an imposing ~ against which the film repeatedly will be measured —Arthur Knight⟩ **syn** see STANDARD

yard tackle *n* **:** a tackle used on the lower yard of a ship; *esp* **:** a heavy double or treble purchase for hoisting

yardwand \'=,=\ *n* [ME *yerde wande*] *archaic* **:** YARDSTICK

[1]**yare** \'ya(a)|ər, 'ye|, |ə; 'yär, 'yȧ(r\ *adj* -ER/-EST [ME, fr. OE *gearu, gearo*; akin to OHG *garo* ready, complete, ON *gerr, gǫrr* ready, perfect, skilled, OHG *garawen* to prepare, OE *gierwan* to prepare, cook and prob. to OE *wearm* warm — more at WARM] **1** *archaic* **:** set for prompt action **:** READY **2** *or* **yar** \'yär, 'yȧ(r\ **a :** characterized by speed and agility **:** NIMBLE, LIVELY **b** *of a ship* **:** easily handled **:** MANEUVERABLE — **yare·ly** *adv, archaic*

[2]**yare** \"\ *adv* [ME, fr. OE *gearo, gearwe*; akin to OE *gearo, gearu* ready] *archaic* **:** QUICKLY

ya·re·ta \yə'rād·ə\ *n* -S [AmerSp, fr. Quechua] **:** any of several densely cushioned resinous Andean herbs of the genera *Azorella* and *Laretia* (family Umbelliferae) commonly used as fuel — called also *llareta*

ya·ri·ya·ri \¦yärē'yärē\ *n* -S [native name in Guiana] **:** any of various lancewoods of the genus *Dugetia* (family Annonaceae)

yark \'yärk\ *var of* YERK

yar·kandi \yär'kändē, -kan-\ *n, pl* **yarkandi** *or* **yarkandis** *cap* **:** a native or inhabitant of Yarkand, an oasis city in the west end of the Tarim Basin of Chinese Turkistan — compare UIGHUR

yar·ke *or* **yar·kee** \'yärkē\ *n* -S [F *yarqué*, of Cariban origin; akin to Galibi *yaracaro* monkey, Macusi *youareka*] **:** SAKI

yarm \'yärm, 'yȧm\ *vi* -ED/-ING/-S [ME *yarmen*, fr. OE *gyrman, grymman*] *dial Brit* **:** to utter a discordant cry **:** SHRIEK, WAIL — used esp. of the cry of an animal

yar·mouth \'yärməth, 'yȧm-\ *adj, usu cap* [fr. *Yarmouth*, locality in Des Moines County, Iowa] **:** belonging to the second interglacial interval during the glacial epoch in No. America

yar·mul·ke *or* **yar·mel·ke** \'yärməlkə, -ȧm-\ *n* -S [Yiddish, fr. Ukrainian & Pol *jarmułka* small hat, skullcap, prob. fr. Turk *yağmurluk* raincoat, fr. *yağmur* rain] **:** a skullcap worn esp. by Orthodox and Conservative Jewish males in the synagogue, the house, and study halls

[1]**yarn** \'yärn, 'yȧn\ *n* -S *often attrib* [ME *yarn, yern*, fr. OE *gearn*; akin to OHG *garn* yarn, ON *gǫrn* gut, Gk *chordē* string, L *haruspex* soothsayer, diviner basing his predictions on inspection of animal entrails, *hernia* rupture, Lith *žarna* intestine, Skt *hirā* vein] **1 a :** a continuous strand often of two or more plies that is composed of carded or combed fibers twisted together by spinning, filaments laid parallel or twisted together, or a single filament, is made from natural or synthetic fibers and filaments or blends of these, and is used for the warp and weft in weaving and for knitting or other interlacings that form cloth **b :** a similar strand of metal, glass, asbestos, paper, or plastic used separately or in blends **c :** THREAD; *esp* **:** a component of a plied thread **d :** ROPE YARN 1 **2 a :** an entertaining narrative of real or fictitious adventures **:** ANECDOTE, STORY ⟨the whodunit, the western, and the space ~ continue to find readers —J.D.Adams⟩; *esp* **:** a tall tale ⟨spun into the narrative a little ~ which he had fabricated last night in bed —O.E.Rölvaag⟩ **b :** CONVERSATION, CHAT ⟨a ~ with the boys on the dock —Anthony Anable⟩ ⟨stopped to have a ~ with me —Eve Langley⟩

[2]**yarn** \"\ *vb* -ED/-ING/-S *vi* **1 :** to tell a yarn ⟨men ~ of the harbor's famous pilots —George Farwell⟩ ⟨all the personal zest of a man ~*ing* about his past —J.D.Hart⟩ **2 :** to have a conversation **:** CHAT, GOSSIP ⟨whistling about the place, ~*ing* with the fishermen at the breakwater —Vance Palmer⟩ ~ *vt* **:** to envelop or pack (as a pipe joint) with yarn

yarn-dye \'=,=\ *vt* **:** to dye before weaving or knitting — distinguished from *piece-dye*

yarn·er \'yärnər, 'yȧnə(r\ *n* -S **1 :** a teller of yarns or tall tales **2 :** a pipelayer who caulks joints (as with oakum or yarn)

yarning iron *n* **:** a blunt caulking iron usu. with an offset blade

yarn man *or* **yarn boy** *n* **:** a stock clerk for textile yarns

yarning iron

yarn number *n* **:** COUNT 8a

yarn over *vi* **:** to make an additional stitch in knitting or crocheting by bringing the yarn forward over the needle or hook

ya·ro·slavl \,yärə'slävəl\ *adj, usu cap* [fr. *Yaroslavl*, U.S.S.R.] **:** of or from the city of Yaroslavl, U.S.S.R. **:** of the kind or style prevalent in Yaroslavl

yarovize *var of* JAROVIZE

yar·pha \'yärfə\ *n* -S [of Scand origin; akin to ON *jǫrfi* gravel, *jǫrth* earth — more at EARTH] *Scot* **:** PEAT BOG

yarr \'yär\ *n* -S [prob. fr. Fris *jīr*] **:** CORN SPURREY

yar·ran \'yarən\ *n* -S [native name in New So. Wales] **1 :** a rather small Australian acacia (*Acacia homalophylla*) that is a minor fodder tree and an important source of firewood and fence posts **2 :** a showy chiefly coastal bastard myall (*Acacia glaucescens*) with somewhat silvery foliage and fluffy spikes of flowers

yar·row \'ya(,)rō, -,rə; -,rəw, -,rō+V\ *n* -S [ME *yarowe, yarwe*, fr. OE *gearwe*; akin to MD *gerwe, garwe* yarrow, OHG *garwa, garawa*] **:** a plant of the genus *Achillea*; *esp* **:** a strong-scented Eurasian herb (*A. millefolium*) widely naturalized in No. America with finely dissected leaves and small white or rarely pink corymbose flowers

ya·ru·ro \yə'rů(,)rō\ *or* **ya·ru·ra** \-,rə\ *n, pl* **yaruro** *or* **yaruros** *or* **yarura** *or* **yaruras** *usu cap* **1 :** an Indian people of the state of Apure in Venezuela **2 :** a member of the Yaruro people

ya·ru·ru \-,rü\ *n* -S [native name in Guiana] **:** the wood of any of various trees of the genus *Aspidosperma* (esp. *A. excelsa*)

yash·mak *also* **yas·mak** \yäsh'mäk, 'yash,mak\ *n* -S [Turk *yaşmak*] **:** a veil worn by Muslim women wrapped around the upper and lower parts of their faces so that only the eyes remain exposed to public view

yasht \'yasht, 'yəsht\ *n* -S [Av *yashtay* adoration] **:** one of the hymns to angels or lesser divinities forming part of the Avesta

yat·a·ghan \'yad·ə,gan, -,gən\ *also* **at·a·ghan** \'ad·ə-\ *n* -S [Turk *yatağan*] **:** a long knife or short saber common among Muslims made without a cross guard and usu. with a double curve to the edge and a nearly straight back

yataghan

yat·a·lite \'yad·ə,līt\ *n* -S [*Yatala*, Queensland, Australia + E *-ite*] **:** a pegmatoid rock composed of amphibole which is poikilitic with magnetite and sphene and may also contain minor amounts of apatite, microcline, and albite

yatch \'yach\ *n* -ES [by alter.] **:** YACHT

[1]**yate** \'yāt\ *Scot var of* GATE

[2]**yate** \"\ *n* -S [native name in western Australia] **1 :** any of various eucalypts (as *Eucalyptus cornuta* and *E. occidentalis*) **2 :** the wood of a yate tree

Yat·ren \'ya·trə̇n\ *trademark* — used for chiniofon

[1]**yat·ter** \'yad·ə(r)\ *n* -S [prob. fr. [1]*yap* + *-ter* (as in *chatter*)] **:** idle talk **:** CHATTER ⟨among the ~ there are these sentences of sudden wisdom —*Times Lit. Supp.*⟩

[2]**yatter** \"\ *vi* -ED/-ING/-S **:** to make idle chatter **:** PRATTLE ⟨the ladies can go right on ~*ing* about . . . the lovely doilies —Relman Morin⟩

yaud \'yȯd, 'yäd\ *n* -S [earlier *yald*, fr. ON *jalda* mare, of Finno-Ugric origin; akin to Mordvin *elde, äldä* mare] *chiefly Scot* **:** MARE

yauld \'yȯl(d), 'yal(d)\ *adj* [origin unknown] *chiefly Scot* **:** being in vigorous health **:** ENERGETIC ⟨if I was young and ~ —John Buchan⟩

yaum·er \'yämər\ *Scot var of* YAMMER

yaup *var of* YAWP

yau·pon *also* **ya·pon** \'yü,pän, 'yȯ,p-\ *or* **ya·pa** \-pä,-pȧ\ *or* **you·pon** \'yü,pän\ *n* -S [Catawba *yopún*, dim. of *yop* tree, shrub] **:** any of several shrubs or trees of the genus *Ilex*; *esp* **:** a holly (*I. vomitoria*) of the southern U.S. with smooth elliptical leaves used as a substitute for tea and esp. formerly in the black drink of the Indians

yau·tia \yau̇'tēə\ *n* -S [AmerSp *yautía*, fr. Taino] **:** any of several aroids chiefly of tropical America or their starchy edible tubers that are cooked and eaten like yams or potatoes: as **a :** a plant of the genus *Xanthosoma* (esp. *X. sagittifolium*) — called also *spoonflower* **b :** TARO

ya·va·pai \,yävə'pī\ *n, pl* **yavapai** *or* **yavapais** *usu cap* **1 a :** an Indian people of central Arizona **b :** a member of such people **2 :** a Yuman language of the Yavapai people

[1]**yaw** \'yȯ\ *n* -S [origin unknown] **1 :** an angular displacement from a straight line or course **:** DEVIATION: as **a :** a movement of a ship by which it temporarily swerves off course **:** SHEER **b :** angular motion about the normal axis of an airplane ⟨checking the plane's characteristics in roll, pitch and ~ —*Boeing Mag.*⟩ **c** (1) **:** the angle formed by the longitudinal axis of a bullet or missile and the tangent to its trajectory (2) **:** the wobble of a bullet or missile rotating in flight **2 :** an erratic sideward motion **:** LURCH ⟨gave a beery ~ in the saddle —R.L.Stevenson⟩

[2]**yaw** \"\ *vb* -ED/-ING/-S *vi* **1 a :** to deviate erratically from a course ⟨vessels ~ in following seas when . . . more or less out of steering control —W.P.Moore⟩ ⟨suddenly the rocket ship ~*s* hard left —Arthur Murray⟩ ⟨fighting the wheel as the jeep ~*ed* from side to side —Frank Schreider⟩ **b :** to veer away from the normal axis ⟨for an instant the muzzle ~*ed* up at the moon —Vincent McHugh⟩ **2 :** to become deflected **:** SWERVE ⟨his mind kept ~*ing* drunkenly —Norman Mailer⟩ ~ *vt* **:** to cause to yaw ⟨twisted us, and ~*ed* us until the helmsman's life was a burden to him —*Outing*⟩

[3]**yaw** \"\ *vb* -ED/-ING/-S [prob. alter. of [1]*yawn*] **:** GAPE, YAWN

[4]**yaw** \"\ *n* -S [back-formation fr. *yaws*] **:** one of the lesions characteristic of yaws — see MOTHER YAW

ya·wa·ta \yə'wäd·ə\ *adj, usu cap* [fr. *Yawata*, Japan] **:** of or from the city of Yawata, Japan **:** of the kind or style prevalent in Yawata

yawing moment *n* [*yawing* fr. pres. part. of [2]*yaw*] **:** a moment that tends to rotate an airplane about its vertical axis ⟨*yawing moment* is positive when its tends to turn the plane to the right and negative when it turns the plane to the left⟩

[1]**yawl** \'yȯl\ *vb* -ED/-ING/-S [ME *yaulen, yallen*, prob. of imit. origin] *dial Brit* **:** HOWL, SCREAM

²yawl \ˈ"\ n -s [LG *jolle, jölle, jelle*] **1 a :** a ship's small boat usu. rowed by four or six oars and often schooner-rigged : JOLLY BOAT **b :** a light fishing boat with stem and stern alike usu. carrying one, two, or three lugsails **2 :** a fore-and-aft rigged sailboat with a mainmast stepped a little farther forward than in a sloop and carrying a mainsail and one or more jibs and with a small mizzenmast far aft usu. placed abaft the rudderpost — compare KETCH

yawl 2

yawmeter \ˈ=,==\ n [¹*yaw* + *-meter*] : an instrument for measuring the angle of yaw of an airplane : a sideslip indicator

¹yawn \ˈyȯn, ˈyän\ vb -ED/-ING/-S [ME *yanen, yanien*, alter. (influenced by *ganen* to gape, yawn, fr. OE *gānian*) of *yenen, yonen, yeonien*, fr. OE *ginian, geonian;* akin to OE *ginan* to yawn, OHG *ginēn, geinōn*, ON *gīna*, L *hiare*, Gk *chainein*, OSlav *zijati*] vi **1 a :** to gape cavernously : present a wide gulf or breach ⟨this *~ing* fissure may plunge 50 feet or more —G.W.Long⟩ ⟨the vast gap that *~ed* between the gentleman officer and the common seaman —Mary A. Hamilton⟩ **b :** to open up ⟨stood staring at the floor, as if gazing into a pit which had *~ed* suddenly before his eyes —Marcia Davenport⟩ **2 a :** to take a deep breath with the jaws widespread usu. as an involuntary reaction to fatigue or boredom ⟨close the book, ~, and go to bed⟩ ⟨both hens and turkeys ~, especially at roosting time —W.P.Blount⟩ **b** *archaic* **:** to stare openmouthed (as in awe or terror) ⟨methinks it should be now a great eclipse . . . and that the affrighted globe should ~ at alteration —Shak.⟩ **~ vt 1** *archaic* **a :** to cause to open ⟨stood beside the murderer's bed, and *~ed* her ghastly wound —Robert Southey⟩ **b :** to make or proffer by opening **2 a :** to utter with a yawn ⟨~ a reply⟩ **b :** to accomplish with or impel by yawns ⟨*~ed* my way through . . . French —Malcolm Cowley⟩ ⟨have long been laughed or *~ed* out of court —A.L.Guérard⟩

²yawn \ˈ"\ n -s **1 :** an unfilled opening : GAP, CAVITY ⟨struck lightly and . . . lay still, staring up at an oblong ~ that closed with a clattering vibration of loose planks —William Faulkner⟩ ⟨leaning . . . over the ~ of a grave to scatter his handful of earth —Elizabeth Bowen⟩ **2 a :** a deep usu. involuntary intake of breath through the wide open mouth ⟨a dull speech greeted with *~s*⟩ ⟨the telltale ~ of the addict who needs a shot —*Time*⟩ **b :** DULLNESS, TEDIUM ⟨their zeal was quickly blunted by the ~ of habit around them —Bruce Marshall⟩

yawn·er \-nə(r)\ n -s : one that yawns

yawn·ful \ˈ=fəl\ adj : inspiring yawns ⟨a ~ book⟩ — **yawn·ful·ly** \-fəlē\ adv

yawning adj [ME *yaning*, fr. pres. part. of *yanen* to yawn] **1 :** wide open : CAVERNOUS, GAPING ⟨a ~ hole⟩ **2 :** showing fatigue or boredom by yawns ⟨a ~ congregation⟩ — **yawn·ing·ly** adv

yawny \-nē\ adj -ER/-EST : full of or inspiring yawns : SOPORIFIC ⟨a ~ audience⟩ ⟨a ~ lecture⟩

¹yawp *or* **yaup** \ˈyȯp\ vi -ED/-ING/-S [ME *yolpen*, prob. fr. past part. of *yelpen* to boast, call out, yelp — more at YELP] **1 a :** to make a raucous noise : BAWL, SQUAWK ⟨*~ed* at the top of her lungs —Maritta Wolff⟩ ⟨a foghorn howled once, twice, and *~ed* into silence again —Leslie Waller⟩ **b :** to raise a clamor : COMPLAIN, YAMMER ⟨a man must have . . . the right to quit his job, and the right to ~ —J.R.Chamberlain⟩ ⟨the doctor *~ed* about economics —Idwal Jones⟩ **2** [alter. of *gaup*] *dial* : GAPE, STARE — **yawp·er** \-pə(r)\ n -s

²yawp *also* **yaup** \ˈ"\ n -s **1 :** a raucous noise : SQUAWK, YELL ⟨broke into barbaric *~s* suggesting colicky infants —*Duncan Aikman*⟩ **2 :** TALK; *esp* : foolish complaining talk ⟨never heard such dang-fool ~ in my life —C.T.Jackson⟩ **3 :** something suggestive of a raucous noise ⟨the existentialist ~ of despair —W.I.Nichols⟩; *specif* : rough vigorous language ⟨sound my barbaric ~ over the roofs of the world —Walt Whitman⟩

yawping n -s [fr. gerund of ¹*yawp*] : a strident or prattling utterance ⟨some of his *~s* are directed against his employees —Charles Lee⟩ ⟨moldy characters and philosophical *~s* about life —*Time*⟩

yawroot \ˈ=,=\ n [⁴*yaw* + *root;* prob. fr. the belief that it cures yaws] : QUEEN'S-DELIGHT

¹yaws *pl of* YAW, *pres 3d sing of* YAW

²yaws \ˈyȯz\ n *pl but sing or pl in constr* [of Cariban origin; akin to Calinogo *Yáya* the disease] : an infectious contagious but not venereal tropical disease that is caused by a spirochete (*Treponema pertenue*) which cannot be distinguished morphologically from the syphilis spirochete (*T. pallidum*) and that is characterized by a primary ulcerating lesion on the skin followed by a secondary stage in which ulcers develop all over the body and by a third stage in which the bones are involved — called also *frambesia*; compare BEJEL

yaws fly n : a chloropid fly that transmits yaws

yawshrub \ˈ=,=\ n [⁴*yaw* + *shrub*] : QUEEN'S-DELIGHT

yawweed \ˈ=,=\ n [⁴*yaw* + *weed*] : a tropical American shrub (*Morinda royoc*) formerly considered a remedy for yaws with small white odorous flowers

yaw yin \ˈyōˈyin\ *also* **yeh jen** \ˈyeˈyən\ n, *pl* **yaw yin** *or* **yaw yins** *usu cap both Ys&J* [Chin (Pek) *yeh³-jen²*, lit., savage people] : CHINGPAW

yax·che \(ˈ)yäshˈchā\ n -s [AmerSp *yaxché*, fr. Maya *yaxche*, *yaaxche*, lit., green tree] : SILK-COTTON TREE

y-axis \ˈ=ˈ==\ n **1 :** the axis of ordinates in a plane Cartesian coordinate system **2 :** one of the three axes in a three-dimensional rectangular coordinate system

ya·ya \yäˈyä\ n -s [AmerSp, of Cariban origin] : any of several tropical American trees: as **a :** a gum-yielding tree (*Protium panamense*) of Panama — called also *copa* **b :** LANCEWOOD 2 **c :** CHAPARRO 3

yazidi *usu cap, var of* YEZIDI

yazoo \ˈya,zü, ˈyä,-\ n, *pl* **yazoo** *or* **yazoos** *usu cap* **1 :** a Tunican people of the lower Yazoo river valley, west central Mississippi **2 :** a member of the Yazoo people

YB *abbr* yearbook

Yb *symbol* ytterbium

y box n, *cap Y* : a box containing three wires of equal resistance joined to a common point and used in connection with a three-phase electrical system to furnish the central point

YC *abbr* yacht club

y chromosome n, *usu cap Y* : a sex chromosome ordinarily occurring only in the male zygote and cells and formerly supposed to carry factors for maleness that are now usu. thought to exist in autosomes — compare X CHROMOSOME

yclept *or* **ycleped** [ME (past part. of *yclepen* to call, name), fr. OE *geclipod*, past part. of *geclipian* to call, name, fr. *ge-*, perfective, associative, and collective prefix (akin to OHG *gi-*, perfective, associative, and collective prefix) + *clipian* to speak, cry out, call — more at CO-, CLEPE] *past part of* CLEPE

y connection n, *cap Y* **1 :** STAR CONNECTION **2 :** SIAMESE 4

y-coordinate \ˈ==ˈ=(=)=\ n **1 :** the ordinate in a plane Cartesian coordinate system **2 :** one of the three coordinates in a three-dimensional rectangular coordinate system

y current n, *usu cap Y* : the current through one branch of the star arrangement of a three-phase circuit

yd *abbr* yard

yday *abbr* yesterday

ydg *abbr* yarding

¹ye \(ˈ)yē, -,yi, *in a few phrases in which it is preserved* .ē *or* i\ *pron* [ME *ye, yhe*, fr. OE *gē* (suppletive 2d pers. nom. pl. of *thū, thu* thou) — more at YOU, THOU] : ¹YOU 1a — used from the earliest times to the late 13th century only as a plural pronoun of the second person in the nominative case including direct address and still surviving archaically and in many dialects in this use alongside of other more recently originated uses ⟨that ~ may be the children of your Father which is in heaven —Mt 5:45 (AV)⟩ ⟨waft, ~ winds, His story —Reginald Heber⟩ ⟨avast, ~ rogues —Frank Yerby⟩; sometimes used without archaic or dialectal flavor in mock invocations ⟨~ gods and little fishes⟩; used from the late 13th century also as a singular pronoun of the second person in the nominative case including direct address, at first only as the appropriate form of address to a person of high social status or to a person not well known to the speaker but later without this limitation except in a few English dialects, and still surviving archaically and in many dialects in this use ⟨My Lord of Gloucester, now ~ grow too hot —Shak.⟩ ⟨sweet mother, do ~ love the child —Alfred Tennyson⟩ ⟨d' ye stand there, knave, and see your master robbed —Charles Reade⟩; used from the late 14th century also as a singular or plural pronoun of the second person in contexts where the objective case form of an inflected pronoun is the one to be expected and still surviving archaically and in many dialects in this use ⟨vain pomp and glory of this world, I hate ~ —Shak.⟩ ⟨I come, . . ., strange news to tell ~ —John Dryden⟩; compare ¹THEE, ¹THOU

²ye \,yē, yi, *or like* ¹THE\ *definite article* [alter. of OE *þē* the; fr. the fact that in some medieval manuscripts the runic letter *þ* (*th*) became indistinguishable from the Roman letter *y* and as the runic letter grew obsolete printers often used the *y* to replace it] *archaic* : THE — often used in business names to suggest an earlier time ⟨*Ye* Olde Gifte Shoppe⟩

YE *abbr, often not cap* yellow edges

¹yea \ˈyā\ *adv* [ME *ye, ya*, fr. OE *gēa, gē;* akin to OHG & ON *jā* yes, Goth *ja, jai*] **1 :** YES — formerly used in answer to a question not involving a negative but now superseded by *yes* except in oral voting **2 :** more than this : not only so but — used to mark addition or substitution of a more explicit or emphatic phrase and thus interchangeable with *nay* ⟨I therein do rejoice, ~, and will rejoice —Phil 1:18 (AV)⟩

²yea \ˈ"\ n -s [ME *ye, ya*, fr. *ye, ya*, adv.] **1 a :** AFFIRMATION, ASSENT ⟨his ~ meant more than the oath of most men⟩ **b** — used interjectionally (as in a college cheer) to express encouragement or gratification ⟨~, team⟩ **2 a :** an affirmative vote **b :** a person casting a yea vote ⟨stood regularly with the *~s* in promoting the welfare state⟩

yeah *any of the vowel-final pronunciations at* ¹YES\ *adv* [by alter.] : YES

yean \ˈyēn\ vb -ED/-ING/-S [ME *yenen*, fr. (assumed) OE *geēanian*, fr. OE *ge-* (perfective & collective prefix) + *ēanian* to yean; akin to L *agnus* lamb, Gk *amnos*, OIr *ūan*, OSlav *agne*] : to bring forth young (as a sheep or a goat) : LAMB

yean·ling \-liŋ, -lēŋ\ n -s *often attrib* [*yean* + *-ling*] **1 :** LAMB ⟨a ~ lamb⟩ **2 :** KID

year \ˈyi(ə)r, ˈyiə\ n -s [ME *yeer, yere*, fr. OE *gēar;* akin to OHG *jār* year, ON *ār*, Goth *jer*, Gk *hōros* year, *hōra* season of the year, time of day, hour, Av *yārə* year, L *ire* to go — more at ISSUE] **1 a :** the period of about 365¼ solar days required for one revolution of the earth around the sun and generally indicated by the return of the sun to the same part of the sky or by the recurrence of the seasons **b :** the time required for the apparent sun to return to an arbitrary fixed or moving reference point in the sky (as the March equinox for the tropical year or a point among the stars for the sidereal year) **c :** the time in which any planet completes a revolution about the sun ⟨the ~ of Jupiter⟩ ⟨the ~ of Saturn⟩ **2 a :** a cycle in the Gregorian calendar having 365 or 366 days divided into 12 months beginning with January and ending with December — compare LEAP YEAR **b :** a major cycle of days in a calendar usu. having some correspondence with the solar or the lunar year or with both **c :** a period of time equal to one year of the Gregorian calendar but beginning at a different time ⟨within a ~⟩ ⟨a ~ from today⟩ — see FISCAL YEAR **3 :** ACADEMIC YEAR **4 a :** a calendar year that belongs to a particular era or system of reckoning or bears a specified number in the sequence of the years of such an era ⟨died in the ~ of Our Lord 1900⟩ ⟨the time was the ~ of the hegira 300⟩ — compare ANNO DOMINI, ANNO LUCIS **b :** a numbered calendar year ⟨omitted to add the ~ when he dated the letter⟩ **5 a :** 12 months of punishment or imprisonment ⟨the judge gave him 15 *~s*⟩ **b :** a remission of temporal or purgatorial punishment for sin to an extent equivalent to one year of canonical penance in the Roman Catholic Church — compare INDULGENCE 1 **6 years** *pl* **:** a time or era marked in some special way : a period taken as a unit notable for a particular characteristic ⟨*~s* of plenty⟩ **7 a :** 12 months that constitute a measure of age or duration ⟨her 21st ~⟩ ⟨a man of 80 *~s*⟩ — often used in combination ⟨a *year*-old child⟩ ⟨a 50-*year* record⟩ **b years** *pl* **:** AGE ⟨a man in *~s* but a child in understanding⟩ **c years** *pl* **:** OLD AGE ⟨he was slipping into *~s* apace —Robert Browning⟩ **8 :** the annual cycle of the seasons in which there is a recurrent period of the growth, ripening, and decay of vegetation **9 :** any of various sometimes vaguely delimited periods of time longer than a calendar year ⟨the international geophysical ~ was fixed at 18 months⟩ — see GREAT YEAR **10 :** CLASS 2e ⟨he was in my ~ at college⟩

ye·a·ra \yäˈärə\ n -s [origin unknown] : POISON OAK b

year and a day n [ME *yere and a day*] : the time allowed in various legal limitations of time for an act or an event to take place so that there shall certainly be an interim of a full year from and including the day an event happens when this period is computed after an event

year-around *var of* YEAR-ROUND

year-bearer \ˈ=,==\ n **1 :** one of four day names in the Maya and Aztec calendars that name a year **2 :** one of the 52 names of days that designate a year in a Maya and Aztec calendar round

yearbook \ˈ=,=\ n : a book published yearly as a report or summary of the statistics or facts of a year and intended as a reference book : a school or college class album : ANNUAL ⟨*~s* giving . . . information about learned societies —H.B. Van Hoesen & F.K.Walter⟩ ⟨the most common publications in the secondary school are . . . the newspaper, the magazine, and the ~ —W.T.Gruhn⟩ ⟨fine pictorial *~s* on furniture and design —Martin James⟩

year class n : the group of young of one kind of animal produced during one year — used chiefly of fishes

year clock n : a clock running for a year on a single winding; *esp* : ANNIVERSARY CLOCK

¹year-end \ˈ=ˈ=\ n : the end of the calendar year

²year-end \ˈ"\ adj : made at the year-end ⟨*year-end* report⟩ : occurring or existing at the year-end ⟨*year-end* upsurge of prices⟩ ⟨*year-end* inventory⟩

¹year·ling \ˈyi(ə)rliŋ, ˈyiəl-, ˈyərl-, ˈyəl-, -lēŋ, -lən\ n -s [ME *yerling*, fr. *yere* year + *-ling*] **1 a :** one (as a child or plant) that is a year old; *esp* : an animal one year old or in the second year of its age — used chiefly of livestock **b :** a racehorse between January 1st of the year after the year in which it was foaled and the next January 1st ranging in actual age from nearly newborn to nearly two years of age **2 :** a member of the next to the lowest class in a military academy (as West Point)

²yearling \ˈ"\ adj : a year old : having passed a first anniversary but not a second

yearlong \ˈ=ˈ=\ adj (or adv) : lasting through a year

¹year·ly \ˈyi(ə)rlē, -iəlē, -li\ adj [ME *yeerly, yerely*, fr. OE *gēarlic*, fr. *gēar* year + *-lic* -ly] : reckoned by the year : occurring, appearing, or being made, done, or acted upon every year or once a year : ANNUAL

²yearly \ˈ"\ adv [ME *yerly, yerely*, fr. OE *gēarlice*, fr. *gēar* year + *-lice* -ly (adv. suffix)] : every year : once a year : from year to year : ANNUALLY ⟨blessings ~ bestowed⟩ ⟨~ will I do this rite —Shak.⟩

yearly meeting n, *usu cap Y&M* **1 :** an organizational unit of the Society of Friends composed of many Quarterly Meetings that is the most comprehensive Quaker administrative group **2 :** a session of a Yearly Meeting

¹yearn \ˈyərn, ˈyə̄n, ˈyəin\ vb -ED/-ING/-S [ME *yernen*, fr. OE *giernan, geornan;* akin to OE *georn* desirous, eager, OHG *gern* eager, willing, *gerōn* to desire, ON *gjarn* eager, willing, *girna* to desire, Goth *-gairns* desirous, *gairnei* wish, L *horiri*, *hortari* to urge, incite, encourage, cheer, Gk *chairein* to rejoice, enjoy, Skt *haryati* he likes, yearns for] vi **1 :** to experience a strong desire or craving ⟨her heart *~ed* for one of the beautifully designed timepieces —David Walden⟩ ⟨young men who *~ed* to succeed at letters —John Mason Brown⟩ ⟨*~ed* after the social and economic setup of the 19th century —R.G. Woolbert⟩ **2 :** to feel tenderness, compassion, or love : become moved or drawn emotionally ⟨*~ed* over her with a father's tenderness and a mother's infinite self-giving⟩ **3 :** to express longing by tone of voice or by that of a musical instrument ⟨his talk *~ed* after something elusive⟩ ⟨the organ *~ed* in the half light⟩ **~ vt 1** *obs* **:** to move to pity, mourning, or compassion : GRIEVE **2 :** to voice in a longing manner : speak or utter so as to express craving or desire ⟨*~ed* out the tender, vivid lyric of an ageless desire⟩ **syn** see LONG

²yearn \ˈ"\ n -s : an eager desire : LONGING, YEARNING

³yearn \ˈ"\ vb -ED/-ING/-S [ME *yernen*, prob. fr. OE *iernan* to run, flow, coagulate — more at RUN] *chiefly Scot* : COAGULATE, CURDLE

yearn·er \ˈyərnər; ˈyə̄nə(r, ˈyəin-\ n -s : one that yearns ⟨*~s* for an absolute government —Russell Lord⟩

yearn·ful \-fəl\ adj [ME *yeornful* eager, anxious, fr. OE *geornful*, fr. *georn* desirous, eager + *-ful*] : full of yearning : MOURNFUL

¹yearning n -s [ME *yerning*, fr. OE *geornung*, fr. *geornan* to yearn + *-ung* -ing] : the act of one that yearns : eager or anxious longing : tender compassion ⟨man's infinite ~ to know the truth about himself —L.C.Eiseley⟩ ⟨the amorous *~s* of lovers for the unattainable —Harrison Smith⟩

²yearn·ing \ˈyērniŋ, -nən\ n -s [ME *yerning*, fr. gerund of *yernen* to curdle] *chiefly Scot* : RENNET

yearn·ing·ly adv : in a yearning manner

year of confusion : the year 46 B.C. when the Julian calendar was introduced 708 years from the founding of Rome

year of grace : a year of the Christian era ⟨down to the present *year of grace*⟩ ⟨the *year of grace* 1955⟩

year-round \ˈ=ˈ=\ *or* **year-around** \ˈ==ˈ=\ adj : effective, employed, or operating for the full year : not seasonal ⟨a *year-round* children's theater —*Newsweek*⟩ ⟨surf-bathing, boating, golf, and tennis are *year-around* enjoyments —*Fortune*⟩

year-round·er \ˈ=ˈ=də(r)\ n : someone or something whose residence, occupation, or use is the same at all seasons

years *pl of* YEAR

year's mind n [ME *yeris minde*, fr. OE *gēargemynd*, fr. *gēar* year + *gemynd* memory, commemoration, mind — more at YEAR, MIND] : a Roman Catholic requiem mass for a deceased person held on or near the anniversary of death or burial — compare MONTH'S MIND

year's purchase n : ²PURCHASE 2b(1)

yeas *pl of* YEA

yea-sayer \ˈ=,=(=)\ n **1 :** one whose attitude is that of confident affirmation ⟨he is a *yea-sayer* who sees all of life's evil, but declares that man is worthy of his name only when he joyously accepts all of life's risks —B.R.Redman⟩ **2 :** YES-MAN

yea-saying \ˈ=ˈ==\ adj : AFFIRMATIVE, POSITIVE ⟨a *yea-saying* culture, noble, proud, and free —*Saturday Rev.*⟩

¹yeast \ˈyēst, *chiefly dial* ˈēst\ n -s [ME *yest*, fr. OE *gist, giest;* akin to ON *jastr* yeast, MHG *jest* foam, OHG *jesan* to ferment, Gk *zestos* boiled, *zein* to boil, seethe, Skt *yasyati* it seethes] **1 a :** a usu. creamy or yellowish surface froth or sediment that occurs esp. in saccharine liquids (as fruit juices or malt worts) in which it promotes alcoholic fermentation, that consists of a suspension of cells of a fungus of the family Saccharomycetaceae, and that is used esp. in the making of alcoholic liquors and as a leaven in baking — see BOTTOM YEAST, TOP YEAST, ZYMASE **b :** a commercial product containing yeast plants packaged either as moist cakes or dry cakes or granules and used esp. as a leaven in baking **c** (1) **:** a minute fungus (esp. *Saccharomyces cerevisiae*) that is present and functionally active in yeast and usu. has little or no mycelium but reproduces by budding (2) **:** any of various similar fungi esp. of the orders Endomycetales and Moniliales **2 :** something resembling the froth of yeast fermentation (as the foam or spume of waves) ⟨they melt into thy ~ of waves —Lord Byron⟩ **3 :** something that causes ferment or activity, creates a lift or drive, or adds vitality ⟨education is . . . the great expression of democratic ~ at work —B.G.Gallagher⟩ ⟨were all seething with the ~ of revolt —J.F.Dobie⟩ ⟨the living ~ of conscience —H.M.Robinson⟩ ⟨had taken the ~ out of me —Hugo Johanson⟩

²yeast \ˈ"\ vb -ED/-ING/-S vi : FERMENT, FROTH **~ vt :** to impregnate with yeast

yeast cake n : a cake of compressed yeast

yeast·i·ly \-təlē, -li\ adv : in a yeasty manner

yeast·i·ness \-tēnəs, -tin-\ n -ES : the quality or state of being yeasty

yeastlike \ˈ=,=\ adj : resembling yeast

yeast nucleic acid n : RIBONUCLEIC ACID

yeast plant *or* **yeast cell** n : an individual plant of a yeast typically consisting of a primary cell bearing one or more buds

yeast spot n : a disease of lima bean, cowpea, and related plants caused by a yeast (*Nematospora phaseoli*) that attacks the seeds within the pods

yeasty \-tē, -ti\ adj -ER/-EST **1 :** of, consisting of, or resembling yeast : having the froth of yeast or one suggesting it ⟨a ~

YEARS OF THREE OF THE PRINCIPAL CALENDARS

CALENDAR	YEAR CHRONOLOGY	YEAR BEGINS	NUMBER OF DAYS common years	NUMBER OF DAYS leap years	LEAP YEARS
GREGORIAN	From Roman year 754, the year immediately following the birth of Christ as placed by Dionysus Exiguus in the 753d year of Rome	Ten days after the winter solstice	365	366	Every fourth year but only those centesimal years divisible by 400
JEWISH	From the Creation as fixed at 3761 B.C.	First new moon after the autumnal equinox. The postexilic year began in the spring with the month Nisan, this now being sometimes called the ecclesiastical year	353 defective 354 regular 355 perfect *or* abundant (There is no regular pattern for defective, regular, and perfect years; adjustments are made so that certain holidays will fall on proper days of the week)	383 384 385	The 3d, 6th, 8th, 11th, 14th, 17th, and 19th years of each 19-year cycle
MUSLIM	From the year of the Hegira, A.D. 622	Retrogresses through the seasons; the year 1 began on Friday, July 16	354	355	The 2d, 5th, 7th, 10th, 13th, 16th, 18th, 21st, 24th, 26th, 29th year of each 30-year cycle

froth covered the mash —C.B.Nordhoff & J.N.Hall› ‹the puddles . . . foamed with a ~ scum —Ellen Glasgow› **2 a :** turbulent with immaturity, incompleteness, or youth **:** not yet settled or formed ‹those ~ years between childhood and maturity —P.E.More› ‹when our American world was young and ~ —Catherine D. Bowen› **b** (1) **:** pregnant with future developments **:** full of the signs of things to come **:** churning with growth ‹the journalism of that ~ decade furnished the springs of modern news techniques —F.L.Mott› (2) **:** marked by deep or massive ferment **:** alive with the processes of change ‹this is a ~ field in which circumstances keep altering cases —R.M. Yoder› ‹the ~ darkness at the mind's base —Bernard DeVoto› **c :** full of vitality, initiative, or resource **:** EBULLIENT, EXUBERANT ‹the reporters were ~ Bohemians —Bruce Catton› ‹the ~ ardor of the famous old Odessa merchants —Esther & Joseph Riwkin› ‹~ and mercurial liberals —*Reporter*› **d :** marked by frothiness or triviality **:** FRIVOLOUS ‹~ chatter›

yeat·man·ite \ˈyātmə,nīt\ *n* -s [Pope *Yeatman* †1953 Am. mining engineer + E *-ite*] **:** a rare mineral $(Mn,Zn)_{16}Sb_2Si_4O_{29}$ consisting of a pseudo-orthorhombic oxide and silicate of manganese, zinc, and antimony

yeats·ian \ˈyātsēən\ *adj, usu cap* [William Butler *Yeats* †1939 Irish poet and dramatist + E *-an*] **:** of or relating to W. B. Yeats or his poetic style or influence ‹*Yeatsian* pentameters —*Times Lit. Supp.*›

yed·da \ˈyedə\ *or* **yed·do** \-e(,)dō\ *n* -s [origin unknown] **:** a natural unsplit straw for hats

yed·do spruce \ˈye(,)dō-\ *n, usu cap Y* [fr. *Yeddo* (*Yedo*), now Tokyo, Japan] **:** an evergreen tree (*Picea jezoensis*) of eastern Asia often cultivated as an ornamental and having dark green leaves that have white bands above and are silvery white beneath — called also *Japanese spruce*

yede *vi* -ED/-ING/-S [obs. E *yede* (past & past part. of E *go*), fr. ME *yede, yeode* (past of *gon, gan* to go), fr. OE *ēode*, 3d pers. past of *gān* to go — more at ISSUE, GO] *obs* **:** GO, PROCEED

yee·la·man \ˈyēləmən\ *n* -s [by alter.] **:** HIELEMAN

yegg \ˈyeg\ *or* **yegg·man** \-mən\ *n, pl* **yeggs** *or* **yeggmen** [origin unknown] **:** SAFECRACKER, ROBBER

yeh \ˈye\ *adv* [by alter.] **:** YES

yeh jen *usu cap Y&J, var of* YAW YIN

yei·bi·chai \ˈyābə,chī\ *n* -s *usu cap* [Navaho *ye'ibeshichai*] **1 :** a Navaho supernatural represented by a masked dancer in an initiation or curative ceremony **2 :** the ceremony performed by Yeibichai dancers

yel *abbr* yellow

yeld \ˈyeld\ *var of* ²EILD

¹yell \ˈyel\ *vb* -ED/-ING/-S [ME *yellen*, fr. OE *giellan*; akin to OHG *gellan* to yell, ON *gjalla*, OE *galan* to sing, scream] *vi* **1 a :** to utter a loud cry, scream, or shout usu. expressive of intense emotion (as of excitement, pain or fear, pleasure or joy) ‹the two boys ~*ed* with fear —Pearl Buck› ‹the crowd ~*ed* and shouted with delight —Sherwood Anderson› ‹the hyenas were ~*ing* like demons› **b :** to make an articulate utterance with a scream or shout ‹hearing him ~ for help with what words he could muster› ‹is ~*ing* across the water to ask who we are› **c :** to give a cheer usu. in unison (as at an athletic contest) ‹we ~*ed* together for the teams —*Duke Univ. Alumni Register*› **2 :** to make a loud strident noise resembling or suggestive of a yell ‹the wind shouts in the sails and ~*s* through the rigging› ‹the brook crashes and ~*s* down the rocky pitch› ‹the locomotive ~*s* in warning and thunders over the crossing› **3 :** to complain or protest with or as if with a yell ‹gives the extremists a chance to ~ —O.W.Holmes †1935› ‹let the opposition ~, we have the vote› **~** *vt* **1 :** to utter or declare with or as if with a yell **:** SHOUT ‹as the students leave they ~ "Merry Christmas" back and forth› ‹able to ~ a warning just in time› ‹the other boys ~ names at him› **2 :** to affect or bring to a specified state or condition by yelling ‹~*ed* up the dogs —Hugh Fosburgh› ‹~ the team to victory› ‹the crows are ~*ing* their heads off›

²yell \"\ *n* -s [ME, fr. *yellen* to yell] **:** an act or instance of yelling: as **a :** an often involuntary scream or shout resulting from intense excitement or strong emotion ‹with ~*s* of fiendish delight the savages greeted their enemy —Francis Birtles› ‹a waiting crowd . . . let out a tumultous ~ of greeting —Carl Sandburg› ‹heard the lacerating ~ of a scared bird shrill in his ear —W.W.Gibson› **b :** a shout consisting of an articulated phrase or statement **c :** a characteristic shout or cry (as in battle) ‹the Apache ~› ‹the rebel ~› **d :** a usu. rhythmic shout or cheer consisting of a specified set of syllables or words used esp. in schools or colleges to encourage or support athletic teams **e :** a noise suggestive of or resembling a yell ‹the hoarse, strident ~ of the siren —Donn Byrne›

yell leader *n* **:** CHEERLEADER

¹yel·low \ˈye(,)lō, |lə; |ləw *or* |lō + V; *dial or NewEng & Brit* + V |lər; *dial* ˈya| (*but* ˈyalə(r) *often occurs in standard speech when "high" precedes*\ *adj* -ER/-EST [ME *yelwe, yelow, yalow*, fr. OE *geolu*; akin to OHG *gelo* yellow, ON *gulr* yellow, OIr *gel* white, L *helvus* light bay, Gk *chlōros* greenish yellow, Skt *hari* yellowish, greenish; basic meaning: shimmer, glow] **1 a :** of the color yellow **:** of a color of the hue of sulfur or of a hue somewhat less red than that of gold **b :** changed to a yellow hue through age, disease (as jaundice), or discoloration **:** YELLOWED, SALLOW ‹~ parchment› ‹~ skin› **c :** having a yellow or mulatto complexion or skin ‹immigration of Orientals raised a false specter of the peril of the ~ races› ‹having had a white father, he is known as a ~ Negro› ‹the ~ girl stopped —R.P.Warren› **2** *archaic* **:** affected with envy **:** JAUNDICED, JEALOUS **3 a :** gaining or holding interest by printing or headlining sensational or scandalous items or ordinary news sensationally distorted ‹tempers might have subsided altogether had not a ~ newspaper . . . exhorted the soldiers to stand for their rights —Dixon Wecter› ‹the same technique of sensationalism that had lured new readers to the ~ journals —H.L.Smith b. 1906› ‹set his newspaper off sharply from the ~ journalism of morbid sensationalism which flowered . . . at the turn of the century —F.L.Mott› **b :** MEAN, DISHONORABLE, COWARDLY ‹the little ~ stain of treason —M.W.Straight› ‹is too ~ to stand up and fight› ‹has a pronounced ~ streak›

²yellow \"\ *vb* -ED/-ING/-S *vt* **:** to make or turn yellow **:** cause to have a yellow tinge or color ‹old clothes and papers that time and neglect have ~*ed*› ‹wild daffodils were ~*ing* the grassy slopes —Victoria Sackville-West› ‹the sun ~*s* the meadow› **~** *vi* **:** to become or turn yellow ‹I let my tobacco ~ for about a week —Caroline Gordon› ‹the leaves ~ in the fall›

³yellow \"\ *n* -s [ME *yelow, yalow*, fr. *yelow, yalow* yellow (adj.)] **1 a :** a color whose hue resembles that of ripe lemons or sunflowers or is that of the portion of the spectrum lying between green and orange **b :** the one of the four psychologically primary hues that is evoked in the normal observer under normal conditions by radiant energy of the wavelength 580 millimicrons **c :** one of the six psychologically primary object colors — compare PRIMARY 4a **d :** one of the subtractive primaries **e :** a pigment or dye that colors yellow **2 :** something that is yellow or is chiefly distinguished by a yellow color: as **a :** a person having yellow skin ‹had engaged blacks, browns, ~*s* about equally —Frances Gaither› **b :** ²SULPHUR **c :** the yolk of an egg **d :** YELLOW SPONGE **3 yellows** *pl* **:** JAUNDICE, WEIL'S DISEASE **4 yellows** *pl* **:** any of several plants: as **a :** YELLOW LADY'S-SLIPPER **b :** CRAMBLING ROCKET **5 yellows** *pl* **:** any of several plant diseases (as of aster, celery, or peach) caused by fungi, bacteria, malnutrition, or esp. by viruses and characterized by yellowing of the foliage and stunting

yellow adder's-tongue *n* **:** DOGTOOTH VIOLET b(1)

yellow alder *n* **:** a tropical American shrubby herb (*Turnera ulmifolia*) with lanceolate oblong leaves and axillary solitary yellow flowers

yellow alert *n* **:** the preliminary stage of alert (as when hostile or unidentified aircraft are nearing a defended area); *also* **:** the signal for this — compare BLUE ALERT, RED ALERT, WHITE ALERT

yellow angelfish *or* **yellow angel** *n* **:** ANGELFISH 2

yellow ant *n* **:** an ant (as some members of the genus *Lasius*) predominantly yellow in color; *esp* **:** the widely distributed ant (*Acanthomyops flavus*) that nests chiefly in open grassland

yellow ash *n* **:** YELLOWWOOD 1a

yellow asphodel *n* **:** an asphodel (*Asphodeline lutea*) with usu. yellow flowers

yellow atrophy *n* **:** ACUTE YELLOW ATROPHY

yellow avens *n* **:** either of two herbs of the genus *Geum* (*G. strictum* and *G. macrophyllum*)

yellow azalea *n* **:** FLAME AZALEA

yellow baboon *n* **:** a long-tailed yellowish African baboon (*Papio cynocephalus*)

yellow bachelor's-button *n* **:** ORANGE MILKWORT

yellowback \ˈ⁼⁼,⁼\ *n* [¹*yellow* + *back*] **1 :** GOLD CERTIFICATE **2 :** a cheap and usu. sensational novel; *esp* **:** one sold in yellow board or paper covers in the late 19th and early 20th centuries **3 :** a freshwater mussel (*Lampsilis anodontoides*) of the Mississippi valley and southeastern U. S. having a heavy shell covered with yellow periostracum and highly valued for mother-of-pearl

yellow balm *n* **:** WHORLED LOOSESTRIFE

yellow balsam *n* **1 :** JEWELWEED b **2 :** a strong-scented West Indian shrub (*Croton flavens*)

yellow-banded hussar \ˈ⁼⁼,⁼⁼-\ *n* **:** an Australian snapper (*Lutjanus amabilis*) that is largely pink with a broad yellow band along each side and is an excellent table fish taken chiefly with hook and line

yellow bark *n* **1 :** CALISAYA BARK **2 :** YELLOW-BARK OAK; *also* **:** the bark of this oak

yellow-bark oak *also* **yellow-barked oak** \ˈ⁼⁼,⁼-\ *n* **:** a black oak (*Quercus velutina*)

yellow bartonia *n* **:** a yellow-flowered screwstem (*Bartonia virginica*) common in eastern No. America

yellow bass *n* **:** a yellow No. American freshwater bass (*Morone interrupta*) with several more or less broken black stripes or bars that is related to and resembles the much larger marine striped bass and is native to the Mississippi drainage from southern Minnesota and Wisconsin to Texas and Louisiana

yellow basswood *n* **:** a common linden (*Tilia glabra*) of No. America

yellow bat *n* **:** a showy southern African insectivorous bat (*Scotophilus nigrita*) with black wings and canary yellow underparts

yellow bear *n* **:** YELLOW WOOLLY BEAR

yellow beardtongue *n* **:** a perennial herb (*Penstemon confertus*) of the Rocky mountain region having showy yellow flowers

yellow bear's-foot *n* **:** a leafcup (*Polymnia uvedalia*)

yellow bedstraw *n* **:** a common yellow-flowered bedstraw (*Galium verum*) — called also *yellow cleavers*

yellow-bellied flycatcher \ˈ⁼⁼,⁼⁼-\ *n* **:** a small flycatcher (*Empidonax flaviventris*) of eastern No. America

yellow-bellied racer *n* **:** BLUE RACER

yellow-bellied sapsucker *or* **yellow-bellied woodpecker** *n* **:** a small woodpecker (*Sphyrapicus varius*) of the eastern U.S. that feeds partly on the sap of trees

yellow-bellied terrapin *n* **:** a terrapin (*Pseudemys scripta*) of the southeastern U.S. having the carapace marked with yellow lines and the plastron yellow or brownish

yellow bells *n pl but sing or pl in constr* **:** any of several plants with bell-shaped yellow flowers: as **a :** DOGTOOTH VIOLET b(1) **b :** CALIFORNIA YELLOW BELLS **c :** YELLOW ELDER

yellowbelly \ˈ⁼⁼,⁼⁼\ *n* [¹*yellow* + *belly*] **1 a :** PUMPKINSEED 1 **b :** SQUAWFISH 1 **c :** CALLOP **d** *NewZeal* **:** any of several flatfishes (as *Ammotretis guntheri*) that are important market fish **e** *southern Africa* **:** a guasa (*Epinephelus guaza*) **2 :** YELLOW BERRY 2 **3 :** one who is yellow **:** COWARD ‹was called a ~ when he would not enlist at the beginning of the war› **4 a :** a person having a yellow skin **b** *Southwest* **:** MEXICAN — usu. used disparagingly ‹two kinds of ethics, one for us and one for the *yellowbellies* across the line —E.L.Jones›

yellow berry *n* **1 yellow berries** *pl* **:** BUCKTHORN BERRIES **2 :** a condition of mature grains of hard wheat resulting from nitrogen deficiency and marked by the occurrence of light yellow opaque soft and starchy kernels among the normally hard dark translucent red amber grains; *also* **:** one of these kernels **3** *usu* **yel·low·berry** \ˈ⁼⁼—*see* BERRY\ **:** PERSIAN BERRY

yellow bile *n* [trans. of Gk *xanthē cholē*] **:** a humor of medieval physiology believed to be secreted by the liver and to cause irascibility — compare BLACK BILE

yellowbill \ˈ⁼⁼,⁼\ *n* [¹*yellow* + *bill*] **:** SCOTER

yellow-billed cuckoo \ˈ⁼⁼,⁼-\ *n* **:** a common No. American cuckoo (*Coccyzus americanus*)

yellow-billed loon *n* **:** a loon (*Gavia adamsi*) found in the northern part of the northern hemisphere

yellow-billed magpie *n* **:** a magpie (*Pica nutalli*) found in California

yellow-billed tropic bird *n* **:** a tropic bird (*Phaëthon lepturus*)

yellow birch *n* **1 :** a No. American birch (*Betula lutea*) with lustrous gray or yellow thin bark **2 :** the hard strong light brown wood of the yellow birch tree used esp. for furniture and buttons

yellowbird \ˈ⁼⁼,⁼\ *n* **1 :** any of various American goldfinches **2 :** YELLOW WARBLER 1a

yellow blight *n* **1 :** a wilt of potatoes caused by a fungus (*Sclerotinia sclerotiorum*) **2 :** WESTERN TOMATO BLIGHT

yellow bluestem *n* **:** a tropical beardgrass (*Andropogon ischaemum*) that is adventive in parts of the U.S. and used as a pasture grass in the dry southern regions

yellow body *n* [trans. of NL *corpus luteum*] **:** CORPUS LUTEUM

yellow book *n, usu cap Y&B* [trans. of F *livre jaune*] **:** an official report of government affairs bound in yellow ‹the Hungarian government issues a *Yellow Book* in which it details its charges of treason —*Current History*›

yellow box *n* **:** a gum tree (*Eucalyptus melliodora*) of southern Australia having yellow inner bark and hard yellowish wood somewhat resembling boxwood — called also *yellow jacket*

yellow boy *n, Brit* **:** a gold coin

yellow-breasted bunting \ˈ⁼⁼,⁼⁼-\ *n* **:** a bunting (*Emberiza aureola*) that is common in northern Russia and Siberia, winters in tropical Asia, and in the adult male is chestnut above with a buff stripe over the eye and a yellow breast crossed by a narrow chestnut band

yellow-breasted chat *n* **:** a large American chat (*Icteria virens*) that is greenish brown above with a bright yellow throat and breast and a white abdomen, that breeds chiefly in the eastern half of the U.S., that winters in Mexico and Central America, and that is noted for its expert mimicking of other birds

yellow bronze *n* **:** BRONZE YELLOW

yellow broom *n* **:** INDIGO BROOM

yellowbrush \ˈ⁼⁼,⁼\ *n* **:** a bright green shrubby plant (*Chrysothamnus viscidiflorus*) of western No. America that bears bright yellow flowers in midsummer

yellow buckeye *n* **:** SWEET BUCKEYE

yellow buckthorn *n* **:** a No. American shrub (*Rhamnus caroliniana*) having leaves yellowish on the lower surface — called also *Indian cherry*

yellow bullhead *n* **:** a yellowish dark-mottled bullhead (*Ameiurus natalis*) widely distributed in central No. America and represented by subspecies in eastern coastal streams

yellow bunting *n* **:** YELLOWHAMMER 1

yellow calla *n* **:** a golden calla (*Zantedeschia elliottiana*) that resembles the common calla and is widely cultivated for its yellow spathes

yellow cancerroot *n* **:** a leafless scaly parasitic herb (*Orobanche fasciculata*) of western No. America having solitary purplish yellow irregular flowers

yellow carabeen *n* **:** CARABEEN

yellow carmine *n* **:** DUTCH ORANGE

yellow cartilage *n* **:** ELASTIC CARTILAGE

yellow cat *or* **yellow catfish** *n* **:** any of several more or less yellow No. American catfishes; *esp* **:** FLATHEAD CATFISH

yellow catechu *or* **yellow cutch** *n* **:** GAMBIER

yellow cedar *n* **1 a :** an evergreen tree (*Chamaecyparis nootkatensis*) of the Pacific coast of No. America often cultivated for ornament; *also* **:** the hard yellow wood of this tree — called also *Alaska cedar* **b :** WESTERN CEDAR 1a **c :** ARBORVITAE 1 **2** *Austral* **:** a sumac (*Rhus rhodanthema*) that yields tannin

yellow cell *n* **:** ZOOXANTHELLA

yellow centaury *n* **1 :** YELLOWWORT **2 :** a Barnaby's thistle (*Centaurea solstitialis*)

yellow chamomile *n* **:** a Eurasian perennial herb (*Anthemis tinctoria*) naturalized in No. America with hairy divided leaves and yellow heads — called also *golden marguerite*

yellow charlock *n* **:** CHARLOCK

yellow chestnut oak *n* **:** CHINQUAPIN OAK b

yellow cinchona *n* **:** CALISAYA BARK

yellow cleavers *n pl but sing or pl in constr* **:** YELLOW BEDSTRAW

yellow clintonia *n* **:** a common woodland herb (*Clintonia borealis*) of temperate regions of No. America with yellow nodding flowers and small round blue fruit

yellow clover *n* **:** either of two hop clovers (*Trifolium aureum* and *T. procumbens*)

yellow clover aphid *n* **:** a plant louse (*Therioaphis trifolii*) that occurs in many parts of the U.S. and is esp. destructive to alfalfa in the southwestern states

yellow cobra *n* **:** CAPE COBRA

yellow cockscomb *n* **:** a rattle (*Rhinanthus crista-galli*)

yellow copperas *n* **:** COPIAPITE

yellow copper ore *n* **:** CHALCOPYRITE

yellow corydalis *n* **:** YELLOW HARLEQUIN

yellow cottonwood *n* **:** a common cottonwood (*Populus deltoides*)

yellow cress *n* **:** a cress with yellow flowers: as **a :** WINTER CRESS **b :** any of several plants (as marsh cress) of the genus *Rorippa*

yellow cross *also* **yellow cross liquid** *n* [so called fr. the symbol used by the Germans in World War I to mark the shells containing it] **:** MUSTARD GAS

yellowcrown \ˈ⁼⁼,⁼\ *n* [¹*yellow* + *crown*] **:** MYRTLE WARBLER

yellow-crowned night heron \ˈ⁼⁼,⁼-\ *n* **:** a night heron (*Nyctanassa violacea*) that has a buffy white crown and is found in the southern U.S. and in So. America

yellow cypress *n* **1 :** YELLOW CEDAR 1a **2 :** a bald cypress (*Taxodium distichum*)

yellow daisy *n* **1 :** BLACK-EYED SUSAN **2 :** ORPIMENT 2

yellow day lily *n* **:** DAY LILY 1

yellow deal *n* **1** *Brit* **:** the wood of the Scotch pine and of a red pine (*Pinus resinosa*) **2 :** the wood of a yellow pine (*Pinus echinata*)

yellow devil *n* **:** any of several yellow-flowered hawkweeds (as *Hieracium pratense* and *H. floribundum*)

yellow dip *n* **:** the oleoresin obtained after the first year trees have been tapped for turpentine

yellow dock *n* **1 :** BITTER DOCK **2 :** CURLED DOCK

yellow dog *n* **1 :** MONGREL, CUR **2 :** a contemptible, worthless, or yellow person ‹any man who didn't stand by his friends . . . was a *yellow dog* —S.H.Adams›

yellow-dog \ˈ⁼⁼¦⁼\ *adj* [*yellow dog*] **1 :** of or relating to a yellow dog or characteristics associated with a yellow dog ‹pursues *yellow-dog* tactics to gain his ends› **2 :** of or relating to opposition to trade unionism or a labor union ‹the Administration's *yellow-dog* injunction has reached the Supreme Court —J.L.Lewis›

yellow-dog contract *n* **:** a contract of employment in which a worker disavows membership in and agrees not to join a labor union during the period of his employment

yellow dwarf *n* **:** any of several plant diseases (as yellow dwarf of potato and onion yellow dwarf) characterized by yellowing of the foliage and stunting

yellow earth *n* **:** impure yellow ocher

yellowed *past of* YELLOW

yellow edge *n* **:** a virus disease of the strawberry characterized chiefly by a marginal chlorosis of the leaf, shortening of the leaf stalk, leaf curling, and dwarfing

yellow eel *n* **:** an eel during the period of growth which varies from about 5 to about 20 years and before it matures as a silver eel — compare ELVER

yellow elder *n* **:** a tropical American shrub or small tree (*Stenolobium stans*) of the family Bignoniaceae that has compound leaves and profuse clusters of yellow funnel-shaped flowers and in the tropics is widely planted for ornament — called also *shower of gold, yellow trumpet flower*

yellow enzyme *n* **:** any of several yellow flavoprotein respiratory enzymes widely distributed in nature: as **a :** a crystallizable enzyme obtained from yeast and constituted of a complex of riboflavin phosphate and a protein — called also *old yellow enzyme, Warburg's yellow enzyme* **b :** an enzyme obtained from yeast and constituted of a complex of flavin adenine dinucleotide and a protein — called also *new yellow enzyme*

yellower *comparative of* YELLOW

yellowest *superlative of* YELLOW

yellow-eye \ˈ⁼⁼,⁼\ *n* [¹*yellow* + *eye*] **:** GOLDENSEAL

yellow-eyed grass \ˈ⁼⁼,⁼-\ *n* **:** a plant of the genus *Xyris*; *esp* **:** any of several such plants of the pine barrens of the southern U.S.

yellow-eyed-grass family *n* **:** XYRIDACEAE

yellow-eyed hawk *n* **:** IGNOBLE HAWK

yellow fat *or* **yellow fat disease** *n* **:** a disease of young ranched mink prob. associated with faulty diet and marked by inflammation of the fatty tissues, subcutaneous edema, and varied visceral lesions — called also *watery hide disease*

yellow fever *n* **:** an acute infectious disease that is characterized by sudden onset, prostration, fever, relatively slow pulse, albuminuria, jaundice, and tendency to hemorrhage esp. from the stomach, that is caused by a virus transmitted by a mosquito, and that occurs esp. in tropical and semitropical areas — called also *yellow jack*

yellow-fever fly *n* **:** a small fly of the genus *Sciara*

yellow-fever mosquito *n* **:** a small dark-colored mosquito (*Aëdes aegypti*) of the warmer parts of the world that is the usual agent in the transmission of yellow fever — compare ANOPHELES, CULEX

yellow fiber *n* **:** ELASTIC FIBER

yellowfin \ˈ⁼⁼,⁼\ *n* [¹*yellow* + *fin*] **1 a** *Scot* **:** TROUT **b** *Brit* **:** a sea trout smolt **2 a :** YELLOWFIN TUNA **b :** YELLOWFIN CROAKER

yellowfin croaker *n* **:** a common croaker (*Umbrina roncador*) of the southern California coast that is grayish or greenish with a metallic brassy luster and is a highly esteemed shallow-water sport fish

yellowfin grouper *n* **:** a medium-sized grouper (*Mycteroperca venenosa*) of the tropical western Atlantic that is olive to grayish or sometimes bright scarlet above, mottled or spotted with red or black along the sides, and yellow or orange at the tips of the pectoral fins

yellow-finned roncador *or* **yellow-fin roncador** \ˈ⁼⁼,⁼-\ *n* **:** YELLOWFIN CROAKER

yellow-fin trout *or* **yellow-finned trout** *n* **:** a large and showy cutthroat trout (*Salmo macdonaldi*) that has yellow fins and is native to Twin Lakes, Colorado

yellowfin tuna *n* **:** either of two tunas (*Neothunnus argentivittatus* and *N. macropterus*) of the Atlantic and of the Pacific respectively that are smaller and finer fleshed than the bluefin

yellow fir *n* **1 :** SCOTCH PINE **2 :** DOUGLAS FIR **3 :** LOWLAND FIR

yellowfish \ˈ⁼⁼,⁼\ *n* **1 :** ATKA MACKEREL **2 :** CONEY 5a **3 :** YELLOWFIN GROUPER

¹yellow flag *n* [¹*yellow* + *flag* (plant)] **:** YELLOW IRIS

²yellow flag *n* [¹*yellow* + *flag* (banner)] **:** QUARANTINE FLAG

yellow flax *n* **:** a yellow-flowered flax or similar plant; *esp* **:** an Indian shrub (*Reinwardtia indica*) having flowers usu. in axillary or terminal clusters

yellow flower *n* **:** CHARLOCK

yellow-flowered watercup \ˈ⁼⁼,⁼-\ *n* **:** HUNTSMAN'S-HORN

yellow foxglove *n* **1** *or* **yellow gerardia :** FALSE FOXGLOVE **2 :** a European yellow-flowered herb (*Digitalis lutea*)

yellow foxtail *n* **:** a common weedy and bristly grass (*Setaria glauca*) found in nearly all temperate countries

yellow fringed orchid *or* **yellow fringed orchis** *n* **:** a terrestrial orchid (*Habenaria ciliaris*) of eastern No. America having lanceolate leaves and showy spikes of yellow or orange fringed flowers

yellow gentian *n* **1 :** a bitterwort (*Gentiana lutea*) of southern Europe having yellow flowers — see GENTIAN 2 **2 :** a gentian (*Dasystephana flavida*) of eastern No. America with yellowish flowers **3 :** AMERICAN COLUMBO

yellow ginger *n* **:** a large yellow-flowered herb (*Hedychium flavum*) that is similar to the white ginger and occurs both wild and cultivated in Hawaii

yellow ginseng *n* **:** BLUE COHOSH

yellow goatfish *n* **:** a goatfish (*Upeneus martinicus*) — compare ²MULLET 2

yellow goatsbeard *n* **:** a European herb (*Tragopogon pratensis*) that is naturalized as a weed in No. America and that has keeled leaves and yellow heads of flowers that close by noon — called also *meadow salsify*

yellow gowan *n, dial Brit* **:** any of several yellow-flowered plants: as **a :** CROWFOOT 1 **b :** a marsh marigold (*Caltha palustris*) **c :** DANDELION 1

yellow granadilla *n* **:** JAMAICA HONEYSUCKLE

yellow grease *n* **:** an inedible fat obtained esp. from the parts of hogs not used in making lard, from condemned animals, or from refuse fat and used as a lubricant — compare WHITE GREASE

yellow-green alga *n* **:** an alga of the division Chrysophyta with the chlorophyll masked by brown or yellow pigment

yellow ground *n* [trans. of Afrik *geelgrond*] **:** kimberlite found in the upper portion of a pipe

yellow grouper *n* **1 :** a grouper (*Mycteroperca olfax*) of the Pacific coast of Central and So. America **2 :** YELLOWFIN GROUPER

yellow grub *n* **:** a larval trematode worm (genus *Clinostomum*) that encysts in the flesh of fishes

yellow grunt *n* **:** a yellow black-banded grunt (*Haemulon sciurus*) used as a food fish and found from Florida to the West Indies and south to Brazil

yellow guayacan *n* **:** BETHABARA

yellow gularis *n* **:** GULARIS a

yellow gum *n* **1 :** any of several Australian eucalypts (as *Eucalyptus gunnii*) **2 :** BLACK GUM 1a

yellow-haired porcupine \'==,=-\ *n* **:** a somewhat yellowish American porcupine (*Erethizon epixanthum*)

yel·low·ham·mer \'==,hamə(r)\ *n* [alter. of earlier *yelambre*, fr. (assumed) ME *yelwambre*, fr. *yelwe* yellow + (assumed) *ambre* yellowhammer, fr. OE *amore;* akin to OS *amer* yellowhammer, OHG *amaro* yellowhammer, *amaro*, *amari* spelt, emmer] **1 :** a common European finch (*Emberiza citrinella*) that in the male is bright yellow on the breast, neck, and sides of the head with the back yellow and brown and the top of the head and the tail quills blackish — called also *yellow bunting* **2 :** YELLOW-SHAFTED FLICKER

yellow harlequin *n* **:** a slender low-branching No. American herb (*Corydalis flavula*) with conspicuously bracted and spurred pale yellow flowers — usu. used in pl.; called also *yellow corydalis*

yellowhead \'==,=\ *n* [[1]*yellow* + *head*] **1 :** BUSH CANARY **2 :** YELLOW-HEADED BLACKBIRD

yellow-headed blackbird \'==,==-\ *n* **:** a large blackbird (*Xanthocephalus xanthocephalus*) of central western No. America that in the male is black with the head and neck orange or yellow

yellow-headed spruce sawfly *n* **:** a No. American sawfly (*Pikonema alaskensis*) that often defoliates spruce in eastern Canada and the northeastern U.S.

yellow-headed tit *n* **:** VERDIN

yellow henbane *n* **:** a ground-cherry (*Physalis viscosa*) found on seabeaches from Virginia to So. America with greenish yellow dark-centered flowers and orange or yellow fruit

yellow hercules *n, usu cap H* **:** HERCULES'-CLUB 1a

yellow honeysuckle *n* **1 :** either of two honeysuckles: **a :** a woody vine (*Lonicera dioica*) of eastern No. America with yellowish green flowers **b :** a twining or loosely climbing shrub (*L. flava*) of the southern U.S. with orange-yellow flowers **2 :** FLAME AZALEA

yellow indian grass *n, usu cap I* **:** WOOD GRASS 1

yellow indian paint *n, usu cap I* **:** GOLDENSEAL 1

yellow indian shoe *n, usu cap I* **:** a yellow lady's-slipper (*Cypripedium parviflorum*)

yellow indigo *n* **:** INDIGO BROOM

yellowing *n* -S [fr. gerund of [2]*yellow*] **:** the process or result of becoming yellow; *specif* **:** a symptom of disease caused by a lack of or a reduced amount of chlorophyll in the foliage of a plant or tree

yellow iris *n* [[1]*yellow*] **:** a common yellow-flowered iris (*Iris pseudacorus*) of Europe and northern Africa that is naturalized in the U.S. and often cultivated — called also *yellow flag, yellow water flag*

yel·low·ish \'yeləw|ish, -lō|, |ēsh\ *adj* [ME *yelowissche*, fr. *yelow* yellow + *-issche, -ish* -ish] **:** somewhat yellow **:** having a tinge of yellow ⟨a ~ green⟩

yellow jack *n* **1 :** YELLOW FEVER **2 :** QUARANTINE FLAG **3 a :** a silvery and golden food fish (*Caranx bartholomaei*) of Florida and the West Indies **b :** the related blue runner

yellow jacket *n* [[1]*yellow* + *jacket*] **1** *or* **yellow hornet :** any of various small yellow-marked social wasps of the family Vespidae that commonly nest in the ground — compare HORNET **2 :** any of several Australian eucalypts with yellowish bark: as **a :** YELLOW BOX **b :** a red gum (*Eucalyptus rostrata*) **3** [so called fr. the color of the capsules] *slang* **:** BARBITURATE 2

yellow jacket

yellow jessamine *also* **yellow jasmine** *n* **1 :** JASMINE 1a(2) **2 :** a twining shrub (*Gelsemium sempervirens*) having evergreen leaves and fragrant yellow flowers with a funnelform corolla — called also *Carolina jessamine*

yellowknife \'==,=\ *n, pl* **yellowknife** *or* **yellowknives** *usu cap* [[1]*yellow* + *knife;* fr. their use of copper implements] **1 :** an Algonquian people living east of Great Slave Lake, Canada, being closely related to the Chipewyan, and speaking the same language **2 :** a member of such people

yellow lady's-slipper *also* **yellow lady-slipper** *n* **:** a yellow-flowered orchid of the genus *Cypripedium* (as *C. calceolus, C. parviflorum*)

yellow lantern *n* **:** SPATTERDOCK 1

yellow late rust *n* **:** a rust of the blackberry caused by a rust fungus (*Kuehneola albida*)

yellow lead ore *n* **:** WULFENITE

yellow leaf *n* **1 :** any of several diseases of plants characterized by chlorosis of the foliage (as cherry leaf spot) **2 :** the latter years of life **:** OLD AGE ⟨my way of life is fall'n into the sere, the *yellow leaf* —Shak.⟩ ⟨fifty-three . . . the *yellow leaf* is upon me —Christopher Isherwood⟩

yellow leaf blight *n* **:** a mosaic disease of cotton

yellow leaf blotch *n* **:** a disease of alfalfa caused by a fungus (*Pyrenopeziza medicaginis*) and characterized by bright yellow or orange spots with small black dots chiefly on the undersides of the leaves

yellow leafcup *n* **:** a roughish hairy leafcup (*Polymnia uvedalia*) with yellow flowers

yellow leaf roll *n* **:** a virus disease of peaches esp. in California characterized by yellowing and upward rolling of the leaf, some scorching on the leaf margins and necrotic spotting, and early dropping of the leaves

yellow-legged goose \'==,=(=)-\ *n* **:** WHITE-FRONTED GOOSE

yellow-legged plover *n* **:** YELLOWLEGS

yellow-leg·ger \'==,legə(r)\ *n* [[1]*yellow* + *leg* + *-er*] **:** YELLOWLEGS

yellowlegs \'==,=\ *n pl but sing or pl in constr* [[1]*yellow* + *legs*, pl. of *leg*] **:** either of two American shore birds that are related to the greenshank and have long yellow legs: **a :** GREATER YELLOWLEGS **b :** LESSER YELLOWLEGS

yellow lemur *n* **:** KINKAJOU

yellow lily *n* **:** MEADOW LILY

yellow linn *n* **:** a cucumber tree (*Magnolia acuminata*)

yellow locust *n* **1 :** LOCUST 3a(2) **2 :** YELLOWWOOD 1a

yellow lotus *or* **yellow nelumbo** *n* **:** AMERICAN LOTUS

yellow lupine *n* **1 :** a European yellow-flowered lupine (*Lupinus luteus*) cultivated as a forage plant **2 :** an annual herb (*Crotalaria retusa*) of tropical Asia that has yellow flowers and is cultivated as a forage crop in the tropics

yel·low·ly *adv* [[1]*yellow* + *-ly*] **:** with a yellow light or color ⟨the brand-new ropes . . . glistened ~ —Adria Langley⟩

yellow mackerel *n* **:** BLUE RUNNER

yellow madder *n* **:** DUTCH PINK 2

yellow mahogany *n* **:** BRAZILIAN MAHOGANY 1

yellow mandarin *n* **:** a low pubescent No. American herb (*Disporum lanuginosum*) found in rich woods and having greenish flowers with narrow segments

yellow maple *n* **:** a variable color averaging a moderate yellowish brown that is lighter, stronger, and slightly redder than Bismarck brown and lighter, stronger, and very slightly yellower than cinnamon brown

yellow-mar·gined leaf-beetle \'==,märjənd-\ *n* [[1]*yellow* + *margin* + *-ed*] **:** a chrysomelid beetle (*Microtheca ochroloma*) that is destructive to crucifers esp. in the southeastern U.S.

yellow marsh saxifrage *n* **:** a slender perennial bog herb (*Saxifraga hirculus*) of the family Saxifragaceae that is found in alpine regions of the northern hemisphere and has a terminal solitary bright yellow red-spotted flower

yellow mealworm *n* **:** a mealworm that is the larva of a beetle (*Tenebrio molitor*)

yellow melilot *n* **:** YELLOW SWEET CLOVER 1

yellow metal *n* **:** MUNTZ METAL

yellow milkweed *n* **:** BUTTERFLY WEED 1

yellow milkwort *n* **:** ORANGE MILKWORT

yellow moccasin flower *or* **yellow noah's-ark** *n, usu cap N* **:** a yellow lady's-slipper (*Cypripedium parviflorum*)

yellow mombin *n* **:** a hog plum (*Spondias mombin*) with yellowish white flowers and yellow fruit

yellow mountain saxifrage *n* **:** a tufted perennial herb (*Saxifraga aizoides*) of alpine regions of the northern hemisphere having ciliate leaves and yellow sometimes orange-spotted corymbose flowers

yellow mustard *n* **:** CHARLOCK

yellow myrtle *n* **1 :** CALIFORNIA LAUREL **2 :** MONEYWORT

yellow-necked caterpillar \'==,=-\ *n* **:** a predominantly black gregarious caterpillar with a yellow thorax, yellow longitudinal stripes, and a covering of white hairs down each side that is the larva of a handmaid moth (*Datana ministra*) and that is often a destructive defoliator of fruit and other deciduous trees and shrubs

yel·low·ness *n* -ES [ME *yelownes*, fr. *yelow* yellow + *-nes* -ness] **:** the quality or state of being yellow

yellow nightshade *n* **:** BUFFALO BUR

yellow-nosed albatross \'==,=-\ *n* **:** an albatross (*Diomedea chlororhynchos*) of southern seas that is distinguished by the narrower black edging of the underwings and by a bright yellow ridgeline on the upper beak

yellow nut grass *n* **:** CHUFA

yellow oak *n* **1 :** a black oak (*Quercus velutina*) **2 :** CHINQUAPIN OAK a

yellow oat grass *also* **yellow oats** *n* **:** a Eurasian grass (*Trisetum flavescens*) with yellow panicles that is sometimes cultivated

yellow ocher *n* [ME *yelu okyr*, fr. *yelow, yelu* yellow + *oker, okyr* ocher] **1 :** a mixture of limonite usu. with clay and silica used as a pigment **2 :** a moderate orange yellow that is yellower and darker than deep chrome yellow — called also *Chinese yellow, English ocher, French ocher, imperial yellow, Italian lake, mineral yellow, ocher yellow, Oxford chrome, Oxford ocher, oxide yellow, permanent yellow, quercitron lake, yellow sienna*

yellow oleander *n* **:** a West Indian shrub or small tree (*Thevetia nereifolia*) with showy clusters of yellow flowers and leaves resembling those of the oleander

yellow owl *n* **:** BARN OWL

yellow oxeye *n* **1 :** CORN MARIGOLD **2 :** BLACK-EYED SUSAN

yellow oxide *also* **yellow oxide of iron** *n* **:** a synthetic pigment consisting essentially of hydrated ferric oxide and similar in color to yellow ocher but more intense

yellow palm warbler *n* **:** a chiefly terrestrial warbler (*Dendroica palmarum hypochrysea*) of eastern No. America that is largely grayish brown above with bright yellow underparts

yellow pareira *also* **yellow pareira brava** *n* **:** a pareira that is the root of a tropical American woody vine (*Abuta amara*), is bright yellow in color and extremely bitter in flavor, and contains some of the same alkaloids as the true pareira — compare WHITE PAREIRA

yellow pa·ril·la \-pə'rilə\ *n* [[1]*yellow* + sarsa*parilla*] **:** CANADA MOONSEED

yellow pea *n* **:** FALSE LUPINE

yellow perch *n* **:** a common No. American perch (*Perca flavescens*) that is yellowish with dark green bands and is an excellent food and sport fish

yellow peril *n, often cap Y&P* **1 :** a danger to Western civilization held to arise from expansion of the power and influence of Oriental peoples (as the Chinese and Japanese) **2 :** a threat to Western living standards developed through the incursion into Western countries of Oriental laborers willing to work for very low wages and under inferior working conditions

yellow phlox *n* **:** WESTERN WALLFLOWER 1

yellow phosphorus *n* **:** WHITE PHOSPHORUS

yellow pickerel *or* **yellow pike** *or* **yellow pikeperch** *n* **:** WALLEYE 4

yellow pickle *n* **:** a nutritional disturbance of cucumbers causing premature ripening

yellow pimpernel *n* **1 :** a perennial herb (*Taenidia integerrima*) of the family Umbelliferae of eastern No. America with ternate leaves and compound umbels of yellow flowers **2 :** WOOD PIMPERNEL

yellow pine *n* **1 :** any of various No. American pines: as **a :** a shortleaf pine (*Pinus echinata*) **b :** LONGLEAF PINE **c :** TABLE-MOUNTAIN PINE **d :** a pitch pine (*Pinus rigida*) **e :** LOBLOLLY PINE 1 **f :** PONDEROSA PINE **g :** ARIZONA PINE **2 :** the wood of a yellow pine

yellow plover *n* **:** GOLDEN PLOVER

yellow plum *n* **:** an often shrubby and somewhat spiny wild plum (*Prunus americana*) with red to yellow fruit — compare AMERICAN PLUM

yellow podzolic soil *or* **yellow soil** *n* **:** any of a group of zonal soils developed under coniferous or mixed forests in warm-temperate moist climates and composed of thin organic and organic-mineral layers resting on a grayish yellow leached layer that in turn rests on a yellow layer

yellow poinciana *n* **:** PRIDE OF BARBADOS

yellow poll *n* **1 :** WIDGEON 1a(1) **2 :** YELLOW WARBLER 1

yellow pond lily *n* **:** SPATTERDOCK

yellow poplar *n* **1 a :** TULIP TREE **b :** TULIPWOOD 1 **2 :** the soft and light but durable wood of the common cucumber tree (*Magnolia acuminata*) of the southeastern U.S.

yellow poppy *n* **1 :** a prickly poppy (*Argemone mexicana*) **2 :** CELANDINE POPPY

yellow precipitate *n* **:** yellow mercuric oxide esp. for use in ophthalmic ointments

yellow prickly ash *n* **:** HERCULES'-CLUB 1a

yellow prussiate of potash : POTASSIUM FERROCYANIDE

yellow prussiate of soda : SODIUM FERROCYANIDE

yellow puccoon *n* **:** GOLDENSEAL 1

yellow pyrites *n* **:** CHALCOPYRITE

yellow rail *n* **:** a very small American rail (*Coturnicops noveboracensis*) of which the lower parts are dull yellow and darkest on the breast and the back is streaked with brownish, yellow, and black color and spotted with white

yellow rain lily *n* **1 :** a bulbous herb (*Zephyranthes texana*) of the prairies of Texas with basal linear leaves and showy yellow or copper-colored purple-striped flowers **2 :** an herb (*Zephyranthes longifolia*) with clear-yellow flowers that is closely related to the Texas plant

yellow rattle *n* **:** RATTLE 3a

yellow redpoll *n* **:** YELLOW PALM WARBLER

yellow-red virosis *n* **:** X-DISEASE d

yellow rocket *n* **:** a winter cress (esp. *Barbarea vulgaris*)

yellow rockrose *also* **yellow rose** *n* **:** SHRUBBY CINQUEFOIL

yellowroot \'==,=\ *n* [[1]*yellow* + *root*] **:** any of several plants with yellow roots: as **a :** SHRUB YELLOWROOT **b :** GOLDENSEAL 1 **c :** a goldthread (*Coptis groenlandica*) **d :** TWINLEAF

yellow root rot *n* [[1]*yellow* + *root rot*] **:** a root rot of fir, spruce, pine, and larch caused by a club fungus (*Sparassis radicata*)

yellow-rumped warbler \'==,=-\ *or* **yellowrump** \'==,=\ *n* **:** MYRTLE WARBLER

yellow rust *n* **:** STRIPE RUST

yellows *pres 3d sing of* YELLOW, *pl of* YELLOW

yellow sage *n* **:** RED SAGE 1

yellow sally *n, usu cap S* **:** a greenish or yellowish European stone fly (genus *Chloroperla*)

yellow sandbox *n* **:** a mature sandbox tree with yellowish wood — compare WHITE SANDBOX

yellow sanders *n* **1 :** any of several tropical American trees or shrubs: as **a :** MOUNTAIN PLUM **b :** a West Indian tree (*Zanthoxylum flavum*) **2 a :** the wood of a yellow sanders **b :** GRANADILLA WOOD 3

yellow sarsaparilla *n* **:** CANADA MOONSEED

yellow scale *n* **:** a scale (*Aonidiella citrina*) that is closely related to the California red scale and attacks citrus in the southwestern U. S., India, and Japan

yellow sedge *n* **1 :** a common sedge (*Carex flava*) with yellowish green culms that is found in No. America and Europe **2 :** YELLOW IRIS

yellowseed \'==,=\ *n* [[1]*yellow* + *seed*] **:** FIELD CRESS

yellow-shafted flicker \'==,==-\ *n* **:** a common woodpecker (*Colaptes auratus*) of eastern No. America conspicuous from its large size and bright symmetrical markings among which are a black crescent on the breast, red nape, white rump, and yellow shafts to the tail and wing feathers — called also *yellowhammer*

yellowshank \'==,=\ *n* [[1]*yellow* + *shank*] **:** YELLOWLEGS

yellowshanks *or* **yellowshins** \'==,=\ *n pl but sing or pl in constr* [[1]*yellow* + *shanks* (pl. of *shank*) or *shins*, pl. of *shin*] **:** YELLOWLEGS

yellow shore crab *n* **:** a shore crab (*Hemigrapsus oregonensis*) of the Pacific coast that generally resembles the purple shore crab but is yellow or gray often with purplish brown or black spots, lacks red on the chelae, and has notably hairy legs

yellow sienna *n* **:** YELLOW OCHER

yel·low·sis \'yelōsəs\ *n, pl* **yellow·ses** \-ō,sēz\ [NL, fr. E [1]*yellow* + NL *-sis*] **:** a photodynamic disease of Scottish sheep marked by dermatitis esp. of the head and face with accumulation of cells and fluid in the subcutaneous spaces and by jaundice — compare GEELDIKKOP

yellow skegs \-'skegz\ *n pl but sing or pl in constr* [[1]*yellow* + E dial. *skegs*, pl. of *skeg* yellow iris, of unknown origin] **:** YELLOW IRIS

yellow snake *n* **:** a West Indian boa (*Epicrates inornatus*) that is common in Jamaica, becomes from 8 to 10 feet long, and has a body that is yellowish or yellowish green mixed with black and anteriorly with black lines

yellow snakeleaf *or* **yellow snowdrop** *n* **:** DOGTOOTH VIOLET

yellow soap *n* **:** a yellow to brown soap used chiefly in laundering; *esp* **:** ROSIN SOAP 1

yellow soft paraffin *n* **:** PETROLATUM a

yellow soil *var of* YELLOW PODZOLIC SOIL

yellow sponge *n* **:** a yellow or brownish short-fibered commercial sponge (*Spongia barbara* or *S. officinalis barbara*) occurring in the Gulf of Mexico and in the Atlantic ocean off the West Indies

[1]**yellow spot** *n* [trans. of NL *macula lutea*] **:** MACULA LUTEA

[2]**yellow spot** *n* [[1]*yellow* + *spot*] **1 :** a small American skipper (*Polites peckius*) of the family Hesperiidae having brownish wings with a large irregular bright-yellow spot on each of the hind wings that is most conspicuous beneath **2 :** TOMATO HORNWORM **3 :** any of several plant diseases characterized by yellow spotting on the foliage: as **a :** TOMATO STREAK **b :** a sugarcane disease that is serious in Australia and is caused by a fungus (*Cercospora kopkei*) **c :** a disease of wheat caused by a fungus (*Helminthosporium tritici-vulgaris*) **d :** a virus disease of pineapple

yellow spruce *n* **1 :** RED SPRUCE **2 :** SITKA SPRUCE **3 :** DOUGLAS FIR

yellow star *n* **1 :** SNEEZEWEED 1a **2 :** SOLAR STAR

yellow star grass *n* **:** a perennial grasslike herb (*Hypoxis hirsuta*) of eastern No. America with loose umbels of yellow star-shaped flowers

yellow star thistle *n* **:** a Barnaby's thistle (*Centaurea solstitialis*)

yellow starwort *n* **:** ELECAMPANE

yellow stone *n* **:** a grayish greenish yellow that is slightly paler than the color hay, paler than absinthe yellow, and greener and duller than dusty yellow — compare YELLOWSTONE

yellowstone \'==,=\ *n* **:** a dark grayish yellow that is redder, stronger, and slightly lighter than California green or olive-sheen and very slightly greener than honey — compare YELLOW STONE

yellow stonecrop *n* **1 :** DWARF HOUSELEEK **2 :** a stonecrop (*Sedum acre*)

yellowstone trout *n, usu cap Y* [fr. *Yellowstone* river & *Yellowstone* Lake, northwest Wyoming] **:** a cutthroat trout of the northern Rocky mountain area that is sometimes distinguished as a separate species (*Salmo lewisi*)

yellow strawberry *n* **:** INDIAN STRAWBERRY 1

yellow stringybark *or* **yellow stringy** *n* **:** any of various stringybarks (esp. *Eucalyptus muelleriana*)

yellow stripe *n* **:** a virus disease of sugarcane characterized by a mottling and striping of the foliage

yellow-striped armyworm \'==,=(=)-\ *n* **:** a caterpillar that is the larva of a noctuid moth (*Prodenia ornithogalli*) and that is a general plant feeder in the western U. S. and a serious pest on cotton in the southern states

yellow stripe rust *n* **:** STRIPE RUST

yellow suckling *or* **yellow suckling clover** *n* **:** a rather small annual hop clover of European origin but widely naturalized and sometimes sown for cover crop or pasture

yellow sugarcane aphid *n* **:** a plant louse (*Sipha flava*) that feeds on sugarcane, grain, and orchard grass in the southern U. S.

yellow swallowtail *n* **:** TIGER SWALLOWTAIL

yellow sweet clover *n* **1 :** a biennial yellow-flowered Eurasian sweet clover (*Melilotus officinalis*) that has aromatic leaves sometimes used as a carminative or flavoring agent, is widely cultivated esp. as a green manure and cover crop, and is naturalized in many parts of the world **2 :** BITTER CLOVER

yellow tacamahac *n* **:** an East Indian tree (*Calophyllum inophyllum*); *also* **:** an oleoresin obtained from this tree

yellowtail \'==,=\ *n, pl* **yellowtail** *or* **yellowtails** [[1]*yellow* + *tail*] **:** any of various fishes having a yellow or yellowish tail: as **a :** an amberfish of the genus *Seriola* — see CALIFORNIA YELLOWTAIL **b :** a mademoiselle (*Bairdiella chrysura*) **c :** RAINBOW RUNNER **d :** PINFISH a **e** *or* **yellowtail snapper :** a common snapper (*Ocyurus chrysurus*) of the tropical western Atlantic and West Indies that is olive above and broadly striped with yellow along the sides and on the tail and highly esteemed for sport and food **f :** SPOT 7 **g** *Austral* **:** a small yellowish green carangid food fish (*Trachurus declivis*) **h :** RUSTY DAB **i :** [1]BUMPER 3

yellowtail rockcod *or* **yellowtail rockfish** *n* **:** a commercially important rockfish (*Sebastodes flavidus*) of the Pacific coast of No. America that is grayish brown above shading to white below and spotted with yellow on the sides and has a yellow tail fin

yellow tang *n* **:** a rockweed (*Ascophyllum nodosum*)

yellow tarweed *n* **:** a sticky annual California herb (*Hemizonia virgata*) of the family Compositae with crowded small leaves and axillary yellow flower heads

yellow teat disease *n* **:** ANAPLASMOSIS

yellow thick head *n* [trans. of Afrik *geeldikkop*] **:** GEELDIKKOP

yellow thistle *n* **:** a thistle (*Cirsium horridulum*) of eastern No. America having yellow heads

yellowthroat \'==,=\ *n* [[1]*yellow* + *throat*] **:** any of several American ground warblers of the genus *Geothlypis; esp* **:** MARYLAND YELLOWTHROAT

yellow-throated marten \'==,==-\ *n* **:** a large strikingly marked yellow and black mustelid mammal (*Charronia flavigula*) of mountainous southern China and Burma

yellow-throated vireo *n* **:** a vireo (*Vireo flavifrons*) of eastern No. America with bright yellow throat and breast

yellow-throated warbler *n* **:** a wood warbler (*Dendroica dominica*) of the southern U. S.

yellow tip *n* [[1]*yellow* + *tip*] **:** a copper deficiency disease of cereals characterized by chlorotic leaf tips and failure of the plants to set seed

yellow tit *n* **:** any of several crested titmice of the genus *Parus* that are natives of southern Asia and have chiefly yellow and green plumage

yellow toadflax *n* **:** a toadflax (*Linaria vulgaris*)

yellowtop \'==,=\ *n* [[1]*yellow* + *top*] **1 a :** any of several goldenrods; *esp* **:** EARLY GOLDENROD — sometimes pl. but sing. in constr. **b :** BITTER CLOVER **c :** GOLDEN CROWNBEARD **2 :** any of several plant diseases characterized by yellowing of the upper foliage: as **a :** a disease of alfalfa of undetermined

cause characterized by a pronounced yellowing of the upper portions of affected plants **b** : a yellowing of alfalfa tops caused by the punctures of the potato leafhopper
yellow trefoil *n* : BLACK MEDIC
yellow trumpet *n* : HUNTSMAN'S-HORN
yellow trumpet flower *n* : YELLOW ELDER
yellow ultramarine *n* : any of various yellow pigments (as barium yellow)
yellow umbil *n* : a yellow lady's-slipper (*Cypripedium parviflorum*)
yellow vetchling *n* : MEADOW PEA
yellow violet *n* : any of several violets with yellow flowers; *esp* : SWEET VIOLET
yellow viper *n* : FER-DE-LANCE
yellow vole *n* : a buff-colored Asiatic vole (*Microtus brandtii*)
yellow wagtail *n* : a wagtail of the genus *Motacilla; esp* : a common Eurasian wagtail (*M. flava*) of which a race (*M. f. tschutschensis*) reaches the coast of northwestern Alaska
yellow warbler *n* **1 a** : a small No. American warbler (*Dendroica petechia*) very common throughout the U. S. and frequently breeding in shade trees in cities and villages and having the male bright yellow with brown streaks on the underparts **b** : any of various related warblers of Central America and the West Indies **2** *dial Eng* : WILLOW WARBLER
yellowware \ˈ≈≈,≈\ *n* : pottery made from buff clay and covered with a yellowish transparent glaze
yellow wart *n* : POTATO WART
yellow wash *n* : a suspension of yellow mercuric oxide in water prepared by adding a solution of mercuric chloride to limewater and used as an antiseptic application to syphilitic sores and in eczema
yellow watercress *n* : a plant of the genus *Rorippa*: as **a** : a Eurasian perennial weedy herb (*R. sylvestris*) naturalized in No. America in wet places and having divided leaves and yellow flowers in loose racemes **b** : MARSH CRESS
yellow water crowfoot *n* : an aquatic buttercup (*Ranunculus flabellaris*) of northern No. America with finely divided leaves and rather showy yellow flowers
yellow water flag *n* : YELLOW IRIS
yellow water lily *n* : a yellow-flowered water lily; *esp* : SPATTERDOCK
yellow wax *n* : any of various yellow waxy substances: as **a** : BEESWAX 2a **b** : a semisolid portion of wax tailings obtained in petroleum distillation
yellow weasel *n* : a large orange-brown kolinsky (*Mustela sibirica*)
yellowweed \ˈ≈≈,≈\ *n* **1** : SNEEZEWEED 1 **2** : any of several goldenrods **3** : ²RAPE 2 **4** : TANSY RAGWORT **5** : DYER'S ROCKET **6** : WINTER CRESS **7** : BALL MUSTARD
yellow willow *n* **1** : GOLDEN WILLOW **2** : a No. American shrub or small tree (*Salix lutea*) having branches and branchlets that are yellow and then become gray and leaves that are yellow-green above
yellow willow herb *n* : a common loosestrife (*Lysimachia vulgaris*)
yellow-winged bat \ˈ≈≈,≈-\ *n* : a tropical African insectivorous bat (genus *Lavia*) having more or less clear yellow wings
yellow-winged sparrow *n* : a grasshopper sparrow (*Ammodramus savannarum pratensis*)
yellowwood \ˈ≈≈,≈\ *n* [¹*yellow* + *wood*] **1** : any of various trees having wood that is yellowish or yielding a yellow extract: as **a** : a tree (*Cladrastis lutea*) of the southern U. S. that has odd-pinnate leaves and showy white fragrant flowers in terminal clusters and heavy hardwood which yields a yellow dye — called also *gopherwood* **b** : OSAGE ORANGE **c** : SWEETLEAF **d** : BUCKTHORN **e** : SMOKE TREE 1 **f** : FLORIDA BOXWOOD **g** : SHRUB YELLOWROOT **h** : any of various West Indian trees or shrubs of the genus *Zanthoxylum; esp* : SATINWOOD 2a(1) **i** : FUSTIC 1a **j** (1) : an Australian tree (*Achronychia laevis*) of the family Rutaceae (2) : SASSAFRAS 3a(2) (3) : an Australian sumac (*Rhus rhodanthema*) that yields a dark yellow wood (4) : LONG JACK **k** : SOUTH AFRICAN YELLOWWOOD; *broadly* : an African tree of the genus *Podocarpus* **l** : any of several trees of the genus *Terminalia* **2** : the wood of a yellowwood tree

yellowwood: leaf, pod, and flowers

yellow wood sorrel *n* : a yellow-flowered plant of the genus *Oxalis*
yellow woolly bear *n* : a woolly bear that is the larva of an ermine moth (*Diacrisia virginica*) and is predominantly yellow in color — called also *yellow bear*
yellowwort \ˈ≈≈,≈\ *n* : a European yellow-flowered bitter herb (*Chlora perfoliata*) of the family Gentianaceae that is sometimes used as a tonic
yellow wove *n* : a cheap blue wove paper
yellow wren *n* **1** : a willow warbler (*Phylloscopus trochilus*) **2** *dial Eng* : WOOD WARBLER 2
yel·lowy \ˈyeləwē\ *adj* [¹*yellow* + *-y*] : YELLOWISH
yellow yam *n, South* : SWEET POTATO
yellow yel·drock \-ˈyeldrək\ *n* [¹*yellow* + E dial. *yeldrock, yeldrick, yeldring* yellowhammer, fr. ¹*yellow*] *dial Brit* : YELLOWHAMMER
yellow yolk *n* : darker yolk that alternates with white yolk and forms the thicker layers of the central yolk mass (as of a bird's egg)
¹**yelm** \ˈyelm\ *n* -s [ME, fr. OE *gelm, gilm* sheaf] *dial Eng* : a bundle of combed straw for thatching
²**yelm** \ˈ"\ *vi* -ED/-ING/-s *dial Eng* : to prepare bundles of straw for thatching
¹**yelp** \ˈyelp, ˈyeu̇p\ *vb* -ED/-ING/-s [ME *yelpen* to boast, call out, fr. OE *gielpan* to boast, exult; akin to OE *gielp* pride, arrogance, praise, OHG *gelph* outcry, revelry, ON *gjalp* boasting, Lith *gulbinti* to praise, and prob. to OE *giellan* to yell — more at YELL] *vi* **1** : to utter a sharp quick cry (as of a hound or turkey) : bark shrilly **2** : to squeal, cry out, or call in shrill sharp manner ⟨ladies and gentlemen who ~ at one another with unmistakable breeding —Wolcott Gibbs⟩ ⟨woodwind cascades that veritably ~ with exuberance —Winthrop Sargeant⟩ ~ *vt* : to utter with a yelp ⟨~*ing* a few phrases in his surprisingly shrill falsetto voice —James Cameron⟩
²**yelp** \ˈ"\ *n* -s **1** : the sharp shrill bark of a dog or other animal **2** : a sharp cry or call : SQUEAL ⟨gave a ~ of alarm⟩
yelp·er \-pə(r)\ *n* -s **1** : one that yelps: as **a** : a yelping dog **b** *dial Eng* : AVOCET **c** *dial* : GREATER YELLOWLEGS **d** *dial Eng* : REDSHANK **1 2** : an instrument used by hunters to produce a call or whistle imitating the yelp of the wild turkey hen **3** : one whose utterance is a sound without sense or resembles a dog's bark ⟨that species of orators called the ~*s* —Sir Walter Scott⟩
yemassee *usu cap, var of* YAMASEE
yem·en \ˈyemən, ˈyām-\ *adj, usu cap* [fr. *Yemen*, country of southwest Arabia] : of or from Yemen : of the kind or style prevalent in Yemen : YEMENI
¹**yem·e·ni** \-nē\ *n* -s *cap* [Ar *yamanī*, fr. *Yaman* Yemen] : YEMENITE
²**yemeni** \ˈ"\ *adj, usu cap* : YEMENITE
¹**yem·en·ite** \-mə,nīt\ *n* -s *cap* [*Yemen* + E *-ite*] : a native or inhabitant of Yemen
²**yemenite** \ˈ"\ *adj, usu cap* : of or relating to Yemen or its inhabitants
¹**yen** \ˈyen\ *n* -s [Jap *en* circle, yen, fr. Chin (Pek) *yüan²* round, circle, dollar] **1** : the basic monetary unit of Japan — see MONEY table **2** : a coin or note representing one yen
²**yen** \ˈ"\ *n* -s [obs. E slang *yen-yen* craving for opium, fr. Chin (Cant) *in-yăn*, fr. *in* opium + *yăn* craving] **1** : an impelling craving for opium or some other narcotic ⟨wanted a fix to get his ~ off⟩ **2** : a strong desire or propensity : LONGING ⟨a ~ to see the world⟩ : URGE ⟨whatever you have a ~ to do — ride, swim, or fish —*Saturday Night*⟩
³**yen** \ˈ"\ *vi* **yenned; yenned; yenning; yens** : to desire intensely : LONG, YEARN
yen·der \ˈyendə(r)\ *dial var of* YONDER
yen-hok \ˈyenˈhäk\ *n* [Chin (Cant) *yin-hŏk*, fr. *in, yin* opium + *hŏk* dipper, ladle] : a needlelike instrument used in the preparation of opium pills
yeni \ˈyenē\ *n* -s [NL (specific epithet of *Calospiza yeni*), of AmerInd origin] : a showy tanager (*Calospiza chilensis* syn. *C. yeni*) of eastern Ecuador, Bolivia, and Peru
yen·i·sei \ˌyenəˈsā\ *n* -s *cap* [fr. *Yenisei* river, western Siberia] : the Uralic language of the Yeniseian people — see URALIC LANGUAGES table
yen·i·sei·an \-āən\ *n* -s *usu cap* [*Yenisei* river, western Siberia + E *-an*] **1** : a member of one of a group of peoples in the Yenisei river country including the Sagai — called also *Yenisei-Ostyak* **2** : a language family spoken in the valley of the Middle Yenisei river in Siberia of which Ket is the only member still spoken
yenisei-ostyak \ˌ≈≈ˈ≈ˈ≈≈,≈\ *n* -s *usu cap Y&O* [*Yenisei* river + E *ostyak*] **1** : YENISEIAN 1 **2** : KET
yen-shee \ˈyenˈshē\ *n* [Chin (Cant) *yin-shi*, fr. *in, yin* opium + *shi* filth, excrement] : the residue formed in the bowl of an opium pipe by smoking
yen·tai \ˈyenˈtī\ *adj, usu cap* [fr. *Yentai* (Chefoo), commercial city of northeast China] : CHEFOO
¹**yeo** \ˈyō\ *dial Brit var of* EWE
²**yeo** *var of* YO
yeo *or* **yeom** *abbr* yeomanry
¹**yeo·man** \ˈyōmən\ *n, pl* **yeomen** [ME *yoman, yeman*, perh. contr. of *yong man, yeng man* young man, attendant, fr. *yong, yeng* young + *man*] **1 a** : an attendant or officer in a royal or noble household performing menial services ⟨~ of the wardrobe⟩; *esp* : one ranking between a sergeant and a groom or between a squire and a page **b** : a person attending or assisting another (as an official) : RETAINER **c** : YEOMAN OF THE GUARD **d** : a seaman, petty officer, or warrant officer (as in the Royal Navy) who assists (as in having charge of stores or signaling procedure) the officer of a particular department **e** : a petty officer (as in the U.S. Navy) who performs clerical duties and is responsible for keeping records and reports and providing information (as on insurance, transportation, or promotions) relating to his department **f** : a clerk who keeps records on board a ship — called also *writer* **2 a** : a small farmer who cultivates his own land; *specif* : one belonging to a class of English freeholders ranking below the gentry and formerly qualified by owning property worth 40 shillings a year to enjoy certain legal privileges (as jury duty) **b** : any person of the social rank of yeoman or of similar rank : a member of the first or most respected class of common people : one of the highest class not entitled to heraldic arms **c** : a member of the British military yeomanry **3** : one that performs great and laborious services ⟨the biscuit pans . . . were the *yeomen* of our kitchen —Alberta Constant⟩
²**yeoman** \ˈ"\ *adj* [ME *yoman, yeman*, fr. *yoman yeman*, n.] **1** : of, relating to, or being a yeoman ⟨of ~ rank⟩ ⟨a ~ farmer⟩ **2** : consisting of yeomen ⟨the ~ class⟩ **3** : characteristic of or befitting a yeoman ⟨a man of big build, of ~ appearance, countrified by nature and wish —*Current Biog.*⟩ **4** : characterized by laborious effort and great usefulness ⟨did ~ service⟩ ⟨performed ~ work⟩ ⟨gave ~ help⟩
yeo·man·ette \ˌyōməˈnet\ *n* -s [¹*yeoman* + *-ette*] : a woman serving as a yeoman in the U.S. naval reserve force during and immediately after World War I
¹**yeo·man·ly** *adj* [¹*yeoman* + *-ly*] **1** : of, relating to, or having the rank of a yeoman **2** : becoming or suitable to a yeoman : STURDY, LOYAL
²**yeo·man·ly** *adv* : in a manner befitting a yeoman : BRAVELY
yeoman of the guard : a member of a military corps attached to the British royal household since the 15th century to guard the sovereign, appointed from retired enlisted men and noncommissioned officers, and divided into two groups serving as ceremonial attendants of the sovereign and as warders of the Tower of London — compare GENTLEMAN-AT-ARMS
yeo·man·ry \ˈyōmənrē, -ri\ *n* -ES [ME *yomanry, yemanry*, fr. *yoman, yeman* yeoman + *-ry*] **1** *obs* : the position or rank of a yeoman **2** : the whole body of yeomen; *specif* : the body of small landed proprietors of the middle class **3** : a British volunteer cavalry force created in 1761 as a home defense force from yeomen and officered by country gentlemen and reorganized in 1907 into part of the territorial force
yeoman usher *n* : the deputy of the black rod
yep \ˈyep\ *or* **yup** \ˈyəp\ *adv* [by alter.] : YES — not often in formal use; compare NOPE
yer \ˌyə(r)\ *or* **yere** \(ˌ)yi(ə)r\ *dial var of* YOUR
-yer — see ²-ER
ye·ra·va \yəˈrävə\ *also* **era·va** \əˈ-\ *n, pl* **yerava** *or* **yeravas** *usu cap* : one of a very dark-skinned people in Coorg prob. of Dravidian origin and formerly subjects of the Kodagu
yerb \ˈyərb\ *dial var of* HERB
yer·ba bue·na \ˈyerbəˈbwānə, ˈyər-\ *n* [Sp, lit., good herb] : a trailing perennial evergreen herb (*Satureia douglasii*) of British Columbia, Idaho, and California that has small white flowers and has been used as an anthelmintic and emmenagogue
yer·bal \yərˈbäl\ *n, pl* **yerba·les** \-äˌlās\ [AmerSp, fr. *yerba*] : a plantation of maté or a district in which it abounds
yerba man·sa \-ˈmän(t)sə; -ˈman-\ *n* [modif. of MexSp *yerba del manso*, lit., farmhouse herb] : a stoloniferous herb (*Anemiopsis californica*) of the family Saururaceae of the western U.S. and Mexico with a pungent rootstock and small spicate flowers subtended by a white involucre suggesting an anemone
yerba ma·té \-ˈmä(ˌ)tā\ *n* [AmerSp *yerba mate*; fr. *yerba* herb, plant (fr. L *herba* grass, herb) + *mate* maté] : MATÉ
yerba reu·ma \-ˈrümə\ *n* [modif. of MexSp *yerbarreuma*, fr. *yerba* herb + *reuma* cold, catarrh, fr. L *rheuma* — more at RHEUM] **1** : a low Californian undershrub (*Frankenia palmeri*) densely covered with small leaves and tiny white flowers **2** : ALKALI HEATH
yerba san·ta \-ˈsäntə, -ˈsan-\ *n* [MexSp, lit., holy herb] : any of several shrubs of the genus *Eriodictyon; esp* : an evergreen shrub (*E. californicum*) of California whose aromatic leaves are used as an expectorant and to mask the bitter taste of various drugs
yer·cum \ˈyərkəm\ *n* -s [Tamil *yerkum*] : MUDAR
¹**yerd** \ˈyərd\ *dial var of* YARD
²**yerd** \ˈ"\ *chiefly Scot var of* EARTH
yere \ˈyi(ə)r\ *dial var of* HERE
yer·e·van *or* **er·e·van** *or* **er·i·van** \ˌyerəˈvän\ *adj, usu cap* [fr. *Yerevan* or *Erevan* or *Erivan*, capital of Armenian S.S.R.] : of or from the city of Yerevan, U.S.S.R. : of the kind or style prevalent in Yerevan
¹**yerk** \ˈyərk\ *vb* -ED/-ING/-s [ME *yerken*] *vt* **1 a** *archaic* : to pull (a stitch) tight in making a shoe **b** *dial* : to bind tightly **2** *dial* **a** : to beat (as with a rod or whip) vigorously : THRASH **b** : to attack (as with harsh words) or excite vigorously : stir up : GOAD **3** *dial* **a** : to cause to move abruptly : JERK, HURL, KICK **b** : to strike up (as a song) **4** *dial* : to begin with zest ~ *vi* **1** *obs* : to lash out with the heels **2** *dial* : to move hastily or suddenly
²**yerk** \ˈ"\ *n* -s **1** *Scot* : THUMP, LASHING, KICK, STAB **2** *dial* : a quick movement : JERK
yer·ra *or* **yer·rah** \ˈyerə\ *interj* [IrGael *a* O + *Dia* God (fr. OIr) + *ara* arrah; akin to L *deus* god — more at DEITY] — used as a mild oath
yert·chuk \ˈyər,chək\ *n* -s [native name in Australia] : a medium sized Australian eucalypt (*Eucalyptus consideniana*) with rough flaky bark and pale gummy timber
¹**yes** \ˈyes, ˈyeu̇, ˈyeə & *a multiplicity of other variants, among them* ˈye, (ˈ)yas, (ˈ)yis, (ˈ)yəs, ˈyə, (ˈ)yās, ˈyi, ˈya(a), ˈya(a)ə, ˈ(y)iə, ˈ(y)eə, ˈyä, ˈä(y)ə, ˈe(y)ə, ˈa(y)ə; *to the variants transcribed as vowel-final, p or a glottal stop may be added*\ *adv* [ME *yes, yis*, fr. OE *gēse, gīse*, prob. fr. *gēa* yea + *sī*, 3d sing. imper. of *bēon* to be (suppletive infinitive) — more at YEA, IS] **1** — used as a function word to express assent or agreement in answer to a question, command, or request ⟨are you ready to leave? *Yes*, I am ready⟩ ⟨~, I will be glad to have lunch with you⟩ ⟨~ I said ~ I will ~ —James Joyce⟩ **2** — used as a function word formerly to constitute and now usu. to introduce correction or contradiction of a negative assertion, direction, or request ⟨you couldn't have meant that. *Yes*, I did mean it⟩ ⟨don't say that! *Yes*, I will⟩ **3 a** — used as a function word to express agreement with the content or implications of a preceding statement ⟨~, I see your point⟩ ⟨~, such a policy would be fatal⟩ **b** — used as a function word to express conditional assent to a statement or proposal subject to or limited by a following objection ⟨this is a good meal. *Yes*, but I prefer my wife's cooking⟩ **4** — used as a function word to emphasize a following affirmative or to introduce a more emphatic, specific, or comprehensive statement ⟨this is a possible, ~, a probable explanation⟩ ⟨a source of inspiration to himself and to his people, ~, to humanity —Ernst Feise⟩ **5** — used as a function word to indicate uncertainty or polite interest or attentiveness ⟨"*Yes?*" he said as he saw the stranger waiting to speak to him⟩
²**yes** \ˈyes\ *n, pl* **yeses** *also* **yesses** **1** : an act or instance of agreeing or assenting by the use of the word *yes* : AFFIRMATION ⟨overcome them with ~*es*, undermine them with grins . . . agree them to death and destruction —Ralph Ellison⟩ **2 a** : an affirmative vote, decision, or opinion ⟨the proposal was carried by a margin of ten ~*es*⟩ **b** *yeses pl* : persons voting in the affirmative ⟨when it was announced that the motion had been defeated, there was a shout of protest from the ~*es*⟩
³**yes** \ˈ"\ *vb* **yessed** *also* **yesed; yessed** *also* **yesed; yessing** *also* **yesing; yesses** *also* **yeses** *vi* : to express agreement or assent ⟨was better at *yessing* than at developing original ideas⟩ ~ *vt* : to give assent to : agree with ⟨all she had to do was ~ him when he was talkin' —Norman Mailer⟩
ye·shi·va *or* **ye·shi·vah** \yəˈshēvə\ *n, pl* **yeshivas** *or* **yeshivahs** *or* **yeshibahs** \-vəz\ *or* **yeshi·voth** *or* **yeshi·vot** *or* **yeshi·both** *or* **yeshi·bot** \yəshēˈvōt, -ōth\ [LHeb *yĕshībhāh*, fr. Heb, sitting, seat] **1** : a school for advanced Talmudic study : a Talmudic academy **2** : an orthodox Jewish rabbinical seminary or college **3** : a Hebrew-English day school providing both secular and religious instruction
yeshiva bocher *n* [Yiddish *yeshive bokher*, lit., yeshiva youth] : BAHUR
yes-man \ˈ≈,≈\ *n, pl* **yes-men** [¹*yes* + *man*] : a person who agrees with everything that is said to him; *esp* : a self-seeker who endorses or supports without criticism every opinion or proposal of an associate or superior : SYCOPHANT, TOADY ⟨depriving himself of the advice of all but timid souls and *yes-men* —*Harper's*⟩ — compare NO-MAN
ye·so \ˈyā(ˌ)sō\ *n* -s [Sp, fr. L *gypsum*] : GYPSUM
yest \ˈyest\ *archaic var of* YEAST
yest *abbr* yesterday
¹**yes·ter** \ˈyestə(r)\ *adj* [*yesterday*] *archaic* : of or relating to yesterday
²**yester** \ˈ"\ *n* -s [by shortening] *chiefly dial* : YESTERDAY
¹**yes·ter·day** \ˈyestə(r)dē, -di, -(r)(ˌ)dā, *rapid* ˈyes(t)dē *or* -di\ *adv* [ME *yisterday, yesterday*, fr. OE *giestran dæg, geostran dæg, gystran dæg*, n. & adv., fr. *giestran* yesterday + *dæg* day; akin to OHG *gestaron* yesterday, ON *ī gær* yesterday, tomorrow, Goth *gistradagis* tomorrow, L *heri* yesterday, Gk *chthes*, Skt *hyas*] **1** : on the day last past : on the day preceding today ⟨the affair took place ~⟩ **2** : at a time not long past : only a short time ago ⟨I was not born ~⟩
²**yesterday** \ˈ"\ *n* [ME *yisterday, yesterday*, fr. OE *geostran dæg*] **1** : the day last past : the day next before the present ⟨had come up into the bows to resume his ~'s toil —C.S. Forester⟩ **2** : recent time : time not long past ⟨nobody comprehended the footwork of a running animal until the ~ of instantaneous photography —R.C.Murphy⟩ ⟨late in the earth's history, a mere geologic ~ —Marjory S. Douglas⟩ **3** : past time — usu. used in pl. ⟨all our ~s have lighted fools the way to dusty death —Shak.⟩ ⟨far back in the dim ~*s* —Stanley Walker⟩ ⟨the beauty they love is all in their tremendous ~ —Mollie Panter-Downes⟩
³**yesterday** \ˈ"\ *adj* : of or relating to yesterday or to a very recent time or period
yes·ter·day·ness *n* -ES : the quality of being yesterday
¹**yes·ter·eve** \ˈyestəˈrēv\ *or* **yes·ter·e·ven** \-vən\ *or* **yes·ter·eve·ning** \-vniŋ\ *adv* [*yester-* (as in *yesterday*) + *eve* or *even* or *evening*] *archaic* : on the evening of yesterday
²**yestereve** \ˈ"\ *or* **yestereven** \ˈ"\ *or* **yesterevening** \ˈ"\ *n, archaic* : the evening of yesterday : the evening last past
¹**yes·ter·morn** \ˈyestərˈmȯ(ə)rn\ *or* **yes·ter·morn·ing** \-ȯrniŋ\ *adv* [*yester-* (as in *yesterday*) + *morn* or *morning*] *archaic* : on the morning of yesterday
²**yestermorn** \ˈ"\ *or* **yestermorning** \ˈ"\ *n, archaic* : the morning of yesterday : the morning of the day last past
yes·tern \ˈyestə(r)n\ *adj* [by alter.] *archaic* : YESTER
¹**yes·ter·night** \ˈyestə(r)ˈnīt\ *adv* [ME *yisternight, yesternight*, fr. OE *gystran niht*, fr. *giestron* yesterday + *niht* night — more at YESTERDAY, NIGHT] *archaic* : on the night last past
²**yesternight** \ˈ"\ *n, archaic* : the night last past
yes·ter·year \ˈyestərˈyi(ə)r, -təˈyiə\ *n* [*yester-* (as in *yesterday*) + *year*] **1** : last year ⟨where are the snows of ~ —D.G. Rossetti⟩ **2** : a period not long past : the recent past ⟨perhaps some of the quiet matrons in the queue were the phrenetic bobby-soxers of ~ —*New Yorker*⟩
²**yesteryear** \ˈ"\ *adv* : in the recent past ⟨library problems . . . are the same today as ~ —H.C.Bauer⟩
¹**yes·treen** \yeˈstrēn\ *adv* [ME(Sc) *yistrevin*, fr. *yisterday* yesterday + *evin* evening, alter. of ME *even*] *chiefly Scot* : on yesterday evening ⟨left here ~ —John Buchan⟩
²**yestreen** \ˈ"\ *n* -s *chiefly Scot* : last evening or night
yesty *abbr* yesterday
¹**yet** \(ˈ)yet\ *usu* -ed·+V\ *adv* [ME *yet, yit, yut*, fr. OE *gīet, gīeta, gȳt*; akin to OFris *ieta, eta, ita* yet] **1 a** : besides what has been considered or mentioned already : in addition : as well : ALSO ⟨had ~ another side to his character —R.A.Hall b.1911⟩ ⟨by ordinary post, as I could furnish ~ another . . . if that went wrong —O.W.Holmes †1935⟩ **b** : EVEN — used as an intensive with comparatives ⟨at a ~ faster speed⟩ ⟨came nearer and ~ nearer⟩ or after *nor* ⟨have never voted for him, nor ~ intend to⟩ **c** : on top of everything else : no less ⟨adjoining rooms with bath and kitchenette ~, at a price that is reasonable indeed —K.L.Wilson⟩ ⟨writes a whole book about them. With pictures, ~ —J.N.Leonard⟩ **2 a** : continuously up to or as late as the present or some specified time : as previously : STILL ⟨animals ~ thrive at the bottom —R.E.Coker⟩ ⟨riches were still respectable, the rise of a millionaire was ~ a romance —Osbert Sitwell⟩ ⟨had developed a great civilization while ~ pagans —Kemp Malone⟩ **b** : up to now : so far : HITHERTO ⟨linguistic evidence has ~ yielded but a scanty return to the historian of culture —Edward Sapir⟩ ⟨there is ~ to be any scientist of any repute who encourages . . . the saucer-prophets —*Saturday Rev.*⟩ **c** : at this or that time : as soon as now ⟨is it time to go ~⟩ ⟨has the mail arrived ~⟩ **d** *archaic* : at length : FINALLY ⟨ere ~ the bees hum about globes of clover —John Keats⟩ **3 a** : at some future time : before all is done : EVENTUALLY ⟨wish to get to him the two blue woolen shirts . . . and will try to do it ~ —Walt Whitman⟩ ⟨could feel in the soft air the flowers that were ~ to show themselves —J.B.Benefield⟩ **b** *archaic* : during the continuance of the present into the future : from now on : HENCEFORTH ⟨~ a little while am I with you, and then I go unto him that sent me —Jn 7:33 (AV)⟩ **4** : HOWEVER, NEVERTHELESS, NOTWITHSTANDING ⟨the verse, which nowhere bursts into a flame of poetry, is ~ economical and tidy —T.S.Eliot⟩ ⟨a life that was austere and which ~ was happy because of its purpose —R.M.Hodesh⟩
²**yet** *conj* [ME *yut, yit*, fr. *yut, yit* yet, adv.] **1** : BUT ⟨a few pretty rivers that look like prime trout water, ~ they are not —Pete Barrett⟩ **2** : THOUGH ⟨my soul, ~ I know not why, hates nothing more than he —Shak.⟩
³**yet** \ˈ"\ *adj* [¹*yet*] : existing or lasting up to the present or a specified time : still continuing ⟨the ~ ruler, but not for long⟩
yet·a·pa \ˈyed·əpə\ *n* -s [prob. of AmerInd origin] : a fork-tailed flycatcher (genus *Gubernetes*) of southern Brazil and Argentina
ye·ti \ˈyetē\ *n* -s [Tibetan] : ABOMINABLE SNOWMAN
yet·ling \ˈyetlən, -liŋ\ *also* **yet·lin** \-lən\ *n* -s [ME *yetling*, fr. *yeten, yetten* to pour, found, cast (fr. OE *gēotan*) + *-ling* — more at FOUND] **1** *chiefly Scot* : a usu. cast-iron pot **2** *chiefly Scot* **a** : something made of cast iron **b** : CAST IRON
yett \ˈyet\ *n* -s [ME, fr. OE *geat* — more at GATE] *chiefly Scot* : GATE
yet·zer \ˈyātsə(r)\ *n, pl* **yet·za·rim** \ˌyātsəˈrēm\ *or* **yetzers** [LHeb *yēṣer*, fr. Heb, form, frame, purpose] : the impulse or inclination with which man is endowed according to Jewish traditional belief
yetzer ha·ra \-ˈhärə\ *n* [LHeb *yēṣer hār'ā* evil inclination] : man's inclination or impulse to evil considered as an essential part of human nature in Jewish traditional belief

1yeuk \ˈyük\ *vi* -ED/-ING/-S [ME (northern) *yykyn, yukyn,* fr. OE *giccan* — more at ITCH] *chiefly Scot* **:** ITCH
2yeuk \"\ *n* -S *chiefly Scot* **:** ITCHING
yeuky \-ki\ *adj* [¹*yeuk* + *-y*] *chiefly Scot* **:** ITCHY
yew \ˈyü\ *n* -S [ME *ew,* fr. OE *ēow, īw;* akin to OHG *īwa* yew, ON *ȳr,* OIr *ēo,* W *ywen,* OSlav *iva* willow] **1 a :** any of numerous shrubs or trees of the genus *Taxus* many of which yield valuable timbers and some of which are widely cultivated for their rich evergreen foliage; *esp* **:** ENGLISH YEW **b :** the wood of a yew; *esp* **:** the heavy fine-grained light brown or red wood of English yew that is valued esp. for cabinetwork, bows, and hoops **2** *archaic* **:** twigs or branches of the yew tree used as symbols of grief **3** *archaic* **:** an archery bow made of yew

twig of yew with ripe fruit

yew·berry \ˈyü- — *see* BERRY\ *n* **:** the fruit of the yew
yew·en \ˈyüən\ *adj* [*yew* + *-en*] *archaic* **:** made of yew
yew family *n* **:** TAXACEAE
yew green *n* **:** a moderate olive green that is yellower, stronger, and slightly lighter than cypress green, greener and darker than holly green (sense 2), and greener, darker, and slightly stronger than Lincoln green
yew pine *n* **:** BLACK SPRUCE 1
yew podocarpus *n* **:** a tree (*Podocarpus macrophyllus* and esp. the variety *P. m. maki*) of China and Japan that is used as an ornamental hedge plant and has lanceolate leaves and gray fissured bark
yew tree *n* [ME *ew tree,* fr. *ew* yew + *tree*] **:** YEW 1a
yez \ˈyēz\ *pron, pl in constr* [¹*ye* + *-s,* n. pl. suffix] *Irish* **:** YOU
yez·i·di \ˈyezədē\ *or* **ya·zi·di** \ˈyäzədē\ *n* -S *usu cap* [prob. of Iranian origin] **:** a member of a syncretistic religious sect inhabiting a small area in Iraq, Syria, and Soviet Armenia, comprising several Kurdish-speaking peoples, and worshiping an angel believed to have been formerly the author of evil but to be now actively good and chief among seven angels to whom the supreme but transcendent God has left the government of the world
yfere *adv* [ME *ifere, yfere, in fere,* prob. fr. *in* + *fere* company, fr. OE *gefēre,* fr. *ge-* associative prefix + derivative of root of *faran* to travel — more at CO-, FARE] *obs* **:** TOGETHER
y-gun \ˈ=,=\ *n, cap Y* [¹*y* + *gun;* fr. its forked shape] **:** an antisubmarine gun having two barrels that form a fork to permit the simultaneous firing of depth charges on each side of the ship on which the gun is mounted
YH *abbr* youth hostel
YHS *var of* IHS
YHWH *also* **YHVH** *or* **JHVH** *or* **JHWH** *or* **IHVH** *n* [Heb *YHWH*] **:** YAHWEH — a transliteration of the tetragrammaton
yid \ˈyid\ *n* -S *usu cap* [Yiddish, fr. MHG *Jude, Jüde,* fr. OHG *Judo, Judeo,* fr. L *Judaeus* — more at JEW] **:** JEW — usu. taken to be offensive
1yid·dish \ˈyidish, -dēsh\ *n* -ES *cap* [Yiddish *yidish,* short for *yidish daytsh,* lit., Jewish German, fr. MHG *jüdisch diutsch,* fr. *jüdisch* Jewish (fr. *Jude* Jew + *-isch* -ish) + *diutsch* German, fr. OHG *diutisc* — more at DUTCH] **:** a High German language spoken by Jews chiefly in eastern Europe and areas to which Jews from eastern Europe have migrated and commonly written in Hebrew characters — called also *Judeo-German;* see INDO-EUROPEAN LANGUAGES table
2yiddish \"\ *adj, usu cap* **1 :** of, relating to, or characteristic of Yiddish ⟨a *Yiddish* word⟩ **2 :** consisting of or written in Yiddish ⟨*Yiddish* newspapers⟩ ⟨*Yiddish* literature⟩
yid·dish·ism \-di,shizəm\ *n* -S *usu cap* [¹*yiddish* + *-ism*] **1 :** a movement characterized by advocacy of the Yiddish language and culture **2 :** a usage, word, phrase, or idiom peculiar to Yiddish
1yid·dish·ist \-shəst\ *n* -S *usu cap* [¹*yiddish* + *-ist*] **:** an adherent of Yiddishism
2yiddishist \"\ *adj, usu cap* **:** of, relating to, or advocating yiddishism ⟨*Yiddishist* schools⟩ ⟨a *Yiddishist* movement⟩
yid·dish·keit \-sh,kīt\ *n* -S *usu cap* [Yiddish *yidishkeyt,* fr. *yidish,* adj., Jewish (fr. MHG *jüdisch*) + *-keyt* -hood, fr. MHG *-keit,* alter. of *-heit,* fr. OHG — more at -HOOD] **:** Jewish character or quality **:** Jewish way of life **:** JEWISHNESS
1yield \ˈyēld, *esp before pause or consonant* ˈyēəld\ *vb* -ED/-ING/-S [ME *yielden, yelden,* fr. OE *gieldan, geldan;* akin to OHG *geltan* to pay, render, requite, ON *gjalda,* Goth *fargildan,* and perh. to OSlav *žlěsti* to pay] *vt* **1** *archaic* **:** to give a reward to **:** RECOMPENSE, REQUITE, REWARD — used chiefly as an expression of gratitude or goodwill ⟨tend me tonight two hours . . . and the gods ~ you for't —*Shak.*⟩ **2 :** to give or render as fitting, rightfully owed, or required ⟨~ him obedience in lawful things —G.P.R.James⟩ **3** *archaic* **:** RETURN 5b ⟨he ~*ed* to this suggestion a ready and rapturous assent —Charles Dickens⟩ **4 a** *archaic* **:** to hand over **:** DELIVER, OFFER, PRESENT ⟨our soul cannot but ~ you forth to public thanks —*Shak.*⟩ **b :** to grant as an act of grace or as a concession **:** give or bestow as a favor ⟨the king ~*ed* the citizens the right of justice —J.R.Green⟩ ⟨refused to ~ passage⟩ **5 :** to give up possession of upon claim or demand: as **a :** to give up (as one's breath, life, or spirit) and so die or expire ⟨~*ed* up the ghost and was gathered unto his people —Gen 49:33 (AV)⟩ **b :** to surrender or relinquish to the physical control of another **:** hand over possession of ⟨refused to ~ the fortress to the enemy⟩ — sometimes used with *up* ⟨the Indians agreed . . . to ~ up their British flags —Grace L. Nute⟩ **c :** to surrender or submit (oneself) to another ⟨each Babylonian woman was in duty bound . . . to ~ herself to a stranger —H.M.Parshley⟩ ⟨emotions do not ~ themselves readily to a verbal pin —Ernest & Pearl Beaglehole⟩ **d :** to give (oneself) up to an inclination, temptation, or habit **:** submit, give over, or incline (oneself) to some influence **:** dedicate or devote (oneself) to something ⟨a temptation to which he ~*ed* himself —H.O.Taylor⟩ ⟨she ~*ed* herself up . . . to the rhythm of a waltz —Victoria Sackville-West⟩ **e** (1) **:** to relinquish one's possession of (as a position of advantage or point of superiority) ⟨~ precedence⟩ ⟨traffic required to ~ right of way⟩ ⟨~*ed* the premiership to his rival⟩ (2) **:** to relinquish (as the floor or a period of allotted speaking time) to another member of a legislative assembly ⟨~ the floor to the senator from Nebraska⟩ **f :** to hand over or resign to the moral control of another **:** give to another the political, economic, or social direction of **:** RELINQUISH ⟨~ sovereignty to an international organization⟩ ⟨~*ed* her heart to another⟩ **6 a** *obs* **:** to acknowledge as being correctly specified **:** ALLOW, CONCEDE ⟨I ~ it just . . . and submit —John Milton⟩ **b** (1) **:** to admit the validity or cogency of ⟨~*ed* the point⟩ ⟨unwilling to ~ the argument⟩ (2) *archaic* **:** CONSENT, AGREE ⟨~*ed* to ask for mercy —Jane West⟩ **c** *obs* **:** to admit to be true **:** concede to be so ⟨hard . . . to ~ they have done amiss —Nicholas Rowe⟩ **7 a :** to bear or bring or put forth as a natural product esp. as a result of cultivation ⟨clover seed . . . ~*s* from 6 to 10 bushels on the cutover lands —*Amer. Guide Series: Minn.*⟩ **b :** to furnish as output or as return or result of expended effort ⟨their soil ~*s* treasures of every kind —H.T.Buckle⟩ **c :** to produce as a result **:** give as a product ⟨this prediction is susceptible of a test which ~*s* a yes or no answer —J.B.Conant⟩ **d :** to give up in response to one's efforts **:** render as the result of the application of skill, persistence, or hard work ⟨words, under the analyses now indicated, ~ the history of their origin —Edward Clodd⟩ — often used with *up* ⟨caves . . . which have not yet ~*ed* up their secrets to the eyes of man —Bill Beatty⟩ **8 :** to give forth **:** DISCHARGE, EMIT ⟨air-swept lindens ~ their scent —Matthew Arnold⟩ **9 a :** to produce or furnish to supply a need **:** provide for use or to serve a purpose **:** AFFORD ⟨cotton can be treated to ~ a series of products —*Industrial & Engineering Chemistry*⟩ ⟨several makes of engine ~ considerably more power —Grenville Manton⟩ ⟨the language too condensed to ~ quotable lines —J.D.Hart⟩ **b :** to give rise to **:** CAUSE, OCCASION ⟨the election ~*ed* only one surprise⟩ **c** (1) **:** to produce as return from an expenditure or investment **:** furnish as profit or interest **:** PAY, RETURN ⟨an investment that now ~*s* him 6 percent⟩ ⟨first steam whaler afloat . . . ~*ed* $151,000 net —*Amer. Guide Series: Conn.*⟩ ⟨it will prosper and ~ a fair return on the . . . investment —Leo Wolman⟩ (2) **:** to produce as revenue **:** bring in ⟨a levy . . . was proposed in order to ~ £4 million —Alzada Comstock⟩ **d** *obs* **:** to present to view **:** EXHIBIT **10 :** to give up (as a run or hit) in baseball ⟨~*ed* a triple to left⟩ ~ *vi* **1 :** to make or give a return **:** be fruitful or productive **:** BEAR, PRODUCE ⟨the impoverished soil would not ~ without application of fertilizers —*Amer. Guide Series: Md.*⟩ ⟨the apple trees did not ~ well this year⟩ **2 :** to give up and cease resistance or contention: as **a :** to surrender and concede being defeated, vanquished, or worsted ⟨the enemy suddenly ~*ed* —M.R.Cohen⟩ **b :** to cease opposition **:** give up the contest **:** SUBMIT, SUCCUMB ⟨after several hours of debate, the opposition ~*ed*⟩ **c :** to cease to withstand the effect of some action ⟨short words which nowhere ~ to analysis —Edward Sapir⟩ ⟨whole passages ~ neatly when translated by shorthand —Fletcher Pratt⟩ **d :** to agree to accept or comply with something **:** exhibit willingness rather than opposition **:** DEFER ⟨~*ed* to the secondary role for which his talent equipped him —Van Wyck Brooks⟩ **3 :** to give way to pressure or influence exerted upon one **:** submit to urging, persuasion, or entreaty **:** consent or agree to something **:** cease opposition or objection to something **:** comply with something ⟨if you ~ to that impulse —T.B.Costain⟩ ⟨~ to the urgent invitation —D.S.Muzzey⟩ ⟨refused to ~ to their demands⟩ ⟨~*s* to her seducer with hardly a struggle —T.S. Eliot⟩ **4 a :** to give way under physical force so as to bend, stretch, or break ⟨the dirt road was so soft it ~*ed* to the foot like a feather bed —*Amer. Guide Series: N.Y. City*⟩ ⟨nylon does not ~ to stretch as readily as rubber yarns —W. E.Shinn⟩ **b :** to lose power of resistance to some physical action or agent (as pressure, friction, or heat) so as to be affected by it ⟨ores that ~ readily to reduction processes —*Amer. Guide Series: Wash.*⟩ ⟨the door suddenly ~*ed* to her hand —Jane Austen⟩ **c :** to permit oneself to be deflected **:** change one's course in deference **:** turn aside ⟨refused to ~ a particle from his resolution⟩ **5 a :** to give place or precedence (as to one having superior right or claim) **:** acknowledge the superiority of someone else ⟨I ~ to no one in my respect for his creative program —R.N.Denney⟩ ⟨the way of life of these peoples must ~ to the culture of the white man —*Current Biog.*⟩ ⟨the acts of New York must ~ to the law of Congress —John Marshall⟩ **b :** to be inferior in some often specified respect ⟨their mutton ~*s* to ours but their beef is excellent —Jonathan Swift⟩ **c :** to give way to or be succeeded by someone or something else ⟨pavements . . . ~*ed* to dirt roads —Giorgio de Santillana⟩ ⟨the cold thin air of the mountains ~*ed* to sweltering heat as they descended —Bernard De Voto⟩ ⟨hard conditions of life . . . ~*ed* to more propitious circumstances —Van Wyck Brooks⟩ **6 :** to relinquish the floor of a legislative assembly (as for a period of time or a question) ⟨~ to the senator from Connecticut⟩

syn SUBMIT, CAPITULATE, SUCCUMB, BOW, DEFER, RELENT: YIELD is a general term referring to any sort of giving in before force, domination, argument, entreaty, appeal ⟨after some further argument I *yielded* the point —W.H.Hudson †1922⟩ ⟨went into the Peace Conference willing to *yield* everything to English interests —H.L.Mencken⟩ ⟨not a man to *yield* weakly —Havelock Ellis⟩ SUBMIT more strongly indicates giving up after conflict, contention, or resistance to the will, control, or disposition of another ⟨not only has faith in divine Providence but *submits* to it humbly —Herbert Agar⟩ ⟨must *submit* ourselves to the will of God —Mary Austin⟩ ⟨tamely *submitted* to the rebuffs —A.T.Quiller-Couch⟩ CAPITULATE centers attention on a definite act of surrendering or giving up to a stronger force or power ⟨how easily we *capitulate* to badges and names, to large societies and dead institutions —R.W. Emerson⟩ ⟨the universities would *capitulate* to a young, vigorous and revolutionary creed, in tune with the Zeitgeist —Walter Moberly⟩ SUCCUMB is likely to indicate utter yielding through weakness or exhaustion ⟨*succumbing* before the barbarian invasions —H.O.Taylor⟩ ⟨presidents who have attempted independent action have soon *succumbed* to the power of the independent action —Ernest Barker⟩ BOW may be used in reference to situations in which a party that has not been vanquished gives in or yields for politic or courteous reasons ⟨their habit of *bowing* to public opinion —Bertrand Russell⟩ ⟨*bowed* to political expediency and requested Blair's resignation —W.E.Smith⟩ ⟨soon learned to *bow* before his wife's more stormy moods —Samuel Butler †1902⟩ DEFER strongly connotes yielding brought about by respect for another or for his position or authority ⟨everybody must *defer* . . . a nation must wait upon her decision, a dean and chapter truckle to her wishes —Victoria Sackville-West⟩ ⟨the banker who was a free man, who ran his own bank in his own way, *deferring* only slightly to the nonsense of the federal bank inspectors —W.A. White⟩ RELENT is used in situations in which a dominant party abates his rigor or mollifies his wrath because of entreaty, consideration, or resurgence of easier nature ⟨might have *relented* and repented having wrung a promise from her —Margaret Deland⟩ **syn** see in addition BEAR, RELINQUISH

2yield \"\ *n* -S *often attrib* [ME *yelde,* fr. *yelden* to yield] **1 :** something (as the amount, quantity, or product) yielded: as **a** (1) **:** the aggregate of products resulting from growth or cultivation ⟨a goodly ~ of fruit —Francis Bacon⟩ ⟨an increased ~ per acre⟩ ⟨~*s* average over twenty pounds of fruit per plant —*Irish Independent*⟩ (2) **:** the aggregate of products resulting from a chemical reaction and usu. expressed as the percentage actually obtained of the amount theoretically possible (3) **:** the amount of explosive energy expended by a nuclear explosion usu. expressed in kilotons of TNT that would produce an explosion resulting in the expending of the same amount of energy **b :** the quantity of a product resulting from exploitation of natural resources ⟨the ~ of a well in barrels of oil⟩ ⟨fishermen . . . are finding that the ~ per hour of trawling is dropping —*Irish Digest*⟩ **c :** the revenue obtained from a tax or levy **d :** the return upon a financial investment usu. expressed as a percentage of cost ⟨the ~ on a bond⟩ ⟨a 4% ~⟩ **e :** the actual or the normal product of a stand of timber **f :** the number of proof gallons of spirit obtained from a bushel of grain in distilling **2 a :** the capacity of yielding produce or other product ⟨a fruit belt owes its abundant ~ to climatic conditions —*Amer. Guide Series: Mich.*⟩ **b :** the capacity to yield under pressure or tension ⟨a material with high ~⟩
yield·able \-dəbəl\ *adj* **:** capable of yielding **:** disposed to yield
yield·ance \-dən(t)s\ *n* -S [¹*yield* + *-ance*] *archaic* **:** the action of yielding **:** COMPLIANCE, CONCESSION, SUBMISSION, SURRENDER ⟨blissful ~ to her sweet allure —Thomas Hardy⟩
yielded *past of* YIELD
yield·er \-də(r)\ *n* -S [ME *yeldere,* fr. *yelden* to yield + *-ere* -er] **:** one that yields: as **a :** one that surrenders, concedes, or gives in ⟨I was not born a ~ —*Shak.*⟩ **b :** something that yields produce or products **:** something that produces or furnishes — usu. used with qualifier ⟨direct taxes . . . proved poor ~*s* —C.L.Jones⟩ ⟨a variety of corn that is established as a good ~⟩
yield gene *n* [²*yield* + *gene*] **:** any of a group of complementary genes no one of which has apparent individual effect; *esp* **:** one that directly or indirectly affects (as by increasing resistance to disease or to drouth) the yield of various field crops
yielding *adj* [fr. pres. part. of ¹*yield*] **1 :** PRODUCTIVE ⟨a new type of wheat — claimed to be extra high ~ —*Wall Street Jour.*⟩ **2 :** inclined to give way (as to pressure) **:** lacking rigidity or stiffness **:** FLEXIBLE ⟨made of a ~ rubber or similar springing material —T.C.J.O'Connell⟩ ⟨a deep ~ mass of leaf mold —*Geog. Jour.*⟩ **3 :** disposed to submit or comply **:** having a tendency to give in, surrender, or agree **:** COMPLIANT, SUBMISSIVE, TRACTABLE ⟨too ~ to make a stand against any encroachment —V.L.Parrington⟩ ⟨too ~ and indecisive a character —Jane Austen⟩
yield·ing·ly *adv* **:** in a yielding manner
yield·ing·ness *n* -ES **:** the quality or state of being yielding ⟨the ~ of the cartilaginous substance —William Paley⟩
yield insurance *n* [²*yield*] **:** insurance that guarantees investors a stated yield on their investment in approved residential housing
yield point *n* **:** a stress sufficiently beyond the elastic limit that the material begins to exhibit plastic properties and continues to deform without further increase of load — used esp. of tension; compare YIELD VALUE
yields *pres 3d sing of* YIELD, *pl of* YIELD
yield strength *n* **:** the stress at which a piece under strain is deformed some definite amount (as 0.1 or 0.2 percent)
yield table *n* **:** a tabulation indicating the volume of wood per unit area of forest to be expected at different ages of the trees
yield value *n* **:** the minimum shearing or normal stress required to produce continuous deformation in a solid
yill \ˈyil\ *chiefly Scot var of* ALE
yill-caup \ˈ=,=\ *n* [*yill* + *caup*] *Scot* **:** a vessel from which ale is drunk
yilt *var of* GILT
1yin \ˈyin\ *chiefly Scot var of* ONE
2yin \"\ *n* -S [Chin (Pek) *yin*¹ dark, feminine principle] **:** the feminine and negative principle (as of passivity, depth, darkness, cold, wetness) in nature that according to traditional Chinese cosmology combines with its opposite yang to produce all that comes to be
yince \ˈyin(t)s\ *chiefly Scot var of* ONCE
ying·kow \ˈyiŋ¦kaů, -kō\ *adj, usu cap* [fr. *Yingkow,* city and port of southern Manchuria] **:** of or from the city of Yingkow, Manchuria **:** of the kind or style prevalent in Yingkow
y-intercept \ˈ=ˈ==,=\ *n* **:** the y-coordinate of the point where a line, curve, or surface intersects the y-axis
1yip \ˈyip\ *vb* **yipped; yipped; yipping; yips** [imit.] *vi* **1 a :** to bark or cry sharply, quickly, and often continuously esp. from eagerness — used chiefly of a dog **b :** to make a sound resembling the yip of a dog **:** utter a short sharp cry **2 :** to complain sharply and loudly **:** SQUEAL ~ *vt* **:** to utter or emit by or as if by yipping
2yip \"\ *n* -S **:** a noise made by or as if by yipping ⟨barked again . . . then tapered off in a long dimenuendo of ~*s* —B.V. Dryer⟩ ⟨let out a ~ of discovery —Emily Hahn⟩ ⟨not another ~ from either complainant —C.W.Morton⟩
1yipe \ˈyīp\ *vi* -ED/-ING/-S [imit.] **:** to cry out sharply esp. from surprise or pain ⟨*yiped* when he touched the hot stove⟩
2yipe \"\ *n* -S **:** a noise made by or as if by yiping ⟨the sudden ~ of a mongrel hurt —Wallace Stegner⟩ — used interjectionally in both sing. and pl.
yip·pee \ˈyipē\ *interj* — used to express exuberant delight or triumph
yird \ˈyərd\ *chiefly Scot var of* EARTH
yirk \ˈyərk\ *Scot var of* YERK
1yirr \ˈyər\ *vi* -ED/-ING/-S [imit.] *Scot* **:** to growl or snarl in the manner of a dog
2yirr \"\ *n* -S *Scot* **:** a sound made by or as if by yirring **:** GROWL, SNARL
yirth \ˈyərth\ *chiefly Scot var of* EARTH
yite \ˈyīt\ *n* -S [origin unknown] *dial Brit* **:** YELLOWHAMMER 1
yiz·kor \ˈyizkə(r)\ *n* -S *often cap* [Heb *yizkōr* remember; fr. the first word of the prayer] **:** a Jewish memorial service or prayer for the dead recited usu. in the synagogue on Yom Kippur, on the last day of Passover, on Shemini Atzereth, and on the second day of Shabuoth
-yl \ˌəl, ˌil, -ˌēl, (*when t, d, or n precedes*) ᵊl; *chiefly Brit* ˌīl\ *n comb form* -S [Gk *hylē* wood, matter; first used in G *benzoyl,* lit., fundamental material of benzoic acid, fr. *benz-* + Gk *hylē* — more at HYLE] **:** chemical radical: as **a :** univalent radical ⟨eth*yl*⟩ ⟨pirid*yl*⟩ ⟨hydrox*yl*⟩ **b :** radical containing oxygen ⟨carbon*yl*⟩ ⟨chrom*yl*⟩ including a few radicals of organic acids ⟨acet*yl*⟩ ⟨glyc*yl*⟩ ⟨succin*yl*⟩; compare -OYL
yl *abbr* yellow
YL *abbr* young lady
ylang-ylang *var of* ILANG-ILANG
yld *abbr* yield
ylem \ˈīləm\ *n* -S [ME, fr. MF *ilem,* prob. fr. ML *hylem,* acc. of *hyle* matter, fr. L, fr. Gk *hylē* — more at HYLE] **:** the primordial first substance from which according to some theories the elements are supposed to be formed; *specif* **:** a primordial gas consisting of neutrons
-ylene \ˌə,lēn, ᵊl,ēn\ *n suffix* -S [*-yl* + *-ene*] **1 :** unsaturated hydrocarbon ⟨piper*ylene*⟩ — compare -ENE **2 :** bivalent radical (phen*ylene* $-C_6H_4-$)
y level *n, usu cap Y* **:** a surveyor's level with a telescope supported in y-shaped rests and as a result capable of being rotated around its own axis or of being taken out of the supports and turned end for end for purposes of adjustment — compare DUMPY LEVEL
-yl·i·dene \ˈilə,dēn, ˌəl-\ *n suffix* -S [ISV *-yl* + *-idene*] **:** bivalent radical derived esp. from a saturated hydrocarbon by removal of two hydrogen atoms from the same carbon atom or by removal of the oxygen atom of an aldehyde ⟨citr*ylidene*⟩ — in the system adopted by the International Union of Pure and Applied Chemistry; compare -IDENE
-yl·i·dyne \ˈilə,dīn, ˌəl-\ *n suffix* -S [ISV *-yl* + *-idyne*] **:** trivalent radical derived esp. from a saturated hydrocarbon by removal of three hydrogen atoms from the same carbon atom ⟨eth*ylidyne* $CH_3C\equiv$⟩ — in the system adopted by the International Union of Pure and Applied Chemistry
y ligament *n, usu cap Y* [¹*y* + *ligament;* fr. its branching] **:** ILIOFEMORAL LIGAMENT
y moth *n, usu cap Y* [so called fr. its y-shaped marking] **:** SILVER Y MOTH
yn *abbr* yen
ynam·bu \ˌēnämˈbü\ *n* -S [Pg *inambu, inhambu,* fr. Tupi *inambú*] **:** a very large tinamou (*Rhynchotus rufescens*) of southern Brazil and Argentina
-yne \ˌīn\ *n suffix* -S [ISV alter. of *-ine*] **:** unsaturated straight-chain hydrocarbon characterized by the presence of one triple bond — in the system adopted by the International Union of Pure and Applied Chemistry to replace the ending *-ine* in this sense ⟨hex*yne*⟩; distinguished from *-ane* and *-ene*
yo *also* **yeo** \ˈyō\ *interj* [ME *yo, io,* interj.] — used esp. by sailors as a signal to commence hauling on a rope
YO *abbr* **1** yarn over **2** year-old
yob \ˈyäb\ *n* -S [back slang for *boy*] *Brit* **:** FELLOW, YOKEL
yock \ˈyäk\ *slang var of* ⁴YAK
yock·er·nut \ˈyäkə(r),nət\ *or* **yock·ey·nut** \-kē,n-\ *n* [*yocker-, yockey-* (prob. irreg. fr. *wankapin*) + *nut*] **:** WATER CHINQUAPIN
yod \ˈyȯd, ˈyōd, ˈyäd\ *n* [prob. fr. *yodh*] **:** the voiced glide or spirant sound \y\ that is the first sound of the English word *yes*
1yo·del *or* **jo·del** \ˈyōdᵊl\ *vb* **yodeled** *or* **yodelled** *or* **yodeled; yodeling** *or* **yodelling** \-d(ᵊ)liŋ\ **yodels** [G *jodeln,* fr. G (southern dial.), fr. G (southern dial.) *jo,* interj.] *vi* **:** to sing in a manner common among the Swiss and Tyrolean mountaineers by suddenly changing from chest voice to head voice or falsetto and the reverse; *also* **:** to shout or call in a similar manner ~ *vt* **:** to sing (a tune) by yodeling
2yodel *or* **jodel** \"\ *n* -S **:** a song or refrain sung by yodeling; *also* **:** a yodeled shout or cry
yo·del·er \-d(ᵊ)lə(r)\ *n* -S **:** one that yodels
yodh *also* **yod** *or* **jod** *or* **iod** \ˈyȯd, ˈyůd\ *n* -S [Heb *yōdh,* lit., hand] **1 :** the 10th letter of the Hebrew alphabet — symbol ׳; see ALPHABET table **2 :** the letter of the Phoenician or of any of various other Semitic alphabets corresponding to Hebrew yodh
yo·ga \ˈyōgə\ *n* -S [Skt, lit., yoking, union, disciplined activity, fr. *yunakti* he yokes — more at YOKE] **1 :** union of the individual self with the universal spirit (as in samadhi) **2** *usu cap* **:** a major orthodox system of Hindu philosophy based on Sankhya but differing from it in being theistic and characterized by the teaching of raja-yoga as a practical method of liberating the self **3 a :** the suppression through progressive discipline (as raja-yoga) of all activity of body, mind, and individual will in order that the self may realize its distinction from them and attain liberation from all pain and suffering **b :** a system of exercises for attaining bodily or mental control and well-being **4 :** a discipline by which the individual prepares himself for liberation of the self and union with the universal spirit — see RAJA-YOGA
yo·ga·ca·ra \ˌyōgəˈkärə\ *n* -S *usu cap* [Skt *yogācāra,* fr. *yoga* + *ācāra* custom, rule of conduct — more at ACHARYA] **1 :** one of the two major philosophical systems of Mahayana Buddhism agreeing with Madhyamika that external objects are unreal but holding that mind is real and that objects which appear to be external and material are in fact ideas or states of consciousness — compare VIJNANAVADA **2** *or* **yo·ga·ca·rin**

\-rən\ [Skt *yogācāra, yogācārin,* fr. *yogācāra* (philosophical system)] **:** an adherent of Yogacara

yogh \ˈyōk, ˈyäk, ˈyȯ\, |k, |g\ *n* -s [ME *yogh, ȝogh, ȝok, ȝoȝ*] **:** a letter ȝ used in Middle English to represent a velar or palatal fricative or \w\ between two vowels the second of which is unstressed

yo·gi \ˈyōgē\ *n* -s [Skt *yogin,* fr. *yoga*] **1** *also* **yo·gin** \-gin\ *or* **jo·gi** \ˈyōgē\ **:** a person who practices yoga; *esp* **:** a Hindu ascetic seeking self-liberation through bodily and mental disciplines (as of posture, breathing, or concentration) and sometimes credited with supernormal powers **2** *or* **yogin** *usu cap* **:** an adherent of Yoga philosophy **3 :** a markedly reflective or mystical person

yo·gic \-gik\ *adj* [*yoga* + *-ic*] **1 :** of or relating to the practice of yoga **2 :** of or relating to philosophic Yoga

yo·gism \-,gizəm\ *n* -s [*yoga* + *-ism*] **1** *usu cap* **:** the teachings of Yoga **2 :** the practice of Yoga

yo·gurt *or* **yo·ghurt** *also* **yo·ghourt** \ˈyōgə(r)t\ *n* -s [Turk *yoğurt*] **:** a fermented slightly acid semisolid food made of whole or skimmed cow's milk and milk solids to which cultures of two bacteria (*Lactobacillus bulgaricus* and *Streptococcus thermophilus*) have been added

yo·him·bé \yəˈhimbā, -bē\ *also* **yo·him·bi** \-bē\ *or* **yo·him·bi·hi** \-bə,hē\ *n* -s [of Bantu origin; akin to Duala *djombé* yohimbé] **:** a tropical African tree (*Corynanthe yohimbe*) of the family Rubiaceae the bark of which yields yohimbine

yo·him·bine \-m,bēn, -bən\ *n* -s [ISV *yohimbé* + *-ine*] **1 :** a crystalline alkaloid $C_{21}H_{26}N_2O_3$ that is the principal alkaloid of yohimbé bark and that has sympathomimetic and hypotensive effects and has been used in the form of its hydrochloride as an aphrodisiac — called also *quebrachine* **2 :** any of several alkaloids isomeric with yohimbine and occurring with it ⟨alpha-*yohimbine*⟩

yo-ho \yōˈhō\ *interj* — used as a signal for effort or to attract attention

yoicks \ˈyȯiks\ *interj* [alter. of *hoicks*] **1** *archaic* — used as a cry of encouragement to foxhounds **2** *archaic* — used to express excitement or exultation

yo·jan \ˈyōjən\ *or* **yo·ja·na** \-jənə\ *n* -s [Hindi & Skt; Hindi *yojan,* fr. Skt *yojana* yoking, distance traversed in one yoking, fr. *yunakti* he yokes — more at YOKE] **:** any of various Hindu units of distance varying from 4 to 10 miles; *esp* **:** a unit equal to about 5 miles

yok \ˈyäk\ *slang var of* ⁴YAK

¹**yoke** \ˈyōk\ *n* -s *see sense 2* [ME *yok,* fr. OE *geoc;* akin to OHG *joh* yoke, ON *ok* yoke, Goth *juk* yoke (of oxen), L *jugum* yoke, *jungere* to join, Gk *zygon* yoke, *zeugnynai* to yoke, join, Skt *yuga* yoke, *yunakti* he yokes, joins] **1 a** (1) **:** a bar or frame of wood by which two draft animals (as oxen) are joined at the heads or necks for working together and esp. for drawing a plow or a load and which is usu. a piece of timber hollowed or made curving near each end, laid on the necks of the oxen, secured in place by a bow passing under and enclosing each neck, and fastened through the timber (2) **:** an arched or curved device formerly laid upon the neck of a defeated person; *also* **:** an arch consisting of a spear resting horizontally upon two upright spears under which a captured foe is compelled to pass as a symbol of submission (3) **:** a frame worn on the neck of an animal (as a cow, pig, or goose) to prevent passage through a fence or hedge (4) **:** a usu. wooden frame fitted to a person's shoulders to carry a load suspended in two equal portions on opposite sides of the body (5) **:** a bar by which the end of the tongue of a wagon or carriage is suspended from the collars of a harness **b :** a tie securing two architectural members together; *specif* **:** the horizontal piece forming the head of a window frame **c** (1) **:** a crosspiece on the head of a boat's rudder to whose ends are attached lines leading forward either to the hands of a steersman or to the drum of a steering wheel so that the boat can be steered farther forward (2) **:** CONTROL COLUMN **d :** a frame or convex piece from which a bell is hung **e :** a clamp or similar piece that embraces two other parts to hold or unite them in their respective or relative positions: as (1) **:** a strap connecting a slide valve to the valve stem (2) **:** the soft iron block or bar (as in a dynamo) permanently connecting the pole pieces of an electromagnet (3) **:** a slotted crosshead used in some steam engines in place of a connecting rod (4) **:** the lower cap on the masthead of a yacht **f :** FIELD FRAME **g :** an assembly that fits around the neck of a cathode ray or picture tube and that contains coils used to control the position of the electron beam in the tube **2** *pl usu* **yoke a :** two animals yoked together ⟨ordinarily drawn by five or six ~ of oxen —W.F.Harris⟩; *also* **:** a pair of animals that work normally together ⟨kept eight ~ of oxen hauling supplies —Marjory S. Douglas⟩ **b** *obs* **:** PAIR, COUPLE **3 a :** an old Kentish unit of land area equal to ¼ sulung **b :** an Austrian cadastral unit equal to 1.42 acres **4 a** (1) **:** an oppressive agency reducing to subjection, submission, humiliation, or servitude ⟨thrown off the ~ of the mother country —C.G.Fenwick⟩ ⟨the young girl would rid herself of her mother's ~ —H.M.Parshley⟩ (2) **:** SERVITUDE, SLAVERY, BONDAGE, SERVICE ⟨my ~ is easy, and my burden is light —Mt 11:30 (RSV)⟩ **b** (1) **:** something that connects or binds **:** RELATIONSHIP, TIE, LINK, BOND ⟨since it recognizes no other truth . . . than its own, it needs must . . . bring everything under one ~ —M.R.Cohen⟩ (2) **:** the matrimonial bond; *esp* **:** one in which the partners are unequal **5 :** a fitted or shaped section of a garment to which a gathered, pleated, or flared section is attached used as the top of a skirt or the shoulder section of any of various garments and esp. of a shirt, blouse, or coat

²**yoke** \"\ *vb* -ED/-ING/-S [ME *yoken,* fr. OE *geocian,* fr. *geoc,* n., yoke — more at ¹YOKE] *vt* **1 a** (1) **:** to put a yoke on **:** join in or with a yoke ⟨continued stolidly *yoking* his oxen —A.C. Whitehead⟩ ⟨an ox . . . had been *yoked* together with a skinny poll-cow —O.E.Rölvaag⟩ (2) **:** to fit a yoke about the neck of (an animal) to prevent passage **b :** to attach a draft animal (as an ox) to ⟨~ a cart⟩; *also* **:** to attach (a draft animal) to something ⟨~ a horse to a cart⟩ **2 :** to couple, join, link, or associate as if by a yoke ⟨*yoked* two goals together in the title of his book —J.D.Hart⟩ ⟨*yoked* to a life and a companionship unvarying —James Boyd⟩ **3** *archaic* **:** to bring into bondage **:** hold in subjection **:** OPPRESS **4 :** to set to a task or operation **:** put to work ⟨*yoked* his great imagination to constant labor —W.R.Nicoll⟩ ~ *vi* **1 :** to be in intimate association **:** become joined or linked esp. in marriage or companionship **:** CONSORT ⟨we'll ~ together, like a double shadow —Shak.⟩ **2** *Scot* **:** to apply oneself vigorously **:** set to work — usu. used with *to*

³**yoke** *var of* YOLK

⁴**yoke** \ˈyōk\ *usu cap* — a communications code word for the letter *y*

yoke bone *n* **:** ZYGOMATIC BONE

yoke elm *n* **1 :** HORNBEAM 1a **2 :** a Himalayan tree (*Carpinus viminea*); *also* **:** its heavy hard wood

yokefellow \ˈ=,=(,)=\ *n* [trans. of Gk *syzygos*] **:** a close associate or companion **:** MATE, FELLOW, PARTNER; *esp* **:** a partner in marriage

yoke-footed \ˈ=;==\ *adj* **:** YOKE-TOED

yo·kel \ˈyōkəl\ *n* -s [perh. fr. E dial. *yokel* green woodpecker, of imit. origin] **:** an unpolished, naïve, or gullible inhabitant of a rural area or of a small town ⟨the legendary ~ who rushed onto the stage to rescue the heroine —Hunter Mead⟩ ⟨evidently peasants, some of them young ~s from the village, no doubt ignorant and stupid —George Santayana⟩ **syn** see BOOR

yo·kel·ish \-k(ə)lish\ *adj* **:** characteristic of or resembling a yokel **:** RUDE, UNCOUTH

yo·kel·ry \-kəlrē, -ri\ *n* -ES **:** gullible unsophisticated country-folk **:** YOKELS

yokemate \ˈ=,=\ *n* **:** YOKEFELLOW

yoke riveter *n* **:** a pneumatic riveter connected by a yoke with a dolly so that the center lines of the two coincide

yokes *pl of* YOKE, *pres 3d sing of* YOKE

yoke-toed \ˈ=;=\ *adj* **:** having two toes in front and two behind **:** ZYGODACTYL ⟨most woodpeckers are *yoke-toed*⟩

yoking *n* -s [fr. gerund of ²*yoke*] **1** *Scot* **:** CONTEST, BOUT **2** *dial Brit* **:** a period of steady work esp. by a plowman and team **3** *slang* **:** a street assault **:** MUGGING

yok·kai·chi \ˈyōˈkīchē\ *adj, usu cap* [*Yokkaichi,* city in southern Honshu, Japan] **:** of or from the city of Yokkaichi, Japan **:** of the kind or style prevalent in Yokkaichi

yo·ko·ha·ma \ˌyōkəˈhämə\ *adj, usu cap* [*Yokohama,* city in southeast Honshu, Japan] **:** of or from the city of Yokohama, Japan **:** of the kind or style prevalent in Yokohama

yokohama bean *n, usu cap Y* **:** a Japanese woody vine (*Mucuna hasjoo*) that is related to the velvet bean and has showy purple flowers in racemes followed by plump ash-colored seeds resembling lima beans; *also* **:** its seed

yokohama fowl *n, usu cap Y* **:** JAPANESE FOWL

yo·ko·su·ka \ˌyōkəˈsükə *also* yəˈkäskə\ *adj, usu cap* [*Yokosuka,* city in southeast Honshu, Japan] **:** of or from the city of Yokosuka, Japan **:** of the kind or style prevalent in Yokosuka

yo·kuts \ˈyō(,)kəts\ *n, pl* **yokuts** [Yokuts, people] **1 a :** an Indian people of the San Joaquin Valley and adjacent Sierra Nevada slopes, California **b :** a member of such people **2 :** a Mariposan language of the Yokuts people **3 :** MARIPOSAN

yol·dia \ˈyōldēə\ *n, cap* [NL, fr. Count *Yoldi* †1852 Span. nobleman in charge of the royal naturalistic collection of Denmark + NL *-ia*] **:** a large genus of small primitive bivalve mollusks (family Nuculamidae) widely distributed in temperate and Arctic seas

yole \ˈyōl\ *n* -s [alter. of *yawl*] **:** a usu. open sailing boat of the Shetland and Orkney islands smaller than a fifie and with usu. one raked mast

yolk \ˈyōk *also* ˈyōlk *dial* ˈyelk *or* ˈyalk\ *or* **yoke** \ˈyōk\ *n* -s [ME *yolke, yelke,* fr. OE *geolca, geoloca,* fr. *geolu* yellow — more at YELLOW] **1 a :** the yellow spheroidal mass of stored food that forms the inner portion of the egg of a bird or reptile and is surrounded by the white — see WHITE YOLK, YELLOW YOLK; EGG illustration **b** *archaic* **:** the whole contents of an ovum which may be distinguished into a protoplasmic formative portion and an ergastric nutritive portion **c :** the material stored in an ovum that supplies food material to the developing embryo, consists chiefly of vitellin, nucleoprotein and other proteins, lecithin, and cholesterol, may be sparse and diffuse (as in a placental mammal) or copious and specif. arranged (as at the center or at one pole of the ovum), and when copious exerts a profound influence on the course of segmentation **2** [prob. alter. of (assumed) ME *yoke,* fr. (assumed) OE *ēowoca;* akin to MD *ieke* yolk (of wool); derivative fr. the root of E ¹*ewe*] **:** oily material permeating wool in the natural state and consisting of wool fat, suint, and debris of various sorts **3** *obs* **:** the best or most important part **:** CENTER, ESSENCE

yolk cell *n* **:** a nucleated cytoplasmic mass that is derived from the egg nucleus of an arthropod and provides nutriment for the developing embryo

yolk cord *n* **:** a slender protoplasmic cord that connects the yolk glands with the egg chambers in an insect (as an aphid)

yolk duct *n* **:** VITELLINE DUCT

yolked \-kt, *often* ,=*in combination*\ *adj* **:** having a yolk — usu. used in combination

yolk fry *n* **:** fry of fish between hatching and complete absorption of the yolk sac

yolk gland *n* **:** VITELLARIUM

yolk nucleus *n* **1 :** a formed body possibly associated with yolk formation present in the cytoplasm of many developing oocytes **2 :** a nucleus in yolk **:** VITELLOPHAG

yolk plate *n* **:** one of the lamellae into which the yolk of the egg of amphibians and various fishes splits

yolk plug *n* **:** a pluglike mass of yolk cells found in the blastopore of the embryos of some vertebrates

yolk sac *n* **:** a membranous sac that is attached to an embryo and encloses food yolk (as in most vertebrates and cephalopods), that is continuous through the vitelline duct with the intestinal cavity of the embryo, that being abundantly supplied with blood vessels is throughout embryonic life and in some forms later the chief organ of nutrition, and that in placental mammals is nearly vestigial and functions chiefly prior to the elaboration of the placenta

yolk-sac placenta *n* **:** a structure in some sharks resembling a placenta, consisting of the vascular embryonic yolk sac wall intimately associated with the vascular maternal uterine or oviducal wall, and serving to nourish the embryo

yolk stalk *n* **:** the narrow tubular stalk connecting the yolk sac with the embryo

yolky \-kē,-ki, *stressed* ˈ==\ *adj* -ER/-EST [*yolk* + *-y*] **1 :** relating to, resembling, or containing yolk **2** [prob. alter. of (assumed) ME *yoky,* fr. OE *ēowocig,* fr. (assumed) OE *ēowoca* yolk (of wool) + OE *-ig* -y — more at YOLK] **:** full of yolk **:** GREASY — used of unwashed wool

yolk yellow *n* **:** a strong yellow that is greener and stronger than gamboge and slightly stronger than light chrome yellow — called also *primuline yellow*

yo·ma·wood \ˈyōmə,-\ *n* [perh. fr. Burmese *youma* mountain range + E *wood*] **:** the wood of an Asiatic padauk and esp. Andaman padauk

yom kip·pur \(ˈ)yōmˈkipər, ¦yəm-, (ˈ)yōm-, (ˈ)yäm-; ¦=ki-¦pù(ə)r\ *n, usu cap Y&K* [Heb *yōm kippūr,* fr. *yōm* day + *kippūr* atonement] **:** a solemn Jewish fast day falling on the 10th day of Tishri and marked by continuous prayer and repentance according to the rites described in Leviticus 16 — called also *Day of Atonement*

yom tob *or* **yom tov** \ˈyō|m(,)təv, ˈyə| *sometimes* |n(,)t-; ¦yōmˈtōv\ *n, pl* **yo·mim to·bim** *or* **yo·mim to·vim** \¦yōmə̄m-ˈtōvəm, yō¦mēmtōˈvēm\ [Heb *yōm ṭōbh,* fr. *yōm* day + *ṭōbh* good] **:** a Jewish holiday or festival

yo·mud \ˈyōməd\ *n, pl* **yomud** *or* **yomuds** *usu cap* **1 :** a Turkoman people inhabiting the Khoresm oasis of Soviet Turkestan **2 :** a member of the Yomud people

¹**yon** \ˈyän, ˈyȯn, ˈyən\ *adj* [ME, fr. OE *geon;* akin to OHG *ienēr, enēr,* adj., that, ON *inn* the, Goth *jains,* adj., that, L *enim,* conj., for, Gk *enē* day after tomorrow, OSlav *onŭ* he, that] **1** *chiefly dial* **:** that or lies some distance away in the indicated place or direction **:** YONDER 2 ⟨the nighest is four miles off, over ~ snowy hills —Herman Melville⟩ **2** *dial* **:** YONDER 1 ⟨friends on the ~ side of the Potomac —Hervey Allen⟩

²**yon** \"\ *pron* [ME, fr. *yon,* adj.] *dial* **:** that or those yonder ⟨marryin' a man like ~ —Neil Munro⟩

³**yon** \"\ *adv* [ME (Sc), fr. ME *yon,* adj.] **:** YONDER ⟨~ the gallows used to clank —A.E.Housman⟩ ⟨palaces here and pleasure domes ~ —John Beaufort⟩ ⟨scattered here and ~ —Calder Willingham⟩

⁴**yon** \ˈyän\ *n* -s [origin unknown] **:** an Indian tree (*Anogeissus acuminata*) of the family Combretaceae with hard heavy yellowish wood that is esp. strong and useful for handles and shafts

yon·cal·la *also* **yon·kal·la** *or* **yon·ka·la** \yänˈkälə\ *n, pl* **yoncalla** *or* **yoncallas** *also* **yonkalla** *or* **yonkallas** *or* **yonkala** *or* **yonkalas** *usu cap* **1 :** a Kalapooian people of southwestern Oregon **2 :** a member of the Yoncalla people

yon·co·pin *also* **yon·ka·pin** *or* **yan·ka·pin** \ˈyäŋkə,pin\ *n* -S [modif. of Ojibwa *wankipin,* lit., crooked root] **:** WATER CHINQUAPIN

¹**yond** \ˈyänd, ˈyȯnd, ˈyənd\ *adv* [ME, fr. OE *geond;* akin to Goth *jaind* to that place, OE *geon,* adj., yonder — more at YON] *archaic* **:** YONDER

²**yond** \"\ *adj* [ME, fr. *yond,* adv.] *dial Brit* **:** YON

³**yond** \"\ *pron* [ME, fr. *yond,* adj.] *Brit* **:** that or those yonder

⁴**yond** \"\ *prep* [short for ²*beyond*] *archaic* **:** BEYOND, PAST

⁵**yond** *adj* [derived fr. ¹*yond* (through misunderstanding of the words *a tygre yond in Ynde,* actually meaning "a tiger yonder in India", in line E1199 of Chaucer's *Canterbury Tales*)] *obs* **:** RAGING

¹**yon·der** \ˈyändə(r) *sometimes* ˈyȯn- *or* ˈyən-\ *adv* [ME, fr. ¹*yond* + *-er* (as in *hider* hither)] **:** at or in that indicated somewhat distant place usu. within sight ⟨off ~ on a high rise —F.B.Gipson⟩ ⟨look way back ~ down the hill —Eudora Welty⟩

²**yonder** \"\ *adj* [ME, fr. *yonder,* adv.] **1 :** farther removed **:** more distant **:** THITHER ⟨a pleasant hay meadow . . . bordered it on the ~ side —Agnes S. Turnbull⟩ **2 :** being at a distance within view or at a place or in a direction known or indicated ⟨could not see any trees save one, way ~ in the stubble field —Jean Stafford⟩ ⟨down at the bottom of that road ~ —Dorothy G. Spicer⟩

³**yonder** \"\ *pron* [¹*yonder*] **:** something that is or is in an indicated somewhat distant place ⟨sending chips from he... —Maristan Chapman⟩

yo·ni \ˈyōnē\ *n* -s [Skt, vulva] **:** a figure representing female genitals serving as the formal symbol under whi... Shakti is worshiped — compare LINGAM — **yo·nic** \-nik\ *adj*

yonker *var of* YOUNKER

yon·kers \ˈyäŋkə(r)z\ *adj, usu cap* [*Yonkers,* city in southeast New York] **:** of or from the city of Yonkers, N.Y. ⟨a *Yonkers* resident⟩ **:** of the kind or style prevalent in Yonkers

yon·kers·ite \-,zīt\ *n* -s *cap* **:** a native or resident of Yonkers, New York

yons *pl of* YON

yont \ˈyänt\ *Scot var of* YOND

¹**yoo-hoo** \ˈyü,hü\ *interj* [origin unknown] — used to attract attention or as a call to persons

²**yoo-hoo** \"\ *vi* -ED/-ING/-S **:** to attract attention or call by or as if by shouting *yoo-hoo* ⟨arrived and *yoo-hooed* at the door —John Selby⟩

yore \ˈyō(ə)r, -ō(ə)r, -ōə, -ō(ə)\ *n* -s [ME, fr. *yore,* adv., long ago, fr. OE *geāra,* fr. *gēar* year — more at YEAR] **:** time past and esp. long since past — usu. used in the phrase *of yore* ⟨prize the region less highly than of ~ —R.A.Billington⟩ ⟨the finishing school of ~ is just about finished —H.R.Allen⟩

¹**york** \ˈyȯ(ə)rk, -ō(ə)k\ *adj, usu cap* [*York,* city in northern England] **1 :** of or from the city of York, England **:** of the kind or style prevalent in York **2** [*Yorkshire, York,* county in northern England] **:** YORKSHIRE

²**york** \"\ *vt* -ED/-ING/-S [back-formation fr. ²*yorker*] **:** to bowl out (a batsman) in cricket with a yorker

york boat *n, usu cap Y* [*York* Factory, trading post in northeast Manitoba, Canada] **:** a large rowboat used for hauling freight on inland waterways in the Canadian Northwest

¹**york·er** \ˈyȯrkər, -ō(ə)kə(r\ *n* -s *cap* [New *York,* state in the eastern U.S. + E *-er*] **1 :** a native or resident of New York esp. in colonial times **2** [*York,* city and county in southern Pennsylvania + E *-er*] **:** a native or resident of York, Pennsylvania or of York county, Pennsylvania

²**yorker** \"\ *n* -s [*York,* county in northern England + E *-er*] **:** a bowled ball in cricket that pitches in or close to the blockhole

³**yorker** \"\ *n* -s [New *York,* city in southeast New York (state) + E *-er;* fr. the popularity of such hogs with butchers in New York City] **:** a light but high-quality well-finished market hog suitable for fresh pork production

yorker brethren *n pl, usu cap Y&B* [¹*yorker* + *brethren;* fr. their origin mainly in York county, Pennsylvania] **:** members of a small body of River Brethren in the U.S. — called also *Old Order Brethren*

york gum *n, usu cap Y* [*York,* town in southwest Western Australia] **:** any of various eucalypts (esp. *Eucalyptus loxophleba* and *E. foecunda*) of Australia having pale brown wood with white markings

york·ish \-kish\ *adj, usu cap* [*York,* English royal house with reigning monarchs 1461–70 and 1471–85 (fr. *York,* city and county in northern England) + E *-ish*] **:** YORKIST

¹**york·ist** \-kəst\ *n* -s *cap* [*York,* English royal house + E *-ist*] **:** a member or supporter of the English royal house of York founded by Richard, Duke of York, in the time of Henry VI and continued by Edward IV, Edward V, and Richard III — compare LANCASTRIAN

²**yorkist** \"\ *adj, usu cap* **:** of or relating to the royal house of York

york rite *n, usu cap Y & often cap R* [*York,* city and county in northern England] **1 :** a ceremonial observed by one of the Masonic systems **2 :** a system or organization that observes the York rite and confers in the U.S. 13 degrees of which the last three are in commanderies of Knights Templar and in England four degrees — compare SCOTTISH RITE

york round *n, usu cap Y* **:** a men's round in archery consisting of 72 arrows fired at 100 yards, 48 at 80 yards, and 24 at 60 yards

york shilling *n, usu cap Y* [New *York,* state in the eastern U.S.] **:** a New York shilling worth about 12½ cents

¹**york·shire** \ˈyȯ(r)k,shi(ə)r, -iə, -,shə(r)\ *adj, usu cap* [*Yorkshire, York,* county in northern England] **:** of or from the county of York, England **:** of the kind or style prevalent in York

²**yorkshire** \"\ *n* -s *usu cap* **1 :** any of several breeds or strains of white swine originated in Yorkshire, England; *esp* **:** LARGE WHITE **2 :** a swine of a Yorkshire breed or strain — compare MIDDLE WHITE

yorkshire bond *n, usu cap Y* **:** FLYING BOND

yorkshire canary *n, usu cap Y* **:** a canary of a variety distinguished by long slim erect build

yorkshire chair *n, usu cap Y* **:** a small chair with knobbed turned legs, straight uprights ending at the top with scrolls, and a broad carved top rail and a wide splat arched above and crescent-cut below made esp. in England in the 17th and 18th centuries

Yorkshire chair

yorkshire coach horse *n, usu cap Y* **:** a large strong bay or brown horse with dark legs, mane, and tail belonging to an English breed derived largely from the Cleveland bay

yorkshire fog *n, usu cap Y* **:** VELVET GRASS

yorkshire grease *n, usu cap Y* **:** wool grease recovered by scouring

yorkshire light *n, usu cap Y* **:** a window made with sashes sliding in one plane as distinguished from hinged casements and with a usu. horizontal movement to avoid the necessity of a weighted sash

york·shire·man \-,mən, -,man, -,maa(ə)n\ *n, pl* **yorkshiremen** *cap* **:** a native or inhabitant of Yorkshire, England

yorkshire pudding *n, usu cap Y* **:** a batter of eggs, flour, and milk baked in meat drippings

yorkshire sanicle *n, usu cap Y* **:** a butterwort (*Pinguicula vulgaris*)

yorkshire terrier *n, usu cap Y* **:** a toy terrier having a compact body and straight silky hair that often trails on the ground and is colored a dark steel blue from the occiput to the root of the tail, a rich golden tan on the head and legs, and a bright tan on the chest

yorkshire tyke *n, usu cap Y* **:** YORKSHIREMAN

york spot *n, usu cap Y* [*York* Imperial, variety of apple developed in York county, Pennsylvania (fr. *York,* county in southern Pennsylvania) + E *spot*] **:** a cork disease of apples

york state *adj, usu cap Y* [New *York,* state in the eastern U.S.] **:** NEW YORK 2

yo·ru·ba \ˈyȯrəbə, ˈyōr-\ *n, pl* **yoruba** *or* **yorubas** *usu cap* **1 a :** a Negro people of the eastern Guinea coast mainly between Dahomey and the lower Niger **b :** a member of such people **2 :** a Kwa language of the Yoruba people

yo·ru·ban \-bən\ *adj, usu cap* **:** of or relating to the Yoruba

yo·shi·no paper \yəˈshē(,)nō-\ *n, usu cap Y* [perh. fr. *Yoshino,* town in central Honshu, Japan] **:** a Japanese tissue made from the fibers of the paper mulberry

¹**you** \(ˈ)yü, yə, yē, *in "you're" usu* & *in "you'll" often* (ˈ)yù; *dial* (ˈ)yō; *the* y & *a preceding* t *are usu* ch (=t+sh) *as in "not you," the* y & *a preceding* d *are usu* j (=d+zh) *as in "did you"*\ *pron* [ME *you, yow,* fr. OE *ēow,* used as dat. & accus. of *gē* you; akin to MD *u* you (used as dat. & accus. of *gi, ge* you), OHG *iu* (used as dat. of *ir* you), ON *ythr* (used as dat. & accus. of *ēr* you), Goth *izwis* (used as dat. & accus. of *jus* you), and prob. to L *vos* you — more at RENDEZVOUS] **1 a :** the one or ones being addressed — used currently and freely as the pronoun of the second person singular or plural in any grammatical relation except that of a possessive; used from Old English times to the 13th or 14th century only as a plural pronoun of the second person in the dative or accusative case as direct or indirect object of a verb or as object of a preposition and still current in this use alongside of other more recently originated uses ⟨I'll meet ~ there, fellows⟩ ⟨we will give ~ ten minutes to disperse⟩ ⟨presents for ~ two⟩; used since the 13th or 14th century also as a singular pronoun of

the second person as direct or indirect object of a verb or as object of a preposition, at first only as the appropriate form of address to a person of high social status or to a person not well known to the speaker but later without this limitation ⟨I shall . . . obey ~, madam —*Shak.*⟩ ⟨can I pour ~ a cup of tea⟩ ⟨a suit tailored just for ~⟩; used since the 14th century also as a plural pronoun of the second person in the nominative case and at any rate since the 16th century also in direct address ⟨~ have among you killed a sweet and innocent lady —*Shak.*⟩ ⟨stand still, ~ ever-moving spheres of heaven —Christopher Marlowe⟩; used since the 15th century also as a singular pronoun of the second person in the nominative case and at any rate since the early 16th century also in direct address, at first only as the appropriate form of address to a person of high social status or to a person not well known to the speaker but later without this limitation ⟨~ shall not go, my lord —*Shak.*⟩ ⟨stop that, ~ little pest⟩; sometimes used as a vague indirect object simply to suggest the concern or involvement of the one or ones being addressed or even with little or no meaning ⟨a civil modest wife, and one . . . that will not miss ~ morning nor evening prayer —*Shak.*⟩ ⟨he could knock ~ off forty Latin verses in an hour —W.M.Thackeray⟩; used like the adjective *your* with a gerund by speakers and writers on all educational levels though disapproved by some grammarians ⟨there is no point in ~ waiting any longer⟩; see YE, YOUR, YOURS; compare THEE, THOU **b** (1) **:** YOURSELVES — used reflexively as indirect object of a verb ⟨build ~ cities —Num 32:24 (AV)⟩ or object of a preposition ⟨divide it between ~⟩ or direct object of a verb ⟨prepare ~, lords —*Shak.*⟩ (2) **:** YOURSELF — used reflexively as indirect object of a verb ⟨you'd better find ~ another place to hang your hat —T.H. Phillips⟩ or object of a preposition ⟨bring your wife with ~⟩ or direct object of a verb ⟨Your Highness shall repose ~ at the Tower —*Shak.*⟩ **2 :** ²ONE 1b(1) ⟨when ~ have summed up all the factors of a man that can be measured ~ have still not described or understood him —A.L.Nickerson⟩ — **for you :** displayed in his, her, its, or their characteristic nature or behavior ⟨he's already forgotten he was hurt — that's a child *for you*⟩ — often used disparagingly ⟨that's a woman driver *for you*⟩ — **to you 1 :** according to the form of a name or title that is proper for you to use ⟨not John, if you don't mind — Mr. Doe *to you*⟩ **2 :** in easily understandable nontechnical language ⟨trinitrotoluene (TNT *to you*)⟩

²**you** \ˈyü\ *n* -s **1 :** a person indistinguishable from the one being addressed ⟨in everything but outward appearance he is another ~⟩ **2 :** the personality of the person being addressed ⟨the real ~⟩

you-all \(ˈ)yü¦ȯl, ˈyȯl\ *pron, chiefly South* **:** YOU — usu. used in addressing two or more persons or sometimes one person as representing also another or others ⟨down here we can always spot Yankees by the way they use *you-all* in the singular —Arthur Gordon⟩ ⟨*you-all* stop arguing among yourselves⟩

¹**young** \ˈyəŋ\ *adj* **youn·ger** \-ŋgə(r)\ **youn·gest** \-ŋgəst\ [ME *yong*, fr. OE *geong*; akin to OHG *jung* young, ON *ungr* young, Goth *jungs* youthful, new, L *juvenis* young, Skt *yuvan*] **1 :** being in the first or relatively early stage of life, growth, or development: as **a :** not long born **:** being in the first part of life **:** not yet arrived at adolescence, maturity, or age ⟨mothers with very ~ children⟩ ⟨a strapping ~*er* brother —R.T.Bird⟩ ⟨~ people⟩ ⟨a ~ family⟩ ⟨a ~ man⟩ ⟨you have but a very few years to be ~ and handsome —Jonathan Swift⟩ ⟨forgot that he was once ~ and passionate —Carl Van Doren⟩ ⟨~ puppies⟩ ⟨a spirited ~ colt⟩; *specif* **:** JUNIOR 1a ⟨the ~ Mr. Smith⟩ ⟨it was ~ Alex who . . . informed his father —Glenway Wescott⟩ **b :** of an early, tender, or desirable age esp. for use as food ⟨fresh ~ lamb⟩ ⟨~ pork⟩ ⟨~ corn on the cob⟩ **c :** being in an early or immature state of development or cultivation ⟨in place of the old will come new ~ scarlet oaks and beech, 10 feet high when planted —P.L.Ritzema⟩ ⟨apple sawfly caterpillars attack the ~ fruit in early summer⟩ ⟨~ shoots of the new grass⟩; *specif* **:** being in an early stage of ripening or fermentation ⟨a ~ cheese⟩ ⟨~ wine⟩ **2 :** having little experience esp. in a newly begun course of action or procedure **:** UNPRACTICED ⟨liked to hide my blunders . . . behind the shield of pretence that I was ~, naïve, inexperienced —*Omnibook*⟩ ⟨was always ~ for liberty . . . of the intellect and spirit —Van Wyck Brooks⟩ ⟨the world was as yet too ~ in science for that —Charlton Laird⟩ **3 a :** newly formed, constructed, or organized **:** recently come into being **:** NEW ⟨she is a ~ ship, capable of outrunning most submarines —Walter Bernstein⟩ ⟨this part of the road is ~*er* than the part farther west —G.R.Stewart⟩ ⟨when the war was ~ —Thomas Wood †1950⟩ ⟨a ~ boom town —*Current Biog.*⟩ ⟨a model for the ~ democracies —*Brit. Bk. News*⟩ ⟨the ~*er* universities —S.P.B. Mais⟩ ⟨the ~ petroleum industry⟩ **b :** being in the early part or phase of a specified development or period of time ⟨a ~ moon —J.B.S.Haldane⟩ ⟨the day was still ~ —Agnes S. Turnbull⟩ ⟨the night is yet ~ —R.H.Croll⟩ **c :** YOUTHFUL 5 ⟨the ~ alluvial soils . . . have not yet developed a profile —R.E.Crist⟩ ⟨streams that have just entered upon their work of erosion . . . are called ~ streams —V.C.Finch & G.T.Trewartha⟩ **4 :** of, relating to, or having the characteristics of youth or a young person ⟨trying to stay ~ as he grows old⟩ ⟨her soft ~ voice —Walter O'Meara⟩ ⟨loves the language enough to want to keep it always ~ and racy —C.E.Montague⟩ ⟨~ for his age⟩ ⟨wearing the ~*est* and giddiest hats they can find —Lois Long⟩ **5 :** simulative of something in its full scale **:** DIMINUTIVE, MINIATURE ⟨under her hands the harpsichord . . . was no small and ancient instrument, but a whole ~ orchestra in sound —Osbert Sitwell⟩ ⟨the heavy rain produced a ~ flood in the street⟩ ⟨his souvenirs form a ~ museum⟩ **6** *usu cap* **:** forming or representing a new or rejuvenated group or movement esp. of a political nature ⟨the *Young* Republicans⟩ ⟨*Young* Germany⟩ ⟨*Young* Italy⟩

²**young** \ˈ"\ *n, pl* **young** *also* **youngs** [ME *yonge*, fr. OE *geonga* (sing.), *geonge*, *geongan* (pl.), fr. *geong*, adj.] **1** *young, pl* **:** those that are young: as **a :** young persons **:** YOUTH ⟨a story for ~ and old⟩ ⟨impart to the ~ the cultural heritage —Thomas Munro⟩ ⟨the ~ have a harder time of it than any previous generation —Hans Weigel⟩ **b :** the offspring of human beings or of animals before or for a short time after birth ⟨parents must think out . . . what this means to their own ~ —Dorothy Barclay⟩ ⟨talking to him as all women talk to their ~ —Farley Mowat⟩ ⟨watching animals . . . with ~ —C.K.Ogden⟩ ⟨bringing forth their ~⟩ **2 :** a single recently born or hatched animal **:** OFFSPRING ⟨producing one ~ each year⟩ — **with young :** PREGNANT — used of a female animal

youngberry \ˈ=,- — *see* BERRY\ *n* [after B. M. *Young fl* 1900 Am. fruit grower who developed it] **:** the large sweet reddish black fruit of a hybrid between a trailing blackberry and a southern dewberry grown in western and southern U.S.; *also* **:** the trailing hybrid bramble

youn·ger \ˈyəŋgə(r)\ *n* -s [ME *yonger*, fr. OE *geongra* disciple, servant, alter. (influenced by *geong*) of *gyngra*, fr. *gyngra*, compar. of *geong* young] **1 :** an inferior in age **:** JUNIOR — usu. used with a possessive pronoun ⟨his sister is several years his ~⟩ **2 a :** a young person **:** OFFSPRING — usu. used in pl. ⟨all the ~*s* are going to the circus with their families⟩ **3 a :** the dealer in a two-handed card game **b :** the partner of the eldest hand in a four-handed partnership game

youn·gest \-gəst\ *n, pl* **youngest** [ME *yongest*, *yongeste*, alter. (influenced by *yong* young) of *yingest*, *yingeste*, fr. OE *gyngesta*, *gyngsta*, fr. *gyngst*, superl. of *geong* young] **:** one that is least old; *esp* **:** the youngest child or member of a family ⟨you can go back to your law office after our ~ grows up —Evelyn Barkins⟩

young fustic *n* **1 :** FUSTET 2 **2 :** the coloring matter that is extracted from fustet dyewood — see DYE table I (under *Natural Brown 1*)

young-helmholtz theory \ˈyəŋˈhelm,hōlts, -ˈheu̇¦-\ *n, usu cap Y&H* [Thomas *Young* †1829 Eng. physician and physicist and Hermann L. F. von *Helmholtz* †1894 Ger. physicist] **:** a theory in color vision: the eye has three separate elements each of which is stimulated by a different primary color

young hyson *n* **:** a hyson tea made from young leaves

young·ish \ˈyəŋish, -ēsh\ *adj* **:** somewhat young **:** more nearly resembling or characteristic of a young person than one of maturity or middle age ⟨a ~ but not adolescent audience —Virgil Thomson⟩ ⟨~ spinsters —*New Yorker*⟩ ⟨prematurely bald, ~ —T.M.Johnson⟩

young lady *n* [ME *yong lady*, fr. *yong* young + *lady*] **:** a usu. unmarried young woman of grace, manners, or distinction ⟨is becoming quite a *young lady*⟩

¹**young·ling** \ˈyəŋliŋ, -lēŋ\ *n* -s [ME *yongling*, fr. OE *geongling*, fr. *geong* young + *-ling*] **:** one that is young: as **a :** a young person **:** YOUTH ⟨a thin blond ~ —D.C.Peattie⟩ ⟨an automobile . . . is no treat to quite a large proportion of our ~*s* —F.A.Swinnerton⟩ **b :** a young animal or offspring of an animal ⟨the ~ rejoined its mother who . . . led her darling away into the tall grass —Roy Bedichek⟩ ⟨nerves . . . so placed in the ~ as to provide for the migration —*Book of Fishes*⟩

²**youngling** \ˈ"\ *adj* **:** YOUNG, YOUTHFUL

young·ly *adv* **1 :** in a young or youthful manner ⟨her . . . dark hair was ~ dressed —Margaret Sloper⟩ **2 :** early in life **:** in youth ⟨had been a passionate and ~ matured girl —Philip Wylie⟩

young man *n* [ME *yong man*, fr. *yong* young + *man*] **1 :** a male youth; *esp* **:** one in early manhood **2 :** a youth employed as a helper **3 :** male sweetheart **:** BEAU ⟨she is entertaining her *young man* this evening⟩

young·ness *n* -ES **:** YOUTHFULNESS

young-old \ˈ=¦=\ *adj* **:** old in years but having the characteristics of youth

young one \ˈyəŋ(w)ən, *dial* -ŋəm *or* ˈyōŋə-\ *n* [ME *yong oon* young person, fr. *yong* young + *oon* one] **1 :** a young human being **:** CHILD, YOUNGSTER ⟨they've got eleven *young ones*, eleven brats now —Elizabeth M. Roberts⟩ **2 :** a young animal

young people *n* **:** the youth usu. between the ages of 12 and 24 ministered to by a Protestant Christian church or denomination; *esp* **:** the organized youth group of a church ⟨the *young people's* meeting⟩ ⟨*young people's* service⟩ ⟨the *young people* have invited the Connecticut valley youth to be their guests —*Springfield (Mass.) Unity News*⟩

youngs *pl of* YOUNG

young's experiment \ˈyəŋz-\ *n, usu cap Y* [after Thomas *Young* †1829 Eng. physician and physicist] **:** an experiment in which light diverging from one slit passes through two narrow slits very close together and then falls on a screen so that a series of parallel bands are observed on the screen because of interference of light from the two slits

young's modulus *n, usu cap Y* **:** the ratio of the tensile stress in a material to the corresponding tensile strain — see MODULUS OF ELASTICITY

young·ster \ˈyəŋztə(r), -ŋ(k)st-\ *n* -s **1 a :** a usu. vigorous or lively young person **:** YOUTH ⟨communities which do not have adequate facilities for the ~ in trouble —J.B.Costello⟩ ⟨tells us . . . of the adolescence of this ~ —H.G.Wells⟩ ⟨a bumper crop of teen-age ~*s* fast ripening into . . . soldiers —*U.S.News & World Report*⟩ **b :** CHILD ⟨the mother with her ~*s* tumbling about her feet⟩ **c :** a person in the relatively early years of manhood or of a career ⟨it is among the ~*s*, aged from 20 to 40, that the flame of confidence burns brightest —Drew Middleton⟩ ⟨only a handful . . . left, most of them ~*s* in their twenties and thirties —*Saturday Rev.*⟩ **d :** an older or aged person retaining the vitality or vigor of youth ⟨a sprightly ~ of eighty, he's still going strong doing six shows a day —*Irish Digest*⟩ **2 a :** a midshipman who has served less than four years — compare OLDSTER 1 **b :** a sophomore at a military academy (as the U.S. Naval Academy) **3 a :** a young mammal, bird, or plant esp. of a domesticated or cultivated breed or type ⟨owners can try out their ~*s* for the first time on a racecourse —Dennis Craig⟩ ⟨one ~ . . . old enough to fly —T.M.Downs⟩ ⟨no trees except for a few hardy ~*s* —Nathaniel Burt⟩ **b youngsters** *pl, dial* **:** the young leaves of the common wintergreen (*Gaultheria procumbens*) **4 :** something newly formed, instituted, or established ⟨ballet . . . was just about a hundred years old, practically a ~ as art forms go —Anatole Chujoy⟩ ⟨joined hands with another promising ~, a journalistic fraternity —*Quill*⟩

youngs·town \ˈyəŋz,tau̇n\ *adj, usu cap* [*Youngstown*, city in northeast Ohio] **:** of or from the city of Youngstown, Ohio ⟨*Youngstown* steel mills⟩ **:** of the kind or style prevalent in Youngstown

young thing *n* [ME *yong thing* young person, fr. *yong* young + *thing* person, living being, thing] **1 :** a young person; *esp* **:** a young woman ⟨sweet *young thing*⟩ **2 :** a young animal; *specif* **:** a horse not yet old enough to be completely trained and ready for use

young turk *n, usu cap Y&T* [*Young Turk*, member of a revolutionary party in Turkey in the early years of the 20th cent.] **:** an insurgent or a member of an insurgent group in a political party **:** LIBERAL, RADICAL ⟨are the *Young Turks* . . . opposed to the ossified conservatism of the older so-called statesmen —John Gunther⟩ ⟨the truculence of the *Young Turks* colliding with the standpat South —Alistair Cooke⟩

youn·ker *or* **yon·ker** \ˈyəŋkə(r)\ *n* -s [D *jonker* young nobleman, young man of high rank, fr. MD *jonchere*, fr. *jonc* young (akin to OE *geong* young) + *here* lord, master (akin to OHG *hērro*, *hēriro* lord, master, fr. *hēriro*, compar. of *hēr* old) — more at YOUNG, HOAR] **1 a :** a young man **:** YOUNGSTER **b :** CHILD **2** *archaic* **:** a junior seaman on board ship

youpon *var of* YAUPON

¹**your** [ME, fr. OE *ēower* (used as gen. of *gē* you); akin to OHG *iuwēr* of you, ON *ythar*, Goth *izwara* of you, OE *ēow* (used as dat. & accus. of *gē* you) — more at YOU] *obs possessive of* YE

²**your** \yə(r), (ˌ)yu̇(ə)r, (ˌ)yō(ə)r, (ˌ)yȯ(ə)r, -ùə, -ōə, -ȯ(ə), *South chiefly substand* (ˌ)yō; *for* t & d + y *see* ¹YOU\ *adj* [ME, fr. OE *ēower*; akin to OHG *iuwēr* your, ON *ythar*, *ythvarr*, Goth *izwar*; derivative fr. the root of E ¹*you*] **1 a :** of or belonging to you or yourself or yourselves as possessor or possessors **:** due to you **:** inherent in you **:** associated or connected with you ⟨~ heart⟩ ⟨~ talents⟩ ⟨~ bodies⟩ **b :** of or relating to you or yourself or yourselves as author or authors, doer or doers, giver or givers, or agent or agents **:** effected by you **:** experienced by you as subject **:** that you are capable of ⟨~ contributions⟩ ⟨with ~ permission⟩ ⟨by ~ assembling here⟩ ⟨working ~ hardest⟩ **c :** of or relating to you or yourself or yourselves as object of an action **:** experienced by you as object ⟨~ discharge from the army⟩ ⟨~ election as the officers for the coming year⟩ **d :** that you have to do with or are supposed to possess or to have knowledge or a share of or some special interest in ⟨you students know ~ geography⟩ — sometimes used with little or no meaning almost as an equivalent to the definite article *the* ⟨~ worm is ~ only emperor for diet —*Shak.*⟩ ⟨if ~ pragmatist-instrumentalist is asked for an opinion —M.B.Smith⟩ **e :** that is esp. significant for you **:** that brings you good fortune or prominence — used with *day* or sometimes with other words indicating a division of time ⟨congratulations on the prizes; this is really ~ day⟩ **2 :** of, belonging to, or relating to one or oneself ⟨when you face the north, east is at ~ right⟩ — compare ¹YOU 2

yourn \(ˈ)yō(ə)rn, (ˈ)yu̇(ə)rn, (ˈ)yȯ(ə)rn, -ùən, -ōən, -ȯ(ə)n; *for* t & d + y *see* ¹YOU\ *pron* [ME *youren*, fr. *youre*, *your* your + *-n* (as in *min* mine)] *dial* **:** YOURS

¹**yours** *pronunciations at* ²YOUR *(except first)* + z\ *pron* [ME *yours*, *youres*, fr. *your* + *-s*, *-es* -'s] **1 a :** your one **:** your ones — used without a following noun as a pronoun equivalent in meaning to the adjective *your* ⟨either my fault or ~⟩ ⟨these tomatoes are ~⟩; often used esp. with an adverbial modifier in the complimentary close of a letter to express the polite fiction that the sender puts himself entirely at the receiver's disposal ⟨~ truly⟩ ⟨~ faithfully⟩ ⟨sincerely ~⟩; often used after *of* to single out one or more members of a class belonging to or connected with the one or ones being addressed ⟨a neighbor of ~⟩ ⟨some favorite records of ~⟩ or merely to identify something or someone as belonging to or connected with the one or ones being addressed without any implication of membership in a more extensive class ⟨that arthritis of ~⟩ ⟨all those cats of ~⟩ ⟨that wry humor of ~⟩ **b :** your family ⟨sending best wishes to you and ~⟩ **c :** your letter ⟨this is in reply to ~ of the 24th⟩ — usu. considered stylistically undesirable **2 :** something belonging to you **:** what belongs to you ⟨all that is mine is ~ —Lk 15:31 (RSV)⟩ **3 :** something belonging to one **:** what belongs to one ⟨when you have worked hard, you naturally want to get the reward that is rightfully ~⟩ — compare ¹YOU 2 — **yours truly :** I, ME, MYSELF ⟨I can take care of *yours truly*⟩ ⟨if it suits you, it's all right with *yours truly*⟩

²**yours** *adj, obs* **:** ²YOUR 1 — used as the first of two modifiers of the same noun

yourself \=ˈ=\ *pron* [ME, fr. ²*your* + *self*, n.] **1 a :** that identical one that is you **:** the self that belongs to you **:** the self that is yours — used at first only in reference to a person of high social status or a person not well known to the speaker ⟨as many, worthy lady, to ~ —*Shak.*⟩ but later without this limitation; used reflexively as object of a preposition or direct or indirect object of a verb ⟨why should you be so cruel to ~ —John Milton⟩ ⟨be careful or you might hurt ~⟩ ⟨how much time do you allow ~ for a shave⟩ or for emphasis in apposition esp. with *you* or *ye* or after an imperative verb ⟨an ice pick which you ~ had bought —Erle Stanley Gardner⟩ ⟨you said the same thing ~⟩ ⟨I'd like to see you do any better ~⟩ ⟨carry the packages ~⟩ or for emphasis instead of nonreflexive *you* as object of a preposition or direct or indirect object of a verb ⟨a method developed . . . by men like ~ —Bernard Bloch⟩ ⟨asked me to give your wife and ~ his best wishes⟩ or for emphasis instead of *you* or instead of *you yourself* as predicate nominative ⟨the only one I am worried about is ~⟩ or in comparisons after *than* or *as* ⟨nobody is better qualified for the job than ~⟩ or as part of a compound subject ⟨we hope your husband and ~ can be there⟩ or in archaic or substandard use as only subject of a verb either in the third person singular form or in the same form that would agree with *you* as subject ⟨I'm all right; how's ~⟩ ⟨~ are tall —Robert Browning⟩ or in absolute constructions ⟨~ a cautious man, you expect caution in others⟩ **b :** your normal, healthy, or sane condition ⟨when you came to ~ again after the accident⟩ **:** your normal, healthy, or sane self ⟨you are not ~ today⟩ **2 :** ONESELF ⟨it is more restful to ride in a car that someone else is driving than to drive a car ~⟩ ⟨the registrant testified that, in his belief, the Bible does believe in defending ~ but not with weapons —J.J.Smith⟩ ⟨the process of coming to ~ after an anesthetic⟩

yourselves \=ˈ=\ *pron pl* [fr. *yourself*, after E *self: selves*] **1 :** those identical ones that are you **:** the selves that belong to you **:** the selves that are yours — used reflexively as object of a preposition or direct or indirect object of a verb ⟨you have a right to be proud of ~⟩ ⟨you need not trouble ~ about that⟩ ⟨so that you children can get ~ a treat⟩ or for emphasis in apposition esp. with *you* or *ye* or after an imperative verb ⟨that ye will not fall upon me ~ —Judg 15:12 (AV)⟩ ⟨do your homework ~⟩ or for emphasis instead of nonreflexive *you* as object of a preposition or direct or indirect object of a verb ⟨here are some presents for your children and also some for ~⟩ or for predicate nominative ⟨it was ~ broke compact and played false —Robert Browning⟩ or in comparisons after *than* or *as* ⟨by my birth I am held no less than ~ to know the limits of honor —P.B.Shelley⟩ or as part of a compound subject ⟨what do your neighbors and ~ think of the new highway⟩ or archaically as only subject of a verb ⟨now ~ have heard these things —Robert Browning⟩ or in absolute constructions ⟨envy me not the chance, ~ more fortunate —Robert Browning⟩ **2 :** the normal, healthy, or sane condition of you persons **:** your normal, healthy, or sane selves ⟨you will feel more like ~ after a good rest⟩

yous *pl of* YOU

youse *or* **yous** \(ˌ)yüz, yəz, yəs, (ˌ)yüs\ *pron* [¹*you* + ¹*-s*] *substand* **:** YOU — usu. used in addressing two or more persons or sometimes one person as representing also another or others ⟨the two of ~ —J.M.Synge⟩ ⟨the rest of ~ —J.A. Hetherington⟩

youth \ˈyüth\ *n, pl* **youths** \-t͟hz,-ths\ *often attrib* [ME *youthe*, fr. OE *geoguth*; akin to MD *joget* youth, OHG *jugund*, Goth *junda* youth, OE *geong* young — more at YOUNG] **1 a :** the time of life when one is young; *esp* **:** the period between childhood and maturity ⟨left two little girls who . . . spent their motherless ~ with their widowed father —Havelock Ellis⟩ ⟨in his ~ . . . combined cotton and dairy farming with acquiring an education —*Current Biog.*⟩ ⟨incongruities of ~ and age —John Galsworthy⟩ **b :** the early period of existence, growth, or development ⟨following its lively ~ the community lapsed into quietude —*Amer. Guide Series: Texas*⟩ ⟨dinosaurian knowledge was still in its ~ —W.E.Swinton⟩ ⟨many potentially sound animals are ruined . . . especially in ~ —*Farming*⟩ **2 a :** a young person; *esp* **:** a young male between the ages of adolescence and maturity ⟨at the age of fourteen the ~ entered . . . the office —A.L.Churchill⟩ ⟨a ~ aged 17 years —*Jour. Amer. Med. Assoc.*⟩ ⟨~*s* with something better than a secondary education —Roy Lewis & Angus Maude⟩ ⟨sold . . . to men, women, ~*s* of both sexes, and even to children —*Amer. Bk. Publishers Council*⟩ **b :** young persons or creatures — usu. pl. in constr. ⟨a future for the ~ who enter the teaching profession —*Education Digest*⟩ ⟨only seven out of ten ~ of high school age are now enrolled —B.H.Alberty⟩ ⟨that American ~ on the nation's campuses is not given . . . disappointment —B.G.Gallagher⟩ **c** *sometimes cap* **:** youth personified or youth in general ⟨~ in its search for life's permanent values —*Brit. Bk. News*⟩ ⟨~ will be served⟩ ⟨for ~ nothing is insurmountable⟩ **3 :** the fresh or vigorous condition or appearance of body, mind, or spirit characteristic of the period between childhood and maturity **:** YOUTHFULNESS ⟨restore an old man to ~ —Sara Jordan⟩ ⟨an inevitable symptom of the city's ~ and vigor —*Amer. Guide Series: Minn.*⟩ ⟨these ancient stories have the perennial ~ of human charm —H.O.Taylor⟩ **4 :** the quality or state of being young ⟨succeeded admirably in spite of his extreme ~ —F.T.Persons⟩ **5 :** the first stage into which a cycle of erosion is commonly divided ⟨all the erosional stages from the features of ~ to those of old age —V.C.Finch & G.T.Trewartha⟩

syn ADOLESCENCE, PUBERTY, PUBESCENCE, YOUTH are frequently used interchangeably to refer to the period between childhood and maturity. YOUTH, the most inclusive of these terms, applies sometimes to the entire period from childhood to maturity, sometimes to the period only between the maturing of the sexual organs and attaining to other types of maturity; more than the other terms YOUTH suggests the vigor, innocence, and ingratiating attributes generally associated with this early period of life and so has come to suggest vigor or fullness of life generally. ADOLESCENCE designates the same period as YOUTH in its most restricted sense, but carries a stronger implication of immaturity, suggesting the inexperience or awkwardness or mental or emotional instability often characteristic of that period of life; in legal use it designates the period from puberty to full legal age or majority. Strictly, PUBERTY designates the age at which the symptoms of sexual maturing appear, as the growth of beard and alteration of voice range in boys or breast development in girls; legally this age is fixed at fourteen for boys and twelve for girls. More broadly, PUBERTY covers the earlier period of adolescence. PUBESCENCE is sometimes used as the equivalent of PUBERTY or more specif. signifies the early years of sexual maturing.

youth-and-old-age \ˈ=ˌ=ˌ=ˈ=\ *n* **:** ZINNIA 2

youth·en \ˈyüthən\ *vb* -ED/-ING/-S *vt* **:** to make youthful in appearance, behavior, or qualities of mind or feeling ~ *vi* **:** to become youthful in appearance or characteristics

youth fellowship *n, often cap Y&F* **:** the organized youth group of a Protestant Christian church or denomination

youth·ful \ˈyüthfəl\ *adj* **1 :** of, relating to, or appropriate for youth or the period of youth ⟨could remember from his ~ enlisted days —J.G.Cozzens⟩ ⟨his ~ optimism and his cheerful trust in men —Katherine McNamara⟩ **2 :** not yet advanced beyond the early stage of growth or development ⟨in the ~ shell the dorsal valve develops a nearly straight posterior . . . margin —J.A.Thomson b. 1881⟩ ⟨a hotbed of ~ plants⟩ ⟨a ~ culture —Stringfellow Barr⟩ **3 :** possessing or characterized by youth **:** not old or mature ⟨~ dancers crowd the floor⟩ ⟨the ~ pitcher handles himself like a veteran⟩ **4 :** having the vitality or freshness of youth **:** FRESH, VIGOROUS ⟨seems a bit dated now . . . but it is skillful, fluent, and ~ —Arthur Berger⟩ ⟨a ~ octogenarian —W.J.Ghent⟩ ⟨of the most brilliant colors and ~ cut —W.M.Thackeray⟩ **5 :** having accomplished or undergone little erosion ⟨high mountain chains of ~ topography —L.C.Reed⟩ ⟨valleys . . . carved by vigorous ~ streams —*Science*⟩ ⟨the ~ volcanic islands —*Jour. of Geol.*⟩ — compare CYCLE OF EROSION

syn JUVENILE, PUERILE, BOYISH, VIRGIN, VIRGINAL, MAIDEN: YOUTHFUL indicates simply a pertinence or appropriateness to youth; it is likely to be benign or appreciative, noncommittal, or extenuating in its suggestion ⟨in old age when the circulation to the skin is lessened, the skin loses its *youthful* appearance —Morris Fishbein⟩ ⟨with bare shoulders and a little necklace, and a light blue sash, she looked the image of *youthful* innocence and girlish happiness —W.M.Thackeray⟩ ⟨*youthful* indiscretions⟩ JUVENILE often stresses the fact of youth and immaturity or of suitability to it; it may be used to stigmatize lack of adult judgment ⟨*juvenile* activities⟩ ⟨*juvenile* fiction⟩ ⟨the majority of the Irish people were only mildly sympathetic with the rebels, and regarded their desperate rebellion as *juvenile* melodrama —Paul Blanshard⟩ ⟨whereas adolescents looked upon this intense absorption as *juvenile* and had much more sophisticated attitudes —J.E.Anderson⟩ PUERILE may factually describe the acts or utterances of a boy or girl, esp. one quite young; it often stigmatizes childish immaturity in situations in which adult maturity can be expected or hoped for ⟨*puerile* digestive upsets⟩ ⟨it was dishonest, it was absurd, and it was *puerile* —Bernard De Voto⟩ ⟨badly constructed, incoherent, *puerile* in conception and presentation, and written in shoddy journalese —D.S.Savage⟩ BOYISH is often used in reference to the attractive or engaging qualities of normal, vigorous, unsophisticated boys ⟨*boyish* ardor⟩ ⟨*boyish* frankness⟩ ⟨had always, in a shy, *boyish* fashion, worshipped his big brother —B.A.Williams⟩ ⟨her features were clear-cut, her neck long and slender, her figure slim and *boyish* —Elizabeth Goudge⟩ VIRGIN stresses inexperience, esp. sexual inexperience, often with accompanying ingenuousness ⟨he was married, and the secret could be given only to a *virgin* youth —W.T.Corlett⟩ ⟨the picture of youth, unprotected innocence, and humble *virgin* simplicity —W.M. Thackeray⟩ VIRGINAL may be closely synonymous with VIRGIN; it is more likely to connote chastened or pure suggestions of virgin inexperience ⟨though she had lost long ago her *virginal* loveliness, she had ripened at middle age into a handsome and fruitful-looking woman —Ellen Glasgow⟩ MAIDEN may be a less frank synonym for VIRGIN ⟨a *maiden* aunt⟩ or it may apply to a first effort ⟨a *maiden* speech⟩ or suggest youthful chaste inexperience ⟨the *maiden* chastity and simplicity of these furnishings⟩ ⟨the young ladies on board, whom . . . the Cambridge lads and their pale-faced tutor avoided with *maiden* coyness —W.M.Thackeray⟩

youth·ful·ly \-fəlē, -li\ *adv* : in a youthful manner ⟨he is still ~ erratic⟩

youth·ful·ness *n* -ES : the quality or state of being youthful

youthful offender *or* **youth offender** *n* : a young lawbreaker usu. between the ages of 16 and 22 who has not committed a crime punishable by death or life imprisonment and toward whom a criminal court may use juvenile court procedures to attempt rehabilitation without imprisonment or other usual penalties

youth group *n* : a group of youths or young persons forming a part or a unit of an organized social, political, or religious institution ⟨the church sponsors a *youth group*⟩ ⟨the *youth groups* held another congress —E.A.Peers⟩

youth·head \ˈyüth,hed, -ü,thed\ *n* [ME *youthede, youthhede,* fr. *youthe, youth* youth + *-hede* -hood (akin to ME *-hod, -had* -hood)] *chiefly Scot* : the state or time of youth

youth·hood \-th,hu̇d\ *n* : the fact, condition, state, or time of being young

youth hostel *n* : HOSTEL 2b

youth hosteler *or* **youth hosteller** *n* **1** : one that stays at a youth hostel while traveling **2** : one that supervises a youth hostel

youth·ly *adj, archaic* : YOUTHFUL

youth movement *n* : a political, religious, or social movement or agitation led by or consisting chiefly of youth or young people and usu. aiming at reform or revolution ⟨ready . . . to join the Nazi *youth movements* —*Brit. Bk. News*⟩ ⟨the liberal section of younger Americans, the type out of whom *youth movements* are made —*Nation*⟩ ⟨basic to all *youth movements* are a deep dissatisfaction with the existing . . . order, a desire to change this order —Hans Kohn⟩ — compare YOUTH GROUP

youth–on–age \ˈ≈,≈ˈ≈\ *n* : PICKABACK PLANT

youths *pl of* YOUTH

youthy \ˈyüthē, -thi\ *adj* -ER/-EST **1** *chiefly Scot* : YOUTHFUL **2** : affecting youthful habits or dress ⟨a ~ lady in her middle sixties⟩

[1]**yow** \ˈyau̇\ *dial Brit var of* YOU

[2]**yow** \ˈ"\ *interj* [ME *yowe*] — used to express excitement, joy, or surprise

[3]**yow** \ˈyō, ˈyau̇\ *dial Brit var of* EWE

[1]**yowl** \ˈyau̇l, *esp before pause or consonant* -au̇əl\ *vb* -ED/-ING/-S [ME *yowlen, youlen,* prob. of imit. origin] *vi* **1** : to utter a loud cry of grief, pain, or distress usu. in a long and mournful fashion : WAIL, HOWL ⟨the dog pacing the fence ~*s* at every step⟩ ⟨the boy caught his finger in an office door and ~*ed* —Daniel Lang⟩ **2** : to complain or protest with or as if with yowls ⟨the children are ~*ing* over who is going first⟩ ⟨the Congressman ~*s* at his party for weak support⟩ ⟨those conditions that guarantee . . . the right to ~ —*Fortune*⟩ ~ *vt* : to utter or express with or as if with yowls ⟨the dog ~*s* his pain to the world⟩

[2]**yowl** \ˈ"\ *n* -S [ME (Sc) *yowle,* fr. ME *yowlen, youlen,* v.] : a loud long mournful wail or howl (as of a dog or cat) ⟨the familiar ~ that, taken up by the pack, is such melodious music —F.G.Turnbull⟩ ⟨giving an occasional ~ of excitement —R.A.W.Hughes⟩ ⟨wild, discordant yells and ~*s* —*Broadway Mag.*⟩ ⟨the raucous ~ of a motorcar's horn —*Hearst's*⟩

[1]**yowt** \ˈyau̇t\ *vi* -ED/-ING/-S [ME (Sc) *yowten,* of imit. origin] *dial Brit* : HOWL, YELP, YELL

[2]**yowt** \ˈ"\ *n* -S *dial Brit* : HOWL, YELL

yo–yo \ˈyō(,)yō\ *n, pl* **yo–yos** *also* **yo–yoes** [native name in the Philippines] : a thick deeply grooved double disk with a string attached to its center that is made to fall and rise to the hand by unwinding and rewinding on the string

YP *abbr* **1** yard patrol **2** yellow pine **3** yield point **4** young people

yper·ite \ˈēpə,rīt\ *n* -S [F *ypérite,* fr. *ypér-* (fr. *Ypres, Ieper,* commune in northwest Belgium where it was used in World War I) + *-ite*] : MUSTARD GAS

y point *n, usu cap Y* : the neutral point for a three-phase electrical circuit

ypointing \iˈ≈≈, ēˈ-\ *adj* [*y-* + *pointing*] *archaic* : pointing or reaching toward a specified thing — usu. used in the phrase *star-ypointing* ⟨or that his hallowed reliques should be hid under a *star-ypointing* pyramid —John Milton⟩

ypon·o·meu·ta \(,)ē,pänəˈmyüd·ə\ *n* cap [NL, prob. irreg. fr. Gk *hyponomeutēs* miner, fr. *hyponomeuein* to undermine, fr. *hyponomos* underground passage, fr. *hyponemesthai* to eat away beneath, fr. *hypo-* + *nemesthai* to take food, graze, pres. middle infin. of *nemein* to pasture — more at NIMBLE] : a genus of black-spotted white moths that is the type of the family Yponomeutidae and that comprises the ermine moths

[1]**ypon·o·meu·tid** \(ˈ)≈ˈ≈≈ˈmyüd·əd\ *adj* [NL *Yponomeutidae*] : of or relating to the Yponomeutidae

[2]**yponomeutid** \ˈ"\ *n* -S [NL *Yponomeutidae*] : a moth of the family Yponomeutidae

ypon·o·meu·ti·dae \-ˈüd·ə,dē\ *n pl, cap* [NL, fr. *Yponomeuta* type genus + *-idae*] : a family of tineoid moths including ermine moths and various brightly colored moths some of which have larvae that are injurious to fruits

y potential *n, usu cap Y* : the potential difference between a terminal and the neutral point of a three-phase armature

yr *abbr* **1** year **2** younger **3** your

yrly *abbr* yearly

yrs *abbr* yours

YS *abbr* **1** yellow spot **2** yield strength **3** young soldier

y's *or* **ys** *pl of* Y

y–shaped \ˈ≈ˌ≈\ *adj, cap Y* : having the shape of a capital Y

yst *abbr* youngest

Yt *symbol* yttrium

y theodolite *n, cap Y* : a theodolite with the telescope supported in y's

yt·ter·bic \iˈtərbik\ *adj* [*ytterbium* + *-ic*] : of, relating to, or containing ytterbium — used esp. of compounds in which this element is trivalent

yt·ter·bi·um \-bēəm\ *n* -S [NL, fr. *Ytterby,* Sweden, where gadolinite is found + NL *-ium*] : a metallic element of the rare-earth group that closely resembles yttrium and occurs with it and other related elements in several minerals (as xenotime and gadolinite) and that forms green salts in which it is bivalent and colorless salts in which it is trivalent — symbol *Yb;* see ELEMENT table

ytterbium metal *n* : YTTRIUM METAL

yt·ter·bous \-bəs\ *adj* [*ytterbium* + *-ous*] : of, relating to, or containing ytterbium — used esp. of compounds in which this element is bivalent

yt·tria \ˈi·trēə\ *n* -S [NL, fr. *yttri-* (irreg. fr. *Ytterby,* Sweden, where gadolinite is found) + *-a*] : yttrium oxide Y_2O_3 obtained as a heavy white powder and used esp. formerly in incandescent gas mantles

yt·tri·a·lite \-ə,līt\ *n* -S [*yttria* + *-lite*] : an olive-green massive mineral $(Y,Gd,Th)_2Si_2O_7$ consisting of a silicate chiefly of thorium, yttrium, and gadolinium

yt·tric \ˈi·trik\ *adj* [ISV *yttrium* + *-ic*] : of, relating to, or containing yttrium

yt·trif·er·ous \i·ˈtrifərəs\ *adj* [ISV *yttrium* + *-ferous*] : bearing or containing yttrium or related elements

yt·tri·um \ˈi·trēəm\ *n* -S [NL, fr. *yttria,* after such pairs as NL *lithia: lithium*] : a trivalent metallic element that is usu. included among the rare-earth metals because it resembles them chemically and occurs with them in several minerals (as gadolinite, xenotime, yttrotantalite, euxenite) — symbol *Y;* see ELEMENT table

yttrium metal *n* : any of a group of metals separable as a group from other metals occurring with them and in addition to yttrium including the rare-earth metals holmium, erbium, thulium, ytterbium, and lutetium and sometimes gadolinium, terbium, and dysprosium — compare TERBIUM METAL

yt·tro·columbite \ˌi·trə+\ *n* [*yttria* + *-o-* + *columbite*] : YTTROTANTALITE

yt·tro·cra·site \ˌ≈≈ˈkrā,sīt\ *n* -S [*yttrium* + *-o-* + *cras-* (fr. Gk *krasis* mixing, combination) + *-ite* — more at CRASIS] : a mineral approximately $(Y,Th,U,Ca)_2(Ti,Fe,W)_4O_{11}$ or $(Y,Th,U,Ca)(Ti,Fe,W)_2O_5(OH)$ consisting of an oxide or basic oxide of the yttrium metals, thorium, uranium, titanium, iron, and tungsten and occurring in pitchy-black orthorhombic crystals (hardness 5.5–6, sp. gr. 4.8)

yt·tro·fluorite \ˌ≈≈+\ *n* [G *yttrofluorit,* fr. *yttr-* (fr. NL *yttrium*) + *-o-* + *fluorit* fluorite, fr. It *fluorite*] : a fluorite containing yttrium earths

yt·tro·tan·ta·lite \"+\ *n* [Sw *yttrotantal* yttrotantalite (fr. *yttr-* — fr. NL *yttria* — + *-o-* + *tantal* tantalum, fr. NL *tantalum*) + E *-ite*] : a mineral $(Fe,Y,U,Ca,etc.)(Cb,Ta,Zr,Sn)O_4$ consisting of a metamict oxide of iron, yttrium, uranium, calcium, columbium, tantalum, zirconium, tin, and other minerals and probably related to samarskite — called also *yttrocolumbite*

[1]**yu·an** \ˈyüən, yüˈän\ *also* **yuan dollar** *n, pl* **yuan** *also* **yuan dollars** [Chin (Pek) *yüan²,* lit., round, circular] **1** : the basic monetary unit of China established in 1914 — see MONEY table **2** : a coin or note representing one yuan

[2]**yuan** \"\ *n, pl* **yuan** *or* **yuans** *usu cap* [Chin (Pek) *yüan⁴,* lit., hall, courtyard] : a department of government in the Nationalist government of China ⟨executive *Yuan*⟩ ⟨legislative *Yuan*⟩ ⟨judicial *Yuan*⟩ ⟨control *Yuan*⟩ ⟨examination *Yuan*⟩

yu·ba \ˈyübə\ *n* -S [perh. native name in Australia] : a messmate (*Eucalyptus obliqua*)

yuca \ˈyükə, ˈyəkə, ˈyu̇kə\ *also* **yuc·ca** \ˈyəkə *sometimes* ˈyükə *or* ˈyu̇kə\ *or* **juca** \ˈyükə, ˈyəkə, ˈyu̇kə\ *n* -S [NL *jucca,* fr. 15th cent. Taino *yuca*] : CASSAVA

yu·ca·tan \ˌyükəˈtan, -ˈtän\ *n* -S [*Yucatán,* peninsula in southeast Mexico] : FRENCH YELLOW

yu·ca·tec \ˈ≈≈,tek\ *also* **yu·ca·te·co** \ˌ≈≈ˈtā(,)kō\ *n, pl* **yucatec** *or* **yucatecs** *usu cap* [Sp *yucateco,* fr. *Yucatán,* peninsula in southeast Mexico] **1 a** : an Indian people of the Yucatán peninsula, Mexico **b** : a member of such people **2** : a Mayan language of the Yucatec people **3** *pl* **yucatecs** [Sp *yucateco,* fr. *Yucatán,* peninsula in southeast Mexico, & *Yucatán,* state in the northern part of Yucatán peninsula] : a native or inhabitant of Yucatán state or of the Yucatán peninsula, Mexico

yu·ca·tec·an \ˌ≈≈ˈtekən\ *adj, usu cap* [Sp *yucateco* + E *-an*] **1** : of or relating to the Yucatec Indians or their language **2** : of or relating to the Yucatecs of Yucatán state or of the Yucatán peninsula, Mexico

yuc·ca \ˈyəkə *sometimes* ˈyükə *or* ˈyu̇kə\ *n* [NL, fr. Sp *yuca,* of unknown origin] **1** *cap* : a genus of American sometimes arborescent plants (family Liliaceae) having long pointed often rigid fibrous-margined leaves on a woody caudex and bearing a large panicle of white blossoms — see ADAM'S NEEDLE, BEAR GRASS 1a, JOSHUA TREE, SOAP PLANT c, SPANISH DAGGER **2** *also* **yuca** \ˈyükə, ˈyəkə, ˈyu̇kə\ -S **a** : any plant of the genus *Yucca* **b** : a flower cluster of one of these plants

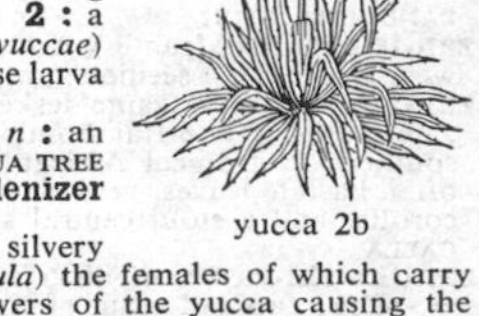

yucca 2b

yucca borer *n* **1** : a California boring weevil (*Scyphophorus yuccae*) **2** : a large butterfly (*Megathymus yuccae*) of the family Hesperiidae whose larva bores in yucca roots

yucca cactus *or* **yucca palm** *n* : an arborescent yucca; *esp* : JOSHUA TREE

yucca fertilizer *or* **yucca pollenizer** *n* : YUCCA MOTH

yucca moth *n* : any of several silvery tineoid moths (genus *Tegeticula*) the females of which carry pollen that fertilizes the flowers of the yucca causing the growth of a seed pod in which the larvae feed

yu·chi *or* **uchee** \ˈyüchē\ *n, pl* **yuchi** *or* **yuchis** *or* **uchee** *or* **uchees** *usu cap* **1 a** : an Indian people of southeastern U.S. **b** : a member of such people **2** : a Uchean language of the Yuchi people **3** : UCHEAN

yuchian *var of* UCHEAN

yueh \ˈyüˈā\ *n, pl* **yueh** *or* **yuehs** *usu cap* [Chin (Pek) *Yüeh⁴*] : one of a group of south China people formerly occupying the coastal provinces from Chekiang southward, having affinities with the early Yao and early Vietnamese, and founding an empire reaching its greatest height at Canton in Kwangtung Province

yueh–chi \-ˈchē\ *or* **yueh–chi–tocharian** *n, pl* **yueh–chi** *or* **yueh–chi–tocharians** *usu cap Y & cap T* : TOCHARIAN

yüeh–p'an \-ˈpän\ *n, pl* **yueh–p'an** *usu cap Y* : a division of the Hsiung-Nu held to be ancestors of the Avars

yuft \ˈyüft\ *n* -S [Russ *yuft', yukht',* perh. fr. Per *juft* pair; fr. the practice of tanning hides in pairs; akin to Av *yuxta-* pair, yoke (of oxen), Skt *yukta* yoke (of oxen), *yunakti* he yokes — more at YOKE] : RUSSIA LEATHER

yu·ga \ˈyu̇gə\ *n* -S [Skt, yoke, pair, race of men, age of the world — more at YOKE] : one of the four ages of a Hindu world cycle each shorter and less righteous than the one preceding — see DVAPARA YUGA, KALI YUGA, KRITA YUGA, TRETA YUGA; compare KALPA, PRALAYA

[1]**yu·go·slav** \ˌyü(,)gōˈsläv, -lav, -lȧv\ *or* **yu·go·slav·ian** \-vēən, -vyən\ *also* **ju·go·slav** \ˌyü(,)gō-\ *or* **ju·go·slav·ian** *n* -S *cap* [*Yugoslav* fr. F *Yougoslave,* fr. G *Jugoslawe,* fr. Serb *jugo-* (fr. *jug* south, fr. OSlav *jugŭ*) + G *Slawe* Slav, fr. ML *Sclavus; Yugoslavian, Jugoslavian* fr. *Yugoslavia, Jugoslavia* + E *-an,* n. suffix; *Jugoslav* fr. G *Jugoslawe* — n. AUGELITE, SLAVE] : a native or inhabitant of Yugoslavia — compare CROATIAN, SOUTH SLAV

[2]**yugoslav** \"\ *or* **yugoslavian** \"\ *also* **jugoslav** \"\ *or* **jugoslavian** \"\ *adj, usu cap* [*Yugoslav, Jugoslav* fr. [1]*Yugoslav, Jugoslav; Yugoslavian, Jugoslavian* fr. *Yugoslavia, Jugoslavia* + E *-an,* adj. suffix] **1** : of, relating to, or characteristic of Yugoslavia **2** : of, relating to, or characteristic of the people of Yugoslavia

yu·go·slav·ia *also* **ju·go·slav·ia** \ˌ≈(,)≈ˈsvēə\ *adj, usu cap* [*Yugoslavia, Jugoslavia,* country in southeast Europe] : of or from Yugoslavia : of the kind or style prevalent in Yugoslavia : YUGOSLAV, YUGOSLAVIAN

yu·go·slav·ic *also* **ju·go·slav·ic** \ˌ≈≈ˈslavik, -läv-, -lȧv-, -vēk\ *adj, usu cap* [[1]*Yugoslav, Jugoslav* + *-ic*] : YUGOSLAV

yu·gur \ˈyügə(r)\ *n, pl* **yugur** *or* **yugurs** *usu cap* **1** : a nomadic pastoral people of northeast Asia **2** : a member of the Yugur people

yu·it \ˈyüət\ *n, pl* **yuit** *or* **yuits** *usu cap* [Esk, men, people] **1** : the Eskimos of Siberia and St. Lawrence Island, Alaska — compare INNUIT **2** : a member of the Yuit people

[1]**yuk** \ˈyək\ *slang var of* [4]YAK

[2]**yuk** \"\ *interj* [imit. (of a sardonic laugh)] — used reduplicatively to express amusement or derision

yu·ka·ghir *or* **yu·ka·gir** \ˌyükəˈgi(ə)r\ *n, pl* **yukaghir** *or* **yukaghirs** *or* **yukagir** *or* **yukagirs** *usu cap* **1 a** : a group of formerly strong mongoloid peoples of northeastern Siberia surviving along the southern tributaries of the Kolyma river above Verkhne Kolymsk and having a culture of the Tungus type **b** : a member of any of such peoples **2 a** : the language of the Yukaghir people **b** : a family of languages of which only Yukaghir is still extant or well-known — see PALEO-SIBERIAN

yuke \ˈyük\ *var of* YEUK

yu·ki \ˈyükē\ *n, pl* **yuki** *or* **yukis** *usu cap* [Wintun, lit., stranger, enemy] **1 a** : an Indian people of the Eel river valley and adjacent Pacific coast, northwestern California **b** : a member of such people **2 a** : a Yukian language of the Yuki and Huchnom peoples **b** : YUKIAN

yu·kian \-kēən\ *n* -S *usu cap* : a language family of northwestern California comprising Yuki and Wappo perhaps related to Hokan

yu·kon \ˈyü,kän\ *adj, usu cap* [*Yukon,* territory in northwest Canada] : of or from Yukon Territory, Canada : of the kind or style prevalent in Yukon Territory

yu·kon·er \-nə(r)\ *n* -S *cap* : a native or inhabitant of the Yukon Territory, Canada

yu·kon·ite \ˈ≈≈,nīt\ *n* -S : ARSENIOSIDERITE

yukon time *or* **yukon standard time** *n, cap Y* : the time of the 9th time zone west of Greenwich that includes the Yukon Territory and part of southern Alaska and is four hours slower than eastern time

yu·lan \ˈyüe,län, -lan\ *n* -S [Chin (Pek) *yü⁴-lan²,* fr. *yü⁴* jade + *lan²* orchid] : a Chinese magnolia (*Magnolia denudata*) with large white very fragrant flowers that appear before the leaves

yule \ˈyül\ *n* -S *often cap, often attrib* [ME *yol, yole,* fr. OE *geōl;* akin to OE *geōla* December or January, ON *jōl* heathen winter feast, yule, Christmas, *ȳlir* month ending near the winter solstice, Goth *jiuleis* (in *fruma jiuleis* November)] : the feast of the nativity of Jesus Christ : CHRISTMAS, CHRISTMASTIDE

yule clog *n, archaic* : YULE LOG

yule log *n, usu cap Y* : a large log formerly brought in with much ceremony and put on the hearth on Christmas Eve as the foundation of the fire ⟨the burning of the *Yule log* and the drinking of wassail —R.E.Meyer⟩

yuletide \ˈ≈,≈\ *n, often cap* : the Christmas season; *esp* : CHRISTMASTIDE

yu·loh \ˈyü,lō\ *n* -S [prob. fr. Chin (Cant) *iū-lǒ* to scull a boat from the stern, fr. *iū* to agitate, shake + *lǒ* oar] : a Chinese sculling oar with a fixed fulcrum

yu·ma \ˈyümə\ *n, pl* **yuma** *or* **yumas** *usu cap* **1 a** : an Indian people of southwestern Arizona and the adjacent parts of Mexico and California **b** : a member of such people **2** : the Yuman language of the Yuma people

[1]**yu·man** \-mən\ *n* -S *usu cap* : a language family of the Hokan stock in Arizona, California, and Mexico comprising Akwa'ala, Cochimi, Cocopa, Diegueño, Havasupai, Kamia, Kiliwa, Maricopa, Mohave, Walapai, Yavapai, and Yuma

[2]**yuman** \"\ *adj, usu cap* **1** : of or relating to Yuman **2** *also* **yu·ma** \-mə\ : PATAYAN

yuma point *n, usu cap Y* [*Yuma* county, northeastern Colorado] : a stone projectile point first found in northeastern Colorado that is not fluted and is longer, narrower, and more painstakingly flaked than the Folsom point

yum·my \ˈyəmē, -mi\ *adj* -ER/-EST [*yum-* (as in *yum-yum*) + *-y*] : highly attractive or pleasing : DELECTABLE ⟨~ flavors like . . . munchy coconut —*advt*⟩ ⟨~ pastel shades —*advt*⟩

yum–yum \ˈyəmˈyəm\ *interj* [imit.] — used to express pleasurable satisfaction esp. in the taste of food

yun \ˈyün\ *n, pl* **yun** *or* **yuns** *usu cap* : a Laotian of the right bank of the Mekong distinguished by tattooing on the body rather than the legs and thighs

yun·ca \ˈyüŋkə\ *or* **yun·ga** \-ŋgə\ *also* **yun·ka** \-ŋkə\ *n, pl* **yunca** *or* **yuncas** *or* **yunga** *or* **yungas** *usu cap* [AmerSp *Yunca, Yunga,* fr. *yunga, yunca* yunga] **1 a** : a group of Indian peoples of the coast of Peru **b** : a member of any of the peoples of this group **2** : the language of the Yunca people now superseded by Quechua and Spanish

yun·can *or* **yun·kan** \-kən\ *adj, usu cap* : relating to or designating the language of the Yunca

yun·ga \ˈyüŋgə\ *n* -S [AmerSp *yunga, yunca,* fr. Quechua] : a densely wooded valley or slope in So. America

yun·gan \ˈyəŋgən\ *n* -S [native name in Queensland, Australia] : DUGONG 2

yun·gas \ˈyüŋgəs\ *n, pl* **yungas** [origin unknown] : a Peruvian rice rat (*Oryzomys mamorae* or *Oryzomys xantheolus*)

[1]**yun·nan·ese** \ˌyünəˈnēz, -nēs\ *also* **yun·nan** \yüˈnan, -nän\ *adj, usu cap* [*yunnanese* fr. *Yunnan,* province in south China + E *-ese; yunnan* fr. *Yunnan,* province in south China] : of or relating to the province of Yunnan, China, or its inhabitants

[2]**yunnanese** \"\ *n, pl* **yunnanese** *cap* : a native or inhabitant of the Chinese province of Yunnan

yup *var of* YEP

yu·pik \ˈyüpik\ *n* -S *usu cap* : an Eskimo-Aleut language of southwestern Alaska

yu·rak \yəˈrak\ *n* -S *cap* **1** : one of the Samoyeds of the arctic coast region from the Yenisei to the White sea **2** : the Uralic language of the Yurak people — see URALIC LANGUAGES table

yu·rok \ˈyu̇,räk, -rək\ *n, pl* **yurok** *also* **yuroks** *usu cap* **1 a** : a Ritwan people of northern California **b** : a member of such people **2** : the language of the Yurok people

yurt \ˈyu̇rt\ *also* **yur·ta** \-tə\ *n* -S [Russ *yurta,* of Turkic origin; akin to Turk *yurt* home, dwelling] : a circular domed tent consisting of skins or felt stretched over a collapsible lattice framework and used by the Kirghiz and other Mongol nomads of Siberia

yu·ruk *or* **ju·ruk** \yəˈru̇k\ *n* -S [Turk *yürük* nomad] **1** *usu cap* : one of a nomadic shepherd people of the mountains of southeastern Anatolia **2** : a Turkish rug from the Konya and Karaman regions, southeastern Anatolia, characterized by bold geometric designs and vivid colors

yu·ru·na \ˌyürəˈnä\ *n, pl* **yuruna** *or* **yurunas** *usu cap* [Tupi, fr. *yurú* mouth + *una* black] **1 a** : a group of Tupian peoples of the Xingú river valley, northern Brazil **b** : a member of any of the peoples of this group **2** : the language of the Yuruna people

y–worm \ˈ≈,≈\ *n, cap Y* [so called fr. the appearance of the large female and small male permanently associated in copulation] : GAPEWORM

1**z** \'zē, *chiefly Brit* 'zed, *archaic or dial* 'izə(r)d\ *n, pl* **z's** *or* **zs** \-ēz, -dz\ *often cap, often attrib* **1 a :** the 26th and last letter of the English alphabet **b :** an instance of this letter printed, written, or otherwise represented **c :** a speech counterpart of orthographic *z* (as *z* in *zone*, *haze* or French *zone*, *seize*) **2 :** a printer's type, a stamp, or some other instrument for reproducing the letter *z* **3 :** someone or something arbitrarily or conveniently designated *z:* as **a :** the 26th in order or class **b :** the 25th in order or class when j is not used **c :** the 23d in order or class when j, v, and w are not used **d :** the third in order or class when x is made the first **4 :** something having the shape of the letter z ⟨a *Z* bar⟩ **5 a :** UNKNOWN QUANTITY 1 **b :** Z-COORDINATE **6 :** a buzzing sound (as of snoring) — usu. used in multiples (as *z-z* or *zzz*)

2**z** *abbr, often cap* **1** zero **2** zinc **3** zloty **4** zone

3**z** *symbol, cap* **1** atomic number **2** impedance **3** zenith distance

'z *like* 4's\ *n* [by alter.] **:** 4's

za·ba·glio·ne \,(d)zäbəl'yōnē\ *also* **za·ba·io·ne** *or* **za·ba·jo·ne** \-bə'y-\ *n* -s [It *zabaglione*, *zabaione* — more at SABAYON] **:** a mixture of eggs, sugar, and wine or fruit juice beaten over hot water until thick and light and served in a glass

za·bra \'zäbrə, 'sä-\ *n* -s [Sp, fr. Catal *atzaura*, fr. Ar *zawraq* small boat] **:** a sailing vessel resembling a small frigate and used chiefly by the Spanish in the 16th and 17th centuries

zab·rze \'zäb,zhā\ *adj, usu cap* [*Zabrze*, city in southwest Poland] **:** of or from the city of Zabrze, Poland **:** of the kind or style prevalent in Zabrze

za·ca·te \zə'käd·ē, sə-\ *n* -s [AmerSp, coarse grass, zacate, fr. Nahuatl *zacatl*] **1 :** forage of grassy plants **:** HERBAGE **2** [PhilSp, fr. AmerSp] *Philippines* **:** RICEGRASS 1

za·ca·teco \,zäkə'tā(,)kō, -te(,)kō, ,sä-\ *also* **za·ca·tec** \,==-'tek\ *n, pl* **zacateco** *or* **zacatecos** *also* **zacatec** *or* **zacatecs** *usu cap* **1 :** a Nahuatlan people of the states of Zacatecas and Durango, Mexico **2 :** a member of the Zacateco people

zac·a·ton \'zakə,tōn, 'sa-\ *n* -s [AmerSp *zacatón* — more at SACATON] **:** any of several grasses with tough wiry stems native to or cultivated in arid or dry regions of the U.S. and adjacent Mexico: as **a :** BROOMROOT **b :** GUINEA GRASS 1 **c :** either of two Mexican grasses (*Epicampes stricta* and *Festuca amplissima*) **d :** SACATON

zacco *var of* ZOCCO

zad \'zad\ *chiefly dial var of* ZED

zad·dik *or* **tzad·dik** *or* **tsad·dik** *also* **za·dik** *or* **tza·dik** *or* **tsa·dik** \'tsädik\ *n, pl* **zad·dik·im** *or* **tzad·dik·im** *or* **tsad·dik·im** *also* **za·dik·im** *or* **tza·dik·im** *or* **tsa·dik·im** \tsä'dikəm, tsä,dē'kēm\ [Heb *ṣaddīq* just, righteous] **1 :** a righteous and saintly person **2 :** the spiritual leader of a modern Hasidic community — compare REBBE

1**za·dok·ite** \'zādə,kīt\ *n* -s *usu cap* [*Zadok*, high priest of Israel during the reign of King David + E *-ite*] **1 :** a Zadokite priest **2 :** a member of the Zadokite sect

2**zadokite** \"\ *adj, usu cap* **1 :** of or relating to Zadok or a line of priests of the highest rank descended from him ⟨the *Zadokite* priesthood⟩ **2 :** of, relating to, or constituting a Jewish rigorist sect seceding from orthodox Judaism and settling in Damascus in the second century B.C.

zaf·fer *or* **zaf·fre** \'zafə(r)\ *also* **zaf·free** \-frē\ *or* **zaf·far** *or* **zaf·fir** \-fə(r)\ *n* -s [It *zaffera*, prob. fr. L *sapphirus* sapphire — more at SAPPHIRE] **1 a :** an impure cobalt oxide obtained as a dark earthy powder usu. by roasting cobaltite or smaltite and used in the manufacture of smalt and as a blue ceramic color **b :** SMALT **2 :** any of various mixtures of zaffer (as with silica or iron oxide)

1**zag** \'zag, -aa(ə)g, -aig\ *n* -s [*-zag* (in *zigzag*)] **1 a :** one of the sharp turns, angles, or alterations in a zigzag course **b :** one of the short straight lines or sections of a zigzag course at an angle to a zig **c :** a movement or direction at an angle to a zig **2 :** ZIG 2

2**zag** \"\ *vi* **zagged; zagged; zagging; zags** [*-zag* (in *zigzag*)] **:** ZIG

za·glos·sus \zə'gläsəs, -glȯs-\ *n, cap* [NL, fr. *za-*, intensive prefix (fr. Gk, fr. *za* through, fr. *dia*) + *-glossus* (fr. Gk *glōssa* tongue) — more at DIA-, GLOSS] **:** a genus of spiny anteaters of New Guinea — see ECHIDNA 1b

za·greb \'zä,greb\ *adj, usu cap* [*Zagreb*, city in northwest Yugoslavia] **:** of or from the city of Zagreb, Yugoslavia **:** of the kind or style prevalent in Zagreb

za·guan \zə'gwän, sə-\ *n* -s [Sp *zaguán* vestibule, entry, fr. Ar *usṭuwān* porch, vestibule, prob. fr. Gk *stoa* portico; akin to Gk *stylos* pillar — more at STEER] **:** a passageway leading from the entrance door to the central patio in houses commonly found in the southwestern U.S. and Mexico

zaidi \'zīdē\ *also* **zaid·ite** \-,dīt\ *n* -s *usu cap* [after *Zaid*, 8th cent. A.D. Muslim leader descended from Muhammad] **:** a member of a Muslim sect of Yemen that constitutes one of the three major branches of Shi'a, recognizes a continuing line of imams descended through Zaid who is the fifth imam, and is closest to sunna in its doctrine

zain *var of* ZAYIN

za·kat \zə'kät\ *also* **za·kah** \-kä\ *n* -s [Ar *zakāt*] **:** an annual alms tax or poor rate that each Muslim is expected to pay as a religious duty and that is used for charitable and religious purposes

za·kus·ka *also* **za·koos·ka** \zə'ku̇skə\ *n, pl* **zakus·ki** \-skē\ *or* **zakuska** [Russ *zakuska*, fr. *zakusit'* to have a snack, fr. *za* for, behind + *-kusit'* (fr. *kus* morsel); akin to Lith dial. *ažu*, *až* for, behind, Arm *z* with regard to, and to Gk *knōdōn* sword, Lith *kąsti* to bite, L *cinis* ashes — more at INCINERATE] **:** HORS D'OEUVRE

1**za·lamb·do·dont** \zə'lamdə,dänt\ *adj* [NL *Zalambdodonta*] **:** of or relating to the Zalambdodonta

2**zalambdodont** \"\ *n* -s [NL *Zalambdodonta*] **:** a mammal of the division Zalambdodonta

za·lamb·do·don·ta \=,=='däntə\ *n pl, cap* [NL, fr. *za-*, intensive prefix + Gk *lambda* (Λ) + NL *-odonta*] *in former classifications* **:** an artificial division of Insectivora comprising the tenrecs and the golden moles which have narrow molars with V-shaped transverse crowns

zal·o·phus \'zaləfəs\ *n, cap* [NL, fr. *za-*, intensive prefix + *-lophus* (fr. Gk *lophos* crest)] **:** a genus of rather small eared seals including the California sea dog

za·ma·cue·ca \,zämə'kwākə, ,sä-\ *n* -s [AmerSp] **:** CUECA

za·man \zə'män, sə-\ *or* **za·mang** \-äŋ\ *n* -s [Sp & Carib; Sp *samán*, fr. Carib *zamang*] **:** RAIN TREE

za·man·do·que \,zämən'dōkē, ,sä-\ *or* **za·man·do·gue** \-ōgē\ *n* -s [MexSp *samandoque*] **:** a Mexican plant (*Hesperaloe funifera*) of the family Liliaceae with long slender leaves that yield a long soft flexible istle fiber

za·mar·ra \zə'märə, sə-\ *n* -s [Sp — more at SAMARRA] **:** a sheepskin coat worn chiefly by Spanish shepherds

zambal *usu cap, var of* SAMBAL

Zam·be·si \zam'bēzē\ *trademark* — used for a direct azo dye; see DYE table I (under *Direct Black 17* and *78*)

zam·be·zian *or* **zam·be·sian** \(')zam¦bēzhən\ *adj, usu cap* [*Zambezi*, *Zambesi*, river in south central and southeast Africa + E *-an*] **:** of or relating to the Zambezi river

zam·bia \'zambēə\ *adj, usu cap* [fr. *Zambia*, country in southern Africa] **:** of or from the country of Zambia **:** of the kind or style prevalent in Zambia

zam·bi·an \-bēən\ *n* -s *cap* [*Zambia*, Africa + E *-an*] **:** a native or inhabitant of Zambia — **zambian** *adj, usu cap*

zam·bo \'z|äm(,)bō, 's|, |am-\ *n* -s [AmerSp, Negro, mulatto — more at SAMBO] **:** a Latin-American of mixed Indian and Negro ancestry

zam·bo·an·ga \,zämbə'wäŋgə, ,sä-\ *adj, usu cap* [*Zamboanga*, city in western Mindanao, Philippines] **:** of or from the city of Zamboanga, Philippines **:** of the kind or style prevalent in Zamboanga

zam·e·nis \'zamənəs\ *n, cap* [NL, modif. of Gk *zamenēs* mighty, raging, fr. *za-*, intensive prefix + *-menēs* (fr. *menos* strength, fierceness, spirit) — more at ZAGLOSSUS, MIND] **:** a large genus of European and Asiatic colubrid snakes closely resembling and in some classifications including a black snake (*Coluber constrictor*) of the U.S.

za·mia \'zāmēə\ *n* [NL, fr. L (in fem. pl. form *zamiae*), MS. var. of *azaniae*, fem. pl. of (assumed) L *azanius*, adj., opening while still on the tree (said of a pinecone), prob. fr. Gk *azainein* to dry up; akin to Gk *azein* to parch — more at ARDOR] **1** *cap* **:** a genus of tropical and subtropical American cycads having a short thick sometimes subterranean caudex, a crown of palmlike leaves, and oblong cones — see COONTIE **2** -s **:** any plant of the genus *Zamia*

za·mi·a·ce·ae \,=='āsē,ē\ *n pl, cap* [NL, fr. *Zamia* + *-aceae*] *in some classifications* **:** a family of cycads that includes the genus *Zamia* and is commonly itself included in Cycadaceae

zam·i·crus \'zaməkrəs\ *n, cap* [NL, fr. *za-*, intensive prefix (fr. Gk) + *-micrus* (fr. Gk *mikros* small); fr. the size of the molars — more at MICR-] **:** a genus of edentates from the Miocene of Argentina related to *Megatherium* but no larger than sloths

zamin·dar *or* **zemin·dar** \zə¦mēn¦där, ¦zamən-, ¦zemən-, ¦zämən-\ *n* -s [Hindi *zamīndār*, fr. Per, fr. *zamīn* land + *-dār* holder; akin to Skt *kṣam* earth, ground — more at HUMBLE, BHUMIDAR] **1 :** a collector of revenues from the cultivators of the land of a specified district for the government of India during the period of Muslim rule **2 :** a feudatory under the British government of India having rights of private property in a large amount of land by paying to the government a fixed substantial revenue raised from the cultivators **3 :** an absentee landlord usu. acting as an intermediary between the cultivators and the government in the period after Indian independence

zamin·da·ri *or* **zamin·da·ry** *or* **zemin·da·ri** *or* **zemin·da·ry** \=,='därē, ,=='d-\ *n, pl* **zamindaris** *or* **zamindaries** *or* **zemindaris** *or* **zemindaries** [Hindi *zamīndārī*, fr. Per, fr. *zamīndār*] **1 :** the system of landholding and revenue collection by zamindars **2 :** the jurisdiction or office of a zamindar **3 :** the land held or administered by a zamindar — compare AMANI

zam·o·rin *also* **zam·o·rine** \¦zamə¦rēn\ *n* -s [Pg *samorim*, fr. Malayalam *sāmūri*, fr. *sāmudri* lord of the sea, fr. Skt *samudra* ocean, fr. *sam* together + *-udra* (akin to Skt *udan* water) — more at SAME, WATER] **:** the Hindu sovereign of Calicut and surrounding territory

za·mouse \zə'müs\ *also* **ga·moos** *or* **ga·mouse** \gə-\ *n, pl* **zamouses** *also* **gamooses** *or* **gamouses** [Ar *jāmūs*] **:** BUSH COW 1

zam·po·gna *or* **zam·po·ña** *also* **sam·po·gna** \(t)säm'pōnyə, zam-\ *n* -s [*zampogna*, *sampogna* fr. It *zampogna*, modif. of LL *symphonia*, a musical instrument, perh. the panpipe, fr. L, harmony of sounds; *zampoña* fr. Sp, modif. of LL *symphonia* — more at SYMPHONY] **1 :** PANPIPE **2 :** BAGPIPE

za·mu·co \zə'mü(,)kō, sə-\ *or* **za·mu·cu** \-kü\ *n, pl* **zamuco** *or* **zamucos** *or* **zamucu** *or* **zamucus** *usu cap* **1 a :** a group of peoples of the northern Chaco **b :** a member of any of such peoples **2 :** the language of the Zamuco peoples

zam·zum·mim \zam'zəməm\ *or* **zam·zum·mims** \-əmz\ *n pl, usu cap* [Heb *zamzummīm*] **:** aboriginal giants reported in the Old Testament to have inhabited the region of Ammon prior to the coming of the Ammonites — compare ANAKIM, EMIM, REPHAIM

zan·cli·dae \'zaŋklə,dē\ *n pl, cap* [NL, fr. *Zanclus*, type genus + *-idae*] **:** a family of marine fishes consisting of the Moorish idols and resembling in many respects the related surgeonfishes but lacking the distinguishing spines of the latter and having above the eyes bony outgrowths resembling horns — compare TEUTHIDIDAE

zan·clus \-ləs\ *n, cap* [NL, fr. Gk *zanklon* sickle] **:** a genus coextensive with the family Zanclidae

zan·de \'zandē\ *or* **zan·deh** \-də\ *n, pl* **zande** *or* **zandes** *or* **zandeh** *or* **zandehs** *usu cap* **1 a :** an African people of considerable prominence in the history and development of the region of the Congo-Sudan frontier esp. over the past century **b :** a member of such people **2 :** an Adamawa-Eastern language of the Zande people spoken in the northern Congo and southwestern Sudan

zan·der \'zandə(r), 'zaan-\ *n, pl* **zander** *or* **zanders** [G *zander*, perh. of Slav origin; akin to Pol *sandacz* zander] **:** a pike perch (*Lucioperca sandra* or *L. lucioperca*) of central Europe related to the walleyed pike

za·ni·ly \'zānᵊlē\ *adv* **:** in a zany manner

za·ni·ness \-nēnəs, -nin-\ *n* -ES **:** the quality or state of being zany ⟨fleeting moments of impulsive ~ —Walter Terry⟩

zan·ja \'zäŋhə, 'sä-\ *n* -s [AmerSp, fr. Sp, ditch, trench] **:** an irrigating canal **:** an irrigation ditch

zan·je·ro \zäŋ'he(,)rō, sä-\ *n* -s [AmerSp, fr. *zanja*] **:** one in charge of water distribution from zanjas

zan·ni \'(d)zänē\ *n, pl* **zanni** *or* **zannis** *usu cap* [It, fr. It dial. (Lombardy) *Zanni*, nickname fr. the name It *Giovanni* John, fr. LL *Joannes* — more at JOHN] **1 :** a madcap clown in masked comedy traditionally from Bergamo, Italy usu. playing the part of a comic servant and indulging in acrobatic antics and tricks — compare PIERROT **2 :** a clown resembling Harlequin

zan·ni·chel·lia \,zanə'kelēə\ *n, cap* [NL, fr. Gian Girolamo *Zannichelli* †1729 Ital. botanist + NL *-ia*] **:** a small genus of aquatic plants (family Potamogetonaceae) of wide distribution having branching capillary stems, small acute leaves, and axillary flowers which with the leaves are orig. enclosed in a hyaline envelope — see HORNED PONDWEED

zan·ni·chel·li·a·ce·ae \,==,=lē'āsē,ē\ [NL, fr. *Zannichellia* + *-aceae*] *syn of* POTAMOGETONACEAE

za·no·nia \zə'nōnēə, -ōnyə\ *n, cap* [NL, fr. Giacomo *Zanoni* †1682 Ital. botanist + NL *-ia*] **:** a genus of Indo-Malayan herbaceous vines (family Cucurbitaceae) with small panicled flowers, 3-valved fruits, and broadly winged seeds — see BANDOLEER FRUIT

zan·te currant \¦zantē-\ *n, usu cap Z* [*Zante*, island in southwest Greece] **:** a seedless grape or raisin

zan·te·des·chia \,zantə'deskēə\ *n, cap* [NL, fr. Giovanni *Zantedeschi* †1846 Ital. botanist + NL *-ia*] **:** a small genus of southern or tropical African aroids with basal long-stalked often hastate leaves, very showy spathes usu. mistaken for a corolla, and a stout central spadix — see CALLA 2, YELLOW CALLA

zan·tho·rhi·za \,zan(t)thə'rīzə\ *n, cap* [NL, irreg. fr. *xanth-* + *-rhiza*] **:** a small genus of No. American low shrubby plants (family Berberidaceae) with purplish brown flowers and very bitter yellow roots

zan·thox·y·la·ce·ae \(,)zan,thäksə'lāsē,ē\ *n pl, cap* [NL, fr. *Zanthoxylum* + *-aceae*] *in some classifications* **:** a family of dicotyledonous plants comprising solely the genus *Zanthoxylum* and being usu. included in Rutaceae

zan·thox·y·lum \='=sələm\ *n* [NL, irreg. fr. *xanth-* + *-xylum*] **1 a** *cap* **:** a genus of widely distributed shrubs or trees (family Rutaceae) having odd-pinnate leaves, small greenish flowers with 2 to 5 pistils, and 2-valved fleshy capsules **b** -s **:** any plant of the genus *Zanthoxylum* **2** -s *also* **xanthoxylum :** the dried bark of prickly ash or hercules'-club formerly used as a diaphoretic and stimulant

zan·ti·ot \'zantēət, -ē,ät\ *or* **zan·ti·ote** \-ē,ōt\ *n* -s *cap* [*Zante*, island in southwest Greece + E *-iot*, *-iote* (as in *cypriot*, *cypriote*)] **:** a native or resident of Zante

1**za·ny** \'zānē, -ni\ *n* -ES [It *zanni* — more at ZANNI] **1 a :** a subordinate fool, clown, acrobat, or mountebank who mimics ludicrously the tricks of his principal **:** an assistant to a mountebank (as in old comedies) **:** MERRY-ANDREW **b :** a usu. professional clown or buffoon **2 :** an assistant or lieutenant attendant upon another; *specif* **:** a slavish follower **:** TOADY — usu. used contemptuously **3** *obs* **:** a wretched or ridiculous imitator **:** a feeble mimic **4 :** one who makes a buffoon or laughingstock of himself to amuse others **5 :** SIMPLETON

2**zany** \"\ *vt* -ED/-ING/-ES *archaic* **:** to play the zany to **:** imitate in the manner of a zany

3**zany** \"\ *adj* -ER/-EST **:** being or having the characteristics of a zany **:** fantastically or irrationally ludicrous **:** mildly insane **:** CRAZY ⟨a ~ sense of humor —*N.Y. Herald Tribune Bk. Rev.*⟩

za·ny·ism \-nē,izəm\ *n* -s **:** a characteristic or practice of a zany **:** BUFFOONERY

zan·za \'zanzə\ *or* **san·sa** \'san(t)sə\ *also* **zan·ze** \'zanzə\ *n* -s [Ar *ṣanj* castanets, cymbals, fr. Per *sanj*] **:** an African musical instrument consisting of graduated sets of tongues of wood or metal inserted into and resonated by a wooden box and sounded by plucking with the fingers or thumbs

zan·zi·bar copal \¦zanzə¦bär, -bȧ(r-\ *n, usu cap Z* [*Zanzibar*, island off the northeast coast of Tanganyika, Tanzania, eastern Africa] **:** a hard copal derived from a tree (*Trachylobium verrucosum*) of the family Leguminosae — called also *anime*

zan·zi·ba·ri \¦==¦bärē\ *n* -s *cap* [Ar *zanjibārīy* of or relating to Zanzibar, fr. *Zanjibār* Zanzibar] **1 :** the Arabic dialect spoken in Zanzibar **2 :** a native or resident of Zanzibar

za·pa·ran \'zäpərən, 'sä-\ *adj, usu cap* **:** of, relating to, or constituting the Zaparo

za·pa·ro \'zäpərō, 'sä-\ *n, pl* **zaparo** *or* **zaparos** *usu cap* **1 a :** a group of peoples of eastern Ecuador and northern Peru **b :** a member of any of such peoples **2 :** the language of the Zaparo people

za·pa·ro·an \,=='rōən\ *n* -s *usu cap* **:** a language family of eastern Ecuador and northern Peru that includes Coronado and Zaparo

za·pa·te·a·do \,zäpətē'ä(,)dō, ,sä-, -ē'au̇\ *n* -s [Sp, fr. *zapatear* to strike with the shoe, tap with the feet, fr. *zapato* shoe — more at SABOT] **1 :** a rhythmic stamping or tapping step characteristic of Spanish dancing **2 :** a Spanish or Latin-American dance marked by the zapateado

za·pa·teo \,=='tā(,)ō\ *n* -s [Sp, fr. *zapatear*] **:** ZAPATEADO 2

za·pa·te·ro \,=='te(,)rō\ *n* -s [Sp, lit., shoemaker, fr. *zapato* shoe] **1 :** a leatherjacket (*Oligoplites saurus*) **2** [AmerSp, fr. Sp] **a :** a tropical American timber tree (*Casearia praecox*) **b :** the wood of this tree — called also *West Indian boxwood*

zap flap \'zap-\ *n* [prob. after Edward F. *Zap*, 20th cent. Am. aeronautical engineer] **:** a split flap in which the hinge axis moves aft as the flap is deflected, thus increasing the area of the wing as well as its camber

1**za·phren·tid** \zə'frentəd\ *adj* [NL *Zaphrentidae*, family of tetracorals in some classifications, fr. *Zaphrentis* + *-idae*] **:** of or relating to the genus *Zaphrentis* or family Zaphrentidae

2**zaphrentid** \"\ *n* -s [NL *Zaphrentidae*] **:** a zaphrentid tetracoral

za·phren·tis \-ntəs\ *n, cap* [NL] **:** a genus (sometimes made the type of the family Zaphrentidae) of solitary cup-shaped tetracorals that are common in Paleozoic formations and have numerous septa radiating from a deep pit in one side of the cup

za·phren·toid \-n·,tȯid\ *adj* [NL *Zaphrentis* + E *-oid*] **:** resembling or related to the genus *Zaphrentis* or family Zaphrentidae

1**zap·o·did** \'zapədəd\ *adj* [NL *Zapodidae*] **:** of or relating to the Zapodidae

2**zapodid** \"\ *n* -s [NL *Zapodidae*] **:** a zapodid rodent

za·pod·i·dae \zə'pädə,dē\ *n pl, cap* [NL, fr. *Zapod-*, *Zapus*, type genus + *-idae*] **:** a widely distributed family of myomorph rodents that includes the jumping mice of No. America and related Old World mice

za·pon fast dye \'zā,pän-\ *n, usu cap Z&F* [*Zapon*, trade name for a lacquer, fr. G *zaponlack*] **:** any of several solvent dyes — see DYE table I (under *Solvent Orange 5*, *Solvent Red 8* and *35*, and *Solvent Yellow 19*)

za·po·ro·zhe \,zäpə'rȯzhə\ *adj, usu cap* [*Zaporozhe*, city in southeast Ukraine, U.S.S.R.] **:** of or from the city of Zaporozhe, U.S.S.R. **:** of the kind or style prevalent in Zaporozhe

za·po·ta gum \zə'pōd·ə-\ *n* [NL *zapota* (specific epithet of the sapodilla *Achras zapota*), fr. Sp *zapote* sapodilla — more at SAPOTA] **:** CHICLE

zapote *var of* SAPOTE

za·po·tec \'zäpə,tek, 'sä-\ *n, pl* **zapotec** *or* **zapotecs** *usu cap* [Sp *Zapoteca*, fr. Nahuatl *Tzapoteca*, lit., people of the land of the sapodillas, fr. *tzapotlan* place of the sapodillas (fr. *tzapotl* sapodilla) + *-teca* (pl. of *-tecatl*, suffix denoting origin)] **1 a :** an Indian people of the state of Oaxaca, Mexico **b :** a member of such people **2 :** a Zapotecan language of the Zapotec people

za·po·tecan \,=='tākən, -tek-\ *n* -s *usu cap* **1 :** a language stock of southern Mexico comprising Chatino and the several languages all known as Zapotec **2 :** the peoples speaking Zapotecan languages

za·pu·pe \zə'pü(,)pē, pə-\ *n* -s [AmerSp] **1 :** any of various Mexican agaves (as *Agave zapupe* and *A. deweyana*) that yield fiber somewhat similar to henequen **2 :** the fiber of a zapupe

za·pus \'zāpəs\ *n, cap* [NL *Zapod-*, *Zapus*, fr. *za-*, intensive prefix + *-pod-*, *-pus* -pus — more at ZAGLOSSUS] **:** the type genus of Zapodidae

za·ra·go·za \¦sȧrȧ¦gō(,)sȧ, ¦thȧrȧ¦gō(,)thȧ\ *adj, usu cap* [*Zaragoza*, *Saragossa*, city in northeastern Spain] **:** SARAGOSSA

za·rah \zə'rä\ *n* -s [origin unknown] **:** KAZOO

zar·a·thus·trian \¦zarə¦thüstrēən\ *also* **zar·a·thus·tric** \-strik\ *adj, usu cap* [*Zarathustra* (Zoroaster) *fl ab* 6th cent. B.C. founder of Zoroastrianism (fr. Av *Zarāthushtra-*) + E *-an* or *-ic*] **:** ZOROASTRIAN

zara·tite \'zärə,tīt, 'zar-\ *n* -s [Sp *zaratita*, fr. Señor *Zarate*, 19th cent. Spaniard + Sp *-ita* -ite] **:** a hydrous basic nickel carbonate $Ni_3(CO_3)(OH)_4.4H_2O$ occurring in emerald-green incrustations or compact masses

za·re·ba *or* **za·ri·ba** *also* **ze·ri·ba** \zə'rēbə\ *n* -s [Ar *zarībah* enclosure, pen] **:** an improvised stockade constructed esp. of thornbushes and used for defense in parts of Africa

zar·e·ma \'zärəmə\ *or* **zar·ma** \-rmə\ *n, usu cap* **:** DYERMA

zarvanism *usu cap, var of* ZERVANISM

zar·zue·la \zärz'wālə, ,zärzə'w-, sär'sw-, ,särsə'w-\ *n* -s [Sp, prob. fr. *La Zarzuela*, royal residence near Madrid where it was first performed] **:** a Spanish opera having spoken dialogue and usu. a comic subject

zastruga *var of* SASTRUGA

zau·ber·flo·te \'tsau̇bə(r),flād·ə, -lōd·ə, *G* -lœtə\ *n* -s [fr. *Die Zauberflöte* (English title *The Magic Flute*), opera first presented in 1791 with music by Wolfgang Amadeus Mozart †1791 Austrian composer and libretto by Emanuel Schikaneder †1812 Ger. theater manager and librettist] **:** a stopped flute pipe-organ stop of harmonic length

zausch·ne·ria \zȯsh'nirēə\ *n* [NL, fr. Johann B. J. *Zauschner* †1799 Bohemian naturalist + NL *-ia*] **1** *cap* **:** a small genus of California perennial herbs (family Onagraceae) with scarlet racemose flowers like those of fuchsia and comose seeds **2** -s **:** any plant of the genus *Zauschneria*

zax \'zaks\ *n* -ES [E dial., alter. of 1*sax*] **:** a tool for trimming and puncturing roofing slates

z-axis \'=,==\ *n* **:** one of the axes in a three-dimensional rectangular coordinate system **:** a line perpendicular to the plane of a polar coordinate system at the pole — compare CYLINDRICAL COORDINATE

za·yin *or* **za·in** \'zäyən, 'zī(y)ən\ *n* -s [Heb *zayin*] **:** the seventh letter of the Hebrew alphabet — symbol ז; see ALPHABET table

z chromosome *n, usu cap Z* **:** a sex chromosome of the kind occurring doubled in the male and singly either with or without a W chromosome in organisms (as moths) in which the female is heterogametic — compare X CHROMOSOME

z-coordinate \'=='=(=)=\ *n* **1 :** one of the three coordinates in a three-dimensional rectangular coordinate system **2 :** the third coordinate in a cylindrical coordinate system

ZD *abbr* zenith distance

zdar·sky tent \'st|ärskē-, 'zd|, zə'd|\ *n, usu cap Z* [after Mathias *Zdarsky* †1940 Austrian skiing expert] **:** an esp. prepared light sheet of cloth that is used for shelter instead of a tent — called also *bivouac sheet*

zdra·vets oil \'zdrävəts-\ *n* [prob. fr. *Zdravets*, town in Bulgaria] **:** geranium oil obtained esp. from a woody-stemmed geranium (*Geranium macrorrhizum*) in Bulgaria and Cyprus

zea \'zēə\ *n* [NL, fr. Gk *zea*, *zeia* single-grained wheat; akin to Skt *yava* barley] **1** *cap* **:** a genus of large grasses having broad ribbon-shaped leaves and monoecious flowers of which the staminate forms an ample terminal panicle and the pistillate is in a sessile axillary spike enveloped by numerous bracts — see INDIAN CORN **2** -s **:** the fresh styles and stigmas of Indian corn formerly used as a diuretic

zeal \'zēl, *esp before pause or consonant* -ēəl\ *n* -s [ME *zele*, fr. LL *zelus*, fr. Gk *zēlos* zeal, emulation, jealousy; akin to Gk (Dor dial.) *zamia* loss and perh. to OIr *āilid* he desires ardently, Russ *yaryĭ* furious, Skt *yāvan* aggressor] **1** *archaic* **:** ardor of feeling taking the form usu. of jealousy or indignation ⟨I the Lord have spoken it in my ~ —Ezek 5:13 (AV)⟩ **2** *obs* **:** ardent desire esp. to do or have something ⟨this doth infer the ~ I had to see him —Shak.⟩ **3 :** impassioned eagerness esp. in favor of a person or a cause **:** active enthusiastic interest mounting to fervor ⟨entered with ~ upon this task —C.S.Sydnor⟩ ⟨a fearless tenacity equivalent to religious ~ —Russell Kirk⟩ **4** *obs* **:** ZEALOT **syn** see PASSION

zea·land·er \'zēləndə(r)\ *n* -s *usu cap* [*Zealand*, *Sjælland*, island in eastern Denmark + E *-er*] **1 :** a native or inhabitant of Zealand in Denmark **2** [*Zealand, Zeeland*, province of southwest Netherlands + E *-er*] : ZEALANDER

zeal·less \'zēlləs\ *adj* : lacking zeal

¹zeal·ot \'zelət, *usu* -əd·+V\ *n* -s [LL *zelotes*, fr. Gk *zēlōtēs*, fr. *zēlos*] **1** *usu cap* : one of a fanatical sect bitterly opposing the Roman domination of Palestine during the great rebellion and the siege of Jerusalem and opposing not only the Romans but other Jewish factions — see SICARIUS **2 a** : one who is zealous : one who embraces a cause and supports it with vigor and enthusiasm **b** : one who is carried away by his zeal : a fanatical partisan **syn** see ENTHUSIAST

²zealot \"\ *adj* : being or characteristic of a zealot

zea·lot·ic \zə'lädik, zē-\ *adj* : of, resembling, or suitable to a zealot : ardently zealous

zeal·ot·ism \'zeləd·,izəm\ *n* -s : ZEALOTRY

zeal·ot·ry \-ə·trē, -ri\ *n* -ES : the character and behavior of a zealot : an excess of zeal : fanatical devotion; *also* : an instance of such behavior or disposition

zeal·ous \'zeləs\ *adj* [ML *zelosus*, fr. LL *zelus* zeal + L *-osus* -ose] : filled with or characterized by zeal : warmly engaged or ardent esp. in behalf of something : marked by a fervent partisanship for a person, a cause, or an ideal ⟨a ~ supporter of the Confederacy —D.Y.Thomas⟩ ⟨impetuous in his enthusiasm, ~ for liberty —G.H.Genzmer⟩

zeal·ous·ly *adv* : in a zealous manner ⟨worked ~ to raise funds⟩

zeal·ous·ness *n* -ES : the quality or state of being zealous

zealous witness *n* : a witness showing partiality for the side that first calls him to the stand in a trial and eagerness to volunteer what he thinks will be advantageous to that side

ze·a·xanthin \,zēə+\ *n* -s [ISV *zea-* (fr. NL *Zea*, genus name of Indian corn) + *xanthin*] : a yellow crystalline carotenoid alcohol $C_{40}H_{54}(OH)_2$ that is isomeric with lutein and occurs widely with it and that is the chief pigment of yellow Indian corn : a dihydroxy β-carotene — compare VIOLAXANTHIN

¹zebra \'zēbrə, *Brit also* 'zeb-\ *n, pl* **zebras** *also* **zebra** [It, fr. Sp *cebra*, fr. OSp *zebra, zebro, enzebro* wild ass, perh. fr. (assumed) VL *eciferus* wild horse, alter. of L *equiferus*, fr. *equus* horse + *ferus* wild — more at EQUINE, FIERCE] **1** : any of several fleet African equine mammals related to the horse and the ass but distinctively and conspicuously patterned in stripes of black or dark brown and white or buff — see BURCHELL'S ZEBRA, GRÉVY'S ZEBRA, MOUNTAIN ZEBRA **2** *or* **zebra butterfly** : a black yellow-striped butterfly (*Heliconius charitonius*) of the family Heliconiidae found in southern Florida and the West Indies **3** : any of various objects bearing stripes like those of the zebra **4 a** : ZEBRA FISH **b** : a small southern African sargo (*Diplodus trifasciatus*) highly esteemed for sport and food

zebra

²zebra \"\ *usu cap* — a communications code word for the letter z

zebra antelope *n* : a small bush antelope (*Cephalophus doriae*) of Liberia that is brown with black cross stripes

zebra-back \'=,=\ *also* **zebra bird** *n* : RED-BELLIED WOODPECKER

zebra caterpillar *n* : a caterpillar that is the larva of an American noctuid moth (*Ceramica picta*), that is light yellow with a broad black stripe on the back and lateral stripes crossed with white, and that feeds on cultivated plants (as cabbages, beets)

zebra civet cat *n* : a banded palm civet (*Hemigalus hardwickii*)

zebra finch *n* : a small Australian weaverbird (*Poephila castanotis* or *Taeniopygia castanotis*) whose plumage is mainly light gray and white but with the upper tail coverts broadly barred black and white and the sides of the head orange-rufous and which is commonly kept in captivity

zebra fish *n* : any of various barred fishes: as **a** : a small Australian sea fish (*Melambaphes zebra*) of the family Girellidae that is olive above and pinkish below with nine dark crossbars **b** : a small dark-barred Canadian variety of the log perch **c** *also* **zebra danio** : a very small blue-and-silver-striped Indian danio (*Brachydanio rerio*) often kept in the tropical aquarium; *also* : any closely related and similarly marked danio

zebra grass *n* : a grass (*Miscanthus sinensis zebrinus*) that has leaves with yellow or white longitudinal stripes

ze·bra·ic \zə'brāik, zē'-, -āek\ *adj* : of the nature of or characteristic of the zebra : ZEBRALIKE

zebralike \'=,=\ *adj* : resembling or suggesting a zebra esp. in color or marking : ZEBRAIC

ze·brano \zə'bra(,)nō\ *or* **ze·brana** \-,nə\ *n* -s [ISV, irreg. fr. ¹*zebra*] : ZEBRAWOOD

zebra parrakeet *n* : BUDGERIGAR

zebra plant *n* : a Brazilian herb (*Calathea zebrina*) with leaves striped green and yellowish white that is widely cultivated as a foliage plant

zebra shark *n* : LEOPARD SHARK c

zebra spider *n* : a European hunting spider (*Salticus scenicus*)

ze·brass \'zē,bras, -aa(ə)s, -ais\ *n* -ES [¹*zebra* + *ass*] : a hybrid produced by breeding a zebra with an ass

zebra swallowtail *n* : a very large swallowtail butterfly (*Papilio marcellus*) of eastern No. America which has greenish white or yellowish white wings barred with black and whose larva feeds on the papaw

zebra-tailed lizard \'=,=,-\ *n* : GRIDIRON-TAILED LIZARD

zebra wolf *also* **zebra opossum** *n* : TASMANIAN WOLF

zebrawood \'=,=\ *n* : any of several trees or shrubs having mottled or striped wood: as **a** : a tropical American and East African tree (*Connarus guianensis*) with strikingly marked hard wood used in cabinetwork **b** : a tropical Asiatic and African shrub (*Guettarda speciosa*) of the family Rubiaceae from the flowers of which a perfume is extracted in India **c** : NAKEDWOOD 2 **d** : MARBLEWOOD 1a **e** : an arariba (*Centrolobium robustum*) **f** : any of various African timber trees (genus *Brachystegia*) with pale golden heartwood uniformly striped with dark brown or black — called also *zingana* **2 a** : the wood of the zebrawood **b** : GONCALO ALVES 2

zebrawood family *n* : CONNARACEAE

ze·bri·na \zə'brīnə\ *n, cap* [NL, fr. G *zebra* (fr. Pg *zébra*, fr. OPg *zevra, zevro* wild ass, perh. fr. assumed VL *eciferus* wild horse) + NL *-ina*; fr. the striped leaves — more at ZEBRA] : a small genus of trailing herbs (family Commelinaceae) of New Mexico and Mexico having ovate or oblong leaves and flowers with sepals and petals united into a tube — see WANDERING JEW 1

ze·brine \'zē,brīn, -,brən\ *adj* [¹*zebra* + *-ine*] : relating to or resembling a zebra : characteristic of a zebra : suggesting a zebra esp. in marking

¹ze·broid \-,brȯid\ *adj* [¹*zebra* + *-oid*] : related to or resembling a zebra

²zebroid \"\ *n* -s : a hybrid between a male zebra and a female horse used as a work animal in some tropical areas because of its docility and its resistance to disease and heat injury

zebru·la \'zēbrələ, 'zeb-\ *or* **ze·brule** \'zē,brül\ *n* -s [*zebrula* alter. (influenced by *-ula*) of *zebrule*, fr. ¹*zebra* + *mule*] : ZEBROID

ze·bu \'zē,byü, -bü\ *n* -s [F *zébu*, perh. modif. of Tibetan *mdzopho* male of a hybrid of the yak bull and the zebu] : an Asiatic ox (*Bos indicus*) domesticated and differentiated into many breeds in India, China, the East Indies, and parts of Africa, used chiefly for draft, for riding, or for milk or flesh, and distinguished from European cattle with which it crosses freely by the presence of a large fleshy hump over the shoulders, a loose skin prolonged into dewlap and folds under the belly, pendulous ears, and marked resistance to the injurious effects of heat and insect attack — compare BRAHMAN

zebu

ze·bub \'zē,bəb\ *n* -s [Ar *dhubāb*] : ZIMB

zebu cattle *n pl* : ZEBUS

zeb·u·lun·ite \'zebyələ,nīt\ *n* -s *usu cap* [*Zebulun*, tenth son of Jacob (Gen 30:20) and ancestor of the tribe (fr. LL *Zabulon*, fr. Heb *Zĕbhūlun*) + E *-ite*] : a member of the Hebrew tribe of Zebulun

zec·chi·no \ze'kē(,)nō, tse-\ *n, pl* **zecchi·ni** \-nē\ *or* **zecchinos** [It — more at SEQUIN] : SEQUIN 1

zech·in *or* **zec·chin** *or* **zec·chine** \'zekən\ *n* -s [It *zecchino*] : SEQUIN 1

zech·stein \'zek,stīn\ *adj, usu cap* [G, lit., mine stone, fr. *zeche* mine (fr. MHG, company, society) + *stein* stone, fr. OHG; akin to OE *teohh* company, society, *teohhian* to determine, propose, OHG *zehōn* to order, arrange, and prob. to Goth *gateihan* to tell — more at DICTION, STONE] : of or relating to a subdivision of the European Permian — see GEOLOGIC TIME table

zed \'zed\ *n* -s [ME, fr. MF *zede*, fr. LL *zeta* zeta, fr. Gk *zēta*] *chiefly Brit* : the letter z

zedakah *n, pl* **zedakoth** *or* **zedakot** *var of* TZEDAKAH

zed·o·ar·ia \,zedə'wa(a)rēə\ *n* -s [ML] : ZEDOARY

zed·o·ary \'=,werē\ *n* -ES [ML *zedoaria, zedoarium*, fr. Ar or Per; Ar *zadwār*, fr. Per] : a fragrant East Indian drug of a warm bitter aromatic taste formerly used in medicine as a stimulant and still used in India and derived from the rhizome of various plants of the genus *Curcuma* (esp. *C. zedoaria*)

zee \'zē\ *n* -s : the letter z

zee·land·er \'zēləndə(r)\ *n* -s *cap* [*Zeeland*, province of southwest Netherlands + E *-er*] : a native or inhabitant of Zeeland in the Netherlands

zee·man effect \'zā,män, 'zēmən-\ *n, usu cap Z* [after Pieter *Zeeman* †1943 Dutch physicist] : a phenomenon that is observed in the emission spectrum when a source of radiation is placed in a magnetic field or observed in the absorption spectrum when an absorbing medium is placed in a magnetic field and that consists of the breaking of single spectral lines into three or more components which are polarized

ze·i·dae \'zēə,dē\ *n pl, cap* [NL *Zeus*, type genus + *-idae*] : a family of marine fishes (order Zeomorphi) comprising the John Dorys

ze·i·form \-ə,fȯrm\ *adj* [NL *Zeus* + E *-iform*] : resembling the Zeidae

zei·gar·nik effect \z|ī'gärnik-, ts|\ *n, usu cap Z* [after Bluma *Zeigarnik*, 20th cent. Ger. psychologist] : the psychological tendency to remember an uncompleted task rather than a completed one

ze·in \'zēən\ *n* -s [NL *Zea* + E *-in*] : a prolamin constituting the principal protein in corn that is usu. obtained as a yellowish powder by extracting corn gluten with aqueous isopropyl alcohol and that is used chiefly in making textile fibers, plastics, printing inks, varnishes and other coatings, and adhesives and sizes

zeit·geist \'tsīt,gīst, 'zīt-\ *n* -s *often cap* [G, fr. *zeit* time (fr. OHG *zīt*) + *geist* spirit, fr. OHG — more at TIDE, GHOST] : the spirit of the time : the general intellectual and moral state or the trend of culture and taste characteristic of an era ⟨the ~ of these centuries . . . operated against the development of a pure science —J.K.Robertson⟩ ⟨speed is a part of our ~; it is basic . . . to our ability to produce —V.E.Leichty⟩

zel·koua \'zelkəwə\ [NL, fr. Georgian *tselkva*] *syn of* ZELKOVA

zel·ko·va \-kəvə\ *n, cap* [NL, fr. Georgian *tselkva*] : a small genus of shrubs and trees (family Ulmaceae) occurring in temperate regions of the Old World and having simple leaves, small apetalous polygamous flowers, and small oblique drupes

¹ze·mi \zə'mē, sə-\ *n, pl* **zemi** *or* **zemis** [Sp *zemi*, fr. Taino *cemi, zemi, zeme*] **1** : a spirit or supernatural being of the aboriginal Tainos of the West Indies **2** : an object believed to be the dwelling of a spirit and to possess magic potency; *esp* : FETISH, IDOL

²ze·mi \'zāmē\ *n, pl* **zemi** *or* **zemis** *usu cap* **1** : a Naga people found chiefly in the Barail area of the Assam-Burma frontier region **2** : a member of the Zemi people

ze·mi·ism \zə'mē,izəm, sə-\ *n* -s [¹*zemi* + *-ism*] : the body of Taino beliefs and practices regarding zemis

zemindar *var of* ZAMINDAR

zemindari *var of* ZAMINDARI

ze·mi·roth *or* **ze·mi·rot** \zə'mē,rōt(h), -ōs\ *n pl* [Heb *zĕmīrōth* (pl.), fr. *zamēr* to sing] : religious songs sung usu. in Hebrew typically around the table at the Sabbath meal

zem·mi \'zemē\ *or* **zem·ni** \-mnē\ *n* -s [Russ dial. (*shchenyuk*) *zemny*, lit., earth puppy, fr. *shchenyuk* puppy + *zemny* of earth, fr. *zemlya* earth; akin to L *humus* earth — more at HUMBLE] : a large eastern European mole rat (*Spalax typhlus*)

zen \'zen\ *n* -s *usu cap* [Jap, religious meditation, fr. Chin (Pek) *ch'an²*, fr. Pali *jhāna*, fr. Skt *dhyāna* — more at DHYANA] **1** *or* **zen buddhism** *usu cap Z&B* : a Japanese school of Mahayana Buddhism that teaches self-discipline, deep meditation, and the attainment of enlightenment by direct intuitive insight into a self-validating transcendent truth beyond all intellectual conceptions and typically expresses its teachings in paradoxical and nonlogical forms — see KOAN, MONDO, SATORI **2** *or* **zen buddhist** *usu cap Z&B* : an adherent of Zen

ze·na·ga \zə'nägə\ *n, pl* **zenaga** *or* **zenagas** *usu cap* **1 a** : a Berber people of southern Morocco with other peoples under the general designation of Moors dominating western Africa in the 11th century and producing the Almoravid Caliphate **b** : a member of such people **2** : the Berber language of the Zenaga people

ze·na·i·da \zə'nāədə\ *n* [NL, fr. *Zénaïde* †1854 cousin and wife of Prince Charles Lucien Bonaparte †1857] **1** *cap* : a genus of tropical American pigeons that has one species (*Zenaida aurita*) reaching the West Indies and formerly the Florida coast and one (*Zenaida asiatica*) occurring in the southwestern United States **2** *or* **zenaida dove** -s : any bird of the genus *Zenaida*

ze·na·i·du·ra \zə,nāə'd(y)ürə\ *n, cap* [NL, fr. *Zenaida* + *-ura*] : a genus of pigeons that includes the common American mourning dove

¹ze·na·na \zə'nänə\ *n* -s [Hindi *zanāna*, fr. Per, fr. *zan* woman; akin to Skt *jani* — more at QUEEN] : the part of a dwelling in which the women of a family are secluded in India and Persia : HAREM, SERAGLIO

²zenana \"\ *adj* : of or relating to zenanas : relating to the women of the zenanas

ze·ner cards \'zēnə(r)-\ *n pl, usu cap Z* [after Karl E. *Zener* †1964 Am. psychologist] : a set of 25 cards that consists of 5 cards of each of 5 kinds bearing a circle, a rectangle, a cross, wavy lines, or a star and that is used in research in extrasensory perception

Zener cards

¹ze·nith \'zēnəth, *chiefly Brit* 'zen-\ *n* -s [ME *cenit, senyth*, fr. MF *cenith*, fr. ML, fr. OSp *zenit*, modif. (prob. due to scribal error) of Ar *samt* (*ar-ra's*) way (of the head)] **1** : the point of the celestial sphere that is vertically above the observer and directly opposite the nadir or that is vertically above any given point on the earth's surface **2 a** : the vault of the sky : the upper region of the heavens **b** : the highest point reached in the heavens by a celestial body **3** : the point of culmination : the greatest height : ACME, PEAK, SUMMIT ⟨classical studies reached their ~ in the twelfth century —H. O.Taylor⟩ ⟨at the ~ of his fame —Alvin Redman⟩ **4** *or* **zenith blue** : a light purplish blue that is redder than lupine and bluer and paler than average periwinkle

²zenith \"\ *adj* : located at or relating to the zenith

ze·nith·al \-thəl\ *adj* **1** : of or relating to the zenith : located at or near the zenith **2** : drawn to show correct directions from the center ⟨a ~ map⟩ : of or relating to zenithal equidistant projection

zenithal equidistant projection *n* : AZIMUTHAL EQUIDISTANT PROJECTION

zenith distance *or* **zenith angle** *n* : the angular distance of a celestial object from the zenith measured by the arc of a vertical circle intercepted between the object and the zenith : the complement of the altitude

zenith eyepiece *n* : an eyepiece or adapter containing a right-angle prism or a plane mirror to reflect the rays from an object near the zenith to the side of a refracting telescope for more convenient observation — called also *diagonal eyepiece*

zenith star *n* : a star that culminates near the zenith

zenith telescope *or* **zenith tube** *n* : a telescope that is installed in a fixed vertical position so that it can be used only to observe stars crossing the meridian near the zenith which is at the center of its field of view and that is used for precise time and latitude determinations

ze·nith·ward \'=,=wə(r)d\ *or* **ze·nith·wards** \-dz\ *adv* [¹*zenith* + *-ward* or *-wards*] : toward the zenith ⟨a ray of everlasting light . . . that had shot itself ~ —Thomas Carlyle⟩

zen·ker's degeneration \'tseŋkə(r)z-, 'ze|\ *n, usu cap Z* [after Friedrich Albert von *Zenker* †1898 Ger. pathologist] : AMYLOIDOSIS

zenker's fluid *n, usu cap Z* [after Konrad *Zenker* †1894 Ger. histologist] : a fixing fluid much used in histological technique and composed of potassium dichromate, mercuric chloride, sodium sulfate, glacial acetic acid, and water

zen·nist \'zenəst\ *n* -s *usu cap* [*zen* + *-ist*] : ZEN 2

ze·no·ni·an \zə'nōnēən\ *adj, usu cap* **1** [L *Zenon-, Zeno* Zeno, 5th cent. B.C. Greek Eleatic philosopher (fr. Gk *Zēnōn*) + E *-ian*] : of or relating to the Eleatic philosopher Zeno, his doctrines, or his paradoxes **2** [L *Zenon-, Zeno* Zeno, 4th & 3d cent. B.C. Greek philosopher and founder of Stoicism, (fr. Gk *Zēnōn*) + E *-ian*] : of or relating to Zeno, the founder of Stoicism

zeno·pho·bia \,zenə'fōbēə\ *n* [by alter.] : XENOPHOBIA

zens *pl of* ZEN

ze·oid \'zē,ȯid\ *adj or n* [NL *Zeoidei*] : ZEOMORPH

ze·oi·dei \zē'ȯidē,ī\ *n pl* [NL, fr. *Zeus* + *-oidei*] *syn of* ZEOMORPHI

ze·o·lite \'zēə,līt\ *n* -s [Sw *zeolit*, fr. Gk *zein* to boil + *-o-* + Sw *-lit* -lite, fr. F -lite; fr. their intumescence under the blowpipe — more at YEAST] **1** : any of a family of hydrous silicates that include several groups (as the monoclinic phillipsite group, the rhombohedral chabazite group, the monoclinic natrolite group, and the monoclinic heulandite group) as well as minerals not yet classified, that are analogous in composition to the feldspars with aluminum, sodium, potassium, and calcium as their chief metals, that occur as secondary minerals in cavities of lavas (as amygdaloidal basalt) and less frequently in granite and gneiss, and that have the capacity to act as cation exchangers or as molecular sieves (hardness usu. 3.5–5.5, sp.gr. 2.0–2.4) **2** : any of various silicates that are processed natural materials (as glauconite or greensand) or synthetic granular sodium aluminum silicates used in water softening and as adsorbents — **ze·o·lit·ic** \¦=='lid·ik\ *adj*

ze·ol·i·ti·za·tion \zē,äləd·ə'zāshən, -əd·,ī'z-\ *n* -s : the act or process of zeolitizing

ze·ol·i·tize \zē'älə,tīz\ *vt* -ED/-ING/-S **1** : to convert into a zeolite **2** : to fill (as the openings in a rock) with zeolites **3** : to treat in a process using zeolite

¹zeo·morph \'zēə,mȯrf\ *adj* [NL *Zeomorphi*] : of or relating to the Zeomorphi

²zeomorph \"\ *n* : a fish of the order Zeomorphi

zeo·mor·phi \,==,'mȯr,fī\ *n pl, cap* [NL, fr. *zeo-* (fr. *Zeus*) + *-morphi*] : a small order of marine bony fishes that in some respects are intermediate between the Berycomorphi and Percomorphi and that include the John Dorys and a few related forms

ze·oph·yl·lite \zē'äfə,līt\ *n* -s [G *zeophyllit*, fr. *zeolit* zeolite + *phyll-* + *-it* -ite; fr. its occurrence in small plates] : a mineral $Ca_4Si_3O_7(OH)_4F_2$ consisting of a basic silicate and fluoride of calcium often containing iron

zep \'zep\ *n* -s *often cap* [by shortening] : ZEPPELIN

Zeph·i·ran \'zefə,ran\ *trademark* — used for benzalkonium chloride

¹zeph·yr \'zefə(r)\ *n* -s [earlier *Zephyrus*, west wind (personified), fr. ME *Zephirus*, fr. L *Zephyrus*, god of the west wind, & *zephyrus* west wind, zephyr, fr. Gk *Zephyros*, god of the west wind, & *zephyros* west wind, zephyr; prob. akin to Gk *zophos* darkness, west] **1 a** : a soft warm breeze from the west **b** : any gentle breeze **2** : any of various lightweight fabrics and articles of clothing (as a small shawl, a duster, or a hat) **3** : a pinkish gray to pale yellowish pink **syn** see WIND

²zephyr \"\ *adj, of a yarn or fabric* : very lightweight, soft, and fine

zeph·yr·an·thes \,zefə'ran,thēz\ *n, cap* [NL, fr. Gk *zephyros* zephyr + NL *-anthes*] : a genus of American bulbous plants (family Amaryllidaceae) having pink, white, or yellowish solitary flowers with broad segments and stamens of different lengths

zeph·yr·e·an \¦zefə¦rēən\ *or* **ze·phyr·ian** \zə'firēən\ *or* **zeph·yr·ous** \'zefərəs\ *adj* [¹*zephyr* + *-ean* or *-ian* or *-ous*] : of the character of, resembling, or suggesting a light breeze

zephyr lily *n* : a plant of the genus *Zephyranthes*; *esp* : a tropical American plant (*Z. carinata*) often cultivated for its rose-red flowers

zep·pe·lin \'zep(ə)lən\ *n* -s *often cap* [after Count Ferdinand von *Zeppelin* †1917 Ger. aeronaut and airship manufacturer] : a rigid airship consisting of a cylindrical trussed and covered frame supported by internal gas cells; *broadly* : AIRSHIP

ze·quin *or* **ze·quine** \ze'kēn, 'zekən, 'zēkwən\ *n* -s [alter. (influenced by It *zecchino*) of *sequin*] : SEQUIN 1

zer·da \'zərdə\ *n* -s [Ar *zerdawā*, prob. of Per origin] : FENNEC

zeriba *var of* ZAREBA

¹ze·ro \'zē(,)rō, 'zi(-\ *n, pl* **zeros** *also* **zeroes** [F or It; F *zéro*, fr. It *zero*, fr. ML *zephirum*, fr. Ar *ṣifr* empty, cipher, zero] **1 a** : the arithmetical symbol 0 or ø denoting the absence of all magnitude or quantity : CIPHER, NAUGHT **b** : a number or element that leaves unchanged any number or element to which it is added: *specif* : the number between the set of all negative numbers and the set of all positive numbers — see NUMBER table **c** : a value of the independent variable of a function that makes it equal to zero ⟨+2 and −2 are ~*s* of $f(x)=x^2-4$⟩ **2 a** (1) : the point of departure in reckoning; *specif* : the point from which the graduation of a scale (as of a thermometer) commences (2) : the temperature represented by the zero mark on a thermometer **b** : ZERO HOUR 1 **c** (1) : the basic setting of the rear sight of a firearm that compensates for inaccuracies of weapon and of firing habits and for elevation required at a given range and that causes the firearm to hit where aimed under normal conditions (2) : the adjustment (as for elevation, windage) required for a gun or other device to achieve accuracy under specific operating conditions **3** : a person or thing that has no importance, influence, or independent existence : NONENTITY, NOBODY, NOTHING, CIPHER **4 a** (1) : a state or condition of total absence or of neutrality between opposites : NOTHING, NAUGHT ⟨a face that registered ~ no matter what happened⟩ ⟨the two eyewitnesses for the State added up to ~, for the defense made mincemeat of their testimony —Ross Colin⟩ ⟨reduce the mortality rate to ~⟩ ⟨hold the reversible reaction of the chemical to ~⟩ (2) : absence of an overt linguistic feature when this absence is itself significant because of the presence of such a feature at corresponding points in the language ⟨some vowel which earlier followed the final consonant but which was later reduced to ~ —R.A.Hall b. 1911⟩ **b** : the lowest point ⟨his spirits fell to ~ —Margaret Kennedy⟩ **5** : something arbitrarily or conveniently designated zero: as **a** : the lowest in order or class ⟨a speech so bad it rated a ~⟩ **b** : the space numbered 0 on a roulette wheel

²zero \"\ *adj* **1** : of, relating to, or being a zero: as **a** : forming a fixed point of departure in reckoning ⟨set the gauge back to the ~ mark⟩ ⟨time zones extending from the ~ meridian⟩ ⟨used the founding date as the ~ year of its era⟩ **b** : having no magnitude or quantity or being intermediate between positive and negative magnitudes or quantities : not any ⟨~ velocity⟩ ⟨~ gravity⟩ ⟨~ angle⟩ ⟨~ lift⟩ ⟨~ toe-in⟩ ⟨~ inches⟩ ⟨~ mass⟩ : NIL ⟨chances of making up the lost time were ~⟩ **c** (1) : ABSENT, LACKING ⟨the ~ modification in the past of *cut* in comparison with *loved, sang*⟩ (2) : having no modified inflectional form : UNMODIFIED ⟨the noun *fish* has a ~ plural *fish* as well as a regular plural *fishes*⟩ **d** (1) : belonging to or being a group or class arbitrarily or conveniently designated zero (2) : of, relating to, or being a logical class having no members : NULL, EMPTY ⟨the ~ denotation of the term *unicorn*⟩ ⟨~ class⟩ **2 a** *of an atmospheric ceiling* : limiting vision to 50 feet or less **b** *of horizontal visibility* **:** limited to 165 feet or less

³**zero** \"\ *vb* -ED/-ING/-ES *vt* **1 :** to adjust (as by firing under test conditions) the zero of — often used with *in* ⟨~*ed* in his rifle at 100 yards⟩ **2 :** to adjust (an instrument or device) to zero value or into synchronism **3 a :** to concentrate firepower (as of mortar or artillery) on the exact range of — usu. used with *in* ⟨it must operate from fixed bases which can be ~*ed* in by the enemy —Carl Spaatz⟩ **b :** to bring to bear on the exact range of a target **:** TRAIN — usu. used with *in* ⟨artillery and mortars were ~*ed* in on all crossroads and avenues of approach —S.J.Tobin⟩ **4 :** to reduce to zero ~ *vi* **1 :** to adjust fire (as of mortars or artillery) on a specific target — usu. used with *in* ⟨an enemy battery that ~*ed* in on the crossroad⟩ **2 :** to move near to or focus attention on a person or thing as if on a target **:** CLOSE — usu. used with *in* ⟨bird-dogs ~*ing* in on coveys of hidden quail —J.N.Leonard⟩ ⟨congressional opponents who ~*ed* in on the bill⟩

¹**zero beat** *n* [²*zero*] **:** a condition in which two radio frequencies are adjusted to equality by first producing beats between them and then reducing the beat frequency to zero — compare HETERODYNE

²**zero beat** *vb* **:** to adjust to zero beat

zero–beat reception *n* [¹*zero beat*] **:** a method of reception with an electron tube in generating condition in exact synchronism with the received wave as determined by zero beat — compare HOMODYNE

zero drift *n* **:** a gradual change in the scale zero of a measuring instrument (as a thermometer or a galvanometer)

zeroes *pl of* ZERO, *pres 3d sing of* ZERO

zero grade *n* **:** the most reduced form of the weak ablaut grade in which the vowel disappears entirely

zero group *n* **:** the group of inert gases having a valence of zero in the periodic table

zero hour *n* **1 a :** the hour at which a previously planned attack or other military operation is started — compare H HOUR **b :** the scheduled time for an action or operation (as the firing of a rocket) to occur or begin — compare COUNTDOWN **2 a :** a time when a vital decision or decisive change in the course of events is impending **:** CRISIS **3 :** the time set as a basis for reckoning the time of day

ze·ro·ize \'zērō,īz, 'zir-\ *vt* -ED/-ING/-S [¹*zero* + *-ize*] **:** to return (as a calculating machine) to zero

zero–lift angle \'⸗(,)⸗,⸗-\ *n* **:** the angle of attack of an airfoil when the lift is zero

zero oil *n* **:** an oil (as a lubricating oil) that becomes too viscous to flow or begins to deposit solid material at a temperature of 0° F by the cold test

zero–order reaction \'⸗(,)⸗,⸗⸗-\ *n* **:** a chemical reaction in which the rate of reaction is constant and independent of the concentration of the reacting substances — compare ORDER OF A REACTION

zero–point energy \'⸗(,)⸗,⸗-\ *n* **:** energy remaining in a substance at the absolute zero of temperature

zero potential *n* **1 :** the ideal potential of a point infinitely distant from all electrification **2 :** the actual potential of the surface of the earth taken as a point of reference — compare GROUND 7b

zeros *pl of* ZERO

zero–sum game \'⸗(,)⸗,⸗-\ *n* **:** a game in which the cumulative winnings equal the cumulative losses

ze·roth \'zē,rōth, 'zi,-\ *adj* [¹*zero* + *-th*] **:** having serial number zero **:** ZERO ⟨a grating spectrum of ~ order⟩ ⟨the ~ power of a number⟩

zerovalent \¦⸗(,)⸗¦⸗⸗\ *adj* [¹*zero* + *valent*] **:** having a valence of zero

zero–zero \¦⸗(,)⸗¦⸗(,)⸗\ *adj* **1 :** characterized by or being atmospheric conditions reducing ceiling and visibility to zero ⟨a *zero-zero* fog⟩ ⟨*zero-zero* weather⟩ **2 :** limited to zero by atmospheric conditions ⟨ceiling and visibility may be unlimited one moment, and *zero-zero* seven minutes later —*All Hands*⟩

zer·van·ism \'zərvə,nizəm\ *also* **zar·van·ism** \'zär-\ *n* -S *usu cap* [*Zervan, Zarvan*, an ancient Iranian god + E *-ian*] **:** an ancient Iranian religion or Zoroastrian heretical sect teaching that infinite time is the originating principle of existence and prior to the dual principles of good and evil held ultimate by orthodox Zoroastrianism and influencing Mithraism

zer·van·ite \-ə,nīt\ *also* **zar·van·ite** \-ə,nīt\ *n* -S *usu cap* [*Zervan, Zarvan* + E *-ite*] **:** an adherent of Zervanism

¹**zest** \'zest\ *n* -S [obs. F *zest* (now *zeste*) orange or lemon peel] **1 :** a piece of the peel or of the thin oily outer skin of an orange or lemon used as flavoring (as for liquor) **2 :** a quality of enhancing enjoyment **:** PIQUANCY ⟨younger children added a ~ and life to the . . . fair —*Springfield (Mass.) Union*⟩ ⟨hot tamales also added ~ to the diet —R.W.Murray⟩ **3 :** keen enjoyment **:** RELISH, GUSTO ⟨years of grinding work . . . had failed to kill her ~ for living —Edna Ferber⟩ ⟨enjoying the meal with full youthful ~ —J.C.Powys⟩ ⟨people who are losing their ~, imagination, joy, and awe, and are filled with boredom —J.B.Priestley⟩

²**zest** \"\ *vt* -ED/-ING/-S **:** to give a relish or flavor to **:** heighten the taste or relish of

zest·ful \'zestfəl\ *adj* [¹*zest* + *-ful*] **:** full of zest **:** marked by keen enjoyment ⟨housecleaning time — that ~ desire to banish clutter —Bernice Caswell⟩ — **zest·ful·ly** \-fəlē, -li\ *adv* — **zest·ful·ness** *n* -ES

zesty \'zestē, -ti\ *adj* [¹*zest* + *-y*] **:** having or characterized by zest **:** PIQUANT

ze·ta \'zād·ə, -ātə *also* 'zē-\ *n* -S [Gk *zēta*, of Sem origin; prob. akin to Heb *ṣādhē* sadhe] **:** the sixth letter of the Greek alphabet — symbol Z or ζ; see ALPHABET table

zeta potential *n* **:** the potential difference across an electric double layer usu. between a solid surface and a liquid — called also *electrokinetic potential;* compare STREAMING POTENTIAL

¹**ze·tet·ic** \zə'ted·ik\ *adj* [Gk *zētētikos*, fr. *zētētos* (verbal of *zētein* to seek for, inquire) + *-ikos* -ic; prob. akin to Skt *diyati* he flies, soars — more at DINO-] **:** proceeding by inquiry

²**zetetic** \"\ *n* -S [Gk *zētētikos*, fr. *zētētikos*, adj.] **:** SKEPTIC, SEEKER; *specif* **:** one of a group of Pyrrhonist philosophers

zet·land \'zetlənd\ *adj, usu cap* [fr. *Zetland*, Scottish county comprising the Shetland islands] **:** of or relating to the county of Zetland, Scotland **:** SHETLAND

zeug·ite \'zü,gīt\ *n* -S [ISV *zeug-* (fr. Gk *zeugnynai* to yoke, join) + *-ite* — more at YOKE] **:** a structure (as a basidium or promycelium) within which the dikaryotic phase of a fungus ends and nuclear fusion occurs

¹**zeu·glo·don** \'züglə,dän\ [NL *Zeuglodont-, Zeuglodon*, fr. Gk *zeuglē* loop or strap of a yoke (fr. *zeugnynai* to yoke) + NL *-odont-, -odon*] *syn of* BASILOSAURUS

²**zeuglodon** \"\ *or* **zeu·glodont** \-nt\ *n* -S **:** any of the extinct slender toothed whales constituting the genus *Basilosaurus*

³**zeuglodon** \"\ *adj* **:** of or relating to the zeuglodons

zeu·glo·don·tia \,⸗⸗'dänch(ē)ə\ *n pl, cap* [NL, fr. *Zeuglodont-, Zeuglodon* + *-ia*] **:** a suborder of Cetacea comprising extinct Eocene and Miocene toothed whales of *Basilosaurus* and related genera — **zeu·glo·don·tian** \,⸗⸗'dänch(ē)ən\ *adj or n*

zeu·glo·don·toid \¦⸗⸗¦dän,tȯid\ *adj* [NL *Zeuglodont-, Zeuglodon* + E *-oid*] **:** ZEUGLODONTIAN

zeu·glop·tera \⸗'glüptərə\ *n pl, cap* [NL, fr. Gk *zeuglē-* loop or strap of a yoke + NL *-ptera*] *in some classifications* **:** an order coextensive with the family Micropterygidae

zeug·ma \'zügmə\ *n* -S [L *zeugmat-, zeugma*, fr. Gk, lit., juncture, joining, fr. *zeugnynai* to yoke, join — more at YOKE] **1 :** the use of a word in the same construction with two adjacent words in the context with only one of which it is appropriate in sense ⟨*they wear a garment like that of the Scythians but a language peculiar to themselves* is an example of ~⟩ — compare SYLLEPSIS **2 :** connection of syllables not permitting diaeresis or caesura in classical prosody **:** CLOSE JUNCTURE — **zeug·mat·ic** \(')züg¦mad·ik, -at|, |ēk\ *adj* — **zeug·mat·i·cal·ly** \|ək(ə)lē, |ēk-, -li\ *adv*

zeu·ner·ite \'zȯinə,rīt\ *n* -S [G *zeunerit*, fr. Gustav *Zeuner* †1907 Ger. physicist and engineer + G *-it* -ite] **:** a mineral $Cu(UO_2)_2(AsO_4)_2.10\text{–}16H_2O$ consisting of a hypothetical hydrous copper uranium arsenate analogous to torbernite, autunite, uranocircite, saléeite, and uranospinite and found in natural specimens that generally prove to be metazeunerite

ze·us \'zēəs\ *n, cap* [NL, fr. L, a kind of fish, fr. Gk *zaios*] **:** the type genus of the family Zeidae

zeu·ze·ra \zü'zirə\ *n, cap* [NL] **:** a genus (the type of the family Zeuzeridae) of moths including the leopard moth and some related moths

zeu·zer·i·dae \zü'zerə,dē\ *n pl, cap* [NL, fr. *Zeuzera*, type genus + *-idae*] **:** a family of moths that is often considered a subfamily of Cossidae and that comprises the leopard moth and other large dull mottled grayish or brownish moths — see XYLEUTES

ZF *abbr* **1** zero frequency **2** zone of fire

ZG *abbr* zoological garden

zhda·nov \'zhdänəf\ *adj, usu cap* [fr. *Zhdanov*, U.S.S.R.] **:** of or from the city of Zhdanov, U.S.S.R. **:** of the kind or style prevalent in Zhdanov

zho *var of* DZO

ZI *abbr* zone of interior

zia *usu cap, var of* SIA

zi·a·met \zē'ä,met\ *n* -S [Turk *ziamat*, fr. Ar *za'āmah*] **:** a fief formerly granted for service in the Turkish army

zi·a·rat \zē'ärət\ *or* **zi·a·ra** \-'ärə\ *n* -S [Hindi *ziyārat* visiting a shrine, pilgrimage, fr. Per, fr. Ar] **:** a tomb of a Muslim saint **:** SHRINE

zib·el·ine *also* **zib·el·line** \'zibə,lēn, -līn\ *n* -S [MF, fr. OIt *zibellino*, of Slav origin; akin to Russ *sobol'* sable — more at SABLE] **1 :** SABLE 2b **2 :** a soft lustrous fabric of wool that is mixed with mohair, alpaca, or camel's hair to form a long silky nap which is pressed down and that is made in various weights for coats, suits, and dresses

zib·et *or* **zib·eth** \'zibət\ *n* -S [It *zibetto* & ML *zibethum*, fr. Ar *zabād* civet perfume] **:** a common Asiatic civet cat (*Viverra zibetha*)

zi·do·ni·an \zī'dōnēən\ *n* -S *cap* [*Zidon* Sidon (fr. Heb *Ṣīdōn*) + E *-an*] **:** SIDONIAN

zie·ger *also* **zi·ger** \'zēgə(r)\ *n* -S [G *zieger*, fr. MHG *ziger* whey, whey cheese — more at SAPSAGO] **:** a cheese made from whey consisting principally of albumin

zie·gler catalyst \'zēglə(r)-\ *n, usu cap Z* [after Karl *Ziegler* *b*1898 Ger. chemistry institute director] **:** a catalyst (as triethyl-aluminum or a complex of a trialkyl-aluminum with titanium tetrachloride) that promotes an ionic type of polymerization of ethylene, propylene, or related olefins at atmospheric pressure with the resultant formation of a relatively high-melting polyethylene, a stereoregular polypropylene, or similar product

zier·vo·gel process \'tsir,fōgəl-\ *n, usu cap Z* [prob. after *Ziervogel*, 19th cent. Ger. metallurgist] **:** a process of extracting silver from its ores by roasting them so as to convert it into sulfate, leaching with water to dissolve the sulfate, and precipitating the silver by means of scrap iron or other reagent

zie·tri·si·kite \,zē·trə'se,kīt\ *n* -S [*Zietrisika*, Moldavia + E *-ite*] **:** a mineral wax resembling ozokerite

zif *also* **ziw** \'zif\ *n* -S *usu cap* [Heb *ziw*] **:** the 2d month of the ancient Hebrew calendar corresponding to Iyar

¹**zig** \'zig\ *n* -S [*zig-* (in *zigzag*)] **1 a :** one of the sharp turns, angles, or alterations in a zigzag course ⟨a zigzag pattern with . . . diamonds planted at each ~ and zag —*New Yorker*⟩ **b :** one of the short straight lines or sections of a zigzag course at an angle to a zag ⟨the stripes making first a ~, then a zag —Lois Long⟩ **c :** a movement or direction at an angle to a zag ⟨~ to the right . . . followed by a zag to the left —*N.Y.Times*⟩ **2 :** a sharp alteration or change of direction (as in a process or policy) ⟨evolutionary ~*s* and zags to adjust to the harshest conditions of nature —Gladwin Hill⟩ ⟨every ~ and zag of the official line —Roy Essoyan⟩

²**zig** \"\ *vi* **zigged; zigged; zigging; zigs** [*zig-* (in *zigzag*)] **:** to execute one of the turns or to follow one of the sections of a zigzag course ⟨*zigged* to the right and zagged back on course —*Monsanto Mag.*⟩ ⟨our policies have *zigged* and zagged too much —H.W.Baldwin⟩

zig·a·de·nus \,zigə'dēnəs\ *n, cap* [NL, alter. of *Zygadenus*, fr. Gk *zygaden* jointly, in pairs, fr. *zygon* yoke, pair — more at YOKE] **:** a genus of herbs (family Liliaceae) of No. America and Asia having basal linear leaves and a terminal panicle of whitish or greenish flowers with a flat spreading perianth — see DEATH CAMAS

zig·gu·rat \'zigə,rat\ *or* **zik·u·rat** *or* **zik·ku·rat** \'zikə-\ *n* -S [Akkadian *ziqqurratu* pinnacle, mountaintop] **:** an ancient Babylonian temple tower consisting of a lofty pyramidal structure built in successive stepped-back stages with outside staircases and a shrine at the top

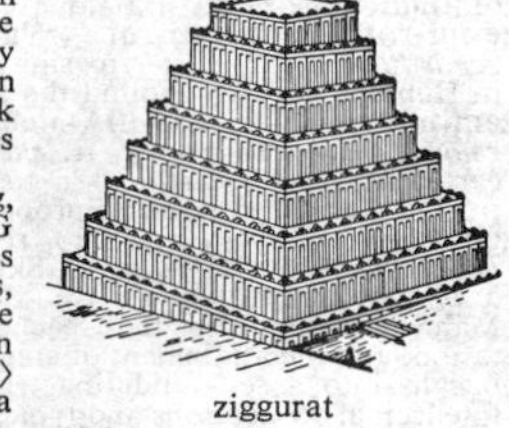
ziggurat

¹**zig·zag** \'zig,zag, -aa(ə)g, -aig\ *n* -S [F, prob. fr. G *zickzack*] **1 :** one of a series of short sharp turns, angles, or alterations in a course ⟨the ~*s* of the mountain roads —Vincent Starrett⟩ ⟨the party line has been a series of violent ~*s* —*Nation*⟩ **2 :** something having the form or character of a series of short sharp turns, angles, or alterations ⟨draw a ~ in the air —Annette Dinsmore⟩ ⟨a blue necktie with cherry red ~*s* —Lawrence Williams⟩: as **a :** a zigzag road or fence ⟨a split⸗rail ~⟩ **b :** a zigzag approach in siege operations to avoid enfilade fire **c :** a molding running in a zigzag line **:** a chevron or series of chevrons

²**zigzag** \"\ *adv* **:** in or by a zigzag path or course ⟨birds . . . flew ~ with a shrill cry —Elizabeth Bowen⟩

³**zigzag** \"\ *also* **zig·zag·gy** \-gē\ *adj* **:** having short sharp turns or angles ⟨a ~ path⟩ ⟨~ stitching⟩

⁴**zigzag** \"\ *vb* **zigzagged; zigzagged; zigzagging; zigzags** *vt* **1 :** to trace a zigzag upon **2 :** to form into a zigzag ⟨office buildings . . . slightly *zigzagged* to fit available ground space —*Amer. Guide Series: Ark.*⟩ ~ *vi* **:** to lie in, proceed along, or consist of a zigzag course ⟨lightning *zigzagging* through the pungent air —William Beebe⟩ ⟨a faint little path that *zigzagged* through ferny undergrowth —G.C.Bestor⟩ ⟨his line of thought suddenly *zigzagged* into the . . . practical —Helen Howe⟩

zigzag clover *n* **:** a European red-flowered clover (*Trifolium medium*) — called also *cow clover*

zigzag endpaper *n* **:** an endpaper made with an accordion fold

zig·zag·ged·ly \(')zig¦zagədlē\ *adv* [*zigzagged* (past part. of ⁴*zigzag*) + *-ly*] **:** in a zigzag manner ⟨skimmed ~ a scant inch from the ground —Lloyd Zimpel⟩

zig·zag·ged·ness \-dnəs\ *n* -ES **:** the quality or state of being zigzag

zig·zag·ger \'zig,zagə(r)\ *n* -S **1 :** one that zigzags **2 :** a sewing machine attachment for appliquéing, cording, or seaming with a zigzag line of stitching

zig·zag·gery \-agərē\ *n* -ES **:** a zigzag method or course

zigzag rule *n* **:** a measuring rule made in sections that fold together

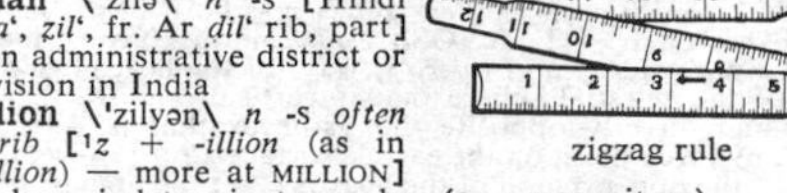
zigzag rule

zikr \'zikər\ *var of* DHIKR

zil·lah \'zilə\ *n* -S [Hindi *zila'*, *zil'*, fr. Ar *dil'* rib, part] **:** an administrative district or division in India

zil·lion \'zilyən\ *n* -S *often attrib* ['z + *-illion* (as in *million*) — more at MILLION] **:** a large indeterminate number ⟨a ~ mosquitoes⟩

zil·lion·aire \,zilyə'na(a)(ə)r, -ne(ə)r, -na(a)ə, -neə, '⸗⸗,⸗\ *n* -S [*zillion* + *-aire* (as in *millionaire*)] **:** one whose wealth is of unspecified millions (as of dollars, pounds, or francs)

zi·mar·ra \zə'märə\ *n* -S [It — more at SIMAR] **:** a black cassock with attached cape and purple sash, buttons, and piping worn esp. in the house by Roman Catholic prelates — called also *simar*

zimb \'zim(b)\ *n* -S [Amharic *zemb, zimb, zenb*] **:** a large two⸗winged fly native to Abyssinia and prob. of the family Tabanidae

zim·ba·lon \'tsimbə,län\ *or* **zim·ba·loon** \-lün\ *n* -S [G *zimbalon*, fr. Hung *cimbalom* — more at CIMBALOM] **:** CIMBALOM

zim·bel \'tsimbəl\ *n* -S [G, fr. OHG *zymbal*, fr. L *cymbalum* — more at CYMBAL] **:** CYMBAL 1b

zim·mer·mann reaction *or* **zim·mer·mann test** \'zimə(r)mən-\ *n, usu cap Z* [after Wilhelm *Zimmermann* *b*1910 Ger. physiological chemist] **:** the formation of a colored mixture on mixing of a ketone, alkali, and *meta*-dinitrobenzene

zim·mi \'zimē\ *var of* DHIMMI

zi·moc·ca \zə'mäkə\ *also* **zimocca sponge** *n* -S [NL] **:** a rather harsh commercial sponge (*Spongia zimocca* or *S. officinalis zimocca*) of a massive more or less conical form occurring in the Mediterranean Sea

¹**zinc** \'ziŋk\ *n* -S *often attrib* [G *zink*, perh. fr. *zinke* point, barb, prong, fr. OHG *zinko;* akin to OHG *zint* point, spike, tine; fr. its forming jags under certain temperatures — more at TINE] **1 :** a bluish white crystalline bivalent metallic element of low to intermediate hardness that is ductile when pure but in the commercial form is brittle at ordinary temperatures and becomes ductile on slight heating, that occurs abundantly in minerals (as sphalerite, zincite, smithsonite, willemite, and franklinite) commonly associated with lead minerals, that is usu. obtained by concentrating the ores, roasting, and either sintering and reducing by heating with coal or coke, distilling and condensing the zinc, and casting the resulting liquid metal into slabs or by leaching the roasted concentrate with dilute sulfuric acid and electrolyzing, that corrodes in moist but not dry air at ordinary temperature and in contact with most common structural metals corrodes sufficiently to protect them, that dissolves in dilute acids to give zinc salts and hydrogen and in hot solutions of sodium hydroxide or potassium hydroxide to give zincates and hydrogen, that is used chiefly as a protective coating for iron and steel, as rolled sheets and strips for roofing and other building purposes, dry batteries, and photoengravers' and printing plates, and in alloys esp. for die⸗casting, and that is a trace element in plant and animal metabolism — symbol *Zn;* see BRASS, GALVANIZED IRON, MOSSY ZINC, SPELTER, ZINC DUST, ZINC OXIDE; ELEMENT table **2 :** a purplish gray that is lighter and slightly bluer than crane, bluer and paler than dove gray or granite, and bluer than cinder gray — called also *cloud gray, gray dawn*

²**zinc** \"\ *vt* **zinced** *or* **zincked; zinced** *or* **zincked; zincing** *or* **zincking; zincs :** to treat or coat with zinc **:** GALVANIZE

zinc alkyl *n* **:** any of a class of organic zinc compounds of the general formula ZnR_2 that are typically colorless mobile liquids giving off poisonous vapors with disagreeable odors that ignite readily in air, that are made usu. by the action of an alkyl iodide (as ethyl iodide) on a zinc-sodium or zinc-copper alloy, and that are very reactive and hence much used in the synthesis of organic compounds ⟨dimethyl-zinc and diethyl⸗zinc are important *zinc alkyls*⟩

zincaluminite \¦⸗⸗¦⸗⸗,⸗\ *n* [*zinc* + *aluminite*] **:** a mineral $Zn_6Al_6(SO_4)_2(OH)_{26}.5H_2O$ consisting of a hydrous basic sulfate of aluminum and zinc

zinc amide *n* **:** an amorphous compound $Zn(NH_2)_2$ obtained by action of ammonia on diethyl-zinc — compare SODIUM AMIDE

zinc ammonium chloride *n* **:** a crystalline salt $ZnCl_2.2NH_4Cl$ or $(NH_4)_2ZnCl_4$ used as a welding, soldering, and galvanizing flux **:** ammonium tetrachloro-zincate

zinc·ate \'ziŋ,kāt\ *n* -S [*zinc* + *-ate*] **:** any of various compounds (as the sodium hydroxo-zincates $Na[Zn(OH)_3].3H_2O$ and $Na_2[Zn(OH)_4].2H_2O$) formed by reaction of zinc oxide or zinc with solutions of alkalies

zinc blende *n* **:** SPHALERITE

zinc bloom *n* [trans. of G *zinkblüte*] **:** HYDROZINCITE

zinc carbonate *n* **:** a crystalline salt $ZnCO_3$ occurring in nature as smithsonite; *also* **:** any of several basic carbonates of zinc occurring as hydrozincite or synthetically prepared and used chiefly as pigments

zinc chloride *n* **:** a poisonous caustic deliquescent readily soluble salt $ZnCl_2$ usu. in the form of granules or fused sticks that is made synthetically (as by reaction of zinc or zinc oxide with hydrochloric acid) and that is used chiefly in preserving and fireproofing wood, in parchmentizing paper and treating textile fibers and fabrics, as a catalyst in organic synthesis, and as a disinfectant and astringent

zinc chromate *n* **1 a :** a yellow crystalline normal salt $ZnCrO_4$ **b :** any of various basic salts; *esp* **:** a golden yellow pigment $4Zn(OH)_2.ZnCrO_4$ used in corrosion-inhibiting priming coats **2 :** ZINC YELLOW — not used systematically

zinc chrome *n* **:** ZINC YELLOW

zinc dust *n* **:** powdery metallic zinc usu. containing zinc oxide in varying amounts that collects as a bluish gray powder during distillation of zinc and that is used chiefly as a reducing agent, as a pigment in corrosion-resistant coatings for iron and steel, and in sherardizing

zinc engraving *n* **1 :** the art or process of photoengraving in zinc **2 :** a zinc linecut or halftone

zinc etching *n* **1 :** the process of making linecuts on zinc **2 :** a zinc linecut

zinc finish *n* **:** the finish obtained when paper is plated between sheets of zinc

zinc flowers *n pl* **:** FLOWERS OF ZINC

zinc gray *n* **:** any of various zinc pigments: as **a :** ZINC DUST **b :** ground sphalerite **c :** a mixture of zinc white with finely divided charcoal or with lithopone, chalk, or other pigments

zinc green *n* **1 :** COBALT GREEN **2 :** any of various green pigments consisting essentially of mixtures of zinc yellow and Prussian blue **3 :** DEEP CHROME GREEN

zinc hydrosulfite *n* **:** a crystallizable salt ZnS_2O_4 made by addition of sulfur dioxide to a warm aqueous slurry of zinc dust (as in the manufacture of sodium hydrosulfite) and used as a bleach; zinc dithionite — not used systematically

zinc·ic \'ziŋkik\ *adj* [ISV *zinc* + *-ic*] **:** relating to, containing, or resembling zinc

zinc·if·er·ous \(')ziŋ¦kif(ə)rəs, (')zin¦si-\ *adj* [ISV *zinc* + *-iferous*] **:** containing or yielding zinc

zinc·i·fi·ca·tion \,ziŋkəfə'kāshən\ *n* -S [fr. *zincify*, after such pairs as E *purify: purification*] **:** the act or process of zincifying

zinc·i·fy \'ziŋkə,fī\ *vt* -ED/-ING/-ES [*zinc* + *-ify*] **:** to coat or impregnate with zinc **:** ZINC, GALVANIZE

zinc·ite \'ziŋ,kīt\ *n* -S [G *zinkit*, fr. *zink* + *-it* -ite] **1 :** a brittle deep-red to orange-yellow hexagonal mineral ZnO consisting of zinc oxide that occurs in massive or granular form (hardness 4–4.5, sp. gr. 5.43–5.7) — called also *red oxide of zinc, red zinc ore* **2 :** an ore of zinc that occurs in New Jersey

zinck·en·ite \'ziŋkə,nīt\ *n* -S [by alter.] **:** ZINKENITE

zincky *or* **zinky** *or* **zincy** \'ziŋkē\ *adj* [*zinc* + *-y*] **:** relating to, containing, or having the appearance of zinc

zin·co \'ziŋ(,)kō\ *n* -S [short for *zincograph*] *Brit* **:** a zinc linecut

zinco– *comb form* [ISV *zinc* + *-o-*] **:** zinc ⟨*zinco*lysis⟩

zin·co·graph \'ziŋkə,graf, -rȧf\ *n* -S [back-formation fr. *zincography*] **1 :** a zinc plate prepared for use in zincography **2 :** a print made by zincography

zin·co·graph·ic \¦⸗⸗¦grafik\ *also* **zin·co·graph·i·cal** \-fəkəl\ *adj* **:** of, relating to, or produced by zincography

zin·cog·ra·phy \ziŋ'kägrəfē\ *n* -ES [ISV *zinco-* + *-graphy*] **1 :** the art or process of engraving or photoengraving letterpress printing surfaces on zinc **2 :** the art or process of preparing planographic printing surfaces on zinc

zinc·oid \'ziŋ,kȯid\ *adj* [*zinc* + *-oid*] **:** of, relating to, or resembling zinc

zinc ointment *n* **:** an ointment that consists of 20 percent of zinc oxide mixed with a petrolatum and white wax base and is used in the treatment of skin diseases

zinc orange *n* **:** a moderate to strong orange that is yellower and lighter than carrot red, lighter than Mars yellow, and slightly redder and less strong than sunburst — called also *cowslip*

zin·co·type \'ziŋkə,tīp\ *n* [*zinco-* + *type*] **:** ZINCOGRAPH

zinc·ous \'ziŋkəs\ *adj* [*zinc* + *-ous*] **:** ZINCIC

zinc oxide *n* **:** an infusible water-insoluble white solid ZnO that turns yellow when heated, that occurs in nature as zincite, that is obtained as a light white powder when zinc is burned, that is produced commercially usu. either by the direct American process of oxidizing zinc vapors during distillation before they have condensed or by the indirect French process of oxidizing the vapors of boiling zinc metal after condensation, and that is used chiefly as a pigment, in compounding rubber, and in pharmaceutical and cosmetic preparations (as ointments and powders) — see FLOWERS OF ZINC, ZINC WHITE

zinc peroxide *n* **:** any of various white to yellowish white powders regarded as mixtures of the peroxide ZnO_2 of zinc,

zinc hydroxide, and zinc carbonate or zinc oxide and used chiefly as disinfectants, astringents, and deodorants because of their ability to release oxygen in contact with moist organic matter

zinc phosphide *n* : a dark gray powdery compound Zn_3P_2 having an odor resembling that of garlic and used as a rodenticide

zincs *pl of* ZINC, *pres 3d sing of* ZINC

zinc silicate *n* : a silicate of zinc; *esp* : the fluorescent crystalline orthosilicate that occurs in nature as willemite, that is made synthetically from zinc oxide and silica or a silicate solution, and that is used in activated form in phosphors

zinc spar *n* : SMITHSONITE

zinc spinel *n* [approximate trans. of F *spinelle zincifère*, lit., zinciferous spinel] : GAHNITE

zinc standard cell *n* : CLARK CELL

zinc stearate *n* : an insoluble salt usu. of commercial stearic acid and usu. containing some zinc oxide that is prepared as a fine bulky powder and is used in ointments and toilet powders, in compounding rubber, and as a drier and flatting agent for paints

zinc sulfate *n* : a crystalline salt $ZnSO_4$ that is usu. obtained by reaction of sulfuric acid with zinc, zinc oxide, or a roasted zinc ore, that normally crystallizes from solutions as the efflorescent heptahydrate occurring also as the mineral goslarite, and that is used chiefly in coagulating baths for viscose rayon, in fertilizers and sprays, in making lithopone and other zinc chemicals, in dyeing and printing, in flotation, and in medicine as an astringent and emetic

zinc sulfide *n* : a fluorescent compound ZnS that occurs in nature as sphalerite and wurtzite, that is obtained synthetically as a white to yellowish powder (as by precipitation with hydrogen sulfide from a solution as a zinc salt), and that is used as a white pigment esp. in the form of lithopone and as a luminous pigment in crystallized activated form — see LUMINOUS PAINT, PHOSPHOR

zinc te·troxy·chromate \-te·¦träksə̇+\ *n* [*tetroxychromate* fr. *tetra-* + *oxy-* + *chromate*] : the basic zinc chromate $4Zn(OH)_2.ZnCrO_4$ — not used systematically

zin·cum \ˈziŋkəm\ *n* -S [NL, fr. G *zink*] : ZINC

zinc vitriol *n* [trans. of NL *vitriolum zinci*] : zinc sulfate heptahydrate

zinc white *n* : zinc oxide that is used as a white pigment (as in house paints, antifouling paints, water colors, enamels, and glazes), that is the whitest of all pigments, and that is permanent and not poisonous but lacks the opacity and covering power of white lead or titanium dioxide

zinc yellow *n* **1** : a greenish yellow pigment that is usu. made by reaction of zinc oxide, potassium dichromate, and sulfuric acid and then has the approximate composition $4ZnO.K_2O.4CrO_3.3H_2O$ of a complex salt and that is used chiefly in corrosion-inhibiting priming coats and in printing inks — called also *zinc chrome* **2** : LIGHT CHROME YELLOW

zin·diq \zinˈdēk\ *n* -S [Ar *zindīq*] : a heretic characterized by an extreme religious infidelity to Islam

zin·eb \ˈzi,neb\ *n* -S [*zinc ethylene-bis-dithiocarbamate*] : an agricultural fungicide $(-CH_2NHCSS)_2Zn$ obtained as a white powder or crystals : zinc ethylene-bis-dithiocarbamate

zin·fan·del \ˈzinfən,del\ *n* -S *often cap* [perh. fr. a European place name] : a red table wine of claret type made from a small black vinifera grape that is grown chiefly in California

¹zing \ˈziŋ\ *n* -S [imit.] **1** : a shrill humming noise ⟨the ~ of machine-gun bullets —F.J.Bell⟩ **2** : LIVELINESS, ENTHUSIASM, VIM ⟨lost its youthful frontier ~ —Joseph Stocker⟩; *also* : a quality that arouses enthusiasm, interest, or vitality ⟨a subtropical ~ to the air —M.F.K.Fisher⟩

²zing \"\ *vi* -ED/-ING/-S : to give forth or to travel with a humming sound ⟨the sound of tires ~*ing* away into the night —Dorothea & S.E.Jones⟩ ⟨played his own twelve-string guitar, and its . . . strings ~*ed* at breakneck time —Frederic Ramsey⟩

zin·ga·na \ˈziŋgənə\ *n* -S [It, fem. of *zingano, zingaro* gypsy; fr. its brown color] : ZEBRAWOOD 1f

zing·el \ˈtsiŋəl\ *n* -S [G, fr. MHG, girth, fr. L *cingulum, cingula* girdle — more at CINGLE] : a small brownish green edible freshwater European perch (*Zingel zingel*) having a round elongated body and a prominent snout

zin·ger·one \ˈzinjə,rōn\ *n* -S [ISV *zinger-* (irreg. fr. NL *Zingiber*) + *-one*] : a pungent crystalline phenolic ketone $C_{11}H_{14}O_3$ present in traces in ginger oil but made synthetically from vanillin and acetone; 4-(3-oxo-butyl)-guaiacol — see SHOGAOL

zin·gi·ber \ˈzinjəbə(r)\ *n* [NL, fr. L, ginger — more at GINGER] **1** *cap* : a genus of tropical Asiatic and Polynesian plants (family Zingiberaceae) having tuberous rootstocks, leafy stems, and a coned cluster of imbricated bracts of which each bract encloses from one to three flowers — see GINGER **2** -S : any plant of the genus *Zingiber*

zin·gi·ber·a·ce·ae \,zinjəbəˈrāsē,ē\ *n pl, cap* [NL, fr. *Zingiber*, type genus + *-aceae*] : a family of tropical monocotyledonous plants (order Musales) consisting of leafy perennial herbs with aromatic rootstocks and very irregular flowers having a single perfect stamen — **zin·gi·ber·a·ceous** \¦==¦rāshəs\ *adj*

zin·gi·ber·a·les \,===ˈrā(,)lēz\ [NL, fr. *Zingiber* + *-ales*] *syn of* MUSALES

zin·gi·ber·ene \ˈ===,rēn\ *n* -S [ISV *zingiber-* (fr. NL *Zingiber*) + *-ene*] : a liquid sesquiterpene hydrocarbon $C_{15}H_{24}$ constituting the chief component of ginger oil

zin·gi·ber·ol \-,rōl, -,rōl\ *n* -S [ISV *zingiber-* (fr. NL *Zingiber*) + *-ol*] : a fragrant liquid sesquiterpenoid alcohol $C_{15}H_{25}OH$ obtained from ginger oil

zinj·an·thro·pus \zinˈjan(t)thrəpəs\ *n* [NL, fr. Ar *Zinj* eastern Africa + NL *-anthropus*] **1** *cap* : a genus of fossil hominids based on a skull found in eastern Africa, characterized by very low brow and large molars, and tentatively assigned to the Lower Pleistocene **2** *pl* **zinjanthro·pi** \-rə,pī\ *or* **zinjanthropuses** : an individual or fossil of the genus *Zinjanthropus*

zin·ke \ˈziŋkə\ *also* **zink** \-k\ *n* -S [G *zinke* point, prong, cornet — more at ZINC] : CORNET 1a

zin·ken·ite \ˈziŋkə,nīt\ *n* -S [G *zinkenit*, fr. J. K. L. *Zinken* †1862 Ger. mineralogist + G *-it* -ite] : a steel-gray mineral $Pb_6Sb_{14}S_{27}$ of metallic luster consisting of a lead antimony sulfide and occurring in orthorhombic crystals and in masses (hardness 3–3.5, sp. gr. 5.30–5.35)

zinky *var of* ZINCKY

zin·nia \ˈzinēə, -nyə *also* ˈzēn-\ *n* [NL, fr. Johann G. *Zinn* †1759 Ger. physician and botanist + NL *-ia*] **1** *cap* : a small genus of tropical American herbs (family Compositae) having showy flower heads with long-lasting ray flowers and floral bracts imbricated in several series **2** -S : any flower or plant of the genus *Zinnia*

zinn·wald·ite \ˈtsin,väl,tīt\ *n* -S [G *zinnwaldit*, fr. *Zinnwald*, Bohemia, its locality + G *-it* -ite] : a pale violet, yellow, brown, or dark gray mineral $K_2(Li,Fe,Al)_6(Si,Al)_8O_{20}(OH,F)_4$ that consists of mica containing iron and lithium

zin·zi·ber \ˈzinzəbə(r)\ [NL, alter. of L *zingiber* ginger] *syn of* ZINGIBER

zin·zi·ber·a·ce·ae \,zinzəbəˈrāsē,ē\ [NL, fr. *Zinziber* + *-aceae*] *syn of* ZINGIBERACEAE

zi·on \ˈzīən\ *n* -S *usu cap* [fr. *Zion*, height in the northeastern part of Jerusalem, Palestine, that was once the site of Solomon's Temple and the seat of government of the kingdom of Judah and that was later identified with Jerusalem and Palestine as the birthplace and spiritual center of Judeo-Christianity and the earthly abode of God, fr. ME *Sion*, fr. OE, fr. LL, fr. Heb *Ṣiyyōn*] **1 a** : the Jewish people : ISRAEL **b** : the Jewish homeland that is symbolic of Judaism or of Jewish national aspiration **2** *also* **si·on** \ˈsīən\ : CITY OF GOD **3** : UTOPIA ⟨sought to set up perpetual *Zions* in the backcountry —W.H.Hale⟩

zioncheck \ˈ==,=\ *n, usu cap* [prob. fr. *Zion* (sense 3) + *check*] : a card game of the contract rummy group

zi·on·ism \ˈzīə,nizəm\ *n* -S *usu cap* [*Zion* (Palestine) + E *-ism*] : a theory, plan, or movement for setting up a Jewish national or religious community in Palestine

¹zi·on·ist \-,nəst\ *also* **zi·on·is·tic** \,zīəˈnistik, -tēk\ *adj, usu cap* [*Zion* + E *-ist* or *-istic*] **1** : of or relating to Zionism **2** : adhering to or advocating Zionism

²zionist \"\ *n* -S *usu cap* : an adherent or supporter of Zionism

¹zi·on·ite \ˈzīə,nīt\ *n* -S *usu cap* [*Zion* (city of God) + E *-ite*] **1** : a citizen of Zion : one of the chosen people of God **2** : RONSDORFER

²zionite \"\ *n* -S *usu cap* [*Zion* (Palestine) + E *-ite*] : a person who favors Zionism : ZIONIST

³zionite \"\ *n* -S *usu cap* [*Zion* City (now Zion, Illinois), religious community of the Christian Catholic Church + E *-ite*] : a follower of John Alexander Dowie (1848–1907) founder of Zion City, Illinois and of the Christian Catholic Church

zi·on·ward \ˈzīənwə(r)d\ *adv, usu cap* : toward Zion : HEAVENWARD

¹zip \ˈzip\ *vb* **zipped; zipped; zipping; zips** [imit. of the sound of an object flying past the hearer] *vi* **1** : to move or act with speed and usu. with force, vigor, or enthusiasm ⟨particles which ~ through outer space with the speed of light —*Newsweek*⟩ ⟨bright-faced waitresses were *zipping* by in trim white-collared uniforms —P.E.Deutschman⟩ **2** : to travel with a sharp hissing or humming sound ⟨rifle fire *zipped* over them —Nevil Shute⟩ ~ *vt* **1** : to impart speed or force to ⟨tunnel which ~s traffic under the . . . mountain —Richard Thruelsen⟩ **2** : to add zest, interest, or life to — often used with *up* ⟨~ up an old folk tune with a little dash of swing —T.D.Clark⟩

²zip \"\ *n* -S **1** : a sudden sharp hissing or sibilant sound (as made by a flying bullet) **2** : ENERGY, VIM, SNAP, FORCE, DASH ⟨~ in his stride and a gleam in his eye —*Phoenix Flame*⟩

³zip \"\ *n* -S *often attrib* [by shortening] **1** *also* **zipp** \"\ *chiefly Brit* : ZIPPER **2** : the act or process of opening or closing a zipper

⁴zip \"\ *vb* **zipped; zipped; zipping; zips** [back-formation fr. ¹*zipper*] *vt* **1 a** : to close or open with a zipper : to fasten or unfasten (an article equipped with a zipper) ⟨my rubber suit *zipped* up to my chin —F.S.Herman⟩ ⟨*zipping* the brief case closed —J.A.Phillips⟩ ⟨*zipped* up my jacket —J.J.Custer⟩ **b** : to cause (a zipper) to open or shut ⟨the top of the zipper still to be *zipped* —*New Yorker*⟩ **2** : to enclose or wrap by fastening a zipper ⟨a dozen children in all, *zipped* and buttoned into their snowsuits —E.J.Kahn⟩ ⟨possessions are securely *zipped* inside —*Harper's Bazaar*⟩ **3** : BUTTON 3 ⟨kept his mouth *zipped* tight for weeks —Carl Sifakis⟩ ~ *vi* **1** : to close or open a zipper ⟨fingers ~ and hook and fasten —Agnes de Mille⟩ **2** : to become or be designed to become open, closed, or attached by means of a zipper ⟨the lining ~s in easily⟩

⁵zip \"\ *n* -S [Maya] : any of a number of small gods known to the ancient Mayas as the supernatural protectors of the deer

zip-fastener \ˈ=,=(=)=\ *n, chiefly Brit* : ZIPPER

zip fuel *n* : a jet or rocket fuel that has a higher heat content than a hydrocarbon fuel

zip gun *n* : a homemade gun that is constructed from a toy pistol or length of pipe, has a firing pin usu. powered by a rubber band, and fires a .22 caliber bullet ⟨teen-age gangs with *zip guns*⟩

¹ziph·i·id \ˈzifēəd\ *adj* [NL *Ziphiidae*] : ZIPHIOID

²ziphiid \"\ *n* -S [NL *Ziphiidae*] : ZIPHIOID

zi·phi·idae \zə̇ˈfīə,dē\ *n pl, cap* [NL, fr. *Ziphius*, type genus + *-idae*] : a family of toothed whales that are 12 to 30 feet long, have the front of the head drawn out so as to suggest a beak and the teeth wanting or reduced to one or two on each side of the lower jaw, and are related to the sperm whales and sometimes esp. formerly included with them in the family Physeteridae

¹ziph·i·oid \ˈzifē,ȯid\ *adj* [NL *Ziphius* + E *-oid*] : of or relating to the Ziphiidae

²ziphioid \"\ *n* -S : a whale of the family Ziphiidae

ziphi·sternum \¦zifə̇+\ *n* [NL, by alter.] : XIPHISTERNUM

ziph·i·us \ˈzifēəs\ *n, cap* [NL, modif. of Gk *xiphios* swordfish, fr. *xiphos* sword] : a genus (the type of the family Ziphiidae) of nearly cosmopolitan beaked whales

zipped *adj* [fr. past part. of ⁴*zip*] : ZIPPERED

zip·pe·ite \ˈtsipə,īt\ *n* -S [G *zippeit*, fr. Franz X. M. *Zippe* †1863 Austrian mineralogist + G *-it* -ite] : a mineral approximately $(UO_2)_2(SO_4)(OH)_2.4H_2O$ consisting of a hydrous basic sulfate of uranium

¹zip·per \ˈzipə(r)\ *n* -S *often attrib* [fr. *Zipper*, a trademark] : a fastener consisting of two rows of metal or plastic teeth on strips of tape for binding to the edges of an opening (as of a garment or bag) and having a sliding piece that closes the opening by drawing the teeth into interlocking position

²zipper \"\ *vt* -ED/-ING/-S : ⁴ZIP

zippered *adj* : equipped with a zipper

zip·py \ˈzipē, -pi\ *adj* -ER/-EST [²*zip* + *-y*] : full of zip : BRISK, SNAPPY

zi·ram \ˈzī,ram\ *n* -S [*zinc* + *-ram* (as in *thiram*)] : a zinc salt $[(CH_3)_2NCSS]_2Zn$ obtained as a white powder or crystals and used as a rubber accelerator and agricultural fungicide; zinc dimethyl-dithiocarbamate — used esp. of the fungicide

zir·con \ˈzər,kän, ˈzə-, ˈzəi-, *sometimes* -,kən\ *n* -S [G *zircon* (now usu. *zirkon*), modif. of F *jargon* jargoon, zircon, fr. It *giargone*] : a tetragonal mineral $ZrSiO_4$ consisting of a zirconium silicate and occurring usu. in square prisms of adamantine luster and brown or grayish color (hardness 7.5, sp. gr. usu. about 4.7) — see HYACINTH, STARLITE

zircon- *comb form* [ISV, fr. NL *zirconia*] : zirconium ⟨*zirconsyenite*⟩

zir·con·ate \ˈzərkə,nāt\ *n* -S [ISV *zircon-* + *-ate*] : any of various compounds (as sodium zirconate Na_2ZrO_3) obtained usu. by heating zirconium oxide and a metal oxide or carbonate

zir·co·nia \(,)zərˈkōnēə, zə'-, zə̄'-, zəi'-\ *n* -S [NL, fr. ISV *zircon* + NL *-ia*, fem. n. suffix] : ZIRCONIUM OXIDE ⟨~ refractories⟩

zir·con·ic \-ˈkänik\ *adj* [ISV *zircon-* + *-ic*] : of, relating to, or containing zirconium

zir·con·if·er·ous \¦zərkəˈnif(ə)rəs\ *adj* [*zircon* + *-iferous*] **1** : containing or yielding zircon **2** [*zircon-* + *-iferous*] : containing or yielding zirconium

zir·co·ni·um \(,)zərˈkōnēəm, zə'-, zə̄'-, zəi'-\ *n* -S [NL, fr. ISV *zircon* + NL *-ium*] : a steel-gray strong ductile high-melting chiefly tetravalent metallic element that occurs widely in combined form esp. in zircon and baddeleyite, that is now obtained usu. from sands containing zircon by heating with carbon and chlorine and passing the volatile zirconium tetrachloride formed into hot molten magnesium or sodium to yield a spongy form of the free metal containing up to three percent of hafnium, that resembles titanium and hafnium chemically and in massive form has good corrosion resistance at ordinary or moderately elevated temperatures, and that is used in spinnerets for viscose rayon, in getters for vacuum tubes, in steel making, and when freed from hafnium in nuclear reactors as a structural material and as a cladding material for uranium because of its ability to allow the passage of low-speed neutrons — symbol *Zr*; see ELEMENT table

zirconium hydride *n* : a gray to black brittle powder ZrH_2 used as a getter in vacuum tubes, as a bonding agent for abrasives and ceramics, in powder metallurgy, and in delay-fuse mixtures in flare shells

zirconium oxide *or* **zirconium dioxide** *n* : a refractory crystalline compound ZrO_2 that occurs in nature as baddeleyite, that is usu. obtained as a heavy hard white insoluble powder by heating zircon with carbon in an arc furnace and burning the product in air, and that is used chiefly in refractories (as crucibles and cements), in thermal and electric insulation, in abrasives, in enamels and glazes as an opacifying pigment, and esp. formerly in incandescent lamps because of its brilliant luminosity when heated — called also *zirconia*

zirconium silicate *n* : a fluorescent crystalline insoluble salt $ZrSiO_4$ that occurs in nature as zircon and can be obtained synthetically by mixing solutions of sodium silicate and a soluble zirconium salt (as zirconium oxychloride), that is decomposed into zirconium oxide at high temperatures, and that is used in refractories, in electric insulation, in abrasives, and in enamels and porcelains

zir·con·oid \ˈzərkə,nȯid\ *n* -S [*zircon* + *-oid*] : a ditetragonal dipyramid

zir·co·nyl \-kənᵊl\ *n* -S [ISV *zircon-* + *-yl*] : the bivalent radical ZrO consisting of zirconium and oxygen ⟨~ chloride is the oxychloride $ZrOCl_2$⟩

zi·ri·co·te \,zirəˈkōtā\ *n* -S [AmerSp] : a tree (*Cordia dodecandra*) of Mexico and Central America having brown wood streaked with dark almost black lines

zirk·ler·ite \ˈzərklə,rīt\ *n* -S [G *zirklerit*, fr. *Zirkler*, 20th cent. Ger. director of mines + G *-it* -ite] : a mineral $(Fe,Mg,Ca)_9Al_4Cl_{18}(OH)_{12}.14H_2O$ consisting of a basic hydrous chloride of iron, magnesium, calcium, and aluminum

zir·phaea \zə(r)ˈfēə\ *n, cap* [NL] : a genus of rock-boring marine bivalve mollusks related to *Pholas*

ziryen *cap, var of* ZYRIAN

¹zith·er \ˈziṯhə(r), ˈzithə(r)\ *also* **zit·tern** \ˈzid·ə(r)n\ *n* -S [*zither* fr. G, fr. OHG *zitera, cithara* cittern, fr. L *cithara*, fr. Gk *kithara*; *zittern* alter. (influenced by *cittern*) of *zither*] : a musical instrument consisting of a shallow soundboard set horizontally before the performer and overlaid with 30 to 40 strings some of which pass over a fretted fingerboard, are stopped with the left hand, and are played by a plectrum on the right thumb to produce the melody and the remainder of which are tuned in fourths and plucked by the fingers of the right hand — compare CITTERN

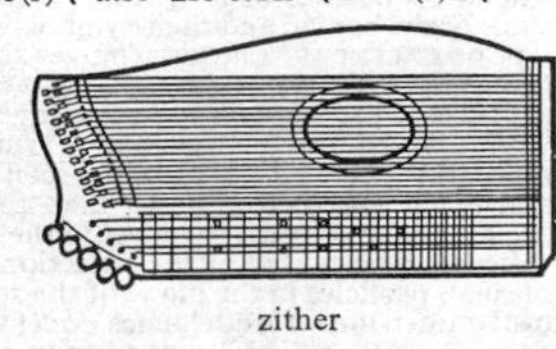

zither

²zither \"\ *vi* -ED/-ING/-S : to play on the zither

zith·er·ist \-ərə̇st\ *n* -S : a player on the zither

ziw *usu cap, var of* ZIF

zi·za·nia \zəˈzānēə\ *n, cap* [NL, fr. LL *zizanium* darnel, cockle, fr. Gk *zizanion*] : a genus of tall monoecious grasses having long flat leaves and ample panicles of one-flowered spikelets — see WILD RICE

ziz·ia \ˈzizēə\ *n, cap* [NL, fr. I. B. *Ziz*, 19th cent. Ger. botanist + NL *-ia*] : a small genus of No. American herbs (family Umbelliferae) with ternately compound leaves, yellow flowers in compound umbels, and flat wingless fruit — see GOLDEN ALEXANDER, GOLDEN MEADOW PARSNIP

ziz·i·phus \ˈzizəfəs\ *n* [NL, fr. L *zizyphus* jujube tree, fr. *zizyphum* jujube — more at JUJUBE] **1** *cap* : a large genus of spiny chiefly tropical American and Asiatic shrubs (family Rhamnaceae) having triple-veined leaves and small cymose flowers with a 2-celled ovary — see CHRIST'S-THORN, JUJUBE, LOTUS TREE **2** -ES : any plant of the genus *Ziziphus*

zi·zith *or* **zi·zit** *or* **tsi·tsith** *or* **tzi·tzith** *also* **si·sith** *or* **tzi·tzis** \ˈtsitsəs, tsēˈtsēt\ *n pl* [Heb *ṣīṣīth*] : the fringes or tassels of entwined cords or threads worn by Jewish males at the 4 corners of the outer garment or on the tallith and the arba kanfoth as reminders of God's commandments in accordance with the scriptural passages Deut 22:12 and Num 15:37–41

zl *abbr* zloty

zlo·ty \ˈzlȯtē, -ti\ *n, pl* **zlotys** *also* **zloty** [Pol *złoty*, lit., golden, fr. *złoto* gold; akin to Russ *zoloto* gold, OHG *gold* — more at GOLD] **1** : the basic monetary unit of Poland — see MONEY table **2** : a coin representing one zloty

Zn *symbol* **1** azimuth **2** zinc

zo- *or* **zoo-** *comb form* [Gk *zō-*, *zōio-*, fr. *zōion*; akin to Gk *zōē* life — more at QUICK] **1** : animal : animal kingdom or kind ⟨*zoology*⟩ ⟨*zoophile*⟩ ⟨*zooid*⟩ ⟨*zoanthropy*⟩ **2** [Gk *zō-*, *zōo-*, alive, fr. *zōos*; akin to Gk *zōē* life] : motile ⟨*zoogonidium*⟩

zoa *pl of* ZOON

-zoa \ˈzōə\ *n pl comb form* [NL, fr. Gk *zōia*, pl. of *zōion*] : animals — in the names of taxa ⟨*Bryozoa*⟩ ⟨*Echinozoa*⟩

zoaea *var of* ZOEA

zo·an·thar·ia \,zōənˈtha(a)rēə\ *n pl, cap* [NL, fr. *Zoanthus* + *-aria*] : a subclass of Anthozoa that comprises forms with a hexamerous arrangement of the usu. simple tentacles or septa or both and that includes most of the recent corals and sea anemones

¹zo·an·thar·i·an \¦==¦tha(a)rēən\ *adj* [NL *Zoantharia* + E *-an*] : of or relating to the Zoantharia

²zoantharian \"\ *n* -S : a coelenterate of the subclass Zoantharia

zo·an·the·ae \zōˈan(t)thē,ē\ [NL] *syn of* ZOANTHIDEA

zo·an·thid \zōˈan(t)thə̇d\ *also* **zo·an·thoid** \-n,thȯid\ *n* -S [*zoanthid* fr. NL *Zoanthidea*; *zoanthoid* fr. NL *Zoanthus* + E *-oid*] : a coelenterate of the order Zoanthidea

zo·an·thid·ea \,zōənˈthidēə\ *n pl, cap* [NL, fr. *Zoanthus* + *-idea*] : a small order of Zoantharia comprising solitary or colonial and mostly epizoic coelenterates resembling small sea anemones but distinguished by absence of a pedal disk and by an arrangement of mesenteries suggesting that of the fossil tetracorals

zo·an·thid·e·an \¦==¦thidēən\ *also* **zo·an·thid** \zōˈan(t)thə̇d\ *adj* [*zoanthidean* fr. NL *Zoanthidea* + E *-an*; *zoanthid* fr. NL *Zoanthidea*] : of or relating to the Zoanthidea

zo·an·tho·deme \zōˈan(t)thə,dēm\ *n* [ISV *zoantho-* (fr. NL *Zoanthus*) + *deme*] : the aggregate of zooids in a compound anthozoan

zo·an·thro·py \zōˈan(t)thrəpē\ *n* -ES [*zo-* + *-anthropy* (as in *lycanthropy*)] : a monomania in which a person believes himself changed into an animal and acts like one

zo·an·thus \zōˈan(t)thəs\ *n, cap* [NL, fr. *zo-* + Gk *anthos* flower — more at ANTHOLOGY] : a large genus (the type of the family Zoanthidae) of zoanthidean colonial polyps that are widely distributed in tropical seas, are united at their bases by stolons, resemble groups of small anemones, and have short, brightly colored tentacles

zo·ar·ces \zōˈärˌsēz\ *n, cap* [NL, fr. Gk *zōarkēs* life-supporting, fr. *zōē* life + *-arkēs* supporting (fr. *arkein* to defend, support) — more at QUICK, ARK] : the type genus of the family Zoarcidae

zo·ar·ci·dae \-rsə,dē\ *n pl, cap* [NL, fr. *Zoarces*, type genus + *-idae*] : a family of chiefly arctic and antarctic blennies comprising the eelpouts

zo·ar·i·al \zōˈa(a)rēəl\ *adj* [NL *zoarium* + E *-al*] : of or relating to a zoarium

zo·ar·ite \ˈzōə,rīt, ˈzōr,īt, ˈzȯ,rīt\ *n* -S *usu cap* [*Zoar*, Ohio + E *-ite*] : a member of a 19th century communal sect of German Protestant separatists and founders of the Zoar Community at Zoar, Ohio in 1817 — called also *Bimelerite, Bimmeler*

zo·ar·i·um \zōˈa(a)rēəm\ *also* **zo·o·ar·i·um** \,zōəˈ-\ *n, pl* **zoar·ia** \-ēə\ [NL, fr. *zo-* + *-arium*] : a colony of colonial bryozoans

zo·ca·lo \ˈzōkə,lō\ *n* -S [MexSp *zócalo*, fr. Sp, socle, fr. It *zoccolo*] : the public square of a Mexican city or town : PLAZA

zoc·co \ˈzä(,)kō\ *or* **zoc·co·lo** \ˈzäkə,lō\ *or* **zac·co** \ˈzä(,)kō\ *n* -S [*zocco* fr. It, sock, socle, fr. L *soccus* sock; *zoccolo* fr. It, sock, wooden shoe, socle, dim. of *zocco*; *zacco* modif. of It *zoccolo* — more at SOCLE] : SOCLE

zo·di·ac \ˈzōdē,ak\ *n* -S [ME, fr. MF *zodiaque*, fr. L *zodiacus*, fr. Gk *zōidiakos*, fr. *zōidiakos*, adj., of carved or painted figures,

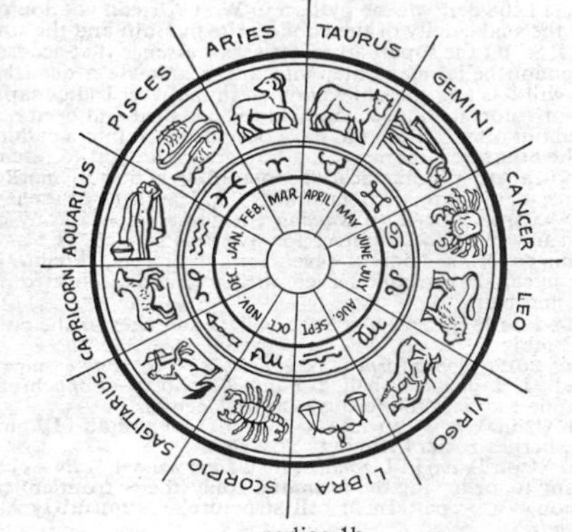

zodiac 1b

of the zodiac, fr. *zōidion* carved or painted figure, sign of the zodiac, dim. of *zōion* living being, animal, figure, image; akin to Gk *zōē* life — more at QUICK] **1 a :** an imaginary belt in the heavens usu. 18 degrees wide that encompasses the apparent paths of all the principal planets except Pluto, that has the ecliptic as its central line, and that is divided into 12 constellations or signs each taken for astrological purposes to extend 30 degrees of longitude **b :** a figure representing the signs of the zodiac and their symbols **2 :** a cyclic course (as of time) **:** CALENDAR, CIRCUIT ⟨moves through a ~ of feasts and fasts —R.W.Emerson⟩

zo·di·a·cal \zō'dīəkəl\ *adj* [*zodiac* + *-al*] **:** of, relating to, or within the zodiac ⟨~ figure⟩ ⟨~ symbols⟩ ⟨~ constellations⟩

zodiacal light *n* **:** a diffuse glow seen in the west after twilight and in the east before dawn that appears wedge-shaped and lies along the ecliptic, is widest in the parts near the sun, and is believed to be caused by the reflection of sunlight from myriads of small particles in the plane of the solar system

zo·di·oph·i·lous \¦zōdē¦äfələs\ *adj* [Gk *zōidion* (dim. of *zōion* animal) + E *-philous*] **:** ZOOPHILIC a

zo·ea *also* **zo·aea** \zō'ēə\ *n, pl* **zo·e·ae** \-ē,ē\ *or* **zoeas** [NL, fr. Gk *zōē* life] **:** an early larval form of decapod crustaceans and esp. of crabs and anomurans that commonly precedes the megalops and that is distinguished by the relatively large cephalothorax commonly bearing three or four long spines, the conspicuous eyes, the relatively large and fringed antennae and mouthparts used for swimming, the rudimentary thoracic appendages, and the long slender abdomen having small or no swimmerets

zo·e·a·form \-'ēə,fȯrm\ *adj* **:** having the form or appearance of a zoea

zo·e·al \-'ēəl\ *adj* **:** of, relating to, or being a zoea ⟨~ forms⟩ ⟨~ stages⟩

zoecial *var of* ZOOECIAL

zoecium *var of* ZOOECIUM

zoell·ner illusion \'tsəlnə(r)-\ *n, usu cap Z* **:** ZÖLLNER ILLUSION

zoellner's lines *n pl, usu cap Z* **:** ZÖLLNER'S LINES

zo·et·ic \zō'edik\ *adj* [Gk *zōē* life + E *-etic*] **:** of or relating to life **:** LIVING, VITAL

zo·e·trope \'zōē,trōp\ *also* **zo·o·trope** \'zōə-\ *n* -s [*zoetrope* fr. *Zoetrope*, a trademark; *zootrope* alter. (influenced by *zo-*) of *zoetrope*] **:** an optical toy in which figures on the inside of a revolving cylinder are viewed through slits in its circumference and appear like a single animated figure

zo·go \'zō(,)gō\ *n* -s [Papuan] **:** something that is sacred or holy to the people of the Torres strait; *esp* **:** a charm or sacred object held to have wonder-working power

zo·ic \'zōik\ *adj* [Gk *zōikos*] **:** of or relating to animals or animal life and action

¹-zo·ic \¦zōik, -ōek\ *adj comb form* [Gk *zōikos* of or pertaining to animals, fr. *zōi-* zo- + *-ikos* -ic] **:** animal **:** having a (specified) animal mode of existence **:** animallike ⟨holo*zoic*⟩ ⟨phanero*zoic*⟩ ⟨copro*zoic*⟩ ⟨cyto*zoic*⟩

²-zoic \"\ *adj comb form* [Gk *zōē* life + E *-ic* — more at QUICK] **:** of or relating to a (specified) geological era ⟨Archeo*zoic*⟩ ⟨Meso*zoic*⟩

zo·id \'zōəd\ *n* -s [*zo-* + *-id*] **:** ZOOID

zo·id·i·oph·i·lous \zō¦idē¦äfələs\ *adj* [Gk *zōidion* (dim. of *zōion* animal) + E *-philous* — more at ZODIAC] **:** ZOOPHILIC a

zo·i·dog·a·mous \¦zōə¦dägəməs\ *adj* [*zoid* + *-o-* + *-gamous*] **:** fertilizing by a spermatozoid or motile cell

zo·i·lus \'zōələs\ *n, pl* **zoiluses** \-səz\ *also* **zoi·li** \-,lī\ *usu cap* [after *Zoilus* 4th cent. B.C. Greek rhetorician and critic who was notable for the severity of his criticisms of Homer's poems] **:** a bitter and usu. enviously carping critic **:** one given to unjust quibbling and faultfinding **:** BELITTLER, CAVILER — compare ARISTARCH, MOMUS

zoi·sia \'zȯisēə, 'zȯizēə, 'zȯishə\ *n, cap* [NL, fr. Karl von *Zois* †1800 Ger. botanist + NL *-ia*] **:** a small genus of Asiatic grasses that have creeping rhizomes, short pointed leaves, and one-flowered spikelets in racemes and that are valued as lawn grasses esp. in warm regions — see ZOYSIA

zois·ite \'zȯi,sīt\ *n* -s [G *zoisit*, fr. Baron Sigismund *Zois* von Edelstein †1819 Slovenian nobleman + G *-it* -ite] **:** an orthorhombic mineral $Ca_2Al_3Si_3O_{12}OH$ consisting of a basic calcium aluminum silicate that is related to epidote and that occurs massive or in prismatic grayish, brown, green, or rose crystals

zois·it·iza·tion \,zȯisəd·ə'zāshən\ *n* -s [*zoisite* + *-ization*] **:** the process of converting feldspar into zoisite — compare SAUSSURITIZATION

¹zo·ism \'zō,izəm\ *n* -s [Gk *zōē* life + E *-ism*] **:** a doctrine that the phenomena of life are due to a peculiar vital principle **:** the theory of élan vital

²zoism \"\ *n* -s [ISV *zo-* + *-ism*] **:** reverence for animal life **:** belief in animal powers and influences

zo·ist \'zōəst\ *n* -s [Gk *zōē* life + E *-ist*] **:** an advocate or adherent of the doctrine of zoism — **zo·is·tic** \zō'istik\ *adj*

zo·kor \'zō,kȯr\ *n* -s [native name in the Altai mountains] **:** a burrowing rodent (*Myotalpa aspalax*) native to the Altai mountains that resembles a mole rat

zo·la·esque \¦zōlə¦esk\ *adj, usu cap* [Émile *Zola* †1902 Fr. novelist + E *-esque*] **:** of, relating to, or suggestive of Zola or his writings

zol·ler·nia \zə'lərnēə\ *n, cap* [NL, irreg. fr. Hugo *Zöller* †1933 Ger. explorer + NL *-ia*] **:** a small genus of Brazilian timber trees (family Leguminosae) with simply pinnate leaves, nearly regular flowers, and a woody legume

zöll·ner illusion \'tsəlnə(r)-\ *n, usu cap Z* [after Johann K. F. *Zöllner* †1882 Ger. physicist] **:** the illusion produced by Zöllner's lines

zöllner's lines *n pl, usu cap Z* [after Johann K. F. *Zöllner* †1882] **:** parallel lines made to appear to converge or diverge by oblique intersections

Zöllner's lines

zoll·ver·ein \'tsōlfə,rīn\ *n* -s *usu cap* [G, fr. *zoll* toll, duty (fr. OHG *zol*) + *verein* union, society — more at TOLL, VEREIN] **:** CUSTOMS UNION

zo·lot·nik \¦zälət¦nēk, -nik\ *n* -s [Russ, fr. *zoloto* gold + *-nik*, n. suffix denoting a thing connected with something specified — more at ZLOTY] **:** a Russian unit of weight equal to 4.266 grams or a small fraction of an ounce

zom·bi *or* **zom·bie** \'zämbē\ *n* -s [of Niger-Congo origin; akin to Kongo & Kimbundu & Tshiluba *nzambi* god, Kongo *zumbi* good-luck fetish, image] **1 a** (1) **:** the deity of the python in West African voodoo cults (2) **:** the snake deity of the voodoo rite in Haiti and the southern U.S. **b :** the supernatural power or essence that according to voodoo belief may enter into and reanimate a dead body **c :** a will-less and speechless human in the West Indies capable only of automatic movement held to have died and been reanimated but often believed to have been drugged into a catalepsy for the hours of interment **2 a :** a person thought to resemble the so-called walking dead **:** DOPE **b :** a person markedly strange or abnormal in mentality, appearance, or behavior **:** CHARACTER, QUEER **c** *Canada* **:** a home-defense army conscript unwilling to volunteer for overseas service **3 :** a very tall mixed drink made of several kinds of rum, liqueur, and fruit juice, shaken and served with ice, and decorated with mint and fruit

zom·bi·ism \-ē,izəm\ *n* -s **:** the beliefs and rites of the cult of the zombi

zon- *or* **zono-** *comb form* [Gk *zōn-*, *zōno-*, fr. *zōnē* — more at ZONE] **1 :** girdle **:** belt **:** band ⟨*Zon*ites⟩ ⟨*Zono*chlorite⟩ **2 :** zone **:** zonal ⟨*zono*ferous⟩ ⟨*zono*plankton⟩

zo·na \'zōnə\ *n, pl* **zo·nae** \-,nē, -,nī\ *or* **zonas** [L, girdle, zone, herpes zoster] **:** HERPES ZOSTER

zon·al \'zōnᵊl\ *adj* [LL *zonalis*, fr. L *zona* zone + *-alis* -al] **:** of, relating to, or having the form of a zone ⟨the ~ frontier⟩ ⟨a ~ division⟩ ⟨a ~ pattern of cell structure⟩ — **zon·al·ly** \-ᵊlē, -ᵊli\ *adv*

zonal equation *n* **:** the mathematical relation that belongs to all the planes of a zone of a crystal and expresses their common position with reference to the axes

zonal geranium *n* **:** FISH GERANIUM

zonal rotation *n* **:** the rotation at unequal rates of the visible surfaces of various astronomical bodies (as the sun, Jupiter, or Saturn)

zonal soil *n* **1 :** a major soil group often classified as a category of the highest rank and generally covering a wide geographic region or zone and embracing soils that are well-developed from the parent material by the normal soil-forming action of climate and living organisms — compare AZONAL SOIL, INTRAZONAL SOIL **2 :** a soil (as many grassland and desert soils) belonging to a major soil group or category

zonal structure *n* **:** a structure characterized by the arrangements (as of color or inclusions) of a crystal in parallel or concentric layers that usu. follow the outline of the crystal and mark the changes that have taken place during its growth

zona pel·lu·ci·da \-pə'lüsədə, -pel'yü-\ *n, pl* **zonae pelluci·dae** \-ə,dē, -,dī\ [NL, transparent zone] **:** the transparent more or less elastic outer layer or envelope of an ovum often traversed by numerous radiating striae

zona ra·di·a·ta \-,rādē'äd·ə, -'ād·ə\ *n, pl* **zonae radia·tae** \-'äd·,ē, -'ād·,ē, -d·,ī\ [NL, radiate zone] **:** ZONA PELLUCIDA; *esp* **:** one having unusually distinct striations

zo·nar·ia \zō'na(a)rēə\ *n pl, cap* [NL, fr. neut. pl. of L *zonarius* of a belt, zonal] *in former classifications* **:** a division of Mammalia comprising forms (as the carnivores and various ungulates) having a zonary placenta

zo·na·ry \'zōnərē, -ri\ *adj* [L *zonarius*, fr. *zona* + *-arius* -ary] **1 :** ZONAL **2** *of a placenta* **:** having villi arranged in a band (as in carnivores and elephants)

zon·ate \'zō,nāt, *usu* -ād·+V\ *also* **zon·at·ed** \-ād·əd\ *adj* [*zonate* fr. NL *zonatus*, fr. L *zona* + *-atus* -ate; *zonated* fr. NL *zonatus* + E *-ed*] **:** marked with zones **:** RINGED, BELTED

zo·na·tion \zō'nāshən\ *n* -s [¹*zone* + *-ation*] **1 :** formation in zones, bands, or concentric layers **:** zonate structure ⟨~ of a growing plant cell⟩ **2 :** arrangement or distribution of kinds of organisms in biogeographic zones ⟨altitudinal ~ of coniferous trees⟩

zon·da \'z|ondə, 's|, |än-\ *n* -s [AmerSp] **:** a hot enervating north wind that sweeps down from the Andes over the Argentine pampas

¹zone \'zōn\ *n* -s [L *zona* girdle, belt, zone, fr. Gk *zōnē*; akin to Gk *zōma* girdle, *zōnnynai* to gird, Lith *juosti* to gird, Av *yasta* encircled, girt] **1 a :** any of five great divisions of the earth's surface with respect to latitude and temperature — see FRIGID ZONE, TEMPERATE ZONE, TORRID ZONE **b :** any division of a planetary surface bounded by two encircling parallels ⟨~s of the sun's surface⟩ **c :** a belt around the heavens bounded usu. by small circles parallel to the equator of the system of coordinates involved ⟨~s of declination in the equatorial system⟩ **d** *obs* **:** the course or range of a celestial body (as the sun) ⟨the sun . . . in the great ~ of heaven —John Milton⟩ **e :** the portion of the surface of a sphere included between two parallel planes **:** the part of a surface of revolution between two planes perpendicular to the axis **f :** a series of faces of a crystal whose intersection lines with each other are all parallel **2** *archaic* **:** GIRDLE, BELT, BAND ⟨how to loose the ~ of virgins —Robert Herrick †1674⟩ **3 :** something that forms a concentric band ⟨surrounding the hub lies the middle ~ . . . largely residential —J.E.Pate⟩: as **a :** any encircling anatomical area or structure; *specif* **:** one of the three regions in the retina of the eye differing in color sensitivity ⟨all hues can be seen with the inner or central ~, blue and yellow with the middle, and only colorless light with the outer⟩ **b** (1) **:** a typically band-formed part of a biogeographic region that usu. has a distinct slope and a markedly uniform climate and supports a similar fauna and flora throughout its extent **:** LIFE ZONE ⟨a marine littoral ~⟩ ⟨the Austral ~⟩ (2) **:** such a zone characterized by the dominance of some life form ⟨the laminarian ~ below low tide⟩ ⟨a broad ~ of elfin woodland⟩ **c :** a belt, layer, or series of layers of earth materials (as rock) characterized by some particular property, action, or content ⟨the ~ of saturation⟩ ⟨the eohippus ~⟩ **4 :** a region or area set off or characterized as distinct from surrounding or adjoining parts ⟨the danger ~⟩ ⟨a ~ of influence⟩ ⟨erogenous ~⟩ ⟨the movement of individuals . . . into and out of the survey ~ —J.M.Mogey⟩ ⟨a ~ of uncertainty and hesitation in . . . foreign policy —*Atlantic*⟩ **5 :** one of the sections or divisions of an area or territory created for a particular purpose ⟨a ~ of military occupation⟩ ⟨divided the country into 10 sales ~s⟩: as **a :** a section of a city that has been zoned **b :** any one of the eight concentric bands of territory centered on any given postal shipment point that is arbitrarily designated as a distance bracket for U.S. parcel post mail so that shipments to all points within it may be charged at a single rate — called also *parcel post zone* **c :** one of the numbered sections into which a large city or metropolitan area is divided in the U.S. postal system so that placing the number after the name of the post office in the address on postal matter facilitates sorting and delivery of the mail — called also *postal delivery zone* **d :** the aggregate of stations in a direction or on a line of railroad situated between various maximum and minimum limits from a point at which a shipment of traffic originates **e :** any distance (as within a circular area or on a single line) within which the same fare is charged by a common carrier ⟨the 20-cent fare ~⟩ **f :** an area on a field of play ⟨the end ~s of a football field⟩ **g :** a stretch of roadway, section of a thoroughfare, or part of a street system in which certain traffic regulations are in force ⟨school ~⟩ ⟨no-parking ~⟩ ⟨no-passing ~⟩ — compare SAFETY ZONE **h :** a space at the curb reserved for the loading and unloading of materials and people ⟨a commercial loading ~⟩ ⟨bus loading ~⟩ **6 :** a row of positions on a punched card of a computer

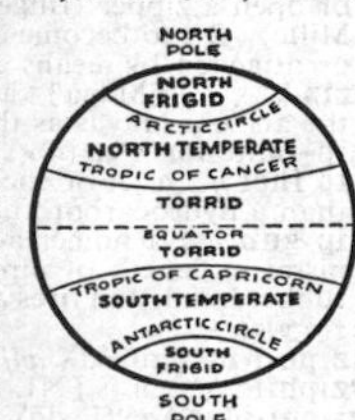

zones 1a

²zone \"\ *vt* -ED/-ING/-S **1 :** to surround with or include within a zone or band **:** ENCIRCLE ⟨waist and . . . bosom agreeably *zoned* —Arnold Bennett⟩ ⟨the . . . horizon is *zoned* with a mellow uniform band of light —E.K.Kane⟩ **2 :** to arrange in or mark off into zones ⟨~s the world into climatic provinces⟩ ⟨*zoned* the house into sleeping, service, and living areas⟩; *specif* **:** to partition (a city, borough, or township) by ordinance into zones or sections reserved for different purposes (as residence, business, or manufacturing or combinations of these) and governed by appropriate building regulations (as of the height and area of all structures) ⟨*zoned* the neighborhood as residential⟩

zone axis *n* **:** a straight line to which all faces of a given zone of a crystal are parallel

zoned \'zōnd\ *adj* [¹*zone* + *-ed*] **:** wearing the zone that is symbolic of virginity **:** VIRGIN, CHASTE ⟨fair ~ damsels —Alexander Pope⟩

zone defense *n* **:** a system of defense in various sports (as basketball and football) in which each defensive player guards an assigned zone or section of the court or field — compare MAN-TO-MAN DEFENSE

zone fire *n* **:** fire (as of artillery) delivered at successive ranges and sometimes with varying deflections to cover surely the area in which the target lies

zone·less \'zōnləs\ *adj* **:** wearing no zone or girdle **:** UNGIRT ⟨reeling goddess with the ~ waist —William Cowper⟩

zone line *n* **:** a line marking the limit or boundary of a zone; *specif* **:** BLUE LINE 2

zone of action : an area of responsibility that is defined by boundaries and assigned to a military unit in any situation involving action (as advance, attack, or retrograde movement) — compare SECTOR

zone of clouds : a belt of clouds prevailing over the ocean near the equator

zone of combined fracture and flow : the part of the earth between the zone of fracture and the zone of flow where the rocks may break or flow according to conditions (as of deformation or strength of the materials)

zone of fire : the area within which a particular military unit is prepared to deliver fire

zone of flow *or* **zone of flowage :** the subsurface part of the earth underlying the zone of fracture and including the larger part of the earth in which the fracturing of rocks is prevented by pressure and all deformation is by a sort of flow

zone of fracture : the part of the earth's crust in which deformation may result in and be accompanied by fracture

zone of interior : the part of the theater of war that is not included within the theater of operations

zone of mobility *or* **zone of weakness :** ASTHENOSPHERE

zone of ro·lan·do \-rō'lan(,)dō, -län-\ *usu cap R* [after Luigi *Rolando* †1831 Ital. anatomist] **:** MOTOR AREA

zone of silence : a region surrounding a source of sound in which because of interference or refraction the sound is inaudible though it can be heard in more distant regions

zone phenomenon *n* **:** the occurrence of prozones in antibody-antigen mixtures

zone plate *n* **:** an optical device that consists of a series of concentric opaque rings of such width that rays from alternate half-period elements are cut off and that has some properties of a converging lens

zone servant *n* **:** a leader of the Jehovah's Witnesses responsible for a particular area within the charge of a regional servant

zone time *n* **:** standard time applied at sea in which the surface of the globe is divided into 24 zones of 15° or one hour each, the 0 zone extends 7½° east and west of the meridian of Greenwich, and the zones are designated by the number of hours that must be applied to the local time to obtain Greenwich time

zo·nif·er·ous \(')zō¦nif(ə)rəs\ *adj* [*zon-* + *-iferous*] **:** having a zone **:** ZONED

zoning *n* -s [fr. gerund of ²*zone*] **:** the act or process of zoning (as in city planning) ⟨~ ordinances⟩ ⟨~ commission⟩

zo·nite \'zō,nīt\ *n* -s [ISV *zon-* + *-ite*] **:** a body segment of a diplopod

zo·ni·tes \zō'nīd·(,)ēz\ *n, cap* [NL, fr. *zon-* + *-ites*] **:** the type genus of the family Zonitidae

¹zo·ni·tid \'zōnəd·əd\ *adj* [NL *Zonitidae*] **:** of or relating to the Zonitidae

²zonitid \"\ *n* -s **:** a snail of the family Zonitidae

zo·nit·i·dae \zō'nid·ə,dē\ *n pl, cap* [NL, fr. *Zonites*, type genus + *-idae*] **:** a family of small terrestrial snails (suborder Stylommatophora) having a thin depressed shell with sharp peristome

zo·ni·toi·des \,zōnə'tȯi(,)dēz\ *n, cap* [NL, fr. *Zonites* + L *-oides* -oid] **:** a genus of usu. small rather flat amber-colored land snails (family Zonitidae) that have a simple lip not turned back

zono- — see ZON-

zo·no·chlo·rite \,zō(,)nō'klōr,īt, -ō,rīt\ *n* -s [*zon-* + *chlor-* + *-ite*] **:** an impure prehnite occurring in green pebbles of banded structure

zo·no·ciliate \¦=(,)=+\ *adj* [*zon-* + *ciliate*] **:** having a band of cilia — used esp. of annelid larvae

zo·no·limnetic \"+\ *adj* [ISV *zon-* + *limnetic*; orig. formed as G *zonolimnetisch*] **:** of or relating to a definite zone in depth — used esp. of freshwater planktonic animals

zo·no·placental \"+\ *adj* [*zon-* + *placental*] **1 :** having a zonary placenta **2 :** of or relating to the Zonaria

zo·no·plac·en·ta·lia \,zō(,)nō,plasᵊn'tālēə\ [NL, fr. *zon-* + *Placentalia*] *syn of* ZONARIA

zo·no·trich·ia \,zōnə'trikēə\ *n, cap* [NL, fr. *zon-* + *trich-* + *-ia*] **:** a genus of rather large New World sparrows (family Fringillidae) occurring chiefly in western No. America and having the upperparts largely brown and the underparts unmarked grayish white — see GAMBEL SPARROW, GOLDEN-CROWNED SPARROW, WHITE-CROWNED SPARROW, WHITE-THROATED SPARROW

zon·ta \'zäntə\ *n* -s *usu cap* [Sioux *zon'-ta* honest, trustworthy] **:** one of an organization of service clubs made up of executive women each of whom is a sole representative of one business or profession in a community

zonu·la \'zōnyələ, 'zän-\ *n, pl* **zonu·lae** \-ə,lē, -,lī\ *or* **zonu·las** [L] **:** ZONULE; *specif* **:** ZONULE OF ZINN

zo·nu·lar \'zōnyələ(r)\ *adj* **:** of or relating to a zonule

zon·ule \'zōn,yül\ *n* -s [L *zonula*, dim. of *zona* girdle, belt, zone — more at ZONE] **1 :** a little zone, belt, or girdle **2 :** the suspensory ligament of the eye

zonule of zinn \-'tsin\ *usu cap 2d Z* [after Johann G. *Zinn* †1759 Ger. physician and botanist] **:** the suspensory ligament of the crystalline lens of the eye

zo·nure \'zōnyə(r)\ *n* -s [NL *Zonurus*] **:** GIRDLE-TAILED LIZARD

zo·nu·ri·dae \zōn'yürə,dē\ [NL, fr. *Zonurus*, type genus (fr. *zon-* + *-urus*) + *-idae*] *syn of* CORDYLIDAE

zoo \'zü\ *n* -s [short for *zoological garden*] **1 :** a zoological garden or collection of living animals usu. for public display **2** *slang* **:** a place (as a prison, shop cafeteria, or railway caboose) in which people are crowded together haphazardly

zoo- — see ZO-

zooarium *var of* ZOARIUM

zoo·benthos \¦zōə+\ *n* [NL, fr. *zo-* + *benthos*] **:** animal life of the benthos

zoo·cecidium \"+\ *n, pl* **zoocecidia** [NL, fr. *zo-* + *cecidium*] **:** a plant gall caused by an animal (as an insect, mite, or nematode worm)

zoo·chlorella \¦zōə+\ *n, pl* **zoochlorellae** [NL, fr. *zo-* + *Chlorella*] **:** any of various minute green algae (genus *Chlorella*) that habitually live symbiotically within the cytoplasm of some protozoans and other invertebrates

zo·o·chore \'zōə,kō(ə)r\ *n* -s [*zo-* + *-chore*] **:** a plant distributed by living animals

zoo·cultural \¦zōə+\ *adj* [*zo-* + *cultural*] **:** ZOOTECHNICAL

zoo·culture \'zōə+,-\ *n* [*zo-* + *culture*] **:** ZOOTECHNY

zoo·e·cial *also* **zo·e·cial** \zō'ēshəl\ *adj* [NL *zooecium*, *zoecium* + E *-al*] **:** of, relating to, or constituting a zooecium

zoo·e·ci·um *also* **zo·e·ci·um** \-shēəm\ *n, pl* **zoo·e·cia** *also* **zoe·cia** \-ēə\ [NL, fr. *zo-* + Gk *oikos* house + NL *-ium* — more at VICINITY] **:** one of the cells or tubes that enclose the feeding zooids of a bryozoan

zoo-ecology \¦zōə+\ *n* **:** a branch of ecology dealing with the relation of animals to their environment and to other animals

zoo·eras·tia \¦zōə¦rastēə\ *n* -s [NL *zooerastia*, fr. *zo-* + *-erastia* (as in *paederastia* pederasty)] **:** BESTIALITY 3

zoo·eras·ty \¦zōə¦e,rastē\ *n* -ES [NL *zooerastia*] **:** ZOOERASTIA

zoo·flagellate \¦zōə+\ *n* [*zo-* + *flagellate*] **:** a member of the Zoomastigina **:** a flagellate protozoan lacking photosynthesis and other plantlike characteristics — compare PLANTLIKE FLAGELLATE

zoo·ful \'zü,fu̇l\ *n* -s **:** enough to fill a zoo

zoo·gamete \¦zōə+\ *n* [ISV *zo-* + *gamete*] **:** a motile gamete esp. of a plant (as an alga)

zo·o·gen·ic \¦zōə¦jenik\ *adj* [ISV *zo-* + *-genic*] **:** caused by or associated with animals or their activities ⟨a ~ virus⟩ ⟨~ fossiliferous rocks⟩

zo·og·e·nous \zō'äjənəs\ *also* **zo·o·ge·ne·ous** \¦zōə¦jēnēəs\ *adj* [*zo-* + *-genous*] **:** ZOOGENIC

zoo·geographer \¦zōə+\ *n* [*zoogeography* + *-er*] **:** a specialist in zoogeography **:** a student of animal distribution

zoo·geographic *also* **zoo·geographical** \"+\ *adj* [*zoogeography* ISV *zoogeography* + *-ic*; *zoogeographical* fr. *zoogeography* + *-ical*] **:** of or relating to zoogeography or to the natural distribution of animals — **zoo·geographically** \"+\ *adv*

zoo·geography \"+\ *n* [ISV *zo-* + *geography*] **:** a branch of biogeography concerned with the geographical distribution of animals and esp. with the determination of the land and marine areas characterized by special groups of animals and the study of the causes and significance of such groups — compare PHYTOGEOGRAPHY

zo·o·glea *also* **zo·o·gloea** \,zōə'glēə\ *n, pl* **zoogleas** \-ēəz\ *or* **zoogle·ae** \-ē,ē\ [NL, fr. *zo-* + MGk *gloia*, *glia* glue — more at CLAY] **:** a gelatinous or mucilaginous mass that is characteristic of the growth of various bacteria when growing in fluid media rich in organic material and is made up of the bodies of the bacteria embedded in a matrix of swollen confluent capsule substance — **zo·o·gle·al** \¦==¦glēəl\ *adj*

zoog·ler \'züglə(r)\ *n* -s [origin unknown] **:** FROGGER 1

zoo·gonidium \¦zōə+\ *n, pl* **zoogonidia** [NL, fr. *zo-* + *gonidium*] **:** an active or motile gonidium **:** SWARM SPORE, ZOOSPORE

zoo·grafting \'zōə+,-\ *n* [*zo-* + *grafting*] **:** the use of animal tissue in surgical grafting

zo·og·ra·pher \zō'ägrəfə(r)\ *n* -s [*zo-* + *-grapher*] *archaic*

: one who describes or depicts animals and their forms and habits

zo·o·graph·ic \¦zōə¦grafik\ *or* **zo·o·graph·i·cal** \-fə̇kəl\ *adj* [*zoography* + *-ic* or *-ical*] **1** : of, relating to, or consisting of graphic or verbal description of animals **2** : ZOOGEOGRAPHIC

zo·og·ra·phy \zō'ägrəfē\ *n* -ES [Gk *zōio-* (fr. *zōion* animal) + E *-graphy* — more at ZOON] **1** : descriptive zoology **2** : ZOOGEOGRAPHY

zo·oid \'zō,ȯid\ *n* -S [*zo-* + *-oid*] : an entity that resembles but is not wholly the same as a separate individual organism: as **a** : an organized body (as a phagocyte or a sperm cell) having locomotion **b** : a more or less independent animal produced (as by fission, proliferation, or strobilation) by other than direct sexual methods and so having an equivocal individuality — used esp. of a single person of a compound organism (as a hydroid, coral, or bryozoan colony) — **zo·oi·dal** \(')zō¦ȯidᵊl\ *adj*

zo·oi·di·oph·i·lous \zō¦ȯidē¦äfələs\ *adj* [prob. alter. of *zoidiophilous*] : ZOOPHILIC a

zooks \'zu̇ks, 'züks\ *interj* [origin unknown] — used as a mild oath

zo·ol·a·ter \zō'äləd·ə(r)\ *n* -S [*zo-* + *-later*] : one that practices zoolatry

zo·ol·a·trous \-lə·trəs\ *adj* [*zoolatry* + *-ous*] : of, relating to, or constituting zoolatry

zo·ol·a·try \-rē\ *n* -ES [NL *zoolatria*, fr. *zo-* + LL *-latria* -latry] **1** : worship directed toward particular kinds of animals often as representative of a natural force, as incarnation of some deity, or as symbolic of some power or protector (as a tribal ancestor) **2** : excessive preoccupation with or devotion to animals and esp. to a domestic pet

zo·ol·o·ger \zō'äləjə(r)\ *n* -S [NL *zoologia* zoology + E *-er*] *archaic* : ZOOLOGIST

zo·o·log·i·cal \¦zōə¦läjə̇kəl, -jēk-, ÷ ¦züə¦-\ *also* **zo·o·log·ic** \-jik, -jēk\ *adj* [*zoology* + *-ical* or *-ic*] **1** : of, relating to, or occupied with zoology **2** : of, relating to, or affecting lower animals often as distinguished from man ⟨~ infections⟩ — **zo·o·log·i·cal·ly** \-jə̇k(ə)lē, -jēk-, -li\ *adv*

zoological garden *n* : a garden or park where wild animals are kept for exhibition

zo·ol·o·gist \zō'äləjə̇st, ÷ zü-\ *n* -S : a specialist in zoology

zo·ol·o·gize \-lə,jīz\ *vb* -ED/-ING/-S *vi* **1** : to study zoology **2** : to collect animals for study ~ *vt* : to subject to zoological investigation

zo·ol·ogy \-ləjē, -ji\ *n* -ES [NL *zoologia*, fr. *zo-* + *-logia* -logy] **1** : a science that deals with animals : a branch of biology concerned with the animal kingdom and its members as individuals and classes and with animal life and animal morphology together with anatomy, histology, and cytology, physiology, embryology, genetics, taxonomy, paleontology, ecology, and various other sciences in whole or in part **2** : a treatise on zoology **3 a** : animal life (as of a region) : FAUNA ⟨the ~ of Australia⟩ **b** : the properties and vital phenomena exhibited by an animal, animal type, or group : animal physiology ⟨the ~ of a crustacean⟩

[1]**zoom** \'züm\ *vb* -ED/-ING/-S [imit.] *vi* **1** : to move with or make a loud but low hum or buzz **2** *of an airplane* : to climb for a short time at an angle greater than that which can be maintained in steady flight so that the machine is carried upward at the expense of its stored kinetic energy **3 a** *of a motion-picture or television camera* : to move toward or away from an object rapidly while keeping the object in focus **b** *of a motion-picture or television image* : to appear to come closer to or to move away from the observer as the result of varying the focal length of the camera lens ~ *vt* : to cause (as a motion-picture or television image) to zoom

[2]**zoom** \"\ *n* -S **1 a** : an act or process of zooming: as (1) : a sudden increase in the upward slope of the flight path of an airplane; *broadly* : a sharp upward movement (as of a business cycle) (2) : a process by which an image is made to grow or to shrink rapidly in the field of view of a motion-picture or television camera **b** : a zooming sound **2** : a cocktail consisting of brandy, honey, and cream shaken in ice and served in a wine glass

zo·o·mas·ti·gida \,zōə,mastə'jīdə\ *or* **zo·o·mas·ti·go·da** \-'gōdə\ *or* **zo·o·mas·ti·go·ta** \-'gōd·ə\ *syn of* ZOOMASTIGINA

zo·o·mas·ti·gi·na \-'jīnə\ *n pl*, *cap* [NL, fr. *zo-* + *mastig-* + *-ina*] : a subclass of Mastigophora that comprises holozoic or saprozoic flagellates lacking chromatophores and stigma and that includes the orders Hypermastigina, Polymastigina, Protomonadina, and Rhizomastigina — compare PHYTOMASTIGINA

zo·om·e·ter \zō'äməd·ə(r)\ *n* [*zo-* + *-meter*] : an animal that because of regularly recurrent parallel fluctuations in population can be used to predict the scarcity or abundance of another animal

zo·o·met·ric \¦zōə¦me·trik\ *or* **zo·o·met·ri·cal** \-rə̇kəl\ *adj* [*zo-* + *-metric* or *metrical*] : designed for the measurement of animals and esp. for the estimation of a measure of bulk (as weight) through determination of some linear measurement (as girth) ⟨a ~ tape⟩

zoo·mimic \¦zōə+\ *adj* [*zo-* + *mimic*] *of a primitive culture* : imitative of animal behavior esp. in the use of animal parts (as teeth and horns) in making tools and weapons

zoom lens *n* : a camera lens in which the focal length and the image size can be varied continuously so that the image remains in focus at all times — called also *varifocal lens*

zo·o·morph \'zōə,mȯrf\ *n* [ISV *zo-* + *-morph*] : something in the form of an animal; *esp* : a conventional image or symbol of a zoomorphized deity or supernatural being

zo·o·mor·phic \¦==¦mȯrfik\ *adj* [ISV *zo-* + *-morphic*] **1** : having the form of often stylized animals ⟨~ writing⟩ **2 a** : of, relating to, or constituting a zoomorphized deity or supernatural being **b** : of, relating to, or like a zoomorph **3** : of or relating to zoomorphism

zo·o·mor·phism \,=='mȯr,fizəm\ *n* -S [ISV *zo-* + *-morphism*] **1** : the representation of deity in the form or with the attributes of the lower animals **2** : the use of animal forms in art or symbolism

zo·o·mor·phize \-,fīz\ *vt* -ED/-ING/-S [*zoomorphic* + *-ize*] : to conceive of or symbolize or represent (a deity or supernatural being) as an animal ⟨*zoomorphizing* their clan founder as a spirit bear so that bears became sacred to the clan⟩

zo·on \'zō,än\ *n*, *pl* **zoa** \'zōə\ [NL, fr. Gk *zōion* animal; akin to Gk *zōē* life — more at QUICK] **1** : the whole product of one fertilized egg whether consisting of a single individual (as a dog), a colony of associated persons (as many hydroids), or an asexually-produced progeny of a sexually-produced individual (as some aphids) — often distinguished from *zooid* **2** : ZOOID — **zo·on·al** \'zōənᵊl\ *adj*

-zoon \"\ *n comb form*, *pl* **-zoa** \"\ [NL, fr. Gk *zōion* animal] : living being : animal : zooid ⟨antho*zoon*⟩ ⟨hemato*zoon*⟩ ⟨spermato*zoon*⟩

zo·on·o·my \zō'änəmē\ *n* -ES [NL *zoonomia*, fr. *zo-* + L *-nomia* -nomy] : PHYSIOLOGY

zo·on·o·sis \zō'änəsə̇s, ,zōə'nōsə̇s\ *n*, *pl* **zoono·ses** \-,sēz\ [NL, fr. *zo-* + *-nosis* (fr. Gk *nosos* disease)] : a disease communicable from animals to man under natural conditions — compare PANZOOTIC

zo·o·not·ic \¦zōə¦näd·ik\ *adj* [fr. NL *zoonosis*, after such pairs as NL *neurosis*: E *neurotic*] : of, relating to, or constituting a zoonosis

zoo·paleontology \¦zōə+\ *n* [*zo-* + *paleontology*] : PALEOZOOLOGY

zoo·parasite \"+\ *n* [*zo-* + *parasite*] : a parasitic animal — **zoo·parasitic** \"+\ *adj*

zoo·pathological \"+\ *adj* [in sense 1, fr. *zoopathology* + *-ical*; in sense 2, fr. *zo-* + *pathological*] **1** : of or relating to zoopathology **2** : pathological to lower animals

zoo·pathology \"+\ *n* [*zo-* + *pathology*] : a branch of pathology dealing with the diseases of the lower animals

zooph *abbr* zoophytological; zoophytology

zo·oph·a·ga \zō'äfəgə\ *n pl*, *cap* [NL, fr. *zo-* + *-phaga*] *in former classifications* : a major division of Mammalia comprising the flesh-eating mammals — **zo·oph·a·gan** \-gən\ *n* -S

zo·o·pha·gin·eae \,zōəfə'jinē,ē\ *n pl*, *cap* [NL, fr. *zo-* + *phag-* + *-ineae*] *in some classifications* : a suborder of Virales comprising animal parasitic viruses

zo·oph·a·gous \zō'äfəgəs\ *adj* [ISV *zo-* + *-phagous*] **1** : feeding on animals : CARNIVOROUS **2** [NL *Zoophaga* + E *-ous*] : of or relating to the Zoophaga

zoo·pharmacological \¦zōə+\ *adj* [*zo-* + *pharmacological*] : of or relating to the pharmacology of animal organs or tissues

zoo·pharmacy \"+\ *n* [*zo-* + *pharmacy*] : veterinary pharmacy

zo·o·phile \'zōə,fīl\ *n* -S [*zo-* + *-phile*] : a zoophilic individual

zoo·phil·ia \,zōə'filēə\ *also* **zo·oph·i·lism** \zō'äfə,lizəm\ *n* -S [*zoophilia* fr. NL, fr. *zo-* + *-philia*; *zoophilism* fr. *zo-* + *phil-* + *-ism*] : the quality or state of being zoophilic; *esp* : an erotic fixation on animals that may result in sexual excitement through real or fancied contact — compare ZOOERASTIA

zo·o·phil·ic \¦zōə¦filik\ *or* **zo·oph·i·lous** \zō'äfələs\ *adj* [*zo-* + *-philic* or *-philous*] : having an attraction to or preference for animals: as **a** *usu zoophilous* : adapted to pollination by animals other than insects — compare ENTOMOPHILOUS **b** : afflicted with sexual zoophilia **c** *of an insect* : preferring lower animals to man as a source of food — compare ANDROPHILIC

zo·oph·i·list \zō'äfələ̇st\ *n* -S [*zo-* + *phil-* + *-ist*] : a lover of animals: **a** : a person concerned with the rights of lower animals and their protection from abuse **b** : one afflicted with zoophilia

zo·oph·i·lite \-fə,līt\ *n* -S [*zo-* + *phil-* + *-ite*] : ZOOPHILIST — **zo·oph·i·lit·ic** \=¦==¦lid·ik\ *adj*

zo·oph·i·ly \zō'äfəlē\ *n* -ES [NL *zoophilia*] : ZOOPHILIA

zoo·phobia \¦zōə+\ *n* [NL, fr. *zo-* + *phobia*] **1** : morbid fear of animals **2** : the fear of animal spirits or of zoomorphized entities — **zo·oph·o·bous** \zō'äfəbəs\ *adj*

zo·o·phor·ic \¦zōə¦fȯrik\ *adj* [L *zoophorus* + E *-ic*] : of, relating to, or employing a zoophorus

zo·oph·o·rus \zō'äfərəs\ *n*, *pl* **zoopho·ri** \-fə,rī\ [L, fr. Gk *zōiophoros*, fr. *zōi-* zo- + *-phoros* -phore] : a frieze having continuous relief sculptures of men or animals or both

zoo·physics \¦zōə+\ *n pl but sing or pl in constr* [*zo-* + *physics*] : the scientific study of the physical principles underlying the structure and uses of the organs of animals

zo·oph·y·ta \zō'äfəd·ə\ *n pl*, *cap* [NL, fr. Gk *zōophyta*, pl. of *zōophyton*] *in former classifications* : an extensive artificial and heterogeneous group of invertebrates mostly incapable of locomotion that commonly includes all or many of the forms distinguished as coelenterates, sponges, bryozoans, echinoderms, protozoans, and worms but is sometimes restricted to coelenterates and sponges or to anthozoans alone

zo·o·phyte \'zōə,fīt\ *n* -S [Gk *zōophyton*, fr. *zō-* zo- + *phyton* plant — more at PHYT-] **1** *obs* : a plant resembling an animal **2** : any of numerous invertebrate animals (as a coral, gorgonian, sea anemone, hydroid, bryozoan, or sponge) more or less resembling plants in appearance or mode of growth; *esp* : one (as many corals and hydroids) that forms a branching arborescent colony attached to a substrate — **zo·o·phyt·ic** \¦==¦fid·ik\ *adj*

zoo·plankter \¦zōə+\ *n* [*zo-* + *plankter*] : a planktonic animal ⟨copepods and other ~*s*⟩

zoo·plankton \"+\ *n* [*zo-* + *plankton*] : animal life of the plankton — **zoo·planktonic** \"+\ *adj*

zo·o·prax·i·scope \,zōə'praksə,skōp\ *n* [*zo-* + *praxis* + *-scope*; fr. the fact that it usu. showed pictures of a moving animal] : a motion-picture projector invented about 1882

zoos *pl of* ZOO

zoo·sperm \'zōə+,-\ *n* [ISV *zo-* + *sperm*] **1** : SPERMATOZOID, SPERMATOZOON **2** : ZOOSPORE

zoo·sporangiophore \¦zōə+\ *n* [*zo-* + *sporangiophore*] : a sporangiophore that bears zoosporangia

zoo·sporangium \"+\ *n*, *pl* **zoosporangia** [NL, fr. *zo-* + *sporangium*] : a spore case or sporangium bearing zoospores

zoo·spore \'zōə+,-\ *n* [ISV *zo-* + *spore*] : an independently motile spore: as **a** (1) : a motile usu. naked and flagellated asexual spore (as of an alga or lower fungus) — called also *swarm spore* (2) : ZOOGONIDIUM **b** : PLANOGAMETE **c** (1) : a flagellated gamete of a foraminiferan (2) : a minute amoeboid or flagellated product of protozoan sporocyst division whether sexual or asexual — **zo·o·spor·ic** \,zōə'spōrik, -pȯr-, -pär-\ *or* **zo·os·po·rous** \zō'äspərəs; ¦zōə¦spōrəs, -pȯr-\ *adj* — **zo·o·spo·rif·er·ous** \,zōəspə'rifərəs, -spōr'if-, -spȯr-\ *adj*

zoo·sporocyst \¦zōə+\ *n* [*zoospore* + *-o-* + *cyst*] : a unicellular zoosporangium — compare SPOROCYST

zo·os·ter·ol \zō'ästə,rȯl, -rōl\ *n* [*zo-* + *sterol*] : any of a group of sterols (as cholesterol or coprostanol) of animal origin — compare PHYTOSTEROL

zo·o·taxy \'zōə,taksē\ *n* -ES [ISV *zo-* + *-taxy*] : zoological taxonomy

zo·o·tech·ni·cal \¦zōə¦teknə̇kəl\ *also* **zo·o·tech·nic** \-nik\ *adj* [*zootechnical* fr. *zootechny* + *-ical*; *zootechnic* ISV *zootechny* + *-ic*] : of or relating to zootechny

zo·o·tech·ni·cian \,==tek'nishən\ *n* [ISV *zootechnic* + *-an*] : a specialist in zootechny

zo·o·technics \,=='tekniks\ *n pl but sing or pl in constr* [*zootechnic* + *-s*] : ZOOTECHNY 1

zo·o·tech·ny \'==,teknē\ *n* -ES [ISV *zo-* + *-techny*; prob. orig. formed as F *zootechnie*] **1** : the scientific art of maintaining and improving animals under domestication including breeding, genetics, nutrition, and housing : the technology of animal husbandry **2** : methods and devices for capturing and utilizing animals esp. as employed by nonliterate people

zo·o·the·ism \'zōə(,)thē,izəm, ,zōə'th-\ *n* [*zo-* + *-theism*] : belief in animal gods — compare ZOOLATRY

zoo·therapy \¦zōə+\ *n* [ISV *zo-* + *therapy*] : veterinary therapeutics

zo·ot·o·my \zō'äd·əmē\ *n* -ES [*zo-* + *-tomy*] **1** : the dissection of animals **2** : animal anatomy esp. as studied on a comparative basis : comparative anatomy

zoo·totemism \¦zōə+\ *n* [*zo-* + *totemism*] : belief in or use of animals as totems

zootrope *var of* ZOETROPE

zo·o·troph·ic \¦zōə·¦träfik\ *adj* [*zo-* + *-trophic*] : HETEROTROPHIC — used esp. by protozoologists

zoot suit \'züt-\ *n* [coined by Harold C. Fox *b* 1910 Amer. clothier and bandleader] : a flashy suit of extreme cut typically consisting of a thigh-length jacket with wide padded shoulders and peg-top trousers tapering to narrow cuffs — **zoot-suiter** \'='==\ *n* -S

zooty \'züd·ē\ *adj* [*zoot* suit + *-y*] : typical of a zoot-suiter : extreme or flashy in manner or style ⟨a ~ haircut⟩

zo·o·type \'zōə,tīp\ *n* [*zo-* + *type*] : an animal serving as a type; *also* : the type so represented — **zo·o·typ·ic** \¦==¦tipik\ *adj*

zo·o·xan·thel·la \,zōəzan'thelə\ *n*, *pl* **zooxanthel·lae** \-ē,lē\ [NL, fr. *zo-* + *xanth-* + *-ella*] : any of various symbiotic dinoflagellates that live within the cells of other organisms (as reef-building coral polyps and some radiolarians and flatworms)

zoo·zoo \'zü,zü\ *n* -S [imit. of its sound] *dial Eng* : RINGDOVE

zop·pa \'tsäpə, 'zä-\ *or* **zop·po** \-pō\ *adj* [It, lit., limping] : SYNCOPATED — used as a direction in music; see ALLA ZOPPA

zo·que \'sōkā\ *n*, *pl* **zoque** \"\ *or* **zo·ques** \-ās\ *usu cap* **1 a** : a Zoquean people of Oaxaca, Chiapas, and Tabasco in Mexico **b** : a member of the Zoque people **2** : the language of the Zoque people

zo·que·an \-āən\ *n*, *pl* **zoquean** *or* **zoqueans** *usu cap* [*Zoque* + E *-an*] **1 a** : a Mexican Indian people of eastern Tabasco and the adjacent districts of Chiapas and Oaxaca **b** : a member of such people **2** : a language stock of southern Mexico that includes Zoque, Mixe, and Popoluca

zo·rap·tera \zə'raptərə\ *n pl*, *cap* [NL, fr. Gk *zōros* pure, sheer + NL *Aptera*] : an order of minute terrestrial commonly apterous insects that are widely distributed in the warmer parts of the world, form a single genus (*Zorotypus*), and are related to the order Corrodentia in which they are often included as a suborder

zor·il \'zȯrə̇l, 'zär-\ *or* **zo·rille** \zə'ril\ *also* **zo·ril·la** \-lə\ *or* **zoril·lo** \-i(,)lō\ *n* -S [F *zorille*, fr. Sp *zorrilla*, *zorrillo*, dim. of *zorra*, *zorro* fox, fr. OSp *zorrar* to drag, of imit. origin] **1** : STRIPED MUISHOND **2** : a North African muishond (*Ictonyx frenata*) related to the striped muishond

zo·ril·la \zə'rilə\ [NL, fr. Sp *zorrilla*] *syn of* ICTONYX

zo·ril·lo \zə'ri(,)lō\ *n* -S [Sp *zorrillo* little fox, skunk, dim. of *zorro* fox] : a tropical American shrub or small tree (*Roupala darienensis*) of the family Proteaceae that has an offensive skunklike odor and is used as a remedy for headache

[1]**zo·ro·as·tri·an** \¦zōrə¦wastrēən, ¦zȯr-, -rō¦a-, -aas-\ *adj*, *usu cap* [*Zoroaster fl ab* 6th cent. B.C. founder of Zoroastrianism (fr. L *Zoroastres*, fr. Gk *Zōroastrēs*, fr. Av *Zarāthushtra-*) + E *-an*] : of or relating to Zoroaster or Zoroastrianism

[2]**zoroastrian** \"\ *n* -S *usu cap* : an adherent of Zoroastrianism — compare GABAR, PARSI

zo·ro·as·tri·an·ism \,=='==ə,nizəm\ *n* -S *cap* : a religion founded in Persia by the prophet Zoroaster teaching the worship of Ahura Mazda as the source of all good and requiring the practice of good thoughts, words, and deeds and the renunciation of evil — compare PARSIISM

zo·ro·ty·pus \,zōrə'tīpəs\ *n*, *cap* [NL, fr. Gk *zōros* pure, sheer + L *typus* type] : the sole genus of the order Zoraptera

zor·ra \'zȯrə\ *n* -S [AmerSp *zorra*, *sorra*] : any of several coarse tropical grasses

zor·tzi·co \zȯ(r)'sē(,)kō\ *n* -S [Basque, fr. *zortzi* eight; fr. its time] : a Basque song or dance in ⅝ time and dotted rhythm

zos·ter \'zōstə(r), 'zäs-\ *n* -S [L, fr. Gk *zōstēr* girdle — more at HERPES ZOSTER] : HERPES ZOSTER

zos·te·ra \zä'stirə\ *n*, *cap* [NL, fr. Gk *zōstēr* girdle, a seaweed] : a small genus of widely distributed marine plants (family Potamogetonaceae) with branching stems, distichous leaves, and monoecious flowers that are borne in a spadix — see EELGRASS

zos·ter·a·ce·ae \,zästə'rāsē,ē\ *n pl*, *cap* [NL, fr. *Zostera* + *-aceae*] *in some classifications* : a family of widely distributed marine or aquatic herbs (order Naiadales) that is nearly or exactly equivalent to Potamogetonaceae

zos·ter·op·i·dae \,zästə'räpə,dē\ *n pl*, *cap* [NL, fr. *Zosterop-*, *Zosterops*, type genus + *-idae*] : a family of passerine birds consisting of the silvereyes

zos·ter·ops \'zästə,räps\ *n*, *cap* [NL, fr. Gk *zōstēr* girdle + *ōp-*, *ōps* eye — more at OPTIC] : the type genus of the family Zosteropidae

zotzil *usu cap*, *var of* TZOTZIL

zou·ave \zü'äv, -'åv, '=,=, 'zwäv, 'zwåv\ *n* -S *usu cap* [F, fr. Berber *Zwāwa*, tribe of Kabyles in the Djurdjura mountains, Algeria] **1** : one of a body of French infantry orig. composed of Algerians that is characterized by a colorful uniform of gaiters, baggy trousers, short and open-fronted jacket, and usu. tasseled cap or turban and by very quick and spirited drill **2** : a member of a body of soldiers (as a volunteer regiment in the army of the U. S. in the Civil War) adopting the dress and drill of the Zouaves

Zouave 1

zounds \'z(w)au̇n(d)z, 'z(w)ün(d)z\ *interj* [euphemism for *God's wounds*] — used as a mild oath

zou-zou *var of* ZU-ZU

zow·ie \'zau̇ē, -au̇i\ *interj* [imit. of the sound of a speeding vehicle] — used to express astonishment, admiration, or delight esp. over something sudden or speedy

[1]**zoy·sia** \'zȯisēə, 'zȯizēə, 'zȯishə\ [NL] *syn of* ZOISIA

[2]**zoysia** \"\ *n* -S : a grass of the genus *Zoisia*: as **a** : MANILA GRASS **b** : KOREAN LAWN GRASS

Zr *symbol* zirconium

ZS *abbr* zoological society

z's *or* **zs** *pl of* Z

ZT *abbr* zone time

z-twist \'=,=\ *n*, *cap Z* : an openband twist

zu·brow·ka \'zübrəvkə\ *n* -S [Pol *żubrówka*, fr. Russ *zubrovka* sweet grass, zubrowka] : a dry straw-colored chiefly Russian liqueur of vodka flavored with herbs

zuc·chet·to \zü'ked·(,)ō\ *n* -S [It, fr. *zucca* gourd, head, fr. LL *cucutia*, a gourd; perh. akin to L *cucurbita* gourd — more at GOURD] : a small round skullcap worn by Roman Catholic ecclesiastics in colors that vary according to the rank of the wearer — compare BIRETTA

zucchetto

zuc·chi·ni \zü'kēnē, -ni *also* -'chē-\ *n*, *pl* **zucchini** *or* **zucchinis** [It, pl. of *zucchino*, dim. of *zucca* gourd] : a summer squash that is characterized by bushy growth and smooth slender cylindrical straight to slightly curved fruits with very dark green or blackish green skin and thick greenish white or creamy white tender flesh and is usu. preferred for table use when from five inches to a foot long — compare COCOZELLE

zu·fo·lo *or* **zuf·fo·lo** \'tsüfə,lō\ *n*, *pl* **zufo·li** *or* **zuffo·li** \-lē\ [It, fr. OIt, whistle, whistling, hiss, fr. (assumed) VL *sufilus*, *sifilus*, fr. L *sibilus*; akin to L *sibilare* to hiss, whistle — more at SIBILANT] : a little flute or flageolet; *esp* : one used to teach birds

zug·zwang \'tsük,tsfäŋ\ *n* -S [G, fr. *zug* pull, tug + *zwang* force, coercion; akin to OHG *ziohan* to pull and *dwingan* to press, oppress, compel — more at TOW, THONG] : the necessity of moving in chess when it is to one's disadvantage

zui·sin \'zȯizᵊn\ *n* -S [perh. of Algonquian origin; akin to Ojibwa *jishib* duck, Pequot *m'shizzeege* sheldrake] : BALDPATE 2

zu'l-hij·ja \zül'hi(,)jä\ *usu cap Z&H*, *var of* DHU'L-HIJJA

zu'l-ka·dah \-'kä(,)dä\ *usu cap Z&K*, *var of* DHU'L-QADAH

[1]**zu·lu** \'zü(,)lü\ *n*, *pl* **zulu** *or* **zulus** *usu cap* **1 a** : a Bantu-speaking Ngoni people of Natal related to the Xhosa and other peoples of southern Africa **b** : a member of the Zulu people **2** : a Bantu language of the Zulu people closely related to Xhosa and Swazi with which it forms the Ngoni group and of considerable literary importance as one of the leading Bantu languages of southern Africa

[2]**zulu** \"\ *n* -S [prob. fr. [1]*zulu*] **1** : a 2-masted Scotch lugger with straight stem, raking and narrow stern, and very lofty fore lug **2 a** : a 19th century U. S. or Canadian railroad car or train carrying immigrants and their possessions **b** : a person or group traveling in a zulu

[3]**zulu** \"\ *usu cap* — a communications code word for the letter *z*

zum·boo·ruk \zəm'bü,rək\ *n* -S [Ar *zanbūrak*, fr. Per *zanbūrah*, fr. *zanbūr* hornet] : a small cannon mounted on a swivel; *esp* : one fired from a rest on the back of a camel

zu·ni \'zünē\ *or* **zu·ñi** \-nyē\ *n*, *pl* **zuni** *or* **zunis** *or* **zuñi** *or* **zuñis** *usu cap* [Sp, fr. Keresan *sïni* middle] **1 a** : a people occupying a pueblo in western New Mexico **b** : a member of the Zuni people **2** : the language of the Zuni people — **zu·ni·an** \-nēən\ *or* **zu·ñi·an** \-nyē-\ *adj*

zu·ni·an \-nēən\ *or* **zu·ñi·an** \-nyē-\ *n*, *pl* **zunian** *or* **zuñian** *usu cap* [*Zuni* + E *-an*] : a language family consisting of Zuni only

zuñi brown *n*, *often cap Z* : AUBURN

zun·yite \'zün,yīt\ *n* -S [*Zuñi* Mine, near Silverton, Colo. + E *-ite*] : a mineral $Al_{13}Si_5O_{20}(OH,F)_{18}Cl$ consisting of a basic silicate, chloride, and fluoride of aluminum and occurring in minute transparent tetrahedrons

zu·rich \'zu̇rik, -rēk\ *or* **zü·rich** \'tsœrik\ *adj*, *usu cap* [fr. *Zurich* or *Zürich*, Switzerland] : of or from the city of Zurich, Switzerland : of the kind or style prevalent in Zurich

zutuhil *or* **zutugil** *usu cap*, *var of* TZUTUHIL

zuur·veldt \'zu̇r,velt\ *n* [Afrik *zuurveld*, fr. MD *zuur*, *suur* sour + *velt*, *veld* field; akin to OE & OHG *sūr* sour — more at SOUR, VELD] : SOURVELD

zu·zim \zü'zēm\ *or* **zu·zims** \-mz\ *n pl*, *usu cap* [Heb *zūzīm*] : ZAMZUMMIM

zu-zu *also* **zou-zou** \'zü,zü\ *n* -S [by shortening & redupl. fr. *zouave*] : a member of a Zouave regiment in the Civil War

zwan·zi·ger \'tsfän(t)sə̇gə(r), 'tsvä-\ *n* -S [G, fr. *zwanzig* twenty, fr. OHG *zweinzug*, fr. *zwein-* (akin to OE *twēgen*, *twā*, *tū* two) + *-zug* group of 10 — more at TWO, EIGHTY] : a former Austrian and German billon coin of 20 kreutzers

zwet·schen·was·ser \'tsfechən,väsə(r), 'tsve-\ *n* -S [G, lit., plum water, fr. *zwetschen* (pl. of *zwetsche* plum) + *wasser* water, fr. OHG *wazzar* — more at WATER] : a colorless plum brandy with a bitter almond taste

zwick·au \'tsfi,kau̇, 'tsvi-\ *adj*, *usu cap* [fr. *Zwickau*, Germany] : of or from the city of Zwickau, Germany : of the kind or style prevalent in Zwickau

zwickau prophet *n, usu cap Z* **:** a member of a 16th century Anabaptist sect centered in Zwickau whose leaders (as Storch and Münzer) claimed prophetic powers

zwie·back \ˈswē,bak, ˈzw-, -wī,- *also* -bäk\ *n, pl* **zwieback** *or* **zwiebacks** [G, lit., twice baked, fr. *zwie-* (fr. OHG *zwi-* twice) + *backen* to bake, fr. OHG *bahhan;* trans. of It *biscotto* biscuit — more at TWI-, BAKE] **:** a usu. sweetened bread enriched with eggs that is first prepared and baked and then sliced and toasted until dry and crisp

zwing·er \ˈtsfiŋə(r), ˈtsvi-\ *n* -S [G, fr. MHG *twinger, zwinger* one that forces or constrains, narrow space between the wall of a castle and the outer walls, fr. *twingen, dwingen* to press, oppress, fr. OHG *dwingan* — more at THONG] **:** a fortress protecting a city

¹**zwing·li·an** \ˈzwiŋ(g)lēən\ *also* **zwing·li·an·ist** \-nəst\ *n* -S *usu cap* [*zwinglian* fr. Ulrich *Zwingli* †1531 Swiss religious reformer + E *-an*, n. suffix; *zwinglianist* fr. ²*zwinglian* + *-ist*] **:** a follower or adherent of Zwingli or Zwinglianism

²**zwinglian** \ˈ"\ *adj, usu cap* [Ulrich *Zwingli* †1531 + E *-an*, adj. suffix] **:** of or relating to Zwingli or Zwinglianism

zwing·li·an·ism \-ēə,nizəm\ *n* -S *usu cap* **:** the teachings of Zwingli; *specif* **:** the doctrine that in the Lord's Supper there is an influence of Christ upon the soul but that the true body of Christ is present by the contemplation of faith and not in essence or reality

zwisch·en·spiel \ˈtsfishən,shpēl, ˈtsvi-\ *n* [G, fr. *zwischen* between (fr. MHG, fr. OHG *zwiskēn*, dat. pl., both, fr. *zwisk*, adj., twofold, fr. an old distributive numeral akin to Goth *tweihnai* two each) + *spiel* play, fr. OHG *spil* — more at BETWIXT, SPIEL] **:** a musical interlude **:** INTERMEZZO

zwit·ter·ion \ˈtsvid·ə,rīən\ *n* [G, fr. *zwitter* hybrid (fr. OHG *zwitaran*, fr. *zwi-* double, twice) + ISV *ion* — more at TWI-] **:** DIPOLAR ION — **zwit·ter·ion·ic** \ˌ==ˌrīˈänik\ *adj*

zyg- *or* **zygo-** *comb form* [NL, fr. Gk, fr. *zygon* — more at YOKE] **1 a :** yoke **:** connecting in the manner of a yoke **:** joining ⟨*zygo*sphene⟩ ⟨*zyg*antrum⟩ ⟨*zygo*neure⟩ **b :** zygomatic ⟨*zyg*ion⟩ **2 :** yoked state or part **:** pair ⟨*zygo*dactyl⟩ ⟨*zygo*dont⟩ **3 :** union **:** fusion **:** zygosis ⟨*zygo*spore⟩ ⟨*zygo*genesis⟩

zyg·a·dene \ˈzigə,dēn, ˈzig-\ *n* -S [NL *Zygadenus*] **:** a plant of the genus *Zigadenus*

zyg·a·de·nine \ˌ==ˈdē,nēn, -,nən\ *n* -S [ISV *zygaden-* (fr. NL *Zygadenus*) + *-ine*] **:** a crystalline alkaloid $C_{27}H_{43}NO_7$ that is obtained from plants of the genera *Zigadenus* and *Veratrum*

zyg·a·de·nus \-ˈdēnəs\ [NL] *syn of* ZIGADENUS

zyg·ae·nid \zīˈjēnəd\ *adj* [NL *Zygaenidae*] **:** of or relating to the Zygaenidae

¹**zy·gae·ni·dae** \-nə,dē\ [NL, fr. *Zygaena* (fr. Gk *zygaina* hammerheaded shark) + *-idae*] *syn of* SPHYRNIDAE

²**zygaenidae** \ˈ"\ *n pl, cap* [NL, fr. *Zygaena*, type genus (fr. Gk *zygaina*) + *-idae*] **:** a family of moths including the foresters, burnet moths, and related moths most of which are brightly colored and day-flying

zy·gan·trum \zīˈgan·trəm, zəˈ-\ *n, pl* **zygan·tra** \-rə\ *also* **zygantrums** [NL, fr. *zyg-* + LL *antrum* cavity of the body — more at ANTRUM] **:** a fossa on the posterior median part of the neural arch of a vertebra (as of a snake) that accommodates the zygosphene of the next vertebra

zyg·apophysis \ˌzig, ˌzigō+\ *n, pl* **zygapophyses** [NL, fr. *zyg-* + *apophysis*] **:** one of the articular processes of the neural arch of a vertebra of which there are usu. two anterior and two posterior

zyg·i·on \ˈzigē,än, ˈzij-\ *n, pl* **zygia** \-ēə\ *also* **zygions** [NL, fr. *zyg-* + *-ion* (as in *gonion*)] **:** a craniometric point at either end of the bizygomatic diameter

zy·gite \ˈzī,jīt\ *n* -S [Gk *zygitēs*, fr. *zygon* yoke, thwart + *-itēs* -ite — more at YOKE] **:** a rower of the middle tier in an ancient trireme or in the upper tier of a bireme

zyg·nema \zigˈnēmə\ *n, cap* [NL, fr. *zyg-* + *-nema*] **:** a genus of common filamentous algae (family Zygnemataceae) having two stellate chromatophores in each cell

zyg·ne·ma·les \ˌzignəˈmā(,)lēz\ [NL, fr. *Zygnema* + *-ales*] *syn of* ZYGNEMATALES

zyg·ne·ma·ta·ce·ae \ˌzig,nēməˈtāsē,ē\ *n pl, cap* [NL, fr. *Zygnemat-*, *Zygnema*, type genus + *-aceae*] **:** a family of common freshwater algae (order Zygnematales) often forming bright green slimy masses in stagnant or running water and consisting of unbranched cylindrical filaments with green chromatophores arranged in spiral bands, stars, or rarely straight bands — see SPIROGYRA, ZYGNEMA — **zyg·ne·ma·ta·ceous** \ˌ==ˌ==ˈtāshəs\ *adj*

zyg·ne·ma·ta·les \-ˈtā(,)lēz\ *n pl, cap* [NL, fr. *Zygnemat-*, *Zygnema* + *-ales*] **:** an order of green algae (class Chlorophyceae) that include the pond scums and desmids, are distinguished by the absence of asexual reproduction and lack of flagellated reproductive structure, and reproduce sexually by fusion of amoeboid gametes — compare AKONTAE

zygo- — see ZYG-

zy·go·cactus \ˌzīgō, ˌzigō+\ *n, cap* [NL, fr. *zyg-* + *Cactus*] **:** a small genus of Brazilian cacti having flat fleshy usu. branched joints, showy red or pink flowers, and red fleshy fruits and including the widely cultivated crab cactus

zy·goc·i·ty \zīˈgäsəd·ē, zəˈ-\ *n* -ES [*zygotic* + *-city* (as in *velocity*)] **:** zygotic condition ⟨rules for the diagnosis of ~ in cattle twins —John Hancock⟩

¹**zy·go·dac·tyl** \ˌzīgōˈdaktəl, ˌzig-\ *or* **zy·go·dac·ty·lous** \-tələs\ *also* **zy·go·dac·tyle** \-tᵊl\ *adj* [NL *zygodactyl, zygodactyle* ISV *zyg-* + *dactyl; zygodactylous* fr. *zyg-* + *-dactylous*] **1 :** having the toes arranged two in front and two behind — used of a bird **2 :** SYNDACTYL ⟨familial occurrence of ~ hands⟩

²**zygodactyl** \ˈ"\ *also* **zygodactyle** \ˈ"\ *n* -S **:** a zygodactyl bird (as a woodpecker or parrot)

zy·go·dac·ty·lae \ˌ==ˈdaktə,lē\ *or* **zy·go·dac·ty·li** \-,lī\ *n pl, cap* [NL, fr. *zyg-* + *-dactylae, -dactyli* (fr. *dactylus* dactyl)] *in former classifications* **:** a group of nonpasserine birds consisting of those having zygodactyl feet

zy·go·dac·tyl·ism \-,lizəm\ *n* -S [*zyg-* + *-dactylism*] **:** the condition of being zygodactyl or of having zygodactyl feet

zy·go·dont \ˈzīgə,dänt, ˈzig-\ *adj* [ISV *zyg-* + *-odont*] **:** having or being molar teeth with four tubercles in which the tubercles are united in pairs by crests

zy·go·genesis \ˌzīgō, ˌzigō+\ *n* [NL, fr. *zyg-* + *genesis*] **:** reproduction by means of specialized germ cells or gametes **:** sexual and biparental reproduction

zy·goid \ˈzī,gȯid, ˈzi,-\ *adj* [*zyg-* + *-oid*] **:** of or relating to a zygote **:** ZYGOTIC

zy·golo·bous \ˌzīgə,lōbəs, (ˈ)zīˈgäləbəs\ *adj* [*zyg-* + *lob-* + *-ous*] *of the prostomium of an annelid worm* **:** not set off by a groove from the first true segment

zy·go·ma \zīˈgōmə, zəˈ-\ *n, pl* **zygoma·ta** \-məd·ə\ *also* **zygomas** [NL, fr. Gk *zygōma*, fr. *zygoun* to yoke, join together, fr. *zygon* yoke — more at YOKE] **1 :** ZYGOMATIC ARCH **2 :** ZYGOMATIC PROCESS a **3 :** ZYGOMATIC BONE

¹**zy·go·mat·ic** \ˌzīgəˈmad·ik, ˌzig-, -at|, |ēk\ *adj* [NL *zygomaticus*, fr. *zygomat-*, *zygoma* + L *-icus* -ic] **:** of, relating to, constituting, or situated in the region of the zygoma and esp. the zygomatic arch as a whole

²**zygomatic** \ˈ"\ *n* -S **:** ZYGOMATIC BONE

zygomatic arch *n* **:** the arch of bone that extends along the front or side of the skull beneath the orbit, is formed in most mammals by the union of the zygomatic bone with the maxillary bone in front and the zygomatic process of the temporal bone behind, and in lower vertebrates may be modified by the addition of other bones or may be duplicated (as in some reptiles) — compare DIAPSIDA

zygomatic bone *n* **:** a bone of the side of the face below the eye that in mammals forms part of the zygomatic arch and part of the orbit and articulates with the temporal, sphenoid, frontal, and maxillary bones and in birds is slender and rodlike and joins the maxilla and quadratojugal **:** a malar bone — called also *cheekbone*

zygomatic muscle *n* **:** a slender band of muscle on either side of the face arising from the zygomatic bone and inserting into the orbicularis oris and skin at the corner of the mouth

zygomatic nerve *n* **:** a branch of the maxillary nerve that divides into a facial branch supplying the skin of the prominent part of the cheek and a temporal branch supplying the skin of the anterior temporal region — called also respectively *zygomaticofacial nerve, zygomaticotemporal nerve*

zygomatico- *comb form* [NL, fr. *zygomaticus* zygomatic] **:** zygomatic and ⟨*zygomatico*maxillary⟩

zy·go·mat·i·co·auricularis \ˌzīgəˈmad·ə̇kō, ˌzig-+\ *n* [NL, fr. *zygomatico-* + *auricularis*] **:** the anterior auricularis muscle

zy·go·mat·i·co·temporal \ˈ"+\ *adj* [*zygomatico-* + *temporal*] **1 :** of, relating to, or uniting the zygomatic arch and the temporal bone ⟨the ~ suture⟩ **2 :** of, relating to, or constituting a foramen in the zygomatic bone that gives passage to the temporal branch of the zygomatic nerve

zygomatic process *n* **:** any of several bony processes that enter into or strengthen the zygomatic arch: as **a :** a long slender process of the temporal or squamosal bone helping to form the zygomatic arch **b :** a process of the zygomatic bone articulating with the temporal bone **c :** a narrow process of the frontal bone articulating with the zygomatic bone **d :** a broad rough process of the maxilla articulating with the zygomatic bone

zygomatic suture *n* **:** the zygomaticotemporal suture

zy·go·mat·i·cus \ˌzīgəˈmad·ə̇kəs, ˌzig-\ *n* -ES [NL, fr. *zygomaticus* zygomatic] **:** ZYGOMATIC MUSCLE

zy·go·max·il·la·re \ˌzīgə,maksəˈla(a)rē, ˌzig-\ *n* -S [NL, fr. *zyg-* + *maxillare*, fr. neut. sing. of L *maxillaris* maxillar] **:** ZYGOMAXILLARY POINT

zy·go·maxillary \ˌzīgō, ˌzigō+\ *adj* [ISV *zyg-* + *maxillary*] **:** of, relating to, or joining the maxilla and zygoma

zygomaxillary point *n* **:** a craniometric point at the lower end of the zygomaticotemporal suture

zy·go·mor·phic \ˌzīgəˈmȯrfik, ˌzig-, -ō(ə)f-, -fēk\ *also* **zy·go·mor·phous** \-fəs\ *adj* [*zyg-* + *-morphic*] **:** bilaterally symmetrical; *specif* **:** capable of division into essentially symmetrical halves by only one longitudinal plane passing through the axis ⟨the ~ pea flower⟩ — compare ACTINOMORPHIC — **zy·go·mor·phism** \ˌ==ˈmȯ(r),fizəm\ *n* -S — **zy·go·mor·phy** \ˌ==,mȯrfē\ *n* -ES

zy·go·my·cete \ˌzīgōˈmī,sēt, ˌzig-, -ō,mīˈsēt\ *n* -S [NL *Zygomycetes*] **:** a fungus of the subclass Zygomycetes

zy·go·my·ce·tes \ˌ==,mīˈsēd·ēz\ *n pl, cap* [NL, fr. *zyg-* + *-mycetes*] **:** a subclass of fungi (class Phycomycetes) distinguished from the Oomycetes by gametangia that are morphologically alike and by sexually produced zygospores — see ENTOMOPHTHORALES, MUCORALES — **zy·go·my·ce·tous** \ˌ==ˌ==ˈsēd·əs\ *adj*

zy·go·my·cet·i·dae \ˌ==,==ˈsed·ə,dē\ [NL, fr. *Zygomycetes* + *-idae*] *syn of* ZYGOMYCETES

zy·go·neure \ˈzīgə,n(y)u̇r, ˈzig-\ *n* -S [*zyg-* + NL *neuron*] **:** a connecting neuron

zy·go·phore \ˈzīgə,fō(ə)r, ˈzig-\ *n* -S [*zyg-* + *-phore*] **:** a specialized hyphal branch giving rise to another that forms the gamete in some molds (family Mucoraceae) — **zy·go·phor·ic** \ˌ==ˈfȯrik\ *adj*

zy·go·phy·ce·ae \ˌzīgōˈfīsē,ē, ˌzig-, -ˈfis-\ *n pl, cap* [NL, fr. *zyg-* + *-phyceae*] *in some esp former classifications* **:** a class that comprises greenish unicellular or filamentous algae having conspicuous chromatophores and multiplying by simple division and by conjugation and that includes the desmids and pond scums and usu. also the diatoms — compare ZYGNEMATALES — **zy·go·phy·ceous** \ˌ==ˈfishəs\ *adj*

zy·go·phyl·la·ce·ae \ˌzīgōfəˈlāsē,ē, ˌzig-\ *n pl, cap* [NL, fr. *Zygophyllum*, type genus + *-aceae*] **:** a family of herbs, shrubs, or trees (order Geraniales) distinguished by pinnate or bifoliolate stipulate leaves and axillary pentamerous flowers — see GUAIACUM 1, TRIBULUS — **zy·go·phyl·la·ceous** \ˌ===ˈlāshəs\ *adj*

zy·go·phyl·lum \ˌzīgəˈfiləm, ˌzig-\ *n, cap* [NL, fr. *zyg-* + *-phyllum*] **:** a genus of Old World shrubs (family Zygophyllaceae) that are distinguished mainly by the opposite bifoliate leaves — see BEAN CAPER

zy·gop·tera \zīˈgäptərə\ *n pl, cap* [NL, fr. *zyg-* + *-ptera*] **:** a suborder of Odonata comprising forms that are distinguished from the typical dragonflies by a slenderer elongated body, by narrow equal wings held upright in repose, and by aquatic larvae that have a pair of paddle-shaped tracheal gills at the apex of the abdomen — see DAMSELFLY; compare ANISOPTERA — **zy·gop·ter·an** \-rən\ *adj or n* — **zy·gop·ter·ous** \-rəs\ *adj*

zy·gop·ter·a·ce·ae \zī,gäptəˈrāsē,ē\ *n pl, cap* [NL, fr. *Zygopteris*, type genus + *-aceae*] **:** a family of primitive Paleozoic ferns of Europe and the U.S. having pinnae in two or four series at an angle to the plane of the leaf blade

zy·gop·ter·i·da·ce·ae \-tərəˈdāsē,ē\ [NL, fr. *Zygopterid-*, *Zygopteris* + *-aceae*] *syn of* ZYGOPTERACEAE

zy·gop·ter·i·des \ˌzīgäpˈterə,dēz\ [NL] *syn of* ZYGOPTERA

zy·gop·ter·is \zīˈgäptərə̇s\ *n, cap* [NL, fr. *zyg-* + *-pteris*] **:** the type genus of Zygopteraceae

zy·go·saccharomyces \ˌzīgō, ˌzigō+\ *n, cap* [NL, fr. *zyg-* + *Saccharomyces*] **:** a genus of yeasts (family Saccharomycetaceae) in which ascospore formation is preceded by conjugation and which is often included in *Saccharomyces*

zy·gose \ˈzī,gōs, ˈzi,-\ *adj* [back-formation fr. *zygosis*] **:** of or relating to zygosis

zy·go·sis \zīˈgōsə̇s, zəˈ-\ *n, pl* **zygo·ses** \-ō,sēz\ [NL, fr. *zyg-* + *-osis*] **:** zygote formation **:** union of gametes **:** CONJUGATION — used esp. in combination; see HETEROZYGOSIS

zy·gos·i·ty \-ˈgäsəd·ē\ *n* -ES [NL *zygosis* + E *-ity*] **:** zygotic quality or characteristics **:** specific inheritance

zy·go·sperm \ˈzīgə, ˈzigə+,-\ *n* [*zyg-* + *sperm*] **:** ZYGOSPORE

zy·go·sphe·nal \ˌzīgōˈsfēnᵊl, ˌzig-\ *adj* **:** of, relating to, or constituting a zygosphene

zy·go·sphene \ˈ==,sfēn\ *n* -S [*zyg-* + Gk *sphēn* wedge — more at SPOON] **:** a median process on the front part of the neural arch of the vertebrae of most snakes and some lizards — see ZYGANTRUM

zy·go·sphere \ˈzīgə, ˈzigə+,-\ *n* [*zyg-* + *sphere*] **:** a plant gamete capable of uniting with a similar one to form a zygospore

zy·go·sporangium *also* **zy·go·sporange** \ˌ==+\ *n, pl* **zygosporangia** *also* **zygosporanges** [NL *zygosporangium*, fr. *zyg-* + *sporangium*] **:** a sporangium in which zygospores are produced

zy·go·spore \ˈ==+,-\ *n* [ISV *zyg-* + *spore*] **:** a plant spore (as in a conjugate alga) that is formed by conjugation of two similar sexual cells, usu. has a thickened and ornamented wall and serves as a resting spore, and ultimately produces the sporophytic phase of the plant — compare OOSPORE — **zy·go·spor·ic** \ˌ==+ˈspȯrik\ *adj*

zy·go·style \ˈzīgə,stīl, ˈzig-\ *n* [*zyg-* + *-style*] **:** the terminal caudal vertebra

zy·go·tax·is \ˌzīgəˈtaksə̇s, ˌzig-\ *n* [NL, fr. *zyg-* + *-taxis*] **:** the attraction between two zygophores or suspensors that is immediately responsible for conjugation

zy·gote \ˈzī,gōt, ˈzi,-, *usu* -ōd·+V\ *n* -S [Gk *zygōtos* yoked, fr. *zygoun* to yoke, join together, fr. *zygon* yoke — more at YOKE] **:** a cell formed by the union of two gametes **:** a fertilized egg **:** ZYGOSPORE; *broadly* **:** the developing individual produced from such a cell

zy·go·tene \ˈzīgə,tēn, ˈzig-\ *n* [ISV *zyg-* + *-tene;* orig. formed as F *zygotène*] **:** the synaptic stage in meiosis in which homologous chromosomes pair intimately

zy·got·ic \(ˌ)zīˈgäd·ik, zəˈg-\ *adj* **:** of, relating to, or existing as a zygote — often used in combination — **zy·got·i·cal·ly** \-d·ə̇k(ə)lē\ *adv*

zy·go·toid \ˈzīgə,tȯid, ˈzig-\ *n* -S [*zygote* + *-oid*] **:** a multinucleate zygospore

-zy·gous \ˌzīgəs, ˌzəgəs, ˌzēgəs\ *adj comb form* [Gk *-zygos*, fr. *zygon* yoke] **1 :** yoked **:** zygomatic ⟨crypto*zygous*⟩ **2 :** having (such) a zygotic constitution ⟨hetero*zygous*⟩

zy·go·zoospore \ˌzīgō, ˌzigō+\ *n* [*zyg-* + *zoospore*] **:** a motile zygospore

zym- *or* **zymo-** *comb form* [NL, fr. Gk, fr. *zymē* — more at ENZYME] **1 :** leaven **:** concerned with fermentation ⟨*zymo*lysis⟩ ⟨*zymo*phosphate⟩ **2 :** ferment **:** enzyme ⟨*zymo*genesis⟩ ⟨*zymo*sthenic⟩

zy·mase \ˈzī,mās\ *n* -S [ISV *zym-* + *-ase*] **:** a complex of enzymes that brings about glycolysis, that was orig. found in yeasts and bacteria and is also present in higher plants and animals, and that may be separated by filtration or dialysis into the apozymase and the coenzyme diphosphopyridine nucleotide

zyme \ˈzīm\ *n* -S [Gk *zymē* leaven, ferment] **:** FERMENT, ENZYME

-zyme \ˌzīm\ *n* -S *comb form* [Gk *zymē* leaven] **:** enzyme ⟨histo*zyme*⟩ ⟨lyso*zymes*⟩

zy·min \ˈzīmə̇n\ *n* -S [*zym-* + *-in*] **1 :** ZYME **2 :** pancreatin prepared as a powder

zy·mo·gen \ˈzīməjən, -,jen\ *n* -S [ISV *zym-* + *-gen*] **:** an inactive protein precursor (as trypsinogen or pepsinogen) of an enzyme esp. a proteolytic enzyme that is secreted in living cells and can be activated by catalysis (as by a kinase or an acid) ⟨~ granules⟩ — called also *proenzyme*

zy·mo·gen·ic \ˌ==ˈjenik\ *adj* [in sense 1, fr. *zym-* + *-genic;* in sense 2, fr. *zymogen* + *-ic*] **1 :** producing fermentation **:** AMYLOLYTIC; *broadly* **:** obtaining energy by amylolytic processes **2 :** of or relating to a zymogen

zy·mog·e·nous \(ˈ)zīˈmäjənəs\ *adj* [*zym-* + *-genous*] **:** ZYMOGENIC

zy·mol·o·gy \zīˈmäləjē, -ji\ *n* -ES [NL *zymologia*, fr. Gk *zym-* (fr. *zymē* leaven) + L *-logia* -logy] **:** a science that deals with fermentation

zy·mo·plas·tic \ˌzīmōˈplastik\ *adj* [*zym-* + *-plastic*] **:** participating in the formation of enzymes — compare THROMBOPLASTIC

zy·mo·san \ˈzīmə,san\ *n* -S [*zymosis* + *-an*] **:** a largely carbohydrate fraction of the yeast cell that is used in the assay of properdin

zy·mo·scope \ˈzīmə,skōp\ *n* [ISV *zym-* + *-scope*] **:** an apparatus for determining the fermenting power of yeast by measuring the amount of carbon dioxide evolved from a given quantity of sugar

zy·mo·sis \zīˈmōsə̇s\ *n, pl* **zymo·ses** \-ō,sēz\ [NL, fr. Gk *zymōsis*, fr. *zymoun* to ferment + *-sis*] **:** FERMENTATION

zy·mos·ter·ol \zīˈmästə,rōl, -rȯl\ *n* [*zym-* + *sterol*] **:** a crystalline unsaturated sterol $C_{27}H_{43}OH$ occurring with ergosterol in yeast fat, resembling ergosterol chemically, and yielding cholestanol on hydrogenation

zy·mos·then·ic \ˌzīməsˈthenik\ *adj* [*zym-* + *sthenic*] **:** strengthening the activity of an enzyme

zy·mot·ic \(ˈ)zīˈmäd·|ik, -ät|, |ēk\ *adj* [Gk *zymōtikos* causing fermentation, fr. *zymōtos* fermented (verbal of *zymoun* to ferment, fr. *zymē* leaven) + *-ikos* -ic — more at ENZYME] **1 :** of, relating to, causing, or caused by fermentation **2 :** of, relating to, constituting, or causing an infectious or contagious disease — **zy·mot·i·cal·ly** \|ə̇k(ə)lē, |ēk-, -li\ *adv*

zy·mur·gy \ˈzī,mərjē\ *n* -ES [*zym-* + *-urgy*] **:** a branch of applied chemistry that deals with fermentation processes (as in wine making or brewing)

zyr·i·an \ˈzirēən\ *n, pl* **zyrian** *or* **zyrians** *cap* [fr. *Zyrian* Autonomous Area (Komi Republic), U.S.S.R.] **1 :** KOMI 1 **2** *also* **zir·yen** \ˈzir,yen, zərˈy-\ [*ziryen* fr. F *zyriène*] **:** the Finno-Ugric language of the Komi people — called also *Komi;* see URALIC LANGUAGES table

zyth·ia \ˈzithēə\ *n, cap* [NL, fr. Gk *zythos* beer, ale (perh. akin to Gk *zymē* leaven) + NL *-ia*] **:** a genus (the type of the family Zythiaceae) of imperfect fungi characterized by white or bright-colored fleshy or waxy pycnidia and hyaline nonseptate spores

zyth·i·a·ce·ae \ˌzitheˈāsē,ē\ *n pl, cap* [NL, fr. *Zythia*, type genus + *-aceae*] **:** a family of imperfect fungi (order Sphaeropsidales) — see ZYTHIA

zy·thum \ˈzīthəm\ *n* -S [L, fr. Gk *zythos*] **:** beer of ancient times: as **a :** beer of ancient Egypt **b :** beer of the northern peoples

zy·zo·mys \ˈzīzə,mis\ *n, cap* [NL, alter. of *Zygomys*, fr. *zyg-* + *-mys*] **:** a genus of small Australian murid rodents characterized externally by short rounded ears and long slightly tufted tail which is usu. all white and by upper molar teeth in which the outermost of the usual three tubercles constituting the cross crests is practically absent

zyz·zo·ge·ton \ˌzizəˈjē,tän\ *n, cap* [NL, fr. *Zyzza*, genus of leafhoppers in former classifications (prob. of imit. origin) + Gk *geitōn* neighbor] **:** a genus of large So. American leafhoppers (family Cicadellidae) having the pronotum tuberculate and the front tibiae grooved

NOAH WEBSTER

OCTOBER 16, 1758 — MAY 28, 1843

THE significance of Noah Webster's *Dictionary* and his *Spelling Book* can be appreciated only when they are viewed against the background spanned by his life. He was born on an eighty-acre Connecticut farm the year before Wolfe's victory on the Plains of Abraham, and lived to see American pioneers penetrate overland into California and Oregon. He was a small boy when the Stamp Act aroused the colonists, and a student at Yale when college classes were dispersed into the interior towns by the menace of British landing parties. He marched with his father against Burgoyne. In 1785, moved by the incompetence of the Confederation of thirteen sovereign states, he wrote a widely circulated argument for national union. In 1787 he issued an influential pamphlet advocating the adoption of the Federal Constitution. From 1793 to 1798 he owned, managed, and edited a daily and a weekly newspaper in New York City, supporting the Federalist policies of Washington and Adams. Living under the first ten presidents, he witnessed the acquisition of Louisiana Territory and Florida, the admission of thirteen additional states, and the approaching annexation of Texas.

Out of the patriotism and nationalism inspired by this sweep of events came the conviction that lusty young America needed its own school books, its own uniform language, and its own intellectual life. Into the attainment of these ends Webster flung himself with insatiable curiosity and indomitable energy. His *Blue-Backed Speller* (which taught not only spelling but pronunciation, common sense, morals, and good citizenship) was partly provoked by his efforts to use Dilworth's English spelling book while he was teaching school in Connecticut, New York, and Philadelphia. His dictionaries (*Compendious*, 1806; *American*, 1828) were suggested partly by his resentment against the ignorance concerning American institutions shown in contemporary British dictionaries. All his life he was a defender and interpreter of the American political "experiment", with all its cultural implications.

His dictionaries and his *Spelling Book* grew out of an intimate and vital familiarity with American life. He knew the farm, the law, the city, the school, and politics. He knew the country as a whole—he had traveled (1785–1786) by horse, by carriage, and by sailing vessel from Massachusetts to South Carolina, persuading state legislatures to pass laws for the protection of copyright. He was a spelling reformer, an orchardist, a gardener, and an experimental scientist. He was admitted to practice before the United States Supreme Court. He became and remained a devoted Calvinistic churchman. He wrote scores of articles, books, and pamphlets on literary, economic, political, philological, practical, and scientific subjects —on banks, epidemics, insurance, the French Revolution, the decomposition of white-lead paint, the Jay Treaty, and the rights of neutral nations in time of war. He edited Governor Winthrop's Journal. He wrote and published a revised and emended version of the Bible.

He assumed all the local duties and responsibilities of a citizen. He was clerk and committeeman of his Hartford school district. He was a member for a time of the General Assembly of Connecticut and for a time of the General Court of Massachusetts. He was councilman and alderman in New Haven and judge of the County Court. In Amherst he was town moderator. He was a director of the Hampshire Bible Society, a vice-president of the Hampshire and Hampden Agricultural Society, and a founder of the Connecticut Academy of Arts and Sciences. He was active in the establishment of both Amherst Academy and Amherst College, and was president of the Board of Trustees of the Academy. In New Haven he campaigned for the introduction of an adequate water supply, and took active part in a movement to plant elms along the streets.

In 1807 he wrote: "I hope to be able to finish my Complete Dictionary. . . . It will require the incessant labor of from three to five years." In 1812 he moved to Amherst, Massachusetts, where for ten years he labored from point to point about the large circular table that held the dictionaries and grammars of twenty languages. In 1824 he sailed to spend a year in the libraries of Paris, London, and Cambridge in order to consult books not available in America. In 1828, at the age of seventy, he at length published *An American Dictionary of the English Language* in a two-volume edition of 2500 copies.

The *American Dictionary* stands practically beyond praise or comparison. The excellence of the definitions has received ample acknowledgment. But some other features of Webster's work have never been adequately recognized: First, the inclusion of thousands of modern technical and scientific terms, making it more than a purely literary dictionary. Second, the discovery of the correct principle for arranging the definitions, with the etymologically primary meaning first. And third, the etymologies, which are mines of pertinent and valuable information, as appears when they are compared, not only with the results of an added century of research, but especially with the scanty or fragmentary treatment of Johnson, Junius, and Skinner, and the speculations of Horne Tooke.

Webster brought out a revised edition of the *Dictionary* in 1841, just before his death. The *Spelling Book* had meanwhile undergone many revisions and improvements. These two books, written to illuminate and explain to the American people both their language and their culture, were his contribution to American civilization.

The publishers and the editors of this latest edition of *Webster's Dictionary* have worked under the constant responsibility of maintaining Noah Webster's standards of integrity and clarity in meeting the needs of the whole modern English-speaking world.